Chicago 7-County street guide

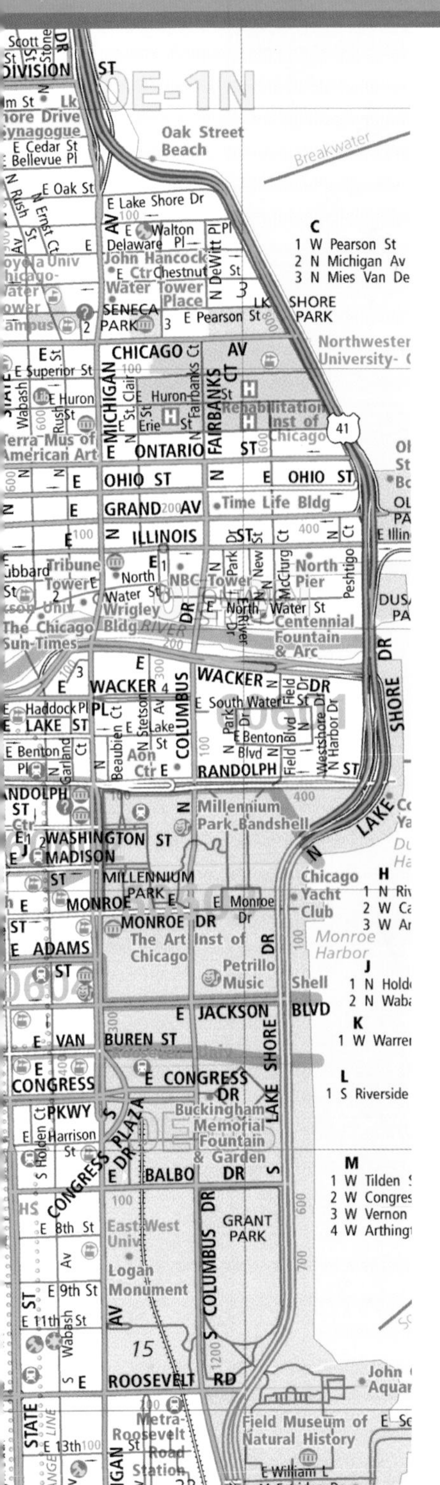

Contents

Introduction

Using Your Street Guide	A
PageFinder™ Map	B
Legend	C
We've Got You Covered	D
Chicago Block Numbers	E

Maps

Downtown Map	F
Street Guide Detail Maps	2349-4031
Vicinity Map	Inside back cover

Lists and Indexes

Cities & Communities Index	1
List of Abbreviations	6
Street Index and Points of Interest Index	7
Comment Card	Last page

RAND McNALLY
Rand McNally Consumer Affairs
P.O. Box 7600
Chicago, IL 60680-9915
randmcnally.com
For comments or suggestions, please call (800) 777-MAPS (-6277)
or email us at:
consumeraffairs@randmcnally.com

Using Your Street Guide

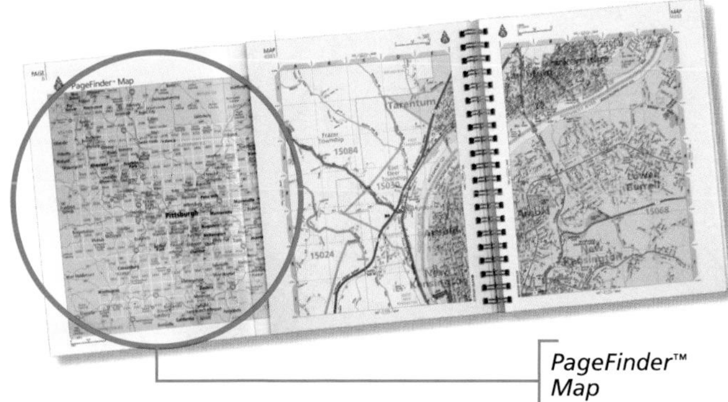

The PageFinder™ Map

> Turn to the PageFinder™ Map. Each of the small squares outlined on this map represents a different map page in the Street Guide.

> Locate the specific part of the Street Guide coverage area that you're interested in.

> Note the appropriate map page number.

> Turn to that map page.

missing pages?

Please note that map pages in this book are numbered according to the PageFinder™ Map. For this reason, your book may look as though it is missing pages. For example, one page might contain map number 15 while the following page contains map number 25.

Use the PageFinder™ Map inside this flap for fast and easy navigation through your Street Guide.

The Maps

> Each map is divided into a grid formed by rows and columns. These rows and columns correspond to letters and numbers running horizontally and vertically along the edges of the map.

> To use a grid reference from the index, search horizontally within the appropriate row and vertically within the appropriate column. The destination can be found within the grid square where the row and column meet.

> Adjacent map pages are indicated by numbers that appear at the top, bottom, and sides of each map.

> The legend explains symbols that appear on the maps.

The Index

> The Street Guide includes separate indexes for streets, schools, parks, shopping centers, golf courses, and other points of interest.

> In the street listings, information is presented in the following order: block number, city, ZIP code, map page number, and grid reference.

STREET Block	City	ZIP	Map#	Grid
BROADWAY DR				
4400	SCH	60646	533	B6
6200	PLA	61644	532	D2
7800	WCH	60656	532	A3

> A grid reference is a letter-number combination (B6 for example) that tells you precisely where to find a particular street or point of interest on a map.

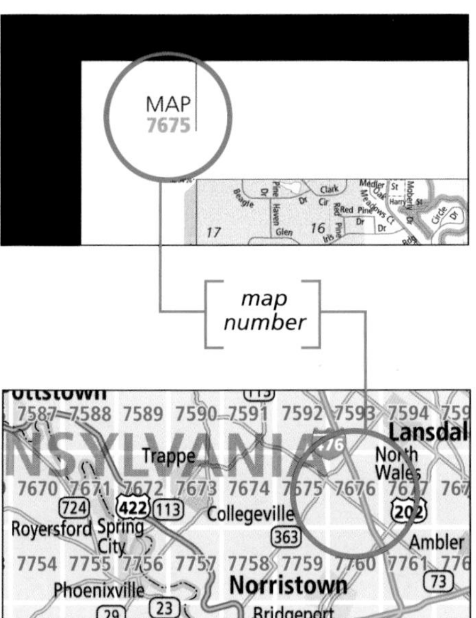

The Chicago Grid

> The entire Chicago Metropolitan area is divided into a grid, which is based on the number of miles distant from point zero, at State and Madison streets in downtown Chicago.

> Example: If you are looking at an MLS listing for a property in grid section 9W-3S, you know that it is nine miles west and three miles south of downtown. Grid coordinates are on every map in this book, including unincorporated areas. Grid locations are also listed with every index entry.

Legend

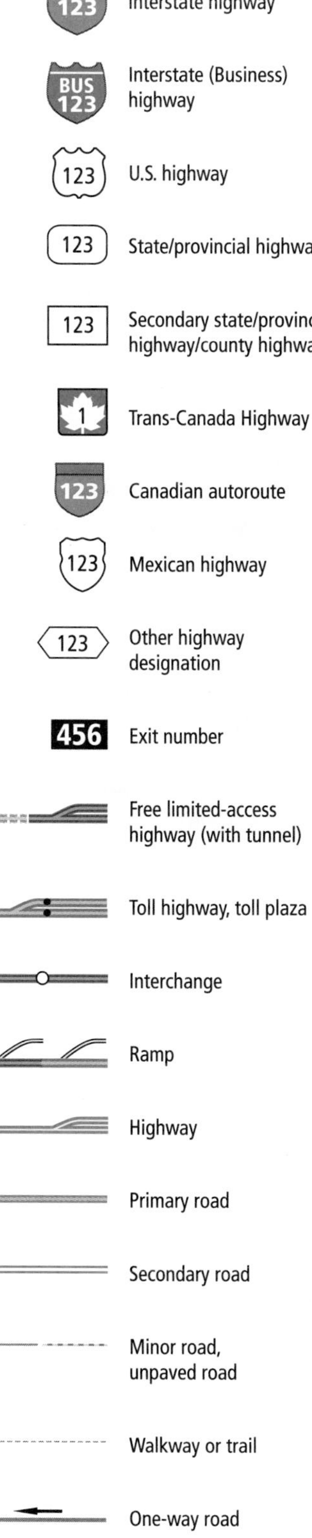

- Interstate highway
- Interstate (Business) highway
- U.S. highway
- State/provincial highway
- Secondary state/provincial highway/county highway
- Trans-Canada Highway
- Canadian autoroute
- Mexican highway
- Other highway designation
- Exit number
- Free limited-access highway (with tunnel)
- Toll highway, toll plaza
- Interchange
- Ramp
- Highway
- Primary road
- Secondary road
- Minor road, unpaved road
- Walkway or trail
- One-way road

- Ferry, waterway
- Levee
- Trolley
- Railroad, station, mass transit line
- Bus station
- Park and ride
- Rest area, service area
- Airport
- 1200 Block number
- International boundary, state boundary
- County boundary
- Township/range boundary, section corner
- 12345 ZIP code boundary, ZIP code
- 4W-2N Chicago Grid Boundary, Chicago Grid
- 45°33'30" 90°33'30" Latitude, longitude
- Hospital
- School
- University or college
- Information/visitor cent welcome center

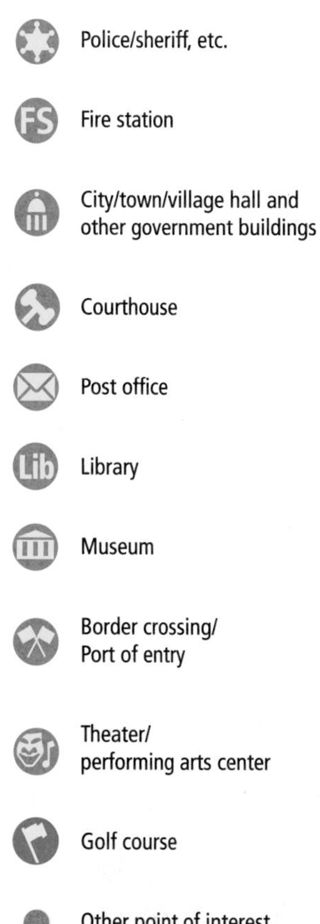

- Police/sheriff, etc.
- Fire station
- City/town/village hall and other government buildings
- Courthouse
- Post office
- Library
- Museum
- Border crossing/ Port of entry
- Theater/ performing arts center
- Golf course
- Other point of interest

we've got you COVERED

Rand McNally's broad selection of products is perfect for your every need. Whether you're looking for the convenience of write-on wipe-off laminated maps, extra maps for every car, or a Road Atlas to plan your next vacation or to use as a reference, Rand McNally has you covered.

Street Guides

Chicago 7-County
Chicago & Cook County
DuPage & Kane Counties
Lake & McHenry Counties
Joliet/ Aurora/ Naperville
Get Around® Chicago Street Atlas
Fort Wayne
South Bend/ Elkhart/ Michiana
Western Michigan

Folded Maps

EasyFinder® Laminated Maps

Illinois
Indiana
Michigan
Chicago North & Downtown
Aurora/ Naperville
North Shore - Evanston/ Highland Park
Chicago South & Downtown
Gurnee/ Waukegan/ Grayslake
Chicago & Vicinity Regional
Fort Wayne, IN
South Bend, IN
Grand Rapids, MI
Kalamazoo, MI
Lansing, MI
Southwest Michigan

Paper Maps

Illinois
Indiana
Michigan
Chicagoland
DuPage County
Chicago Streets
Aurora/ Naperville/ Fox River Valley
Joliet/ North Will County
North Lake County/ Chain of Lakes
South Lake County
Northwest Suburban Cook County
McHenry County
Chicago & Vicinity Regional
Fort Wayne, IN
Lafayette/ West Lafayette, IN
Michigan City/ La Porte, IN
Muncie/ Marion/ Kokomo/ Richmond, IN
Northwest Indiana
South Bend, IN
Benton Harbor/ St. Joseph, MI
Grand Rapids, MI
Kalamazoo/ Battle Creek, MI
Lansing, MI
Muskegon/ Holland, MI

Road Atlases

Road Atlas
Road Atlas & Travel Guide
Large Scale Road Atlas
Midsize Road Atlas
Deluxe Midsize Road Atlas
Pocket Road Atlas

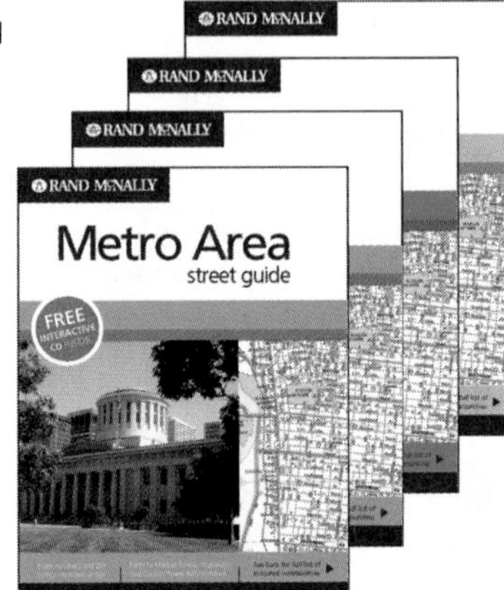

Wherever Rand McNally products are sold or at
www.randmcnally.com

Chicago Block Numbers

This page explains the block-numbering system used in the city of Chicago. This system should not be confused with the grid system that Rand McNally uses throughout the Chicago 7-County Street Guide — see page A for details

For the most part, streets in Chicago lie in a grid pattern, and the intersection of State and Madison streets is designated as the city center. Madison Street, running east and west, and State Street, running north and south, represent the base lines, or axis, from which all block and house numbers are determined.

Generally, block numbers in Chicago ascend in all directions by multiples of 100. Chicago street names and block numbers extend into some but not all neighboring suburbs. Here is a list of the major streets in Chicago along with their distance from the base line in both miles and block numbers.

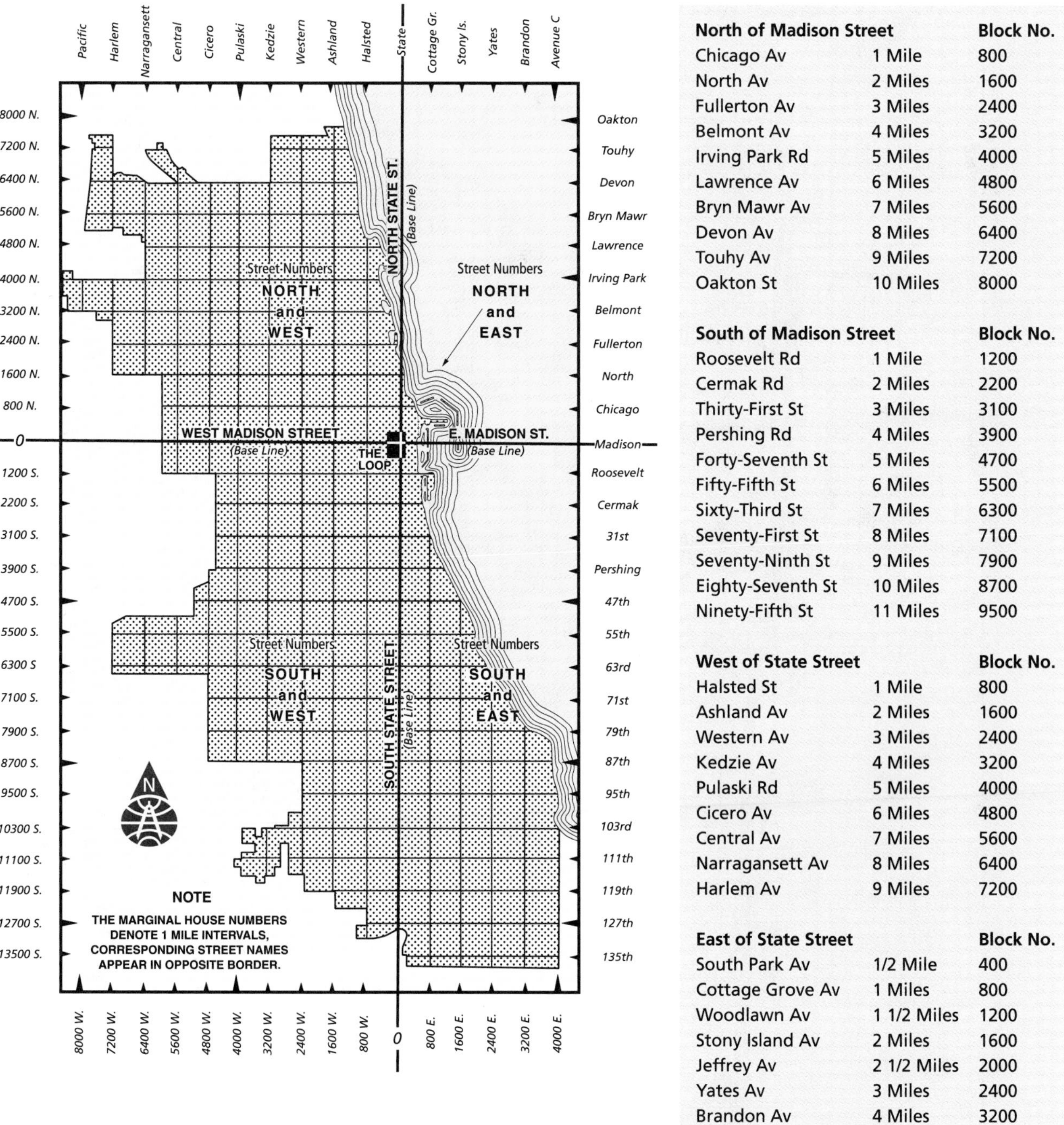

North of Madison Street		Block No.
Chicago Av	1 Mile	800
North Av	2 Miles	1600
Fullerton Av	3 Miles	2400
Belmont Av	4 Miles	3200
Irving Park Rd	5 Miles	4000
Lawrence Av	6 Miles	4800
Bryn Mawr Av	7 Miles	5600
Devon Av	8 Miles	6400
Touhy Av	9 Miles	7200
Oakton St	10 Miles	8000

South of Madison Street		Block No.
Roosevelt Rd	1 Mile	1200
Cermak Rd	2 Miles	2200
Thirty-First St	3 Miles	3100
Pershing Rd	4 Miles	3900
Forty-Seventh St	5 Miles	4700
Fifty-Fifth St	6 Miles	5500
Sixty-Third St	7 Miles	6300
Seventy-First St	8 Miles	7100
Seventy-Ninth St	9 Miles	7900
Eighty-Seventh St	10 Miles	8700
Ninety-Fifth St	11 Miles	9500

West of State Street		Block No.
Halsted St	1 Mile	800
Ashland Av	2 Miles	1600
Western Av	3 Miles	2400
Kedzie Av	4 Miles	3200
Pulaski Rd	5 Miles	4000
Cicero Av	6 Miles	4800
Central Av	7 Miles	5600
Narragansett Av	8 Miles	6400
Harlem Av	9 Miles	7200

East of State Street		Block No.
South Park Av	1/2 Mile	400
Cottage Grove Av	1 Miles	800
Woodlawn Av	1 1/2 Miles	1200
Stony Island Av	2 Miles	1600
Jeffrey Av	2 1/2 Miles	2000
Yates Av	3 Miles	2400
Brandon Av	4 Miles	3200

Downtown Chicago

1 2 3 4 5 6 7

A B C D E

Note: This grid references this map only

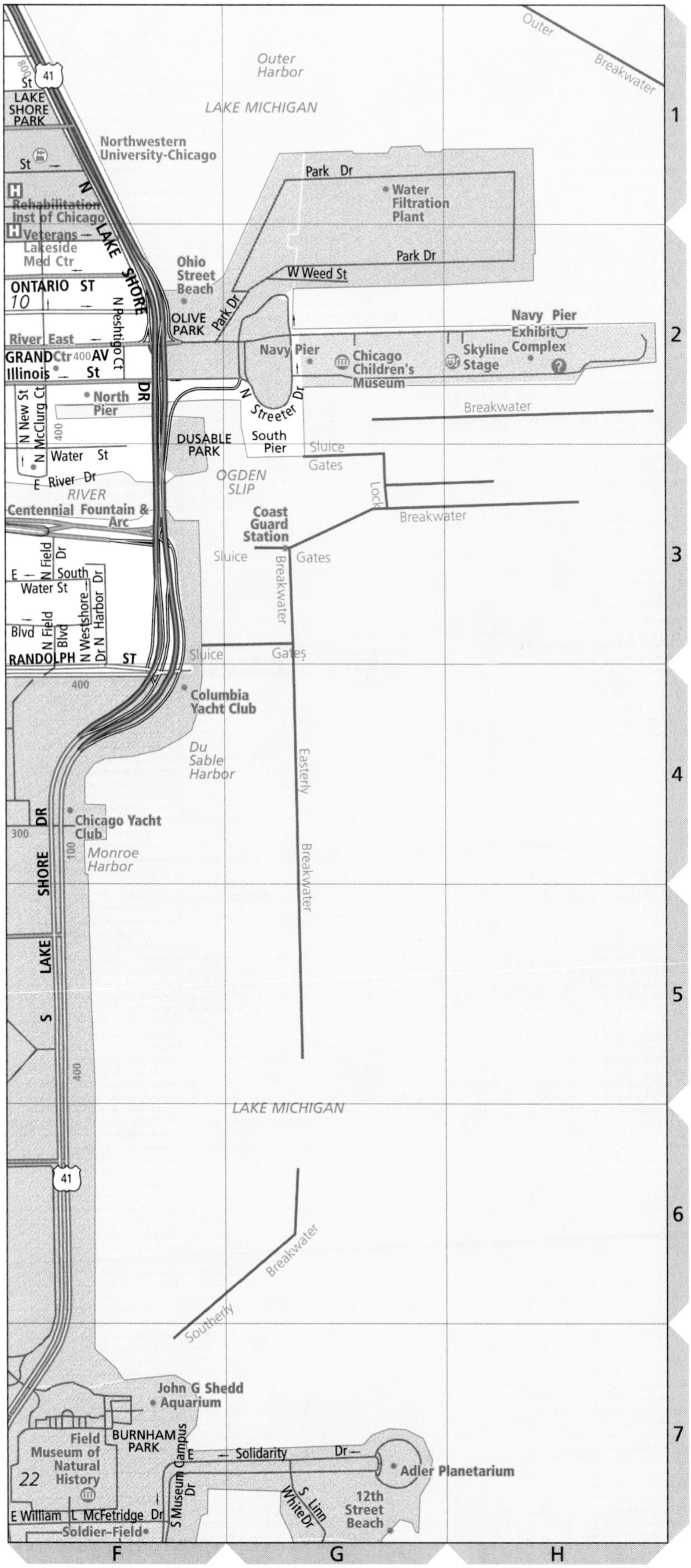

Points of Interest

Place	Grid
Adler Planetarium	G7
Aon Center	E3
AT&T Corporate Center	C4
Buckingham Memorial Fountain & Garden	E5
Burnham Park	E7
Carbide & Carbon Building	D3
Chicago Avenue Water Tower & Pumping Station	E1
Chicago Center for Performing Arts	A1
Chicago Children's Museum	G2
Chicago City Hall	D4
Chicago Mercantile Exchange	C4
Chicago Symphony Orchestra Hall	E5
Chicago Theatre	D3
Chicago Union Station	C5
City College of Chicago-Harold Washington College	D3
Civic Opera House	C4
Coast Guard Station	G3
Columbia College	E6
Cook County Building	C4
Cook County Circuit Court	D3
Cook County Circuit Court	D4
Cook County Circuit Court	D7
Cook County Circuit Court	E7
Daley Civic Center	D4
Dearborn Station	D6
Equitable Building	E3
Field Museum of Natural History	F7
Fine Arts Building	D5
First National Bank Plaza	D4
Four Seasons-Ritz Carlton Chicago	E1
Grant Park	E6
Greyhound-Chicago	B5
Harold Washington Library Center	D5
Hilton Chicago & Towers	D6
Illinois Center	E3
Illinois Supreme Court	C3
Jane Addams Hull-House Museum	A6
John G Shedd Aquarium	F7
John Hancock Center	E1
Loews-House of Blues Hotel	D3
Loyola University Chicago-Water Tower Campus	D1
Marina City	D3
Merchandise Mart	C3
Metra-Blue Line-LaSalle Station	D5
Metra-Chicago Station	C5
Metra-Millennium Station	E4
Metra-Ogilvie Transportation Center	B4
Metra-Roosevelt Road Station	E7
Metra-Van Buren Street Station	E5
Midwest Stock Exchange	C5
Navy Pier	G2
Navy Pier Exhibit Complex	H2
NBC Tower	E2
North Pier	F2
Northwestern Memorial Hospital	E1
Northwestern University-Chicago	F1
One Financial Place	D5
Petrillo Music Shell	E4
Prudential Building	E3
Roosevelt University	E5
Sears Tower	C5
Soldier Field	F7
Stone Container Building	E3
The Art Institute of Chicago	E4
The Chicago Sun-Times	D3
The Palmer House Hilton	D4
Tribune Tower	D2
United States Courthouse	D5
University of Illinois at Chicago	A6
Washington Square Park	D1
Water Tower Place	E1
Wrigley Building	D3

1 in. = 1400 ft.

0 0.25 0.5

miles

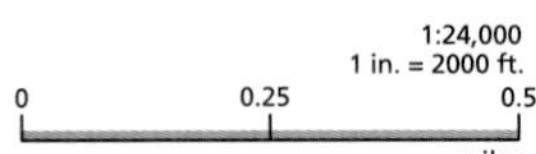

SEE B MAP

SEE B MAP

SEE 2350 MAP

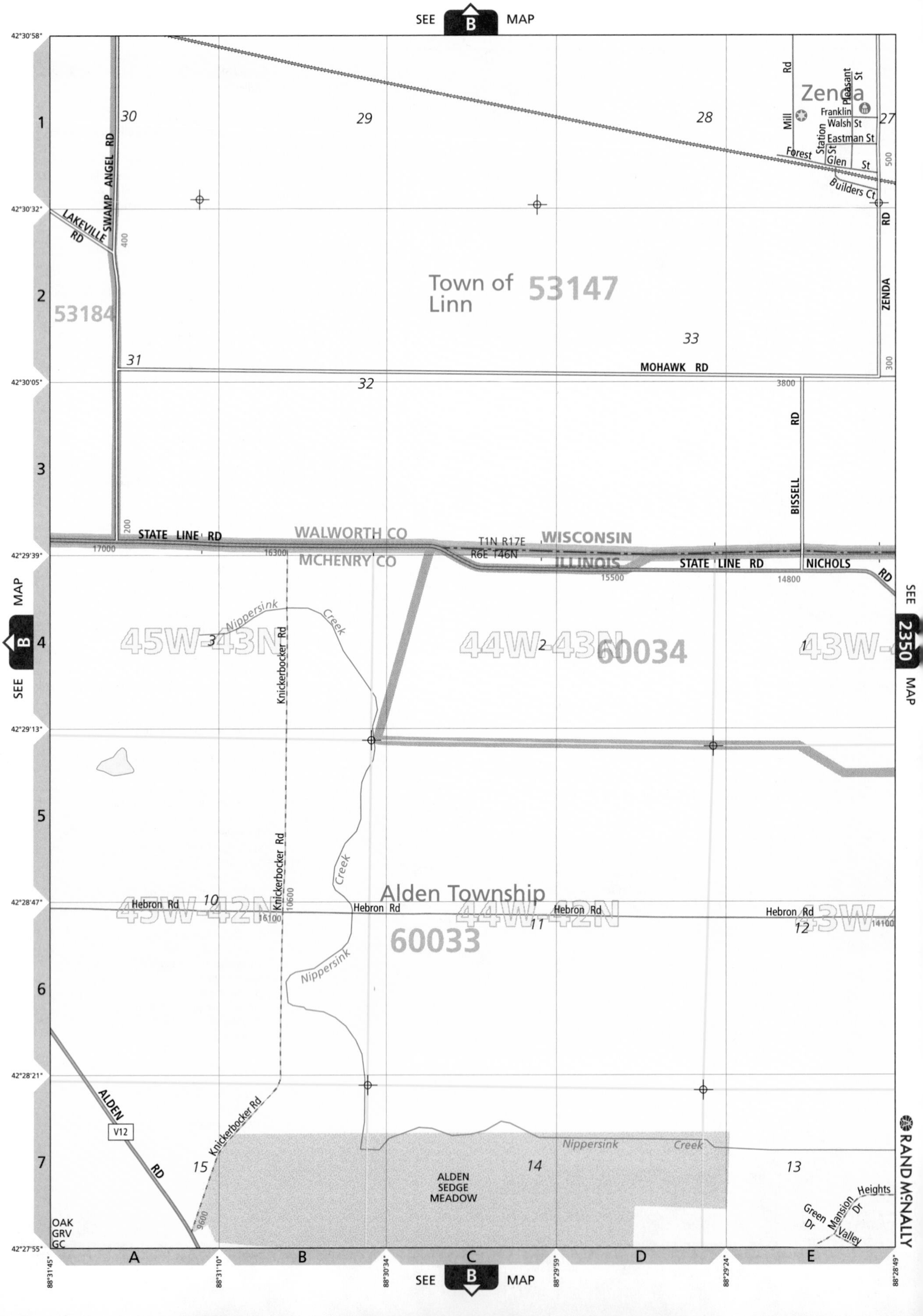

1:24,000
1 in. = 2000 ft.
0 0.25 0.5
miles

SEE B MAP

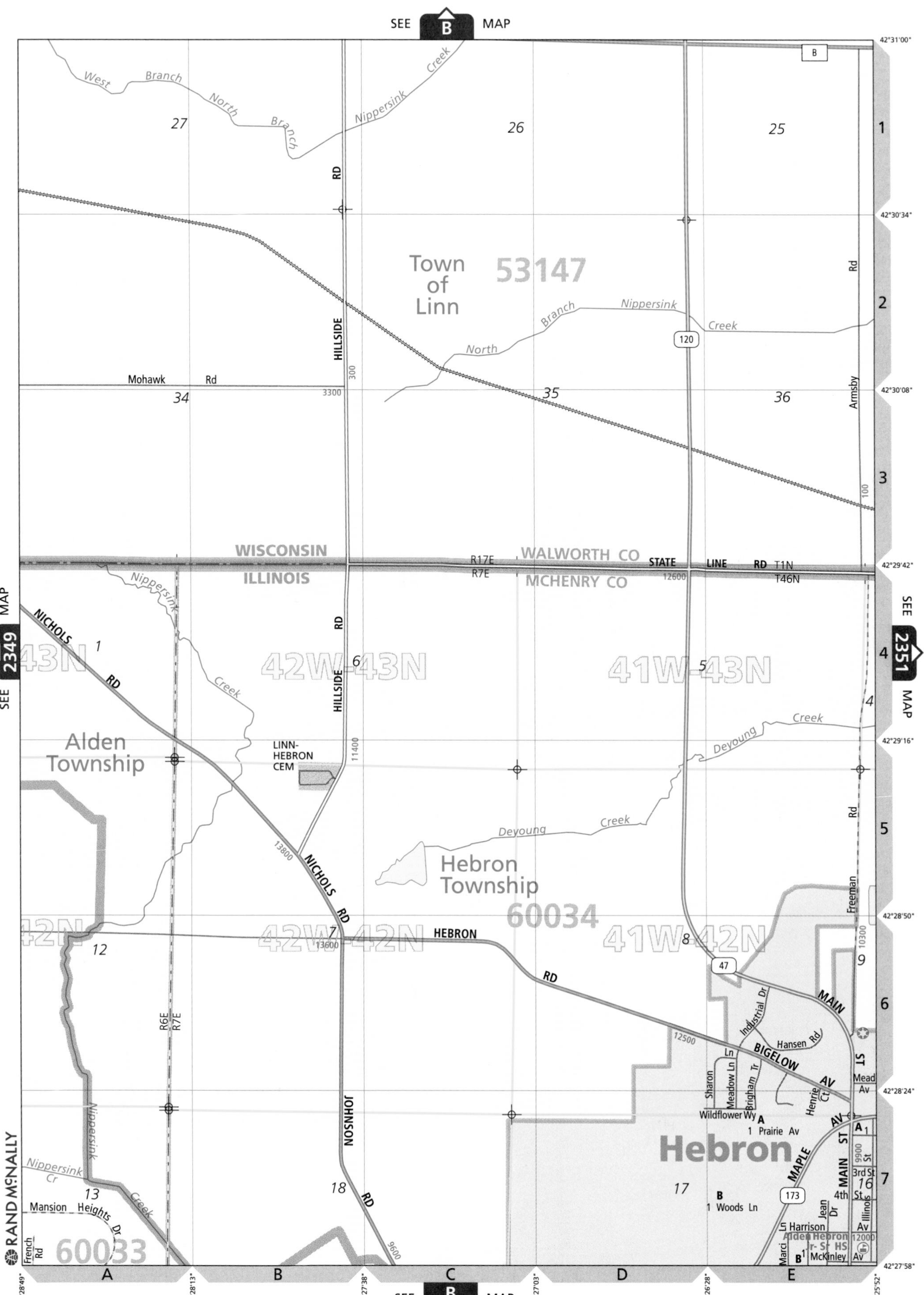

SEE MAP 2349

SEE MAP 2351

SEE B MAP

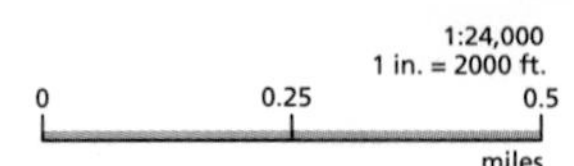

SEE B MAP

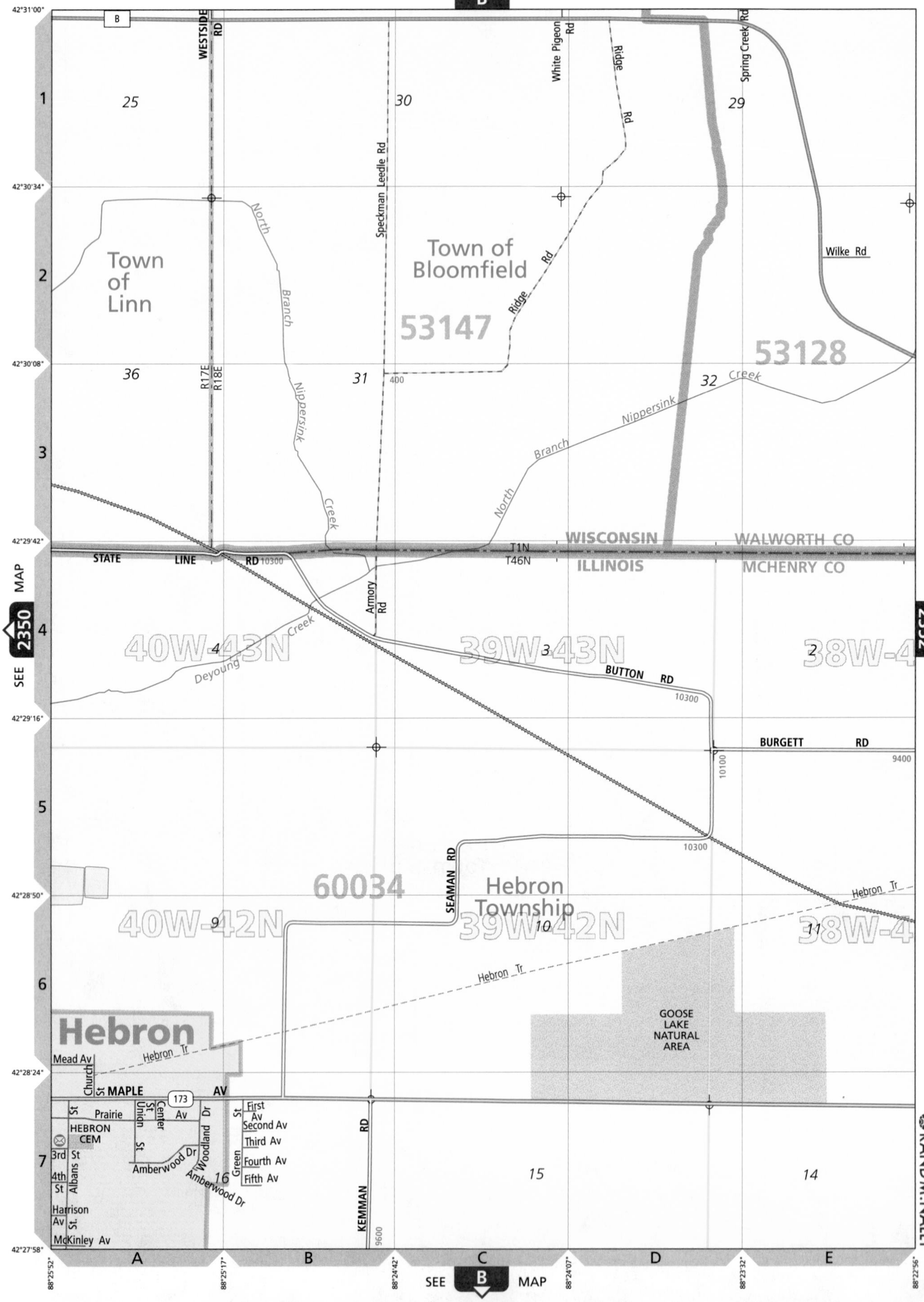

SEE 2350 MAP

SEE 2352 MAP

SEE B MAP

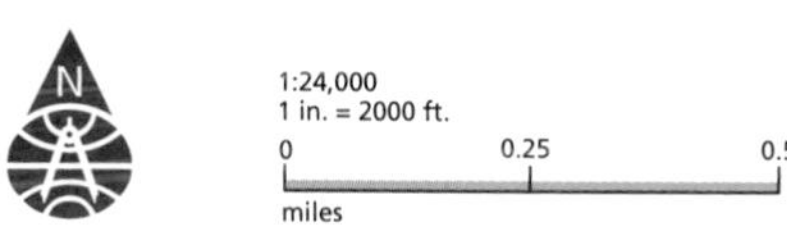

SEE B MAP

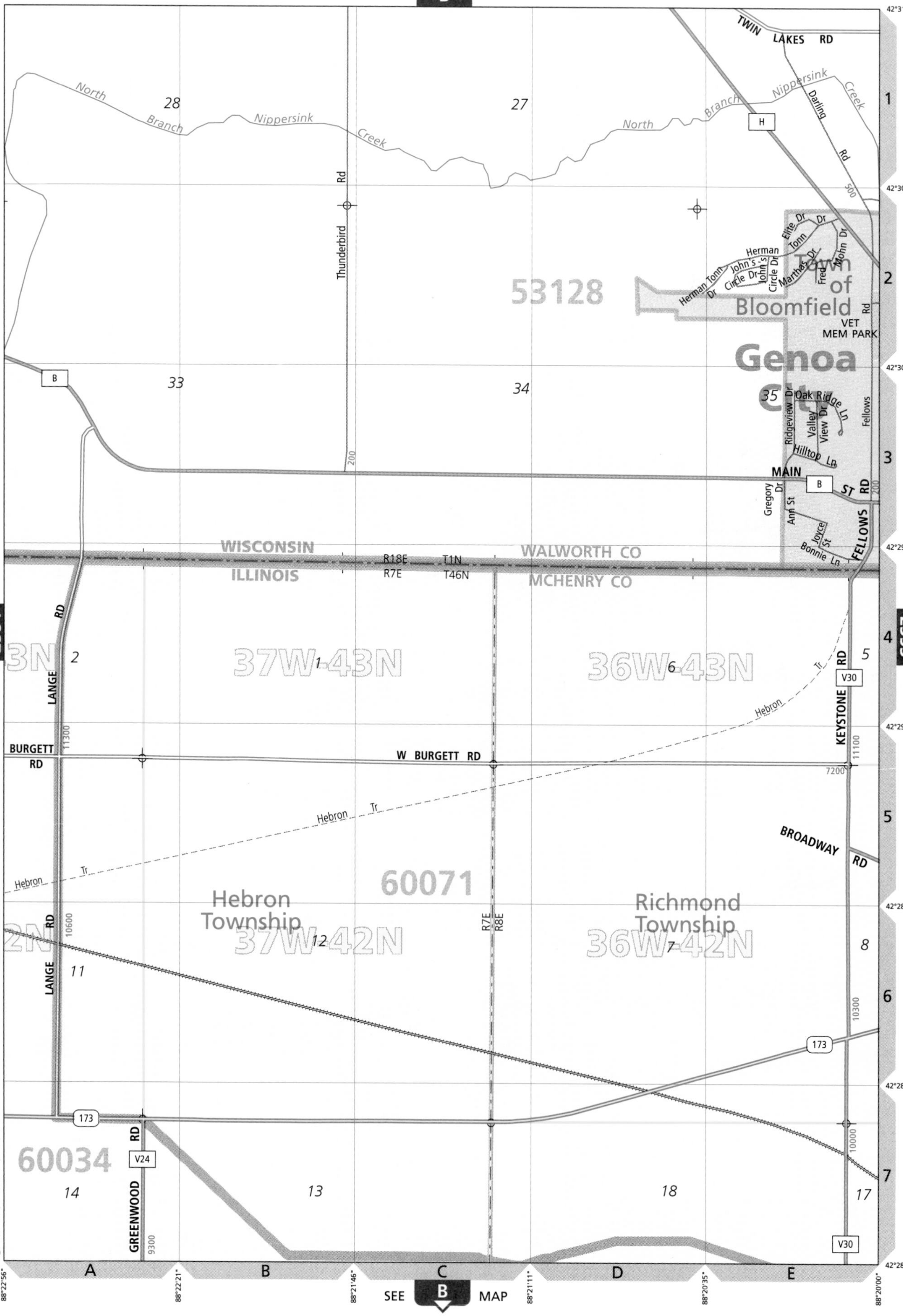

42°31'02"
TWIN LAKES RD
North Branch Nippersink Creek
28
27
Darling Rd
H
Thunderbird Rd
500
42°30'36"
53128
Town of Bloomfield
Elite Dr
Tonn Dr
Mohn Dr
Herman Tonn Dr
Herman
John's Dr
John's Circle Dr
Circle Dr
Marthas Dr
Fred Rd
VET MEM PARK
Genoa City
42°30'10"
B
33
34
35
Oak Ridge Ln
Ridgeview Dr
Valley View Dr
Fellows
Hilltop Ln
200
MAIN ST
B
RD
Gregory Dr
Ann St
Joyce St
Bonnie Ln
FELLOWS
42°29'44"
WISCONSIN
ILLINOIS
R18E
R7E
T1N
T46N
WALWORTH CO
MCHENRY CO

SEE MAP 2351

SEE MAP 2353

LANGE RD
3N
2
37W-43N
1
36W-43N
6
5
KEYSTONE RD
V30
Hebron Tr
42°29'18"
BURGETT RD
11300
W BURGETT RD
11100
7200
BROADWAY RD
60071
Hebron Township
Richmond Township
42°28'52"
2N
37W-42N
12
R7E
R8E
36W-42N
7
8
LANGE RD
10600
11
10300
173
42°28'26"
173
10000
60034
GREENWOOD RD
V24
14
13
18
17
9300
V30
42°28'00"
A
B
C
D
E
88°22'56"
88°22'21"
88°21'46"
88°21'11"
88°20'35"
88°20'00"
1
2
3
4
5
6
7

SEE B MAP

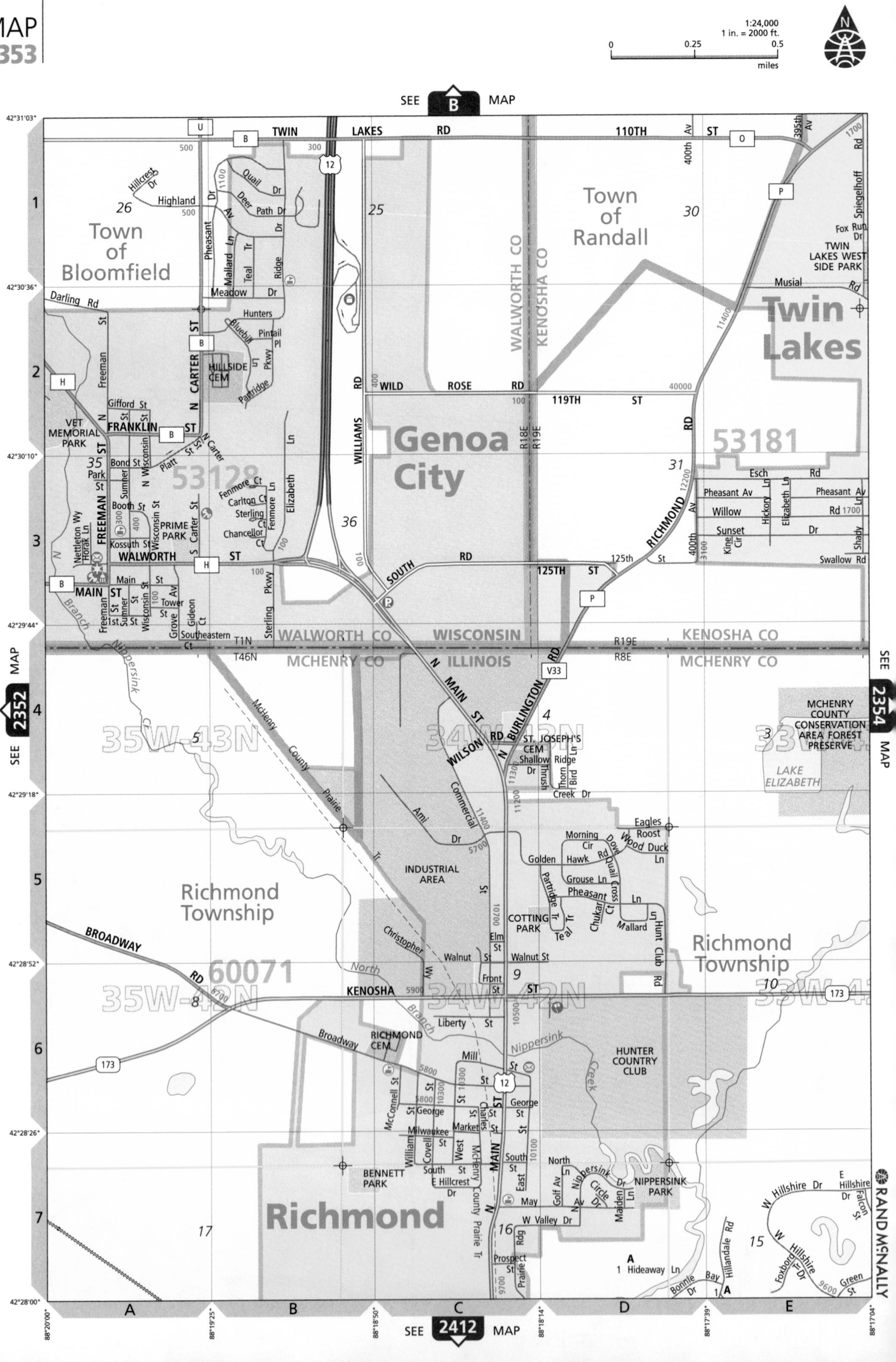

1:24,000
1 in. = 2000 ft.
0 0.25 0.5
miles

SEE B MAP

SEE 2352 MAP
SEE 2354 MAP
SEE 2412 MAP

1:24,000
1 in. = 2000 ft.
0 0.25 0.5
miles

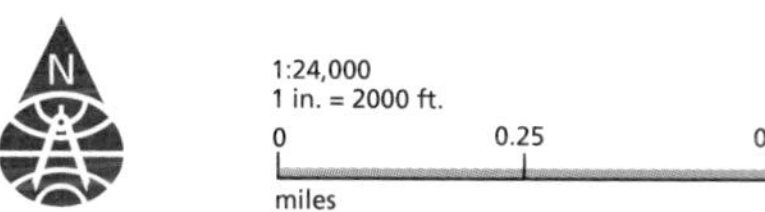

SEE B MAP
SEE 2353 MAP
SEE 2355 MAP
SEE 2413 MAP
Twin Lakes
Town of Randall
Richmond Township
Spring Grove
53181
60081
60071
WISCONSIN
ILLINOIS
KENOSHA CO
MCHENRY CO
32W-43N
31W-43N
32W-42N
31W-42N
LAKE MARY
LAKE ELIZABETH
TWIN LAKES WEST SIDE PARK
PARK
MILLENNIUM PARK
Lake Elizabeth Manor Marina
MCHENRY COUNTY CONSERVATION AREA FOREST PRESERVE
WASHINGTON CEM
SPRING DALE PARK
STATE LINE RD
E LAKESHORE DR
WILMOT RD
110TH ST
116TH ST
360TH AV
374TH AV
LAKEVIEW RD
N SOLON RD
N CLARK RD
WINN RD
ENGLISH PRAIRIE RD
Zarnstorff Rd
West Park Dr
Lower Horseshoe Dr
Spring Dr
Hawthorn Dr
Evergreen Ln
Walnut Rd
Christie Ln
Beach Rd
Lynne Dr
Grandview Ln
Cobblestone Ct
Kriwiel Dr
Blackhawk Tr
Schoors Ln
Richmond Park Dr
Howden Rd
Sunnyside Av
Grant St
Lincoln Av
Harding Av
Taft St
Overlook Dr
Sandpiper Ct
Morning Dove Ln
Partridge Ct
Cardinal Ln
Hawk Ln
Red
Musial Rd
Lucille Av
Haegele Av
Pearl Ct
Catherine Av
Porter St
Anna
Haerle
First St
Second St
Steinert Rd
Dietrich Dr
Skinner Dr
Esch Rd
Pheasant Av
Willow Rd
Sunset Dr
Swallow Rd
Lakeshore Wy
Zerfas Dr
Fox Run Dr
Timber Ridge Ct
Hawks Point Tr
Sequoia Ct
Magnolia Dr
Forest Ridge Dr
Cypress Dr
Redwood Ct
Lang Rd
Fox Bluff Ln
Falcon Ln
Steeplechase Ct
Steeplechase Ln
Ascot Ln
W Hunters Ln
Hunters Ct
Meadowdale Cir
Spring Dale Dr
Bonner
Heritage Pth
Serenity
Preservation Wy
E Hillshire Dr
Falcon
Green St
T1N
T46N
R19E
R8E
R9E
EM
Z
C
HM
CK
V37
V40
173
A
B
C
D
E
1
2
3
4
5
6
7
RAND McNALLY

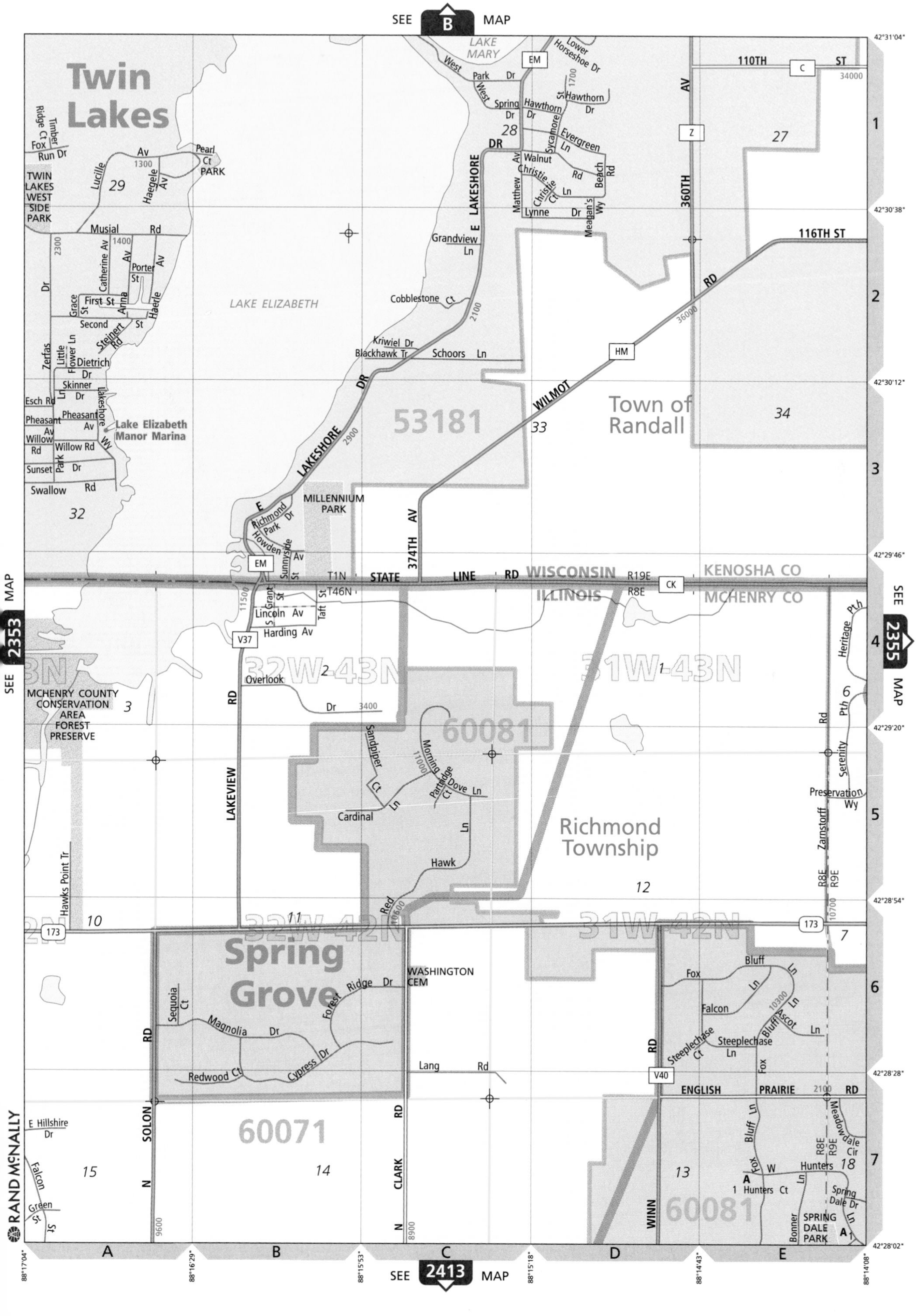

1:24,000
1 in. = 2000 ft.
0 0.25 0.5
miles

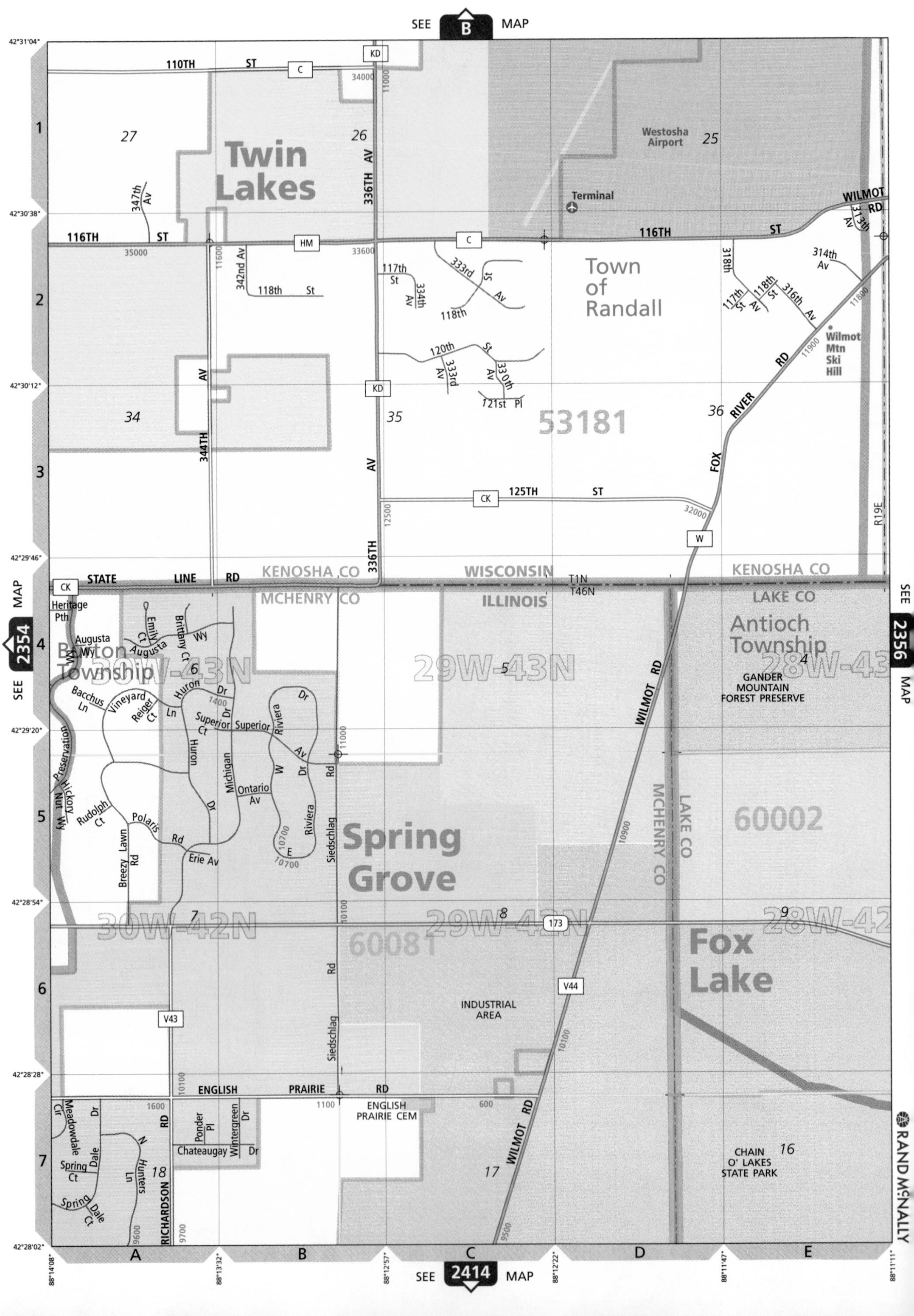

SEE B MAP

110TH ST
C
KD
34000
11000
27
26
Twin Lakes
336TH AV
347th Av
Westosha Airport
25
Terminal
WILMOT RD
313th Av
116TH ST
HM
C
116TH ST
35000
11600
33600
342nd Av
118th St
117th St
334th Av
333rd St
Av
118th
Town of Randall
318th Av
314th Av
117th St Av
118th St
316th Av
11800
Wilmot Mtn Ski Hill
11900
120th St
333rd Av
330th Av
121st Pl
KD
AV
34
35
53181
36
FOX RIVER RD
344TH
AV
CK
125TH ST
12500
32000
W
R19E
336TH
CK
STATE LINE RD
KENOSHA CO
WISCONSIN
T1N T46N
KENOSHA CO
MCHENRY CO
ILLINOIS
LAKE CO
Heritage Pth
Augusta Wy
Emily Ct
Brittany Ct
Wy
Augusta
Burton Township
30W-43N
6
29W-43N
5
Antioch Township
28W-43N
4
GANDER MOUNTAIN FOREST PRESERVE
WILMOT RD
Bacchus Ln
Vineyard
Reiger Ct
Ln
Huron Dr
1400
Dr
Superior Ct
Superior
Riviera
Dr
Av
11000
Preservation
Hickory Nut Wy
Huron
Michigan
W
Dr
Rd
Ontario Av
Dr
Riviera
E
10700
10700
Siedschlag
Rudolph Ct
Polaris Rd
Breezy Lawn Rd
Erie Av
Spring Grove
MCHENRY CO
LAKE CO
10900
60002
30W-42N
7
29W-42N
8
173
28W-42N
9
10100
60081
Fox Lake
Rd
V44
INDUSTRIAL AREA
V43
Siedschlag
10100
10100
ENGLISH PRAIRIE RD
Meadowdale Cir
Dr
1600
RD
Ponder Pl
Wintergreen Dr
1100
ENGLISH PRAIRIE CEM
600
WILMOT RD
Chateaugay Dr
Spring Dale Ct
N Hunters Ln
18
17
CHAIN O' LAKES STATE PARK
16
Spring Dale Ct
RICHARDSON
9600
9700
9500

1
2
3
4
5
6
7
A B C D E

42°31'04"
42°30'38"
42°30'12"
42°29'46"
42°29'20"
42°28'54"
42°28'28"
42°28'02"
88°14'08"
88°13'32"
88°12'57"
88°12'22"
88°11'47"
88°11'11"

SEE 2354 MAP
SEE 2356 MAP
SEE 2414 MAP

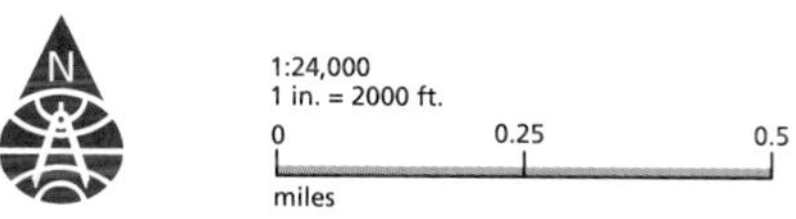

SEE B MAP

Wilmot
Town of Salem
53179
53192
53105
Kenosha Co Fairgrounds
Wilmot Speedway
Wilmot Union HS
CAMP LAKE
PEAT LAKE STATE NATURAL AREA
PEAT LAKE
KENOSHA CO
LAKE CO
WISCONSIN
ILLINOIS
T1N
T46N
27W-43N
26W-43N
GANDER MOUNTAIN FOREST PRESERVE
60002
Antioch Township
Fox Lake
27W-42N
26W-42N
CHANNEL LAKE
CHAIN O'LAKES STATE PARK
FOX RIVER
60081
Spiros East Marina
LAKE MARIE

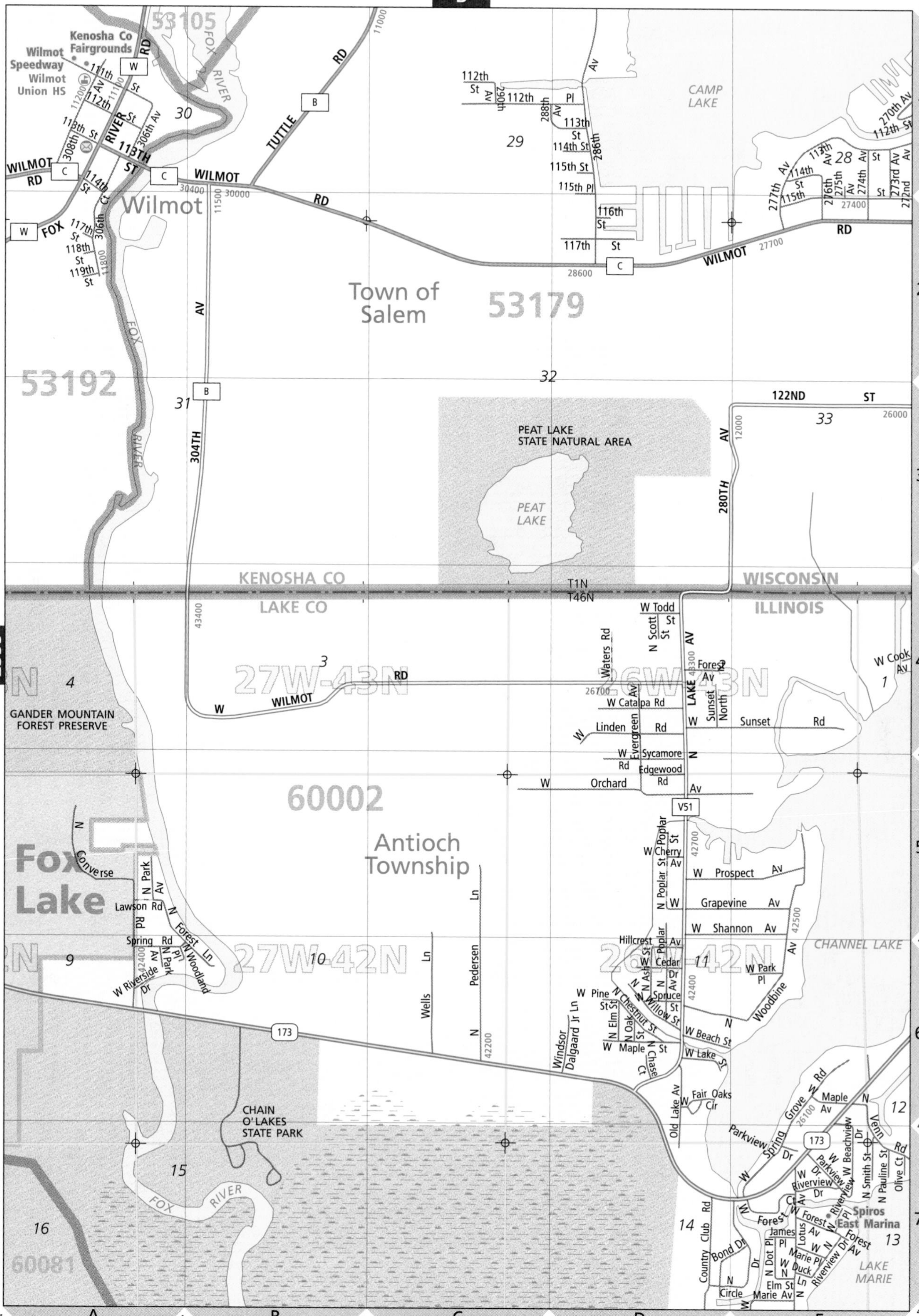

SEE 2355 MAP

SEE 2357 MAP

SEE 2415 MAP

1:24,000
1 in. = 2000 ft.
0 0.25 0.5
miles

SEE B MAP

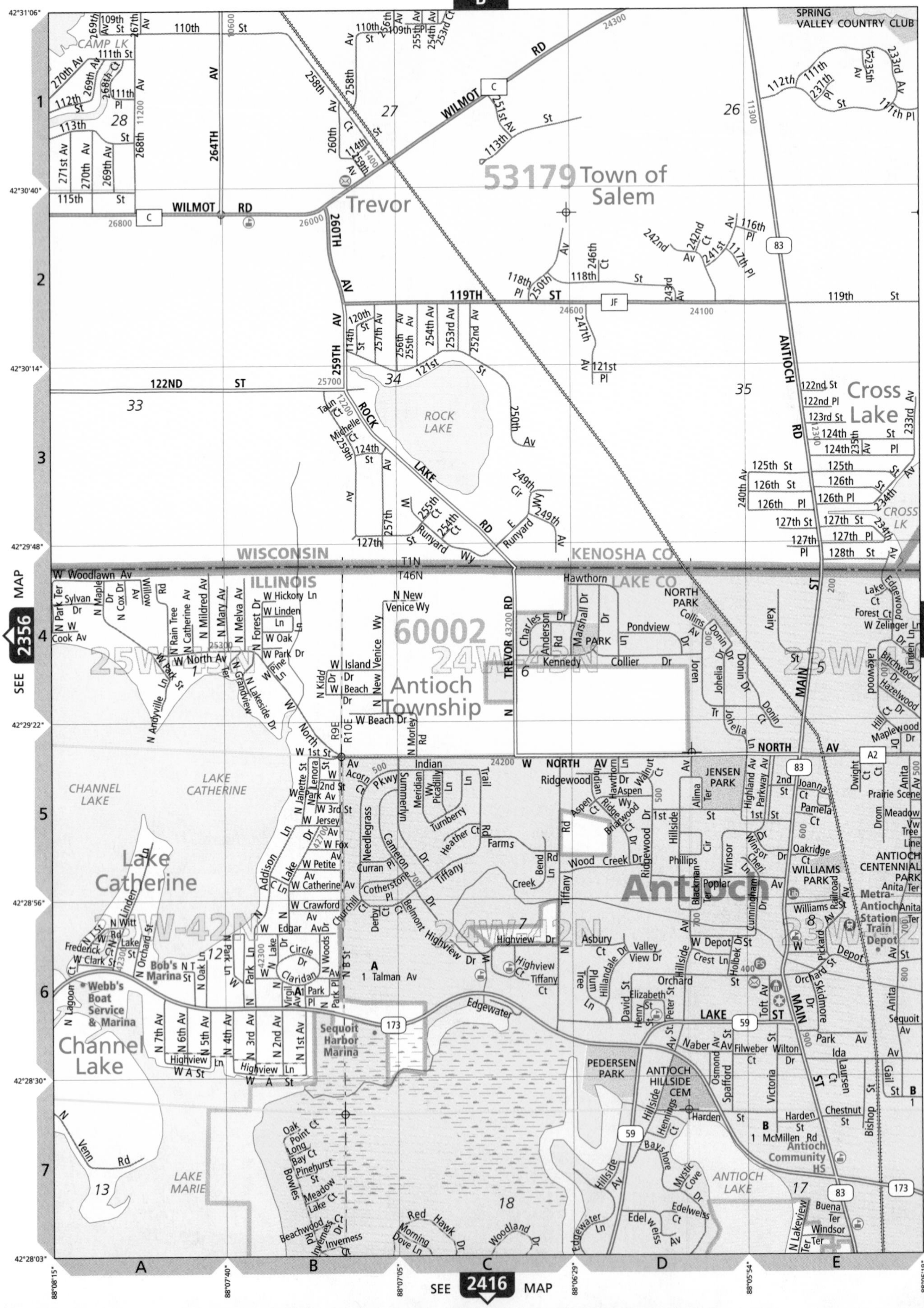

WILMOT RD
Trevor
53179 Town of Salem
119TH ST
122ND ST
ROCK LAKE
ROCK LAKE RD
ANTIOCH RD
Cross Lake
SPRING VALLEY COUNTRY CLUB
WISCONSIN
KENOSHA CO
ILLINOIS
LAKE CO
60002
Antioch Township
TREVOR RD
NORTH AV
Antioch
Lake Catherine
Channel Lake
LAKE MARIE
ANTIOCH LAKE
MAIN ST
LAKE ST
PEDERSEN PARK
JENSEN PARK
NORTH PARK
WILLIAMS PARK
ANTIOCH CENTENNIAL PARK
ANTIOCH HILLSIDE CEM
Antioch Community HS
Sequoit Harbor Marina
Bob's Marina
Webb's Boat Service & Marina
Metra-Antioch Station Train Depot

SEE 2356 MAP
SEE 2358 MAP
SEE 2416 MAP

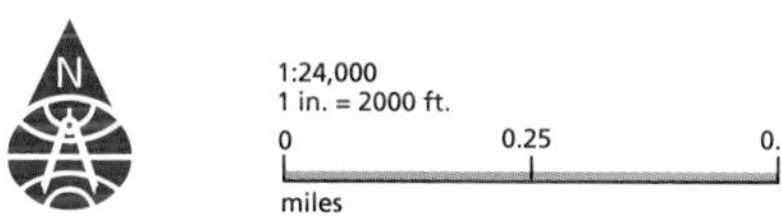

SEE B MAP

Town of Salem

Town of Bristol

53179

53104

Voltz Lake

VOLTZ LAKE

LAKE SHANGRI LA

BENET LAKE

Lake Shangrila

Benet Lake

CROSS LAKE

SPRING VALLEY CC

116TH ST

WISCONSIN

ILLINOIS

KENOSHA CO

LAKE CO

T1N

T46N

128TH ST

22W-43N

21W-43N

22W-42N

21W-42N

Antioch Township

Antioch

60002

MCGREAL LK

RED WING SLOUGH

SILVER LAKE

ANTIOCH CENTENNIAL PARK

SPRENGER PARK

N DEEP LAKE RD

NELSON RD

224TH AV

208TH AV

210TH AV

124TH ST

W NORTH AV

NORTH AV

A

1 Hazelwood Dr

2 Prairie Scene

3 Meadow Vw

B

1 Sequoit Av

2 Ida Av

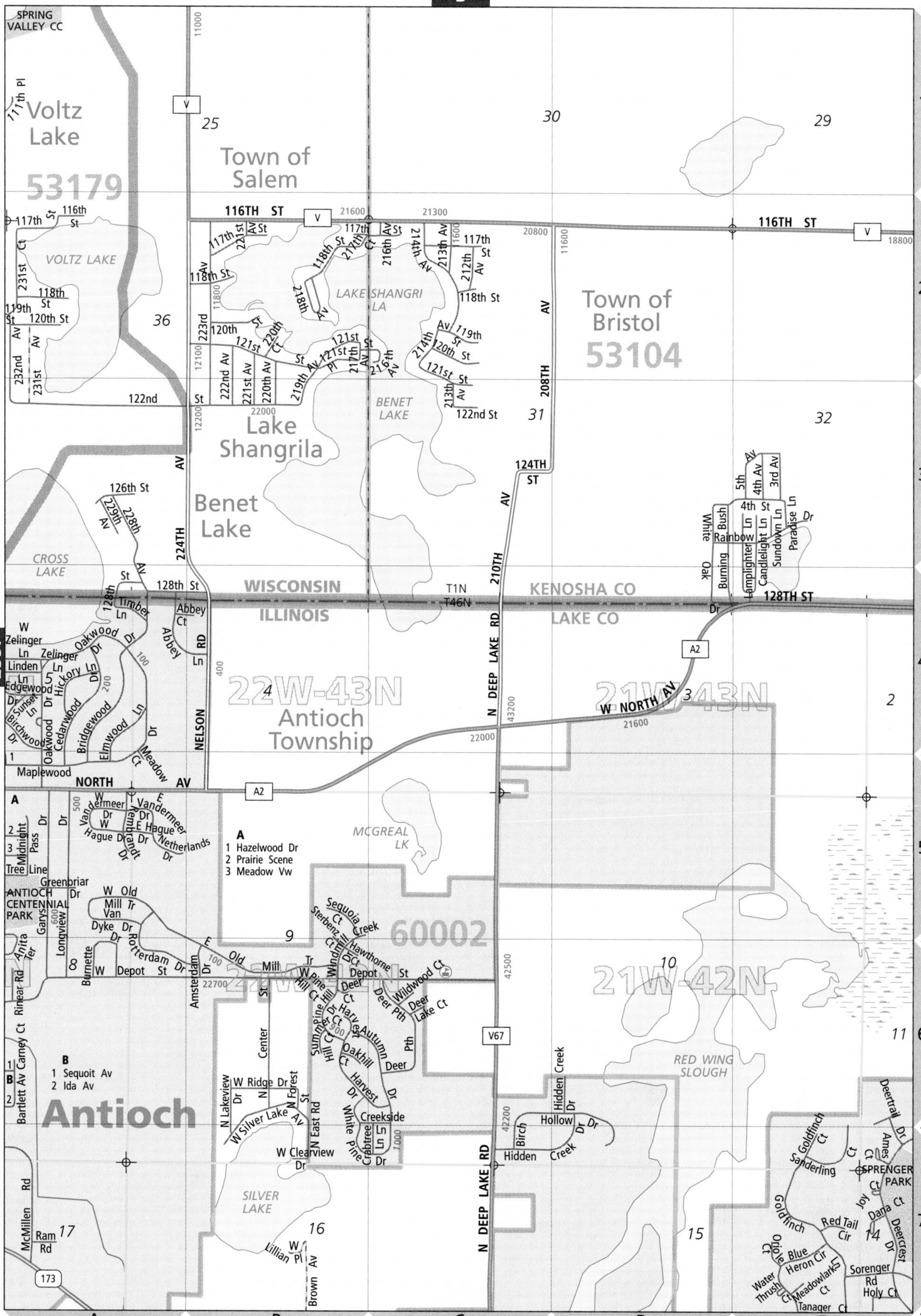

SEE 2357 MAP

SEE 2359 MAP

SEE 2417 MAP

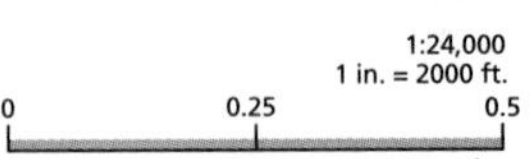

SEE B MAP

42°31'07"
42°30'41"
42°30'15"
42°29'49"
42°29'23"
42°28'57"
42°28'31"
42°28'05"

1
2
3
4
5
6
7

WINFIELD RD
Q
16800
BRISTOL RD
29
28
27
53104
Dutch Gap Canal
V
116TH ST
11500
HORTON RD
15200
119th St
183rd Av
182nd Av
187th Av
11900
CJ
Town of Bristol
53142
120th St
12000
185th Av
121st St
12100
122nd St
32
33
34
MUD LAKE
BRISTOL RD
Pikeville
A2
128TH ST
T1N
T46N
W STATE LINE RD
WISCONSIN
ILLINOIS
KENOSHA CO
LAKE CO
WG
18500
PINE DUNES FOR PRES
20W-43N
2
19W-43N
1
6
18W-4
N CRAWFORD RD
Mill Creek
Brighton Farm Rd
Antioch Township
12
60002
DEER LAKE
HICKORY UNION CEM
Newport Township
7
20W-42N
11
19W-42N
W EDWARDS RD
18W-4
18500
45
R10E
R11E
Antioch
Kevington Dr
Kimberly Ln
Christine Dr
Neuhaven Dr
Dr
Scott Ln
MacKenzie Ct
Devon
Deercrest
MARY'S PARK
Bradford
Ashlyn Ln
Sandy Dr
Moore Dr
SPRENGER PARK
Natalie Ct
Ln Ct
Mark Ct
Park View Dr
Anthony Ct
Jerome Ct
Jerome Ct
Brian Ct
1
3
2
A
Kathleen Dr

A
1 Sorenger Rd
2 Brian Ct W
3 Walker Dr

N Tammi Ter
S
Pedersen Dr
W Pedersen Dr S
14
13
18
N CRAWFORD RD
W Woodmere Ter
Burr Hollow Dr
41700

A
B
C
D
E

88°02'23"
88°01'47"
88°01'12"
88°00'37"
88°00'02"
87°59'26"

SEE 2358 MAP

SEE 2360 MAP

SEE 2418 MAP

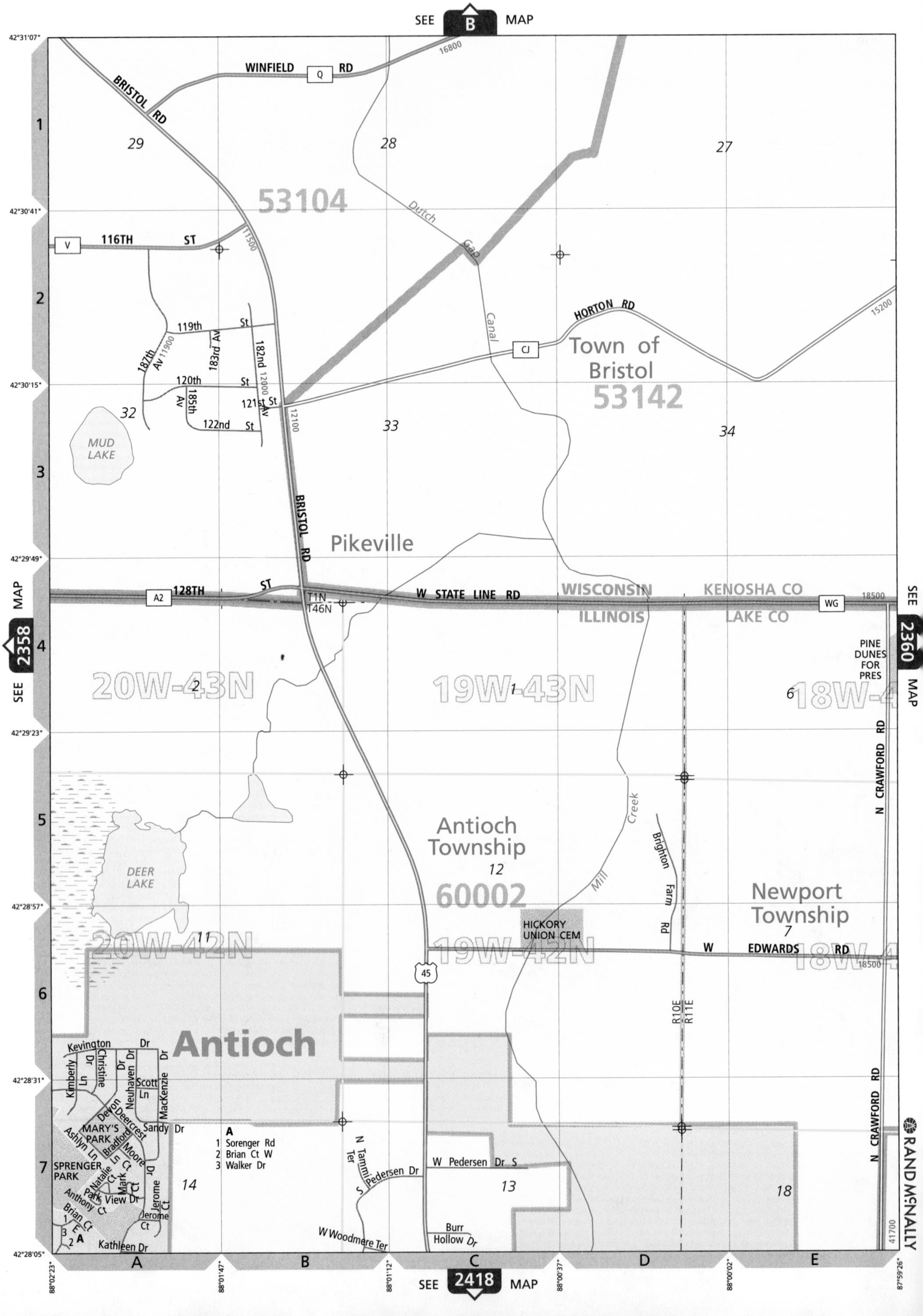

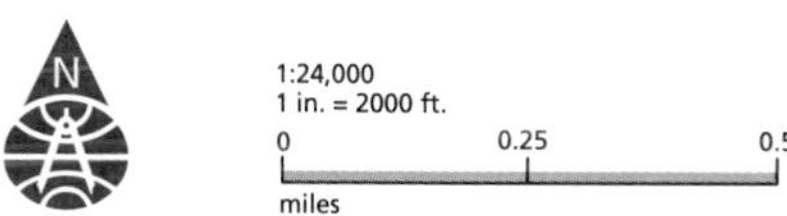

SEE B MAP
SEE 2359 MAP
SEE 2361 MAP
SEE 2419 MAP

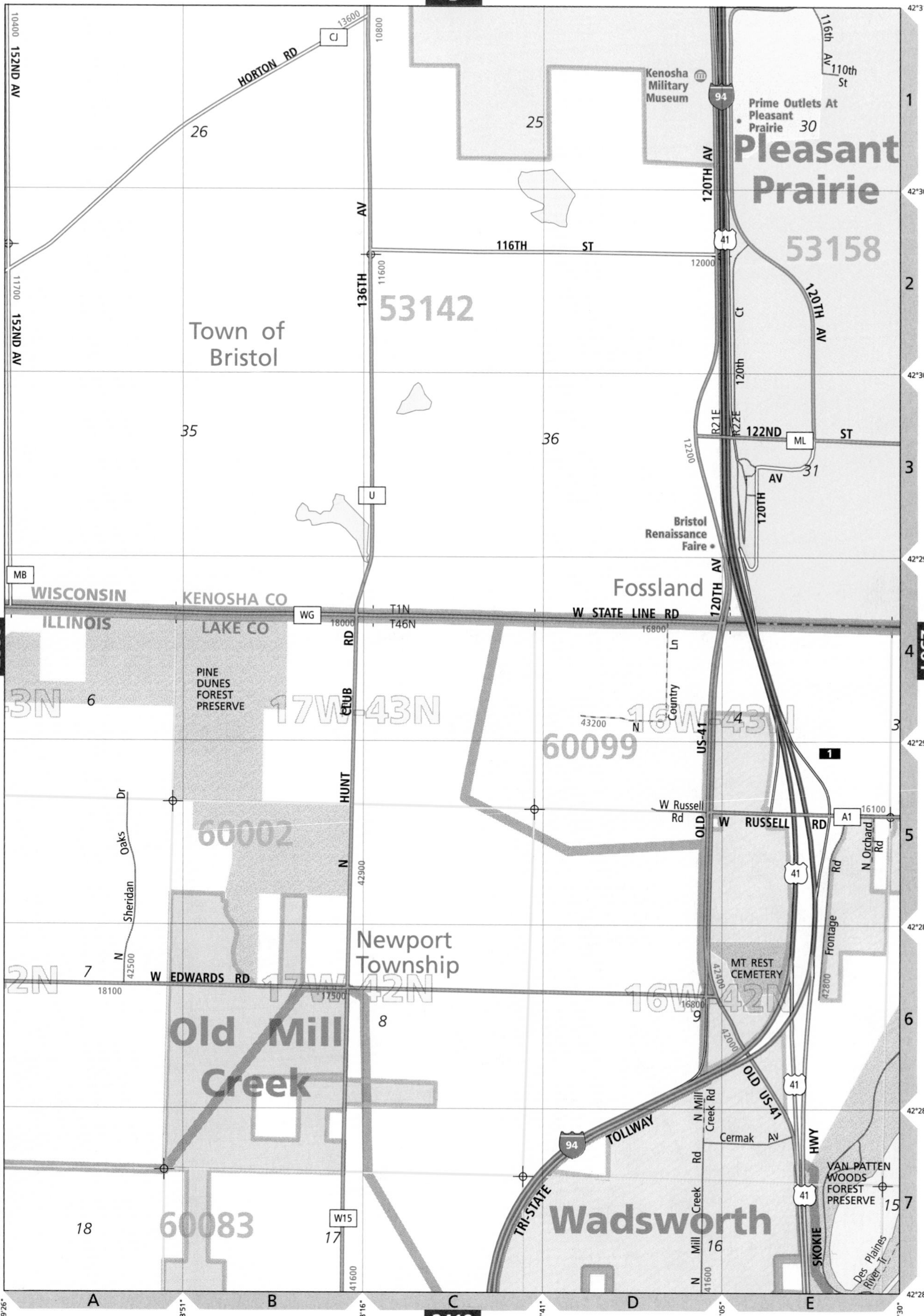

Town of Bristol
Pleasant Prairie
Fossland
Newport Township
Old Mill Creek
Wadsworth

Kenosha Military Museum
Prime Outlets At Pleasant Prairie
Bristol Renaissance Faire
PINE DUNES FOREST PRESERVE
MT REST CEMETERY
VAN PATTEN WOODS FOREST PRESERVE

WISCONSIN
ILLINOIS
KENOSHA CO
LAKE CO

152ND AV
HORTON RD
136TH AV
116TH ST
120TH AV
122ND ST
W STATE LINE RD
N HUNT CLUB RD
W RUSSELL RD
OLD US-41
W EDWARDS RD
TRI-STATE TOLLWAY
SKOKIE HWY
N Mill Creek Rd
Cermak Av
N Sheridan Oaks Dr
Country Ln
Frontage Rd
N Orchard Rd
116th Av
110th St
Des Plaines River Tr

53142
53158
60099
60002
60083

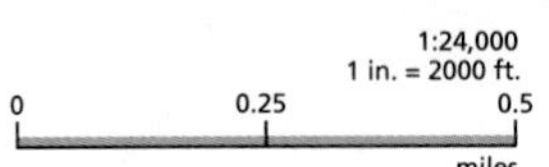

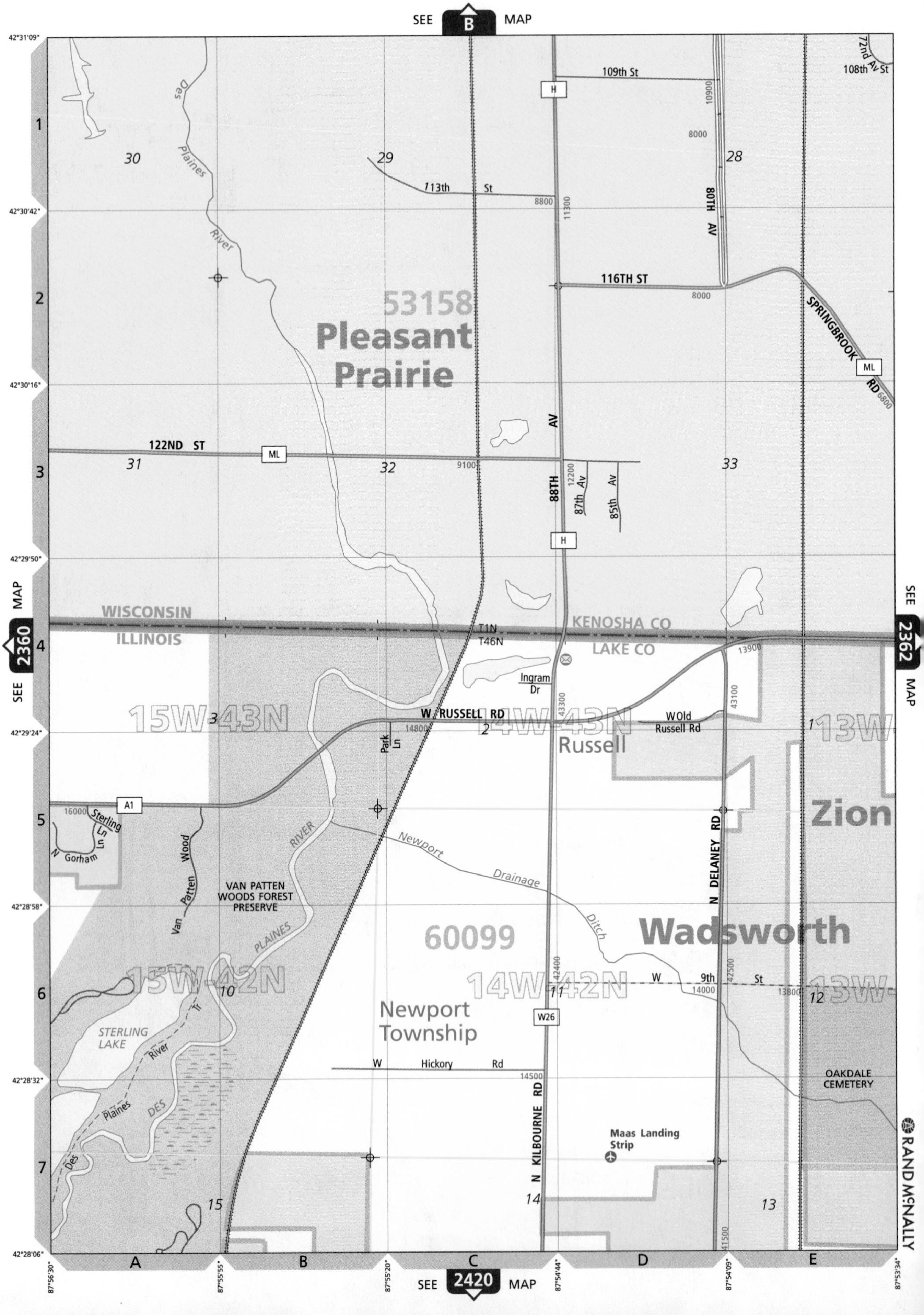

SEE B MAP

SEE 2360 MAP
SEE 2362 MAP
SEE 2420 MAP

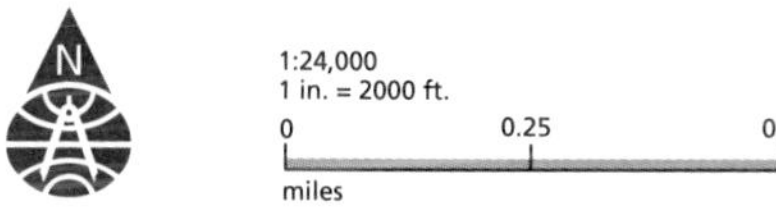

SEE B MAP

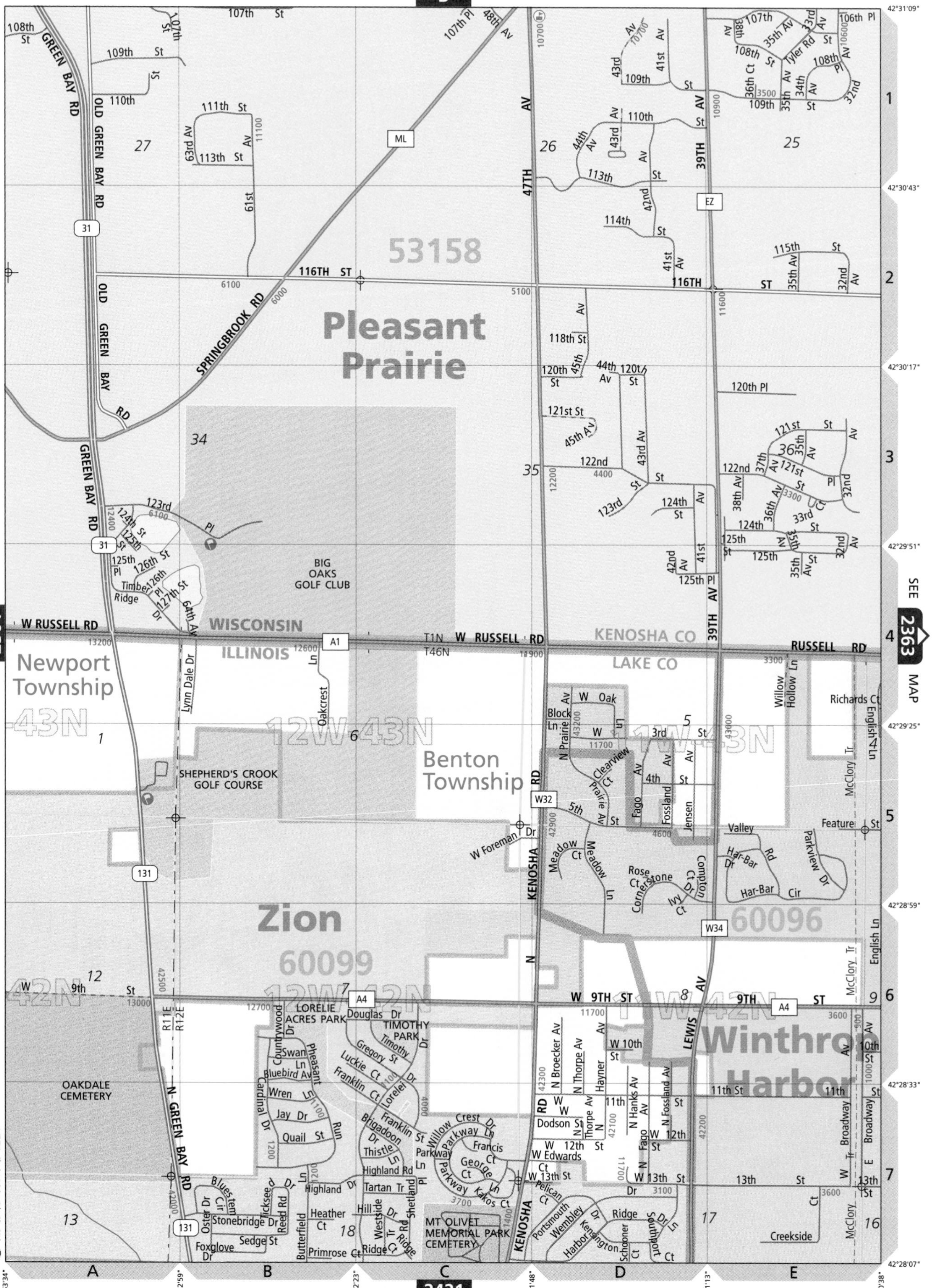

SEE 2361 MAP

SEE 2363 MAP

Pleasant Prairie

53158

WISCONSIN

ILLINOIS

KENOSHA CO

LAKE CO

Newport Township

Benton Township

Zion

60099

60096

Winthrop Harbor

BIG OAKS GOLF CLUB

SHEPHERD'S CROOK GOLF COURSE

OAKDALE CEMETERY

MT OLIVET MEMORIAL PARK CEMETERY

LORELIE ACRES PARK

TIMOTHY PARK

W RUSSELL RD

116TH ST

SPRINGBROOK RD

GREEN BAY RD

OLD GREEN BAY RD

47TH AV

39TH AV

LEWIS AV

KENOSHA RD

W 9TH ST

N GREEN BAY RD

T1N

T46N

12W 43N

11W 43N

12W 42N

11W 42N

R11E

R12E

1 2 3 4 5 6 7

A B C D E

SEE 2421 MAP

1:24,000
1 in. = 2000 ft.
0 0.25 0.5
miles

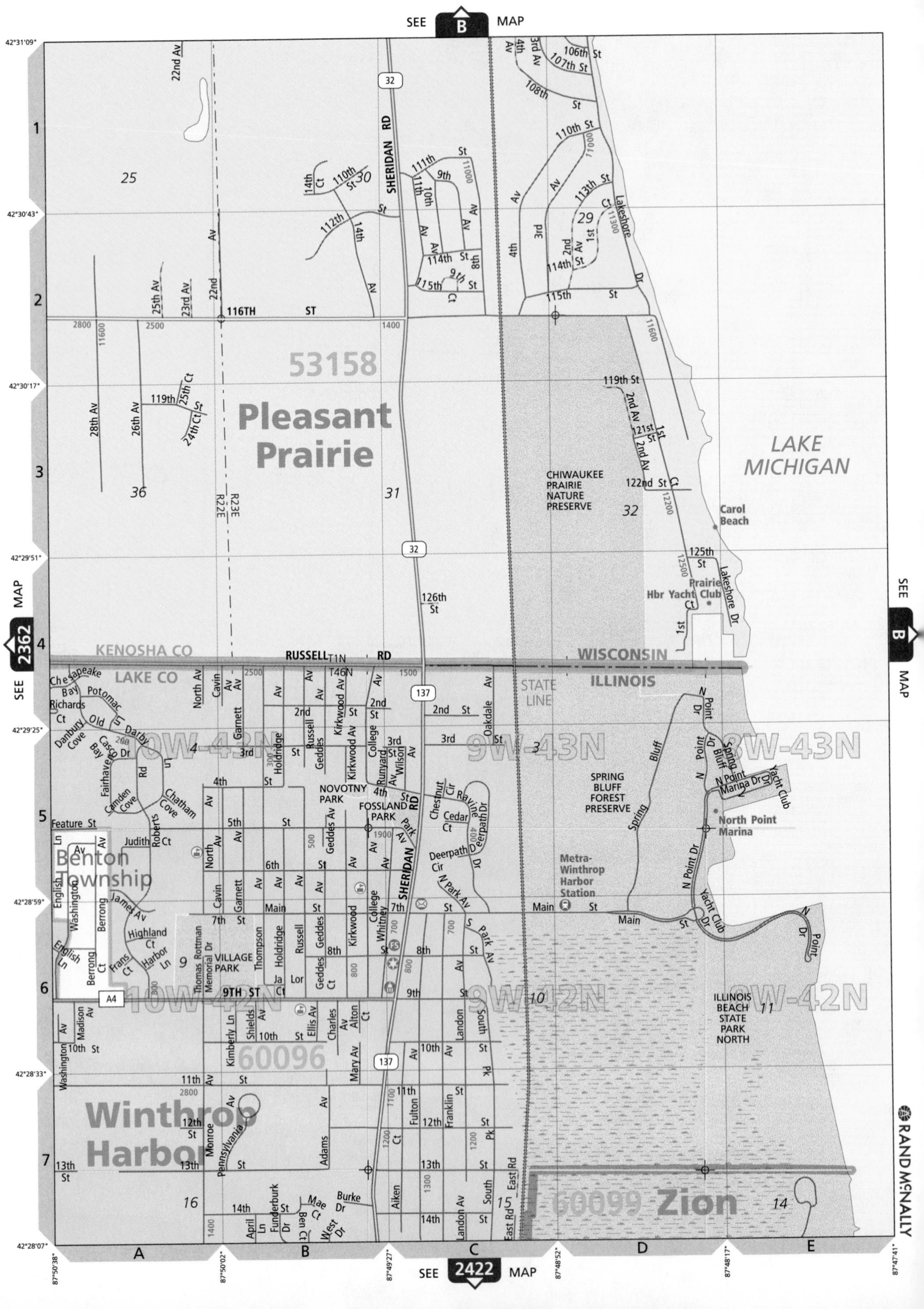

SEE B MAP

SEE 2362 MAP

SEE B MAP

A B C D E

1 2 3 4 5 6 7

SEE 2422 MAP

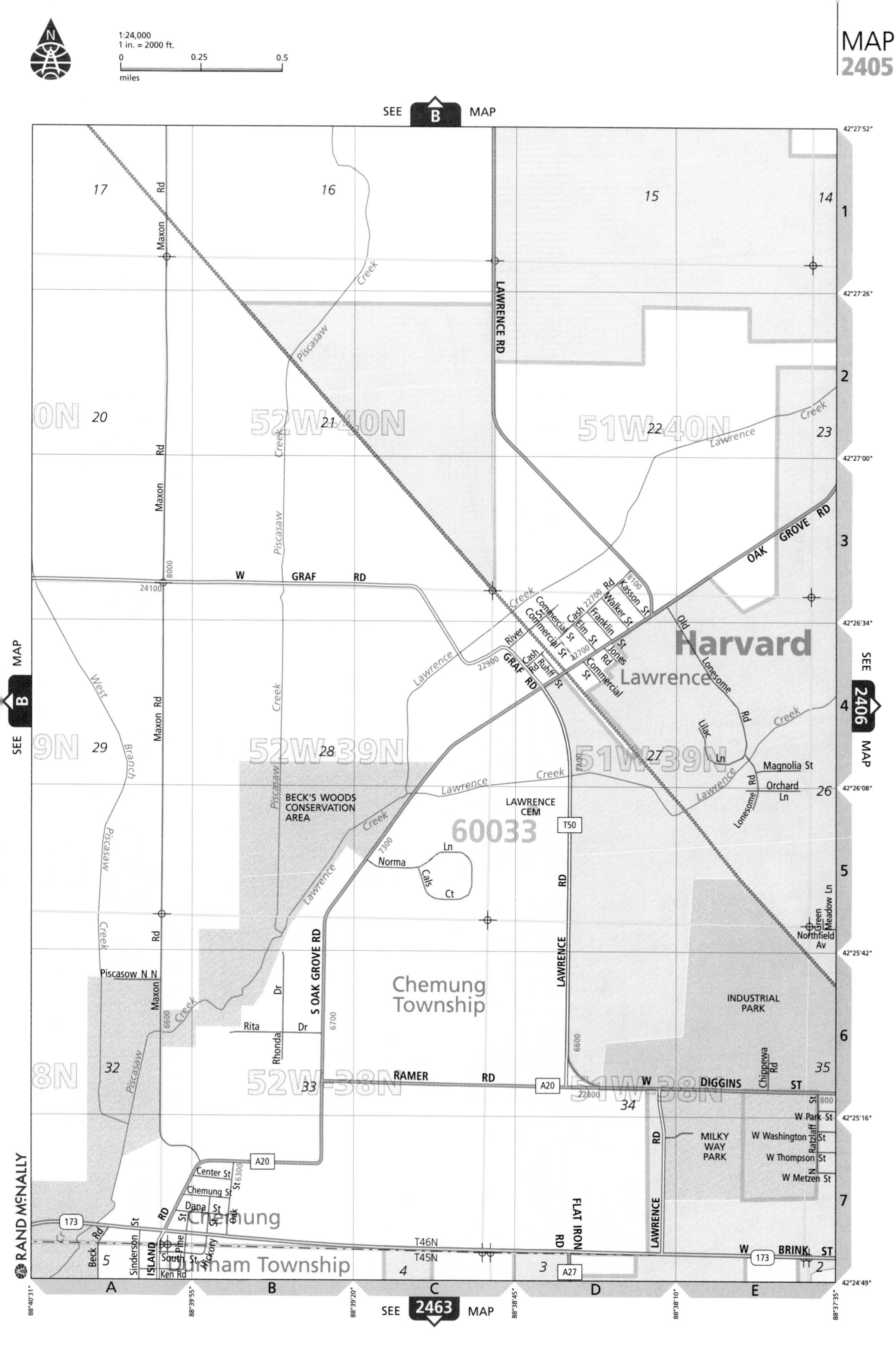

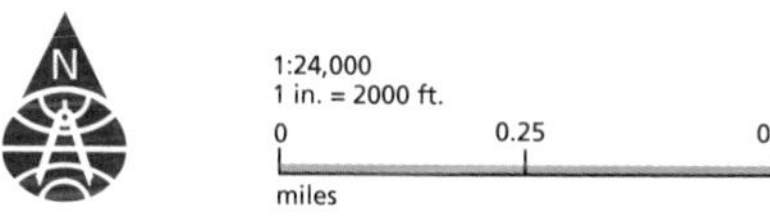

SEE B MAP

SEE B MAP

SEE 2406 MAP

SEE 2463 MAP

1:24,000
1 in. = 2000 ft.
0 0.25 0.5
miles

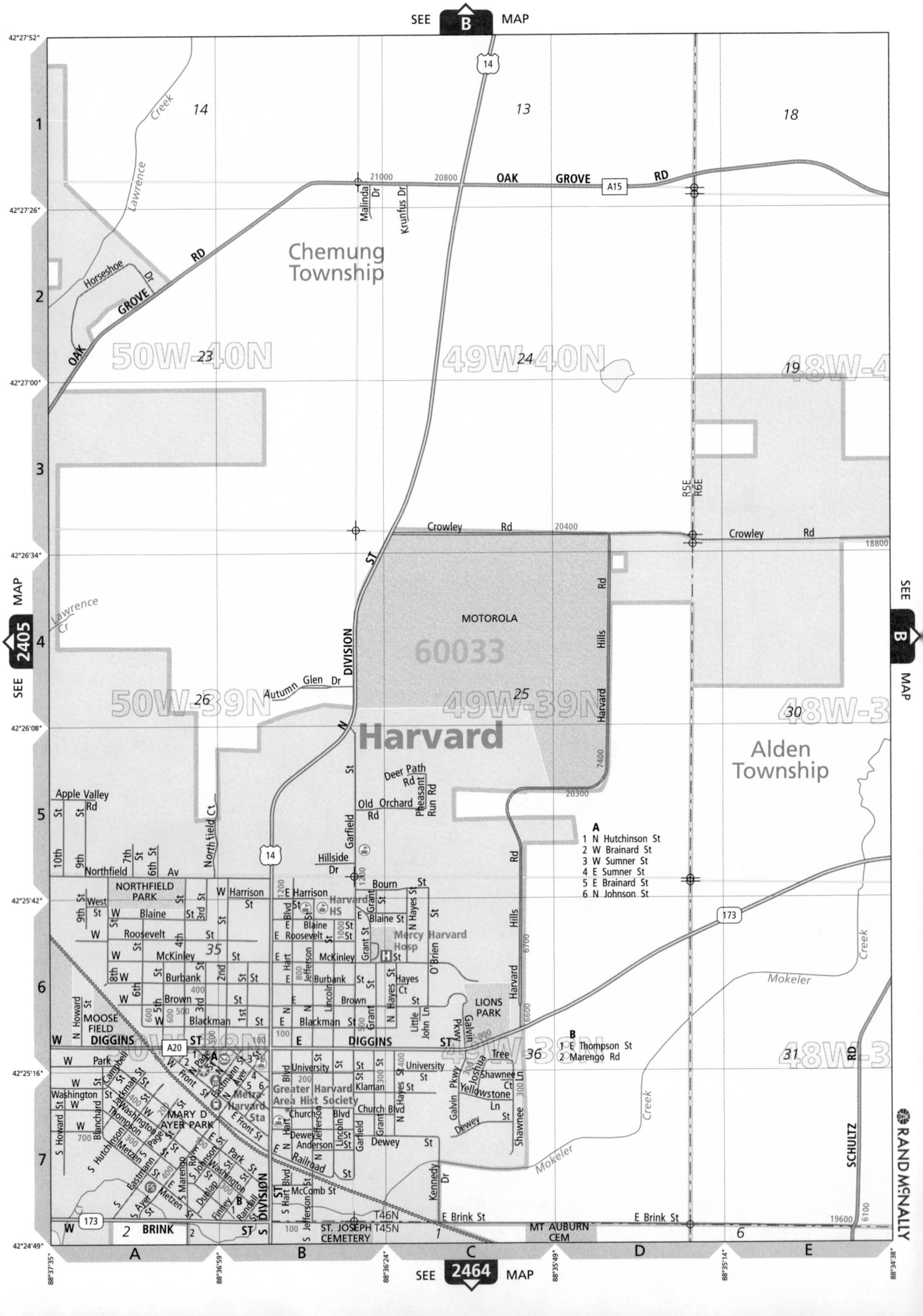

SEE B MAP

Chemung Township

Harvard

Alden Township

MOTOROLA

60033

A
1 N Hutchinson St
2 W Brainard St
3 W Sumner St
4 E Sumner St
5 E Brainard St
6 N Johnson St

B
1 E Thompson St
2 Marengo Rd

SEE 2405 MAP

SEE B MAP

SEE 2464 MAP

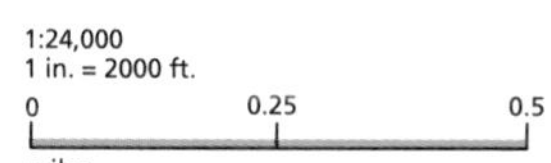

SEE 2353 MAP

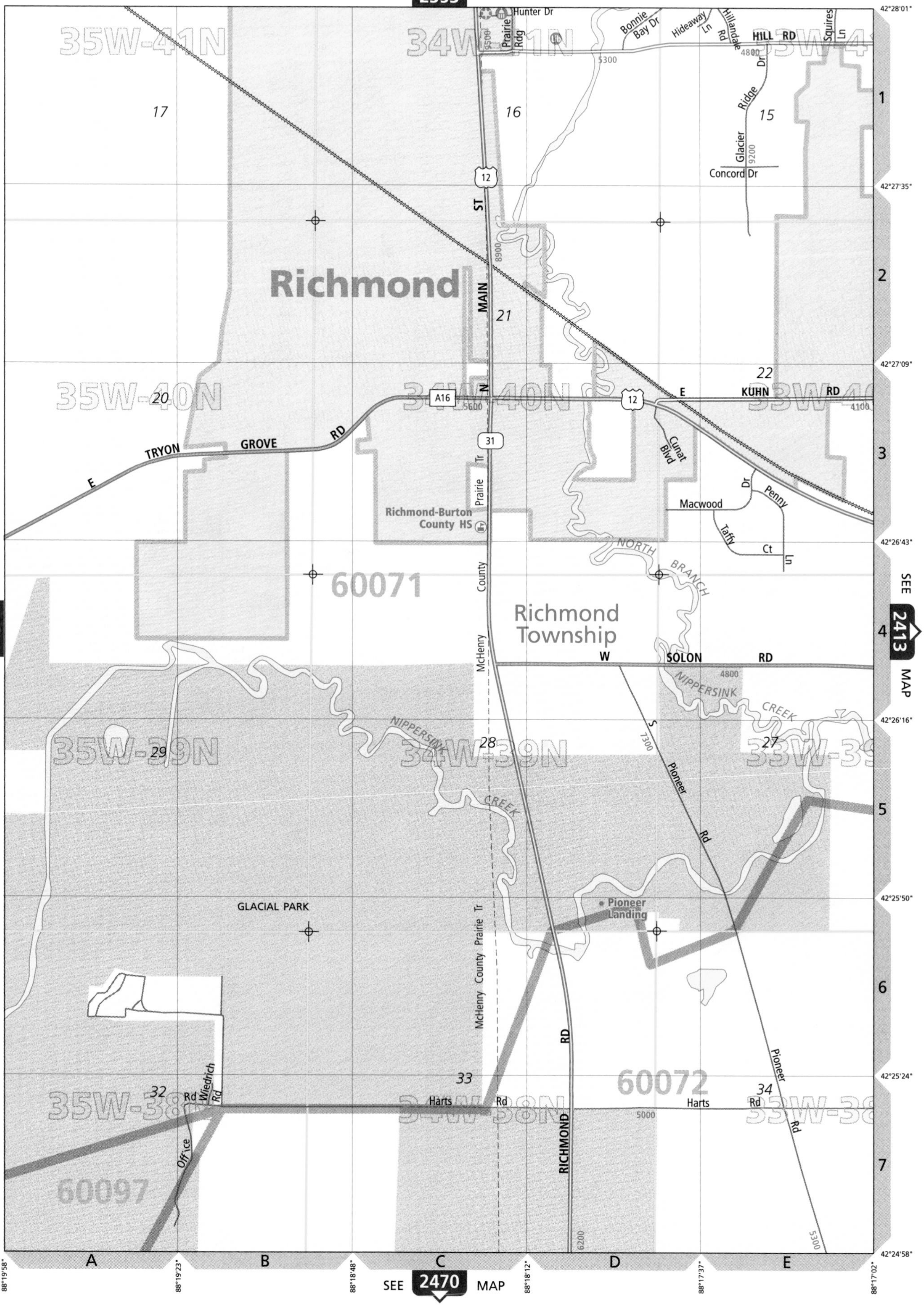

SEE B MAP

SEE 2413 MAP

SEE 2470 MAP

1:24,000
1 in. = 2000 ft.
0 0.25 0.5
miles

SEE 2354 MAP

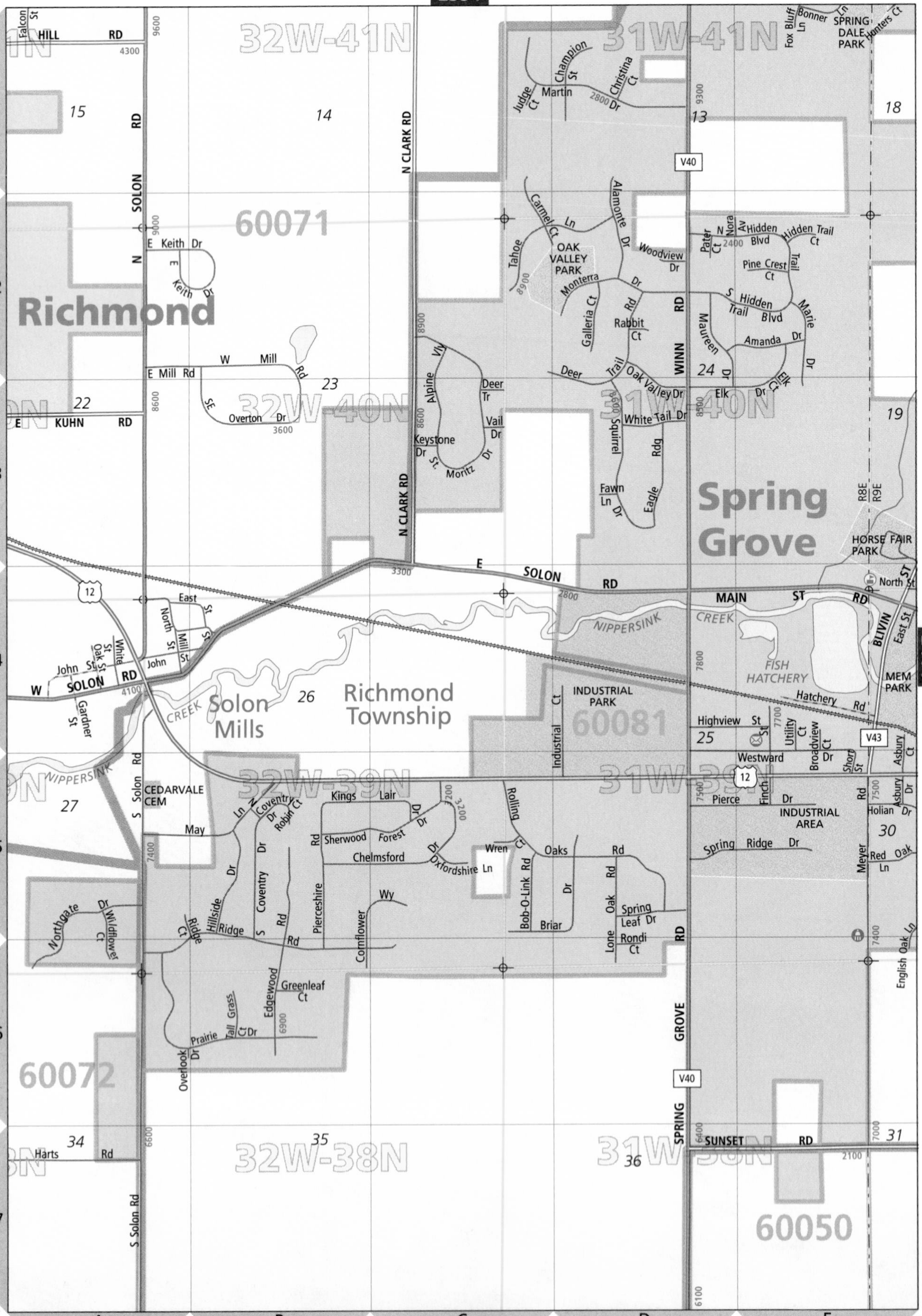

SEE 2412 MAP
SEE 2414 MAP
SEE 2471 MAP

1:24,000
1 in. = 2000 ft.
0 0.25 0.5
miles

SEE 2355 MAP

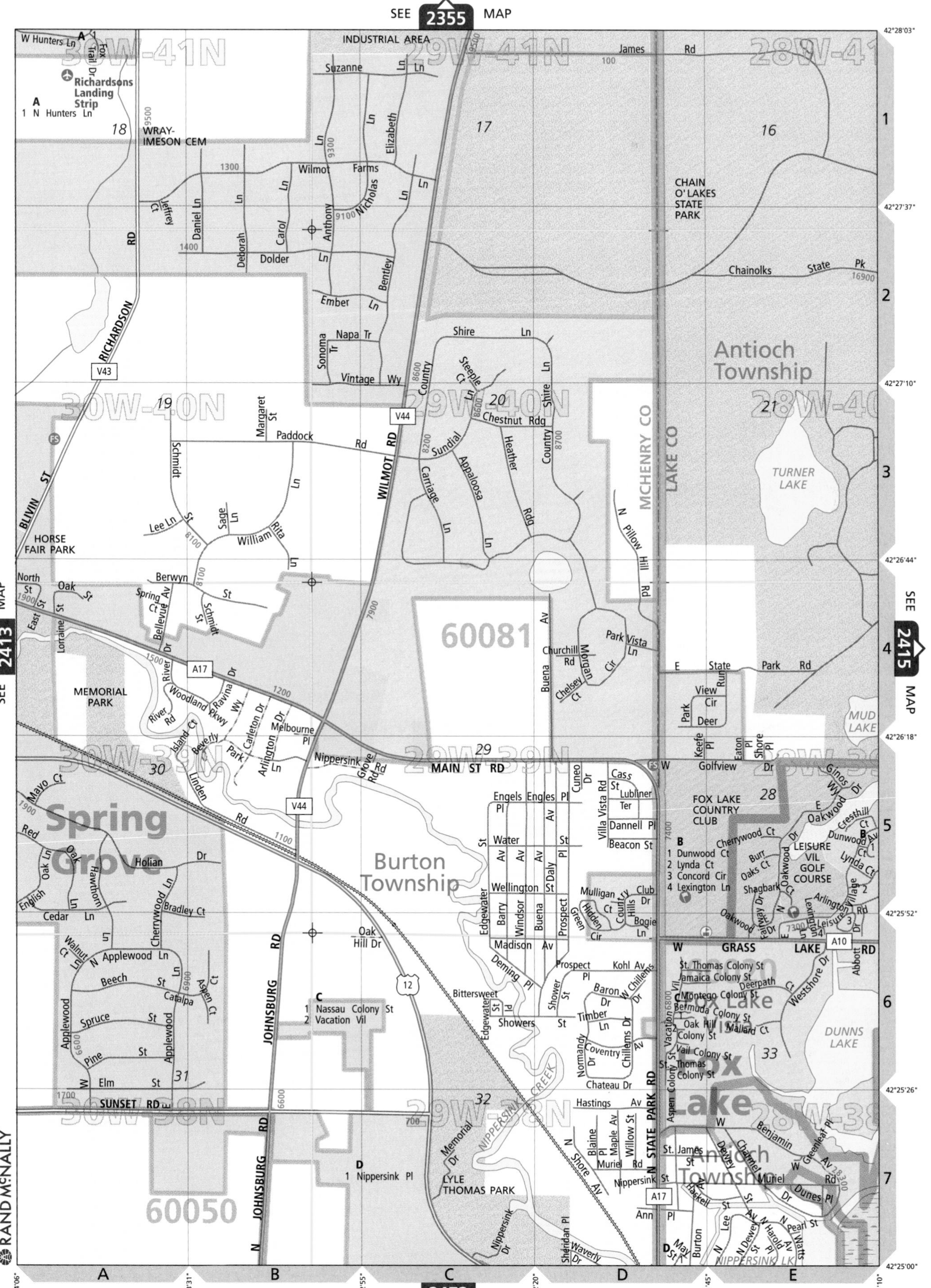

SEE 2413 MAP
SEE 2415 MAP
SEE 2472 MAP

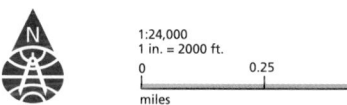

1:24,000
1 in. = 2000 ft.
0 0.25 0.5
miles

SEE 2356 MAP

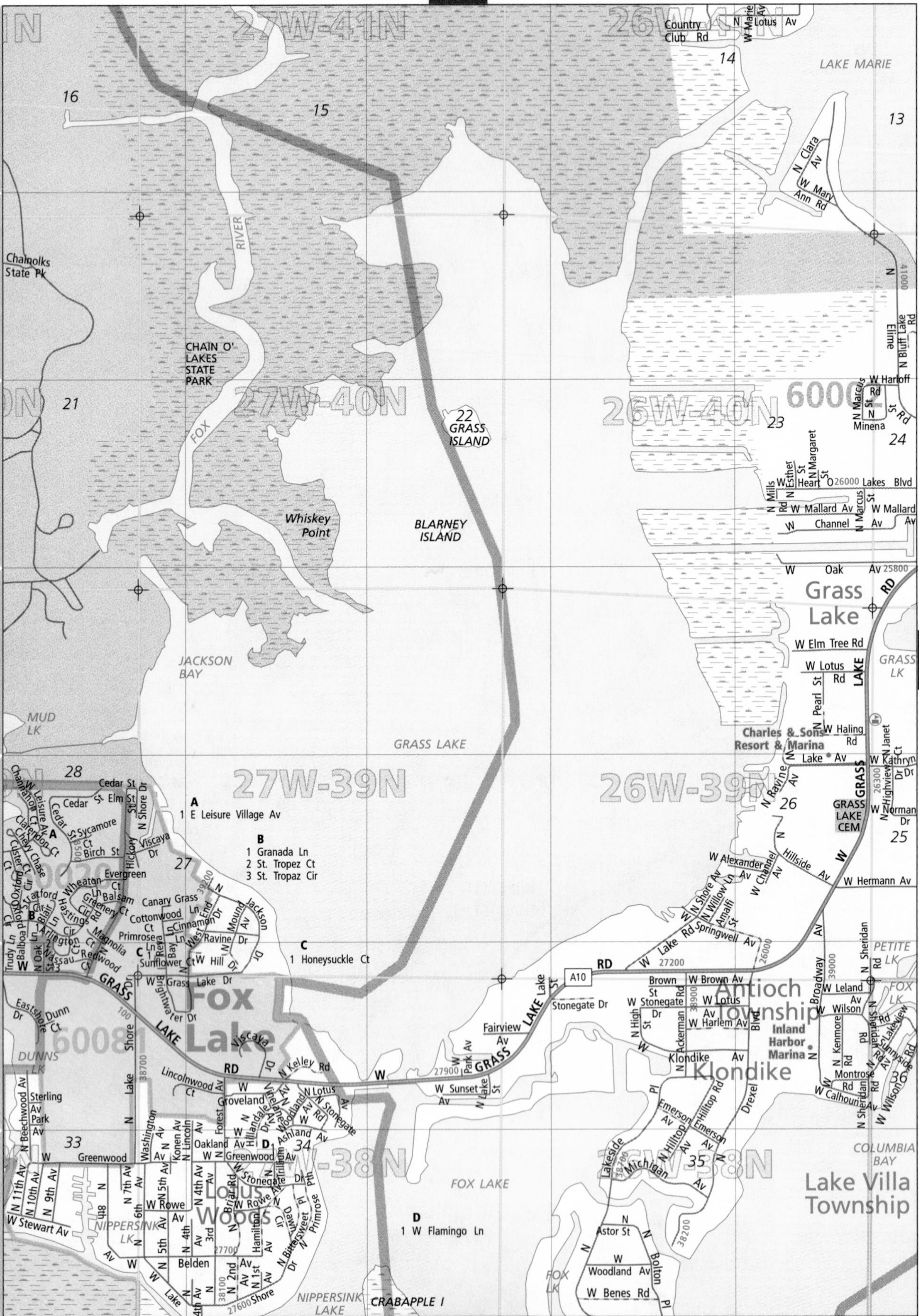

SEE 2414 MAP

SEE 2416 MAP

A
1 E Leisure Village Av

B
1 Granada Ln
2 St. Tropez Ct
3 St. Tropaz Cir

C
1 Honeysuckle Ct

D
1 W Flamingo Ln

Chain O' Lakes State Park
Grass Lake
Fox Lake
Antioch Township
Klondike
Lotus Woods
Lake Villa Township
Charles & Sons Resort & Marina
Inland Harbor Marina
Grass Lake Cem

SEE 2473 MAP

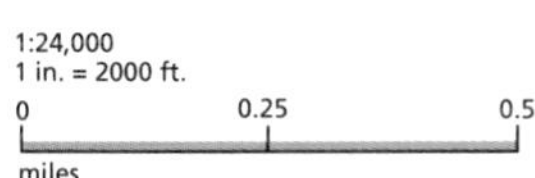

SEE 2357 MAP

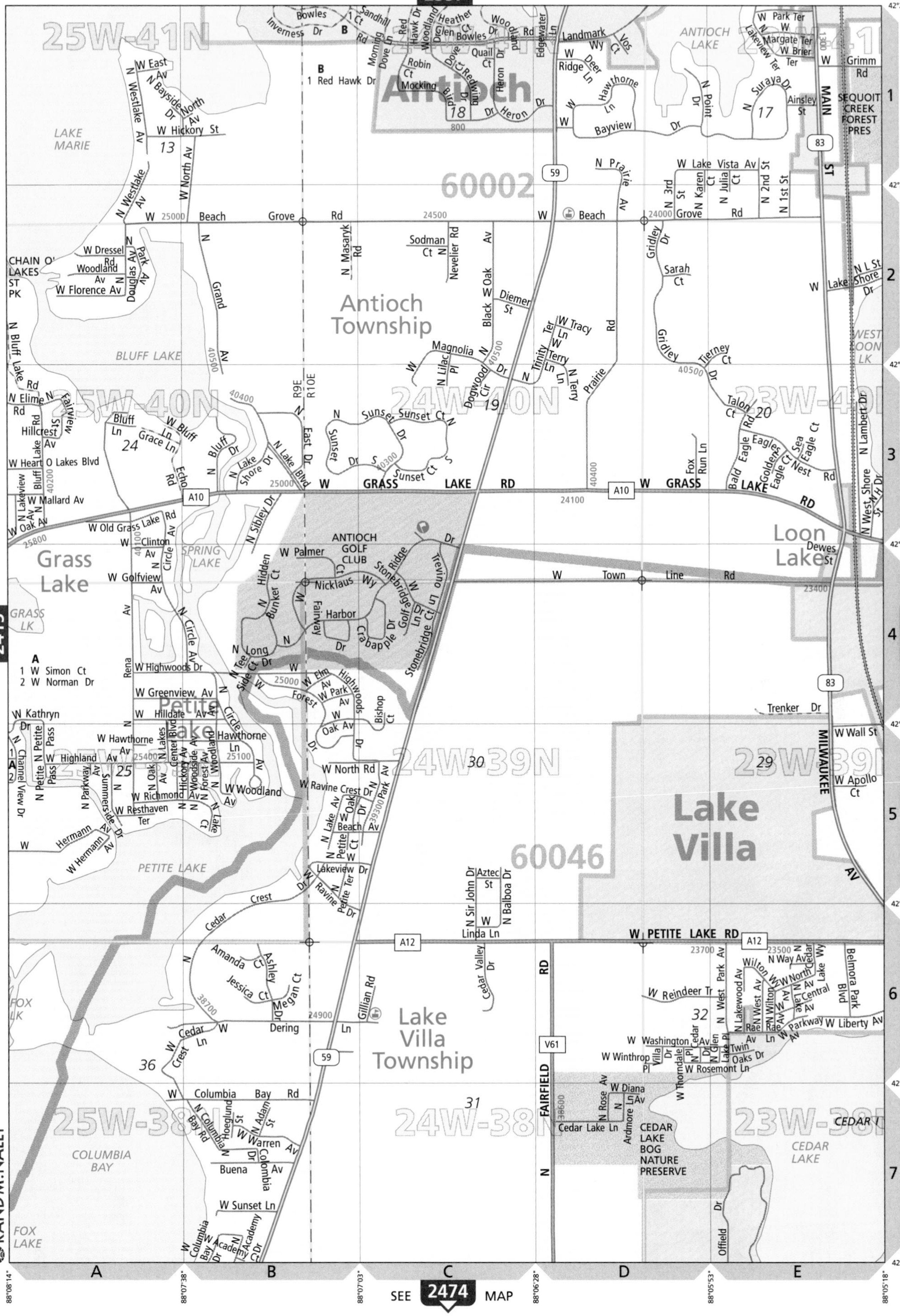

Antioch
Antioch Township
Lake Villa
Lake Villa Township
Grass Lake
Loon Lake
60002
60046
25W-41N
25W-40N
24W-40N
23W-40N
24W-39N
23W-39N
25W-38N
24W-38N
23W-38N
LAKE MARIE
BLUFF LAKE
PETITE LAKE
COLUMBIA BAY
FOX LAKE
CEDAR LAKE
ANTIOCH LAKE
SPRING LAKE
ANTIOCH GOLF CLUB
CHAIN O' LAKES ST PK
SEQUOIT CREEK FOREST PRES
CEDAR LAKE BOG NATURE PRESERVE
W GRASS LAKE RD
W Beach Grove Rd
W Town Line Rd
W PETITE LAKE RD
N MAIN ST
MILWAUKEE AV
N FAIRFIELD RD
W Columbia Bay Rd
W Dering Ln

A
1 W Simon Ct
2 W Norman Dr

B
1 Red Hawk Dr

SEE 2415 MAP
SEE 2417 MAP
SEE 2474 MAP

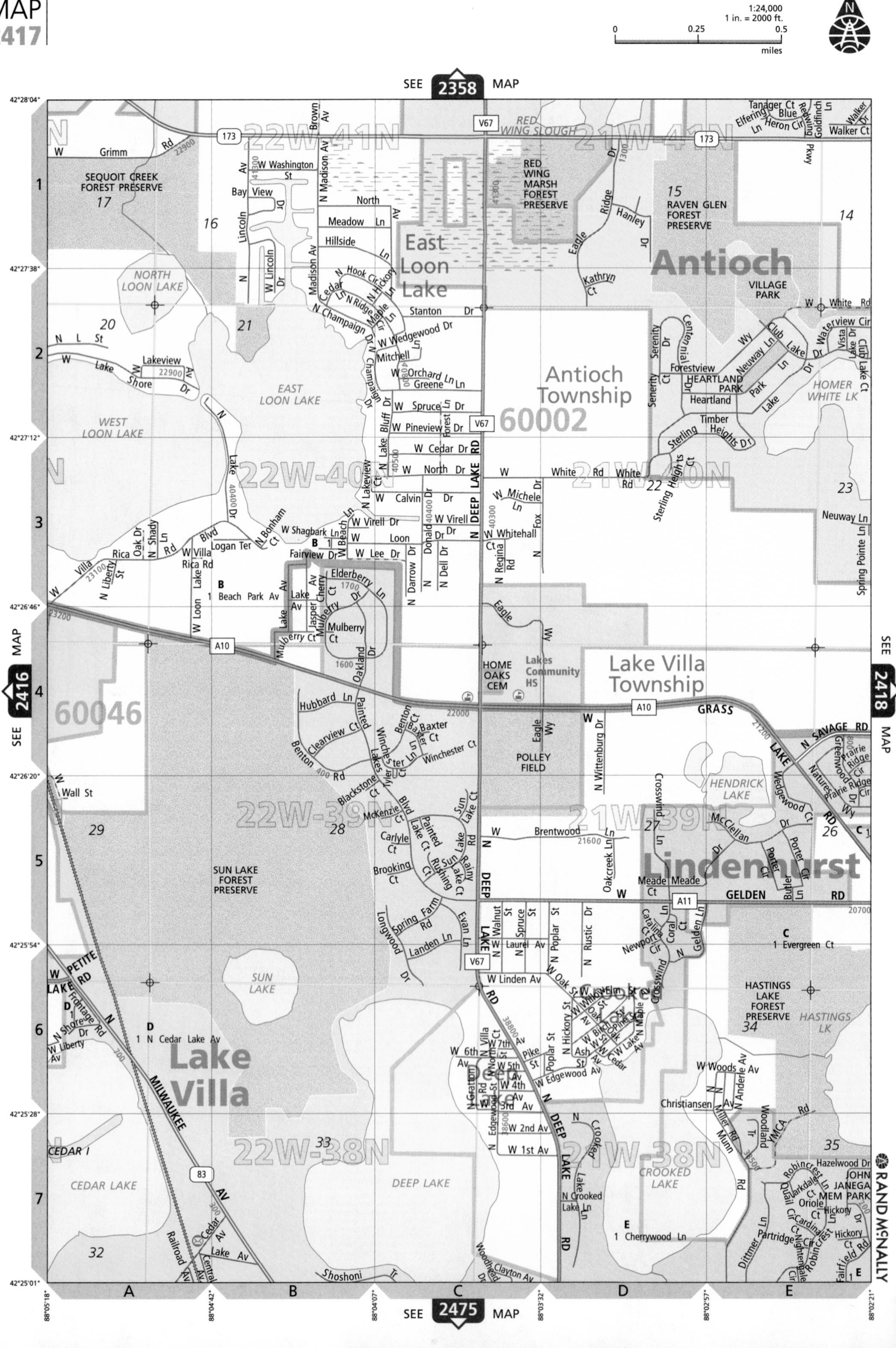

1:24,000
1 in. = 2000 ft.
0 0.25 0.5
miles

SEE 2358 MAP

SEE 2416 MAP

SEE 2418 MAP

SEE 2475 MAP

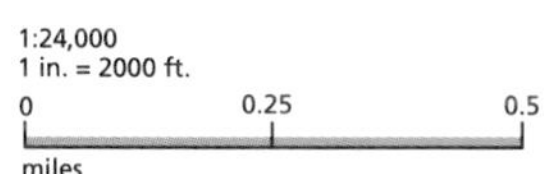

SEE 2359 MAP

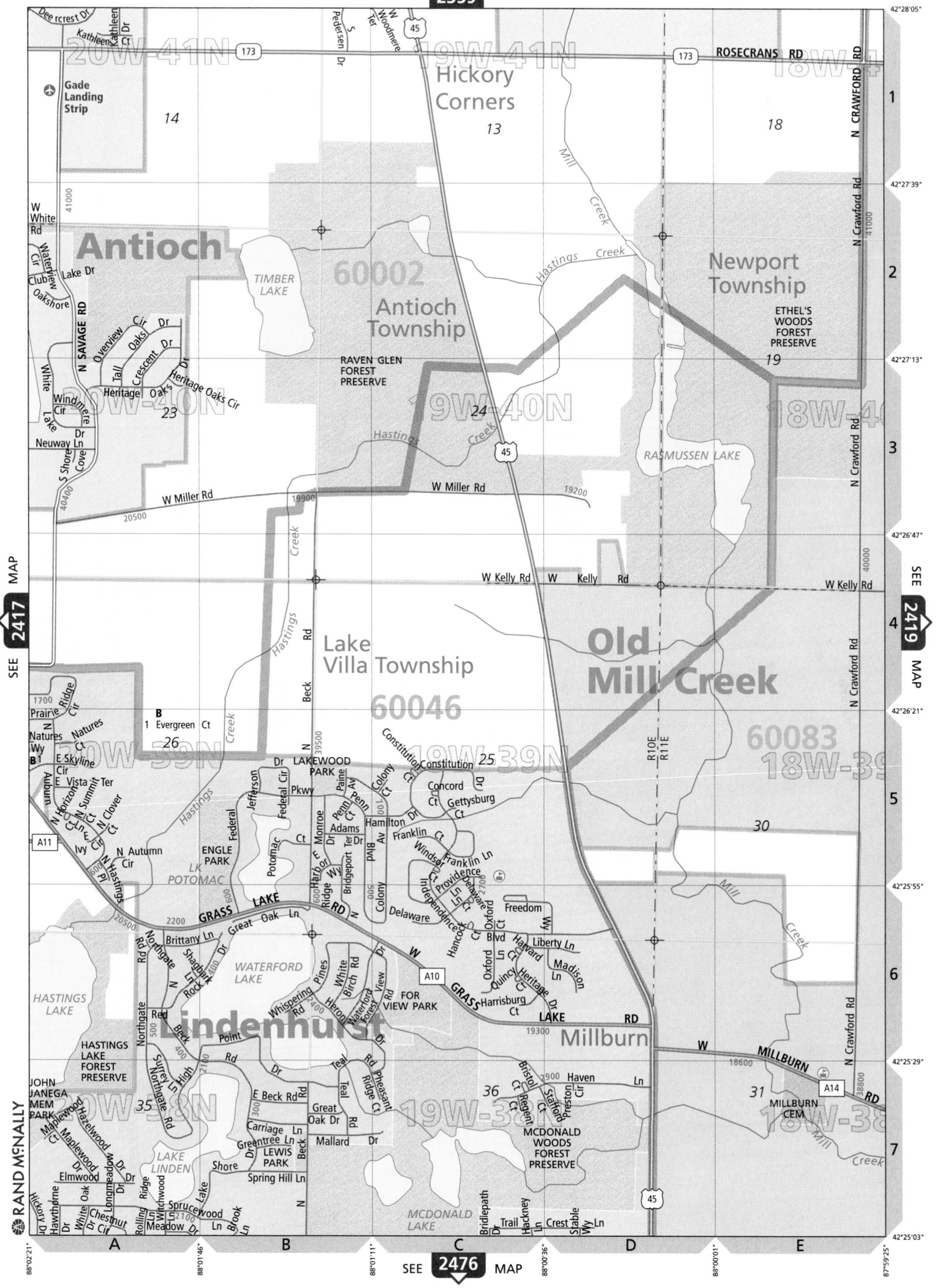

SEE 2417 MAP

SEE 2419 MAP

SEE 2476 MAP

Antioch

Hickory Corners

Antioch Township

Newport Township

Lake Villa Township

Old Mill Creek

Lindenhurst

Millburn

1:24,000
1 in. = 2000 ft.
0 0.25 0.5
miles

SEE 2360 MAP

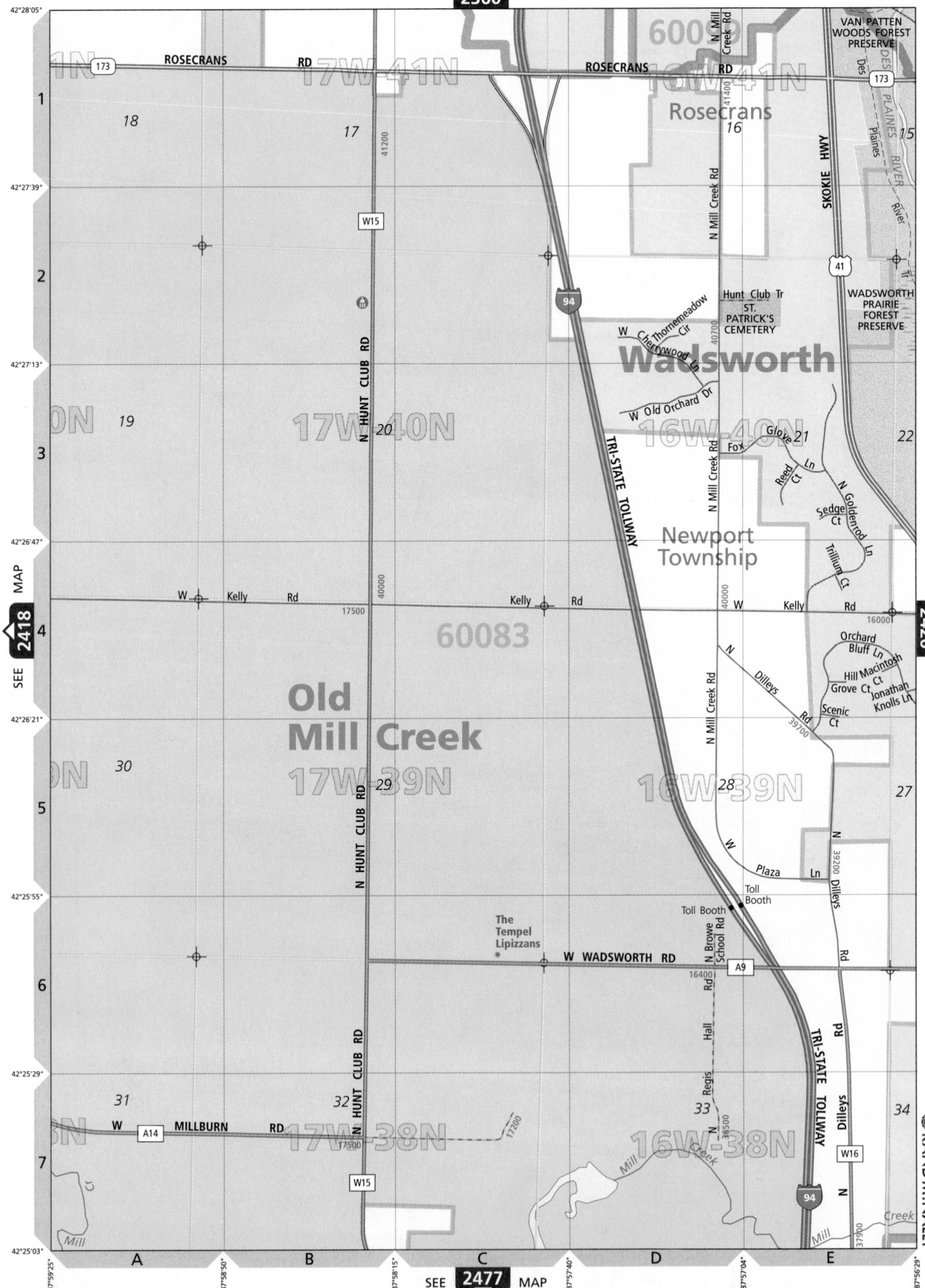

SEE 2418 MAP

SEE 2420 MAP

SEE 2477 MAP

1:24,000
1 in. = 2000 ft.
0 0.25 0.5
miles

SEE 2361 MAP

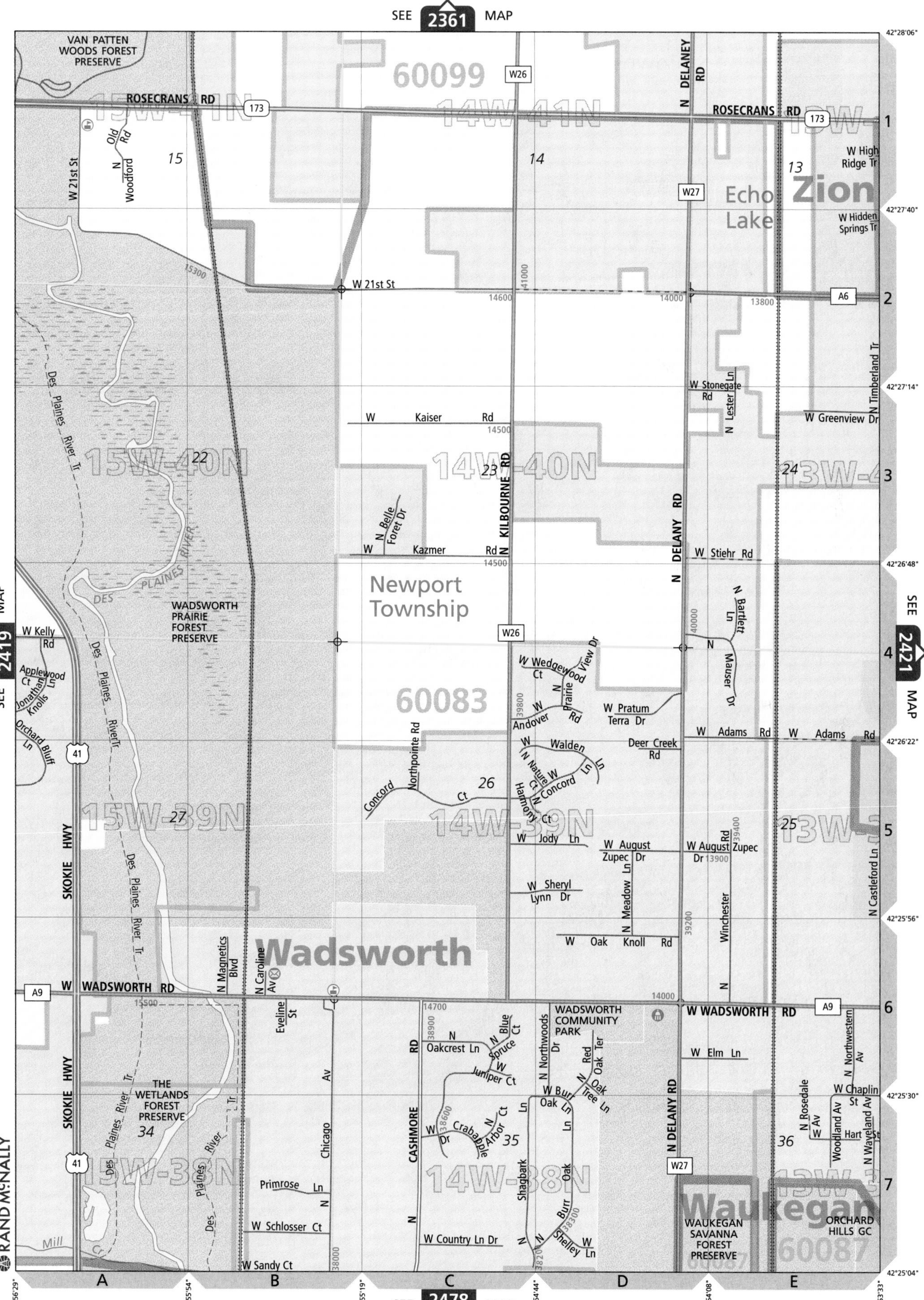

SEE 2419 MAP

SEE 2421 MAP

SEE 2478 MAP

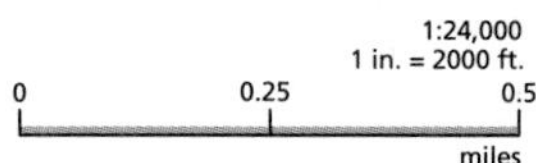

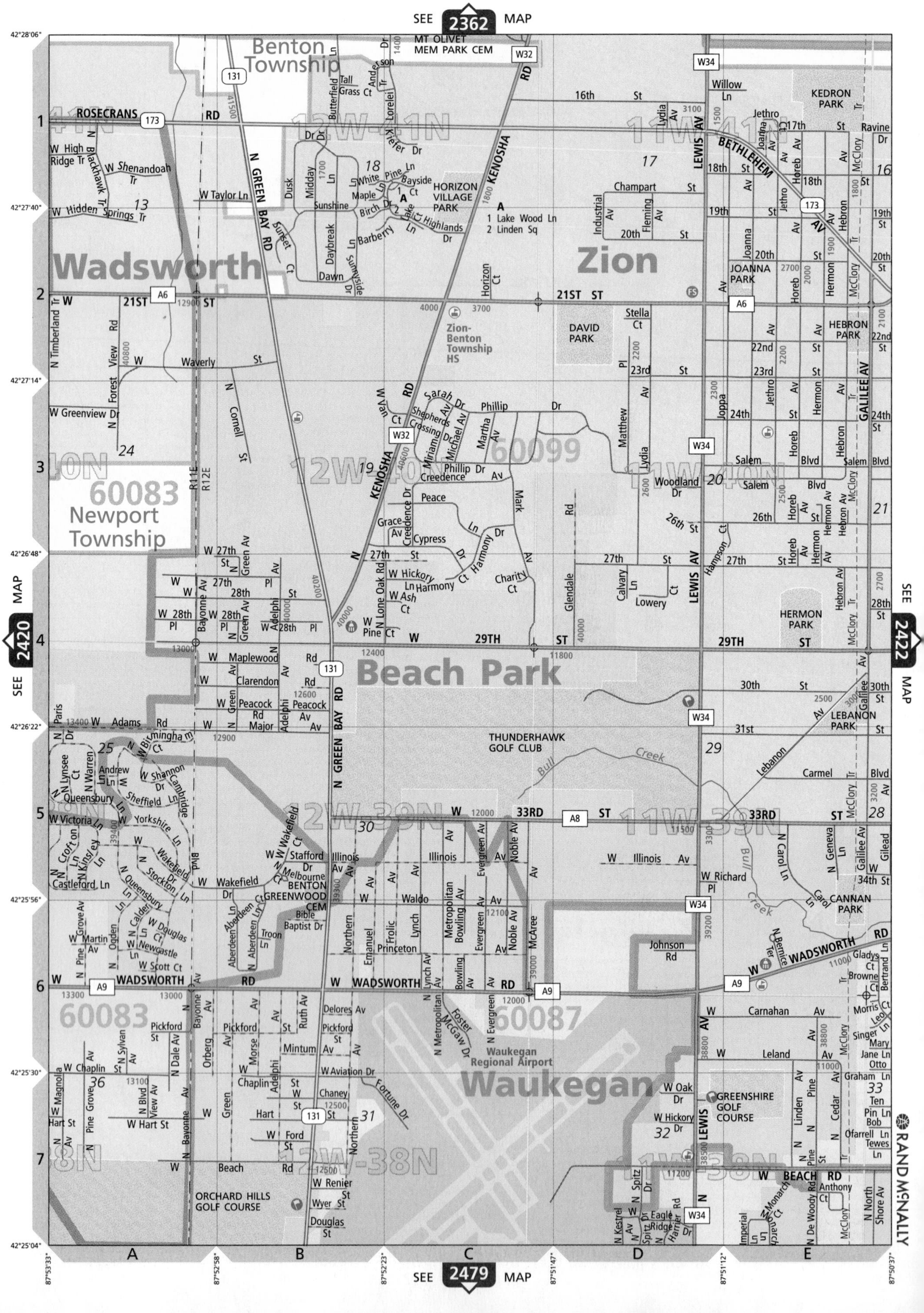

1:24,000
1 in. = 2000 ft.
0 0.25 0.5
miles
N
SEE 2362 MAP
SEE 2479 MAP
SEE 2420 MAP
SEE 2422 MAP
42°28'06"
42°27'40"
42°27'14"
42°26'48"
42°26'22"
42°25'56"
42°25'30"
42°25'04"
87°53'33"
87°52'58"
87°52'23"
87°51'47"
87°51'12"
87°50'37"
A
B
C
D
E
1
2
3
4
5
6
7
Benton Township
Wadsworth
Zion
Beach Park
Waukegan
Newport Township
60083
60099
60087
12W-41N
11W-41N
12W-40N
11W-40N
12W-39N
11W-39N
12W-38N
11W-38N
R11E
R12E
MT OLIVET MEM PARK CEM
HORIZON VILLAGE PARK
A
1 Lake Wood Ln
2 Linden Sq
KEDRON PARK
JOANNA PARK
DAVID PARK
HEBRON PARK
Zion-Benton Township HS
HERMON PARK
LEBANON PARK
THUNDERHAWK GOLF CLUB
BENTON GREENWOOD CEM
CANNAN PARK
Waukegan Regional Airport
GREENSHIRE GOLF COURSE
ORCHARD HILLS GOLF COURSE
ROSECRANS RD
N GREEN BAY RD
KENOSHA RD
LEWIS AV
BETHLEHEM AV
21ST ST
29TH ST
33RD ST
WADSWORTH RD
BEACH RD
GALILEE AV
131
173
W32
W34
A6
A8
A9
Bull Creek
Willow Ln
16th St
17th St
18th St
19th St
20th St
22nd St
23rd St
24th St
26th St
27th St
28th St
30th St
31st St
Salem Blvd
Carmel Blvd
Phillip Dr
W Taylor Ln
W Hidden Springs Tr
W Shenandoah Tr
W High Ridge Tr
Waverly St
W Greenview Dr
Cornell St
W Maplewood Rd
Clarendon Rd
Peacock Rd
Major Av
W Adams Rd
Queensbury Ln
Yorkshire Ln
Wakefield Dr
Castleford Ln
W Illinois Av
W Richard Pl
Johnson Rd
Carnahan Av
Leland Av
Pickford St
W Chaplin St
Mintum Av
W Aviation Dr
Fortune Dr
W Hart St
Beach Rd
W Renier St
Wyer St
Douglas St
W Oak Dr
W Hickory Dr
Eagle Ridge Dr
Imperial Ln
N De Woody Rd
N North Shore Av
Lebanon Av
N Carol Ln
Graham Ln
Gladys Ct
13
16
17
18
19
20
21
24
25
28
29
30
31
32
33
36
RAND McNALLY

1:24,000
1 in. = 2000 ft.
0 0.25 0.5
miles

SEE 2363 MAP

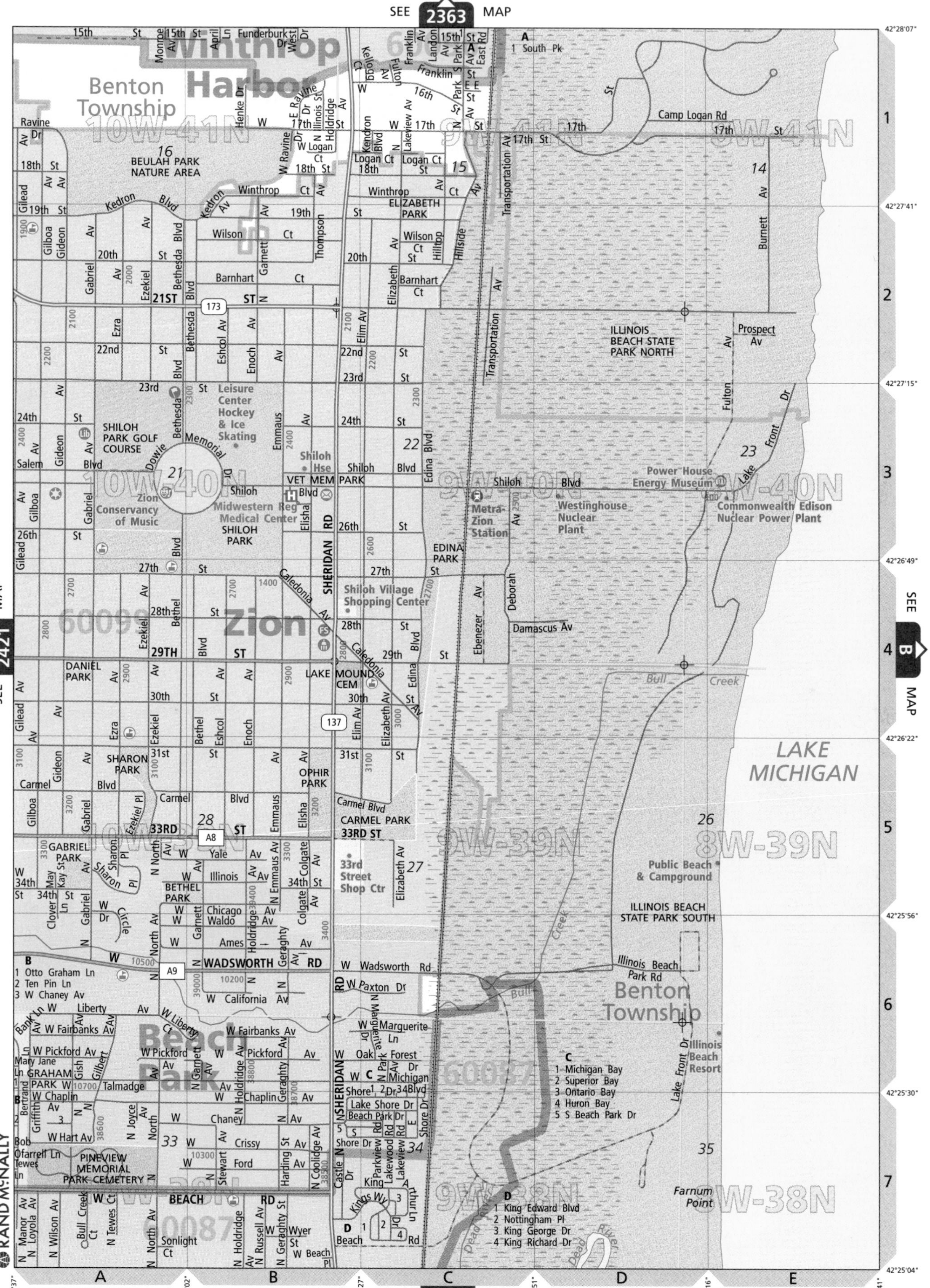

SEE 2421 MAP

SEE B MAP

SEE 2480 MAP

1:24,000
1 in. = 2000 ft.
0 0.25 0.5
miles

SEE 2405 MAP

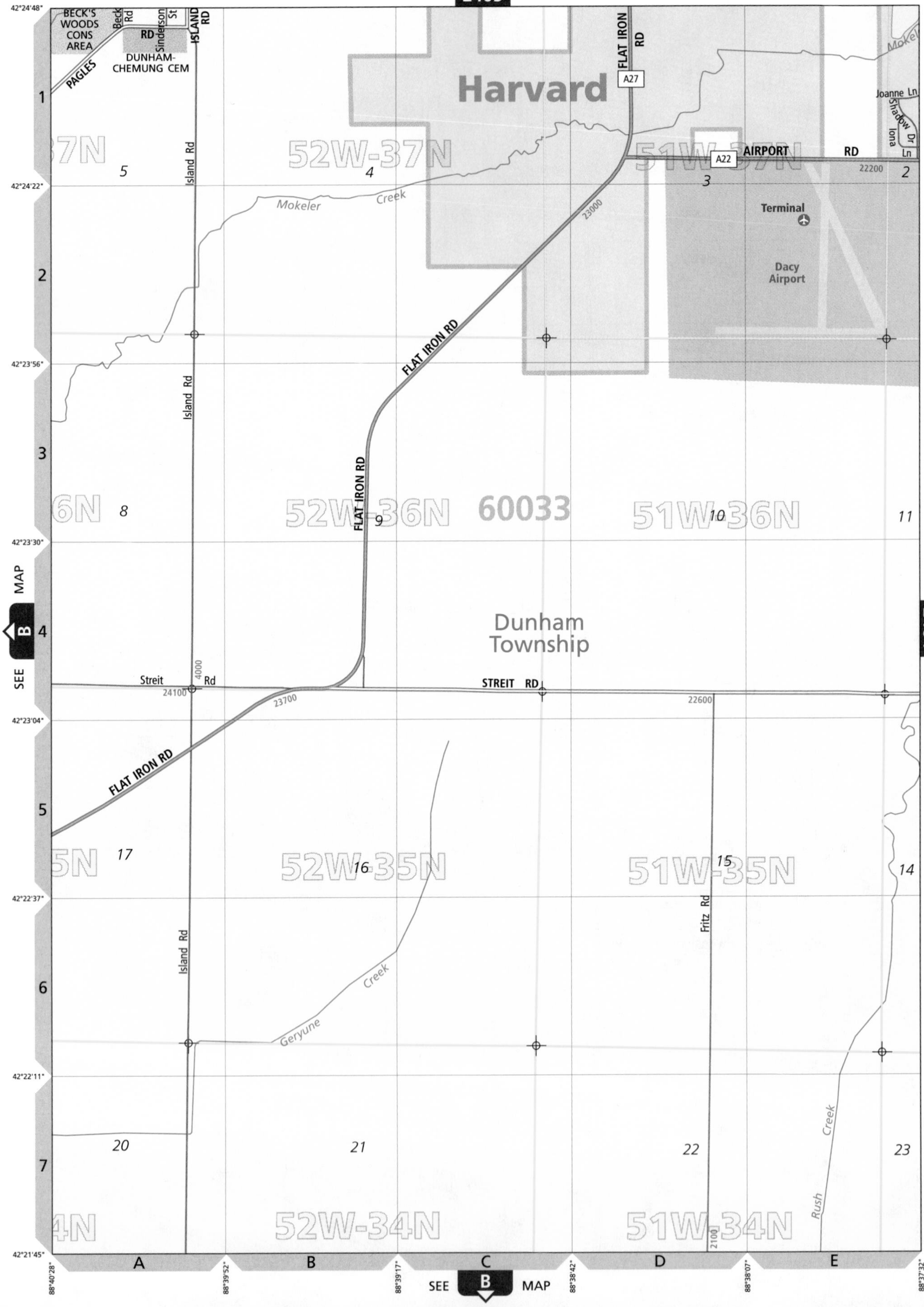

Harvard
BECK'S WOODS CONS AREA
Beck Rd
Sinderson St
ISLAND RD
PAGLES RD
DUNHAM-CHEMUNG CEM
FLAT IRON RD
A27
Mokeler Creek
Joanne Ln
Shadow Dr
Iona Ln
AIRPORT RD
A22
22200
23000
Terminal
Dacy Airport
52W-37N
51W-37N
Island Rd
52W-36N
60033
51W-36N
Dunham Township
Streit Rd
4000
24100
23700
STREIT RD
22600
52W-35N
51W-35N
Fritz Rd
Geryune Creek
Rush Creek
52W-34N
51W-34N
2100

5 4 3 2
8 9 10 11
17 16 15 14
20 21 22 23

A B C D E
1 2 3 4 5 6 7

SEE B MAP

SEE 2464 MAP

SEE B MAP

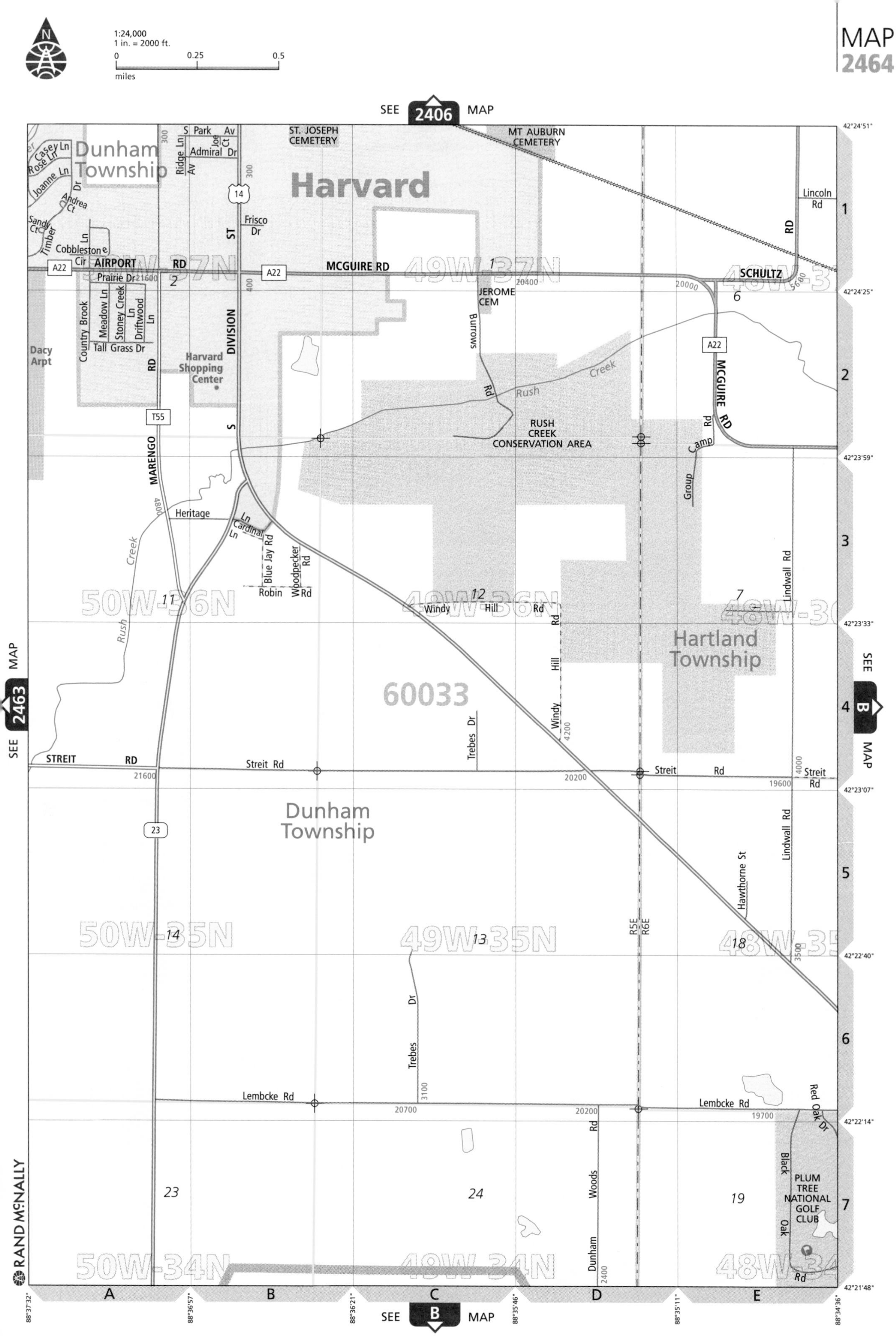

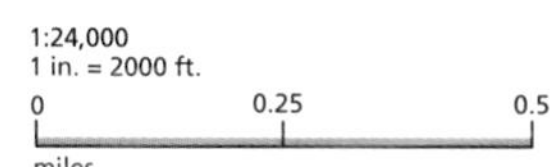

SEE 2406 MAP

Harvard
Dunham Township
Hartland Township
Dunham Township
60033
ST. JOSEPH CEMETERY
MT AUBURN CEMETERY
JEROME CEM
RUSH CREEK CONSERVATION AREA
Harvard Shopping Center
Dacy Arpt
PLUM TREE NATIONAL GOLF CLUB
MCGUIRE RD
AIRPORT RD
DIVISION ST
MARENGO RD
STREIT RD
Streit Rd
Lembcke Rd
Windy Hill Rd
Trebes Dr
Woods Rd
Dunham Rd
Lindwall Rd
Hawthorne St
Group Camp Rd
Burrows Rd
SCHULTZ RD
Lincoln Rd
Rush Creek
Heritage
Cardinal Ln
Blue Jay Rd
Woodpecker Rd
Robin Rd
Frisco Dr
Park Av
Admiral Dr
Joe Ct
Ridge Ln Av
Casey Ln
Rose Ln
Joanne Ln
Andrea Ct
Sandy Ct
Timber Dr
Cobblestone Cir
Prairie Dr
Country Brook
Meadow Ln
Stoney Creek Ln
Driftwood Ln
Tall Grass Dr
Red Oak Dr
Black Oak Rd
50W-37N
49W-37N
48W-37N
50W-36N
49W-36N
48W-36N
50W-35N
49W-35N
48W-35N
50W-34N
49W-34N
48W-34N
R5E R6E

SEE MAP 2463

SEE B MAP

SEE B MAP

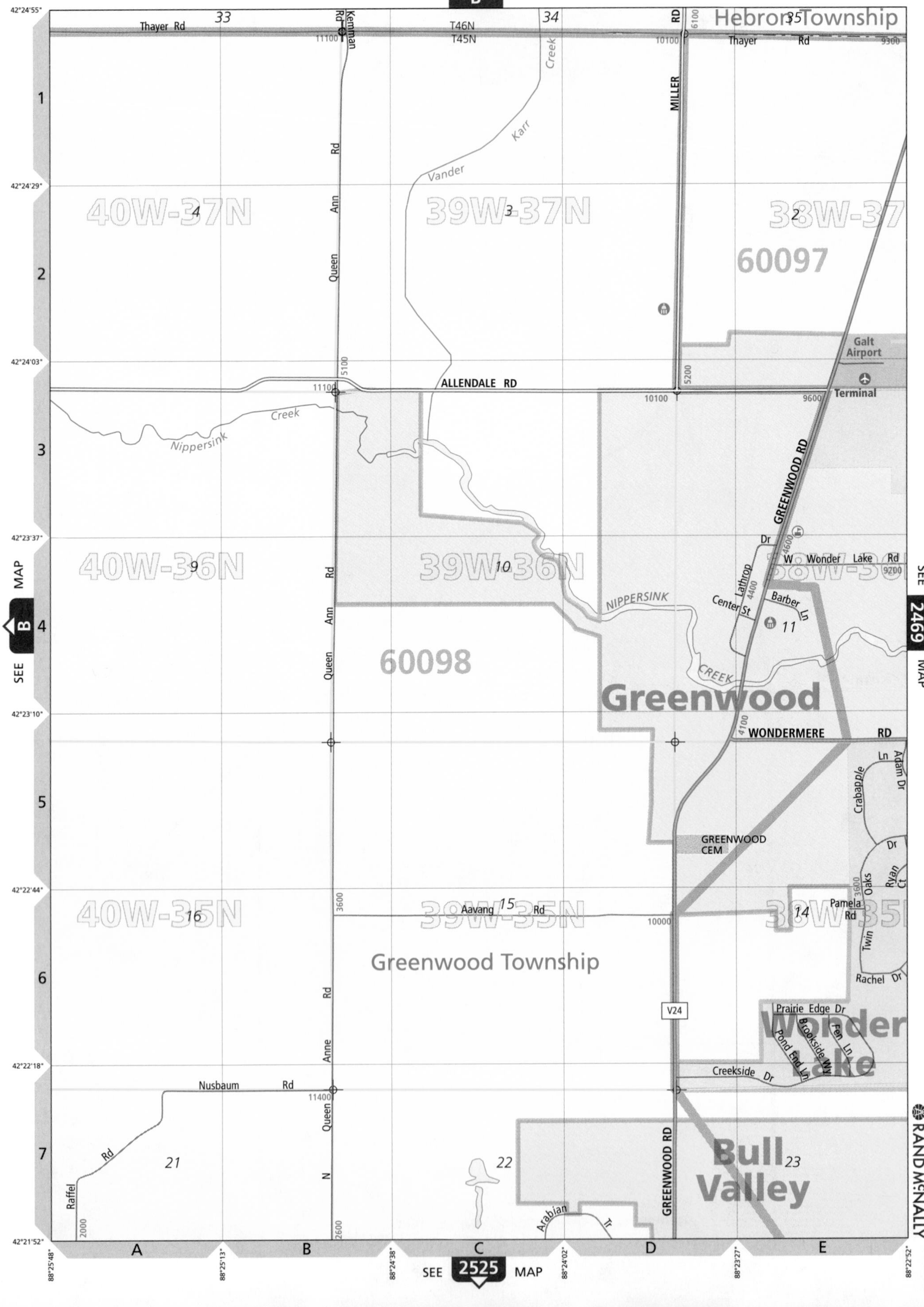

1:24,000
1 in. = 2000 ft.
0 0.25 0.5
miles

SEE B MAP

Thayer Rd
33
Kemman Rd
T46N
T45N
34
Vander Karr Creek
MILLER RD
Hebron Township
35
Thayer Rd
40W-37N
4
Queen Ann Rd
39W-37N
3
38W-37
2
60097
Galt Airport
Terminal
ALLENDALE RD
Nippersink Creek
GREENWOOD RD
40W-36N
9
39W-36N
10
Lathrop
Dr
W Wonder Lake Rd
Barber Ln
Center St
NIPPERSINK CREEK
11
60098
Greenwood
WONDERMERE RD
Adam Dr
Crabapple Ln
GREENWOOD CEM
Ryan Ct
Oaks Dr
40W-35N
16
39W-35N
15
Aavang Rd
38W-35N
14
Pamela Rd
Twin
Greenwood Township
Rachel Dr
V24
Prairie Edge Dr
Wonder Lake
Brookside Wy
Fen Ln
Pond End Ln
Creekside Dr
Nusbaum Rd
N Queen Anne Rd
Raffel Rd
21
22
Bull Valley
23
Arabian Tr

SEE B MAP

SEE 2469 MAP

SEE 2525 MAP

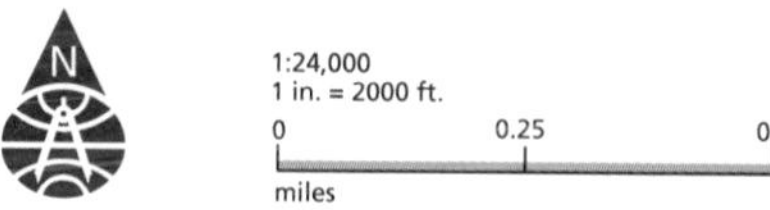

SEE B MAP

SEE 2468 MAP

SEE 2470 MAP

Hebron Township
Richmond Township
Greenwood Township
Greenwood
Galt Airport
Hickory Falls
Wonder Woods
White Oaks Bay
Ringwood
McHenry Township
Wonder Lake
Bull Valley
Highland Shores
Wooded Shores
Oakwood Shores
Shore Hills
Wonder View
GLACIAL PARK
JACOBSON PARK
HARRISON-BENWELL PARK
CHRIST THE KING CEM
Wonder Lake Marina
WONDER LAKE
NIPPERSINK CREEK
37W-37N
36W-37N
37W-36N
36W-36N
37W-35N
36W-35N
60097
T46N
T45N
R7E
R8E
HOWE RD
GREENWOOD RD
BARNARD MILL RD
WONDER LAKE RD
W WONDER LAKE RD
WONDERMERE RD
THOMPSON RD
MCCULLOM LAKE RD
HANCOCK DR
E WONDER LAKE RD

42°24'57"
42°24'31"
42°24'05"
42°23'39"
42°23'13"
42°22'47"
42°22'21"
42°21'54"
88°22'52"
88°22'17"
88°21'42"
88°21'06"
88°20'31"
88°19'56"

A B C D E
1 2 3 4 5 6 7

SEE 2526 MAP

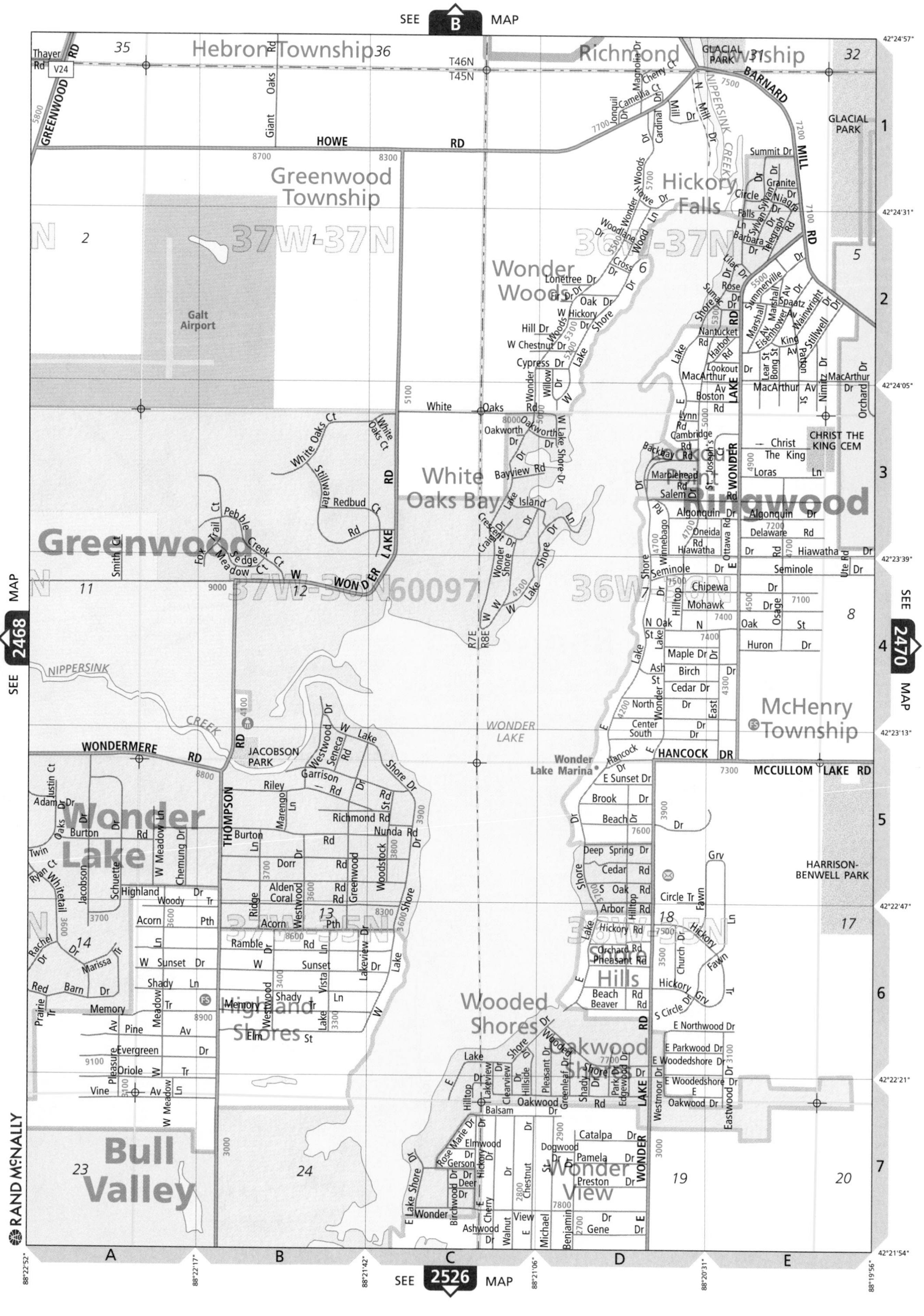

1:24,000
1 in. = 2000 ft.
0 0.25 0.5
miles

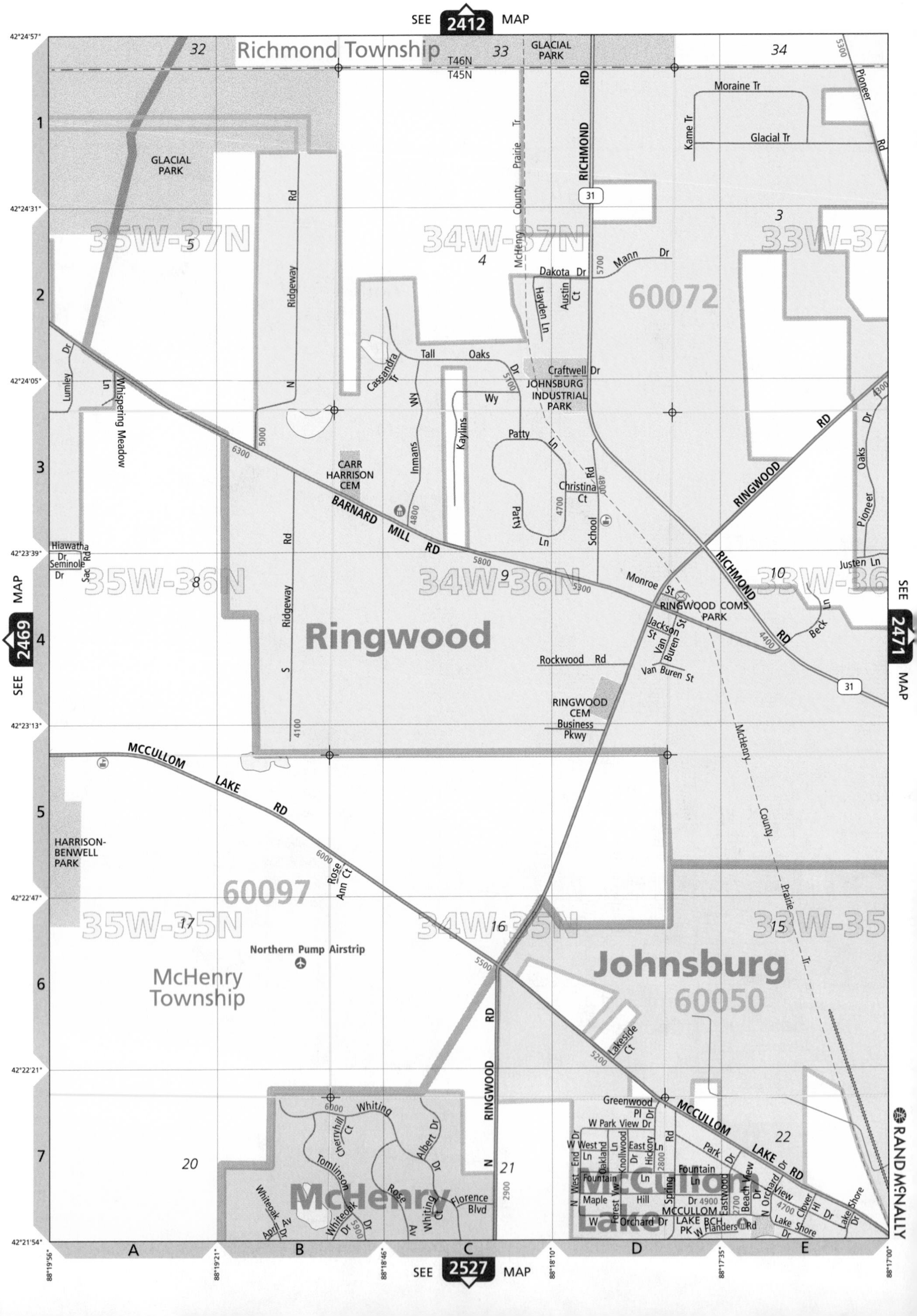

SEE 2412 MAP

Richmond Township
GLACIAL PARK
T46N
T45N
Moraine Tr
Glacial Tr
Kame Tr
Pioneer Rd
RICHMOND RD
McHenry County Prairie Tr
Ridgeway Rd
N Ridgeway Rd
S Ridgeway Rd
35W-37N
34W-37N
33W-37
Dakota Dr
Mann Dr
Hayden Ln
Austin Ct
60072
Lumley Dr
Whispering Meadow Ln
Cassandra Tr
Tall Oaks Dr
Inmans Wy
Kaylins Wy
Craftwell Dr
JOHNSBURG INDUSTRIAL PARK
Patty Ln
Christina Ct
School Rd
CARR HARRISON CEM
BARNARD MILL RD
RINGWOOD RD
Oaks Dr
Pioneer
Justen Ln
Hiawatha Dr
Seminole Dr
Sac Rd
35W-36N
34W-36N
33W-36
Monroe St
RINGWOOD COMS PARK
Jackson St
Van Buren St
Beck Ln
Ringwood
Rockwood Rd
RINGWOOD CEM
Business Pkwy
MCCULLOM LAKE RD
HARRISON-BENWELL PARK
Rose Ann Ct
60097
35W-35N
34W-35N
33W-35
Northern Pump Airstrip
McHenry Township
Johnsburg
60050
Lakeside Ct
RINGWOOD RD
N RINGWOOD RD
Whiting Ct
Cherryhill Ct
Albert Dr
Tomlinson Dr
Rose Av
Whiting Ct
Florence Blvd
Whiteoak Dr
April Av
McHenry
Greenwood Pl
W Park View Dr
W West End Dr
Oakland Ln
Knollwood Dr
East Ln
Hickory Dr
Park Dr
Fountain Ln
Spring Dr
Eastwood Dr
Beach View Dr
N Orchard Dr
Orchard View Dr
Clover Dr
Hi Dr
Lake Shore Dr
Maple Ln
Hill Ln
W Orchard Dr
MCCULLOM LAKE BCH PK
W Flanders Rd
Forest Vw
McCullom Lake
McHenry County Prairie Tr

SEE 2469 MAP
SEE 2471 MAP
SEE 2527 MAP

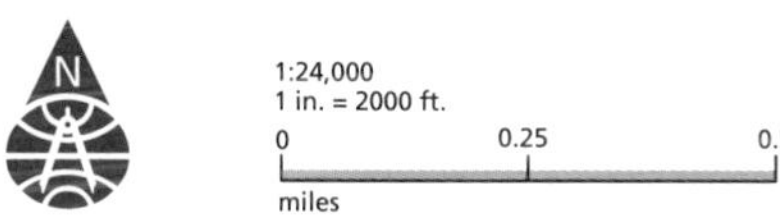

SEE 2413 MAP

Richmond Township
McHenry Township
Ringwood
Johnsburg
McHenry
60081
60072
60050
60051
32W-37N
31W-37N
32W-36N
31W-36N
32W-35N
31W-35N
Miller Rd
W Ringwood Rd
Spring Grove Rd
Richmond Rd
Johnsburg Rd
N Chapel Hill Rd
N Riverside Dr
Pioneer Rd
Solon Rd
HILLER PARK
ALBERT A ADAM'S PARK
ST. JOHN THE BAPTIST CEM
JOHNSBURG COMM CLUB
Johnsburg HS
Dutch Creek
Fox River
A
1 River Terrace Dr
2 Linden Av
B
1 Kendall Cross

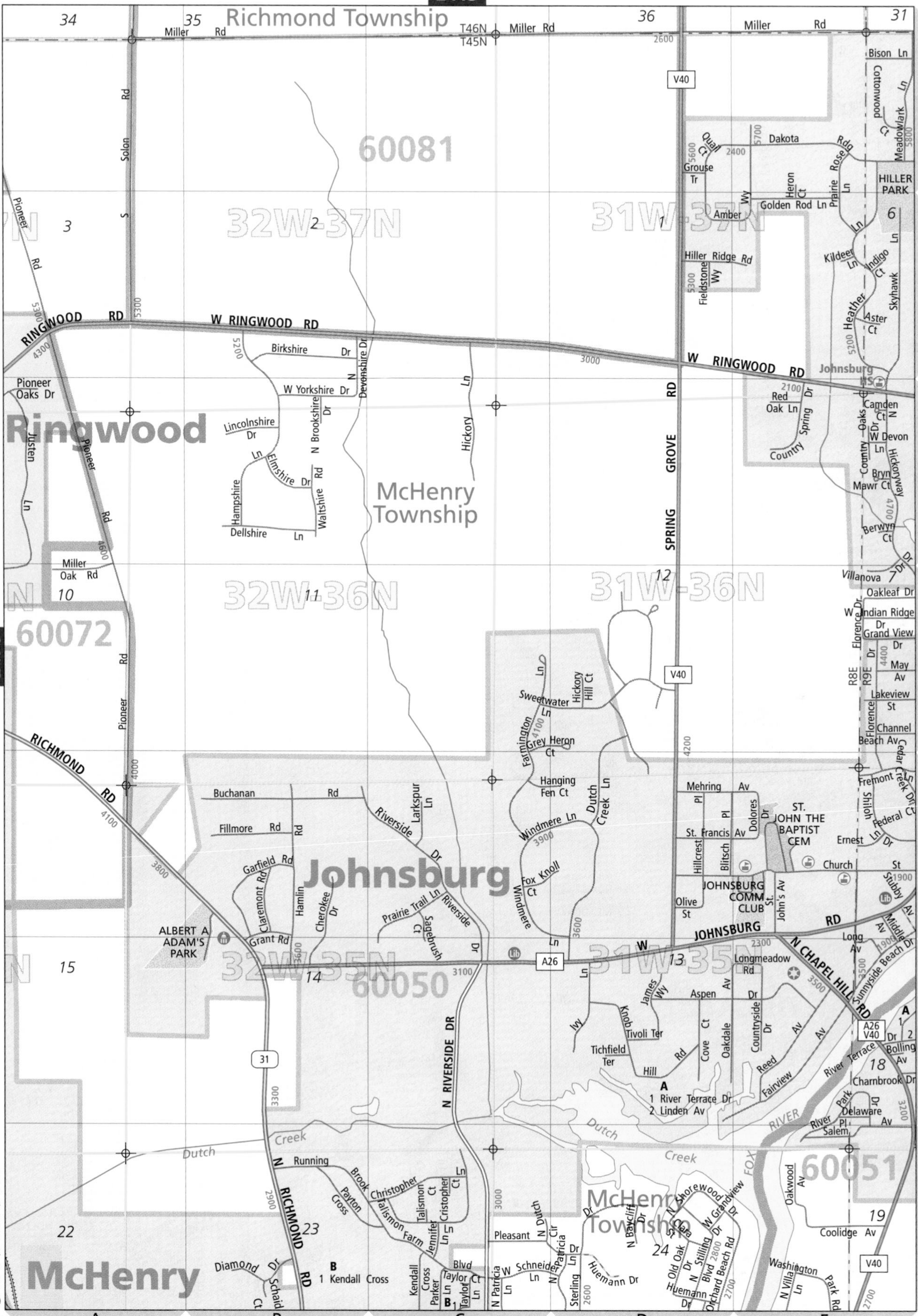

SEE 2470 MAP

SEE 2472 MAP

SEE 2528 MAP

1:24,000
1 in. = 2000 ft.
0 0.25 0.5
miles

SEE 2414 MAP

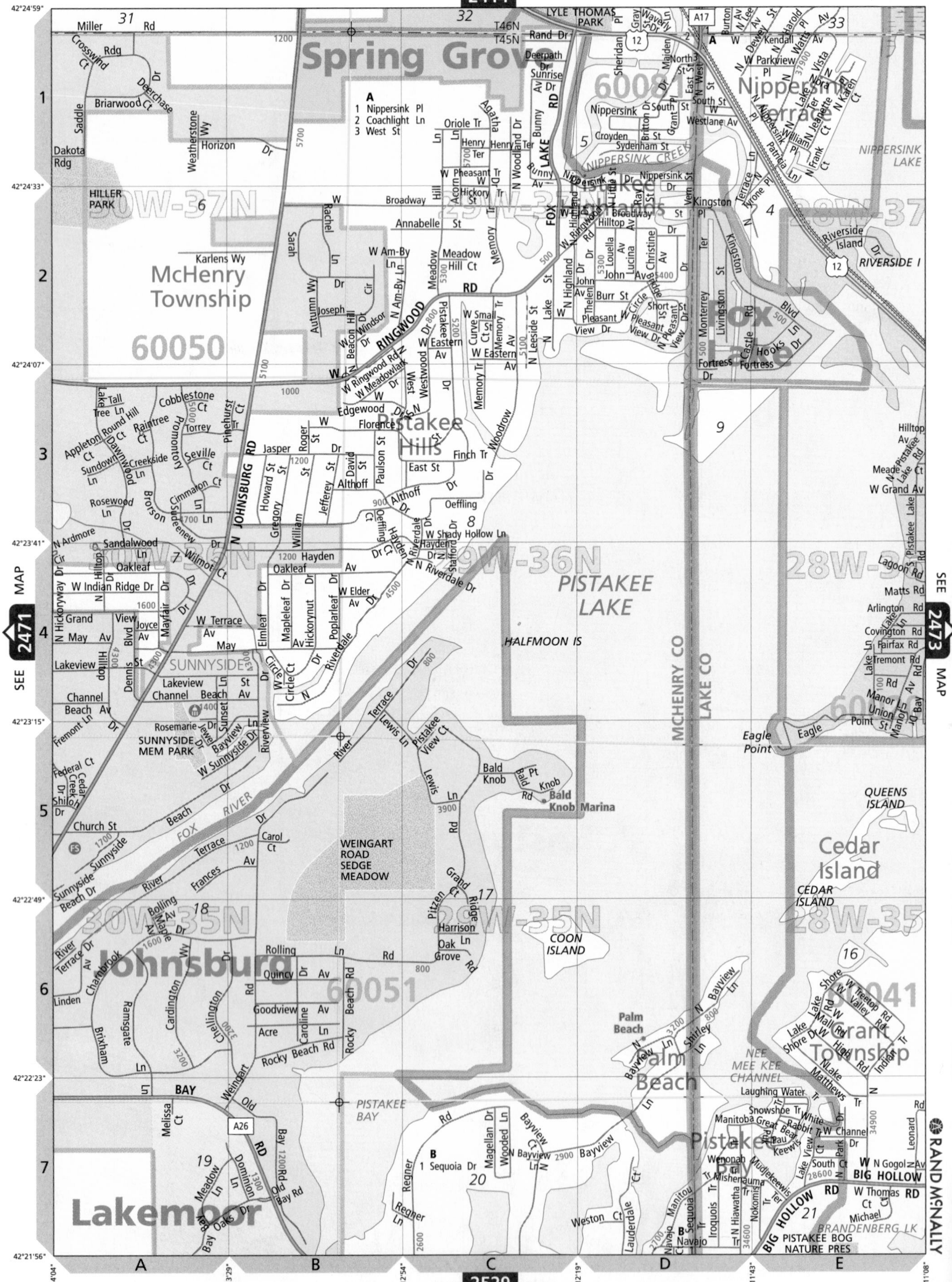

SEE 2471 MAP

SEE 2473 MAP

SEE 2529 MAP

Spring Grove

McHenry Township

60050

Nippersink Terrace

60081

Pistakee Highlands

Fox Lake

Pistakee Hills

Johnsburg

60051

Lakemoor

Cedar Island

Grant Township

60041

Palm Beach

Pistakee Bay

PISTAKEE LAKE

NIPPERSINK LAKE

HALFMOON IS

COON ISLAND

QUEENS ISLAND

CEDAR ISLAND

RIVERSIDE I

FOX RIVER

PISTAKEE BAY

NEE MEE KEE CHANNEL

BRANDENBERG LK

HILLER PARK

LYLE THOMAS PARK

SUNNYSIDE MEM PARK

WEINGART ROAD SEDGE MEADOW

PISTAKEE BOG NATURE PRES

Bald Knob Marina

Palm Beach

Eagle Point

SUNNYSIDE

MCHENRY CO

LAKE CO

30W-37N
29W-37N
28W-37N
30W-36N
29W-36N
28W-36N
30W-35N
29W-35N
28W-35N

T46N
T45N

A
1 Nippersink Pl
2 Coachlight Ln
3 West St

B
1 Sequoia Dr

Miller Rd · Crosswind Ct · Rdg · Deerchase Ct · Dr · Briarwood Ct · Saddle · Dakota Rdg · Weatherstone Wy · Horizon Dr · Karlens Wy · W Broadway · Rachel · Sarah · Annabelle St · Autumn Wy · Joseph · Ln · Dr · Cir · W Am-By Ln · N Am-By Ln · Meadow Hill Ct · Oriole Tr · Henry Ter · Agatha · W Pheasant Tr · Hickory St · Acorn · W Ringwood Rd · W Meadowlark · Westwood Dr · Pistakee · W Eastern Av · Curve Ct · W Small St · Memory Tr · N Leeside St · Lake St · N Highland Dr · N Woodland Dr · Bunny Av · FOX LAKE RD · Rand Dr · Deerpath Dr · Sunrise · Nippersink Dr · Croyden St · Sydenham St · Nippersink Creek · South St · Westlane Av · Kingston Pl · Broadway St · Hilltop · Louella Av · Lucina · Christine Av · John Av · Burr St · Thelen · Pleasant View Dr · W Circle Dr · Short St · Monterrey · Livingston St · Castle Rd · Hooks Dr · Fortress Dr · Blvd · N Dewey · W Parkview Pl · Kendall Av · Watts · Vista · Harold · N Karen Ct · N Jeanette Ct · Frank Ct · Patricia · William · Tyrone Pl · Terrace · Riverside Island Dr · Gray St · Waverly · Sheridan Pl · Maiden · North St · East St · West St · Burton · N Lee · Vern St

Tall Tree Ln · Cobblestone Ct · Appleton Round Hill Ct · Raintree Ct · Torrey · Pinehurst Ct · Promontory · Sundown Ln · Dawnwood · Creekside Ln · Seville Ct · Rosewood Ln · Bronson · Cimmaron Ct · Sandalwood Ln · N Ardmore Cir · Wilmot Ct · Oakleaf · W Indian Ridge Dr · N Hickoryway Dr · Grand View · May Av · Joyce Av · Mayfair · Lakeview Ct · Dennis St · Channel Beach Av · Fremont Ln · Rosemarie · Sunset · Bayview · Riverview · W Sunnyside Dr · Federal Ct · Cedar Creek Dr · Shiloh Dr · Church St · Sunnyside Beach Dr · N JOHNSBURG RD · Jasper · Roger St · Howard St · Gregory · William · Jefferey St · David St · Althoff Dr · Paulson St · Edgewood · Florence · East St · Finch Tr · Woodrow Dr · Oeffling Dr · Hayden Dr · W Shady Hollow Ln · N Riverdale Dr · Stafford · W Elder Av · Hayden Av · Elmleaf · Mapleleaf Dr · Hickorynut · Poplarleaf Dr · W Terrace Av · Circle Ct · Riverdale · River Terrace Dr · Lewis Ln · Pistakee View Ct · Bald Knob Pt · Bald Knob Rd · Beach Dr · Carol Ct · Frances Av · Bolling Av · Maple Dr · Grand Ridge Ct · Pitzen Ct · Harrison · Oak Grove Rd · Rolling Ln Rd · Quincy Dr · Goodview Av · Caroline · Acre Ln · Rocky Beach Rd · River Terrace Dr · Chambrook · Cardington · Chellington · Ramsgate · Brixham · Linden · BAY RD · Weingart · Old Bay Rd · Melissa Ct · Meadow Ln · Dominion · Oaks Dr · Bay · Regner Rd · Magellan Dr · Wooded Ln · N Bayview Ln · Bayview Ct · Weston Ct · Lauderdale Ct · N Bayview Ln · Shirley Ln · Laughing Water · Snowshoe Tr · Manitoba · Great Bear · White Rabbit Tr · W Channel Dr · Keewis · Lake View · South Ct · Wenonah · Mishe Nahma · Mudjekeewis · Navajo · Sequoia · Iroquois · N Hiawatha · Nokomis · Manitou · W Treetop Rd · Valley · Lake Shore Dr · Mall Rd · W High · N Lake · Matthews · Indian Tr · N Park Dr · W N Gogol · BIG HOLLOW RD · W Thomas Ct · Michael · Leonard · Hilltop Av · N Pistakee Lake Rd · Meade Ct · W Grand Av · Lagoon Rd · Matts Rd · Arlington Rd · Covington Rd · Fairfax Rd · Fremont Rd · Manor Ln · Union Point St · Eagle · Bay

A17 · A26 · 12

42°24'59" · 42°24'33" · 42°24'07" · 42°23'41" · 42°23'15" · 42°22'49" · 42°22'23" · 42°21'56"

88°14'04" · 88°13'29" · 88°12'54" · 88°12'19" · 88°11'43" · 88°11'08"

A B C D E

1 2 3 4 5 6 7

1:24,000
1 in. = 2000 ft.
0 0.25 0.5
miles

SEE 2415 MAP

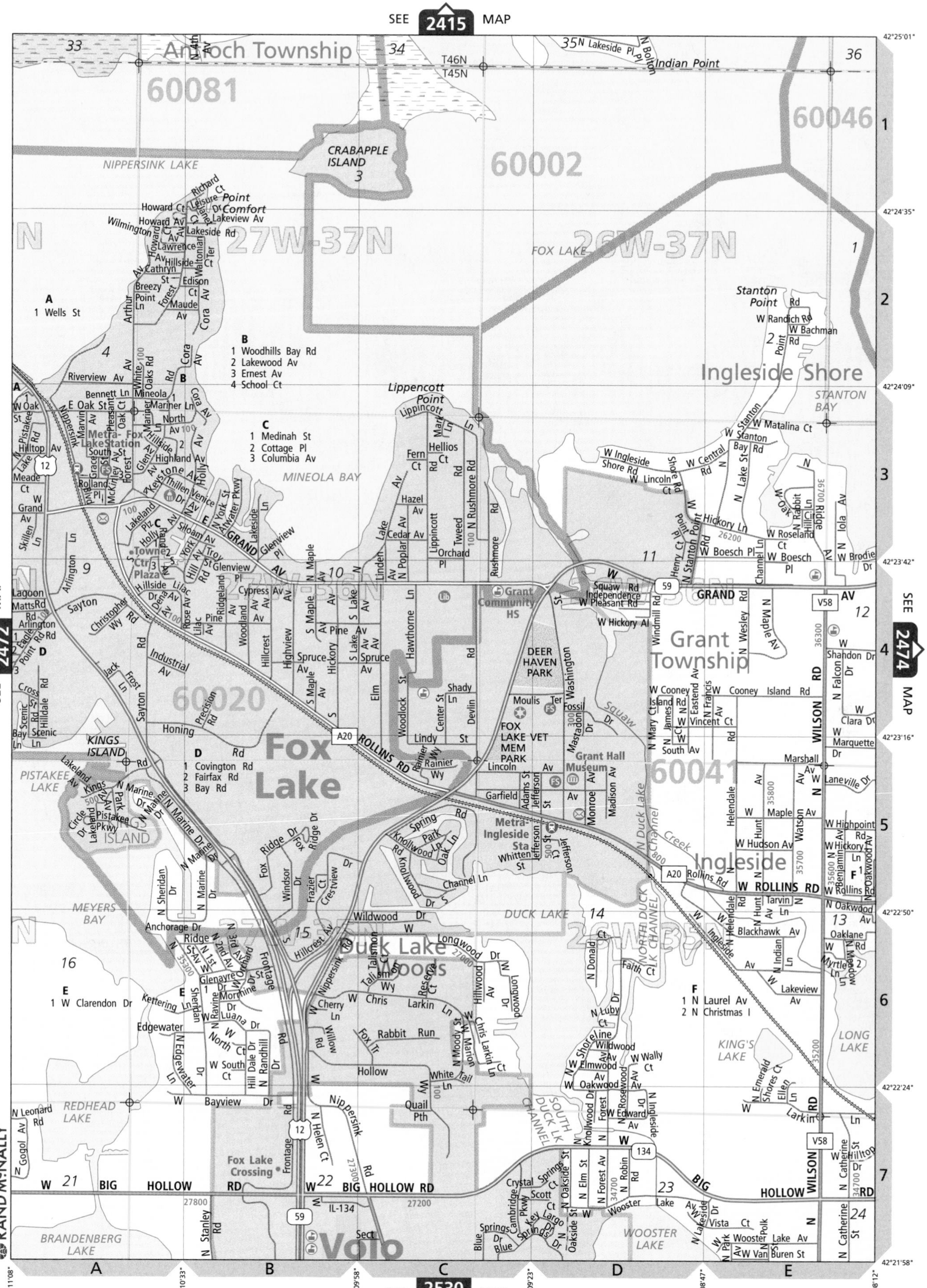

Antioch Township
60081
60046
60002
NIPPERSINK LAKE
CRABAPPLE ISLAND
27W-37N
26W-37N
FOX LAKE
Point Comfort
Stanton Point
Ingleside Shore
STANTON BAY
Lippencott Point
MINEOLA BAY
Indian Point
T46N
T45N
A
1 Wells St
B
1 Woodhills Bay Rd
2 Lakewood Av
3 Ernest Av
4 School Ct
C
1 Medinah St
2 Cottage Pl
3 Columbia Av
D
1 Covington Rd
2 Fairfax Rd
3 Bay Rd
E
1 W Clarendon Dr
F
1 N Laurel Av
2 N Christmas I
Metra- Fox Lake Station
Towne Ctr Plaza
GRAND AV
Grant Community HS
Grant Township
DEER HAVEN PARK
FOX LAKE VET MEM PARK
Grant Hall Museum
60020
60041
Fox Lake
KINGS ISLAND
PISTAKEE LAKE
MEYERS BAY
ROLLINS RD
Metra- Ingleside Sta
Ingleside
W ROLLINS RD
DUCK LAKE
Duck Lake Woods
NORTH DUCK LK CHANNEL
SOUTH DUCK LK CHANNEL
KING'S LAKE
LONG LAKE
REDHEAD LAKE
BRANDENBERG LAKE
WOOSTER LAKE
Fox Lake Crossing
W BIG HOLLOW RD
BIG HOLLOW RD
WILSON RD
Volo
RAND McNALLY

SEE 2472 MAP
SEE 2474 MAP
SEE 2530 MAP

1:24,000
1 in. = 2000 ft.
0 0.25 0.5
miles

SEE 2416 MAP

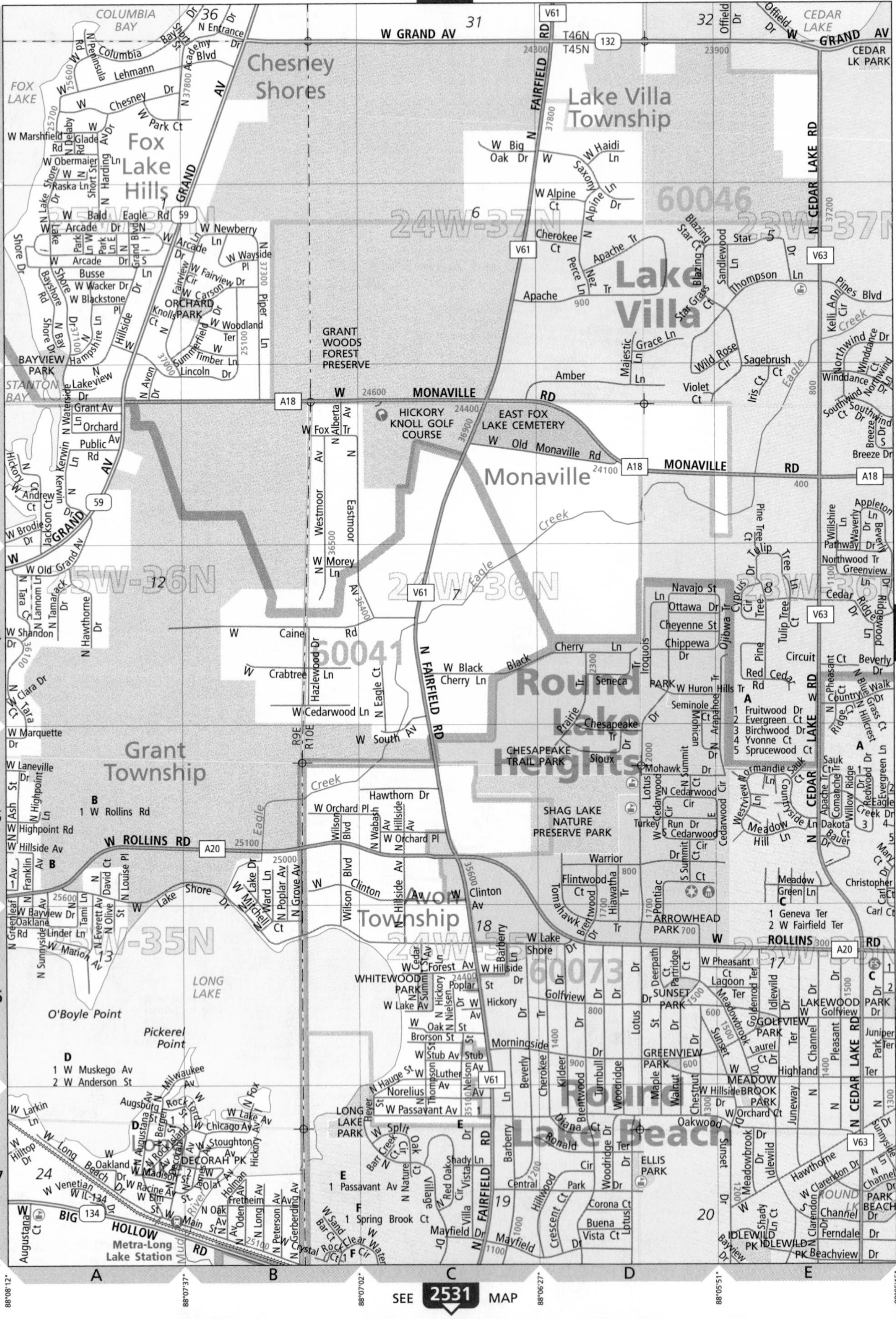

SEE 2473 MAP

SEE 2475 MAP

Chesney Shores

Fox Lake Hills

Lake Villa Township

Lake Villa

GRANT WOODS FOREST PRESERVE

HICKORY KNOLL GOLF COURSE

EAST FOX LAKE CEMETERY

Monaville

Grant Township

Round Lake Heights

CHESAPEAKE TRAIL PARK

SHAG LAKE NATURE PRESERVE PARK

Avon Township

Round Lake Beach

LONG LAKE

O'Boyle Point

Pickerel Point

Metra-Long Lake Station

COLUMBIA BAY

FOX LAKE

STANTON BAY

CEDAR LAKE

CEDAR LK PARK

BAYVIEW PARK

ORCHARD PARK

ARROWHEAD PARK

WHITEWOOD PARK

SUNSET PARK

GREENVIEW PARK

MEADOWBROOK PARK

LAKEWOOD PARK

GOLFVIEW PARK

LONG LAKE PARK

ELLIS PARK

DECORAH PK

IDLEWILD PK

ROUND LK PARK BEACH

W GRAND AV

W MONAVILLE RD

W ROLLINS RD

N FAIRFIELD RD

N CEDAR LAKE RD

BIG HOLLOW RD

24W-37N

23W-37N

25W-36N

24W-36N

23W-36N

25W-35N

24W-35N

23W-35N

60046

60041

60073

T46N
T45N

R9E
R10E

A
1 Fruitwood Dr
2 Evergreen Ct
3 Birchwood Dr
4 Yvonne Ct
5 Sprucewood Ct

B
1 W Rollins Rd

C
1 Geneva Ter
2 W Fairfield Ter

D
1 W Muskego Av
2 W Anderson St

E
1 Passavant Av

F
1 Spring Brook Ct

42°25'01"
42°24'35"
42°24'09"
42°23'42"
42°23'16"
42°22'50"
42°22'24"
42°21'58"

88°08'12"
88°07'37"
88°07'02"
88°06'27"
88°05'51"
88°05'16"

A B C D E

1 2 3 4 5 6 7

SEE 2531 MAP

1:24,000
1 in. = 2000 ft.
0 0.25 0.5
miles

SEE 2417 MAP

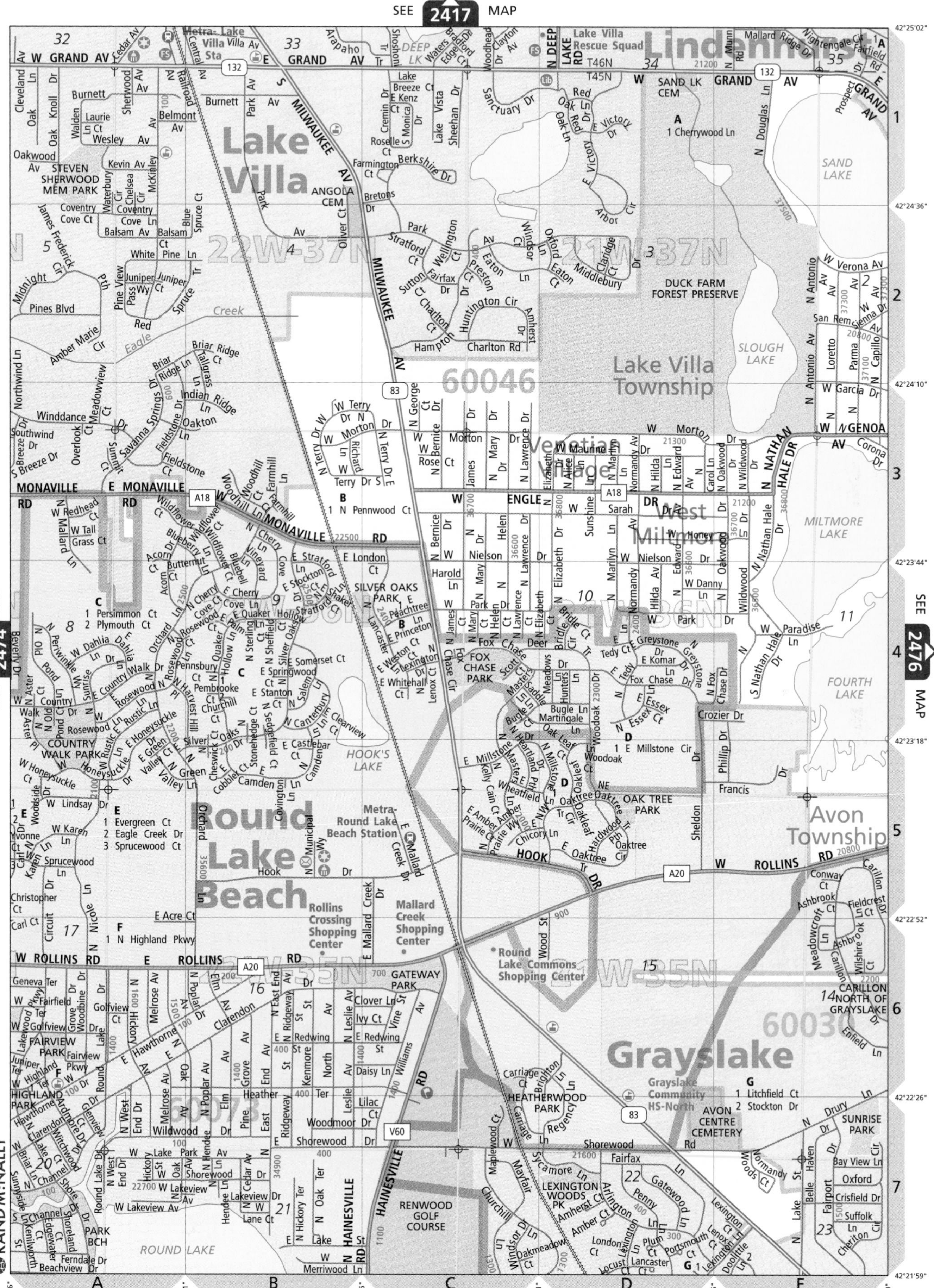

SEE 2474 MAP

SEE 2476 MAP

SEE 2532 MAP

1:24,000
1 in. = 2000 ft.
0 0.25 0.5
miles

SEE 2418 MAP

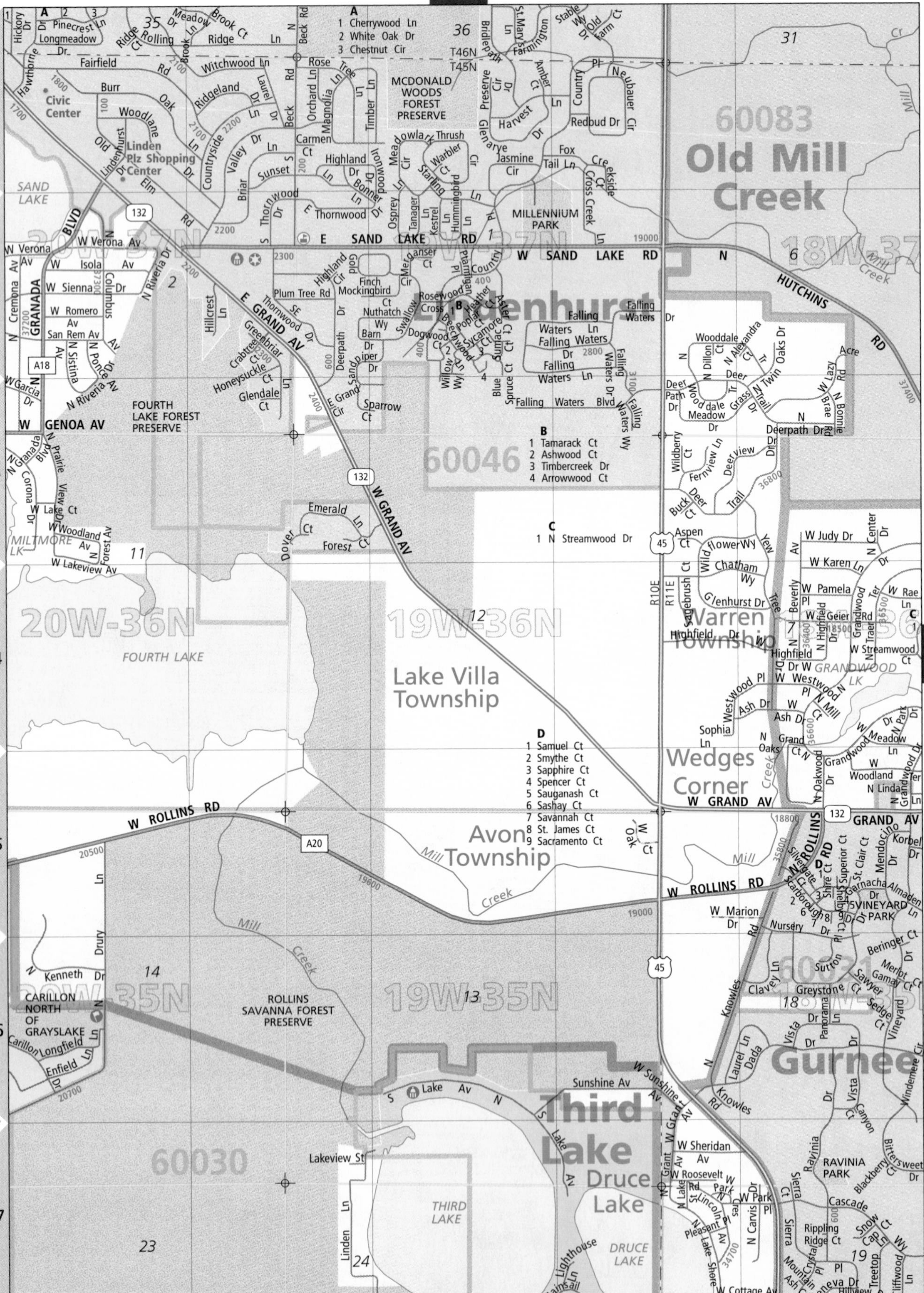

SEE 2475 MAP

SEE 2477 MAP

SEE 2533 MAP

A
1 Cherrywood Ln
2 White Oak Dr
3 Chestnut Cir

B
1 Tamarack Ct
2 Ashwood Ct
3 Timbercreek Dr
4 Arrowwood Ct

C
1 N Streamwood Dr

D
1 Samuel Ct
2 Smythe Ct
3 Sapphire Ct
4 Spencer Ct
5 Sauganash Ct
6 Sashay Ct
7 Savannah Ct
8 St. James Ct
9 Sacramento Ct

Lindenhurst

Old Mill Creek

60083

60046

60030

Lake Villa Township

Avon Township

Warren Township

Wedges Corner

Gurnee

Third Lake

Druce Lake

MCDONALD WOODS FOREST PRESERVE

FOURTH LAKE FOREST PRESERVE

ROLLINS SAVANNA FOREST PRESERVE

MILLENNIUM PARK

Civic Center

Linden Plz Shopping Center

CARILLON NORTH OF GRAYSLAKE

VINEYARD PARK

RAVINIA PARK

FOURTH LAKE

SAND LAKE

THIRD LAKE

DRUCE LAKE

MILTMORE LK

GRANDWOOD LK

20W-37N

19W-37N

18W-37N

20W-36N

19W-36N

20W-35N

19W-35N

T46N

T45N

R10E

R11E

E SAND LAKE RD

W SAND LAKE RD

W ROLLINS RD

W GRAND AV

E GRAND AV

HUTCHINS RD

GRANADA BLVD

W GENOA AV

Mill Creek

42°25'02"
42°24'36"
42°24'10"
42°23'44"
42°23'18"
42°22'52"
42°22'26"
42°21'59"

88°02'20"
88°01'45"
88°01'10"
88°00'35"
87°59'59"
87°59'24"

A B C D E

1 2 3 4 5 6 7

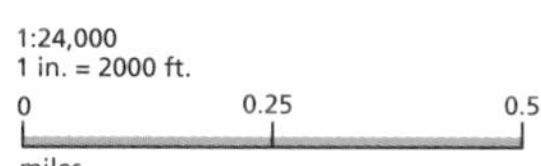

SEE 2419 MAP

Old Mill Creek
60083
Warren Township
Newport Township
Wadsworth
Grandwood Park
Gurnee
Stonebrook
Orchard Valley
60031

WESTGATE NATURE PRESERVE
PASTURE PARK
WESTGATE PARK
Gurnee Mills Mall
Stonebrook Coms Plaza
Grand Hunt Shopping Center
Rinkside Family Entertainment Center
CONCORD OAKS PARK
WARREN CEMETERY
Grand Tri- State Business Park
BITTERSWEET GOLF CLUB
HUNT CLUB COMMUNITY PARK
TIMBER WOODS PARK
SIX FLAGS GREAT AMERICA
NORTH RIDGE PLZ

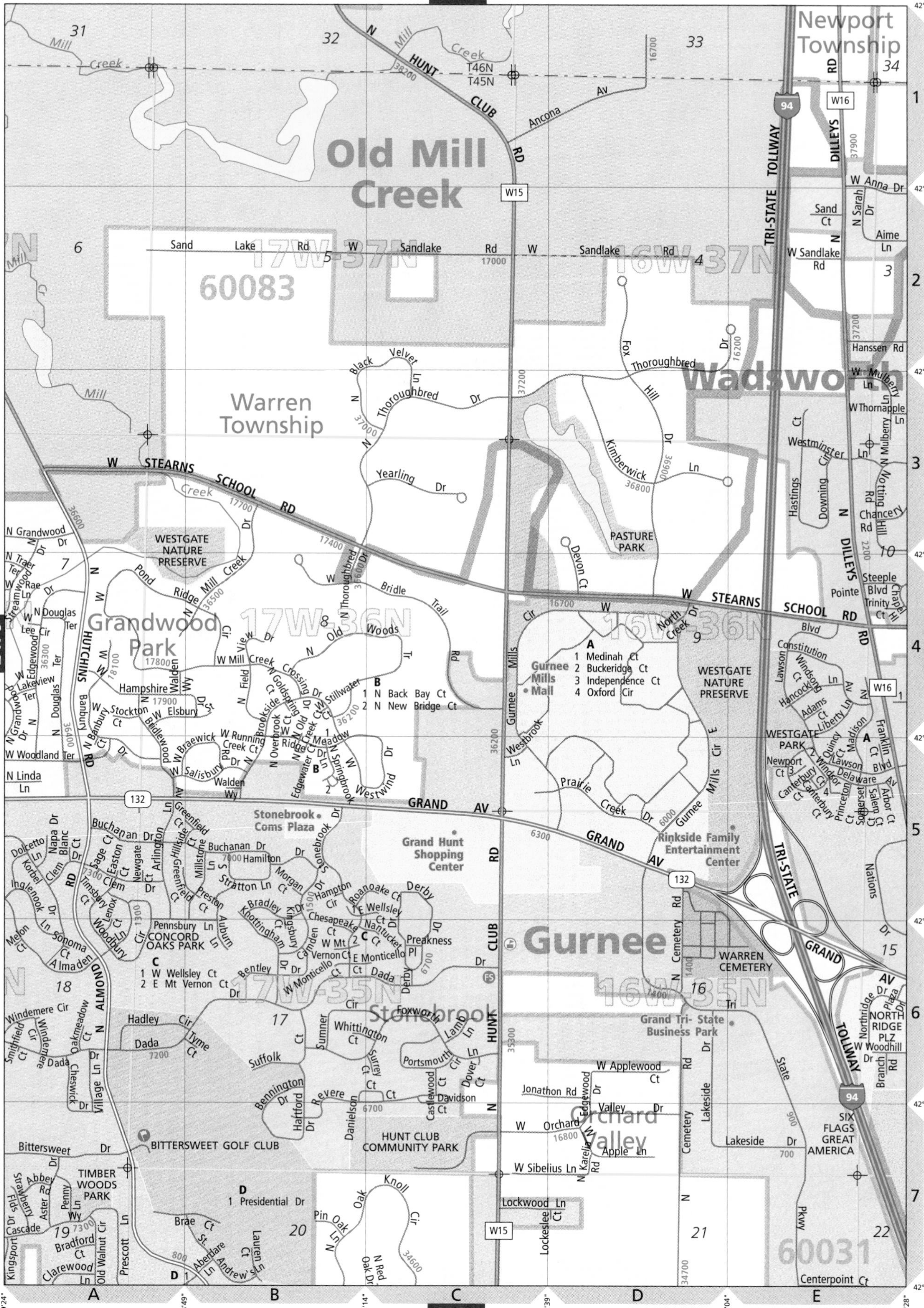

TRI-STATE TOLLWAY
N HUNT CLUB RD
W STEARNS SCHOOL RD
GRAND AV
N HUTCHINS RD
N ALMOND RD
N DILLEYS RD

A
1 Medinah Ct
2 Buckeridge Ct
3 Independence Ct
4 Oxford Cir

B
1 N Back Bay Ct
2 N New Bridge Ct

C
1 W Wellsley Ct
2 E Mt Vernon Ct

D
1 Presidential Dr

SEE 2476 MAP

SEE 2478 MAP

SEE 2534 MAP

1:24,000
1 in. = 2000 ft.
0 0.25 0.5
miles

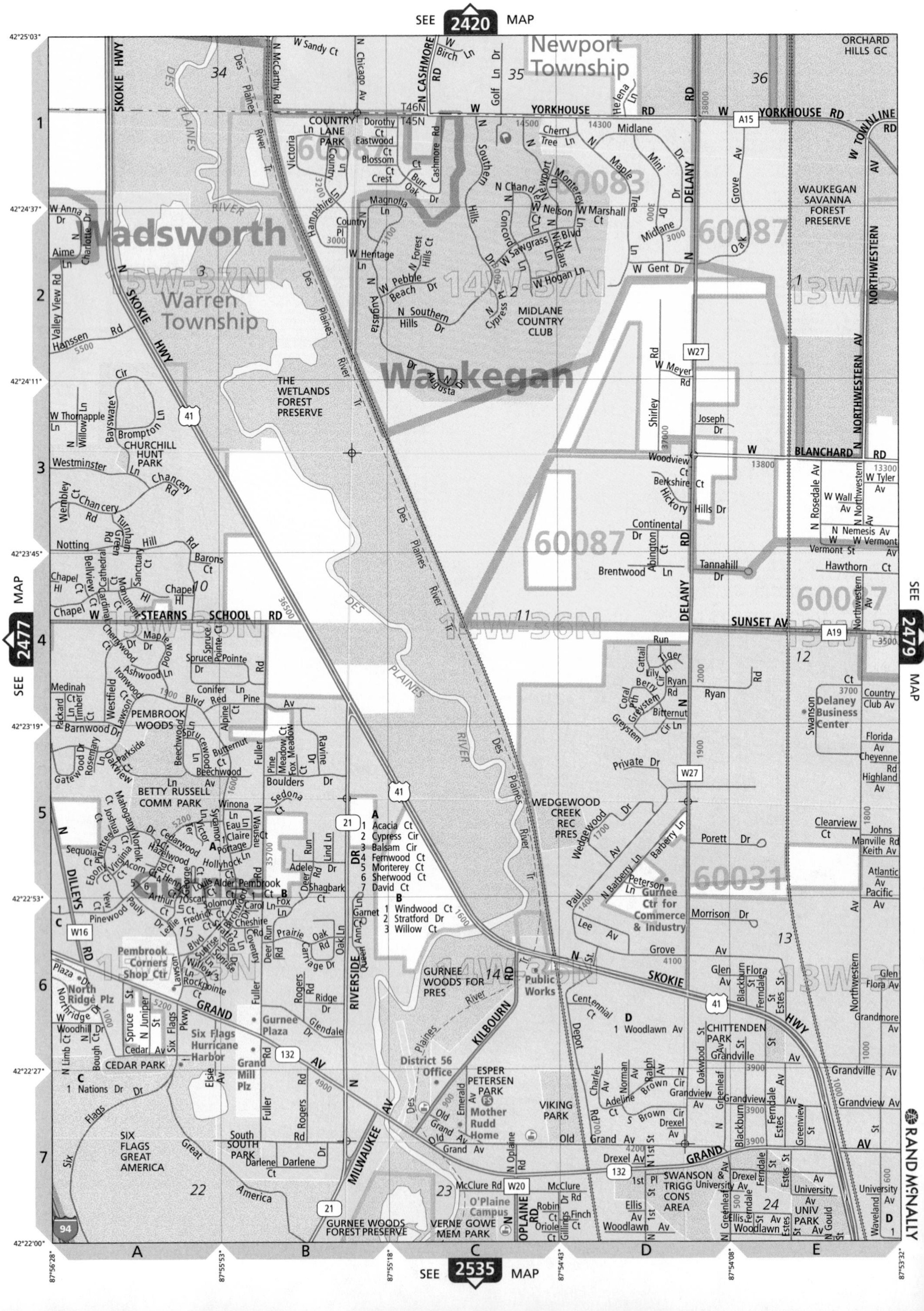

SEE 2420 MAP

Newport Township
Wadsworth
Warren Township
Waukegan
Gurnee

ORCHARD HILLS GC
WAUKEGAN SAVANNA FOREST PRESERVE
COUNTRY LANE PARK
MIDLANE COUNTRY CLUB
THE WETLANDS FOREST PRESERVE
CHURCHILL HUNT PARK
PEMBROOK WOODS
BETTY RUSSELL COMM PARK
WEDGEWOOD CREEK REC PRES
Gurnee Ctr for Commerce & Industry
Delaney Business Center
GURNEE WOODS FOR PRES
Public Works
Pembrook Corners Shop Ctr
North Ridge Plz
Six Flags Hurricane Harbor
Gurnee Plaza
Grand Mill Plz
CEDAR PARK
SIX FLAGS GREAT AMERICA
SOUTH PARK
District 56 Office
ESPER PETERSEN PARK
Mother Rudd Home
VIKING PARK
CHITTENDEN PARK
SWANSON & TRIGG CONS AREA
UNIV PARK
O'Plaine Campus
VERNE GOWE MEM PARK
GURNEE WOODS FOREST PRESERVE

SKOKIE HWY
YORKHOUSE RD
DELANY RD
STEARNS SCHOOL RD
SUNSET AV
BLANCHARD RD
NORTHWESTERN AV
TOWNLINE RD
DILLEYS RD
GRAND AV
MILWAUKEE AV
RIVERSIDE DR
KILBOURN RD
OPLAINE RD
DES PLAINES RIVER

A
1 Acacia Ct
2 Cypress Cir
3 Balsam Cir
4 Fernwood Ct
5 Monterey Ct
6 Sherwood Ct
7 David Ct

B
1 Windwood Ct
2 Stratford Dr
3 Willow Ct

C
1 Nations Dr

D
1 Woodlawn Av

60083
60087
60031

15W-37N
14W-37N
15W-36N
14W-36N
13W-36N

A B C D E
1 2 3 4 5 6 7

SEE 2477 MAP
SEE 2479 MAP
SEE 2535 MAP

RAND McNALLY

1:24,000
1 in. = 2000 ft.
0 0.25 0.5
miles

SEE 2421 MAP

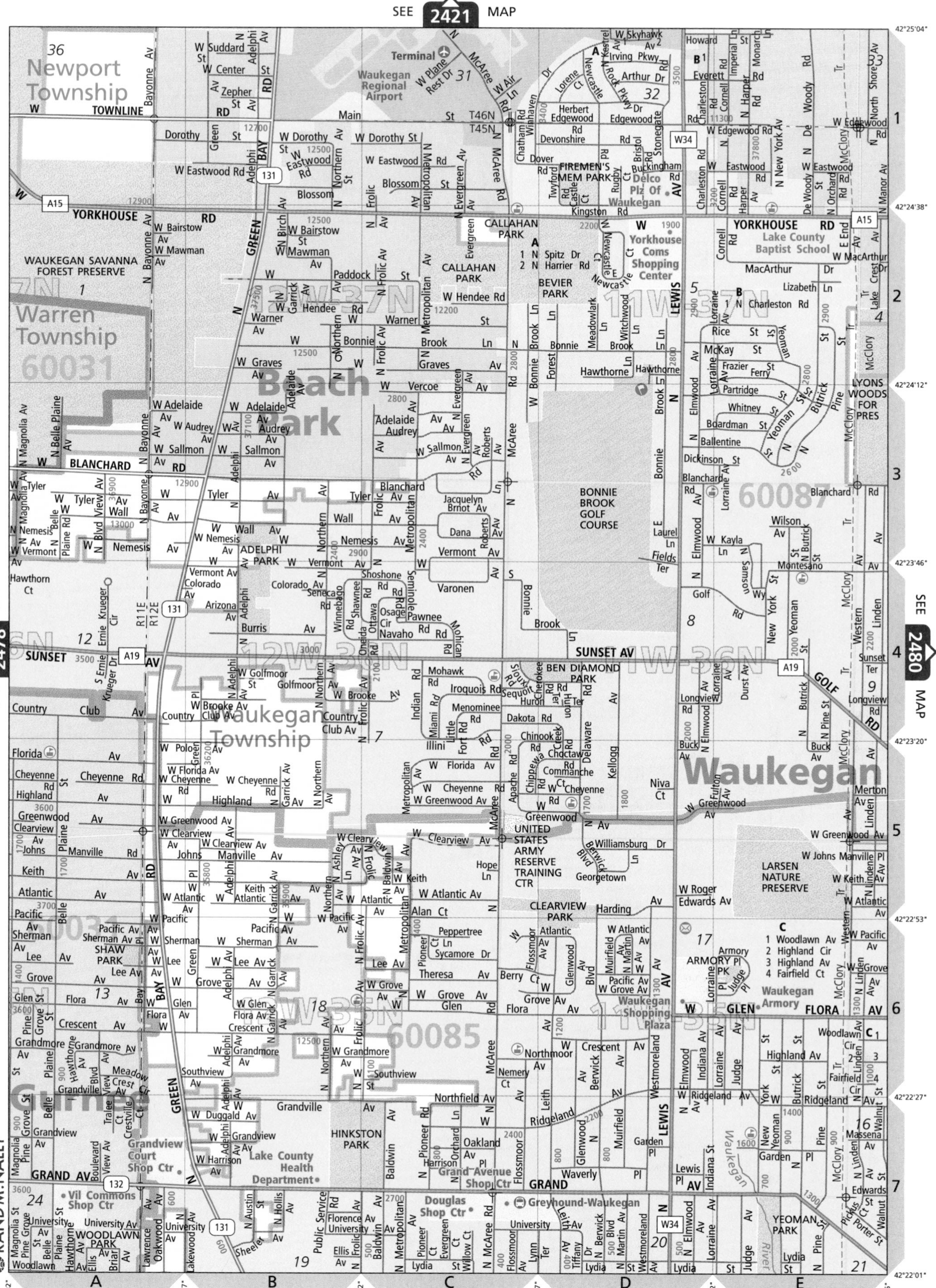

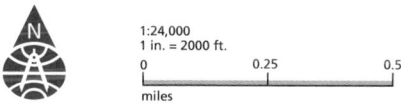

SEE 2478 MAP
SEE 2480 MAP
SEE 2536 MAP

1:24,000
1 in. = 2000 ft.
0 0.25 0.5
miles

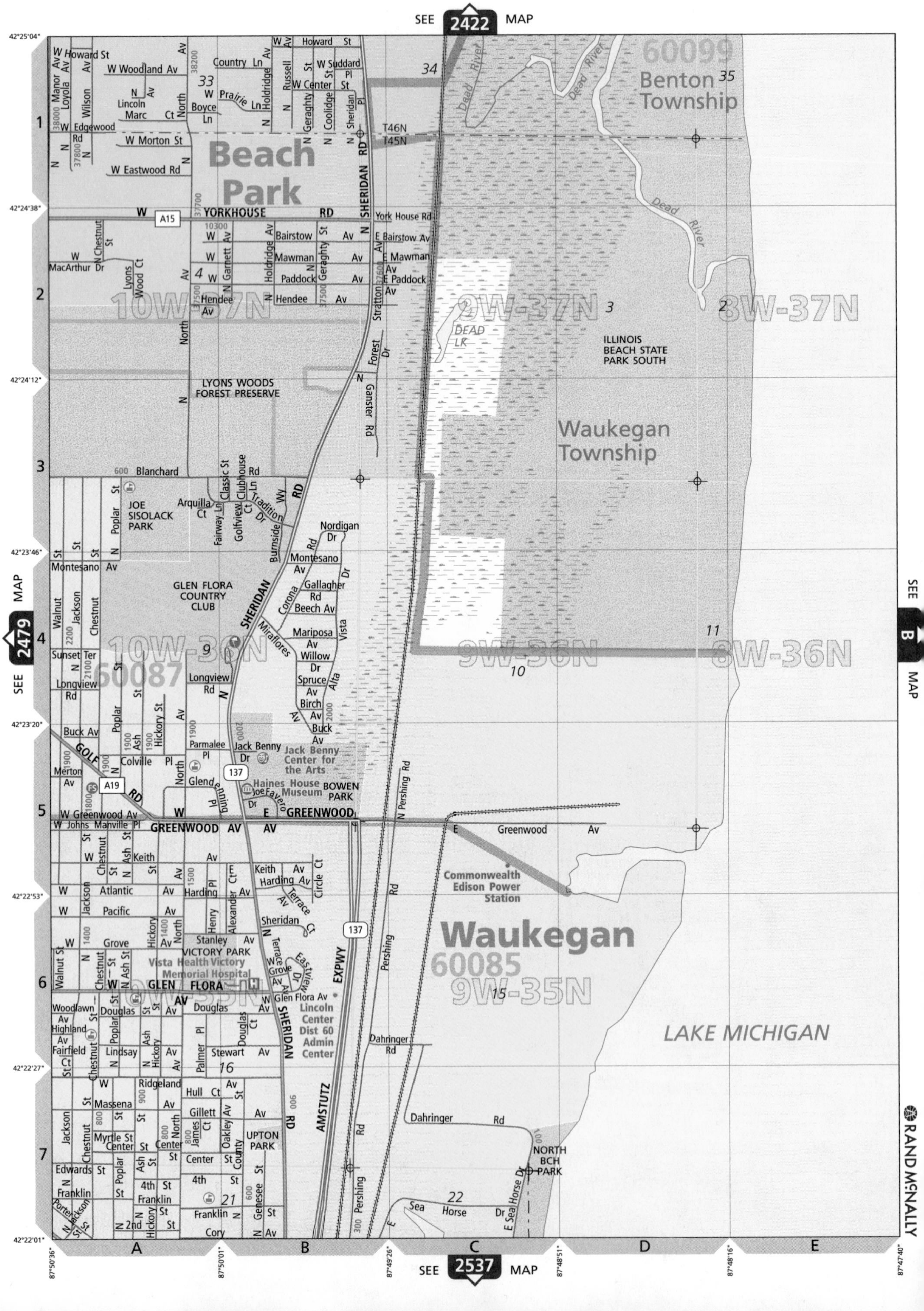

SEE 2422 MAP

SEE 2479 MAP

SEE B MAP

SEE 2537 MAP

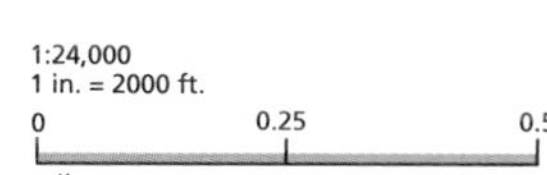

SEE B MAP

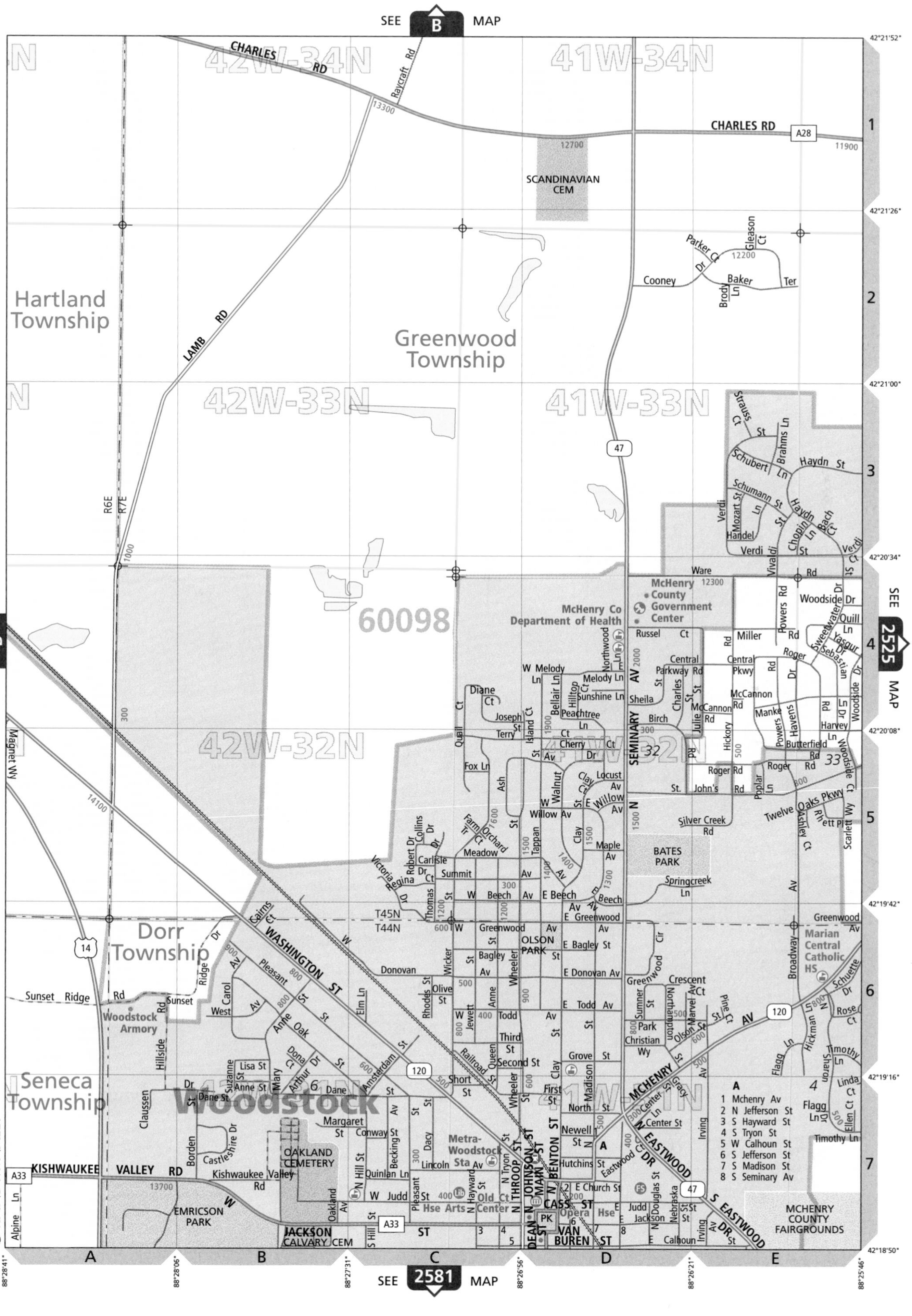

SEE B MAP

SEE 2525 MAP

SEE 2581 MAP

Hartland Township

Greenwood Township

Dorr Township

Seneca Township

Woodstock

60098

SCANDINAVIAN CEM

McHenry County Government Center

McHenry Co Department of Health

BATES PARK

OLSON PARK

Marian Central Catholic HS

Woodstock Armory

OAKLAND CEMETERY

EMRICSON PARK

JACKSON CALVARY CEM

Metra-Woodstock Sta

Old Ct Hse Arts Center

Opera Hse

MCHENRY COUNTY FAIRGROUNDS

CHARLES RD

LAMB RD

WASHINGTON ST

KISHWAUKEE VALLEY RD

MCHENRY AV

EASTWOOD DR

SEMINARY AV

A
1 Mchenry Av
2 N Jefferson St
3 S Hayward St
4 S Tryon St
5 W Calhoun St
6 S Jefferson St
7 S Madison St
8 S Seminary Av

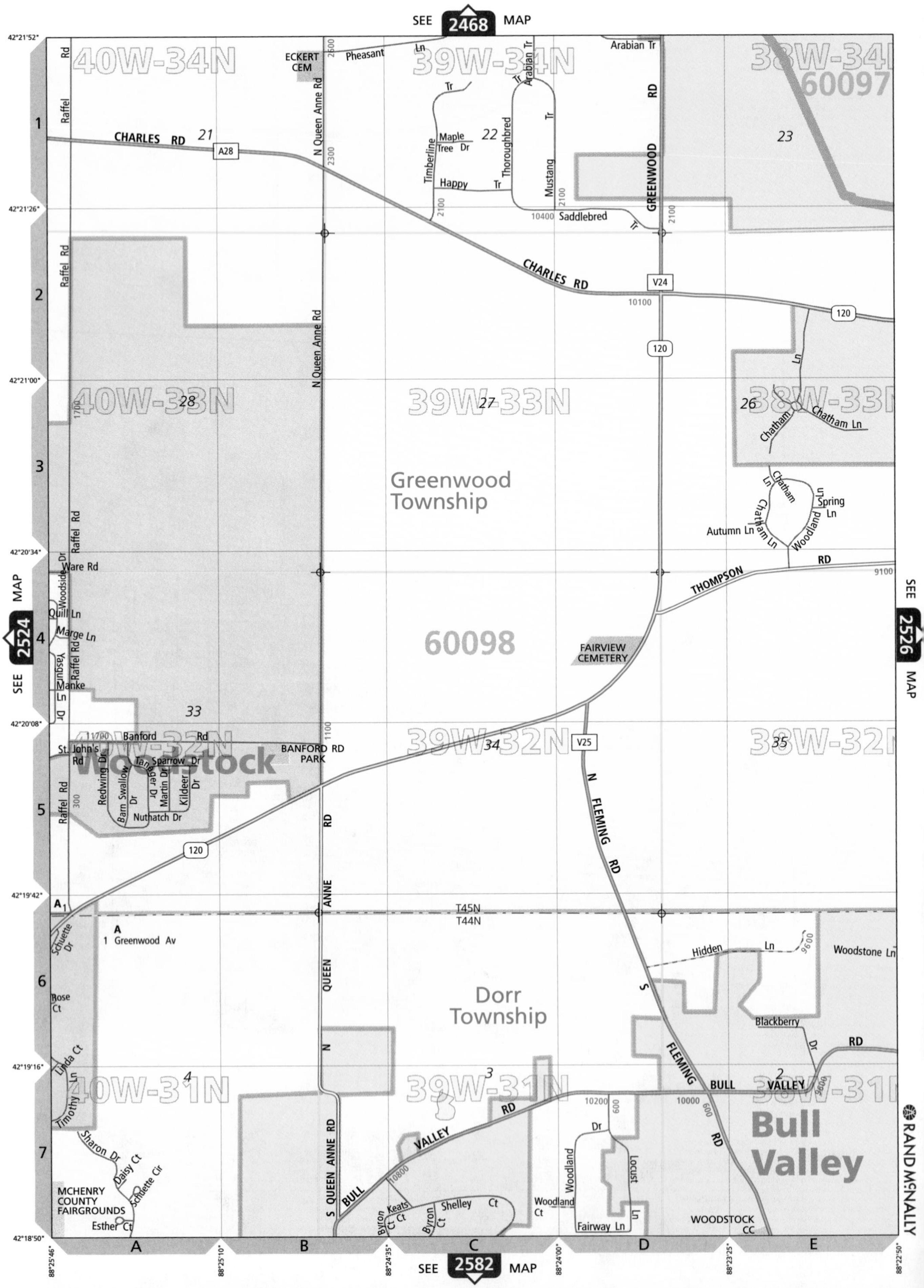

1:24,000
1 in. = 2000 ft.
0 0.25 0.5
miles

SEE 2468 MAP

SEE 2524 MAP

SEE 2526 MAP

SEE 2582 MAP

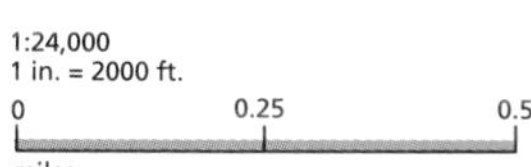

SEE 2469 MAP

Wonder Lake
37W-34N
36W-34N
Pine Needle Pass
Shadow Ln
23
24
19
20
THOMPSON RD
Basswood Dr
Cherry Dr
Walnut Dr
Chestnut Dr
E Chestnut Dr
St
Benjamin Dr
Lucy Dr
Maplewood Dr
E WONDER LAKE RD
Highview Dr
7900
E Meadow Ln
Lakeview Dr
Walnut Dr
S Chestnut Dr
Michael Dr
Pinoak
S Maplewood Dr
McHenry Township
60097
OSTEND CEM
120
1900
Bull Ridge Dr
Black Oak Dr
1700
Ginko Ct
Burr Oak Dr
1600
26
25
30
29
37W-33N
36W-33N
Marshland Wy
Hogbac Rd
Burr Oak Ct
Greenwood Township
60050
R7E
R8E
Boone Creek
1500
9100
N RIDGE RD
1100
N VALLEY HILL RD
7500
Burning Tree Dr
7100
Burning Tree Cir
McHenry
Eagle Point Dr
Timber Tr
Rd
800
Woodridge Tr
Ridgeway Tr
Glen
Colony Tr
Deer Run Tr
500
Silver
600
Deerwood Tr
60098
N COLD SPRINGS RD
Cambridge Ct
N Concord Dr
Bennington Ct
35
36
31
32
37W-32N
36W-32N
Forest Oak Dr
W Trey Rd
Trey Rd
N DRAPER RD
200
Breckenridge Ct
Wilmington Ct
Concord Dr
8400
Sudburg Ct
N Swarthmore Rd
Waterford Dr
Farmstead Dr
T45N
T44N
Woodstone Ln
S COLD SPRINGS RD
Tipperary Ct
Swarthmore Rd
7900
Nunda Township
Wexford Ct
Westgate St
E
Hythe Cir
Whitaker Ct
Millburne Ct
Gln
Stirlingshire Ct
McAndrews Dr
S DRAPER RD
300
High Meadow Ln
High Meadow Dr
2
1
6
5
Boone Creek
S VALLEY HILL RD
S RIDGE RD
Bull Valley
BULL VALLEY RD
37W-31N
36W-31N
8600
600
8000
7100
1200
Orchard Valley Dr
N CHERRY VALLEY RD
Boone Creek Ct
Stonewier Pt
BOONE CREEK GOLF CLUB
Saddle Creek Tr
Dorr Township
42°21'54"
42°21'28"
42°21'02"
42°20'36"
42°20'10"
42°19'44"
42°19'18"
42°18'52"
88°22'50"
88°22'15"
88°21'40"
88°21'04"
88°20'29"
88°19'54"
1
2
3
4
5
6
7
A
B
C
D
E

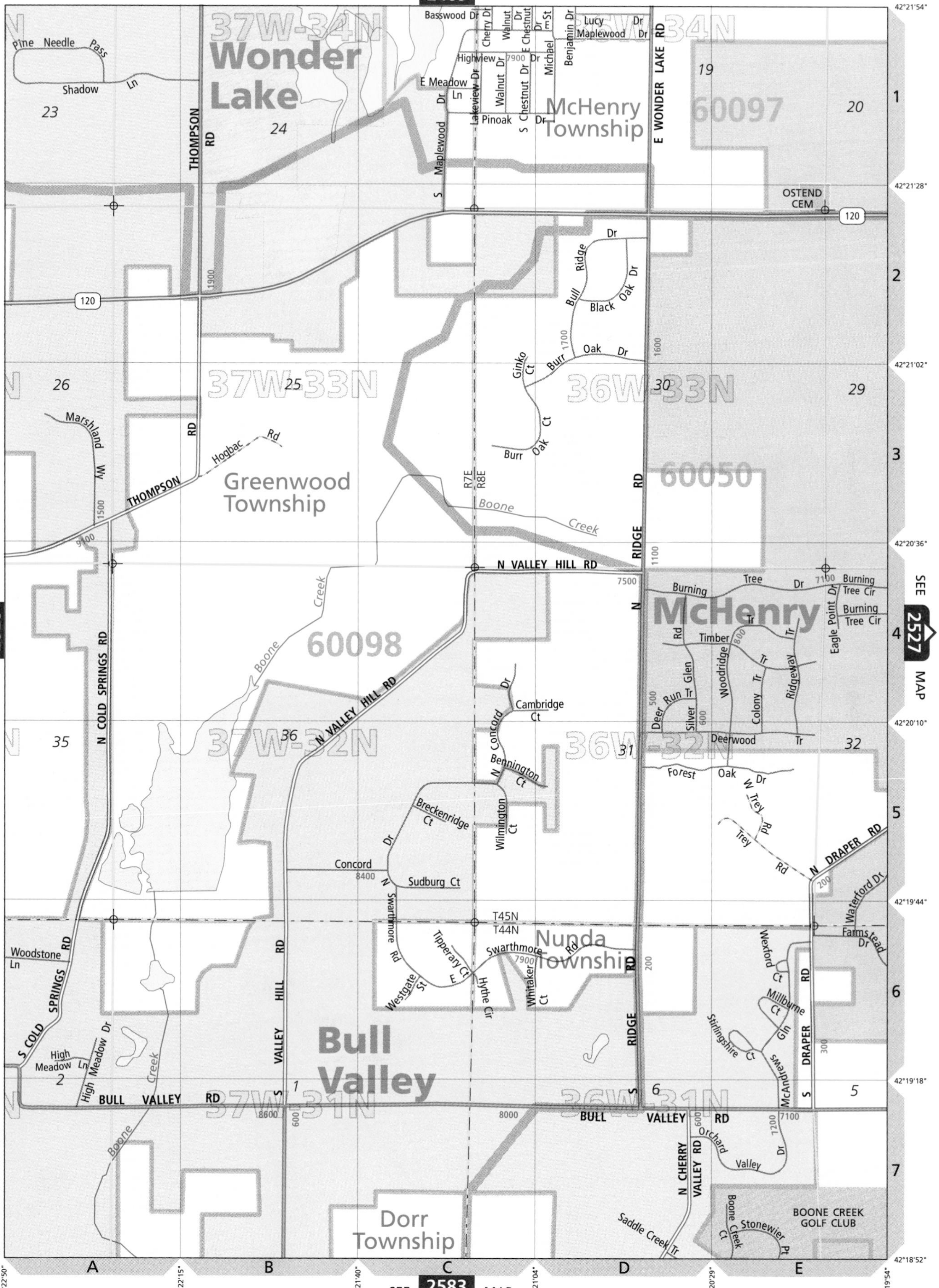

SEE 2525 MAP

SEE 2527 MAP

SEE 2583 MAP

1:24,000
1 in. = 2000 ft.
0 0.25 0.5
miles

SEE 2470 MAP

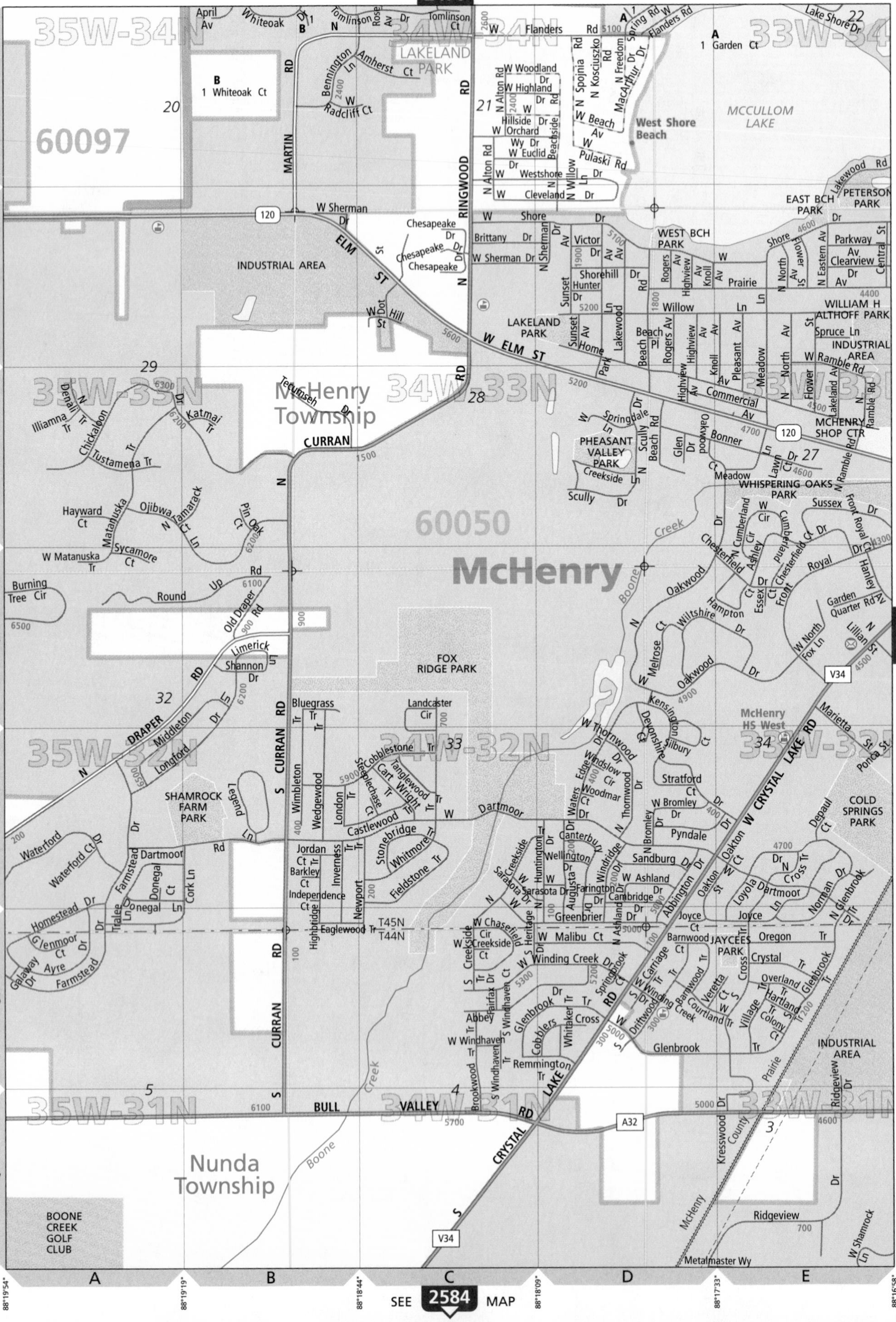

35W-34N
34W-34N
33W-34N
LAKELAND PARK
60097
B 1 Whiteoak Ct
A 1 Garden Ct
MCCULLOM LAKE
West Shore Beach
EAST BCH PARK
PETERSON PARK
WEST BCH PARK
INDUSTRIAL AREA
LAKELAND PARK
WILLIAM H ALTHOFF PARK
INDUSTRIAL AREA
McHenry Township
35W-33N
34W-33N
33W-33N
MCHENRY SHOP CTR
PHEASANT VALLEY PARK
WHISPERING OAKS PARK
60050
McHenry
FOX RIDGE PARK
McHenry HS West
35W-32N
34W-32N
33W-32N
SHAMROCK FARM PARK
COLD SPRINGS PARK
JAYCEES PARK
T45N
T44N
INDUSTRIAL AREA
35W-31N
34W-31N
33W-31N
Nunda Township
BOONE CREEK GOLF CLUB

W Sherman Dr, ELM ST, W ELM ST, RINGWOOD RD, MARTIN RD, CURRAN RD, S CURRAN RD, N DRAPER RD, W Dartmoor Dr, W CRYSTAL LAKE RD, S CRYSTAL LAKE RD, BULL VALLEY RD, Boone Creek, Ridgeview Dr, Metalmaster Wy

120
V34
A32

SEE 2526 MAP

SEE 2528 MAP

A B C D E
1 2 3 4 5 6 7

42°21'54" 42°21'28" 42°21'02" 42°20'36" 42°20'10" 42°19'44" 42°19'18" 42°18'52"
88°19'54" 88°19'19" 88°18'44" 88°18'09" 88°17'33" 88°16'58"

SEE 2584 MAP

1:24,000
1 in. = 2000 ft.
0 0.25 0.5
miles

SEE 2471 MAP

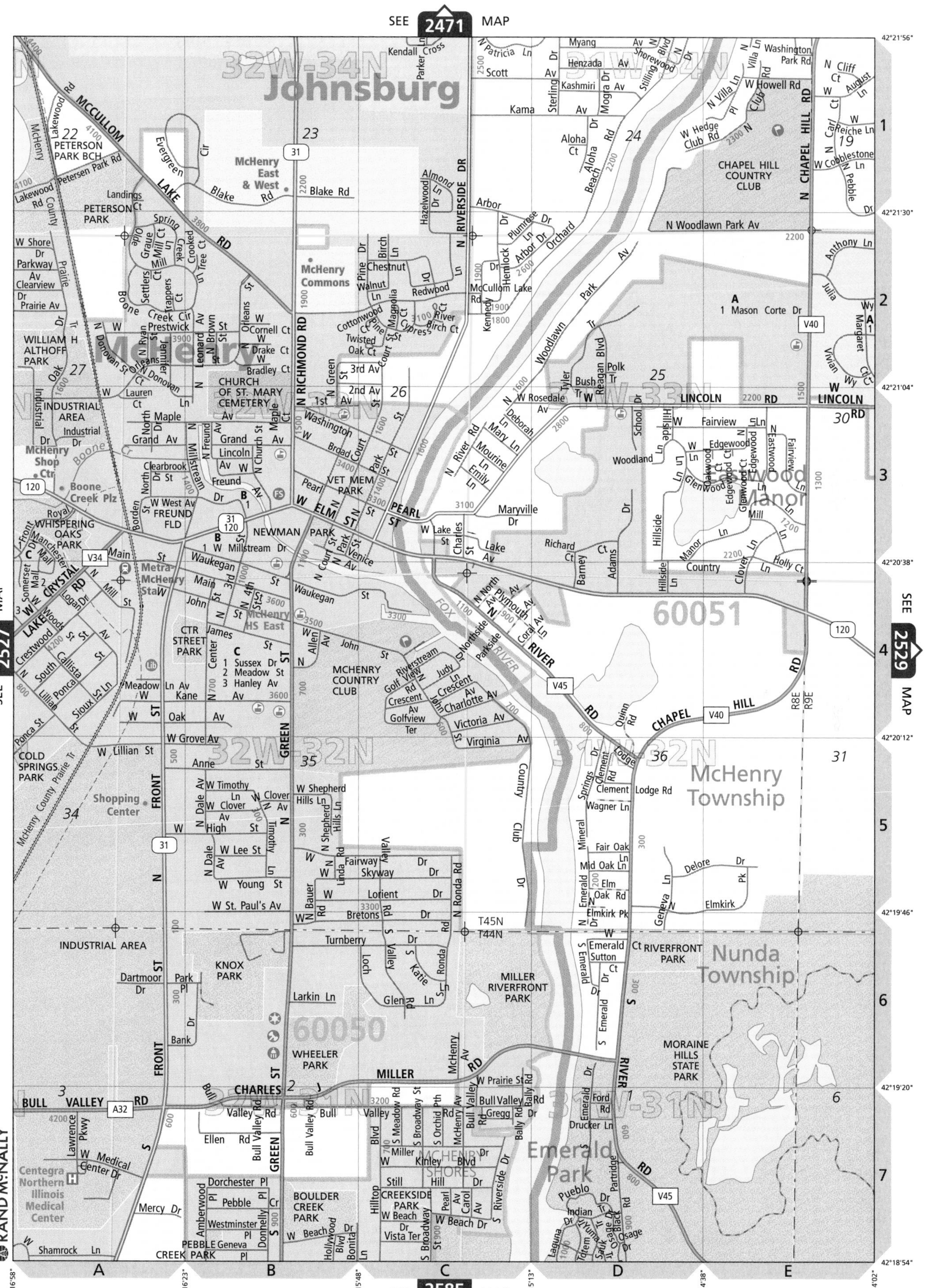

SEE 2527 MAP
SEE 2529 MAP
SEE 2585 MAP

RAND McNALLY

1:24,000
1 in. = 2000 ft.
0 0.25 0.5
miles

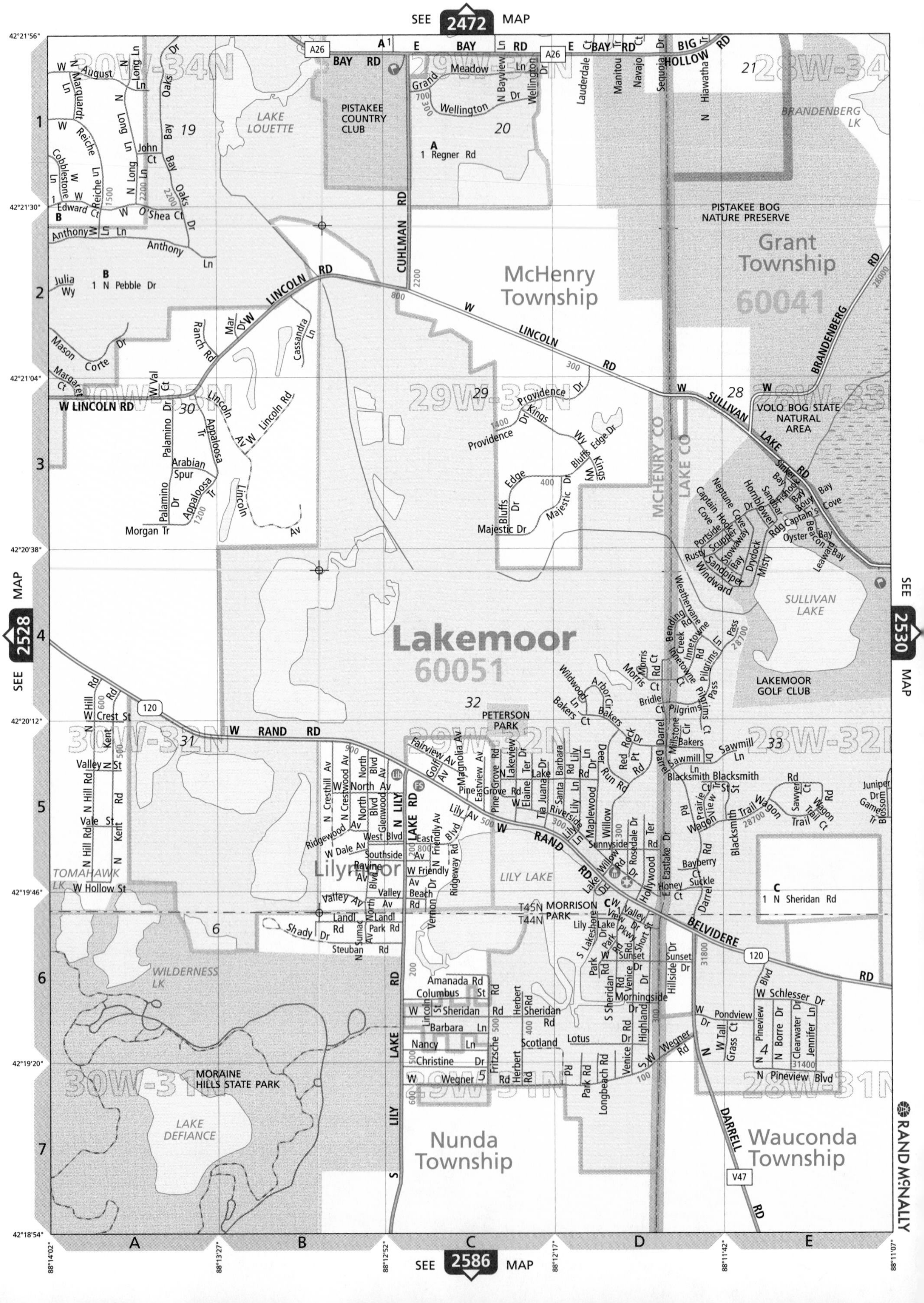

SEE 2472 MAP

SEE 2528 MAP

SEE 2530 MAP

SEE 2586 MAP

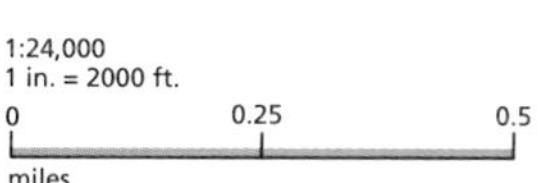

SEE 2473 MAP

Volo
Fox Lake
Round Lake
Lakemoor
Grant Township
Wauconda Township
VOLO BOG STATE NATURAL AREA
LAKEMOOR GOLF CLUB
MARL FLAT FOREST PRESERVE
BAXTER TECHNOLOGY PARK
SINGING HILLS FOREST PRESERVE
GRANT CEM
Volo Auto Mus
BRANDENBERG LAKE
WOOSTER LAKE
FISH LAKE
W BRANDENBERG RD
W SULLIVAN LAKE RD
MOLIDOR RD
W NIPPERSINK RD
W NIPPERSINK AV
N FISH LAKE RD
N WILSON RD
BELVIDERE RD
VOLO VILLAGE RD
N FOX LAKE RD
N GILMER RD
27W-34N
26W-34N
27W-33N
26W-33N
27W-32N
26W-32N
27W-31N
26W-31N
60041
60073
60030
60051
T45N
T44N

A
1 N Barberry Rd
2 N Goldenrod Rd

B
1 Spring Valley Ct

C
1 W Forest Cove Dr

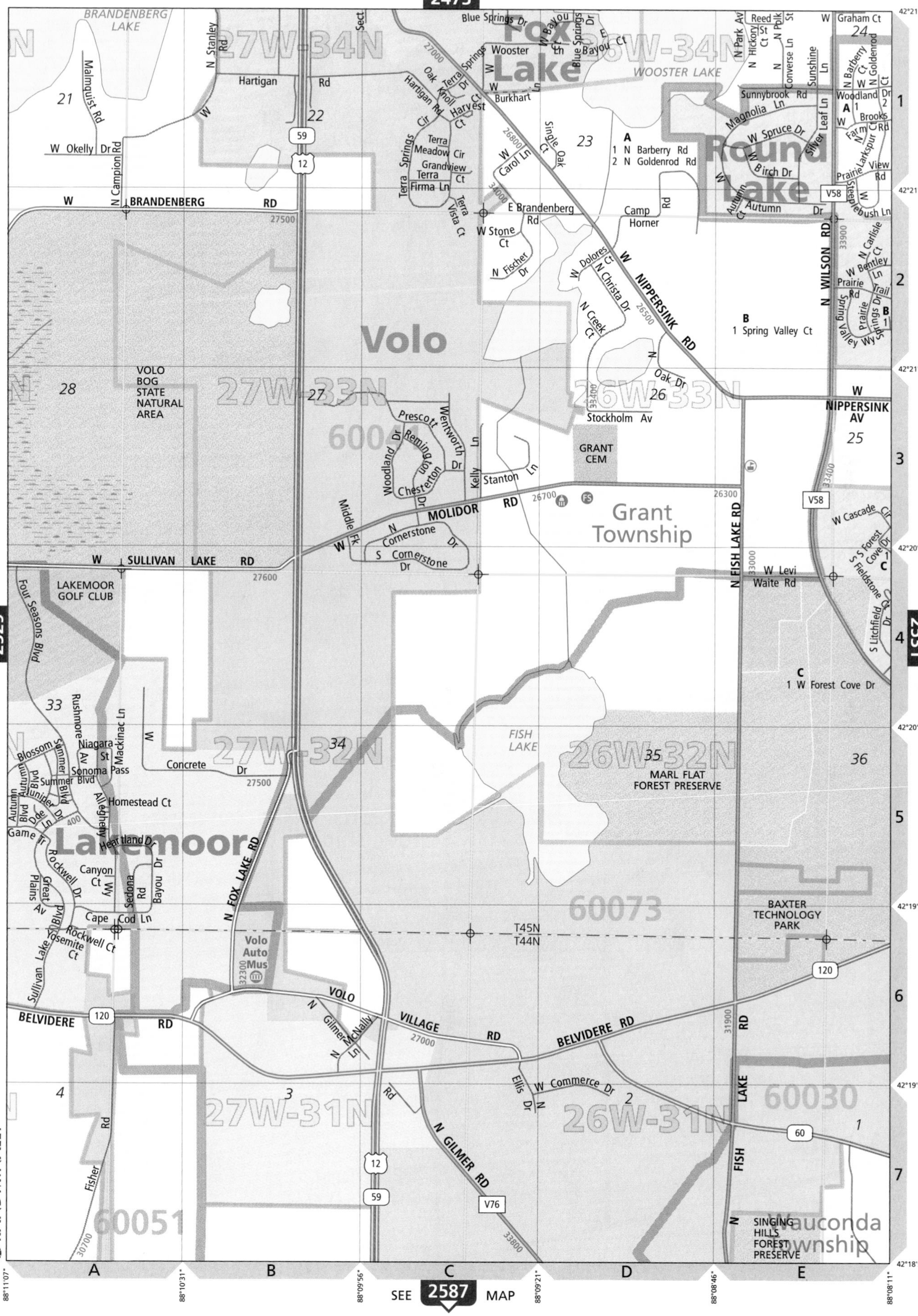

SEE 2529 MAP

SEE 2531 MAP

SEE 2587 MAP

1:24,000
1 in. = 2000 ft.
0 0.25 0.5
miles

SEE 2474 MAP

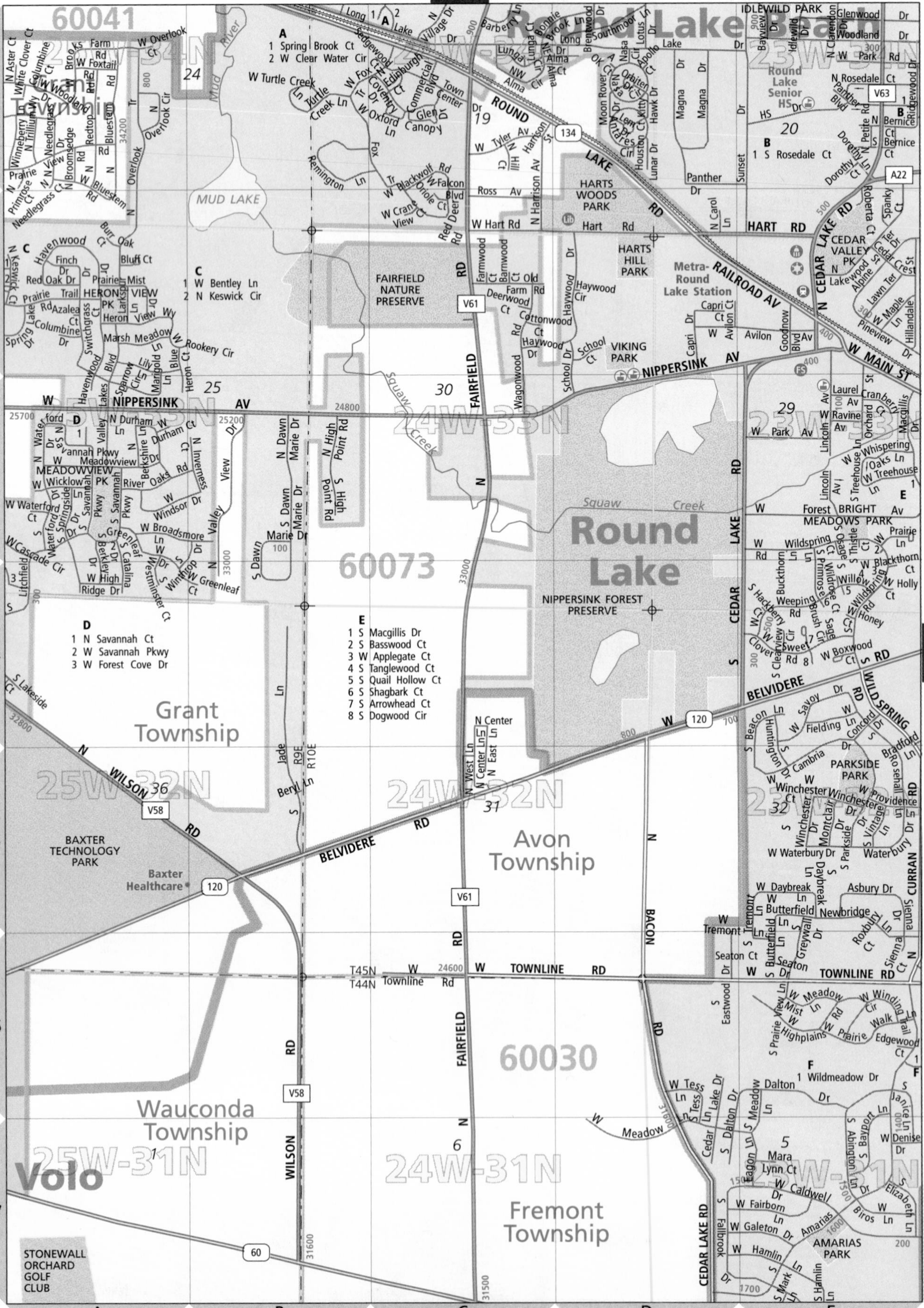

Round Lake Beach

Round Lake

Grant Township

Avon Township

Wauconda Township

Fremont Township

Volo

60041

60073

60030

A
1 Spring Brook Ct
2 W Clear Water Cir

B
1 S Rosedale Ct

C
1 W Bentley Ln
2 N Keswick Cir

D
1 N Savannah Ct
2 W Savannah Pkwy
3 W Forest Cove Dr

E
1 S Macgillis Dr
2 S Basswood Ct
3 W Applegate Ct
4 S Tanglewood Ct
5 S Quail Hollow Ct
6 S Shagbark Ct
7 S Arrowhead Ct
8 S Dogwood Cir

F
1 Wildmeadow Dr

FAIRFIELD NATURE PRESERVE

NIPPERSINK FOREST PRESERVE

HARTS WOODS PARK

HARTS HILL PARK

VIKING PARK

CEDAR VALLEY PK

HERON VIEW PK

MEADOWVIEW PK

BRIGHT MEADOWS PARK

PARKSIDE PARK

AMARIAS PARK

IDLEWILD PARK

Round Lake Senior HS

Metra-Round Lake Station

MUD LAKE

BAXTER TECHNOLOGY PARK

Baxter Healthcare

STONEWALL ORCHARD GOLF CLUB

SEE 2530 MAP

SEE 2532 MAP

SEE 2588 MAP

1:24,000
1 in. = 2000 ft.
0 0.25 0.5
miles

SEE 2475 MAP

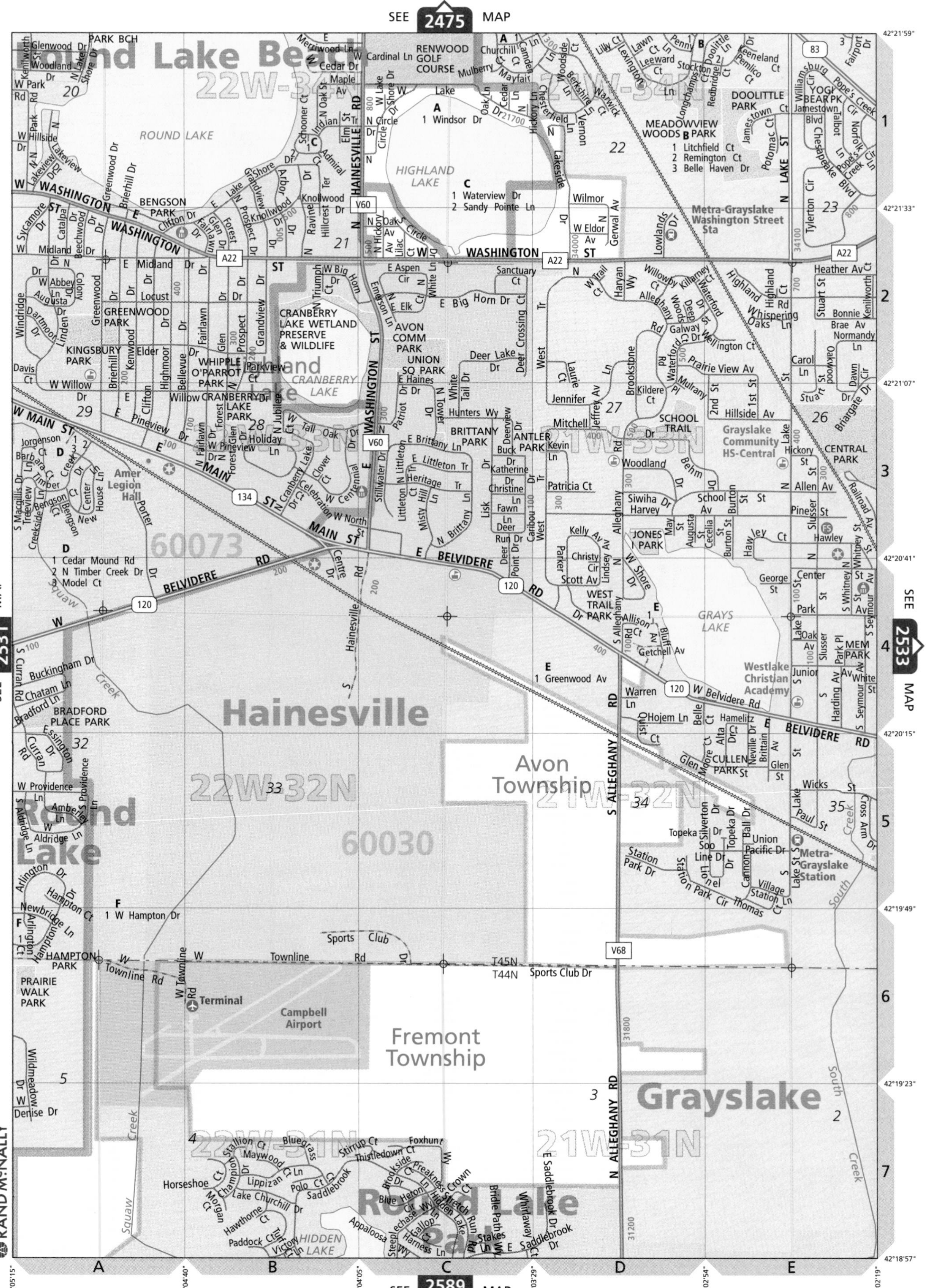

SEE 2531 MAP

SEE 2533 MAP

SEE 2589 MAP

1:24,000
1 in. = 2000 ft.
0 0.25 0.5
miles

SEE 2476 MAP

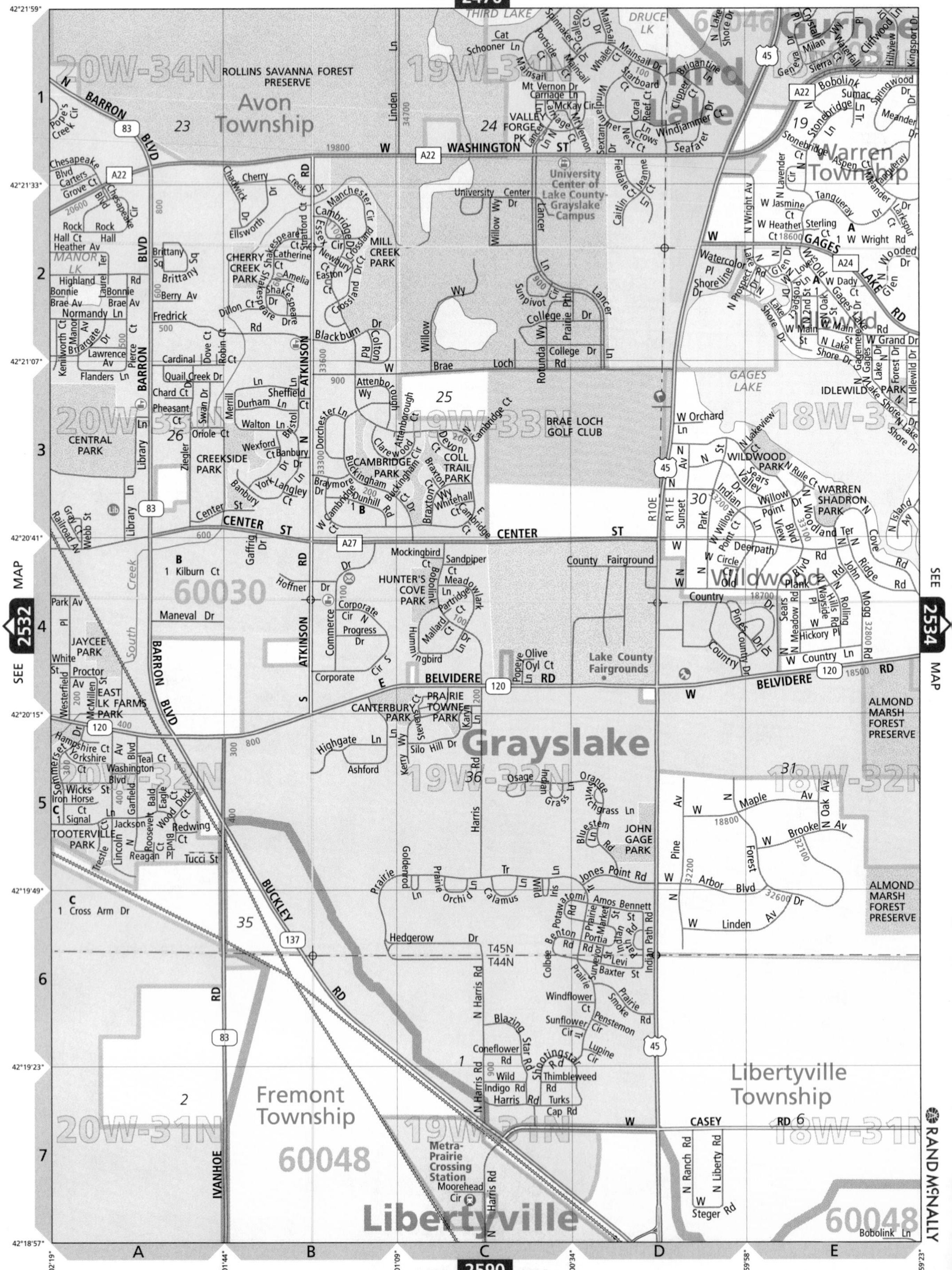

SEE 2532 MAP

SEE 2534 MAP

SEE 2590 MAP

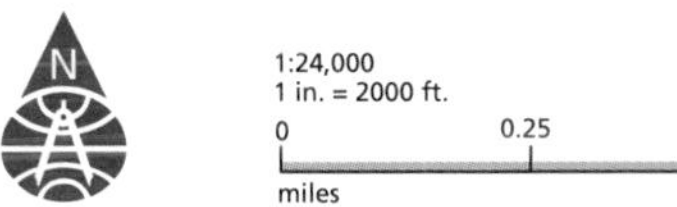

SEE 2477 MAP

SEE 2533 MAP

SEE 2535 MAP

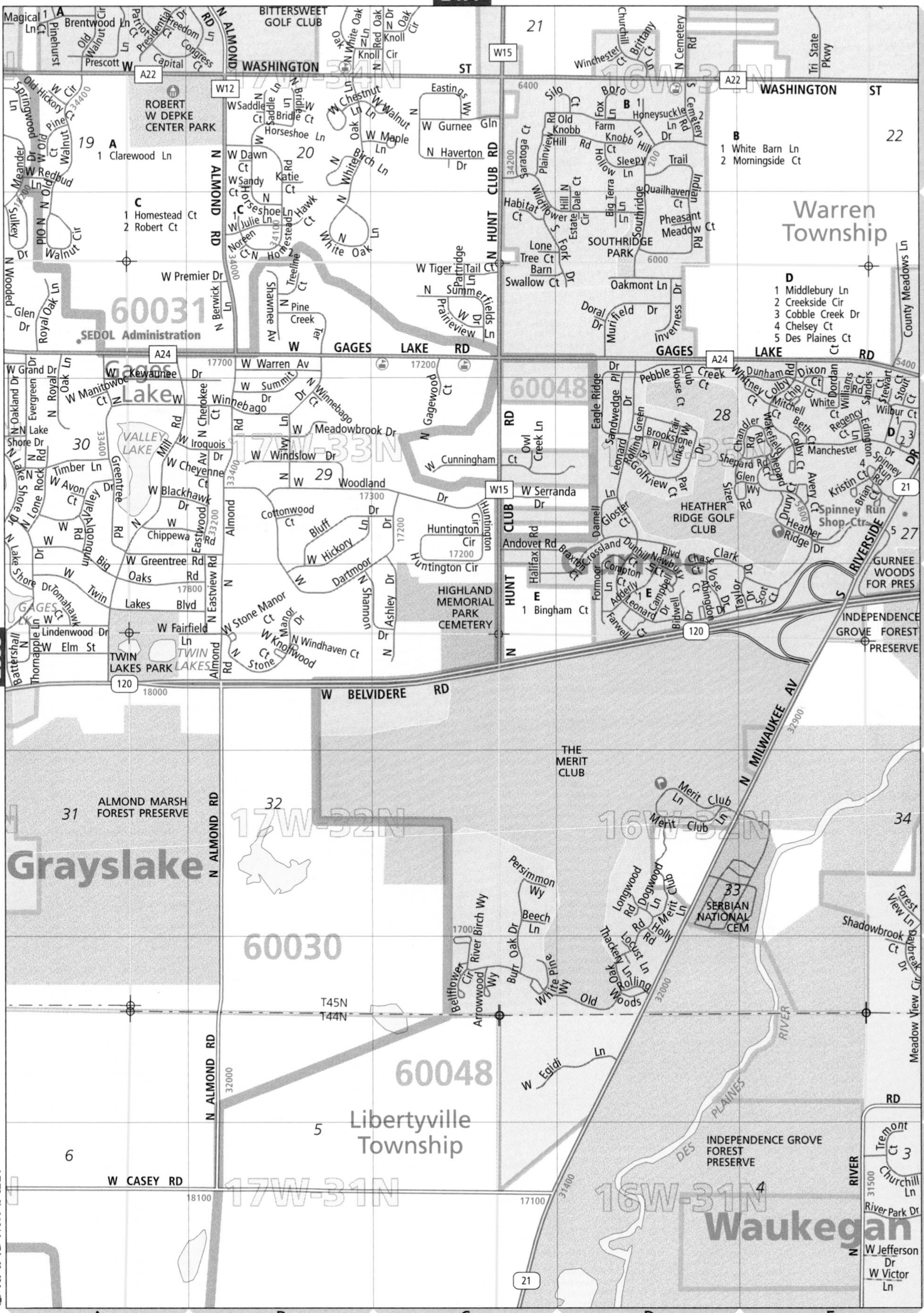

SEE 2591 MAP

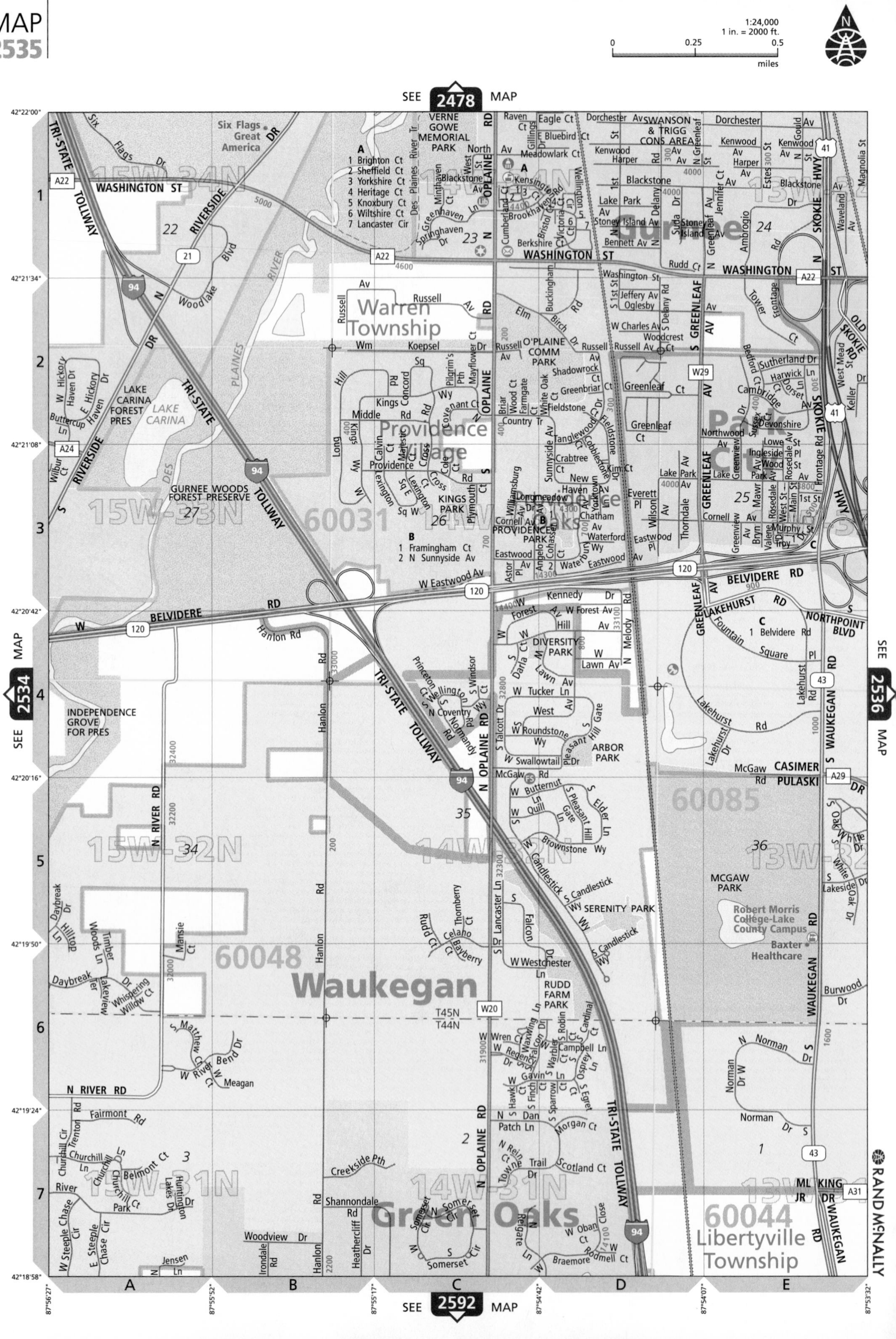

1:24,000
1 in. = 2000 ft.
0 0.25 0.5
miles

SEE 2478 MAP

SEE 2534 MAP

SEE 2536 MAP

Six Flags Great America

VERNE GOWE MEMORIAL PARK

SWANSON & TRIGG CONS AREA

A
1 Brighton Ct
2 Sheffield Ct
3 Yorkshire Ct
4 Heritage Ct
5 Knoxbury Ct
6 Wiltshire Ct
7 Lancaster Cir

Gurnee

Warren Township

O'PLAINE COMM PARK

LAKE CARINA FOREST PRES

LAKE CARINA

Providence Village

GURNEE WOODS FOREST PRESERVE

KINGS PARK

PROVIDENCE PARK

B
1 Framingham Ct
2 N Sunnyside Av

15W-34N
14W-34N
13W-34N
15W-33N
14W-33N
13W-33N
15W-32N
14W-32N
13W-32N
15W-31N
14W-31N
13W-31N

60031
60048
60085
60044

Park City

C
1 Belvidere Rd

TRI-STATE TOLLWAY
WASHINGTON ST
BELVIDERE RD
N OPLAINE RD
S GREENLEAF AV
SKOKIE HWY
WAUKEGAN RD
N RIVER RD
NORTHPOINT BLVD
CASIMER PULASKI DR
ML KING JR DR

INDEPENDENCE GROVE FOR PRES

DIVERSITY PARK

ARBOR PARK

SERENITY PARK

MCGAW PARK

Robert Morris College-Lake County Campus

Baxter Healthcare

RUDD FARM PARK

Waukegan

T45N
T44N

Green Oaks

Libertyville Township

A B C D E

1 2 3 4 5 6 7

42°22'00" 42°21'34" 42°21'08" 42°20'42" 42°20'16" 42°19'50" 42°19'24" 42°18'58"

87°56'27" 87°55'52" 87°55'17" 87°54'42" 87°54'07" 87°53'32"

SEE 2592 MAP

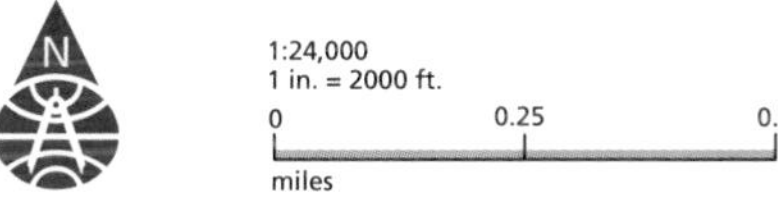

SEE 2479 MAP

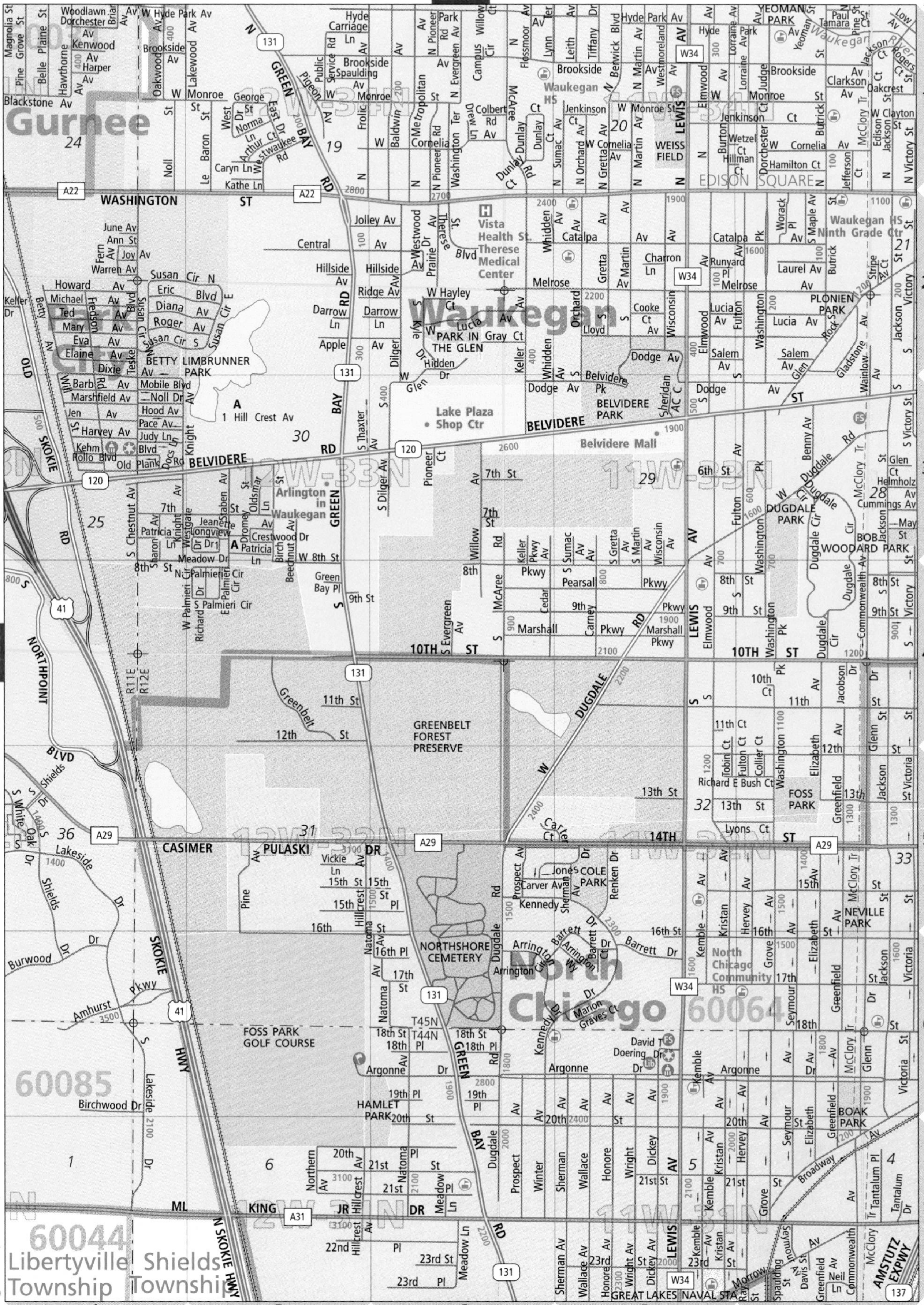

SEE 2535 MAP

SEE 2537 MAP

Gurnee

Park City

Waukegan

North Chicago 60064

60085

60044

Libertyville Township

Shields Township

EDISON SQUARE

WASHINGTON ST

BELVIDERE ST

10TH ST

14TH ST

CASIMER PULASKI DR

ML KING JR DR

GREEN BAY RD

LEWIS AV

SKOKIE HWY

NORTHPOINT BLVD

OLD SKOKIE RD

AMSTUTZ EXPWY

W DUGDALE RD

Waukegan HS

Vista Health St. Therese Medical Center

Lake Plaza Shop Ctr

Belvidere Mall

BETTY LIMBRUNNER PARK

PARK IN THE GLEN

BELVIDERE PARK

DUGDALE PARK

BOB JACKSON WOODARD PARK

PLONIEN PARK

YEOMAN PARK

WEISS FIELD

Arlington in Waukegan

Waukegan HS Ninth Grade Ctr

GREENBELT FOREST PRESERVE

FOSS PARK

COLE PARK

NEVILLE PARK

NORTHSHORE CEMETERY

North Chicago Community HS

FOSS PARK GOLF COURSE

HAMLET PARK

BOAK PARK

GREAT LAKES NAVAL STA

12W-34N

11W-34N

12W-33N

11W-33N

12W-32N

11W-32N

12W-31N

11W-31N

T45N

T44N

R11E

R12E

1 2 3 4 5 6 7

A B C D E

42°22'01"

42°21'35"

42°21'09"

42°20'43"

42°20'17"

42°19'51"

42°19'25"

42°18'59"

87°53'32"

87°52'57"

87°52'21"

87°51'46"

87°51'11"

87°50'36"

SEE 2593 MAP

1:24,000
1 in. = 2000 ft.
0 0.25 0.5
miles

SEE 2480 MAP

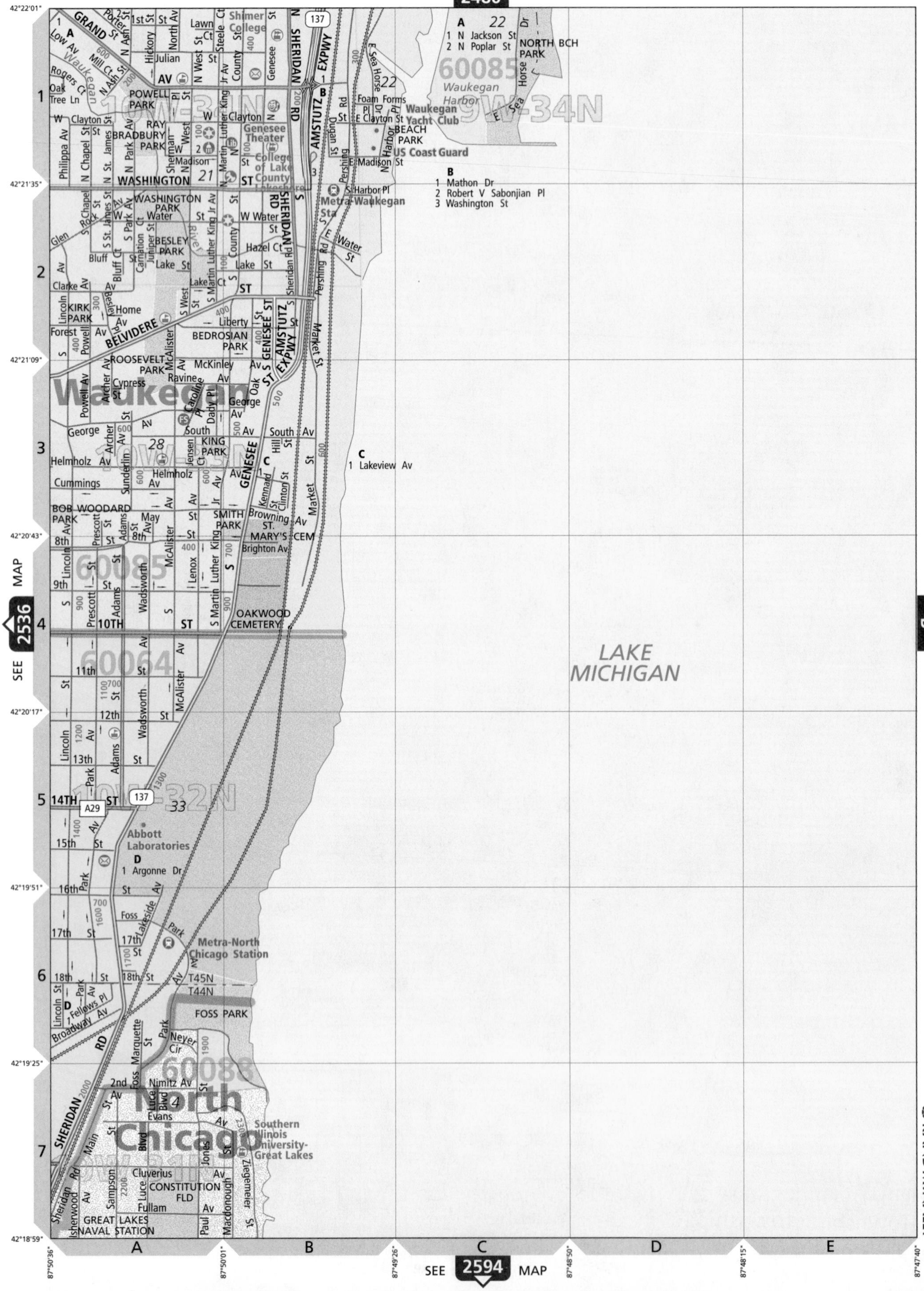

A
1 N Jackson St
2 N Poplar St

B
1 Mathon Dr
2 Robert V Sabonjian Pl
3 Washington St

C
1 Lakeview Av

D
1 Argonne Dr

Waukegan

North Chicago

LAKE MICHIGAN

Waukegan Harbor

Waukegan Yacht Club

US Coast Guard

NORTH BCH PARK

BEACH PARK

Shimer College

Genesee Theater

College of Lake County Lakeshore

Metra-Waukegan Sta

POWELL PARK

RAY BRADBURY PARK

WASHINGTON PARK

BESLEY PARK

KIRK PARK

BEDROSIAN PARK

ROOSEVELT PARK

KING PARK

BOB WOODARD PARK

SMITH PARK

ST. MARY'S CEM

OAKWOOD CEMETERY

Abbott Laboratories

Metra-North Chicago Station

FOSS PARK

Southern Illinois University-Great Lakes

CONSTITUTION FLD

GREAT LAKES NAVAL STATION

60085 60064 60088

10W-34N 9W-34N 10W-33N 10W-32N 9W-31N

T45N T44N

GRAND AV · WASHINGTON ST · BELVIDERE ST · GENESEE ST · AMSTUTZ EXPWY · SHERIDAN RD · 10TH ST · 14TH ST

42°22'01" 42°21'35" 42°21'09" 42°20'43" 42°20'17" 42°19'51" 42°19'25" 42°18'59"

87°50'36" 87°50'01" 87°49'26" 87°48'50" 87°48'15" 87°47'40"

A B C D E

1 2 3 4 5 6 7

SEE 2536 MAP

SEE B MAP

SEE 2594 MAP

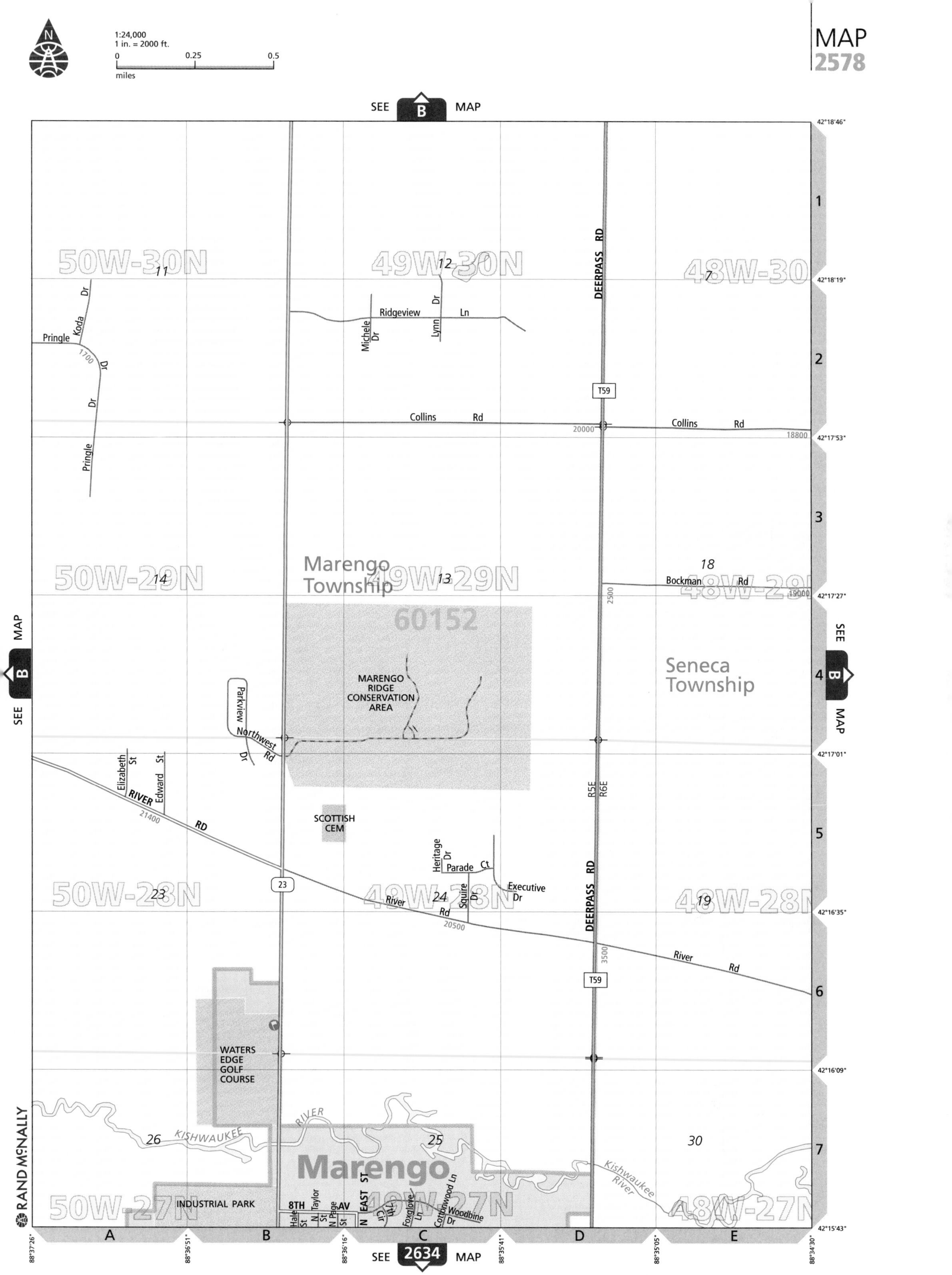

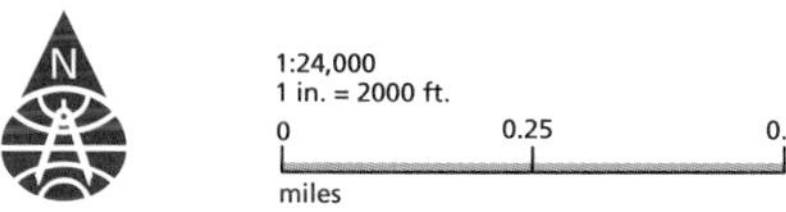

SEE B MAP

SEE B MAP

SEE B MAP

SEE 2634 MAP

1:24,000
1 in. = 2000 ft.
0 0.25 0.5
miles

SEE 2524 MAP

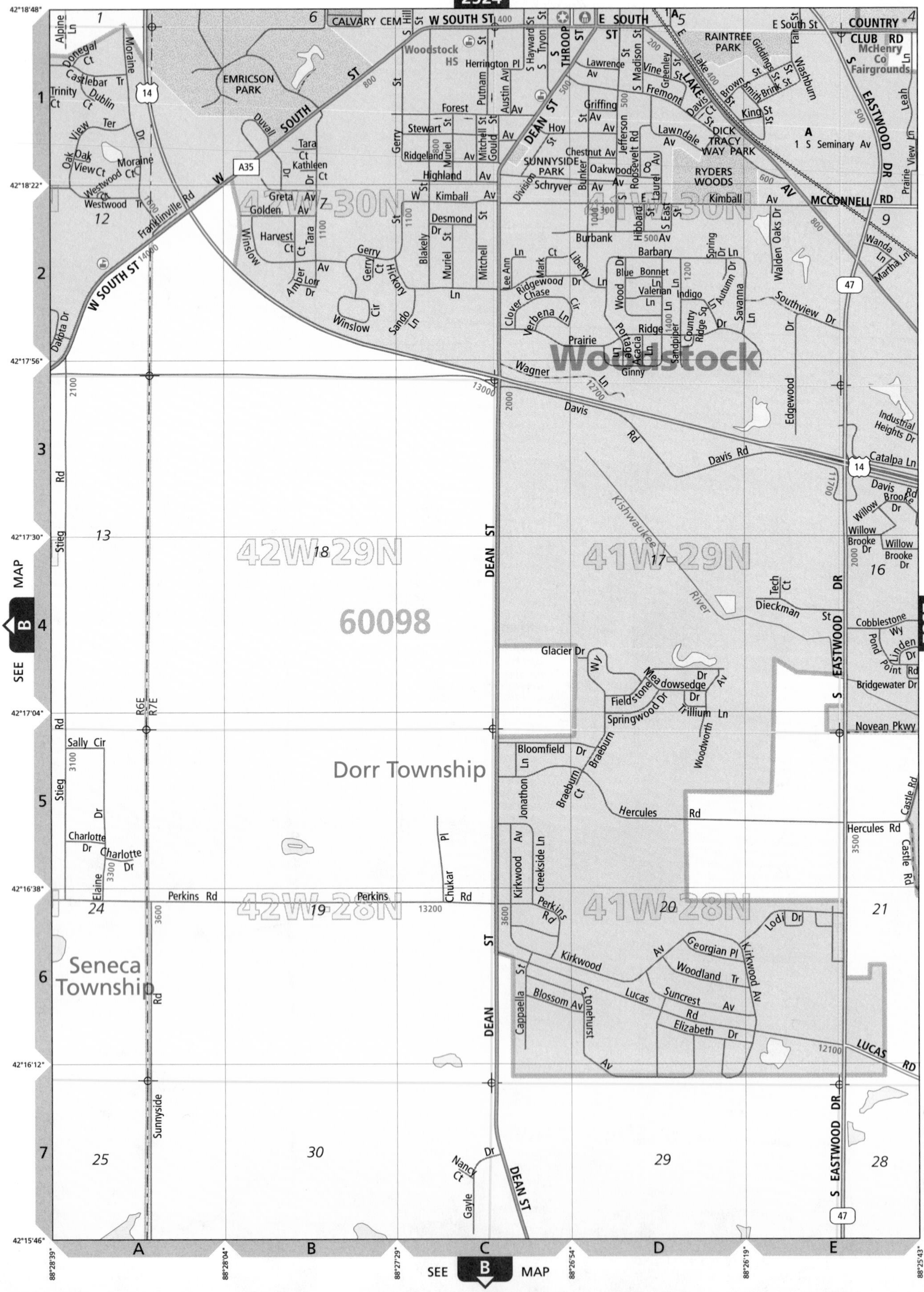

SEE B MAP
SEE 2582 MAP
SEE B MAP

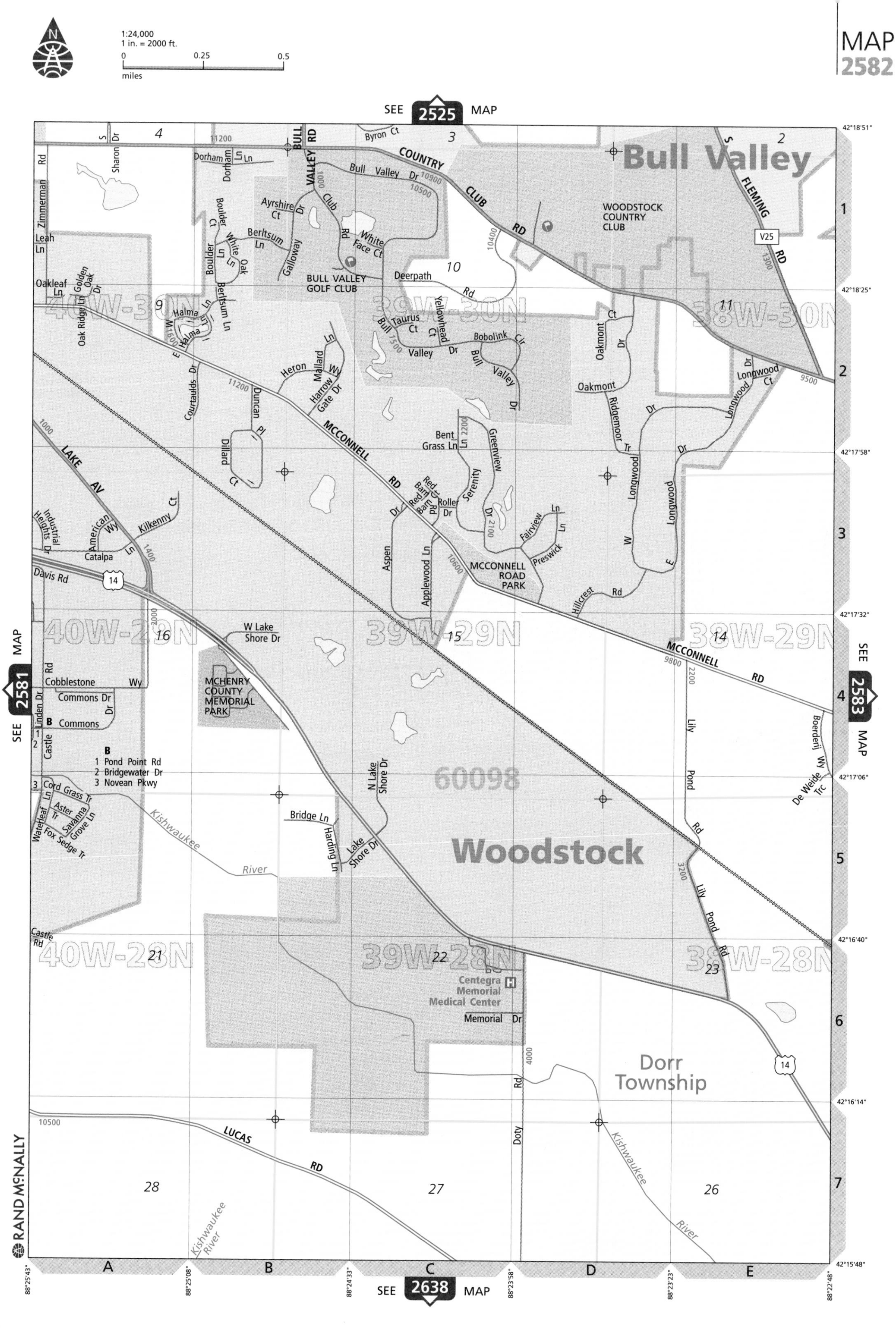

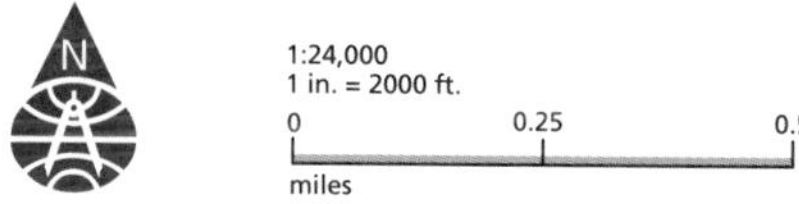

SEE 2525 MAP

SEE 2581 MAP
SEE 2583 MAP
SEE 2638 MAP

1:24,000
1 in. = 2000 ft.
0 0.25 0.5
miles

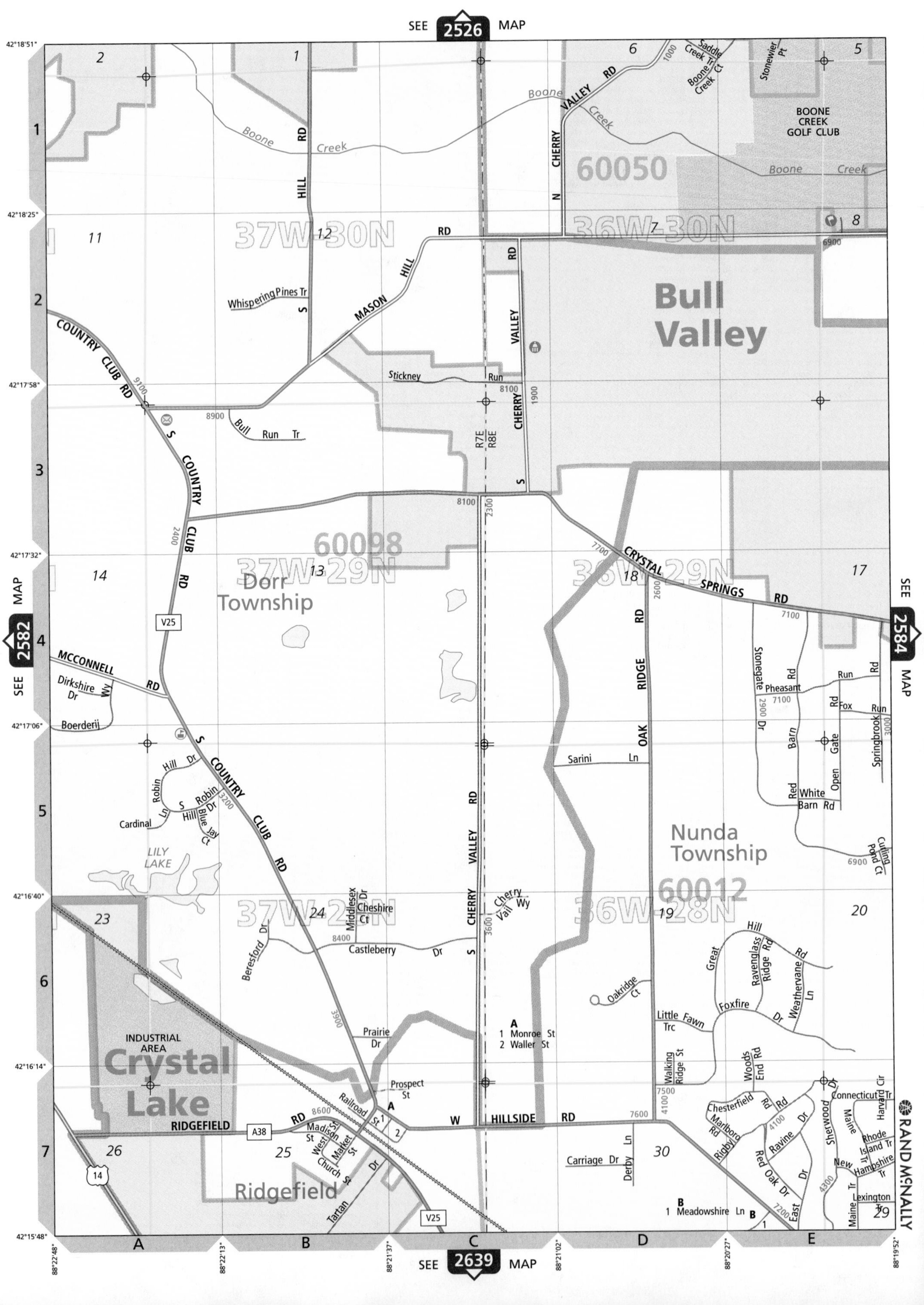

SEE 2526 MAP
SEE 2582 MAP
SEE 2584 MAP
SEE 2639 MAP
Bull Valley
Crystal Lake
Ridgefield
Dorr Township
Nunda Township
BOONE CREEK GOLF CLUB
INDUSTRIAL AREA
LILY LAKE
60050
60098
60012
37W-30N
36W-30N
37W-29N
36W-29N
37W-28N
36W-28N
R7E
R8E
Boone Creek
HILL RD
S HILL RD
MASON HILL RD
Whispering Pines Tr
COUNTRY CLUB RD
S COUNTRY CLUB RD
N CHERRY VALLEY RD
S CHERRY VALLEY RD
Saddle Creek Tr
Boone Creek Ct
Stonewier Pt
Stickney Run
Bull Run Tr
CRYSTAL SPRINGS RD
OAK RIDGE RD
MCCONNELL RD
Dirkshire Dr
Wy
Boerderij
Robin Hill Dr
S Robin Hill Dr
Cardinal Ln
Blue Jay Ct
Sarini Ln
Stonegate Rd
Pheasant Run Rd
Fox Run
Springbrook
Red Barn Rd
Open Gate
White Barn Rd
Cutting Pond Ct
Middlesex Dr
Cheshire Ct
Cherry Vail Wy
Beresford Dr
Castleberry Dr
Great Hill Rd
Ravenglass Ridge Rd
Weathervane Ln
Oakridge Ct
Foxfire Dr
Little Fawn Trc
Walking Ridge St
Woods End Rd
Prairie Dr
Prospect St
Railroad St
A
1 Monroe St
2 Waller St
W HILLSIDE RD
RIDGEFIELD RD
Madison St
West St
Market St
Church St
Tartan Dr
Carriage Dr
Derby Ln
Chesterfield Rd
Marlboro Rd
Rigby
Red Oak Dr
Ravine Dr
East
Sherwood Dr
Connecticut Tr
Harvard Cir
Maine
Rhode Island Tr
New Hampshire Tr
Maine Tr
Lexington Tr
B
1 Meadowshire Ln
V25
A38
14
1000
9100
8900
8100
1900
2300
2400
7700
2600
7100
2900
3000
6900
3200
3600
8400
3900
8600
7600
7500
4100
4300
7200
1 2 3 4 5 6 7
A B C D E
1 2 5 6 7 8 11 12 13 14 17 18 19 20 23 24 25 26 29 30
42°18'51" 42°18'25" 42°17'58" 42°17'32" 42°17'06" 42°16'40" 42°16'14" 42°15'48"
88°22'48" 88°22'13" 88°21'37" 88°21'02" 88°20'27" 88°19'52"
RAND McNALLY

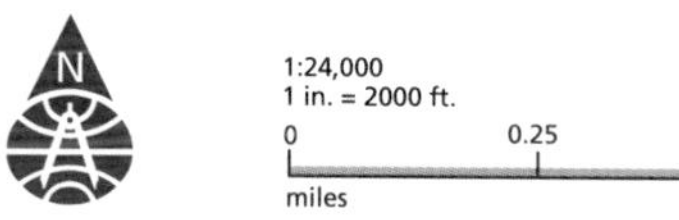

SEE 2527 MAP

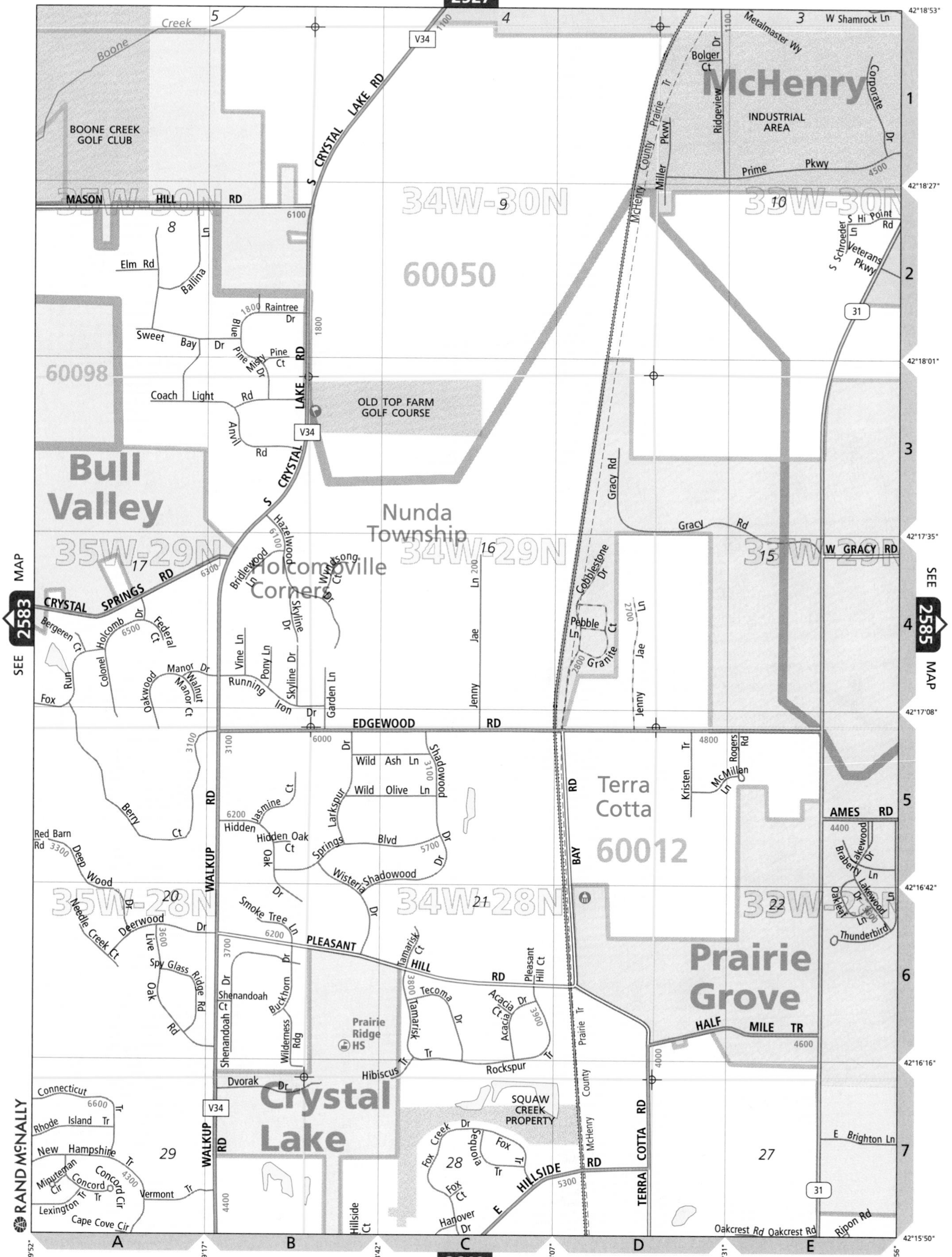

SEE 2583 MAP

SEE 2585 MAP

SEE 2640 MAP

1:24,000
1 in. = 2000 ft.
0 0.25 0.5
miles

SEE 2528 MAP

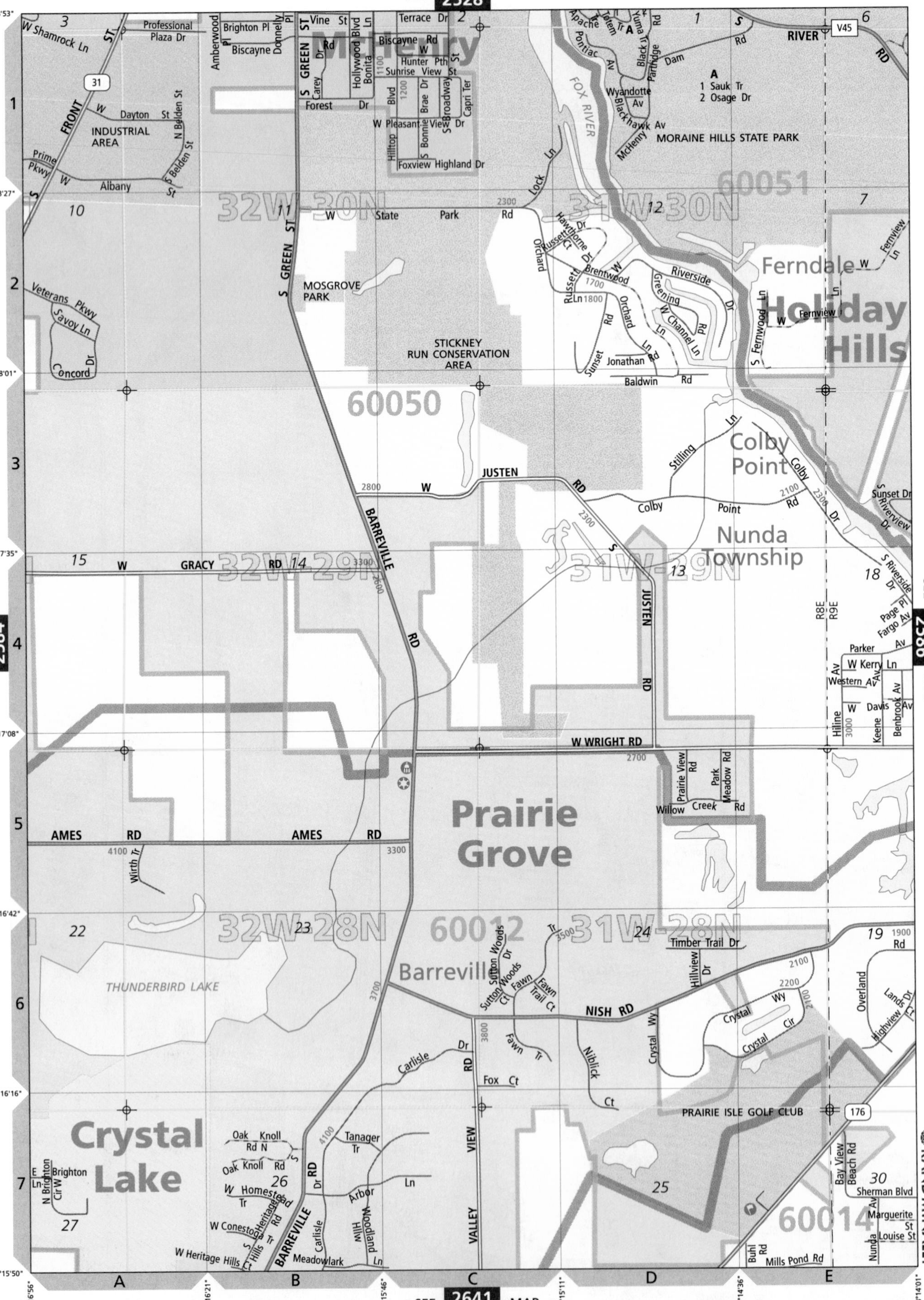

SEE MAP 2584

SEE 2586 MAP

McHenry
INDUSTRIAL AREA
MOSGROVE PARK
STICKNEY RUN CONSERVATION AREA
MORAINE HILLS STATE PARK
FOX RIVER
Ferndale
Holiday Hills
Colby Point
Nunda Township
Prairie Grove
Barreville
Crystal Lake
THUNDERBIRD LAKE
PRAIRIE ISLE GOLF CLUB

A
1 Sauk Tr
2 Osage Dr

SEE 2641 MAP

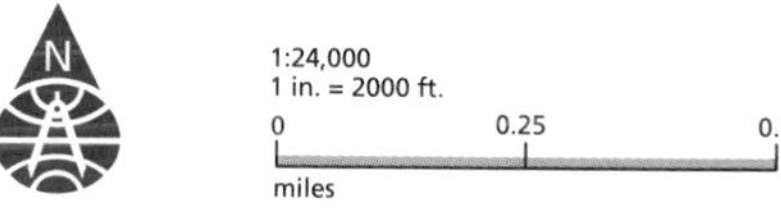

SEE 2529 MAP

MORAINE HILLS STATE PARK

Nunda Township

FISHER FAMILY PARK

Holiday Hills

Wauconda Township

30W-30N

29W-30N

28W-30N

60051

GRISWOLD LAKE

HIGHWOOD LK

McHENRY CO

LAKE CO

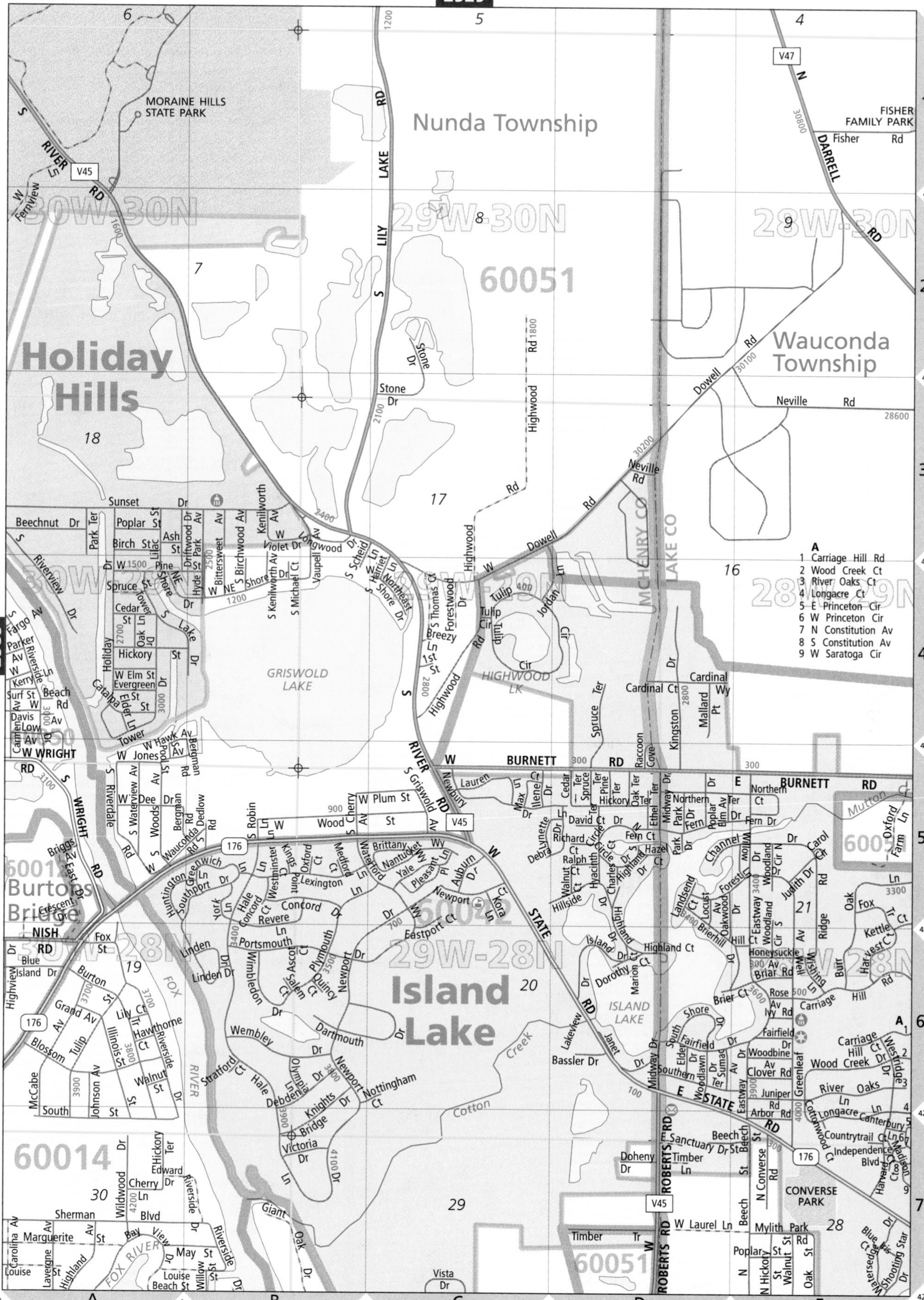

SEE 2585 MAP

SEE 2587 MAP

A
1 Carriage Hill Rd
2 Wood Creek Ct
3 River Oaks Ct
4 Longacre Ct
5 E Princeton Cir
6 W Princeton Cir
7 N Constitution Av
8 S Constitution Av
9 W Saratoga Cir

60012

Burtons Bridge

60042

29W-28N

Island Lake

ISLAND LAKE

FOX RIVER

60014

CONVERSE PARK

60051

SEE 2642 MAP

1:24,000
1 in. = 2000 ft.
0 0.25 0.5
miles

SEE 2530 MAP 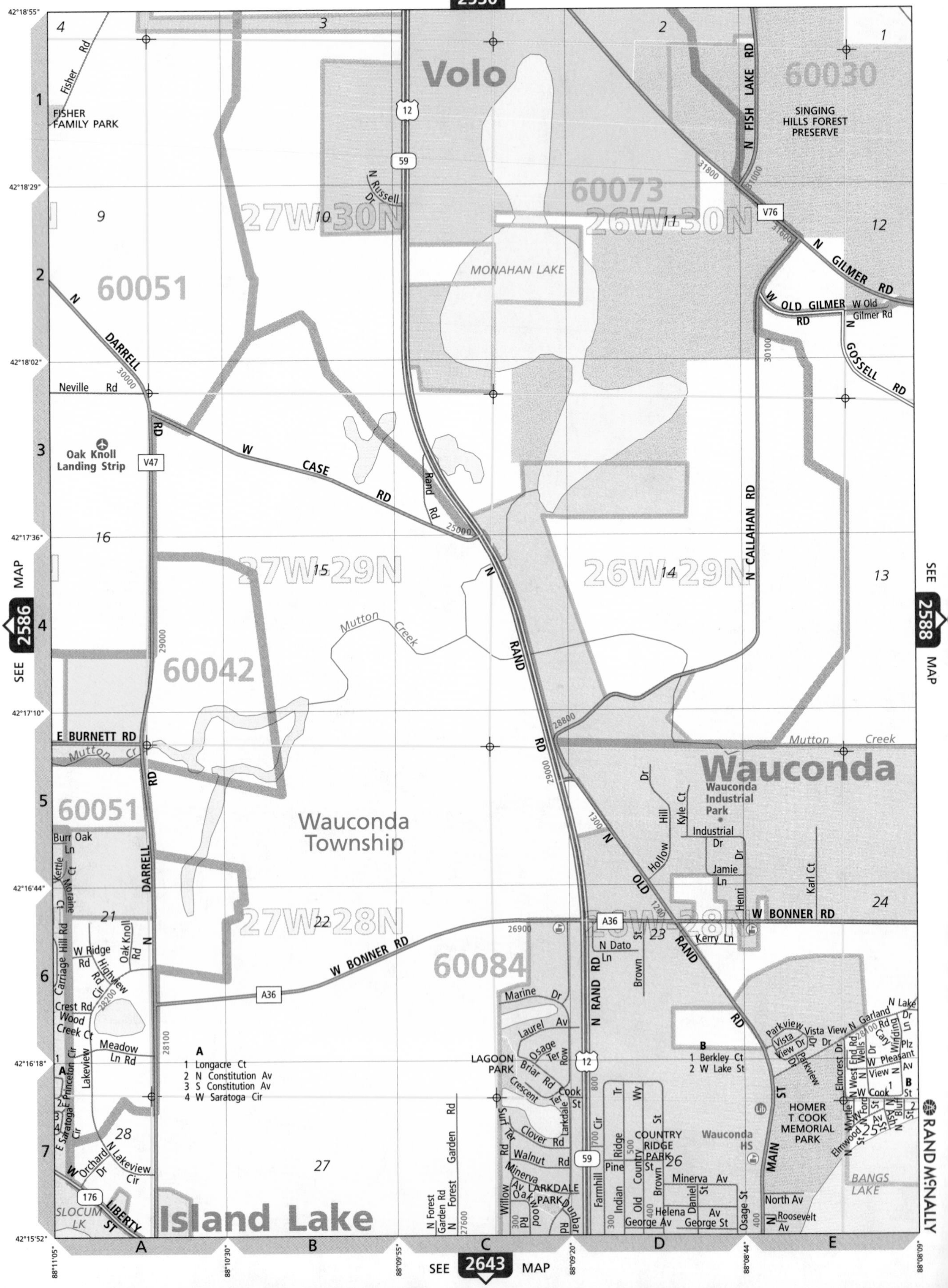
SEE 2586 MAP
SEE 2588 MAP
SEE 2643 MAP

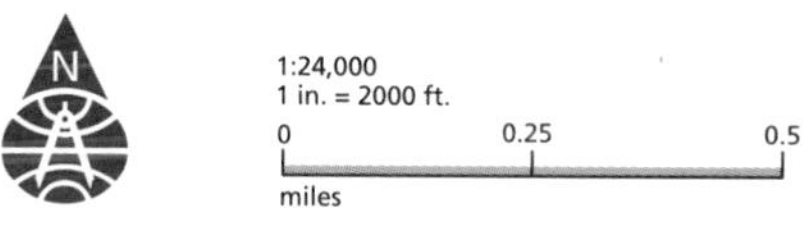

SEE 2531 MAP

Round Lake
LAKEWOOD GRV PARK
KRISTINA PARK
60073
LAKE HELEN
STONEWALL ORCHARD GOLF CLUB
SINGING HILLS FOREST PRESERVE
FIELDBROOK PARK
25W-30N
24W-30N
23W-30N
60030
W CHARDON RD
N FAIRFIELD RD
N GILMER RD
Wauconda
FISHHOOK PARK
Fremont Township
N GOSSELL RD
25W-29N
24W-29N
23W-29N
Wauconda Township
RAYS LAKE
RAYS LAKE FOREST PRESERVE
LAKE FAIRFIELD
ORCHARD HILLS PARK
60084
LAKE NAPA SUWE
Landing Strip
W Lake Fairfield Ln
WATERSTONE PARK
60060
LAKEWOOD FOREST PRESERVE
E BONNER RD
25W-28N
24W-28N
23W-28N
BANGS LAKE
MAIMAN'S LAKE SHORE PARK
FOUR WINDS GOLF COURSE

A
1 Bacon Rd

B
1 Marina Ct
2 Edgewater Ln

A B C D E
1 2 3 4 5 6 7

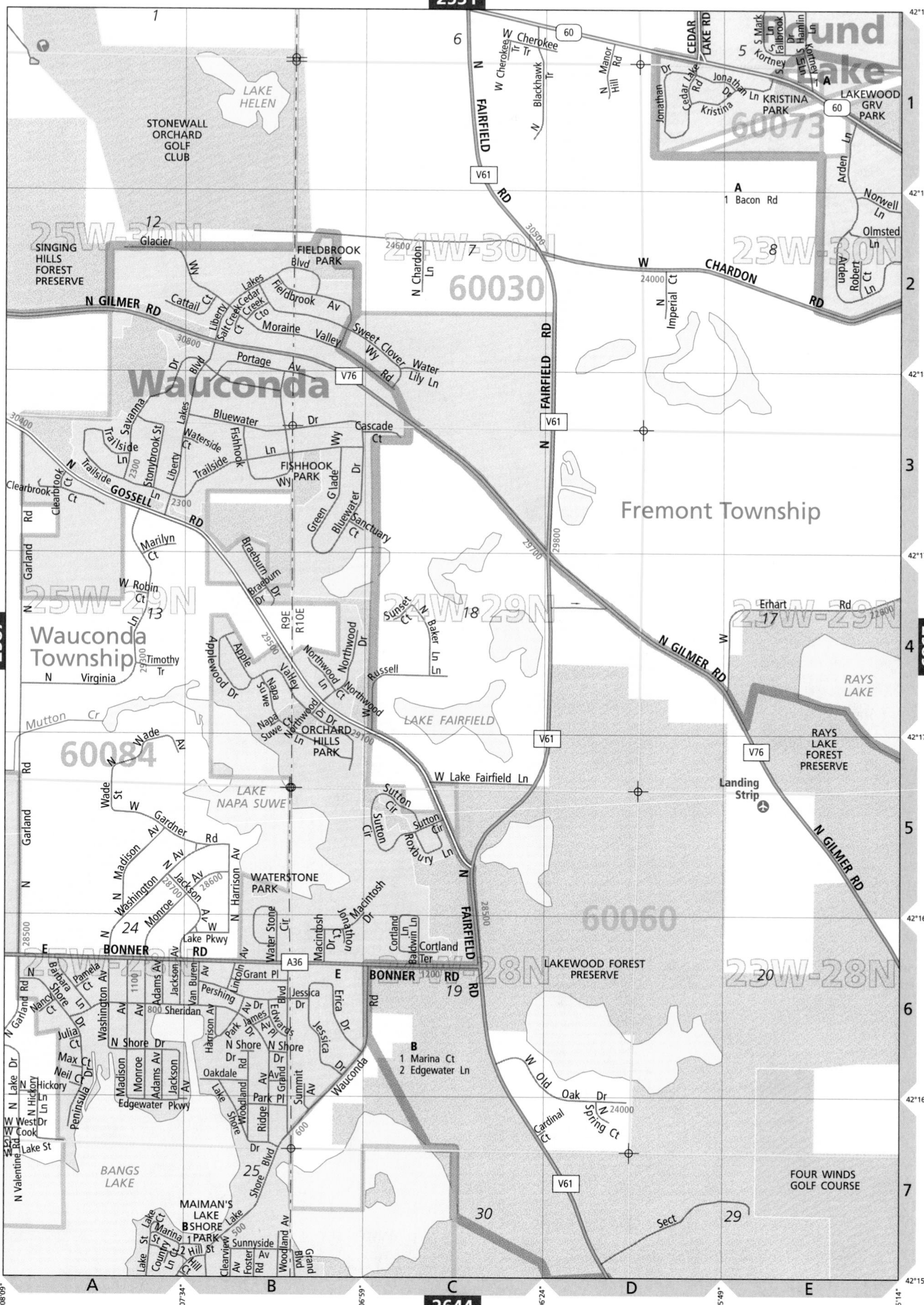

SEE 2587 MAP
SEE 2589 MAP
SEE 2644 MAP

1:24,000
1 in. = 2000 ft.
0 0.25 0.5
miles

SEE 2532 MAP

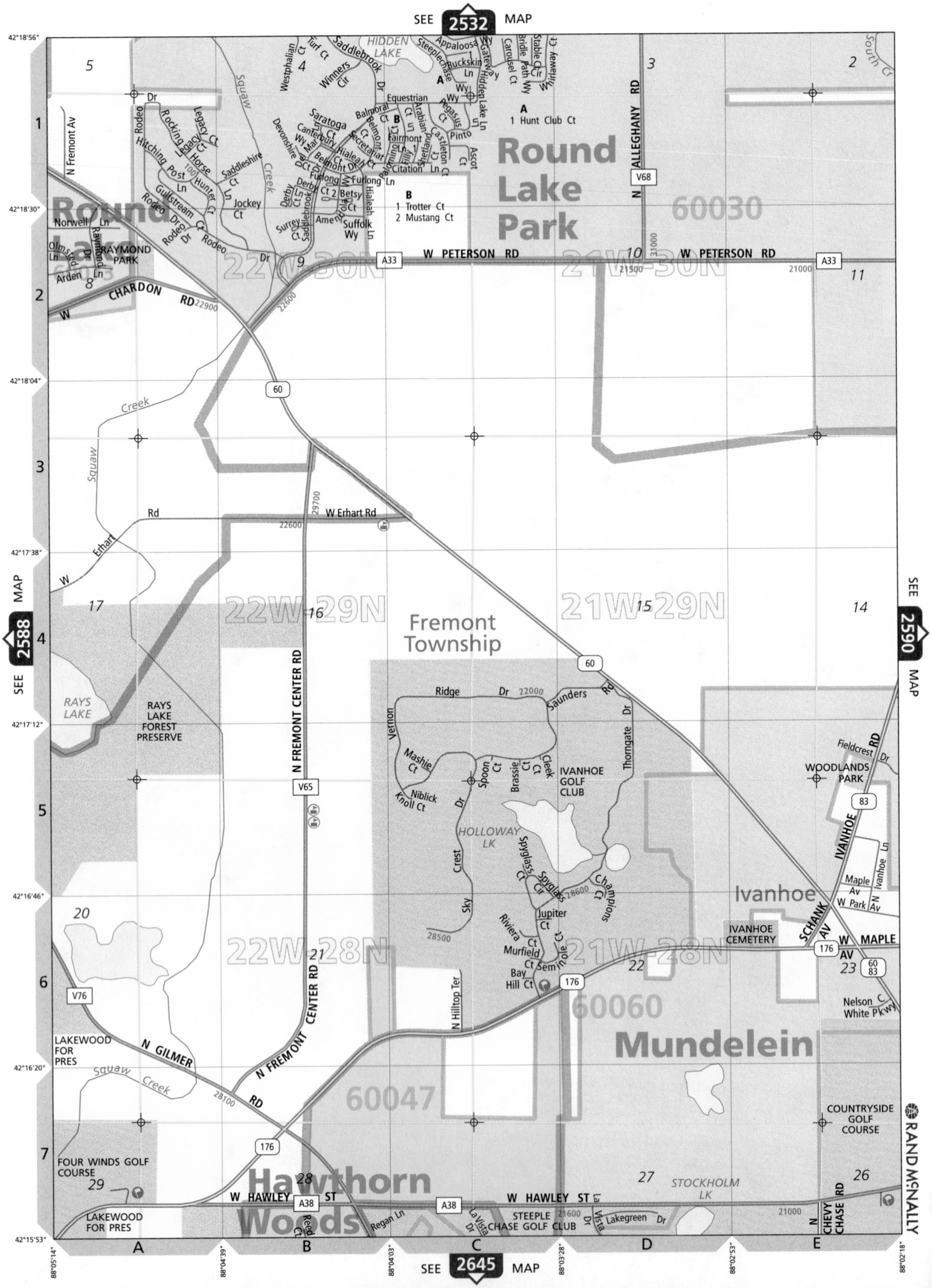

SEE 2588 MAP

SEE 2590 MAP

SEE 2645 MAP

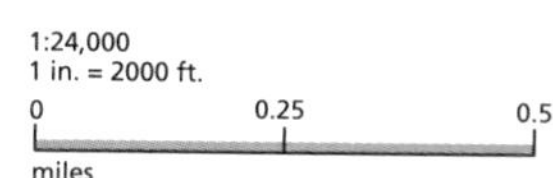

SEE 2533 MAP

Grayslake
Round Lake Park
Fremont Township
Libertyville
Libertyville Township
North Hills
Mundelein
60030
60048
VILLAGE GREEN COUNTRY CLUB
KEITH MIONE COMMUNITY PARK
LONG MEADOW PARK
LEO LEATHERS PARK
LOCH LOMOND
ST. MARY'S LAKE
PINE MEADOW GOLF CLUB
COUNTRYSIDE GOLF COURSE
SANDBURG PARK
MEM PARK
LINCOLN PARK
SCOTT BROWN PARK
Libertyville Sports Complex
Mundelein HS
Metra-Mundelein Station

SEE 2589 MAP

SEE 2591 MAP

SEE 2646 MAP

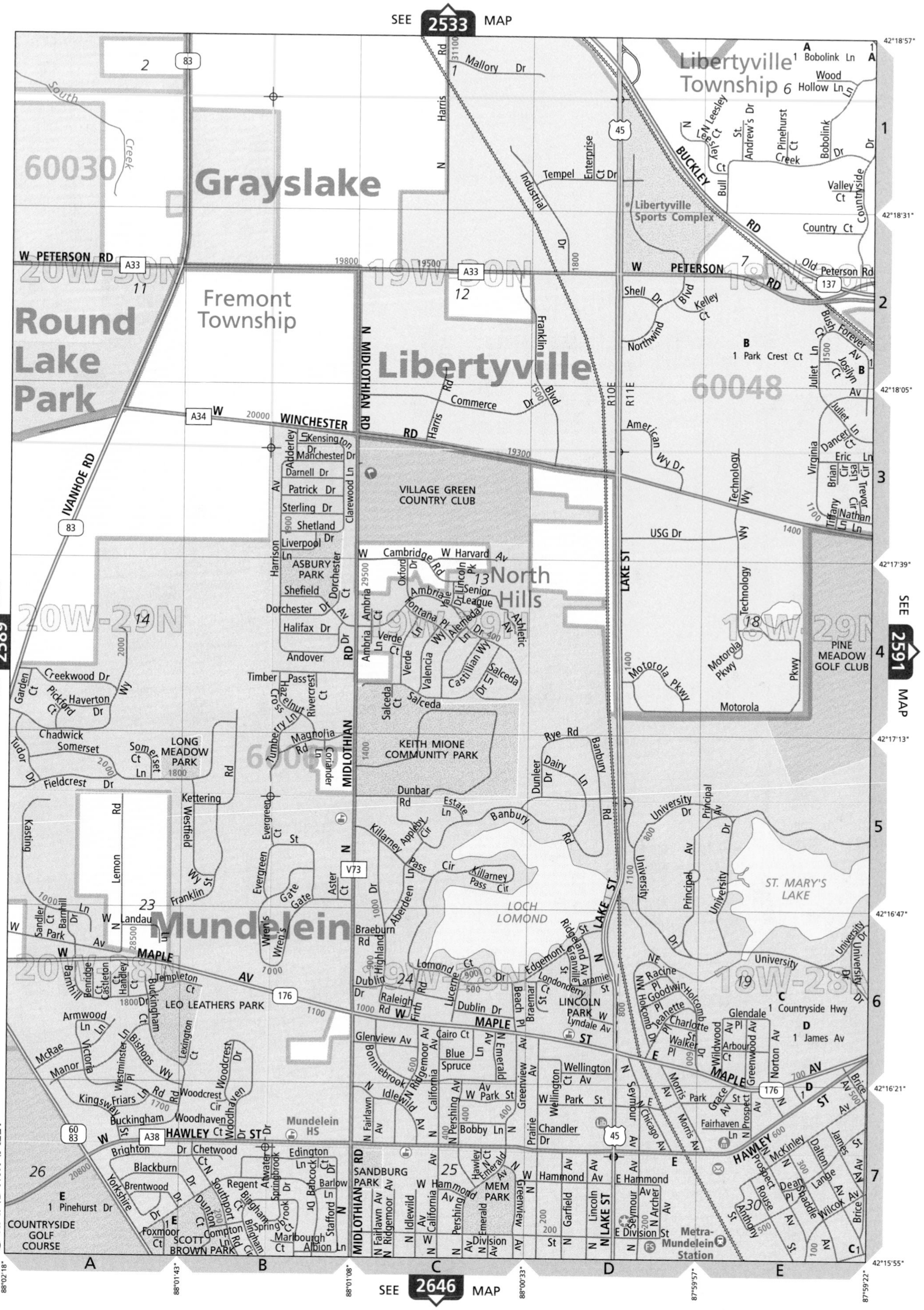

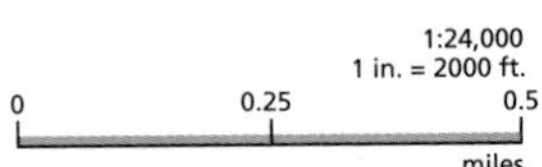

SEE 2534 MAP

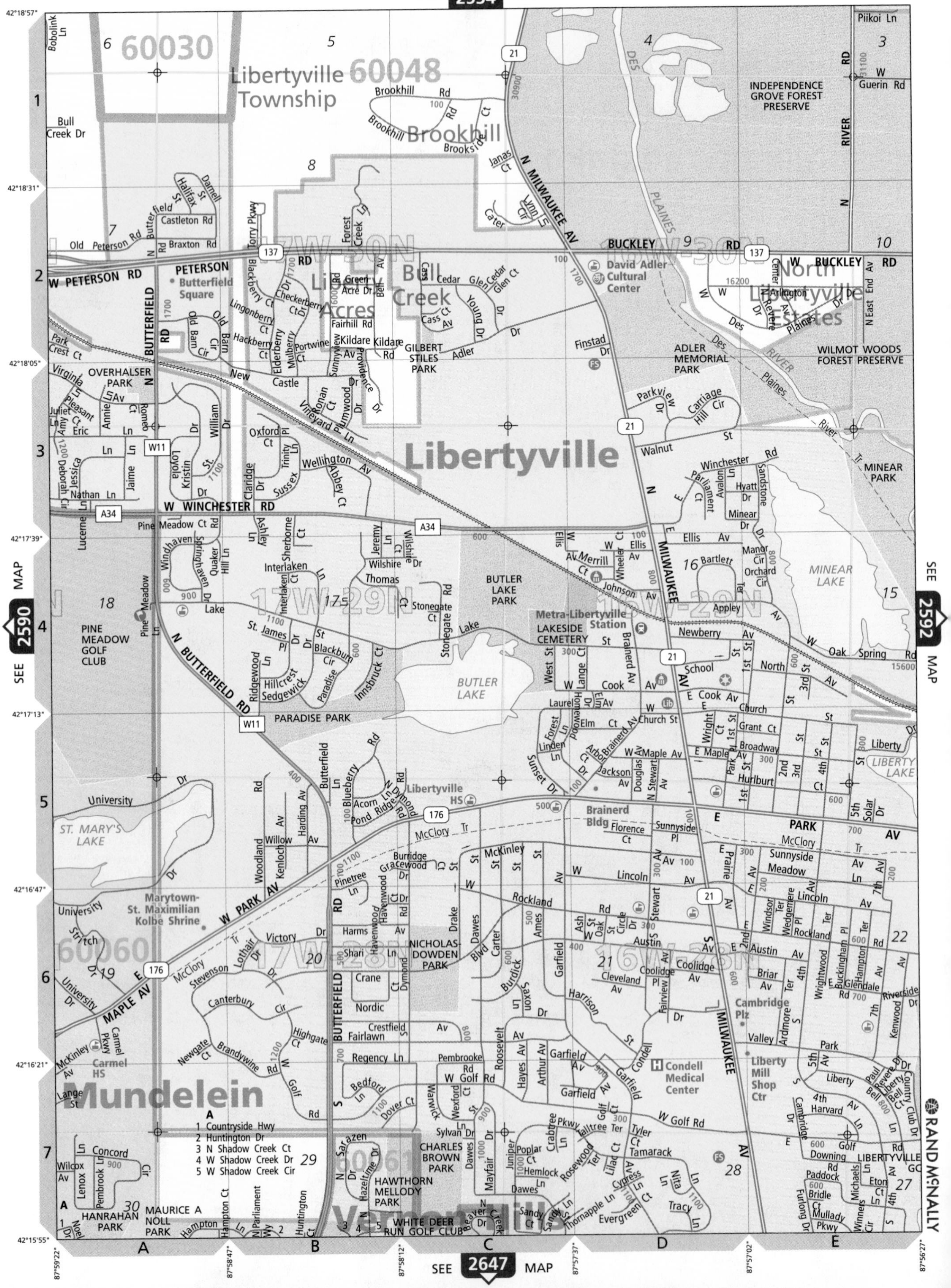

SEE 2590 MAP

SEE 2592 MAP

Libertyville Township

60030

60048

60060

60061

Libertyville

Mundelein

Vernon Hills

Brookhill

Liberty Acres

Bull Creek

North Libertyville Estates

17W-30N

16W-30N

17W-29N

16W-29N

17W-28N

16W-28N

INDEPENDENCE GROVE FOREST PRESERVE

WILMOT WOODS FOREST PRESERVE

ADLER MEMORIAL PARK

David Adler Cultural Center

GILBERT STILES PARK

OVERHALSER PARK

Butterfield Square

MINEAR PARK

MINEAR LAKE

BUTLER LAKE PARK

BUTLER LAKE

Metra-Libertyville Station

LAKESIDE CEMETERY

PINE MEADOW GOLF CLUB

PARADISE PARK

Libertyville HS

Brainerd Bldg

ST. MARY'S LAKE

Marytown-St. Maximilian Kolbe Shrine

NICHOLAS-DOWDEN PARK

Cambridge Plz

Liberty Mill Shop Ctr

Condell Medical Center

LIBERTY LAKE

Carmel HS

CHARLES BROWN PARK

HAWTHORN MELLODY PARK

HANRAHAN PARK

MAURICE A NOLL PARK

WHITE DEER RUN GOLF CLUB

LIBERTYVILLE GC

A
1 Countryside Hwy
2 Huntington Dr
3 N Shadow Creek Ct
4 W Shadow Creek Dr
5 W Shadow Creek Cir

SEE 2647 MAP

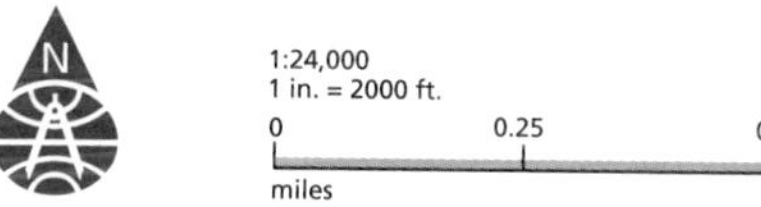

SEE 2535 MAP

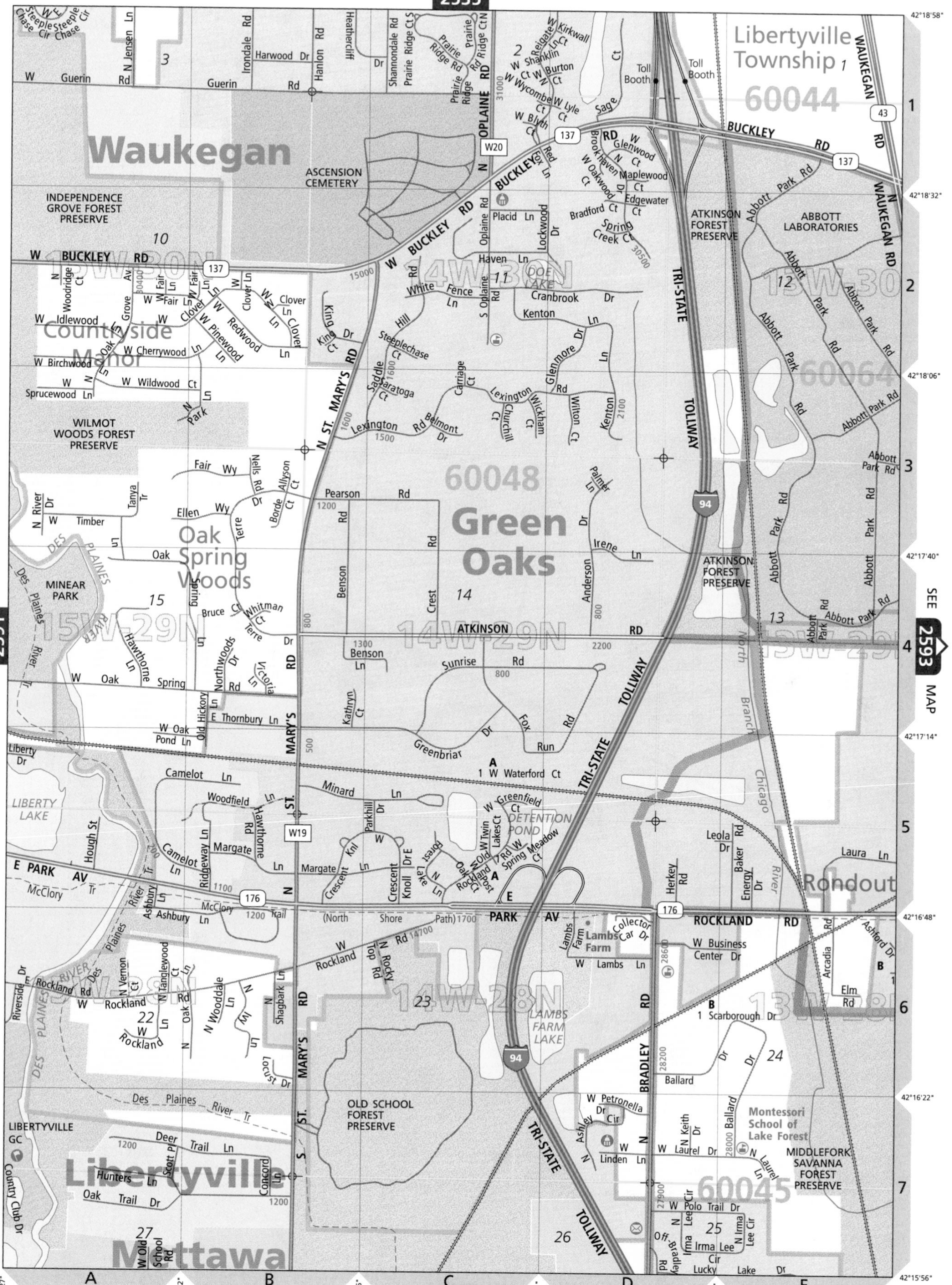

SEE 2591 MAP

SEE 2593 MAP

SEE 2648 MAP

1:24,000
1 in. = 2000 ft.
0 0.25 0.5
miles

SEE 2536 MAP

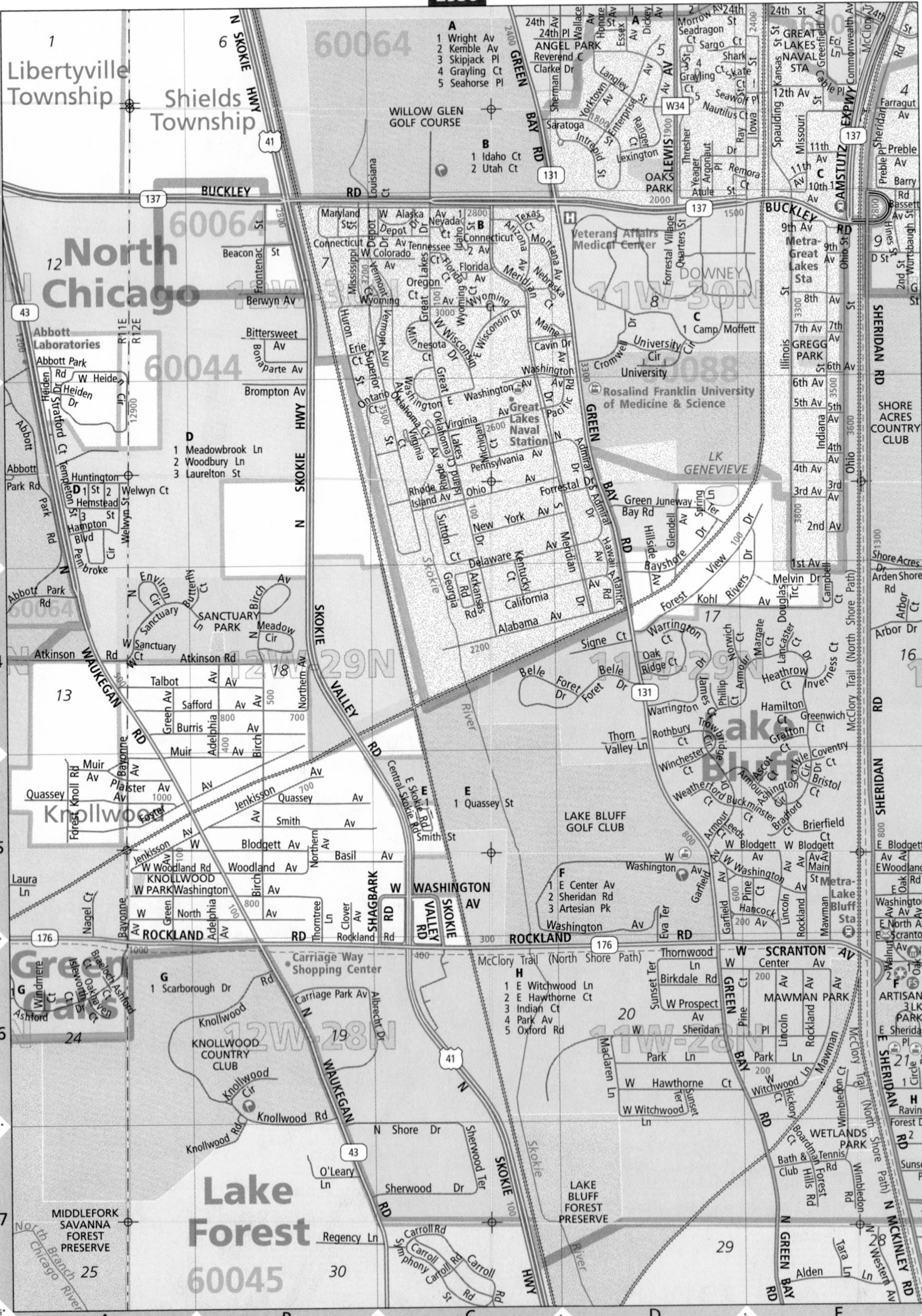

SEE 2592 MAP

SEE 2594 MAP

SEE 2649 MAP

1:24,000
1 in. = 2000 ft.
0 0.25 0.5
miles

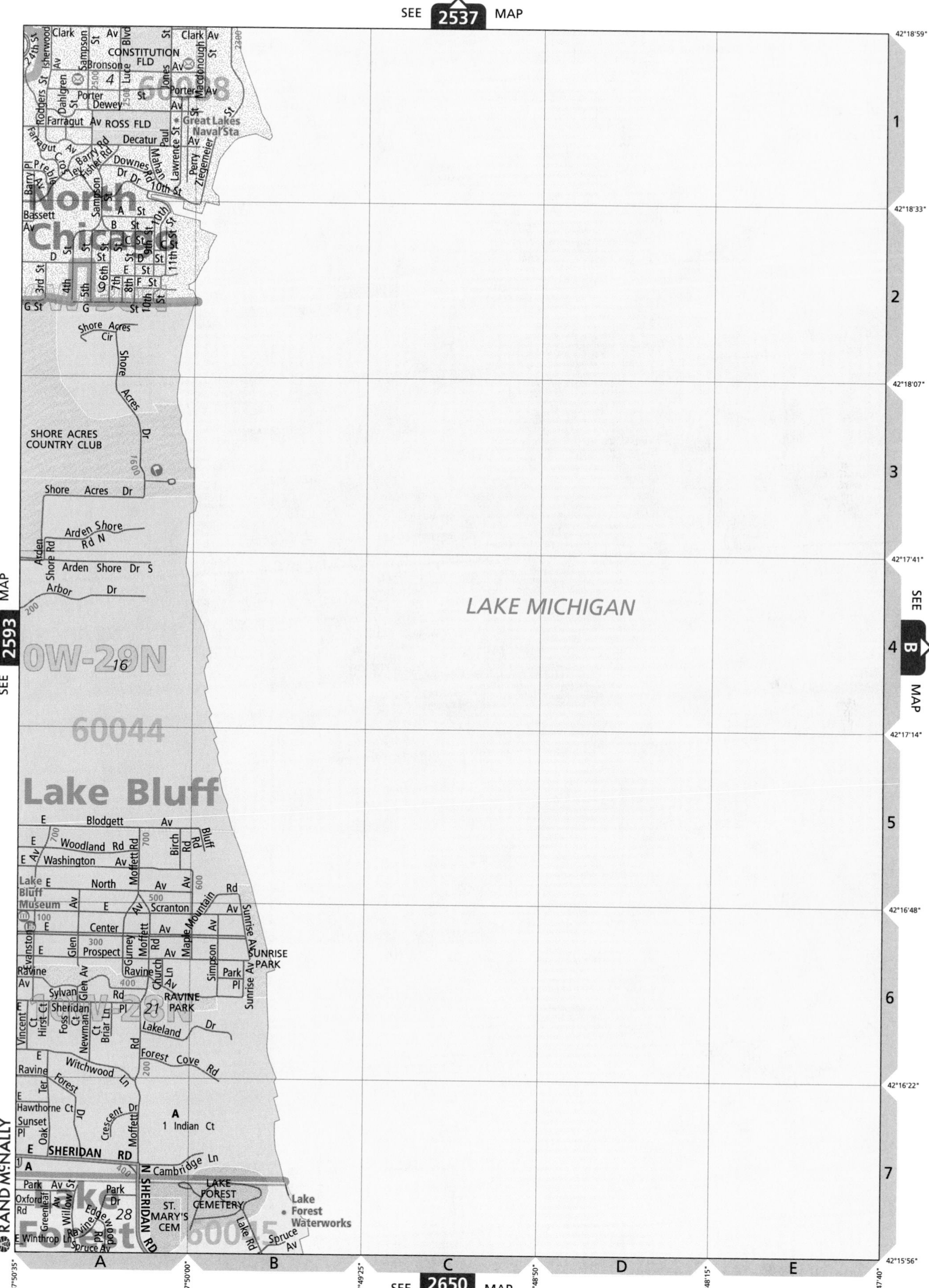

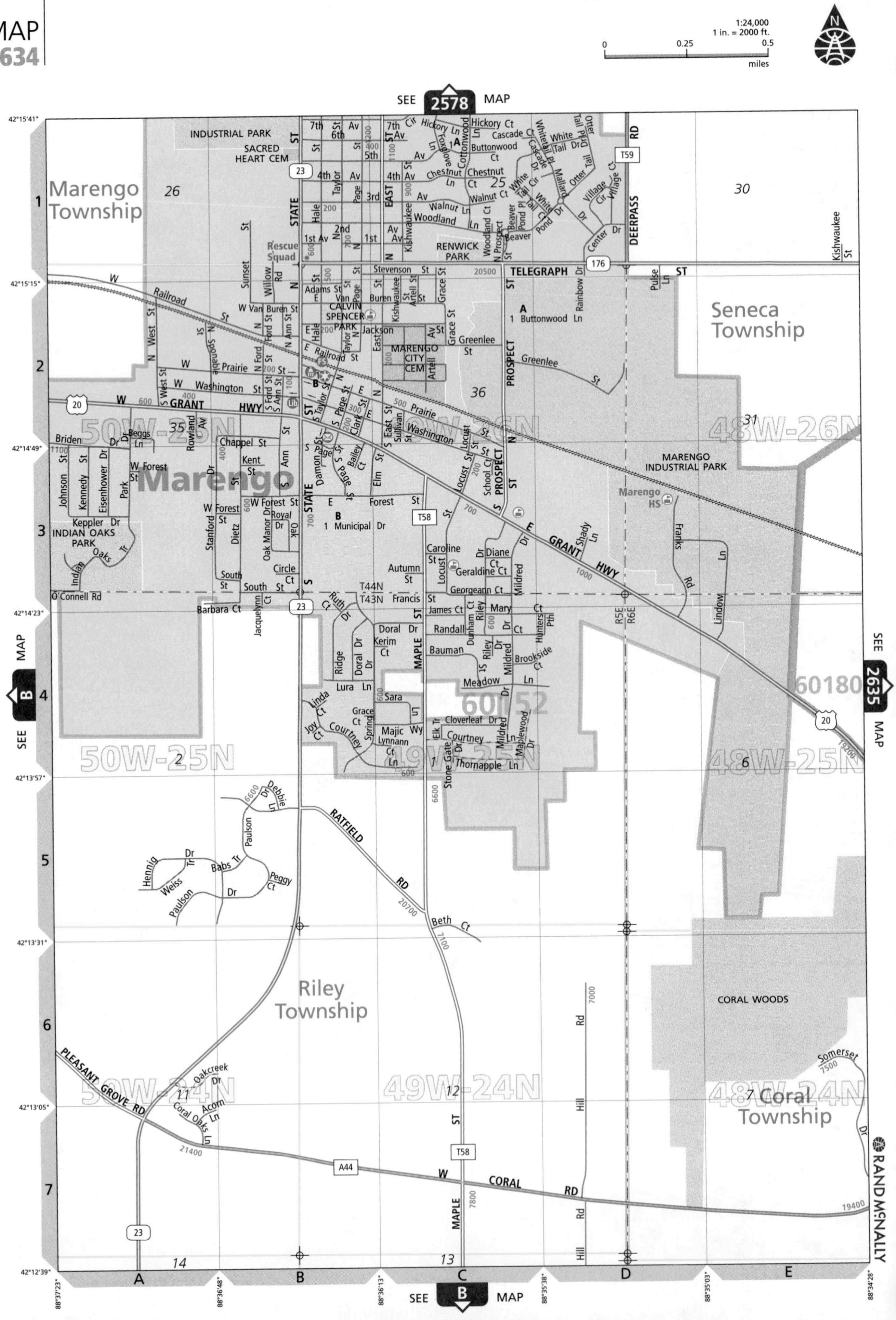

1:24,000
1 in. = 2000 ft.
0 0.25 0.5
miles

SEE 2578 MAP

SEE B MAP

SEE 2635 MAP

SEE B MAP

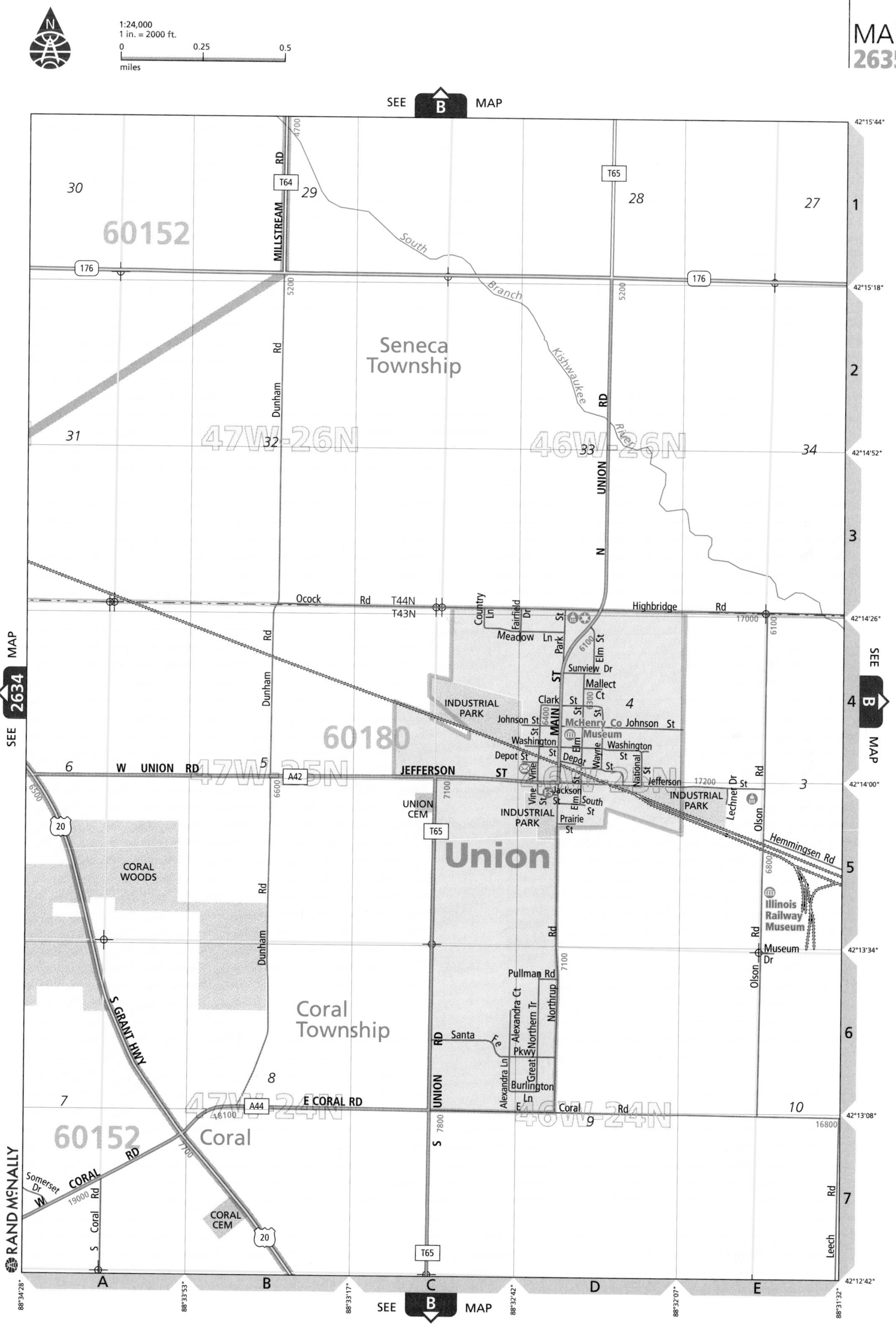

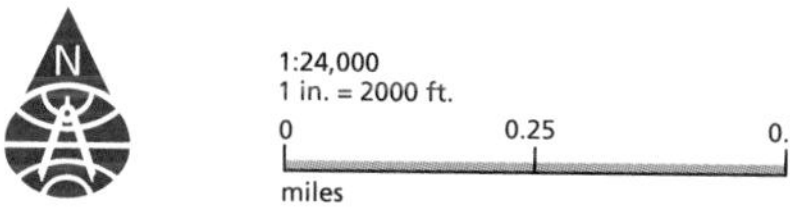

SEE B MAP

30
29
28
27
60152
MILLSTREAM RD
T64
T65
176
South Branch Kishwaukee River
Seneca Township
Dunham Rd
31
32
33
34
47W-26N
46W-26N
N UNION RD
Ocock Rd T44N T43N
Highbridge Rd
17000
6100
Country Ln
Fairfield Dr
Meadow Ln
Park St
Elm St
Sunview Dr
Mallect Ct
INDUSTRIAL PARK
Clark St
Johnson St
MAIN ST
McHenry Co Museum
Washington St
Depot St
Wayne St
National St
Jefferson
17200
60180
6
W UNION RD
5
47W-25N
A42
JEFFERSON ST
UNION CEM
Vine St
Jackson St
South St
Prairie St
INDUSTRIAL PARK
Lechner Dr
Olson Rd
3
4
Hemmingsen Rd
Union
20
CORAL WOODS
Illinois Railway Museum
Museum Dr
Pullman Rd
Northrup Rd
Alexandra Ct
Northern Tr
Santa Fe Pkwy
Great
Alexandra Ln
Burlington Ln
S GRANT HWY
Coral Township
8
7
47W-24N
A44
E CORAL RD
18100
UNION RD
E Coral Rd
46W-24N
9
10
16800
60152
Coral
W CORAL RD
Somerset Dr
19000
S Coral Rd
CORAL CEM
7800
T65
Leech Rd

SEE 2634 MAP
SEE B MAP
SEE B MAP

42°15'44"
42°15'18"
42°14'52"
42°14'26"
42°14'00"
42°13'34"
42°13'08"
42°12'42"
88°34'28"
88°33'53"
88°33'17"
88°32'42"
88°32'07"
88°31'32"
A B C D E
1 2 3 4 5 6 7

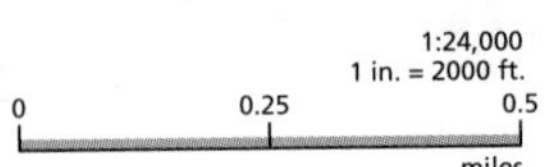

SEE 2582 MAP

Crystal Lake
Lakewood
Dorr Township
Grafton Township
Huntley
CRAIG WOODS EXECUTIVE GOLF CLUB
CRYSTAL WOODS GOLF CLUB
TURNBERRY COUNTRY CLUB
RED TAIL GOLF CLUB

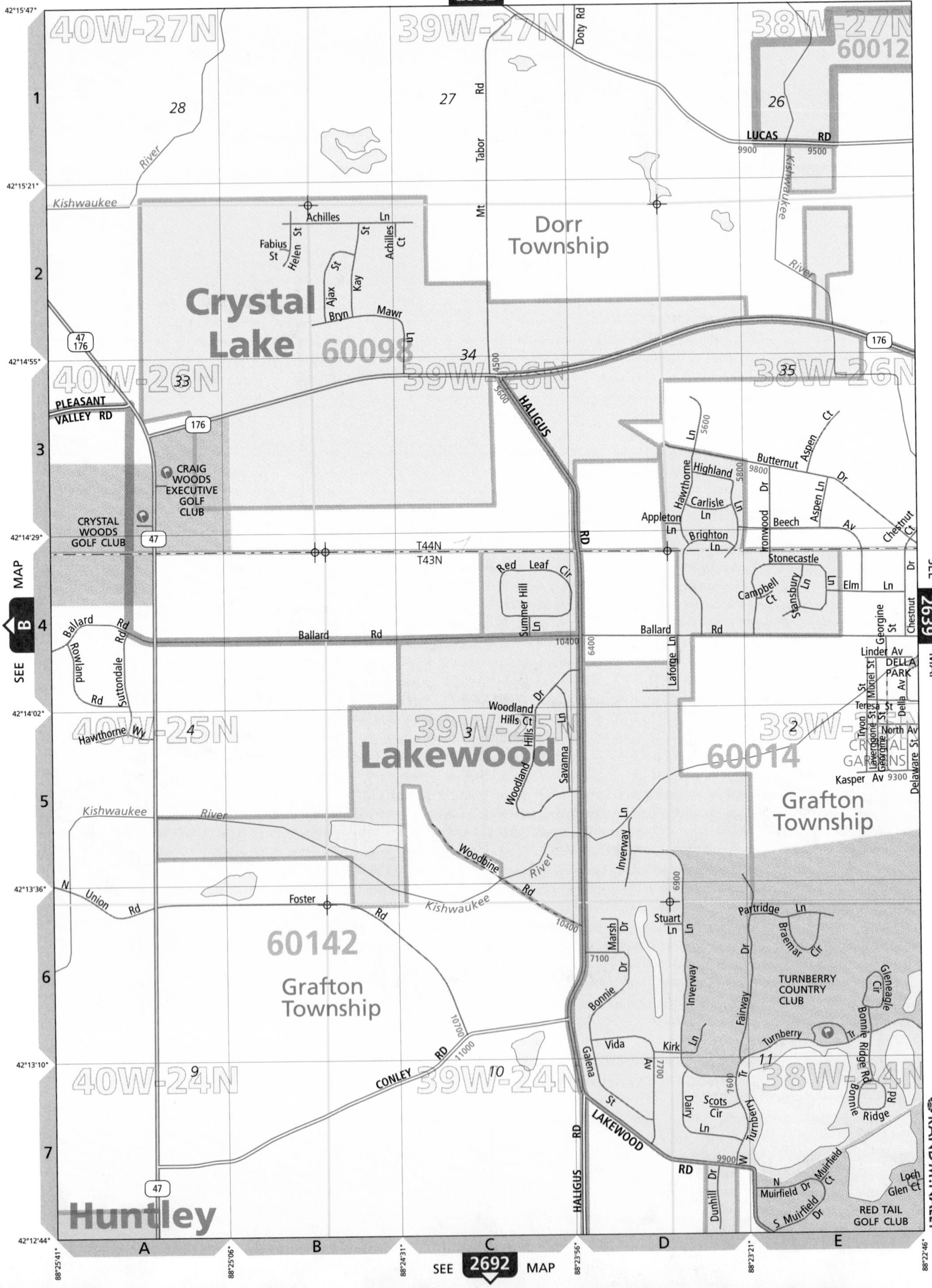

SEE B MAP
SEE 2639 MAP
SEE 2692 MAP

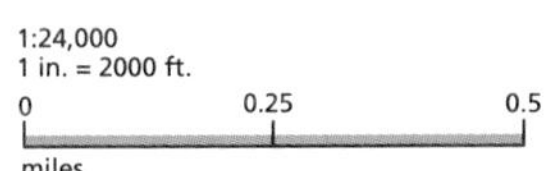

SEE 2583 MAP

Nunda Township

Dorr Township

Crystal Lake

Lakewood

Grafton Township

RIDGEFIELD CEMETERY

CRYSTAL LAKE MEMORIAL PARK

McHenry County College

LIPPOLD PARK

COMMERCIAL PARK

BUTTERNUT PRES

DELLA PARK

EDGEWATER PARK

CRYSTAL COVE

CRYSTAL LAKE

NORTH SHORE

MCCORMICK PARK

Main Beach

MAIN BEACH PARK

CRYSTAL LAKE CEM

McHenry Co Music Center

TURNBERRY COUNTRY CLUB

CRYSTAL LAKE COUNTRY CLUB

LADD PARK

CRESS CREEK PROPERTY

FOUR COLONIES PARK

HILL FARM PARK

KNAACK PARK

RED TAIL GOLF CLUB

60012

60098

60014

37W-27N

36W-27N

37W-26N

36W-26N

37W-25N

36W-25N

37W-24N

36W-24N

T44N
T43N
R7E R8E

A
1 Sherwood Dr
2 Maine Tr

B
1 Cress Creek Ter

C
1 Wellington Dr

D
1 Stonehedge Ct

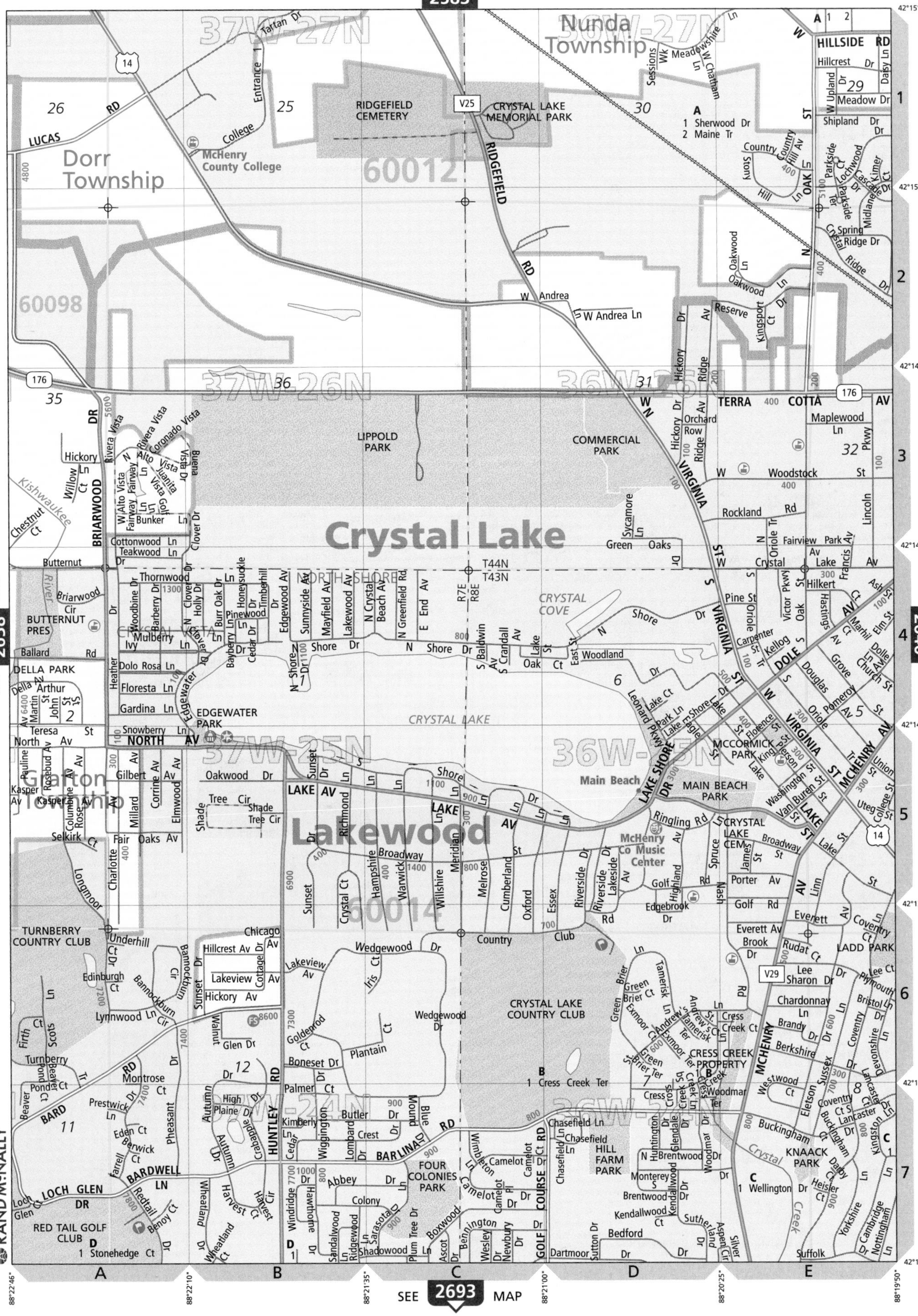

SEE 2638 MAP

SEE 2640 MAP

SEE 2693 MAP

1:24,000
1 in. = 2000 ft.
0 0.25 0.5
miles

SEE 2584 MAP

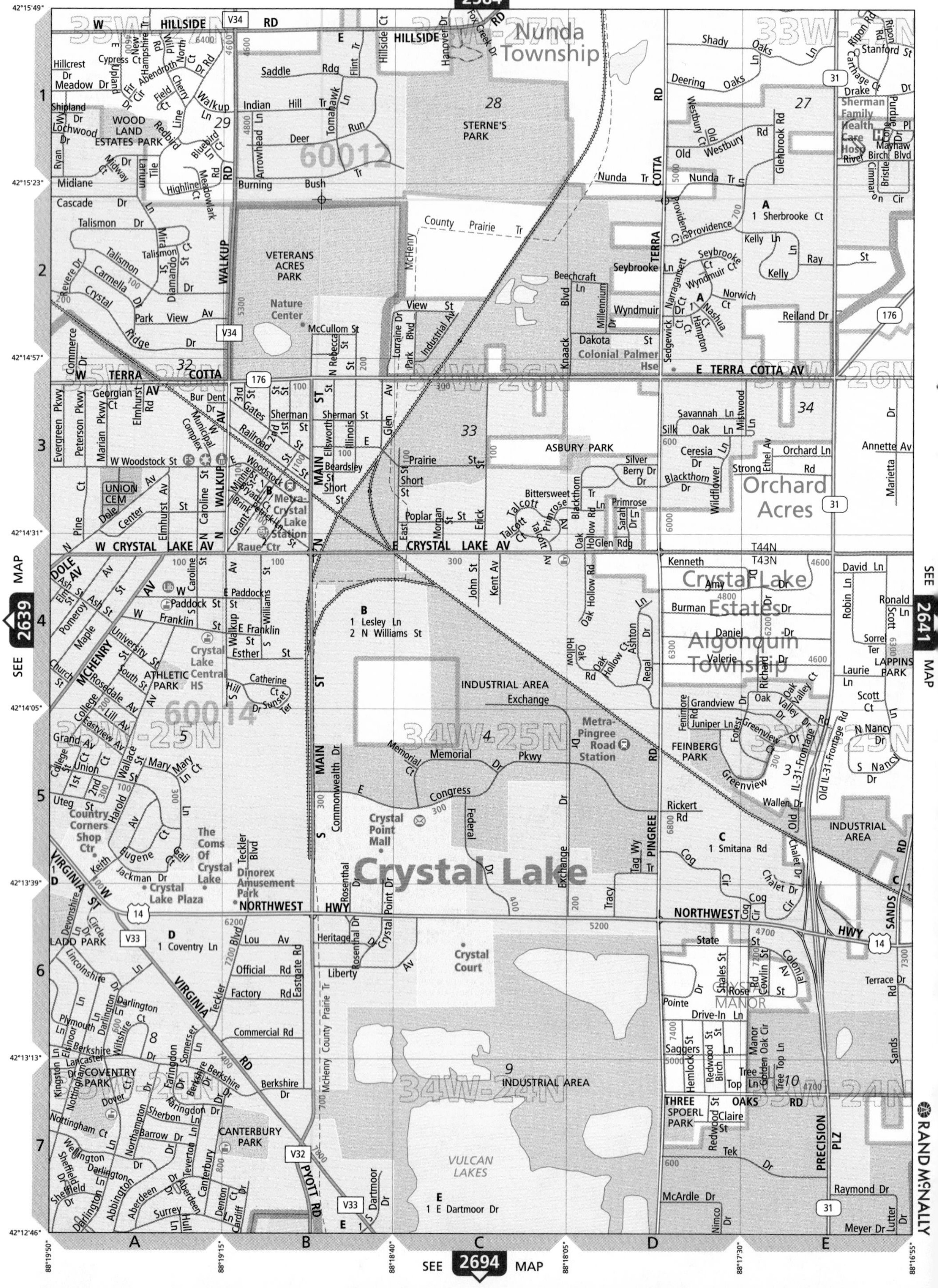

SEE 2639 MAP

SEE 2641 MAP

Nunda Township

Orchard Acres

Crystal Lake Estates

Algonquin Township

Crystal Lake

STERNE'S PARK

VETERANS ACRES PARK

Nature Center

WOOD LAND ESTATES PARK

ASBURY PARK

UNION CEM

Municipal Complex

Metra-Crystal Lake Station

Raue Ctr

Crystal Lake Central HS

ATHLETIC PARK

INDUSTRIAL AREA

Metra-Pingree Road Station

FEINBERG PARK

LAPPINS PARK

Sherman Family Health Care Hosp

Colonial Palmer Hse

Country Corners Shop Ctr

The Coms Of Crystal Lake

Dinorex Amusement Park

Crystal Lake Plaza

Crystal Point Mall

Crystal Court

LADD PARK

COVENTRY PARK

CANTERBURY PARK

THREE OAKS SPOERL PARK

GAYS MANOR

VULCAN LAKES

60012

60014

35W-27N 34W-27N 33W-27N

35W-26N 34W-26N 33W-26N

35W-25N 34W-25N 33W-25N

35W-24N 34W-24N 33W-24N

T44N
T43N

W HILLSIDE RD

E HILLSIDE RD

WALKUP RD

TERRA COTTA RD

W TERRA COTTA AV

E TERRA COTTA AV

W CRYSTAL LAKE AV

E CRYSTAL LAKE AV

MAIN ST

S MAIN ST

MCHENRY AV

PINGREE RD

NORTHWEST HWY

VIRGINIA ST

VIRGINIA RD

PYOTT RD

SANDS RD

PRECISION PLZ

THREE OAKS RD

McHenry County Prairie Tr

A 1 Sherbrooke Ct

B 1 Lesley Ln 2 N Williams St

C 1 Smitana Rd

D 1 Coventry Ln

E 1 E Dartmoor Dr

42°15'49" 42°15'23" 42°14'57" 42°14'31" 42°14'05" 42°13'39" 42°13'13" 42°12'46"

88°19'50" 88°19'15" 88°18'40" 88°18'05" 88°17'30" 88°16'55"

A B C D E

1 2 3 4 5 6 7

SEE 2694 MAP

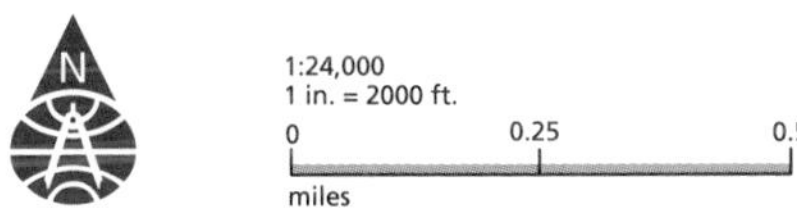

SEE 2585 MAP

SEE 2640 MAP

SEE 2642 MAP

A
1 S Heritage Hills Rd
2 Carlisle Dr

B
1 Blue Ct

C
1 Northlane Rd

D
1 Silver Lakes Rd

D
1 Oakdale Ter

E
1 Bur Oak Ct

Prairie Grove
Nunda Township
Oakwood Hills
Lake Killarney
Silver Lake
Algonquin Township
Crystal Lake
Cary

PRAIRIE GROVE CEMETERY
OAKWOOD HILLS FEN CONSERVATION AREA
OAKWOOD HILLS PARK
CHALET HILLS GOLF CLUB
SILVER LAKE
LAKE KILLARNEY
LK KILLARNEY PARK
WYNDWOOD PARK
INDUSTRIAL AREA
THE HOLLOWS CONSERVATION AREA
LAKE ATWOOD
WEST LAKE
LIONS PARK
BRITTANY PARK
FOXFORD HILLS GOLF CLUB
CARY-GROVE PARK
Cary-Grove Community HS
JAYCEE PARK
JAMESWAY PARK
CANDLEWOOD PARK
THREE OAKS PARK
WILLIAM KAPER SR PARK
Christian Community Theater
Cary Square

32W-27N
31W-27N
32W-26N
31W-26N
32W-25N
31W-25N
32W-24N
31W-24N

60014
60013

T44N
T43N
R8E
R9E

42°15'51"
42°15'25"
42°14'59"
42°14'33"
42°14'07"
42°13'41"
42°13'14"
42°12'48"

88°16'55"
88°16'19"
88°15'44"
88°15'09"
88°14'34"
88°13'59"

A B C D E
1 2 3 4 5 6 7

SEE 2695 MAP

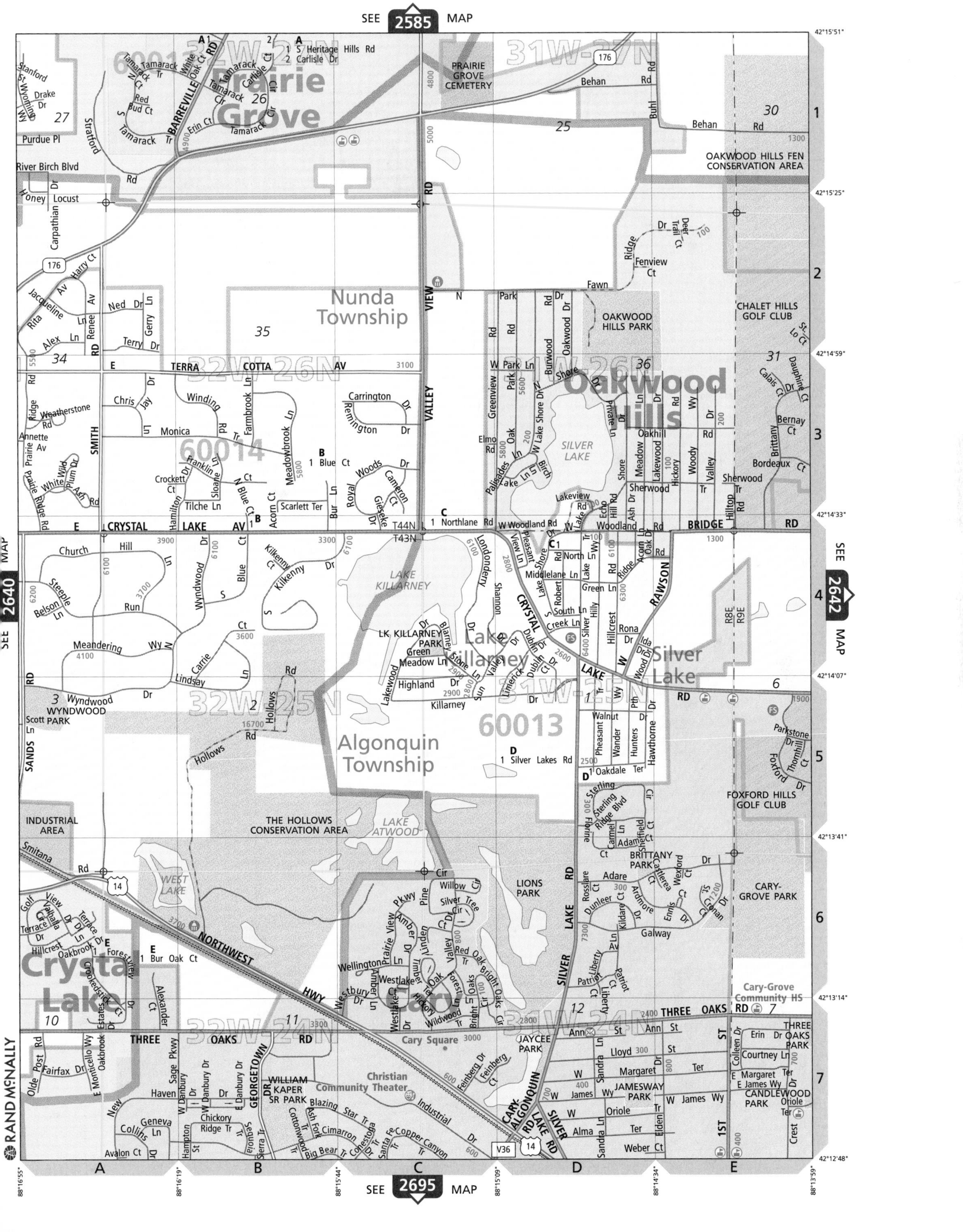

1:24,000
1 in. = 2000 ft.
0 0.25 0.5
miles

SEE 2586 MAP

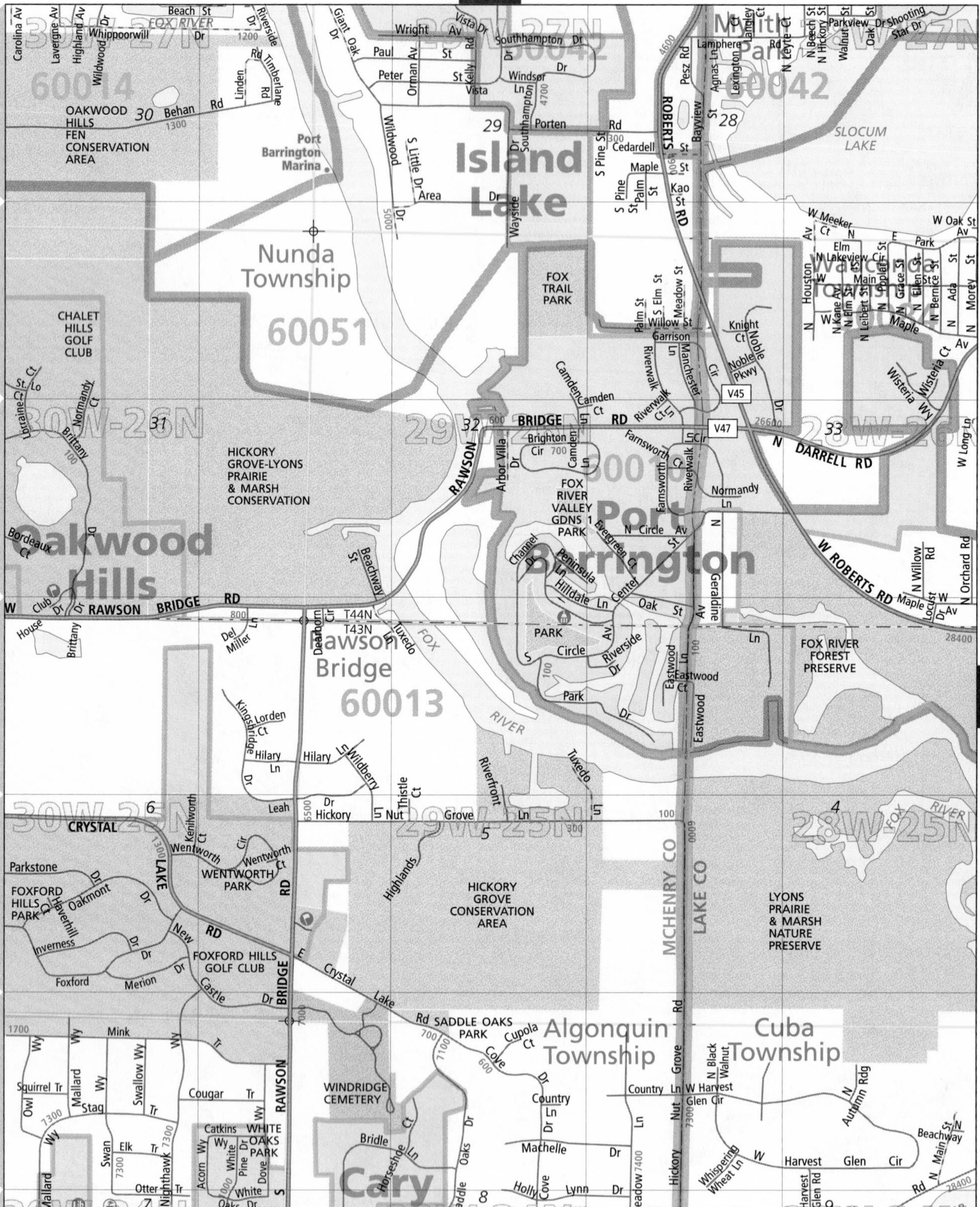

SEE 2641 MAP
SEE 2643 MAP
SEE 2696 MAP

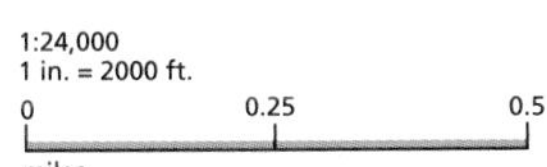

SEE 2587 MAP

SEE 2642 MAP

SEE 2644 MAP

60042
Island Lake
27W-27N
Forest Gardens
176
W LIBERTY
Wauconda
26W-27N
SLOCUM LAKE
28
27
26
25
Williams Park
Wauconda Township
60084
BANGS LAKE
SLOCUM LAKE RD
W SLOCUM LAKE RD
W Slocum Lake Rd
12
59
RAND RD
MAIN ST
E LIBERTY ST
OSAGE PARK
MEM PARK
A
1 High St
2 Lakeview Av
3 Wilson Av
MEADOWVIEW PARK
SADDLEWOOD PARK
N ANDERSON RD
BARRINGTON RD
S RAND RD
W IVANHOE RD
OAK GROVE PARK
27W-26N
26W-26N
33
34
35
36
LAKE LAKELAND
LAKE FAIRVIEW
Lake Barrington
FOX RIVER FOREST PRESERVE
N BARRINGTON RD
T44N
T43N
ROBERTS RD
V45
NORTH TOWER LAKE
DAVLINS PND
Port Barrington
RIVER RD
27W-25N
26W-25N
4
3
2
1
60010
LYONS PRAIRIE & MARSH NATURE PRES
REST I
PLAY I
DUCK I
TOWER LAKE
DEVIL'S I
SNAKE I
The Market Place
60013
GRASSY LAKE FOREST PRESERVE
V50
FOX RIVER
Tower Lakes
V49
KELSEY RD
LAKE BARRINGTON
59
BARRINGTON BOG NATURE PRES
27W-24N
26W-24N
9
10
11
12
Cuba Township
C
1 Lake Barrington Shrs
2 Foxwood Ln
LAKE BARRINGTON SHORES GOLF CLUB
B
1 Cutter Ln
KELSEY RD
RIVER RD

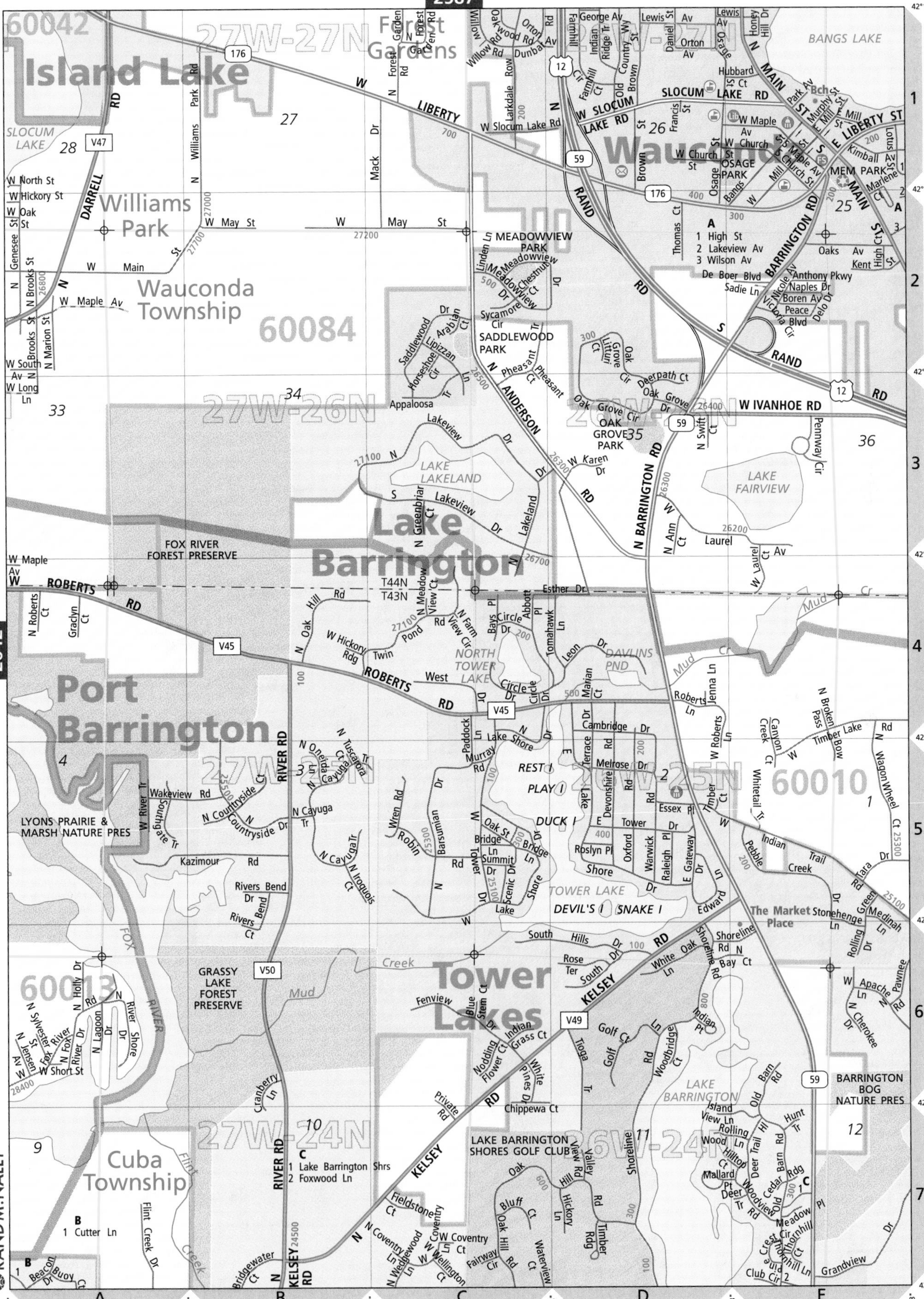

Grid columns: A B C D E
Grid rows: 1 2 3 4 5 6 7

42°15'53" 42°15'27" 42°15'01" 42°14'34" 42°14'08" 42°13'42" 42°13'16" 42°12'50"
88°11'03" 88°10'28" 88°09'53" 88°09'18" 88°08'43" 88°08'08"

SEE 2697 MAP

1:24,000
1 in. = 2000 ft.
0 0.25 0.5
miles

SEE 2588 MAP

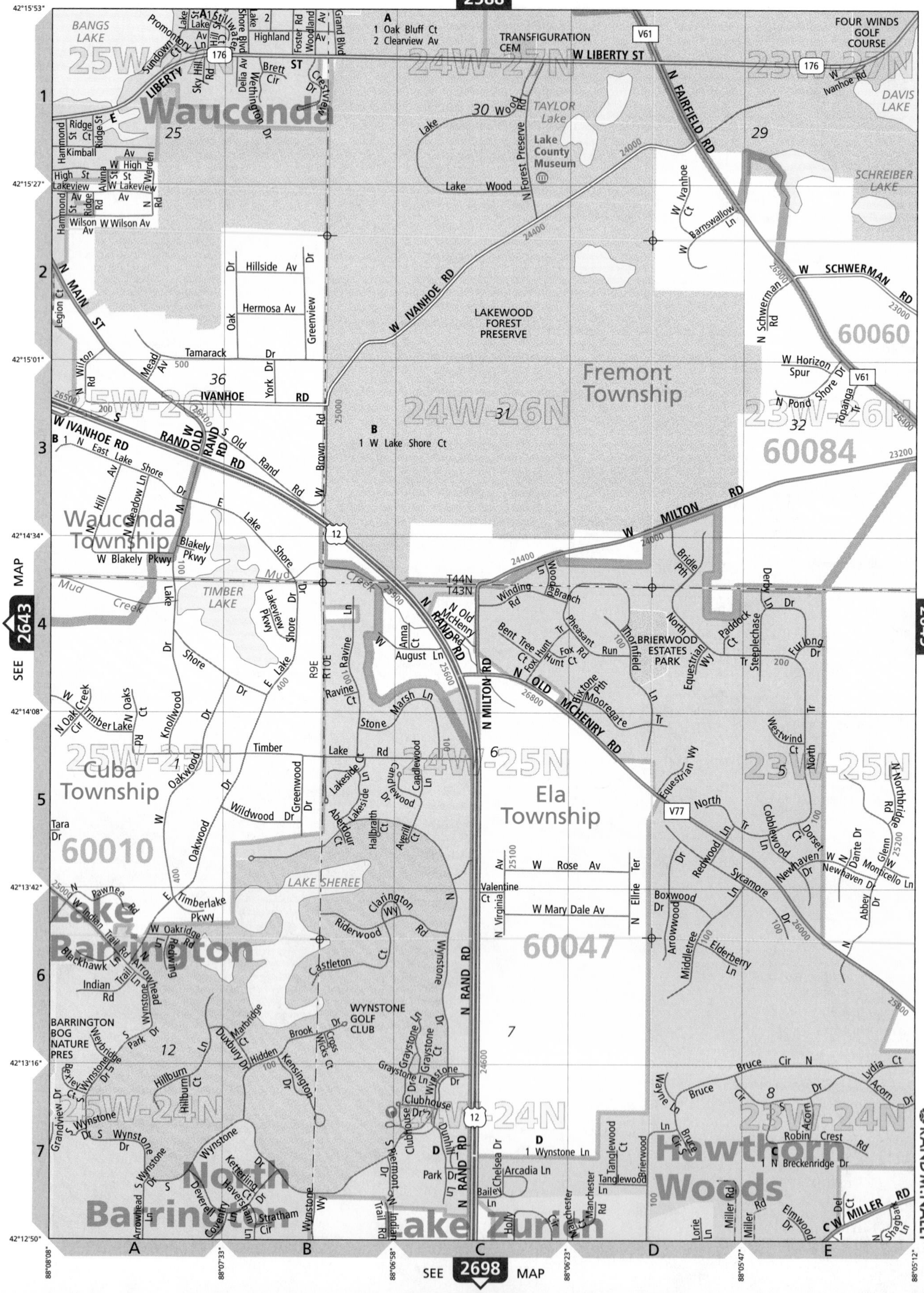

Wauconda
Fremont Township
Wauconda Township
Cuba Township
Ela Township
Lake Barrington
North Barrington
Lake Zurich
Hawthorn Woods

LAKEWOOD FOREST PRESERVE
TRANSFIGURATION CEM
Lake County Museum
FOUR WINDS GOLF COURSE
BRIERWOOD ESTATES PARK
WYNSTONE GOLF CLUB
BARRINGTON BOG NATURE PRES

BANGS LAKE
TAYLOR Lake
DAVIS LAKE
SCHREIBER LAKE
TIMBER LAKE
LAKE SHEREE

60060
60084
60010
60047

A
1 Oak Bluff Ct
2 Clearview Av

B
1 W Lake Shore Ct

B
1 N East Lake Shore Dr

D
1 Wynstone Ln

C
1 N Breckenridge Dr

SEE 2643 MAP

SEE 2645 MAP

SEE 2698 MAP

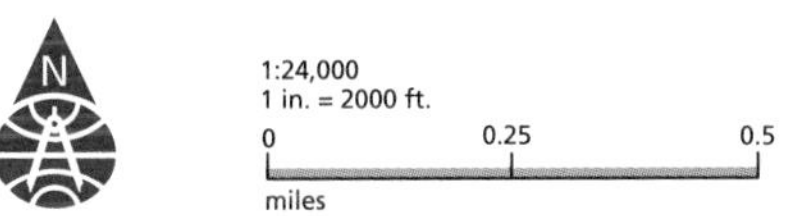

SEE 2589 MAP

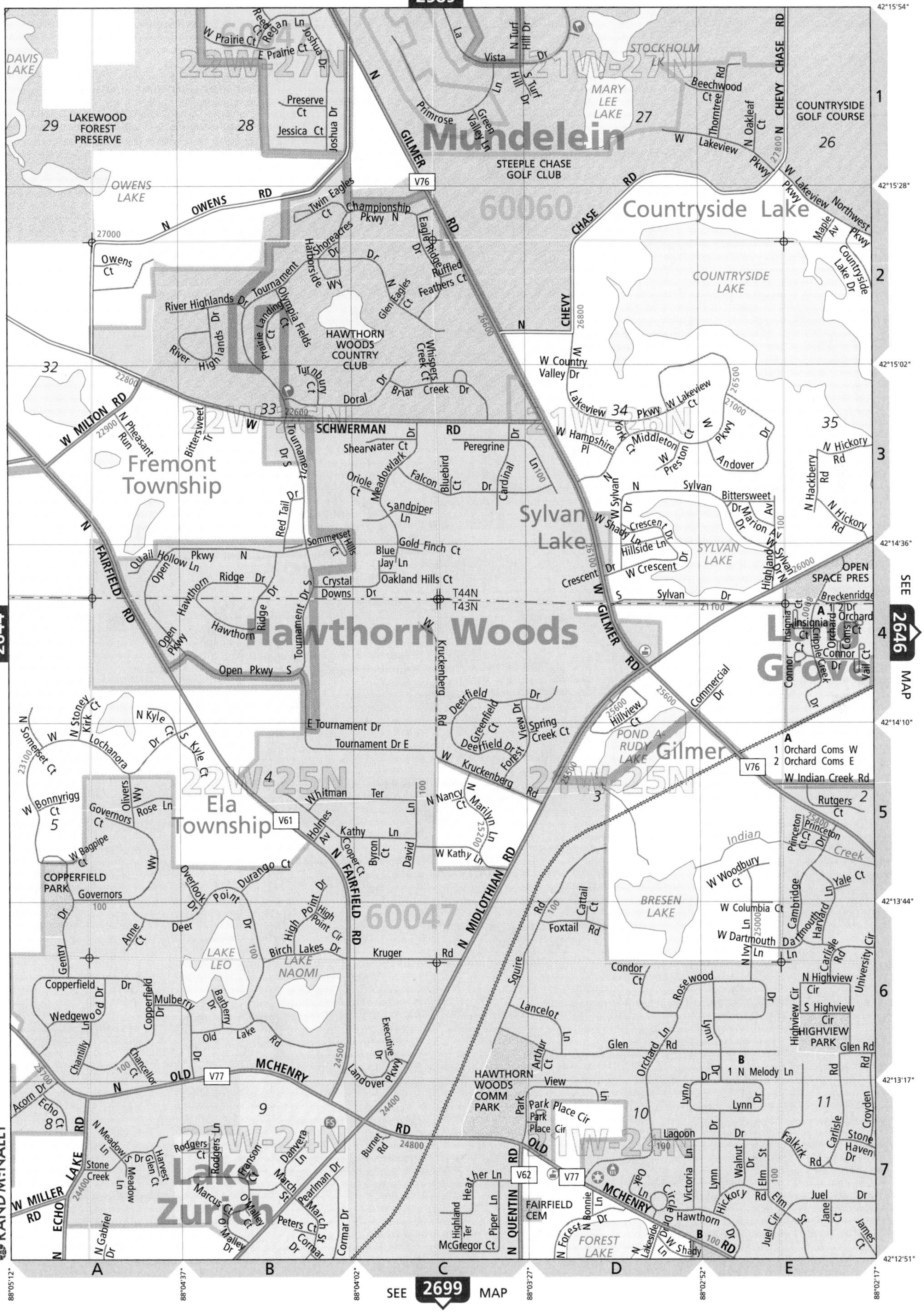

SEE 2644 MAP

SEE 2646 MAP

Mundelein

Hawthorn Woods

Long Grove

Lake Zurich

Gilmer

Sylvan Lake

Countryside Lake

Fremont Township

Ela Township

60060

60047

22W-27N

21W-27N

22W-26N

21W-26N

22W-25N

21W-25N

21W-24N

LAKEWOOD FOREST PRESERVE

STEEPLE CHASE GOLF CLUB

COUNTRYSIDE GOLF COURSE

HAWTHORN WOODS COUNTRY CLUB

HAWTHORN WOODS COMM PARK

COPPERFIELD PARK

HIGHVIEW PARK

OPEN SPACE PRES

FAIRFIELD CEM

DAVIS LAKE

OWENS LAKE

STOCKHOLM LK

MARY LEE LAKE

COUNTRYSIDE LAKE

SYLVAN LAKE

POND A RUDY LAKE

BRESEN LAKE

LAKE LEO

LAKE NAOMI

FOREST LAKE

Indian Creek

N GILMER RD

N CHEVY CHASE RD

N OWENS RD

W MILTON RD

SCHWERMAN RD

N FAIRFIELD RD

N MIDLOTHIAN RD

OLD MCHENRY RD

N QUENTIN RD

N ECHO LAKE RD

W MILLER RD

V76

V61

V77

V62

A
1 Orchard Coms W
2 Orchard Coms E

B
1 N Melody Ln

T44N
T43N

A B C D E

1 2 3 4 5 6 7

42°15'54"
42°15'28"
42°15'02"
42°14'36"
42°14'10"
42°13'44"
42°13'17"
42°12'51"

88°05'12"
88°04'37"
88°04'02"
88°03'27"
88°02'52"
88°02'17"

SEE 2699 MAP

1:24,000
1 in. = 2000 ft.
0 0.25 0.5
miles

SEE 2590 MAP

SEE 2645 MAP

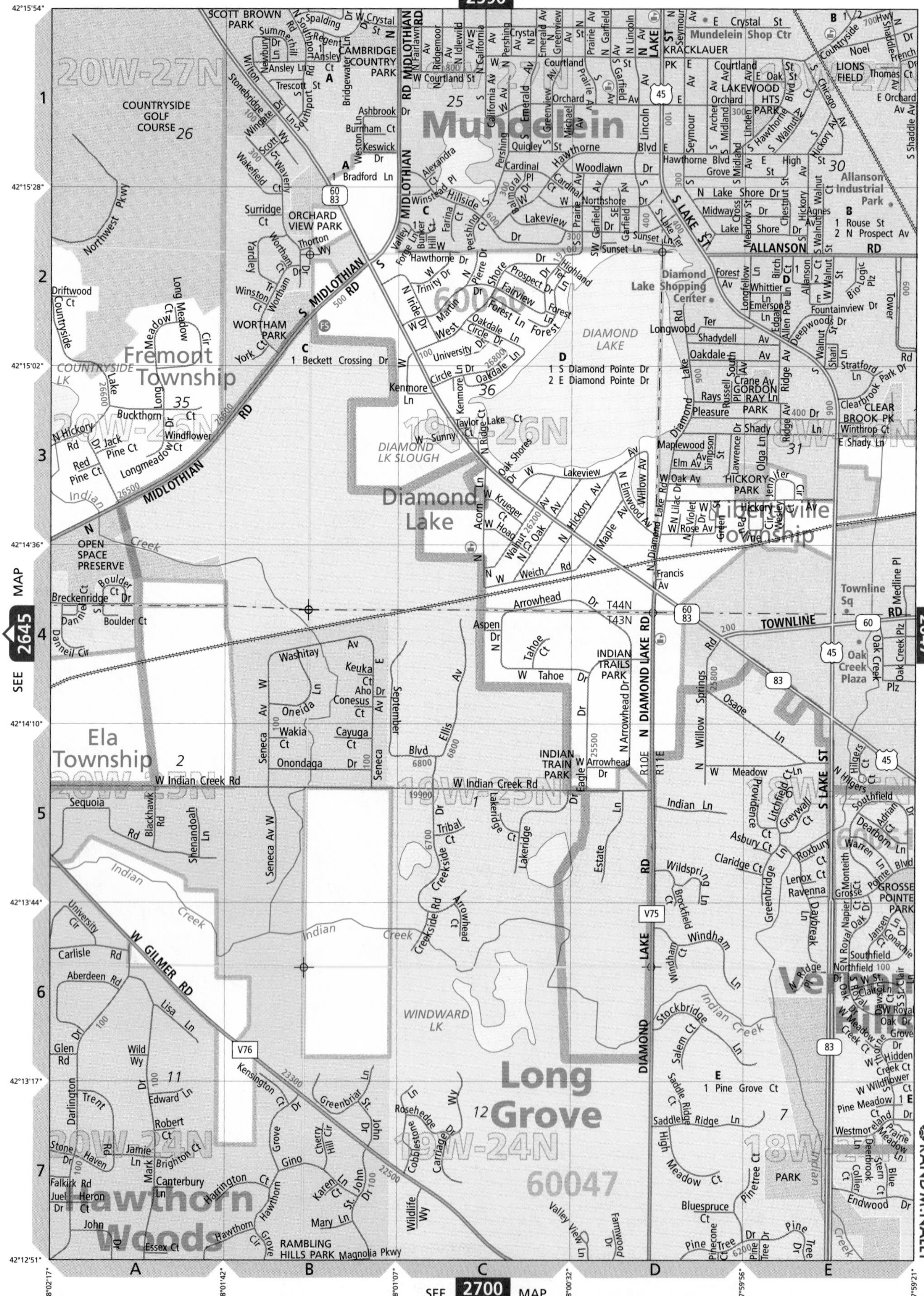

SEE 2647 MAP

Mundelein
Fremont Township
Diamond Lake
Libertyville Township
Ela Township
Long Grove
Hawthorn Woods
Vernon Hills

COUNTRYSIDE GOLF COURSE
CAMBRIDGE COUNTRY PARK
SCOTT BROWN PARK
ORCHARD VIEW PARK
WORTHAM PARK
KRACKLAUER PK
LAKEWOOD HTS PARK
LIONS FIELD
Allanson Industrial Park
Diamond Lake Shopping Center
Mundelein Shop Ctr
GORDON RAY PARK
CLEAR BROOK PK
HICKORY PARK
OPEN SPACE PRESERVE
INDIAN TRAILS PARK
INDIAN TRAIN PARK
Townline Sq
Oak Creek Plaza
GROSSE POINTE PARK
RAMBLING HILLS PARK
PARK

DIAMOND LAKE
DIAMOND LK SLOUGH
COUNTRYSIDE LK
WINDWARD LK
Indian Creek

60060
60047

20W-27N
19W-27N
18W-27N
20W-26N
19W-26N
18W-26N
20W-25N
19W-25N
18W-25N
20W-24N
19W-24N
18W-24N

T44N
T43N
R10E
R11E

S MIDLOTHIAN RD
MIDLOTHIAN RD
N MIDLOTHIAN RD
N LAKE ST
S LAKE ST
ALLANSON RD
TOWNLINE RD
N DIAMOND LAKE RD
DIAMOND LAKE RD
W GILMER RD
W Indian Creek Rd
Hawthorne Blvd
Lake Shore Dr
Northwest Pkwy
Arrowhead Dr
Weich Rd
Magnolia Pkwy

42°15'54"
42°15'28"
42°15'02"
42°14'36"
42°14'10"
42°13'44"
42°13'17"
42°12'51"

88°02'17"
88°01'42"
88°01'07"
88°00'32"
87°59'56"
87°59'21"

A B C D E
1 2 3 4 5 6 7

SEE 2700 MAP

1:24,000
1 in. = 2000 ft.
0 0.25 0.5
miles

SEE 2591 MAP

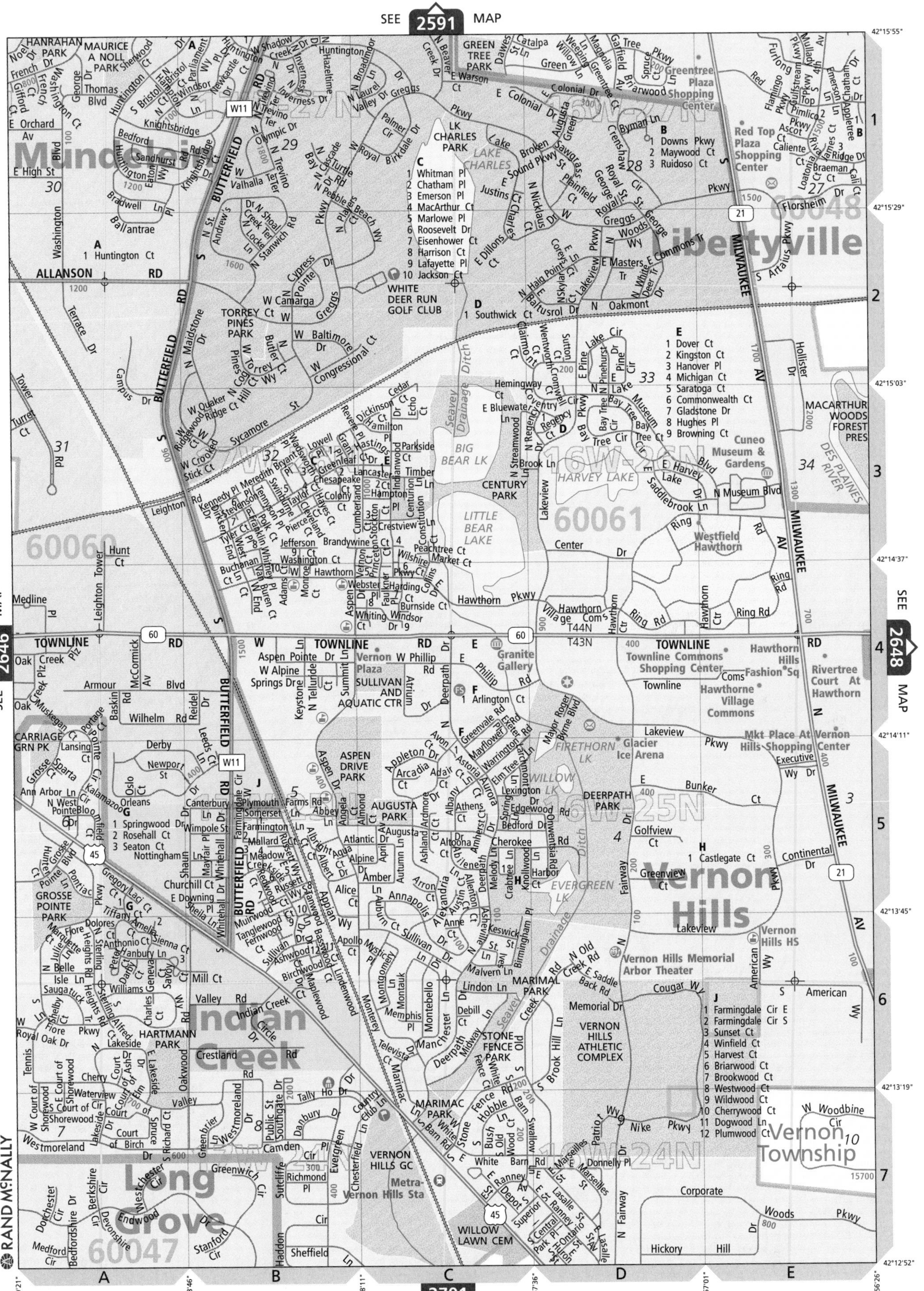

SEE 2646 MAP
SEE 2648 MAP
SEE 2701 MAP

1:24,000
1 in. = 2000 ft.
0 0.25 0.5
miles

SEE 2592 MAP

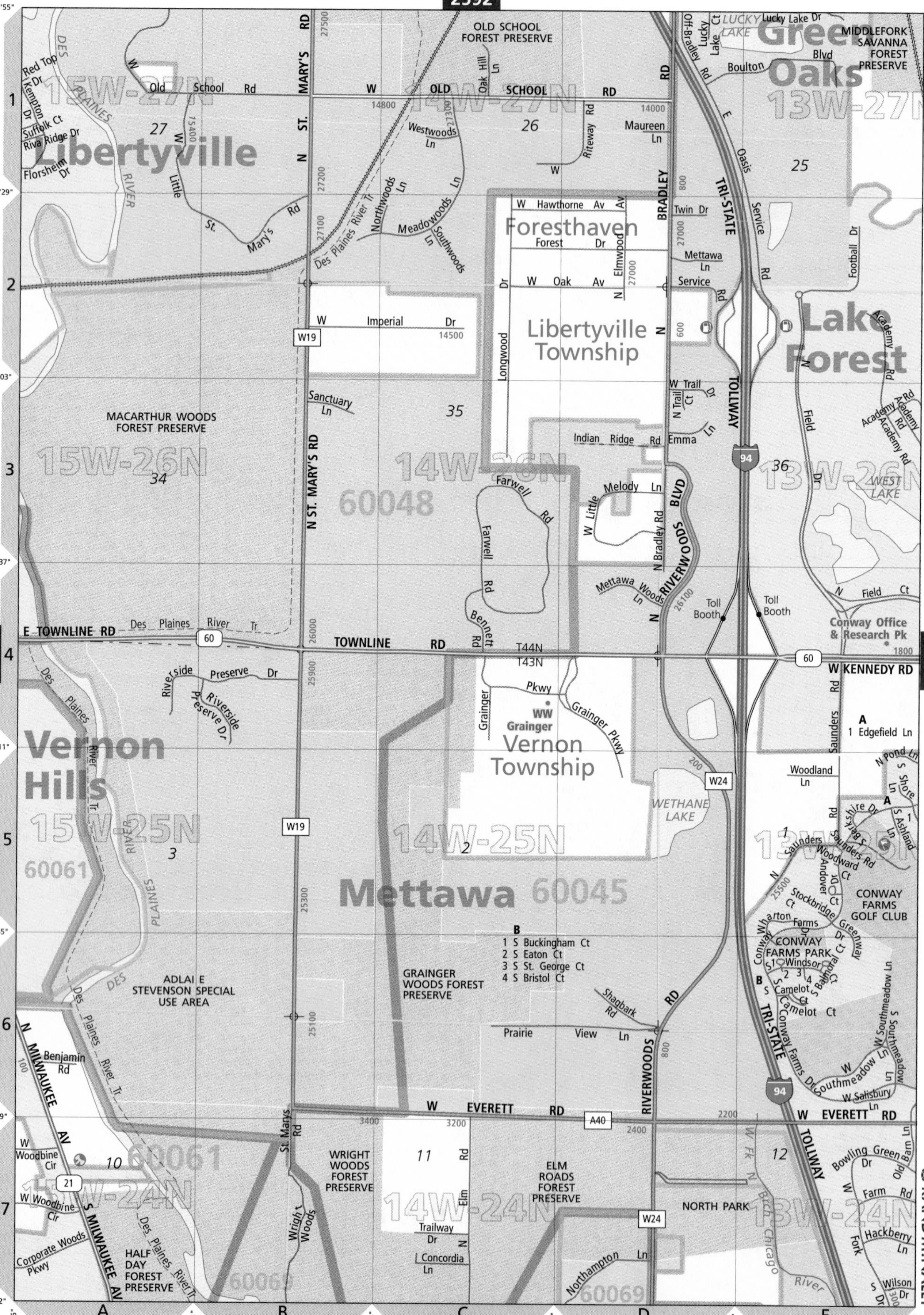

42°15'55"
42°15'29"
42°15'03"
42°14'37"
42°14'11"
42°13'45"
42°13'19"
42°12'52"

1
2
3
4
5
6
7

OLD SCHOOL FOREST PRESERVE
Red Top Dr
Kempton Dr
Suffolk Ct
Riva Ridge Dr
Florsheim Dr
W Old School Rd
W OLD SCHOOL RD
15W-27N
14W-27N
13W-27N
Libertyville
DES PLAINES RIVER
27
26
25
15400
14800
14000
27500
27300
27200
27100
N ST. MARY'S RD
Oak Hill Ln
Westwoods Ln
Riteway Rd
Maureen Ln
W Little St. Mary's Rd
Northwoods Ln
Meadowoods Ln
Southwoods Ln
Des Plaines River Tr
Green Oaks
LUCKY LAKE
Lucky Lake Dr
Lucky Lake Ct
Off-Bradley Rd
Boulton Blvd
MIDDLEFORK SAVANNA FOREST PRESERVE
E Oasis Service Rd
TRI-STATE TOLLWAY
BRADLEY RD
800
W Hawthorne Av
Foresthaven
Forest Dr
Elmwood Av
W Oak Av
27000
Twin Dr
Mettawa Ln
Service Rd
Football Dr
W Imperial Dr
14500
W19
Libertyville Township
Longwood Dr
600
Lake Forest
Academy Rd
Sanctuary Ln
MACARTHUR WOODS FOREST PRESERVE
35
W Trail Dr
N Trail Ct
Indian Ridge Rd
Emma Ln
Field Dr
Academy Rd
15W-26N
14W-26N
13W-26N
34
36
60048
N ST. MARY'S RD
Farwell Rd
Melody Ln
W Little Melody Ln
94
WEST LAKE
N Bradley Rd
N RIVERWOODS BLVD
Mettawa Woods Ln
26100
Toll Booth
Toll Booth
N Field Ct
Conway Office & Research Pk
1800
Bennett Rd
E TOWNLINE RD
Des Plaines River Tr
60
26000
TOWNLINE RD
T44N
T43N
W KENNEDY RD
25900
Riverside Preserve Dr
Riverside Preserve Dr
Grainger Pkwy
WW Grainger
Grainger Pkwy
Saunders Rd
A
1 Edgefield Ln
Vernon Hills
Des Plaines River Tr
Vernon Township
200
W24
N Pond Ln
S Shore Ln
Woodland Ln
WETHANE LAKE
A
S Berkshire Dr
S Ashland Ln
15W-25N
14W-25N
13W-25N
3
2
1
60061
W19
S Saunders Rd
Woodward Ct
Andover Ct
Mettawa
60045
N Saunders Rd
25500
Stockbridge Ct
CONWAY FARMS GOLF CLUB
25300
Wharton Ct
Farms Dr
Greenway
B
1 S Buckingham Ct
2 S Eaton Ct
3 S St. George Ct
4 S Bristol Ct
CONWAY FARMS PARK
S Windsor Ct
Balmoral Ct
DES PLAINES
ADLAI E STEVENSON SPECIAL USE AREA
GRAINGER WOODS FOREST PRESERVE
Shagbark Rd
RIVERWOODS RD
B
S Camelot Ct
S Camelot Ct
Conway Farms Dr
S Southmeadow Ln
W Southmeadow Ln
25100
Prairie View Ln
N MILWAUKEE AV
100
Benjamin Rd
Des Plaines River Tr
800
W Southmeadow Ln
W Salisbury Ln
W EVERETT RD
A40
3400
3200
2400
2200
W EVERETT RD
St. Marys Rd
W Woodbine Cir
10
60061
11
Elm Rd
WRIGHT WOODS FOREST PRESERVE
ELM ROADS FOREST PRESERVE
12
W FK N Br Chicago River
Bowling Green Dr
Old Barn Ln
21
W Woodbine Cir
15W-24N
14W-24N
13W-24N
NORTH PARK
W Farm Rd
Wright Woods
Trailway Dr
W24
S MILWAUKEE AV
Corporate Woods Pkwy
Des Plaines River Tr
HALF DAY FOREST PRESERVE
Concordia Ln
Northampton Ln
Fork Ln
Hackberry Ln
60069
60069
S Wilson Dr
300

A B C D E

87°56'26" 87°55'51" 87°55'16" 87°54'40" 87°54'05" 87°53'30"

SEE 2647 MAP
SEE 2649 MAP
SEE 2702 MAP

1:24,000
1 in. = 2000 ft.
0 0.25 0.5
miles

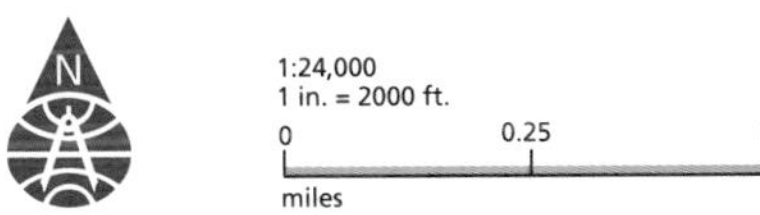

SEE 2593 MAP

Libertyville Township
Vernon Township
Lake Forest
60045
12W-27N
11W-27N
12W-26N
11W-26N
12W-25N
11W-25N
12W-24N
11W-24N
T44N
T43N
R11E
R12E
MIDDLEFORK SAVANNA FOREST PRESERVE
LAKE BLUFF FOR PRES
DEERPATH GOLF COURSE
DEERPATH COMMUNITY PARK
ONWENTSIA CLUB
Lake Forest Academy
Lake Forest Graduate School of Management
ROUTE 60 PARK
CONWAY FARMS GOLF CLUB
Lake Forest Hospital
Sunset Corners Shop Ctr
Metra-Lake Forest Station
WEST LAKE FOREST
EVERETT PARK
ST. PATRICK CEM
PRAIRIE WOLF FOREST PRESERVE
NORTHCROFT PARK
BUENA PARK
WAVELAND PARK
WEST PARK
WEST LAKE
EAST LAKE
N WAUKEGAN RD
S WAUKEGAN RD
TELEGRAPH RD
SKOKIE HWY
S SKOKIE HWY
GREEN BAY RD
W KENNEDY RD
DEERPATH RD
E DEERPATH RD
W WESTLEIGH RD
E WESTLEIGH RD
W EVERETT RD
OLD ELM RD
S RIDGE RD
N Westmoreland Rd
North Branch Chicago River
Skokie River
A
1 Harvard Ct
2 Stanford Ct
B
1 E Illinois Rd
C
1 W Mallard Ln
2 W Sandpiper Ln
D
1 Conway Farms Dr
E
1 Settlers Sq
2 Lynette Dr
F
1 Kimberly Ln

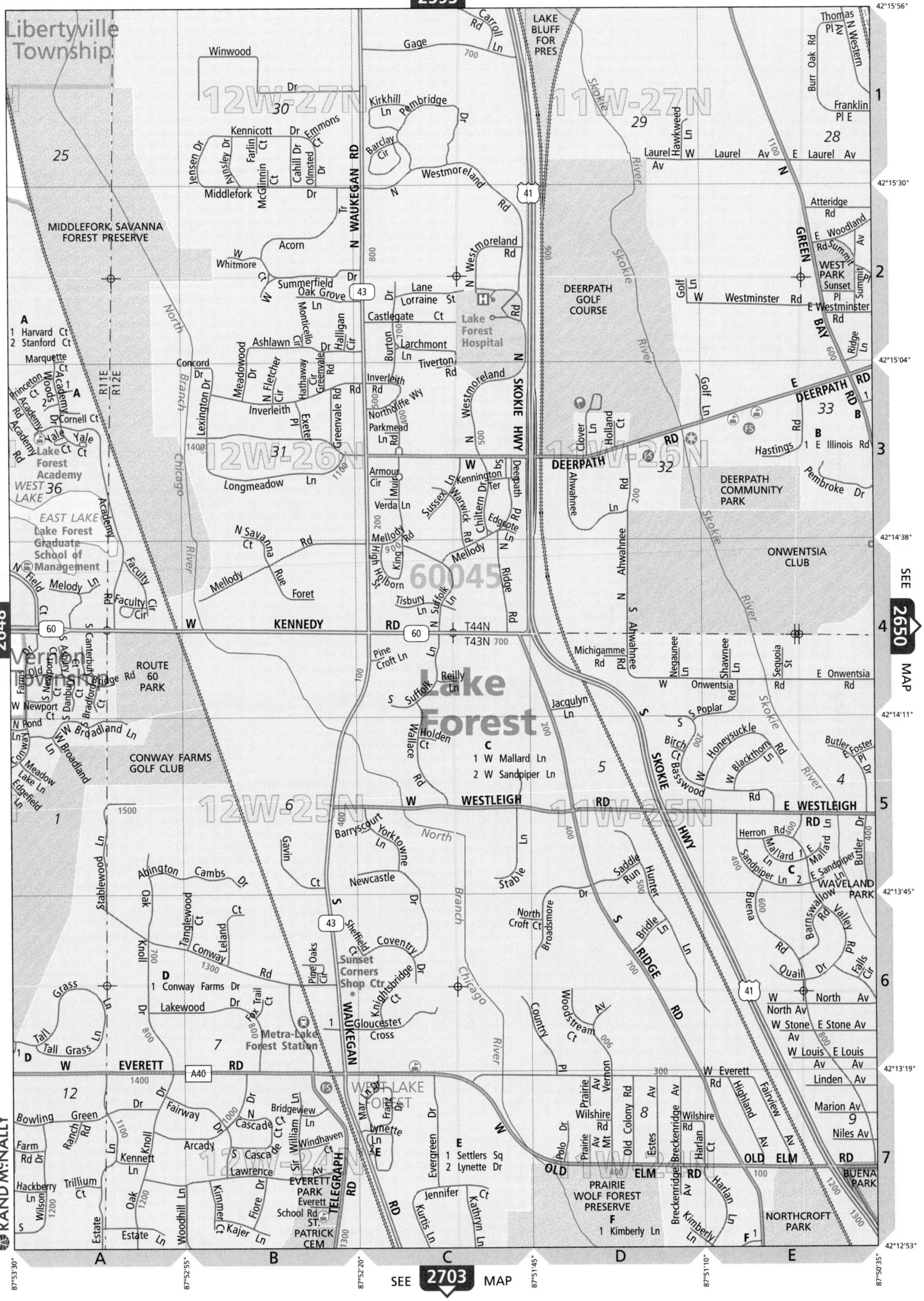

SEE 2648 MAP
SEE 2650 MAP
SEE 2703 MAP

1:24,000
1 in. = 2000 ft.
0 0.25 0.5
miles

SEE 2594 MAP

SEE 2649 MAP

SEE B MAP

SEE 2704 MAP

A B C D E
1 2 3 4 5 6 7

42°15'56" 42°15'30" 42°15'04" 42°14'38" 42°14'11" 42°13'45" 42°13'19" 42°12'53"
87°50'35" 87°50'00" 87°49'25" 87°48'49" 87°48'14" 87°47'39"

RAND McNALLY

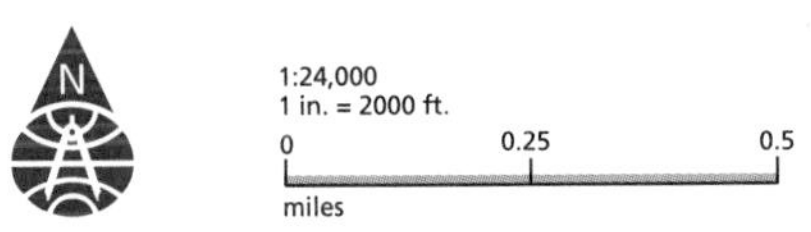

SEE B MAP

Grafton Township

Coral Township

Huntley

60142

42W-23N
41W-23N
42W-22N
41W-22N
42W-21N
41W-21N

R6E R7E

7 8 9 13 16 17 18 19 20 21 24 25 28 29 30 31 32 33 36

Frohling Rd
Adamson Rd
Adamson Rd
S Union Rd
Coyne Station Rd
Ernesti Rd
Ernesti Rd
Sawyer St
Ackman Rd
Sinnett St
Ramschell St
Keating Dr
Donahue Dr
Enstrom Ln
Enstrom Ct
Kalsow Ln
Malone St
Talamore Blvd
Davis Ln
Hawley Ln
Connor Ln
Blvd St
Baumgartner St
Field
Williams Dr
Founders
Cummings
Brunschon Ln
Williams Dr
S Union Rd
Dieckman Rd
South Branch Kishwaukee River
1 Church Rd
Ruth Ct
MARENGO RD
A47
Oakleaf Ln
Oakland Ct
Oakcrest
Wolf Dr
Dr
North St
4th St
Union
Special Plz
Borden St
Bonnie Brae Rd
Janice Dr
Janice
Dr
B ST
W MAIN STREET RD
A47
HARMONY RD
A49
Huntley HS
Wernecke Rd
Windsor Ct
Windsor Dr
HEMMER RD
WHISPER CREEK GOLF CLUB
Greenway Dr
Nelson Dr
Maplewood Av
Heatherdale Ln
Bellflower Ln
Norfolk Dr
Stonewater Dr
Big Horn Dr
Cross Dr
Primrose Ct
Summerview
Wildrose Dr
W Coventry Ln
1 Morning Glory Ln
Kreutzer Rd
Fitzgerald Ln
Lions Chase Ct
Nicollet Ln
Lions Chase Ln
Richmond Ln
Lasalle Ln
Carver Ln
1 E Coral St
BETSEY WARRINGTON PARK
Sunset Ln
Heinz Av
Lincoln Av
Mill St
DEICKE PARK
VINE ST
47

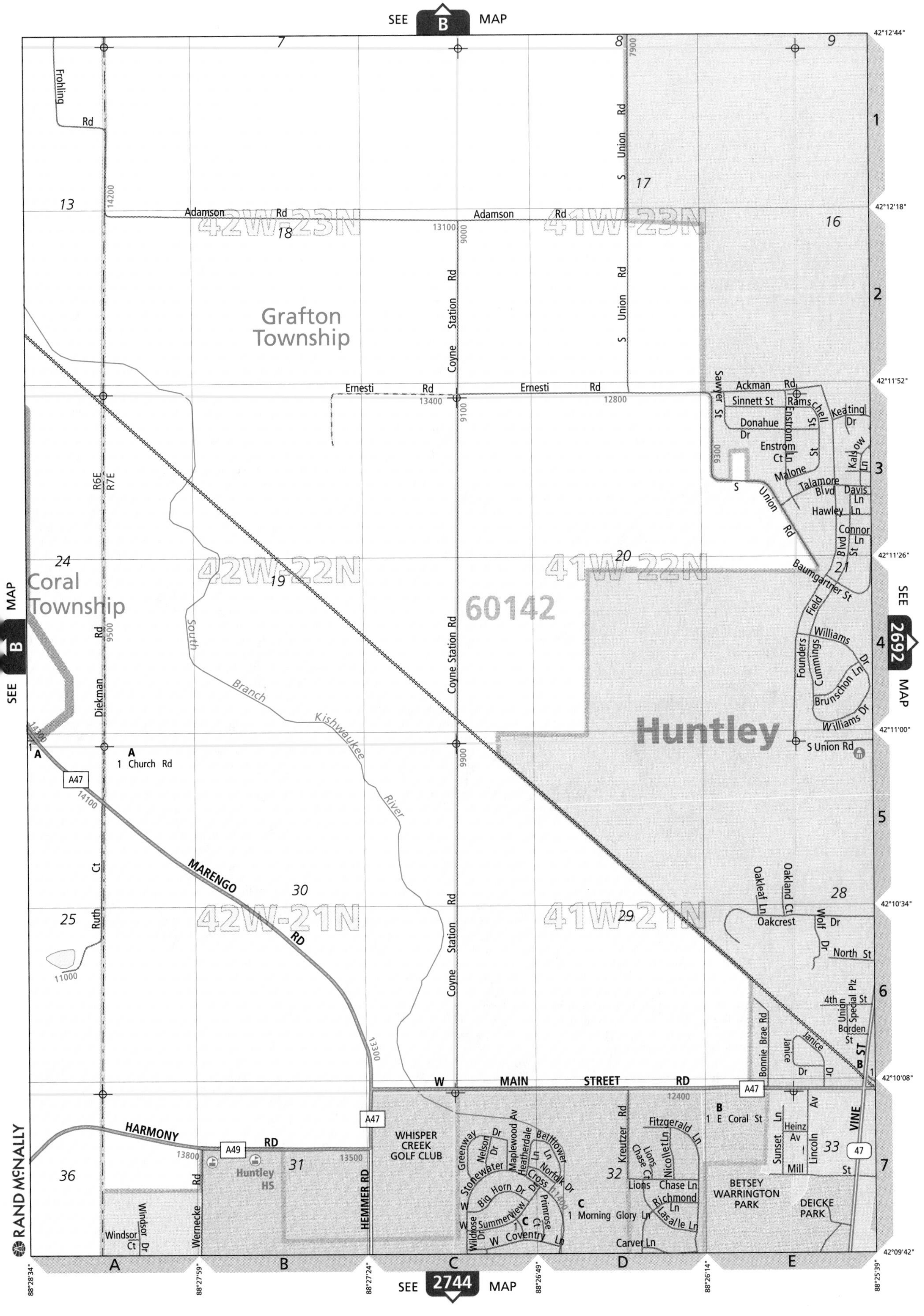

14200 9500 9000 13100 9100 13400 12800 7900 9300 14300 14100 9900 11000 13300 13800 13500 11400 12400

42°12'44"
42°12'18"
42°11'52"
42°11'26"
42°11'00"
42°10'34"
42°10'08"
42°09'42"

88°28'34"
88°27'59"
88°27'24"
88°26'49"
88°26'14"
88°25'39"

A B C D E
1 2 3 4 5 6 7

SEE 2692 MAP

SEE 2744 MAP

1:24,000
1 in. = 2000 ft.
0 0.25 0.5 miles

SEE 2638 MAP

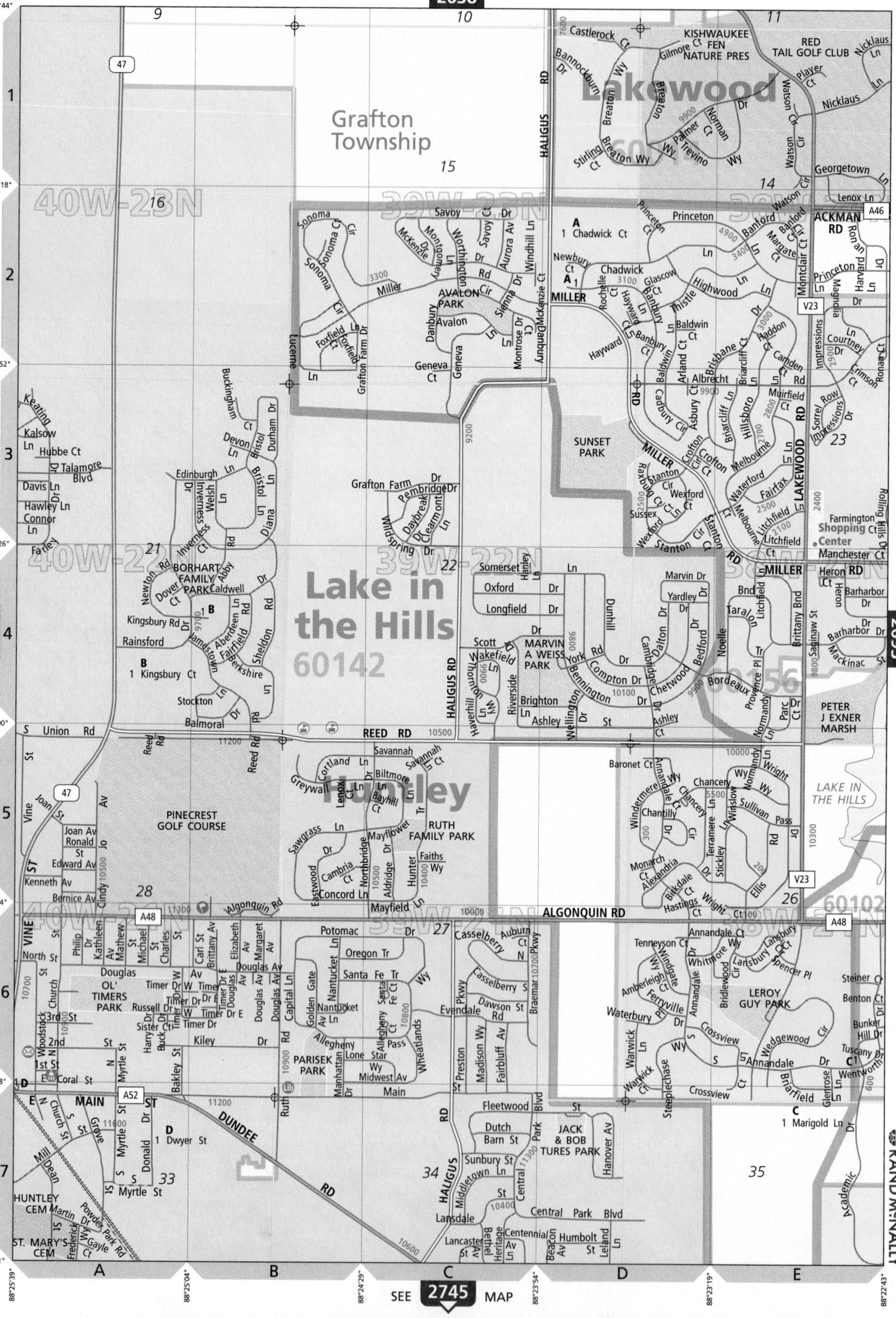

SEE 2691 MAP

SEE 2693 MAP

SEE 2745 MAP

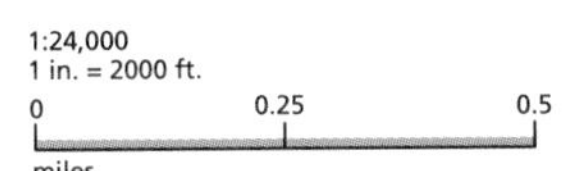

SEE 2639 MAP

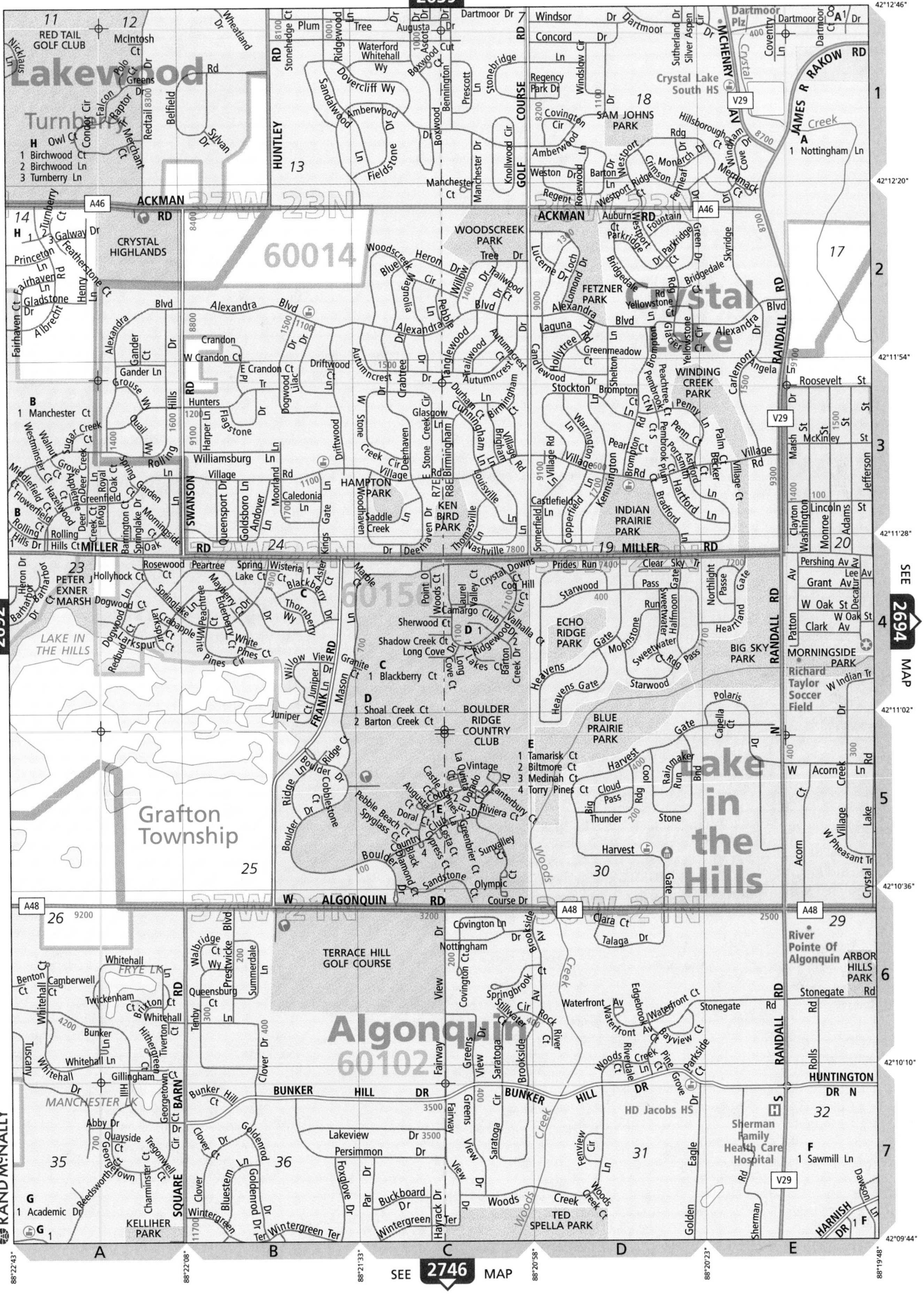

SEE 2692 MAP

SEE 2694 MAP

SEE 2746 MAP

Lakewood

Turnberry

Crystal Lake

Lake in the Hills

Grafton Township

Algonquin

60014

60156

60102

37W 23N

36W 23N

37W 22N

36W 22N

37W 21N

36W 21N

RED TAIL GOLF CLUB

CRYSTAL HIGHLANDS

Crystal Lake South HS

SAM JOHNS PARK

WOODSCREEK PARK

FETZNER PARK

WINDING CREEK PARK

HAMPTON PARK

KEN BIRD PARK

INDIAN PRAIRIE PARK

PETER J EXNER MARSH

LAKE IN THE HILLS

BOULDER RIDGE COUNTRY CLUB

ECHO RIDGE PARK

BIG SKY PARK

BLUE PRAIRIE PARK

MORNINGSIDE PARK

Richard Taylor Soccer Field

TERRACE HILL GOLF COURSE

River Pointe Of Algonquin

ARBOR HILLS PARK

HD Jacobs HS

Sherman Family Health Care Hospital

TED SPELLA PARK

KELLIHER PARK

FRYE LK

MANCHESTER LK

Dartmoor Plz

ACKMAN RD

MILLER RD

W ALGONQUIN RD

BUNKER HILL DR

RANDALL RD

HUNTLEY RD

GOLF COURSE RD

MCHENRY AV

JAMES R RAKOW RD

SWANSON RD

FRANK RD

BARN SQUARE

HUNTINGTON DR N

HARNISH DR

A46

A48

V29

H
1 Birchwood Ct
2 Birchwood Ln
3 Turnberry Ln

A
1 Nottingham Ln

B
1 Manchester Ct

C
1 Blackberry Ct

D
1 Shoal Creek Ct
2 Barton Creek Ct

E
1 Tamarisk Ct
2 Biltmore Ct
3 Medinah Ct
4 Torry Pines Ct

F
1 Sawmill Ln

G
1 Academic Dr

A B C D E

1 2 3 4 5 6 7

42°12'46"

42°12'20"

42°11'54"

42°11'28"

42°11'02"

42°10'36"

42°10'10"

42°09'44"

88°22'43"

88°22'08"

88°21'33"

88°20'58"

88°20'23"

88°19'48"

1:24,000
1 in. = 2000 ft.
0 0.25 0.5
miles

SEE 2640 MAP

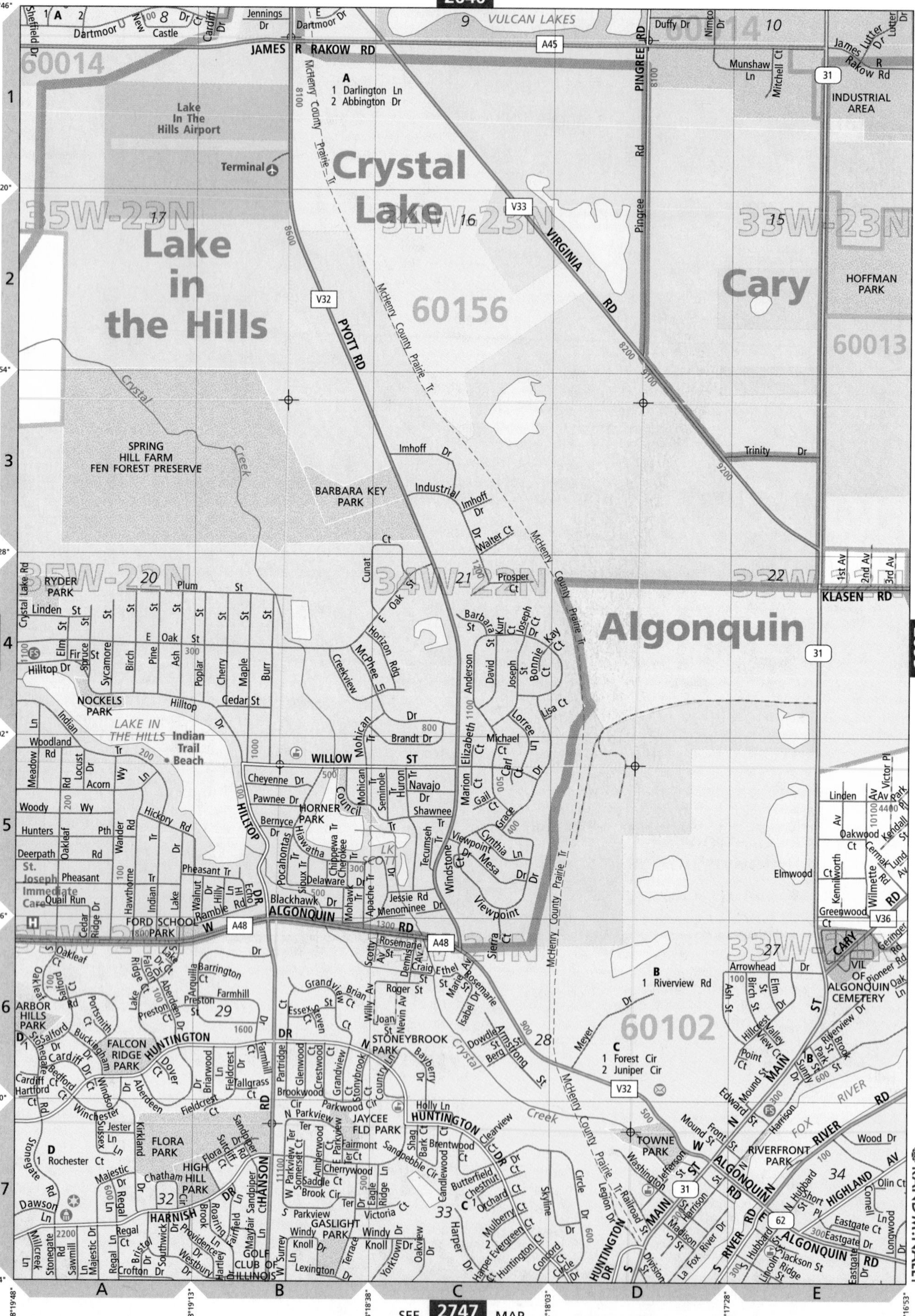

Crystal Lake

Lake in the Hills

Cary

Algonquin

Lake In The Hills Airport

SPRING HILL FARM FEN FOREST PRESERVE

BARBARA KEY PARK

HOFFMAN PARK

INDUSTRIAL AREA

NOCKELS PARK

RYDER PARK

HORNER PARK

FORD SCHOOL PARK

ARBOR HILLS PARK

FALCON RIDGE PARK

FLORA PARK

HIGH HILL PARK

STONEYBROOK PARK

JAYCEE FLD PARK

GASLIGHT PARK

GOLF CLUB OF ILLINOIS

TOWNE PARK

RIVERFRONT PARK

VIL OF ALGONQUIN CEMETERY

A
1 Darlington Ln
2 Abbington Dr

B
1 Riverview Rd

C
1 Forest Cir
2 Juniper Cir

D
1 Rochester Ct

SEE 2693 MAP

SEE 2695 MAP

SEE 2747 MAP

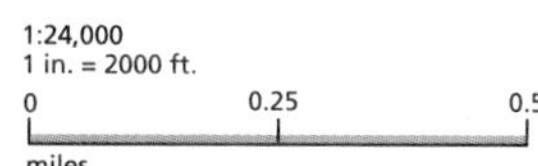

SEE 2641 MAP

Cary

Trout Valley

Fox River Grove

Turner Camp

Haegers Bend

Algonquin Township

Algonquin

Barrington Hills

60013

60021

60102

60010

32W-22N

31W-22N

32W-21N

31W-21N

HOFFMAN PARK

CAMBRIA PARK

HAMPTON PARK

GREENFIELDS PARK

CARY VET PARK

CARY CEM

Metra Cary Sta

CARY COUNTRY CLUB

FOX RIVER PARK

SPRING CREEK PARK

ST. JOHN'S CEMETERY

PRESIDENTIAL PARK

HOLDER MEM PARK

Root Spring

Cary Creek

Spring Creek

FOX RIVER

W MAIN ST

E MAIN ST

CRYSTAL ST

CARY-ALGONQUIN RD

CARY RD

KLASEN RD

ALGONQUIN RD

N RIVER RD

CHAPEL RD

CHURCH RD

HAEGERS BEND RD

HIGHLAND AV

SPRING CREEK RD

GEORGETOWN DR

1ST ST

V36

14

62

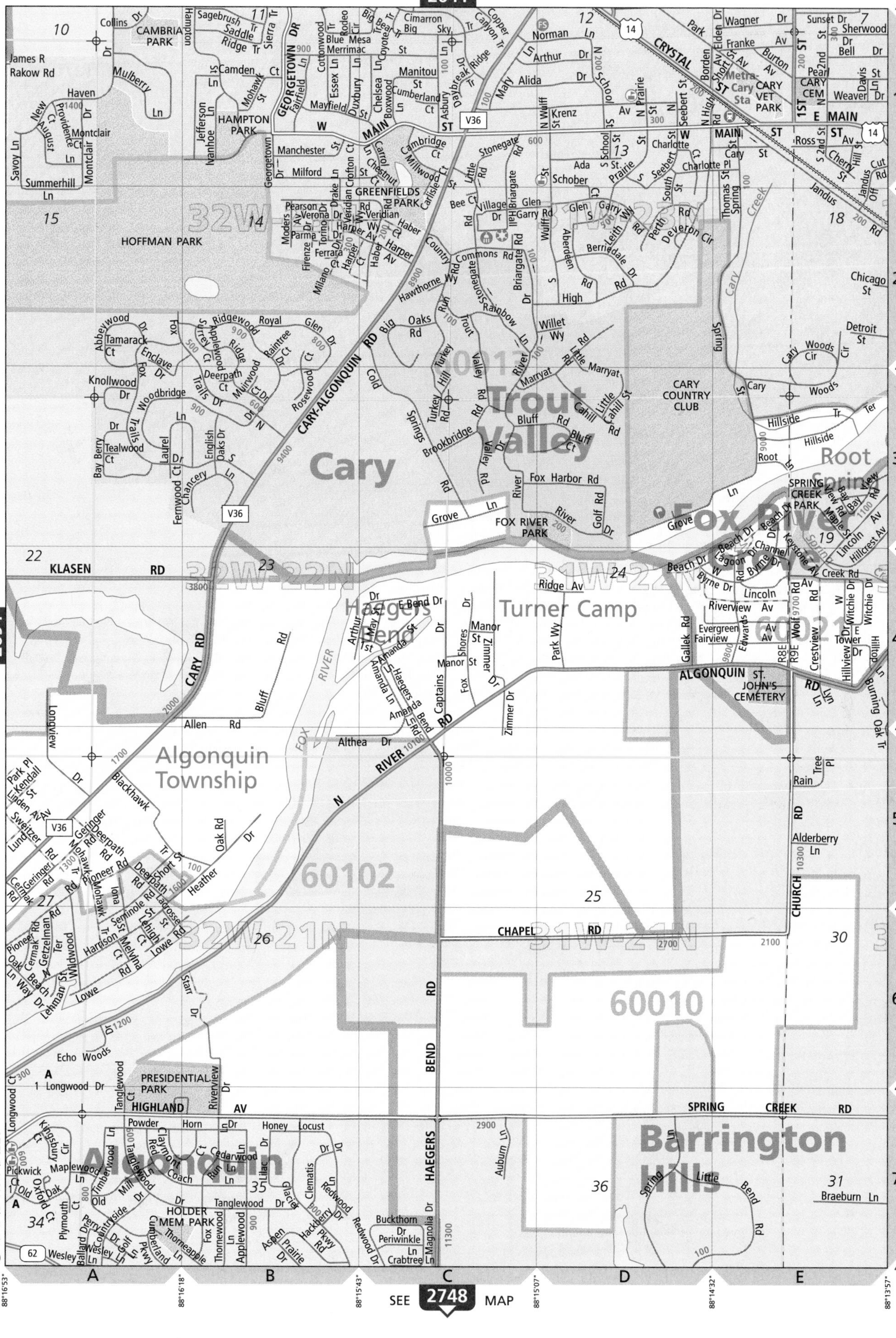

SEE 2694 MAP

SEE 2696 MAP

SEE 2748 MAP

A B C D E

1 2 3 4 5 6 7

42°12'48" 42°12'22" 42°11'56" 42°11'30" 42°11'04" 42°10'38" 42°10'12" 42°09'46"

88°16'53" 88°16'18" 88°15'43" 88°15'07" 88°14'32" 88°13'57"

1:24,000
1 in. = 2000 ft.
0 0.25 0.5
miles

SEE 2642 MAP

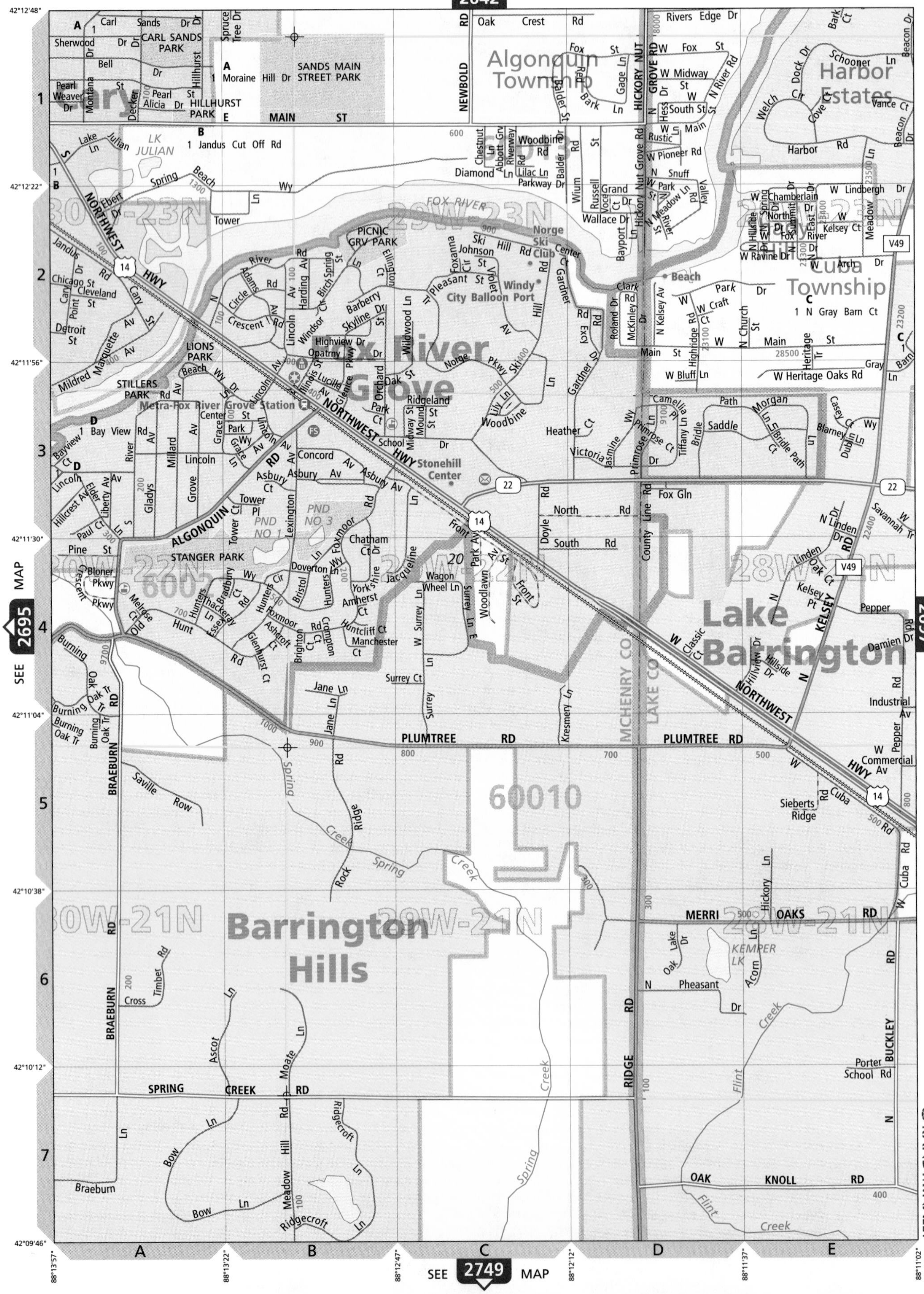

SEE 2695 MAP

SEE 2697 MAP

Cary

CARL SANDS PARK

HILLHURST PARK

SANDS MAIN STREET PARK

LK JULIAN

Algonquin Township

Harbor Estates

Cuba Township

Fox River Grove

LIONS PARK

STILLERS PARK

PICNIC GRV PARK

Metra-Fox River Grove Station

Norge Ski Club

Windy City Balloon Port

Stonehill Center

STANGER PARK

PND NO 1

PND NO 3

FOX RIVER

Lake Barrington

Barrington Hills

KEMPER LK

60010

NORTHWEST HWY

ALGONQUIN RD

PLUMTREE RD

MERRI OAKS RD

SPRING CREEK RD

OAK KNOLL RD

BRAEBURN RD

RIDGE RD

BUCKLEY RD

NEWBOLD RD

HICKORY NUT GROVE RD

KELSEY RD

MCHENRY CO

LAKE CO

30W-23N

29W-23N

28W-23N

30W-22N

29W-22N

28W-22N

30W-21N

29W-21N

28W-21N

SEE 2749 MAP

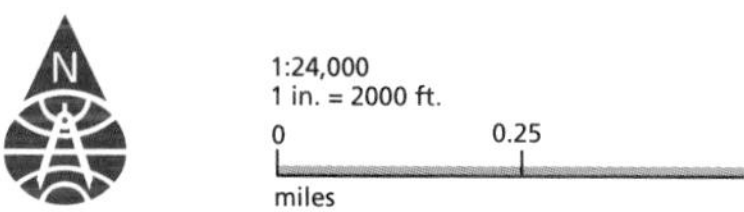

SEE 2643 MAP

Beacon Dr
Buoy Ct
9
Flint Creek Dr
Bridgewater Ct
10
W Kensington Ct
Longmeadow Ct
Oak Hill Rd
LK BARRINGTON SHORES GOLF CLUB
Shoreline Rd
Barn Rd
Old
59
12
Schooner Ct
N Hurdale Ln
V49
RD
W MILLER RD
A42
Shoreline
11
MILLER RD
Vance Ct
KELSEY
Alice Ln
N OLD
24000
N Pointe Ct
Rd
N Wedgewood
A
1 Waterview Ct
LK BARRINGTON
600
Border Ln
Lakeview Pl
300
ETON PARK
1
B
1 Harbor Rd
Flint Creek
Lookout Pointe
N McGraw Ct
Hillfarm Ct
Rd
Hillfarm
23800
GRASSY LAKE FOREST PRESERVE
Wooded
Ln
Glen Cir
Oxford
Brookside
Woodland
Dr
Dr
Rd
Eton
Woodbine Pl
500
Crooked Ln
200
Dr
BARRINGTON RD
23700
23500
16
15
27W-23N
Old Barrington Ct
RD
GRASSY LAKE
14
26W-23N
Golfview
13
Crestview Ln
Drain
Lake
Grayshire Ln
Chesapeake Dr
N Longview Pt
W Lakeridge Dr
Lakeview Dr
Vista Ln
Flint
BILTMORE COUNTRY CLUB
2
FLINT LAKE
100
Dr
Grassy
Dr
Wienecke Ct
North Barrington
59
Gray Barn Ln
N Gray Barn Ct
Woodland
West Ln
100
East Ln
Golfview Ln
100
Signal Hill Rd
500
600
Osage Dr
Mohawk Dr
Seminole Dr
Iroquois Dr
Castleview Ct
Creek
STONEHENGE GOLF CLUB
H
Advocate Good Shepherd Hospital
N OLD BARRINGTON RD
100
VIL WILDLIFE REFUGE
Onondaga Dr
3
W Savannah Tr
Savannah Tr
Flint
Century Oaks Dr
Century Oaks Dr
Savannah Ct
Trillium Ct
Cherry Hill Dr
21
27W-22N
26W-22N
22
24
22
23
W Driftwood Ct
Savannah Tr
E Savannah 27500
W Brookside Ct
Brookside Wy
NW Brookside Wy
60010
100
Haverton Wy
Damien Dr
Lake Barrington
W Apple Tree Ln
RD
N Edgemond Ln
26100
Haverton Conservation Area
4
Industrial Av
Creek
W Henry Ln
N Countryside Ln
Bertha Ln
22000
BARRINGTON
22000
N
22000
W Flynn Creek Dr
27100
W Scott Rd
W Scott Rd
W Commercial Av
N HARBOR RD
W Country Estates Rd
Cuba Township
5
Flint
OLD
Crest Hill Dr
C
1 W Drake Rd
2 W Chatham Rd
C
W Flynn Creek Dr
Countryside Ln
N
W Sunset Ln
W
Crown Rd
Chatham Rd
28
27W-21N
W
21500
N
CUBA RD
21500
WHITE MEM CEM
25
ST
27
27000
26500
26W-21N
26
25800
NORTHWEST
RD
W Falkirk Cir
21300
N
Fox Hollow Dr
Elizabeth Ln
6
HWY
Grant St
Grant St
W Glenbarr Ln
Border Rd
Laurine Dr
Ln
HOUGH
Barrington Hills
25th St
N 24th St
23rd St
St
St
21200
St
HART
St
Highland
21st
20th
19th Rd
21100
N Taylor Ln
St
St
Prestwick
N Prestwick Dr
D
1 Commonwealth Ct
2 Sycamore Rd
W Sunset Rd
N Elizabeth
N Columbus Dr
14
N 22nd St
N
N 18th St
N
14th St
Dr
W
Hippler Rd
W
N
Taylor Rd
Lincoln
Brandt Rd
E Providence Rd
Rub of the Green Ln
The Foundry Of Barrington Shop Ctr
13th
N Scott Av
N Cumnor Av
BARRINGTON HILLS COUNTRY CLUB
E
1 Old Hart Rd
W Merton Rd
Carriage Tr
Hampstead Ct
7
Bisque Dr
Dormy Ln
RD
HART RD
16th St
35
26200
N Exmoor Av
36
59
33
OAK KNOLL RD
300
34
Flint Creek
Paganica Dr
Oakwood Dr
Norther Av
Western
N Scott Av
W Roslyn Rd
20800
Roslyn Rd
Covington Dr
D
HART RD
Cumnor
Barrington
Bryant Av
Prospect Av
Sunny Ln
Pine Rd
700 800
E 1
W Waverly Rd
E
2

A B C D E
1 2 3 4 5 6 7

42°12'50"
42°12'24"
42°11'58"
42°11'32"
42°11'06"
42°10'40"
42°10'13"
42°09'47"
88°11'02"
88°10'27"
88°09'52"
88°09'17"
88°08'42"
88°08'07"

SEE 2696 MAP

SEE 2698 MAP

SEE 2750 MAP

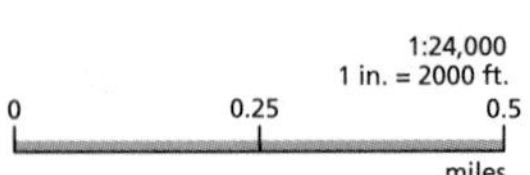

SEE 2644 MAP

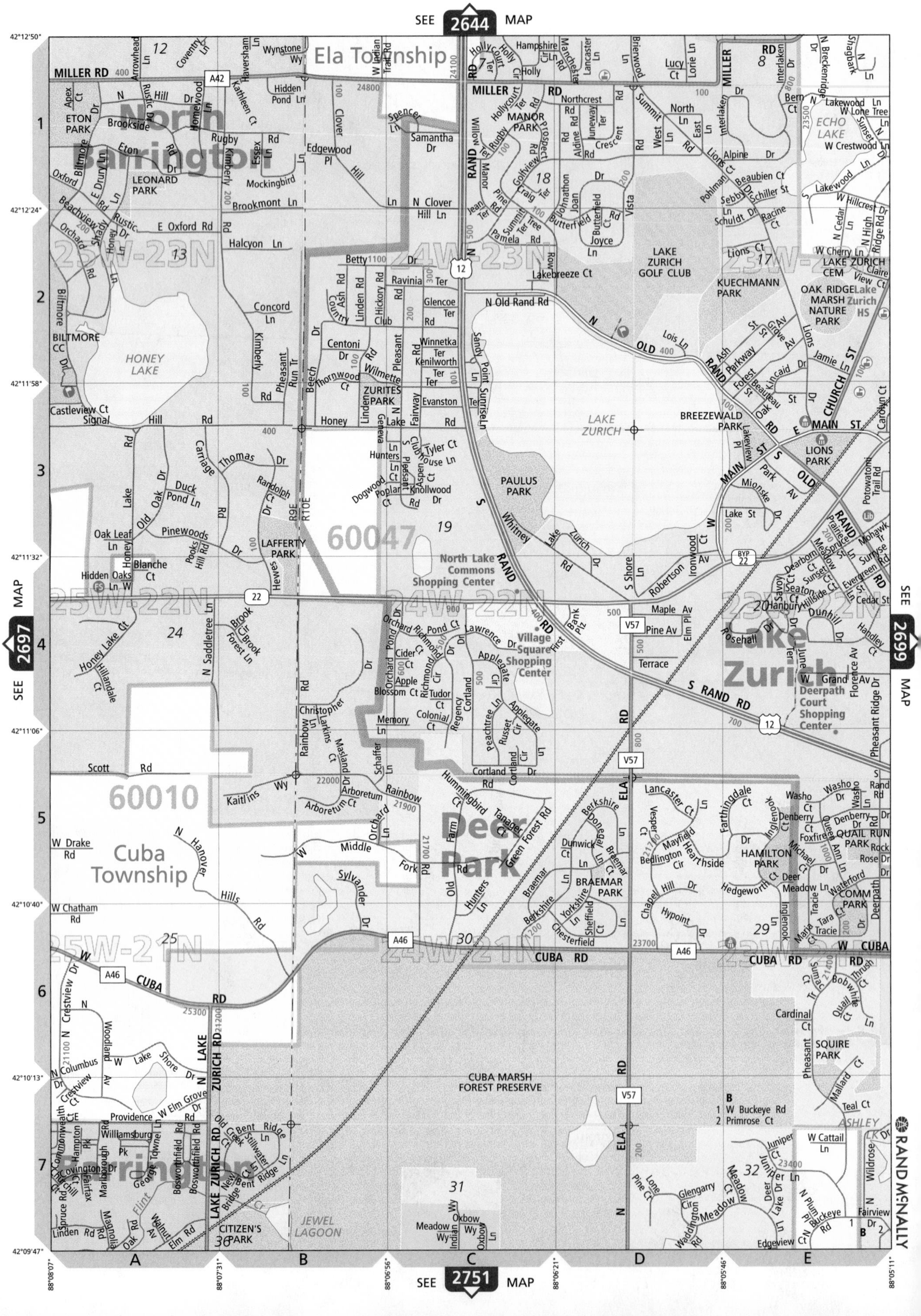

SEE 2697 MAP

SEE 2699 MAP

SEE 2751 MAP

North Barrington
Ela Township
Lake Zurich
Deer Park
Cuba Township
Barrington
LAKE ZURICH
HONEY LAKE
CUBA MARSH FOREST PRESERVE
LAKE ZURICH GOLF CLUB
PAULUS PARK
North Lake Commons Shopping Center
Village Square Shopping Center
Deerpath Court Shopping Center
60047
60010

B
1 W Buckeye Rd
2 Primrose Ct

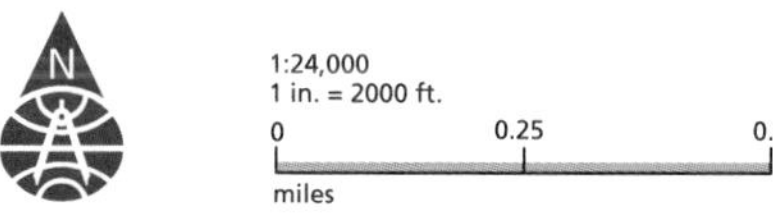

SEE 2645 MAP

Hawthorn Woods

Forest Lake

Lake Zurich

Ela Township

60047

22W-23N

21W-23N

22W-22N

21W-22N

22W-21N

21W-21N

Long Grove

Kildeer

Deer Park

60010

60074

Quentin Road Christian School

KEMPER LAKES GOLF CLUB

KEMPER LAKE

LAKE ZURICH CEM

OLD MILL GROVE PARK

KNOX PARK

BRISTOL TRAILS PARK

SARAH ADAMS PARK

CHESTNUT CORNERS-HUNTERS CREEK PARK

BUFFALO CREEK PARK

WARWICK PARK

SPARROW RIDGE PARK

KILDEER NATURE CTR

COUNTRYSIDE WEST PARK

CENTRAL SLOUGH

ASHLEY LK

KELLEY LK

N QUENTIN RD

MAIN ST

CUBA RD

RAND RD

OLD MCHENRY RD

LONG GROVE RD

N MIDLOTHIAN RD

LAKEWOOD LN

A
1 Cedar St

B
1 S Rand Rd

C
1 Greenbay Ct
2 Bushrun Ct
3 Lexington Ln W

SEE 2698 MAP

SEE 2700 MAP

A B C D E

1 2 3 4 5 6 7

42°12'51" 42°12'25" 42°11'59" 42°11'33" 42°11'07" 42°10'41" 42°10'15" 42°09'49"

88°05'11" 88°04'36" 88°04'01" 88°03'26" 88°02'51" 88°02'16"

SEE 2752 MAP

1:24,000
1 in. = 2000 ft.
0 0.25 0.5
miles

SEE 2646 MAP

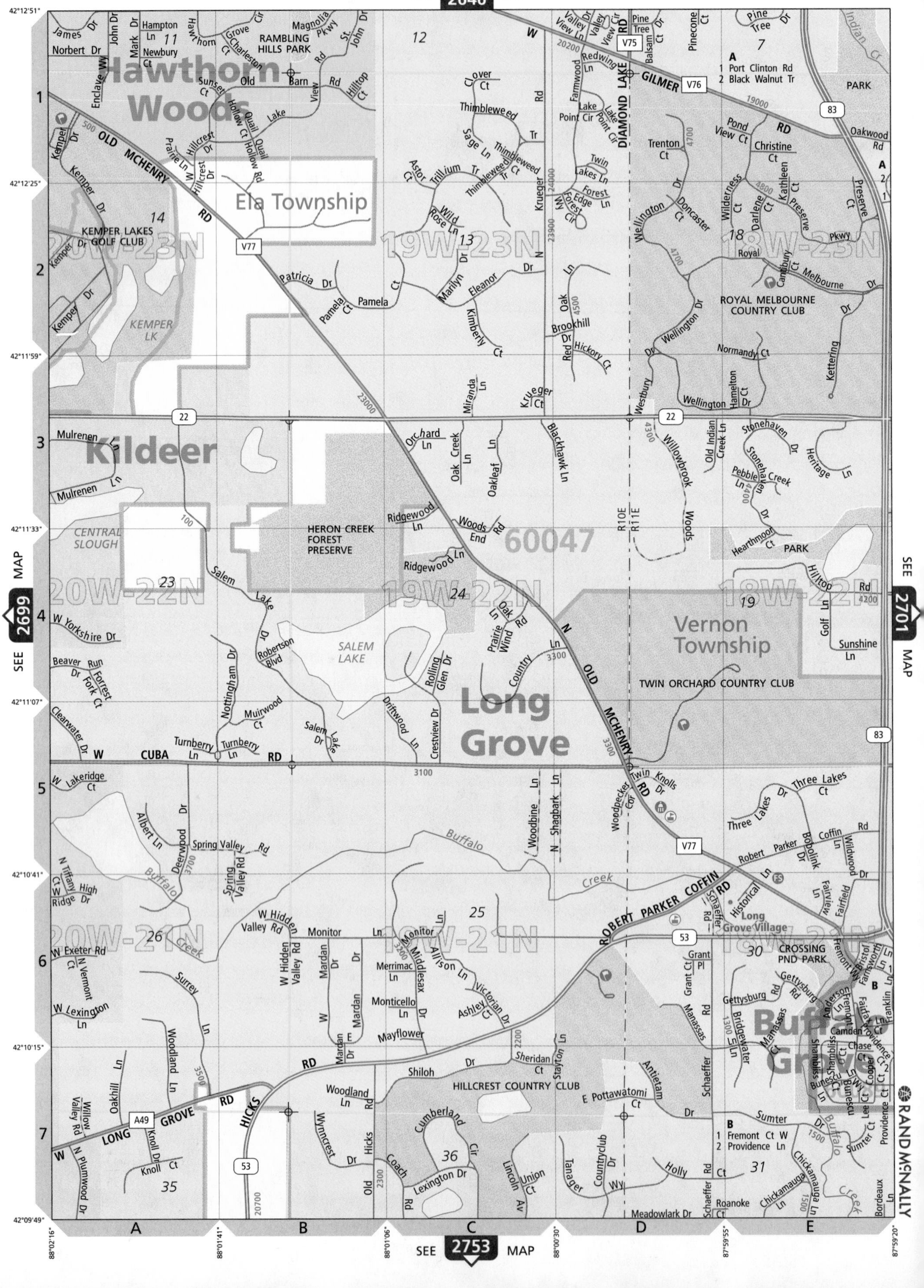

Hawthorn Woods
RAMBLING HILLS PARK
Ela Township
KEMPER LAKES GOLF CLUB
KEMPER LK
20W-23N
19W-23N
18W-23N
ROYAL MELBOURNE COUNTRY CLUB
PARK
Kildeer
CENTRAL SLOUGH
HERON CREEK FOREST PRESERVE
60047
R10E
R11E
20W-22N
19W-22N
18W-22N
SALEM LAKE
Vernon Township
TWIN ORCHARD COUNTRY CLUB
Long Grove
20W-21N
19W-21N
18W-21N
Long Grove Village
CROSSING PND PARK
Buffalo Grove
HILLCREST COUNTRY CLUB

James Dr, Norbert Dr, John Dr, Mark Dr, Hampton Ln, Newbury Ct, Enclave Wy, Hawthorn Ct, Grove Cir, Charleston Ct, Magnolia Pkwy, St. John Dr, Sunset Ct, Old Barn Rd, View Rd, Hilltop Ct, Hollow Ct, Quail Hollow Rd, Quail Lake, Hillcrest Dr, Prairie Ln, Kempel Dr, Kemper Dr, OLD MCHENRY RD, Clover Ct, Thimbleweed Tr, Thimbleweed Ct, Sage Ln, Astor Ct, Trillium Tr, Wild Rose Ln, Marilyn Dr, Eleanor Dr, Kimberly Ct, Patricia Dr, Pamela Ct, Pamela Ct, Krueger Rd, Farmwood Ln, Redwing Ln, Lake Point Cir, Lake Point Ct, Twin Lakes Ln, Forest Edge Ln, Forest Wy, Forest Cir, Oak Ln, Brookhill Dr, Red Oak Ln, Hickory Ct, Valley View Ln, Valley Dr, View Cir, DIAMOND LAKE RD, W GILMER RD, Pine Tree Ct, Balsam Ct, Pinecone Ct, Pine Tree Dr, Pond View Ct, Trenton Ct, Christine Ct, Oakwood Rd, Wellington Dr, Doncaster Ct, Wilderness Ct, Darlene Ct, Kathleen Ct, Preserve Pkwy, Preserve Ct, Royal Melbourne Dr, Canbury Ct, Normandy Ct, Kettering Dr, Westbury Dr, Hamelton Ct, Miranda Ln, Krueger Ct

A
1 Port Clinton Rd
2 Black Walnut Tr

Mulrenen Ln, Mulrenen Ln, Orchard Ln, Oak Creek Ln, Oakleaf Ln, Blackhawk Ln, Willowbrook Woods, Old Indian Creek Ln, Stonehaven Dr, Heritage Ln, Pebble Creek Ln, Hearthmoor Ct, Hilltop Rd, Golf Ln, Sunshine Ln, Ridgewood Ln, Woods End Rd, Salem Lake Dr, Robertson Blvd, Nottingham Dr, Muirwood Ct, Salem Lake Dr, Driftwood Ln, Crestview Dr, Rolling Glen Dr, Oak Ln, Prairie Wind Rd, Country Ln, N OLD MCHENRY RD, W Yorkshire Dr, Beaver Run Dr, Forrest Fork Ct, Clearwater Dr, Turnberry Ln, W CUBA RD

W Lakeridge Ct, Albert Ln, Deerwood Dr, Spring Valley Rd, N Tiffany Ct, W High Ridge Dr, Woodbine Ln, N Shagbark Ln, Woodpecker Cor, Twin Knolls Dr, Three Lakes Dr, Three Lakes Ct, Robert Parker Coffin Rd, Bobolink Dr, Wildwood Dr, Fairview Ln, Fairfield Ln, Schaefer Rd, Historical Ln, Buffalo Creek, W Hidden Valley Rd, Monitor Ln, W Exeter Rd, N Vermont Ct, Surrey Ln, W Lexington Ln, W Mardan Dr, Merrimac Ln, Middlesax Dr, Allison Ln, Victorian Dr, Ashley Ct, Monticello Ln, Mayflower, Mardan Ct, Grant Ct, Grant Pl, Gettysburg Rd, Gettysburg Ct, Fremont Wy, Bristol Ln, Farnsworth Ln, Anderson Ct, Fairfax Ln, Franklin Ln, Camden Ct, Chase Ct, Providence Ct, Manassas Rd, Manassas Ct, Bridgewater Ln, Shambliss Ln, Bunescu Ct, Lee Ct, Cooper Ct

Oakhill Ln, Woodland Ln, Willow Valley Rd, W LONG GROVE RD, Knoll Dr, Knoll Ct, N Plumwood Dr, HICKS RD, Woodland Ln, Wynncrest Dr, Old Hicks Rd, Coach Rd, Shiloh Dr, Sheridan Ct, Stayton Ln, Cumberland Cir, Lexington Dr, Lincoln Av, Union Ct, Tanager Wy, Countryclub Dr, E Pottawatomi Ct, Antietam Dr, Schaeffer Rd, Holly Ct, Sumter Dr, Chickamauga Ln, Roanoke Ct, Meadowlark Dr, Bordeaux Ln

B
1 Fremont Ct W
2 Providence Ln

11, 12, 7, 14, 13, 18, 23, 24, 19, 26, 25, 30, 35, 36, 31

V75, V76, V77, 83, 22, 53, A49

500, 20200, 19000, 4700, 4800, 24000, 23900, 4500, 23000, 4300, 4400, 4200, 100, 3300, 3100, 3700, 3500, 3200, 2200, 2300, 20700, 1300, 1500

1 2 3 4 5 6 7
A B C D E

42°12'51" 42°12'25" 42°11'59" 42°11'33" 42°11'07" 42°10'41" 42°10'15" 42°09'49"
88°02'16" 88°01'41" 88°01'06" 88°00'30" 87°59'55" 87°59'20"

SEE 2699 MAP

SEE 2701 MAP

SEE 2753 MAP

1:24,000
1 in. = 2000 ft.
0 0.25 0.5
miles

SEE 2647 MAP

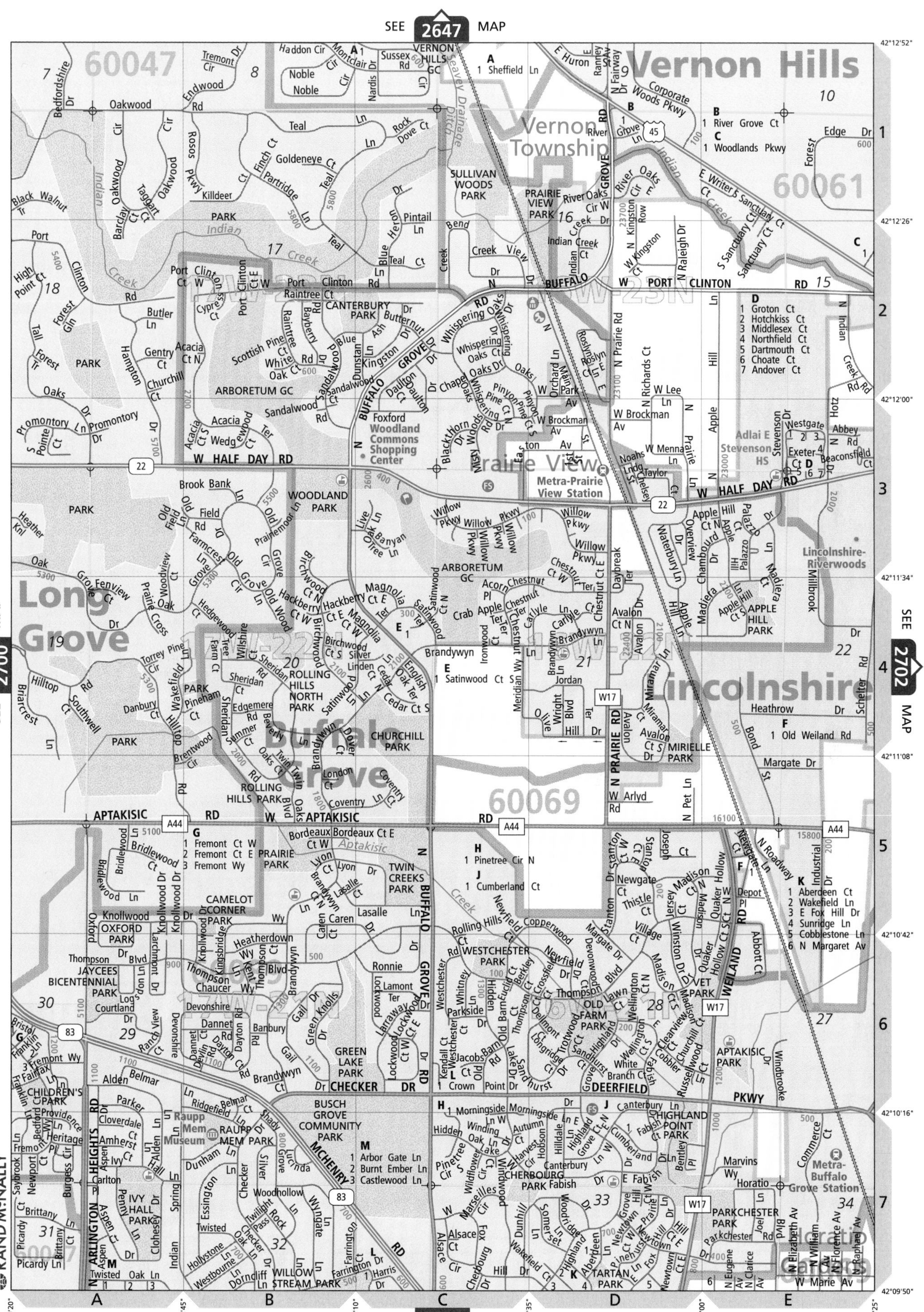

SEE 2700 MAP
SEE 2702 MAP
SEE 2754 MAP

1:24,000
1 in. = 2000 ft.

0 0.25 0.5
miles

SEE 2648 MAP

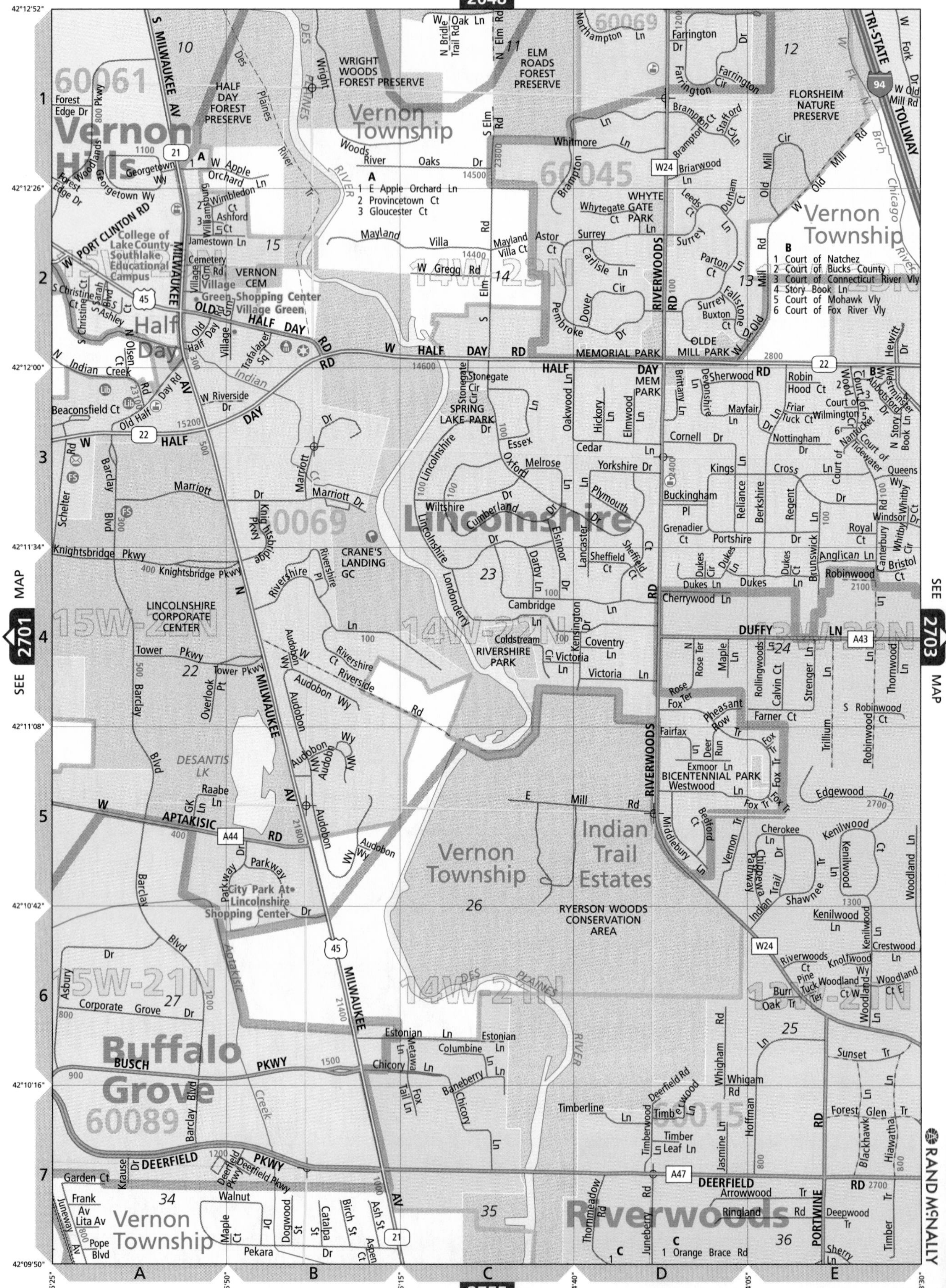

SEE 2701 MAP

SEE 2703 MAP

A
1 E Apple Orchard Ln
2 Provincetown Ct
3 Gloucester Ct

B
1 Court of Natchez
2 Court of Bucks County
3 Court of Connecticut River Vly
4 Story Book Ln
5 Court of Mohawk Vly
6 Court of Fox River Vly

C
1 Orange Brace Rd

Vernon Hills
Half Day
Lincolnshire
Vernon Township
Indian Trail Estates
Buffalo Grove
Riverwoods

SEE 2755 MAP

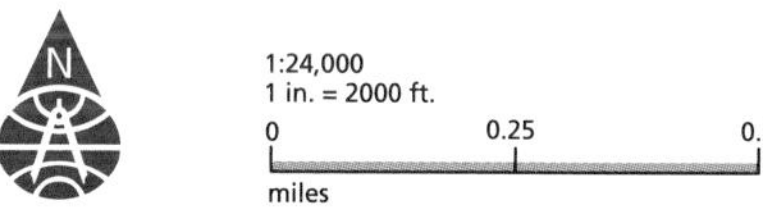

SEE 2649 MAP

Lake Forest
Everett Park
60045
Prairie Wolf Forest Preserve
Northcroft Park
Walter E Heller Nature Preserve
Walter E Heller Nature Center
Del Mar Woods
12W-23N
11W-23N
Half Day Rd
Trinity International University
Bannockburn Green Shopping Center
Lincolnshire
Bannockburn
Highland Park
60035
Balzer Park
Riverwoods
12W-22N
11W-22N
60015
Duffy Ln
Deerfield HS
Bannockburn Forest Preserve
Tri-State Tollway
Waukegan Rd
Telegraph Rd
Trinity Blumberg Park
West Deerfield Township
Woodland Park
Lake Eleanor
Ravinia Green Country Club
Deerfield Golf Club
12W-21N
11W-21N
Deerfield
Jaycee Memorial Park
Clavey Park
James C Mitchell Park
Maplewood Park
Metra-Deerfield Sta
Jewett Park
Riverwoods Rd
Deerfield Rd
Saunders Rd
Wilmot Rd
Wilmot Park
Deerfield Square
Deerfield Cem

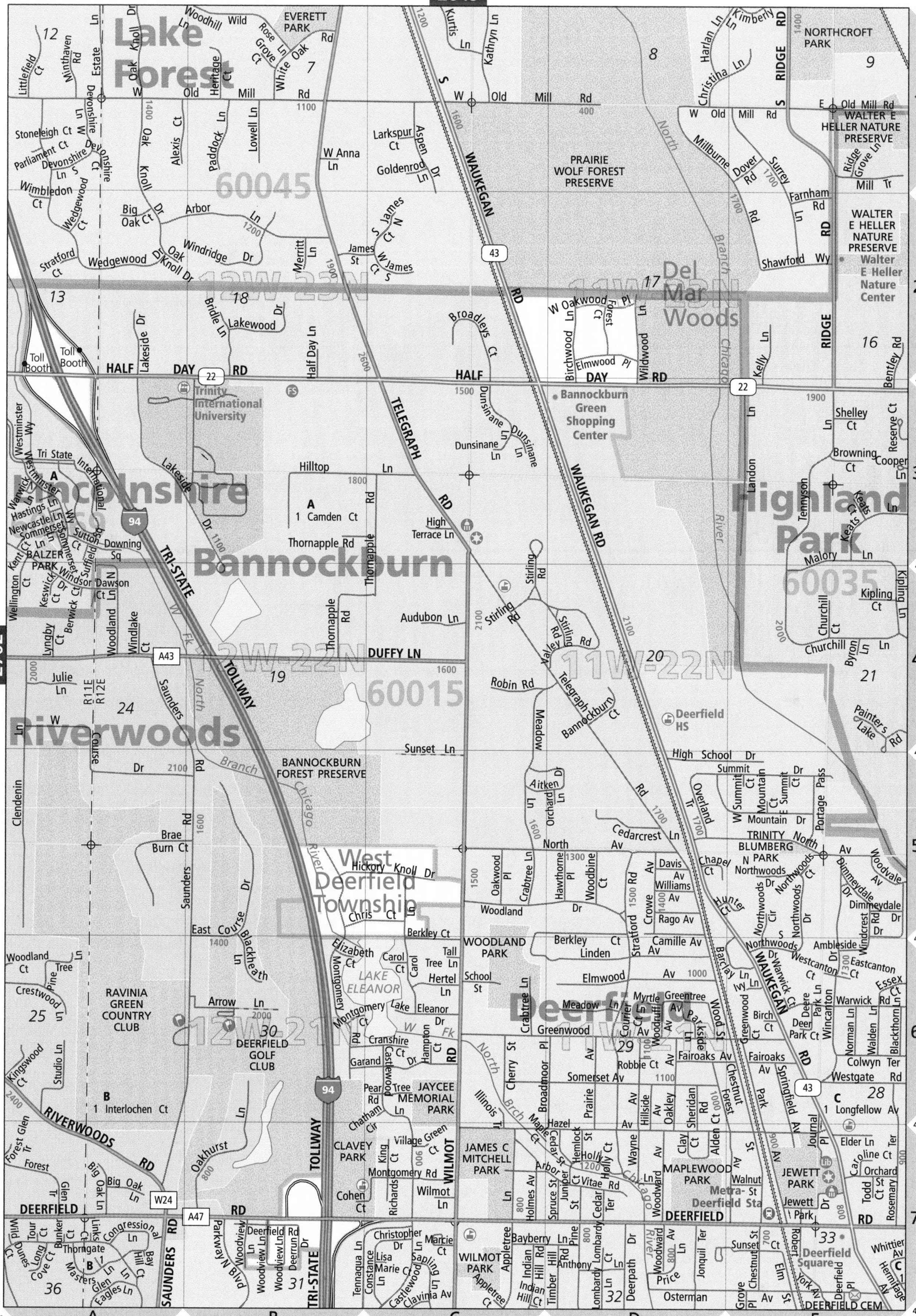

SEE 2702 MAP

SEE 2704 MAP

SEE 2756 MAP

42°12'53"
42°12'27"
42°12'01"
42°11'35"
42°11'09"
42°10'43"
42°10'17"
42°09'50"
87°53'30"
87°52'54"
87°52'19"
87°51'44"
87°51'09"
87°50'34"

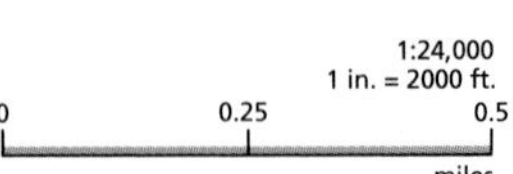

SEE 2650 MAP

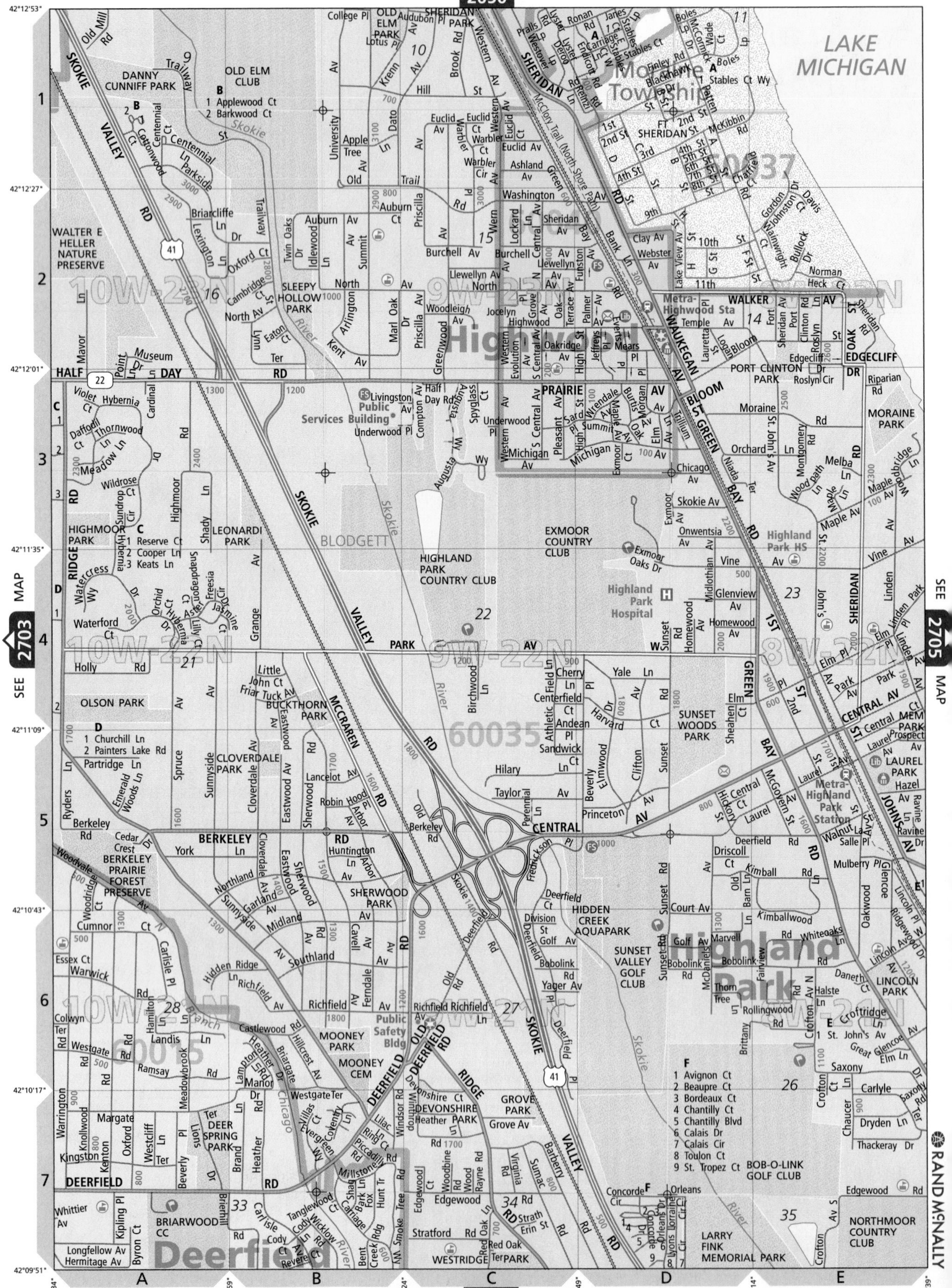

SEE 2703 MAP

SEE 2705 MAP

LAKE MICHIGAN

Highwood

Highland Park

Deerfield

Moraine Township

OLD ELM CLUB
DANNY CUNNIFF PARK
WALTER E HELLER NATURE PRESERVE
SLEEPY HOLLOW PARK
HIGHMOOR PARK
LEONARDI PARK
BLODGETT
HIGHLAND PARK COUNTRY CLUB
EXMOOR COUNTRY CLUB
Highland Park Hospital
Highland Park HS
MORAINE PARK
PORT CLINTON PARK
OLSON PARK
BUCKTHORN PARK
CLOVERDALE PARK
SUNSET WOODS PARK
LAUREL PARK
MEM PARK
BERKELEY PRAIRIE FOREST PRESERVE
SHERWOOD PARK
HIDDEN CREEK AQUAPARK
SUNSET VALLEY GOLF CLUB
LINCOLN PARK
MOONEY PARK
MOONEY CEM
DEER SPRING PARK
DEVONSHIRE PARK
GROVE PARK
BRIARWOOD CC
BOB-O-LINK GOLF CLUB
LARRY FINK MEMORIAL PARK
NORTHMOOR COUNTRY CLUB
WESTRIDGE PARK
Livingston Public Services Building
Public Safety Bldg
Metra-Highwood Sta
Metra-Highland Park Station

A
1 St. Johns Av
1 Stables Ct Wy

B
1 Applewood Ct
2 Barkwood Ct

C
1 Reserve Ct
2 Cooper Ln
3 Keats Ln

D
1 Churchill Ln
2 Painters Lake Rd

E
1 St. John's Av

F
1 Avignon Ct
2 Beaupre Ct
3 Bordeaux Ct
4 Chantilly Ct
5 Chantilly Blvd
6 Calais Dr
7 Calais Cir
8 Toulon Ct
9 St. Tropez Ct

10W-22N
9W-22N
8W-22N
10W-21N
9W-21N
8W-21N

60037
60035
60015

SKOKIE VALLEY RD
HALF DAY RD
PARK AV
CENTRAL AV
BERKELEY RD
DEERFIELD RD
SHERIDAN RD
GREEN BAY RD
WAUKEGAN AV
RIDGE RD

42°12'53"
42°12'27"
42°12'01"
42°11'35"
42°11'09"
42°10'43"
42°10'17"
42°09'51"

87°50'34"
87°49'59"
87°49'24"
87°48'49"
87°48'14"
87°47'39"

RAND McNALLY

SEE 2757 MAP

1:24,000
1 in. = 2000 ft.
0 0.25 0.5
miles

SEE B MAP

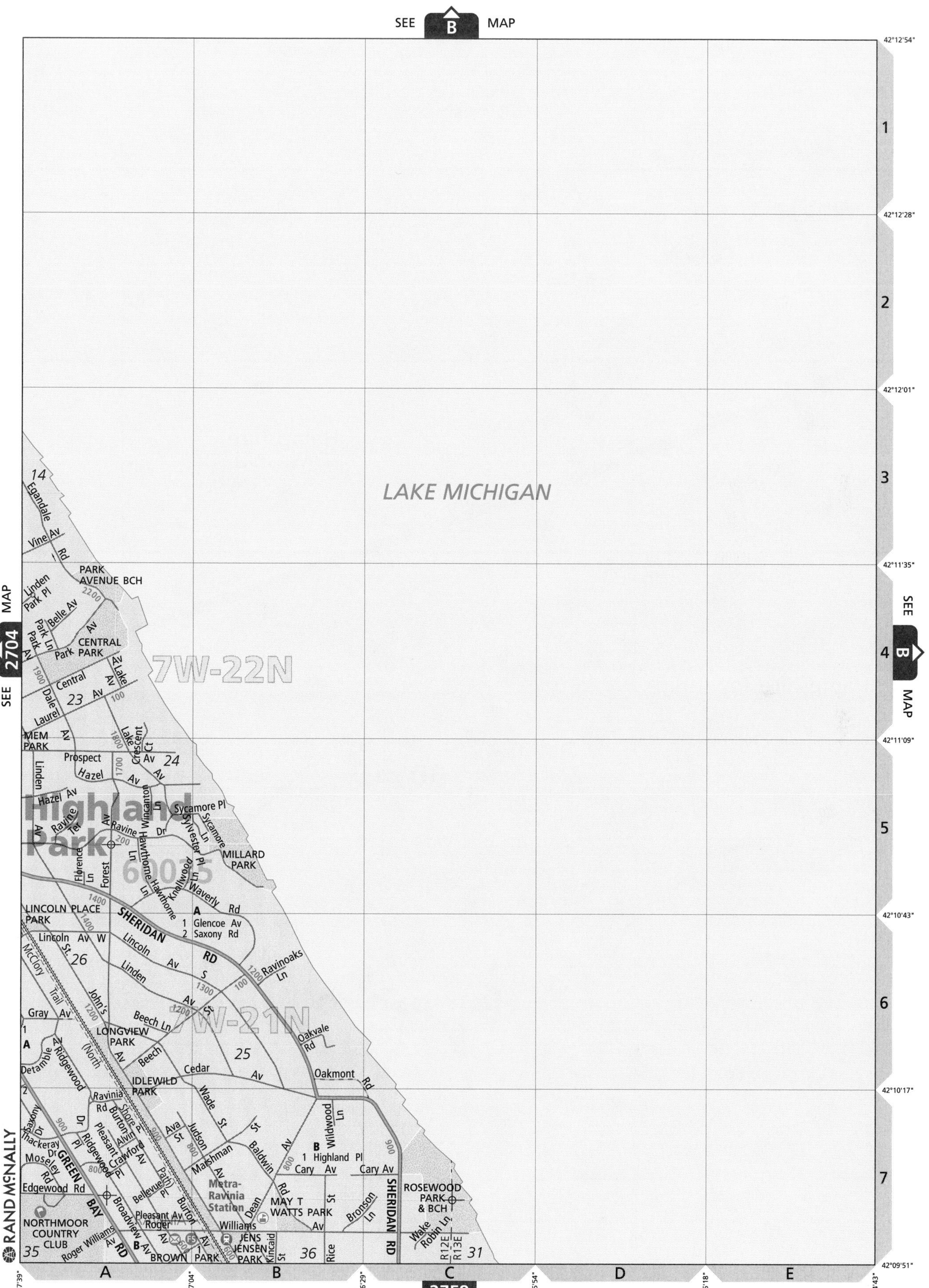

42°12'54" 42°12'28" 42°12'01" 42°11'35" 42°11'09" 42°10'43" 42°10'17" 42°09'51"

87°47'39" 87°47'04" 87°46'29" 87°45'54" 87°45'18" 87°44'43"

A B C D E

1 2 3 4 5 6 7

SEE 2704 MAP

SEE B MAP

SEE 2758 MAP

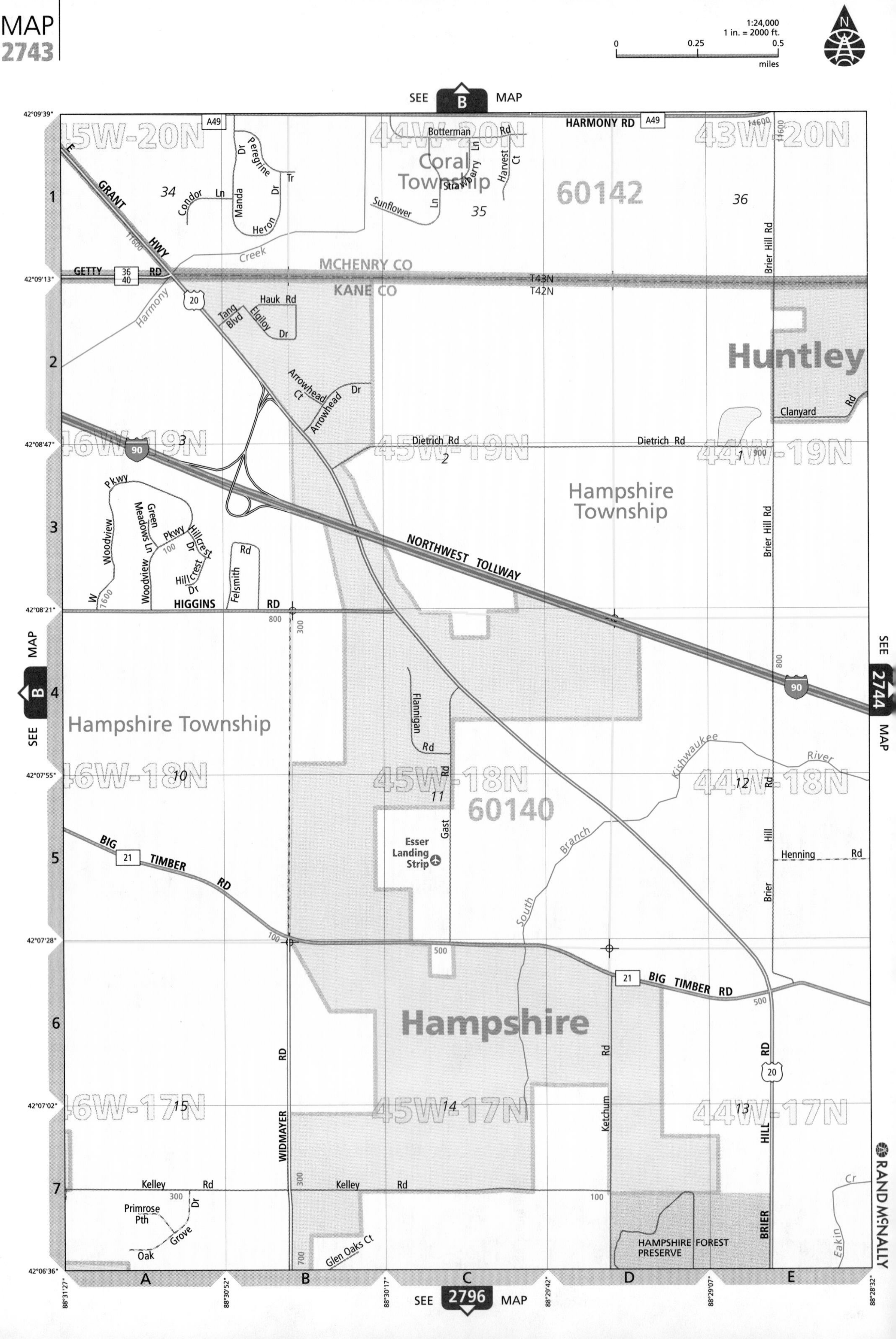

1:24,000
1 in. = 2000 ft.
0 0.25 0.5
miles

SEE B MAP

42°09'39"
A49
HARMONY RD
A49
14600
45W-20N
44W-20N
43W-20N
Botterman Rd
Peregrine Dr
Tr
Manda Dr
Heron
Condor Ln
34
Coral Township
Strawberry Ln
Harvest Ct
Sunflower Ln
35
60142
36
1
GRANT HWY
E
11600
Creek
Brier Hill Rd
GETTY 36 40 RD
42°09'13"
MCHENRY CO
KANE CO
T43N
T42N
Harmony
20
Hauk Rd
Tang Blvd
Elgiloy Dr
2
Huntley
Arrowhead Ct
Arrowhead Dr
Clanyard Rd
42°08'47"
46W-19N
90
3
45W-19N
Dietrich Rd
2
Dietrich Rd
44W-19N
1
900
Pkwy
Green Meadows Ln
Pkwy
Hillcrest Dr
Hillcrest Dr
100
Woodview
Woodview
W
7600
Rd
Felsmith
Hampshire Township
3
Brier Hill Rd
NORTHWEST TOLLWAY
HIGGINS RD
42°08'21"
800
300
800
90
SEE 2744 MAP
SEE B MAP
4
Flannigan Rd
Hampshire Township
42°07'55"
46W-18N
10
45W-18N
11
Gast Rd
60140
Kishwaukee River
44W-18N
12
Brier Hill Rd
Branch
Esser Landing Strip
5
BIG 21 TIMBER RD
Henning Rd
South
42°07'28"
100
500
21 BIG TIMBER RD
500
6
Hampshire
WIDMAYER RD
Ketchum Rd
BRIER HILL RD
20
42°07'02"
46W-17N
15
45W-17N
14
44W-17N
13
7
Kelley Rd
300
Kelley Rd
100
Cr
Primrose Pth
300
Dr
Grove
Oak
700
Glen Oaks Ct
HAMPSHIRE FOREST PRESERVE
Eakin
42°06'36"
A B C D E
88°31'27" 88°30'52" 88°30'17" 88°29'42" 88°29'07" 88°28'32"

SEE 2796 MAP

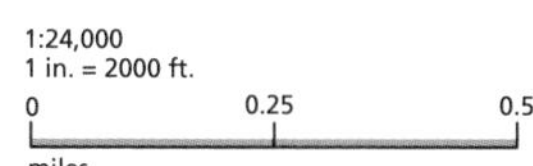

SEE 2691 MAP
SEE 2743 MAP
SEE 2745 MAP
SEE 2797 MAP

Huntley

Coral Township

Rutland Township

MCHENRY CO
KANE CO

BETSEY WARRINGTON PARK

DEICKE PARK

WHISPER CREEK GOLF CLUB

Prime Outlets-Huntley

60142
60140

42W-20N
43W-19N
42W-19N
43W-18N
42W-18N
43W-17N
42W-17N

T43N
T42N
R6E
R7E

NORTHWEST TOLLWAY
FREEMAN RD
BIG TIMBER RD
SUN CITY BLVD
DEL WEBB BLVD
COUNTRYVIEW BLVD
HEMMER RD

Kishwaukee River
Kishwaukee River S Brch
S Branch Kishwaukee River
Eakin Creek

Sterling Ln, Sunderlin Dr, Verbend Pth, Sunderlin Dr, Windsor Dr, Ludbury Ct, Ludbury Rdg, Chatfield Cross, Borhart Dr, Bloomfield Dr, Westmore Dr, Wernecke Rd, Wilshire, Wilshire Ct, Chestnut Ln, Kirkland Dr, Shady Ln, Barton Av, Burham St, Honeysuckle, Wildwood Dr, Winterberry Ln, Delaney Rd, Bonaire Rd, Tanglewood Ln, Evergreen Ln, Wembley Dr, Messiner Dr, Nealy Rd, Morgan Dr, Denell Dr, Lehigh St, Wy, Nottingham Ln, Essex Ln, Greenbrier Dr, Stonebridge Ln, Kensington Dr, Sedgewick Dr, Wildrose Dr, W Stratford Ln, Bittersweet, Jasmine Ln, Lilac Ln, Summer Ln, Ridge, Bull Ridge Dr, W Kishwaukee, W Tall Grass Tr, Meadow, Brookwood, Deer Cross Ln, River Terrace, Richmond Ln, Clark Ln, Kinzie Ln, Fitzgerald Ln, Plymouth Ln, Elliot Ln, W Riverview Ct, Stonewater Dr, Milbrook Dr, W Rock Springs Ln, W Willow Creek Ln, W River Park Dr, Spring Creek Dr, Sweetwater Ln, Gardner Dr, Latham, Hideaway, Fallow Dr, Dakota, Fields, Wildflower Ln, Juneberry Ln, Moonlight Ridge Ct, Regency Pkwy, Princeton Pkwy, Princeton Dr, Princeton Dr, Kreutzer Rd, Dean St, Grove Rd, Tuliptree, Hickory Ct, Plum Laurel Ln, Black Oak Tr, Clanyard, Palisades Av, Chanwahon Rd, Red Hills Rd, Starved Rock Pl, Beaver Dam Ln, Moraine Hills Dr, Island Tr, Dixon Springs Ln, Wedgemere, Arlington Rolling Meadows, Flowerwood Ln, Fieldstone Dr, W Hampton Ct, Castle Rock Dr, Green Meadow Ct, Glenwood Dr, Cadence Dr, Rockton Tr, Longmeadow Dr, Green Meadow Av, Traverse Ct, Muir Dr, Woodgrove Dr, Roosevelt Ct, Timber Creek, Westridge Ct, Forestview Ct, Woodland Dr, Stone Hill Dr, Meadow View Ct, Penefield Ln, Patriot Wy, Sage Dr, Dearborn Ct, Dearborn Tr, Crestview, Briargate Dr, Prime Pointe Ct, Eakin Creek Ct, Drendel Rd, Shirley Ln, Drendel Rd, Sun City Blvd, Cold Springs Dr, Elmwood Ct, Boxwood Ct, Birdie, Golfview, Mulberry Ct, Highland Dr, Eagle Ridge Ln, Hill, Oak Grove Dr, Sycamore Ct, Horseshoe Ct, Saddle Ct, Tall Oak Ct, W Whispering Oak Ct, W Pheasant Ridge Dr, Ash Ct, Scenic Tr Rdg, Acorn Ct, Applewood Dr, Winding Creek Lp, Cherry Hill Ln, Rock Creek Cir, Farm Hill Dr, Rock Creek Cir, Wood Ridge Dr, W Fox Run, W Prairie Dr, Stone Creek Ct, Springs, Powers Rd, Oak Creek Pkwy, Village Green Dr, Robert Rd, W Suzanne Rd, W Thomas Rd, Beverly Blvd, Whittingham Ln, Hennig Rd, Freeman Rd, W Wisconsin Cir, W Illinois Dr, Iowa Ct, Indiana Ct, Pennsylvania Av, Michigan Av, White Tail Ln, Quail Ridge Dr, Foxtail, Deerpath Ct, Windy Ln, Songbird Ln, Prairie Dr, Jim Dhamer Dr, George Bush Ct, Quality Dr, Henning Rd, Sandwald Rd, Automall Dr, Van Acker Rd, Manning Rd, Reinking Rd

A 1, B 1, C 1, A 1 W Hampton Ct, B 1 Castle Rock Dr, C 1 Whittingham Ln

47, 63, 90, 21

1, 2, 3, 4, 5, 6, 7
A, B, C, D, E

36, 31, 32, 33, 1, 6, 5, 4, 12, 7, 8, 9, 13, 18, 17, 16

42°09'41"
42°09'15"
42°08'49"
42°08'23"
42°07'57"
42°07'31"
42°07'05"
42°06'39"
88°28'32"
88°27'57"
88°27'22"
88°26'47"
88°26'12"
88°25'37"

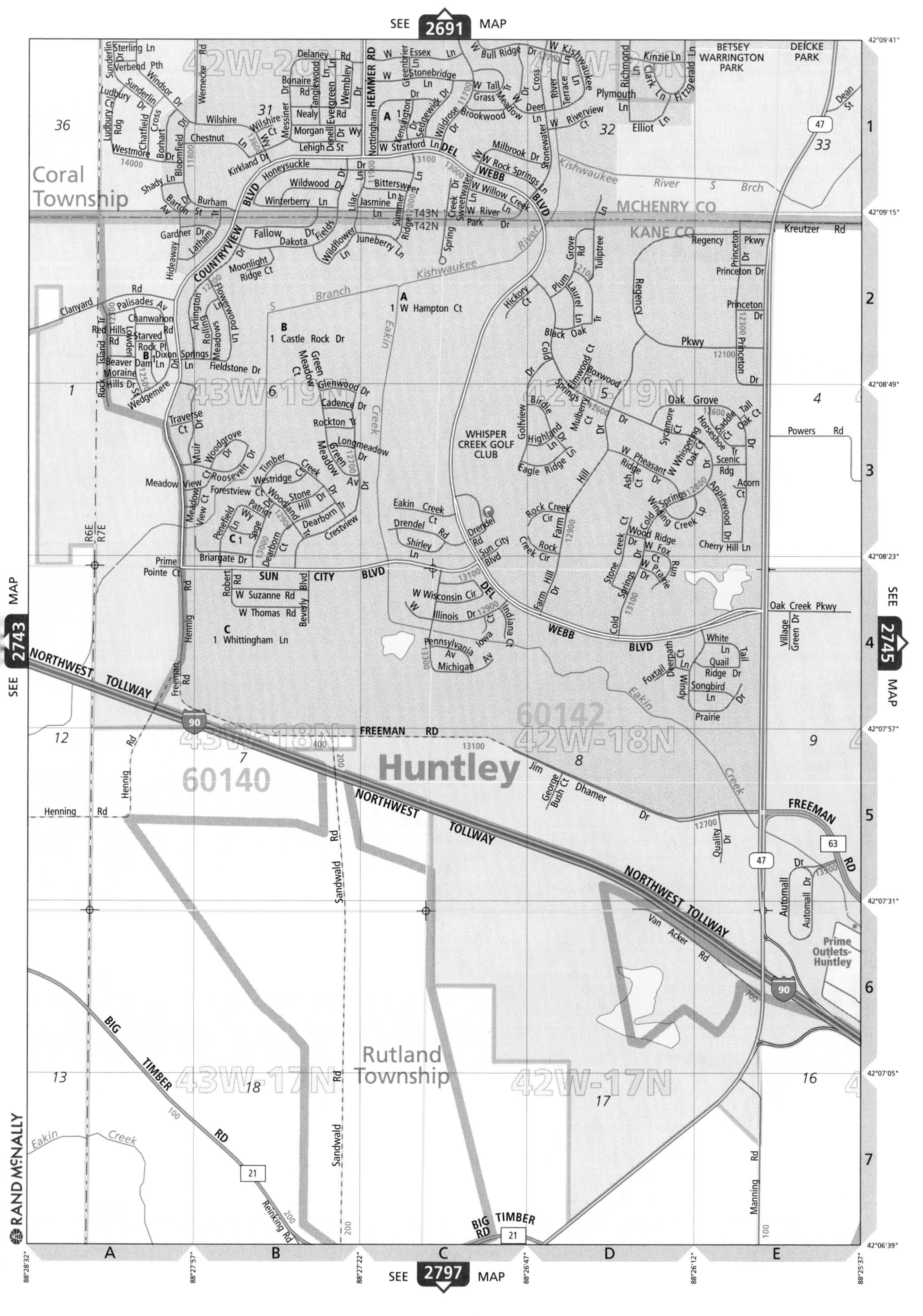

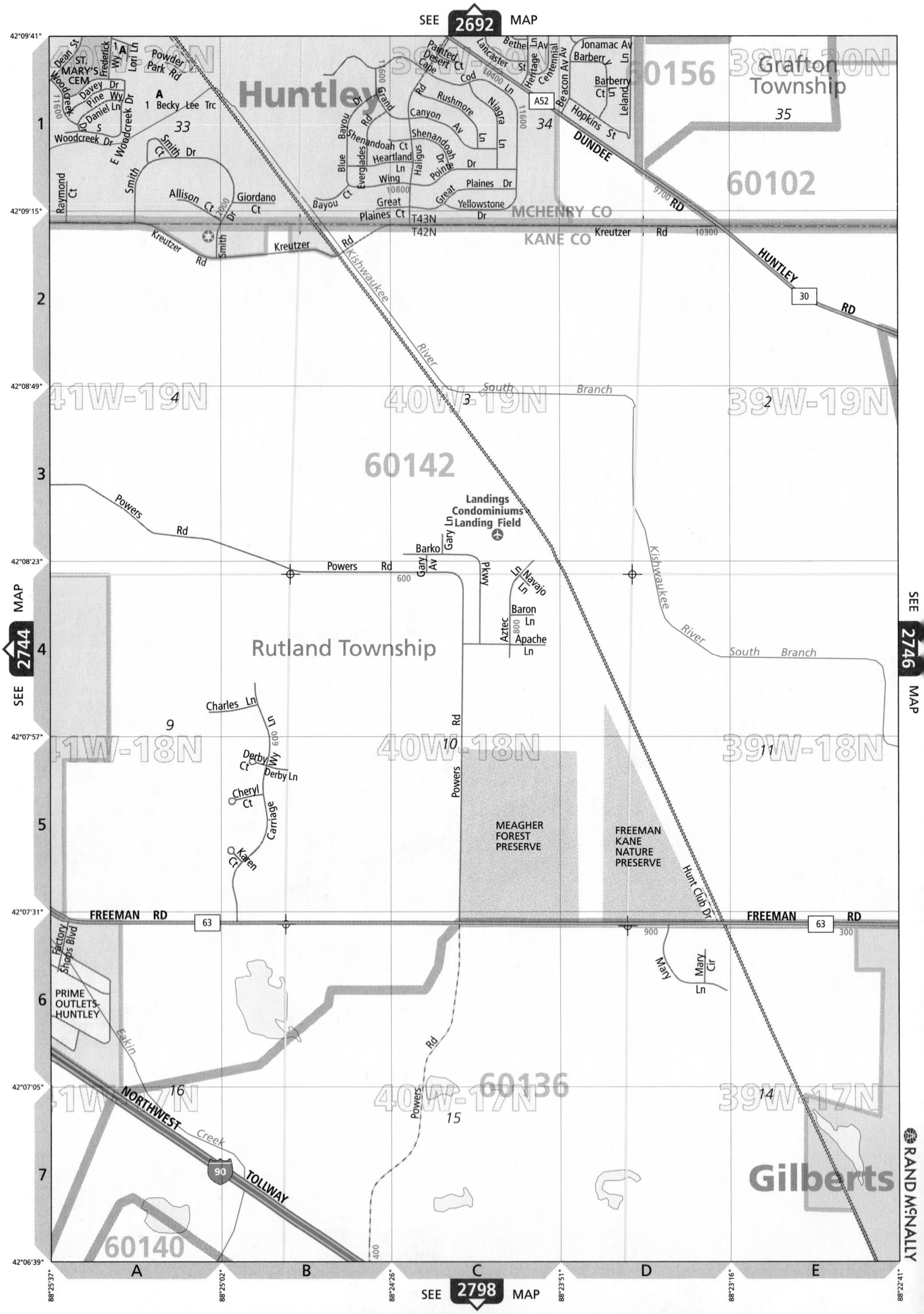

1:24,000
1 in. = 2000 ft.
0
0.25
0.5
miles
SEE 2692 MAP
SEE 2744 MAP
SEE 2746 MAP
SEE 2798 MAP
Huntley
Grafton Township
Rutland Township
Gilberts
60156
60102
60142
60136
60140
MCHENRY CO
KANE CO
T43N
T42N
ST. MARY'S CEM
Landings Condominiums Landing Field
MEAGHER FOREST PRESERVE
FREEMAN KANE NATURE PRESERVE
PRIME OUTLETS-HUNTLEY
DUNDEE RD
HUNTLEY RD
FREEMAN RD
NORTHWEST TOLLWAY
Kishwaukee River
South Branch
Powers Rd
Kreutzer Rd
Hunt Club Dr
Factory Shops Blvd
Eakin Creek
Charles Ln
Derby Wy
Derby Ln
Cheryl Ct
Carriage Ln
Karen Ct
Barko
Gary Ln
Gary Av
Pkwy
Navajo Ln
Baron Ln
Aztec
Apache Ln
Mary Ln
Mary Cir
Allison Ct
Giordano Ct
Smith Dr
Smith Ct
Raymond Ct
Woodcreek Dr
E Woodcreek Dr
Becky Lee Trc
Powder Park Rd
Dean St
Frederick Wy
Lori Ln
Davey Dr
Pine Wy
Daniel Ln
Grand Dr
Bayou Rd
Blue Bayou Ct
Everglades
Shenandoah Ct
Heartland Ln
Wing
Haligus
Great Plaines Ct
Great Plaines Dr
Yellowstone Dr
Canyon Av
Rushmore Ln
Niagara Ln
Shenandoah Dr
Pointe Dr
Painted Desert Ct
Cape Cod
Lancaster St
Bethel Av
Heritage Ln
Centennial
Beacon Av
Jonamac Av
Barberry Ln
Barberry Ct
Leland
Hopkins St
A52
30
63
90
33
34
35
4
3
2
9
10
11
16
15
14
41W-19N
40W-19N
39W-19N
41W-18N
40W-18N
39W-18N
40W-17N
39W-17N
A
B
C
D
E
1
2
3
4
5
6
7
RAND McNALLY

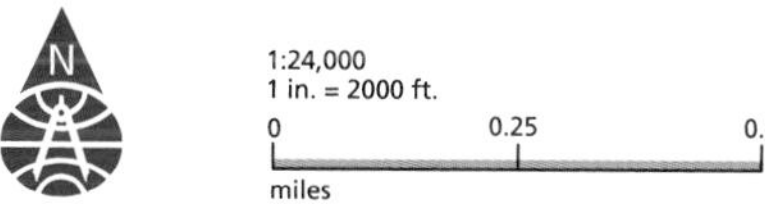

SEE 2693 MAP

Algonquin

Algonquin Township

Grafton Township

Dundee Township

Rutland Township

Kimball Farms

Carpentersville

Gilberts

KELLIHER PARK

TED SPELLA PARK

BINNIE WOODS FOREST PRESERVE

RANDALL OAKS GOLF CLUB

RANDALL OAKS PARK

Algonquin Commons

MCHENRY CO

KANE CO

T43N
T42N

R7E R8E

60142 60102 60118 60110 60136

37W-20N 36W-20N 38W-19N 37W-19N 38W-18N 37W-18N 38W-17N 37W-17N

A
1 Robinwood Dr

B
1 Dellwood Ct
2 Stonegate Rd
3 Cedar Grove Ct

C
1 Northgate Ct
2 Abbeywood Ct

HUNTLEY RD

GALLIGAN RD

BARN SQUARE RD

RANDALL RD

N COUNTY LINE RD

LONGMEADOW PKWY

FREEMAN RD

BINNIE RD

SEE 2745 MAP

SEE 2747 MAP

A B C D E

1 2 3 4 5 6 7

SEE 2799 MAP

1:24,000
1 in. = 2000 ft.
0 0.25 0.5
miles

SEE 2694 MAP

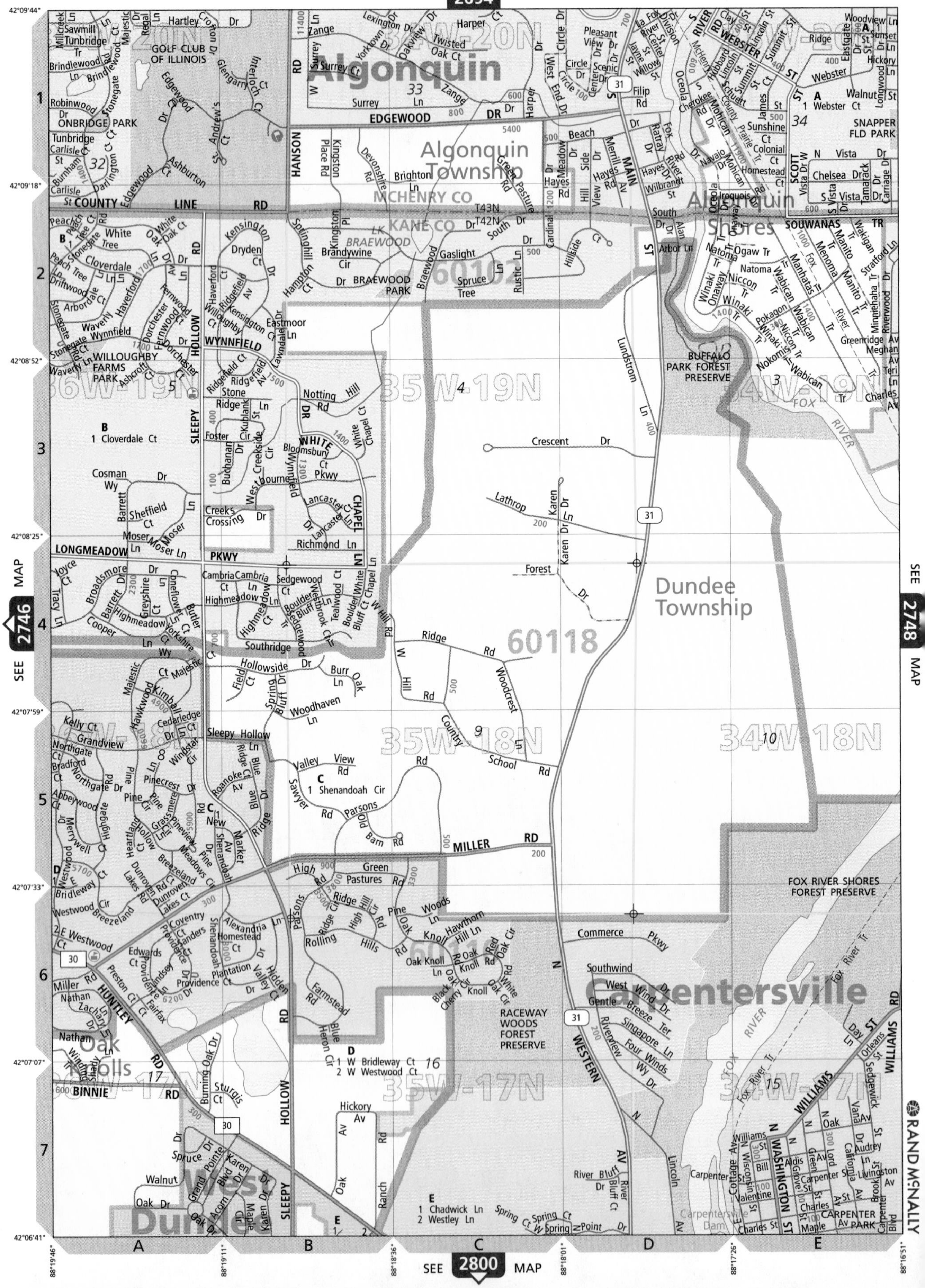

Algonquin

Algonquin Township

Algonquin Shores

Dundee Township

Carpentersville

West Dundee

Oak Knolls

GOLF CLUB OF ILLINOIS

ONBRIDGE PARK

WILLOUGHBY FARMS PARK

BRAEWOOD PARK

SNAPPER FLD PARK

BUFFALO PARK FOREST PRESERVE

FOX RIVER SHORES FOREST PRESERVE

RACEWAY WOODS FOREST PRESERVE

CARPENTER PARK

MCHENRY CO

KANE CO

T43N
T42N

60102

60118

60110

34W-20N

35W-19N

34W-19N

35W-18N

34W-18N

35W-17N

34W-17N

A
1 Webster Ct

B
1 Cloverdale Ct

C
1 Shenandoah Cir

D
1 W Bridleway Ct
2 W Westwood Ct

E
1 Chadwick Ln
2 Westley Ln

SEE 2746 MAP

SEE 2748 MAP

SEE 2800 MAP

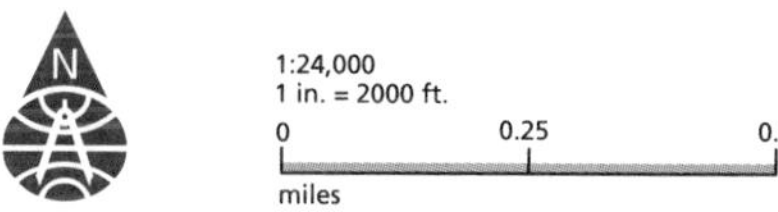

SEE 2695 MAP

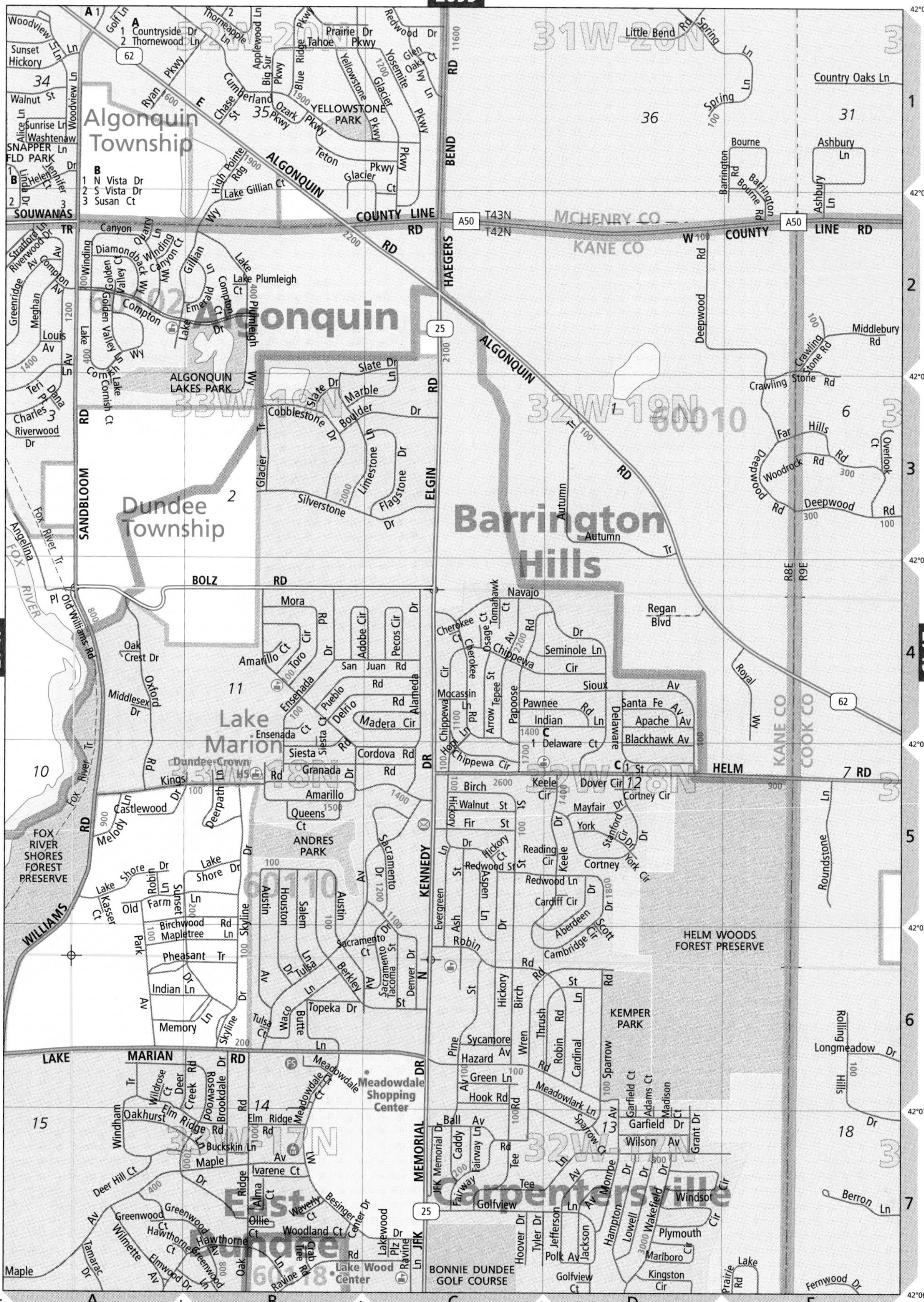

SEE 2747 MAP

SEE 2749 MAP

Algonquin

Algonquin Township

Dundee Township

Barrington Hills

Lake Marion

East Dundee

Carpentersville

McHENRY CO

KANE CO

COOK CO

T43N

T42N

R8E

R9E

31W-20N

32W-20N

33W-19N

32W-19N

33W-18N

32W-18N

33W-17N

32W-17N

60102

60010

60110

60118

COUNTY LINE RD

W COUNTY LINE RD

SOUWANAS TR

ALGONQUIN RD

HAEGERS BEND RD

ELGIN RD

SANDBLOOM RD

BOLZ RD

HELM RD

LAKE MARIAN RD

KENNEDY DR

MEMORIAL DR

WILLIAMS RD

FOX RIVER

YELLOWSTONE PARK

SNAPPER FLD PARK

ALGONQUIN LAKES PARK

ANDRES PARK

KEMPER PARK

FOX RIVER SHORES FOREST PRESERVE

HELM WOODS FOREST PRESERVE

Meadowdale Shopping Center

Dundee-Crown HS

Lake Wood Center

BONNIE DUNDEE GOLF COURSE

A
1 Countryside Dr
2 Thornewood Ln

B
1 N Vista Dr
2 S Vista Dr
3 Susan Ct

1 Delaware Ct

1 St

A50

62

25

1
2
3
4
5
6
7

A
B
C
D
E

42°09'46"
42°09'20"
42°08'53"
42°08'27"
42°08'01"
42°07'35"
42°07'09"
42°06'43"

88°16'51"
88°16'16"
88°15'41"
88°15'06"
88°14'31"
88°13'56"

SEE 2801 MAP

1:24,000
1 in. = 2000 ft.
0 0.25 0.5
miles

SEE 2696 MAP

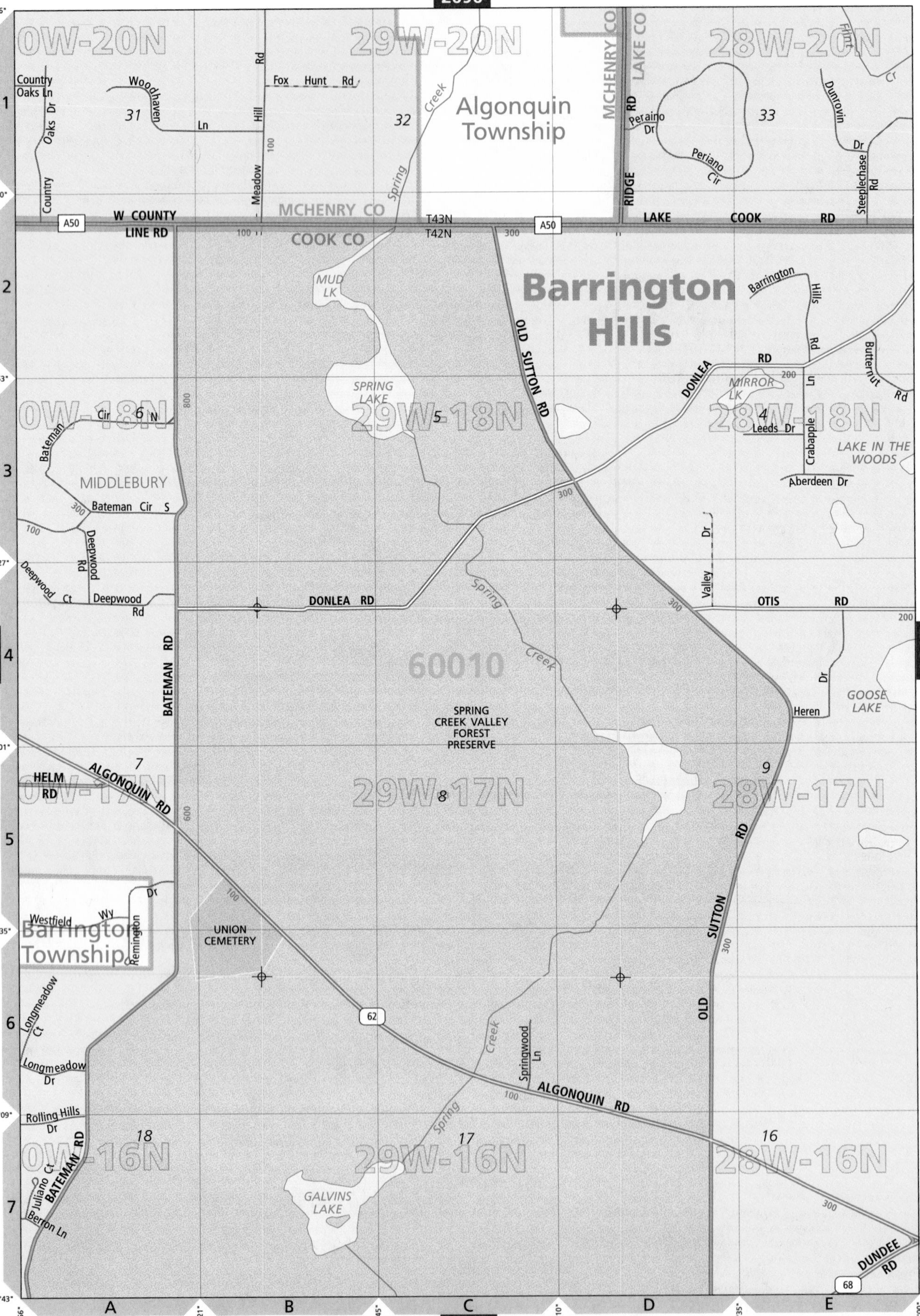

SEE 2748 MAP

SEE 2750 MAP

SEE 2802 MAP

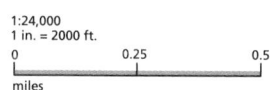

1:24,000
1 in. = 2000 ft.
0 0.25 0.5
miles

SEE 2697 MAP

Cuba Township
27W-20N
26W-20N
OAK KNOLL RD
NORTHWEST HWY
14
Steeplechase Rd
33
34
35
36
BARRINGTON HILLS COUNTRY CLUB
C
1 E Liberty St
2 Washington St
3 Franklin St
4 Barrington Commons Ct
5 Catlow Ct
6 Garfield St
A
1 Cumnor Av
2 Western
B
1 Sycamore Rd
BARRINGTON PARK DISTRICT GC
LANGENDORF PARK
ROSS LK
OLD HART RD
HART RD
HOUGH ST
Barrington HS
Barrington Shopping Center
Barrington Ice House
Station Mall
LAKE COOK RD
LAKE CO
COOK CO
T43N
T42N
D
1 Park Av
2 E Station St
3 E Lake St
4 E Lincoln Av
5 E Russell St
6 E Hillside Av
DONLEA RD
Three Lakes Rd
LACEY LAKE
TWIN LAKES
LK MELISSA
DANA LK
Dana Ln
Caesar Dr
Butternut Rd
Hart Hills Rd
Oakdene Dr E
Marmon Ln
Oakdene Dr W
Oakdene Dr
EVERGREEN CEMETERY
27W-18N
26W-18N
Barrington Hills
Barrington
LK IN THE WOODS
ORCHARD LAKE
60010
Sandalwood Ln
Windrush Ln
OTIS RD
HAWLEY WOODS RD
HAWTHORNE LAKE
Hawthorne Ln
HAWTHORNE RD
DUNDEE AV
STEPHANIE LK
GOOSE LAKE
BRINKER RD
Heron Ln
Hawthorne Ln
Goose Lake Dr
Hills & Dales Rd
Round Barn Rd
HAWLEY LAKE
KEENE LAKE
HEATHER LK
59
27W-17N
26W-17N
West Ln
Lakeview Ln
Jennifer Ct
BARRINGTON RD
JFK Health World
DUNDEE RD
68
E
1 Bridgestone Ct
Stone Canyon Wy
OLD DUNDEE RD
NEW SUTTON RD
LA BUYS LAKE
Inverness
CRABTREE FOREST PRESERVE
27W-16N
26W-16N
Barrington Township
BRINKER RD
BRADWELL RD
F
1 Torrin Rocks Cove
ALGONQUIN RD
62
CRABTREE LAKE
Stover Rd
RAND McNALLY

SEE 2749 MAP
SEE 2751 MAP
SEE 2803 MAP

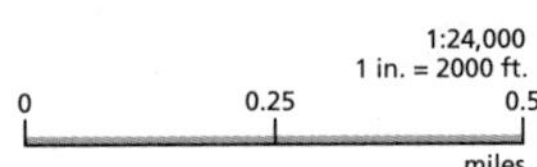

SEE 2698 MAP

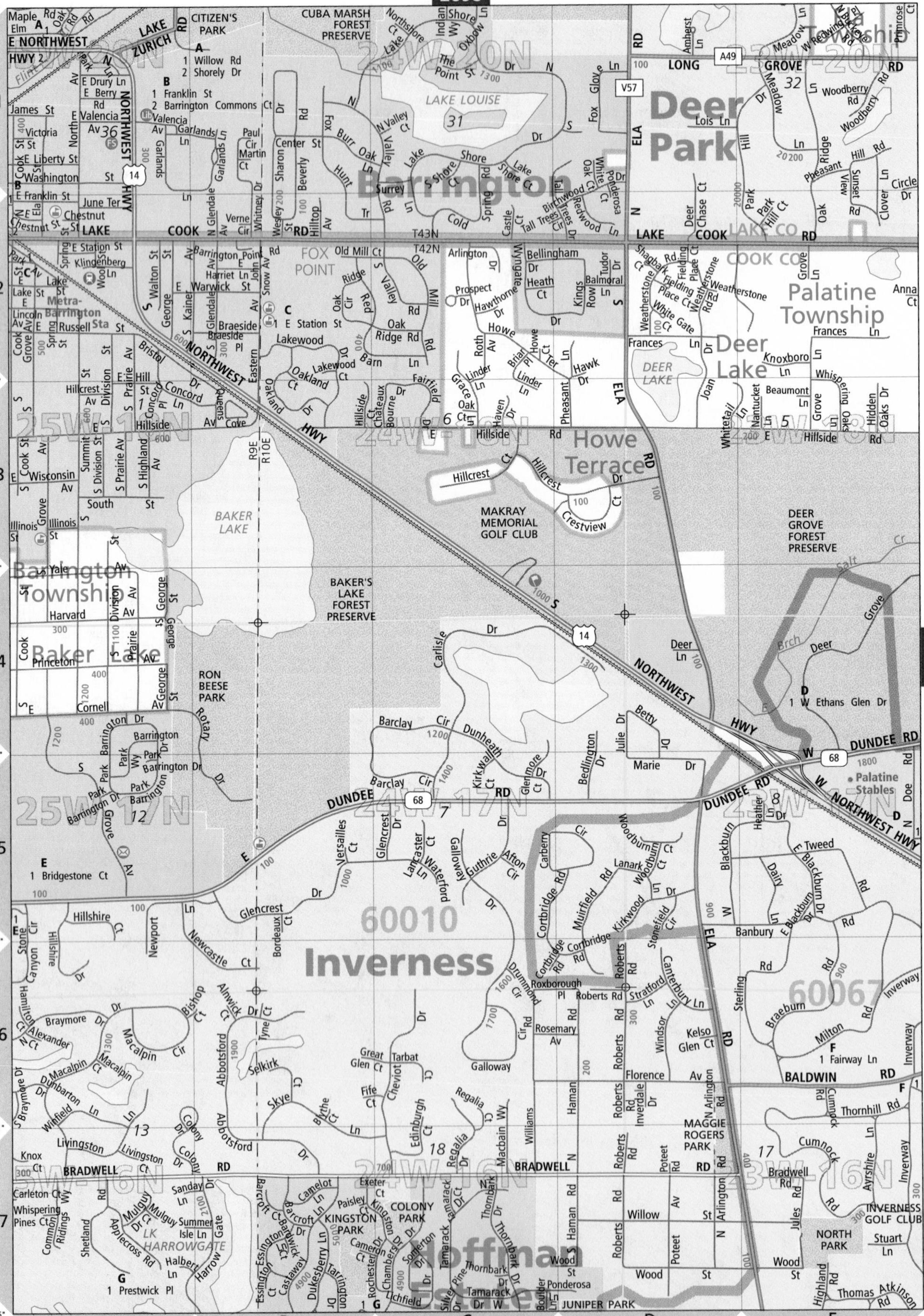

SEE 2750 MAP

SEE 2752 MAP

Barrington

Deer Park

Palatine Township

Barrington Township

Baker Lake

Inverness

60010

60067

Hoffman Estates

Deer Lake

Howe Terrace

LAKE LOUISE

BAKER LAKE

CUBA MARSH FOREST PRESERVE

BAKER'S LAKE FOREST PRESERVE

DEER GROVE FOREST PRESERVE

MAKRAY MEMORIAL GOLF CLUB

INVERNESS GOLF CLUB

CITIZEN'S PARK

RON BEESE PARK

KINGSTON PARK

COLONY PARK

MAGGIE ROGERS PARK

NORTH PARK

JUNIPER PARK

FOX POINT

LK HARROWGATE

Palatine Stables

NORTHWEST HWY

LAKE COOK RD

DUNDEE RD

ELA RD

LONG GROVE RD

BALDWIN RD

BRADWELL RD

LAKE ZURICH RD

A
1 Willow Rd
2 Shorely Dr

B
1 Franklin St
2 Barrington Commons Ct

C
1 E Station St

D
1 W Ethans Glen Dr

E
1 Bridgestone Ct

F
1 Fairway Ln

G
1 Prestwick Pl

A B C D E

1 2 3 4 5 6 7

SEE 2804 MAP

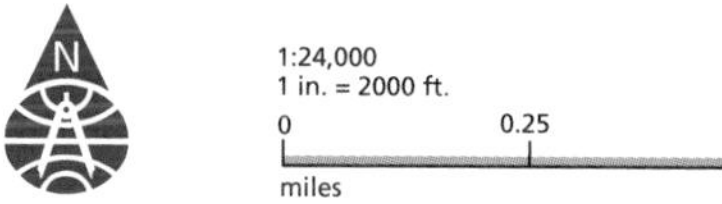

SEE 2699 MAP

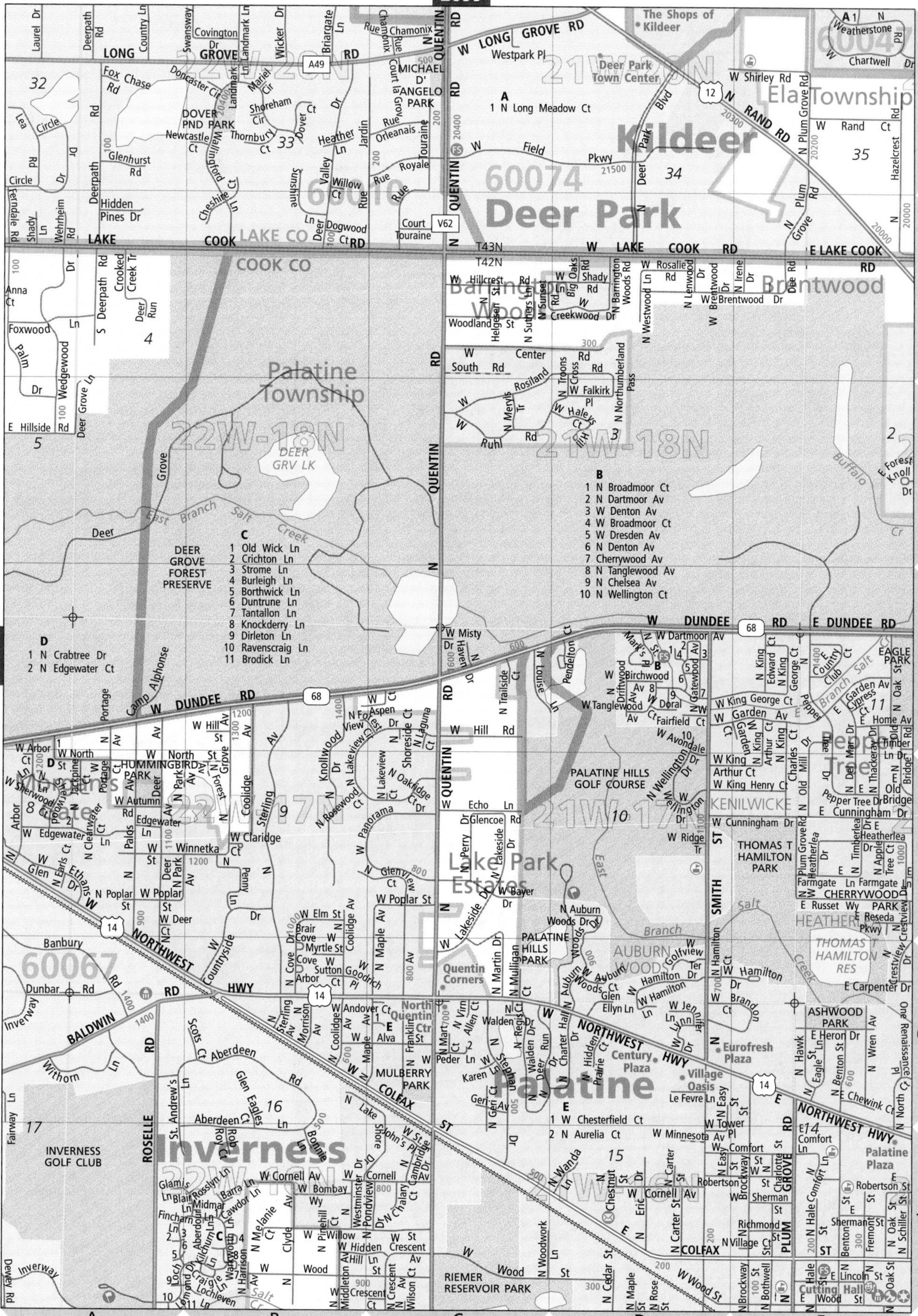

SEE 2751 MAP

SEE 2753 MAP

SEE 2805 MAP

A
1 N Long Meadow Ct

B
1 N Broadmoor Ct
2 N Dartmoor Av
3 W Denton Av
4 W Broadmoor Ct
5 W Dresden Av
6 N Denton Av
7 Cherrywood Av
8 N Tanglewood Av
9 N Chelsea Av
10 N Wellington Ct

C
1 Old Wick Ln
2 Crichton Ln
3 Strome Ln
4 Burleigh Ln
5 Borthwick Ln
6 Duntrune Ln
7 Tantallon Ln
8 Knockderry Ln
9 Dirleton Ln
10 Ravenscraig Ln
11 Brodick Ln

D
1 N Crabtree Dr
2 N Edgewater Ct

E
1 W Chesterfield Ct
2 N Aurelia Ct

Kildeer
Deer Park
Ela Township
Palatine Township
Palatine
Inverness
Lake Park Estates
Brentwood
Barrington Woods
Pepper Tree
DEER GROVE FOREST PRESERVE
PALATINE HILLS GOLF COURSE
INVERNESS GOLF CLUB
THOMAS T HAMILTON PARK
RIEMER RESERVOIR PARK
LAKE CO
COOK CO
W LONG GROVE RD
W LAKE COOK RD
W DUNDEE RD
NORTHWEST HWY
N QUENTIN RD
N SMITH ST
ROSELLE RD
BALDWIN RD
COLFAX ST
N PLUM GROVE RD

RAND McNALLY

1:24,000
1 in. = 2000 ft.
0 0.25 0.5
miles

SEE 2700 MAP

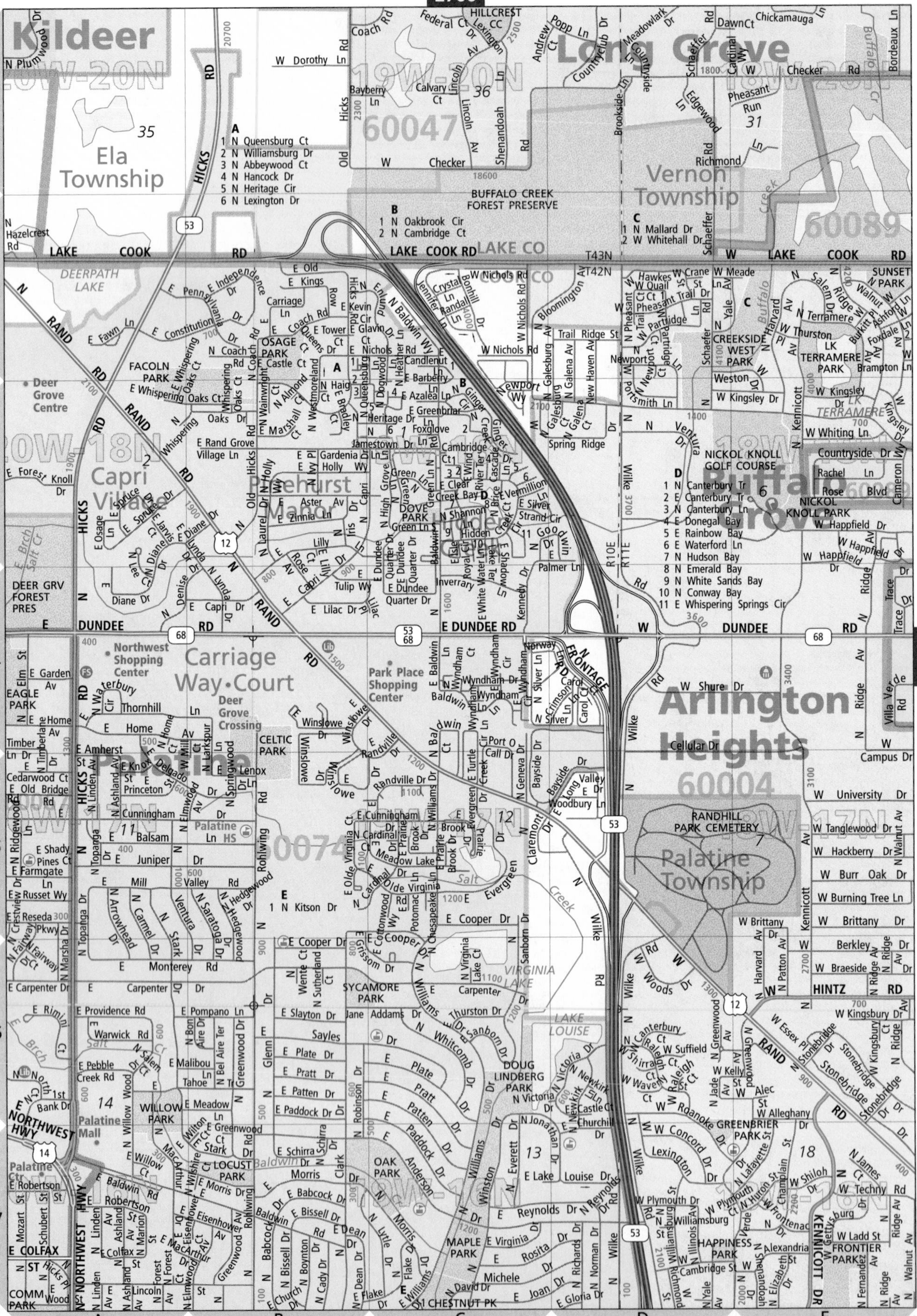

Kildeer
Long Grove
Ela Township
Vernon Township
Buffalo Grove
Arlington Heights
Palatine
Palatine Township

A
1 N Queensburg Ct
2 N Williamsburg Dr
3 N Abbeywood Ct
4 N Hancock Dr
5 N Heritage Cir
6 N Lexington Dr

B
1 N Oakbrook Cir
2 N Cambridge Ct

C
1 N Mallard Dr
2 W Whitehall Dr

D
1 N Canterbury Ct
2 E Canterbury Tr
3 N Canterbury Ln
4 E Donegal Bay
5 E Rainbow Bay
6 E Waterford Ln
7 N Hudson Bay
8 N Emerald Bay
9 N White Sands Bay
10 N Conway Bay
11 E Whispering Springs Cir

E
1 N Kitson Dr

SEE 2752 MAP

SEE 2754 MAP

SEE 2806 MAP

RAND McNALLY

1:24,000
1 in. = 2000 ft.
0 0.25 0.5
miles

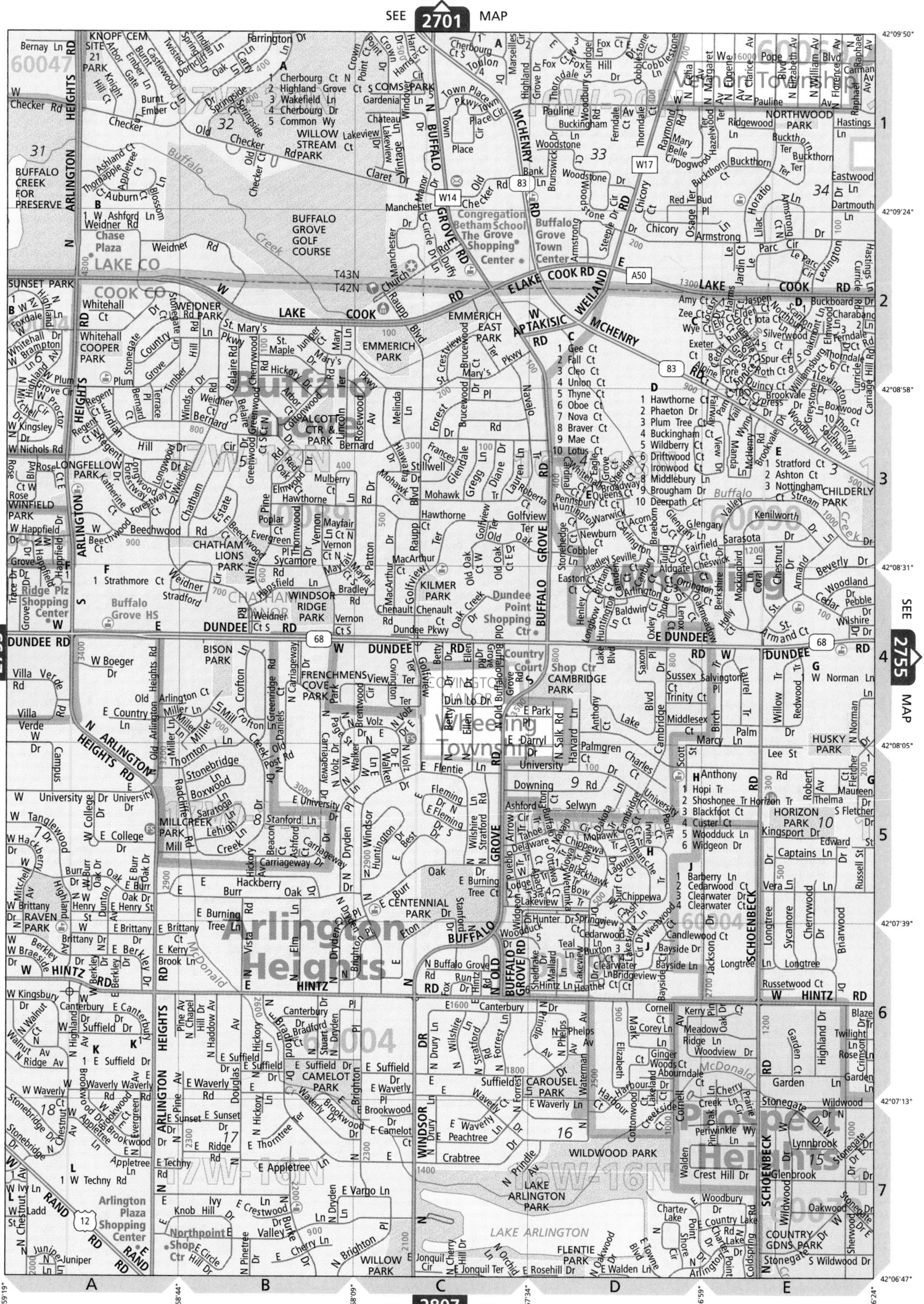

1:24,000
1 in. = 2000 ft.
0 0.25 0.5
miles

SEE 2702 MAP

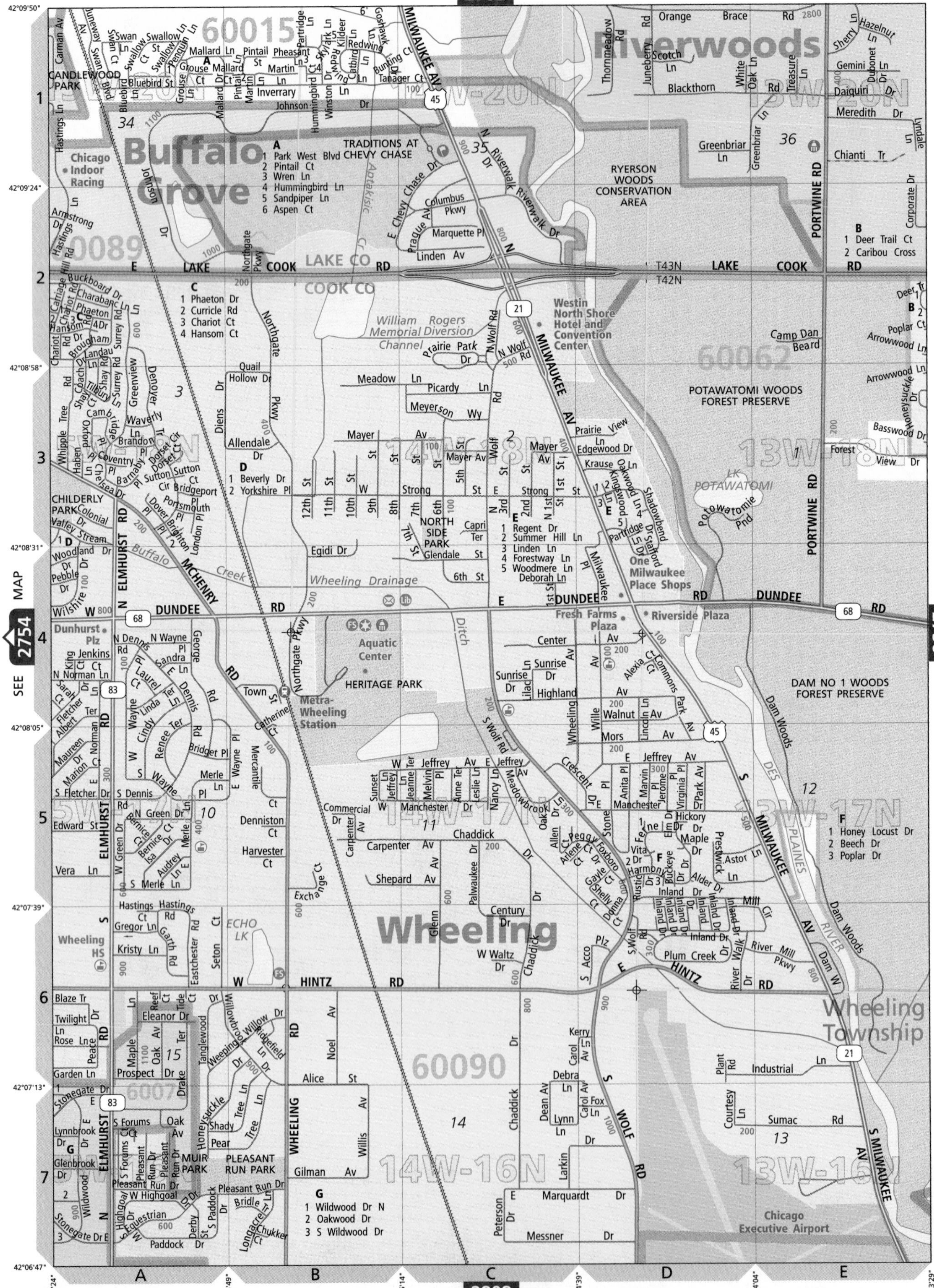

Buffalo Grove

Riverwoods

Wheeling

Wheeling Township

60015 60089 60062 60090 60070

Chicago Indoor Racing

TRADITIONS AT CHEVY CHASE

RYERSON WOODS CONSERVATION AREA

POTAWATOMI WOODS FOREST PRESERVE

DAM NO 1 WOODS FOREST PRESERVE

Westin North Shore Hotel and Convention Center

One Milwaukee Place Shops

Fresh Farms Plaza

Riverside Plaza

Aquatic Center

HERITAGE PARK

Metra-Wheeling Station

NORTH SIDE PARK

Dunhurst Plz

Wheeling HS

MUIR PARK

PLEASANT RUN PARK

CHILDERLY PARK

CANDLEWOOD PARK

Chicago Executive Airport

LAKE CO
COOK CO

William Rogers Memorial Diversion Channel

Wheeling Drainage Ditch

A
1 Park West Blvd
2 Pintail Ct
3 Wren Ln
4 Hummingbird Ln
5 Sandpiper Ln
6 Aspen Ct

B
1 Deer Trail Ct
2 Caribou Cross

C
1 Phaeton Dr
2 Curricle Rd
3 Chariot Ct
4 Hansom Ct

D
1 Beverly Dr
2 Yorkshire Pl

E
1 Regent Dr
2 Summer Hill Ln
3 Linden Ln
4 Forestway Ln
5 Woodmere Ln

F
1 Honey Locust Dr
2 Beech Dr
3 Poplar Dr

G
1 Wildwood Dr N
2 Oakwood Dr
3 S Wildwood Dr

SEE 2754 MAP

SEE 2756 MAP

SEE 2808 MAP

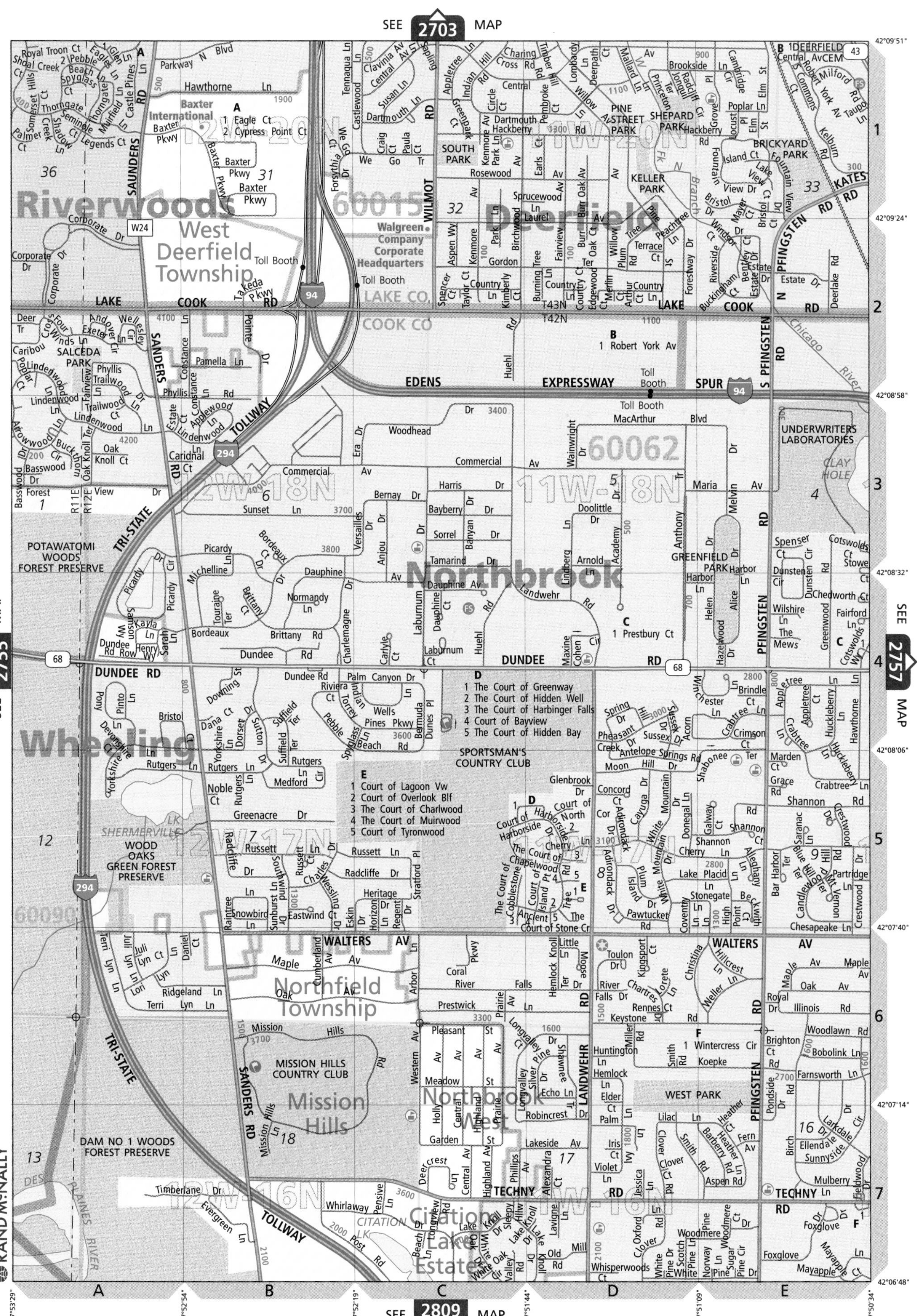
1:24,000
1 in. = 2000 ft.
0 0.25 0.5
miles
SEE 2703 MAP
SEE 2755 MAP
SEE 2757 MAP
SEE 2809 MAP
Riverwoods
Deerfield
Northbrook
Wheeling
West Deerfield Township
Northfield Township
Mission Hills
Northbrook West
Citation Lake Estates
POTAWATOMI WOODS FOREST PRESERVE
WOOD OAKS GREEN FOREST PRESERVE
DAM NO 1 WOODS FOREST PRESERVE
SPORTSMAN'S COUNTRY CLUB
MISSION HILLS COUNTRY CLUB
UNDERWRITERS LABORATORIES
Walgreen Company Corporate Headquarters
Baxter International
EDENS EXPRESSWAY SPUR
TRI-STATE TOLLWAY
LAKE COOK RD
DUNDEE RD
WALTERS AV
TECHNY RD
PFINGSTEN RD
SANDERS RD
60015
60062
60090
RAND McNALLY

1:24,000
1 in. = 2000 ft.
0 0.25 0.5
miles

SEE 2704 MAP

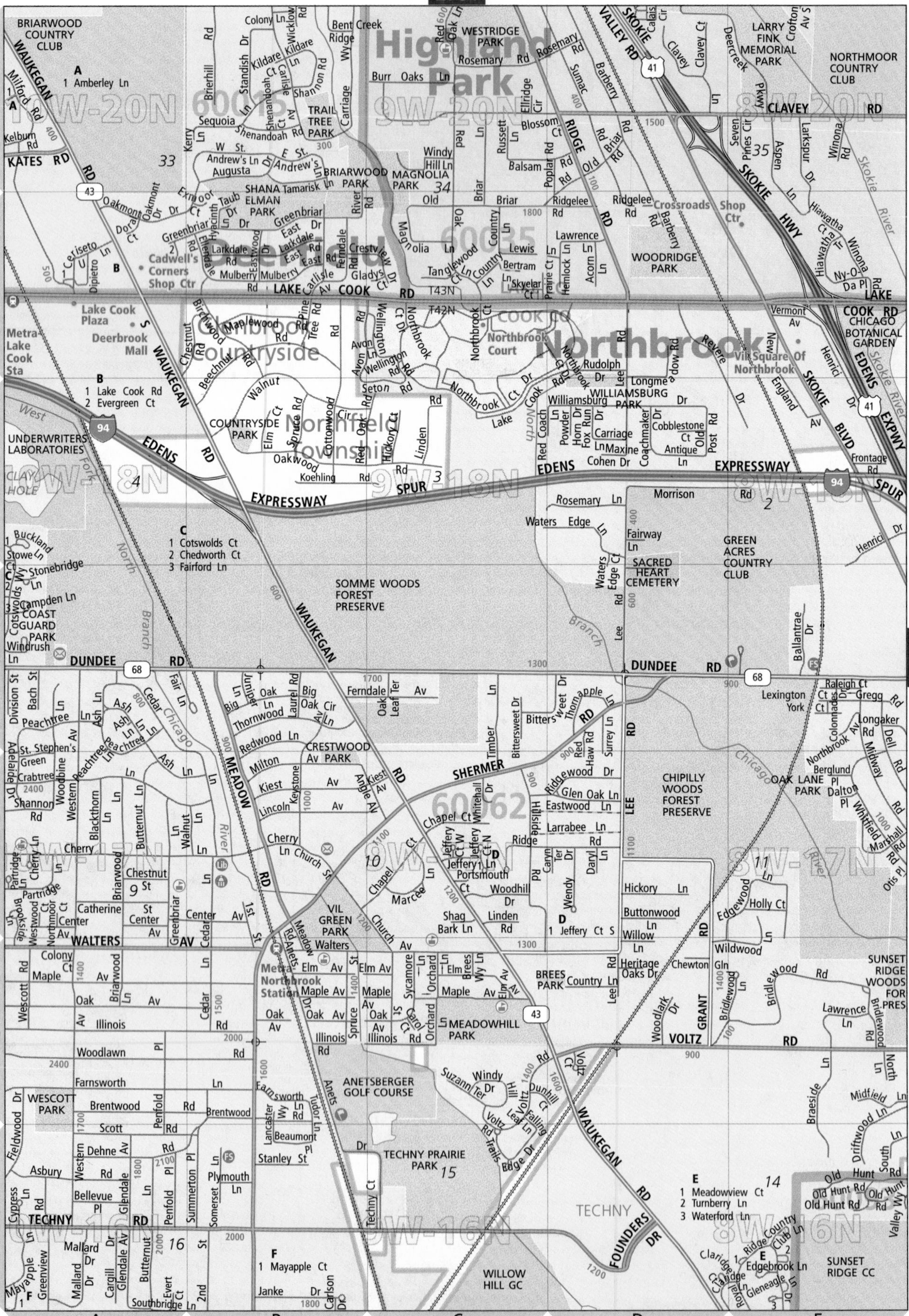

A
1 Amberley Ln

B
1 Lake Cook Rd
2 Evergreen Ct

C
1 Cotswolds Ct
2 Chedworth Ct
3 Fairford Ln

D
1 Jeffery Ct S

E
1 Meadowview Ct
2 Turnberry Ln
3 Waterford Ln

F
1 Mayapple Ct

SEE 2756 MAP

SEE 2758 MAP

SEE 2810 MAP

1:24,000
1 in. = 2000 ft.
0 0.25 0.5
miles

SEE 2705 MAP

SEE 2757 MAP

SEE 2759 MAP

SEE 2811 MAP

1:24,000
1 in. = 2000 ft.
0 0.25 0.5
miles

SEE B MAP

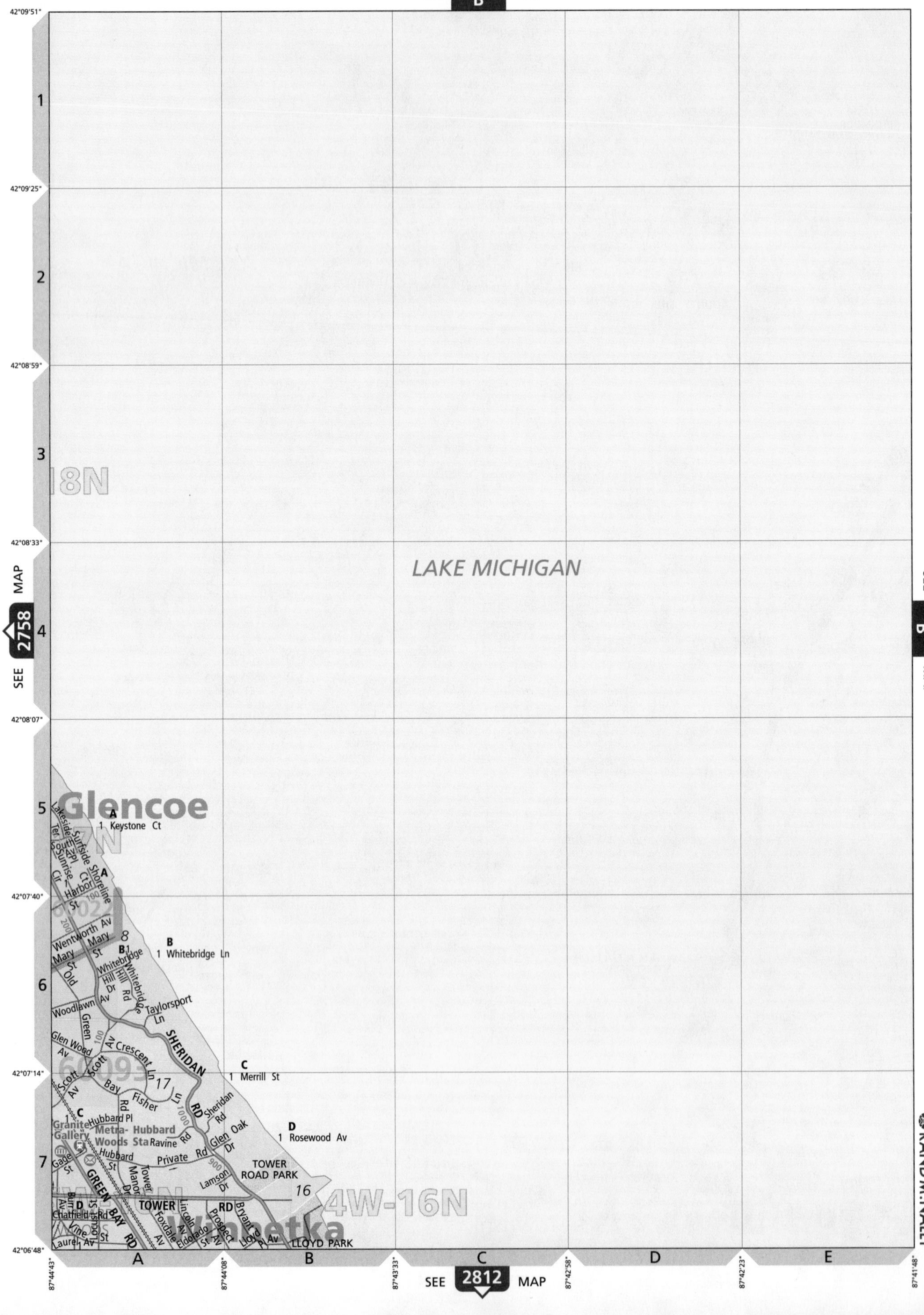

42°09'51" 42°09'25" 42°08'59" 42°08'33" 42°08'07" 42°07'40" 42°07'14" 42°06'48"

87°44'43" 87°44'08" 87°43'33" 87°42'58" 87°42'23" 87°41'48"

A B C D E

1 2 3 4 5 6 7

SEE 2758 MAP

SEE B MAP

SEE 2812 MAP

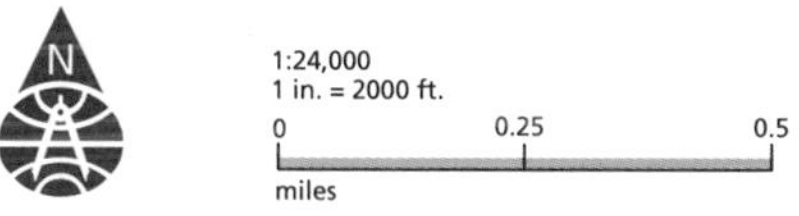

SEE B MAP

Hampshire

60140

Hampshire Township

Burlington Township

48W-16N
47W-16N
48W-15N
47W-15N
48W-14N
47W-14N
48W-13N
47W-13N

T42N
T41N

19 20 21 22 15
30 29 28 27
31 32 33 34
5 4 3 2

WALKER RD
FRENCH RD
LENSCHOW RD
BURLINGTON RD
W OAK KNOLL DR
E OAK KNOLL DR
ALLEN RD
HARMONY RD
N STATE ST
S STATE ST
GETZELMAN RD
WARNER ST
E WASHINGTON AV
E PANAMA AV
W Terwilliger
Burlington Creek
Hampshire Creek

HAMPSHIRE CTR CEM
BRUCE REAM MEMORIAL PARK
Hampshire Middle-High School

W Meadowdale Cir
E Meadowdale Cir
Savanna Dr
Stonegate Cir
Cardinal Wy
Wild Prairie Pointe
Jessamine Dr
Campion
W Klick St
N West St
Mill
N Center St
N East St
Av
N Park St
Brandt Dr
E Keyes Av
W Rinn Av
W Jefferson
Oak Av
Park St
W Jackson Av
Prairie Av
S Park St
A
1 S Walnut Pl
S Klick St
Edgewood Av
Maple Pl
S Ash Pl
E Jefferson Av
E Jackson Av
Elm St
Baldwin Pl
Grove Av
E South Av
Panama Av
E Highland Av
E High Av
S St
Hillcrest Av
Jake Ln
Julie Ln
Robert
Old
Mill Ln
Casey Ln
Paige Ln
Bruce Ln
S Elizabeth
Prairieview Pkwy
Fox Run Ln
Whitetail Cir
Fieldstone Ln
Sawgrass Ln
Woodside Ter
Clover Cir
Bluestem Ln
Hampshire
W Brookedge Dr
Timber Ln
W Duchess Ln
Red Hawk Rd
Peregine Wy
Prairieview Pkwy
Barn Owl Dr
Schmidt Dr
Schmidt Cir
Maxwell Cir
Nicholas Dr
Jack Cir
Dylan Dr
Brittany Cir
Pheasant Ct
Old Oak Ct
Coyote Ct
Coyote Tr
Hill Ln
Oak
Pheasant Tr
Shirewood Farm Rd
Red Barn Rd

1
2
3
4
5
6
7

A B C D E

42°06'36"
42°06'10"
42°05'44"
42°05'18"
42°04'52"
42°04'26"
42°04'00"
42°03'34"

88°34'20"
88°33'45"
88°33'10"
88°32'35"
88°32'00"
88°31'25"

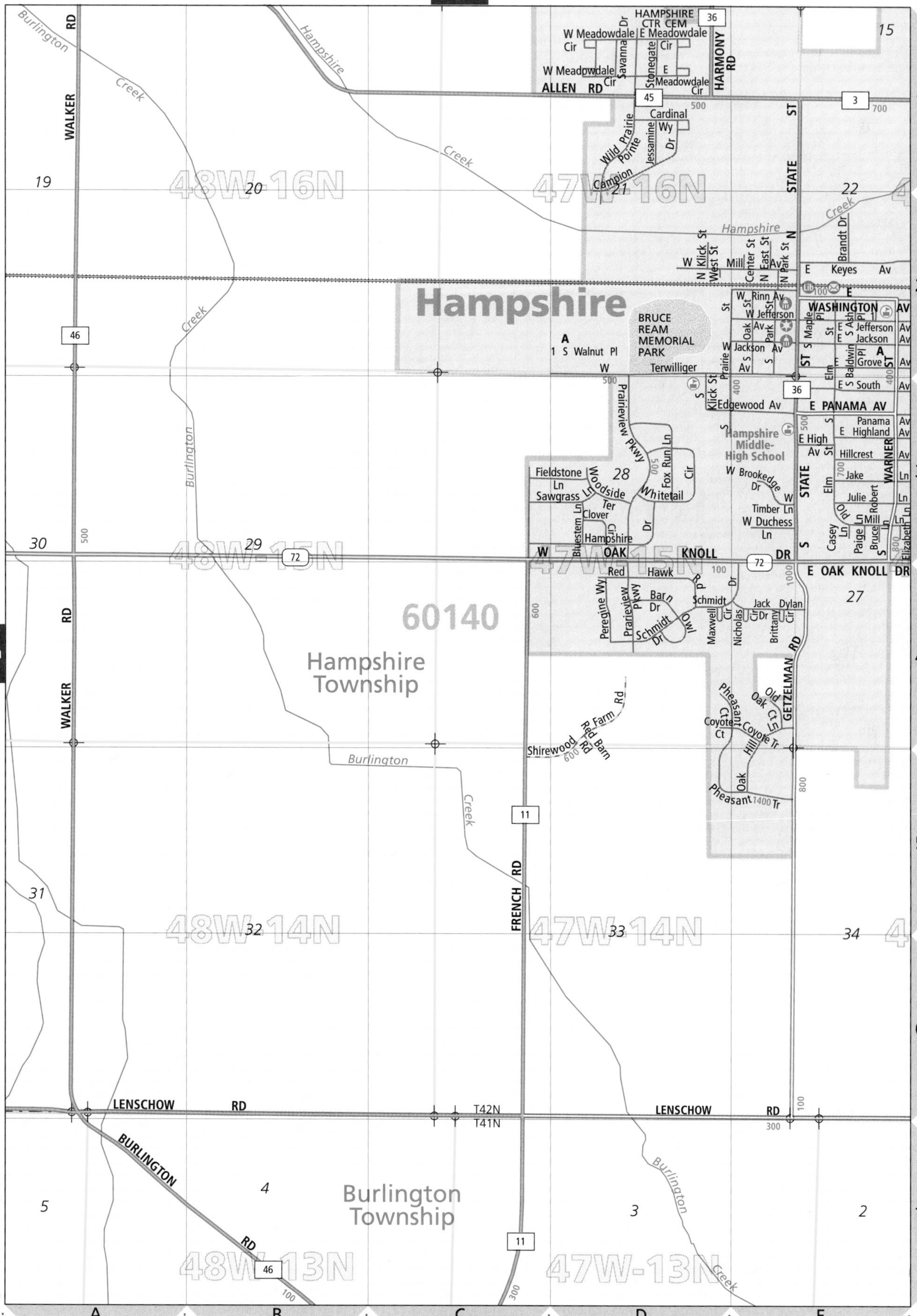

SEE B MAP

SEE 2796 MAP

SEE B MAP

RAND McNALLY

1:24,000
1 in. = 2000 ft.
0 0.25 0.5
miles

SEE 2743 MAP

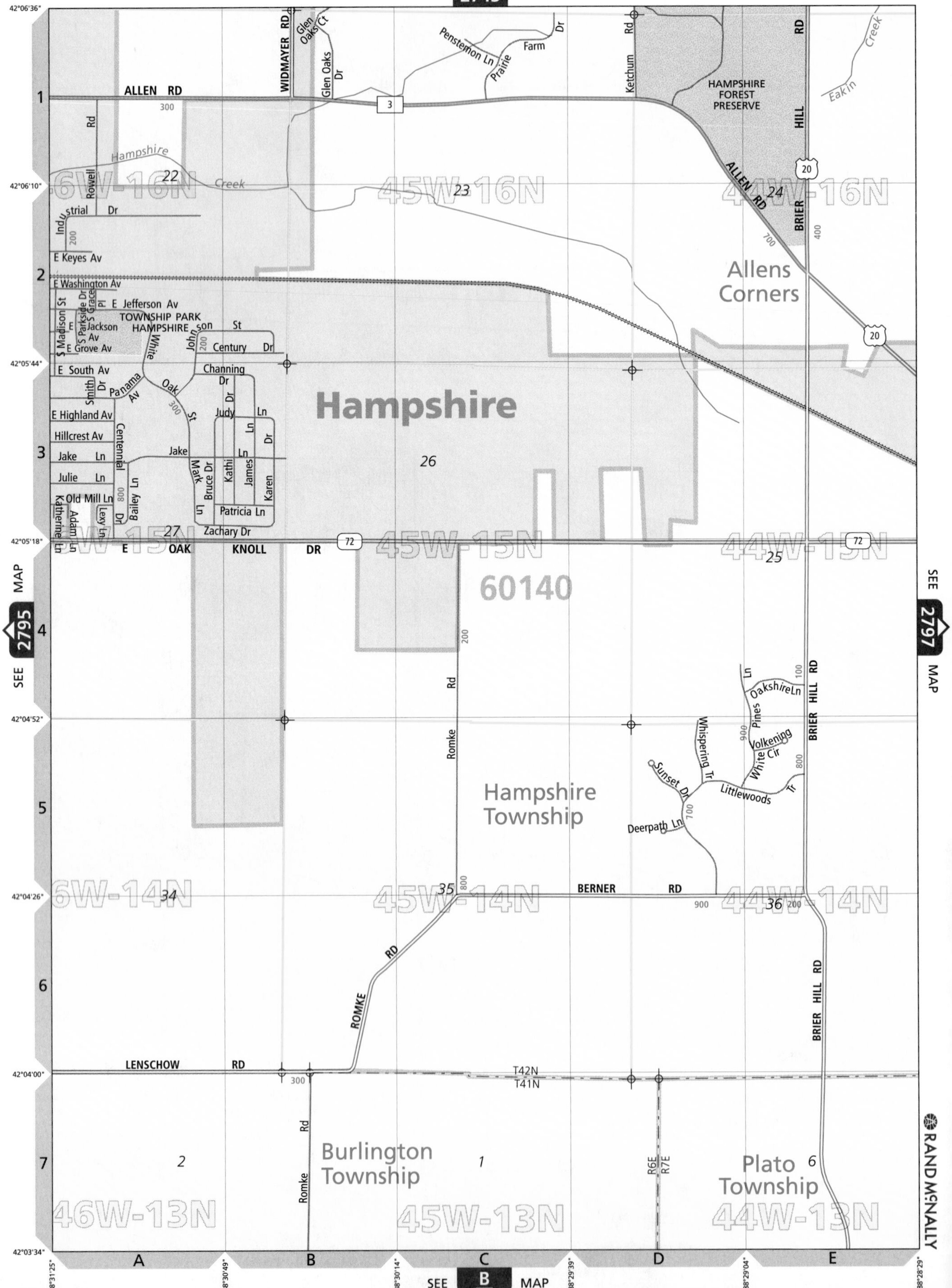

SEE 2795 MAP

SEE 2797 MAP

SEE B MAP

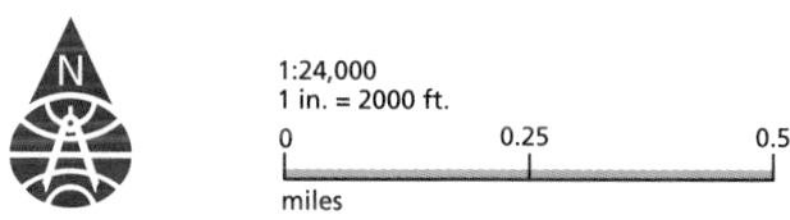

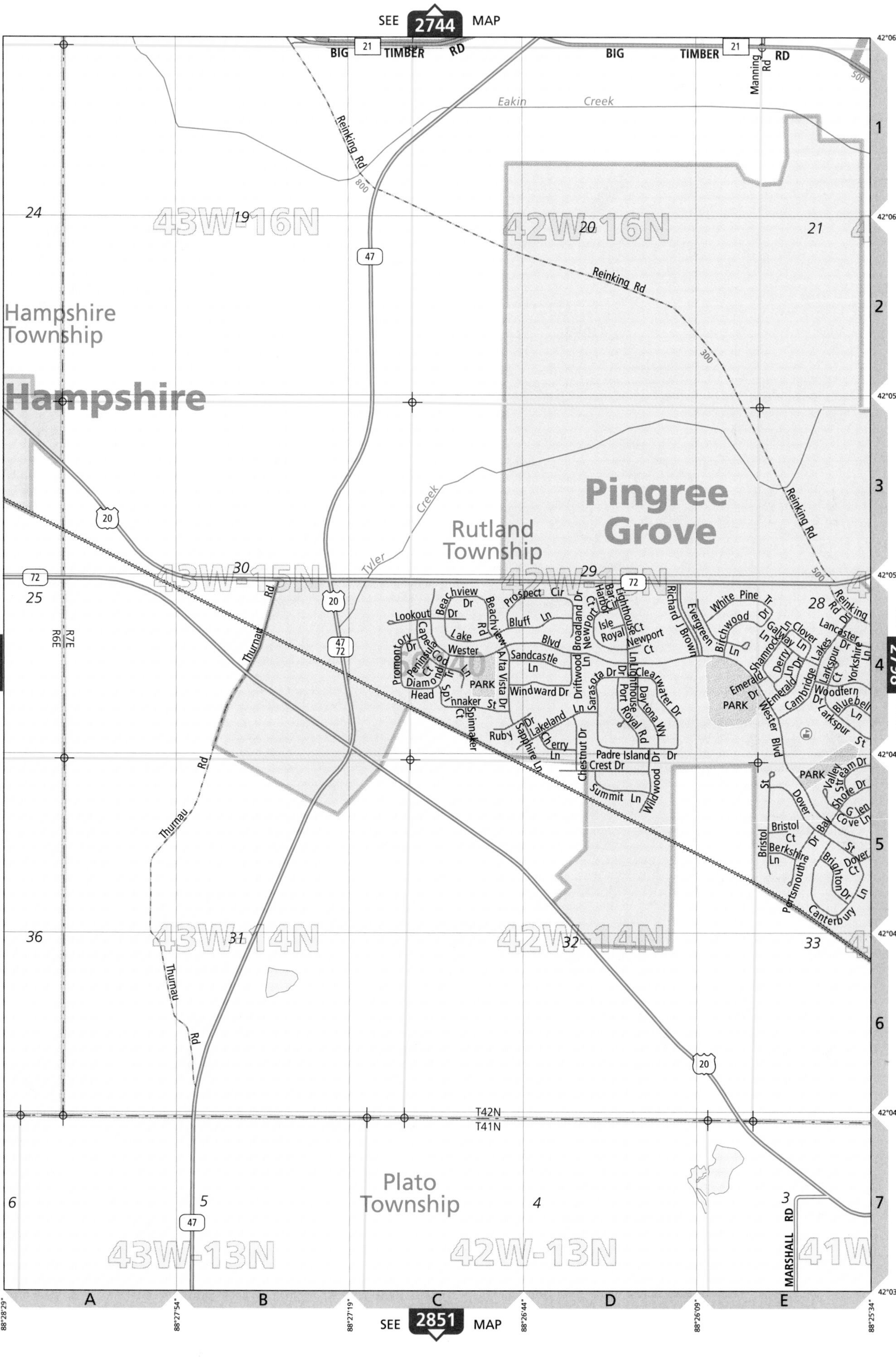

SEE 2744 MAP

BIG TIMBER RD
Manning Rd
Eakin Creek
Reinking Rd
43W-16N
42W-16N
Hampshire Township
Hampshire
Pingree Grove
Rutland Township
Tyler Creek
43W-15N
42W-15N
Thurnau Rd
Richard J Brown
Evergreen
White Pine Tr
Birchwood Dr
Lookout Dr
Beachview Dr
Prospect Cir
Bluff Ln
Lake Blvd
Wester
Sandcastle Ln
Windward Dr
Broadland Dr
Driftwood Ln
Newport Ct
Isle Royal Ct
Lighthouse Ln
Clearwater Dr
Daytona Wy
Port Royal Rd
Padre Island Dr
Crest Dr
Summit Ln
Wildwood Dr
Chestnut Dr
Sarasota Dr
Lakeland Ln
Cherry Ln
Sapphire Ln
Ruby Dr
Spinnaker St
Spinnaker Ct
PARK
Diamond Head
Peninsula Ct
Cape Cod Tr
Promontory Dr
Emerald Dr
Shamrock Ln
Galway Ln
Clover Ct
Derry Ln
Lancaster Rd
Cambridge Lakes Dr
Larkspur Dr
Yorkshire Ct
Woodfern Dr
Bluebell Ln
Larkspur St
Wester Blvd
Valley Stream Dr
Shore Dr
Glen Cove Ln
Dover Bay Dr
Bristol St
Bristol Ct
Berkshire Ln
Portsmouthe Dr
Brighton Dr
Dover Ct
Canterbury Ln
43W-14N
42W-14N
T42N
T41N
Plato Township
MARSHALL RD
43W-13N
42W-13N
41W
R7E
R6E

SEE 2796 MAP
SEE 2798 MAP
SEE 2851 MAP

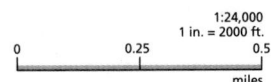

1:24,000
1 in. = 2000 ft.
0 0.25 0.5
miles

SEE 2745 MAP

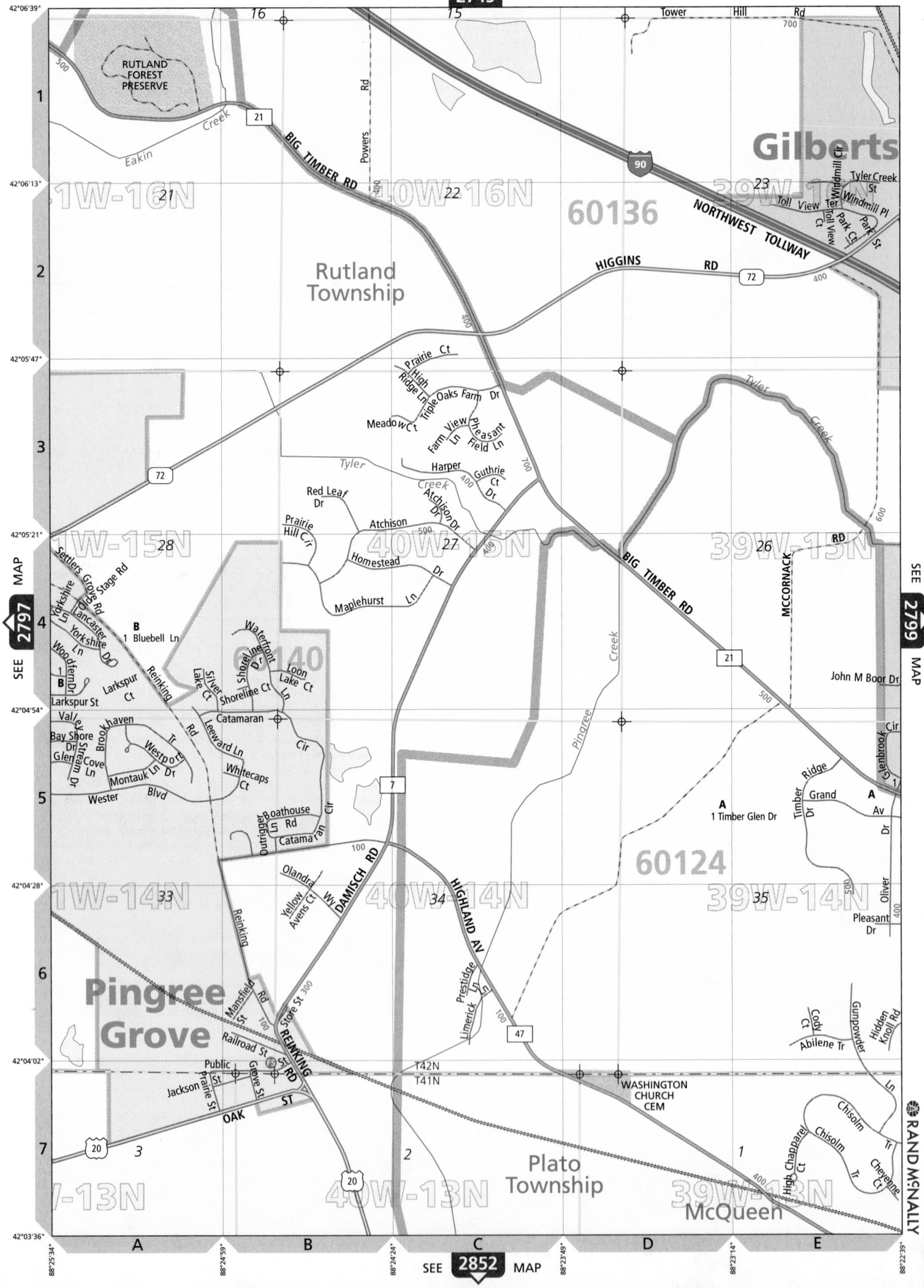

SEE 2797 MAP

SEE 2799 MAP

SEE 2852 MAP

RUTLAND FOREST PRESERVE
Gilberts
Rutland Township
Pingree Grove
Plato Township
McQueen
60136
60140
60124
BIG TIMBER RD
NORTHWEST TOLLWAY
HIGGINS RD
HIGHLAND AV
DAMISCH RD
REINKING RD
OAK ST
MCCORNACK RD
WASHINGTON CHURCH CEM
A 1 Timber Glen Dr
B 1 Bluebell Ln

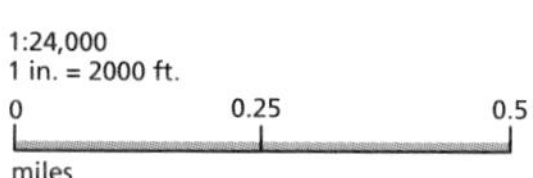

SEE 2746 MAP

A
1 Matteson St
2 Jackson St

Waitcus Park
Gilberts
60118
Dundee Township
Countryview Estates
West Dundee
Sleepy Hollow
60136
Rutland Township
Elgin
Northwest Business Park
Northwest Corporate Park
Mem Park
St. Mary's Cem
Northwest Tollway
Toll Booth
Toll Booth
Higgins Rd
Tyrrell Rd
Randall Rd
Mason Rd
Big Timber Rd
Coombs Rd
Galligan Rd

B
1 Appaloosa Ct
2 Palomino Ct

38W-16N
37W-16N
38W-15N
37W-15N
38W-14N
37W-14N
38W-13N
37W-13N
36W-13N

T42N
T41N
R7E
R8E

60124
60123
Burnidge-Paul Wolff Forest Preserve
Big Timber Camp
Burnidge Woods Park
Plato Township
Wildwood Valley
Elgin Township

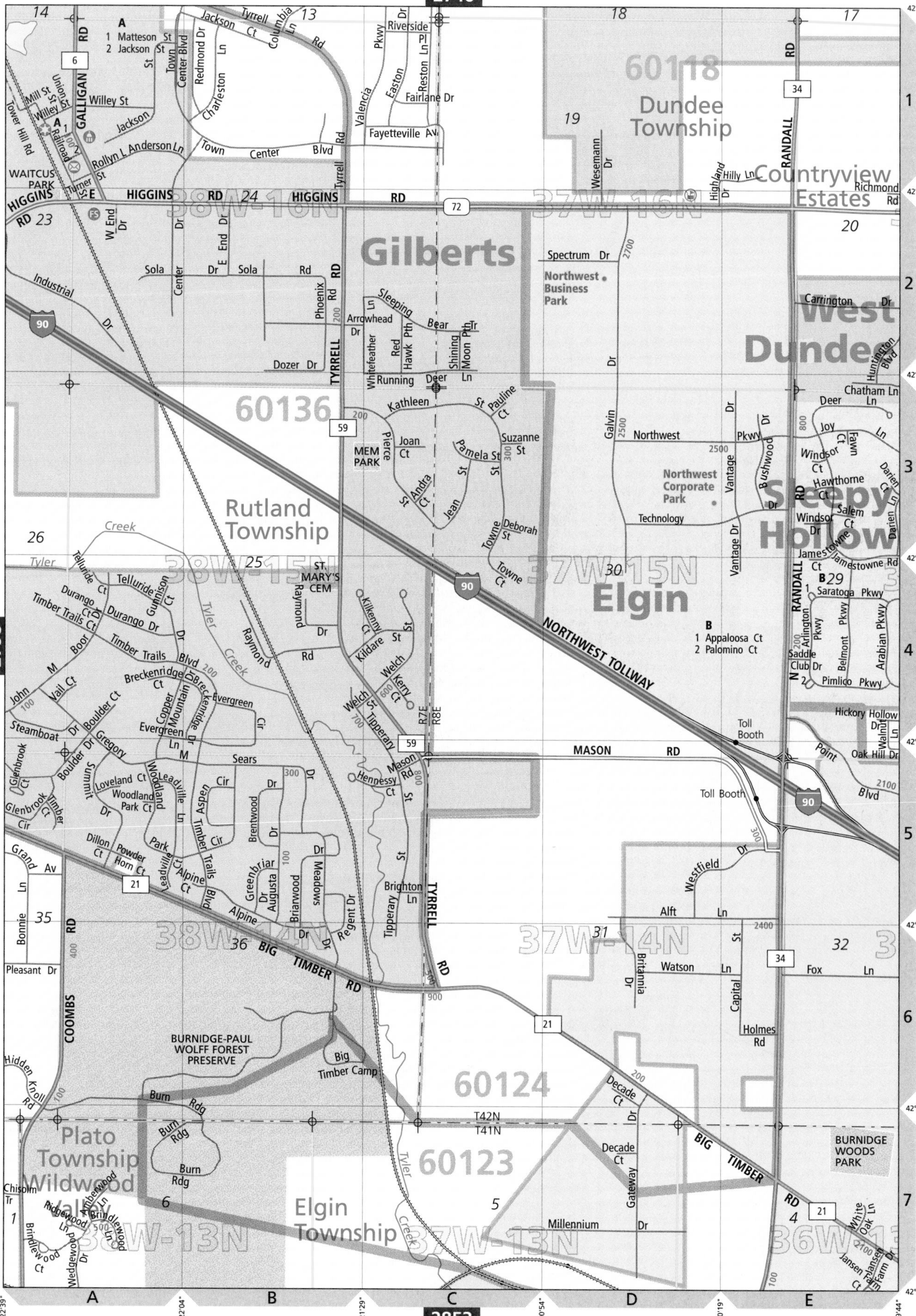

SEE 2798 MAP

SEE 2800 MAP

42°06'41"
42°06'15"
42°05'49"
42°05'23"
42°04'57"
42°04'31"
42°04'05"
42°03'38"

88°22'39"
88°22'04"
88°21'29"
88°20'54"
88°20'19"
88°19'44"

SEE 2853 MAP

1:24,000
1 in. = 2000 ft.
0 0.25 0.5
miles

SEE 2747 MAP

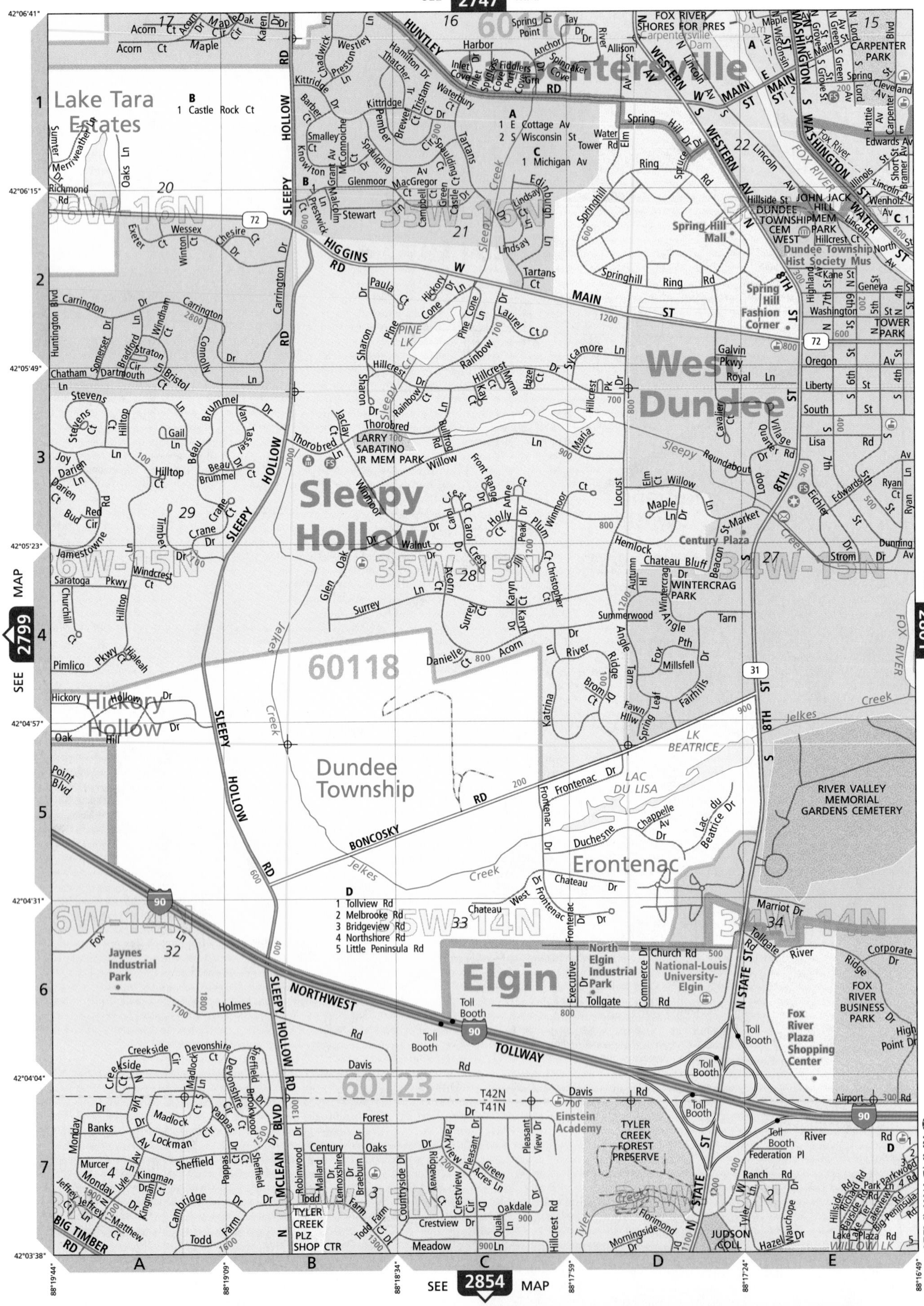

Carpentersville
Lake Tara Estates
West Dundee
Sleepy Hollow
Hickory Hollow
Dundee Township
Frontenac
Elgin

FOX RIVER SHORES FOR PRES
CARPENTER PARK
JOHN JACK HILL MEM PARK
DUNDEE TOWNSHIP CEM
Dundee Township Hist Society Mus
Spring Hill Mall
Spring Hill Fashion Corner
TOWER PARK
LARRY SABATINO JR MEM PARK
Century Plaza
WINTERCRAG PARK
LK BEATRICE
LAC DU LISA
RIVER VALLEY MEMORIAL GARDENS CEMETERY
Jaynes Industrial Park
North Elgin Industrial Park
National-Louis University-Elgin
FOX RIVER BUSINESS PARK
Fox River Plaza Shopping Center
Einstein Academy
TYLER CREEK FOREST PRESERVE
TYLER CREEK PLZ SHOP CTR
JUDSON COLL

60110
60118
60123

A
1 E Cottage Av
2 S Wisconsin St

B
1 Castle Rock Ct

C
1 Michigan Av

D
1 Tollview Rd
2 Melbrooke Rd
3 Bridgeview Rd
4 Northshore Rd
5 Little Peninsula Rd

SEE 2799 MAP

SEE 2801 MAP

SEE 2854 MAP

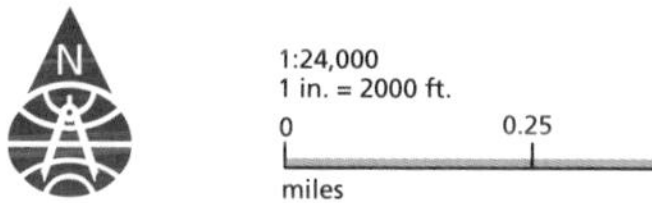

SEE 2748 MAP

Carpentersville

East Dundee

Barrington Hills

West Dundee

Hoffman Estates

Elgin

Dundee Township

Hanover Township

MAX MCGRAW WILDLIFE FOUNDATION

BONNIE DUNDEE GOLF COURSE

GOLFVIEW PARK

SPRING CREEK VALLEY FOR PRES

SPRING CREEK VALLEY FOREST PRESERVE

MAX FREEMAN MEM PARK

LIONS PARK

CARMEN GARCIA MEM ARBORETUM PARK

WILLIAM ALDIS SR PARK

SOUTH END PARK

RIVER VALLEY MEM GDNS CEM

DUNDEE TOWNSHIP CEMETERY EAST

FOX RIVER BUSINESS PARK

VOYAGEUR LNDG FOREST PRES

TROUT PARK

Comm Unit School District 300 Board of Education

Dolphin Cove Family Aquatic

Clearwater Theater

Haeger Pottery Factory

Summit School

River Valley Square

A
1 Springwood Cir

B
1 Entrance Rd
2 Cheryl Ln
3 Willow Lake Rd
4 Big Peninsula Rd
5 Little Peninsula Rd

D
1 Geneva St

B
1 Exit
2 Rd
3 Northshore
4 Rd

32W-16N

33W-16N

33W-15N

32W-15N

33W-14N

32W-14N

KANE CO

COOK CO

NORTHWEST TOLLWAY

SEE 2800 MAP

SEE 2802 MAP

A B C D E

SEE 2855 MAP

1:24,000
1 in. = 2000 ft.
0 0.25 0.5
miles

SEE 2749 MAP

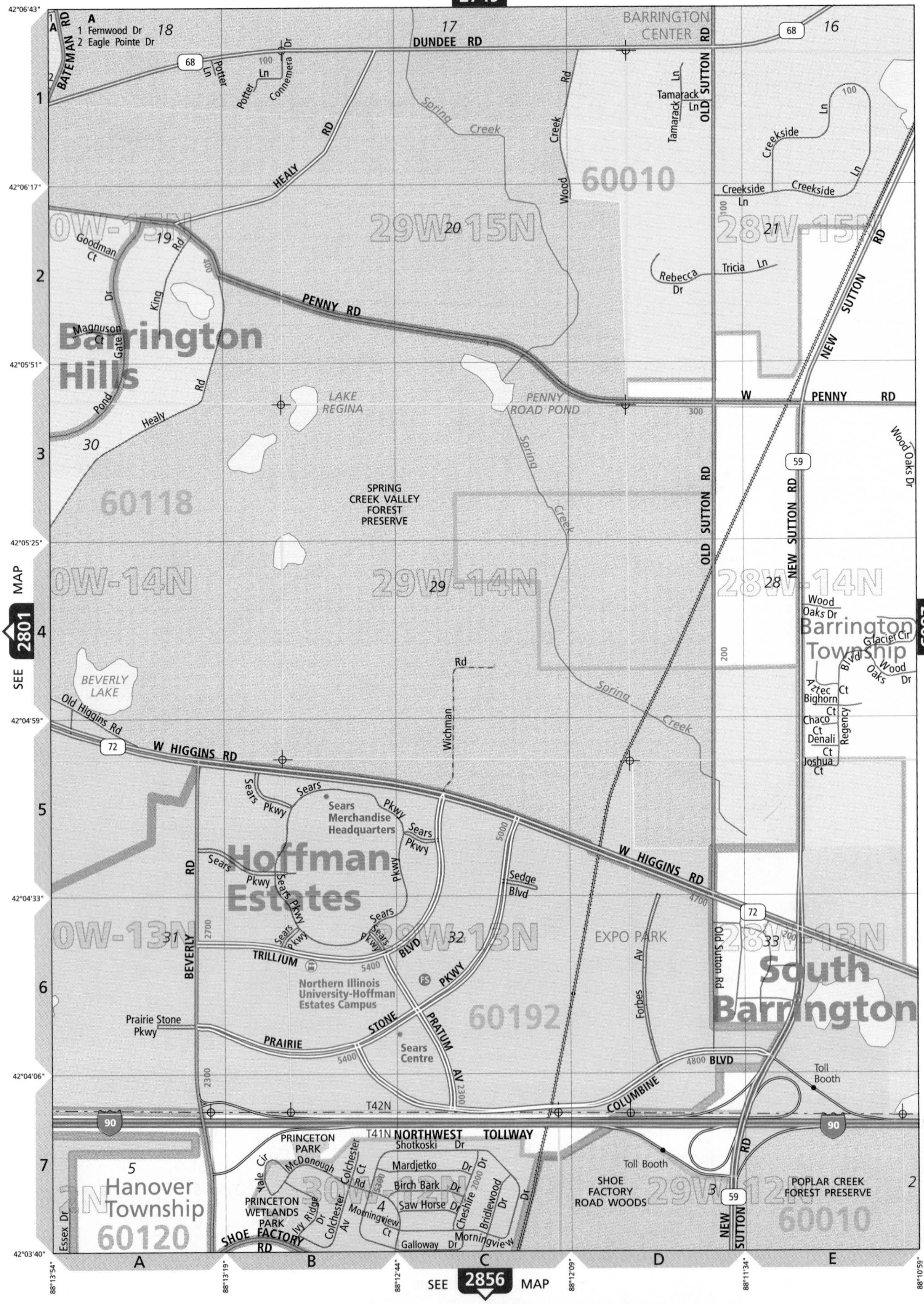

SEE 2801 MAP

SEE 2803 MAP

SEE 2856 MAP

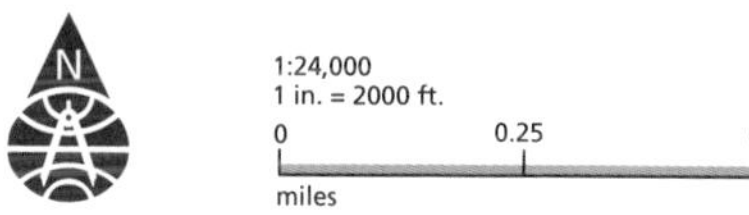

SEE 2750 MAP

Barrington Hills
Inverness
South Barrington
Barrington Township
Hoffman Estates

CRABTREE LAKE
Crabtree Nature Center
CRABTREE FOREST PRESERVE
ALEXANDER STILLMAN NATURE CENTER
MARVIN DUNTEMAN PARK
LAKE ROSE
LAKE ADALYN
Beach
South Barrington Executive Center
South Barrington Office Center
POPLAR CREEK FOREST PRESERVE
Toll Booth
PARK

E PALATINE RD
W PALATINE RD
ALGONQUIN RD
W PENNY RD
E PENNY RD
W MUNDHANK RD
E MUNDHANK RD
BARTLETT RD
S BARRINGTON RD
N BARRINGTON RD
W HIGGINS RD
NORTHWEST TOLLWAY
W CENTRAL RD
LAKEWOOD BLVD
HASSELL RD
SHOE FACTORY RD
GREENSPOINT PKWY
NEW SUTTON RD

60010
60192
27W-15N
26W-15N
27W-14N
26W-14N
27W-13N
26W-13N
28W-12N
27W-12N
26W-12N
T42N
T41N
R9E
R10E

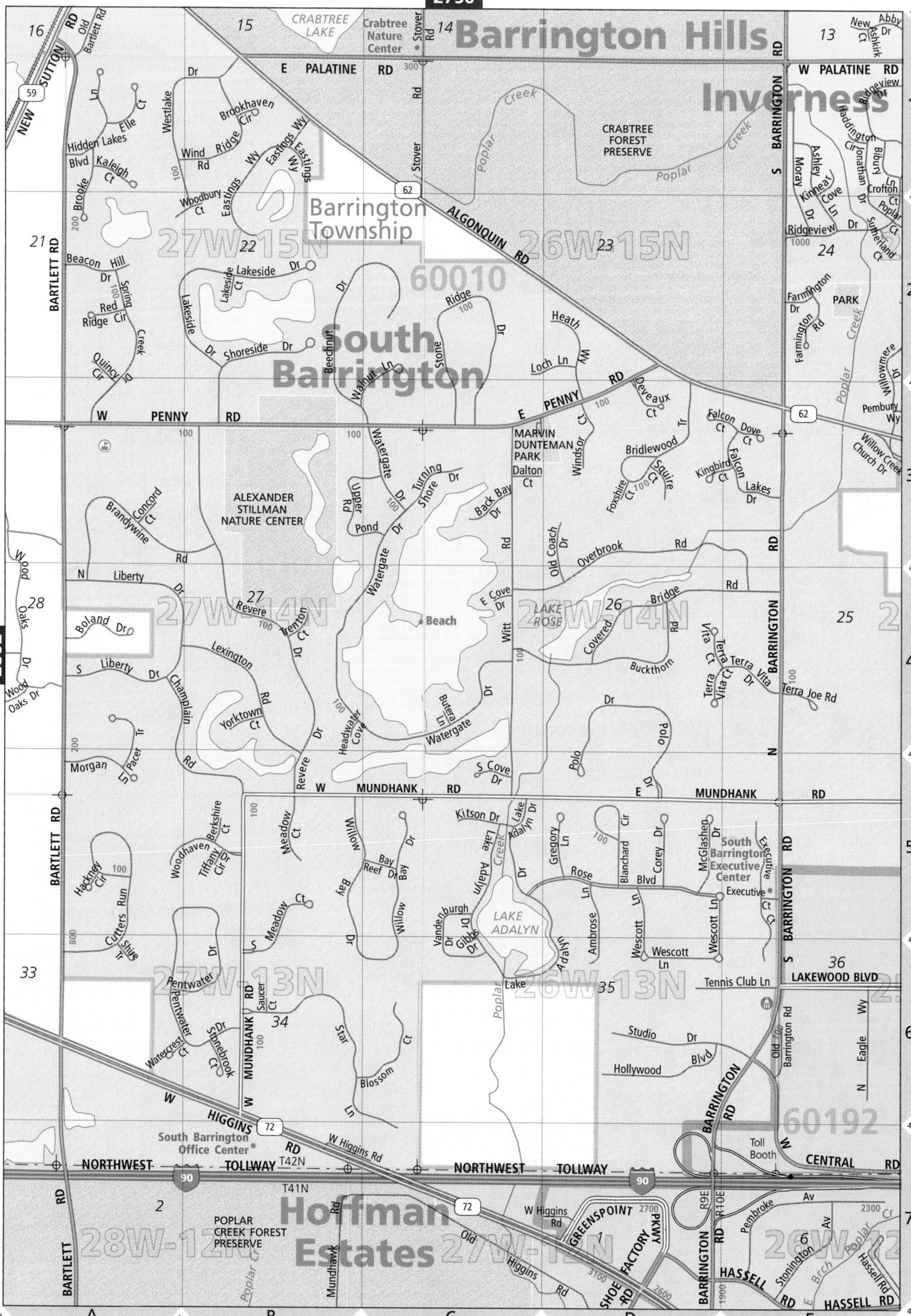

SEE 2802 MAP

SEE 2804 MAP

SEE 2857 MAP

A B C D E
1 2 3 4 5 6 7

42°06'45" 42°06'19" 42°05'52" 42°05'26" 42°05'00" 42°04'34" 42°04'08" 42°03'42"
88°10'59" 88°10'24" 88°09'49" 88°09'14" 88°08'39" 88°08'04"

1:24,000
1 in. = 2000 ft.
0 0.25 0.5
miles

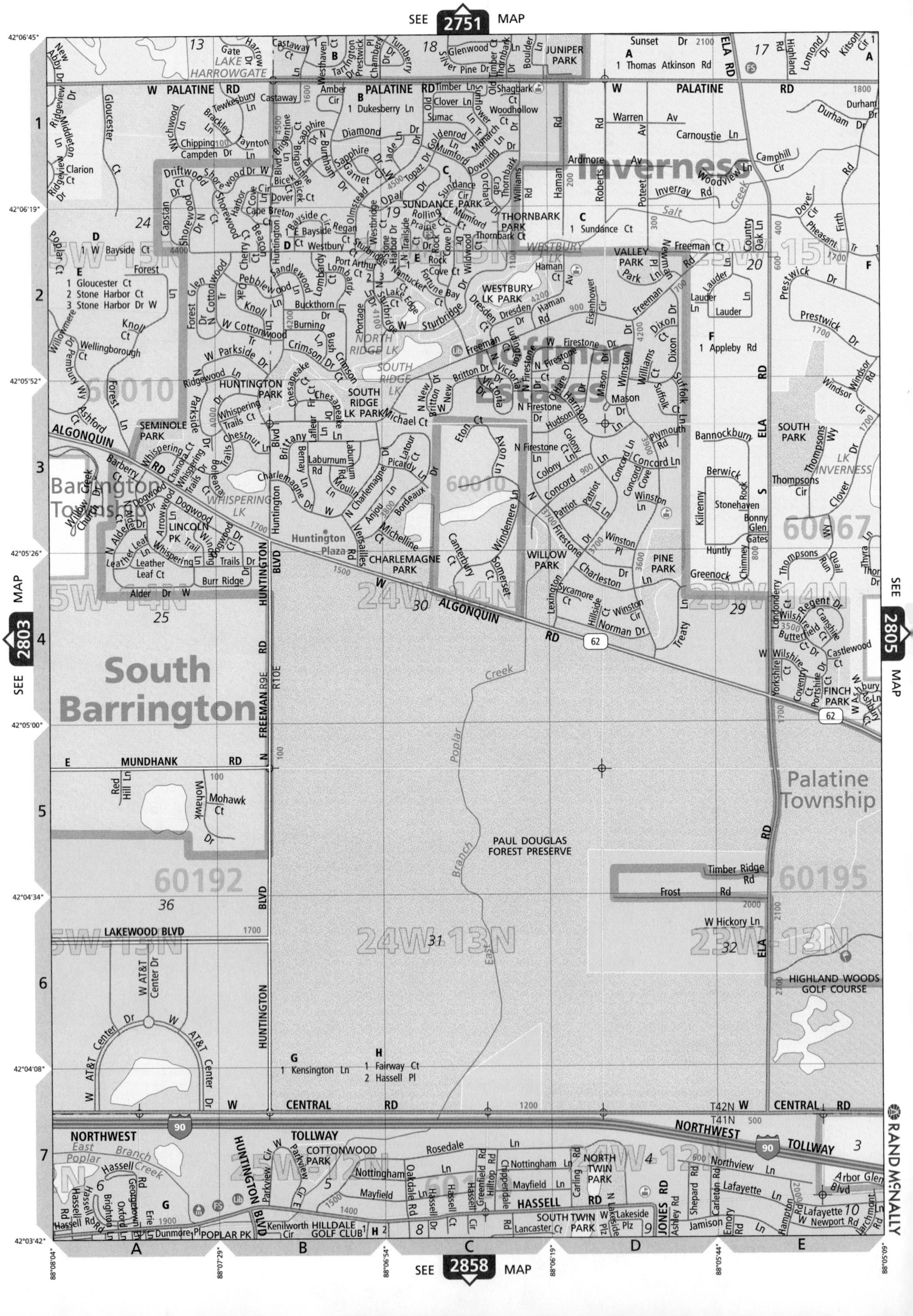

SEE 2751 MAP

SEE 2803 MAP

SEE 2805 MAP

SEE 2858 MAP

A
1 Thomas Atkinson Rd

B
1 Dukesberry Ln

C
1 Sundance Ct

D
1 W Bayside Ct

D
1 E Bayside Ct

E
1 Gloucester Ct
2 Stone Harbor Ct
3 Stone Harbor Dr W

F
1 Appleby Rd

G
1 Kensington Ln

H
1 Fairway Ct
2 Hassell Pl

Inverness

Hoffman Estates

South Barrington

Barrington Township

Palatine Township

PAUL DOUGLAS FOREST PRESERVE

HIGHLAND WOODS GOLF COURSE

HILLDALE GOLF CLUB

W PALATINE RD

ALGONQUIN RD

W ALGONQUIN RD

HUNTINGTON BLVD

N FREEMAN RD

ELA RD

MUNDHANK RD

LAKEWOOD BLVD

W CENTRAL RD

NORTHWEST TOLLWAY

HASSELL RD

JONES RD

60010

60067

60192

60195

25W-15N

24W-15N

23W-15N

25W-14N

24W-14N

23W-14N

25W-13N

24W-13N

23W-13N

25W-12N

24W-12N

T42N

T41N

R9E

R10E

A B C D E

1 2 3 4 5 6 7

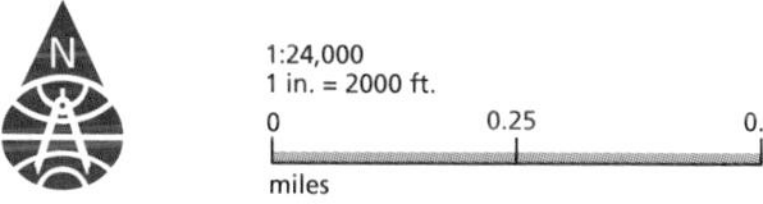

SEE 2752 MAP

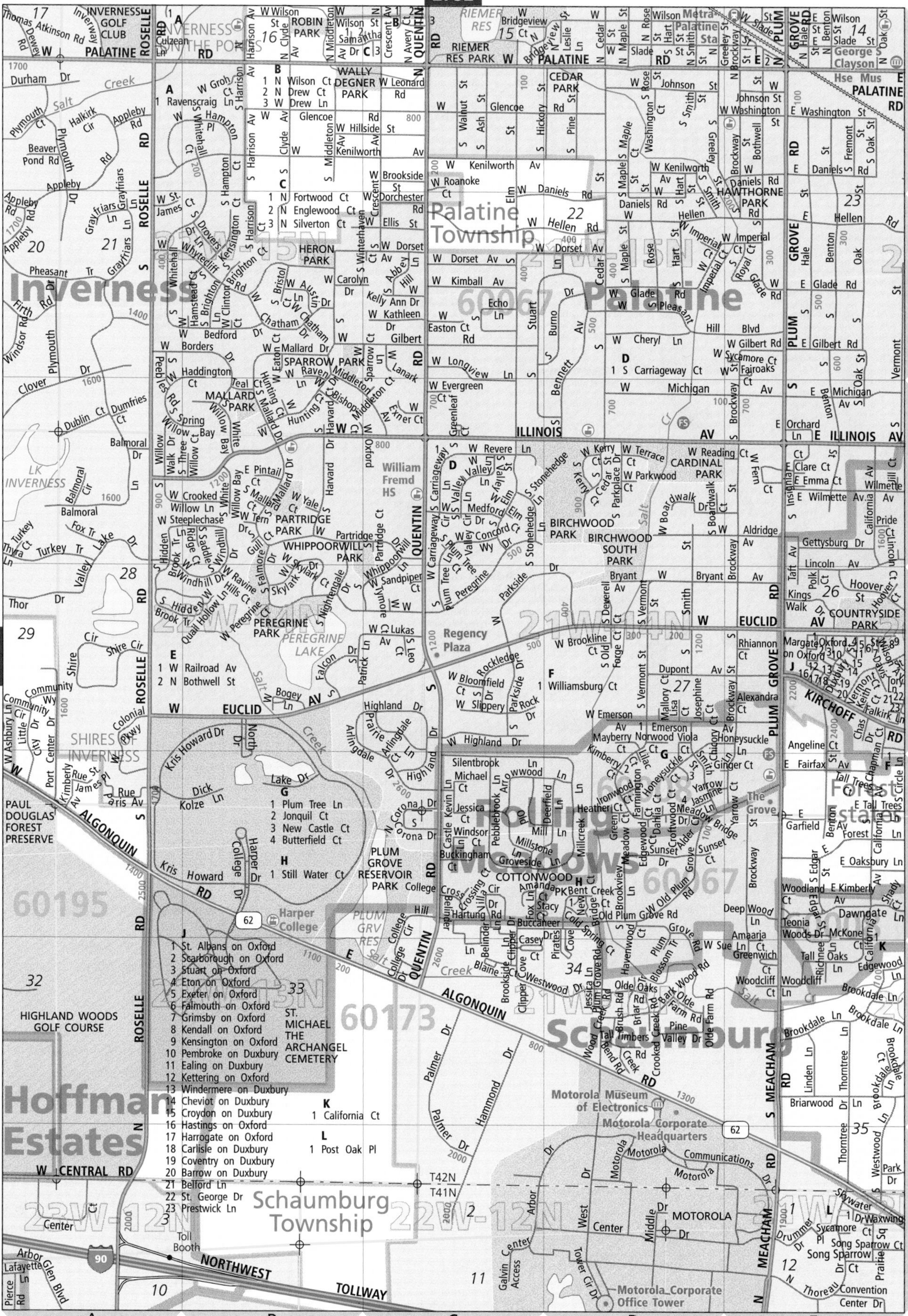

SEE 2804 MAP

SEE 2806 MAP

Inverness

Palatine

Palatine Township

Rolling Meadows

Schaumburg

Hoffman Estates

Schaumburg Township

A
1 Ravenscraig Ln

B
1 N Wilson Ct
2 N Drew Ct
3 W Drew Ln

C
1 N Fortwood Ct
2 N Englewood Ct
3 N Silverton Ct

D
1 S Carriageway Ct

E
1 W Railroad Av
2 N Bothwell St

G
1 Plum Tree Ln
2 Jonquil Ct
3 New Castle Ct
4 Butterfield Ct

H
1 Still Water Ct

J
1 St. Albans on Oxford
2 Scarborough on Oxford
3 Stuart on Oxford
4 Eton on Oxford
5 Exeter on Oxford
6 Falmouth on Oxford
7 Grimsby on Oxford
8 Kendall on Oxford
9 Kensington on Oxford
10 Pembroke on Duxbury
11 Ealing on Duxbury
12 Kettering on Oxford
13 Windermere on Duxbury
14 Cheviot on Duxbury
15 Croydon on Duxbury
16 Hastings on Oxford
17 Harrogate on Oxford
18 Carlisle on Duxbury
19 Coventry on Duxbury
20 Barrow on Duxbury
21 Belford Ln
22 St. George Dr
23 Prestwick Ln

K
1 California Ct

L
1 Post Oak Pl

SEE 2859 MAP

1:24,000
1 in. = 2000 ft.
0 0.25 0.5
miles

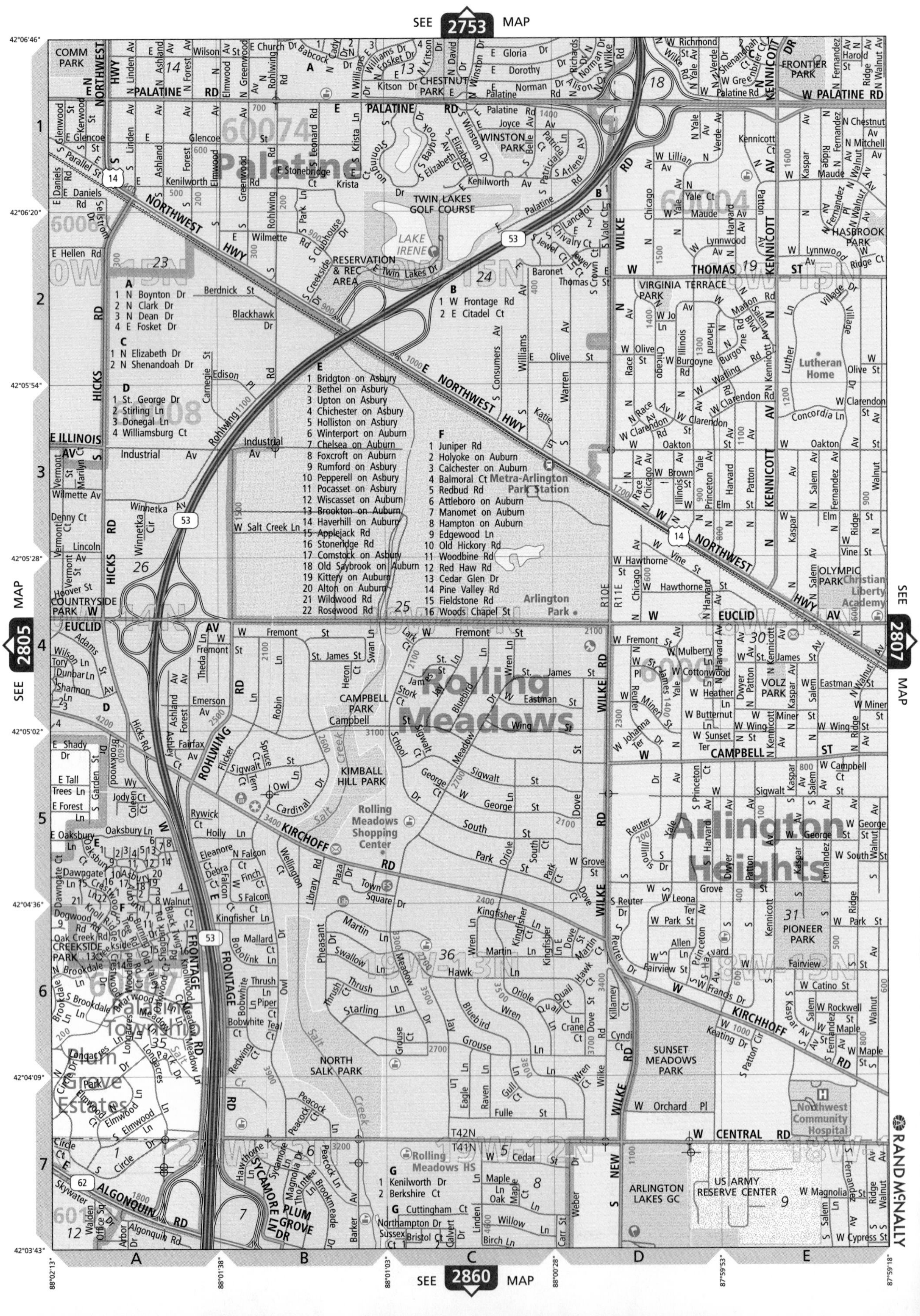

SEE 2753 MAP

Palatine 60074

Rolling Meadows

Arlington Heights

Palatine Township

Plum Grove Estates

A
1 N Boynton Dr
2 N Clark Dr
3 N Dean Dr
4 E Fosket Dr

B
1 W Frontage Rd
2 E Citadel Ct

C
1 N Elizabeth Dr
2 N Shenandoah Dr

D
1 St. George Dr
2 Stirling Ln
3 Donegal Ln
4 Williamsburg Ct

E
1 Bridgton on Asbury
2 Bethel on Asbury
3 Upton on Asbury
4 Chichester on Asbury
5 Holliston on Asbury
6 Winterport on Auburn
7 Chelsea on Auburn
8 Foxcroft on Asbury
9 Rumford on Asbury
10 Pepperell on Asbury
11 Pocasset on Asbury
12 Wiscasset on Auburn
13 Brookton on Auburn
14 Haverhill on Auburn
15 Applejack Rd
16 Stoneridge Rd
17 Comstock on Asbury
18 Old Saybrook on Auburn
19 Kittery on Auburn
20 Alton on Auburn
21 Wildwood Rd
22 Rosewood Rd

F
1 Juniper Rd
2 Holyoke on Auburn
3 Calchester on Auburn
4 Balmoral Ct
5 Redbud Rd
6 Attleboro on Auburn
7 Manomet on Auburn
8 Hampton on Auburn
9 Edgewood Ln
10 Old Hickory Rd
11 Woodbine Rd
12 Red Haw Rd
13 Cedar Glen Dr
14 Pine Valley Rd
15 Fieldstone Rd
16 Woods Chapel St

G
1 Kenilworth Dr
2 Berkshire Ct

SEE 2805 MAP

SEE 2807 MAP

SEE 2860 MAP

1:24,000
1 in. = 2000 ft.
0 0.25 0.5
miles

SEE 2754 MAP

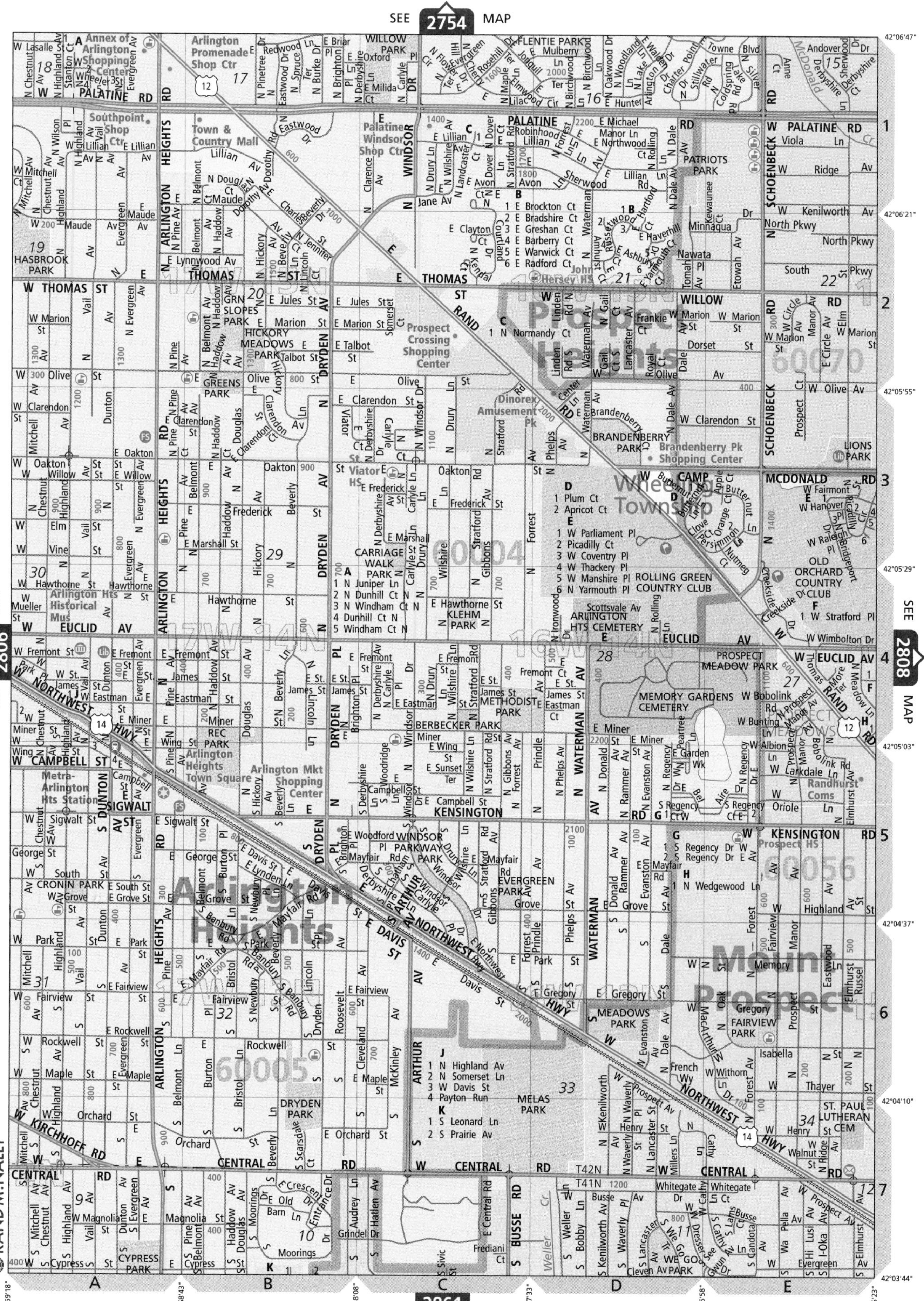

SEE 2806 MAP

SEE 2808 MAP

SEE 2861 MAP

1:24,000
1 in. = 2000 ft.
0 0.25 0.5
miles

SEE 2755 MAP

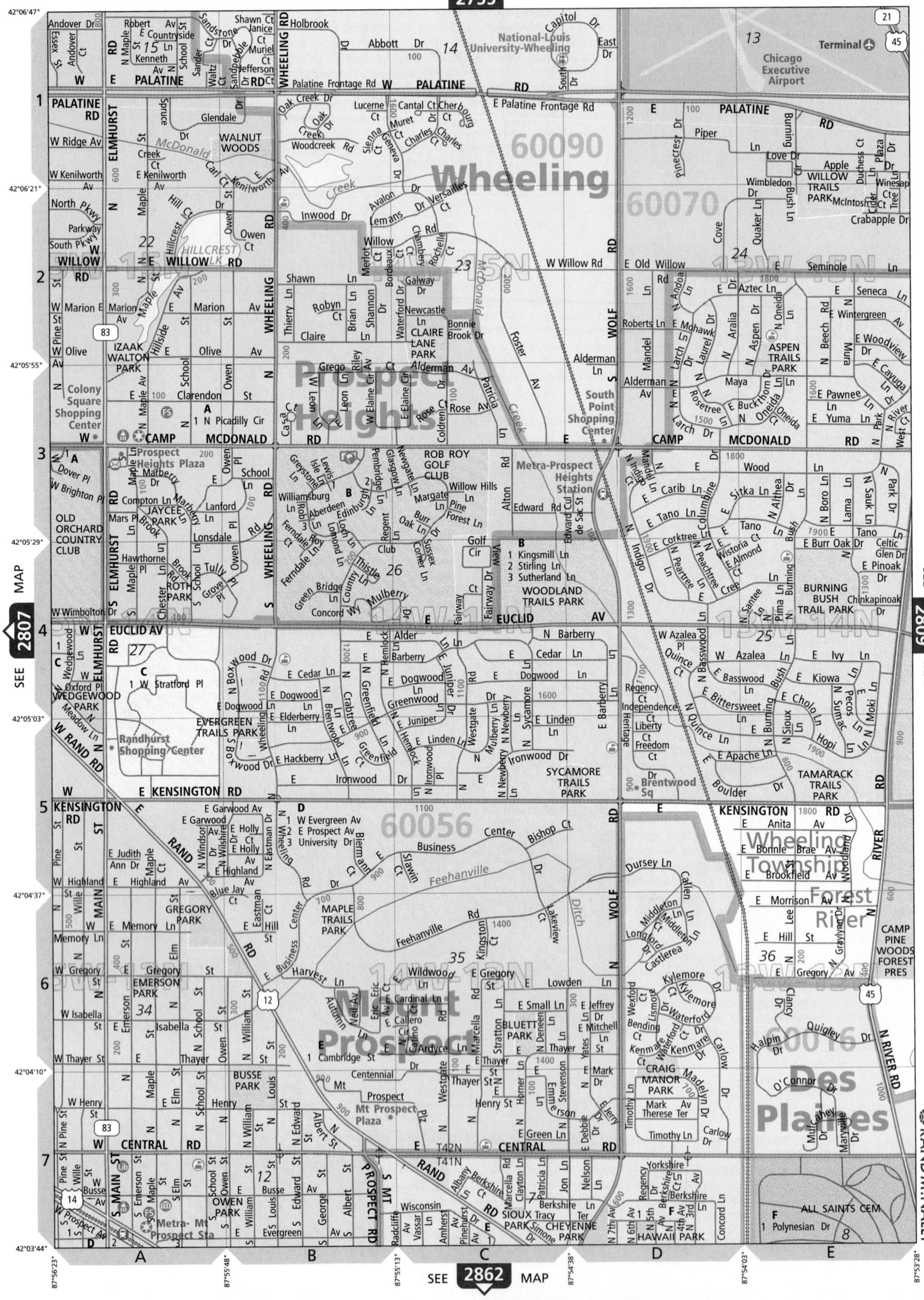

SEE 2807 MAP

SEE 2809 MAP

Wheeling
60090
60070
Prospect Heights
60056
Mount Prospect
Wheeling Township
Forest River
Des Plaines
60016

National-Louis University-Wheeling
Chicago Executive Airport
Terminal
WALNUT WOODS
HILLCREST LK
IZAAK WALTON PARK
Colony Square Shopping Center
CLAIRE LANE PARK
ASPEN TRAILS PARK
WILLOW TRAILS PARK
South Point Shopping Center
Prospect Heights Plaza
JAYCEE PARK
OLD ORCHARD COUNTRY CLUB
ROTH PARK
ROB ROY GOLF CLUB
Metra-Prospect Heights Station
WOODLAND TRAILS PARK
BURNING BUSH TRAIL PARK
WEDGEWOOD PARK
Randhurst Shopping Center
EVERGREEN TRAILS PARK
SYCAMORE TRAILS PARK
Brentwood Sq
TAMARACK TRAILS PARK
GREGORY PARK
MAPLE TRAILS PARK
CAMP PINE WOODS FOREST PRES
EMERSON PARK
BLUETT PARK
CRAIG MANOR PARK
BUSSE PARK
Mt Prospect Plaza
OWEN PARK
Metra-Mt Prospect Sta
SIOUX PARK
CHEYENNE PARK
HAWAII PARK
ALL SAINTS CEM

A: 1 N Picadilly Cir
B: 1 Kingsmill Ln, 2 Stirling Ln, 3 Sutherland Ln
C: 1 W Stratford Pl
D: 1 W Evergreen Av, 2 E Prospect Av, 3 University Dr
E: 1 Cambridge St
F: 1 Polynesian Dr

PALATINE RD
WILLOW RD
CAMP MCDONALD RD
EUCLID AV
KENSINGTON RD
CENTRAL RD
ELMHURST RD
WHEELING RD
WOLF RD
RAND RD
MAIN ST
PROSPECT RD
N RIVER RD
RIVER RD

42°06'47"
42°06'21"
42°05'55"
42°05'29"
42°05'03"
42°04'37"
42°04'10"
42°03'44"
87°56'23"
87°55'48"
87°55'13"
87°54'38"
87°54'03"
87°53'28"

A B C D E
1 2 3 4 5 6 7

SEE 2862 MAP

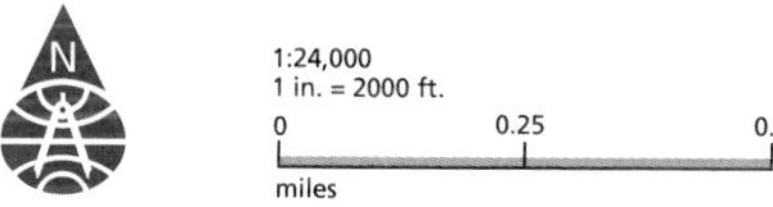

SEE 2756 MAP

DAM NO 1 WOODS FOREST PRESERVE

ALLYSON WOODS FOREST PRESERVE

Prospect Heights

Allstate

INDIAN RIDGE PARK

STONEGATE PARK

Northbrook

HAWTHORNE GLEN PARK

Plaza Del Prado

WILLOW PARK

Glenbrook Hospital

Glenbrook South HS

LAKE AVENUE WOODS FOREST PRESERVE

NORTHFIELD WOODS

INDIAN TRAIL PARK

Glenview

Glenview Estates

Wheeling Township

The Grove

THE GROVE

Nixon's Greenwood-Central

Zenith Electronics

FLICK PARK

GOLDEN ACRES

CAMP PINE WOODS FOREST PRESERVE

BECK LAKE

Northfield Township

COUNTRYSIDE PARK

Triumvera

OAKTON COMMUNITY COLLEGE-DES PLAINES CAMPUS

ALL SAINTS CEM

Des Plaines

Cobblestone

Maine Township

RIDGEWOOD CEMETERY

60090 · 60070 · 60062 · 60025 · 60056 · 60016

12W-15N · 11W-15N · 12W-14N · 11W-14N · 12W-13N · 11W-13N · T42N · T41N · R11E · R12E

WILLOW RD · MILWAUKEE AV · PALATINE RD · SANDERS RD · TRI-STATE TOLLWAY · LANDWEHR RD · PFINGSTEN RD · LAKE AV · GLENVIEW RD · CENTRAL RD · DEARLOVE RD · RIVER RD · E RIVER RD · N EAST RIVER RD · CULLIGAN PKWY · WINKLEMAN RD

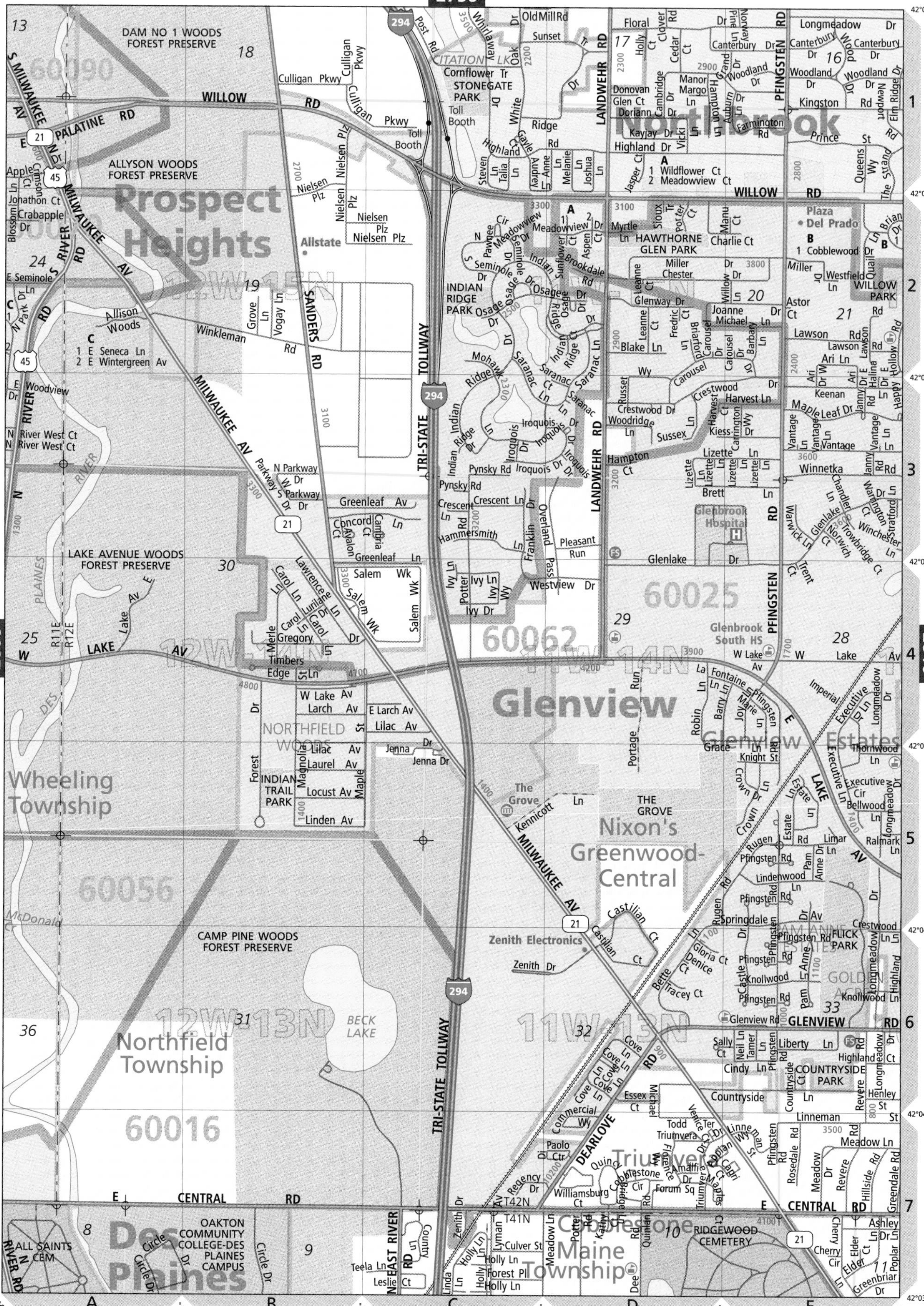

SEE 2808 MAP

SEE 2810 MAP

SEE 2863 MAP

42°06'48" · 42°06'22" · 42°05'56" · 42°05'30" · 42°05'03" · 42°04'37" · 42°04'11" · 42°03'45"

87°53'28" · 87°52'53" · 87°52'18" · 87°51'43" · 87°51'08" · 87°50'33"

A · B · C · D · E

1 · 2 · 3 · 4 · 5 · 6 · 7

1:24,000
1 in. = 2000 ft.
0 0.25 0.5
miles

SEE 2757 MAP

SEE 2809 MAP

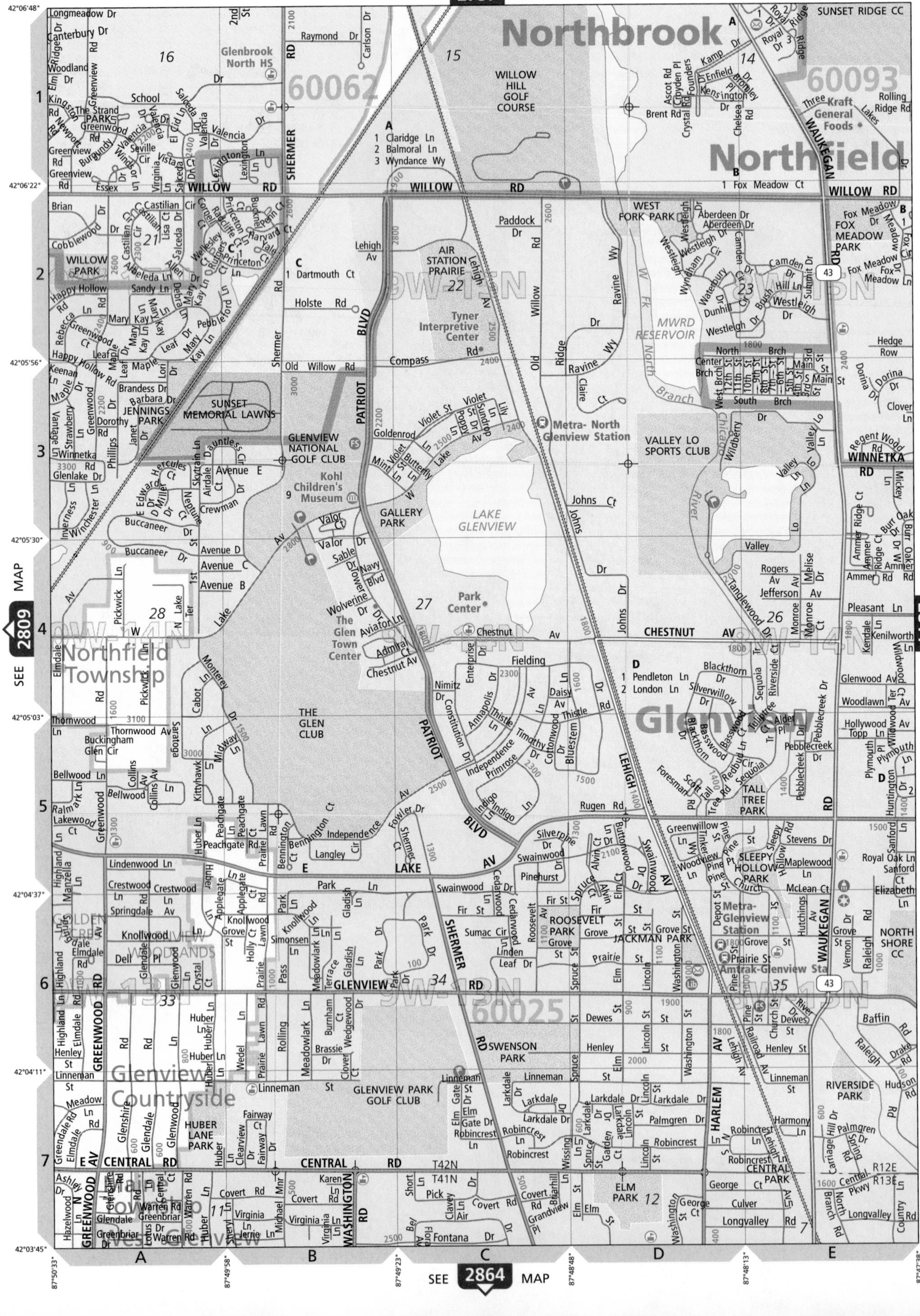

SEE 2811 MAP

SEE 2864 MAP

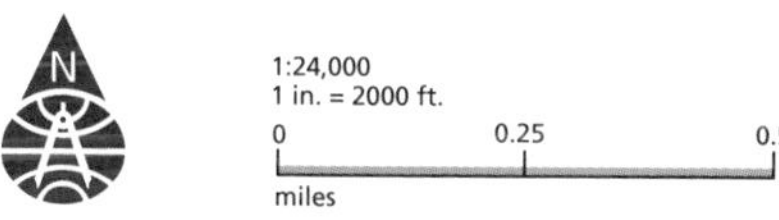

SEE 2758 MAP

Winnetka

Northfield

Wilmette

Glenview

Golf

Skokie

Northfield Township

New Trier Township

SUNSET RIDGE COUNTRY CLUB

WINNETKA GOLF CLUB

WILLIAM N ERICKSON FOREST PRESERVE

SKOKIE LAGOONS

WEST ELM STREET PARK

WILLOW PARK

CLARKSON PARK

NORTHFIELD PARK

CROW ISLAND WOODS

COLE PARK

New Trier HS- Northfield Campus

WILMETTE GOLF CLUB

Loyola Academy

Edens Plaza

NORTH SHORE COUNTRY CLUB

BLUE STAR MEMORIAL WOODS

HIBBARD PARK

North Shore Theater of Wilmette

HARMS WOODS FOREST PRESERVE

CUNLIFF PARK

LAWLER PARK

A
1 Crooked Creek Ln

B
1 Walnut Av
2 Hollendale Villa

C
1 Regent Wood Rd

D
1 Birchwood Ct

E
1 Hudson Rd

F
1 Russett Ln
2 Peach Pkwy

G
1 Crabtree Ln

WILLOW RD · WINNETKA RD · LAKE AV · GLENVIEW RD · OLD ORCHARD RD · ILLINOIS RD · EDENS EXPWY · SKOKIE RD · SKOKIE BLVD · HIBBARD RD · HAPP RD · WAGNER RD · HARMS RD · SUNSET RIDGE RD · CENTRAL AV · FORESTWAY DR · LARAMIE AV · WILMETTE AV · HILL RD

SEE 2810 MAP

SEE 2812 MAP

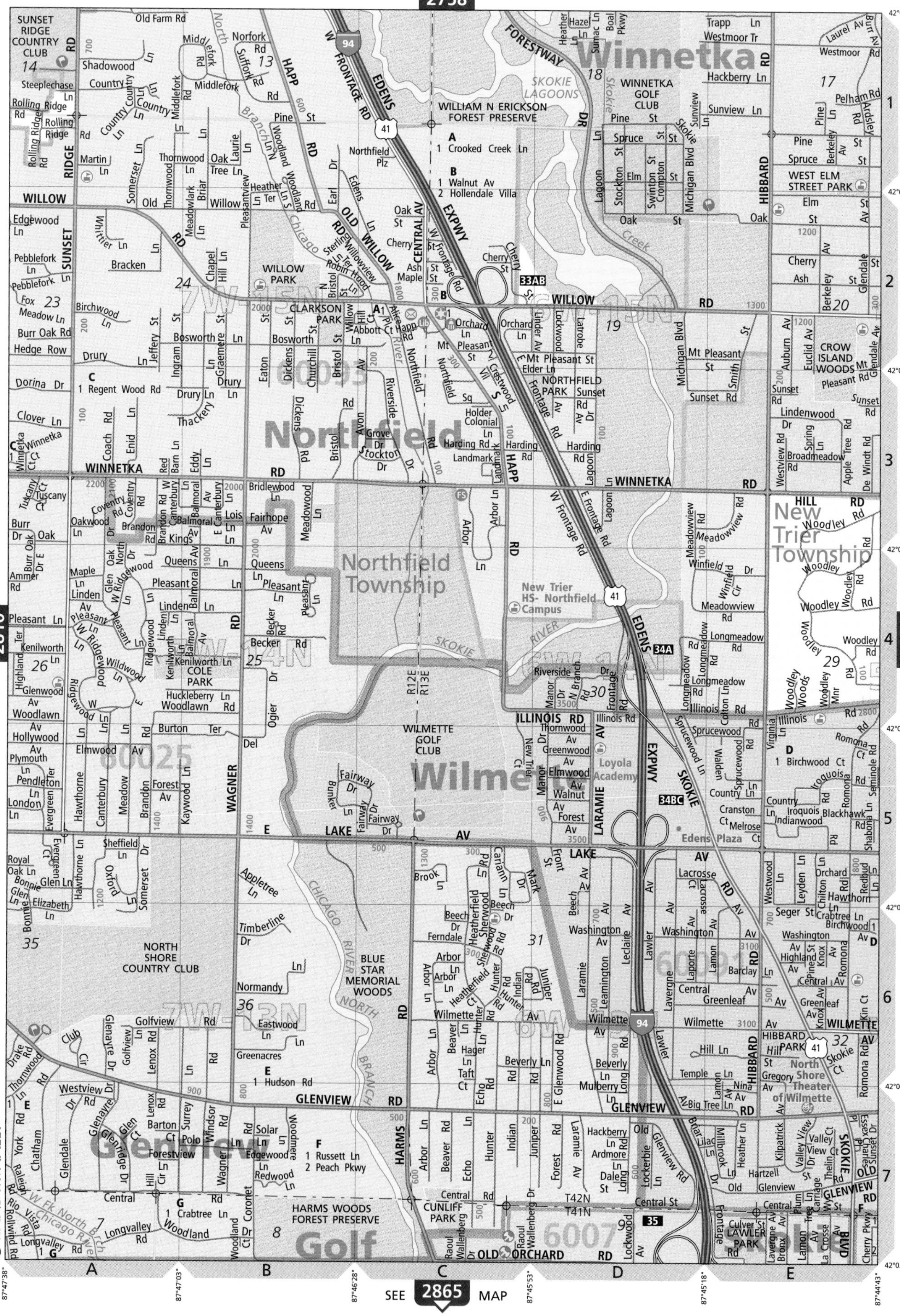

SEE 2865 MAP

1:24,000
1 in. = 2000 ft.
0 0.25 0.5
miles

SEE 2759 MAP

SEE 2811 MAP

SEE 2813 MAP

LAKE MICHIGAN

Winnetka

Kenilworth

Wilmette

Evanston

Skokie

New Trier Township

A
1 Eldorado St
2 Lloyd Pl

B
1 Green Bay Rd

C
1 Richmond Rd

D
1 Michigan Av

E
1 Russett Ln
2 Peach Pkwy

F
1 Wellington Ct

SEE 2866 MAP

1:24,000
1 in. = 2000 ft.
0 0.25 0.5
miles

SEE B MAP

SEE 2812 MAP

SEE B MAP

SEE 2867 MAP

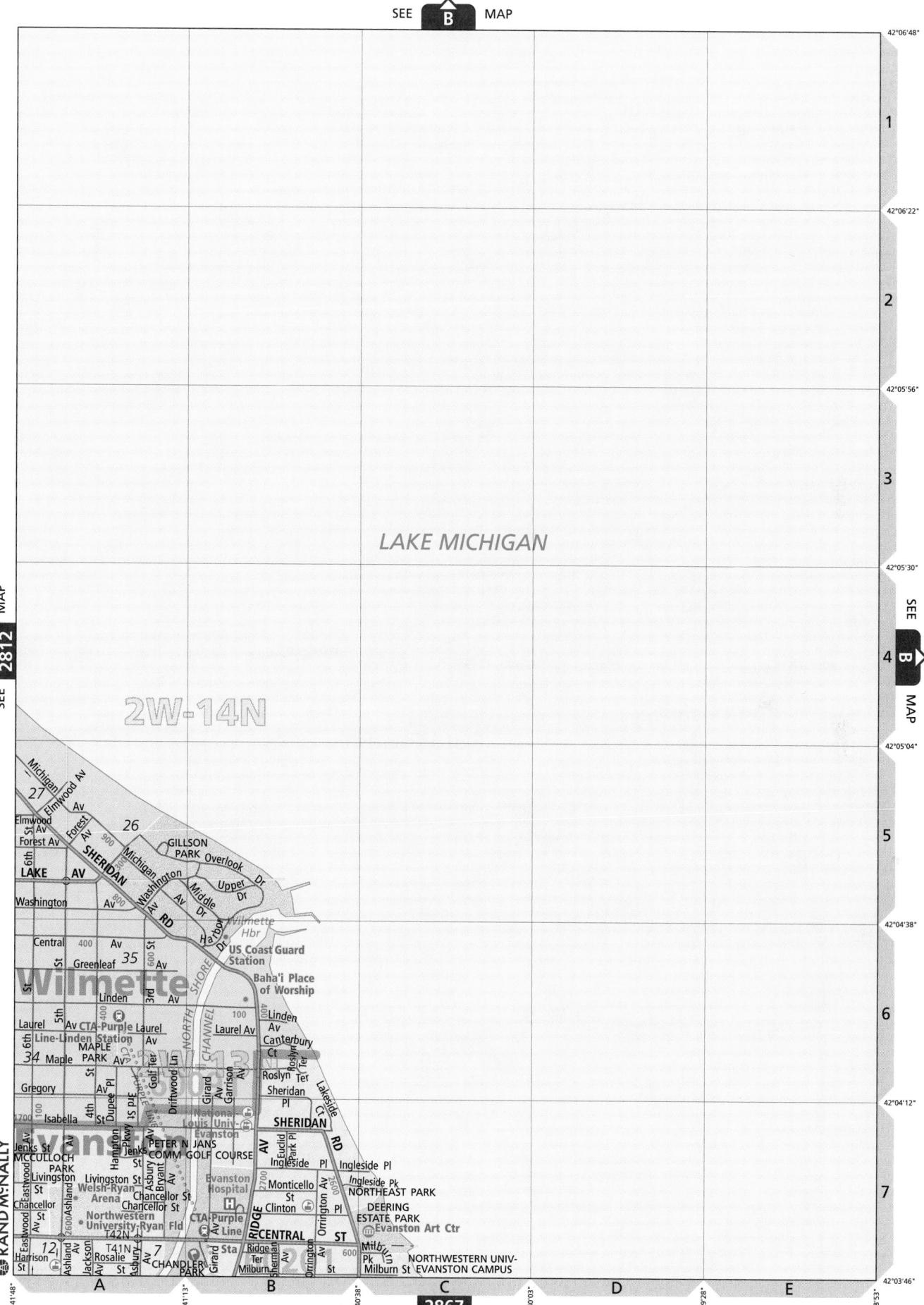

1:24,000
1 in. = 2000 ft.
0 0.25 0.5
miles

SEE 2797 MAP

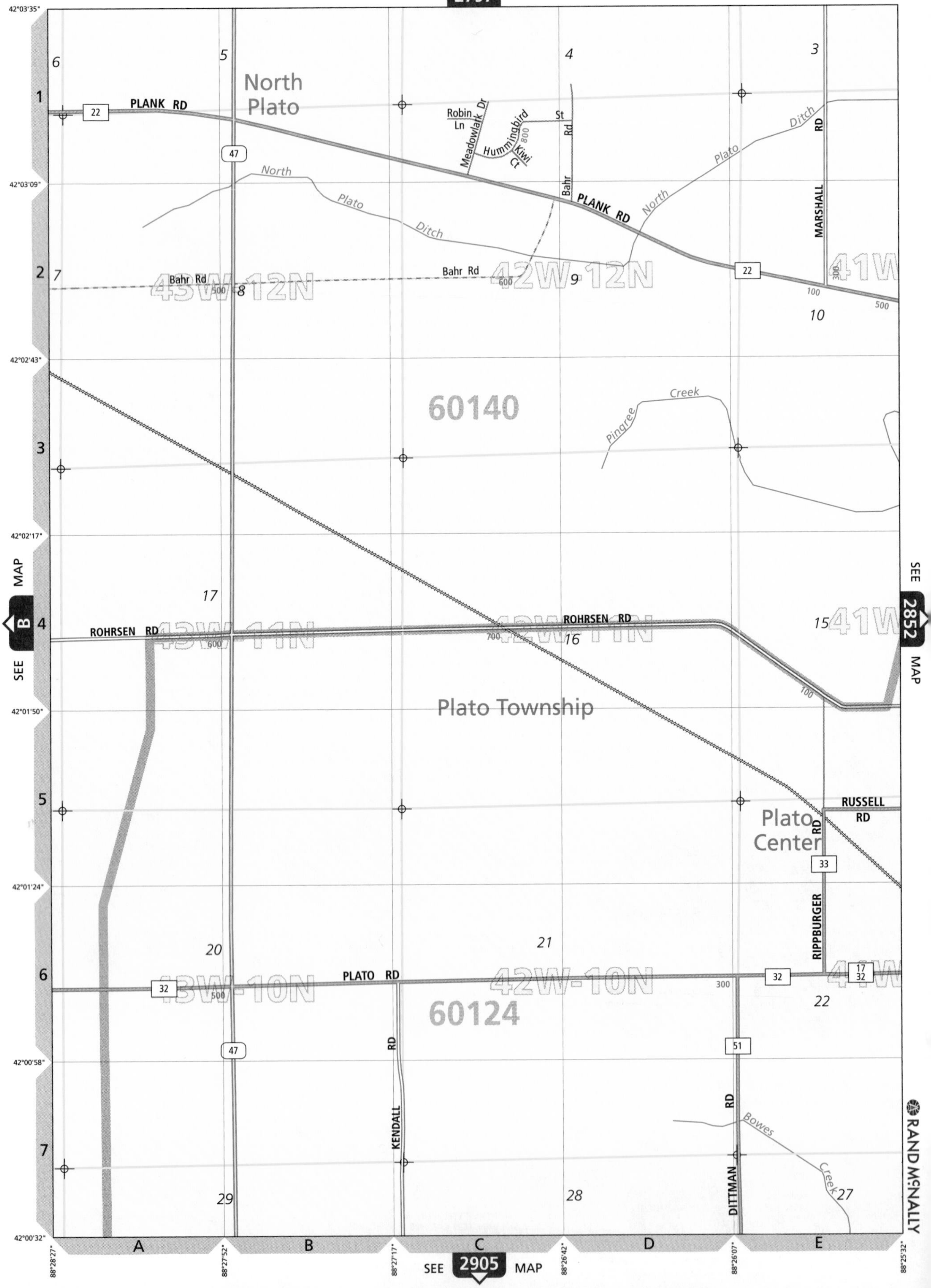

SEE B MAP

SEE 2852 MAP

SEE 2905 MAP

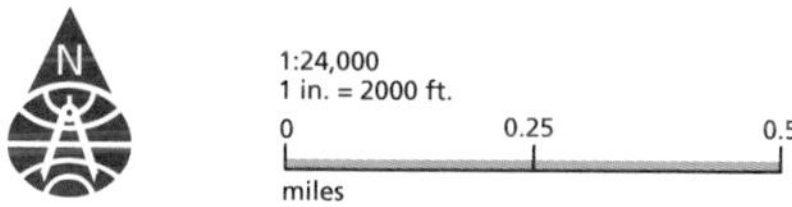

SEE 2798 MAP

Plato Township

60140

60124

Montague Forest

FITCHIE CREEK FOREST PRESERVE

Northwest Baptist Academy

PLANK RD

RUSSELL RD

MUIRHEAD RD

ROHRSEN RD

PLATO RD

BOWES RD

CRAWFORD RD

CORRON RD

NESLER RD

HIGHLAND AV

Switzer Rd

Pingree Rd

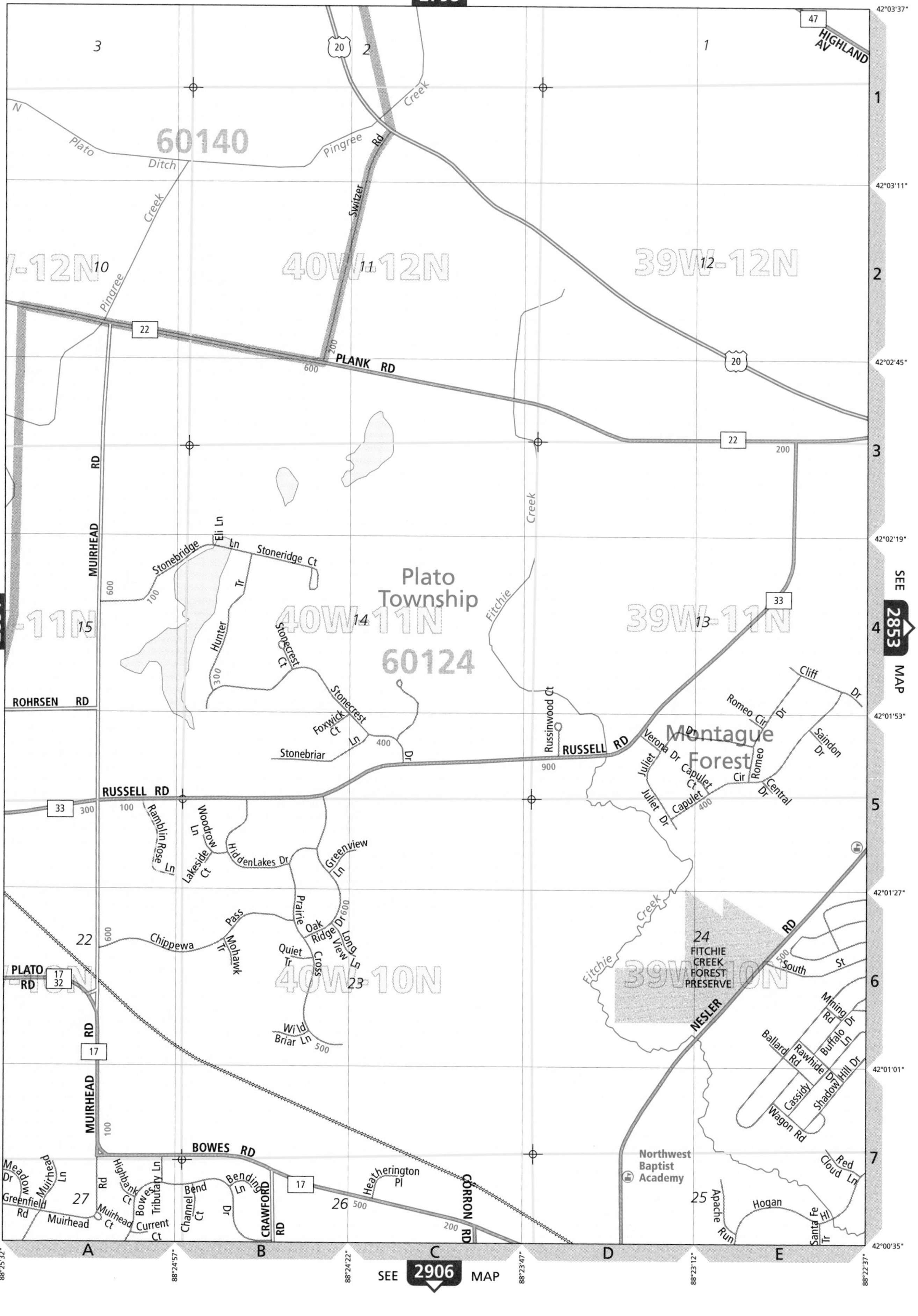

SEE 2851 MAP

SEE 2853 MAP

SEE 2906 MAP

1:24,000
1 in. = 2000 ft.
0 0.25 0.5
miles

SEE 2799 MAP

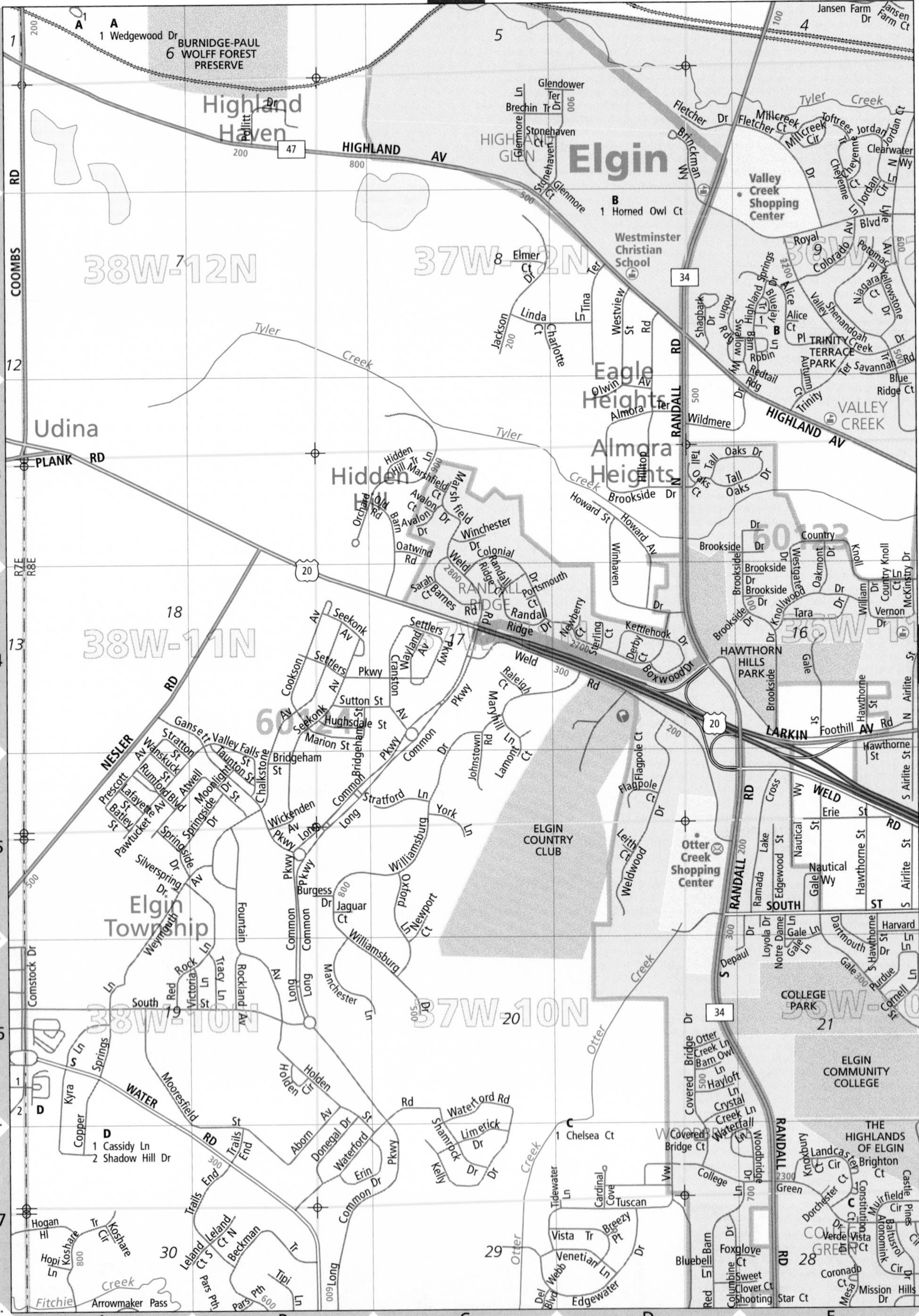

SEE 2852 MAP

SEE 2854 MAP

A
1 Wedgewood Dr

B
1 Horned Owl Ct

C
1 Chelsea Ct

D
1 Cassidy Ln
2 Shadow Hill Dr

BURNIDGE-PAUL WOLFF FOREST PRESERVE

Highland Haven

HIGHLAND GLEN

Elgin

Valley Creek Shopping Center

Westminster Christian School

TRINITY TERRACE PARK

VALLEY CREEK

Eagle Heights

Almora Heights

Udina

Hidden Hill

RANDALL RIDGE

HAWTHORN HILLS PARK

ELGIN COUNTRY CLUB

Otter Creek Shopping Center

Elgin Township

COLLEGE PARK

ELGIN COMMUNITY COLLEGE

THE HIGHLANDS OF ELGIN

WOODBRIDGE

COUNTRY GREEN

38W-12N
37W-12N
36W-12N
38W-11N
37W-11N
36W-11N
38W-10N
37W-10N
36W-10N

60123
60124

HIGHLAND AV
COOMBS RD
PLANK RD
NESLER RD
RANDALL RD
LARKIN AV
WELD RD
SOUTH ST
WATER RD

SEE 2907 MAP

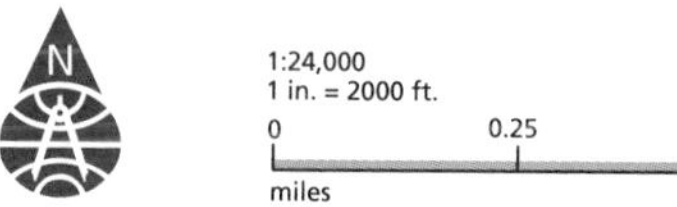

SEE 2800 MAP

SEE 2853 MAP

SEE 2855 MAP

B
1 Dexter Av
2 North St
3 Division St
4 E Highland Av
5 Grove Ct
6 N Grove Av
7 DuPage St
8 Wellington Av

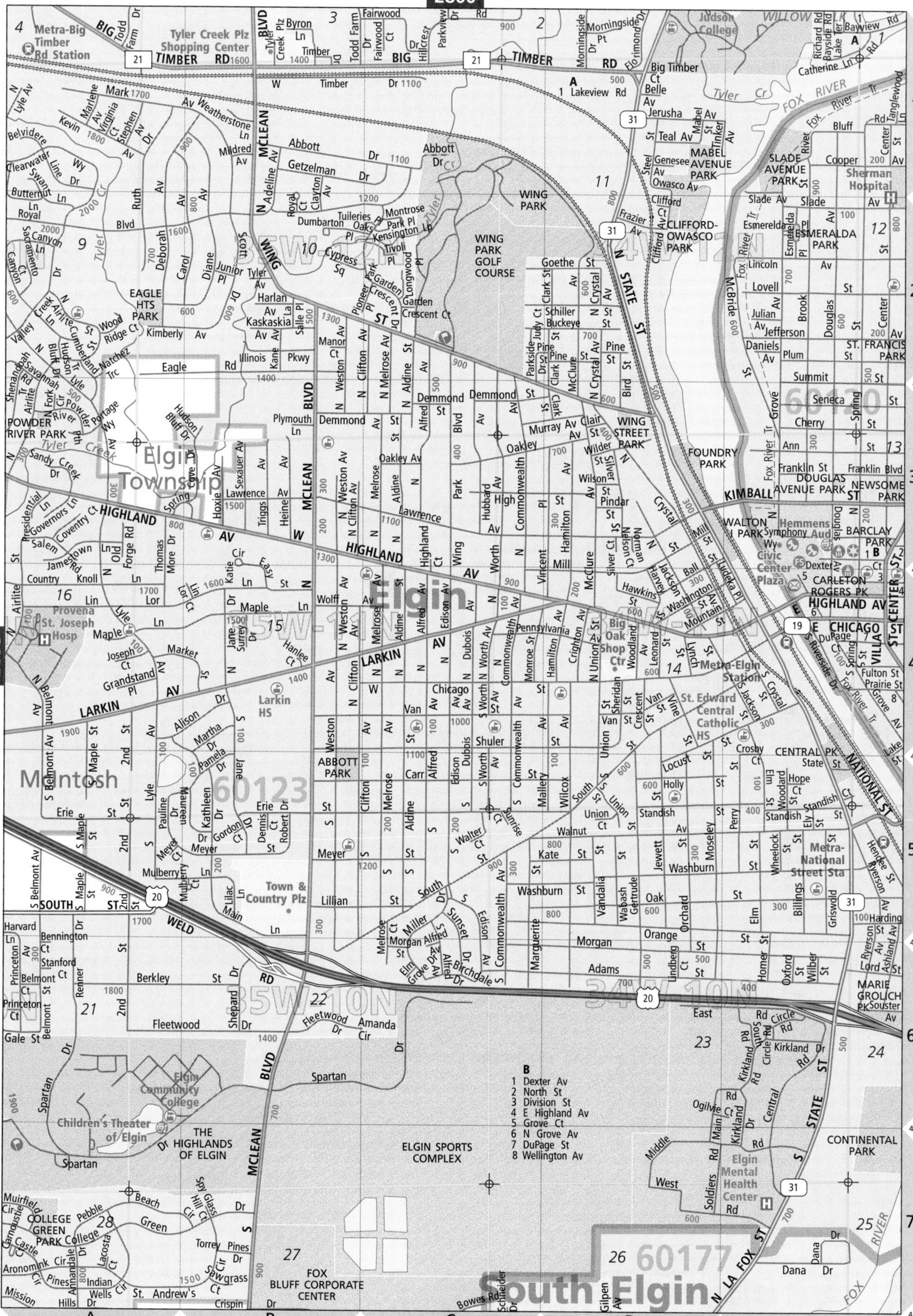

Elgin

South Elgin

Elgin Township

McIntosh

ELGIN SPORTS COMPLEX

FOX BLUFF CORPORATE CENTER

SEE 2908 MAP

1:24,000
1 in. = 2000 ft.
0 0.25 0.5
miles

SEE 2801 MAP

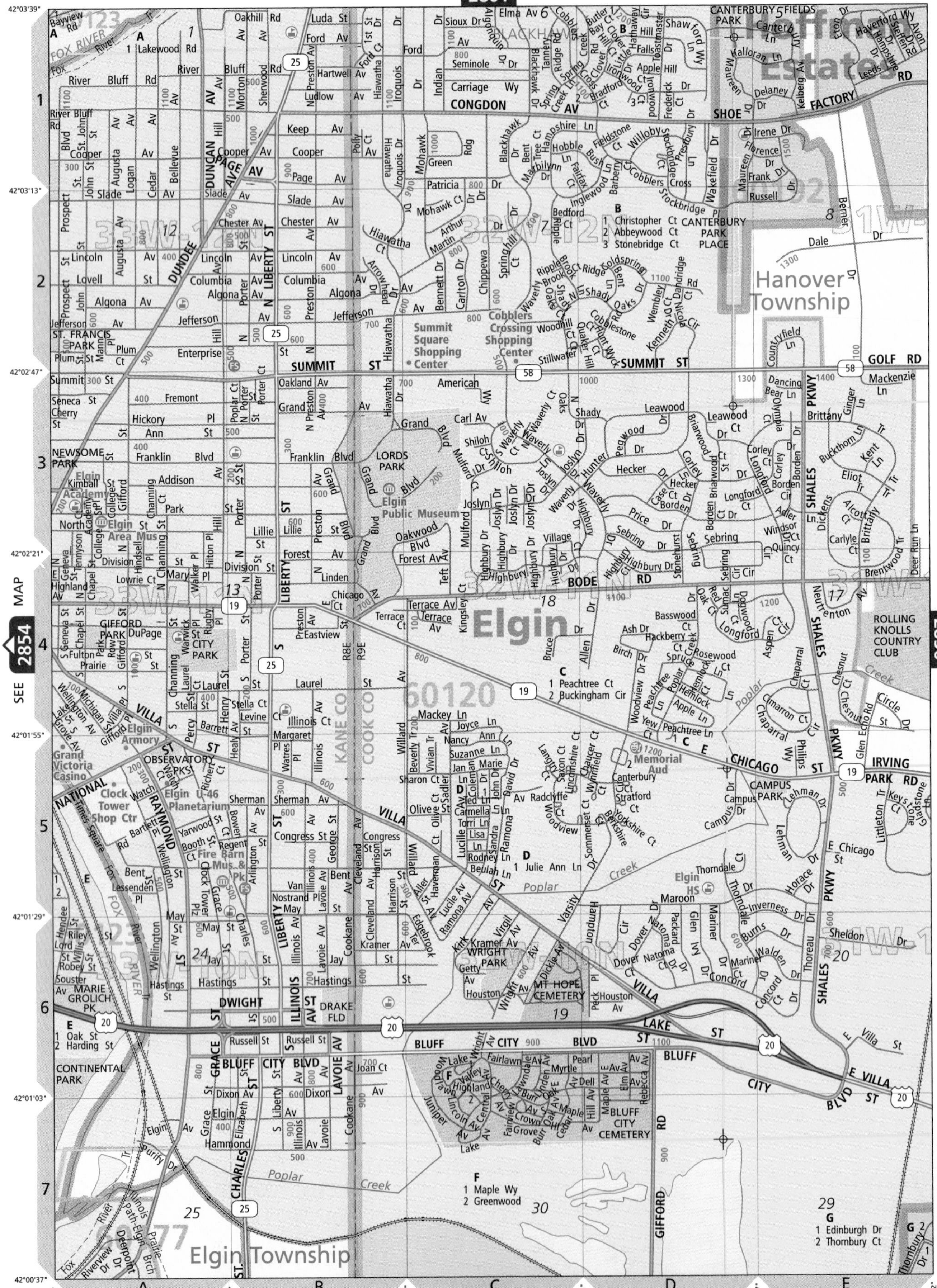

Elgin

Hoffman Estates

Hanover Township

Elgin Township

60120

ROLLING KNOLLS COUNTRY CLUB

A
1 Lakewood Rd

B
1 Christopher Ct
2 Abbeywood Ct
3 Stonebridge Ct

C
1 Peachtree Ct
2 Buckingham Cir

D
1 Julie Ann Ln

E
1 Oak St
2 Harding St

F
1 Maple Wy
2 Greenwood

G
1 Edinburgh Dr
2 Thornbury Ct

SEE 2854 MAP

SEE 2856 MAP

SEE 2909 MAP

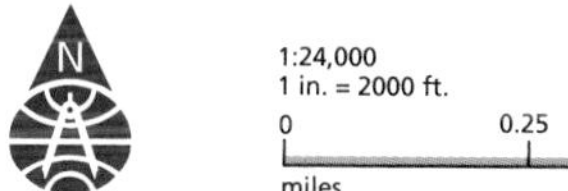

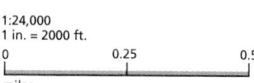

1:24,000
1 in. = 2000 ft.
0 0.25 0.5
miles

SEE 2802 MAP

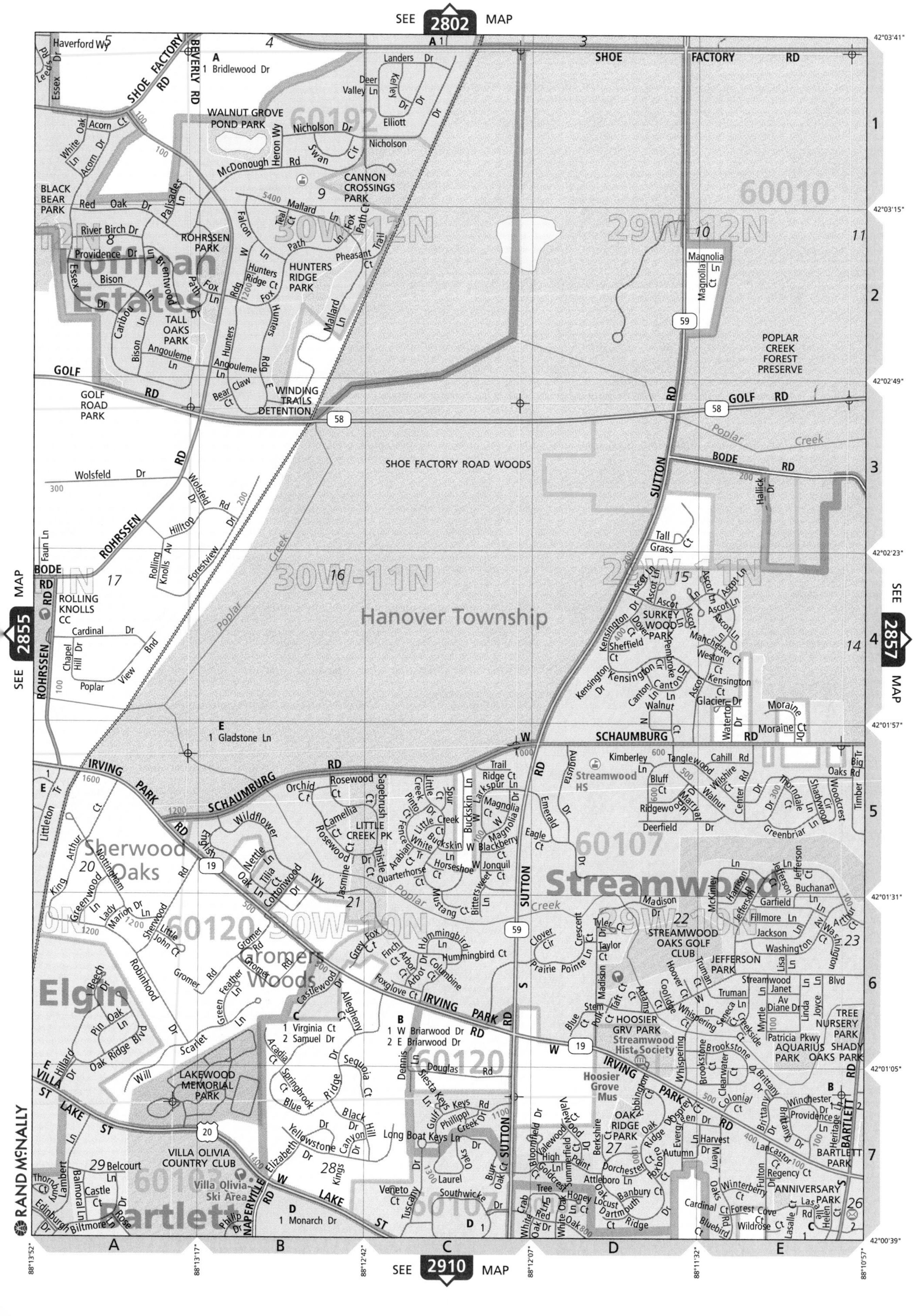

SEE 2855 MAP

SEE 2857 MAP

SEE 2910 MAP

42°03'41" 42°03'15" 42°02'49" 42°02'23" 42°01'57" 42°01'31" 42°01'05" 42°00'39"

88°13'52" 88°13'17" 88°12'42" 88°12'07" 88°11'32" 88°10'57"

A B C D E

1 2 3 4 5 6 7

SHOE FACTORY RD
GOLF RD
BODE RD
SUTTON RD
ROHRSSEN RD
BEVERLY RD
IRVING PARK RD
SCHAUMBURG RD
W SCHAUMBURG RD
W IRVING PARK RD
W LAKE ST
LAKE ST
VILLA ST
NAPERVILLE RD
BARTLETT RD

Hoffman Estates
Streamwood
Elgin
Bartlett
Sherwood Oaks
Gromers Woods
Hanover Township

30W-12N
29W-12N
30W-11N
29W-11N
30W-10N
29W-10N

60192
60010
60107
60120
60103

WALNUT GROVE POND PARK
CANNON CROSSINGS PARK
BLACK BEAR PARK
ROHRSSEN PARK
HUNTERS RIDGE PARK
TALL OAKS PARK
GOLF ROAD PARK
WINDING TRAILS DETENTION
POPLAR CREEK FOREST PRESERVE
SHOE FACTORY ROAD WOODS
ROLLING KNOLLS CC
SURKEY WOOD PARK
LITTLE CREEK PK
Streamwood HS
STREAMWOOD OAKS GOLF CLUB
JEFFERSON PARK
HOOSIER GRV PARK
Streamwood Hist. Society
Hoosier Grove Mus
AQUARIUS PARK
TREE NURSERY PARK
SHADY OAKS PARK
OAK RIDGE PARK
BARTLETT PARK
ANNIVERSARY PARK
LAKEWOOD MEMORIAL PARK
VILLA OLIVIA COUNTRY CLUB
Villa Olivia Ski Area

A
1 Bridlewood Dr

B
1 W Briarwood Dr
2 E Briarwood Dr

C
1 Virginia Ct
2 Samuel Dr

D
1 Monarch Dr

E
1 Gladstone Ln

Poplar Creek

1:24,000
1 in. = 2000 ft.
0 0.25 0.5
miles

SEE 2803 MAP

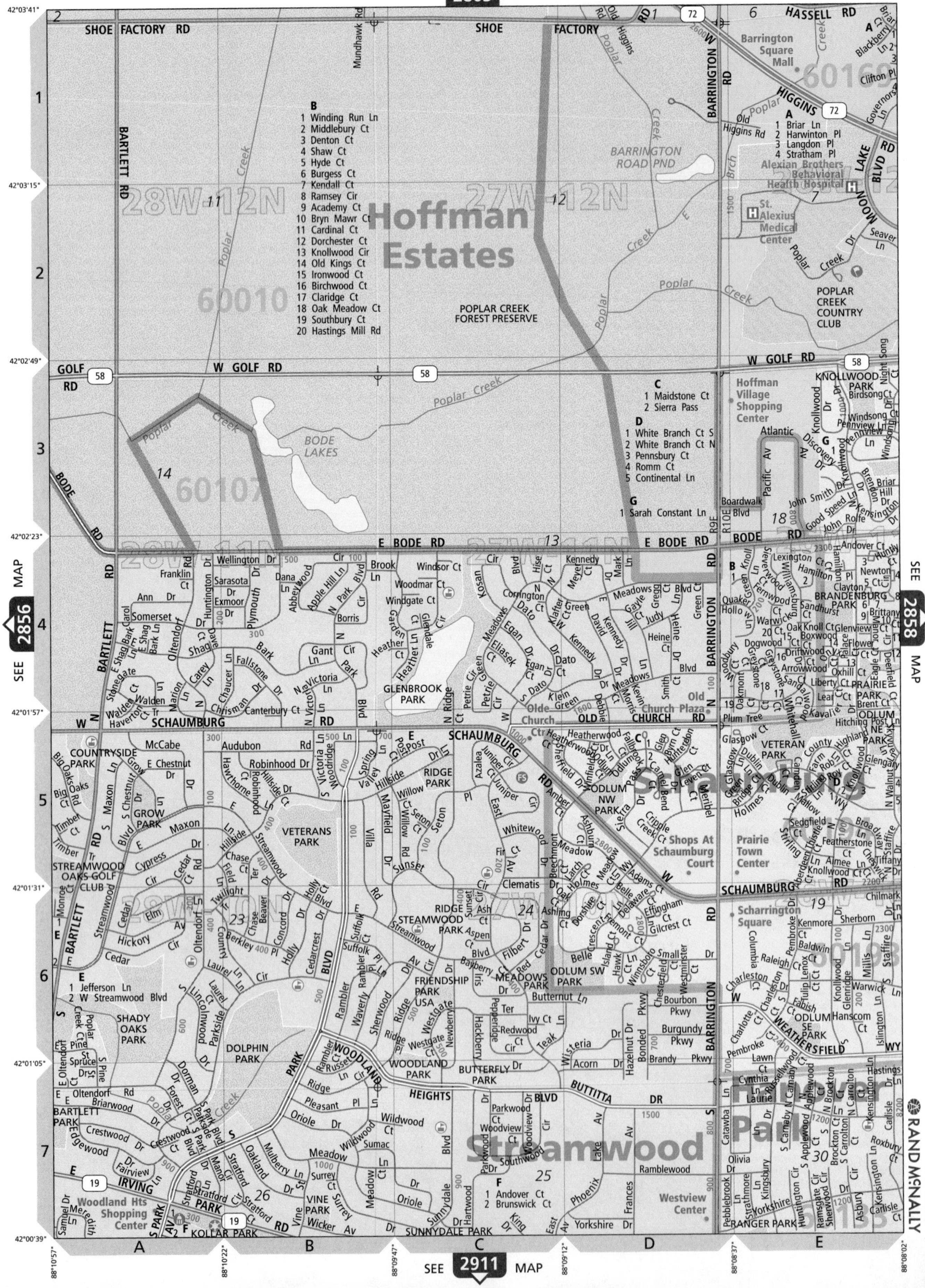

Hoffman Estates

B
1 Winding Run Ln
2 Middlebury Ct
3 Denton Ct
4 Shaw Ct
5 Hyde Ct
6 Burgess Ct
7 Kendall Ct
8 Ramsey Cir
9 Academy Ct
10 Bryn Mawr Ct
11 Cardinal Ct
12 Dorchester Ct
13 Knollwood Cir
14 Old Kings Ct
15 Ironwood Ct
16 Birchwood Ct
17 Claridge Ct
18 Oak Meadow Ct
19 Southbury Ct
20 Hastings Mill Rd

A
1 Briar Ln
2 Harwinton Pl
3 Langdon Pl
4 Stratham Pl

C
1 Maidstone Ct
2 Sierra Pass

D
1 White Branch Ct S
2 White Branch Ct N
3 Pennsbury Ct
4 Romm Ct
5 Continental Ln

G
1 Sarah Constant Ln

E
1 Jefferson Ln
2 W Streamwood Blvd

F
1 Andover Ct
2 Brunswick Ct

POPLAR CREEK FOREST PRESERVE

Schaumburg

Streamwood

Hanover Park

SEE 2856 MAP

SEE 2858 MAP

SEE 2911 MAP

1:24,000
1 in. = 2000 ft.
0 0.25 0.5
miles

SEE 2804 MAP

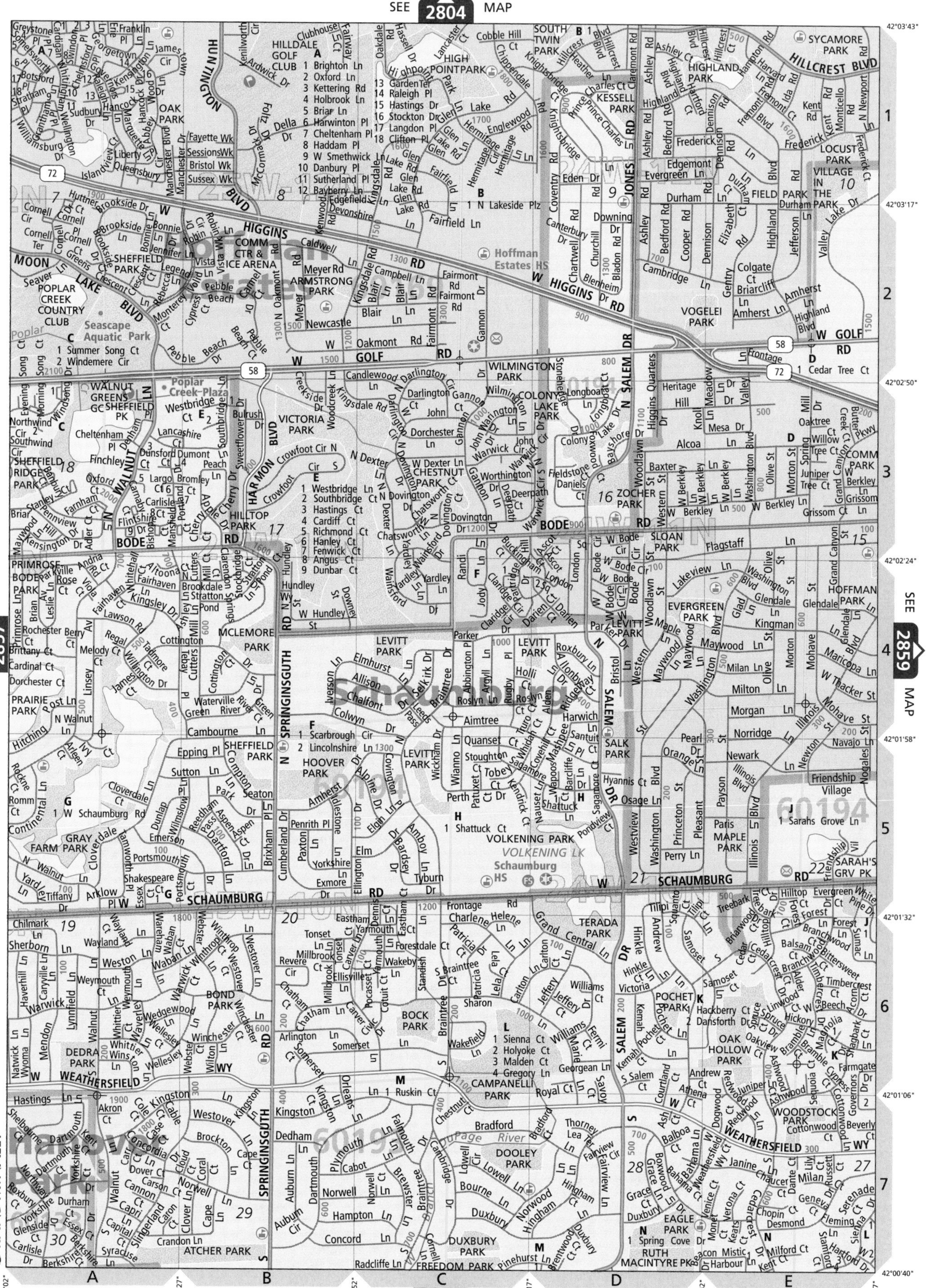

SEE 2857 MAP

SEE 2859 MAP

SEE 2912 MAP

1:24,000
1 in. = 2000 ft.
0 0.25 0.5
miles

SEE 2805 MAP

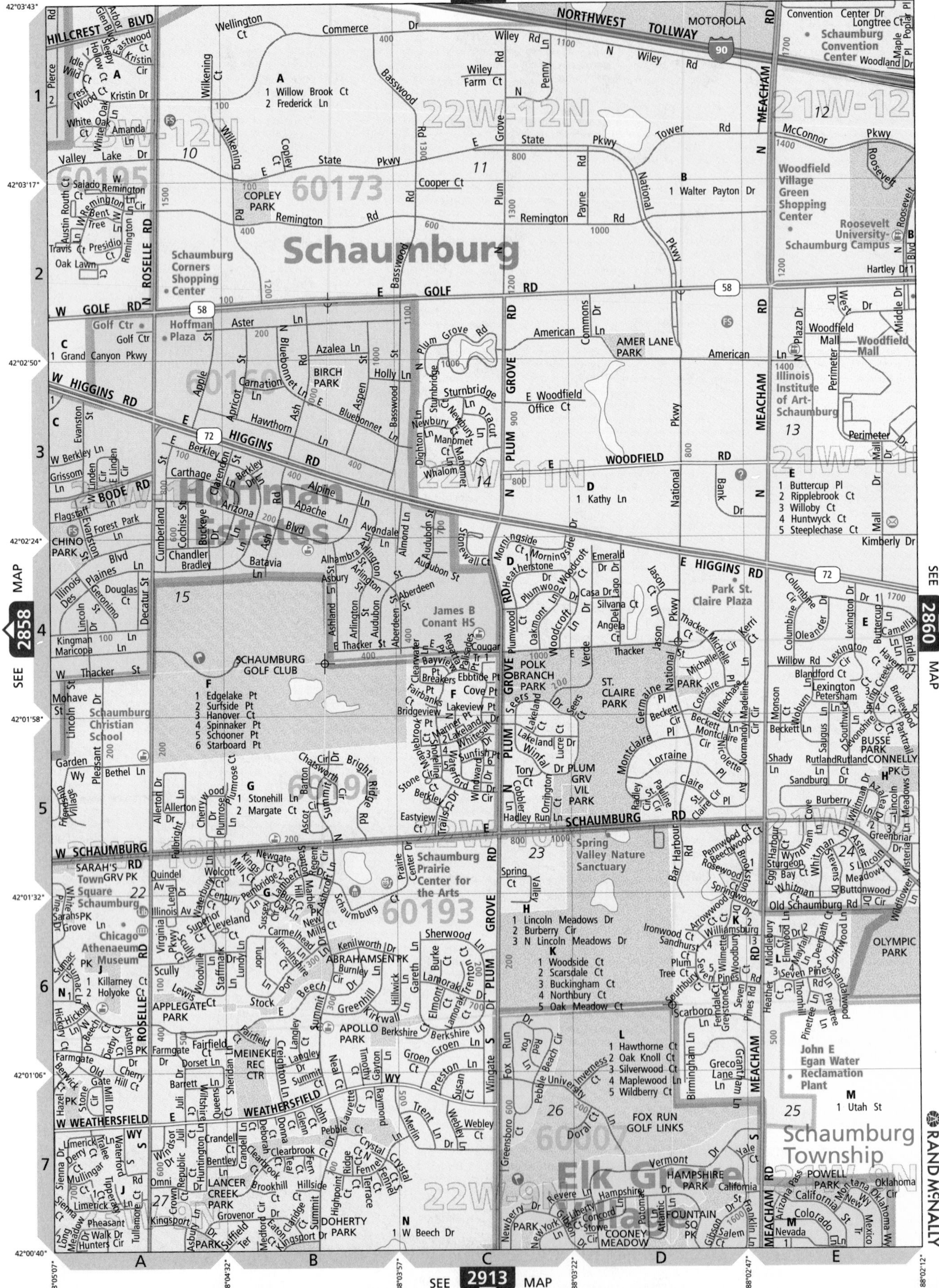

Schaumburg

Hoffman Estates

Elk Grove Village

Schaumburg Township

A
1 Willow Brook Ct
2 Frederick Ln

B
1 Walter Payton Dr

C
1 Grand Canyon Pkwy

D
1 Kathy Ln

E
1 Buttercup Pl
2 Ripplebrook Ct
3 Willoby Ct
4 Huntwyck Ct
5 Steeplechase Ct

F
1 Edgelake Pt
2 Surfside Pt
3 Hanover Ct
4 Spinnaker Pt
5 Schooner Pt
6 Starboard Pt

G
1 Stonehill Ln
2 Margate Ct

H
1 Lincoln Meadows Dr
2 Burberry Cir
3 N Lincoln Meadows Dr

J
1 Killarney Ct
2 Holyoke Ct

K
1 Woodside Ct
2 Scarsdale Ct
3 Buckingham Ct
4 Northbury Ct
5 Oak Meadow Ct

L
1 Hawthorne Ct
2 Oak Knoll Ct
3 Silverwood Ct
4 Maplewood Ln
5 Wildberry Ct

M
1 Utah St

N
1 W Beech Dr

Schaumburg Corners Shopping Center
Woodfield Village Green Shopping Center
Roosevelt University-Schaumburg Campus
Schaumburg Convention Center
Woodfield Mall
Illinois Institute of Art-Schaumburg
James B Conant HS
Schaumburg Golf Club
Schaumburg Christian School
Schaumburg Prairie Center for the Arts
Spring Valley Nature Sanctuary
Chicago Athenaeum Museum
John E Egan Water Reclamation Plant
Fox Run Golf Links
Olympic Park

SEE 2858 MAP

SEE 2860 MAP

SEE 2913 MAP

1:24,000
1 in. = 2000 ft.
0 0.25 0.5
miles

SEE 2806 MAP

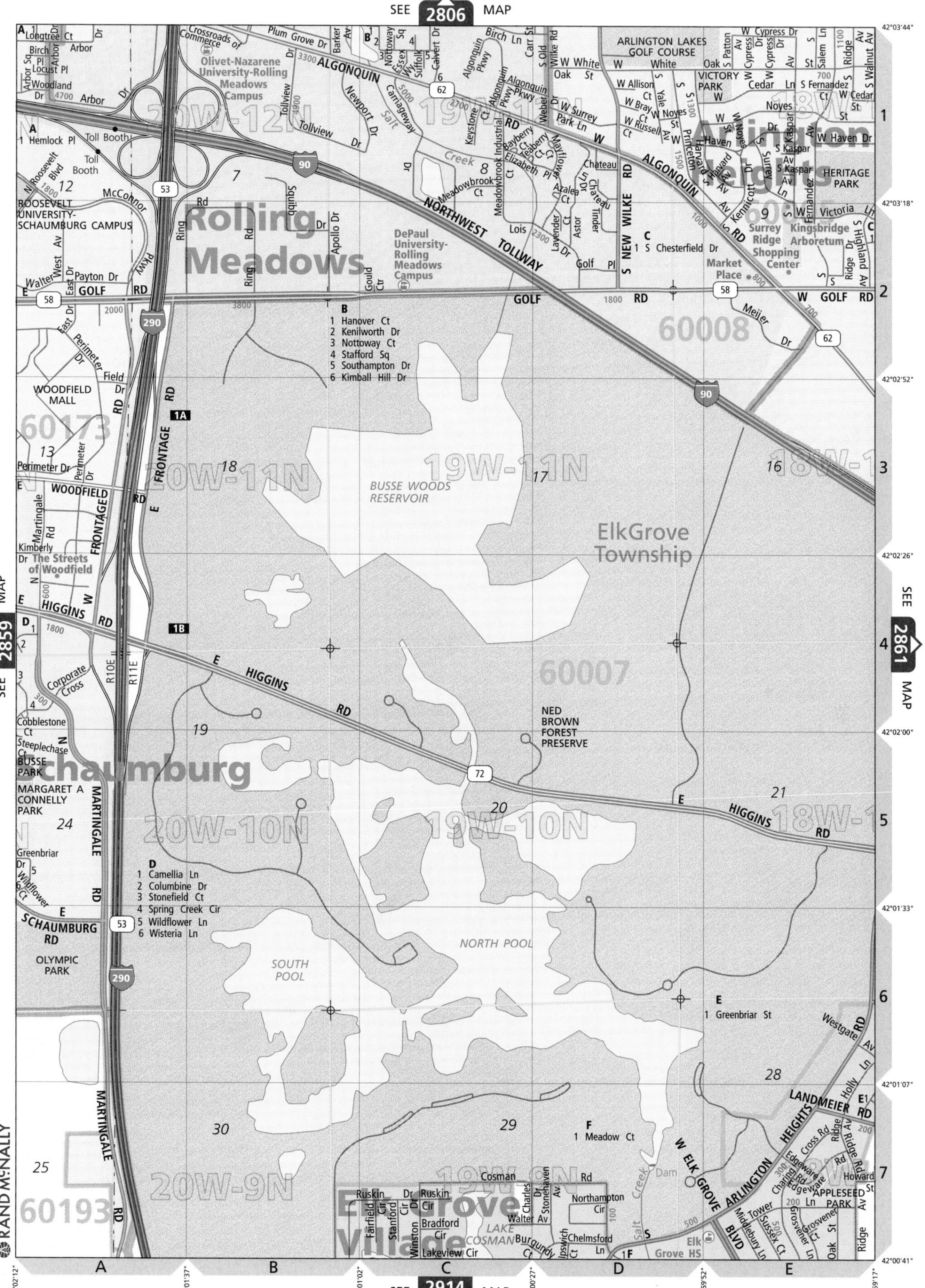

SEE 2859 MAP

SEE 2861 MAP

SEE 2914 MAP

1:24,000
1 in. = 2000 ft.
0 0.25 0.5
miles

SEE 2807 MAP

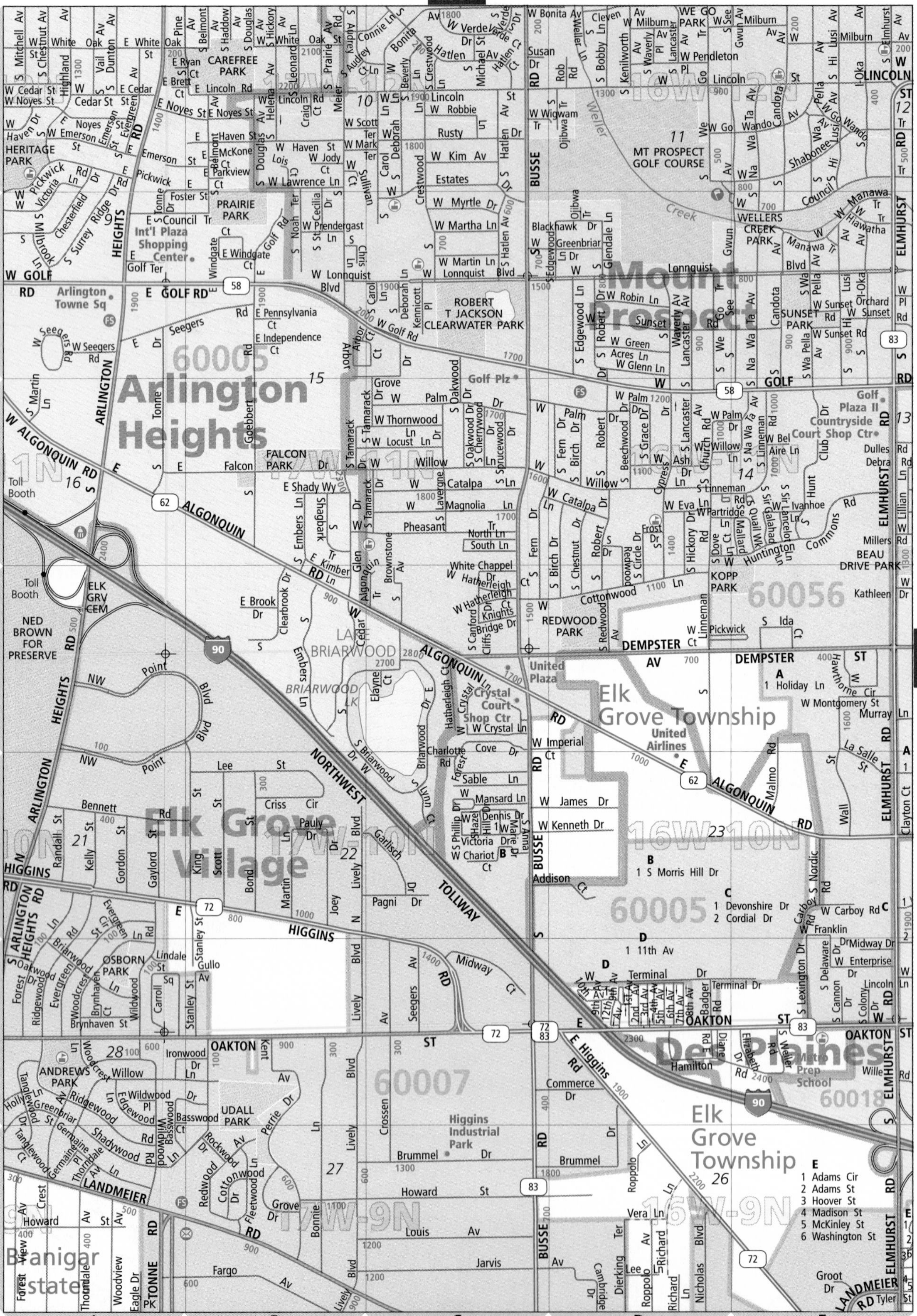

Arlington Heights

Mount Prospect

Elk Grove Village

Des Plaines

Elk Grove Township

60005

60056

60007

60018

MT PROSPECT GOLF COURSE

ROBERT T JACKSON CLEARWATER PARK

NED BROWN FOR PRESERVE

Higgins Industrial Park

United Airlines

Int'l Plaza Shopping Center

Arlington Towne Sq

Golf Plz

Golf Plaza II

Countryside Court Shop Ctr

United Plaza

Crystal Court Shop Ctr

ALGONQUIN RD

NORTHWEST TOLLWAY

HIGGINS

OAKTON ST

DEMPSTER

GOLF RD

ARLINGTON HEIGHTS RD

BUSSE RD

ELMHURST RD

LANDMEIER RD

A
1 Holiday Ln

B
1 S Morris Hill Dr

C
1 Devonshire Dr
2 Cordial Dr

D
1 11th Av

E
1 Adams Cir
2 Adams St
3 Hoover St
4 Madison St
5 McKinley St
6 Washington St

SEE 2860 MAP

SEE 2862 MAP

SEE 2915 MAP

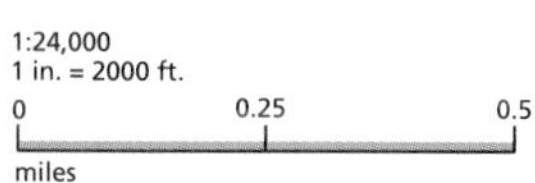

SEE 2808 MAP

Mount Prospect

Des Plaines

Elk Grove Township

NORTHWEST HWY
MT PROSPECT RD
WOLF RD
GOLF RD
STATE ST
BROADWAY
RAND RD
THACKER ST
DEMPSTER ST
ALGONQUIN RD
OAKTON ST
HOWARD AV
MANNHEIM RD
LEE ST
GRACELAND AV
MINER ST
NORTHWEST TOLLWAY
LINCOLN ST
MAIN ST
WILLE RD

LIONS PARK
DIMUCCI PARK
CHEYENNE PARK
CHIPPEWA PARK
CORNELL PARK
ALL SAINTS CEMETERY
FOREST PRESERVE
SUNRISE PARK
NORTHSHIRE PARK
BLACKHAWK PARK
Metra-Cumberland Sta
COUNTRYSIDE PARK
BRENTWOOD PARK
TOMAHAWK PARK
CUMBERLAND TERRACE PARK
MANOR PARK
WEST PARK
BEAU DRIVE PARK
Brentwood Baptist Christian Academy
WAYCINDEN PARK
EINSTEIN PARK
WESTFIELD PARK
PRAIRIE LAKES PARK
MOUNTAIN VIEW PARK
The Willows Academy
FRIENDSHIP PARK CONSERVATORY
DEVONSHIRE PARK
The Oaks Of Des Plaines Shop Ctr
Maine West HS
METRO-MAJESKI ATHLETIC FIELDS
LAKE PARK
LAKE PARK GOLF COURSE
LAKE OPEKA

60056
60016
60018

A
1 College Dr
2 University Dr
3 Village Dr

B
1 Simone Dr

C
1 S Inner Circle Dr

D
1 Little Path Rd

E
1 Ashland Av
2 Campbell Av
3 Whitcomb Av

F
1 Adams Cir

1 2 3 4 5 6 7

A B C D E

42°03'45"
42°03'19"
42°02'53"
42°02'26"
42°02'00"
42°01'34"
42°01'08"
42°00'42"

87°56'22"
87°55'47"
87°55'12"
87°54'37"
87°54'02"
87°53'27"

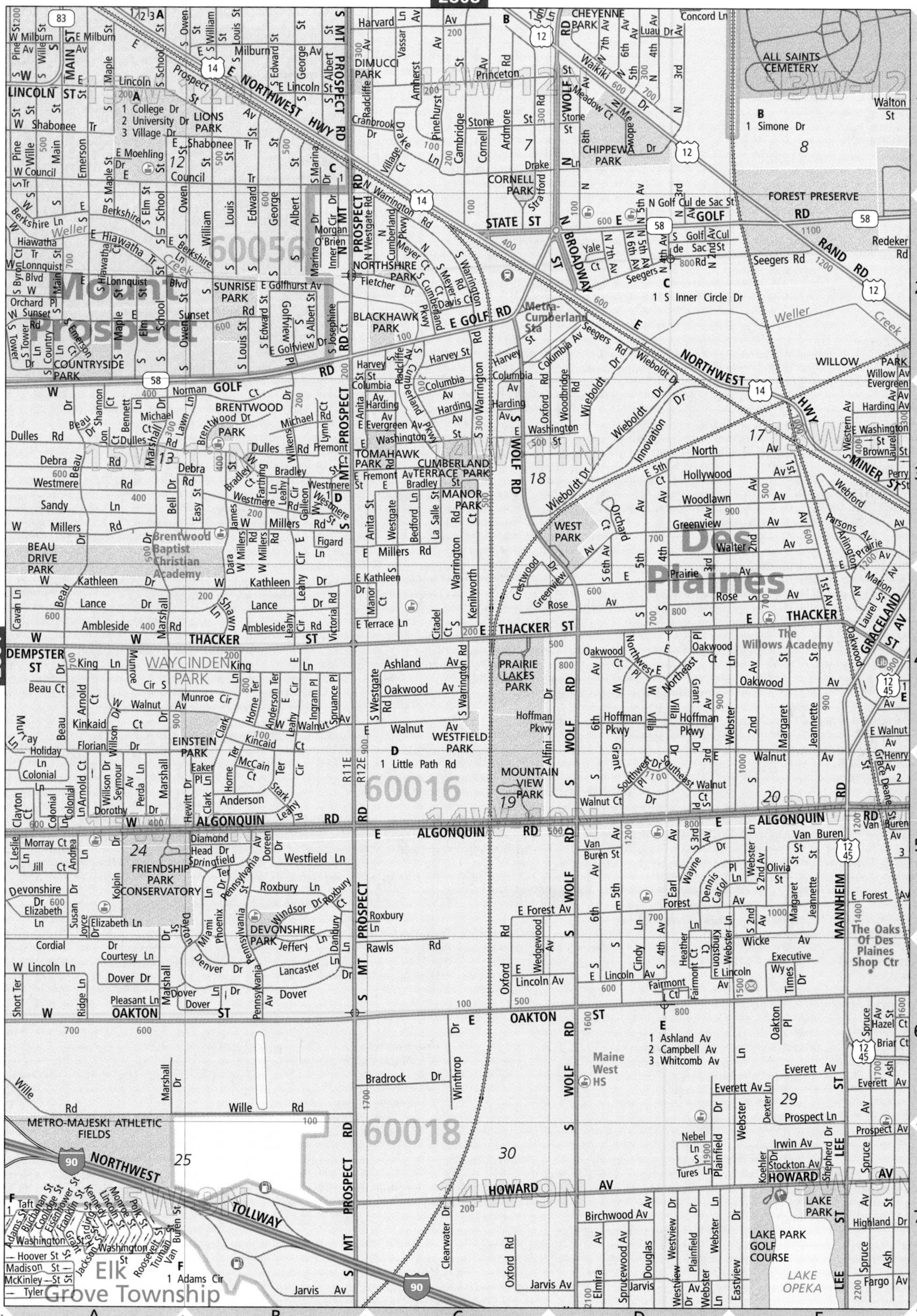

SEE 2861 MAP

SEE 2863 MAP

SEE 2916 MAP

1:24,000
1 in. = 2000 ft.
0 0.25 0.5
miles

SEE 2809 MAP

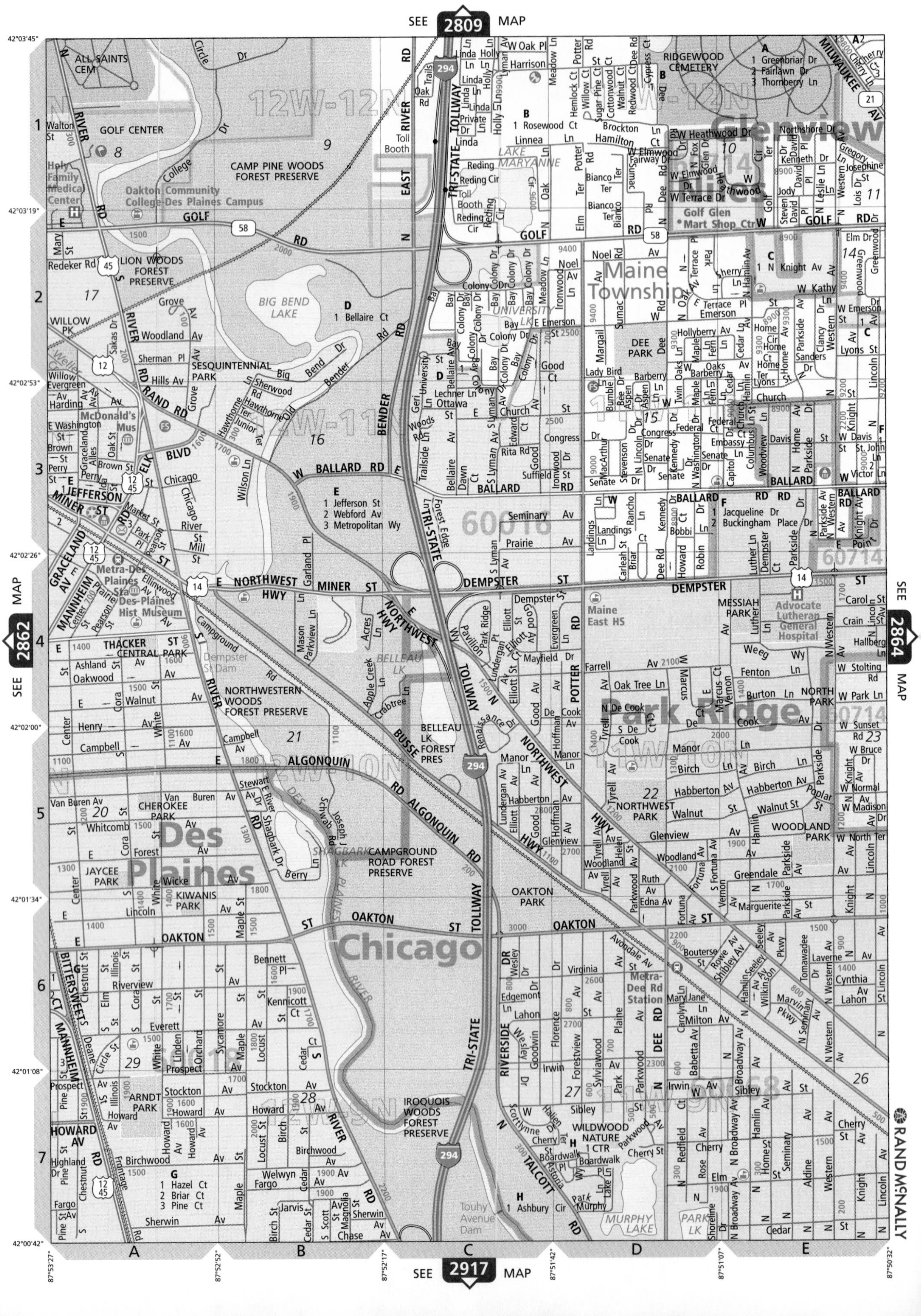

SEE 2862 MAP

SEE 2864 MAP

SEE 2917 MAP

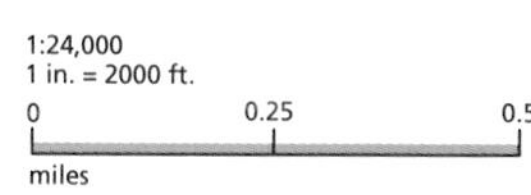

SEE 2810 MAP

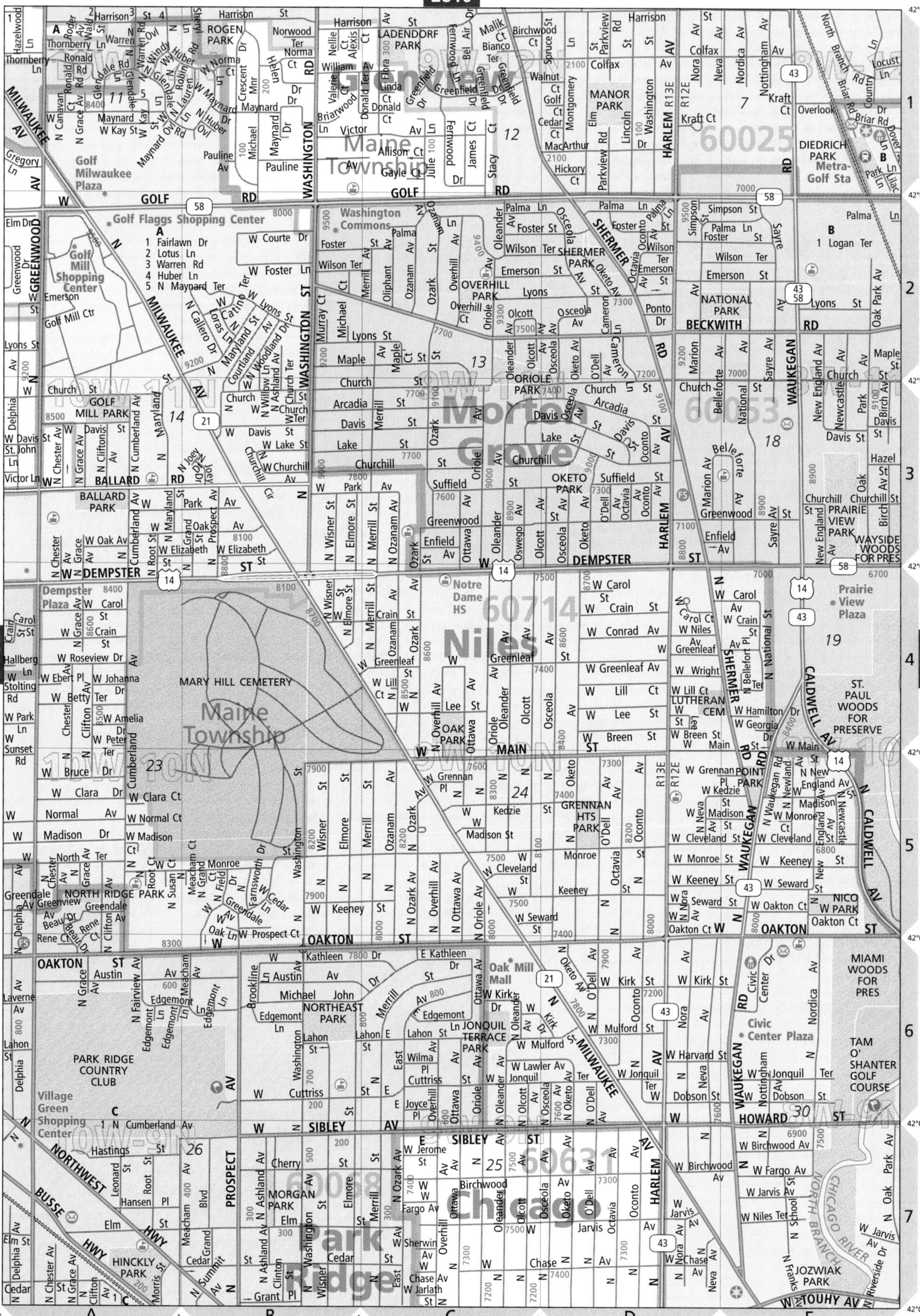

SEE 2863 MAP

SEE 2865 MAP

Glenview

Maine Township

Morton Grove

Niles

Park Ridge

Chicago

A
1 Fairlawn Dr
2 Lotus Ln
3 Warren Rd
4 Huber Ln
5 N Maynard Ter

B
1 Logan Ter

C
1 N Cumberland Av

A B C D E

1 2 3 4 5 6 7

SEE 2918 MAP

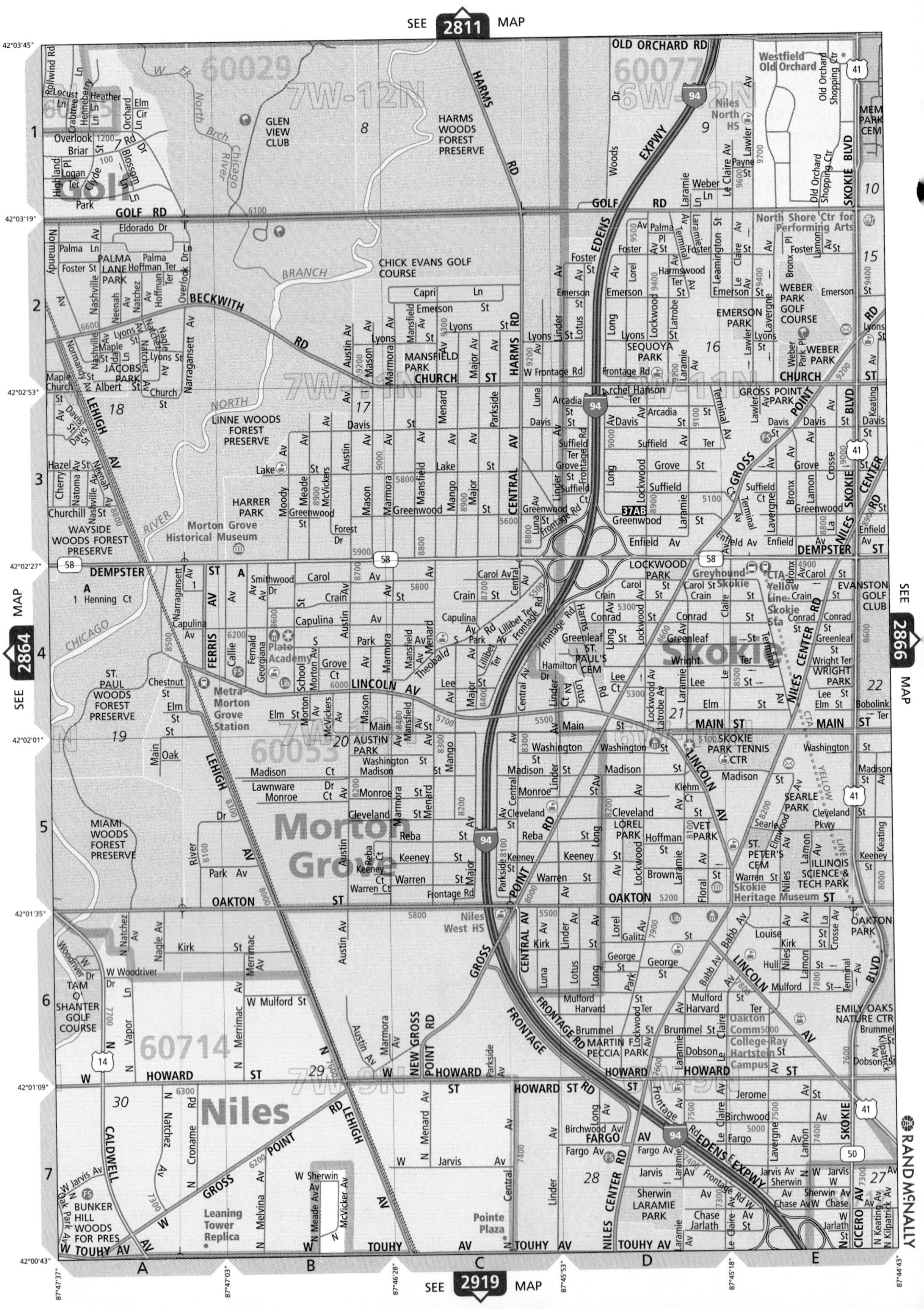

1:24,000
1 in. = 2000 ft.
0 0.25 0.5
miles

SEE 2811 MAP

SEE 2864 MAP

SEE 2866 MAP

SEE 2919 MAP

Golf
Morton Grove
Niles
Skokie

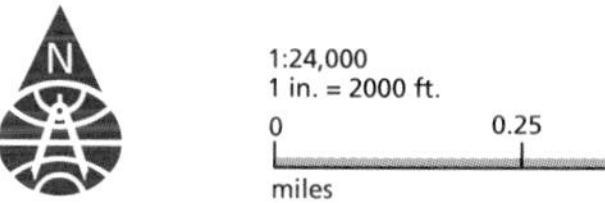

SEE 2812 MAP

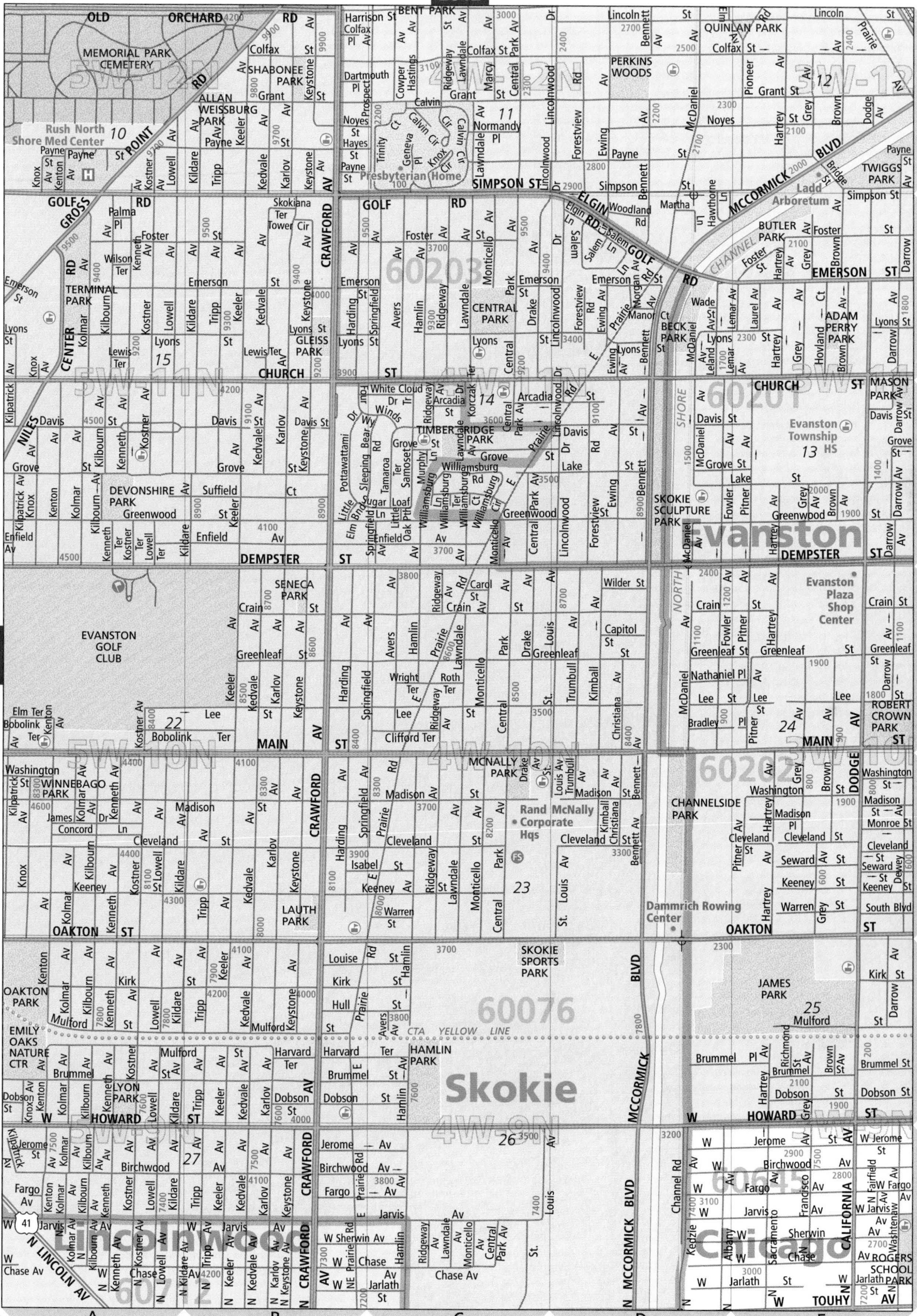

SEE 2865 MAP

SEE 2867 MAP

Evanston

Skokie

Lincolnwood

Chicago

MEMORIAL PARK CEMETERY
SHABONEE PARK
ALLAN WEISSBURG PARK
Rush North Shore Med Center
Presbyterian Home
PERKINS WOODS
QUINLAN PARK
TWIGGS PARK
Ladd Arboretum
BUTLER PARK
TERMINAL PARK
GLEISS PARK
CENTRAL PARK
BECK PARK
ADAM PERRY PARK
MASON PARK
TIMBER RIDGE PARK
DEVONSHIRE PARK
SKOKIE SCULPTURE PARK
Evanston Township HS
EVANSTON GOLF CLUB
SENECA PARK
Evanston Plaza Shop Center
ROBERT CROWN PARK
WINNEBAGO PARK
MCNALLY PARK
Rand McNally Corporate Hqs
CHANNELSIDE PARK
LAUTH PARK
Dammrich Rowing Center
SKOKIE SPORTS PARK
OAKTON PARK
JAMES PARK
EMILY OAKS NATURE CTR
HAMLIN PARK
LYON PARK
ROGERS SCHOOL PARK

OLD ORCHARD RD
GOLF RD
GROSS POINT RD
SIMPSON ST
MCCORMICK BLVD
ELGIN RD
CENTER RD
NILES
CHURCH ST
DEMPSTER ST
MAIN ST
OAKTON ST
HOWARD ST
TOUHY AV
CRAWFORD AV
N LINCOLN AV
CALIFORNIA AV
DODGE AV
NORTH SHORE CHANNEL
CTA YELLOW LINE

60203
60201
60202
60076
60645
60712

5W-12N
4W-12N
3W-12
5W-11N
4W-11N
3W-11
5W-10N
4W-10N
3W-10N
5W-9N
4W-9N
3W-9N

42°03'46"
42°03'20"
42°02'53"
42°02'27"
42°02'01"
42°01'35"
42°01'09"
42°00'43"

87°44'43"
87°44'08"
87°43'33"
87°42'58"
87°42'23"
87°41'48"

A
B
C
D
E

1
2
3
4
5
6
7

SEE 2920 MAP

1:24,000
1 in. = 2000 ft.
0 0.25 0.5
miles

SEE 2813 MAP

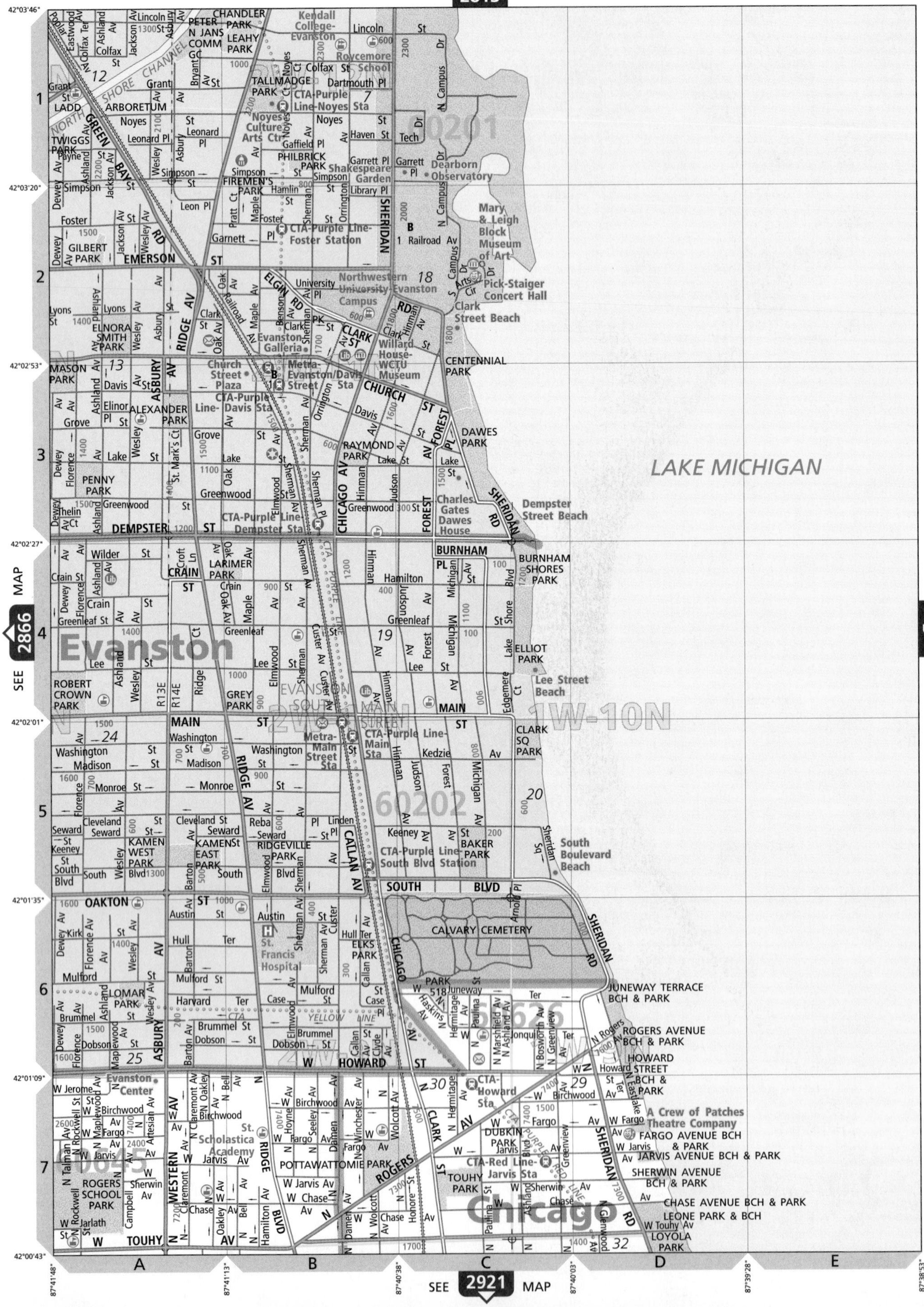

SEE 2866 MAP

SEE B MAP

LAKE MICHIGAN

Evanston

Chicago

60201

60202

60626

60645

1W-10N

Northwestern University-Evanston Campus

Kendall College-Evanston

Roycemore School

Noyes Culture Arts Ctr

Shakespeare Garden

Dearborn Observatory

Mary & Leigh Block Museum of Art

Pick-Staiger Concert Hall

Clark Street Beach

Evanston Galleria

Willard House-WCTU Museum

Church Street Plaza

CTA-Purple Line-Noyes Sta

CTA-Purple Line-Foster Station

CTA-Purple Line-Davis Sta

Metra-Evanston/Davis Street Sta

CTA-Purple Line-Dempster Sta

CTA-Purple Line-Main Sta

Metra-Main Street Sta

CTA-Purple Line South Blvd Station

CTA-Howard Sta

CTA-Red Line-Jarvis Sta

Charles Gates Dawes House

Dempster Street Beach

Lee Street Beach

South Boulevard Beach

St. Francis Hospital

CALVARY CEMETERY

Evanston Center

St. Scholastica Academy

A Crew of Patches Theatre Company

JUNEWAY TERRACE BCH & PARK

ROGERS AVENUE BCH & PARK

HOWARD STREET BCH & PARK

FARGO AVENUE BCH & PARK

JARVIS AVENUE BCH & PARK

SHERWIN AVENUE BCH & PARK

CHASE AVENUE BCH & PARK

LEONE PARK & BCH

LOYOLA PARK

42°03'46" 42°03'20" 42°02'53" 42°02'27" 42°02'01" 42°01'35" 42°01'09" 42°00'43"

87°41'48" 87°41'13" 87°40'38" 87°40'03" 87°39'28" 87°38'53"

A B C D E

1 2 3 4 5 6 7

1:24,000
1 in. = 2000 ft.
0 0.25 0.5
miles

SEE 2851 MAP

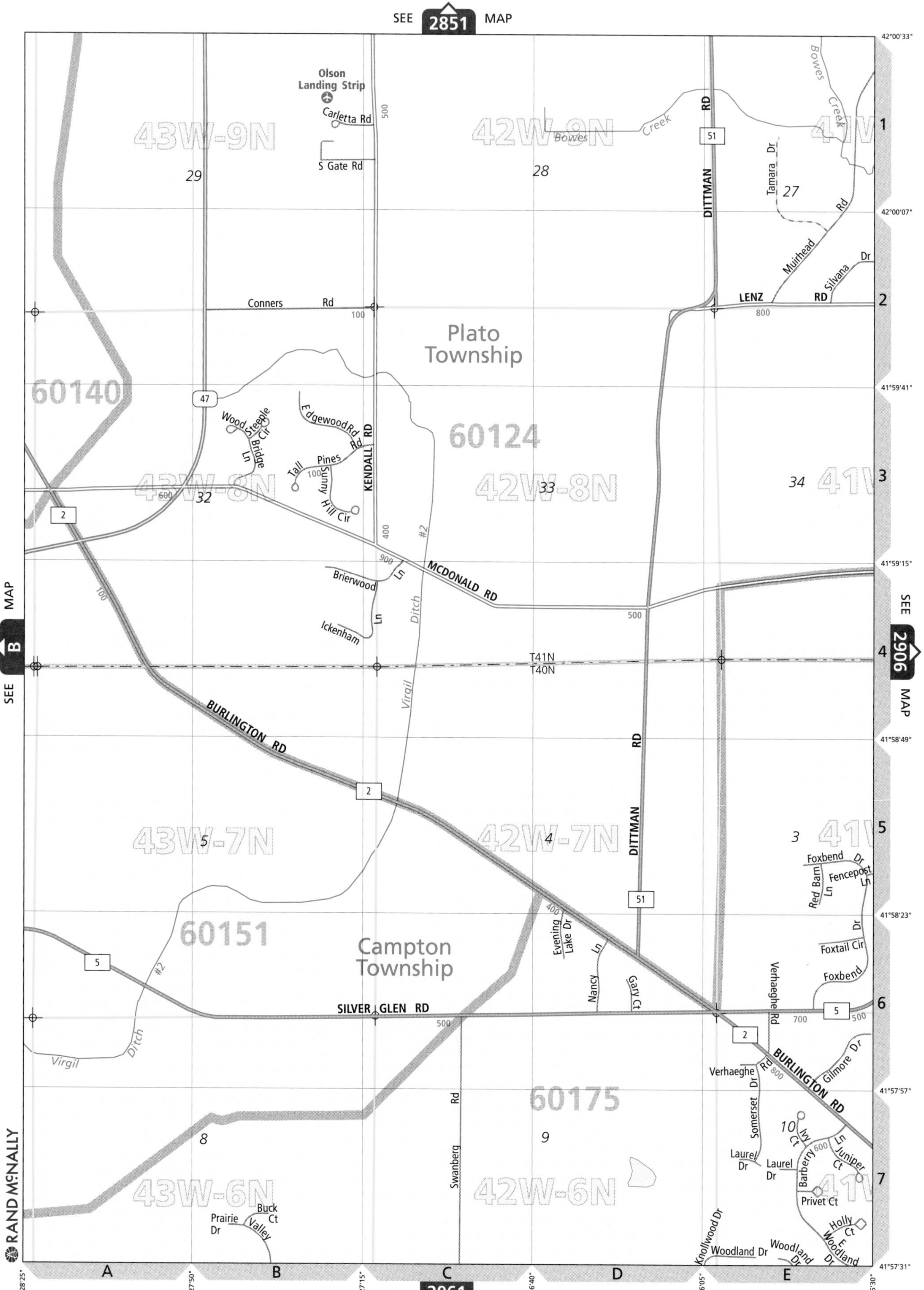

SEE B MAP

SEE 2906 MAP

SEE 2961 MAP

1:24,000
1 in. = 2000 ft.
0 0.25 0.5
miles

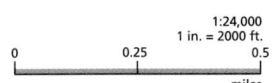

SEE 2852 MAP

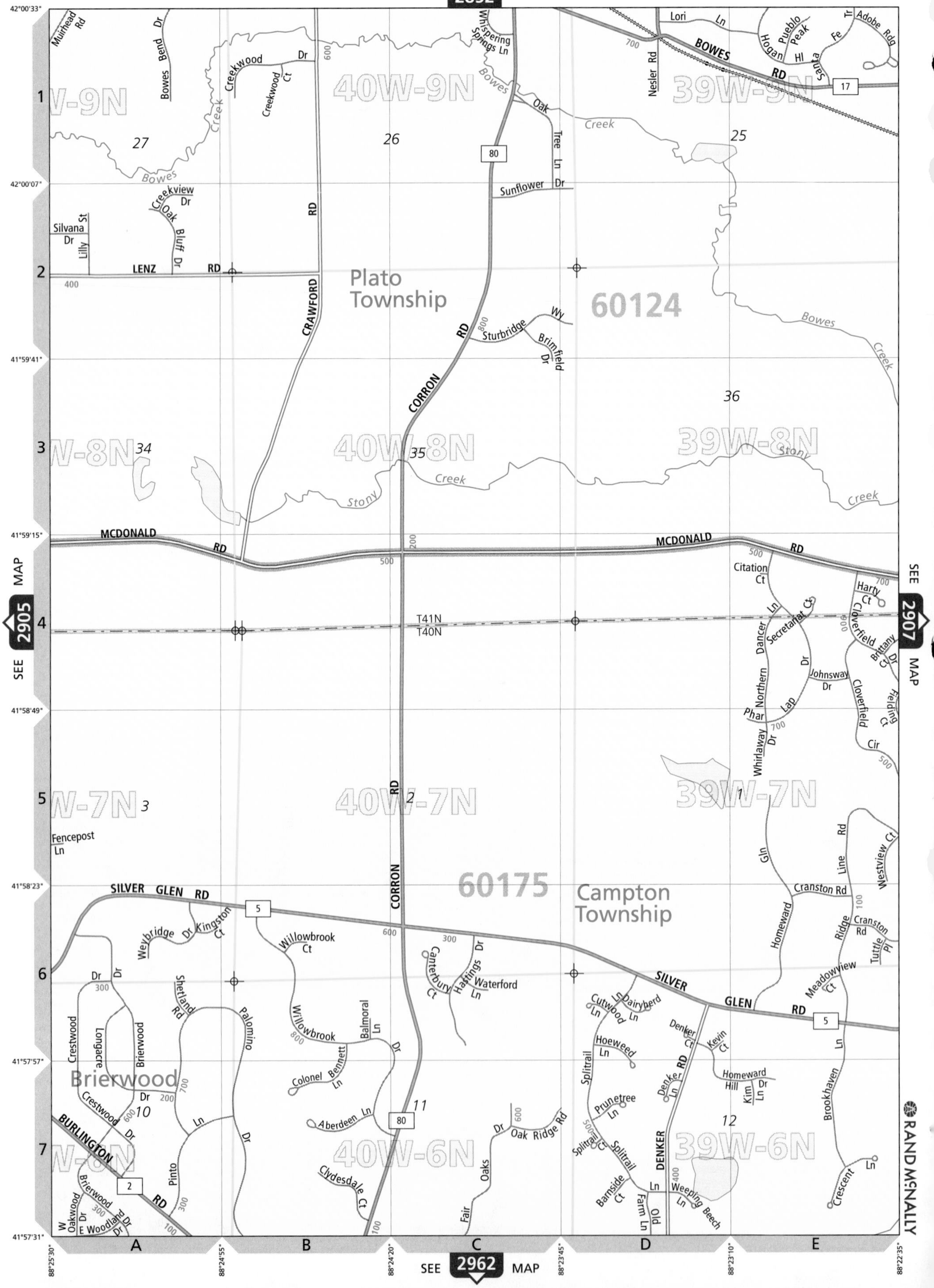

SEE 2905 MAP
SEE 2907 MAP
SEE 2962 MAP

1:24,000
1 in. = 2000 ft.
0 0.25 0.5
miles

SEE 2853 MAP

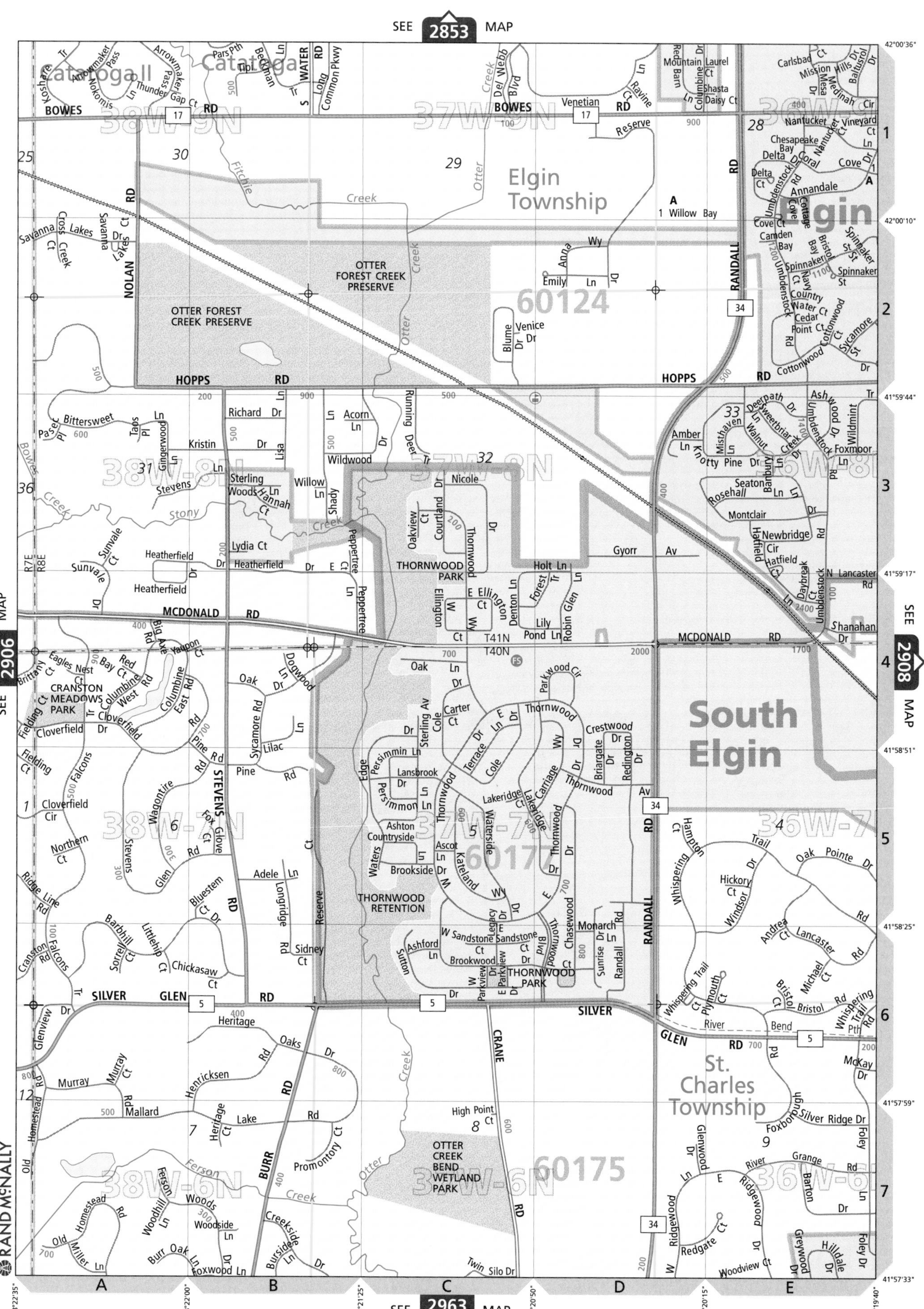

SEE 2906 MAP
SEE 2908 MAP
SEE 2963 MAP

1:24,000
1 in. = 2000 ft.
0 0.25 0.5
miles

SEE 2854 MAP

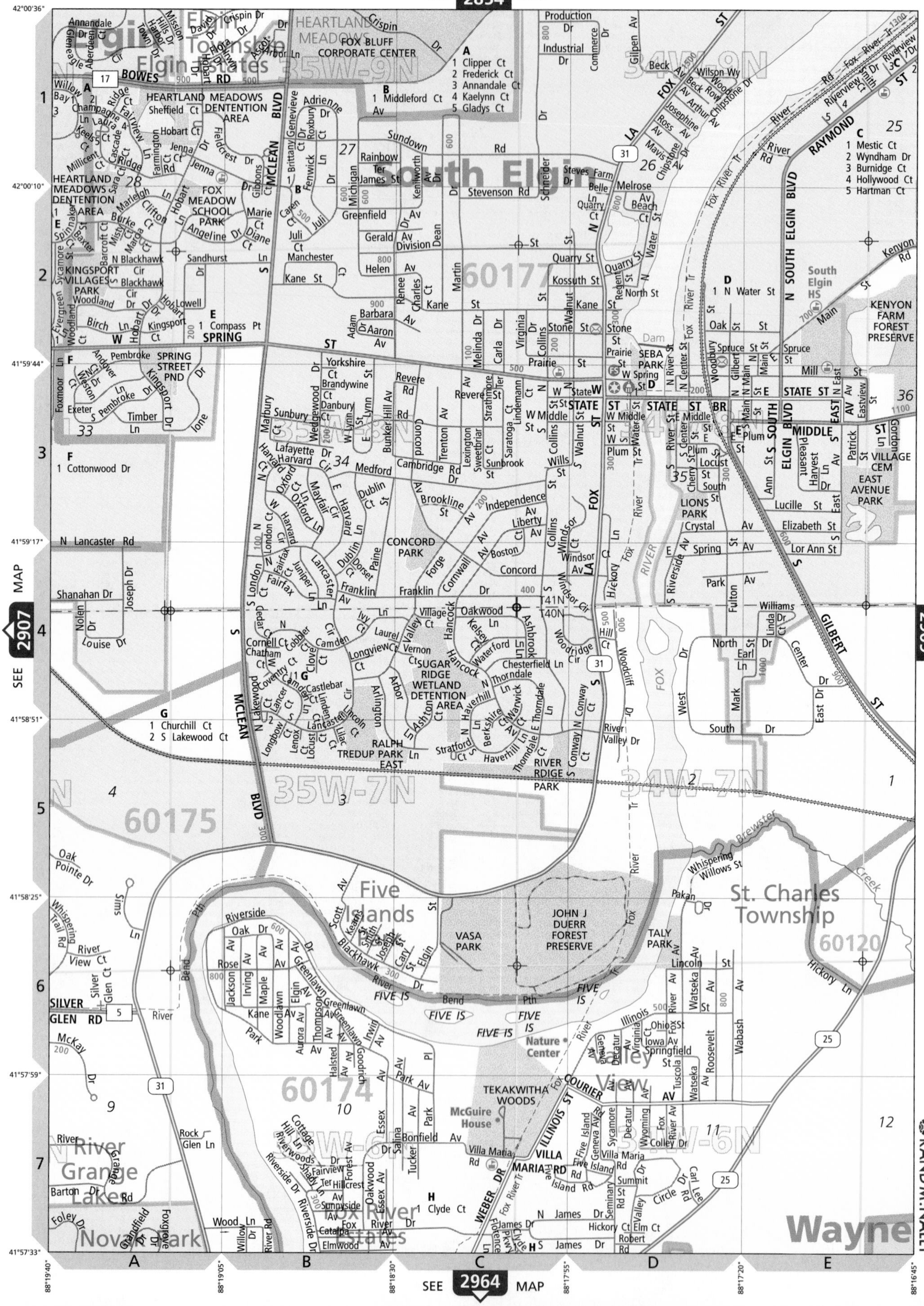

A
1 Clipper Ct
2 Frederick Ct
3 Annandale Ct
4 Kaelynn Ct
5 Gladys Ct

B
1 Middleford Ct

C
1 Mestic Ct
2 Wyndham Dr
3 Burnidge Ct
4 Hollywood Ct
5 Hartman Ct

D
1 N Water St

E
1 Compass Pt

F
1 Cottonwood Dr

G
1 Churchill Ct
2 S Lakewood Ct

H
1 Clyde Ct

South Elgin
St. Charles Township
Wayne

SEE 2907 MAP

SEE 2909 MAP

SEE 2964 MAP

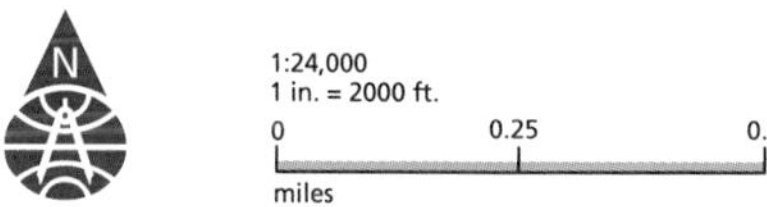

SEE 2855 MAP

South Elgin
Elgin Township
Elgin
Hanover Township
Bartlett
St. Charles Township
Wayne Township
Wayne

33W-9N
32W-9N
31W-9N
33W-8N
32W-8N
31W-8N
33W-7N
32W-7N
31W-7N
33W-6N
32W-6N
31W-6N

60177
60120
60103
60184

A
1 Riverview Dr
2 Moody Ct
3 Carlton Ct

RAYMOND ST
Wyndham Dr
Richmond Cir
Deerpoint Dr
Prairie Point Dr
Illinois Prairie Path-Elgin Brch
ST. CHARLES ST
25
Kenyon Rd
KENYON FARM FOREST PRESERVE
S Barry Rd
Comiskey Rd
Vulcan Blvd
GIFFORD RD
Blue Heron Cir
Angelico Ln
Kingfisher Rd
Blue Heron Wy
Veronica Cir
Primrose Ln
Primrose Ct
Sunflower Ln
Sundrop Ct
Osprey Ct
Fountain Grass Ct
Fountain Grass Cir
Spaulding Rd
Gasket Dr
Thornbury Dr
Versailles Ln
Lambert Ln
Ivory Ln
12th Av
11th Av
10th Av
9th Av
8th Av
7th Av
6th Av
5th Av
4th Av
3rd Av
2nd Av
1st
James Dr
Mable Ln
Laurie Ln
Helen Dr
Jones Dr
Carlino Dr
Daves Ct
Joseph Ct
Prairie Path Dr
3rd Ct
E MIDDLE ST
61
W BARTLETT RD
Bartlett Pointe Dr
Norwich Dr
Woodhaven Dr
Providence Dr
Grovetown Dr
Fieldcrest Dr
Prescott Dr
Weston Ct
Hearthstone Dr
Westridge Blvd
Faircroft Rd
Moorehead Dr
Cummings Dr
Norwich Dr
Ridgemore Dr
Cedarfield Dr
Troutman Dr
Carroll Wy
Southfield Dr
Remington Dr
Edgewater Dr
Butler
Burton
Dallas Dr
Rushmore Dr
Bennington Ln
Stanton Dr
Carey Wy
Barnett Ln
Ruzich Dr
Dyer Dr
Lanyon Dr
Ariana Dr
Lillian Pl
Silbury Dr
Southwind Blvd
EAST AVENUE PARK
COOK CO
DUPAGE CO
T41N
T40N
R8E
R9E
KANE CO
DUPAGE CO
JAMES PATE PHILLIP STATE PARK
Hecht Dr
Hecht Ct
BREWSTER CREEK BUSINESS PARK
Brewster Creek Blvd
S GILBERT ST
DUNHAM RD
STEARNS RD
29
LITTLE WOODS CEM
Coblestone Ln
Brewster Creek
Brewster Creek Cir
Ashley Ln
Woodmere Ln
Hub Rd
Shagbark Ln
Sulky Rd
Surrey Rd
Rochefort Ln
19
PRATT'S WAYNE WOODS FOREST PRESERVE
CATFISH POND
HORSETAIL PND
BEAVER SLOUGH
PICKEREL LAKE
Main Dr
POWIS RD
Model Airfield Rd

25 30 29 36 31 32 1 6 5 12 7 8

1 2 3 4 5 6 7
A B C D E

42°00'38"
42°00'12"
41°59'45"
41°59'19"
41°58'53"
41°58'27"
41°58'01"
41°57'35"
88°16'45"
88°16'10"
88°15'35"
88°15'00"
88°14'25"
88°13'51"

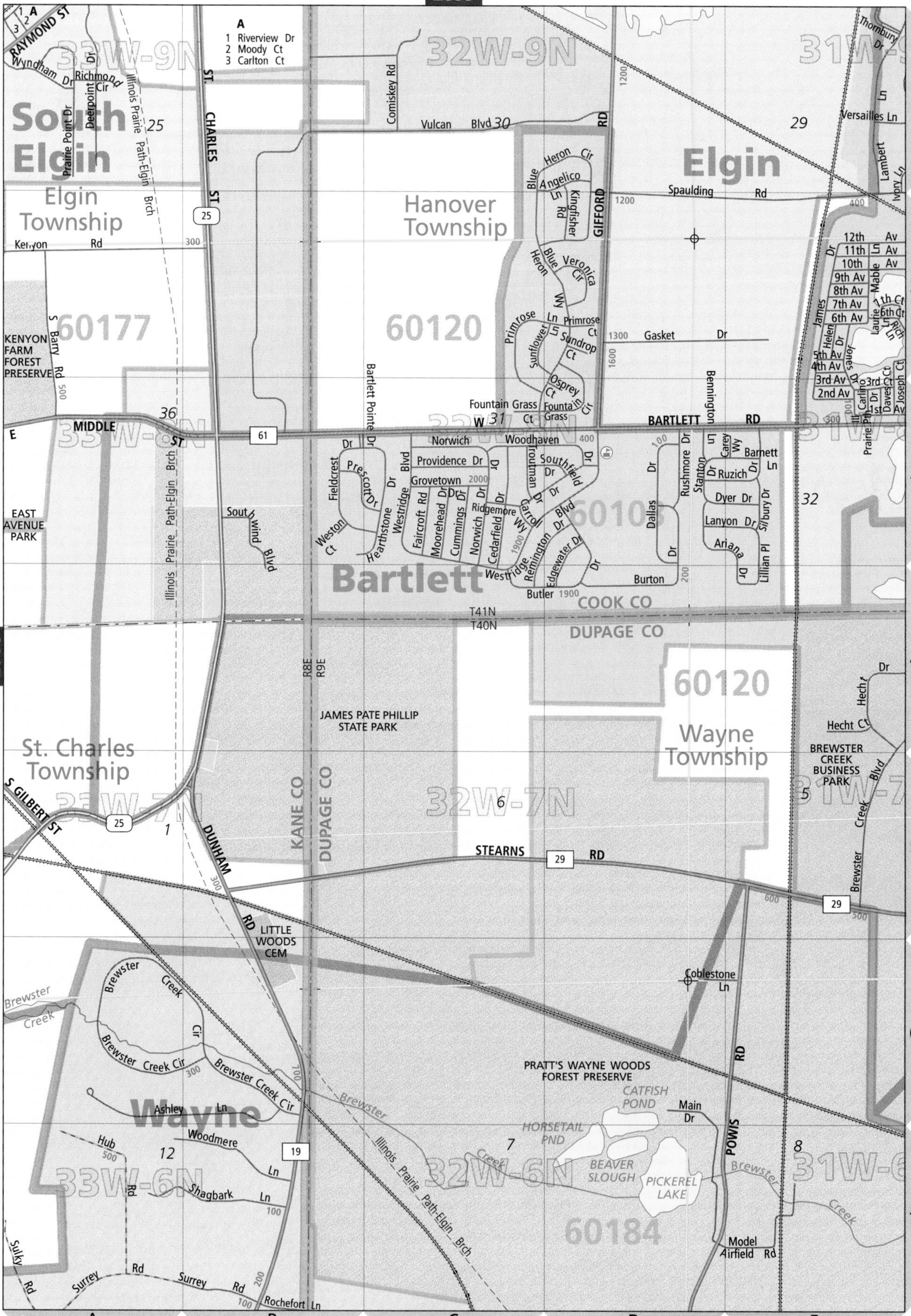

SEE 2908 MAP

SEE 2910 MAP

SEE 2965 MAP

1:24,000
1 in. = 2000 ft.
0 0.25 0.5
miles

SEE 2856 MAP

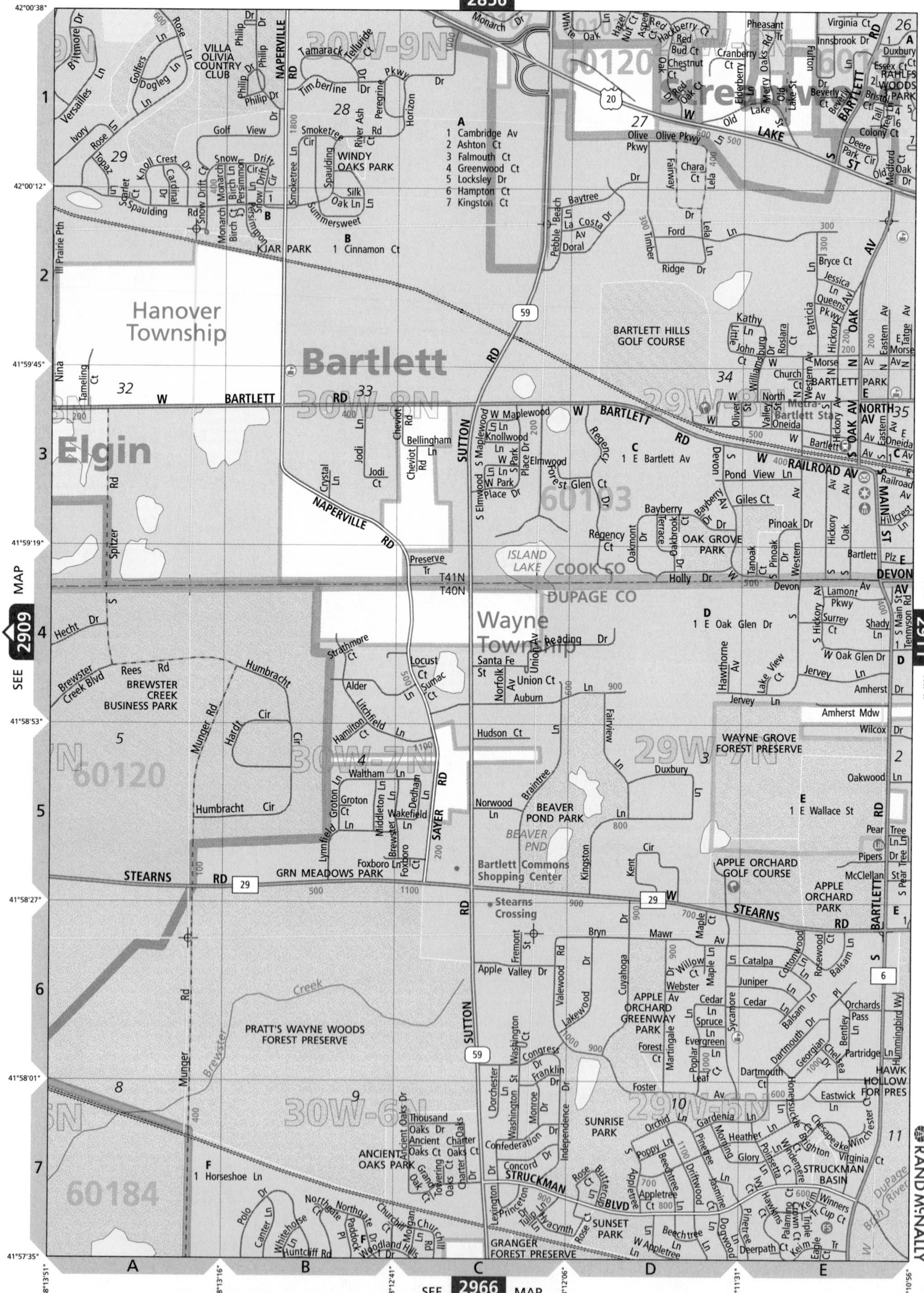

SEE 2909 MAP

SEE 2911 MAP

RAND McNALLY

SEE 2966 MAP

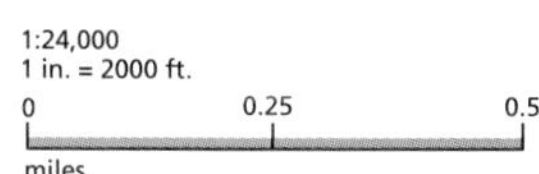

SEE 2857 MAP

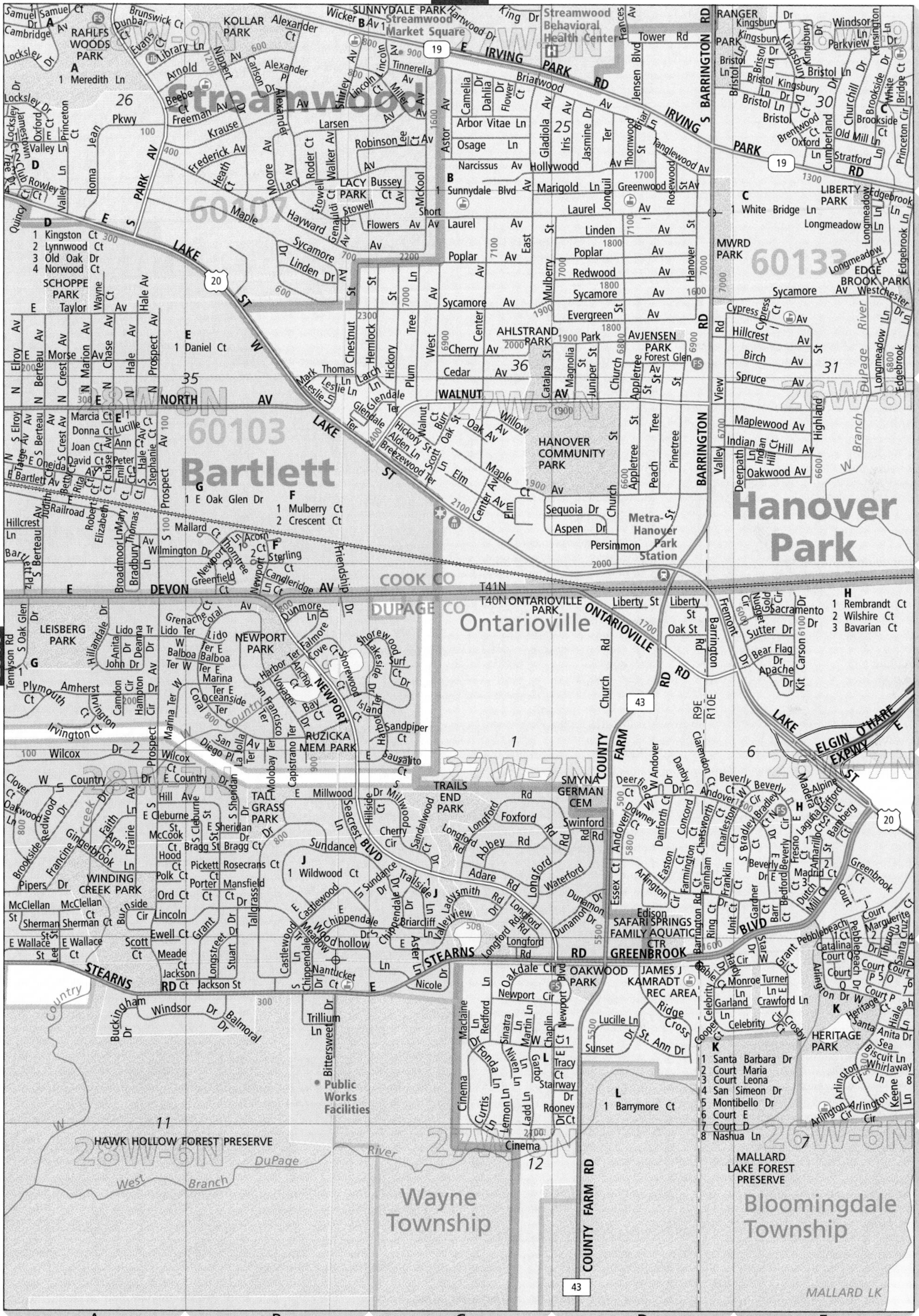

SEE 2910 MAP

SEE 2912 MAP

Streamwood

Bartlett

Hanover Park

Ontarioville

Wayne Township

Bloomingdale Township

60107

60103

60133

COOK CO

DUPAGE CO

T41N
T40N

R9E
R10E

28W-9N
27W-9N
26W-9N
28W-8N
27W-8N
26W-8N
28W-7N
27W-7N
26W-7N
28W-6N
27W-6N
26W-6N

RAHLFS WOODS PARK
KOLLAR PARK
SUNNYDALE PARK
Streamwood Market Square
Streamwood Behavioral Health Center
RANGER PARK
LACY PARK
LIBERTY PARK
MWRD PARK
EDGE BROOK PARK
SCHOPPE PARK
AHLSTRAND PARK
JENSEN PARK
HANOVER COMMUNITY PARK
Metra-Hanover Park Station
ONTARIOVILLE PARK
LEISBERG PARK
NEWPORT PARK
RUZICKA MEM PARK
TALL GRASS PARK
TRAILS END PARK
SMYNA GERMAN CEM
WINDING CREEK PARK
SAFARI SPRINGS FAMILY AQUATIC CTR
OAKWOOD PARK
JAMES J KAMRADT REC AREA
HERITAGE PARK
Public Works Facilities
HAWK HOLLOW FOREST PRESERVE
MALLARD LAKE FOREST PRESERVE
MALLARD LK

IRVING PARK RD
LAKE ST
S BARRINGTON RD
NORTH AV
DEVON AV
ONTARIOVILLE RD
COUNTY FARM RD
STEARNS RD
GREENBROOK BLVD
SEACREST BLVD
ELGIN O'HARE EXPWY
W Branch DuPage River

A
1 Meredith Ln

B
1 Sunnydale Blvd

C
1 White Bridge Ln

D
1 Kingston Ct
2 Lynnwood Ct
3 Old Oak Dr
4 Norwood Ct

E
1 Daniel Ct

F
1 Mulberry Ct
2 Crescent Ct

G
1 E Oak Glen Dr

H
1 Rembrandt Ct
2 Wilshire Ct
3 Bavarian Ct

J
1 Wildwood Ct

K
1 Santa Barbara Dr
2 Court Maria
3 Court Leona
4 San Simeon Dr
5 Montibello Dr
6 Court E
7 Court D
8 Nashua Ln

L
1 Barrymore Ct

42°00'39"
42°00'13"
41°59'47"
41°59'21"
41°58'55"
41°58'29"
41°58'03"
41°57'37"

88°10'56"
88°10'21"
88°09'46"
88°09'11"
88°08'36"
88°08'01"

A B C D E

1 2 3 4 5 6 7

SEE 2967 MAP

1:24,000
1 in. = 2000 ft.
0 0.25 0.5
miles

SEE 2858 MAP

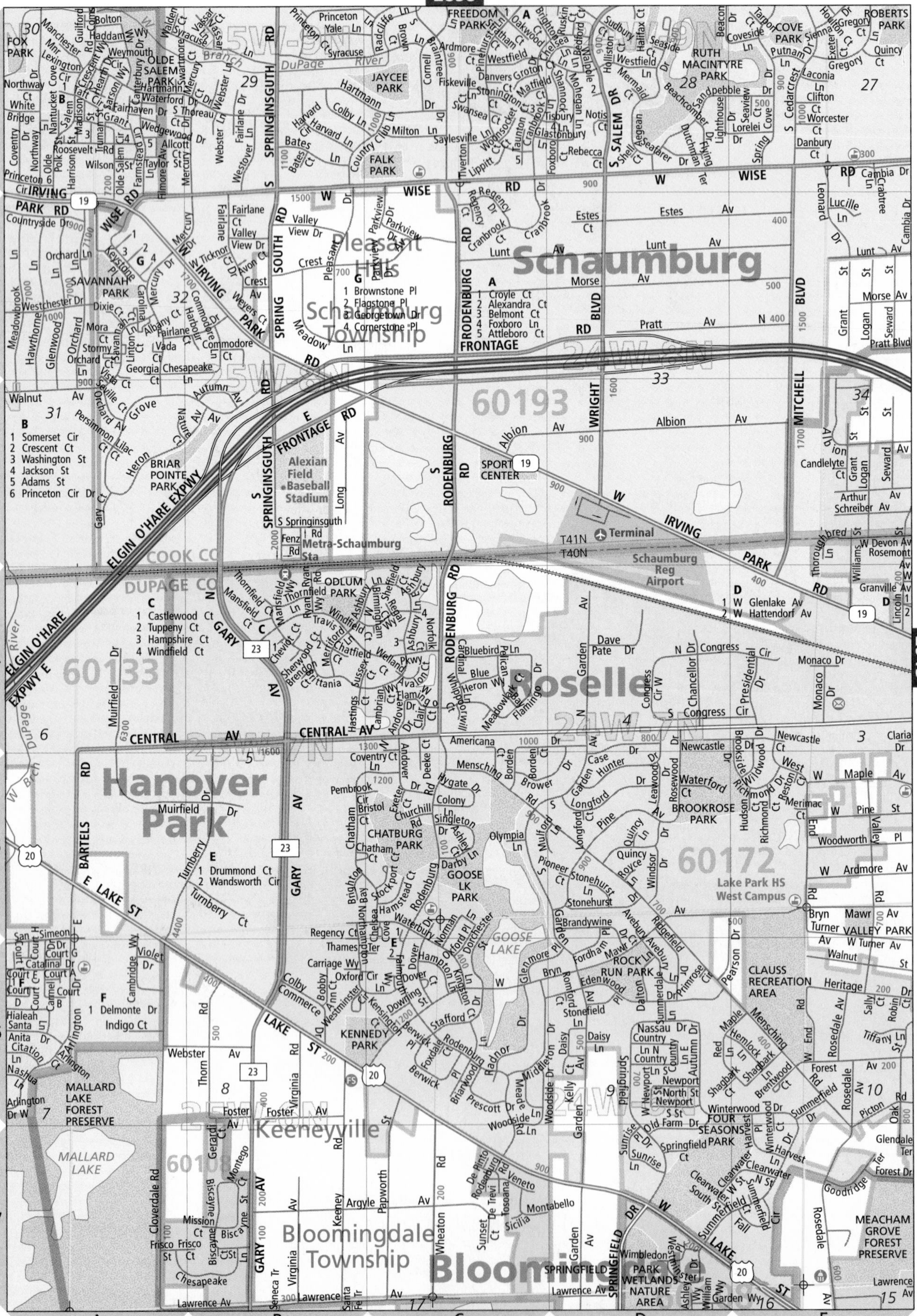

SEE 2911 MAP

SEE 2913 MAP

Schaumburg

Schaumburg Township

Roselle

Hanover Park

Keeneyville

Bloomingdale Township

Bloomingdale

60193

60133

60172

60108

ELGIN O'HARE EXPWY

W IRVING PARK RD

WISE RD

S SPRINGINSGUTH RD

S RODENBURG RD

GARY AV

CENTRAL AV

E LAKE ST

W LAKE ST

Alexian Field Baseball Stadium

Metra-Schaumburg Sta

Schaumburg Reg Airport

MALLARD LAKE FOREST PRESERVE

MEACHAM GROVE FOREST PRESERVE

CLAUSS RECREATION AREA

Lake Park HS West Campus

SPRINGFIELD PARK WETLANDS NATURE AREA

COOK CO

DUPAGE CO

T41N
T40N

A B C D E

1 2 3 4 5 6 7

SEE 2968 MAP

RAND McNALLY

1:24,000
1 in. = 2000 ft.
0 0.25 0.5
miles

SEE 2859 MAP

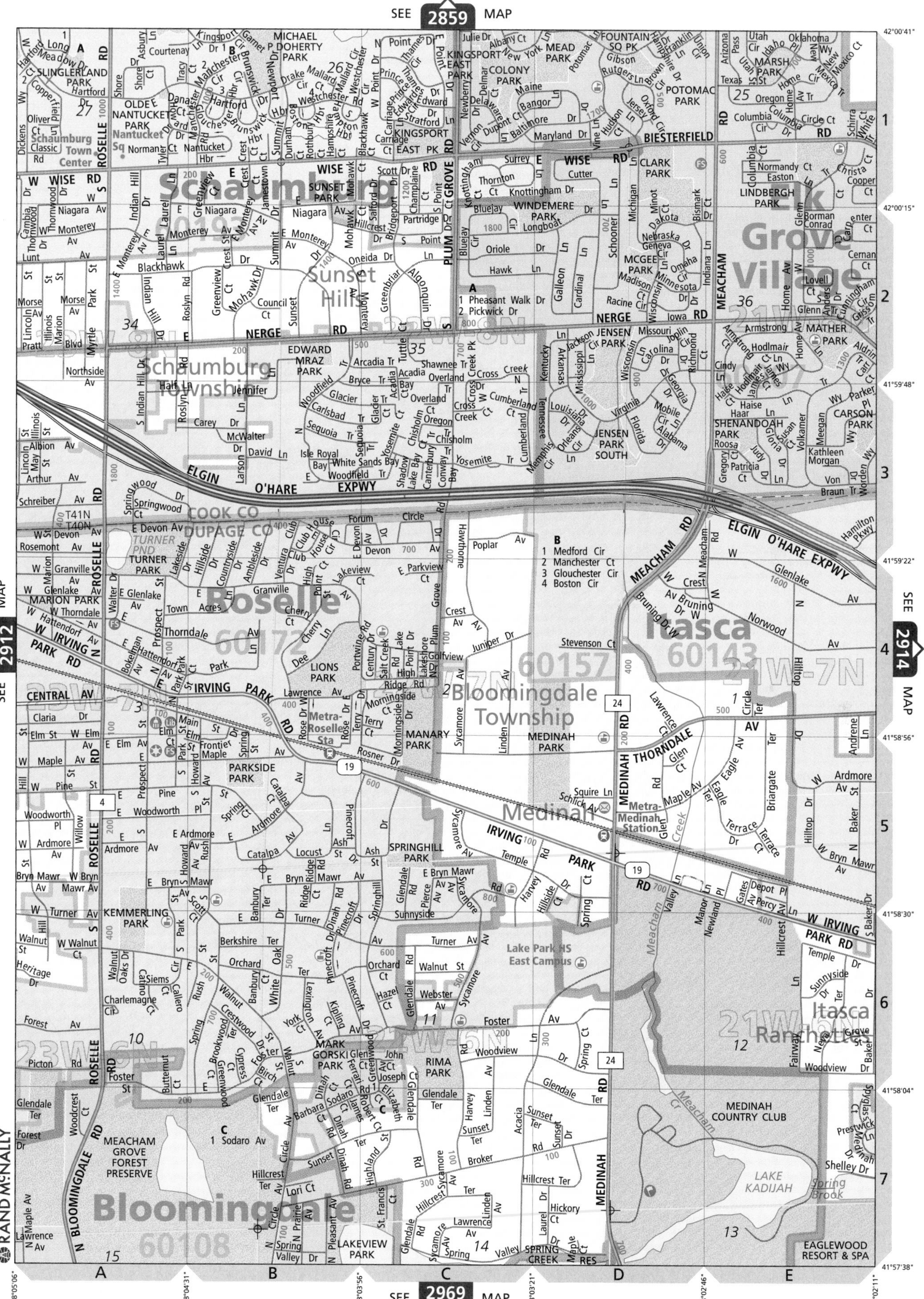

SEE 2912 MAP

SEE 2914 MAP

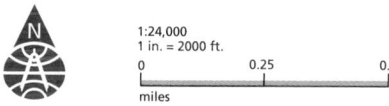

SEE 2969 MAP

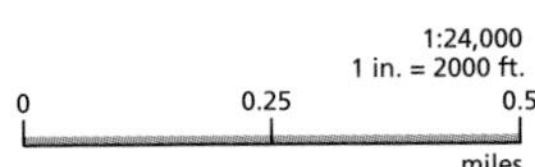

SEE 2860 MAP

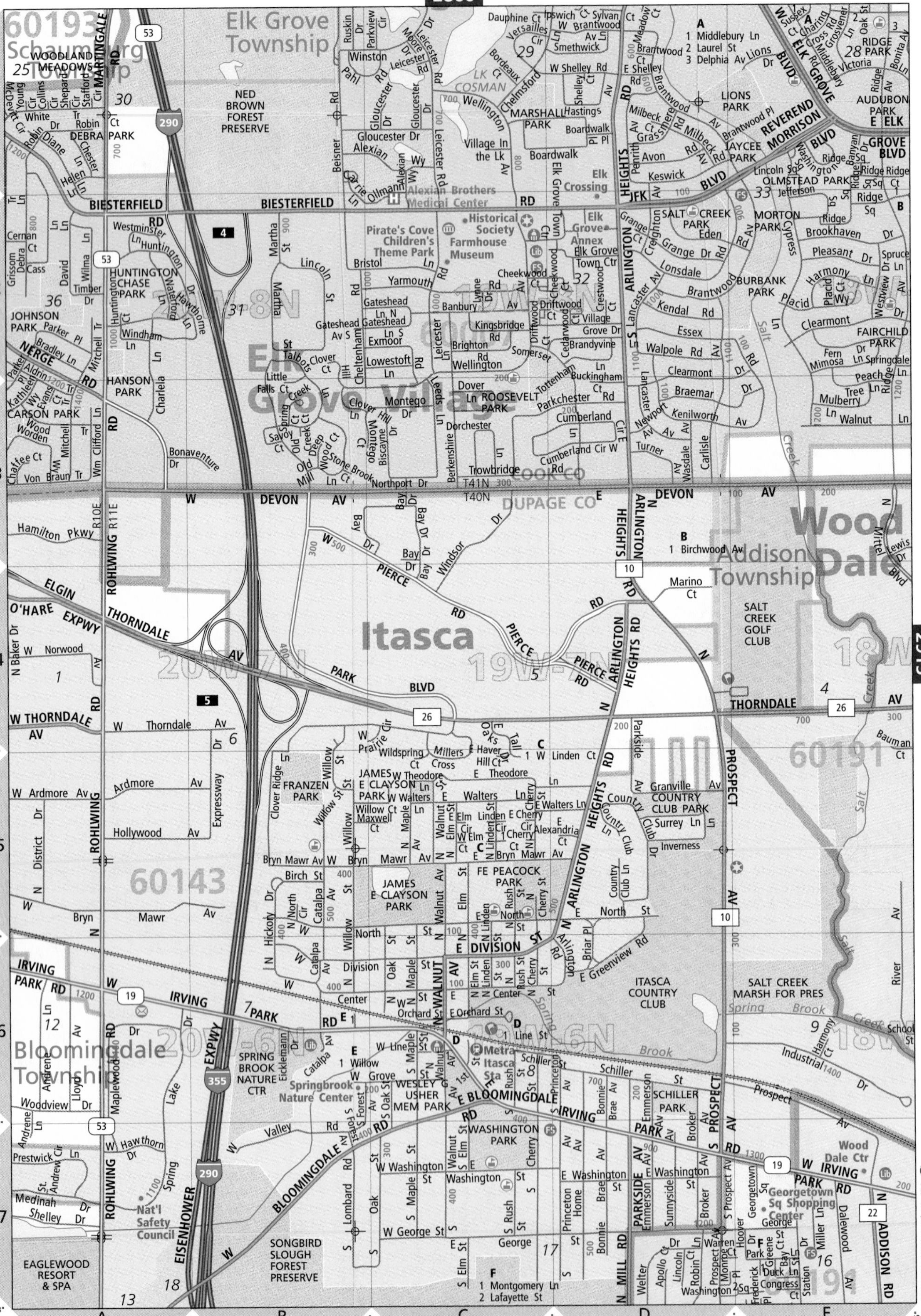

SEE 2913 MAP

SEE 2915 MAP

Elk Grove Township

Schaumburg Township

Elk Grove Village

Itasca

Addison Township

Wood Dale

Bloomingdale Township

A
1 Middlebury Ln
2 Laurel St
3 Delphia Av

B
1 Birchwood Av

C
1 W Linden Ct

D
1 Line St

E
1 Willow

F
1 Montgomery Ln
2 Lafayette St

NED BROWN FOREST PRESERVE

ALEXIAN BROTHERS MEDICAL CENTER

SALT CREEK GOLF CLUB

ITASCA COUNTRY CLUB

SALT CREEK MARSH FOR PRES

SPRING BROOK NATURE CTR

SONGBIRD SLOUGH FOREST PRESERVE

EAGLEWOOD RESORT & SPA

Nat'l Safety Council

Georgetown Sq Shopping Center

COOK CO
DUPAGE CO

A B C D E

1 2 3 4 5 6 7

SEE 2970 MAP

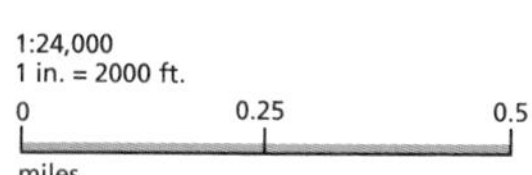

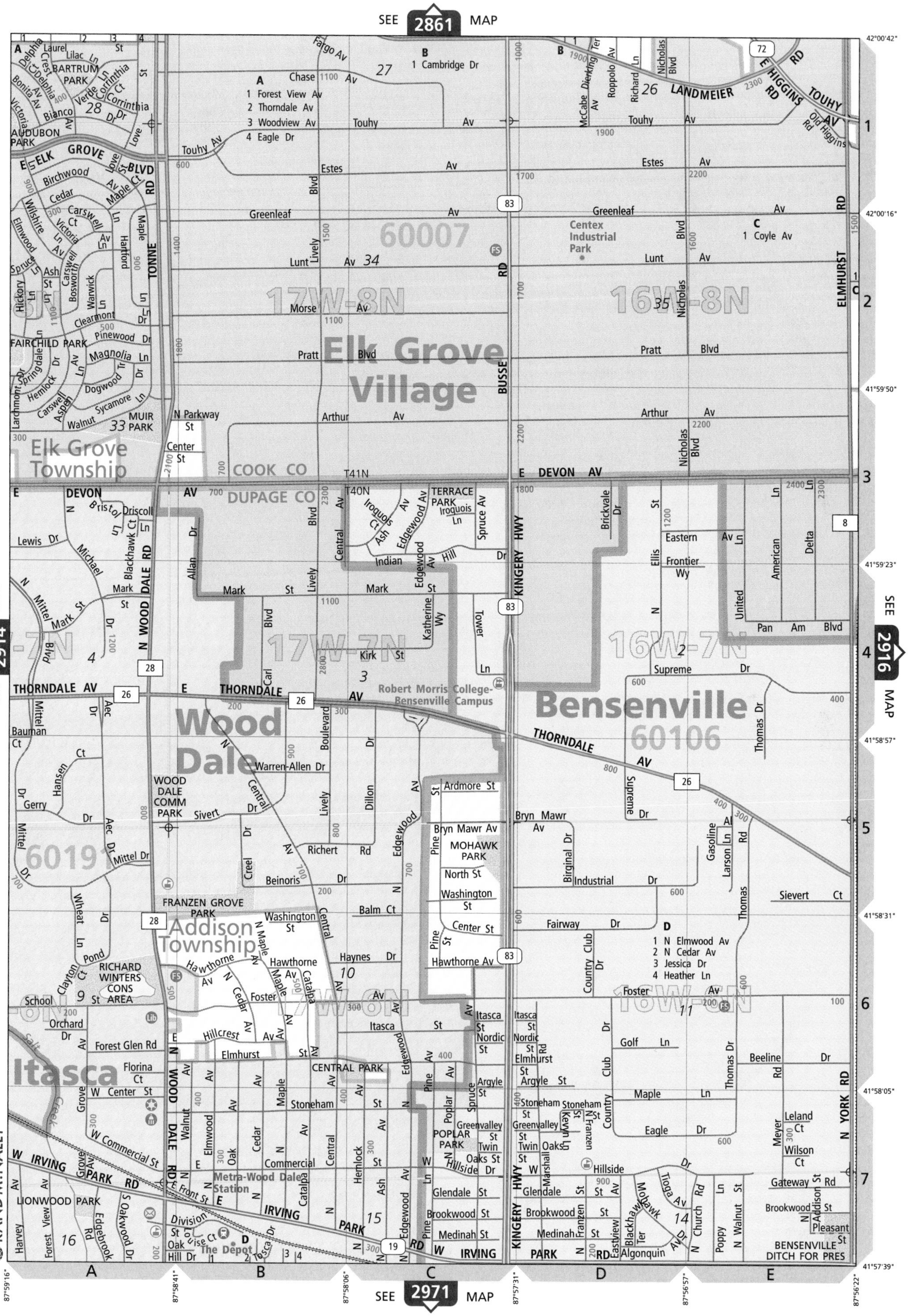

SEE 2861 MAP

SEE 2914 MAP

SEE 2916 MAP

SEE 2971 MAP

Elk Grove Village
60007
17W-8N
16W-8N
Elk Grove Township
COOK CO
DUPAGE CO
T41N
T40N
17W-7N
16W-7N
Wood Dale
Bensenville
60106
60191
Addison Township
Itasca
17W-6N
16W-6N

A
1 Forest View Av
2 Thorndale Av
3 Woodview Av
4 Eagle Dr

B
1 Cambridge Dr

C
1 Coyle Av

D
1 N Elmwood Av
2 N Cedar Av
3 Jessica Dr
4 Heather Ln

BARTRUM PARK
AUDUBON PARK
FAIRCHILD PARK
MUIR PARK
Centex Industrial Park
TERRACE PARK
Robert Morris College-Bensenville Campus
WOOD DALE COMM PARK
MOHAWK PARK
FRANZEN GROVE PARK
RICHARD WINTERS CONS AREA
CENTRAL PARK
POPLAR PARK
LIONWOOD PARK
Metra-Wood Dale Station
The Depot
BENSENVILLE DITCH FOR PRES

E ELK GROVE BLVD
TONNE RD
BUSSE RD
KINGERY HWY
LANDMEIER RD
E HIGGINS RD
TOUHY AV
ELMHURST RD
E DEVON AV
N WOOD DALE RD
THORNDALE AV
E THORNDALE AV
W IRVING PARK RD
IRVING PARK RD
N YORK RD
Touhy Av
Estes Av
Greenleaf Av
Lunt Av
Morse Av
Pratt Blvd
Arthur Av
Lively Blvd
Nicholas Blvd
Mark St
Kirk St
Central Av
Supreme Dr
Pan Am Blvd
Industrial Dr
Fairway Dr
Foster Av
Itasca St
Irving Park Rd

28 27 34 33 26 35 4 3 2 9 10 11 16 15

83 72 8 28 26 19

1 2 3 4 5 6 7
A B C D E

42°00'42"
42°00'16"
41°59'50"
41°59'23"
41°58'57"
41°58'31"
41°58'05"
41°57'39"
87°59'16"
87°58'41"
87°58'06"
87°57'31"
87°56'57"
87°56'22"

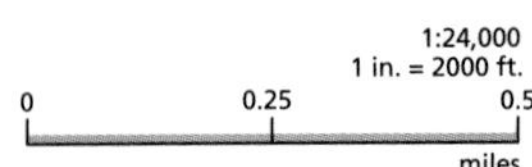

SEE 2862 MAP

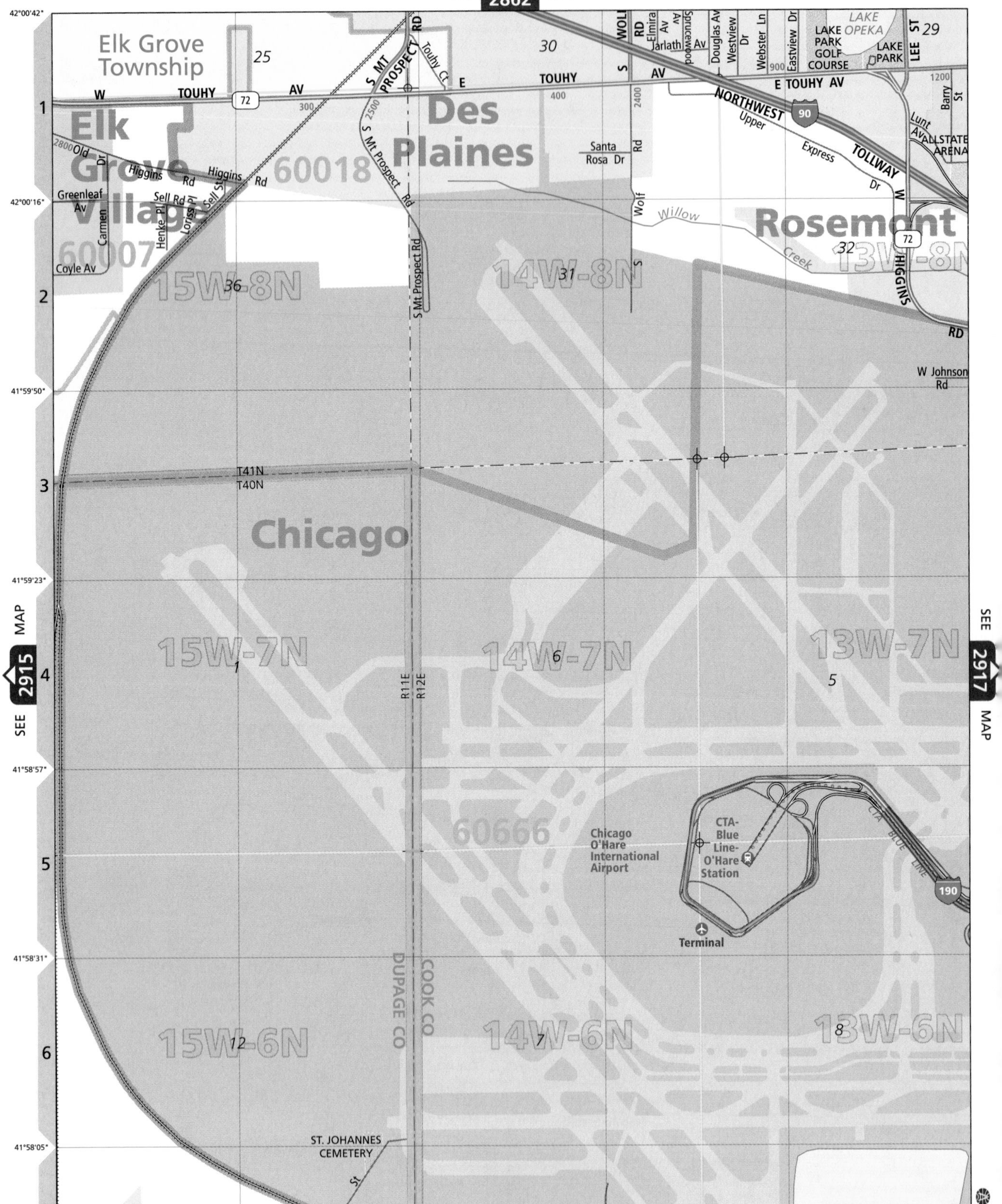

SEE 2915 MAP

SEE 2917 MAP

Elk Grove Township
Elk Grove Village
60007
Des Plaines
60018
Rosemont
Chicago
60666
60106
Bensenville

W TOUHY AV
72
E TOUHY AV
300
400
900
1200
2400
2500
2800
Old Higgins Rd
Higgins Rd
Greenleaf Av
Sell Rd
Sell St
Henke Pl
Loriss Pl
Carmen Dr
Coyle Av
S MT PROSPECT RD
S Mt Prospect Rd
Touhy Ct
S WOLF RD
Wolf Rd
Elmira Av
Jarlath Av
Sprucewood Av
Douglas Av
Westview Dr
Webster Ln
Eastview Dr
LAKE OPEKA
LAKE PARK GOLF COURSE
LAKE PARK
LEE ST
Barry St
Lunt Av
ALLSTATE ARENA
Santa Rosa Dr
NORTHWEST TOLLWAY
90
Upper Express Dr
W HIGGINS RD
Willow Creek
W Johnson Rd

15W-8N
14W-8N
13W-8N
15W-7N
14W-7N
13W-7N
15W-6N
14W-6N
13W-6N
25
30
29
36
31
32
1
6
5
12
7
8
13
18
17

T41N
T40N
R11E
R12E
DUPAGE CO
COOK CO

Chicago O'Hare International Airport
CTA-Blue Line-O'Hare Station
CTA BLUE LINE
190
Terminal

ST. JOHANNES CEMETERY
Division St
RESTHAVEN CEM
E Hillside Dr
Garden Av
Orchard Av
BENSENVILLE DITCH FOR PRES
O'Hare Cargo Area Rd
N Access Rd
Post Office Rd
LAKE O'HARE
Crystal Creek

42°00'42"
42°00'16"
41°59'50"
41°59'23"
41°58'57"
41°58'31"
41°58'05"
41°57'39"
87°56'22"
87°55'47"
87°55'12"
87°54'37"
87°54'02"
87°53'27"

A B C D E
1 2 3 4 5 6 7

SEE 2972 MAP

1:24,000
1 in. = 2000 ft.
0 0.25 0.5
miles

SEE 2863 MAP

SEE 2916 MAP

SEE 2918 MAP

SEE 2973 MAP

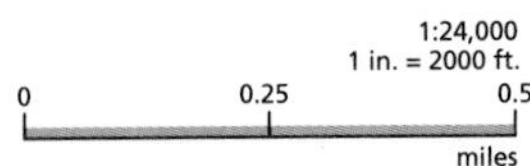

SEE 2864 MAP

Park Ridge
Niles
Norridge
Harwood Heights
Chicago
Leyden Township
Maine Township
Norwood Park Township
60068
60631
60656
60706
10W-8N
9W-8N
8W-8N
10W-7N
9W-7N
8W-7N
10W-6N
9W-6N
8W-6N
TOUHY AV
BELLE PLAINE AV
DEVON AV
TALCOTT RD
HIGGINS RD
KENNEDY EXPWY
NORTHWEST HWY
CUMBERLAND AV
CANFIELD AV
HARLEM AV
FOSTER AV
LAWRENCE AV
GUNNISON ST
MILWAUKEE AV
OZANAM AV
BRYN MAWR AV
Resurrection HS
Resurrection Medical Center
Metra-Park Ridge Sta
Metra-Edison Pk Station
Metra-Norwood Park Station
CTA-Blue Line-Cumberland
CTA-Blue Line-Harlem Sta
Harlem-Foster Shopping Center
Harwood Commons
Holiday Plaza Shopping Center
Ridgemoor CC
St. Adalbert Cemetery
Union Ridge Cem
Pioneer Park
Brooks Park
Edison Park
Olympia Park
Mon Park
South Park
Jaycee Park
Seminole Park
Oriole Park
Norridge Park
Myrtle Grv Park
Centennial Park
Norwood Circle Park
Norwood Plgnd Park
Miami Woods For Pres
Bunker Hill Woods For Pres
Greyhound-Chicago

SEE 2917 MAP
SEE 2919 MAP
SEE 2974 MAP

1:24,000
1 in. = 2000 ft.
0 0.25 0.5
miles

SEE 2865 MAP

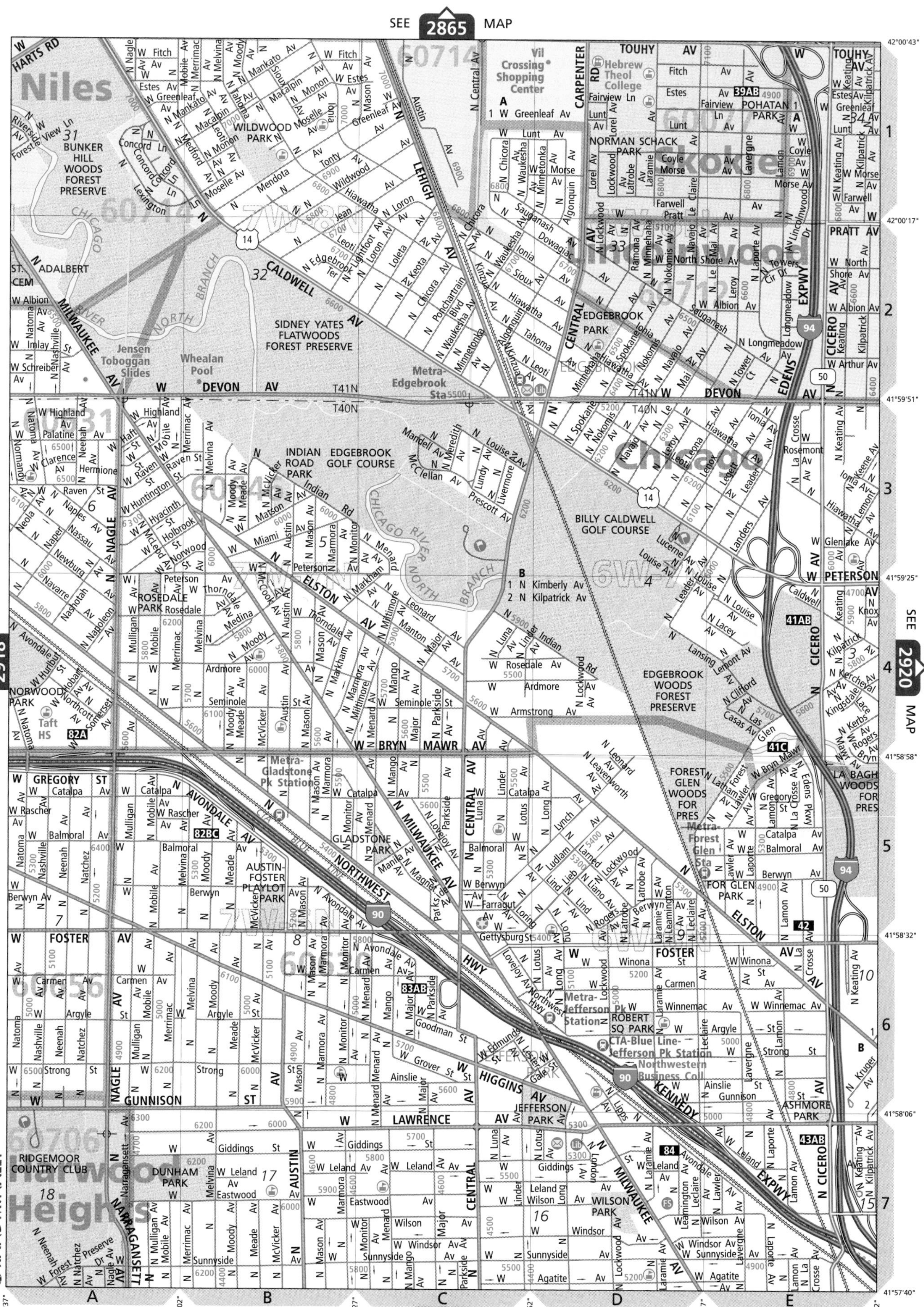

SEE 2975 MAP

1:24,000
1 in. = 2000 ft.
0 0.25 0.5
miles

SEE 2866 MAP

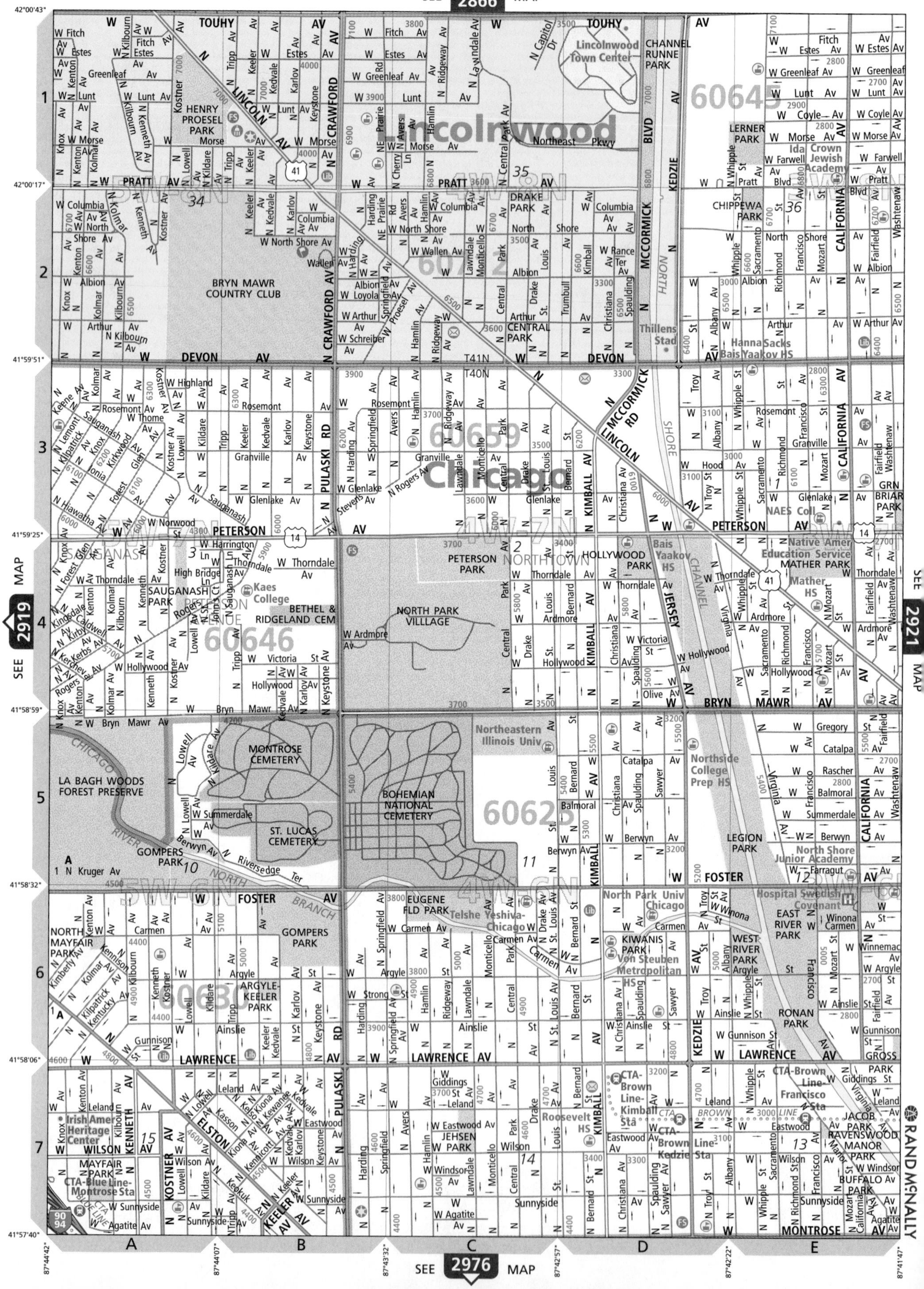

42°00'43"

Lincolnwood

Chicago

HENRY PROESEL PARK
BRYN MAWR COUNTRY CLUB
Lincolnwood Town Center
CHANNEL RUNNE PARK
LERNER PARK
Ida Crown Jewish Academy
CHIPPEWA PARK
DRAKE PARK
CENTRAL PARK
Thillens Stad
Hanna Sacks Bais Yaakov HS
NAES Coll
GRN BRIAR PARK
SAUGANASH PARK
PETERSON PARK
NORTHTOWN
HOLLYWOOD PARK
Bais Yaakov HS
Native Amer Education Service
MATHER PARK
Mather HS
Kaes College
BETHEL & RIDGELAND CEM
NORTH PARK VILLAGE
Northeastern Illinois Univ
MONTROSE CEMETERY
LA BAGH WOODS FOREST PRESERVE
BOHEMIAN NATIONAL CEMETERY
ST. LUCAS CEMETERY
GOMPERS PARK
Northside College Prep HS
LEGION PARK
North Shore Junior Academy
EUGENE FLD PARK
Telshe Yeshiva-Chicago
North Park Univ Chicago
Hospital Swedish Covenant
EAST RIVER PARK
NORTH MAYFAIR PARK
ARGYLE-KEELER PARK
KIWANIS PARK
Von Steuben Metropolitan HS
WEST RIVER PARK
RONAN PARK
Irish Amer Heritage Center
MAYFAIR PARK
CTA-Blue Line-Montrose Sta
JEHSEN W PARK
Roosevelt HS
CTA-Brown Line-Kimball Sta
CTA-Brown Line-Kedzie Sta
CTA-Brown Line-Francisco Sta
JACOB PARK
RAVENSWOOD MANOR PARK
BUFFALO PARK

60645
60712
60659
60646
60625
60630

5W-8N
4W-8N
5W-7N
1W-7N
5W-6N
4W-6N

TOUHY AV
PRATT AV
DEVON AV
PETERSON AV
BRYN MAWR AV
FOSTER AV
LAWRENCE AV
MONTROSE AV
LINCOLN AV
CRAWFORD AV
PULASKI RD
MCCORMICK BLVD
KEDZIE AV
KIMBALL AV
CALIFORNIA AV
JERSEY AV
ELSTON AV
KOSTNER AV
KENNETH AV
KEELER AV
NORTH SHORE CHANNEL
CHICAGO RIVER NORTH BRANCH

SEE 2919 MAP

SEE 2921 MAP

1 2 3 4 5 6 7

A B C D E

87°44'42" 87°44'07" 87°43'32" 87°42'57" 87°42'22" 87°41'47"

SEE 2976 MAP

1:24,000
1 in. = 2000 ft.
0 0.25 0.5
miles

SEE 2867 MAP

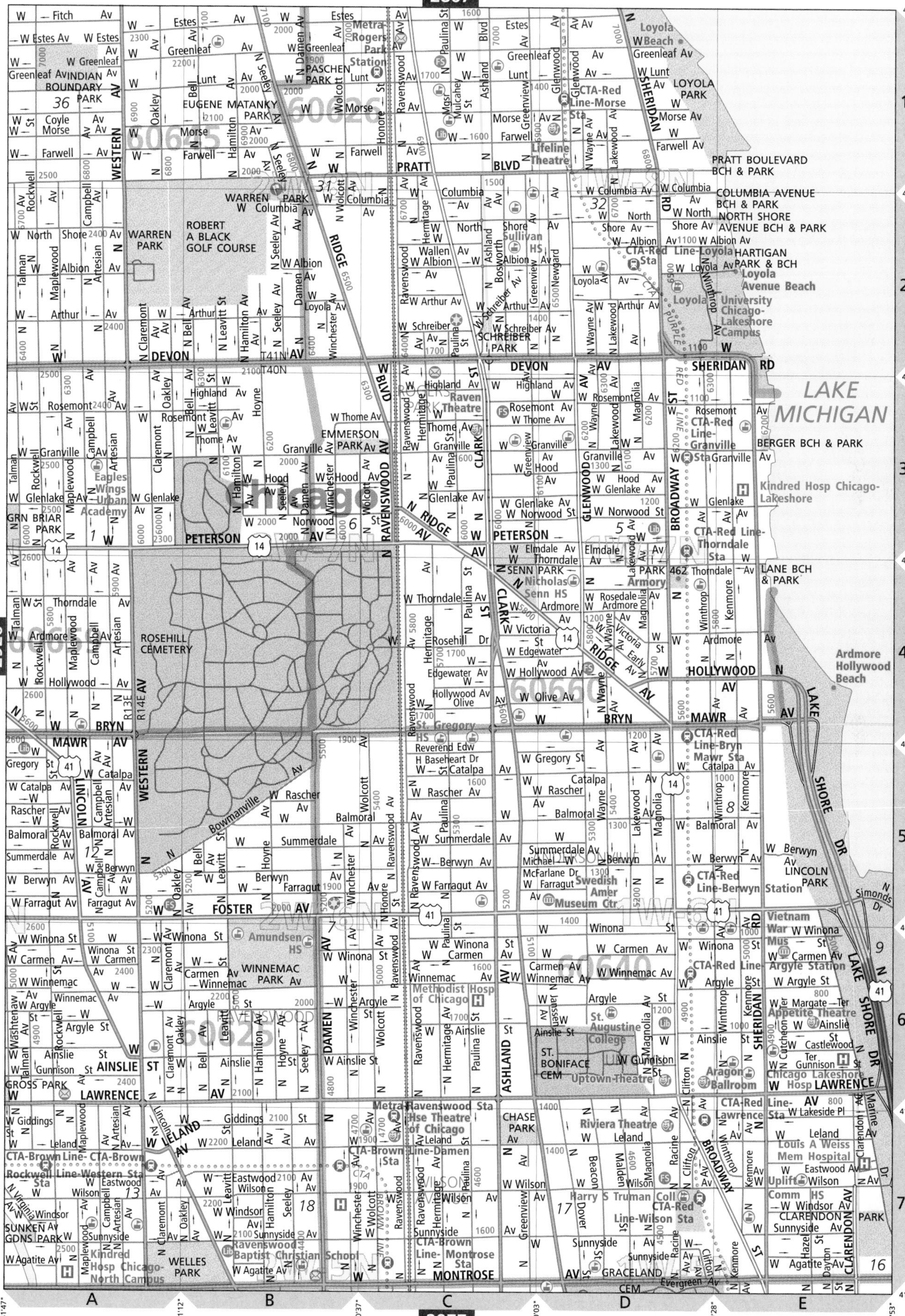

SEE 2920 MAP

SEE 2922 MAP

Chicago

LAKE MICHIGAN

INDIAN BOUNDARY PARK
EUGENE MATANKY PARK
PASCHEN PARK
Metra-Rogers Park Station
LOYOLA PARK
Loyola Beach
CTA-Red Line-Morse Sta
Lifeline Theatre
PRATT BOULEVARD BCH & PARK
WARREN PARK
ROBERT A BLACK GOLF COURSE
COLUMBIA AVENUE BCH & PARK
NORTH SHORE AVENUE BCH & PARK
HARTIGAN PARK & BCH
Loyola Avenue Beach
Sullivan HS
CTA-Red Line-Loyola Sta
Loyola University Chicago-Lakeshore Campus
SCHREIBER PARK
DEVON
SHERIDAN RD
Raven Theatre
EMMERSON PARK
Eagles Wings Urban Academy
GRN BRIAR PARK
CTA-Red Line-Granville Sta
BERGER BCH & PARK
Kindred Hosp Chicago-Lakeshore
PETERSON
CTA-Red Line-Thorndale Sta
LANE BCH & PARK
SENN PARK
Nicholas Senn HS
PARK 462 Armory
ROSEHILL CEMETERY
Ardmore Hollywood Beach
HOLLYWOOD
BRYN MAWR AV
St. Gregory HS
CTA-Red Line-Bryn Mawr Sta
LAKE SHORE DR
LINCOLN PARK
CTA-Red Line-Berwyn Station
Swedish Amer Museum Ctr
FOSTER AV
Amundsen HS
WINNEMAC PARK
Vietnam War Mus
CTA-Red Line-Argyle Station
Methodist Hosp of Chicago
Appetite Theatre
St. Augustine College
ST. BONIFACE CEM
Uptown Theatre
Aragon Ballroom
Chicago Lakeshore Hosp
AINSLIE ST
GROSS PARK
LAWRENCE AV
CTA-Red Line-Lawrence Sta
Metra-Ravenswood Sta
Hse Theatre of Chicago
CHASE PARK
Riviera Theatre
Louis A Weiss Mem Hospital
CTA-Brown Line-Rockwell Sta
CTA-Brown Line-Western Sta
CTA-Brown Line-Damen Sta
Uplift Comm HS
Harry S Truman Coll
CTA-Red Line-Wilson Sta
CLARENDON PARK
SUNKEN GDNS PARK
Kindred Hosp Chicago-North Campus
WELLES PARK
Ravenswood Baptist Christian School
CTA-Brown Line-Montrose Sta
MONTROSE
GRACELAND CEM

A B C D E
1 2 3 4 5 6 7

SEE 2977 MAP

1:24,000
1 in. = 2000 ft.
0 0.25 0.5
miles

SEE B MAP

42°00'43"
42°00'17"
41°59'51"
41°59'25"
41°58'59"
41°58'33"
41°58'06"
41°57'40"

1
2
3
4
5
6
7

LAKE MICHIGAN

Foster Avenue Beach
W Foster Dr
0W-6N
N Simonds
9
W LAWRENCE AV
Lawrence-Wilson Dr
N LAKE SHORE DR
W Wilson Av
41
16
60640
Chicago
Montrose-Wilson Beach
LINCOLN PARK
W Montrose Harbor Dr
W Montrose Av
N Marine Dr
60613
MONTROSE HARBOR

SEE 2921 MAP

SEE B MAP

A B C D E

87°38'53" 87°38'18" 87°37'43" 87°37'08" 87°36'33" 87°35'58"

SEE 2978 MAP

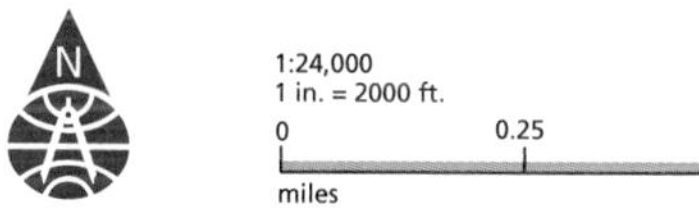

SEE 2905 MAP

The Knolls
Empire Hills
Kingswood
60175
Meadowview
Windings
Lily Lake
Mary Meadows
Brookside
Foxfield
Campton Township
60119
60151
CAMPTON PARK
CAMPTON FOREST PRESERVE
43W-5N
42W-5N
41W
43W-4N
42W-4N
43W-3N
42W-3N

EMPIRE RD
69
64
47
ANDERSON RD
CAMPTON HILLS DR
BEITH RD
TOWN HALL RD
Great Western Tr
Ferson Creek
Mill Creek

Gopher Ct
Badger Ct
Valley Dr
Otter Ln
Prairie
Beaver Ln
Beaver Ct
Creekside Ct
Swanberg Rd
Knollwood Dr
White Oak Ln
Esther Ln
Woodland Dr
E Woodland Dr
Boxwood Ln
Margie Ln
Kettlehook Ct
Timber Ln
Harvest Ct
Castle Dr
Dominion Dr
Campton Ridge Dr
Audubon Ct
Arboretum Ln
Kingswood Dr
Nuthatch Ct
Ravine Dr
Forest Glen Ln
Tanager Ct
Jensen
Ironwood Ct
Eagle Ct
Cranberry Ln
Lost View
Meadowlark Ct
Sylvan Ln
Copperwood Dr
Copperwood Ln
Quail Ct
Jens Ln
Steeple Chase
Hawthorne Ct
Redbud Ct
Hidden Springs Ct
Retreat Ct
Harvest
Paddock
Bridle Ct
Fox Moor Dr
Leslie Ct
Coleman Ln
Heather Ln
Hazelwood Ct
Hazelwood Tr
Cornwall Dr
Clover Ct
Fox Hill Ct
Fox Wilds Dr
Fox Wilds Ct
Meadowview
Fescue Ct
Hanson Rd
Campton Ct
Sanctuary Ln
Ferson Ct
Hunters Rdg
Hunters Hill Dr
Oak Hill Dr
Hunters Ln
Hunters Ct
Hill Dr
Forest Trails Ct
Hunters Dr
W Carol Dr
Mary Ct
W Mary Dr
E Mary Dr
Carol Dr
Westwoods Ct
Westwoods Dr
Chaffield Dr
Brookside West Dr
N Circle Dr
Circle Dr
Griffin Ln
Snowbird Ct
Forpre Tr
Campton Forpre Tr
Golden Oaks Ln
Wayne Dr
Barlow Dr
Kildeer Ln
Mohican Ln
Fenimore Ln
Deerslayer Dr
Uncas Ln
Parthfinder Dr
Hawkeye Ct
Chalfedon Ct
Blue Larkspur Ln
Whirlaway Ct
Whirlaway
Council Ct
Citation Dr
Fairfeno
Chateaugay Ct
Venetian Wy
Hawk Cir
Foxfield Ct
Hunter Ct
Windsor Ct
Falcon Ln
Arrowhead Dr
Foxfield Dr
Derby Ln
East Dr
Lin's Ln
Country View Ln
Farmview Rd
High Point Ln
High Point Ct
Far View Rd
Woodcrest Ct
Springwood Ln
Town Hall Rd
N Bowgren Cir
S Bowgren Cir

8
9
10
15
16
17
20
21
22
27
28
29
32
33
34

41°57'31"
41°57'05"
41°56'39"
41°56'12"
41°55'46"
41°55'20"
41°54'54"
41°54'28"
88°28'22"
88°27'47"
88°27'12"
88°26'37"
88°26'02"
88°25'28"

A
B
C
D
E
1
2
3
4
5
6
7

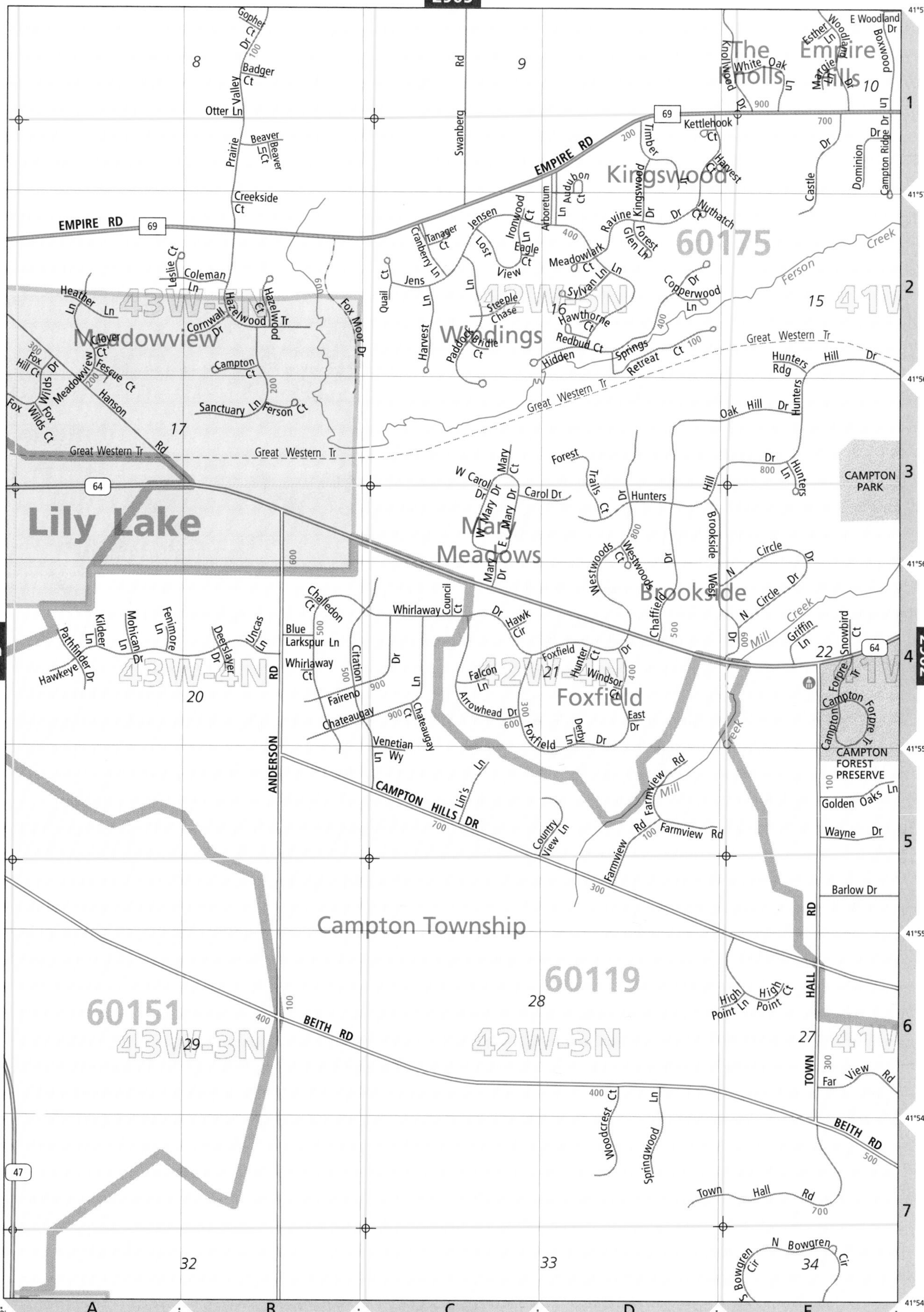

SEE B MAP
SEE 2962 MAP
SEE 3017 MAP

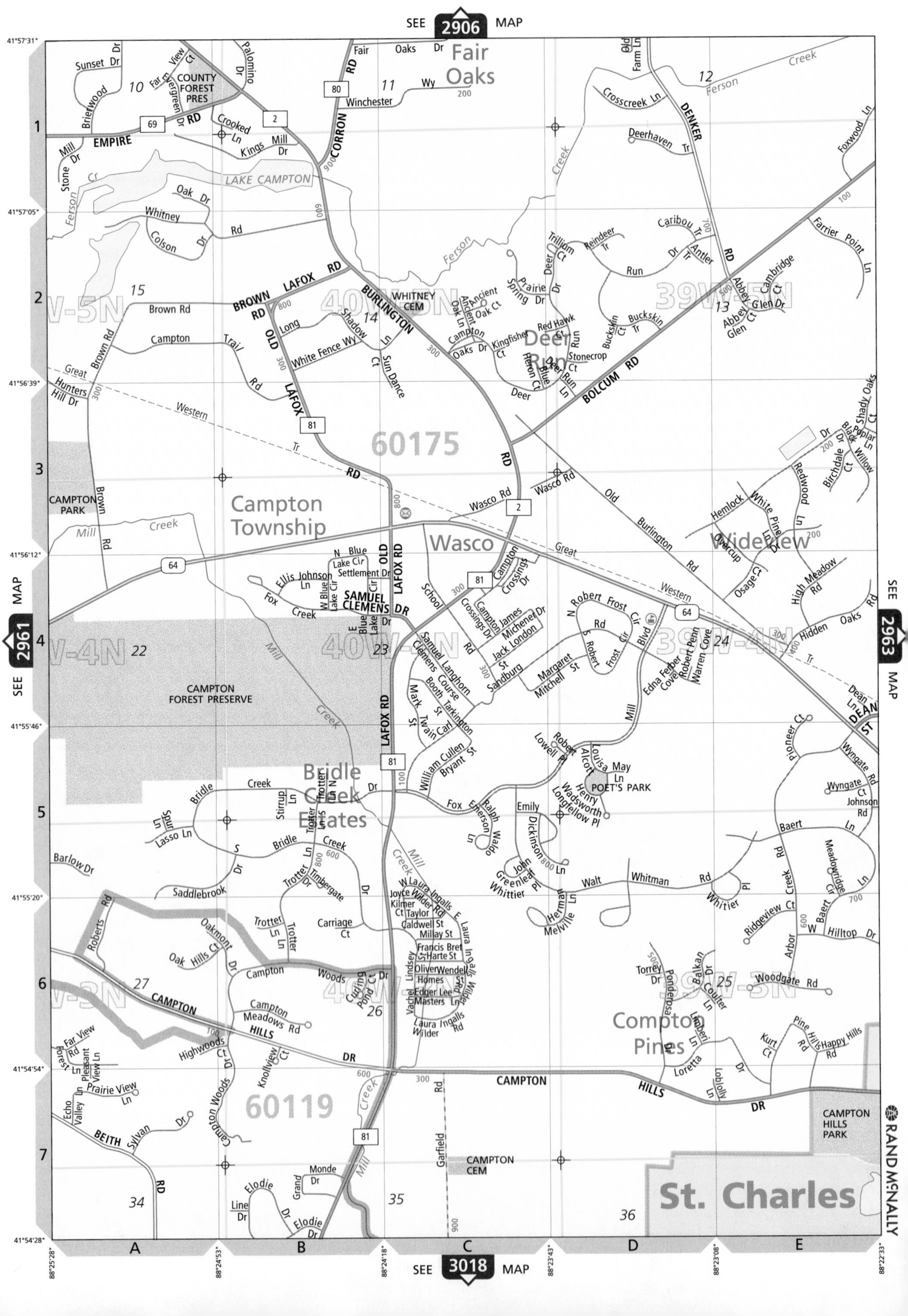

1:24,000
1 in. = 2000 ft.
0 0.25 0.5
miles

SEE 2906 MAP

Fair Oaks
COUNTY FOREST PRES
LAKE CAMPTON
WHITNEY CEM
Deer Run
60175
Campton Township
CAMPTON PARK
Wasco
Wildeview
CAMPTON FOREST PRESERVE
Bridle Creek Estates
POET'S PARK
Compton Pines
60119
CAMPTON CEM
CAMPTON HILLS PARK
St. Charles

EMPIRE RD
CORRON RD
DENKER RD
BROWN LAFOX RD
OLD LAFOX RD
BURLINGTON RD
BOLCUM RD
LAFOX RD
SAMUEL CLEMENS DR
OLD LAFOX RD
CAMPTON HILLS DR
BEITH RD
DEAN ST

SEE 2961 MAP
SEE 2963 MAP
SEE 3018 MAP

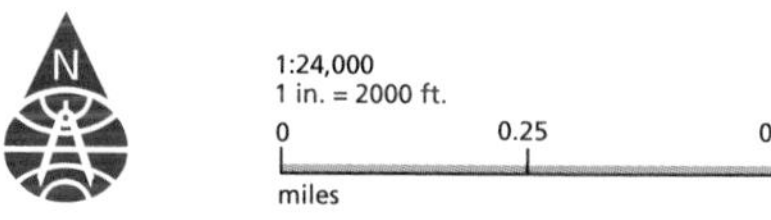

SEE 2907 MAP

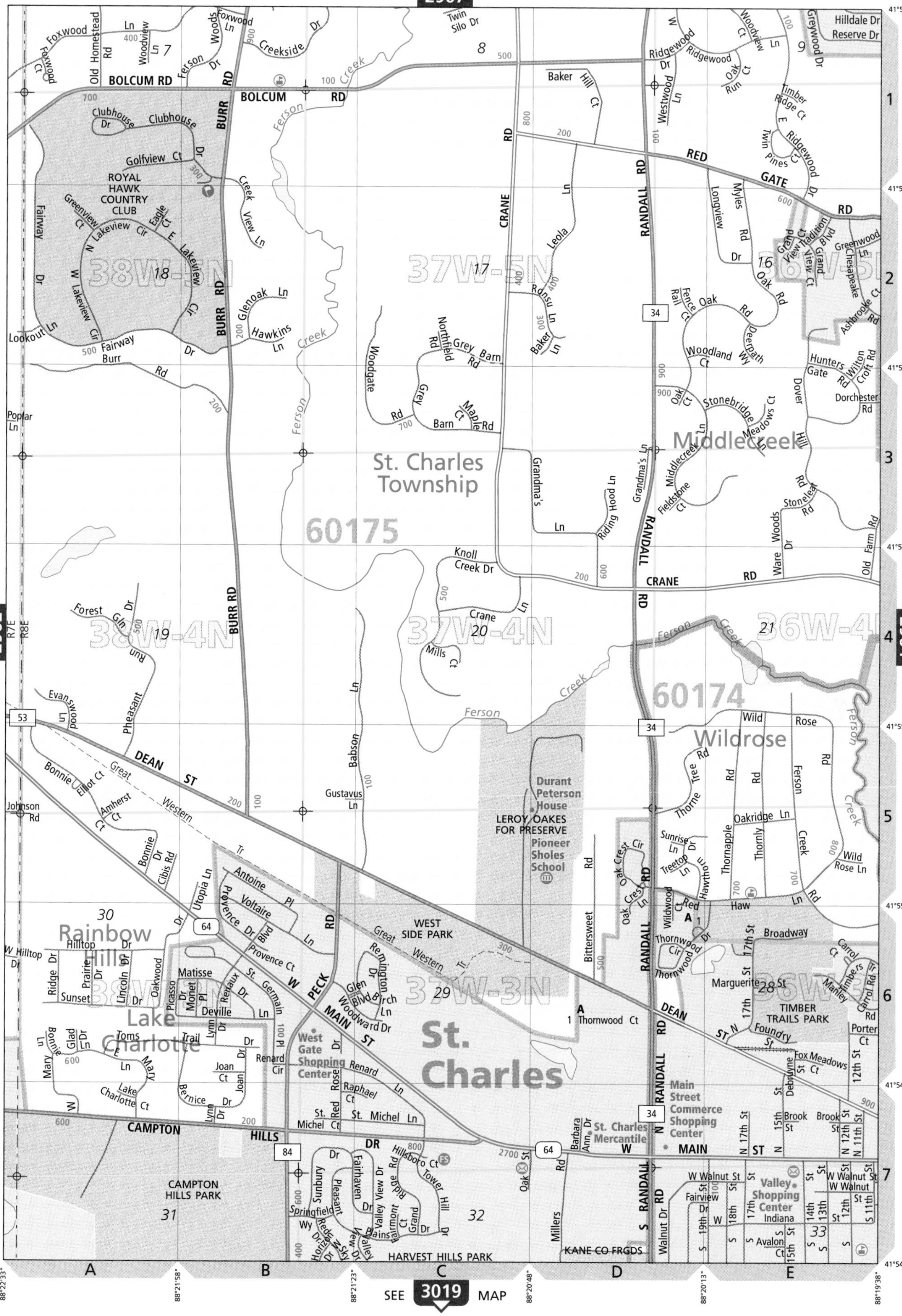

SEE 2962 MAP

SEE 2964 MAP

St. Charles Township

60175

60174

Middlecreek

Wildrose

Rainbow Hills

Lake Charlotte

St. Charles

ROYAL HAWK COUNTRY CLUB

38W-5N 18
37W-5N 17
36W-5N 16
38W-4N 19
37W-4N 20
36W-4N 21
38W-3N 30
37W-3N 29
36W-3N 28
31
32
33
7
8
9

BOLCUM RD
BURR RD
CRANE RD
RANDALL RD
RED GATE RD
DEAN ST
W MAIN ST
CAMPTON HILLS DR
PECK RD

Durant Peterson House
LEROY OAKES FOR PRESERVE
Pioneer Sholes School
WEST SIDE PARK
West Gate Shopping Center
Main Street Commerce Shopping Center
St. Charles Mercantile
Valley Shopping Center
TIMBER TRAILS PARK
CAMPTON HILLS PARK
HARVEST HILLS PARK
KANE CO FRGDS

Ferson Creek
Great Western Tr

1 2 3 4 5 6 7
A B C D E

41°57'33" 41°57'07" 41°56'41" 41°56'15" 41°55'49" 41°55'23" 41°54'56" 41°54'30"

88°22'33" 88°21'58" 88°21'23" 88°20'48" 88°20'13" 88°19'38"

SEE 3019 MAP

1:24,000
1 in. = 2000 ft.
0 0.25 0.5
miles

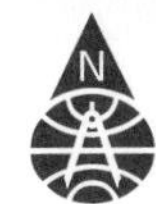

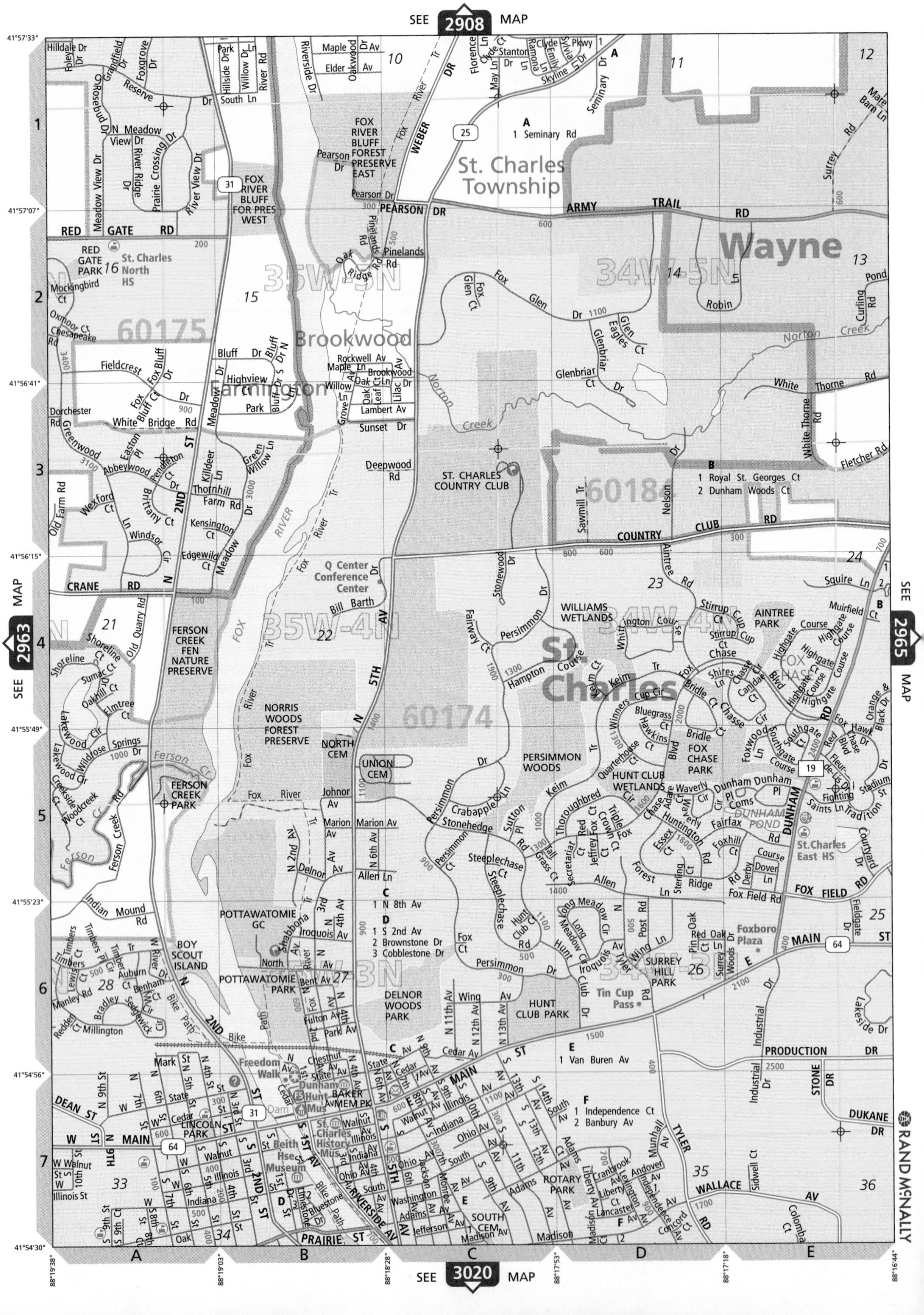

SEE 2908 MAP
SEE 2963 MAP
SEE 2965 MAP
SEE 3020 MAP
41°57'33"
41°57'07"
41°56'41"
41°56'15"
41°55'49"
41°55'23"
41°54'56"
41°54'30"
88°19'38"
88°19'03"
88°18'28"
88°17'53"
88°17'18"
88°16'44"
A
B
C
D
E
1
2
3
4
5
6
7
St. Charles Township
Wayne
Brookwood
Farmington
St. Charles
35W-5N
34W-5N
35W-4N
34W-4N
35W-3N
34W-3N
60175
60184
60174
A
1 Seminary Rd
B
1 Royal St. Georges Ct
2 Dunham Woods Ct
C
1 N 8th Av
D
1 S 2nd Av
2 Brownstone Dr
3 Cobblestone Dr
E
1 Van Buren Av
F
1 Independence Ct
2 Banbury Av
FOX RIVER BLUFF FOREST PRESERVE EAST
FOX RIVER BLUFF FOR PRES WEST
RED GATE PARK
St. Charles North HS
ST. CHARLES COUNTRY CLUB
Q Center Conference Center
FERSON CREEK FEN NATURE PRESERVE
NORRIS WOODS FOREST PRESERVE
NORTH CEM
UNION CEM
WILLIAMS WETLANDS
AINTREE PARK
FOX CHASE PARK
PERSIMMON WOODS
HUNT CLUB WETLANDS
DUNHAM POND
St.Charles East HS
FERSON CREEK PARK
BOY SCOUT ISLAND
POTTAWATOMIE GC
POTTAWATOMIE PARK
DELNOR WOODS PARK
HUNT CLUB PARK
SURREY HILL PARK
Tin Cup Pass
Foxboro Plaza
Freedom Walk
Dunham Hunt Mus
BAKER MEM PK
LINCOLN PARK
St. Charles History Mus
Beith Hse Museum
ROTARY PARK
SOUTH CEM
RED GATE RD
PEARSON DR
ARMY TRAIL RD
COUNTRY CLUB RD
CRANE RD
N 2ND ST
N 5TH AV
WEBER DR
DUNHAM RD
FOX FIELD RD
MAIN ST
W MAIN ST
DEAN ST
PRODUCTION DR
STONE DR
DUKANE DR
TYLER RD
WALLACE AV
PRAIRIE ST
RIVERSIDE AV
S 2ND ST
S 1ST AV
S 5TH AV
N 9TH
Fox River
Norton Creek
Ferson Cr
Fox River Tr
25
31
19
64
RAND McNALLY

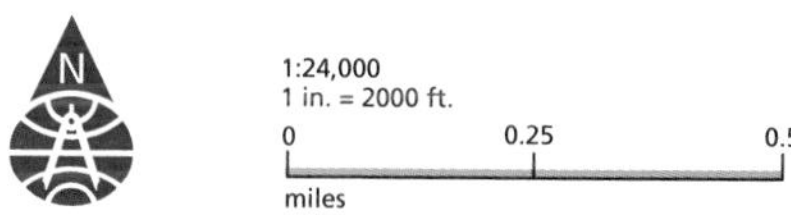

SEE 2909 MAP

Wayne
60184
West Chicago
60185
St. Charles
St. Charles Township
Wayne Township
33W-5N
32W-5N
31W-5
33W-4
32W-4
31W-4
33W-3N
32W-3N
31W-3N
60174

Dunham Castle
MISTY MEADOWS NATURAL AREA
ROYAL FOX GOLF CLUB
KINGSWOOD WETLAND
MAJESTIC OAKS WETLAND
MAJESTIC OAKS PARK
CHARLEMAGNE KINGSWOOD PK
CORNERSTONE LAKES PARK
PRATT'S WAYNE WOODS FOREST PRESERVE
Norris Cultural Arts Ctr
Foxfield Commons
Stuarts Crossing Shopping Center
Charlestowne Mall
Main Street Commons
East Gate Commons
Pheasant Run Resort & Convention Center
PHEASANT RUN GOLF COURSE
DuPage Airport
KANE CO
DUPAGE CO
Illinois Prairie Path-Elgin Brch
Norton Creek

ARMY TRAIL RD
DUNHAM RD
KIRK RD
SMITH RD
POWIS RD
KAUTZ RD
FOX FIELD RD
E MAIN ST
NORTH AV
PRODUCTION DR
OHIO AV
DUKANE DR
Illinois Av
Tower Rd
Keil Rd
Stern Av
Swenson Av
Aviation Av
DuPage Dr
Mare Barn Ln
Railroad St
Honey Hill Dr
Smith Rd
Nancy Ln
Percheron

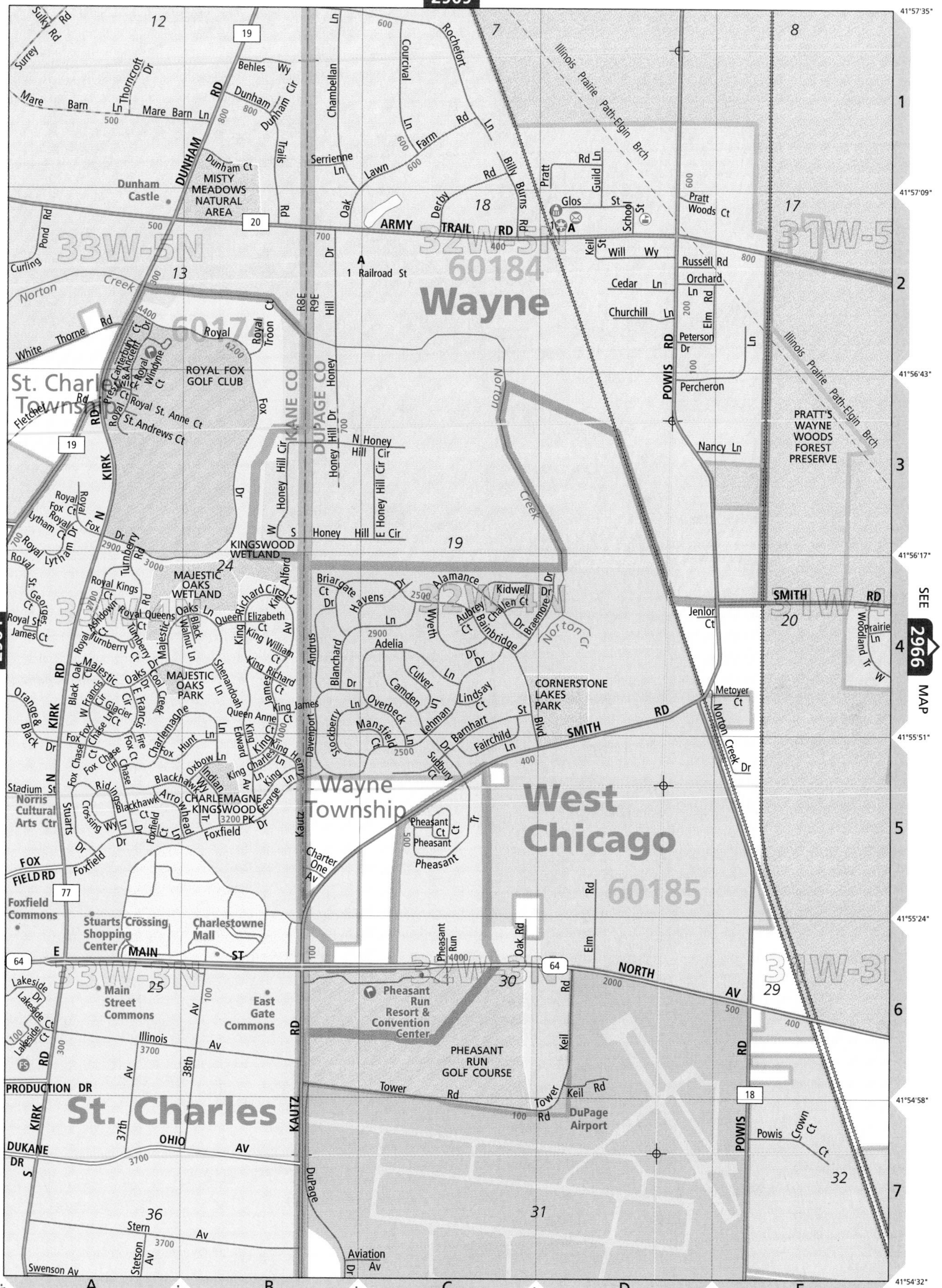

19
20
77
64
18

12 7 8 13 18 17 24 19 20 25 30 29 36 31 32

1 2 3 4 5 6 7
A B C D E

41°57'35"
41°57'09"
41°56'43"
41°56'17"
41°55'51"
41°55'24"
41°54'58"
41°54'32"
88°16'44"
88°16'09"
88°15'34"
88°14'59"
88°14'24"
88°13'49"

SEE 2964 MAP

SEE 2966 MAP

SEE 3021 MAP

1:24,000
1 in. = 2000 ft.
0 0.25 0.5 miles

SEE 2910 MAP

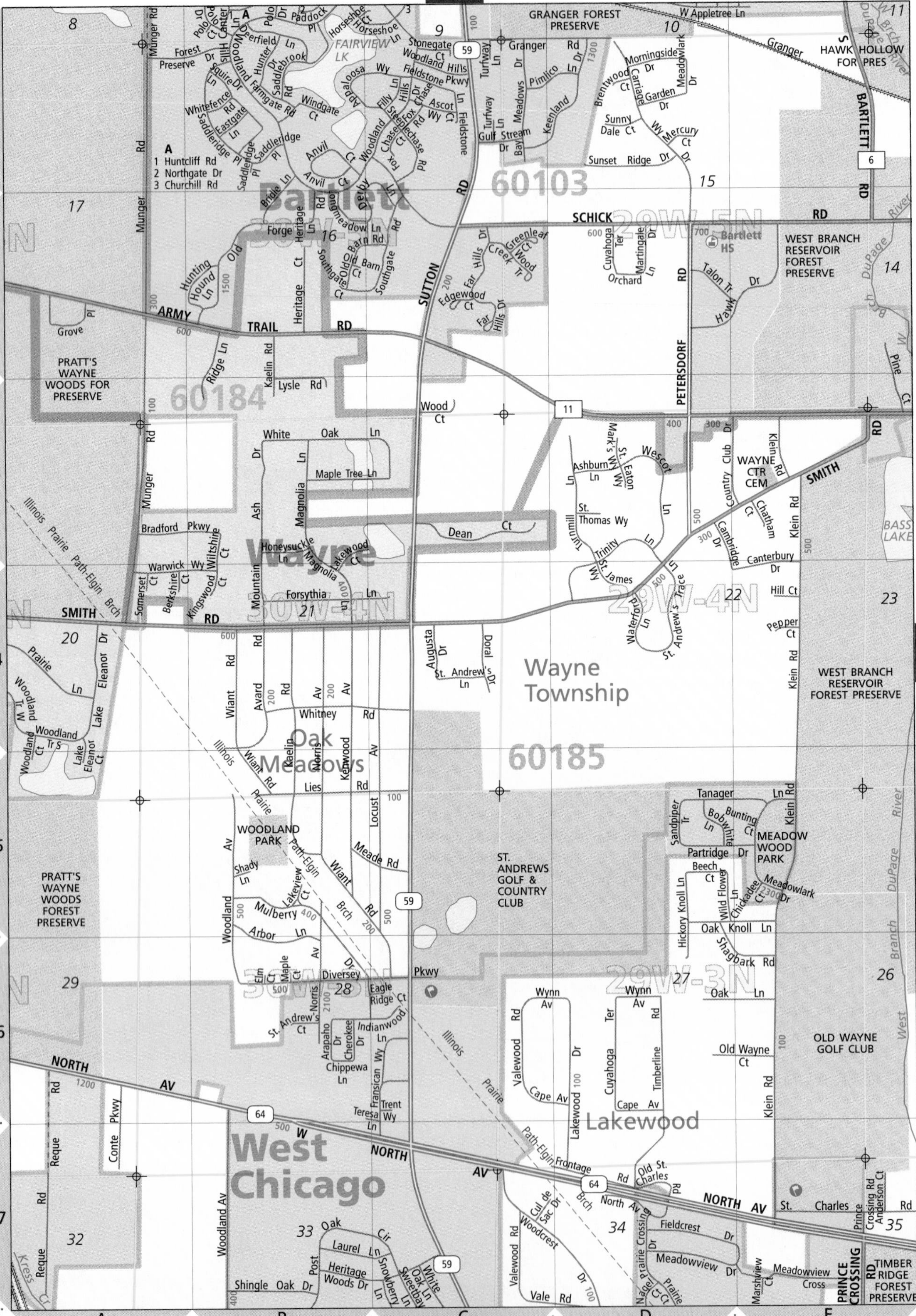

SEE 2965 MAP

SEE 2967 MAP

SEE 3022 MAP

1:24,000
1 in. = 2000 ft.
0 0.25 0.5
miles

SEE 2911 MAP

SEE 2966 MAP
SEE 2968 MAP
SEE 3023 MAP

1:24,000
1 in. = 2000 ft.
0 0.25 0.5
miles

SEE 2912 MAP

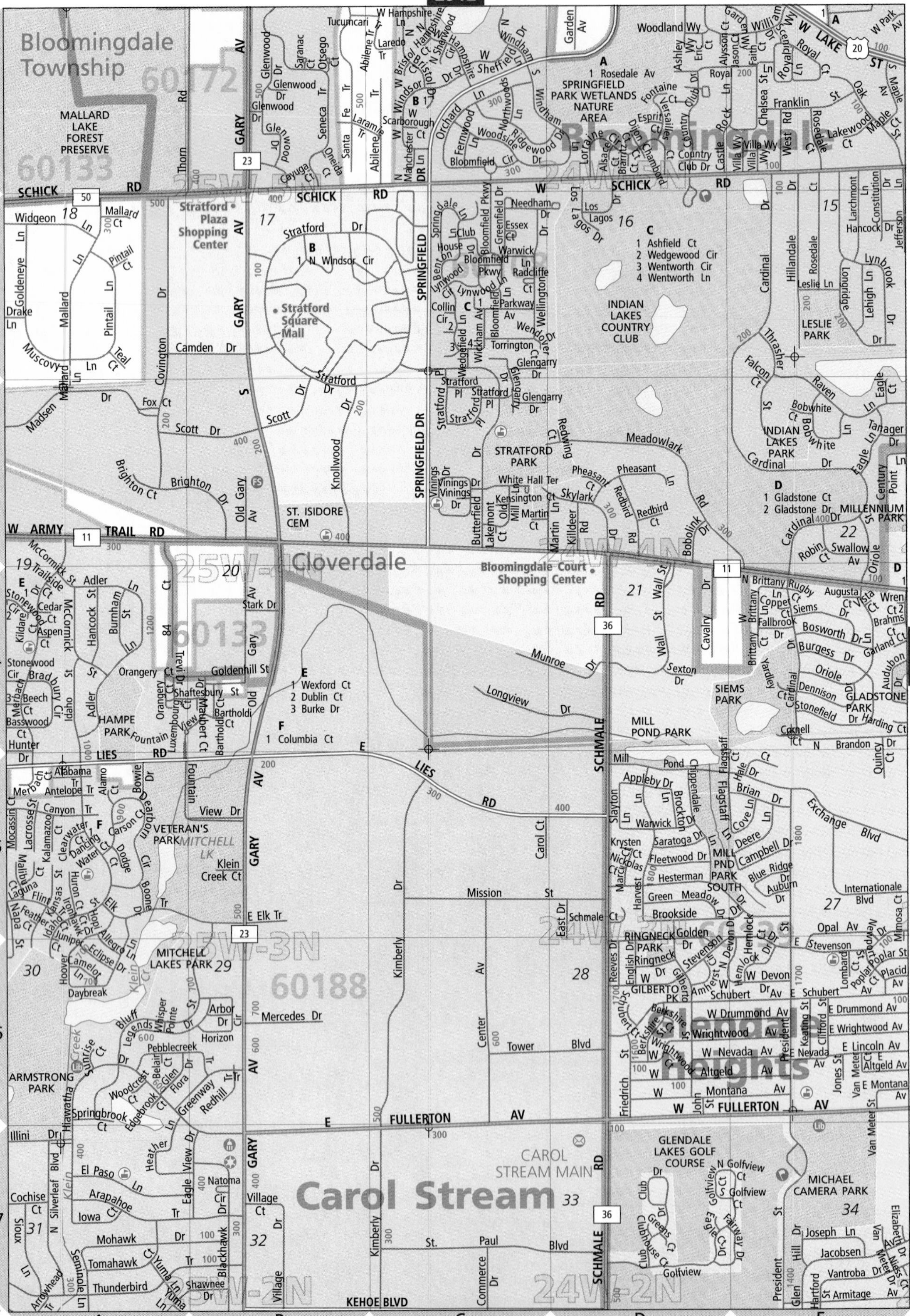

Bloomingdale Township

60172

60133

MALLARD LAKE FOREST PRESERVE

Bloomingdale

SPRINGFIELD PARK WETLANDS NATURE AREA

A
1 Rosedale Av

B
1 N Windsor Cir

C
1 Ashfield Ct
2 Wedgewood Cir
3 Wentworth Cir
4 Wentworth Ln

D
1 Gladstone Ct
2 Gladstone Dr

E
1 Wexford Ct
2 Dublin Ct
3 Burke Dr

F
1 Columbia Ct

Stratford Plaza Shopping Center

Stratford Square Mall

INDIAN LAKES COUNTRY CLUB

LESLIE PARK

INDIAN LAKES PARK

STRATFORD PARK

MILLENNIUM PARK

ST. ISIDORE CEM

Cloverdale

Bloomingdale Court Shopping Center

HAMPE PARK

SIEMS PARK

GLADSTONE PARK

MILL POND PARK

VETERAN'S PARK

MITCHELL LK

MILL PND PARK SOUTH

RINGNECK PARK

GILBERTO PK

MITCHELL LAKES PARK

60188

Glendale Heights

ARMSTRONG PARK

GLENDALE LAKES GOLF COURSE

MICHAEL CAMERA PARK

CAROL STREAM MAIN

Carol Stream

SCHICK RD

W ARMY TRAIL RD

LIES RD

E FULLERTON AV

KEHOE BLVD

GARY AV

SPRINGFIELD DR

SCHMALE RD

25W-5N

24W-5N

25W-4N

24W-4N

25W-3N

24W-3N

25W-2N

24W-2N

SEE 2967 MAP

SEE 2969 MAP

SEE 3024 MAP

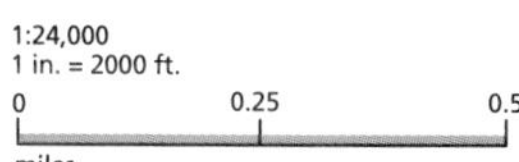

SEE 2913 MAP

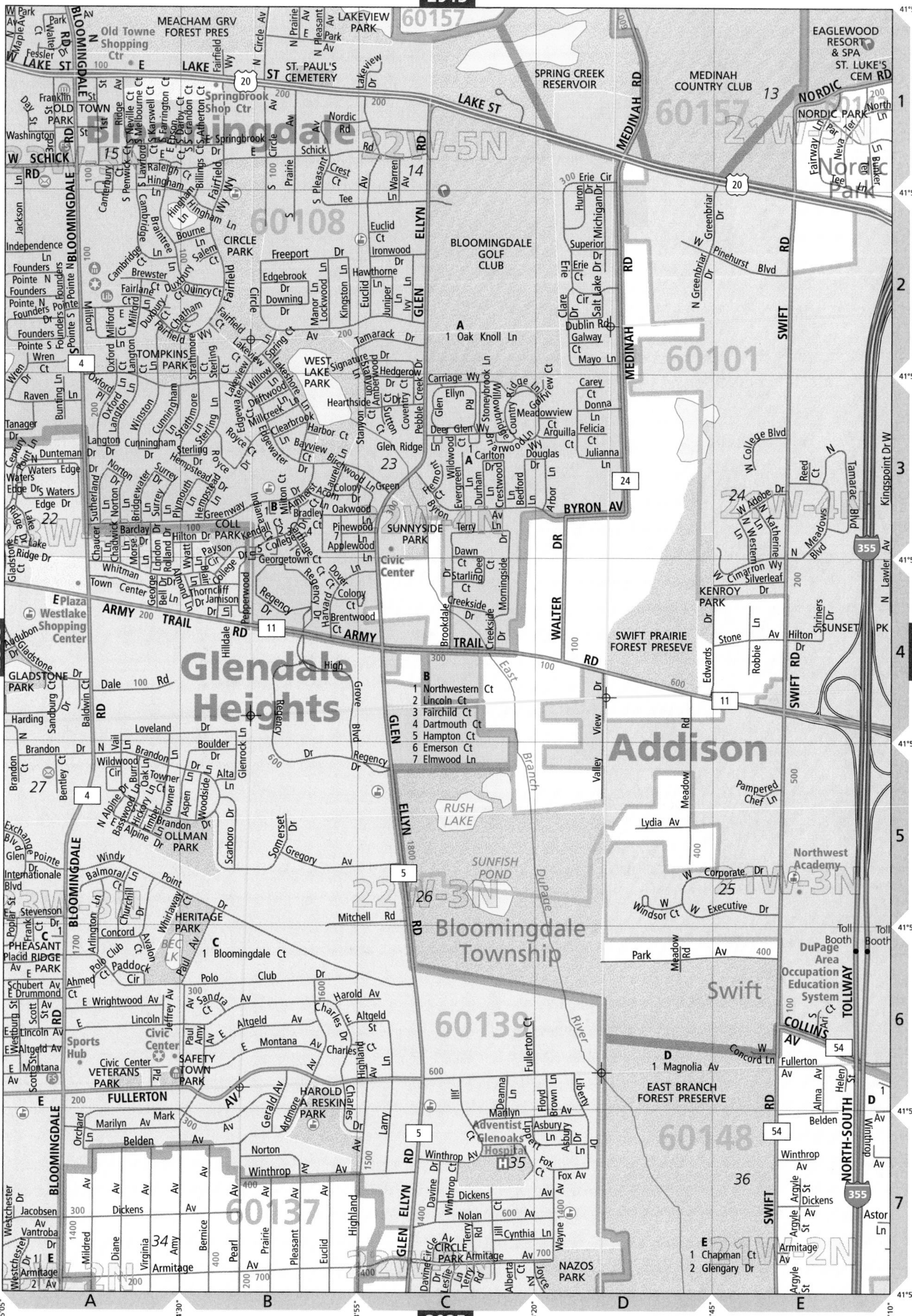

SEE 2968 MAP

SEE 2970 MAP

Bloomingdale

Glendale Heights

Addison

Swift

Bloomingdale Township

A
1 Oak Knoll Ln

B
1 Northwestern Ct
2 Lincoln Ct
3 Fairchild Ct
4 Dartmouth Ct
5 Hampton Ct
6 Emerson Ct
7 Elmwood Ln

C
1 Bloomingdale Ct

D
1 Magnolia Av

E
1 Chapman Ct
2 Glengary Dr

41°57'38" 41°57'12" 41°56'46" 41°56'20" 41°55'54" 41°55'27" 41°55'01" 41°54'35"

88°05'05" 88°04'30" 88°03'55" 88°03'20" 88°02'45" 88°02'10"

A B C D E

1 2 3 4 5 6 7

SEE 3025 MAP

1:24,000
1 in. = 2000 ft.
0 0.25 0.5
miles

SEE 2914 MAP

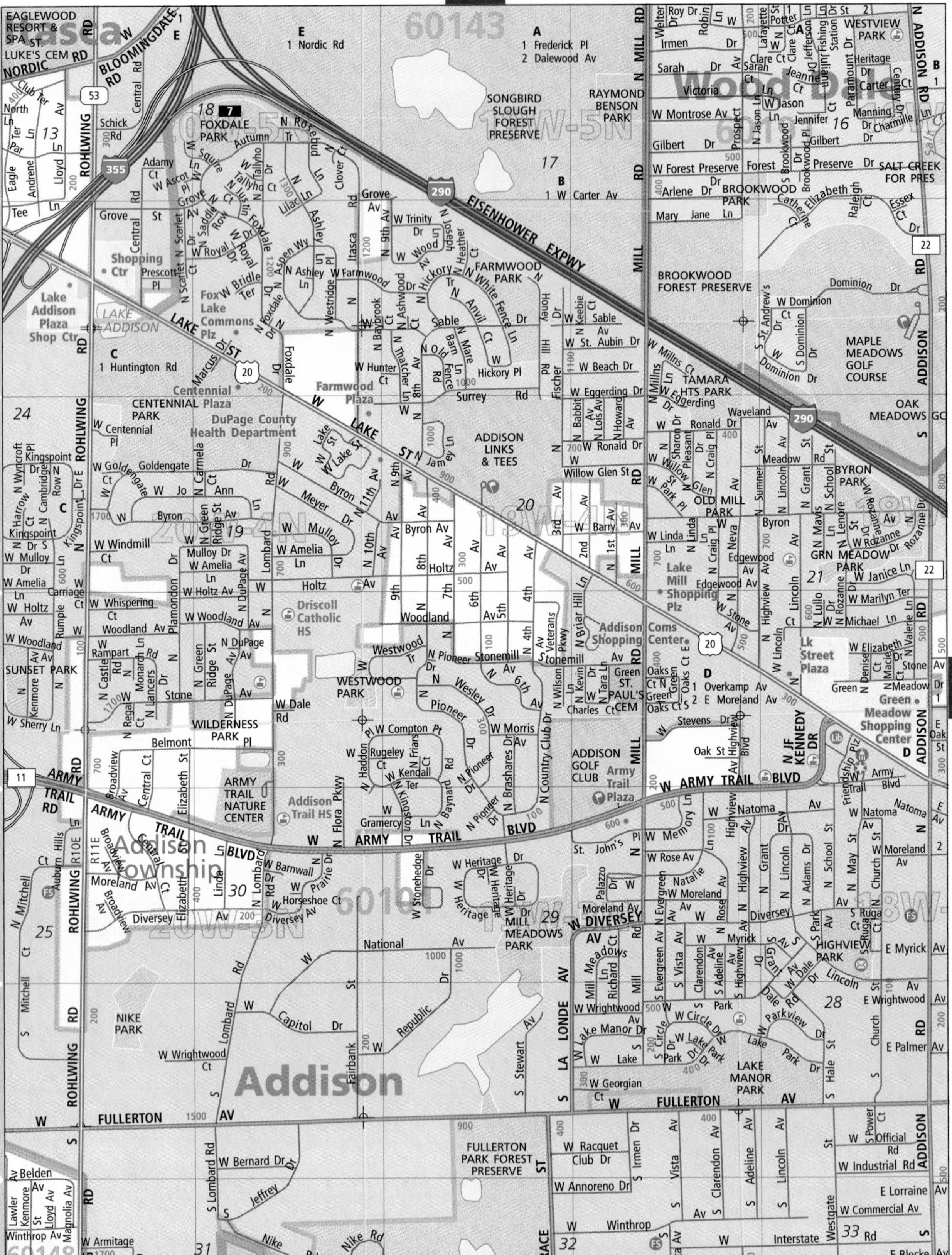

SEE 2969 MAP

SEE 2971 MAP

EAGLEWOOD RESORT & SPA
ST. LUKE'S CEM
Itasca
60143
Wood Dale
FOXDALE PARK
SONGBIRD SLOUGH FOREST PRESERVE
RAYMOND BENSON PARK
WESTVIEW PARK
SALT CREEK FOR PRES
BROOKWOOD PARK
BROOKWOOD FOREST PRESERVE
EISENHOWER EXPWY
Shopping Ctr
Lake Addison Plaza Shop Ctr
LAKE ADDISON
Fox Lake Commons Plz
FARMWOOD PARK
Farmwood Plaza
Centennial Plaza
CENTENNIAL PARK
DuPage County Health Department
ADDISON LINKS & TEES
TAMARA HTS PARK
MAPLE MEADOWS GOLF COURSE
OAK MEADOWS GC
OLD MILL PARK
BYRON PARK
Lake Mill Shopping Plz
GRN MEADOW PARK
Driscoll Catholic HS
Addison Shopping Center
Addison Coms Center
Lk Street Plaza
Green Meadow Shopping Center
SUNSET PARK
WESTWOOD PARK
ST. PAUL'S CEM
WILDERNESS PARK
ADDISON GOLF CLUB
Army Trail Plaza
ARMY TRAIL NATURE CENTER
Addison Trail HS
ARMY TRAIL BLVD
Addison Township
60101
MILL MEADOWS PARK
HIGHVIEW PARK
NIKE PARK
LAKE MANOR PARK
Addison
FULLERTON AV
FULLERTON PARK FOREST PRESERVE
LOMBARD INDUSTRIAL PARK
60148
Lombard
20W-5N
19W-5N
20W-4N
19W-4N
18W-4N
20W-3N
19W-3N
18W-3N
20W-2N
19W-2N
18W-2N

SEE 3026 MAP

1:24,000
1 in. = 2000 ft.
0 0.25 0.5
miles

SEE 2915 MAP

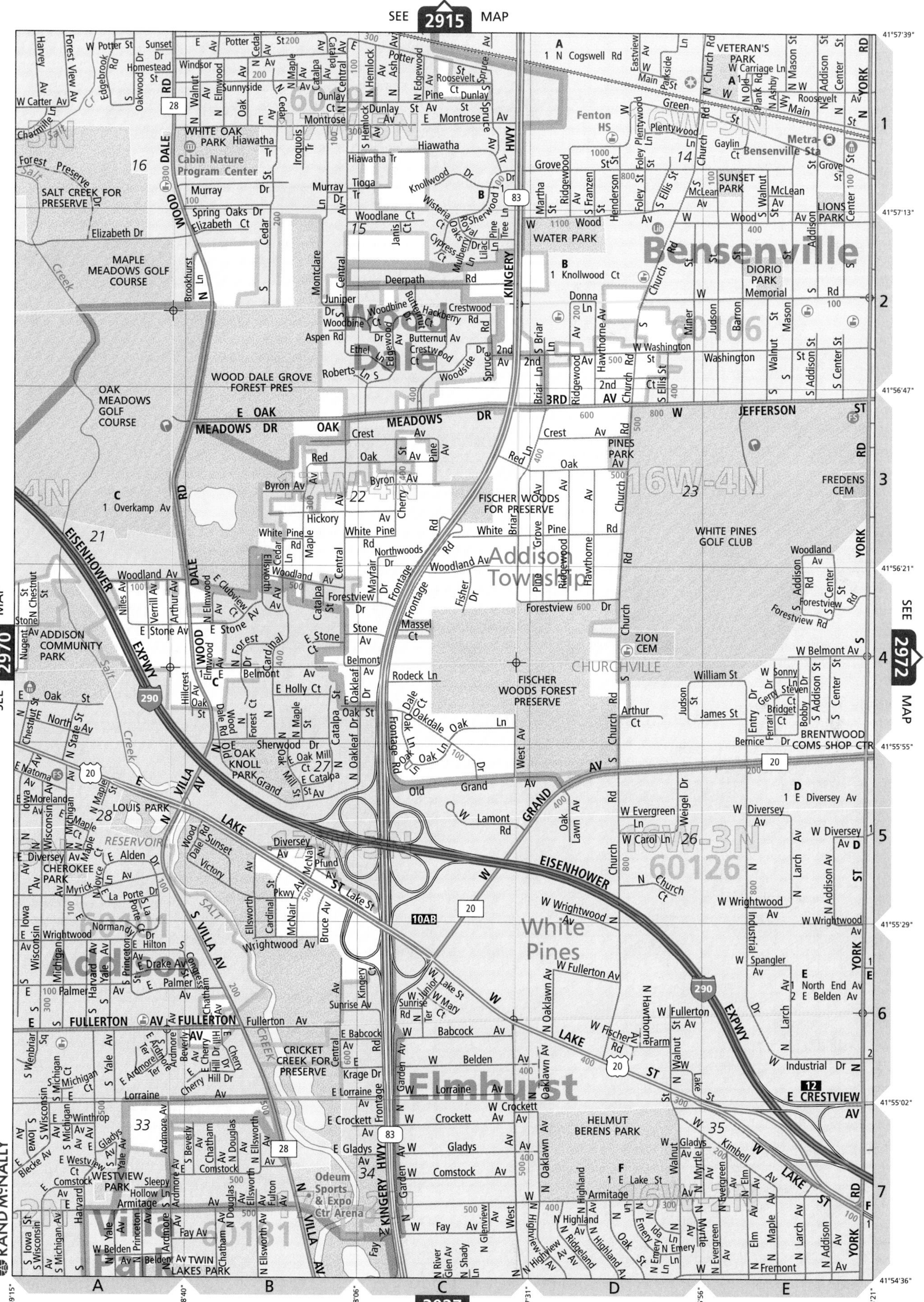

SEE 2970 MAP
SEE 2972 MAP
SEE 3027 MAP

RAND McNALLY

1:24,000
1 in. = 2000 ft.
0 0.25 0.5
miles

SEE 2916 MAP

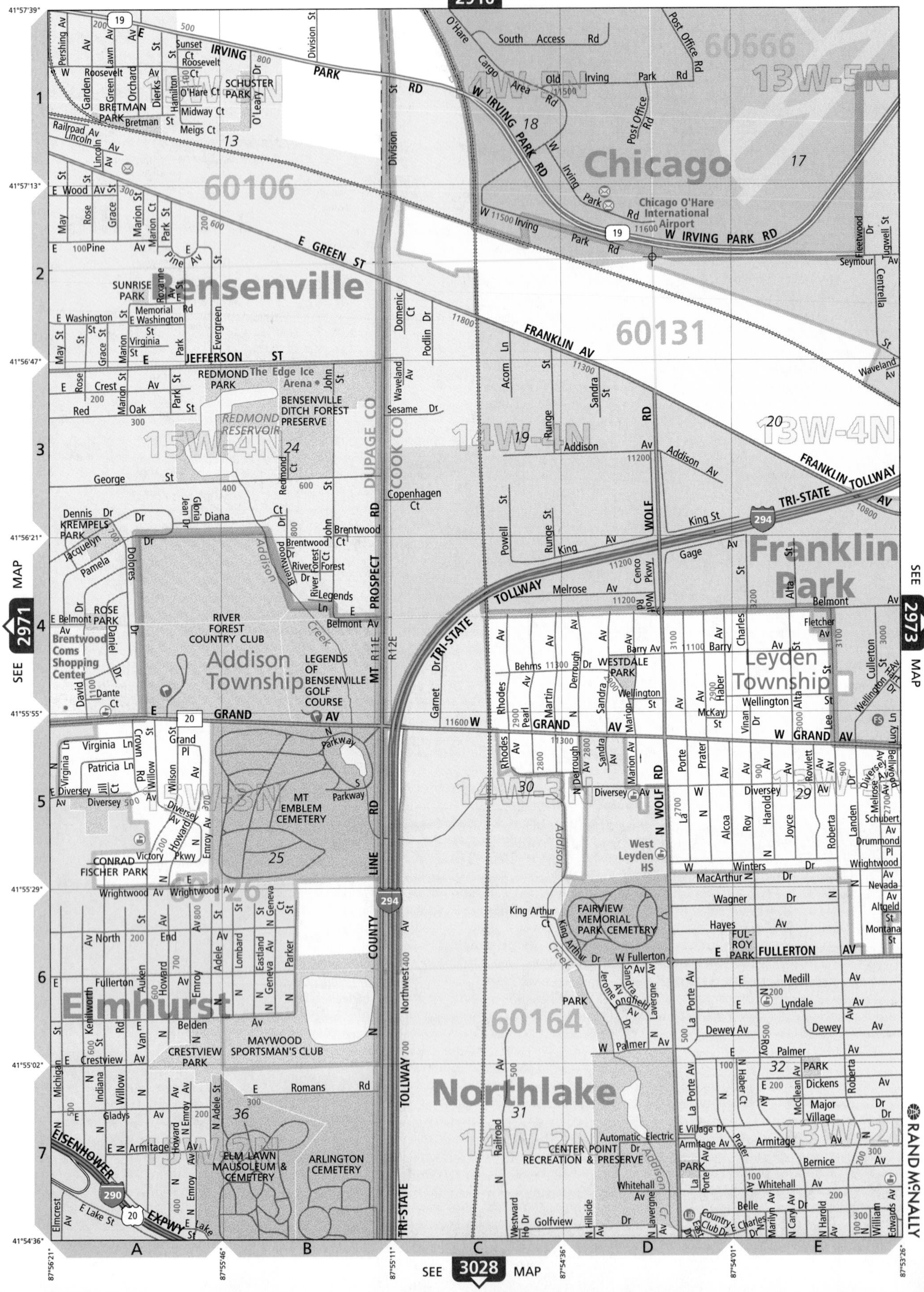

SEE 2971 MAP

SEE 2973 MAP

Bensenville
Chicago
Chicago O'Hare International Airport
Franklin Park
Leyden Township
Addison Township
Elmhurst
Northlake

60106
60666
60131
60126
60164

SCHUSTER PARK
BRETMAN PARK
SUNRISE PARK
REDMOND PARK
The Edge Ice Arena
BENSENVILLE DITCH FOREST PRESERVE
REDMOND RESERVOIR
KREMPELS PARK
ROSE PARK
Brentwood Coms Shopping Center
RIVER FOREST COUNTRY CLUB
LEGENDS OF BENSENVILLE GOLF COURSE
MT EMBLEM CEMETERY
CONRAD FISCHER PARK
CRESTVIEW PARK
MAYWOOD SPORTSMAN'S CLUB
ELM LAWN MAUSOLEUM & CEMETERY
ARLINGTON CEMETERY
WESTDALE PARK
West Leyden HS
FAIRVIEW MEMORIAL PARK CEMETERY
FUL-ROY PARK
CENTER POINT RECREATION & PRESERVE
PARK

IRVING PARK RD
E GREEN ST
FRANKLIN AV
JEFFERSON ST
FRANKLIN TOLLWAY
TRI-STATE TOLLWAY
GRAND AV
FULLERTON AV
EISENHOWER EXPWY
MT PROSPECT RD
COUNTY LINE RD
N WOLF RD
DUPAGE CO
COOK CO
R11E
R12E

15W-5N
14W-5N
13W-5N
15W-4N
14W-4N
13W-4N
15W-3N
14W-3N
13W-3N
15W-2N
14W-2N
13W-2N

41°57'39"
41°57'13"
41°56'47"
41°56'21"
41°55'55"
41°55'29"
41°55'02"
41°54'36"
87°56'21"
87°55'46"
87°55'11"
87°54'36"
87°54'01"
87°53'26"

1 2 3 4 5 6 7
A B C D E

SEE 3028 MAP

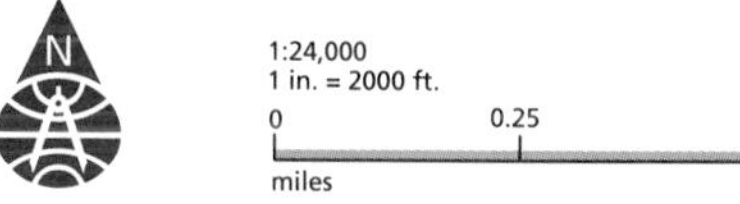

SEE 2917 MAP

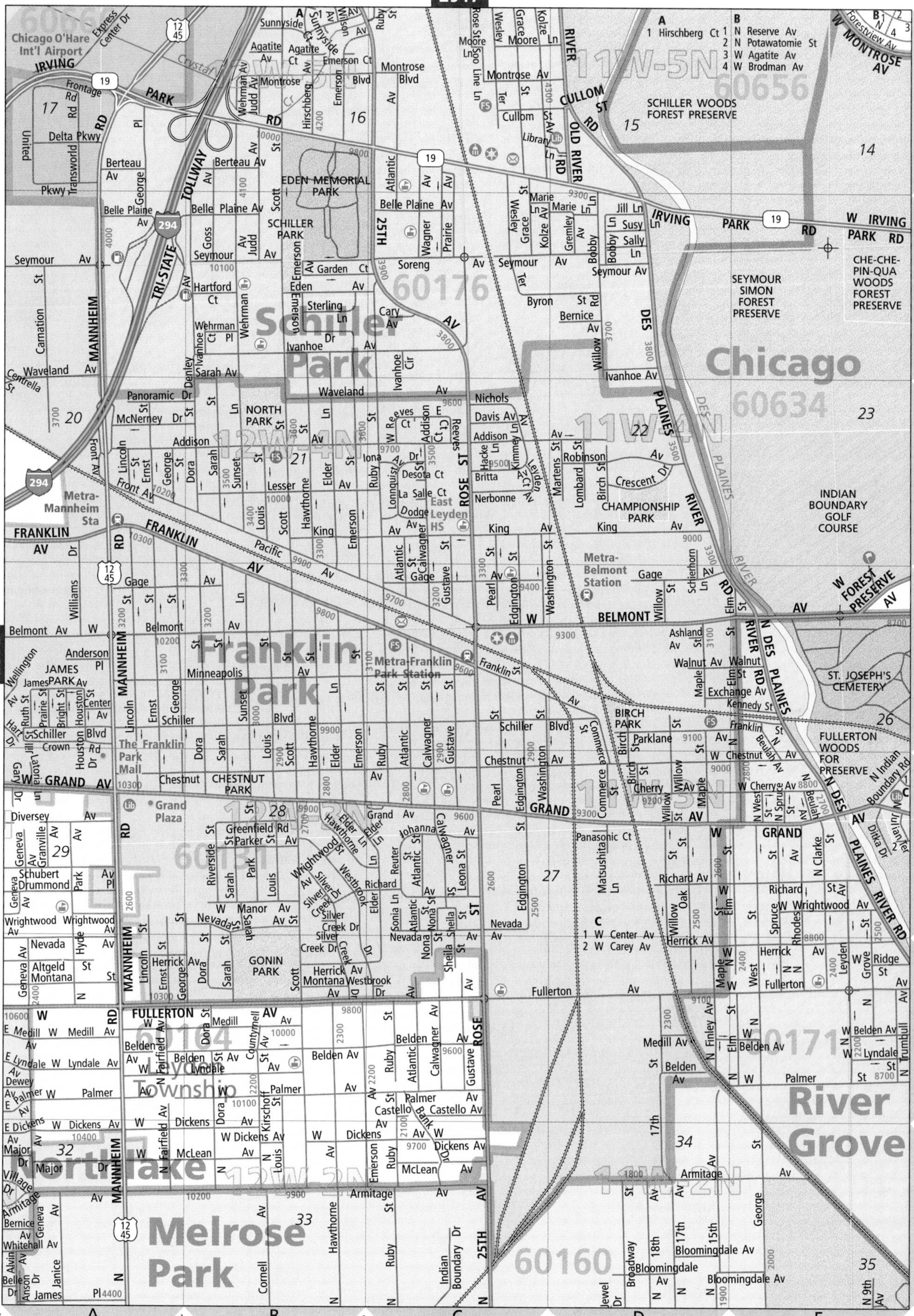

SEE 2972 MAP

SEE 2974 MAP

SEE 3029 MAP

1:24,000
1 in. = 2000 ft.
0 0.25 0.5
miles

SEE 2918 MAP

SEE 2973 MAP

SEE 2975 MAP

41°57'40"
41°57'14"
41°56'48"
41°56'21"
41°55'55"
41°55'29"
41°55'03"
41°54'37"

1
2
3
4
5
6
7

Norridge
Chicago
River Grove
Elmwood Park

WESTLAWN CEMETERY
ACACIA CEMETERY
IRVING PARK BOULEVARD CEM
SCHILLER WOODS FOR PRESERVE
SCHILLER PND
CHE-CHE-PIN-QUA WOODS FOREST PRESERVE
SEYMOUR SIMON FOREST PRESERVE
INDIAN BOUNDARY GOLF COURSE
HIAWATHA PARK
ST. JOSEPH'S CEMETERY
FULLERTON WOODS FOR PRES
ELMWOOD MEMORIAL CEMETERY
Guerin Prep HS
Elmwood Park HS
OAK PARK COUNTRY CLUB
FULLERTON WOODS FOREST PRESERVE
KIDDIELAND PARK
Triton College
Cernan Earth & Space Center
Metra-River Grove Station
Metra-Elmwood Park Station
Metra-Mont Clare Sta
Metra-Mars Sta
Ridgewood Community HS
Harlem-Irving Plaza
Norridge Commons
Chicago-Read Mental Health Center
MT OLIVE CEMETERY
ROSEMONT CEM
SHABBONA PARK
BELL PARK
RUTHERFORD PARK
SAYRE PK
Chicago Shriners Hosp
DUNNING

MONTROSE AV
IRVING PARK RD
ADDISON ST
BELMONT AV
DIVERSEY AV
GRAND AV
FULLERTON AV
W FOREST PRESERVE AV
CUMBERLAND AV
THATCHER AV
HARLEM AV
OAK PARK AV
DES PLAINES RIVER RD
1ST AV
5TH AV
CANFIELD AV
DES PLAINES RIVER

60656
60706
60634
60171
60707
60160

10W-5N
9W-5N
10W-4N
9W-4N
9W-3N
10W-2N
9W-2N

A
B
C
D
E

87°50'31"
87°49'56"
87°49'21"
87°48'47"
87°48'12"
87°47'37"

SEE 3030 MAP

1:24,000
1 in. = 2000 ft.
0 0.25 0.5
miles

SEE 2919 MAP

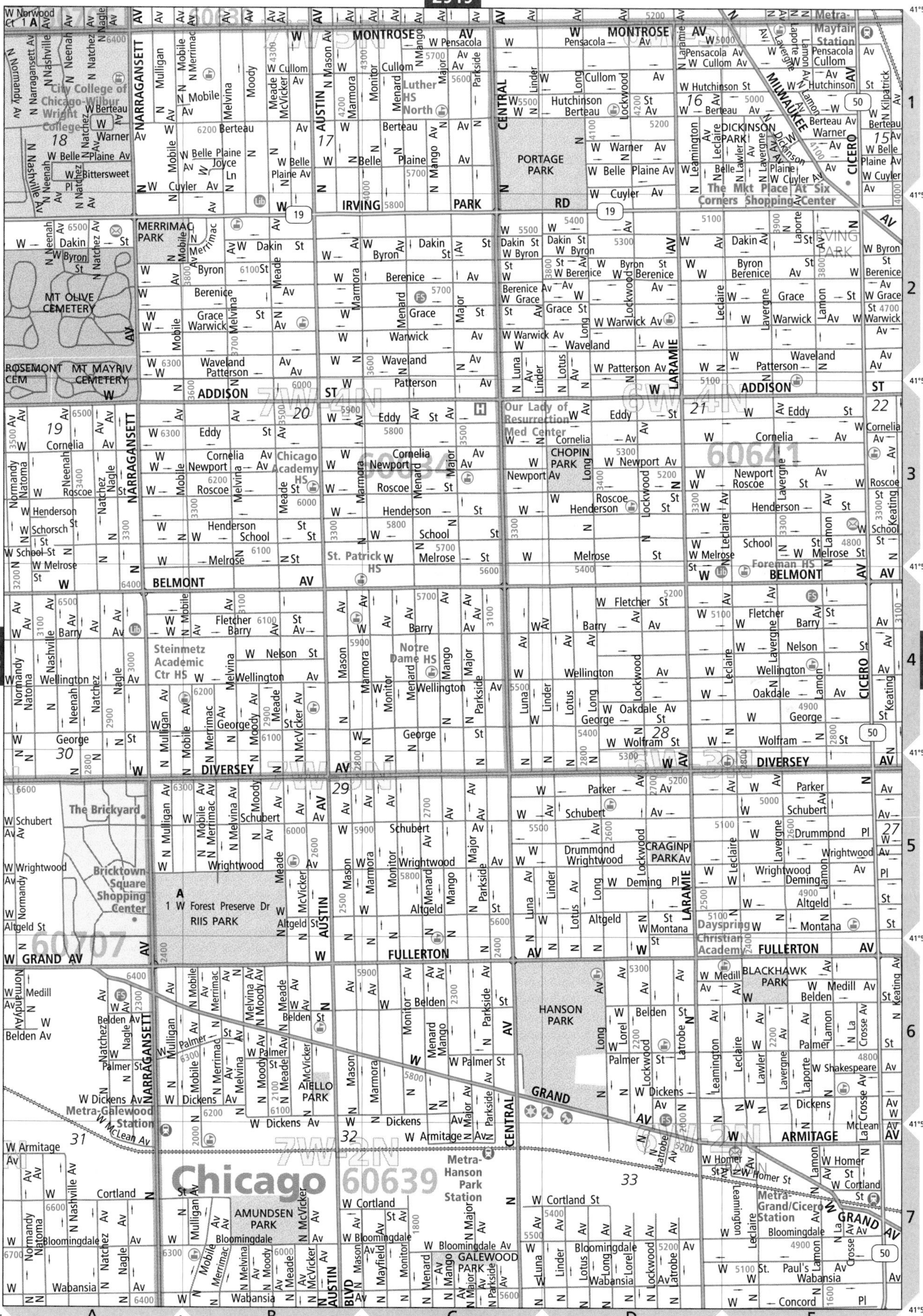

SEE 2974 MAP

SEE 2976 MAP

SEE 3031 MAP

MONTROSE AV
IRVING PARK RD
ADDISON ST
BELMONT AV
DIVERSEY AV
FULLERTON AV
W GRAND AV
ARMITAGE
NARRAGANSETT
AUSTIN
CENTRAL
LARAMIE
CICERO
MILWAUKEE

City College of Chicago-Wilbur Wright College
Luther HS North
PORTAGE PARK
Metra-Mayfair Station
DICKINSON PARK
The Mkt Place At Six Corners Shopping Center
MERRIMAC PARK
MT OLIVE CEMETERY
ROSEMONT CEM
MT MAYRIV CEMETERY
Our Lady of Resurrection Med Center
CHOPIN PARK
Chicago Academy HS
St. Patrick HS
Foreman HS
Steinmetz Academic Ctr HS
Notre Dame HS
The Brickyard
Bricktown Square Shopping Center
RIIS PARK
CRAGIN PARK
Dayspring Christian Academy
BLACKHAWK PARK
HANSON PARK
AIELLO PARK
Metra-Galewood Station
Metra-Hanson Park Station
AMUNDSEN PARK
GALEWOOD PARK
Metra-Grand/Cicero Station
Chicago 60639
60707
60634
60641

7W-4N
6W-4N
7W-3N
6W-3N
7W-2N
6W-2N

41°57'40"
41°57'14"
41°56'48"
41°56'22"
41°55'56"
41°55'30"
41°55'04"
41°54'38"
87°47'37"
87°47'02"
87°46'27"
87°45'52"
87°45'17"
87°44'42"

A B C D E
1 2 3 4 5 6 7

1:24,000
1 in. = 2000 ft.
0 0.25 0.5
miles

SEE 2920 MAP

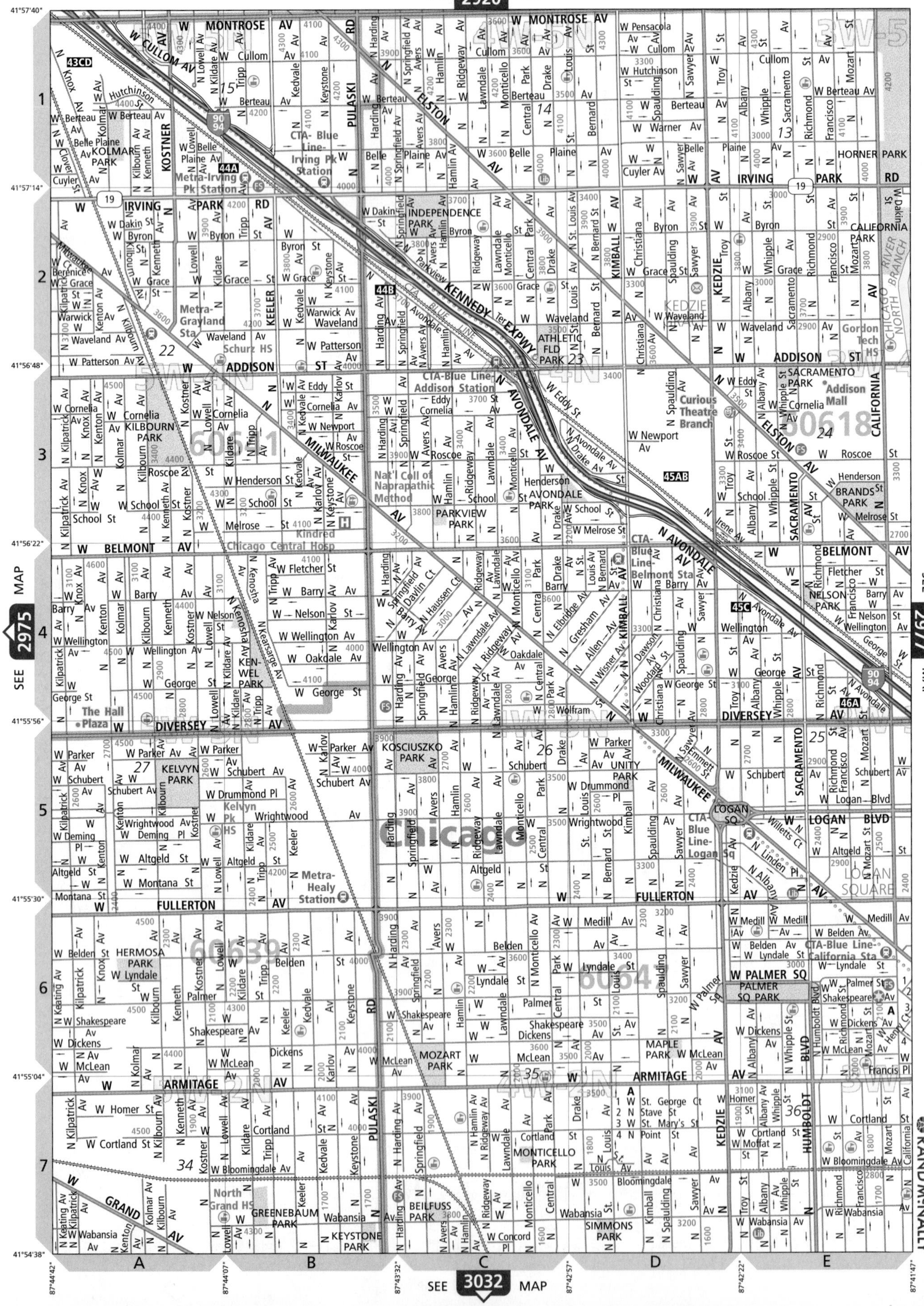

SEE 2975 MAP

SEE 2977 MAP

41°57'40"
41°57'14"
41°56'48"
41°56'22"
41°55'56"
41°55'30"
41°55'04"
41°54'38"

1
2
3
4
5
6
7

W MONTROSE AV
W IRVING PARK RD
W ADDISON ST
W BELMONT AV
W DIVERSEY AV
W FULLERTON AV
W ARMITAGE AV
GRAND AV

KOSTNER
PULASKI
KEELER
KIMBALL
KEDZIE
SACRAMENTO
CALIFORNIA
HUMBOLDT BLVD
N ELSTON AV
N MILWAUKEE AV
N AVONDALE AV
KENNEDY EXPWY
W LOGAN BLVD
W PALMER SQ

Chicago

KOLMAR PARK
INDEPENDENCE PARK
CALIFORNIA PARK
ATHLETIC FLD PARK
KILBOURN PARK
PARKVIEW PARK
AVONDALE PARK
SACRAMENTO PARK
BRANDS PARK
KEN-WEL PARK
NELSON PARK
KOSCIUSZKO PARK
KELVYN PARK
UNITY PARK
HERMOSA PARK
PALMER SQ PARK
MOZART PARK
MAPLE PARK
MONTICELLO PARK
GREENEBAUM PARK
BEILFUSS PARK
KEYSTONE PARK
SIMMONS PARK
LOGAN SQUARE
HORNER PARK

Metra-Irving Pk Station
CTA-Blue Line-Irving Pk Station
Metra-Grayland Sta
CTA-Blue Line Addison Station
CTA-Blue Line-Belmont Sta
CTA-Blue Line-Logan Sq
CTA-Blue Line-California Sta
Metra-Healy Station
Schurz HS
Gordon Tech HS
Kelvyn Pk HS
North Grand HS
Nat'l Coll of Naprapathic Method
Kindred Chicago Central Hosp
Curious Theatre Branch
Addison Mall
The Hall Plaza
CHICAGO RIVER NORTH BRANCH

60618
60641
60639
60647

A B C D E

87°44'42"
87°44'07"
87°43'32"
87°42'57"
87°42'22"
87°41'47"

SEE 3032 MAP

1:24,000
1 in. = 2000 ft.
0 0.25 0.5
miles

SEE 2921 MAP

SEE 2976 MAP
SEE 2978 MAP
SEE 3033 MAP

RAND McNALLY

1:24,000
1 in. = 2000 ft.
0 0.25 0.5
miles

SEE 2922 MAP

A
1 W Junior Ter
2 W Hutchinson St
3 W Bittersweet Pl

B
1 N Sheridan Rd

C
1 N Childrens Plz

D
1 N Crilly Ct
2 W Willow St

E
1 N St. Michael's Ct

F
1 N Wieland St
2 N Sandburg Ter
3 N Dearborn Pkwy
4 N Astor St

LAKE MICHIGAN

MONTROSE HBR
LINCOLN PARK
Lycee Francais de Chicago
SYDNEY R MAROVITZ GC
Prologue Alt HS
Bird Sanctuary
BELMONT HARBOR
Our Lady of Mt Carmel Church
Chicago Yacht Club
Lakeshore Theater
St. Joseph Hospital
Century Shopping Center
Elks Nat'l Hqs & Mem Bldg
Governor Oglesby Mon
NORTH POND
Chicago Theatre for Young Audiences
St. Clement's Church
Peggy Notebaert Nature Museum
Children's Mem Hospital
Lincoln Park Conservatory
Chicago
Victory Gdns Theater
Lincoln Park Hospital
Francis Parker School
DIVERSEY Parker HBR LAGOON
OZ PARK
Lincoln Park Zoo
Lincoln Park HS
Chicago Academy of Sci
Farm in the Zoo
SOUTH PND
BAULER PARK
Midwest Buddhist Temple
Louis Sullivan Row Houses
Lincoln Mon
North Avenue Beach
Royal George Theatre
St. Michael's Church
Chicago Hist Society
Latin School of Chicago
Second City
Free Associates Theater
North Blvd

LAKE SHORE DR
N SHERIDAN RD
BELMONT AV
DIVERSEY PKWY
FULLERTON PKWY
N CANNON DR
N STOCKTON DR
N LINCOLN AV
N CLARK ST
ARMITAGE AV
NORTH AV
W LA SALLE DR
W NORTH BLVD

41°57'40" 41°57'14" 41°56'48" 41°56'22" 41°55'56" 41°55'30" 41°55'04" 41°54'38"

87°38'53" 87°38'18" 87°37'43" 87°37'08" 87°36'33" 87°35'58"

SEE 2977 MAP

SEE B MAP

SEE 3034 MAP

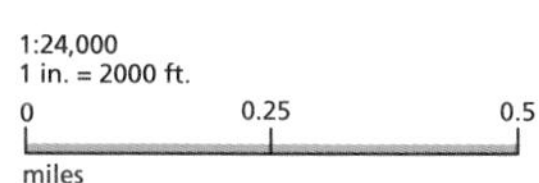

SEE 2961 MAP

Campton Township

Elburn

Stillmeadow

Blackberry Township

60119

Winden Oak

42W-2N
43W-2N
43W-1N
42W-1N
41W
43W-0N
42W-0N
43W-0S
42W-0S

T40N
T39N

ST. GALL CEM
BLACKBERRY CEM
LIBERTY PARK
HERITAGE PARK
HUGHES CREEK GOLF CLUB
JOHNSON'S MOUND FOREST PRESERVE
Broadview Academy

KESLINGER RD
HUGHES RD
POULEY RD
ANDERSON RD
MAIN ST
HARLEY RD
SMITH RD
GREEN RD
Forest Preserve Rd

A 1 N Bowgren Cir

Ream Dr, Collins Dr, Snow Dr, Walker Ct, Walker, 1st St, Conley Dr, Hoyt Dr, Westlake Dr, Tiller St, Shepherd Ln, Anderson Rd, Center, Wright St, E 1st St, Warne Ct, Morrill Ln, Valley Dr, Gee Ct, Prairie Valley Ct, Sharp Ct, Weston Ct, Conley Ct, Downing, Drover St, Prairie, Laverne St, Valley Dr, Highland, Highview Ct, Downing St, Ridge, E Birch St, Maple Ct, Erickson Ct, E Willow St, 3rd, E Lilac St, E Reader St, 2nd St, 4th St, Hicks Dr, Paul St, E Pierce St, Dempsey Dr, E Shannon St, E North St, E Nebraska St, Kansas St, South St, Swain St, E Oak Dr

Bowgren Cir, Bowgren Dr, Meadowsweet Dr, Still Meadows Ln, Stargrass Ln, Pennycress Ct, Northway Dr, Denali Ct, Denali Rd, Blackberry Creek

Gray Av, Liberty St, Stoffa Av, Holbrook Av, Kindberg Ct, President St, Berry Av, Kendall St, Liberty Dr, Republic, Patriot, Robinson, Wise, Oakwood Dr, Sears, Freedom Cir, Cline Rd, Reeves St, Cline Av, Anderson Rd, Veteran, Motz St, Blackberry Creek Dr, Turnbull, Clark Av, Bowdish St, Griffith Av, Pattee Av, Swan Dr, Motz St, Corrigan St, Griffith Av, Remington Av, Founder Dr, Citizen Av, Spalding Av, Seaton, Anderson, Avon Ct, Melbourne St, Corrigan St, Soldier Ct, Creek Dr, Souders St, Lance Av, Fairfield, Beed Av, Lakin Av, Independence, Setter St, Wheeler Av, Dodson Av, Independence Av, Fairfield Dr, Carolyn Ct, Spring Valley Dr, Swinton Ct, Kenmar Dr, Kenmar Ln, Kenmar Ct, Sorrel Dr, Rowe Rd, Rowe, Timbercrest Dr, Whispering Oaks Dr, Autumn Woods Ln

1 2 3 4 5 6 7
A B C D E

SEE MAP B
SEE 3018 MAP
SEE 3075 MAP

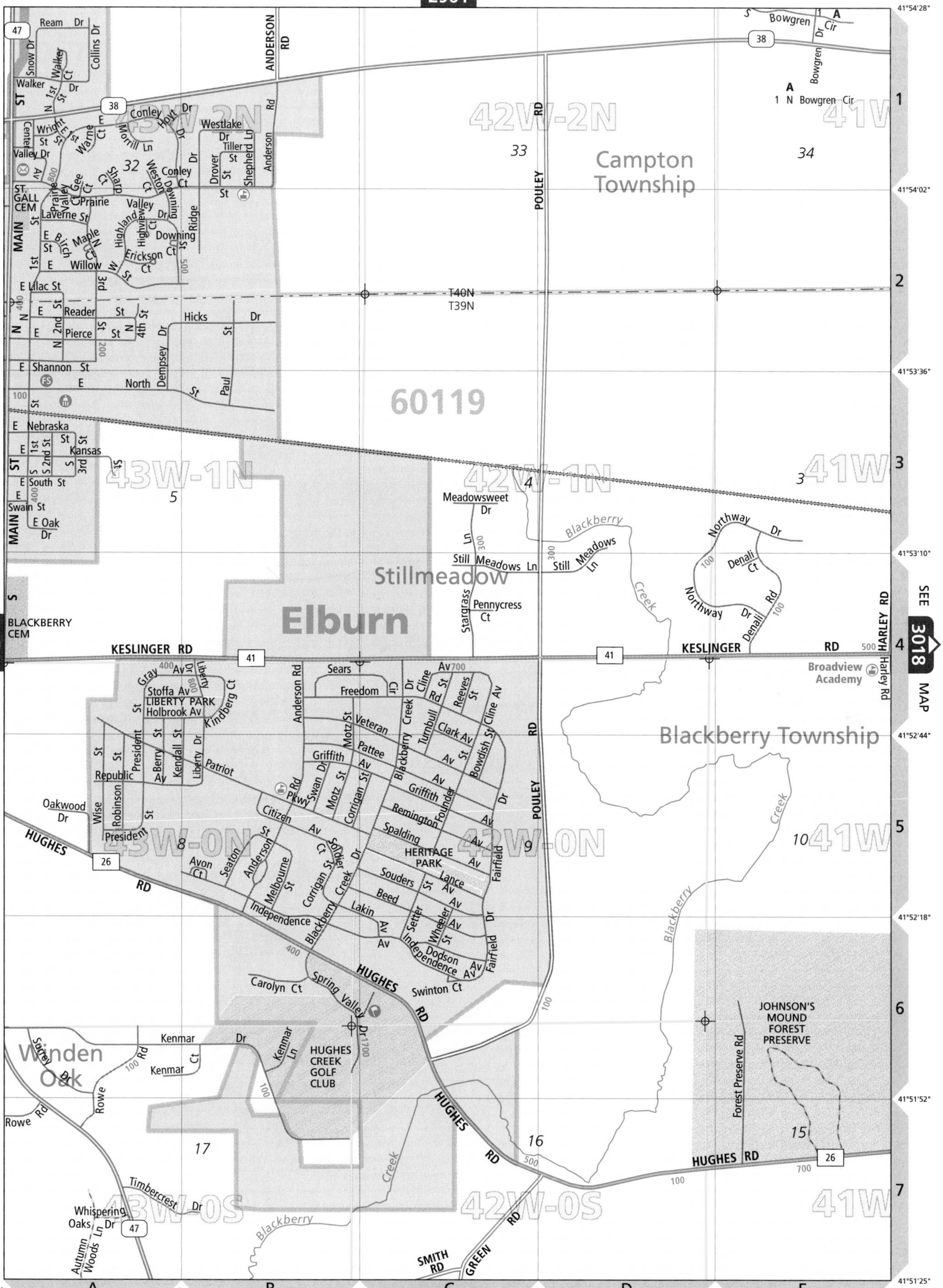

1:24,000
1 in. = 2000 ft.
0 0.25 0.5
miles

SEE 2962 MAP

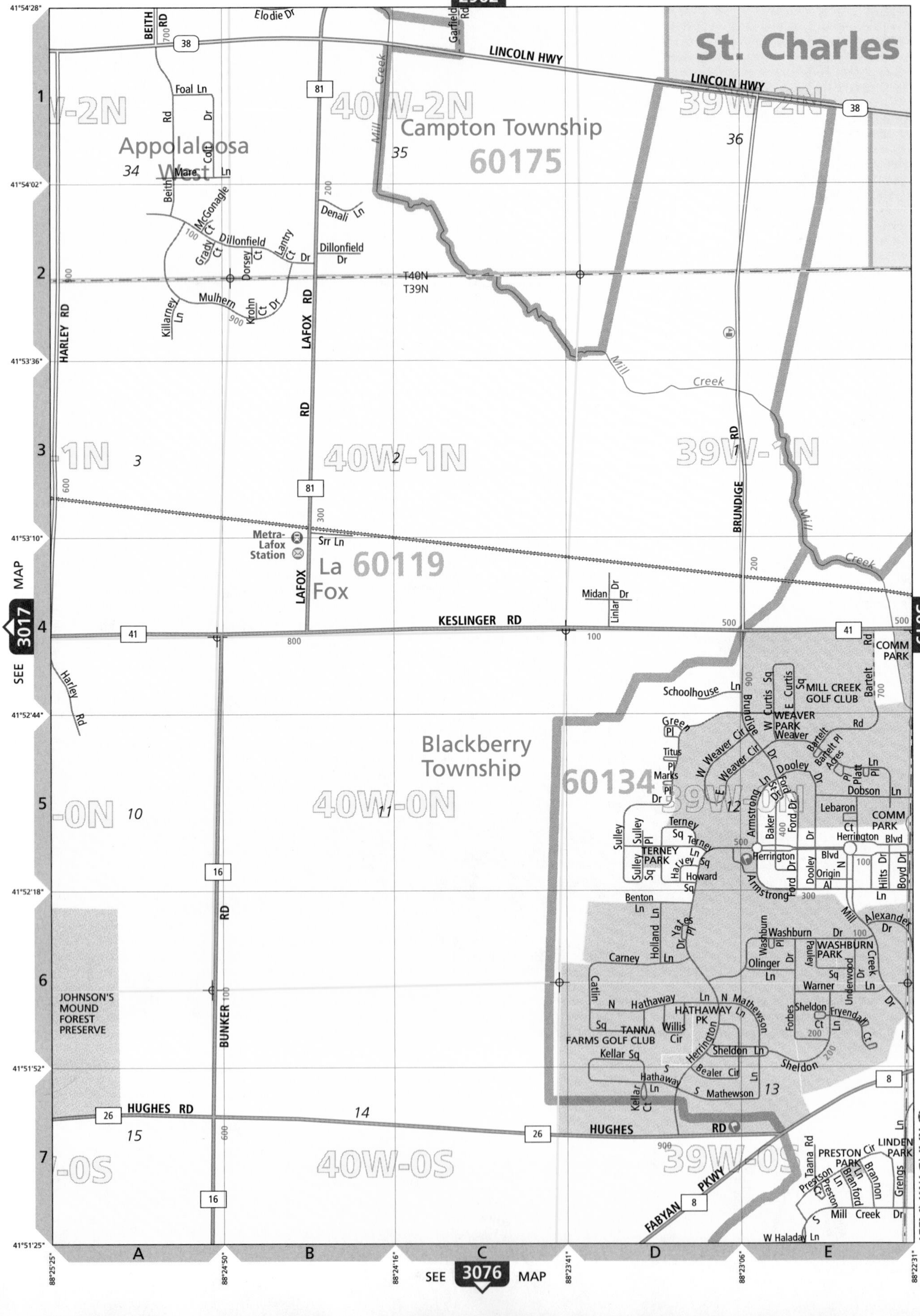

SEE 3017 MAP

SEE 3019 MAP

A B C D E

SEE 3076 MAP

1:24,000
1 in. = 2000 ft.
0 0.25 0.5
miles

SEE 2963 MAP

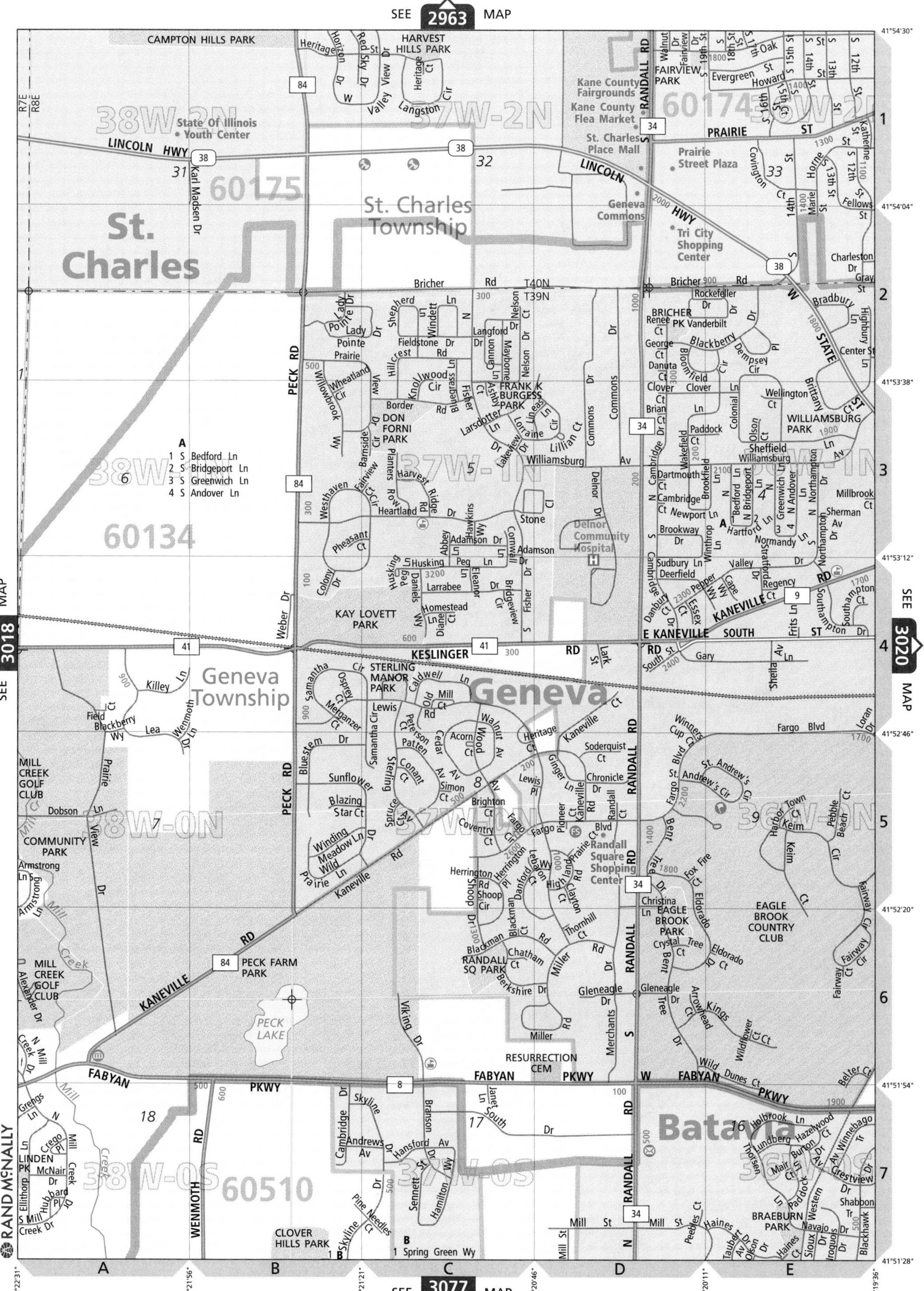

SEE 3018 MAP
SEE 3020 MAP
SEE 3077 MAP

1:24,000
1 in. = 2000 ft.
0 0.25 0.5
miles

SEE 2964 MAP

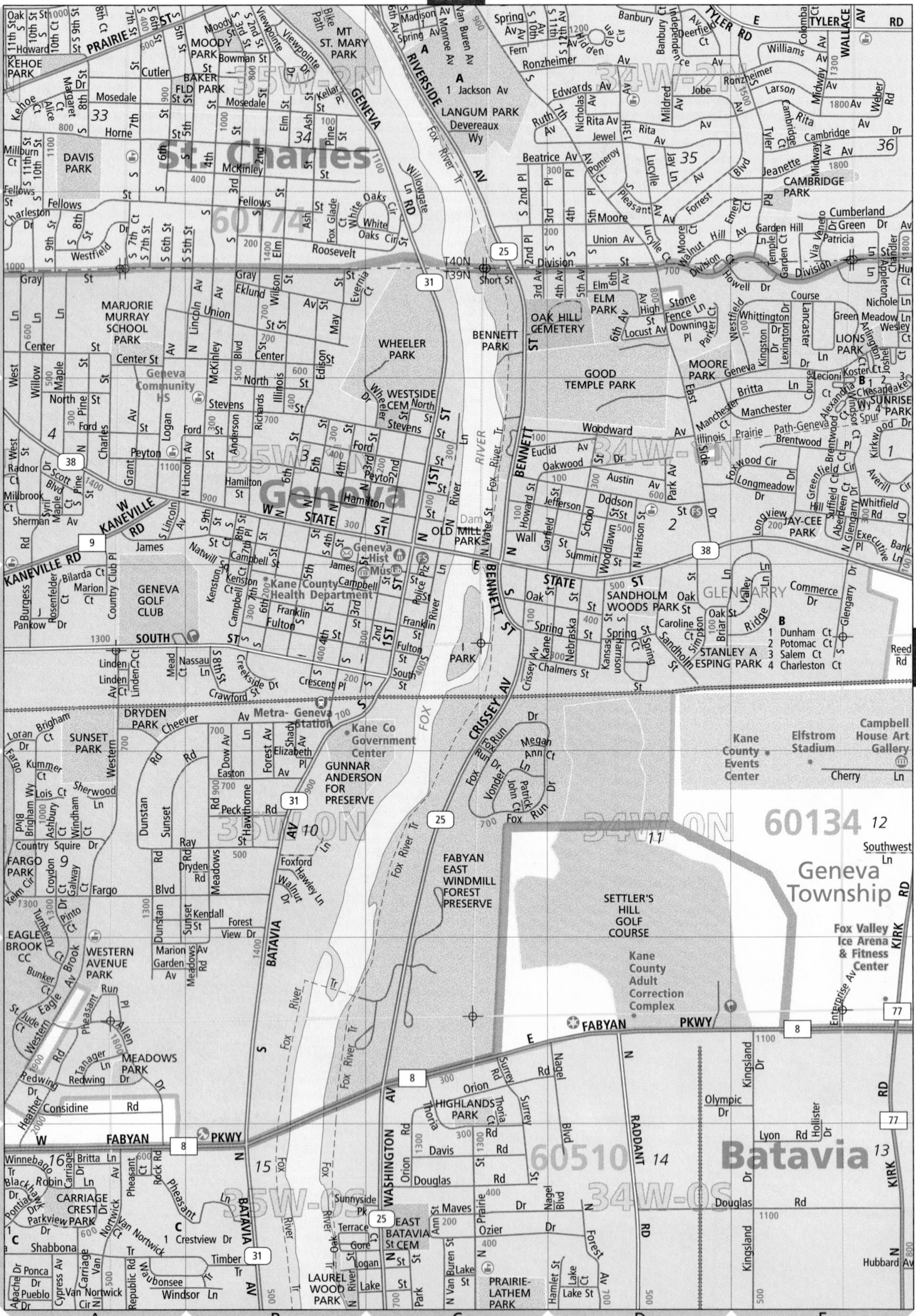

St. Charles
60174
35W-2N
34W-2N
Geneva
35W-1N
34W-1N
35W-0N
34W-0N
60134
Geneva Township
60510
Batavia
35W-0S
34W-0S

MT ST. MARY PARK
MOODY PARK
BAKER FLD PARK
KEHOE PARK
DAVIS PARK
LANGUM PARK
CAMBRIDGE PARK
MARJORIE MURRAY SCHOOL PARK
Geneva Community HS
WHEELER PARK
WESTSIDE CEM
BENNETT PARK
OAK HILL CEMETERY
ELM PARK
GOOD TEMPLE PARK
MOORE PARK
LIONS PARK
SUNRISE PARK
JAY-CEE PARK
OLD MILL PARK
Geneva Hist Mus
Kane County Health Department
GENEVA GOLF CLUB
SANDHOLM WOODS PARK
GLENGARRY
STANLEY A ESPING PARK
I PARK
DRYDEN PARK
Metra-Geneva Station
SUNSET PARK
Kane Co Government Center
GUNNAR ANDERSON FOR PRESERVE
Kane County Events Center
Elfstrom Stadium
Campbell House Art Gallery
FARGO PARK
FABYAN EAST WINDMILL FOREST PRESERVE
SETTLER'S HILL GOLF COURSE
Kane County Adult Correction Complex
Fox Valley Ice Arena & Fitness Center
EAGLE BROOK CC
WESTERN AVENUE PARK
MEADOWS PARK
HIGHLANDS PARK
CARRIAGE CREST PARK
EAST BATAVIA CEM
LAUREL WOOD PARK
PRAIRIE-LATHEM PARK
FOX RIVER

SEE 3019 MAP
SEE 3021 MAP

RAND McNALLY

SEE 3078 MAP

1:24,000
1 in. = 2000 ft.
0 0.25 0.5
miles

SEE 2965 MAP

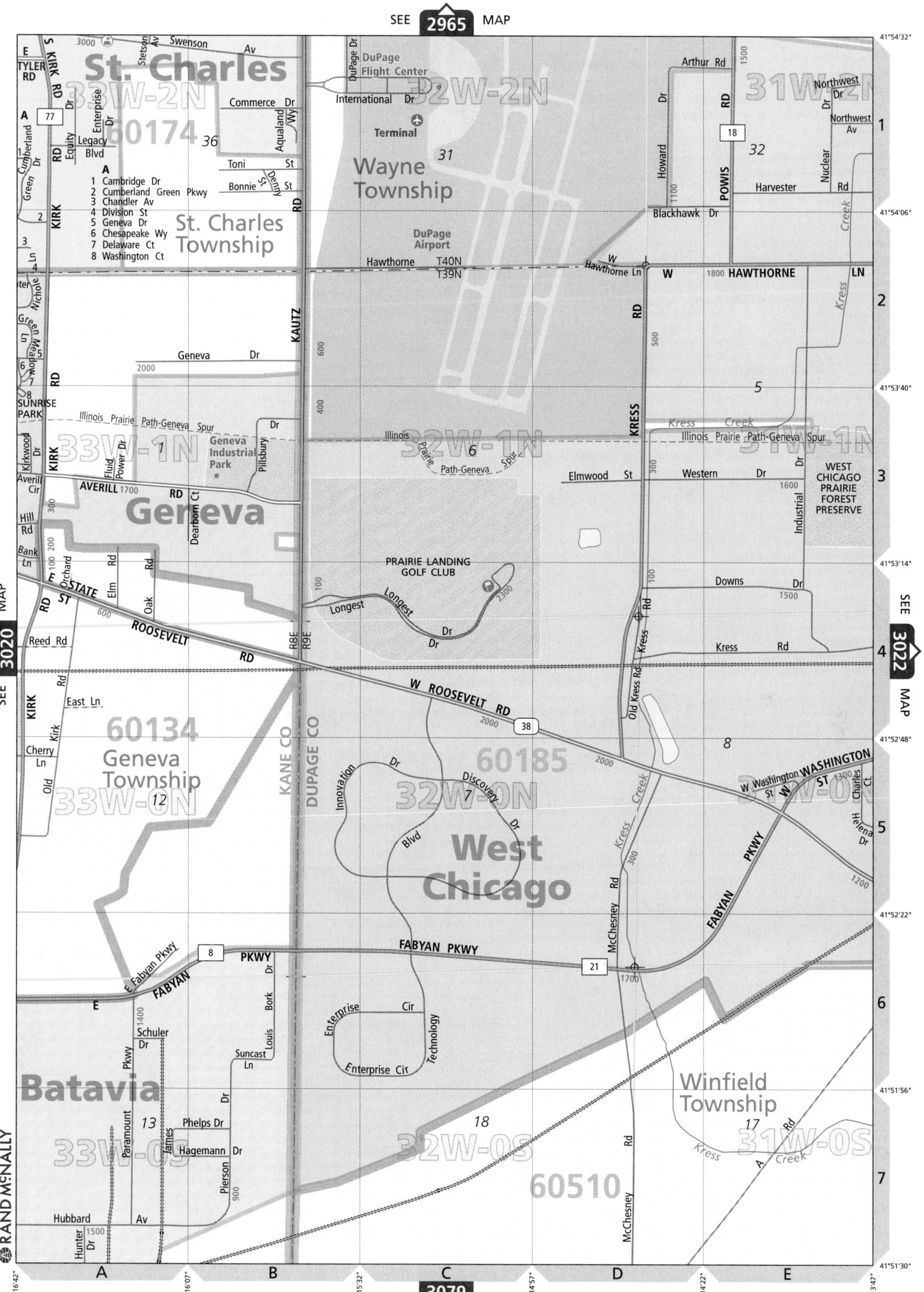

SEE 3020 MAP
SEE 3022 MAP
SEE 3079 MAP

1:24,000
1 in. = 2000 ft.
0 0.25 0.5
miles

SEE 2966 MAP

West Chicago

McQueen

Wayne Township

TIMBER RIDGE FOREST PRESERVE

WEST CHICAGO PRAIRIE FOREST PRESERVE

REED PARK

GLEN OAK CEM

OAKWOOD CEM

West Chicago City Mus

Kruse House Museum

Metra-West Chicago Sta

Community HS

CALVARY CEMETERY

EASTON PARK

PIONEER PARK

High Lake

Whiskey Creek

WEST DUPAGE WOODS FOREST PRESERVE

MANVILLE OAKS PARK

Winfield Township

60185

60510

60190

30W-2N 29W-2N 30W-1N 29W-1N 30W-0N 29W-0N 30W-0S 29W-0S

T40N T39N

W HAWTHORNE LN — E HAWTHORNE LN

W WASHINGTON ST — WASHINGTON ST

GENEVA ST — GENEVA RD

W ROOSEVELT RD — E ROOSEVELT RD

NELTNOR BLVD

JOLIET ST

PRINCE CROSSING RD

HIGHLAKE RD

Illinois Prairie Path-Geneva Spur

Illinois Prairie Path-Elgin

Great Western Tr

Kress Creek

West Branch DuPage River

A
1 N Aurora St
2 S Aurora St

1 2 3 4 5 6 7

A B C D E

41°54'32" 41°54'06" 41°53'40" 41°53'14" 41°52'48" 41°52'22" 41°51'56" 41°51'30"

88°13'47" 88°13'12" 88°12'37" 88°12'02" 88°11'28" 88°10'53"

SEE 3021 MAP

SEE 3023 MAP

SEE 3080 MAP

RAND McNALLY

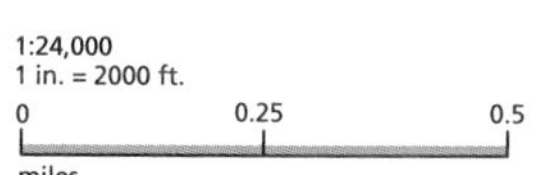

SEE 2967 MAP

SEE 3022 MAP

SEE 3024 MAP

SEE 3081 MAP

41°54'34"
41°54'08"
41°53'42"
41°53'16"
41°52'50"
41°52'23"
41°51'57"
41°51'31"

88°10'53"
88°10'18"
88°09'43"
88°09'08"
88°08'33"
88°07'58"

A B C D E
1 2 3 4 5 6 7

Wayne Township
Carol Stream
Bloomingdale Township
Winfield Township
West Chicago
Milton Township
Winfield
Wheaton
Pleasant Hill
Jewell Road
North Woods
Geneva Road

28W-2N
27W-2N
26W-2N
28W-1N
27W-1N
26W-1N
28W-0N
27W-0N
26W-0N
28W-0S
27W-0S
26W-0S

60188
60185
60187
60190

T40N
T39N
R9E
R10E

MCCASLIN PARK
O'RAHILLY VOLUNTEER PARK
RED HAWK PARK
KLEIN CREEK GOLF CLUB
Kline Creek Farm
TIMBER RIDGE FOREST PRESERVE
PRAIRIE TRAIL PARK
HERITAGE PLEASANT HILL PARK
WINFIELD ESTATES PARK
OAKWOOD PARK
WINFIELD MOUNDS FOREST PRESERVE
Central DuPage Hosp
RIVERSIDE PARK
Metra-Winfield Station
CREEKSIDE PARK
WEST DUPAGE WOODS FOREST PRESERVE
FOUNDERS PARK
EAST STREET PARK
LINCOLN MARSH NAT AREA
DuPage County Fairgrounds
DuPage Co Health Department
FIREFIGHTERS PARK
SPRING LAKE
HIGH LAKE

Great Western Tr
Illinois Prairie Path-Elgin Brch
Illinois Prairie Path-Geneva Spur
West Branch DuPage River
Klein Creek
Winfield Cr

NORTH AV
ST. CHARLES RD
COUNTY FARM RD
N COUNTY FARM RD
S COUNTY FARM RD
GENEVA RD
WINFIELD RD
HIGHLAKE RD
JEWELL RD
GARYS MILL RD
PLEASANT HILL RD
KUHN RD
National St
Indian Knoll Rd
Hawthorne Ln
Roosevelt Rd

A
1 Houghton Ct
2 Houghton Ln

B
1 Meadowview Ct

C
1 Church St
2 Chicago Av

1:24,000
1 in. = 2000 ft.
0 0.25 0.5
miles

SEE 2968 MAP

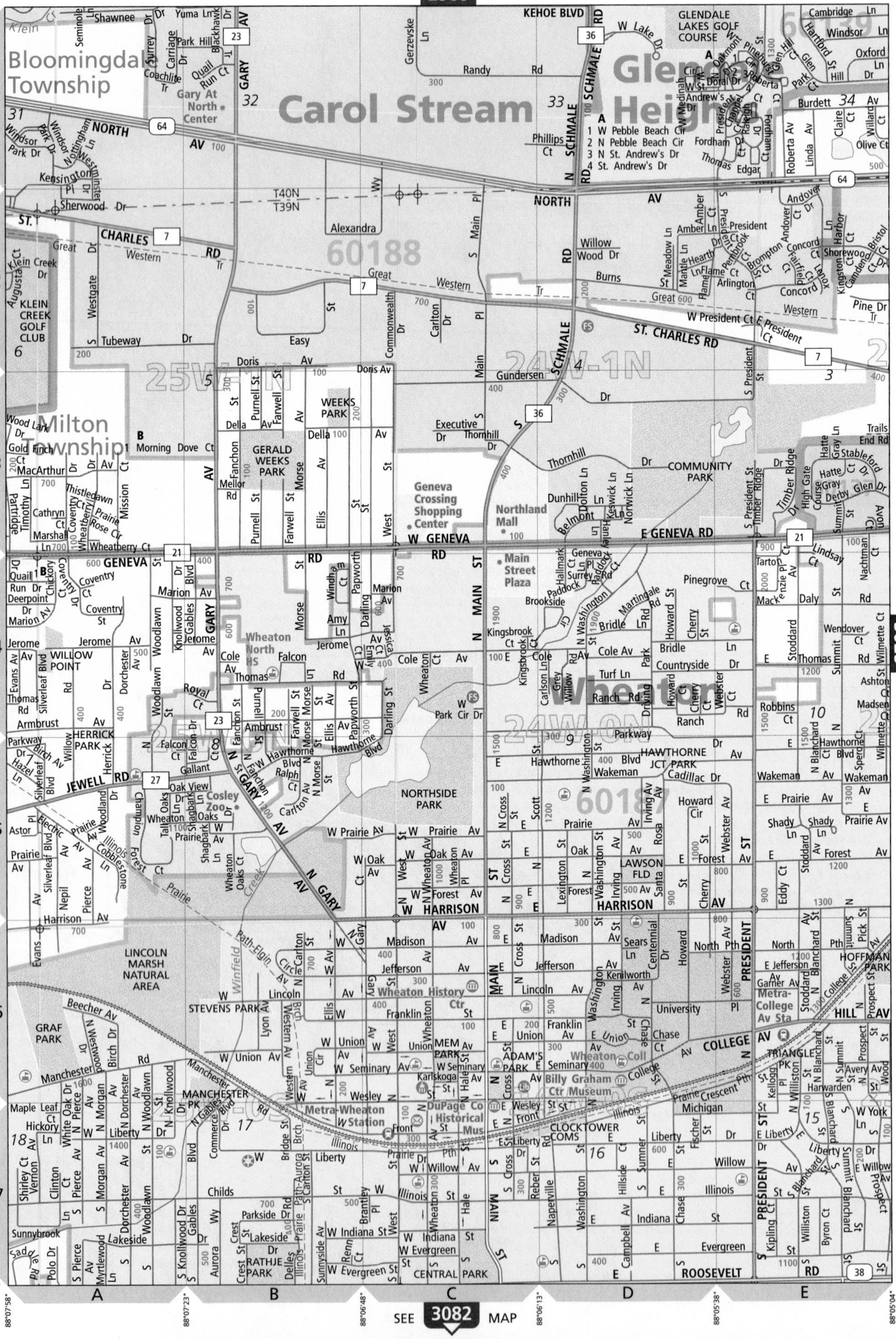

Bloomingdale Township

Carol Stream

Glendale Heights

Milton Township

Wheaton

60188

60187

60139

25W-1N

24W-1N

24W-0N

A
1 W Pebble Beach Cir
2 N Pebble Beach Cir
3 N St. Andrew's Dr
4 St. Andrew's Dr

GLENDALE LAKES GOLF COURSE

KLEIN CREEK GOLF CLUB

Gary At North Center

WEEKS PARK

GERALD WEEKS PARK

Geneva Crossing Shopping Center

Northland Mall

Main Street Plaza

COMMUNITY PARK

Wheaton North HS

WILLOW POINT

HERRICK PARK

Cosley Zoo

NORTHSIDE PARK

HAWTHORNE JCT PARK

LAWSON FLD

LINCOLN MARSH NATURAL AREA

GRAF PARK

STEVENS PARK

MANCHESTER PK

Wheaton History Ctr

MEM PARK

ADAM'S PARK

Wheaton Coll

Billy Graham Ctr Museum

Metra-Wheaton Station

DuPage Co Historical Mus

CLOCKTOWER COMS

RATHJE PARK

CENTRAL PARK

TRIANGLE PK

HOFFMAN PARK

Metra-College Av Sta

NORTH AV

ST. CHARLES RD

GENEVA RD

JEWELL RD

N GARY AV

SCHMALE RD

N MAIN ST

HARRISON AV

COLLEGE AV

PRESIDENT ST

ROOSEVELT RD

HILL AV

SEE 3023 MAP

SEE 3025 MAP

SEE 3082 MAP

A B C D E
1 2 3 4 5 6 7

41°54'34" 41°54'08" 41°53'42" 41°53'16" 41°52'50" 41°52'23" 41°51'57" 41°51'31"

88°07'58" 88°07'23" 88°06'48" 88°06'13" 88°05'38" 88°05'03"

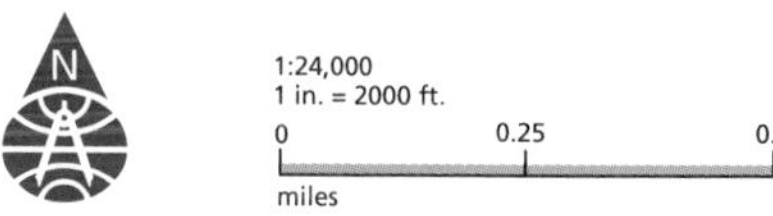

SEE 2969 MAP

SEE 3024 MAP

SEE 3026 MAP

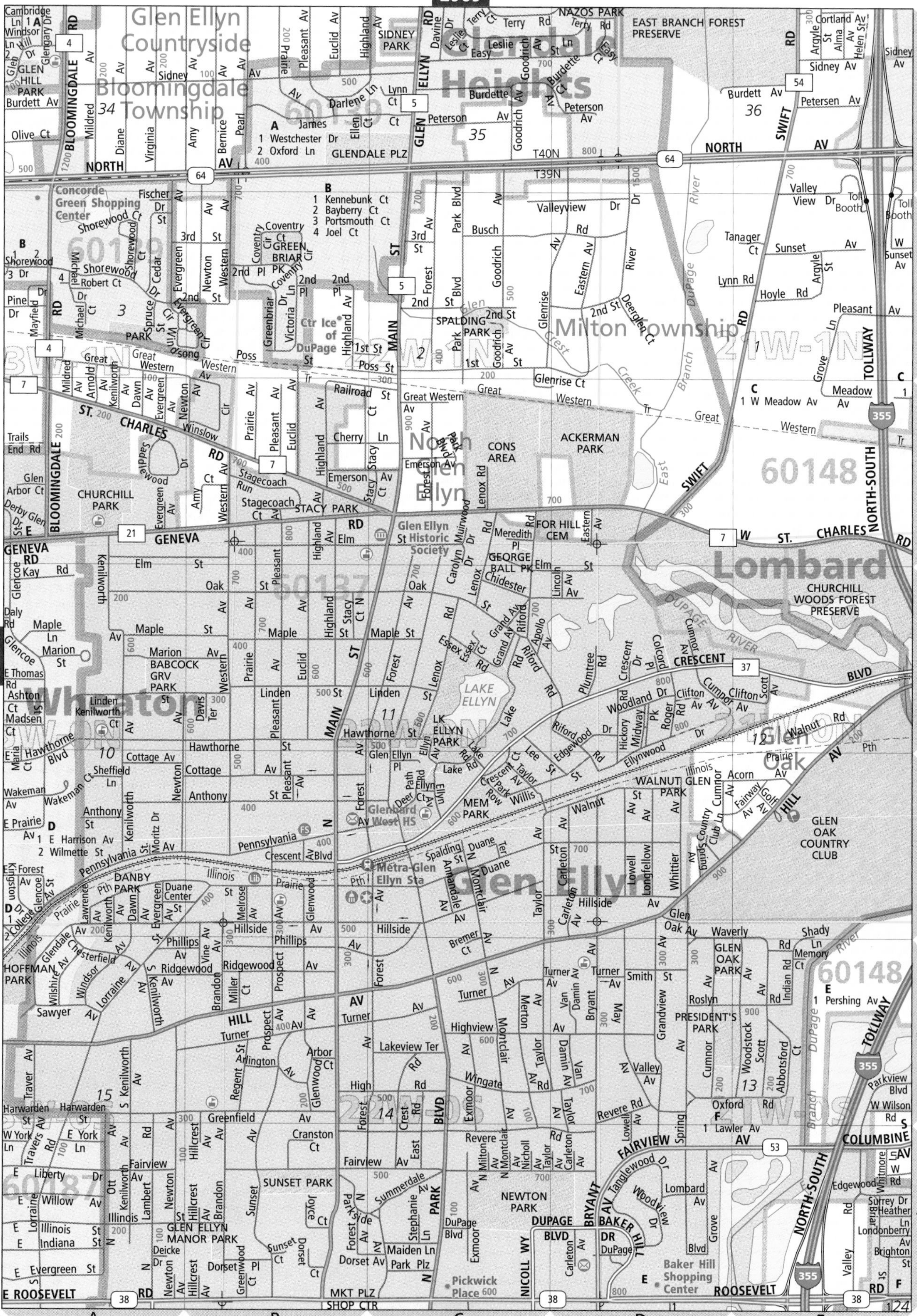

Glen Ellyn Countryside

Glendale Heights

Bloomingdale Township

Milton Township

North Glen Ellyn

Glen Ellyn

Lombard

Wheaton

Glen Oak

EAST BRANCH FOREST PRESERVE

CHURCHILL WOODS FOREST PRESERVE

GLEN OAK COUNTRY CLUB

ACKERMAN PARK

CONS AREA

CHURCHILL PARK

STACY PARK

SPALDING PARK

SIDNEY PARK

NAZOS PARK

GLEN HILL PARK

GEORGE BALL PK

FOR HILL CEM

BABCOCK GRV PARK

LK ELLYN PARK

LAKE ELLYN

MEM PARK

WALNUT GLEN PARK

DANBY PARK

HOFFMAN PARK

GLEN OAK PARK

PRESIDENT'S PARK

SUNSET PARK

NEWTON PARK

GLEN ELLYN MANOR PARK

Concorde Green Shopping Center

Baker Hill Shopping Center

Glen Ellyn St Historic Society

Glenbard West HS

Metra-Glen Ellyn Sta

Ctr Ice of DuPage

Pickwick Place

GLENDALE PLZ

MKT PLZ

SHOP CTR

NORTH AV

ST. CHARLES RD

GENEVA RD

CRESCENT BLVD

HILL AV

ROOSEVELT RD

MAIN ST

PARK BLVD

BLOOMINGDALE RD

SWIFT RD

NORTH-SOUTH TOLLWAY

DUPAGE BLVD

FAIRVIEW AV

60139 60137 60148 60187

3W-1N 22W-1N 21W-1N 23W-0N 22W-0N 21W-0N 22W-0S 21W-0S

T40N T39N

A B C D E

1 2 3 4 5 6 7

41°54'35" 41°54'09" 41°53'43" 41°53'17" 41°52'51" 41°52'25" 41°51'59" 41°51'33"

88°05'04" 88°04'29" 88°03'54" 88°03'19" 88°02'44" 88°02'09"

SEE 3083 MAP

1:24,000
1 in. = 2000 ft.
0 0.25 0.5
miles

SEE 2970 MAP

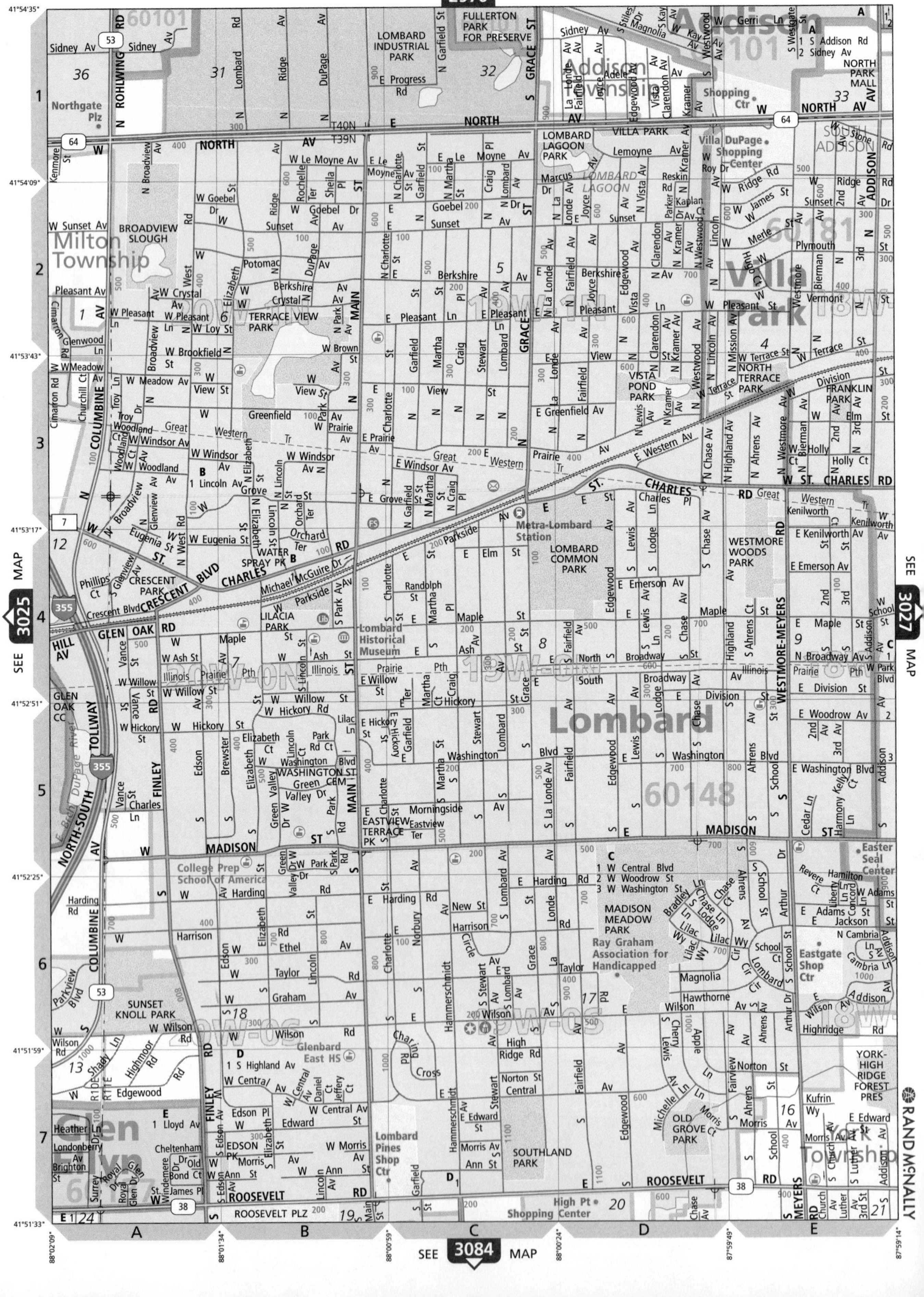

SEE 3025 MAP

SEE 3027 MAP

SEE 3084 MAP

41°54'35" 41°54'09" 41°53'43" 41°53'17" 41°52'51" 41°52'25" 41°51'59" 41°51'33"

88°02'09" 88°01'34" 88°00'59" 88°00'24" 87°59'49" 87°59'14"

A B C D E

1 2 3 4 5 6 7

Addison
Addison Township
Villa Park
Milton Township
Lombard
Glen Ellyn
York Township
60101 60181 60148 60137

LOMBARD INDUSTRIAL PARK
FULLERTON PARK FOR PRESERVE
NORTH PARK MALL
Shopping Ctr
Northgate Plz
LOMBARD LAGOON PARK
Villa DuPage Shopping Center
BROADVIEW SLOUGH
TERRACE VIEW PARK
VISTA POND PARK
NORTH TERRACE PARK
FRANKLIN PARK
Metra-Lombard Station
LOMBARD COMMON PARK
WESTMORE WOODS PARK
CRESCENT PARK
WATER SPRAY PK
LILACIA PARK
Lombard Historical Museum
GLEN OAK CC
WASHINGTON ST GREEN CEM
EASTVIEW TERRACE PK
College Prep School of America
MADISON MEADOW PARK
Ray Graham Association for Handicapped
Easter Seal Center
Eastgate Shop Ctr
SUNSET KNOLL PARK
Glenbard East HS
YORK-HIGH RIDGE FOREST PRES
OLD GROVE PARK
SOUTHLAND PARK
Lombard Pines Shop Ctr
EDSON PK
High Pt Shopping Center
NORTH-SOUTH TOLLWAY
NORTH AV
ST. CHARLES RD
MADISON ST
ROOSEVELT RD
ROOSEVELT PLZ
GLEN OAK RD
CRESCENT BLVD
MAIN ST
GRACE ST
FINLEY RD
COLUMBINE AV
WESTMORE-MEYERS RD

A: 1 S Addison Rd, 2 Sidney Av
B: 1 Lincoln Av
C: 1 W Central Blvd, 2 W Woodrow St, 3 W Washington St
D: 1 S Highland Av
E: 1 Lloyd Av

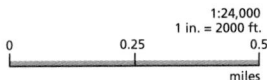

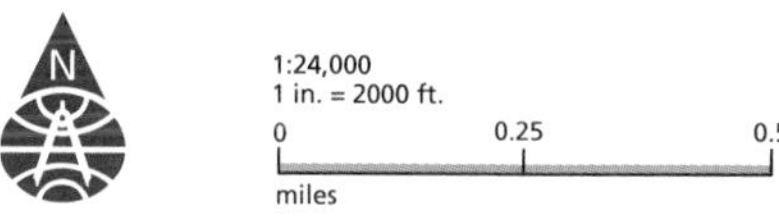

SEE 2971 MAP

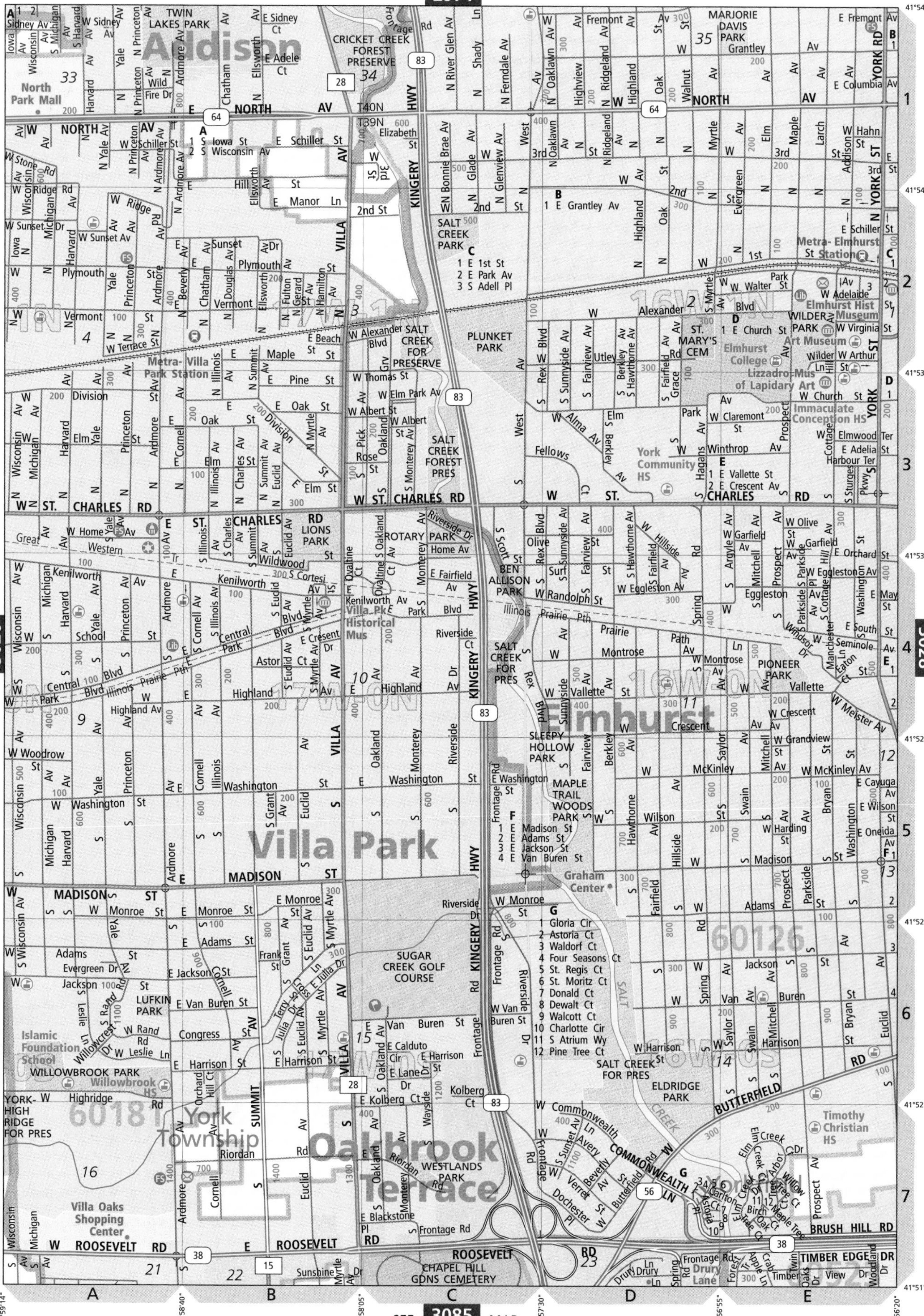

SEE 3026 MAP

SEE 3028 MAP

Addison

Villa Park

Elmhurst

Oakbrook Terrace

York Township

TWIN LAKES PARK

CRICKET CREEK FOREST PRESERVE

MARJORIE DAVIS PARK

North Park Mall

SALT CREEK PARK

Metra- Villa Park Station

Metra- Elmhurst Station

Elmhurst Hist Museum

WILDER PARK

Art Museum

ST. MARY'S CEM

Elmhurst College

Lizzadro Mus of Lapidary Art

Immaculate Conception HS

PLUNKET PARK

SALT CREEK FOR PRESERVE

SALT CREEK FOREST PRES

York Community HS

LIONS PARK

ROTARY PARK

BEN ALLISON PARK

Villa Pk Historical Mus

SALT CREEK FOR PRES

PIONEER PARK

SLEEPY HOLLOW PARK

MAPLE TRAIL WOODS PARK

Graham Center

SUGAR CREEK GOLF COURSE

LUFKIN PARK

Islamic Foundation School

WILLOWBROOK PARK

Willowbrook HS

YORK-HIGH RIDGE FOR PRES

SALT CREEK FOR PRES

ELDRIDGE PARK

Timothy Christian HS

WESTLANDS PARK

Villa Oaks Shopping Center

CHAPEL HILL GDNS CEMETERY

Drury Lane

Great Western Tr

Illinois Prairie Pth

NORTH AV

ST. CHARLES RD

MADISON ST

ROOSEVELT RD

KINGERY HWY

VILLA AV

YORK ST

YORK RD

BUTTERFIELD RD

COMMONWEALTH LN

BRUSH HILL RD

TIMBER EDGE DR

SUMMIT

60181

60126

T40N
T39N

A 1 S Iowa St
2 S Wisconsin Av

B 1 E Grantley Av

C 1 E 1st St
2 E Park Av
3 S Adell Pl

D 1 E Church St

E 1 E Vallette St
2 E Crescent Av

F 1 E Madison St
2 E Adams St
3 E Jackson St
4 E Van Buren St

G 1 Gloria Cir
2 Astoria Ct
3 Waldorf Ct
4 Four Seasons Ct
5 St. Regis Ct
6 St. Moritz Ct
7 Donald Ct
8 Dewalt Ct
9 Walcott Ct
10 Charlotte Cir
11 S Atrium Wy
12 Pine Tree Ct

A B C D E

1 2 3 4 5 6 7

41°54'36" 41°54'10" 41°53'44" 41°53'18" 41°52'52" 41°52'26" 41°52'00" 41°51'34"

87°59'14" 87°58'40" 87°58'05" 87°57'30" 87°56'55" 87°56'20"

SEE 3085 MAP

1:24,000
1 in. = 2000 ft.
0 0.25 0.5
miles

SEE 2972 MAP

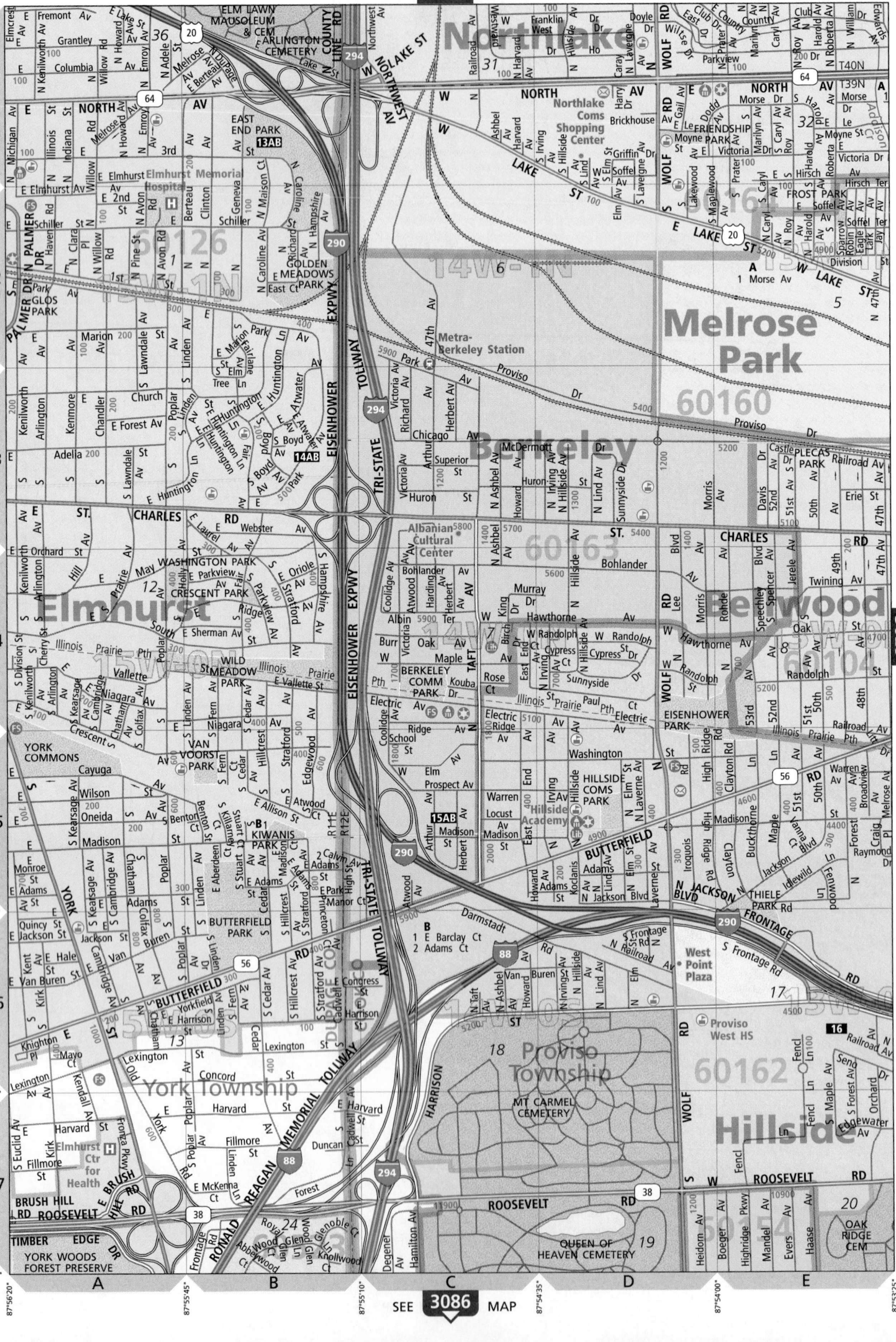

Northlake
Melrose Park
Berkeley
Elmhurst
Bellwood
York Township
Proviso Township
Hillside

60126
60160
60163
60104
60162
60164

15W-1N
14W-1N
13W-1N
15W-0N
14W-0N
13W-0N
15W-0S
14W-0S
13W-0S

ELM LAWN MAUSOLEUM & CEM
ARLINGTON CEMETERY
MT CARMEL CEMETERY
QUEEN OF HEAVEN CEMETERY
OAK RIDGE CEM
YORK WOODS FOREST PRESERVE
Elmhurst Memorial Hospital
Elmhurst Ctr for Health
Metra-Berkeley Station
Albanian Cultural Center
Northlake Coms Shopping Center
West Point Plaza
Proviso West HS
Hillside Academy
YORK COMMONS
EAST END PARK
GOLDEN MEADOWS PARK
GLOS PARK
WASHINGTON PARK
CRESCENT PARK
WILD MEADOW PARK
VAN VOORST PARK
KIWANIS PARK
BUTTERFIELD PARK
BERKELEY COMM PARK
HILLSIDE COMS PARK
EISENHOWER PARK
FRIENDSHIP PARK
FROST PARK
PLECAS PARK
THIELE PARK

EISENHOWER EXPWY
TRI-STATE TOLLWAY
RONALD REAGAN MEMORIAL TOLLWAY
NORTH AV
LAKE ST
ST. CHARLES RD
BUTTERFIELD RD
ROOSEVELT RD
WOLF RD
YORK ST
HARRISON ST
BRUSH HILL RD
TIMBER EDGE DR
COUNTY LINE RD
NORTHWEST AV
N JACKSON BLVD
FRONTAGE RD

20 64 290 294 88 56 38

1 2 3 4 5 6 7
A B C D E

41°54'36" 41°54'10" 41°53'44" 41°53'18" 41°52'52" 41°52'26" 41°52'00" 41°51'34"
87°56'20" 87°55'45" 87°55'10" 87°54'35" 87°54'00" 87°53'25"

SEE 3027 MAP

SEE 3029 MAP

SEE 3086 MAP

1:24,000
1 in. = 2000 ft.
0 0.25 0.5
miles

SEE 2973 MAP

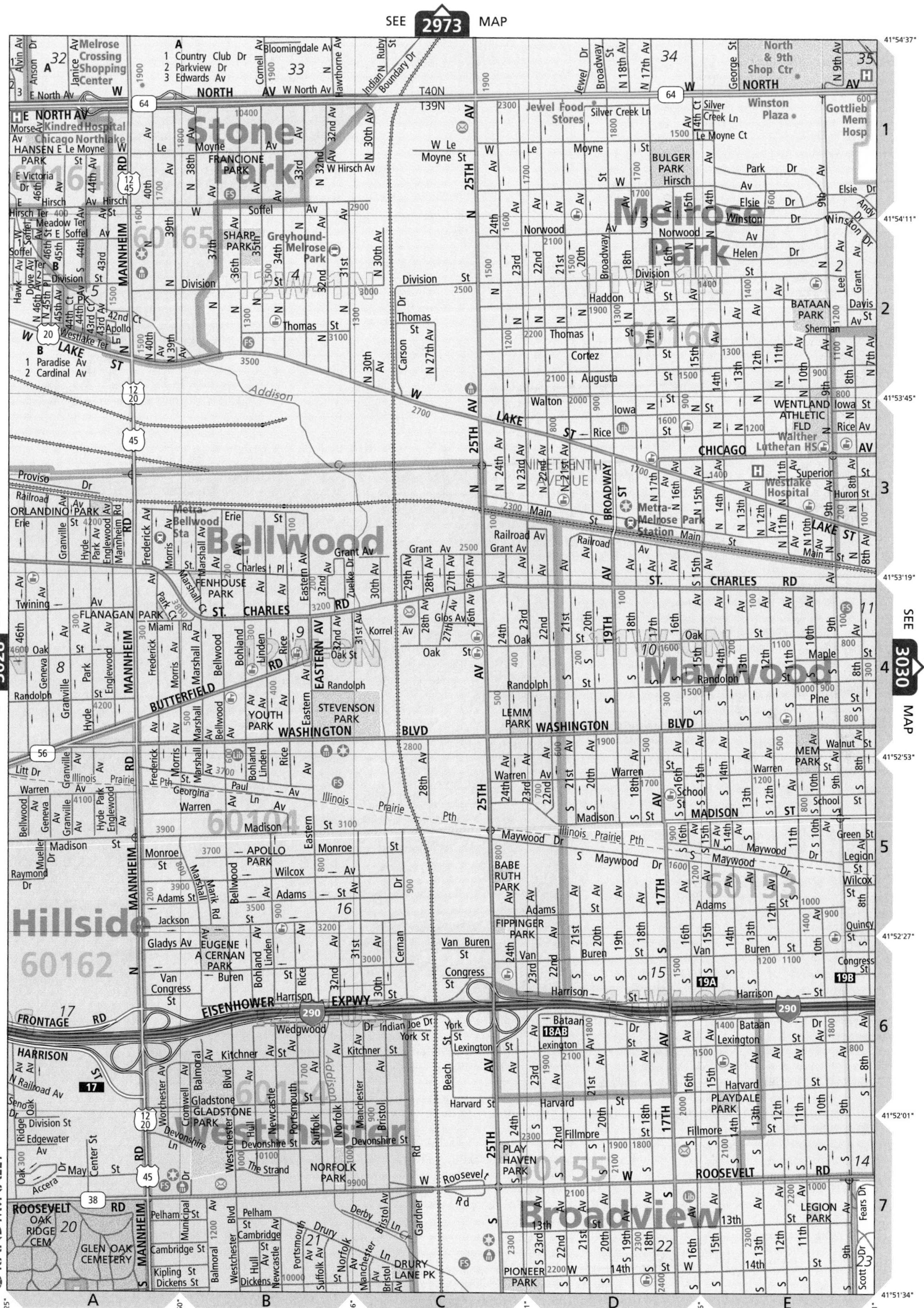

SEE 3028 MAP

SEE 3030 MAP

SEE 3087 MAP

1:24,000
1 in. = 2000 ft.
0 0.25 0.5
miles

SEE 2974 MAP

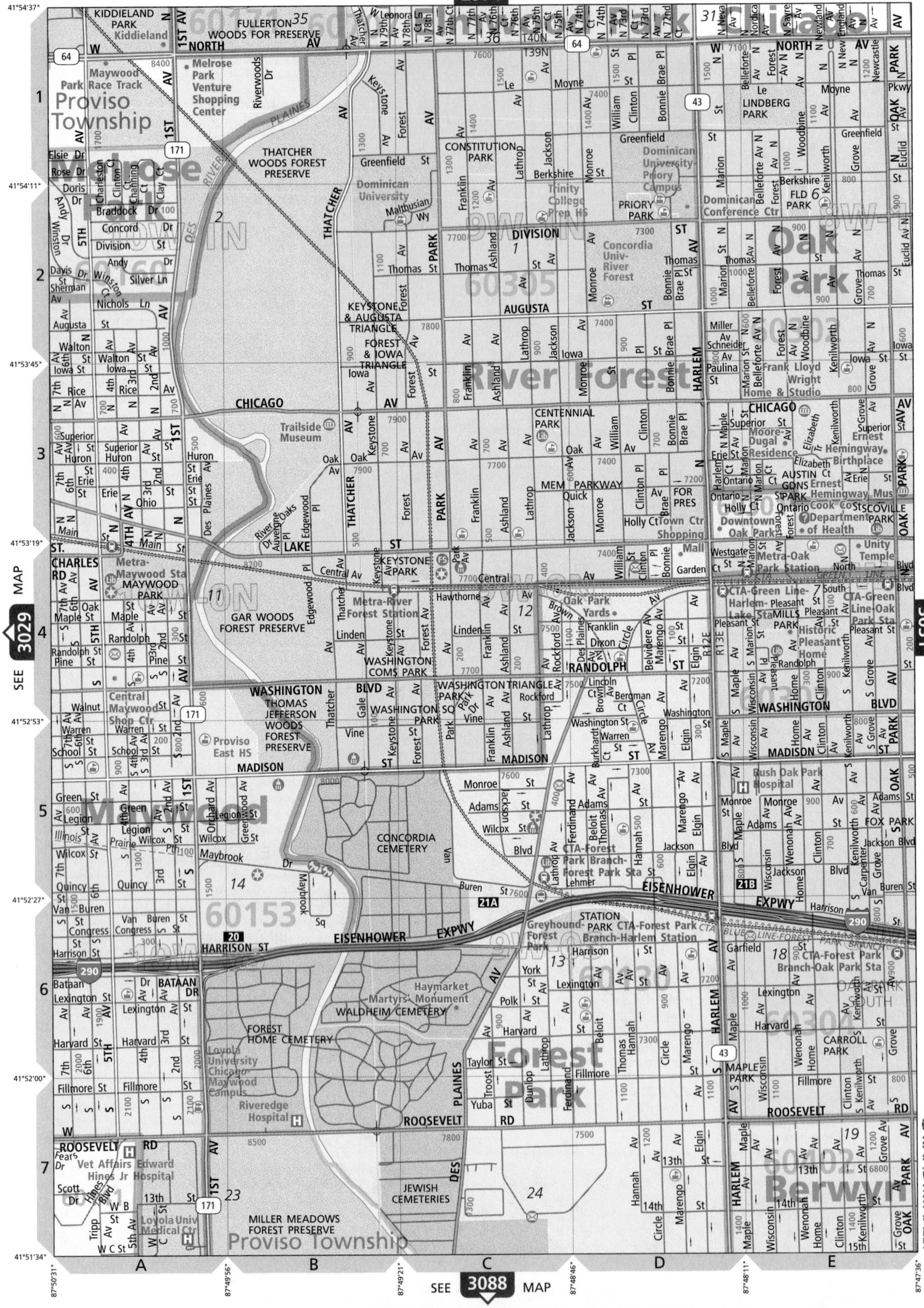

SEE 3029 MAP

SEE 3031 MAP

41°54'37"
41°54'11"
41°53'45"
41°53'19"
41°52'53"
41°52'27"
41°52'00"
41°51'34"

1
2
3
4
5
6
7

Melrose Park
Proviso Township
Maywood
River Forest
Oak Park
Forest Park
Berwyn
Chicago
Elmwood Park

Kiddieland Park
Maywood Park Race Track
Melrose Park Venture Shopping Center
Thatcher Woods Forest Preserve
Dominican University
Constitution Park
Trinity College Prep HS
Dominican University Priory Campus
Priory Park
Dominican Conference Ctr
Concordia Univ-River Forest
Lindberg Park
Keystone & Augusta Triangle
Forest & Iowa Triangle
Frank Lloyd Wright Home & Studio
Trailside Museum
Centennial Park
Moore-Dugal Residence
Ernest Hemingway Birthplace
Austin Gdns Park
Ernest Hemingway Mus
Cook Co Department of Health
Scoville Park
Unity Temple
Downtown Oak Park
Town Ctr Shopping Mall
Maywood Park
Metra-Maywood Sta
Keystone Park
Metra-River Forest Station
Oak Park Yards
Gar Woods Forest Preserve
Metra-Oak Park Station
CTA-Green Line-Harlem-Lake Sta
CTA-Green Line-Oak Park Sta
Mills Park
Historic Pleasant Home
Washington Coms Park
Washington Triangle Park
Washington Sq Park
Thomas Jefferson Woods Forest Preserve
Central Maywood Shop Ctr
Proviso East HS
Concordia Cemetery
Rush Oak Park Hospital
Fox Park
CTA-Forest Park Branch-Forest Park Sta
Greyhound-Forest Park Station
CTA-Forest Park Branch-Harlem Station
CTA-Forest Park Branch-Oak Park Sta
Haymarket Martyrs' Monument
Waldheim Cemetery
Forest Home Cemetery
Loyola University Chicago-Maywood Campus
Riveredge Hospital
Carroll Park
Maple Park
Vet Affairs Edward Hines Jr Hospital
Loyola Univ Medical Ctr
Jewish Cemeteries
Miller Meadows Forest Preserve

Eisenhower Expwy
North Av
Chicago Av
Lake St
Washington Blvd
Madison St
Roosevelt Rd
Harlem Av
Des Plaines River

A B C D E

87°50'31" 87°49'56" 87°49'21" 87°48'46" 87°48'11" 87°47'36"

SEE 3088 MAP

1:24,000
1 in. = 2000 ft.
0 0.25 0.5
miles

SEE 2975 MAP

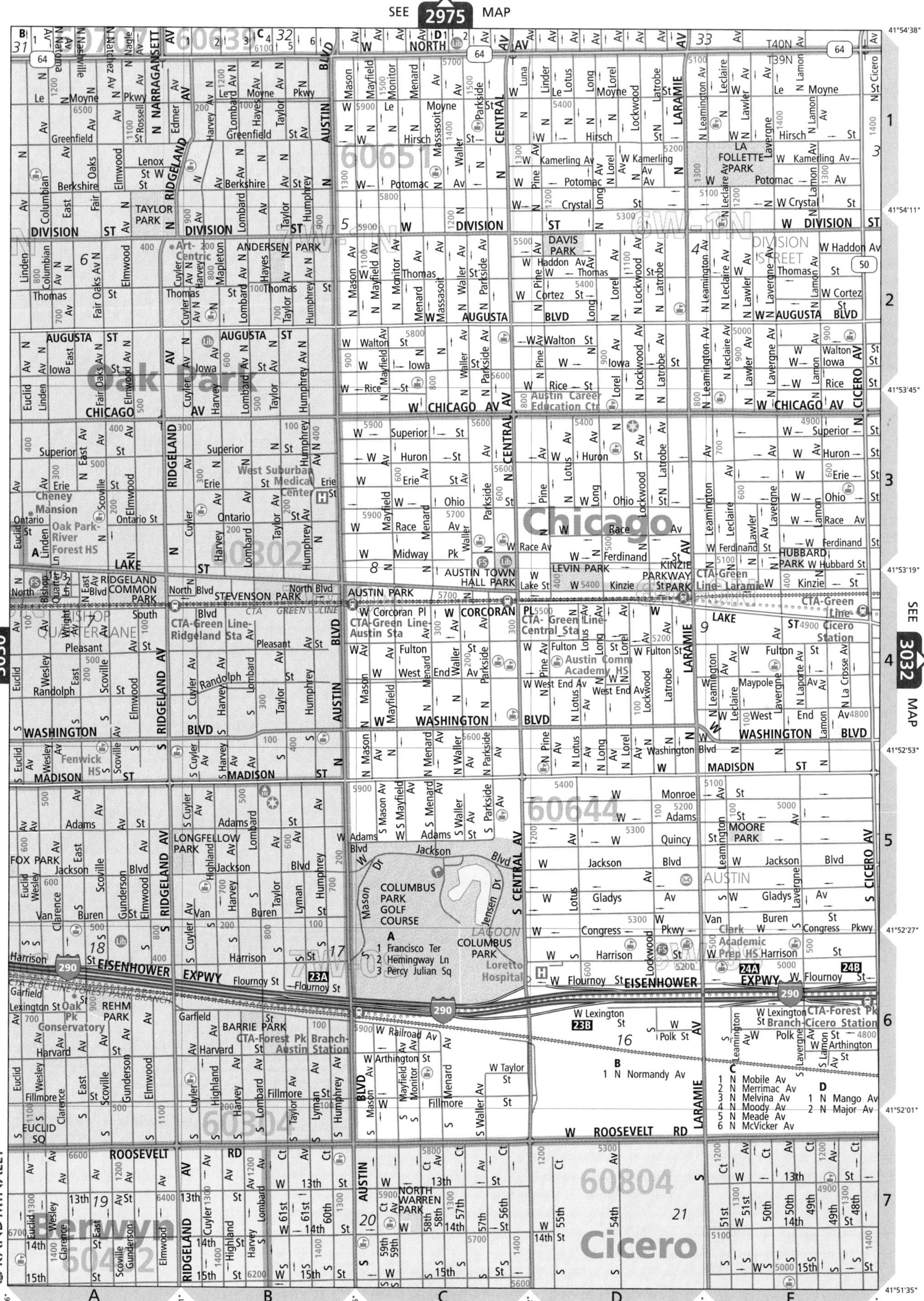

SEE 3030 MAP

SEE 3032 MAP

SEE 3089 MAP

1:24,000
1 in. = 2000 ft.
0 0.25 0.5
miles

SEE 2976 MAP

Chicago

A
1 N Lowell Av

B
1 N Drake Av

C
1 W Le Moyne St
2 W Evergreen Av

D
1 W Haddon Av

E
1 W Fulton Dr

F
1 W Randolph St

G
1 S Independence Blvd

Cicero

SEE 3031 MAP

SEE 3033 MAP

SEE 3090 MAP

1:24,000
1 in. = 2000 ft.
0 0.25 0.5
miles

SEE 2977 MAP

SEE 3091 MAP

1:24,000
1 in. = 2000 ft.
0 0.25 0.5
miles

SEE 2978 MAP

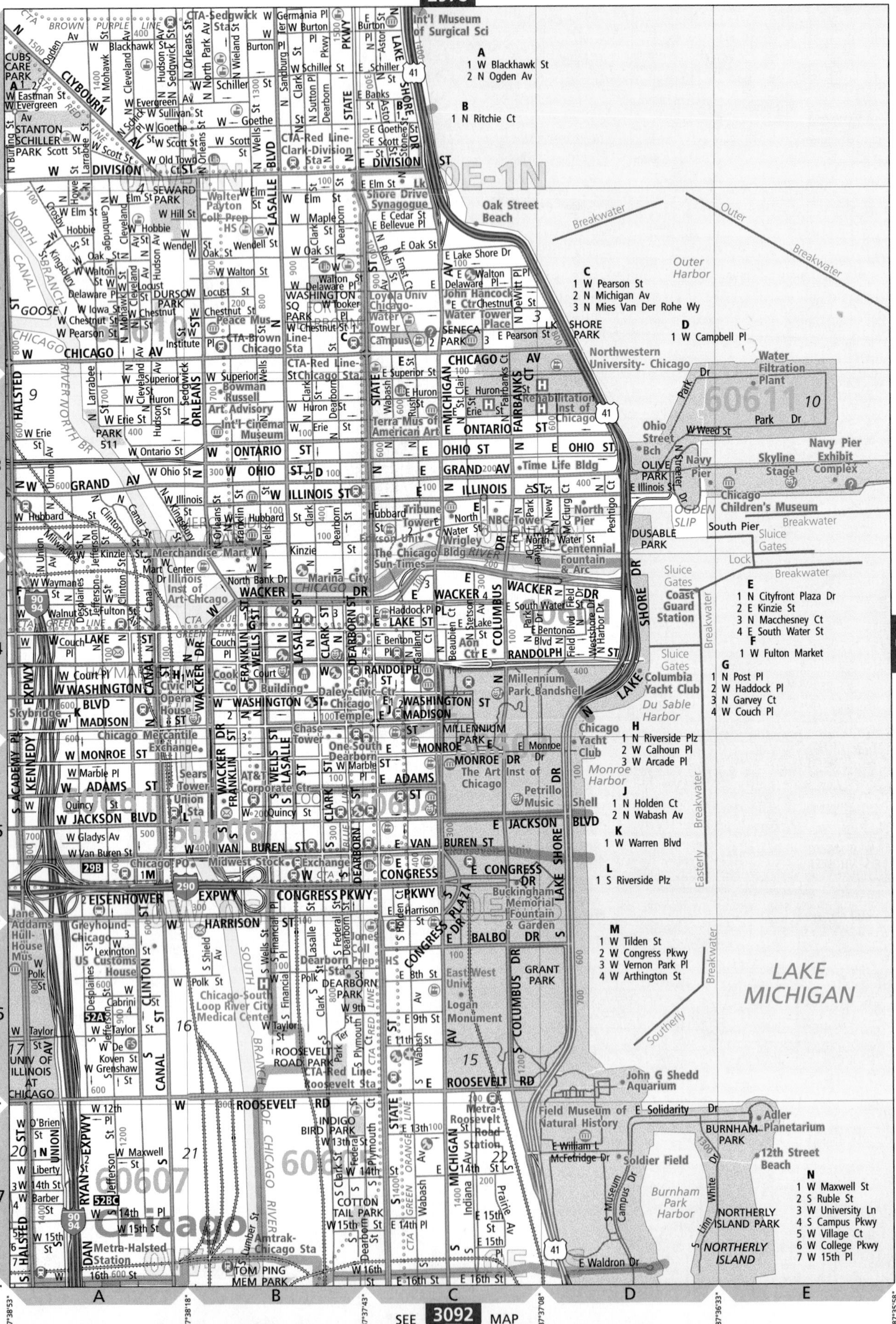

SEE 3033 MAP

SEE B MAP

A
1 W Blackhawk St
2 N Ogden Av

B
1 N Ritchie Ct

C
1 W Pearson St
2 N Michigan Av
3 N Mies Van Der Rohe Wy

D
1 W Campbell Pl

E
1 N Cityfront Plaza Dr
2 E Kinzie St
3 N Macchesney Ct
4 E South Water St

F
1 W Fulton Market

G
1 N Post Pl
2 W Haddock Pl
3 N Garvey Ct
4 W Couch Pl

H
1 N Riverside Plz
2 W Calhoun Pl
3 W Arcade Pl

J
1 N Holden Ct
2 N Wabash Av

K
1 W Warren Blvd

L
1 S Riverside Plz

M
1 W Tilden St
2 W Congress Pkwy
3 W Vernon Park Pl
4 W Arthington St

N
1 W Maxwell St
2 S Ruble St
3 W University Ln
4 S Campus Pkwy
5 W Village Ct
6 W College Pkwy
7 W 15th Pl

LAKE MICHIGAN

Chicago

60610 60611 60654 60661 60606 60604 60605 60607

SEE 3092 MAP

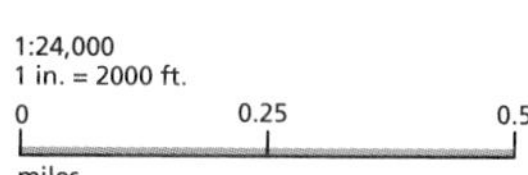

SEE 3017 MAP

SEE B MAP

SEE 3076 MAP

SEE 3135 MAP

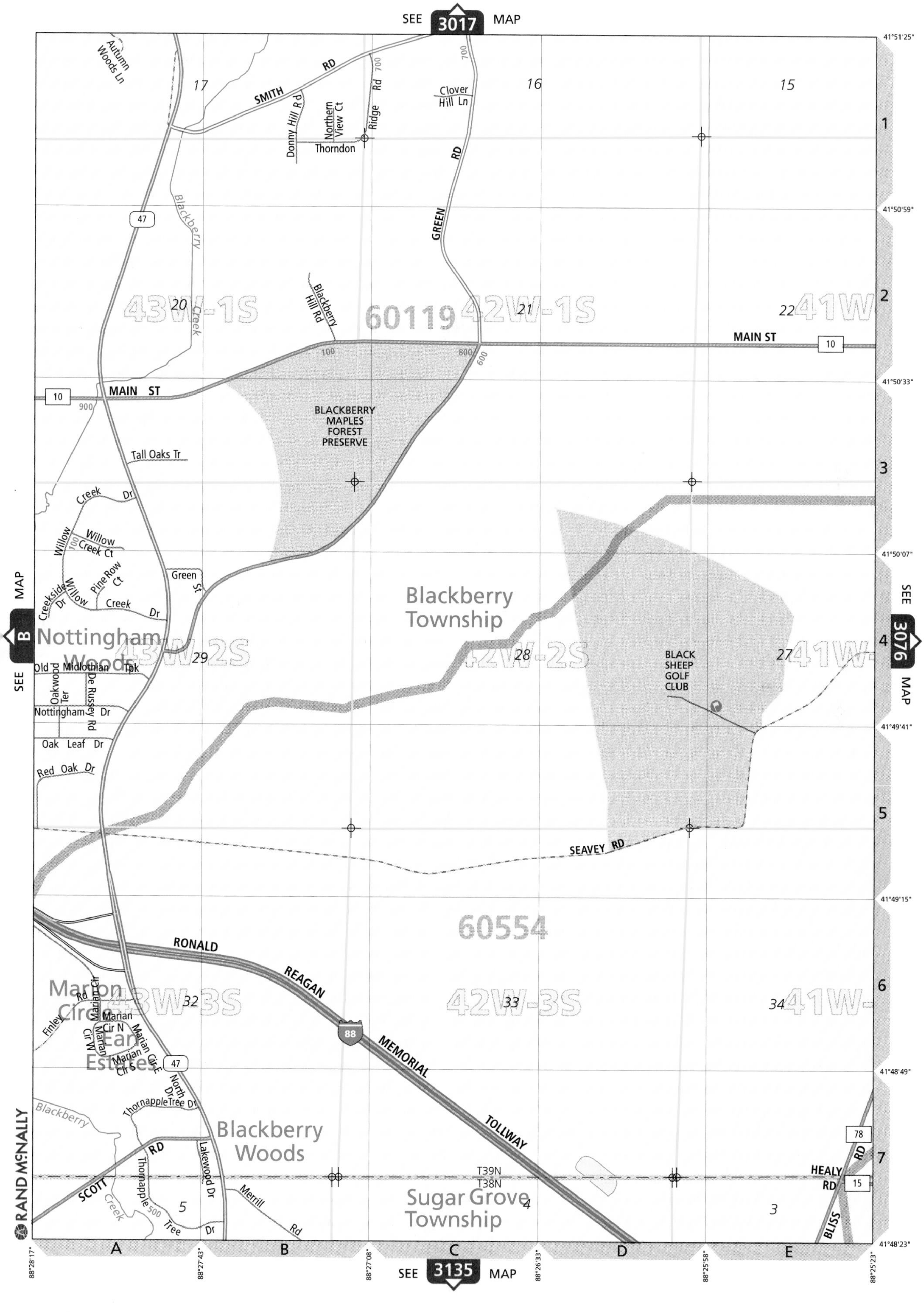

1:24,000
1 in. = 2000 ft.
0 0.25 0.5
miles

SEE 3018 MAP

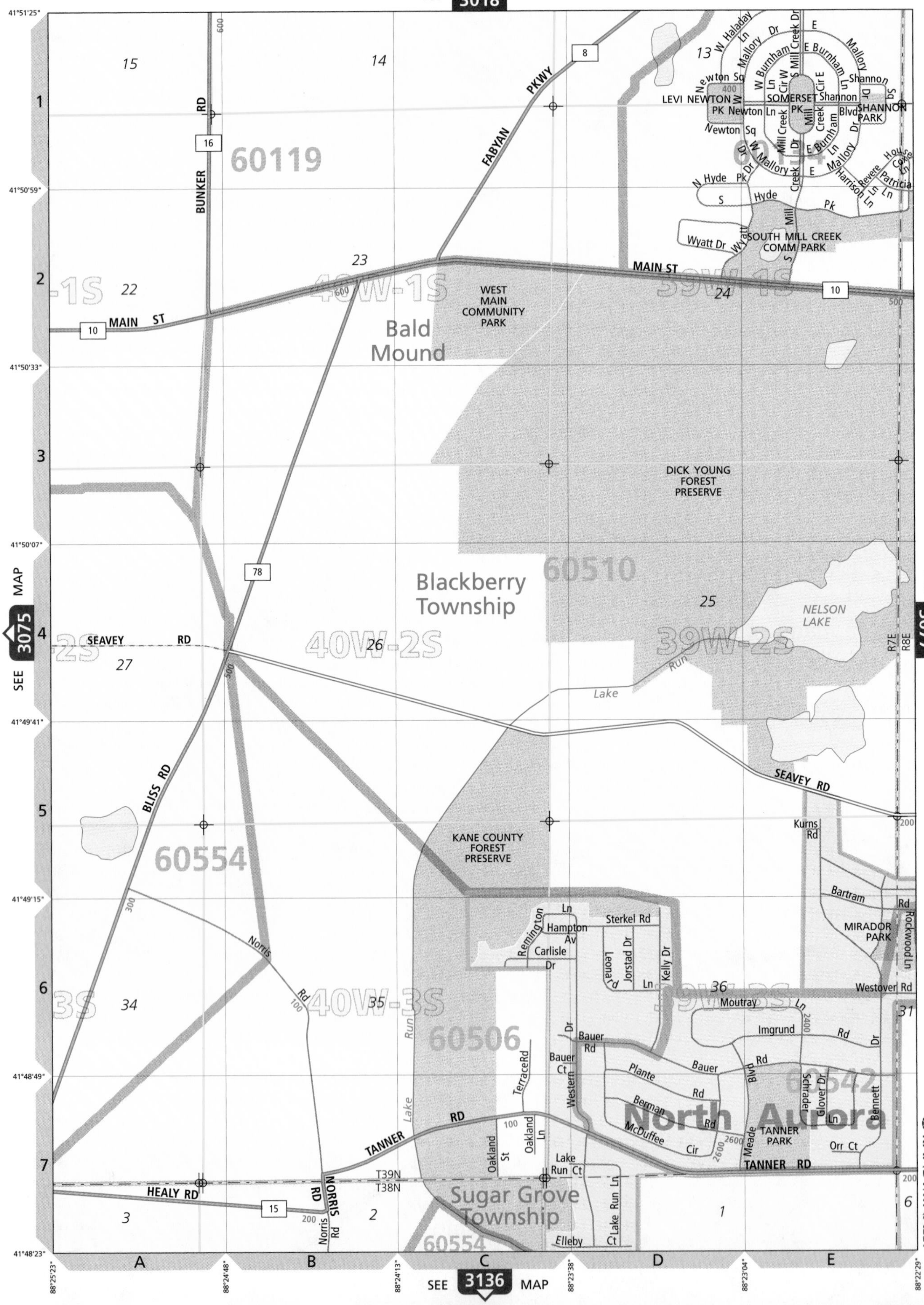

SEE 3075 MAP

SEE 3077 MAP

SEE 3136 MAP

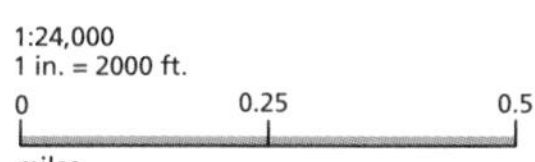

SEE 3019 MAP

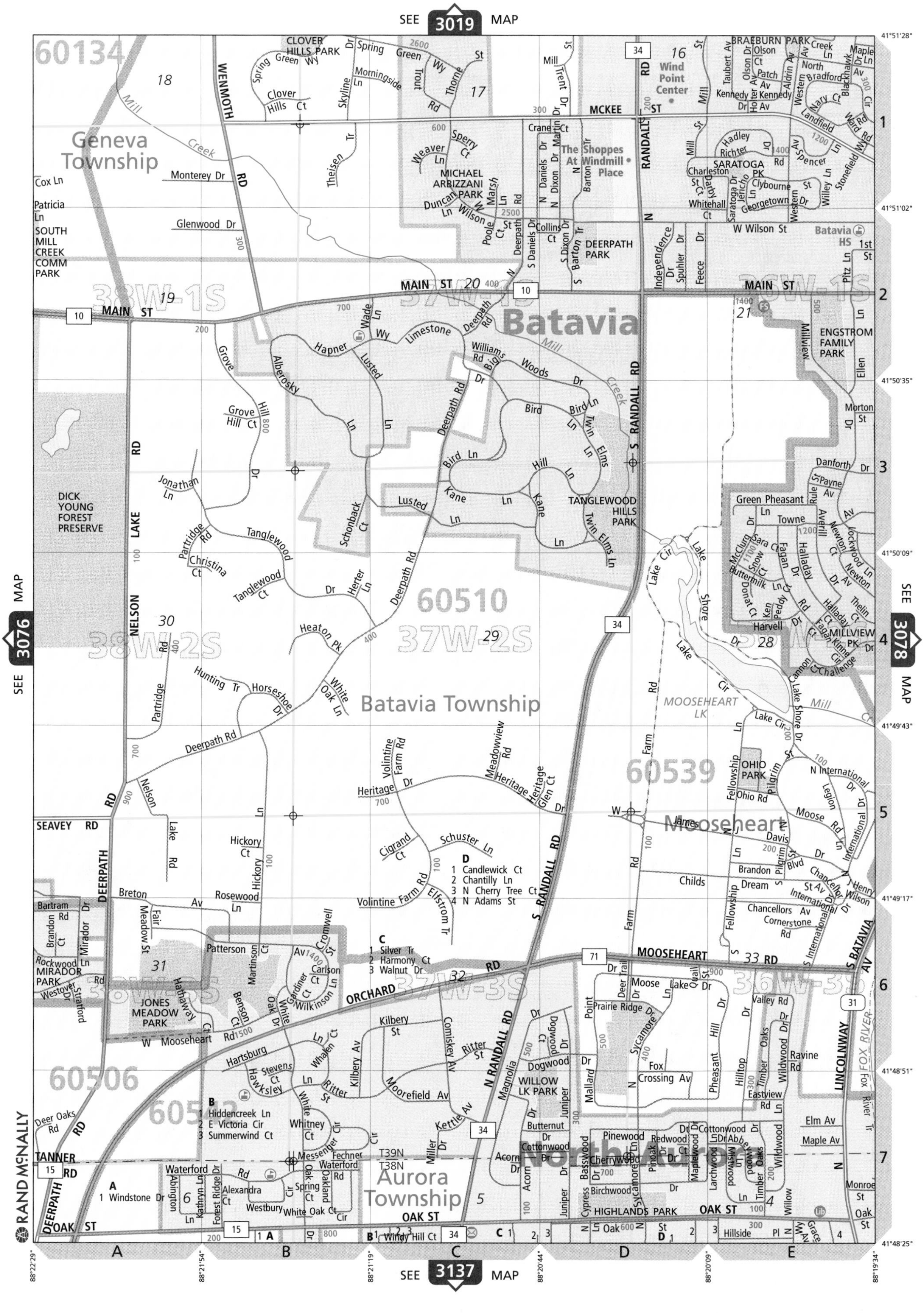

SEE 3076 MAP

SEE 3078 MAP

Geneva Township

Batavia

Batavia Township

Mooseheart

North Aurora

Aurora Township

60134

60510

60539

60506

60542

A
1 Windstone Dr

B
1 Hiddencreek Ln
2 E Victoria Cir
3 Summerwind Ct

C
1 Silver Tr
2 Harmony Ct
3 Walnut Dr

D
1 Candlewick Ct
2 Chantilly Ln
3 N Cherry Tree Ct
4 N Adams St

SEE 3137 MAP

1:24,000
1 in. = 2000 ft.
0 0.25 0.5
miles

SEE 3020 MAP

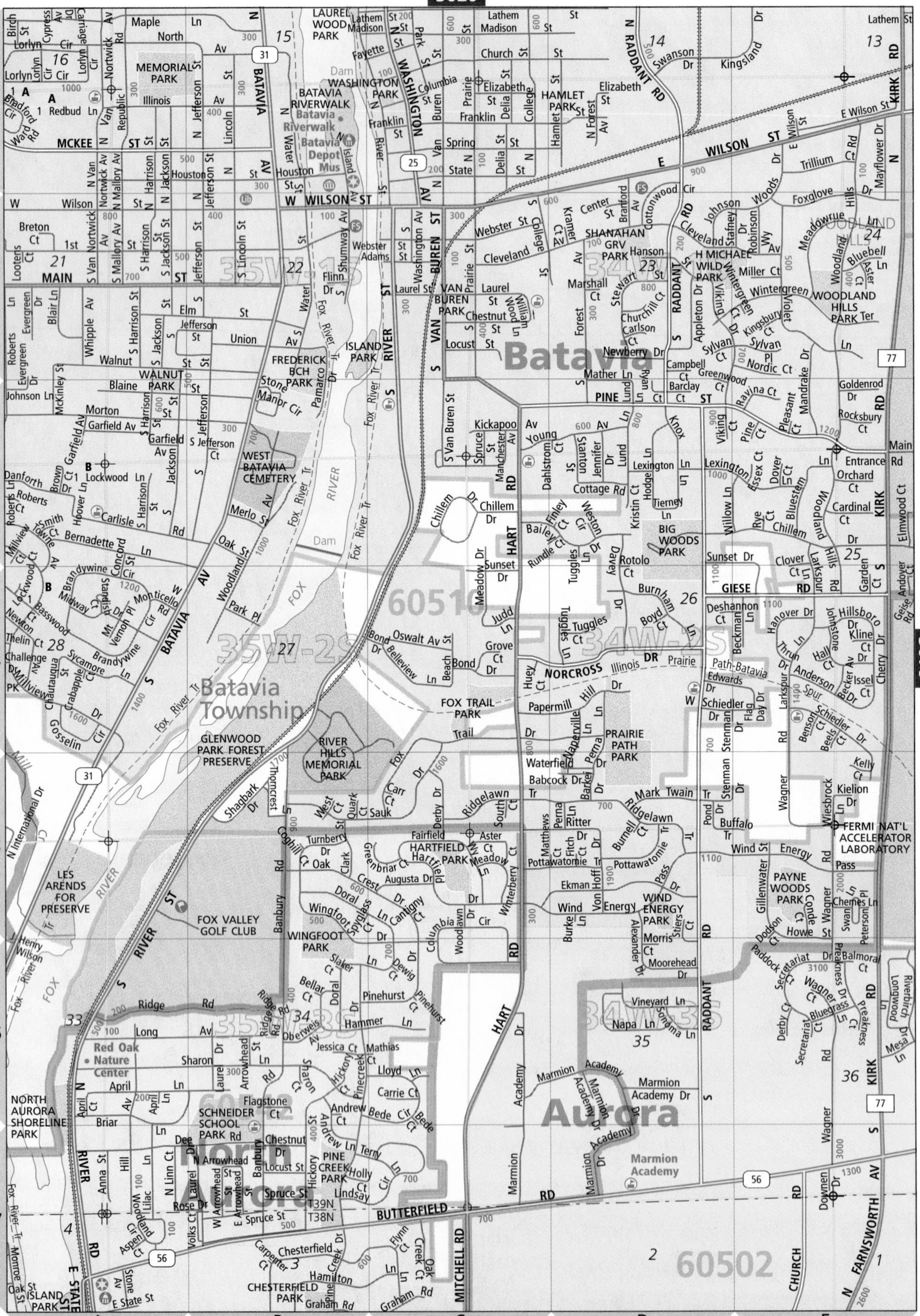

Batavia

Batavia Township

Aurora

North Aurora

60510

60502

BATAVIA RIVERWALK

WASHINGTON PARK

MEMORIAL PARK

HAMLET PARK

SHANAHAN GRV PARK

H MICHAEL WILD PARK

WOODLAND HILLS PARK

VAN BUREN PARK

ISLAND PARK

FREDERICK BCH PARK

WALNUT PARK

WEST BATAVIA CEMETERY

BIG WOODS PARK

FOX TRAIL PARK

PRAIRIE PATH PARK

GLENWOOD PARK FOREST PRESERVE

RIVER HILLS MEMORIAL PARK

HARTFIELD PARK

WIND ENERGY PARK

PAYNE WOODS PARK

FERMI NAT'L ACCELERATOR LABORATORY

LES ARENDS FOR PRESERVE

FOX VALLEY GOLF CLUB

WINGFOOT PARK

Red Oak Nature Center

NORTH AURORA SHORELINE PARK

SCHNEIDER SCHOOL PARK

PINE CREEK PARK

Marmion Academy

CHESTERFIELD PARK

ISLAND PARK

SEE 3077 MAP

SEE 3079 MAP

SEE 3138 MAP

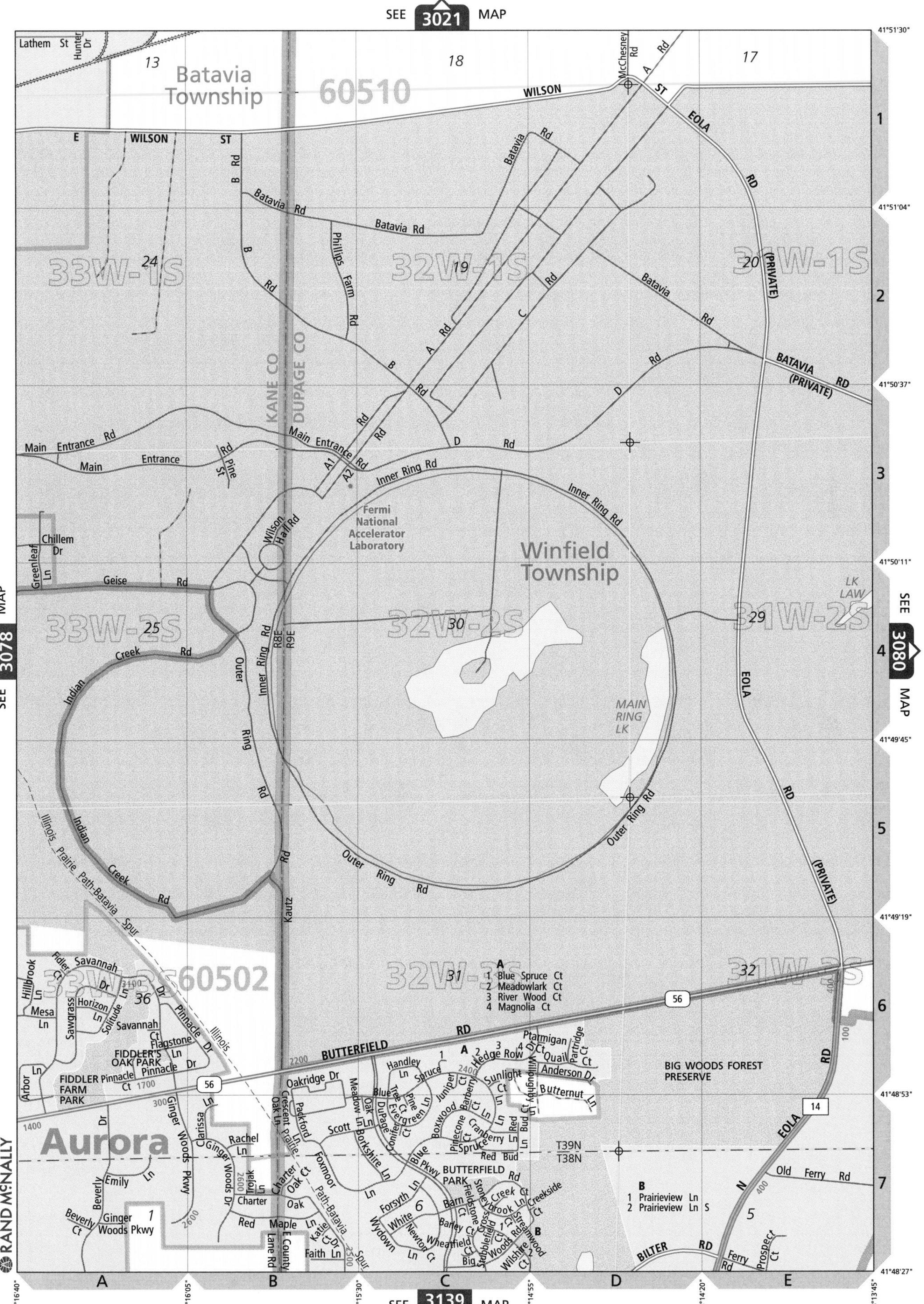
1:24,000
1 in. = 2000 ft.
0 0.25 0.5
miles
SEE 3021 MAP
SEE 3078 MAP
SEE 3080 MAP
SEE 3139 MAP
Batavia Township
60510
Winfield Township
Fermi National Accelerator Laboratory
KANE CO
DUPAGE CO
E WILSON ST
Batavia Rd
Phillips Farm Rd
Main Entrance Rd
Inner Ring Rd
Outer Ring Rd
Geise Rd
Indian Creek Rd
EOLA RD (PRIVATE)
BATAVIA RD (PRIVATE)
Kautz Rd
MAIN RING LK
LK LAW
60502
Aurora
BUTTERFIELD RD
BIG WOODS FOREST PRESERVE
FIDDLER'S OAK PARK
FIDDLER FARM PARK
BUTTERFIELD PARK
Illinois Prairie Path-Batavia Spur
A
1 Blue Spruce Ct
2 Meadowlark Ct
3 River Wood Ct
4 Magnolia Ct
B
1 Prairieview Ln
2 Prairieview Ln S
T39N
T38N
RAND McNALLY

1:24,000
1 in. = 2000 ft.
0 0.25 0.5
miles

SEE 3022 MAP

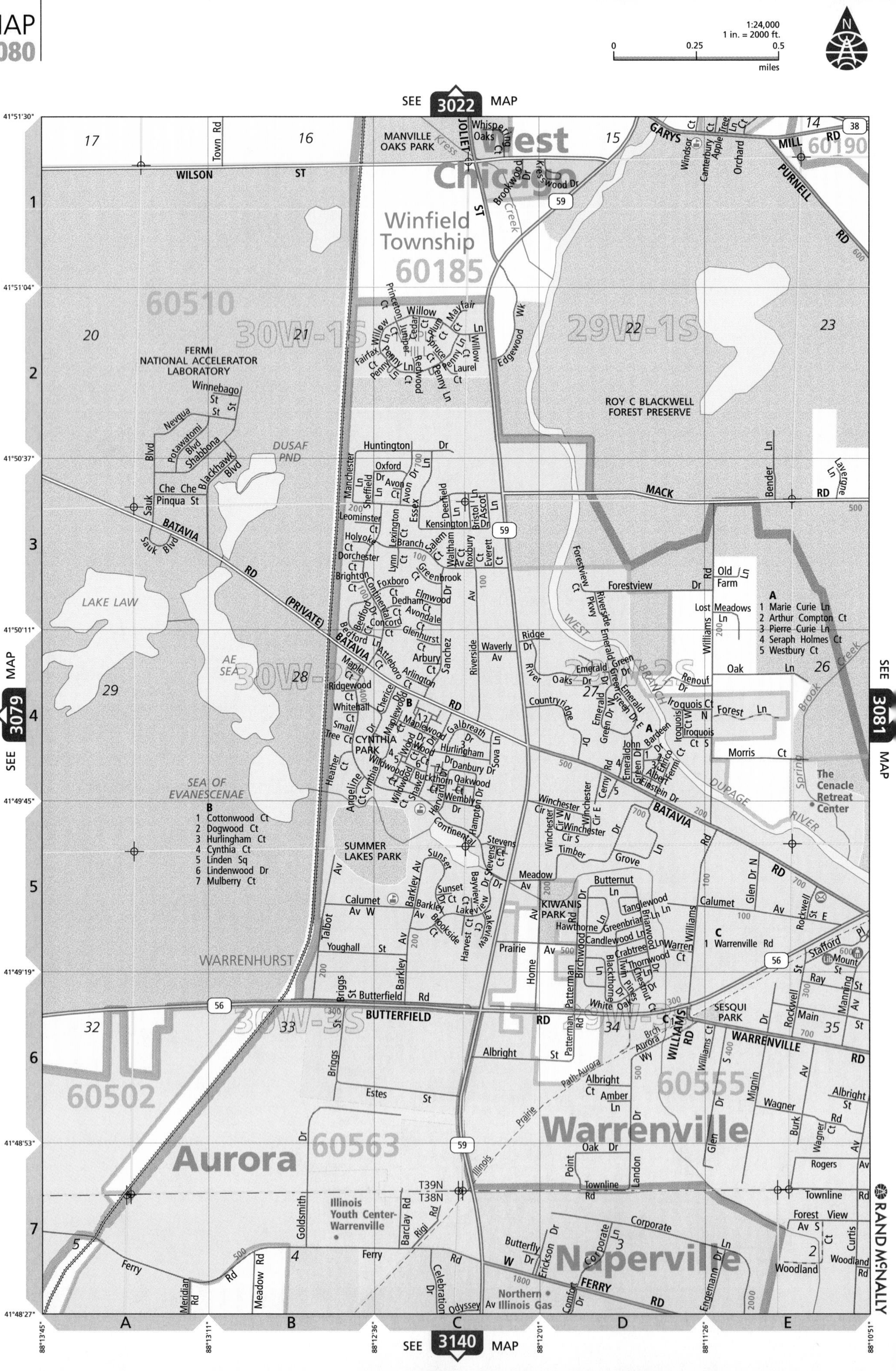

SEE 3079 MAP

SEE 3081 MAP

SEE 3140 MAP

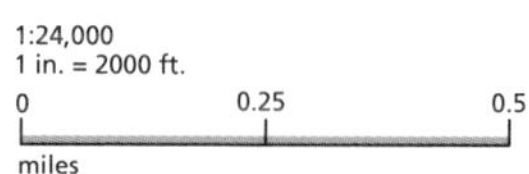

SEE 3023 MAP

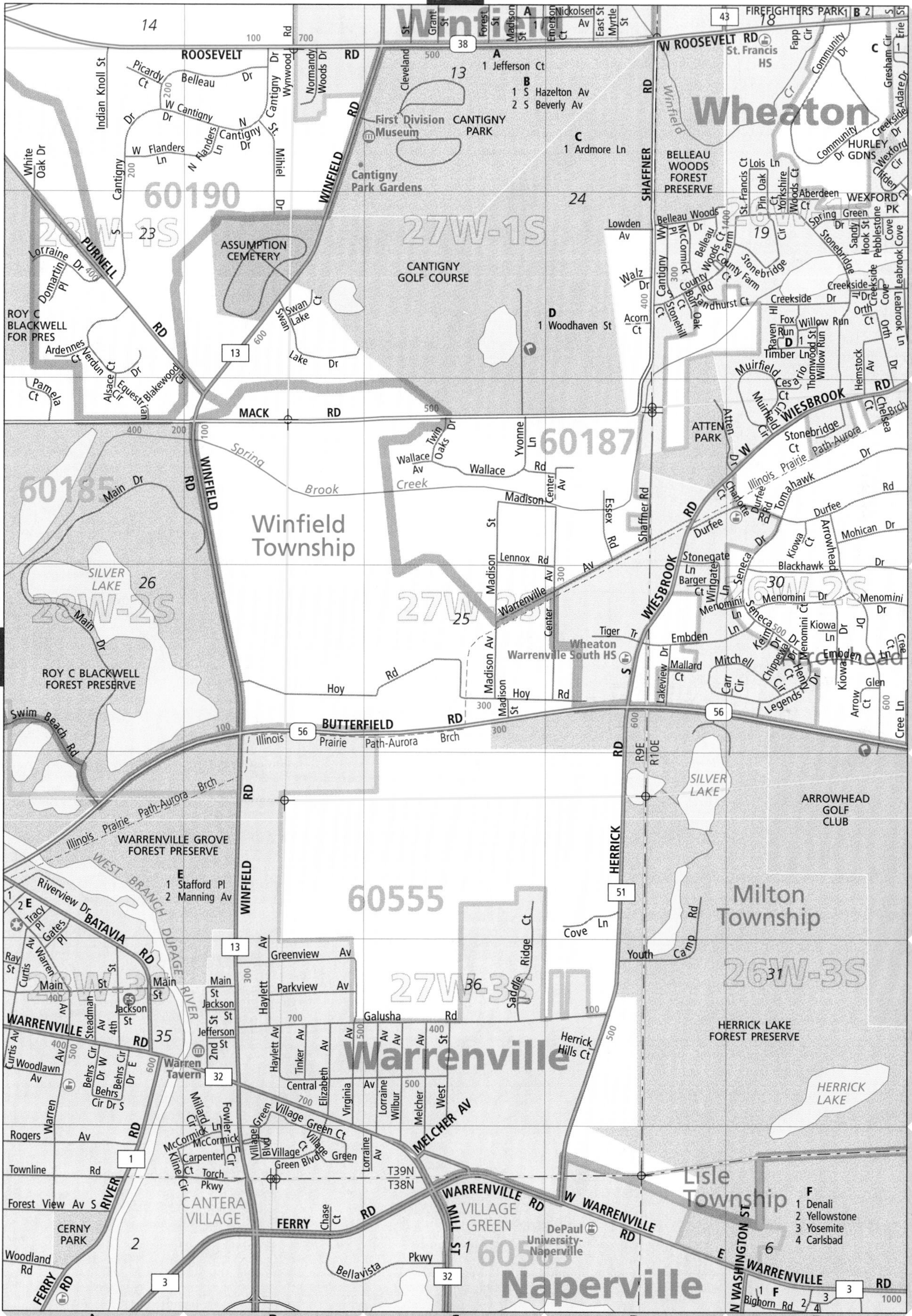

SEE 3080 MAP

SEE 3082 MAP

SEE 3141 MAP

1:24,000
1 in. = 2000 ft.
0 0.25 0.5
miles

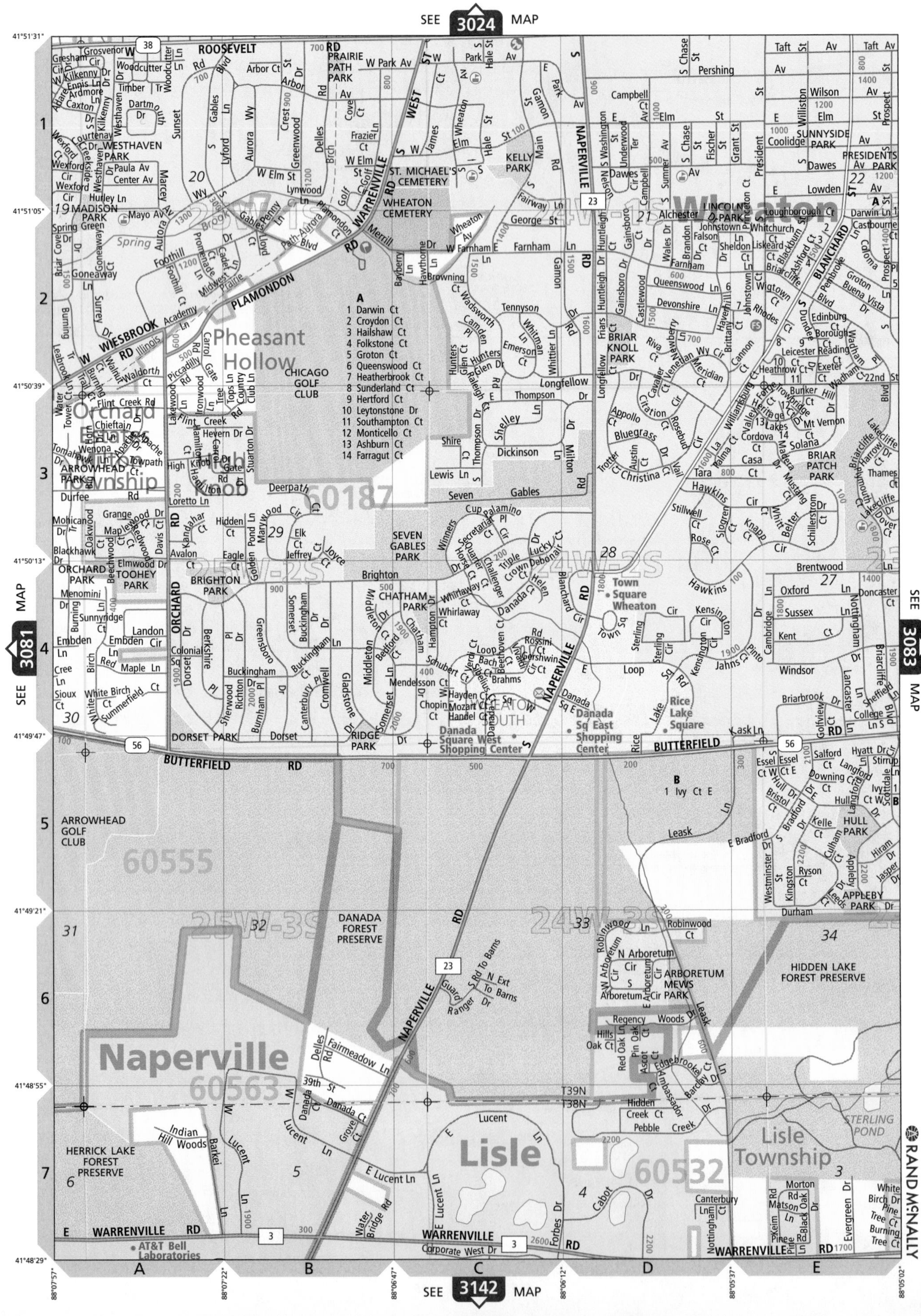

SEE 3024 MAP
SEE 3081 MAP
SEE 3083 MAP
SEE 3142 MAP
ROOSEVELT RD
PRAIRIE PATH PARK
WESTHAVEN PARK
MADISON PARK
KELLY PARK
ST. MICHAEL'S CEMETERY
WHEATON CEMETERY
Wheaton
LINCOLN PARK
SUNNYSIDE PARK
PRESIDENTS PARK
BRIAR KNOLL PARK
BRIAR PATCH PARK
Pheasant Hollow
CHICAGO GOLF CLUB
Orchard Estates
Milton Township
ARROWHEAD PARK
Hull Knob
SEVEN GABLES PARK
ORCHARD PARK
TOOHEY PARK
BRIGHTON PARK
CHATHAM PARK
Town Square Wheaton
Rice Lake Square
Danada Square West Shopping Center
Danada Sq East Shopping Center
DORSET PARK
RIDGE PARK
BUTTERFIELD RD
ARROWHEAD GOLF CLUB
60555
60187
60563
60532
HULL PARK
APPLEBY PARK
DANADA FOREST PRESERVE
HIDDEN LAKE FOREST PRESERVE
ARBORETUM MEWS PARK
Naperville
HERRICK LAKE FOREST PRESERVE
Lisle
Lisle Township
STERLING POND
NAPERVILLE RD
WARRENVILLE RD
AT&T Bell Laboratories
T39N
T38N
A
1 Darwin Ct
2 Croydon Ct
3 Hailshaw Ct
4 Folkstone Ct
5 Groton Ct
6 Queenswood Ct
7 Heatherbrook Ct
8 Sunderland Ct
9 Hertford Ct
10 Leytonstone Dr
11 Southampton Ct
12 Monticello Ct
13 Ashburn Ct
14 Farragut Ct
B
1 Ivy Ct E
A B C D E
1 2 3 4 5 6 7
RAND McNALLY

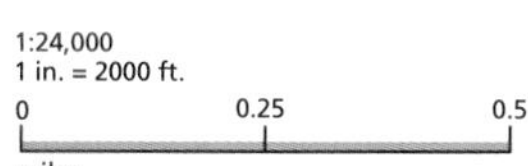

SEE 3025 MAP

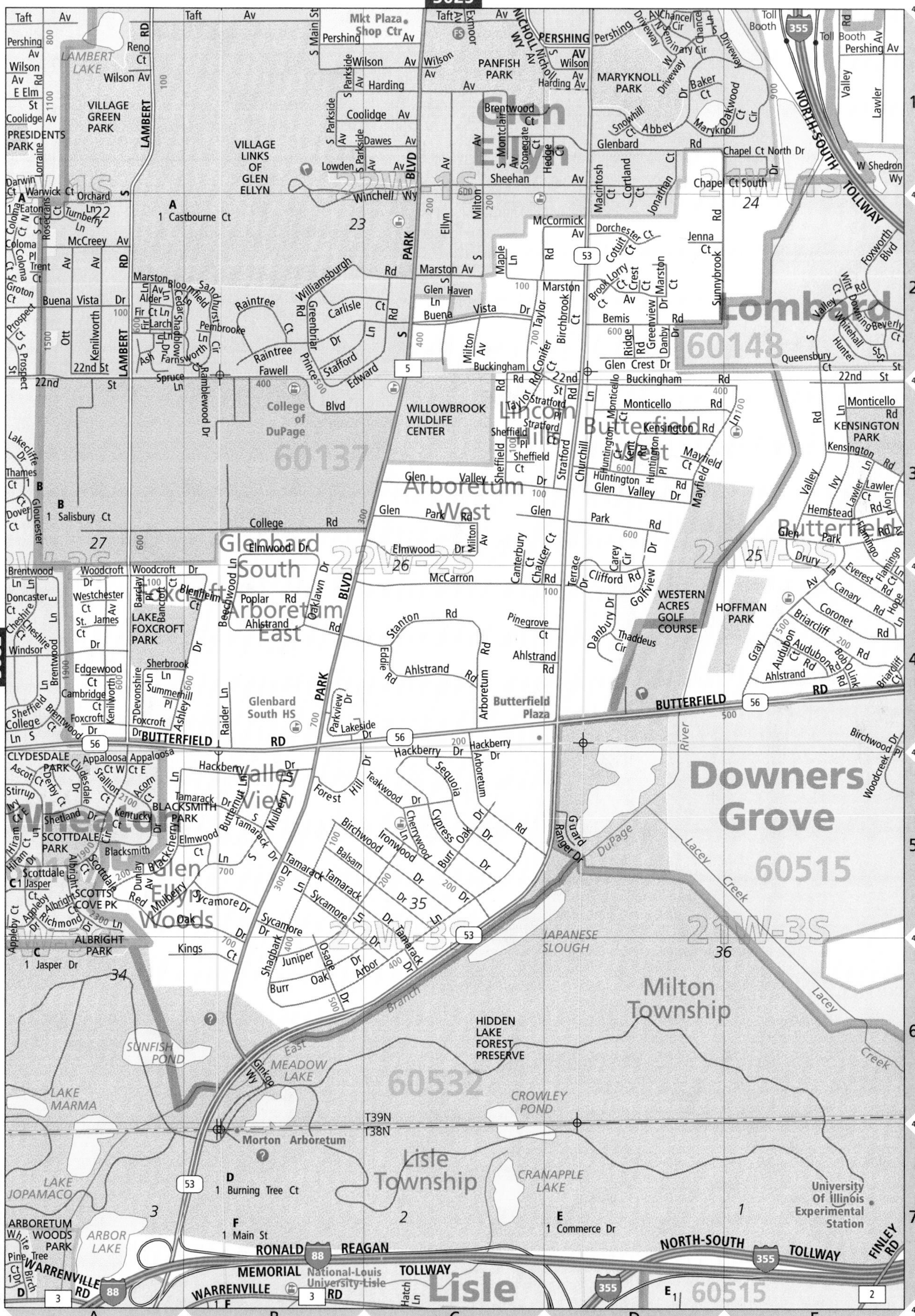

SEE 3082 MAP

SEE 3084 MAP

Glen Ellyn

Lombard 60148

Wheaton

Downers Grove 60515

Lisle 60515

60137

60532

Milton Township

Lisle Township

VILLAGE GREEN PARK

PRESIDENTS PARK

VILLAGE LINKS OF GLEN ELLYN

PANFISH PARK

MARYKNOLL PARK

College of DuPage

WILLOWBROOK WILDLIFE CENTER

Lincoln Hills

Butterfield West

Arboretum West

Glenbard South

Foxcroft

Arboretum East

LAKE FOXCROFT PARK

Glenbard South HS

Butterfield Plaza

WESTERN ACRES GOLF COURSE

HOFFMAN PARK

KENSINGTON PARK

Valley View

BLACKSMITH PARK

CLYDESDALE PARK

SCOTTDALE PARK

SCOTTS COVE PK

ALBRIGHT PARK

Glen Ellyn Woods

JAPANESE SLOUGH

HIDDEN LAKE FOREST PRESERVE

SUNFISH POND

MEADOW LAKE

LAKE MARMA

CROWLEY POND

Morton Arboretum

LAKE JOPAMACO

CRANAPPLE LAKE

ARBORETUM WOODS PARK

ARBOR LAKE

University Of Illinois Experimental Station

National-Louis University-Lisle

Mkt Plaza Shop Ctr

NORTH-SOUTH TOLLWAY

RONALD REAGAN MEMORIAL TOLLWAY

BUTTERFIELD RD

PARK BLVD

LAMBERT RD

22nd St

College Rd

WARRENVILLE RD

FINLEY RD

East Branch DuPage River

Lacey Creek

22W-1S 21W-1S 22W-2S 21W-2S 22W-3S 21W-3S

T39N T38N

A 1 Castbourne Ct

B 1 Salisbury Ct

C 1 Jasper Dr

D 1 Burning Tree Ct

E 1 Commerce Dr

F 1 Main St

41°51'33" 41°51'07" 41°50'40" 41°50'14" 41°49'48" 41°49'22" 41°48'56" 41°48'30"

88°05'02" 88°04'27" 88°03'53" 88°03'18" 88°02'43" 88°02'08"

A B C D E

1 2 3 4 5 6 7

SEE 3143 MAP

1:24,000
1 in. = 2000 ft.
0 0.25 0.5
miles

SEE 3026 MAP

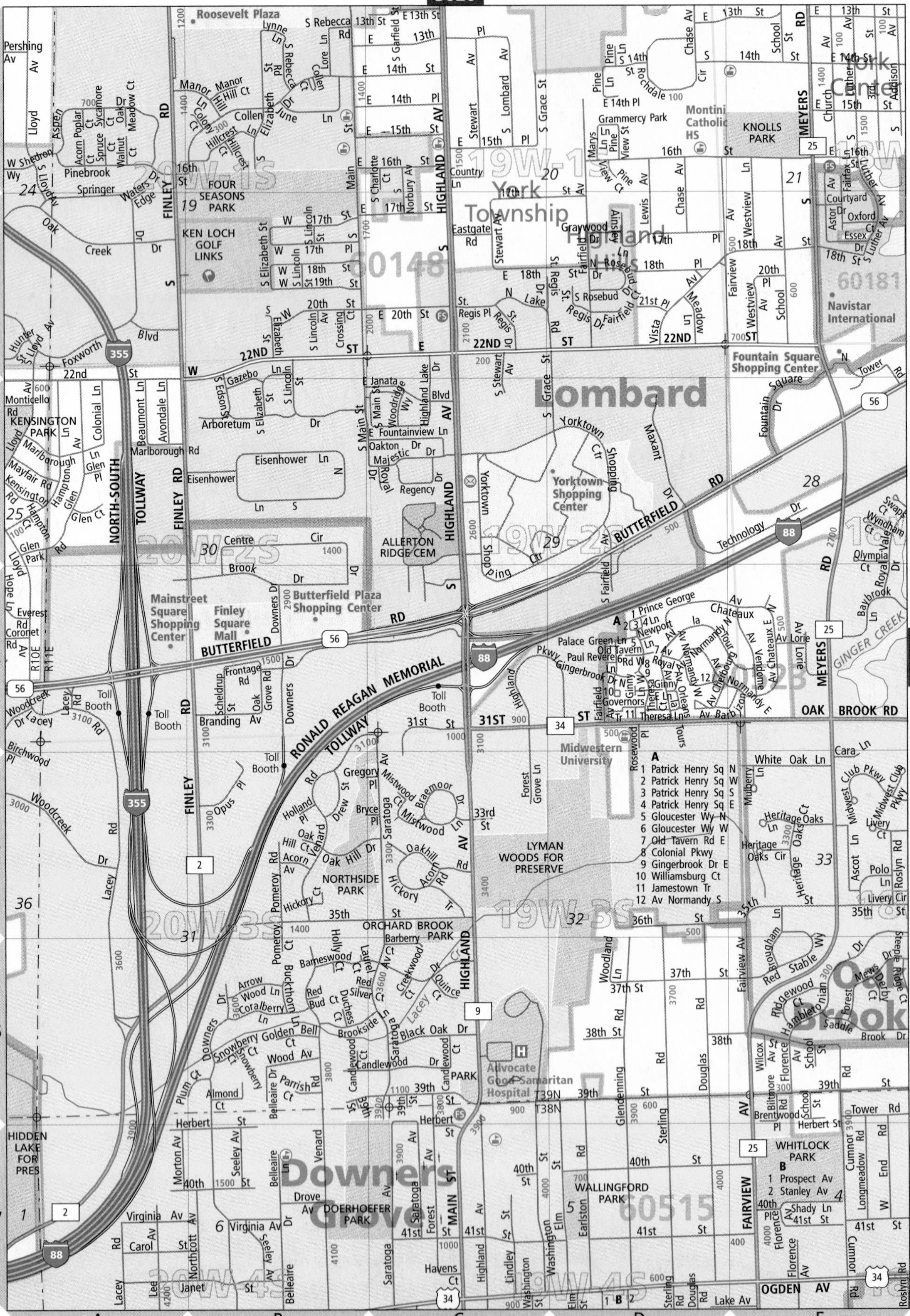

Lombard

York Township

Highland Hills

Downers Grove

Oak Brook

York Center

60148

60181

60515

Roosevelt Plaza

FOUR SEASONS PARK

KEN LOCH GOLF LINKS

KENSINGTON PARK

KNOLLS PARK

Montini Catholic HS

Navistar International

Fountain Square Shopping Center

Yorktown Shopping Center

ALLERTON RIDGE CEM

Mainstreet Square Shopping Center

Finley Square Mall

Butterfield Plaza Shopping Center

Midwestern University

NORTHSIDE PARK

ORCHARD BROOK PARK

LYMAN WOODS FOR PRESERVE

Advocate Good Samaritan Hospital

HIDDEN LAKE FOR PRES

DOERHOEFER PARK

WALLINGFORD PARK

WHITLOCK PARK

NORTH-SOUTH TOLLWAY

RONALD REAGAN MEMORIAL TOLLWAY

BUTTERFIELD RD

OAK BROOK RD

OGDEN AV

FINLEY RD

HIGHLAND AV

MAIN ST

MEYERS RD

FAIRVIEW AV

22ND ST

31ST ST

A
1 Patrick Henry Sq N
2 Patrick Henry Sq W
3 Patrick Henry Sq S
4 Patrick Henry Sq E
5 Gloucester Wy N
6 Gloucester Wy W
7 Old Tavern Rd E
8 Colonial Pkwy
9 Gingerbrook Dr E
10 Williamsburg Ct
11 Jamestown Tr
12 Av Normandy S

B
1 Prospect Av
2 Stanley Av

SEE 3083 MAP

SEE 3085 MAP

SEE 3144 MAP

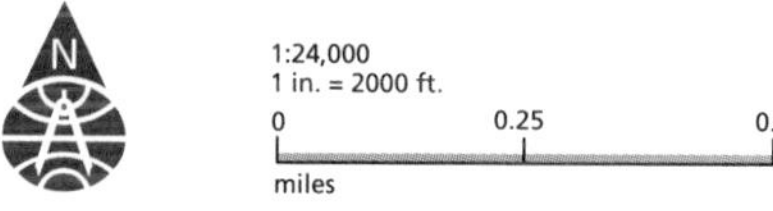

SEE 3027 MAP

Oakbrook Terrace
York Township
Oak Brook
Westmont
Downers Grove Township
Clarendon Hills
Hinsdale

CHAPEL HILL GARDENS CEMETERY
Oakbrook Terrace Tower
Oakbrook Court
Greyhound-Oak Brook
Oakbrook Shopping Center
McDonald Plaza
DOROTHY DRENNON PARK
TERRACE VIEW PARK
The Shops At Oak Brook
Toll Booth
RONALD REAGAN MEMORIAL TOLLWAY
BUTLER NATIONAL GOLF CLUB
TEAL LAKE
CENTRAL PARK
OAK BROOK GOLF CLUB
BUTTERFIELD COUNTRY CLUB
FULLERSBURG WOODS FOR PRES
MAYS LAKE FOREST PRESERVE
MAYS LAKES
Mayslake Retirement Vil
SADDLE BROOK PARK
WILLOW CREST GOLF CLUB
Westmont HS
OAKWOOD PARK
BLACKHAWK PARK
TY WARNER PARK
LAKE CHARLES
Inland Meeting & Expo Center
HINSDALE GOLF CLUB
St. James Crossing
BRONSWOOD CEMETERY
Downers Grove Marketplace

BUTTERFIELD RD
22ND ST
OAK BROOK RD
MIDWEST RD
SUMMIT AV
KINGERY HWY
MID AMERICA PLZ
JORIE BLVD
SPRING RD
ADAMS RD
CASS AV
OGDEN AV
35th St
39th St
KINGERY EXPWY HWY

B 1 Briarwood Pass
C 1 Tartan Lakes Wy
D 1 Hambletonian Dr 2 Saddle Brook Dr
A 1 S Michigan Av 2 S Ardmore Av

60181
60523
60559
60521
60514
17W-1S
16W-1S
17W-2S
16W-2S
17W-3S
16W-3S
17W-4S
16W-4S
T39N
T38N

41°51'34"
41°51'08"
41°50'41"
41°50'15"
41°49'49"
41°49'23"
41°48'57"
41°48'31"
87°59'13"
87°58'39"
87°58'04"
87°57'29"
87°56'54"
87°56'19"

A B C D E
1 2 3 4 5 6 7

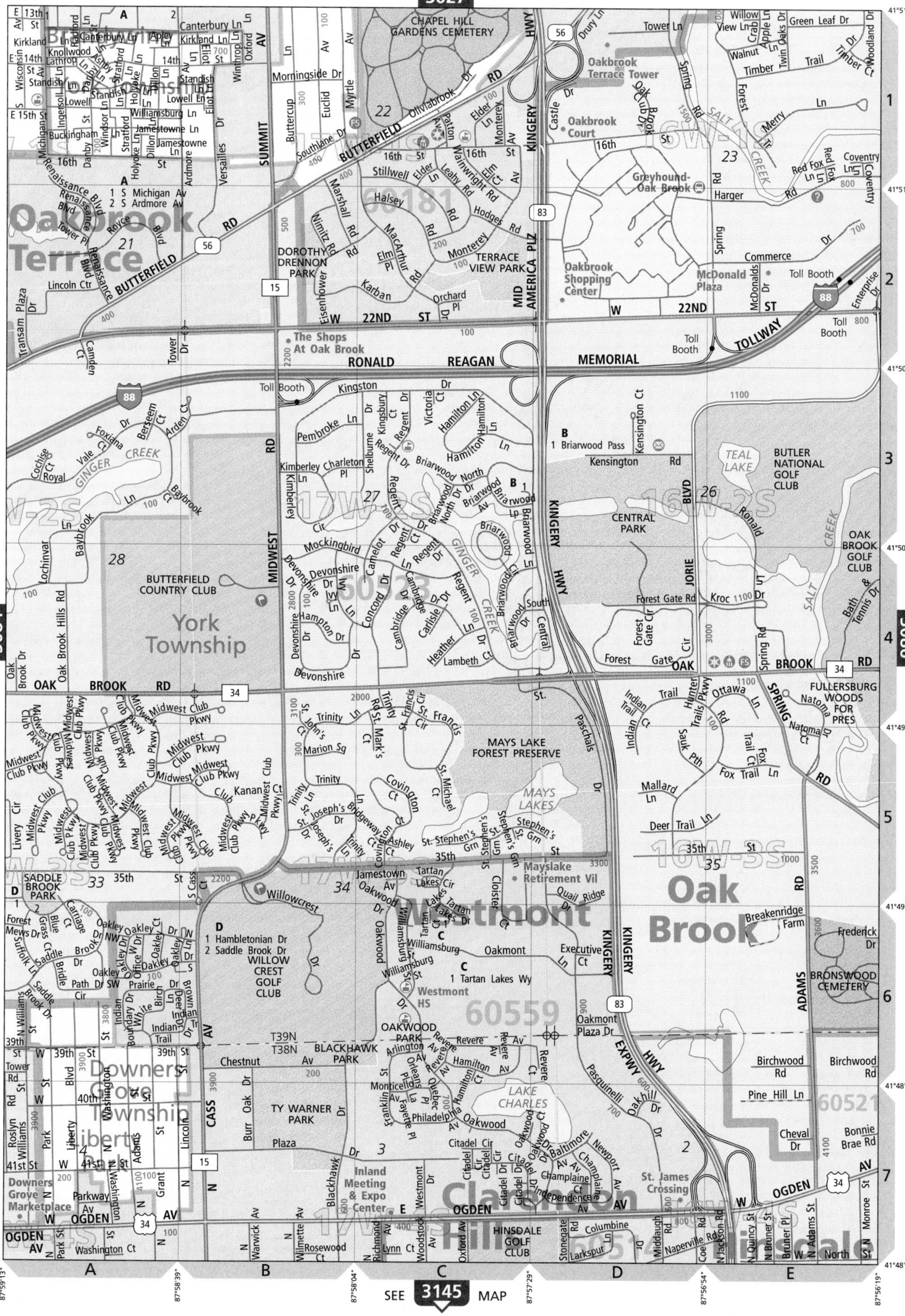

SEE 3084 MAP
SEE 3086 MAP
SEE 3145 MAP

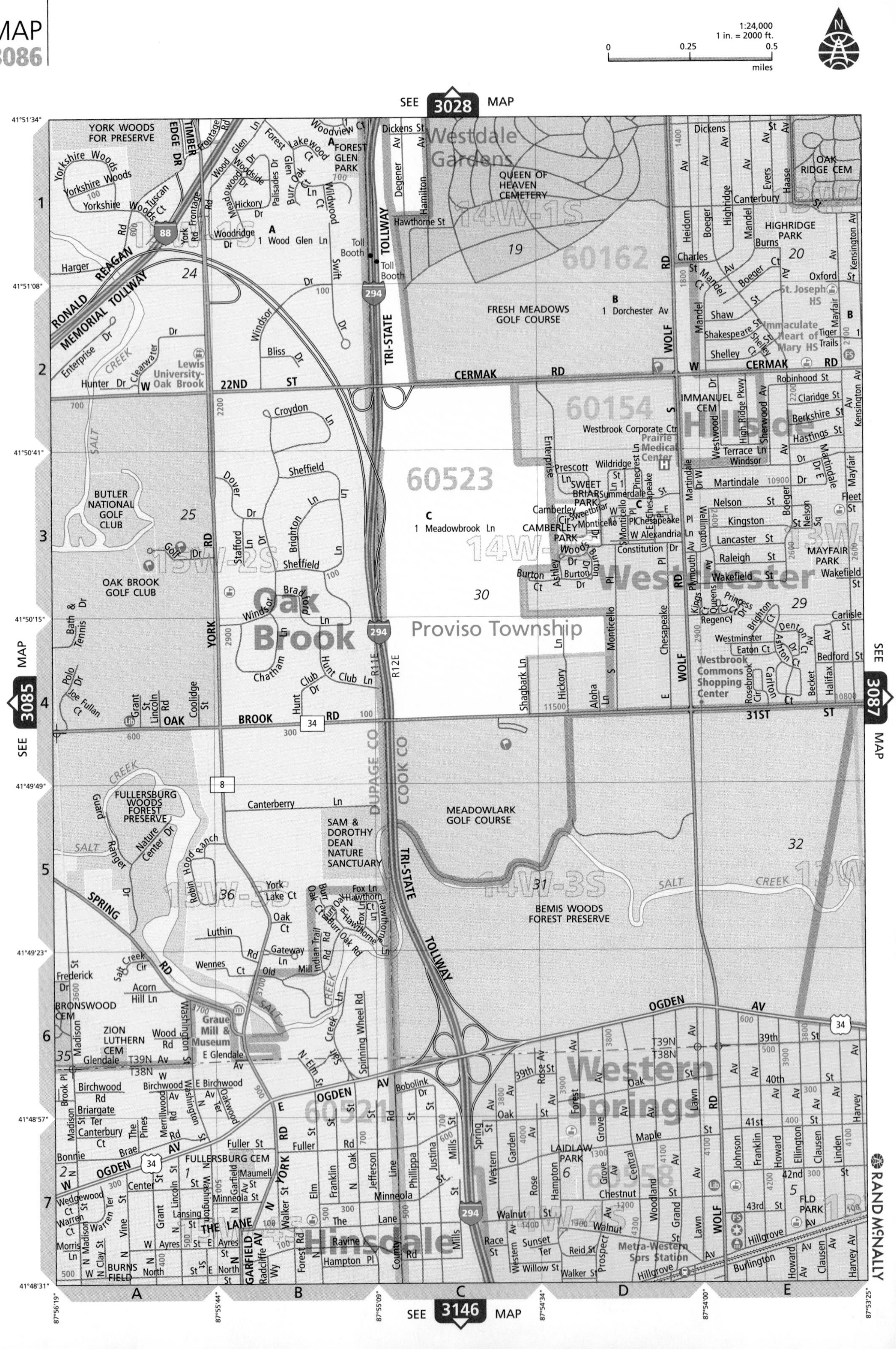

1:24,000
1 in. = 2000 ft.
0 0.25 0.5 miles

SEE 3028 MAP
SEE 3085 MAP
SEE 3087 MAP
SEE 3146 MAP

YORK WOODS FOR PRESERVE
FOREST GLEN PARK
Westdale Gardens
QUEEN OF HEAVEN CEMETERY
OAK RIDGE CEM
HIGHRIDGE PARK
60162
FRESH MEADOWS GOLF COURSE
St. Joseph HS
Immaculate Heart of Mary HS
Lewis University-Oak Brook
RONALD REAGAN MEMORIAL TOLLWAY
TRI-STATE TOLLWAY
CERMAK RD
22ND ST
60154
IMMANUEL CEM
Hillside
Westbrook Corporate Ctr
Prairie Medical Center
60523
SWEET BRIAR PARK
CAMBERLEY PARK
BUTLER NATIONAL GOLF CLUB
OAK BROOK GOLF CLUB
Oak Brook
Proviso Township
Westchester
MAYFAIR PARK
Westbrook Commons Shopping Center
OAK BROOK RD
31ST ST
FULLERSBURG WOODS FOREST PRESERVE
SAM & DOROTHY DEAN NATURE SANCTUARY
MEADOWLARK GOLF COURSE
BEMIS WOODS FOREST PRESERVE
SALT CREEK
SPRING RD
BRONSWOOD CEM
ZION LUTHERN CEM
Graue Mill & Museum
OGDEN AV
Western Springs
60521
60558
LAIDLAW PARK
FLD PARK
FULLERSBURG CEM
BURNS FIELD
Hinsdale
Metra-Western Sprs Station
DUPAGE CO
COOK CO

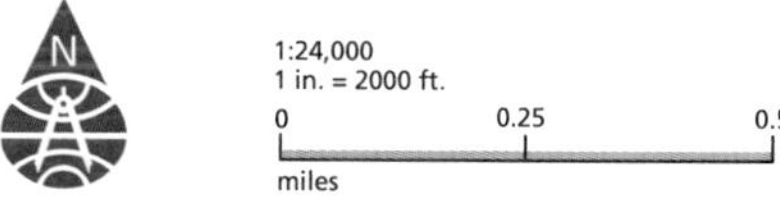

SEE 3029 MAP

Westchester
60154
Broadview
60155
North Riverside
Proviso Township
WESTCHESTER WOODS FOREST PRESERVE
26TH STREET WOODS FOREST PRESERVE
BREZINA WOODS FOR PRESERVE
PARKHOLM CEM
HANESWORTH PARK
WILLIAM G YENA PARK
CANDY CANE PARK
BROOKFIELD WOODS FOREST PRESERVE
POSSUM HOLLOW WOODS FOREST PRESERVE
ROBIN HOOD PARK
LA GRANGE PARK WOODS FOREST PRESERVE
BEMIS WOODS FOREST PRESERVE
BROOKFIELD ZOO-CHICAGO ZOOLOGICAL PARK
ZOO WOODS FOR PRES
STONE MONROE PARK
60525
La Grange Park
MADIN PARK
KIWANIS PARK
60513
MEM PARK
BCH OAK PARK
The Village Market
Nazareth Academy
Door County Maritime Museum
SHAWMUT PARK
Metra-Congress Park Station
Metra-Brookfield Station
La Grange
Brookfield
Amtrak-La Grange Sta
Metra-Stone Av Station
Lyons Township High School-North
GILBERT PARK
ELM PARK
EHLERT PARK
OAK RIDGE CEM
GLEN OAK CEM
COMMUNITY PARK
SCHROEDER PARK
MENORAH GARDENS CEMETERY
Broadview Vil Square Shopping Center
BEVERLY PARK

A
1 39th St
2 40th St
3 42nd St
4 Hillgrove Av

B
1 N Tilden Av

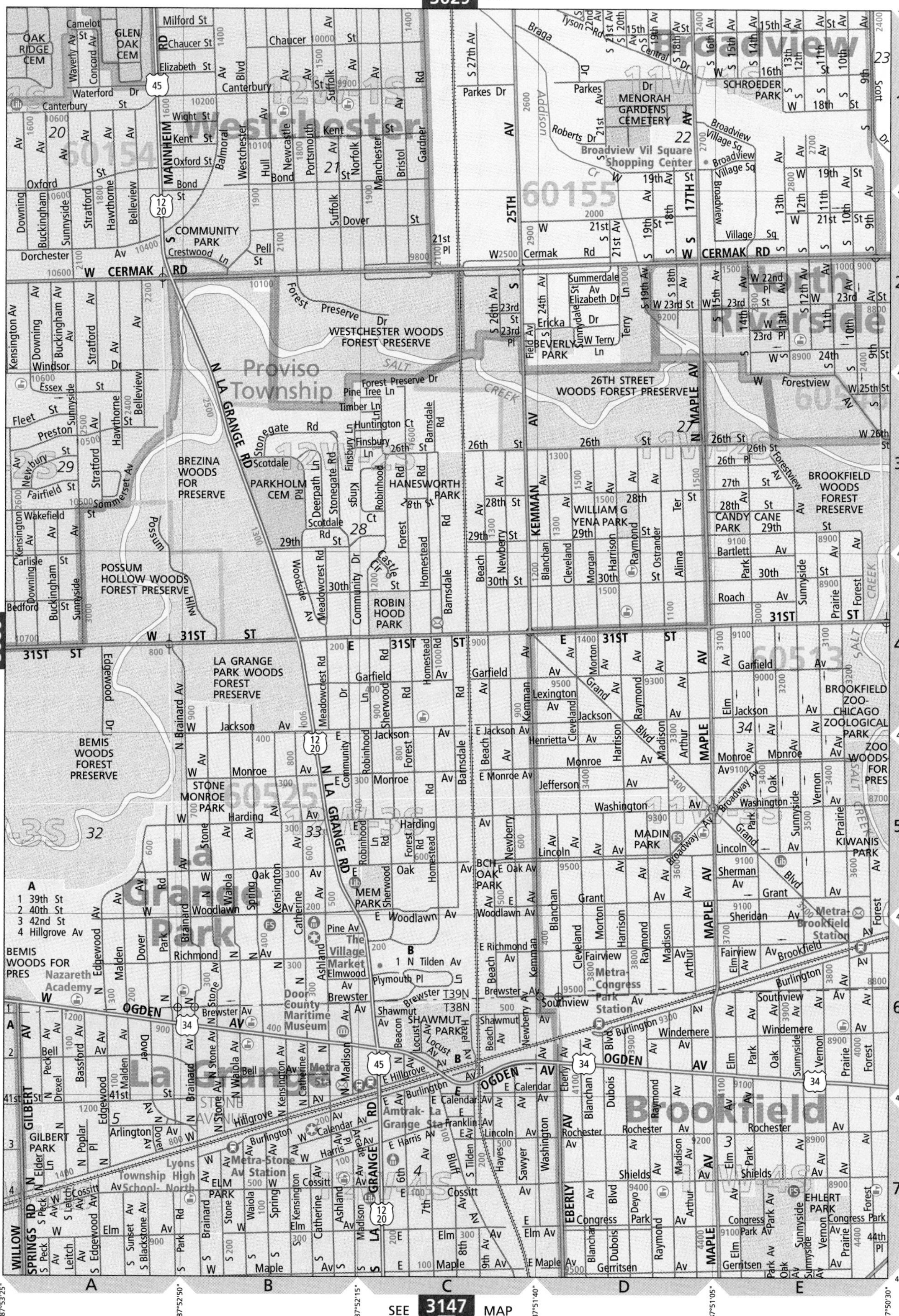

SEE 3086 MAP

SEE 3088 MAP

SEE 3147 MAP

1:24,000
1 in. = 2000 ft.
0 0.25 0.5 miles

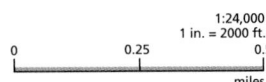

SEE 3030 MAP

SEE 3087 MAP

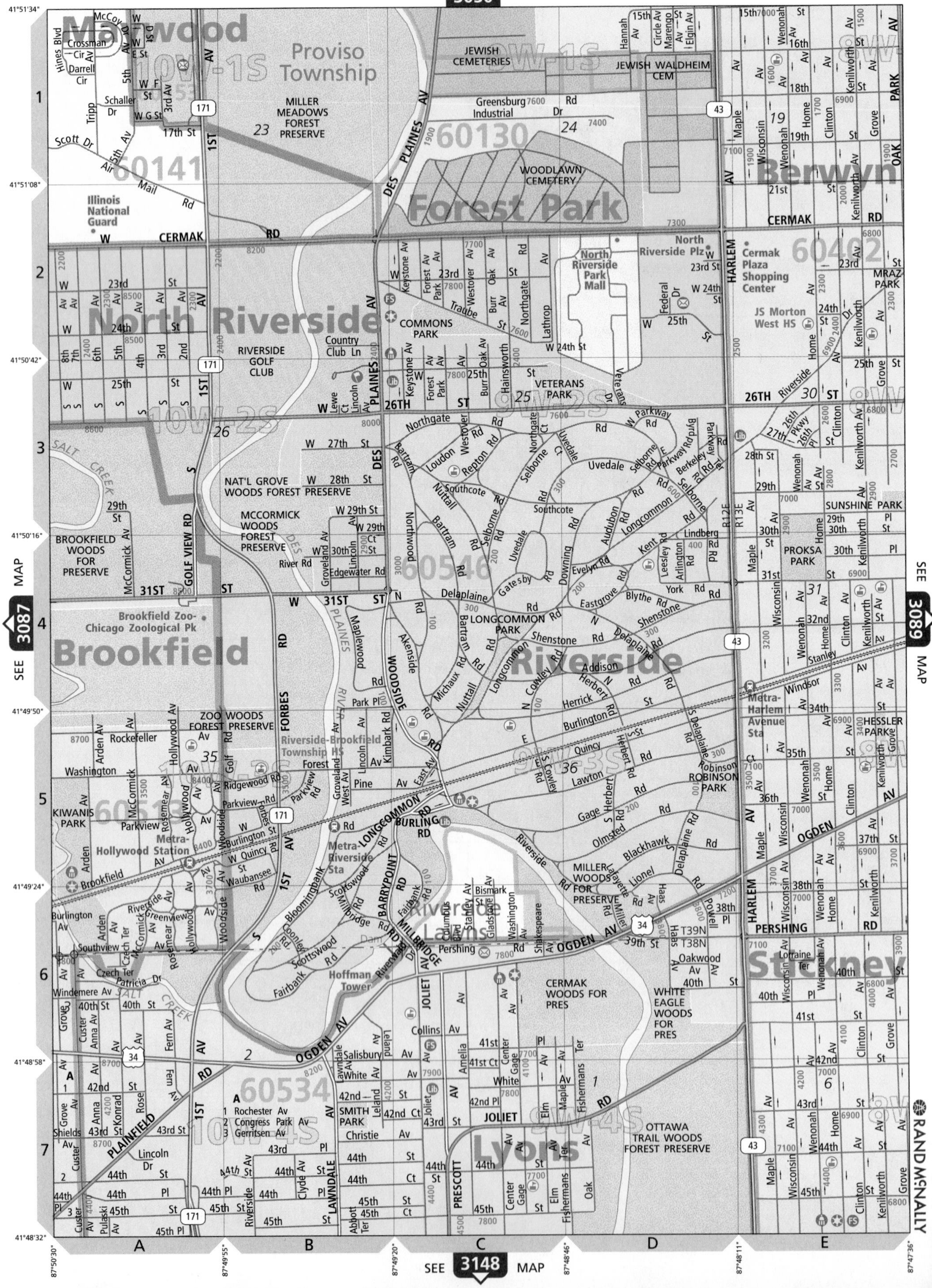

SEE 3089 MAP

Maywood
Proviso Township
MILLER MEADOWS FOREST PRESERVE
JEWISH CEMETERIES
JEWISH WALDHEIM CEM
WOODLAWN CEMETERY
Forest Park
Berwyn
Illinois National Guard
North Riverside
North Riverside Park Mall
Cermak Plaza Shopping Center
JS Morton West HS
MRAZ PARK
COMMONS PARK
RIVERSIDE GOLF CLUB
VETERANS PARK
NAT'L GROVE WOODS FOREST PRESERVE
MCCORMICK WOODS FOREST PRESERVE
BROOKFIELD WOODS FOR PRESERVE
SUNSHINE PARK
PROKSA PARK
Brookfield Zoo-Chicago Zoological Pk
Brookfield
LONGCOMMON PARK
Riverside
ZOO WOODS FOREST PRESERVE
Riverside-Brookfield Township HS
HESSLER PARK
Metra-Harlem Avenue Sta
ROBINSON PARK
KIWANIS PARK
Metra-Hollywood Station
Metra-Riverside Sta
MILLER WOODS FOR PRESERVE
Riverside Lawns
Hoffman Tower
CERMAK WOODS FOR PRES
WHITE EAGLE WOODS FOR PRES
Stickney
SMITH PARK
Lyons
OTTAWA TRAIL WOODS FOREST PRESERVE

SEE 3148 MAP

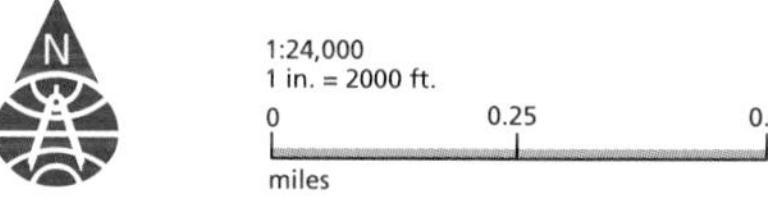

SEE 3031 MAP

Berwyn

Cicero

Stickney

Stickney Township

Forest View

Chicago

60804

60402

60638

NORTH CLYDE PARK

WARREN PARK

PARKHOLME PARK

Cicero Stadium

CTA-Cermak Branch-54-Cermak Station

CTA BLUE LINE-CERMAK BRANCH

JS Morton East HS

WEST MORTON PARK

MORTON PARK

Metra-Cicero Sta

Cicero Yard

CLYDE PARK

HAWTHORNE PARK

JANURA PARK

BERGUIN REC & FIELD PARK

Metra-Lavergne Sta

Metra-Berwyn Station

MacNeal Hospital

COLUMBUS PARK

MANOR PARK

SMIRZ PARK

KOLAR PARK

FREEDOM PARK

Morton College

Chicago Motor Speedway

Hawthorne Race Course

VETERAN'S MEMORIAL PARK

MT AUBURN CEMETERY

LECLAIRE HEARST PARK

CERMAK RD

26TH ST

W OGDEN AV

PERSHING RD

STEVENSON EXPWY

SANITARY & SHIP CANAL

DRAINAGE CANAL

Bank Rd

OAK PARK AV

RIDGELAND AV

AUSTIN BLVD

CENTRAL AV

S LARAMIE AV

49TH AV

T39N

T38N

7W-1S

6W-1S

7W-2S

6W-2S

7W-3S

6W-3S

7W-4S

6W-4S

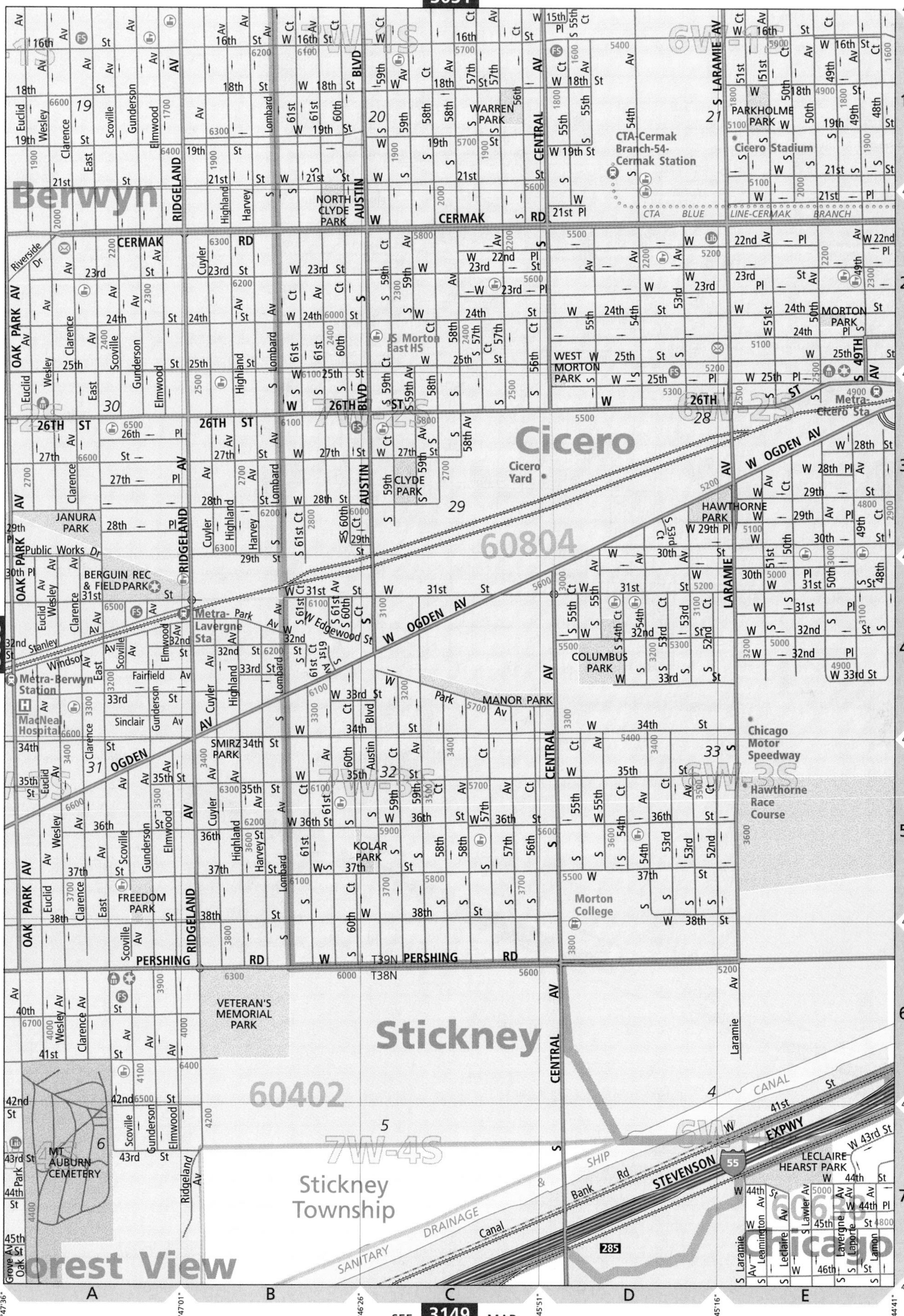

SEE 3088 MAP

SEE 3090 MAP

SEE 3149 MAP

A B C D E

1 2 3 4 5 6 7

41°51'35" 41°51'09" 41°50'43" 41°50'17" 41°49'50" 41°49'24" 41°48'58" 41°48'32"

87°47'36" 87°47'01" 87°46'26" 87°45'51" 87°45'16" 87°44'41"

1:24,000
1 in. = 2000 ft.
0 0.25 0.5
miles

SEE 3032 MAP

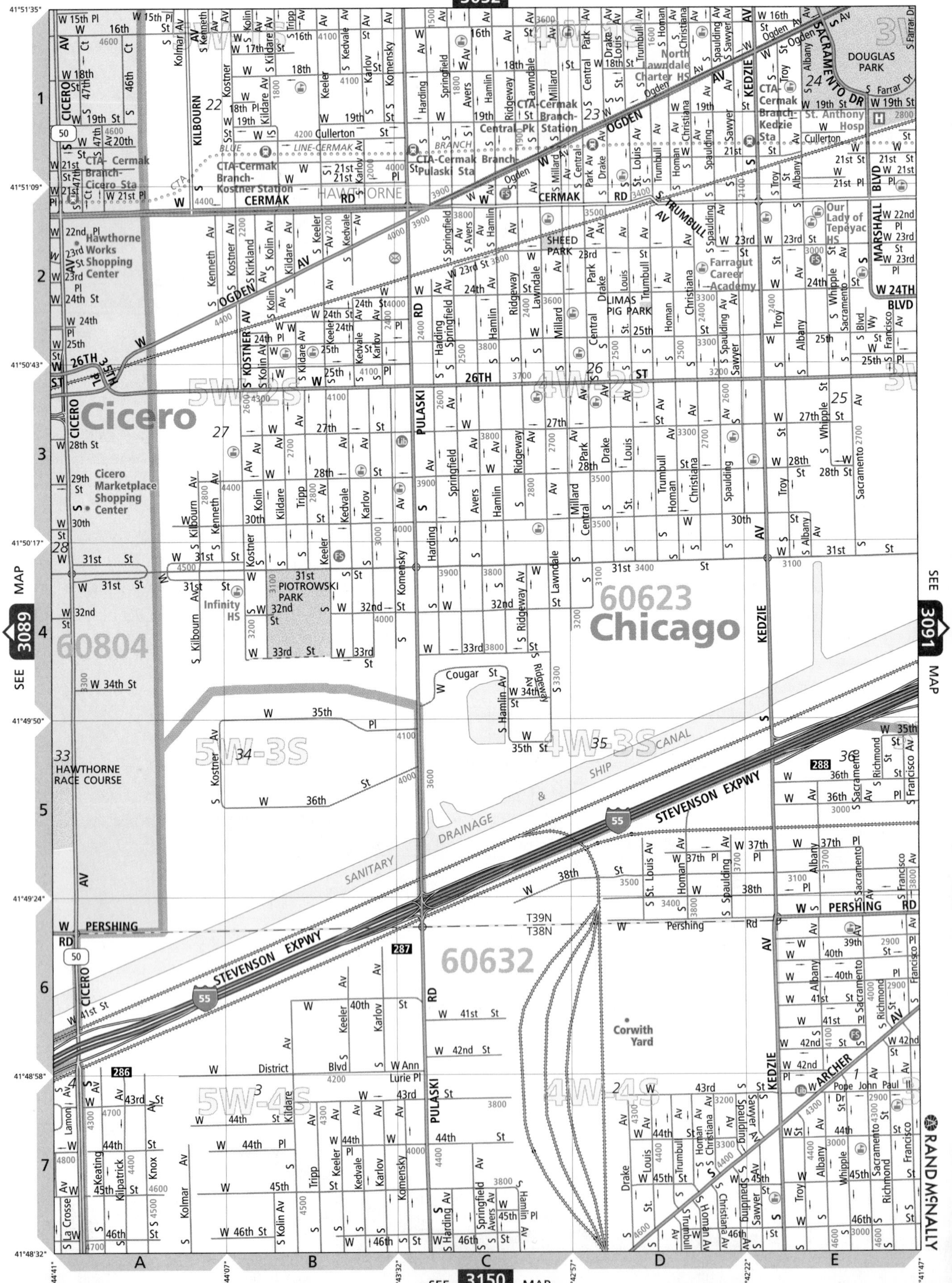

Cicero

Chicago

60804

60623

60632

CICERO AV
KILBOURN AV
KOSTNER AV
PULASKI RD
KEDZIE AV
SACRAMENTO DR
MARSHALL BLVD
OGDEN AV
CERMAK RD
26TH ST
31st St
PERSHING RD
STEVENSON EXPWY
ARCHER AV
W 24TH BLVD
TRUMBULL AV

DOUGLAS PARK
St. Anthony Hosp
CTA-Cermak Branch-Cicero Sta
CTA-Cermak Branch-Kostner Station
CTA-Cermak Branch-Pulaski Sta
CTA-Cermak Branch-Central Pk Station
CTA-Cermak Branch-Kedzie Sta
North Lawndale Charter HS
HAWTHORNE
Hawthorne Works Shopping Center
SHEED PARK
LIMAS PIG PARK
Farragut Career Academy
Our Lady of Tepeyac HS
Cicero Marketplace Shopping Center
PIOTROWSKI PARK
Infinity HS
HAWTHORNE RACE COURSE
SANITARY DRAINAGE & SHIP CANAL
Corwith Yard
T39N
T38N

5W-2S
4W-2S
5W-3S
4W-3S
5W-4S
4W-4S

A B C D E
1 2 3 4 5 6 7

SEE 3089 MAP

SEE 3091 MAP

SEE 3150 MAP

1:24,000
1 in. = 2000 ft.
0 0.25 0.5
miles

SEE 3033 MAP

SEE 3090 MAP
SEE 3092 MAP
SEE 3151 MAP

1:24,000
1 in. = 2000 ft.
0 0.25 0.5
miles

SEE 3034 MAP

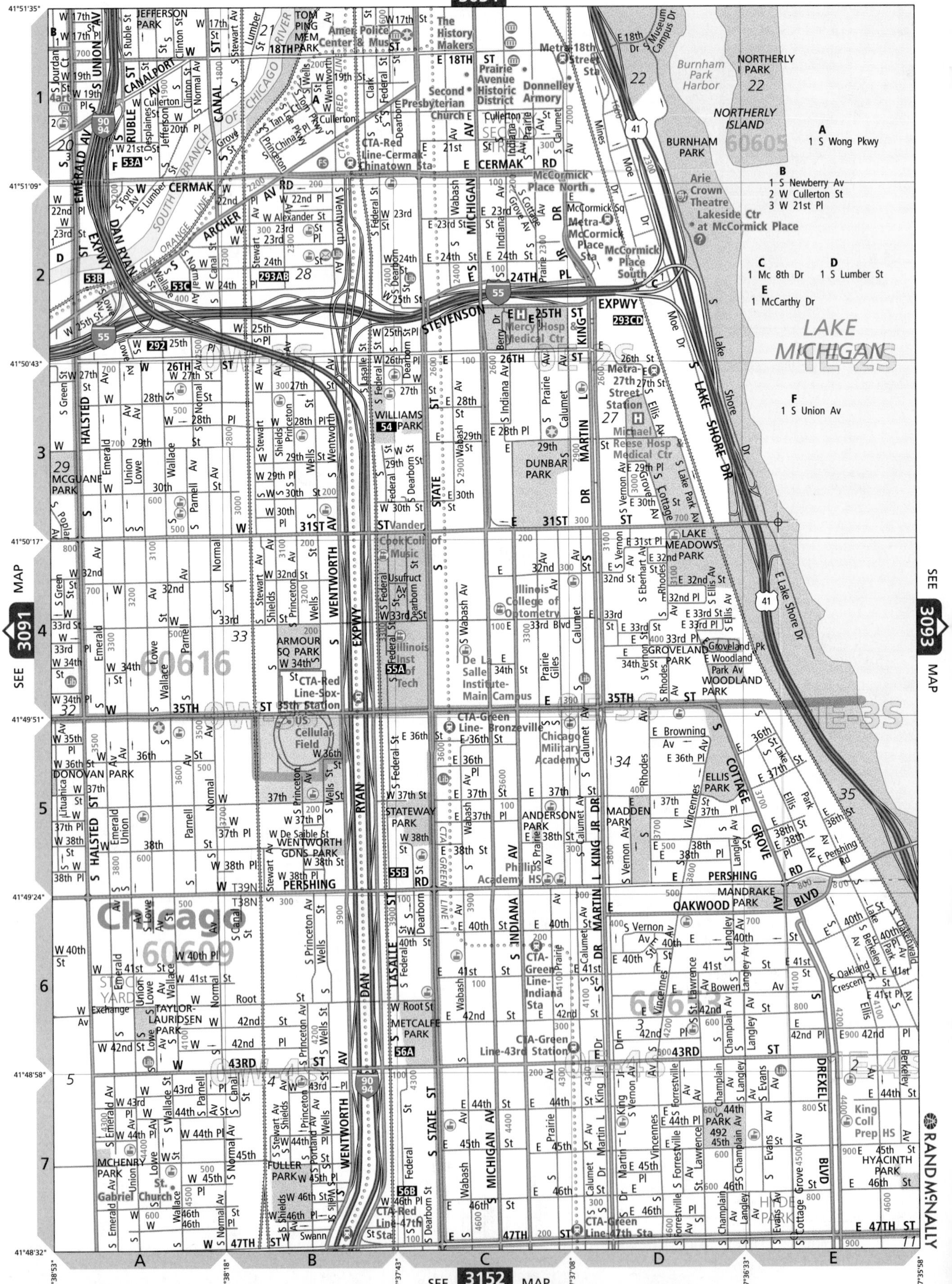

SEE 3091 MAP

SEE 3093 MAP

A
1 S Wong Pkwy

B
1 S Newberry Av
2 W Cullerton St
3 W 21st Pl

C
1 Mc 8th Dr

D
1 S Lumber St

E
1 McCarthy Dr

F
1 S Union Av

LAKE MICHIGAN

Chicago 60609

SEE 3152 MAP

1:24,000
1 in. = 2000 ft.
0 0.25 0.5
miles

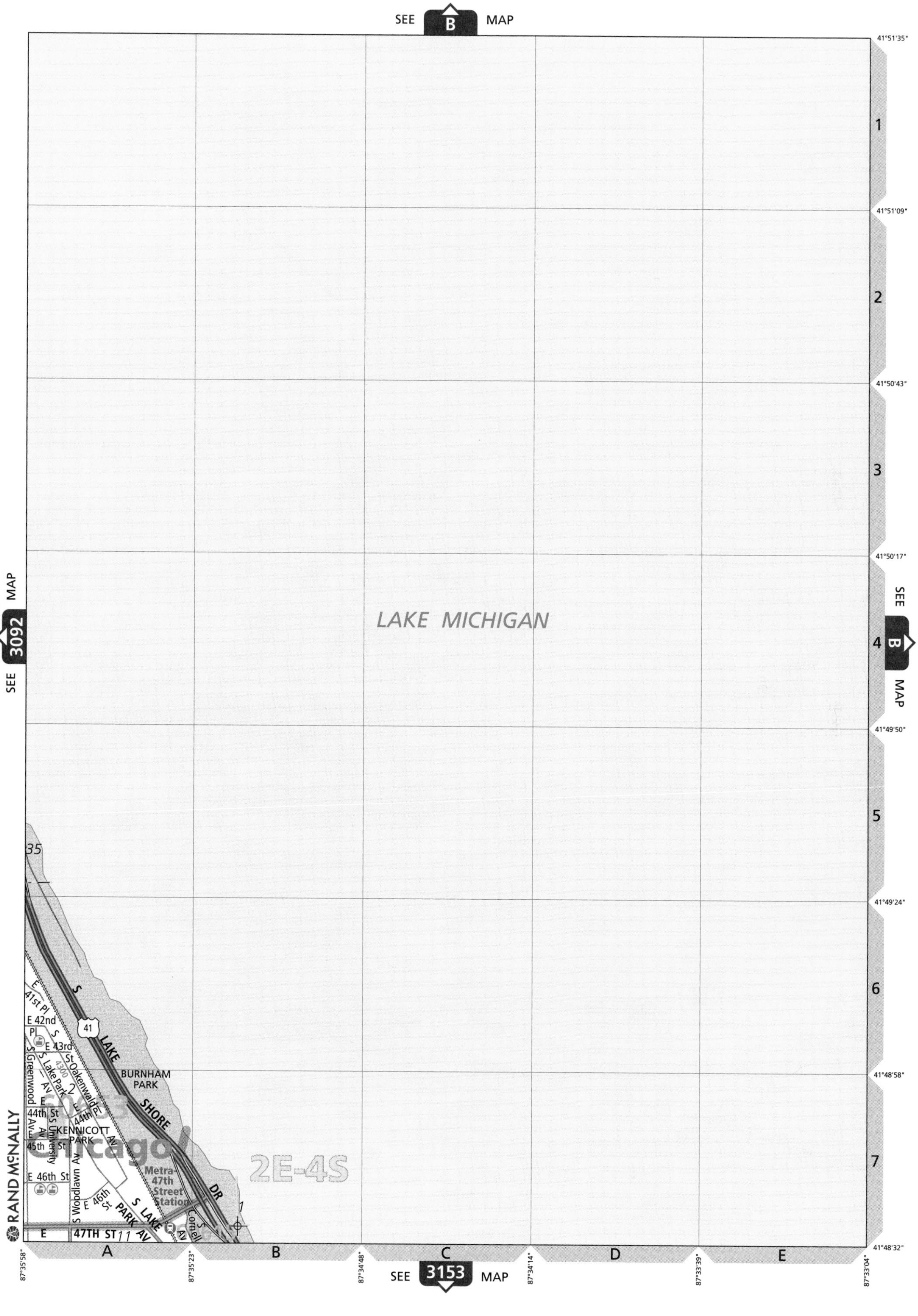

SEE B MAP

SEE 3092 MAP

SEE B MAP

SEE 3153 MAP

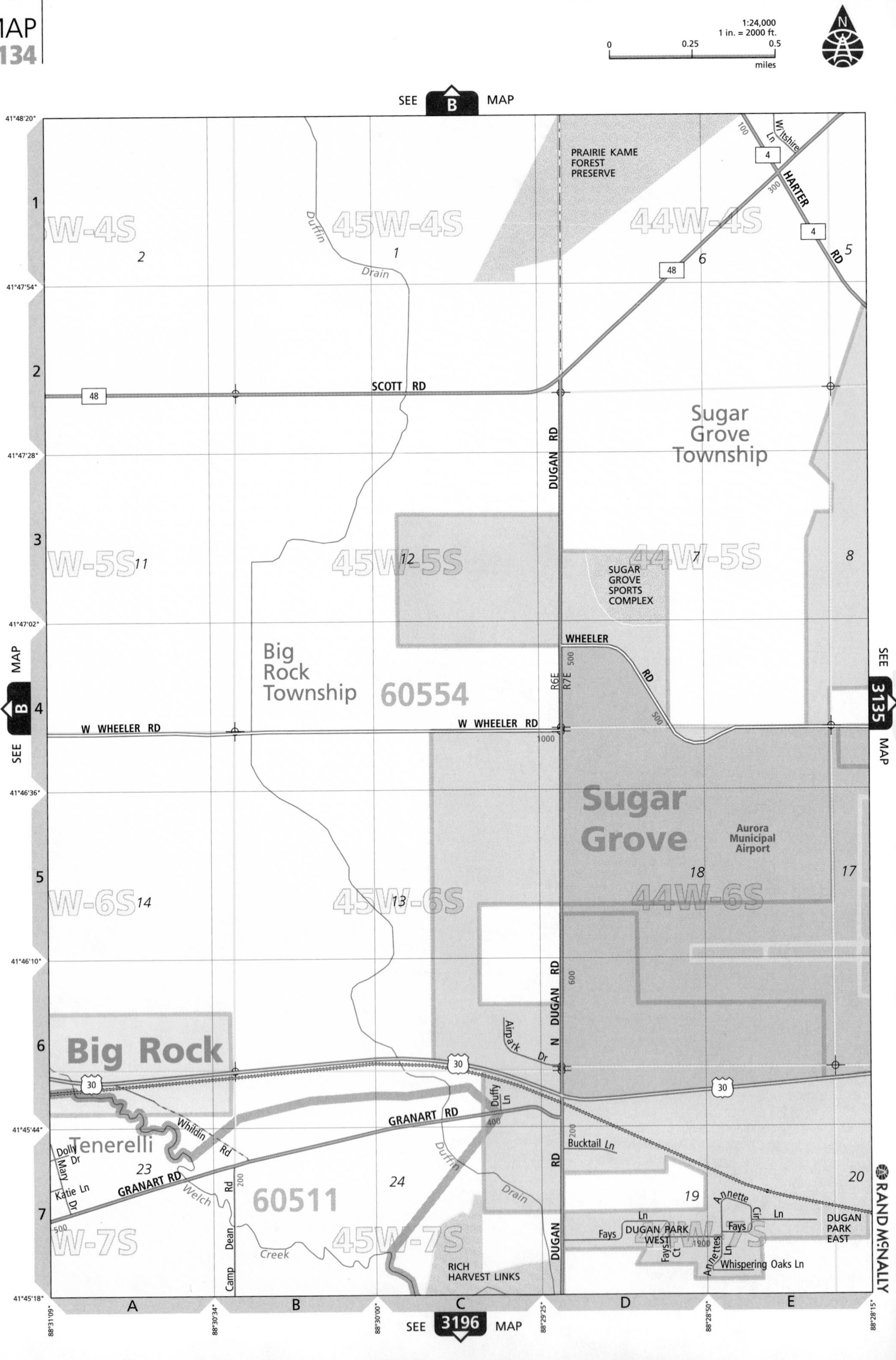

1:24,000
1 in. = 2000 ft.
0 0.25 0.5
miles

SEE B MAP

PRAIRIE KAME FOREST PRESERVE

45W-4S
44W-4S
Duffin Drain
SCOTT RD
DUGAN RD
HARTER RD
Wiltshire Ln
Sugar Grove Township
45W-5S
44W-5S
SUGAR GROVE SPORTS COMPLEX
WHEELER RD
Big Rock Township
60554
R6E R7E
W WHEELER RD
Sugar Grove
Aurora Municipal Airport
45W-6S
44W-6S
N DUGAN RD
Airpark Dr
Big Rock
Tenerelli
Whildin Rd
GRANART RD
Duffy Ln
Bucktail Ln
Dolly Dr
Mary Dr
Katie Ln
Welch Creek
Camp Dean Rd
60511
45W-7S
Duffin Drain
RICH HARVEST LINKS
Annette Cir
Fays Ln
Fays Ct
Annettes Ln
DUGAN PARK WEST
DUGAN PARK EAST
Whispering Oaks Ln
44W-7S

SEE 3135 MAP

SEE 3196 MAP

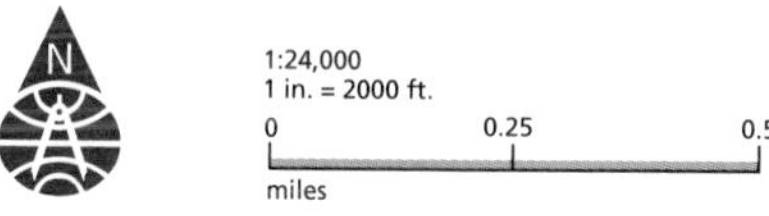

SEE 3075 MAP

Sugar Grove Township

Sugar Grove

60554

60506

43W-4S
42W-4S
43W-5S
42W-5S
43W-6S
42W-6S
43W-7S
42W-7S
41W-7

47
88
RONALD REAGAN MEMORIAL TOLLWAY
BLISS RD
Old Oaks Rd
Merrill Rd
Blackberry Creek
Wheatfield Av
Denny Rd
Denny St
Redbud Ln
Hunters Ridge Ln
Pine St
Cherry St
Oak
Hickory St
Chestnut Hill Ln
Chestnut Hill Ct
Hannaford Dr
Birch St
Willow St
Elm
Spruce
Windstone Ct
Windstone Dr
Stonehill Ln
SUGAR GROVE CEM
Waubonsee Community College-Sugar Grove
HANNAFORD WOODS FOREST PRESERVE
HARTER RD
4
Old Harter Rd
Stamford Pl
Abbey Ct
Pembridge Pl
New Bond
Cornwall Cir
Tudor Ct
Edgewood Dr
Queens Gate
Carlisle Ct
Evergreen Wild Ginger Rd
Courtney Cir
Haverhill Ct
Fairlee Ct
Windsor
Merrill
Woodbury Ct
Kingsman Ct
Brighton Dr
Greenfield Rd
Greenfield Manor
Black Walnut Ct
Hill Pl
Sheffield Cir
Douglas Dr
Shelburne Ln
Hanover Ln
Laura Ln
Merrill New Rd
Penny Ln
Green Heron Ln
Green Hills Ct
Glengarry Dr
Normandie Dr
Hillcrest
Saddlewood
Hardwick Ct
NORMANDIE PARK
Heaton Ct
Windwood Dr
Windwood Ct
Winthrop
New Rd
Briargate Dr
Briargate Cir
HANKES RD
Blackberry Ct
Fairfax Cir
Braeburn Cir
Quarry Cir
Cedar Gate Cir
BLISS CREEK GOLF CLUB
KEDEKA RD
78
BLISS WOODS FOREST PRESERVE
Virgil Gilman Nature Tr
WAUBONSEE DR
HEARTLAND DR
Cardinal Dr
WHEELER RD
Carriage Hill Ct
Westbourne Dr
Westbourne Av
Caledonian Av
Vale Dr
Hampsted Av
Sutton Av
Sutton Ct
WINDSOR WEST PARK
Oxford Av
Chesney
W Park Av
N Division Dr
Division Dr
Capitol Dr
Whitfield Dr
Belle
PARK
Vue Ln
Chatsworth Av
St. James Pkwy
Exeter Ln
Somerset Dr
Brompton Dr
Carlton Mews
Hampton Ct
Berkshire Ln
Berkshire Ct
Regency Blvd
E Park Av
E GALENA BLVD
Aurora Municipal Airport
Air Classics Museum
Veterans Memorial Pkwy
Terminal
30
56
Meadows Dr
Meadows Ct
Terry Dr
Monna St
Indigo Dr
Ridgeview Ln
Snow St
Municipal Dr
Bastian Dr
Yolane Ln
Yolane Ct
VOLUNTEER PARK
Sugar Ln
Richard St
Frontage Rd
Cross St
STRUBLER PARK
Neil Rd
Joy St
Joy Ct
Stanley
Patricia Ln
Calkins Dr
McCannon St
Main St
Arbor Av
Chelsea Av
Maple
West St
Grove St
WR KECK PARK
Railroad St
W 1st St
Bedford Av
Dover Ct
Bristol Ct
SHEFFIELD PLAINS PARK
CHELSEA PARK
Prairie St
1
2
3
4
5
6
7
8
9
10
15
16
17
20
21
22

A
B
C
D
E
1
2
3
4
5
6
7

41°48'23"
41°47'57"
41°47'31"
41°47'04"
41°46'38"
41°46'12"
41°45'46"
41°45'20"
88°28'15"
88°27'40"
88°27'05"
88°26'31"
88°25'56"
88°25'21"

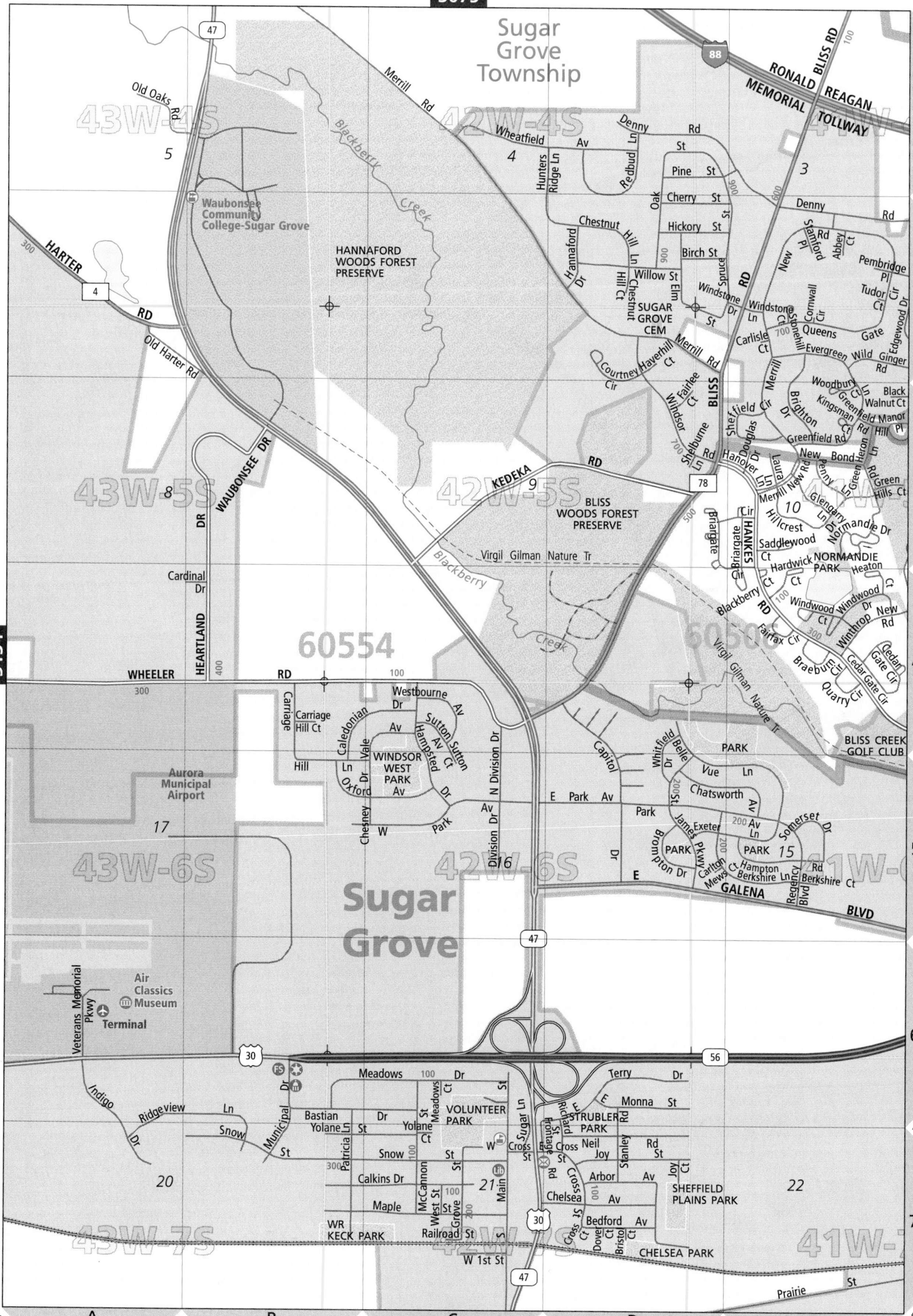

SEE 3134 MAP

SEE 3136 MAP

SEE 3197 MAP

1:24,000
1 in. = 2000 ft.
0 0.25 0.5
miles

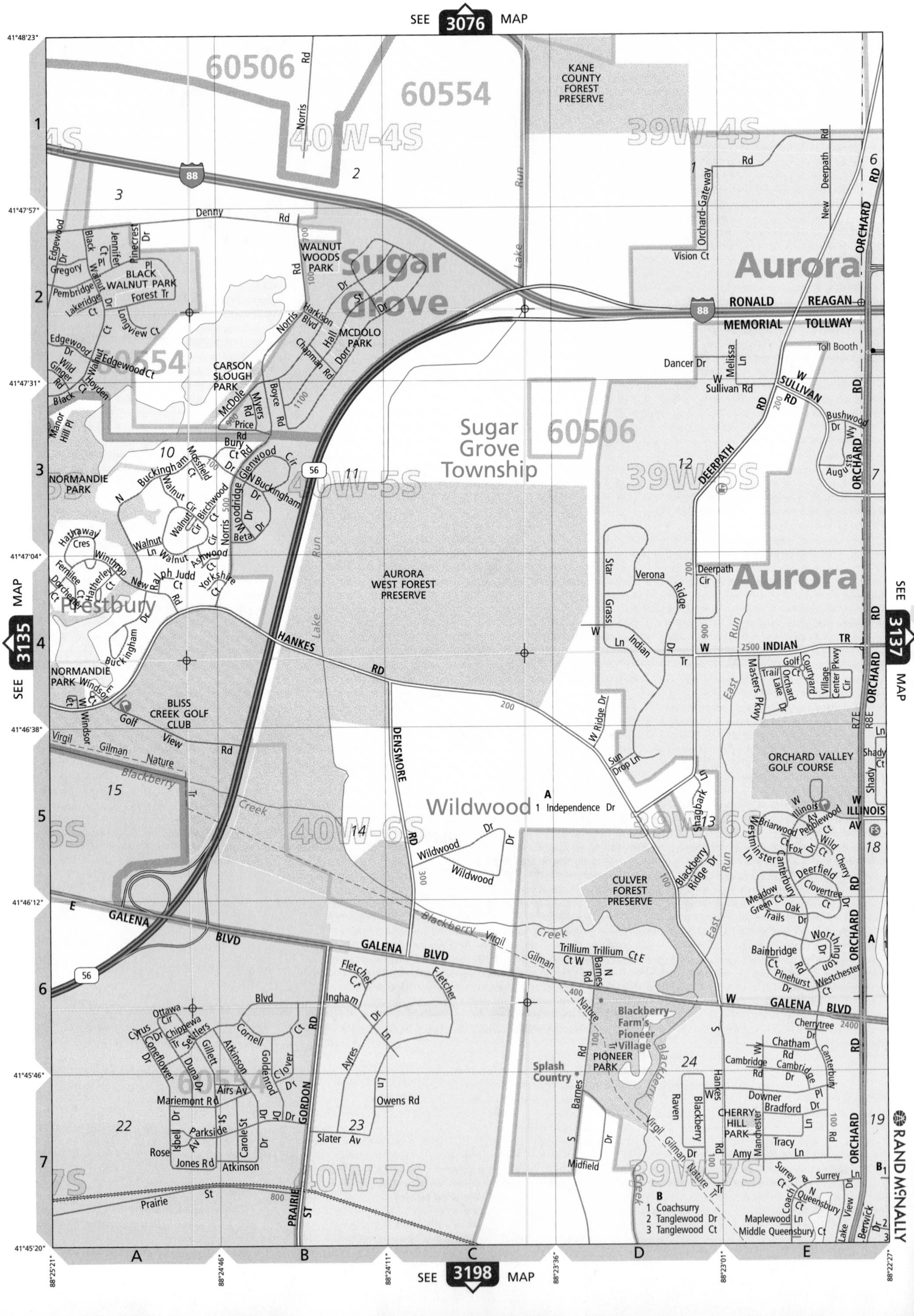

SEE 3076 MAP

SEE 3135 MAP

SEE 3137 MAP

SEE 3198 MAP

1:24,000
1 in. = 2000 ft.
0 0.25 0.5
miles

SEE 3077 MAP

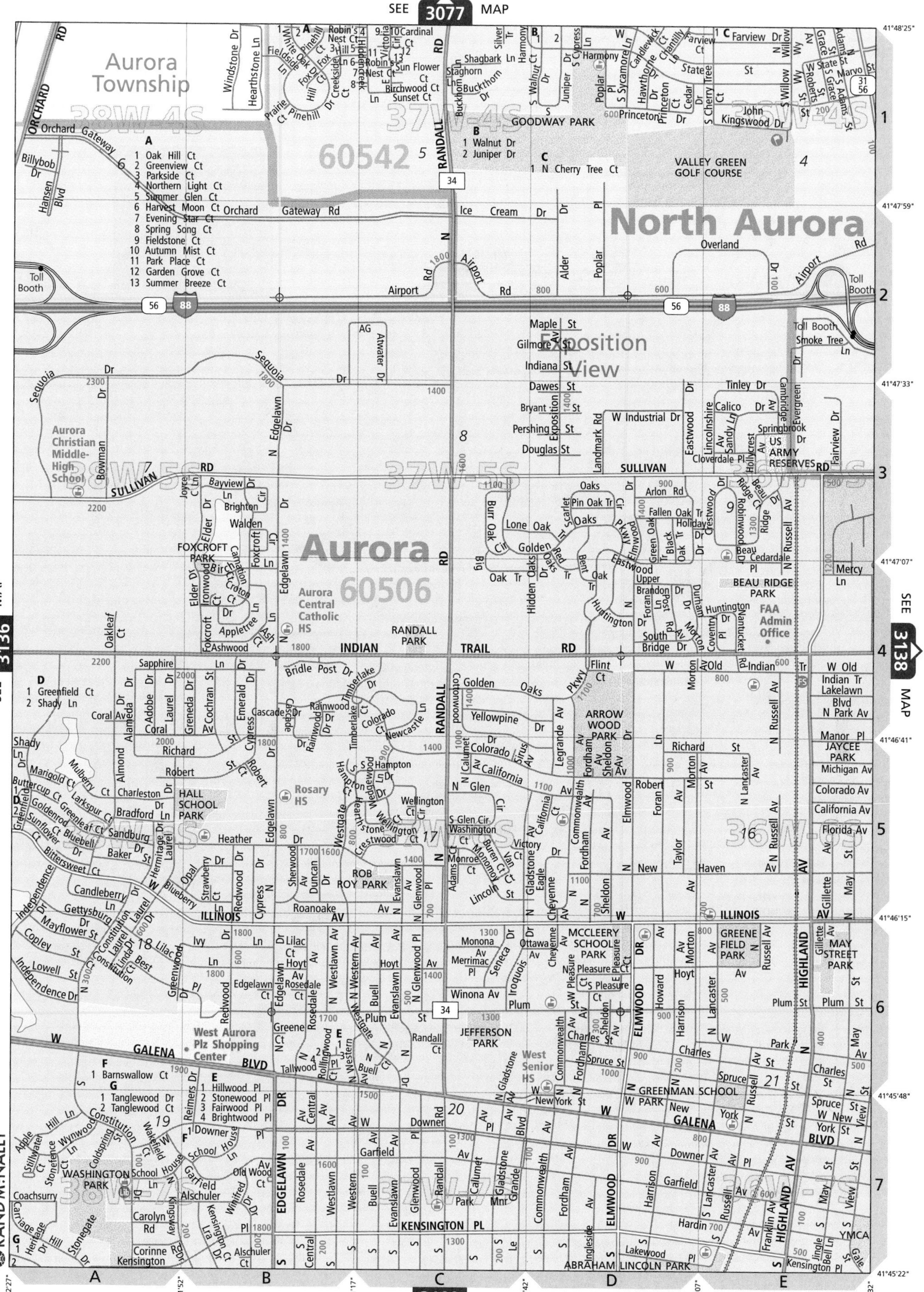

41°48'25" 41°47'59" 41°47'33" 41°47'07" 41°46'41" 41°46'15" 41°45'48" 41°45'22"
88°22'27" 88°21'52" 88°21'17" 88°20'42" 88°20'07" 88°19'32"

SEE 3136 MAP
SEE 3138 MAP
SEE 3199 MAP

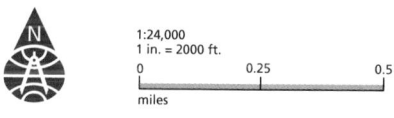

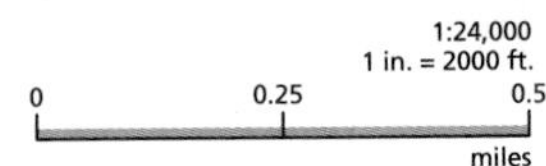

SEE 3078 MAP

North Aurora
60542
35W-4S
34W-4S
60502
Aurora
60504
60506
60505
35W-5S
35W-6S
35W-7S
34W-5S
34W-6S
34W-7S
Aurora Township
Chicago Premium Outlets
Chesterfield Park
Church Road Park
St. Joseph Cemetery
Provena Mercy Center
Indian Trail I Park
Aurora Commons Shopping Center
Convention Center
Calvary Cem
St. Michael Cemetery
Northgate Shopping Center
Illinois Avenue Park
Garfield Park
Simmons School Park
Pigeon Hill Park
McCullough Park
West Aurora Cem
Vet Mem Park
Solfisburg Park
North River Street Park
Aurora Hist-Museum
Tanner Hse
Wilder Park
Walter Payton Museum
Aurora Armory
Metra-Aurora Station
Waubonsee Comm College-Aurora
Hollywood Casino-Aurora
Lincoln Mini Park
East Aurora Cem
Edna M Rollins Park
St. Nicholas Cem
Ronald Reagan Memorial Tollway
Indian Trail Rd
Fox River
Indian Creek
Lincolnway
Sullivan Rd
Mitchell Rd
Church Rd
Farnsworth Av
Broadway
Lake St
River St
Illinois Av
Galena Blvd
New York St
Molitor Rd
Bilter Rd
Corporate Blvd
Sheffer Rd
Forest Av
Aurora Av

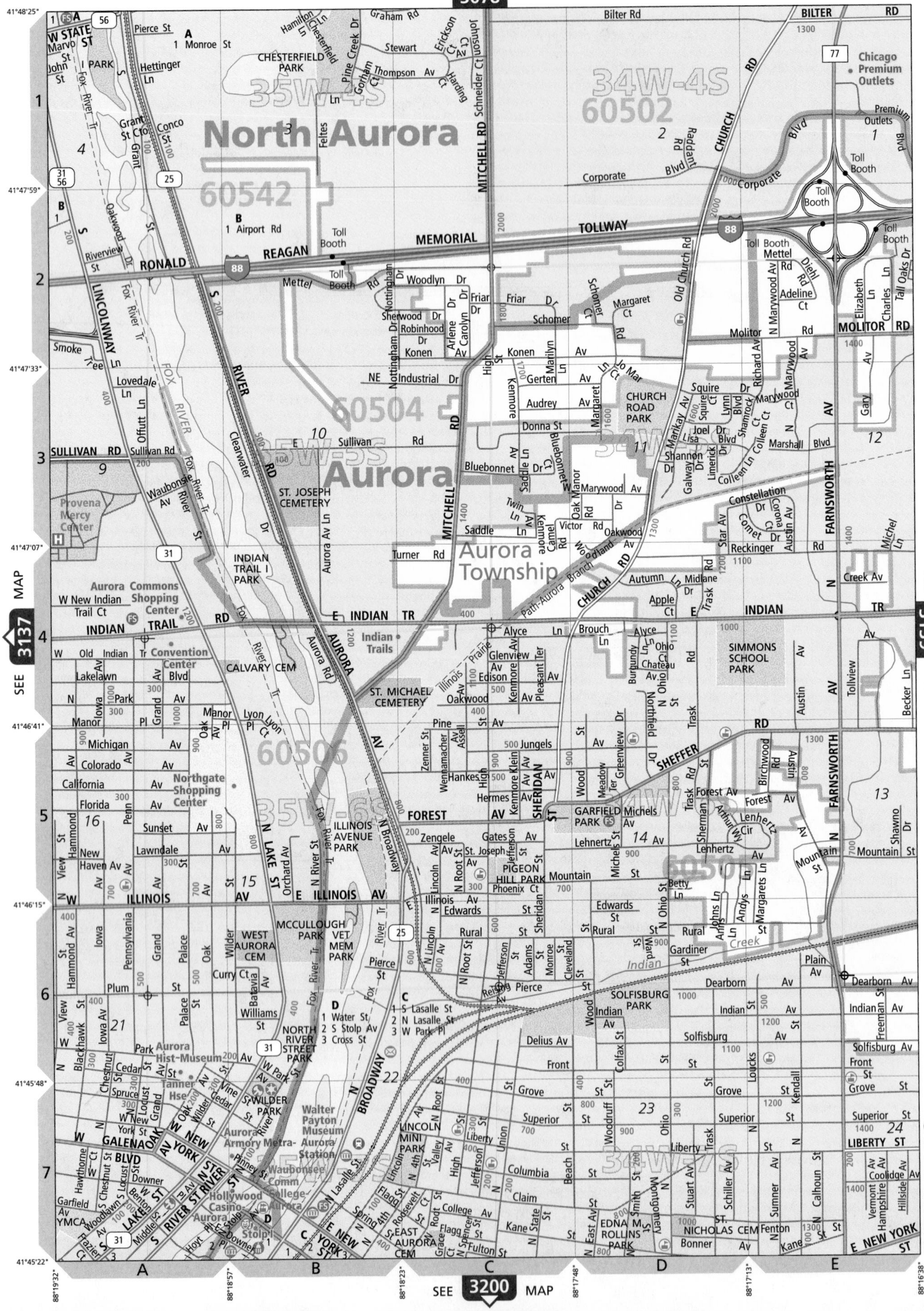

SEE 3137 MAP
SEE 3139 MAP
SEE 3200 MAP

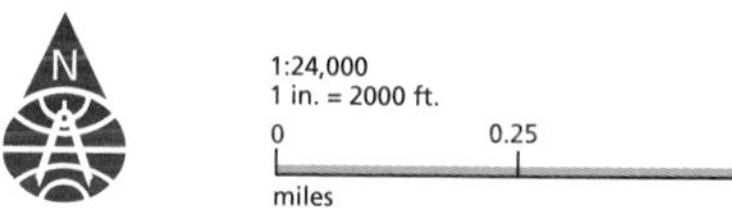

SEE 3079 MAP

SEE 3138 MAP

SEE 3140 MAP

Aurora Township

BIG WOODS FOREST PRESERVE

RONALD REAGAN MEMORIAL TOLLWAY

Country Lake

Naperville Township

Naperville

STONEBRIDGE COUNTRY CLUB

BIRMINGHAM PARK

O'DONNELL PARK

INDIAN CREEK PARK

ASBURY PARK

Eola

Aurora

60504

60563

60505

60502

A
1 DuPage Pkwy
2 Country Oaks Ct
3 Wingate Ct
4 Devonshire Ct

B
1 Cane Garden Cir
2 Sandpebble Ln
3 Kimberly Ct
4 Jasmine Ct
5 Half Moon Cir
6 Persimmon Ct
7 Shadybrook Ln
8 St. Anne's Ct

C
1 Hidden Pond Cir

E
1 Edgewood Av
2 Woodland Av

SEE 3201 MAP

1:24,000
1 in. = 2000 ft.
0 0.25 0.5
miles

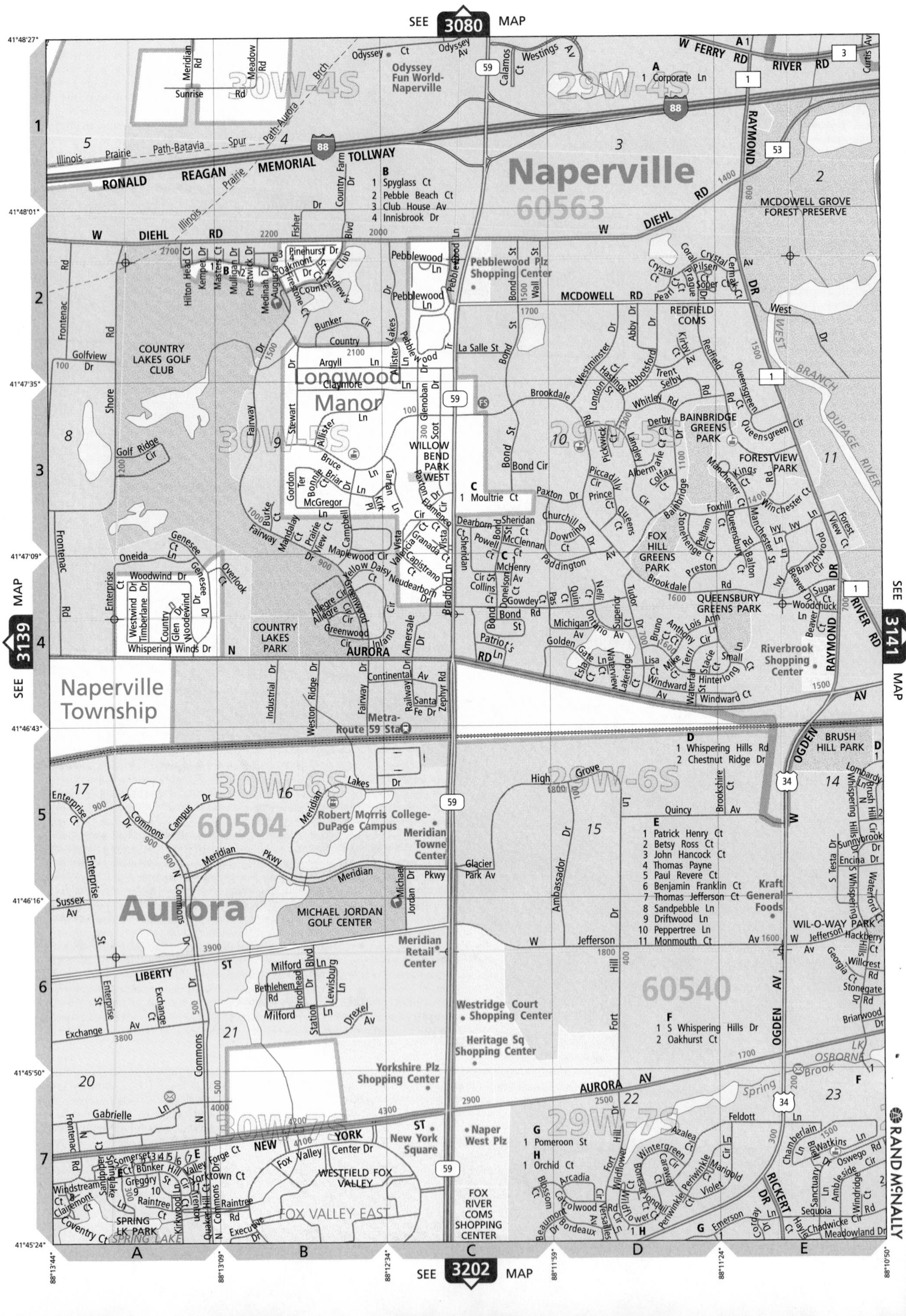

SEE 3080 MAP

SEE 3139 MAP

SEE 3141 MAP

Naperville
60563

Naperville Township

Aurora
60504
60540

Odyssey Fun World-Naperville

RONALD REAGAN MEMORIAL TOLLWAY

COUNTRY LAKES GOLF CLUB

Longwood Manor

WILLOW BEND PARK WEST

COUNTRY LAKES PARK

MCDOWELL GROVE FOREST PRESERVE

REDFIELD COMS

BAINBRIDGE GREENS PARK

FORESTVIEW PARK

FOX HILL GREENS PARK

QUEENSBURY GREENS PARK

Riverbrook Shopping Center

Pebblewood Plz Shopping Center

Metra-Route 59 Sta

Robert Morris College-DuPage Campus

Meridian Towne Center

MICHAEL JORDAN GOLF CENTER

Meridian Retail Center

Westridge Court Shopping Center

Heritage Sq Shopping Center

Yorkshire Plz Shopping Center

Naper West Plz

New York Square

WESTFIELD FOX VALLEY

FOX VALLEY EAST

FOX RIVER COMS SHOPPING CENTER

SPRING LK PARK

BRUSH HILL PARK

WIL-O-WAY PARK

Kraft General Foods

A
1 Corporate Ln

B
1 Spyglass Ct
2 Pebble Beach Ct
3 Club House Av
4 Innisbrook Dr

C
1 Moultrie Ct

D
1 Whispering Hills Rd
2 Chestnut Ridge Dr

E
1 Patrick Henry Ct
2 Betsy Ross Ct
3 John Hancock Ct
4 Thomas Payne
5 Paul Revere Ct
6 Benjamin Franklin Ct
7 Thomas Jefferson Ct
8 Sandpebble Ln
9 Driftwood Ln
10 Peppertree Ln
11 Monmouth Ct

F
1 S Whispering Hills Dr
2 Oakhurst Ct

G
1 Pomeroon St

H
1 Orchid Ct

SEE 3202 MAP

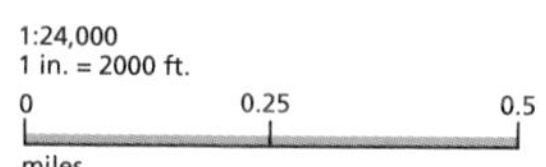

SEE 3081 MAP

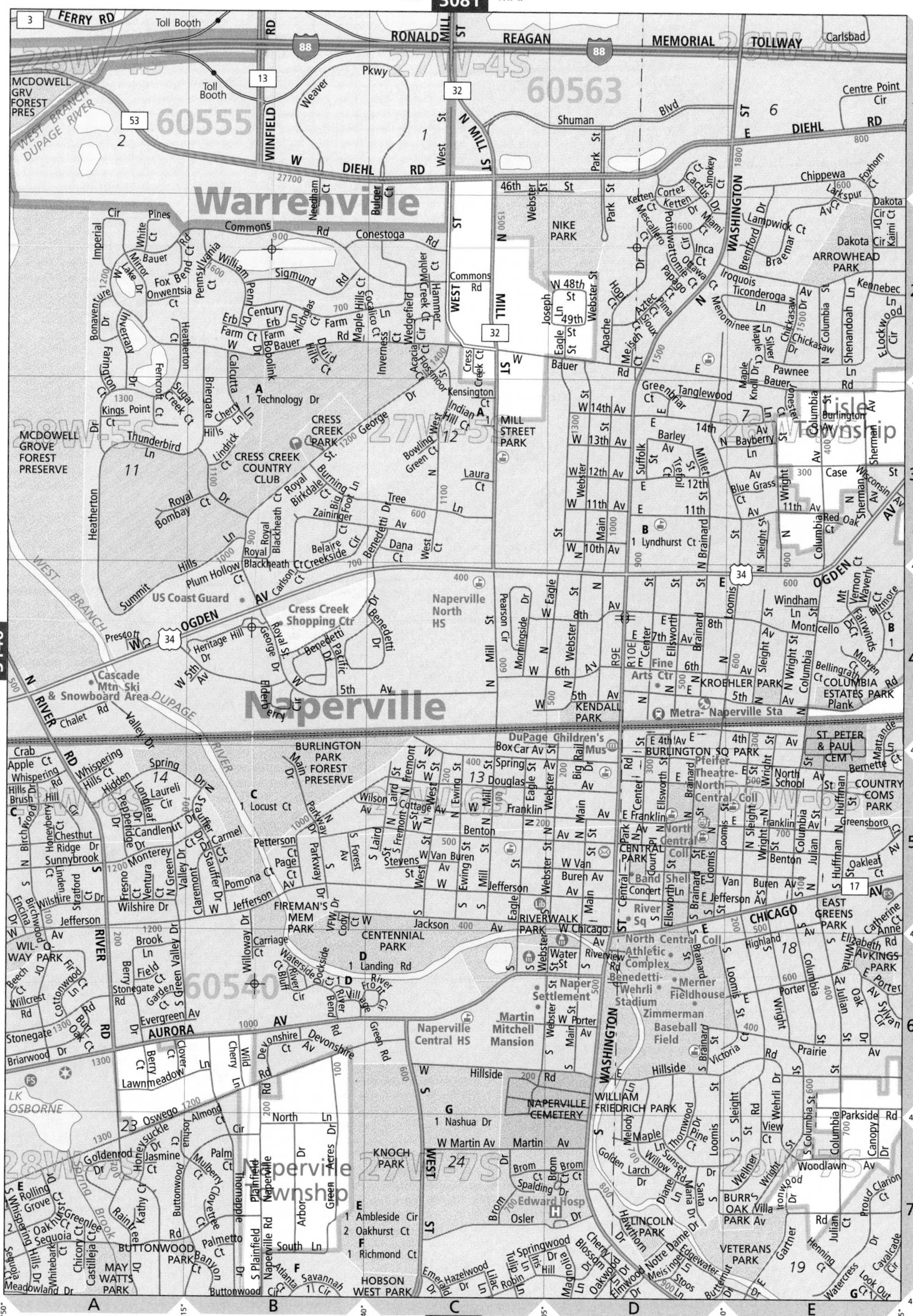

SEE 3140 MAP

SEE 3142 MAP

Warrenville

Naperville

60555

60563

60540

Lisle Township

Naperville Township

MCDOWELL GRV FOREST PRES

MCDOWELL GROVE FOREST PRESERVE

CRESS CREEK COUNTRY CLUB

CRESS CREEK PARK

NIKE PARK

ARROWHEAD PARK

MILL STREET PARK

Naperville North HS

Cress Creek Shopping Ctr

US Coast Guard

Cascade Mtn Ski & Snowboard Area

KENDALL PARK

Metra- Naperville Sta

BURLINGTON PARK FOREST PRESERVE

DuPage Children's Mus

BURLINGTON SQ PARK

ST PETER & PAUL CEM

COUNTRY COMS PARK

North Central Coll

Pfeifer Theatre- North Central Coll

FIREMAN'S MEM PARK

CENTENNIAL PARK

RIVERWALK PARK

CENTRAL PARK

Band Shell Concert

River Sq

Fine Arts Ctr

KROEHLER PARK

COLUMBIA ESTATES PARK

EAST GREENS PARK

KINGS PARK

WIL-O-WAY PARK

Naper Settlement

Martin Mitchell Mansion

Naperville Central HS

Benedetti-Wehrli Stadium

Merner Fieldhouse

Zimmerman Baseball Field

North Central Coll Athletic Complex

WILLIAM FRIEDRICH PARK

NAPERVILLE CEMETERY

Edward Hosp

KNOCH PARK

LINCOLN PARK

BURR OAK PARK

VETERANS PARK

BUTTONWOOD PARK

MAY WATTS PARK

HOBSON WEST PARK

LK OSBORNE

WEST BRANCH DUPAGE RIVER

RONALD REAGAN MEMORIAL TOLLWAY

FERRY RD

W DIEHL RD

E DIEHL RD

OGDEN AV

AURORA AV

CHICAGO AV

N RIVER RD

WASHINGTON ST

WEST ST

MILL ST

WINFIELD RD

A
B
C
D
E

1
2
3
4
5
6
7

41°48'29"
41°48'02"
41°47'36"
41°47'10"
41°46'44"
41°46'18"
41°45'52"
41°45'26"

88°10'50"
88°10'15"
88°09'40"
88°09'05"
88°08'30"
88°07'55"

RAND McNALLY

SEE 3203 MAP

1:24,000
1 in. = 2000 ft.
0 0.25 0.5
miles

SEE 3082 MAP

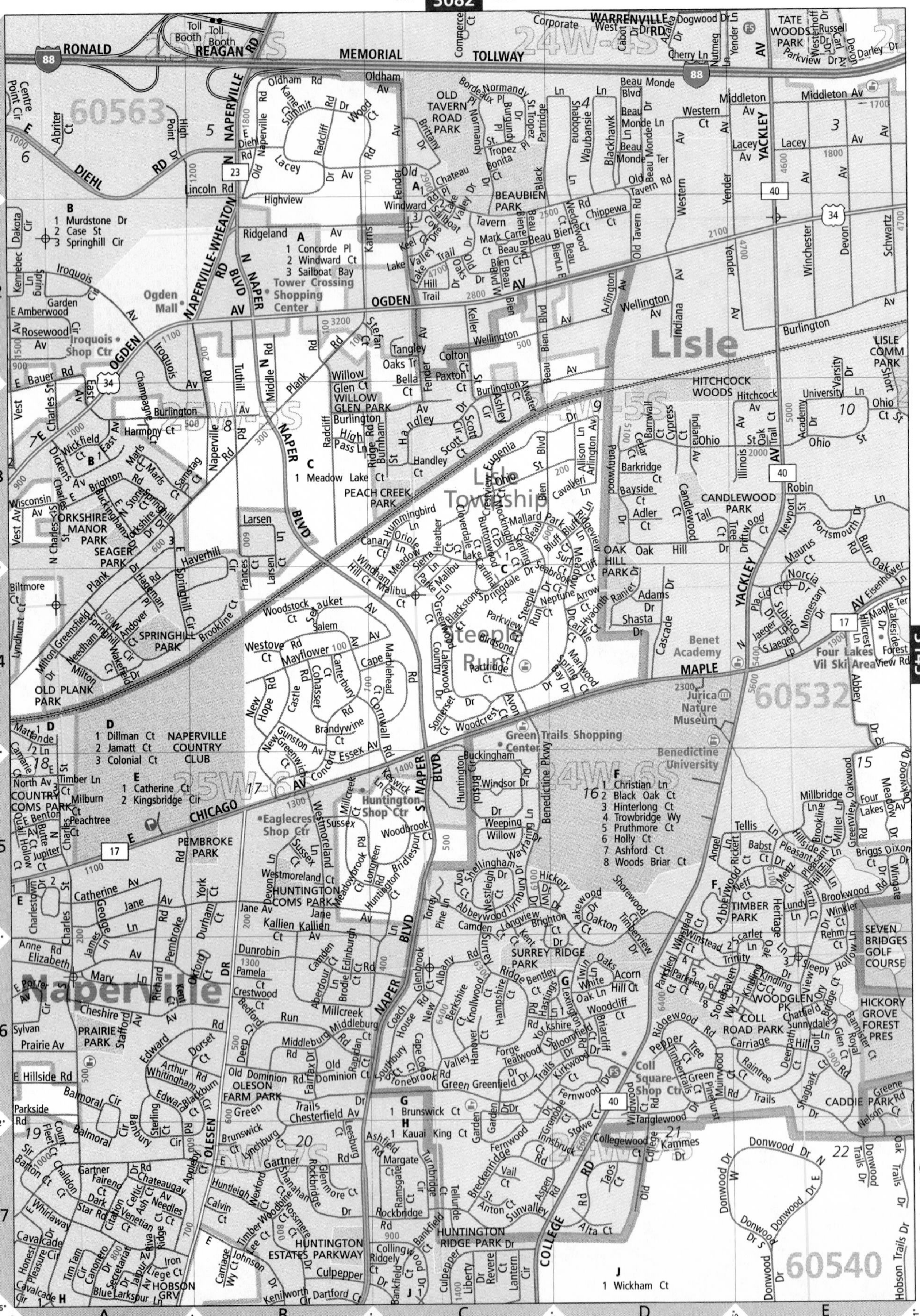

SEE 3141 MAP

SEE 3143 MAP

SEE 3204 MAP

RONALD REAGAN MEMORIAL TOLLWAY

WARRENVILLE RD

Lisle

Naperville

Lisle Township

Steeple Run

A
1 Concorde Pl
2 Windward Ct
3 Sailboat Bay

B
1 Murdstone Dr
2 Case St
3 Springhill Cir

C
1 Meadow Lake Ct

D
1 Dillman Ct
2 Jamatt Ct
3 Colonial Ct

E
1 Catherine Ct
2 Kingsbridge Cir

F
1 Christian Ln
2 Black Oak Ct
3 Hinterlong Ct
4 Trowbridge Wy
5 Pruthmore Ct
6 Holly Ct
7 Ashford Ct
8 Woods Briar Ct

G
1 Brunswick Ct

H
1 Kauai King Ct

J
1 Wickham Ct

OLD TAVERN ROAD PARK
BEAUBIEN PARK
Tower Crossing Shopping Center
Ogden Mall
Iroquois Shop Ctr
WILLOW GLEN PARK
PEACH CREEK PARK
YORKSHIRE MANOR PARK
SEAGER PARK
SPRINGHILL PARK
OLD PLANK PARK
NAPERVILLE COUNTRY CLUB
COUNTRY COMS PARK
Eaglecrest Shop Ctr
Huntington Shop Ctr
PEMBROKE PARK
HUNTINGTON COMS PARK
Green Trails Shopping Center
HITCHCOCK WOODS
CANDLEWOOD PARK
OAK HILL PARK
Benet Academy
Four Lakes Vil Ski Area
Jurica Nature Museum
Benedictine University
LISLE COMM PARK
TATE WOODS PARK
TIMBER PARK
SEVEN BRIDGES GOLF COURSE
WOODGLEN PK
HICKORY GROVE FOREST PRES
COLL ROAD PARK
SURREY RIDGE PARK
PRAIRIE PARK
OLESON FARM PARK
Coll Square Shop Ctr
CADDIE PARK
HUNTINGTON ESTATES PARKWAY
HUNTINGTON RIDGE PARK
HOBSON GRV

60563
60532
60540

24W-4S
24W-5S
25W-5S
24W-6S
25W-6S
25W-7S
24W-7S

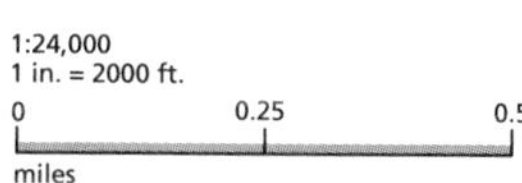

SEE 3083 MAP

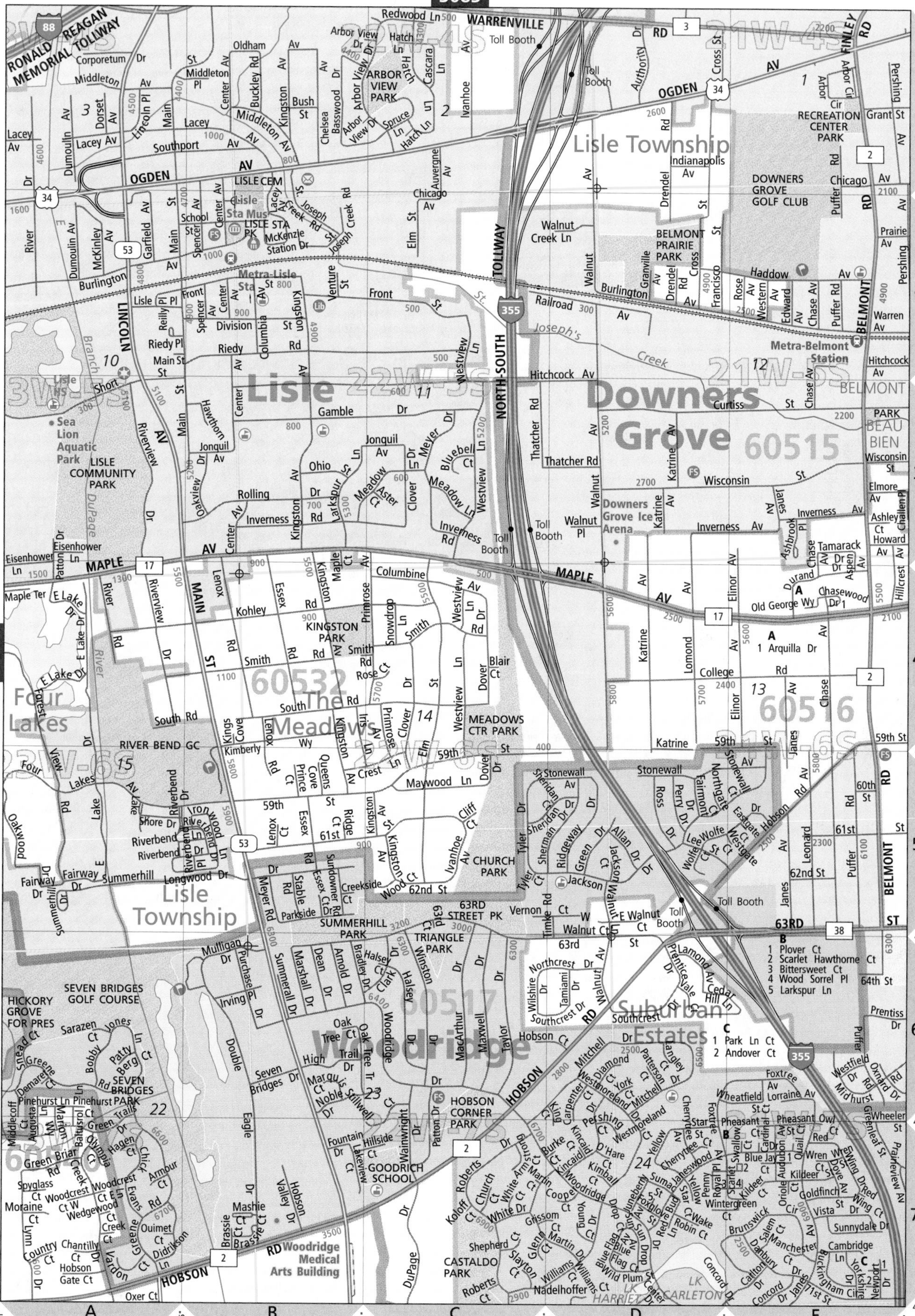

SEE 3142 MAP

SEE 3144 MAP

Lisle

Downers Grove 60515

Lisle Township

60532

The Meadows

60516

60517

Woodridge

Suburban Estates

Four Lakes

A
1 Arquilla Dr

B
1 Plover Ct
2 Scarlet Hawthorne Ct
3 Bittersweet Ct
4 Wood Sorrel Pl
5 Larkspur Ln

C
1 Park Ln Ct
2 Andover Ct

SEE 3205 MAP

1:24,000
1 in. = 2000 ft.
0 0.25 0.5
miles

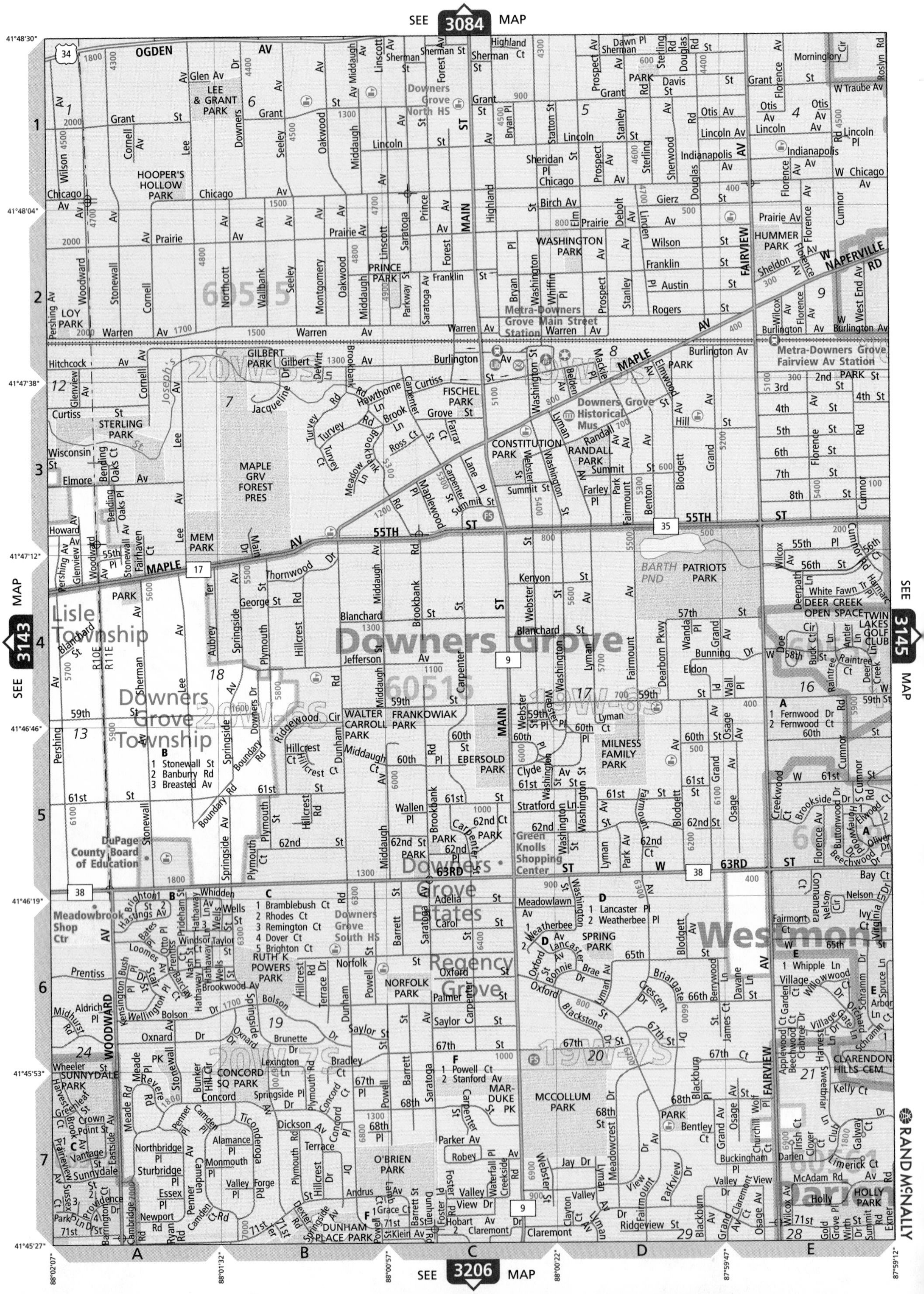

SEE 3084 MAP

SEE 3143 MAP

SEE 3145 MAP

SEE 3206 MAP

1:24,000
1 in. = 2000 ft.
0 0.25 0.5
miles

SEE 3085 MAP

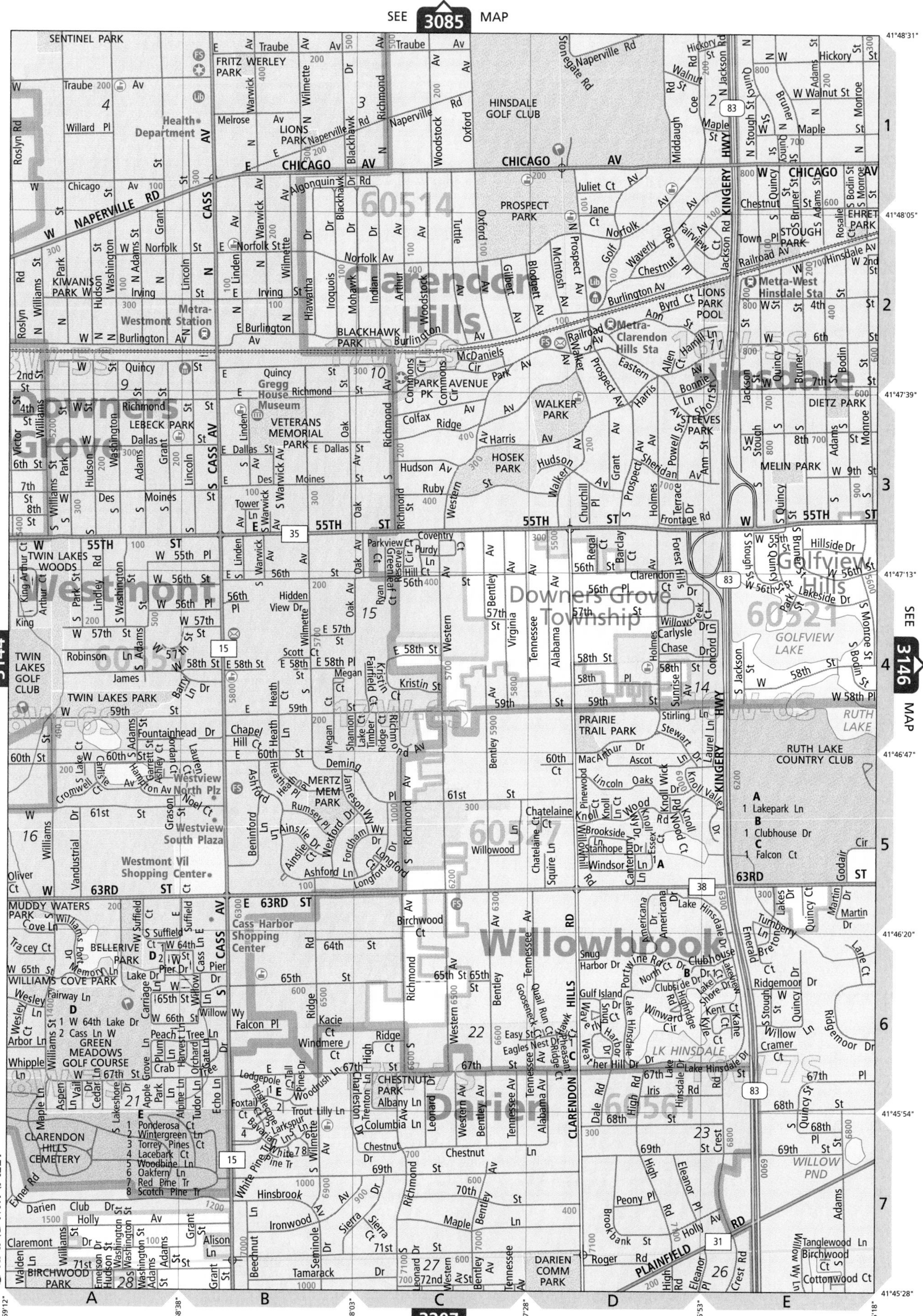

SEE 3144 MAP
SEE 3146 MAP
SEE 3207 MAP

1:24,000
1 in. = 2000 ft.
0 0.25 0.5
miles

SEE 3086 MAP

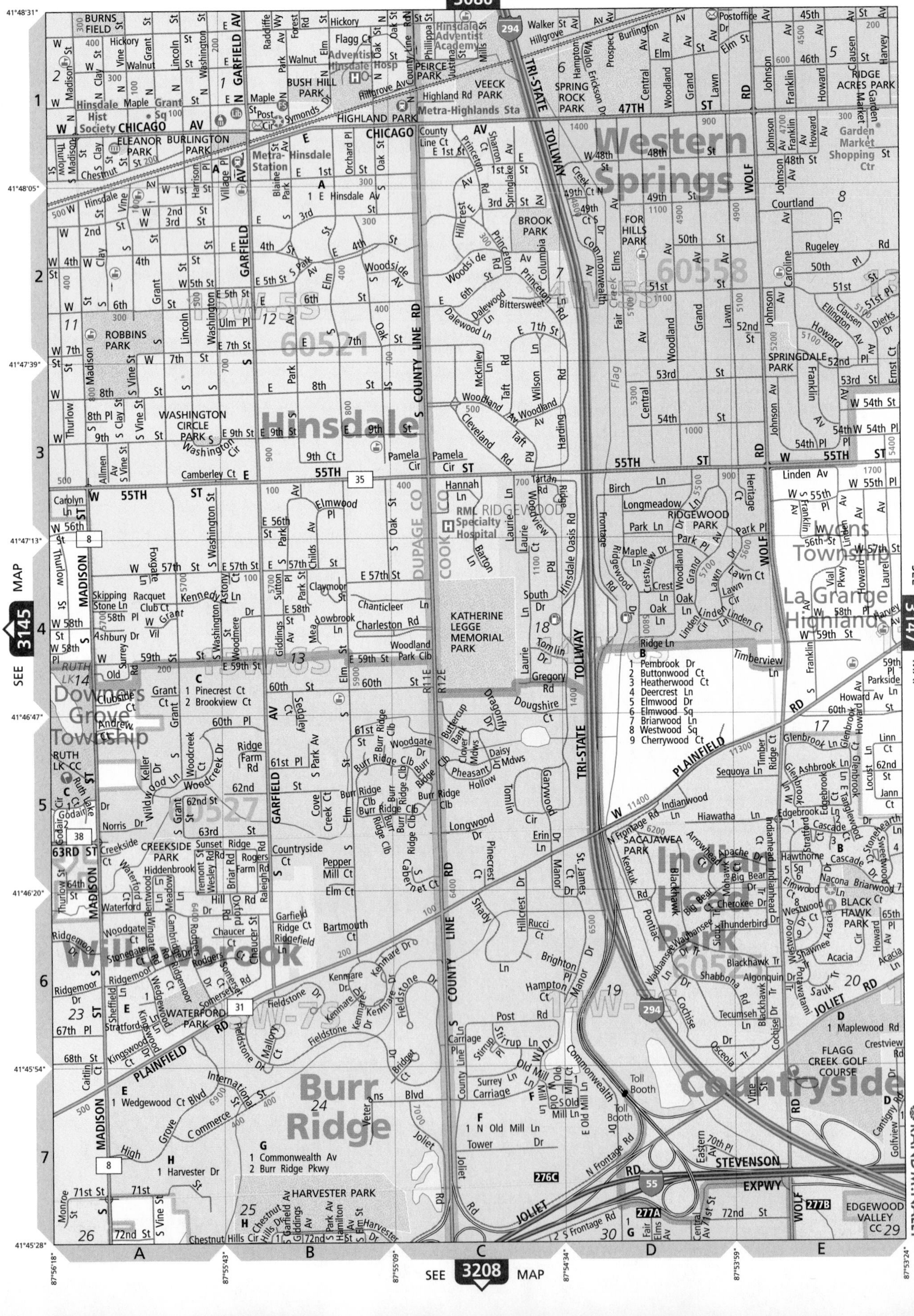

SEE 3145 MAP

SEE 3147 MAP

Hinsdale
Western Springs
La Grange Highlands
Lyons Township
Downers Grove Township
Willowbrook
Burr Ridge
Indian Head Park
Countryside

60521
60558
60527

DUPAGE CO
COOK CO

TRI-STATE TOLLWAY
294
STEVENSON EXPWY
55
JOLIET RD
PLAINFIELD RD
COUNTY LINE RD
GARFIELD AV
MADISON ST
WOLF RD
CHICAGO AV
55TH ST
47TH ST
63RD ST

Hinsdale Adventist Academy
Adventist Hinsdale Hosp
RML Specialty Hospital
Hinsdale Hist Society
Metra-Hinsdale Station
Metra-Highlands Sta
Katherine Legge Memorial Park
Robbins Park
Washington Circle Park
Brook Park
Bush Hill Park
Pierce Park
Veeck Park
Highland Park
Eleanor Park
Burlington Park
For Hills Park
Spring Rock Park
Springdale Park
Ridge Acres Park
Garden Market Shopping Ctr
Ridgewood Park
Creekside Park
Waterford Park
Sacajawea Park
Black Hawk Park
Harvester Park
Flagg Creek Golf Course
Edgewood Valley CC
Ruth Lk CC
Toll Booth

41°48'31"
41°48'05"
41°47'39"
41°47'13"
41°46'47"
41°46'20"
41°45'54"
41°45'28"
87°56'18"
87°55'43"
87°55'09"
87°54'34"
87°53'59"
87°53'24"

A B C D E
1 2 3 4 5 6 7

SEE 3208 MAP

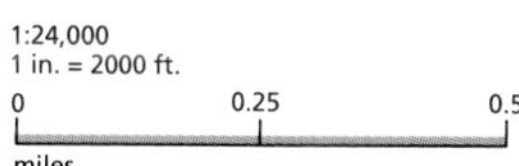

SEE 3087 MAP

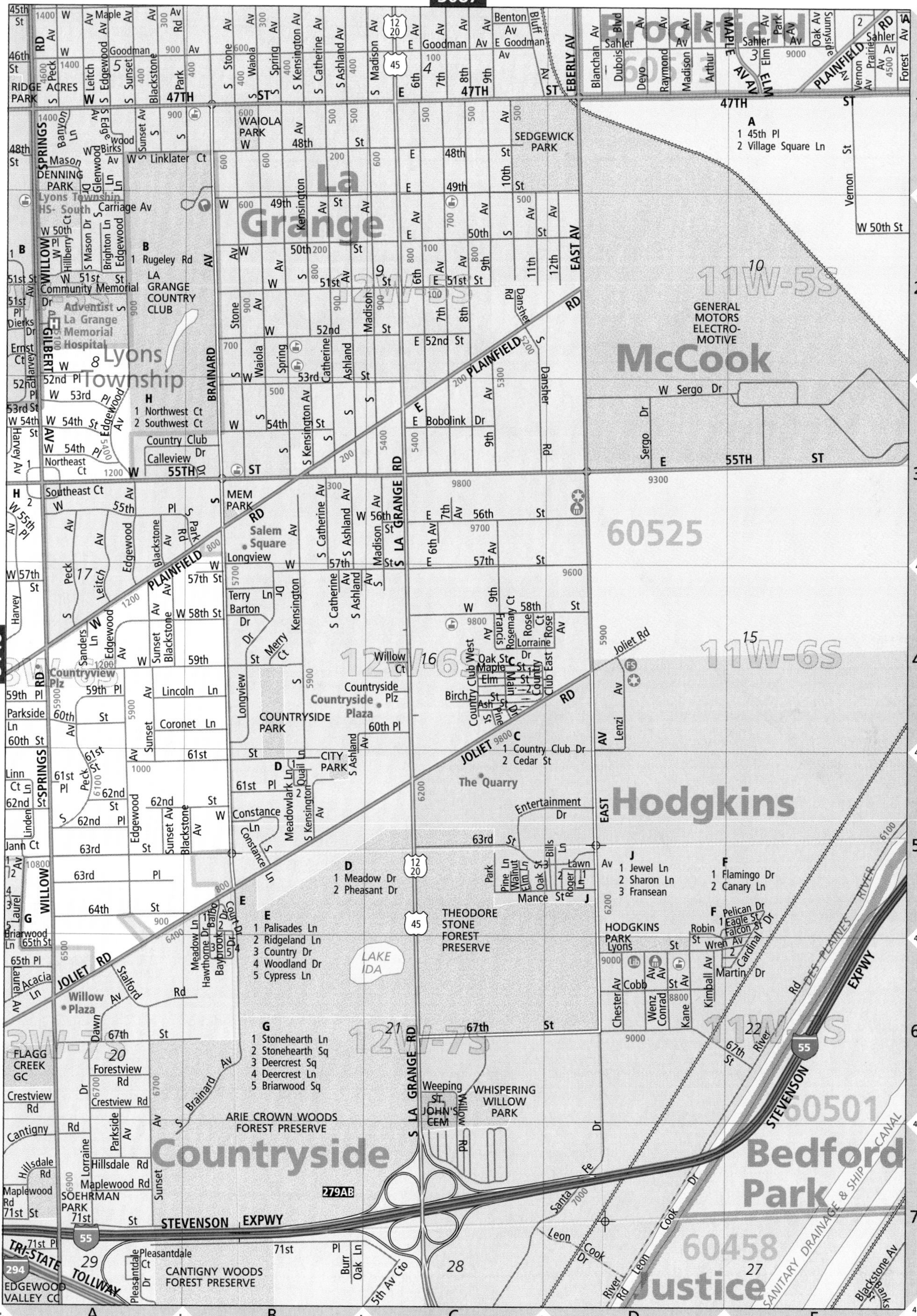

SEE 3146 MAP

SEE 3148 MAP

Brookfield

60513

La Grange

Lyons Township

McCook

60525

Hodgkins

Countryside

Bedford Park

60501

60458

Justice

RIDGE ACRES PARK

DENNING PARK

Lyons Township HS- South

LA GRANGE COUNTRY CLUB

Community Memorial

Adventist La Grange Memorial Hospital

WAIOLA PARK

SEDGEWICK PARK

GENERAL MOTORS ELECTRO-MOTIVE

MEM PARK

Salem Square

Countryview Plz

Countryside Plz

Countryside Plaza

COUNTRYSIDE PARK

CITY PARK

The Quarry

THEODORE STONE FOREST PRESERVE

LAKE IDA

HODGKINS PARK

Willow Plaza

FLAGG CREEK GC

ARIE CROWN WOODS FOREST PRESERVE

WHISPERING WILLOW PARK

ST JOHN'S CEM

SOEHRMAN PARK

CANTIGNY WOODS FOREST PRESERVE

EDGEWOOD VALLEY CC

STEVENSON EXPWY

TRI-STATE TOLLWAY

SANITARY DRAINAGE & SHIP CANAL

DES PLAINES RIVER

11W-5S

12W-5S

11W-6S

12W-6S

12W-7S

11W-7S

A
1 45th Pl
2 Village Square Ln

B
1 Rugeley Rd

C
1 Country Club Dr
2 Cedar St

D
1 Meadow Dr
2 Pheasant Dr

E
1 Palisades Ln
2 Ridgeland Ln
3 Country Dr
4 Woodland Dr
5 Cypress Ln

F
1 Flamingo Dr
2 Canary Ln

G
1 Stonehearth Ln
2 Stonehearth Sq
3 Deercrest Sq
4 Deercrest Ln
5 Briarwood Sq

H
1 Northwest Ct
2 Southwest Ct

J
1 Jewel Ln
2 Sharon Ln
3 Fransean

41°48'32"
41°48'06"
41°47'40"
41°47'13"
41°46'47"
41°46'21"
41°45'55"
41°45'29"

87°53'24"
87°52'49"
87°52'14"
87°51'39"
87°51'05"
87°50'30"

A B C D E

1 2 3 4 5 6 7

SEE 3209 MAP

1:24,000
1 in. = 2000 ft.
0 0.25 0.5
miles

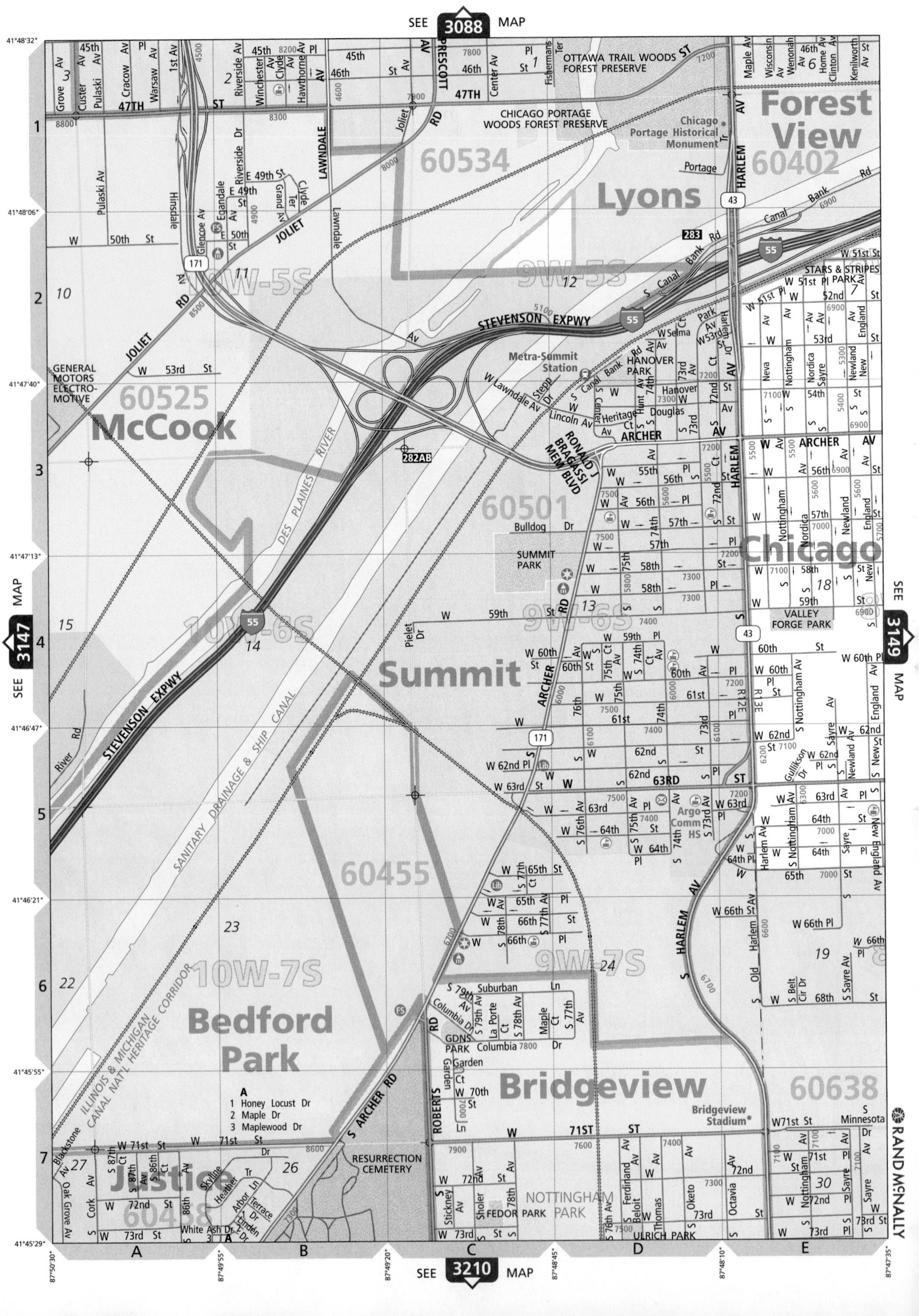

SEE 3088 MAP

SEE 3147 MAP

SEE 3149 MAP

SEE 3210 MAP

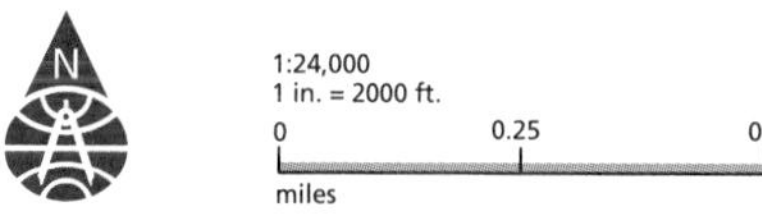

SEE 3089 MAP

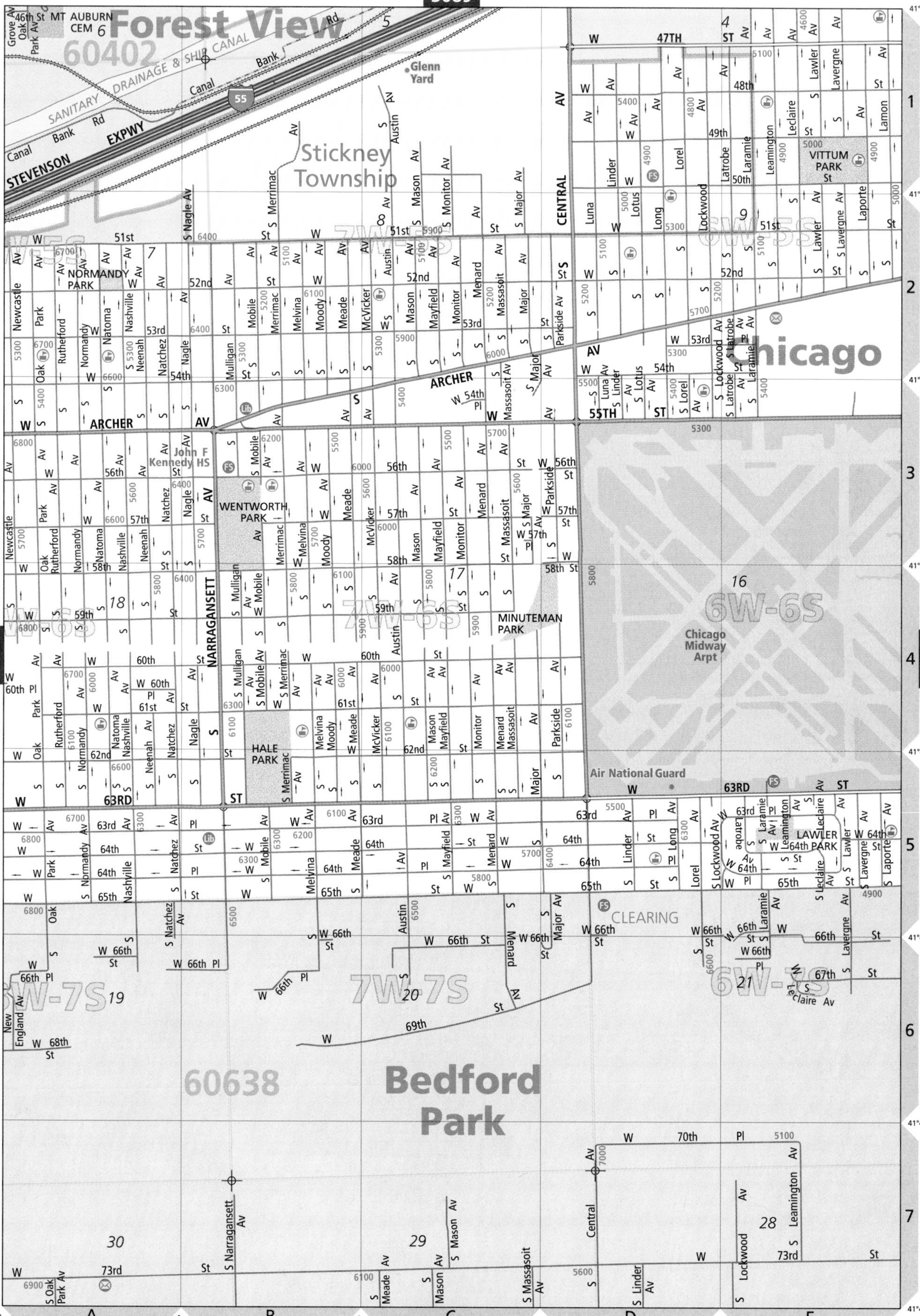

SEE 3148 MAP

SEE 3150 MAP

Forest View
60402
MT AUBURN CEM
Stickney Township
Glenn Yard
SANITARY DRAINAGE & SHIP CANAL
STEVENSON EXPWY
55
NORMANDY PARK
John F Kennedy HS
WENTWORTH PARK
HALE PARK
MINUTEMAN PARK
VITTUM PARK
LAWLER PARK
Chicago
Chicago Midway Arpt
Air National Guard
CLEARING
Bedford Park
60638
W 47TH ST
W 51st St
W 55TH ST
ARCHER AV
NARRAGANSETT AV
CENTRAL AV
W 63RD ST
W 65th St
W 69th St
W 70th Pl
W 73rd St
7W-5S
6W-5S
7W-6S
6W-6S
7W-7S
6W-7S

	A	B	C	D	E
1					
2					
3					
4					
5					
6					
7					

41°48'32" 41°48'06" 41°47'40" 41°47'14" 41°46'48" 41°46'22" 41°45'56" 41°45'29"

87°47'35" 87°47'01" 87°46'26" 87°45'51" 87°45'16" 87°44'41"

SEE 3211 MAP

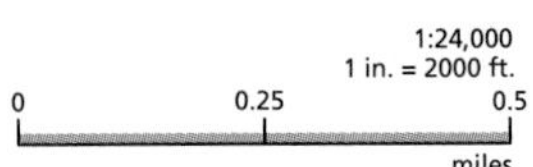

SEE 3090 MAP

SEE 3149 MAP

SEE 3151 MAP

Chicago

Bedford Park

60632

60638

60629

ARCHER PARK

CURIE PARK

Curie Metropolitan HS

Midway Square

CTA-Orange Line-Pulaski Station

CTA-Orange Line-Kedzie Station

STROHACKER PARK

ELSDON

Hancock HS

Hancock College Prep

SENKA PARK

PASTEUR PARK

CTA-Orange Line-Midway Sta

Chicago Midway Arpt

Terminal

Administration Bldg

CITY PARK 61st

Hubbard HS

CHICAGO LAWN

PARK 528

Balzekas Mus of Lithuanian Culture

WEST LAWN PARK

PARK 484

MARQUETTE PARK GOLF COURSE

MARQUETTE PARK

Bedford City Sq

Tootsie Roll Industries

CICERO AV

PULASKI RD

KEDZIE AV

ARCHER AV

47TH ST

55TH ST

59TH ST

63RD ST

MARQUETTE RD

71ST ST

S STATE RD

A B C D E

1 2 3 4 5 6 7

41°48'32" 41°48'06" 41°47'40" 41°47'14" 41°46'48" 41°46'22" 41°45'56" 41°45'29"

87°44'41" 87°44'06" 87°43'31" 87°42'57" 87°42'22" 87°41'47"

SEE 3212 MAP

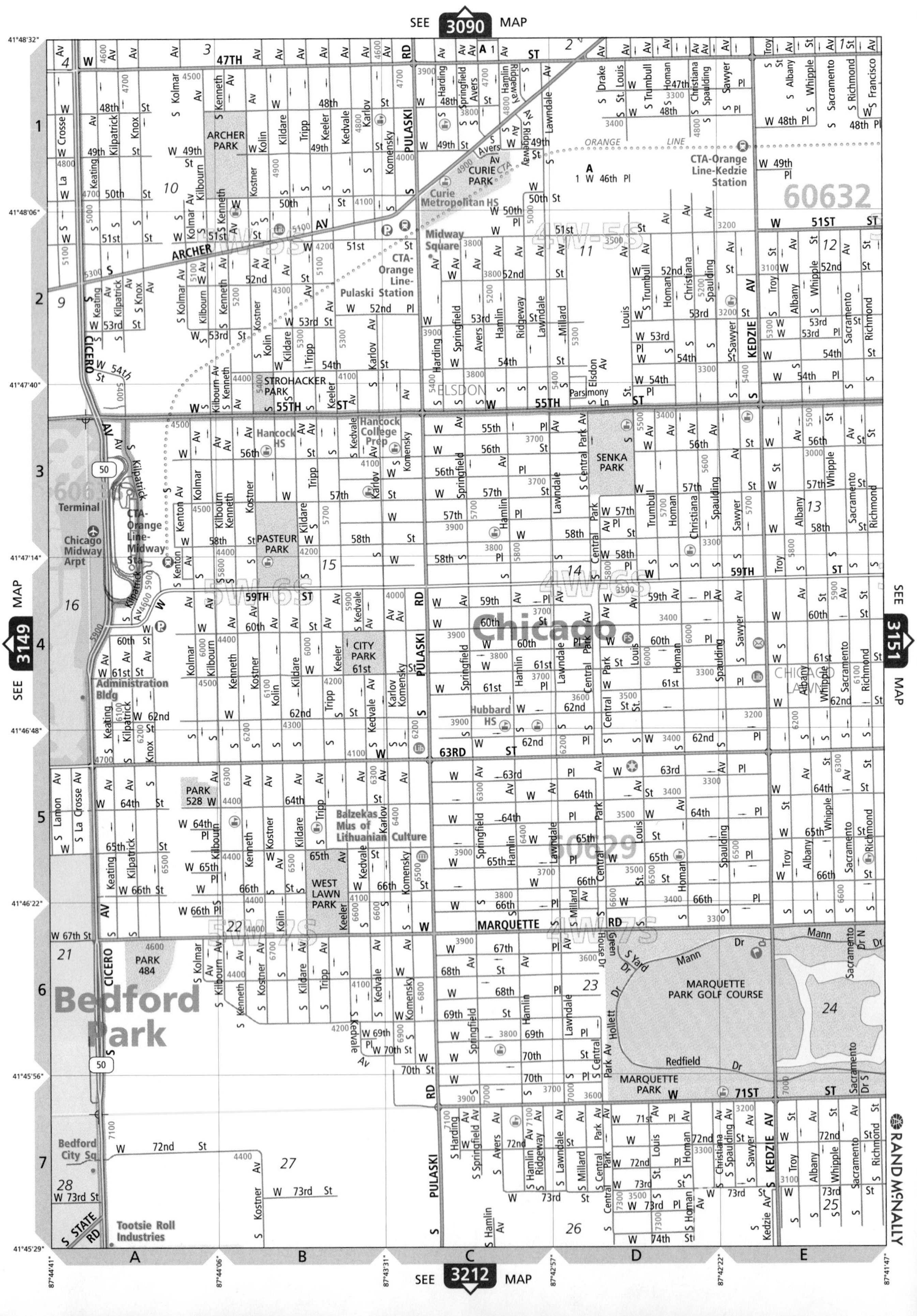

1:24,000
1 in. = 2000 ft.
0 0.25 0.5
miles

SEE 3091 MAP

SEE 3150 MAP

SEE 3152 MAP

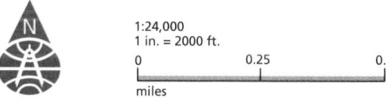

SEE 3213 MAP

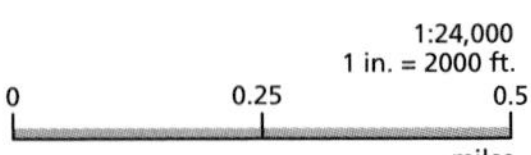

SEE 3092 MAP

Chicago

60609
60615
60621
60637
60619

W 47TH ST
W 51ST ST
GARFIELD BLVD
E GARFIELD BLVD
W 59TH ST
E 59TH ST
MIDWAY PLAISANCE
W 63RD ST
E 63RD ST
W 63RD PKWY
MARQUETTE RD
W 71ST ST
E 71ST ST
W 74TH ST
E 75TH ST
E 55TH ST
E 67TH ST
E HYDE PARK BLVD
S HALSTED ST
S WENTWORTH AV
S STATE ST
S INDIANA AV
S MICHIGAN AV
S DR MARTIN L KING JR DR
S COTTAGE GROVE AV
S DREXEL BLVD
S LAWRENCE AV
S LAFAYETTE AV
S VINCENNES AV
S PARNELL AV
S NORMAL BLVD
S YALE AV
S WELLS ST
DAN RYAN EXPWY
CHICAGO SKWY

Tilden Achievement Academy
O'Toole Athletic Field
WAGNER PARK
LOWE PARK
TAYLOR PARK
Du Sable HS
Hales Franciscan HS
Provident Hospital of Cook County
Dyett Academic Ctr
General Jones Armory
Chicago Osteopathic Hosp & Medical Ctr
CTA-Green Line-51st Sta
CTA-Red Line-Garfield Sta
CTA-Green Line-Garfield Sta
ACE Technical Charter HS
WILLOW PARK
STOUT PARK
Rose Garden
WASHINGTON PARK
Du Sable Mus of African American History
LAGOON
Court Theatre-University of Chicago
Hope College Preparatory HS
HOPE PARK
SHERWOOD PARK
University of Chicago Med Ctr
Univ of Chicago
MIDWAY PLAISANCE PARK
Midway Studios
JACKSON PARK
Englewood Academy HS
CTA-Ashland Branch-Halsted Sta
CTA-Red Line-63rd Sta
CTA-Green Line-King Drive Station
CTA-Green Line-E 63rd-Cottage Grv Station
ENGLEWOOD
St. Bernard Hosp & Health Care Center
NORMAL PARK
Robeson HS
City Coll of Chicago-Kennedy King Coll
CTA-Red Line-69th Sta
OAKWOODS CEMETERY
LILY GDNS PARK
HAMILTON PARK
MEM PARK
MEYERING PARK

1 2 3 4 5 6 7
A B C D E

SEE 3151 MAP
SEE 3153 MAP
SEE 3214 MAP

1:24,000
1 in. = 2000 ft.
0 0.25 0.5
miles

SEE 3093 MAP

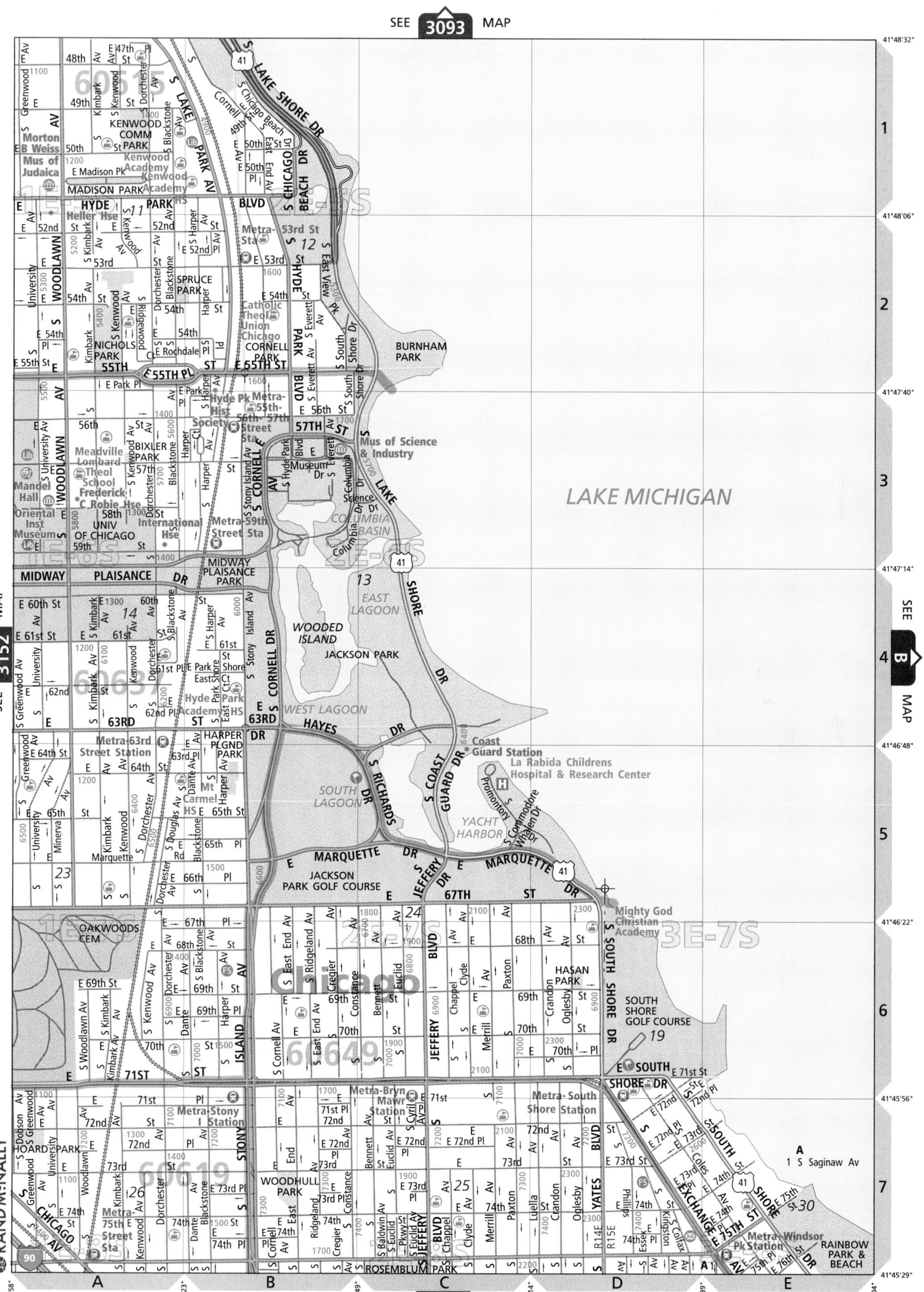

SEE 3152 MAP
SEE B MAP
SEE 3215 MAP

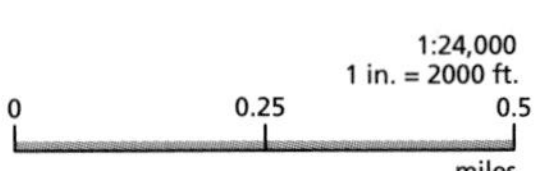

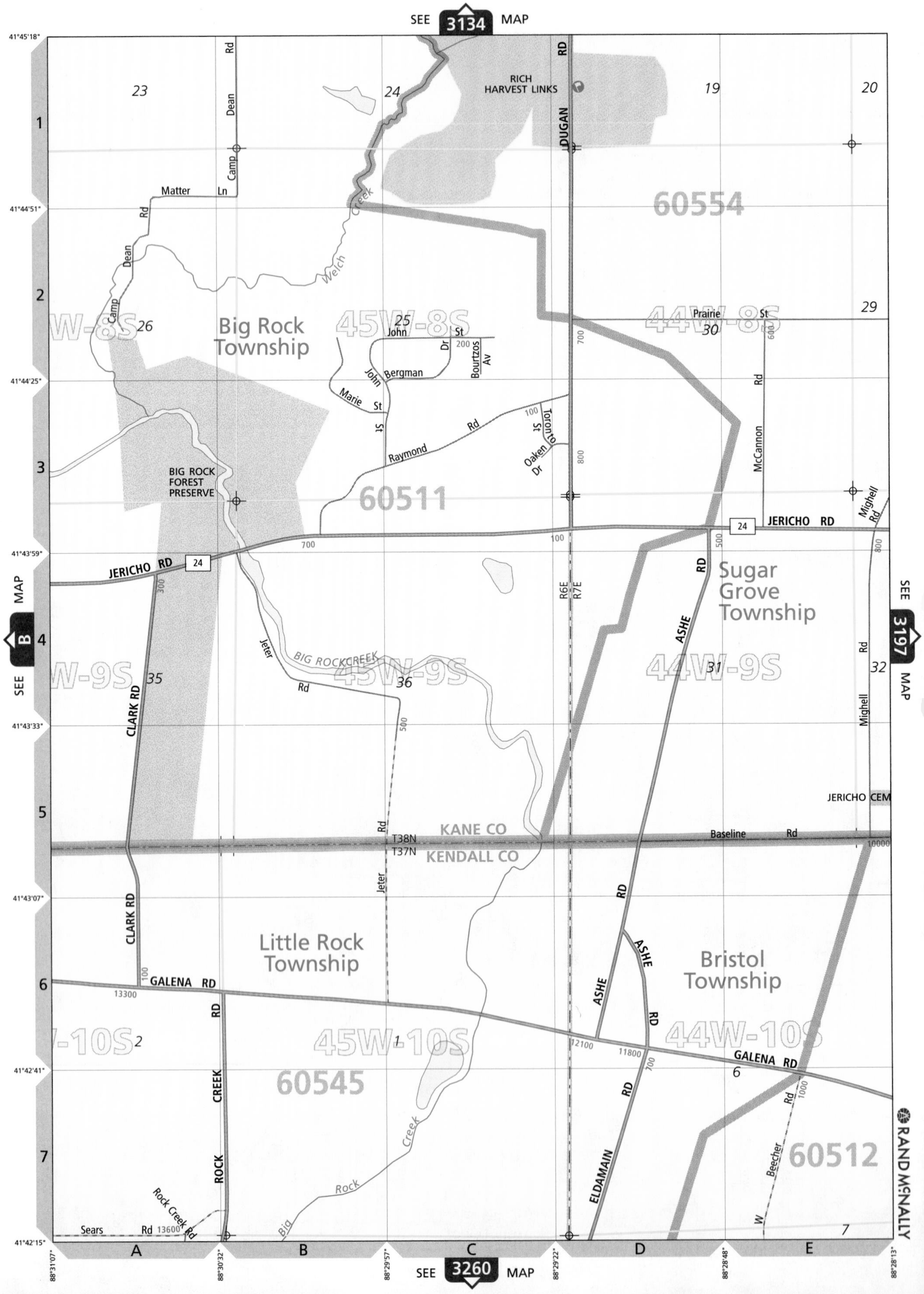

SEE 3134 MAP

RICH HARVEST LINKS

60554

Big Rock Township

60511

BIG ROCK FOREST PRESERVE

JERICHO RD

Sugar Grove Township

KANE CO

KENDALL CO

Little Rock Township

Bristol Township

60545

60512

JERICHO CEM

SEE 3197 MAP

SEE B MAP

SEE 3260 MAP

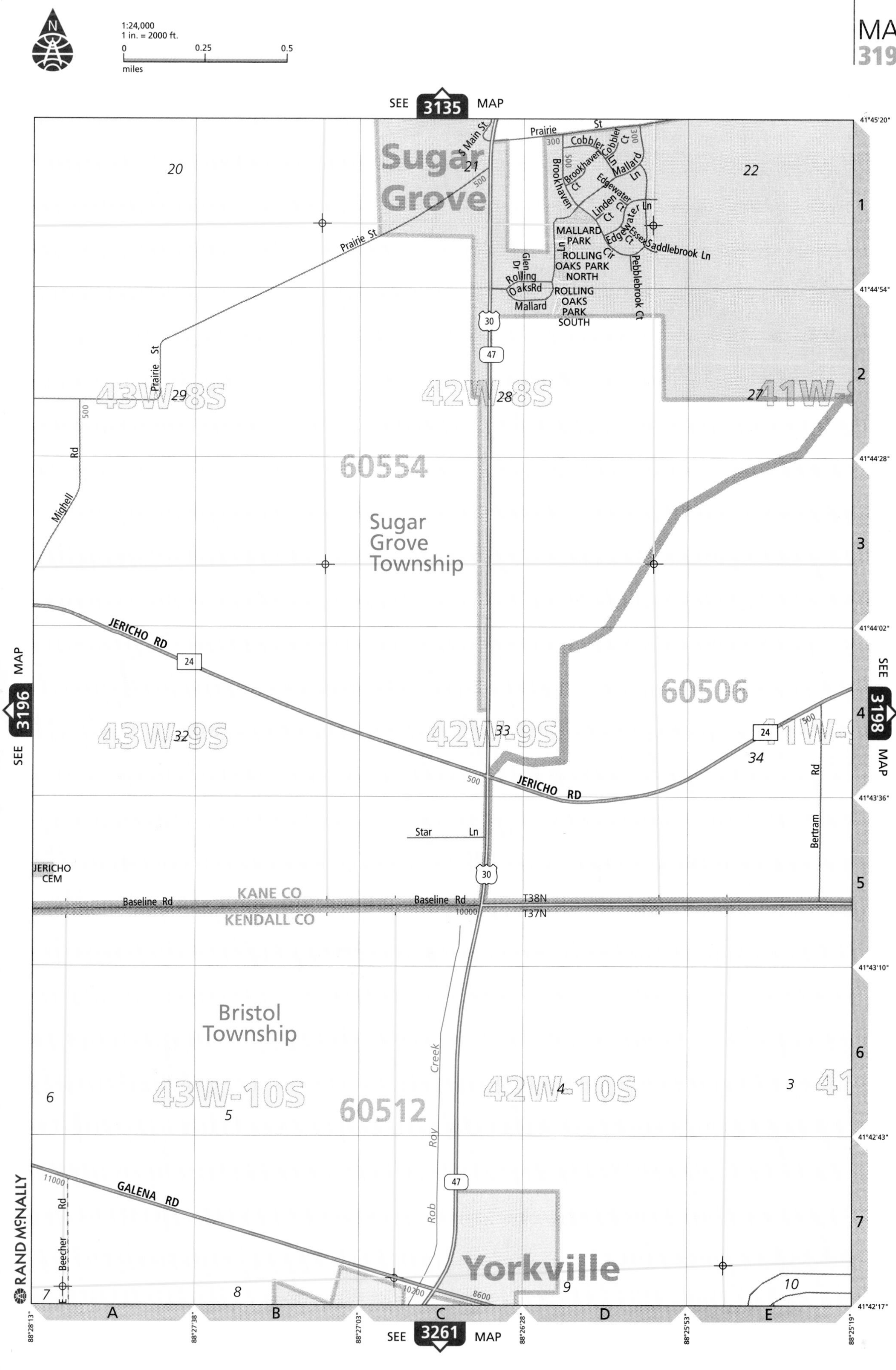

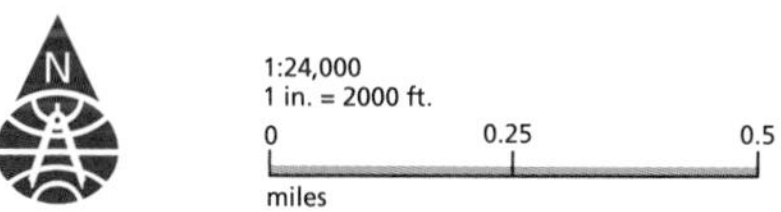

N
1:24,000
1 in. = 2000 ft.
0
0.25
0.5
miles
SEE 3135 MAP
SEE 3196 MAP
SEE 3198 MAP
SEE 3261 MAP
Sugar Grove
Sugar Grove Township
Bristol Township
Yorkville
60554
60506
60512
43W-8S
42W-8S
41W-8S
43W-9S
42W-9S
41W-9S
43W-10S
42W-10S
20
21
22
27
28
29
32
33
34
3
4
5
6
7
8
9
10
Prairie St
S Main St
Cobbler Ct
Cobbler Ln
Brookhaven Ct
Brookhaven
Mallard Ln
Edgewater Ct
Linden Ct
Edgewater Ln
Essex Ct
Edgewater Cir
Saddlebrook Ln
Pebblebrook Ct
MALLARD PARK
ROLLING OAKS PARK NORTH
ROLLING OAKS PARK SOUTH
Glen Dr
Rolling Oaks Rd
Mallard
Mighell Rd
JERICHO RD
Bertram Rd
Star Ln
JERICHO CEM
Baseline Rd
KANE CO
KENDALL CO
T38N
T37N
Rob Roy Creek
GALENA RD
Beecher Rd
E
300
500
10000
10200
11000
8600
24
30
47
A
B
C
D
E
1
2
3
4
5
6
7
41°45'20"
41°44'54"
41°44'28"
41°44'02"
41°43'36"
41°43'10"
41°42'43"
41°42'17"
88°28'13"
88°27'38"
88°27'03"
88°26'28"
88°25'53"
88°25'19"
RAND McNALLY

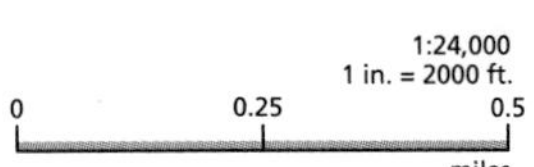

1:24,000
1 in. = 2000 ft.
0 0.25 0.5
miles

SEE 3136 MAP
SEE 3197 MAP
SEE 3199 MAP
SEE 3262 MAP
Sugar Grove
Sugar Grove Township
Aurora
Montgomery
Countryside
Bristol Township
Oswego
KANE CO
KENDALL CO
T38N
T37N
60554
60506
60538
60512
60543
40W-8S
39W-8S
40W-9S
39W-9S
40W-10S
39W-10S
ROBERT I STUART SPORTS COMPLEX
JERICHO LAKE
JERICHO LAKE PARK
PRAIRIE ST
JERICHO RD
ORCHARD RD
AUCUTT RD
GALENA RD
Gordon Rd
S Barnes Rd
Blackberry Creek
A
1 Wyckwood Dr
2 Taliesin Dr
3 Sans Souci Dr
B
1 Whitlock Ct
2 Fitchome St
C
1 S Concord Dr
RAND McNALLY
41°45'20"
41°44'54"
41°44'28"
41°44'02"
41°43'36"
41°43'10"
41°42'43"
41°42'17"
88°25'19"
88°24'44"
88°24'09"
88°23'34"
88°22'59"
88°22'24"

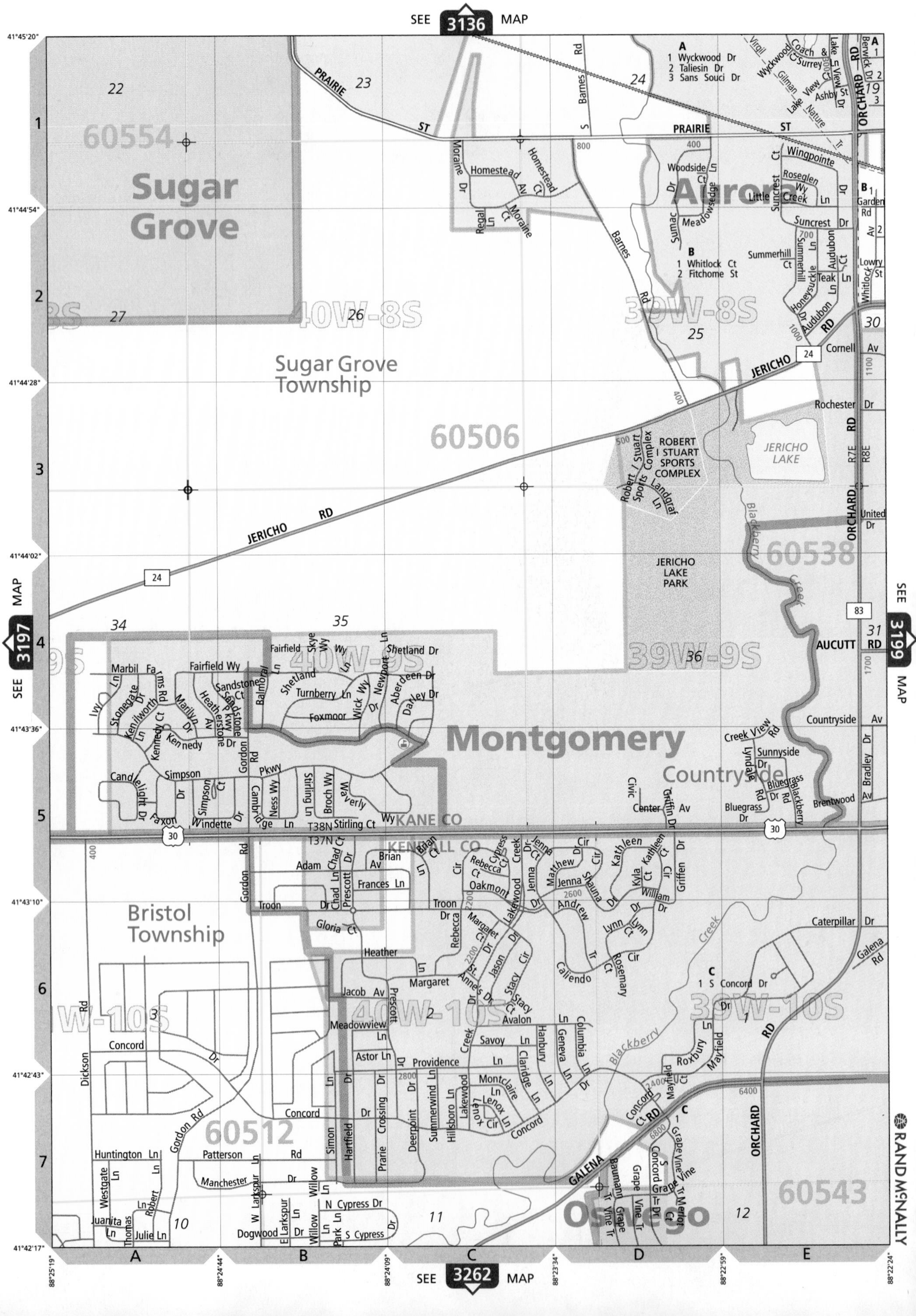

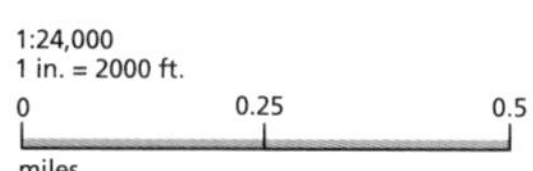

SEE 3137 MAP

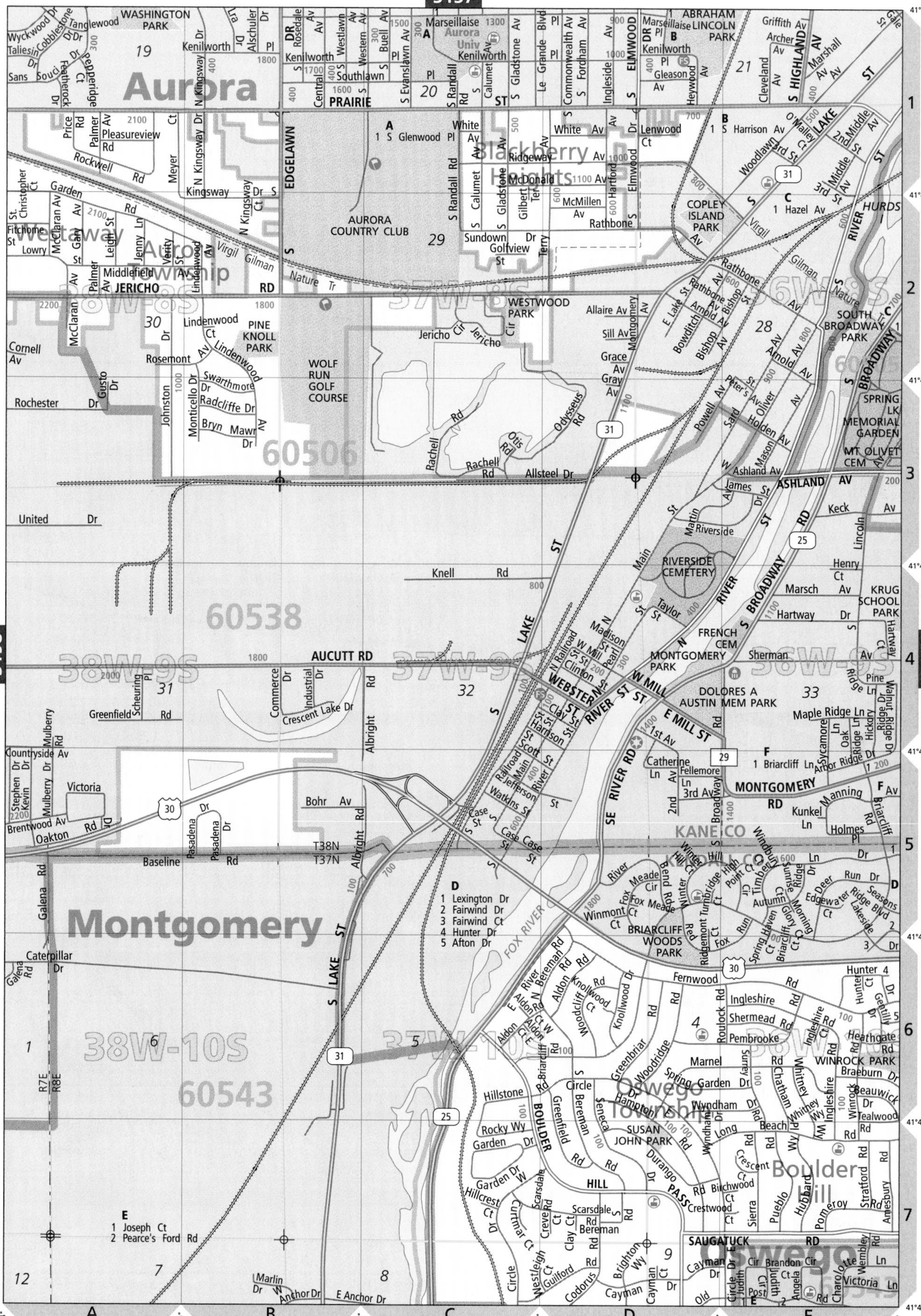

SEE 3198 MAP

SEE 3200 MAP

SEE 3263 MAP

Aurora

Montgomery

Boulder Hill

Oswego

Aurora Township

Oswego Township

Blackberry Heights

WASHINGTON PARK

ABRAHAM LINCOLN PARK

Aurora Univ

AURORA COUNTRY CLUB

COPLEY ISLAND PARK

WESTWOOD PARK

PINE KNOLL PARK

WOLF RUN GOLF COURSE

SOUTH BROADWAY PARK

SPRING LK MEMORIAL GARDEN

MT OLIVET CEM

RIVERSIDE CEMETERY

FRENCH CEM

MONTGOMERY PARK

DOLORES A AUSTIN MEM PARK

KRUG SCHOOL PARK

BRIARCLIFF WOODS PARK

WINROCK PARK

SUSAN JOHN PARK

KANE CO

KENDALL CO

FOX RIVER

60506

60538

60543

38W-8S

37W-8S

36W-8S

38W-9S

37W-9S

36W-9S

38W-10S

37W-10S

36W-10S

T38N

T37N

R7E

R8E

A
1 S Glenwood Pl

B
1 S Harrison Av

C
1 Hazel Av

D
1 Lexington Dr
2 Fairwind Dr
3 Fairwind Ct
4 Hunter Dr
5 Afton Dr

E
1 Joseph Ct
2 Pearce's Ford Rd

F
1 Briarcliff Ln

41°45'22"

41°44'56"

41°44'30"

41°44'04"

41°43'38"

41°43'12"

41°42'46"

41°42'20"

88°22'24"

88°21'50"

88°21'15"

88°20'40"

88°20'05"

88°19'30"

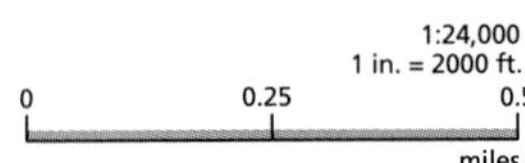

SEE 3138 MAP

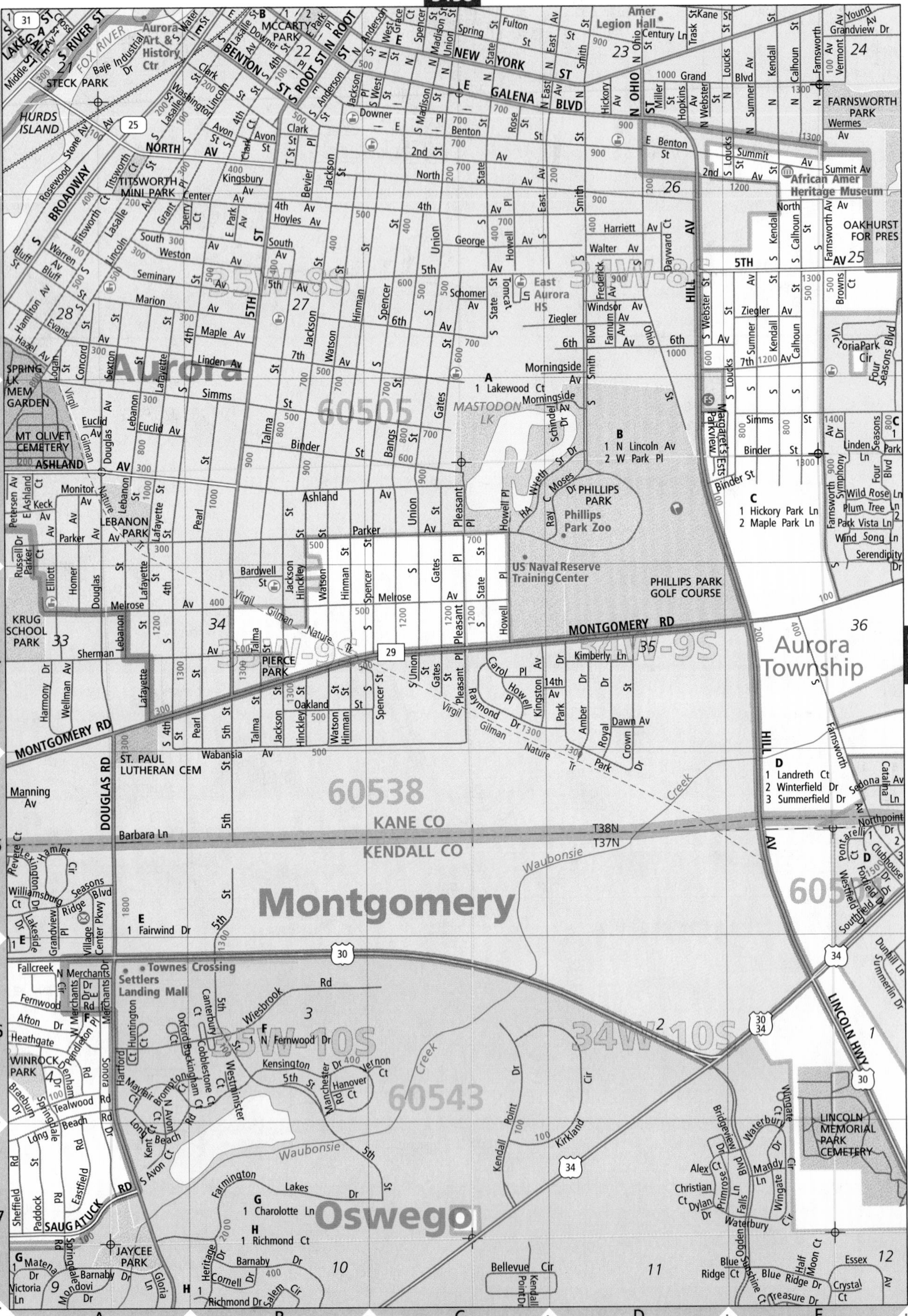

SEE 3199 MAP

SEE 3201 MAP

Aurora

Montgomery

Oswego

Aurora Township

KANE CO

KENDALL CO

60505

60538

60543

A
1 Lakewood Ct

B
1 N Lincoln Av
2 W Park Pl

C
1 Hickory Park Ln
2 Maple Park Ln

D
1 Landreth Ct
2 Winterfield Dr
3 Summerfield Dr

E
1 Fairwind Dr

F
1 N Fernwood Dr

G
1 Charolotte Ln

H
1 Richmond Ct

PHILLIPS PARK

Phillips Park Zoo

PHILLIPS PARK GOLF COURSE

US Naval Reserve Training Center

East Aurora HS

MT OLIVET CEMETERY

SPRING LK MEM GARDEN

ST. PAUL LUTHERAN CEM

LINCOLN MEMORIAL PARK CEMETERY

Settlers Landing Mall

Towns Crossing

African Amer Heritage Museum

Aurora Art & History Ctr

Amer Legion Hall

FARNSWORTH PARK

OAKHURST FOR PRES

KRUG SCHOOL PARK

LEBANON PARK

PIERCE PARK

TITSWORTH MINI PARK

STECK PARK

HURDS ISLAND

MCCARTY PARK

WINROCK PARK

JAYCEE PARK

A B C D E

1 2 3 4 5 6 7

SEE 3264 MAP

1:24,000
1 in. = 2000 ft.
0 0.25 0.5
miles

SEE 3139 MAP

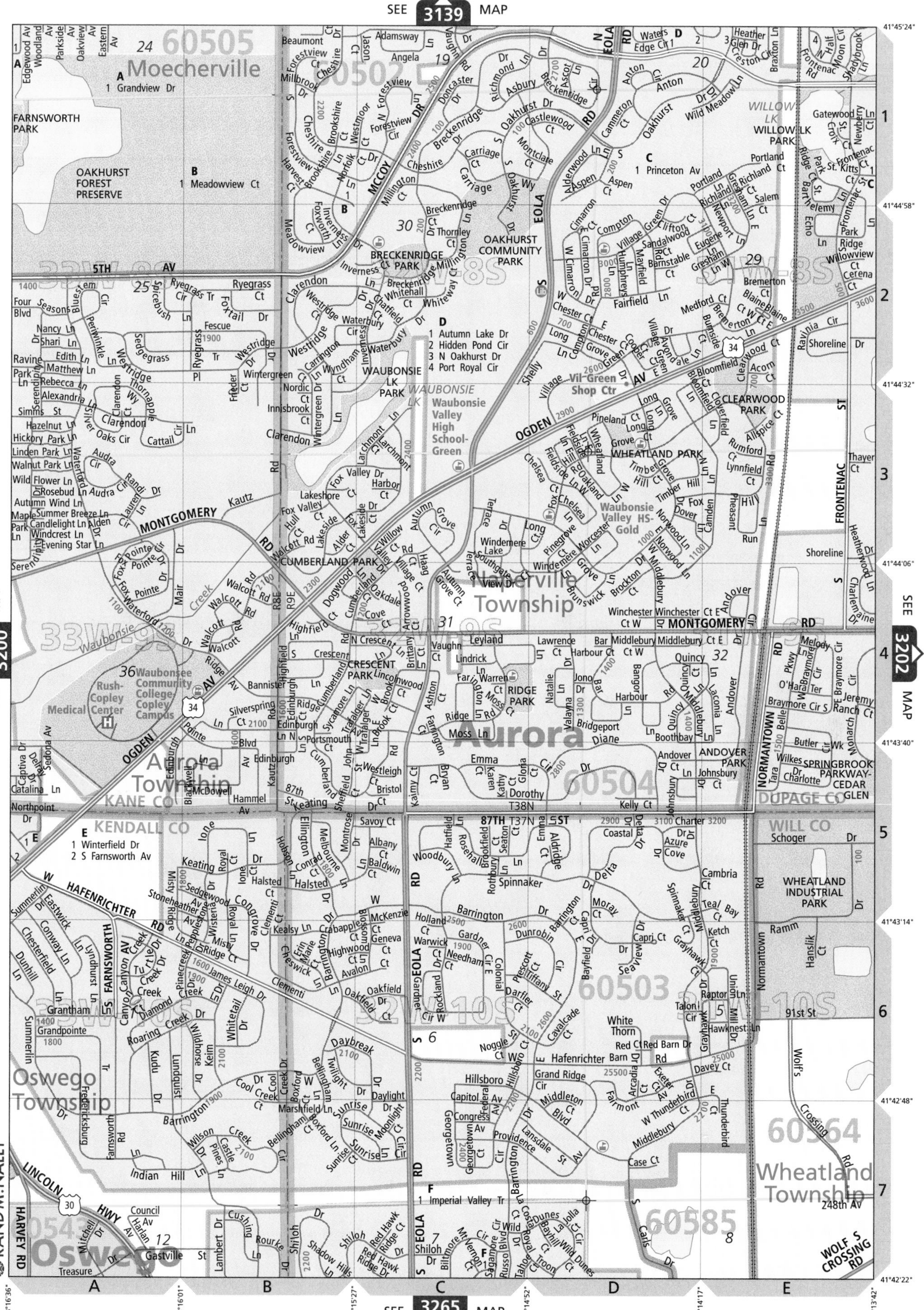

SEE 3200 MAP

SEE 3202 MAP

SEE 3265 MAP

1:24,000
1 in. = 2000 ft.
0 0.25 0.5
miles

SEE 3140 MAP

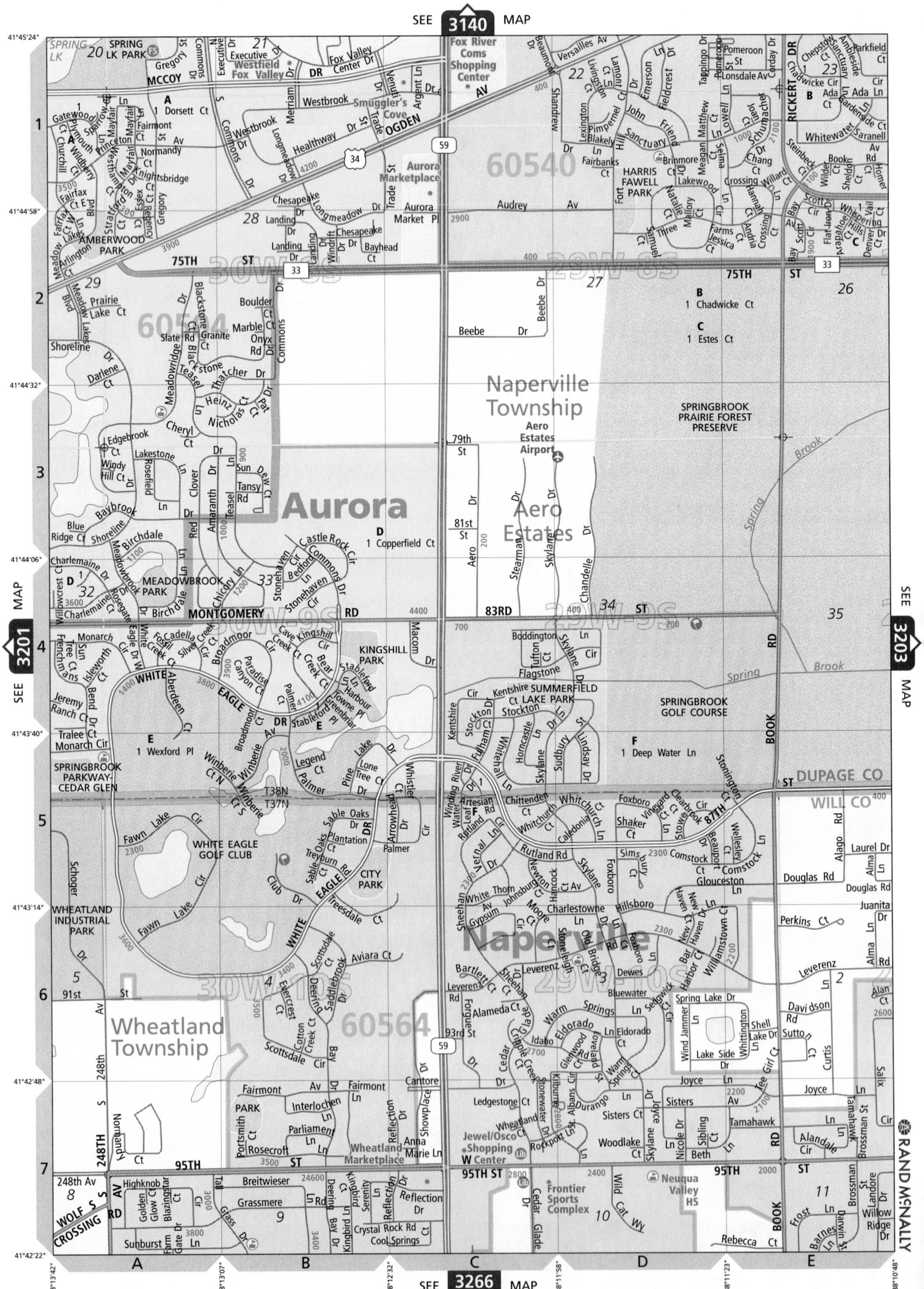

SEE 3201 MAP

SEE 3203 MAP

SEE 3266 MAP

Aurora

Naperville

Naperville Township

Wheatland Township

Aero Estates

Aero Estates Airport

SPRINGBROOK PRAIRIE FOREST PRESERVE

SPRINGBROOK GOLF COURSE

WHITE EAGLE GOLF CLUB

WHEATLAND INDUSTRIAL PARK

SPRINGBROOK PARKWAY-CEDAR GLEN

MEADOWBROOK PARK

KINGSHILL PARK

SUMMERFIELD LAKE PARK

HARRIS FAWELL PARK

AMBERWOOD PARK

SPRING LK PARK

CITY PARK

FAIRMONT PARK

Westfield Fox Valley

Fox River Coms Shopping Center

Smuggler's Cove

Aurora Marketplace

Wheatland Marketplace

Jewel/Osco Shopping Center

Frontier Sports Complex

Neuqua Valley HS

DUPAGE CO

WILL CO

60540

60564

A
1 Dorsett Ct

B
1 Chadwicke Ct

C
1 Estes Ct

D
1 Copperfield Ct

E
1 Wexford Pl

F
1 Deep Water Ln

MCCOY DR
OGDEN AV
75TH ST
83RD ST
MONTGOMERY RD
WHITE EAGLE DR
95TH ST
248TH AV
WOLF CROSSING RD
BOOK RD
RICKERT DR
87TH ST

41°45'24"
41°44'58"
41°44'32"
41°44'06"
41°43'40"
41°43'14"
41°42'48"
41°42'22"

88°13'42"
88°13'07"
88°12'32"
88°11'58"
88°11'23"
88°10'48"

1:24,000
1 in. = 2000 ft.
0 0.25 0.5
miles

SEE 3141 MAP

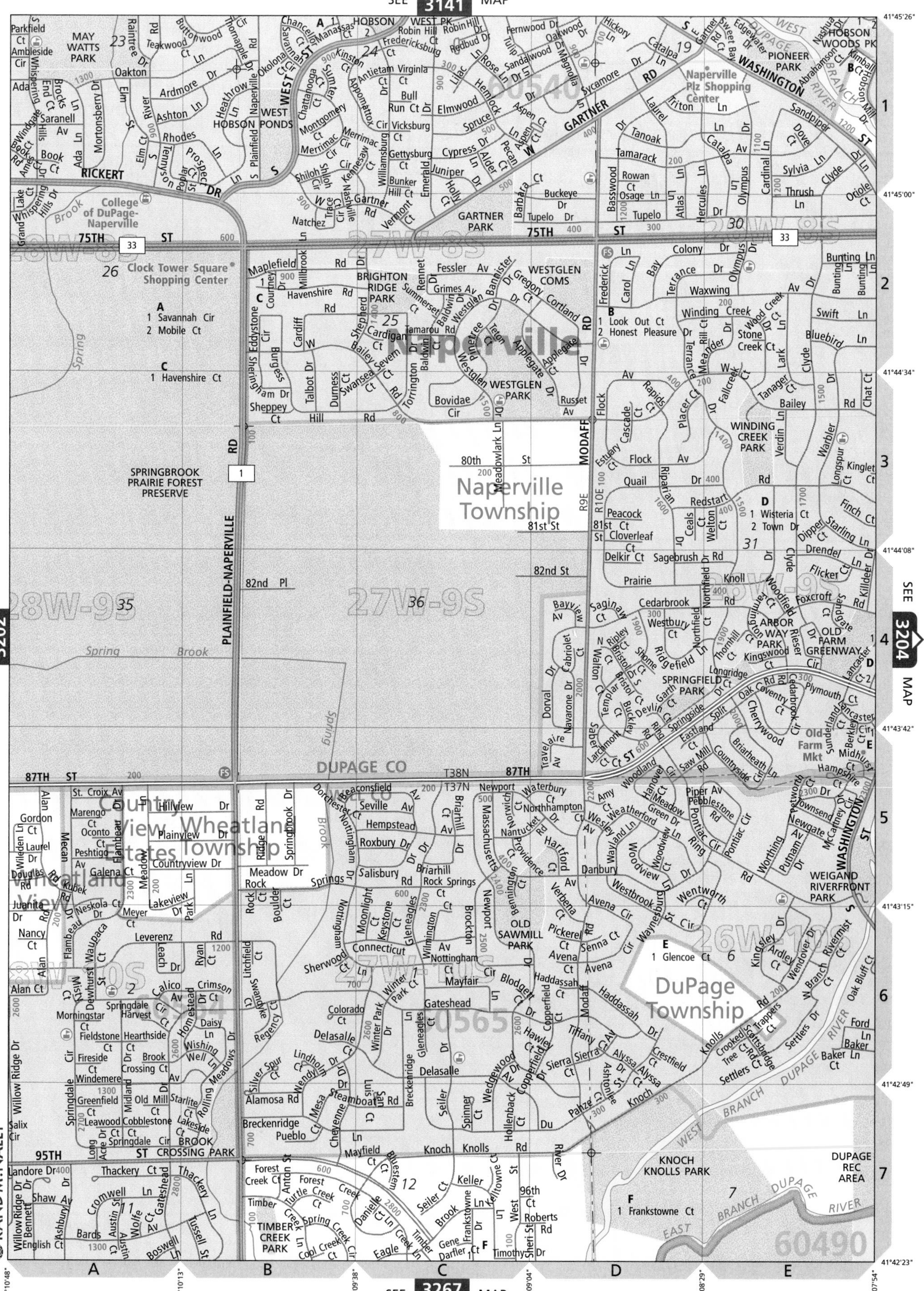

A B C D E
1 2 3 4 5 6 7

41°45'26" 41°45'00" 41°44'34" 41°44'08" 41°43'42" 41°43'15" 41°42'49" 41°42'23"
88°10'48" 88°10'13" 88°09'38" 88°09'04" 88°08'29" 88°07'54"

SEE 3202 MAP
SEE 3204 MAP
SEE 3267 MAP

1:24,000
1 in. = 2000 ft.
0 0.25 0.5
miles

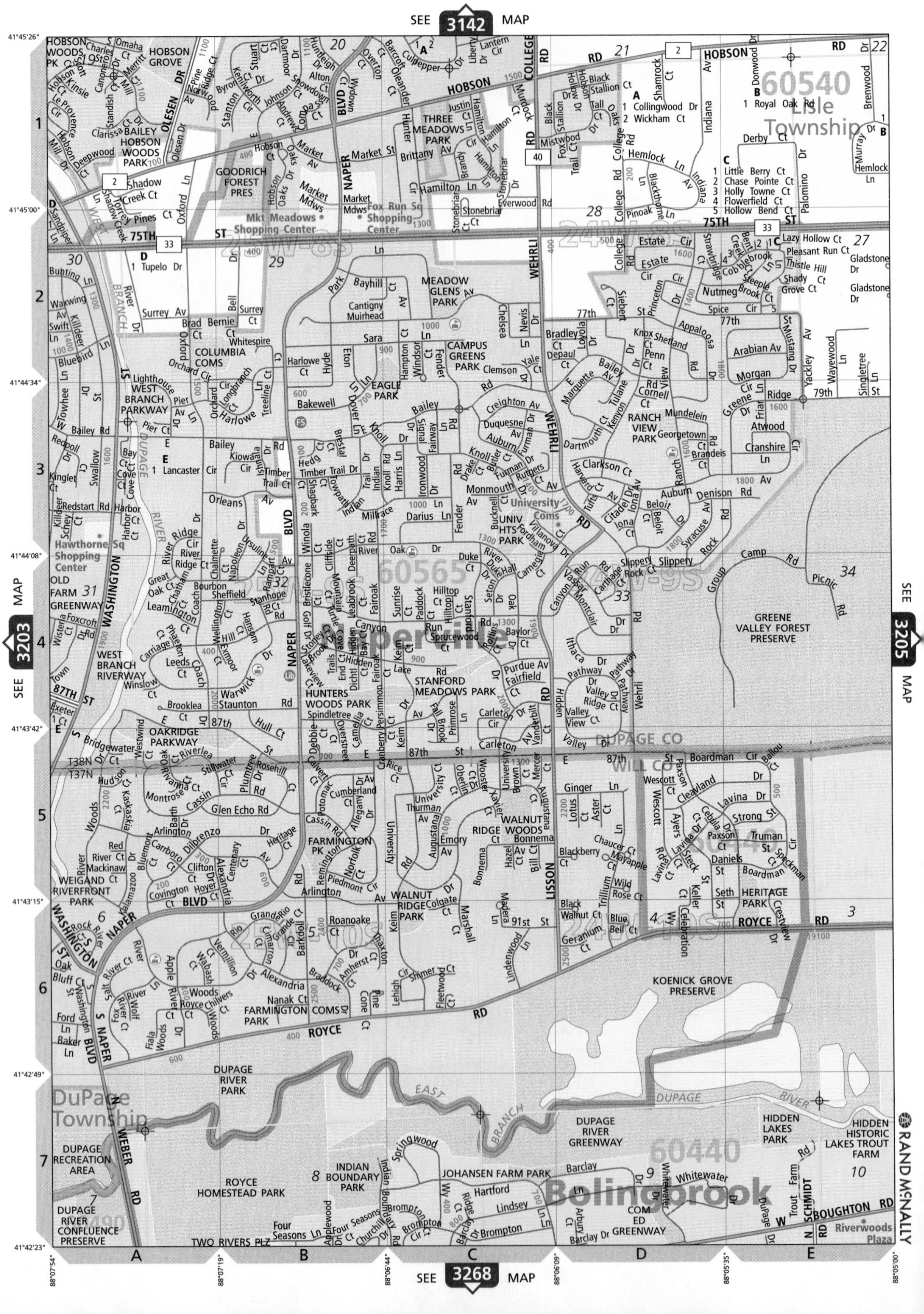

SEE 3142 MAP

A
1 Culpepper Cir
2 Liberty Ct

A
1 Collingwood Dr
2 Wickham Ct

B
1 Royal Oak Rd

C
1 Little Berry Ct
2 Chase Pointe Ct
3 Holly Towne Ct
4 Flowerfield Ct
5 Hollow Bend Ct

C
1 Lazy Hollow Ct
Pleasant Run Ct

D
1 Tupelo Dr

E
1 Lancaster Cir

60540
Lisle Township

HOBSON WOODS PK
HOBSON GROVE
BAILEY HOBSON WOODS PARK
GOODRICH FOREST PRES
THREE MEADOWS PARK
Mkt Meadows Shopping Center
Fox Run Sq Shopping Center
MEADOW GLENS PARK
CAMPUS GREENS PARK
COLUMBIA COMS
WEST BRANCH PARKWAY
EAGLE PARK
RANCH VIEW PARK
University Coms
UNIV HTS PARK
Hawthorne Sq Shopping Center
OLD FARM GREENWAY
WEST BRANCH RIVERWAY
60565
Naperville
HUNTERS WOODS PARK
STANFORD MEADOWS PARK
GREENE VALLEY FOREST PRESERVE
OAKRIDGE PARKWAY
DUPAGE CO
WILL CO
T38N
T37N
FARMINGTON PK
RIDGE WOODS PARK
WALNUT RIDGE PARK
WEIGAND RIVERFRONT PARK
HERITAGE PARK
60440
FARMINGTON COMS PARK
KOENICK GROVE PRESERVE
DUPAGE RIVER PARK
DuPage Township
DUPAGE RIVER GREENWAY
HIDDEN LAKES PARK
HIDDEN HISTORIC LAKES TROUT FARM
DUPAGE RECREATION AREA
INDIAN BOUNDARY PARK
JOHANSEN FARM PARK
ROYCE HOMESTEAD PARK
DUPAGE RIVER CONFLUENCE PRESERVE
COM ED GREENWAY
Bolingbrook
Riverwoods Plaza

SEE 3203 MAP

SEE 3205 MAP

SEE 3268 MAP

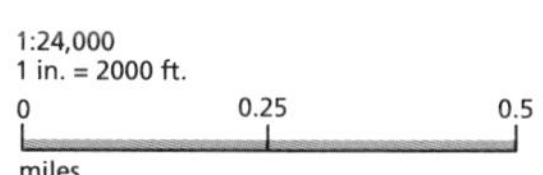

SEE 3143 MAP

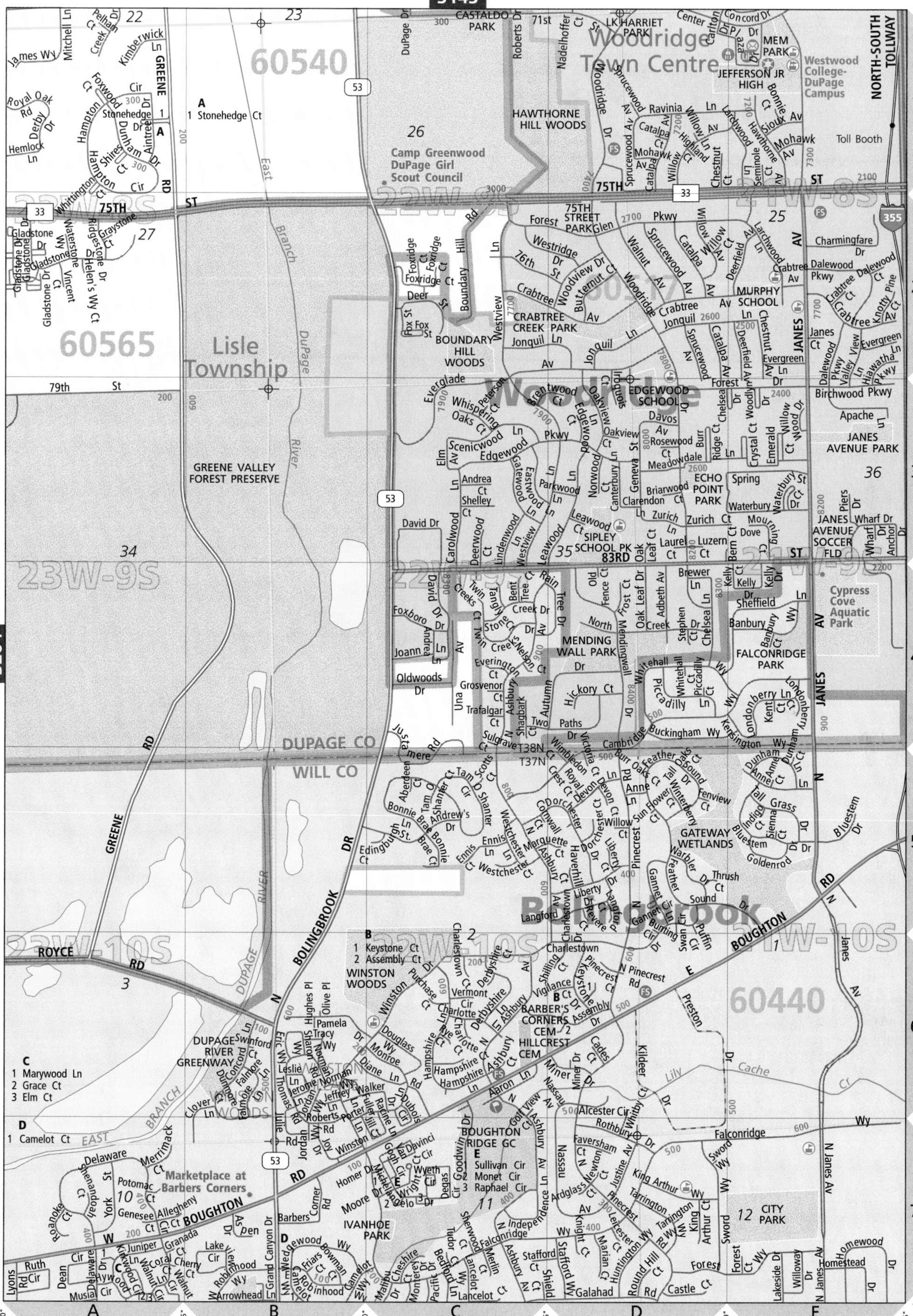

SEE 3204 MAP

SEE 3206 MAP

Woodridge Town Centre
CASTALDO PARK
LK HARRIET PARK
MEM PARK
JEFFERSON JR HIGH
Westwood College-DuPage Campus
NORTH-SOUTH TOLLWAY
Toll Booth
HAWTHORNE HILL WOODS
Camp Greenwood DuPage Girl Scout Council
60540
60565
60517
60440
75TH STREET PARK
MURPHY SCHOOL
CRABTREE CREEK PARK
BOUNDARY HILL WOODS
Lisle Township
Woodridge
EDGEWOOD SCHOOL
JANES AVENUE PARK
ECHO POINT PARK
SIPLEY SCHOOL PK
JANES AVENUE SOCCER FLD
GREENE VALLEY FOREST PRESERVE
Cypress Cove Aquatic Park
MENDING WALL PARK
FALCONRIDGE PARK
DUPAGE CO
WILL CO
T38N
T37N
GATEWAY WETLANDS
Bolingbrook
WINSTON WOODS
BARBER'S CORNERS CEM
HILLCREST CEM
DUPAGE RIVER GREENWAY
BOUGHTON RIDGE GC
Marketplace at Barbers Corners
IVANHOE PARK
CITY PARK

A
1 Stonehedge Ct

B
1 Keystone Ct
2 Assembly Ct

C
1 Marywood Ln
2 Grace Ct
3 Elm Ct

D
1 Camelot Ct

E
1 Sullivan Cir
2 Monet Cir
3 Raphael Cir

RAND McNALLY

SEE 3269 MAP

1:24,000
1 in. = 2000 ft.
0 0.25 0.5
miles

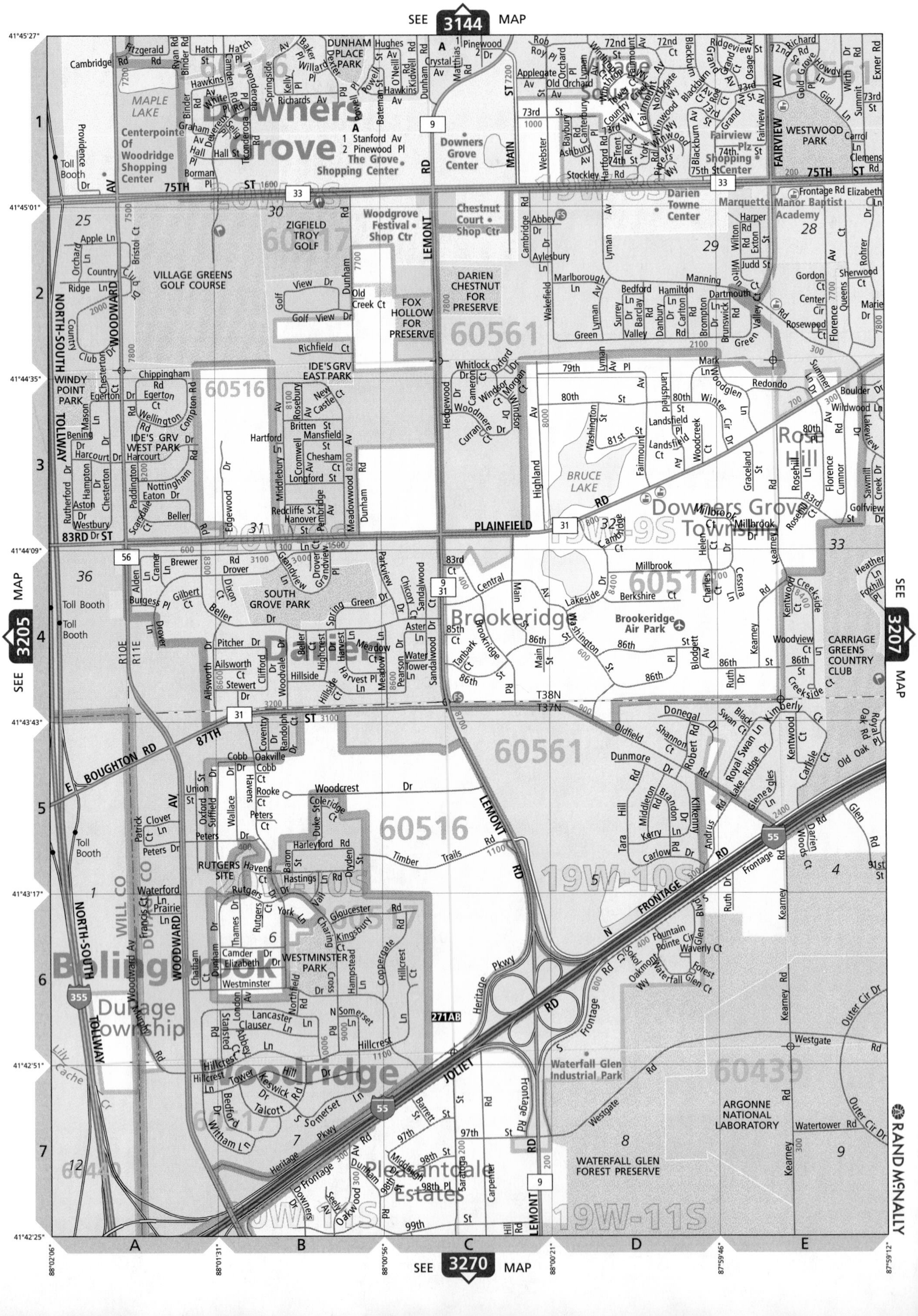

SEE 3144 MAP

41°45'27"
41°45'01"
41°44'35"
41°44'09"
41°43'43"
41°43'17"
41°42'51"
41°42'25"

Downers Grove
Darien
Brookeridge
Bolingbrook
Woodridge
DuPage Township
Downers Grove Township
Rose Hill
Pleasantdale Estates

Centerpointe Of Woodridge Shopping Center
The Grove Shopping Center
Downers Grove Center
Village Square
Fairview Plz Shopping Center
Westwood Park
Darien Towne Center
Marquette Manor Baptist Academy
Zigfield Troy Golf
Woodgrove Festival Shop Ctr
Chestnut Court Shop Ctr
Village Greens Golf Course
Fox Hollow For Preserve
Darien Chestnut For Preserve
Ide's Grv East Park
Ide's Grv West Park
Windy Point Park
Maple Lake
Bruce Lake
South Grove Park
Brookeridge Air Park
Carriage Greens Country Club
Rutgers Site
Westminster Park
Waterfall Glen Industrial Park
Argonne National Laboratory
Waterfall Glen Forest Preserve
Toll Booth

75TH ST
PLAINFIELD RD
83RD ST
87TH ST
BOUGHTON RD
LEMONT RD
JOLIET RD
N FRONTAGE RD
WOODWARD AV
FAIRVIEW AV
MAIN ST
NORTH-SOUTH TOLLWAY
WILL CO
DUPAGE CO
T38N
T37N
R10E
R11E

60516
60517
60561
60439
60440

19W-8S
20W-8S
19W-9S
20W-9S
19W-10S
20W-10S
19W-11S
20W-11S

25 30 29 28 36 31 32 33 1 6 5 4 12 7 8 9

1 2 3 4 5 6 7
A B C D E

SEE 3205 MAP

SEE 3207 MAP

SEE 3270 MAP

88°02'06"
88°01'31"
88°00'56"
88°00'21"
87°59'46"
87°59'12"

1:24,000
1 in. = 2000 ft.
0 0.25 0.5
miles

SEE 3145 MAP

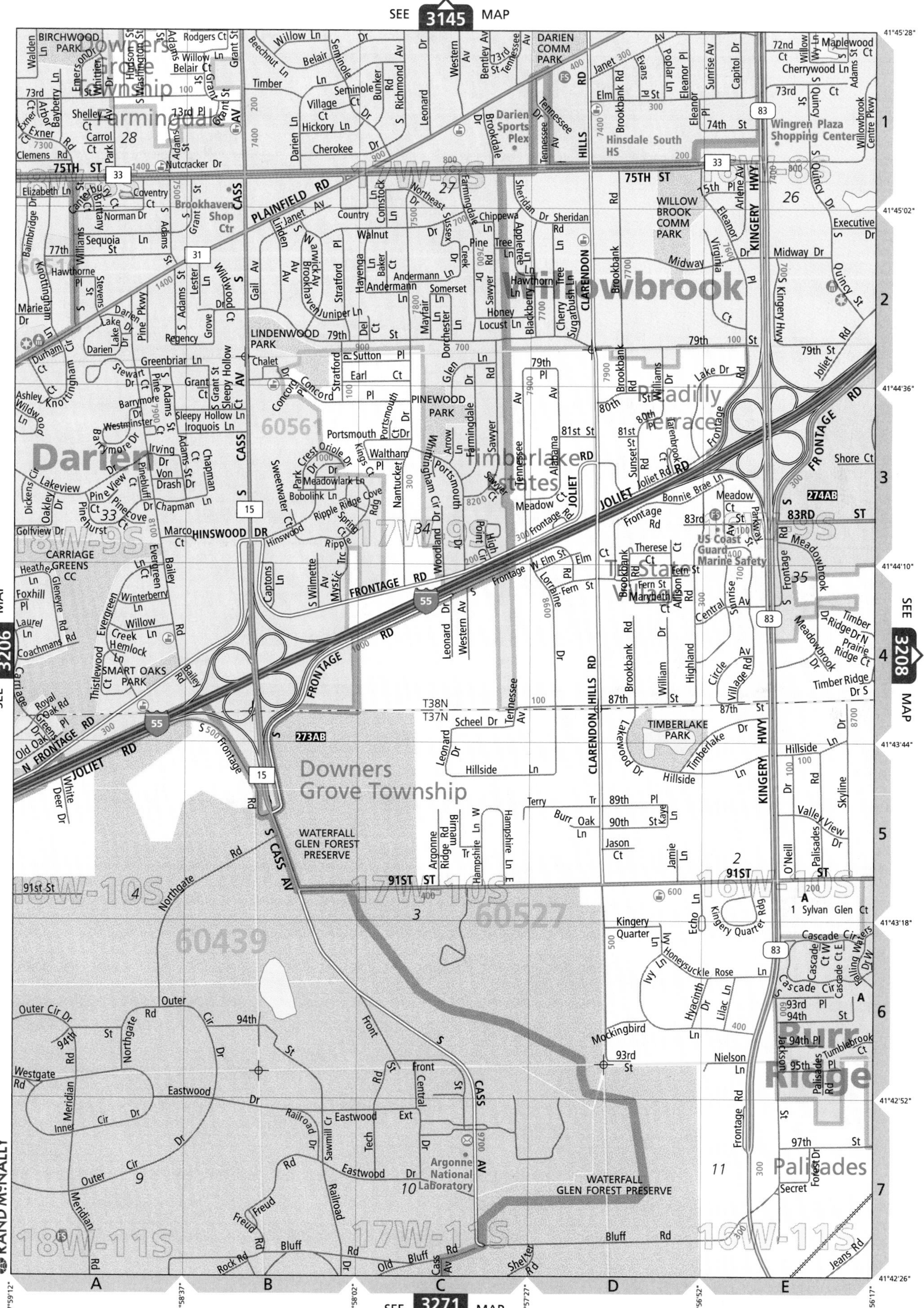

SEE 3206 MAP
SEE 3208 MAP
SEE 3271 MAP

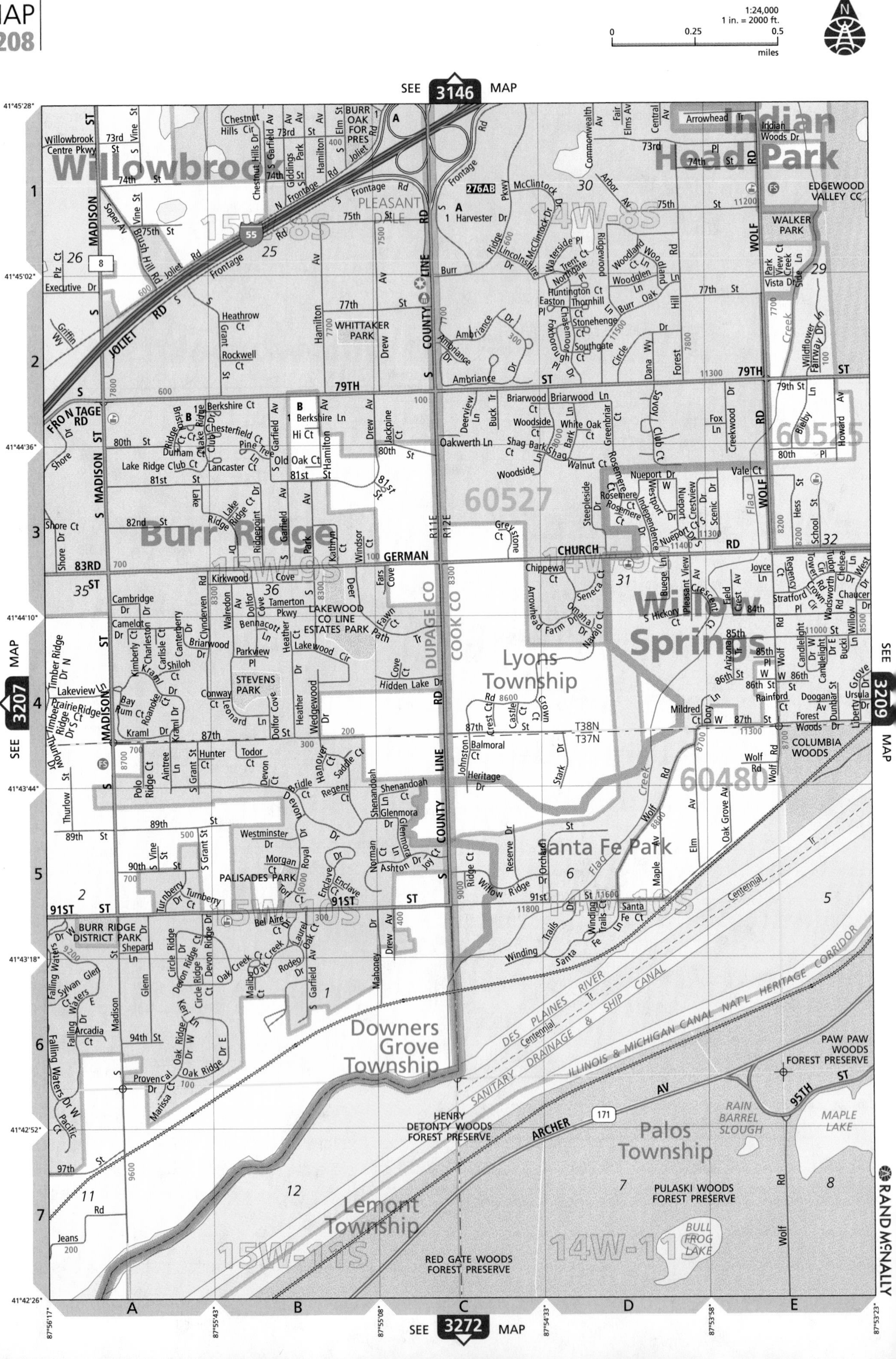

1:24,000
1 in. = 2000 ft.
0 0.25 0.5
miles

SEE 3146 MAP

SEE 3207 MAP

SEE 3209 MAP

Willowbrook
Indian Head Park
Burr Ridge
Willow Springs
Lyons Township
Downers Grove Township
Lemont Township
Palos Township
Santa Fe Park
PLEASANT DALE
WHITTAKER PARK
LAKEWOOD CO LINE ESTATES PARK
STEVENS PARK
PALISADES PARK
BURR RIDGE DISTRICT PARK
EDGEWOOD VALLEY CC
WALKER PARK
COLUMBIA WOODS
PAW PAW WOODS FOREST PRESERVE
HENRY DETONTY WOODS FOREST PRESERVE
PULASKI WOODS FOREST PRESERVE
RED GATE WOODS FOREST PRESERVE
BURR OAK FOR PRES
RAIN BARREL SLOUGH
MAPLE LAKE
BULL FROG LAKE
DES PLAINES RIVER
SANITARY DRAINAGE & SHIP CANAL
ILLINOIS & MICHIGAN CANAL NAT'L HERITAGE CORRIDOR
60527
60525
60480
15W-8S
14W-8S
15W-9S
14W-9S
15W-10S
14W-10S
15W-11S
14W-11S
T38N
T37N
R11E
R12E
DUPAGE CO
COOK CO

SEE 3272 MAP

1:24,000
1 in. = 2000 ft.
0 0.25 0.5
miles

SEE 3147 MAP

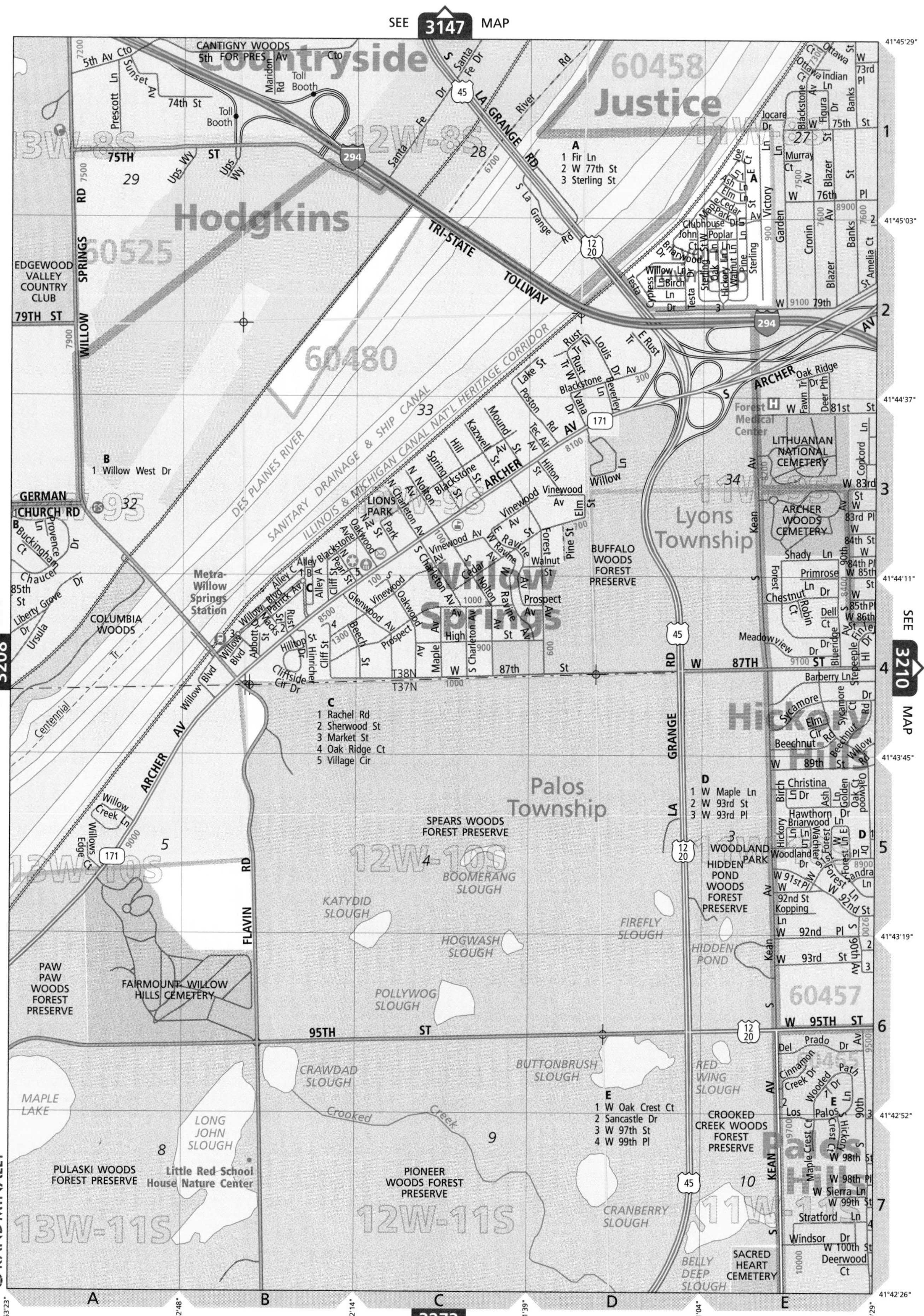

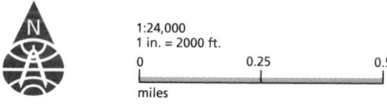

SEE 3208 MAP
SEE 3210 MAP
SEE 3273 MAP

1:24,000
1 in. = 2000 ft.
0 0.25 0.5
miles

SEE 3148 MAP

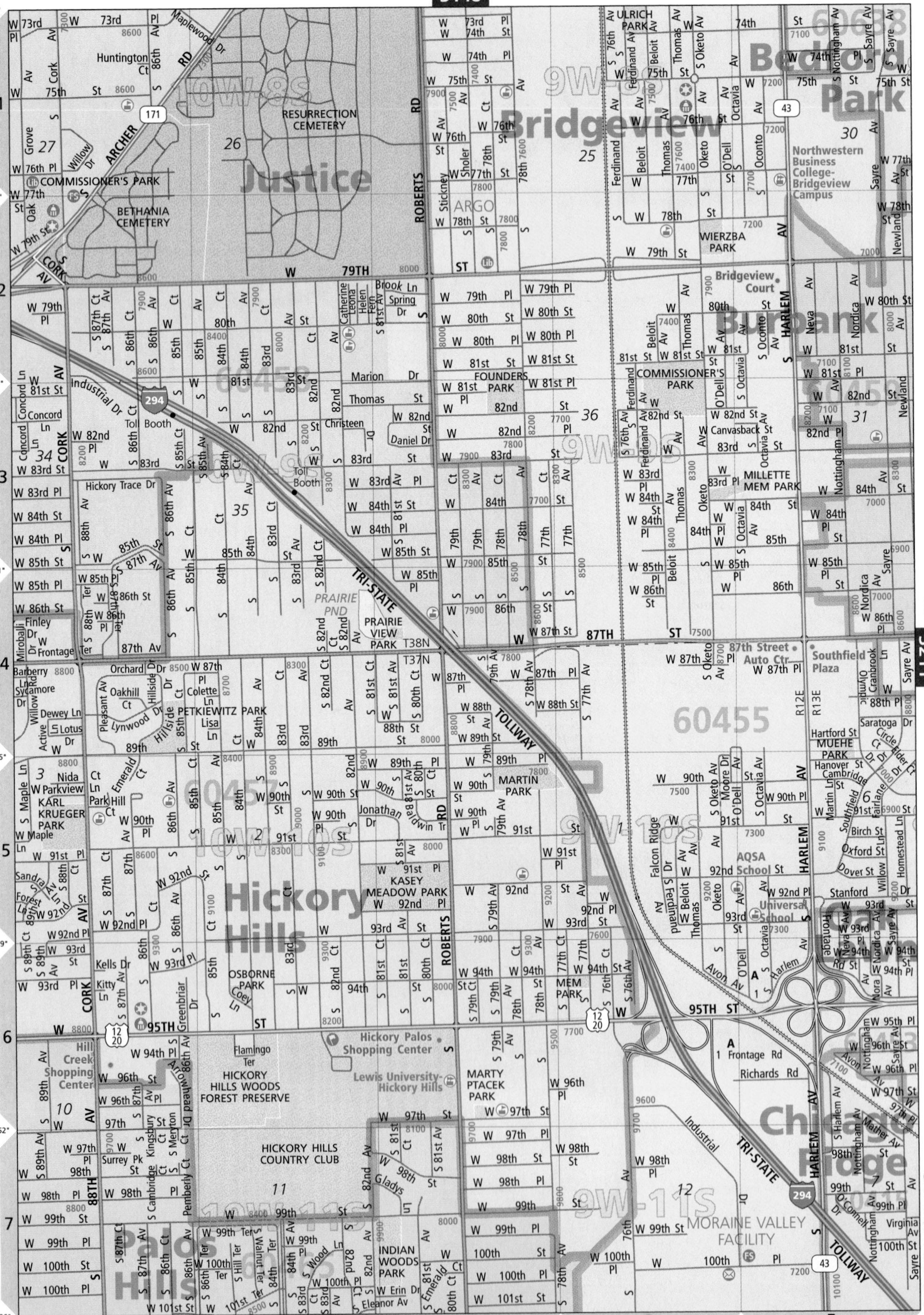

SEE 3209 MAP

SEE 3211 MAP

SEE 3274 MAP

1:24,000
1 in. = 2000 ft.
0 0.25 0.5
miles

SEE 3149 MAP

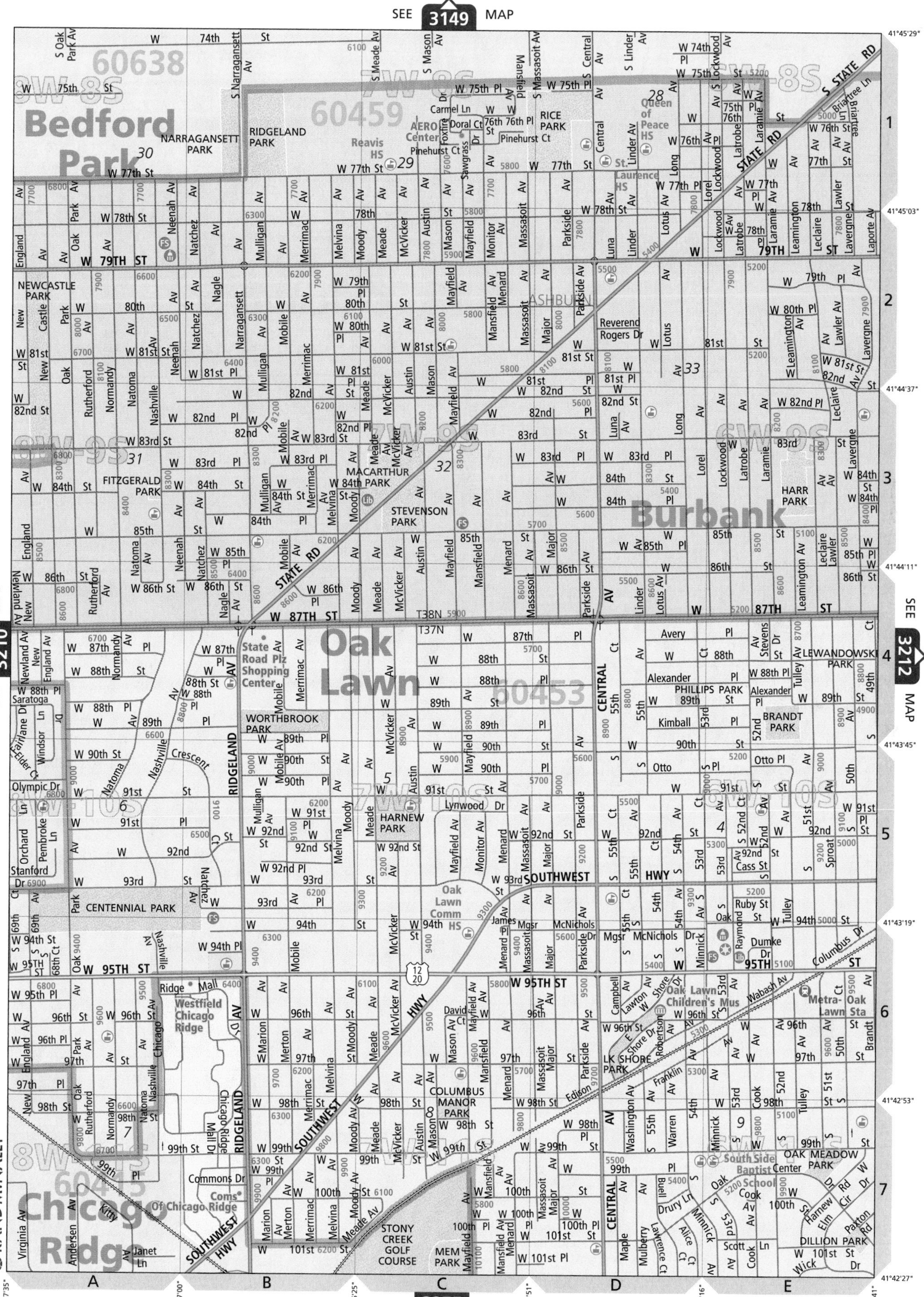

SEE 3210 MAP
SEE 3212 MAP
SEE 3275 MAP

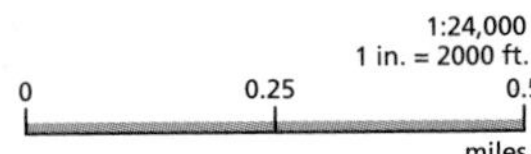

SEE 3150 MAP

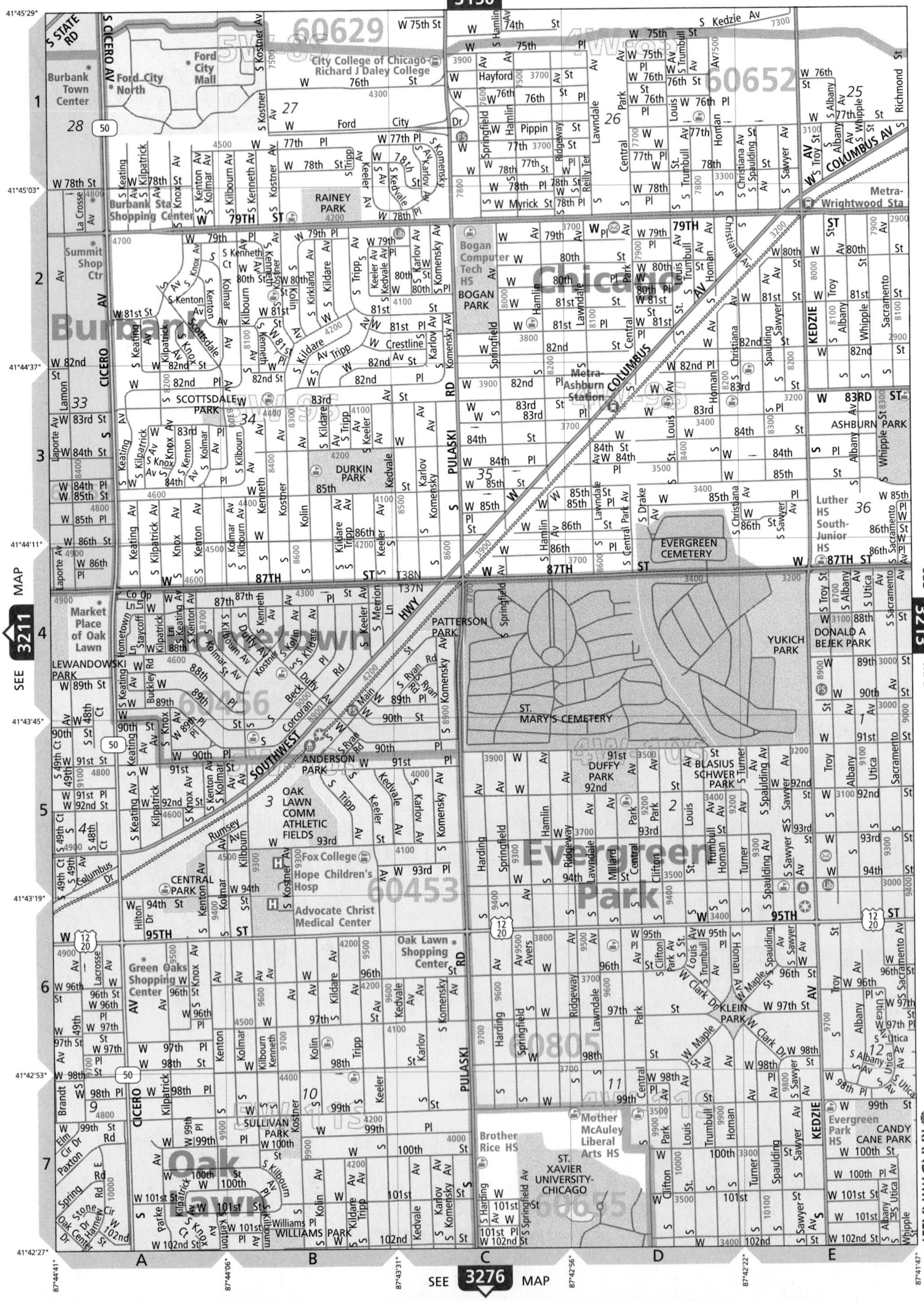

SEE 3211 MAP

SEE 3213 MAP

Burbank
Burbank Town Center
Ford City North
Ford City Mall
City College of Chicago-Richard J Daley College
Rainey Park
Burbank Sta Shopping Center
Summit Shop Ctr
Chicago
Bogan Computer Tech HS
Bogan Park
Metra-Ashburn Station
Metra-Wrightwood Sta
Ashburn Park
Scottsdale Park
Durkin Park
Luther HS South-Junior HS
Evergreen Cemetery
Hometown
Market Place of Oak Lawn
Lewandowski Park
Patterson Park
St. Mary's Cemetery
Yukich Park
Donald A Bejek Park
Anderson Park
Oak Lawn Comm Athletic Fields
Fox College
Hope Children's Hosp
Advocate Christ Medical Center
Central Park
Duffy Park
Blasius Schwer Park
Evergreen Park
Green Oaks Shopping Center
Oak Lawn Shopping Center
Klein Park
Sullivan Park
Williams Park
Oak Lawn
Brother Rice HS
Mother McAuley Liberal Arts HS
St. Xavier University-Chicago
Evergreen Park HS
Candy Cane Park

60629 60652 60456 60453 60805 60655

S Cicero Av · S Pulaski Rd · S Kedzie Av · W 79th St · W 87th St · W 95th St · Southwest Hwy · Columbus Av

T38N T37N

41°45'29" 41°45'03" 41°44'37" 41°44'11" 41°43'45" 41°43'19" 41°42'53" 41°42'27"

87°44'41" 87°44'06" 87°43'31" 87°42'56" 87°42'22" 87°41'47"

A B C D E

1 2 3 4 5 6 7

SEE 3276 MAP

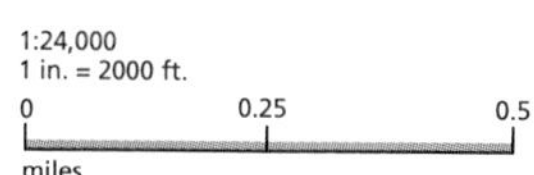

SEE 3151 MAP

W 75TH ST · W 76TH ST · W 77TH ST · W 78TH ST · W 79TH ST · W 80TH ST · W 81ST ST · W 82ND ST · W 83RD ST · W 84TH ST · W 85TH ST · W 86TH ST · W 87TH ST · W 88TH ST · W 89TH ST · W 90TH ST · W 91ST ST · W 92ND ST · W 93RD ST · W 94TH ST · W 95TH ST · W 96TH ST · W 97TH ST · W 98TH ST · W 99TH ST · W 100TH ST · W 101ST ST · W 102ND ST

S WESTERN AV · S DAMEN AV · S ASHLAND AV · S RACINE AV · S VINCENNES AV · BEVERLY AV · W COLUMBUS AV · S LONGWOOD DR · S PROSPECT AV · S CHARLES ST · S WINSTON AV · MALTA AV

60629 · 60652 · 60620 · 60805 · 60655 · 60643

ASHLAND AVENUE · HAWTHORNE PARK · St. Rita of Cascia HS · AUBURN PARK · DAWES PARK · Calumet Academy HS · O'HALLAREN PARK · FOSTER PARK · ASHBURN PARK · DAN RYAN WOODS FOREST PRESERVE · Chicago · MARSHFIELD PARK · BEVERLY COUNTRY CLUB · NORTHEAST PARK · Metra-Brainerd Station · PLEASANT PARKWAY PARK · MAGGIE COSME PARK · Metra-91st Street Sta · BRAINERD PARK · EVERGREEN COUNTRY CLUB · Little Co of Mary Hospital & Health Care Ctr · Fairway Plaza · Metra-95th Street Sta · Evergreen Park · The Plaza · Yards Plaza · RIDGE PARK · Chicago Intl Charter School-Longwood · Metra-95th Street Sta · OAKDALE PARK · Metra-99th Street Station · HURLEY PARK · BEVERLY PARK · GRAVER PARK

T38N · T37N · R13E · R14E

A
1 S Racine Av
2 W 101st Pl
3 W 102nd Pl

A · B · C · D · E
1 · 2 · 3 · 4 · 5 · 6 · 7

41°45'30" · 41°45'04" · 41°44'37" · 41°44'11" · 41°43'45" · 41°43'19" · 41°42'53" · 41°42'27"
87°41'47" · 87°41'12" · 87°40'37" · 87°40'02" · 87°39'27" · 87°38'53"

SEE 3212 MAP

SEE 3214 MAP

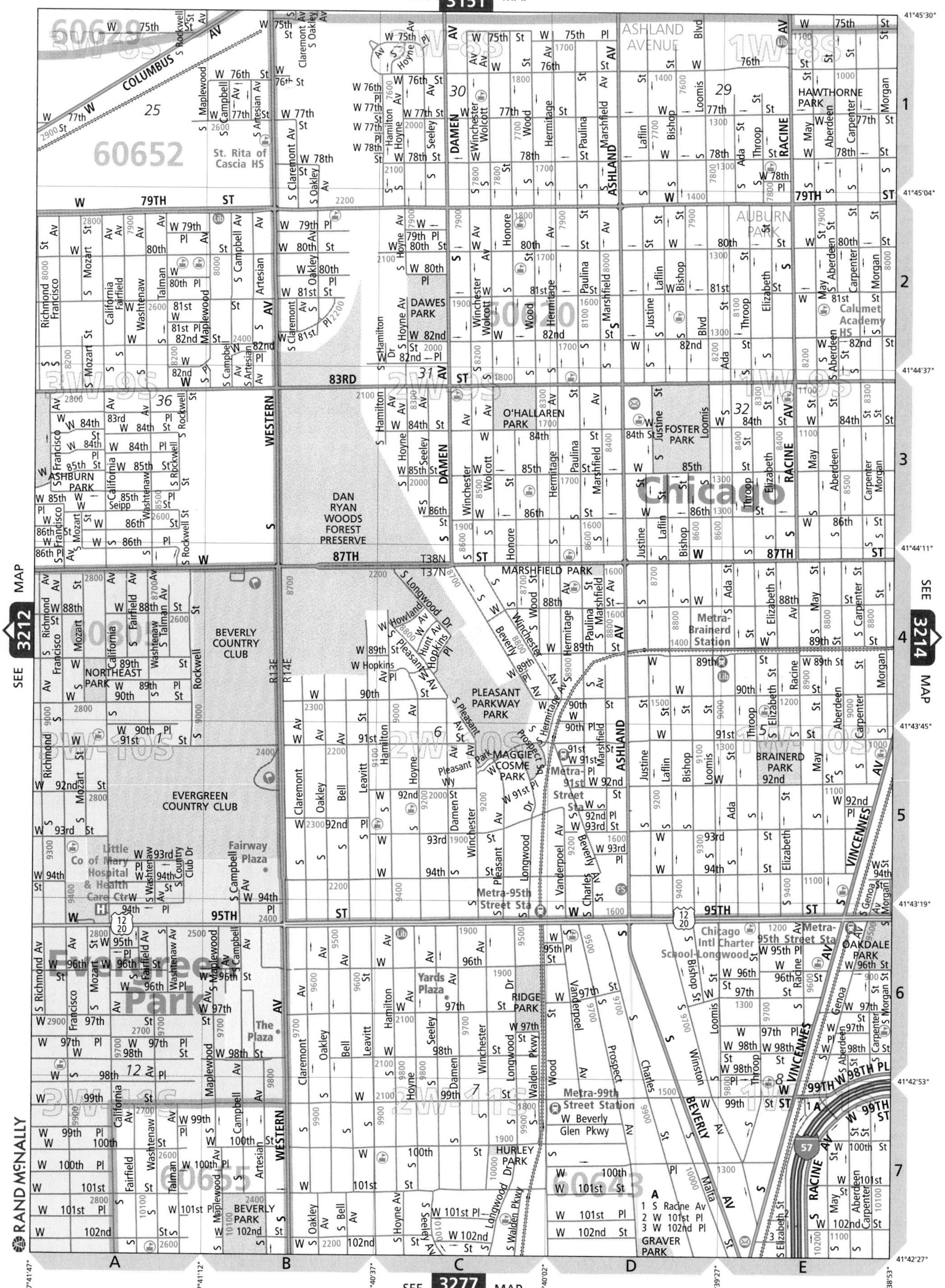

SEE 3277 MAP

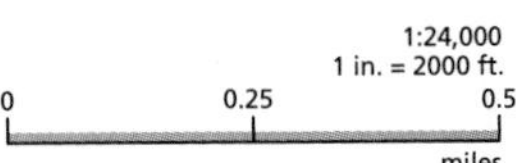

SEE 3152 MAP

SEE 3213 MAP

SEE 3215 MAP

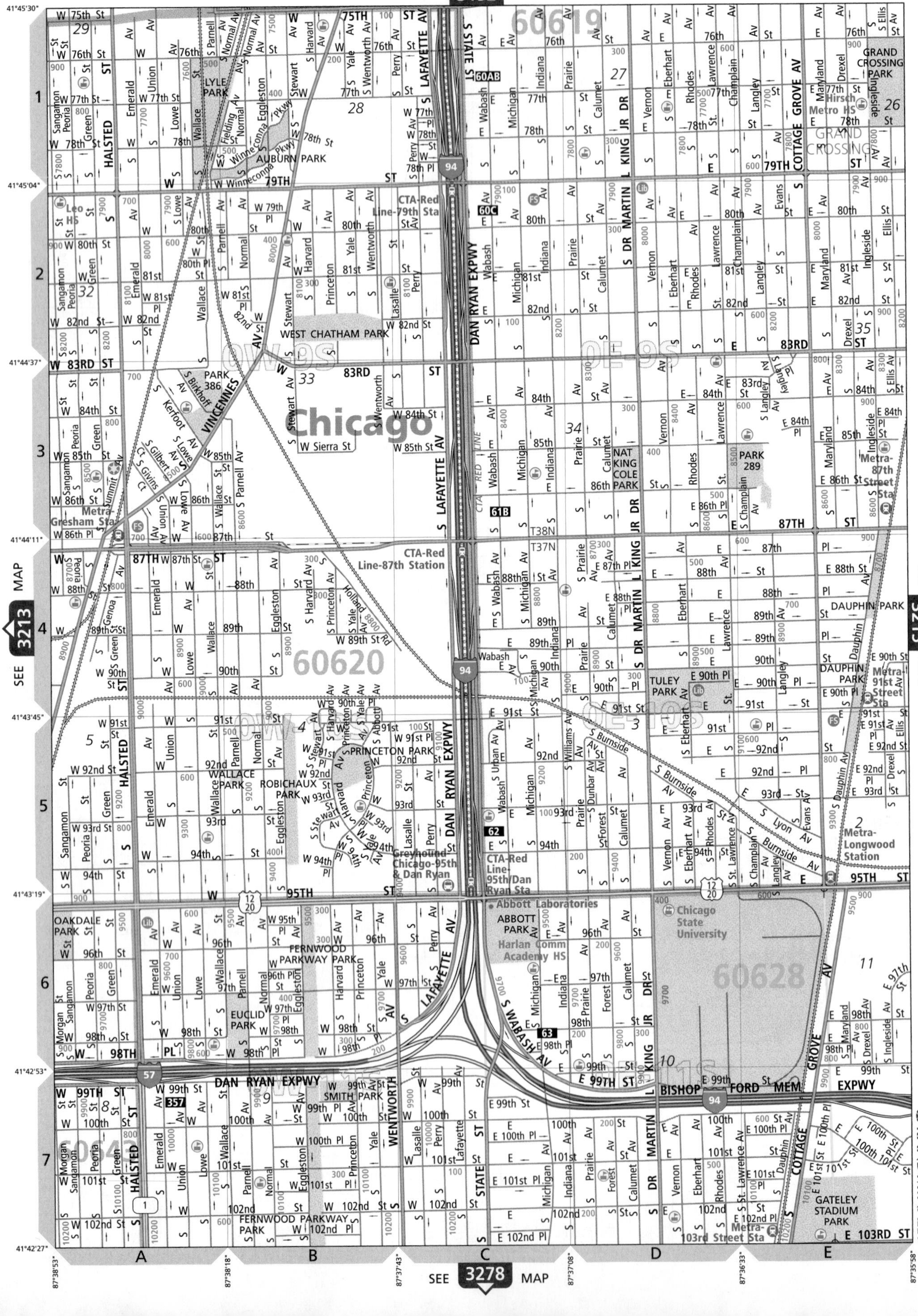

Chicago

60619
60620
60628
60643

DAN RYAN EXPWY
BISHOP FORD MEM EXPWY
HALSTED ST
VINCENNES AV
S STATE ST
S LAFAYETTE AV
S DR MARTIN L KING JR DR
COTTAGE GROVE AV
W 75TH ST
79TH ST
83RD ST
87TH ST
95TH ST
E 103RD ST

LYLE PARK
AUBURN PARK
WEST CHATHAM PARK
PARK 386
NAT KING COLE PARK
PARK 289
GRAND CROSSING PARK
GRAND CROSSING
Hirsch Metro HS
Leo HS
Metra-Gresham Sta
CTA-Red Line-79th Sta
CTA-Red Line-87th Station
DAUPHIN PARK
TULEY PARK
Metra-91st Street Sta
Metra-87th Street Sta
PRINCETON PARK
WALLACE PARK
ROBICHAUX PARK
Greyhound Chicago-95th & Dan Ryan
CTA-Red Line-95th/Dan Ryan Sta
Metra-Longwood Station
Abbott Laboratories
ABBOTT PARK
Harlan Comm Academy HS
Chicago State University
OAKDALE PARK
FERNWOOD PARKWAY PARK
EUCLID PARK
SMITH PARK
FERNWOOD PARKWAY PARK
Metra-103rd Street Sta
GATELEY STADIUM PARK

41°45'30"
41°45'04"
41°44'37"
41°44'11"
41°43'45"
41°43'19"
41°42'53"
41°42'27"
87°38'53"
87°38'18"
87°37'43"
87°37'08"
87°36'33"
87°35'58"

A B C D E
1 2 3 4 5 6 7

SEE 3278 MAP

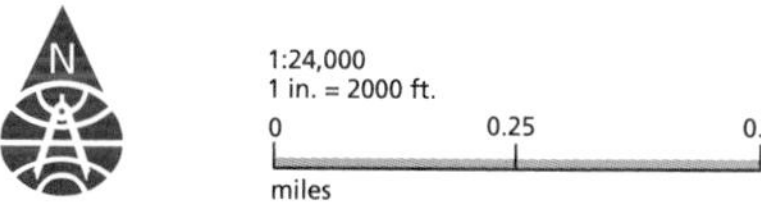

SEE 3153 MAP

SEE 3214 MAP

SEE 3216 MAP

SEE 3279 MAP

A
1 E Cheltenham Pl
2 S Commercial Av

Chicago

60619
60649
60617
60628

AVALON PARK
ADAMS PARK
ESSEX PARK
GRAND CROSSING PARK
ROSEMBLUM PARK
SOUTH SHORE
RAINBOW PARK & BCH
ECKERSALL PARK
Eckersall Stad
STONEY ISLAND PARK
BESSEMER PARK
BURNSIDE PARK
BURNSIDE
DOUGHERTY PARK
MERRILL PARK
BENSLEY PARK
VET PARK
TRUMBULL PARK

Jackson Pk Hosp & Med Ctr
School of Tech HS
HS of the Arts
New Regal Theatre
Metra-79th Street Station
Metra-83rd Street Station
Metra-Cheltenham Sta
Metra-83rd Street Sta
South Shore Hospital
Chicago Vocational Career Academy
Bowen HS
BEST Academy
Advocate Trinity Hospital
Olive Harvey College
Toll Booth

CHICAGO SKWY
ANTHONY AV
BISHOP FORD MEMORIAL EXPWY
S STONY ISLAND AV
STONY ISLAND EXT
JEFFERY BLVD
YATES BLVD
EXCHANGE AV
S SOUTH SHORE DR
COMMERCIAL AV
COLFAX AV
TORRENCE AV
S CONSTANCE AV
VAN VLISSINGEN RD
E 79TH ST
83RD ST
87TH ST
E 95TH ST
99TH
100TH ST
E 103RD ST

T38N
T37N
R14E
R15E

1E-9S
2E-9S
3E-9S
1E-10S
2E-10S
3E-10S
1E-11S
2E-11S
3E-11S

A B C D E
1 2 3 4 5 6 7

41°45'29"
41°45'03"
41°44'37"
41°44'11"
41°43'45"
41°43'19"
41°42'53"
41°42'27"

87°35'58"
87°35'24"
87°34'49"
87°34'14"
87°33'39"
87°33'04"

1:24,000
1 in. = 2000 ft.
0 0.25 0.5
miles

SEE B MAP

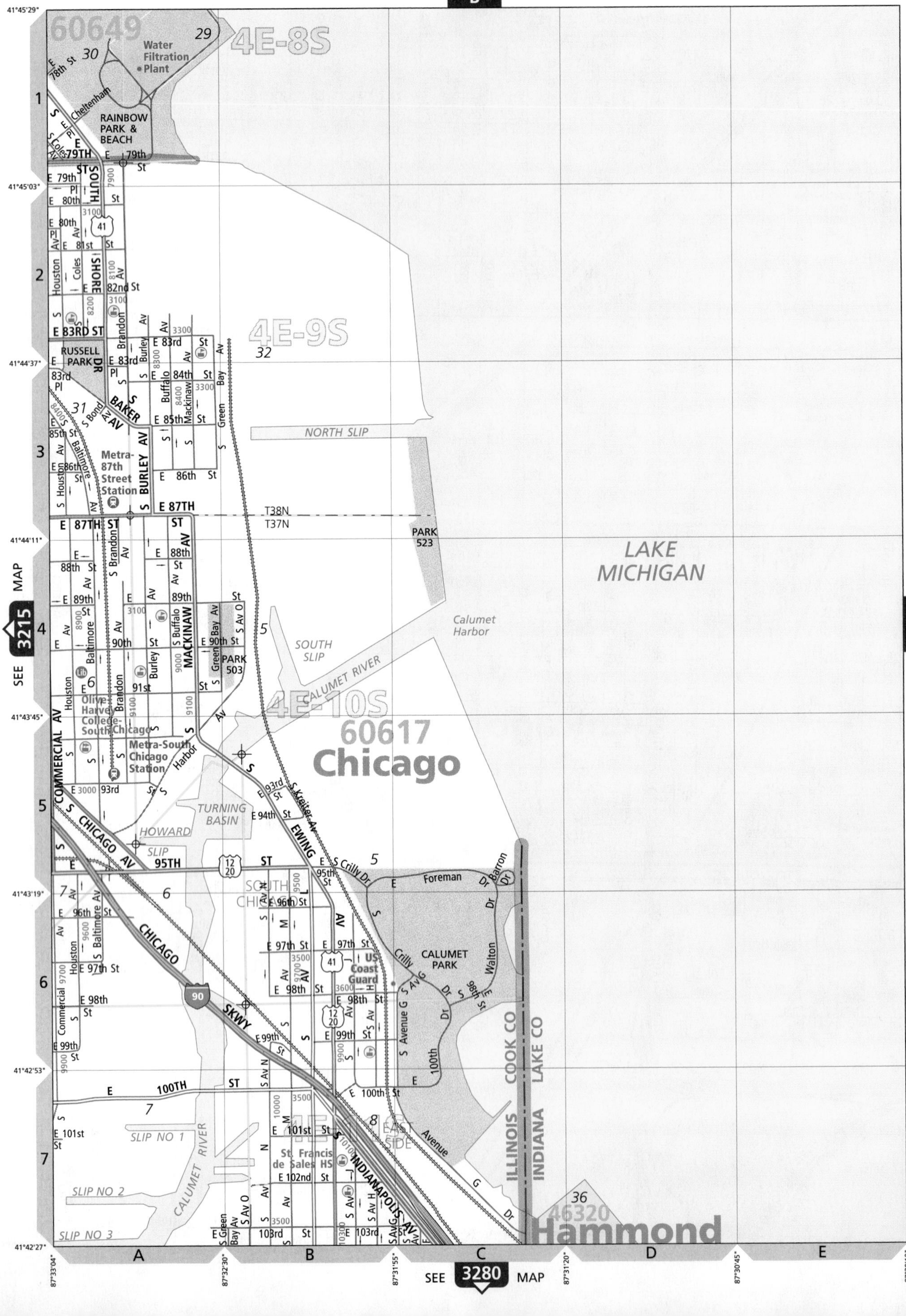

60649
4E-8S
Water Filtration Plant
RAINBOW PARK & BEACH
E 79TH ST
SOUTH SHORE DR
E 83RD ST
RUSSELL PARK
4E-9S
NORTH SLIP
S BAKER AV
S BURLEY AV
Metra-87th Street Station
E 87TH ST
T38N
T37N
PARK 523
LAKE MICHIGAN
Calumet Harbor
SOUTH SLIP
S MACKINAW AV
PARK 503
CALUMET RIVER
4E-10S
60617
Chicago
Olive-Harvey College-South Chicago
Metra-South Chicago Station
COMMERCIAL AV
S CHICAGO AV
TURNING BASIN
HOWARD SLIP
S EWING AV
E 95TH ST
SOUTH CHICAGO
CALUMET PARK
US Coast Guard
CHICAGO SKWY
E 100TH ST
SLIP NO 1
SLIP NO 2
SLIP NO 3
CALUMET RIVER
St Francis de Sales HS
EAST SIDE
S INDIANAPOLIS AV
COOK CO
LAKE CO
ILLINOIS
INDIANA
46320
Hammond

SEE 3215 MAP

SEE B MAP

A B C D E

SEE 3280 MAP

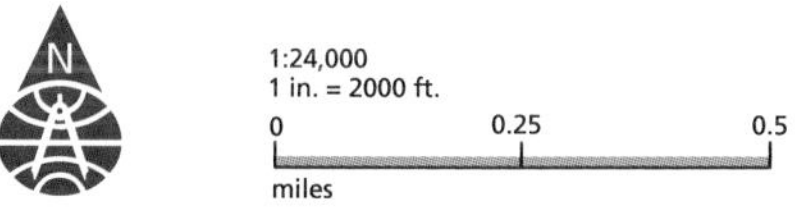

SEE B MAP

E SANDWICH RD
51W-11S
12
50W-11S
Smith Rd
7
Tyler Rd
49W-11S
8
Creek Rd
Little Rock Creek
Coy Rd
Miller Rd
Cook Rd
60545
51W-12S
13
50W-12S
18
49W-12S
17
Sandwich Township
R6E R5E
Little Rock Township
Wagner Rd
Sedgewick Rd
Sedgewick Rd
KENDALL CO
DEKALB CO
Huntsman Trails
51W-13S
24
50W-13S
19
49W-13S
20
Frazier Rd
Pratt Rd
60548
William Ln
Sandra Ct
Frazier Ct
Woodland Dr
Laurie Rd
Laurie Rd
Whitetail Ln
Deer
LATHAM ST
Sandhurst
Run
Bender St
E Knights Rd
E Pleasant Av
JAMES KNIGHT PARK
Anthony Ln
Bauer Ct
Daniel Ln
PATRIOT'S PARK
Red Fox Cir
Kramer
Reimann
Sandwich
Sandy Bluff Rd
30
29
25
E Arnold St
Elm St
Roberts Rd
Lillian Ln
E McQuown St
E Taylor St
Duvick Av
51W-14S
50W-14S
49W-14S
34

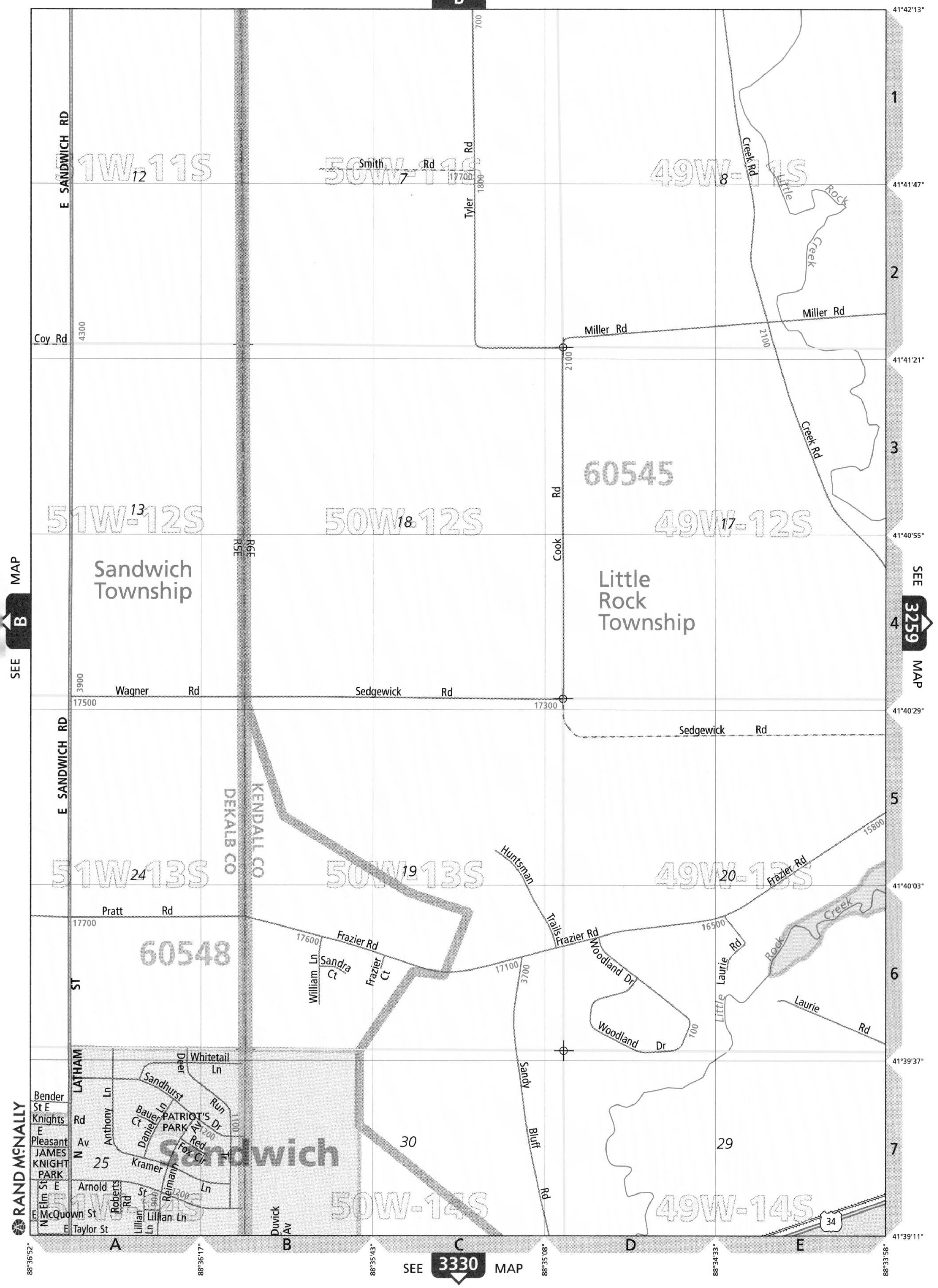

SEE 3259 MAP

SEE 3330 MAP

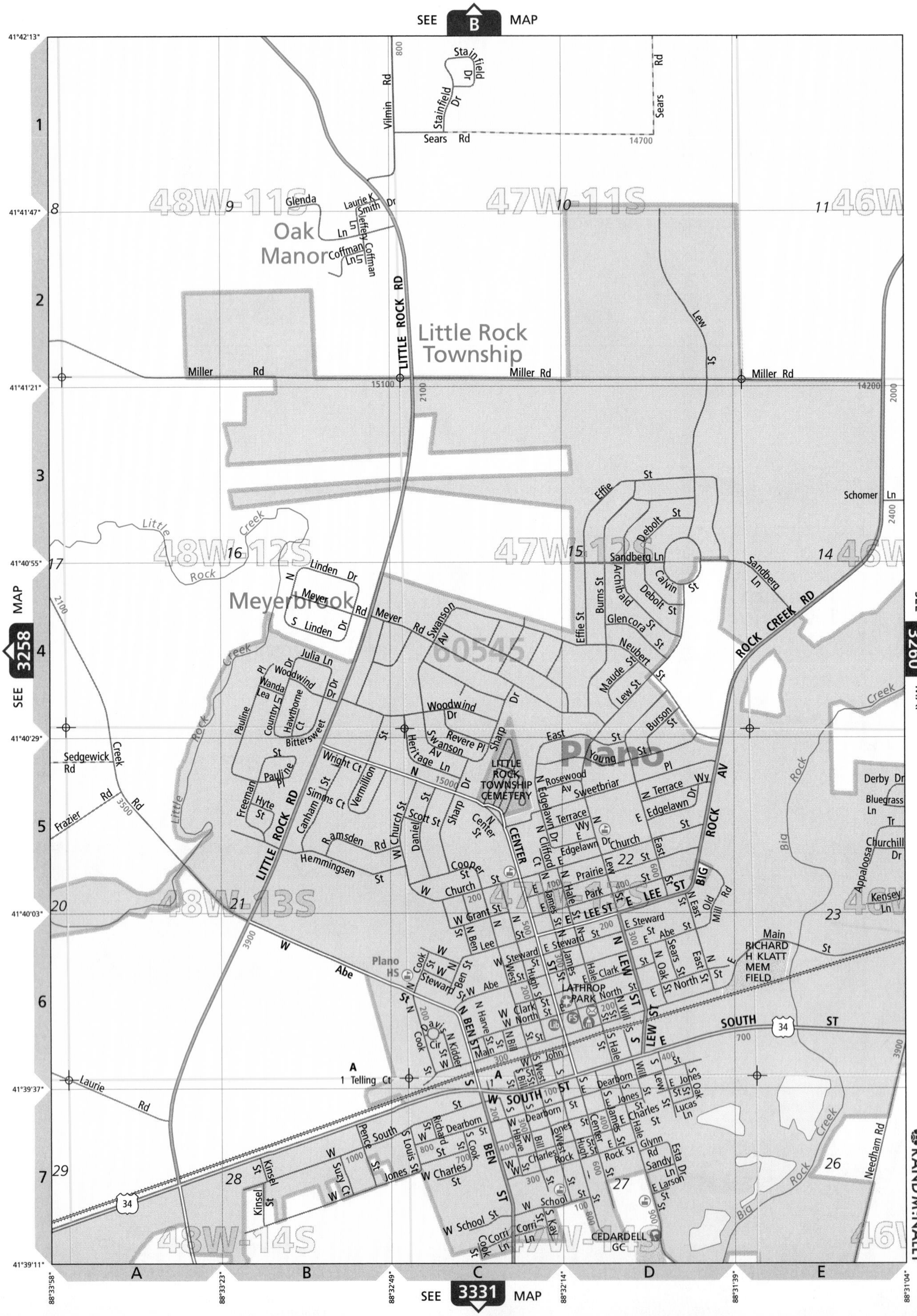

1:24,000
1 in. = 2000 ft.
0 0.25 0.5
miles

SEE B MAP

SEE 3258 MAP

SEE 3260 MAP

SEE 3331 MAP

RAND McNALLY

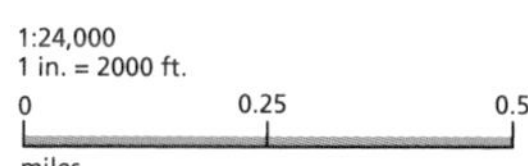

SEE 3196 MAP

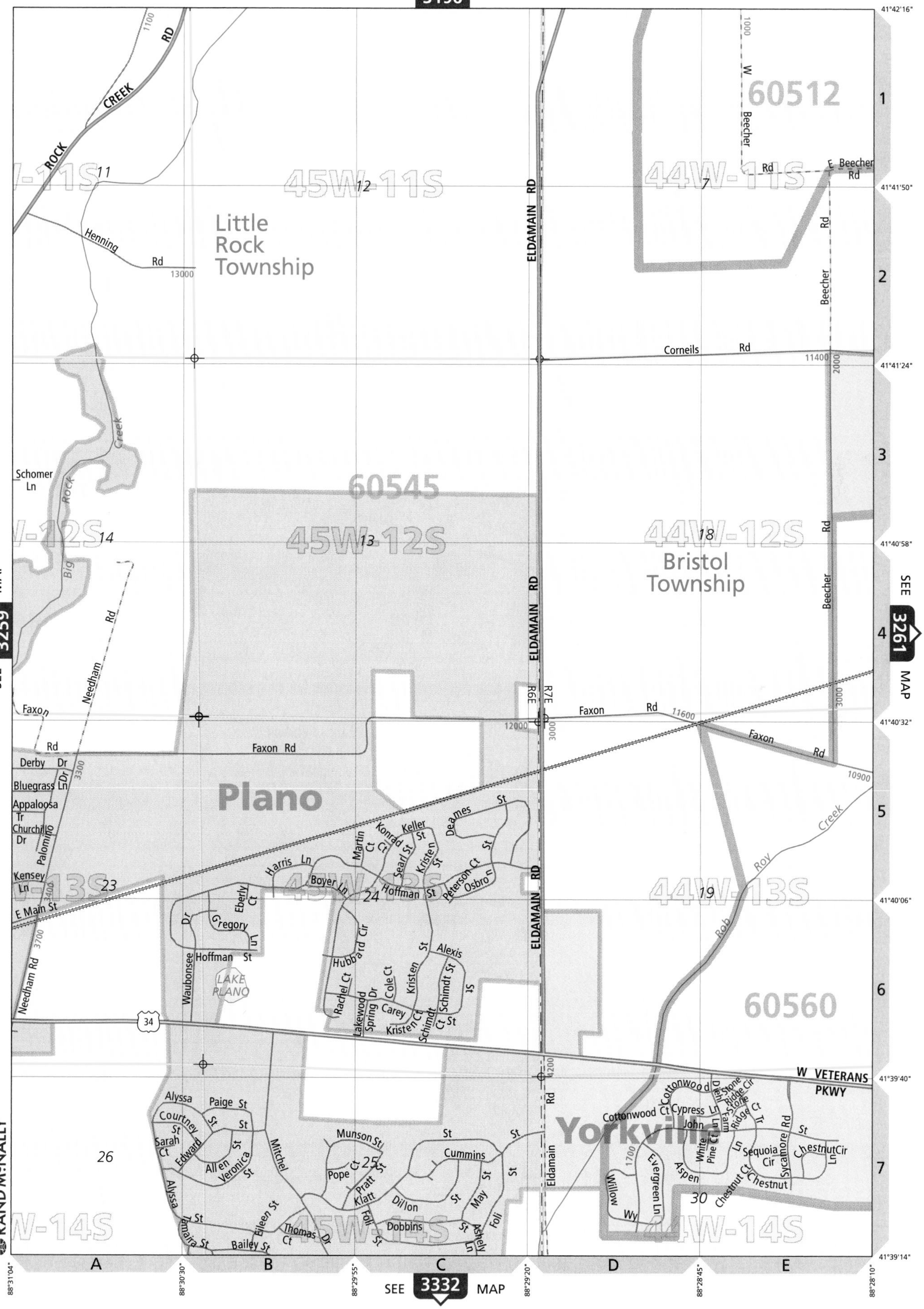

SEE 3259 MAP

SEE 3261 MAP

SEE 3332 MAP

1:24,000
1 in. = 2000 ft.
0 0.25 0.5
miles

SEE 3197 MAP

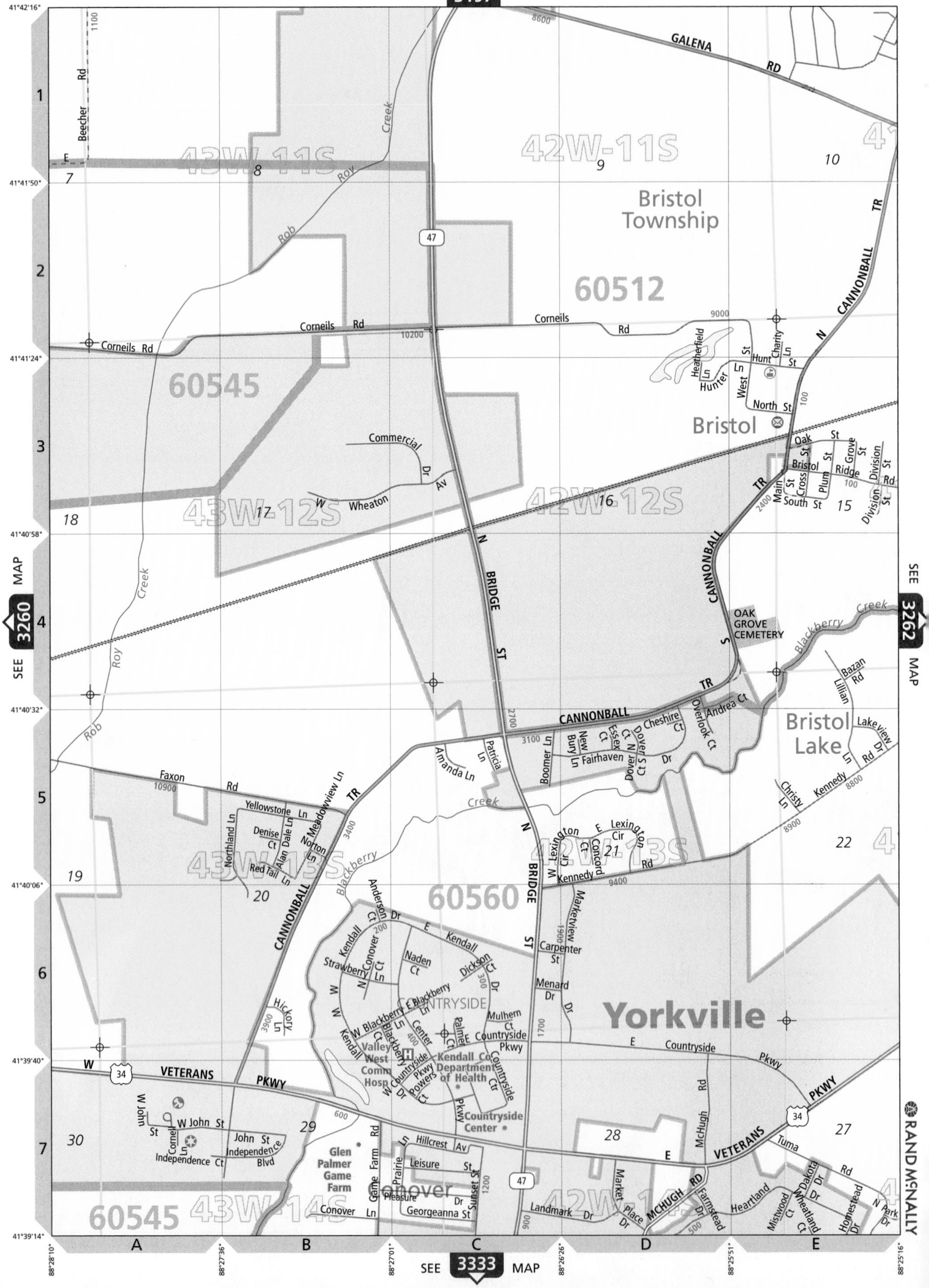

SEE 3260 MAP

SEE 3262 MAP

SEE 3333 MAP

Bristol Township
Bristol
Bristol Lake
Yorkville
60512
60545
60560
42W-11S
43W-11S
42W-12S
43W-12S
42W-13S
43W-13S
42W-14S
43W-14S

GALENA RD
Corneils Rd
Beecher Rd
Rob Roy Creek
Blackberry Creek
Commercial Dr
W Wheaton Av
N BRIDGE ST
N CANNONBALL TR
S CANNONBALL TR
CANNONBALL TR
Faxon Rd
W VETERANS PKWY
E VETERANS PKWY
E Countryside Pkwy
McHugh Rd
Heatherfield Ln
Hunter Ln
Hunt St
Charity Ln
West St
North St
Oak St
Bristol St
Grove St
Division St
Ridge Rd
Main St
Cross St
Plum St
South St
OAK GROVE CEMETERY
Bazan Rd
Lillian Ln
Lakeview Dr
Kennedy Rd
Christy Ln
Andrea Ct
Overlook Ct
Cheshire Ct
Dover Ct N
Dover Ct S
Essex Ct
Concord Ct
New Bury Ln
Fairhaven Dr
Boomer Ln
Patricia Ln
Amanda Ln
W Lexington Cir
E Lexington Cir
Kennedy Rd
Marketview Dr
Carpenter St
Menard Dr
Yellowstone Ln
Meadowview Ln
Northland Ln
Denise Ct
Alan Dale Ln
Norton Ln
Red Tail Ln
Anderson Ct
Anderson Dr
E Kendall Dr
W Kendall Dr
Conover Ct
Naden Ct
Dickson Ct
Strawberry Ln
N Conover Ln
E Blackberry Ln
W Blackberry Ln
Center Pkwy
Palmer Ct
Mulhern Ct
E Countryside Pkwy
W Countryside Pkwy
Countryside Ctr
Powers Ct
Blackberry Dr
COUNTRYSIDE
Hickory Ln
Valley West Comm Hosp
Kendall Co Department of Health
Countryside Center
W John St
John St
Cornell Ln
Independence Ct
Independence Blvd
Glen Palmer Game Farm
Game Farm Rd
Prairie Ln
Hillcrest Av
Leisure St
Pleasure Dr
Sunset St
Conover Ln
Georgeanna St
Landmark Dr
Market Place Dr
MCHUGH RD
Farmstead Dr
Heartland Dr
Mistwood Ct
Wheatland Ct
Dakota Dr
Tuma Rd
Homestead Dr
N Park Dr
Conover

1 2 3 4 5 6 7
A B C D E
7 8 9 10 15 16 17 18 19 20 21 22 27 28 29 30

41°42'16" 41°41'50" 41°41'24" 41°40'58" 41°40'32" 41°40'06" 41°39'40" 41°39'14"
88°28'10" 88°27'36" 88°27'01" 88°26'26" 88°25'51" 88°25'16"

1:24,000
1 in. = 2000 ft.
0 0.25 0.5
miles

SEE 3198 MAP

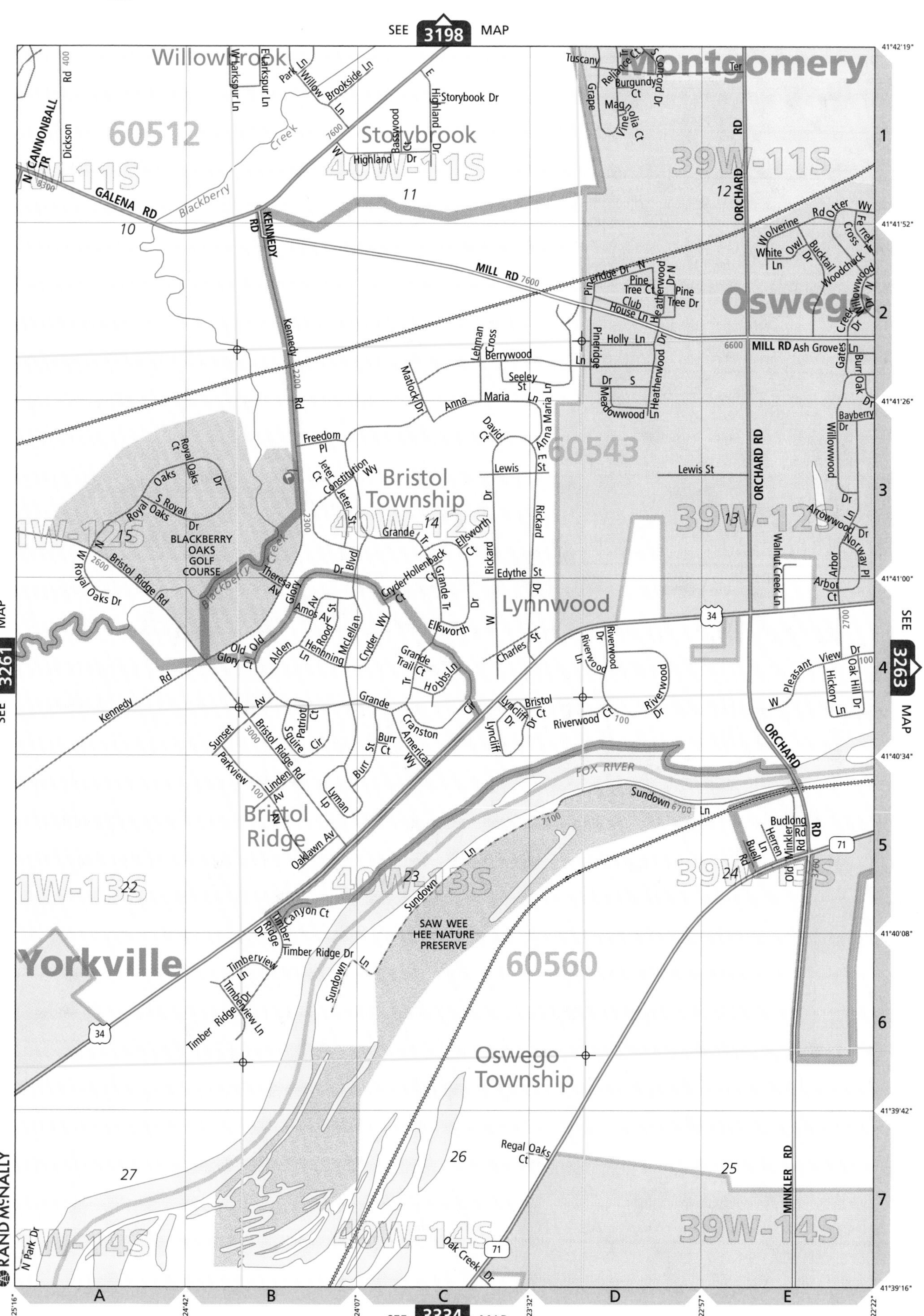

SEE 3261 MAP
SEE 3263 MAP
SEE 3334 MAP

RAND McNALLY

1:24,000
1 in. = 2000 ft.
0 0.25 0.5
miles

SEE 3199 MAP

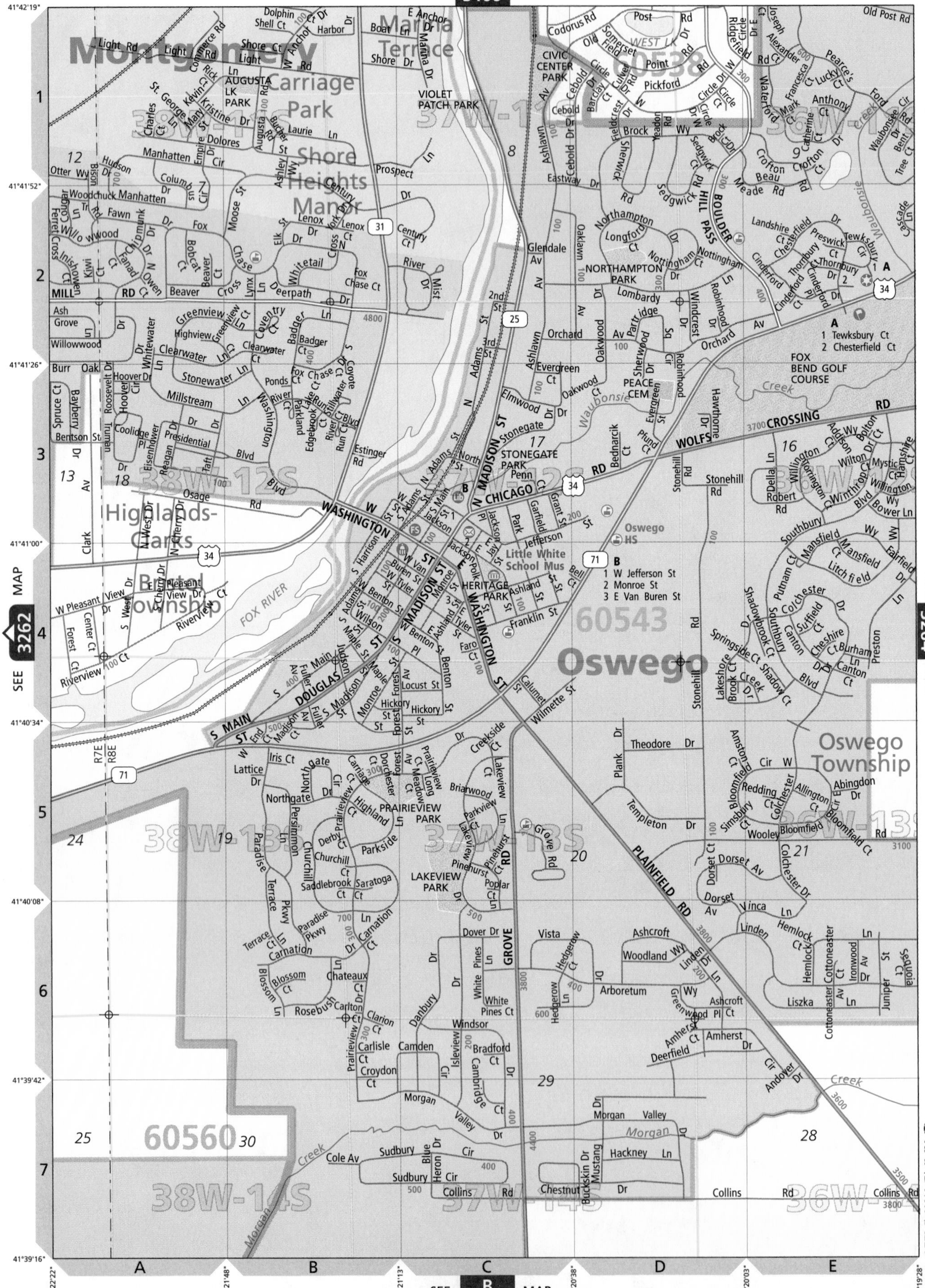

Montgomery

Oswego

Oswego Township

Bristol Township

Highlands-Oaks

Carriage Park

Shore Heights Manor

Marina Terrace

A
1 Tewksbury Ct
2 Chesterfield Ct

B
1 W Jefferson St
2 Monroe St
3 E Van Buren St

SEE 3262 MAP

SEE 3264 MAP

SEE B MAP

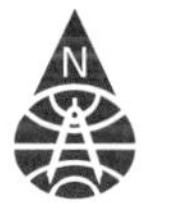

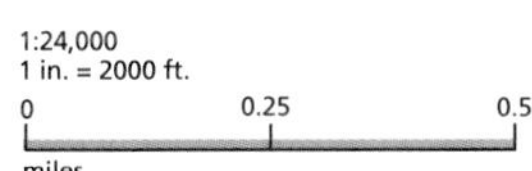

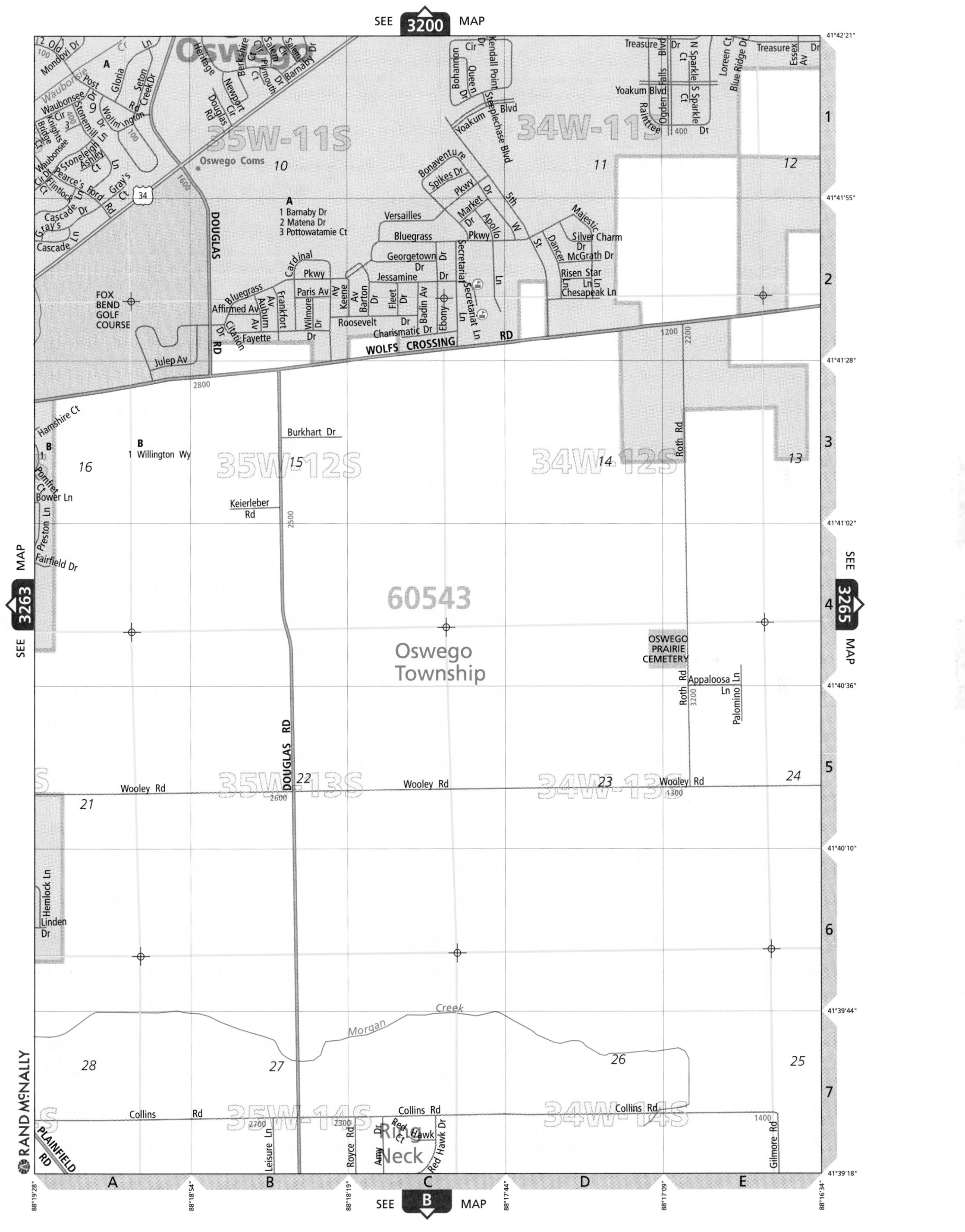

1:24,000
1 in. = 2000 ft.
0 0.25 0.5
miles
SEE 3200 MAP
SEE MAP 3263
SEE 3265 MAP
SEE B MAP
Oswego
35W-11S
34W-11S
35W-12S
34W-12S
35W-13S
34W-13S
35W-14S
34W-14S
60543
Oswego Township
Oswego Coms
FOX BEND GOLF COURSE
OSWEGO PRAIRIE CEMETERY
Ring Neck
A
1 Barnaby Dr
2 Matena Dr
3 Pottowatamie Ct
B
1 Willington Wy
DOUGLAS RD
WOLFS CROSSING RD
PLAINFIELD RD
Wooley Rd
Collins Rd
Roth Rd
Gilmore Rd
Morgan Creek
Treasure Dr
Yoakum Blvd
Steeplechase Blvd
5th St
Bluegrass
Versailles
Georgetown Dr
Jessamine Dr
Cardinal Pkwy
Roosevelt Dr
Charismatic Dr
Secretariat Ln
Burkhart Dr
Keierleber Rd
Hamshire Ct
Bower Ln
Preston Ln
Fairfield Dr
Hemlock Ln
Linden Dr
Appaloosa Ln
Palomino Ln
Leisure Ln
Royce Rd
Amy Dr
Red Hawk Dr
Julep Av
Fayette Dr
Majestic
Silver Charm Dr
McGrath Dr
Risen Star Ln
Chesapeake Ln
A B C D E
1 2 3 4 5 6 7

1:24,000
1 in. = 2000 ft.
0 0.25 0.5 miles

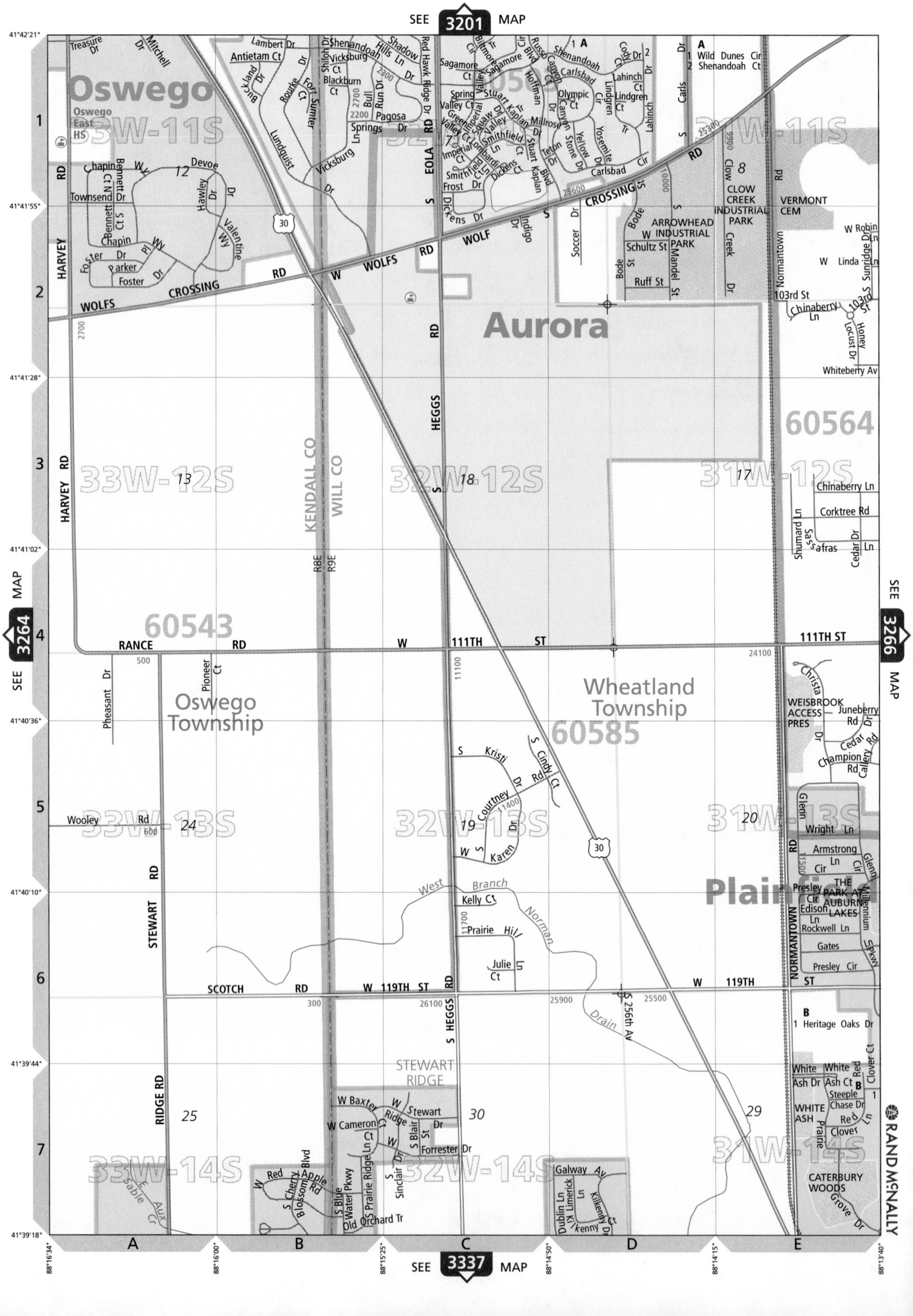

SEE 3201 MAP

SEE 3264 MAP

SEE 3266 MAP

SEE 3337 MAP

1:24,000
1 in. = 2000 ft.
0 0.25 0.5
miles

SEE 3202 MAP

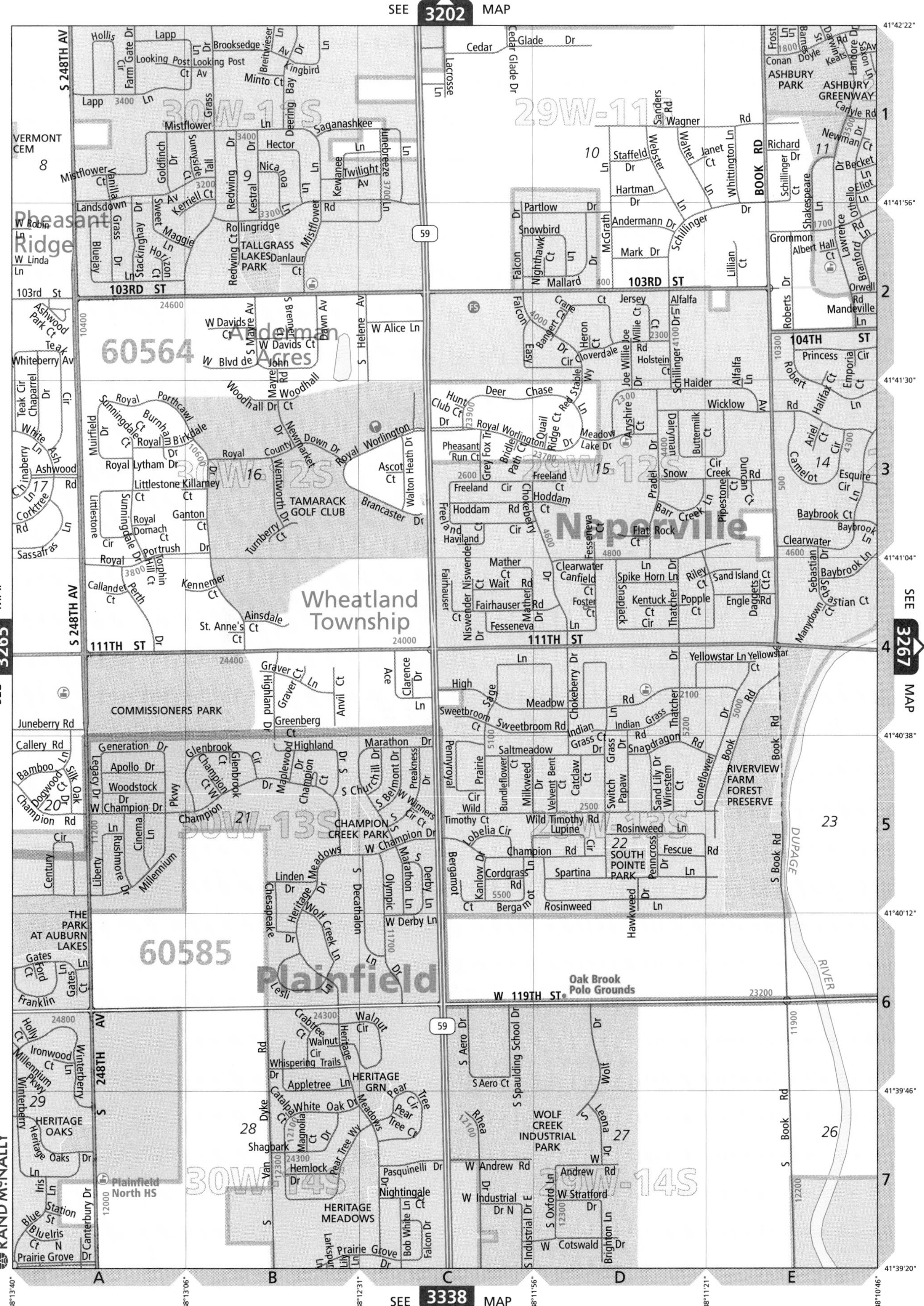

SEE 3265 MAP
SEE 3267 MAP
SEE 3338 MAP

1:24,000
1 in. = 2000 ft.
0 0.25 0.5
miles

SEE 3203 MAP

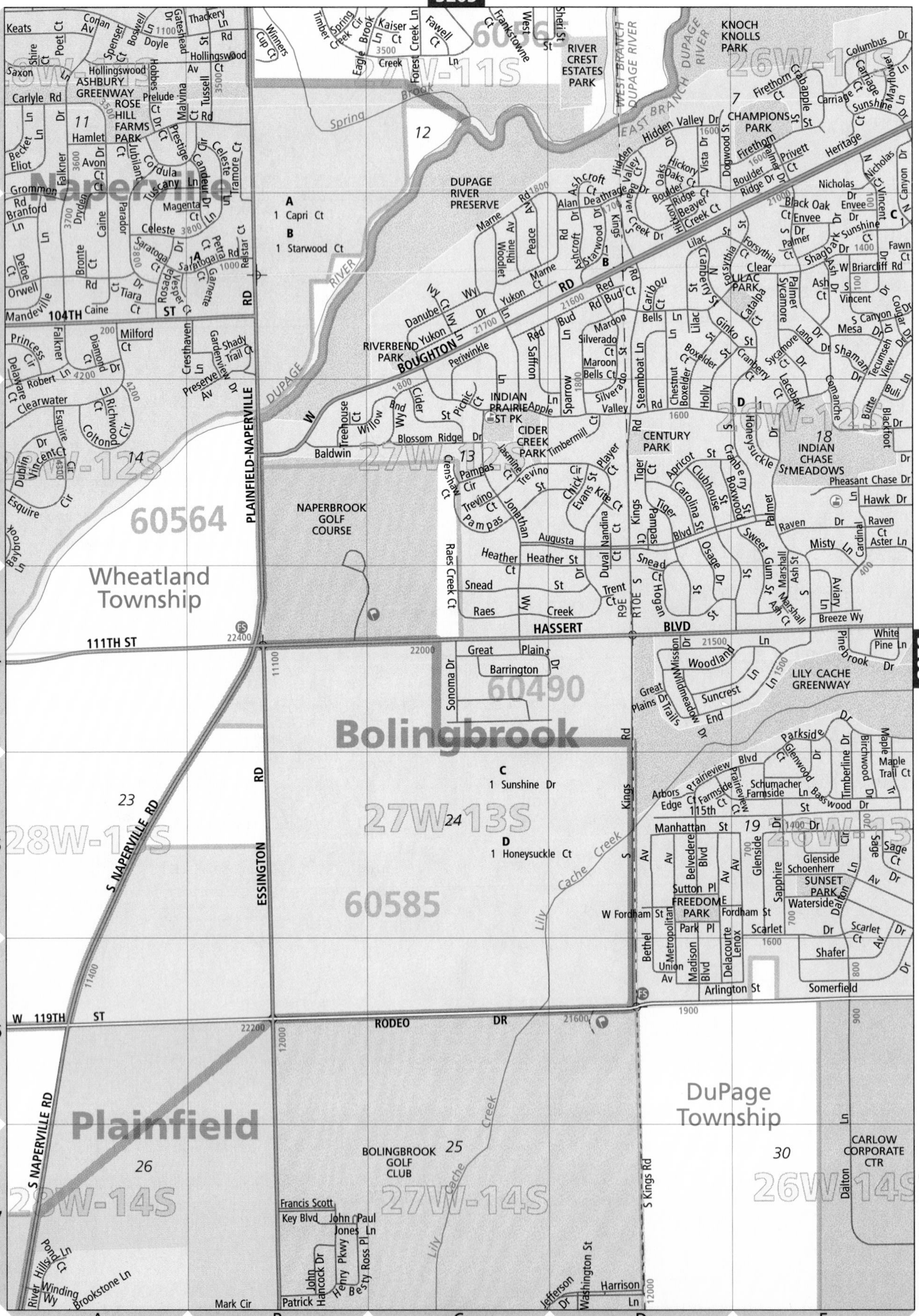

SEE 3266 MAP

SEE 3268 MAP

SEE 3339 MAP

A 1 Capri Ct
B 1 Starwood Ct
C 1 Sunshine Dr
D 1 Honeysuckle Ct

Naperville

Wheatland Township

Bolingbrook

Plainfield

DuPage Township

60564

60565

60490

60585

28W-12S

28W-13S

28W-14S

27W-11S

27W-12S

27W-13S

27W-14S

26W-11S

26W-12S

26W-13S

26W-14S

ASHBURY GREENWAY

ROSE HILL FARMS PARK

DUPAGE RIVER PRESERVE

RIVER CREST ESTATES PARK

KNOCH KNOLLS PARK

CHAMPIONS PARK

RIVERBEND PARK

INDIAN PRAIRIE ST PK

CIDER CREEK PARK

CENTURY PARK

LILAC PARK

INDIAN CHASE MEADOWS

NAPERBROOK GOLF COURSE

LILY CACHE GREENWAY

SUNSET PARK

FREEDOM PARK

BOLINGBROOK GOLF CLUB

CARLOW CORPORATE CTR

W BOUGHTON RD

PLAINFIELD-NAPERVILLE RD

111TH ST

HASSERT BLVD

104TH ST

ESSINGTON RD

S NAPERVILLE RD

W 119TH ST

RODEO DR

S Kings Rd

DUPAGE RIVER

WEST BRANCH DUPAGE RIVER

EAST BRANCH DUPAGE RIVER

Spring Brook

Lily Cache Creek

1:24,000
1 in. = 2000 ft.
0 0.25 0.5
miles

SEE 3204 MAP

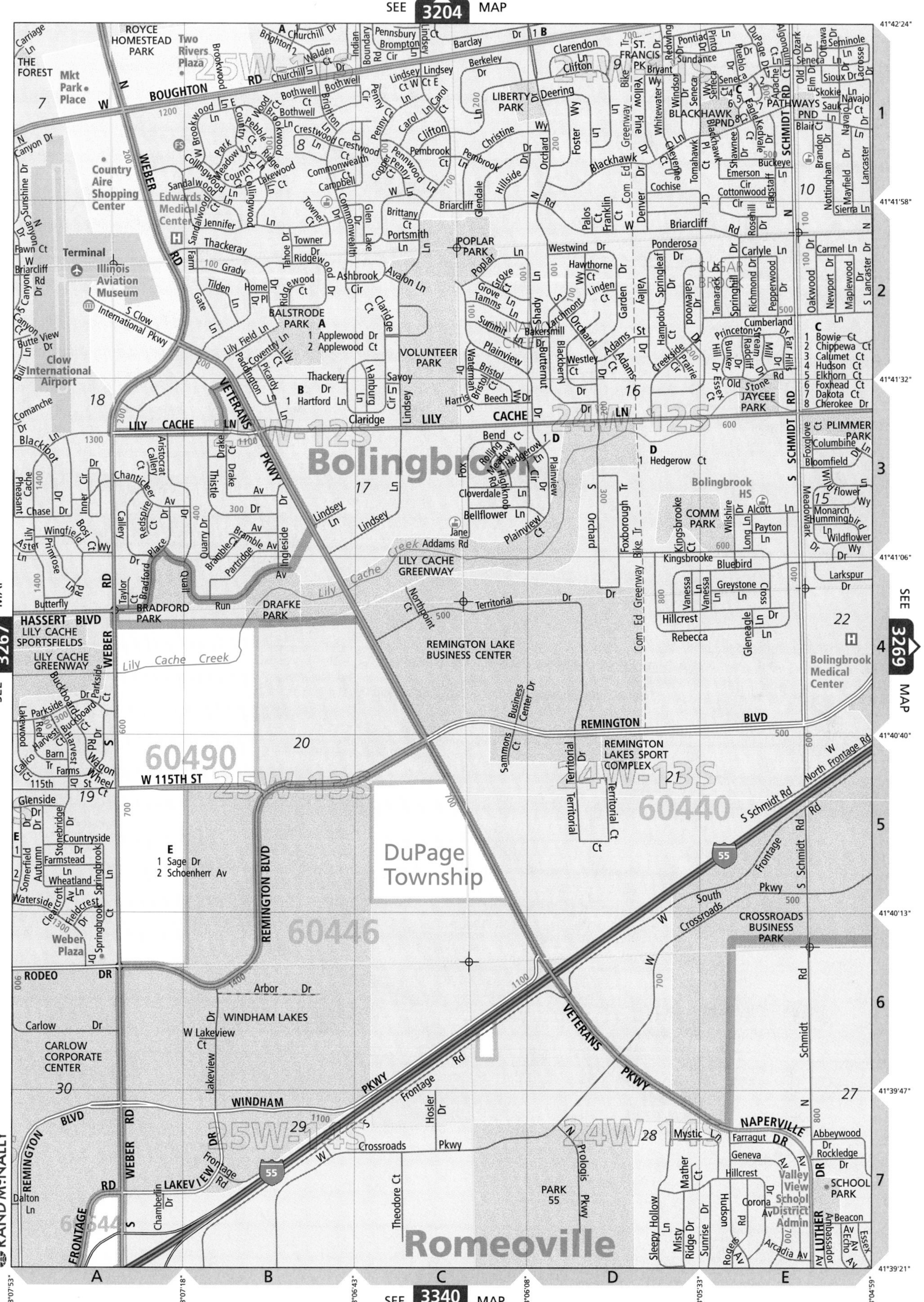

SEE 3267 MAP
SEE 3269 MAP
SEE 3340 MAP

1:24,000
1 in. = 2000 ft.
0 0.25 0.5
miles

SEE 3205 MAP

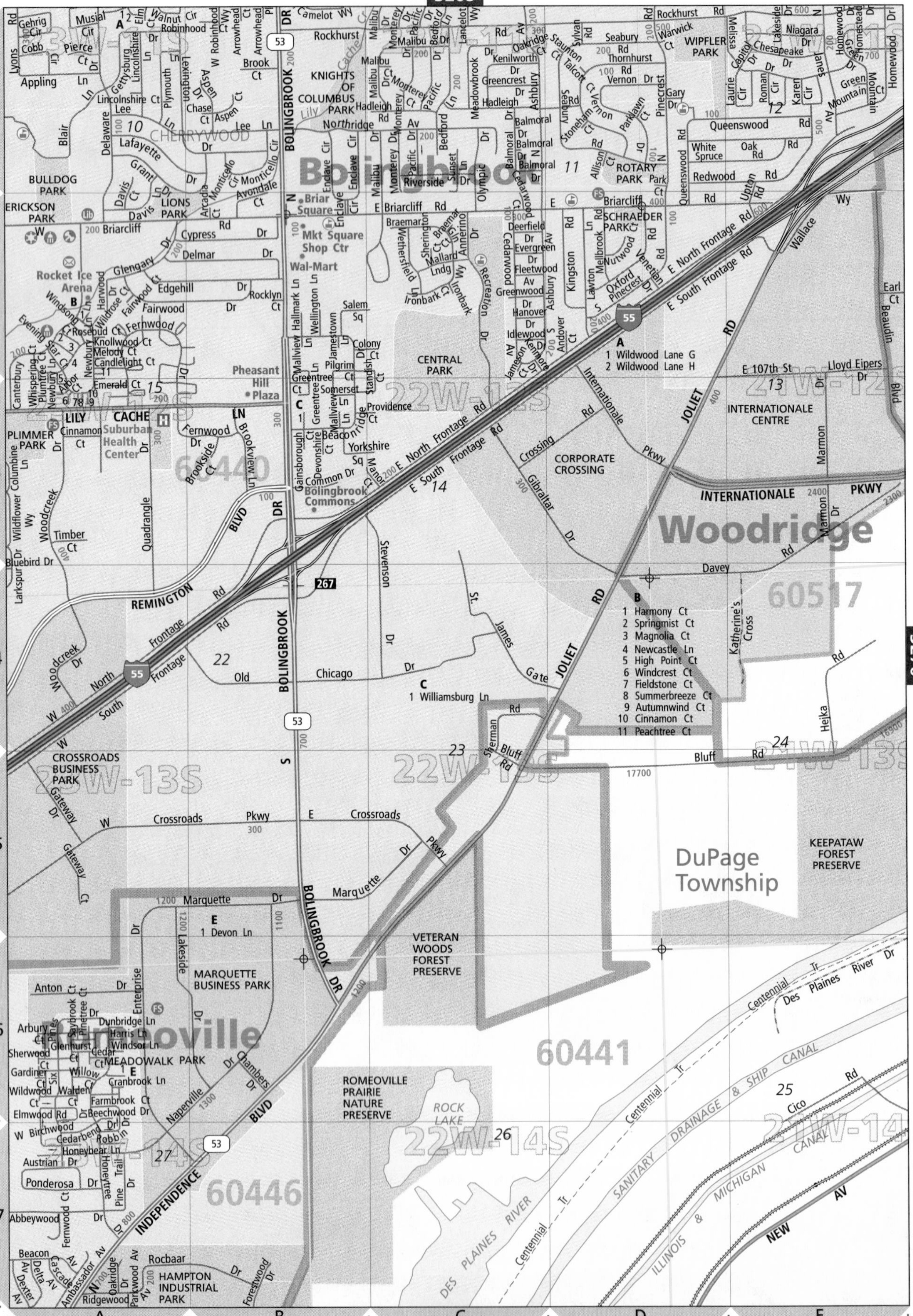

SEE 3268 MAP

SEE 3270 MAP

Bolingbrook

Woodridge

Romeoville

DuPage Township

KNIGHTS OF COLUMBUS PARK

BULLDOG PARK

ERICKSON PARK

LIONS PARK

Briar Square

Mkt Square Shop Ctr

Wal-Mart

Rocket Ice Arena

Pheasant Hill Plaza

CENTRAL PARK

ROTARY PARK

WIPFLER PARK

SCHRAEDER PARK

LILY CACHE

PLIMMER PARK

Suburban Health Center

Bolingbrook Commons

CORPORATE CROSSING

INTERNATIONALE CENTRE

CROSSROADS BUSINESS PARK

MARQUETTE BUSINESS PARK

VETERAN WOODS FOREST PRESERVE

KEEPATAW FOREST PRESERVE

ROMEOVILLE PRAIRIE NATURE PRESERVE

ROCK LAKE

MEADOWALK PARK

HAMPTON INDUSTRIAL PARK

DES PLAINES RIVER

SANITARY DRAINAGE & SHIP CANAL

ILLINOIS & MICHIGAN CANAL

60440

60517

60441

60446

A
1 Wildwood Lane G
2 Wildwood Lane H

B
1 Harmony Ct
2 Springmist Ct
3 Magnolia Ct
4 Newcastle Ln
5 High Point Ct
6 Windcrest Ct
7 Fieldstone Ct
8 Summerbreeze Ct
9 Autumnwind Ct
10 Cinnamon Ct
11 Peachtree Ct

C
1 Williamsburg Ln

E
1 Devon Ln

A B C D E

1 2 3 4 5 6 7

41°42'24" 41°41'58" 41°41'32" 41°41'06" 41°40'40" 41°40'13" 41°39'47" 41°39'21"

88°04'59" 88°04'24" 88°03'49" 88°03'14" 88°02'39" 88°02'05"

RAND McNALLY

SEE 3341 MAP

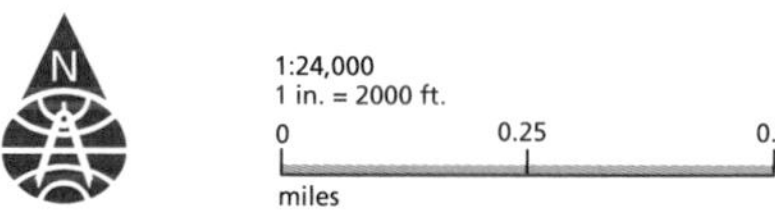

SEE 3206 MAP

JOLIET RD
Frontage Rd
WOODWARD AV
Downers Dr
Oakwood Av
Meadow Ln
Dunham Rd
Midhaugh Dr
Saratoga St
Carpenter Rd
Hill Rd
Pleasantdale Dr
101st St
55
269
12
7
8
9
ARGONNE NATIONAL LABORATORY
Kearney Rd
Bluff Rd
Werch Dr
103rd St
Patrick Rd
60517
INTERNATIONALE CENTRE BUSINESS PARK
Rising Ct
Argonne Dr
Argonne Woods Dr
Woodside Dr
Deerpath
Deerpath Ln
9
INTERNATIONALE CENTRE
Internationale Pkwy
PKWY
Earl Ct
NORTH-SOUTH TOLLWAY
INTERNATIONALE
MOREY DR
Woodridge
INTERNATIONALE ESTATES PARK
Aspen Ln
Stonebridge Wy
Naples Ln
Rothenburg Rd
WATERFALL GLEN FOREST PRESERVE
18
Davey Rd
20W-12S
19W-12S
17
16
13
355
FOREST VIEW PARK
Laura Ln
Alexander Dr
Deans Cove
Whitney Ln
Christopher Dr
Hillcrest Ln
MURPHY RD
109TH ST
Quarry Rd
Beaudin Blvd
Downers Grove Township
Knoebel Dr
Hill Rd
Bluff Rd
Railroad Dr
WILL CO
DUPAGE CO
Linden Cir
Oak Bluff Ct
Sycamore Ct
Oak Ct Ln
Dystrup Rd
Carpenter St
Bluff Rd
DUPAGE CO
COOK CO
LEMONT RD
WOODRIDGE FOREST PRESERVE
R10E
R11E
Lemont Township
Centennial Tr
Bank Rd
Old Lemont Rd
Canal
Black Partridge
W Bluff Rd
GOOSE LAKE
Bluff Rd
WOODRIDGE FOREST PRESERVE
Centennial Tr
STATE ST
20W-13S
19
RIVER
Rd
19W-13S
20
21
24
WILL CO
COOK CO
DES PLAINES
Des Plaines River Dr
Donohoe
Stephen St
River Rd
Pruxne St
Wheeler Dr
KEEPATAW FOREST PRESERVE
Centennial Tr
Metra-Lemont Station
Park Dr
GENERAL FRY'S LNDG
Talcot St
Mayfair Ct
Lenox Ct
SANITARY DRAINAGE & SHIP CANAL
Industrial
MAIN ST
ILLINOIS ST
Lemont HS
Centennial Tr
Des Plaines River Dr
E NEW AV
LOCKPORT ST
STEPHEN ST
McCARTHY RD
Hilltop Dr
Lindsay Ct
ILLINOIS & MICHIGAN CANAL
Timberline Dr
Old Quarry Rd
Bridge Rd
Brown Dr
W Division St
W Custer St
E Division St
E Custer St
E Logan St
THE BOWL
Division Ct
Custer St
Sobieski St
Moczygemba St
Pulawski St
Czacki St
Ledochowski St
McCarthy St
Kruk St
Tomaszewski St
Harasek St
W NEW AV
TIMBERLINE PARK
60439
Logan
Ridge Av
Kettering Ln
Walnut St
Chestnut St
Hickory St
East St
Evergreen Dr
Cedar Ct
Spruce Ct
Lemont
Eureka Av
Short St
S Main St
Lintz St
Hillview Ct
Schultz St
Houston St
NORTH-SOUTH TOLLWAY
Losey Ct
Norton Av
Oak Ct
Freehauf St
Keepataw Dr
S NEW AV
Cicero Rd
25
30
20W-14S
Aspen Ct
Peiffer Av
W Peiffer Av
29
Rosehill Dr
Glenview Ln
28
Berkley Ln
STATE ST
Cherokee
Kim Pl
ST. ALPHONSUS CEM
60441
Province Dr
Stratton Dr
Briarcliffe
Thornberry Dr
Doolin
Jacqueline Ct
Edgewood Rd
Hermes St
Walter St
Florence St
Weimer Av
Lemont Plz
Keepataw
Kip
Crestview Dr
Forest Ln
Durham Rd
Covington Ln
Overton Dr
DuPage Township
Wilshire Ct
Bond Dr
Toll Booth
Deborah Dr
Roberta Dr
Rose Ct
Wend St
Erin Ln
Meagan Ln
Warner Cir
CYRIL & METHODIUS CEM
Glenys
Gillian St
Alpine Ln
Norwalk
COVINGTON KNOLLS PARK
Windsor Ct
Sterling Dr
Dowdell Dr
Smith Rd
355
127TH ST
ST. MATHEW CEM
W 127TH ST
B
1 St. Andrew's Ct
2 Ashbury Dr
3 Chestnut Cross
33

A B C D E
1 2 3 4 5 6 7

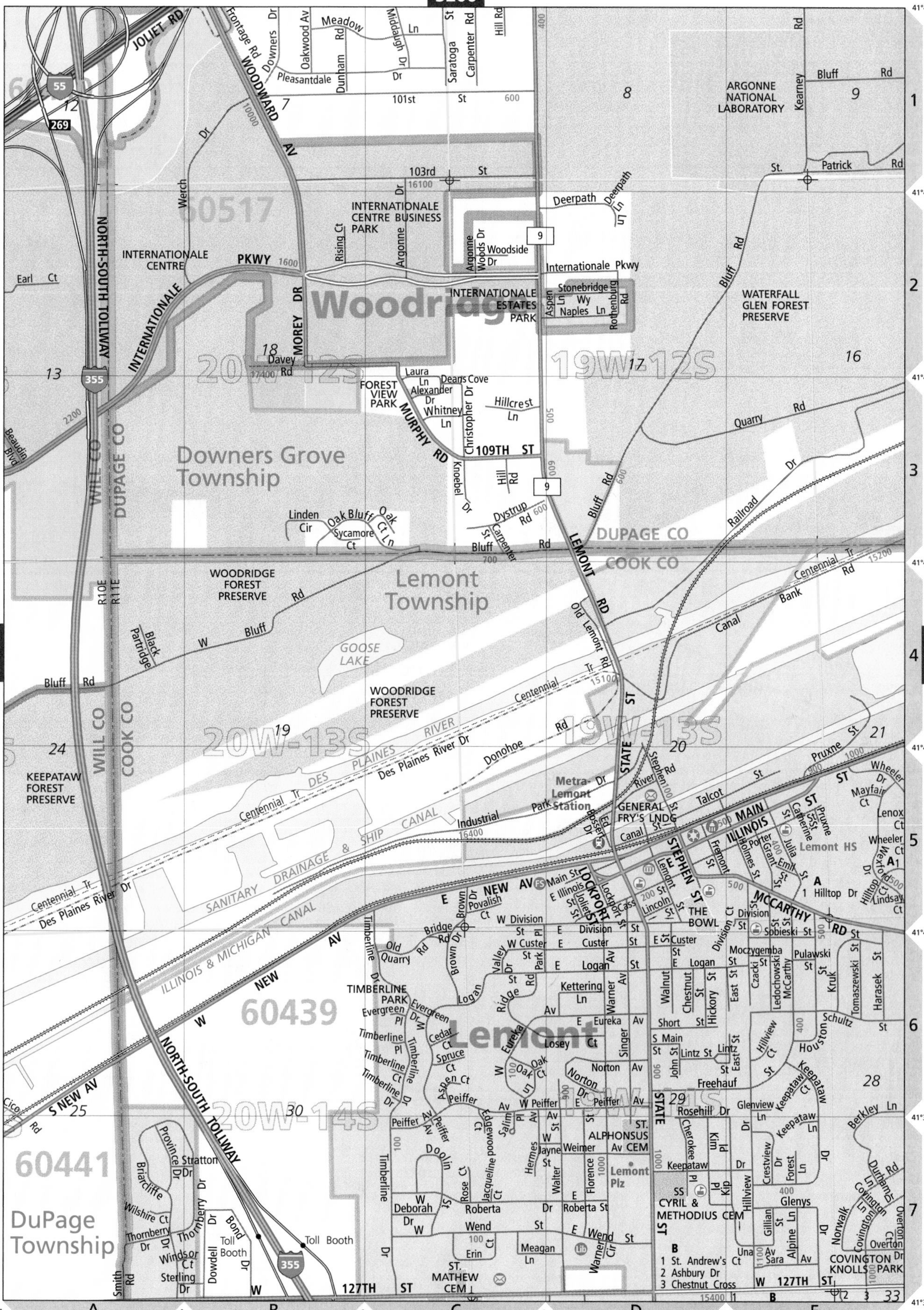

SEE 3269 MAP
SEE 3271 MAP
SEE 3342 MAP

41°42'25" 41°41'59" 41°41'33" 41°41'07" 41°40'41" 41°40'15" 41°39'49" 41°39'22"
88°02'05" 88°01'30" 88°00'55" 88°00'20" 87°59'45" 87°59'11"

1:24,000
1 in. = 2000 ft.
0 0.25 0.5 miles

SEE 3207 MAP

ARGONNE NATIONAL LABORATORY
WATERFALL GLEN FOREST PRESERVE
ST. PATRICK'S CEM
Downers Grove Township
60527
60439
Lemont
Lemont Township
DES PLAINES RIVER
SANITARY DRAINAGE & SHIP CANAL
ILLINOIS & MICHIGAN CANAL
CALUMET SAG CHANNEL
ILLINOIS & MICHIGAN CANAL NAT'L HERITAGE CORRIDOR
DUPAGE CO
COOK CO
KINGERY HWY
MAIN ST
S ARCHER AV
MCCARTHY RD
WALKER RD
DERBY RD
Parker Rd
Mt Assisi Academy
Slovenian Cultural Center
Mother Teresa Home
A
1 St. Bonaventure Ct
2 St. Claire Ct
3 St. Joseph Ct
B
1 Lenox Ct
2 Lenox St
3 Wheeler Ct
COG HILL GOLF & COUNTRY CLUB
MT VERNON MEMORIAL ESTATES
RUFFLED FEATHERS GOLF COURSE
GLENEAGLES COUNTRY CLUB
NORTHVIEW PARK
LITHUANIAN WORLD CTR
COVINGTON KNOLLS PK
W 127TH ST
18W-12S
17W-12S
16W-12S
18W-13S
17W-13S
16W-13S
18W-14S
17W-14S
16W-14S
RAND McNALLY

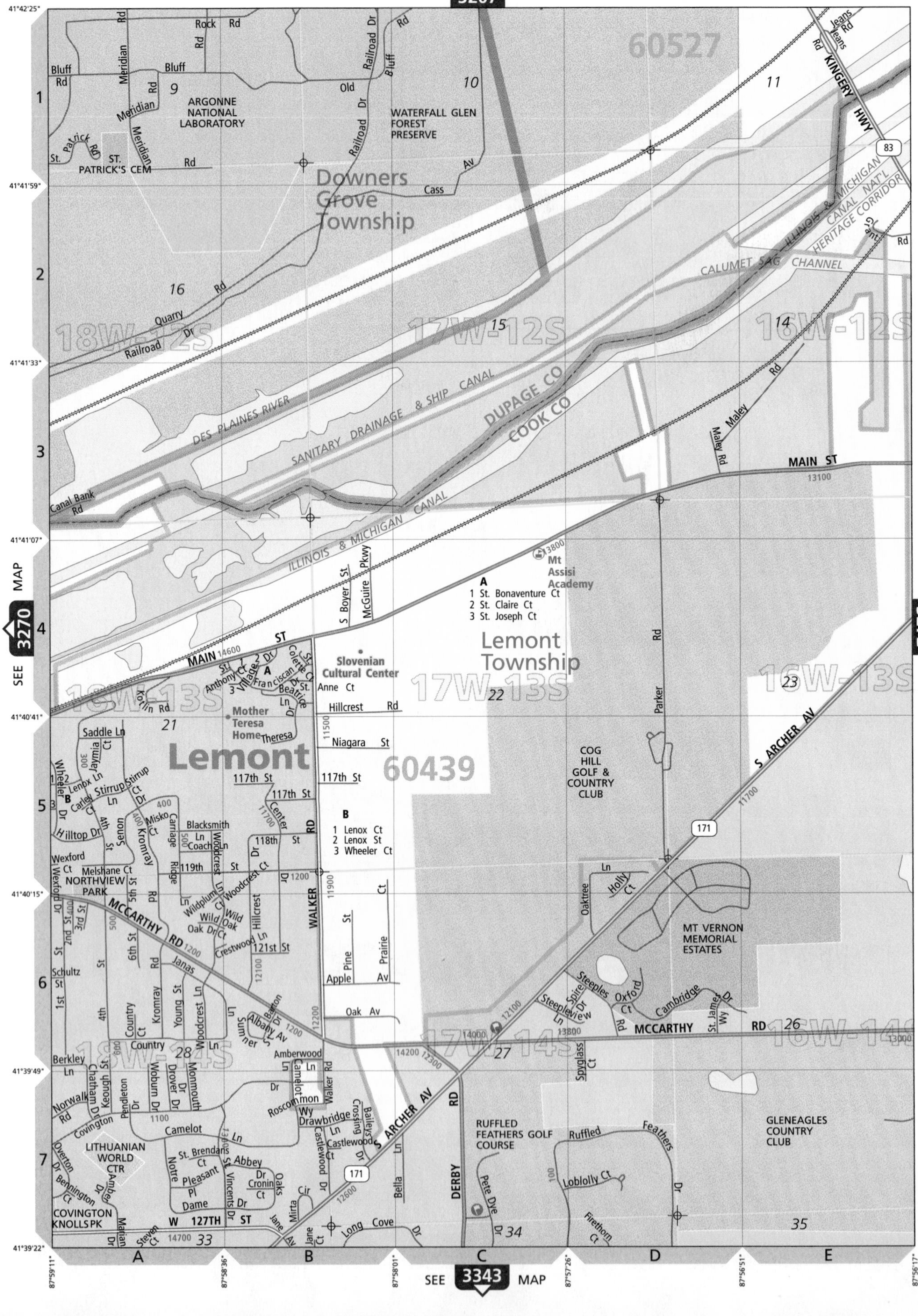

SEE 3270 MAP

SEE 3272 MAP

SEE 3343 MAP

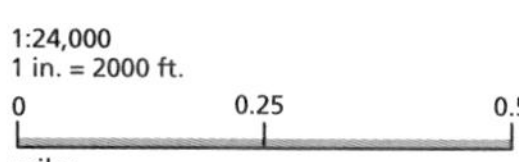

SEE 3208 MAP

SEE 3271 MAP

SEE 3273 MAP

SEE 3344 MAP

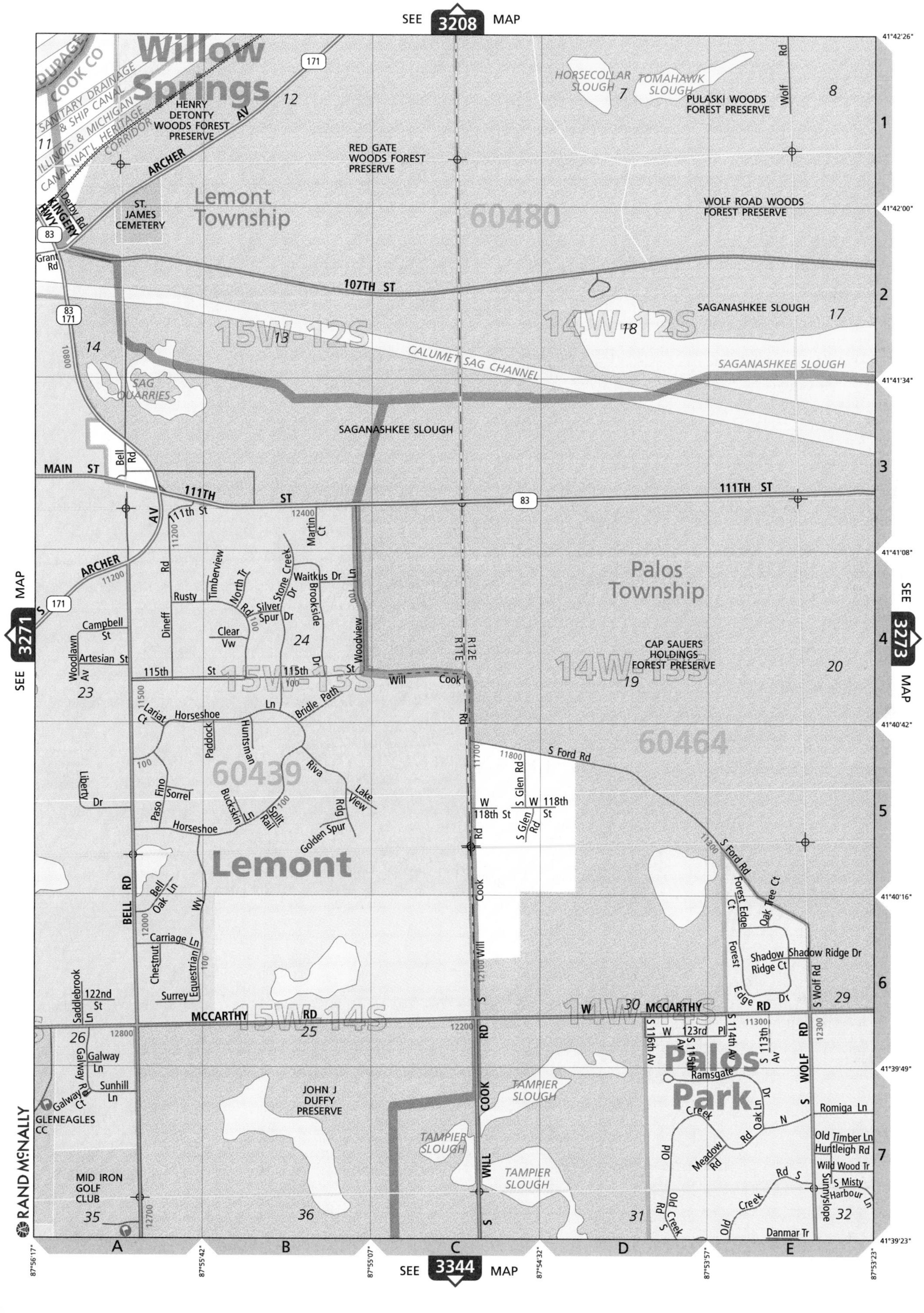

1:24,000
1 in. = 2000 ft.
0 0.25 0.5
miles

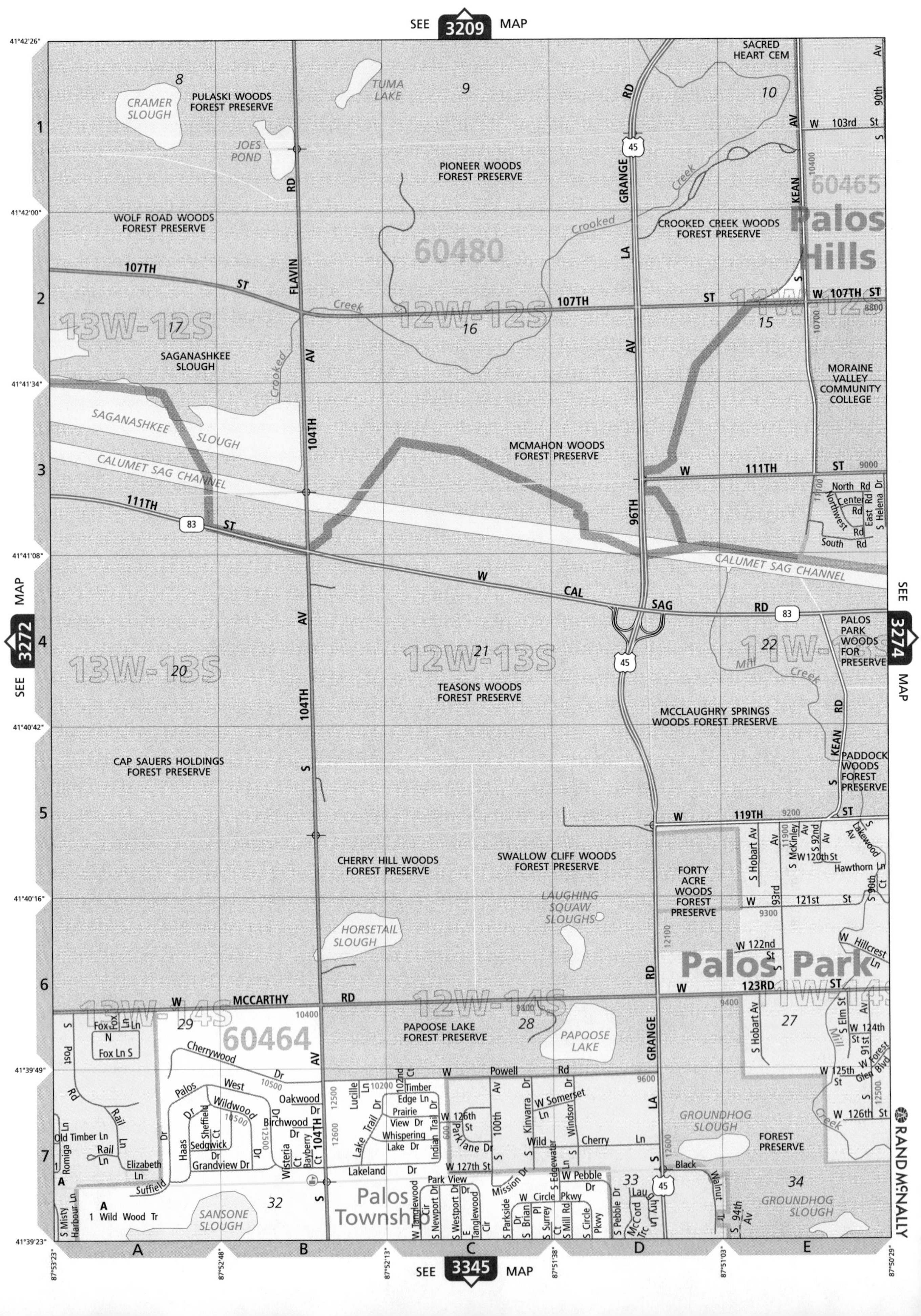

SEE 3209 MAP

SEE 3272 MAP

SEE 3274 MAP

SEE 3345 MAP

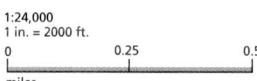

1:24,000
1 in. = 2000 ft.
0 0.25 0.5
miles

SEE 3210 MAP

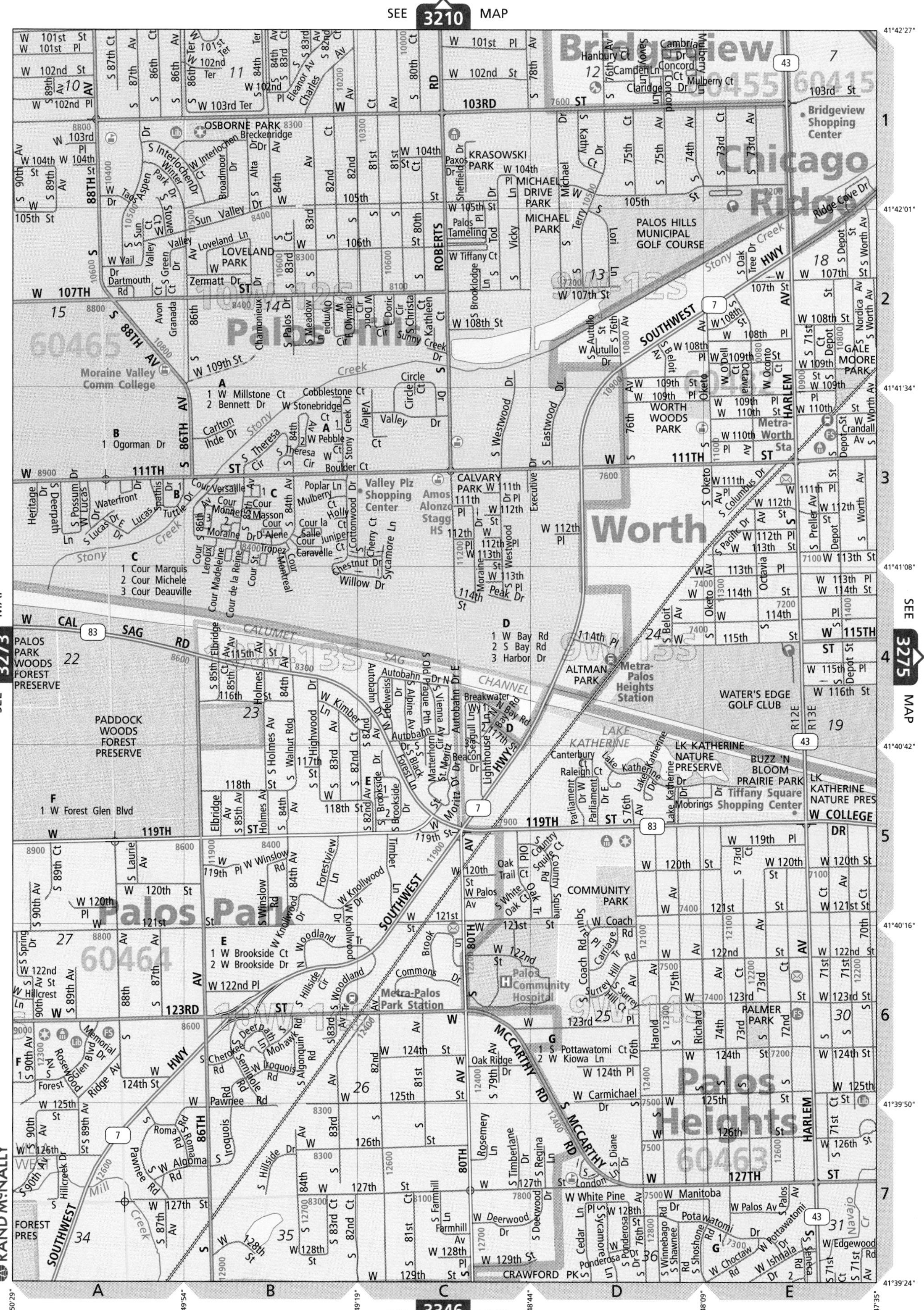

SEE 3273 MAP
SEE 3275 MAP
SEE 3346 MAP

1:24,000
1 in. = 2000 ft.
0 0.25 0.5
miles

SEE 3211 MAP

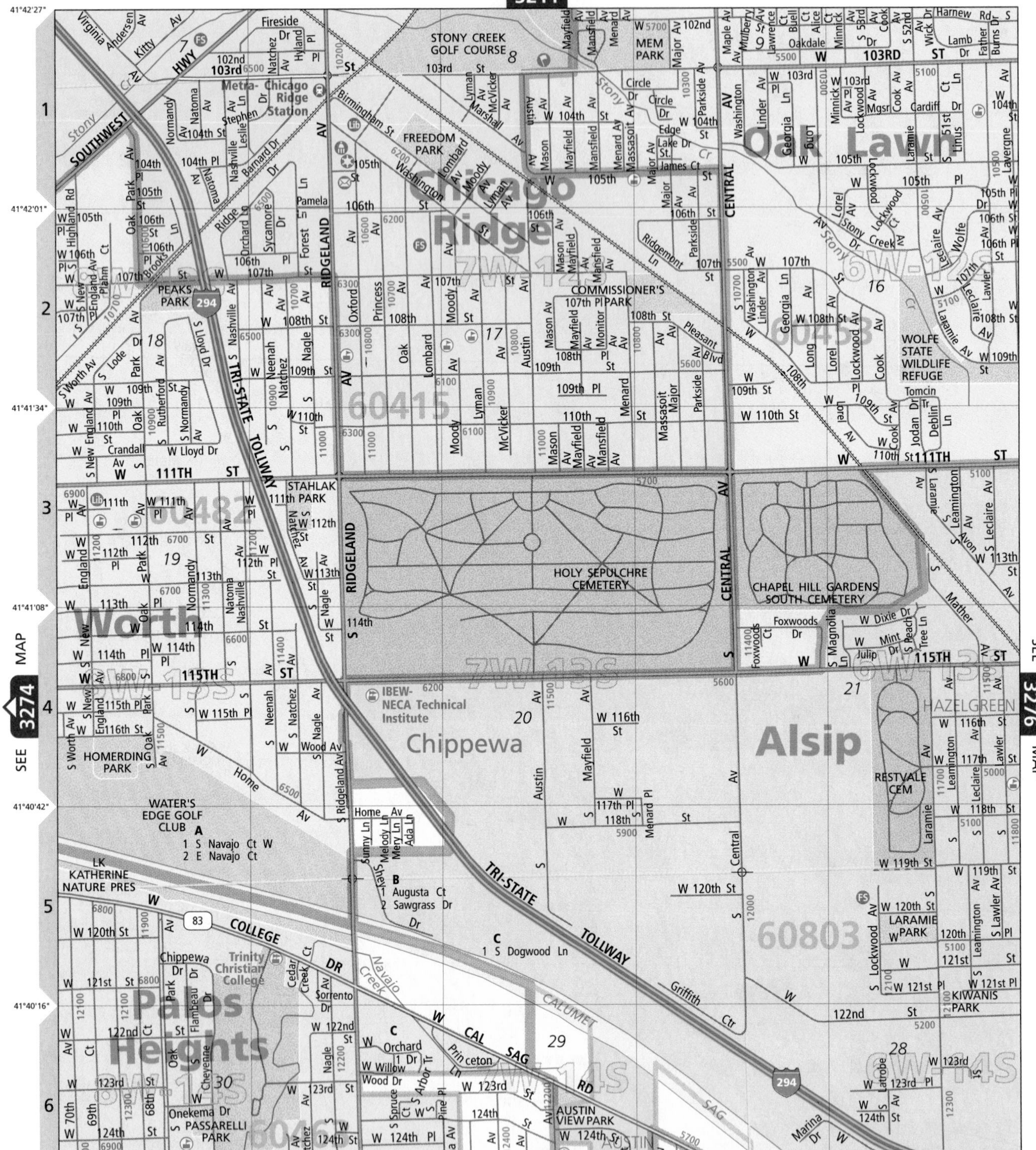

STONY CREEK GOLF COURSE
MEM PARK
Metra-Chicago Ridge Station
FREEDOM PARK
Chicago Ridge
Oak Lawn
PEAKS PARK
COMMISSIONER'S PARK
WOLFE STATE WILDLIFE REFUGE
STAHLAK 111th PARK
Worth
HOLY SEPULCHRE CEMETERY
CHAPEL HILL GARDENS SOUTH CEMETERY
HOMERDING PARK
IBEW-NECA Technical Institute
Chippewa
Alsip
HAZELGREEN
RESTVALE CEM
WATER'S EDGE GOLF CLUB
A
1 S Navajo Ct W
2 E Navajo Ct
LK KATHERINE NATURE PRES
B
1 Augusta Ct
2 Sawgrass Dr
C
1 S Dogwood Ln
Trinity Christian College
LARAMIE PARK
KIWANIS PARK
Palos Heights
PASSARELLI PARK
AUSTIN VIEW PARK
MEYERS PARK
Indian Trails Shop Ctr
Worth Township
PLAYFIELD PARK
Crestwood
TRI-STATE TOLLWAY
SOUTHWEST HWY
COLLEGE DR
CAL SAG RD
CALUMET SAG CHANNEL
111TH ST
115TH ST
127TH ST
103RD ST
RIDGELAND AV
CENTRAL AV

SEE 3274 MAP

SEE 3276 MAP

SEE 3347 MAP

RAND McNALLY

1:24,000
1 in. = 2000 ft.
0 0.25 0.5
miles

SEE 3212 MAP

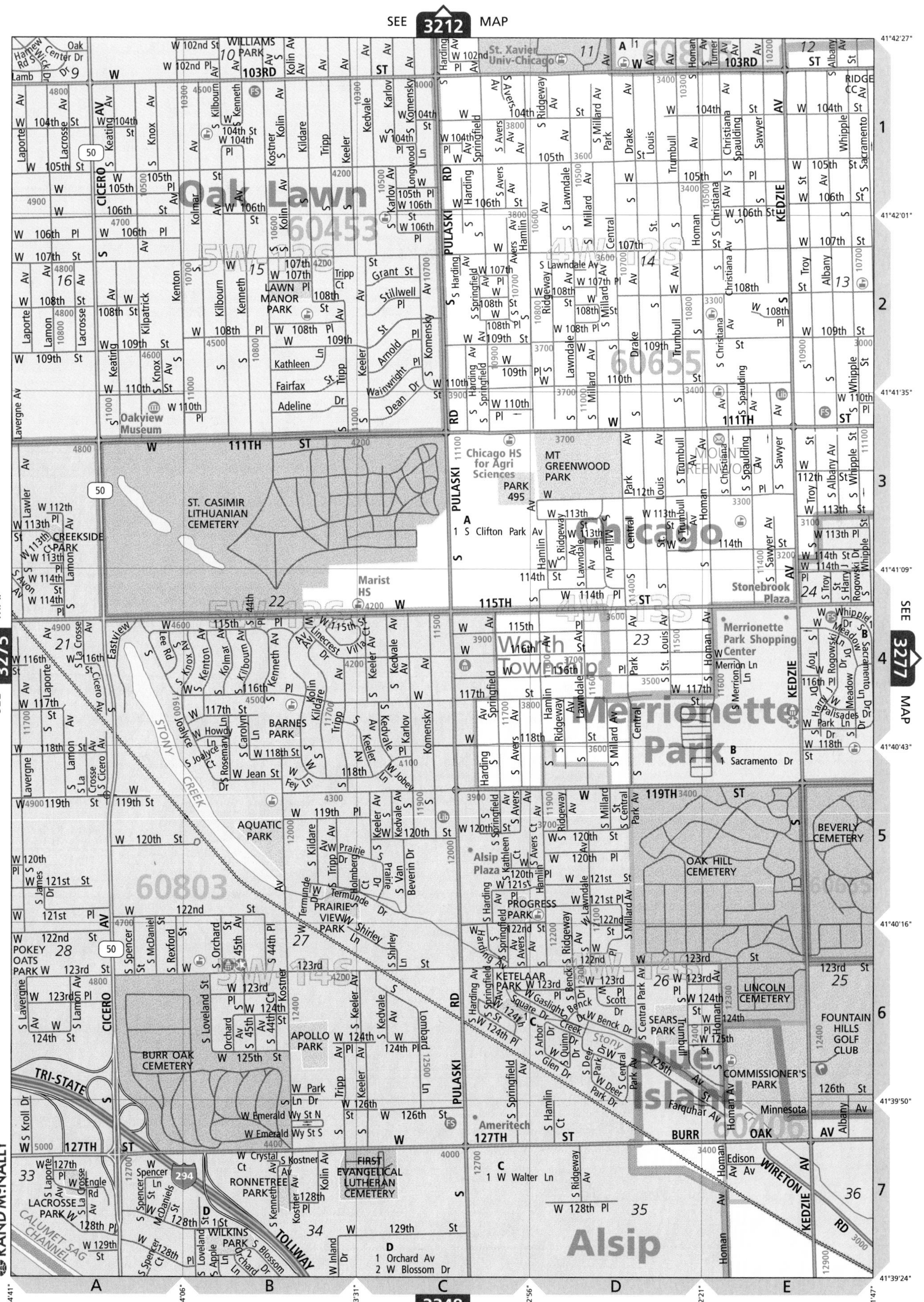

SEE 3275 MAP
SEE 3277 MAP
SEE 3348 MAP

1:24,000
1 in. = 2000 ft.
0 0.25 0.5
miles

SEE 3213 MAP

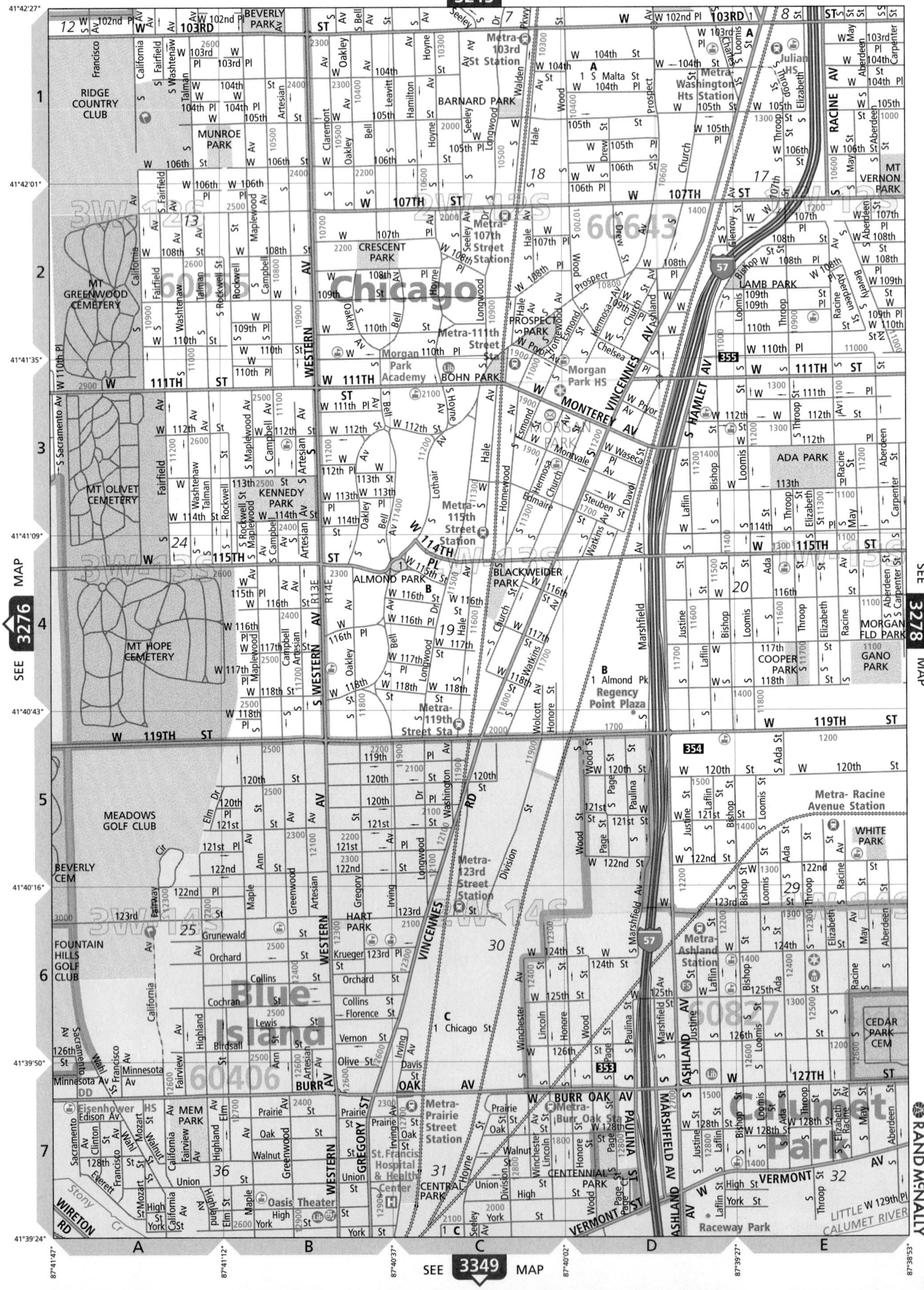

SEE 3276 MAP

SEE 3278 MAP

SEE 3349 MAP

Chicago

Blue Island

Calumet Park

RIDGE COUNTRY CLUB
MUNROE PARK
BARNARD PARK
Metra-103rd St Station
Metra-Washington Hts Station
Julian HS
MT VERNON PARK
CRESCENT PARK
Metra-107th Street Station
MT GREENWOOD CEMETERY
PROSPECT PARK
Metra-111th Street Sta
Morgan Park Academy
BOHN PARK
Morgan Park HS
LAMB PARK
MT OLIVET CEMETERY
KENNEDY PARK
MORGAN PARK
ADA PARK
Metra-115th Street Station
ALMOND PARK
BLACKWEIDER PARK
MT HOPE CEMETERY
COOPER PARK
MORGAN FLD PARK
GANO PARK
Regency Point Plaza
Metra-119th Street Sta
MEADOWS GOLF CLUB
Metra-Racine Avenue Station
WHITE PARK
BEVERLY CEM
Metra-123rd Street Station
HART PARK
FOUNTAIN HILLS GOLF CLUB
Metra-Ashland Station
CEDAR PARK CEM
MEM PARK
Eisenhower HS
Metra-Prairie Street Station
Metra-Burr Oak Sta
St.Francis Hospital & Health Center
Oasis Theater
CENTRAL PARK
CENTENNIAL PARK
Raceway Park
LITTLE CALUMET RIVER

60643
60655
60827
60406

1:24,000
1 in. = 2000 ft.
0 0.25 0.5
miles

SEE 3214 MAP

SEE 3277 MAP
SEE 3279 MAP

A B C D E

SEE 3350 MAP

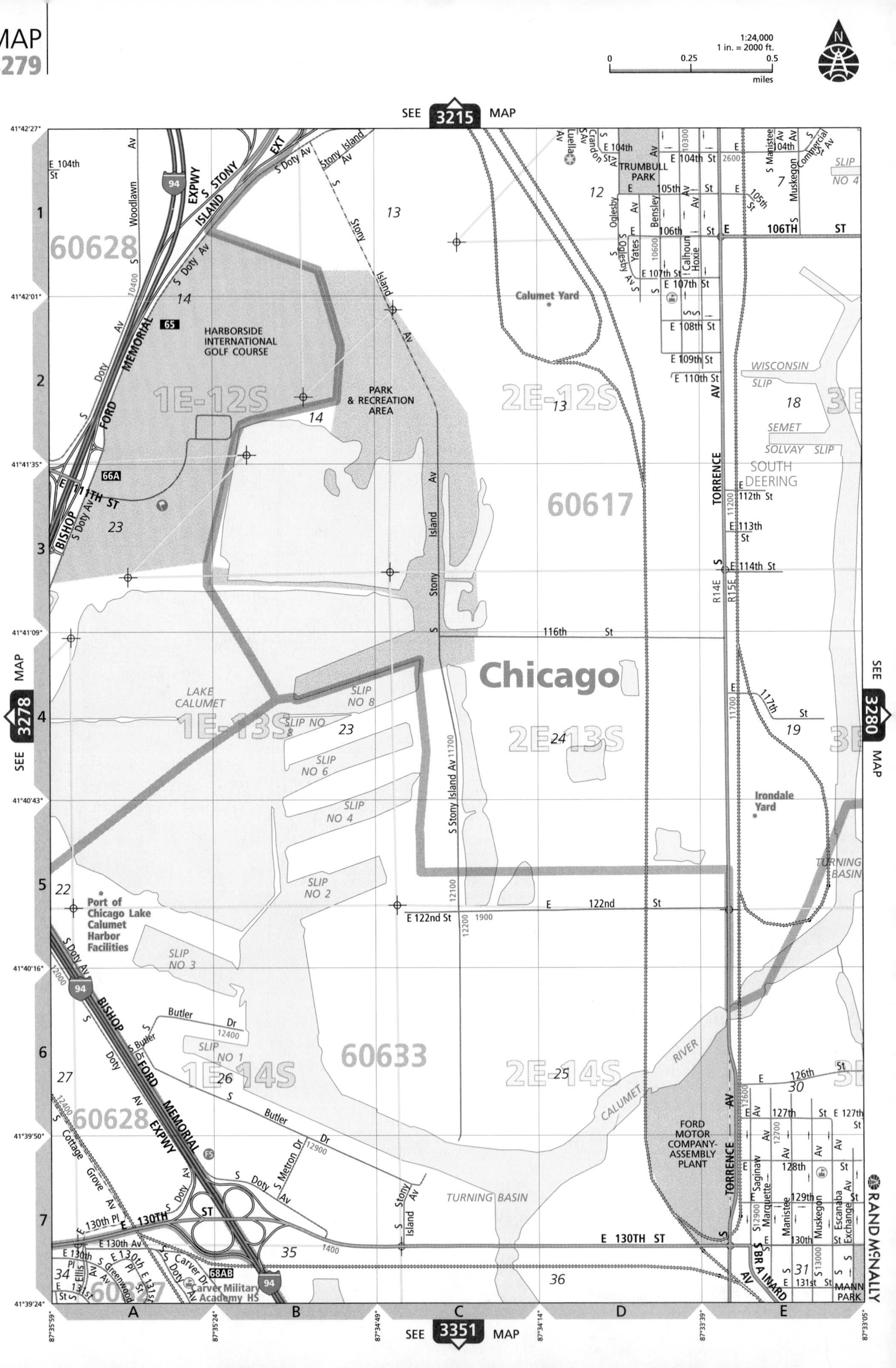

1:24,000
1 in. = 2000 ft.
0 0.25 0.5
miles
N
SEE 3215 MAP
SEE 3278 MAP
SEE 3280 MAP
SEE 3351 MAP
Chicago
HARBORSIDE INTERNATIONAL GOLF COURSE
PARK & RECREATION AREA
Calumet Yard
TRUMBULL PARK
SOUTH DEERING
LAKE CALUMET
Irondale Yard
Port of Chicago Lake Calumet Harbor Facilities
FORD MOTOR COMPANY-ASSEMBLY PLANT
Carver Military Academy HS
MANN PARK
CALUMET RIVER
TURNING BASIN
WISCONSIN SLIP
SEMET SLIP
SOLVAY SLIP
SLIP NO 1
SLIP NO 2
SLIP NO 3
SLIP NO 4
SLIP NO 6
SLIP NO 8
60628
60617
60633
60827
1E-12S
2E-12S
1E-13S
2E-13S
1E-14S
2E-14S
R14E
R15E
S STONY ISLAND EXPWY
I-94
BISHOP FORD MEMORIAL EXPWY
S Stony Island Av
S Doty Av
TORRENCE AV
E 106TH ST
E 130TH ST
E 111TH ST
116th St
E 122nd St
Butler Dr
S Woodlawn Av
S Cottage Grove Av
S Metron Dr
E 104th St
E 105th St
E 107th St
E 108th St
E 109th St
E 110th St
E 112th St
E 113th St
E 114th St
E 117th St
E 126th St
E 127th St
E 128th St
E 129th St
E 130th St
E 131st St
S Brainard Av
S Saginaw Av
S Marquette Av
S Manistee Av
S Muskegon Av
S Escanaba Av
S Exchange Av
S Commercial Av
S Oglesby Av
S Bensley Av
S Yates Av
S Calhoun Av
S Hoxie Av
S Crandon Av
S Luella Av
S Ellis Av
S Greenwood Av
S Carver Dr
E 130th Pl
65
66A
68AB
A B C D E
1 2 3 4 5 6 7
41°42'27"
41°42'01"
41°41'35"
41°41'09"
41°40'43"
41°40'16"
41°39'50"
41°39'24"
87°35'59"
87°35'24"
87°34'49"
87°34'14"
87°33'39"
87°33'05"
RAND McNALLY

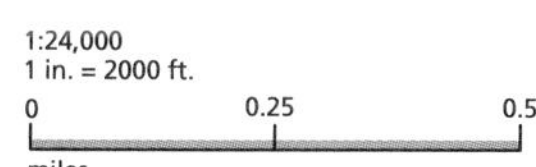

SEE 3216 MAP

SEE 3279 MAP

SEE B MAP

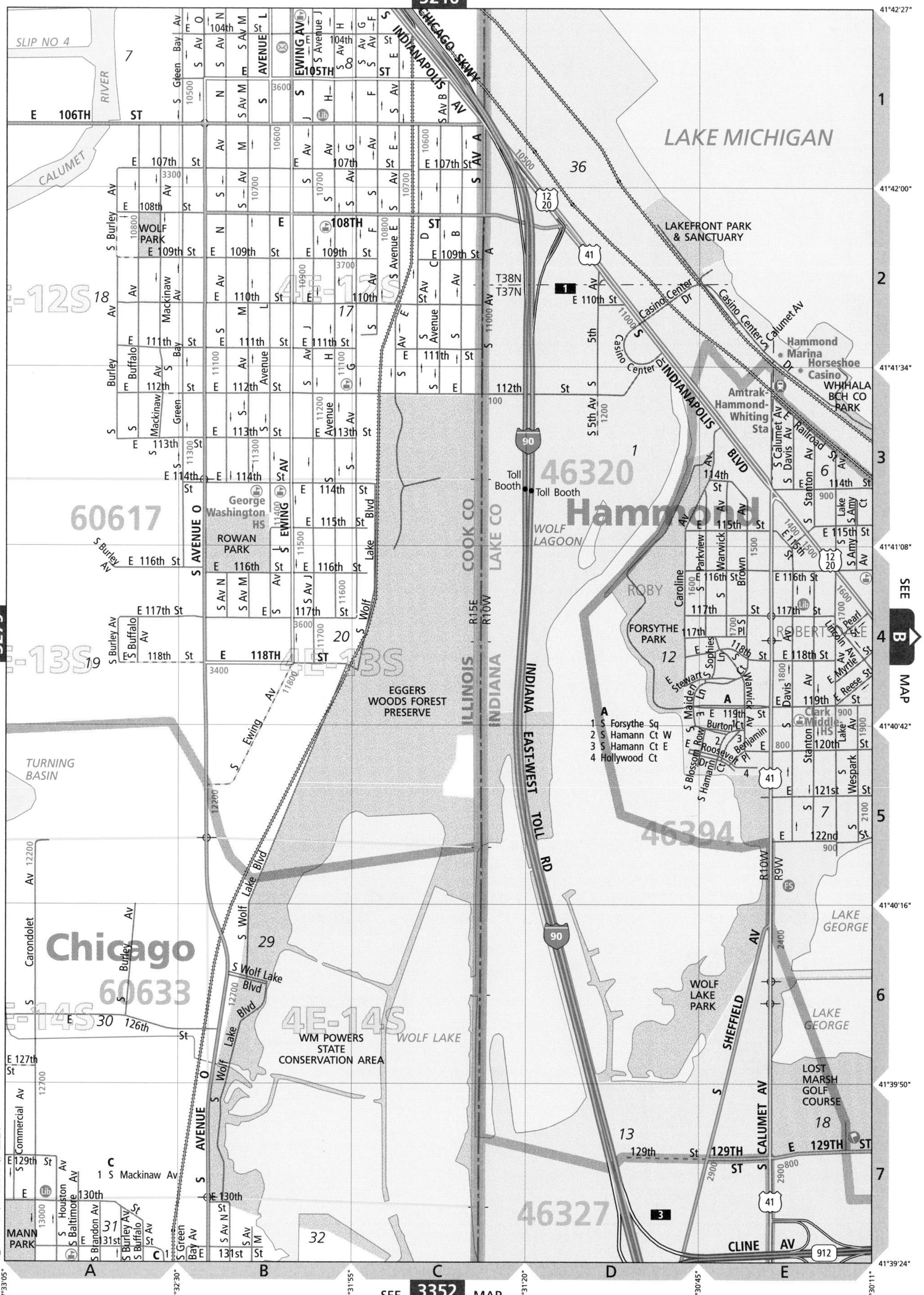

SEE 3352 MAP

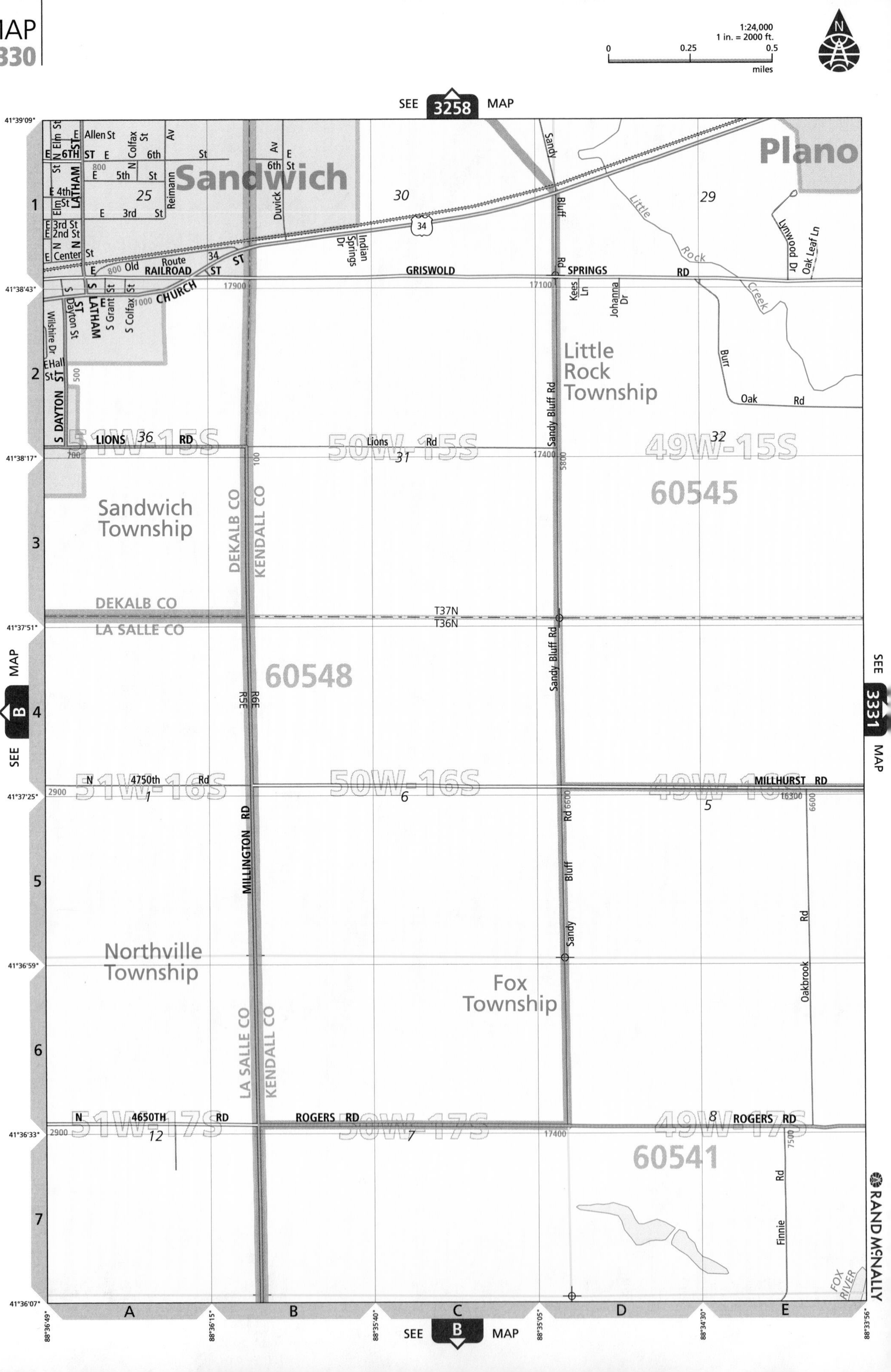

1:24,000
1 in. = 2000 ft.
0 0.25 0.5
miles
N
SEE 3258 MAP
SEE 3331 MAP
SEE B MAP
SEE B MAP
Sandwich
Plano
Little Rock Township
Sandwich Township
Northville Township
Fox Township
60545
60548
60541
51W-15S
50W-15S
49W-15S
51W-16S
50W-16S
49W-16S
51W-17S
50W-17S
49W-17S
25
30
29
36
31
32
1
6
5
12
7
8
DEKALB CO
KENDALL CO
LA SALLE CO
T37N
T36N
R6E
R5E
Allen St
E 6TH ST
E 6th St
E 5th St
E 4th St
E 3rd St
E 2nd St
E Center St
N Elm St
N Colfax St
N LATHAM ST
Reimann Av
Duvick Av
E 6th St
34
Old Route 34
E RAILROAD ST
CHURCH ST
S Dayton St
S LATHAM
S Grant St
S Colfax St
Wilshire Dr
E Hall St
S DAYTON ST
Indian Springs Dr
GRISWOLD SPRINGS RD
Sandy Bluff Rd
Kees Ln
Johanna Dr
Little Rock Creek
Lynwood Dr
Oak Leaf Ln
Burr Oak Rd
LIONS RD
Lions Rd
N 4750th Rd
MILLHURST RD
MILLINGTON RD
Oakbrook Rd
N 4650TH RD
ROGERS RD
Finnie Rd
FOX RIVER
800
1000
17900
17100
500
700
100
17400
5800
2900
16300
6600
7500
41°39'09"
41°38'43"
41°38'17"
41°37'51"
41°37'25"
41°36'59"
41°36'33"
41°36'07"
88°36'49"
88°36'15"
88°35'40"
88°35'05"
88°34'30"
88°33'56"
A B C D E
1 2 3 4 5 6 7
RAND McNALLY

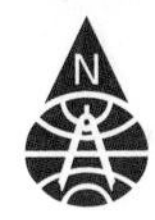

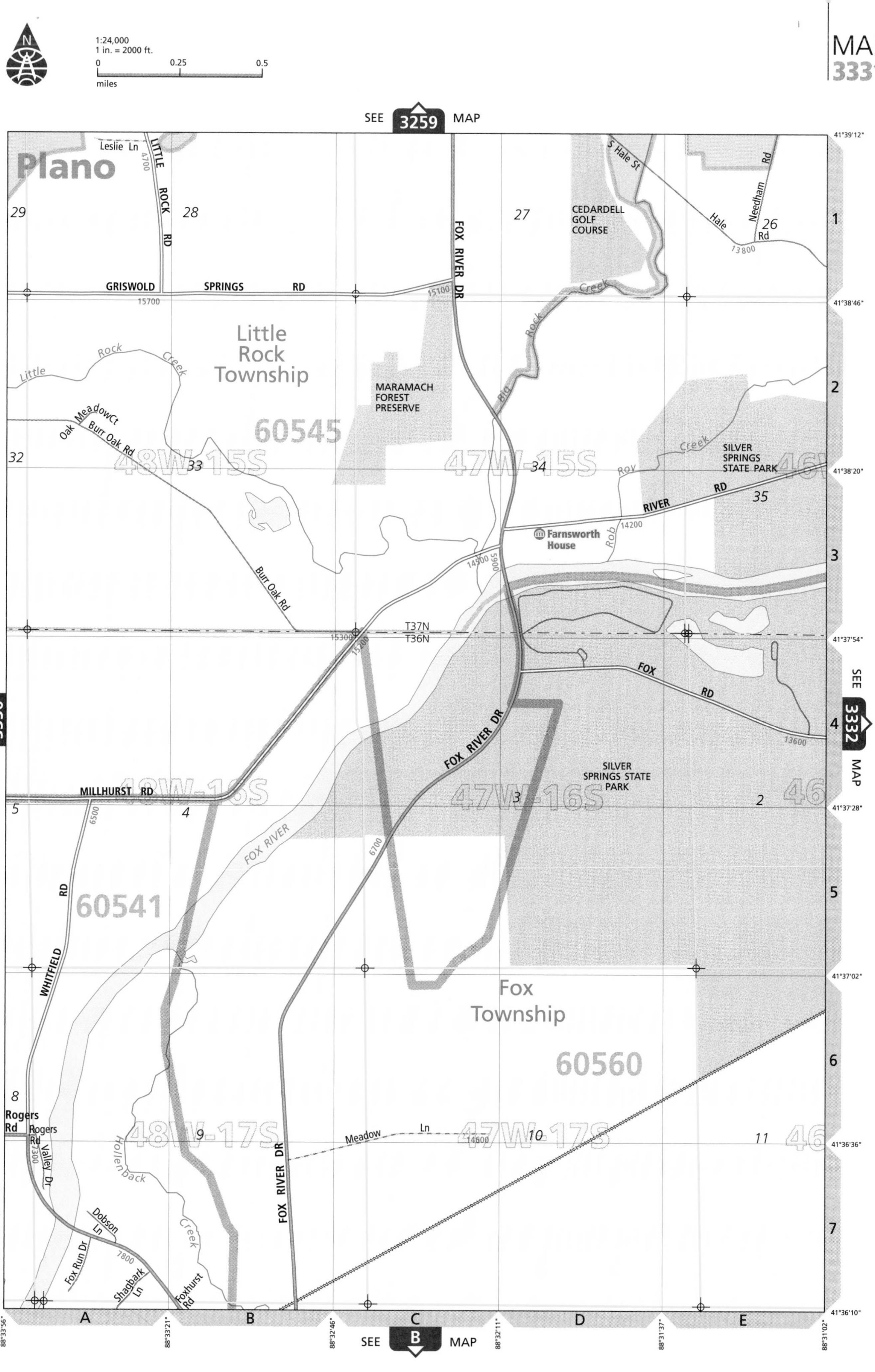

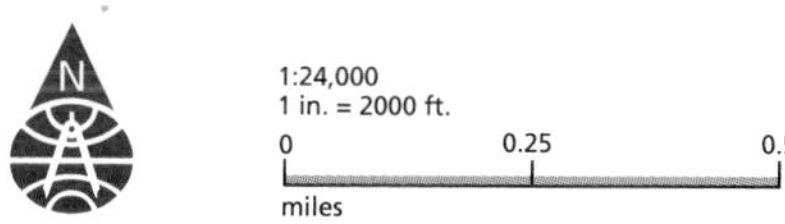

SEE 3259 MAP
SEE 3330 MAP
SEE 3332 MAP
SEE B MAP

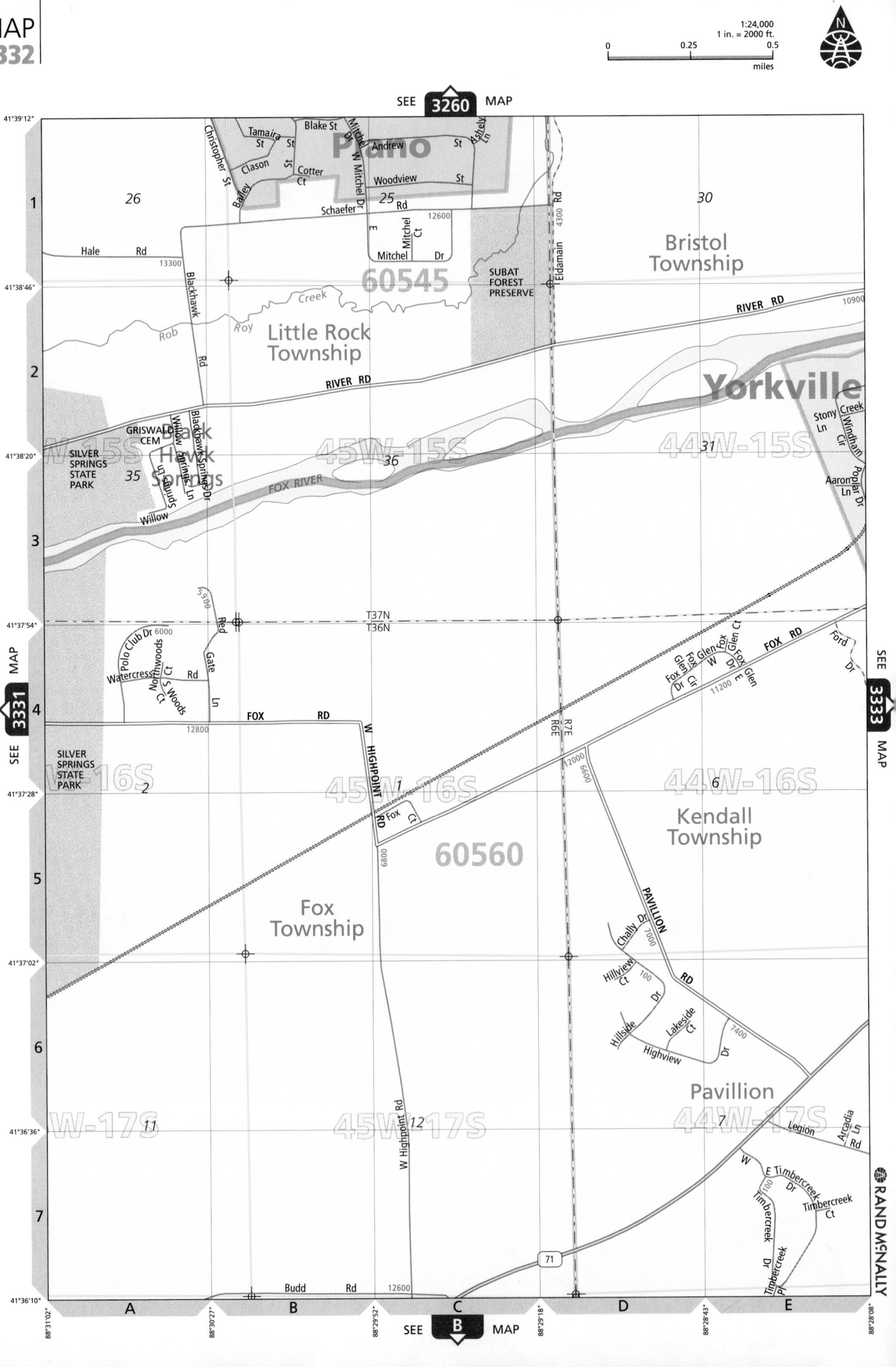

1:24,000
1 in. = 2000 ft.
0 0.25 0.5
miles

SEE 3260 MAP

SEE 3331 MAP

SEE 3333 MAP

SEE B MAP

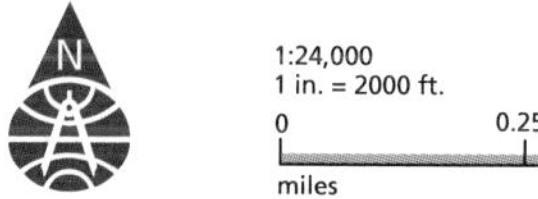

SEE 3261 MAP

60545
Bristol Township

Yorkville HS

ELMWOOD CEM

Wacker

FOX RIVER

Oswego Township

Kendall County Government Center

Kendall Township

T37N
T36N

60560

HARRIS FOREST PRESERVE

Yorkville

43W-15S
42W-15S
43W-16S
42W-16S
43W-17S
42W-17S

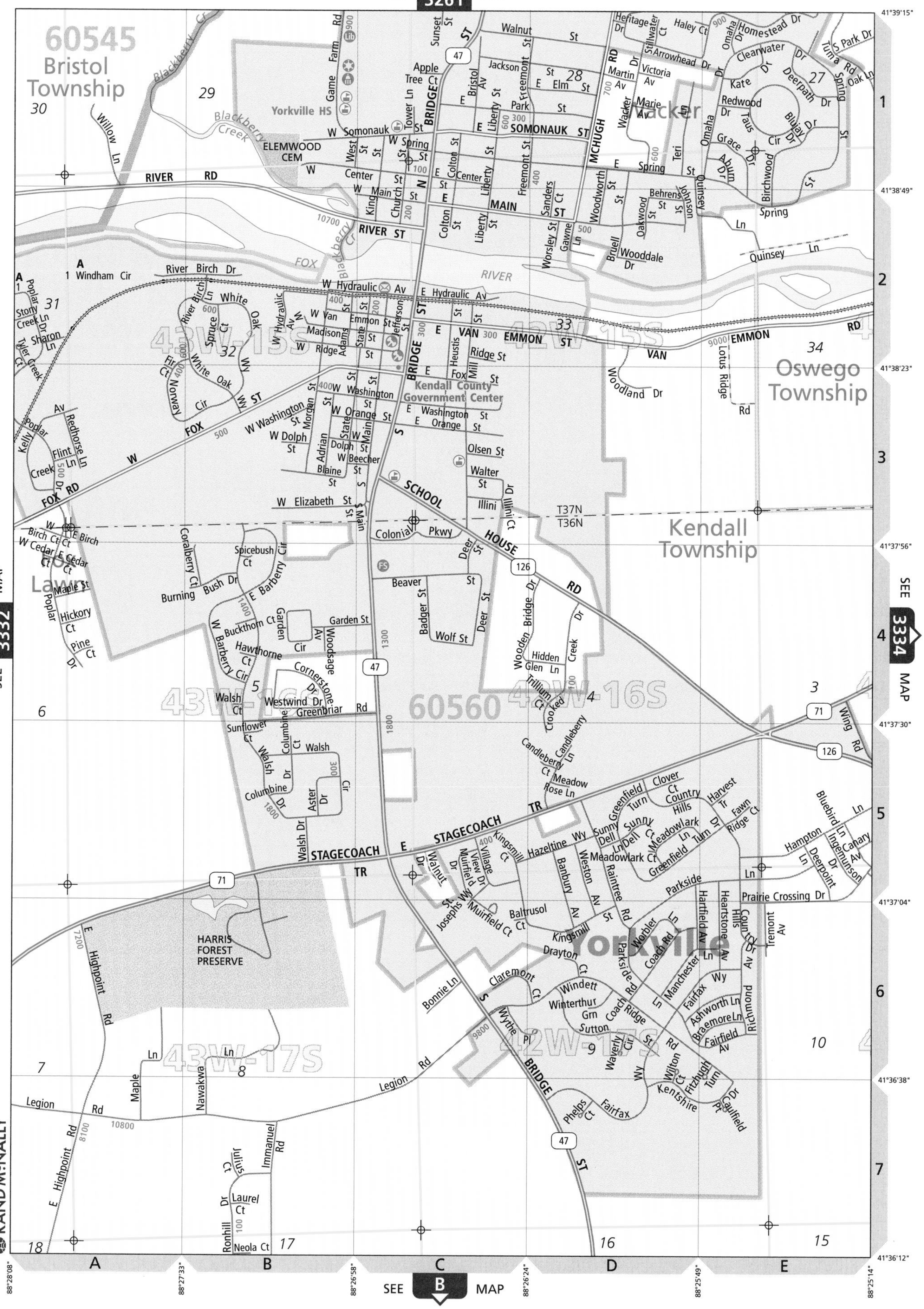

SEE 3332 MAP

SEE 3334 MAP

SEE B MAP

1:24,000
1 in. = 2000 ft.
0 0.25 0.5
miles

SEE 3262 MAP

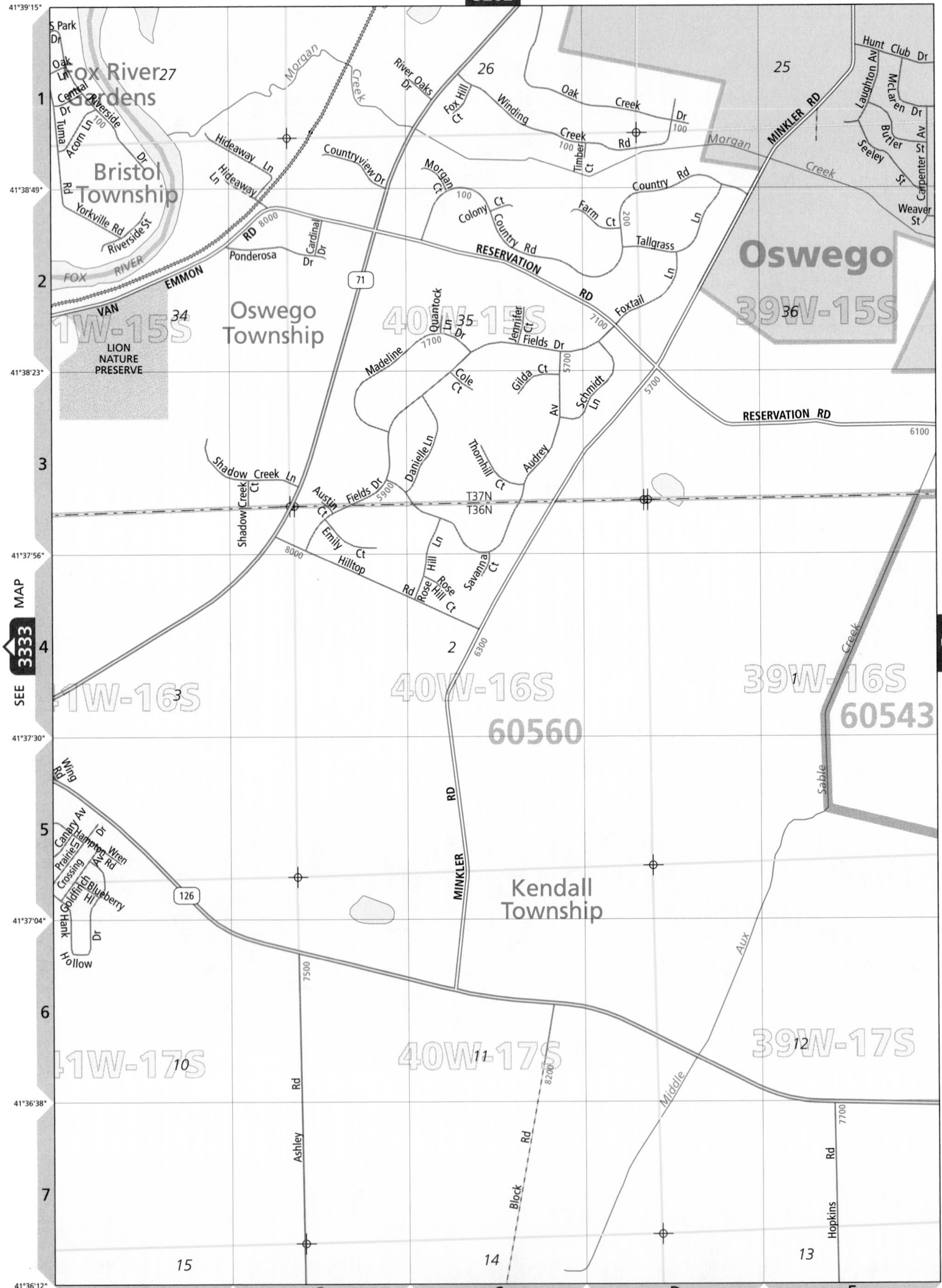

SEE 3333 MAP

SEE B MAP

SEE B MAP

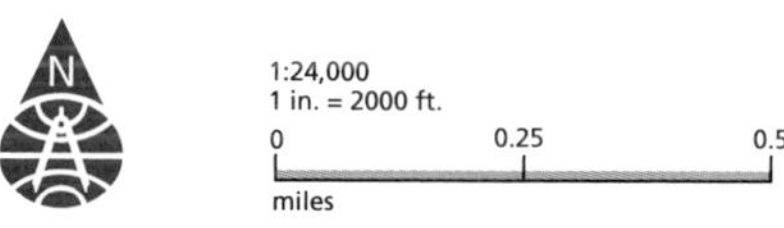

SEE 3265 MAP

Oswego Township
W Vincent Dr
S Cherry Blossom Ln
S Bluewater Pkwy
CHATHAM SQ
S Elizabeth Ln
S Blvd
W Chatham Dr
W Milestone Dr
Elizabeth Ct
S Willowgate
Poplar Cross
RIDGE RD
25
30
S HEGGS RD
12000
Dublin Ln
Kildare Dr
Kilkenny Dr
Tr
Roundstone Av
KING'S BRIDGE ESTATES
Wheatland Township
29
A
1 Canterbury Dr
NORMANTOWN RD
Blue Iris Ct S
Canterbury Ct
Blue Iris Ln
30
SIMONS RD
W 127TH RD
W 127TH ST
26200
500
Wild Rye Ct
Timber Wood Wy
Timber Wood Cir
Pines
Poplar Cross
Grande
Blvd
WHEATLAND
W 128th St
12700
26000
Meadowland Cir
Skyline Dr
Stony Man Ct
Shenandoah
NORTHWEST COMMUNITY PARK
Trelliage Av
25100
Terrace
Meadow
Dr
TURTLE CREEK
Grotto Ct
Persimmon Ct
Bower Ct
Juniper Ct
Pavilion
Blvd
Partree Pl
Ln
Summerhouse Dr
White Pine Wy
Conifer Wy
Cypress Ln
Peppertree
Rustic Wood Ln
Timber Wood Cir
Thornwood Blvd
White Cedar Dr
Tall Spruce Dr
Alpine Wy
Silverleaf Dr
Grande Poplar Ct
Park Ct
Silverleaf Blvd
Elizabeth
Hadfield
Elaine
129th St
12900
Shelly
Hawks Bill Ln
Hawks Bill Ct
Skyline
SHENANDOAH
13000
Pastoral
Staggs Leap Tr
12900
Rock Fish
NORMAN GREENWAY
Ln
W 131st St
Dr
33W-15S
36
32W-15S
31
31W-15S
32
Sunderlin Rd
Vermette Rd
Augusta Ct
Ln
Whispering Woods Ct
Whispering
Woods Cir
Skyline Ct N
Skyline Ct S
Cinnamon
Cinnamon Ct
Blue Bell Ct
Northland
Tiger Lily
Blue Bell Ln
Cir
Wheat Dr
25200
Ambrose Rd
Jacob Fry Dr
Shreffler Dr
Flagg Dr
Blakely
Dr
GRANDE PARK
Thornwood Wy
Oakcrest Ln
Lilywoods Wy
Forestview Wy
GRANDE PARK
Campbell
Woods Wy
Skyline
Taylor St
Dr
Prairie Pond
Blakely
Dr
NATURE'S CROSSING
Grill
Mary Lee Ct
WALKERS GRV PARK
WALKERS GROVE
Rd
Grande Park Blvd
Birch Wy
Rustling
Grande Ct
Lindengate Ct
Morning Mist Pl
Mapleview Dr
13400
DUNMORE ESTATES
Ross Ln
Birdseye Ct
PRAIRIE PONDS
Dr
Red Star Dr
W
Monroe Dr
Lee Ct
Jones Ct
Barn
Basswood Cir
Summergrove Dr
Lindengate Cir
60585
Skyline
Kerr Ct
DUNMOOR ESTATES
Dr
Sunnymere
Blakely Ct
Gateway
Sunnymere Ct
Sunflower Ct
Cir
NORMAN GREENWAY
W Latham Ct
Branch
Round
1800
13400
W PAYDON RD
W 135TH ST
T37N
W 135TH ST
Ashgate
Basswood Wy
6300
T36N
25900
2000
B
1 Diana Ct
Chelsea Ln
Marigold
Savanna
B
Diane Ln
Ashgate Wy
Arborview Blvd
Basswood Cir
Arborview
Cross
RIDGE
Plainfield
Meadow
Brett
St
Dr
PLAINFIELD RD
800
Norman
Spruce Ln
Rd
Michele Dr
60543
Sandra Ln
33W-16S
1
R8E
R9E
32W-16S
6
Drain
Ln
Madison St
31W-16S
5
Trillium
Knoll Rd
Meadow Briar Ln
143rd St
KENDALL CO
WILL CO
143rd St
60544
PRAIRIE KNOLL
RD
Thornberry Dr
Ct
Thornberry Cir
Thornberry Ct
Fieldbrook Dr
Meadow
Rock
Chimney Ct
Thornberry Dr
Ln
Johnson Rd
1200
6200
W 143rd St
1900
14500
Government
Springfield Ct
General Dr
Jefferson Av
Independence Dr
Brigade Ln
Declaration Dr
Dr
PLAINFIELD-OSWEGO
Presidential Av
Na-Au-Say Township
Independence
Scott Dr
Scott Ct
Rd
Capital
Colonial
Grant Ct
Gettysburg Rd
Gettysburg Ct
Ln
33W-17S
12
32W-17S
7
31W-17S
8
Steiner
Bicentennial
Ct
Pkwy
Constitution Ct
Liberty
Grove
Cavalry Ct
Blvd
Federal
Plainfield Township
S
Cir
Meadow
Patriot Ct
Colonial Pkwy
Freedom Wy
Soldier Ct N
1800
W Betty Ln
Viking Blvd
W Andy Ct S
126
W
LOCKPORT
ST
25600
Willow Ln
Willow Dr
Dr W
E
Sandbank Dr
Sandbank Dr
13
S COUNTY LINE RD
18
DRAUDEN RD
17
W Sunshine Cir
Ct
N Clover
N Meadow
N Poppy
Lnm
N Daisy Ct
100
300

A B C D E
1 2 3 4 5 6 7

41°39'19"
41°38'53"
41°38'27"
41°38'01"
41°37'35"
41°37'08"
41°36'42"
41°36'16"
88°16'33"
88°15'58"
88°15'23"
88°14'48"
88°14'14"
88°13'39"

SEE B MAP

SEE 3338 MAP

SEE 3415 MAP

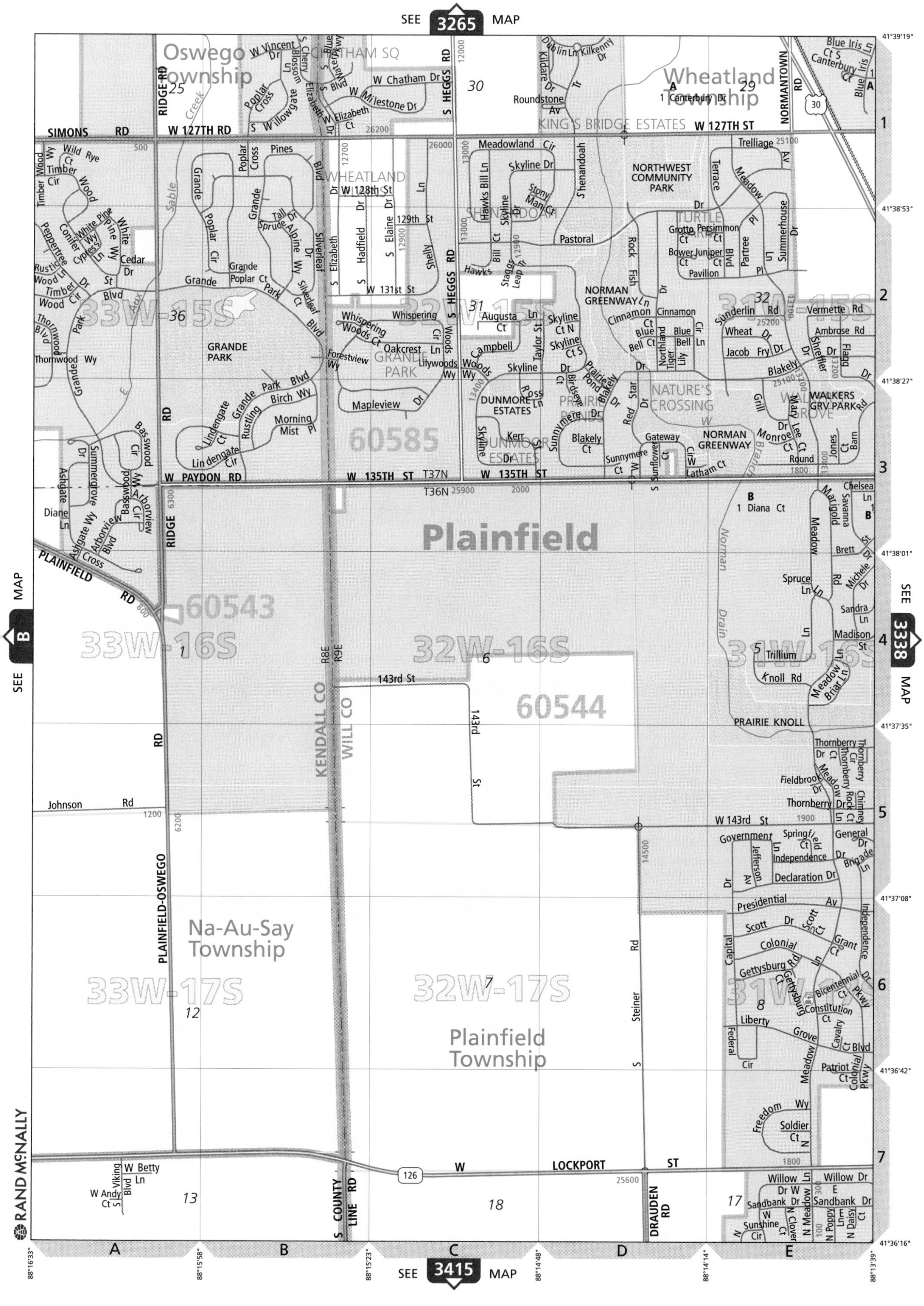

1:24,000
1 in. = 2000 ft.
0 0.25 0.5
miles

SEE 3266 MAP

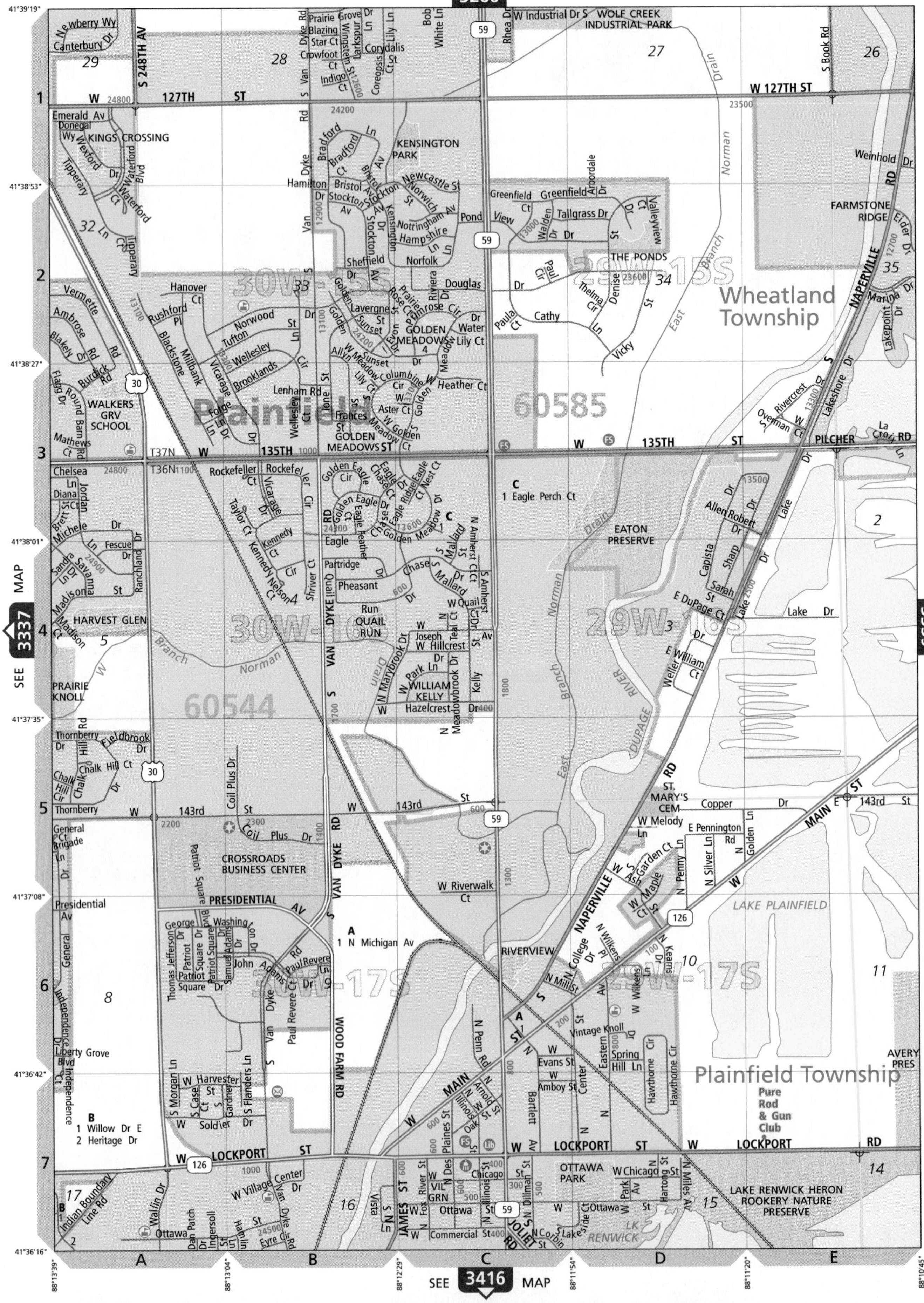

SEE 3337 MAP

SEE 3339 MAP

W 127TH ST
W 135TH ST
W 143rd St
LOCKPORT ST
PILCHER RD
NAPERVILLE RD
S VAN DYKE RD
WOOD FARM RD
S 248TH AV
W MAIN ST
JAMES ST
JOLIET RD
WOLF CREEK INDUSTRIAL PARK
KINGS CROSSING
KENSINGTON PARK
GOLDEN MEADOWS
THE PONDS
FARMSTONE RIDGE
WALKERS GRV SCHOOL
HARVEST GLEN
PRAIRIE KNOLL
QUAIL RUN
WILLIAM KELLY
EATON PRESERVE
ST. MARY'S CEM
CROSSROADS BUSINESS CENTER
RIVERVIEW
VIL GRN
OTTAWA PARK
LAKE RENWICK HERON ROOKERY NATURE PRESERVE
LK RENWICK
LAKE PLAINFIELD
AVERY PRES
Pure Rod & Gun Club
Plainfield
Wheatland Township
Plainfield Township
60585
60544
30W-15S
29W-15S
30W-16S
29W-16S
30W-17S
29W-17S
DUPAGE RIVER
East Branch
Norman Drain
W Branch Norman

A
1 N Michigan Av

B
1 Willow Dr E
2 Heritage Dr

C
1 Eagle Perch Ct

1 2 3 4 5 6 7
A B C D E

41°39'19" 41°38'53" 41°38'27" 41°38'01" 41°37'35" 41°37'08" 41°36'42" 41°36'16"
88°13'39" 88°13'04" 88°12'29" 88°11'54" 88°11'20" 88°10'45"

SEE 3416 MAP

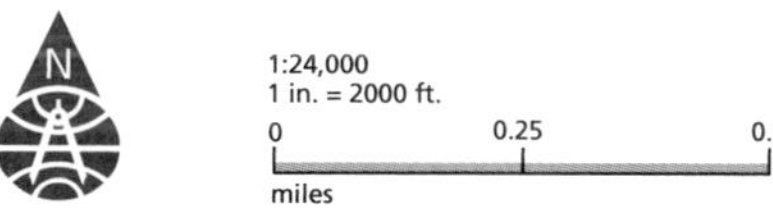

1:24,000
1 in. = 2000 ft.
0 0.25 0.5
miles

SEE 3267 MAP

Bolingbrook
Plainfield
Romeoville
Wheatland Township
DuPage Township
Plainfield Township
Lockport Township
60544
60585
60446
60490
27W-15S
28W-15S
26W-15S
28W-16S
27W-16S
26W-16S
28W-17S
27W-17S
26W-17S
BOLINGBROOK GOLF CLUB
CARLOW CORPORATE CTR
RIVER HILLS PARK
PRAIRIE TRAILS PARK
FARMSTONE RIDGE
Hickory Hills Rod & Gun Club
WATER'S RIDGE
THE RESERVE
BRUCE PONTI COMM PARK
LINKS AT CARILLON
WESLAKE PARK WEST
WESLAKE PARK
OAK PARK SPORTSMEN CLUB
BUDLER PARK
ROTARY PARK
INDEPENDENCE PARK
WESGLEN PARK
CENTURY PK
AVERY PRESERVE
FOUR SEASONS PARK SPORTS COMPLEX
LAKE RENWICK HERON ROOKERY NATURE PRESERVE
WILL COUNTY PRESERVE
REAGAN BLVD
REMINGTON BLVD
NORMANTOWN RD
SW Frontage Rd
NAPERVILLE RD
ESSINGTON RD
PILCHER RD
135TH ST
W 135th St
W MAIN ST
E 143rd St
S BUDLER RD
LAKEWOOD
W TAYLOR RD
FALLS DR
W LOCKPORT RD
W AIRPORT RD
Frontage Rd
T37N
T36N
R9E
R10E
A
1 Glenview Ct
2 Pebblestone Wy
3 River Hills Ct
4 Brookstone Ln
B
1 S Jonesport Cir
2 S Portage Ct
3 W Juneau Ct
4 W Petoskey Ct
C
1 Faulkner Ct
2 S Gladstone Ct
3 S Georgetown Dr
D
1 Freesia Dr
E
1 S Mt Pleasant Ct
2 W Ocala Ct
3 W Norwich Ct
4 S Manassas Ln
F
1 Pembrooke Ct
2 Parkview W
3 Sutcliffe Ct
4 Sedgewicke Ct
G
1 Gleneagle Dr
H
1 Parkview Cir
2 Wood Hill Dr
3 Cherrywood Ct
A
B
C
D
E
1
2
3
4
5
6
7
41°39'21"
41°38'54"
41°38'28"
41°38'02"
41°37'36"
41°37'10"
41°36'44"
41°36'18"
88°10'45"
88°10'10"
88°09'35"
88°09'01"
88°08'26"
88°07'51"

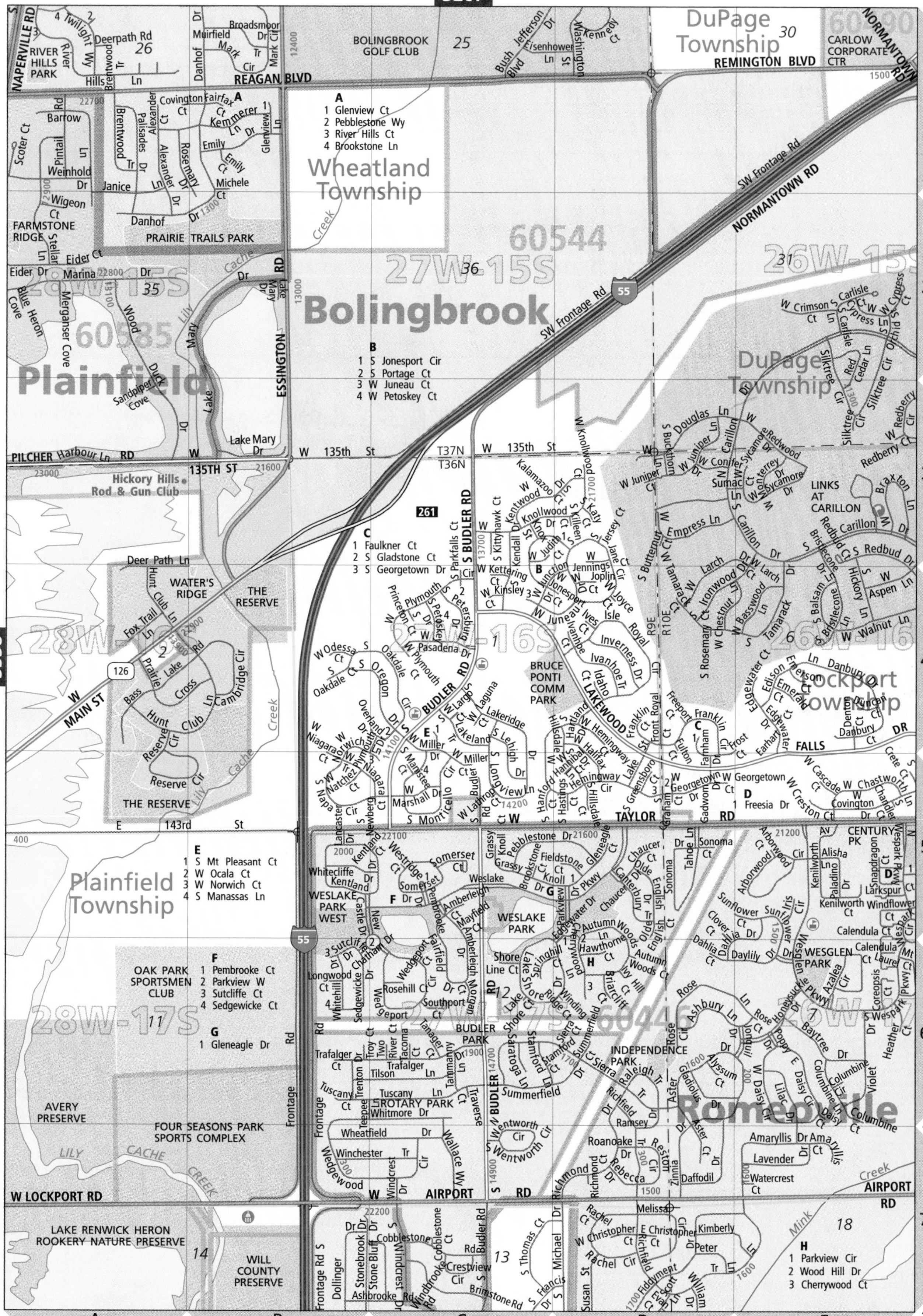

SEE 3338 MAP
SEE 3340 MAP
SEE 3417 MAP

1:24,000
1 in. = 2000 ft.
0 0.25 0.5
miles

SEE 3268 MAP

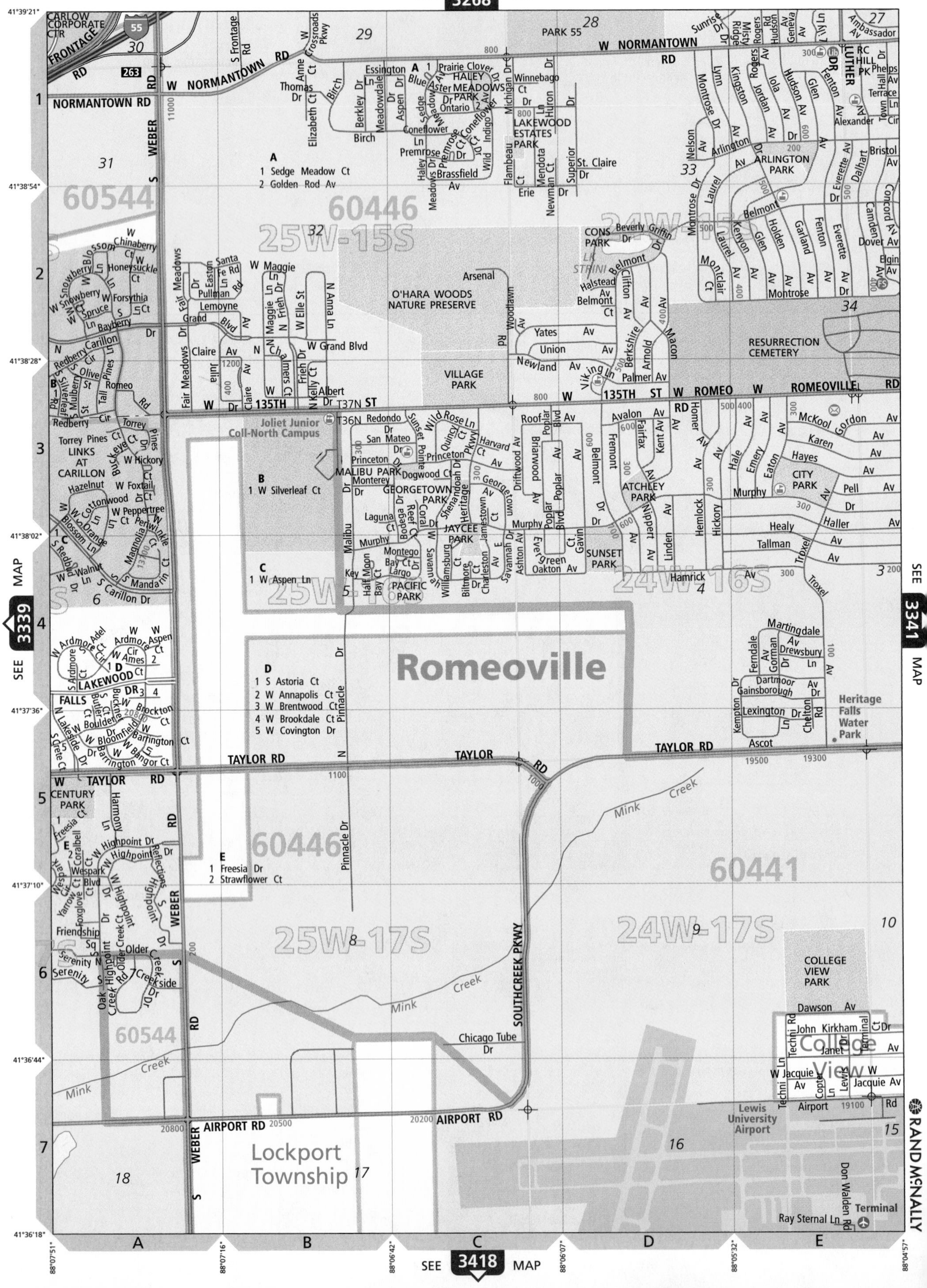

A
1 Sedge Meadow Ct
2 Golden Rod Av

B
1 W Silverleaf Ct

C
1 W Aspen Ln

D
1 S Astoria Ct
2 W Annapolis Ct
3 W Brentwood Ct
4 W Brookdale Ct
5 W Covington Dr

E
1 Freesia Dr
2 Strawflower Ct

Romeoville

Lockport Township

CARLOW CORPORATE CTR
W NORMANTOWN RD
NORMANTOWN RD
S WEBER RD
HALEY MEADOWS PARK
LAKEWOOD ESTATES PARK
PARK 55
ARLINGTON PARK
CONS PARK
O'HARA WOODS NATURE PRESERVE
VILLAGE PARK
RESURRECTION CEMETERY
W 135TH ST
W ROMEO RD
W ROMEOVILLE RD
Joliet Junior Coll-North Campus
MALIBU PARK
GEORGETOWN PARK
JAYCEE PARK
PACIFIC PARK
SUNSET PARK
ATCHLEY PARK
CITY PARK
TORREY PINES LINKS AT CARILLON
LAKEWOOD FALLS
TAYLOR RD
CENTURY PARK
SOUTHCREEK PKWY
Mink Creek
Chicago Tube Dr
Heritage Falls Water Park
COLLEGE VIEW PARK
College View
Lewis University Airport
AIRPORT RD
Terminal
Ray Sternal Ln
Don Walden Rd

60544
60446
60441
25W-15S
24W-15S
25W-16S
24W-16S
25W-17S
24W-17S

SEE 3339 MAP
SEE 3341 MAP
SEE 3418 MAP

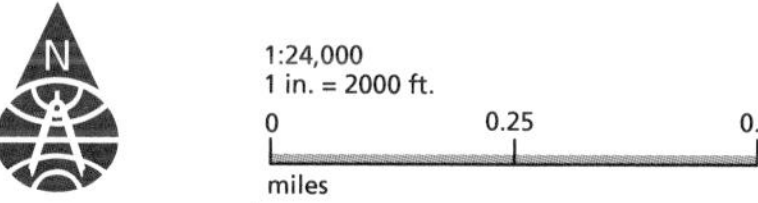

SEE 3269 MAP

Romeoville
Lockport
DuPage Township
Lockport Township
ROMEOVILLE PRAIRIE NATURE PRESERVE
ISLE A LA CACHE FOREST PRESERVE
Isle A La Cache Museum
BIG RUN GOLF CLUB
LOCKPORT GOLF & REC CLUB
CALVARY CEM
RESURRECTION CEM
MURPHY PARK
HAMPTON INDUSTRIAL PARK
Romeoville HS
Lewis Univ Arpt
Lewis University
60446
60441
W 127TH ST
W ROMEOVILLE RD
E ROMEO RD
W 135TH ST
W 143rd St
W 145th St
W 147th St
W 151ST ST
N INDEPENDENCE BLVD
S INDEPENDENCE BLVD
NEW AV
High Rd
ARCHER AV
STATE ST
SANITARY & SHIP CANAL
ILLINOIS & MICHIGAN CANAL
DES PLAINES RIVER
Long Run
Centennial Tr
TAYLOR RD
NAPERVILLE RD
53
171
T37N
T36N

B
1 Gordon Av
2 Hayes Av
3 Pell Av
4 Larsen Cir

A
1 Ambassador Av

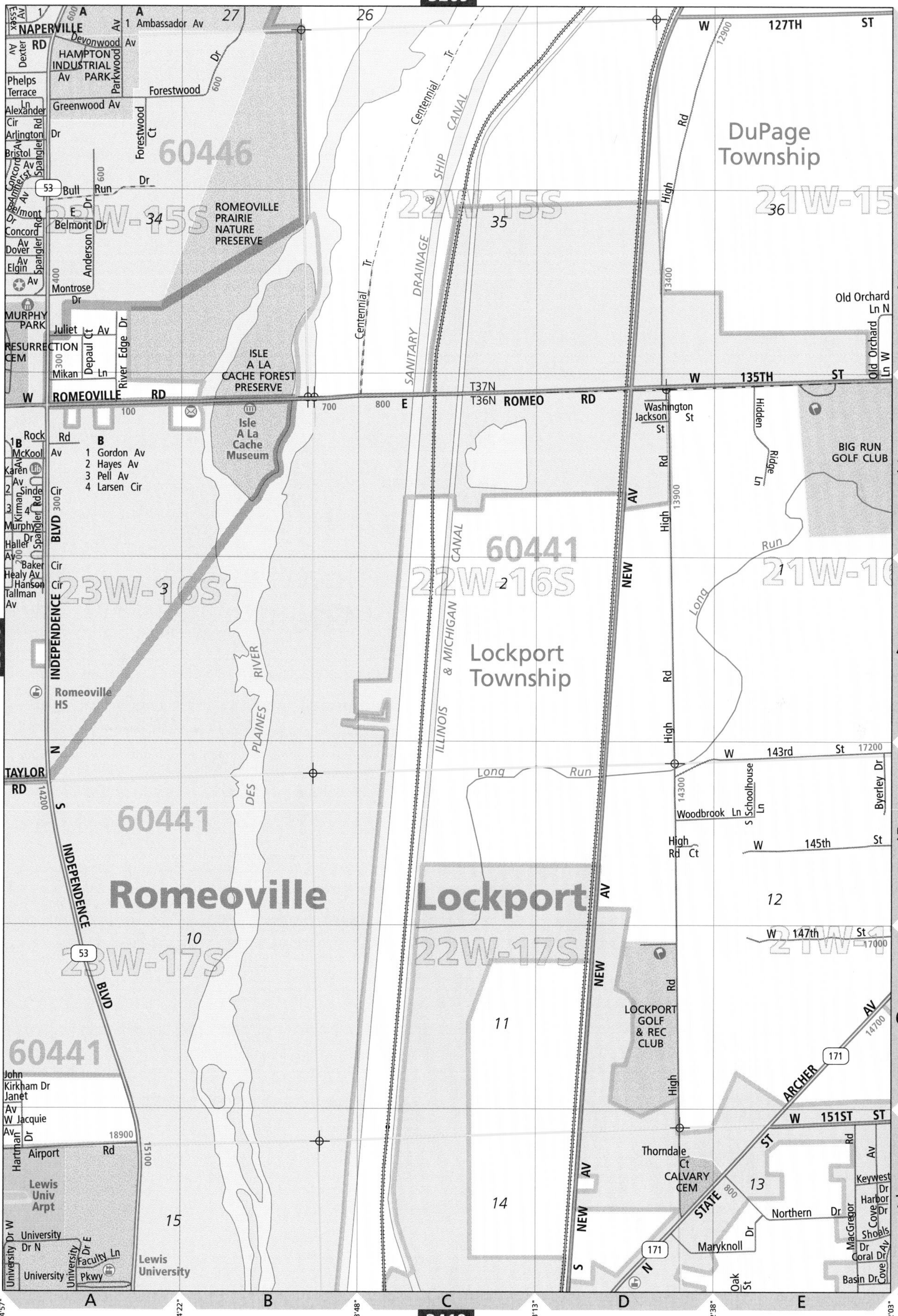

SEE 3340 MAP

SEE 3342 MAP

SEE 3419 MAP

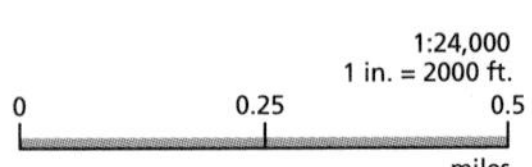

SEE 3270 MAP

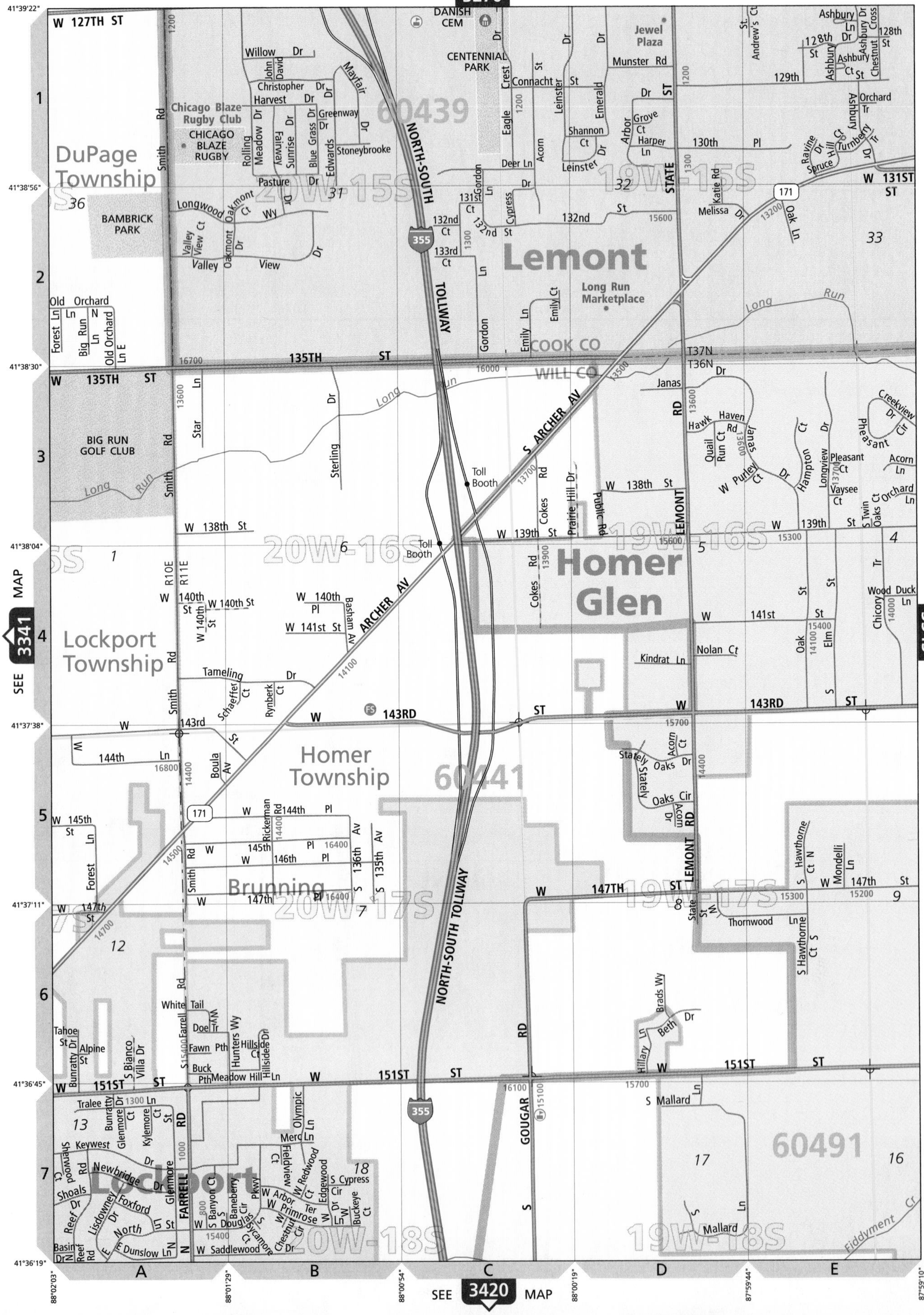

SEE 3341 MAP

SEE 3343 MAP

SEE 3420 MAP

DuPage Township

Lockport Township

Homer Township

Lemont

Homer Glen

Lockport

Brunning

60439

60441

60491

20W-15S 19W-15S 20W-16S 19W-16S 20W-17S 19W-17S 20W-18S 19W-18S

COOK CO

WILL CO

T37N T36N

R10E R11E

DANISH CEM

CENTENNIAL PARK

Jewel Plaza

Chicago Blaze Rugby Club

CHICAGO BLAZE RUGBY

BAMBRICK PARK

Long Run Marketplace

BIG RUN GOLF CLUB

Toll Booth

W 127TH ST

W 135TH ST

135TH ST

W 143RD ST

143RD ST

W 147TH ST

W 151ST ST

W 131ST ST

NORTH-SOUTH TOLLWAY

S ARCHER AV

ARCHER AV

STATE RD

LEMONT RD

SMITH RD

FARRELL RD

S GOUGAR RD

Long Run

355

171

41°39'22" 41°38'56" 41°38'30" 41°38'04" 41°37'38" 41°37'11" 41°36'45" 41°36'19"

88°02'03" 88°01'29" 88°00'54" 88°00'19" 87°59'44" 87°59'10"

A B C D E

1 2 3 4 5 6 7

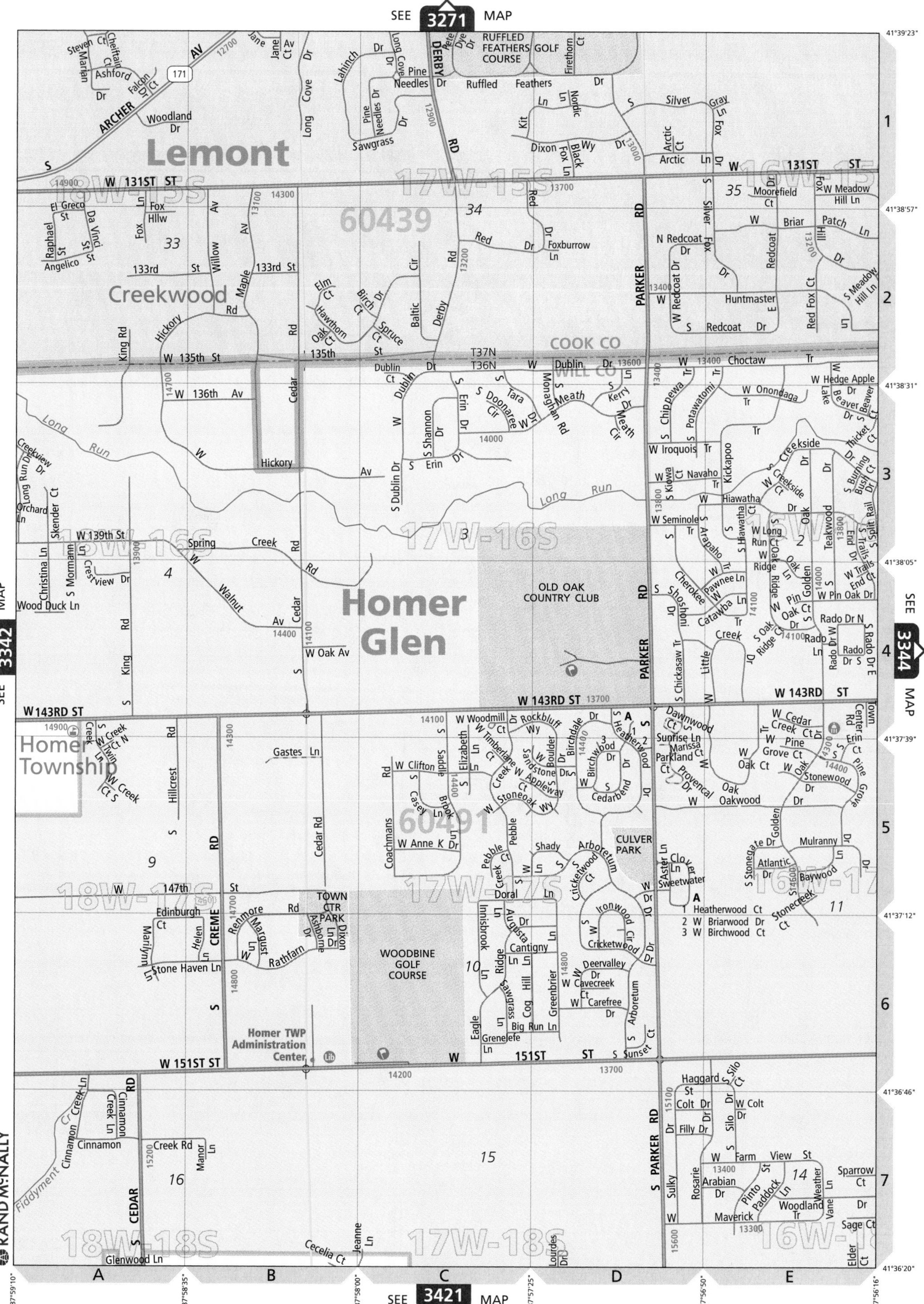

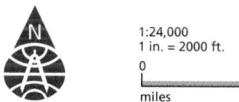

1:24,000
1 in. = 2000 ft.
0 0.25 0.5
miles
SEE 3271 MAP
SEE 3342 MAP
SEE 3344 MAP
SEE 3421 MAP
Lemont
Creekwood
Homer Glen
Homer Township
60439
60491
RUFFLED FEATHERS GOLF COURSE
OLD OAK COUNTRY CLUB
WOODBINE GOLF COURSE
CULVER PARK
TOWN CTR PARK
Homer TWP Administration Center
COOK CO
WILL CO
T37N
T36N
W 131ST ST
W 135th St
W 143RD ST
W 151ST ST
S PARKER RD
S CEDAR RD
S CREME RD
DERBY RD
ARCHER AV
Long Run
1 W Heatherwood Ct
2 W Briarwood Dr
3 W Birchwood Ct
RAND McNALLY

1:24,000
1 in. = 2000 ft.
0 0.25 0.5
miles

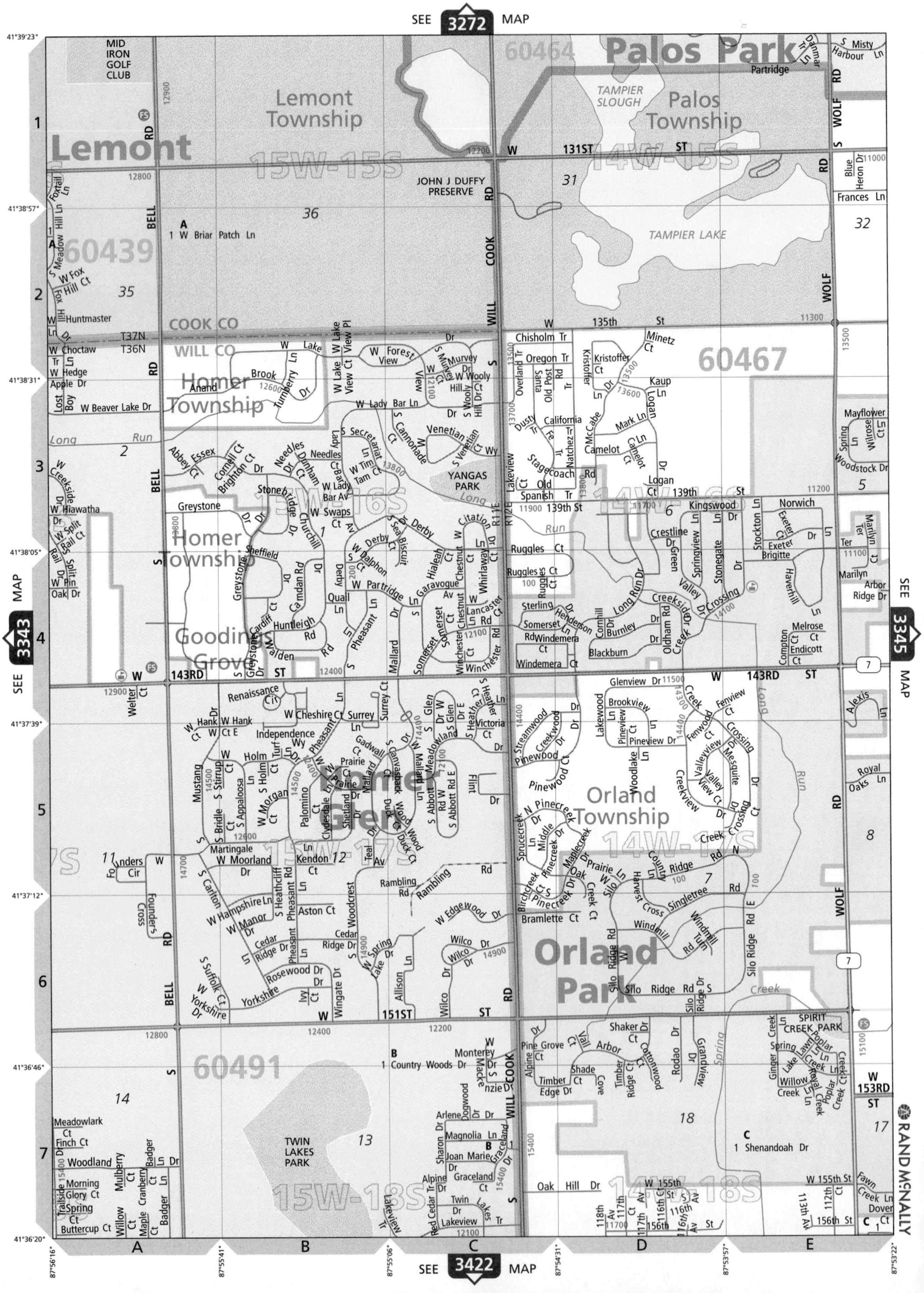

SEE 3272 MAP

SEE 3343 MAP

SEE 3345 MAP

SEE 3422 MAP

1:24,000
1 in. = 2000 ft.
0 0.25 0.5
miles

SEE 3273 MAP

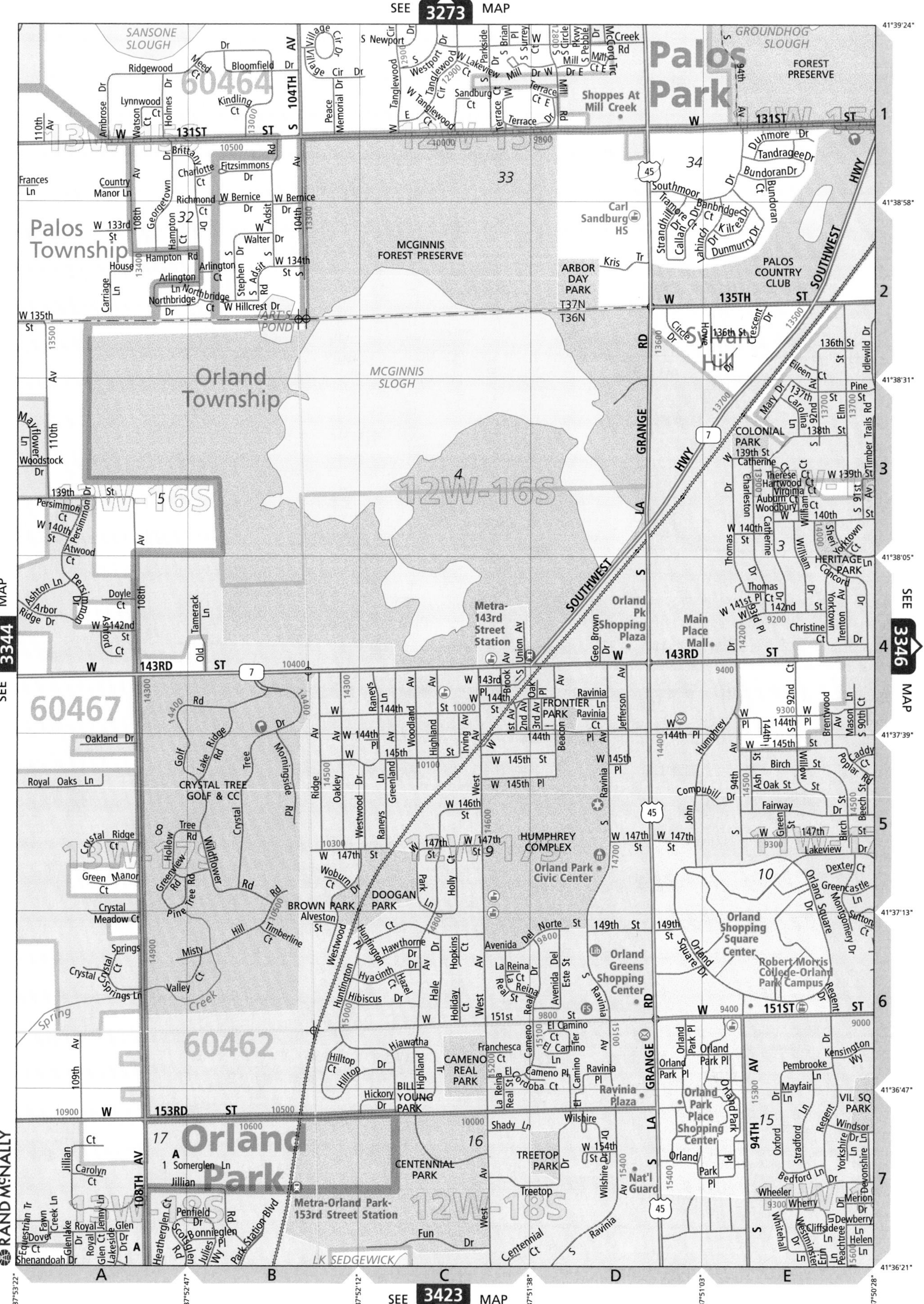

SEE 3344 MAP

SEE 3346 MAP

SEE 3423 MAP

1:24,000
1 in. = 2000 ft.
0 0.25 0.5
miles

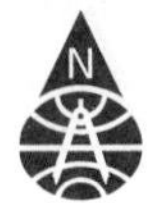

SEE 3274 MAP

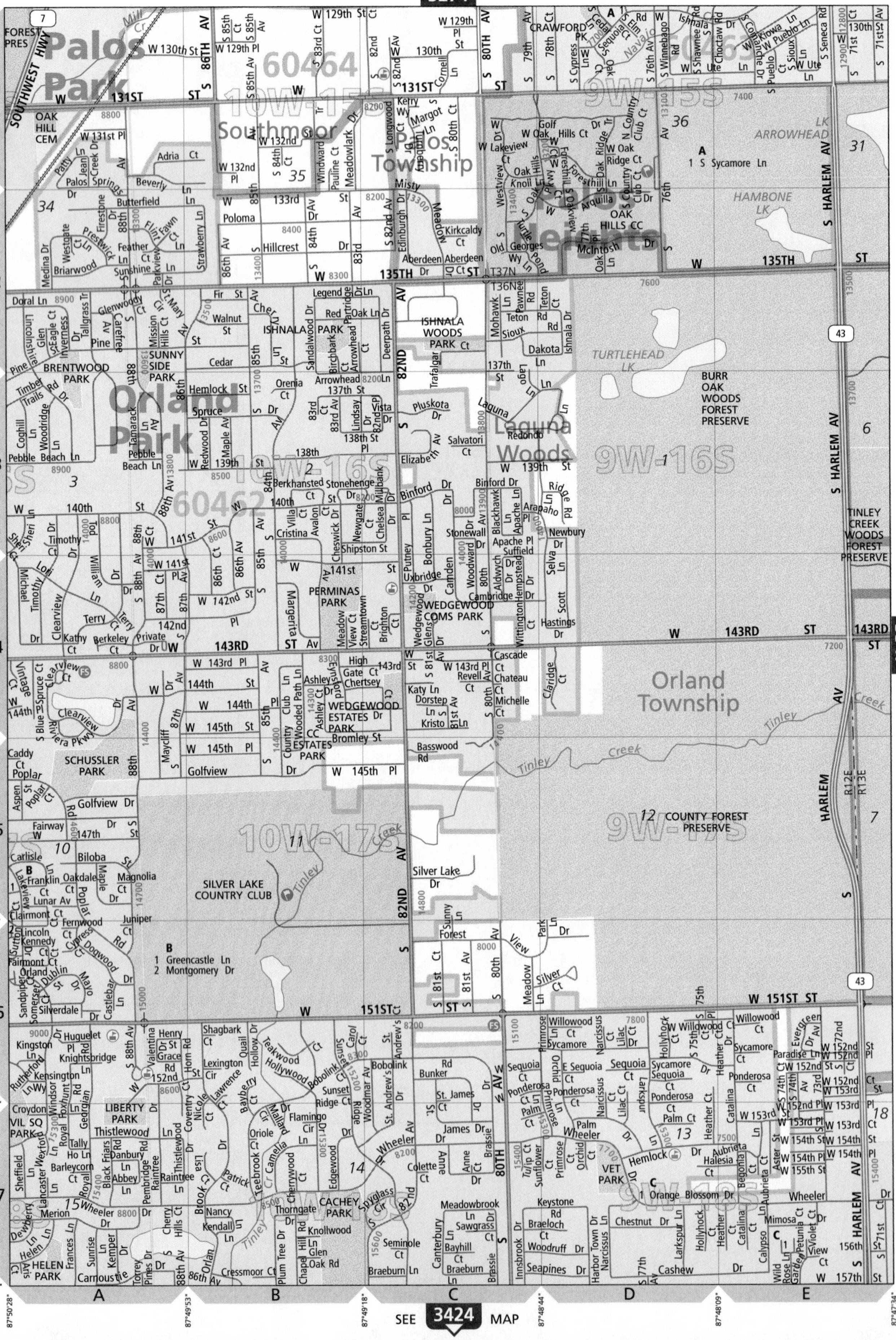

Palos Park
Southmoor
Palos Township
Palos Heights
Orland Park
Laguna Woods
Orland Township
60464
60463
60462
10W-15S
9W-15S
10W-16S
9W-16S
10W-17S
9W-17S
10W-18S
9W-18S
SOUTHWEST HWY
W 131ST ST
W 135TH ST
W 143RD ST
W 151ST ST
S 82ND AV
S 80TH AV
S HARLEM AV
S 86TH AV
88th Av
OAK HILL CEM
OAK HILLS CC
LK ARROWHEAD
HAMBONE LK
TURTLEHEAD LK
BURR OAK WOODS FOREST PRESERVE
TINLEY CREEK WOODS FOREST PRESERVE
COUNTY FOREST PRESERVE
ISHNALA WOODS PARK
ISHNALA PARK
SUNNY SIDE PARK
BRENTWOOD PARK
PERMINAS PARK
WEDGEWOOD COMS PARK
WEDGEWOOD ESTATES PARK
CC ESTATES PARK
SCHUSSLER PARK
SILVER LAKE COUNTRY CLUB
LIBERTY PARK
VIL SQ PARK
CACHEY PARK
VET PARK
HELEN PARK
Tinley Creek
Mill Cr
FOREST PRES
A 1 S Sycamore Ln
B 1 Greencastle Ln 2 Montgomery Dr
R12E R13E
43
7
41°39'24"
41°38'58"
41°38'31"
41°38'05"
41°37'39"
41°37'13"
41°36'47"
41°36'21"
87°50'28"
87°49'53"
87°49'18"
87°48'44"
87°48'09"
87°47'34"
A
B
C
D
E
1
2
3
4
5
6
7

SEE 3345 MAP

SEE 3347 MAP

SEE 3424 MAP

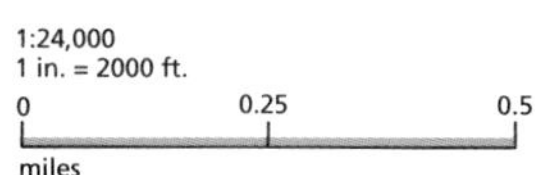

SEE 3275 MAP

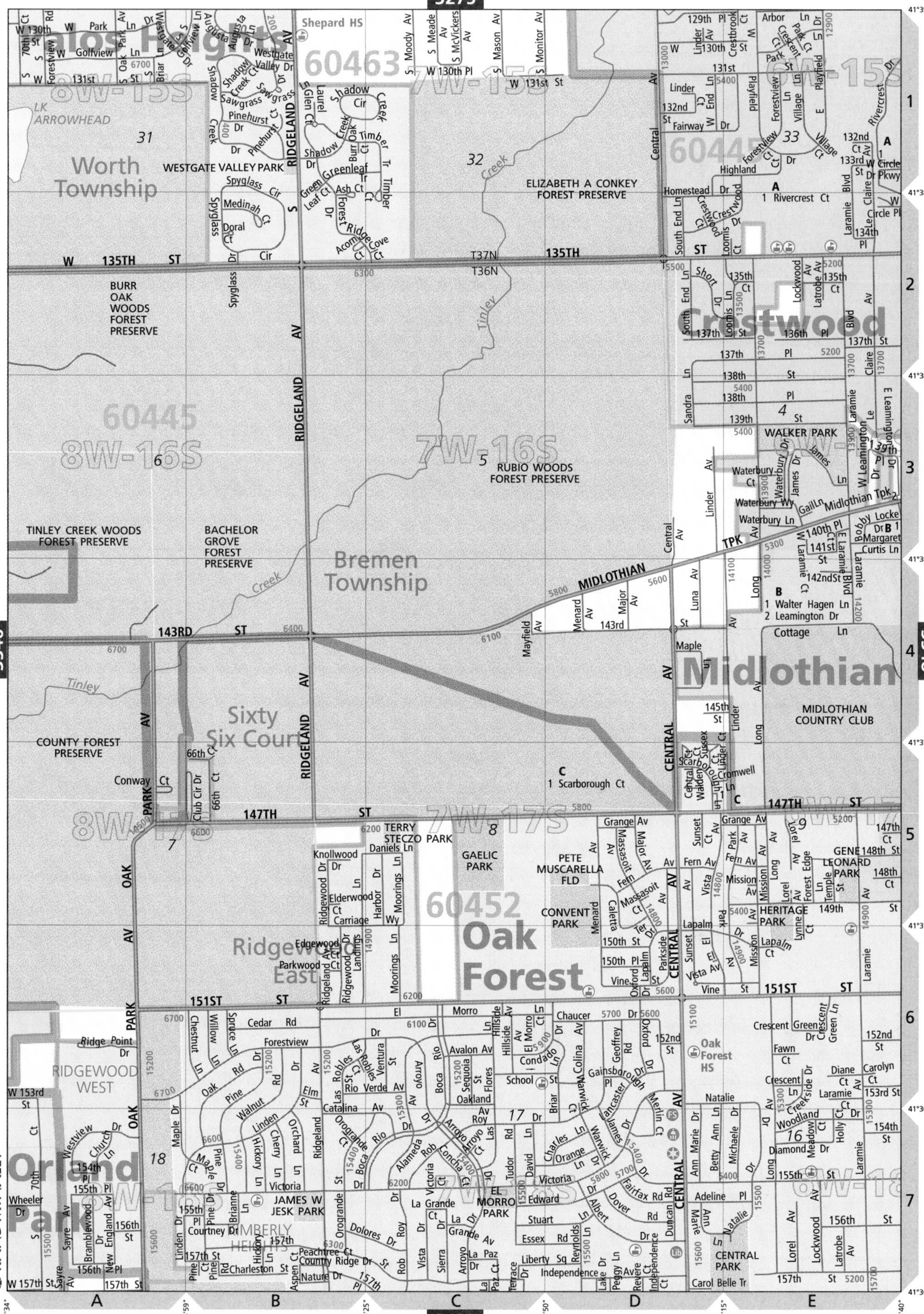

SEE 3346 MAP

SEE 3348 MAP

Palos Heights
60463
8W-15S
7W-15S
6W-15S
Shepard HS
LK ARROWHEAD
31
32
33
Worth Township
WESTGATE VALLEY PARK
ELIZABETH A CONKEY FOREST PRESERVE
60445
A
1 Rivercrest Ct
W 135TH ST
135TH ST
T37N
T36N
BURR OAK WOODS FOREST PRESERVE
Crestwood
60445
8W-16S
6
7W-16S
5
RUBIO WOODS FOREST PRESERVE
4
WALKER PARK
TINLEY CREEK WOODS FOREST PRESERVE
BACHELOR GROVE FOREST PRESERVE
Bremen Township
RIDGELAND AV
MIDLOTHIAN TPK
B
1 Walter Hagen Ln
2 Leamington Dr
143RD ST
Midlothian
MIDLOTHIAN COUNTRY CLUB
Sixty Six Court
COUNTY FOREST PRESERVE
C
1 Scarborough Ct
CENTRAL AV
OAK PARK AV
147TH ST
8W-17S
7
7W-17S
8
TERRY STECZO PARK
GAELIC PARK
PETE MUSCARELLA FLD
9
GENE LEONARD PARK
HERITAGE PARK
60452
CONVENT PARK
Oak Forest
Ridgewood East
151ST ST
RIDGEWOOD WEST
Oak Forest HS
17
16
18
Orland Park
8W-18S
JAMES W JESK PARK
TIMBERLY HEIGHTS
EL MORRO PARK
7W-18S
6W-18S
CENTRAL PARK
W 157th St
157th St

	A	B	C	D	E	
41°39'24"						1
41°38'58"						2
41°38'32"						3
41°38'06"						4
41°37'40"						5
41°37'14"						6
41°36'48"						7
41°36'21"						

87°47'34" 87°46'59" 87°46'25" 87°45'50" 87°45'15" 87°44'40"

SEE 3425 MAP

1:24,000
1 in. = 2000 ft.
0 0.25 0.5
miles

SEE 3276 MAP

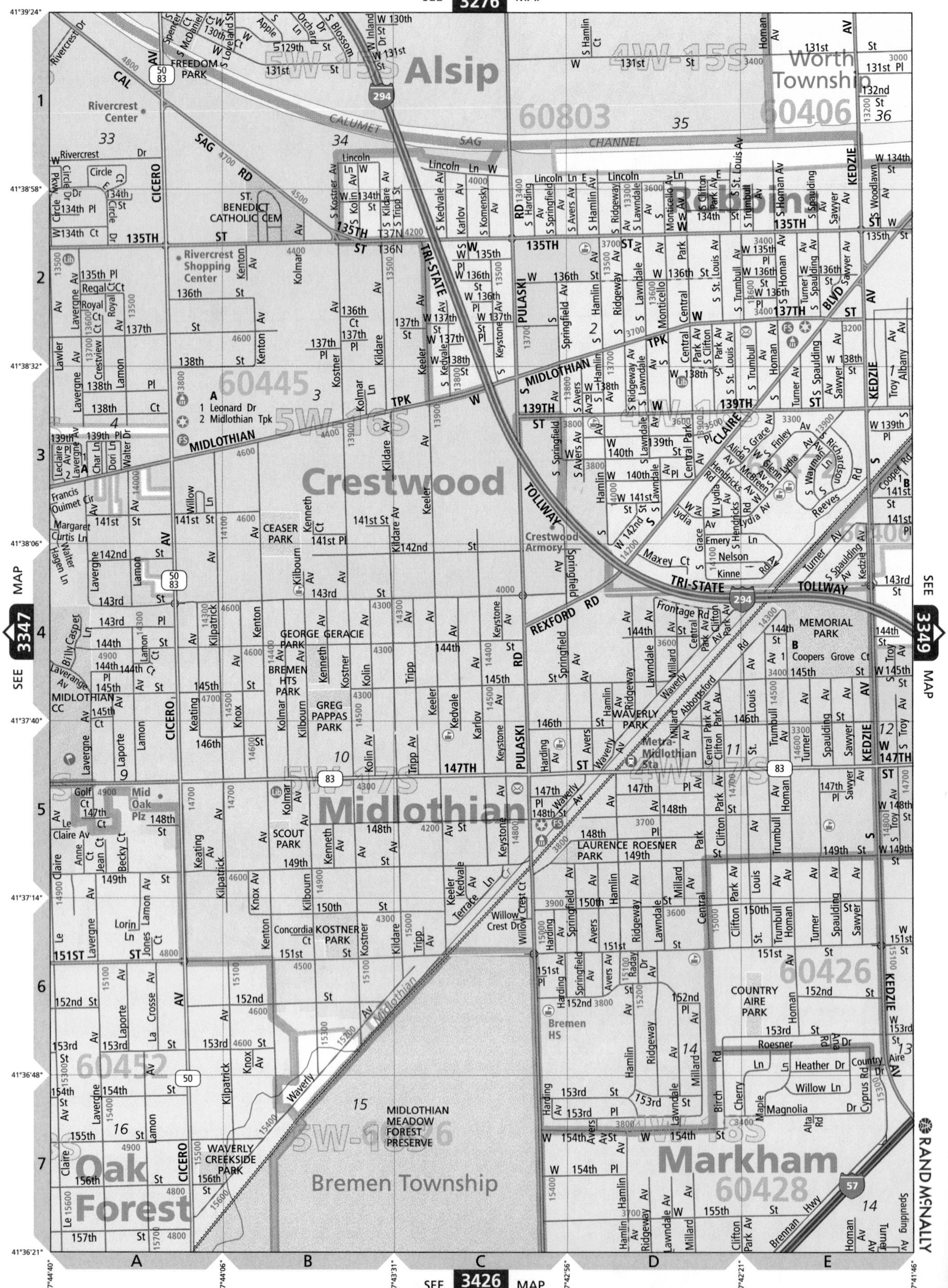

Alsip
60803
4W-15S
5W-15S
Worth Township
60406
131st St
CALUMET SAG CHANNEL
FREEDOM PARK
Rivercrest Center
ST. BENEDICT CATHOLIC CEM
Robbins
135TH ST
Rivercrest Shopping Center
60445
5W-16S
Crestwood
MIDLOTHIAN TPK
TRI-STATE TOLLWAY
CICERO AV
PULASKI RD
KEDZIE AV
CLAIRE BLVD
1 Leonard Dr
2 Midlothian Tpk
CEASER PARK
Crestwood Armory
REXFORD RD
GEORGE GERACIE PARK
BREMEN HTS PARK
GREG PAPPAS PARK
MIDLOTHIAN CC
WAVERLY PARK
Metra-Midlothian Sta
MEMORIAL PARK
1 Coopers Grove Ct
147TH ST
Midlothian
5W-17S
4W-17S
Mid Oak Plz
SCOUT PARK
LAURENCE ROESNER PARK
KOSTNER PARK
Concordia Ct
Willow Crest Dr
151ST ST
60426
COUNTRY AIRE PARK
Bremen HS
60452
MIDLOTHIAN MEADOW FOREST PRESERVE
5W-18S
4W-18S
WAVERLY CREEKSIDE PARK
Oak Forest
Bremen Township
Markham
60428
Brennan Hwy
RAND McNALLY

SEE 3347 MAP
SEE 3349 MAP

A B C D E
1 2 3 4 5 6 7

SEE 3426 MAP

1:24,000
1 in. = 2000 ft.
0 0.25 0.5
miles

SEE 3277 MAP

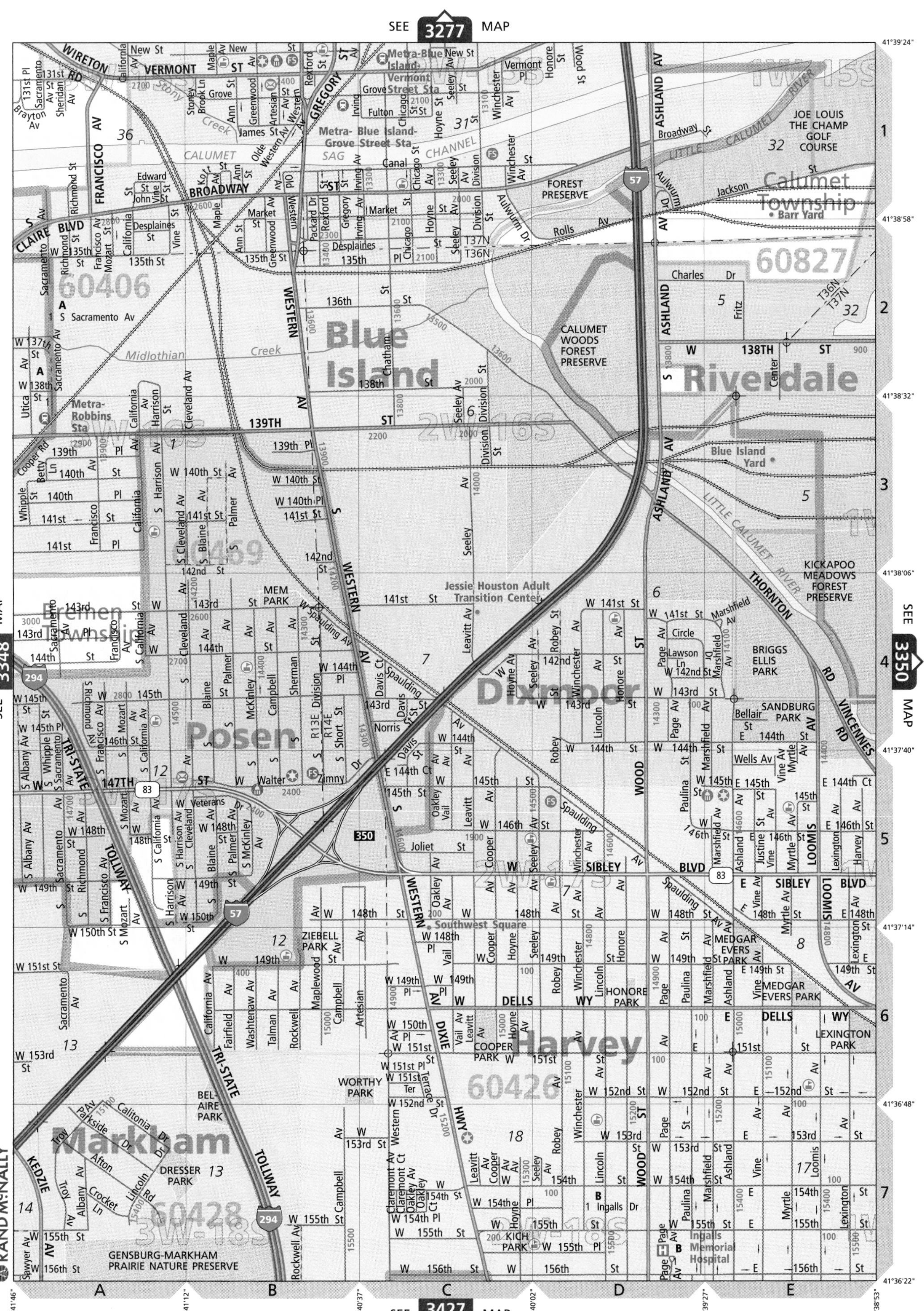

SEE 3427 MAP

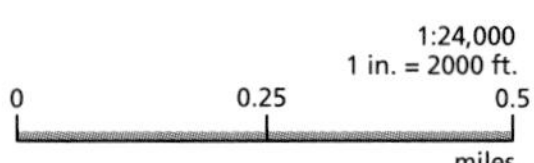

1:24,000
1 in. = 2000 ft.
0 0.25 0.5
miles

SEE 3278 MAP

SEE 3349 MAP

SEE 3351 MAP

SEE 3428 MAP

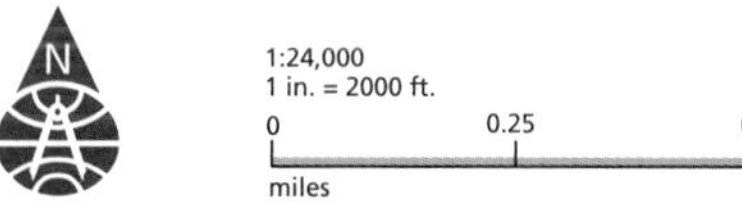

SEE 3279 MAP

Chicago
60633
60827
Dolton
60419
60409
Burnham
Calumet City
South Holland
60473
Thornton Township

A
1 S Manistee Av
2 S Muskegon Av
3 E 133rd St

B
1 MacArthur Ct

C
1 S Martha Av

BISHOP FORD MEMORIAL EXPWY
FLATFOOT LK
BEAUBIEN WOODS FOREST PRESERVE
CARVER PARK
LITTLE CALUMET RIVER
CALUMET RIVER
GRAND CALUMET RIVER
Thomas J O'Brien Lock & Dam
Sunset Bay Marina
Croissant Marina
A1 Millennium Marina
LK COTTAGE GROVE
NEEDLES PARK
KANDY KANE PARK
BLACKSTONE PARK
DOWNEY PARK
MEADOWLANE PARK
Kmart Plaza
Thornridge HS
Sibley Crossing Shop Ctr
LAMPLIGHTER PARK
CITY PARK
OAKLAND CEMETERY
TRIANGLE PARK
Almar Plaza
COMMISSIONER'S PARK
SHABBONA WOODS FOREST PRESERVE
CLAYHOLE WOODS FOREST PRESERVE
RIVERFRONT PARK
LITTLE CALUMET PARK
PACESETTER PARK
RIVERVIEW PARK
GOUWENS PARK
FOREST PRESERVE
MANN PARK

E 134th St
E 138th St
E MAIN ST
DOLTON AV
DOLTON RD
LINCOLN AV
E SIBLEY BLVD
E STATE ST
MICHIGAN CITY RD
E 154TH ST
PULASKI RD
S TORRENCE AV
COTTAGE GROVE AV
GREENWOOD RD
DORCHESTER
S BRAINARD AV

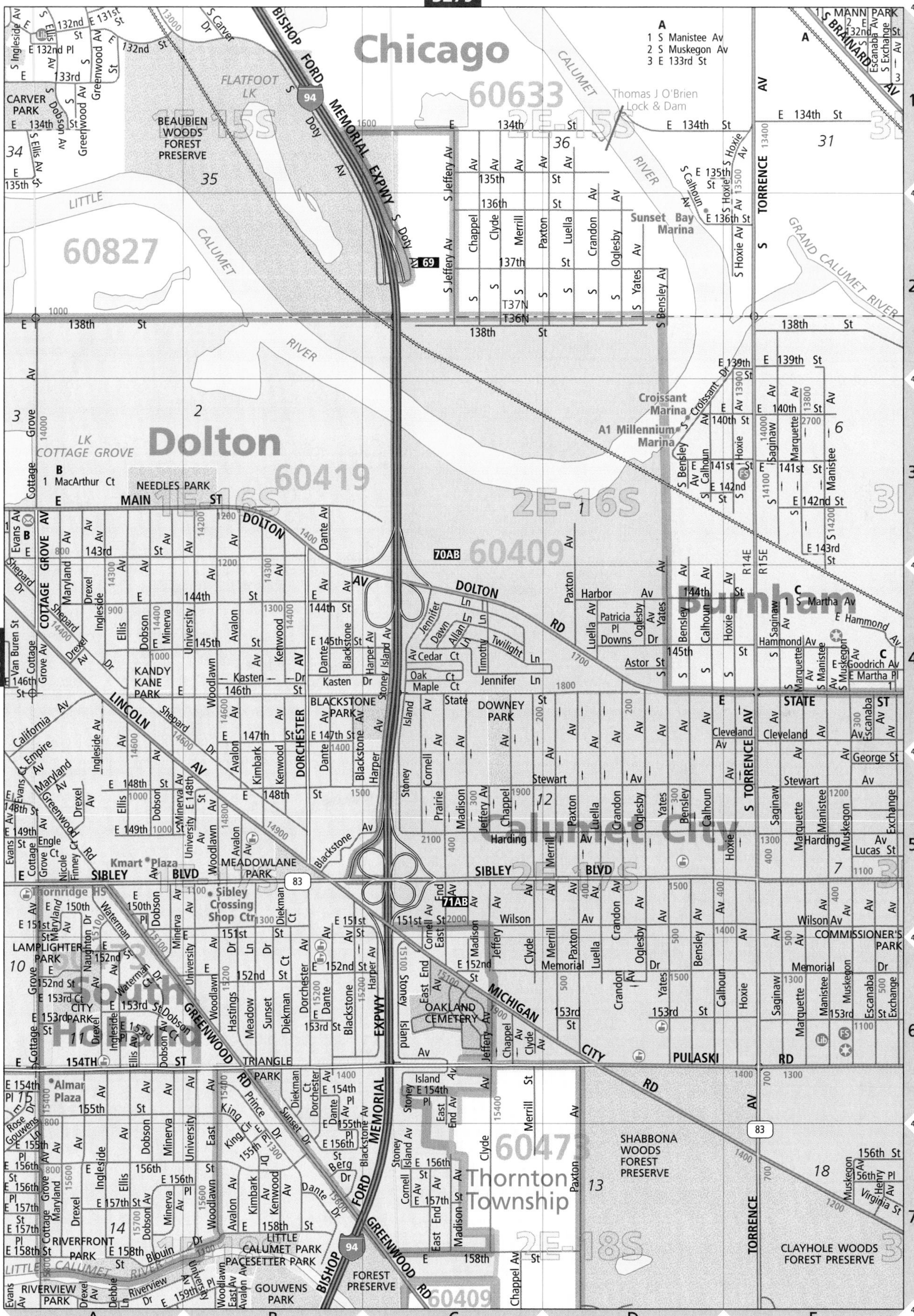

SEE 3350 MAP

SEE 3352 MAP

SEE 3429 MAP

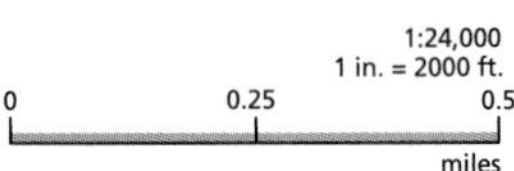

SEE 3280 MAP

SEE 3351 MAP

SEE B MAP

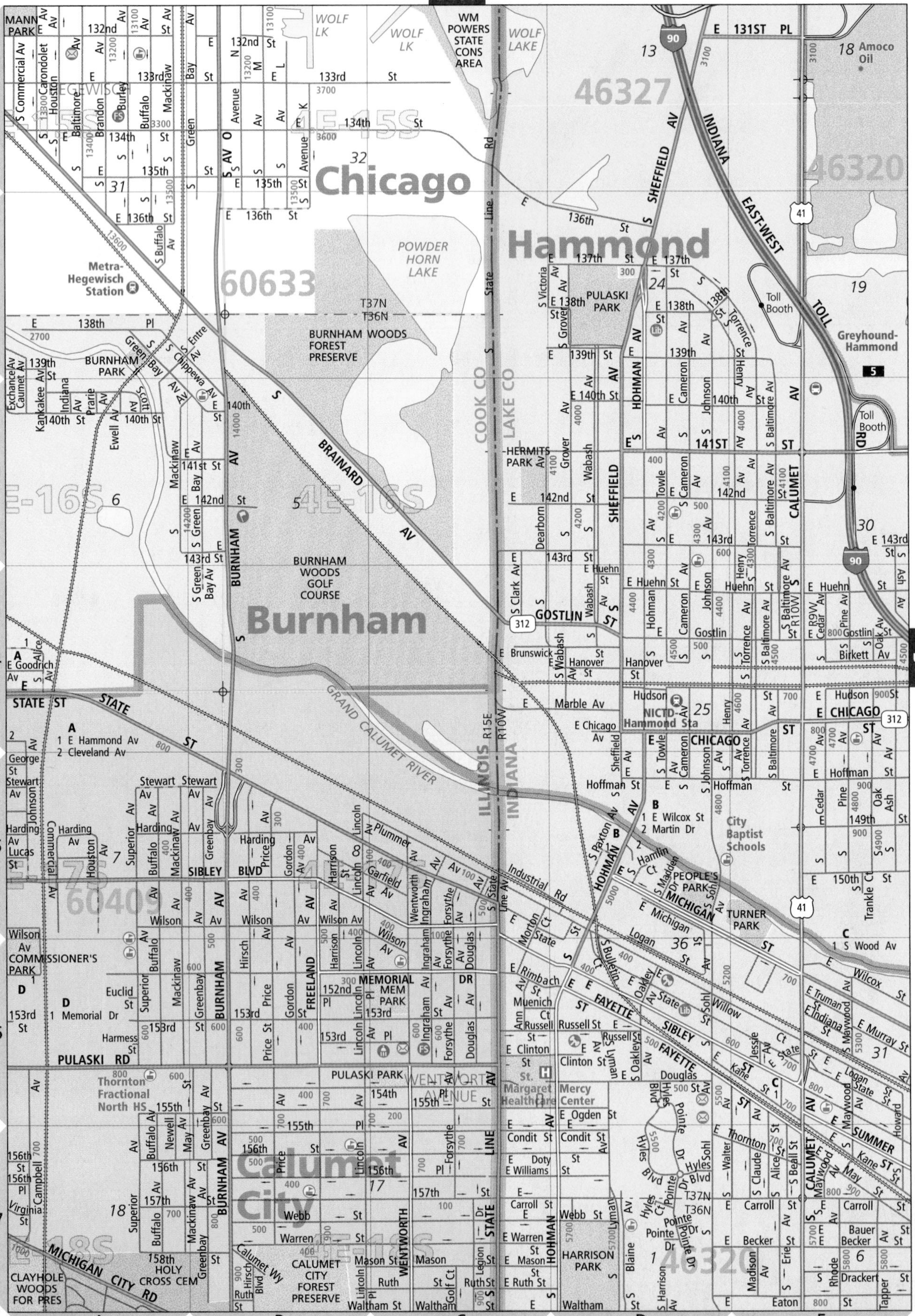

Chicago

Hammond

Burnham

Calumet City

60633

46327

46320

60409

WOLF LAKE

POWDER HORN LAKE

WM POWERS STATE CONS AREA

BURNHAM WOODS FOREST PRESERVE

BURNHAM WOODS GOLF COURSE

BURNHAM PARK

HEGEWISCH

Metra-Hegewisch Station

PULASKI PARK

HERMITS PARK

COMMISSIONER'S PARK

MEMORIAL MEM PARK

PULASKI PARK

Thornton Fractional North HS

HOLY CROSS CEM

CALUMET CITY FOREST PRESERVE

CLAYHOLE WOODS FOR PRES

St. Margaret Healthcare

Mercy Center

HARRISON PARK

NICTD-Hammond Sta

City Baptist Schools

PEOPLE'S PARK

TURNER PARK

Greyhound-Hammond

Amoco Oil

Toll Booth

GRAND CALUMET RIVER

COOK CO

LAKE CO

ILLINOIS

INDIANA

R15E

R10W

T37N

T36N

A
1 E Hammond Av
2 Cleveland Av

B
1 E Wilcox St
2 Martin Dr

C
1 S Wood Av

D
1 Memorial Dr

SEE 3430 MAP

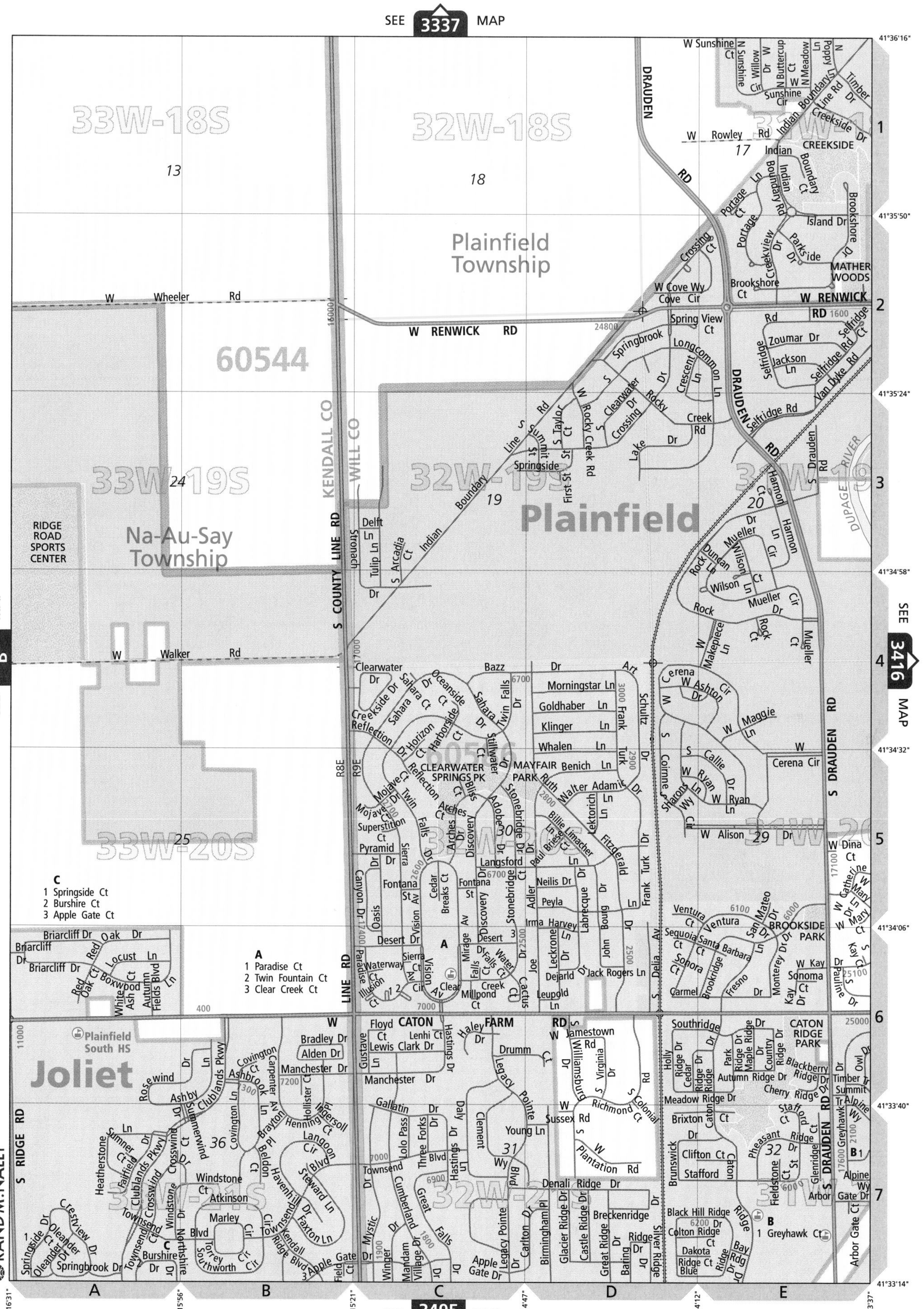
1:24,000
1 in. = 2000 ft.
0 0.25 0.5
miles
SEE 3337 MAP
SEE 3416 MAP
SEE 3495 MAP
33W-18S
32W-18S
33W-19S
32W-19S
33W-20S
32W-20S
33W-21S
32W-21S
31W-19S
31W-20S
31W-21S
Plainfield Township
Na-Au-Say Township
Plainfield
Joliet
60544
60586
RIDGE ROAD SPORTS CENTER
CLEARWATER SPRINGS PK
MAYFAIR PARK
CREEKSIDE
MATHER WOODS
BROOKSIDE PARK
CATON RIDGE PARK
Plainfield South HS
KENDALL CO
WILL CO
S COUNTY LINE RD
DRAUDEN RD
S DRAUDEN RD
W RENWICK RD
W Wheeler Rd
W Walker Rd
W CATON FARM RD
Indian Boundary Line Rd
DUPAGE RIVER
S RIDGE RD
A
1 Paradise Ct
2 Twin Fountain Ct
3 Clear Creek Ct
B
1 Greyhawk Ct
C
1 Springside Ct
2 Burshire Ct
3 Apple Gate Ct
A B C D E
1 2 3 4 5 6 7
41°36'16"
41°35'50"
41°35'24"
41°34'58"
41°34'32"
41°34'06"
41°33'40"
41°33'14"
88°16'31"
88°15'56"
88°15'21"
88°14'47"
88°14'12"
88°13'37"
RAND McNALLY

1:24,000
1 in. = 2000 ft.
0 0.25 0.5
miles

SEE 3338 MAP

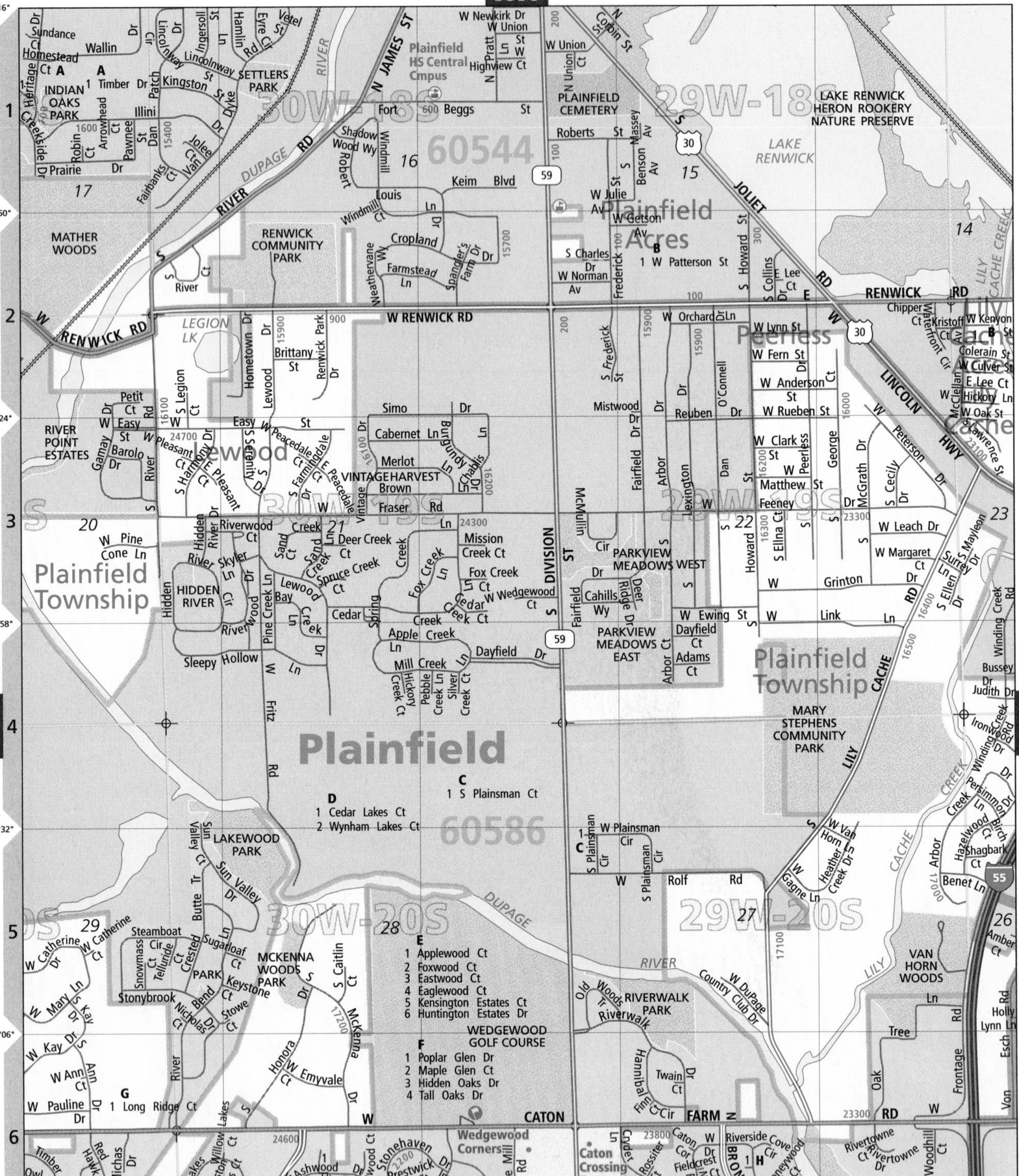

SEE 3415 MAP

A
1 Timber Dr

B
1 W Patterson St

C
1 S Plainsman Ct

D
1 Cedar Lakes Ct
2 Wynham Lakes Ct

E
1 Applewood Ct
2 Foxwood Ct
3 Eastwood Ct
4 Eaglewood Ct
5 Kensington Estates Ct
6 Huntington Estates Dr

F
1 Poplar Glen Dr
2 Maple Glen Ct
3 Hidden Oaks Dr
4 Tall Oaks Dr

G
1 Long Ridge Ct

H
1 Old Meadow Ct

J
1 Squires Mill Rd

Plainfield

60544

60586

SEE 3496 MAP

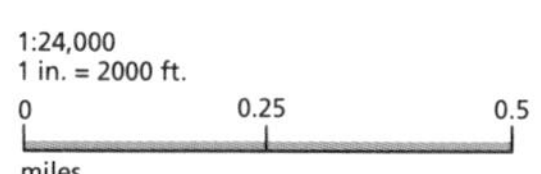

SEE 3339 MAP

LAKE RENWICK HERON ROOKERY NATURE PRESERVE

WILL COUNTY PRESERVE

Plainfield Fishing Resort

MISTWOOD GOLF CLUB

Romeoville

60544

W RENWICK RD

E RENWICK RD

Plainfield Township

OLD RENWICK TRAIL PARK

Plainfield

Pinecrest

60435

60441

Westfield Louis Joliet Mall

60431

DIVISION ST

W DIVISION ST

HENNEPIN DR

PLAINFIELD

Coynes

Lockport Township

60403

Crystal Lawns

W CATON FARM RD

CATON FARM RD

Westriver Crossing

Joliet

JOHN LEACH MEM PARK

Fiday View

Crest Hill

THEODORE MARSH PRES

ESSINGTON RD

GAYLORD RD

A
1 Tomahawk Lake Ct
2 Silver Moon Lake Wy

B
1 Sunset Ct
2 Sunrise Ct

C
1 Carnation Dr
2 Orchid Ln
3 Morning Glory Ln

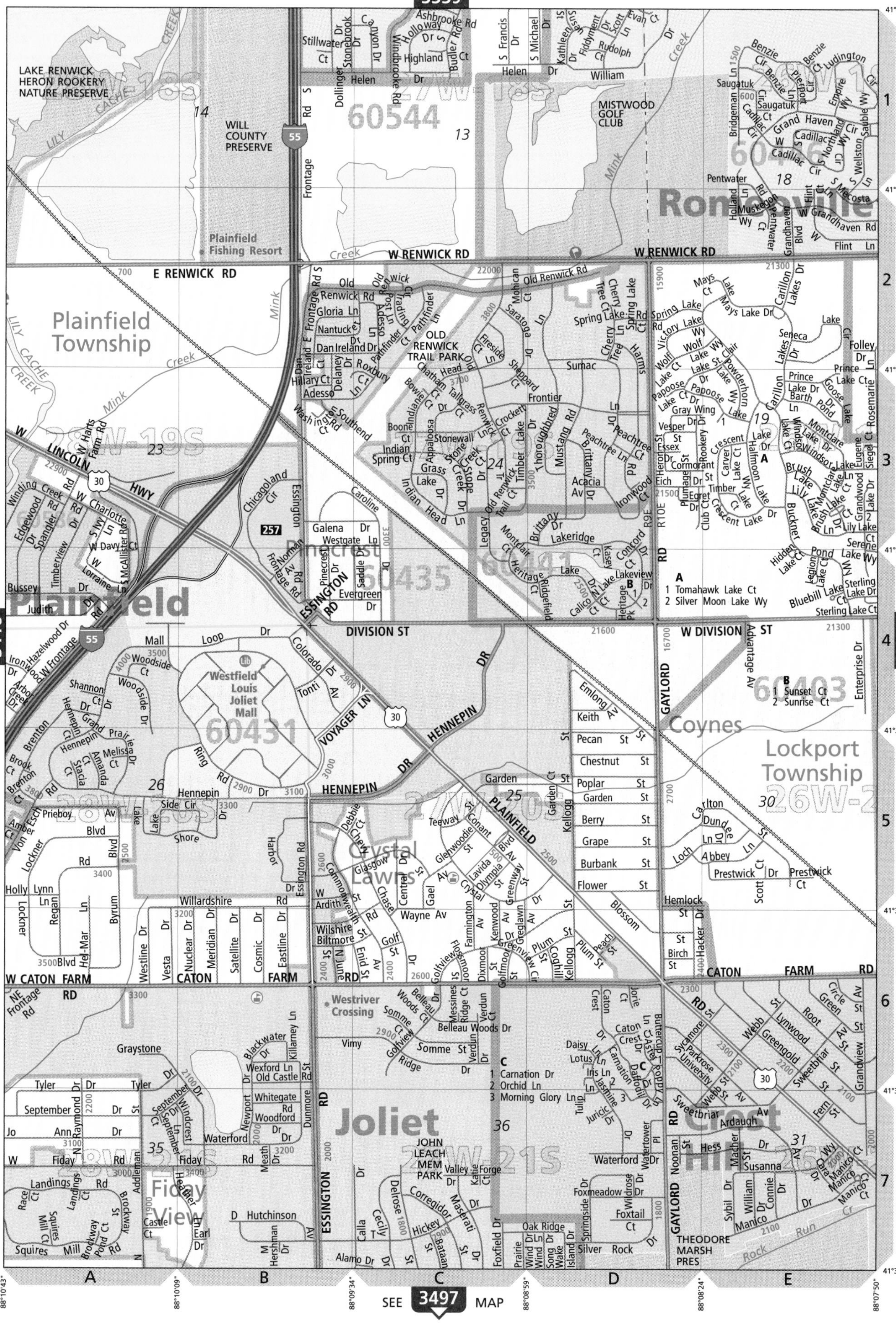

SEE 3416 MAP

SEE 3418 MAP

SEE 3497 MAP

1:24,000
1 in. = 2000 ft.
0 0.25 0.5
miles

SEE 3340 MAP

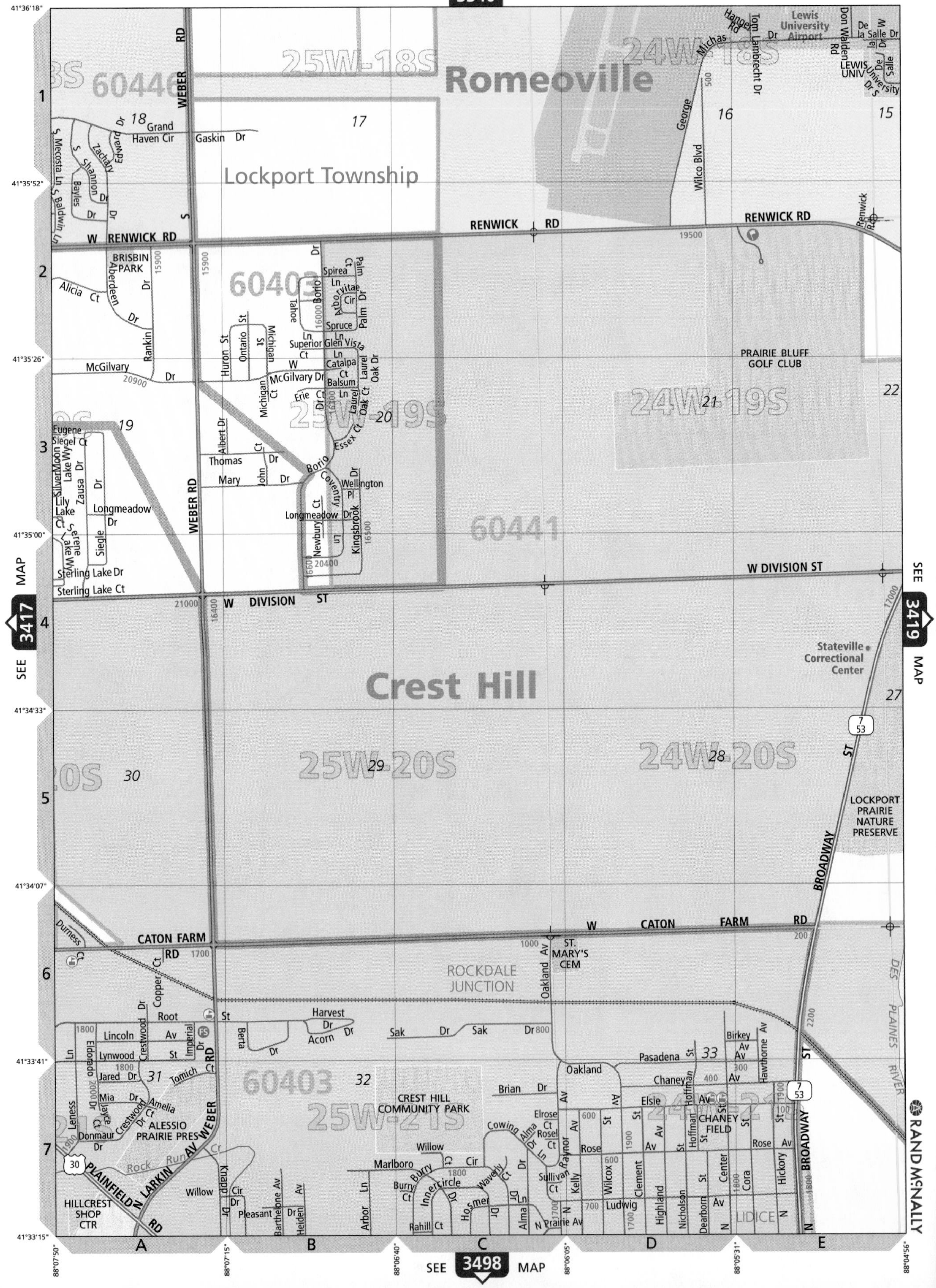

SEE 3417 MAP

SEE 3419 MAP

Romeoville
Lockport Township
Crest Hill
Lewis University Airport
LEWIS UNIV
PRAIRIE BLUFF GOLF CLUB
Stateville Correctional Center
LOCKPORT PRAIRIE NATURE PRESERVE
BRISBIN PARK
ROCKDALE JUNCTION
ST. MARY'S CEM
CREST HILL COMMUNITY PARK
CHANEY FIELD
ALESSIO PRAIRIE PRES
HILLCREST SHOP CTR
LIDICE
DES PLAINES RIVER

60446
60403
60441
25W-18S
24W-18S
25W-19S
24W-19S
25W-20S
24W-20S
25W-21S
24W-21S

WEBER RD
S WEBER RD
W RENWICK RD
RENWICK RD
W DIVISION ST
W CATON FARM RD
CATON FARM RD
BROADWAY ST
PLAINFIELD N LARKIN AV
Michas Dr
Hangar Rd
Tom Lambrecht Dr
Don Walden Rd
De la Salle Dr
University Dr S
George Wilco Blvd
Grand Haven Cir
Gaskin Dr
S Mecosta Ln
S Baldwin Ln
S Shannon Dr
Zachary Dr
Edward Dr
Bayles Dr
Aberdeen Dr
Alicia Ct
Rankin Dr
McGilvary Dr
Huron St
Ontario St
Michigan St
Michigan Ct
Tahoe Ln
Superior Ct
W McGilvary Dr
Borio Dr
Spirea Ln
Arborvitae Cir
Palm Ct
Palm Dr
Spruce Ln
Glen Vista
Catalpa Ln
Balsum Ct
Laurel Ln
Laurel Oak Dr
Oak Ct
Erie Ct
Essex Ct
Albert Dr
Thomas Ct
Mary Dr
John Dr
Coventry Dr
Wellington Pl
Kingsbrook Dr
Longmeadow Dr
Newbury Ct
Eugene Siegel Ct
Silver Moon Lake Wy
Zausa Dr
Lily Lake Ct
Serene Lake Wy
Siegle Dr
Sterling Lake Dr
Sterling Lake Ct
Durness Ct
Copper Ct
Crestwood Dr
Root St
Lincoln Av
Lynwood St
Imperial Av
Eldorado Dr
Jared Dr
Tomich Ct
Mia Dr
Amelia Ct
Jayce Ct
Crestwood Dr
Leness Ln
Donmaur Dr
Rock Run Cr
Harvest Dr
Acorn Dr
Berta Dr
Sak Dr
Oakland Av
Oakland
Pasadena St
Birkey Av
Hawthorne Av
Chaney Av
Hoffman St
Elsie Av
Brian Dr
Elrose Ct
Rosel Ct
Cowing Alma Dr
Raynor Av
Rose Av
Sullivan Ct
Kelly St
Wilcox St
Clement Av
Highland Av
Nicholson St
Dearborn St
Center St
Cora St
Hickory St
Ludwig
Prairie Av
Willow Cir
Marlboro Ct
Burry Ct
Innercircle Dr
Hosmer Dr
Waverly Ct
Rahill Ct
Arbor Ln
Knapp Dr
Willow Cir
Pleasant Dr
Barthelone Av
Heiden Av
Alma Ln

1 2 3 4 5 6 7
A B C D E

SEE 3498 MAP

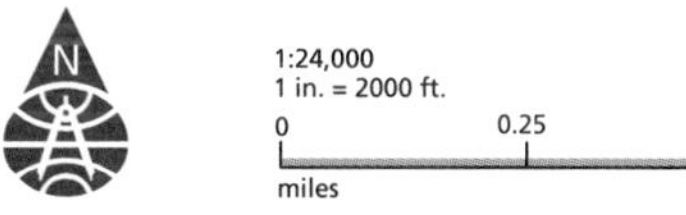

SEE 3341 MAP

Romeoville

Lockport

Crest Hill

Dellwood Highlands

Fairmont

Bonnie Brea

Lockport Township

60441

60432

LEWIS UNIVERSITY

LOCKPORT PRAIRIE NATURE PRESERVE

DELLWOOD WEST PARK

DELLWOOD PARK

LEGION PARK

BONNIE BRAE PARK

WEST SIDE PARK

LOCKPORT CEMETERY

RUSSIAN CEM

ATHLETIC FIELD

SOUTH LOCKPORT

LAMBS WOODS FOR PRES

AF HILL PARK

MT CALVARY CEM

Fitzpatrick House

Illinois & Michigan Canal

Illinois State Mus

Gaylord Bldg

Pioneer Settlement

Will Co Hist Society

Central Sq Building

Lockport Station

Lockport Township HS-Central

DES PLAINES RIVER

SANITARY DRAINAGE & SHIP CANAL

ILLINOIS & MICHIGAN CANAL

RENWICK RD

BROADWAY ST

W 9TH ST

E 9TH ST

THORNTON ST

S STATE ST

S NEW AV

GARFIELD AV

E DIVISION ST

W Division St

S BRIGGS ST

W BRUCE RD

W Oak Av

B
1 Clinton St
2 W 11th St
3 W 12th St
4 W 13th St

A
1 De la Salle Dr

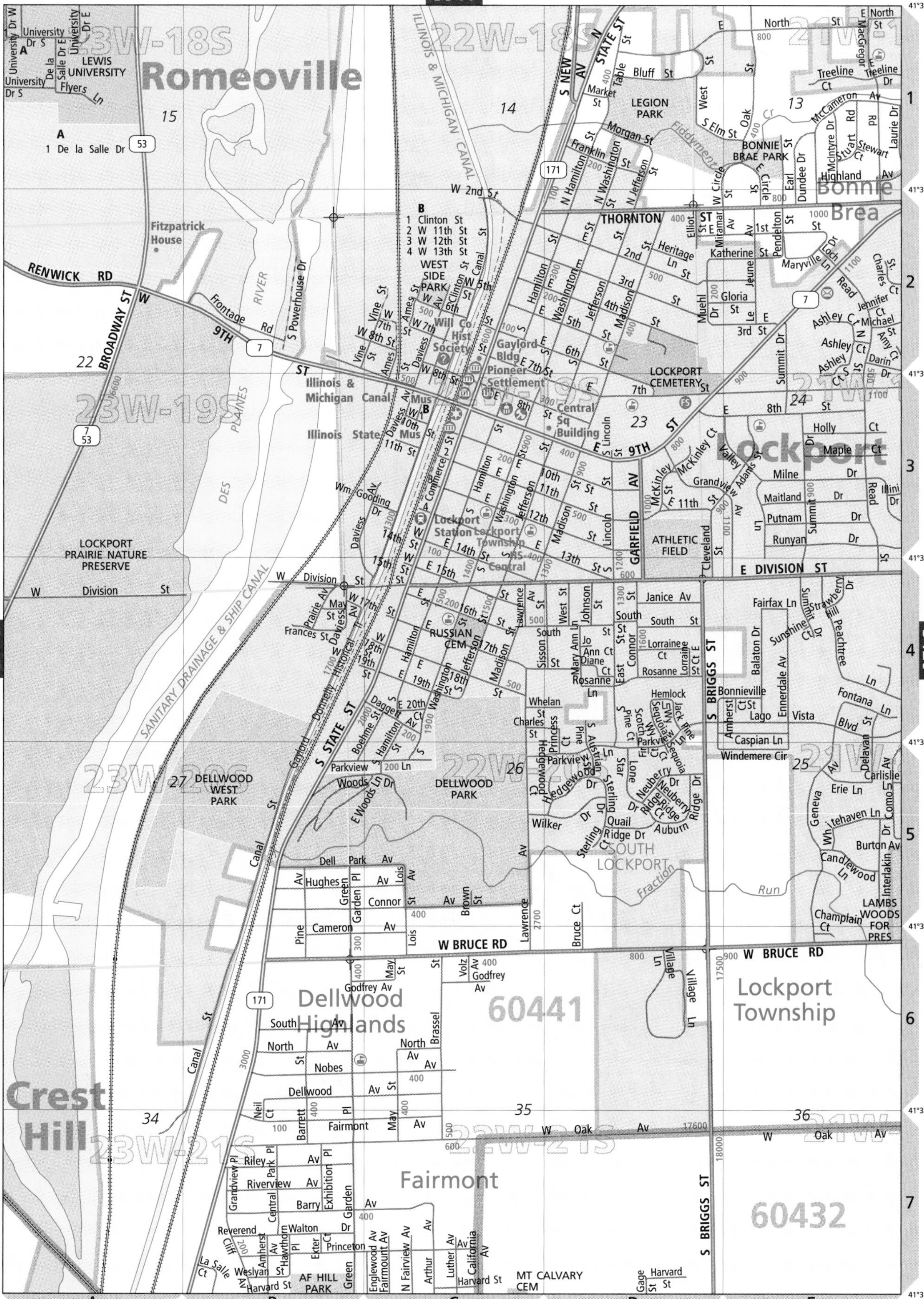

SEE 3418 MAP

SEE 3420 MAP

SEE 3499 MAP

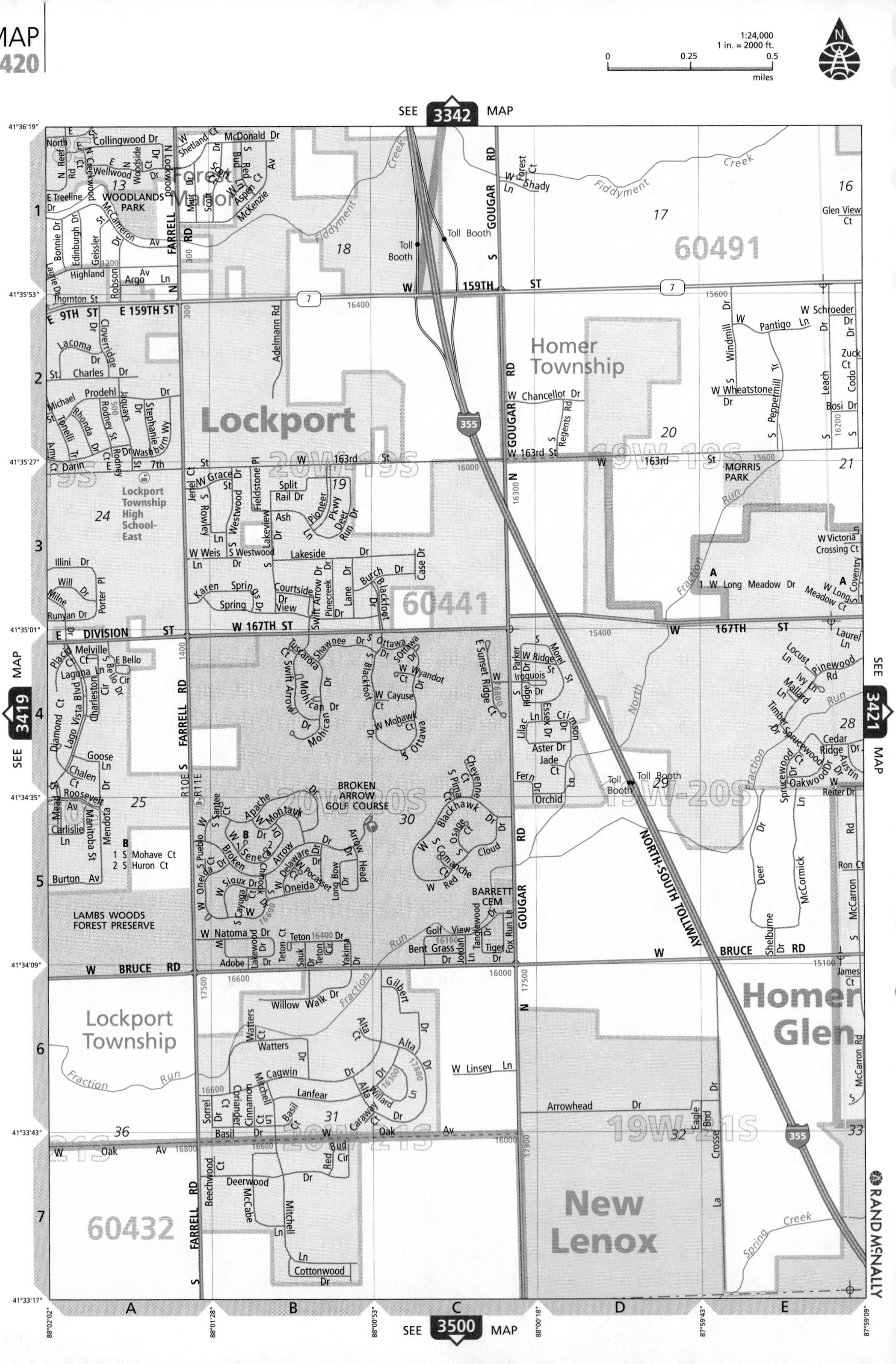

1:24,000
1 in. = 2000 ft.
0 — 0.25 — 0.5
miles

SEE 3342 MAP

SEE 3419 MAP

SEE 3421 MAP

Lockport
Homer Township
Lockport Township
Homer Glen
New Lenox
Forest Manor
WOODLANDS PARK
MORRIS PARK
Lockport Township High School-East
BROKEN ARROW GOLF COURSE
BARRETT CEM
LAMBS WOODS FOREST PRESERVE

60491
60441
60432

W 159TH ST
E 159TH ST
E 9TH ST
W 163rd St
W 167TH ST
E DIVISION ST
W BRUCE RD
W Oak Av
FARRELL RD
S GOUGAR RD
N GOUGAR RD
NORTH-SOUTH TOLLWAY
Toll Booth

Fiddyment Creek
Fraction Run
North Run
Spring Creek

B
1 S Mohave Ct
2 S Huron Ct

A
1 W Long Meadow Dr

20W-19S
19W-19S
20W-20S
19W-20S
20W-21S
19W-21S

41°36'19"
41°35'53"
41°35'27"
41°35'01"
41°34'35"
41°34'09"
41°33'43"
41°33'17"

88°02'02" 88°01'28" 88°00'53" 88°00'18" 87°59'43" 87°59'08"

A B C D E
1 2 3 4 5 6 7

RAND McNALLY

SEE 3500 MAP

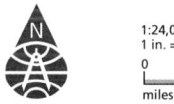

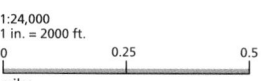

1:24,000
1 in. = 2000 ft.
0 0.25 0.5
miles

SEE 3343 MAP

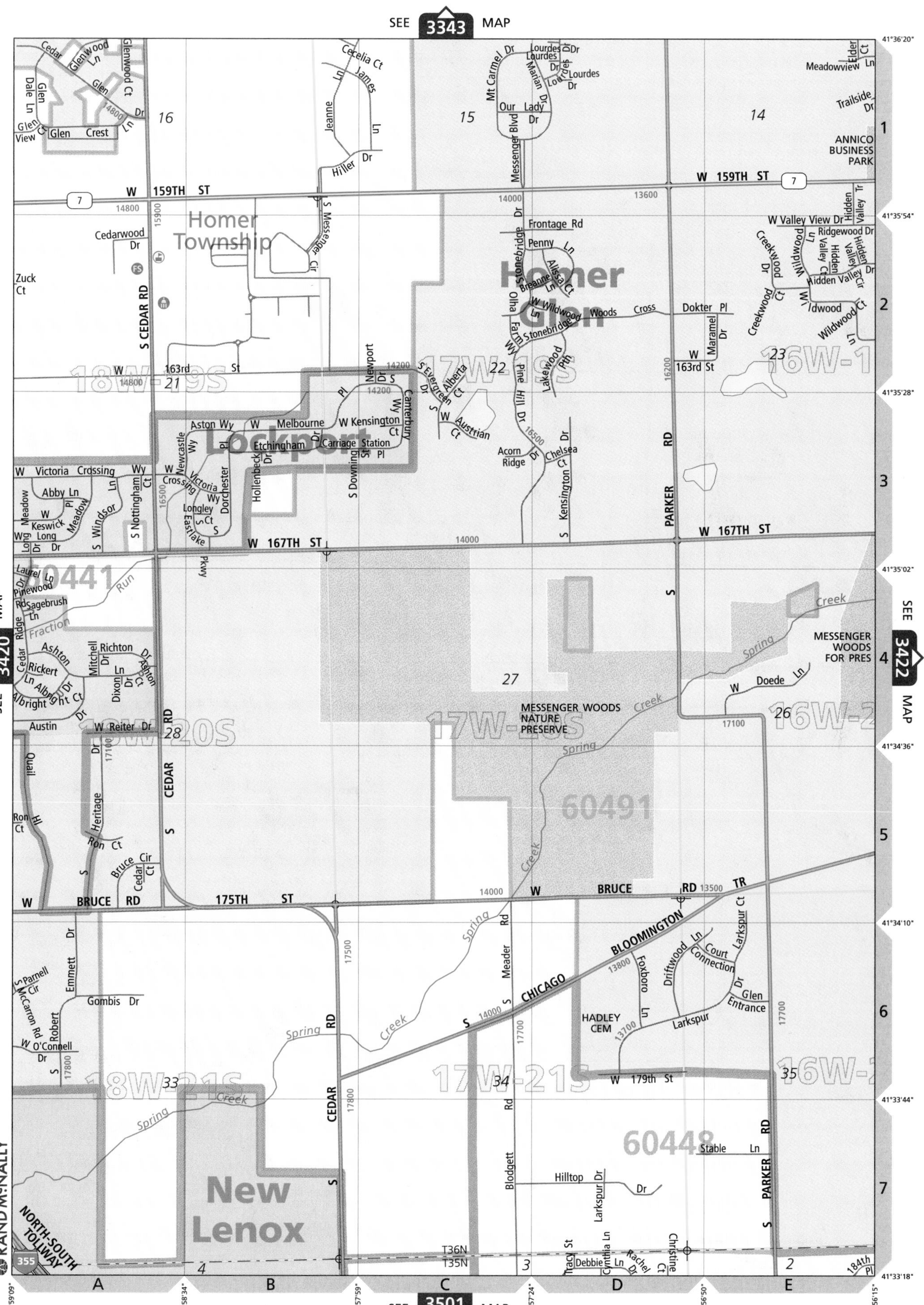

SEE 3420 MAP
SEE 3422 MAP
SEE 3501 MAP

1:24,000
1 in. = 2000 ft.
0 0.25 0.5
miles

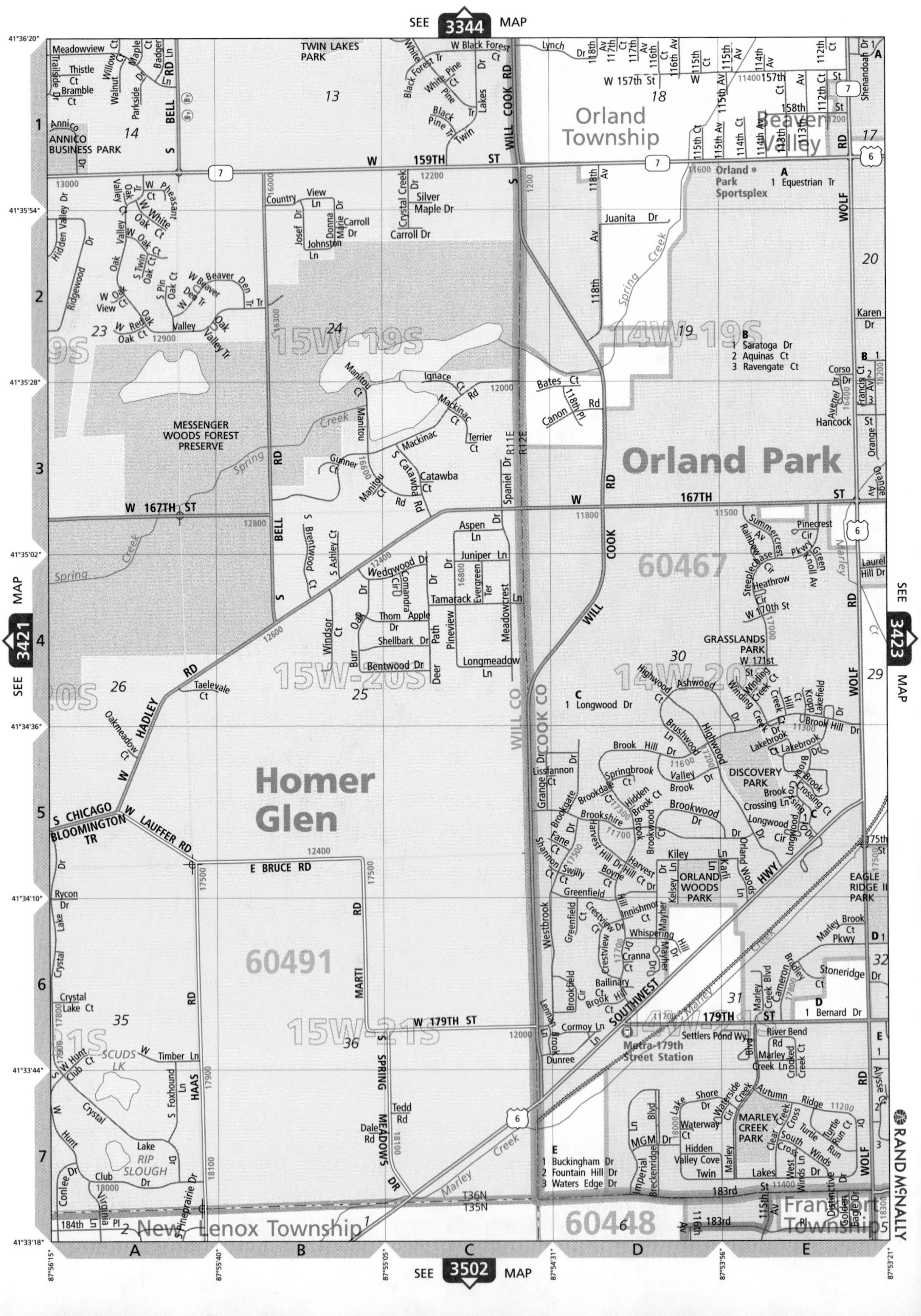

SEE 3344 MAP

Orland Township

Orland Park

Homer Glen

Orland Park Sportsplex

MESSENGER WOODS FOREST PRESERVE

TWIN LAKES PARK

ANNICO BUSINESS PARK

GRASSLANDS PARK

DISCOVERY PARK

ORLAND WOODS PARK

EAGLE RIDGE II PARK

MARLEY CREEK PARK

Metra-179th Street Station

New Lenox Township

Frankfort Township

60467

60491

60448

A
1 Equestrian Tr

B
1 Saratoga Dr
2 Aquinas Ct
3 Ravengate Ct

C
1 Longwood Dr

D
1 Bernard Dr

E
1 Buckingham Dr
2 Fountain Hill Dr
3 Waters Edge Dr

SEE 3421 MAP

SEE 3423 MAP

SEE 3502 MAP

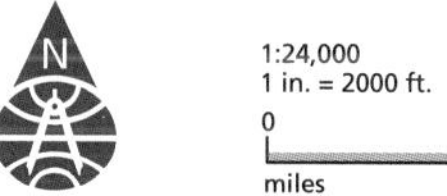

1:24,000
1 in. = 2000 ft.
0 0.25 0.5
miles

SEE 3345 MAP

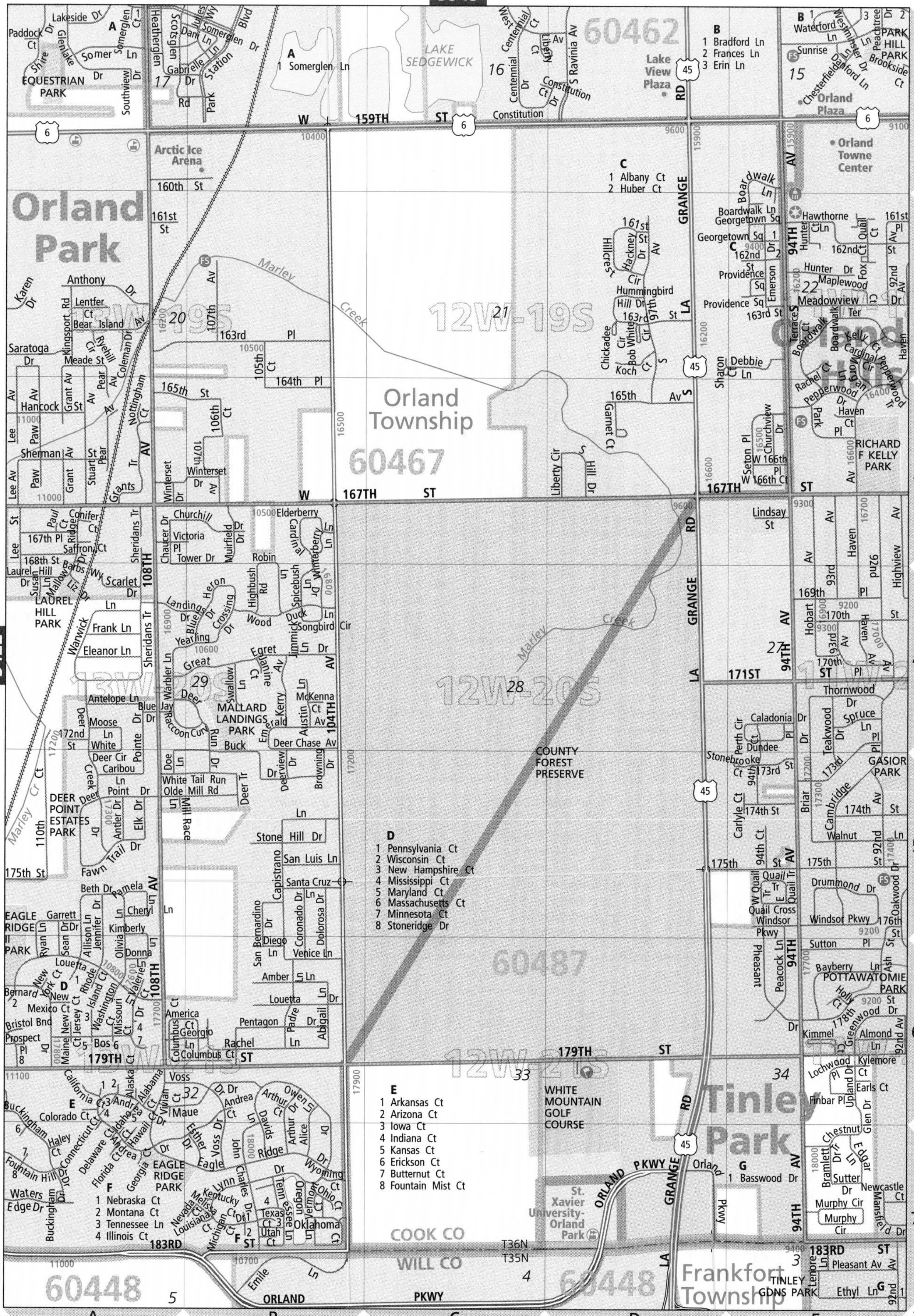

SEE 3422 MAP

SEE 3424 MAP

SEE 3503 MAP

A
1 Somerglen Ln

B
1 Bradford Ln
2 Frances Ln
3 Erin Ln

C
1 Albany Ct
2 Huber Ct

D
1 Pennsylvania Ct
2 Wisconsin Ct
3 New Hampshire Ct
4 Mississippi Ct
5 Maryland Ct
6 Massachusetts Ct
7 Minnesota Ct
8 Stoneridge Dr

E
1 Arkansas Ct
2 Arizona Ct
3 Iowa Ct
4 Indiana Ct
5 Kansas Ct
6 Erickson Ct
7 Butternut Ct
8 Fountain Mist Ct

F
1 Nebraska Ct
2 Montana Ct
3 Tennessee Ln
4 Illinois Ct

G
1 Basswood Dr

Orland Park
Orland Township
Orland Hills
Tinley Park
Frankfort Township
COOK CO
WILL CO
T36N
T35N
60462
60467
60487
60448
12W-19S
12W-20S
12W-21S
EQUESTRIAN PARK
LAKE SEDGEWICK
Lake View Plaza
Orland Plaza
Orland Towne Center
Arctic Ice Arena
RICHARD F KELLY PARK
LAUREL HILL PARK
MALLARD LANDINGS PARK
DEER POINT ESTATES PARK
EAGLE RIDGE II PARK
EAGLE RIDGE PARK
COUNTY FOREST PRESERVE
GASIOR PARK
POTTAWATOMIE PARK
WHITE MOUNTAIN GOLF COURSE
St. Xavier University-Orland Park
TINLEY GDNS PARK
W 159TH ST
W 167TH ST
179TH ST
183RD ST
LA GRANGE RD
94TH AV
108TH AV
104TH AV
ORLAND PKWY
Marley Creek

41°36'21"
41°35'55"
41°35'29"
41°35'03"
41°34'37"
41°34'11"
41°33'44"
41°33'18"
87°53'21"
87°52'46"
87°52'12"
87°51'37"
87°51'02"
87°50'27"

1:24,000
1 in. = 2000 ft.
0 0.25 0.5
miles

SEE 3346 MAP

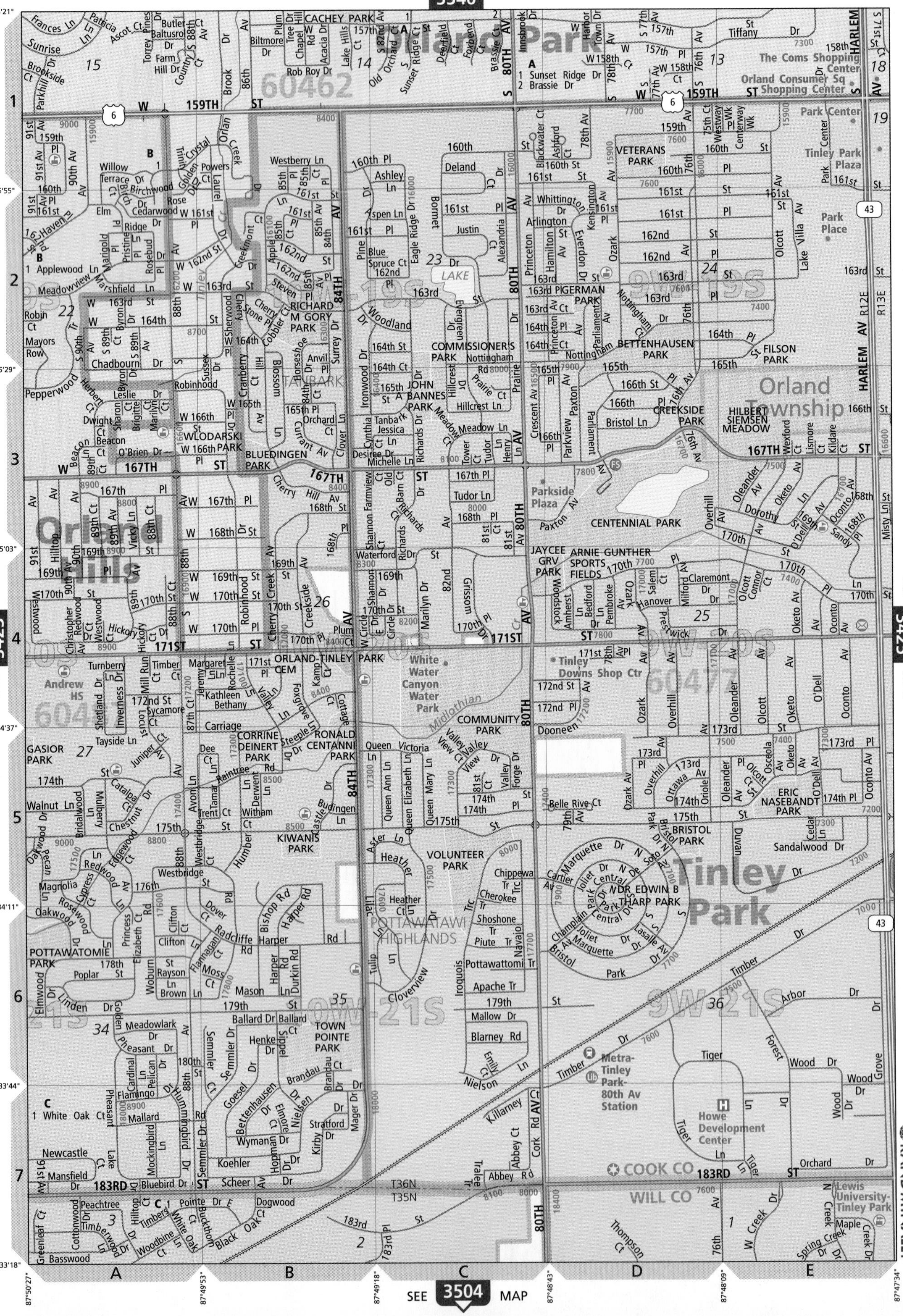

SEE 3423 MAP

SEE 3425 MAP

Orland Park
60462
Orland Hills
60477
Tinley Park
Orland Township
COOK CO
WILL CO
T36N
T35N
R12E
R13E
9W-19S
9W-20S
9W-21S

W 159TH ST
167TH ST
171ST ST
175th St
183RD ST
84TH AV
80TH AV
HARLEM AV

CACHEY PARK
The Coms Shopping Center
Orland Consumer Sq Shopping Center
Park Center
Tinley Park Plaza
Park Place
VETERANS PARK
RICHARD M GORY PARK
PIGERMAN PARK
BETTENHAUSEN PARK
COMMISSIONER'S PARK
FILSON PARK
JOHN A BANNES PARK
WLODARSKI PARK
BLUEDINGEN PARK
CREEKSIDE PARK
HILBERT SIEMSEN MEADOW
Parkside Plaza
CENTENNIAL PARK
JAYCEE GRV PARK
ARNIE GUNTHER SPORTS FIELDS
ORLAND-TINLEY CEM
Andrew HS
White Water Canyon Water Park
Tinley Downs Shop Ctr
COMMUNITY PARK
GASIOR PARK
CORRINE DEINERT PARK
RONALD CENTANNI PARK
KIWANIS PARK
VOLUNTEER PARK
ERIC NASEBANDT PARK
BRISTOL PARK
DR EDWIN B THARP PARK
POTTAWATOMIE PARK
POTTAWATAWI HIGHLANDS
TOWN POINTE PARK
Metra-Tinley Park-80th Av Station
Howe Development Center
Lewis University-Tinley Park

A 1 Sunset Ridge Dr 2 Brassie Dr
B 1 Applewood Ln
C 1 White Oak Ct

41°36'21" 41°35'55" 41°35'29" 41°35'03" 41°34'37" 41°34'11" 41°33'44" 41°33'18"
87°50'27" 87°49'53" 87°49'18" 87°48'43" 87°48'09" 87°47'34"

A B C D E
1 2 3 4 5 6 7

SEE 3504 MAP

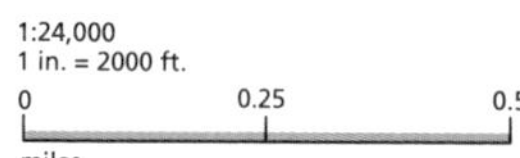

SEE 3347 MAP

Oak Forest
60452
18
17
16
W 159TH ST
159TH ST
159TH ST
Sayre Av
157th Pl
New England Av
S 71st Ct
Ridgeland Av
Sara Ann Ln
Jon Rd
Joann Ln
157th Pl
Jillann Dr
Rob Roy Dr
Bret Dr
Rob Roy Ct
Heron Dr
Arroyo Dr
La Paz Ct
Terrace Dr
Brookwood Dr
Coty Ct
Thomas Ln
158th St
Reynolds Pl
Lake Dr
Pebble Ln
Revere Ct
Oak Creek Shopping Center
CENTRAL PARK
Lorel Av
Laramie Av
158th St
Oak For Commons Shopping Center
159TH ST

Brementowne Mall
COUNTY FOREST PRESERVE
GEORGE W DUNNE NATIONAL GOLF COURSE
A
1 Dennis Ct
Bremen Township
LAGOON PARK
Leslie Ln
Vera Ct
Jamie Ln
Aimee
Margie Ln
Beth Ct
Abbe Ct
Babette Ct
Mary Ann Ct
Pamela Ct
Janet Dr
Ellen Ct
Debra Ct
FRIENDLY OAKS PARK
160th St
161st St
162nd St
Lockwood
Latrobe Av
Shadow Creek Ct
161st St
163rd St
21

161st St
Centennial Cir
Irenes Courtyard
Julias Courtyard
Margarets Courtyard
Plymouth Ct
Lexington Ct
BICENTENNIAL PARK
Kingston Ct
163rd St
Brementowne Dr
ST. BONIFACE PK
19
163rd Pl
163rd Pl
James St
7W-19S
20
Jody Dr
Ln
Mark Ln
Ann
Leslie
Patricia Av
Austin Av
Kimberly Dr
Gaynelle Rd
166th St
Fulton Ter
Kingston
Chelsea Rd
Birchwood Rd
Sussex Rd
Crown Rd
Oxford Ln
Winston Dr
Manchester St
Hunter Tr
Maplewood Ct
Cobble Stone Ct
Olde Gatehouse Rd
Coachwood Tr
Charnswood Dr
166th St
Laverne Ln
Theresa Ln
167TH ST
Oak Park Av
164th St
164th Pl
164th Pl
165th St
165th Pl
Terrace Dr
Skyline Dr
Clark Ln
65th Ct
65th Av
64th Ct
Tinley Park
166th St
Fairfax Ct
167TH ST
YANKEE WOODS FOREST PRESERVE
MIDLOTHIAN RESERVOIR
CENTRAL AV
167TH ST

Westwind Ct
Westwind Dr
168th St
Crystal Ct
Parkside Dr
Maple Ln
Riverside Dr
Hubbard Ln
Glenview Dr
Ravinia Dr
Pine Point Dr
LEWIS PARK
Normandy Dr
Honey Ln
Arcadia Dr
Carlsbad Dr
Barbara Av
Scott Ct
LANCASTER WOODS PARK
Laura Ln
Gaynelle Rd
Beverly Av
Jennifer Rd
Andres Av
Jacquelyn Ct
Marie Dr
Anne Dr
Brittney Ln
LUTHERAN CEM
Helen Ct
Sandidge Ct
Lakeside Dr
Lake Bluff Dr
Hillside Pl
Lakewood Dr
Trout View Ct
Gentry Ln
Christopher Ct
Debra Av
Autumn Dr
Barbara Ln
Midlothian Creek
Forest Dr
Willow Dr
View Dr
169th St
169th St
170th St
Sayre Av
England Av
ST. MIHIEL FOREST PRESERVE
B
1 Deerpath Rd
2 Elmwood Rd
3 Greentree Rd
4 Hawthorne Rd
Aldersyde Rd
Bellaire Rd
Newport Ct
Coulter Rd
169th St
170th Pl
Thackeray Av
Forest Tr
170th Pl
Laramie Av
Martha Ln
29
30

171ST ST
Tinley Pk Commons Shop Ctr
172nd St
172nd St
MEM PARK
VOGT WOODS COMM PARK
OAK FOREST AV
7W-20S
171st Pl
Bonnie Tr
Bonnie Tr W
Belle St
Bonnie Tr E
April Ct
Kathleen Ct
Danielle Ct
Jessica Dr
Harcourt St
JAMES A MALECKY PARK
28
Lockwood Av
YANKEE WOODS FOREST PRESERVE
Parkside Av
173rd St
Christopher Dr
Nicholas Ct
Metra- Tinley Pk Station
North St
South St
173rd Pl
Vogt St
173rd Pl
174th St
174th Pl
Tinley Pk Historical Society
Vogt Visual Arts Ctr
174th Pl
175th St
175TH ST
174th St
28
George Brennan Hwy

HICKORY ST
175th St
175th Pl
176th St
176th Pl
176th St
Tinley Park HS
60477
RIDGELAND AV
177th St
177th St
177th St
62nd Av
33
RAUHOFF PARK
177th Pl
HIRSCH PARK
178th St
178th St
Highland Av
31
179th St
179th St
32
7W-21S
345AB
33
MEM SCHOOL PARK
179th Pl
180th Ct
180th St
Jeanette Ct
180th St
180th Pl
181st St
Live Oak Ct
Royal Oak Ct
Pin Oak Ct
TINLEY CREEK FOREST PRESERVE
CENTRAL AV
Eagle Ct
White Tailed Ln
Martin
France Cir
Rita Rd
181st Pl
182nd St
182nd Pl
C
1 Pine Wood Ct
32
MOLINE EXPWY
80
182nd Ct
Glen Cir
Swilly
183RD ST
183RD ST
Elliott Av
Como Ct
Zurich Ct
Millennium Cir
Convention Center Dr
Bellagio Cir
Pointe Dr
Pond View Dr
Pinewood Ln
Lakeview Cir
Scotch Pine Dr
Pine Lake Dr
Cone Dr
Pine Ridge Dr
Misty Pines Dr
Misty Pine Ct
Union Drainage Ditch
T36N
T35N
183RD ST
Rich Township
6
5
5
4
HARLEM AV

1 2 3 4 5 6 7
A B C D E

41°36'21"
41°35'55"
41°35'29"
41°35'03"
41°34'37"
41°34'11"
41°33'45"
41°33'19"
87°47'34"
87°46'59"
87°46'24"
87°45'50"
87°45'15"
87°44'40"

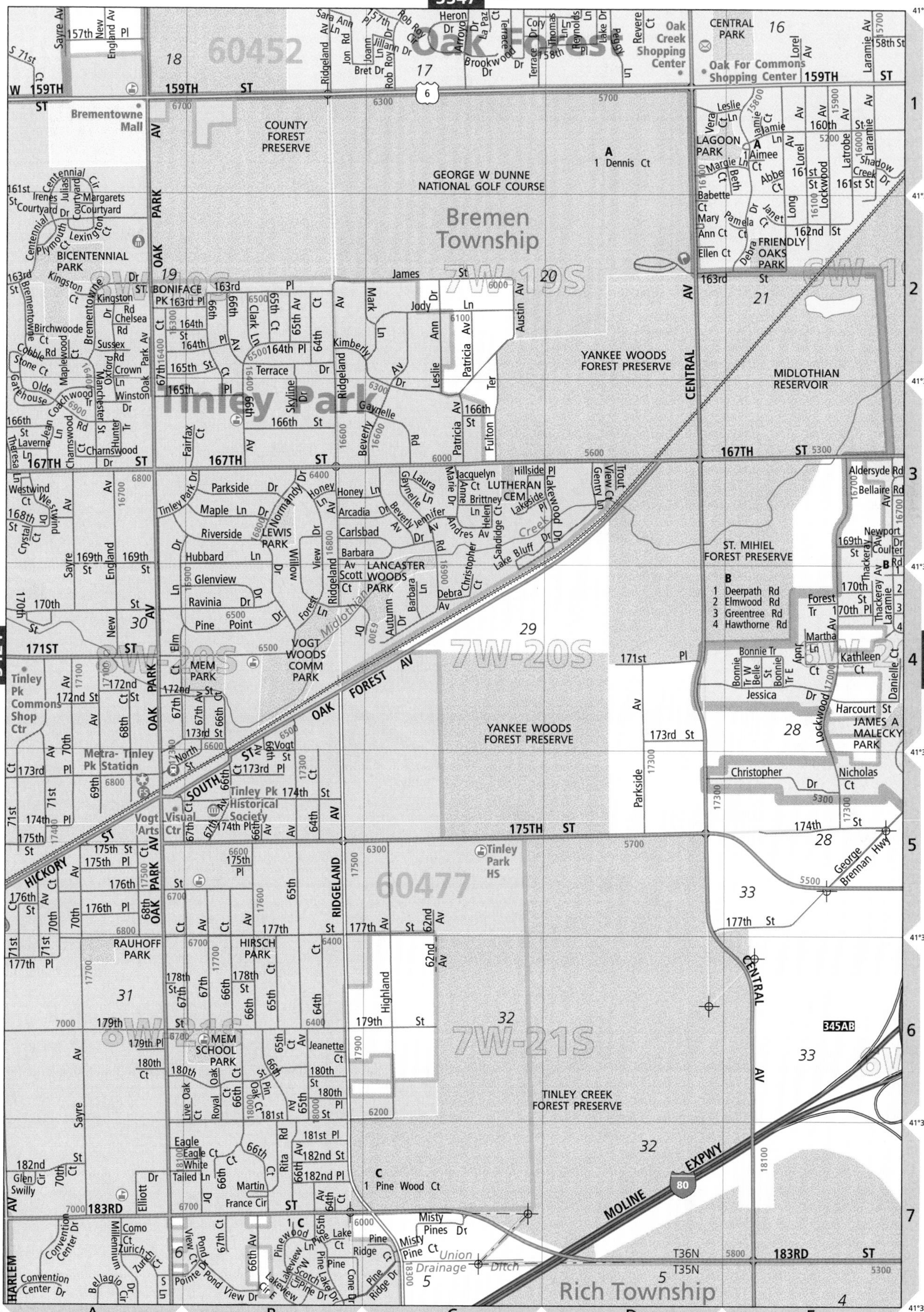

SEE 3424 MAP

SEE 3426 MAP

SEE 3505 MAP

1:24,000
1 in. = 2000 ft.
0 0.25 0.5
miles

SEE 3348 MAP

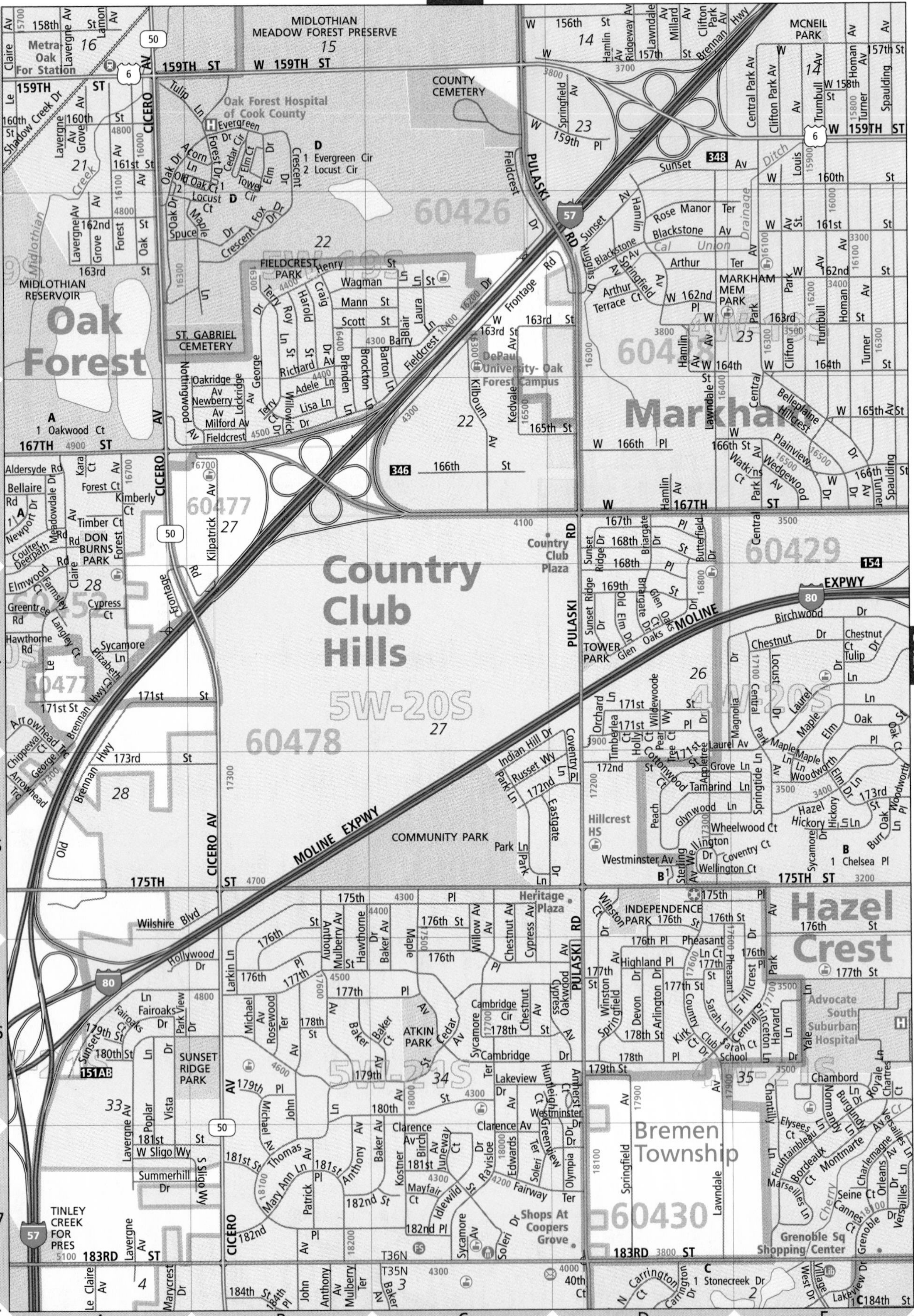

SEE 3425 MAP

SEE 3427 MAP

Oak Forest

Country Club Hills

Markham

Hazel Crest

MIDLOTHIAN MEADOW FOREST PRESERVE

Oak Forest Hospital of Cook County

COUNTY CEMETERY

ST. GABRIEL CEMETERY

MIDLOTHIAN RESERVOIR

FIELDCREST PARK

DON BURNS PARK

DePaul University- Oak Forest Campus

MARKHAM MEM PARK

MCNEIL PARK

TOWER PARK

Country Club Plaza

COMMUNITY PARK

Hillcrest HS

INDEPENDENCE PARK

Heritage Plaza

SUNSET RIDGE PARK

ATKIN PARK

Advocate South Suburban Hospital

Bremen Township

Shops At Coopers Grove

Grenoble Sq Shopping Center

TINLEY CREEK FOR PRES

Metra-Oak For Station

MOLINE EXPWY

CICERO AV

PULASKI RD

159TH ST

167TH ST

175TH ST

183RD ST

60426 60428 60429 60477 60478 60452 60430

5W-19S 4W-19S 5W-20S 4W-20S 5W-21S 4W-21S

A 1 Oakwood Ct

B 1 Chelsea Pl

C 1 Stonecreek Dr

D 1 Evergreen Cir 2 Locust Cir

A B C D E

1 2 3 4 5 6 7

SEE 3506 MAP

RAND McNALLY

1:24,000
1 in. = 2000 ft.
0 0.25 0.5
miles

SEE 3349 MAP

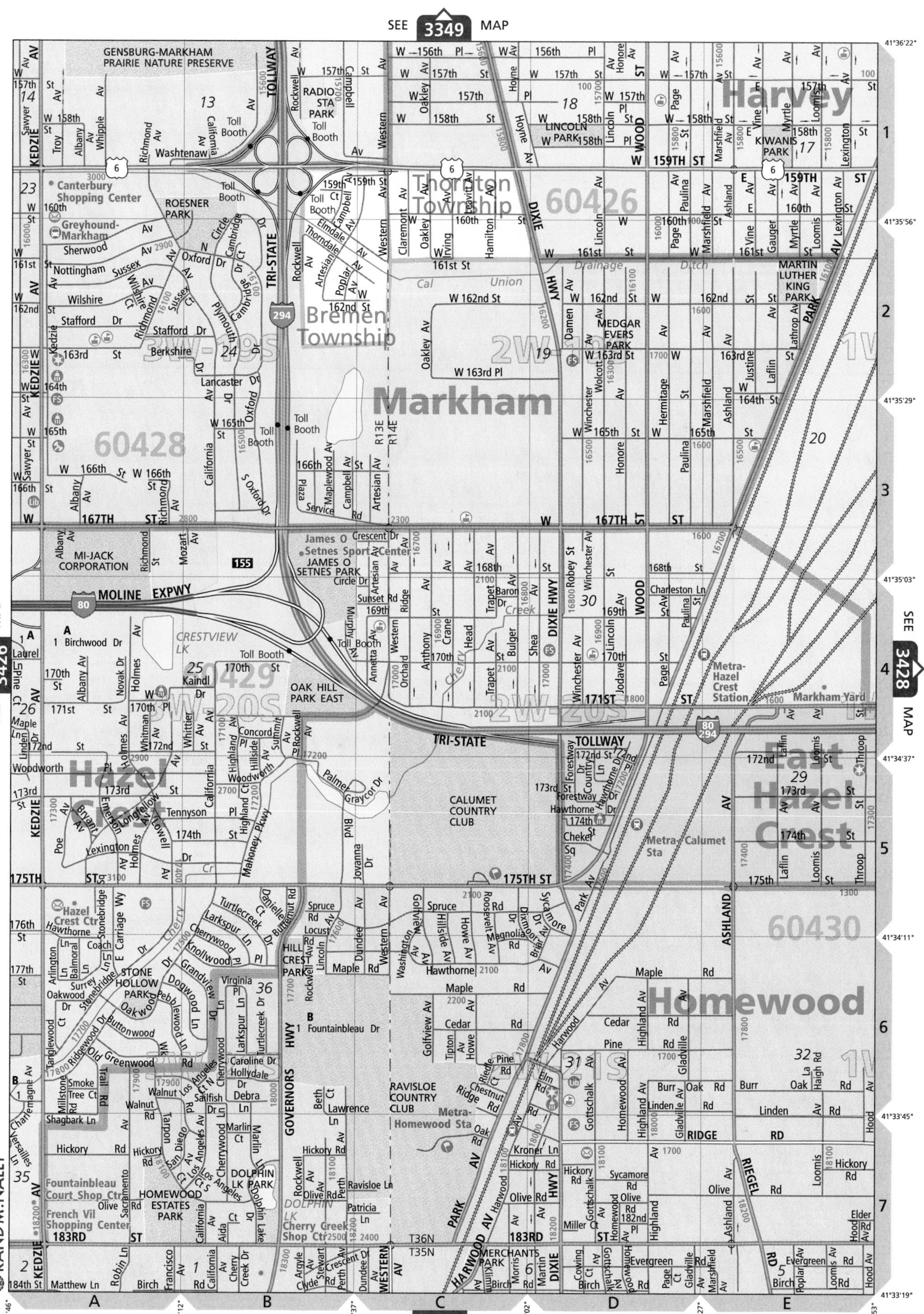

SEE 3426 MAP
SEE 3428 MAP
SEE 3507 MAP

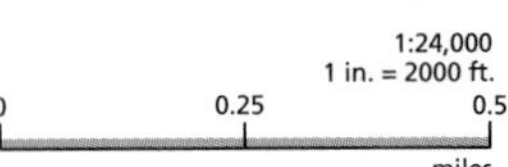

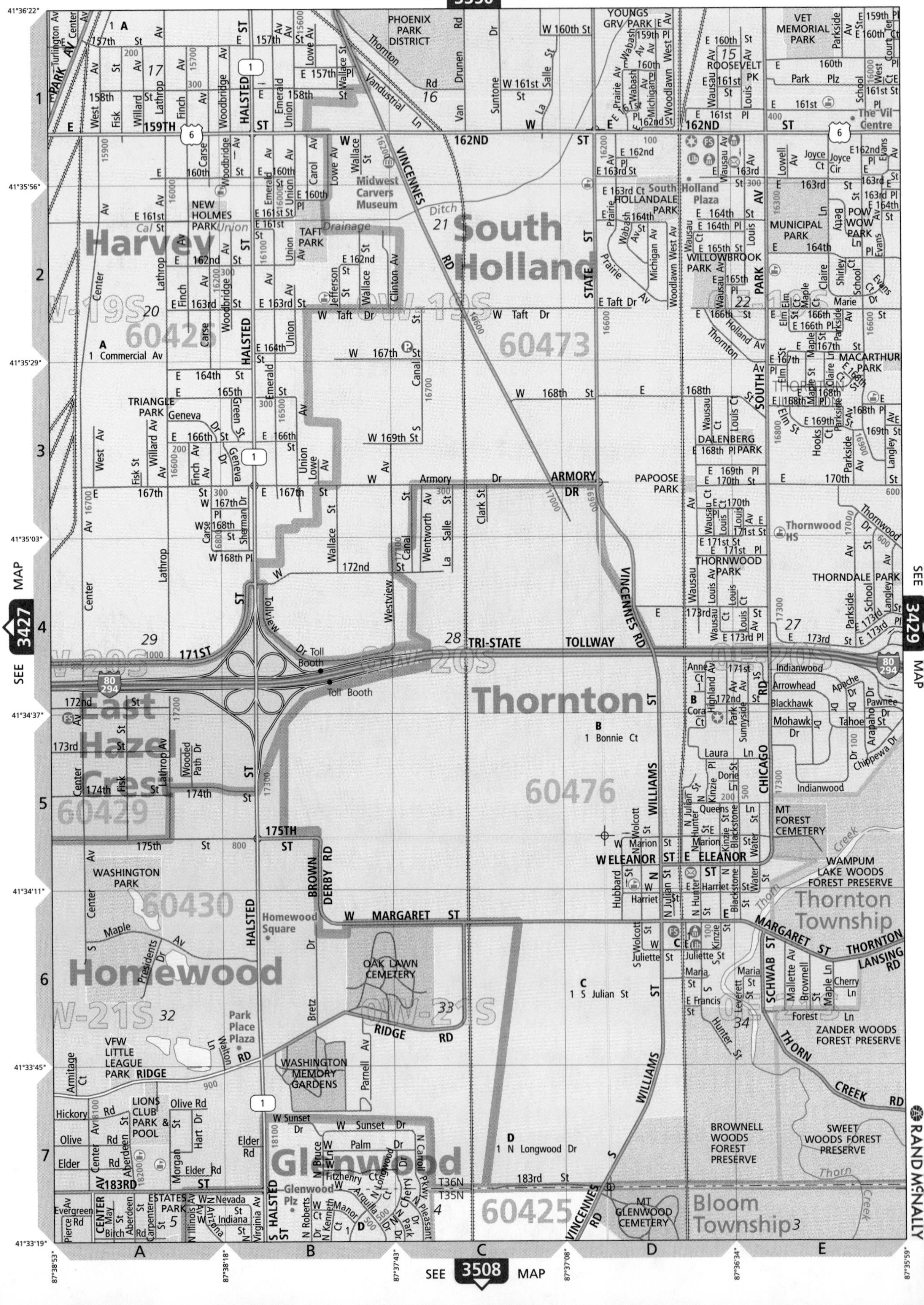

SEE 3350 MAP

Harvey

South Holland

East Hazel Crest

Thornton

Homewood

Glenwood

Thornton Township

Bloom Township

60425

60473

60429

60476

60430

TRI-STATE TOLLWAY

VINCENNES RD

HALSTED ST

162ND ST

159TH ST

175TH ST

183RD ST

WILLIAMS ST

CHICAGO RD

STATE ST

SOUTH PARK AV

ARMORY DR

W MARGARET ST

RIDGE RD

THORN CREEK RD

THORNTON LANSING RD

SEE 3427 MAP

SEE 3429 MAP

SEE 3508 MAP

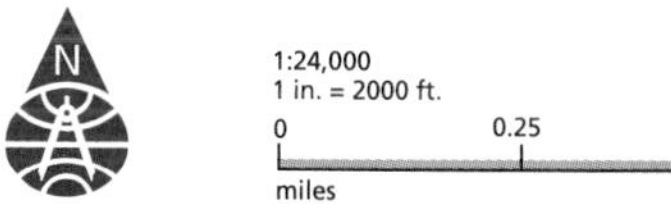

SEE 3351 MAP

Calumet City

South Holland

Lansing

Thornton Township

Bloom Township

GOUWENS PARK

FOREST PRES

GREEN PARK

Sand Ridge Nature Center

SHABBONA WOODS FOREST PRESERVE

CLAYHOLE WOODS FOR PRESERVE

GREEN LK

Pacesetter Park Plaza

River Oaks West Shopping Center

River Oaks Shopping Center

RIVER OAKS GOLF COURSE

THE PARK OF RIVER OAKS

MAICACH PARK

PIONEER PARK

MACARTHUR PARK

TERRACE VIEW PARK

RIVERFRONT PARK

The Landings

River Place Shop Center

THORNDALE PARK

THORNCREEK PARK

THORN LK

VOLBRECHT PARK

FOREST PRES

PAARLBERG PARK

Hist Society

Lansing Commons

TRI-STATE TOLLWAY

KINGERY EXPWY

BISHOP FORD MEMORIAL EXPWY

LITTLE CALUMET RIVER

THORN CREEK

WAMPUM LAKE

WAMPUM LAKE WOODS FOREST PRESERVE

Lansing Square

Eisenhower Center

LAN-OAK PARK

OAK RIDGE CEM

OAK GLEN LUTHERAN CEM

Illiana Christian HS

ZANDER WOODS FOREST PRESERVE

VAN LATEN PARK

KIWANIS PARK

OAK GLEN

LIONS PARK

SWEET WOODS FOR PRESERVE

JURGENSEN WOODS FOR PRESERVE

LANSING WOODS FOREST PRESERVE

LANSING WOODS FOR PRESERVE

159TH ST

170th St

LANSING RD

THORNTON

RIDGE RD

TORRENCE AV

STONEY ISLAND AV

186TH ST

60409

60473

60438

60476

60411

60425

1E-19S

2E-19S

1E-20S

1E-21S

2E-21S

T36N

T35N

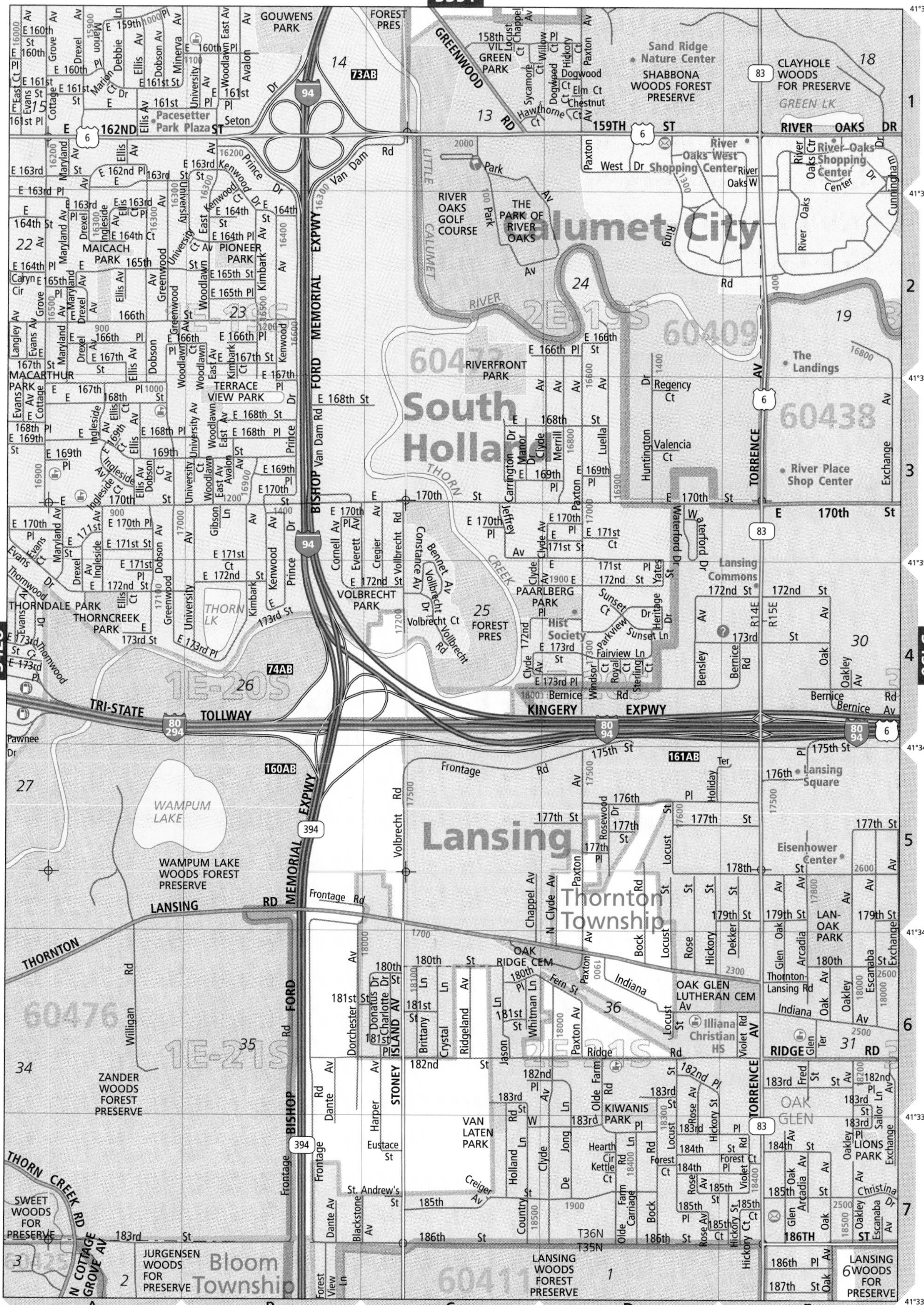

SEE 3428 MAP

SEE 3430 MAP

SEE 3509 MAP

A B C D E

1 2 3 4 5 6 7

41°36'21"

41°35'55"

41°35'29"

41°35'03"

41°34'37"

41°34'11"

41°33'45"

41°33'19"

87°35'59"

87°35'24"

87°34'49"

87°34'15"

87°33'40"

87°33'05"

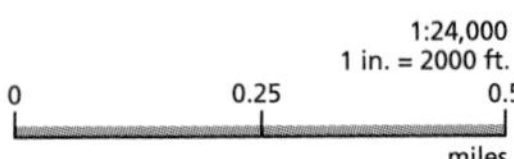

SEE 3352 MAP

SEE 3429 MAP

SEE B MAP

Calumet City

Hammond

Lansing

Munster

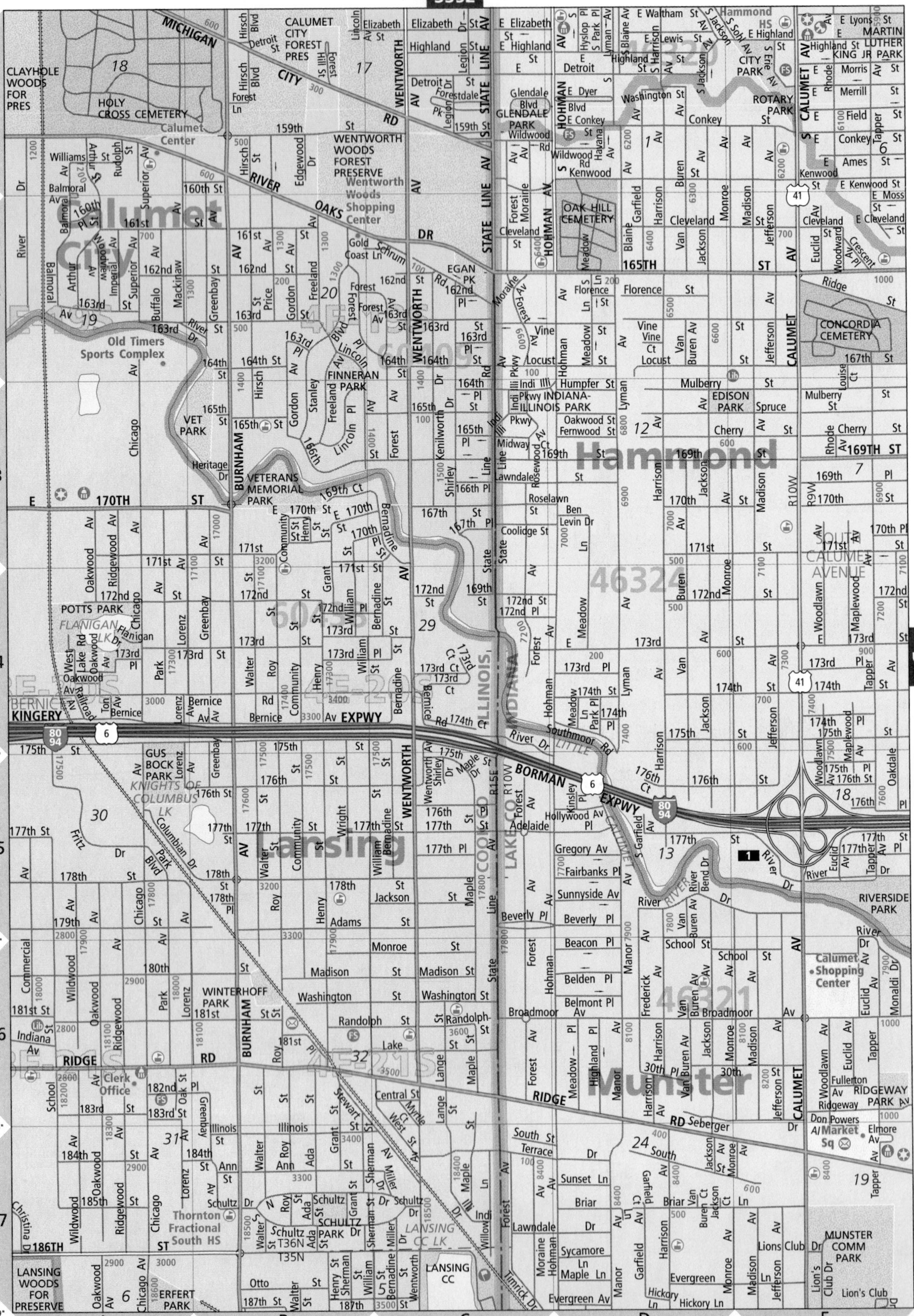

CLAYHOLE WOODS FOR PRES

HOLY CROSS CEMETERY

Calumet Center

CALUMET CITY FOREST PRES

WENTWORTH WOODS FOREST PRESERVE

Wentworth Woods Shopping Center

GLENDALE PARK

OAK HILL CEMETERY

Hammond HS

CITY PARK

ROTARY PARK

MARTIN LUTHER KING JR PARK

CONCORDIA CEMETERY

Old Timers Sports Complex

VET PARK

VETERANS MEMORIAL PARK

FINNERAN PARK

INDIANA-ILLINOIS PARK

EDISON PARK

POTTS PARK

FLANIGAN LK

GUS BOCK PARK

KNIGHTS OF COLUMBUS LK

WINTERHOFF PARK

RIVERSIDE PARK

Calumet Shopping Center

Clerk Office

RIDGEWAY PARK

Market Sq

Thornton Fractional South HS

SCHULTZ PARK

LANSING CC LK

LANSING CC

LANSING WOODS FOR PRESERVE

ERFERT PARK

MUNSTER COMM PARK

Lion's Club

46320

46324

46321

60409

60438

ILLINOIS

INDIANA

COOK CO

LAKE CO

MICHIGAN CITY RD

RIVER OAKS DR

STATE LINE AV

WENTWORTH AV

BURNHAM AV

CALUMET AV

HOHMAN AV

165TH ST

169TH ST

E 170TH ST

KINGERY EXPWY

BORMAN EXPWY

RIDGE RD

186TH ST

LITTLE CALUMET RIVER

41°36'21"

41°35'55"

41°35'29"

41°35'03"

41°34'37"

41°34'11"

41°33'45"

41°33'19"

87°33'05"

87°32'30"

87°31'56"

87°31'21"

87°30'46"

87°30'12"

1 2 3 4 5 6 7

A B C D E

RAND McNALLY

SEE 3510 MAP

1:24,000
1 in. = 2000 ft.
0 0.25 0.5
miles

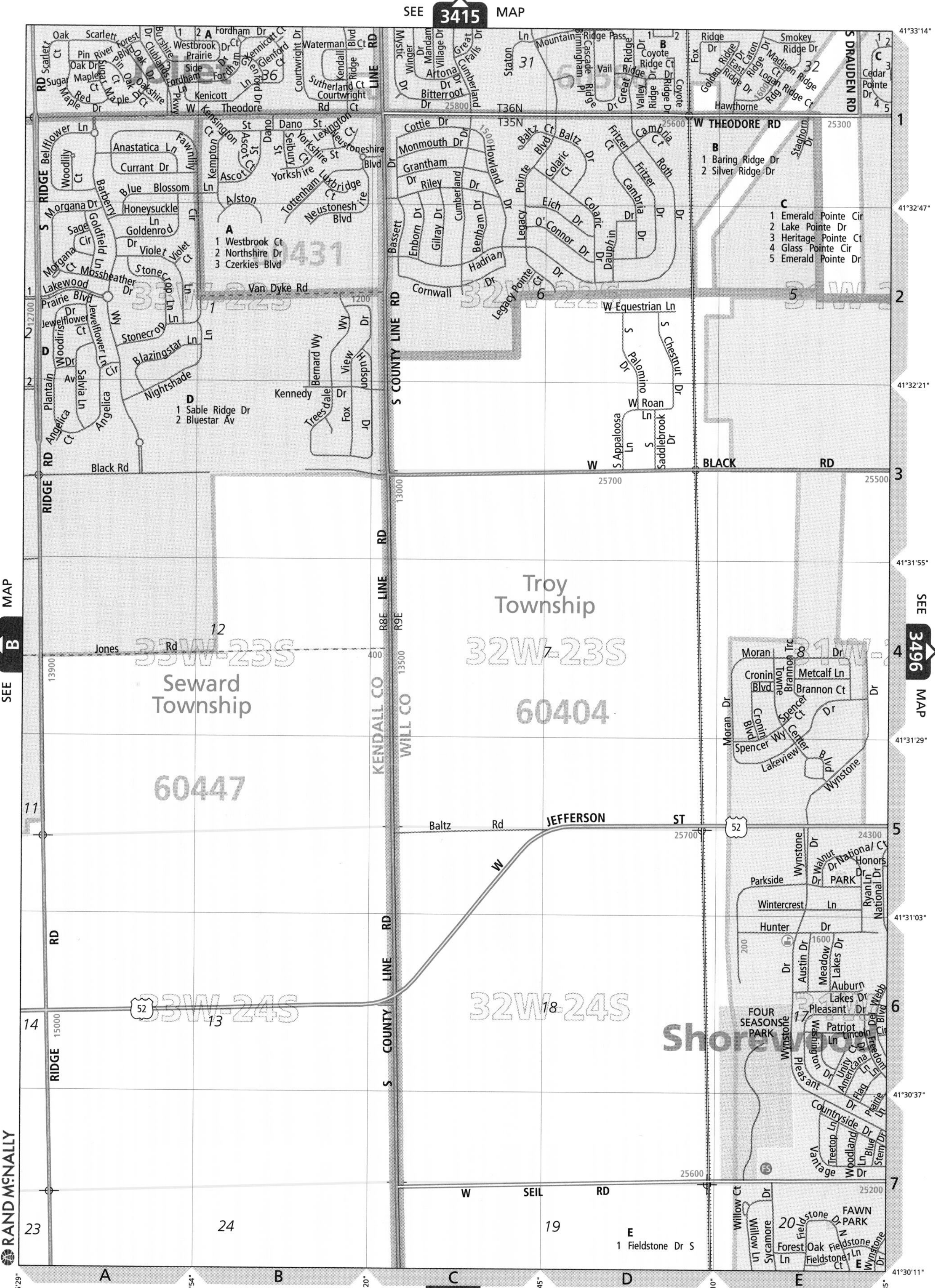

1:24,000
1 in. = 2000 ft.
0 0.25 0.5
miles

SEE 3416 MAP

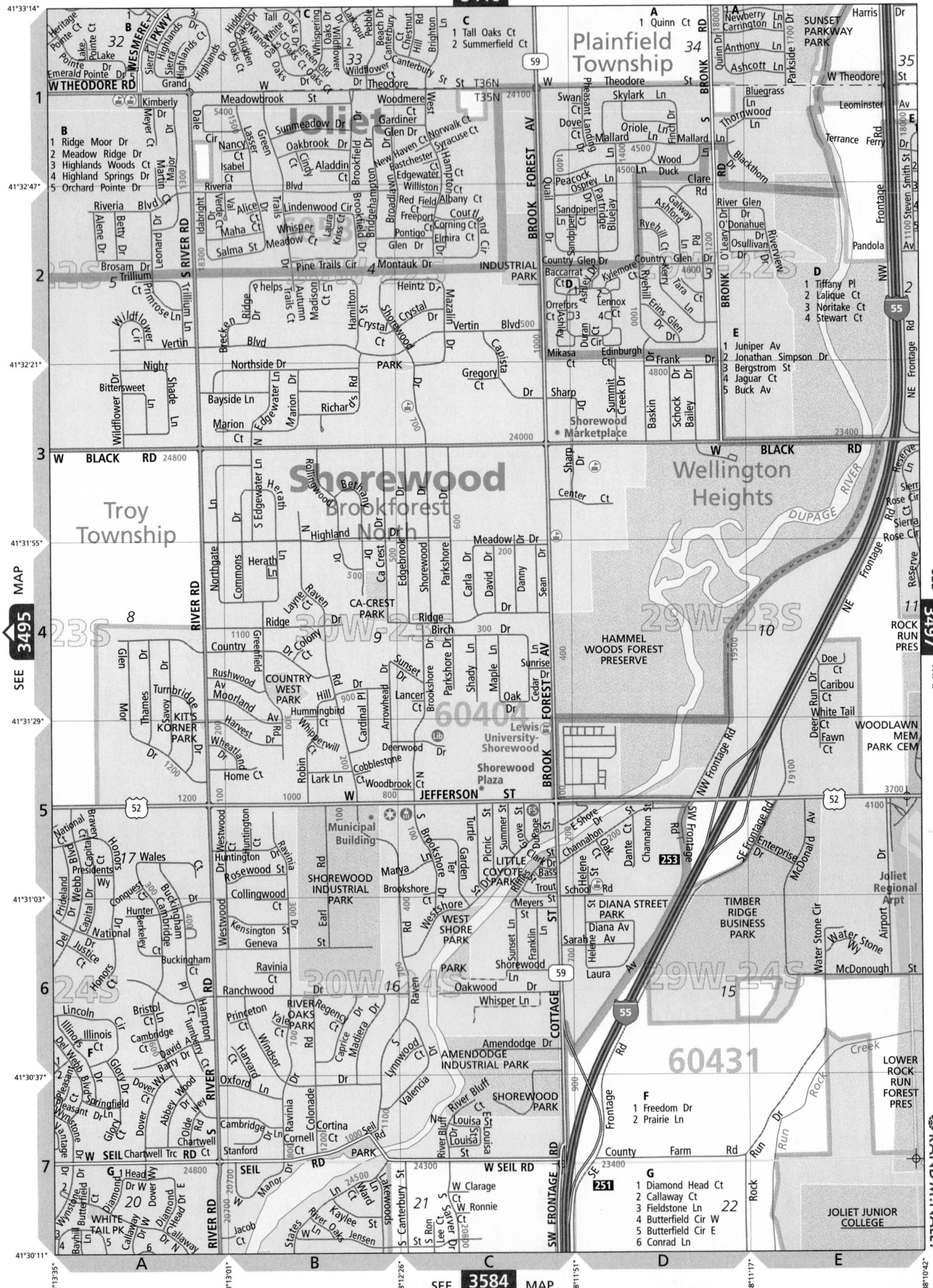

A
1 Quinn Ct

B
1 Ridge Moor Dr
2 Meadow Ridge Dr
3 Highlands Woods Ct
4 Highland Springs Dr
5 Orchard Pointe Dr

C
1 Tall Oaks Ct
2 Summerfield Ct

D
1 Tiffany Pl
2 Lalique Ct
3 Noritake Ct
4 Stewart Ct

E
1 Juniper Av
2 Jonathan Simpson Dr
3 Bergstrom St
4 Jaguar Ct
5 Buck Av

F
1 Freedom Dr
2 Prairie Ln

G
1 Diamond Head Ct
2 Callaway Ct
3 Fieldstone Ln
4 Butterfield Cir W
5 Butterfield Cir E
6 Conrad Ln

Joliet

Plainfield Township

SUNSET PARKWAY PARK

INDUSTRIAL PARK

Shorewood

Shorewood Marketplace

Brookforest North

Troy Township

Wellington Heights

CA-CREST PARK

HAMMEL WOODS FOREST PRESERVE

COUNTRY WEST PARK

KIT'S KORNER PARK

Lewis University-Shorewood

Shorewood Plaza

ROCK RUN PRES

WOODLAWN MEM PARK CEM

60404

Municipal Building

SHOREWOOD INDUSTRIAL PARK

LITTLE COYOTE PARK

DIANA STREET PARK

TIMBER RIDGE BUSINESS PARK

Joliet Regional Arpt

WEST SHORE PARK

RIVER OAKS PARK

AMENDODGE INDUSTRIAL PARK

SHOREWOOD PARK

60431

LOWER ROCK RUN FOREST PRES

JOLIET JUNIOR COLLEGE

DUPAGE RIVER

W BLACK RD

W JEFFERSON ST

W SEIL RD

RIVER RD

BROOK FOREST AV

SEE 3495 MAP

SEE 3497 MAP

SEE 3584 MAP

A B C D E

RAND McNALLY

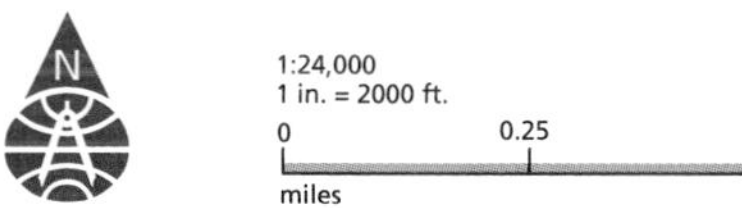

SEE 3417 MAP

Plainfield Township

Crest Hill

Rooney Heights

Timberline

Troy Township

Joliet

Joliet Township

Rockdale

THEODORE MARSH PRESERVE

ROCK RUN PRESERVE

HOLY CROSS CEM

PAUL E BRIESE PARK

TWIN CREEK PARK

JENNIFER ANN VOOTS PARK

BOB FOWLER MEM SOCCER FIELDS

JOHN H LEACH PARK

WOODLAWN MEMORIAL PARK CEMETERY

HILLS OF REST CEMETERY

Provena St. Joseph Medical Center

Joliet Regional Airport

INWOOD PARK

Joliet Mem Stadium

Joliet Armory

INWOOD GOLF CLUB

Maycrest Shopping Center

LOWER ROCK RUN FOR PRESERVE

Illinois State Boy's Detention Center

OAK LEAF CENTER BUSINESS PARK

COUNTY FARM CEM

COLL PARK Pavilion

JOLIET JUNIOR COLLEGE

THEODORE ST

BLACK RD

W JEFFERSON ST

MCDONOUGH ST

W INGALLS AV

W GLENWOOD AV

ESSINGTON RD

129TH INFANTRY DR

HOUBOLT RD

GAYLORD RD

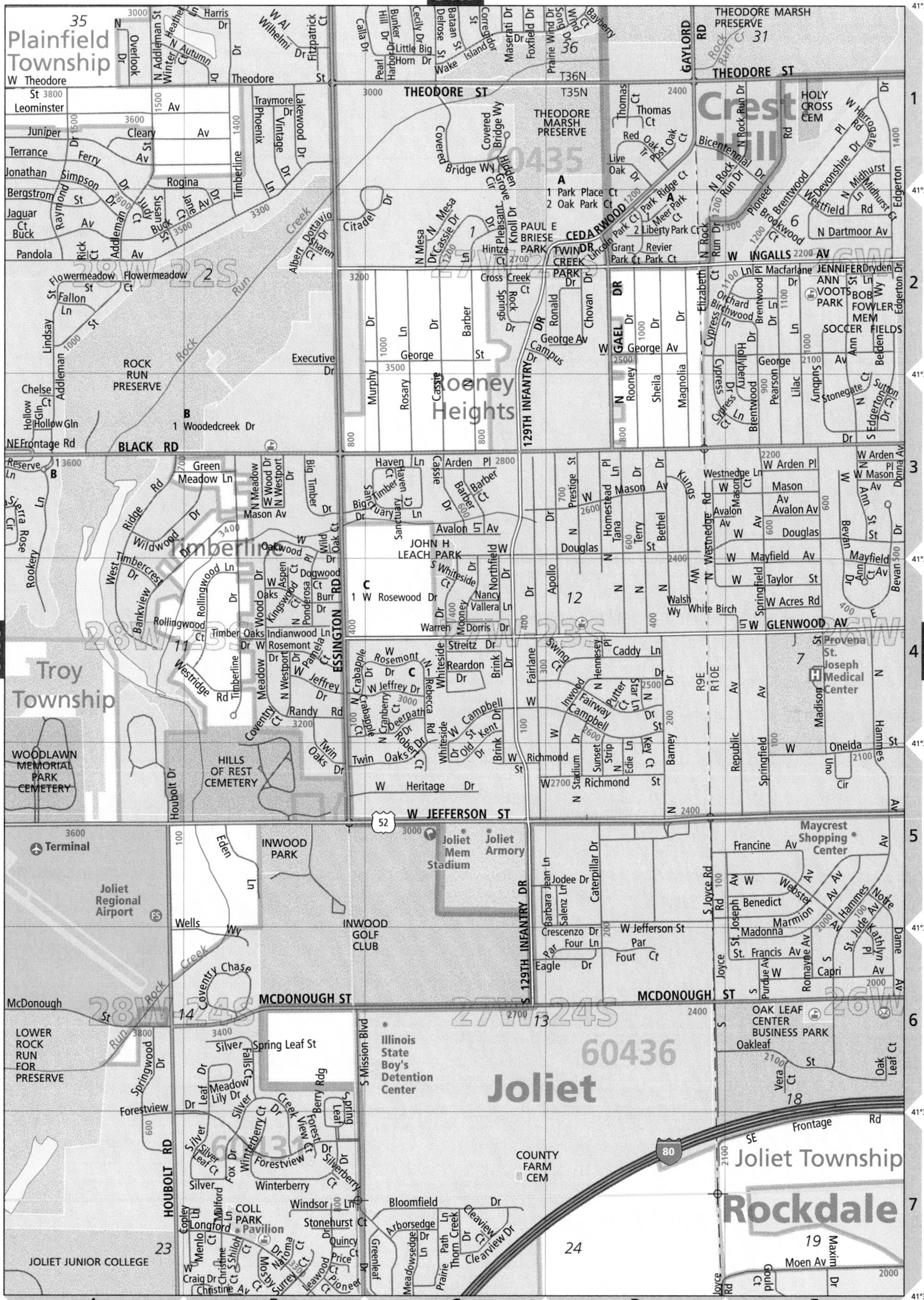

SEE 3496 MAP

SEE 3498 MAP

SEE 3585 MAP

1:24,000
1 in. = 2000 ft.
0 0.25 0.5
miles

SEE 3418 MAP

SEE 3497 MAP

SEE 3499 MAP

Joliet
Crest Hill
Rockdale
Joliet Township

B
1 N Des Plaines St
2 S Broadway St

A
1 Cherrywood Ct
2 Carousel Ct

SEE 3586 MAP

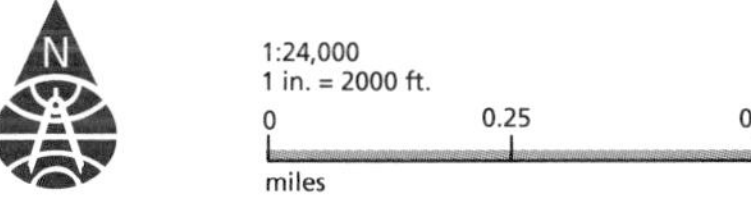

SEE 3419 MAP

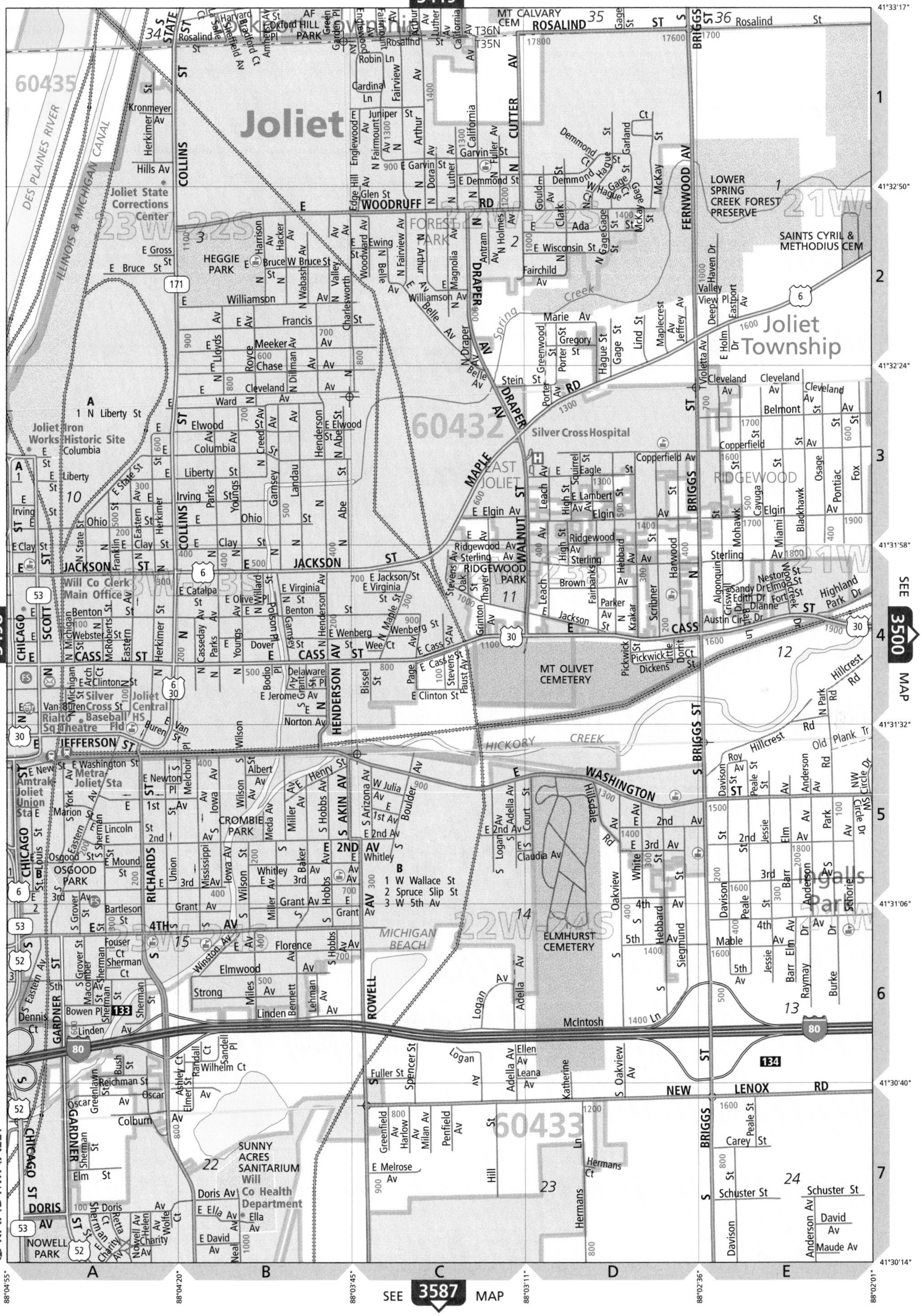

SEE 3498 MAP

SEE 3500 MAP

Joliet

Joliet Township

Joliet State Corrections Center

Joliet Iron Works Historic Site

Will Co Clerk Main Office

Silver Cross Field

Joliet Central HS

Rialto Sq Theatre

Baseball Fld

Metra-Joliet Sta

Amtrak-Joliet Union Sta

Silver Cross Hospital

MT OLIVET CEMETERY

ELMHURST CEMETERY

MT CALVARY CEM

SAINTS CYRIL & METHODIUS CEM

LOWER SPRING CREEK FOREST PRESERVE

SUNNY ACRES SANITARIUM

Will Co Health Department

HEGGIE PARK

CROMBIE PARK

OSGOOD PARK

RIDGEWOOD PARK

NOWELL PARK

FOREST PARK

EAST JOLIET

RIDGEWOOD

Ingalls Park

MICHIGAN BEACH

HILL PARK

DES PLAINES RIVER

ILLINOIS & MICHIGAN CANAL

Spring Creek

HICKORY CREEK

60435

60432

60433

T36N

T35N

23W-22S

22W-22S

21W-22S

23W-23S

22W-23S

21W-23S

23W-24S

22W-24S

21W-24S

A
1 N Liberty St

B
1 W Wallace St
2 Spruce Slip St
3 W 5th Av

ROSALIND ST

E WOODRUFF RD

JACKSON ST

E CASS ST

JEFFERSON ST

E WASHINGTON

4TH AV

2ND AV

NEW LENOX RD

MAPLE RD

DRAPER AV

COLLINS ST

S STATE ST

CHICAGO ST

SCOTT ST

RICHARDS ST

GARDNER ST

HENDERSON AV

S AKIN AV

ROWELL AV

WALNUT ST

CUTTER AV

FERNWOOD AV

BRIGGS ST

S BRIGGS ST

DORIS AV

McIntosh Ln

6

30

52

53

80

171

133

134

A B C D E

1 2 3 4 5 6 7

41°33'17"

41°32'50"

41°32'24"

41°31'58"

41°31'32"

41°31'06"

41°30'40"

41°30'14"

88°04'55"

88°04'20"

88°03'45"

88°03'11"

88°02'36"

88°02'01"

SEE 3587 MAP

1:24,000
1 in. = 2000 ft.
0 0.25 0.5
miles

SEE 3420 MAP

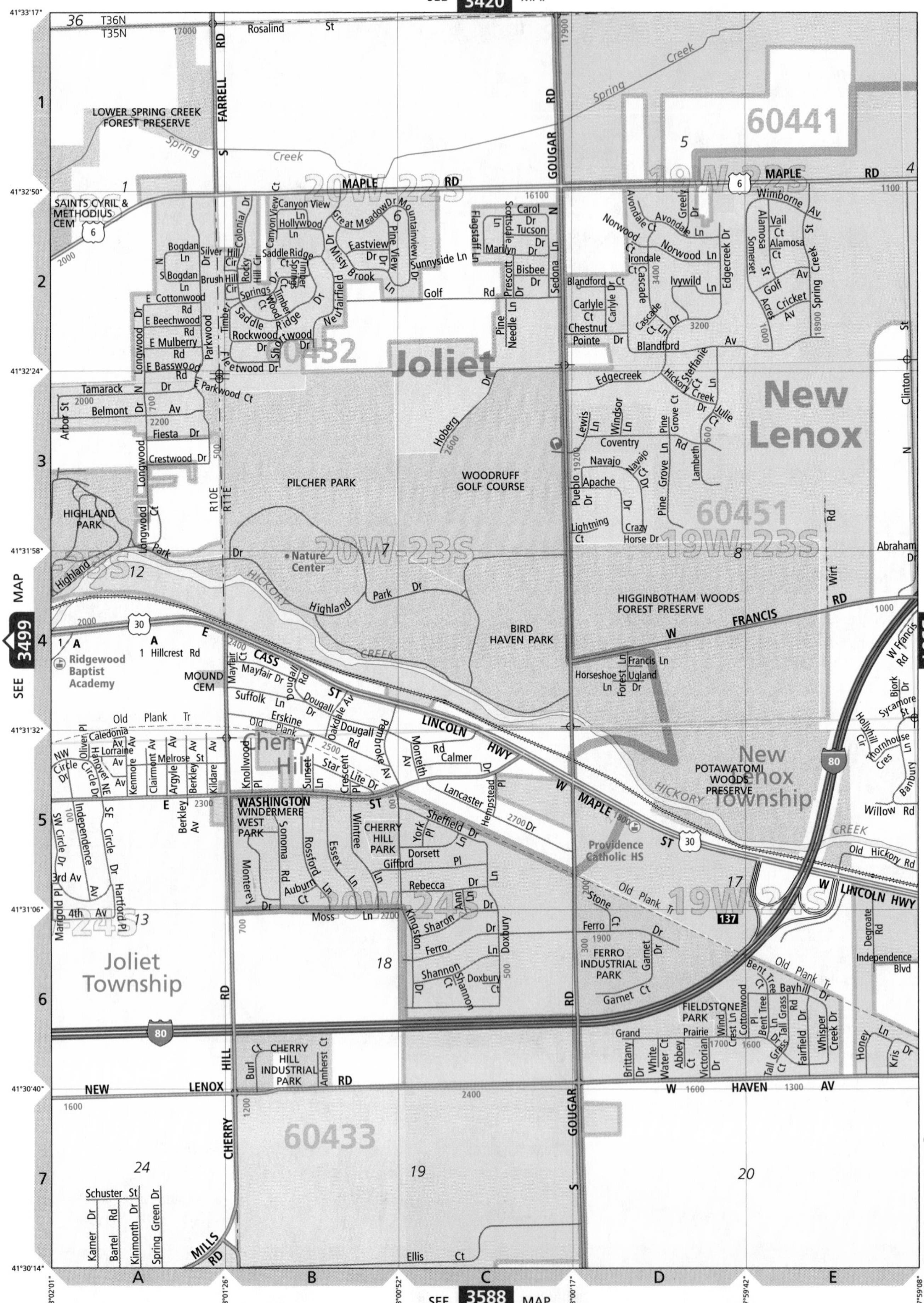

SEE 3499 MAP

SEE 3501 MAP

SEE 3588 MAP

1:24,000
1 in. = 2000 ft.
0 0.25 0.5
miles

SEE 3421 MAP

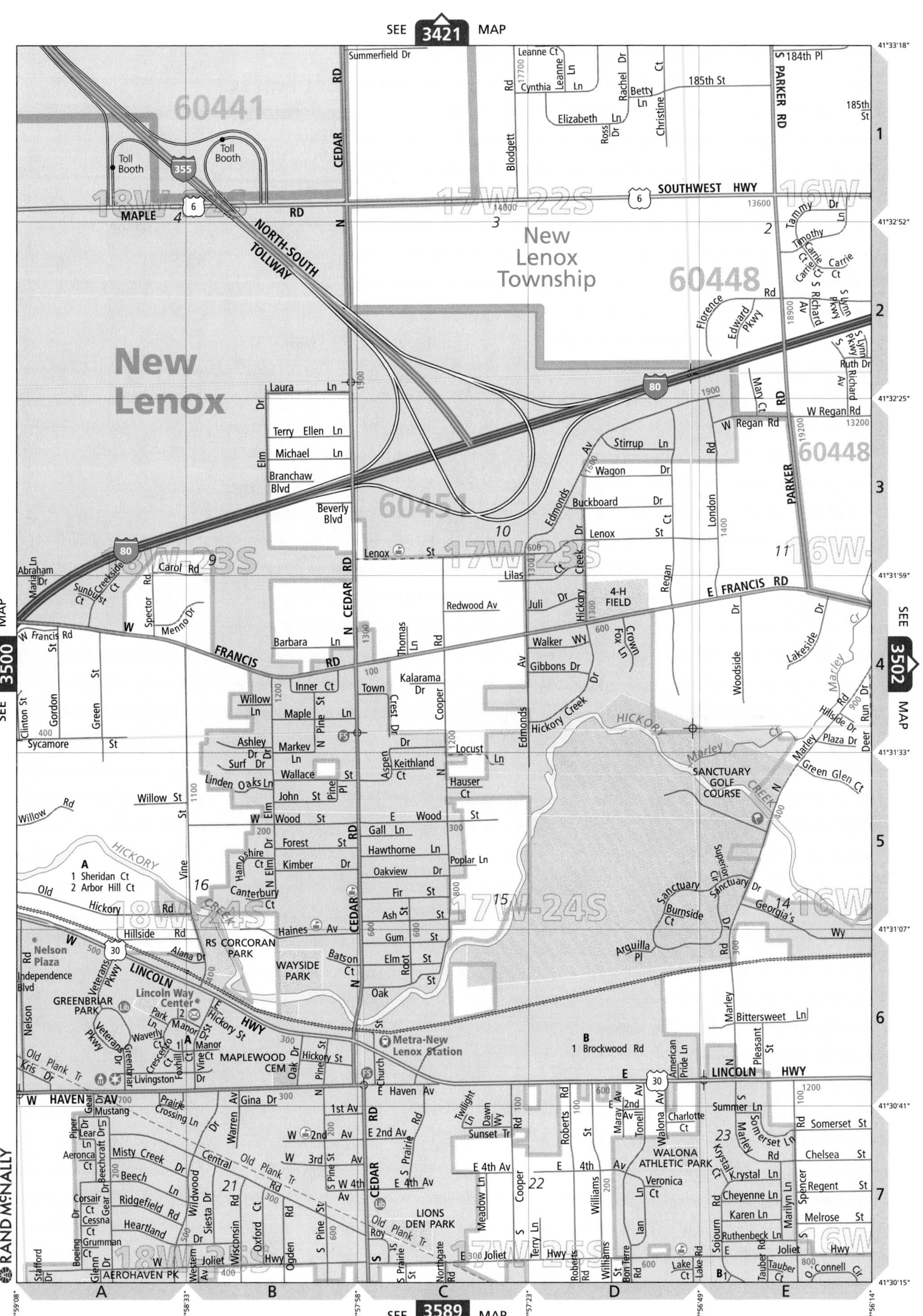

SEE 3500 MAP
SEE 3502 MAP
SEE 3589 MAP

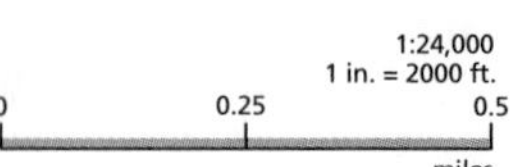

SEE 3422 MAP

New Lenox Township

Orland Park 60467

Frankfort Township

Marley

Mokena 60448

Gilletts

Lincolnwood Hills

New Lenox 60451

WILLOW RUN GOLF COURSE

HALEY PARK

BUSKE PARK

MARSHALL CEM

WILLOWVIEW PARK

HICKORY CREEK FOREST PRESERVE

SCHOOLHOUSE MANOR PARK

Lincoln-Way Central HS

A
1 Granite Dr
2 Revere Rd
3 Bryant Rd
4 Parker St
5 St. Mary's Rd

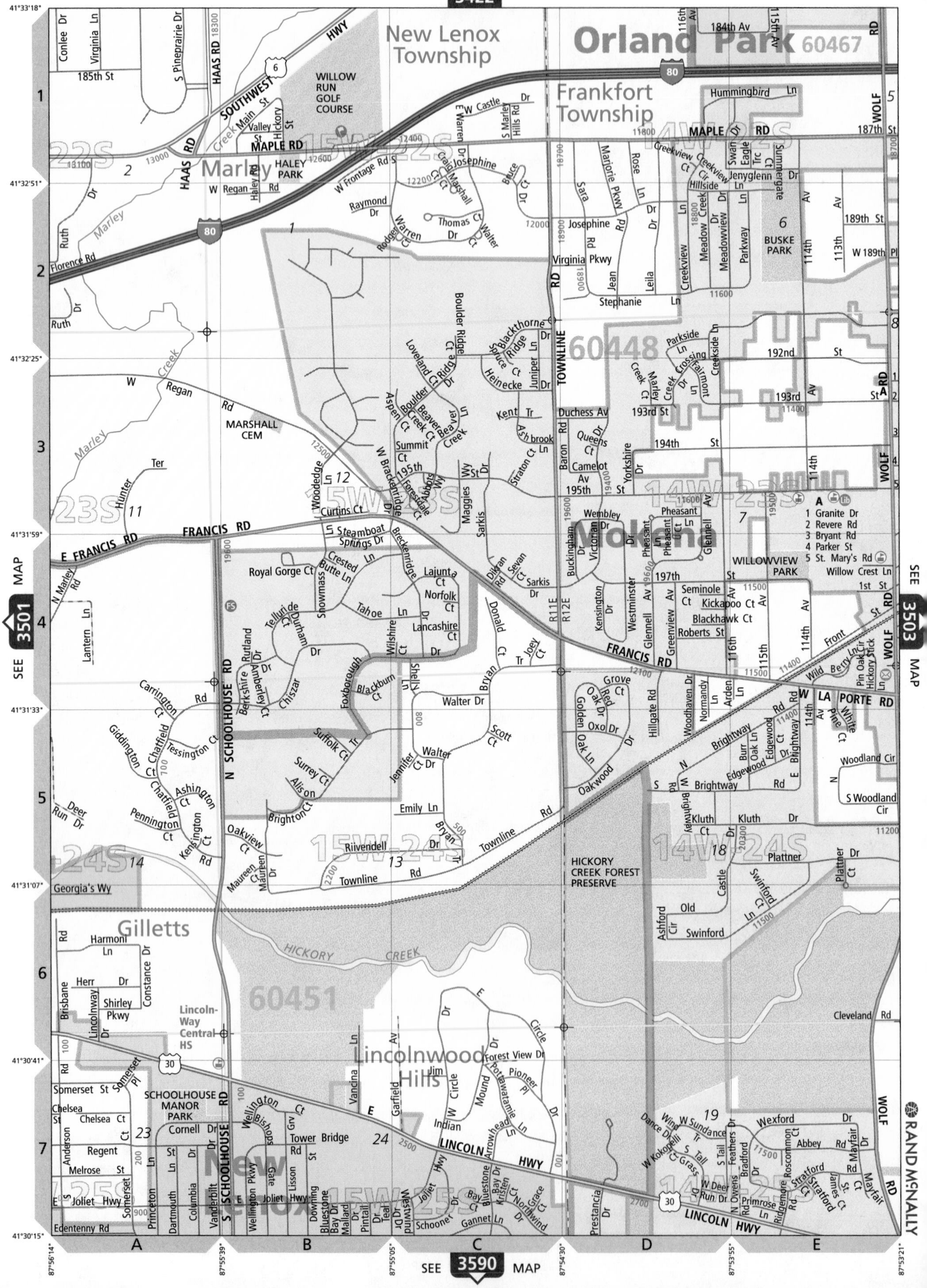

SEE 3501 MAP

SEE 3503 MAP

SEE 3590 MAP

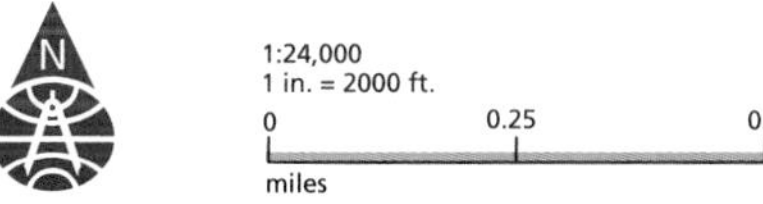

SEE 3423 MAP

Orland Park

MOLINE EXPWY

Frankfort Township

Mokena

60448

Arbury Hills

A
1 W Westinghouse Ct
2 W Huntington Ct
3 W Pullman Ct
4 W Stanford Ct

MARLEY CREEK PARK

Olivieri Business Park

Mokena Crossings Business Pk

Hickory Creek Ctr

Hickory Creek Station

HECHT PARK

ST. MARY'S CEM

YUNKER PARK

GRN MEADOWS PARK

GRASMERE PARK

NORMAL TOWERS INDUSTRIAL PARK

Metra-Mokena Sta

Hickory Creek Marketplace

VAN HORNE WOODS FOREST PRESERVE

MOKENA COMM PARK

ST. JOHN'S CEM

Frankfort Township

The Vineyards Shopping Center

60423

TANGLEWOOD PARK

Environmental Learning Center

Lincoln-Way East HS

Frankfort Town Ctr

FRANKFORT CEM

Crossing Shop Ctr Frankfort

LINCOLN MEADOWS PARK

Frankfort

B
1 Brookridge Ct
2 Washington Pkwy

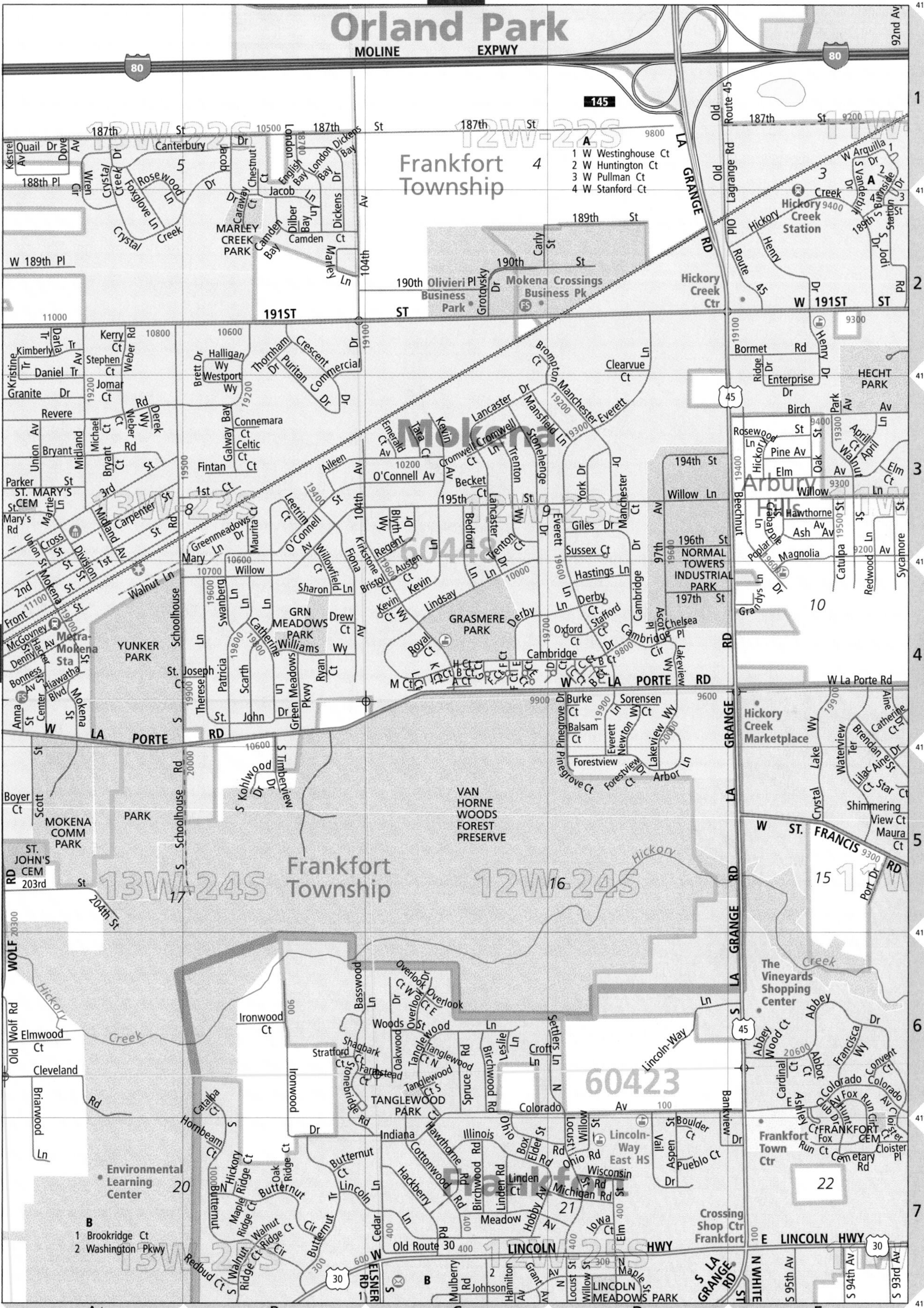

SEE 3502 MAP

SEE 3504 MAP

SEE 3591 MAP

1:24,000
1 in. = 2000 ft.
0 0.25 0.5
miles

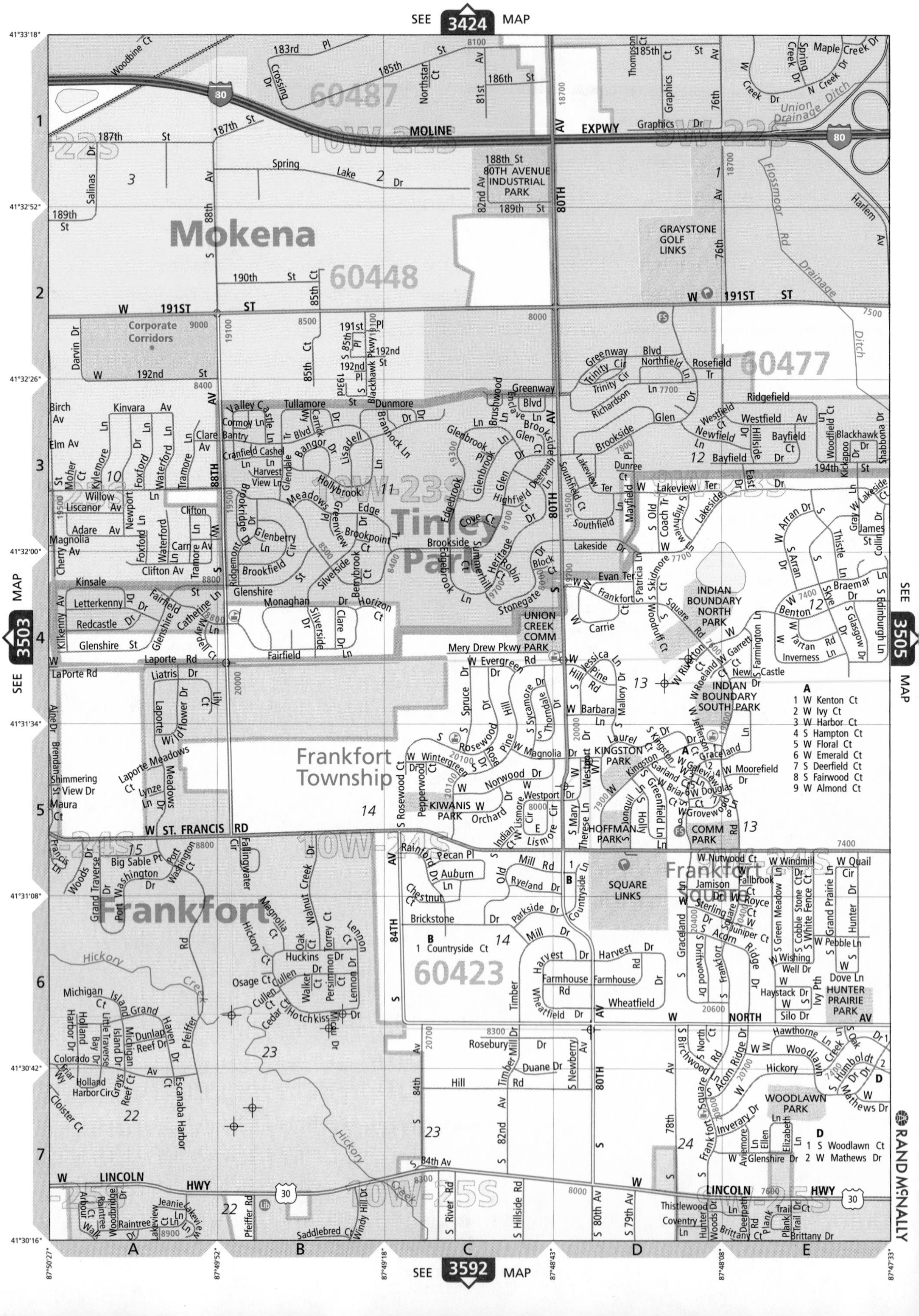

SEE 3424 MAP

SEE 3503 MAP

SEE 3505 MAP

SEE 3592 MAP

Mokena

Tinley Park

Frankfort Township

Frankfort

Frankfort Square

60487 60448 60477 60423

80TH AVENUE INDUSTRIAL PARK

GRAYSTONE GOLF LINKS

Corporate Corridors

UNION CREEK COMM PARK

INDIAN BOUNDARY NORTH PARK

INDIAN BOUNDARY SOUTH PARK

KINGSTON PARK

KIWANIS PARK

HOFFMAN PARK

COMM PARK

SQUARE LINKS

HUNTER PRAIRIE PARK

WOODLAWN PARK

A
1 W Kenton Ct
2 W Ivy Ct
3 W Harbor Ct
4 S Hampton Ct
5 W Floral Ct
6 W Emerald Ct
7 S Deerfield Ct
8 S Fairwood Ct
9 W Almond Ct

B
1 Countryside Ct

D
1 S Woodlawn Ct
2 W Mathews Dr

1:24,000
1 in. = 2000 ft.
0 0.25 0.5
miles

SEE 3425 MAP

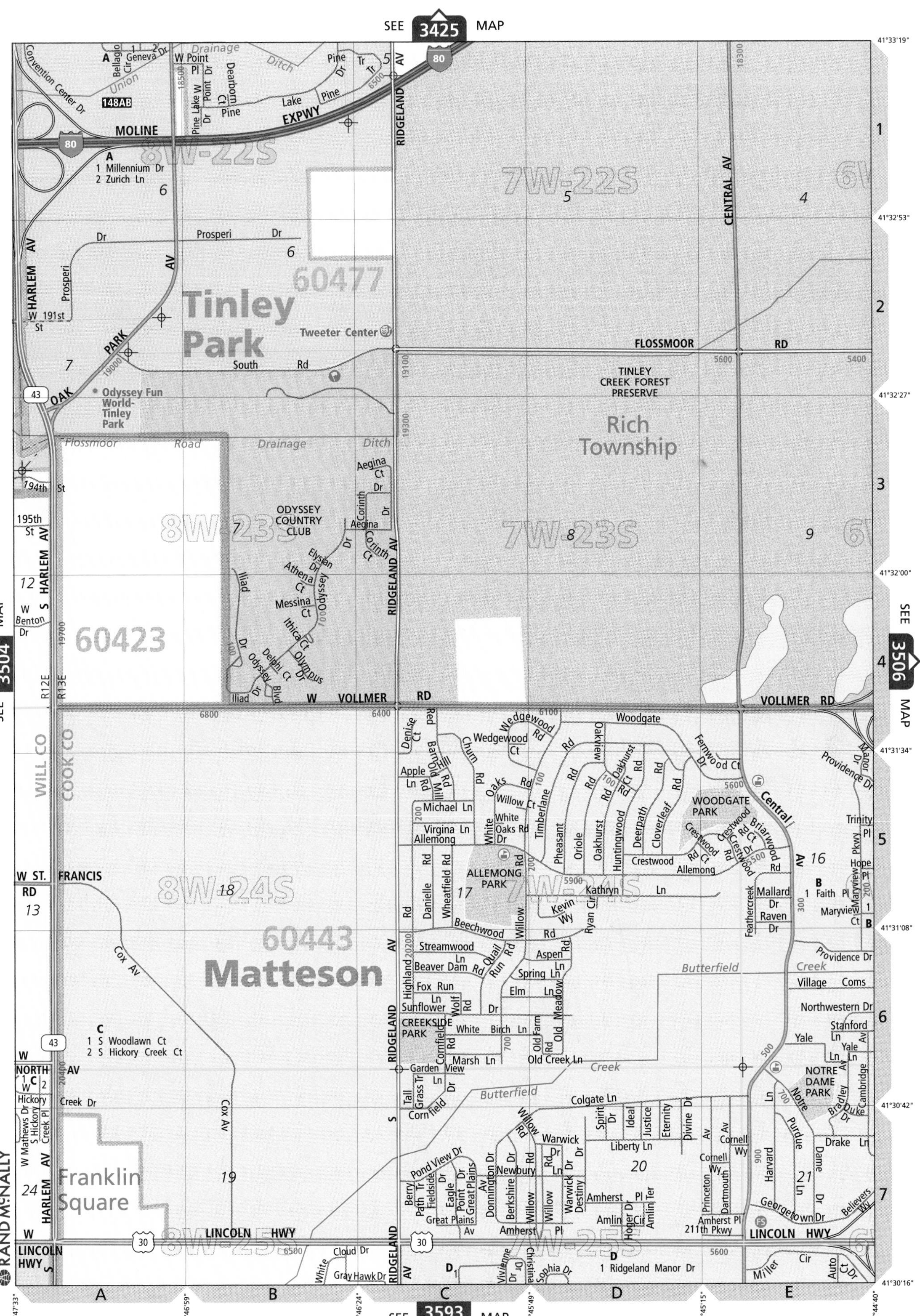

SEE 3504 MAP

SEE 3506 MAP

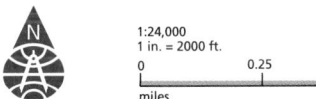

SEE 3593 MAP

1:24,000
1 in. = 2000 ft.
0 0.25 0.5
miles

SEE 3426 MAP

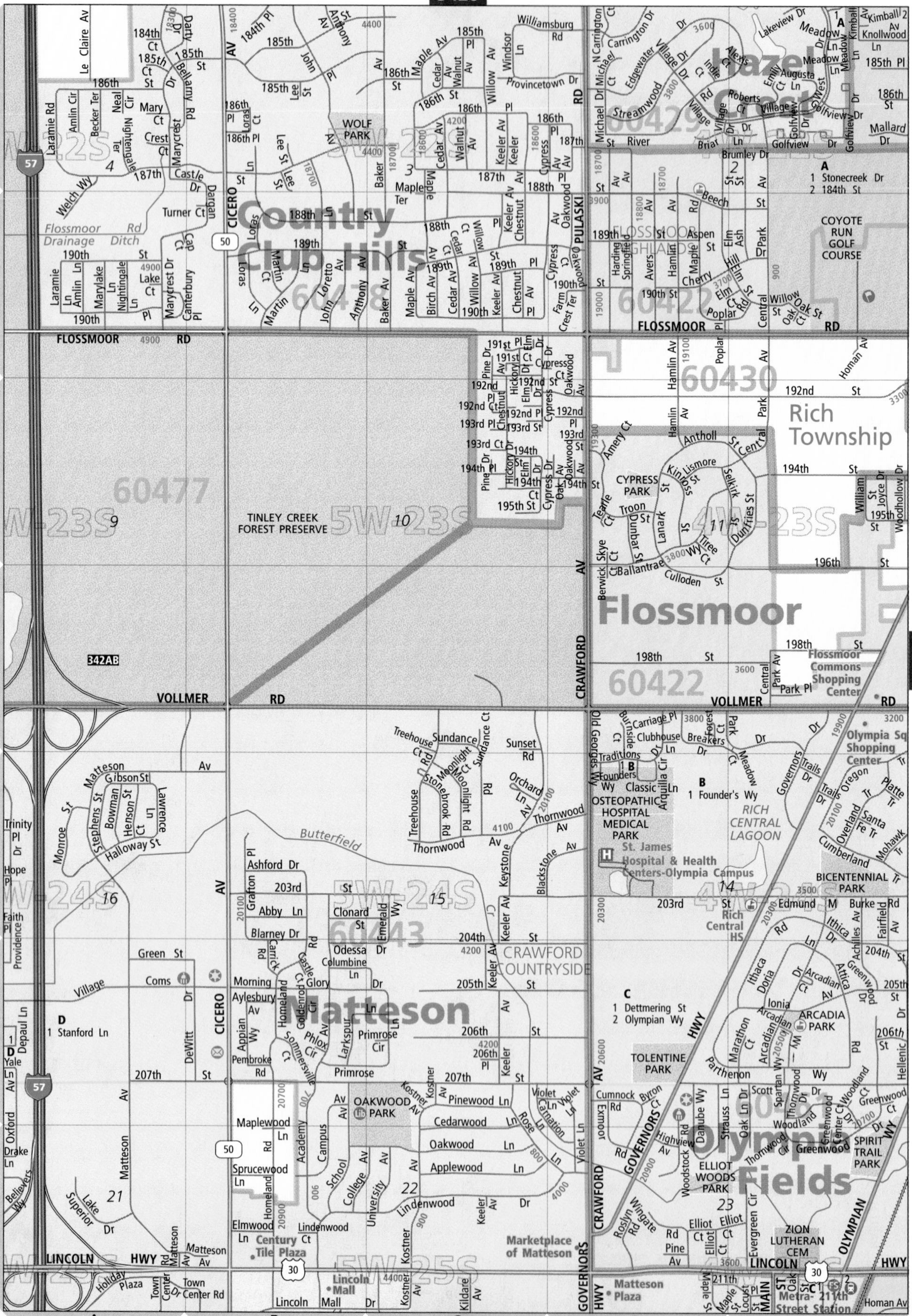

SEE 3505 MAP

SEE 3507 MAP

Country Club Hills
60478
WOLF PARK
Hazel Crest
60429
FLOSSMOOR HIGHLANDS
60422
COYOTE RUN GOLF COURSE
A
1 Stonecreek Dr
2 184th St
FLOSSMOOR RD
60430
Rich Township
CYPRESS PARK
60477
TINLEY CREEK FOREST PRESERVE
Flossmoor
Flossmoor Commons Shopping Center
VOLLMER RD
CICERO AV
PULASKI RD
CRAWFORD AV
342AB
B
1 Founder's Wy
OSTEOPATHIC HOSPITAL MEDICAL PARK
St. James Hospital & Health Centers-Olympia Campus
RICH CENTRAL LAGOON
Olympia Sq Shopping Center
BICENTENNIAL PARK
Rich Central HS
CRAWFORD COUNTRYSIDE
60443
Matteson
C
1 Dettmering St
2 Olympian Wy
ARCADIA PARK
TOLENTINE PARK
D
1 Stanford Ln
OAKWOOD PARK
SPIRIT TRAIL PARK
ELLIOT WOODS PARK
Olympia Fields
Marketplace of Matteson
Century Tile Plaza
Lincoln Mall
Matteson Plaza
ZION LUTHERAN CEM
Metra- 211th Street Station
LINCOLN HWY
GOVERNORS HWY
OLYMPIAN WY

41°33'19" 41°32'53" 41°32'27" 41°32'00" 41°31'34" 41°31'08" 41°30'42" 41°30'16"
87°44'40" 87°44'05" 87°43'30" 87°42'56" 87°42'21" 87°41'46"

A B C D E
1 2 3 4 5 6 7

SEE 3594 MAP

1:24,000
1 in. = 2000 ft.
0 0.25 0.5
miles

SEE 3427 MAP

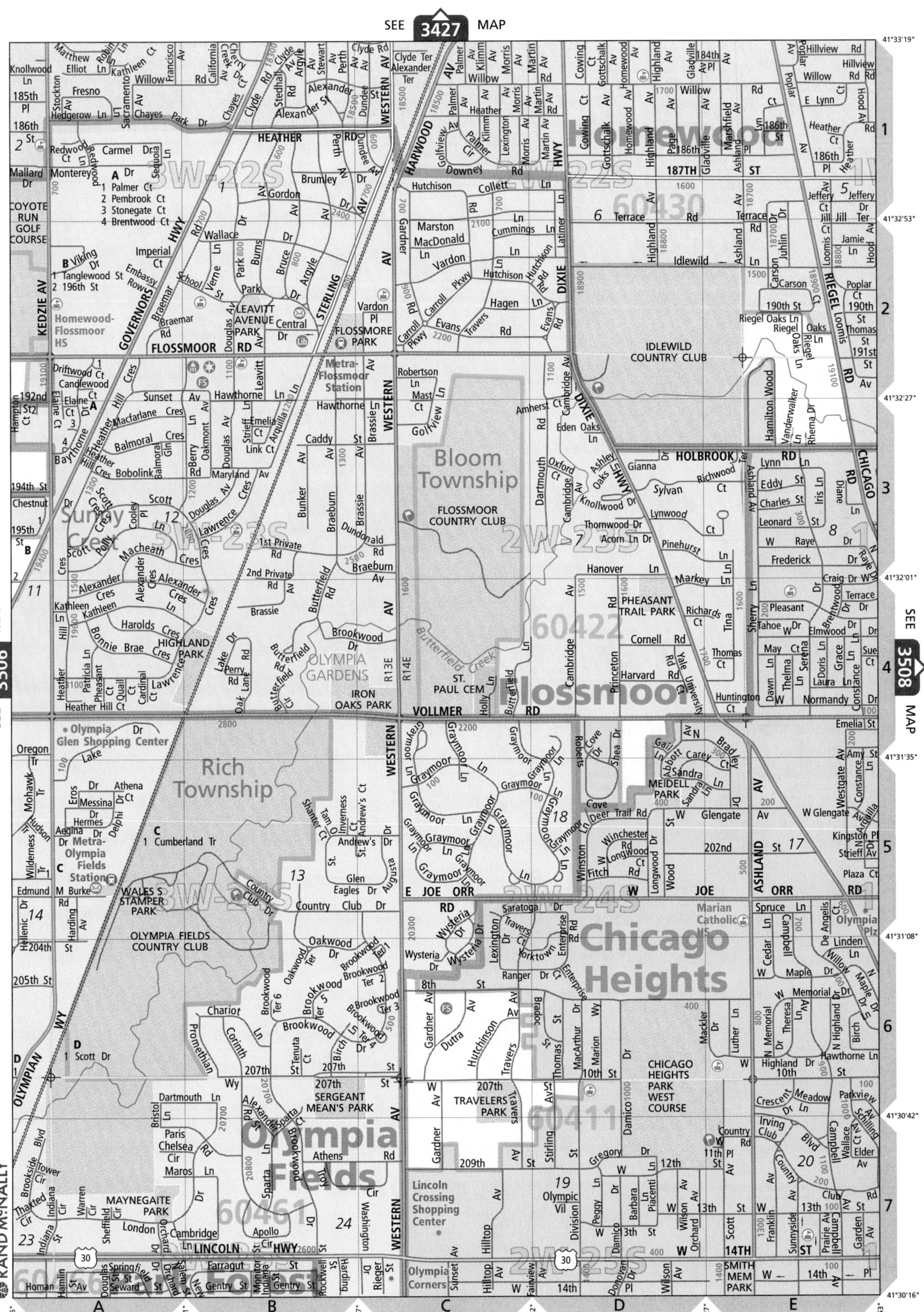

SEE 3506 MAP
SEE 3508 MAP
SEE 3595 MAP

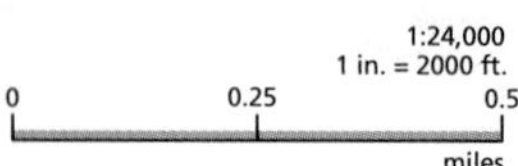

SEE 3428 MAP

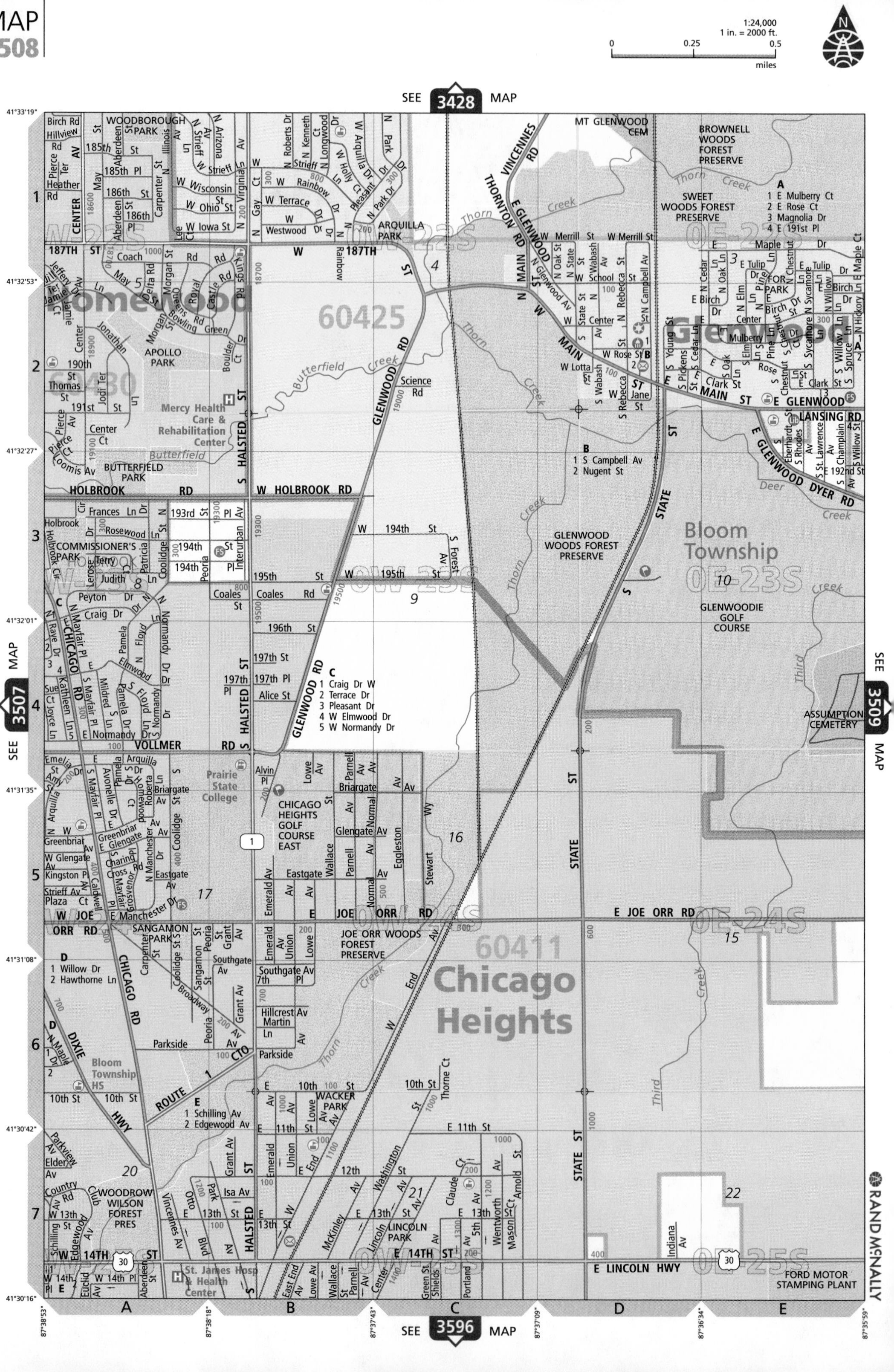

SEE 3507 MAP

SEE 3509 MAP

SEE 3596 MAP

Homewood

Glenwood

Chicago Heights

Bloom Township

60425

60430

60411

WOODBOROUGH PARK

ARQUILLA PARK

MT GLENWOOD CEM

BROWNELL WOODS FOREST PRESERVE

SWEET WOODS FOREST PRESERVE

FOR PARK

APOLLO PARK

Mercy Health Care & Rehabilitation Center

BUTTERFIELD PARK

COMMISSIONER'S PARK

GLENWOOD WOODS FOREST PRESERVE

GLENWOODIE GOLF COURSE

ASSUMPTION CEMETERY

Prairie State College

CHICAGO HEIGHTS GOLF COURSE EAST

SANGAMON PARK

JOE ORR WOODS FOREST PRESERVE

Bloom Township HS

WACKER PARK

WOODROW WILSON FOREST PRES

LINCOLN PARK

St. James Hosp & Health Center

FORD MOTOR STAMPING PLANT

W 187TH ST

HOLBROOK RD

W HOLBROOK RD

VOLLMER RD

W JOE ORR RD

E JOE ORR RD

E LINCOLN HWY

W 14TH ST

E 14TH ST

S HALSTED ST

GLENWOOD RD

STATE ST

CHICAGO RD

DIXIE HWY

ROUTE 1 CTO

THORNTON RD

VINCENNES RD

E GLENWOOD LANSING RD

E GLENWOOD DYER RD

MAIN ST

A
1 E Mulberry Ct
2 E Rose Ct
3 Magnolia Dr
4 E 191st Pl

B
1 S Campbell Av
2 Nugent St

C
1 Craig Dr W
2 Terrace Dr
3 Pleasant Dr
4 W Elmwood Dr
5 W Normandy Dr

D
1 Willow Dr
2 Hawthorne Ln

E
1 Schilling Av
2 Edgewood Av

41°33'19"
41°32'53"
41°32'27"
41°32'01"
41°31'35"
41°31'08"
41°30'42"
41°30'16"

87°38'53"
87°38'18"
87°37'43"
87°37'09"
87°36'34"
87°35'59"

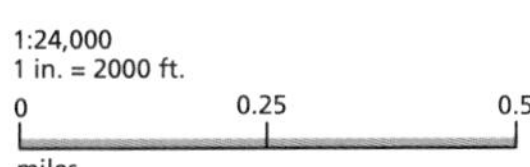

SEE 3429 MAP

SWEET WOODS FOREST PRESERVE

JURGENSEN WOODS FOREST PRESERVE

LANSING WOODS FOREST PRESERVE

60476

1E-22S

2E-22S

N COTTAGE GROVE AV

BISHOP FORD MEMORIAL EXPWY

STONEY ISLAND AV

TORRENCE AV

GLENWOOD LANSING RD

HICKORY GLEN PARK

Glenwood

GLENWOOD DYER RD

GLENWOODIE GC

ASSUMPTION CEM

60425

1E-23S

2E-23S

Lynwood

LYNWOOD

Lynwood Center

60411

E JOE ORR RD

1E-24S

2E-24S

Bloom Township

RAINBOW PARK

Ford Heights

E LINCOLN HWY

1E-25S

2E-25S

Sauk Village

FORD MOTOR STAMPING PLANT

SEE 3508 MAP

SEE 3510 MAP

SEE 3597 MAP

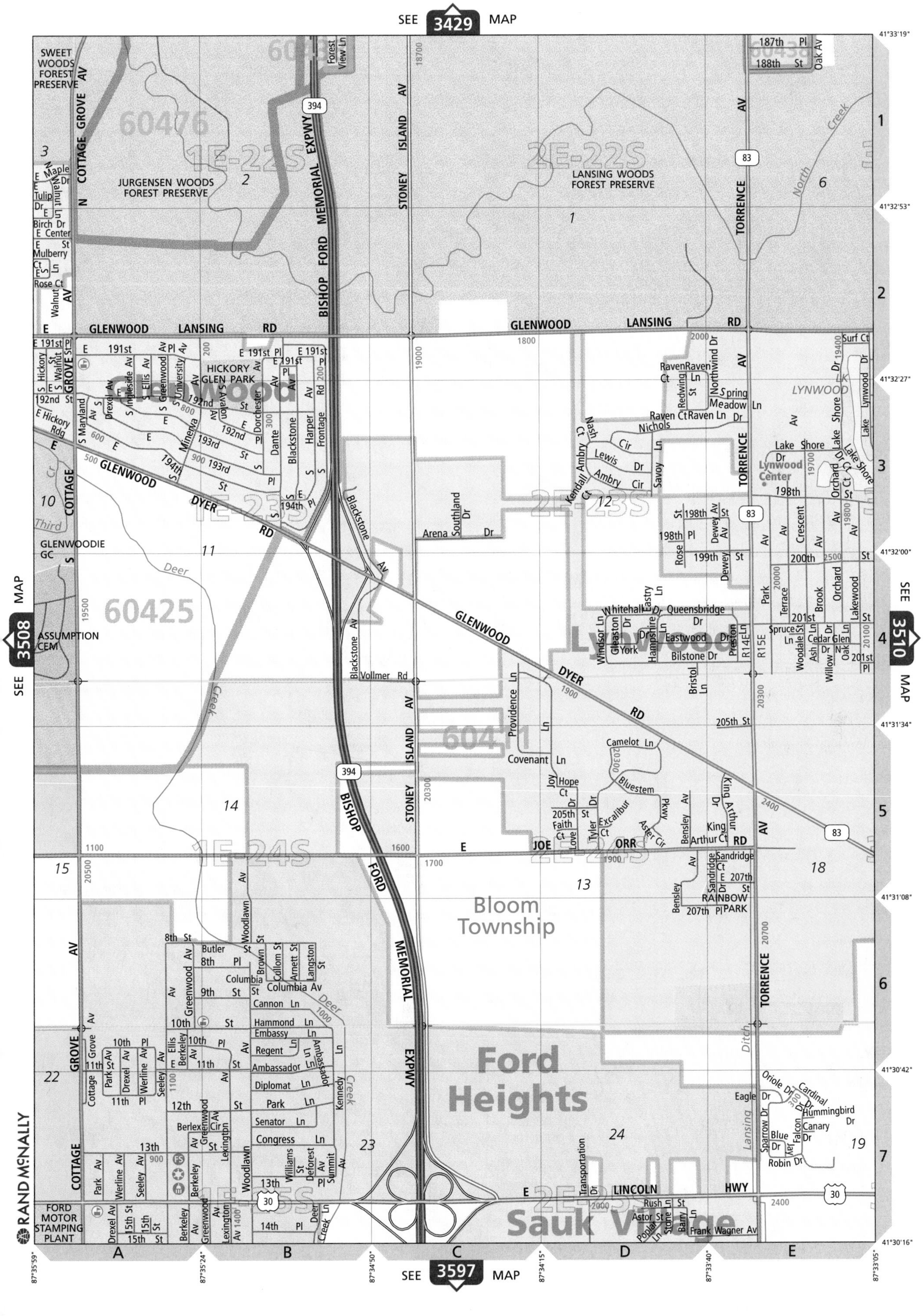

1:24,000
1 in. = 2000 ft.
0 0.25 0.5
miles

SEE 3430 MAP

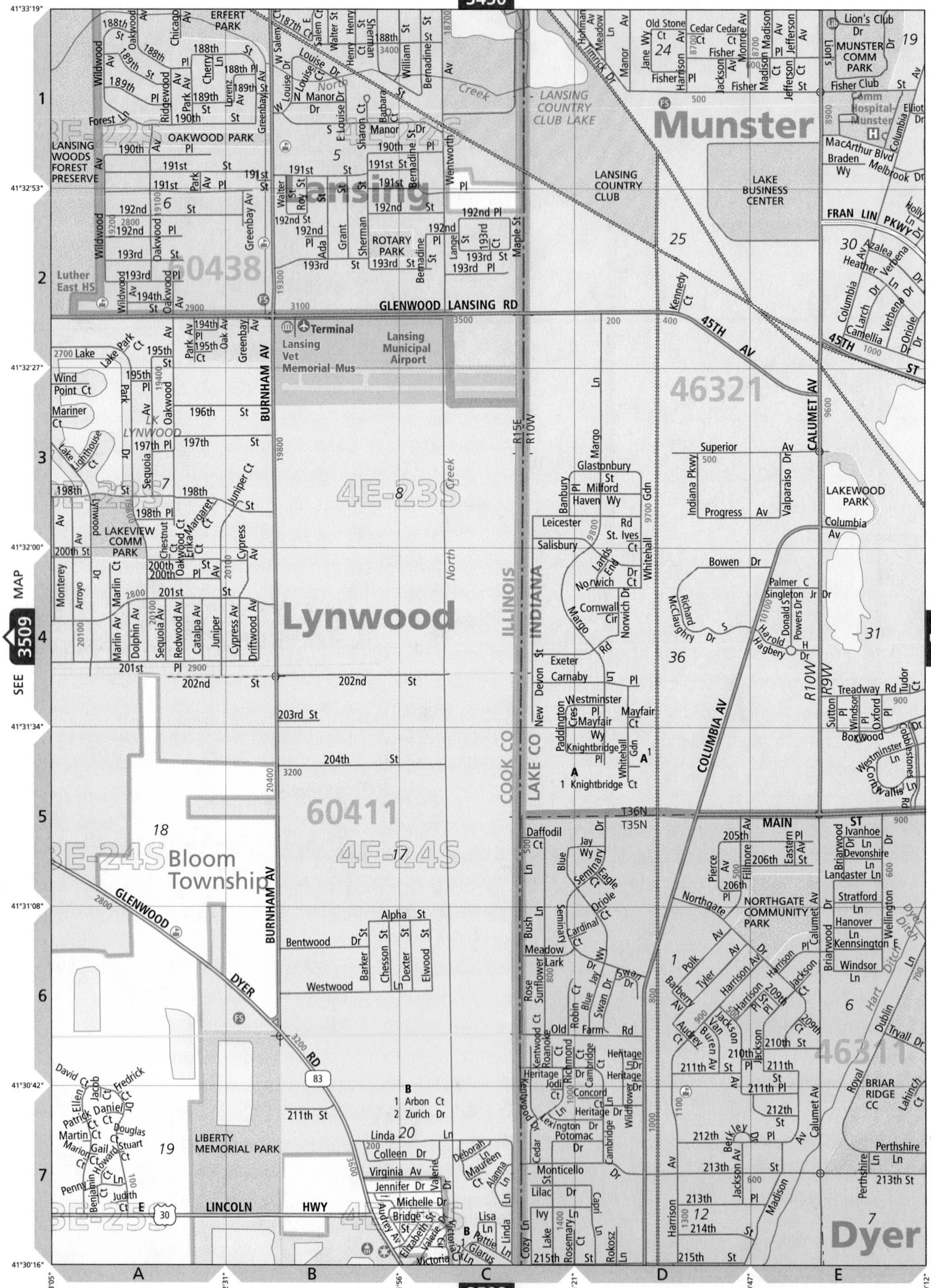

Munster
Lansing
Lynwood
Dyer
Bloom Township

ERFERT PARK
OAKWOOD PARK
LANSING WOODS FOREST PRESERVE
ROTARY PARK
LANSING COUNTRY CLUB LAKE
LANSING COUNTRY CLUB
LAKE BUSINESS CENTER
MUNSTER COMM PARK
Lion's Club Dr
Comm Hospital-Munster
Luther East HS
Terminal
Lansing Vet Memorial Mus
Lansing Municipal Airport
LK LYNWOOD
LAKEVIEW COMM PARK
LAKEWOOD PARK
NORTHGATE COMMUNITY PARK
LIBERTY MEMORIAL PARK
BRIAR RIDGE CC

GLENWOOD LANSING RD
45TH AV
BURNHAM AV
CALUMET AV
COLUMBIA AV
MAIN ST
GLENWOOD DYER RD
LINCOLN HWY
FRAN LIN PKWY

ILLINOIS
INDIANA
COOK CO
LAKE CO
R15E R10W
R10W R9W
T36N T35N

60438
60411
46321
46311

4E-22S
4E-23S
4E-24S
3E-22S
3E-23S
3E-24S

A
1 Knightbridge Ct

B
1 Arbon Ct
2 Zurich Dr

SEE 3509 MAP

SEE B MAP

A B C D E
1 2 3 4 5 6 7

41°33'19" 41°32'53" 41°32'27" 41°32'00" 41°31'34" 41°31'08" 41°30'42" 41°30'16"
87°33'05" 87°32'31" 87°31'56" 87°31'21" 87°30'47" 87°30'12"

SEE 3598 MAP

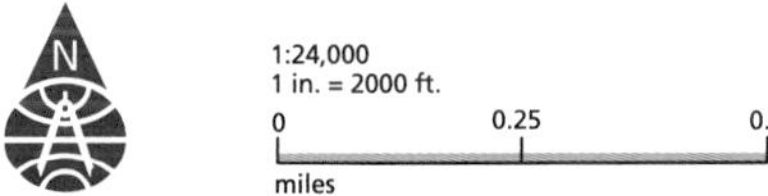

SEE 3495 MAP

Shorewood

Seward Township

Troy Township

Channahon Township

Minooka

60404

60447

KENDALL CO

GRUNDY CO

WILL CO

W MOUND RD

W SHEPLEY RD

HOLT RD

S COUNTY LINE RD

RIDGE RD

Ingolsby Rd

Canal Rd N

DUPAGE RIVER

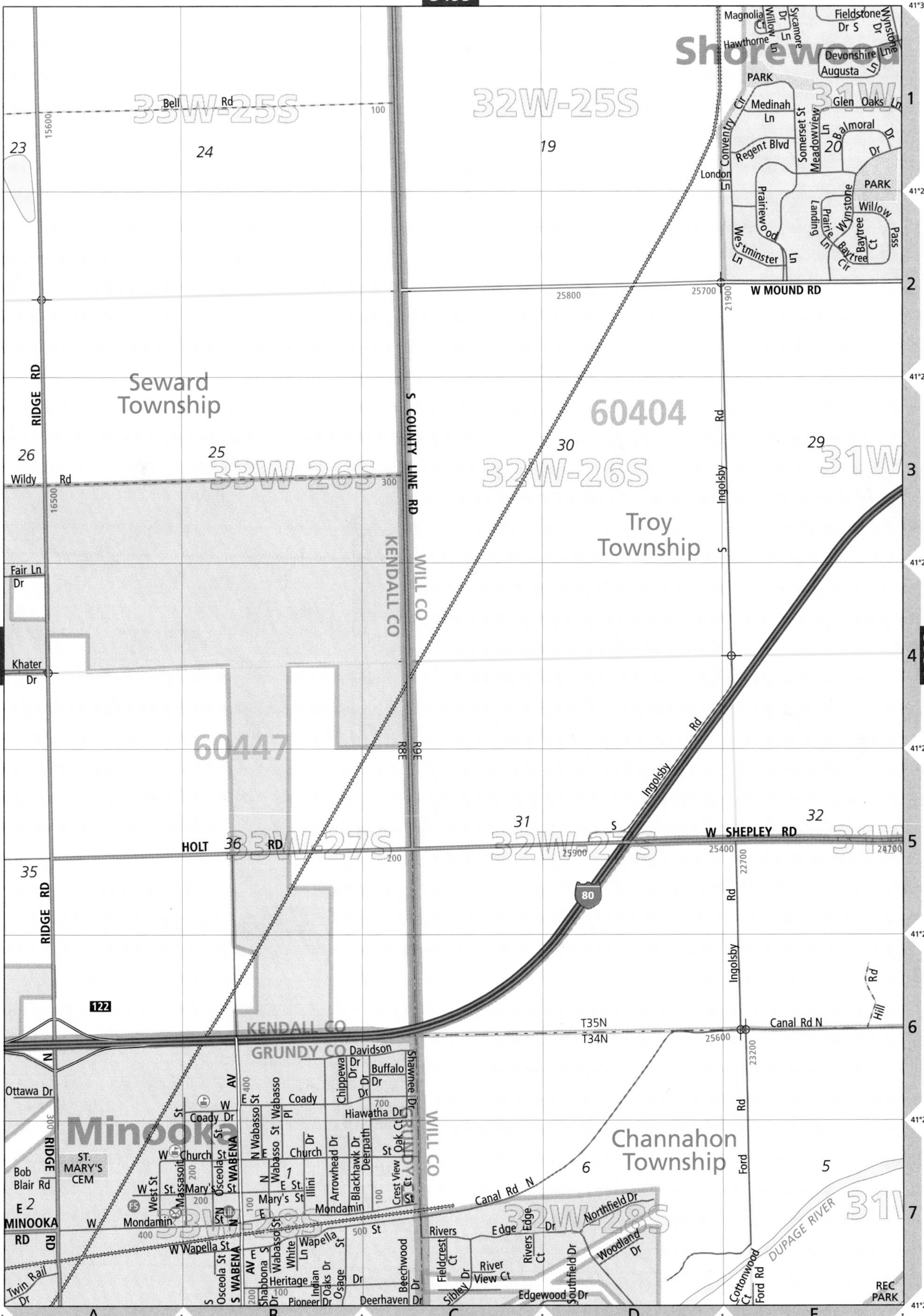

SEE B MAP

SEE 3584 MAP

SEE 3672 MAP

1:24,000
1 in. = 2000 ft.
0 0.25 0.5
miles

SEE 3496 MAP

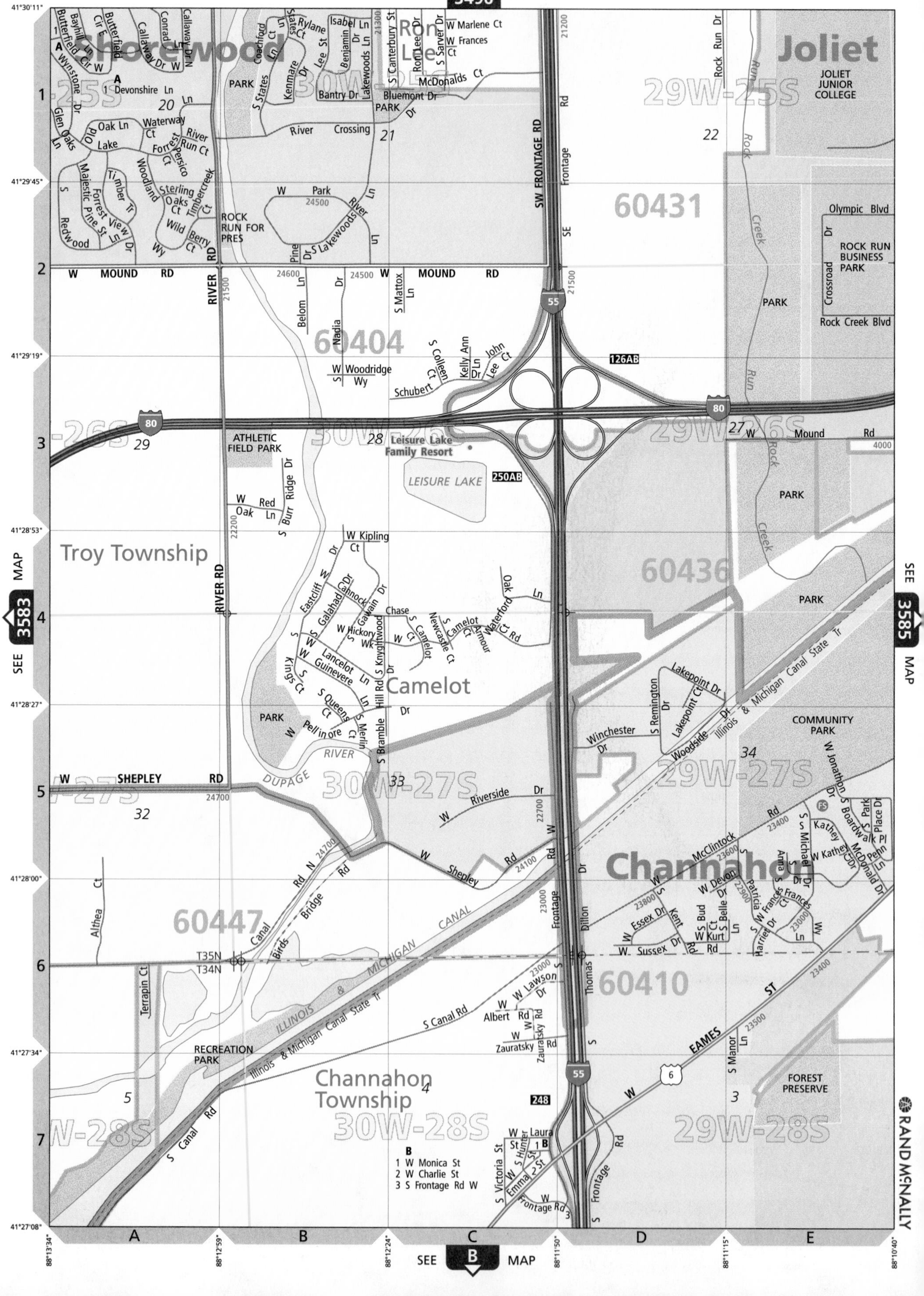

SEE 3583 MAP

SEE 3585 MAP

SEE B MAP

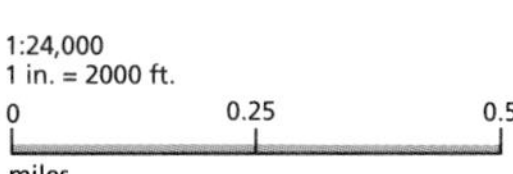

SEE 3497 MAP

Joliet

Rockdale

Channahon

Troy Township

Joliet Township

Channahon Township

Jackson Township

Joliet Junior College

SOUTHFIELD BUSINESS PARK

ROCK RUN BUSINESS PARK

CROWN TRYGG INDUSTRIAL PARK

Splash Station Waterpark

Empress Casino-Joliet

LOWER ROCK RUN PRESERVE

PARK

COMM PARK

Challenge Park

ILLINOIS & MICHIGAN CANAL

Illinois & Michigan Canal State Tr

DES PLAINES RIVER

A
1 Surrey Ct
2 S Mission Blvd

S Louise Ln, S Loren Dr, W Christine Ct, Christine Av, Jerald Dr, Leawood Ct, Leawood Dr, Cathy Ct, Karen Ct, Karen Dr, Longford Dr, Greenleaf Dr, Meadowsedge Ln, Trailsend Ln, Centennial Dr, Olympic Blvd, Corporate Dr, Riverboat Center Blvd, Riverboat Center Dr, Commerce Ln, Rock Creek Blvd, HOUBOLT RD, EMPRESS RD, W Mound Rd, W Mound Ct, Joyce Rd, Gould Ct, Maxim Dr, CHANNAHON RD, Terry Dr, Reeves Rd, Yish Indian Tr, Empress Dr, Alexandria Dr, W Laraway Rd, W Marylou Av, S Donna Av, W Karl Av, Carrie Av, Deal Av, Joseph Av, W McClintock Rd, W EAMES ST, W Andrew Av, W Schweizer Rd, Schweizer Rd, S Youngs Rd, S Vetter Rd

60431, 60436, 60410, 60421

28W-25S, 27W-25S, 26W, 28W-26S, 27W-26S, 28W-27S, 27W-27S, 28W-28S, 27W-28S

R9E, R10E, T35N, T34N

1, 2, 3, 6, 19, 23, 24, 25, 26, 30, 31, 35, 36

80, 6, 127

41°30'13", 41°29'46", 41°29'20", 41°28'54", 41°28'28", 41°28'02", 41°27'36", 41°27'10"

88°10'40", 88°10'06", 88°09'31", 88°08'56", 88°08'22", 88°07'47"

A B C D E

1 2 3 4 5 6 7

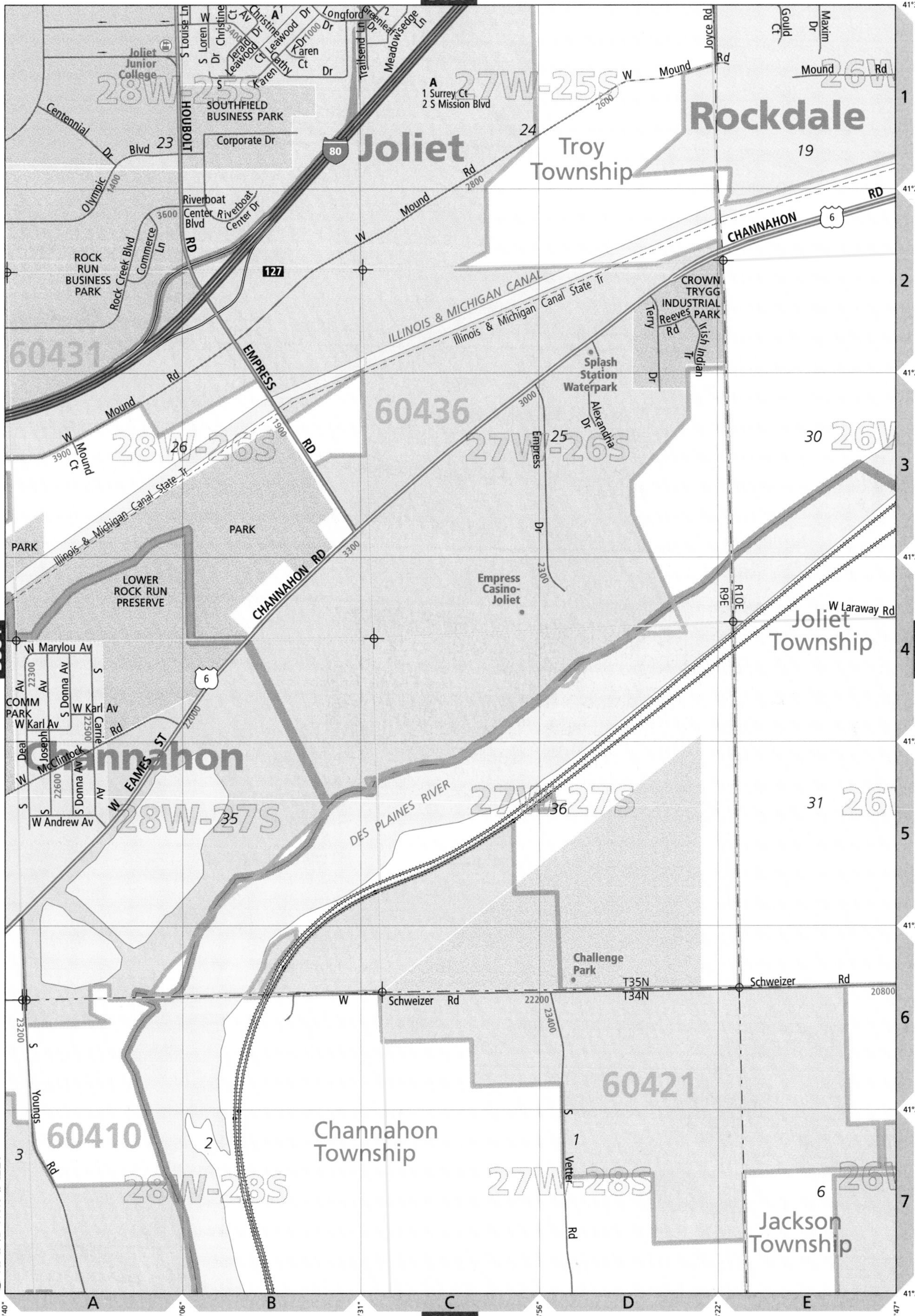

SEE 3584 MAP

SEE 3586 MAP

SEE 3674 MAP

1:24,000
1 in. = 2000 ft.
0 0.25 0.5
miles

SEE 3498 MAP

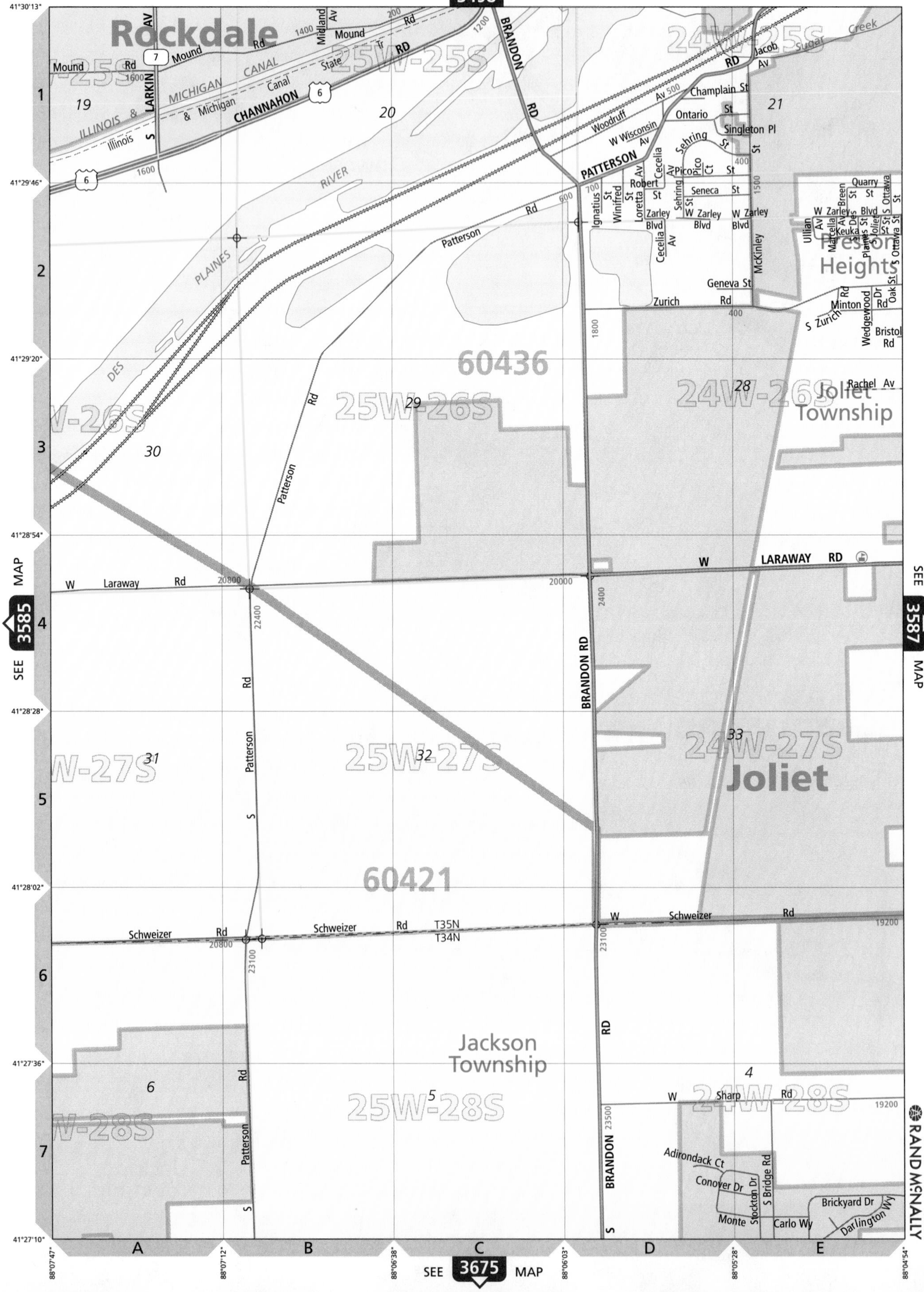

SEE 3585 MAP

SEE 3587 MAP

SEE 3675 MAP

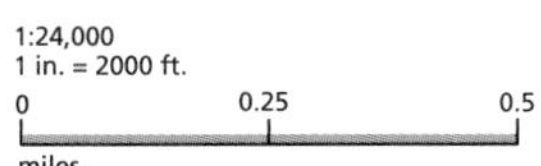

SEE 3499 MAP

SEE MAP 3586

SEE MAP 3588

SEE B MAP

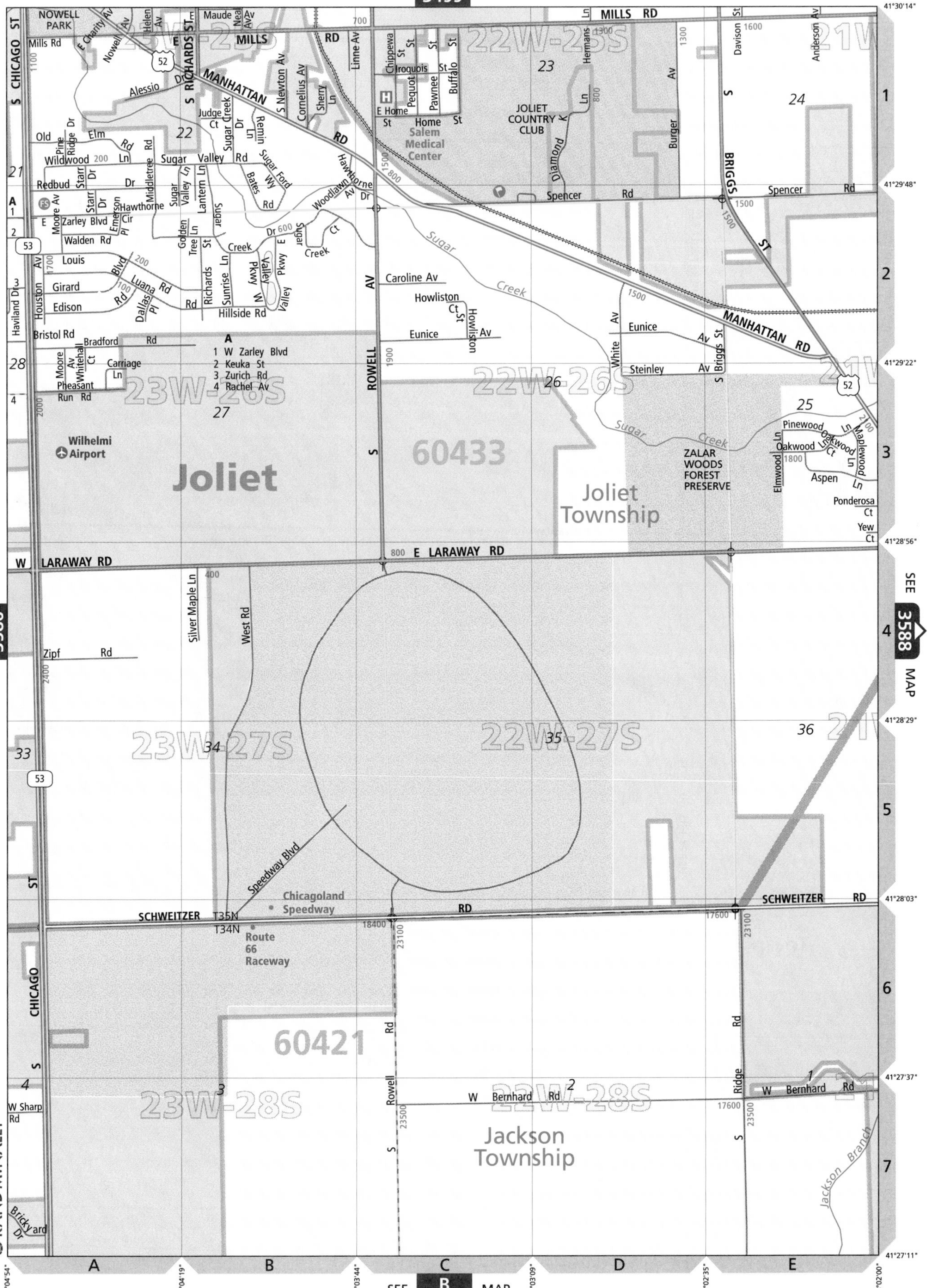

1:24,000
1 in. = 2000 ft.
0 0.25 0.5
miles

SEE 3500 MAP

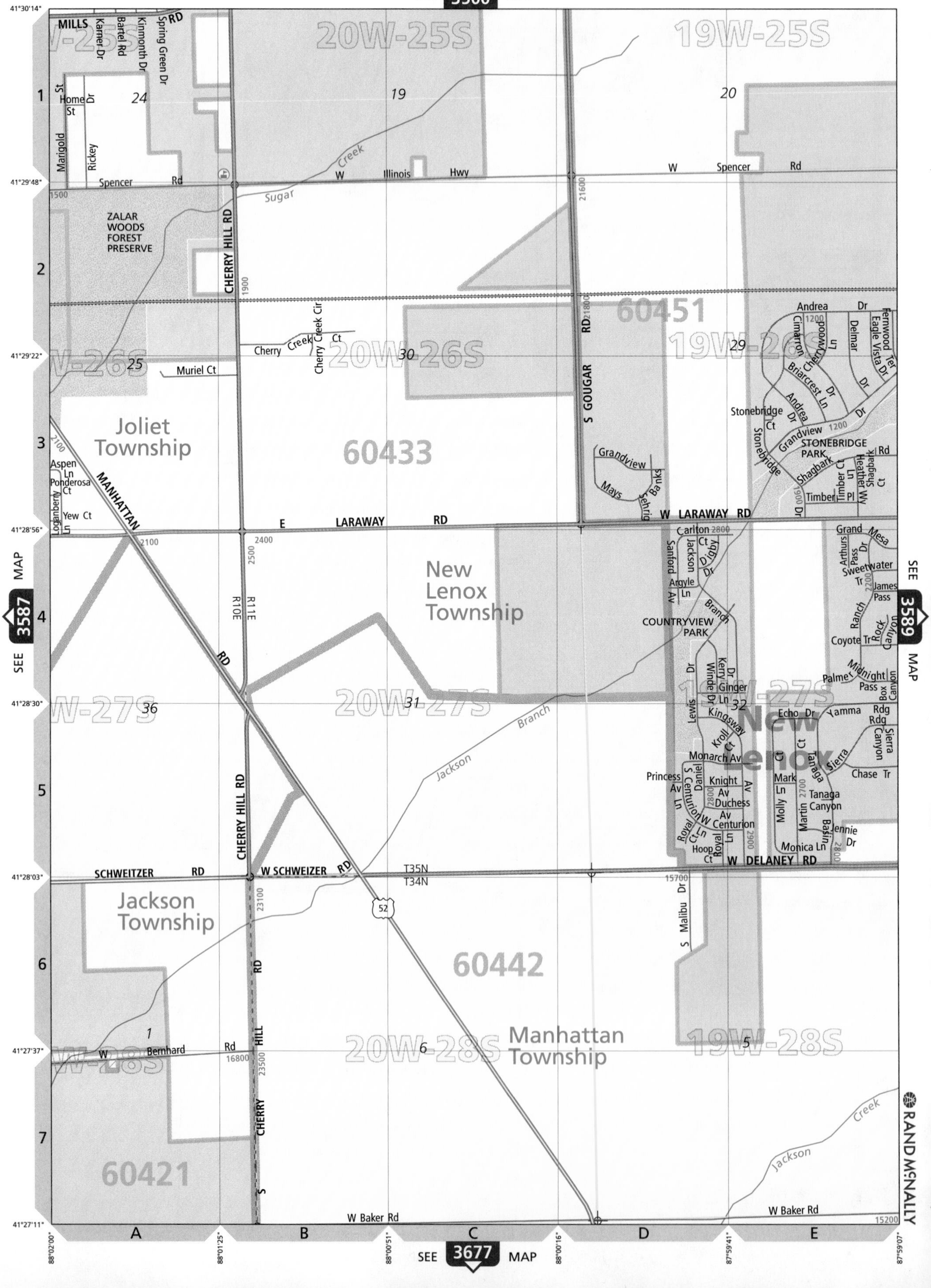

SEE 3587 MAP

SEE 3589 MAP

Joliet Township

New Lenox Township

Jackson Township

Manhattan Township

New Lenox

ZALAR WOODS FOREST PRESERVE

STONEBRIDGE PARK

COUNTRYVIEW PARK

60433

60451

60442

60421

20W-25S 19W-25S 20W-26S 19W-26S 20W-27S 19W-27S 20W-28S 19W-28S

CHERRY HILL RD

S GOUGAR RD

MANHATTAN RD

E LARAWAY RD

W LARAWAY RD

SCHWEITZER RD

W SCHWEIZER RD

W DELANEY RD

W Spencer Rd

W Illinois Hwy

W Bernhard Rd

W Baker Rd

A B C D E

SEE 3677 MAP

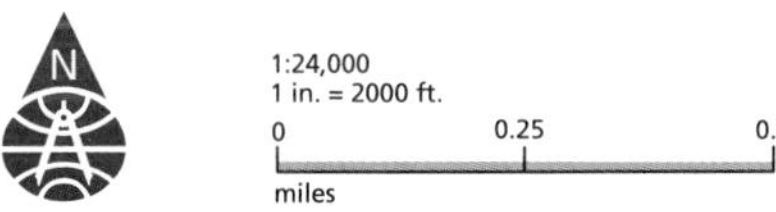

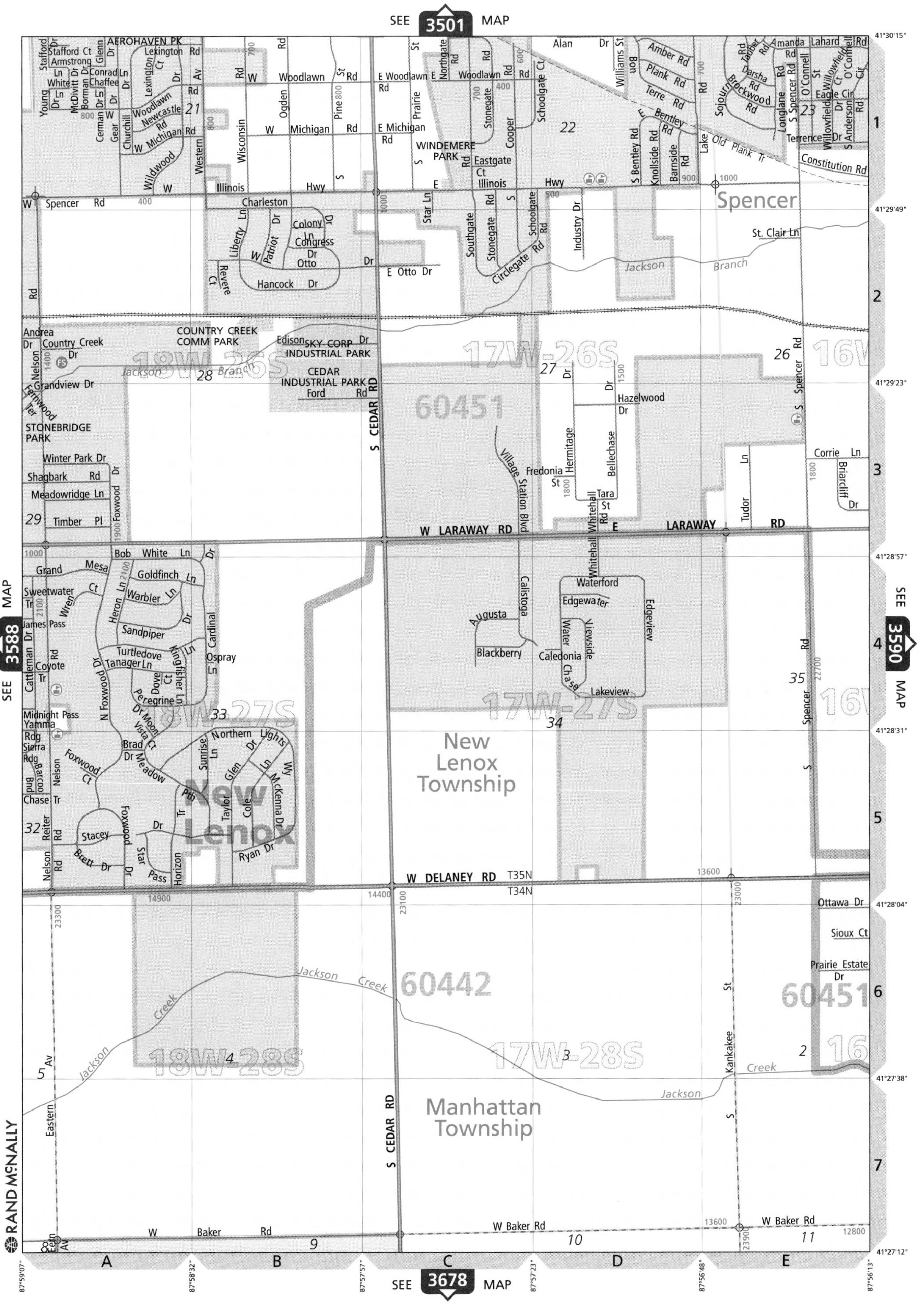

SEE 3501 MAP

SEE 3588 MAP

SEE 3590 MAP

SEE 3678 MAP

1:24,000
1 in. = 2000 ft.
0 0.25 0.5
miles

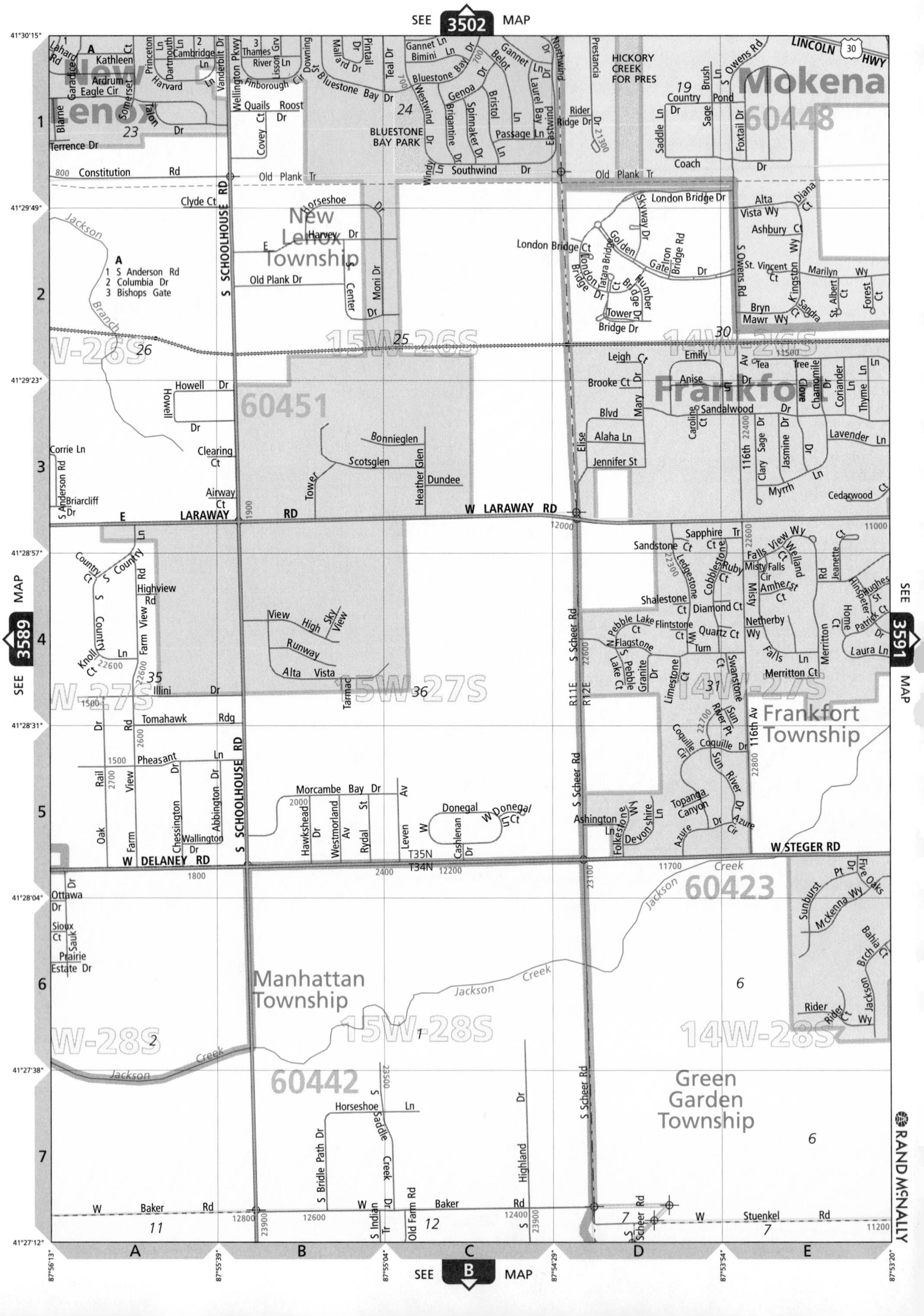

SEE 3502 MAP
SEE 3589 MAP
SEE 3591 MAP
SEE B MAP
New Lenox
Mokena
60448
Frankfort
Frankfort Township
New Lenox Township
Manhattan Township
Green Garden Township
60451
60423
60442
HICKORY CREEK FOR PRES
BLUESTONE BAY PARK
LINCOLN HWY
30
Constitution Rd
Old Plank Tr
S SCHOOLHOUSE RD
E LARAWAY RD
W LARAWAY RD
W DELANEY RD
W STEGER RD
W Baker Rd
W Stuenkel Rd
S Scheer Rd
S Owens Rd
116th Av
Wellington Pkwy
Vanderbilt Dr
Southwind Dr
London Bridge Dr
Golden Gate Dr
Sandalwood Dr
Lavender Ln
Jackson Creek
Jackson Branch
15W-26S
14W-26S
15W-27S
14W-27S
15W-28S
14W-28S
R11E
R12E
T35N
T34N
A
1 S Anderson Rd
2 Columbia Dr
3 Bishops Gate
A B C D E
1 2 3 4 5 6 7
41°30'15"
41°29'49"
41°29'23"
41°28'57"
41°28'31"
41°28'04"
41°27'38"
41°27'12"
87°56'13"
87°55'39"
87°55'04"
87°54'29"
87°53'54"
87°53'20"
RAND McNALLY

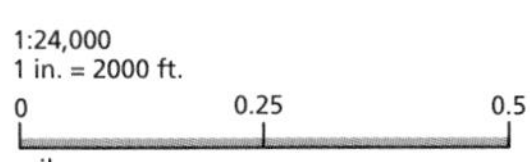

SEE 3503 MAP

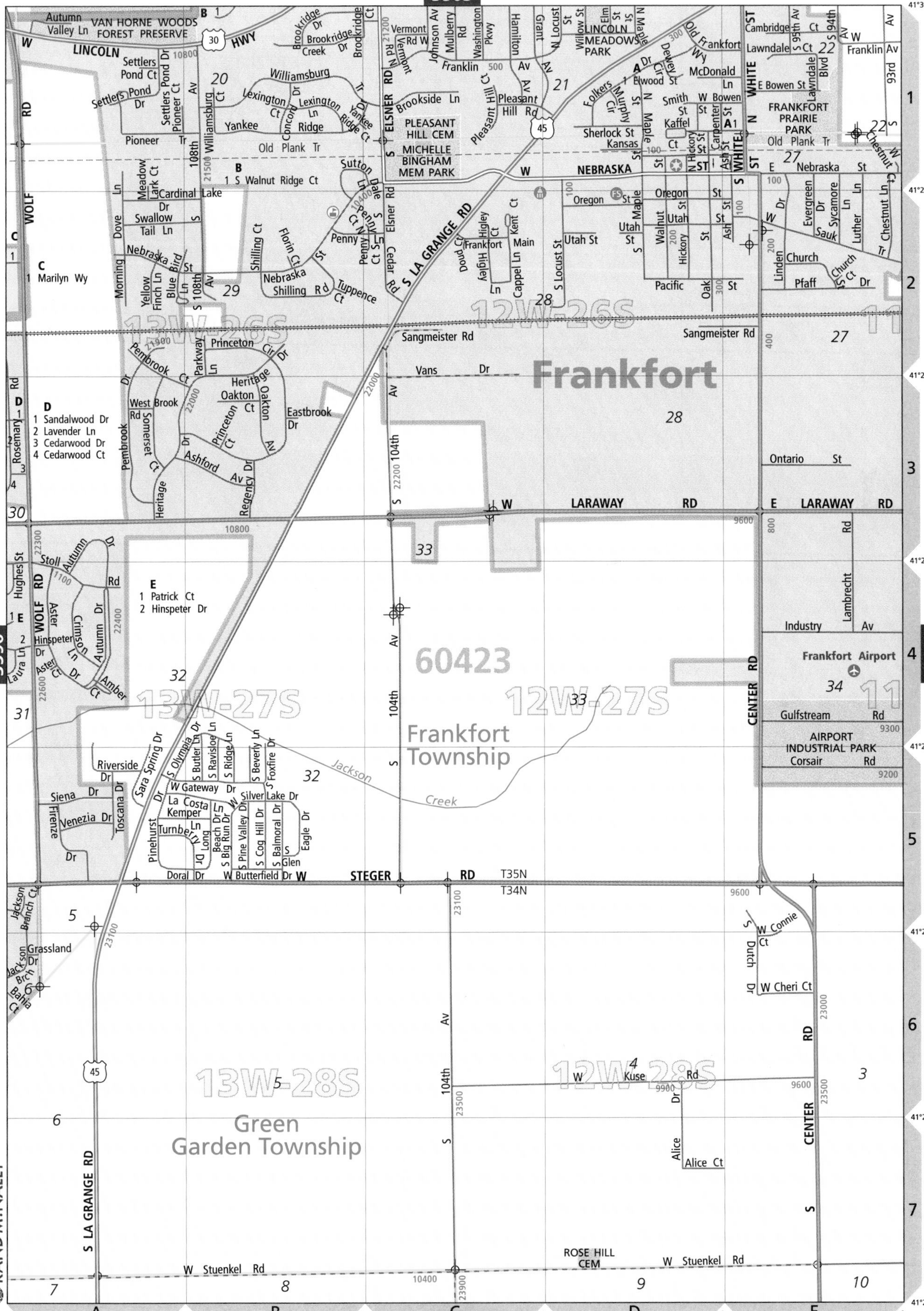

SEE 3590 MAP

SEE 3592 MAP

SEE B MAP

41°30'16" 41°29'50" 41°29'23" 41°28'57" 41°28'31" 41°28'05" 41°27'39" 41°27'13"

87°53'20" 87°52'45" 87°52'10" 87°51'36" 87°51'01" 87°50'26"

A B C D E

1 2 3 4 5 6 7

Frankfort

Frankfort Township

Green Garden Township

60423

VAN HORNE WOODS FOREST PRESERVE

LINCOLN MEADOWS PARK

PLEASANT HILL CEM

MICHELLE BINGHAM MEM PARK

FRANKFORT PRAIRIE PARK

Frankfort Airport

AIRPORT INDUSTRIAL PARK

ROSE HILL CEM

W LINCOLN HWY

W NEBRASKA ST

W LARAWAY RD

E LARAWAY RD

W STEGER RD

W Stuenkel Rd

W Kuse Rd

S LA GRANGE RD

WOLF RD

CENTER RD

S 104th Av

S ELSNER RD

WHITE ST

Sangmeister Rd

Jackson Creek

T35N

T34N

13W-26S 12W-26S 13W-27S 12W-27S 13W-28S 12W-28S

A
1 S Walnut Ridge Ct

B
1 S Walnut Ridge Ct

C
1 Marilyn Wy

D
1 Sandalwood Dr
2 Lavender Ln
3 Cedarwood Dr
4 Cedarwood Ct

E
1 Patrick Ct
2 Hinspeter Dr

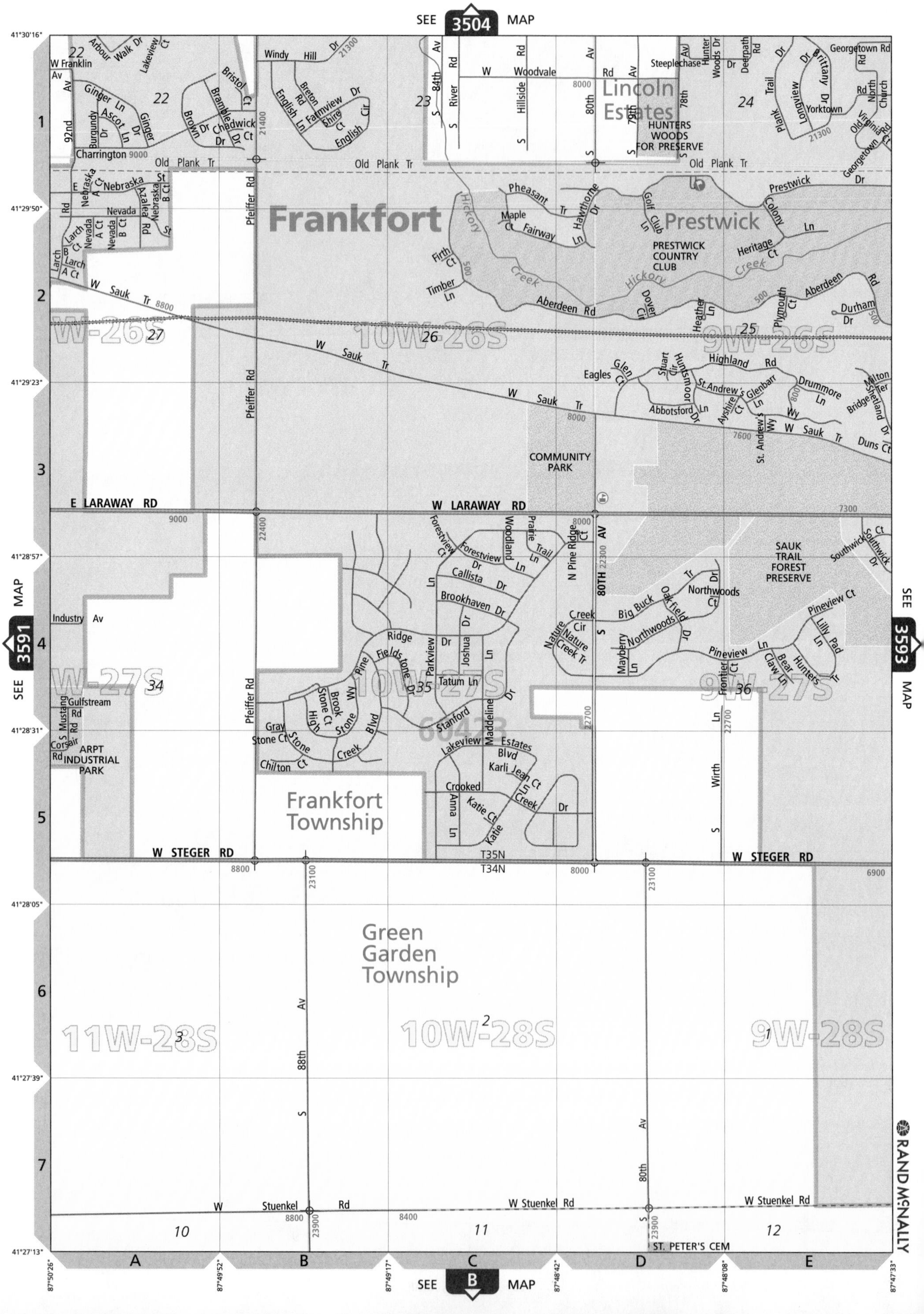

1:24,000
1 in. = 2000 ft.
0 0.25 0.5
miles
N
SEE 3504 MAP
SEE 3591 MAP
SEE 3593 MAP
SEE B MAP
Frankfort
Lincoln Estates
HUNTERS WOODS FOR PRESERVE
Prestwick
PRESTWICK COUNTRY CLUB
COMMUNITY PARK
SAUK TRAIL FOREST PRESERVE
ARPT INDUSTRIAL PARK
Frankfort Township
Green Garden Township
ST. PETER'S CEM
Old Plank Tr
W Sauk Tr
E LARAWAY RD
W LARAWAY RD
W STEGER RD
W Stuenkel Rd
Pfeiffer Rd
S 80TH AV
S 88th Av
S 80th Av
S Wirth Ln
Hickory Creek
10W-26S
9W-26S
W-26S
W-27S
10W-27S
9W-27S
11W-28S
10W-28S
9W-28S
60423
T35N
T34N
A B C D E
1 2 3 4 5 6 7
RAND McNALLY

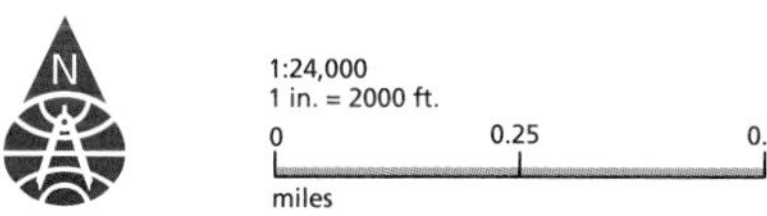

SEE 3505 MAP

A
1 Yorktown Rd
2 Georgetown Coms

B
1 Hearthside Dr

C
1 Milton Bridge Ter
2 Duns Ct

D
1 Kara St

Matteson

Richton Park

Rich Township

Frankfort

University Park

Monee Township

Green Garden Township

SAUK TRAIL FOREST PRESERVE

GOVERNORS GATEWAY INDUSTRIAL PARK

PRESTWICK CC

60443

60471

60423

60449

8W-26S

7W-26S

8W-27S

7W-27S

8W-28S

7W-28S

WILL CO

COOK CO

R12E

R13E

T35N

T34N

S HARLEM AV

RIDGELAND AV

CENTRAL AV

SAUK TR

W LARAWAY RD

W STEGER RD

W Stuenkel Rd

Old Plank Tr

University Pkwy

Hickory Creek

Butterfield Creek

Georgetown Rd, Virginia Ct, Prestwick Dr, S Harlem Av, Golf View Ln, Aberdeen Rd, Bridle Path, White Cloud Dr, Blue Sky Ln, Patricia Dr, Pasture Side Tr, Old Plank Blvd, Harvest Ln, Barn Owl Dr, Gray Hawk Dr, Shannon Av, Karlin Ct, Taylor Ct, Whitney Ct, Megan Ct, Vivienne Av, Victoria Ct, Christina Dr, Sophia, Alessandra Dr, Patricia Ln, Olivia Ct, Auto Ct, Miller Cir, Wild Rock Ter, Tullamore Ter, Blackthorn, Briarbranch Ter, Pleasant Rd, Windmere Cir, N Windmere, Knollwood Cir, Timber Ridge, Candlegate Cir, Brushwood Dr, Thistle Ct, Hedgewick Ct, Heathermead Rd, Burlwood Ct, Greensward Wy, Prairie Rd, Moorfield, Woodbine Ter, Chapparal Ter, Huntsbridge, Ivy Log Ter, Thorntree Ter, Hickory Glen, Tanglewood Rd, Petunia Cir, Crocus Ln, Buttercup Ln, Hyacinth Ln, Marigold Cir, Lilac Ln, Maplebrook Dr, Aster Ln, Begonia Ln, Poppy Ln, Pansey Cir, Tulip Ln, Daffodil Ln, Hibiscus Cir, Troon Cir, Shetland Dr, W Sauk Tr, Southwick Ct, Southwick Dr, Ryan, Trevor Cir, Brianne Ct, Ojai Dr, Palo Alto, Redondo Dr, Oxnard Ct, Tiburon St, Ventura Dove, Buena Vista Blvd, Alamitos Dr, Hildago Dr, Hilda go Ct, Arroyo St, Bohlmann Pkwy, Imperial Dr, Arquilla Dr, Kara Ln, Imperial Ct, Northwind Dr, Bentgrass Av, Greenfield Blvd, Crosswind, Sawgrass Dr, Westwind Dr, Deana Ln, Southwind Dr

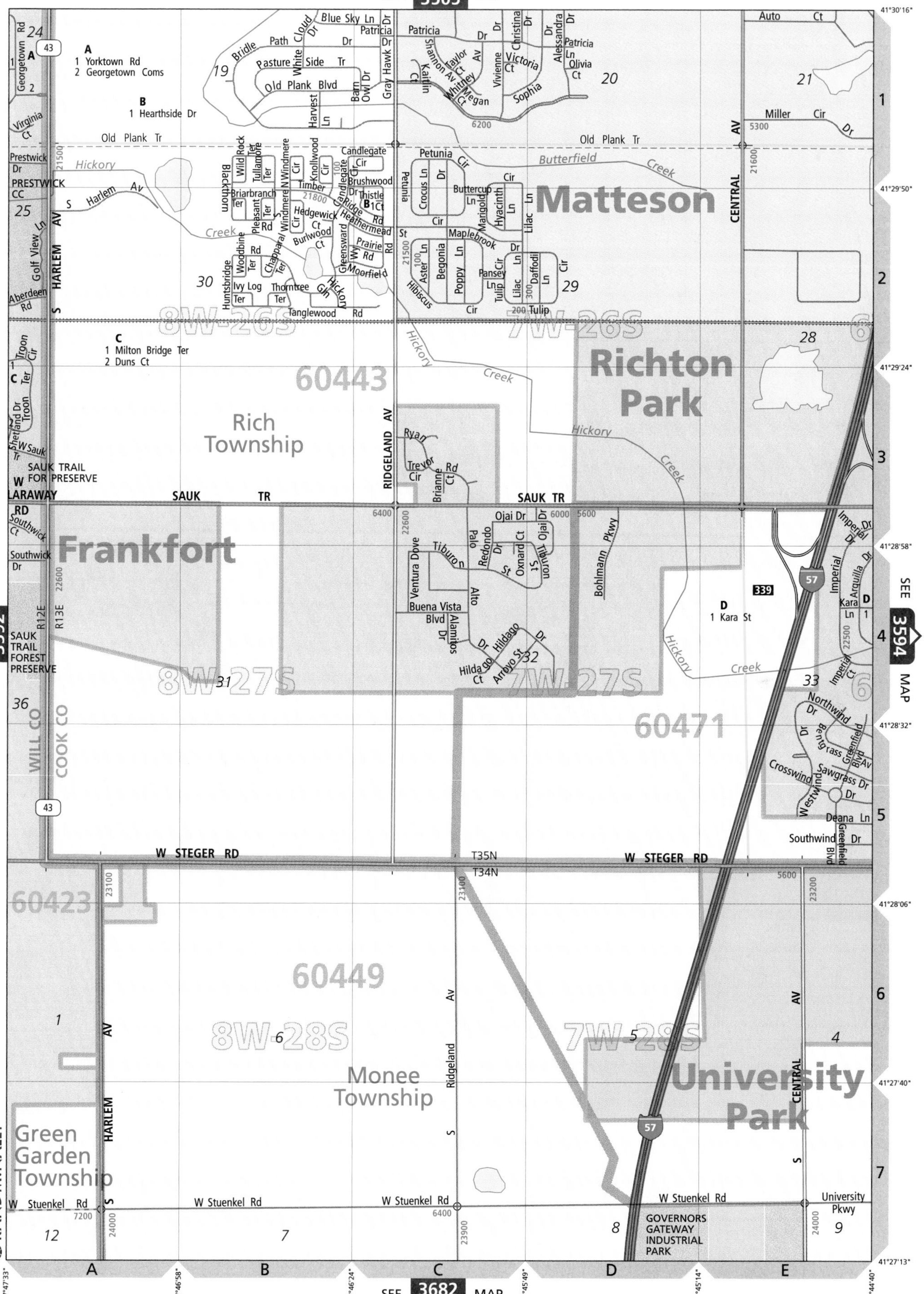

SEE 3592 MAP

SEE 3594 MAP

SEE 3682 MAP

41°30'16" 41°29'50" 41°29'24" 41°28'58" 41°28'32" 41°28'06" 41°27'40" 41°27'13"

87°47'33" 87°46'58" 87°46'24" 87°45'49" 87°45'14" 87°44'40"

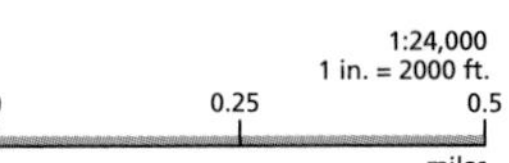

SEE 3506 MAP

Matteson
60443
Richton Park
Rich Township
60471
Park Forest
University Park
60449
Monee Township
60466
60417

Matteson Town Center
LINCOLN MALL
GOVERNORS TRAIL PARK
Metra-Matteson Station
MEM PARK
WINNEBAGO PARK
GLAESER PARK
Rich South HS
SAUK SCHOOL PARK
LAKE GEORGE
KLAWITTER PARK
PIERCE PARK
Governors Plaza
Metra-Richton Pk Station
KEOKUK PARK
SOMONAUK PARK
Haedtler Landing Strip
Metra-University Park Station
UNIVERSITY GOLF CLUB
THORN CREEK WOODS NATURE PRESERVE
Thorn Creek Woods Nature Center
GOVERNORS STATE UNIVERSITY

A
1 Olympian Wy

B
1 Jackson St
2 Wildflower Rd

C
1 Lioncrest Ct
2 St. Ives Ct

CICERO AV
S CICERO AV
GOVERNORS HWY
MAIN ST
SAUK TR
STEGER RD
W STEGER RD
UNIVERSITY PKWY
W STUENKEL RD
OLD MONEE RD
STEGER-MONEE RD
Old Plank Road Tr
Old Plank Tr
Gateway Dr
Holiday Plaza Dr
Town Center Rd
Lincoln Mall Dr
Kildare Ct
St. Lawrence Av
Washington Av
Keeler Av
Richton Rd
Charleston Rd
Sumpter Dr
Richmond Ct
Euclid Av
Maple Av
Poplar Av
Birchwood Rd
Clark Dr
Andover Dr
Arlington Dr
Greenbriar Ln
Karlov Av
Lincoln Blvd
Jefferson
Farmington
Crescent
Imperial Dr
Monterey Dr
Hickory Creek Dr
Northwind Dr
Bentgrass Av
Sawgrass Dr
Southwind Dr
Polk St
Davis Av
Dewey Av
Tamarack St
Crawford Av
Central Av
Hawthorne Dr
Nauvoo St
Shabbona
Topeka St
Tampa St
Talala St
Pine Trace Ct
University Cross
Oak Hill Dr
Homan Av
Illinois St
Chase St
Dettmering St
Oak St
212th
213th
214th
215th
216th St
217th
218th
219th St

COOK CO
WILL CO
T35N
T34N
6W-26S
5W-26S
4W-26S
6W-27S
5W-27S
4W-27S
6W-28S
5W-28S
4W-28S

41°30'16"
41°29'50"
41°29'24"
41°28'58"
41°28'32"
41°28'06"
41°27'40"
41°27'13"
87°44'40"
87°44'05"
87°43'30"
87°42'55"
87°42'21"
87°41'46"

A B C D E
1 2 3 4 5 6 7

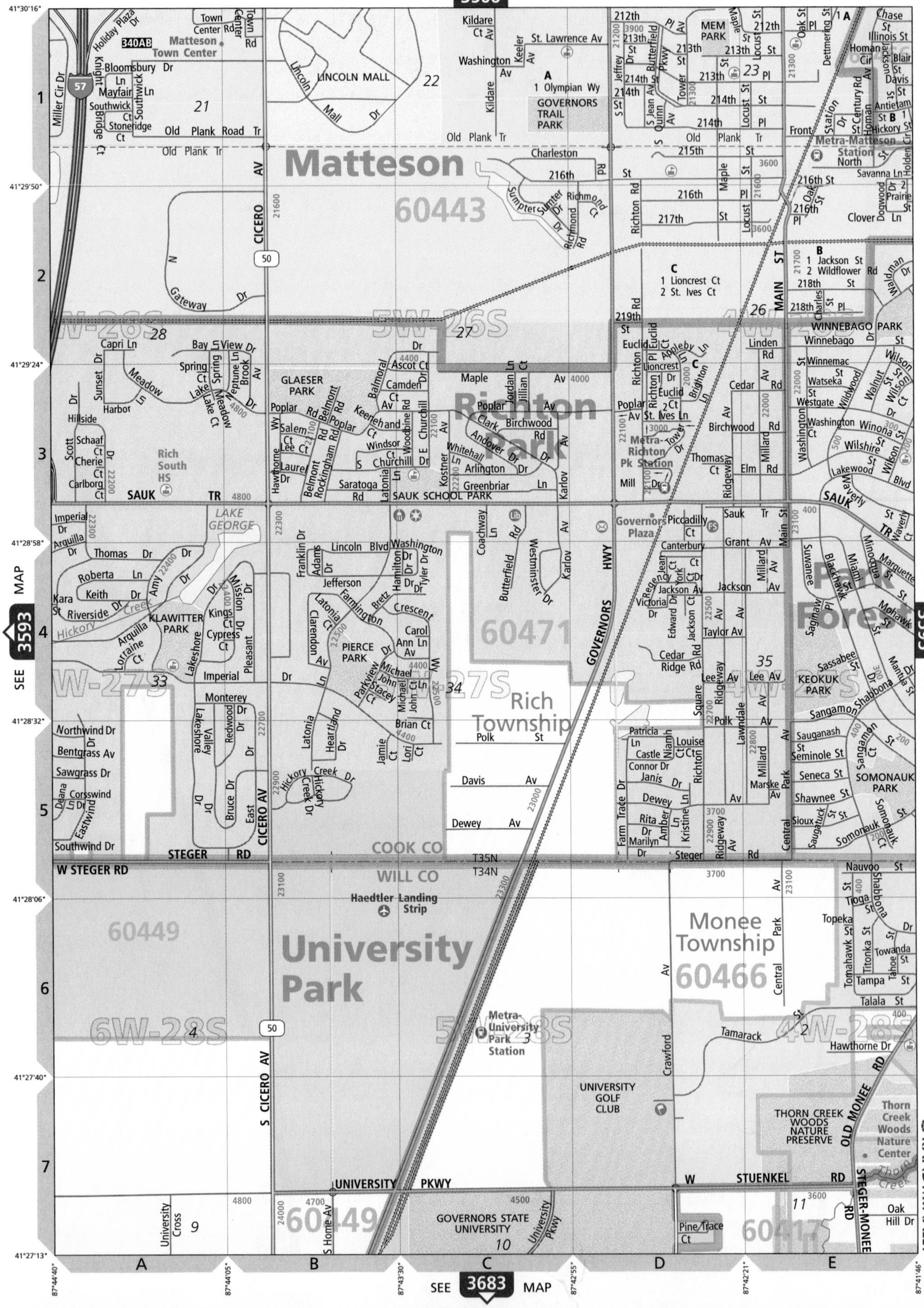

SEE 3593 MAP
SEE 3595 MAP
SEE 3683 MAP

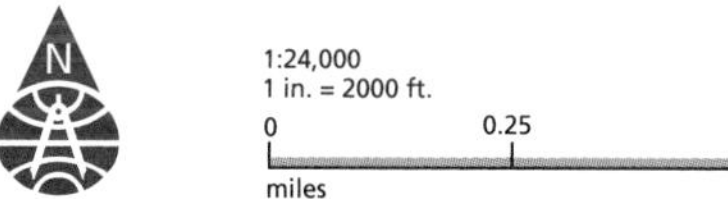

SEE 3507 MAP

Park Forest

Chicago Heights

South Chicago Heights

Steger

University Park

Bloom Township

Monee Township

Crete Township

INDIANA PARK

ILLINOIS PARK

LOGAN PARK

Elizabeth Ludeman Development Center

DOMINIC J SESTO PARK

CORNET PARK

SMITH MEM PARK

INDIAN HILL WOODS FOREST PRESERVE

ALGONQUIN PARK

EASTGATE PARK

Norwood Square Shopping Center

WINNEBAGO PARK

CENTRAL PARK

KROTIAK PARK

VET MEM PARK

PARK FOREST AQUA CENTER

Freedom Hall Nathan Manilow Theatre

Illinois Theatre Center

Illinois Philharmonic Orchestra

ST. ANNE'S CEM

Rich East HS

CEDAR PARK

MURPHY PARK

MEM PARK

SAUK TRAIL WOODS FOREST PRESERVE

SAUK LAKE

SCHUBERTS WOODS FOREST PRESERVE

KINGS GROVE FOREST PRESERVE

MARQUETTE PARK

ONARGA PARK

SOMONAUK PARK

Park Forest Academy

SHABBONA PARK

CALVARY CEM

COOK CO

WILL CO

LAUREL PARK

THORN CREEK WOODS NATURE PRESERVE

DEER CREEK FOR PRES

W 26TH ST

WESTERN AV

SAUK TR

MONEE RD

OLD MONEE RD

W STEGER RD

RICHTON RD

W SAUK TR

60443

60411

60466

60475

60417

3W-26S

2W-26S

3W-27S

2W-27S

3W-28S

2W-28S

T35N

T34N

R13E

R14E

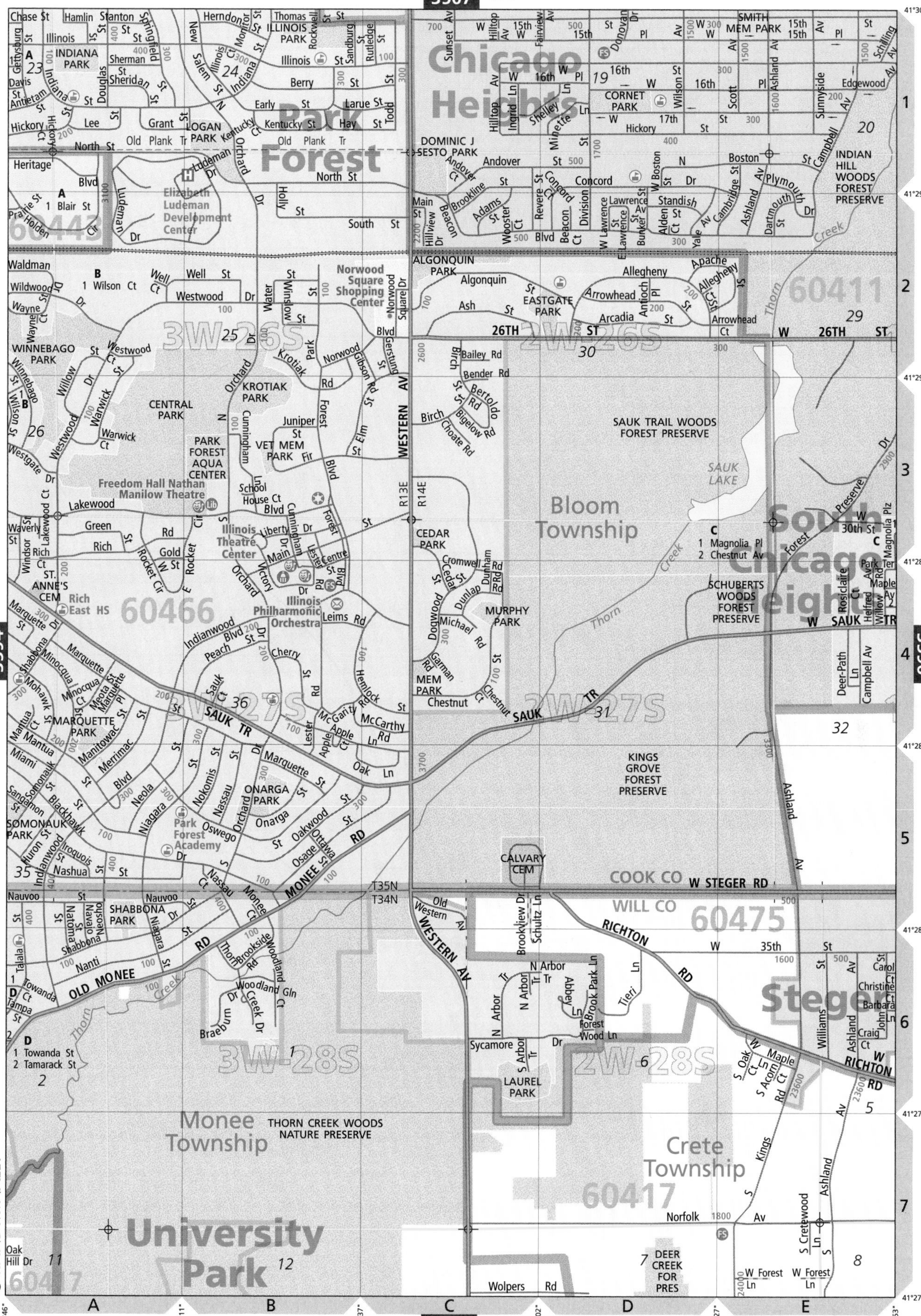

SEE 3594 MAP

SEE 3596 MAP

SEE 3684 MAP

1:24,000
1 in. = 2000 ft.
0 0.25 0.5
miles

SEE 3508 MAP

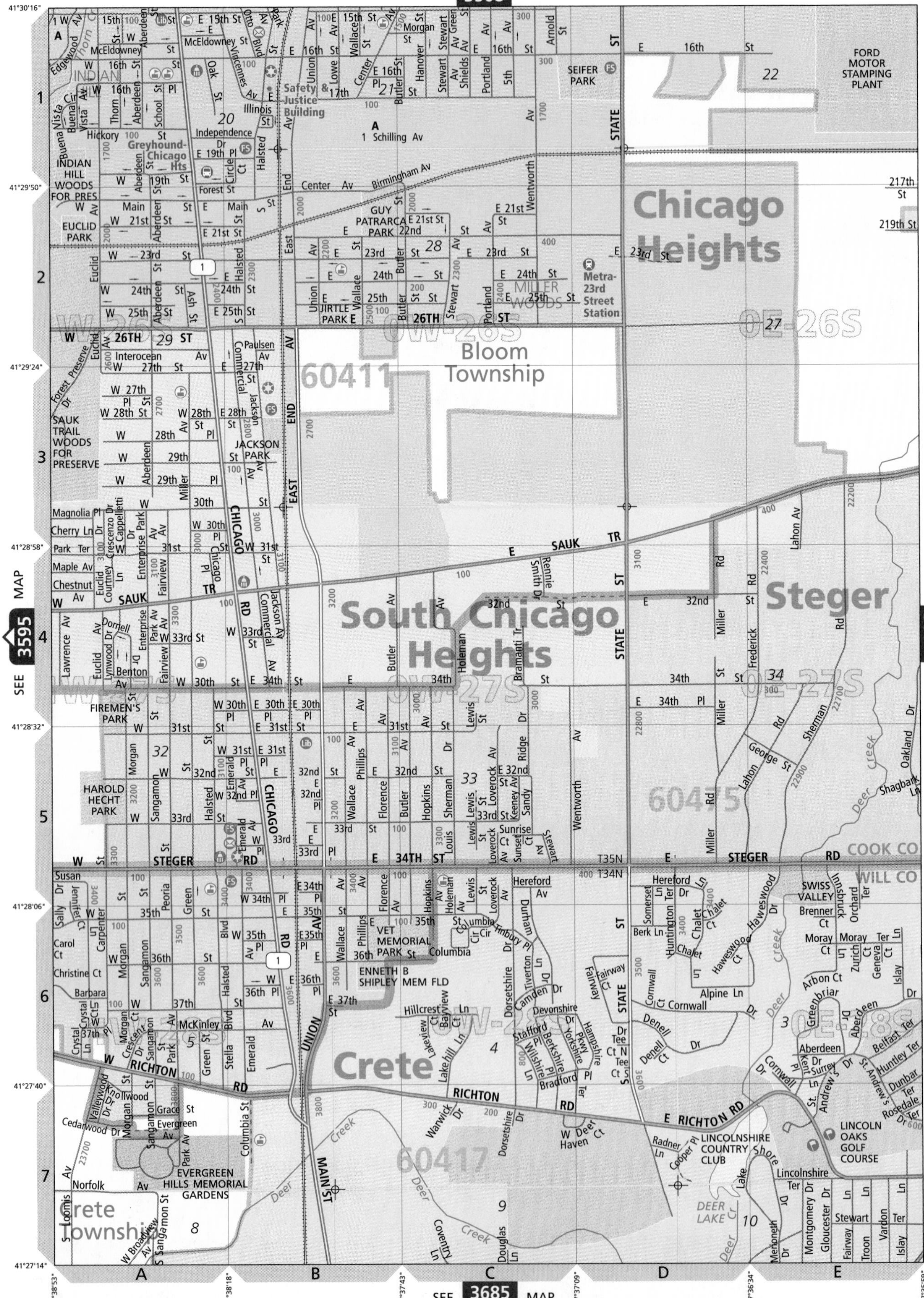

SEE 3595 MAP

SEE 3597 MAP

Chicago Heights

South Chicago Heights

Steger

Crete

Crete Township

Bloom Township

60411

60475

60417

0W-26S 0E-26S 0W-27S 0E-27S 0W-28S 0E-28S

COOK CO

WILL CO

T35N T34N

FORD MOTOR STAMPING PLANT

SEIFER PARK

Safety & Justice Building

Greyhound-Chicago Hts

INDIAN HILL WOODS FOR PRES

EUCLID PARK

GUY PATRARCA PARK

JIRTLE PARK

MILLER WOODS

Metra-23rd Street Station

JACKSON PARK

SAUK TRAIL WOODS FOR PRESERVE

FIREMEN'S PARK

HAROLD HECHT PARK

VET MEMORIAL PARK

ENNETH B SHIPLEY MEM FLD

SWISS VALLEY

EVERGREEN HILLS MEMORIAL GARDENS

LINCOLNSHIRE COUNTRY CLUB

LINCOLN OAKS GOLF COURSE

DEER LAKE

Deer Creek

E 16th St, W 26TH ST, E 26TH ST, E SAUK TR, W SAUK TR, W STEGER RD, E STEGER RD, E 34TH ST, W RICHTON RD, E RICHTON RD, CHICAGO RD, EAST END AV, STATE ST, UNION AV, MAIN ST, Birmingham Av, Center Av, Schilling Av

41°30'16" 41°29'50" 41°29'24" 41°28'58" 41°28'32" 41°28'06" 41°27'40" 41°27'14"

87°38'53" 87°38'18" 87°37'43" 87°37'09" 87°36'34" 87°35'59"

1 2 3 4 5 6 7

A B C D E

SEE 3685 MAP

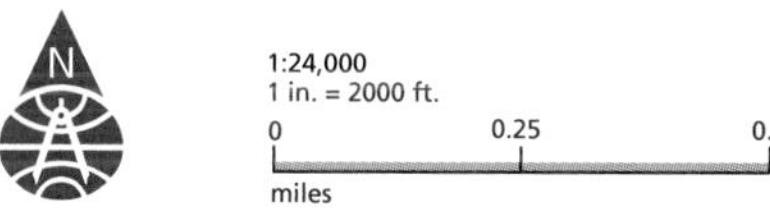

SEE 3509 MAP

SEE 3596 MAP

SEE 3598 MAP

Ford Heights

Sauk Village

Steger

Crete

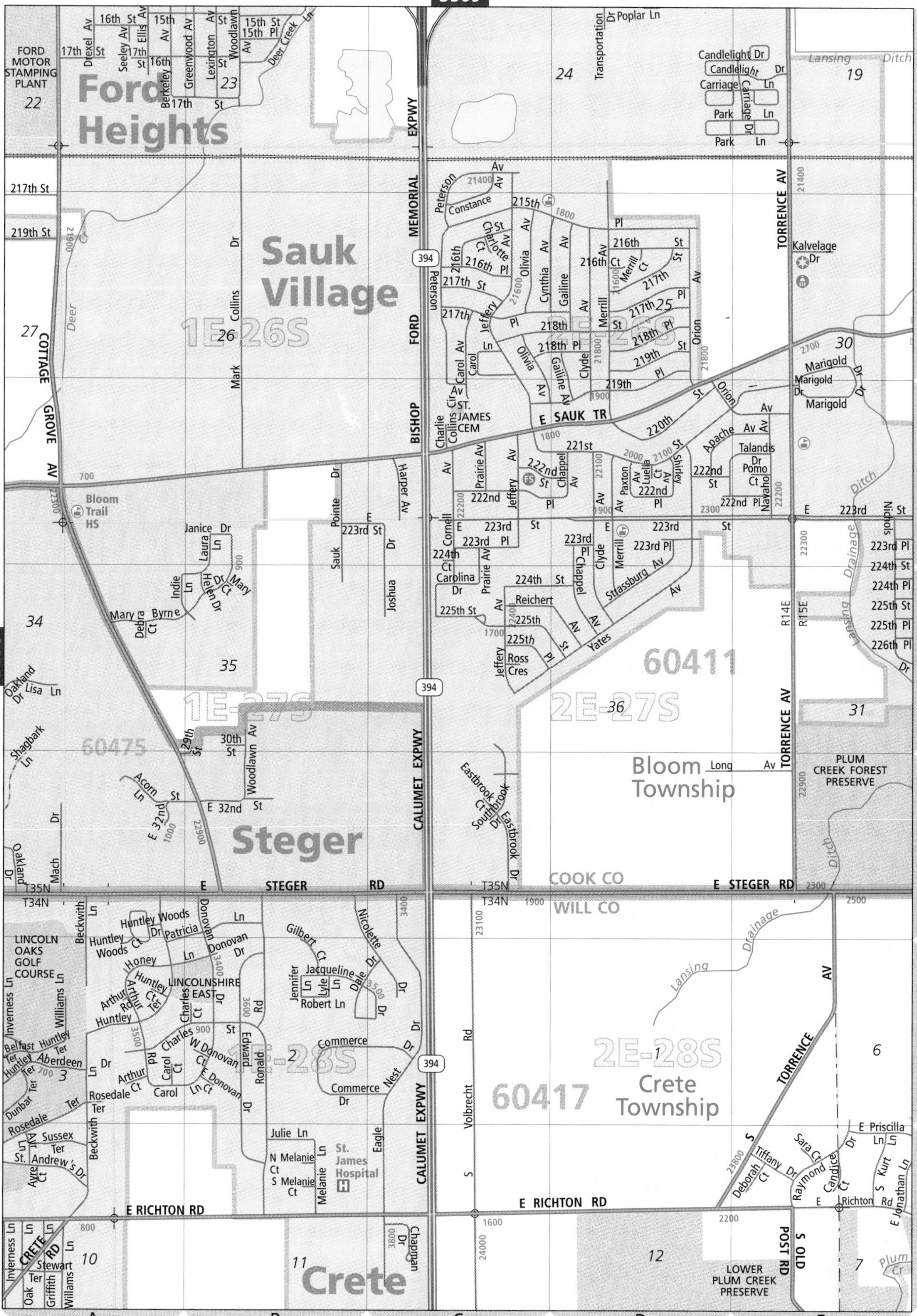

Bloom Township

Crete Township

SEE 3686 MAP

1:24,000
1 in. = 2000 ft.
0 0.25 0.5
miles

SEE 3510 MAP

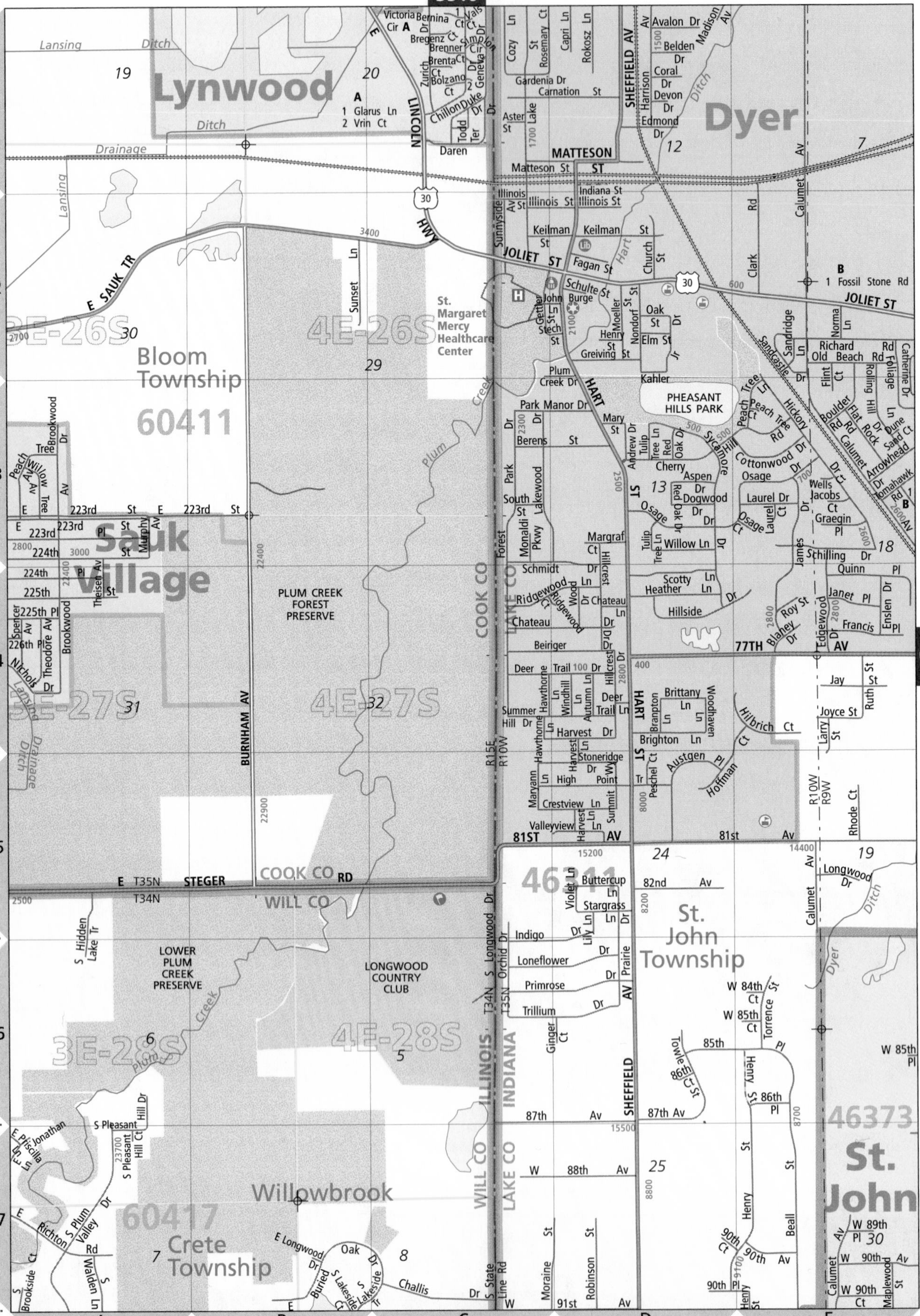

SEE 3597 MAP

SEE B MAP

SEE 3687 MAP

1:24,000
1 in. = 2000 ft.
0 0.25 0.5
miles

SEE 3583 MAP

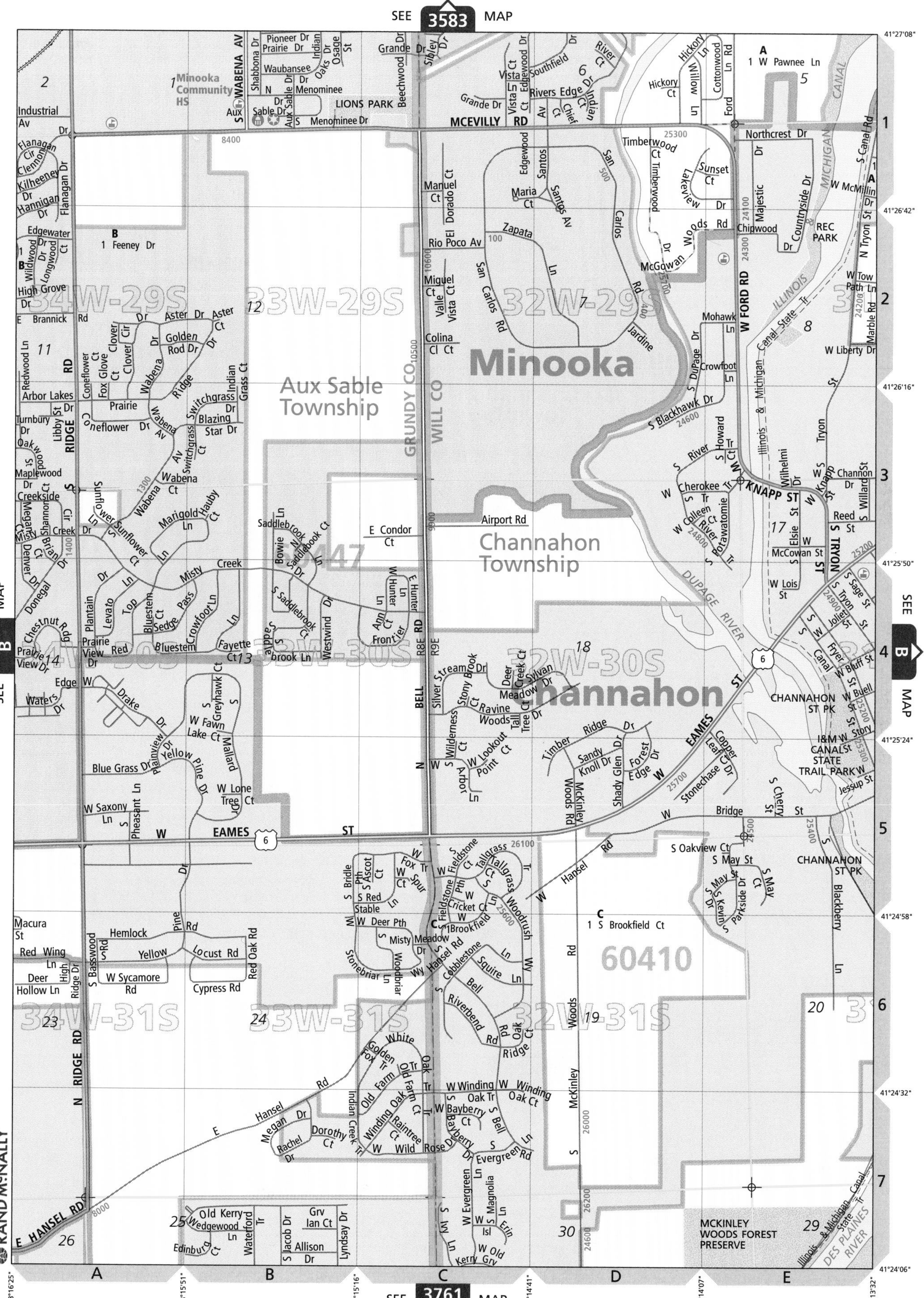

SEE B MAP

SEE B MAP

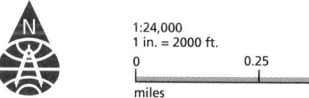

SEE 3761 MAP

1:24,000
1 in. = 2000 ft.
0 0.25 0.5
miles

SEE 3585 MAP

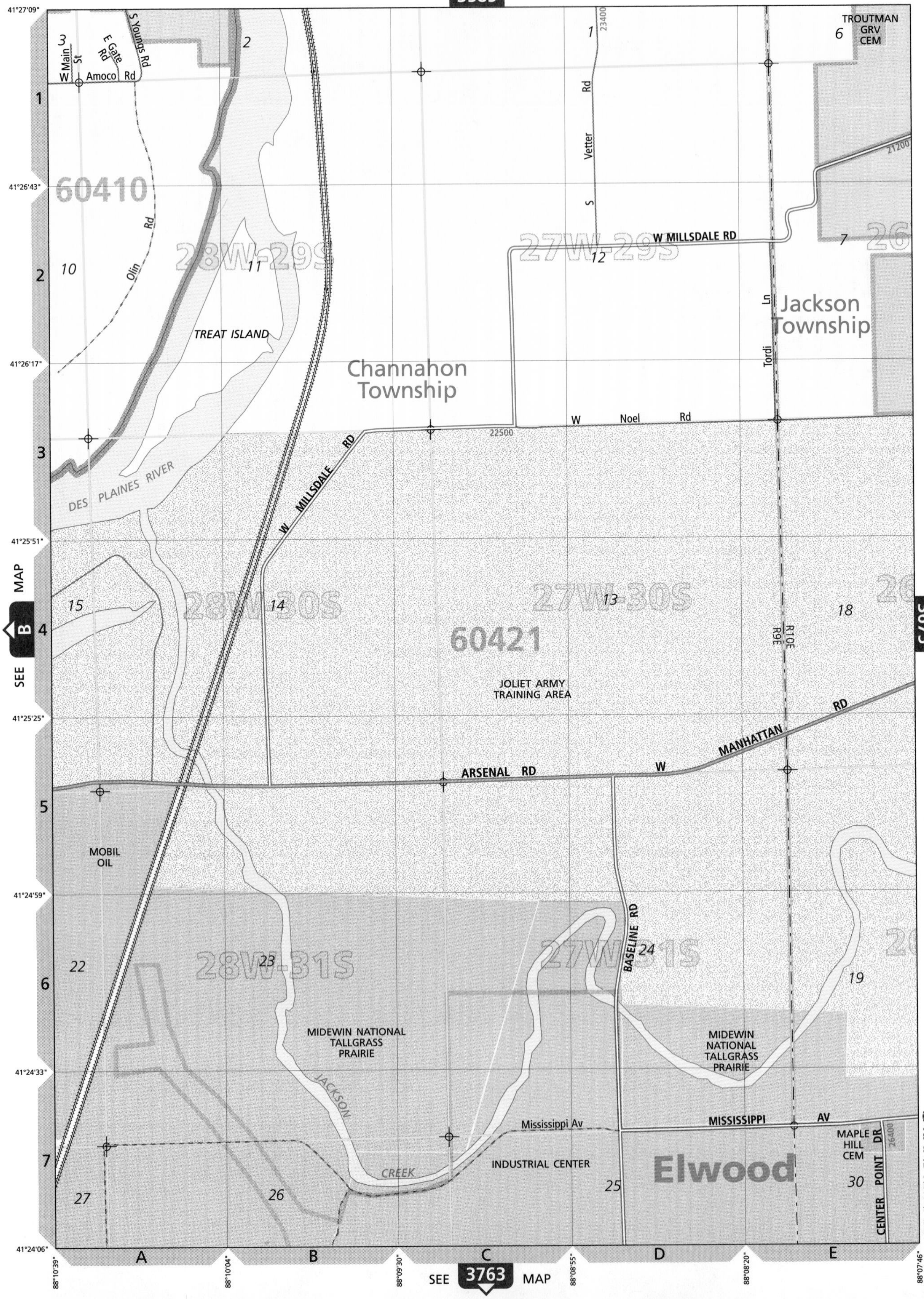

SEE B MAP

SEE 3675 MAP

SEE 3763 MAP

1:24,000
1 in. = 2000 ft.
0 0.25 0.5
miles

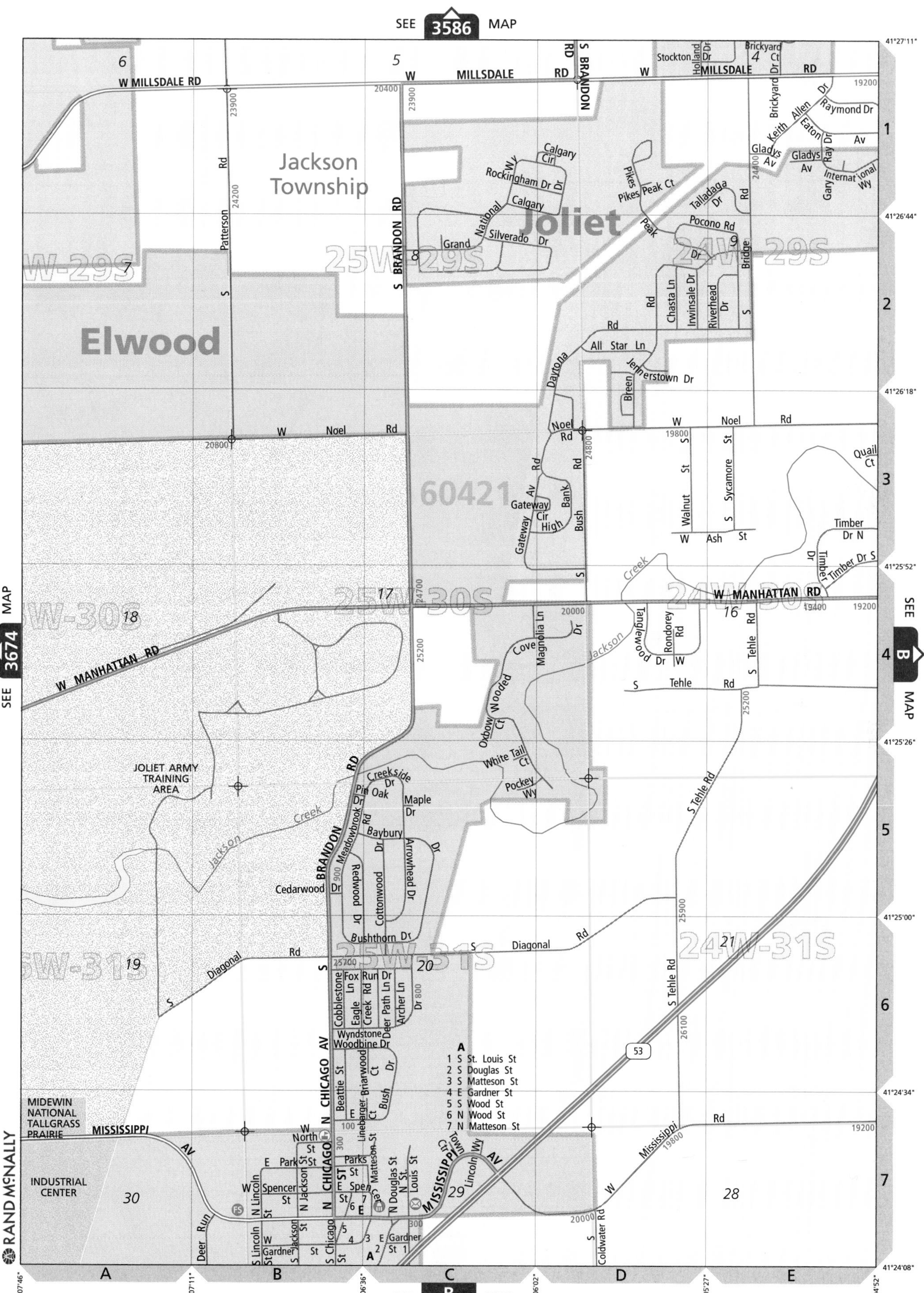

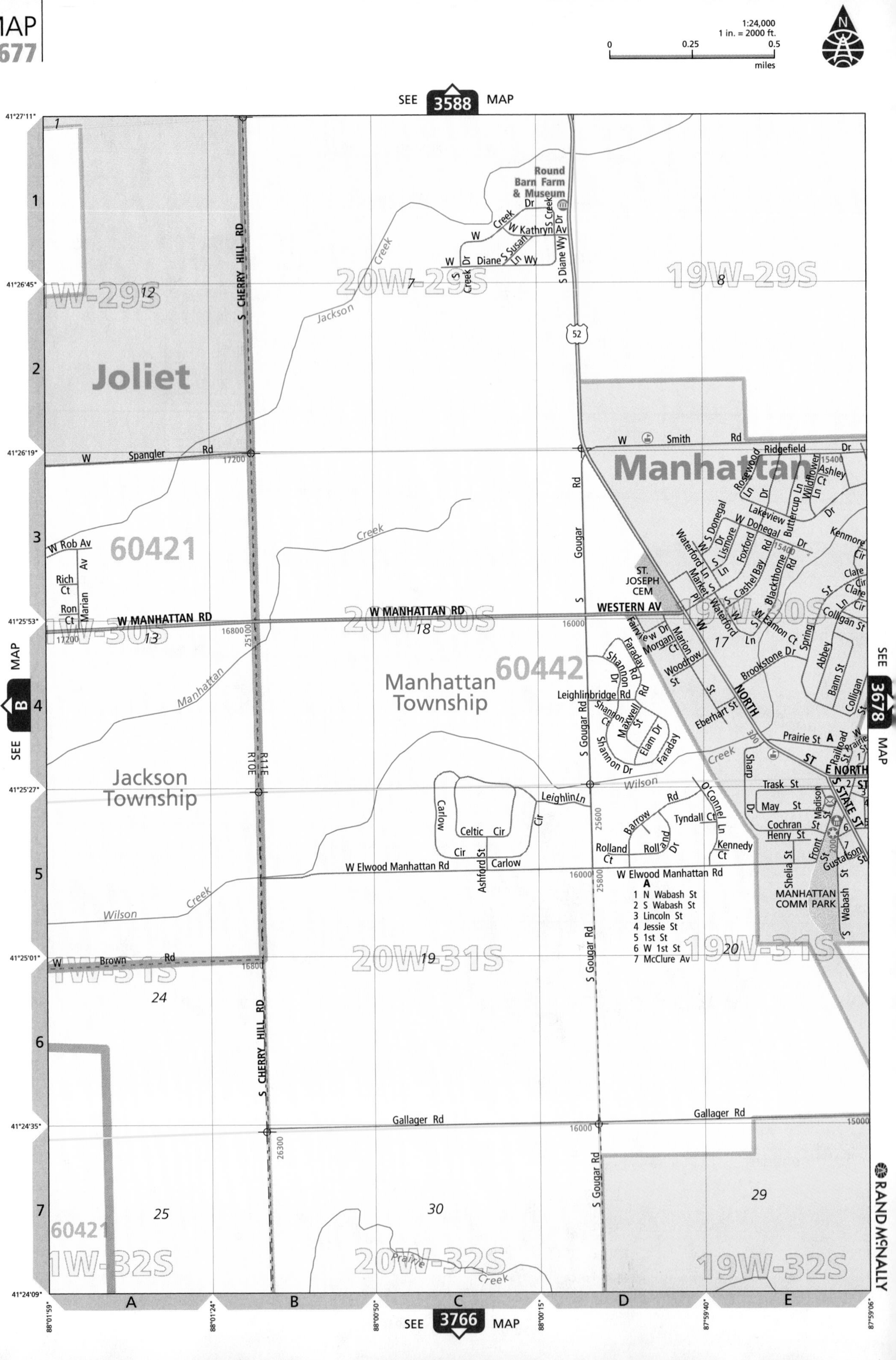

1:24,000
1 in. = 2000 ft.
0 0.25 0.5
miles

SEE 3588 MAP

Joliet

Manhattan

Round Barn Farm & Museum

Jackson Township

Manhattan Township

60421

60442

20W-29S
19W-29S
20W-30S
19W-30S
20W-31S
19W-31S
20W-32S
19W-32S

S CHERRY HILL RD
W Spangler Rd
W MANHATTAN RD
W Brown Rd
Gallager Rd
W Elwood Manhattan Rd
S Gougar Rd
WESTERN AV
W Smith Rd
S Diane Wy
W Kathryn Av
W Creek Dr
W Diane Dr
S Susan Ln
W Rob Av
Rich Ct
Ron Ct
Marian Av
Jackson Creek
Manhattan Creek
Wilson Creek
Prairie Creek
ST. JOSEPH CEM
MANHATTAN COMM PARK
Ridgefield Dr
Rosewood Ln
Lakeview Dr
W Donegal Dr
Kenmore Cir
Clare Cir
Colligan Ln
Abbey Ln
Bann St
Brookstone Dr
W Eamon Ct
Shannon Dr
Faraday Rd
Leighlinbridge Rd
Maxwell St
Elam Dr
Leighlin Ln
Carlow Cir
Celtic Cir
Ashford St
Barrow Ct
Rolland Ct
Rolland Dr
Tyndall Ct
O'Connel Ln
Kennedy Ct
Woodrow St
Marion Ct
Morgan Ct
Eberhart St
NORTH ST
S STATE ST
Prairie St
Trask St
May St
Cochran St
Henry St
Shelia St
Wabash St
Gustafson St
R11E R10E

A
1 N Wabash St
2 S Wabash St
3 Lincoln St
4 Jessie St
5 1st St
6 W 1st St
7 McClure Av

A B C D E
1 2 3 4 5 6 7

SEE B MAP

SEE 3678 MAP

SEE 3766 MAP

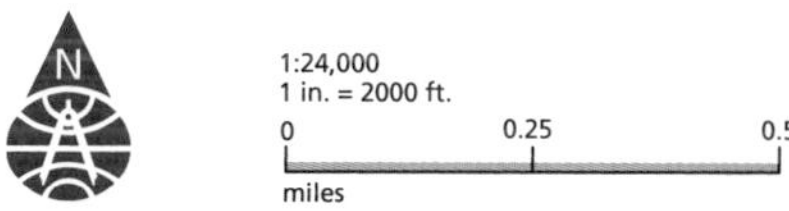

1:24,000
1 in. = 2000 ft.
0 0.25 0.5
miles

SEE 3589 MAP
SEE 3677 MAP
SEE B MAP
SEE 3767 MAP
Manhattan
Manhattan Township
60442
18W-29S
17W-29S
18W-30S
17W-30S
18W-31S
17W-31S
18W-32S
17W-32S
W Smith Rd
W Carriage Ln
S Kankakee St
S CEDAR RD
W MANHATTAN MONEE RD
NORTH ST
Gallager Rd
W Bruns Rd
W Haley Rd
Redstone Dr
Wilson Creek
Prairie Creek
S STATE ST
Eastern Av
Fern Av
Lakeview Dr
Abbey Ln
Kenmore Cir
Clare Cir
Colligan St
Thelma St
Jessie St
Prairie St
N Park St
N Eastern Av
Whitson St
1st St
2nd St
3rd St
Park St
Eastern St
Lee St
Kay St
Jan St
Julianne Ct
Julianne Dr
Brett Ct
Terri Ct
Briar Ct
Andrea Dr
Bryan Dr
Francis Ct
Calla Dr
52
A B C D E
1 2 3 4 5 6 7
41°27'12"
41°26'46"
41°26'20"
41°25'54"
41°25'28"
41°25'02"
41°24'36"
41°24'10"
87°59'06"
87°58'31"
87°57'56"
87°57'22"
87°56'47"
87°56'12"
RAND McNALLY

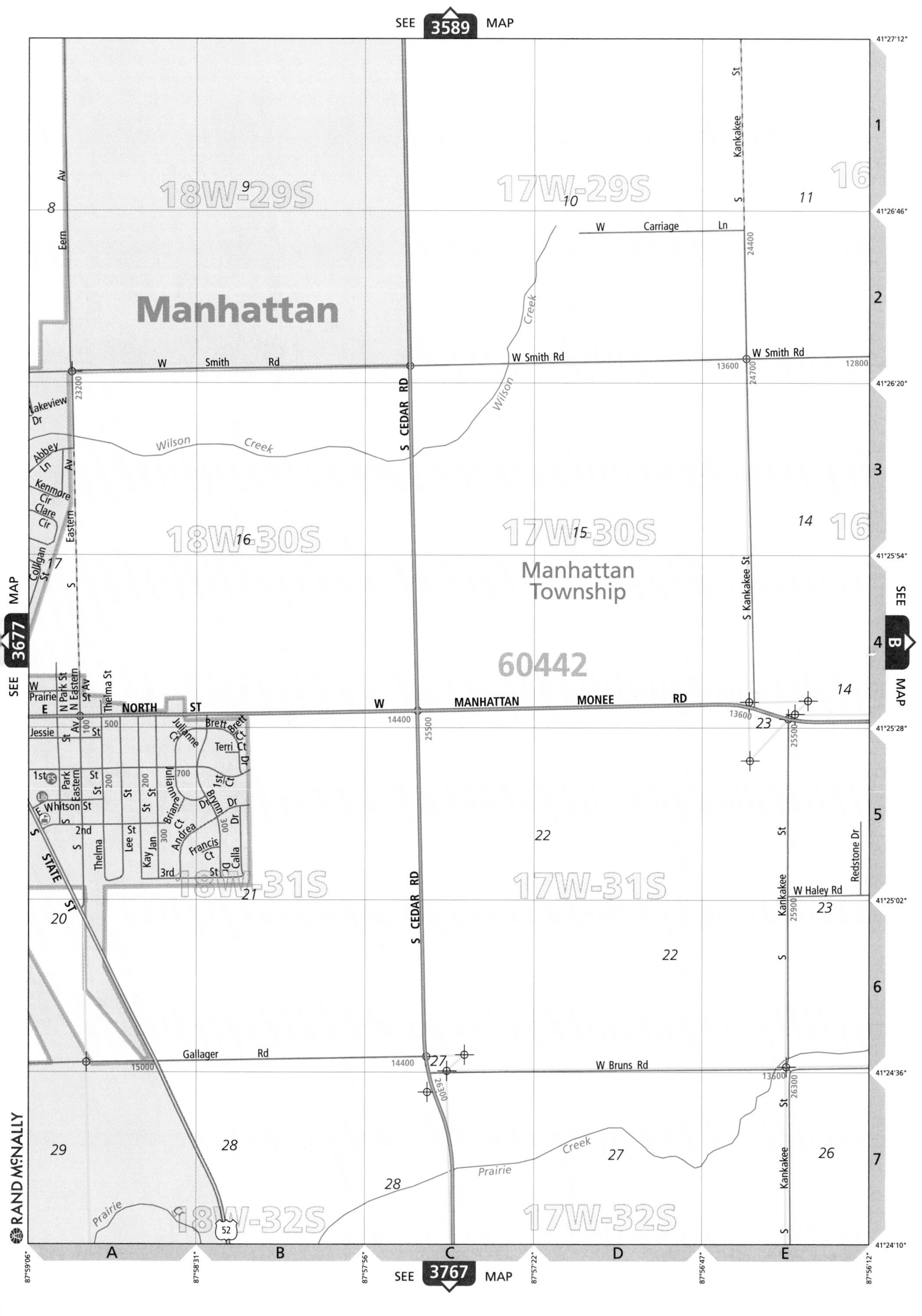

1:24,000
1 in. = 2000 ft.
0 0.25 0.5
miles

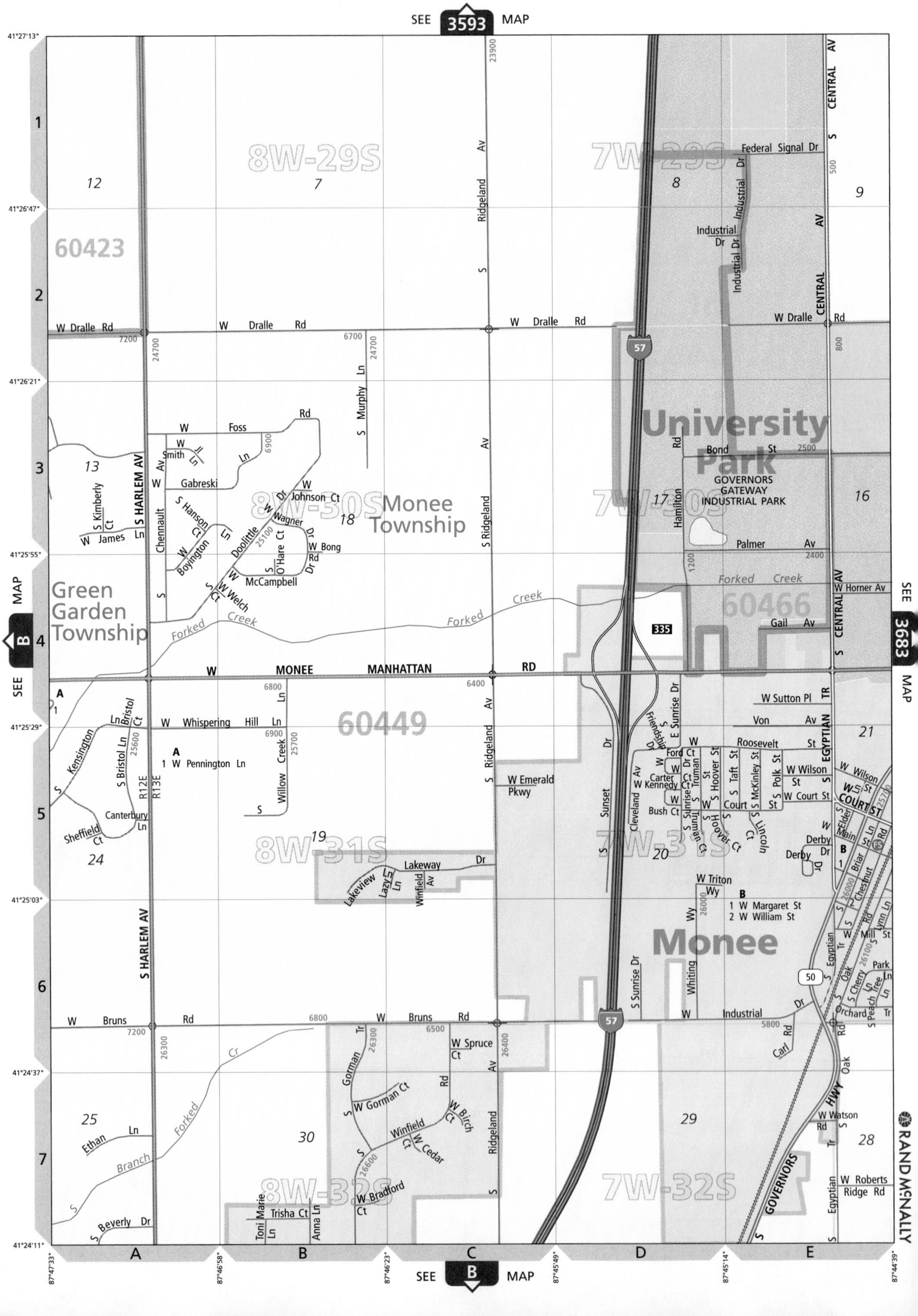

SEE 3593 MAP

SEE B MAP
SEE 3683 MAP
SEE B MAP

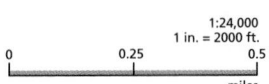

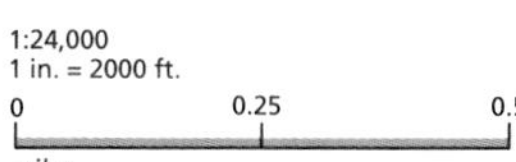

SEE 3594 MAP

SEE MAP 3682

SEE 3684 MAP

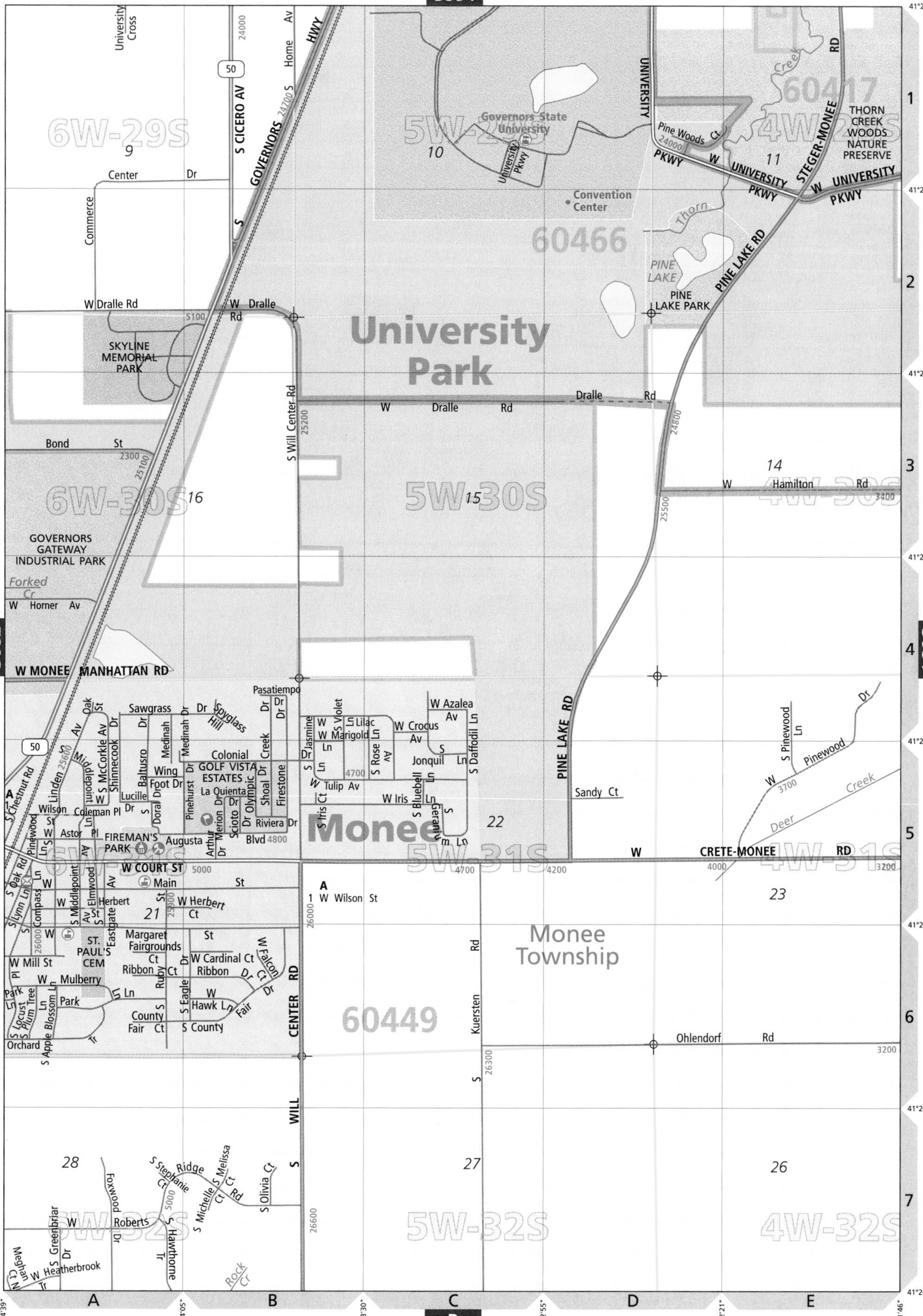

University Park

Monee

Monee Township

Governors State University

Convention Center

SKYLINE MEMORIAL PARK

GOVERNORS GATEWAY INDUSTRIAL PARK

THORN CREEK WOODS NATURE PRESERVE

PINE LAKE

PINE LAKE PARK

GOLF VISTA ESTATES

FIREMAN'S PARK

ST. PAUL'S CEM

60417
60466
60449

6W-29S
5W-29S
4W-29S
6W-30S
5W-30S
4W-30S
6W-31S
5W-31S
4W-31S
6W-32S
5W-32S
4W-32S

9
10
11
14
15
16
21
22
23
26
27
28

S GOVERNORS HWY
S CICERO AV
50
UNIVERSITY PKWY
W UNIVERSITY PKWY
STEGER-MONEE RD
PINE LAKE RD
W Dralle Rd
W Dralle Rd
S Will Center Rd
S WILL CENTER RD
W Hamilton Rd
W MONEE MANHATTAN RD
W CRETE-MONEE RD
W COURT ST
S Kuersten Rd
Ohlendorf Rd
Sandy Ct
W Pinewood Dr
S Pinewood Ln
Deer Creek
Thorn Creek
Forked Cr
Rock Cr
Pine Woods Ct
University Cross
Center Dr
Commerce
S Home Av
Bond St
W Horner Av
W Wilson St
W Roberts
W Heatherbrook Tr
S Greenbriar Dr
Foxwood Dr
S Hawthorne Tr
S Stephanie Ridge Ct
S Melissa Ct Rd
S Michelle Ct
S Olivia Ct
Meghan Ct

A
B
C
D
E
1
2
3
4
5
6
7

41°27'14"
41°26'47"
41°26'21"
41°25'55"
41°25'29"
41°25'03"
41°24'37"
41°24'11"
87°44'39"
87°44'05"
87°43'30"
87°42'55"
87°42'21"
87°41'46"

SEE B MAP

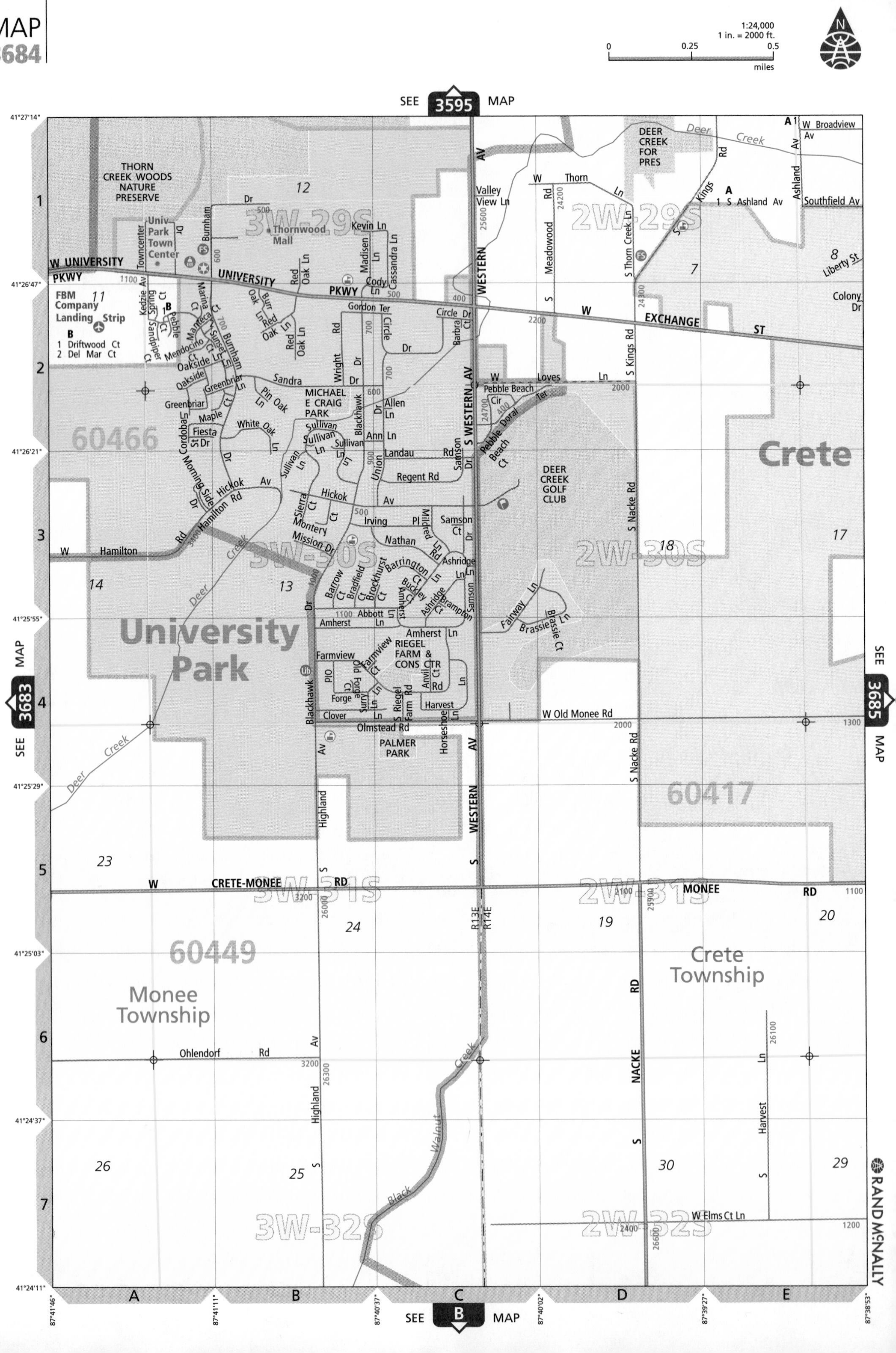

1:24,000
1 in. = 2000 ft.
0 0.25 0.5
miles

SEE 3595 MAP

SEE 3683 MAP

SEE 3685 MAP

SEE B MAP

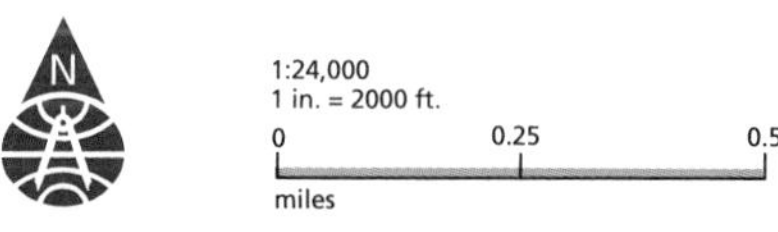

SEE 3596 MAP

1W-29S
0W-29S
0E-29S
8
9
10
W EXCHANGE ST
E EXCHANGE ST
MAIN ST
CRETE RD
Crete-Monee HS
CRETE PARK
ADAMS CEM
CRETE CEM
HERITAGE PARK
Lincoln Dr
Grant Blvd
Greenwood Ter
Oakwood Dr
Milburn
Joe Orr Rd
Wingate
Hubbard
Herman
Brackman Av
Crete Blvd
Naoma
Orchard Dr
W Farm St

1W-30S
0W-30S
0E-30S
17
16
15
W BURVILLE RD
E BURVILLE RD
TRINITY CEM
ZION CEM
60417
Crete
Hartmann Dr
Munz Rd
E Munz Rd
S STATE ST
W Old Monee Rd
S Sangamon St
7th St

1W-31S
0W-31S
0E-31S
20
21
22
MONEE RD
W MONEE RD
S DIXIE HWY
Round House Rd
W Windsor Av
W Kent Av
Crete Township

Balmoral Park Race Track
CALUMET EXPWY
394
E BEMES RD
Old Mud Rd
29
28
27
1W-32S
0W-32S
0E-32S
W Elms Ct Ln
W ELMS CT LN
BALMORAL WOODS COUNTRY CLUB
GOODENOW GROVE
60401
Plum Creek
W Auburn Ln
Arlington Ln
S Melrose Ln
S Balmoral Woods Dr

41°27'14"
41°26'47"
41°26'21"
41°25'55"
41°25'29"
41°25'03"
41°24'37"
41°24'11"
87°38'53"
87°38'18"
87°37'43"
87°37'09"
87°36'34"
87°35'59"

1 2 3 4 5 6 7
A B C D E

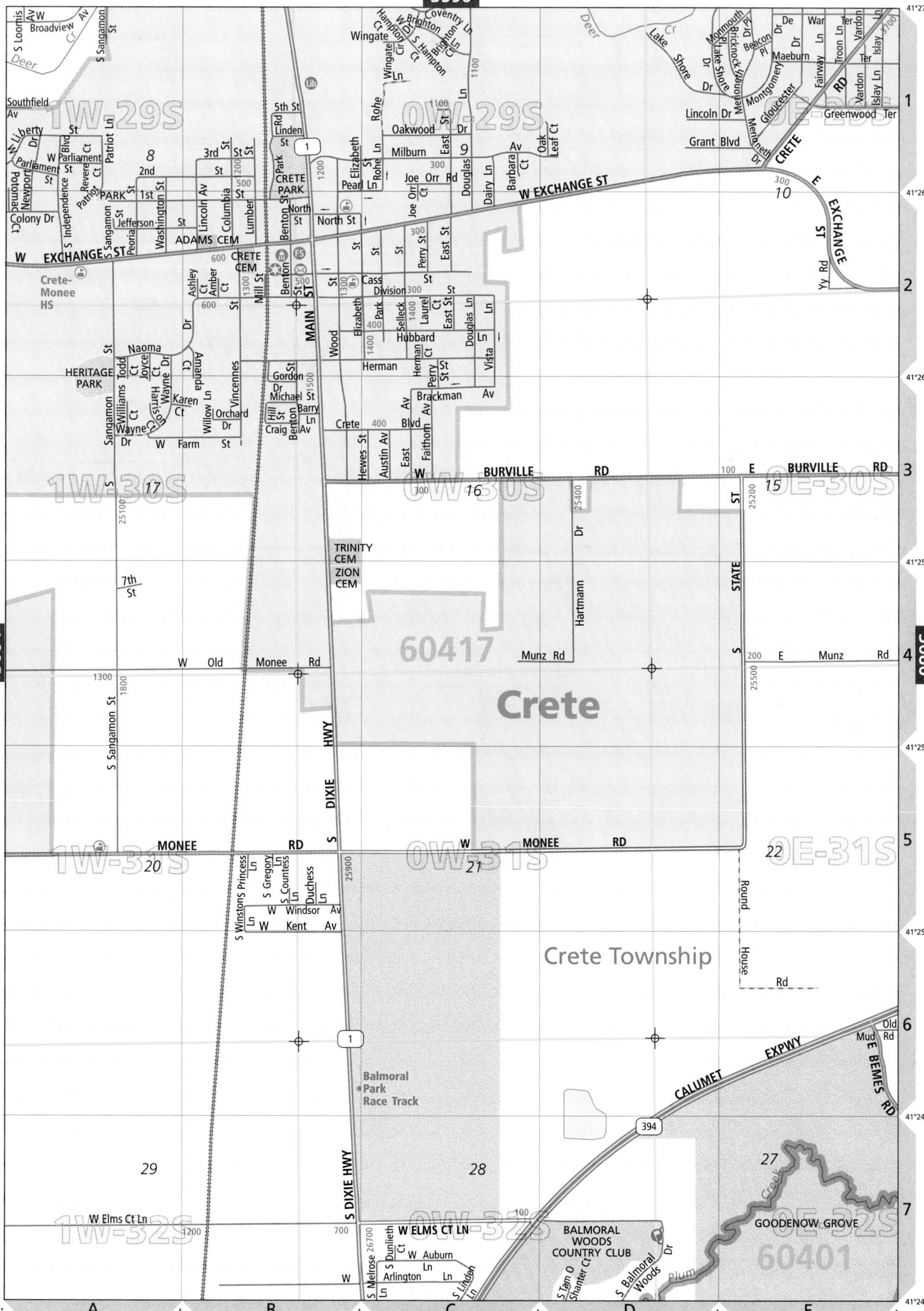

SEE 3684 MAP
SEE 3686 MAP
SEE 3774 MAP

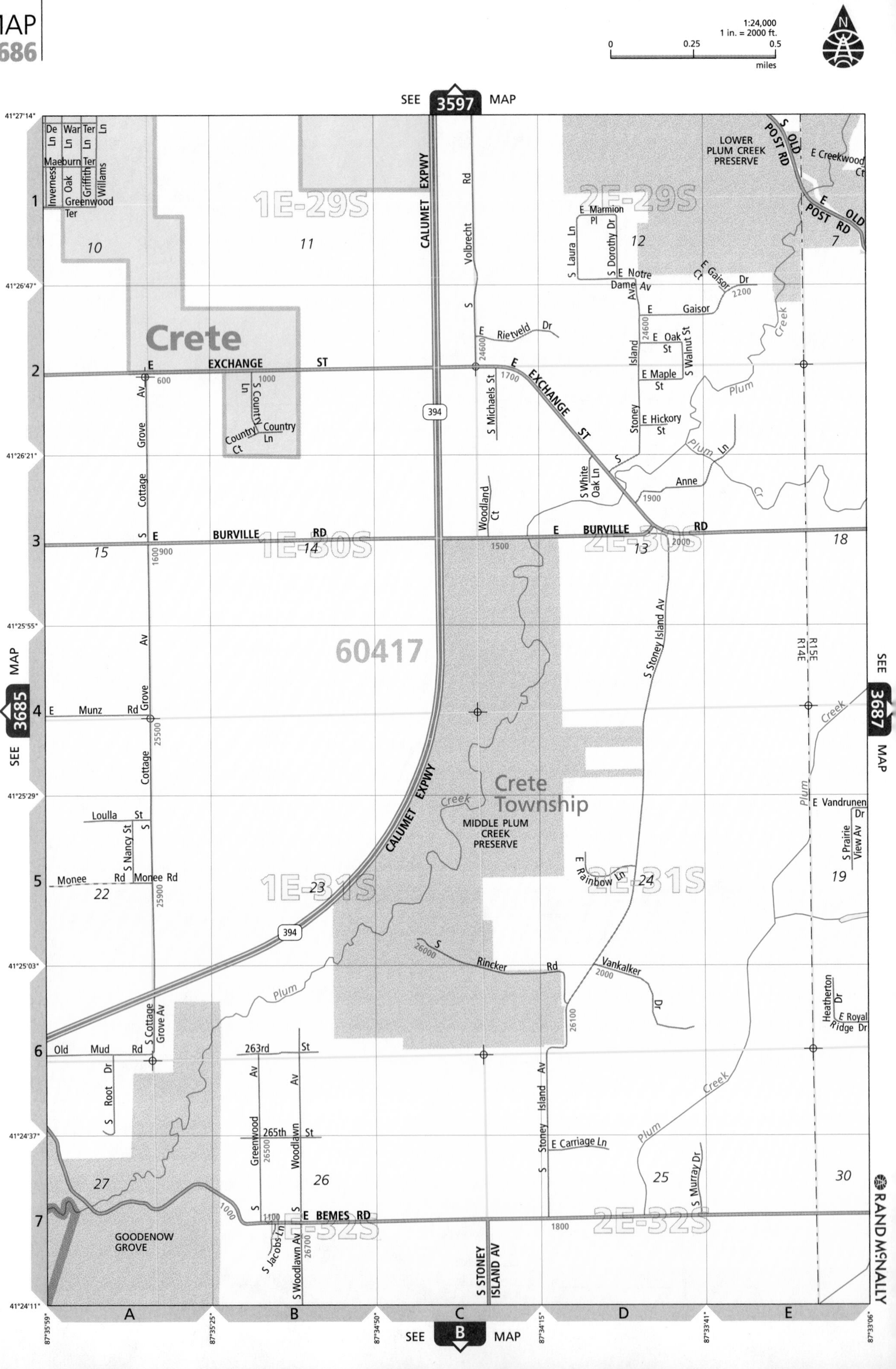

1:24,000
1 in. = 2000 ft.
0 0.25 0.5
miles

SEE 3597 MAP

SEE 3685 MAP
SEE 3687 MAP
SEE B MAP

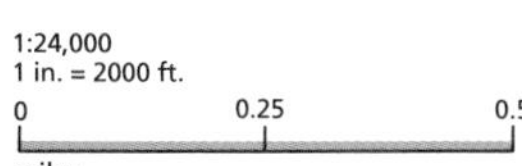

SEE 3598 MAP

SEE 3686 MAP

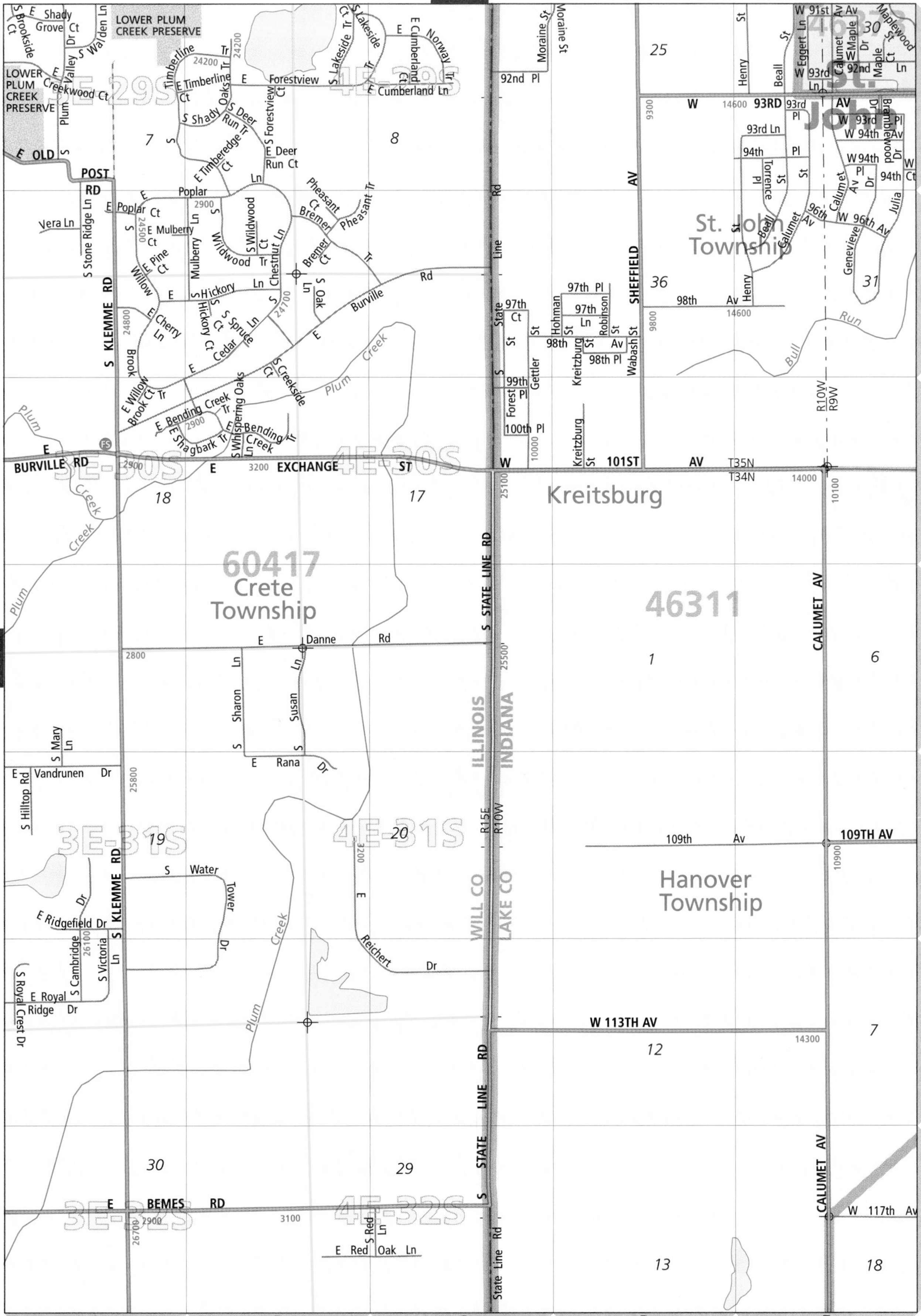

SEE B MAP

SEE B MAP

1:24,000
1 in. = 2000 ft.
0 0.25 0.5
miles

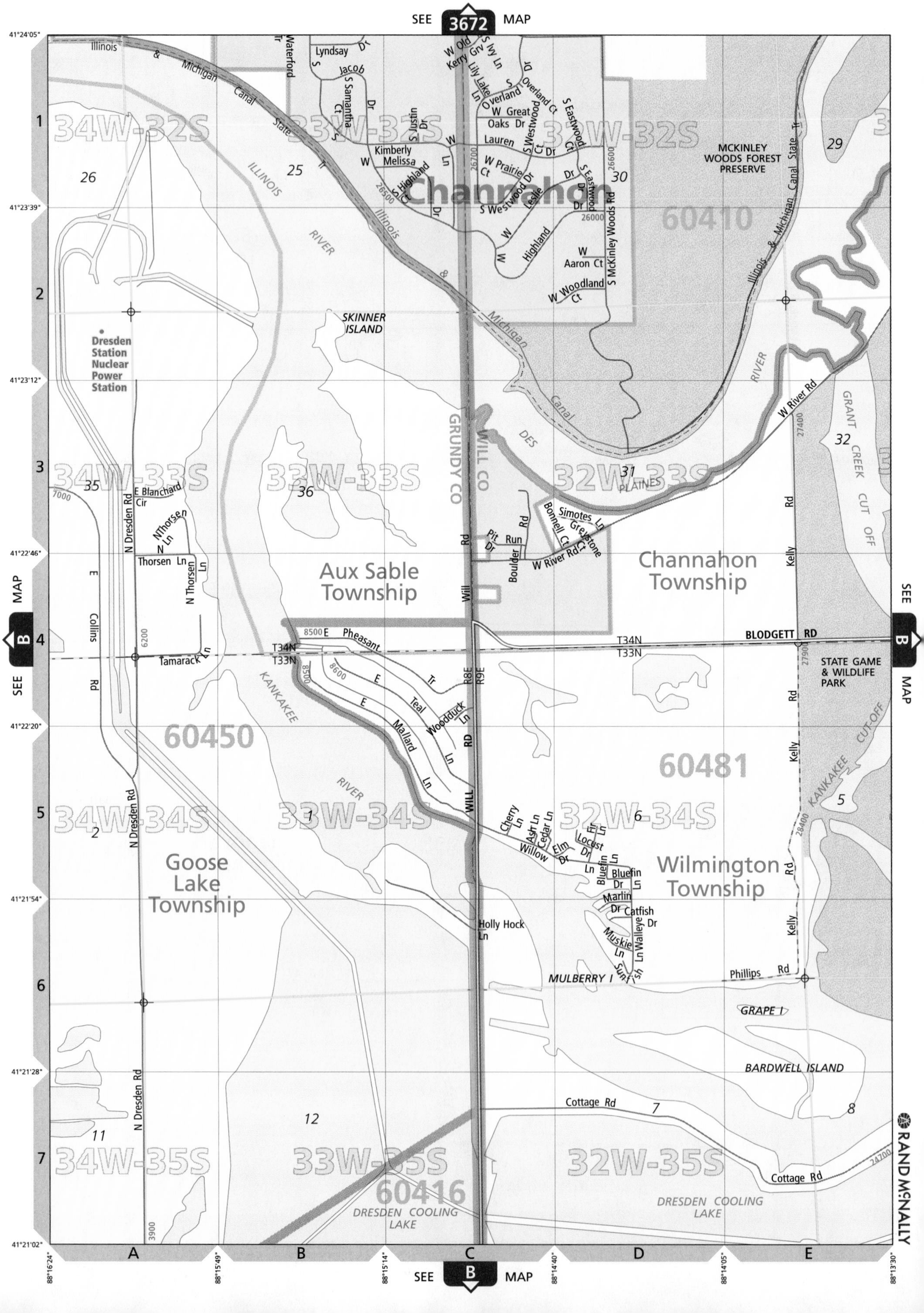

SEE 3672 MAP

Channahon
Aux Sable Township
Channahon Township
Goose Lake Township
Wilmington Township
MCKINLEY WOODS FOREST PRESERVE
STATE GAME & WILDLIFE PARK
Dresden Station Nuclear Power Station
SKINNER ISLAND
MULBERRY I
GRAPE I
BARDWELL ISLAND
DRESDEN COOLING LAKE
GRUNDY CO
WILL CO
60410
60450
60481
60416
Illinois & Michigan Canal State Tr
ILLINOIS RIVER
DES PLAINES RIVER
KANKAKEE RIVER
GRANT CREEK CUT OFF
KANKAKEE CUT-OFF
Blodgett Rd
T34N
T33N
R8E
R9E

SEE B MAP

1:24,000
1 in. = 2000 ft.
0 0.25 0.5
miles

SEE 3674 MAP

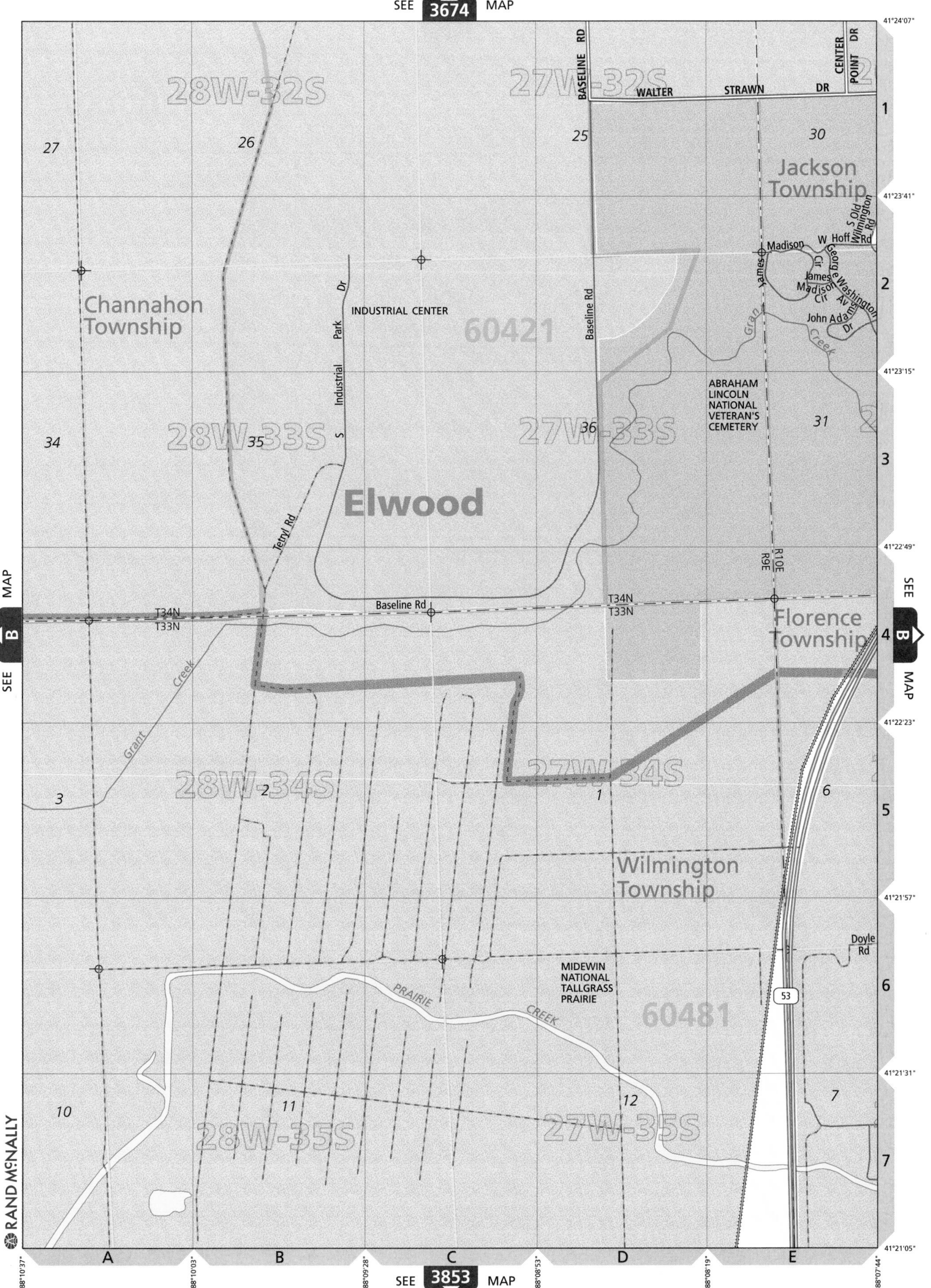

SEE B MAP

SEE B MAP

SEE 3853 MAP

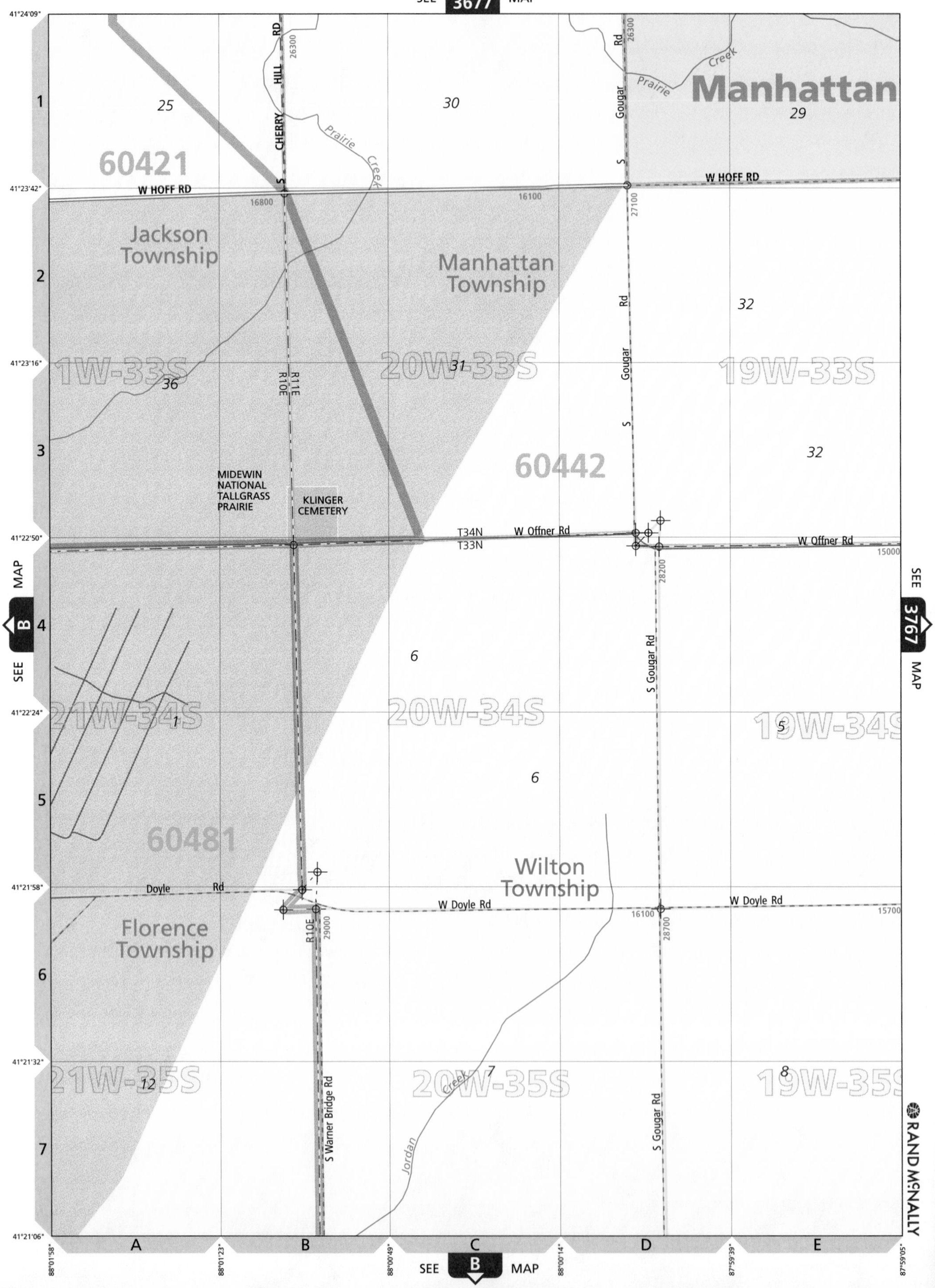

1:24,000
1 in. = 2000 ft.
0 0.25 0.5
miles

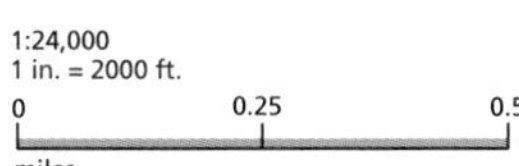

SEE 3678 MAP

Manhattan
Prairie Cr
Prairie Creek
29
28
27
26
W HOFF RD
52
W PAULING RD
W PAULING RD
S CEDAR RD
S Kankakee St
26300
13600
27100
Manhattan Township
18W-33S
33
17W-33S
34
32
35
S Walsh Rd
Johnson Landing Strip
W Offner Rd
T34N
T33N
W Offner Rd
Elevator Rd
T34N
T33N
Elevator Rd
W Offner Rd
15000
14400
27900
13700
13600
60442
S Wallingford Rd
S Walsh Rd
28200
18W-34S
4
17W-34S
3
5
2
W Draves Rd
14000
W Domagalla St
LAUGHTON PRESERVE
Forked Creek
Wilton Township
W Doyle Rd
W Doyle Rd
15700
14700
28600
West Branch
10
LAUGHTON PRESERVE
18W-35S
9
17W-35S
Forked Creek
8
11
S Walsh Rd
S CEDAR RD
Wallingford Tr
S Quigley Rd
Wilton Center
Joliet Rd
W JOLIET RD

1
2
3
4
5
6
7
A
B
C
D
E

41°24'10"
41°23'43"
41°23'17"
41°22'51"
41°22'25"
41°21'59"
41°21'33"
41°21'07"
87°59'05"
87°58'30"
87°57'55"
87°57'21"
87°56'46"
87°56'12"

SEE 3766 MAP

SEE B MAP

SEE B MAP

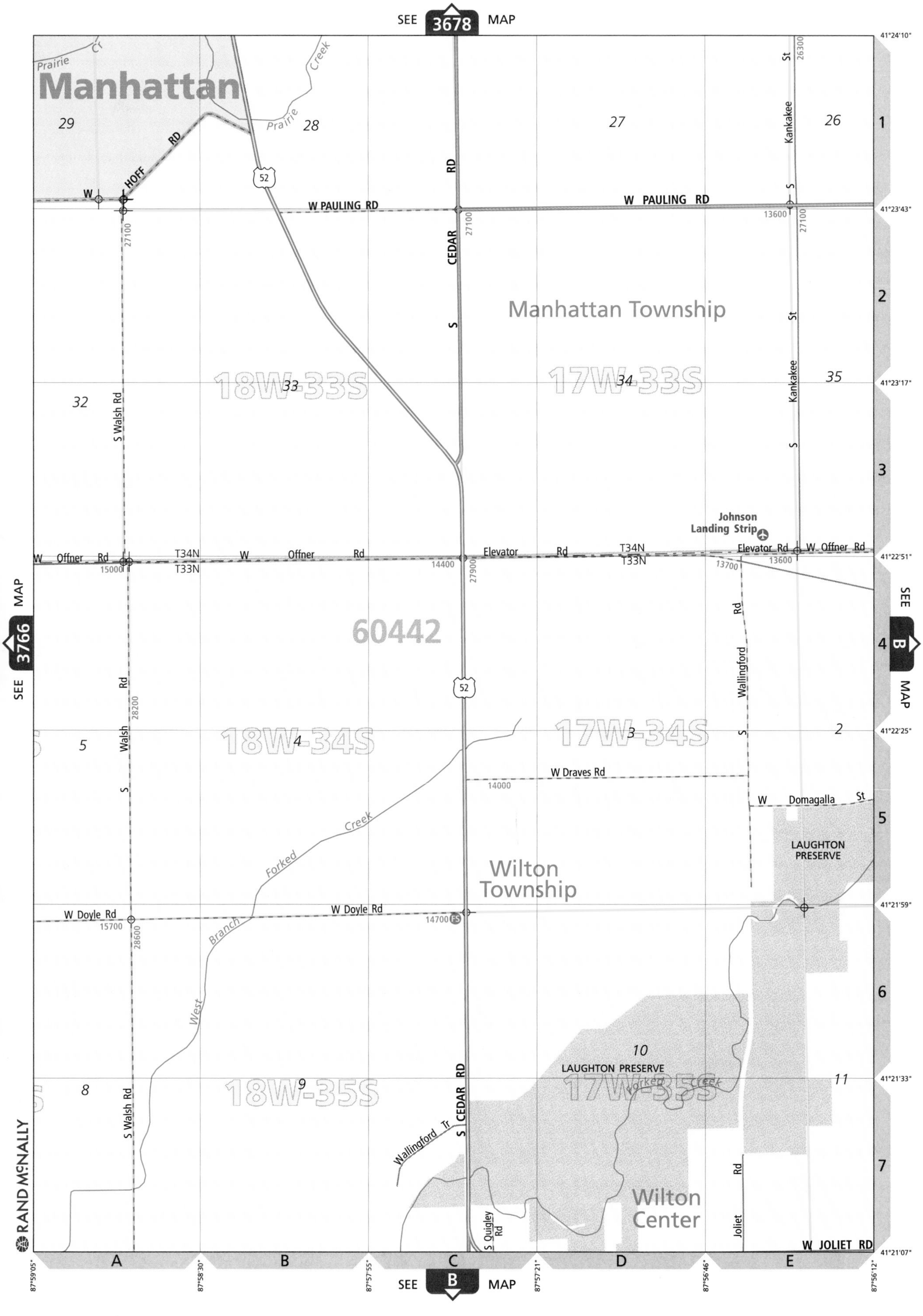

1:24,000
1 in. = 2000 ft.
0 0.25 0.5
miles

SEE 3685 MAP

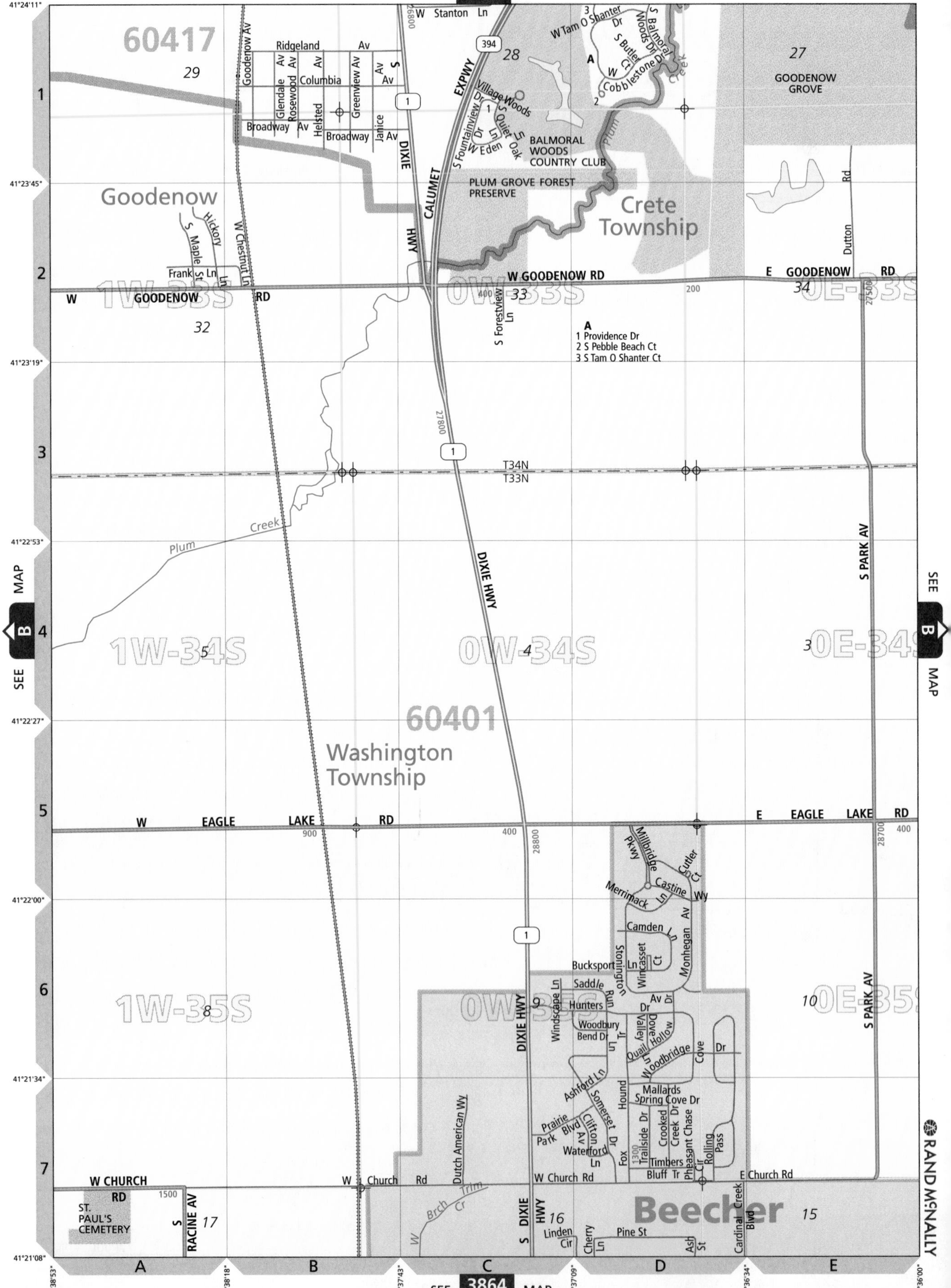

SEE B MAP

SEE B MAP

SEE 3864 MAP

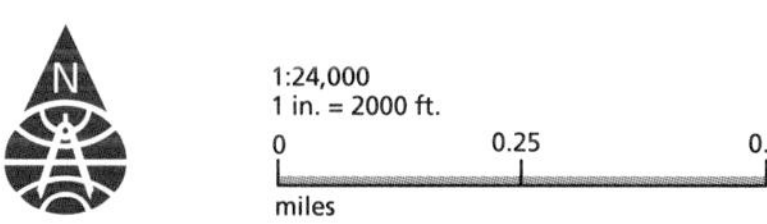

SEE 3763 MAP

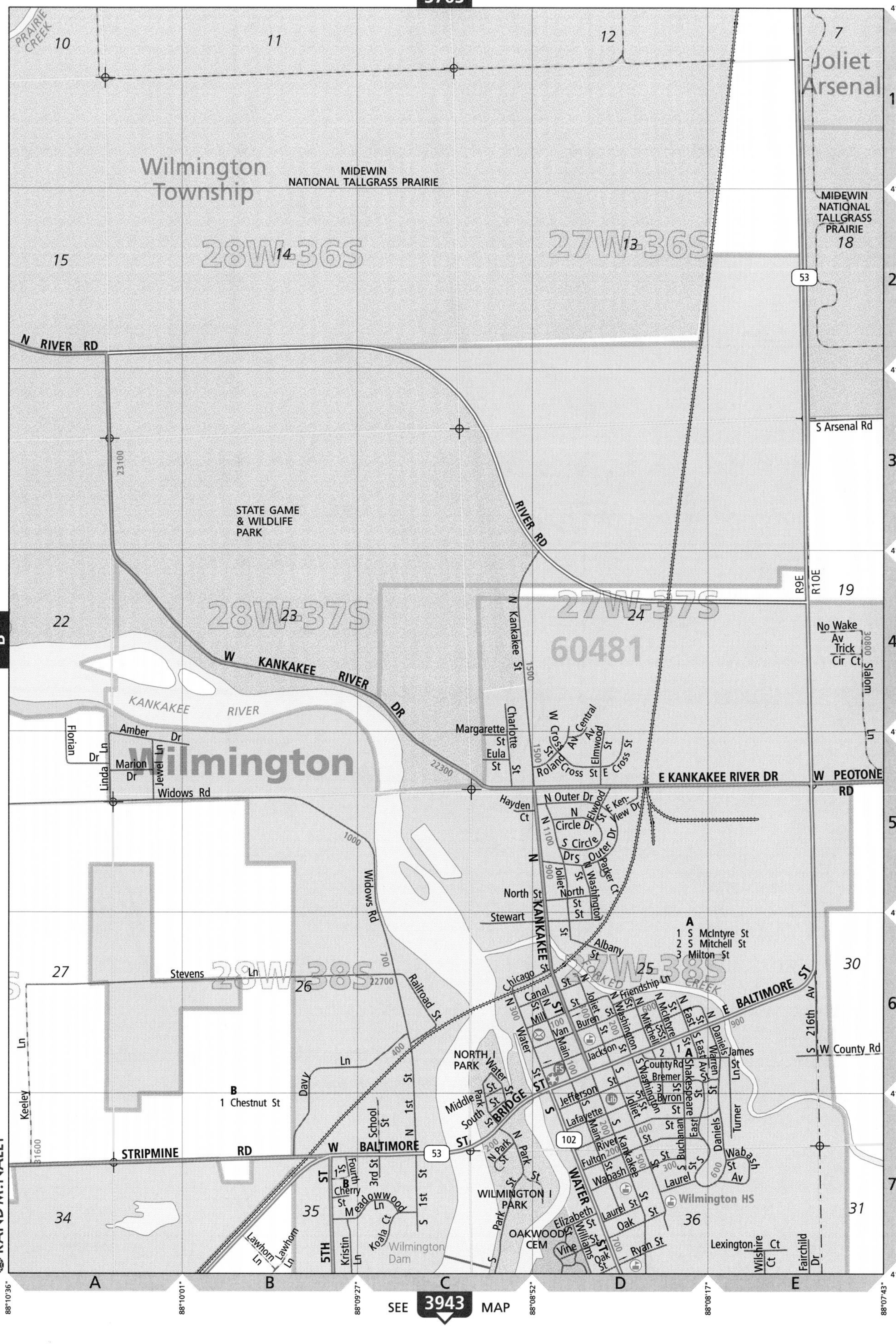

Wilmington Township
MIDEWIN NATIONAL TALLGRASS PRAIRIE
Joliet Arsenal
MIDEWIN NATIONAL TALLGRASS PRAIRIE
28W-36S
27W-36S
N RIVER RD
RIVER RD
S Arsenal Rd
STATE GAME & WILDLIFE PARK
28W-37S
27W-37S
60481
W KANKAKEE RIVER DR
KANKAKEE RIVER
Wilmington
E KANKAKEE RIVER DR
W PEOTONE RD
No Wake Av
Trick Cir Ct
Slalom Ln
Widows Rd
Widows Rd
N KANKAKEE ST
28W-38S
27W-38S
Stevens Ln
Railroad St
E BALTIMORE ST
W County Rd
216th Av
A
1 S McIntyre St
2 S Mitchell St
3 Milton St
B
1 Chestnut St
STRIPMINE RD
W BALTIMORE ST
BRIDGE ST
NORTH I PARK
WILMINGTON I PARK
OAKWOOD CEM
Wilmington HS
Wilmington Dam
Lexington Ct
Fairchild Dr

SEE 3943 MAP

SEE B MAP

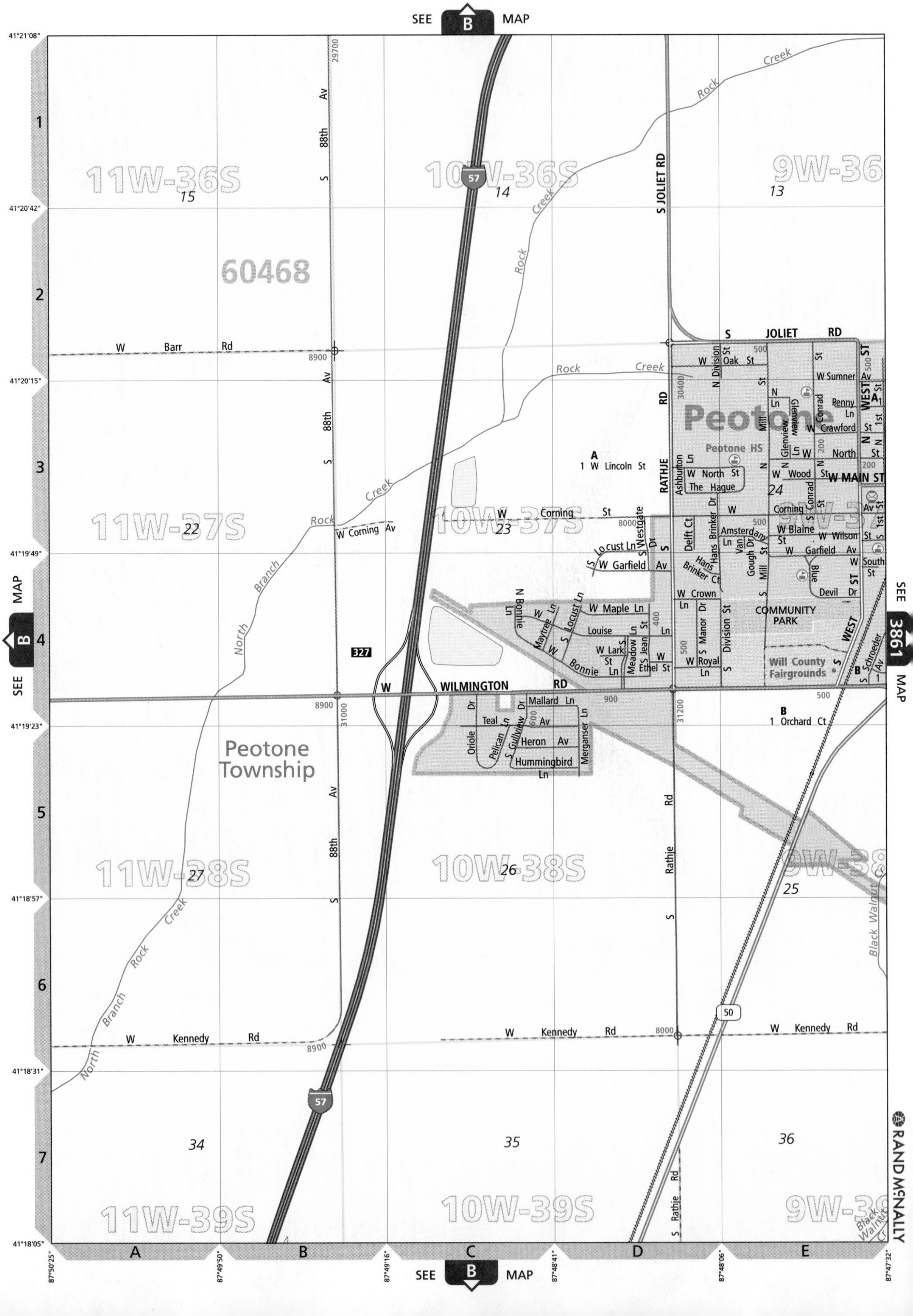

1:24,000
1 in. = 2000 ft.
0 0.25 0.5
miles

SEE B MAP

SEE B MAP

SEE 3861 MAP

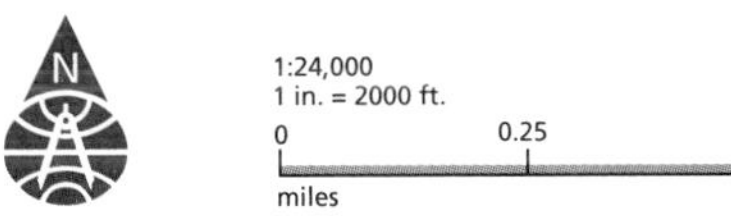

SEE B MAP

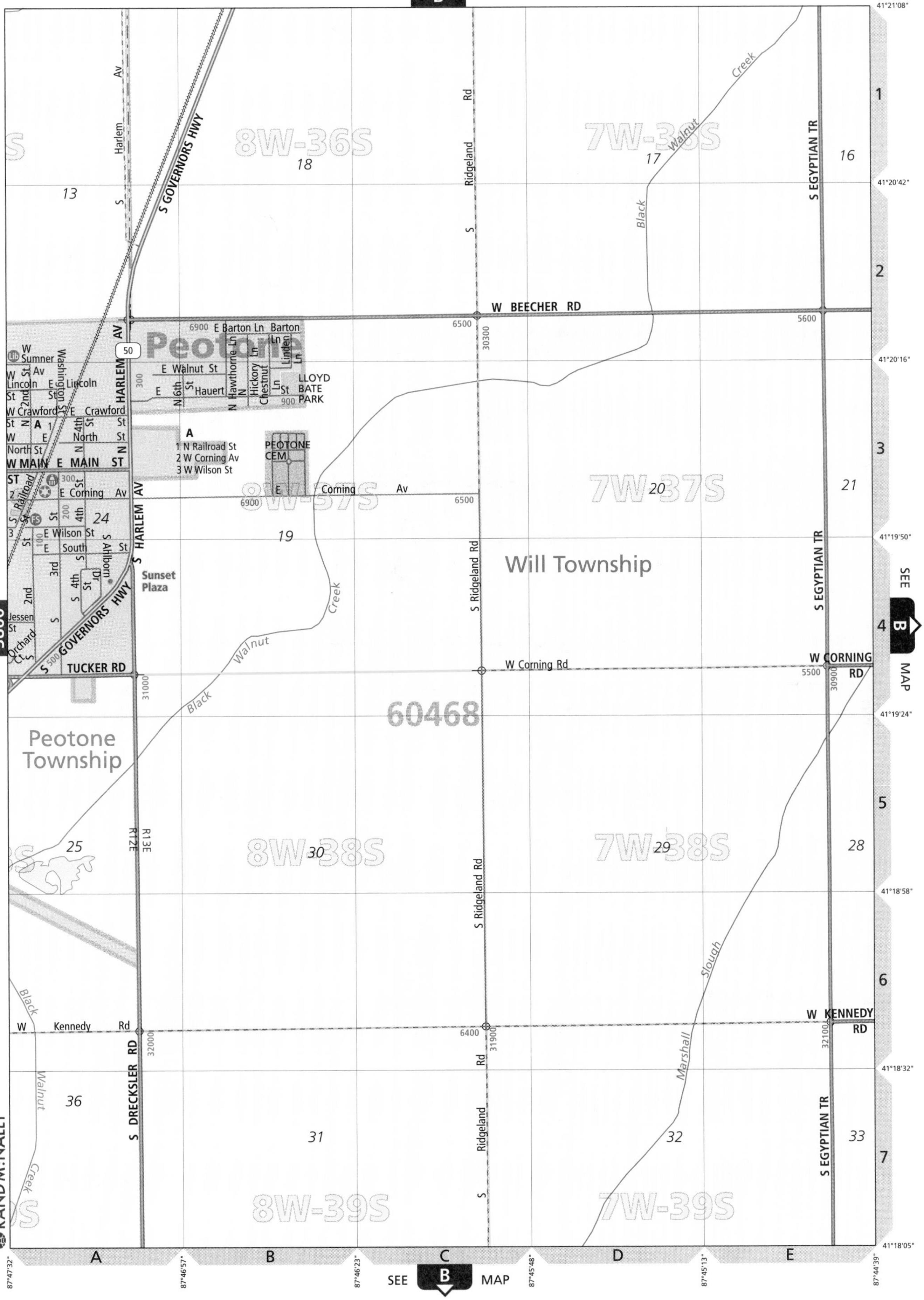

SEE 3860 MAP

SEE B MAP

SEE B MAP

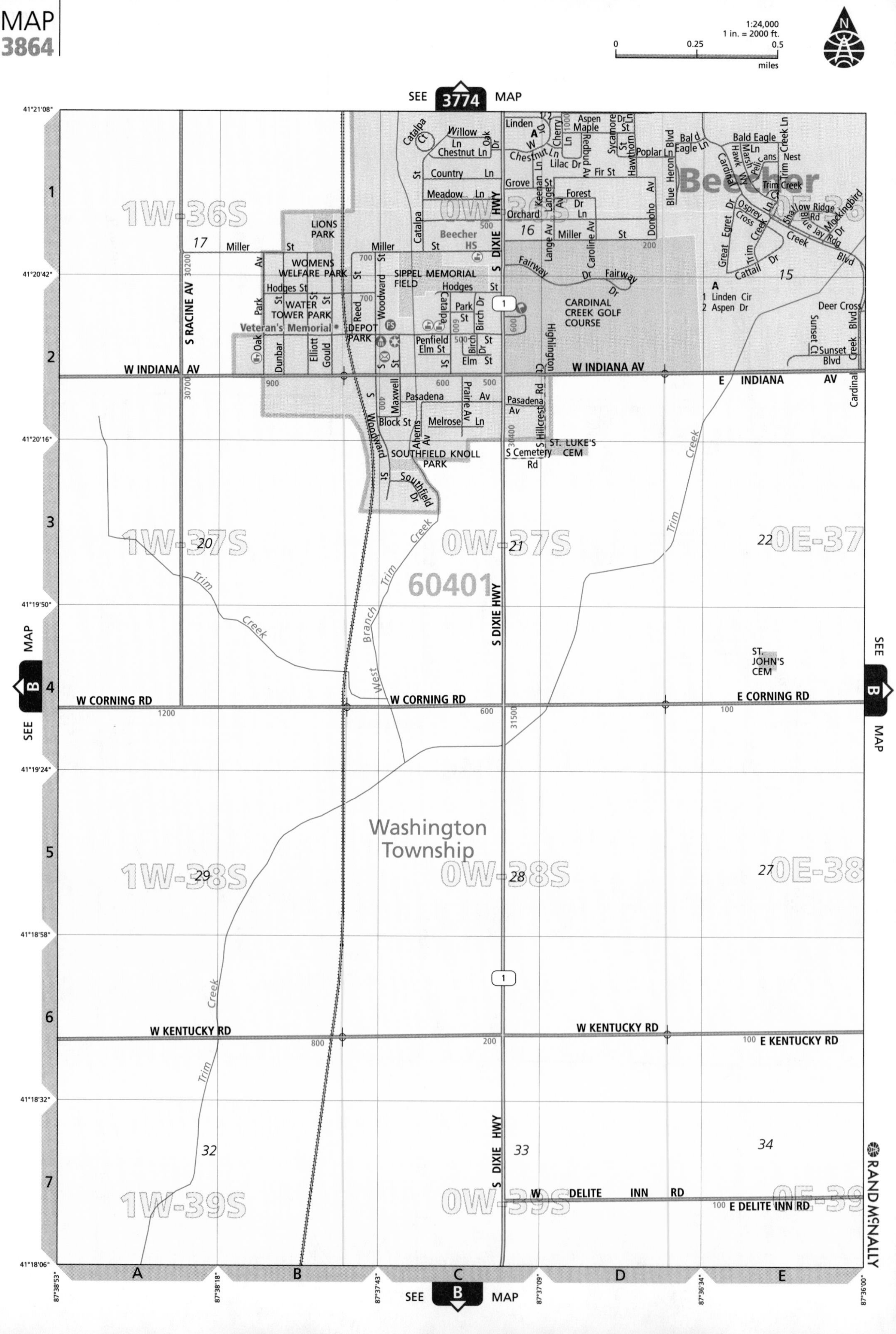

1:24,000
1 in. = 2000 ft.
0 0.25 0.5
miles

SEE 3774 MAP

Beecher

Washington Township

60401

1W-36S 0W-36S 0E-36
1W-37S 0W-37S 0E-37
1W-38S 0W-38S 0E-38
1W-39S 0W-39S 0E-39

17 16 15 20 21 22 29 28 27 32 33 34

W INDIANA AV
E INDIANA AV
W CORNING RD
E CORNING RD
W KENTUCKY RD
E KENTUCKY RD
W DELITE INN RD
E DELITE INN RD
S DIXIE HWY
S RACINE AV

LIONS PARK
WOMENS WELFARE PARK
WATER TOWER PARK
Veteran's Memorial
DEPOT PARK
SIPPEL MEMORIAL FIELD
Beecher HS
CARDINAL CREEK GOLF COURSE
SOUTHFIELD KNOLL PARK
ST. LUKE'S CEM
ST. JOHN'S CEM

Miller St
Hodges St
Penfield St
Elm St
Pasadena Av
Block St
Melrose Ln
Prairie Av
Ahearns Av
S Woodward St
Southfield Dr
Maxwell
Oak St
Dunbar St
Elliott St
Gould St
Reed St
Park St
Birch Dr
Catalpa St
Catalpa Ct
Willow Ln
Chestnut Ln
Oak Dr
Country Ln
Meadow Ln
Linden Dr
Chestnut Ln
Grove Ln
Orchard Ln
Keenan Ln
Lange Av
Cherry Ln
Lilac Dr
Aspen Maple
Redbud Av
Sycamore Dr
Fir St
Hawthorn St
Poplar Ln
Blue Heron Blvd
Bald Eagle Ln
Donoho Av
Forest Dr
Miller St
Caroline Av
Fairway Dr
Highlington Ct
Hillcrest Rd
S Cemetery Rd
Pasadena Av
Bald Eagle Ln
Marsh Hawk Wy
Pelicans Nest
Trim Creek Ln
Cardinal
Trim Creek Ct
Osprey Cross
Great Egret Dr
Shallow Ridge Rd
Blue Jay Rdg
Mockingbird Dr
Trim Creek Blvd
Cattail Dr
Deer Cross
Sunset Ct
Sunset Blvd
Creek Blvd
Cardinal

A
1 Linden Cir
2 Aspen Dr

Trim Creek
West Branch Trim Creek

700 900 600 500 1200 100 800 200 30200 30700 30400 31500

1

41°21'08" 41°20'42" 41°20'16" 41°19'50" 41°19'24" 41°18'58" 41°18'32" 41°18'06"
87°38'53" 87°38'18" 87°37'43" 87°37'09" 87°36'34" 87°36'00"

1 2 3 4 5 6 7
A B C D E

SEE B MAP
SEE B MAP
SEE B MAP

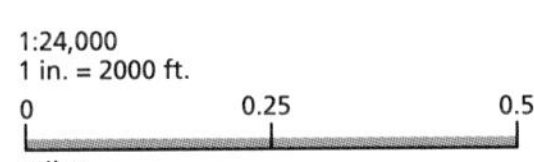

SEE B MAP

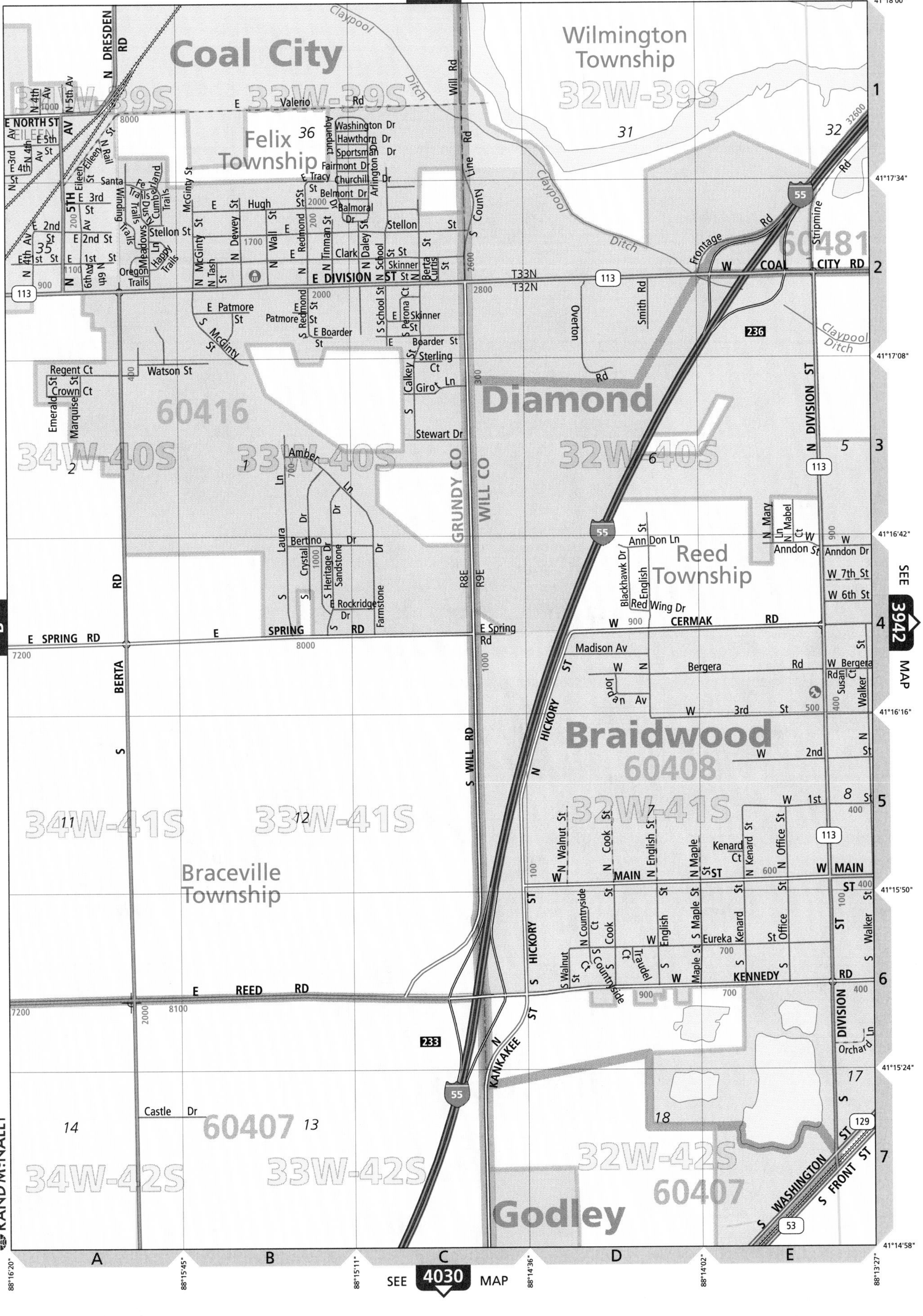

Coal City
Wilmington Township
Felix Township
Diamond
Reed Township
Braidwood
60408
Braceville Township
Godley
60416
60481
60407
33W-39S
32W-39S
34W-40S
33W-40S
32W-40S
34W-41S
33W-41S
32W-41S
34W-42S
33W-42S
32W-42S

N DRESDEN RD
E Valerio Rd
E NORTH ST
E DIVISION ST
W COAL CITY RD
E Patmore St
Watson St
Regent Ct
Crown Ct
Emerald St
Marquise St
Stewart Dr
Amber Ln
Laura Ln
Bertino Dr
Crystal Dr
S Heritage Dr
Sandstone Dr
E Rockridge Dr
Farmstone Dr
E SPRING RD
E Spring Rd
S BERTA RD
S WILL RD
GRUNDY CO
WILL CO
R8E
R9E
T33N
T32N
Overton Rd
Smith Rd
Frontage Rd
Stripmine Rd
Claypool Ditch
County Line Rd
Will Rd
W CERMAK RD
Madison Av
W Bergera Rd
Jordan Av
W 3rd St
W 2nd St
W 1st St
N HICKORY ST
N DIVISION ST
S DIVISION ST
W MAIN ST
W KENNEDY RD
E REED RD
N KANKAKEE ST
S WASHINGTON ST
S FRONT ST
Castle Dr
Orchard Ln
Ann Don Ln
Anndon Dr
W 7th St
W 6th St
Red Wing Dr
Blackhawk Dr
N English St
Eureka St
Kenard Ct
N Office St
S Walker St
Susan Ct

113
55
129
53
233
236

1
2
3
4
5
6
7
A
B
C
D
E

41°18'00"
41°17'34"
41°17'08"
41°16'42"
41°16'16"
41°15'50"
41°15'24"
41°14'58"
88°16'20"
88°15'45"
88°15'11"
88°14'36"
88°14'02"
88°13'27"

SEE B MAP

SEE 3942 MAP

SEE 4030 MAP

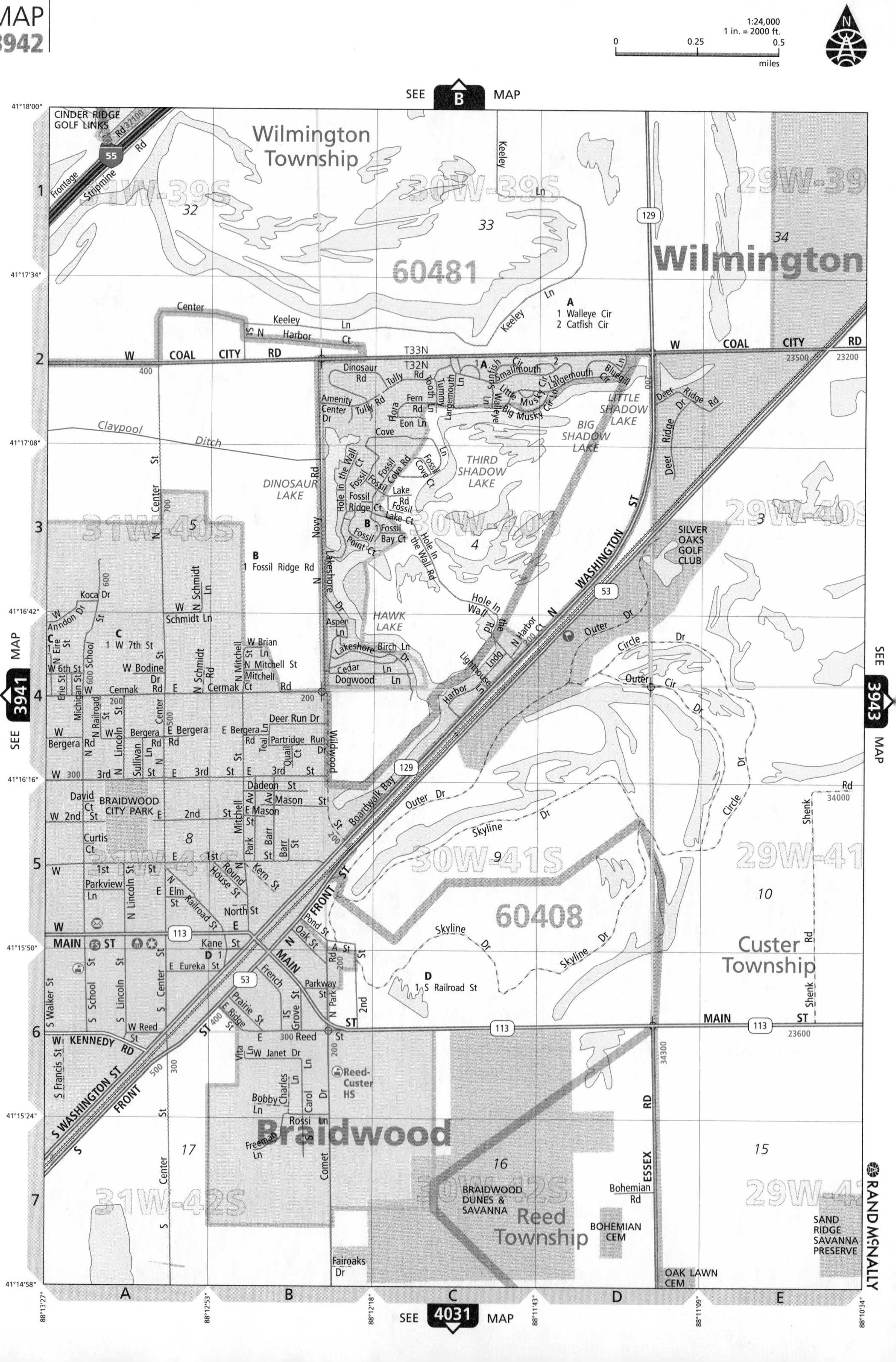

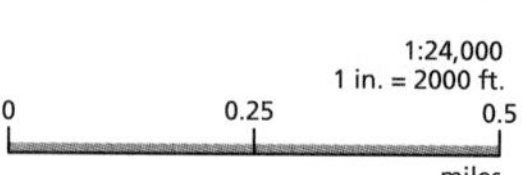

SEE B MAP

CINDER RIDGE GOLF LINKS

Wilmington Township

Wilmington

60481

31W-39S 30W-39S 29W-39S

32 33 34

Frontage Rd
Stripmine Rd 32100
55
Keeley Ln
129

A
1 Walleye Cir
2 Catfish Cir

Center
Keeley Ln
S N Harbor Ct

W COAL CITY RD 400
W COAL CITY RD 23500 23200
T33N
T32N

Dinosaur Rd
Tully Rd
Tooth Ln
Tummy Ln
Largemouth Ln
Sunfish Cir
Smallmouth
Largemouth Cir
Bluegill Ln
Little Musky Cir
Big Musky Cir
Walleye Ln
Amenity Center Dr
Flora
Fern Rd
Eon Ln
Cove
Deer Ridge Rd
Deer Ridge Dr
LITTLE SHADOW LAKE
BIG SHADOW LAKE
THIRD SHADOW LAKE

Claypool Ditch

DINOSAUR LAKE

Hole In the Wall Ct
Fossil Cove Rd
Fossil Cove Ct
Fossil Ct
Fossil Ridge Ct
Lake Rd
Fossil Lake Ct
Fossil Bay Ct
Fossil Point Ct
Hole In the Wall Rd

B
1 Fossil Ridge Rd

N Novy Rd
N Center St 700

31W-40S 30W-40S 29W-40S

5 4 3

N WASHINGTON ST 200
53
SILVER OAKS GOLF CLUB

Koca Dr
W Anndon Dr
W Schmidt Ln
N Schmidt Ln
600

C
1 W 7th St

N Eire St
W 6th St
Erie St
Michigan St
School St 600
W Bodine Dr
N Schmidt Rd
N Mitchell Ct
W Brian Ln
N Mitchell St
Mitchell Ct
Cermak Rd
E Cermak Rd
200

Lakeshore Dr
Aspen Ln
HAWK LAKE
Lakeshore Birch Ln
Dr
Cedar Ln
Dogwood Ln

Hole In the Wall Rd
N Harbor 200 Ct
Lighthouse Lndg
Harbor Ln
Outer Dr
Circle Dr
Outer Cir
Dr

W Bergera Rd
N Railroad St
W Lincoln Ln
Bergera Rd
N Center St
500
E Bergera Rd
E Bergera Ln
Deer Run Dr
Partridge Run Dr
Teal Ln
Quail Ct
Wildwood
N Sullivan Ln
W 300 3rd St
E 3rd St
E 3rd St
129

41°16'16"

David Ct
BRAIDWOOD CITY PARK
W 2nd St
E 2nd St
Dadeon St
Mason St
E Mason St
N Mitchell Av
Park Av
Barr St
Barr St
Curtis Ct
8
Boardwalk Bay
St 200
Outer Dr
Skyline Dr
Circle Dr

31W-41S 30W-41S 29W-41S

9 10

W 1st St
E 1st St
Round House St
Kern St
Parkview Ln
N Lincoln St
N Elm St
Railroad St
North St
FRONT ST
60408

W MAIN ST
113
E MAIN
Kane St
D 1
E Eureka St
Oak St
Pond St
Rd A St
St
Skyline Dr
Skyline Dr

D
1 S Railroad St

Custer Township

Shenk Rd
Rd 34000
Shenk Rd

S Walker St
S School St
S Lincoln St
S Center St
53
French
Prairie St
E Ridge St
Grove St
Parkway St
N Park
2nd
W Reed St
W KENNEDY RD
FRONT ST 400
E 300 Reed St 200
MAIN ST 113
MAIN ST 113 23600
34300

S Francis St
S WASHINGTON ST
FRONT 500
300 St
Vita
W Janet Dr
Ln
Reed-Custer HS
Bobby Ln
Charles Ln
Carol Dr
Rossi Ln
Braidwood
Freeman Ln
Comet St
S Center St

17 16 15

ESSEX RD

31W-42S 30W-42S 29W-42S

BRAIDWOOD DUNES & SAVANNA
Reed Township
Bohemian Rd
BOHEMIAN CEM
Fairoaks Dr
OAK LAWN CEM
SAND RIDGE SAVANNA PRESERVE

1 2 3 4 5 6 7

A B C D E

41°18'00"
41°17'34"
41°17'08"
41°16'42"
41°16'16"
41°15'50"
41°15'24"
41°14'58"

88°13'27"
88°12'53"
88°12'18"
88°11'43"
88°11'09"
88°10'34"

SEE 3941 MAP

SEE 3943 MAP

SEE 4031 MAP

1:24,000
1 in. = 2000 ft.
0 0.25 0.5
miles

SEE 3853 MAP

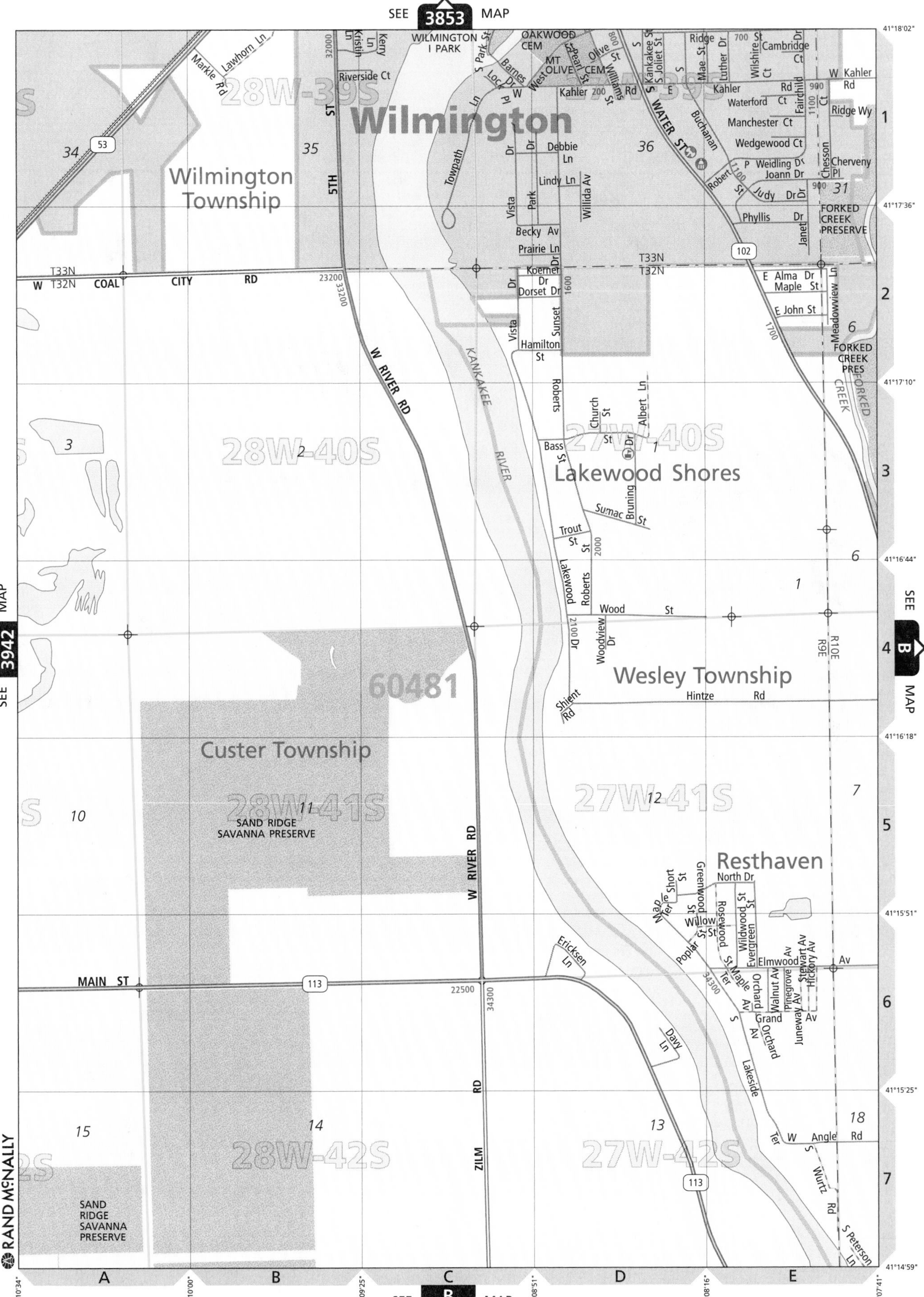

SEE 3942 MAP

SEE B MAP

SEE B MAP

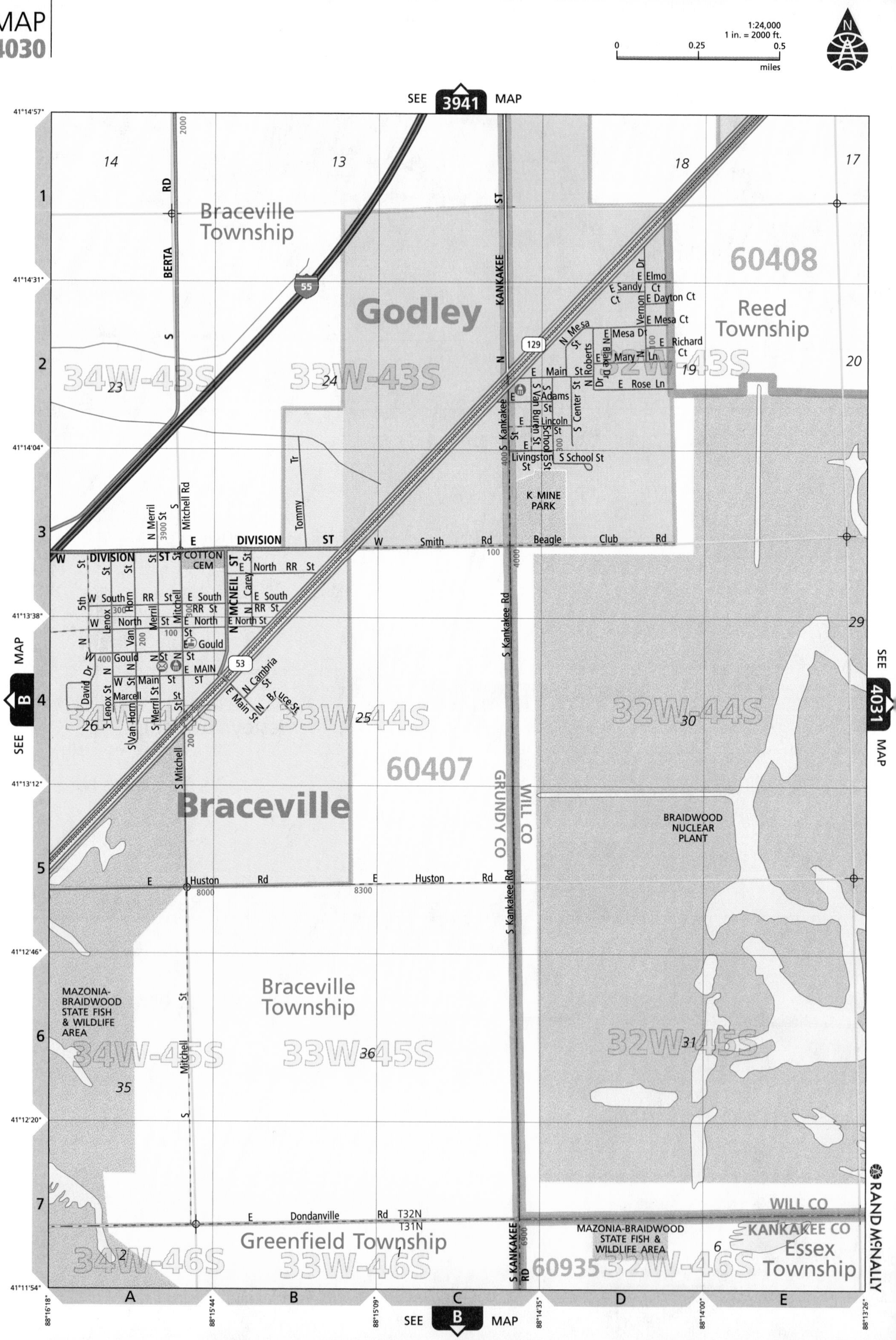

1:24,000
1 in. = 2000 ft.
0 0.25 0.5
miles

SEE 3941 MAP

SEE B MAP

SEE 4031 MAP

SEE B MAP

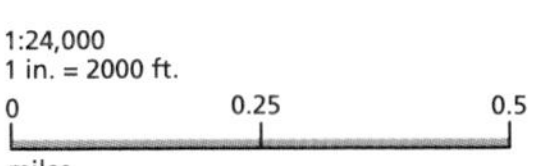

SEE 3942 MAP

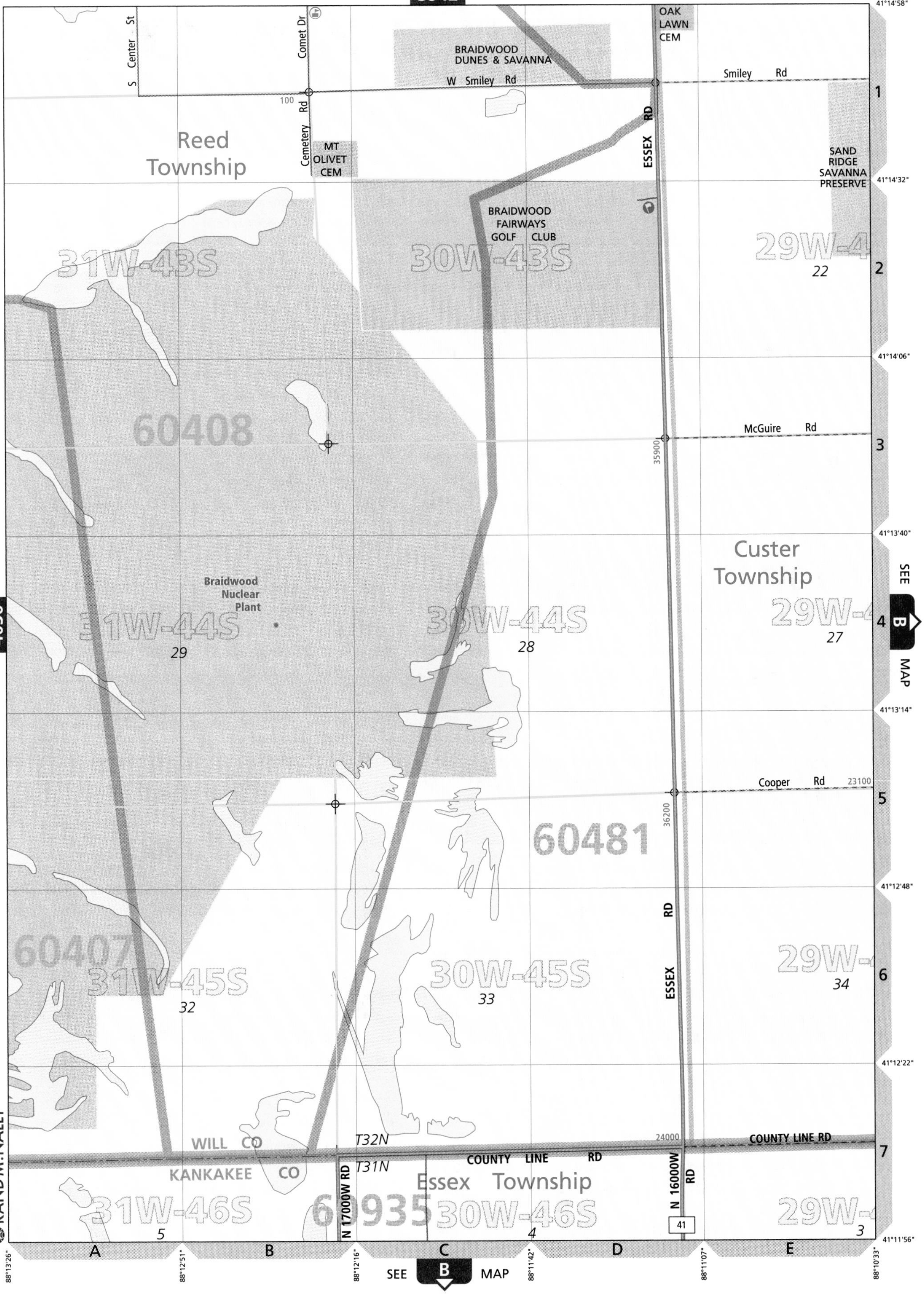

SEE 4030 MAP

SEE B MAP

SEE B MAP

Cities and Communities

Community Name	Abbr.	County	ZIP Code	Map Page
* Addison	ADSN	DuPage	60101	2970
Addison Township	AddT	Cook	60007	2914
Addison Township	AddT	DuPage	60126	2971
Aero Estates		DuPage	60564	3202
Alden Township	AdnT	McHenry	60033	2349
* Algonquin	ALGN	Kane	60102	2746
* Algonquin	ALGN	McHenry	60102	2694
Algonquin Shores		McHenry	60102	2747
Algonquin Township	AlqT	McHenry	60014	2641
Allens Corners		Kane	60140	2796
Almora Heights		Kane	60124	2853
* Alsip	ALSP	Cook	60803	3276
Anderman Acres		Will	60564	3266
* Antioch	ANTH	Lake	60002	2357
Antioch Township	AntT	Lake	60002	2415
Appaloosa West		Kane	60119	3018
Arboretum East		DuPage	60137	3083
Arboretum West		DuPage	60137	3083
Arbury Hills		Will	60448	3503
* Arlington Heights	ANHT	Cook	60005	2861
Arrowhead		DuPage	60187	3081
* Aurora	AURA	Will	60503	3265
* Aurora	AURA	Kane	60505	3138
* Aurora	AURA	Kendall	60503	3265
* Aurora	AURA	DuPage	60502	3139
Aurora Township	AraT	Kane	60505	3200
Aurora Township	AraT	DuPage	60502	3139
Aux Sable Township	AxST	Grundy	60450	3761
Avon Township	AvnT	Lake	60046	2476
Baker Lake		Cook	60010	2751
Bald Mound		Kane	60510	3076
* Bannockburn	BKBN	Lake	60015	2703
Barreville		McHenry	60012	2585
* Barrington	BRTN	Lake	60010	2751
* Barrington	BRTN	Cook	60010	2750
* Barrington Hills	BNHL	Cook	60010	2750
* Barrington Hills	BNHL	McHenry	60010	2696
* Barrington Hills	BNHL	Lake	60010	2696
* Barrington Hills	BNHL	Kane	60010	2748
Barrington Township	BrnT	Cook	60118	2802
Barrington Woods		Cook	60074	2752
* Bartlett	BRLT	DuPage	60103	2910
* Bartlett	BRLT	Cook	60103	2910
* Bartlett	BRLT	Kane	60120	2909
* Batavia	BTVA	Kane	60510	3078
Batavia Township	BtvT	Kane	60510	3079
* Beach Park	BHPK	Lake	60099	2421
Beaver Valley		Cook	60467	3422
* Bedford Park	BDPK	Cook	60501	3148
* Beecher	BCHR	Will	60401	3864
* Bellwood	BLWD	Cook	60104	3029
Benet Lake		Kenosha	53104	2358
* Bensenville	BNVL	Cook	60131	2972
* Bensenville	BNVL	DuPage	60106	2971
Benton Township	BtnT	Lake	60099	2422
* Berkeley	BKLY	Cook	60163	3028
* Berwyn	BRWN	Cook	60402	3089
* Big Rock	BGRK	Kane	60554	3134
Big Rock Township	BRkT	Kane	60511	3196
Blackberry Heights		Kane	60506	3199
Blackberry Township	BbyT	Kane	60119	3018
Blackberry Woods		Kane	60554	3075
Black Hawk Springs		Kendall	60545	3332
Bloomfield, Town of	BfdT	Walworth	53128	2352
* Bloomingdale	BMDL	DuPage	60108	2969
Bloomingdale Twp	BmdT	DuPage	60108	2912
Bloom Township	BlmT	Cook	60411	3598
* Blue Island	BLID	Cook	60406	3349
* Bolingbrook	BGBK	DuPage	60440	3205
* Bolingbrook	BGBK	Will	60440	3269
Bonnie Brea		Will	60441	3419
Boulder Hill		Kendall	60538	3199
* Braceville	BCVL	Grundy	60407	4030
Braceville Township	BvlT	Grundy	60407	4030
* Braidwood	BDWD	Will	60408	3942
Brandywine		DuPage	60181	3085
Branigar Estates		Cook	60007	2861
Bremen Township	BmnT	Cook	60426	3426
Brentwood		Cook	60074	2752
* Bridgeview	BGVW	Cook	60455	3210
Bridle Creek Estates		Kane	60175	2962
Brierwood		Kane	60175	2906
Bristol		Kendall	60512	3261
Bristol, Town of	BtlT	Kenosha	53142	2360
Bristol Lake		Kendall	60560	3261
Bristol Ridge		Kendall	60560	3262
Bristol Township	BtlT	Kendall	60512	3197
* Broadview	BDVW	Cook	60155	3029
Brookeridge		DuPage	60516	3206
* Brookfield	BKFD	Cook	60513	3088
Brookforest North		Will	60404	3496
Brookhill		Lake	60048	2591
Brookside		Kane	60175	2961
Brookwood		Kane	60174	2964
Brunning		Will	60441	3342
* Buffalo Grove	BFGV	Cook	60089	2754
* Buffalo Grove	BFGV	Lake	60089	2701
Bull Creek		Lake	60048	2591
* Bull Valley	BLVY	McHenry	60098	2583
* Burbank	BRBK	Cook	60459	3211
Burlington Township	BrlT	Kane	60140	2795
* Burnham	BNHM	Cook	60633	3352
* Burr Ridge	BRRG	Cook	60527	3208
* Burr Ridge	BRRG	DuPage	60527	3208
Burtons Bridge		McHenry	60050	2586
Burton Township	BtnT	McHenry	60050	2414
Butterfield		DuPage	60148	3083
Butterfield West		DuPage	60137	3083
* Calumet City	CTCY	Cook	60409	3352
* Calumet Park	CTPK	Cook	60827	3277
Calumet Township	ClmT	Cook	60827	3349
Camelot		Will	60404	3584
Campton Township	CmpT	Kane	60175	2961
Capri Village		Cook	60074	2753
* Carol Stream	CLSM	DuPage	60188	2968
* Carpentersville	CPVL	Kane	60110	2748
Carriage Park		Kendall	60543	3263
Carriage Way Court		Cook	60074	2753
* Cary	CRY	McHenry	60013	2695
Catatoga		Kane	60124	2907
Catatoga II		Kane	60124	2907
Cedar Island		Lake	60041	2472
* Channahon	CNHN	Grundy	60447	3672
* Channahon	CNHN	Will	60410	3672
Channahon Township	CnhT	Will	60421	3674
Channel Lake		Lake	60002	2357
Chemung		McHenry	60033	2405
Chemung Township	CmgT	McHenry	60033	2406
Cherry Hill		Will	60433	3500
Chesney Shores		Lake	60046	2474
* Chicago	CHCG	DuPage	60666	2916
* Chicago	CHCG	Cook	60602	3034
* Chicago Heights	CHHT	Cook	60411	3596
* Chicago Ridge	CHRG	Cook	60415	3275
Chippewa		Cook	60803	3275
* Cicero	CCRO	Cook	60804	3089
Citation Lake Estates		Cook	60062	2756
* Clarendon Hills	CNHL	DuPage	60514	3145
Cloverdale		DuPage	60108	2968
* Coal City	CLCY	Grundy	60416	3941
* Coal City	CLCY	Will	60416	3941
Cobblestone		Cook	60016	2809
Colby Point		McHenry	60050	2585
College View		Will	60441	3340
Compton Pines		Kane	60175	2962
Conover		Kendall	60560	3261
--Cook County	CokC			
Coral		McHenry	60180	2635
Coral Township	CrlT	McHenry	60180	2635
* Country Club Hills	CCHL	Cook	60478	3426
Country Lake		DuPage	60563	3139
Countryside		Kane	60506	3198
* Countryside	CTSD	Cook	60525	3147
Countryside Lake		Lake	60060	2645
Countryside Manor		Lake	60048	2592
Country View Estates		Will	60564	3203
Countryview Estates		Kane	60118	2799
Coynes		Will	60435	3417
Creekwood		Cook	60439	3343
* Crest Hill	CTHL	Will	60403	3498
* Crestwood	CTWD	Cook	60445	3348
* Crete	CRTE	Will	60417	3685
Crete Township	CteT	Will	60417	3686
Crooked Lake		Lake	60046	2417
Cross Lake		Kenosha	53179	2357

*Indicates incorporated city

Cities and Communities

Community Name	Abbr.	County	ZIP Code	Map Page
* Crystal Lake	CLLK	McHenry	60014	2640
Crystal Lake Estates		McHenry	60014	2640
Crystal Lawns		Will	60435	3417
Cuba Township	CbaT	Lake	60013	2642
Custer Township	CstT	Will	60481	3943
* Darien	DRN	DuPage	60516	3207
Deep Lake		Lake	60046	2417
* Deerfield	DRFD	Cook	60015	2756
* Deerfield	DRFD	Lake	60015	2703
Deer Lake		Cook	60010	2751
* Deer Park	DRPK	Lake	60010	2698
Deer Run		Kane	60175	2962
--DeKalb County	DKbC			
Dellwood Highlands		Will	60441	3419
Del Mar Woods		Lake	60015	2703
* Des Plaines	DSPN	Cook	60016	2863
* Diamond	DMND	Grundy	60416	3941
* Diamond	DMND	Will	60416	3941
Diamond Lake		Lake	60060	2646
* Dixmoor	DXMR	Cook	60426	3349
* Dolton	DLTN	Cook	60419	3350
Dorr Township	DrrT	McHenry	60098	2581
* Downers Grove	DRGV	DuPage	60515	3144
Downers Grove Estates		DuPage	60516	3144
Downers Grove Twp	DGvT	DuPage	60527	3207
Druce Lake		Lake	60046	2476
Duck Lake Woods		Lake	60041	2473
Dundee Township	DndT	Kane	60118	2801
Dunham Township	DhmT	McHenry	60033	2464
--DuPage County	DPgC			
DuPage Township	DPgT	Will	60441	3269
DuPage Township	DPgT	DuPage	60517	3206
* Dyer	DYR	Lake	46311	3598
Eagle Heights		Kane	60124	2853
Earl Estates		Kane	60554	3075
* East Dundee	EDND	Cook	60118	2801
* East Dundee	EDND	Kane	60118	2801
* East Hazel Crest	EHZC	Cook	60429	3427
East Loon Lake		Lake	60002	2417
Eastwood Manor		McHenry	60051	2528
Echo Lake		Lake	60099	2420
Ela Township	ElaT	Lake	60060	2645
* Elburn	ELBN	Kane	60119	3017
* Elgin	ELGN	Cook	60120	2855
* Elgin	ELGN	Kane	60120	2854
Elgin Estates		Kane	60123	2908
Elgin Township	ElgT	Cook	60120	2909
Elgin Township	ElgT	Kane	60124	2907
Elk Grove Township	EGvT	Cook	60018	2916
* Elk Grove Village	EGVV	DuPage	60007	2915
* Elk Grove Village	EGVV	Cook	60007	2914
* Elmhurst	EMHT	DuPage	60126	3028
* Elmhurst	EMHT	Cook	60162	3028
* Elmwood Park	EDPK	Cook	60707	2974
* Elwood	ELWD	Will	60421	3675
Emerald Park		McHenry	60051	2528
Empire Hills		Kane	60175	2961
Eola		DuPage	60502	3139
Erontenac		Kane	60118	2800
Essex Township	EsxT	Kankakee	60935	4031
* Evanston	EVTN	Cook	60201	2867
* Evergreen Park	ENGN	Cook	60805	3212
Exposition View		Kane	60506	3137
Fairmont		Will	60441	3419
Fair Oaks		DuPage	60185	2967
Fair Oaks		Kane	60175	2962
Farmingdale		DuPage	60561	3207
Farmington		Kane	60175	2964
Felix Township	FlxT	Grundy	60416	3941
Ferndale		McHenry	60051	2585
Fiday View		Will	60431	3417
Five Islands Park		Kane	60177	2908
Florence Township	FrnT	Will	60481	3766
* Flossmoor	FSMR	Cook	60422	3507
* Ford Heights	FDHT	Cook	60411	3509
Forest Estates		Cook	60067	2805
Forest Gardens		Lake	60084	2643
Foresthaven		Lake	60045	2648
Forest Lake		Lake	60047	2699
Forest Manor		Will	60441	3420
* Forest Park	FTPK	Cook	60130	3030
Forest River		Cook	60056	2808
* Forest View	FTVW	Cook	60402	3088
Fort Sheridan		Lake	60037	2650
Fossland		Lake	60099	2360
Four Lakes		DuPage	60532	3143
Foxcroft		DuPage	60137	3083
Foxfield		Kane	60175	2961
* Fox Lake	FXLK	Lake	60020	2473
* Fox Lake	FXLK	McHenry	60081	2355
Fox Lake Hills		Lake	60046	2474
Fox Lake Vista		Lake	60020	2414
Fox Lawn		Kendall	60560	3333
Fox River Estates		Kane	60174	2908
Fox River Gardens		Kendall	60560	3334
* Fox River Grove	FRGV	Lake	60021	2696
* Fox River Grove	FRGV	McHenry	60021	2696
Fox Township	FoxT	Kendall	60560	3332
* Frankfort	FKFT	Cook	60443	3593
* Frankfort	FKFT	Will	60423	3591
Frankfort Square		Will	60423	3504
Frankfort Township	FftT	Will	60448	3503
* Franklin Park	FNPK	Cook	60131	2973
Franklin Square		Will	60423	3505
Fremont Township	FmtT	Lake	60060	2588
Gages Lake		Lake	60030	2534
* Geneva	GNVA	Kane	60134	3020
Geneva Road		DuPage	60190	3023
Geneva Township	GnvT	Kane	60510	3077
* Genoa City	GNCY	Walworth	53128	2353
* Gilberts	GLBT	Kane	60136	2799
Gilletts		Will	60451	3502
Gilmer		Lake	60047	2645
Glenbard South		DuPage	60137	3083
Glenbrook Countryside		Cook	60062	2757
* Glencoe	GLNC	Cook	60022	2758
* Glendale Heights	GLHT	DuPage	60139	2969
* Glen Ellyn	GNEN	DuPage	60137	3025
Glen Ellyn Countryside		DuPage	60137	3025
Glen Ellyn Woods		DuPage	60137	3083
Glen Oak		DuPage	60137	3025
* Glenview	GNVW	Cook	60025	2810
Glenview Countryside		Cook	60025	2810
Glenview Estates		Cook	60025	2809
* Glenwood	GNWD	Cook	60425	3508
* Godley	GDLY	Grundy	60407	4030
* Godley	GDLY	Will	60407	4030
* Golf	GLF	Cook	60029	2864
Golfview Hills		DuPage	60521	3145
Goodenow		Will	60401	3774
Goodings Grove		Will	60491	3344
Goose Lake Township	GLkT	Grundy	60450	3761
Grafton Township	GfnT	McHenry	60142	2691
Grandwood Park		Lake	60031	2477
Grant Township	GrtT	Lake	60041	2530
Grass Lake		Lake	60002	2416
* Grayslake	GYLK	Lake	60030	2532
Greenfield Township	GflT	Grundy	60407	4030
Green Garden Twp	GGnT	Will	60423	3591
* Green Oaks	GNOK	Lake	60048	2592
* Greenwood	GNWD	McHenry	60098	2468
Greenwood Township	GwdT	McHenry	60098	2468
Gromers Woods		Cook	60120	2856
--Grundy County	GdyC			
* Gurnee	GRNE	Lake	60031	2535
Haegers Bend		McHenry	60102	2695
* Hainesville	HNVL	Lake	60073	2532
Half Day		Lake	60061	2702
* Hammond	HMND	Lake	46320	3430
* Hampshire	HPSR	Kane	60140	2795
Hampshire Township	HshT	Kane	60140	2796
* Hanover Park	HRPK	Cook	60133	2911
* Hanover Park	HRPK	DuPage	60133	2911
Hanover Township	HnrT	Cook	60120	2855
Hanover Township	HnrT	Lake	46311	3687
Harbor Estates		Lake	60010	2696
Hartland Township	HtdT	McHenry	60033	2464
* Harvard	HRVD	McHenry	60033	2406
* Harvey	HRVY	Cook	60426	3350
* Harwood Heights	HDHT	Cook	60706	2918
* Hawthorn Woods	HNWD	Lake	60047	2645
* Hazel Crest	HLCT	Cook	60429	3427
* Hebron	HBRN	McHenry	60034	2350
Hebron Township	HbnT	McHenry	60034	2351
Hickory Corners		Lake	60002	2418

*Indicates incorporated city

Cities and Communities

Community Name	Abbr.	County	ZIP Code	Map Page
Hickory Falls		McHenry	60097	2469
* Hickory Hills	HYHL	Cook	60457	3210
Hickory Hollow		Kane	60118	2800
Hidden Creek		Cook	60074	2753
Hidden Hill		Kane	60124	2853
High Knob		DuPage	60187	3082
High Lake		DuPage	60185	3022
Highland Haven		Kane	60124	2853
Highland Hills		DuPage	60148	3084
Highland Lake		Lake	60030	2532
* Highland Park	HDPK	Lake	60035	2704
Highlands-Clarks		Kendall	60543	3263
Highland Shores		McHenry	60097	2469
* Highwood	HIWD	Lake	60040	2704
* Hillside	HLSD	Cook	60162	3028
* Hinsdale	HNDL	DuPage	60521	3146
* Hinsdale	HNDL	Cook	60521	3146
* Hodgkins	HGKN	Cook	60525	3147
* Hoffman Estates	HFET	Cook	60169	2804
* Hoffman Estates	HFET	Kane	60118	2801
Holcombville Corners		McHenry	60012	2584
* Holiday Hills	HHLL	McHenry	60051	2586
* Homer Glen	HMGN	Will	60491	3343
Homer Township	HmrT	Will	60491	3421
* Hometown	HMTN	Cook	60456	3212
* Homewood	HMWD	Cook	60430	3427
Horatio Gardens		Lake	60069	2701
Howe Terrace		Cook	60010	2751
* Huntley	HTLY	Kane	60142	2744
* Huntley	HTLY	McHenry	60142	2692
Idlewild		Lake	60030	2533
* Indian Creek	INCK	Lake	60061	2647
* Indian Head Park	IHPK	Cook	60525	3146
Indian Trail Estates		Lake	60069	2702
Ingalls Park		Will	60433	3499
Ingleside		Lake	60041	2473
Ingleside Shore		Lake	60041	2473
* Inverness	IVNS	Cook	60067	2752
* Island Lake	ISLK	Lake	60042	2586
* Island Lake	ISLK	McHenry	60042	2586
* Itasca	ITSC	DuPage	60143	2914
Itasca Ranchettes		DuPage	60143	2913
Ivanhoe		Lake	60060	2589
Jackson Township	JknT	Will	60421	3675
Jewell Road		DuPage	60187	3023
* Johnsburg	JNBG	McHenry	60050	2472
* Joliet	JLET	Will	60432	3498
* Joliet	JLET	Kendall	60586	3415
Joliet Arsenal		Will	60481	3853
Joliet Township	JltT	Will	60421	3586
* Justice	JSTC	Cook	60458	3210
--Kane County	KneC			
--Kankakee County	KkeC			
Keeneyville		DuPage	60172	2912
--Kendall County	KdlC			
Kendall Township	KdlT	Kendall	60560	3334
* Kenilworth	KLWH	Cook	60043	2812
--Kenosha County	KnhC			
* Kildeer	KLDR	Lake	60047	2699
Kimball Farms		Kane	60110	2746
Kingswood		Kane	60175	2961
Klondike		Lake	60002	2415
Knollwood		Lake	60044	2593
Kreitsburg		Lake	46311	3687
La Fox		Kane	60119	3018
* La Grange	LGNG	Cook	60525	3087
La Grange Highlands		Cook	60525	3146
* La Grange Park	LGPK	Cook	60525	3087
Laguna Woods		Cook	60462	3346
* Lake Barrington	LKBN	Lake	60010	2697
* Lake Bluff	LKBF	Lake	60044	2593
Lake Catherine		Lake	60002	2357
Lake Charlotte		Kane	60175	2963
--Lake County	LkeC			
* Lake Forest	LKFT	Lake	60045	2650
* Lake in the Hills	LIHL	McHenry	60156	2693
Lake Killarney		McHenry	60013	2641
Lake Marion		Kane	60110	2748
* Lakemoor	LKMR	McHenry	60051	2529
* Lakemoor	LKMR	Lake	60051	2529
Lake Park Estates		Cook	60067	2752
Lake Shangri-La		Kenosha	53104	2358
Lake Tara Estates		Kane	60118	2800
* Lake Villa	LKVL	Lake	60046	2475
Lake Villa Township	LkvT	Lake	60046	2476
Lakewood		DuPage	60185	2966
* Lakewood	LKWD	McHenry	60014	2639
Lakewood Shores		Will	60481	3943
* Lake Zurich	LKZH	Lake	60047	2698
* Lansing	LNSG	Cook	60438	3430
--La Salle County	LaSC			
Lawrence		McHenry	60033	2405
* Lemont	LMNT	Cook	60439	3270
* Lemont	LMNT	DuPage	60527	3271
Lemont Township	LmnT	Cook	60480	3272
Lewood		Will	60586	3416
Leyden Township	LydT	Cook	60164	2973
Liberty Acres		Lake	60048	2591
Liberty Park		DuPage	60559	3085
* Libertyville	LYVL	Lake	60048	2591
Libertyville Township	LbvT	Lake	60044	2592
Lily Cache		Will	60544	3416
Lily Cache Acres		Will	60544	3416
* Lily Lake	LYLK	Kane	60175	2961
Lilymoor		McHenry	60051	2529
Lincoln Estates		Will	60423	3592
Lincoln Hills		DuPage	60137	3083
* Lincolnshire	LNSH	Lake	60069	2702
* Lincolnwood	LNWD	Cook	60712	2920
Lincolnwood Hills		Will	60451	3502
* Lindenhurst	LNHT	Lake	60046	2476
Linn, Town of	LinT	Walworth	53147	2349
* Lisle	LSLE	DuPage	60532	3143
Lisle Township	LslT	DuPage	60565	3205
Little Rock Township	LtRT	Kendall	60545	3258
* Lockport	LKPT	Will	60441	3419
Lockport Township	LktT	Will	60403	3417
* Lombard	LMBD	DuPage	60148	3026
* Long Grove	LGGV	Lake	60047	2700
Long Lake		Lake	60041	2474
Longwood Manor		DuPage	60563	3140
Lookout Point		McHenry	60097	2469
Loon Lake		Lake	60002	2416
Lotus Woods		Lake	60081	2415
Lynnwood		Kendall	60543	3262
* Lynwood	LYWD	Cook	60411	3510
* Lyons	LYNS	Cook	60534	3088
Lyons Township	LynT	Cook	60480	3209
Maine Township	MaiT	Cook	60068	2863
* Manhattan	MHTN	Will	60442	3677
Manhattan Township	MhtT	Will	60442	3767
* Marengo	MRGO	McHenry	60152	2634
Marengo Township	MngT	McHenry	60152	2634
Marina Terrace		Kendall	60543	3263
Marion Circle		Kane	60554	3075
* Markham	MKHM	Cook	60428	3427
Marley		Will	60448	3502
Mary Meadows		Kane	60175	2961
* Matteson	MTSN	Cook	60443	3506
* Maywood	MYWD	Cook	60153	3030
* McCook	MCCK	Cook	60525	3148
* McCullom Lake	MCLK	McHenry	60050	2470
* McHenry	MHRY	McHenry	60050	2528
--McHenry County	McHC			
McHenry Township	MchT	McHenry	60050	2471
McIntosh		Kane	60123	2854
McQueen		Kane	60124	2798
McQueen		DuPage	60185	3022
Meadowview		Kane	60175	2961
Medinah		DuPage	60157	2913
* Melrose Park	MLPK	Cook	60160	3029
* Merrionette Park	MTPK	Cook	60803	3276
* Mettawa	MTWA	Lake	60048	2648
Meyerbrook		Kendall	60545	3259
Middlecreek		Kane	60175	2963
* Midlothian	MDLN	Cook	60445	3348
Millburn		Lake	60046	2418
Milton Township	MltT	DuPage	60137	3083
* Minooka	MNKA	Grundy	60447	3672
* Minooka	MNKA	Will	60447	3672
* Minooka	MNKA	Kendall	60447	3583
Mission Hills		Cook	60062	2756
Moecherville		Kane	60505	3201
* Mokena	MKNA	Will	60448	3503
Monaville		Lake	60046	2474

*Indicates incorporated city

Cities and Communities

Community Name	Abbr.	County	ZIP Code	Map Page
* Monee	MONE	Will	60449	3683
Monee Township	MonT	Will	60449	3684
Montague Forest		Kane	60124	2852
* Montgomery	MTGY	Kendall	60543	3199
* Montgomery	MTGY	Kane	60538	3199
Mooseheart		Kane	60539	3077
Moraine Township	MrnT	Lake	60037	2704
Morgan's Gate		Cook	60067	2752
* Morton Grove	MNGV	Cook	60053	2865
* Mt Prospect	MPPT	Cook	60056	2808
* Mundelein	MDLN	Lake	60060	2590
* Munster	MNSR	Lake	46321	3430
Mylith Park		Lake	60042	2642
Na-Au-Say Township	NasT	Kendall	60544	3415
Na-Au-Say Township	NasT	Will	60544	3337
* Naperville	NPVL	Will	60564	3202
* Naperville	NPVL	DuPage	60540	3141
Naperville Township	NpvT	DuPage	60540	3141
* New Lenox	NLNX	Will	60451	3501
New Lenox Township	NlxT	Will	60451	3590
Newport Township	NptT	Lake	60002	2360
New Trier Township	NTrT	Cook	60093	2812
* Niles	NLES	Cook	60714	2864
Nippersink Terrace		Lake	60081	2472
Nixon's Grnwd-Central		Cook	60025	2809
Nordic Park		DuPage	60143	2969
* Norridge	NRDG	Cook	60706	2974
* North Aurora	NARA	Kane	60542	3078
* North Barrington	NBRN	Lake	60010	2697
* Northbrook	NHBK	Cook	60062	2757
Northbrook West		Cook	60062	2756
* North Chicago	NCHI	Lake	60064	2536
* Northfield	NHFD	Cook	60093	2811
Northfield Township	NfdT	Cook	60025	2809
North Glen Ellyn		DuPage	60137	3025
North Hills		Lake	60060	2590
* Northlake	NHLK	Cook	60164	3028
North Libertyville Ests		Lake	60048	2591
North Plato		Kane	60140	2851
* North Riverside	NRIV	Cook	60546	3088
Northville Township	NvlT	La Salle	60548	3330
North Woods		DuPage	60185	3023
Norwood Park Twp	NpkT	Cook	60656	2918
Nottingham Woods		Kane	60119	3075
Novak Park		Kane	60175	2964
Nunda Township	NndT	McHenry	60012	2584
* Oak Brook	OKBK	DuPage	60523	3085
* Oakbrook Terrace	OKTR	DuPage	60181	3085
* Oak Forest	OKFT	Cook	60452	3347
Oak Knolls		Kane	60118	2747
* Oak Lawn	OKLN	Cook	60453	3211
Oak Manor		Kendall	60545	3259
Oak Meadows		DuPage	60185	2966
* Oak Park	OKPK	Cook	60304	3031
Oak Spring Woods		Lake	60048	2592
* Oakwood Hills	ODHL	McHenry	60013	2641
Oakwood Shores		McHenry	60097	2469
* Old Mill Creek	OMCK	Lake	60083	2419
* Olympia Fields	OMFD	Cook	60461	3506
Ontarioville		DuPage	60133	2911
Orchard Acres		McHenry	60014	2640
Orchard Estates		DuPage	60187	3082
Orchard Valley		Lake	60031	2477
* Orland Hills	ODHL	Cook	60487	3423
* Orland Park	ODPK	Will	60448	3503
* Orland Park	ODPK	Cook	60462	3345
Orland Township	OrlT	Cook	60467	3344
* Oswego	OSWG	Kendall	60543	3263
Oswego Township	OswT	Kendall	60543	3264
* Palatine	PLTN	Cook	60067	2752
Palatine Township	PltT	Cook	60074	2752
Palisades		DuPage	60527	3208
Palm Beach		Lake	60051	2472
* Palos Heights	PSHT	Cook	60463	3274
* Palos Hills	PSHL	Cook	60465	3274
* Palos Park	PSPK	Cook	60464	3274
Palos Township	PlsT	Cook	60464	3273
* Park City	PKCY	Lake	60085	2536
* Park Forest	PKFT	Cook	60466	3595
* Park Forest	PKFT	Will	60466	3594
* Park Ridge	PKRG	Cook	60068	2918
Pavillion		Kendall	60560	3332
Peerless		Will	60586	3416
* Peotone	PTON	Will	60468	3861
Peotone Township	PtnT	Will	60468	3861
Pepper Tree		Cook	60067	2752
Petite Lake		Lake	60002	2416
Pheasant Hollow		DuPage	60187	3082
Pheasant Ridge		Will	60564	3266
* Phoenix	PHNX	Cook	60426	3350
Picadilly Terrace		DuPage	60527	3207
Pikeville		Kenosha	53142	2359
Pinecrest		Will	60435	3417
Pinehurst Manor		Cook	60074	2753
* Pingree Grove	PGGV	Kane	60140	2797
Pistakee Bay		Lake	60051	2472
Pistakee Highlands		McHenry	60050	2472
Pistakee Hills		McHenry	60050	2472
* Plainfield	PNFD	Kendall	60585	3337
* Plainfield	PNFD	Will	60544	3338
Plainfield Acres		Will	60544	3416
Plainfield Township	PnfT	Will	60544	3339
* Plano	PLNO	Kendall	60545	3259
Plato Center		Kane	60124	2851
Plato Township	PltT	Kane	60124	2852
Pleasantdale Estates		DuPage	60439	3206
Pleasant Hill		DuPage	60187	3023
Pleasant Hills		Cook	60193	2912
* Pleasant Prairie	PTPR	Kenosha	53158	2362
Plum Grove Estates		Cook	60067	2806
* Port Barrington	PTBR	McHenry	60010	2642
* Port Barrington	PTBR	Lake	60010	2643
* Posen	POSN	Cook	60469	3349
* Prairie Grove	PRGV	McHenry	60012	2585
Prairie View		Lake	60069	2701
Prestbury		Kane	60506	3136
Preston Heights		Will	60436	3587
Prestwick		Will	60423	3592
* Prospect Heights	PTHT	Cook	60070	2808
Providence Oaks		Lake	60031	2535
Providence Village		Lake	60031	2535
Proviso Township	PvsT	Cook	60558	3086
Rainbow Hills		Kane	60175	2963
Randall, Town of	RdlT	Kenosha	53181	2355
Rawson Bridge		McHenry	60013	2642
Reed Township	RedT	Will	60408	4031
Regency Grove		DuPage	60516	3144
Resthaven		Will	60481	3943
* Richmond	RHMD	McHenry	60071	2412
Richmond Township	RcmT	McHenry	60071	2352
* Richton Park	RNPK	Cook	60471	3594
Rich Township	RchT	Cook	60443	3593
Ridgefield		McHenry	60012	2583
Ridgewood East		Cook	60452	3347
Riley Township	RlyT	McHenry	60152	2634
Ring Neck		Kendall	60543	3264
* Ringwood	RGWD	McHenry	60072	2470
* Riverdale	RVDL	Cook	60827	3350
* River Forest	RVFT	Cook	60305	3030
River Grange Lakes		Kane	60175	2908
* River Grove	RVGV	Cook	60171	2974
* Riverside	RVSD	Cook	60546	3088
Riverside Lawns		Cook	60534	3088
Riverside Township	RvsT	Cook	60534	3088
* Riverwoods	RVWD	Lake	60015	2755
* Robbins	RBBN	Cook	60472	3348
* Rockdale	RKDL	Will	60436	3498
* Rolling Meadows	RGMW	Cook	60008	2806
* Romeoville	RMVL	Will	60446	3341
Rondout		Lake	60044	2592
Ron Lee		Will	60404	3584
Rooney Heights		Will	60435	3497
Root Spring		McHenry	60013	2695
Rosecrans		Lake	60083	2419
Rose Hill		DuPage	60516	3206
* Roselle	ROSL	DuPage	60172	2913
* Roselle	ROSL	Cook	60172	2913
* Rosemont	RSMT	Cook	60018	2917
* Round Lake	RDLK	Lake	60073	2531
* Round Lake Beach	RLKB	Lake	60073	2475
* Round Lake Heights	RLKH	Lake	60073	2474
* Round Lake Park	RLKP	Lake	60073	2532
Russell		Lake	60099	2361
Rutland Township	RtdT	Kane	60142	2745
* St. Charles	SCRL	DuPage	60174	2965

*Indicates incorporated city

Cities and Communities

Community Name	Abbr.	County	ZIP Code	Map Page
* St. Charles	SCRL	Kane	60174	2964
St. Charles Township	SchT	Kane	60175	2907
* St. John	SJHN	Lake	46373	3598
St. John Township	SjnT	Lake	46311	3687
Salem, Town of	SlmT	Kenosha	53179	2357
* Sandwich	SDWH	Kendall	60548	3258
* Sandwich	SDWH	DeKalb	60548	3330
Sandwich Township	SdwT	DeKalb	60548	3258
Santa Fe Park		Cook	60480	3208
* Sauk Village	SLVL	Cook	60411	3597
* Schaumburg	SMBG	Cook	60193	2859
* Schaumburg	SMBG	DuPage	60172	2912
Schaumburg Township	SmbT	Cook	60193	2913
* Schiller Park	SRPK	Cook	60176	2973
Seneca Township	SenT	McHenry	60180	2635
Seward Township	SwdT	Kendall	60447	3495
Shady Hill		Lake	60010	2696
Sherwood Oaks		Cook	60120	2856
Shields Township	ShdT	Lake	60044	2593
Shore Heights Manor		Kendall	60543	3263
Shore Hills		McHenry	60097	2469
* Shorewood	SRWD	Will	60404	3496
Silver Lake		McHenry	60013	2641
Sixty Six Court		Cook	60452	3347
* Skokie	SKOK	Cook	60077	2865
* Sleepy Hollow	SYHW	Kane	60118	2800
Solon Mills		McHenry	60071	2413
* South Barrington	SBTN	Cook	60010	2803
* South Chicago Hts	SCHT	Cook	60411	3596
* South Elgin	SEGN	Kane	60177	2908
* South Holland	SHLD	Cook	60473	3428
Southmoor		Cook	60464	3346
Spencer		Will	60451	3589
* Spring Grove	SPGV	McHenry	60081	2413
Steeple Run		DuPage	60540	3142
* Steger	STGR	Cook	60475	3596
* Steger	STGR	Will	60475	3596
* Stickney	SKNY	Cook	60402	3089
Stickney Township	StkT	Cook	60402	3089
Stillmeadow		Kane	60119	3017
Stonebrook		Lake	60031	2477
* Stone Park	SNPK	Cook	60165	3029
Storybrook		Kendall	60512	3262
* Streamwood	SMWD	Cook	60107	2857
Suburban Estates		DuPage	60517	3143
* Sugar Grove	SRGV	Kane	60554	3135
Sugar Grove Township	SgrT	Kane	60554	3197
* Summit	SMMT	Cook	60501	3148
Sunny Crest		Cook	60422	3507
Sunset Hills		Cook	60193	2913
Swift		DuPage	60148	2969
Sylvan Hill		Cook	60462	3345
Sylvan Lake		Lake	60060	2645
Tenerelli		Kane	60511	3134
Terra Cotta		McHenry	60012	2584
The Knolls		Kane	60175	2961
The Meadows		DuPage	60532	3143
* Third Lake	TDLK	Lake	60030	2476
* Thornton	TNTN	Cook	60476	3428
Thornton Township	ThtT	Cook	60476	3429
Timberlake Estates		DuPage	60527	3207
Timberline		Will	60431	3497
Timber Ridge		DuPage	60185	2967
* Tinley Park	TYPK	Will	60477	3504
* Tinley Park	TYPK	Cook	60477	3425
* Tower Lakes	TRLK	Lake	60010	2643
Trevor		Kenosha	53179	2357
Tri-State Village		DuPage	60527	3207
Triumvera		Cook	60025	2809
* Trout Valley	TVLY	McHenry	60013	2695
Troy Township	TroT	Will	60404	3583
Turnberry		McHenry	60014	2693
Turner Camp		McHenry	60102	2695
* Twin Lakes	TNLK	Kenosha	53181	2354
Udina		Kane	60124	2853
* Union	UNON	McHenry	60180	2635
* University Park	UYPK	Cook	60471	3594
* University Park	UYPK	Will	60466	3684
Valley View		Kane	60174	2908
Valley View		DuPage	60137	3083
Venetian Village		Lake	60046	2475
* Vernon Hills	VNHL	Lake	60061	2647
Vernon Township	VrnT	Lake	60045	2648
Village Square		DuPage	60516	3206
* Villa Park	VLPK	DuPage	60181	3027
* Volo	VOLO	Lake	60073	2587
Voltz Lake		Kenosha	53179	2358
Wacker		Kendall	60560	3333
* Wadsworth	WDWH	Lake	60083	2420
--Walworth County	WthC			
Warren Township	WrnT	Lake	60031	2534
* Warrenville	WNVL	DuPage	60555	3080
Wasco		Kane	60175	2962
Washington Township	WshT	Will	60401	3864
* Wauconda	WCDA	Lake	60084	2643
Wauconda Township	WcnT	Lake	60073	2587
* Waukegan	WKGN	Lake	60085	2537
Waukegan Township	WkgT	Lake	60099	2480
* Wayne	WYNE	DuPage	60184	2965
* Wayne	WYNE	Kane	60184	2909
Wayne Center		DuPage	60103	2967
Wayne Township	WynT	DuPage	60185	2967
Wedges Corner		Lake	60046	2476
Wellington Heights		Will	60404	3496
Wesley Township	WslT	Will	60481	3943
Westaway		Kane	60506	3199
* Westchester	WSTR	Cook	60154	3029
* West Chicago	WCHI	DuPage	60185	3022
Westdale Gardens		Cook	60126	3086
West Deerfield Twp	WdfT	Lake	60015	2703
* West Dundee	WDND	Kane	60118	2801
* Western Springs	WNSP	Cook	60558	3086
West Glenview		Cook	60025	2810
West Miltmore		Lake	60046	2475
* Westmont	WTMT	DuPage	60559	3145
Wheatland Township	WldT	Will	60585	3266
Wheatland View		Will	60564	3203
* Wheaton	WHTN	DuPage	60187	3024
* Wheeling	WLNG	Cook	60090	2755
* Wheeling	WLNG	Lake	60089	2754
Wheeling Township	WhlT	Cook	60056	2808
Whiskey Creek		DuPage	60185	3022
White Oaks Bay		McHenry	60097	2469
White Pines		DuPage	60126	2971
Wideview		Kane	60175	2962
Wildrose		Kane	60174	2963
Wildwood		Lake	60030	2533
Wildwood		Kane	60506	3136
Wildwood Valley		Kane	60124	2799
--Will County	WilC			
Williams Park		Lake	60084	2643
Willowbrook		Will	60417	3598
Willowbrook		Kendall	60512	3262
* Willowbrook	WLBK	DuPage	60527	3207
* Willow Springs	WLSP	Cook	60480	3209
Will Township	WllT	Will	60468	3861
* Wilmette	WLMT	Cook	60091	2812
* Wilmington	WMTN	Will	60481	3943
Wilmington Township	WmTp	Will	60481	3763
Wilmot		Kenosha	53192	2356
Wilton Township	WltT	Will	60442	3767
Winden Oak		Kane	60119	3017
Windings		Kane	60175	2961
* Winfield	WNFD	DuPage	60190	3023
Winfield Township	WnfT	DuPage	60510	3079
* Winnetka	WNKA	Cook	60093	2812
* Winthrop Harbor	WPHR	Lake	60096	2363
* Wonder Lake	WRLK	McHenry	60097	2469
Wonder View		McHenry	60097	2469
Wonder Woods		McHenry	60097	2469
* Wood Dale	WDDL	DuPage	60191	2915
Wooded Shores		McHenry	60097	2469
* Woodridge	WDRG	Will	60517	3270
* Woodridge	WDRG	DuPage	60517	3205
Woodridge Twn Cntre		DuPage	60517	3205
* Woodstock	WDSK	McHenry	60098	2581
* Worth	WRTH	Cook	60482	3274
Worth Township	WthT	Cook	60463	3275
York Center		DuPage	60148	3084
Yorkfield		DuPage	60126	3027
York Township	YkTp	DuPage	60126	3028
* Yorkville	YKVL	Kendall	60560	3333
Zenda		Walworth	53147	2349
* Zion	ZION	Lake	60099	2422

*Indicates incorporated city

List of Abbreviations

Admin	Administration
Agri	Agricultural
Ag	Agriculture
AFB	Air Force Base
Arpt	Airport
Al	Alley
Amer	American
Anx	Annex
Arc	Arcade
Arch	Archaeological
Aud	Auditorium
Avd	Avenida
Av	Avenue
Bfld	Battlefield
Bch	Beach
Bnd	Bend
Bio	Biological
Blf	Bluff
Blvd	Boulevard
Brch	Branch
Br	Bridge
Brk	Brook
Bldg	Building
Bur	Bureau
Byp	Bypass
Bywy	Byway
Cl	Calle
Cljn	Callejon
Cmto	Caminito
Cm	Camino
Cap	Capitol
Cath	Cathedral
Cswy	Causeway
Cem	Cemetery
Ctr	Center
Ctr	Centre
Cir	Circle
Crlo	Circulo
CH	City Hall
Clf	Cliff
Clfs	Cliffs
Clb	Club
Cltr	Cluster
Col	Coliseum
Coll	College
Com	Common
Coms	Commons
Comm	Community
Co.	Company
Cons	Conservation
Conv & Vis Bur	Convention and Visitors Bureau
Cor	Corner
Cors	Corners
Corp	Corporation
Corr	Corridor
Cte	Corte
CC	Country Club
Co	County
Ct	Court
Ct Hse	Court House
Cts	Courts
Cr	Creek
Cres	Crescent
Cross	Crossing
Curv	Curve
Cto	Cut Off
Dept	Department
Dev	Development
Diag	Diagonal
Div	Division
Dr	Drive
Drwy	Driveway
E	East
El	Elevation
Env	Environmental
Est	Estate
Ests	Estates
Exh	Exhibition
Expm	Experimental
Expo	Exposition
Expwy	Expressway
Ext	Extension
Frgds	Fairgrounds
ft	Feet
Fy	Ferry
Fld	Field
Flds	Fields
Flt	Flat
Flts	Flats
For	Forest
Fk	Fork
Ft	Fort
Found	Foundation
Frwy	Freeway
Gdn	Garden
Gdns	Gardens
Gen Hosp	General Hospital
Gln	Glen
GC	Golf Course
Grn	Green
Grds	Grounds
Grv	Grove
Hbr	Harbor/Harbour
Hvn	Haven
HQs	Headquarters
Ht	Height
Hts	Heights
HS	High School
Hwy	Highway
Hl	Hill
Hls	Hills
Hist	Historical
Hllw	Hollow
Hosp	Hospital
Hse	House
Ind Res	Indian Reservation
Info	Information
Inst	Institute
Int'l	International
I	Island
Is	Islands
Isl	Isle
Jct	Junction
Knl	Knoll
Knls	Knolls
Lk	Lake
Lndg	Landing
Ln	Lane
Lib	Library
Ldg	Lodge
Lp	Loop
Mnr	Manor
Mkt	Market
Mdw	Meadow
Mdws	Meadows
Med	Medical
Mem	Memorial
Metro	Metropolitan
Mw	Mews
Mil	Military
Ml	Mill
Mls	Mills
Mon	Monument
Mtwy	Motorway
Mnd	Mound
Mnds	Mounds
Mt	Mount
Mtn	Mountain
Mtns	Mountains
Mun	Municipal
Mus	Museum
Nat'l	National
Nat'l For	National Forest
Nat'l Hist Pk	National Historic Park
Nat'l Hist Site	National Historic Site
Nat'l Mon	National Monument
Nat'l Park	National Park
Nat'l Rec Area	National Recreation Area
Nat'l Wld Ref	National Wildlife Refuge
Nat	Natural
NAS	Naval Air Station
Nk	Nook
N	North
Orch	Orchard
Ohwy	Outer Highway
Ovl	Oval
Ovlk	Overlook
Ovps	Overpass
Pk	Park
Pkwy	Parkway
Pas	Paseo
Psg	Passage
Pass	Passenger
Pth	Path
Pn	Pine
Pns	Pines
Pl	Place
Pln	Plain
Plns	Plains
Plgnd	Playground
Plz	Plaza
Pt	Point
Pnd	Pond
PO	Post Office
Pres	Preserve
Prov	Provincial
Rwy	Railway
Rec	Recreation
Reg	Regional
Res	Reservoir
Rst	Rest
Rdg	Ridge
Rd	Road
Rds	Roads
St.	Saint
Ste.	Sainte
Sci	Science
Sci	Sciences
Sci	Scientific
Shop Ctr	Shopping Center
Shr	Shore
Shrs	Shores
Skwy	Skyway
S	South
Spr	Spring
Sprs	Springs
Sq	Square
Stad	Stadium
St For	State Forest
St Hist Site	State Historic Site
St Nat Area	State Natural Area
St Pk	State Park
St Rec Area	State Recreation Area
Sta	Station
St	Street
Smt	Summit
Sys	Systems
Tech	Technical
Tech	Technological
Tech	Technology
Ter	Terrace
Terr	Territory
Theol	Theological
Thwy	Throughway
Toll Fy	Toll Ferry
TIC	Tourist Information Center
Trc	Trace
Trfwy	Trafficway
Tr	Trail
Tun	Tunnel
Tpk	Turnpike
Unps	Underpass
Univ	University
Vly	Valley
Vet	Veterans
Vw	View
Vil	Village
Wk	Walk
Wall	Wall
Wy	Way
W	West
WMA	Wildlife Management Area

Chicago 7-County Street Index

HIGHWAYS

- **ALT** - Alternate Route
- **BIA** - Bureau of Indian Affairs
- **BUS** - Business Route
- **CO** - County Highway/Road
- **FM** - Farm To Market Road
- **HIST** - Historic Highway
- **I** - Interstate Highway
- **LP** - State Loop
- **PK** - Park & Recreation Road
- **PROV** - Provincial Highway
- **RTE** - Other Route
- **SPR** - State Spur
- **SR** - State Route/Highway
- **TCH** - Trans-Canada Highway
- **US** - United States Highway

STREET Block	City	ZIP	Map#	CGS	Grid
CO-1					
10	NPVL	60563	3141	28W-6S	A4
10	WNVL	60555	3081	28W-3S	A7
100	NPVL	60564	3203	27W-9S	B3
100	NPVL	60565	3203	28W-9S	B3
100	NpvT	60564	3203	28W-9S	B3
100	NpvT	60565	3203	28W-9S	B4
300	NPVL	60563	3140	29W-4S	E1
CO-1 Ferry Rd					
200	WNVL	60555	3081	28W-4S	A7
CO-1 Plainfield-Naperville Rd					
100	NPVL	60564	3203	28W-9S	B3
100	NPVL	60565	3203	28W-9S	B3
100	NpvT	60564	3203	28W-9S	B3
400	NpvT	60565	3203	27W-8S	B3
CO-1 Raymond Dr					
300	NPVL	60563	3140	29W-4S	E1
CO-1 River Rd					
10	NPVL	60563	3140	28W-5S	E4
10	NPVL	60563	3141	28W-6S	A4
10	WNVL	60555	3081	28W-3S	A7
CO-2					
10	CmpT	60124	2905	43W-7N	B5
10	CmpT	60151	2905	43W-7N	B5
10	CmpT	60175	2905	41W-6N	E6
10	CmpT	60175	2962	40W-6N	B1
10	DRGV	60515	3083	21W-4S	E7
10	DRGV	60532	3083	21W-4S	E7
10	LslT	60517	3143	22W-7S	C7
10	LslT	60532	3083	21W-4S	E7
10	LslT	60532	3084	21W-4S	A7
10	LslT	60540	3143	23W-7S	B7
10	LslT	60540	3204	26W-8S	A1
10	PltT	60124	2905	43W-7N	C5
10	PltT	60151	2905	43W-7N	C5
10	WDRG	60517	3143	23W-7S	B7
100	CmpT	60175	2906	41W-6N	A7
100	NPVL	60540	3204	25W-8S	C1
100	WDRG	60540	3143	23W-7S	A7
400	LslT	60565	3204	25W-8S	B1
400	NPVL	60565	3204	25W-8S	B1
400	PltT	60140	2905	43W-7N	C5
500	LslT	60540	3205	23W-7S	A1
3000	DRGV	60515	3084	20W-3S	B5
4400	DRGV	60515	3143	21W-4S	E1
5600	DRGV	60516	3143	21W-6S	E4
5600	LslT	60515	3143	21W-6S	E4
5600	LslT	60516	3143	21W-6S	E4
CO-2 Belmont Rd					
4400	DRGV	60515	3143	21W-4S	E1
5600	DRGV	60516	3143	21W-6S	E4
5600	LslT	60515	3143	21W-6S	E4
5600	LslT	60516	3143	21W-6S	E4
CO-2 Burlington Rd					
10	CmpT	60124	2905	43W-7N	B5
10	CmpT	60151	2905	43W-7N	B5
10	CmpT	60175	2905	41W-6N	E6
10	CmpT	60175	2962	40W-6N	B1
10	PltT	60124	2905	43W-7N	C5
10	PltT	60151	2905	43W-7N	C5
100	CmpT	60175	2906	41W-6N	A7
400	PltT	60140	2905	43W-7N	C5
CO-2 Finley Rd					
-	DRGV	60515	3143	21W-4S	E1
10	DRGV	60515	3083	21W-4S	E7
10	DRGV	60532	3083	21W-4S	E7
10	LslT	60532	3083	21W-4S	E7
10	LslT	60532	3084	21W-4S	A7
3000	DRGV	60515	3084	20W-3S	B5
CO-2 Hobson Rd					
10	LslT	60517	3143	22W-7S	C7
10	LslT	60540	3143	23W-7S	B7
10	LslT	60540	3204	26W-8S	A1
10	WDRG	60517	3143	23W-7S	B7
100	NPVL	60540	3204	25W-8S	C1
100	WDRG	60540	3143	23W-7S	A7
400	LslT	60565	3204	25W-8S	B1
400	NPVL	60565	3204	25W-8S	B1
500	LslT	60540	3205	23W-7S	A1
2200	DRGV	60516	3143	21W-6S	E4
2200	LslT	60516	3143	21W-6S	E4
CO-3					
10	HPSR	60140	2795	46W-16N	E1
10	HPSR	60140	2796	45W-16N	B1
10	HshT	60140	2796	45W-16N	B1
10	NPVL	60532	3082	25W-4S	B7
10	NPVL	60563	3082	25W-4S	B7
100	LslT	60563	3081	26W-4S	D7
300	NPVL	60555	3140	28W-4S	E1
300	NPVL	60563	3140	28W-4S	E1
300	WNVL	60555	3081	26W-4S	E7
300	WNVL	60555	3140	28W-4S	E1
300	WNVL	60563	3140	28W-4S	E1
400	DRGV	60532	3143	22W-4S	D1
400	LSLE	60532	3143	21W-4S	D1
400	LslT	60532	3143	21W-4S	D1
400	NPVL	60555	3081	26W-4S	E7
400	NPVL	60563	3081	26W-4S	E7
400	WNVL	60563	3081	27W-3S	C7
500	LslT	60563	3082	25W-4S	B7
500	WNVL	60555	3141	28W-4S	A1
700	LSLE	60532	3083	23W-4S	E7
1400	LSLE	60532	3083	23W-4S	A7
1400	LslT	60532	3083	23W-4S	A7
1600	LslT	60532	3082	23W-4S	E7
2100	LSLE	60532	3142	24W-4S	D1
2200	DRGV	60515	3143	21W-4S	E1
2600	LSLE	60515	3143	21W-4S	D1
CO-3 Allen Rd					
10	HPSR	60140	2795	46W-16N	E1
10	HPSR	60140	2796	45W-16N	B1
10	HshT	60140	2796	45W-16N	B1
CO-3 Ferry Rd					
-	WNVL	60555	3081	28W-4S	A7
-	WNVL	60555	3141	28W-4S	A1
CO-3 River Rd					
300	NPVL	60555	3140	28W-4S	E1
300	NPVL	60563	3140	28W-4S	E1
300	WNVL	60555	3140	28W-4S	E1
300	WNVL	60563	3140	28W-4S	E1
500	WNVL	60555	3141	28W-4S	A1
CO-3 Warrenville Rd					
10	LSLE	60532	3082	25W-4S	B7
10	NPVL	60532	3082	25W-4S	B7
10	NPVL	60563	3082	25W-4S	B7
200	WNVL	60563	3081	27W-4S	D7
300	WNVL	60555	3081	26W-4S	E7
400	DRGV	60532	3143	22W-4S	D1
400	LSLE	60532	3143	21W-4S	D1
400	LslT	60532	3143	21W-4S	D1
400	NPVL	60555	3081	26W-4S	E7
400	NPVL	60563	3081	26W-4S	E7
500	LslT	60563	3082	25W-4S	B7
1400	LSLE	60532	3083	23W-4S	A7
1400	LslT	60532	3083	23W-4S	A7
1600	LslT	60532	3082	23W-4S	E7
2100	LSLE	60532	3142	24W-4S	D1
2200	DRGV	60515	3143	21W-4S	E1
2600	LSLE	60515	3143	21W-4S	D1
CO-3 E Warrenville Rd					
1000	LslT	60563	3081	26W-4S	E7
1000	NPVL	60563	3081	26W-4S	E7
1000	NPVL	60563	3082	26W-4S	A7
1100	LslT	60563	3082	25W-4S	A7
CO-3 W Warrenville Rd					
100	LslT	60563	3081	26W-4S	D7
100	NPVL	60555	3081	27W-4S	D7
100	NPVL	60563	3081	27W-4S	D7
100	WNVL	60555	3081	27W-4S	D7
100	WNVL	60563	3081	27W-4S	D7
CO-4					
10	GNEN	60137	3025	23W-1N	A3
10	GNEN	60187	3025	23W-1N	A3
10	ROSL	60172	2913	23W-7N	A5
10	WHTN	60187	3025	23W-1N	A3
100	BMDL	60108	2913	23W-5N	A7
100	BMDL	60108	2969	23W-4N	A2
100	MltT	60137	3025	23W-1N	A3
100	MltT	60188	3025	23W-1N	A3
100	SgrT	60554	3134	44W-4S	E1
200	BMDL	60139	2969	23W-4N	A3
200	BMDL	60172	2913	23W-6N	A6
300	GLHT	60137	3025	23W-2N	A1
300	GLHT	60139	3025	23W-2N	A1
300	MltT	60139	3025	23W-1N	A2
300	ROSL	60108	2913	23W-6N	A6
300	SgrT	60554	3135	43W-4S	A2
300	SRGV	60554	3134	43W-4S	E2
300	SRGV	60554	3135	43W-4S	A2
1200	BmdT	60137	3025	23W-2N	A1
1200	BmdT	60139	3025	23W-2N	A1
1200	BmdT	60188	3025	23W-2N	A1
1400	BmdT	60137	2969	23W-2N	A7
1400	BmdT	60139	2969	23W-2N	A7
1400	GLHT	60137	2969	23W-2N	A7
1400	GLHT	60139	2969	23W-2N	A7
2100	GLHT	60108	2969	23W-4N	A3
CO-4 Bloomingdale Rd					
10	GNEN	60137	3025	23W-1N	A3
10	GNEN	60187	3025	23W-1N	A3
10	WHTN	60187	3025	23W-1N	A3
100	MltT	60137	3025	23W-1N	A3
100	MltT	60188	3025	23W-1N	A3
300	GLHT	60137	3025	23W-2N	A1
300	GLHT	60139	3025	23W-2N	A1
300	MltT	60139	3025	23W-1N	A2
1200	BmdT	60137	3025	23W-2N	A1
1200	BmdT	60139	3025	23W-2N	A1
1200	BmdT	60188	3025	23W-2N	A1
1400	BmdT	60137	2969	23W-2N	A7
1400	BmdT	60139	2969	23W-2N	A7
1400	GLHT	60137	2969	23W-2N	A7
1400	GLHT	60139	2969	23W-2N	A7
2100	BMDL	60108	2969	23W-4N	A3
2100	BMDL	60139	2969	23W-4N	A3
2100	GLHT	60108	2969	23W-4N	A3
CO-4 N Bloomingdale Rd					
100	BMDL	60108	2913	23W-5N	A7
100	BMDL	60108	2969	23W-4N	A2
200	BMDL	60172	2913	23W-6N	A6
CO-4 S Bloomingdale Rd					
-	GLHT	60139	2969	23W-4N	A3
100	BMDL	60108	2969	23W-5N	A1
200	BMDL	60139	2969	23W-4N	A3
CO-4 Harter Rd					
100	SgrT	60554	3134	44W-4S	E1
300	SgrT	60554	3135	43W-4S	A2
300	SRGV	60554	3134	43W-4S	E2
300	SRGV	60554	3135	43W-4S	A2
CO-4 Roselle Rd					
300	BMDL	60108	2913	23W-6N	A6
300	BMDL	60172	2913	23W-6N	A6
300	ROSL	60108	2913	23W-6N	A6
300	ROSL	60172	2913	23W-6N	A6
CO-4 N Roselle Rd					
300	ROSL	60172	2913	23W-7N	A3
CO-4 S Roselle Rd					
10	ROSL	60172	2913	23W-7N	A5
700	BMDL	60108	2913	23W-6N	A6
700	ROSL	60108	2913	23W-6N	A6
CO-5					
10	CmpT	60124	2905	42W-7N	E6
10	CmpT	60151	2905	41W-6N	E6
10	CmpT	60175	2905	42W-7N	D6
10	CmpT	60175	2906	40W-7N	B6
10	MltT	60137	3083	22W-1S	C2
10	SchT	60175	2907	38W-6N	B6
10	SchT	60177	2907	38W-6N	B6
10	SEGN	60177	2907	38W-6N	B6
100	GLHT	60139	3025	22W-1N	C2
100	SchT	60175	2908	36W-6N	A6
200	GNEN	60137	3083	22W-1S	C2
300	BMDL	60108	2969	22W-3N	C5
300	BMDL	60139	2969	22W-3N	C5
300	GLHT	60139	2969	22W-3N	C5
300	MltT	60137	3025	22W-1N	C2
400	BmdT	60101	2969	22W-3N	C6
400	BmdT	60139	2969	22W-3N	C6
400	GLHT	60101	2969	22W-3N	C6
400	MltT	60532	3083	22W-3S	B6
500	GLHT	60137	3025	22W-1N	C2
500	MltT	60139	3025	22W-1N	C2
700	CmpT	60175	2907	38W-6N	A6
700	SEGN	60175	2907	38W-6N	B6
800	GNEN	60137	3025	22W-1N	C3
1300	BmdT	60139	3025	22W-2N	C1
CO-5 Glen Ellyn Rd					
-	GLHT	60137	3025	22W-1N	C1
100	GLHT	60139	3025	22W-2N	C1
300	BMDL	60108	2969	22W-3N	C5
300	BMDL	60139	2969	22W-3N	C5
300	GLHT	60139	2969	22W-3N	C5
400	BmdT	60101	2969	22W-3N	C6
400	BmdT	60139	2969	22W-3N	C6
400	GLHT	60101	2969	22W-3N	C6
1300	BmdT	60139	3025	22W-2N	C1
CO-5 Main St					
300	MltT	60137	3025	22W-1N	C2
500	GLHT	60137	3025	22W-1N	C2
500	GLHT	60139	3025	22W-1N	C2
500	MltT	60139	3025	22W-1N	C2
CO-5 N Main St					
800	GNEN	60137	3025	22W-1N	C3
800	MltT	60137	3025	22W-1N	C3
CO-5 Park Blvd					
10	MltT	60137	3083	22W-3S	B5
200	GNEN	60137	3083	22W-2S	C3
400	MltT	60532	3083	22W-3S	B6
CO-5 S Park Blvd					
400	GNEN	60137	3083	22W-1S	C2
400	MltT	60137	3083	22W-1S	C2
CO-5 Silver Glen Rd					
10	CmpT	60124	2905	42W-7N	E6
10	CmpT	60151	2905	41W-6N	E6
10	CmpT	60175	2905	42W-7N	D6
10	CmpT	60175	2906	40W-7N	B6
10	SchT	60175	2907	38W-6N	B6
10	SchT	60177	2907	38W-6N	B6
10	SEGN	60177	2907	38W-6N	B6
100	SchT	60175	2908	36W-6N	A6
700	CmpT	60175	2907	38W-6N	A6
700	SEGN	60175	2907	38W-6N	B6
CO-6					
10	GLBT	60118	2746	39W-18N	A4
10	GLBT	60136	2746	38W-17N	A7
10	GLBT	60136	2799	38W-16N	A1
10	RtdT	60118	2746	39W-17N	A7
10	RtdT	60136	2746	39W-18N	A4
10	RtdT	60142	2746	39W-18N	A4
200	WynT	60103	2910	28W-7N	E5
400	BRLT	60103	2910	28W-6N	E6
400	BRLT	60103	2966	28W-5N	E1
400	WynT	60103	2966	28W-5N	E1
CO-6 S Bartlett Rd					
200	WynT	60103	2910	28W-7N	E5
400	BRLT	60103	2910	28W-6N	E6
400	BRLT	60103	2966	28W-5N	E1
400	WynT	60103	2966	28W-5N	E1
CO-6 Galligan Rd					
10	GLBT	60118	2746	39W-18N	A4
10	GLBT	60136	2746	39W-17N	A7
10	GLBT	60136	2799	39W-16N	A1
10	RtdT	60118	2746	39W-17N	A7
10	RtdT	60136	2746	39W-18N	A4
10	RtdT	60142	2746	39W-18N	A4
CO-7					
10	BmdT	60188	3023	26W-2N	E2
10	BmdT	60188	3024	25W-1N	A2
10	CLSM	60188	3023	26W-2N	E2
10	CLSM	60188	3024	23W-1N	E2
10	GNEN	60137	3025	22W-1N	B3
10	MltT	60188	3024	23W-1N	E2
10	PGGV	60140	2798	40W-14N	B6
10	PltT	60140	2798	40W-13N	B7
10	RtdT	60140	2798	40W-14N	C5
10	WynT	60188	3023	27W-2N	D1
100	WynT	60185	3023	27W-2N	C1
300	MltT	60188	3025	23W-1N	A3
400	LMBD	60148	3025	21W-0N	E3
400	MltT	60137	3025	21W-0N	D3
400	MltT	60148	3025	21W-1N	D3
600	LMBD	60148	3026	21W-0N	A3
600	MltT	60148	3026	21W-0N	A3
CO-7 Damisch Rd					
10	PGGV	60140	2798	40W-14N	B6
10	RtdT	60140	2798	40W-14N	B5
CO-7 Geneva Rd					
500	GNEN	60137	3025	22W-1N	C3
500	MltT	60137	3025	22W-1N	C3
CO-7 Reinking Rd					
10	PGGV	60140	2798	40W-14N	B7
10	PltT	60140	2798	40W-13N	B7
CO-7 St. Charles Rd					
10	BmdT	60188	3023	26W-2N	E2
10	BmdT	60188	3024	25W-1N	A2
10	CLSM	60188	3023	26W-2N	E2
10	CLSM	60188	3024	25W-1N	A2
10	MltT	60188	3024	23W-1N	E2
10	WynT	60188	3023	27W-2N	D1
100	WynT	60185	3023	27W-2N	C1
300	MltT	60188	3025	23W-1N	A3
400	LMBD	60148	3025	21W-0N	E3
400	MltT	60137	3025	21W-0N	D3
400	MltT	60148	3025	21W-1N	D3
600	GNEN	60137	3025	21W-0N	D3
CO-7 W St. Charles Rd					
600	LMBD	60148	3026	21W-0N	A3
600	MltT	60148	3026	21W-0N	A3
700	LMBD	60148	3025	21W-0N	E3
700	MltT	60148	3025	21W-0N	E3
CO-8					
10	BbyT	60134	3018	39W-0S	D7
10	BTVA	60134	3019	37W-0S	C6
10	BTVA	60134	3020	35W-0S	B7
10	BTVA	60510	3019	37W-0S	C6
10	BTVA	60510	3020	34W-0S	E6
10	GNVA	60134	3020	35W-0S	C6
10	GNVA	60510	3020	35W-0S	C6
10	GnvT	60134	3018	39W-0S	E7
10	GnvT	60134	3019	37W-0S	C7
10	GnvT	60134	3020	34W-0S	E6
100	BbyT	60119	3076	39W-0S	D1
100	BbyT	60510	3076	40W-1S	C2
100	GNVA	60134	3019	37W-0S	D6
100	GnvT	60510	3019	37W-0S	C7
200	BNVL	60106	2915	15W-5N	E7
300	BbyT	60119	3018	39W-0S	D7
300	CHCG	60106	2915	15W-5N	E7
300	GnvT	60510	3020	34W-0S	C6
800	EGVV	60106	2915	15W-7N	E4
1400	BTVA	60510	3021	33W-0N	B6
1400	GnvT	60134	3021	33W-0S	A6
1400	GnvT	60510	3021	33W-0N	B6
1800	WCHI	60185	3021	33W-0N	B6
2300	EGvT	60007	2915	16W-7N	E3
2300	EGVV	60007	2915	16W-7N	E3
2700	OKBK	60523	3086	15W-3S	B5
3600	HNDL	60521	3086	15W-3S	B6
3700	OKBK	60521	3086	15W-3S	B6
5400	DGvT	60521	3146	16W-6S	A3
5400	HNDL	60521	3146	15W-7S	A7
5800	DGvT	60527	3146	16W-6S	A4
5900	BRRG	60527	3146	16W-6S	A5
6300	WLBK	60527	3146	15W-7S	A5
7200	DGvT	60527	3208	15W-8S	A1
7200	WLBK	60527	3208	16W-8S	A1
7600	BRRG	60527	3208	15W-8S	A2
CO-8 Elmhurst Rd					
2300	EGvT	60007	2915	16W-7N	E3
2300	EGVV	60007	2915	16W-7N	E3
CO-8 Fabyan Pkwy					
10	BbyT	60134	3018	39W-0S	D7
10	BTVA	60134	3019	37W-0S	C6
10	BTVA	60510	3019	37W-0S	C6
10	GnvT	60134	3018	39W-0S	E7
10	GnvT	60134	3019	37W-0S	C7
100	BbyT	60119	3076	39W-0S	D1
100	BbyT	60510	3076	40W-1S	C2
100	GNVA	60134	3019	37W-0S	D6
100	GnvT	60510	3019	37W-0S	C7
300	BbyT	60119	3018	39W-0S	D7
CO-8 E Fabyan Pkwy					
-	BTVA	60134	3020	35W-0S	B6
10	BTVA	60510	3020	34W-0S	E6
10	GNVA	60134	3020	35W-0S	C6
10	GNVA	60510	3020	35W-0S	C6
300	GnvT	60510	3020	34W-0S	C6
1100	GnvT	60134	3020	34W-0S	E6
1400	BTVA	60510	3021	33W-0N	B6
1400	GnvT	60134	3021	33W-0S	A6
1400	GnvT	60510	3021	33W-0N	B6
1800	WCHI	60185	3021	33W-0N	B6
CO-8 W Fabyan Pkwy					
-	GnvT	60510	3019	36W-0S	D6
10	BTVA	60134	3020	35W-0S	B7
10	BTVA	60510	3020	35W-0S	B7
10	GNVA	60134	3020	35W-0S	B7
10	GnvT	60134	3020	35W-0S	A7
800	GnvT	60510	3020	36W-0S	A7
1000	BTVA	60134	3019	36W-0S	E7
1000	BTVA	60510	3019	36W-0S	E7
1000	GNVA	60134	3019	36W-0S	E7
1000	GnvT	60134	3019	36W-0S	E7
CO-8 S Madison St					
5400	DGvT	60521	3146	16W-6S	A3
5400	HNDL	60521	3146	15W-7S	A7
5800	DGvT	60527	3146	16W-6S	A4
5900	BRRG	60527	3146	16W-6S	A5
6300	WLBK	60527	3146	15W-7S	A5
7200	DGvT	60527	3208	16W-8S	A1
7200	WLBK	60527	3208	16W-8S	A1
7600	BRRG	60527	3208	15W-8S	A2
CO-8 York Rd					
2700	OKBK	60523	3086	15W-3S	B5
3600	HNDL	60521	3086	15W-3S	B6
3700	OKBK	60521	3086	15W-3S	B6
CO-8 N York Rd					
200	BNVL	60106	2915	15W-5N	E7
300	CHCG	60106	2915	15W-5N	E7
800	EGVV	60007	2915	15W-7N	E4
800	EGVV	60106	2915	15W-7N	E4
CO-9					
10	DGvT	60439	3270	19W-12S	C1
10	DRGV	60516	3144	19W-6S	C4
10	WDRG	60439	3270	19W-12S	C3
10	WDRG	60517	3270	19W-12S	C3
200	DGvT	60439	3206	19W-11S	C7
200	DGvT	60517	3270	19W-12S	D3
200	DRN	60439	3206	19W-11S	C7
500	LMNT	60439	3270	19W-12S	C3
700	DGvT	60516	3206	19W-11S	C7
700	DGvT	60561	3206	19W-11S	C7
700	DRN	60516	3206	19W-11S	C7
700	DRN	60561	3206	19W-11S	C7
1100	GNVA	60134	3020	36W-1N	A3
1700	GNVA	60134	3019	36W-1N	E4
2900	LMBD	60148	3084	19W-2S	C4
2900	LMBD	60515	3084	19W-2S	C4
2900	YkTp	60148	3084	19W-2S	C4
2900	YkTp	60515	3084	19W-2S	C4
3200	DRGV	60515	3084	19W-3S	C6
5500	DRGV	60515	3144	19W-6S	C4
7100	DRGV	60516	3206	19W-8S	C1
7300	WDRG	60516	3206	19W-8S	C1
7500	DRN	60517	3206	19W-8S	C2
7500	WDRG	60517	3206	19W-8S	C2
7500	WDRG	60561	3206	19W-8S	C2
7600	DGvT	60517	3206	19W-8S	C2
CO-9 Highland Av					
2900	LMBD	60148	3084	19W-2S	C4
2900	LMBD	60515	3084	19W-2S	C4
2900	YkTp	60148	3084	19W-2S	C4
2900	YkTp	60515	3084	19W-2S	C4
3200	DRGV	60515	3084	19W-3S	C6
CO-9 Kaneville Rd					
1500	GNVA	60134	3020	36W-1N	A3
1700	GNVA	60134	3019	36W-1N	E4
CO-9 W Kaneville Rd					
1100	GNVA	60134	3020	36W-1N	A3
CO-9 Lemont Rd					
10	DGvT	60439	3270	19W-12S	C1
10	WDRG	60439	3270	19W-12S	C3
10	WDRG	60517	3270	19W-12S	C3
200	DGvT	60439	3206	19W-11S	C7
200	DGvT	60517	3270	19W-12S	C3
200	DRN	60439	3206	19W-11S	C7
500	LMNT	60439	3270	19W-12S	C3
700	DGvT	60516	3206	19W-11S	C7
700	DGvT	60561	3206	19W-11S	C7
700	DRN	60516	3206	19W-11S	C7
700	DRN	60561	3206	19W-11S	C7
7200	DRGV	60516	3206	19W-8S	C1
7300	WDRG	60516	3206	19W-8S	C1
7500	DRN	60517	3206	19W-8S	C2
7500	WDRG	60517	3206	19W-8S	C2
7500	WDRG	60561	3206	19W-8S	C2
7600	DGvT	60517	3206	19W-8S	C2
CO-9 Main St					
10	DRGV	60516	3144	19W-6S	C4
3900	DRGV	60515	3084	19W-4S	C6
5500	DRGV	60515	3144	19W-6S	C4
7100	DRGV	60516	3206	19W-8S	C1
CO-10					
-	AddT	60191	2914	19W-7N	D4
-	ITSC	60191	2914	19W-7N	D4
10	BbyT	60119	3075	43W-1S	A3
10	BbyT	60119	3076	41W-1S	A2
10	BbyT	60134	3076	39W-1S	E2
10	BbyT	60510	3076	41W-1S	A2
10	BTVA	60510	3077	37W-1S	C2
10	BtvT	60510	3077	37W-1S	C2
10	ITSC	60143	2914	18W-6N	D5
200	BtvT	60134	3077	38W-1S	A2
200	WDDL	60143	2914	19W-6N	D7
200	WDDL	60191	2914	19W-6N	D7
300	AddT	60143	2914	19W-7N	D4
500	BtvT	60134	3076	38W-1S	E2
500	BtvT	60510	3076	38W-1S	E2
1200	EGVV	60007	2914	19W-7N	D4
2000	BTVA	60539	3077	36W-1S	D2
2000	BtvT	60539	3077	36W-1S	D2
CO-10 N Arlington Heights Rd					
1200	AddT	60143	2914	19W-7N	D4
1200	EGVV	60007	2914	19W-7N	D4
1200	ITSC	60143	2914	19W-7N	D4
CO-10 Main St					
10	BbyT	60119	3075	43W-1S	A3
10	BbyT	60119	3076	41W-1S	A2
10	BbyT	60134	3076	39W-1S	E2
10	BbyT	60510	3076	41W-1S	A2
10	BTVA	60510	3077	37W-1S	C2
10	BtvT	60510	3077	37W-1S	C2
200	BtvT	60134	3077	38W-1S	A2
500	BtvT	60134	3076	38W-1S	E2
500	BtvT	60510	3076	38W-1S	E2
2000	BTVA	60539	3077	36W-1S	D2
2000	BtvT	60539	3077	36W-1S	D2
CO-10 N Prospect Av					
-	AddT	60191	2914	19W-7N	D4
-	ITSC	60191	2914	19W-7N	D4
10	ITSC	60143	2914	19W-6N	D5
300	AddT	60143	2914	18W-7N	D5
CO-10 S Prospect Av					
100	ITSC	60143	2914	18W-6N	D6
200	WDDL	60143	2914	19W-6N	D7
200	WDDL	60191	2914	19W-6N	D7
CO-11					
-	ADSN	60101	2969	21W-3N	E4
10	AddT	60101	2970	21W-3N	A5
10	ADSN	60101	2970	21W-3N	A4
10	BMDL	60101	2969	22W-4N	D4
10	BmdT	60101	2969	22W-4N	D4
10	BmdT	60101	2970	21W-3N	A5
10	BRLT	60103	2966	29W-5N	D3
10	BrlT	60140	2795	47W-14N	C6
10	BRLT	60185	2966	29W-4N	E3
10	GLHT	60139	2969	22W-4N	B4
10	HPSR	60140	2795	47W-15N	C4
10	HshT	60140	2795	47W-13N	C7
10	WynT	60103	2966	29W-4N	E3
10	WynT	60185	2966	29W-4N	E3
100	BMDL	60108	2968	24W-4N	D4
100	BMDL	60108	2969	22W-4N	B4
100	BMDL	60139	2968	23W-4N	E4
100	BmdT	60108	2969	22W-4N	C4
100	GLHT	60108	2968	24W-4N	D4
100	GLHT	60139	2968	24W-4N	D4
200	BmdT	60108	2968	25W-4N	A3
200	BmdT	60188	2968	25W-4N	A3
200	CLSM	60108	2968	25W-4N	A3
200	CLSM	60188	2968	25W-4N	A3
200	WYNE	60103	2966	30W-5N	B2
200	WYNE	60184	2966	29W-5N	D3
300	BMDL	60139	2969	22W-4N	B4
300	BmdT	60139	2969	22W-4N	C4
300	BRLT	60103	2967	28W-4N	B3
300	CLSM	60103	2967	28W-4N	B3
300	CLSM	60188	2967	26W-4N	E3
300	GLHT	60108	2969	22W-4N	B4
300	WynT	60184	2966	29W-5N	D3
400	BMDL	60108	2967	26W-4N	E3
400	BMDL	60133	2968	25W-4N	B3
400	BmdT	60108	2967	26W-4N	E3
400	BmdT	60133	2968	25W-4N	B3
400	BmdT	60188	2967	26W-4N	E3
400	CLSM	60108	2967	26W-4N	E3
400	WynT	60103	2967	28W-4N	A3
400	WynT	60185	2967	28W-4N	A3
500	BRLT	60184	2966	29W-5N	D3
500	BRLT	60185	2967	28W-4N	A3
500	HRPK	60108	2967	26W-4N	E3
500	HRPK	60133	2967	28W-4N	B3
500	HRPK	60188	2967	26W-4N	E3
700	CLSM	60133	2967	28W-4N	B3
1300	BRLT	60188	2967	28W-4N	B3
1300	HRPK	60103	2967	28W-4N	B3
CO-11 Army Trail Rd					
-	ADSN	60101	2969	21W-3N	E4
10	AddT	60101	2970	20W-3N	A5
10	ADSN	60101	2970	21W-3N	A4
10	BMDL	60101	2969	22W-4N	D4
10	BmdT	60101	2969	22W-4N	D4
10	BmdT	60101	2970	21W-3N	A5
10	BRLT	60103	2966	29W-5N	D3
10	BRLT	60185	2966	29W-4N	E3
10	WynT	60103	2966	29W-4N	E3
10	WynT	60185	2966	29W-4N	E3
100	BMDL	60108	2969	22W-4N	B4
100	BmdT	60108	2969	22W-4N	C4
200	WYNE	60103	2966	30W-5N	B2
200	WYNE	60184	2966	29W-5N	D3
300	BMDL	60139	2969	22W-4N	B4
300	BmdT	60139	2969	22W-4N	C4
300	BRLT	60103	2967	28W-4N	A3
300	CLSM	60103	2967	28W-4N	A3
300	CLSM	60188	2967	28W-4N	A3
300	WynT	60184	2966	29W-5N	D3
400	GLHT	60139	2969	22W-4N	B4
400	WynT	60103	2967	28W-4N	A3
400	WynT	60185	2967	28W-4N	A3
500	BRLT	60184	2966	29W-5N	D3
500	BRLT	60185	2967	28W-4N	A3
500	GLHT	60108	2969	22W-4N	B4
CO-11 E Army Trail Rd					
10	GLHT	60139	2969	23W-4N	B4
100	BMDL	60108	2968	23W-4N	E4
100	BMDL	60139	2968	23W-4N	E4
100	GLHT	60108	2968	23W-4N	E4
100	GLHT	60139	2968	23W-4N	E4
300	BMDL	60108	2969	23W-4N	B4
300	BMDL	60139	2969	23W-4N	B4
300	GLHT	60108	2969	23W-4N	B4
CO-11 W Army Trail Rd					
100	BMDL	60108	2968	24W-4N	D4
100	BMDL	60139	2968	23W-4N	E4
100	GLHT	60108	2968	24W-4N	D4
100	GLHT	60139	2968	24W-4N	D4
200	BmdT	60108	2968	25W-4N	A3
200	BmdT	60188	2968	25W-4N	A3
200	CLSM	60108	2968	25W-4N	A3
200	CLSM	60188	2968	25W-4N	A3
400	BMDL	60108	2967	26W-4N	E3
400	BMDL	60133	2968	25W-4N	B3
400	BmdT	60108	2967	26W-4N	E3
400	BmdT	60133	2968	25W-4N	B3
400	BmdT	60188	2967	26W-4N	E3
400	CLSM	60108	2967	26W-4N	E3
400	CLSM	60188	2967	26W-4N	E3
500	HRPK	60108	2967	26W-4N	E3
500	HRPK	60133	2967	28W-4N	B3
500	HRPK	60188	2967	26W-4N	E3
700	CLSM	60133	2967	28W-4N	B3
1300	BRLT	60103	2967	28W-4N	B3
1300	BRLT	60188	2967	28W-4N	B3
1300	CLSM	60103	2967	28W-4N	B3
1300	HRPK	60103	2967	28W-4N	B3
CO-11 French Rd					
10	BrlT	60140	2795	47W-14N	C6

STREET Block	City	ZIP	Map#	CGS	Grid
CO-11 French Rd					
10	HPSR	60140	2795	47W-15N	C4
10	HshT	60140	2795	47W-13N	C7
CO-13					
-	NPVL	60555	3141	28W-4S	B1
-	NPVL	60563	3141	28W-4S	B1
10	WNFD	60190	3023	27W-0N	C6
10	WnfT	60555	3081	28W-3S	B6
100	WNFD	60190	3081	27W-1S	C1
100	WnfT	60185	3081	28W-3S	B6
100	WnfT	60187	3081	27W-1S	B1
100	WnfT	60190	3081	27W-1S	C1
300	WNFD	60185	3023	27W-0N	C5
300	WnfT	60185	3023	27W-0N	C5
300	WnfT	60190	3023	27W-0N	C5
900	NPVL	60563	3140	29W-5S	E2
3600	WNVL	60555	3141	28W-4S	B1
4200	WNVL	60555	3081	28W-1S	B2
CO-13 W Diehl Rd					
-	WNVL	60555	3141	28W-4S	B1
CO-13 Ferry Rd					
-	WNVL	60555	3081	28W-4S	B7
CO-13 Raymond Dr					
900	NPVL	60563	3140	29W-5S	E2
CO-13 River Rd					
100	WNVL	60555	3081	28W-4S	A7
CO-13 Winfield Rd					
-	NPVL	60555	3141	28W-4S	B1
-	NPVL	60563	3141	28W-4S	B1
10	WNFD	60190	3023	27W-0N	C6
10	WnfT	60555	3081	28W-3S	B6
100	WNFD	60190	3081	27W-1S	C1
100	WnfT	60185	3081	28W-3S	B6
100	WnfT	60187	3081	27W-1S	B1
100	WnfT	60190	3081	27W-1S	C1
300	WNFD	60185	3023	27W-0N	C5
300	WnfT	60185	3023	27W-0N	C5
300	WnfT	60190	3023	27W-0N	C5
3600	WNVL	60555	3141	28W-4S	B1
4200	WNVL	60555	3081	28W-1S	B2
CO-14					
10	AURA	60502	3139	31W-7S	D6
10	NpvT	60502	3139	31W-7S	D6
10	NpvT	60563	3139	31W-5S	D2
100	AURA	60502	3079	31W-3S	E7
100	AURA	60510	3079	31W-3S	E7
100	AURA	60563	3139	31W-5S	D3
100	WnfT	60510	3079	31W-3S	E7
300	AURA	60504	3139	31W-7S	D7
CO-14 N Eola Rd					
10	NpvT	60502	3139	31W-7S	D6
10	NpvT	60563	3139	31W-5S	D2
100	AURA	60502	3079	31W-3S	E7
100	AURA	60502	3139	31W-5S	D3
100	AURA	60510	3079	31W-3S	E7
100	AURA	60563	3139	31W-5S	D3
100	WnfT	60510	3079	31W-3S	E7
300	AURA	60504	3139	31W-7S	D7
CO-15					
-	DGvT	60439	3207	17W-10S	B5
-	DGvT	60527	3207	17W-10S	B5
-	DGvT	60561	3207	17W-10S	B5
10	AraT	60506	3077	38W-4S	B7
10	BbyT	60506	3076	40W-4S	B7
10	BtvT	60506	3077	38W-4S	B7
10	NARA	60506	3076	40W-3S	C7
10	OKTR	60181	3027	17W-1S	B7
10	OKTR	60181	3085	17W-1S	B2
10	SgrT	60506	3076	40W-4S	B7
10	VLPK	60181	3027	17W-1S	B7
10	YkTp	60181	3085	17W-1S	B2
200	AraT	60506	3076	38W-3S	E7
200	AraT	60542	3077	38W-4S	A7
200	BtvT	60506	3076	38W-3S	E7
200	DRN	60561	3207	17W-10S	B5
200	NARA	60542	3076	39W-3S	E7
200	NARA	60542	3077	38W-4S	A7
200	SgrT	60506	3075	41W-4S	E7
200	SgrT	60554	3075	41W-4S	E7
400	OKBK	60523	3085	17W-1S	B2
400	OKTR	60523	3085	17W-1S	B2
400	WTMT	60559	3145	17W-6S	B4
500	OKBK	60181	3085	17W-1S	B2
600	WTMT	60559	3085	17W-4S	B7
700	DGvT	60561	3145	17W-7S	B7
700	DRN	60561	3145	17W-7S	B7
2300	YkTp	60523	3085	17W-2S	B3
3400	OKBK	60559	3085	17W-3S	B5
3500	WTMT	60523	3085	17W-3S	B6
6600	DRN	60559	3145	17W-7S	B6
6600	WTMT	60561	3145	17W-7S	B6
CO-15 N Cass Av					
600	WTMT	60559	3085	17W-4S	B7
CO-15 S Cass Av					
-	DGvT	60439	3207	17W-10S	B5
-	DGvT	60527	3207	17W-10S	B5
200	DGvT	60561	3207	17W-8S	B1
200	DRN	60561	3207	17W-10S	B5
400	WTMT	60559	3145	18W-6S	B4
700	DGvT	60561	3145	17W-7S	B7
700	DRN	60561	3145	17W-7S	B7
6600	DRN	60559	3145	17W-7S	B6
6600	WTMT	60561	3145	17W-7S	B6
CO-15 Deerpath Rd					
10	AraT	60506	3077	38W-4S	A7
10	BtvT	60506	3077	38W-4S	A7
CO-15 Healy Rd					
200	SgrT	60506	3075	41W-4S	E7
200	SgrT	60506	3076	40W-4S	B7
200	SgrT	60554	3075	41W-4S	E7
CO-15 Midwest Rd					
2200	OKBK	60181	3085	17W-2S	B2
2200	OKBK	60523	3085	17W-2S	B2
2300	YkTp	60523	3085	17W-2S	B3
3400	OKBK	60559	3085	17W-3S	B5
3500	WTMT	60523	3085	17W-3S	B6
3500	WTMT	60559	3085	17W-3S	B5
CO-15 Norris Rd					
10	BbyT	60506	3076	40W-3S	B7
10	SgrT	60506	3076	40W-4S	B7
CO-15 Oak St					
200	AraT	60506	3077	38W-4S	A7
200	AraT	60542	3077	38W-4S	A7
200	NARA	60542	3077	38W-4S	A7
CO-15 Summit Av					
10	OKTR	60181	3027	17W-1S	B7
10	OKTR	60181	3085	17W-1S	B2
10	VLPK	60181	3027	17W-1S	B7
10	YkTp	60181	3085	17W-1S	B2
400	OKBK	60523	3085	17W-1S	B2
400	OKTR	60523	3085	17W-1S	B2
500	OKBK	60181	3085	17W-1S	B2
CO-15 Tanner Rd					
-	AraT	60506	3077	38W-4S	B7
-	BtvT	60506	3077	38W-4S	B7
10	BbyT	60506	3076	40W-4S	B7
CO-15 Tanner Rd					
10	NARA	60506	3076	40W-3S	C7
200	AraT	60506	3076	38W-3S	E7
200	BtvT	60506	3076	38W-3S	E7
200	NARA	60542	3076	39W-3S	E7
200	SgrT	60506	3076	39W-3S	E7
CO-16					
100	BbyT	60119	3018	40W-0N	A5
600	BbyT	60119	3076	41W-1S	A1
600	BbyT	60510	3076	41W-1S	A1
CO-16 Bunker Rd					
100	BbyT	60119	3018	40W-0N	A5
600	BbyT	60119	3076	41W-1S	A1
600	BbyT	60510	3076	41W-1S	A1
CO-17					
10	ELGN	60123	2908	36W-9N	A1
10	ELGN	60177	2908	36W-9N	A1
10	ElgT	60124	2907	37W-9N	D1
10	PltT	60124	2852	40W-9N	B7
10	PltT	60124	2906	39W-9N	E1
10	SEGN	60123	2908	36W-9N	A1
10	SEGN	60177	2908	36W-9N	A1
400	ELGN	60123	2907	37W-9N	D1
400	ELGN	60124	2907	36W-9N	E1
400	ElgT	60123	2907	36W-9N	E1
400	PltT	60124	2851	41W-10N	E6
500	ElgT	60123	2908	35W-9N	B1
500	ElgT	60177	2908	35W-9N	A1
500	LSLE	60532	3142	23W-6S	E4
500	LSLE	60532	3143	23W-5S	A4
500	LSLE	60540	3142	24W-6S	C4
500	LslT	60532	3143	22W-5S	C4
500	LslT	60540	3142	24W-6S	C4
500	NPVL	60532	3142	24W-6S	C4
500	NPVL	60540	3142	24W-6S	C4
700	PltT	60124	2907	39W-9N	A1
800	NPVL	60540	3141	26W-6S	E5
1400	DRGV	60515	3144	20W-6S	A4
1400	DRGV	60516	3144	20W-6S	A4
1500	LslT	60532	3142	23W-6S	E4
1700	DGvT	60515	3144	20W-6S	A4
1700	DGvT	60516	3144	20W-6S	A4
1900	LslT	60515	3144	20W-6S	A4
1900	LslT	60516	3144	20W-6S	A4
2200	LslT	60515	3143	21W-6S	E4
2200	LslT	60516	3143	21W-6S	E4
2600	DRGV	60515	3143	21W-6S	D4
2800	DRGV	60516	3143	22W-6S	D4
CO-17 Bowes Rd					
10	ELGN	60123	2908	36W-9N	A1
10	ELGN	60177	2908	36W-9N	A1
10	ElgT	60124	2907	37W-9N	D1
10	PltT	60124	2852	41W-10N	A7
10	PltT	60124	2906	39W-9N	E1
10	SEGN	60123	2908	36W-9N	A1
10	SEGN	60177	2908	36W-9N	A1
400	ELGN	60123	2907	37W-9N	D1
400	ELGN	60124	2907	36W-9N	E1
400	ElgT	60123	2907	36W-9N	E1
500	ElgT	60123	2908	35W-9N	B1
500	ElgT	60177	2908	35W-9N	A1
700	PltT	60124	2907	39W-9N	A1
CO-17 E Chicago Av					
800	NPVL	60540	3141	26W-6S	E5
1000	NPVL	60540	3142	26W-6S	A5
1100	LslT	60540	3142	25W-6S	A5
CO-17 Maple Av					
500	LSLE	60532	3142	23W-6S	E4
500	LSLE	60532	3143	23W-5S	A4
500	LSLE	60540	3142	24W-6S	C4
500	LslT	60532	3143	22W-5S	C4
500	LslT	60540	3142	24W-6S	C4
500	NPVL	60532	3142	24W-6S	C4
500	NPVL	60540	3142	24W-6S	C4
1400	DRGV	60515	3144	20W-6S	A4
1400	DRGV	60516	3144	20W-6S	A4
1500	LslT	60532	3142	23W-6S	E4
1700	DGvT	60515	3144	20W-6S	A4
1700	DGvT	60516	3144	20W-6S	A4
1900	LslT	60515	3144	20W-6S	A4
1900	LslT	60516	3144	20W-6S	A4
2200	LslT	60516	3143	21W-6S	E4
2600	DRGV	60516	3143	21W-6S	D4
2800	DRGV	60515	3143	22W-6S	D4
2800	LslT	60515	3143	22W-6S	D4
CO-17 Muirhead Rd					
10	PltT	60124	2852	40W-9N	B7
CO-17 Plato Rd					
400	PltT	60124	2851	41W-10N	E6
400	PltT	60124	2852	41W-10N	A6
CO-18					
10	WCHI	60185	3021	31W-2N	E1
100	WCHI	60185	2965	31W-3N	E6
100	WynT	60185	2965	31W-3N	E6
300	WnfT	60185	3021	31W-1N	D3
1100	WynT	60185	3021	31W-2N	E1
CO-18 W Hawthorne Ln					
1700	WCHI	60185	3021	31W-2N	D2
1800	WnfT	60185	3021	31W-1N	D2
CO-18 Kress Rd					
10	WCHI	60185	3021	32W-0N	D4
300	WnfT	60185	3021	31W-1N	D3
CO-18 Powis Rd					
100	WCHI	60185	2965	31W-3N	E6
100	WynT	60185	2965	31W-3N	E6
700	WCHI	60185	3021	31W-2N	E1
1100	WynT	60185	3021	31W-2N	E1
CO-19					
-	SchT	60103	2909	33W-7N	B5
10	SchT	60174	2965	33W-4N	A3
10	SchT	60184	2965	33W-4N	A3
10	SCRL	60174	2964	34W-4N	E5
10	SCRL	60174	2965	33W-4N	A3
10	SCRL	60184	2965	33W-4N	A3
10	WYNE	60120	2909	33W-7N	B6
10	WYNE	60174	2965	33W-4N	A3
10	WYNE	60184	2909	33W-6N	B7
10	WYNE	60184	2965	33W-6N	B1
200	BRLT	60120	2909	33W-7N	B5
200	SchT	60120	2909	33W-7N	B5
500	SchT	60174	2964	34W-4N	E5
CO-19 Dunham Rd					
-	SchT	60103	2909	33W-7N	B5
10	SchT	60174	2965	33W-4N	A3
10	SchT	60184	2965	33W-4N	A3
10	SCRL	60174	2964	34W-4N	E5
10	SCRL	60174	2965	33W-4N	A3
10	SCRL	60184	2965	33W-4N	A3
10	WYNE	60120	2909	33W-7N	B6
10	WYNE	60174	2965	33W-4N	A3
10	WYNE	60184	2909	33W-6N	B7
10	WYNE	60184	2965	33W-6N	B1
200	BRLT	60120	2909	33W-7N	B5
200	SchT	60120	2909	33W-7N	B5
500	SchT	60174	2964	34W-4N	E5
CO-20					
10	BNVL	60106	2971	16W-3N	E5
10	BNVL	60106	2972	15W-3N	A5
10	EMHT	60106	2971	16W-3N	E5
10	EMHT	60106	2972	15W-3N	A5
10	EMHT	60126	2971	17W-3N	C5
10	EMHT	60126	2972	15W-3N	A5
100	AddT	60106	2972	15W-3N	A5
100	AddT	60126	2972	15W-3N	A5
100	FNPK	60131	2972	15W-3N	B5
100	FNPK	60164	2972	15W-3N	B5
100	LydT	60164	2972	15W-3N	B5
100	WYNE	60184	2965	33W-5N	B2
300	AddT	60106	2971	16W-3N	D5
CO-20 Army Trail Rd					
100	WYNE	60184	2965	33W-5N	B2
CO-20 E Grand Av					
10	BNVL	60106	2972	15W-3N	A5
10	EMHT	60106	2972	15W-3N	A5
10	EMHT	60126	2972	15W-3N	A5
100	AddT	60106	2972	15W-3N	A5
100	AddT	60126	2972	15W-3N	A5
100	FNPK	60131	2972	15W-3N	B5
100	FNPK	60164	2972	15W-3N	B5
100	LydT	60164	2972	15W-3N	B5
CO-20 W Grand Av					
10	BNVL	60106	2971	16W-3N	E5
10	EMHT	60106	2971	16W-3N	E5
10	EMHT	60126	2971	17W-3N	C5
300	AddT	60106	2971	16W-3N	D5
CO-21					
10	DndT	60124	2799	37W-14N	D7
10	ELGN	60124	2799	37W-14N	D6
10	ElgT	60124	2799	36W-13N	D7
10	GLBT	60124	2799	36W-13N	E7
10	GLBT	60136	2799	36W-13N	E7
10	HPSR	60140	2743	46W-18N	A5
10	HshT	60140	2743	46W-18N	A5
10	HshT	60140	2744	43W-17N	B7
10	MltT	60187	3023	27W-1N	D3
10	MltT	60187	3024	25W-0N	C3
10	MltT	60188	3023	26W-1N	E3
10	MltT	60188	3024	25W-0N	C3
10	MltT	60190	3023	27W-1N	D3
10	RtdT	60124	2799	36W-13N	E7
10	RtdT	60136	2798	39W-15N	D4
10	RtdT	60136	2799	38W-14N	C6
10	RtdT	60140	2744	43W-17N	B7
10	RtdT	60140	2797	42W-16N	E1
10	RtdT	60140	2798	39W-15N	D4
10	RtdT	60142	2744	42W-17N	C7
10	RtdT	60142	2797	43W-17N	C1
10	WNFD	60187	3023	26W-1N	E3
10	WNFD	60188	3023	26W-1N	E3
10	WNFD	60190	3023	26W-1N	E4
10	WnfT	60185	3023	26W-1N	E4
10	WnfT	60187	3023	27W-1N	D3
10	WnfT	60190	3023	26W-1N	E4
100	CLSM	60188	3024	24W-0N	C3
100	GNEN	60137	3024	23W-0N	E3
100	GNEN	60137	3025	23W-1N	A3
100	GNEN	60187	3025	23W-1N	A3
100	GNEN	60188	3024	23W-1N	E3
100	WHTN	60137	3024	23W-1N	E3
100	WHTN	60187	3024	23W-0N	E3
100	WHTN	60187	3025	23W-1N	A3
100	WHTN	60188	3024	23W-1N	E3
100	WNFD	60185	3023	26W-1N	E4
200	DndT	60136	2799	37W-14N	C6
200	GLBT	60124	2798	39W-14N	E5
200	GLBT	60136	2798	39W-14N	E5
200	RtdT	60124	2798	39W-14N	E5
300	ELGN	60123	2800	36W-13N	A7
300	MltT	60137	3025	23W-1N	A3
500	ELGN	60123	2854	35W-12N	C1
500	RtdT	60136	2797	41W-16N	E1
600	WCHI	60185	3021	32W-0S	D6
700	BTVA	60510	3021	32W-0N	B6
700	GnvT	60510	3021	32W-0N	B6
700	WCHI	60185	3022	28W-0N	E4
700	WnfT	60185	3022	28W-0N	E4
800	ELGN	60123	2799	36W-13N	E7
800	ElgT	60123	2799	36W-13N	E7
CO-21 Big Timber Rd					
10	DndT	60124	2799	37W-14N	D7
10	ELGN	60124	2799	37W-14N	D6
10	ElgT	60124	2799	36W-13N	D7
10	GLBT	60124	2799	36W-13N	E7
10	GLBT	60136	2799	36W-13N	E7
10	HPSR	60140	2743	46W-18N	A5
10	HshT	60140	2743	46W-18N	A5
10	HshT	60140	2744	43W-17N	B7
10	RtdT	60124	2799	36W-13N	E7
10	RtdT	60136	2798	39W-15N	D4
10	RtdT	60136	2799	38W-14N	C6
10	RtdT	60140	2744	43W-17N	B7
10	RtdT	60140	2797	42W-16N	E1
10	RtdT	60140	2798	39W-15N	D4
10	RtdT	60142	2744	42W-17N	C7
10	RtdT	60142	2797	43W-17N	C1
200	DndT	60136	2799	37W-14N	C6
200	GLBT	60124	2798	39W-14N	E5
200	GLBT	60136	2798	39W-14N	E5
200	RtdT	60124	2798	39W-14N	E5
300	ELGN	60123	2800	36W-13N	A7
500	ELGN	60123	2854	35W-12N	C1
500	RtdT	60136	2797	41W-16N	E1
800	ELGN	60123	2799	36W-13N	E7
800	ElgT	60123	2799	36W-13N	E7
CO-21 Fabyan Pkwy					
600	WCHI	60185	3021	32W-0S	D6
700	BTVA	60510	3021	32W-0N	B6
700	GnvT	60510	3021	32W-0N	B6
CO-21 Geneva Rd					
10	MltT	60187	3023	27W-1N	D3
10	MltT	60187	3024	25W-0N	C3
10	MltT	60188	3023	26W-1N	E3
10	MltT	60188	3024	25W-0N	C3
10	MltT	60190	3023	27W-1N	D3
10	WNFD	60187	3023	26W-1N	E3
10	WNFD	60188	3023	26W-1N	E3
10	WNFD	60190	3023	26W-1N	E4
10	WnfT	60185	3023	26W-1N	E4
10	WnfT	60187	3023	27W-1N	D3
10	WnfT	60190	3023	26W-1N	E4
100	WNFD	60185	3023	26W-1N	E4
200	GNEN	60137	3025	23W-1N	A3
200	GNEN	60187	3025	23W-1N	A3
200	WHTN	60187	3024	25W-1N	B3
300	MltT	60137	3025	23W-1N	A3
700	WCHI	60185	3022	28W-0N	E4
700	WnfT	60185	3022	28W-0N	E4
CO-21 E Geneva Rd					
100	CLSM	60188	3024	24W-0N	C3
100	GNEN	60137	3024	23W-0N	E3
CO-21 E Geneva Rd					
100	GNEN	60137	3025	23W-1N	A3
100	GNEN	60187	3025	23W-1N	A3
100	GNEN	60188	3024	23W-1N	E3
100	MltT	60188	3024	23W-1N	E3
100	WHTN	60137	3024	23W-1N	E3
100	WHTN	60187	3024	23W-0N	E3
100	WHTN	60187	3025	23W-1N	A3
100	WHTN	60188	3024	23W-1N	E3
600	MltT	60187	3024	23W-0N	E3
CO-21 W Geneva Rd					
100	MltT	60187	3024	24W-0N	C3
100	MltT	60188	3024	24W-0N	C3
100	WHTN	60187	3024	24W-0N	C3
100	WHTN	60188	3024	24W-0N	C3
CO-22					
10	PltT	60124	2852	39W-12N	E3
10	PltT	60140	2851	41W-12N	E2
10	PltT	60140	2852	39W-12N	E3
100	WDDL	60191	2970	18W-5N	E2
200	ADSN	60191	2970	18W-5N	E2
200	WDDL	60191	2914	18W-6N	E7
300	AddT	60101	2970	18W-4N	E4
300	ADSN	60101	2970	18W-4N	E3
700	ElgT	60124	2853	38W-12N	A3
700	PltT	60124	2853	38W-12N	A3
CO-22 N Addison Rd					
100	WDDL	60191	2970	18W-5N	E1
200	WDDL	60191	2914	18W-6N	E7
300	AddT	60101	2970	18W-4N	E4
300	ADSN	60101	2970	18W-4N	E3
800	ADSN	60191	2970	18W-4N	E3
CO-22 S Addison Rd					
-	ADSN	60101	2970	18W-4N	E3
100	WDDL	60191	2970	18W-5N	E2
200	ADSN	60191	2970	18W-5N	E2
CO-22 Plank Rd					
10	PltT	60124	2852	39W-12N	E3
10	PltT	60140	2851	41W-12N	E2
10	PltT	60140	2852	39W-12N	E3
700	ElgT	60124	2853	38W-12N	A3
700	PltT	60124	2853	38W-12N	A3
CO-23					
-	BMDL	60188	2968	25W-4N	B4
-	HRPK	60133	2912	25W-7N	B4
-	HRPK	60172	2912	25W-6N	B6
-	ROSL	60133	2912	25W-6N	B6
10	BMDL	60108	2912	25W-6N	B7
10	BMDL	60172	2912	25W-6N	B7
10	BmdT	60108	2912	25W-6N	B7
10	BmdT	60172	2912	25W-6N	B7
10	LSLE	60532	3082	25W-4S	B7
10	LSLE	60563	3082	25W-4S	B7
10	LslT	60563	3082	25W-4S	B7
10	MltT	60187	3024	25W-1N	B3
10	MltT	60187	3082	24W-3S	C5
10	MltT	60188	3024	25W-1N	B3
10	MltT	60563	3082	25W-3S	B7
10	NPVL	60532	3082	25W-4S	B7
10	NPVL	60563	3082	25W-4S	B7
10	WHTN	60187	3024	25W-1N	B3
10	WHTN	60187	3082	24W-3S	C6
100	BMDL	60108	2968	25W-3N	B5
100	BMDL	60172	2968	25W-3N	B5
100	CLSM	60188	3024	25W-2N	B1
100	LslT	60532	3082	25W-4S	B7
200	BMDL	60133	2968	25W-4N	B3
200	ROSL	60172	2912	25W-6N	B6
200	SMBG	60172	2912	25W-6N	B6
200	SMBG	60193	2912	25W-6N	B6
300	CLSM	60188	2968	25W-2N	B7
400	LSLE	60532	3142	25W-4S	B1
400	LSLE	60563	3142	25W-4S	B1
400	LslT	60563	3142	25W-4S	B1
400	NPVL	60532	3142	25W-4S	B1
400	NPVL	60563	3142	25W-4S	B1
500	BmdT	60172	2968	25W-5N	B1
1100	CLSM	60133	2968	25W-4N	B4
CO-23 Gary Av					
-	BMDL	60108	2968	25W-4N	B3
-	BMDL	60133	2968	25W-4N	B3
-	BMDL	60188	2968	25W-4N	B4
-	HRPK	60133	2912	25W-7N	B5
-	ROSL	60133	2912	25W-6N	B6
10	BMDL	60108	2912	25W-6N	B7
10	BMDL	60172	2912	25W-6N	B7
10	BmdT	60108	2912	25W-6N	B7
10	BmdT	60172	2912	25W-6N	B7
10	MltT	60187	3024	25W-1N	B3
10	MltT	60188	3024	25W-1N	B3
10	WHTN	60187	3024	25W-1N	B3
100	CLSM	60188	3024	25W-2N	B1
300	CLSM	60188	2968	25W-2N	B7
400	BMDL	60172	2968	25W-5N	B1
500	BmdT	60172	2968	25W-5N	B1
500	HRPK	60172	2912	25W-6N	B6
500	ROSL	60172	2912	25W-6N	B6
1100	CLSM	60133	2968	25W-4N	B4
CO-23 N Gary Av					
-	CLSM	60188	3024	25W-2N	B1
-	HRPK	60133	2912	25W-7N	B4
-	HRPK	60172	2912	25W-7N	B4
200	ROSL	60172	2912	25W-6N	B6
200	SMBG	60172	2912	25W-6N	B6
200	SMBG	60193	2912	25W-6N	B6
1500	MltT	60187	3024	25W-0N	B5
1500	WHTN	60187	3024	25W-0N	B5
CO-23 S Gary Av					
100	BMDL	60108	2968	25W-3N	B5
100	BMDL	60172	2968	25W-3N	B5
200	BMDL	60133	2968	25W-4N	B3
CO-23 N Naper Blvd					
-	LslT	60563	3142	25W-4S	B2
1500	NPVL	60563	3142	25W-4S	B1
CO-23 Naperville Rd					
10	LSLE	60532	3082	25W-4S	B7
10	LSLE	60563	3082	25W-4S	B7
10	LslT	60563	3082	25W-4S	B7
10	MltT	60187	3082	24W-3S	C5
10	MltT	60563	3082	25W-3S	B7
10	NPVL	60532	3082	25W-4S	B7
10	NPVL	60563	3082	25W-4S	B7
10	WHTN	60187	3082	24W-3S	C5
100	LslT	60532	3082	25W-4S	B7
400	LSLE	60532	3142	25W-4S	B1
400	LSLE	60563	3142	25W-4S	B1
400	LslT	60563	3142	25W-4S	B1
400	NPVL	60532	3142	25W-4S	B1
400	NPVL	60563	3142	25W-4S	B1
CO-23 N Naperville Rd					
1600	LslT	60563	3142	25W-4S	B2
1600	NPVL	60563	3142	25W-4S	B2
CO-23 S Naperville Rd					
700	WHTN	60187	3082	24W-3S	C6
2000	MltT	60187	3082	24W-3S	C5
CO-24					
-	EGVV	60143	2913	21W-7N	E3
10	AURA	60506	3198	39W-8S	E2
10	BMDL	60101	2969	22W-4N	D3
10	BMDL	60108	2969	21W-5N	D2
10	BMDL	60157	2913	22W-5N	D7
10	BmdT	60101	2969	21W-5N	D2
10	BmdT	60143	2913	22W-7N	D5
10	BmdT	60157	2913	22W-6N	D7
10	BRkT	60511	3196	44W-9S	D3
10	MTGY	60506	3198	39W-8S	E2
10	SgrT	60506	3197	41W-9S	E4
10	SgrT	60506	3198	39W-8S	E2
10	SgrT	60511	3196	46W-9S	A4
10	SgrT	60554	3196	46W-9S	A4
10	SgrT	60554	3197	43W-9S	A4
300	ITSC	60143	2913	22W-6N	D6
300	ITSC	60157	2913	22W-6N	D6
300	ROSL	60143	2913	22W-7N	D4
300	ROSL	60157	2913	22W-7N	D4
400	BMDL	60157	2969	21W-4N	D3
400	BmdT	60108	2969	21W-4N	D3
400	BmdT	60157	2969	21W-4N	D3
700	BMDL	60101	2913	21W-5N	D7
2400	AraT	60506	3198	39W-8S	E2
2400	AraT	60538	3198	39W-8S	E2
2400	AURA	60538	3198	39W-8S	E2
2400	MTGY	60538	3198	39W-8S	E2
CO-24 Byron Av					
10	BMDL	60101	2969	22W-4N	D3
10	BMDL	60108	2969	22W-4N	D3
10	BmdT	60101	2969	22W-4N	D3
700	BmdT	60108	2969	21W-4N	D3
CO-24 Jericho Rd					
10	AURA	60506	3198	39W-8S	E2
10	BRkT	60511	3196	44W-9S	D3
10	MTGY	60506	3198	39W-8S	E2
10	SgrT	60506	3197	41W-9S	E4
10	SgrT	60506	3198	39W-8S	E2
10	SgrT	60511	3196	46W-9S	A4
10	SgrT	60554	3196	46W-9S	A4
10	SgrT	60554	3197	43W-9S	A4
2400	AraT	60506	3198	39W-8S	E2
2400	AraT	60538	3198	39W-8S	E2
2400	AURA	60538	3198	39W-8S	E2
2400	MTGY	60538	3198	39W-8S	E2
CO-24 Meacham Rd					
-	EGVV	60143	2913	21W-7N	D3
-	ITSC	60143	2913	21W-7N	D3
-	ITSC	60157	2913	21W-7N	D3
CO-24 Medinah Rd					
10	BMDL	60101	2969	21W-5N	D2
10	BMDL	60108	2969	21W-5N	D2
10	BMDL	60157	2913	22W-5N	D7
10	BmdT	60101	2969	21W-5N	D2
10	BmdT	60143	2913	22W-7N	D5
10	BmdT	60157	2913	22W-6N	D7
300	ITSC	60143	2913	22W-6N	D6
300	ITSC	60157	2913	22W-6N	D6
300	ROSL	60143	2913	22W-7N	D4
300	ROSL	60157	2913	22W-7N	D4
400	BMDL	60157	2969	21W-4N	D3
400	BmdT	60108	2969	21W-4N	D3
400	BmdT	60157	2969	21W-4N	D3
700	BMDL	60101	2913	21W-5N	D7
CO-24 Walter Dr					
100	BMDL	60101	2969	22W-4N	D3
100	BMDL	60108	2969	22W-4N	D3
100	BmdT	60101	2969	22W-4N	D4
CO-25					
1200	YkTp	60148	3026	18W-1S	E7
1300	YkTp	60148	3084	18W-1S	E1
1600	OKTR	60181	3084	18W-1S	E1
1600	YkTp	60181	3084	18W-1S	E1
2000	YkTp	60523	3084	18W-2S	E2
2700	OKBK	60523	3084	18W-2S	E4
3800	DRGV	60515	3084	18W-3S	E6
3800	YkTp	60515	3084	18W-3S	E6
CO-25 Fairview Av					
3800	DRGV	60515	3084	18W-3S	E6
3800	OKBK	60523	3084	18W-3S	E6
3800	YkTp	60515	3084	18W-3S	E6
3800	YkTp	60523	3084	18W-3S	E6
CO-25 Meyers Rd					
-	YkTp	60148	3084	18W-2S	E2
-	YkTp	60181	3084	18W-2S	E2
-	YkTp	60515	3084	18W-3S	E6
2700	OKBK	60523	3084	18W-2S	E4
2700	YkTp	60523	3084	18W-2S	E3
CO-25 S Meyers Rd					
1200	YkTp	60148	3026	18W-1S	E7
1300	YkTp	60148	3084	18W-1S	E1
1600	OKTR	60181	3084	18W-1S	E1
1600	YkTp	60181	3084	18W-1S	E1
2000	YkTp	60523	3084	18W-2S	E2
CO-26					
10	AddT	60143	2914	19W-7N	D4
10	AddT	60191	2914	19W-7N	D4
10	BbyT	60119	3017	43W-0N	A5
10	BbyT	60119	3018	41W-0S	A7
10	BNVL	60106	2915	16W-6N	E5
10	CHCG	60106	2915	16W-6N	E5
10	ITSC	60191	2914	19W-7N	D4
10	WDDL	60191	2915	18W-7N	A4
100	EGVV	60007	2915	17W-7N	B4
300	EGVV	60191	2915	17W-7N	C4
300	ITSC	60143	2914	18W-7N	E4
300	WDDL	60143	2914	18W-7N	E4
300	WDDL	60191	2914	18W-7N	E4
400	ELBN	60119	3017	43W-0N	A5
500	BNVL	60191	2915	17W-7N	C4
500	EGVV	60106	2915	17W-7N	C4
800	BbyT	60134	3018	39W-0S	E7
CO-26 Hughes Rd					
10	BbyT	60119	3017	43W-0N	A5
10	BbyT	60119	3018	41W-0S	A7
400	ELBN	60119	3017	43W-0N	A5
800	BbyT	60134	3018	39W-0S	E7
CO-26 Thorndale Av					
-	BNVL	60191	2915	17W-7N	C4
10	AddT	60143	2914	19W-7N	D4
10	AddT	60191	2914	19W-7N	D4
10	BNVL	60106	2915	16W-6N	E5
10	CHCG	60106	2915	16W-6N	E5
10	ITSC	60191	2914	19W-7N	D4
10	WDDL	60191	2915	18W-7N	A4
300	ITSC	60143	2914	18W-7N	E4
300	WDDL	60143	2914	18W-7N	E4
300	WDDL	60191	2914	18W-7N	E4
CO-26 E Thorndale Av					
10	WDDL	60191	2915	16W-7N	D5
100	EGVV	60007	2915	17W-7N	B4
300	EGVV	60191	2915	17W-7N	C4
500	BNVL	60106	2915	17W-7N	C4
500	BNVL	60191	2915	17W-7N	C4
500	EGVV	60106	2915	17W-7N	C4

Chicago 7-County Street Index

STREET Block	City	ZIP	Map#	CGS	Grid
CO-27					
10	MltT	60187	3023	26W-0N	E5
10	MltT	60187	3024	26W-0N	A5
10	MltT	60190	3023	26W-0N	E5
10	WNFD	60187	3023	26W-0N	E5
10	WNFD	60190	3023	26W-0N	E5
10	WnfT	60185	3023	28W-0N	A5
10	WnfT	60190	3023	28W-0N	A5
300	WCHI	60185	3022	28W-0N	E4
300	WnfT	60185	3022	29W-0N	E4
600	WHTN	60187	3024	25W-0N	A5
CO-27 Highlake Rd					
10	WnfT	60185	3023	28W-0N	A5
10	WnfT	60190	3023	28W-0N	A5
500	WNFD	60190	3023	27W-0S	C6
700	WCHI	60185	3022	28W-0N	E5
700	WnfT	60185	3022	28W-0N	E5
CO-27 Jewell Rd					
10	MltT	60187	3023	26W-0N	E5
10	MltT	60187	3024	26W-0N	A5
10	MltT	60190	3023	26W-0N	E5
10	WNFD	60187	3023	26W-0N	E5
10	WNFD	60190	3023	26W-0N	E5
600	WHTN	60187	3024	25W-0N	A5
CO-27 Prince Crossing Rd					
300	WCHI	60185	3022	29W-0N	E4
300	WnfT	60185	3022	29W-0N	E4
CO-28					
-	EGvT	60007	2915	18W-7N	A4
-	EGVV	60007	2915	18W-7N	A4
-	WDDL	60007	2915	18W-7N	A4
10	AddT	60101	2971	17W-2N	B7
10	AddT	60191	2971	17W-4N	B2
10	ADSN	60101	2971	17W-2N	B7
10	ADSN	60191	2971	17W-5N	B2
10	WDDL	60191	2971	17W-5N	A1
100	AddT	60106	2971	17W-4N	B4
200	WDDL	60191	2915	18W-7N	A4
400	AddT	60181	2971	17W-2N	B7
400	AddT	60191	2915	17W-6N	A6
400	ADSN	60181	2971	17W-2N	B7
400	VLPK	60101	2971	17W-2N	B7
500	ADSN	60106	2971	17W-4N	B3
800	VLPK	60181	3027	17W-2N	B1
900	VLPK	60181	2971	17W-2N	B7
1400	EGVV	60191	2915	18W-7N	A4
CO-28 N Villa Av					
10	AddT	60101	2971	17W-3N	A5
400	ADSN	60101	2971	17W-3N	B5
800	VLPK	60181	3027	17W-2N	B1
900	VLPK	60101	2971	17W-2N	B7
900	VLPK	60181	2971	17W-2N	B7
CO-28 S Villa Av					
10	AddT	60101	2971	17W-2N	B7
10	ADSN	60101	2971	17W-2N	B7
400	AddT	60181	2971	17W-2N	B7
400	ADSN	60181	2971	17W-2N	B7
400	VLPK	60101	2971	17W-2N	B7
CO-28 Wood Dale Rd					
-	AddT	60101	2971	17W-3N	A5
3200	ADSN	60101	2971	17W-3N	A5
CO-28 N Wood Dale Rd					
-	EGvT	60007	2915	18W-7N	A4
-	EGVV	60007	2915	18W-7N	A4
-	WDDL	60007	2915	18W-7N	A4
10	AddT	60101	2971	17W-4N	B4
10	AddT	60191	2971	17W-4N	B2
10	ADSN	60101	2971	17W-4N	B2
10	ADSN	60191	2971	17W-5N	B2
10	WDDL	60191	2971	18W-5N	A1
100	AddT	60106	2971	17W-4N	B4
200	WDDL	60191	2915	18W-7N	A4
400	AddT	60191	2915	17W-6N	A6
500	ADSN	60106	2971	17W-4N	B3
1400	EGVV	60191	2915	18W-7N	A4
CO-29					
-	HRPK	60103	2911	27W-7N	C6
10	BRLT	60103	2910	30W-7N	B5
10	BRLT	60103	2911	27W-7N	D6
10	BRLT	60120	2909	32W-7N	D5
10	BRLT	60120	2910	31W-7N	A5
10	BRLT	60133	2911	27W-7N	D6
10	BRLT	60184	2909	31W-7N	E5
10	MTGY	60538	3199	36W-9S	E5
10	SchT	60120	2909	32W-7N	D5
10	WynT	60120	2909	32W-7N	D5
10	WynT	60184	2909	31W-7N	E5
200	MTGY	60538	3200	35W-9S	C4
200	WynT	60103	2911	27W-6N	B6
300	AURA	60505	3200	35W-9S	A4
300	MTGY	60505	3200	35W-9S	C4
500	AraT	60505	3200	35W-9S	C4
500	AraT	60538	3200	35W-9S	C4
1300	BmdT	60133	2911	26W-7N	E5
1300	HRPK	60133	2911	26W-7N	E5
1400	AraT	60504	3200	34W-9S	E4
1400	AURA	60504	3200	34W-9S	E4
1400	MTGY	60504	3200	34W-9S	E4
CO-29 S Broadway Rd					
1300	MTGY	60538	3199	36W-9S	E5
CO-29 Greenbrook Blvd					
10	BRLT	60103	2911	27W-7N	D6
10	BRLT	60133	2911	27W-7N	D6
10	HRPK	60133	2911	27W-7N	D6
1300	BmdT	60133	2911	26W-7N	E5
CO-29 E Mill St					
10	MTGY	60538	3199	36W-9S	D4
CO-29 Montgomery Rd					
100	MTGY	60538	3199	36W-9S	D5
200	MTGY	60538	3200	35W-9S	C4
300	AURA	60505	3200	35W-9S	A4
300	MTGY	60505	3200	35W-9S	C4
500	AraT	60505	3200	35W-9S	C4
500	AraT	60538	3200	35W-9S	C4
1400	AraT	60504	3200	34W-9S	E4
1400	AURA	60504	3200	34W-9S	E4
1400	MTGY	60504	3200	34W-9S	E4
CO-29 Stearns Rd					
10	BRLT	60103	2910	30W-7N	A5
10	BRLT	60120	2909	32W-7N	D5
10	BRLT	60120	2910	31W-7N	A5
10	BRLT	60184	2909	31W-7N	E5
10	SchT	60120	2909	32W-7N	D5
10	WynT	60120	2909	32W-7N	D5
10	WynT	60184	2909	31W-7N	E5
100	BRLT	60103	2911	28W-6N	B6
500	WynT	60103	2911	28W-6N	A6
CO-29 E Stearns Rd					
-	BRLT	60133	2911	27W-7N	D6
-	HRPK	60103	2911	27W-7N	C6
-	HRPK	60133	2911	27W-7N	C6
200	BRLT	60103	2911	27W-6N	B6
200	WynT	60103	2911	27W-6N	B6
CO-29 W Stearns Rd					
100	BRLT	60103	2910	30W-7N	B5
500	BRLT	60120	2910	30W-7N	A5
CO-30					
10	CPVL	60110	2746	39W-19N	A2
10	CPVL	60118	2746	39W-19N	A2
10	DndT	60110	2746	39W-19N	A2
10	DndT	60118	2746	39W-19N	A2
10	RtdT	60118	2746	39W-19N	A2
10	RtdT	60142	2746	39W-19N	A2
200	CPVL	60110	2800	34W-16N	D1
200	CPVL	60118	2800	35W-16N	D1
200	RtdT	60118	2745	39W-19N	E2
200	RtdT	60142	2745	39W-19N	E2
200	WDND	60118	2800	35W-16N	D1
300	CPVL	60110	2747	36W-17N	A6
300	DndT	60118	2747	36W-17N	A7
300	WDND	60118	2747	36W-17N	A7
500	GfnT	60102	2745	39W-19N	E2
500	GfnT	60142	2745	39W-19N	E2
500	RtdT	60102	2745	39W-19N	E2
CO-30 Huntley Rd					
10	CPVL	60110	2746	39W-19N	A2
10	CPVL	60118	2746	39W-19N	A2
10	DndT	60110	2746	39W-19N	A2
10	DndT	60118	2746	39W-19N	A2
10	RtdT	60118	2746	39W-19N	A2
10	RtdT	60142	2746	39W-19N	A2
200	RtdT	60118	2745	39W-19N	E2
200	RtdT	60142	2745	39W-19N	E2
300	CPVL	60110	2747	36W-17N	A6
300	DndT	60118	2747	36W-17N	A7
300	WDND	60118	2747	36W-17N	A7
500	GfnT	60102	2745	39W-19N	E2
500	GfnT	60142	2745	39W-19N	E2
500	RtdT	60102	2745	39W-19N	E2
CO-30 W Main St					
200	CPVL	60110	2800	34W-16N	D1
200	CPVL	60118	2800	35W-16N	D1
200	WDND	60118	2800	35W-16N	D1
CO-31					
10	DRGV	60516	3206	19W-9S	D3
10	DRGV	60561	3206	19W-9S	D3
10	DRN	60516	3206	19W-9S	D3
10	DRN	60561	3206	20W-10S	B4
100	BRRG	60527	3146	15W-7S	B6
100	DRN	60527	3145	16W-7S	E7
100	DRN	60561	3145	16W-7S	E7
100	WLBK	60527	3145	16W-7S	E7
100	WLBK	60527	3146	15W-7S	B6
100	WLBK	60561	3145	16W-7S	E7
200	DGvT	60516	3206	20W-10S	B4
300	DRN	60561	3207	18W-8S	B2
400	DRN	60527	3207	17W-8S	D1
400	WLBK	60527	3207	17W-8S	D1
400	WLBK	60561	3207	17W-8S	D1
500	DGvT	60561	3206	19W-9S	C3
1500	DRGV	60516	3207	18W-8S	A2
1500	DRN	60561	3207	18W-8S	A2
1600	DGvT	60517	3206	20W-10S	B4
1600	WDRG	60517	3206	20W-10S	B4
1600	WDRG	60561	3206	20W-10S	B4
1700	DRGV	60561	3207	18W-9S	A2
3200	DRN	60517	3206	20W-10S	B4
CO-31 87th St					
1600	DGvT	60516	3206	20W-10S	B4
1600	DGvT	60517	3206	20W-10S	B4
1600	DGvT	60561	3206	20W-10S	B4
1600	DRN	60561	3206	20W-10S	B4
1600	WDRG	60517	3206	20W-10S	B4
1600	WDRG	60561	3206	20W-10S	B4
2800	DRN	60516	3206	20W-10S	B4
3200	DRN	60517	3206	20W-10S	B4
CO-31 Lemont Rd					
700	DGvT	60516	3206	20W-9S	C4
700	DGvT	60561	3206	20W-9S	C4
700	DRN	60516	3206	20W-9S	C4
700	DRN	60561	3206	20W-9S	C4
8300	DGvT	60517	3206	20W-9S	C3
8300	DRN	60517	3206	20W-9S	C3
CO-31 Plainfield Rd					
-	DGvT	60517	3206	19W-9S	C3
-	DRN	60517	3206	19W-9S	C3
10	DRGV	60516	3206	19W-9S	D3
10	DRGV	60561	3206	19W-9S	D3
10	DRN	60516	3206	19W-9S	D3
10	DRN	60561	3206	19W-9S	D3
100	BRRG	60527	3146	15W-7S	B6
100	DRN	60527	3145	16W-7S	E7
100	DRN	60561	3145	16W-7S	E7
100	WLBK	60527	3145	16W-7S	E7
100	WLBK	60527	3146	15W-7S	B6
100	WLBK	60561	3145	16W-7S	E7
200	DGvT	60516	3206	18W-9S	E3
300	DRN	60561	3207	18W-8S	B2
400	DRN	60527	3207	17W-8S	D1
400	WLBK	60527	3207	17W-8S	D1
400	WLBK	60561	3207	17W-8S	D1
500	DGvT	60561	3206	19W-9S	C3
1500	DRGV	60516	3207	18W-8S	A2
1500	DRN	60516	3207	18W-8S	A2
1700	DRGV	60561	3207	18W-9S	A2
CO-32					
-	NPVL	60555	3081	27W-4S	C7
-	NPVL	60563	3081	27W-4S	C7
-	WNVL	60563	3081	27W-4S	C7
10	NPVL	60563	3141	27W-4S	C1
10	PltT	60124	2851	43W-10N	A6
10	PltT	60140	2851	43W-10N	A6
10	WNVL	60555	3141	27W-4S	C1
10	WNVL	60563	3141	27W-4S	C1
100	WNVL	60555	3081	28W-3S	B6
400	PltT	60124	2852	41W-10N	A6
1400	NpvT	60563	3141	27W-5S	C2
CO-32 Mill St					
-	NPVL	60555	3081	27W-4S	C7
-	NPVL	60563	3081	27W-4S	C7
-	WNVL	60555	3081	27W-4S	C7
-	WNVL	60563	3081	27W-4S	C7
10	NPVL	60563	3141	27W-4S	C1
10	WNVL	60555	3141	27W-4S	C1
10	WNVL	60563	3141	27W-4S	C1
CO-32 N Mill St					
900	NPVL	60563	3141	27W-5S	C3
1400	NpvT	60563	3141	27W-5S	C2
1900	WNVL	60555	3141	27W-4S	C1
1900	WNVL	60563	3141	27W-4S	C1
CO-32 Plato Rd					
10	PltT	60124	2851	43W-10N	A6
10	PltT	60140	2851	43W-10N	A6
400	PltT	60124	2852	41W-10N	A6
CO-32 Warrenville Rd					
-	NPVL	60555	3081	27W-4S	C7
-	NPVL	60563	3081	27W-4S	C7
-	WNVL	60563	3081	27W-4S	C7
100	WNVL	60555	3081	28W-3S	B6
CO-33					
-	NPVL	60540	3203	28W-8S	A2
-	NPVL	60565	3203	26W-8S	E2
CO-33					
-	NpvT	60564	3203	27W-8S	B2
10	LslT	60540	3204	25W-8S	A2
10	LslT	60565	3204	25W-8S	A2
10	NPVL	60540	3204	25W-8S	C2
10	NPVL	60565	3204	25W-8S	A2
10	PltT	60124	2852	41W-10N	A5
10	WLBK	60527	3207	16W-8S	E1
100	DRN	60527	3207	16W-8S	D1
100	DRN	60561	3207	16W-8S	E1
200	DRGV	60561	3206	18W-8S	E1
200	DRN	60516	3206	19W-8S	E1
200	DRN	60561	3206	18W-8S	E1
300	PltT	60124	2851	41W-10N	E5
400	DGvT	60516	3206	19W-8S	C1
400	DRGV	60516	3206	20W-8S	B1
400	LslT	60540	3205	23W-8S	A2
400	LslT	60565	3205	23W-8S	A2
400	NPVL	60540	3202	29W-8S	D2
400	NPVL	60564	3202	29W-8S	D2
400	NpvT	60564	3202	29W-8S	D2
400	WLBK	60561	3207	17W-8S	D1
600	AURA	60504	3202	30W-8S	B2
600	AURA	60540	3202	30W-8S	C2
600	AURA	60564	3202	30W-8S	C2
600	NpvT	60504	3202	30W-8S	C2
1000	WDRG	60516	3206	20W-8S	C1
1100	NPVL	60564	3203	28W-8S	B2
1500	DRGV	60516	3207	18W-8S	A1
1500	DRN	60516	3207	18W-8S	A1
1700	WDRG	60517	3206	20W-8S	A1
2100	WDRG	60517	3205	21W-8S	D2
2900	LslT	60517	3205	22W-8S	D2
CO-33 75th St					
-	AURA	60504	3202	28W-8S	E2
-	AURA	60564	3202	30W-8S	B2
-	NPVL	60540	3203	28W-8S	A2
-	NPVL	60564	3203	27W-8S	B2
-	NPVL	60565	3203	28W-8S	A2
-	NpvT	60504	3202	30W-8S	B2
-	NpvT	60564	3203	27W-8S	B2
10	LslT	60540	3204	25W-8S	A2
10	LslT	60565	3204	24W-8S	E2
10	NPVL	60540	3204	25W-8S	C2
10	NPVL	60565	3204	25W-8S	A2
10	WLBK	60527	3207	16W-8S	E1
100	DRN	60527	3207	16W-8S	D1
100	DRN	60561	3207	16W-8S	E1
200	DRGV	60516	3206	19W-8S	E1
200	DRN	60516	3206	19W-8S	E1
300	DRN	60561	3206	19W-8S	E1
400	DGvT	60516	3206	19W-8S	C1
400	DRGV	60561	3206	19W-8S	E1
400	DRN	60561	3206	19W-8S	E1
400	LslT	60565	3205	23W-8S	A2
400	NPVL	60540	3202	29W-8S	D2
400	NPVL	60564	3202	29W-8S	D2
400	NpvT	60564	3202	29W-8S	C2
400	WLBK	60561	3207	17W-8S	D1
500	LslT	60540	3205	22W-8S	B2
500	WDRG	60516	3206	19W-8S	C1
600	AURA	60540	3202	30W-8S	C2
600	NpvT	60564	3203	28W-8S	A2
1000	WDRG	60517	3206	20W-8S	C1
1500	DRGV	60516	3207	18W-8S	A1
1500	DRN	60516	3207	18W-8S	A1
2100	WDRG	60517	3205	23W-8S	A2
2900	LslT	60517	3205	22W-8S	B2
CO-33 Rippburger Rd					
700	PltT	60124	2851	41W-10N	E6
CO-33 Russell Rd					
10	PltT	60124	2852	41W-10N	A5
300	PltT	60124	2851	41W-10N	E5
CO-34					
-	BtvT	60542	3077	37W-3S	C6
-	DndT	60123	2799	37W-14N	E6
-	NARA	60506	3137	37W-4S	C2
-	NARA	60539	3077	37W-3S	C6
-	NARA	60542	3137	37W-4S	C1
10	ALGN	60102	2746	36W-19N	E3
10	ALGN	60118	2746	36W-19N	E3
10	AraT	60542	3077	37W-4S	C7
10	AURA	60506	3137	37W-4S	C1
10	BTVA	60510	3077	37W-2S	D4
10	BTVA	60539	3077	37W-2S	D4
10	BtvT	60539	3077	37W-2S	D4
10	DndT	60102	2746	36W-19N	E3
10	DndT	60118	2746	37W-19N	E2
10	DndT	60118	2799	37W-16N	E1
10	DndT	60124	2799	37W-14N	E6
10	ELGN	60118	2799	37W-14N	E6
10	ELGN	60123	2799	37W-14N	E6
10	ELGN	60123	2853	37W-12N	D2
10	ELGN	60123	2907	37W-6N	D7
10	ELGN	60124	2799	37W-14N	E6
10	ELGN	60124	2853	37W-12N	D2
10	ELGN	60124	2907	37W-6N	D7
10	ElgT	60123	2799	36W-13N	E7
10	ElgT	60123	2853	37W-12N	D2
10	ElgT	60123	2907	37W-6N	D7
10	ElgT	60124	2799	36W-13N	E7
10	ElgT	60124	2853	37W-12N	D2
10	ElgT	60124	2907	37W-6N	D7
10	NARA	60542	3077	37W-4S	C7
10	SchT	60174	2963	36W-5N	D2
10	SchT	60175	2963	37W-5N	D2
10	SCRL	60174	2963	36W-2N	D7
10	SCRL	60175	2963	36W-2N	D7
10	SYHW	60118	2799	37W-14N	E6
10	WDND	60118	2746	37W-17N	E7
10	WDND	60118	2799	37W-16N	E3
100	OKBK	60523	3086	15W-3S	B4
100	PvsT	60523	3086	15W-2S	C4
100	SCRL	60134	3019	37W-2N	D1
100	SCRL	60174	3019	37W-2N	D1
100	SCRL	60175	3019	37W-2N	D1
200	BTVA	60510	3019	37W-0S	D7
200	BtvT	60510	3077	37W-2S	D4
200	GNVA	60134	3019	36W-2N	D1
200	SchT	60175	2907	37W-6N	D7
200	SEGN	60175	2907	36W-8N	D3
200	SEGN	60177	2907	37W-6N	D7
200	SYHW	60124	2799	37W-15N	E4
300	CPVL	60110	2746	36W-19N	E2
300	CPVL	60118	2746	36W-17N	E7
300	SchT	60174	3019	36W-2N	D1
300	SchT	60175	3019	36W-2N	D1
300	SEGN	60175	2907	36W-8N	D4
300	WDND	60110	2746	36W-17N	E7
400	GnvT	60134	3019	37W-0S	D7
400	GnvT	60510	3019	37W-0S	D7
500	BTVA	60134	3019	37W-0S	D7
500	DRGV	60515	3084	19W-2S	D4
500	DRGV	60523	3084	19W-2S	D4
500	OKBK	60523	3084	19W-3S	D4
500	YkTp	60515	3084	19W-2S	D4
500	YkTp	60523	3084	19W-3S	D4
800	OKBK	60523	3085	17W-3S	B4
CO-34					
900	GNVA	60174	3019	37W-2N	D1
1700	AURA	60542	3137	37W-5S	C2
2000	YkTp	60523	3085	17W-2S	B4
2300	DndT	60110	2746	37W-19N	E2
CO-34 31st St					
500	DRGV	60515	3084	19W-2S	D4
500	DRGV	60523	3084	19W-2S	D4
500	OKBK	60523	3084	18W-2S	E4
500	YkTp	60515	3084	19W-2S	D4
500	YkTp	60523	3084	19W-2S	D4
CO-34 Oak Brook Rd					
100	OKBK	60523	3086	15W-3S	B4
100	PvsT	60523	3086	15W-2S	C4
800	OKBK	60523	3085	17W-3S	B4
2000	YkTp	60523	3085	17W-2S	B4
2800	OKBK	60523	3084	19W-3S	D4
3000	DRGV	60523	3084	18W-2S	E4
3000	YkTp	60523	3084	19W-3S	D4
CO-34 Randall Rd					
-	SCRL	60174	2963	36W-3N	D5
-	SCRL	60175	2963	36W-3N	D5
10	ALGN	60102	2746	36W-19N	E3
10	ALGN	60118	2746	36W-19N	E3
10	DndT	60102	2746	36W-19N	E3
10	DndT	60118	2746	37W-19N	E2
10	DndT	60118	2799	37W-16N	E1
10	ELGN	60123	2853	36W-9N	E7
10	ELGN	60123	2907	37W-6N	D7
10	ELGN	60124	2799	37W-16N	E2
10	ELGN	60124	2853	36W-9N	E7
10	ELGN	60124	2907	37W-6N	D7
10	ElgT	60123	2907	37W-6N	D7
10	ElgT	60124	2853	36W-9N	E7
10	ElgT	60124	2907	37W-6N	D7
10	SchT	60174	2963	37W-5N	D2
10	SchT	60175	2963	37W-5N	D2
10	WDND	60118	2746	37W-17N	E7
10	WDND	60118	2799	37W-16N	E1
100	SCRL	60134	3019	37W-2N	D1
100	SCRL	60174	3019	37W-2N	D1
100	SCRL	60175	3019	37W-2N	D1
200	GNVA	60134	3019	37W-2N	D1
200	SchT	60175	2907	37W-6N	D7
200	SEGN	60124	2907	36W-8N	D3
200	SEGN	60177	2907	37W-6N	D7
300	CPVL	60110	2746	37W-19N	E2
300	CPVL	60118	2746	36W-17N	E7
300	SEGN	60175	2907	36W-8N	D4
300	WDND	60110	2746	36W-17N	E7
900	GNVA	60174	3019	37W-2N	D1
2300	DndT	60110	2746	37W-19N	E2
CO-34 N Randall Rd					
-	BtvT	60510	3077	37W-3S	C6
-	BtvT	60539	3077	37W-3S	C6
-	BtvT	60542	3077	37W-3S	C6
-	DndT	60123	2799	37W-14N	E6
-	NARA	60506	3137	37W-4S	C2
-	NARA	60539	3077	37W-3S	C6
-	NARA	60542	3137	37W-4S	C1
10	AraT	60542	3077	37W-4S	C7
10	AURA	60506	3137	37W-4S	C1
10	BTVA	60510	3077	37W-1S	D1
10	DndT	60124	2799	37W-14N	E6
10	ELGN	60118	2799	37W-14N	E6
10	ELGN	60123	2799	37W-14N	E6
10	ELGN	60123	2853	37W-12N	D2
10	ELGN	60124	2799	37W-14N	E6
10	ElgT	60123	2799	36W-13N	E7
10	ElgT	60123	2853	37W-12N	D2
10	ElgT	60124	2799	36W-13N	E7
10	ElgT	60124	2853	37W-12N	D2
10	NARA	60542	3077	37W-4S	C7
10	SYHW	60118	2799	37W-14N	E6
10	WDND	60118	2799	37W-16N	E3
100	SCRL	60174	2963	37W-3N	D7
100	SCRL	60175	2963	37W-3N	D7
200	BTVA	60510	3019	37W-0S	D7
200	DndT	60118	2799	37W-16N	E2
200	SYHW	60124	2799	37W-15N	E4
300	SchT	60174	2963	36W-3N	D6
300	SchT	60175	2963	36W-3N	D6
400	GnvT	60134	3019	37W-0S	D7
400	GnvT	60510	3019	37W-0S	D7
500	BTVA	60134	3019	37W-0S	D7
500	ELGN	60124	2853	37W-12N	D2
500	GNVA	60134	3019	37W-0S	D7
1700	AURA	60542	3137	37W-5S	C2
CO-34 S Randall Rd					
-	BtvT	60542	3077	37W-3S	C6
-	NARA	60539	3077	37W-3S	C6
-	NARA	60542	3077	37W-3S	C6
10	BTVA	60510	3077	37W-2S	D4
10	BTVA	60539	3077	37W-2S	D4
10	BtvT	60539	3077	37W-2S	D4
10	SchT	60174	2963	36W-2N	D7
10	SchT	60175	2963	36W-2N	D7
10	SCRL	60174	2963	36W-2N	D7
10	SCRL	60175	2963	36W-2N	D7
100	ELGN	60123	2853	36W-11N	E5
100	ELGN	60124	2853	36W-11N	E5
200	BtvT	60510	3077	37W-2S	D4
300	SchT	60174	3019	36W-2N	D1
300	SchT	60175	3019	36W-2N	D1
300	SCRL	60174	3019	36W-2N	D1
300	SCRL	60175	3019	36W-2N	D1
1400	GNVA	60134	3019	36W-0N	D5
1500	ALGN	60102	2746	36W-19N	E2
1800	BTVA	60134	3019	37W-0S	D6
1800	BTVA	60510	3019	37W-0S	D6
1800	GnvT	60134	3019	37W-0S	D6
1800	GnvT	60510	3019	37W-0S	D6
CO-35					
-	CNHL	60521	3145	16W-6S	E3
10	WTMT	60559	3145	17W-5S	B3
100	CNHL	60514	3145	16W-5S	D3
100	DRGV	60515	3144	19W-6S	D3
100	DRGV	60516	3144	19W-6S	D3
100	DRGV	60559	3144	19W-6S	D3
100	WTMT	60559	3144	19W-6S	D3
200	DGvT	60514	3145	17W-5S	D3
300	DRGV	60515	3145	18W-5S	A3
300	DRGV	60559	3145	18W-5S	A3
300	WTMT	60514	3145	17W-5S	C3
300	WTMT	60515	3145	18W-5S	A3
400	HNDL	60521	3146	15W-6S	B3
500	DGvT	60521	3145	17W-6S	B3
500	HNDL	60521	3145	17W-6S	B3
CO-35 55th St					
-	CNHL	60521	3145	16W-6S	E3
-	DGvT	60521	3145	16W-6S	E3
-	DRGV	60515	3145	18W-5S	A3
-	DRGV	60559	3145	18W-5S	A3
-	HNDL	60521	3145	16W-6S	E3
-	WTMT	60559	3145	18W-5S	A3
100	CNHL	60514	3145	16W-5S	D3
CO-35 55th St					
100	DRGV	60515	3144	19W-6S	D3
100	DRGV	60516	3144	19W-6S	D3
100	DRGV	60559	3144	19W-6S	D3
100	WTMT	60559	3144	19W-6S	D3
200	DGvT	60514	3145	17W-5S	D3
CO-35 E 55th St					
10	HNDL	60521	3146	15W-6S	B3
10	WTMT	60559	3145	17W-5S	B3
300	CNHL	60514	3145	17W-5S	C3
300	WTMT	60514	3145	17W-5S	C3
CO-35 W 55th St					
-	CNHL	60514	3145	16W-6S	E3
-	CNHL	60521	3145	16W-6S	E3
10	HNDL	60521	3146	15W-5S	A3
10	WTMT	60559	3145	18W-5S	B3
300	DRGV	60515	3145	18W-5S	A3
300	DRGV	60559	3145	18W-5S	A3
300	WTMT	60515	3145	18W-5S	A3
500	DGvT	60521	3145	17W-6S	B3
500	HNDL	60521	3145	17W-6S	B3
CO-36					
-	BMDL	60188	2968	24W-4N	D4
-	CLSM	60108	2968	24W-4N	D4
-	CrlT	60140	2743	45W-20N	A1
-	CrlT	60142	2743	45W-20N	A1
-	HPSR	60140	2743	45W-20N	A1
-	HshT	60140	2743	45W-20N	A1
10	BMDL	60108	2968	24W-4N	D4
10	BMDL	60139	2968	24W-4N	D4
10	GLHT	60108	2968	24W-4N	D4
10	GLHT	60139	2968	24W-4N	D4
10	HPSR	60140	2795	46W-15N	E3
10	HshT	60140	2795	47W-16N	D1
100	CLSM	60139	3024	24W-2N	D1
100	CLSM	60188	2968	24W-3N	D6
100	CLSM	60188	3024	24W-1N	D3
100	GLHT	60139	3024	24W-2N	D1
100	GLHT	60188	2968	24W-3N	D6
100	GLHT	60188	3024	24W-2N	D1
200	MltT	60188	3024	24W-1N	C3
400	WHTN	60188	3024	24W-1N	C3
1800	CLSM	60139	2968	24W-3N	D5
2200	WHTN	60187	3024	24W-1N	C3
CO-36 Allen Rd					
10	HPSR	60140	2795	47W-16N	E1
CO-36 Getty Rd					
-	CrlT	60140	2743	45W-20N	A1
-	CrlT	60142	2743	45W-20N	A1
-	HPSR	60140	2743	45W-20N	A1
-	HshT	60140	2743	45W-20N	A1
CO-36 Harmony Rd					
10	HPSR	60140	2795	47W-16N	D1
10	HshT	60140	2795	47W-16N	D1
CO-36 N Main St					
2200	CLSM	60188	3024	24W-1N	C3
2200	MltT	60188	3024	24W-1N	C3
2200	WHTN	60187	3024	24W-1N	C3
2200	WHTN	60188	3024	24W-1N	C3
CO-36 Schmale Rd					
-	BMDL	60188	2968	24W-4N	D4
-	CLSM	60108	2968	24W-4N	D4
10	BMDL	60108	2968	24W-4N	D4
10	BMDL	60139	2968	24W-4N	D4
10	GLHT	60108	2968	24W-4N	D4
10	GLHT	60139	2968	24W-4N	D4
100	CLSM	60188	2968	24W-3N	D6
100	CLSM	60188	3024	24W-2N	D1
100	GLHT	60188	2968	24W-3N	D6
400	CLSM	60139	3024	24W-2N	D1
400	GLHT	60139	3024	24W-2N	D1
400	GLHT	60188	3024	24W-2N	D1
1800	CLSM	60139	2968	24W-3N	D5
CO-36 N Schmale Rd					
100	CLSM	60139	3024	24W-2N	D1
100	CLSM	60188	3024	24W-2N	D1
100	GLHT	60139	3024	24W-2N	D1
100	GLHT	60188	3024	24W-2N	D1
CO-36 S Schmale Rd					
100	CLSM	60188	3024	24W-1N	C3
100	GLHT	60188	3024	24W-1N	D2
200	MltT	60188	3024	24W-1N	C3
400	WHTN	60188	3024	24W-1N	C3
CO-36 N State St					
100	HPSR	60140	2795	47W-15N	E3
CO-36 S State St					
100	HPSR	60140	2795	46W-16N	E2
CO-37					
200	GNEN	60137	3025	21W-0N	E4
200	LMBD	60137	3025	21W-0N	E4
200	LMBD	60148	3025	21W-0N	E4
200	MltT	60137	3025	21W-0N	E4
CO-37 Crescent Blvd					
200	GNEN	60137	3025	21W-0N	E4
200	LMBD	60137	3025	21W-0N	E4
200	LMBD	60148	3025	21W-0N	E4
200	MltT	60137	3025	21W-0N	E4
CO-38					
-	LslT	60517	3143	21W-6S	E5
10	DGvT	60527	3145	16W-6S	E5
10	DGvT	60527	3146	16W-6S	A5
10	WLBK	60527	3145	16W-6S	E5
10	WLBK	60527	3146	16W-6S	A5
10	WTMT	60527	3145	17W-6S	B5
10	WTMT	60559	3145	16W-7S	D5
400	DGvT	60516	3144	19W-6S	E5
400	DGvT	60559	3145	17W-6S	C5
400	DRGV	60516	3144	19W-6S	E5
400	WTMT	60516	3144	19W-6S	E5
400	WTMT	60559	3144	21W-7S	A5
1900	LslT	60516	3144	20W-7S	A5
2100	DRGV	60516	3143	21W-7S	E5
2100	LslT	60516	3143	21W-7S	E5
2200	WDRG	60516	3143	21W-7S	E5
2200	WDRG	60517	3143	21W-7S	E5
CO-38 63rd St					
-	LslT	60517	3143	21W-7S	E5
10	DGvT	60527	3145	16W-6S	E5
10	DGvT	60527	3146	16W-6S	A5
10	WLBK	60527	3145	16W-6S	E5
10	WLBK	60527	3146	16W-6S	A5
400	DGvT	60559	3145	17W-6S	C5
400	WTMT	60527	3145	17W-6S	C5
400	WTMT	60559	3145	17W-6S	C5
800	DRGV	60516	3144	19W-6S	D5
1400	DGvT	60516	3144	20W-7S	B5
1900	LslT	60516	3144	20W-7S	A5
2100	DRGV	60516	3143	21W-7S	E5
2100	LslT	60516	3143	21W-7S	E5
2200	WDRG	60516	3143	21W-7S	E5
2200	WDRG	60517	3143	21W-7S	E5
CO-38 E 63rd St					
10	WTMT	60527	3145	17W-6S	B5
10	WTMT	60559	3145	17W-6S	B5
CO-38 W 63rd St					
10	WTMT	60559	3145	16W-7S	D5

Chicago 7-County Street Index

STREET Block	City	ZIP	Map#	CGS	Grid
CO-38 W 63rd St					
400	DGvT	60516	3144	19W-6S	E5
400	DRGV	60516	3144	19W-6S	E5
400	WTMT	60516	3144	19W-6S	E5
400	WTMT	60559	3144	21W-7S	A5
CO-38 Hobson Rd					
-	LslT	60517	3143	21W-7S	D6
-	WDRG	60517	3143	21W-7S	D6
CO-40					
-	CrlT	60140	2743	45W-20N	A1
-	CrlT	60142	2743	45W-20N	A1
-	HPSR	60140	2743	45W-20N	A1
-	HshT	60140	2743	45W-20N	A1
-	LslT	60532	3142	24W-7S	C7
-	LslT	60540	3142	24W-7S	C7
-	NPVL	60532	3142	24W-7S	C7
-	NPVL	60540	3142	24W-7S	C7
10	BNHL	60010	2801	32W-16N	E1
10	BNHL	60118	2801	32W-16N	E1
10	CPVL	60110	2801	32W-16N	E1
10	CPVL	60118	2801	32W-16N	E1
10	EDND	60110	2801	32W-16N	E1
10	EDND	60118	2801	32W-16N	E1
100	LslT	60540	3204	24W-8S	C1
100	NPVL	60540	3204	24W-8S	C1
200	LslT	60565	3204	24W-8S	C2
4300	LSLE	60532	3142	24W-7S	D6
CO-40 College Rd					
-	LslT	60532	3142	24W-7S	C7
-	LslT	60540	3142	24W-7S	C7
-	LslT	60540	3204	24W-7S	C1
-	NPVL	60532	3142	24W-7S	C7
-	NPVL	60540	3142	24W-7S	C7
-	NPVL	60540	3204	24W-7S	C1
5600	LSLE	60532	3142	24W-6S	E4
CO-40 Getty Rd					
-	CrlT	60140	2743	45W-20N	A1
-	CrlT	60142	2743	45W-20N	A1
-	HPSR	60140	2743	45W-20N	A1
-	HshT	60140	2743	45W-20N	A1
CO-40 Penny Rd					
10	BNHL	60010	2801	32W-16N	E1
10	BNHL	60118	2801	32W-16N	E1
10	CPVL	60110	2801	32W-16N	E1
10	CPVL	60118	2801	32W-16N	E1
10	EDND	60110	2801	32W-16N	E1
10	EDND	60118	2801	32W-16N	E1
CO-40 Wehrli Rd					
100	LslT	60540	3204	24W-8S	C1
100	NPVL	60540	3204	24W-8S	C1
200	LslT	60565	3204	24W-8S	C2
CO-40 Yackley Av					
4300	LSLE	60532	3142	24W-7S	D6
CO-41					
10	BbyT	60119	3017	42W-1N	D4
10	BbyT	60119	3018	39W-1N	E4
10	BbyT	60134	3018	39W-0N	E4
10	ELBN	60119	3017	42W-1N	D4
10	GNVA	60134	3019	38W-0N	A4
10	GnvT	60134	3019	38W-0N	A4
500	BbyT	60134	3019	38W-1N	A4
2200	DRGV	60516	3143	21W-6S	E4
2200	LslT	60516	3143	21W-6S	E4
6700	EsxT	60481	4031	30W-46S	D7
6700	EsxT	60935	4031	30W-46S	D7
6700	RedT	60481	4031	30W-46S	D7
CO-41 N 16000W Rd					
6700	EsxT	60481	4031	30W-46S	D7
6700	EsxT	60935	4031	30W-46S	D7
6700	RedT	60481	4031	30W-46S	D7
CO-41 Hobson Rd					
2200	DRGV	60516	3143	21W-6S	E4
2200	LslT	60516	3143	21W-6S	E4
CO-41 Keslinger Rd					
10	BbyT	60119	3017	42W-1N	D4
10	BbyT	60119	3018	39W-1N	E4
10	BbyT	60134	3018	39W-0N	E4
10	ELBN	60119	3017	42W-1N	D4
10	GNVA	60134	3019	38W-0N	A4
10	GnvT	60134	3019	38W-0N	A4
500	BbyT	60134	3019	38W-1N	A4
CO-43					
10	HRPK	60133	2911	27W-6N	D7
10	HRPK	60133	2967	27W-3N	D6
10	MltT	60187	3023	27W-1N	D3
10	MltT	60190	3023	27W-1N	D3
10	WHTN	60187	3023	27W-1N	D3
10	WNFD	60190	3023	26W-0N	D6
10	WnfT	60185	3023	27W-2N	D2
10	WynT	60133	2911	27W-6N	D7
10	WynT	60133	2967	27W-6N	D1
10	WynT	60185	3023	27W-2N	D1
100	WNFD	60185	3023	27W-1N	D3
100	WnfT	60190	3023	27W-1N	D3
300	CLSM	60185	2967	27W-2N	D7
300	CLSM	60188	2967	27W-2N	D7
300	WynT	60185	2967	27W-2N	D7
300	WynT	60188	2967	27W-2N	D7
400	WHTN	60187	3081	26W-0S	D1
500	BRLT	60103	2911	27W-7N	D5
500	BRLT	60133	2911	27W-7N	D5
500	HRPK	60103	2911	27W-7N	D5
1200	CLSM	60133	2967	27W-4N	D3
CO-43 County Farm Rd					
-	CLSM	60133	2967	27W-4N	D3
10	HRPK	60133	2911	27W-6N	D7
10	HRPK	60133	2967	27W-3N	D6
10	MltT	60187	3023	26W-0S	D6
10	MltT	60190	3023	26W-0N	D6
10	WHTN	60187	3023	26W-0S	D6
10	WNFD	60190	3023	26W-0N	D6
10	WnfT	60185	3023	27W-2N	D2
10	WynT	60133	2911	27W-6N	D7
10	WynT	60133	2967	27W-6N	D1
10	WynT	60185	3023	27W-2N	D1
100	WNFD	60185	3023	27W-1N	D3
100	WnfT	60190	3023	27W-1N	D3
300	CLSM	60185	2967	27W-2N	D7
300	CLSM	60188	2967	27W-2N	D7
300	WynT	60185	2967	27W-2N	D7
300	WynT	60188	2967	27W-2N	D7
500	BRLT	60103	2911	27W-7N	D5
500	BRLT	60133	2911	27W-7N	D5
500	HRPK	60103	2911	27W-7N	D5
CO-43 N County Farm Rd					
-	CLSM	60185	2967	27W-3N	D7
-	MltT	60187	3023	27W-1N	D3
-	MltT	60190	3023	27W-1N	D3
-	WynT	60185	2967	27W-3N	D7
-	WynT	60188	2967	27W-3N	D7
100	WHTN	60187	3023	27W-1N	D3
900	CLSM	60188	2967	27W-3N	D5
1200	CLSM	60133	2967	27W-4N	D3
1200	HRPK	60133	2967	27W-4N	D3
CO-43 S County Farm Rd					
100	WHTN	60187	3023	26W-0S	D7
400	WHTN	60187	3081	26W-0S	D1
CO-45					
10	HshT	60140	2795	47W-16N	D1
500	HPSR	60140	2795	47W-16N	D1
CO-45 Allen Rd					
10	HshT	60140	2795	47W-16N	D1
500	HPSR	60140	2795	47W-16N	D1
CO-46					
10	BrlT	60140	2795	48W-13N	B7
10	HshT	60140	2795	48W-13N	B7
CO-46 Burlington Rd					
100	BrlT	60140	2795	48W-13N	B7
100	HshT	60140	2795	48W-13N	B7
CO-46 Walker Rd					
10	BrlT	60140	2795	48W-14N	A6
10	HshT	60140	2795	49W-16N	A2
CO-47					
10	ELGN	60123	2853	37W-12N	D2
10	ELGN	60124	2853	37W-12N	D2
10	ElgT	60123	2853	37W-12N	D2
10	ElgT	60124	2853	38W-12N	B1
10	PltT	60124	2798	39W-13N	D7
10	PltT	60124	2852	39W-13N	E1
10	PltT	60124	2853	38W-12N	B1
10	RtdT	60124	2798	40W-14N	C6
10	RtdT	60140	2798	40W-14N	C6
CO-47 Highland Av					
10	ELGN	60123	2853	37W-12N	D2
10	ELGN	60124	2853	37W-12N	D2
10	ElgT	60123	2853	37W-12N	D2
10	ElgT	60124	2853	38W-12N	B1
10	PltT	60124	2798	39W-13N	D7
10	PltT	60124	2852	39W-13N	E1
10	PltT	60124	2853	38W-12N	B1
10	RtdT	60124	2798	40W-14N	C6
200	RtdT	60140	2798	40W-14N	C6
CO-48					
10	BRkT	60554	3134	44W-4S	D1
10	SgrT	60554	3134	44W-4S	D1
CO-48 Scott Rd					
10	BRkT	60554	3134	44W-4S	D1
10	SgrT	60554	3134	44W-4S	D1
CO-50					
100	HRPK	60133	2967	27W-5N	D2
400	BMDL	60108	2968	25W-5N	A2
400	BMDL	60172	2968	25W-5N	A2
400	BmdT	60108	2967	26W-5N	E2
400	BmdT	60133	2967	26W-5N	E2
400	BmdT	60172	2968	25W-5N	A2
500	BmdT	60108	2968	25W-5N	A2
500	BmdT	60133	2968	25W-5N	A2
500	WynT	60133	2967	26W-5N	D2
CO-50 Schick Rd					
100	HRPK	60133	2967	27W-5N	D2
400	BMDL	60108	2968	25W-5N	A2
400	BMDL	60172	2968	25W-5N	A2
400	BmdT	60108	2967	26W-5N	E2
400	BmdT	60133	2967	26W-5N	E2
400	BmdT	60172	2968	25W-5N	A2
500	BmdT	60108	2968	25W-5N	A2
500	BmdT	60133	2968	25W-5N	A2
500	WynT	60133	2967	26W-5N	D2
CO-51					
10	CmpT	60124	2905	42W-8N	D4
10	NPVL	60555	3081	27W-4S	D7
10	NPVL	60563	3081	27W-4S	D7
10	PltT	60124	2851	41W-10N	E6
10	PltT	60124	2905	42W-7N	D5
10	WnfT	60555	3081	27W-3S	D5
10	WNVL	60555	3081	27W-4S	D7
10	WNVL	60563	3081	27W-4S	D7
400	CmpT	60175	2905	42W-7N	D6
600	WHTN	60187	3081	27W-2S	D4
600	WnfT	60187	3081	27W-2S	D4
CO-51 Dittman Rd					
10	CmpT	60124	2905	42W-8N	D4
10	PltT	60124	2851	42W-10N	D6
10	PltT	60124	2905	42W-7N	D5
400	CmpT	60175	2905	42W-7N	D6
CO-51 Herrick Rd					
10	NPVL	60555	3081	27W-4S	D7
10	NPVL	60563	3081	27W-4S	D7
10	WnfT	60555	3081	27W-3S	D5
10	WNVL	60555	3081	27W-4S	D7
10	WNVL	60563	3081	27W-4S	D7
600	WHTN	60187	3081	27W-2S	D4
600	WnfT	60187	3081	27W-2S	D4
CO-53					
-	NPVL	60563	3140	29W-4S	E1
10	CmpT	60175	2962	39W-4N	E5
800	CmpT	60175	2963	38W-4N	A4
800	SchT	60175	2963	39W-4N	A4
27500	NpvT	60563	3141	27W-4S	C1
27500	WNVL	60563	3141	27W-4S	C1
28200	NPVL	60563	3141	28W-4S	A1
28200	WNVL	60555	3141	28W-4S	A1
CO-53 Dean St					
10	CmpT	60175	2962	39W-4N	E5
800	CmpT	60175	2963	39W-4N	A4
800	SchT	60175	2963	39W-4N	A4
CO-53 W Diehl Rd					
-	NPVL	60563	3140	29W-4S	E1
27500	NpvT	60563	3141	27W-4S	C1
27500	WNVL	60563	3141	27W-4S	C1
28200	NPVL	60563	3141	28W-4S	A1
28200	WNVL	60555	3141	28W-4S	A1
CO-54					
-	BmdT	60101	2969	21W-3N	E6
-	MltT	60148	3025	21W-1N	E1
10	ADSN	60101	2969	21W-2N	E7
10	BmdT	60148	2969	21W-2N	E7
10	BmdT	60148	3025	21W-2N	E1
CO-54 Collins Av					
-	ADSN	60101	2969	21W-3N	E6
-	BmdT	60101	2969	21W-3N	E6
-	BmdT	60148	2969	21W-3N	E6
CO-54 Swift Rd					
-	MltT	60148	3025	21W-1N	E1
10	ADSN	60101	2969	21W-2N	E7
10	BmdT	60101	2969	21W-2N	E7
10	BmdT	60148	2969	21W-2N	E7
10	BmdT	60148	3025	21W-2N	E1
CO-56					
7500	WDRG	60517	3206	21W-9S	A4
8300	DRN	60517	3206	20W-9S	A4
8300	DRN	60561	3206	21W-9S	A4
CO-56 Woodward Av					
7500	WDRG	60517	3206	21W-9S	A4
8300	DRN	60517	3206	21W-9S	A4
8300	DRN	60561	3206	21W-9S	A4
CO-59					
10	GLBT	60136	2799	38W-15N	C5
10	RtdT	60136	2799	38W-16N	B3
200	RtdT	60118	2799	38W-16N	B2
500	DndT	60124	2799	38W-15N	C5
500	DndT	60136	2799	37W-14N	C6
500	GLBT	60124	2799	38W-15N	C5
CO-59 Tyrrell Rd					
10	GLBT	60136	2799	38W-15N	C5
10	RtdT	60136	2799	38W-16N	B3
200	RtdT	60118	2799	38W-16N	B2
500	DndT	60124	2799	38W-15N	C5
500	DndT	60136	2799	37W-14N	C6
500	GLBT	60124	2799	38W-15N	C5
CO-61					
2100	BRLT	60103	2909	33W-8N	B3
2100	BRLT	60120	2909	33W-8N	B3
2100	HnrT	60120	2909	33W-8N	B3
2100	SEGN	60103	2909	33W-8N	B3
2100	SEGN	60120	2909	33W-8N	B3
2100	SEGN	60177	2909	33W-8N	B3
CO-61 W Bartlett Rd					
2100	BRLT	60103	2909	33W-8N	B3
2100	BRLT	60120	2909	33W-8N	B3
2100	HnrT	60120	2909	33W-8N	B3
2100	SEGN	60103	2909	33W-8N	B3
2100	SEGN	60120	2909	33W-8N	B3
2100	SEGN	60177	2909	33W-8N	B3
CO-63					
10	HTLY	60142	2744	41W-18N	E5
10	RtdT	60136	2745	39W-17N	E6
10	RtdT	60142	2745	39W-17N	E6
100	GLBT	60118	2746	39W-17N	A6
100	GLBT	60136	2745	39W-17N	E6
100	GLBT	60136	2746	39W-17N	A6
100	GLBT	60142	2745	39W-17N	E6
100	GLBT	60142	2746	39W-17N	A6
100	RtdT	60118	2746	39W-17N	A6
100	RtdT	60136	2746	39W-17N	A6
100	RtdT	60142	2746	39W-17N	A6
700	HTLY	60142	2745	41W-18N	A6
CO-63 Freeman Rd					
10	HTLY	60142	2744	41W-18N	E5
10	RtdT	60136	2745	39W-17N	E6
10	RtdT	60142	2745	39W-17N	E6
100	GLBT	60118	2746	39W-17N	A6
100	GLBT	60136	2745	39W-17N	E6
100	GLBT	60136	2746	39W-17N	A6
100	GLBT	60142	2745	39W-17N	E6
100	GLBT	60142	2746	39W-17N	A6
100	RtdT	60118	2746	39W-17N	A6
100	RtdT	60136	2746	39W-17N	A6
100	RtdT	60142	2746	39W-17N	A6
400	HTLY	60142	2745	41W-18N	A6
CO-69					
10	CmpT	60175	2961	43W-5N	A2
10	CmpT	60175	2962	41W-6N	A1
CO-69 Empire Rd					
10	CmpT	60175	2961	43W-5N	A2
10	CmpT	60175	2962	41W-6N	A1
CO-71					
10	BtvT	60539	3077	37W-3S	D6
10	BtvT	60542	3077	37W-3S	D6
10	NARA	60542	3077	37W-3S	D6
200	BtvT	60510	3077	37W-3S	C6
200	NARA	60539	3077	37W-3S	D6
CO-71 Mooseheart Rd					
10	BtvT	60539	3077	37W-3S	D6
10	BtvT	60542	3077	37W-3S	D6
10	NARA	60542	3077	37W-3S	D6
200	BtvT	60510	3077	37W-3S	C6
200	NARA	60539	3077	37W-3S	D6
CO-74					
-	JLET	60433	3587	23W-26S	A4
-	JLET	60436	3587	23W-26S	A4
-	JltT	60433	3587	23W-26S	A4
-	JltT	60436	3587	23W-26S	A4
CO-77					
-	BTVA	60502	3078	33W-2S	E5
-	BtvT	60502	3078	33W-3S	E5
-	SchT	60174	2965	33W-5N	A3
-	SchT	60184	2965	33W-5N	A3
10	BTVA	60510	3078	33W-3S	E6
10	BtvT	60510	3078	33W-3S	E6
10	GNVA	60134	3021	33W-2N	A2
10	GnvT	60134	3021	33W-2N	A2
10	SCRL	60134	3021	33W-2N	A2
10	SCRL	60174	3021	33W-2N	A1
100	GNVA	60185	3021	33W-1N	A4
100	GnvT	60185	3021	33W-1N	A4
300	SCRL	60174	2965	33W-3N	A5
600	BTVA	60510	3020	33W-0S	E7
1200	GnvT	60134	3020	33W-0S	E7
2300	AraT	60504	3138	34W-4S	E1
2300	AURA	60502	3138	33W-4S	E1
2300	AURA	60504	3138	34W-4S	E1
2600	AURA	60502	3078	33W-4S	E7
CO-77 N Farnsworth Av					
2300	AraT	60504	3138	34W-4S	E1
2300	AURA	60502	3138	34W-4S	E1
2300	AURA	60504	3138	34W-4S	E1
2600	AURA	60502	3078	33W-4S	E7
CO-77 Kirk Rd					
-	BTVA	60510	3020	33W-0S	E7
-	GnvT	60134	3020	33W-0S	E7
10	GNVA	60134	3021	33W-2N	A2
10	GnvT	60134	3021	33W-2N	A2
10	SCRL	60134	3021	33W-2N	A2
10	SCRL	60174	3021	33W-2N	A2
100	GNVA	60185	3021	33W-1N	A4
100	GnvT	60185	3021	33W-1N	A4
CO-77 N Kirk Rd					
-	SchT	60174	2965	33W-5N	A3
-	SchT	60184	2965	33W-5N	A3
-	SCRL	60174	2965	33W-3N	A5
10	BTVA	60510	3078	33W-1S	E1
600	BTVA	60510	3020	33W-0S	E7
1200	GnvT	60134	3020	33W-0S	E6
CO-77 S Kirk Rd					
-	AURA	60502	3078	33W-3S	E6
-	BTVA	60502	3078	33W-2S	E5
-	BtvT	60502	3078	33W-3S	E5
10	BTVA	60510	3078	33W-3S	E6
10	BtvT	60510	3078	33W-3S	E6
300	SCRL	60174	2965	33W-3N	A6
700	SCRL	60174	3021	33W-2N	A1
CO-78					
10	BbyT	60506	3076	40W-2S	B4
10	BbyT	60510	3076	40W-2S	B4
10	BbyT	60554	3076	40W-2S	B4
10	SgrT	60554	3135	41W-5S	D3
10	SRGV	60506	3135	42W-6S	D4
10	SRGV	60554	3135	41W-5S	D3
100	SgrT	60506	3075	41W-3S	E7
100	SgrT	60506	3135	41W-5S	D3
100	SgrT	60554	3075	41W-3S	E7
300	BbyT	60506	3075	41W-3S	E7
300	BbyT	60554	3075	41W-3S	E7
500	BbyT	60119	3076	40W-2S	B4
CO-78 Bliss Rd					
10	BbyT	60506	3076	40W-2S	B4
10	BbyT	60510	3076	40W-2S	B4
10	BbyT	60554	3076	40W-2S	B4
10	SgrT	60554	3135	41W-5S	D3
10	SRGV	60506	3135	42W-6S	D4
10	SRGV	60554	3135	41W-5S	D3
100	SgrT	60506	3075	41W-3S	E7
100	SgrT	60506	3135	41W-5S	D3
100	SgrT	60554	3075	41W-3S	E7
300	BbyT	60506	3075	41W-3S	E7
300	BbyT	60554	3075	41W-3S	E7
500	BbyT	60119	3076	40W-2S	B4
CO-80					
10	CmpT	60175	2906	40W-6N	C7
10	CmpT	60175	2962	40W-6N	B1
10	PltT	60124	2906	40W-9N	C2
10	PltT	60175	2906	40W-8N	C4
CO-80 Corron Rd					
10	CmpT	60175	2906	40W-6N	C7
10	CmpT	60175	2962	40W-6N	B1
10	PltT	60124	2906	40W-9N	C2
10	PltT	60175	2906	40W-8N	C4
CO-81					
10	BbyT	60119	3018	40W-1N	B4
10	CmpT	60119	3018	40W-2N	B1
10	CmpT	60175	2962	40W-3N	B7
200	CmpT	60119	2962	40W-3N	B7
CO-81 Brown Rd					
800	CmpT	60175	2962	40W-5N	B2
CO-81 Lafox Rd					
10	BbyT	60119	3018	40W-1N	B4
10	CmpT	60119	3018	40W-2N	B1
10	CmpT	60175	2962	40W-3N	C5
200	CmpT	60119	2962	40W-3N	B7
CO-81 Old Lafox Rd					
10	CmpT	60175	2962	40W-3N	B7
CO-83					
1100	AraT	60506	3198	38W-9S	E4
1100	AraT	60538	3198	39W-9S	E4
1100	AURA	60506	3198	39W-9S	E4
1100	AURA	60538	3198	39W-9S	E4
1100	MTGY	60506	3198	39W-9S	E4
1100	MTGY	60538	3198	39W-9S	E4
CO-83 Orchard Rd					
1100	AraT	60506	3198	39W-9S	E4
1100	AraT	60538	3198	39W-9S	E4
1100	AURA	60506	3198	39W-9S	E4
1100	AURA	60538	3198	39W-9S	E4
1100	MTGY	60506	3198	39W-9S	E4
1100	MTGY	60538	3198	39W-9S	E4
CO-84					
10	GNVA	60134	3019	38W-2N	B1
10	GnvT	60134	3019	38W-2N	B1
400	SCRL	60175	2963	38W-3N	B7
900	GnvT	60175	3019	37W-1N	B2
900	SchT	60175	3019	37W-1N	B2
900	SCRL	60175	3019	37W-1N	B2
CO-84 Kaneville Rd					
10	GNVA	60134	3019	37W-0N	B6
10	GnvT	60134	3019	38W-0N	A6
CO-84 Peck Rd					
10	GNVA	60134	3019	38W-2N	B1
10	GnvT	60134	3019	38W-2N	B1
400	SCRL	60175	2963	38W-3N	B7
900	GnvT	60175	3019	37W-1N	B2
900	SchT	60175	3019	37W-1N	B2
900	SCRL	60175	3019	37W-1N	B2
CO-A1					
11900	BtnT	53158	2362	12W-43N	B4
11900	BtnT	60099	2362	12W-43N	B4
11900	PTPR	53158	2362	12W-43N	B4
12600	PTPR	60099	2362	12W-43N	B4
13000	NptT	53158	2362	13W-43N	A4
13000	NptT	60099	2362	13W-43N	A4
13400	NptT	60099	2361	15W-42N	A5
13400	PTPR	53158	2361	15W-42N	A5
13400	WDWH	53158	2361	15W-42N	A5
13400	WDWH	60099	2361	15W-42N	A5
13400	ZION	60099	2361	15W-42N	A5
13800	PTPR	60099	2361	15W-42N	A5
16100	NptT	60099	2360	16W-42N	E5
16100	WDWH	60099	2360	16W-42N	E5
CO-A1 W Russell Rd					
11900	BtnT	53158	2362	12W-43N	B4
11900	BtnT	60099	2362	12W-43N	B4
11900	PTPR	53158	2362	12W-43N	B4
12600	PTPR	60099	2362	12W-43N	B4
13000	NptT	53158	2362	13W-43N	A4
13000	NptT	60099	2362	13W-43N	A4
13400	NptT	60099	2361	15W-42N	A5
13400	PTPR	53158	2361	15W-42N	A5
13400	WDWH	53158	2361	15W-42N	A5
13400	WDWH	60099	2361	15W-42N	A5
13400	ZION	60099	2361	15W-42N	A5
13800	PTPR	60099	2361	15W-42N	A5
16100	NptT	60099	2360	16W-42N	E5
16100	WDWH	60099	2360	16W-42N	E5
CO-A2					
10	ANTH	60002	2358	21W-43N	D4
10	AntT	60002	2358	22W-43N	B5
200	ANTH	60002	2357	23W-42N	E5
18100	AntT	60002	2359	20W-43N	A4
18100	BtlT	53104	2359	20W-43N	A4
18100	BtlT	53142	2359		B4
18100	BtlT	60002	2359	20W-43N	A4
18400	AntT	53104	2358	20W-43N	E4
18400	AntT	53104	2359	20W-43N	A4
18400	BtlT	53104	2358	20W-43N	E4
21400	BtlT	60002	2358	21W-43N	E4
CO-A2 128th St					
18100	AntT	60002	2359	20W-43N	A4
18100	BtlT	53104	2359	20W-43N	A4
18100	BtlT	53142	2359		B4
18100	BtlT	60002	2359	20W-43N	A4
18400	AntT	53104	2358	20W-43N	E4
18400	AntT	53104	2359	20W-43N	A4
18400	AntT	60002	2358	20W-43N	E4
18400	BtlT	53104	2358	20W-43N	E4
CO-A2 North Av					
10	ANTH	60002	2358	21W-43N	D4
10	AntT	60002	2358	22W-43N	B5
200	ANTH	60002	2357	23W-42N	E5
CO-A2 W North Av					
21400	ANTH	60002	2358	21W-43N	D4
21400	AntT	53104	2358	21W-43N	E4
21400	AntT	60002	2358	21W-43N	E4
21400	BtlT	53104	2358	21W-43N	E4
21400	BtlT	60002	2358	21W-43N	E4
CO-A4					
-	HNVL	60030	2532	22W-33N	C3
1900	WPHR	60096	2363	10W-42N	A6
3100	BtnT	60096	2363	10W-42N	A6
3400	BtnT	60096	2362	11W-42N	E6
3400	WPHR	60096	2362	11W-42N	E6
11600	BtnT	60099	2362	12W-42N	C6
11600	WPHR	60099	2362	11W-42N	D6
11700	ZION	60099	2362	12W-42N	C6
CO-A4 9th St					
1900	WPHR	60096	2363	10W-42N	A6
3100	BtnT	60096	2363	10W-42N	A6
3400	BtnT	60096	2362	11W-42N	E6
3400	WPHR	60096	2362	11W-42N	E6
CO-A4 W 9th St					
11400	BtnT	60096	2362	11W-42N	D6
11400	WPHR	60096	2362	11W-42N	D6
11600	BtnT	60099	2362	12W-42N	C6
11600	WPHR	60099	2362	11W-42N	D6
11700	ZION	60099	2362	12W-42N	C6
CO-A6					
2700	ZION	60099	2421	11W-40N	E2
3600	BHPK	60099	2421	12W-41N	C2
4600	BtnT	60099	2421	12W-41N	B2
4800	WDWH	60099	2421	12W-41N	B2
12800	WDWH	60083	2421	11W-40N	E2
13400	BtnT	60083	2420	13W-40N	E2
13400	BtnT	60099	2420	13W-40N	E2
13400	WDWH	60083	2420	13W-40N	E2
13400	ZION	60099	2420	13W-41N	E2
13800	NptT	60083	2420	13W-40N	E2
CO-A6 21st St					
2700	ZION	60099	2421	11W-41N	E2
3600	BHPK	60099	2421	12W-41N	C2
4600	BtnT	60099	2421	12W-41N	B2
4800	WDWH	60099	2421	12W-41N	B2
CO-A6 W 21st St					
12800	BHPK	60099	2421	12W-41N	B2
12800	BtnT	60099	2421	12W-41N	B2
12800	WDWH	60083	2421	11W-40N	E2
12800	WDWH	60099	2421	12W-41N	A2
13200	ZION	60099	2421	11W-40N	E2
13400	BtnT	60083	2420	13W-40N	E2
13400	BtnT	60099	2420	13W-40N	E2
13400	WDWH	60083	2420	13W-40N	E2
13400	ZION	60099	2420	13W-41N	E2
13800	NptT	60083	2420	13W-40N	E2
CO-A7					
100	BtnT	60081	2414	29W-39N	D5
100	FXLK	60081	2414	28W-39N	D5
7000	FXLK	60020	2414	28W-39N	D6
CO-A7 Main St Rd					
100	BtnT	60081	2414	29W-39N	D5
100	FXLK	60081	2414	29W-39N	D5
CO-A7 N State Park Rd					
7000	BtnT	60081	2414	28W-39N	D6
7000	FXLK	60020	2414	28W-39N	D6
7000	FXLK	60081	2414	28W-39N	D6
CO-A8					
1200	ZION	60099	2422	10W-39N	B5
2300	ZION	60099	2421	11W-39N	D5
2400	BHPK	60099	2421	11W-39N	D5
12000	BHPK	60087	2421	12W-39N	C5
CO-A8 33rd St					
1200	ZION	60099	2422	10W-39N	B5
2300	ZION	60099	2421	11W-39N	D5
2400	BHPK	60099	2421	11W-39N	D5
CO-A8 W 33rd St					
11500	BHPK	60099	2421	11W-39N	D5
11500	ZION	60099	2421	11W-39N	D5
12000	BHPK	60087	2421	12W-39N	C5
CO-A9					
2200	BHPK	60087	2421	11W-38N	D6
2200	BHPK	60099	2421	13W-38N	A6
2200	WKGN	60087	2421	11W-39N	D6
2200	WKGN	60099	2421	13W-38N	A6
4000	NptT	60083	2420	13W-39N	E6
4000	WDWH	60083	2420	15W-38N	A6
10000	BHPK	60099	2422	10W-39N	A6
12600	BHPK	60083	2421	12W-39N	A6
12600	WDWH	60083	2421	12W-39N	A6
15800	NptT	60083	2419	16W-38N	D6
15800	WDWH	60083	2419	15W-39N	E6
16100	OMCK	60083	2419	16W-38N	D6
CO-A9 W Wadsworth Rd					
2200	BHPK	60087	2421	11W-38N	D6
2200	BHPK	60099	2421	13W-38N	A6
2200	WKGN	60087	2421	11W-39N	D6
2200	WKGN	60099	2421	13W-38N	A6
4000	NptT	60083	2420	13W-39N	E6
4000	WDWH	60083	2420	15W-38N	A6
10000	BHPK	60099	2422	10W-39N	A6
12600	BHPK	60083	2421	12W-39N	A6
12600	WDWH	60083	2421	12W-39N	A6
15800	NptT	60083	2419	16W-38N	D6
15800	WDWH	60083	2419	15W-39N	E6
16100	OMCK	60083	2419	16W-38N	D6
CO-A10					
100	FXLK	60020	2415	28W-38N	A6
100	FXLK	60081	2415	28W-38N	A6
600	FXLK	60020	2414	28W-38N	E6
2000	LkvT	60046	2418	19W-38N	C6
2000	LNHT	60046	2418	19W-38N	C6
19000	OMCK	60046	2418	19W-38N	D6
19000	OMCK	60083	2418	19W-38N	D6
20700	LkvT	60046	2417	22W-39N	B4
20700	LNHT	60046	2417	22W-39N	B4
21200	LkvT	60002	2417	21W-39N	D4
21600	LKVL	60002	2417	21W-39N	C4
21600	LKVL	60046	2417	21W-39N	C4
22700	AntT	60002	2417	22W-40N	A4
22700	AntT	60046	2417	22W-40N	A4
23300	AntT	60002	2416	25W-40N	B3
23300	LKVL	60002	2416	23W-40N	E3
25800	AntT	60002	2415	26W-38N	D6
27700	AntT	60081	2415	27W-38N	B6
29600	BtnT	60081	2414	28W-38N	E6
29600	FXLK	60081	2414	28W-38N	E6
CO-A10 Grass Lake Rd					
2000	LkvT	60046	2418	20W-39N	A6
2000	LNHT	60046	2418	20W-39N	A6
CO-A10 W Grass Lake Rd					
100	FXLK	60020	2415	28W-38N	A6
100	FXLK	60081	2415	28W-38N	A6
600	FXLK	60020	2414	28W-38N	E6
19000	OMCK	60046	2418	19W-38N	D6
19000	OMCK	60083	2418	19W-38N	D6
20700	LkvT	60046	2417	22W-39N	B4
20700	LkvT	60046	2418	19W-38N	C6
20700	LNHT	60046	2417	22W-39N	B4
20700	LNHT	60046	2418	19W-38N	C6
21200	LkvT	60002	2417	21W-39N	D4
21600	LKVL	60002	2417	21W-39N	C4
21600	LKVL	60046	2417	21W-39N	C4
22700	AntT	60002	2417	22W-40N	A4
22700	AntT	60046	2417	22W-40N	A4
23300	AntT	60002	2416	25W-40N	B3
23300	LKVL	60002	2416	23W-40N	E3
25800	AntT	60002	2415	26W-38N	D6
27700	AntT	60081	2415	27W-38N	B6
29600	BtnT	60081	2414	28W-38N	E6
29600	FXLK	60081	2414	28W-38N	E6

STREET Block	City	ZIP	Map#	CGS	Grid
CO-A11					
20700	LkvT	60046	2417	21W-39N	D5
20700	LkvT	60046	2418	20W-39N	A5
20700	LNHT	60046	2417	21W-39N	E5
20700	LNHT	60046	2418	20W-39N	A5
21900	LKVL	60046	2417	22W-39N	C5
CO-A11 W Gelden Rd					
20700	LkvT	60046	2417	21W-39N	D5
20700	LkvT	60046	2418	20W-39N	A5
20700	LNHT	60046	2417	21W-39N	E5
20700	LNHT	60046	2418	20W-39N	A5
21900	LKVL	60046	2417	22W-39N	C5
CO-A12					
-	LKVL	60046	2417	23W-39N	A6
-	LkvT	60046	2417	23W-39N	A6
23400	LKVL	60046	2416	24W-38N	C6
23400	LkvT	60046	2416	24W-38N	C6
CO-A12 W Petite Lake Rd					
-	LKVL	60046	2417	23W-39N	A6
-	LkvT	60046	2417	23W-39N	A6
23400	LKVL	60046	2416	24W-38N	C6
23400	LkvT	60046	2416	24W-38N	C6
CO-A14					
17500	OMCK	60083	2419	18W-38N	A7
18400	OMCK	60083	2418	18W-38N	E7
18600	LNHT	60046	2418	18W-38N	E7
18600	OMCK	60046	2418	18W-38N	E7
CO-A14 W Millburn Rd					
17500	OMCK	60083	2419	18W-38N	A7
18400	OMCK	60083	2418	18W-38N	E7
18600	LNHT	60046	2418	18W-38N	E7
18600	OMCK	60046	2418	18W-38N	E7
CO-A15					
1200	BHPK	60087	2479	11W-37N	E2
1200	WKGN	60087	2479	10W-37N	E2
2500	WkgT	60087	2479	12W-37N	C2
3300	WKGN	60087	2478	13W-37N	E1
3300	WrnT	60087	2479	11W-37N	E2
3500	NptT	60083	2478	13W-37N	E1
10000	BHPK	60087	2480	10W-37N	A2
13900	WDWH	60083	2478	14W-38N	D1
13900	WDWH	60087	2478	13W-38N	D1
13900	WKGN	60083	2478	14W-38N	D1
19300	AdnT	60033	2406	49W-40N	D1
19900	CmgT	60033	2406	49W-40N	D1
CO-A15 Oak Grove Rd					
19300	AdnT	60033	2406	49W-40N	D1
19900	CmgT	60033	2406	49W-40N	D1
CO-A15 W Yorkhouse Rd					
1200	BHPK	60087	2479	11W-37N	E2
1200	WKGN	60087	2479	11W-37N	E2
2500	WkgT	60087	2479	12W-37N	C2
3300	WKGN	60087	2478	13W-37N	E1
3300	WrnT	60087	2479	11W-37N	E2
3500	NptT	60083	2478	13W-37N	E1
10000	BHPK	60087	2480	10W-37N	A2
13900	WDWH	60083	2478	14W-38N	D1
13900	WDWH	60087	2478	13W-38N	D1
13900	WKGN	60083	2478	14W-38N	D1
CO-A16					
5600	RcmT	60071	2412	34W-40N	C3
5600	RHMD	60071	2412	34W-40N	C3
CO-A16 E Tryon Grove Rd					
5600	RcmT	60071	2412	34W-40N	C3
5600	RHMD	60071	2412	34W-40N	C3
CO-A17					
-	MchT	60081	2472	29W-37N	D1
200	FXLK	60081	2414	29W-39N	D5
500	SPGV	60081	2414	30W-39N	B4
1900	SPGV	60081	2413	30W-39N	E4
6100	AntT	60081	2472	29W-38N	D1
6100	BtnT	60081	2472	29W-38N	D1
6100	GrtT	60081	2472	29W-38N	D1
6500	AntT	60081	2414	29W-38N	D7
6500	BtnT	60081	2414	29W-38N	D7
6500	FXLK	60020	2414	29W-38N	D7
CO-A17 Main St Rd					
200	BtnT	60081	2414	30W-39N	B4
200	FXLK	60081	2414	29W-39N	D5
500	SPGV	60081	2414	30W-39N	B4
1900	SPGV	60081	2413	30W-39N	E4
CO-A17 N State Park Rd					
-	MchT	60081	2472	29W-37N	D1
6100	AntT	60081	2472	29W-38N	D1
6100	BtnT	60081	2472	29W-38N	D1
6100	GrtT	60081	2472	29W-38N	D1
6500	AntT	60081	2414	29W-38N	D7
6500	BtnT	60081	2414	29W-38N	D7
6500	FXLK	60020	2414	29W-38N	D7
6500	FXLK	60081	2414	29W-38N	D7
CO-A18					
10	LKVL	60046	2475	22W-36N	B3
10	LKVL	60073	2475	23W-36N	A3
10	LkvT	60046	2475	22W-36N	B3
10	LkvT	60073	2475	22W-36N	A3
10	RLKB	60046	2475	22W-36N	A3
10	RLKB	60073	2475	23W-36N	A3
200	LKVL	60046	2474	24W-36N	D3
300	LkvT	60046	2476	20W-37N	A2
300	LNHT	60046	2476	20W-37N	A2
400	LkvT	60046	2474	24W-36N	D3
24800	GrtT	60046	2474	25W-37N	B3
25400	GrtT	60041	2474	25W-37N	A3
25400	LkvT	60041	2474	25W-37N	A3
CO-A18 W Engle Dr					
21100	LkvT	60046	2475	21W-36N	E3
CO-A18 W Genoa Av					
20600	LkvT	60046	2476	20W-37N	A3
20700	LkvT	60046	2475	21W-36N	D3
CO-A18 N Granada Blvd					
300	LkvT	60046	2476	20W-37N	A2
300	LNHT	60046	2476	20W-37N	A2
CO-A18 Monaville Rd					
10	LKVL	60046	2475	23W-36N	A3
10	LKVL	60073	2475	23W-36N	A3
10	RLKB	60073	2475	23W-36N	A3
200	LKVL	60046	2474	23W-36N	E3
400	LkvT	60046	2474	23W-36N	E3
CO-A18 E Monaville Rd					
10	LKVL	60046	2475	22W-36N	B3
10	LKVL	60073	2475	23W-36N	A3
10	LkvT	60046	2475	22W-36N	B3
10	LkvT	60073	2475	22W-36N	A3
10	RLKB	60046	2475	23W-36N	A3
10	RLKB	60073	2475	23W-36N	A3
CO-A18 W Monaville Rd					
22400	LkvT	60046	2475	22W-36N	B3
22400	RLKB	60046	2475	22W-36N	B3
22400	RLKB	60073	2475	22W-36N	B3
22500	LkvT	60073	2475	22W-36N	B3
22600	LKVL	60046	2475	22W-36N	B3
22600	LKVL	60073	2475	22W-36N	B3
23700	LKVL	60046	2474	24W-36N	D3
23700	LkvT	60046	2474	24W-36N	D3
24800	GrtT	60046	2474	25W-37N	B3
25400	GrtT	60041	2474	25W-37N	A3
CO-A18 W Monaville Rd					
25400	LkvT	60041	2474	25W-37N	A3
CO-A18 N Nathan Hale Dr					
36800	LkvT	60046	2475	21W-36N	E3
CO-A19					
300	WKGN	60085	2480	10W-36N	B5
300	WKGN	60087	2480	10W-36N	A5
1100	WKGN	60087	2479	11W-36N	E4
3500	GRNE	60031	2478	13W-36N	E4
3500	WKGN	60087	2478	13W-36N	E4
3800	WrnT	60031	2478	13W-36N	D4
3800	WrnT	60087	2478	13W-36N	D4
CO-A19 Golf Rd					
-	WKGN	60085	2480	10W-36N	A5
700	WKGN	60087	2480	10W-36N	A5
1100	WKGN	60087	2479	10W-36N	E4
CO-A19 W Greenwood Av					
300	WKGN	60085	2480	10W-36N	B5
300	WKGN	60087	2480	10W-36N	B5
CO-A19 Sunset Av					
1400	WKGN	60087	2479	11W-36N	E4
3500	GRNE	60031	2478	13W-36N	E4
3500	WKGN	60087	2478	13W-36N	E4
3800	WrnT	60031	2478	13W-36N	D4
3800	WrnT	60087	2478	13W-36N	D4
CO-A20					
-	GRNE	60031	2476	18W-35N	E5
-	WrnT	60031	2476	18W-35N	E5
10	FXLK	60020	2473	27W-36N	B5
10	RLKB	60073	2475	22W-35N	B6
200	RLKB	60073	2474	23W-35N	E6
400	FXLK	60041	2473	26W-35N	C5
500	HRVD	60033	2406	50W-38N	A6
500	RLKH	60073	2474	23W-35N	E6
600	GrtT	60041	2473	26W-35N	D5
700	RLKB	60046	2475	22W-35N	C6
900	GYLK	60046	2475	21W-35N	D5
1000	AvnT	60073	2474	23W-35N	E6
1000	CmgT	60033	2405	52W-38N	B7
1000	HRVD	60033	2405	51W-38N	E6
19000	AvnT	60046	2476	19W-35N	B5
19000	WrnT	60046	2476	19W-35N	D5
20500	AvnT	60046	2475	21W-35N	D5
20500	GYLK	60030	2475	21W-35N	D5
20500	GYLK	60030	2476	20W-35N	A5
24800	GrtT	60041	2474	23W-35N	E6
24800	GrtT	60073	2474	23W-35N	E6
CO-A20 W Diggins St					
500	HRVD	60033	2406	50W-38N	A6
1000	CmgT	60033	2405	51W-38N	E6
1000	HRVD	60033	2405	51W-38N	E6
CO-A20 E Grand Av					
10	FXLK	60020	2473	28W-36N	A3
CO-A20 S Oak Grove Rd					
6100	CmgT	60033	2405	52W-38N	A7
CO-A20 Ramer Rd					
22800	CmgT	60033	2405	52W-38N	B7
22800	HRVD	60033	2405	51W-38N	D6
CO-A20 Rollins Rd					
10	FXLK	60020	2473	27W-36N	B5
400	FXLK	60041	2473	26W-35N	C5
600	GrtT	60041	2473	26W-35N	D5
CO-A20 E Rollins Rd					
10	RLKB	60073	2475	22W-35N	A6
700	RLKB	60046	2475	22W-35N	C6
900	GYLK	60046	2475	21W-35N	D5
CO-A20 N Rollins Rd					
-	GRNE	60031	2476	18W-35N	E5
-	WrnT	60031	2476	18W-35N	E5
-	WrnT	60046	2476	18W-35N	E5
CO-A20 W Rollins Rd					
-	GRNE	60031	2476	18W-35N	E5
10	RLKB	60073	2475	22W-35N	B6
200	RLKB	60073	2474	23W-35N	E6
500	RLKH	60073	2474	23W-35N	E6
1000	AvnT	60073	2474	23W-35N	E6
19000	AvnT	60046	2476	19W-35N	B5
19000	WrnT	60046	2476	19W-35N	D5
20500	AvnT	60046	2475	21W-35N	D5
20500	GYLK	60030	2475	21W-35N	D5
20500	GYLK	60030	2476	20W-35N	A5
20800	GYLK	60046	2475	21W-35N	E5
21300	RLKB	60046	2475	21W-35N	D5
24800	GrtT	60041	2474	23W-35N	E6
24800	GrtT	60073	2474	23W-35N	E6
25900	GrtT	60041	2473	26W-35N	D5
CO-A22					
10	RDLK	60073	2532	23W-34N	A2
10	RLKP	60073	2532	22W-34N	B2
100	HRVD	60033	2464	50W-37N	B1
100	RDLK	60073	2531	23W-34N	E1
400	HNVL	60030	2532	21W-33N	D2
400	HNVL	60030	2532	22W-34N	B2
3000	PKCY	60085	2536	12W-33N	B2
3000	WKGN	60085	2536	12W-33N	B2
3400	GRNE	60031	2536	13W-34N	A2
3400	GRNE	60085	2536	13W-34N	A2
3900	GRNE	60031	2535	14W-34N	C1
4300	WrnT	60031	2535	14W-34N	C1
6000	GRNE	60031	2534	16W-34N	D1
6000	WrnT	60031	2534	16W-34N	D1
13700	PKCY	60085	2535	14W-34N	C1
18200	WrnT	60030	2534	18W-34N	A1
18300	GRNE	60031	2533	18W-34N	E1
18300	WrnT	60030	2533	18W-34N	E1
18300	WrnT	60031	2533	18W-34N	E1
18500	GRNE	60030	2533	18W-34N	E1
18700	HtdT	60033	2464	48W-37N	E2
18700	TDLK	60030	2533	18W-34N	E1
18900	GYLK	60030	2533	20W-34N	A1
18900	TDLK	60031	2533	18W-34N	D1
19400	AvnT	60030	2533	20W-34N	A1
20100	DhmT	60033	2464	48W-37N	E2
20700	GYLK	60030	2532	21W-33N	D2
21600	AvnT	60030	2532	21W-33N	D2
21700	AvnT	60073	2532	21W-33N	D2
22000	DhmT	60033	2463	51W-37N	D1
22000	HRVD	60033	2463	51W-37N	D1
CO-A22 Airport Rd					
100	HRVD	60033	2464	50W-37N	A1
21600	DhmT	60033	2464	50W-37N	A1
22000	DhmT	60033	2463	51W-37N	D1
22000	HRVD	60033	2463	51W-37N	D1
CO-A22 McGuire Rd					
18700	HtdT	60033	2464	48W-37N	E2
20100	DhmT	60033	2464	48W-37N	E2
20100	HRVD	60033	2464	50W-37N	B1
CO-A22 Washington St					
3000	PKCY	60085	2536	12W-33N	B2
3000	WKGN	60085	2536	12W-33N	B2
3400	GRNE	60031	2536	13W-34N	A2
3400	GRNE	60085	2536	13W-34N	A2
3900	GRNE	60031	2535	14W-34N	C1
4300	WrnT	60031	2535	14W-34N	C1
6000	GRNE	60031	2534	16W-34N	D1
6000	WrnT	60031	2534	16W-34N	D1
CO-A22 Washington St					
13700	PKCY	60085	2535	14W-34N	C1
CO-A22 E Washington St					
10	RDLK	60073	2532	23W-34N	A2
10	RLKP	60073	2532	22W-34N	B2
400	HNVL	60030	2532	22W-34N	B2
400	HNVL	60073	2532	22W-34N	B2
CO-A22 W Washington St					
10	RDLK	60073	2532	23W-34N	A2
10	RLKP	60073	2532	23W-34N	A2
100	RDLK	60073	2531	23W-34N	E1
17000	GRNE	60031	2534	17W-34N	C1
17000	WrnT	60031	2534	17W-34N	C1
18200	WrnT	60030	2534	18W-34N	A1
18300	GRNE	60031	2533	18W-34N	E1
18300	WrnT	60030	2533	18W-34N	E1
18300	WrnT	60031	2533	18W-34N	E1
18500	GRNE	60030	2533	18W-34N	E1
18700	TDLK	60030	2533	18W-34N	E1
18900	GYLK	60030	2533	20W-34N	A1
18900	TDLK	60031	2533	18W-34N	D1
19400	AvnT	60030	2533	20W-34N	A1
20700	GYLK	60030	2532	21W-33N	D2
21600	AvnT	60030	2532	21W-33N	D2
21700	AvnT	60073	2532	21W-33N	D2
21700	HNVL	60030	2532	21W-33N	D2
CO-A24					
5400	GRNE	60031	2534	15W-33N	E2
5400	GRNE	60031	2535	15W-33N	A3
5400	WrnT	60031	2534	15W-33N	E2
5700	GRNE	60048	2534	16W-33N	D2
17100	WrnT	60030	2534	16W-33N	D2
17100	WrnT	60048	2534	16W-33N	C2
18400	WrnT	60030	2533	18W-33N	E2
18700	GYLK	60030	2533	18W-34N	D2
18800	TDLK	60030	2533	18W-34N	D2
CO-A24 Gages Lake Rd					
5400	GRNE	60031	2534	15W-33N	E2
5400	GRNE	60031	2535	15W-33N	A3
5400	WrnT	60031	2534	15W-33N	E2
5700	GRNE	60048	2534	16W-33N	D2
CO-A24 W Gages Lake Rd					
17100	GRNE	60031	2534	16W-33N	C2
17100	GRNE	60048	2534	16W-33N	C2
17100	WrnT	60030	2534	16W-33N	D2
17100	WrnT	60031	2534	16W-33N	C2
17100	WrnT	60048	2534	16W-33N	C2
18400	WrnT	60030	2533	18W-33N	E2
18700	GYLK	60030	2533	18W-34N	D2
18800	TDLK	60030	2533	18W-34N	D2
CO-A26					
100	GrtT	60051	2529	29W-34N	D1
100	MchT	60051	2529	29W-34N	C1
300	LKMR	60051	2529	29W-34N	C1
900	JNBG	60051	2529	30W-34N	B1
1100	JNBG	60051	2472	30W-34N	B7
1100	LKMR	60051	2472	30W-34N	B7
2300	JNBG	60050	2471	31W-35N	C6
3100	JNBG	60051	2471	30W-35N	E7
CO-A26 Bay Rd					
900	JNBG	60051	2529	30W-34N	B1
900	LKMR	60051	2529	30W-34N	B1
900	MchT	60051	2529	30W-34N	B1
1100	JNBG	60051	2472	30W-34N	B7
1100	LKMR	60051	2472	30W-34N	B7
CO-A26 E Bay Rd					
100	GrtT	60051	2529	29W-34N	D1
100	MchT	60051	2529	29W-34N	C1
300	LKMR	60051	2529	29W-34N	C1
CO-A26 N Chapel Hill Rd					
3100	JNBG	60051	2471	30W-35N	E7
3500	JNBG	60051	2471	31W-35N	E6
CO-A26 W Johnsburg Rd					
2300	JNBG	60050	2471	31W-35N	C6
CO-A27					
-	AvnT	60030	2533	19W-33N	B4
500	GYLK	60030	2533	19W-33N	B4
5600	HRVD	60033	2463	51W-37N	D1
22800	CmgT	60033	2405	51W-37N	D7
22800	DhmT	60033	2405	51W-37N	D7
22800	HRVD	60033	2405	51W-37N	D7
23000	DhmT	60033	2463	52W-36N	B3
CO-A27 Center St					
-	AvnT	60030	2533	19W-33N	B4
500	GYLK	60030	2533	19W-33N	B4
CO-A27 Flat Iron Rd					
5600	HRVD	60033	2463	51W-37N	D1
22800	CmgT	60033	2405	51W-37N	D7
22800	DhmT	60033	2405	51W-37N	D7
22800	HRVD	60033	2405	51W-37N	D7
23000	DhmT	60033	2463	52W-36N	B3
CO-A27 Streit Rd					
23500	DhmT	60033	2463	52W-36N	B4
CO-A28					
10100	GwdT	60098	2525	40W-34N	B1
11900	GwdT	60098	2524	41W-34N	E1
CO-A28 Charles Rd					
10100	GwdT	60098	2525	40W-34N	B1
11900	GwdT	60098	2524	41W-34N	E1
CO-A29					
-	WKGN	60064	2536	12W-32N	C5
-	WKGN	60085	2536	13W-32N	E5
-	WrnT	60085	2535	13W-32N	E5
600	NCHI	60064	2537	10W-32N	A5
1000	NCHI	60064	2536	12W-32N	C5
1100	WKGN	60085	2536	12W-32N	C5
CO-A29 14th St					
600	NCHI	60064	2537	10W-32N	A5
1000	NCHI	60064	2536	10W-32N	E5
1100	WKGN	60085	2536	10W-32N	E5
CO-A29 Casimer Pulaski Dr					
-	WKGN	60064	2536	12W-32N	C5
-	WKGN	60085	2535	13W-32N	E5
-	WKGN	60085	2536	12W-32N	C5
-	WrnT	60085	2535	13W-32N	E5
3100	NCHI	60064	2536	12W-32N	C5
CO-A31					
-	LbvT	60044	2535	13W-31N	E7
-	LbvT	60044	2536	12W-31N	B7
-	WKGN	60044	2535	13W-31N	E7
-	WKGN	60085	2536	12W-31N	B7
3100	NCHI	60064	2536	12W-31N	B7
3100	ShdT	60044	2536	12W-31N	B7
CO-A31 ML King Jr Dr					
-	LbvT	60044	2535	13W-31N	E7
-	LbvT	60044	2536	12W-31N	B7
-	WKGN	60085	2535	13W-31N	E7
-	WKGN	60085	2536	12W-31N	B7
3100	NCHI	60064	2536	12W-31N	B7
3100	ShdT	60044	2536	12W-31N	B7
CO-A32					
4000	MHRY	60050	2528	32W-31N	A7
4000	NndT	60050	2528	32W-31N	A7
4200	MHRY	60050	2527	34W-31N	D7
4600	NndT	60050	2527	34W-31N	D7
CO-A32 Bull Valley Rd					
4000	MHRY	60050	2528	33W-31N	A7
4000	NndT	60050	2528	32W-31N	A7
4200	MHRY	60050	2527	34W-31N	D7
4600	NndT	60050	2527	34W-31N	D7
CO-A33					
-	LbvT	60048	2591	18W-30N	A2
-	LYVL	60048	2590	18W-30N	E2
-	LYVL	60048	2591	18W-30N	A2
200	WDSK	60098	2524	42W-31N	C7
1800	LbvT	60048	2590	18W-30N	E2
13700	SenT	60098	2524	43W-31N	A7
19200	FmtT	60048	2590	19W-30N	D2
19500	FmtT	60060	2590	19W-30N	C2
19800	FmtT	60030	2590	20W-30N	A2
19800	GYLK	60030	2590	20W-30N	A2
19800	GYLK	60048	2590	20W-30N	B2
19800	RLKP	60030	2590	20W-30N	A2
20700	FmtT	60030	2589	20W-30N	E2
20700	GYLK	60030	2589	20W-30N	E2
20700	RLKP	60030	2589	20W-30N	E2
21500	FmtT	60060	2589	21W-30N	D2
22000	RLKP	60060	2589	22W-30N	B2
CO-A33 W Jackson St					
200	WDSK	60098	2524	42W-31N	C7
CO-A33 Kishwaukee Valley Rd					
1100	WDSK	60098	2524	42W-31N	B7
13700	SenT	60098	2524	43W-31N	A7
CO-A33 W Peterson Rd					
-	LbvT	60048	2590	18W-30N	E2
-	LbvT	60048	2591	18W-30N	A2
-	LYVL	60048	2591	18W-30N	A2
1800	LYVL	60048	2590	18W-30N	E2
19200	FmtT	60048	2590	19W-30N	D2
19500	FmtT	60060	2590	19W-30N	C2
19800	FmtT	60030	2590	20W-30N	A2
19800	GYLK	60030	2590	20W-30N	A2
19800	GYLK	60048	2590	20W-30N	B2
19800	RLKP	60030	2590	20W-30N	A2
20700	FmtT	60030	2589	20W-30N	E2
20700	GYLK	60030	2589	20W-30N	E2
20700	RLKP	60030	2589	20W-30N	E2
21500	FmtT	60060	2589	21W-30N	D2
22000	RLKP	60060	2589	22W-30N	B2
CO-A34					
-	LbvT	60048	2591	17W-29N	B3
-	LYVL	60060	2591	17W-29N	C3
-	MDLN	60048	2591	17W-29N	C3
-	MDLN	60060	2591	17W-29N	C3
100	LYVL	60048	2591	17W-29N	C3
1400	LYVL	60048	2590	20W-30N	B3
1400	LYVL	60060	2590	20W-30N	B3
1400	MDLN	60048	2590	18W-29N	E3
1400	MDLN	60060	2590	18W-29N	E3
19100	FmtT	60048	2590	20W-30N	B3
19100	FmtT	60060	2590	20W-30N	B3
20000	RLKP	60030	2590	20W-30N	A3
CO-A34 W Winchester Rd					
-	LbvT	60048	2591	17W-29N	B3
-	LYVL	60060	2591	17W-29N	C3
-	MDLN	60060	2591	17W-29N	C3
100	LYVL	60048	2591	17W-29N	C3
1400	LYVL	60048	2590	20W-30N	B3
1400	LYVL	60060	2590	20W-30N	B3
1400	MDLN	60048	2590	18W-29N	E3
1400	MDLN	60060	2590	18W-29N	E3
19100	FmtT	60048	2590	20W-30N	B3
19100	FmtT	60060	2590	20W-30N	B3
20000	RLKP	60030	2590	20W-30N	A3
CO-A35					
100	WDSK	60098	2581	42W-30N	B1
1100	DrrT	60098	2581	42W-30N	B1
14000	SenT	60098	2581	43W-30N	A2
CO-A35 W South St					
100	WDSK	60098	2581	42W-30N	B1
1100	DrrT	60098	2581	42W-30N	B1
14000	SenT	60098	2581	43W-30N	A2
CO-A36					
100	WCDA	60084	2587	26W-28N	D6
600	WCDA	60084	2588	24W-28N	B6
600	WcnT	60084	2587	27W-28N	B6
600	WcnT	60084	2588	25W-28N	B6
1100	FmtT	60060	2588	24W-28N	C6
1100	WCDA	60060	2588	24W-28N	C6
1200	FmtT	60084	2588	24W-28N	C6
27000	WcnT	60051	2587	27W-28N	A6
CO-A36 E Bonner Rd					
600	WCDA	60084	2588	25W-28N	B6
600	WcnT	60084	2588	25W-28N	B6
1100	FmtT	60060	2588	24W-28N	C6
1100	WCDA	60060	2588	24W-28N	C6
1200	FmtT	60084	2588	24W-28N	C6
CO-A36 W Bonner Rd					
600	WCDA	60084	2587	27W-28N	B6
600	WcnT	60084	2587	27W-28N	B6
27000	WcnT	60051	2587	27W-28N	A6
CO-A38					
10	MDLN	60060	2590	20W-28N	A7
200	FmtT	60060	2589	22W-27N	B7
200	HNWD	60047	2589	22W-27N	B7
200	HNWD	60060	2589	22W-27N	B7
1800	FmtT	60060	2590	20W-27N	A7
8500	DrrT	60012	2583	37W-27N	B7
8600	CLLK	60012	2583	37W-27N	B7
8900	DrrT	60098	2583	38W-27N	A7
20800	MDLN	60060	2589	21W-27N	E7
21700	FmtT	60047	2589	22W-27N	C7
21700	MDLN	60047	2589	22W-27N	C7
CO-A38 E Hawley St					
10	MDLN	60060	2590	20W-28N	A7
CO-A38 W Hawley St					
10	MDLN	60060	2590	19W-28N	D7
200	FmtT	60060	2589	22W-27N	B7
200	HNWD	60047	2589	22W-27N	B7
200	HNWD	60060	2589	22W-27N	B7
1800	FmtT	60060	2590	20W-27N	A7
20800	MDLN	60060	2589	21W-27N	E7
21700	FmtT	60047	2589	22W-27N	C7
21700	MDLN	60047	2589	22W-27N	C7
CO-A38 Ridgefield Rd					
8500	DrrT	60012	2583	37W-27N	B7
8600	CLLK	60012	2583	37W-27N	B7
8900	DrrT	60098	2583	38W-27N	A7
CO-A40					
1000	LKFT	60045	2649	12W-24N	B7
1800	LKFT	60045	2648	13W-24N	E7
1800	VrnT	60045	2648	14W-24N	D7
2100	MTWA	60045	2648	14W-24N	D7
3200	MTWA	60048	2648	14W-24N	D7
3400	VrnT	60048	2648	14W-24N	D7
CO-A40 W Everett Rd					
1000	LKFT	60045	2649	12W-24N	B7
1800	LKFT	60045	2648	13W-24N	E7
1800	VrnT	60045	2648	14W-24N	D7
2100	MTWA	60045	2648	14W-24N	D7
CO-A40 W Everett Rd					
3200	MTWA	60048	2648	14W-24N	D7
3400	VrnT	60048	2648	14W-24N	D7
CO-A42					
-	UNON	60180	2635	47W-25N	B5
300	NBRN	60010	2698	25W-23N	A1
500	LKBN	60010	2697	26W-24N	D1
500	LKBN	60010	2698	25W-24N	A1
500	NBRN	60010	2697	26W-24N	D1
18700	CrlT	60152	2635	48W-25N	A4
18700	CrlT	60180	2635	47W-25N	B5
24600	ElaT	60010	2698	25W-23N	A1
24600	ElaT	60047	2698	24W-24N	C1
24600	LKZH	60047	2698	24W-24N	C1
CO-A42 Miller Rd					
300	NBRN	60010	2698	25W-23N	A1
500	LKBN	60010	2697	25W-24N	E1
500	LKBN	60010	2698	25W-24N	A1
500	NBRN	60010	2697	25W-24N	E1
24600	ElaT	60010	2698	25W-23N	A1
24600	ElaT	60047	2698	24W-24N	C1
24600	LKZH	60047	2698	24W-24N	C1
CO-A42 W Miller Rd					
500	LKBN	60010	2697	26W-24N	D1
500	NBRN	60010	2697	26W-24N	D1
CO-A42 W Union Rd					
-	UNON	60180	2635	47W-25N	B5
18700	CrlT	60152	2635	48W-25N	A4
18700	CrlT	60180	2635	47W-25N	B5
CO-A43					
-	BKBN	60015	2703	12W-22N	B4
2000	RVWD	60015	2703	12W-22N	A4
2600	RVWD	60015	2702	13W-22N	E4
2800	LNSH	60015	2702	13W-22N	E4
2800	LNSH	60069	2702	13W-22N	E4
CO-A43 Duffy Ln					
-	BKBN	60015	2703	12W-22N	B4
2000	RVWD	60015	2703	12W-22N	A4
2600	RVWD	60015	2702	13W-22N	E4
2800	LNSH	60015	2702	13W-22N	E4
2800	LNSH	60069	2702	13W-22N	E4
CO-A44					
-	LGGV	60047	2700	18W-22N	E5
-	UNON	60180	2635	47W-24N	C6
-	VrnT	60047	2700	18W-22N	E5
-	VrnT	60069	2702	14W-21N	B5
400	BFGV	60069	2701	17W-22N	C5
400	BFGV	60089	2701	17W-22N	C5
400	BFGV	60089	2702	15W-21N	A5
400	LNSH	60069	2702	15W-21N	A5
400	LNSH	60089	2702	15W-21N	A5
400	VrnT	60069	2701	17W-22N	C5
500	BFGV	60069	2702	15W-21N	B5
1200	BFGV	60047	2701	17W-22N	B5
1200	LGGV	60047	2701	17W-21N	A5
1200	LGGV	60089	2701	17W-22N	B5
15600	LNSH	60069	2701	15W-21N	E5
16100	VrnT	60089	2701	16W-22N	E5
18100	CrlT	60152	2635	47W-24N	A7
18100	CrlT	60180	2635	47W-24N	B6
19200	CrlT	60152	2634	48W-24N	E7
19700	RlyT	60152	2634	49W-24N	B7
CO-A44 Aptakisic Rd					
-	LGGV	60047	2700	18W-22N	E5
-	VrnT	60047	2700	18W-22N	E5
5100	BFGV	60047	2701	17W-22N	B5
5100	BFGV	60089	2701	17W-22N	B5
5100	LGGV	60047	2701	17W-21N	A5
5100	LGGV	60089	2701	17W-22N	B5
CO-A44 W Aptakisic Rd					
-	VrnT	60069	2702	14W-21N	B5
400	BFGV	60069	2701	17W-22N	C5
400	BFGV	60089	2701	17W-22N	C5
400	BFGV	60089	2702	15W-21N	A5
400	LNSH	60069	2702	15W-21N	A5
400	LNSH	60089	2702	15W-21N	A5
400	VrnT	60069	2701	17W-22N	C5
500	BFGV	60069	2702	15W-21N	A5
1200	BFGV	60047	2701	17W-22N	B5
1200	LGGV	60047	2701	17W-22N	B5
1200	LGGV	60089	2701	17W-22N	B5
15600	LNSH	60069	2701	15W-21N	E5
16100	VrnT	60089	2701	16W-22N	E5
CO-A44 E Coral Rd					
-	UNON	60180	2635	47W-24N	C6
18100	CrlT	60152	2635	47W-24N	A7
18100	CrlT	60180	2635	47W-24N	B6
CO-A44 W Coral Rd					
18800	CrlT	60152	2635	47W-24N	A7
18800	CrlT	60180	2635	47W-24N	A7
19200	CrlT	60152	2634	48W-24N	E7
19700	RlyT	60152	2634	49W-24N	B7
CO-A45					
-	AlqT	60014	2694	33W-23N	E1
-	CLLK	60156	2694	34W-23N	B1
-	LIHL	60156	2694	34W-23N	B1
1000	CLLK	60014	2694	34W-23N	C1
1000	LIHL	60014	2694	34W-23N	C1
CO-A45 James R Rakow Rd					
-	AlqT	60014	2694	33W-23N	E1
-	CLLK	60156	2694	34W-23N	B1
-	LIHL	60156	2694	34W-23N	B1
1000	CLLK	60014	2694	34W-23N	C1
1000	LIHL	60014	2694	34W-23N	C1
CO-A46					
100	LKZH	60010	2699	23W-21N	A6
100	LKZH	60047	2699	23W-21N	A6
400	CLLK	60014	2693	36W-23N	E2
400	DRPK	60010	2698	23W-21N	D6
400	LKZH	60010	2698	23W-21N	E6
400	LKZH	60047	2698	23W-21N	E6
7800	GfnT	60014	2693	38W-23N	A2
8100	GfnT	60156	2693	37W-23N	B2
8900	LKWD	60014	2693	37W-23N	B2
9300	GfnT	60014	2692	38W-23N	E2
9300	GfnT	60156	2692	38W-23N	E2
9300	LIHL	60156	2692	38W-23N	E2
9300	LKWD	60014	2692	38W-23N	E2
9300	LKWD	60156	2693	37W-23N	A2
23700	ElaT	60010	2698	25W-21N	A6
25200	CbaT	60010	2698	25W-21N	B6
CO-A46 Ackman Rd					
7700	CLLK	60014	2693	38W-23N	A2
7800	GfnT	60014	2693	38W-23N	A2
8100	GfnT	60156	2693	37W-23N	B2
8900	LKWD	60014	2693	37W-23N	B2
9300	GfnT	60014	2692	38W-23N	E2
9300	GfnT	60156	2692	38W-23N	E2
9300	LIHL	60156	2692	38W-23N	E2
9300	LKWD	60014	2692	38W-23N	E2
9300	LKWD	60156	2693	37W-23N	A2
CO-A46 Cuba Rd					
-	CbaT	60010	2698	24W-21N	B6
23500	DRPK	60010	2698	23W-21N	D6
23500	LKZH	60010	2698	23W-21N	E6
23500	LKZH	60047	2698	23W-21N	E6

Chicago 7-County Street Index

STREET Block	City	ZIP	Map#	CGS	Grid
CO-A46 Cuba Rd					
23700	ElaT	60010	2698	25W-21N	A6
CO-A46 W Cuba Rd					
100	LKZH	60010	2699	23W-21N	A6
100	LKZH	60047	2699	23W-21N	A6
400	DRPK	60010	2698	23W-21N	E6
400	LKZH	60010	2698	23W-21N	E6
400	LKZH	60047	2698	23W-21N	E6
25200	CbaT	60010	2698	25W-21N	B6
CO-A47					
400	BFGV	60089	2701	16W-21N	E6
400	HDPK	60035	2704	8W-22N	E4
400	VrnT	60089	2701	16W-21N	E6
1600	DRFD	60015	2703	12W-20N	B7
1700	WdfT	60015	2703	12W-21N	C7
2100	RVWD	60015	2703	12W-20N	B7
2300	RVWD	60015	2702	13W-20N	D7
3700	BFGV	60089	2702	13W-20N	D7
11500	GfnT	60142	2691	42W-20N	C7
11900	HTLY	60142	2691	41W-21N	E7
13300	CrlT	60142	2691	43W-21N	A5
14100	CrlT	60180	2691	43W-21N	A5
CO-A47 Central Av					
400	HDPK	60035	2704	8W-22N	E4
CO-A47 Deerfield Pkwy					
-	BFGV	60089	2702	13W-20N	D7
-	RVWD	60015	2702	13W-20N	D7
400	BFGV	60089	2701	16W-21N	E6
400	VrnT	60089	2701	16W-21N	E6
CO-A47 Deerfield Rd					
1600	DRFD	60015	2703	12W-20N	B7
1700	WdfT	60015	2703	12W-21N	C7
2100	RVWD	60015	2703	12W-20N	B7
2300	RVWD	60015	2702	13W-21N	E7
3700	BFGV	60089	2702	14W-21N	B7
CO-A47 Harmony Rd					
11500	GfnT	60142	2691	42W-20N	B7
CO-A47 W Main Street Rd					
11900	HTLY	60142	2691	41W-21N	E7
12100	GfnT	60142	2691	41W-21N	E7
CO-A47 Marengo Rd					
13300	CrlT	60142	2691	43W-21N	A5
13300	GfnT	60142	2691	42W-21N	B6
14100	CrlT	60180	2691	43W-21N	A5
CO-A48					
1100	ALGN	60102	2694	35W-21N	B6
1100	ALGN	60156	2694	35W-21N	B6
1100	LIHL	60102	2694	34W-21N	C6
1100	LIHL	60156	2694	35W-21N	B6
2400	LIHL	60102	2693	35W-21N	E6
2400	LIHL	60156	2693	35W-21N	E6
2500	ALGN	60156	2693	36W-21N	D6
3700	GfnT	60156	2693	36W-21N	D6
9100	ALGN	60102	2693	38W-21N	A6
9100	GfnT	60102	2693	38W-21N	A6
9400	ALGN	60102	2692	38W-21N	E6
9400	GfnT	60102	2692	38W-21N	E6
9400	LIHL	60156	2692	38W-21N	E6
10000	GfnT	60142	2692	39W-21N	C6
10000	GfnT	60156	2692	39W-21N	C6
10000	HTLY	60142	2692	40W-21N	A6
CO-A48 Algonquin Rd					
9100	ALGN	60102	2693	38W-21N	A6
9100	GfnT	60102	2693	38W-21N	A6
9400	ALGN	60102	2692	38W-21N	E6
9400	GfnT	60102	2692	38W-21N	E6
9400	LIHL	60156	2692	38W-21N	E6
10000	GfnT	60142	2692	39W-21N	C6
10000	GfnT	60156	2692	39W-21N	C6
10000	HTLY	60142	2692	40W-21N	A6
CO-A48 W Algonquin Rd					
1100	ALGN	60102	2694	35W-21N	B6
1100	ALGN	60156	2694	35W-21N	B6
1100	LIHL	60102	2694	34W-21N	C6
1100	LIHL	60156	2694	35W-21N	B6
2400	LIHL	60102	2693	35W-21N	E6
2500	ALGN	60102	2693	36W-21N	D6
2500	ALGN	60156	2693	36W-21N	D6
2500	LIHL	60102	2693	36W-21N	D6
3700	GfnT	60156	2693	36W-21N	D6
CO-A49					
10	DRPK	60010	2752	22W-20N	B1
100	BRTN	60010	2751	23W-20N	D1
100	DRPK	60010	2751	23W-20N	D1
100	ElaT	60010	2751	23W-20N	E1
500	DRPK	60074	2752	22W-20N	C1
3400	ElaT	60047	2700	20W-20N	A7
3400	LGGV	60047	2700	20W-20N	A7
3500	KLDR	60047	2700	20W-20N	A7
13500	GfnT	60142	2691	42W-20N	B7
13500	HTLY	60142	2691	42W-20N	B7
13900	CrlT	60142	2691	43W-20N	A7
14600	CrlT	60142	2743	45W-20N	A1
20700	KLDR	60047	2699	20W-20N	E7
21400	ElaT	60074	2699	21W-20N	D7
21600	ElaT	60074	2752	21W-20N	D1
CO-A49 Harmony Rd					
13500	GfnT	60142	2691	42W-20N	B7
13500	HTLY	60142	2691	42W-20N	B7
13900	CrlT	60142	2691	43W-20N	A7
14600	CrlT	60142	2743	45W-20N	A1
CO-A49 Long Grove Rd					
10	DRPK	60010	2752	22W-20N	B1
100	BRTN	60010	2751	23W-20N	D1
100	DRPK	60010	2751	23W-20N	D1
100	ElaT	60010	2751	23W-20N	E1
500	DRPK	60074	2752	22W-20N	C1
CO-A49 W Long Grove Rd					
3400	ElaT	60047	2700	20W-20N	A7
3400	LGGV	60047	2700	20W-20N	A7
3500	KLDR	60047	2700	20W-20N	A7
20700	KLDR	60047	2699	20W-20N	E7
21400	ElaT	60074	2699	21W-20N	D7
21600	DRPK	60074	2752	21W-20N	D1
21600	ElaT	60074	2752	21W-20N	D1
21700	DRPK	60010	2752	21W-20N	C1
CO-A50					
10	BNHL	60010	2749	30W-18N	A2
100	ALGN	60102	2748	32W-19N	E2
100	BFGV	60089	2754	16W-20N	D2
100	BNHL	60010	2748	32W-19N	E2
100	BNHL	60102	2748	32W-19N	E2
100	WLNG	60089	2754	16W-20N	D2
300	AlqT	60010	2749	29W-20N	D2
1300	WLNG	60090	2754	16W-20N	D2
2000	AlqT	60102	2748	32W-20N	B2
CO-A50 County Line Rd					
2000	ALGN	60102	2748	32W-20N	B2
2000	AlqT	60102	2748	32W-20N	B2
2200	BNHL	60010	2748	32W-20N	C2
2200	BNHL	60102	2748	32W-20N	C2
CO-A50 W County Line Rd					
10	BNHL	60010	2749	30W-18N	A2
100	ALGN	60102	2748	32W-19N	E2
100	BNHL	60010	2748	32W-19N	E2
100	BNHL	60102	2748	32W-19N	E2
300	AlqT	60010	2749	29W-20N	D2
CO-A50 E Lake Cook Rd					
100	BFGV	60089	2754	16W-20N	D2
100	WLNG	60089	2754	16W-20N	D2
1300	WLNG	60090	2754	16W-20N	D2
CO-A52					
10	GfnT	60102	2745	38W-20N	D2
10	RtdT	60102	2745	38W-20N	D2
10	RtdT	60142	2745	38W-20N	D2
9700	GfnT	60156	2745	39W-20N	D1
10300	GfnT	60142	2745	39W-20N	C1
10300	HTLY	60142	2745	39W-20N	C1
10600	HTLY	60142	2692	40W-20N	A7
10700	GfnT	60142	2692	39W-20N	B7
11800	HTLY	60142	2691	40W-21N	E7
CO-A52 Dundee Rd					
10	GfnT	60102	2745	38W-20N	D2
10	RtdT	60102	2745	38W-20N	D2
10	RtdT	60142	2745	38W-20N	D2
9700	GfnT	60156	2745	39W-20N	D1
10300	GfnT	60142	2745	39W-20N	C1
10300	HTLY	60142	2745	39W-20N	C1
10600	HTLY	60142	2692	39W-20N	C7
10700	GfnT	60142	2692	39W-20N	B7
CO-A52 E Main St					
11300	HTLY	60142	2692	40W-20N	A7
11800	HTLY	60142	2691	40W-21N	E7
CO-B					
100	BfdT	53128	2353		A2
100	GNCY	53128	2353		A2
100	RdlT	53128	2353		B1
800	BfdT	53128	2352		A3
800	GNCY	53128	2352		E3
1600	BfdT	53128	2351		E2
1900	BfdT	53147	2351		A1
2300	LinT	53147	2351		A1
2700	LinT	53147	2350		E1
11000	SlmT	53179	2356		B3
11500	AntT	53179	2356		B3
11500	AntT	60002	2356		B3
CO-B 304th Av					
11500	AntT	53179	2356		B3
11500	AntT	60002	2356		B3
11500	SlmT	53179	2356		B3
CO-B N Carter St					
700	GNCY	53128	2353		A2
900	BfdT	53128	2353		A2
CO-B Franklin St					
300	GNCY	53128	2353		A2
CO-B Freeman St					
200	GNCY	53128	2353		A3
CO-B Main St					
700	GNCY	53128	2353		A3
800	BfdT	53128	2352		E3
800	GNCY	53128	2352		E3
CO-B Tuttle Rd					
11000	SlmT	53179	2356		B1
CO-B Twin Lakes Rd					
100	BfdT	53128	2353		B1
100	GNCY	53128	2353		B1
100	RdlT	53128	2353		B1
CO-B Wilmot Rd					
30000	SlmT	53179	2356		B1
CO-C					
11000	RdlT	53181	2355		B1
11000	TNLK	53181	2355		B1
11300	SlmT	53192	2356		A1
24300	SlmT	53179	2357		C1
27200	SlmT	53179	2356		D2
31200	RdlT	53192	2355		E1
34000	RdlT	53181	2354		E1
34000	TNLK	53181	2354		E1
CO-C 110th St					
34000	RdlT	53181	2354		E1
34000	RdlT	53181	2355		B1
34000	TNLK	53181	2354		E1
34000	TNLK	53181	2355		B1
CO-C 113th St					
30500	SlmT	53179	2356		A1
30500	SlmT	53192	2356		A1
CO-C 114th St					
30700	SlmT	53192	2356		A1
CO-C 116th St					
31600	RdlT	53181	2355		C2
31800	TNLK	53181	2355		C2
CO-C 336th Av					
11000	RdlT	53181	2355		B2
11000	TNLK	53181	2355		B1
CO-C Fox River Rd					
11300	SlmT	53192	2356		A1
CO-C Wilmot Rd					
24300	SlmT	53179	2357		C1
27200	SlmT	53179	2356		D2
30800	SlmT	53192	2356		A1
31200	RdlT	53181	2355		E1
31200	RdlT	53192	2355		E1
CO-CJ					
13600	BtlT	53142	2360		B1
15200	BtlT	53142	2359		C2
17200	BtlT	53104	2359		B3
CO-CJ Horton Rd					
13600	BtlT	53142	2360		B1
15200	BtlT	53142	2359		C2
17200	BtlT	53104	2359		B3
CO-CK					
900	BtnT	60081	2355	30W-43N	A4
900	RdlT	53181	2355		C3
900	RdlT	60081	2355	29W-43N	B4
1000	SPGV	60081	2355	30W-43N	B4
1400	BtnT	60071	2355	30W-43N	A4
1600	BtnT	53181	2354	31W-43N	D4
1600	BtnT	60071	2354	31W-43N	D4
1600	RcmT	53181	2354	31W-43N	D4
1600	RcmT	60071	2354	31W-43N	D4
1600	RcmT	60081	2354	31W-43N	D4
1600	RdlT	53181	2354	31W-43N	D4
1600	RdlT	60071	2354	31W-43N	D4
1600	RdlT	60081	2354	31W-43N	D4
CO-CK 125th St					
32000	RdlT	53181	2355		C3
CO-CK 336th Av					
12500	RdlT	53181	2355		B3
12700	BtnT	60081	2355		B4
12700	RdlT	60081	2355		B4
CO-CK State Line Rd					
900	BtnT	60081	2355	30W-43N	A4
900	RdlT	53181	2355	30W-43N	A4
900	RdlT	60081	2355	29W-43N	B4
1000	SPGV	60081	2355	30W-43N	B4
1400	BtnT	60071	2355	30W-43N	A4
1600	BtnT	53181	2354	31W-43N	D4
1600	BtnT	60071	2354	31W-43N	D4
1600	RcmT	53181	2354	31W-43N	D4
1600	RcmT	60071	2354	31W-43N	D4
1600	RcmT	60081	2354	31W-43N	D4
1600	RdlT	53181	2354	31W-43N	D4
1600	RdlT	60071	2354	31W-43N	D4
1600	RdlT	60081	2354	31W-43N	D4
CO-EM					
1700	TNLK	53181	2354		B4
3100	RcmT	60071	2354		B4
3100	TNLK	60071	2354		B4
CO-EM E Lakeshore Dr					
1700	TNLK	53181	2354		B4
3100	RcmT	60071	2354		B4
3100	TNLK	60071	2354		B4
CO-EZ					
10400	PTPR	53158	2362		E2
12600	BtnT	53158	2362		E4
12600	BtnT	60096	2362		E4
12600	BtnT	60099	2362		E4
CO-EZ 39th Av					
10400	PTPR	53158	2362		D2
12600	BtnT	53158	2362		E4
12600	BtnT	60096	2362		E4
12600	BtnT	60099	2362		E4
CO-G					
2400	ANTH	60002	2357	23W-43N	E4
CO-G Donin Dr					
2400	ANTH	60002	2357	23W-43N	E4
CO-H					
-	BfdT	53128	2353		B3
100	GNCY	53128	2353		A2
500	BfdT	53128	2352		E1
500	GNCY	53128	2352		E2
10500	PTPR	53158	2361		D3
12200	NptT	60099	2361		D3
12200	PTPR	60099	2361		D3
CO-H 88th Av					
10500	PTPR	53158	2361		D3
12200	NptT	60099	2361		D3
12200	PTPR	60099	2361		D3
CO-H Freeman St					
300	GNCY	53128	2353		A3
CO-H Walworth St					
100	GNCY	53128	2353		A3
CO-HM					
12600	RcmT	60081	2354		C4
12600	RdlT	53181	2354		D2
12600	RdlT	60081	2354		C4
33600	RdlT	53181	2355		B2
33600	TNLK	53181	2355		B2
35000	TNLK	53181	2354		D2
CO-HM 116th St					
33600	RdlT	53181	2355		B2
33600	TNLK	53181	2355		B2
35000	RdlT	53181	2354		E2
35000	TNLK	53181	2354		E2
CO-HM 374th Av					
12600	RcmT	60081	2354		C4
12600	RdlT	53181	2354		C3
12600	RdlT	60081	2354		C4
CO-HM Wilmot Rd					
35600	RdlT	53181	2354		D2
35600	TNLK	53181	2354		D2
CO-JF					
23800	SlmT	53179	2357		D2
CO-JF 119th St					
23800	SlmT	53179	2357		E2
CO-JF 260th Av					
-	SlmT	53179	2357		D2
CO-JI					
32500	GRNE	60031	2477	16W-37N	E3
CO-JI Hastings Ct					
32500	GRNE	60031	2477	16W-37N	E3
CO-KD					
9800	RdlT	53181	2355		B1
9800	TNLK	53181	2355		B3
12700	BtnT	60081	2355		B4
12700	RdlT	60081	2355		B4
CO-KD 336th Av					
9800	RdlT	53181	2355		B1
9800	TNLK	53181	2355		B3
12700	BtnT	60081	2355		B4
12700	RdlT	60081	2355		B4
CO-MB					
6800	GRNE	60031	2477	16W-36N	E3
10400	BtlT	53142	2360		A4
11700	BtlT	60002	2360		A4
11700	NptT	60002	2360		A4
CO-MB 152nd Av					
10400	BtlT	53142	2360		A4
11700	BtlT	60002	2360		A4
11700	NptT	60002	2360		A4
CO-MB Westminster Ln					
6800	GRNE	60031	2477	16W-36N	E3
CO-ML					
-	BtlT	53142	2360		E3
4800	PTPR	53158	2362		C1
6800	PTPR	53158	2361		B3
9100	PTPR	53158	2360		E3
CO-ML 88th Av					
11600	PTPR	53158	2361		D2
CO-ML 116th St					
8000	PTPR	53158	2361		D2
CO-ML 122nd St					
-	BtlT	53142	2360		E3
8800	PTPR	53158	2361		B3
9100	PTPR	53158	2360		E3
CO-ML Springbrook Rd					
4800	PTPR	53158	2362		C1
6800	PTPR	53158	2361		E2
CO-O					
1700	TNLK	53181	2353		E1
39500	RdlT	53128	2353		E1
39500	TNLK	53128	2353		E1
40000	BfdT	53128	2353		E1
CO-O 110th St					
39500	RdlT	53128	2353		E1
39500	TNLK	53128	2353		E1
39500	TNLK	53181	2353		E1
40000	BfdT	53128	2353		E1
CO-O Richmond Rd					
1700	TNLK	53181	2353		E1
CO-P					
1700	TNLK	53181	2353		E1
1800	RdlT	53128	2353		E1
1800	RdlT	53181	2353		E1
1800	TNLK	53128	2353		E1
12500	RcmT	60071	2353		D4
12500	RHMD	60071	2353		D4
12500	TNLK	60071	2353		D4
CO-P Richmond Rd					
1700	TNLK	53181	2353		E1
1800	RdlT	53128	2353		E1
1800	RdlT	53181	2353		E1
1800	TNLK	53128	2353		E1
12500	RcmT	60071	2353		D4
12500	RHMD	60071	2353		D4
12500	TNLK	60071	2353		D4
CO-Q					
16800	BtlT	53104	2359		B1
CO-Q Winfield Rd					
16800	BtlT	53104	2359		B1
CO-T50					
6600	CmgT	60033	2405	51W-39N	D5
6600	HRVD	60033	2405	51W-39N	D5
CO-T50 Lawrence Rd					
6600	CmgT	60033	2405	51W-39N	D5
6600	HRVD	60033	2405	51W-39N	D5
CO-T50 Oak Grove Rd					
22600	CmgT	60033	2405	51W-39N	D3
22600	HRVD	60033	2405	51W-39N	D3
CO-T55					
4600	DhmT	60033	2464	50W-37N	A2
5000	HRVD	60033	2464	50W-37N	A2
CO-T55 Marengo Rd					
4600	DhmT	60033	2464	50W-37N	A2
5000	HRVD	60033	2464	50W-37N	A2
CO-T58					
300	MRGO	60152	2634	49W-24N	C7
6300	RlyT	60152	2634	49W-25N	C4
CO-T58 Maple St					
300	MRGO	60152	2634	49W-24N	C7
6300	RlyT	60152	2634	49W-25N	C4
CO-T59					
1100	MngT	60152	2578	49W-28N	D6
1100	SenT	60152	2578	49W-28N	D6
3500	MRGO	60152	2578	49W-28N	D6
4700	MngT	60152	2634	49W-27N	D1
4700	MRGO	60152	2634	49W-27N	D1
4700	SenT	60152	2634	49W-27N	D1
CO-T59 Deerpass Rd					
1100	MngT	60152	2578	49W-28N	D6
1100	SenT	60152	2578	49W-28N	D6
3500	MRGO	60152	2578	49W-28N	D6
4700	MngT	60152	2634	49W-27N	D1
4700	MRGO	60152	2634	49W-27N	D1
4700	SenT	60152	2634	49W-27N	D1
CO-T64					
4700	SenT	60152	2635	47W-27N	B1
4700	SenT	60180	2635	47W-27N	B1
CO-T64 Millstream Rd					
4700	SenT	60152	2635	47W-27N	B1
4700	SenT	60180	2635	47W-27N	B1
CO-T65					
4700	SenT	60180	2635	46W-27N	D1
5100	UNON	60180	2635	47W-24N	C7
6600	CrlT	60180	2635	47W-25N	C5
CO-T65 Jefferson St					
17700	UNON	60180	2635	47W-24N	C7
CO-T65 Main St					
6000	UNON	60180	2635	46W-25N	D4
CO-T65 N Union Rd					
4700	SenT	60180	2635	46W-27N	D1
5100	UNON	60180	2635	46W-26N	D3
CO-T65 S Union Rd					
6600	CrlT	60180	2635	47W-25N	C5
6600	UNON	60180	2635	47W-25N	C5
CO-T65 W Union Rd					
-	CrlT	60180	2635	46W-25N	C4
-	UNON	60180	2635	46W-25N	C4
CO-U					
-	GNCY	53128	2353		A2
500	BfdT	53128	2353		A1
10400	BtlT	53142	2360		C3
12600	NptT	53142	2360		B4
12600	NptT	60002	2360		B4
CO-U 136th Av					
10400	BtlT	53142	2360		C3
12600	NptT	53142	2360		B4
12600	NptT	60002	2360		B4
CO-U N Carter St					
-	GNCY	53128	2353		A2
CO-V					
11000	SlmT	53104	2358		B1
18200	BtlT	53104	2359		A2
18800	BtlT	53104	2358		B2
CO-V 116th St					
18200	BtlT	53104	2359		A2
18800	BtlT	53104	2358		B2
21600	SlmT	53104	2358		B2
CO-V 224th Av					
11000	SlmT	53104	2358		B1
CO-V12					
9600	AdnT	60033	2349	45W-41N	A7
CO-V12 Alden Rd					
9600	AdnT	60033	2349	45W-41N	A7
CO-V23					
-	GfnT	60014	2692	38W-23N	E2
-	LKWD	60014	2692	38W-23N	E2
2400	LIHL	60156	2692	38W-21N	E5
9800	GfnT	60156	2692	38W-22N	E4
10300	GfnT	60102	2692	38W-21N	E6
CO-V23 Lakewood Rd					
-	GfnT	60014	2692	38W-23N	E2
-	LKWD	60014	2692	38W-23N	E2
2400	LIHL	60156	2692	38W-21N	E5
9800	GfnT	60156	2692	38W-22N	E4
10300	GfnT	60102	2692	38W-21N	E6
CO-V24					
1900	GwdT	60098	2525	39W-33N	D2
2100	BLVY	60098	2525	39W-34N	D1
2700	BLVY	60098	2468	39W-34N	D7
2700	GwdT	60097	2468	39W-35N	D6
2700	GwdT	60098	2468	39W-35N	D6
2700	WRLK	60097	2468	39W-35N	D6
2700	WRLK	60098	2468	39W-34N	D7
3100	GNWD	60097	2468	39W-35N	D6
3100	GNWD	60098	2468	39W-35N	D6
5800	GwdT	60097	2469	38W-37N	A1
5800	HbnT	60034	2469	38W-37N	A1
5800	HbnT	60097	2469	38W-37N	A1
9300	HbnT	60034	2352	38W-41N	A7
9300	HbnT	60071	2352	38W-41N	A7
CO-V24 Greenwood Rd					
1900	GwdT	60098	2525	39W-33N	D2
2100	BLVY	60098	2525	39W-34N	D1
2700	BLVY	60098	2468	39W-34N	D7
2700	GwdT	60097	2468	39W-35N	D6
2700	GwdT	60098	2468	39W-35N	D6
2700	WRLK	60097	2468	39W-35N	D6
2700	WRLK	60098	2468	39W-34N	D7
3100	GNWD	60097	2468	39W-35N	D6
3100	GNWD	60098	2468	39W-35N	D6
5800	GwdT	60097	2469	38W-37N	A1
5800	HbnT	60034	2469	38W-37N	A1
5800	HbnT	60097	2469	38W-37N	A1
9300	HbnT	60034	2352	38W-41N	A7
9300	HbnT	60071	2352	38W-41N	A7
CO-V25					
10	DrrT	60098	2525	39W-32N	D5
10	GwdT	60098	2525	39W-32N	D5
200	BLVY	60098	2525	39W-32N	D5
900	BLVY	60098	2582	38W-30N	E1
900	DrrT	60098	2582	38W-30N	E1
CO-V25					
2100	DrrT	60098	2583	37W-29N	A4
4000	DrrT	60012	2583	37W-27N	C7
7800	CLLK	60012	2639	37W-27N	C1
7800	NndT	60012	2639	37W-27N	C1
8000	DrrT	60012	2639	37W-27N	C1
8100	CLLK	60012	2583	37W-27N	C7
CO-V25 Country Club Rd					
9100	DrrT	60098	2583	37W-29N	A4
CO-V25 S Country Club Rd					
2100	DrrT	60098	2583	37W-29N	A3
4000	DrrT	60012	2583	37W-27N	C7
CO-V25 N Fleming Rd					
10	GwdT	60098	2525	39W-32N	D5
CO-V25 S Fleming Rd					
10	DrrT	60098	2525	39W-32N	D5
10	GwdT	60098	2525	39W-32N	D6
200	BLVY	60098	2525	39W-32N	D5
900	BLVY	60098	2582	38W-30N	E1
900	DrrT	60098	2582	38W-30N	E1
CO-V25 Ridgefield Rd					
7800	CLLK	60012	2639	37W-27N	C1
7800	NndT	60012	2639	37W-27N	C1
8000	DrrT	60012	2639	37W-27N	C1
8100	CLLK	60012	2583	37W-27N	C7
8100	DrrT	60012	2583	37W-27N	C7
CO-V29					
10	ALGN	60102	2693	36W-21N	E6
10	LIHL	60102	2693	36W-21N	E6
10	LIHL	60156	2693	36W-20N	E7
300	CLLK	60014	2693	36W-24N	E6
1000	CLLK	60014	2693	36W-23N	E1
8700	AlqT	60014	2693	36W-20N	E7
9000	AlqT	60156	2693	36W-20N	E7
9100	CLLK	60156	2693	36W-20N	E7
9100	LIHL	60014	2693	36W-20N	E7
11100	AlqT	60102	2746	36W-20N	E1
11900	ALGN	60102	2746	36W-20N	E1
CO-V29 McHenry Av					
300	CLLK	60014	2639	36W-24N	E6
1000	CLLK	60014	2693	36W-23N	E1
CO-V29 Randall Rd					
8700	AlqT	60014	2693	36W-20N	E7
8700	CLLK	60014	2693	36W-20N	E7
9000	AlqT	60156	2693	36W-20N	E7
9100	CLLK	60156	2693	36W-20N	E7
9100	LIHL	60014	2693	36W-20N	E7
9100	LIHL	60156	2693	36W-20N	E7
CO-V29 N Randall Rd					
-	CLLK	60014	2693	36W-22N	E4
-	CLLK	60156	2693	36W-22N	E4
10	ALGN	60102	2693	36W-21N	E6
10	LIHL	60102	2693	36W-21N	E6
10	LIHL	60156	2693	36W-21N	E5
CO-V29 S Randall Rd					
10	ALGN	60102	2693	36W-21N	E6
10	LIHL	60102	2693	36W-21N	E6
10	LIHL	60156	2693	36W-21N	E6
11100	AlqT	60102	2746	36W-20N	E1
11900	ALGN	60102	2746	36W-20N	E1
CO-V30					
9400	RcmT	60071	2352	36W-41N	E7
11300	GNCY	53128	2352	35W-43N	E4
11300	GNCY	60071	2352	35W-43N	E4
CO-V30 Keystone Rd					
10300	RcmT	60071	2352	36W-43N	E4
11300	GNCY	53128	2352	35W-43N	E4
11300	GNCY	60071	2352	35W-43N	E4
CO-V32					
100	LIHL	60156	2694	34W-23N	B2
400	ALGN	60102	2694	34W-21N	D6
600	CLLK	60014	2640	35W-24N	B7
800	CLLK	60156	2640	35W-24N	B7
800	LIHL	60156	2640	35W-24N	B7
8000	CLLK	60156	2694	35W-24N	B1
CO-V32 W Algonquin Rd					
400	ALGN	60102	2694	34W-21N	D6
1100	LIHL	60156	2694	34W-21N	C6
CO-V32 S Main St					
600	CLLK	60014	2640	35W-24N	B6
CO-V32 Pyott Rd					
100	ALGN	60102	2694	34W-21N	C6
100	LIHL	60156	2694	34W-23N	B2
800	CLLK	60014	2640	35W-24N	B7
800	CLLK	60156	2640	35W-24N	B7
800	LIHL	60156	2640	35W-24N	B7
8000	CLLK	60156	2694	35W-24N	B1
CO-V33					
10	CLLK	60014	2640	35W-24N	A6
8000	CLLK	60014	2694	34W-23N	C2
8000	LIHL	60014	2694	34W-23N	C2
8200	CLLK	60156	2694	34W-23N	C1
8200	LIHL	60156	2694	34W-23N	C2
9200	ALGN	60013	2694	33W-22N	E3
9200	AlqT	60013	2694	33W-22N	E3
11300	RcmT	60071	2353	34W-43N	D4
11300	RHMD	60071	2353	34W-43N	D4
11400	RdlT	53181	2353	34W-43N	D4
11400	TNLK	53128	2353	34W-43N	D4
11400	TNLK	53181	2353	34W-43N	D4
11400	TNLK	60071	2353	34W-43N	D4
CO-V33 N Burlington Rd					
11300	RcmT	60071	2353	34W-43N	D4
11300	RHMD	60071	2353	34W-43N	D4
11400	RdlT	53181	2353	34W-43N	D4
11400	TNLK	53128	2353	34W-43N	D4
11400	TNLK	53181	2353	34W-43N	D4
11400	TNLK	60071	2353	34W-43N	D4
CO-V33 Virginia Rd					
10	CLLK	60014	2640	35W-24N	A6
8000	CLLK	60014	2694	34W-23N	C2
8000	LIHL	60014	2694	34W-23N	C2
8200	CLLK	60156	2694	34W-23N	C1
8200	LIHL	60156	2694	34W-23N	C2
9200	ALGN	60013	2694	33W-22N	E3
9200	AlqT	60013	2694	33W-22N	E3
CO-V34					
100	MHRY	60050	2527	34W-31N	C7
300	CLLK	60012	2640	35W-26N	B2
300	CLLK	60014	2640	35W-26N	B3
300	NndT	60050	2527	34W-31N	D6
500	BLVY	60050	2584	34W-30N	C1
500	MHRY	60050	2584	34W-30N	C1
2100	NndT	60050	2584	35W-29N	B3
2300	NndT	60012	2584	35W-27N	B7
2400	BLVY	60012	2584	35W-29N	B4
4000	MHRY	60050	2528	33W-33N	A4
4100	CLLK	60012	2584	35W-28N	B7
4400	NndT	60012	2640	35W-26N	A2
CO-V34 S Crystal Lake Rd					
200	MHRY	60050	2527	34W-31N	D6
300	NndT	60050	2527	34W-31N	D6
500	BLVY	60050	2584	34W-30N	C1
500	MHRY	60050	2584	34W-30N	C1
500	NndT	60050	2584	34W-30N	C1
2100	NndT	60012	2584	35W-29N	B3

Chicago 7-County Street Index

STREET Block	City	ZIP	Map#	CGS	Grid
CO-V34 S Crystal Lake Rd					
2400	BLVY	60012	2584	35W-29N	B4
CO-V34 W Crystal Lake Rd					
4000	MHRY	60050	2528	33W-33N	A4
4300	MHRY	60050	2527	34W-31N	C7
CO-V34 Walkup Rd					
300	CLLK	60012	2640	35W-26N	A2
300	CLLK	60014	2640	35W-26N	B3
2600	BLVY	60012	2584	35W-29N	B4
2600	NndT	60012	2584	35W-27N	B7
4100	CLLK	60012	2584	35W-28N	B7
4400	NndT	60012	2640	35W-26N	A2
CO-V36					
100	CRY	60013	2695	33W-21N	A5
200	TVLY	60013	2695	32W-23N	C2
400	CRY	60013	2641	31W-24N	D7
900	ALGN	60102	2694	33W-21N	E6
1000	AlqT	60102	2694	33W-21N	E6
1300	AlqT	60102	2695	33W-21N	A5
1700	ALGN	60013	2695	32W-22N	A4
2000	CRY	60102	2695	32W-22N	B4
CO-V36 Cary Rd					
900	ALGN	60102	2694	33W-21N	E6
1000	AlqT	60102	2694	33W-21N	E6
1300	AlqT	60102	2695	33W-21N	A5
1700	ALGN	60013	2695	32W-22N	A4
2000	CRY	60102	2695	32W-22N	B4
2200	CRY	60013	2695	32W-22N	B3
CO-V36 Cary-Algonquin Rd					
-	ALGN	60013	2695	32W-22N	B3
-	CRY	60102	2695	32W-22N	B3
100	CRY	60013	2695	33W-21N	A5
200	TVLY	60013	2695	32W-23N	C2
400	CRY	60013	2641	31W-24N	C7
CO-V37					
10500	RcmT	60071	2354	32W-43N	B4
10500	SPGV	60081	2354	32W-42N	B6
11500	TNLK	53181	2354	32W-43N	B4
11500	TNLK	60071	2354	32W-43N	B4
CO-V37 Lakeview Rd					
10500	RcmT	60071	2354	32W-43N	B4
10500	SPGV	60081	2354	32W-42N	B6
11500	TNLK	53181	2354	32W-43N	B4
11500	TNLK	60071	2354	32W-43N	B4
CO-V40					
1000	MchT	60051	2528	31W-32N	E4
1000	MHRY	60051	2528	31W-32N	E4
1500	LKMR	60051	2528	31W-32N	E4
2300	JNBG	60050	2471	31W-37N	D1
2700	MchT	60051	2471	30W-34N	E7
2900	JNBG	60051	2471	30W-34N	E7
4100	MchT	60050	2471	31W-37N	D1
5000	MchT	60081	2471	31W-37N	D1
5300	JNBG	60081	2471	31W-37N	D1
5600	RcmT	60050	2471	31W-37N	D1
5600	RcmT	60081	2471	31W-37N	D1
6100	RcmT	60050	2413	31W-38N	D7
6100	RcmT	60081	2413	31W-41N	D1
6300	SPGV	60081	2413	31W-41N	D1
9700	RcmT	60071	2354	31W-42N	D7
9700	SPGV	60071	2354	31W-42N	D7
9700	SPGV	60081	2354	31W-42N	D7
CO-V40 Chapel Hill Rd					
-	MchT	60051	2528	31W-32N	E4
-	MHRY	60051	2528	30W-32N	E4
CO-V40 N Chapel Hill Rd					
1000	MchT	60051	2528	31W-32N	E4
1000	MHRY	60051	2528	31W-32N	E4
1500	LKMR	60051	2528	31W-32N	E4
2700	MchT	60051	2471	30W-34N	E7
2900	JNBG	60051	2471	30W-34N	E7
3500	JNBG	60050	2471	31W-35N	E6
CO-V40 W Johnsburg Rd					
2300	JNBG	60050	2471	31W-35N	D6
CO-V40 Spring Grove Rd					
3600	JNBG	60050	2471	31W-37N	D1
4100	MchT	60050	2471	31W-37N	D1
5000	MchT	60081	2471	31W-37N	D1
5300	JNBG	60081	2471	31W-37N	D1
5600	RcmT	60050	2471	31W-37N	D1
5600	RcmT	60081	2471	31W-37N	D1
6100	RcmT	60050	2413	31W-38N	D7
6100	RcmT	60081	2413	31W-38N	D7
6300	SPGV	60081	2413	31W-38N	D7
CO-V40 Winn Rd					
7600	SPGV	60081	2413	31W-41N	D1
7800	RcmT	60081	2413	31W-41N	D1
9700	RcmT	60071	2354	31W-42N	D7
9700	SPGV	60071	2354	31W-42N	D7
9700	SPGV	60081	2354	31W-42N	D7
CO-V43					
7600	SPGV	60081	2413	30W-39N	E4
8400	BtnT	60081	2414	30W-40N	A2
8400	SPGV	60081	2414	30W-40N	A2
9700	BtnT	60081	2355	30W-42N	A6
9700	SPGV	60081	2355	30W-42N	A6
CO-V43 Blivin St					
-	BtnT	60081	2414	30W-40N	A3
-	SPGV	60081	2414	30W-40N	A3
7600	SPGV	60081	2413	31W-39N	E4
CO-V43 Richardson Rd					
8400	BtnT	60081	2414	30W-40N	A2
8400	SPGV	60081	2414	30W-40N	A2
9700	BtnT	60081	2355	30W-42N	A6
9700	SPGV	60081	2355	30W-42N	A6
CO-V44					
7300	BtnT	60081	2414	30W-39N	B5
7600	SPGV	60081	2414	30W-39N	B5
7700	FXLK	60081	2414	29W-39N	B4
9500	FXLK	60081	2355	29W-42N	D6
10000	BtnT	60081	2355	29W-42N	D6
10900	AntT	60002	2355	29W-43N	D4
10900	FXLK	60002	2355	29W-43N	D4
CO-V44 Wilmot Rd					
7300	BtnT	60081	2414	30W-39N	B5
7600	SPGV	60081	2414	30W-39N	B5
7700	FXLK	60081	2414	29W-39N	B4
9500	FXLK	60081	2355	29W-42N	D6
10000	BtnT	60081	2355	29W-42N	D6
10900	AntT	60002	2355	29W-43N	D4
10900	FXLK	60002	2355	29W-43N	D4
CO-V45					
-	ISLK	60051	2586	29W-28N	C5
100	MchT	60051	2528	31W-31N	D7
100	NndT	60051	2528	31W-32N	D6
200	TRLK	60010	2643	26W-25N	D4
900	NndT	60051	2585	30W-30N	E1
1000	MHRY	60051	2528	32W-33N	C4
1500	HHLL	60051	2586	30W-30N	A2
1500	NndT	60051	2586	29W-28N	C5
4000	ISLK	60042	2586	29W-27N	D7
4000	NndT	60042	2586	29W-27N	D7
4100	WcnT	60042	2586	29W-27N	D7
4600	NndT	60042	2642	29W-27N	D1
4600	NndT	60051	2642	29W-27N	D1
5000	WcnT	60010	2642	28W-26N	D2
27100	LKBN	60010	2643	27W-25N	C4
27700	CbaT	60010	2643	26W-25N	C4
28100	WcnT	60010	2643	26W-25N	C4
28300	PTBR	60010	2643	26W-25N	C4
28400	PTBR	60010	2642	28W-26N	D2
28700	WcnT	60084	2642	28W-26N	D2
28800	PTBR	60084	2642	28W-26N	D3
CO-V45 N River Rd					
100	MchT	60051	2528	31W-31N	D7
100	NndT	60051	2528	31W-32N	D6
1000	MHRY	60051	2528	32W-33N	C4
CO-V45 S River Rd					
-	ISLK	60042	2586	29W-28N	C5
-	ISLK	60051	2586	29W-28N	C5
100	NndT	60051	2528	31W-31N	D6
900	NndT	60051	2585	30W-30N	E1
1500	HHLL	60051	2586	30W-30N	A2
1500	NndT	60051	2586	29W-28N	C5
3100	NndT	60042	2586	29W-29N	C5
CO-V45 Roberts Rd					
-	PTBR	60010	2642	28W-26N	D2
-	WcnT	60084	2642	28W-26N	D2
200	TRLK	60010	2643	26W-25N	D4
4000	ISLK	60042	2586	29W-27N	D7
4000	NndT	60042	2586	29W-27N	D7
4100	WcnT	60042	2586	29W-27N	D7
4600	NndT	60042	2642	29W-27N	D1
4600	NndT	60051	2642	29W-27N	D1
5000	WcnT	60010	2642	28W-26N	D2
27100	LKBN	60010	2643	27W-25N	C4
27700	CbaT	60010	2643	27W-25N	B4
CO-V45 W Roberts Rd					
28000	CbaT	60010	2643	26W-25N	C4
28000	LKBN	60010	2643	27W-25N	A4
28100	WcnT	60010	2643	26W-25N	C4
28300	PTBR	60010	2643	26W-25N	C4
28400	PTBR	60010	2642	28W-25N	E4
28400	WcnT	60010	2642	28W-25N	E4
28700	WcnT	60084	2642	28W-26N	E3
28800	PTBR	60084	2642	28W-26N	D3
29000	NndT	60042	2586	29W-27N	D7
29000	NndT	60042	2642	29W-27N	D1
29000	NndT	60051	2586	29W-27N	D7
29000	NndT	60051	2642	29W-27N	D1
29000	WcnT	60042	2586	29W-27N	D7
29400	ISLK	60042	2586	29W-27N	D7
29400	ISLK	60051	2586	29W-27N	D7
CO-V47					
26600	PTBR	60010	2642	28W-26N	D3
26600	WcnT	60010	2642	28W-26N	D3
26600	WcnT	60084	2642	28W-26N	D3
26700	WcnT	60084	2643	28W-27N	A1
26900	ISLK	60042	2643	28W-27N	A1
26900	WcnT	60042	2643	28W-27N	A1
27300	ISLK	60084	2643	27W-27N	A1
27600	ISLK	60084	2587	28W-29N	A3
27600	WcnT	60084	2587	28W-29N	A3
27800	WcnT	60051	2587	27W-28N	A7
28300	ISLK	60042	2587	28W-28N	A5
28300	ISLK	60051	2587	27W-28N	A5
28300	WcnT	60042	2587	28W-28N	A5
30000	WcnT	60051	2586	28W-30N	E1
30800	LKMR	60051	2529	28W-31N	E7
30800	WcnT	60051	2529	28W-31N	E7
CO-V47 N Darrell Rd					
26600	PTBR	60010	2642	28W-26N	D3
26600	WcnT	60010	2642	28W-26N	D3
26600	WcnT	60084	2642	28W-26N	E3
26700	WcnT	60084	2643	28W-27N	A1
26900	ISLK	60042	2643	28W-27N	A1
26900	WcnT	60042	2643	28W-27N	A1
27300	ISLK	60084	2643	27W-27N	A1
27600	ISLK	60084	2587	28W-29N	A3
27600	WcnT	60084	2587	28W-29N	A3
27800	WcnT	60051	2587	27W-28N	A7
28300	ISLK	60042	2587	28W-28N	A5
28300	ISLK	60051	2587	27W-28N	A5
28300	WcnT	60042	2587	28W-28N	A5
30000	WcnT	60051	2586	28W-30N	E1
30800	LKMR	60051	2529	28W-31N	E7
30800	WcnT	60051	2529	28W-31N	E7
CO-V47 Rawson Bridge Rd					
-	PTBR	60010	2642	28W-26N	D3
-	WcnT	60010	2642	28W-26N	D3
-	WcnT	60084	2642	28W-26N	D3
CO-V49					
200	LKBN	60010	2643	26W-24N	D6
200	TRLK	60010	2643	26W-24N	D6
22000	CbaT	60010	2696	28W-22N	E4
22000	LKBN	60010	2696	28W-22N	E4
23500	LKBN	60010	2697	27W-23N	A1
23800	CbaT	60010	2697	27W-23N	A1
24100	CbaT	60010	2643	27W-24N	C7
CO-V49 Kelsey Rd					
200	LKBN	60010	2643	26W-24N	D6
200	TRLK	60010	2643	26W-24N	D6
CO-V49 N Kelsey Rd					
22000	CbaT	60010	2696	28W-22N	E4
22000	LKBN	60010	2696	28W-22N	E4
23500	LKBN	60010	2697	27W-23N	A1
23800	CbaT	60010	2697	27W-23N	A1
24100	CbaT	60010	2643	27W-24N	C7
24100	LKBN	60010	2643	27W-24N	B7
24300	TRLK	60010	2643	27W-24N	C7
CO-V50					
100	LKBN	60010	2643	27W-24N	B6
CO-V50 River Rd					
100	LKBN	60010	2643	27W-24N	B6
CO-V51					
-	GYLK	60030	2533	20W-33N	A3
42000	AntT	60002	2356	26W-42N	D5
43400	AntT	53179	2356	26W-43N	D4
43400	SlmT	53179	2356	26W-43N	D4
CO-V51 Center St					
-	GYLK	60030	2533	20W-33N	A3
CO-V51 N Lake Av					
42000	AntT	60002	2356	26W-42N	D5
43400	AntT	53179	2356	26W-43N	D4
43400	SlmT	53179	2356	26W-43N	D4
CO-V57					
-	ElaT	60010	2698	24W-21N	D6
10	BRTN	60010	2751	24W-20N	D1
10	DRPK	60010	2751	24W-20N	D1
10	ElaT	60010	2751	24W-20N	D1
10	PltT	60010	2751	24W-20N	D1
100	DRPK	60010	2698	24W-20N	D7
400	LKZH	60047	2698	24W-22N	D4
800	LKZH	60010	2698	24W-22N	D5
CO-V57 Ela Rd					
-	ElaT	60010	2698	24W-21N	D6
400	LKZH	60047	2698	24W-22N	D4
800	DRPK	60010	2698	24W-22N	D4
800	LKZH	60010	2698	24W-22N	D5
CO-V57 N Ela Rd					
10	BRTN	60010	2751	24W-20N	D1
10	DRPK	60010	2751	24W-20N	D1
10	ElaT	60010	2751	24W-20N	D1
10	PltT	60010	2751	24W-20N	D1
100	DRPK	60010	2698	24W-20N	D7
CO-V58					
300	GrtT	60041	2530	26W-33N	E3
300	RDLK	60041	2530	26W-33N	E2
300	RDLK	60073	2530	26W-33N	E3
31600	GrtT	60030	2531	25W-31N	B6
31600	GrtT	60073	2531	25W-31N	B6
31600	RDLK	60073	2531	25W-31N	B6
31600	WcnT	60030	2531	25W-31N	B6
32800	GrtT	60073	2530	26W-33N	E3
34600	GrtT	60041	2473	26W-34N	E7
CO-V58 Wilson Rd					
31600	GrtT	60030	2531	25W-31N	B6
31600	GrtT	60073	2531	25W-31N	B6
31600	RDLK	60073	2531	25W-31N	B6
31600	WcnT	60030	2531	25W-31N	B6
CO-V58 N Wilson Rd					
300	GrtT	60041	2530	26W-33N	E3
300	RDLK	60041	2530	26W-33N	E2
300	RDLK	60073	2530	26W-33N	E3
32500	GrtT	60030	2531	25W-32N	A5
32500	GrtT	60073	2531	25W-32N	A5
32500	RDLK	60073	2531	25W-32N	A5
32800	GrtT	60073	2530	26W-33N	E3
34600	GrtT	60041	2473	26W-34N	E7
CO-V60					
10	HNVL	60030	2532	22W-33N	C3
100	HNVL	60073	2532	22W-33N	C3
500	AvnT	60030	2532	22W-33N	C3
500	RLKP	60073	2532	22W-33N	C3
600	AvnT	60073	2532	22W-34N	C1
800	RLKB	60073	2532	22W-34N	C1
1100	RLKB	60030	2475	22W-35N	C7
1100	RLKB	60073	2475	22W-35N	C7
CO-V60 Hainesville Rd					
1100	RLKB	60030	2475	22W-35N	C7
1100	RLKB	60073	2475	22W-35N	C7
CO-V60 N Hainesville Rd					
10	HNVL	60030	2532	22W-33N	C3
100	HNVL	60073	2532	22W-33N	C3
500	AvnT	60030	2532	22W-33N	C3
500	RLKP	60073	2532	22W-33N	C3
600	AvnT	60073	2532	22W-34N	C1
800	RLKB	60073	2532	22W-34N	C1
34600	RLKB	60073	2475	22W-34N	C7
CO-V61					
10	AvnT	60073	2531	24W-33N	C2
10	ElaT	60047	2645	22W-25N	B5
10	HNWD	60047	2645	22W-25N	B5
10	LKZH	60047	2645	22W-24N	B7
10	RDLK	60073	2531	24W-33N	C2
800	RLKB	60073	2531	24W-34N	C1
900	RLKB	60073	2474	24W-34N	C7
1200	AvnT	60073	2474	24W-35N	C7
1200	FmtT	60060	2588	24W-30N	C1
1200	WCDA	60060	2588	24W-30N	C1
1200	WCDA	60084	2588	24W-30N	C1
25700	HNWD	60060	2645	22W-25N	A4
25800	FmtT	60047	2645	22W-26N	A4
25800	FmtT	60060	2645	23W-26N	A3
25800	FmtT	60084	2645	23W-26N	A3
26400	FmtT	60060	2644	24W-27N	D1
26400	FmtT	60084	2644	24W-27N	D1
27200	FmtT	60084	2588	24W-27N	D7
29500	FmtT	60030	2588	24W-29N	D4
29500	WCDA	60030	2588	24W-29N	D4
31500	FmtT	60030	2531	24W-31N	C7
31600	AvnT	60030	2531	24W-32N	C6
32600	RDLK	60030	2531	24W-32N	C4
35400	RLKH	60073	2474	24W-35N	C6
35900	LkvT	60041	2474	24W-37N	C2
35900	LkvT	60073	2474	24W-35N	C5
36800	LKVL	60046	2474	24W-37N	C3
36800	LkvT	60046	2474	24W-36N	C3
38000	LkvT	60046	2416	24W-38N	D6
CO-V61 N Fairfield Rd					
10	AvnT	60073	2531	24W-33N	C2
10	ElaT	60047	2645	22W-25N	B5
10	HNWD	60047	2645	22W-25N	B5
10	LKZH	60047	2645	22W-24N	B7
10	RDLK	60073	2531	24W-33N	C2
800	RLKB	60073	2531	24W-34N	C1
900	RLKB	60073	2474	24W-34N	C7
1200	AvnT	60073	2474	24W-35N	C7
1200	FmtT	60060	2588	24W-30N	C1
1200	WCDA	60060	2588	24W-30N	C1
1200	WCDA	60084	2588	24W-30N	C1
25700	HNWD	60060	2645	22W-25N	A4
25800	FmtT	60047	2645	22W-26N	A4
25800	FmtT	60060	2645	23W-26N	A3
25800	FmtT	60084	2645	23W-26N	A3
26400	FmtT	60060	2644	24W-27N	D1
26400	FmtT	60084	2644	24W-27N	D1
27200	FmtT	60084	2588	24W-27N	D7
29500	FmtT	60030	2588	24W-29N	D4
29500	WCDA	60030	2588	24W-29N	D4
31500	FmtT	60030	2531	24W-31N	C7
31600	AvnT	60030	2531	24W-32N	C6
32600	RDLK	60030	2531	24W-32N	C4
35400	RLKH	60073	2474	24W-35N	C6
35900	LkvT	60041	2474	24W-37N	C2
35900	LkvT	60073	2474	24W-35N	C5
36800	LKVL	60046	2474	24W-37N	C3
36800	LkvT	60046	2474	24W-36N	C3
38000	LkvT	60046	2416	24W-38N	D6
CO-V62					
20000	DRPK	60010	2752	22W-20N	C2
20000	DRPK	60074	2752	22W-20N	C2
20000	PltT	60010	2752	22W-20N	C2
20000	PltT	60074	2752	22W-20N	C2
20600	DRPK	60047	2752	22W-20N	C2
20600	DRPK	60074	2699	22W-20N	C7
20600	ElaT	60047	2699	21W-23N	C2
20600	KLDR	60047	2699	21W-21N	C6
20600	KLDR	60074	2752	22W-20N	C2
20800	ElaT	60074	2699	21W-21N	C6
20800	KLDR	60074	2699	21W-21N	C6
21600	LKZH	60047	2699	21W-23N	C2
23500	HNWD	60047	2699	21W-23N	C2
24200	ElaT	60047	2645	21W-24N	C7
24200	HNWD	60047	2645	21W-24N	C7
CO-V62 Quentin Rd					
21300	KLDR	60047	2699	21W-21N	C6
21600	LKZH	60047	2699	21W-21N	C5
CO-V62 N Quentin Rd					
20000	DRPK	60010	2752	22W-20N	C2
20000	DRPK	60074	2752	22W-20N	C2
20000	PltT	60010	2752	22W-20N	C2
20000	PltT	60074	2752	22W-20N	C2
20600	DRPK	60047	2752	22W-20N	C2
20600	DRPK	60074	2699	22W-20N	C7
20600	ElaT	60047	2699	21W-21N	C6
20600	KLDR	60047	2699	21W-21N	C6
20600	KLDR	60074	2752	22W-20N	C2
20800	ElaT	60074	2699	21W-21N	C6
20800	KLDR	60074	2699	21W-21N	C6
22000	LKZH	60047	2699	21W-23N	C2
23500	HNWD	60047	2699	21W-23N	C2
24200	ElaT	60047	2645	21W-24N	C7
24200	HNWD	60047	2645	21W-24N	C7
CO-V63					
10	LKVL	60046	2474	23W-37N	E2
10	LkvT	60046	2474	23W-37N	E1
200	RDLK	60073	2531	23W-34N	E1
800	RLKB	60073	2531	23W-34N	E1
1000	RLKB	60073	2474	23W-34N	E7
1300	LKVL	60073	2474	23W-36N	E4
1300	RLKB	60046	2474	23W-36N	E4
CO-V63 N Cedar Lake Rd					
10	LKVL	60046	2474	23W-37N	E2
10	LkvT	60046	2474	23W-37N	E1
200	RDLK	60073	2531	23W-34N	E1
800	RLKB	60073	2531	23W-34N	E1
1000	RLKB	60073	2474	23W-34N	E7
1300	LKVL	60073	2474	23W-36N	E4
1300	RLKB	60046	2474	23W-36N	E4
CO-V65					
28000	FmtT	60060	2589	22W-28N	B5
28900	FmtT	60030	2589	22W-29N	B3
CO-V65 N Fremont Center Rd					
28000	FmtT	60060	2589	22W-28N	B5
28900	FmtT	60030	2589	22W-29N	B3
CO-V67					
38200	LKVL	60046	2417	22W-39N	C6
38200	LKVL	60046	2475	21W-38N	D1
38200	LkvT	60046	2417	22W-39N	C6
38200	LNHT	60046	2417	21W-38N	D7
38200	LNHT	60046	2475	21W-38N	D1
40100	AntT	60002	2417	22W-40N	C4
40100	LKVL	60002	2417	22W-39N	C6
40100	LkvT	60002	2417	22W-39N	C6
40900	ANTH	60002	2417	22W-40N	C2
41700	ANTH	60002	2358	22W-42N	C6
41700	AntT	60002	2358	22W-42N	C6
43200	BtlT	53104	2358	22W-43N	C4
43200	BtlT	60002	2358	22W-43N	C4
CO-V67 N Deep Lake Rd					
38200	LKVL	60046	2417	22W-39N	C6
38200	LKVL	60046	2475	21W-38N	D1
38200	LkvT	60046	2417	22W-39N	C6
38200	LNHT	60046	2417	21W-38N	D7
38200	LNHT	60046	2475	21W-38N	D1
40100	AntT	60002	2417	22W-40N	C4
40100	LKVL	60002	2417	22W-39N	C6
40100	LkvT	60002	2417	22W-39N	C6
40900	ANTH	60002	2417	22W-40N	C2
41700	ANTH	60002	2358	22W-42N	C6
41700	AntT	60002	2358	22W-42N	C6
43200	BtlT	53104	2358	22W-43N	C4
43200	BtlT	60002	2358	22W-43N	C4
CO-V68					
200	AvnT	60030	2532	21W-32N	D6
200	GYLK	60030	2532	21W-32N	D6
31000	FmtT	60030	2589	21W-30N	D1
31000	RLKP	60030	2589	21W-30N	D1
31200	FmtT	60030	2532	21W-31N	D7
31200	RLKP	60030	2532	21W-31N	D7
CO-V68 N Alleghany Rd					
31000	FmtT	60030	2589	21W-30N	D1
31000	RLKP	60030	2589	21W-30N	D1
31200	FmtT	60030	2532	21W-31N	D7
31200	GYLK	60030	2532	21W-31N	D7
31200	RLKP	60030	2532	21W-31N	D7
31800	AvnT	60030	2532	21W-31N	D6
CO-V68 S Alleghany Rd					
200	AvnT	60030	2532	21W-32N	D6
200	GYLK	60030	2532	21W-32N	D6
CO-V69					
10	BFGV	60089	2754	18W-20N	A2
100	ANHT	60004	2754	17W-20N	A2
100	VrnT	60004	2754	17W-20N	A2
100	VrnT	60089	2754	17W-20N	A2
300	BFGV	60047	2754	17W-20N	A1
300	LGGV	60047	2754	18W-20N	A1
300	VrnT	60047	2754	17W-20N	A1
400	BFGV	60047	2701	18W-20N	A7
400	BFGV	60089	2701	18W-20N	A7
400	LGGV	60047	2701	18W-20N	A7
400	LGGV	60089	2701	18W-20N	A7
CO-V69 N Arlington Heights Rd					
10	BFGV	60089	2754	18W-20N	A2
100	ANHT	60004	2754	17W-20N	A2
100	VrnT	60004	2754	17W-20N	A2
100	VrnT	60089	2754	17W-20N	A2
300	BFGV	60047	2754	17W-20N	A1
300	LGGV	60047	2754	17W-20N	A1
300	VrnT	60047	2754	18W-20N	A1
400	BFGV	60047	2701	18W-20N	A7
400	BFGV	60089	2701	18W-20N	A7
400	LGGV	60047	2701	18W-20N	A7
400	LGGV	60089	2701	18W-20N	A7
CO-V73					
700	FmtT	60060	2590	19W-28N	B5
700	MDLN	60060	2590	19W-28N	B5
2300	FmtT	60048	2590	19W-30N	C3
2300	LYVL	60048	2590	19W-30N	C3
2300	LYVL	60060	2590	19W-30N	C3
CO-V73 N Midlothian Rd					
700	FmtT	60060	2590	19W-28N	B5
700	MDLN	60060	2590	19W-28N	B5
2300	FmtT	60048	2590	19W-30N	C3
2300	LYVL	60048	2590	19W-30N	C3
2300	LYVL	60060	2590	19W-30N	C3
CO-V75					
6300	LGGV	60047	2646	19W-24N	D7
6300	LGGV	60047	2700	19W-24N	D1
6500	LGGV	60060	2646	19W-24N	D6
6700	ElaT	60047	2646	19W-25N	D5
6700	ElaT	60060	2646	19W-25N	D6
6700	VrnT	60047	2646	19W-25N	D5
6700	VrnT	60060	2646	19W-25N	D6
25700	FmtT	60060	2646	19W-25N	D6
25700	LbvT	60060	2646	19W-25N	D6
CO-V75 Diamond Lake Rd					
-	ElaT	60060	2646	19W-25N	D5
6300	LGGV	60047	2646	19W-24N	D7
6300	LGGV	60047	2700	19W-24N	D1
6500	LGGV	60060	2646	19W-24N	D6
CO-V75 N Diamond Lake Rd					
6700	ElaT	60047	2646	19W-25N	D5
6700	ElaT	60060	2646	19W-25N	D6
6700	LGGV	60047	2646	19W-25N	D5
6700	LGGV	60060	2646	19W-25N	D6
6700	VrnT	60047	2646	19W-25N	D5
6700	VrnT	60060	2646	19W-25N	D6
25700	FmtT	60060	2646	19W-25N	D6
25700	LbvT	60060	2646	19W-25N	D6
CO-V76					
100	ElaT	60047	2645	22W-27N	C1
100	ElaT	60060	2645	22W-27N	C1
100	HNWD	60047	2645	21W-25N	D4
100	HNWD	60060	2645	21W-25N	D4
18700	LGGV	60047	2700	18W-23N	D1
21300	LGGV	60047	2646	19W-24N	C7
22500	HNWD	60047	2646	20W-24N	B6
23300	ElaT	60047	2646	20W-24N	B6
26000	FmtT	60047	2645	21W-26N	D4
26000	FmtT	60060	2645	21W-26N	D4
27100	MDLN	60060	2645	22W-27N	C1
27600	HNWD	60047	2589	22W-27N	B7
27600	HNWD	60060	2589	22W-27N	B7
27700	FmtT	60060	2589	23W-28N	A6
28100	FmtT	60060	2588	23W-29N	E5
29100	FmtT	60030	2588	24W-30N	B3
29500	WCDA	60030	2588	24W-30N	B3
29700	FmtT	60084	2588	24W-30N	B3
29700	WCDA	60060	2588	24W-30N	B3
29700	WCDA	60084	2588	24W-30N	B3
30800	WcnT	60030	2587	26W-30N	E2
30800	WcnT	60030	2588	25W-30N	A2
30800	WcnT	60073	2587	26W-30N	E2
30800	WcnT	60084	2587	26W-30N	E2
30800	WcnT	60084	2588	25W-30N	A2
31800	VOLO	60073	2587	26W-30N	D1
32600	VOLO	60073	2530	26W-31N	C7
33800	LKMR	60073	2530	26W-31N	C7
CO-V76 N Gilmer Rd					
26500	FmtT	60047	2645	21W-26N	C3
26500	FmtT	60060	2645	21W-26N	C3
26500	HNWD	60047	2645	21W-26N	C2
26500	HNWD	60060	2645	21W-26N	D3
27100	MDLN	60060	2645	22W-27N	C1
27600	HNWD	60047	2589	22W-27N	B7
27600	HNWD	60060	2589	22W-27N	B7
27700	FmtT	60060	2589	23W-28N	A6
28100	FmtT	60060	2588	23W-29N	E5
29100	FmtT	60030	2588	24W-30N	B3
29500	WCDA	60030	2588	24W-30N	B3
29700	FmtT	60084	2588	24W-30N	B3
29700	WCDA	60060	2588	24W-30N	B3
29700	WCDA	60084	2588	24W-30N	B3
30800	WcnT	60030	2587	26W-30N	E2
30800	WcnT	60030	2588	25W-30N	A2
30800	WcnT	60073	2587	26W-30N	E2
30800	WcnT	60084	2587	26W-30N	E2
30800	WcnT	60084	2588	25W-30N	A2
31800	VOLO	60073	2587	26W-30N	D1
32600	VOLO	60073	2530	26W-31N	C7
33800	LKMR	60073	2530	26W-31N	C7
CO-V76 W Gilmer Rd					
100	ElaT	60047	2645	22W-27N	C1
100	ElaT	60060	2645	22W-27N	C1
100	HNWD	60047	2645	21W-25N	D4
100	HNWD	60060	2645	21W-25N	D4
18700	LGGV	60047	2700	18W-23N	D1
21300	LGGV	60047	2646	19W-24N	C7
22500	HNWD	60047	2646	20W-24N	B6
23300	ElaT	60047	2646	20W-24N	B6
26000	FmtT	60047	2645	21W-26N	D4
26000	FmtT	60060	2645	21W-26N	D4
CO-V77					
100	ElaT	60047	2645	21W-24N	D7
100	HNWD	60047	2645	22W-24N	B6
100	HNWD	60047	2699	20W-23N	E1
100	KLDR	60047	2645	21W-24N	D7
100	KLDR	60047	2699	20W-23N	E1
100	LGGV	60047	2700	18W-21N	D5
500	ElaT	60047	2700	18W-21N	D5
500	HNWD	60047	2700	20W-23N	A1
500	KLDR	60047	2700	20W-23N	A1
1100	BFGV	60047	2700	18W-21N	E6
1100	BFGV	60089	2700	18W-21N	E6
1100	LGGV	60089	2700	18W-21N	E6
24900	LKZH	60047	2645	22W-24N	B6
25800	ElaT	60047	2644	23W-25N	D5
25800	HNWD	60047	2644	23W-24N	E6
CO-V77 Old McHenry Rd					
-	LGGV	60047	2700	20W-23N	B2
100	ElaT	60047	2645	21W-24N	D7
100	HNWD	60047	2645	21W-24N	D7
100	HNWD	60047	2699	20W-23N	E1
100	KLDR	60047	2645	21W-24N	D7
100	KLDR	60047	2699	20W-23N	E1
500	ElaT	60047	2700	20W-23N	A1
500	HNWD	60047	2700	20W-23N	A1
500	KLDR	60047	2700	20W-23N	A1
CO-V77 N Old McHenry Rd					
100	LGGV	60047	2700	18W-21N	D5
1100	BFGV	60047	2700	18W-21N	E6
1100	BFGV	60089	2700	18W-21N	E6
1100	LGGV	60089	2700	18W-21N	E6
3300	ElaT	60047	2700	18W-21N	D5
24500	ElaT	60047	2645	21W-24N	C7
24500	HNWD	60047	2645	22W-24N	B6
24900	LKZH	60047	2645	22W-24N	B6
25800	ElaT	60047	2644	23W-25N	D5
25800	HNWD	60047	2644	23W-24N	E6
CO-W					
-	AntT	60002	2355		D3
-	RdlT	60002	2355		D3
10200	SlmT	53105	2356		A1
10200	SlmT	53192	2356		A2
11700	RdlT	53181	2355		D3
11700	RdlT	53192	2355		E2
CO-W Fox River Rd					
-	AntT	60002	2355		D3
-	RdlT	60002	2355		D3
10200	SlmT	53105	2356		A1
10200	SlmT	53192	2356		A2
11700	RdlT	53181	2355		D3
11700	RdlT	53192	2355		E2
CO-W11					
-	LbvT	60060	2591	17W-28N	B7
-	LbvT	60061	2591	17W-27N	B7
-	MDLN	60061	2591	17W-27N	B7
-	VNHL	60061	2591	17W-28N	B7
100	INCK	60061	2647	17W-25N	B6
100	LYVL	60048	2591	17W-29N	B5
100	MDLN	60060	2647	17W-27N	B1
100	MDLN	60061	2647	17W-27N	B1
100	VNHL	60060	2647	17W-25N	B6
100	VNHL	60061	2647	17W-27N	B1
500	MDLN	60060	2591	17W-29N	B5
600	LYVL	60060	2591	17W-29N	B5
1300	LbvT	60048	2591	17W-30N	A3
CO-W11 Butterfield Rd					
100	INCK	60061	2647	17W-25N	B6
100	MDLN	60060	2647	17W-25N	B6
100	MDLN	60061	2647	17W-25N	B6
100	VNHL	60060	2647	17W-25N	B6
100	VNHL	60061	2647	17W-25N	B6
CO-W11 N Butterfield Rd					
100	LYVL	60048	2591	17W-29N	B5

STREET Block	City	ZIP	Map#	CGS	Grid
CO-W11 N Butterfield Rd					
500	MDLN	60060	2591	17W-29N	B5
600	LYVL	60060	2591	17W-29N	B5
1300	LbvT	60048	2591	17W-30N	A3
CO-W11 S Butterfield Rd					
-	LbvT	60060	2591	17W-28N	B7
-	LbvT	60061	2591	17W-27N	B7
-	MDLN	60060	2591	17W-27N	B7
-	MDLN	60061	2591	17W-27N	B7
-	VNHL	60061	2591	17W-28N	B7
100	LYVL	60048	2591	17W-28N	B5
400	MDLN	60060	2647	17W-27N	B1
400	MDLN	60061	2647	17W-27N	B1
400	VNHL	60061	2647	17W-27N	B1
900	VNHL	60060	2647	17W-26N	A3
CO-W12					
-	WrnT	60030	2534	17W-34N	B1
34000	WrnT	60031	2534	17W-34N	B1
34300	GRNE	60031	2534	17W-34N	B1
CO-W12 N Almond Rd					
-	WrnT	60030	2534	17W-34N	B1
34000	WrnT	60031	2534	17W-34N	B1
34300	GRNE	60031	2534	17W-34N	B1
CO-W14					
-	VrnT	60089	2701	17W-22N	C4
10	BFGV	60089	2754	16W-20N	C1
600	BFGV	60089	2701	16W-20N	C7
1600	BFGV	60069	2701	17W-21N	C5
1600	VrnT	60069	2701	17W-22N	C5
CO-W14 N Buffalo Grove Rd					
-	VrnT	60089	2701	17W-22N	C4
10	BFGV	60089	2754	16W-20N	C1
600	BFGV	60089	2701	16W-20N	C7
1600	BFGV	60069	2701	17W-21N	C5
1600	VrnT	60069	2701	17W-22N	C5
CO-W15					
1100	GRNE	60031	2477	17W-35N	C5
33000	GRNE	60031	2534	17W-33N	C3
33000	WrnT	60030	2534	17W-33N	C3
33000	WrnT	60031	2534	17W-33N	C3
33000	WrnT	60048	2534	17W-33N	C3
33200	GRNE	60030	2534	17W-33N	C3
33200	GRNE	60048	2534	17W-33N	C3
34500	WrnT	60031	2477	17W-34N	C7
36600	WrnT	60083	2477	17W-37N	C3
37200	OMCK	60083	2477	17W-34N	C7
38200	NptT	60083	2419	17W-38N	B7
38200	NptT	60083	2477	17W-34N	C7
38200	OMCK	60083	2419	17W-38N	B7
41600	NptT	60002	2360	17W-41N	B7
41600	NptT	60083	2360	17W-41N	B7
41600	OMCK	60083	2360	17W-42N	B7
43400	BtlT	53142	2360	17W-43N	B4
43400	NptT	53142	2360	17W-43N	B4
CO-W15 N Hunt Club Rd					
1100	GRNE	60031	2477	17W-35N	C5
33000	GRNE	60031	2534	17W-33N	C3
33000	WrnT	60030	2534	17W-33N	C3
33000	WrnT	60031	2534	17W-33N	C3
33000	WrnT	60048	2534	17W-33N	C3
33200	GRNE	60030	2534	17W-33N	C3
33200	GRNE	60048	2534	17W-33N	C3
34500	WrnT	60031	2477	17W-34N	C7
36600	WrnT	60083	2477	17W-37N	C3
37200	OMCK	60083	2477	17W-34N	C7
38200	NptT	60083	2419	17W-38N	B7
38200	NptT	60083	2477	17W-34N	C7
38200	OMCK	60083	2419	17W-38N	B7
41600	NptT	60002	2360	17W-41N	B7
41600	NptT	60083	2360	17W-41N	B7
41600	OMCK	60083	2360	17W-42N	B7
43400	BtlT	53142	2360	17W-43N	B4
43400	NptT	53142	2360	17W-43N	B4
CO-W16					
1400	GRNE	60031	2478	15W-35N	A6
1400	WrnT	60031	2478	15W-35N	A6
1700	GRNE	60031	2477	15W-35N	E5
2000	WrnT	60031	2477	15W-36N	E4
2400	WDWH	60031	2477	16W-37N	E3
2700	WDWH	60083	2477	15W-36N	E4
37200	WrnT	60083	2477	15W-36N	E4
37900	NptT	60083	2419	16W-38N	E7
37900	NptT	60083	2477	15W-36N	E4
CO-W16 N Dilleys Rd					
1400	GRNE	60031	2478	15W-35N	A6
1400	WrnT	60031	2478	15W-35N	A6
1700	GRNE	60031	2477	15W-35N	E5
2000	WrnT	60031	2477	15W-36N	E4
2400	WDWH	60031	2477	16W-37N	E3
2700	WDWH	60083	2477	15W-36N	E4
37200	WrnT	60083	2477	15W-36N	E4
37900	NptT	60083	2419	16W-38N	E7
37900	NptT	60083	2477	15W-36N	E4
CO-W17					
100	BFGV	60089	2754	16W-20N	D1
100	WLNG	60089	2754	16W-20N	D2
300	BFGV	60069	2754	16W-20N	D1
300	VrnT	60069	2754	16W-20N	D1
300	VrnT	60089	2754	16W-20N	D1
1200	BFGV	60069	2701	16W-21N	E6
1600	VrnT	60089	2701	16W-21N	E6
22000	BFGV	60089	2701	16W-22N	D4
22000	VrnT	60069	2701	16W-22N	D4
CO-W17 N Prairie Rd					
22000	BFGV	60069	2701	16W-22N	D4
22000	BFGV	60089	2701	16W-22N	D4
22000	VrnT	60069	2701	16W-22N	D4
22000	VrnT	60089	2701	16W-22N	D4
CO-W17 Weiland Rd					
100	BFGV	60089	2754	16W-20N	D1
100	WLNG	60089	2754	16W-20N	D2
300	BFGV	60069	2754	16W-20N	D1
300	VrnT	60069	2754	16W-20N	D1
300	VrnT	60089	2754	16W-20N	D1
800	BFGV	60089	2701	16W-20N	D7
1200	BFGV	60069	2701	16W-21N	E6
1600	VrnT	60069	2701	16W-21N	E6
1600	VrnT	60089	2701	16W-21N	E6
CO-W19					
100	GNOK	60048	2592	15W-28N	B5
100	LYVL	60048	2592	15W-28N	B5
200	LbvT	60048	2592	15W-28N	B5
400	MTWA	60048	2592	15W-28N	B6
25000	MTWA	60045	2648	14W-24N	B6
25000	MTWA	60048	2648	15W-25N	B5
25000	VrnT	60045	2648	14W-24N	B6
25000	VrnT	60048	2648	14W-24N	B6
26100	LbvT	60048	2648	15W-26N	B2
CO-W19 N St. Mary's Rd					
100	GNOK	60048	2592	15W-28N	B5
100	LYVL	60048	2592	15W-28N	B5
600	LbvT	60048	2592	15W-28N	B5
25000	MTWA	60045	2648	14W-24N	B6
25000	MTWA	60048	2648	15W-25N	B5
25000	VrnT	60045	2648	14W-24N	B6
25000	VrnT	60048	2648	14W-24N	B6
CO-W19 N St. Mary's Rd					
26100	LbvT	60048	2648	15W-26N	B2
27500	MTWA	60048	2592	15W-27N	B7
CO-W19 S St. Mary's Rd					
200	GNOK	60048	2592	15W-28N	B6
200	LbvT	60048	2592	15W-28N	B6
200	LYVL	60048	2592	15W-28N	B6
400	MTWA	60048	2592	15W-28N	B6
CO-W20					
10	GRNE	60031	2535	14W-32N	C6
10	WrnT	60031	2535	14W-34N	C1
400	GRNE	60031	2478	14W-34N	C7
1000	WKGN	60031	2535	14W-33N	C4
1000	WKGN	60085	2535	14W-33N	C4
30900	GNOK	60048	2592	14W-30N	C1
31000	GNOK	60048	2535	14W-31N	C7
31500	WKGN	60048	2535	14W-31N	C7
32300	WrnT	60048	2535	14W-32N	C5
32300	WrnT	60085	2535	14W-32N	C5
CO-W20 N Oplaine Rd					
10	GRNE	60031	2535	14W-34N	C1
10	WrnT	60031	2535	14W-34N	C1
400	GRNE	60031	2478	14W-34N	C7
30900	GNOK	60048	2592	14W-30N	C1
31000	GNOK	60048	2535	14W-31N	C7
31500	WKGN	60048	2535	14W-31N	C7
32300	WKGN	60085	2535	14W-32N	C5
32300	WrnT	60048	2535	14W-32N	C5
32300	WrnT	60085	2535	14W-32N	C5
32800	WKGN	60031	2535	14W-33N	C4
CO-W20 S Oplaine Rd					
10	GRNE	60031	2535	14W-32N	C6
10	WrnT	60031	2535	14W-34N	C1
1000	WKGN	60031	2535	14W-33N	C4
1000	WKGN	60085	2535	14W-33N	C4
CO-W24					
10	LNSH	60045	2702	14W-23N	D2
10	LNSH	60069	2702	13W-21N	E6
10	MTWA	60045	2648	13W-25N	D5
10	NHBK	60015	2756	12W-20N	A2
10	NHBK	60062	2756	12W-20N	A2
10	RVWD	60015	2702	13W-22N	D4
10	RVWD	60015	2756	12W-20N	A2
10	WdfT	60015	2756	12W-20N	A2
400	DRFD	60015	2756	12W-20N	A1
600	DRFD	60015	2703	12W-20N	A7
600	RVWD	60015	2703	12W-21N	A7
800	VrnT	60045	2648	14W-24N	D6
1000	LNSH	60045	2648	14W-24N	D7
1000	LNSH	60069	2648	14W-24N	D7
2100	LNSH	60015	2702	14W-22N	D4
3000	VrnT	60015	2702	13W-21N	D6
CO-W24 Riverwoods Rd					
10	LNSH	60045	2702	14W-23N	D2
10	LNSH	60069	2702	13W-21N	E6
10	MTWA	60045	2648	13W-25N	D5
10	RVWD	60015	2702	13W-22N	D4
800	VrnT	60045	2648	14W-24N	D6
1000	LNSH	60045	2648	14W-24N	D7
1000	LNSH	60069	2648	14W-24N	D7
2100	LNSH	60015	2702	14W-22N	D4
2200	RVWD	60015	2703	12W-21N	A7
3000	VrnT	60015	2702	13W-21N	D6
CO-W24 Saunders Rd					
10	NHBK	60015	2756	12W-20N	A2
10	NHBK	60062	2756	12W-20N	A2
10	RVWD	60015	2756	12W-20N	A2
10	WdfT	60015	2756	12W-20N	A2
400	DRFD	60015	2756	12W-20N	A1
600	DRFD	60015	2703	12W-20N	A7
600	RVWD	60015	2703	12W-20N	A7
CO-W26					
39000	WDWH	60083	2420	14W-41N	C1
39600	NptT	60083	2420	14W-41N	C1
41000	NptT	60099	2420	14W-41N	C1
41500	NptT	60099	2361	14W-42N	C6
41500	WDWH	60099	2361	14W-41N	C7
43300	PTPR	53158	2361	14W-42N	C6
43300	PTPR	60099	2361	14W-42N	C6
CO-W26 N Kilbourne Rd					
39000	WDWH	60083	2420	14W-41N	C1
39600	NptT	60083	2420	14W-41N	C1
41000	NptT	60099	2420	14W-41N	C1
41500	NptT	60099	2361	14W-42N	C6
41500	WDWH	60099	2361	14W-41N	C7
43300	PTPR	53158	2361	14W-42N	C6
43300	PTPR	60099	2361	14W-42N	C6
CO-W27					
1100	GRNE	60031	2478	14W-36N	D5
1400	WrnT	60031	2478	14W-36N	D5
2100	WKGN	60087	2478	14W-36N	D4
2100	WrnT	60087	2478	14W-36N	D4
2200	WKGN	60031	2478	14W-36N	D4
3000	WDWH	60083	2478	14W-37N	D1
3000	WDWH	60087	2478	14W-37N	D1
3000	WKGN	60083	2478	14W-37N	D2
38000	WDWH	60083	2420	14W-38N	D7
38000	WDWH	60087	2420	14W-38N	D7
38000	WKGN	60083	2420	14W-38N	D7
38000	WKGN	60087	2420	14W-38N	D7
39900	NptT	60083	2420	14W-41N	D1
41000	WDWH	60099	2420	14W-41N	D1
43300	NptT	60099	2361	14W-43N	D4
CO-W27 N Delaney Rd					
43300	NptT	60099	2361	14W-43N	D4
CO-W27 N Delany Rd					
1100	GRNE	60031	2478	14W-36N	D5
1400	WrnT	60031	2478	14W-36N	D5
2100	WKGN	60087	2478	14W-36N	D4
2100	WrnT	60087	2478	14W-36N	D4
2200	WKGN	60031	2478	14W-36N	D4
3000	WDWH	60083	2478	14W-37N	D1
3000	WDWH	60087	2478	14W-37N	D1
3000	WKGN	60083	2478	14W-37N	D2
38000	WDWH	60083	2420	14W-38N	D7
38000	WDWH	60087	2420	14W-38N	D7
38000	WKGN	60083	2420	14W-38N	D7
38000	WKGN	60087	2420	14W-38N	D7
39900	NptT	60083	2420	14W-41N	D1
41000	WDWH	60099	2420	14W-41N	D1
CO-W29					
-	WKGN	60085	2535	13W-33N	D3
10	GRNE	60031	2535	13W-33N	D2
10	WrnT	60031	2535	13W-33N	D2
200	PKCY	60085	2535	13W-34N	D2
CO-W29 Greenleaf Av					
-	WKGN	60085	2535	13W-33N	D3
300	GRNE	60031	2535	13W-33N	D2
300	PKCY	60085	2535	13W-33N	D2
300	WrnT	60031	2535	13W-33N	D2
CO-W29 S Greenleaf Av					
10	GRNE	60031	2535	13W-33N	D2
10	WrnT	60031	2535	13W-33N	D2
200	PKCY	60085	2535	13W-34N	D2
CO-W32					
400	BtnT	53158	2362	11W-43N	D4
CO-W32					
400	BtnT	60099	2362	11W-43N	D5
400	PTPR	53158	2362	11W-43N	D4
400	WPHR	60099	2362	11W-43N	D5
800	ZION	60099	2362	11W-42N	D6
1500	BtnT	60099	2421	12W-41N	C1
1500	ZION	60099	2421	12W-41N	C1
1900	BHPK	60099	2421	12W-41N	C1
42800	WPHR	60096	2362	11W-43N	D5
CO-W32 Kenosha Rd					
1200	BtnT	60099	2362	11W-42N	C7
1200	ZION	60099	2362	11W-42N	C7
1500	BtnT	60099	2421	12W-41N	C1
1500	ZION	60099	2421	12W-41N	C1
1900	BHPK	60099	2421	12W-41N	C2
CO-W32 N Kenosha Rd					
400	BtnT	53158	2362	11W-43N	D4
400	BtnT	60099	2362	11W-43N	D5
400	PTPR	53158	2362	11W-43N	D4
400	WPHR	60099	2362	11W-43N	D5
800	ZION	60099	2362	11W-42N	D6
40000	BHPK	60099	2421	12W-41N	C1
40000	ZION	60099	2421	12W-40N	B3
42800	WPHR	60096	2362	11W-43N	D5
CO-W34					
-	BtnT	60099	2421	11W-41N	D1
-	WPHR	60096	2421	11W-41N	D1
10	WKGN	60085	2536	11W-34N	D1
400	BtnT	60096	2362	11W-42N	E6
400	BtnT	60099	2362	11W-42N	D6
400	WPHR	60096	2362	11W-42N	D6
400	WPHR	60099	2362	11W-42N	D6
500	WKGN	60085	2479	11W-34N	D7
1100	ZION	60096	2362	11W-42N	D7
1100	ZION	60099	2362	11W-42N	D7
1300	NCHI	60064	2536	11W-32N	D5
1500	ZION	60099	2421	11W-41N	D1
2300	NCHI	60064	2593	11W-31N	D1
2300	NCHI	60088	2593	11W-31N	D1
3100	BHPK	60099	2421	11W-39N	D5
3200	BHPK	60087	2479	11W-37N	D1
3200	WKGN	60087	2479	11W-37N	D1
3400	WKGN	60087	2421	11W-39N	D6
3400	WKGN	60099	2421	11W-39N	D6
3800	BHPK	60087	2421	11W-38N	D7
43300	BtnT	53158	2362	11W-43N	E4
43300	PTPR	53158	2362	11W-43N	E4
CO-W34 Lewis Av					
-	BtnT	60099	2421	11W-41N	D1
-	WPHR	60096	2421	11W-41N	D1
400	BtnT	60096	2362	11W-42N	D6
400	BtnT	60099	2362	11W-42N	D6
400	WPHR	60096	2362	11W-42N	D6
400	WPHR	60099	2362	11W-42N	D6
1100	ZION	60096	2362	11W-42N	D7
1100	ZION	60099	2362	11W-42N	D7
1400	NCHI	60064	2536	11W-32N	D5
1400	WKGN	60085	2536	11W-32N	D5
1500	ZION	60099	2421	11W-41N	D1
2300	NCHI	60064	2593	11W-31N	D1
2300	NCHI	60088	2593	11W-31N	D1
3100	BHPK	60099	2421	11W-39N	D5
3400	WKGN	60087	2421	11W-39N	D6
3400	WKGN	60099	2421	11W-39N	D6
43300	BtnT	53158	2362	11W-43N	E4
43300	PTPR	53158	2362	11W-43N	E4
CO-W34 N Lewis Av					
10	WKGN	60085	2536	11W-34N	D1
500	WKGN	60085	2479	11W-34N	D7
3200	BHPK	60087	2479	11W-37N	D1
3200	WKGN	60087	2479	11W-37N	D1
3700	WKGN	60087	2421	11W-38N	D7
3800	BHPK	60087	2421	11W-38N	D7
3800	BHPK	60099	2421	11W-38N	D7
39200	WKGN	60099	2421	11W-39N	D6
CO-W34 S Lewis Av					
10	WKGN	60085	2536	11W-34N	D2
1300	NCHI	60064	2536	11W-32N	D5
CO-WG					
15200	BtlT	53142	2360	17W-43N	B4
15200	BtlT	60002	2360	17W-43N	B4
15200	NptT	60002	2360	17W-43N	B4
16500	BtlT	60099	2360	16W-43N	D4
16500	NptT	53142	2360	16W-43N	D4
16500	NptT	60099	2360	16W-43N	D4
17900	AntT	60002	2359	18W-43N	E4
17900	BtlT	53104	2359	18W-43N	E4
17900	BtlT	53142	2359	18W-43N	E4
18500	BtlT	60002	2359	18W-43N	E4
18500	NptT	53142	2359	18W-43N	D4
18500	NptT	60002	2359	18W-43N	E4
CO-WG 128th St					
-	BtlT	53142	2360	16W-43N	E4
-	BtlT	60099	2360	16W-43N	E4
-	NptT	60099	2360	16W-43N	E4
17900	AntT	60002	2359	18W-43N	E4
17900	BtlT	53104	2359	18W-43N	E4
17900	BtlT	53142	2359	18W-43N	E4
CO-WG W State Line Rd					
15200	BtlT	53142	2360	17W-43N	B4
15200	BtlT	60002	2360	17W-43N	B4
15200	NptT	60002	2360	17W-43N	B4
16500	BtlT	60099	2360	16W-43N	D4
16500	NptT	53142	2360	16W-43N	D4
16500	NptT	60099	2360	16W-43N	D4
18500	AntT	60002	2359	19W-43N	D4
18500	BtlT	53142	2359	19W-43N	D4
18500	BtlT	60002	2359	18W-43N	E4
18500	NptT	53142	2359	18W-43N	D4
18500	NptT	60002	2359	18W-43N	E4
19800	BtlT	53104	2359		B4
CO-Z					
-	RdlT	53181	2354		D2
1600	TNLK	53181	2354		D1
CO-Z 360th Av					
-	RdlT	53181	2354		D2
-	TNLK	53181	2354		D1
CO-Z Wilmot Av					
1600	TNLK	53181	2354		D1
I-55					
-	BCVL	-	4030	33W-43S	B2
-	BDPK	-	3147	13W-8S	A7
-	BDPK	-	3148	10W-6S	A4
-	BDWD	-	3941	32W-39S	E2
-	BGBK	-	3268	24W-13S	E5
-	BGBK	-	3269	23W-13S	A4
-	BGBK	-	3270	21W-11S	A1
-	BGBK	-	3339	27W-15S	D2
-	BRRG	-	3146	14W-8S	D7
-	BRRG	-	3207	18W-10S	A4
-	BRRG	-	3208	15W-8S	B1
-	BvlT	-	3941	32W-41S	C6
-	BvlT	-	4030	33W-43S	B2
-	CHCG	-	3089	6W-4S	E6
-	CHCG	-	3090	5W-4S	A6
-	CHCG	-	3091	3W-3S	A4
I-55					
-	CHCG	-	3092	0W-2S	A2
-	CNHN	-	3584	30W-27S	C4
-	CTSD	-	3146	14W-8S	D7
-	CTSD	-	3147	12W-7S	B7
-	DGvT	-	3206	20W-11S	B7
-	DGvT	-	3207	16W-9S	D3
-	DGvT	-	3270	21W-11S	A1
-	DMND	-	3941	31W-39S	E2
-	DPgT	-	3268	24W-14S	C6
-	DPgT	-	3269	22W-12S	D2
-	DPgT	-	3270	21W-11S	A1
-	DRN	-	3206	20W-11S	B7
-	DRN	-	3207	18W-9S	B4
-	FTVW	-	3089	6W-4S	E7
-	FTVW	-	3148	10W-6S	B4
-	FTVW	-	3149	7W-5S	B1
-	GDLY	-	4030	33W-43S	B2
-	HGKN	-	3147	13W-8S	A7
-	IHPK	-	3146	14W-8S	D7
-	JLET	-	3416	28W-21S	E6
-	JLET	-	3417	28W-18S	B1
-	JLET	-	3496	28W-23S	E2
-	PNFD	-	3339	27W-15S	D2
-	PNFD	-	3417	28W-18S	B1
-	PnfT	-	3339	28W-17S	B6
-	PnfT	-	3416	28W-21S	E7
-	PnfT	-	3417	28W-18S	B1
-	PnfT	-	3496	29W-22S	E2
-	RedT	-	3941	32W-39S	E2
-	RMVL	-	3268	25W-14S	B7
-	RMVL	-	3339	26W-15S	D2
-	RMVL	-	3340	26W-14S	A1
-	SKNY	-	3089	6W-4S	E7
-	SMMT	-	3148	9W-5S	D2
-	SRWD	-	3496	29W-23S	E3
-	StkT	-	3089	6W-4S	E7
-	TroT	-	3496	29W-24S	D5
-	TroT	-	3584	30W-27S	C4
-	WDRG	-	3206	20W-11S	B7
-	WDRG	-	3270	21W-11S	A1
-	WLBK	-	3207	18W-10S	A4
-	WLBK	-	3208	15W-8S	B1
-	WldT	-	3339	27W-15S	C3
-	WmTp	-	3941	31W-39S	E1
-	WmTp	-	3942	31W-39S	A1
I-55 Joliet Rd					
-	BGBK	-	3270	20W-11S	A1
-	BRRG	-	3146	14W-8S	D7
-	BRRG	-	3207	18W-10S	A4
-	BRRG	-	3208	15W-8S	B1
-	DGvT	-	3206	20W-11S	B7
-	DGvT	-	3207	16W-9S	D3
-	DGvT	-	3270	21W-11S	A1
-	DPgT	-	3270	20W-11S	A1
-	DRN	-	3206	19W-10S	E5
-	DRN	-	3207	18W-9S	B4
-	IHPK	-	3146	14W-7S	D7
-	WDRG	-	3206	20W-11S	C7
-	WDRG	-	3270	21W-11S	A1
-	WLBK	-	3207	18W-10S	A4
-	WLBK	-	3208	15W-8S	B1
I-55 Stevenson Expwy					
-	BDPK	-	3147	11W-7S	E6
-	BDPK	-	3148	10W-6S	A4
-	CHCG	-	3089	6W-4S	E6
-	CHCG	-	3090	4W-3S	D5
-	CHCG	-	3091	3W-3S	A4
-	CHCG	-	3092	0E-2S	C2
-	CTSD	-	3146	14W-8S	D7
-	CTSD	-	3147	12W-7S	C7
-	FTVW	-	3089	6W-4S	E7
-	FTVW	-	3148	10W-6S	B4
-	FTVW	-	3149	7W-5S	B1
-	HGKN	-	3147	13W-8S	A7
-	IHPK	-	3146	14W-8S	D7
-	SKNY	-	3089	6W-4S	E7
-	SMMT	-	3148	10W-6S	B4
-	StkT	-	3089	6W-4S	E7
I-57					
-	BLID	-	3277	2W-14S	D5
-	BLID	-	3349	2W-15S	D1
-	BmnT	-	3349	3W-17S	A6
-	BmnT	-	3425	6W-21S	E6
-	BmnT	-	3426	5W-20S	B4
-	CCHL	-	3426	6W-20S	A5
-	CCHL	-	3506	6W-22S	A1
-	CHCG	-	3213	1W-11S	E7
-	CHCG	-	3214	0W-11S	A7
-	CHCG	-	3277	1W-12S	D2
-	ClmT	-	3349	2W-15S	D1
-	CTPK	-	3277	2W-14S	D6
-	DXMR	-	3349	3W-17S	B5
-	MKHM	-	3348	4W-18S	E7
-	MKHM	-	3349	3W-17S	A6
-	MKHM	-	3426	5W-19S	C2
-	MONE	-	3682	7W-30S	D2
-	MonT	-	3593	7W-28S	D7
-	MonT	-	3682	7W-29S	D2
-	MTSN	-	3506	6W-23S	A4
-	MTSN	-	3594	6W-25S	A1
-	OKFT	-	3426	5W-19S	C2
-	POSN	-	3349	2W-17S	C5
-	PtnT	-	3860	11W-39S	B7
-	RchT	-	3426	6W-22S	A7
-	RchT	-	3506	6W-23S	A1
-	RchT	-	3593	7W-28S	D7
-	RNPK	-	3593	6W-26S	E3
-	RNPK	-	3594	6W-26S	A2
-	RVDL	-	3349	2W-15S	D1
-	UYPK	-	3593	7W-28S	D6
-	UYPK	-	3682	7W-30S	D3
I-57 Dan Ryan Expwy					
-	CHCG	-	3214	1W-11S	A7
I-80					
-	AxST	-	3583	34W-27S	A6
-	BmnT	-	3425	7W-21S	D7
-	BmnT	-	3426	6W-21S	A6
-	CCHL	-	3426	6W-21S	A6
-	EHZC	-	3427	1W-20S	E4
-	EHZC	-	3428	0W-20S	C4
-	FftT	-	3502	14W-22S	D1
-	FftT	-	3503	13W-22S	A1
-	FftT	-	3504	9W-22S	D1
-	HLCT	-	3426	6W-21S	A6
-	HLCT	-	3427	3W-20S	C4
-	HMND	-	3430		D5
-	JLET	-	3497	27W-24S	D7
-	JLET	-	3498	24W-24S	E6
-	JLET	-	3499	23W-24S	A6
-	JLET	-	3584	29W-26S	D3
-	JLET	-	3585	28W-25S	B1
-	JltT	-	3499	21W-24S	E6
-	JltT	-	3500	21W-24S	A6
-	LNSG	-	3429	2E-20S	C4
-	LNSG	-	3430	3E-20S	A4
I-80					
-	MKHM	-	3427	3W-20S	A4
-	MKNA	-	3503	12W-22S	D1
-	MKNA	-	3504	10W-22S	A1
-	MNKA	-	3583	33W-27S	C6
-	MNSR	-	3430	4E-20S	C4
-	NLNX	-	3500	19W-24S	E5
-	NLNX	-	3501	17W-23S	D2
-	NlxT	-	3500	19W-24S	E5
-	NlxT	-	3501	18W-23S	A3
-	NlxT	-	3502	15W-22S	A2
-	ODPK	-	3502	14W-22S	D1
-	ODPK	-	3503	13W-22S	B1
-	RchT	-	3425	7W-21S	D7
-	RchT	-	3505	7W-22S	C1
-	RKDL	-	3498	25W-24S	B6
-	SHLD	-	3428	0E-20S	D4
-	SHLD	-	3429	0E-20S	A4
-	SwdT	-	3583	32W-27S	C6
-	ThtT	-	3429	2E-20S	C4
-	TNTN	-	3428	0E-20S	D4
-	TroT	-	3497	27W-24S	D7
-	TroT	-	3583	32W-27S	D5
-	TroT	-	3584	29W-26S	E3
-	TYPK	-	3503	11W-22S	E1
-	TYPK	-	3504	11W-22S	A1
-	TYPK	-	3505	7W-22S	C1
I-80 Borman Expwy					
-	HMND	-	3430		D5
-	LNSG	-	3430		C5
-	MNSR	-	3430		C4
I-80 Kingery Expwy					
-	LNSG	-	3429	2E-20S	C4
-	LNSG	-	3430	3E-20S	B4
-	MNSR	-	3430	4E-20S	C4
-	ThtT	-	3429	2E-20S	C4
I-80 Moline Expwy					
-	BmnT	-	3425	7W-21S	D7
-	BmnT	-	3426	6W-21S	A6
-	CCHL	-	3426	4W-20S	E4
-	FftT	-	3503	11W-22S	E1
-	FftT	-	3504	9W-22S	D1
-	HLCT	-	3426	6W-21S	A6
-	HLCT	-	3427	3W-20S	A4
-	MKHM	-	3427	3W-20S	A4
-	MKNA	-	3503	12W-22S	D1
-	MKNA	-	3504	10W-22S	A1
-	ODPK	-	3503	12W-22S	D1
-	RchT	-	3425	7W-21S	D7
-	RchT	-	3505	7W-22S	C1
-	TYPK	-	3503	11W-22S	E1
-	TYPK	-	3504	11W-22S	A1
-	TYPK	-	3505	7W-22S	C1
I-80 Tri-State Tollway					
-	EHZC	-	3427	1W-20S	E4
-	EHZC	-	3428	0W-20S	C4
-	HLCT	-	3427	3W-20S	C4
-	LNSG	-	3429	2E-20S	C4
-	SHLD	-	3428	0E-20S	D4
-	SHLD	-	3429	0E-20S	A4
-	ThtT	-	3429	0E-20S	A4
-	TNTN	-	3428	0E-20S	D4
I-88					
-	AraT	-	3138	34W-4S	D2
-	AraT	-	3139	32W-4S	B2
-	AURA	-	3136	38W-5S	E2
-	AURA	-	3137	36W-5S	E2
-	AURA	-	3138	36W-5S	A2
-	AURA	-	3139	33W-4S	A2
-	BbyT	-	3075	42W-3S	B6
-	DRGV	-	3083	21W-4S	D7
-	DRGV	-	3084	21W-4S	A7
-	EMHT	-	3028	14W-0S	C6
-	HLSD	-	3028	14W-0S	C6
-	LMBD	-	3084	19W-2S	D4
-	LSLE	-	3083	23W-4S	A7
-	LSLE	-	3142	25W-4S	B1
-	LSLE	-	3143	23W-4S	A1
-	LslT	-	3083	21W-4S	D7
-	LslT	-	3084	21W-4S	A7
-	LslT	-	3142	23W-4S	E1
-	LslT	-	3143	23W-4S	A1
-	NARA	-	3137	38W-5S	A2
-	NARA	-	3138	35W-4S	B2
-	NPVL	-	3140	30W-4S	B1
-	NPVL	-	3141	28W-4S	B1
-	NPVL	-	3142	25W-4S	B1
-	NpvT	-	3139	31W-4S	E1
-	NpvT	-	3140	29W-4S	D1
-	OKBK	-	3028	15W-1S	B7
-	OKBK	-	3084	20W-4S	A7
-	OKBK	-	3085	18W-2S	A3
-	OKBK	-	3086	15W-1S	A1
-	PvsT	-	3028	14W-0S	C6
-	SgrT	-	3075	42W-4S	D7
-	SgrT	-	3135	41W-4S	D1
-	SgrT	-	3136	39W-5S	D2
-	SRGV	-	3135	41W-4S	D1
-	SRGV	-	3136	40W-4S	C2
-	WNVL	-	3141	27W-4S	D1
-	YkTp	-	3028	15W-0S	B7
-	YkTp	-	3084	18W-2S	E3
-	YkTp	-	3086	15W-1S	B1
I-88 Ronald Reagan Mem Tollway					
-	AraT	-	3138	35W-4S	B2
-	AraT	-	3139	32W-4S	B2
-	AURA	-	3136	38W-5S	E2
-	AURA	-	3137	36W-5S	E2
-	AURA	-	3138	36W-5S	A2
-	AURA	-	3139	33W-4S	A2
-	BbyT	-	3075	42W-3S	B6
-	DRGV	-	3083	21W-4S	D7
-	DRGV	-	3084	21W-4S	A7
-	EMHT	-	3028	14W-0S	C6
-	HLSD	-	3028	14W-0S	C6
-	LMBD	-	3084	20W-4S	A7
-	LSLE	-	3083	23W-4S	A7
-	LSLE	-	3142	25W-4S	B1
-	LSLE	-	3143	23W-4S	A1
-	LslT	-	3083	21W-4S	D7
-	LslT	-	3084	21W-4S	A7
-	LslT	-	3142	23W-4S	E1
-	LslT	-	3143	23W-4S	A1
-	NARA	-	3137	38W-5S	A2
-	NARA	-	3138	35W-4S	B2
-	NPVL	-	3140	30W-4S	B1
-	NPVL	-	3141	27W-4S	D1
-	NPVL	-	3142	25W-4S	B1
-	NpvT	-	3139	31W-4S	E1
-	NpvT	-	3140	29W-4S	D1
-	OKBK	-	3028	15W-1S	B7
-	OKBK	-	3084	18W-2S	E3
-	OKBK	-	3085	18W-2S	A3
-	OKBK	-	3086	15W-1S	A1
-	PvsT	-	3028	14W-0S	C6

STREET Block	City	ZIP	Map#	CGS	Grid
I-88 Ronald Reagan Mem Tollway					
-	SgrT	-	3075	42W-4S	D7
-	SgrT	-	3135	41W-4S	D1
-	SgrT	-	3136	41W-4S	A1
-	SRGV	-	3135	41W-4S	D1
-	SRGV	-	3136	40W-4S	C2
-	WNVL	-	3141	27W-4S	D1
-	YkTp	-	3028	15W-1S	B7
-	YkTp	-	3084	20W-4S	A7
-	YkTp	-	3086	15W-1S	B1
I-90					
-	ANHT	-	2860	18W-11N	E3
-	ANHT	-	2861	17W-10N	B4
-	CHCG	-	2916	13W-8N	E1
-	CHCG	-	2917	11W-7N	D4
-	CHCG	-	2918	8W-6N	E5
-	CHCG	-	2919	7W-6N	C5
-	CHCG	-	2920	5W-5N	A7
-	CHCG	-	2976	5W-5N	A1
-	CHCG	-	2977	3W-3N	A4
-	CHCG	-	3033	1W-0N	E3
-	CHCG	-	3034	0W-0S	A5
-	CHCG	-	3092	0W-2S	B3
-	CHCG	-	3152	0W-5S	B1
-	CHCG	-	3153	1E-8S	A7
-	CHCG	-	3215	1E-8S	A1
-	CHCG	-	3216	3E-10S	A6
-	CHCG	-	3280	4E-11S	C1
-	DndT	-	2799	36W-14N	E5
-	DndT	-	2800	35W-14N	B6
-	DSPN	-	2861	16W-9N	E6
-	DSPN	-	2862	14W-9N	C7
-	DSPN	-	2916	13W-8N	E1
-	DSPN	-	2917	12W-8N	B2
-	EGvT	-	2860	18W-11N	D3
-	EGvT	-	2861	16W-9N	E6
-	EGvT	-	2862	15W-9N	A7
-	EGVV	-	2861	16W-10N	D6
-	ELGN	-	2799	36W-14N	E5
-	ELGN	-	2800	35W-14N	B6
-	ELGN	-	2801	33W-13N	A7
-	ElgT	-	2801	33W-13N	B7
-	GLBT	-	2798	39W-16N	D2
-	GLBT	-	2799	37W-15N	C4
-	HFET	-	2802	29W-12N	D7
-	HFET	-	2803	28W-12N	B7
-	HFET	-	2804	24W-12N	E7
-	HMND	-	3280		D3
-	HMND	-	3352		E4
-	HnrT	-	2801	32W-12N	C7
-	HnrT	-	2802	30W-12N	C7
-	HPSR	-	2743	46W-19N	A3
-	HshT	-	2743	44W-18N	E4
-	HshT	-	2744	41W-17N	E6
-	HTLY	-	2744	43W-18N	A4
-	HTLY	-	2745	41W-17N	A7
-	MPPT	-	2861	17W-10N	C5
-	RGMW	-	2859	21W-12N	E1
-	RGMW	-	2860	20W-12N	B1
-	RSMT	-	2916	13W-8N	E1
-	RSMT	-	2917	11W-7N	D4
-	RtdT	-	2744	43W-18N	A4
-	RtdT	-	2745	41W-17N	A7
-	RtdT	-	2798	39W-16N	D1
-	RtdT	-	2799	38W-15N	A3
-	SMBG	-	2804	24W-12N	E7
-	SMBG	-	2805	23W-12N	B7
-	SMBG	-	2859	21W-12N	D1
-	SmbT	-	2805	23W-12N	B7
-	SmbT	-	2859	21W-12N	D1
I-90 Chicago Skwy					
-	CHCG	-	3152	0E-7S	E6
-	CHCG	-	3153	1E-8S	A7
-	CHCG	-	3215	3E-10S	E5
-	CHCG	-	3216	3E-10S	A6
-	CHCG	-	3280	4E-11S	C1
-	HMND	-	3280	4E-11S	C1
I-90 Chicago Skwy W					
-	CHCG	-	3152	0E-7S	D6
-	CHCG	-	3215	3E-10S	D4
I-90 Dan Ryan Expwy					
-	CHCG	-	3034	0W-0S	A5
-	CHCG	-	3092	0W-4S	B7
-	CHCG	-	3152	0W-5S	B1
I-90 Indiana East-West Toll Rd					
-	CHCG	-	3280		C1
-	HMND	-	3280		D7
-	HMND	-	3352		E2
I-90 Kennedy Expwy					
-	CHCG	-	2917	10W-7N	E4
-	CHCG	-	2918	8W-6N	E5
-	CHCG	-	2919	6W-6N	D6
-	CHCG	-	2920	5W-5N	A7
-	CHCG	-	2976	4W-4N	B2
-	CHCG	-	2977	3W-3N	A4
-	CHCG	-	3033	1W-0N	E3
-	CHCG	-	3034	0W-0N	A4
I-90 Kennedy Expwy E					
-	CHCG	-	2919	7W-6N	C6
I-90 Northwest Tollway					
-	ANHT	-	2860	18W-11N	D3
-	ANHT	-	2861	17W-10N	B4
-	CHCG	-	2916	13W-8N	E1
-	CHCG	-	2917	11W-7N	D4
-	DndT	-	2799	36W-14N	E5
-	DndT	-	2800	36W-14N	A6
-	DSPN	-	2861	16W-9N	E6
-	DSPN	-	2862	15W-9N	A7
-	DSPN	-	2916	13W-8N	E1
-	DSPN	-	2917	12W-8N	B2
-	EGvT	-	2860	18W-11N	D3
-	EGvT	-	2861	16W-10N	D6
-	EGvT	-	2862	15W-9N	A7
-	EGVV	-	2861	17W-10N	B4
-	ELGN	-	2799	36W-14N	E5
-	ELGN	-	2800	36W-14N	A6
-	ELGN	-	2801	32W-12N	C7
-	ElgT	-	2801	33W-13N	A7
-	GLBT	-	2798	39W-16N	D2
-	GLBT	-	2799	37W-15N	C4
-	HFET	-	2802	29W-12N	D7
-	HFET	-	2803	27W-12N	D7
-	HFET	-	2804	24W-12N	E7
-	HnrT	-	2801	32W-12N	C7
-	HnrT	-	2802	31W-12N	A7
-	HPSR	-	2743	46W-19N	A3
-	HshT	-	2743	44W-18N	E4
-	HshT	-	2744	43W-18N	A4
-	HTLY	-	2744	41W-17N	E6
-	HTLY	-	2745	41W-17N	A6
-	MPPT	-	2861	17W-10N	C5
-	RGMW	-	2859	21W-12N	E1
-	RGMW	-	2860	20W-12N	B1
-	RSMT	-	2916	13W-8N	E1
-	RSMT	-	2917	11W-7N	D4
-	RtdT	-	2744	41W-17N	E6
-	RtdT	-	2745	41W-17N	A7
-	RtdT	-	2798	39W-16N	D1
-	RtdT	-	2799	38W-15N	A3
-	SMBG	-	2804	24W-12N	E7
-	SMBG	-	2805	23W-12N	A7
-	SMBG	-	2859	21W-12N	D1
-	SmbT	-	2805	23W-12N	B7
-	SmbT	-	2859	21W-12N	D1
I-94					
-	BKBN	-	2703	12W-22N	A3
-	BtlT	-	2360		E4
-	CHCG	-	2919	5W-5N	E7
-	CHCG	-	2920	5W-5N	A7
-	CHCG	-	2976	5W-5N	B1
-	CHCG	-	2977	3W-3N	A4
-	CHCG	-	3033	1W-0N	E3
-	CHCG	-	3034	0W-0N	A4
-	CHCG	-	3092	0W-2S	B3
-	CHCG	-	3152	0W-7S	C5
-	CHCG	-	3214	0W-10S	C6
-	CHCG	-	3215	1E-11S	A7
-	CHCG	-	3278	0E-14S	E5
-	CHCG	-	3279	1E-14S	B7
-	CHCG	-	3351	1E-15S	B1
-	CTCY	-	3351	1E-17S	C4
-	DLTN	-	3351	1E-17S	C5
-	DRFD	-	2703	12W-21N	B5
-	DRFD	-	2756	12W-20N	B1
-	DRFD	-	2757	10W-18N	A3
-	GLNC	-	2758	7W-16N	B7
-	GNOK	-	2535	14W-31N	D6
-	GNOK	-	2592	13W-29N	D3
-	GNOK	-	2648	13W-27N	D1
-	GNVW	-	2811	6W-13N	D6
-	GRNE	-	2477	16W-37N	E1
-	GRNE	-	2535	15W-34N	A2
-	HMND	-	3430		D5
-	LbvT	-	2535	14W-31N	D7
-	LbvT	-	2592	13W-29N	D3
-	LbvT	-	2648	14W-27N	D1
-	LKFT	-	2648	13W-24N	E6
-	LKFT	-	2702	13W-24N	E1
-	LKFT	-	2703	13W-23N	A2
-	LNSG	-	3429	2E-20S	C4
-	LNSG	-	3430	3E-20S	A4
-	LNSH	-	2703	12W-22N	A3
-	LNWD	-	2919	5W-6N	E5
-	MNGV	-	2865	6W-10N	D4
-	MNSR	-	3430		D5
-	MTWA	-	2592	14W-28N	D7
-	MTWA	-	2648	14W-27N	D1
-	NfdT	-	2756	12W-20N	B2
-	NfdT	-	2757	8W-18N	E3
-	NfdT	-	2758	7W-17N	B6
-	NfdT	-	2811	7W-15N	C1
-	NHBK	-	2756	11W-18N	E3
-	NHBK	-	2757	10W-18N	A3
-	NHBK	-	2758	7W-17N	B6
-	NHFD	-	2758	7W-16N	B7
-	NHFD	-	2811	6W-13N	D6
-	NptT	-	2360		D1
-	NptT	-	2419	17W-41N	C1
-	NptT	-	2477	16W-38N	E1
-	NtrT	-	2758	7W-18N	A4
-	NtrT	-	2811	6W-14N	D4
-	OMCK	-	2419	17W-41N	C1
-	OMCK	-	2477	16W-38N	E1
-	PTPR	-	2360		D1
-	RVWD	-	2703	12W-22N	B4
-	SHLD	-	3351	1E-18S	B7
-	SHLD	-	3429	1E-18S	B1
-	SKOK	-	2811	6W-13N	E7
-	SKOK	-	2865	6W-10N	D4
-	SKOK	-	2919	6W-8N	E1
-	ThtT	-	3429	1E-20S	B4
-	VrnT	-	2648	13W-24N	E6
-	VrnT	-	2702	13W-23N	E1
-	VrnT	-	2703	12W-21N	B6
-	WdfT	-	2703	12W-21N	B6
-	WdfT	-	2756	12W-20N	B2
-	WDWH	-	2360	16W-42N	E6
-	WDWH	-	2419	17W-41N	C1
-	WDWH	-	2477	16W-37N	E1
-	WKGN	-	2535	14W-33N	C4
-	WLMT	-	2811	6W-13N	D6
-	WrnT	-	2477	16W-37N	E1
-	WrnT	-	2478	15W-34N	A7
-	WrnT	-	2535	14W-32N	C5
I-94 Bishop Ford Mem Expwy					
-	CHCG	-	3214	0W-11S	C6
-	CHCG	-	3215	1E-11S	A7
-	CHCG	-	3278	0E-14S	E5
-	CHCG	-	3279	1E-15S	B7
-	CHCG	-	3351	1E-15S	B1
-	CTCY	-	3351	2E-16S	C3
-	DLTN	-	3351	2E-16S	C2
-	SHLD	-	3351	1E-18S	C7
-	SHLD	-	3429	1E-20S	B3
I-94 Borman Expwy					
-	HMND	-	3430		D5
-	LNSG	-	3430		C5
-	MNSR	-	3430		D5
I-94 Dan Ryan Expwy					
-	CHCG	-	3034	0W-0S	A5
-	CHCG	-	3092	0W-4S	B7
-	CHCG	-	3152	0W-8S	C7
-	CHCG	-	3214	0W-10S	C6
I-94 Dan Ryan Expwy E					
-	CHCG	-	3152	0W-7S	C5
I-94 Dan Ryan Expwy W					
-	CHCG	-	3152	0W-7S	C5
I-94 Edens Expwy					
-	CHCG	-	2919	6W-8N	E3
-	CHCG	-	2920	5W-5N	A7
-	GLNC	-	2758	7W-16N	B7
-	GNVW	-	2811	6W-13N	D6
-	LNWD	-	2919	6W-8N	E2
-	MNGV	-	2865	7W-10N	C5
-	NfdT	-	2811	7W-15N	C1
-	NHBK	-	2758	7W-18N	A4
-	NHFD	-	2758	7W-16N	B7
-	NHFD	-	2811	6W-14N	D4
-	NtrT	-	2758	7W-18N	A4
-	NtrT	-	2811	6W-14N	D4
-	SKOK	-	2811	6W-13N	E7
-	SKOK	-	2865	6W-12N	D1
-	SKOK	-	2919	6W-8N	E1
-	WLMT	-	2811	6W-14N	D4
I-94 Edens Expressway Spur					
-	DRFD	-	2756	11W-18N	E3
-	DRFD	-	2757	10W-18N	A3
-	NfdT	-	2756	12W-18N	B2
-	NfdT	-	2757	10W-18N	A3
-	NfdT	-	2758	7W-17N	B6
-	NHBK	-	2756	11W-18N	E3
-	NHBK	-	2757	8W-18N	E3
-	NHBK	-	2758	7W-17N	B6
-	WdfT	-	2756	12W-20N	B2
I-94 Edens Expressway Spur E					
-	NfdT	-	2756	12W-20N	B2
-	NfdT	-	2757	10W-18N	A3
-	NHBK	-	2757	8W-18N	E3
-	WdfT	-	2756	12W-20N	B2
I-94 Edens Expressway Spur W					
-	DRFD	-	2756	12W-20N	B1
-	NfdT	-	2757	10W-18N	A3
-	WdfT	-	2756	12W-20N	B1
I-94 Kennedy Expwy					
-	CHCG	-	2920	5W-5N	A7
-	CHCG	-	2976	4W-4N	B2
-	CHCG	-	2977	2W-2N	C6
-	CHCG	-	3033	1W-0N	E3
-	CHCG	-	3034	0W-0N	A4
I-94 Kingery Expwy					
-	LNSG	-	3429	3E-20S	E4
-	LNSG	-	3430	3E-20S	B4
-	MNSR	-	3430	4E-20S	C4
-	SHLD	-	3429	1E-18S	B1
-	ThtT	-	3429	2E-20S	C4
I-94 Tri-State Tollway					
-	BKBN	-	2703	12W-22N	A3
-	DRFD	-	2703	12W-21N	B5
-	DRFD	-	2756	12W-20N	B1
-	GNOK	-	2535	14W-31N	D6
-	GNOK	-	2592	14W-28N	C6
-	GNOK	-	2648	13W-27N	D1
-	GRNE	-	2477	16W-37N	E1
-	GRNE	-	2535	15W-34N	A2
-	LbvT	-	2535	14W-31N	D7
-	LbvT	-	2592	13W-29N	D3
-	LbvT	-	2648	13W-26N	E2
-	LKFT	-	2648	13W-24N	E6
-	LKFT	-	2702	13W-24N	E1
-	LKFT	-	2703	13W-23N	A2
-	LNSH	-	2703	12W-21N	B6
-	MTWA	-	2592	14W-28N	D7
-	MTWA	-	2648	13W-27N	D1
-	NptT	-	2360	16W-42N	D6
-	NptT	-	2419	17W-41N	C1
-	NptT	-	2477	16W-38N	E1
-	OMCK	-	2419	17W-41N	C1
-	OMCK	-	2477	16W-38N	E1
-	RVWD	-	2703	12W-22N	A3
-	VrnT	-	2648	13W-24N	E6
-	VrnT	-	2702	13W-23N	E1
-	VrnT	-	2703	12W-21N	B6
-	WdfT	-	2703	12W-22N	A3
-	WdfT	-	2756	12W-20N	B2
-	WDWH	-	2360	16W-42N	E6
-	WDWH	-	2419	16W-38N	E7
-	WDWH	-	2477	16W-37N	E1
-	WKGN	-	2535	14W-31N	D6
-	WrnT	-	2477	16W-38N	E1
-	WrnT	-	2478	15W-34N	A7
-	WrnT	-	2535	14W-32N	C5
I-190					
-	CHCG	-	2917	10W-7N	E4
-	CHCG	60666	2916	13W-6N	E5
-	RSMT	-	2917	11W-7N	E4
I-290					
-	AddT	-	2971	18W-3N	A4
-	ADSN	-	2914	20W-6N	B7
-	ADSN	-	2970	18W-4N	E3
-	ADSN	-	2971	18W-3N	A4
-	BDVW	-	3029	11W-0S	C6
-	BKLY	-	3028	14W-0S	C5
-	BLWD	-	3029	12W-0S	B6
-	CHCG	-	3031	7W-0S	C6
-	CHCG	-	3032	5W-0S	A6
-	CHCG	-	3033	1W-0S	D5
-	CHCG	-	3034	0W-0S	A5
-	EGvT	-	2860	20W-9N	A7
-	EGvT	-	2914	20W-8N	A1
-	EGVV	-	2914	20W-6N	B7
-	EMHT	-	2971	17W-3N	C5
-	EMHT	-	2972	15W-2N	A7
-	EMHT	-	3028	14W-1N	B2
-	FTPK	-	3030	8W-0S	E6
-	HLSD	-	3028	14W-0S	C5
-	HLSD	-	3029	12W-0S	A6
-	ITSC	-	2914	20W-8N	B3
-	MYWD	-	3029	11W-0S	D6
-	MYWD	-	3030	10W-0S	A6
-	NHLK	-	3028	15W-1N	B1
-	OKPK	-	3030	8W-0S	E6
-	OKPK	-	3031	7W-0S	C6
-	PvsT	-	3028	14W-0S	C6
-	RGMW	-	2860	20W-12N	A1
-	SMBG	-	2860	21W-10N	A5
-	WDDL	-	2970	18W-4N	E3
-	WSTR	-	3029	12W-0S	C6
I-290 Eisenhower Expwy					
-	AddT	-	2971	18W-3N	A4
-	ADSN	-	2914	20W-5N	A7
-	ADSN	-	2970	18W-4N	E3
-	ADSN	-	2971	16W-3N	D6
-	BDVW	-	3029	11W-0S	C6
-	BKLY	-	3028	14W-0N	B5
-	BLWD	-	3029	11W-0S	C6
-	CHCG	-	3031	7W-0S	C6
-	CHCG	-	3032	3W-0S	E5
-	CHCG	-	3033	1W-0S	E5
-	CHCG	-	3034	0W-0S	A5
-	EMHT	-	2971	17W-3N	C5
-	EMHT	-	2972	15W-2N	A7
-	EMHT	-	3028	15W-0N	B3
-	FTPK	-	3030	8W-0S	E6
-	HLSD	-	3028	13W-0S	E6
-	HLSD	-	3029	12W-0S	A6
-	ITSC	-	2914	20W-5N	A7
-	MYWD	-	3029	12W-0S	B6
-	MYWD	-	3030	10W-0S	A6
-	NHLK	-	3028	15W-1N	B1
-	OKPK	-	3030	10W-0S	A6
-	OKPK	-	3031	7W-0S	C6
-	PvsT	-	3028	14W-0S	C6
-	WDDL	-	2970	18W-4N	E3
-	WSTR	-	3029	12W-0S	C6
I-294					
-	ALSP	-	3275	7W-14S	C5
-	ALSP	-	3276	5W-15S	A7
-	ALSP	-	3348	5W-15S	B1
-	BGVW	-	3210	9W-11S	E7
-	BKLY	-	3028	14W-1N	C3
-	BmnT	-	3348	4W-17S	E4
-	BmnT	-	3349	3W-17S	A5
-	BRRG	-	3146	14W-6S	D4
-	CHCG	-	2863	12W-9N	C7
-	CHCG	-	2917	12W-6N	B6
-	CHRG	-	3210	9W-11S	E7
-	CHRG	-	3274	8W-11S	E1
-	CHRG	-	3275	6W-14S	D6
-	CTSD	-	3146	13W-8S	E7
-	CTSD	-	3147	13W-8S	A7
-	CTSD	-	3209	13W-8S	A1
-	CTWD	-	3348	4W-17S	D4
-	DRFD	-	2756	12W-18N	B2
-	DSPN	-	2863	12W-10N	C4
-	DSPN	-	2917	12W-8N	C2
-	EHZC	-	3427	1W-20S	E4
-	EHZC	-	3428	0W-20S	C4
-	EMHT	-	3028	14W-0S	C6
-	FNPK	-	2972	14W-3N	B6
-	FNPK	-	2973	13W-4N	A3
-	GNVW	-	2809	12W-16N	C1
-	HGKN	-	3209	12W-8S	B1
-	HLCT	-	3427	3W-19S	B3
-	HLSD	-	3028	14W-0S	C6
-	HNDL	-	3086	14W-3S	C6
-	HNDL	-	3146	14W-7S	D6
-	HYHL	-	3210	10W-9S	B3
-	IHPK	-	3146	14W-7S	D6
-	JSTC	-	3209	11W-9S	E2
-	JSTC	-	3210	9W-9S	C4
-	LNSG	-	3429	2E-20S	D4
-	LNSG	-	3430	3E-20S	A4
-	LydT	-	2972	14W-3N	B6
-	LydT	-	2973	13W-4N	A3
-	LynT	-	3086	14W-3S	C6
-	LynT	-	3146	14W-6S	D5
-	LynT	-	3147	13W-8S	A7
-	LynT	-	3209	12W-8S	D2
-	MaiT	-	2809	11W-13N	C7
-	MaiT	-	2863	12W-12N	C1
-	MDLN	-	3348	4W-16S	D4
-	MKHM	-	3349	3W-17S	B6
-	MKHM	-	3427	3W-19S	B2
-	NfdT	-	2756	13W-17N	A5
-	NfdT	-	2809	11W-13N	C6
-	NHBK	-	2756	12W-18N	B3
-	NHBK	-	2809	12W-16N	C1
-	NHLK	-	2972	14W-2N	B6
-	NHLK	-	3028	14W-2N	B1
-	OKBK	-	3086	14W-1S	B2
-	PKRG	-	2863	12W-10N	C5
-	POSN	-	3349	3W-17S	A5
-	PvsT	-	3028	14W-0S	C7
-	PvsT	-	3086	14W-3S	C6
-	RBBN	-	3348	5W-15S	B1
-	RSMT	-	2917	11W-7N	C3
-	SHLD	-	3428	0E-20S	D4
-	SHLD	-	3429	0E-20S	A4
-	SRPK	-	2917	12W-6N	C6
-	SRPK	-	2973	12W-5N	A2
-	ThtT	-	3429	0E-20S	A4
-	TNTN	-	3428	0W-20S	C4
-	WdfT	-	2756	13W-17N	A5
-	WhlT	-	2756	12W-18N	A4
-	WLNG	-	2756	12W-18N	A4
-	WLSP	-	3209	12W-8S	C1
-	WNSP	-	3086	14W-3S	C6
-	WNSP	-	3146	14W-7S	D6
-	WRTH	-	3275	6W-14S	D6
-	WthT	-	3275	7W-13S	B4
I-294 Kingery Expwy					
-	LNSG	-	3429	3E-20S	E4
-	LNSG	-	3430	3E-20S	A4
-	ThtT	-	3429	2E-20S	C4
I-294 Tri-State Tollway					
-	ALSP	-	3275	7W-13S	C5
-	ALSP	-	3276	5W-15S	A7
-	ALSP	-	3348	5W-15S	B1
-	BGVW	-	3210	9W-10S	D5
-	BKLY	-	3028	14W-0S	C6
-	BmnT	-	3348	4W-17S	E4
-	BmnT	-	3349	3W-17S	B6
-	BRRG	-	3146	14W-7S	D6
-	CHCG	-	2863	12W-9N	C7
-	CHCG	-	2917	12W-6N	B6
-	CHRG	-	3210	9W-11S	E7
-	CHRG	-	3274	8W-11S	E1
-	CHRG	-	3275	6W-14S	D6
-	CTSD	-	3146	13W-8S	E7
-	CTSD	-	3147	13W-8S	A7
-	CTSD	-	3209	13W-8S	A1
-	CTWD	-	3348	5W-15S	B1
-	DRFD	-	2756	12W-18N	B2
-	DSPN	-	2863	12W-10N	C4
-	DSPN	-	2917	12W-6N	B6
-	EHZC	-	3427	1W-20S	E4
-	EHZC	-	3428	0W-20S	C4
-	EMHT	-	3028	14W-0S	C6
-	FNPK	-	2972	14W-3N	B6
-	FNPK	-	2973	13W-4N	A3
-	GNVW	-	2809	11W-13N	C6
-	HGKN	-	3209	12W-8S	C1
-	HLCT	-	3427	3W-20S	C4
-	HLSD	-	3028	14W-0S	C6
-	HNDL	-	3086	14W-3S	C6
-	HNDL	-	3146	14W-7S	D6
-	HYHL	-	3210	10W-9S	B3
-	IHPK	-	3146	14W-7S	D6
-	JSTC	-	3209	11W-9S	E2
-	JSTC	-	3210	10W-9S	A3
-	LNSG	-	3429	2E-20S	C4
-	LydT	-	2972	14W-3N	B6
-	LydT	-	2973	13W-4N	A3
-	LynT	-	3086	14W-3S	C6
-	LynT	-	3146	14W-6S	D4
-	LynT	-	3147	13W-8S	A7
-	LynT	-	3209	12W-8S	D2
-	MaiT	-	2809	11W-13N	C7
-	MaiT	-	2863	12W-12N	C1
-	MDLN	-	3348	4W-16S	D4
-	MKHM	-	3349	3W-17S	B6
-	MKHM	-	3427	3W-19S	B2
-	NfdT	-	2756	13W-17N	A5
-	NfdT	-	2809	11W-13N	C6
-	NHBK	-	2756	12W-18N	B3
-	NHBK	-	2809	12W-16N	C1
-	NHLK	-	2972	14W-2N	B6
-	NHLK	-	3028	14W-2N	B1
-	OKBK	-	3086	15W-1S	B2
-	PKRG	-	2863	12W-10N	C4
-	POSN	-	3349	3W-17S	A4
-	PvsT	-	3028	14W-0S	C7
-	PvsT	-	3086	15W-1S	B2
-	RBBN	-	3348	5W-15S	B1
-	RSMT	-	2917	11W-7N	C3
-	SHLD	-	3428	0E-20S	D4
-	SHLD	-	3429	0E-20S	A4
-	SRPK	-	2917	12W-5N	B7
-	SRPK	-	2973	12W-5N	A2
-	ThtT	-	3429	1E-20S	B4
-	TNTN	-	3428	0W-20S	C4
-	WdfT	-	2756	13W-17N	A5
-	WhlT	-	2756	12W-18N	A4
-	WLNG	-	2756	12W-18N	A4
-	WLSP	-	3209	11W-9S	E2
-	WNSP	-	3086	14W-4S	C6
-	WNSP	-	3146	14W-7S	D6
-	WRTH	-	3275	8W-12S	A2
-	WthT	-	3275	7W-13S	B4
I-355					
-	ADSN	-	2914	20W-6N	B7
-	ADSN	-	2969	21W-4N	E3
-	ADSN	-	2970	20W-5N	A1
-	BGBK	-	3206	21W-10S	A6
-	BGBK	-	3270	20W-14S	B7
-	BmdT	-	2969	21W-3N	E6
-	BmdT	-	2970	20W-5N	A1
-	BmdT	-	3025	21W-2N	E1
-	DPgT	-	3270	20W-14S	B7
-	DRGV	-	3083	21W-4S	D7
-	DRGV	-	3084	20W-2S	A3
-	DRGV	-	3143	22W-6S	C4
-	GNEN	-	3025	21W-0S	E7
-	HmrT	-	3342	20W-18S	C7
-	HmrT	-	3420	19W-21S	E7
-	ITSC	-	2914	20W-6N	B6
-	LKPT	-	3342	20W-18S	C7
-	LKPT	-	3420	19W-21S	E7
-	LMBD	-	3025	21W-0S	E7
-	LMBD	-	3026	21W-0N	A5
-	LMBD	-	3083	21W-1S	E1
-	LMBD	-	3084	20W-2S	A3
-	LMNT	-	3270	20W-14S	B7
-	LMNT	-	3342	20W-18S	C7
-	LSLE	-	3083	21W-4S	E7
-	LSLE	-	3143	22W-4S	D1
-	LslT	-	3083	21W-4S	D7
-	LslT	-	3084	21W-4S	A7
-	LslT	-	3143	22W-6S	D4
-	MltT	-	3025	21W-1N	E3
-	MltT	-	3026	21W-0N	A4
-	MltT	-	3083	21W-1S	E1
-	NLNX	-	3420	19W-21S	E7
-	NLNX	-	3421	18W-22S	A7
-	NLNX	-	3501	18W-22S	A1
-	WDRG	-	3143	21W-7S	E6
-	WDRG	-	3205	21W-8S	E2
-	WDRG	-	3206	21W-9S	A4
-	WDRG	-	3270	20W-14S	B7
-	YkTp	-	3084	20W-1S	A2
I-355 North-South Tollway					
-	ADSN	-	2969	21W-2N	E6
-	BGBK	-	3206	21W-10S	A6
-	BGBK	-	3270	20W-14S	B7
-	BmdT	-	2969	21W-2N	E6
-	BmdT	-	3025	21W-2N	E1
-	DPgT	-	3270	20W-14S	B7
-	DRGV	-	3083	21W-4S	D7
-	DRGV	-	3084	20W-2S	A3
-	DRGV	-	3143	22W-5S	C3
-	GNEN	-	3025	21W-0S	E7
-	HmrT	-	3342	20W-18S	C7
-	HmrT	-	3420	19W-21S	E7
-	LKPT	-	3342	20W-18S	C7
-	LKPT	-	3420	19W-21S	E7
-	LMBD	-	3025	21W-0S	E6
-	LMBD	-	3026	21W-0N	A5
-	LMBD	-	3083	21W-1S	E1
-	LMBD	-	3084	20W-1S	A2
-	LMNT	-	3270	20W-14S	B7
-	LMNT	-	3342	20W-18S	C7
-	LSLE	-	3083	21W-4S	E7
-	LSLE	-	3143	22W-4S	D1
-	LslT	-	3083	21W-4S	E7
-	LslT	-	3084	21W-4S	A7
-	LslT	-	3143	22W-5S	C2
-	MltT	-	3025	21W-0S	E7
-	MltT	-	3026	21W-0N	A4
-	MltT	-	3083	21W-1S	E1
-	NLNX	-	3420	19W-21S	E7
-	NLNX	-	3421	18W-22S	A7
-	NLNX	-	3501	18W-22S	A1
-	WDRG	-	3143	22W-6S	D5
-	WDRG	-	3205	21W-8S	E2
-	WDRG	-	3206	21W-9S	A3
-	WDRG	-	3270	20W-14S	B7
-	YkTp	-	3084	20W-1S	A2
SR-1					
-	EHZC	60426	3428	0W-20S	B4
-	EHZC	60473	3428	0W-20S	B4
-	PHNX	60426	3350	1W-18S	B7
-	RVDL	60827	3278	0W-15S	A7
100	CHHT	60411	3508	1W-23S	B4
300	BCHR	60401	3864	0W-36S	C2
300	WshT	60401	3864	0W-37S	C2
800	CRTE	60417	3596	1W-28S	B7
800	CRTE	60417	3685	0W-29S	B1
1100	BCHR	60401	3774	0W-35S	C6
1500	CHHT	60411	3596	1W-28S	B6
1500	CteT	60417	3685	0W-32S	B6
2500	SCHT	60411	3596	1W-26S	A2
3000	SCHT	60475	3596	1W-27S	B4
3000	STGR	60475	3596	1W-27S	B4
3700	CRTE	60475	3596	1W-28S	B7
9900	CHCG	60628	3214	0W-11S	A7
9900	CHCG	60643	3214	1W-11S	A7
10300	CHCG	60628	3278	0W-13S	A3
10300	CHCG	60643	3278	1W-13S	A3
12200	CTPK	60628	3278	1W-14S	A6
12200	CTPK	60643	3278	1W-14S	A6
12200	CTPK	60827	3278	1W-14S	A6
13100	RVDL	60827	3350	1W-17S	A6
14300	HRVY	60426	3350	0W-18S	B7
14300	HRVY	60827	3350	1W-16S	A4
15600	HRVY	60426	3428	0W-21S	B7
16900	SHLD	60426	3428	0W-20S	B4
16900	SHLD	60473	3428	0W-20S	B4
17100	EHZC	60429	3428	0W-20S	B5
17300	EHZC	60430	3428	0W-20S	B5
17300	HMWD	60429	3428	0W-20S	B5
17300	HMWD	60430	3428	0W-20S	B5
18000	GNWD	60425	3428	0W-21S	B7
18000	HMWD	60425	3428	0W-21S	B7
18300	GNWD	60425	3508	0W-24S	B5
18500	HMWD	60425	3508	1W-24S	B5
18500	HMWD	60430	3508	1W-24S	B5
19100	BlmT	60411	3508	1W-23S	B3
19100	GNWD	60411	3508	1W-23S	B3
26700	CteT	60417	3774	0W-32S	C1
27500	CteT	60401	3774	0W-33S	C3
27600	WshT	60401	3774	0W-35S	C6
SR-1 Chicago Rd					
1100	CHHT	60411	3508	1W-25S	A7
1500	CHHT	60411	3596	1W-28S	B6

Chicago 7-County Street Index

STREET Block	City	ZIP	Map#	CGS	Grid
SR-1 Chicago Rd					
2500	SCHT	60411	3596	1W-26S	A2
3000	SCHT	60475	3596	1W-27S	B4
3000	STGR	60475	3596	1W-27S	B4
3700	CRTE	60417	3596	1W-28S	B7
3700	CRTE	60475	3596	1W-28S	B7
SR-1 Dixie Hwy					
-	CteT	60417	3774	0W-32S	C1
27500	CteT	60401	3774	0W-33S	C3
27600	WshT	60401	3774	0W-35S	C6
28600	BCHR	60401	3774	0W-35S	C6
SR-1 S Dixie Hwy					
300	BCHR	60401	3864	0W-36S	C2
300	WshT	60401	3864	0W-37S	C2
1100	BCHR	60401	3774	0W-36S	C7
25300	CRTE	60417	3685	0W-30S	B4
25300	CteT	60417	3685	0W-32S	B6
26700	CteT	60417	3774	0W-32S	C1
26900	CteT	60401	3774	0W-33S	C2
SR-1 Halsted St					
-	EHZC	60426	3428	0W-20S	B4
-	EHZC	60473	3428	0W-20S	B4
14300	HRVY	60426	3350	1W-17S	A4
14300	HRVY	60827	3350	1W-16S	A4
14300	RVDL	60827	3350	1W-16S	A4
15200	PHNX	60426	3350	0W-18S	B7
15600	HRVY	60426	3428	1W-21S	B7
16900	SHLD	60426	3428	0W-20S	B4
16900	SHLD	60473	3428	0W-20S	B4
17100	EHZC	60429	3428	0W-20S	B5
17300	EHZC	60430	3428	0W-20S	B5
17300	HMWD	60429	3428	0W-20S	B5
17300	HMWD	60430	3428	0W-20S	B5
18000	GNWD	60425	3428	0W-21S	B7
18000	HMWD	60425	3428	0W-21S	B7
SR-1 S Halsted St					
-	RVDL	60827	3278	0W-15S	A7
100	CHHT	60411	3508	1W-23S	B4
9900	CHCG	60628	3214	1W-11S	A7
9900	CHCG	60643	3214	1W-11S	A7
10300	CHCG	60628	3278	1W-13S	A3
10300	CHCG	60643	3278	1W-13S	A3
12200	CTPK	60628	3278	1W-14S	A6
12200	CTPK	60643	3278	1W-14S	A6
12200	CTPK	60827	3278	1W-14S	A6
13100	RVDL	60827	3350	1W-17S	A6
14500	HRVY	60426	3350	1W-16S	A4
14500	HRVY	60827	3350	1W-16S	A4
18300	GNWD	60425	3428	0W-22S	B7
18300	GNWD	60425	3508	1W-24S	B5
18300	HMWD	60430	3428	0W-22S	B7
18500	HMWD	60425	3508	1W-24S	B5
18500	HMWD	60430	3508	1W-24S	B5
19100	BlmT	60411	3508	1W-23S	B3
19100	GNWD	60411	3508	1W-23S	B3
SR-1 Main St					
800	CRTE	60417	3596	1W-28S	B7
800	CRTE	60417	3685	0W-29S	B1
1500	CteT	60417	3685	0W-30S	B3
SR-1 Route 1 Cto					
-	CHHT	60411	3508	1W-24S	B6
SR-1 Vincennes Rd					
-	PHNX	60426	3350	1W-18S	B7
14900	HRVY	60426	3350	1W-18S	B7
SR-7					
-	JltT	60436	3586	26W-25S	A1
10	JLET	60435	3498	26W-23S	A4
10	JLET	60436	3498	26W-23S	A5
10	LKPT	60441	3419	22W-19S	C3
200	CTHL	60403	3498	25W-22S	C1
200	CTHL	60435	3498	24W-21S	E1
500	LktT	60441	3419	23W-19S	B2
600	JltT	60436	3498	26W-24S	A7
600	RKDL	60436	3498	26W-25S	A7
1200	JLET	60403	3498	26W-22S	A1
1200	LKPT	60441	3420	21W-18S	A2
1200	LktT	60441	3420	21W-18S	A2
1200	RKDL	60436	3586	26W-25S	A1
1300	HmrT	60441	3420	21W-18S	A2
1600	LktT	60435	3498	24W-21S	E1
1700	CTHL	60403	3418	24W-21S	E7
1700	CTHL	60435	3418	24W-21S	E7
1800	LktT	60435	3418	24W-21S	E7
2000	CTHL	60441	3418	24W-21S	E6
9800	ODPK	60462	3345	11W-16S	E3
10600	CHRG	60415	3274	9W-12S	E2
10600	CHRG	60482	3274	9W-12S	E2
10600	OrlT	60462	3345	11W-16S	E3
10600	WRTH	60415	3274	9W-12S	E2
10600	WRTH	60482	3274	9W-12S	E2
10700	ODPK	60467	3345	13W-16S	A4
10700	OrlT	60467	3345	13W-16S	A4
10800	PSHL	60465	3274	9W-13S	C5
10800	PSHL	60482	3274	9W-12S	D2
10900	ODPK	60467	3344	13W-17S	E6
10900	OrlT	60467	3344	14W-17S	E6
11200	ODPK	60467	3422	15W-19S	B1
11200	OrlT	60467	3422	15W-19S	B1
11200	PSHT	60465	3274	9W-13S	C5
11400	PSHT	60463	3274	9W-13S	C5
11800	HMGN	60491	3422	14W-18S	C1
11800	PSHT	60464	3274	9W-13S	C5
11800	PSPK	60464	3274	11W-14S	A7
12600	PlsT	60464	3346	11W-15S	A1
12600	PSPK	60464	3346	11W-15S	A1
13000	HMGN	60491	3421	18W-19S	A1
13000	ODPK	60462	3346	11W-15S	A1
13000	PlsT	60462	3346	11W-15S	A1
13000	PSPK	60462	3346	11W-15S	A1
13100	PlsT	60462	3345	11W-16S	E3
13900	HmrT	60491	3421	17W-18S	C1
14800	HmrT	60491	3420	20W-19S	B2
15800	RMVL	60441	3419	23W-19S	B2
16000	LKPT	60491	3420	20W-19S	C2
16200	CTHL	60441	3419	23W-19S	A2
17000	LktT	60441	3418	24W-20S	E5
SR-7 E 9th St					
-	LKPT	60441	3420	21W-19S	A2
100	LKPT	60441	3419	22W-19S	C3
1100	LktT	60441	3419	21W-19S	E2
SR-7 W 9th St					
-	RMVL	60441	3419	23W-19S	B2
10	LKPT	60441	3419	22W-19S	C3
500	LktT	60441	3419	23W-19S	B2
SR-7 W 143rd St					
9800	ODPK	60462	3345	12W-16S	C4
10600	OrlT	60462	3345	13W-16S	B4
10700	ODPK	60467	3345	13W-16S	A4
10700	OrlT	60467	3345	13W-16S	A4
10900	ODPK	60467	3344	14W-17S	E6
10900	OrlT	60467	3344	14W-17S	E6
SR-7 E 159th St					
1200	LKPT	60441	3420	21W-18S	A2
1200	LktT	60441	3420	21W-18S	A2
1300	HmrT	60441	3420	21W-18S	A2
SR-7 W 159th St					
11200	ODPK	60467	3422	14W-18S	E1
11200	OrlT	60467	3422	14W-18S	E1
11800	HMGN	60491	3422	14W-18S	C1
13000	HMGN	60491	3421	18W-19S	A1
13900	HmrT	60491	3421	17W-18S	C1
14800	HmrT	60491	3420	20W-19S	B2
15400	HmrT	60441	3420	19W-19S	C1
16000	LKPT	60441	3420	20W-19S	C2
16000	LKPT	60491	3420	20W-19S	C2
16600	LktT	60441	3420	20W-18S	A2
SR-7 Broadway St					
2100	CTHL	60403	3418	24W-21S	E6
2100	CTHL	60435	3418	24W-21S	E6
2100	CTHL	60441	3418	24W-21S	E6
2100	LktT	60435	3418	24W-21S	E6
15800	LktT	60441	3419	23W-19S	A2
15800	RMVL	60441	3419	23W-19S	A2
16200	CTHL	60441	3419	23W-19S	A2
17000	LktT	60441	3418	24W-20S	E5
SR-7 N Broadway St					
1600	CTHL	60403	3498	24W-21S	E1
1600	CTHL	60435	3498	24W-21S	E1
1600	JLET	60435	3498	24W-21S	E1
1600	LktT	60435	3498	24W-21S	E1
1700	CTHL	60403	3418	24W-21S	E7
1700	CTHL	60435	3418	24W-21S	E7
1800	LktT	60435	3418	24W-21S	E7
2000	CTHL	60441	3418	24W-21S	E6
SR-7 N Larkin Av					
10	JLET	60435	3498	26W-23S	A4
10	JLET	60436	3498	26W-23S	A5
1200	JLET	60403	3498	26W-22S	A1
SR-7 S Larkin Av					
-	JltT	60436	3586	26W-25S	A1
10	JLET	60435	3498	26W-24S	A5
10	JLET	60436	3498	26W-24S	A5
600	JltT	60436	3498	26W-24S	A7
600	RKDL	60436	3498	26W-25S	A7
1200	RKDL	60436	3586	26W-25S	A1
SR-7 Southwest Hwy					
10600	CHRG	60415	3274	9W-12S	E2
10600	CHRG	60482	3274	9W-12S	E2
10600	WRTH	60415	3274	9W-12S	E2
10600	WRTH	60482	3274	9W-12S	E2
10800	PSHL	60465	3274	9W-13S	C5
10800	PSHL	60482	3274	9W-12S	D2
11200	PSHT	60465	3274	9W-13S	C5
11400	PSHT	60463	3274	9W-13S	C5
11800	PSHT	60464	3274	9W-13S	C5
11800	PSPK	60464	3274	11W-14S	A7
12600	PlsT	60464	3346	11W-15S	A1
12600	PSPK	60464	3346	11W-15S	A1
13000	ODPK	60462	3346	11W-15S	A1
13000	PlsT	60462	3346	11W-15S	A1
13000	PSPK	60462	3346	11W-15S	A1
13100	ODPK	60462	3345	11W-16S	E3
13100	OrlT	60462	3345	11W-16S	E3
13100	PlsT	60462	3345	11W-16S	E3
SR-7 Theodore St					
200	CTHL	60403	3498	25W-22S	C1
200	CTHL	60435	3498	24W-21S	E1
200	JLET	60435	3498	25W-22S	C1
1400	JLET	60403	3498	25W-21S	B1
SR-7 Wolf Rd					
14300	ODPK	60467	3344	13W-17S	E4
14300	OrlT	60467	3344	13W-17S	E4
15600	ODPK	60467	3422	15W-19S	B1
15600	OrlT	60467	3422	15W-19S	B1
SR-19					
-	CHCG	60176	2973	12W-5N	C1
-	CHCG	60634	2973	12W-5N	C1
-	CHCG	60666	2973	12W-5N	A1
-	FNPK	60131	2972	14W-5N	D2
-	FNPK	60131	2973	13W-5N	A1
-	FNPK	60666	2972	13W-5N	E2
-	SRPK	60666	2973	12W-5N	A1
10	BmdT	60143	2913	22W-6N	D5
10	BmdT	60143	2914	18W-6N	E7
10	BmdT	60157	2913	22W-6N	D5
10	BNVL	60106	2915	16W-5N	E7
10	BNVL	60106	2972	15W-5N	A1
10	ELGN	60120	2854	34W-11N	E4
10	HnrT	60107	2856	30W-10N	B5
10	HnrT	60120	2856	30W-10N	B5
10	ITSC	60143	2914	18W-6N	E7
10	ROSL	60172	2913	21W-6N	D5
10	SMWD	60107	2856	30W-10N	B5
10	SMWD	60107	2857	28W-9N	A7
100	ELGN	60123	2854	34W-11N	E4
100	ROSL	60172	2912	23W-7N	E4
100	SMBG	60172	2912	23W-7N	E4
100	SMWD	60120	2856	30W-10N	B5
100	WDDL	60191	2915	17W-5N	C7
200	WDDL	60191	2914	18W-6N	E7
300	ELGN	60120	2855	33W-11N	B4
400	CHCG	60106	2972	15W-5N	A1
400	ITSC	60143	2913	21W-6N	E6
400	ITSC	60191	2914	18W-6N	E7
400	ROSL	60157	2913	22W-7N	C5
400	SMBG	60193	2912	24W-7N	D3
400	WDDL	60143	2914	18W-6N	E7
600	CHCG	60613	2978	0W-4N	A1
700	CHCG	60613	2977	3W-4N	A2
700	SmbT	60193	2912	25W-8N	B2
800	HRPK	60133	2912	24W-8N	C3
800	SMBG	60133	2912	26W-9N	A2
800	SMWD	60107	2911	27W-9N	C1
900	BNVL	60131	2972	14W-5N	B1
900	CHCG	60131	2972	14W-5N	D2
900	HRPK	60107	2911	27W-9N	C1
900	HRPK	60133	2911	27W-9N	C1
900	SMWD	60133	2911	27W-9N	C1
1400	HnrT	60120	2855	31W-10N	E5
1600	ELGN	60120	2856	31W-10N	A5
1900	CHCG	60618	2977	2W-5N	B1
2700	CHCG	60618	2976	3W-4N	E2
3900	CHCG	60641	2976	5W-4N	A2
4600	CHCG	60641	2975	7W-4N	B2
5500	CHCG	60634	2975	6W-5N	C2
6600	CHCG	60634	2974	8W-4N	D2
7100	NRDG	60634	2974	8W-5N	D2
7100	NRDG	60706	2974	8W-5N	D2
7300	CHCG	60706	2974	9W-4N	D2
9200	SRPK	60176	2973	12W-5N	A1
11500	CHCG	60666	2972	14W-5N	D2
SR-19 E Chicago St					
-	ELGN	60123	2854	34W-11N	E4
10	ELGN	60120	2854	34W-11N	E4
300	ELGN	60120	2855	33W-11N	B4
1400	HnrT	60120	2855	31W-10N	E5
SR-19 W Chicago St					
100	ELGN	60123	2854	34W-11N	E4
SR-19 Irving Park Rd					
-	CHCG	60176	2973	12W-5N	C1
-	CHCG	60634	2973	12W-5N	C1
-	CHCG	60666	2973	12W-5N	A1
-	ELGN	60120	2855	31W-10N	E5
-	FNPK	60131	2973	13W-5N	A1
-	HnrT	60120	2855	31W-10N	E5
-	ROSL	60157	2913	22W-7N	C5
-	ROSL	60172	2913	22W-7N	C5
-	SRPK	60666	2973	12W-5N	A1
10	BmdT	60143	2913	22W-6N	D5
10	BmdT	60143	2914	18W-6N	E7
10	BmdT	60157	2913	22W-6N	D5
10	HnrT	60107	2856	30W-10N	B5
10	HnrT	60120	2856	30W-10N	B5
10	ITSC	60143	2914	18W-6N	E7
100	SMWD	60107	2856	30W-10N	B5
100	SMWD	60120	2856	30W-10N	B5
400	ITSC	60143	2913	21W-6N	E6
800	HRPK	60133	2912	24W-8N	C3
800	SMBG	60133	2912	26W-9N	A2
1200	HRPK	60133	2911	27W-9N	C1
1600	ELGN	60120	2856	31W-10N	A5
1700	HRPK	60107	2911	27W-9N	D1
1700	SMWD	60107	2911	27W-9N	D1
1700	SMWD	60133	2911	27W-9N	D1
9200	SRPK	60176	2973	12W-5N	A1
SR-19 E Irving Park Rd					
10	BNVL	60106	2972	15W-5N	A1
10	ROSL	60172	2913	23W-7N	A4
10	SMWD	60107	2857	28W-9N	A7
100	ITSC	60143	2914	19W-6N	C6
100	WDDL	60191	2915	17W-5N	B7
400	BmdT	60157	2913	22W-7N	C5
400	BNVL	60106	2915	17W-5N	C7
400	CHCG	60106	2972	15W-5N	A1
400	ROSL	60157	2913	22W-7N	C5
800	SMWD	60107	2911	27W-9N	C1
900	BNVL	60131	2972	14W-5N	B1
900	CHCG	60131	2972	14W-5N	B1
900	HRPK	60107	2911	27W-9N	C1
900	HRPK	60133	2911	27W-9N	C1
900	SMWD	60133	2911	27W-9N	C1
1100	WDDL	60143	2914	19W-6N	D7
1200	WDDL	60191	2914	19W-6N	D7
1300	ITSC	60191	2914	18W-6N	E7
11500	CHCG	60666	2972	14W-5N	C1
SR-19 W Irving Park Rd					
-	BNVL	60131	2972	14W-5N	C1
-	CHCG	60131	2972	14W-5N	D2
-	CHCG	60176	2973	11W-5N	E2
-	CHCG	60634	2973	10W-5N	E2
-	CHCG	60666	2972	14W-5N	D2
-	FNPK	60131	2972	14W-5N	D2
-	FNPK	60666	2972	13W-5N	E2
10	BNVL	60106	2915	16W-5N	E7
10	ROSL	60172	2913	21W-6N	D5
10	SMWD	60107	2856	29W-10N	D6
100	ROSL	60172	2912	23W-7N	E4
100	SMBG	60172	2912	23W-7N	E4
100	WDDL	60191	2915	17W-5N	C7
200	ITSC	60143	2914	19W-6N	C6
200	WDDL	60191	2914	18W-6N	E7
400	ITSC	60191	2914	18W-6N	E7
400	SMBG	60193	2912	24W-7N	D3
400	WDDL	60143	2914	18W-6N	E7
600	CHCG	60613	2978	0W-5N	A1
700	CHCG	60613	2977	3W-4N	A2
700	HnrT	60107	2856	29W-10N	D6
700	SmbT	60193	2912	25W-8N	B2
900	HnrT	60120	2856	29W-10N	C6
900	SMWD	60120	2856	29W-10N	C6
1200	BmdT	60143	2914	21W-6N	A6
1400	BmdT	60143	2913	21W-6N	E6
1400	ITSC	60143	2913	21W-6N	E6
1800	SMBG	60133	2912	25W-8N	A2
1900	CHCG	60618	2977	2W-5N	B1
1900	HRPK	60133	2912	25W-9N	A2
2700	CHCG	60618	2976	3W-4N	E2
3900	CHCG	60641	2976	5W-4N	A2
4600	CHCG	60641	2975	7W-4N	B2
5500	CHCG	60634	2975	6W-5N	C2
6600	CHCG	60634	2974	8W-4N	D2
7100	NRDG	60634	2974	8W-5N	D2
7100	NRDG	60706	2974	8W-5N	D2
7300	CHCG	60706	2974	9W-4N	D2
SR-19 N Recreation Dr					
-	CHCG	60613	2978	0W-4N	A1
SR-21					
-	VrnT	60061	2647	15W-25N	E6
-	WrnT	60031	2478	15W-35N	B5
10	VNHL	60061	2648	15W-24N	A7
10	VrnT	60061	2648	15W-24N	A7
100	LNSH	60061	2702	15W-23N	A2
100	LNSH	60069	2702	15W-23N	A1
100	LYVL	60048	2591	16W-29N	D4
100	MTWA	60048	2647	15W-25N	E6
100	VNHL	60061	2647	15W-25N	E5
100	VNHL	60061	2702	15W-24N	A1
100	VNHL	60069	2702	15W-23N	A2
100	VrnT	60061	2702	15W-24N	A1
300	GRNE	60031	2535	15W-34N	A1
300	VrnT	60069	2702	15W-23N	A2
500	GRNE	60031	2478	14W-35N	B5
500	MaiT	60016	2809	10W-13N	E7
500	MaiT	60025	2809	10W-13N	E7
500	NfdT	60016	2809	10W-13N	E7
500	NfdT	60025	2809	11W-13N	E7
500	PTHT	60062	2809	13W-15N	A1
500	PTHT	60070	2809	13W-15N	A1
500	PTHT	60090	2809	13W-15N	A1
500	WhlT	60062	2809	13W-15N	A1
500	WhlT	60090	2809	13W-15N	A1
500	WLNG	60090	2755	13W-16N	E6
600	WhlT	60090	2755	13W-17N	E5
700	GNVW	60025	2809	11W-13N	D6
700	GRNE	60031	2534	16W-31N	C7
800	BFGV	60090	2755	14W-20N	C2
900	BFGV	60089	2755	14W-20N	C1
900	VrnT	60015	2755	14W-20N	C1
900	VrnT	60062	2755	14W-20N	C1
900	VrnT	60089	2755	14W-20N	C1
1000	BFGV	60089	2702	14W-20N	B7
1000	LYVL	60048	2647	15W-25N	E5
1000	PTHT	60070	2755	13W-16N	E7
1000	PTHT	60070	2808	13W-16N	E1
1000	RVWD	60015	2702	14W-20N	B7
1000	RVWD	60015	2755	14W-20N	C1
1000	VrnT	60015	2702	14W-20N	B7
1000	WhlT	60090	2808	13W-16N	E1
1400	LNSH	60015	2702	14W-21N	B6
1600	GNVW	60062	2809	12W-14N	C4
1600	VNHL	60048	2647	16W-26N	E2
1700	LbvT	60048	2591	16W-30N	D2
1800	NfdT	60062	2809	12W-14N	C4
7500	CHCG	60631	2864	9W-9N	D7
7500	CHCG	60714	2864	9W-9N	D7
7500	NLES	60631	2864	9W-9N	D7
7500	NLES	60714	2864	9W-9N	D6
8300	MaiT	60714	2864	9W-10N	C5
9500	MaiT	60016	2864	10W-11N	A2
9600	GNVW	60025	2864	10W-12N	A1
9600	MaiT	60025	2864	10W-12N	A1
9600	NLES	60025	2864	10W-12N	A1
9700	GNVW	60025	2863	10W-12N	E1
9700	MaiT	60025	2863	10W-12N	E1
9800	MaiT	60016	2863	10W-12N	E1
31000	LbvT	60048	2534	16W-31N	C7
31400	WKGN	60048	2534	16W-31N	D6
32000	GRNE	60048	2534	16W-32N	D6
32200	WrnT	60048	2534	16W-32N	D5
SR-21 Milwaukee Av					
-	LYVL	60048	2647	16W-26N	E3
-	VNHL	60061	2647	16W-26N	E3
100	LNSH	60061	2702	15W-23N	A2
100	LNSH	60069	2702	15W-23N	A1
100	VNHL	60061	2702	15W-23N	A2
100	VNHL	60069	2702	15W-23N	A2
200	VrnT	60061	2702	15W-23N	A2
300	VrnT	60069	2702	15W-23N	A2
500	MaiT	60016	2809	10W-13N	E7
500	MaiT	60025	2809	10W-13N	E7
500	NfdT	60016	2809	10W-13N	E7
500	NfdT	60025	2809	11W-13N	E7
700	GNVW	60025	2809	11W-13N	D6
900	BFGV	60089	2755	14W-20N	C1
900	VrnT	60015	2755	14W-20N	C1
900	VrnT	60062	2755	14W-20N	C1
900	VrnT	60089	2755	14W-20N	C1
1000	BFGV	60089	2702	14W-20N	B7
1000	RVWD	60015	2702	14W-20N	B7
1000	RVWD	60015	2755	14W-20N	C1
1000	VrnT	60015	2702	14W-20N	B7
1400	LNSH	60015	2702	14W-21N	B6
1600	GNVW	60062	2809	12W-14N	C4
1800	NfdT	60062	2809	12W-14N	C4
2800	PTHT	60062	2809	12W-15N	A2
2800	PTHT	60070	2809	12W-15N	A2
9700	GNVW	60025	2863	10W-12N	E1
9700	GNVW	60025	2864	10W-12N	A1
9700	MaiT	60016	2864	10W-12N	A1
9700	MaiT	60025	2863	10W-12N	E1
9700	MaiT	60025	2864	10W-12N	A1
9700	MaiT	60714	2864	10W-12N	A1
9700	NLES	60025	2864	10W-12N	A1
9700	NLES	60714	2864	10W-12N	A1
9800	MaiT	60016	2863	10W-12N	E1
20400	BFGV	60090	2755	14W-20N	C1
SR-21 N Milwaukee Av					
-	NfdT	60062	2809	12W-15N	A2
-	VrnT	60061	2647	15W-25N	E6
10	VNHL	60061	2648	15W-24N	A7
10	VrnT	60061	2648	15W-24N	A7
100	LYVL	60048	2591	16W-29N	D4
100	MTWA	60048	2647	15W-25N	E6
100	VNHL	60061	2647	15W-25N	E6
500	PTHT	60062	2809	13W-15N	A1
500	PTHT	60070	2809	13W-15N	A1
500	PTHT	60090	2809	13W-15N	A1
500	WhlT	60062	2809	13W-15N	A1
500	WhlT	60090	2809	13W-15N	A1
500	WLNG	60090	2755	13W-16N	E6
800	BFGV	60090	2755	14W-20N	C2
900	BFGV	60089	2755	14W-20N	C1
900	VrnT	60062	2755	14W-20N	C1
900	VrnT	60089	2755	14W-20N	C1
1700	LbvT	60048	2591	16W-30N	D2
7500	CHCG	60631	2864	9W-9N	D7
7500	CHCG	60714	2864	9W-9N	D7
7500	NLES	60631	2864	9W-9N	D7
7500	NLES	60714	2864	9W-9N	D6
8300	MaiT	60714	2864	9W-10N	C5
9500	MaiT	60016	2864	10W-11N	A2
9600	GNVW	60025	2864	10W-12N	A1
9600	MaiT	60025	2864	10W-12N	A1
9600	NLES	60025	2864	10W-12N	A1
21800	LNSH	60069	2702	15W-21N	B5
21800	VrnT	60069	2702	14W-21N	B5
31000	LbvT	60048	2534	16W-31N	C7
31400	WKGN	60048	2534	16W-31N	D6
32200	WrnT	60048	2534	16W-32N	D5
32700	GRNE	60048	2534	16W-32N	E5
SR-21 S Milwaukee Av					
10	WLNG	60090	2755	14W-18N	D4
100	LYVL	60048	2591	16W-28N	D5
100	VNHL	60061	2648	15W-24N	A7
100	VNHL	60061	2702	15W-24N	A1
100	VrnT	60061	2648	15W-24N	A7
100	VrnT	60061	2702	15W-24N	A1
600	WhlT	60090	2755	13W-17N	E5
1000	LYVL	60048	2647	15W-25N	E5
1000	PTHT	60070	2755	13W-16N	E7
1000	PTHT	60070	2808	13W-16N	E1
1000	PTHT	60070	2809	13W-16N	A1
1000	PTHT	60090	2809	13W-16N	A1
1000	WhlT	60090	2808	13W-16N	E1
1000	WhlT	60090	2809	13W-16N	A1
1200	VNHL	60061	2647	15W-25N	E5
1600	VNHL	60048	2647	16W-26N	E2
SR-21 N Riverside Dr					
-	WrnT	60031	2478	15W-35N	B5
300	GRNE	60031	2535	15W-34N	B1
500	GRNE	60031	2478	15W-35N	B5
SR-21 S Riverside Dr					
-	GRNE	60031	2535	15W-34N	A1
-	GRNE	60048	2534	16W-33N	E4
700	GRNE	60031	2534	16W-31N	C7
SR-22					
-	CbaT	60010	2696	29W-22N	C3
-	CbaT	60010	2697	26W-22N	D4
-	CbaT	60010	2698	25W-22N	A4
-	ElaT	60047	2700	18W-22N	D3
-	KLDR	60047	2700	18W-22N	D3
-	LGGV	60047	2700	18W-23N	D3
-	LGGV	60089	2701	17W-23N	B3
-	LKBN	60010	2696	29W-22N	C3
-	LKBN	60010	2697	28W-22N	A3
-	NBRN	60010	2697	26W-22N	D4
-	VrnT	60089	2701	16W-22N	D3
10	LNSH	60045	2702	14W-23N	C2
10	LNSH	60069	2702	13W-23N	E2
10	VrnT	60069	2702	13W-23N	E2
100	BFGV	60069	2701	16W-22N	C3
100	BFGV	60089	2701	16W-22N	C3
100	VrnT	60069	2701	16W-22N	C3
200	LKZH	60047	2699	23W-23N	A3
400	LNSH	60069	2701	15W-22N	E3
500	LKZH	60047	2698	24W-22N	D4
700	ElaT	60047	2699	22W-22N	B3
800	HDPK	60035	2703	11W-23N	E3
800	WdfT	60015	2703	11W-23N	D3
1000	FRGV	60010	2696	29W-22N	D3
1000	FRGV	60021	2696	29W-22N	C3
1000	LKZH	60010	2698	24W-22N	C4
1100	BKBN	60015	2703	11W-23N	D3
1300	HDPK	60035	2704	10W-23N	A3
2200	VrnT	60015	2703	13W-23N	A2
2300	LNSH	60069	2703	12W-23N	B3
2300	VrnT	60069	2703	12W-23N	B3
5500	BFGV	60047	2701	17W-23N	A3
5500	LGGV	60047	2701	17W-22N	A3
21400	KLDR	60047	2699	22W-22N	B3
23100	ElaT	60010	2698	24W-22N	B4
23100	ElaT	60047	2698	24W-22N	B4
23100	NBRN	60010	2698	25W-22N	B4
SR-22 BYP					
300	LKZH	60047	2698	23W-22N	E4
SR-22 Half Day Rd					
10	LNSH	60045	2702	14W-23N	C2
10	LNSH	60069	2702	14W-23N	C2
10	VrnT	60069	2702	13W-23N	D2
800	HDPK	60035	2703	11W-23N	E3
800	WdfT	60015	2703	11W-23N	D3
1100	BKBN	60015	2703	11W-23N	D3
1300	HDPK	60035	2704	10W-23N	A3
2200	VrnT	60015	2703	13W-23N	A2
2300	LNSH	60069	2703	12W-23N	B3
2300	VrnT	60069	2703	12W-23N	B3
SR-22 W Half Day Rd					
-	LGGV	60089	2701	17W-23N	B3
-	VrnT	60089	2701	16W-22N	D3
10	LNSH	60069	2702	13W-23N	E2
100	BFGV	60069	2701	16W-22N	C3
100	BFGV	60089	2701	16W-22N	C3
100	VrnT	60069	2701	16W-22N	C3
400	LNSH	60069	2701	15W-22N	E3
5500	BFGV	60047	2701	17W-23N	A3
5500	LGGV	60047	2701	17W-22N	A3
14400	LNSH	60045	2702	14W-23N	C2
14500	VrnT	60069	2702	13W-23N	E2
SR-22 Main St					
21400	KLDR	60047	2699	21W-23N	D3
21500	ElaT	60047	2699	21W-23N	D3
SR-22 W Main St					
-	LKZH	60047	2698	24W-22N	C4
SR-23					
-	HRVD	60033	2464	50W-35N	A5
-	MngT	60152	2578	50W-28N	B5
100	MRGO	60152	2634	49W-25N	B3
1100	RlyT	60152	2634	50W-25N	B3
1400	MRGO	60152	2578	50W-27N	B7
2000	DhmT	60033	2464	50W-35N	A5
SR-23 N State St					
-	MngT	60152	2578	50W-27N	B7
100	MRGO	60152	2634	50W-25N	B3
1400	MRGO	60152	2578	50W-27N	B7
SR-23 S State St					
100	MRGO	60152	2634	50W-26N	B2
1100	RlyT	60152	2634	50W-25N	B3
SR-25					
10	AURA	60505	3138	35W-7S	B7
10	AURA	60505	3200	35W-8S	A1
10	BTVA	60510	3078	35W-1S	C1
10	CPVL	60110	2748	33W-19N	C2
10	CPVL	60110	2801	33W-16N	C2
10	EDND	60110	2801	33W-16N	C2
10	EDND	60118	2801	33W-16N	C2
10	ELGN	60120	2855	33W-11N	B4
10	GNVA	60134	3020	34W-1N	C3
10	NARA	60542	3078	36W-4S	A7
10	NARA	60542	3138	35W-4S	A1
10	OSWG	60543	3263	37W-12S	C2
10	SchT	60120	2908	34W-6N	D7
10	SchT	60120	2909	33W-7N	A5
10	SchT	60174	2964	34W-6N	D1
10	SCRL	60174	2964	35W-5N	C1
100	AURA	60542	3138	35W-4S	A1
100	BNHL	60110	2748	32W-19N	C2
200	AURA	60504	3138	35W-4S	A1
200	EDND	60110	2748	33W-17N	C7
200	NARA	60504	3138	35W-4S	A1
200	SchT	60174	2908	34W-6N	D7
300	BtvT	60510	3078	35W-2S	C4
300	WYNE	60174	2964	35W-5N	C2
400	BRLT	60120	2909	33W-9N	B1
400	BRLT	60177	2909	33W-9N	B1
400	ElgT	60120	2909	33W-9N	B1
400	ElgT	60177	2909	33W-9N	B2
400	SchT	60103	2909	33W-7N	A5
400	SchT	60177	2909	33W-7N	A5
400	SEGN	60120	2909	33W-9N	B1
400	SEGN	60177	2909	33W-9N	B1
500	BRLT	60103	2909	33W-7N	B4
500	NARA	60510	3078	36W-3S	A6
500	OswT	60538	3199	37W-10S	C7
500	OswT	60538	3263	37W-11S	C1
500	OswT	60543	3199	37W-10S	C7
500	OswT	60543	3263	37W-12S	C2
600	DndT	60118	2801	33W-14N	C6
600	SEGN	60103	2909	33W-8N	B3
700	AURA	60505	3199	36W-9S	E3
800	BTVA	60510	3020	35W-0S	C7
800	MTGY	60505	3199	36W-8S	E3
800	MTGY	60538	3199	36W-8S	E3
800	SCRL	60134	3020	34W-1N	C2
800	SCRL	60174	3020	35W-0N	C5
900	AURA	60506	3138	35W-6S	B4
900	ElgT	60120	2855	33W-9N	B7
900	ElgT	60177	2855	33W-9N	B7
1200	GNVA	60510	3020	35W-0S	C6
1300	ELGN	60120	2801	33W-14N	C6
1500	DndT	60120	2801	33W-14N	C6
1500	ELGN	60118	2801	33W-14N	C6
1900	DndT	60110	2748	32W-19N	C2
2100	ALGN	60102	2748	32W-19N	C2
2100	ALGN	60110	2748	32W-19N	C2
2100	BNHL	60010	2748	32W-19N	C2
2100	BNHL	60102	2748	32W-19N	C2
SR-25 N 5th Av					
10	SCRL	60174	2964	35W-3N	B7
SR-25 S 5th Av					
10	SCRL	60174	2964	35W-3N	B7
SR-25 Aurora Av					
700	AURA	60505	3138	35W-6S	C5
900	AURA	60504	3138	35W-6S	B4
900	AURA	60506	3138	35W-6S	B4
1100	AURA	60542	3138	35W-5S	B4
SR-25 N Bennett St					
10	GNVA	60134	3020	34W-1N	C3
800	SCRL	60134	3020	34W-1N	C2
800	SCRL	60174	3020	34W-1N	C2
SR-25 S Bennett St					
10	GNVA	60134	3020	34W-1N	C4
SR-25 Bluff City Blvd					
500	ELGN	60120	2855	33W-10N	B6
SR-25 N Broadway					
10	AURA	60505	3138	35W-7S	B7

STREET Block	City	ZIP	Map#	CGS	Grid
SR-25 S Broadway					
10	AURA	60505	3138	35W-7S	B7
10	AURA	60505	3200	35W-8S	A1
700	AURA	60505	3199	36W-9S	E3
800	MTGY	60505	3199	36W-8S	E3
800	MTGY	60538	3199	36W-8S	E3
SR-25 S Broadway Rd					
1000	AURA	60505	3199	36W-8S	E3
1000	MTGY	60505	3199	36W-8S	E3
1000	MTGY	60538	3199	36W-9S	E3
SR-25 Crissey Av					
-	BTVA	60510	3020	35W-0S	C6
-	GNVA	60510	3020	35W-0S	C6
200	GNVA	60134	3020	34W-1N	C4
SR-25 Dundee Av					
10	CPVL	60110	2801	33W-16N	C2
10	EDND	60110	2801	33W-16N	C2
10	EDND	60118	2801	33W-16N	C2
600	DndT	60118	2801	33W-14N	C6
1100	ELGN	60120	2855	33W-12N	B1
1300	ELGN	60120	2801	33W-14N	C6
1500	DndT	60120	2801	33W-14N	C6
1500	ELGN	60118	2801	33W-14N	C6
SR-25 Elgin Rd					
1600	BNHL	60110	2748	33W-19N	C2
1600	CPVL	60110	2748	33W-19N	C2
1900	DndT	60110	2748	32W-19N	C2
2100	ALGN	60102	2748	32W-19N	C2
2100	ALGN	60110	2748	32W-19N	C2
2100	BNHL	60010	2748	32W-19N	C2
2100	BNHL	60102	2748	32W-19N	C2
SR-25 JFK Memorial Dr					
-	EDND	60118	2801	33W-16N	C1
10	CPVL	60110	2748	33W-17N	C6
200	EDND	60110	2748	33W-17N	C7
800	CPVL	60110	2801	33W-16N	C1
800	EDND	60110	2801	33W-16N	C1
SR-25 N Kennedy Dr					
10	CPVL	60110	2748	33W-17N	C6
100	BNHL	60110	2748	33W-18N	C4
SR-25 N Liberty St					
10	ELGN	60120	2855	33W-11N	B4
SR-25 S Liberty St					
10	ELGN	60120	2855	33W-11N	B4
SR-25 N Madison St					
10	OSWG	60543	3263	37W-12S	C3
SR-25 N River Rd					
10	NARA	60542	3078	36W-4S	A7
500	NARA	60510	3078	36W-3S	A6
SR-25 S River Rd					
10	NARA	60542	3138	35W-4S	A1
100	AURA	60542	3138	35W-4S	A1
200	AURA	60504	3138	35W-4S	A1
200	NARA	60504	3138	35W-4S	A1
SR-25 SE River Rd					
1300	MTGY	60538	3199	36W-9S	D4
1800	OswT	60538	3199	37W-10S	D5
SR-25 S River St					
10	BTVA	60510	3078	35W-1S	C2
300	BtvT	60510	3078	35W-2S	C4
2000	NARA	60510	3078	35W-3S	A5
2500	NARA	60542	3078	36W-3S	A6
SR-25 Riverside Av					
900	SCRL	60174	3020	35W-0N	C5
1800	GNVA	60134	3020	34W-2N	C2
1800	SCRL	60134	3020	34W-2N	C2
SR-25 St. Charles St					
800	ELGN	60120	2855	33W-10N	B6
900	ElgT	60120	2855	33W-9N	B7
900	ElgT	60177	2855	33W-9N	B7
1100	ElgT	60120	2909	33W-9N	B1
1100	ElgT	60177	2909	33W-9N	B1
SR-25 N Washington Av					
10	BTVA	60510	3078	35W-1S	C1
800	BTVA	60510	3020	35W-0S	C7
1200	GNVA	60134	3020	35W-0S	C6
1200	GNVA	60510	3020	35W-0S	C6
SR-25 E Wilson St					
100	BTVA	60510	3078	35W-1S	C2
SR-31					
-	ALGN	60013	2694	33W-22N	E3
-	AlqT	60013	2694	33W-22N	E3
-	AlqT	60014	2640	33W-26N	E3
-	AlqT	60014	2694	33W-23N	E1
-	CLLK	60012	2584	33W-30N	E2
-	CLLK	60012	2640	33W-27N	E1
-	CLLK	60013	2694	33W-23N	E1
-	CLLK	60014	2694	33W-24N	E1
-	CRY	60013	2694	33W-23N	E2
-	CRY	60014	2694	33W-23N	E3
-	DndT	60118	2800	34W-15N	E4
-	LIHL	60013	2694	33W-22N	E4
-	LIHL	60014	2694	33W-23N	E2
-	LIHL	60102	2694	33W-23N	E1
-	LIHL	60156	2694	33W-22N	E3
-	MHRY	60050	2584	33W-30N	E2
-	NndT	60012	2584	33W-30N	E2
-	NndT	60012	2640	33W-27N	E1
-	NndT	60014	2640	33W-26N	E3
-	NndT	60050	2584	33W-28N	E5
-	PRGV	60012	2584	33W-28N	E5
-	PRGV	60050	2584	33W-29N	E3
10	ALGN	60102	2694	33W-23N	E1
10	AURA	60506	3138	36W-7S	A7
10	BTVA	60510	3078	35W-0S	B1
10	CLLK	60014	2640	33W-24N	E7
10	CPVL	60110	2800	34W-15N	E4
10	CPVL	60118	2800	34W-15N	E4
10	DndT	60118	2747	34W-19N	D4
10	ELGN	60123	2854	34W-9N	E7
10	GNVA	60134	3020	35W-1N	C3
10	NARA	60542	3077	36W-4S	E7
10	NARA	60542	3137	36W-4S	E1
10	SchT	60174	2964	35W-5N	B1
10	SchT	60175	2964	35W-5N	B1
10	SchT	60177	2908	34W-7N	C5
10	SCRL	60174	2964	35W-3N	B7
10	SCRL	60175	2964	35W-5N	B1
10	SEGN	60177	2908	34W-7N	D4
100	AURA	60506	3200	36W-7S	A1
100	CPVL	60110	2747	35W-17N	C6
100	MHRY	60050	2528	32W-32N	A5
100	MTGY	60538	3199	37W-8S	D3
100	MTGY	60543	3199	37W-10S	B6
100	NARA	60542	3138	35W-5S	A4
100	WDND	60110	2800	34W-15N	E4
100	WDND	60118	2800	34W-15N	E4
200	AURA	60542	3138	35W-5S	A4
200	BtvT	60510	3077	36W-3S	E6
200	BtvT	60510	3078	36W-3S	A6
200	BtvT	60539	3077	36W-3S	E6
200	BtvT	60539	3078	36W-3S	A6
200	BtvT	60542	3077	36W-3S	E6
200	SchT	60175	2908	35W-6N	A7
200	SCRL	60175	2908	35W-6N	A7
300	AURA	60506	3199	37W-8S	D3
SR-31					
400	NndT	60050	2528	32W-31N	A7
400	SEGN	60175	2908	35W-7N	B5
500	BTVA	60510	3020	35W-0S	B7
500	SCRL	60174	3020	35W-1N	C2
600	BTVA	60134	3020	35W-0S	B7
700	SEGN	60123	2854	34W-9N	E7
1000	AlqT	60102	2694	33W-23N	E1
1000	MHRY	60050	2585	33W-30N	A1
1000	MTGY	60506	3199	37W-8S	D3
1000	NndT	60050	2585	33W-30N	A1
1100	AraT	60506	3199	37W-8S	D3
1100	ELGN	60123	2800	34W-13N	D7
1300	MTGY	60543	3263	37W-11S	B2
1400	ALGN	60102	2747	34W-20N	D1
1400	DndT	60102	2747	34W-20N	D1
1500	ELGN	60177	2854	34W-9N	E7
1500	ELGN	60177	2908	34W-9N	D1
1500	SEGN	60123	2854	34W-9N	E7
1700	DndT	60123	2800	34W-14N	E6
1700	WDND	60123	2800	34W-14N	E6
1900	MchT	60050	2528	32W-33N	B2
1900	OSWG	60543	3263	37W-11S	B2
2500	JNBG	60050	2528	32W-34N	B1
2700	JNBG	60050	2471	32W-35N	B6
2700	MchT	60050	2471	32W-34N	B7
3900	JNBG	60072	2471	32W-35N	A5
3900	MchT	60072	2471	32W-35N	A5
4100	RGWD	60072	2470	33W-36N	E4
4100	RGWD	60072	2471	33W-36N	A4
4400	MchT	60072	2470	33W-36N	E4
5700	RcmT	60072	2470	33W-36N	E4
6200	RcmT	60072	2412	34W-38N	D7
6600	RcmT	60071	2412	34W-38N	D6
7800	RHMD	60071	2412	34W-40N	C3
10400	PTPR	53158	2362		A4
12600	NptT	53158	2362		A4
12600	NptT	60099	2362		A4
SR-31 N 1st St					
10	GNVA	60134	3020	35W-1N	C3
500	SCRL	60174	3020	35W-2N	C2
SR-31 S 1st St					
10	GNVA	60134	3020	35W-1N	C3
SR-31 N 2nd St					
10	SCRL	60174	2964	35W-3N	B7
2700	SchT	60174	2964	35W-5N	B1
2700	SCRL	60175	2964	35W-5N	B1
SR-31 S 2nd St					
10	SCRL	60174	2964	35W-3N	B7
SR-31 N 8th St					
100	WDND	60118	2800	34W-15N	E4
400	CPVL	60110	2800	34W-15N	E4
400	CPVL	60118	2800	34W-15N	E4
400	WDND	60110	2800	34W-15N	E4
SR-31 S 8th St					
-	DndT	60118	2800	34W-15N	E4
100	WDND	60118	2800	34W-16N	E2
SR-31 N Batavia Av					
10	BTVA	60510	3078	35W-0S	B1
500	BTVA	60510	3020	35W-0S	B7
600	BTVA	60134	3020	35W-0S	B7
600	GNVA	60134	3020	35W-0S	B7
SR-31 S Batavia Av					
10	BTVA	60510	3078	35W-1S	B2
200	BtvT	60510	3077	36W-3S	E6
200	BtvT	60510	3078	36W-3S	A6
200	BtvT	60539	3077	36W-3S	E6
200	BtvT	60539	3078	36W-3S	A6
200	BtvT	60542	3077	36W-3S	E6
600	GNVA	60134	3020	35W-0N	B4
SR-31 W Elm St					
3600	MHRY	60050	2528	32W-33N	B3
SR-31 N Front St					
100	MHRY	60050	2528	32W-32N	A5
SR-31 S Front St					
100	MHRY	60050	2528	32W-31N	A6
400	NndT	60050	2528	32W-31N	A7
1000	MHRY	60050	2585	33W-30N	A1
1000	NndT	60050	2585	33W-30N	A1
SR-31 Gale St					
100	AURA	60506	3200	36W-7S	A1
SR-31 Geneva Rd					
600	SCRL	60174	2964	35W-2N	B7
600	SCRL	60174	3020	35W-1N	C2
1300	GNVA	60134	3020	35W-2N	C2
SR-31 Green Bay Rd					
10400	PTPR	53158	2362		A4
12600	NptT	53158	2362		A4
12600	NptT	60099	2362		A4
SR-31 N La Fox St					
10	SEGN	60177	2908	34W-7N	D4
1500	ELGN	60123	2854	34W-9N	E7
1500	ELGN	60177	2854	34W-9N	E7
1500	ELGN	60177	2908	34W-9N	D1
1500	SEGN	60123	2854	34W-9N	E7
1500	SEGN	60177	2854	34W-9N	E7
SR-31 S La Fox St					
10	SEGN	60177	2908	34W-8N	D3
400	SchT	60177	2908	34W-7N	D4
SR-31 N Lake St					
10	AURA	60506	3138	35W-7S	A7
1300	AURA	60542	3138	36W-5S	A3
1300	NARA	60542	3138	36W-5S	A3
SR-31 S Lake St					
10	AURA	60506	3138	35W-7S	A7
100	MTGY	60538	3199	37W-8S	D3
100	MTGY	60543	3199	37W-10S	B6
200	AURA	60506	3200	36W-7S	A1
300	AURA	60506	3199	37W-8S	D3
1000	MTGY	60506	3199	37W-8S	D3
1100	AraT	60506	3199	37W-8S	D3
SR-31 N Lincoln Hwy					
-	NARA	60542	3137	36W-4S	E1
SR-31 N Lincolnway					
10	NARA	60542	3077	36W-4S	E7
10	NARA	60542	3137	36W-4S	E1
200	BtvT	60510	3077	36W-3S	E6
200	BtvT	60539	3077	36W-3S	E6
200	BtvT	60542	3077	36W-3S	E6
SR-31 S Lincolnway					
10	NARA	60542	3137	36W-4S	E1
100	NARA	60542	3138	35W-5S	A4
200	AURA	60542	3138	35W-5S	A4
400	AURA	60506	3138	35W-5S	A4
SR-31 N Main St					
10	ALGN	60102	2694	33W-20N	D7
1000	AlqT	60102	2694	33W-21N	E6
SR-31 S Main St					
10	ALGN	60102	2694	33W-20N	D7
1400	ALGN	60102	2747	34W-20N	D1
1400	DndT	60102	2747	34W-20N	D1
1500	DndT	60118	2747	34W-19N	D2
SR-31 W New York St					
100	AURA	60506	3138	36W-7S	A7
SR-31 Precision Plz					
10	CLLK	60014	2640	33W-24N	E7
SR-31 Richmond Rd					
4100	JNBG	60050	2471	33W-35N	A5
4100	JNBG	60072	2471	33W-35N	A5
4100	MchT	60072	2471	33W-35N	A5
4100	RGWD	60072	2470	33W-36N	E4
4100	RGWD	60072	2471	33W-36N	A4
4400	MchT	60072	2470	33W-36N	E4
5700	RcmT	60072	2470	33W-36N	E4
6200	RcmT	60072	2412	34W-38N	D7
6600	RcmT	60071	2412	34W-38N	D6
SR-31 N Richmond Rd					
1300	MHRY	60050	2528	32W-34N	B1
1900	MchT	60050	2528	32W-33N	B2
2500	JNBG	60050	2528	32W-34N	B1
2700	JNBG	60050	2471	32W-35N	B6
2700	MchT	60050	2471	32W-34N	B7
3900	JNBG	60072	2471	32W-35N	A5
3900	MchT	60072	2471	32W-35N	A5
SR-31 N River St					
10	AURA	60506	3138	35W-7S	A7
SR-31 S River St					
10	AURA	60506	3138	35W-7S	A7
100	AURA	60506	3200	36W-7S	A1
SR-31 N State St					
10	ELGN	60123	2854	34W-9N	E7
1100	ELGN	60123	2800	34W-13N	D7
1700	DndT	60123	2800	34W-14N	E6
1700	WDND	60118	2800	34W-14N	E6
1700	WDND	60123	2800	34W-14N	E6
SR-31 S State St					
10	ELGN	60123	2854	34W-11N	E4
700	SEGN	60123	2854	34W-9N	E7
2100	WDND	60118	2800	34W-14N	E6
SR-31 N Western Av					
-	DndT	60118	2747	35W-17N	C6
10	CPVL	60110	2800	34W-16N	D1
100	CPVL	60110	2747	35W-17N	D7
SR-31 S Western Av					
10	CPVL	60110	2800	34W-16N	D1
10	CPVL	60118	2800	34W-16N	D1
100	WDND	60110	2800	34W-16N	E2
100	WDND	60118	2800	34W-16N	E2
SR-32					
10400	PTPR	53158	2363		C3
12700	WPHR	53158	2363		C4
12700	WPHR	60096	2363		C4
SR-32 Sheridan Rd					
10400	PTPR	53158	2363		C3
12700	WPHR	53158	2363		C4
12700	WPHR	60096	2363		C4
SR-38					
-	CmpT	60151	3017	43W-2N	A1
-	ELBN	60151	3017	43W-2N	A1
-	EMHT	60126	3027	17W-1S	B7
-	EMHT	60126	3028	15W-1S	B7
-	EMHT	60181	3027	17W-1S	B7
-	EMHT	60523	3027	16W-1S	E7
-	EMHT	60523	3028	15W-1S	A7
-	OKBK	60126	3028	15W-1S	A7
-	OKBK	60181	3027	16W-1S	E7
-	OKBK	60523	3027	16W-1S	E7
-	OKBK	60523	3028	15W-1S	A7
-	OKTR	60126	3027	17W-1S	B7
-	YkTp	60126	3028	15W-1S	B7
-	YkTp	60523	3028	14W-1S	B7
10	CmpT	60119	3017	43W-2N	A1
10	CmpT	60119	3018	39W-2N	E1
10	CmpT	60175	3018	39W-2N	E1
10	ELBN	60119	3017	43W-2N	B1
10	GNVA	60134	3020	36W-1N	A3
10	GnvT	60134	3021	32W-0N	C4
10	GnvT	60185	3021	32W-0N	C4
10	LMBD	60148	3026	18W-0S	E7
10	OKTR	60181	3027	17W-1S	B7
10	SCRL	60119	3018	39W-2N	E1
10	SCRL	60175	3018	39W-2N	E1
10	WCHI	60185	3021	33W-0N	B4
10	WCHI	60185	3022	30W-0S	A6
10	WHTN	60187	3081	27W-1S	C1
10	WHTN	60190	3081	27W-1S	D1
10	WNFD	60187	3081	27W-1S	D1
10	WNFD	60190	3081	27W-1S	D1
10	WnfT	60185	3022	29W-0S	E7
10	WnfT	60187	3081	27W-1S	D1
10	WnfT	60190	3022	28W-0S	E7
10	WnfT	60190	3081	27W-1S	D1
10	YkTp	60148	3026	18W-0S	E7
100	WHTN	60187	3024	23W-0S	E7
100	WHTN	60187	3082	25W-1S	A1
200	GNEN	60137	3025	23W-1S	A7
200	GNEN	60187	3025	23W-0S	A7
200	SchT	60175	3019	37W-2N	C1
200	SCRL	60175	3019	37W-2N	D1
200	WHTN	60187	3025	23W-0S	A7
300	VLPK	60181	3027	17W-1S	C7
300	YkTp	60148	3027	18W-0S	A7
300	YkTp	60181	3027	18W-0S	A7
400	GNEN	60137	3026	20W-0S	A7
400	GNEN	60148	3026	20W-0S	A7
400	WnfT	60510	3022	30W-0S	B6
600	GNVA	60134	3021	32W-0N	C4
600	GNVA	60185	3021	32W-0N	C4
600	WCHI	60510	3022	30W-0S	B6
600	WnfT	60190	3080	28W-0S	E1
700	GNEN	60148	3025	23W-1S	A7
700	MltT	60148	3025	23W-1S	A7
700	MltT	60148	3026	20W-0S	A7
900	MltT	60137	3025	21W-1S	E7
1200	GnvT	60134	3020	33W-1N	E4
1400	SCRL	60174	3019	36W-2N	E2
1600	MltT	60187	3082	25W-1S	A1
1700	GNVA	60134	3019	36W-2N	E2
1800	WHTN	60137	3025	23W-0S	A7
1900	MltT	60187	3081	27W-1S	C1
1900	SCRL	60134	3019	36W-1N	E2
4000	HLSD	60162	3029	13W-1S	A7
4000	PvsT	60162	3029	13W-1S	A7
4000	WSTR	60154	3029	13W-0S	A7
4000	WSTR	60162	3029	13W-0S	A7
4300	HLSD	60162	3028	14W-1S	D7
4300	PvsT	60162	3028	14W-1S	D7
4400	HLSD	60154	3028	13W-0S	E7
4400	WSTR	60154	3028	13W-0S	E7
4400	WSTR	60162	3028	13W-0S	E7
11900	PvsT	60126	3028	15W-1S	B7
SR-38 Lincoln Hwy					
-	SchT	60175	3019	38W-2N	B1
10	CmpT	60119	3018	39W-2N	E1
10	CmpT	60175	3018	39W-2N	E1
10	SCRL	60119	3018	39W-2N	E1
10	SCRL	60175	3018	39W-2N	E1
1400	SCRL	60174	3019	36W-2N	E2
3800	SCRL	60175	3019	38W-2N	A1
SR-38 Roosevelt Rd					
-	EMHT	60126	3027	17W-1S	B7
-	EMHT	60126	3028	15W-1S	B7
SR-38 Roosevelt Rd					
-	EMHT	60181	3027	17W-1S	B7
-	EMHT	60523	3027	16W-1S	E7
-	EMHT	60523	3028	15W-1S	A7
-	HLSD	60154	3028	13W-0S	D7
-	OKBK	60126	3028	15W-1S	A7
-	OKBK	60181	3027	16W-1S	E7
-	OKBK	60523	3028	15W-1S	A7
-	OKTR	60126	3027	17W-1S	B7
-	WHTN	60137	3025	23W-0S	A7
-	WSTR	60162	3028	13W-0S	D7
-	YkTp	60126	3028	15W-1S	B7
-	YkTp	60523	3028	14W-1S	B7
10	GnvT	60134	3021	33W-0N	B4
10	GnvT	60185	3021	33W-0N	B4
10	WCHI	60185	3021	33W-0N	B4
10	WCHI	60185	3022	29W-0S	E7
10	WHTN	60187	3081	27W-1S	D1
10	WHTN	60190	3081	27W-1S	D1
10	WNFD	60187	3081	27W-1S	D1
10	WNFD	60190	3081	27W-1S	D1
10	WnfT	60185	3022	29W-0S	E7
10	WnfT	60187	3081	27W-1S	D1
10	WnfT	60190	3022	28W-0S	E7
10	WnfT	60190	3081	27W-1S	D1
100	YkTp	60181	3027	17W-1S	C7
200	GNEN	60137	3025	21W-1S	E7
200	GNEN	60187	3025	23W-0S	A7
200	OKTR	60181	3027	17W-1S	B7
200	VLPK	60181	3027	17W-1S	C7
200	WHTN	60187	3025	23W-0S	A7
600	WnfT	60190	3080	28W-0S	E1
900	MltT	60137	3025	21W-1S	E7
1000	GNEN	60148	3025	21W-0S	E7
1000	MltT	60148	3025	21W-0S	E7
4000	HLSD	60162	3029	13W-1S	A7
4000	PvsT	60162	3029	13W-1S	A7
4000	WSTR	60154	3029	13W-0S	A7
4000	WSTR	60162	3029	13W-0S	A7
4300	HLSD	60162	3028	14W-1S	D7
4300	PvsT	60162	3028	14W-1S	D7
4400	WSTR	60154	3028	13W-0S	E7
11900	PvsT	60126	3028	15W-1S	B7
SR-38 E Roosevelt Rd					
10	LMBD	60148	3026	18W-0S	E7
10	OKTR	60181	3027	17W-0S	B7
10	VLPK	60181	3027	17W-1S	C7
10	YkTp	60148	3026	18W-0S	E7
100	WCHI	60185	3022	29W-0S	C7
100	WHTN	60187	3024	23W-0S	E7
200	WnfT	60185	3022	29W-0S	C7
1600	WHTN	60187	3025	23W-0S	A7
1800	GNEN	60137	3025	23W-0S	A7
1800	GNEN	60187	3025	23W-0S	A7
1800	WHTN	60137	3025	23W-0S	A7
SR-38 W Roosevelt Rd					
-	GnvT	60134	3021	32W-0N	B4
-	GnvT	60185	3021	32W-0N	B4
-	MltT	60137	3025	21W-0S	E7
10	LMBD	60148	3026	20W-0S	B7
10	VLPK	60181	3027	18W-0S	A7
100	WCHI	60185	3022	30W-0S	A6
100	WHTN	60187	3082	25W-1S	A1
100	WnfT	60185	3022	30W-0S	C6
300	YkTp	60148	3027	18W-0S	A7
300	YkTp	60181	3027	18W-0S	A7
400	GNEN	60137	3026	20W-0S	A7
400	GNEN	60148	3026	20W-0S	A7
400	WnfT	60510	3022	30W-0S	B6
600	WCHI	60510	3022	30W-0S	B6
700	GNEN	60137	3025	23W-1S	A7
700	GNEN	60148	3025	23W-1S	A7
700	MltT	60148	3025	23W-1S	A7
700	MltT	60148	3026	20W-0S	A7
1200	WCHI	60185	3021	31W-0N	E5
1600	MltT	60187	3082	25W-1S	A1
1900	MltT	60187	3081	27W-1S	C1
1900	WHTN	60187	3081	27W-1S	C1
2100	WHTN	60190	3081	26W-1S	D1
2100	WNFD	60190	3081	26W-1S	D1
2100	WnfT	60187	3081	26W-1S	D1
2100	WnfT	60190	3081	26W-1S	D1
10900	HLSD	60154	3028	13W-0S	E7
10900	HLSD	60162	3028	13W-0S	E7
10900	WSTR	60154	3028	13W-0S	E7
10900	WSTR	60162	3028	13W-0S	E7
SR-38 E State St					
10	GNVA	60134	3020	35W-1N	C3
600	GNVA	60134	3021	32W-0N	C4
600	GNVA	60185	3021	32W-0N	C4
600	GnvT	60134	3021	32W-0N	C4
600	GnvT	60185	3021	32W-0N	C4
1200	GnvT	60134	3020	33W-1N	E4
SR-38 W State St					
10	GNVA	60134	3020	36W-1N	A3
1700	GNVA	60134	3019	36W-2N	E2
1900	SCRL	60134	3019	36W-1N	E2
1900	SCRL	60174	3019	36W-1N	E2
SR-43					
-	BGVW	60453	3210	8W-10S	E6
-	FTVW	60534	3148	9W-5S	E1
-	NCHI	60044	2592	13W-30N	E1
-	OKLN	60415	3210	8W-11S	E6
-	OKLN	60453	3210	8W-11S	E6
-	OKLN	60455	3210	8W-11S	E6
-	PKCY	60085	2535	13W-33N	E4
-	PlsT	60463	3346	9W-16S	E2
-	SMMT	60534	3148	8W-5S	E2
-	TYPK	60423	3505	8W-23S	A3
10	DRFD	60015	2757	10W-20N	A2
10	DRFD	60062	2757	10W-20N	A2
10	FTPK	60130	3030	8W-0N	D4
10	FTPK	60302	3030	9W-0N	D5
10	FTPK	60304	3030	9W-0N	D5
10	GNVW	60025	2864	8W-12N	E1
10	GNVW	60053	2864	8W-12N	E2
10	LKBF	60044	2593	12W-28N	B6
10	LKFT	60044	2593	12W-28N	B6
10	LKFT	60045	2593	12W-28N	B6
10	LKFT	60045	2649	12W-25N	B6
10	MNGV	60025	2864	8W-12N	E1
10	MNGV	60053	2864	8W-10N	E4
10	NfdT	60062	2757	10W-18N	A2
10	OKPK	60130	3030	8W-0N	D4
10	OKPK	60302	3030	8W-0N	D6
10	OKPK	60304	3030	9W-0N	D5
10	ShdT	60044	2593	12W-28N	B5
100	GNVW	60025	2810	8W-13N	E6
100	GNVW	60093	2810	8W-15N	E3
100	NHFD	60025	2810	8W-15N	E3
100	NHFD	60093	2810	8W-15N	E2
300	NHBK	60062	2810	8W-15N	E2
400	OKPK	60301	3030	8W-0N	D4
400	OKPK	60305	3030	9W-0S	D6
400	RVFT	60301	3030	8W-0N	D4
SR-43					
400	RVFT	60302	3030	9W-0S	D6
400	RVFT	60305	3030	9W-0S	D6
600	DRFD	60015	2703	11W-21N	E6
600	DRFD	60015	2756	10W-20N	E1
600	NHBK	60062	2757	9W-18N	B4
700	LbvT	60044	2593	13W-29N	A3
700	NCHI	60044	2593	13W-30N	A2
800	WKGN	60085	2535	13W-33N	E4
1000	WrnT	60085	2535	13W-32N	E4
1100	BRWN	60130	3030	8W-0S	D7
1100	BRWN	60304	3030	8W-0S	D7
1100	BRWN	60402	3030	8W-0S	D7
1200	LKFT	60045	2703	11W-23N	C2
1200	NCHI	60064	2593	13W-30N	A2
1300	LbvT	60044	2592	13W-30N	E1
1300	LbvT	60064	2592	13W-30N	E2
1500	BRWN	60130	3088	9W-1S	D1
1500	BRWN	60402	3088	9W-1S	D1
1500	CHCG	60302	3030	8W-1N	D1
1500	CHCG	60707	3030	8W-1N	D1
1500	EDPK	60707	3030	8W-1N	D1
1500	FTPK	60130	3088	8W-1S	D1
1500	NRIV	60130	3088	9W-1S	D1
1500	RVFT	60707	3030	8W-1N	D1
1600	BKBN	60015	2703	11W-23N	C2
1600	BKBN	60045	2703	11W-23N	C2
1600	WdfT	60015	2703	11W-23N	C2
1600	WdfT	60045	2703	11W-23N	C2
1700	CHCG	60707	2974	8W-2N	D7
1700	EDPK	60707	2974	8W-2N	D7
1700	LKBF	60045	2593	12W-28N	B7
2100	BRWN	60546	3088	9W-1S	D2
2100	LbvT	60044	2535	13W-31N	E7
2100	NHFD	60062	2810	8W-16N	E1
2100	NRIV	60546	3088	9W-1S	D2
2500	RVSD	60546	3088	9W-2S	D3
2700	CHCG	60634	2974	8W-3N	D5
2800	RVSD	60402	3088	9W-2S	D3
3600	LYNS	60402	3088	8W-3S	E5
3600	LYNS	60534	3088	8W-3S	E5
3600	LYNS	60546	3088	8W-3S	E5
3800	SKNY	60402	3088	8W-3S	E6
3900	NRDG	60634	2974	9W-3N	D5
3900	NRDG	60706	2974	9W-3N	D5
4200	SKNY	60534	3088	8W-4S	E7
4400	FTVW	60402	3088	8W-4S	E7
4400	FTVW	60534	3088	8W-4S	E7
4400	HDHT	60706	2918	8W-5N	D7
4400	NRDG	60706	2918	8W-5N	D7
4600	FTVW	60402	3148	9W-5S	E1
4600	LYNS	60534	3148	8W-4S	E1
4700	CHCG	60656	2918	8W-6N	D7
4700	CHCG	60706	2918	8W-6N	D7
4700	HDHT	60656	2918	8W-6N	D7
5100	CHCG	60402	3148	9W-5S	E1
5100	CHCG	60501	3148	9W-5S	E1
5100	CHCG	60638	3148	9W-5S	E1
5100	FTVW	60501	3148	9W-5S	E1
5300	SMMT	60501	3148	8W-6S	E4
5600	CHCG	60631	2918	8W-6N	D6
6300	BDPK	60501	3148	8W-7S	E5
6300	BDPK	60638	3148	8W-7S	E5
6500	CHCG	60714	2918	9W-6N	D6
6500	NLES	60714	2918	9W-6N	D6
6700	BGVW	60455	3148	9W-7S	E6
6700	BGVW	60501	3148	9W-7S	E6
6700	BGVW	60638	3148	9W-7S	E6
6800	BDPK	60455	3148	9W-7S	E7
7000	NLES	60714	2864	8W-10N	E5
7200	CHCG	60631	2864	8W-9N	D7
7200	CHCG	60714	2864	8W-9N	D7
7300	BDPK	60638	3210	8W-8S	E1
7300	BGVW	60455	3210	8W-8S	E1
7300	BGVW	60638	3210	8W-8S	E1
7500	NLES	60631	2864	8W-9N	D7
7700	BGVW	60459	3210	8W-8S	E2
7700	BRBK	60455	3210	8W-8S	E2
7700	BRBK	60459	3210	8W-8S	E2
8300	MNGV	60714	2864	8W-10N	E5
9800	BGVW	60415	3210	8W-11S	E7
9800	CHRG	60415	3210	8W-11S	E7
9900	CHRG	60455	3210	8W-11S	E7
10100	BGVW	60415	3274	8W-11S	E1
10100	BGVW	60455	3274	8W-11S	E1
10100	CHRG	60415	3274	8W-15S	E7
10100	PSHL	60415	3274	8W-11S	E1
10100	PSHL	60455	3274	8W-11S	E1
10100	PSHL	60465	3274	8W-11S	E1
10400	WRTH	60415	3274	9W-15S	E7
10400	WRTH	60482	3274	9W-15S	E7
10500	CHRG	60482	3274	9W-15S	E7
11600	PSHT	60463	3274	8W-13S	E5
11600	WRTH	60463	3274	8W-13S	E5
12800	PSHT	60463	3346	9W-16S	E2
12900	WthT	60463	3346	9W-16S	E2
13500	BmnT	60445	3346	8W-17S	E6
13500	BmnT	60462	3346	9W-17S	E6
13500	OrlT	60462	3346	9W-16S	E2
13500	WthT	60445	3346	9W-16S	E2
13500	WthT	60462	3346	9W-16S	E2
14100	BmnT	60452	3346	9W-17S	E4
14100	OrlT	60445	3346	9W-16S	E4
14100	OrlT	60452	3346	9W-16S	E4
15100	ODPK	60462	3346	9W-18S	E6
15300	OKFT	60462	3346	9W-18S	E7
15700	ODPK	60462	3424	9W-18S	E1
15800	TYPK	60477	3424	9W-19S	E1
16300	OrlT	60477	3424	9W-19S	E2
18200	TYPK	60477	3425	8W-21S	A7
19300	FftT	60477	3505	9W-23S	A3
19300	TYPK	60477	3505	8W-23S	A3
19700	FftT	60423	3505	9W-24S	A6
19700	MTSN	60443	3505	8W-23S	A3
19700	RchT	60423	3505	9W-24S	A6
20600	FKFT	60423	3505	8W-25S	A7
20600	RchT	60443	3505	8W-25S	A7
21500	FKFT	60423	3593	9W-27S	A5
21500	RchT	60443	3593	9W-27S	A5
22400	FKFT	60443	3593	8W-27S	A5
29500	LbvT	60064	2593	13W-29N	A4
SR-43 Harlem Av					
-	CHCG	60402	3148	8W-5S	E2
-	CHCG	60501	3148	8W-5S	E2
-	CHCG	60638	3148	8W-5S	E2
-	FftT	60477	3505	9W-23S	A2
-	FTVW	60402	3148	9W-5S	E1
-	FTVW	60501	3148	8W-5S	E2
-	LYNS	60534	3148	9W-5S	E1
-	SMMT	60501	3148	9W-5S	E2
-	SMMT	60534	3148	9W-5S	E2
-	TYPK	60477	3505	8W-22S	A1
1100	BRWN	60130	3030	8W-0S	D7
1100	BRWN	60304	3030	8W-0S	D7
1100	BRWN	60402	3030	8W-0S	D7
1100	FTPK	60130	3030	8W-0S	D7

STREET Block	City	ZIP	Map#	CGS	Grid
SR-43 Harlem Av					
1100	OKPK	60130	3030	8W-0S	D7
1100	OKPK	60304	3030	8W-0S	D7
1500	BRWN	60130	3088	9W-1S	D1
1500	BRWN	60402	3088	9W-1S	D1
1500	FTPK	60130	3088	8W-1S	D1
1500	NRIV	60130	3088	9W-1S	D1
2100	BRWN	60546	3088	9W-1S	D2
2100	NRIV	60546	3088	9W-1S	D2
2500	RVSD	60546	3088	9W-2S	D3
2800	RVSD	60402	3088	9W-2S	D3
3600	LYNS	60402	3088	8W-3S	E5
3600	LYNS	60534	3088	8W-3S	E5
3600	LYNS	60546	3088	8W-3S	E5
3800	SKNY	60402	3088	8W-3S	E6
4200	SKNY	60534	3088	8W-4S	E7
4400	FTVW	60402	3088	8W-4S	E7
4400	FTVW	60534	3088	8W-4S	E7
4600	FTVW	60534	3148	8W-4S	E1
15900	ODPK	60462	3424	9W-19S	E1
15900	TYPK	60477	3424	9W-19S	E2
16300	OrlT	60477	3424	8W-19S	E2
18200	TYPK	60477	3425	8W-21S	A7
SR-43 N Harlem Av					
10	FTPK	60130	3030	8W-0N	D4
10	FTPK	60302	3030	9W-0N	D5
10	FTPK	60304	3030	9W-0N	D5
10	OKPK	60130	3030	8W-0N	D4
10	OKPK	60302	3030	9W-0S	D6
10	OKPK	60304	3030	9W-0N	D5
400	OKPK	60301	3030	8W-0N	D4
400	OKPK	60305	3030	9W-0S	D6
400	RVFT	60301	3030	8W-0N	D4
400	RVFT	60302	3030	9W-0S	D6
400	RVFT	60305	3030	9W-0S	D6
1500	CHCG	60302	3030	8W-1N	D1
1500	CHCG	60707	3030	8W-1N	D1
1500	EDPK	60707	3030	8W-1N	D1
1500	RVFT	60707	3030	8W-1N	D1
1700	CHCG	60707	2974	8W-2N	D7
1700	EDPK	60707	2974	8W-2N	D7
2700	CHCG	60634	2974	9W-3N	D5
3900	NRDG	60634	2974	9W-3N	D5
3900	NRDG	60706	2974	9W-3N	D5
4400	HDHT	60706	2918	8W-5N	D7
4400	NRDG	60706	2918	8W-5N	D7
4700	CHCG	60656	2918	8W-6N	D7
4700	CHCG	60706	2918	8W-6N	D7
4700	HDHT	60656	2918	8W-6N	D7
5600	CHCG	60631	2918	9W-6N	D6
6500	CHCG	60714	2918	9W-6N	D6
6500	NLES	60714	2918	9W-6N	D6
7200	CHCG	60631	2864	8W-9N	D7
7200	CHCG	60714	2864	8W-9N	D7
7200	NLES	60714	2864	8W-9N	D7
7500	NLES	60631	2864	8W-9N	D7
SR-43 S Harlem Av					
-	BGVW	60453	3210	8W-10S	E6
-	FftT	60477	3505	9W-23S	A3
-	OKLN	60415	3210	8W-11S	E6
-	OKLN	60453	3210	8W-11S	E6
-	OKLN	60455	3210	8W-11S	E6
-	PlsT	60463	3346	9W-16S	E2
-	SMMT	60534	3148	9W-5S	E2
-	TYPK	60423	3505	8W-23S	A3
-	TYPK	60477	3505	8W-23S	A3
10	FTPK	60130	3030	9W-0S	D5
10	FTPK	60302	3030	9W-0S	D5
10	FTPK	60304	3030	9W-0S	D5
10	OKPK	60302	3030	9W-0S	D5
10	OKPK	60304	3030	9W-0S	D5
700	OKPK	60130	3030	9W-0S	D6
5100	CHCG	60402	3148	9W-5S	E1
5100	CHCG	60501	3148	9W-5S	E1
5100	CHCG	60638	3148	9W-5S	E1
5100	FTVW	60402	3148	9W-5S	E1
5100	FTVW	60501	3148	9W-5S	E1
5100	SMMT	60501	3148	9W-5S	E1
6300	BDPK	60501	3148	8W-7S	E5
6300	BDPK	60638	3148	8W-7S	E5
6700	BGVW	60455	3148	9W-7S	E6
6700	BGVW	60501	3148	9W-7S	E6
6700	BGVW	60638	3148	9W-7S	E6
6800	BDPK	60455	3148	9W-7S	E7
7300	BDPK	60638	3210	8W-8S	E1
7300	BGVW	60455	3210	9W-8S	E1
7300	BGVW	60638	3210	9W-8S	E1
7700	BGVW	60459	3210	8W-8S	E2
7700	BRBK	60455	3210	8W-8S	E2
7700	BRBK	60459	3210	8W-8S	E2
9800	BGVW	60415	3210	8W-11S	E7
9800	CHRG	60415	3210	8W-11S	E7
9900	CHRG	60455	3210	8W-11S	E7
10100	BGVW	60415	3274	8W-11S	E1
10100	BGVW	60455	3274	8W-11S	E1
10100	CHRG	60415	3274	9W-15S	E7
10100	PSHL	60415	3274	8W-11S	E1
10100	PSHL	60455	3274	8W-11S	E1
10100	PSHL	60465	3274	8W-11S	E1
10400	WRTH	60415	3274	9W-15S	E7
10400	WRTH	60482	3274	9W-15S	E7
10500	CHRG	60482	3274	9W-15S	E7
11600	PSHT	60463	3274	8W-13S	E5
11600	WRTH	60463	3274	8W-13S	E5
12800	PSHT	60463	3346	9W-16S	E2
13500	BmnT	60445	3346	9W-17S	E6
13500	BmnT	60462	3346	9W-16S	E2
13500	WthT	60445	3346	9W-17S	E6
13500	WthT	60462	3346	9W-16S	E2
13500	WthT	60463	3346	9W-17S	E6
13700	OrlT	60462	3346	8W-16S	E3
14100	BmnT	60452	3346	8W-16S	E4
14100	OrlT	60445	3346	8W-16S	E4
14100	OrlT	60452	3346	9W-17S	E4
15100	ODPK	60462	3346	9W-18S	E6
15200	OKFT	60462	3346	9W-18S	E6
15700	ODPK	60462	3424	9W-18S	E1
15800	TYPK	60477	3424	9W-18S	E1
19700	FftT	60423	3505	9W-24S	A6
19700	MTSN	60443	3505	9W-24S	A6
19700	RchT	60423	3505	9W-24S	A6
20600	FKFT	60423	3505	8W-25S	A7
20600	RchT	60423	3505	8W-25S	A7
21500	FKFT	60423	3593	9W-27S	A5
21500	RchT	60443	3593	9W-27S	A5
22400	FKFT	60443	3593	9W-27S	A5
SR-43 W Oakton St					
7000	NLES	60714	2864	8W-10N	E5
SR-43 Waukegan Rd					
-	LbvT	60044	2535	13W-31N	E7
-	WKGN	60085	2535	13W-31N	E7
10	DRFD	60015	2757	10W-20N	A2
10	DRFD	60062	2757	10W-20N	A2
10	GNVW	60025	2864	8W-12N	E1
10	GNVW	60053	2864	8W-12N	E2
10	MNGV	60025	2864	8W-12N	E1
10	MNGV	60053	2864	8W-10N	E4
100	GNVW	60025	2810	8W-13N	E6
100	GNVW	60093	2810	8W-15N	E3
100	NHFD	60025	2810	8W-15N	E3
100	NHFD	60093	2810	8W-15N	E2
300	NHBK	60062	2810	8W-15N	E2
400	NfdT	60062	2757	10W-18N	B3
600	DRFD	60015	2703	11W-21N	E6
600	DRFD	60015	2756	10W-20N	E1
600	NHBK	60062	2757	9W-18N	B4
1300	LbvT	60044	2592	13W-30N	E1
1300	LbvT	60064	2592	13W-30N	E2
1300	NCHI	60044	2592	13W-30N	E2
1600	BKBN	60015	2703	11W-22N	D5
2100	NHFD	60062	2810	8W-16N	E1
2100	WdfT	60015	2703	11W-23N	C3
8400	MNGV	60714	2864	8W-10N	E4
8400	NLES	60714	2864	8W-10N	E4
SR-43 N Waukegan Rd					
10	LKBF	60044	2593	12W-28N	B6
10	LKFT	60044	2593	12W-28N	B6
10	LKFT	60045	2593	12W-28N	B6
10	LKFT	60045	2649	12W-25N	B6
10	ShdT	60044	2593	12W-28N	B5
700	LbvT	60044	2593	13W-29N	A3
700	NCHI	60044	2593	13W-30N	A2
1200	NCHI	60064	2593	13W-30N	A2
1700	LKBF	60045	2593	12W-28N	B7
8000	NLES	60714	2864	8W-10N	E5
8300	MNGV	60053	2864	8W-10N	E5
8300	MNGV	60714	2864	8W-10N	E5
29500	LbvT	60064	2593	13W-29N	A4
SR-43 S Waukegan Rd					
-	PKCY	60085	2535	13W-33N	E4
10	DRFD	60015	2757	10W-18N	A2
10	DRFD	60062	2757	10W-18N	A2
10	LKFT	60045	2649	12W-25N	C4
10	NfdT	60062	2757	10W-18N	A2
800	WKGN	60085	2535	13W-33N	E4
1000	WrnT	60085	2535	13W-32N	E4
1200	LKFT	60045	2703	11W-23N	C2
1600	BKBN	60015	2703	11W-23N	C2
1600	BKBN	60045	2703	11W-23N	C2
1600	WdfT	60015	2703	11W-23N	C2
1600	WdfT	60045	2703	11W-23N	C2
2100	LbvT	60044	2535	13W-31N	E7
SR-47					
-	BRkT	60554	3135	42W-7S	C7
-	BRkT	60554	3197	42W-7S	C1
-	CLLK	60098	2638	40W-26N	A3
-	DrrT	60098	2638	40W-26N	A4
-	DrrT	60142	2638	40W-26N	A3
-	GfnT	60098	2638	40W-26N	A4
-	GfnT	60142	2638	40W-25N	A4
-	GfnT	60142	2692	40W-23N	A1
-	HTLY	60140	2744	41W-17N	E6
-	HTLY	60142	2638	40W-24N	A7
-	HTLY	60142	2744	42W-18N	E5
-	LIHL	60142	2692	40W-23N	A1
-	LKWD	60142	2638	40W-25N	A5
-	RtdT	60140	2744	42W-17N	E6
-	RtdT	60142	2744	42W-18N	E5
-	YKVL	60512	3197	42W-10S	C7
10	ELBN	60119	3017	43W-2N	A1
10	PGGV	60140	2797	43W-14N	B5
10	PltT	60124	2851	43W-10N	B6
10	PltT	60124	2905	43W-8N	B3
10	PltT	60151	2905	43W-8N	A3
10	RtdT	60140	2797	43W-13N	B7
10	SgrT	60506	3197	42W-10S	C7
10	SgrT	60554	3197	42W-10S	C7
10	SRGV	60554	3197	42W-8S	C2
10	WDSK	60098	2524	41W-31N	D3
100	BbyT	60119	3075	43W-3S	A6
100	SgrT	60554	3075	43W-4S	B7
100	YKVL	60560	3333	43W-16S	C4
200	CmpT	60151	2961	43W-3N	A7
200	PltT	60140	2797	43W-13N	B7
200	PltT	60140	2851	43W-12N	B1
200	SgrT	60554	3135	42W-7S	C7
200	SRGV	60554	3135	42W-7S	C7
200	WDSK	60098	2581	40W-30N	E2
300	BbyT	60119	3017	43W-0S	A7
600	CmpT	60119	3017	43W-2N	A1
600	CmpT	60151	3017	43W-2N	A1
600	ELBN	60151	2961	43W-2N	A7
600	ELBN	60151	3017	43W-2N	A1
800	BtlT	60512	3197	42W-10S	C7
900	BbyT	60554	3075	43W-3S	A5
1100	YKVL	60560	3261	42W-14S	C7
1200	BtlT	60560	3261	42W-14S	C7
1300	KdlT	60560	3333	43W-16S	C4
2000	BtlT	60512	3261	42W-14S	C7
2000	YKVL	60512	3261	42W-14S	C7
2000	YKVL	60545	3261	42W-14S	C7
2100	GwdT	60098	2524	41W-33N	D4
2800	DrrT	60098	2581	40W-29N	E5
9600	HBRN	60034	2350	41W-41N	E7
10300	HbnT	60034	2350	41W-42N	E6
10400	HTLY	60142	2692	40W-21N	A5
10800	HTLY	60142	2691	40W-20N	E7
11500	HbnT	53147	2350	41W-42N	E6
11500	LinT	53147	2350	41W-42N	E6
SR-47 N Bridge St					
100	YKVL	60560	3333	42W-15S	C2
1100	YKVL	60560	3261	42W-14S	C7
1200	BtlT	60560	3261	42W-14S	C7
2400	YKVL	60512	3261	42W-13S	C5
2600	BtlT	60512	3261	42W-12S	C3
SR-47 S Bridge St					
100	YKVL	60560	3333	43W-16S	C4
1300	KdlT	60560	3333	43W-16S	C4
SR-47 N Eastwood Dr					
10	WDSK	60098	2524	41W-31N	E7
SR-47 S Eastwood Dr					
10	WDSK	60098	2524	41W-31N	E7
200	WDSK	60098	2581	40W-30N	E2
2800	DrrT	60098	2581	40W-29N	E5
SR-47 Main St					
-	HbnT	60034	2350	41W-42N	E6
9600	HBRN	60034	2350	41W-41N	E7
SR-47 N Main St					
100	ELBN	60119	3017	44W-1N	A3
600	CmpT	60119	3017	43W-2N	A1
600	CmpT	60151	3017	43W-2N	A1
600	ELBN	60151	3017	43W-2N	A1
SR-47 S Main St					
10	ELBN	60119	3017	44W-1N	A3
100	BbyT	60119	3017	44W-1N	A3
SR-47 N Seminary Av					
600	WDSK	60098	2524	41W-33N	D3
2100	GwdT	60098	2524	41W-33N	D4
SR-47 Vine St					
10400	HTLY	60142	2692	40W-21N	A5
10800	HTLY	60142	2691	40W-21N	E6
SR-50					
-	CTWD	60803	3348	5W-15S	A1
-	LNHT	60046	2418	19W-38N	C6
-	MonT	60466	3683	6W-29S	B2
-	PtnT	60468	3860	9W-38S	E6
-	PTON	60468	3860	9W-38S	E6
-	UYPK	60466	3683	6W-29S	B2
10	CHCG	60644	3031	5W-0N	E5
100	PTON	60468	3861	9W-37S	A2
100	WlIT	60468	3861	9W-37S	A2
300	PtnT	60468	3861	8W-37S	A2
700	CHCG	60651	3031	5W-1N	E2
800	CHCG	60644	3032	5W-0S	A6
1000	CCRO	60804	3032	5W-0S	A7
1000	CHCG	60804	3032	5W-0S	A7
1500	CCRO	60804	3090	5W-1S	A1
1500	CHCG	60639	3031	5W-1N	E1
1600	CHCG	60639	2975	5W-2N	E7
2700	CHCG	60641	2975	5W-5N	E1
3400	SKNY	60804	3090	5W-3S	A5
3500	GRNE	60031	2477	16W-36N	E3
3700	CCRO	60632	3090	5W-3S	A6
3700	CHCG	60632	3090	5W-3S	A6
3700	CHCG	60804	3090	5W-3S	A6
4200	CHCG	60638	3090	6W-4S	A7
4300	CHCG	60630	2975	5W-5N	E1
4400	CHCG	60630	2919	5W-5N	E7
4600	CHCG	60632	3150	5W-6S	A3
4600	CHCG	60638	3150	5W-6S	A3
5600	CHCG	60646	2919	6W-7N	E4
6100	CHCG	60629	3150	6W-7S	A6
6300	CHCG	60712	2919	6W-7N	E3
6300	LNWD	60712	2919	6W-6N	E5
6400	BDPK	60638	3150	5W-7S	A6
6700	BDPK	60629	3150	5W-7S	A7
7200	LNWD	60712	2865	6W-9N	E7
7300	SKOK	60077	2865	6W-9N	E7
7300	SKOK	60712	2865	6W-9N	E7
7400	BDPK	60638	3212	5W-8S	A1
7400	BRBK	60459	3212	5W-8S	A1
7400	CHCG	60629	3212	5W-8S	A1
7400	CHCG	60638	3212	5W-8S	A1
7400	CHCG	60652	3212	6W-8S	A1
7500	SKOK	60076	2865	5W-9N	E7
7700	CHCG	60459	3212	6W-8S	A1
8600	HMTN	60453	3212	6W-9S	A4
8600	HMTN	60456	3212	6W-9S	A4
8600	HMTN	60459	3212	6W-9S	A4
8600	HMTN	60652	3212	6W-9S	A4
8600	OKLN	60453	3212	6W-9S	A4
8600	OKLN	60459	3212	6W-9S	A4
8900	OKLN	60456	3212	6W-10S	A4
10200	OKLN	60453	3276	5W-13S	A3
11000	ALSP	60453	3276	5W-12S	A3
11000	ALSP	60655	3276	5W-12S	A3
11000	ALSP	60803	3276	5W-12S	A3
11000	CHCG	60453	3276	5W-12S	A3
11000	CHCG	60655	3276	5W-12S	A3
11100	CHCG	60803	3276	5W-13S	A4
13100	ALSP	60803	3348	5W-15S	A1
13100	CTWD	60445	3348	5W-15S	A1
13900	BmnT	60445	3348	5W-16S	A3
14300	MDLN	60445	3348	5W-18S	A7
14700	MDLN	60452	3348	6W-18S	A7
14800	OKFT	60452	3348	5W-17S	A5
14900	OKFT	60445	3348	5W-17S	A6
15700	BmnT	60426	3426	5W-21S	B7
15700	BmnT	60452	3426	6W-21S	B7
15700	OKFT	60426	3426	5W-18S	A1
15700	OKFT	60452	3426	6W-21S	B7
16700	BmnT	60477	3426	5W-20S	A3
17000	BmnT	60478	3426	6W-20S	B4
17000	CCHL	60477	3426	6W-20S	B4
17000	CCHL	60478	3426	6W-20S	B4
18400	CCHL	60478	3506	6W-25S	B7
18800	CCHL	60477	3506	5W-22S	B2
18800	RchT	60477	3506	5W-22S	B2
19900	MTSN	60443	3506	6W-24S	B4
19900	RchT	60443	3506	6W-24S	B4
21100	MTSN	60443	3594	6W-26S	B2
21900	RNPK	60471	3594	6W-26S	B2
22700	UYPK	60471	3594	6W-27S	B5
22900	UYPK	60449	3594	6W-27S	B5
23100	MonT	60449	3594	6W-28S	B7
24000	MonT	60449	3683	6W-31S	A5
25100	UYPK	60449	3683	6W-30S	A3
25300	MONE	60449	3683	6W-30S	A4
25600	MONE	60449	3682	7W-31S	E6
26200	MonT	60449	3682	7W-32S	E7
SR-50 Cicero Av					
-	ALSP	60803	3348	5W-15S	A1
-	CTWD	60803	3348	5W-15S	A1
13100	CTWD	60445	3348	5W-15S	A1
13900	BmnT	60445	3348	5W-16S	A3
14300	MDLN	60445	3348	6W-18S	A7
14700	MDLN	60452	3348	6W-18S	A7
14800	OKFT	60452	3348	5W-17S	A5
14900	OKFT	60445	3348	5W-17S	A6
15700	BmnT	60426	3426	6W-21S	B7
15700	BmnT	60452	3426	6W-21S	B7
15700	OKFT	60426	3426	5W-18S	A1
15700	OKFT	60452	3426	6W-21S	B7
16700	BmnT	60477	3426	5W-20S	A3
17000	BmnT	60478	3426	6W-20S	B4
17000	CCHL	60477	3426	6W-20S	B4
17000	CCHL	60478	3426	6W-20S	B4
18400	CCHL	60478	3506	6W-25S	B7
18800	CCHL	60477	3506	5W-22S	B2
18800	RchT	60477	3506	5W-22S	B2
19900	MTSN	60443	3506	6W-24S	B4
19900	RchT	60443	3506	6W-24S	B4
21100	MTSN	60443	3594	6W-26S	B2
21900	RNPK	60471	3594	6W-26S	B2
22700	UYPK	60471	3594	6W-27S	B5
22900	UYPK	60449	3594	6W-27S	B5
SR-50 N Cicero Av					
10	CHCG	60644	3031	5W-0N	E5
700	CHCG	60651	3031	6W-1N	E2
1500	CHCG	60639	3031	5W-1N	E1
1600	CHCG	60639	2975	5W-2N	E7
2700	CHCG	60641	2975	6W-5N	E1
4300	CHCG	60630	2975	5W-5N	E1
4400	CHCG	60630	2919	5W-5N	E7
5600	CHCG	60646	2919	6W-7N	E4
6300	CHCG	60712	2919	6W-7N	E3
6300	LNWD	60712	2919	6W-6N	E5
7200	LNWD	60712	2865	6W-9N	E7
7300	SKOK	60077	2865	6W-9N	E7
7300	SKOK	60712	2865	6W-9N	E7
SR-50 S Cicero Av					
-	CTWD	60445	3348	5W-15S	A1
-	CTWD	60803	3348	5W-15S	A1
-	MonT	60466	3683	6W-29S	B2
-	UYPK	60466	3683	6W-29S	B2
10	CHCG	60644	3031	5W-0S	E5
800	CHCG	60644	3032	5W-0S	A6
1000	CCRO	60804	3032	5W-0S	A7
1000	CHCG	60804	3032	5W-0S	A7
1500	CCRO	60804	3090	5W-1S	A1
3400	SKNY	60804	3090	5W-3S	A5
3700	CCRO	60632	3090	5W-3S	A6
3700	CHCG	60804	3090	5W-3S	A6
4200	CHCG	60632	3090	6W-4S	A7
4200	CHCG	60638	3090	5W-4S	A7
4600	CHCG	60632	3150	5W-6S	A3
4600	CHCG	60638	3150	5W-6S	A3
6100	CHCG	60629	3150	6W-7S	A6
6400	BDPK	60638	3150	6W-7S	A6
7100	BDPK	60629	3150	5W-8S	A7
7400	BDPK	60638	3212	5W-8S	A1
7400	BRBK	60459	3212	6W-8S	A1
7400	CHCG	60629	3212	5W-8S	A1
7400	CHCG	60638	3212	5W-8S	A1
7400	CHCG	60652	3212	6W-8S	A1
7700	CHCG	60459	3212	6W-8S	A1
8600	HMTN	60453	3212	6W-9S	A4
8600	HMTN	60456	3212	6W-9S	A4
8600	HMTN	60459	3212	6W-9S	A4
8600	HMTN	60652	3212	6W-9S	A4
8600	OKLN	60453	3212	6W-9S	A4
8600	OKLN	60459	3212	6W-9S	A4
8900	OKLN	60456	3212	6W-10S	A4
10200	OKLN	60453	3276	6W-13S	A3
11000	ALSP	60453	3276	5W-12S	A3
11000	ALSP	60655	3276	5W-12S	A3
11000	ALSP	60803	3276	5W-12S	A3
11000	CHCG	60453	3276	5W-12S	A3
11000	CHCG	60655	3276	5W-12S	A3
11100	CHCG	60803	3276	5W-13S	A4
13100	ALSP	60803	3348	5W-15S	A1
23100	MonT	60449	3594	6W-28S	B7
23100	RNPK	60471	3594	6W-28S	B5
23100	UYPK	60449	3594	6W-28S	B6
23100	UYPK	60471	3594	6W-28S	B5
24000	MonT	60449	3683	6W-31S	A5
SR-50 S Governors Hwy					
-	MonT	60466	3683	6W-29S	B2
-	UYPK	60466	3683	6W-29S	B2
400	PTON	60468	3861	9W-37S	A4
400	WlIT	60468	3861	9W-37S	A4
600	PtnT	60468	3861	9W-37S	A4
25100	MonT	60449	3683	6W-30S	A3
25100	UYPK	60449	3683	6W-30S	A3
25300	MONE	60449	3683	6W-30S	A4
25600	MONE	60449	3682	7W-31S	E6
26200	MonT	60449	3682	7W-32S	E7
SR-50 N Harlem Av					
100	PTON	60468	3861	9W-37S	A2
200	WlIT	60468	3861	9W-37S	A2
300	PtnT	60468	3861	9W-37S	A2
SR-50 S Harlem Av					
100	PTON	60468	3861	8W-37S	A3
100	WlIT	60468	3861	8W-37S	A3
SR-50 Hastings Ct					
3500	GRNE	60031	2477	16W-36N	E3
SR-50 Oxford Ln					
-	LNHT	60046	2418	19W-38N	C6
SR-50 Skokie Blvd					
7400	LNWD	60712	2865	6W-9N	E7
7400	SKOK	60077	2865	6W-9N	E7
7400	SKOK	60712	2865	6W-9N	E7
7500	SKOK	60076	2865	6W-9N	E7
SR-53					
-	ANHT	-	2753	18W-16N	D7
-	ANHT	-	2806	19W-15N	B2
-	BCVL	60407	4030	33W-44S	B3
-	BFGV	60047	2700	18W-21N	D6
-	BFGV	60089	2700	18W-21N	D6
-	BvlT	60407	4030	33W-43S	B3
-	CstT	60481	3942	30W-40S	D3
-	DRGV	60137	3083	22W-2S	D4
-	DRGV	60515	3083	22W-2S	D4
-	EGvT	-	2860	20W-12N	A1
-	EGvT	-	2914	20W-9N	A1
-	ELWD	60421	3675	25W-32S	C7
-	FrnT	60421	3763	27W-35S	E6
-	FrnT	60481	3763	27W-35S	E6
-	FrnT	60481	3853	26W-36S	E2
-	GDLY	60407	4030	33W-44S	B4
-	GNEN	60137	3083	22W-1S	D1
-	LGGV	60089	2700	18W-21N	D6
-	LSLE	60532	3083	23W-4S	A7
-	LslT	60517	3205	22W-8S	B1
-	LslT	60532	3083	23W-4S	B7
-	LslT	60540	3143	22W-7S	B7
-	LslT	60540	3205	22W-8S	B1
-	LslT	60565	3205	22W-8S	B1
-	MltT	60137	3083	22W-3S	C6
-	MltT	60515	3083	22W-2S	D4
-	MltT	60532	3083	22W-3S	B6
-	PLTN	-	2753	19W-17N	D5
-	PLTN	-	2806	19W-15N	C2
-	PltT	-	2753	18W-16N	D7
-	PltT	-	2806	20W-13N	A6
-	RedT	60408	4030	32W-42S	E1
-	RGMW	-	2806	19W-15N	B2
-	RGMW	-	2860	20W-12N	A1
-	SMBG	-	2806	20W-12N	A7
-	SMBG	-	2860	20W-12N	A1
-	WDRG	60517	3205	22W-8S	B1
-	WDRG	60565	3205	22W-8S	B1
-	WMTN	60481	3853	27W-36S	E2
-	WMTN	60481	3942	29W-39S	E2
-	WMTN	60481	3943	29W-39S	A1
-	WmTp	60481	3763	26W-35S	E7
-	WmTp	60481	3853	27W-36S	E2
-	WmTp	60481	3942	29W-39S	E2
-	WmTp	60481	3943	29W-39S	A1
10	ADSN	60101	2970	20W-4N	A4
10	BmdT	60101	2970	20W-4N	A4
10	BmdT	60143	2914	20W-6N	A7
10	GNEN	60137	3025	21W-0S	E7
10	ITSC	60143	2914	20W-6N	A7
10	JLET	60432	3498	24W-23S	E5
10	JLET	60432	3499	23W-23S	A4
10	JLET	60436	3498	24W-23S	E5
10	LktT	60446	3341	23W-16S	A4
10	LMBD	60148	3026	21W-0S	A6
10	RMVL	60441	3341	23W-17S	A6
10	RMVL	60446	3341	23W-16S	A4
100	AddT	60101	2970	20W-5N	A2
100	ADSN	60143	2970	20W-5N	A1
100	BDWD	60408	3942	31W-41S	B6
100	BGBK	60440	3269	22W-11S	B1
100	BmdT	60143	2970	21W-5N	A1
100	JLET	60435	3498	24W-23S	E3
200	JLET	60433	3499	23W-24S	A6
200	JLET	60436	3499	24W-24S	A6
200	RedT	60408	3942	31W-41S	B5
200	RedT	60481	3942	30W-40S	D3
300	BGBK	60440	3205	23W-11S	B7
300	DPgT	60441	3341	23W-15S	A3
300	DPgT	60446	3341	23W-15S	A3
300	MltT	60148	3026	21W-1N	A2
400	BmdT	60108	2970	20W-2N	A6
400	ITSC	60143	2970	21W-5N	A1
500	YkTp	60148	3026	21W-0N	A5
600	DPgT	60440	3205	22W-10S	B5
600	JltT	60436	3499	23W-25S	A7
700	ADSN	60148	2970	20W-2N	A7
700	RedT	60408	3941	32W-42S	E7
700	RMVL	60446	3269	23W-14S	B7
800	ADSN	60101	3026	20W-2N	A1
800	ADSN	60148	3026	21W-2N	A1
800	EGVV	60007	2914	20W-8N	A2
900	JLET	60433	3587	23W-25S	A1
900	JLET	60436	3587	24W-25S	A1
900	JltT	60433	3587	23W-26S	A2
900	JltT	60436	3587	24W-26S	A2
1000	AddT	60148	3026	20W-2N	A1
1000	ITSC	60007	2914	21W-8N	A3
1000	MltT	60148	3025	21W-0S	E7
1100	AddT	60143	2914	21W-7N	A4
1100	GNEN	60148	3025	21W-0S	E7
1100	LGGV	60047	2700	18W-21N	D6
1100	LMBD	60148	3025	21W-0S	E7
1600	CTHL	60403	3498	24W-21S	E1
1600	CTHL	60435	3498	24W-21S	E1
1600	LktT	60435	3498	24W-21S	E1
1700	CTHL	60403	3418	24W-21S	E7
1700	CTHL	60435	3418	24W-21S	E7
1800	LktT	60435	3418	24W-21S	E7
2000	CTHL	60441	3418	24W-21S	E6
2300	ElaT	60047	2753	20W-18N	A2
2300	ElaT	60074	2753	20W-18N	A2
2300	LGGV	60047	2753	20W-18N	A2
2300	LGGV	60074	2753	20W-18N	A2
2400	JLET	60421	3587	23W-27S	A6
3000	JknT	60421	3587	23W-28S	A6
4300	LSLE	60532	3143	23W-6S	B5
5400	LslT	60532	3143	23W-5S	A3
6100	WDRG	60517	3143	22W-6S	B5
6200	LslT	60517	3143	22W-6S	B5
14200	LktT	60441	3341	23W-17S	A6
15700	LktT	60441	3419	23W-18S	A1
15700	RMVL	60441	3419	23W-18S	A1
16200	CTHL	60441	3419	23W-19S	A2
17000	LktT	60441	3418	24W-20S	E5
20700	ElaT	60047	2700	20W-20N	B7
25600	JknT	60421	3675	24W-31S	D6
SR-53 EXT					
-	ANHT	-	2753	19W-18N	C3
-	ElaT	-	2753	19W-18N	C2
-	PLTN	-	2753	19W-18N	C3
-	PltT	-	2753	19W-18N	D3
SR-53 E Baltimore St					
100	WMTN	60481	3853	27W-38S	D6
SR-53 W Baltimore St					
200	WMTN	60481	3853	27W-38S	C7
SR-53 Biesterfield Rd					
1000	EGVV	60007	2914	21W-8N	A2
SR-53 Bolingbrook Dr					
-	BGBK	60440	3269	22W-13S	B6
-	RMVL	60446	3269	22W-13S	B6
SR-53 N Bolingbrook Dr					
-	LslT	60565	3205	22W-10S	C5
100	BGBK	60440	3269	23W-11S	B1
300	BGBK	60440	3205	23W-11S	B7
600	DPgT	60440	3205	22W-10S	B5
SR-53 S Bolingbrook Dr					
-	RMVL	60446	3269	23W-13S	B5
500	BGBK	60440	3269	23W-13S	B4
SR-53 Bridge St					
100	WMTN	60481	3853	28W-39S	C7
SR-53 Broadway St					
2100	CTHL	60403	3418	24W-21S	E6
2100	CTHL	60435	3418	24W-21S	E6
2100	CTHL	60441	3418	24W-21S	E6
2100	LktT	60435	3418	24W-21S	E6
15700	LktT	60441	3419	23W-18S	A1
15700	RMVL	60441	3419	23W-18S	A1
16200	CTHL	60441	3419	23W-19S	A2
17000	LktT	60441	3418	24W-20S	E5
SR-53 N Broadway St					
700	JLET	60435	3498	24W-23S	E3
1600	CTHL	60403	3498	24W-21S	E1
1600	CTHL	60435	3498	24W-21S	E1
1600	LktT	60435	3498	24W-21S	E1
1700	CTHL	60403	3418	24W-21S	E7
1700	CTHL	60435	3418	24W-21S	E7
1800	LktT	60435	3418	24W-21S	E7
2000	CTHL	60441	3418	24W-21S	E6
SR-53 Bryant Av					
10	GNEN	60137	3025	22W-0S	D7
SR-53 N Chicago St					
500	JLET	60432	3499	23W-23S	A3
SR-53 S Chicago St					
-	JknT	60421	3587	23W-28S	A7
-	JLET	60432	3499	23W-23S	A5
-	JLET	60436	3498	24W-24S	E5
200	JLET	60433	3499	24W-24S	A6
600	JLET	60436	3499	24W-24S	A7
600	JltT	60436	3499	23W-25S	A7
900	JLET	60433	3587	23W-25S	A1
900	JLET	60436	3587	23W-25S	A1
900	JltT	60433	3587	24W-26S	A2
900	JltT	60436	3587	24W-26S	A2
2400	JLET	60421	3587	23W-27S	A6
SR-53 E Columbia St					
10	JLET	60432	3499	23W-23S	A4
SR-53 N Columbine Av					
10	LMBD	60148	3026	21W-0N	A3
300	MltT	60148	3026	21W-1N	A2
SR-53 S Columbine Av					
10	LMBD	60148	3026	21W-0S	A6
500	MltT	60148	3026	21W-0N	A5
500	YkTp	60148	3026	21W-0N	A5
1000	MltT	60148	3025	21W-0S	E7
1100	GNEN	60137	3025	21W-0S	E7
1100	GNEN	60148	3025	21W-0S	E7
1100	LMBD	60148	3025	21W-0S	E7
SR-53 E Dundee Rd					
-	PltT	60004	2753	19W-18N	D4
900	PLTN	60074	2753	19W-18N	B4
1500	PltT	60074	2753	19W-18N	C4
SR-53 W Dundee Rd					
-	ANHT	60004	2753	19W-18N	D4
-	PltT	60004	2753	19W-18N	D4
-	PltT	60074	2753	19W-18N	D4
SR-53 Fairview Av					
-	GNEN	60137	3025	21W-0S	E7
-	GNEN	60148	3025	21W-0S	E7
-	LMBD	60148	3025	21W-0S	E7
-	MltT	60148	3025	21W-0S	E7
SR-53 N Front St					
100	BDWD	60408	3942	31W-41S	B5

STREET Block	City	ZIP	Map#	CGS	Grid
SR-53 N Front St					
200	RedT	60408	3942	31W-41S	B5
200	RedT	60481	3942	30W-41S	B5
SR-53 S Front St					
100	BDWD	60408	3942	31W-41S	B6
300	RedT	60408	3942	31W-41S	B6
700	RedT	60408	3941	32W-42S	E7
SR-53 Hicks Rd					
2700	ElaT	60047	2753	20W-20N	A2
2700	ElaT	60074	2753	20W-20N	A2
2700	LGGV	60047	2753	20W-20N	A2
2700	LGGV	60074	2753	20W-20N	A2
2700	PLTN	60074	2753	20W-20N	A2
20700	ElaT	60047	2700	20W-20N	B7
20700	LGGV	60047	2700	20W-21N	B7
SR-53 N Hicks Rd					
2100	PLTN	60074	2753	20W-20N	A2
2300	ElaT	60047	2753	20W-18N	A2
2300	ElaT	60074	2753	20W-18N	A2
2300	LGGV	60047	2753	20W-18N	A2
2300	LGGV	60074	2753	20W-18N	A2
SR-53 N Independence Blvd					
10	LktT	60446	3341	23W-16S	A4
10	RMVL	60441	3341	23W-16S	A5
10	RMVL	60446	3341	23W-16S	A4
300	DPgT	60441	3341	23W-15S	A3
300	DPgT	60446	3341	23W-15S	A3
700	RMVL	60446	3269	23W-14S	B7
SR-53 S Independence Blvd					
14200	LktT	60441	3341	23W-17S	A6
14200	RMVL	60441	3341	23W-17S	A6
14200	RMVL	60446	3341	23W-16S	A5
SR-53 W Jackson St					
10	JLET	60432	3498	24W-23S	E4
SR-53 Lincoln Av					
-	LSLE	60532	3083	23W-4S	A7
-	LslT	60532	3083	23W-4S	A7
4300	LSLE	60532	3143	23W-6S	B5
SR-53 Main St					
5200	LSLE	60532	3143	23W-5S	A3
5400	LslT	60532	3143	23W-5S	A3
SR-53 N Ottawa St					
10	JLET	60436	3498	24W-23S	E5
400	JLET	60432	3498	24W-23S	E5
SR-53 S Ottawa St					
10	JLET	60432	3498	24W-23S	E5
10	JLET	60436	3498	24W-24S	E5
SR-53 Rand Rd					
2000	PLTN	60074	2753	20W-18N	A3
SR-53 N Rand Rd					
1600	PLTN	60074	2753	19W-18N	B4
SR-53 Rohlwing Rd					
10	ADSN	60101	2970	20W-4N	A4
10	BmdT	60143	2914	20W-6N	A7
100	AddT	60101	2970	20W-5N	A2
100	ADSN	60143	2970	21W-5N	A1
100	BmdT	60101	2970	20W-5N	A2
100	BmdT	60143	2970	21W-5N	A1
400	ITSC	60143	2970	21W-5N	A1
800	EGVV	60007	2914	21W-8N	A2
1000	ITSC	60007	2914	21W-8N	A3
1000	ITSC	60143	2914	21W-8N	A3
1100	AddT	60143	2914	21W-7N	A4
SR-53 N Rohlwing Rd					
200	AddT	60101	2970	20W-4N	A3
200	ADSN	60101	2970	20W-4N	A3
200	BmdT	60143	2914	20W-6N	A6
200	ITSC	60143	2914	20W-6N	A6
500	BmdT	60148	2970	20W-2N	A7
600	BmdT	60101	2970	20W-4N	A3
700	ADSN	60148	2970	20W-2N	A7
800	ADSN	60101	3026	21W-2N	A1
800	ADSN	60148	3026	21W-2N	A1
800	LMBD	60148	3026	21W-2N	A1
1000	AddT	60148	3026	20W-2N	A1
1000	ADSN	60143	2970	20W-5N	A2
1000	BmdT	60143	2970	20W-5N	A2
SR-53 S Rohlwing Rd					
300	ADSN	60101	2970	20W-3N	A6
300	BmdT	60101	2970	20W-3N	A6
400	BmdT	60148	2970	20W-2N	A6
SR-53 W Ruby St					
100	JLET	60432	3498	24W-23S	E3
100	JLET	60435	3498	24W-23S	E3
SR-53 N Scott St					
10	JLET	60432	3499	23W-23S	A5
10	JLET	60433	3499	23W-23S	A5
SR-53 E Washington St					
10	JLET	60432	3499	23W-23S	A5
10	JLET	60433	3499	23W-23S	A5
10	JLET	60436	3499	23W-23S	A5
SR-56					
-	AURA	-	3136	38W-5S	E2
-	AURA	-	3137	38W-5S	A2
-	EMHT	60181	3027	16W-1S	D7
-	OKTR	60181	3027	16W-1S	D7
-	SgrT	-	3135	41W-7S	D6
-	SgrT	-	3136	41W-6S	A6
-	SRGV	-	3135	41W-7S	D6
-	SRGV	-	3136	41W-6S	A6
-	WnfT	60563	3080	30W-3S	B6
10	AURA	60502	3079	33W-3S	B6
10	AURA	60510	3079	33W-3S	B6
10	BtvT	60502	3079	33W-3S	B6
10	DRGV	60137	3083	22W-2S	D4
10	MltT	60137	3083	22W-2S	C4
10	MltT	60187	3082	24W-3S	E5
10	MltT	60515	3083	22W-2S	D4
10	MltT	60555	3082	25W-3S	A5
10	NARA	60542	3078	36W-4S	A7
10	NARA	60542	3137	36W-4S	E1
10	NARA	60542	3138	36W-4S	A1
10	OKTR	60181	3085	17W-1S	B2
10	WHTN	60187	3081	27W-2S	B4
10	WHTN	60187	3082	23W-3S	E5
10	WHTN	60187	3083	23W-2S	A4
10	WHTN	60555	3082	25W-3S	B5
10	WnfT	60185	3081	28W-2S	B4
10	WnfT	60510	3079	31W-3S	E6
10	WnfT	60555	3081	27W-2S	B4
10	WNVL	60555	3080	29W-3S	E5
10	WNVL	60555	3081	28W-2S	B4
100	AraT	60510	3078	35W-4S	C7
100	AraT	60542	3078	35W-4S	C7
100	EMHT	60126	3027	16W-0S	D7
100	EMHT	60126	3028	15W-0S	A6
100	MltT	60187	3081	27W-2S	B4
100	MltT	60187	3083	23W-2S	A4
100	MltT	60555	3081	27W-2S	B4
100	NARA	60510	3078	35W-4S	C7
100	WNVL	60185	3081	28W-2S	A5
100	WNVL	60563	3080	30W-3S	C6
100	YkTp	60181	3085	17W-1S	B2
200	AURA	60542	3138	36W-4S	A2
200	WHTN	60137	3083	23W-2S	A4
300	AURA	60563	3080	30W-3S	B6

STREET Block	City	ZIP	Map#	CGS	Grid
SR-56					
400	WnfT	60555	3080	29W-3S	D6
500	BKLY	60162	3028	15W-0S	B6
500	BKLY	60163	3028	15W-0S	B6
500	EMHT	60162	3028	15W-0S	B6
500	OKBK	60181	3085	18W-2S	A2
500	OKBK	60523	3085	17W-1S	B2
500	OKTR	60523	3085	17W-1S	B2
500	WHTN	60555	3081	27W-2S	B4
500	WnfT	60187	3081	27W-2S	B4
500	YkTp	60148	3084	19W-2S	D3
500	YkTp	60523	3084	20W-2S	B4
600	AraT	60502	3078	34W-4S	C7
600	AURA	60502	3078	35W-4S	A7
600	AURA	60510	3078	34W-3S	C7
600	NARA	60502	3078	34W-4S	C7
700	AURA	60502	3080	30W-3S	B6
700	AURA	60510	3080	31W-3S	A6
700	OKBK	60148	3084	19W-2S	E3
700	OKBK	60523	3084	20W-2S	B4
700	WnfT	60502	3080	30W-3S	B6
700	WnfT	60510	3080	30W-3S	B6
800	DRGV	60148	3084	21W-2S	A4
800	DRGV	60515	3084	21W-2S	A4
800	MltT	60148	3084	21W-2S	A4
800	MltT	60515	3084	21W-2S	A4
1000	LMBD	60148	3084	19W-2S	C4
1000	LMBD	60515	3084	19W-2S	C4
2000	DRGV	60515	3083	23W-2S	A4
2100	DRGV	60148	3083	21W-2S	E4
2100	MltT	60148	3083	21W-2S	E4
2700	YkTp	60523	3085	18W-2S	A3
4000	BLWD	60104	3029	13W-0N	A5
4000	BLWD	60162	3029	12W-0N	A4
4000	HLSD	60162	3029	13W-0N	A5
4100	HLSD	60104	3029	13W-0N	A5
4300	BLWD	60104	3028	13W-0N	E5
4300	BLWD	60162	3028	13W-0N	E5
4300	HLSD	60162	3028	13W-0N	E5
5200	HLSD	60163	3028	14W-0S	C5
SR-56 Butterfield Rd					
-	WnfT	60563	3080	30W-3S	B6
10	AURA	60502	3079	33W-3S	B6
10	AURA	60510	3079	33W-3S	B6
10	BtvT	60502	3079	33W-3S	B6
10	DRGV	60137	3083	22W-2S	D4
10	MltT	60137	3083	22W-2S	C4
10	MltT	60187	3082	24W-3S	E5
10	MltT	60515	3083	22W-2S	D4
10	MltT	60555	3082	25W-3S	A5
10	OKTR	60181	3085	17W-1S	B2
10	WHTN	60187	3081	27W-2S	B4
10	WHTN	60187	3082	23W-3S	E5
10	WHTN	60187	3083	23W-2S	A4
10	WHTN	60555	3082	25W-3S	B5
10	WnfT	60185	3081	28W-2S	B4
10	WnfT	60510	3079	31W-3S	E6
10	WnfT	60555	3081	27W-2S	B4
10	WNVL	60555	3080	29W-3S	E5
10	WNVL	60555	3081	28W-2S	B4
100	AraT	60510	3078	35W-4S	C7
100	AraT	60542	3078	35W-4S	C7
100	MltT	60187	3081	27W-2S	B4
100	MltT	60187	3083	23W-2S	A4
100	MltT	60555	3081	27W-2S	B4
100	NARA	60510	3078	35W-4S	C7
100	NARA	60542	3078	35W-4S	C7
100	WNVL	60185	3081	28W-2S	A5
100	WNVL	60563	3080	30W-3S	C6
100	YkTp	60181	3085	17W-1S	B2
200	WHTN	60137	3083	23W-2S	A4
300	AURA	60563	3080	30W-3S	B6
400	WnfT	60555	3080	29W-3S	D6
500	OKBK	60181	3085	18W-2S	A2
500	OKBK	60523	3085	17W-1S	B2
500	OKTR	60523	3085	17W-1S	B2
500	WHTN	60555	3081	27W-2S	B4
500	WnfT	60187	3081	27W-2S	B4
500	YkTp	60148	3084	19W-2S	D3
500	YkTp	60523	3084	20W-2S	B4
600	AraT	60502	3078	34W-4S	C7
600	AURA	60502	3078	35W-4S	A7
600	AURA	60510	3078	34W-3S	C7
600	NARA	60502	3078	34W-4S	C7
700	AURA	60502	3080	30W-3S	B6
700	AURA	60510	3080	31W-3S	A6
700	OKBK	60148	3084	19W-2S	E3
700	OKBK	60523	3084	20W-2S	B4
700	WnfT	60502	3080	30W-3S	B6
700	WnfT	60510	3080	30W-3S	B6
800	DRGV	60148	3084	21W-2S	A4
800	DRGV	60515	3084	21W-2S	A4
800	MltT	60148	3084	21W-2S	A4
800	MltT	60515	3084	21W-2S	A4
1000	LMBD	60148	3084	19W-2S	C4
1000	LMBD	60515	3084	19W-2S	C4
2000	DRGV	60515	3083	23W-2S	A4
2100	DRGV	60148	3083	21W-2S	E4
2100	MltT	60148	3083	21W-2S	E4
2700	YkTp	60523	3085	18W-2S	A3
4000	BLWD	60104	3029	13W-0N	A5
4000	HLSD	60162	3029	13W-0N	A5
4100	HLSD	60104	3029	13W-0N	A5
4200	BLWD	60162	3029	13W-0N	A5
4300	BLWD	60104	3028	13W-0N	E5
4300	BLWD	60162	3028	13W-0N	E5
4300	HLSD	60162	3028	13W-0N	E5
5200	BKLY	60163	3028	14W-0S	C5
5200	HLSD	60163	3028	14W-0S	C5
5900	BKLY	60162	3028	14W-0S	C5
5900	EMHT	60162	3028	14W-0S	C6
6000	EMHT	60126	3028	14W-0S	B6
SR-56 E Butterfield Rd					
-	LMBD	60148	3084	19W-2S	D3
100	EMHT	60126	3027	16W-0S	D7
100	EMHT	60126	3028	15W-0S	A6
500	BKLY	60126	3028	15W-0S	B6
500	BKLY	60163	3028	15W-0S	B6
500	EMHT	60162	3028	15W-0S	B6
SR-56 W Butterfield Rd					
-	EMHT	60181	3027	16W-1S	D7
-	OKTR	60181	3027	16W-1S	D7
100	EMHT	60126	3027	16W-0S	E6
SR-56 N Lincoln Hwy					
-	NARA	60542	3137	36W-4S	E1
SR-56 S Lincolnway					
10	NARA	60542	3137	36W-4S	E1
100	NARA	60542	3138	36W-4S	A1
200	AURA	60542	3138	36W-4S	A2
SR-56 R Reagan Mem Tollway					
-	AURA	-	3136	38W-5S	E2
-	AURA	-	3137	38W-5S	A2
-	NARA	-	3137	36W-5S	E2
-	SgrT	-	3136	41W-6S	A6
SR-56 E State St					
10	NARA	60542	3078	36W-4S	A7

STREET Block	City	ZIP	Map#	CGS	Grid
SR-56 E State St					
10	NARA	60542	3138	36W-4S	A1
SR-56 W State St					
-	NARA	60542	3138	36W-4S	A1
SR-56 Washington Blvd					
4000	BLWD	60104	3029	12W-0N	A4
4000	BLWD	60162	3029	12W-0N	A4
4000	HLSD	60162	3029	13W-0N	A4
4100	HLSD	60104	3029	13W-0N	A4
SR-58					
-	HFET	60010	2856	29W-11N	E3
-	HFET	60010	2857	27W-12N	C3
-	HFET	60120	2856	29W-11N	E3
10	ANHT	60005	2861	17W-11N	B2
10	HFET	60169	2859	23W-12N	A2
10	HFET	60173	2859	23W-12N	A2
10	HFET	60195	2859	23W-12N	A2
10	MPPT	60016	2862	15W-11N	A3
10	MPPT	60056	2862	15W-11N	A3
10	SMBG	60169	2859	23W-12N	A2
10	SMBG	60195	2859	23W-12N	A2
300	DSPN	60016	2861	16W-11N	E3
300	DSPN	60056	2862	15W-11N	B2
300	HFET	60169	2858	25W-11N	B2
300	HFET	60195	2858	23W-12N	E2
300	MPPT	60016	2861	16W-11N	E3
300	MPPT	60056	2861	16W-11N	D3
300	SMBG	60169	2858	24W-11N	E2
300	SMBG	60195	2858	24W-11N	E2
500	ANHT	60005	2860	18W-11N	E2
500	DSPN	60016	2862	13W-12N	E2
500	HFET	60192	2856	30W-11N	B3
500	HnrT	60120	2856	30W-11N	B3
500	HnrT	60192	2856	30W-11N	B3
600	ELGN	60120	2855	32W-12N	C3
600	MPPT	60005	2861	17W-11N	B2
600	SMBG	60194	2858	24W-12N	D2
700	RGMW	60008	2860	21W-11N	A2
900	HFET	60194	2858	24W-12N	D2
1300	DSPN	60016	2863	12W-12N	B2
1300	HnrT	60120	2855	32W-12N	C3
1400	SMBG	60173	2859	23W-11N	A2
1700	GNVW	60025	2864	10W-11N	B2
1700	GNVW	60053	2864	10W-11N	B2
1700	MaiT	60016	2863	12W-12N	B2
1700	MNGV	60053	2864	8W-10N	E4
2000	RGMW	60173	2860	20W-12N	A2
2000	SMBG	60173	2860	20W-12N	A2
2100	EGvT	60007	2860	21W-11N	A2
2100	HFET	60169	2857	27W-11N	C3
2100	HFET	60194	2857	27W-11N	C3
2100	RGMW	60007	2860	19W-12N	C2
2100	SMBG	60194	2857	27W-11N	C3
2200	EGvT	60008	2860	21W-11N	A2
2400	MaiT	60025	2864	9W-12N	C2
2400	MaiT	60053	2864	9W-12N	C2
2500	MaiT	60714	2864	9W-12N	B2
4800	SKOK	60076	2865	6W-11N	E4
4800	SKOK	60077	2865	6W-11N	E4
5600	MNGV	60053	2865	8W-10N	A4
6900	MNGV	60025	2864	8W-12N	E2
8000	NLES	60714	2864	10W-12N	B2
8100	MaiT	60016	2864	10W-12N	A2
8500	NLES	60016	2864	10W-12N	A2
8700	MaiT	60714	2863	11W-12N	E2
8700	NLES	60016	2863	11W-12N	E2
8700	NLES	60714	2863	11W-12N	E2
SR-58 Dempster St					
4800	SKOK	60076	2865	6W-11N	E4
4800	SKOK	60077	2865	6W-11N	E4
5600	MNGV	60053	2865	8W-10N	A4
6700	MNGV	60053	2864	8W-10N	E4
SR-58 Golf Rd					
-	ELGN	60120	2855	31W-12N	E3
-	HFET	60010	2856	29W-11N	E3
-	HFET	60010	2857	28W-12N	A3
-	HFET	60120	2856	29W-11N	E3
-	HnrT	60120	2855	31W-12N	E3
-	RGMW	60173	2860	20W-12N	A2
-	SMBG	60173	2860	20W-12N	A2
500	HFET	60192	2856	30W-11N	B3
500	HnrT	60120	2856	30W-11N	B3
500	HnrT	60192	2856	30W-11N	B3
1100	ANHT	60005	2860	18W-12N	A2
1100	RGMW	60008	2860	21W-11N	A2
1700	GNVW	60025	2864	10W-11N	B2
1700	GNVW	60053	2864	10W-11N	B2
1700	MNGV	60053	2864	10W-11N	B2
2100	EGvT	60007	2860	21W-11N	A2
2100	RGMW	60007	2860	19W-12N	C2
2200	EGvT	60008	2860	21W-11N	A2
2400	MaiT	60025	2864	9W-12N	C2
2400	MaiT	60053	2864	9W-12N	C2
2500	MaiT	60714	2864	9W-12N	B2
6900	MNGV	60025	2864	8W-12N	E2
9200	MaiT	60016	2863	11W-12N	D2
9200	NLES	60016	2863	11W-12N	D2
9200	NLES	60714	2863	11W-12N	D2
9500	DSPN	60016	2863	11W-12N	C2
SR-58 E Golf Rd					
10	ANHT	60005	2861	17W-11N	B2
10	HFET	60169	2859	23W-12N	A2
10	HFET	60173	2859	23W-12N	A2
10	HFET	60195	2859	23W-12N	A2
10	SMBG	60169	2859	23W-12N	A2
10	SMBG	60195	2859	23W-12N	A2
500	DSPN	60016	2862	13W-12N	E2
600	MPPT	60005	2861	17W-11N	B2
600	MPPT	60056	2861	17W-11N	B2
1300	DSPN	60016	2863	12W-12N	B2
1400	SMBG	60173	2859	23W-11N	A2
1700	MaiT	60016	2863	12W-12N	B2
2000	EGvT	60007	2860	20W-11N	A2
2000	EGvT	60008	2860	20W-11N	A2
2000	RGMW	60008	2860	20W-12N	A2
2000	RGMW	60173	2860	20W-12N	A2
2000	SMBG	60173	2860	20W-12N	A2
SR-58 W Golf Rd					
-	HFET	60010	2857	27W-12N	C3
10	DSPN	60016	2862	15W-11N	A3
10	HFET	60169	2859	23W-12N	A2
10	HFET	60173	2859	23W-12N	A2
10	HFET	60195	2859	23W-12N	A2
10	MPPT	60016	2862	15W-11N	A3
10	MPPT	60056	2862	15W-11N	A3
10	SMBG	60169	2859	23W-12N	A2
10	SMBG	60173	2859	23W-12N	A2
10	SMBG	60195	2859	23W-12N	A2
300	DSPN	60016	2861	16W-11N	E3
300	DSPN	60056	2862	15W-11N	B2
300	HFET	60169	2858	25W-11N	B2
300	HFET	60195	2858	23W-12N	E2
300	MPPT	60016	2861	16W-11N	E3
300	MPPT	60056	2861	16W-11N	D3
300	SMBG	60169	2858	24W-11N	E2
300	SMBG	60195	2858	24W-11N	E2

STREET Block	City	ZIP	Map#	CGS	Grid
SR-58 W Golf Rd					
500	ANHT	60005	2860	18W-11N	E2
700	RGMW	60008	2860	18W-12N	E2
900	HFET	60194	2858	24W-12N	D2
1600	SMBG	60194	2858	25W-12N	B2
2000	ANHT	60005	2861	17W-11N	B2
2000	MPPT	60005	2861	17W-11N	B2
2100	HFET	60169	2857	27W-11N	C3
2100	HFET	60194	2857	27W-11N	C3
2100	SMBG	60194	2857	27W-11N	C3
8000	MaiT	60025	2864	10W-12N	B2
8000	MaiT	60053	2864	10W-12N	B2
8000	MaiT	60714	2864	10W-12N	B2
8000	MNGV	60053	2864	10W-12N	B2
8000	NLES	60714	2864	10W-12N	B2
8100	MaiT	60016	2864	10W-12N	A2
8500	NLES	60016	2864	10W-12N	A2
8700	MaiT	60016	2863	10W-12N	E2
8700	MaiT	60714	2863	11W-12N	E2
8700	NLES	60016	2863	11W-12N	E2
8700	NLES	60714	2863	11W-12N	E2
SR-58 Summit St					
600	ELGN	60120	2855	32W-12N	C3
1300	HnrT	60120	2855	32W-12N	C3
SR-58 Waukegan Rd					
8800	MNGV	60053	2864	8W-11N	E3
9500	GNVW	60025	2864	8W-11N	E2
9500	GNVW	60053	2864	8W-11N	E2
9500	MNGV	60025	2864	8W-11N	E2
SR-59					
-	ANTH	60002	2416	24W-41N	D1
-	AntT	60002	2416	24W-38N	B6
-	AntT	60046	2416	24W-38N	B6
-	AURA	60504	3140	29W-7S	C7
-	AURA	60504	3202	29W-8S	C1
-	AURA	60540	3140	30W-7S	C6
-	AURA	60540	3202	30W-8S	C1
-	AURA	60555	3080	30W-3S	C6
-	AURA	60563	3080	30W-3S	C6
-	AURA	60563	3140	29W-6S	C5
-	BNHL	60010	2803	28W-15N	A1
-	BRLT	60103	2856	29W-9N	C7
-	BRLT	60107	2856	30W-9N	C7
-	BRLT	60120	2856	30W-9N	C7
-	BRLT	60120	2910	30W-6N	C6
-	BrnT	60010	2803	28W-15N	A1
-	BrnT	60192	2802	28W-13N	E6
-	CbaT	60010	2643	26W-24N	E6
-	FXLK	60041	2530	27W-34N	B1
-	GrtT	60041	2474	25W-36N	A3
-	GrtT	60041	2530	27W-34N	B1
-	GrtT	60073	2530	27W-32N	B5
-	HFET	60010	2856	29W-12N	D1
-	HnrT	60010	2802	29W-12N	D7
-	JLET	60404	3496	30W-21S	C1
-	LKBN	60010	2643	26W-24N	E6
-	LKBN	60010	2697	26W-24N	E1
-	LKMR	60041	2530	27W-32N	B5
-	LKMR	60073	2530	27W-31N	C7
-	LkvT	60002	2416	24W-40N	C4
-	LkvT	60041	2474	25W-37N	A3
-	LkvT	60046	2416	24W-40N	C4
-	LkvT	60046	2474	25W-38N	B1
-	NBRN	60010	2643	26W-24N	E7
-	NBRN	60010	2697	26W-23N	E2
-	NPVL	60504	3140	30W-7S	C7
-	NPVL	60504	3202	30W-8S	C1
-	NPVL	60540	3140	29W-6S	C5
-	NPVL	60540	3202	30W-8S	C1
-	NPVL	60563	3080	29W-3S	C7
-	NPVL	60563	3140	30W-6S	C5
-	NPVL	60564	3202	29W-8S	C2
-	NPVL	60585	3266	29W-13S	C4
-	NpvT	60540	3140	30W-6S	C5
-	NpvT	60563	3140	30W-6S	C5
-	NpvT	60564	3202	29W-8S	C2
-	PnfT	60586	3496	30W-21S	C1
-	SMWD	60103	2856	29W-9N	C7
-	SMWD	60103	2910	30W-9N	C1
-	SMWD	60107	2910	30W-9N	C1
-	SMWD	60120	2910	30W-9N	C1
-	VOLO	60041	2530	27W-32N	B5
-	VOLO	60073	2530	27W-32N	B5
-	VOLO	60073	2587	27W-31N	C1
-	WCHI	60185	2966	30W-3N	C6
-	WCHI	60185	3080	29W-1S	D1
-	WcnT	60073	2530	27W-31N	C7
-	WnfT	60185	3080	29W-1S	D1
-	WnfT	60555	3080	29W-3S	C5
-	WNVL	60185	3080	29W-1S	C2
-	WNVL	60555	3080	30W-3S	C7
-	WNVL	60563	3080	30W-3S	C6
-	WYNE	60103	2966	30W-4N	C3
-	WynT	60185	3022	30W-2N	C1
10	BNHL	60010	2750	27W-16N	A7
10	BRLT	60103	2910	30W-6N	C6
10	BRLT	60103	2966	30W-5N	C1
10	BRTN	60010	2750	25W-18N	E2
10	HnrT	60107	2856	29W-12N	D2
10	HnrT	60120	2856	29W-12N	D2
10	PNFD	60544	3416	29W-19S	C4
10	SMWD	60107	2856	29W-12N	D2
10	SMWD	60120	2856	29W-12N	D2
10	WldT	60564	3202	29W-10S	C6
10	WYNE	60184	2966	30W-2N	C7
10	WynT	60103	2910	30W-8N	C4
10	WynT	60103	2966	30W-2N	C7
10	WynT	60184	2966	30W-2N	C7
100	BrnT	60010	2750	27W-16N	B6
100	PNFD	60586	3416	29W-18S	C2
100	PnfT	60544	3416	29W-18S	C2
100	SRWD	60404	3496	30W-21S	C1
100	SRWD	60431	3496	29W-23S	C5
100	WCHI	60185	3022	29W-1N	D4
200	HFET	60107	2856	29W-11N	D3
200	HFET	60120	2856	29W-11N	D3
200	WnfT	60185	3022	29W-2N	C1
300	ANTH	60002	2357	24W-41N	D7
300	PNFD	60544	3338	29W-18S	C7
400	NPVL	60564	3266	29W-13S	C3
400	NpvT	60564	3202	29W-8S	C2
400	WldT	60564	3266	30W-11S	C2
500	FXLK	60020	2473	26W-36N	D4
500	FXLK	60041	2473	26W-36N	D4
500	WYNE	60185	2966	30W-4N	C3
500	WynT	60185	2966	30W-4N	C3
600	WCDA	60084	2587	26W-27N	D7
700	AURA	60564	3202	29W-9S	C5
700	BNHL	60010	2802	28W-14N	E5
700	BNHL	60118	2802	28W-14N	E4
700	BrnT	60010	2802	28W-14N	E3
700	BrnT	60118	2802	28W-14N	E3
700	BRTN	60010	2697	25W-20N	E7
700	CbaT	60010	2697	25W-20N	E7
800	TroT	60404	3496	29W-24S	C6
800	TroT	60431	3496	29W-24S	C6

STREET Block	City	ZIP	Map#	CGS	Grid
SR-59					
800	WcnT	60084	2587	26W-28N	D6
900	JLET	60431	3496	30W-21S	C1
1000	PnfT	60544	3338	29W-17S	C6
1100	JLET	60586	3496	30W-21S	C1
2500	HFET	60010	2802	29W-12N	D7
2500	HFET	60192	2802	28W-13N	E6
2500	SBTN	60010	2802	28W-13N	E6
2800	PNFD	60585	3338	30W-18S	C7
12100	PNFD	60585	3266	29W-14S	C6
12100	WldT	60585	3266	29W-14S	C6
12200	WldT	60585	3338	29W-14S	C1
16500	PnfT	60586	3416	29W-19S	C4
17200	JLET	60586	3416	30W-20S	C5
25900	CbaT	60084	2643	26W-26N	D4
25900	TRLK	60010	2643	26W-24N	E6
25900	TRLK	60084	2643	26W-26N	D4
25900	WcnT	60084	2643	26W-26N	D3
26000	GrtT	60041	2473	26W-36N	E4
26300	WCDA	60084	2643	26W-26N	D3
29000	WCDA	60073	2587	26W-29N	C5
29500	WcnT	60073	2587	27W-29N	C4
SR-59 N Barrington Rd					
25900	CbaT	60084	2643	26W-26N	D4
25900	TRLK	60010	2643	26W-26N	D4
25900	TRLK	60084	2643	26W-26N	D3
25900	WcnT	60084	2643	26W-26N	D3
26300	WCDA	60084	2643	26W-26N	D3
SR-59 Brook Forest Av					
-	JLET	60404	3496	30W-21S	C1
-	PnfT	60586	3496	30W-21S	C1
100	SRWD	60404	3496	30W-21S	C1
100	SRWD	60431	3496	29W-23S	C5
900	JLET	60431	3496	30W-21S	C1
1100	JLET	60586	3496	30W-21S	C1
SR-59 Cottage St					
100	SRWD	60404	3496	29W-24S	C5
100	SRWD	60431	3496	29W-24S	C5
800	TroT	60404	3496	29W-24S	C6
800	TroT	60431	3496	29W-24S	C6
SR-59 S Division St					
-	PNFD	60586	3416	29W-19S	C3
SR-59 Grand Av					
-	GrtT	60041	2474	25W-37N	A3
-	LkvT	60041	2474	25W-37N	A3
-	LkvT	60046	2474	25W-37N	B1
SR-59 E Grand Av					
500	FXLK	60020	2473	26W-36N	D4
500	FXLK	60041	2473	26W-36N	D4
SR-59 W Grand Av					
-	GrtT	60041	2474	25W-36N	A3
26000	GrtT	60041	2473	26W-36N	E4
26200	FXLK	60041	2473	26W-36N	D4
26500	FXLK	60020	2473	26W-36N	D4
SR-59 Hawthorne Rd					
10	BNHL	60010	2750	25W-18N	E3
10	BRTN	60010	2750	25W-18N	E3
SR-59 N Hough St					
-	NBRN	60010	2697	25W-22N	E4
100	BRTN	60010	2750	25W-20N	E2
700	BRTN	60010	2697	25W-20N	E7
700	CbaT	60010	2697	25W-20N	E7
SR-59 S Hough St					
100	BRTN	60010	2750	25W-18N	E2
SR-59 Lake St					
300	ANTH	60002	2357	24W-41N	D7
SR-59 N Neltnor Blvd					
100	WCHI	60185	3022	29W-1N	D4
300	WnfT	60185	3022	29W-2N	C1
SR-59 S Neltnor Blvd					
100	WCHI	60185	3022	29W-0N	D4
200	WnfT	60185	3022	29W-0N	D5
SR-59 New Sutton Rd					
-	BNHL	60010	2803	28W-15N	A1
-	BrnT	60010	2803	28W-15N	A1
-	BrnT	60192	2802	28W-13N	E6
-	HnrT	60010	2802	29W-12N	D7
100	BNHL	60010	2750	27W-16N	A7
100	BrnT	60010	2750	27W-16N	B6
700	BNHL	60010	2802	28W-14N	E5
700	BNHL	60118	2802	28W-14N	E4
700	BrnT	60010	2802	28W-14N	E3
700	BrnT	60118	2802	28W-14N	E3
2500	HFET	60010	2802	29W-12N	D7
2500	HFET	60192	2802	28W-13N	E6
2700	SBTN	60010	2802	28W-13N	E6
SR-59 N Rand Rd					
200	WCDA	60084	2643	26W-27N	D1
200	WcnT	60084	2643	26W-26N	D2
600	WCDA	60084	2587	26W-27N	D7
800	WcnT	60084	2587	26W-28N	D6
29000	WCDA	60073	2587	26W-29N	C5
29500	WcnT	60073	2587	27W-29N	C4
SR-59 S Rand Rd					
400	WCDA	60084	2643	26W-26N	D2
400	WcnT	60084	2643	26W-26N	D2
SR-59 Sutton Rd					
-	BRLT	60103	2856	29W-9N	C7
-	BRLT	60107	2856	30W-9N	C7
-	BRLT	60120	2856	30W-9N	C7
-	BRLT	60120	2910	30W-6N	C6
-	HFET	60010	2856	29W-12N	D1
-	SMWD	60103	2856	29W-9N	C7
-	SMWD	60103	2910	30W-9N	C1
-	SMWD	60107	2910	30W-9N	C1
-	SMWD	60120	2910	30W-9N	C1
10	BRLT	60103	2910	30W-6N	C6
10	BRLT	60103	2966	30W-5N	C1
10	WYNE	60184	2966	30W-5N	C3
10	WynT	60103	2910	30W-8N	C4
10	WynT	60103	2966	30W-5N	C2
10	WynT	60184	2966	30W-5N	C3
200	HFET	60107	2856	29W-11N	D3
200	HFET	60120	2856	29W-11N	D3
200	HnrT	60107	2856	29W-12N	D2
200	HnrT	60120	2856	29W-12N	D2
200	SMWD	60107	2856	29W-12N	D2
200	SMWD	60120	2856	29W-12N	D2
SR-59 S Sutton Rd					
10	HnrT	60107	2856	29W-11N	D5
10	HnrT	60120	2856	29W-11N	D5
10	SMWD	60107	2856	29W-10N	D5
10	SMWD	60120	2856	29W-11N	D5
SR-60					
-	FmtT	60030	2531	24W-31N	C7
-	FmtT	60030	2588	23W-30N	E1
-	FmtT	60030	2589	21W-29N	D4
-	FmtT	60060	2589	21W-29N	D4
-	FmtT	60060	2590	20W-28N	A6
-	FmtT	60073	2588	23W-30N	E1
-	FmtT	60073	2589	23W-30N	A1
-	LbvT	60045	2648	13W-25N	E4
-	LbvT	60060	2646	18W-26N	D4
-	LGGV	60047	2646	19W-26N	C3
-	MDLN	60060	2589	20W-28N	E6
-	MDLN	60060	2590	20W-28N	A6

STREET Block	City	ZIP	Map#	CGS	Grid
SR-60					
-	MTWA	60045	2648	14W-26N	D4
-	MTWA	60048	2648	15W-26N	A4
-	RDLK	60030	2588	23W-30N	E1
-	RDLK	60030	2589	23W-30N	A2
-	RDLK	60073	2588	23W-30N	E1
-	RDLK	60073	2589	23W-30N	A1
-	RLKP	60030	2589	22W-30N	B3
-	RLKP	60060	2589	22W-30N	B3
-	VNHL	60061	2648	15W-26N	B4
-	VOLO	60030	2530	26W-31N	E7
-	VOLO	60030	2531	25W-31N	B7
-	VOLO	60073	2530	26W-31N	E7
-	VrnT	60045	2649	13W-26N	A4
-	VrnT	60048	2648	15W-26N	B4
-	VrnT	60060	2646	18W-26N	D4
-	WcnT	60030	2530	26W-31N	E7
-	WcnT	60030	2531	25W-31N	B7
10	VNHL	60061	2647	16W-26N	C4
200	MDLN	60060	2646	18W-25N	E4
400	MDLN	60060	2647	17W-25N	A4
400	VNHL	60060	2647	17W-26N	B4
700	FmtT	60060	2646	19W-26N	B2
700	LKFT	60045	2649	12W-25N	C4
700	VrnT	60048	2647	15W-26N	E4
1800	LKFT	60045	2648	13W-25N	E4
1800	VrnT	60045	2648	13W-25N	E4
SR-60 W Kennedy Rd					
-	LbvT	60045	2648	13W-25N	E4
-	VrnT	60045	2649	13W-25N	A4
700	LKFT	60045	2649	12W-25N	C4
1800	LKFT	60045	2648	13W-25N	E4
1800	VrnT	60045	2648	13W-25N	E4
SR-60 Townline Rd					
-	LbvT	60045	2648	13W-26N	E4
-	LKFT	60045	2648	13W-26N	E4
-	MTWA	60045	2648	14W-26N	D4
-	MTWA	60048	2648	15W-26N	A4
-	VNHL	60061	2648	15W-26N	A4
-	VrnT	60045	2648	13W-26N	D4
-	VrnT	60048	2648	14W-26N	D4
200	MDLN	60060	2646	18W-25N	E4
800	MDLN	60060	2647	17W-25N	A4
1300	VNHL	60060	2647	17W-26N	B4
1500	VNHL	60061	2647	17W-26N	B4
SR-60 E Townline Rd					
-	VNHL	60061	2648	15W-26N	B4
-	VrnT	60048	2648	15W-26N	B4
10	VNHL	60061	2647	16W-26N	C4
700	VrnT	60048	2647	15W-26N	E4
SR-60 W Townline Rd					
10	VNHL	60061	2647	17W-26N	C4
400	MDLN	60060	2647	17W-26N	B4
400	VNHL	60060	2647	17W-26N	B4
SR-62					
-	RGMW	60067	2806	20W-12N	A7
10	ALGN	60102	2694	33W-20N	E7
10	ANHT	60005	2861	18W-11N	A3
10	BNHL	60010	2750	27W-16N	A7
10	BNHL	60010	2803	27W-15N	C1
10	BrnT	60010	2750	27W-16N	A7
10	BrnT	60010	2803	27W-15N	C1
10	SBTN	60010	2803	27W-15N	C1
100	ALGN	60102	2748	32W-19N	C2
100	ALGN	60110	2748	32W-19N	C2
100	BNHL	60010	2748	32W-20N	A1
100	BNHL	60010	2749	29W-16N	B6
100	BNHL	60102	2748	32W-19N	C2
100	BNHL	60110	2748	32W-19N	C2
200	PLTN	60067	2805	22W-13N	B6
200	PltT	60173	2805	22W-13N	B6
200	SMBG	60173	2805	22W-13N	B6
300	DSPN	60016	2861	16W-10N	E5
300	DSPN	60018	2861	16W-10N	E5
300	MPPT	60016	2861	16W-10N	E5
300	MPPT	60018	2861	16W-10N	E5
300	MPPT	60056	2861	16W-10N	E5
400	ANHT	60005	2860	18W-11N	E2
400	ANHT	60008	2860	18W-11N	E2
500	EGvT	60005	2861	16W-10N	E5
500	EGvT	60056	2861	16W-10N	E5
700	HFET	60067	2804	23W-14N	E4
700	HFET	60192	2804	23W-14N	E4
700	PltT	60067	2804	23W-14N	E4
700	PltT	60192	2804	23W-14N	E4
700	PltT	60195	2804	23W-14N	E4
700	RGMW	60008	2860	18W-11N	E2
800	ALGN	60102	2695	33W-20N	A7
1000	RGMW	60005	2860	18W-11N	E2
1300	SBTN	60010	2804	23W-14N	E4
1300	SBTN	60192	2804	23W-14N	E4
1400	HFET	60010	2804	23W-14N	E4
1400	PltT	60067	2805	21W-13N	E7
1400	PltT	60195	2805	21W-13N	E7
1500	MPPT	60005	2861	16W-10N	E5
1500	SMBG	60067	2805	20W-13N	E7
1600	IVNS	60067	2804	23W-14N	E5
1600	IVNS	60067	2805	21W-13N	E7
1600	IVNS	60195	2804	23W-14N	E5
1700	ANHT	60056	2861	17W-11N	C4
1700	SMBG	60067	2806	21W-12N	A7
1700	SMBG	60173	2806	21W-12N	A7
1800	HFET	60195	2804	23W-14N	E4
1900	AlqT	60102	2748	32W-20N	B2
2000	RGMW	60008	2806	21W-12N	A7
2000	RGMW	60173	2806	21W-12N	A7
2000	SMBG	60008	2806	21W-12N	A7
SR-62 Algonquin Rd					
-	HFET	60010	2804	23W-14N	E4
-	HFET	60192	2804	23W-14N	E4
-	RGMW	60008	2806	20W-12N	A7
-	SBTN	60010	2804	23W-14N	E4
-	SBTN	60192	2804	23W-14N	E4
10	BNHL	60010	2750	27W-16N	A7
10	BNHL	60010	2803	27W-15N	C1
10	BrnT	60010	2750	27W-16N	A7
10	BrnT	60010	2803	27W-15N	C1
10	SBTN	60010	2803	27W-15N	C1
100	ALGN	60102	2748	32W-19N	C2
100	ALGN	60110	2748	32W-19N	C2
100	BNHL	60010	2748	32W-20N	A1
100	BNHL	60010	2749	29W-16N	B6
100	BNHL	60102	2748	32W-19N	C2
100	BNHL	60110	2748	32W-19N	C2
2200	ANHT	60005	2860	19W-12N	D1
2200	ANHT	60008	2860	19W-12N	D1
2200	RGMW	60005	2860	19W-12N	D1
2200	RGMW	60008	2860	19W-12N	C1
SR-62 E Algonquin Rd					
-	RGMW	60067	2806	20W-12N	A7
10	ALGN	60102	2694	33W-20N	E7
10	ANHT	60005	2861	18W-11N	A3
200	PLTN	60067	2805	22W-13N	B6
200	PltT	60173	2805	22W-13N	B6
200	SMBG	60173	2805	22W-13N	B6
800	ALGN	60102	2695	33W-20N	A7
SR-62 E Algonquin Rd					
1000	EGvT	60005	2861	16W-10N	D5
1000	EGvT	60056	2861	16W-10N	D5
1500	MPPT	60005	2861	16W-10N	E5
1500	PltT	60067	2805	20W-13N	E7
1500	SMBG	60067	2805	20W-13N	E7
1600	MPPT	60056	2861	16W-10N	E5
1700	SMBG	60067	2806	21W-12N	A7
1700	SMBG	60173	2806	21W-12N	A7
1900	ALGN	60102	2748	32W-20N	B2
1900	AlqT	60102	2748	32W-20N	B2
2000	RGMW	60008	2806	21W-12N	A7
2000	RGMW	60173	2806	21W-12N	A7
2000	SMBG	60008	2806	21W-12N	A7
2200	ALGN	60110	2748	33W-19N	C2
2200	BNHL	60010	2748	33W-19N	C2
2200	BNHL	60102	2748	33W-19N	C2
2200	BNHL	60110	2748	33W-19N	C2
SR-62 W Algonquin Rd					
10	ALGN	60102	2694	33W-20N	E7
10	ANHT	60005	2861	18W-11N	A3
300	DSPN	60016	2861	16W-10N	E5
300	DSPN	60018	2861	16W-10N	E5
300	MPPT	60016	2861	16W-10N	E5
300	MPPT	60018	2861	16W-10N	E5
300	MPPT	60056	2861	16W-10N	E5
400	ANHT	60005	2860	18W-11N	E2
400	ANHT	60008	2860	18W-11N	E2
500	EGvT	60056	2861	16W-10N	E5
700	HFET	60067	2804	23W-14N	E4
700	HFET	60192	2804	23W-14N	D4
700	PltT	60067	2804	23W-14N	E4
700	PltT	60192	2804	23W-14N	E4
700	PltT	60195	2804	23W-14N	E4
700	RGMW	60008	2860	18W-11N	E2
1000	RGMW	60005	2860	18W-11N	E2
1100	PLTN	60067	2805	22W-13N	B6
1100	PltT	60173	2805	22W-13N	B6
1100	SMBG	60173	2805	22W-13N	B6
1300	SBTN	60010	2804	24W-14N	C4
1300	SBTN	60192	2804	24W-14N	C4
1400	HFET	60010	2804	24W-14N	C4
1400	PltT	60067	2805	21W-13N	E7
1400	PltT	60195	2805	21W-13N	E7
1500	EGvT	60005	2861	16W-10N	D4
1600	IVNS	60067	2804	23W-14N	E5
1600	IVNS	60067	2805	21W-13N	E7
1600	IVNS	60195	2804	23W-14N	E5
1700	ANHT	60056	2861	17W-11N	C4
1700	MPPT	60005	2861	17W-10N	C4
1800	HFET	60195	2804	23W-14N	E4
SR-64					
-	ADSN	60148	3026	18W-2N	D1
-	CHCG	60614	2978	0W-1N	A7
-	CLSM	60139	3024	24W-2N	D1
-	EMHT	60126	3028	14W-1N	B1
-	MLPK	60164	3029	12W-1N	A1
-	NHLK	60160	3029	13W-2N	A1
-	NHLK	60164	3029	13W-1N	A1
-	NHLK	60165	3029	13W-1N	A1
-	SNPK	60164	3029	12W-1N	A1
10	BmdT	60137	3025	23W-1N	B1
10	BmdT	60139	3025	23W-1N	A1
10	CLSM	60188	3023	26W-2N	D1
10	CmpT	60119	2961	42W-4N	D4
10	CmpT	60175	2961	41W-4N	E4
10	CmpT	60175	2962	41W-4N	A4
10	GLHT	60139	3024	23W-1N	E1
10	GLHT	60139	3025	23W-1N	B1
10	LMBD	60148	3025	21W-1N	E1
10	LMBD	60148	3026	21W-1N	A1
10	LYLK	60151	2961	43W-4N	A3
10	MltT	60148	3025	21W-1N	E1
10	NHLK	60164	3028	15W-1N	A1
10	SCRL	60174	2964	35W-3N	B7
10	VLPK	60181	3027	17W-2N	B1
10	WCHI	60185	2965	32W-3N	D6
10	WCHI	60185	2966	29W-2N	D7
10	WynT	60185	2965	32W-3N	D6
10	WynT	60185	2966	30W-3N	B6
10	WynT	60185	2967	28W-2N	B7
10	WynT	60185	3023	27W-2N	C1
10	WynT	60188	3023	27W-2N	D1
10	YkTp	60181	3027	17W-2N	A1
100	BmdT	60188	3024	25W-2N	A1
100	CHCG	60610	2978	0W-2N	B7
100	EMHT	60126	3027	17W-1N	B1
100	GLHT	60137	3025	21W-1N	D1
100	SCRL	60185	2965	32W-3N	D6
200	ADSN	60181	3026	18W-2N	E1
200	BmdT	60188	3023	26W-2N	E1
200	MltT	60137	3025	22W-1N	C1
200	VLPK	60101	3026	18W-2N	E1
300	AddT	60148	3026	21W-1N	A1
300	SchT	60175	2963	37W-3N	D7
300	VLPK	60181	3026	18W-1N	E1
400	BmdT	60148	3025	21W-2N	E1
400	BmdT	60188	3025	23W-2N	A1
400	CLSM	60188	3024	25W-2N	A1
400	CmpT	60175	2963	37W-3N	D7
400	GLHT	60148	3025	21W-1N	D1
400	GLHT	60188	3025	23W-2N	A1
400	LYLK	60175	2961	43W-4N	A3
400	VLPK	60126	3027	17W-2N	B1
400	VLPK	60148	3026	19W-2N	D1
400	YkTp	60126	3027	17W-2N	B1
500	ADSN	60101	3026	18W-1N	E1
500	MLPK	60160	3030	10W-2N	A1
500	PvsT	60160	3030	10W-1N	A1
500	WCHI	60185	2967	28W-2N	B7
600	MLPK	60160	3029	12W-1N	A1
700	CHCG	60610	2977	1W-1N	E7
700	CHCG	60614	2977	1W-1N	E7
700	CHCG	60622	2977	1W-1N	E7
700	GLHT	60188	3024	23W-2N	E1
1100	SCRL	60174	2963	36W-3N	E7
1900	CHCG	60622	3033	3W-1N	A1
1900	CHCG	60647	3033	3W-1N	A1
1900	SCRL	60175	2963	36W-3N	D7
2500	MLPK	60165	3029	12W-1N	A1
2500	SNPK	60160	3029	12W-1N	A1
2500	SNPK	60165	3029	12W-1N	A1
2800	CHCG	60622	3032	3W-1N	E1
2800	CHCG	60647	3032	3W-1N	E1
2800	SCRL	60174	2965	33W-3N	A6
3100	CHCG	60651	3032	3W-2N	D1
3900	CHCG	60639	3032	4W-2N	B1
4700	CHCG	60639	3031	8W-1N	A1
4700	CHCG	60651	3031	8W-1N	A1
5900	OKPK	60302	3031	7W-2N	B1
5900	OKPK	60639	3031	7W-2N	B1
5900	OKPK	60651	3031	7W-2N	B1
6000	CHCG	60302	3031	7W-2N	B1
6300	CHCG	60707	3031	7W-2N	A1
6700	CHCG	60302	3030	8W-2N	E1
6700	CHCG	60707	3030	10W-1N	A1
SR-64					
6700	OKPK	60302	3030	10W-1N	A1
7100	EDPK	60707	3030	8W-2N	D1
7100	OKPK	60305	3030	8W-2N	D1
7100	RVFT	60305	3030	8W-2N	D1
7100	RVFT	60707	3030	8W-2N	D1
8300	RVFT	60160	3030	10W-1N	B1
8300	RVFT	60171	3030	10W-1N	B1
8300	RVGV	60171	3030	10W-1N	B1
8400	MLPK	60171	3030	10W-1N	A1
8400	RVGV	60160	3030	10W-2N	A1
SR-64 W Eugenie St					
100	CHCG	60614	2978	0W-2N	B7
SR-64 N Lasalle Dr					
1600	CHCG	60610	2978	0W-2N	B7
1600	CHCG	60614	2978	0W-2N	B7
SR-64 W La Salle Dr					
-	CHCG	60614	2978	0W-1N	A7
SR-64 E Main St					
10	SCRL	60174	2964	35W-3N	B7
400	SCRL	60185	2965	32W-3N	C6
400	WynT	60185	2965	32W-3N	C6
2800	SCRL	60174	2965	33W-3N	A6
SR-64 W Main St					
10	SCRL	60174	2964	35W-3N	B7
1100	SCRL	60174	2963	36W-3N	E7
1900	SCRL	60175	2963	36W-3N	D7
3700	SchT	60175	2963	38W-3N	B6
SR-64 North Av					
-	CLSM	60139	3024	24W-2N	D1
-	SCRL	60174	2965	33W-3N	A6
10	BmdT	60137	3025	23W-1N	B1
10	BmdT	60139	3025	23W-1N	A1
10	BmdT	60188	3023	26W-2N	E1
10	BmdT	60188	3025	23W-1N	A1
10	CLSM	60188	3023	26W-2N	D1
10	GLHT	60139	3024	23W-1N	E1
10	GLHT	60139	3025	23W-1N	B1
10	GLHT	60188	3025	23W-1N	A1
10	MltT	60148	3025	21W-1N	E1
10	WCHI	60185	2965	32W-3N	D6
10	WCHI	60185	2966	29W-2N	D7
10	WynT	60185	2965	32W-3N	D6
10	WynT	60185	2966	30W-3N	B6
10	WynT	60185	2967	28W-2N	B7
10	WynT	60185	3023	26W-2N	D1
10	WynT	60188	3023	27W-2N	D1
100	BmdT	60188	3024	25W-2N	A1
100	SCRL	60185	2965	32W-3N	D6
200	MltT	60137	3025	22W-1N	C1
300	GLHT	60137	3025	23W-1N	B1
400	BmdT	60148	3025	21W-2N	E1
400	CLSM	60188	3024	25W-2N	A1
400	GLHT	60148	3025	21W-2N	D1
400	LMBD	60148	3025	21W-2N	E1
500	WCHI	60185	2967	28W-2N	B7
700	GLHT	60188	3024	23W-2N	E1
SR-64 E North Av					
-	MLPK	60160	3029	13W-2N	A1
-	MLPK	60164	3029	13W-2N	A1
-	NHLK	60160	3029	13W-2N	A1
-	NHLK	60164	3028	15W-1N	B1
-	NHLK	60164	3029	13W-1N	A1
-	NHLK	60165	3029	13W-1N	A1
-	SNPK	60164	3029	13W-1N	A1
10	LMBD	60148	3026	19W-1N	C1
10	VLPK	60181	3027	17W-2N	B1
10	YkTp	60181	3027	17W-2N	A1
100	EMHT	60126	3027	17W-1N	B1
100	EMHT	60126	3028	15W-1N	A1
400	VLPK	60126	3027	17W-2N	B1
400	VLPK	60148	3026	19W-2N	D1
400	YkTp	60126	3027	17W-2N	B1
600	AddT	60148	3026	19W-2N	D1
SR-64 W North Av					
-	ADSN	60148	3026	18W-2N	D1
-	EMHT	60126	3028	14W-2N	B1
-	LMBD	60148	3025	21W-2N	E1
-	MLPK	60164	3029	12W-2N	A1
-	SNPK	60164	3029	12W-1N	A1
-	VLPK	60148	3026	18W-2N	D1
10	LMBD	60148	3026	21W-1N	A1
10	NHLK	60164	3028	13W-1N	E1
10	VLPK	60181	3027	18W-2N	A1
100	CHCG	60610	2978	0W-2N	B7
100	CHCG	60614	2978	0W-2N	B7
100	EMHT	60126	3027	16W-2N	E1
100	WCHI	60185	2966	30W-3N	C7
100	WynT	60185	2966	29W-3N	C7
200	ADSN	60181	3026	18W-2N	E1
200	VLPK	60101	3026	18W-2N	E1
300	AddT	60148	3026	21W-1N	A1
300	VLPK	60181	3026	18W-1N	E1
500	ADSN	60101	3026	18W-1N	E1
500	MLPK	60160	3030	10W-2N	A1
500	PvsT	60160	3030	10W-2N	A1
600	MLPK	60160	3029	12W-1N	A1
600	VLPK	60126	3027	17W-2N	C1
600	YkTp	60126	3027	17W-2N	C1
700	CHCG	60610	2977	1W-1N	E7
700	CHCG	60614	2977	1W-1N	E7
700	CHCG	60622	2977	1W-1N	E7
1900	CHCG	60622	3033	3W-1N	A1
1900	CHCG	60647	3033	3W-1N	A1
2500	MLPK	60165	3029	12W-1N	A1
2500	SNPK	60160	3029	12W-1N	A1
2500	SNPK	60165	3029	12W-1N	A1
2800	CHCG	60622	3032	3W-1N	E1
2800	CHCG	60647	3032	3W-1N	E1
3100	CHCG	60651	3032	3W-2N	D1
3900	CHCG	60639	3032	4W-2N	B1
4700	CHCG	60639	3031	8W-1N	A1
4700	CHCG	60651	3031	8W-1N	A1
5900	OKPK	60302	3031	7W-2N	B1
5900	OKPK	60639	3031	7W-2N	B1
5900	OKPK	60651	3031	7W-2N	B1
6000	CHCG	60302	3031	7W-2N	B1
6300	CHCG	60707	3031	7W-2N	A1
6700	CHCG	60302	3030	8W-2N	E1
6700	CHCG	60707	3030	10W-1N	A1
6700	OKPK	60302	3030	10W-1N	A1
7100	EDPK	60707	3030	8W-2N	D1
7100	OKPK	60305	3030	8W-2N	D1
7100	RVFT	60305	3030	8W-2N	D1
7100	RVFT	60707	3030	8W-2N	D1
8300	RVFT	60160	3030	10W-1N	B1
8300	RVFT	60171	3030	10W-1N	B1
8300	RVGV	60160	3030	10W-2N	A1
8400	MLPK	60171	3030	10W-1N	A1
8400	RVGV	60171	3030	10W-2N	A1
SR-68					
-	BFGV	60004	2754	15W-18N	E4
-	BNHL	60010	2801	30W-15N	E1
-	CPVL	60118	2801	32W-16N	D1
-	GLNC	60062	2758	8W-17N	A4
-	NtrT	60062	2758	8W-17N	A4
SR-68					
-	PltT	60004	2753	19W-18N	D4
-	WhlT	60062	2755	13W-18N	E4
-	WhlT	60062	2756	13W-18N	A4
-	WhlT	60090	2755	13W-18N	E4
-	WhlT	60090	2756	13W-18N	A4
-	WLNG	60062	2755	13W-18N	E4
-	WLNG	60090	2756	13W-18N	A4
10	BFGV	60089	2754	15W-18N	E4
10	BFGV	60090	2754	16W-18N	D4
10	BNHL	60010	2750	26W-17N	D5
10	BRTN	60010	2750	26W-17N	D5
10	BRTN	60010	2751	25W-17N	A5
10	IVNS	60010	2750	26W-17N	D5
10	IVNS	60010	2751	25W-17N	A5
10	PLTN	60067	2752	21W-18N	E4
10	PLTN	60067	2753	20W-17N	A4
10	PLTN	60074	2752	20W-18N	E4
10	PLTN	60074	2753	20W-17N	A4
10	PltT	60074	2752	21W-18N	E4
10	PltT	60074	2753	20W-17N	A4
10	WLNG	60089	2754	16W-18N	D4
10	WLNG	60090	2754	16W-18N	D4
10	WLNG	60090	2755	13W-18N	E4
100	BNHL	60010	2802	30W-15N	A1
100	BrnT	60010	2750	27W-16N	A7
100	EDND	60118	2801	32W-16N	D1
100	IVNS	60067	2751	23W-17N	D5
100	PltT	60067	2753	20W-18N	A4
200	BNHL	60010	2749	28W-16N	E7
200	DndT	60118	2801	32W-16N	D1
400	ANHT	60004	2754	15W-18N	E4
400	NHBK	60062	2758	8W-17N	A4
500	CPVL	60110	2801	33W-16N	C2
500	EDND	60110	2801	33W-16N	C2
500	NHBK	60062	2757	8W-17N	E4
700	ANHT	60004	2753	18W-17N	E4
700	BFGV	60089	2753	18W-17N	E4
700	PltT	60067	2752	21W-17N	C4
1000	ANHT	60089	2754	17W-18N	A4
1200	PltT	60010	2752	22W-17N	A4
1500	PLTN	60010	2752	23W-17N	A4
1700	PLTN	60010	2751	24W-17N	C5
1700	PLTN	60067	2751	24W-17N	C5
1700	PltT	60010	2751	24W-17N	C5
1800	PltT	60067	2751	23W-17N	E5
2500	NHBK	60062	2756	10W-18N	E4
4100	NfdT	60062	2756	13W-18N	A4
SR-68 Algonquin Rd					
100	BNHL	60010	2750	27W-16N	A7
100	BrnT	60010	2750	27W-16N	A7
SR-68 Barrington Av					
500	CPVL	60110	2801	33W-16N	C2
500	DndT	60118	2801	33W-16N	B2
500	EDND	60110	2801	33W-16N	C2
500	EDND	60118	2801	33W-16N	B2
SR-68 Dundee Rd					
-	BNHL	60010	2801	30W-15N	E1
-	BRTN	60010	2750	25W-17N	E5
-	CPVL	60110	2801	32W-16N	D1
-	CPVL	60118	2801	32W-16N	D1
-	EDND	60110	2801	30W-15N	E1
-	EDND	60118	2801	32W-16N	D1
-	GLNC	60062	2758	8W-17N	A4
-	IVNS	60010	2750	25W-17N	E5
-	NtrT	60062	2758	8W-17N	A4
-	PLTN	60067	2751	23W-17N	E5
-	PltT	60067	2751	23W-17N	E5
-	WhlT	60062	2755	13W-18N	E4
-	WhlT	60062	2756	13W-18N	A4
-	WhlT	60090	2755	13W-18N	E4
-	WhlT	60090	2756	13W-18N	A4
-	WLNG	60062	2755	13W-18N	E4
-	WLNG	60090	2755	13W-18N	E4
-	WLNG	60090	2756	13W-18N	A4
10	BNHL	60010	2750	26W-17N	D5
100	BNHL	60010	2802	30W-15N	A1
200	BNHL	60010	2749	28W-16N	E7
400	NHBK	60062	2758	8W-17N	A4
500	NHBK	60062	2757	8W-17N	E4
2000	IVNS	60010	2751	23W-17N	D5
2000	IVNS	60067	2751	23W-17N	D5
2000	PltT	60010	2751	23W-17N	E5
2500	NHBK	60062	2756	10W-18N	E4
4100	NfdT	60062	2756	13W-18N	A4
SR-68 E Dundee Rd					
-	BFGV	60004	2754	15W-18N	E4
-	PltT	60004	2753	19W-18N	D4
-	WhlT	60062	2755	13W-18N	E4
-	WLNG	60062	2755	13W-18N	E4
10	BRTN	60010	2750	26W-17N	D5
10	BRTN	60010	2751	25W-17N	A5
10	IVNS	60010	2750	26W-17N	D5
10	IVNS	60010	2751	25W-17N	A5
10	PLTN	60067	2752	20W-18N	E4
10	PLTN	60067	2753	20W-17N	A4
10	PLTN	60074	2752	20W-18N	E4
10	PLTN	60074	2753	20W-17N	A4
10	PltT	60074	2752	20W-18N	E4
10	PltT	60074	2753	20W-17N	A4
10	WLNG	60090	2755	13W-18N	E4
100	IVNS	60067	2751	23W-17N	D5
100	PltT	60067	2753	20W-18N	A4
300	BFGV	60090	2754	16W-18N	D4
600	ANHT	60004	2754	15W-18N	E4
600	BFGV	60089	2754	15W-18N	E4
1000	ANHT	60089	2754	17W-18N	A4
SR-68 W Dundee Rd					
-	PltT	60004	2753	19W-18N	D4
-	PltT	60074	2753	19W-18N	D4
10	BFGV	60089	2754	16W-18N	C4
10	BFGV	60090	2754	16W-18N	D4
10	WLNG	60089	2754	16W-18N	D4
10	WLNG	60090	2755	14W-18N	C4
100	PLTN	60067	2752	21W-18N	E4
100	PltT	60074	2752	21W-18N	E4
500	PLTN	60074	2752	21W-17N	C4
700	ANHT	60004	2753	18W-17N	E4
700	BFGV	60089	2753	18W-17N	E4
700	PltT	60067	2752	21W-17N	C4
800	WLNG	60090	2754	15W-18N	E4
1200	ANHT	60004	2754	17W-18N	A4
1200	ANHT	60089	2754	17W-18N	A4
1200	PltT	60010	2752	22W-17N	A4
1500	PLTN	60010	2752	23W-17N	A4
1700	PLTN	60010	2751	24W-17N	C5
1700	PLTN	60067	2751	24W-17N	C5
1700	PltT	60010	2751	24W-17N	C5
1800	PltT	60067	2751	23W-17N	E5
SR-68 New Sutton Rd					
100	BNHL	60010	2750	26W-17N	C6
100	BrnT	60010	2750	27W-16N	B6
SR-68 Penny Av					
100	EDND	60118	2801	32W-16N	D1
200	DndT	60118	2801	32W-16N	D1
SR-71					
100	KdlT	60560	3333	41W-16S	E4
100	YKVL	60560	3333	41W-16S	E4
4000	OSWG	60543	3263	38W-13S	A5
5000	OswT	60543	3263	38W-13S	A5
5600	OSWG	60543	3262	39W-13S	E5
5600	OswT	60543	3262	39W-13S	E5
5600	OswT	60560	3262	40W-14S	C7
6600	OSWG	60560	3262	40W-14S	C7
7300	OswT	60560	3334	40W-14S	C1
7900	KdlT	60560	3334	40W-15S	B2
11000	KdlT	60560	3332	45W-17S	D7
11600	FoxT	60560	3332	45W-17S	C7
SR-71 Stagecoach Tr					
-	KdlT	60560	3333	43W-16S	B5
-	YKVL	60560	3333	43W-16S	B5
SR-71 E Stagecoach Tr					
100	KdlT	60560	3333	42W-16S	C5
100	YKVL	60560	3333	43W-16S	C5
SR-72					
-	CHCG	60018	2916	13W-8N	E1
-	DndT	60118	2800	36W-16N	B2
-	DndT	60136	2799	37W-16N	C2
-	HFET	60118	2801	32W-15N	E4
-	HFET	60192	2802	28W-13N	E6
-	HshT	60140	2797	44W-15N	A4
-	PGGV	60140	2797	44W-15N	A4
-	PGGV	60140	2798	41W-15N	A3
-	RtdT	60140	2797	44W-15N	A4
-	SMBG	60007	2860	20W-11N	A4
10	BrnT	60010	2803	27W-13N	A6
10	DSPN	60018	2916	15W-8N	B1
10	EDND	60118	2801	32W-15N	E4
10	EGvT	60007	2861	16W-9N	E7
10	EGvT	60018	2916	15W-8N	B1
10	EGVV	60007	2861	17W-10N	B5
10	GLBT	60136	2798	39W-16N	E2
10	GLBT	60136	2799	38W-16N	A2
10	HFET	60169	2859	21W-11N	E4
10	HFET	60195	2859	21W-11N	E4
10	HPSR	60140	2796	46W-15N	A3
10	HshT	60140	2796	44W-15N	E4
10	MaiT	60018	2916	14W-8N	C1
10	RtdT	60136	2798	39W-16N	E2
10	RtdT	60140	2798	39W-16N	E2
10	SBTN	60010	2803	27W-13N	B7
10	WDND	60118	2801	33W-16N	A2
100	HPSR	60140	2795	48W-15N	B3
100	HshT	60140	2795	48W-15N	B3
100	SMBG	60169	2859	23W-11N	A3
100	SMBG	60195	2859	23W-11N	A3
200	BrnT	60010	2802	28W-13N	E6
200	HFET	60010	2802	28W-13N	D5
200	HFET	60118	2802	28W-13N	E6
200	HFET	60169	2858	24W-11N	E2
200	HFET	60195	2858	23W-11N	E3
200	SBTN	60010	2802	28W-13N	E6
200	SMBG	60195	2858	23W-11N	E3
300	CHCG	60007	2916	15W-8N	A1
400	DndT	60118	2801	32W-15N	E4
400	WDND	60118	2800	36W-16N	B2
500	RtdT	60118	2799	38W-16N	B2
500	RtdT	60136	2799	38W-16N	B2
500	SMBG	60194	2858	24W-12N	D2
600	HFET	60173	2859	22W-11N	C3
600	SMBG	60169	2858	24W-12N	D2
600	SMBG	60173	2859	22W-11N	C3
700	CHCG	60631	2918	9W-7N	D5
700	PKRG	60068	2918	10W-7N	B4
700	PKRG	60631	2918	10W-7N	A4
900	SYHW	60118	2800	35W-16N	D2
1000	HFET	60194	2858	24W-12N	D2
1500	CHCG	60018	2917	11W-7N	E4
1500	CHCG	60068	2917	11W-7N	E4
1500	CHCG	60631	2917	11W-7N	E4
1500	PKRG	60068	2917	11W-7N	E4
1500	PKRG	60631	2917	11W-7N	E4
1700	SMBG	60173	2860	19W-10N	C5
1800	EGvT	60007	2860	20W-11N	A4
2000	PKRG	60018	2917	11W-7N	D4
2200	HFET	60169	2857	27W-12N	D1
2400	EGVV	60007	2915	16W-9N	E1
2500	DndT	60118	2799	37W-16N	C2
2500	DndT	60124	2799	37W-16N	D2
2500	EGVV	60007	2915	16W-9N	E1
2500	EGvT	60018	2915	16W-9N	E1
2500	ELGN	60118	2799	37W-16N	C2
2500	ELGN	60124	2799	37W-16N	C2
2600	HFET	60010	2857	26W-12N	E1
2600	HFET	60169	2803	27W-12N	D7
2800	EGVV	60007	2916	15W-8N	A1
2800	EGVV	60018	2915	15W-8N	E1
2800	EGVV	60018	2916	15W-8N	A1
2900	HFET	60010	2803	27W-12N	D7
7200	CHCG	60656	2918	9W-7N	D5
7700	CHCG	60068	2918	10W-7N	B4
9300	RSMT	60018	2917	12W-7N	C3
9300	RSMT	60068	2917	11W-7N	D4
9600	DSPN	60018	2917	12W-7N	C3
10200	CHCG	60666	2917	13W-8N	A2
10200	RSMT	60666	2917	12W-8N	A2
10700	CHCG	60666	2916	13W-8N	E2
10700	RSMT	60018	2916	13W-8N	E2
10700	RSMT	60666	2916	13W-8N	E2
SR-72 W Higgins Av					
7200	CHCG	60631	2918	9W-7N	D5
7200	CHCG	60656	2918	9W-7N	D5
SR-72 Higgins Rd					
-	DndT	60118	2800	36W-16N	B2
-	DndT	60136	2799	37W-16N	C2
-	EGvT	60007	2860	18W-10N	E5
-	SYHW	60118	2800	35W-16N	B2
-	WDND	60118	2800	35W-16N	B2
10	GLBT	60136	2798	39W-16N	E2
10	RtdT	60136	2798	40W-16N	C2
10	RtdT	60140	2798	40W-16N	C2
500	GLBT	60136	2799	38W-16N	B2
500	RtdT	60118	2799	38W-16N	B2
500	RtdT	60136	2799	38W-16N	B2
700	CHCG	60631	2918	10W-7N	A4
700	PKRG	60068	2918	10W-7N	A4
700	PKRG	60631	2918	10W-7N	A4
1500	CHCG	60068	2917	11W-7N	E4
1500	CHCG	60631	2917	11W-7N	E4
1500	PKRG	60068	2917	11W-7N	E4
1500	PKRG	60631	2917	11W-7N	E4
2000	PKRG	60018	2917	11W-7N	D4
2500	DndT	60118	2799	37W-16N	C2
2500	DndT	60124	2799	37W-16N	D2
2500	ELGN	60118	2799	37W-16N	C2
2500	ELGN	60124	2799	37W-16N	C2
SR-72 E Higgins Rd					
-	EGvT	60007	2860	20W-11N	A4
-	SMBG	60007	2860	20W-11N	A4
10	EGvT	60007	2861	17W-10N	B5

STREET Block	City	ZIP	Map#	CGS	Grid
SR-72 E Higgins Rd					
10	EGVV	60007	2861	17W-9N	C6
10	GLBT	60136	2799	38W-16N	A2
10	HFET	60169	2859	23W-11N	A3
600	HFET	60173	2859	22W-11N	C3
600	SMBG	60169	2859	22W-11N	C3
600	SMBG	60173	2859	22W-11N	C3
1700	SMBG	60173	2860	19W-10N	C5
2400	EGVV	60007	2915	16W-9N	E1
2600	EGvT	60007	2915	16W-9N	E1
SR-72 W Higgins Rd					
-	CHCG	60018	2916	13W-8N	E1
-	DSPN	60018	2916	13W-8N	E1
-	EDND	60118	2801	30W-14N	E4
-	HFET	60118	2801	30W-14N	E4
-	HFET	60192	2802	28W-13N	E6
-	PKRG	60018	2917	11W-7N	D4
-	PKRG	60068	2917	11W-7N	D4
10	BrnT	60010	2803	27W-13N	A6
10	HFET	60169	2859	21W-11N	E4
10	HFET	60195	2859	21W-11N	E4
10	SBTN	60010	2803	27W-13N	B7
100	SMBG	60169	2859	23W-11N	A3
100	SMBG	60195	2859	23W-11N	A3
200	BrnT	60010	2802	28W-13N	E6
200	HFET	60010	2802	28W-13N	D5
200	HFET	60118	2802	28W-13N	E6
200	HFET	60195	2858	23W-11N	E3
200	SBTN	60010	2802	28W-13N	E6
200	SMBG	60195	2858	23W-11N	E3
500	SMBG	60194	2858	24W-12N	D2
600	HFET	60169	2858	26W-12N	A1
600	SMBG	60169	2858	24W-12N	D2
1000	HFET	60194	2858	24W-12N	D2
2200	HFET	60169	2857	27W-12N	D1
2600	HFET	60010	2857	26W-12N	E1
2600	HFET	60169	2803	27W-12N	D7
2900	HFET	60010	2803	27W-12N	D7
7700	PKRG	60631	2918	9W-7N	B4
8300	CHCG	60068	2918	10W-7N	B4
8300	CHCG	60631	2918	10W-7N	B4
8300	PKRG	60068	2918	10W-7N	B4
8400	CHCG	60018	2917	10W-7N	E4
8400	CHCG	60068	2917	10W-7N	E4
8400	CHCG	60631	2917	10W-7N	E4
8400	PKRG	60631	2917	10W-7N	E4
9300	RSMT	60018	2917	12W-7N	C3
9300	RSMT	60068	2917	11W-7N	D4
9600	DSPN	60018	2917	12W-7N	C3
10200	CHCG	60666	2917	13W-8N	A2
10200	RSMT	60666	2917	12W-8N	A2
10700	CHCG	60666	2916	13W-8N	E2
10700	RSMT	60018	2916	13W-8N	E2
10700	RSMT	60666	2916	13W-8N	E2
SR-72 E Main St					
-	HFET	60118	2801	32W-15N	E4
10	EDND	60118	2801	32W-15N	E4
400	DndT	60118	2801	32W-15N	E4
SR-72 W Main St					
10	EDND	60118	2801	33W-16N	A2
10	WDND	60118	2801	33W-16N	A2
400	WDND	60118	2800	34W-16N	E2
900	SYHW	60118	2800	35W-16N	D2
SR-72 E Oak Knoll Dr					
10	HPSR	60140	2796	46W-15N	A3
10	HshT	60140	2796	46W-15N	A3
100	HPSR	60140	2795	48W-15N	B3
100	HshT	60140	2795	48W-15N	B3
SR-72 W Oak Knoll Dr					
100	HPSR	60140	2795	47W-15N	E3
100	HshT	60140	2795	47W-15N	C3
SR-72 Oakton St					
1500	EGVV	60007	2861	17W-9N	C6
1800	EGvT	60007	2861	16W-9N	D6
SR-72 N Oriole Av					
-	CHCG	60631	2918	9W-7N	C4
SR-72 Touhy Av					
2500	EGvT	60007	2915	16W-9N	E1
2500	EGvT	60018	2915	16W-9N	E1
2500	EGVV	60007	2915	16W-9N	E1
SR-72 E Touhy Av					
200	CHCG	60018	2916	14W-8N	C1
200	DSPN	60018	2916	15W-8N	B1
200	MaiT	60018	2916	14W-8N	C1
SR-72 W Touhy Av					
10	DSPN	60018	2916	14W-8N	B1
10	EGvT	60018	2916	15W-8N	B1
10	MaiT	60018	2916	14W-8N	C1
300	CHCG	60007	2916	15W-8N	A1
300	CHCG	60018	2916	15W-8N	A1
2800	EGvT	60007	2915	15W-8N	E1
2800	EGvT	60018	2915	15W-8N	E1
2800	EGVV	60007	2915	15W-8N	E1
2800	EGVV	60007	2916	15W-8N	A1
2800	EGVV	60018	2915	15W-8N	E1
2800	EGVV	60018	2916	15W-8N	A1
SR-83					
-	AddT	60101	2971	17W-3N	C5
-	AddT	60106	2971	17W-4N	C4
-	AddT	60191	2971	17W-4N	C2
-	ADSN	60101	2971	17W-3N	C4
-	ADSN	60106	2971	17W-3N	C4
-	ADSN	60126	2971	17W-2N	C7
-	AvnT	60048	2533	20W-32N	A5
-	BFGV	60047	2700	18W-21N	E6
-	BFGV	60089	2700	18W-21N	E6
-	BNVL	60007	2915	16W-7N	C4
-	BNVL	60106	2971	17W-2N	C7
-	BNVL	60191	2971	16W-5N	C1
-	CNHL	60514	3085	16W-4S	E7
-	CNHL	60514	3145	16W-6S	E4
-	CNHL	60521	3085	16W-4S	E7
-	CNHL	60521	3145	16W-4S	E1
-	CNHL	60527	3145	16W-6S	E4
-	CTWD	60803	3348	5W-15S	A1
-	DGvT	60439	3271	16W-11S	E1
-	DGvT	60514	3145	16W-6S	E4
-	DGvT	60521	3145	16W-6S	E4
-	DGvT	60527	3271	16W-12S	E1
-	EMHT	60101	2971	17W-2N	C7
-	EMHT	60126	2971	17W-3N	C5
-	EMHT	60126	3027	17W-0N	C4
-	EMHT	60181	3027	17W-0S	C7
-	FmtT	60030	2533	20W-31N	A6
-	FmtT	60030	2590	20W-31N	B1
-	FmtT	60048	2533	20W-31N	A7
-	FmtT	60048	2590	20W-31N	A1
-	FmtT	60060	2589	20W-28N	E5
-	FmtT	60060	2590	20W-29N	A3
-	GYLK	60030	2590	20W-30N	B1
-	GYLK	60048	2533	20W-32N	A5
-	GYLK	60048	2590	20W-30N	B1
-	HNDL	60521	3145	16W-7S	E6
-	LbvT	60060	2646	18W-26N	D4
-	LGGV	60047	2646	18W-25N	E4
-	LGGV	60060	2646	18W-25N	E4

STREET Block	City	ZIP	Map#	CGS	Grid
SR-83					
-	LGGV	60061	2646	18W-25N	E5
-	LGGV	60089	2700	18W-21N	E6
-	LGGV	60089	2701	18W-21N	A6
-	LKVL	60002	2416	23W-40N	E4
-	LKVL	60046	2416	23W-39N	E4
-	LkvT	60046	2416	23W-39N	E4
-	LkvT	60046	2475	21W-35N	D7
-	LkvT	60073	2475	22W-36N	C3
-	LmnT	60439	3271	16W-11S	E1
-	MDLN	60047	2646	18W-25N	E4
-	MDLN	60060	2589	20W-28N	E5
-	MDLN	60060	2590	20W-29N	A3
-	OKBK	60181	3085	16W-1S	D2
-	OKBK	60521	3085	16W-3S	D6
-	OKTR	60126	3027	17W-0S	C7
-	OKTR	60181	3027	17W-0S	C7
-	OKTR	60523	3085	16W-1S	D2
-	PlsT	60464	3272	14W-12S	D3
-	PlsT	60480	3273	13W-13S	A3
-	RLKB	60073	2475	22W-36N	C3
-	RLKP	60030	2590	20W-30N	A2
-	VLPK	60126	2971	17W-2N	C7
-	VLPK	60126	3027	17W-0S	C6
-	VLPK	60181	3027	17W-0N	C3
-	VNHL	60047	2646	18W-24N	E6
-	VrnT	60060	2646	18W-26N	D4
-	WDDL	60106	2971	17W-2N	C7
-	WDDL	60191	2971	17W-5N	C1
-	WTMT	60514	3085	16W-4S	E7
-	WTMT	60521	3085	16W-4S	E7
10	BFGV	60089	2754	16W-20N	C1
10	DGvT	60527	3207	16W-10S	E6
10	DLTN	60419	3350	0E-17S	E5
10	GYLK	60030	2533	20W-34N	A1
10	HRVY	60426	3349	2W-17S	E5
10	LKVL	60046	2475	21W-35N	D7
10	MPPT	60056	2808	15W-14N	A3
10	MPPT	60070	2808	15W-14N	A3
10	OKTR	60181	3085	16W-1S	D2
10	PTHT	60056	2808	15W-14N	A3
10	PTHT	60070	2808	15W-13N	A7
10	SHLD	60419	3350	0E-17S	E5
10	SHLD	60473	3350	0E-17S	E5
10	WLBK	60527	3207	16W-9S	E4
10	WLNG	60090	2755	15W-16N	A7
100	DLTN	60473	3350	0E-17S	D5
100	DXMR	60426	3349	2W-17S	D5
100	HRVY	60426	3350	1W-17S	A5
100	LKVL	60046	2417	22W-38N	A7
200	ANTH	53179	2357	23W-42N	E5
200	ANTH	60002	2357	23W-42N	E5
200	EGVV	60007	2861	17W-9N	C7
200	MPPT	60056	2862	15W-12N	A1
200	SHLD	60426	3350	0W-17S	C5
200	SlmT	53179	2357	23W-42N	E5
400	BNVL	60106	2915	16W-6N	C6
400	BRRG	60527	3207	16W-9S	E4
400	CTCY	60409	3351	3E-18S	E7
400	HRVY	60419	3350	0W-17S	B5
400	MPPT	60056	2861	16W-9N	E6
500	WLNG	60090	2754	15W-18N	E3
600	BFGV	60089	2701	18W-21N	A6
600	DSPN	60016	2861	15W-11N	E3
600	EGvT	60007	2861	17W-9N	C7
600	HNDL	60521	3085	16W-4S	D6
600	HNDL	60559	3085	16W-4S	D6
600	MPPT	60016	2861	15W-11N	E3
600	OKBK	60523	3085	16W-1S	D2
600	OKBK	60559	3085	16W-4S	D6
600	WTMT	60559	3085	16W-4S	D6
700	DLTN	60419	3351	0E-17S	A5
700	DLTN	60473	3351	1E-17S	A5
700	FmtT	60060	2646	19W-26N	B2
700	MDLN	60060	2646	18W-25N	E4
800	LkvT	60046	2417	22W-38N	A7
800	SHLD	60419	3351	1E-17S	A5
800	SHLD	60473	3351	1E-17S	A5
900	CTCY	60409	3429	3E-21S	E7
900	DSPN	60018	2861	16W-9N	E6
900	EGvT	60005	2861	16W-9N	E6
900	EGVV	60007	2915	16W-8N	C1
900	MPPT	60005	2861	16W-9N	E6
900	MPPT	60018	2861	16W-9N	E6
900	PTHT	60070	2755	15W-16N	A7
900	PTHT	60090	2755	15W-17N	A6
900	WLNG	60089	2754	16W-18N	D2
900	WTMT	60523	3085	16W-3S	D6
1200	ANTH	60002	2416	23W-41N	E1
1200	AntT	60002	2357	23W-41N	E7
1200	AntT	60002	2416	23W-41N	E1
1400	CTCY	60438	3429	3E-19S	E3
1400	DLTN	60409	3351	1E-17S	B5
1400	LNSG	60409	3429	3E-19S	E2
1400	LNSG	60438	3429	3E-19S	E3
1900	EGVV	60005	2861	16W-9N	D6
2200	POSN	60426	3349	2W-17S	C5
2200	POSN	60469	3349	3W-17S	A5
2400	BlmT	60411	3510	4E-25S	B6
2400	LYWD	60411	3509	2E-23S	E3
2400	LYWD	60411	3510	4E-25S	B6
3100	MDLN	60445	3348	3W-17S	E5
3100	POSN	60445	3348	3W-17S	E5
3100	POSN	60469	3348	5W-17S	B5
4200	LGGV	60047	2700	18W-23N	E1
4200	VrnT	60047	2700	18W-22N	E5
4800	ALSP	60803	3276	5W-14S	A7
5100	ALSP	60803	3275	8W-14S	A5
5200	ALSP	60445	3275	6W-14S	E7
5200	CTWD	60445	3275	6W-14S	E7
5500	ALSP	60463	3275	8W-14S	A5
5500	WthT	60463	3275	6W-14S	D6
5500	WthT	60803	3275	8W-14S	A5
6200	WLBK	60527	3145	16W-6S	E5
6300	DGvT	60527	3145	16W-6S	E5
6300	PSHT	60463	3275	8W-14S	A5
6300	VNHL	60061	2646	18W-24N	E6
6600	DRN	60527	3145	16W-7S	E6
6700	DRN	60561	3145	16W-7S	E6
6700	WLBK	60561	3145	16W-7S	E6
7000	PSHT	60463	3274	9W-14S	D5
7100	DRN	60527	3207	16W-8S	E1
7200	DRN	60561	3207	16W-8S	E1
7900	PSHT	60464	3274	9W-13S	C5
7900	PSPK	60464	3274	9W-13S	C5
8500	PlsT	60464	3274	11W-13S	A4
8600	PlsT	60464	3273	11W-13S	E4
10800	LMNT	60439	3272	14W-13S	C3
12200	LMNT	60464	3272	15W-12S	B3
13100	ALSP	60803	3348	5W-15S	A1
13100	CTWD	60445	3348	5W-15S	A1
13900	BmnT	60445	3348	5W-16S	A3
18500	BlmT	60411	3429	3E-21S	E7
18500	LNSG	60411	3429	3E-21S	E7
19000	BlmT	60411	3509	3E-22S	E3
19000	LNSG	60411	3509	3E-22S	E1

STREET Block	City	ZIP	Map#	CGS	Grid
SR-83					
19000	LNSG	60438	3509	3E-22S	E1
34200	AvnT	60030	2533	20W-34N	A1
34400	GYLK	60030	2532	20W-34N	E1
34600	AvnT	60030	2475	21W-34N	E7
34600	GYLK	60030	2475	21W-34N	E7
34800	GYLK	60046	2475	21W-35N	D7
34800	RLKB	60046	2475	21W-35N	D7
SR-83 111th St					
-	PlsT	60464	3272	14W-12S	D3
-	PlsT	60464	3273	13W-13S	A3
-	PlsT	60480	3273	13W-13S	A3
12200	LMNT	60439	3272	14W-13S	C3
12200	LmnT	60464	3272	15W-12S	B3
SR-83 119th St					
7400	PSHT	60463	3274	9W-14S	D5
7900	PSHT	60464	3274	9W-13S	C5
7900	PSPK	60464	3274	9W-13S	C5
SR-83 W 127th St					
4800	ALSP	60803	3276	5W-14S	A7
5100	ALSP	60803	3275	6W-14S	E7
5200	ALSP	60445	3275	6W-14S	E7
5200	CTWD	60445	3275	6W-14S	E7
SR-83 147th St					
3200	MDLN	60445	3348	4W-17S	E5
3200	POSN	60445	3348	4W-17S	E5
3200	POSN	60469	3348	4W-17S	E5
SR-83 W 147th St					
2300	DXMR	60426	3349	2W-17S	C5
2300	HRVY	60426	3349	2W-17S	C5
2300	POSN	60426	3349	3W-17S	C5
2300	POSN	60469	3349	3W-17S	A5
3100	MDLN	60445	3348	3W-17S	E5
3100	POSN	60445	3348	3W-17S	E5
3100	POSN	60469	3348	5W-17S	B5
SR-83 Antioch Rd					
10900	SlmT	53179	2357	23W-42N	E5
12700	ANTH	53179	2357	23W-42N	E5
12700	ANTH	60002	2357	23W-42N	E5
SR-83 S Archer Av					
10800	LMNT	60439	3272	16W-12S	A3
SR-83 Barron Blvd					
-	AvnT	60030	2533	20W-32N	A5
-	AvnT	60048	2533	20W-32N	A5
-	GYLK	60048	2533	20W-32N	A5
10	GYLK	60030	2533	20W-34N	A1
SR-83 N Barron Blvd					
34200	AvnT	60030	2533	20W-34N	A1
34200	GYLK	60030	2533	20W-34N	A1
SR-83 Busse Rd					
200	EGVV	60007	2861	17W-9N	C7
600	EGvT	60007	2861	17W-9N	C7
900	EGVV	60007	2915	17W-8N	C1
1000	BNVL	60106	2915	16W-7N	C4
SR-83 W Cal Sag Rd					
-	PlsT	60480	3273	12W-13S	B3
-	PSHT	60463	3275	7W-14S	B5
5400	ALSP	60445	3275	6W-14S	E7
5400	ALSP	60803	3275	8W-14S	A5
5400	CTWD	60445	3275	6W-14S	E7
5500	ALSP	60463	3275	8W-14S	A5
5500	WthT	60463	3275	6W-14S	D6
5500	WthT	60803	3275	8W-14S	A5
8000	PSHT	60463	3274	10W-13S	C5
8000	PSHT	60464	3274	10W-13S	C5
8000	PSPK	60464	3274	10W-13S	C5
8500	PlsT	60464	3274	11W-13S	A4
8600	PlsT	60464	3273	11W-13S	E4
SR-83 Cicero Av					
-	ALSP	60803	3348	5W-15S	A1
-	CTWD	60803	3348	5W-15S	A1
13100	CTWD	60445	3348	5W-15S	A1
13900	BmnT	60445	3348	5W-16S	A3
14300	MDLN	60445	3348	5W-17S	A4
SR-83 S Cicero Av					
-	CTWD	60445	3348	5W-15S	A1
-	CTWD	60803	3348	5W-15S	A1
12700	ALSP	60803	3276	6W-15S	A7
13100	ALSP	60803	3348	5W-15S	A1
SR-83 W College Dr					
6300	PSHT	60463	3275	8W-14S	B5
6300	WthT	60463	3275	8W-14S	B5
7400	PSHT	60463	3274	9W-13S	E5
7900	PSHT	60464	3274	9W-13S	C5
7900	PSPK	60464	3274	9W-13S	C5
SR-83 Elmhurst Rd					
600	MPPT	60016	2861	15W-11N	E3
900	DSPN	60016	2861	15W-10N	E4
900	MPPT	60056	2861	15W-10N	E4
SR-83 N Elmhurst Rd					
10	MPPT	60056	2808	15W-15N	A3
10	MPPT	60070	2808	15W-15N	A3
10	PTHT	60070	2808	15W-13N	A7
10	WLNG	60090	2755	15W-18N	A4
900	PTHT	60070	2755	15W-16N	A7
1000	PTHT	60090	2755	15W-16N	A7
1100	PTHT	60056	2808	15W-14N	A4
SR-83 S Elmhurst Rd					
10	MPPT	60056	2808	15W-14N	A3
10	MPPT	60070	2808	15W-14N	A3
10	PTHT	60056	2808	15W-14N	A3
10	PTHT	60070	2808	15W-14N	A3
10	WLNG	60090	2755	15W-18N	A4
400	MPPT	60056	2861	16W-9N	E6
800	MPPT	60016	2861	15W-10N	E4
900	DSPN	60016	2861	15W-11N	E3
900	PTHT	60090	2755	15W-17N	A6
1400	DSPN	60018	2861	15W-10N	E6
1400	MPPT	60018	2861	15W-10N	E6
SR-83 Glenwood Dyer Rd					
2400	BlmT	60411	3510	4E-25S	B6
2400	LYWD	60411	3509	3E-24S	E5
2400	LYWD	60411	3510	4E-25S	B6
SR-83 Ivanhoe Rd					
-	AvnT	60030	2533	20W-32N	A5
-	AvnT	60048	2533	20W-32N	A5
-	FmtT	60030	2533	20W-31N	A6
-	FmtT	60030	2590	20W-31N	A1
-	FmtT	60048	2533	20W-31N	A7
-	FmtT	60048	2590	20W-31N	A1
-	FmtT	60060	2589	20W-28N	E5
-	FmtT	60060	2590	20W-29N	A3
-	GYLK	60030	2533	20W-32N	A5
-	GYLK	60030	2590	20W-30N	B1
-	GYLK	60048	2533	20W-32N	A5
-	GYLK	60048	2590	20W-30N	B1
-	MDLN	60060	2589	20W-28N	E5
-	MDLN	60060	2590	20W-29N	A3
-	RLKP	60030	2590	20W-30N	A2
SR-83 Kingery Expwy					
600	HNDL	60521	3085	16W-4S	D6
600	HNDL	60559	3085	16W-4S	D6
600	OKBK	60523	3085	16W-4S	D6
600	OKBK	60559	3085	16W-4S	D6
600	WTMT	60559	3085	16W-4S	D6
900	WTMT	60523	3085	16W-3S	D6

STREET Block	City	ZIP	Map#	CGS	Grid
SR-83 Kingery Hwy					
-	AddT	60101	2971	17W-3N	C5
-	AddT	60106	2971	17W-4N	C4
-	AddT	60191	2971	17W-4N	C2
-	ADSN	60101	2971	17W-3N	C4
-	ADSN	60106	2971	17W-3N	C4
-	ADSN	60126	2971	17W-2N	C7
-	BNVL	60007	2915	16W-7N	C4
-	BNVL	60106	2971	17W-2N	C7
-	BNVL	60191	2971	16W-5N	C1
-	CNHL	60514	3085	16W-4S	E7
-	CNHL	60514	3145	16W-4S	E1
-	CNHL	60521	3085	16W-4S	E7
-	CNHL	60521	3145	16W-7S	E6
-	CNHL	60527	3145	16W-6S	E4
-	DGvT	60439	3271	16W-11S	E1
-	DGvT	60514	3145	16W-6S	E4
-	DGvT	60521	3145	16W-6S	E4
-	DGvT	60527	3271	16W-12S	E1
-	EGVV	60007	2915	17W-6N	C6
-	EMHT	60101	2971	17W-3N	C6
-	EMHT	60126	2971	17W-2N	C7
-	EMHT	60126	3027	17W-0N	C4
-	EMHT	60181	3027	17W-0S	C7
-	HNDL	60521	3085	16W-3S	D6
-	HNDL	60521	3145	16W-7S	E6
-	HNDL	60559	3085	16W-3S	D6
-	LmnT	60439	3271	16W-11S	E1
-	LmnT	60439	3272	16W-12S	A2
-	OKBK	60181	3085	16W-1S	D2
-	OKBK	60521	3085	16W-3S	D6
-	OKBK	60523	3085	16W-3S	D6
-	OKBK	60559	3085	16W-3S	D6
-	OKTR	60126	3027	17W-0S	C7
-	OKTR	60181	3027	17W-0S	C7
-	OKTR	60523	3085	16W-3S	D6
-	VLPK	60126	2971	17W-2N	C7
-	VLPK	60126	3027	17W-0N	C3
-	VLPK	60181	3027	17W-0N	C3
-	WDDL	60106	2971	17W-2N	C7
-	WDDL	60191	2971	17W-5N	C1
-	WTMT	60514	3085	16W-4S	E7
-	WTMT	60521	3085	16W-4S	E7
-	WTMT	60523	3085	16W-3S	D6
-	WTMT	60559	3085	16W-4S	D7
300	DGvT	60527	3207	16W-11S	E7
400	BNVL	60106	2915	17W-6N	C6
400	BRRG	60527	3207	16W-9S	E4
6300	DGvT	60527	3145	16W-6S	E5
6300	WLBK	60527	3145	16W-7S	E5
6600	DRN	60527	3145	16W-7S	E6
6600	WLBK	60561	3145	16W-7S	E6
6700	DRN	60561	3145	16W-7S	E6
7100	WLBK	60527	3207	16W-10S	E6
7200	DRN	60527	3207	16W-8S	E1
7200	DRN	60561	3207	16W-8S	E1
SR-83 S Kingery Hwy					
7600	WLBK	60527	3207	16W-8S	E2
SR-83 W Lincoln St					
-	MPPT	60056	2861	15W-12N	E1
-	MPPT	60056	2862	15W-12N	A1
SR-83 Main St					
200	ANTH	53179	2357	23W-43N	E4
200	ANTH	60002	2357	23W-43N	E4
200	SlmT	53179	2357	23W-43N	E4
1200	ANTH	60002	2416	23W-41N	E1
1200	AntT	60002	2357	23W-41N	E7
1200	AntT	60002	2416	23W-41N	E1
SR-83 N Main St					
10	MPPT	60056	2808	15W-13N	A7
SR-83 S Main St					
10	MPPT	60056	2808	15W-12N	A7
200	MPPT	60056	2862	15W-12N	A1
SR-83 McHenry Rd					
10	BFGV	60089	2754	16W-18N	D2
400	WLNG	60090	2755	15W-16N	A7
500	WLNG	60090	2754	15W-18N	E3
600	BFGV	60089	2701	17W-20N	B7
900	WLNG	60089	2754	16W-18N	D2
SR-83 Mid America Plz					
10	OKTR	60181	3085	16W-1S	D2
SR-83 Milwaukee Av					
-	AntT	60002	2416	23W-39N	E4
-	LKVL	60002	2416	23W-39N	E4
-	LKVL	60046	2416	23W-39N	E4
-	LKVL	60046	2417	22W-38N	A7
-	LKVL	60046	2475	21W-35N	D7
-	LkvT	60046	2416	23W-39N	E4
-	LkvT	60046	2417	22W-38N	A7
-	LkvT	60046	2475	21W-35N	D7
-	LkvT	60073	2475	22W-36N	C3
-	RLKB	60046	2475	21W-35N	C6
-	RLKB	60073	2475	22W-36N	C3
SR-83 N Milwaukee Av					
-	LKVL	60046	2475	22W-38N	B1
100	LKVL	60046	2417	22W-38N	B7
800	LkvT	60046	2417	23W-39N	A6
SR-83 S Milwaukee Av					
10	LKVL	60046	2475	22W-37N	B1
SR-83 Oakton St					
1800	EGvT	60007	2861	16W-9N	D6
1800	EGVV	60007	2861	16W-9N	C6
1900	EGvT	60005	2861	16W-9N	D6
1900	EGVV	60005	2861	16W-9N	D6
SR-83 E Oakton St					
2200	EGvT	60005	2861	16W-9N	D6
2200	EGvT	60007	2861	16W-9N	D6
2200	EGVV	60005	2861	16W-9N	D6
2200	EGVV	60007	2861	16W-9N	D6
2300	MPPT	60005	2861	16W-9N	D6
2500	MPPT	60056	2861	16W-9N	E6
2600	DSPN	60018	2861	16W-9N	E6
2600	MPPT	60018	2861	16W-9N	E6
SR-83 W Oakton St					
900	DSPN	60018	2861	16W-9N	E6
900	EGvT	60005	2861	16W-9N	E6
900	MPPT	60005	2861	16W-9N	E6
900	MPPT	60018	2861	16W-9N	E6
900	MPPT	60056	2861	16W-9N	E6
SR-83 Sibley Blvd					
-	DLTN	60409	3351	1E-17S	C5
-	DLTN	60419	3351	1E-17S	C5
1400	CTCY	60409	3351	2E-18S	E7
SR-83 E Sibley Blvd					
10	HRVY	60426	3349	1W-17S	E5
10	SHLD	60419	3350	0E-17S	D5
10	SHLD	60473	3350	0E-17S	D5
100	DLTN	60473	3350	0E-17S	D5
100	HRVY	60426	3350	1W-17S	A5
400	DLTN	60419	3350	0W-17S	B5
400	HRVY	60419	3350	0W-17S	B5
500	SHLD	60426	3350	0W-17S	C5
700	DLTN	60419	3351	0E-17S	A5
700	DLTN	60473	3351	1E-17S	A5
800	SHLD	60419	3351	1E-17S	A5

STREET Block	City	ZIP	Map#	CGS	Grid
SR-83 E Sibley Blvd					
800	SHLD	60473	3351	1E-17S	A5
1400	DLTN	60409	3351	1E-17S	B5
SR-83 W Sibley Blvd					
10	DLTN	60419	3350	0E-17S	E5
10	HRVY	60426	3349	1W-17S	E5
10	SHLD	60419	3350	0E-17S	E5
10	SHLD	60473	3350	0E-17S	E5
100	DXMR	60426	3349	2W-17S	D5
200	HRVY	60426	3350	0W-17S	C5
200	SHLD	60426	3350	0W-17S	C5
2200	POSN	60426	3349	2W-17S	C5
2200	POSN	60469	3349	2W-17S	C5
SR-83 Torrence Av					
400	CTCY	60409	3351	3E-17S	E5
900	CTCY	60409	3429	2E-21S	E7
1400	CTCY	60438	3429	3E-19S	E3
1400	LNSG	60409	3429	3E-19S	E2
1400	LNSG	60438	3429	3E-19S	E3
18500	BlmT	60411	3429	3E-21S	E7
18500	LNSG	60411	3429	3E-21S	E7
19000	BlmT	60411	3509	2E-23S	E3
19000	LNSG	60411	3509	3E-22S	E1
19000	LNSG	60438	3509	3E-22S	E1
19300	LYWD	60411	3509	2E-23S	E3
SR-102					
100	WMTN	60481	3853	27W-38S	D7
800	WMTN	60481	3943	27W-39S	E2
1200	WslT	60481	3943	27W-40S	E2
SR-102 S Water St					
100	WMTN	60481	3853	27W-38S	D7
800	WMTN	60481	3943	27W-39S	E2
1200	WslT	60481	3943	27W-40S	E2
SR-113					
100	BDWD	60408	3941	32W-41S	E5
100	BDWD	60408	3942	30W-42S	C6
400	RedT	60408	3942	31W-41S	B6
500	BDWD	60481	3941	31W-39S	E2
500	RedT	60408	3941	32W-41S	E5
500	WmTp	60481	3941	31W-39S	E2
800	BvlT	60416	3941	34W-39S	A2
800	CLCY	60416	3941	34W-39S	A2
900	DMND	60416	3941	34W-39S	A2
2900	DMND	60408	3941	32W-39S	D2
2900	DMND	60481	3941	32W-39S	D2
22100	CstT	60481	3943	27W-42S	D7
22500	CstT	60481	3942	29W-41S	E6
23600	RedT	60481	3942	29W-41S	D6
SR-113 W Coal City Rd					
-	DMND	60408	3941	32W-39S	E2
-	DMND	60416	3941	32W-39S	E2
-	DMND	60481	3941	32W-39S	E2
500	BDWD	60408	3941	31W-39S	E2
500	BDWD	60481	3941	31W-39S	E2
500	RedT	60408	3941	31W-39S	E2
500	WmTp	60481	3941	31W-39S	E2
SR-113 E Division St					
800	BvlT	60416	3941	34W-39S	A2
800	CLCY	60416	3941	34W-39S	A2
900	DMND	60416	3941	34W-39S	A2
2900	DMND	60408	3941	32W-39S	D2
2900	DMND	60481	3941	32W-39S	D2
SR-113 N Division St					
100	BDWD	60408	3941	32W-41S	E5
500	RedT	60408	3941	32W-41S	E5
1100	BDWD	60481	3941	31W-40S	E2
1100	WmTp	60481	3941	31W-40S	E2
SR-113 Main St					
22500	CstT	60481	3942	29W-41S	E6
22500	CstT	60481	3943	28W-41S	B6
23600	RedT	60408	3942	29W-41S	D6
23600	RedT	60481	3942	29W-41S	D6
SR-113 E Main St					
100	BDWD	60408	3942	30W-42S	C6
400	RedT	60408	3942	31W-41S	B6
SR-113 W Main St					
100	BDWD	60408	3942	31W-41S	A5
400	BDWD	60408	3941	31W-41S	E5
SR-120					
-	GRNE	60031	2534	15W-33N	E4
-	GRNE	60048	2534	16W-33N	D4
-	GrtT	60030	2531	24W-32N	B5
-	GrtT	60073	2530	26W-31N	E6
-	GrtT	60073	2531	24W-32N	B5
-	LKMR	60041	2530	27W-31N	A6
-	LKMR	60051	2530	28W-31N	A6
-	LKMR	60073	2530	27W-31N	B6
-	MchT	60097	2527	35W-33N	A2
-	MHRY	60050	2526	35W-33N	E2
-	MHRY	60097	2526	35W-33N	E2
-	MHRY	60097	2527	35W-33N	A2
-	PKCY	60085	2535	13W-33N	D3
-	VOLO	60051	2530	27W-31N	A6
-	VOLO	60073	2530	26W-31N	E6
-	VOLO	60073	2531	25W-32N	A6
-	WcnT	60051	2530	28W-31N	A6
-	WcnT	60073	2530	27W-31N	A6
-	WrnT	60030	2534	17W-32N	B4
-	WrnT	60031	2534	15W-33N	E4
-	WrnT	60048	2534	18W-32N	A4
-	WrnT	60048	2535	15W-33N	B4
10	GYLK	60030	2532	21W-32N	E4
10	HNVL	60030	2532	22W-33N	A4
10	HNVL	60073	2532	22W-33N	A4
10	WDSK	60098	2524	42W-31N	C6
100	HbnT	53147	2350		D4
100	HbnT	60034	2350		D4
100	LinT	53147	2350		D2
100	LKMR	60051	2529	30W-32N	A4
100	RDLK	60073	2532	23W-32N	A4
100	RLKP	60030	2532	23W-32N	A4
100	RLKP	60073	2532	23W-32N	A4
100	WcnT	60051	2529	29W-31N	D6
100	WKGN	60085	2537	10W-33N	B2
300	AvnT	60030	2532	21W-32N	D4
400	GYLK	60030	2533	19W-32N	C4
500	MchT	60051	2529	30W-32N	A4
700	AvnT	60030	2531	23W-32N	D4
700	AvnT	60030	2533	20W-32N	A5
700	AvnT	60073	2531	24W-32N	D4
700	RDLK	60073	2531	23W-32N	D4
800	DrrT	60098	2524	42W-31N	C6
800	GwdT	60098	2524	42W-31N	C6
1200	GwdT	60098	2525	40W-32N	A5
1200	WDSK	60098	2525	40W-32N	A5
2000	WrnT	60030	2533	19W-32N	C4
2600	WKGN	60085	2536	12W-33N	C3
2900	PKCY	60085	2536	13W-33N	A3
3300	MchT	60051	2528	32W-33N	C3
3300	MHRY	60050	2528	30W-32N	E4
3300	MHRY	60051	2528	32W-33N	C3
3800	WKGN	60085	2535	13W-33N	D3
4200	GRNE	60031	2535	14W-33N	D3
4200	WKGN	60031	2535	14W-33N	D3
4300	MHRY	60050	2527	35W-33N	B2
4400	WrnT	60031	2535	14W-33N	C3

STREET Block	City	ZIP	Map#	CGS	Grid
SR-120					
5200	MchT	60050	2527	34W-33N	C2
7800	BLVY	60097	2526	35W-33N	E2
7800	BLVY	60098	2526	35W-33N	E2
7800	GwdT	60098	2526	35W-33N	E2
7800	MchT	60050	2526	36W-33N	D2
7800	MchT	60097	2526	36W-33N	D2
7800	MchT	60098	2526	36W-33N	D2
7800	WRLK	60098	2526	37W-33N	B2
8700	BLVY	60098	2525	38W-33N	E2
13900	HtdT	60098	2524	42W-32N	A5
18000	GYLK	60030	2534	18W-32N	A4
SR-120 Belvidere Rd					
-	AvnT	60030	2531	24W-32N	C5
-	AvnT	60073	2531	24W-32N	C5
-	GRNE	60031	2535	14W-33N	D3
-	GrtT	60030	2531	24W-32N	B5
-	GrtT	60073	2530	26W-31N	E6
-	GrtT	60073	2531	24W-32N	B5
-	LKMR	60041	2530	27W-31N	A6
-	LKMR	60051	2529	28W-31N	D6
-	LKMR	60051	2530	28W-31N	A6
-	LKMR	60073	2530	27W-31N	B6
-	PKCY	60085	2535	13W-33N	D3
-	RDLK	60073	2531	24W-32N	C5
-	VOLO	60051	2530	27W-31N	A6
-	VOLO	60073	2530	26W-31N	E6
-	VOLO	60073	2531	25W-32N	A6
-	WcnT	60051	2529	28W-31N	E6
-	WcnT	60051	2530	28W-31N	A6
-	WcnT	60073	2530	27W-31N	A6
-	WKGN	60031	2535	14W-33N	D3
2900	PKCY	60085	2536	13W-33N	A3
2900	WKGN	60085	2536	13W-33N	A3
3800	WKGN	60085	2535	13W-33N	D3
SR-120 E Belvidere Rd					
-	GYLK	60030	2532	21W-33N	C4
10	HNVL	60030	2532	22W-33N	C3
400	GYLK	60030	2533	20W-32N	A5
700	AvnT	60030	2533	20W-32N	A5
SR-120 W Belvidere Rd					
-	GRNE	60031	2534	15W-33N	E4
-	GRNE	60048	2534	16W-33N	D4
-	WrnT	60030	2534	17W-32N	B4
-	WrnT	60031	2534	15W-33N	E4
-	WrnT	60048	2534	18W-32N	A4
-	WrnT	60048	2535	15W-33N	B4
10	GYLK	60030	2532	21W-32N	E4
10	HNVL	60030	2532	22W-33N	A4
10	HNVL	60073	2532	22W-33N	A4
100	RDLK	60073	2532	23W-32N	A4
100	RLKP	60030	2532	23W-32N	A4
100	RLKP	60073	2532	23W-32N	A4
300	AvnT	60030	2532	21W-32N	D4
700	AvnT	60030	2531	23W-32N	D4
700	AvnT	60073	2531	24W-32N	D4
700	RDLK	60073	2531	23W-32N	D4
1800	AvnT	60030	2533	18W-32N	D4
1800	GYLK	60030	2533	19W-32N	C4
2000	WrnT	60030	2533	19W-32N	C4
4200	GRNE	60031	2535	14W-33N	D3
4200	WKGN	60031	2535	14W-33N	D3
4200	WKGN	60085	2535	14W-33N	D3
4400	WrnT	60031	2535	14W-33N	C3
18000	GYLK	60030	2534	18W-32N	A4
SR-120 Belvidere St					
100	WKGN	60085	2537	10W-33N	B2
2600	WKGN	60085	2536	12W-33N	C3
SR-120 E Church St					
100	WDSK	60098	2524	41W-31N	D7
SR-120 W Church St					
10	WDSK	60098	2524	41W-31N	D7
SR-120 Elm St					
-	MchT	60050	2527	34W-33N	B2
-	MHRY	60050	2527	34W-33N	B2
SR-120 W Elm St					
3300	MchT	60051	2528	32W-33N	C3
3300	MHRY	60050	2528	30W-32N	E4
3300	MHRY	60051	2528	32W-33N	C3
4300	MHRY	60050	2527	35W-33N	B2
5200	MchT	60050	2527	34W-33N	C2
SR-120 N Madison St					
300	WDSK	60098	2524	41W-31N	D7
SR-120 McHenry Av					
200	WDSK	60098	2524	41W-31N	D7
SR-120 W Rand Rd					
100	LKMR	60051	2529	30W-32N	A4
100	WcnT	60051	2529	29W-31N	D6
500	MchT	60050	2529	30W-32N	A4
SR-120 Washington St					
10	WDSK	60098	2524	42W-31N	C6
800	DrrT	60098	2524	42W-31N	C6
800	GwdT	60098	2524	42W-31N	C6
13900	HtdT	60098	2524	42W-32N	A5
SR-126					
10	PNFD	60544	3338	30W-18S	A7
10	PnfT	60544	3338	29W-17S	D6
100	YKVL	60560	3333	41W-16S	E5
400	PNFD	60544	3339	28W-16S	A4
400	PnfT	60544	3339	28W-16S	A4
700	NasT	60543	3337	32W-18S	C7
700	NasT	60544	3337	32W-18S	C7
1700	PNFD	60544	3337	31W-17S	E7
1700	PnfT	60544	3337	31W-17S	E7
5000	KdlT	60560	3334	41W-17S	A5
8000	YKVL	60560	3334	41W-17S	A5
8700	KdlT	60560	3333	41W-16S	E5
24000	PnfT	60543	3337	32W-17S	B7
SR-126 W Lockport St					
700	PNFD	60544	3338	30W-18S	A7
1000	PnfT	60544	3338	30W-18S	A7
1700	PNFD	60544	3337	31W-17S	E7
1700	PnfT	60544	3337	31W-17S	E7
24000	NasT	60543	3337	32W-17S	B7
24000	NasT	60544	3337	32W-17S	B7
24000	PnfT	60543	3337	32W-17S	B7
SR-126 W Main St					
10	PNFD	60544	3338	29W-17S	D6
10	PnfT	60544	3338	29W-17S	D6
400	PNFD	60544	3339	28W-16S	A4
400	PnfT	60544	3339	28W-16S	A4
SR-126 School House Rd					
100	YKVL	60560	3333	41W-16S	E5
SR-129					
-	BCVL	60407	4030	33W-43S	B3
-	BDWD	60407	4030	32W-43S	C2
-	GDLY	60407	4030	32W-43S	C2
-	RedT	60407	4030	32W-43S	C2
100	BDWD	60408	3942	30W-41S	C4
100	RedT	60481	3942	30W-41S	C4
200	RedT	60408	3942	30W-39S	D1
200	WMTN	60481	3942	30W-39S	D1
200	WmTp	60408	3942	30W-39S	D1
200	WmTp	60481	3942	30W-39S	D1
400	BDWD	60407	3941	31W-42S	E7
400	BDWD	60408	3941	31W-42S	E7
SR-129					
400	RedT	60407	3941	31W-42S	E7
400	RedT	60408	3941	31W-42S	E7
SR-129 N Washington St					
100	BDWD	60408	3942	30W-41S	C4
100	RedT	60481	3942	30W-41S	C4
200	RedT	60408	3942	30W-40S	D3
200	WMTN	60481	3942	29W-40S	D2
200	WmTp	60408	3942	29W-40S	D2
200	WmTp	60481	3942	29W-40S	D2
SR-129 S Washington St					
100	BDWD	60408	3942	31W-41S	A6
300	RedT	60408	3942	31W-42S	A7
400	BDWD	60407	3941	31W-42S	E7
400	BDWD	60408	3941	31W-42S	E7
400	RedT	60407	3941	31W-42S	E7
400	RedT	60408	3941	31W-42S	E7
SR-131					
10	WKGN	60085	2536	12W-33N	B3
400	WKGN	60085	2479	12W-33N	B7
600	LKBF	60044	2593	11W-28N	D5
700	WkgT	60085	2479	12W-35N	B7
900	NCHI	60064	2536	12W-33N	B4
900	WKGN	60064	2536	12W-33N	B4
1000	NCHI	60044	2593	11W-29N	D4
1000	NCHI	60088	2593	11W-30N	C1
1000	ShdT	60044	2593	11W-29N	D4
1000	ShdT	60088	2593	11W-29N	D4
1400	WkgT	60031	2479	12W-35N	A6
2100	WKGN	60087	2479	12W-36N	A4
2100	WkgT	60087	2479	12W-36N	A4
2400	NCHI	60064	2593	11W-30N	C1
36900	BHPK	60087	2479	12W-36N	A4
38300	BHPK	60087	2421	12W-38N	B7
38300	WKGN	60087	2421	12W-38N	B7
39000	BHPK	60083	2421	12W-39N	B6
39000	BHPK	60099	2421	12W-39N	B4
40800	BtnT	60099	2421	12W-40N	B2
40800	WDWH	60099	2421	12W-40N	B2
41000	ZION	60099	2421	12W-41N	B2
41700	ZION	60099	2362	12W-41N	A7
42000	BtnT	60099	2362	13W-42N	A7
42500	NptT	60099	2362	12W-41N	B7
43400	NptT	53158	2362	13W-43N	A4
43400	PTPR	53158	2362	13W-43N	A4
SR-131 Green Bay Rd					
600	LKBF	60044	2593	11W-28N	D5
1000	NCHI	60044	2593	11W-29N	D4
1000	NCHI	60064	2536	12W-32N	B5
1000	NCHI	60088	2593	11W-30N	C1
1000	ShdT	60044	2593	11W-29N	D4
1000	ShdT	60088	2593	11W-29N	D4
1000	WKGN	60064	2536	12W-32N	B4
1000	WKGN	60085	2536	12W-32N	B4
2400	NCHI	60064	2593	11W-30N	C1
SR-131 N Green Bay Rd					
10	WKGN	60085	2536	12W-33N	B1
400	WKGN	60085	2479	12W-33N	B7
700	WkgT	60085	2479	12W-35N	B7
1400	WkgT	60031	2479	12W-35N	A6
2100	WKGN	60087	2479	12W-36N	A4
2100	WkgT	60087	2479	12W-36N	A4
36900	BHPK	60087	2479	12W-36N	A4
38300	BHPK	60087	2421	12W-38N	B7
38300	WKGN	60087	2421	12W-38N	B7
39000	BHPK	60083	2421	12W-39N	B6
39000	BHPK	60099	2421	12W-39N	B4
40800	BtnT	60099	2421	12W-40N	B2
40800	WDWH	60099	2421	12W-40N	B2
41000	ZION	60099	2421	12W-41N	B2
41700	ZION	60099	2362	12W-41N	A7
42000	BtnT	60099	2362	13W-42N	A7
42500	NptT	60099	2362	12W-41N	A7
43400	NptT	53158	2362	13W-43N	A4
43400	PTPR	53158	2362	13W-43N	A4
SR-131 S Green Bay Rd					
10	WKGN	60085	2536	12W-33N	B3
900	NCHI	60064	2536	12W-33N	B4
900	WKGN	60064	2536	12W-33N	B4
SR-132					
-	WKGN	60085	2537	10W-34N	B1
10	LKVL	60046	2475	21W-37N	E1
200	LKVL	60046	2474	24W-37N	D1
400	LkvT	60046	2474	23W-38N	E1
800	LNHT	60046	2475	21W-38N	D1
1000	LkvT	60046	2475	21W-38N	D1
1700	LNHT	60046	2476	20W-37N	A2
2000	LkvT	60046	2476	20W-37N	A2
3300	GRNE	60031	2479	13W-34N	A7
3300	WKGN	60031	2479	12W-35N	A7
3300	WKGN	60085	2479	12W-35N	A7
3700	GRNE	60031	2478	14W-34N	D7
5300	WrnT	60031	2478	15W-35N	A6
5800	WrnT	60031	2477	18W-35N	A5
6000	GRNE	60031	2477	18W-35N	A5
7600	GRNE	60031	2476	18W-36N	E5
7600	WrnT	60031	2476	18W-36N	E5
18700	WrnT	60046	2476	18W-36N	E5
SR-132 Grand Av					
-	WKGN	60085	2537	10W-34N	B1
3300	GRNE	60031	2479	13W-34N	A7
3300	WKGN	60031	2479	12W-35N	A7
3300	WKGN	60085	2479	12W-35N	A7
3700	GRNE	60031	2478	14W-34N	D7
5300	WrnT	60031	2478	15W-35N	A6
5800	WrnT	60031	2477	18W-35N	A5
6000	GRNE	60031	2477	18W-35N	A5
7600	GRNE	60031	2476	18W-36N	E5
7600	WrnT	60031	2476	18W-36N	E5
SR-132 E Grand Av					
10	LKVL	60046	2475	22W-38N	A1
1000	LkvT	60046	2475	21W-38N	D1
1700	LNHT	60046	2475	20W-37N	E1
1700	LNHT	60046	2476	20W-37N	A2
2000	LkvT	60046	2476	20W-37N	A2
SR-132 W Grand Av					
10	LKVL	60046	2475	21W-37N	E1
200	LKVL	60046	2474	24W-37N	D1
400	LkvT	60046	2474	23W-38N	E1
18400	GRNE	60031	2476	18W-36N	E5
18400	WrnT	60031	2476	18W-36N	E5
18700	WrnT	60046	2476	18W-36N	E5
18900	LkvT	60046	2476	18W-36N	D5
19400	LNHT	60046	2476	19W-36N	C3
20800	LkvT	60046	2475	20W-37N	E1
20800	LNHT	60046	2475	20W-37N	E1
SR-134					
-	GrtT	60041	2474	25W-34N	A7
-	GrtT	60041	2531	25W-34N	B1
-	RDLK	60073	2474	25W-34N	B7
10	RLKP	60073	2532	22W-33N	B3
100	HNVL	60073	2532	22W-33N	A3
100	RDLK	60073	2532	22W-33N	B3
200	RDLK	60073	2531	23W-33N	E3
300	HNVL	60030	2532	22W-33N	B3
500	AvnT	60073	2531	24W-34N	D1
SR-134					
27200	FXLK	60041	2473	27W-34N	C7
27200	GrtT	60041	2473	26W-34N	D7
SR-134 W Big Hollow Rd					
-	GrtT	60041	2474	25W-34N	A7
-	RDLK	60073	2474	25W-34N	B7
27200	FXLK	60041	2473	27W-34N	C7
27200	GrtT	60041	2473	26W-34N	D7
SR-134 E Main St					
10	RLKP	60073	2532	22W-33N	A3
100	HNVL	60073	2532	22W-33N	A3
300	HNVL	60030	2532	22W-33N	B3
SR-134 W Main St					
10	RLKP	60073	2532	22W-33N	B3
100	RDLK	60073	2532	22W-33N	B3
SR-134 Nippersink Av					
200	RDLK	60073	2531	23W-33N	E3
SR-134 Railroad Av					
300	RDLK	60073	2531	23W-33N	E2
500	AvnT	60073	2531	23W-34N	D2
SR-134 Round Lake Rd					
-	AvnT	60073	2531	24W-34N	D1
-	RDLK	60073	2531	24W-34N	C1
SR-137					
-	AvnT	60030	2533	20W-32N	B6
-	AvnT	60048	2533	20W-32N	B6
-	FmtT	60048	2533	19W-31N	B6
-	FmtT	60048	2590	18W-30N	E2
-	GNOK	60044	2592	15W-30N	B2
-	GYLK	60030	2533	20W-32N	B6
-	GYLK	60048	2533	20W-32N	B6
-	LbvT	60044	2592	13W-30N	E1
-	LbvT	60044	2593	13W-30N	A1
-	LbvT	60048	2590	19W-31N	D1
-	LbvT	60064	2592	13W-30N	E1
-	LYVL	60048	2590	19W-31N	D1
-	NCHI	60044	2592	13W-30N	E1
-	NCHI	60044	2593	12W-30N	B2
-	NCHI	60064	2536	10W-31N	E7
-	ShdT	60088	2593	12W-30N	A2
-	WKGN	60085	2480	10W-35N	B6
-	WKGN	60087	2480	10W-35N	B6
10	LYVL	60048	2591	17W-30N	B2
100	PTPR	53158	2363	9W-43N	C4
100	WPHR	53158	2363	9W-43N	C4
100	WPHR	60096	2363	9W-42N	B6
300	LbvT	60048	2591	16W-30N	E2
500	WKGN	60085	2537	10W-34N	B1
900	NCHI	60064	2537	10W-32N	A5
1100	LbvT	60048	2592	15W-30N	A2
1400	BtnT	60096	2422	9W-41N	B1
1400	BtnT	60099	2422	9W-41N	B1
1400	WPHR	60096	2422	9W-41N	B1
1500	NCHI	60088	2593	12W-30N	A2
1700	ZION	60099	2422	10W-39N	B4
2000	NCHI	60064	2593	12W-30N	A2
2100	GNOK	60048	2592	15W-30N	B2
2500	BHPK	60087	2480	10W-36N	B3
2500	WkgT	60087	2480	10W-36N	B3
3400	BHPK	60099	2422	10W-39N	B6
3400	ShdT	60044	2593	12W-30N	A2
3400	ShdT	60064	2593	12W-30N	A2
37800	BHPK	60099	2480	9W-37N	B1
38200	BHPK	60087	2422	9W-38N	B7
SR-137 Amstutz Expwy					
-	NCHI	60044	2593	11W-30N	E2
-	NCHI	60064	2536	10W-31N	E7
-	NCHI	60064	2537	10W-31N	A7
-	NCHI	60064	2593	10W-31N	E1
-	NCHI	60088	2593	11W-30N	E1
-	WKGN	60085	2480	10W-35N	B6
-	WKGN	60085	2537	10W-34N	B1
-	WKGN	60087	2480	10W-35N	B6
SR-137 S Amstutz Expwy					
-	WKGN	60085	2537	10W-33N	B3
SR-137 Buckley Rd					
-	AvnT	60030	2533	20W-32N	B6
-	AvnT	60048	2533	20W-32N	B6
-	FmtT	60048	2533	19W-31N	B6
-	FmtT	60048	2590	18W-30N	E2
-	GNOK	60044	2592	15W-30N	B2
-	GYLK	60030	2533	20W-32N	B6
-	GYLK	60048	2533	20W-32N	B6
-	LbvT	60044	2592	13W-30N	E1
-	LbvT	60044	2593	13W-30N	A1
-	LbvT	60048	2590	19W-31N	D1
-	LbvT	60064	2592	13W-30N	E1
-	LYVL	60048	2590	19W-31N	D1
-	NCHI	60044	2592	13W-30N	E1
-	ShdT	60088	2593	12W-30N	A2
10	LbvT	60048	2591	16W-30N	D2
10	LYVL	60048	2591	16W-30N	D2
1500	NCHI	60088	2593	12W-30N	A2
2000	NCHI	60064	2593	12W-30N	A2
2100	GNOK	60048	2592	15W-30N	B2
3400	ShdT	60044	2593	12W-30N	A2
3400	ShdT	60064	2593	12W-30N	A2
3500	NCHI	60044	2593	12W-30N	A2
SR-137 W Buckley Rd					
1100	LbvT	60048	2592	15W-30N	A2
14400	GNOK	60048	2592	14W-30N	C1
15700	LbvT	60048	2591	15W-30N	E2
SR-137 S Genesee St					
500	WKGN	60085	2537	10W-33N	B3
900	NCHI	60064	2537	10W-33N	B4
SR-137 E Greenwood Av					
10	WKGN	60085	2480	10W-36N	B5
10	WKGN	60087	2480	10W-36N	B5
SR-137 Peterson Rd					
300	LbvT	60048	2591	16W-30N	E2
300	LYVL	60048	2591	16W-30N	E2
SR-137 W Peterson Rd					
-	LbvT	60048	2591	18W-30N	A2
-	LYVL	60048	2591	18W-30N	A2
SR-137 Sheridan Rd					
-	WKGN	60085	2537	10W-32N	A4
100	PTPR	53158	2363	9W-43N	C4
100	WPHR	53158	2363	9W-43N	C4
100	WPHR	60096	2363	9W-42N	B6
1000	NCHI	60064	2537	10W-32N	A5
1400	BtnT	60096	2422	9W-41N	B1
1400	BtnT	60099	2422	9W-41N	B1
1400	WPHR	60096	2422	9W-41N	B1
1700	ZION	60099	2422	10W-39N	B4
3400	BHPK	60099	2422	10W-39N	B6
SR-137 N Sheridan Rd					
1800	WKGN	60085	2480	10W-36N	B5
1800	WKGN	60087	2480	10W-36N	B5
2500	BHPK	60087	2480	10W-36N	B3
2500	WkgT	60087	2480	10W-36N	B3
37800	BHPK	60099	2480	9W-37N	B1
38200	BHPK	60087	2422	9W-38N	B7
38400	BHPK	60099	2422	10W-38N	B7
SR-142					
-	NptT	60099	2360	16W-43N	D5
-	WDWH	60099	2360	16W-43N	D5
SR-142 W Russell Rd					
-	NptT	60099	2360	16W-43N	D5
-	WDWH	60099	2360	16W-43N	D5
SR-158					
4400	BHPK	60099	2421	13W-39N	A5
SR-158 N Lynsee Ct					
4600	BHPK	60099	2421	13W-39N	A5
SR-158 N Queensbury Ln					
4400	BHPK	60099	2421	13W-39N	A5
SR-171					
-	CHCG	60068	2918	10W-6N	A5
-	JSTC	60458	3209	11W-9S	D3
-	JSTC	60480	3209	11W-9S	E2
-	LmnT	60480	3208	15W-11S	C7
-	LmnT	60480	3272	15W-11S	B1
-	LYNS	60534	3148	10W-4S	A1
-	MCCK	60525	3148	10W-5S	A2
-	MCCK	60534	3148	10W-4S	A1
-	MYWD	60130	3088	10W-3S	B5
-	MYWD	60153	3088	10W-3S	B5
-	PKRG	60068	2918	10W-6N	A5
-	PlsT	60480	3208	14W-11S	D6
-	PvsT	60130	3088	10W-3S	B5
-	PvsT	60153	3030	10W-0S	A7
-	PvsT	60153	3088	10W-3S	B5
-	SMMT	60525	3148	10W-5S	B2
10	MYWD	60153	3030	10W-0N	A4
100	LKPT	60441	3419	22W-18S	D1
100	RVFT	60305	3030	10W-0N	A4
200	LktT	60441	3419	22W-18S	D1
400	JLET	60432	3499	23W-22S	A2
600	LKPT	60441	3341	21W-17S	E6
700	MLPK	60153	3030	10W-1N	A2
700	MLPK	60160	3030	10W-1N	A1
1400	JLET	60441	3499	23W-21S	A1
1400	JltT	60432	3499	23W-22S	A1
1400	LktT	60432	3499	23W-21S	A1
1400	LktT	60441	3499	23W-21S	A1
1600	MLPK	60160	2974	10W-2N	A7
1600	MLPK	60171	3030	10W-2N	A1
1600	PvsT	60160	3030	10W-1N	A1
1600	RVGV	60160	2974	10W-2N	A7
1600	RVGV	60160	3030	10W-2N	A1
1600	RVGV	60171	2974	10W-2N	A7
1600	RVGV	60171	3030	10W-2N	A1
1700	FTPK	60130	3030	10W-0S	A6
1700	FTPK	60153	3030	10W-0S	A6
1700	MYWD	60130	3030	10W-0S	A6
2100	PvsT	60130	3030	10W-1S	A7
2200	NRIV	60141	3088	10W-2S	A2
2200	NRIV	60546	3088	10W-2S	A2
2200	PvsT	60141	3088	10W-3S	B5
2500	BKFD	60546	3088	10W-2S	A3
3000	RVGV	60634	2974	10W-3N	A4
3500	RVSD	60546	3088	10W-3S	B5
3700	CHCG	60634	2974	10W-2N	A6
3900	BKFD	60513	3088	10W-4S	B6
3900	LYNS	60534	3088	10W-4S	A7
3900	RVSD	60513	3088	10W-4S	B6
4200	CHCG	60656	2974	10W-2N	A6
4200	CHCG	60706	2974	10W-2N	A6
4200	NRDG	60706	2974	10W-2N	A6
4600	CHCG	60656	2918	10W-5N	A7
4600	CHCG	60706	2918	10W-5N	A7
4600	NRDG	60656	2918	10W-5N	A7
4600	NRDG	60706	2918	10W-5N	A7
5500	CHCG	60631	2918	10W-6N	A5
5500	SMMT	60501	3148	9W-6S	C5
6300	BDPK	60501	3148	9W-7S	C5
6600	BDPK	60455	3148	9W-7S	C6
6700	BGVW	60455	3148	9W-7S	C6
6700	BGVW	60501	3148	9W-7S	C6
6800	BDPK	60458	3148	9W-7S	C6
6800	BGVW	60458	3148	9W-7S	C6
7000	JSTC	60458	3148	10W-7S	B7
7000	JSTC	60501	3148	10W-7S	B7
7300	JSTC	60458	3210	10W-8S	A1
8000	WLSP	60480	3209	11W-9S	D3
9000	PlsT	60480	3209	13W-10S	A5
10800	LMNT	60439	3272	16W-13S	A4
11300	LMNT	60439	3271	17W-14S	B7
12700	LMNT	60439	3343	18W-15S	A1
12900	LMNT	60439	3342	18W-15S	E1
13400	HMGN	60439	3342	19W-15S	D2
13400	HMGN	60491	3342	19W-15S	D2
13500	HMGN	60441	3342	19W-16S	D3
13500	HmrT	60441	3342	20W-17S	A5
13500	HmrT	60491	3342	20W-17S	A5
14400	LktT	60441	3342	20W-17S	A5
14500	LKPT	60441	3342	21W-17S	A5
14700	LktT	60441	3341	21W-17S	E6
SR-171 1st Av					
-	FTPK	60130	3030	10W-1S	A7
-	FTPK	60153	3030	10W-1S	A7
-	MYWD	60130	3088	10W-3S	B5
-	MYWD	60153	3088	10W-3S	B5
-	NRIV	60141	3088	10W-1S	A2
-	NRIV	60546	3088	10W-2S	A2
-	PvsT	60130	3088	10W-3S	B5
-	PvsT	60141	3088	10W-3S	B5
-	PvsT	60153	3030	10W-1S	A7
-	PvsT	60153	3088	10W-3S	B5
1900	MLPK	60160	3030	10W-1N	A1
1900	MLPK	60171	3030	10W-1N	A1
1900	PvsT	60160	3030	10W-1N	A1
1900	RVGV	60160	3030	10W-2N	A1
1900	RVGV	60171	3030	10W-2N	A1
2100	MYWD	60130	3030	10W-1S	A7
2100	MYWD	60153	3030	10W-1S	A7
2100	PvsT	60130	3030	10W-1S	A7
3900	BKFD	60513	3088	10W-4S	B6
3900	LYNS	60534	3088	10W-4S	A6
3900	RVSD	60513	3088	10W-4S	B6
3900	RVSD	60546	3088	10W-4S	B6
SR-171 N 1st Av					
10	MYWD	60153	3030	10W-0N	A4
700	MLPK	60153	3030	10W-1N	A2
700	MLPK	60160	3030	10W-1N	A1
700	RVFT	60305	3030	10W-1N	A3
1600	MLPK	60160	2974	10W-2N	A7
1600	MLPK	60171	3030	10W-2N	A1
1600	PvsT	60160	3030	10W-1N	A1
1600	RVGV	60160	2974	10W-2N	A7
1600	RVGV	60160	3030	10W-2N	A1
1600	RVGV	60171	2974	10W-2N	A7
1600	RVGV	60171	3030	10W-2N	A1
SR-171 S 1st Av					
-	BKFD	60513	3088	10W-2S	A3
-	LYNS	60534	3088	10W-3S	B6
-	PvsT	60130	3030	10W-0S	A7
-	PvsT	60153	3030	10W-0S	A7
-	RVSD	60513	3088	10W-3S	B6
-	RVSD	60546	3088	10W-2S	B4
100	MYWD	60153	3030	10W-0N	A4
100	RVFT	60305	3030	10W-0N	A4
1700	FTPK	60130	3030	10W-0S	A6
SR-171 S 1st Av					
1700	FTPK	60153	3030	10W-0S	A6
1700	MYWD	60130	3030	10W-0S	A6
2200	NRIV	60141	3088	10W-2S	A2
2200	NRIV	60546	3088	10W-2S	A2
2200	PvsT	60141	3088	10W-1S	A2
2500	BKFD	60546	3088	10W-2S	A3
SR-171 Archer Av					
-	JSTC	60458	3209	11W-9S	E2
-	JSTC	60480	3209	11W-9S	E2
-	LmnT	60439	3272	15W-11S	B1
-	LmnT	60439	3208	15W-11S	C7
-	LmnT	60480	3272	15W-11S	B1
-	PlsT	60480	3208	14W-11S	D6
8000	WLSP	60480	3209	11W-9S	D3
9000	PlsT	60480	3209	13W-10S	A5
13900	HmrT	60441	3342	20W-17S	A5
13900	HmrT	60491	3342	20W-17S	A5
14400	LktT	60441	3342	20W-17S	A5
14500	LKPT	60441	3342	21W-17S	A5
14700	LKPT	60441	3341	21W-17S	E6
14700	LktT	60441	3341	21W-17S	E6
SR-171 S Archer Av					
-	JSTC	60458	3209	11W-9S	D3
-	JSTC	60458	3210	11W-8S	A2
-	JSTC	60480	3209	11W-9S	E2
-	WLSP	60480	3209	11W-9S	E2
10800	LMNT	60439	3272	16W-13S	A4
11300	LMNT	60439	3271	17W-14S	B7
12700	LMNT	60439	3343	18W-15S	A1
12900	LMNT	60439	3342	18W-15S	E1
13400	HMGN	60439	3342	19W-15S	D2
13400	HMGN	60491	3342	19W-15S	D2
13500	HMGN	60441	3342	19W-16S	D3
13500	HmrT	60441	3342	19W-16S	D3
13500	HmrT	60491	3342	19W-16S	D3
SR-171 S Archer Rd					
5500	SMMT	60501	3148	9W-6S	C5
6300	BDPK	60501	3148	9W-7S	C5
6600	BDPK	60455	3148	9W-7S	C6
6700	BGVW	60455	3148	9W-7S	C6
6700	BGVW	60501	3148	9W-7S	C6
6800	BDPK	60458	3148	9W-7S	C6
6800	BGVW	60458	3148	9W-7S	C6
7000	JSTC	60458	3148	10W-7S	B7
7000	JSTC	60501	3148	10W-7S	B7
7300	JSTC	60458	3210	10W-8S	A1
SR-171 Collins St					
1000	JLET	60432	3499	23W-22S	A2
1400	JLET	60441	3499	23W-21S	A1
1400	JltT	60432	3499	23W-22S	A1
1400	LktT	60432	3499	23W-21S	A1
1400	LktT	60441	3499	23W-21S	A1
SR-171 N Collins St					
400	JLET	60432	3499	23W-23S	A4
SR-171 N Cumberland Av					
-	CHCG	60068	2918	10W-6N	A5
-	PKRG	60068	2918	10W-6N	A5
3200	RVGV	60171	2974	10W-4N	A4
3200	RVGV	60634	2974	10W-4N	A4
3700	CHCG	60634	2974	10W-2N	A6
4200	CHCG	60656	2974	10W-2N	A6
4200	CHCG	60706	2974	10W-2N	A6
4200	NRDG	60706	2974	10W-2N	A6
4600	CHCG	60656	2918	10W-5N	A7
4600	CHCG	60706	2918	10W-5N	A7
4600	NRDG	60656	2918	10W-5N	A7
4600	NRDG	60706	2918	10W-5N	A7
5500	CHCG	60631	2918	10W-6N	A5
SR-171 Forbes Rd					
-	NRIV	60546	3088	10W-3S	B4
-	RVSD	60546	3088	10W-3S	B4
SR-171 RJ Bragassi Mem Blvd					
-	SMMT	60501	3148	9W-6S	D3
SR-171 N State St					
100	LKPT	60441	3419	22W-18S	D1
200	LktT	60441	3419	22W-18S	D1
600	LKPT	60441	3341	21W-17S	E6
SR-171 S State St					
100	LKPT	60441	3419	23W-21S	B6
2300	LktT	60441	3419	23W-20S	B5
3500	JLET	60432	3499	23W-21S	A1
3500	JLET	60441	3499	23W-21S	A1
3500	JltT	60432	3499	23W-21S	A1
3500	LktT	60432	3499	23W-21S	A1
3500	LktT	60441	3499	23W-21S	A1
SR-171 N Thatcher Av					
2500	RVGV	60171	2974	10W-3N	A5
3000	CHCG	60634	2974	10W-3N	A4
3000	RVGV	60634	2974	10W-3N	A4
SR-173					
-	AdnT	60033	2406	48W-38N	E6
-	ANTH	60002	2357	25W-42N	B6
-	ANTH	60002	2358	23W-41N	A7
-	ANTH	60002	2417	21W-41N	D1
-	ANTH	60002	2418	18W-41N	D1
-	AntT	60002	2356	26W-41N	E7
-	AntT	60002	2357	23W-41N	E7
-	AntT	60002	2358	23W-41N	A7
-	AntT	60002	2417	21W-41N	D1
-	AntT	60002	2418	18W-41N	D1
-	BtnT	60071	2354	31W-42N	E6
-	BtnT	60071	2355	30W-42N	A6
-	BtnT	60081	2355	30W-42N	A6
-	BtnT	60083	2420	13W-41N	E1
-	BtnT	60099	2420	13W-41N	E1
-	BtnT	60099	2421	12W-41N	B1
-	CmgT	60033	2406	48W-38N	D6
-	FXLK	60002	2355	29W-42N	C6
-	FXLK	60002	2356	28W-42N	A6
-	FXLK	60081	2355	29W-42N	C6
-	NptT	60002	2418	18W-41N	D1
-	NptT	60002	2419	17W-41N	C1
-	NptT	60083	2418	18W-41N	D1
-	NptT	60083	2419	18W-41N	A1
-	NptT	60083	2420	15W-41N	B1
-	NptT	60099	2420	15W-41N	B1
-	OMCK	60083	2418	18W-41N	D1
-	OMCK	60083	2419	18W-41N	A1
-	RcmT	60071	2352	36W-42N	E6
-	RcmT	60071	2354	31W-42N	E6
-	RcmT	60081	2354	32W-42N	C6
-	SPGV	60071	2354	32W-42N	A6
-	SPGV	60081	2354	31W-42N	E6
-	SPGV	60081	2355	29W-42N	C6
-	WDWH	60083	2419	16W-41N	D1
-	WDWH	60083	2420	13W-41N	E1
-	WDWH	60083	2421	11W-41N	E2
-	WDWH	60099	2419	17W-41N	C1
-	WDWH	60099	2420	13W-41N	E1
-	WDWH	60099	2421	11W-41N	E2
-	ZION	60099	2420	13W-41N	E1
100	DhmT	60033	2406	50W-37N	A7
100	HRVD	60033	2406	50W-37N	A7
800	DhmT	60033	2405	51W-38N	E7
800	HRVD	60033	2405	50W-38N	E7

STREET Block	City	ZIP	Map#	CGS	Grid
SR-173					
1200	ZION	60099	2422	10W-41N	B2
3100	ZION	60099	2421	11W-41N	D1
5300	RcmT	60071	2353	35W-42N	A6
5300	RHMD	60071	2353	34W-42N	D6
9300	HbnT	60034	2351	40W-41N	A7
9300	HbnT	60034	2352	38W-42N	A7
9300	HbnT	60071	2352	38W-42N	A7
11400	HBRN	60034	2351	40W-42N	A7
12000	HBRN	60034	2350	41W-41N	E7
23000	CmgT	60033	2405	51W-37N	E7
SR-173 21st St					
1200	ZION	60099	2422	10W-41N	B2
SR-173 Bethlehem Av					
-	ZION	60099	2421	11W-41N	E1
SR-173 W Brink St					
100	DhmT	60033	2406	50W-37N	A7
100	HRVD	60033	2406	50W-37N	A7
800	DhmT	60033	2405	51W-38N	E7
800	HRVD	60033	2405	50W-38N	E7
SR-173 E Diggins St					
100	HRVD	60033	2406	50W-38N	B6
SR-173 N Division St					
100	HRVD	60033	2406	50W-38N	B7
SR-173 S Division St					
100	HRVD	60033	2406	50W-38N	B7
SR-173 Kenosha St					
5300	RcmT	60071	2353	34W-42N	D6
5300	RHMD	60071	2353	34W-42N	D6
SR-173 Maple Av					
11300	HbnT	60034	2351	40W-41N	A7
11400	HBRN	60034	2351	40W-42N	A7
12000	HBRN	60034	2350	41W-41N	E7
SR-173 Rosecrans Rd					
-	ANTH	60002	2418	18W-41N	D1
-	AntT	60002	2418	18W-41N	D1
-	BtnT	60083	2420	13W-41N	E1
-	BtnT	60099	2420	13W-41N	E1
-	BtnT	60099	2421	12W-41N	B1
-	NptT	60002	2418	18W-41N	D1
-	NptT	60002	2419	17W-41N	C1
-	NptT	60083	2418	18W-41N	D1
-	NptT	60083	2419	18W-41N	A1
-	NptT	60083	2420	15W-41N	B1
-	NptT	60099	2420	15W-41N	B1
-	OMCK	60083	2418	18W-41N	D1
-	OMCK	60083	2419	18W-41N	A1
-	WDWH	60083	2419	16W-41N	D1
-	WDWH	60083	2420	13W-41N	E1
-	WDWH	60083	2421	11W-41N	E2
-	WDWH	60099	2419	17W-41N	C1
-	WDWH	60099	2420	13W-41N	E1
-	WDWH	60099	2421	11W-41N	E2
-	ZION	60099	2420	13W-41N	E1
SR-176					
-	DrrT	60142	2638	40W-26N	A3
-	FmtT	60047	2589	22W-28N	B6
-	FmtT	60060	2644	23W-27N	E1
-	GNOK	60045	2592	14W-28N	D5
-	HNWD	60047	2589	21W-28N	D6
-	HNWD	60060	2589	22W-28N	C6
-	ISLK	60042	2587	28W-27N	A7
-	ISLK	60042	2643	28W-27N	A1
-	ISLK	60084	2587	28W-27N	A7
-	ISLK	60084	2643	27W-27N	B1
-	LKBF	60044	2593	11W-28N	E6
-	WcnT	60042	2587	28W-27N	A7
-	WcnT	60042	2643	28W-27N	A1
-	WcnT	60084	2587	28W-27N	A7
10	CLLK	60012	2640	33W-26N	E2
10	CLLK	60014	2640	33W-26N	E2
10	MDLN	60060	2590	19W-28N	B6
100	ISLK	60042	2586	28W-27N	E7
100	LYVL	60048	2591	18W-28N	A6
100	MRGO	60152	2634	49W-26N	D1
100	WCDA	60084	2643	26W-27N	D2
200	CLLK	60014	2639	38W-26N	A3
300	NndT	60012	2640	34W-26N	C3
300	NndT	60014	2639	35W-26N	E3
300	NndT	60014	2640	33W-26N	E2
300	ShdT	60044	2593	12W-28N	C6
300	WCDA	60084	2644	23W-27N	E1
400	WcnT	60042	2586	28W-28N	E7
600	CLLK	60012	2639	36W-26N	D3
600	ISLK	60051	2586	28W-27N	E7
600	LKFT	60044	2593	12W-28N	B6
600	LKFT	60045	2593	12W-28N	B6
600	NndT	60012	2639	36W-26N	D3
600	NndT	60042	2586	29W-28N	C5
600	NndT	60051	2586	28W-27N	E7
600	WcnT	60084	2643	27W-27N	B1
800	LYVL	60048	2592	15W-28N	B5
900	MDLN	60060	2591	18W-28N	A6
1000	FmtT	60060	2590	19W-28N	B6
1000	FmtT	60084	2644	24W-27N	B1
1000	GNOK	60044	2593	11W-28N	D6
1000	LbvT	60048	2592	13W-28N	D5
1000	WcnT	60084	2644	25W-27N	B1
1100	GNOK	60048	2592	13W-28N	D5
1300	GNOK	60044	2592	13W-28N	E5
1300	LbvT	60044	2592	13W-28N	E5
1500	LbvT	60045	2592	13W-28N	E5
1600	NndT	60012	2586	30W-28N	A6
1600	NndT	60014	2586	30W-28N	A6
1600	NndT	60050	2586	30W-28N	A5
1900	FmtT	60060	2589	22W-27N	B7
1900	MDLN	60060	2589	20W-28N	E6
2000	NndT	60012	2585	30W-27N	E7
2000	NndT	60014	2585	30W-27N	E7
2000	PRGV	60014	2585	30W-27N	E7
2400	NndT	60014	2641	31W-27N	D1
2400	PRGV	60014	2641	31W-27N	D1
3000	NndT	60013	2641	31W-27N	C1
3000	PRGV	60013	2641	31W-27N	C1
3200	PRGV	60012	2641	32W-27N	B1
3500	CLLK	60012	2641	32W-27N	B1
3800	CLLK	60014	2641	32W-26N	A2
8200	DrrT	60014	2639	37W-26N	C3
9100	CLLK	60014	2638	38W-26N	E2
9100	CLLK	60098	2638	38W-26N	E2
9100	CLLK	60098	2639	38W-26N	A3
9100	DrrT	60014	2638	38W-26N	E2
9100	DrrT	60098	2638	38W-26N	E2
9100	DrrT	60098	2639	38W-26N	A3
18600	SenT	60152	2634	48W-27N	E1
18600	SenT	60152	2635	47W-27N	A1
18600	SenT	60180	2635	46W-27N	E1
SR-176 E Liberty St					
100	WCDA	60084	2643	25W-27N	E1
300	WCDA	60084	2644	23W-27N	E1
1000	FmtT	60084	2644	24W-27N	B1
1000	WcnT	60084	2644	25W-27N	B1
SR-176 W Liberty St					
-	FmtT	60060	2644	23W-27N	D1
-	FmtT	60084	2644	24W-27N	C1
-	ISLK	60042	2587	28W-27N	A7
SR-176 W Liberty St					
-	ISLK	60042	2643	28W-27N	A1
-	ISLK	60084	2587	28W-27N	A7
-	ISLK	60084	2643	27W-27N	B1
-	WcnT	60042	2587	28W-27N	A7
-	WcnT	60042	2643	28W-27N	A1
-	WcnT	60084	2587	28W-27N	A7
100	WCDA	60084	2643	26W-27N	D2
600	WcnT	60084	2643	27W-27N	B1
SR-176 E Maple Av					
10	MDLN	60060	2590	18W-28N	D6
900	MDLN	60060	2591	18W-28N	A6
1000	LYVL	60048	2591	18W-28N	A6
SR-176 W Maple Av					
1100	FmtT	60060	2590	19W-28N	B6
1100	MDLN	60060	2590	19W-28N	B6
1900	FmtT	60060	2589	21W-28N	E6
1900	MDLN	60060	2589	21W-28N	E6
SR-176 W Maple St					
10	MDLN	60060	2590	19W-28N	D6
1000	FmtT	60060	2590	19W-28N	C6
SR-176 E Park Av					
-	GNOK	60044	2592	14W-28N	D5
-	GNOK	60045	2592	14W-28N	D5
100	LYVL	60048	2591	16W-28N	D5
800	LYVL	60048	2592	15W-28N	B5
1000	LbvT	60048	2592	13W-28N	D5
1100	GNOK	60048	2592	13W-28N	D5
SR-176 W Park Av					
100	LYVL	60048	2591	18W-28N	A6
1500	MDLN	60060	2591	17W-28N	A6
SR-176 Rockland Rd					
10	LKBF	60044	2593	11W-28N	D6
300	ShdT	60044	2593	12W-28N	C6
600	LKFT	60044	2593	12W-28N	B6
600	LKFT	60045	2593	12W-28N	B6
1000	GNOK	60044	2593	11W-28N	D6
1300	GNOK	60045	2592	13W-28N	E5
1300	LbvT	60044	2592	13W-28N	E5
1500	GNOK	60045	2592	13W-28N	E5
1500	LbvT	60045	2592	13W-28N	E5
SR-176 W Scranton Av					
-	LKBF	60044	2593	11W-28N	E6
SR-176 E State Rd					
100	ISLK	60042	2586	28W-28N	D6
400	WcnT	60042	2586	28W-28N	E7
SR-176 W State Rd					
100	ISLK	60042	2586	29W-28N	D6
600	ISLK	60051	2586	29W-28N	C5
600	NndT	60042	2586	29W-28N	C5
600	NndT	60051	2586	29W-28N	C5
SR-176 Telegraph St					
100	MRGO	60152	2634	49W-26N	D1
20000	SenT	60152	2634	48W-27N	D1
SR-176 E Terra Cotta Av					
10	CLLK	60012	2640	35W-26N	B3
10	CLLK	60014	2640	35W-26N	B3
300	NndT	60012	2640	34W-26N	C3
300	NndT	60014	2640	34W-26N	C3
SR-176 W Terra Cotta Av					
10	CLLK	60012	2640	35W-26N	A3
10	CLLK	60014	2640	35W-26N	A3
200	CLLK	60014	2639	38W-26N	A3
300	NndT	60012	2639	35W-26N	E3
600	CLLK	60012	2639	36W-26N	D3
600	NndT	60012	2639	36W-26N	D3
SR-312					
10	BNHM	60633	3352		C4
800	HMND	46327	3352		E4
SR-312 E Chicago St					
800	HMND	46327	3352		E4
SR-312 Gostlin St					
10	BNHM	60633	3352		C4
10	HMND	46327	3352		C4
SR-394					
-	BlmT	-	3429	1E-21S	B7
-	BlmT	-	3509	1E-24S	B5
-	BlmT	-	3597	1E-26S	C2
-	CRTE	60417	3597	1E-28S	C6
-	CRTE	60417	3686	1E-30S	C2
-	CteT	60401	3774	0W-33S	C2
-	CteT	60417	3597	1E-28S	C6
-	CteT	60417	3685	0W-32S	D7
-	CteT	60417	3686	1E-31S	B5
-	CteT	60417	3774	0W-32S	C1
-	FDHT	-	3509	1E-24S	C6
-	GNWD	-	3509	1E-22S	B2
-	LYWD	-	3509	1E-23S	B4
-	SHLD	-	3429	1E-20S	B5
-	SLVL	60411	3597	1E-27S	C4
-	STGR	60411	3597	1E-27S	C4
-	STGR	60475	3597	1E-27S	C4
-	ThtT	-	3429	1E-20S	B4
SR-394 Bishop Ford Mem Expwy					
-	BlmT	-	3429	1E-21S	B7
-	BlmT	-	3509	1E-24S	B5
-	BlmT	-	3597	1E-26S	C2
-	FDHT	-	3509	1E-24S	C6
-	GNWD	-	3509	1E-22S	B2
-	LYWD	-	3509	1E-23S	B3
-	SHLD	-	3429	1E-20S	B5
-	SLVL	60411	3597	1E-26S	C2
-	ThtT	-	3429	1E-20S	B4
SR-394 Calumet Expwy					
-	CRTE	60417	3597	1E-28S	C6
-	CRTE	60417	3686	1E-30S	C2
-	CteT	60401	3774	0W-33S	C2
-	CteT	60417	3597	1E-28S	C6
-	CteT	60417	3685	0W-32S	D7
-	CteT	60417	3686	1E-30S	C2
-	CteT	60417	3774	0W-32S	C1
-	SLVL	60411	3597	1E-27S	C4
-	STGR	60411	3597	1E-28S	C6
-	STGR	60475	3597	1E-27S	C4
SR-394 Kingery Expwy					
-	SHLD		3429	1E-20S	B3
SR-912					
-	HMND	-	3280		E7
SR-912 Cline Av					
-	HMND	-	3280		E7
US-6					
-	HMGN	60448	3422	15W-21S	C7
-	HMND	-	3430		D5
-	LNSG	-	3429	3E-20S	E4
-	LNSG	-	3430		D5
-	MNSR	-	3430		D5
-	NlxT	60448	3422	15W-21S	C7
-	SHLD	60409	3429	1E-19S	C1
10	HRVY	60426	3427	1W-18S	E1
10	JLET	60432	3498	24W-24S	E5
10	JLET	60432	3499	23W-23S	A4
10	JLET	60433	3499	23W-24S	A5
10	JLET	60436	3498	24W-25S	D7
10	JLET	60436	3499	23W-24S	A5
10	SHLD	60473	3428	0E-19S	E1
100	HRVY	60426	3428	1W-18S	A1
US-6					
200	HRVY	60428	3427	2W-18S	C1
200	MKHM	60428	3427	2W-19S	C1
200	NLNX	60451	3500	19W-22S	D1
200	NLNX	60451	3501	18W-22S	A1
200	NlxT	60448	3501	17W-22S	D1
200	NlxT	60451	3501	18W-22S	B1
200	ThtT	60428	3427	2W-18S	C1
300	HRVY	60473	3428	0W-18S	B1
300	SHLD	60426	3428	0W-18S	B1
400	JltT	60432	3499	23W-23S	B4
600	JltT	60436	3498	24W-24S	D7
700	RKDL	60436	3498	25W-25S	C7
700	SHLD	60473	3429	0E-18S	A1
1100	CTCY	60409	3429	3E-19S	E3
1200	JltT	60436	3586	26W-25S	A2
1300	JLET	60441	3500	19W-22S	D1
1300	JLET	60451	3500	19W-22S	D1
1300	NLNX	60441	3500	19W-22S	D1
1300	NlxT	60441	3500	19W-22S	D1
1300	NlxT	60451	3500	19W-22S	D1
1400	CTCY	60438	3429	3E-19S	E3
1400	LNSG	60409	3429	3E-19S	E2
1600	JLET	60436	3585	28W-27S	B4
1600	JltT	60436	3585	28W-27S	B4
1600	RKDL	60436	3586	25W-25S	B1
2000	JLET	60432	3500	21W-22S	A2
2000	JltT	60432	3500	21W-22S	A2
2300	BmnT	60428	3427	2W-19S	C1
2300	MKHM	60426	3427	2W-19S	C1
3200	TroT	60436	3585	28W-26S	B3
3300	MKHM	60428	3426	4W-19S	E1
3400	JLET	60410	3585	28W-27S	B4
3800	BmnT	60426	3426	4W-19S	E1
3800	MKHM	60426	3426	4W-19S	E1
4700	BmnT	60452	3426	5W-18S	A1
4700	OKFT	60426	3426	5W-18S	B1
4700	OKFT	60452	3426	5W-18S	B1
5100	OKFT	60452	3425	7W-19S	C1
5400	BmnT	60452	3425	6W-18S	D1
5400	BmnT	60477	3425	6W-18S	D1
6400	TYPK	60477	3425	8W-19S	B1
6700	TYPK	60452	3425	8W-19S	A1
6900	ODPK	60462	3425	8W-19S	A1
6900	ODPK	60477	3425	8W-19S	A1
7100	ODPK	60462	3424	11W-19S	A1
7100	TYPK	60462	3424	11W-19S	A1
7200	ODPK	60477	3424	9W-19S	E1
7600	TYPK	60462	3424	9W-18S	D1
8000	TYPK	60487	3424	10W-19S	B1
8700	ODHL	60462	3424	10W-19S	A1
8700	ODHL	60487	3424	10W-19S	A1
8700	ODPK	60487	3424	10W-19S	A1
9100	ODHL	60487	3423	11W-19S	E1
9100	ODPK	60462	3423	11W-19S	E1
9200	ODHL	60462	3423	11W-19S	E1
9300	ODPK	60467	3423	11W-19S	E1
9900	OrlT	60462	3423	12W-18S	C1
9900	OrlT	60467	3423	12W-18S	C1
10800	ODPK	60467	3422	13W-19S	E1
10800	OrlT	60467	3422	13W-19S	E1
13000	NlxT	60448	3502	15W-22S	B1
15800	NlxT	60432	3500	19W-22S	C1
17900	HMGN	60491	3422	14W-21S	C7
22000	CNHN	60410	3585	28W-27S	A5
23000	CnhT	60410	3585	28W-27S	A5
23200	CNHN	60410	3584	29W-28S	D7
23200	CnhT	60410	3584	29W-28S	D7
23200	JLET	60410	3584	29W-28S	D7
25800	CnhT	60410	3672	32W-30S	D5
26100	AxST	60447	3672	32W-30S	C5
26100	CNHN	60410	3672	33W-30S	B5
26100	CNHN	60447	3672	32W-30S	C5
27100	AxST	60410	3672	33W-30S	A5
27100	MNKA	60447	3672	33W-30S	A5
US-6 159th St					
-	SHLD	60409	3429	1E-19S	C1
-	SHLD	60473	3429	1E-19S	C1
1400	CTCY	60409	3429	2E-18S	E1
4700	BmnT	60426	3426	5W-18S	B1
4700	BmnT	60452	3426	5W-18S	A1
4700	OKFT	60426	3426	5W-18S	B1
4700	OKFT	60452	3426	5W-18S	B1
5100	OKFT	60452	3425	7W-19S	C1
5400	BmnT	60452	3425	6W-18S	D1
5400	BmnT	60477	3425	6W-18S	D1
6400	TYPK	60477	3425	8W-19S	B1
6700	TYPK	60452	3425	8W-19S	A1
6900	ODPK	60462	3425	8W-19S	A1
6900	ODPK	60477	3425	8W-19S	A1
US-6 E 159th St					
10	HRVY	60426	3427	1W-18S	E1
100	HRVY	60426	3428	1W-18S	A1
300	HRVY	60473	3428	0W-18S	B1
300	SHLD	60426	3428	0W-18S	B1
300	SHLD	60473	3428	0W-18S	B1
US-6 W 159th St					
-	OKFT	60426	3426	5W-18S	B1
-	OKFT	60452	3426	5W-18S	B1
10	HRVY	60426	3427	2W-18S	E1
200	HRVY	60428	3427	2W-18S	C1
200	MKHM	60428	3427	2W-19S	C1
200	ThtT	60428	3427	2W-18S	C1
2300	BmnT	60428	3427	2W-19S	C1
2300	MKHM	60426	3427	2W-19S	C1
3300	MKHM	60428	3426	4W-19S	E1
3800	BmnT	60426	3426	4W-19S	E1
3800	MKHM	60426	3426	4W-19S	E1
7000	ODPK	60462	3425	8W-19S	A1
7000	ODPK	60477	3425	8W-19S	A1
7000	TYPK	60477	3425	8W-19S	A1
7100	ODPK	60462	3424	11W-19S	A1
7100	TYPK	60477	3424	11W-19S	A1
7200	ODPK	60477	3424	9W-19S	E1
7600	TYPK	60462	3424	9W-18S	D1
8000	TYPK	60487	3424	10W-19S	B1
8700	ODHL	60462	3424	10W-19S	A1
8700	ODHL	60487	3424	10W-19S	A1
8700	ODPK	60487	3424	10W-19S	A1
9100	ODHL	60487	3423	11W-19S	E1
9100	ODPK	60462	3423	11W-19S	E1
9200	ODHL	60462	3423	11W-19S	E1
9300	ODPK	60467	3423	11W-19S	E1
9900	OrlT	60462	3423	12W-18S	C1
9900	OrlT	60467	3423	12W-18S	C1
10800	ODPK	60467	3422	13W-18S	E1
10800	OrlT	60467	3422	13W-18S	E1
US-6 E 162nd St					
10	SHLD	60473	3428	0E-19S	D1
700	SHLD	60473	3429	0E-18S	A1
US-6 W 162nd St					
10	SHLD	60473	3428	0E-19S	E1
500	HRVY	60426	3428	0W-18S	B1
500	HRVY	60473	3428	0W-18S	B1
500	SHLD	60426	3428	0W-18S	B1
US-6 Borman Expwy					
-	HMND	-	3430		D5
-	LNSG	-	3430		D5
-	MNSR	-	3430		D5
US-6 E Cass St					
10	JLET	60432	3499	23W-23S	A4
US-6 Channahon Rd					
-	JltT	60436	3498	25W-25S	C7
-	RKDL	60436	3498	25W-25S	C7
1200	JltT	60436	3586	26W-25S	A2
1600	JLET	60436	3585	28W-27S	B4
1600	JltT	60436	3585	28W-27S	B4
1600	RKDL	60436	3586	25W-25S	B1
3200	TroT	60436	3585	28W-26S	B3
3400	JLET	60410	3585	28W-27S	B4
US-6 S Chicago St					
-	JLET	60432	3499	23W-23S	A5
-	JLET	60436	3498	24W-24S	E5
10	JLET	60433	3499	23W-24S	A5
10	JLET	60436	3499	23W-24S	A5
US-6 N Collins St					
10	JLET	60432	3499	23W-23S	A5
US-6 W Eames St					
22000	CNHN	60410	3585	28W-27S	A5
22000	JLET	60410	3585	28W-27S	A5
23000	CnhT	60410	3585	28W-27S	A5
23200	CNHN	60410	3584	29W-28S	D7
23200	CnhT	60410	3584	29W-28S	D7
23200	JLET	60410	3584	29W-28S	D7
25300	CNHN	60410	3672	31W-30S	E4
25800	CnhT	60410	3672	32W-30S	D5
26100	AxST	60447	3672	32W-30S	C5
26100	CNHN	60447	3672	32W-30S	C5
27100	AxST	60410	3672	33W-30S	A5
27100	MNKA	60447	3672	33W-30S	A5
US-6 E Jackson St					
400	JLET	60432	3499	23W-23S	B4
US-6 E Jefferson St					
10	JLET	60432	3499	23W-23S	A5
US-6 Kingery Expwy					
-	LNSG	-	3429	3E-20S	E4
-	LNSG	-	3430	3E-20S	A4
-	MNSR	-	3430	4E-20S	C4
US-6 Maple Rd					
200	NLNX	60451	3500	19W-22S	D1
200	NLNX	60451	3501	18W-22S	A1
200	NlxT	60448	3501	18W-22S	B1
200	NlxT	60451	3501	18W-22S	B1
400	JLET	60432	3499	22W-23S	C3
400	JltT	60432	3499	23W-23S	B4
1300	JLET	60441	3500	19W-22S	D1
1300	JLET	60451	3500	19W-22S	D1
1300	NLNX	60441	3500	19W-22S	D1
1300	NlxT	60441	3500	19W-22S	D1
1300	NlxT	60451	3500	19W-22S	D1
2000	JLET	60432	3500	21W-22S	A2
2000	JltT	60432	3500	21W-22S	A2
15800	NlxT	60432	3500	19W-22S	C1
US-6 W McDonough St					
10	JLET	60436	3498	24W-24S	E6
US-6 N Ottawa St					
10	JLET	60432	3498	24W-24S	E5
10	JLET	60436	3498	24W-23S	E5
US-6 S Ottawa St					
10	JLET	60432	3498	24W-23S	E5
10	JLET	60436	3498	24W-24S	E5
US-6 Railroad St					
400	JLET	60436	3498	24W-25S	D7
600	JltT	60436	3498	24W-24S	D7
700	RKDL	60436	3498	25W-25S	C7
US-6 N Scott St					
10	JLET	60432	3499	23W-23S	A5
10	JLET	60433	3499	23W-23S	A5
US-6 Southwest Hwy					
-	HMGN	60448	3422	15W-21S	C7
-	NlxT	60448	3422	15W-21S	C7
11300	ODPK	60467	3422	14W-21S	E5
13000	NlxT	60448	3502	15W-22S	B1
13100	NlxT	60448	3501	17W-22S	D1
14000	NLNX	60451	3501	17W-22S	B1
14000	NlxT	60451	3501	17W-22S	C1
17700	OrlT	60467	3422	14W-21S	D6
17900	HMGN	60491	3422	14W-21S	C7
US-6 Torrence Av					
1100	CTCY	60409	3429	3E-19S	E3
1400	CTCY	60438	3429	3E-19S	E3
1400	LNSG	60409	3429	3E-19S	E2
1400	LNSG	60438	3429	3E-19S	E3
US-6 E Washington St					
10	JLET	60432	3499	23W-23S	A5
10	JLET	60433	3499	23W-23S	A5
10	JLET	60436	3499	23W-23S	A5
US-6 Wolf Rd					
15900	ODPK	60467	3422	13W-19S	E1
15900	OrlT	60467	3422	13W-19S	E1
US-12					
-	ANHT	60074	2753	19W-17N	D5
-	BfdT	53128	2353	34W-42N	C6
-	BGVW	60453	3210	8W-10S	E6
-	BGVW	60455	3210	8W-10S	E6
-	BGVW	60457	3210	9W-11S	D6
-	BtnT	60050	2472	29W-38N	C1
-	BtnT	60081	2414	29W-38N	C6
-	BtnT	60081	2472	29W-38N	C1
-	CHCG	60176	2917	12W-6N	B6
-	CHCG	60617	3216	4E-11S	B7
-	CHCG	60666	2973	12W-5N	B1
-	CTSD	60525	3147	12W-8S	C7
-	FXLK	60020	2472	28W-37N	E2
-	FXLK	60020	2473	28W-36N	A3
-	FXLK	60041	2473	27W-34N	B7
-	FXLK	60041	2530	27W-34N	B1
-	GNCY		2353		B1
-	GrtT	60020	2473	27W-34N	B7
-	GrtT	60041	2473	27W-35N	B7
-	GrtT	60041	2530	27W-34N	B1
-	GrtT	60073	2530	27W-32N	B5
-	GrtT	60081	2472	29W-37N	D1
-	HGKN	60525	3209	12W-8S	C1
-	HYHL	60455	3210	9W-11S	D6
-	LKMR	60041	2530	27W-32N	B5
-	LKMR	60073	2530	27W-31N	C7
-	LynT	60458	3209	11W-8S	D2
-	LynT	60480	3209	11W-9S	D3
-	LynT	60525	3209	11W-8S	D2
-	MchT	60050	2472	29W-38N	D1
-	MchT	60081	2472	29W-37N	D1
-	OKLN	60453	3210	8W-10S	E6
-	OKLN	60455	3210	8W-10S	E6
-	RcmT	53128	2353		C4
-	RHMD	60071	2353		C4
-	SPGV	60050	2414	29W-38N	C7
-	SPGV	60050	2472	29W-38N	C1
-	SPGV	60081	2413	32W-39N	B5
-	SPGV	60081	2414	29W-38N	C7
-	SPGV	60081	2472	29W-38N	C1
US-12					
-	SRPK	60176	2917	12W-5N	B7
-	SRPK	60176	2973	12W-5N	B1
-	VOLO	60041	2530	27W-32N	B5
-	VOLO	60073	2530	27W-32N	B5
-	VOLO	60073	2587	27W-31N	C1
-	WcnT	60073	2530	27W-31N	C7
-	WcnT	60073	2587	27W-30N	C2
-	WLSP	60458	3209	11W-9S	D2
-	WLSP	60480	3209	11W-8S	D2
-	WLSP	60525	3209	12W-8S	C1
10	ANHT	60004	2754	17W-16N	A7
10	BLWD	60104	3029	12W-0N	A3
10	BLWD	60160	3029	12W-1N	A3
10	CHCG	60619	3214	0E-10S	C6
10	CHCG	60620	3214	0E-10S	C6
10	CHCG	60628	3214	0W-11S	C6
10	DRPK	60010	2699	22W-21N	B7
10	DRPK	60047	2699	22W-21N	B7
10	DSPN	60016	2808	14W-12N	C7
10	HLSD	60104	3029	12W-0S	A6
10	HLSD	60154	3029	12W-0S	A6
10	HLSD	60162	3029	12W-0S	A6
10	KLDR	60010	2699	22W-21N	B7
10	KLDR	60047	2699	22W-21N	B7
10	LGNG	60525	3087	12W-4S	C6
10	LKZH	60010	2699	22W-21N	B6
10	LKZH	60047	2698	24W-23N	C2
10	LKZH	60047	2699	21W-20N	C7
10	MLPK	60160	3029	12W-1N	A3
10	MPPT	60016	2808	14W-12N	C7
10	MPPT	60056	2808	15W-13N	B6
10	WSTR	60154	3029	12W-0S	A6
100	BLWD	60162	3029	12W-0S	A5
100	LGPK	60525	3087	12W-4S	C6
100	WSTR	60162	3029	12W-0S	A7
200	ANHT	60004	2807	15W-14N	E4
200	WCDA	60084	2643	25W-26N	E3
200	WcnT	60084	2643	26W-27N	D1
300	DSPN	60016	2862	13W-11N	E2
300	LGNG	60525	3147	12W-4S	C1
300	MPPT	60056	2807	15W-14N	E4
300	PvsT	60162	3029	12W-0S	A7
400	ANHT	60004	2753	18W-17N	E6
600	ANHT	60056	2807	15W-14N	E4
600	DRPK	60074	2699	21W-20N	C7
600	DRPK	60074	2752	21W-20N	D1
600	ElaT	60047	2699	21W-20N	C7
600	ElaT	60074	2699	21W-20N	D7
600	ElaT	60074	2752	21W-20N	D1
600	KLDR	60074	2699	21W-20N	C7
600	WCDA	60084	2587	26W-28N	D7
700	CHCG	60643	3214	0W-10S	A6
700	ElaT	60010	2698	24W-23N	C1
700	MPPT	60004	2807	16W-14N	E4
800	ElaT	60047	2698	24W-23N	C1
800	WcnT	60084	2587	26W-28N	D6
900	CHCG	60619	3215	1E-10S	A5
900	CHCG	60628	3215	1E-10S	A5
900	CHCG	60643	3213	1W-10S	E6
900	ElaT	60047	2644	24W-24N	C7
900	NBRN	60047	2644	24W-24N	C7
1000	CHCG	60620	3213	1W-10S	E6
1000	DSPN	60018	2862	13W-10N	E5
1000	HMND	46320	3280		D3
1000	HMND	46394	3280		E4
1000	PvsT	60525	3087	12W-3S	B4
1200	DSPN	60016	2863	13W-11N	A2
1200	PLTN	60074	2753	20W-18N	B3
1200	PltT	60004	2753	18W-17N	D6
1200	PltT	60074	2753	19W-17N	D5
1200	PTHT	60004	2807	17W-15N	C2
1400	PvsT	60162	3087	12W-1S	A1
1400	WSTR	60154	3087	12W-1S	A1
1400	WSTR	60162	3087	12W-1S	A1
1500	CHCG	60617	3215	1E-10S	B5
1500	SNPK	60160	3029	12W-1N	A2
1500	SNPK	60165	3029	12W-1N	A2
1700	DSPN	60018	2863	13W-9N	A6
1800	MLPK	60160	3029	12W-1N	A1
1800	MLPK	60165	3029	12W-1N	A1
1800	SNPK	60164	3029	12W-1N	A1
2000	DSPN	60018	2917	13W-9N	A1
2000	LydT	60160	2973	12W-2N	A7
2000	LydT	60164	2973	12W-2N	A7
2000	MLPK	60160	2973	12W-2N	A7
2000	NHLK	60160	2973	12W-2N	A7
2000	NHLK	60164	2973	12W-2N	A7
2000	RSMT	60018	2917	13W-9N	A1
2100	PvsT	60154	3087	12W-1S	A2
2300	CHCG	60805	3213	2W-10S	B6
2300	ENGN	60805	3213	2W-10S	B6
2300	LydT	60131	2973	12W-2N	A6
2300	PltT	60074	2752	20W-18N	E2
2400	FNPK	60131	2973	13W-3N	A6
2400	WhlT	60004	2807	16W-14N	D3
2600	FNPK	60164	2973	13W-3N	A5
2900	CHCG	60018	2917	12W-8N	A2
2900	ENGN	60805	3212	3W-10S	E6
3700	FNPK	60176	2973	13W-4N	A3
3700	SRPK	60131	2973	13W-4N	A3
3900	ENGN	60453	3212	4W-10S	C6
3900	OKLN	60453	3212	4W-10S	C6
4100	RcmT	60071	2413	33W-40N	A4
4100	RcmT	60081	2413	32W-39N	A4
4300	RcmT	60071	2412	34W-40N	D3
4300	RHMD	60071	2412	34W-40N	D3
4900	OKLN	60453	3211	6W-10S	E6
6000	HGKN	60525	3147	12W-6S	C5
6300	CHRG	60415	3211	7W-10S	B6
6300	CHRG	60453	3211	7W-10S	B6
6300	OKLN	60415	3211	7W-10S	B6
6400	CHCG	60666	2917	12W-8N	A3
6400	RSMT	60666	2917	12W-8N	A3
7600	HYHL	60457	3210	9W-11S	D6
8700	HYHL	60465	3210	10W-10S	A6
8700	PSHL	60457	3210	10W-10S	A6
8700	PSHL	60465	3210	10W-10S	A6
8900	HYHL	60457	3209	11W-10S	E6
8900	HYHL	60465	3209	11W-10S	E6
8900	PSHL	60465	3209	11W-10S	E6
9000	PlsT	60457	3209	11W-10S	E6
9000	PlsT	60465	3209	11W-10S	E6
9000	PlsT	60480	3209	11W-10S	E6
9000	PSHL	60457	3209	11W-10S	E6
10500	CHCG	60617	3280		C1
10500	HMND	60617	3280	4E-11S	C1
11200	RcmT	60071	2353	34W-43N	C5
11500	GNCY	60071	2353	34W-43N	C4
20200	KLDR	60074	2752	21W-20N	E1
20400	KLDR	60047	2752	21W-20N	E1
24000	ElaT	60010	2644	24W-24N	C7
24000	NBRN	60010	2644	24W-24N	C7
24200	HNWD	60047	2644	24W-24N	C7
24200	LKZH	60047	2644	24W-24N	C7
25800	ElaT	60084	2644	24W-25N	C4

Block	City	ZIP	Map#	CGS	Grid
US-12					
25900	FmtT	60084	2644	24W-26N	B4
25900	WcnT	60010	2644	25W-26N	B3
25900	WcnT	60084	2644	25W-26N	B3
26400	WCDA	60084	2644	25W-26N	A3
29000	WCDA	60073	2587	26W-29N	C5
US-12 95th St					
-	HYHL	60457	3209	11W-10S	E6
-	PlsT	60457	3209	11W-10S	E6
-	PlsT	60465	3209	11W-10S	E6
-	PlsT	60480	3209	11W-10S	E6
-	PSHL	60457	3209	11W-10S	E6
-	PSHL	60465	3209	11W-10S	E6
US-12 E 95th St					
10	CHCG	60619	3214	0E-10S	C6
10	CHCG	60620	3214	0E-10S	C6
10	CHCG	60628	3214	0E-10S	C6
900	CHCG	60619	3215	1E-10S	A5
900	CHCG	60628	3215	1E-10S	A5
1500	CHCG	60617	3215	1E-10S	B5
3000	CHCG	60617	3216	3E-11S	A5
US-12 W 95th St					
-	BGVW	60453	3210	8W-10S	E6
-	BGVW	60455	3210	8W-10S	E6
-	BGVW	60457	3210	9W-11S	D6
-	CHCG	60619	3214	0W-10S	C6
-	HYHL	60455	3210	9W-11S	D6
-	OKLN	60453	3210	8W-10S	E6
-	OKLN	60455	3210	8W-10S	E6
10	CHCG	60620	3214	0W-10S	C6
10	CHCG	60628	3214	0W-11S	C6
700	CHCG	60643	3214	0W-10S	A6
1000	CHCG	60620	3213	1W-10S	E6
2300	CHCG	60805	3213	2W-10S	B6
2300	ENGN	60805	3213	2W-10S	B6
2400	CHCG	60643	3213	3W-10S	B6
2900	ENGN	60805	3212	3W-10S	E6
3900	ENGN	60453	3212	4W-10S	C6
3900	OKLN	60453	3212	4W-10S	C6
4900	OKLN	60453	3211	6W-10S	E6
6300	CHRG	60415	3211	7W-10S	B6
6300	CHRG	60453	3211	7W-10S	B6
6300	OKLN	60415	3211	7W-10S	B6
7600	HYHL	60457	3210	9W-11S	D6
8700	HYHL	60465	3210	10W-10S	A6
8700	PSHL	60457	3210	10W-10S	A6
8700	PSHL	60465	3210	10W-10S	A6
8900	HYHL	60457	3209	11W-10S	E6
8900	HYHL	60465	3209	11W-10S	E6
8900	PSHL	60465	3209	11W-10S	E6
9000	PlsT	60457	3209	11W-10S	E6
9000	PlsT	60465	3209	11W-10S	E6
9000	PlsT	60480	3209	11W-10S	E6
9000	PSHL	60457	3209	11W-10S	E6
US-12 S Ewing Av					
9500	CHCG	60617	3216	4E-10S	B5
US-12 Graceland Av					
800	DSPN	60016	2862	13W-10N	E4
US-12 S Indianapolis Av					
-	CHCG	60617	3280	4E-11S	C1
-	HMND	60617	3280	4E-11S	C1
10000	CHCG	60617	3216	4E-11S	B7
10600	HMND	46320	3280	4E-11S	C1
US-12 S Indianapolis Blvd					
1000	HMND	46320	3280		D3
1000	HMND	46394	3280		E4
10500	CHCG	60617	3280		C1
10500	HMND	60617	3280	4E-11S	C1
US-12 La Grange Rd					
-	LynT	60458	3209	11W-8S	D2
-	LynT	60480	3209	11W-9S	D3
-	LynT	60525	3209	11W-8S	D2
-	PlsT	60480	3209	11W-9S	D4
-	WLSP	60458	3209	11W-9S	D2
-	WLSP	60480	3209	11W-8S	D2
-	WLSP	60525	3209	12W-8S	D1
US-12 N La Grange Rd					
-	PvsT	60154	3087	12W-2S	A2
-	WSTR	60154	3087	12W-2S	A2
10	LGNG	60525	3087	12W-4S	C6
100	LGPK	60525	3087	12W-4S	C6
1000	PvsT	60525	3087	12W-3S	B4
US-12 S La Grange Rd					
-	CTSD	60525	3147	12W-8S	C7
-	HGKN	60525	3209	12W-8S	C1
-	WLSP	60525	3209	12W-8S	C1
10	LGNG	60525	3087	12W-4S	C7
300	LGNG	60525	3147	12W-4S	C1
6000	HGKN	60525	3147	12W-6S	C5
US-12 N Main St					
8600	RcmT	60071	2412	34W-40N	C3
8600	RHMD	60071	2412	34W-41N	C1
9700	RHMD	60071	2353	34W-41N	C7
11200	RcmT	60071	2353	34W-43N	C5
11500	GNCY	53128	2353	34W-43N	C4
11500	GNCY	60071	2353	34W-43N	C4
11500	RcmT	53128	2353	34W-43N	C4
US-12 Mannheim Rd					
-	CHCG	60176	2917	12W-6N	B6
-	CHCG	60666	2973	12W-5N	B1
-	DSPN	60016	2863	13W-11N	A3
-	SRPK	60176	2917	12W-6N	B6
10	BLWD	60104	3029	12W-0N	A3
10	BLWD	60160	3029	12W-1N	A3
10	MLPK	60160	3029	12W-1N	A3
500	BLWD	60162	3029	12W-0N	A4
500	HLSD	60162	3029	12W-0N	A4
1000	DSPN	60016	2862	13W-10N	E5
1000	DSPN	60018	2862	13W-10N	E5
1700	DSPN	60018	2863	13W-9N	A6
2000	DSPN	60018	2917	13W-9N	A1
2000	RSMT	60018	2917	13W-9N	A1
2400	FNPK	60131	2973	13W-3N	A6
2400	LydT	60131	2973	13W-3N	A6
2400	LydT	60164	2973	13W-3N	A6
2600	FNPK	60164	2973	13W-3N	A5
2900	CHCG	60018	2917	12W-8N	A2
3700	FNPK	60176	2973	13W-4N	A3
3700	SRPK	60131	2973	13W-4N	A3
3700	SRPK	60176	2973	13W-4N	A3
6400	CHCG	60666	2917	12W-8N	A3
6400	RSMT	60666	2917	12W-8N	A3
US-12 N Mannheim Rd					
-	BLWD	60104	3029	12W-1N	A3
-	BLWD	60160	3029	12W-1N	A3
-	HLSD	60154	3029	12W-0S	A6
-	WSTR	60154	3029	12W-0S	A6
10	HLSD	60104	3029	12W-0S	A6
10	HLSD	60162	3029	12W-0S	A6
100	BLWD	60162	3029	12W-0S	A5
1500	MLPK	60160	3029	12W-1N	A2
1500	SNPK	60160	3029	12W-1N	A2
1500	SNPK	60165	3029	12W-1N	A2
1800	MLPK	60164	3029	12W-1N	A1
1800	MLPK	60165	3029	12W-1N	A1
1800	SNPK	60164	3029	12W-1N	A1
US-12 N Mannheim Rd					
2000	LydT	60160	2973	12W-2N	A7
2000	LydT	60164	2973	12W-2N	A7
2000	MLPK	60160	2973	12W-2N	A7
2000	NHLK	60160	2973	12W-2N	A7
2000	NHLK	60164	2973	12W-2N	A7
2300	LydT	60131	2973	12W-2N	A6
US-12 S Mannheim Rd					
-	BLWD	60104	3029	12W-0S	A6
-	HLSD	60104	3029	12W-0S	A6
10	HLSD	60154	3029	12W-0S	A6
10	HLSD	60162	3029	12W-0S	A6
10	WSTR	60154	3029	12W-0S	A6
100	WSTR	60162	3029	12W-0S	A7
300	PvsT	60162	3029	12W-0S	A7
1400	PvsT	60162	3087	12W-1S	A1
1400	WSTR	60154	3087	12W-1S	A1
1400	WSTR	60162	3087	12W-1S	A1
2100	PvsT	60154	3087	12W-1S	A2
2100	PvsT	60525	3087	12W-1S	A2
US-12 Rand Rd					
10	DRPK	60010	2699	22W-21N	B7
10	DRPK	60047	2699	22W-21N	B7
10	DSPN	60016	2808	14W-12N	C7
10	KLDR	60010	2699	22W-21N	B7
10	KLDR	60047	2699	22W-21N	B7
10	LKZH	60010	2699	22W-21N	B6
10	MPPT	60016	2808	14W-12N	C7
10	MPPT	60056	2808	14W-12N	C7
300	DSPN	60016	2862	13W-11N	E2
300	LKZH	60047	2699	22W-21N	B6
600	DRPK	60074	2699	21W-20N	C7
600	DRPK	60074	2752	21W-20N	D1
600	ElaT	60047	2699	21W-20N	C7
600	ElaT	60074	2699	21W-20N	D7
600	ElaT	60074	2752	21W-20N	D1
600	KLDR	60074	2699	21W-20N	C7
1200	DSPN	60016	2863	13W-11N	A2
2000	PLTN	60074	2753	20W-18N	A3
US-12 E Rand Rd					
10	ANHT	60004	2754	17W-16N	A7
10	MPPT	60056	2808	15W-13N	A5
200	ANHT	60004	2807	15W-14N	E4
900	DSPN	60016	2808	14W-13N	B7
900	MPPT	60016	2808	14W-13N	B7
1200	PTHT	60004	2807	17W-15N	C2
2400	MPPT	60004	2807	16W-14N	D3
2400	MPPT	60056	2807	16W-14N	D3
2400	WhlT	60004	2807	16W-14N	D3
2500	ANHT	60056	2807	16W-14N	E4
US-12 N Rand Rd					
-	WcnT	60073	2587	27W-29N	C4
10	LKZH	60047	2698	24W-23N	C1
200	WCDA	60084	2643	26W-26N	D2
200	WcnT	60084	2643	26W-26N	D2
600	WCDA	60084	2587	27W-30N	C1
700	ElaT	60010	2698	24W-23N	C1
700	ElaT	60047	2698	24W-23N	C1
800	WcnT	60084	2587	26W-28N	D6
900	ElaT	60047	2644	24W-24N	C7
900	NBRN	60047	2644	24W-24N	C7
1200	PLTN	60074	2753	20W-18N	B3
2100	PltT	60074	2753	20W-18N	A2
2300	DRPK	60074	2752	20W-18N	E2
2300	ElaT	60074	2752	20W-18N	E2
2300	PltT	60074	2752	20W-18N	E2
20200	KLDR	60074	2752	21W-20N	E1
20400	KLDR	60047	2752	21W-20N	D1
24000	ElaT	60010	2644	24W-24N	C7
24000	NBRN	60010	2644	24W-24N	C7
24200	HNWD	60047	2644	24W-24N	C7
24200	LKZH	60047	2644	24W-24N	C7
25800	ElaT	60084	2644	24W-25N	C4
25900	FmtT	60084	2644	24W-26N	B4
25900	WcnT	60010	2644	25W-26N	B3
25900	WcnT	60084	2644	25W-26N	B3
29000	WCDA	60073	2587	26W-29N	C5
US-12 S Rand Rd					
10	LKZH	60047	2698	23W-22N	E5
400	WCDA	60084	2643	26W-27N	D1
900	LKZH	60047	2699	21W-20N	C7
1100	KLDR	60047	2699	22W-21N	A5
1100	LKZH	60010	2699	22W-21N	B6
26400	WCDA	60084	2644	25W-26N	A3
26400	WcnT	60010	2644	25W-26N	A3
26400	WcnT	60084	2644	25W-26N	A3
26500	WcnT	60084	2643	25W-26N	E3
US-12 W Rand Rd					
-	ANHT	60074	2753	19W-17N	D5
-	PltT	60074	2753	19W-17N	D5
10	ANHT	60004	2754	17W-16N	A7
10	MPPT	60056	2808	15W-13N	B6
300	MPPT	60056	2807	15W-14N	E4
400	ANHT	60004	2753	18W-17N	D6
600	ANHT	60056	2807	15W-14N	E4
700	ANHT	60004	2807	16W-14N	E4
700	MPPT	60004	2807	16W-14N	E4
1200	PltT	60004	2753	18W-17N	D6
US-12 S River Rd					
-	DSPN	60016	2863	13W-11N	A3
US-14					
-	DSPN	60068	2863	12W-10N	C4
-	HtdT	60033	2464	48W-35N	E5
-	NLES	60053	2865	8W-9N	A6
-	PltT	60067	2751	23W-17N	E5
-	SenT	60098	2581	43W-30N	A1
10	AlqT	60013	2696	30W-23N	A2
10	ANHT	60004	2807	17W-14N	A4
10	ANHT	60005	2807	17W-14N	A4
10	CLLK	60014	2639	37W-27N	A1
10	CRY	60013	2641	31W-24N	D7
10	CRY	60013	2695	31W-24N	A1
10	CRY	60013	2696	30W-23N	A2
10	DSPN	60016	2862	14W-12N	C1
10	FRGV	60013	2696	30W-23N	A2
10	FRGV	60021	2696	29W-22N	C3
10	MPPT	60016	2862	14W-12N	B1
10	MPPT	60056	2808	15W-12N	A7
10	MPPT	60056	2862	13W-11N	E3
10	PLTN	60067	2752	22W-17N	A5
10	PLTN	60067	2806	18W-14N	D3
10	PLTN	60074	2806	18W-14N	D3
100	BRTN	60010	2751	24W-17N	D4
100	CLLK	60014	2640	35W-24N	A6
100	HRVD	60033	2406	50W-38N	B7
100	NndT	60012	2639	36W-26N	D3
100	PLTN	60074	2753	20W-16N	A7
200	MPPT	60056	2807	15W-12N	E7
200	PLTN	60067	2753	20W-16N	A7
300	HRVD	60033	2464	50W-37N	B1
500	ANHT	60004	2806	18W-14N	E4
500	ANHT	60005	2806	18W-14N	E4
500	BRTN	60010	2697	26W-20N	D7
500	BRTN	60010	2750	26W-20N	D1
500	PltT	60067	2752	21W-16N	C6
800	AlqT	60013	2641	32W-24N	B7
US-14					
800	AlqT	60014	2641	31W-24N	D7
800	CbaT	60010	2697	27W-21N	B7
800	CRY	60014	2641	31W-24N	D7
800	DhmT	60033	2464	50W-37N	B2
900	LKBN	60010	2697	28W-21N	A5
1000	FRGV	60010	2696	29W-22N	D4
1000	LKBN	60010	2696	28W-21N	E5
1000	LKBN	60021	2696	29W-22N	D4
1100	PltT	60010	2751	23W-17N	D4
1200	NLES	60714	2863	10W-10N	E4
1200	NLES	60714	2864	8W-10N	E4
1200	PKRG	60068	2863	10W-10N	E4
1200	PKRG	60068	2864	10W-10N	A4
1200	PKRG	60714	2863	10W-10N	E4
1200	PKRG	60714	2864	10W-10N	A4
1300	DrrT	60098	2524	43W-31N	A6
1300	DSPN	60016	2863	12W-11N	A4
1300	SenT	60098	2524	43W-31N	A6
1300	WDSK	60098	2524	43W-31N	A6
1500	NLES	60068	2863	11W-11N	E4
1500	PLTN	60067	2751	23W-17N	E5
1700	CHCG	60660	2921	2W-7N	B3
1800	ANHT	60074	2806	19W-14N	D3
1800	CmgT	60033	2406	50W-39N	B5
1900	CHCG	60659	2921	2W-7N	B3
2000	MaiT	60016	2863	11W-11N	D4
2000	PKRG	60016	2863	11W-11N	D4
2700	CHCG	60659	2920	3W-7N	E3
3800	CHCG	60646	2920	4W-7N	B4
4100	CLLK	60014	2641	33W-24N	A6
4400	AlqT	60014	2640	33W-24N	E6
4700	CHCG	60646	2919	6W-7N	D3
5200	CHCG	60640	2921	1W-6N	D5
6800	CHCG	60714	2919	7W-8N	B1
6800	NLES	60714	2919	7W-8N	B1
6900	MNGV	60053	2864	8W-10N	E4
7000	NLES	60053	2864	8W-10N	E4
7100	MNGV	60714	2864	8W-11N	D4
7200	CHCG	60646	2865	8W-9N	A7
7200	CHCG	60714	2865	8W-9N	A7
7200	NLES	60646	2865	8W-9N	A7
7200	NLES	60714	2865	8W-9N	A6
7800	CLLK	60012	2639	36W-26N	C2
7900	DrrT	60012	2639	37W-26N	C2
7900	DrrT	60014	2639	37W-26N	C2
7900	MNGV	60053	2865	8W-9N	A6
7900	MNGV	60714	2865	8W-9N	A6
9000	CLLK	60012	2583	38W-27N	A7
9000	DrrT	60098	2583	38W-27N	A7
9200	WDSK	60098	2582	38W-28N	E6
11400	DrrT	60098	2582	40W-29N	B4
12200	WDSK	60098	2581	40W-29N	E3
13200	DrrT	60098	2581	43W-30N	A1
14300	HtdT	60098	2524	43W-31N	A6
28700	CbaT	60010	2696	28W-22N	D4
US-14 N Broadway St					
5200	CHCG	60640	2921	1W-6N	D5
5500	CHCG	60660	2921	1W-6N	D4
US-14 Caldwell Av					
7900	MNGV	60053	2864	8W-10N	E4
7900	NLES	60714	2864	8W-10N	E4
US-14 N Caldwell Av					
-	NLES	60053	2865	8W-9N	A6
6000	CHCG	60646	2919	6W-7N	D3
6800	CHCG	60714	2919	7W-8N	B1
6800	NLES	60714	2919	7W-8N	B1
7200	CHCG	60646	2865	8W-9N	A7
7200	CHCG	60714	2865	8W-9N	A7
7200	NLES	60646	2865	8W-9N	A7
7200	NLES	60714	2865	8W-9N	A6
7900	MNGV	60053	2865	8W-9N	A6
7900	MNGV	60714	2865	8W-9N	A6
8000	MNGV	60053	2864	8W-10N	E5
8000	MNGV	60714	2864	8W-10N	E5
8000	NLES	60714	2864	8W-10N	E5
US-14 Crystal St					
10	CRY	60013	2695	31W-23N	E1
US-14 Dempster St					
-	DSPN	60068	2863	12W-10N	C4
1200	NLES	60714	2863	10W-10N	C7
1200	PKRG	60068	2863	10W-10N	E4
1200	PKRG	60068	2864	10W-10N	A4
1200	PKRG	60714	2863	10W-10N	E4
1200	PKRG	60714	2864	10W-10N	A4
1500	NLES	60068	2863	11W-11N	E4
2000	MaiT	60016	2863	11W-11N	D4
2000	PKRG	60016	2863	11W-11N	D4
2300	DSPN	60016	2863	12W-10N	C4
6900	MNGV	60053	2864	8W-10N	E4
7000	NLES	60053	2864	8W-10N	E4
7000	NLES	60714	2864	8W-10N	E4
US-14 W Dempster St					
7000	MNGV	60053	2864	8W-11N	E4
7000	NLES	60053	2864	8W-11N	E4
7000	NLES	60714	2864	8W-11N	E4
7100	MNGV	60714	2864	8W-11N	D4
8500	PKRG	60068	2864	10W-10N	A4
8500	PKRG	60714	2864	10W-10N	A4
US-14 N Division St					
100	HRVD	60033	2406	50W-38N	B7
1800	CmgT	60033	2406	50W-39N	B4
US-14 S Division St					
100	HRVD	60033	2406	50W-38N	B7
300	HRVD	60033	2464	50W-37N	B1
800	DhmT	60033	2464	50W-37N	B2
US-14 E Main St					
10	CRY	60013	2695	30W-23N	E1
US-14 W Main St					
10	CRY	60013	2695	31W-23N	E1
US-14 Miner St					
1200	DSPN	60016	2862	13W-11N	E3
1300	DSPN	60016	2863	12W-11N	A4
US-14 Northwest Hwy					
-	CbaT	60010	2696	29W-22N	D4
-	CRY	60013	2696	30W-23N	A2
10	AlqT	60013	2696	30W-23N	A2
10	CRY	60013	2641	31W-24N	D7
10	CRY	60013	2695	31W-24N	D1
10	FRGV	60013	2696	30W-23N	A2
10	FRGV	60021	2696	29W-22N	C3
800	AlqT	60013	2641	32W-24N	B7
800	AlqT	60014	2641	31W-24N	D7
800	CRY	60014	2641	31W-24N	D7
1000	FRGV	60010	2696	29W-22N	D4
1000	LKBN	60010	2696	29W-22N	D4
1000	LKBN	60021	2696	29W-22N	D4
4100	CLLK	60014	2641	33W-24N	A6
4400	AlqT	60014	2640	33W-24N	E6
4400	CLLK	60014	2640	33W-24N	E6
US-14 E Northwest Hwy					
10	ANHT	60004	2807	17W-14N	A4
10	ANHT	60005	2807	17W-14N	A4
10	DSPN	60016	2862	14W-12N	C1
10	MPPT	60016	2862	14W-12N	B1
10	MPPT	60056	2808	15W-12N	A7
US-14 E Northwest Hwy					
10	MPPT	60056	2862	13W-11N	E3
10	PLTN	60067	2752	20W-16N	E6
100	BRTN	60010	2751	25W-20N	A1
200	PLTN	60067	2753	20W-16N	A7
400	PLTN	60067	2806	20W-15N	A1
400	PLTN	60074	2806	20W-15N	A1
1700	DSPN	60016	2863	12W-11N	A4
2100	MPPT	60056	2807	16W-13N	D6
US-14 N Northwest Hwy					
10	PLTN	60067	2806	20W-16N	A1
10	PLTN	60074	2806	20W-16N	A1
100	BRTN	60010	2751	25W-20N	A2
100	PLTN	60074	2753	20W-16N	A7
300	PLTN	60067	2753	20W-16N	A7
US-14 S Northwest Hwy					
-	PLTN	60067	2751	23W-17N	E5
-	PltT	60067	2751	23W-17N	E5
10	CRY	60013	2695	30W-23N	E1
10	CRY	60013	2696	30W-23N	A2
10	PLTN	60067	2806	18W-14N	D3
10	PLTN	60074	2806	18W-14N	D3
100	AlqT	60013	2696	30W-23N	A2
100	BRTN	60010	2751	24W-17N	D4
100	FRGV	60013	2696	30W-23N	A2
1100	PltT	60010	2751	23W-17N	D4
US-14 W Northwest Hwy					
-	FRGV	60010	2696	28W-22N	D4
-	PltT	60010	2751	23W-17N	E5
-	PltT	60067	2751	23W-17N	E5
10	ANHT	60004	2807	17W-14N	A4
10	ANHT	60005	2807	17W-14N	A4
10	MPPT	60056	2808	15W-12N	A7
10	PLTN	60067	2752	22W-17N	A5
200	MPPT	60056	2807	15W-12N	E7
500	ANHT	60004	2806	18W-14N	E4
500	ANHT	60005	2806	18W-14N	E4
500	BRTN	60010	2697	26W-20N	D7
500	BRTN	60010	2750	26W-20N	D1
500	PltT	60067	2752	21W-16N	C6
800	CbaT	60010	2697	27W-21N	B7
900	LKBN	60010	2697	28W-21N	A5
1500	PLTN	60067	2751	23W-17N	E5
1800	ANHT	60074	2806	19W-14N	D3
1800	PLTN	60074	2806	19W-14N	D3
28300	LKBN	60010	2696	28W-21N	E5
28700	CbaT	60010	2696	28W-22N	D4
28900	FRGV	60021	2696	28W-22N	D4
28900	LKBN	60021	2696	28W-22N	D4
US-14 W Peterson Av					
1700	CHCG	60660	2921	2W-7N	B3
1900	CHCG	60659	2921	2W-7N	B3
2700	CHCG	60659	2920	3W-7N	E3
3800	CHCG	60646	2920	4W-7N	B4
4700	CHCG	60646	2919	5W-7N	E4
US-14 N Ridge Av					
5600	CHCG	60640	2921	1W-7N	D4
5600	CHCG	60660	2921	1W-7N	D4
US-14 N Virginia St					
10	CLLK	60014	2639	37W-27N	A1
100	NndT	60012	2639	36W-26N	D3
US-14 S Virginia St					
10	CLLK	60014	2639	36W-25N	D4
US-14 W Virginia St					
100	CLLK	60014	2640	35W-24N	A6
200	CLLK	60014	2639	35W-25N	E5
US-14 Waukegan Rd					
8500	MNGV	60053	2864	8W-10N	E4
US-20					
-	BGVW	60453	3210	8W-10S	E6
-	BGVW	60455	3210	8W-10S	E6
-	BGVW	60457	3210	9W-11S	D6
-	ELGN	-	2853	37W-11N	D4
-	ELGN	-	2854	35W-10N	A5
-	ELGN	-	2855	33W-10N	A6
-	ElgT	-	2853	36W-11N	E5
-	ElgT	-	2854	35W-10N	A5
-	EMHT	-	2972	15W-2N	A7
-	EMHT	-	3028	15W-2N	B1
-	HGKN	60525	3147	12W-8S	C7
-	HGKN	60525	3209	12W-8S	C1
-	HYHL	60455	3210	9W-11S	D6
-	LynT	60458	3209	11W-8S	D2
-	LynT	60480	3209	11W-9S	D3
-	LynT	60525	3209	11W-8S	D2
-	OKLN	60453	3210	8W-10S	E6
-	OKLN	60455	3210	8W-10S	E6
-	PlsT	60480	3209	11W-9S	D4
-	SMWD	60120	2910	30W-9N	C1
-	WLSP	60458	3209	11W-9S	D2
-	WLSP	60480	3209	11W-8S	D2
-	WLSP	60525	3209	12W-8S	C1
10	AddT	60101	2970	21W-5N	A2
10	ADSN	60101	2970	20W-4N	B2
10	ADSN	60101	2971	18W-3N	A5
10	ADSN	60143	2970	21W-5N	A2
10	BLWD	60104	3029	12W-0N	A3
10	BLWD	60160	3029	12W-1N	A3
10	BMDL	60101	2969	22W-5N	D1
10	BMDL	60108	2969	23W-5N	B1
10	BmdT	60101	2969	21W-5N	E1
10	BmdT	60101	2970	20W-4N	B2
10	BmdT	60143	2970	20W-4N	B2
10	BmdT	60172	2912	25W-6N	C6
10	CHCG	60619	3214	0E-10S	C6
10	CHCG	60620	3214	0E-10S	C6
10	CHCG	60628	3214	0W-11S	C6
10	ElgT	60124	2853	38W-11N	B4
10	HLSD	60104	3029	12W-0S	A6
10	HLSD	60154	3029	12W-0S	A6
10	HLSD	60162	3029	12W-0S	A6
10	HPSR	60140	2743	44W-17N	E6
10	HPSR	60140	2796	44W-16N	E2
10	HPSR	60140	2797	43W-15N	B4
10	HshT	60140	2743	46W-19N	A2
10	HshT	60140	2796	44W-16N	E2
10	HshT	60140	2797	43W-15N	B4
10	LGNG	60525	3087	12W-4S	C6
10	MLPK	60160	3028	13W-1N	E2
10	MLPK	60160	3029	13W-1N	A2
10	NHLK	60164	3028	13W-1N	E2
10	PGGV	60140	2797	43W-14N	C5
10	PGGV	60140	2798	40W-13N	B7
10	PltT	60124	2852	39W-12N	D2
10	PltT	60140	2798	40W-13N	B7
10	PltT	60140	2852	39W-12N	E3
10	ROSL	60172	2912	24W-6N	E7
10	RtdT	60140	2797	43W-15N	B4
10	WSTR	60154	3029	12W-0S	A6
100	ADSN	60101	2969	21W-5N	E1
100	BLWD	60162	3029	12W-0S	A5
100	BMDL	60108	2968	23W-5N	E1
100	BmdT	60108	2968	23W-5N	E1
100	BmdT	60143	2969	21W-5N	E2
100	BRLT	60103	2910	29W-9N	D1
100	BRLT	60103	2911	28W-8N	B2
US-20					
100	BRLT	60107	2910	29W-9N	D1
100	LGPK	60525	3087	12W-4S	C6
100	MRGO	60152	2634	50W-26N	A2
100	SMWD	60103	2910	28W-9N	E2
100	SMWD	60103	2911	28W-8N	B2
100	SMWD	60107	2910	29W-9N	D1
100	SMWD	60107	2911	28W-8N	B2
100	WSTR	60162	3029	12W-0S	A7
200	AddT	60101	2971	17W-3N	A5
200	AddT	60143	2970	20W-5N	A2
200	BMDL	60108	2912	24W-6N	E7
200	BMDL	60172	2912	24W-6N	E7
200	BmdT	60108	2912	24W-5N	E7
200	BmdT	60133	2911	26W-7N	E5
200	BRLT	60107	2911	28W-9N	A2
200	ELGN	60123	2853	36W-11N	D4
200	HRPK	60133	2911	26W-7N	E5
200	ROSL	60108	2912	24W-6N	E7
300	EMHT	60101	2971	17W-3N	C6
300	EMHT	60126	2971	16W-2N	D6
300	HRPK	60133	2912	26W-7N	A5
300	HRPK	60172	2912	25W-6N	B6
300	LGNG	60525	3147	12W-4S	C1
300	PvsT	60162	3029	12W-0S	A7
400	BmdT	60133	2912	26W-7N	A5
400	BmdT	60157	2969	21W-5N	E1
500	BRLT	60120	2910	29W-9N	D1
500	HnrT	60103	2910	29W-9N	D1
500	HnrT	60120	2910	29W-9N	D1
500	PltT	60140	2797	41W-13N	E7
600	HRPK	60103	2911	28W-8N	B2
700	CHCG	60643	3214	0W-10S	A6
700	PltT	60124	2853	38W-12N	A3
800	CrlT	60140	2743	46W-19N	A2
800	CrlT	60142	2743	46W-19N	A2
900	CHCG	60619	3215	1E-10S	A5
900	CHCG	60620	3213	1W-10S	E6
900	CHCG	60628	3215	1E-10S	A5
1000	CHCG	60643	3213	1W-10S	E6
1000	HMND	46320	3280		D3
1000	HMND	46394	3280		E4
1000	PvsT	60525	3087	12W-3S	B4
1100	BRLT	60103	2856	30W-9N	B7
1100	BRLT	60107	2856	30W-9N	B7
1100	HnrT	60107	2856	30W-9N	B7
1100	SMWD	60107	2856	30W-9N	C7
1400	BRLT	60120	2856	30W-9N	B7
1400	HnrT	60120	2856	30W-9N	B7
1400	PvsT	60162	3087	12W-1S	A1
1400	WSTR	60154	3087	12W-1S	A1
1400	WSTR	60162	3087	12W-1S	A1
1500	CHCG	60617	3215	1E-10S	B5
1500	ELGN	60120	2856	30W-9N	B7
1600	ELGN	60103	2856	31W-10N	A7
2100	PvsT	60154	3087	12W-1S	A2
2200	BRLT	60133	2911	27W-8N	C3
2300	CHCG	60805	3213	2W-11S	B6
2400	ENGN	60805	3213	3W-10S	B6
2900	ENGN	60805	3212	3W-10S	E6
3000	CHCG	60617	3216	3E-11S	A5
3900	ENGN	60453	3212	4W-10S	C6
3900	OKLN	60453	3212	4W-10S	C6
4100	MLPK	60165	3029	13W-1N	A2
4100	SNPK	60160	3029	13W-1N	A2
4100	SNPK	60165	3029	13W-1N	A2
4900	OKLN	60453	3211	6W-10S	E6
5200	CTSD	60525	3147	12W-5S	C3
6300	CHRG	60415	3211	7W-10S	B6
6300	CHRG	60453	3211	7W-10S	B6
6300	OKLN	60415	3211	7W-10S	B6
6500	CrlT	60152	2635	47W-24N	B7
6500	CrlT	60180	2635	47W-24N	B7
7600	HYHL	60457	3210	9W-11S	D6
8700	HYHL	60465	3210	10W-10S	A6
8700	PSHL	60457	3210	10W-10S	A6
8700	PSHL	60465	3210	10W-10S	A6
8900	HYHL	60457	3209	11W-10S	E6
8900	HYHL	60465	3209	11W-10S	E6
8900	PSHL	60465	3209	11W-10S	E6
9000	PlsT	60457	3209	11W-10S	E6
9000	PlsT	60465	3209	11W-10S	E6
9000	PSHL	60457	3209	11W-10S	E6
10300	CHCG	60617	3280	4E-11S	C1
10500	HMND	60617	3280	4E-11S	C1
19200	CrlT	60152	2634	48W-25N	E4
19200	CrlT	60180	2634	48W-25N	E4
US-20 BUS					
-	ELGN	60120	2855	32W-10N	D6
US-20 95th St					
-	HYHL	60457	3209	11W-10S	E6
-	PlsT	60457	3209	11W-10S	E6
-	PlsT	60465	3209	11W-10S	E6
-	PlsT	60480	3209	11W-10S	E6
-	PSHL	60457	3209	11W-10S	E6
-	PSHL	60465	3209	11W-10S	E6
US-20 E 95th St					
10	CHCG	60619	3214	0E-10S	C6
10	CHCG	60620	3214	0E-10S	C6
10	CHCG	60628	3214	0E-10S	C6
900	CHCG	60619	3215	1E-10S	A5
900	CHCG	60628	3215	1E-10S	A5
1500	CHCG	60617	3215	1E-10S	B5
3000	CHCG	60617	3216	3E-11S	A5
US-20 W 95th St					
-	BGVW	60453	3210	8W-10S	E6
-	BGVW	60455	3210	8W-10S	E6
-	BGVW	60457	3210	9W-11S	D6
-	CHCG	60619	3214	0W-10S	C6
-	HYHL	60455	3210	9W-11S	D6
-	OKLN	60453	3210	8W-10S	E6
-	OKLN	60455	3210	8W-10S	E6
10	CHCG	60620	3214	0W-11S	C6
10	CHCG	60628	3214	0W-10S	C6
700	CHCG	60643	3214	0W-10S	A6
1000	CHCG	60620	3213	1W-10S	E6
2300	CHCG	60805	3213	2W-10S	B6
2400	CHCG	60643	3213	3W-10S	B6
2400	ENGN	60805	3213	3W-10S	B6
2900	ENGN	60805	3212	3W-10S	E6
3900	ENGN	60453	3212	4W-10S	C6
3900	OKLN	60453	3212	4W-10S	C6
4900	OKLN	60453	3211	6W-10S	E6
6300	CHRG	60415	3211	7W-10S	B6
6300	CHRG	60453	3211	7W-10S	B6
6300	OKLN	60415	3211	7W-10S	B6
7600	HYHL	60457	3210	9W-11S	D6
8700	HYHL	60465	3210	10W-10S	A6
8700	PSHL	60457	3210	10W-10S	A6
8700	PSHL	60465	3210	10W-10S	A6
8900	HYHL	60457	3209	11W-10S	E6
8900	HYHL	60465	3209	11W-10S	E6
8900	PSHL	60465	3209	11W-10S	E6
9000	PlsT	60457	3209	11W-10S	E6
9000	PlsT	60465	3209	11W-10S	E6
9000	PlsT	60480	3209	11W-10S	E6

STREET Block City ZIP Map# CGS Grid

US-20 W 95th St
9000 PSHL 60457 3209 11W-10S E6
US-20 Brier Hill Rd
10 HshT 60140 2743 44W-17N E6
400 HshT 60140 2796 44W-16N E2
US-20 Eisenhower Expwy
- EMHT - 2971 16W-2N E7
- EMHT - 2972 15W-2N A7
- EMHT - 3028 15W-2N B1
US-20 S Ewing Av
9500 CHCG 60617 3216 4E-10S B5
US-20 E Grant Hwy
100 MRGO 60152 2634 49W-26N B2
11400 CrlT 60140 2743 45W-20N A1
11400 CrlT 60142 2743 45W-20N A1
11600 HPSR 60140 2743 45W-20N A1
11600 HshT 60140 2743 45W-20N A1
19200 CrlT 60152 2634 48W-25N E4
19200 CrlT 60180 2634 48W-25N E4
US-20 S Grant Hwy
6500 CrlT 60152 2635 47W-24N B7
6500 CrlT 60180 2635 47W-24N B7
US-20 W Grant Hwy
100 MRGO 60152 2634 50W-26N A2
US-20 S Indianapolis Av
- CHCG 60617 3280 4E-11S C1
- HMND 60617 3280 4E-11S C1
10000 CHCG 60617 3216 4E-11S B7
10600 HMND 46320 3280 4E-11S C1
US-20 S Indianapolis Blvd
1000 HMND 46320 3280 D3
1000 HMND 46394 3280 E4
10500 CHCG 60617 3280 C1
10500 HMND 60617 3280 4E-11S C1
US-20 La Grange Rd
- LynT 60458 3209 11W-8S D2
- LynT 60480 3209 11W-9S D3
- LynT 60525 3209 11W-8S D2
- PlsT 60480 3209 11W-9S D4
- WLSP 60458 3209 11W-9S D2
- WLSP 60480 3209 11W-8S D2
- WLSP 60525 3209 12W-8S D2
US-20 N La Grange Rd
- PvsT 60154 3087 12W-2S A2
- WSTR 60154 3087 12W-2S A2
10 LGNG 60525 3087 12W-4S C6
100 LGPK 60525 3087 12W-4S C6
1000 PvsT 60525 3087 12W-3S B4
US-20 S La Grange Rd
- HGKN 60525 3147 12W-8S C7
- HGKN 60525 3209 12W-8S C1
- WLSP 60525 3209 12W-8S C1
10 LGNG 60525 3087 12W-4S C7
300 LGNG 60525 3147 12W-4S C1
5200 CTSD 60525 3147 12W-5S C3
US-20 Lake St
- AddT 60101 2971 17W-3N B5
- BmdT 60133 2911 26W-7N E5
- BRLT 60103 2856 31W-9N A7
- BRLT 60120 2856 31W-9N A7
- ELGN - 2855 32W-10N D6
- ELGN 60103 2856 31W-10N A7
- ELGN 60120 2856 31W-10N A7
- HnrT 60120 2856 31W-9N A7
10 AddT 60101 2970 21W-5N A2
10 ADSN 60101 2970 20W-4N B2
10 ADSN 60143 2970 21W-5N A2
10 BMDL 60101 2969 22W-5N D1
10 BmdT 60101 2969 21W-5N E1
10 BmdT 60101 2970 20W-4N B2
10 BmdT 60143 2970 20W-4N B2
10 BmdT 60172 2912 25W-6N C6
10 ROSL 60172 2912 25W-6N C6
100 ADSN 60101 2969 21W-5N E1
100 BMDL 60108 2969 22W-5N D1
100 BmdT 60143 2969 21W-5N E2
200 AddT 60143 2970 20W-5N A2
200 HRPK 60133 2911 26W-7N E5
300 HRPK 60133 2912 25W-6N B6
300 HRPK 60172 2912 25W-6N B6
400 BmdT 60133 2912 25W-6N A6
400 BmdT 60157 2969 21W-5N E1
600 BMDL 60108 2912 24W-6N D7
600 BMDL 60172 2912 24W-6N D7
US-20 E Lake St
10 ADSN 60101 2971 18W-3N A5
10 MLPK 60160 3028 13W-1N E2
10 NHLK 60164 3028 13W-1N D2
100 BMDL 60108 2969 23W-5N A1
100 BRLT 60103 2910 28W-9N E2
100 BRLT 60103 2911 28W-8N B2
100 BRLT 60107 2910 28W-9N E1
100 SMWD 60103 2910 28W-9N E2
100 SMWD 60103 2911 28W-8N B2
100 SMWD 60107 2910 28W-9N E2
100 SMWD 60107 2911 28W-8N B2
200 AddT 60101 2971 17W-3N A5
200 BRLT 60107 2911 28W-9N A2
300 EMHT 60101 2971 17W-3N C6
300 EMHT 60126 2971 17W-3N C6
1000 BmdT 60133 2911 26W-7N E5
1000 BmdT 60133 2912 26W-7N A5
1000 HRPK 60133 2911 26W-7N E5
1000 HRPK 60133 2912 26W-7N A5
US-20 W Lake St
- EMHT 60101 2971 17W-3N C6
- SMWD 60120 2910 30W-9N C1
10 ADSN 60101 2970 18W-3N E4
10 NHLK 60164 3028 13W-1N E2
100 AddT 60101 2970 20W-4N B3
100 BMDL 60108 2968 23W-5N E1
100 BMDL 60108 2969 23W-5N B1
100 BmdT 60108 2968 23W-5N E1
200 BMDL 60108 2912 24W-6N E7
200 BMDL 60172 2912 24W-6N E7
200 BmdT 60108 2912 24W-5N E7
200 ROSL 60108 2912 24W-6N E7
200 ROSL 60172 2912 24W-6N E7
300 AddT 60101 2971 17W-3N C6
300 EMHT 60126 2971 16W-2N D6
500 BRLT 60103 2910 29W-9N D1
500 BRLT 60107 2910 29W-9N D1
500 BRLT 60120 2910 29W-9N D1
500 HnrT 60103 2910 29W-9N D1
500 HnrT 60120 2910 29W-9N D1
500 SMWD 60107 2910 29W-9N D1
600 BRLT 60103 2911 28W-8N B2
600 HRPK 60103 2911 28W-8N B2
600 HRPK 60133 2911 28W-8N B2
600 SMWD 60107 2911 28W-8N B2
1100 BRLT 60103 2856 30W-9N B7
1100 BRLT 60107 2856 30W-9N B7
1100 HnrT 60107 2856 30W-9N B7
1100 SMWD 60107 2856 30W-9N C7
1400 BRLT 60120 2856 30W-9N B7
1400 HnrT 60120 2856 30W-9N B7

US-20 W Lake St
2200 BRLT 60133 2911 27W-8N C3
4100 MLPK 60160 3029 13W-1N A2
4100 MLPK 60165 3029 13W-1N A2
4100 SNPK 60160 3029 13W-1N A2
4100 SNPK 60165 3029 13W-1N A2
4700 MLPK 60160 3028 13W-1N E2
US-20 Mannheim Rd
10 BLWD 60104 3029 12W-0N A3
10 BLWD 60160 3029 12W-1N A3
10 MLPK 60160 3029 12W-1N A3
500 BLWD 60162 3029 12W-0N A4
500 HLSD 60162 3029 12W-0N A4
US-20 N Mannheim Rd
- BLWD 60104 3029 12W-1N A3
- BLWD 60160 3029 12W-1N A3
- HLSD 60154 3029 12W-0S A6
- MLPK 60160 3029 12W-1N A2
- SNPK 60160 3029 12W-1N A2
- SNPK 60165 3029 12W-1N A2
- WSTR 60154 3029 12W-0S A6
10 HLSD 60104 3029 12W-0S A6
10 HLSD 60162 3029 12W-0S A6
100 BLWD 60162 3029 12W-0S A5
US-20 S Mannheim Rd
- BLWD 60104 3029 12W-0S A6
- HLSD 60104 3029 12W-0S A6
10 HLSD 60154 3029 12W-0S A6
10 HLSD 60162 3029 12W-0S A6
10 WSTR 60154 3029 12W-0S A6
100 WSTR 60162 3029 12W-0S A7
300 PvsT 60162 3029 12W-0S A7
1400 PvsT 60162 3087 12W-1S A1
1400 WSTR 60154 3087 12W-1S A1
1400 WSTR 60162 3087 12W-1S A1
2100 PvsT 60154 3087 12W-1S A2
2100 PvsT 60525 3087 12W-1S A2
US-20 Oak St
10 PGGV 60140 2798 40W-13N B7
10 PltT 60140 2798 40W-13N B7
US-20 Villa St
- ELGN - 2855 31W-10N E6
US-20 BUS Villa St
- ELGN 60120 2855 32W-10N D6
US-20 E Villa St
1500 ELGN 60120 2855 31W-10N E7
1500 ELGN 60120 2856 30W-9N B7
1600 ELGN 60103 2856 31W-10N A7
US-30
- AraT 60538 3199 38W-9S B5
- AURA 60543 3265 32W-12S C3
- AURA 60585 3265 32W-12S C3
- BRKT 60554 3135 42W-7S C7
- BRKT 60554 3197 42W-7S C1
- BtlT 60512 3198 40W-9S B5
- BtlT 60538 3198 40W-9S B5
- MTGY 60506 3198 39W-9S D5
- MTGY 60538 3198 41W-10S A5
- MTGY 60538 3198 36W-10S E6
- OswT 60538 3199 37W-10S D5
- PNFD 60585 3338 31W-15S A3
- SgrT 60506 3198 41W-9S A5
- SgrT 60538 3198 41W-9S A5
- SgrT 60554 3134 45W-6S C6
- SRGV - 3135 43W-7S B6
- WldT 60585 3265 33W-11S B2
- WldT 60585 3337 31W-14S E1
- WldT 60585 3338 31W-15S A3
10 BlmT 60411 3598 D2
10 CHHT 60411 3508 0E-25S E7
10 DYR 46311 3598 C2
10 FKFT 60423 3503 13W-25S B7
10 JLET 60432 3498 24W-23S E5
10 JLET 60432 3499 23W-23S A5
10 PNFD 60544 3416 29W-18S D1
10 SgrT 60506 3197 42W-9S C5
10 SgrT 60554 3197 42W-9S C5
10 SRGV 60554 3197 42W-8S C2
100 CHHT 60411 3507 1W-25S E7
100 FftT 60423 3503 13W-25S B7
100 JLET 60435 3498 24W-23S E5
200 SgrT 60554 3135 43W-7S B6
300 BGRK 60554 3134 46W-7S A6
300 BlmT 60411 3508 0E-25S E7
300 BRKT 60554 3134 45W-6S B6
300 MTGY 60503 3200 33W-10S E6
300 MTGY 60504 3200 33W-10S E6
300 MTGY 60538 3200 33W-10S E6
300 OswT 60503 3200 33W-10S E6
300 OswT 60504 3200 33W-10S E6
300 OswT 60538 3200 33W-10S E6
300 OswT 60543 3200 33W-10S E6
300 PNFD 60544 3338 31W-15S A3
300 PNFD 60586 3416 29W-18S D1
300 SRGV 60554 3134 45W-6S C6
400 OSWG 60538 3200 35W-10S B6
400 OSWG 60543 3200 35W-10S B6
700 OMFD 60461 3507 3W-25S A7
800 BtlT 60512 3197 42W-9S C5
800 CHHT 60411 3509 1E-25S A7
800 FDHT 60411 3509 1E-25S A7
800 JltT 60432 3499 21W-23S E4
900 FKFT 60423 3591 13W-25S B1
1000 MTGY 60543 3200 34W-10S E6
1000 NLNX 60451 3501 17W-25S D6
1000 NlxT 60451 3501 17W-25S D6
1000 OSWG 60543 3201 33W-11S A7
1000 OswT 60503 3201 33W-11S A7
1000 OswT 60543 3201 33W-11S A7
1000 PnfT 60544 3338 30W-16S A5
1100 NLNX 60451 3500 19W-24S D5
1100 NlxT 60451 3500 19W-24S D5
1100 OSWG 60503 3265 33W-11S B2
1100 OSWG 60543 3265 33W-11S B1
1100 OswT 60503 3265 33W-11S B1
1100 OswT 60543 3265 33W-11S B2
1200 NLNX 60451 3502 16W-25S A7
1200 NlxT 60451 3502 16W-25S A7
1400 BlmT 60411 3509 3E-25S E7
1400 NLNX 60433 3500 19W-24S D5
1400 NlxT 60432 3500 21W-23S A4
1500 CTHL 60403 3498 25W-22S A1
1500 JLET 60403 3498 25W-22S A1
1600 CTHL 60403 3418 26W-21S A7
1700 SLVL 60411 3509 3E-25S E7
1800 JLET 60433 3499 21W-23S E4
1800 JltT 60433 3499 21W-23S E4
1900 JltT 60432 3500 21W-23S A4
1900 JltT 60433 3500 21W-23S A4
2000 CTHL 60403 3417 26W-21S E7
2000 NlxT 60433 3500 21W-23S A4
2200 WldT 60543 3265 33W-11S B2
2300 CTHL 60435 3417 26W-21S D6
2300 LktT 60435 3417 26W-20S D6
2300 PnfT 60435 3417 26W-20S D6
2400 BlmT 60411 3510 3E-25S A7

US-30
2400 JLET 60435 3417 27W-20S D5
2500 JLET 60432 3500 20W-23S B4
2500 PKFT 60466 3507 3W-25S A7
2600 JLET 60431 3417 26W-21S E6
2700 FftT 60448 3502 14W-25S D7
2700 FftT 60451 3502 14W-25S D7
2700 MKNA 60448 3502 14W-25S D7
2700 MKNA 60451 3502 14W-25S D7
2800 LYWD 60411 3510 3E-25S A7
3200 MTSN 60443 3506 4W-25S E7
3200 MTSN 60466 3506 4W-25S E7
3200 OMFD 60461 3506 4W-25S E7
3200 PKFT 60466 3506 4W-25S E7
5300 MTSN 60443 3505 7W-25S C7
6200 RchT 60443 3505 7W-25S C7
6700 FftT 60423 3505 8W-25S A7
6700 FKFT 60423 3505 8W-25S A7
7400 FftT 60423 3504 9W-25S E7
7400 FKFT 60423 3504 9W-25S E7
11100 MKNA 60448 3591 13W-25S B1
11200 MKNA 60448 3590 14W-25S E1
21400 LYWD 60411 3598 D2
22800 JLET 60544 3417 26W-21S E6
22800 JLET 60586 3417 26W-21S E6
22800 PnfT 60544 3417 28W-19S A3
22800 PnfT 60586 3417 28W-19S A3
22900 PNFD 60586 3417 28W-19S A3
23000 PnfT 60544 3416 29W-18S D1
23000 PnfT 60586 3416 29W-18S D1
US-30 E 14th St
10 CHHT 60411 3508 1W-25S A7
300 BlmT 60411 3508 0W-25S D7
US-30 W 14th St
10 CHHT 60411 3508 1W-25S A7
100 CHHT 60411 3507 1W-25S E7
700 OMFD 60461 3507 2W-25S C7
US-30 E Cass St
10 JLET 60432 3499 21W-23S E4
800 JltT 60432 3499 21W-23S E4
1800 JLET 60433 3499 21W-23S E4
1800 JltT 60433 3499 21W-23S E4
1900 JltT 60432 3500 21W-23S A4
1900 JltT 60433 3500 21W-23S A4
2000 NlxT 60432 3500 21W-23S A4
2000 NlxT 60433 3500 21W-23S A4
2500 JLET 60432 3500 20W-23S B4
US-30 W Cass St
10 JLET 60432 3498 24W-23S E4
100 JLET 60435 3498 24W-23S E4
US-30 N Center St
100 JLET 60435 3498 24W-23S E4
US-30 N Collins St
10 JLET 60432 3499 23W-23S A5
US-30 E Jefferson St
10 JLET 60432 3499 23W-23S A5
US-30 W Jefferson St
10 JLET 60432 3498 24W-23S E5
200 JLET 60435 3498 24W-23S E5
US-30 S Joliet Rd
10 PNFD 60544 3416 29W-18S D1
300 PNFD 60544 3338 29W-18S C7
300 PNFD 60586 3416 29W-18S E2
US-30 Joliet St
10 BlmT 60411 3598 C2
10 DYR 46311 3598 C2
US-30 Lincoln Hwy
- CHHT 60411 3507 3W-25S C7
- JLET 60431 3417 28W-19S B4
- JLET 60432 3500 20W-23S C4
- JLET 60435 3417 28W-19S B4
- NLNX 60433 3500 20W-24S C5
- NLNX 60451 3500 19W-24S C5
- NlxT 60432 3500 20W-24S C5
- NlxT 60433 3500 20W-23S C4
- NlxT 60451 3500 19W-24S C5
- OswT 60503 3201 33W-11S A7
- OswT 60543 3201 33W-11S A7
300 MTGY 60503 3200 33W-10S E6
300 MTGY 60504 3200 33W-10S E6
300 MTGY 60538 3200 33W-10S E6
300 OswT 60503 3200 33W-10S E6
300 OswT 60504 3200 33W-10S E6
300 OswT 60538 3200 33W-10S E6
300 OswT 60543 3200 33W-10S E6
2400 OMFD 60461 3507 3W-25S A7
2500 PKFT 60466 3507 3W-25S A7
3200 MTSN 60443 3506 4W-25S E7
3200 MTSN 60466 3506 4W-25S E7
3200 OMFD 60461 3506 4W-25S E7
3200 PKFT 60466 3506 4W-25S E7
5300 MTSN 60443 3505 7W-25S C7
6200 RchT 60443 3505 7W-25S C7
6700 FftT 60423 3505 8W-25S A7
6700 FKFT 60423 3505 8W-25S A7
11200 FKFT 60423 3591 13W-25S B1
11200 MKNA 60448 3502 14W-25S E7
11200 MKNA 60448 3590 14W-25S E1
11200 MKNA 60448 3591 13W-25S B1
US-30 E Lincoln Hwy
10 FKFT 60423 3503 11W-25S E7
100 FftT 60423 3503 11W-25S E7
400 BlmT 60411 3508 0E-25S E7
400 CHHT 60411 3508 0E-25S E7
400 NLNX 60451 3501 17W-24S D6
400 NlxT 60451 3501 17W-24S D6
800 CHHT 60411 3509 1E-25S A7
800 FDHT 60411 3509 1E-25S A7
1200 NLNX 60451 3502 16W-25S A7
1200 NlxT 60451 3502 16W-25S A7
1400 BlmT 60411 3509 3E-25S E7
1700 SLVL 60411 3509 3E-25S E7
2400 BlmT 60411 3510 3E-25S A7
2700 FftT 60448 3502 14W-25S D7
2700 FftT 60451 3502 14W-25S D7
2700 MKNA 60448 3502 14W-25S D7
2700 MKNA 60451 3502 14W-25S D7
2800 LYWD 60411 3510 3E-25S A7
21400 BlmT 60411 3598 D2
21400 LYWD 60411 3598 D2
US-30 W Lincoln Hwy
- JLET 60431 3417 26W-21S E6
900 FKFT 60423 3591 13W-25S B1
1000 NLNX 60451 3501 17W-25S D6
1000 NlxT 60451 3501 17W-25S D6
1100 NLNX 60451 3500 19W-24S E5
1100 NlxT 60451 3500 19W-24S E5
1300 NLNX 60451 3500 19W-24S E5
7200 FftT 60423 3505 9W-25S A7
7200 FKFT 60423 3505 9W-25S A7
7200 RchT 60443 3505 9W-25S A7
7400 FftT 60423 3504 9W-25S E7
7400 FKFT 60423 3504 9W-25S E7
9200 FftT 60423 3503 13W-25S B7
9200 FKFT 60423 3503 13W-25S B7
11100 MKNA 60448 3591 14W-25S A1
22800 JLET 60544 3417 26W-21S E6

US-30 W Lincoln Hwy
22800 JLET 60586 3417 26W-21S E6
22800 PnfT 60544 3417 28W-19S A3
22800 PnfT 60586 3417 28W-19S A3
22900 PNFD 60586 3417 28W-19S A3
23000 PNFD 60544 3416 29W-18S D1
23000 PNFD 60586 3416 29W-18S D1
23000 PnfT 60544 3416 29W-18S D1
23000 PnfT 60586 3416 29W-18S D1
US-30 W Lockport St
400 PNFD 60544 3338 30W-17S C7
1000 PnfT 60544 3338 30W-17S A7
US-30 W Maple St
1400 NLNX 60433 3500 19W-24S D5
1400 NLNX 60451 3500 19W-24S D5
1400 NlxT 60432 3500 19W-24S D5
1400 NlxT 60451 3500 19W-24S D5
US-30 Plainfield Rd
400 JLET 60435 3498 25W-22S B1
1500 CTHL 60403 3498 25W-22S A1
1500 JLET 60403 3498 25W-22S A1
1600 CTHL 60403 3418 26W-21S A7
2000 CTHL 60403 3417 26W-21S E7
2300 CTHL 60435 3417 26W-21S D6
2300 LktT 60435 3417 26W-20S D6
2300 PnfT 60435 3417 26W-20S D6
2400 JLET 60435 3417 27W-20S D5
2600 JLET 60431 3417 27W-20S C5
US-30 E Sauk Tr
3600 BlmT 60411 3598 4E-26S C2
3600 DYR 46311 3598 4E-26S C2
US-30 US Highway 34
1200 MTGY 60538 3200 34W-10S E6
1200 MTGY 60543 3200 34W-10S E6
1200 OSWG 60538 3200 34W-10S E6
1200 OSWG 60543 3200 34W-10S E6
1200 OswT 60543 3200 34W-10S E6
US-30 US Route 30
- MTGY 60538 3199 37W-9S B5
US-30 W Western Av
200 JLET 60432 3498 24W-23S E4
200 JLET 60435 3498 24W-23S E5
US-34
- LtRT 60545 3258 49W-14S E7
- LtRT 60545 3259 48W-14S C7
- LtRT 60545 3330 50W-14S C1
- MTGY 60543 3263 38W-12S B3
- OswT 60543 3263 37W-12S B3
- PLNO 60545 3258 49W-14S E7
- YKVL 60560 3262 41W-13S A6
10 BtlT 60560 3261 43W-14S A7
10 DGvT 60559 3085 18W-4S B7
10 DRGV 60515 3084 18W-4S E7
10 DRGV 60515 3085 18W-4S A7
10 LGNG 60525 3087 12W-4S C6
10 LGPK 60525 3087 13W-4S B6
10 LGPK 60558 3087 13W-4S B6
10 LSLE 60563 3142 25W-5S B2
10 LslT 60563 3142 25W-5S B2
10 NPVL 60540 3140 29W-7S D7
10 NPVL 60540 3202 29W-7S D1
10 NPVL 60563 3141 28W-6S A4
10 NPVL 60563 3142 25W-5S B2
10 OSWG 60543 3263 38W-12S A4
10 PLNO 60545 3259 46W-13S E6
10 PvsT 60525 3087 13W-4S B6
10 PvsT 60558 3087 13W-4S B6
10 WNSP 60558 3087 13W-4S B6
10 WTMT 60514 3084 18W-4S E7
10 WTMT 60515 3085 18W-4S A7
10 WTMT 60559 3084 18W-4S E7
10 WTMT 60559 3085 17W-4S B7
10 YKVL 60560 3261 43W-14S A7
100 CNHL 60514 3085 16W-4S D7
100 CNHL 60559 3085 16W-4S D7
100 LSLE 60532 3142 23W-5S E2
100 PvsT 60525 3086 13W-3S E6
100 PvsT 60558 3086 15W-4S A7
100 WNSP 60558 3086 15W-4S A7
100 WTMT 60514 3085 16W-4S D7
300 NpvT 60504 3201 32W-9S C3
400 AURA 60540 3202 29W-8S C1
400 HNDL 60521 3086 15W-4S C6
400 LSLE 60532 3143 22W-4S C1
400 LslT 60532 3143 22W-4S C1
400 LynT 60521 3086 15W-4S C6
400 LynT 60558 3086 15W-4S C6
500 HNDL 60521 3085 16W-4S E7
600 AraT 60504 3201 33W-10S A5
600 AURA 60503 3201 33W-10S A5
600 OswT 60503 3201 33W-10S A5
600 OswT 60504 3201 33W-10S A5
600 SDWH 60548 3330 51W-15S A2
700 AURA 60503 3200 33W-10S E6
700 AURA 60504 3200 34W-10S E6
700 LtRT 60545 3260 46W-13S A6
700 PLNO 60545 3260 46W-13S A6
800 CNHL 60521 3085 16W-4S E7
800 MTGY 60503 3200 34W-10S E6
800 MTGY 60504 3200 34W-10S E6
800 MTGY 60538 3200 34W-10S D7
800 OswT 60503 3200 34W-10S E6
800 OswT 60538 3200 34W-10S E6
800 OswT 60543 3200 34W-10S E6
800 WTMT 60521 3085 16W-4S E7
1000 MTGY 60543 3200 34W-10S D7
1000 OSWG 60538 3200 34W-10S D7
1000 OSWG 60543 3200 34W-10S D7
1000 SdwT 60548 3330 51W-15S A2
1200 DRGV 60515 3144 21W-4S A1
1300 NPVL 60563 3140 28W-6S E5
1400 LtRT 60548 3330 51W-14S B1
1500 WNSP 60525 3087 13W-3S A6
2000 DRGV 60515 3143 23W-4S A2
2100 AURA 60504 3201 33W-9S B4
2200 OSWG 60543 3264 35W-11S A2
2500 LslT 60515 3143 21W-4S D1
2700 DRGV 60532 3143 22W-4S D1
3600 AURA 60504 3202 30W-8S B1
4300 NPVL 60504 3202 30W-8S C1
5000 BtlT 60543 3262 38W-12S B3
6000 BtlT 60543 3262 39W-12S E4
6000 OSWG 60543 3262 39W-12S E4
7200 BRWN 60402 3088 9W-3S D6
7200 BtlT 60560 3262 40W-13S C4
7200 LYNS 60402 3088 9W-3S D6
7200 LYNS 60534 3088 9W-3S D6
7200 LYNS 60546 3088 9W-3S D6
7200 RVSD 60402 3088 9W-3S D6
7200 RVSD 60546 3088 9W-3S D6
8700 BKFD 60513 3088 10W-4S A6
8700 BKFD 60534 3088 10W-4S A6
8800 BKFD 60513 3087 11W-4S E6
9500 BKFD 60525 3087 11W-4S D6
11400 BtlT 60560 3260 44W-14S E6

US-34
11400 YKVL 60560 3260 44W-14S E6
11900 BtlT 60545 3260 44W-13S D6
11900 YKVL 60545 3260 44W-13S D6
US-34 Chicago Rd
10 OSWG 60543 3263 37W-12S C3
US-34 E Church St
600 SDWH 60548 3330 51W-15S A2
1000 SdwT 60548 3330 51W-15S A2
1400 LtRT 60548 3330 51W-14S B1
US-34 S Madison St
10 OSWG 60543 3263 37W-12S C3
US-34 Ogden Av
- HNDL 60521 3086 14W-3S C6
- LynT 60521 3086 14W-3S C6
- LynT 60558 3086 14W-3S C6
- NPVL 60563 3140 28W-6S E5
- OswT 60503 3201 33W-9S A5
- OswT 60504 3201 33W-9S A5
10 DRGV 60515 3084 18W-4S E7
10 DRGV 60515 3085 18W-4S A7
10 LGPK 60525 3087 13W-4S B6
10 LGPK 60558 3087 13W-4S B6
10 LSLE 60563 3142 25W-5S B2
10 LslT 60563 3142 25W-5S B2
10 NPVL 60540 3140 29W-7S D7
10 NPVL 60540 3202 29W-7S D1
10 NPVL 60563 3142 25W-5S B2
10 PvsT 60525 3087 13W-4S B6
10 PvsT 60558 3087 13W-4S B6
10 WNSP 60558 3087 13W-4S B6
10 WTMT 60515 3084 18W-4S E7
10 WTMT 60515 3085 18W-4S A7
10 WTMT 60559 3084 18W-4S E7
10 WTMT 60559 3085 18W-4S A7
100 LSLE 60532 3142 23W-5S E2
100 PvsT 60525 3086 13W-3S E6
100 PvsT 60558 3086 15W-4S A7
100 WNSP 60558 3086 15W-4S A7
400 AURA 60540 3202 29W-8S C1
400 LSLE 60532 3143 22W-4S C1
400 LslT 60532 3143 22W-4S C1
1200 DRGV 60515 3144 21W-4S A1
1900 AraT 60504 3201 33W-9S A5
2000 DRGV 60515 3143 23W-4S A2
2100 AURA 60504 3201 33W-9S B4
2400 NpvT 60504 3201 32W-9S C3
2500 LslT 60515 3143 21W-4S D1
2700 DRGV 60532 3143 22W-4S D1
3600 AURA 60504 3202 30W-8S B1
4300 NPVL 60504 3202 30W-8S C1
7200 BRWN 60402 3088 9W-3S D6
7200 LYNS 60402 3088 9W-3S D6
7200 LYNS 60534 3088 9W-3S D6
7200 LYNS 60546 3088 9W-3S D6
7200 RVSD 60402 3088 9W-3S D6
7200 RVSD 60546 3088 9W-3S D6
8700 BKFD 60513 3088 10W-4S A6
8700 BKFD 60534 3088 10W-4S A6
8800 BKFD 60513 3087 11W-4S E6
9500 BKFD 60525 3087 11W-4S D6
9500 LGNG 60525 3087 11W-4S D6
US-34 E Ogden Av
10 LGNG 60525 3087 12W-4S C6
10 NPVL 60563 3141 28W-6S A4
10 WTMT 60559 3085 17W-4S B7
100 CNHL 60514 3085 16W-4S D7
100 CNHL 60559 3085 16W-4S D7
100 WTMT 60514 3085 16W-4S D7
400 HNDL 60521 3086 15W-4S C6
400 LynT 60521 3086 15W-4S C6
400 LynT 60558 3086 15W-4S C6
800 CNHL 60521 3085 16W-4S E7
800 HNDL 60521 3085 16W-4S E7
800 WTMT 60521 3085 16W-4S E7
1000 LslT 60563 3142 25W-5S A3
1000 NPVL 60563 3142 26W-5S A3
1400 LSLE 60563 3142 25W-5S B2
9600 BKFD 60513 3087 12W-4S D6
9600 BKFD 60525 3087 12W-4S D6
US-34 W Ogden Av
- CNHL 60514 3085 16W-4S E7
- CNHL 60521 3085 16W-4S E7
- WTMT 60514 3085 16W-4S E7
- WTMT 60521 3085 16W-4S E7
- WTMT 60559 3085 16W-4S E7
10 DGvT 60559 3085 18W-4S B7
10 HNDL 60521 3086 15W-4S A7
10 LGNG 60525 3087 12W-4S C6
10 NPVL 60563 3141 27W-5S D4
300 DRGV 60515 3085 18W-4S A7
300 WTMT 60515 3085 18W-4S A7
500 HNDL 60521 3085 16W-4S E7
1200 LGPK 60525 3087 13W-3S A6
1300 NPVL 60563 3140 29W-6S E5
1500 LGPK 60558 3087 13W-3S A6
1500 NPVL 60540 3140 28W-6S E5
1500 WNSP 60525 3087 13W-3S A6
1500 WNSP 60558 3087 13W-3S A6
1600 PvsT 60525 3087 13W-3S A6
1600 PvsT 60558 3087 13W-3S A6
US-34 E South St
10 PLNO 60545 3259 46W-13S E6
700 LtRT 60545 3260 46W-13S A6
700 PLNO 60545 3260 46W-13S A6
US-34 W South St
10 PLNO 60545 3259 47W-14S D6
US-34 US Highway 34
1200 MTGY 60538 3200 34W-10S D7
1200 MTGY 60543 3200 34W-10S D7
1200 OSWG 60538 3200 34W-10S D7
1200 OSWG 60543 3200 34W-10S D7
1200 OswT 60543 3200 34W-10S E6
7200 BtlT 60543 3262 40W-13S C4
7200 BtlT 60560 3262 40W-13S C4
US-34 E Veterans Pkwy
10 BtlT 60560 3261 42W-14S D7
10 YKVL 60560 3261 42W-14S C7
US-34 W Veterans Pkwy
- BtlT 60560 3260 44W-14S E7
- YKVL 60560 3260 44W-14S E7
10 BtlT 60560 3261 43W-14S A7
10 YKVL 60560 3261 43W-14S A7
200 BtlT 60560 3261 43W-14S A7
US-34 W Washington St
- OswT 60543 3263 37W-12S B3
10 OSWG 60543 3263 37W-12S C4
US-41
- BtlT - 2360 E4
- CHCG - 2921 0W-6N E6
- CHCG - 2922 0W-5N A7
- CHCG - 2978 0W-3N B4
- CHCG - 3034 0E-1N C1
- CHCG - 3092 0E-1S D1
- CHCG - 3093 1E-4S A1
- CHCG - 3153 2E-5S B1
- CokC - 3034 0E-0N D3

STREET Block	City	ZIP	Map#	CGS	Grid
US-41					
-	CokC	60637	3153	2E-6S	C3
-	GLNC	-	2758	7W-16N	B7
-	HDPK	60035	2757	8W-20N	D1
-	NCHI	60064	2536	13W-32N	A4
-	NCHI	60085	2536	12W-32N	A5
-	NfdT	-	2757	8W-18N	E3
-	NfdT	-	2811	7W-15N	C1
-	NHBK	-	2757	8W-18N	E3
-	NHBK	-	2758	7W-17N	A4
-	NHFD	-	2758	7W-16N	B7
-	NHFD	-	2811	6W-14N	D4
-	NptT	60031	2420	15W-38N	A7
-	NptT	60031	2478	15W-38N	A1
-	NptT	60083	2360	16W-41N	E7
-	NptT	60083	2419	16W-40N	E2
-	NptT	60083	2420	15W-40N	A4
-	NptT	60099	2360	16W-42N	E6
-	NtrT	-	2758	7W-18N	A4
-	NtrT	-	2811	6W-14N	D4
-	PKCY	-	2535	13W-33N	E2
-	PKCY	-	2536	13W-33N	A4
-	PTPR	-	2360		E1
-	ShdT	60044	2536	12W-31N	B7
-	WDWH	60031	2420	15W-39N	A5
-	WDWH	60083	2360	16W-41N	E7
-	WDWH	60083	2419	16W-40N	E2
-	WDWH	60083	2420	15W-38N	A7
-	WDWH	60099	2360	16W-42N	E6
-	WKGN	-	2535	13W-33N	E3
-	WKGN	60064	2536	12W-32N	A5
-	WKGN	60085	2536	13W-33N	A4
-	WLMT	60093	2811	5W-13N	E6
10	CHCG	60601	3034	0E-1S	D7
10	CHCG	60603	3034	0E-1S	D7
100	CHCG	60604	3034	0E-0S	D5
100	LKFT	60044	2593	11W-28N	C7
100	ShdT	60044	2593	12W-28N	C6
300	CHCG	60605	3034	0E-0S	D5
300	GRNE	60031	2535	13W-34N	E1
300	LKBF	60044	2593	11W-28N	C6
300	LKFT	60045	2593	11W-28N	C7
500	HDPK	60035	2704	9W-21N	C6
900	LKFT	60045	2649	11W-24N	E6
1000	GRNE	60031	2478	13W-35N	D6
1000	HMND	46320	3280		D2
1000	HMND	46394	3280		E7
1100	NCHI	60088	2593	12W-30N	B2
1200	LKFT	60035	2649	10W-24N	E7
1200	LKFT	60035	2650	10W-24N	A7
1200	LKFT	60045	2650	10W-24N	A7
1200	WrnT	60031	2478	14W-36N	C5
1400	ShdT	60088	2593	12W-30N	B2
1500	CHCG	60616	3034	0E-1S	D7
1900	CHCG	60625	2921	2W-6N	B5
2000	CHCG	60637	3153	2E-7S	D5
2000	CHCG	60649	3153	2E-7S	C5
2300	WDWH	60031	2478	15W-37N	A2
2500	HMND	46327	3280		E7
2800	NCHI	60044	2593	12W-28N	C6
2800	NCHI	60064	2593	12W-28N	C6
2800	ShdT	60064	2593	12W-28N	C6
3000	HMND	46320	3352		E5
3000	HMND	46327	3352		E5
3200	CHCG	60617	3216	4E-10S	B6
3300	LKFT	60035	2704	10W-24N	A1
3300	LKFT	60045	2704	10W-24N	A1
5500	CHCG	60659	2921	1W-6N	E5
5600	CHCG	60659	2920	3W-7N	E4
5900	HMND	46320	3430		E2
6100	HMND	46324	3430		E2
6300	LNWD	60659	2920	4W-7N	C3
6300	LNWD	60712	2920	3W-7N	E4
7200	LNWD	60076	2866	5W-9N	A7
7200	LNWD	60712	2866	5W-9N	A7
7200	SKOK	60076	2866	5W-9N	A7
7200	SKOK	60712	2866	5W-9N	A7
7500	SKOK	60076	2865	5W-9N	E7
7500	SKOK	60077	2865	5W-9N	E7
7700	CHCG	60649	3215	3E-8S	E1
7800	CHCG	60649	3216	3E-8S	A1
10000	SKOK	60076	2811	5W-12N	E7
10000	SKOK	60077	2811	5W-12N	E7
10000	WLMT	60076	2811	6W-12N	E7
10000	WLMT	60077	2811	6W-12N	E7
10000	WLMT	60091	2811	5W-13N	E6
10500	CHCG	60617	3280		C1
10500	HMND	60617	3280	4E-11S	C1
US-41 E 85th St					
3200	CHCG	60617	3216	4E-9S	A3
US-41 E 87th St					
3200	CHCG	60617	3216	4E-9S	A3
US-41 S Baker Av					
8400	CHCG	60617	3216	3E-9S	A3
US-41 Borman Expwy					
-	HMND	-	3430		E5
US-41 S Burley Av					
8500	CHCG	60617	3216	4E-9S	A3
US-41 Calumet Av					
6200	HMND	46320	3430		E1
6200	HMND	46324	3430		E1
US-41 S Calumet Av					
1400	HMND	46394	3280		E7
2100	HMND	46320	3280		E5
2500	HMND	46327	3280		E7
3000	HMND	46320	3352		E5
3000	HMND	46327	3352		E5
5900	HMND	46320	3430		E2
6100	HMND	46324	3430		E2
US-41 S Coast Guard Dr					
6400	CHCG	60637	3153	2E-7S	C5
6400	CHCG	60649	3153	2E-7S	C5
US-41 Edens Expwy					
-	GLNC	-	2758	7W-16N	B7
-	HDPK	-	2757	8W-20N	E2
-	NfdT	-	2757	8W-18N	E2
-	NfdT	-	2811	7W-15N	C1
-	NHBK	-	2757	8W-18N	E3
-	NHBK	-	2758	7W-17N	A4
-	NHFD	-	2758	7W-16N	B7
-	NHFD	-	2811	6W-14N	D4
-	NtrT	-	2758	7W-18N	A4
-	NtrT	-	2811	6W-14N	D4
US-41 S Ewing Av					
9200	CHCG	60617	3216	4E-10S	A5
US-41 W Foster Av					
900	CHCG	60640	2921	1W-6N	E5
1900	CHCG	60625	2921	2W-6N	B5
US-41 S Indianapolis Av					
-	HMND	46320	3280	4E-11S	C1
-	HMND	60617	3280	4E-11S	C1
10000	CHCG	60617	3216	4E-11S	B7
10300	CHCG	60617	3280	4E-11S	C1
US-41 S Indianapolis Blvd					
1000	HMND	46320	3280		D2
1000	HMND	46394	3280		D3
10500	CHCG	60617	3280		C1
10500	HMND	60617	3280	4E-11S	C1
US-41 N Lake Shore Dr					
-	CHCG	-	2921	0W-6N	E6
-	CHCG	-	2922	0W-5N	A7
-	CHCG	-	2978	0W-3N	B4
-	CHCG	-	3034	0E-1N	C1
-	CokC	-	3034	0E-0N	D3
US-41 S Lake Shore Dr					
-	CHCG	-	3092	1E-3S	E4
-	CHCG	-	3093	1E-4S	A6
-	CHCG	-	3153	2E-5S	B1
-	CokC	60637	3153	2E-6S	C3
10	CHCG	60601	3034	0E-1S	D7
10	CHCG	60603	3034	0E-1S	D7
100	CHCG	60604	3034	0E-0S	D5
300	CHCG	60605	3034	0E-0S	D5
1500	CHCG	60616	3034	0E-1S	D7
5300	CHCG	60637	3153	2E-7S	D5
US-41 Lincoln Av					
7400	LNWD	60076	2866	5W-9N	A7
7400	LNWD	60712	2866	5W-9N	A7
7400	SKOK	60076	2866	5W-9N	A7
7400	SKOK	60712	2866	5W-9N	A7
7500	SKOK	60076	2865	5W-9N	E7
7500	SKOK	60077	2865	5W-9N	E7
US-41 N Lincoln Av					
5200	CHCG	60625	2921	3W-6N	A5
5500	CHCG	60659	2921	1W-6N	D5
5600	CHCG	60659	2920	3W-7N	E4
6300	LNWD	60659	2920	4W-7N	C3
6300	LNWD	60712	2920	3W-7N	E4
7200	LNWD	60076	2866	5W-9N	A7
7200	LNWD	60712	2866	5W-9N	A7
7200	SKOK	60076	2866	5W-9N	A7
7200	SKOK	60712	2866	5W-9N	A7
US-41 S Mackinaw Av					
8700	CHCG	60617	3216	4E-10S	B6
US-41 E Marquette Dr					
2000	CHCG	60637	3153	2E-7S	C5
2000	CHCG	60649	3153	2E-7S	C5
US-41 Skokie Blvd					
7500	SKOK	60076	2865	5W-9N	E7
7500	SKOK	60077	2865	5W-9N	E7
10000	SKOK	60076	2811	5W-12N	E7
10000	SKOK	60077	2811	5W-12N	E7
10000	WLMT	60076	2811	6W-12N	E7
10000	WLMT	60077	2811	6W-12N	E7
10000	WLMT	60091	2811	5W-13N	E7
US-41 Skokie Hwy					
-	GRNE	60031	2535	13W-34N	E1
-	HDPK	-	2757	8W-18N	E3
-	NCHI	60064	2536	13W-32N	A4
-	NCHI	60085	2536	12W-32N	A6
-	NfdT	-	2757	8W-20N	D1
-	NHBK	-	2757	8W-18N	E3
-	NptT	60031	2420	15W-39N	A5
-	NptT	60031	2478	15W-38N	A1
-	NptT	60083	2360	16W-41N	E7
-	NptT	60083	2419	16W-40N	E2
-	NptT	60083	2420	15W-40N	A4
-	NptT	60099	2360	16W-42N	E6
-	PKCY	-	2535	13W-33N	E2
-	PKCY	-	2536	13W-33N	A4
-	ShdT	60044	2536	12W-31N	B7
-	WDWH	60031	2420	15W-39N	A5
-	WDWH	60031	2478	15W-38N	A1
-	WDWH	60083	2360	16W-41N	E7
-	WDWH	60083	2419	16W-40N	E2
-	WDWH	60083	2420	15W-39N	A5
-	WDWH	60099	2360	16W-42N	E6
-	WKGN	-	2535	13W-33N	E3
-	WKGN	60064	2536	12W-32N	A5
-	WKGN	60085	2536	13W-33N	A4
-	WrnT	60031	2478	15W-37N	A1
US-41 N Skokie Hwy					
-	NCHI	60064	2536	12W-31N	B7
-	ShdT	60044	2536	12W-31N	B7
-	WDWH	60031	2478	15W-37N	A2
-	WKGN	60085	2536	12W-31N	B7
100	LKFT	60045	2593	11W-28N	C7
300	GRNE	60031	2535	13W-34N	E1
300	LKFT	60044	2593	11W-28N	C7
900	LKFT	60045	2649	11W-24N	E6
1000	GRNE	60031	2478	13W-35N	D6
1100	NCHI	60088	2593	12W-30N	B2
1300	WrnT	60031	2478	15W-37N	A3
1400	ShdT	60088	2593	12W-30N	B2
2800	NCHI	60044	2593	12W-28N	C6
2800	NCHI	60064	2593	12W-28N	C6
2800	ShdT	60044	2593	12W-28N	C6
2800	ShdT	60064	2593	12W-28N	C6
3600	LKBF	60044	2593	12W-29N	B4
US-41 S Skokie Hwy					
1200	LKFT	60035	2650	10W-24N	A7
1200	LKFT	60045	2649	10W-24N	E7
1200	LKFT	60045	2650	10W-24N	A7
3300	LKFT	60035	2649	10W-24N	E7
US-41 Skokie Rd					
-	NHFD	60093	2811	5W-13N	E6
-	SKOK	60076	2811	5W-13N	E7
-	SKOK	60077	2811	5W-13N	E7
-	WLMT	60076	2811	5W-13N	E7
-	WLMT	60077	2811	5W-13N	E7
-	WLMT	60091	2811	5W-13N	E6
-	WLMT	60093	2811	5W-13N	E6
US-41 Skokie Valley Rd					
-	HDPK	60035	2757	9W-20N	D1
-	LKBF	60044	2593	12W-29N	C5
-	ShdT	60044	2593	12W-29N	C5
500	HDPK	60035	2704	10W-23N	A2
3100	LKFT	60045	2704	10W-24N	A1
3300	LKFT	60035	2704	10W-24N	A1
US-41 E South Shore Dr					
2400	CHCG	60649	3153	3E-7S	D6
US-41 S South Shore Dr					
6700	CHCG	60637	3153	2E-7S	D5
6700	CHCG	60649	3153	2E-7S	D5
7700	CHCG	60649	3215	3E-8S	E1
7800	CHCG	60617	3216	3E-8S	A1
7800	CHCG	60649	3216	3E-8S	A1
US-45					
-	ANTH	60002	2359	19W-42N	C6
-	AntT	60002	2418	19W-41N	C1
-	AntT	60046	2418	19W-40N	C3
-	AvnT	60046	2476	19W-35N	D5
-	BtlT	60002	2359		B4
-	CHCG	60176	2917	12W-6N	B6
-	CHCG	60666	2917	12W-7N	A3
-	CHCG	60666	2973	12W-5N	B1
-	GRNE	60031	2476	18W-35N	D6
-	GRNE	60031	2477	16W-36N	E3
-	GRNE	60046	2476	18W-34N	E7
-	GRNE	60046	2533	18W-34N	E1
-	HGKN	60525	3147	12W-8S	C7
-	HGKN	60525	3209	12W-8S	C1
-	LbvT	60048	2590	19W-31N	D1
-	LkvT	60046	2418	19W-39N	D5
-	LkvT	60046	2476	19W-36N	D3
-	LkvT	60083	2418	19W-39N	D5
-	LNHT	60046	2418	19W-38N	D7
-	LNHT	60046	2476	19W-36N	D3
-	LNHT	60083	2418	19W-39N	D5
-	LynT	60458	3209	12W-8S	C1
-	LynT	60480	3209	12W-8S	C1
-	LynT	60525	3209	11W-8S	D2
-	MKNA	60448	3423	12W-22S	D7
-	OMCK	60046	2418	19W-38N	D7
-	OMCK	60046	2476	19W-37N	D1
-	OMCK	60083	2418	19W-38N	D7
-	OMCK	60083	2476	19W-38N	D1
-	PlsT	60465	3273	12W-13S	D4
-	PlsT	60480	3209	11W-11S	D7
-	PlsT	60480	3273	12W-13S	D4
-	SRPK	60176	2917	12W-6N	B6
-	SRPK	60176	2973	12W-5N	B1
-	TDLK	60046	2533	18W-34N	E1
-	VNHL	60061	2701	16W-23N	D1
-	VrnT	60061	2647	16W-24N	C7
-	VrnT	60061	2701	16W-24N	D1
-	VrnT	60069	2701	16W-24N	D1
-	WLSP	60458	3209	12W-8S	C1
-	WLSP	60480	3209	11W-9S	D4
-	WLSP	60525	3209	12W-8S	C1
-	WrnT	60031	2476	18W-34N	E7
-	WrnT	60046	2476	19W-36N	D3
-	WrnT	60046	2533	18W-34N	E1
10	AvnT	60030	2533	18W-33N	D4
10	BLWD	60104	3029	12W-1N	A3
10	BLWD	60160	3029	13W-1N	A3
10	DSPN	60016	2863	13W-11N	A2
10	FKFT	60423	3503	12W-25S	E7
10	GYLK	60030	2533	18W-34N	E1
10	HLSD	60104	3029	12W-0S	A6
10	HLSD	60154	3029	12W-0S	A6
10	HLSD	60162	3029	12W-0S	A7
10	LGNG	60525	3087	12W-4S	C6
10	MDLN	60060	2646	18W-25N	E4
10	MLPK	60160	3029	13W-1N	A3
10	WSTR	60154	3029	13W-0S	A7
100	BLWD	60162	3029	12W-0S	A5
100	LGPK	60525	3087	12W-4S	C6
100	MaiT	60016	2863	13W-12N	A1
100	MDLN	60060	2590	19W-28N	D7
100	WSTR	60162	3029	13W-0S	A7
200	FKFT	60423	3591	14W-28S	A6
200	INCK	60060	2647	18W-25N	A5
200	INCK	60061	2647	18W-25N	A5
200	LNSH	60061	2702	15W-23N	A2
200	LNSH	60069	2702	15W-23N	A2
200	MDLN	60060	2647	17W-25N	B6
200	MDLN	60061	2647	17W-25N	B6
200	VNHL	60060	2647	17W-25N	B6
200	VNHL	60061	2647	16W-24N	C7
200	VNHL	60061	2702	15W-23N	A2
200	VNHL	60069	2702	15W-23N	A2
200	VrnT	60061	2702	15W-23N	A2
300	LGNG	60525	3147	12W-4S	C1
300	PvsT	60162	3029	12W-0S	A7
300	VrnT	60069	2702	15W-23N	A2
400	WhlT	60056	2808	13W-13N	E6
500	PTHT	60062	2809	13W-15N	A1
500	PTHT	60070	2809	13W-15N	A1
500	PTHT	60090	2809	13W-15N	A1
500	WhlT	60062	2809	13W-15N	A1
500	WhlT	60090	2809	13W-15N	A1
500	WLNG	60090	2755	13W-17N	D5
600	FftT	60423	3503	11W-25S	E6
600	MPPT	60056	2808	13W-13N	E6
600	WhlT	60025	2808	13W-13N	E6
600	WhlT	60090	2755	13W-17N	E5
700	DSPN	60016	2808	13W-12N	E7
700	DSPN	60016	2809	13W-12N	A7
700	MaiT	60016	2808	13W-12N	E7
700	MaiT	60016	2809	13W-12N	A7
700	WrnT	60030	2533	18W-32N	D5
800	BFGV	60090	2755	14W-20N	C2
900	BFGV	60089	2755	14W-20N	C1
900	MPPT	60025	2808	13W-14N	E5
900	VrnT	60015	2755	14W-20N	C1
900	VrnT	60062	2755	14W-20N	C1
900	VrnT	60089	2755	14W-20N	C1
1000	BFGV	60089	2702	14W-20N	B7
1000	DSPN	60016	2862	13W-10N	E5
1000	DSPN	60018	2862	13W-10N	E5
1000	LbvT	60060	2646	18W-26N	E3
1000	PTHT	60070	2755	13W-16N	E7
1000	PTHT	60070	2808	13W-16N	E1
1000	PvsT	60525	3087	12W-3S	B4
1000	RVWD	60015	2702	14W-20N	B7
1000	RVWD	60015	2755	14W-20N	C1
1000	VrnT	60015	2702	14W-20N	B7
1000	WhlT	60090	2808	13W-16N	E1
1200	FmtT	60048	2590	18W-30N	D1
1200	FmtT	60060	2590	19W-29N	D4
1200	LYVL	60048	2590	19W-30N	D1
1200	MDLN	60048	2590	19W-29N	D4
1200	MPPT	60056	2809	13W-15N	A2
1200	WhlT	60056	2809	13W-15N	A2
1300	WhlT	60025	2809	13W-14N	A3
1400	LNSH	60015	2702	14W-21N	B6
1400	PvsT	60162	3087	12W-1S	A1
1400	WSTR	60154	3087	12W-1S	A1
1400	WSTR	60162	3087	12W-1S	A1
1500	SNPK	60160	3029	12W-1N	A2
1500	SNPK	60165	3029	12W-1N	A2
1700	DSPN	60018	2863	13W-9N	A6
1800	MLPK	60164	3029	12W-1N	A1
1800	MLPK	60165	3029	12W-1N	A1
1800	SNPK	60164	3029	12W-1N	A1
2000	DSPN	60018	2917	13W-9N	A1
2000	LydT	60160	2973	12W-2N	A7
2000	LydT	60164	2973	12W-2N	A7
2000	MLPK	60160	2973	12W-2N	A7
2000	NHLK	60160	2973	12W-2N	A7
2000	NHLK	60164	2973	12W-2N	A7
2000	RSMT	60018	2917	13W-9N	A1
2100	PvsT	60154	3087	12W-1S	A2
2300	LydT	60131	2973	12W-2N	A6
2400	FNPK	60131	2973	13W-3N	A6
2600	FNPK	60164	2973	13W-3N	A5
2900	CHCG	60018	2917	12W-8N	A2
3700	FNPK	60176	2973	13W-4N	A3
3700	SRPK	60131	2973	13W-4N	A3
5200	CTSD	60525	3147	12W-5S	C3
6400	RSMT	60666	2917	12W-8N	A3
10700	BtlT	53104	2359	19W-42N	C6
11800	PlsT	60464	3273	11W-15S	D7
11800	PSPK	60464	3273	12W-15S	D7
11900	BtlT	53142	2359		B3
12400	AntT	60002	2359		B4
12700	PSPK	60464	3345	11W-15S	D1
13000	PlsT	60462	3345	11W-15S	D1
13000	PSPK	60462	3345	11W-15S	D1
13400	OrlT	60462	3345	11W-15S	D2
13500	ODPK	60462	3345	11W-16S	D2
15700	ODPK	60462	3423	12W-18S	D1
15800	ODPK	60467	3423	11W-20S	D5
16600	ODHL	60467	3423	12W-19S	D3
16600	ODHL	60487	3423	12W-19S	D3
16600	OrlT	60467	3423	12W-19S	D3
17500	OrlT	60487	3423	11W-21S	D6
17500	TYPK	60487	3423	11W-21S	D5
18200	FftT	60448	3423	12W-21S	D7
18200	ODPK	60448	3423	12W-21S	D7
18200	ODPK	60487	3423	12W-21S	D7
18200	TYPK	60448	3423	12W-21S	D7
19100	MKNA	60448	3503	12W-24S	E6
19200	FftT	60448	3503	12W-24S	E6
19800	FKFT	60448	3503	11W-23S	E4
19800	MKNA	60423	3503	11W-23S	E4
21800	FftT	60423	3591	14W-28S	A6
22900	GGnT	60423	3591	14W-28S	A6
31100	FmtT	60048	2533	19W-31N	D7
31200	LbvT	60030	2533	19W-31N	D7
31200	LbvT	60048	2533	19W-31N	D7
33800	TDLK	60030	2533	18W-34N	E1
34200	TDLK	60031	2533	18W-34N	D1
34200	WrnT	60031	2533	18W-34N	D1
34300	GRNE	60031	2533	18W-34N	E1
US-45 96th Av					
-	PlsT	60464	3273	12W-13S	D4
-	PlsT	60465	3273	12W-13S	D4
-	PlsT	60480	3273	12W-13S	D4
US-45 Bristol Rd					
-	BtlT	60002	2359		B4
10700	BtlT	53104	2359	19W-42N	C6
11900	BtlT	53142	2359		B3
12400	AntT	60002	2359		B4
US-45 N Des Plaines River Rd					
-	DSPN	60016	2808	13W-13N	E6
-	WhlT	60056	2808	13W-13N	E6
US-45 Downing Cir					
-	GRNE	60031	2477	16W-36N	E3
US-45 Graceland Av					
800	DSPN	60016	2862	13W-10N	E4
US-45 La Grange Rd					
-	LynT	60458	3209	12W-8S	C1
-	LynT	60480	3209	12W-8S	C1
-	LynT	60525	3209	11W-8S	D2
-	MKNA	60448	3423	12W-22S	D7
-	PlsT	60480	3209	11W-11S	D7
-	PlsT	60480	3273	12W-12S	D1
-	WLSP	60458	3209	12W-8S	C1
-	WLSP	60480	3209	12W-8S	C1
-	WLSP	60525	3209	12W-8S	D2
16700	ODHL	60467	3423	11W-20S	D3
16700	ODHL	60487	3423	11W-20S	D3
16700	ODPK	60467	3423	11W-20S	D3
16700	OrlT	60467	3423	11W-20S	D3
16700	OrlT	60487	3423	11W-20S	D3
16900	TYPK	60487	3423	11W-20S	D4
18200	FftT	60448	3423	12W-21S	D7
18200	ODPK	60448	3423	12W-21S	D7
18200	ODPK	60487	3423	12W-21S	D7
18200	TYPK	60448	3423	12W-21S	D7
19100	MKNA	60448	3503	12W-24S	E6
19200	FftT	60448	3503	12W-24S	E6
19800	FKFT	60423	3503	11W-23S	E4
19800	FKFT	60448	3503	11W-23S	E4
19800	MKNA	60423	3503	11W-23S	E4
US-45 N La Grange Rd					
-	PvsT	60154	3087	12W-2S	A2
-	WSTR	60154	3087	12W-2S	A2
10	LGNG	60525	3087	12W-4S	C6
100	FKFT	60423	3503	11W-25S	E7
100	LGPK	60525	3087	12W-4S	C6
600	FftT	60423	3503	11W-25S	E6
1000	PvsT	60525	3087	12W-3S	B4
US-45 S La Grange Rd					
-	CTSD	60525	3147	12W-8S	C7
-	HGKN	60525	3209	12W-8S	C1
-	PlsT	60480	3273	12W-13S	D4
-	WLSP	60525	3209	12W-8S	C1
10	LGNG	60525	3087	12W-4S	C7
200	FKFT	60423	3591	14W-28S	A6
300	LGNG	60525	3147	12W-4S	C1
6000	HGKN	60525	3147	12W-6S	C5
11800	PlsT	60464	3273	12W-15S	D7
11800	PSPK	60464	3273	12W-15S	D7
12700	PSPK	60464	3345	12W-15S	D1
13000	PlsT	60462	3345	11W-15S	D1
13000	PSPK	60462	3345	11W-15S	D1
13400	OrlT	60462	3345	11W-15S	D2
13500	ODPK	60462	3345	11W-16S	D2
15700	ODPK	60462	3423	12W-18S	D1
15800	ODPK	60467	3423	12W-20S	D5
16600	ODHL	60467	3423	12W-19S	D3
16600	ODHL	60487	3423	12W-19S	D3
16600	ODPK	60487	3423	12W-19S	D3
16600	OrlT	60467	3423	12W-19S	D3
16600	OrlT	60487	3423	12W-19S	D3
20000	FKFT	60423	3503	11W-24S	E5
20000	FKFT	60448	3503	11W-24S	E5
20600	FftT	60423	3503	12W-24S	E6
21800	FftT	60423	3591	14W-28S	A6
22900	GGnT	60423	3591	14W-28S	A6
US-45 Lake St					
1000	MDLN	60060	2590	19W-28N	D5
1200	FmtT	60048	2590	19W-29N	D4
1200	FmtT	60060	2590	19W-29N	D4
1200	LYVL	60048	2590	19W-29N	D4
1200	MDLN	60048	2590	19W-29N	D4
US-45 N Lake St					
10	MDLN	60060	2646	19W-27N	D1
100	MDLN	60060	2590	19W-28N	D7
1200	FmtT	60048	2590	18W-29N	D4
1200	FmtT	60060	2590	18W-29N	D4
1200	LYVL	60048	2590	18W-29N	D4
1200	MDLN	60048	2590	18W-29N	D4
US-45 S Lake St					
10	MDLN	60060	2646	18W-25N	E4
1000	LbvT	60060	2646	18W-26N	E3
US-45 Mannheim Rd					
-	CHCG	60176	2917	12W-6N	B6
-	CHCG	60666	2917	12W-7N	A3
-	CHCG	60666	2973	12W-5N	B1
-	DSPN	60016	2863	13W-11N	A3
-	SRPK	60176	2917	12W-6N	B6
-	SRPK	60176	2973	12W-5N	B1
10	BLWD	60104	3029	12W-0N	A3
10	BLWD	60160	3029	12W-1N	A3
10	MLPK	60160	3029	12W-1N	A3
500	BLWD	60162	3029	12W-0N	A4
500	HLSD	60162	3029	12W-0N	A4
1000	DSPN	60016	2862	13W-10N	E5
1000	DSPN	60018	2862	13W-10N	E5
1700	DSPN	60018	2863	13W-9N	A6
2000	DSPN	60018	2917	13W-9N	A1
2000	RSMT	60018	2917	13W-9N	A1
2400	FNPK	60131	2973	13W-3N	A6
2400	LydT	60131	2973	13W-3N	A6
2400	LydT	60164	2973	13W-3N	A6
2600	FNPK	60164	2973	13W-3N	A5
2900	CHCG	60018	2917	12W-8N	A2
3700	FNPK	60176	2973	13W-4N	A3
3700	SRPK	60131	2973	13W-4N	A3
6400	RSMT	60666	2917	12W-8N	A3
US-45 N Mannheim Rd					
-	BLWD	60104	3029	13W-1N	A3
-	BLWD	60160	3029	13W-1N	A3
-	HLSD	60154	3029	12W-0S	A6
-	WSTR	60154	3029	12W-0S	A6
10	HLSD	60104	3029	12W-0S	A6
10	HLSD	60162	3029	12W-0S	A6
100	BLWD	60162	3029	12W-0S	A5
1500	MLPK	60160	3029	13W-1N	A3
1500	SNPK	60160	3029	12W-1N	A2
1500	SNPK	60165	3029	12W-1N	A2
1800	MLPK	60164	3029	12W-1N	A1
1800	MLPK	60165	3029	12W-1N	A1
1800	SNPK	60164	3029	12W-1N	A1
2000	LydT	60160	2973	12W-2N	A7
2000	LydT	60164	2973	12W-2N	A7
2000	MLPK	60160	2973	12W-2N	A7
2000	NHLK	60160	2973	12W-2N	A7
2000	NHLK	60164	2973	12W-2N	A7
2300	LydT	60131	2973	12W-2N	A6
US-45 S Mannheim Rd					
-	BLWD	60104	3029	12W-0S	A6
-	HLSD	60104	3029	12W-0S	A6
10	HLSD	60154	3029	12W-0S	A6
10	HLSD	60162	3029	13W-0S	A7
10	WSTR	60154	3029	13W-0S	A7
100	WSTR	60162	3029	13W-0S	A7
300	PvsT	60162	3029	12W-0S	A7
1400	PvsT	60162	3087	12W-1S	A1
1400	WSTR	60154	3087	13W-1S	A1
1400	WSTR	60162	3087	12W-1S	A1
2100	PvsT	60154	3087	12W-1S	A2
2100	PvsT	60525	3087	12W-1S	A2
US-45 Milwaukee Av					
200	LNSH	60061	2702	15W-23N	A2
200	LNSH	60069	2702	15W-23N	A2
200	VNHL	60061	2702	15W-23N	A2
200	VNHL	60069	2702	15W-23N	A2
200	VrnT	60061	2702	15W-23N	A2
300	VrnT	60069	2702	15W-23N	A2
900	BFGV	60089	2755	14W-20N	C1
900	VrnT	60015	2755	14W-20N	C1
900	VrnT	60062	2755	14W-20N	C1
900	VrnT	60089	2755	14W-20N	C1
1000	BFGV	60089	2702	14W-20N	B7
1000	RVWD	60015	2702	14W-20N	B7
1000	RVWD	60015	2755	14W-20N	C1
1000	VrnT	60015	2702	14W-20N	B7
1400	LNSH	60015	2702	14W-21N	B6
20400	BFGV	60090	2755	14W-20N	C1
US-45 N Milwaukee Av					
500	PTHT	60062	2809	13W-15N	A1
500	PTHT	60070	2809	13W-15N	A1
500	PTHT	60090	2809	13W-15N	A1
500	WhlT	60062	2809	13W-15N	A1
500	WhlT	60090	2809	13W-15N	A1
500	WLNG	60090	2755	13W-17N	D5
800	BFGV	60090	2755	14W-20N	C2
900	BFGV	60089	2755	14W-20N	C1
900	VrnT	60062	2755	14W-20N	C1
900	VrnT	60089	2755	14W-20N	C1
21800	LNSH	60069	2702	15W-21N	B5
21800	VrnT	60069	2702	14W-21N	B5
US-45 S Milwaukee Av					
10	WLNG	60090	2755	14W-18N	D4
600	WhlT	60090	2755	13W-17N	E5
1000	PTHT	60070	2755	13W-16N	E7
1000	PTHT	60070	2808	13W-16N	E1
1000	PTHT	60070	2809	13W-16N	A1
1000	PTHT	60090	2809	13W-16N	A1
1000	WhlT	60090	2808	13W-16N	E1
1000	WhlT	60090	2809	13W-16N	A1
US-45 N River Rd					
10	DSPN	60016	2863	13W-12N	A2
100	MaiT	60016	2863	13W-12N	A1
400	WhlT	60056	2808	13W-13N	E6
600	MPPT	60056	2808	13W-13N	E6
600	WhlT	60025	2808	13W-13N	E6
700	DSPN	60016	2808	13W-12N	E7
700	DSPN	60016	2809	13W-12N	A7
700	MaiT	60016	2808	13W-12N	E7
700	MaiT	60016	2809	13W-12N	A7
900	MPPT	60025	2808	13W-14N	E5
1300	MPPT	60056	2809	13W-14N	A3
1300	WhlT	60025	2809	13W-14N	A3
1300	WhlT	60056	2809	13W-14N	A3
1300	WhlT	60062	2809	13W-14N	A3
1500	PTHT	60070	2809	13W-15N	A2
US-45 S River Rd					
10	DSPN	60016	2863	13W-11N	A2
1200	MPPT	60056	2809	13W-15N	A2
1200	PTHT	60070	2809	12W-15N	A2
1200	WhlT	60056	2809	13W-15N	A2
1200	WhlT	60062	2809	13W-15N	A2
US-45 US Highway 45					
400	AvnT	60030	2533	18W-32N	D4
400	GYLK	60030	2533	18W-32N	D5
700	WrnT	60030	2533	18W-32N	D5
US-45 N US Highway 45					
31100	FmtT	60048	2533	19W-31N	D7
31100	LbvT	60048	2533	19W-31N	D7
31200	GYLK	60030	2533	19W-31N	D7
31200	LbvT	60030	2533	19W-31N	D7
32000	WrnT	60030	2533	18W-32N	D5
US-52					
-	MHTN	60442	3767	17W-34S	C4
-	MhtT	60442	3588	20W-27S	B5
-	NlxT	60421	3588	20W-27S	B5
-	NlxT	60433	3588	21W-27S	B5
-	NlxT	60442	3588	20W-27S	B5
10	JLET	60433	3587	23W-25S	A1
10	JLET	60436	3498	26W-24S	A5
10	JltT	60433	3587	23W-25S	A1
10	JltT	60436	3499	23W-25S	A7
10	SwdT	60447	3495	33W-24S	A6
10	TroT	60404	3495	31W-23S	E5
100	MHTN	60442	3677	20W-29S	D2
100	SRWD	60404	3496	30W-23S	C5
100	SRWD	60431	3496	30W-23S	C5
300	MHTN	60442	3678	18W-32S	B7
400	JLET	60433	3499	23W-24S	A6
500	MhtT	60442	3677	20W-29S	D2

Block	City	ZIP	Map#	CGS	Grid
US-52					
500	MhtT	60442	3678	19W-31S	A5
600	JLET	60436	3499	23W-25S	A7
800	JLET	60435	3498	26W-24S	A5
1200	TroT	60404	3496	31W-23S	A5
1800	JLET	60435	3497	27W-24S	C5
1800	JLET	60436	3497	27W-24S	C5
2100	JltT	60421	3588	20W-28S	B6
2100	JltT	60433	3588	20W-28S	B6
2800	JLET	60431	3497	27W-23S	C5
3200	TroT	60431	3497	28W-23S	B5
3700	JLET	60431	3496	31W-24S	A5
3700	TroT	60431	3496	31W-24S	A5
24200	SRWD	60404	3495	31W-24S	E5
27700	MhtT	60442	3767	18W-34S	C4
27800	WltT	60442	3767	17W-33S	C3
US-52 S Cedar Rd					
27700	MhtT	60442	3767	17W-33S	C3
27800	WltT	60442	3767	17W-33S	C3
US-52 S Chicago St					
-	JLET	60436	3498	24W-24S	E6
400	JLET	60433	3499	24W-24S	A6
400	JLET	60436	3499	24W-24S	A6
600	JltT	60436	3499	23W-25S	A7
US-52 Doris Av					
10	JLET	60433	3499	23W-25S	A7
10	JLET	60436	3499	23W-25S	A7
10	JltT	60436	3499	23W-25S	A7
US-52 Gardner St					
1000	JLET	60433	3499	23W-25S	A7
1000	JLET	60436	3499	23W-25S	A7
1100	JLET	60433	3587	23W-25S	A1
1100	JltT	60433	3587	23W-25S	A1
US-52 W Jefferson St					
-	SwdT	60447	3495	32W-24S	C6
100	SRWD	60404	3496	30W-23S	C5
100	SRWD	60431	3496	30W-23S	C5
800	JLET	60435	3498	26W-24S	A5
800	JLET	60436	3498	26W-24S	A5
1200	TroT	60404	3496	31W-23S	A5
1800	JLET	60435	3497	27W-24S	C5
1800	JLET	60436	3497	27W-24S	C5
2800	JLET	60431	3497	27W-23S	C5
3200	TroT	60431	3497	28W-23S	B5
3700	JLET	60431	3496	31W-24S	A5
3700	TroT	60431	3496	31W-24S	A5
24200	SRWD	60404	3495	31W-23S	E5
24200	TroT	60404	3495	31W-23S	E5
US-52 W Joliet Rd					
13000	WltT	60442	3767	16W-35S	E7
US-52 Manhattan Rd					
10	JLET	60433	3587	23W-25S	A1
10	JltT	60433	3587	23W-25S	A1
2100	JltT	60421	3588	20W-28S	B6
2100	JltT	60433	3588	20W-28S	B6
US-52 W McDonough St					
10	JLET	60436	3498	24W-24S	E6
US-52 W North St					
100	MHTN	60442	3677	19W-30S	E4
500	MhtT	60442	3677	19W-30S	D3
US-52 S Raynor Av					
-	JLET	60435	3498	24W-23S	D5
10	JLET	60436	3498	24W-24S	D5
US-52 S State St					
100	MHTN	60442	3677	19W-31S	E4
300	MHTN	60442	3678	18W-32S	B7
500	MhtT	60442	3678	19W-31S	A5

A

Block	City	ZIP	Map#	CGS	Grid
A Ct					
10100	MKNA	60448	3503	12W-23S	C4
A Rd					
-	WnfT	60510	3021	31W-0S	E7
-	WnfT	60510	3022	31W-0S	A6
-	WnfT	60510	3079	32W-1S	C2
A St					
-	HDPK	60037	2704	8W-23N	D1
-	RedT	60408	3942	30W-41S	B6
300	NCHI	60088	2594	10W-30N	A2
W A St					
25400	AntT	60002	2357	25W-42N	A6
A1 Rd					
-	WnfT	60510	3079	32W-2S	B3
A2 Rd					
-	WnfT	60510	3079	32W-2S	B3
Aaron Av					
800	SEGN	60177	2908	35W-8N	B2
W Aaron Ct					
26000	CNHN	60410	3761	32W-32S	D2
Aaron Ln					
-	YKVL	60560	3332	44W-15S	E3
300	BGBK	60440	3205	22W-10S	C6
Aavang Rd					
10000	GNWD	60097	2468	39W-35N	C6
10000	GNWD	60098	2468	39W-35N	C6
10000	GwdT	60097	2468	39W-35N	C6
10000	GwdT	60098	2468	39W-35N	C6
Abbe Ct					
5400	OKFT	60452	3425	6W-19S	E1
Abbey Cir					
2100	JLET	60586	3416	29W-21S	E7
Abbey Ct					
-	HMGN	60491	3344	15W-16S	A3
10	NLNX	60451	3500	19W-24S	D6
10	WDRG	60517	3206	20W-10S	B6
300	ANTH	60002	2358	22W-43N	A4
900	SRGV	60554	3135	41W-4S	E2
1100	LYVL	60048	2591	17W-29N	B3
8000	TYPK	60477	3424	10W-21S	C7
N Abbey Ct					
21900	KLDR	60047	2699	22W-21N	C5
Abbey Dr					
-	FftT	60423	3503	11W-24S	E6
800	GNEN	60137	3083	21W-1S	D1
1000	CLLK	60014	2639	37W-24N	B7
2500	DRN	60561	3206	19W-8S	C2
5200	MHRY	60050	2527	34W-31N	C6
5500	LSLE	60532	3142	23W-6S	E4
5500	LslT	60532	3142	23W-6S	E4
20400	FKFT	60423	3503	11W-24S	E6
Abbey Ln					
-	MHTN	60442	3678	19W-30S	A3
-	MhtT	60442	3678	19W-30S	A3
10	PKFT	60466	3595	2W-28S	D6
100	GNVA	60134	3019	37W-1N	C3
200	ANTH	60002	2358	22W-43N	B4
200	AntT	60002	2358	22W-43N	B4
200	SlmT	53104	2358	22W-43N	A4
200	SlmT	60002	2358	22W-43N	A4
300	VNHL	60061	2647	17W-25N	B5
8800	ODPK	60462	3346	11W-18S	A7
21400	LktT	60403	3417	26W-20S	E5
24900	MHTN	60442	3677	19W-30S	E4
W Abbey Ln					
10	RLKP	60073	2532	23W-33N	A2

Block	City	ZIP	Map#	CGS	Grid
Abbey Rd					
-	FftT	60448	3502	14W-25S	E7
10	LNSH	60069	2701	15W-23N	E3
500	BRLT	60103	2911	27W-7N	C5
7400	GRNE	60031	2477	18W-34N	A7
8000	TYPK	60477	3424	10W-21S	C7
11200	MKNA	60448	3502	14W-25S	E7
Abbey Glen Ct					
400	CmpT	60175	2962	39W-5N	E2
Abbey Glen Dr					
400	CmpT	60175	2962	39W-5N	E2
N Abbey Glenn Dr					
24900	ElaT	60047	2644	23W-25N	E6
24900	HNWD	60047	2644	23W-24N	E6
S Abbey Hill Ln					
400	PLTN	60067	2805	22W-15N	C2
Abbey Oaks Dr					
1200	LMNT	60439	3271	18W-14S	B7
Abbeywood Cir					
100	SMWD	60107	2857	28W-11N	B4
Abbey Wood Ct					
20600	FKFT	60423	3503	11W-24S	E6
Abbeywood Ct					
500	OKBK	60523	3028	15W-1S	B7
1000	ELGN	60120	2855	32W-12N	D2
3500	CPVL	60110	2746	37W-18N	D5
3500	CPVL	60110	2747	36W-18N	A5
N Abbeywood Ct					
2100	PLTN	60074	2753	20W-20N	B1
Abbey Wood Dr					
700	SRWD	60404	3496	31W-24S	A7
Abbeywood Dr					
-	LslT	60532	3142	24W-6S	C5
-	LslT	60540	3142	24W-6S	C5
10	RMVL	60446	3268	23W-14S	E7
10	RMVL	60446	3269	23W-14S	A7
200	SCRL	60175	2964	36W-4N	A3
500	CRY	60013	2695	32W-23N	A2
2200	LSLE	60532	3142	24W-6S	C5
Abbey Wood Ln					
-	HFET	60169	2858	25W-12N	A1
Abbeywood Ln					
200	NARA	60542	3077	36W-3S	E7
Abbington Ct					
10	SMWD	60107	2856	29W-9N	D7
Abbington Dr					
800	CLLK	60014	2640	35W-24N	A7
1000	CLLK	60014	2694	34W-23N	B1
2700	NlxT	60451	3590	16W-27S	B5
4900	MHRY	60050	2527	33W-32N	D6
Abbington Ln					
-	BmdT	60188	2967	26W-4N	E4
-	CLSM	60188	2967	26W-4N	E4
Abbington Pl					
400	SMBG	60194	2858	24W-11N	C4
Abbot Ct					
20700	FKFT	60423	3503	11W-24S	E6
Abbots Wy					
19500	MKNA	60448	3502	15W-23S	C3
Abbotsford Ct					
200	GNEN	60137	3025	21W-0S	E6
Abbotsford Dr					
10	LNSH	60069	2702	13W-23N	E3
1500	NPVL	60563	3140	29W-5S	D3
1900	IVNS	60010	2751	25W-16N	B6
2000	HFET	60010	2751	24W-16N	B7
Abbotsford Ln					
900	FKFT	60423	3592	9W-26S	D3
Abbotsford Rd					
10	KLWH	60043	2812	4W-14N	C3
10	WNKA	60043	2812	4W-14N	C3
10	WNKA	60093	2812	4W-14N	C4
Abbott Av					
200	CHHT	60411	3507	2W-24S	D5
200	FSMR	60422	3507	2W-24S	D5
S Abbott Av					
9000	CHCG	60620	3214	0W-10S	B5
Abbott Ct					
-	BFGV	60069	2701	16W-21N	E6
-	BFGV	60089	2701	16W-21N	E5
-	VrnT	60069	2701	16W-21N	E5
1800	NHFD	60093	2811	7W-15N	B2
Abbott Dr					
-	FXLK	60020	2414	28W-38N	E6
100	WLNG	60090	2808	14W-16N	B1
1000	ELGN	60123	2854	35W-12N	C1
Abbott Grv					
8300	AlqT	60013	2696	29W-23N	C1
Abbott Ln					
1000	UYPK	60466	3684	3W-30S	B3
Abbott Pl					
200	LKBN	60010	2643	26W-25N	C4
200	LKBN	60084	2643	26W-25N	C4
200	TRLK	60010	2643	26W-25N	C4
S Abbott Rd E					
14400	HMGN	60491	3344	15W-17S	C5
S Abbott Rd W					
14500	HMGN	60491	3344	15W-17S	C5
Abbott St					
100	WLSP	60480	3209	12W-9S	B4
Abbott Ter					
4500	LYNS	60534	3088	10W-4S	B7
Abbott Park Rd					
-	GNOK	60044	2592	13W-29N	E4
-	LbvT	60044	2592	13W-30N	E2
-	LbvT	60064	2592	13W-29N	E4
-	LbvT	60064	2593	13W-29N	A4
-	NCHI	60044	2592	13W-29N	E4
-	NCHI	60044	2593	13W-29N	A4
-	NCHI	60064	2592	13W-29N	E4
100	LbvT	60044	2593	13W-30N	A2
Abbottsford Rd					
14300	MDLN	60445	3348	4W-17S	D4
Abby Dr					
-	ALGN	60102	2693	38W-20N	A7
1600	NPVL	60563	3140	29W-5S	D2
Abby Ln					
4600	MTSN	60443	3506	5W-24S	B5
14900	LKPT	60441	3421	18W-19S	A3
Abby Rd					
-	HTLY	60142	2692	40W-22N	B4
E Abe St					
10	PLNO	60545	3259	47W-13S	D6
N Abe St					
600	JLET	60432	3499	23W-23S	B3
W Abe St					
10	PLNO	60545	3259	48W-13S	B6
700	LtRT	60545	3259	48W-13S	B6
Abendroth Dr					
6400	NndT	60012	2640	35W-27N	A1
Aberdare Ln					
-	GRNE	60031	2477	17W-34N	B7
Aberdeen Ct					
10	BFGV	60089	2701	15W-21N	E5
10	SMBG	60194	2857	26W-10N	E6
100	GNVA	60134	3020	34W-1N	E3

Block	City	ZIP	Map#	CGS	Grid
Aberdeen Ct					
300	BRLT	60103	2967	28W-5N	B2
800	BGBK	60440	3205	22W-10S	C5
900	ELGN	60123	2908	36W-9N	A1
1400	AURA	60564	3202	30W-9S	A4
2100	HRPK	60133	2967	27W-5N	C1
2100	WHTN	60187	3081	26W-1S	E2
8000	PSHT	60464	3346	10W-15S	C2
39200	BHPK	60083	2421	12W-39N	B6
E Aberdeen Ct					
300	EMHT	60126	3028	15W-0S	B5
Aberdeen Dr					
-	MTGY	60506	3198	40W-9S	C4
-	MTGY	60538	3198	40W-9S	C4
100	ALGN	60102	2694	35W-21N	A6
100	EDND	60118	2801	33W-16N	C2
200	BNHL	60010	2749	28W-18N	E3
400	CRTE	60417	3596	0E-28S	E6
600	CRTE	60417	3597	0E-28S	A6
800	CLLK	60014	2640	35W-24N	A7
1800	GNVW	60025	2810	8W-15N	D2
2100	CPVL	60110	2748	32W-18N	D6
8100	PSHT	60464	3346	10W-15S	C2
15900	LktT	60441	3418	26W-19S	A2
15900	RMVL	60441	3418	26W-19S	A2
15900	RMVL	60446	3418	26W-19S	A2
Aberdeen Ln					
-	BHPK	60083	2421	12W-39N	B6
500	PTHT	60070	2808	14W-14N	B3
600	BFGV	60089	2701	16W-20N	D7
600	CmpT	60175	2906	40W-6N	B7
1000	IVNS	60067	2752	22W-16N	B7
1000	MDLN	60060	2590	19W-28N	C6
9600	HTLY	60142	2692	40W-22N	B4
N Aberdeen Ln					
39000	BHPK	60083	2421	12W-39N	B6
Aberdeen Rd					
10	HNWD	60047	2646	20W-24N	A6
200	CRY	60013	2695	31W-23N	D2
500	FKFT	60423	3592	9W-26S	E2
500	FKFT	60423	3593	9W-26S	A2
500	IVNS	60067	2752	22W-16N	B6
500	RchT	60443	3593	9W-26S	A2
Aberdeen St					
500	HFET	60169	2859	22W-11N	C4
1400	CHHT	60411	3508	1W-25S	A7
1400	CHHT	60411	3596	1W-25S	A1
2500	SCHT	60411	3596	1W-26S	A3
18100	HMWD	60430	3428	1W-22S	A7
18400	HMWD	60430	3508	1W-22S	A1
N Aberdeen St					
10	CHCG	60607	3033	1W-0N	E4
700	CHCG	60622	3033	2W-0S	C5
S Aberdeen St					
10	CHCG	60607	3033	1W-0S	E5
1400	CHCG	60608	3033	1W-1S	E7
3100	CHCG	60608	3091	1W-3S	E4
3400	CHCG	60609	3091	1W-3S	E4
4700	CHCG	60609	3151	1W-6S	E3
5500	CHCG	60621	3151	1W-8S	E7
7500	CHCG	60620	3213	1W-9S	E2
7500	CHCG	60621	3213	1W-8S	E1
9800	CHCG	60643	3213	1W-11S	E6
10300	CHCG	60643	3277	1W-12S	E1
12700	CTPK	60643	3277	1W-15S	E7
12700	CTPK	60827	3277	1W-15S	E7
Aberdour Ct					
10	NBRN	60010	2644	24W-25N	B5
Aberdour Ln					
100	IVNS	60067	2752	22W-16N	B7
300	NPVL	60540	3142	25W-7S	B6
Abigail Ln					
17700	ODPK	60467	3423	13W-21S	B6
Abilene Ln					
200	VNHL	60061	2647	16W-25N	C5
Abilene Tr					
300	RtdT	60124	2798	39W-14N	E6
400	BMDL	60108	2968	25W-5N	C1
700	BmdT	60108	2968	25W-5N	C1
Abingdon Av					
100	KLWH	60043	2812	3W-14N	E4
Abingdon Ct					
900	GRNE	60031	2534	16W-33N	D4
Abingdon Dr					
-	OSWG	60543	3263	36W-13S	E5
Abington Ct					
2200	WKGN	60087	2478	14W-36N	D4
Abington Ln					
100	NARA	60542	3077	38W-4S	A7
S Abington Ln					
1300	RDLK	60073	2531	23W-31N	E7
Abington Cambs Dr					
1200	LKFT	60045	2649	12W-25N	A5
Abington Woods Dr					
300	AURA	60502	3139	32W-7S	B7
Aborn Av					
600	ElgT	60124	2853	38W-10N	B7
Abourndale Ct					
1400	PTHT	60070	2754	16W-16N	D6
1400	PTHT	60090	2754	16W-16N	D6
1400	WLNG	60090	2754	16W-16N	D6
Abraham Dr					
-	NLNX	60451	3500	19W-23S	E3
-	NLNX	60451	3501	18W-23S	A3
-	NlxT	60451	3500	19W-23S	E3
Abrahamson Ct					
400	LslT	60540	3203	26W-8S	E1
400	NPVL	60540	3203	26W-8S	E1
Abriter Ct					
1800	NPVL	60563	3142	25W-4S	A1
Aburn Dr					
-	YKVL	60560	3333	42W-15S	E1
Acacia Av					
-	JLET	60435	3417	27W-19S	D3
Acacia Cir					
100	IHPK	60525	3146	13W-7S	E6
Acacia Ct					
1400	NPVL	60563	3141	27W-5S	C2
5200	GRNE	60031	2478	14W-35N	B5
5500	NndT	60012	2584	34W-28N	C6
Acacia Ct N					
2900	BFGV	60089	2701	17W-23N	A2
Acacia Ct S					
2700	BFGV	60089	2701	17W-23N	B3
Acacia Dr					
100	IHPK	60525	3146	13W-7S	E6
3800	NndT	60012	2584	34W-28N	C6
15700	ODPK	60462	3424	10W-18S	B1
Acacia Ln					
10	BmdT	60143	2913	22W-6N	C7
10	BmdT	60157	2913	22W-6N	C7
10	ROSL	60143	2913	22W-6N	C7
10	ROSL	60157	2913	22W-6N	C7
1500	WDSK	60098	2581	41W-30N	D3
1600	CTSD	60525	3147	13W-7S	A6
1600	IHPK	60525	3147	13W-7S	A6

Block	City	ZIP	Map#	CGS	Grid
Acacia Ln					
1700	IHPK	60525	3146	13W-7S	E6
Acacia Ter					
2600	BFGV	60047	2701	17W-23N	B3
2600	BFGV	60089	2701	17W-23N	B3
2600	LGGV	60047	2701	17W-23N	B3
Academic Dr					
600	ALGN	60102	2692	38W-20N	E7
600	ALGN	60102	2693	38W-20N	A7
600	ALGN	60102	2746	37W-20N	A1
600	GfnT	60102	2692	38W-20N	E7
800	GfnT	60102	2746	37W-20N	A1
Academy Av					
500	MTSN	60443	3506	5W-25S	B7
Academy Ct					
600	SMBG	60194	2857	28W-12N	B2
W Academy Ct					
25100	LkvT	60046	2416	25W-38N	B7
Academy Dr					
400	NHBK	60062	2756	11W-18N	D3
500	LSLE	60532	3142	23W-5S	E3
N Academy Dr					
37700	LkvT	60046	2474	25W-37N	B1
38100	LkvT	60046	2416	25W-38N	B7
Academy Ln					
800	WCHI	60185	3022	29W-1N	E2
1200	MltT	60187	3082	25W-1S	A2
1200	WHTN	60187	3082	25W-1S	A2
Academy Pl					
200	ELGN	60120	2855	33W-11N	A3
S Academy Pl					
10	CHCG	60607	3034	0W-0S	A5
Academy Rd					
-	LKFT	60045	2648	13W-26N	E3
-	LKFT	60045	2649	13W-26N	A3
Academy Woods Dr					
500	LKFT	60045	2649	13W-26N	A3
Acadia Ct					
10	HnrT	60107	2856	30W-10N	B6
600	ROSL	60172	2913	22W-8N	C3
Acadia Bay					
600	ROSL	60172	2913	22W-8N	C2
Accera Dr					
10	HLSD	60162	3029	13W-0S	A7
N Access Rd					
-	CHCG	60666	2916	14W-5N	C7
S Acco Plz					
700	WLNG	60090	2755	14W-17N	D6
Ace Ln					
800	WldT	60564	3266	30W-13S	C4
Achilles Av					
20300	OMFD	60461	3506	4W-24S	E6
Achilles Ct					
-	CLLK	60098	2638	39W-26N	C2
Achilles Ln					
-	CLLK	60098	2638	39W-26N	B2
N Ackerman Rd					
38700	AntT	60002	2415	26W-38N	D6
Ackman Rd					
-	GfnT	60142	2691	41W-23N	E3
-	HTLY	60142	2691	41W-23N	E3
400	CLLK	60014	2693	37W-23N	A2
7800	GfnT	60014	2693	37W-23N	A2
8100	GfnT	60156	2693	37W-23N	B2
8900	LKWD	60014	2693	37W-23N	B2
9300	GfnT	60014	2692	38W-23N	E2
9300	GfnT	60156	2692	38W-23N	E2
9300	LIHL	60156	2692	38W-23N	E2
9300	LKWD	60014	2692	38W-23N	E2
9300	LKWD	60156	2693	37W-23N	A2
Ackman Rd CO-A46					
7700	CLLK	60014	2693	37W-23N	A2
7800	GfnT	60014	2693	37W-23N	A2
8100	GfnT	60156	2693	37W-23N	B2
8900	LKWD	60014	2693	37W-23N	B2
9300	GfnT	60014	2692	38W-23N	E2
9300	GfnT	60156	2692	38W-23N	E2
9300	LIHL	60156	2692	38W-23N	E2
9300	LKWD	60014	2692	38W-23N	E2
9300	LKWD	60156	2693	37W-23N	A2
W Acme Dr					
100	RVDL	60827	3350	0W-15S	C1
Acorn Av					
400	MltT	60137	3025	21W-0N	E5
1400	DRGV	60515	3084	20W-3S	B5
Acorn Ct					
-	ALGN	60102	2693	35W-21N	E5
-	LIHL	60102	2693	35W-21N	E5
-	LIHL	60156	2693	35W-21N	E5
-	WDND	60118	2800	36W-16N	A1
10	RLKB	60073	2475	22W-36N	A3
200	SMBG	60193	2858	23W-10N	E6
500	ANTH	60002	2357	24W-42N	B5
700	BRLT	60103	2911	28W-8N	B3
1200	SYHW	60118	2800	35W-15N	C4
1500	GRNE	60031	2478	15W-35N	A5
1500	LMBD	60148	3084	20W-1S	A1
1500	WLNG	60090	2754	16W-18N	D3
2100	WHTN	60187	3081	27W-1S	D2
2100	WHTN	60187	3083	23W-3S	A5
2100	WnfT	60187	3081	27W-1S	D2
2600	GNVA	60134	3019	37W-0N	C5
3200	AURA	60504	3201	31W-8S	E2
5000	HFET	60192	2856	31W-12N	A1
6000	NndT	60014	2641	32W-26N	B4
12100	HTLY	60142	2744	42W-19N	E3
13300	PSHT	60463	3347	7W-15S	B2
14300	HMGN	60491	3342	19W-17S	D5
N Acorn Ct					
21600	KLDR	60047	2699	21W-21N	D6
S Acorn Ct					
23500	CteT	60417	3595	2W-28S	E6
Acorn Dr					
10	HNWD	60047	2644	23W-24N	E7
10	HNWD	60047	2645	23W-24N	A7
100	NARA	60542	3077	37W-4S	C7
200	SMWD	60107	2857	27W-10N	D7
800	SYHW	60118	2800	35W-15N	C4
1200	CTHL	60403	3418	25W-21S	B6
1300	WDND	60118	2747	36W-17N	B7
1600	HFET	60192	2856	31W-12N	A1
2400	RLKB	60073	2475	22W-36N	A4
2600	WDND	60118	2800	36W-17N	A1
14500	HMGN	60491	3342	19W-17S	D5
Acorn Ln					
-	BmnT	60426	3426	5W-19S	B1
10	AlqT	60013	2641	31W-25N	D4
10	BNHL	60010	2696	28W-21N	E6
10	BtlT	60560	3334	41W-15S	A1
10	HDPK	60035	2757	9W-20N	D2
10	LIHL	60156	2694	35W-21N	A5
10	ODHL	60013	2641	31W-25N	D4
10	STGR	60475	3597	1E-27S	A5
100	BMDL	60108	2969	22W-4N	B3
100	LYVL	60048	2591	17W-28N	B5
800	ElgT	60124	2907	37W-8N	B3

Block	City	ZIP	Map#	CGS	Grid
Acorn Ln					
2800	NHBK	60062	2756	11W-17N	D4
3600	FNPK	60131	2972	14W-4N	C3
3600	LydT	60131	2972	14W-4N	C3
5600	MchT	60050	2472	29W-37N	C2
7600	RlyT	60152	2634	50W-24N	A7
15000	HMGN	60491	3342	18W-16S	E3
N Acorn Ln					
26100	FmtT	60060	2646	19W-26N	C3
26100	LGGV	60047	2646	19W-26N	C4
W Acorn Ln					
10	LIHL	60156	2693	35W-21N	E5
Acorn Pl					
2300	BFGV	60089	2701	16W-22N	C4
Acorn Pth					
8300	GwdT	60097	2469	37W-35N	A6
8300	WRLK	60097	2469	38W-35N	A6
Acorn Rd					
3400	DRGV	60515	3084	19W-3S	C5
Acorn St					
1200	LMNT	60439	3342	19W-15S	C1
Acorn Tr					
900	LKFT	60045	2649	12W-27N	B2
Acorn Wy					
1000	CRY	60013	2642	30W-24N	B6
Acorn Hill Ct					
2400	LSLE	60532	3142	24W-7S	D6
Acorn Hill Ln					
500	OKBK	60523	3086	15W-3S	A6
1000	WCHI	60185	3022	30W-2N	B1
Acorn Ln Dr					
1800	FSMR	60422	3507	2W-23S	D3
Acorn Ridge Dr					
13900	HMGN	60491	3421	17W-19S	C3
S Acorn Ridge Dr					
20400	FftT	60423	3504	9W-25S	E7
E Acre Ct					
22700	RLKB	60073	2475	22W-35N	A6
Acre Ln					
1100	JNBG	60051	2472	30W-35N	B6
Acres Ln					
800	DSPN	60016	2863	12W-10N	B4
Acres Pl					
100	BbyT	60134	3018	39W-0N	E5
W Acres Rd					
1700	JLET	60435	3498	26W-23S	A4
2200	JLET	60435	3497	26W-23S	E4
Active Ln					
8800	HYHL	60457	3210	11W-10S	A4
Ada Ct					
1700	NPVL	60540	3202	28W-8S	E1
Ada Ln					
-	WthT	60482	3275	7W-13S	B5
900	NPVL	60540	3203	28W-8S	A1
1500	NPVL	60540	3202	28W-8S	E1
Ada St					
400	CRY	60013	2695	31W-23N	D1
18200	LNSG	60438	3430	4E-21S	B7
19100	LNSG	60438	3510	4E-22S	B2
E Ada St					
1200	JLET	60432	3499	22W-22S	D2
1400	JltT	60432	3499	22W-22S	D2
N Ada St					
400	CHCG	60607	3033	1W-0N	D3
400	CHCG	60622	3033	1W-0N	D3
1600	CHCG	60622	2977	1W-2N	D7
26500	WcnT	60084	2642	28W-26N	E2
S Ada St					
600	CHCG	60607	3033	1W-0S	D6
4700	CHCG	60609	3151	1W-5S	D1
5500	CHCG	60636	3151	1W-6S	D4
7600	CHCG	60620	3213	1W-8S	E1
9400	CHCG	60643	3213	1W-10S	E6
11200	CHCG	60643	3277	1W-13S	E4
12200	CTPK	60643	3277	1W-14S	E6
12300	CTPK	60827	3277	1W-15S	E7
Adair Ct					
100	VNHL	60061	2647	17W-25N	C5
Adam Av					
2800	BtlT	60538	3198	40W-10S	B5
2800	MTGY	60538	3198	40W-10S	B5
2900	BtlT	60512	3198	41W-10S	B5
Adam Ct					
300	CRY	60013	2641	31W-25N	D6
Adam Dr					
300	SEGN	60177	2908	35W-8N	B2
3900	WRLK	60097	2469	38W-35N	A5
4000	GNWD	60097	2468	38W-35N	E5
4000	WRLK	60097	2468	38W-35N	E5
Adam Ln					
500	CLSM	60188	2967	26W-3N	D6
800	HPSR	60140	2796	46W-15N	A3
800	HshT	60140	2796	46W-15N	A3
N Adam St					
38400	LkvT	60046	2416	25W-38N	B7
Adams Av					
100	FRGV	60021	2696	30W-23N	B2
300	GLNC	60022	2758	6W-17N	D5
900	SCRL	60174	2964	34W-2N	C7
1000	WPHR	60096	2363	10W-42N	B7
1100	WCDA	60084	2588	25W-28N	A6
1100	WcnT	60084	2588	25W-28N	A6
W Adams Blvd					
-	CHCG	60644	3031	7W-0S	B5
-	OKPK	60304	3031	7W-0S	B5
Adams Cir					
10	EGvT	60018	2861	16W-9N	E7
10	EGvT	60018	2862	15W-9N	A7
Adams Ct					
10	SMWD	60107	2856	29W-10N	D6
500	EMHT	60126	3028	14W-0S	C6
700	AURA	60506	3137	37W-6S	C5
700	BGBK	60440	3268	24W-12S	D2
900	VNHL	60061	2647	17W-26N	B4
1000	CPVL	60110	2748	32W-17N	D7
1300	SCRL	60174	2964	34W-2N	D7
1900	GRNE	60031	2477	16W-36N	E4
2800	SMBG	60193	2857	27W-10N	D5
23600	PNFD	60586	3416	29W-19S	D4
Adams Dr					
500	CPVL	60110	2746	37W-17N	C6
500	DndT	60110	2746	37W-17N	C6
500	DndT	60118	2746	37W-17N	C6
1100	MchT	60051	2528	31W-32N	D4
1100	MHRY	60051	2528	31W-33N	D4
2400	LNHT	60046	2418	19W-39N	B5
2400	LSLE	60532	3142	24W-6S	E4
22400	RNPK	60471	3594	5W-27S	B4
N Adams Dr					
10	ADSN	60101	2970	18W-3N	E5
Adams Rd					
3300	OKBK	60523	3085	16W-3S	E6
3600	HNDL	60521	3085	16W-3S	E6
3600	HNDL	60523	3085	16W-3S	E6
3600	OKBK	60521	3085	16W-3S	E6

STREET Block	City	ZIP	Map#	CGS	Grid
W Adams Rd					
13000	BHPK	60083	2421	13W-39N	A5
13000	BHPK	60099	2421	13W-39N	A4
13200	WDWH	60083	2421	13W-39N	A4
13400	BHPK	60099	2420	13W-39N	E4
13400	WDWH	60083	2420	13W-39N	E4
13500	NptT	60083	2420	13W-39N	E4
Adams St					
-	DGvT	60561	3145	18W-8S	A7
-	HLSD	60162	3028	14W-0S	D5
-	SMBG	60133	2912	26W-8N	A3
-	SMBG	60193	2912	26W-8N	A3
10	BTVA	60510	3078	35W-1S	C2
10	CHCG	60644	3031	7W-0S	B5
10	DGvT	60561	3207	18W-8S	A1
10	EDND	60118	2801	34W-16N	A1
10	EGvT	60018	2861	16W-9N	E7
10	EGvT	60018	2862	15W-9N	A7
10	OKPK	60304	3031	8W-0S	A5
100	FXLK	60041	2473	26W-35N	C5
100	MRGO	60152	2634	49W-26N	B2
200	ELGN	60123	2854	34W-10N	D6
200	YKVL	60560	3333	43W-15S	B2
400	DLTN	60419	3350	0E-16S	D3
600	AURA	60505	3138	34W-6S	C6
600	BGBK	60440	3268	24W-12S	D2
600	HRPK	60133	2912	26W-8N	A3
700	WKGN	60085	2537	10W-33N	A3
800	LKPT	60441	3419	21W-19S	E3
800	OKPK	60304	3030	8W-0S	E5
900	MYWD	60153	3029	11W-0S	D5
900	NCHI	60064	2537	10W-32N	A5
1300	LIHL	60156	2693	35W-22N	E4
1500	AlqT	60156	2693	35W-22N	E3
1900	CHHT	60411	3595	2W-26S	C2
2000	RGMW	60008	2806	20W-14N	A4
2900	BLWD	60104	3029	12W-0S	B5
3200	LNSG	60438	3430	4E-21S	B5
3800	BLWD	60162	3029	12W-0S	A5
3800	HLSD	60162	3029	12W-0S	A5
7200	FTPK	60130	3030	9W-0S	C5
7200	FTPK	60304	3030	9W-0S	D5
8100	DRN	60561	3207	18W-9S	A3
E Adams St					
10	CHCG	60603	3034	0E-0S	C5
10	CHCG	60604	3034	0E-0S	C5
10	GDLY	60407	4030	32W-43S	D2
10	VLPK	60181	3027	17W-0S	B6
100	EMHT	60126	3027	16W-0N	C5
100	EMHT	60126	3028	15W-0S	A5
500	BKLY	60163	3028	15W-0S	B5
1000	LMBD	60148	3026	18W-0S	E6
1100	LMBD	60181	3026	18W-0S	E6
1100	VLPK	60181	3026	18W-0S	E6
N Adams St					
10	HNDL	60521	3145	16W-4S	E1
10	NARA	60542	3077	37W-3S	C6
10	NARA	60542	3137	36W-4S	E1
10	WTMT	60559	3145	18W-5S	A2
100	OSWG	60543	3263	37W-12S	C3
400	HNDL	60521	3085	16W-4S	E7
3900	DGvT	60559	3085	18W-4S	A7
3900	WTMT	60559	3085	18W-4S	A7
S Adams St					
10	HNDL	60521	3145	16W-5S	E1
10	NARA	60542	3137	36W-4S	E1
10	OSWG	60543	3263	37W-12S	C3
800	WTMT	60559	3145	18W-6S	A4
6800	WLBK	60527	3145	16W-7S	E7
7200	WLBK	60527	3207	16W-8S	E1
7800	DRN	60561	3207	18W-8S	A2
W Adams St					
10	CHCG	60603	3034	0W-0S	A5
10	CHCG	60604	3034	0W-0S	A5
10	VLPK	60181	3027	18W-0S	A6
100	CHCG	60606	3034	0W-0S	B5
100	EMHT	60126	3027	16W-0S	E5
300	LMBD	60148	3026	18W-0S	E6
300	LMBD	60181	3026	18W-0S	E6
300	VLPK	60181	3026	18W-0S	E6
400	CHCG	60661	3034	0W-0S	A5
700	CHCG	60607	3034	0W-0S	A5
800	CHCG	60607	3033	1W-0S	D5
1500	CHCG	60612	3033	2W-0S	B5
2800	CHCG	60612	3032	3W-0S	E5
3200	CHCG	60624	3032	4W-0S	D5
4600	CHCG	60644	3032	5W-0S	A5
4800	CHCG	60644	3031	6W-0S	D5
Adamson Dr					
2800	GNVA	60134	3019	37W-1N	C3
Adamson Rd					
-	HTLY	60142	2691	41W-23N	C2
13100	CrlT	60142	2691	42W-23N	A2
13100	GfnT	60142	2691	41W-23N	C2
Adamsway Dr					
2300	AURA	60502	3201	32W-7S	C1
2500	AURA	60502	3139	32W-7S	C7
2500	NpvT	60502	3201	32W-7S	C1
Adamy Ct					
-	ADSN	60143	2970	20W-5N	A1
Adare Av					
9000	MKNA	60448	3504	11W-23S	A3
Adare Ct					
1100	SCRL	60174	2964	34W-3N	D5
Adare Dr					
-	MltT	60187	3082	26W-1S	A1
10	AlqT	60013	2641	31W-24N	D6
10	CRY	60013	2641	31W-24N	D6
900	WHTN	60187	3081	26W-1S	E1
900	WHTN	60187	3082	26W-1S	A1
Adare Rd					
500	BRLT	60103	2911	27W-7N	C5
Adbeth Av					
8300	WDRG	60517	3205	21W-9S	D4
Adderley Ln					
-	FmtT	60060	2590	19W-29N	B3
-	MDLN	60060	2590	19W-29N	B3
Adderly Ln					
800	GRNE	60031	2534	16W-33N	D4
Addison Av					
-	LMBD	60181	3026	18W-0S	E6
-	VLPK	60181	3026	18W-0S	E6
800	LMBD	60148	3026	18W-0S	E6
9400	FNPK	60131	2973	12W-4N	A3
11000	FNPK	60131	2972	13W-4N	D3
N Addison Av					
10	AddT	60101	3026	18W-2N	E1
10	AddT	60181	3026	18W-2N	E1
10	ADSN	60101	3026	18W-2N	E1
10	VLPK	60181	3026	18W-1N	E2
100	EMHT	60126	3027	16W-1N	E1
800	EMHT	60126	2971	16W-3N	E5
S Addison Av					
10	YkTp	60148	3026	18W-0S	E7
10	YkTp	60148	3084	18W-1S	E1
200	LMBD	60148	3026	18W-0N	E4
300	LMBD	60181	3026	18W-0N	E5
300	VLPK	60181	3026	18W-0N	E5
Addison Ct					
-	OSWG	60543	3263	36W-12S	E3
1000	EGvT	60005	2861	16W-10N	C5
1000	EGvT	60056	2861	16W-10N	C5
1000	MPPT	60005	2861	16W-10N	C5
1000	MPPT	60056	2861	16W-10N	C5
9600	FNPK	60131	2973	12W-4N	C3
W Addison Dr					
-	CHCG	60613	2978	0W-4N	A2
N Addison Ln					
42300	AntT	60002	2357	25W-42N	B5
Addison Rd					
100	RVSD	60546	3088	9W-3S	D4
300	BRWN	60402	3088	9W-3S	D4
300	RVSD	60402	3088	9W-3S	D4
N Addison Rd					
10	ADSN	60101	2970	18W-3N	E4
100	WDDL	60191	2970	18W-5N	E1
200	WDDL	60191	2914	18W-5N	E7
300	AddT	60101	2970	18W-4N	E4
800	ADSN	60191	2970	18W-4N	E3
N Addison Rd CO-22					
100	WDDL	60191	2970	18W-5N	E1
200	WDDL	60191	2914	18W-6N	E7
300	AddT	60101	2970	18W-4N	E4
300	ADSN	60101	2970	18W-3N	E4
800	ADSN	60191	2970	18W-4N	E3
S Addison Rd					
10	ADSN	60101	2970	18W-2N	E6
100	WDDL	60191	2970	18W-4N	E2
200	ADSN	60191	2970	18W-5N	E2
700	AddT	60101	2970	18W-2N	E7
700	BNVL	60106	2971	16W-4N	E4
800	AddT	60101	3026	18W-2N	E1
800	AddT	60181	3026	18W-2N	E1
800	ADSN	60101	3026	18W-2N	E1
S Addison Rd CO-22					
-	ADSN	60101	2970	18W-4N	E3
100	WDDL	60191	2970	18W-4N	E2
200	ADSN	60191	2970	18W-5N	E2
Addison St					
400	ELGN	60120	2855	33W-11N	A3
N Addison St					
-	BNVL	60106	2915	16W-5N	E7
10	BNVL	60106	2971	16W-5N	E1
S Addison St					
10	BNVL	60106	2971	16W-5N	E2
W Addison St					
500	CHCG	60613	2978	0W-4N	A2
500	CHCG	60657	2978	0W-4N	A2
700	CHCG	60613	2977	2W-4N	C2
700	CHCG	60657	2977	2W-4N	C2
1900	CHCG	60618	2977	2W-4N	B2
2600	CHCG	60618	2976	3W-4N	E2
3900	CHCG	60641	2976	4W-4N	B3
4700	CHCG	60641	2975	6W-4N	E3
5500	CHCG	60634	2975	6W-4N	C3
6700	CHCG	60634	2974	10W-4N	A3
Addleman St					
1200	JLET	60431	3497	28W-22S	A2
1400	PnfT	60431	3497	28W-22S	A1
N Addleman St					
1600	JLET	60431	3497	28W-21S	A1
1600	PnfT	60431	3497	28W-21S	A1
1800	JLET	60431	3417	28W-21S	A7
1800	PnfT	60431	3417	28W-21S	A7
S Adel Ct					
14000	LktT	60544	3340	26W-16S	A4
Adelaide Av					
2700	BHPK	60087	2479	12W-37N	C3
2700	WKGN	60087	2479	12W-37N	C3
W Adelaide Av					
12900	BHPK	60087	2479	12W-37N	A3
12900	WrnT	60087	2479	12W-37N	A3
Adelaide Dr					
900	NHBK	60062	2757	10W-17N	A4
Adelaide Pl					
10	LNSG	60438	3430		C5
10	MNSR	46321	3430		C5
W Adelaide St					
100	EMHT	60126	3027	16W-1N	E2
Adele Av					
10	AddT	60101	3026	19W-2N	D1
10	AddT	60148	3026	19W-2N	D1
10	ADSN	60101	3026	19W-2N	D1
10	ADSN	60148	3026	19W-2N	D1
E Adele Ct					
200	ADSN	60181	3027	17W-2N	B1
200	VLPK	60181	3027	17W-2N	B1
Adele Dr					
4900	GRNE	60031	2478	15W-35N	B5
Adele Ln					
10	SchT	60175	2907	38W-7N	B5
4400	OKFT	60452	3426	5W-19S	B3
N Adele St					
300	EMHT	60126	3028	15W-2N	A1
700	EMHT	60126	2972	15W-3N	B6
Adelia Ln					
2400	WCHI	60185	2965	32W-4N	C4
Adelia St					
1000	DRGV	60516	3144	19W-7S	C6
E Adelia St					
100	EMHT	60126	3027	16W-1N	E3
100	EMHT	60126	3028	15W-1N	A3
Adeline Av					
800	ELGN	60123	2854	35W-12N	B2
S Adeline Av					
10	ADSN	60101	2970	19W-3N	D5
Adeline Ct					
1300	AraT	60505	3138	34W-5S	E2
4200	GRNE	60031	2478	14W-35N	D7
Adeline Dr					
4200	OKLN	60453	3276	5W-12S	B3
Adeline Pl					
5400	OKFT	60452	3347	6W-18S	D7
S Adell Pl					
100	EMHT	60126	3027	17W-1N	C2
Adella Av					
400	JLET	60433	3499	22W-24S	C6
400	JltT	60433	3499	22W-24S	C6
S Adella Av					
100	JLET	60433	3499	22W-24S	C5
Adelmann Rd					
-	LKPT	60441	3420	20W-19S	B2
Adelphi Av					
-	BHPK	60087	2421	12W-38N	B7
-	BHPK	60087	2479	12W-37N	B1
-	BHPK	60099	2421	12W-39N	B5
-	WKGN	60087	2421	12W-38N	B7
-	WKGN	60087	2479	12W-37N	B1
700	WKGN	60085	2479	12W-35N	B7
35800	WkgT	60085	2479	12W-35N	B5
35900	WkgT	60087	2479	12W-35N	B5
N Adelphi Av					
2200	WKGN	60087	2479	12W-36N	B4
2200	WkgT	60087	2479	12W-36N	B4
38200	BHPK	60087	2479	12W-38N	B1
39900	BHPK	60099	2421	12W-40N	B4
Adelphia Av					
10	LKFT	60044	2593	12W-28N	B5
10	LKFT	60045	2593	12W-28N	B6
400	ShdT	60044	2593	12W-29N	B5
600	LKBF	60044	2593	12W-29N	B4
Adesso Ln					
-	PnfT	60435	3417	27W-19S	B3
-	PnfT	60544	3417	27W-19S	B3
3100	JLET	60435	3417	27W-19S	B3
Adirondack Ct					
-	JLET	60421	3586	24W-28S	D7
Adirondack Dr					
1100	NHBK	60062	2756	11W-17N	D5
Adler Ct					
800	SMBG	60194	2858	26W-11N	A3
2300	LSLE	60532	3142	24W-5S	D3
Adler Dr					
100	LYVL	60048	2591	17W-30N	C2
Adler Ln					
1000	CLSM	60188	2968	25W-4N	A4
1300	ELGN	60120	2855	31W-11N	E3
Adler St					
700	JLET	60436	3498	24W-24S	E7
Admiral Ct					
700	RLKP	60073	2532	22W-34N	B1
1700	GNVW	60025	2810	9W-14N	B4
Admiral Dr					
100	HRVD	60033	2464	50W-37N	B1
N Admiral Dr					
2500	NCHI	60088	2593	11W-30N	D3
S Admiral Dr					
2100	NCHI	60088	2593	11W-29N	D3
Adobe Cir					
100	CPVL	60110	2748	33W-18N	C4
Adobe Ct					
600	CLSM	60188	2967	26W-3N	E6
Adobe Dr					
1000	AURA	60506	3137	38W-6S	A4
2700	JLET	60586	3415	32W-20S	C5
W Adobe Dr					
2100	ADSN	60101	2969	21W-4N	E3
16600	LKPT	60441	3420	20W-20S	B6
Adobe Rdg					
100	PltT	60124	2906	39W-9N	E1
Adria Ct					
8600	ODPK	60462	3346	10W-15S	A1
Adrian Ct					
300	VNHL	60061	2646	18W-25N	E5
Adrian St					
700	YKVL	60560	3333	43W-15S	B3
Adrienne Dr					
1000	SEGN	60177	2908	35W-9N	B1
S Adsit Rd					
13100	PlsT	60462	3345	13W-15S	B2
13100	PlsT	60464	3345	13W-15S	B2
Advantage Av					
16700	LktT	60403	3417	26W-20S	E4
16700	LktT	60435	3417	26W-20S	E4
Aec Dr					
-	WDDL	60191	2915	18W-7N	A4
Aegean Dr					
900	SMBG	60193	2912	24W-9N	D1
Aegina Ct					
10	TYPK	60477	3505	8W-23S	C3
Aegina Dr					
-	OMFD	60461	3507	3W-24S	A5
10	TYPK	60477	3505	8W-23S	B3
S Aero Ct					
23800	WldT	60585	3266	29W-14S	C6
Aero Dr					
10	NpvT	60564	3202	29W-9S	C4
200	NPVL	60564	3202	29W-9S	C4
S Aero Dr					
11900	WldT	60564	3266	29W-14S	C6
11900	WldT	60585	3266	29W-14S	C6
Aeronca Ct					
800	NLNX	60451	3501	18W-25S	A7
Affirmed Av					
500	OSWG	60543	3264	35W-12S	B2
Afton Cir					
1400	IVNS	60010	2751	24W-17N	C5
Afton Dr					
10	OswT	60538	3199	37W-10S	C6
10	OswT	60538	3200	36W-10S	A6
Afton Rd					
15200	MKHM	60428	3349	3W-18S	A7
Agatha Dr					
5600	McHT	60050	2472	29W-37N	C1
Agatite Av					
10000	SRPK	60176	2973	12W-5N	B1
W Agatite Av					
-	CHCG	60706	2974	10W-5N	A1
-	NRDG	60706	2974	10W-5N	A1
800	CHCG	60640	2921	1W-5N	E7
2100	CHCG	60625	2921	2W-5N	B7
2700	CHCG	60625	2920	3W-5N	E7
4500	CHCG	60630	2920	5W-5N	A7
5000	CHCG	60630	2919	6W-5N	D7
7000	HDHT	60706	2918	8W-5N	E7
7000	NRDG	60706	2918	8W-5N	D7
8400	CHCG	60656	2974	10W-5N	A1
8500	CHCG	60656	2973	11W-5N	E1
Agatite Ct					
9900	SRPK	60176	2973	12W-5N	B1
AG Atwater Dr					
-	AURA	60506	3137	37W-5S	C2
Agnes Av					
600	MDLN	60060	2646	18W-27N	E2
W Agnes Av					
1200	JLET	60435	3498	25W-22S	B2
Aherns Av					
300	BCHR	60401	3864	0W-37S	C3
S Ahlborn Dr					
400	PTON	60468	3861	9W-37S	A4
Ahlstrand Rd					
200	MltT	60148	3083	21W-2S	E4
500	MltT	60137	3083	22W-2S	B4
Ahmed Ct					
-	GLHT	60139	2969	23W-3N	A6
Aho Dr					
10	HNWD	60047	2646	19W-25N	B4
10	LGGV	60047	2646	19W-25N	B4
N Ahrens Av					
10	LMBD	60148	3026	18W-1N	E3
S Ahrens Av					
1000	LMBD	60148	3026	18W-0S	E7
1000	YkTp	60148	3026	18W-0S	E7
S Ahrens Ct					
200	LMBD	60148	3026	18W-0N	E4
Ahwahnee Ln					
200	LKFT	60045	2649	11W-26N	D3
N Ahwahnee Rd					
10	LKFT	60045	2649	11W-26N	D4
S Ahwahnee Rd					
10	LKFT	60045	2649	11W-26N	D4
Aida Ct					
-	HMWD	60430	3427	3W-21S	B7
Aiken Ct					
1200	WPHR	60096	2363	9W-41N	C7
Aileen Av					
10200	MKNA	60448	3503	13W-23S	B3
Ailsworth Ct					
3200	DRN	60561	3206	20W-9S	B4
Ailsworth Dr					
8500	DRN	60561	3206	20W-9S	A4
Aime Ln					
15800	WDWH	60031	2478	15W-37N	A2
15800	WDWH	60083	2477	15W-37N	E2
15800	WDWH	60083	2478	15W-37N	A2
Aimee Ct					
5400	OKFT	60452	3425	6W-19S	E1
Aimee Ln					
2300	SMBG	60194	2857	26W-10N	E5
Aimtree Pl					
800	SMBG	60194	2858	24W-10N	C4
Aine Dr					
19900	FftT	60423	3503	11W-24S	E4
19900	FftT	60448	3503	11W-23S	E4
19900	FKFT	60423	3503	11W-24S	E4
19900	FKFT	60423	3504	11W-24S	A4
Ainsdale Ct					
24300	WldT	60564	3266	30W-12S	B4
Ainsley Dr					
100	WCHI	60185	3022	30W-2N	C2
Ainsley Ln					
1600	LMBD	60148	3084	19W-1S	D2
1600	YkTp	60148	3084	19W-1S	D2
Ainsley St					
-	ANTH	60002	2416	23W-41N	E1
-	AntT	60002	2416	23W-41N	E1
Ainslie Ct					
100	WTMT	60559	3145	17W-6S	B5
Ainslie Dr					
100	WTMT	60559	3145	17W-6S	B5
Ainslie St					
9400	SRPK	60176	2917	11W-6N	C7
W Ainslie St					
800	CHCG	60640	2921	1W-6N	E6
2400	CHCG	60625	2921	3W-6N	A6
2700	CHCG	60625	2920	3W-6N	E6
3900	CHCG	60630	2920	5W-6N	A6
4800	CHCG	60630	2919	6W-6N	E6
7200	CHCG	60656	2918	9W-6N	C6
7200	HDHT	60656	2918	9W-6N	C6
7200	HDHT	60706	2918	9W-6N	C6
8600	NRDG	60706	2917	10W-6N	E6
8600	NRDG	60706	2918	10W-6N	A6
8700	CHCG	60706	2917	10W-6N	E6
Aintree Dr					
100	LslT	60540	3205	23W-8S	A1
Aintree Ln					
8700	BRRG	60527	3208	15W-10S	A4
Aintree Rd					
10	SCRL	60174	2964	34W-4N	D3
10	WYNE	60174	2964	34W-4N	D3
10	WYNE	60184	2964	34W-4N	D3
W Air Ln					
2400	WKGN	60087	2479	12W-38N	C1
Airdale Ct					
200	GNVW	60025	2810	10W-14N	A3
N Airlite St					
10	ELGN	60123	2853	36W-11N	E4
300	ELGN	60123	2854	36W-12N	A2
300	ElgT	60123	2854	36W-11N	A3
S Airlite St					
10	ELGN	60123	2853	36W-11N	E5
700	ElgT	60123	2853	36W-10N	E5
Air Mail Rd					
-	PvsT	60141	3088	10W-1S	A1
Airpark Dr					
1000	SRGV	60554	3134	45W-6S	C6
Airport Dr					
10	JLET	60431	3496	29W-24S	E6
10	TroT	60431	3496	29W-24S	E6
Airport Rd					
10	AURA	60542	3137	37W-4S	C2
10	DndT	60123	2801	33W-13N	A7
10	ELGN	60123	2800	34W-13N	E7
10	ELGN	60123	2801	33W-13N	A7
10	ElgT	60123	2801	33W-13N	A7
10	NARA	60542	3137	37W-4S	C2
10	NARA	60542	3138	35W-4S	B2
100	HRVD	60033	2464	50W-37N	A1
1500	RMVL	60446	3339	26W-17S	E7
1800	AURA	60506	3137	37W-4S	C2
1800	NARA	60506	3137	37W-4S	C2
18900	LktT	60441	3341	23W-18S	A7
18900	RMVL	60441	3341	23W-18S	A7
19100	RMVL	60441	3340	24W-18S	E7
19800	LktT	60441	3340	25W-18S	C7
19800	RMVL	60446	3340	25W-18S	C7
20500	LktT	60446	3340	25W-18S	C7
20500	RMVL	60544	3340	25W-18S	C7
20900	PnfT	60446	3339	27W-17S	D7
20900	PnfT	60544	3339	27W-17S	D7
21600	DhmT	60033	2464	50W-37N	A1
22000	DhmT	60033	2463	51W-37N	E1
22000	HRVD	60033	2463	51W-37N	D1
26200	AxST	60447	3672	32W-30S	C3
26200	CnhT	60410	3672	32W-30S	C3
Airport Rd CO-A22					
100	HRVD	60033	2464	50W-37N	A1
21600	DhmT	60033	2464	50W-37N	A1
22000	DhmT	60033	2463	51W-37N	D1
22000	HRVD	60033	2463	51W-37N	D1
W Airport Rd					
20900	PnfT	60446	3339	27W-17S	C7
20900	PnfT	60544	3339	27W-17S	C7
20900	RMVL	60446	3339	27W-17S	C7
20900	RMVL	60544	3339	27W-17S	C7
Airs Av					
-	SRGV	60554	3136	40W-7S	B7
Airway Ct					
1900	NLNX	60451	3590	16W-26S	A3
1900	NlxT	60451	3590	16W-26S	A3
Aitken Dr					
1300	BKBN	60015	2703	11W-22N	C5
Ajax St					
-	CLLK	60098	2638	39W-26N	B2
Akenside Rd					
10	RVSD	60546	3088	9W-3S	C4
S Akin Av					
10	JLET	60433	3499	23W-24S	B5
Akron Ct					
1900	SMBG	60193	2858	25W-9N	A7
Alabama Av					
2100	NCHI	60088	2593	11W-29N	C4
5500	CNHL	60514	3145	17W-6S	D4
5500	DGvT	60514	3145	17W-6S	D4
5500	WLBK	60514	3145	17W-6S	D4
5800	WLBK	60527	3145	17W-6S	D4
6700	DRN	60527	3145	17W-7S	D7
6700	DRN	60561	3145	17W-7S	D7
7900	DGvT	60527	3207	17W-9S	D3
Alabama Ct					
17900	ODPK	60467	3423	13W-21S	A6
Alabama Dr					
1000	EGVV	60007	2913	21W-8N	D3
Alabama Tr					
300	BmdT	60188	2968	26W-3N	A5
300	CLSM	60188	2968	26W-3N	A5
Aladdin Ct					
5200	JLET	60586	3496	30W-22S	B1
Alago Rd					
10	NpvT	60564	3202	28W-10S	E5
10	WldT	60564	3202	28W-10S	E5
Alaha Ln					
11800	FKFT	60423	3590	14W-26S	D3
Alamance Dr					
2300	WCHI	60185	2965	32W-4N	C4
Alamance Pl					
1600	DRGV	60516	3144	20W-7S	A7
Alameda Av					
15200	OKFT	60452	3347	7W-18S	C7
Alameda Ct					
2800	NPVL	60564	3202	29W-10S	C6
Alameda Dr					
10	CPVL	60110	2748	33W-18N	C4
1000	AURA	60506	3137	38W-6S	A5
Alamitos Dr					
-	RNPK	60443	3593	7W-27S	C4
Alamo Ct					
900	CLSM	60188	2968	25W-3N	A5
Alamo Dr					
3100	JLET	60435	3417	27W-21S	B7
Alamonte Dr					
8900	SPGV	60081	2413	31W-41N	D1
Alamosa Ct					
3700	JLET	60451	3500	19W-22S	E2
Alamosa Rd					
800	NPVL	60565	3203	27W-10S	B7
Alamosa St					
900	JLET	60451	3500	19W-22S	E2
900	NLNX	60451	3500	19W-22S	E2
Alan Ct					
1600	NPVL	60564	3202	28W-10S	E6
1600	NPVL	60564	3203	28W-10S	A6
2700	WKGN	60085	2479	12W-35N	C5
2700	WkgT	60085	2479	12W-35N	C5
Alan Dr					
10	ALGN	60102	2747	34W-19N	D2
10	DndT	60102	2747	34W-19N	D2
10	DndT	60118	2747	34W-19N	D2
400	NlxT	60451	3589	17W-25S	D1
Alan Rd					
10	NpvT	60564	3203	28W-10S	A5
10	WldT	60564	3203	28W-10S	A5
300	NPVL	60564	3203	28W-10S	A6
Alana Dr					
300	NLNX	60451	3501	18W-24S	A6
300	NlxT	60451	3501	18W-24S	A6
Alandale Cir					
2700	NPVL	60564	3202	28W-10S	E7
Alan Dale Ln					
-	BtlT	60560	3261	43W-13S	B5
2100	YKVL	60560	3261	43W-13S	B5
Alan Deathrage Dr					
1700	BGBK	60490	3267	27W-11S	D2
N Alann Dr					
800	JLET	60435	3498	26W-22S	A2
Alanna Ln					
400	LYWD	60411	3510	4E-25S	C7
W Alaska Av					
1900	NCHI	60088	2593	12W-30N	C2
Alaska Ct					
17900	ODPK	60467	3423	13W-21S	A6
Albany					
-	ALSP	60406	3276	3W-14S	E7
-	ALSP	60803	3276	3W-14S	E7
-	BLID	60406	3276	3W-14S	E7
Albany Av					
14500	LMNT	60439	3271	18W-14S	B6
15300	MKHM	60428	3349	3W-18S	A7
16600	HLCT	60428	3427	3W-19S	A3
16600	MKHM	60428	3427	3W-19S	A3
16700	HLCT	60429	3427	3W-20S	A3
N Albany Av					
600	CHCG	60622	3032	3W-0N	E3
800	CHCG	60612	3032	3W-1N	E2
2300	CHCG	60647	2976	3W-3N	E5
3200	CHCG	60618	2976	3W-4N	E3
4400	CHCG	60618	2920	3W-5N	E7
4400	CHCG	60625	2920	3W-5N	E7
6000	CHCG	60659	2920	3W-7N	D3
6300	CHCG	60645	2920	3W-7N	D3
7200	CHCG	60645	2866	3W-9N	E7
7500	EVTN	60202	2866	3W-9N	E7
S Albany Av					
-	ENGN	60652	3212	3W-10S	E4
10	CHCG	60612	3032	3W-0S	E5
1100	CHCG	60623	3032	3W-1S	E7
1600	CHCG	60623	3090	3W-1S	E1
3600	CHCG	60632	3090	3W-3S	E5
5100	CHCG	60632	3150	3W-6S	E3
7100	CHCG	60629	3150	3W-8S	E7
7600	CHCG	60652	3212	3W-8S	E1
8700	ENGN	60805	3212	3W-10S	E5
10200	CHCG	60655	3276	3W-11S	E1
10200	ENGN	60805	3276	3W-11S	E1
11200	MTPK	60655	3276	3W-13S	E3
11200	MTPK	60803	3276	3W-13S	E3
13600	RBBN	60472	3348	3W-16S	E3
14500	POSN	60469	3349	3W-17S	A5
14700	MKHM	60428	3349	3W-17S	A5
14700	POSN	60428	3349	3W-17S	A5
Albany Ct					
1400	SMBG	60193	2912	25W-8N	A2
1800	EGVV	60007	2913	22W-9N	C1
2400	AURA	60503	3201	32W-10S	C5
5000	JLET	60586	3496	30W-22S	C2
9400	ODPK	60467	3423	12W-19S	D1
N Albany Dr					
1500	CHCG	60622	3032	3W-1N	E1
1500	CHCG	60647	3032	3W-1N	E1
Albany Ln					
300	VNHL	60061	2647	16W-25N	C5
600	DSPN	60016	2808	14W-12N	C7
800	DRN	60561	3145	17W-7S	C6
Albany St					
-	WMTN	60481	3853	27W-38S	D6
W Albany St					
3900	MHRY	60050	2585	33W-30N	A1

STREET Block	City	ZIP	Map#	CGS	Grid
Albermarle Ct					
1600	NPVL	60563	3140	29W-5S	D3
Alberosky Ln					
-	BTVA	60510	3077	38W-1S	B2
-	BtvT	60510	3077	38W-1S	B2
Albert Av					
500	JLET	60433	3499	23W-24S	B5
Albert Dr					
200	VNHL	60061	2647	17W-25N	B5
500	DndT	60118	2801	32W-14N	C5
2900	MHRY	60050	2470	34W-34N	C7
5600	OKFT	60452	3347	7W-18S	D7
16300	LktT	60441	3418	25W-19S	B3
W Albert Dr					
1100	RMVL	60446	3340	25W-15S	B3
Albert Ln					
1800	WslT	60481	3943	27W-40S	D3
3700	LGGV	60047	2700	20W-21N	A5
W Albert Rd					
23200	CnhT	60410	3584	30W-28S	C6
Albert St					
6400	MNGV	60053	2865	8W-11N	A2
N Albert St					
10	MPPT	60056	2808	14W-13N	B7
S Albert St					
10	MPPT	60056	2808	15W-12N	B7
200	MPPT	60056	2862	15W-12N	B1
W Albert St					
600	EMHT	60126	3027	17W-1N	C3
600	VLPK	60126	3027	17W-1N	B3
600	VLPK	60181	3027	17W-1N	B3
Albert Ter					
200	WLNG	60090	2755	15W-17N	A5
N Alberta Av					
36900	LKVL	60046	2474	24W-36N	B3
36900	LkvT	60046	2474	24W-36N	B3
Alberta Ct					
1300	GLHT	60139	2969	22W-2N	C7
S Alberta Ct					
16300	HMGN	60491	3421	17W-19S	C2
Albert Dottavio Dr					
1200	JLET	60431	3497	28W-22S	B2
1200	JLET	60435	3497	28W-22S	B2
Albert Einstein Dr					
300	WNVL	60555	3080	29W-2S	D4
Albert Hall Ct					
1700	NPVL	60564	3266	28W-11S	E2
Albin Ter					
5800	BKLY	60163	3028	14W-0N	C4
Albion Av					
10	CHCG	60068	2918	10W-8N	B2
10	CHCG	60631	2918	10W-8N	B2
10	PKRG	60068	2918	10W-8N	B2
10	ROSL	60172	2913	23W-8N	A3
10	SmbT	60172	2913	23W-8N	A3
200	ROSL	60172	2912	24W-8N	E3
200	SmbT	60172	2912	24W-8N	E3
500	SMBG	60172	2912	24W-8N	E3
500	SMBG	60193	2912	24W-8N	D3
1300	PKRG	60068	2917	11W-8N	E2
W Albion Av					
1000	CHCG	60626	2921	1W-8N	D2
1900	CHCG	60645	2921	2W-8N	B2
2600	CHCG	60645	2920	3W-8N	E2
3100	LNWD	60645	2920	3W-8N	D2
3300	LNWD	60712	2920	4W-8N	C2
4900	LNWD	60712	2919	6W-8N	E2
6500	CHCG	60631	2919	8W-8N	A2
6500	CHCG	60714	2919	8W-8N	A2
6500	NLES	60631	2919	8W-8N	A2
6500	NLES	60714	2919	8W-8N	A2
6900	NLES	60631	2918	8W-8N	D2
7200	CHCG	60631	2918	9W-8N	D2
7200	CHCG	60714	2918	9W-8N	D2
7200	NLES	60714	2918	9W-8N	D2
Albion Ln					
1100	MDLN	60060	2590	19W-27N	B7
W Albion Ln					
600	ANHT	60004	2807	15W-14N	E5
600	MPPT	60004	2807	16W-14N	E5
600	MPPT	60056	2807	16W-14N	E5
Albrecht Dr					
10	LKBF	60044	2593	12W-28N	B6
900	LKBF	60045	2593	12W-28N	B6
900	LKFT	60044	2593	12W-28N	B6
900	LKFT	60045	2593	12W-28N	B6
Albrecht Rd					
-	GfnT	60014	2693	38W-23N	A2
-	GfnT	60156	2693	38W-23N	A2
-	LIHL	60156	2693	38W-23N	A2
-	LKWD	60014	2693	38W-23N	A2
9900	LIHL	60156	2692	38W-23N	D3
Albright Ct					
300	VNHL	60061	2647	17W-25N	B5
400	WNVL	60555	3080	29W-3S	D6
1800	WHTN	60187	3083	23W-3S	A5
15000	LKPT	60441	3421	18W-20S	A4
Albright Dr					
15000	LKPT	60441	3421	18W-20S	A4
Albright Ln					
2200	WHTN	60187	3083	23W-3S	A5
Albright Rd					
10	MTGY	60543	3199	37W-10S	B5
1800	MTGY	60538	3199	37W-9S	C4
Albright St					
500	WnfT	60555	3080	29W-3S	C6
500	WNVL	60555	3080	29W-3S	C6
600	WNVL	60563	3080	29W-3S	C6
Alcester Cir					
400	BGBK	60440	3205	22W-10S	D6
Alchester Dr					
500	WHTN	60187	3082	24W-1S	D2
Alcoa Av					
800	LydT	60164	2972	13W-3N	D5
Alcoa Ln					
400	HFET	60169	2858	24W-11N	D3
700	SMBG	60194	2858	24W-11N	D3
Alcott Ct					
100	ELGN	60120	2855	31W-11N	E3
Alcott Ln					
500	BGBK	60440	3268	24W-12S	E3
Alden Av					
-	BtlT	60560	3262	40W-12S	B4
Alden Cir					
1800	AURA	60504	3201	33W-9S	A3
Alden Ct					
300	CHHT	60411	3595	2W-26S	D2
900	DRFD	60015	2703	11W-21N	D7
Alden Dr					
2300	JLET	60586	3415	33W-21S	B6
E Alden Dr					
10	ADSN	60101	2971	18W-3N	A5
Alden Ln					
10	LKFT	60045	2593	11W-27N	E7
300	SMBG	60194	2858	24W-11N	D4
900	BFGV	60089	2701	17W-21N	A6
2200	HRPK	60133	2911	27W-8N	C3
2800	DSPN	60018	2917	12W-8N	B2
8300	DRN	60561	3206	20W-9S	A4
Alden Rd					
8300	WRLK	60097	2469	37W-35N	B5
9600	AdnT	60033	2349	45W-41N	A7
Alden Rd CO-V12					
9600	AdnT	60033	2349	45W-41N	A7
Alder Ct					
100	RGMW	60008	2805	21W-13N	D5
200	SMBG	60193	2858	24W-10N	E6
2300	AURA	60504	3201	32W-9S	B3
5100	GRNE	60031	2478	15W-35N	A5
N Alder Ct					
3700	HFET	60192	2804	25W-14N	A3
Alder Dr					
100	NARA	60542	3137	37W-4S	D2
200	AURA	60542	3137	37W-4S	D2
400	WLNG	60090	2755	13W-17N	D5
N Alder Dr					
3600	HFET	60192	2804	25W-14N	A3
Alder Dr W					
1800	HFET	60192	2804	25W-14N	A4
Alder Ln					
-	BRLT	60120	2910	30W-7N	B4
300	GNEN	60137	3083	23W-1S	A2
1000	NPVL	60540	3203	27W-8S	C1
1100	BRLT	60103	2910	30W-7N	B4
E Alder Ln					
900	MPPT	60056	2808	14W-14N	C4
Alder Pl					
1500	GNVW	60025	2810	8W-14N	E5
Alderberry Ln					
10	BNHL	60010	2695	30W-21N	E5
Alderman Av					
800	PTHT	60070	2808	14W-15N	C3
1000	WLNG	60070	2808	13W-15N	D3
1000	WLNG	60090	2808	13W-15N	D3
1200	MPPT	60056	2808	13W-15N	D3
Alderman Ln					
200	PTHT	60070	2808	14W-15N	D3
200	WLNG	60070	2808	14W-15N	D3
200	WLNG	60090	2808	14W-15N	D3
Aldersyde Rd					
5000	OKFT	60452	3426	6W-20S	A3
5100	OKFT	60452	3425	6W-20S	E3
Alderwood Ln					
100	AURA	60504	3201	32W-8S	D1
Aldgate Ct					
1400	WLNG	60090	2754	16W-18N	D4
N Aldine Av					
10	PKRG	60068	2917	11W-8N	E1
200	PKRG	60068	2863	11W-9N	E7
S Aldine Av					
800	PKRG	60068	2917	11W-8N	E2
W Aldine Av					
400	CHCG	60657	2978	0W-4N	A3
600	CHCG	60657	2977	1W-4N	E3
Aldine Rd					
10	LKZH	60047	2698	24W-23N	D1
N Aldine St					
400	ELGN	60123	2854	35W-12N	C3
S Aldine St					
10	ELGN	60123	2854	35W-10N	C5
Aldis Dr					
100	DndT	60118	2801	33W-16N	B2
100	EDND	60118	2801	33W-16N	B2
Aldon Ct E					
10	OswT	60538	3199	37W-10S	C6
Aldon Ct W					
10	OswT	60538	3199	37W-10S	C6
Aldon Rd					
10	OswT	60538	3199	37W-10S	D6
Aldrich Dr					
2100	JLET	60586	3416	29W-21S	D6
Aldrich Pl					
2000	DRGV	60516	3144	21W-7S	A6
W Aldridge Av					
10	PLTN	60067	2805	21W-14N	E3
10	RGMW	60008	2805	21W-14N	E3
10	RGMW	60067	2805	21W-14N	E3
Aldridge Ct					
1700	AURA	60503	3201	32W-10S	D5
Aldridge Dr					
10300	HTLY	60142	2692	39W-21N	C5
S Aldridge Ln					
700	RDLK	60073	2532	23W-32N	A5
W Aldridge Ln					
10	RDLK	60073	2532	23W-32N	A5
Aldrin Av					
200	BTVA	60510	3077	36W-0S	E1
Aldrin Tr					
1200	EGVV	60007	2914	21W-8N	A2
1300	EGVV	60007	2913	21W-8N	E2
Aldwych Dr					
14100	ODPK	60462	3346	9W-16S	C4
W Alec St					
1100	ANHT	60004	2753	18W-16N	E6
Alemeda Ln					
1500	MDLN	60060	2590	19W-29N	C4
Alena Dr					
600	WCHI	60185	3022	28W-1N	E3
600	WnfT	60185	3022	28W-1N	E3
Alene Dr					
1200	JLET	60586	3496	31W-22S	A2
Alessandra Dr					
21100	MTSN	60443	3593	7W-25S	D1
Alessio Dr					
100	JLET	60433	3587	23W-25S	A1
100	JltT	60433	3587	23W-25S	A1
Aleut Tr					
400	CLSM	60188	2967	26W-3N	E5
Alex Ct					
10	OSWG	60543	3200	34W-10S	D7
Alex Ln					
4200	NndT	60014	2641	33W-26N	A2
Alexander Av					
1100	SMWD	60107	2911	28W-9N	B1
W Alexander Av					
26100	AntT	60002	2415	26W-39N	D5
W Alexander Blvd					
200	EMHT	60126	3027	16W-1N	D2
600	VLPK	60126	3027	17W-1N	B2
600	VLPK	60181	3027	17W-1N	B2
Alexander Cir					
10	RMVL	60446	3340	24W-15S	E1
10	RMVL	60446	3341	23W-15S	A1
Alexander Cres					
2900	FSMR	60422	3507	3W-23S	A4
Alexander Ct					
10	BGBK	60490	3339	28W-15S	A1
100	OSWG	60543	3263	36W-11S	E1
500	IVNS	60010	2751	25W-16N	A6
1000	CRY	60013	2641	32W-24N	A6
1100	SMWD	60107	2911	28W-9N	B1
1400	WKGN	60085	2480	10W-35N	B6
Alexander Dr					
10	GnvT	60134	3018	38W-0N	E6
10	GnvT	60134	3019	38W-0N	A6
100	BbyT	60134	3018	39W-0N	E6
1200	DGvT	60439	3270	20W-12S	C3
1300	BGBK	60490	3339	28W-15S	A1
2000	BTVA	60510	3078	34W-3S	D5
Alexander Pl					
1200	SMWD	60107	2911	28W-9N	B1
5200	OKLN	60453	3211	6W-10S	D4
Alexander St					
2400	HMWD	60430	3507	3W-22S	B1
20700	OMFD	60461	3507	3W-25S	B6
W Alexander St					
200	CHCG	60616	3092	0W-2S	B2
Alexander Ter					
2300	HMWD	60430	3507	2W-22S	C1
Alexandra Blvd					
-	AlqT	60014	2693	36W-23N	E2
600	CLLK	60014	2693	37W-23N	C2
Alexandra Ct					
-	NHBK	60062	2756	11W-16N	D7
-	UNON	60180	2635	46W-24N	D6
10	MDLN	60060	2646	19W-27N	C1
200	NARA	60542	3077	38W-4S	B7
900	SMBG	60193	2912	24W-8N	C2
4800	RGMW	60008	2805	21W-14N	E4
4800	RGMW	60067	2805	21W-14N	E4
N Alexandra Ct					
37100	WmT	60046	2476	18W-37N	E2
Alexandra Ln					
-	UNON	60180	2635	46W-24N	C6
Alexandra Wy					
100	CLSM	60188	3024	25W-1N	B2
Alexandria Ct					
1200	GNVA	60134	3020	34W-1N	E3
E Alexandria Ct					
500	ITSC	60143	2914	19W-7N	C5
Alexandria Dr					
10	VNHL	60061	2647	17W-25N	C6
500	NPVL	60565	3204	25W-10S	B6
1700	JLET	60436	3585	27W-26S	D3
5400	LIHL	60156	2692	38W-21N	D5
8000	TYPK	60477	3424	10W-19S	C2
Alexandria Ln					
1700	AURA	60504	3201	33W-8S	A3
5400	CPVL	60110	2747	36W-17N	B6
W Alexandria Ln					
11200	WSTR	60154	3086	14W-2S	D3
W Alexandria St					
900	ANHT	60004	2753	18W-16N	E7
Alexia Ct					
300	WLNG	60090	2755	14W-17N	D4
Alexian Wy					
600	EGVV	60007	2914	19W-8N	B1
Alexis Ct					
300	MaiT	60025	2864	9W-12N	B1
1600	LKFT	60045	2703	12W-23N	A1
18500	HLCT	60429	3506	4W-22S	E1
Alexis Ln					
11100	ODPK	60467	3344	13W-17S	E4
Alexis St					
-	PLNO	60545	3260	45W-13S	C6
Alfalfa Ln					
-	NPVL	60564	3266	29W-12S	D2
Alfini Dr					
800	DSPN	60016	2862	14W-10N	D5
Alft Ln					
2400	ELGN	60123	2799	37W-14N	D5
2400	ELGN	60124	2799	37W-14N	D5
2500	DndT	60124	2799	37W-14N	D5
Alfred Av					
-	ELGN	60123	2854	35W-10N	C6
N Alfred Av					
300	ELGN	60123	2854	35W-12N	C3
S Alfred Av					
10	ELGN	60123	2854	35W-11N	C5
Alfred Ct					
10	VNHL	60061	2647	17W-24N	A6
Alger St					
1500	DSPN	60018	2917	12W-8N	A2
1500	RSMT	60018	2917	12W-8N	A2
W Algoma Rd					
8600	PSPK	60464	3274	10W-14S	A7
Algona Av					
500	ELGN	60120	2855	33W-12N	A2
Algonquin Av					
700	BNVL	60106	2915	16W-5N	D7
N Algonquin Av					
6800	CHCG	60646	2919	6W-8N	D2
Algonquin Ct					
200	BGBK	60440	3268	24W-11S	E1
Algonquin Dr					
10	IHPK	60525	3146	14W-7S	E6
1100	ELGN	60120	2855	32W-12N	C1
1200	ELGN	60120	2801	32W-12N	C7
1400	ROSL	60172	2913	22W-8N	C2
1400	ROSL	60193	2913	22W-8N	C2
1400	SMBG	60193	2913	22W-8N	C2
1400	SmbT	60193	2913	22W-8N	C2
7100	MchT	60097	2469	36W-36N	D3
Algonquin Pkwy					
2200	ANHT	60005	2860	19W-12N	C1
2200	ANHT	60008	2860	19W-12N	C1
2300	RGMW	60008	2860	19W-12N	C1
Algonquin Rd					
-	HFET	60010	2804	25W-14N	A3
-	HFET	60192	2804	25W-14N	A3
-	PKRG	60068	2863	12W-10N	C5
-	SBTN	60010	2804	25W-14N	A3
-	SBTN	60192	2804	25W-14N	A3
10	AlqT	60010	2695	30W-22N	E4
10	AlqT	60021	2695	31W-22N	D4
10	BNHL	60010	2695	30W-22N	E4
10	BNHL	60010	2750	28W-16N	A7
10	BNHL	60010	2803	26W-15N	C2
10	BNHL	60021	2695	31W-22N	D4
10	BrnT	60010	2750	27W-16N	A7
10	BrnT	60010	2803	26W-15N	C2
10	CNHL	60514	3145	17W-5S	B1
10	SBTN	60010	2803	26W-15N	C2
100	ALGN	60102	2748	32W-19N	C2
100	ALGN	60110	2748	32W-19N	C2
100	BNHL	60010	2748	32W-19N	C2
100	BNHL	60010	2749	30W-17N	A5
100	BNHL	60102	2748	32W-19N	C2
100	BNHL	60110	2748	32W-19N	C2
200	AlqT	60010	2696	30W-22N	A4
200	AlqT	60021	2696	30W-22N	A4
200	AlqT	60102	2695	31W-22N	C4
200	BNHL	60010	2696	30W-22N	A4
200	BNHL	60021	2696	30W-22N	A4
200	CHCG	60068	2863	12W-10N	C5
200	DSPN	60016	2863	12W-10N	C5
400	FRGV	60021	2696	30W-22N	A4
1500	BNHL	60102	2695	31W-22N	D4
2200	ANHT	60005	2860	19W-12N	D1
2200	ANHT	60008	2860	19W-12N	D1
2200	RGMW	60005	2860	19W-12N	D1
2200	RGMW	60008	2860	19W-12N	C1
3900	RGMW	60008	2806	21W-12N	A7
9100	ALGN	60102	2693	38W-21N	A6
9100	GfnT	60102	2693	38W-21N	A6
9400	ALGN	60102	2692	38W-21N	E6
9400	GfnT	60102	2692	38W-21N	E6
9400	LIHL	60156	2692	39W-21N	D6
10000	GfnT	60142	2692	39W-21N	C6
10000	GfnT	60156	2692	39W-21N	C6
11100	HTLY	60142	2692	40W-21N	B6
33200	WrnT	60030	2534	18W-33N	A3
Algonquin Rd CO-A48					
9100	ALGN	60102	2693	38W-21N	A6
9100	GfnT	60102	2693	38W-21N	A6
9400	ALGN	60102	2692	38W-21N	E6
9400	GfnT	60102	2692	38W-21N	E6
9400	LIHL	60156	2692	39W-21N	D6
10000	GfnT	60142	2692	39W-21N	C6
10000	GfnT	60156	2692	39W-21N	C6
10000	HTLY	60142	2692	39W-21N	C6
Algonquin Rd SR-62					
-	HFET	60010	2804	25W-14N	A3
-	HFET	60192	2804	25W-14N	A3
-	RGMW	60008	2806	20W-12N	A7
-	SBTN	60010	2804	25W-14N	A3
-	SBTN	60192	2804	25W-14N	A3
10	BNHL	60010	2750	28W-16N	A7
10	BNHL	60010	2803	26W-15N	C2
10	BrnT	60010	2750	27W-16N	A7
10	BrnT	60010	2803	26W-15N	C2
10	SBTN	60010	2803	26W-15N	C2
100	ALGN	60102	2748	32W-19N	C2
100	ALGN	60110	2748	32W-19N	C2
100	BNHL	60010	2748	32W-19N	C2
100	BNHL	60010	2749	30W-17N	A5
100	BNHL	60102	2748	32W-19N	C2
100	BNHL	60110	2748	32W-19N	C2
2200	ANHT	60005	2860	19W-12N	D1
2200	ANHT	60008	2860	19W-12N	D1
2200	RGMW	60005	2860	19W-12N	D1
2200	RGMW	60008	2860	19W-12N	C1
Algonquin Rd SR-68					
100	BNHL	60010	2750	28W-16N	A7
100	BrnT	60010	2750	27W-16N	A7
E Algonquin Rd					
-	RGMW	60067	2806	20W-12N	A7
10	ALGN	60102	2694	33W-20N	E7
10	ANHT	60005	2861	17W-11N	B3
10	DSPN	60016	2862	14W-10N	C5
10	DSPN	60018	2862	14W-10N	C5
200	PLTN	60067	2805	21W-13N	C6
200	PltT	60173	2805	21W-13N	C6
200	SMBG	60173	2805	21W-13N	C6
800	ALGN	60102	2695	33W-20N	A7
1000	EGvT	60005	2861	16W-10N	D5
1000	EGvT	60056	2861	16W-10N	D5
1200	DSPN	60016	2863	12W-10N	B5
1200	DSPN	60018	2863	13W-10N	A5
1500	MPPT	60005	2861	16W-10N	E5
1500	PltT	60067	2805	20W-13N	E7
1500	SMBG	60067	2805	20W-13N	E7
1600	MPPT	60056	2861	16W-10N	E5
1700	SMBG	60067	2806	21W-12N	A7
1700	SMBG	60173	2806	21W-12N	A7
1900	ALGN	60102	2748	32W-20N	B1
1900	AlqT	60102	2748	32W-20N	B1
2000	CHCG	60068	2863	12W-10N	C5
2000	RGMW	60008	2806	21W-12N	A7
2000	RGMW	60173	2806	21W-12N	A7
2000	SMBG	60008	2806	21W-12N	A7
2200	ALGN	60110	2748	33W-19N	C2
2200	BNHL	60010	2748	33W-19N	C2
2200	BNHL	60102	2748	33W-19N	C2
2200	BNHL	60110	2748	33W-19N	C2
E Algonquin Rd SR-62					
-	RGMW	60067	2806	20W-12N	A7
10	ALGN	60102	2694	33W-20N	E7
10	ANHT	60005	2861	17W-11N	A3
200	PLTN	60067	2805	21W-13N	C6
200	PltT	60173	2805	21W-13N	C6
200	SMBG	60173	2805	21W-13N	C6
800	ALGN	60102	2695	33W-20N	A7
1000	EGvT	60005	2861	16W-10N	D5
1000	EGvT	60056	2861	16W-10N	D5
1500	MPPT	60005	2861	16W-10N	E5
1500	PltT	60067	2805	20W-13N	E7
1500	SMBG	60067	2805	20W-13N	E7
1600	MPPT	60056	2861	16W-10N	E5
1700	SMBG	60067	2806	21W-12N	A7
1700	SMBG	60173	2806	21W-12N	A7
1900	ALGN	60102	2748	32W-20N	B1
1900	AlqT	60102	2748	32W-20N	B1
2000	RGMW	60008	2806	21W-12N	A7
2000	RGMW	60173	2806	21W-12N	A7
2000	SMBG	60008	2806	21W-12N	A7
2200	ALGN	60110	2748	33W-19N	C2
2200	BNHL	60010	2748	33W-19N	C2
2200	BNHL	60102	2748	33W-19N	C2
2200	BNHL	60110	2748	33W-19N	C2
S Algonquin Rd					
12300	PSPK	60464	3274	10W-14S	B6
W Algonquin Rd					
10	ALGN	60102	2694	34W-21N	B5
10	ANHT	60005	2861	18W-11N	A3
10	DSPN	60016	2862	15W-10N	B5
10	DSPN	60018	2862	15W-10N	B5
300	DSPN	60016	2861	16W-10N	E5
300	DSPN	60018	2861	16W-10N	E5
300	MPPT	60016	2861	16W-10N	E5
300	MPPT	60018	2861	16W-10N	E5
400	ANHT	60005	2860	19W-12N	D1
400	ANHT	60008	2860	19W-12N	D1
500	EGvT	60056	2861	16W-10N	E5
700	HFET	60067	2804	23W-14N	E4
700	HFET	60192	2804	24W-14N	C4
700	PltT	60067	2804	23W-14N	E4
700	PltT	60192	2804	23W-14N	E4
700	PltT	60195	2804	23W-14N	E4
700	RGMW	60008	2860	19W-12N	D1
1000	RGMW	60005	2860	19W-12N	D1
1100	ALGN	60156	2694	35W-21N	B5
1100	LIHL	60102	2694	34W-21N	C6
1100	LIHL	60156	2694	35W-21N	B5
1100	PLTN	60067	2805	22W-13N	B6
1100	PltT	60173	2805	22W-13N	B6
1100	SMBG	60173	2805	22W-13N	B6
1300	SBTN	60010	2804	24W-14N	C4
1300	SBTN	60192	2804	24W-14N	C4
1400	HFET	60010	2804	24W-14N	C4
1400	PltT	60067	2805	22W-13N	A5
1400	PltT	60195	2805	22W-13N	A5
1500	EGvT	60005	2861	16W-10N	D4
1500	MPPT	60056	2861	17W-10N	C4
1600	IVNS	60067	2804	23W-14N	E5
1600	IVNS	60067	2805	22W-13N	A5
1600	IVNS	60195	2804	23W-14N	E5
1700	ANHT	60056	2861	17W-10N	C4
1700	MPPT	60005	2861	17W-10N	C4
1800	HFET	60195	2804	23W-14N	E4
2300	ALGN	60102	2693	37W-21N	B6
2300	LIHL	60102	2693	37W-21N	B6
2300	LIHL	60156	2693	37W-21N	B6
2500	ALGN	60156	2693	36W-21N	D6
3700	GfnT	60156	2693	37W-21N	B6
3900	GfnT	60102	2693	37W-21N	B6
W Algonquin Rd CO-A48					
1100	ALGN	60102	2694	35W-21N	B5
1100	ALGN	60156	2694	35W-21N	B5
1100	LIHL	60102	2694	34W-21N	C6
1100	LIHL	60156	2694	35W-21N	B5
2500	ALGN	60102	2693	37W-21N	B6
2500	ALGN	60156	2693	36W-21N	D6
2500	LIHL	60102	2693	37W-21N	B6
2500	LIHL	60156	2693	37W-21N	B6
3700	GfnT	60156	2693	37W-21N	B6
W Algonquin Rd CO-V32					
400	ALGN	60102	2694	33W-20N	D7
1100	LIHL	60156	2694	34W-21N	C6
W Algonquin Rd SR-62					
10	ALGN	60102	2694	33W-20N	D7
10	ANHT	60005	2861	18W-11N	A3
300	DSPN	60016	2861	16W-10N	E5
300	DSPN	60018	2861	16W-10N	E5
300	MPPT	60016	2861	16W-10N	E5
300	MPPT	60018	2861	16W-10N	E5
400	ANHT	60005	2860	19W-12N	D1
400	ANHT	60008	2860	19W-12N	D1
500	EGvT	60056	2861	16W-10N	E5
700	HFET	60067	2804	23W-14N	E4
700	HFET	60192	2804	24W-14N	C4
700	PltT	60067	2804	23W-14N	E4
700	PltT	60192	2804	23W-14N	E4
700	PltT	60195	2804	23W-14N	E4
700	RGMW	60008	2860	19W-12N	D1
1000	RGMW	60005	2860	19W-12N	D1
1100	PLTN	60067	2805	22W-13N	B6
1100	PltT	60173	2805	22W-13N	B6
1100	SMBG	60173	2805	22W-13N	B6
1300	SBTN	60010	2804	24W-14N	C4
1300	SBTN	60192	2804	24W-14N	C4
1400	HFET	60010	2804	24W-14N	C4
1400	PltT	60067	2805	22W-13N	A5
1400	PltT	60195	2805	22W-13N	A5
1500	EGvT	60005	2861	16W-10N	D4
1500	MPPT	60056	2861	17W-10N	C4
1600	IVNS	60067	2804	23W-14N	E5
1600	IVNS	60067	2805	22W-13N	A5
1600	IVNS	60195	2804	23W-14N	E5
1700	ANHT	60056	2861	17W-10N	C4
1700	MPPT	60005	2861	17W-10N	C4
1800	HFET	60195	2804	23W-14N	E4
Algonquin St					
100	PKFT	60466	3595	2W-26S	C2
200	JLET	60432	3499	21W-23S	E4
200	JltT	60432	3499	21W-23S	E4
Algonquin Tr					
-	ANHT	60005	2861	17W-11N	C4
-	ANHT	60056	2861	17W-11N	C4
-	MPPT	60056	2861	17W-11N	C4
Alhambra Ln					
600	HFET	60169	2859	22W-11N	B4
S Alice Av					
14500	BNHM	60633	3352	3E-16S	A4
14500	CTCY	60409	3352	3E-16S	A4
14500	CTCY	60633	3352	3E-16S	A4
Alice Ct					
300	VNHL	60061	2647	17W-25N	B5
600	ELGN	60123	2853	36W-12N	E2
900	SCRL	60174	3020	36W-2N	A1
5400	JLET	60586	3496	30W-22S	B2
9800	GGnT	60423	3591	12W-28S	D7
10000	OKLN	60453	3211	6W-11S	D7
10000	OKLN	60453	3275	6W-11S	D1
Alice Dr					
400	NHBK	60062	2756	11W-18N	E4
23600	GGnT	60423	3591	12W-28S	D7
Alice Ln					
10	ALGN	60102	2748	33W-20N	A1
10	CbaT	60010	2697	27W-23N	A1
10	LKBN	60010	2697	27W-23N	A1
17900	ODPK	60467	3423	13W-21S	B7
N Alice Ln					
36800	LkvT	60046	2475	21W-36N	D3
W Alice Ln					
24000	NPVL	60564	3266	30W-12S	C2
24000	WldT	60564	3266	30W-12S	C2
Alice Pl					
300	NHFD	60093	2811	7W-15N	C2
500	ELGN	60123	2853	36W-12N	E2
Alice St					
200	WLNG	60090	2755	14W-16N	B6
700	BlmT	60411	3508	0W-23S	B4
700	CHHT	60411	3508	0W-23S	B4
S Alice St					
5500	HMND	46320	3352		E7
Alicia Ct					
21000	LktT	60441	3418	26W-19S	A2
Alicia Dr					
300	CRY	60013	2696	30W-23N	A1
Alida Av					
-	RBBN	60472	3348	4W-16S	D3
Alida Dr					
500	CRY	60013	2695	31W-23N	C1
Alima Ter					
500	ANTH	60002	2357	23W-42N	D5
1100	BKFD	60513	3087	11W-2S	D4
1100	LGPK	60513	3087	11W-2S	D4
1100	LGPK	60525	3087	11W-2S	D4
1500	PvsT	60525	3087	11W-2S	D4
Alisha Ln					
1500	RMVL	60446	3339	26W-17S	E5
Alison Dr					
1500	ELGN	60123	2854	35W-11N	A4
E Alison Dr					
1500	ANHT	60004	2806	19W-16N	D1
1500	PLTN	60074	2806	19W-16N	D1
W Alison Dr					
25300	PNFD	60586	3415	31W-20S	E5
Alison Ln					
700	CLSM	60188	2967	26W-3N	E6
1200	DRN	60561	3145	18W-7S	B7
2700	WLMT	60091	2812	5W-13N	A6
Alison Tr					
20000	MKNA	60448	3502	15W-24S	B5
20000	MKNA	60451	3502	15W-24S	B5

STREET Block	City	ZIP	Map#	CGS	Grid
Alison Tr					
20000	NlxT	60451	3502	15W-24S	C5
Alissa Ct					
16000	HMGN	60491	3421	17W-19S	D2
Allaire Av					
900	AURA	60506	3199	37W-8S	D2
Allan Dr					
1400	EGVV	60007	2915	17W-7N	B4
1400	EGVV	60191	2915	17W-7N	B4
1400	WDDL	60007	2915	17W-7N	B4
1400	WDDL	60191	2915	17W-7N	B4
6100	WDRG	60517	3143	21W-6S	D5
Allan Ln					
10	CTCY	60409	3351	2E-16S	C4
Allanson Ct					
600	MDLN	60060	2646	18W-26N	E2
Allanson Rd					
200	MDLN	60060	2646	18W-27N	E2
900	MDLN	60060	2647	18W-27N	A2
900	VNHL	60060	2647	18W-27N	A2
1300	VNHL	60061	2647	17W-27N	B2
Allcott Ct					
1800	SMBG	60193	2912	25W-9N	A1
Allegany Dr					
2200	NPVL	60565	3204	25W-10S	B5
W Alleghany Dr					
900	ANHT	60004	2753	18W-16N	E6
Alleghany Ln					
1200	NHBK	60062	2756	11W-17N	E5
Alleghany Rd					
500	GYLK	60030	2532	21W-33N	D2
N Alleghany Rd					
31000	FmtT	60030	2589	21W-30N	D1
31000	RLKP	60030	2589	21W-30N	D1
31200	FmtT	60030	2532	21W-31N	D7
31200	GYLK	60030	2532	21W-31N	D7
31200	RLKP	60030	2532	21W-31N	D7
31800	AvnT	60030	2532	21W-31N	D7
N Alleghany Rd CO-V68					
31000	FmtT	60030	2589	21W-30N	D1
31000	RLKP	60030	2589	21W-30N	D1
31200	FmtT	60030	2532	21W-31N	D7
31200	GYLK	60030	2532	21W-31N	D7
31200	RLKP	60030	2532	21W-31N	D7
31800	AvnT	60030	2532	21W-31N	D7
S Alleghany Rd					
100	AvnT	60030	2532	21W-32N	D5
100	GYLK	60030	2532	21W-32N	D5
S Alleghany Rd CO-V68					
200	AvnT	60030	2532	21W-32N	D5
200	GYLK	60030	2532	21W-32N	D5
Allegheny Ct					
10	BGBK	60440	3205	23W-11S	A7
10	HnrT	60107	2856	30W-10N	B6
10	PKFT	60466	3595	2W-26S	D2
700	CLSM	60188	2967	27W-2N	C7
10600	HTLY	60142	2692	39W-21N	C6
Allegheny St					
200	BlmT	60466	3595	2W-26S	D2
200	PKFT	60466	3595	2W-26S	D2
Allegheny Wy					
-	LKMR	60041	2530	28W-32N	A5
-	LKMR	60051	2530	28W-32N	A5
Allegheny Pass					
10600	HTLY	60142	2692	39W-21N	B6
Allegre Cir					
2100	NPVL	60563	3140	30W-5S	B4
Allegro Ln					
200	CLSM	60188	2968	25W-3N	A5
Allemong Dr					
5500	MTSN	60443	3505	7W-24S	C5
Allen Av					
10	GYLK	60030	2532	20W-33N	E3
1000	WCHI	60185	3022	29W-0S	C6
9700	RSMT	60018	2917	12W-6N	B6
N Allen Av					
800	MHRY	60050	2528	32W-32N	B4
2900	CHCG	60618	2976	4W-3N	D4
Allen Ct					
100	CNHL	60514	3145	16W-5S	D2
400	WLNG	60090	2755	14W-17N	C5
Allen Dr					
10	ELGN	60120	2855	32W-11N	D4
1700	GNVA	60134	3020	35W-0S	A6
1700	GnvT	60134	3020	36W-0S	A6
2100	BTVA	60134	3020	35W-0S	A7
2100	BTVA	60510	3020	35W-0S	A7
2200	NHBK	60062	2810	10W-15N	A2
Allen Ln					
500	SCRL	60174	2964	35W-3N	B5
500	UYPK	60466	3684	3W-30S	C2
S Allen Ln					
500	ANHT	60005	2806	18W-13N	D6
Allen Rd					
-	ALGN	60013	2695	32W-22N	B5
-	AlqT	60102	2695	32W-22N	B5
10	HPSR	60140	2795	47W-16N	E1
10	HPSR	60140	2796	46W-16N	A1
10	HshT	60140	2795	47W-16N	C1
10	HshT	60140	2796	46W-16N	A1
Allen Rd CO-3					
10	HPSR	60140	2795	47W-16N	E1
10	HPSR	60140	2796	46W-16N	A1
10	HshT	60140	2796	46W-16N	A1
Allen Rd CO-36					
10	HPSR	60140	2795	47W-16N	E1
Allen Rd CO-45					
10	HshT	60140	2795	47W-16N	C1
500	HPSR	60140	2795	47W-16N	D1
Allen St					
-	PLNO	60545	3260	45W-14S	B7
E Allen St					
700	SDWH	60548	3330	51W-14S	A1
W Allen St					
10	JLET	60436	3498	24W-24S	E5
Allendale Dr					
400	WLNG	60090	2755	15W-18N	B3
Allendale Rd					
9600	GNWD	60097	2468	39W-37N	C3
9600	GNWD	60098	2468	39W-37N	C3
9600	GwdT	60097	2468	39W-37N	C3
9600	GwdT	60098	2468	39W-37N	C3
9600	WRLK	60097	2468	39W-37N	C3
Allen Robert Dr					
23300	PNFD	60544	3338	29W-16S	D3
23300	PnfT	60544	3338	29W-16S	D3
Allenton Ct					
100	VNHL	60061	2647	16W-25N	C5
Aller St					
500	ELGN	60120	2855	32W-10N	C5
Allerton Dr					
100	SMBG	60194	2859	23W-10N	A5
Alles Av					
300	DSPN	60016	2863	13W-11N	A3
Alles Rd					
700	WNKA	60093	2812	5W-15N	A3
Alley A					
-	WLSP	60480	3209	12W-9S	B4
Alley B					
-	WLSP	60480	3209	12W-9S	B3
Alley C					
-	WLSP	60480	3209	12W-9S	B4
Allington Ct					
100	OSWG	60543	3263	36W-13S	E5
Allison Ct					
100	BGBK	60440	3269	22W-11S	D1
300	GYLK	60030	2532	21W-32N	D4
400	DGvT	60527	3207	16W-9S	D4
2500	MaiT	60025	2864	9W-12N	C1
11200	HTLY	60142	2745	40W-20N	A1
W Allison Ct					
1400	ANHT	60005	2860	19W-12N	D1
Allison Dr					
26600	CNHN	60410	3672	33W-32S	B7
Allison Ln					
400	LslT	60540	3142	24W-5S	D3
1200	SMBG	60194	2858	25W-11N	B4
3200	LGGV	60047	2700	19W-21N	C6
14900	HMGN	60491	3344	15W-17S	C6
17500	ODPK	60467	3423	13W-21S	A6
Allison St					
10	CPVL	60110	2800	35W-16N	D1
E Allison St					
300	EMHT	60126	3028	15W-0N	B5
Allison Woods					
10000	NfdT	60062	2809	12W-15N	A2
10000	PTHT	60062	2809	12W-15N	A2
Allister Ln					
200	NPVL	60563	3140	30W-5S	C2
200	NpvT	60563	3140	30W-5S	C2
Allmen Av					
900	HNDL	60521	3146	15W-5S	A3
Allonby Dr					
400	SMBG	60194	2858	24W-11N	D4
S Allport St					
1600	CHCG	60608	3091	1W-1S	D1
Allspice Ct					
3200	AURA	60504	3201	31W-8S	E3
All Star Ln					
-	JLET	60421	3675	24W-29S	D2
Allsteel Dr					
10	MTGY	60506	3199	37W-8S	C3
10	MTGY	60538	3199	37W-8S	C3
Allyn St					
13200	PNFD	60585	3338	30W-15S	B2
Allyson Ct					
1400	LbvT	60048	2592	15W-29N	B3
Alma Av					
200	BmdT	60148	3025	21W-2N	E1
400	EMHT	60126	3027	16W-1N	D3
700	BmdT	60148	2969	21W-2N	E6
NE Alma Cir					
800	RDLK	60073	2531	24W-34N	C1
800	RLKB	60073	2531	24W-34N	C1
NW Alma Cir					
800	AvnT	60073	2531	24W-34N	C1
800	RDLK	60073	2531	24W-34N	C1
800	RLKB	60073	2531	24W-34N	C1
Alma Ct					
700	CPVL	60110	2748	33W-17N	B7
900	RDLK	60073	2531	24W-34N	D1
Alma Dr					
1700	CTHL	60403	3498	25W-21S	C1
1900	CTHL	60403	3418	25W-21S	C7
E Alma Dr					
900	WslT	60481	3943	27W-40S	E2
Alma Ln					
100	WldT	60564	3202	28W-10S	E5
Alma Ter					
100	CRY	60013	2641	31W-24N	D7
Almaden Ln					
1200	GRNE	60031	2477	18W-35N	A5
1500	GRNE	60031	2476	18W-35N	E5
Almond Ct					
300	VNHL	60061	2647	17W-25N	C5
1100	NPVL	60540	3141	28W-7S	B7
1500	DRGV	60515	3084	20W-3S	B6
E Almond Ct					
1800	MPPT	60056	2808	13W-14N	D4
N Almond Ct					
2000	PLTN	60074	2753	19W-18N	B3
W Almond Ct					
7700	FftT	60423	3504	9W-24S	E5
Almond Dr					
700	AURA	60506	3137	38W-6S	A5
Almond Ln					
600	HFET	60169	2859	22W-11N	C4
2100	GLHT	60139	2969	23W-4N	A4
3100	MHRY	60050	2528	32W-34N	C1
9200	TYPK	60487	3423	11W-21S	E6
Almond Pk					
-	CHCG	60643	3277	2W-13S	D4
Almond Rd					
8800	WrnT	60030	2534	17W-32N	B4
N Almond Rd					
800	GRNE	60031	2477	18W-35N	A6
31500	LbvT	60030	2534	17W-31N	B7
31500	LbvT	60048	2534	17W-31N	B7
33000	WrnT	60030	2534	17W-33N	B3
33600	WrnT	60031	2534	17W-34N	B1
34300	GRNE	60031	2534	17W-34N	B1
N Almond Rd CO-W12					
-	WrnT	60030	2534	17W-34N	B1
34000	WrnT	60031	2534	17W-34N	B1
34300	GRNE	60031	2534	17W-34N	B1
Almora Ter					
10	ElgT	60123	2853	37W-12N	D3
10	ElgT	60124	2853	37W-12N	D3
Alnwick Ct					
600	IVNS	60010	2751	25W-17N	B6
Aloha Ct					
2700	MchT	60050	2528	31W-34N	D1
Aloha Dr					
2200	MchT	60050	2528	31W-34N	D1
Aloha Ln					
10	PvsT	60558	3086	14W-2S	D4
10	WSTR	60523	3086	14W-2S	D4
10	WSTR	60558	3086	14W-2S	D4
Alpha St					
-	LYWD	60411	3510	4E-24S	B6
S Alpine Av					
11500	PSPK	60464	3274	10W-13S	C4
Alpine Ct					
200	GLBT	60136	2799	38W-14N	A5
1300	HRPK	60133	2911	26W-7N	E5
1300	WLNG	60090	2754	16W-18N	D2
1900	GRNE	60031	2478	15W-36N	B5
W Alpine Ct					
24100	LkvT	60046	2474	24W-37N	D2
Alpine Dr					
100	LKZH	60047	2698	23W-23N	E1
100	SMBG	60194	2858	25W-10N	C5
200	GLBT	60136	2799	38W-14N	B5
200	VNHL	60061	2647	17W-25N	B5
300	RDLK	60073	2531	23W-33N	E2
12100	HMGN	60491	3344	15W-18S	C7
15100	ODPK	60467	3344	14W-18S	C7
E Alpine Dr					
200	GLHT	60139	2969	23W-3N	A5
N Alpine Dr					
1800	GLHT	60139	2969	23W-3N	A5
S Alpine Dr					
12500	ALSP	60445	3275	6W-14S	D7
12500	ALSP	60803	3275	6W-14S	D7
12500	CTWD	60445	3275	6W-14S	D7
12500	WthT	60463	3275	6W-14S	D7
12500	WthT	60803	3275	6W-14S	D7
Alpine Ln					
-	DSPN	60018	2917	12W-8N	B2
10	CRTE	60417	3596	0E-28S	D6
300	HFET	60169	2859	23W-11N	B3
400	WLMT	60091	2812	4W-13N	B6
800	SenT	60098	2524	43W-31N	A7
800	SenT	60098	2581	43W-30N	A1
1100	LMNT	60439	3270	19W-14S	E7
6700	WTMT	60559	3145	18W-7S	B7
N Alpine Ln					
37500	LKVL	60046	2474	24W-37N	D2
37500	LkvT	60046	2474	24W-37N	D2
Alpine St					
-	LKPT	60441	3342	21W-17S	A6
Alpine Vly					
8500	SPGV	60081	2413	32W-40N	C3
Alpine Wy					
2000	JLET	60586	3416	31W-21S	A7
5900	JLET	60586	3415	31W-21S	E7
12900	PNFD	60585	3337	33W-15S	B2
W Alpine Springs Dr					
200	VNHL	60061	2647	17W-25N	B4
Alsace Cir					
600	BFGV	60089	2701	16W-20N	C7
Alsace Ct					
100	BMDL	60108	2968	24W-5N	D1
700	BFGV	60089	2701	16W-20N	C7
700	WnfT	60190	3081	28W-1S	A3
Alschuler Ct					
200	AURA	60506	3137	38W-7S	B7
Alschuler Dr					
100	AURA	60506	3137	38W-7S	B7
200	AURA	60506	3199	38W-7S	B1
Alston					
-	JLET	60431	3495	33W-22S	B1
Alta Ct					
2500	LSLE	60532	3142	24W-7S	D7
17600	LKPT	60441	3420	20W-21S	B6
Alta Dr					
300	GYLK	60030	2532	21W-32N	E5
17600	LKPT	60441	3420	20W-21S	C6
S Alta Dr					
10300	PSHL	60465	3274	10W-12S	B1
Alta Ln					
300	GLHT	60139	2969	23W-3N	B5
600	WNFD	60190	3023	27W-0N	D4
Alta Rd					
15400	MKHM	60428	3348	4W-18S	E7
Alta St					
3100	FNPK	60164	2972	13W-3N	E4
3200	FNPK	60131	2972	13W-4N	E4
3200	LydT	60164	2972	13W-4N	E4
Alta Vista					
-	NLNX	60451	3590	15W-27S	B4
Alta Vista Dr					
-	PGGV	60140	2797	42W-15N	C4
2000	WKGN	60087	2480	10W-36N	B4
N Alta Vista Ter					
3800	CHCG	60613	2977	1W-4N	E2
Alta Vista Wy					
-	FftT	60423	3590	14W-26S	E1
-	FftT	60448	3590	14W-26S	E1
-	MKNA	60448	3590	14W-26S	E1
E Altgeld Av					
10	GLHT	60139	2968	23W-3N	E6
300	GLHT	60139	2969	22W-3N	B6
W Altgeld Av					
10	GLHT	60139	2968	24W-3N	D6
Altgeld St					
10500	LydT	60164	2973	13W-3N	A6
10600	LydT	60164	2972	13W-3N	E6
10600	NHLK	60164	2972	13W-3N	E6
E Altgeld St					
500	GLHT	60139	2969	22W-3N	C6
W Altgeld St					
800	CHCG	60614	2977	1W-3N	D5
2400	CHCG	60647	2977	3W-3N	A5
3200	CHCG	60647	2976	4W-3N	C5
4400	CHCG	60639	2976	5W-3N	A5
4800	CHCG	60639	2975	7W-3N	B5
6700	CHCG	60707	2975	8W-3N	A5
7200	CHCG	60707	2974	9W-3N	D5
7200	EDPK	60707	2974	9W-3N	D5
Althea Ct					
22800	CnhT	60447	3584	31W-27S	A6
22800	TroT	60447	3584	31W-27S	A6
Althea Dr					
3200	AlqT	60102	2695	32W-22N	B5
N Althea Dr					
1400	MPPT	60056	2808	13W-14N	E3
Althoff Dr					
700	MchT	60050	2472	30W-36N	B3
Alton Ct					
500	CLSM	60188	2967	27W-3N	D7
900	WPHR	60096	2363	10W-42N	B6
1000	NPVL	60540	3204	25W-8S	B1
Alton Rd					
10	PTHT	60070	2808	14W-14N	C3
100	MPPT	60056	2808	14W-14N	C3
N Alton Rd					
2300	MchT	60050	2527	34W-34N	C1
Alton on Auburn					
10	RGMW	60008	2806	19W-14N	B4
Altoona Ct					
10	VNHL	60061	2647	17W-25N	C5
1800	SMBG	60194	2858	25W-11N	A4
N Alto Vista					
500	DrrT	60014	2639	37W-26N	A3
8800	CLLK	60014	2639	37W-26N	A3
W Alto Vista					
5800	DrrT	60014	2639	37W-26N	A3
W Alva St					
800	PLTN	60067	2752	22W-16N	C6
Alveston St					
10300	ODPK	60462	3345	13W-17S	B6
Alvin Av					
100	MLPK	60160	2973	13W-2N	A7
100	MLPK	60164	2973	13W-2N	A7
100	NHLK	60160	2973	13W-2N	A7
100	NHLK	60160	3029	13W-2N	A1
100	NHLK	60164	2973	13W-2N	A7
100	NHLK	60164	3029	13W-2N	A1
Alvin Ct					
1200	GNVW	60025	2810	9W-13N	D5
Alvin Pl					
-	CHHT	60411	3508	0W-24S	B4
500	HDPK	60035	2705	7W-21N	A7
Alvina St					
-	WCDA	60084	2644	25W-27N	A2
-	WcnT	60084	2644	25W-27N	A2
W Al Wilhelmi Dr					
3200	JLET	60431	3497	28W-21S	B1
3200	JLET	60435	3497	28W-21S	B1
Alyce Ln					
500	AURA	60505	3138	34W-6S	C4
600	AraT	60505	3138	34W-6S	C4
Alyssa Ct					
2800	NPVL	60565	3203	26W-10S	D6
Alyssa Dr					
2700	NPVL	60565	3203	26W-10S	D6
Alyssa St					
-	LtRT	60545	3260	46W-14S	A7
-	PLNO	60545	3260	46W-14S	A7
Alysse Ct					
18000	ODPK	60467	3422	13W-21S	E7
Alysson Ct					
200	BMDL	60108	2968	24W-5N	E1
Alyssum Ct					
200	RMVL	60446	3339	26W-17S	D6
Amaarja Ct					
4800	RGMW	60067	2805	21W-13N	E5
Amalfi Dr					
400	NfdT	60025	2809	11W-13N	D7
Amalfi St					
38700	AntT	60002	2415	26W-39N	D5
Amanda Rd					
400	LKMR	60051	2529	29W-31N	C6
400	NndT	60051	2529	29W-31N	C6
Amanda Cir					
1100	ELGN	60123	2854	35W-10N	C6
Amanda Ct					
10	CRTE	60417	3685	1W-30S	B2
2800	JLET	60431	3417	28W-20S	A5
5500	RGMW	60008	2805	21W-13N	C5
25100	LkvT	60046	2416	25W-38N	B6
Amanda Dr					
2300	SPGV	60081	2413	31W-40N	E2
Amanda Ln					
-	SMBG	60173	2859	23W-12N	A1
-	SMBG	60195	2859	23W-12N	A1
10	BtlT	60560	3261	42W-13S	C5
9800	AlqT	60102	2695	32W-22N	C4
Amanda Rd					
700	NLNX	60451	3589	16W-25S	E1
Amaranth Dr					
900	AURA	60504	3202	30W-9S	A3
900	AURA	60564	3202	30W-9S	A3
S Amarias Dr					
1300	RDLK	60073	2531	23W-31N	E7
1700	FmtT	60030	2531	23W-31N	D7
Amarillo Ct					
400	CPVL	60110	2748	33W-18N	B4
Amarillo Dr					
10	CPVL	60110	2748	33W-18N	B5
Amarillo St					
-	HRPK	60133	2911	26W-7N	E5
Amaryllis Ct					
300	RMVL	60446	3339	26W-17S	E7
Amaryllis Dr					
1500	RMVL	60446	3339	26W-17S	E7
Ambassador Av					
10	RMVL	60446	3269	23W-14S	A7
10	RMVL	60446	3341	23W-14S	A1
100	RMVL	60446	3268	23W-14S	E7
100	RMVL	60446	3340	23W-14S	E1
Ambassador Ct					
3800	LSLE	60532	3082	24W-3S	D6
Ambassador Dr					
100	NPVL	60540	3140	29W-6S	D6
Ambassador Ln					
1500	FDHT	60411	3509	1E-25S	B6
Amber Cir					
4700	HFET	60192	2804	24W-15N	B1
Amber Ct					
10	CRTE	60417	3685	1W-29S	B2
10	LNHT	60046	2476	19W-37N	C1
10	SMBG	60193	2857	27W-10N	C5
100	CLSM	60188	3024	24W-1N	D2
100	WCHI	60185	3022	29W-2N	C1
1100	WDSK	60098	2581	42W-30N	B2
1300	GYLK	60030	2475	21W-34N	D7
2600	ALGN	60102	2746	37W-19N	D2
3800	JLET	60586	3416	28W-20S	E5
3800	JLET	60586	3417	28W-20S	A5
3800	PnfT	60431	3417	28W-20S	A5
3800	PnfT	60586	3417	28W-20S	A5
22500	FKFT	60423	3591	13W-27S	A4
Amber Dr					
1000	LMNT	60439	3271	18W-14S	A7
1100	CRY	60013	2641	32W-24N	C6
1300	MTGY	60538	3200	34W-9S	D4
1300	WMTN	60481	3853	28W-37S	A5
Amber Ln					
-	CRY	60013	2641	32W-24N	C6
200	VNHL	60061	2647	17W-25N	C5
400	WNVL	60555	3080	29W-3S	D6
600	CLSM	60188	3024	24W-1N	D2
600	GLHT	60188	3024	24W-1N	D2
800	LKVL	60046	2474	24W-37N	D3
900	LkvT	60046	2474	24W-37N	C3
1900	DMND	60416	3941	33W-40S	B3
2400	ELGN	60123	2907	36W-8N	D3
2600	ALGN	60102	2746	37W-19N	D2
10400	ODPK	60467	3423	13W-21S	B6
23000	RNPK	60471	3594	4W-27S	D5
Amber Rd					
700	NLNX	60451	3589	17W-25S	D1
Amber Wy					
5500	JNBG	60050	2471	31W-37N	D2
Amberleigh Ct					
10	LIHL	60156	2692	39W-21N	D6
1900	RMVL	60446	3339	27W-17S	C5
Amberleigh Dr					
100	RMVL	60446	3339	27W-17S	C5
Amberley Ct					
19900	MKNA	60448	3502	15W-23S	B4
Amberley Ln					
10	RDLK	60073	2532	23W-32N	A5
400	DRFD	60015	2757	10W-20N	A1
N Amberly Dr					
20600	KLDR	60047	2699	21W-20N	E7
Amber Marie Cir					
-	LKVL	60046	2475	23W-37N	A2
E Amber Prairie Ct					
800	RLKB	60046	2475	21W-35N	C5
N Amber Prairie Wy					
1900	RLKB	60046	2475	21W-35N	C5
1900	RLKB	60073	2475	21W-35N	C5
E Amberwood Cir					
900	NPVL	60563	3142	26W-5S	A2
Amberwood Ct					
200	BMDL	60108	2969	22W-4N	C3
400	ALGN	60102	2694	34W-20N	B7
Amberwood Dr					
-	GfnT	60014	2693	37W-23N	C2
900	CLLK	60014	2693	37W-23N	C1
11600	HBRN	60034	2351	40W-41N	A7
Amberwood Ln					
10	ElgT	60124	2799	38W-13N	A7
1400	LMNT	60439	3271	18W-14S	B6
Amberwood Pl					
800	MHRY	60050	2528	32W-31N	B7
900	MHRY	60050	2585	32W-30N	B1
Ambleside Cir					
1400	NPVL	60540	3140	28W-7S	E7
1400	NPVL	60540	3141	27W-7S	B7
1500	NPVL	60540	3202	28W-7S	E1
1600	NPVL	60540	3203	28W-7S	A1
Ambleside Dr					
10	WNFD	60190	3023	27W-0N	B6
10	WnfT	60190	3023	27W-0N	B6
300	ROSL	60172	2913	23W-7N	B4
700	DRFD	60015	2703	11W-21N	E6
Ambleside Rd					
200	DSPN	60016	2862	15W-11N	A4
Amboy Ln					
10	SMBG	60194	2858	25W-10N	C5
W Amboy St					
200	PNFD	60544	3338	29W-17S	C7
Ambria Ct					
1700	MDLN	60060	2590	19W-29N	C4
Ambria Dr					
100	MDLN	60060	2590	19W-29N	C4
Ambria Ln					
1600	MDLN	60060	2590	19W-29N	C4
Ambriance Dr					
10	BRRG	60527	3208	14W-8S	C2
Ambrogio Dr					
10	GRNE	60031	2535	13W-34N	E1
Ambrose Dr					
13000	PlsT	60464	3345	13W-15S	A1
13000	PlsT	60467	3345	13W-15S	A1
Ambrose Ln					
10	SBTN	60010	2803	26W-13N	D6
Ambrose Rd					
24800	PNFD	60585	3337	31W-15S	E2
24800	PNFD	60585	3338	31W-15S	A2
Ambrust Av					
10	MltT	60187	3024	25W-0N	B4
10	WHTN	60187	3024	25W-0N	B4
Ambry Cir					
-	LYWD	60411	3509	2E-23S	D3
N Am-By Ln					
5200	MchT	60050	2472	29W-37N	B2
W Am-By Ln					
900	JNBG	60050	2472	29W-37N	B2
900	MchT	60050	2472	29W-37N	B2
Amelia Av					
3900	LYNS	60534	3088	9W-4S	C7
Amelia Ct					
800	GYLK	60030	2533	20W-33N	B2
1100	INCK	60061	2647	17W-25N	A6
1700	CTHL	60403	3418	26W-21S	A7
7800	JSTC	60458	3209	11W-8S	E2
W Amelia Dr					
8400	MaiT	60714	2864	10W-10N	A4
8400	NLES	60714	2864	10W-10N	A4
W Amelia Ln					
1300	ADSN	60101	2970	20W-4N	B3
Amendodge Dr					
200	SRWD	60404	3496	30W-24S	C6
200	SRWD	60431	3496	30W-24S	C6
200	TroT	60431	3496	30W-24S	C6
Amendola Wy					
200	RLKP	60030	2589	22W-30N	B2
Amenity Center Dr					
-	BDWD	60481	3942	30W-40S	B2
-	RedT	60408	3942	30W-40S	B2
-	RedT	60481	3942	30W-40S	B2
America Ct					
17800	ODPK	60467	3423	13W-21S	A6
American Ln					
800	SMBG	60173	2859	21W-11N	D2
2300	EGVV	60007	2915	16W-7N	E4
American Wy					
-	BtlT	60543	3262	40W-13S	C4
-	BtlT	60560	3262	40W-13S	C4
-	VNHL	60061	2647	16W-24N	E6
-	VrnT	60061	2647	16W-24N	E6
-	WDSK	60098	2582	40W-29N	A3
10	ELGN	60120	2855	32W-12N	C3
900	EDND	60118	2801	33W-15N	B3
S American Wy					
-	VNHL	60061	2647	15W-24N	E6
-	VrnT	60061	2647	15W-24N	E6
Americana Ct					
10	ROSL	60172	2912	24W-7N	C4
Americana Dr					
6300	WLBK	60527	3145	16W-7S	D6
Americana Ln					
-	SRWD	60404	3495	31W-24S	E6
American Pride Ln					
100	NLNX	60451	3501	17W-24S	D6
100	NlxT	60451	3501	17W-24S	D6
American Wy Dr					
1200	LYVL	60048	2590	18W-30N	D3
Amersale Dr					
600	NPVL	60563	3140	30W-6S	C4
600	NpvT	60563	3140	30W-6S	C4
Amery Ct					
1300	FSMR	60422	3506	4W-23S	D3
W Ames Av					
10000	BHPK	60099	2422	10W-39N	B6
10000	ZION	60099	2422	10W-39N	B6
Ames Ct					
1000	ANTH	60002	2358	20W-42N	E7
1100	NPVL	60540	3203	28W-8S	A1
W Ames Ct					
20800	LktT	60544	3340	26W-16S	A4
Ames Rd					
3300	NndT	60012	2585	32W-28N	A5
3300	PRGV	60012	2585	33W-28N	A5
4100	PRGV	60012	2584	33W-28N	E5
Ames St					
300	LYVL	60048	2591	16W-28N	C6
500	LKPT	60441	3419	22W-19S	C2
E Ames St					
800	HMND	46320	3430		E1
Amesbury Rd					
10	OswT	60538	3199	36W-10S	E7

STREET Block City ZIP Map# CGS Grid

Amherst Av
100 DSPN 60016 2862 14W-12N C1
100 LktT 60441 3419 23W-21S B7
400 LktT 60441 3499 23W-21S A4
500 DSPN 60016 2808 14W-12N C7
500 JLET 60432 3499 23W-21S B1
500 RMVL 60446 3341 23W-15S A2
Amherst Cir
100 OSWG 60543 3263 36W-14S D6
1700 GLHT 60139 2968 24W-3N D6
Amherst Ct
- FKFT 60423 3590 14W-27S E4
- LKPT 60441 3419 21W-20S E4
10 BFGV 60089 2701 17W-21N A7
10 FRGV 60021 2696 29W-22N B4
10 SchT 60175 2963 38W-4N A5
200 BMDL 60108 2969 22W-4N B3
200 OSWG 60543 3263 37W-14S D6
300 VNHL 60061 2647 16W-25N C5
800 NPVL 60565 3204 25W-10S B6
1100 LKZH 60047 2699 22W-22N C5
1300 GYLK 60030 2475 21W-34N D7
2000 FSMR 60422 3507 2W-23S C3
5700 MHRY 60050 2527 34W-34N C1
17900 CCHL 60478 3426 5W-21S D6
20600 JLET 60433 3500 20W-24S B6
20600 NlxT 60433 3500 20W-24S B6
N Amherst Ct
2500 PNFD 60544 3338 30W-16S C3
S Amherst Ct
2500 PNFD 60544 3338 30W-16S C4
Amherst Dr
100 BRLT 60103 2910 29W-7N E4
100 BRLT 60103 2911 28W-7N A4
500 LKVL 60046 2475 21W-37N C2
1300 SMBG 60194 2858 25W-10N B5
Amherst Ln
400 HFET 60169 2858 24W-12N E2
400 HFET 60195 2858 24W-12N E2
400 SMBG 60195 2858 24W-12N E2
1000 UYPK 60449 3684 3W-30S B4
1000 UYPK 60466 3684 3W-30S B4
17000 TYPK 60477 3424 9W-20S D4
20500 DRPK 60010 2751 23W-20N D1
Amherst Mdw
100 BRLT 60103 2910 29W-7N E4
100 WynT 60103 2910 29W-7N E4
Amherst Pl
5700 MTSN 60443 3505 7W-25S D7
E Amherst St
300 PLTN 60067 2753 20W-17N A5
300 PLTN 60074 2753 20W-17N A5
E Amhurst Ct
2200 ANHT 60004 2807 16W-15N D2
Amhurst Ln
900 WLMT 60091 2812 4W-14N B5
Amhurst Pkwy
3400 NCHI 60064 2536 12W-32N A6
3400 NCHI 60085 2536 12W-32N A6
3500 WKGN 60085 2536 13W-32N A6
Ami Dr
5700 RHMD 60071 2353 34W-43N C5
Amli Ct
800 AURA 60502 3139 32W-6S D6
Amli Dr
2700 AURA 60502 3139 32W-7S D6
Amli Ln
2700 AURA 60502 3139 32W-7S D6
Amlin Cir
5700 MTSN 60443 3505 7W-25S D7
18600 CCHL 60478 3506 6W-22S A1
Amlin Ln
19000 CCHL 60478 3506 6W-22S A2
Amlin Ter
1000 MTSN 60443 3505 7W-25S D7
Ammer Rd
1400 GNVW 60025 2810 8W-14N E4
1400 GNVW 60025 2811 8W-14N A4
Ammer Ridge Ct
1900 GNVW 60025 2810 8W-14N E4
W Amoco Rd
23400 CnhT 60410 3674 28W-28S A1
Amos Av
- BtlT 60543 3262 40W-12S B4
- BtlT 60560 3262 40W-12S B4
Amos Bennett St
1500 GYLK 60030 2533 19W-32N D6
Amsterdam Dr
700 ANTH 60002 2358 22W-42N B6
Amsterdam Ln
500 PTON 60468 3860 9W-37S E3
Amsterdam St
500 WDSK 60098 2524 42W-31N C7
Amston Ct
- OSWG 60543 3263 36W-13S D5
Amstutz Expwy
- NCHI 60044 2593 11W-30N E2
- NCHI 60064 2536 10W-31N E7
- NCHI 60064 2537 10W-31N A7
- NCHI 60064 2593 11W-30N E2
- NCHI 60088 2593 11W-30N E2
- WKGN 60085 2480 10W-35N B7
- WKGN 60085 2537 10W-34N B1
- WKGN 60087 2480 10W-35N B7
Amstutz Expwy SR-137
- NCHI 60044 2593 11W-30N E2
- NCHI 60064 2536 10W-31N E7
- NCHI 60064 2537 10W-31N A7
- NCHI 60064 2593 11W-30N E2
- NCHI 60088 2593 11W-30N E2
- WKGN 60085 2480 10W-35N B7
- WKGN 60085 2537 10W-34N B1
- WKGN 60087 2480 10W-35N B7
S Amstutz Expwy
- WKGN 60085 2537 10W-33N B2
S Amstutz Expwy SR-137
- WKGN 60085 2537 10W-33N B2
Amy Av
10 BmdT 60137 3025 23W-2N B1
400 BmdT 60137 2969 23W-2N B7
500 GLHT 60137 2969 23W-2N B7
500 GLHT 60139 2969 23W-2N A7
S Amy Av
1500 HMND 46394 3280 E4
Amy Ct
300 GNEN 60137 3025 23W-1N B3
300 MltT 60137 3025 23W-1N B3
300 NPVL 60565 3203 26W-10S D5
500 LKPT 60441 3419 21W-19S E2
500 LKPT 60441 3420 21W-19S A2
1300 WLNG 60090 2754 16W-18N D2
S Amy Ct
1400 HMND 46394 3280 E3
Amy Dr
10 OswT 60543 3264 35W-14S C7
4500 AlqT 60014 2640 33W-25N D4
4500 NndT 60014 2640 33W-26N E4
4800 CLLK 60014 2640 33W-25N D4
22400 RNPK 60471 3594 6W-27S A4
Amy Ln
500 MltT 60187 3024 25W-0N B4
500 WHTN 60187 3024 25W-0N B4
1200 LYVL 60048 2591 18W-30N A3
2300 AURA 60506 3136 39W-7S E7
N Amy Ln
21600 KLDR 60047 2699 21W-22N D4
Amy St
100 CHHT 60411 3507 1W-24S E5
100 CHHT 60411 3508 1W-24S A4
Ana Rd
- MKHM 60426 3348 4W-18S E6
- MKHM 60428 3348 4W-18S E6
Anand Brook Dr
12400 HmrT 60491 3344 15W-16S A3
12600 HMGN 60491 3344 15W-16S A3
Anastatica Ln
- JLET 60447 3495 33W-22S A1
Anchor Ct
800 BRLT 60103 2911 28W-7N B4
Anchor Dr
300 CPVL 60110 2800 35W-16N C1
8200 WDRG 60517 3205 21W-9S E3
E Anchor Dr
10 MTGY 60543 3199 37W-11S B7
10 MTGY 60543 3263 37W-11S C1
N Anchor Dr
3200 CHCG 60618 2977 3W-4N A3
W Anchor Dr
10 MTGY 60543 3199 37W-11S B7
10 MTGY 60543 3263 38W-11S B1
Anchorage Dr
27800 GrtT 60020 2473 27W-35N A6
Ancient Oak Ct
200 CmpT 60175 2962 40W-5N C2
Ancient Oak Ln
400 CmpT 60175 2962 40W-5N C2
Ancient Oaks Ct
1100 BRLT 60103 2910 30W-6N C7
Ancient Oaks Dr
1100 BRLT 60103 2910 30W-6N C7
Ancient Oaks Rd
- WCHI 60185 2967 28W-2N A7
- WynT 60185 2967 28W-2N A7
400 WCHI 60185 3023 28W-2N A1
400 WynT 60185 3023 28W-2N A1
Ancient Tree Rd
- NHBK 60062 2756 11W-17N C5
Ancona Av
16700 OMCK 60083 2477 16W-37N C1
W Ancona St
- CHCG 60622 3033 2W-0S C5
Andean Pl
1000 HDPK 60035 2704 9W-22N C4
N Anderle Av
- LkvT 60046 2417 21W-38N E6
Andermann Dr
200 WldT 60564 3266 29W-11S D2
Andermann Ln
700 DRN 60561 3207 17W-8S C2
Anders Dr
- EGVV 60007 2913 21W-8N E2
Andersen Av
9900 CHRG 60415 3211 8W-11S A7
9900 CHRG 60415 3275 8W-11S A1
Anderson Av
10 JltT 60433 3499 21W-24S E5
1100 JltT 60433 3587 21W-25S E1
Anderson Blvd
10 GNVA 60134 3020 35W-1N B3
800 SCRL 60134 3020 35W-1N B3
800 SCRL 60174 3020 35W-1N B3
Anderson Ct
100 YKVL 60560 3261 43W-13S B6
700 WynT 60185 2966 28W-2N E7
Anderson Dr
10 AURA 60502 3079 32W-3S D6
10 WnfT 60502 3079 32W-3S D6
500 LIHL 60156 2694 34W-22N C4
500 RMVL 60446 3341 23W-15S A2
800 GNOK 60048 2592 14W-29N D4
1200 BTVA 60510 3078 34W-2S E4
E Anderson Dr
800 PLTN 60074 2753 19W-16N C7
1500 ANHT 60004 2753 18W-16N D7
Anderson Ln
1500 BFGV 60089 2700 18W-21N E6
Anderson Pl
10400 FNPK 60131 2973 13W-3N A4
Anderson Rd
10 CmpT 60119 2961 43W-4N B5
10 CmpT 60119 3017 43W-2N B1
10 CmpT 60151 2961 43W-4N B5
300 ANTH 60002 2357 24W-43N C4
400 LKFT 60037 2650 9W-24N C7
400 LKFT 60045 2650 9W-24N C7
600 LYLK 60175 2961 43W-4N B4
1100 ELBN 60119 3017 43W-0N B4
N Anderson Rd
26000 WcnT 60084 2643 26W-26N C3
26300 LKBN 60084 2643 26W-26N C3
26500 WCDA 60084 2643 26W-26N C3
S Anderson Rd
100 NLNX 60451 3502 16W-25S A7
100 NlxT 60451 3502 16W-25S A7
700 NLNX 60451 3589 16W-25S E1
700 NLNX 60451 3590 16W-26S A1
1700 NlxT 60451 3590 16W-26S A3
Anderson St
300 HRVD 60033 2406 50W-38N B7
N Anderson St
10 AURA 60505 3200 35W-7S C1
S Anderson St
10 AURA 60505 3200 35W-8S B1
W Anderson St
23400 PnfT 60586 3416 29W-19S D2
23500 PNFD 60586 3416 29W-19S D2
25200 GrtT 60041 2474 25W-35N A6
Anderson Ter
200 DSPN 60016 2862 15W-10N B5
Anderson Ter E
800 DSPN 60016 2862 15W-10N B4
Anderson Tr
1500 ZION 60099 2421 12W-41N B1
N Andoa Ln
1800 MPPT 60056 2808 13W-15N D2
1800 PTHT 60070 2808 13W-15N D2
Andover Av
1500 SCRL 60174 2964 34W-2N D7
Andover Cir
10 NHBK 60062 2756 12W-18N A2
1100 AURA 60504 3201 31W-9S E4
Andover Ct
10 LNSH 60069 2701 16W-23N E2
10 SEGN 60177 2908 36W-8N A2
200 BGBK 60440 3269 22W-12S D2
300 SMWD 60107 2857 27W-9N C7
400 LKFT 60045 2648 13W-25N E5
700 BTVA 60502 3078 33W-2S E4
700 BTVA 60510 3078 33W-2S E4
700 BtvT 60502 3078 33W-2S E4
800 PTHT 60070 2808 15W-16N A1
1100 GLHT 60188 3024 23W-1N E2
1100 NPVL 60563 3142 25W-6S A4
1800 CHHT 60411 3595 2W-26S C1
2200 SMBG 60194 2857 26W-11N E4
3100 AURA 60504 3201 31W-9S D5
7000 WDRG 60517 3143 21W-7S E6
W Andover Ct
900 PLTN 60067 2752 22W-16N B6
Andover Dr
- OSWG 60543 3263 36W-14S E7
- OswT 60543 3263 36W-14S E7
10 PTHT 60070 2808 15W-16N A1
10 ROSL 60172 2912 25W-7N C4
100 BmdT 60188 3024 23W-1N E1
100 CLSM 60188 3024 23W-1N E2
100 GLHT 60188 3024 23W-1N E2
100 PTHT 60070 2807 15W-16N E1
1100 MDLN 60060 2590 19W-29N B4
1300 AURA 60504 3201 31W-9S E4
4200 RNPK 60471 3594 5W-26S C3
N Andover Dr
10 ROSL 60172 2912 25W-7N C4
W Andover Dr
5900 HRPK 60133 2911 27W-7N D5
21000 FmtT 60060 2645 21W-26N E3
Andover Dr E
1500 HRPK 60133 2911 26W-7N D5
Andover Dr W
5800 HRPK 60133 2911 27W-7N D5
Andover Ln
- LIHL 60156 2693 37W-22N B3
1700 CLLK 60014 2693 37W-22N B3
N Andover Ln
10 GNVA 60134 3019 36W-1N E3
S Andover Ln
10 GNVA 60134 3019 38W-1N B3
Andover Rd
6300 GRNE 60031 2534 16W-33N C3
6400 WrnT 60030 2534 16W-33N C3
6400 WrnT 60031 2534 16W-33N C3
N Andover Rd
21000 KLDR 60047 2699 21W-21N E6
W Andover Rd
14200 WDWH 60083 2420 14W-39N C4
14300 NptT 60083 2420 14W-39N C4
Andover St
500 CHHT 60411 3595 2W-26S C1
Andra Ct
300 GLBT 60136 2799 38W-15N C3
Andrea Ct
400 HRVD 60033 2464 50W-37N A1
600 SchT 60175 2907 36W-7N E6
600 YKVL 60512 3261 42W-13S D5
600 YKVL 60560 3261 42W-13S D5
3100 WDRG 60517 3205 22W-9S C3
10600 ODPK 60467 3423 13W-21S B6
Andrea Dr
- MhtT 60442 3678 18W-31S A5
300 MHTN 60442 3678 18W-31S A5
1000 NLNX 60451 3588 19W-26S E2
1000 NLNX 60451 3589 19W-26S A2
10600 ODPK 60467 3423 13W-21S A6
Andrea Ln
- LslT 60517 3205 22W-9S C4
1200 DSPN 60016 2862 15W-10N A5
1200 DSPN 60018 2862 15W-10N A5
8400 WDRG 60517 3205 22W-9S C4
W Andrea Ln
7600 NndT 60012 2639 36W-26N D2
Andrene Ln
10 BmdT 60143 2914 21W-6N A6
200 BmdT 60143 2913 21W-7N E5
200 BmdT 60143 2970 21W-5N A1
200 ITSC 60143 2913 21W-7N E5
Andres Av
6000 TYPK 60477 3425 7W-20S C3
W Andrew Av
23000 CNHN 60410 3585 28W-27S A5
Andrew Ct
10 DGvT 60527 3146 15W-6S A5
200 NARA 60542 3078 35W-3S B6
600 SMBG 60193 2858 24W-9N D6
1700 LGGV 60047 2753 19W-20N C1
W Andrew Ct
25700 GrtT 60041 2474 25W-36N A3
Andrew Dr
2400 DYR 46311 3598 D3
Andrew Ln
- BHPK 60083 2421 13W-39N A5
10 HFET 60169 2858 24W-10N D6
10 SMBG 60169 2858 24W-10N D6
10 SMBG 60193 2858 24W-10N D6
200 NARA 60542 3078 35W-3S B6
400 LKZH 60047 2699 22W-22N A3
600 CLSM 60188 2967 26W-3N D6
W Andrew Rd
23800 PNFD 60585 3266 29W-14S C7
23800 WldT 60585 3266 29W-14S C7
Andrew St
- LtRT 60545 3332 45W-14S C1
12300 PLNO 60545 3332 45W-14S C1
Andrew Tr
2200 MTGY 60538 3198 40W-10S D6
Andrews Av
2700 BTVA 60510 3019 37W-0S B7
Andrews Ct
1000 NPVL 60540 3204 25W-8S B1
Andria Ct
1200 NPVL 60540 3202 29W-8S E2
2000 SMBG 60194 2858 26W-11N A4
Andrus Av
1200 DRGV 60516 3144 20W-7S B7
Andrus Dr
2800 WCHI 60185 2965 32W-4N B4
Andrus Rd
200 DGvT 60516 3206 19W-10S D5
200 DGvT 60561 3206 19W-10S D5
200 DRN 60516 3206 19W-10S D5
200 DRN 60561 3206 19W-10S D5
W Andy Ct
10 NasT 60544 3337 33W-18S A7
Andy Dr
100 MLPK 60160 3030 10W-1N A2
600 MLPK 60160 3029 10W-1N E1
Andy Ln
1800 DSPN 60018 2917 12W-8N B2
Andys Ln
10 AraT 60505 3138 34W-6S D6
10 AURA 60505 3138 34W-6S D6
N Andyville Ln
43100 AntT 60002 2357 25W-43N A5
Anets Dr
100 NfdT 60062 2757 9W-16N C7
100 NHBK 60062 2757 9W-16N B6
Angas Ln
4600 NndT 60042 2642 29W-27N D1
4600 WcnT 60042 2642 29W-27N D1
Angel Ln
6000 LSLE 60532 3142 24W-6S D5
Angela Cir
200 OSWG 60543 3199 36W-11S E7
Angela Ct
300 VNHL 60061 2647 17W-25N B5
1000 SMBG 60173 2859 22W-11N D4
Angela Ln
- AlqT 60014 2693 36W-23N E3
- AlqT 60156 2693 36W-23N E3
- CLLK 60014 2693 36W-23N E3
2300 AURA 60502 3201 32W-7S C1
Angelica Cir
800 JLET 60447 3495 33W-22S A3
Angelica Ct
800 JLET 60447 3495 33W-22S A3
Angelico Ln
1900 BRLT 60103 2909 32W-9N D1
Angelico St
14900 LMNT 60439 3343 18W-15S A2
Angelina Pl
10 ALGN 60102 2748 34W-19N A3
10 DndT 60102 2748 34W-19N A3
Angeline Ct
600 WNVL 60555 3080 30W-2S B5
4600 PltT 60067 2805 20W-14N E4
4600 RGMW 60067 2805 20W-14N E4
Angeline Dr
1200 SEGN 60177 2908 35W-9N A2
Angelo Av
600 GRNE 60031 2535 14W-33N D3
Angle Av
1000 NHBK 60062 2757 9W-17N B5
W Angle Rd
21400 WslT 60481 3943 27W-42S E7
Angle Tarn
900 WDND 60118 2800 35W-15N D4
1200 SYHW 60118 2800 35W-15N D4
Anglican Ln
10 LNSH 60069 2702 13W-22N E4
Angouleme Ln
5600 HFET 60192 2856 30W-12N B2
Angus Ct
1800 SMBG 60194 2858 25W-11N B4
Anise Dr
11500 FKFT 60423 3590 14W-26S D3
Anita Av
300 ANTH 60002 2357 23W-42N E6
E Anita Av
100 WhlT 60056 2808 13W-13N E5
Anita Dr
400 BRLT 60103 2911 28W-7N A4
Anita Pl
300 WLNG 60090 2755 14W-17N D5
Anita St
100 RKDL 60436 3498 25W-25S C7
200 DSPN 60016 2862 14W-11N B3
Anita Ter
200 ANTH 60002 2357 23W-42N E5
200 ANTH 60002 2358 23W-42N A6
Anjou Dr
300 NHBK 60062 2756 12W-18N C3
Anjou Ln
3700 HFET 60192 2804 24W-14N B3
Ann Av
5200 HMND 46320 3352 C6
Ann Ct
- MNKA 60447 3672 33W-30S C4
100 BRLT 60103 2911 28W-8N A3
500 JLET 60435 3497 26W-23S E4
N Ann Ct
26100 WcnT 60084 2643 26W-26N D3
W Ann Ct
25000 PnfT 60586 3416 31W-20S A6
S Ann Dr
17300 PnfT 60586 3416 31W-20S A6
17400 JLET 60586 3416 31W-20S A6
Ann Ln
400 NLNX 60451 3500 20W-24S C5
600 UYPK 60466 3684 3W-30S B2
Ann Pl
- AntT 60081 2414 29W-38N D7
- BtnT 60081 2414 29W-38N D7
Ann St
- LMBD 60148 3026 19W-0S C7
10 ELGN 60120 2854 34W-11N E3
100 CNHL 60514 3145 16W-5S D2
100 CRY 60013 2641 31W-24N D7
100 SEGN 60177 2908 34W-8N E3
100 WCHI 60185 3022 30W-0N B5
200 ELGN 60120 2855 33W-11N A3
500 DLTN 60419 3350 0E-16S E4
900 BfdT 53128 2352 E3
900 BTVA 60510 3020 35W-0S C7
900 GNCY 53128 2352 E3
3100 LNSG 60438 3430 3E-21S B7
3400 GRNE 60085 2536 13W-34N A2
3400 PKCY 60085 2536 13W-34N A2
11900 BLID 60406 3277 3W-14S B5
11900 BLID 60655 3277 3W-14S B5
11900 CHCG 60655 3277 3W-14S B5
13100 BLID 60406 3349 3W-15S B1
N Ann St
200 MRGO 60152 2634 50W-26N B2
600 JLET 60435 3497 26W-23S E3
S Ann St
100 MRGO 60152 2634 50W-26N B3
W Ann St
10 LMBD 60148 3026 20W-0S B7
300 GNEN 60137 3026 20W-0S A7
300 GNEN 60148 3026 20W-0S A7
Anna Av
2300 TNLK 53181 2354 A2
4000 LYNS 60534 3088 10W-4S A7
Anna Ct
- PltT 60010 2751 23W-18N E2
- PltT 60010 2752 23W-18N A2
25700 ElaT 60047 2644 24W-25N C4
S Anna Dr
22800 CNHN 60410 3584 29W-27S E5
W Anna Dr
15800 WDWH 60083 2477 16W-37N E1
15800 WDWH 60083 2478 15W-37N A2
Anna Ln
22900 FKFT 60423 3592 10W-27S C5
26300 MONE 60449 3682 8W-32S B7
26300 MonT 60449 3682 8W-32S B7
N Anna Ln
400 RMVL 60446 3340 25W-15S B2
W Anna Ln
1000 LKFT 60045 2703 12W-23N B1
Anna St
100 NARA 60542 3078 35W-3S A7
19900 MKNA 60448 3503 13W-24S A4
Anna Wy
2400 ElgT 60124 2907 37W-9N D2
Annabelle St
700 MchT 60050 2472 29W-37N B2
Anna Maria Ln
10 BtlT 60543 3262 40W-12S C3
S Anna Marie Dr
1800 MPPT 60056 2861 17W-10N C5
Anna Marie Ln
- NPVL 60564 3202 30W-10S C7
- WldT 60564 3202 30W-10S C7
Annandale Av
400 GNEN 60137 3025 22W-0N C5
Annandale Ct
10 LIHL 60156 2692 38W-21N D6
2200 ELGN 60123 2908 35W-9N C1
Annandale Dr
- HTLY 60142 2692 38W-21N D5
- HTLY 60156 2692 38W-21N D5
100 LIHL 60156 2692 38W-21N D5
800 ELGN 60123 2854 36W-9N A7
900 ELGN 60123 2908 36W-9N A1
1000 ELGN 60123 2907 36W-9N E1
S Annandale Dr
100 LIHL 60156 2692 38W-21N D6
W Annapolis Ct
20800 LktT 60544 3340 25W-16S B4
Annapolis Dr
10 VNHL 60061 2647 17W-25N C5
1500 GNVW 60025 2810 9W-14N C5
Ann Arbor Ln
800 VNHL 60061 2647 18W-25N A5
W Anndon Dr
25400 BDWD 60408 3941 31W-40S E4
25400 BDWD 60408 3942 31W-40S A4
25400 RedT 60408 3941 31W-40S E4
Ann Don Ln
900 RedT 60408 3941 32W-40S D4
W Anndon St
500 BDWD 60408 3941 32W-40S E4
500 RedT 60408 3941 32W-40S E4
Anne Ct
- RMVL 60446 3340 25W-15S B1
10 HNWD 60047 2645 22W-25N A6
100 TNTN 60476 3428 0E-20S D4
100 VNHL 60061 2647 16W-25N C6
300 ANHT 60004 2807 15W-16N E1
300 PTHT 60004 2807 15W-16N E1
300 PTHT 60070 2807 15W-16N E1
600 BGBK 60440 3205 21W-10S E5
1100 SYHW 60118 2800 35W-15N C3
8000 ODPK 60462 3346 10W-18S C7
10400 RSMT 60018 2917 13W-8N A1
14800 OKFT 60452 3348 6W-17S A5
Anne Dr
8000 ODPK 60462 3346 10W-18S C7
Anne Ln
600 BGBK 60440 3205 21W-10S E5
1900 CteT 60417 3686 2E-30S D3
2500 NHBK 60062 2809 11W-15N D1
Anne Rd
900 NPVL 60540 3141 26W-6S E5
900 NPVL 60540 3142 26W-6S A6
Anne St
700 WDSK 60098 2524 42W-31N B7
3600 MHRY 60050 2528 32W-32N B5
Anne Ter
300 WLNG 60090 2755 14W-17N C5
W Anne K Dr
14000 HMGN 60491 3343 17W-17S C5
Anne Marie Dr
16700 TYPK 60477 3425 7W-20S C3
Annerino Dr
- BGBK 60440 3269 22W-12S C2
Annetta Av
16900 HLCT 60429 3427 3W-20S C4
Annette Av
4300 NndT 60014 2641 33W-26N A3
4400 NndT 60014 2640 33W-26N E3
Annette Cir
1900 SRGV 60554 3134 44W-7S E7
Annettes Ln
300 SRGV 60554 3134 44W-7S E7
Annico Dr
15700 HMGN 60491 3422 16W-18S A1
Annie Ln
1300 LYVL 60048 2591 18W-30N A3
W Ann Lurie Pl
4000 CHCG 60632 3090 5W-4S C6
Ann Marie Dr
15300 OKFT 60452 3347 6W-18S D7
Ann Marie Ln
5500 OKFT 60452 3347 6W-18S D7
W Annoreno Dr
700 AddT 60101 2970 19W-2N D7
700 ADSN 60101 2970 19W-2N C7
Anns Ln
10 AraT 60505 3138 34W-6S D6
Ansley Ct
1300 MDLN 60060 2646 19W-27N B1
Ansley Ln
1300 MDLN 60060 2646 20W-27N B1
Anson Dr
1900 MLPK 60160 3029 13W-2N A1
1900 MLPK 60164 3029 13W-2N A1
1900 NHLK 60160 3029 13W-2N A1
1900 NHLK 60164 3029 13W-2N A1
2000 MLPK 60160 2973 13W-2N A7
2000 MLPK 60164 2973 13W-2N A7
2000 NHLK 60160 2973 13W-2N A7
2000 NHLK 60164 2973 13W-2N A7
Antares Cir
100 RDLK 60073 2531 24W-34N D1
Antelope Ln
10800 ODPK 60467 3423 13W-20S A4
Antelope Tr
300 CLSM 60188 2968 26W-3N A5
Antelope Springs Rd
3000 NHBK 60062 2756 11W-17N D5
Antholl St
3600 FSMR 60422 3506 4W-23S D3
N Anthon Av
4500 CHCG 60656 2918 10W-5N A7
4700 CHCG 60706 2918 10W-5N A7
4700 NRDG 60706 2918 10W-5N A7

Chicago 7-County Street Index

STREET Block	City	ZIP	Map#	CGS	Grid
Anthonio Ct					
900	INCK	60061	2647	17W-25N	A6
Anthony Av					
16700	HLCT	60428	3427	2W-20S	C4
16700	HLCT	60429	3427	2W-20S	C4
16700	MKHM	60428	3427	2W-20S	C4
17500	CCHL	60478	3426	5W-21S	B5
18300	CCHL	60478	3506	5W-22S	B1
18900	CCHL	60477	3506	5W-22S	B2
18900	RchT	60477	3506	5W-22S	B2
S Anthony Av					
-	CHCG	60619	3152	1E-8S	E7
6800	CHCG	60637	3152	0E-7S	D6
7700	CHCG	60619	3215	1E-8S	A1
8000	CHCG	60617	3215	3E-10S	E5
Anthony Ct					
200	BFGV	60089	2754	16W-17N	D4
400	OSWG	60543	3263	36W-11S	E1
800	NPVL	60563	3140	29W-6S	D4
1200	ANTH	60002	2359	20W-41N	A7
1300	BHPK	60087	2421	11W-38N	E7
1300	WKGN	60087	2421	11W-38N	E7
Anthony Dr					
10800	ODPK	60467	3423	13W-19S	A2
Anthony Ln					
1100	SDWH	60548	3258	51W-14S	A7
1200	DRFD	60015	2703	11W-20N	D7
1400	LKMR	60051	2529	30W-33N	A2
1400	SdwT	60548	3258	51W-14S	A7
1800	LKMR	60051	2528	30W-33N	E2
4200	JLET	60586	3496	29W-21S	D1
8900	SPGV	60081	2414	29W-40N	B2
9500	FXLK	60081	2414	29W-40N	B2
Anthony Pkwy					
100	WcnT	60084	2643	26W-26N	E2
Anthony Rd					
200	BFGV	60089	2754	16W-17N	E5
400	WLNG	60089	2754	16W-17N	D5
400	WLNG	60090	2754	16W-17N	D5
Anthony St					
100	WHTN	60137	3025	23W-0N	A5
100	WHTN	60187	3025	23W-0N	A5
200	GNEN	60137	3025	23W-0N	B5
200	MDLN	60060	2590	18W-27N	E7
Anthony Tr					
200	NHBK	60062	2756	11W-18N	D3
Antietam Ct					
700	NPVL	60540	3203	27W-8S	C1
1900	AURA	60503	3265	33W-11S	B1
Antietam Dr					
1200	LGGV	60047	2700	18W-21N	D7
Antietam St					
500	MTSN	60443	3594	4W-25S	E1
500	MTSN	60466	3594	4W-25S	E1
500	PKFT	60466	3594	4W-25S	E1
500	PKFT	60466	3595	4W-25S	A1
Antigo Tr					
1200	CLSM	60188	2967	28W-4N	B3
Antioch Pl					
10	PKFT	60466	3595	2W-26S	D2
Antioch Rd					
10900	SlmT	53179	2357		E2
12700	ANTH	53179	2357		E2
12700	ANTH	60002	2357		E2
Antioch Rd SR-83					
10900	SlmT	53179	2357		E2
12700	ANTH	53179	2357		E2
12700	ANTH	60002	2357		E2
Antique Ln					
1000	NHBK	60062	2757	8W-18N	D3
Antler Dr					
17300	ODPK	60467	3423	13W-20S	A5
Antler Ln					
5700	WTMT	60559	3144	18W-6S	E4
Antler Tr					
500	CmpT	60175	2962	39W-5N	D2
Antoine Pl					
3400	SCRL	60175	2963	38W-3N	B5
Anton Cir					
3000	AURA	60504	3201	31W-7S	D1
Anton Dr					
100	RMVL	60446	3269	23W-14S	A6
3000	AURA	60504	3201	31W-8S	D1
Anton St					
3100	WldT	60565	3203	27W-11S	B7
N Antonio Av					
37400	LkvT	60046	2475	21W-37N	E2
Antram Av					
1000	JLET	60432	3499	22W-22S	C2
Anvil Ct					
1200	UYPK	60466	3684	3W-30S	C4
1400	BRLT	60103	2966	30W-5N	B1
11100	WldT	60564	3266	30W-13S	B4
N Anvil Ct					
11100	ADSN	60101	2970	19W-5N	C2
Anvil Pl					
8400	TYPK	60487	3424	10W-19S	B2
Anvil Rd					
6100	NndT	60012	2584	35W-29N	B3
A OK Ct					
300	RDLK	60073	2531	24W-34N	D1
Apache Av					
500	CPVL	60110	2748	32W-18N	D4
2400	SLVL	60411	3597	2E-26S	D3
Apache Ct					
200	BGBK	60440	3268	24W-11S	E1
700	LKZH	60047	2699	22W-22N	B5
Apache Dr					
10	MhlT	60187	3082	25W-2S	A3
10	TNTN	60476	3428	0E-20S	E4
400	JLET	60451	3500	19W-23S	D3
500	BTVA	60510	3020	36W-0S	A7
1400	HRPK	60133	2911	26W-7N	E4
1500	NPVL	60563	3141	27W-5S	D2
3200	JLET	60432	3500	19W-23S	D3
4600	IHPK	60525	3146	14W-7S	D5
W Apache Dr					
16500	LKPT	60441	3420	20W-20S	B5
Apache Ln					
200	RtdT	60142	2745	40W-18N	C4
300	HFET	60169	2859	23W-11N	B3
500	CLSM	60188	2967	26W-2N	E7
2200	WDRG	60517	3205	21W-9S	E3
13900	ODPK	60462	3346	9W-16S	C3
E Apache Ln					
1800	MPPT	60056	2808	13W-14N	D5
W Apache Ln					
25700	LKBN	60010	2643	25W-24N	E6
Apache Pl					
7900	ODPK	60462	3346	9W-16S	C3
Apache Rd					
1800	WKGN	60087	2479	11W-36N	C5
Apache Run					
700	PltT	60124	2852	39W-9N	E7
Apache St					
10	PKFT	60466	3595	2W-26S	D2
Apache Tr					
-	ALGN	60102	2694	34W-21N	B6
-	LIHL	60102	2694	34W-21N	B6
200	LIHL	60156	2694	34W-21N	C5
500	LKVL	60046	2474	24W-37N	D2
500	WLNG	60090	2754	16W-17N	D5
1900	RLKB	60073	2474	23W-35N	E5
2600	NndT	60051	2585	31W-31N	D1
8000	TYPK	60477	3424	10W-21S	C6
Apex Ct					
-	NBRN	60010	2698	25W-23N	A1
Apley Ln					
10	YkTp	60181	3085	18W-1S	A1
100	VLPK	60181	3085	18W-1S	A1
Apollo Av					
-	GNEN	60137	3025	22W-0N	C4
Apollo Cir					
2600	OMFD	60461	3507	3W-25S	B7
Apollo Ct					
200	WDDL	60191	2914	19W-5N	D7
300	RDLK	60073	2531	24W-34N	D1
300	VNHL	60061	2647	17W-25N	B6
W Apollo Ct					
23300	LKVL	60046	2416	23W-39N	E5
23300	LkvT	60046	2416	23W-39N	E5
Apollo Dr					
-	EGvT	60007	2860	19W-12N	B2
400	JLET	60435	3497	27W-23S	D4
5600	EGvT	60008	2860	19W-12N	B2
5600	RGMW	60008	2860	19W-12N	B2
24600	PNFD	60585	3266	30W-13S	A5
Apollo Ln					
700	OSWG	60543	3264	34W-11S	C2
4200	SNPK	60165	3029	13W-1N	A2
Appaloosa Ct					
900	SYHW	60118	2799	37W-15N	D4
Appaloosa Ct E					
2100	WHTN	60187	3083	23W-3S	A5
Appaloosa Ct W					
2000	WHTN	60187	3083	23W-3S	A5
Appaloosa Dr					
1800	NPVL	60565	3204	24W-8S	D2
3600	JLET	60435	3417	27W-19S	C3
Appaloosa Ln					
10	OswT	60543	3264	34W-13S	E4
8200	FXLK	60081	2414	29W-40N	C3
S Appaloosa Ln					
14400	HMGN	60491	3344	15W-17S	B5
18900	TroT	60404	3495	32W-22S	D3
Appaloosa Tr					
-	PLNO	60545	3259	46W-13S	E5
-	PLNO	60545	3260	46W-13S	A5
500	CLSM	60188	2967	26W-3N	E6
700	WCDA	60084	2643	27W-26N	C3
1200	MchT	60051	2529	30W-33N	A3
Appaloosa Wy					
1200	BRLT	60103	2966	30W-5N	B1
3100	RLKP	60030	2532	22W-31N	B7
3100	RLKP	60030	2589	22W-31N	C1
Appian Wy					
100	VNHL	60061	2647	17W-25N	B5
500	MTSN	60443	3506	5W-24S	B6
3800	NfdT	60025	2809	11W-13N	D7
Apple Av					
100	LmnT	60439	3271	17W-14S	B6
2800	WKGN	60085	2536	12W-33N	B2
Apple Ct					
10	PKFT	60466	3595	3W-27S	B5
900	AURA	60505	3138	34W-5S	D4
1400	MPPT	60056	2807	16W-14N	E3
Apple Dr					
800	PTHT	60070	2808	13W-15N	E1
800	SMBG	60194	2858	25W-11N	B3
900	PTHT	60062	2809	13W-15N	A1
900	PTHT	60070	2809	13W-15N	A1
900	PTHT	60090	2809	13W-15N	A1
900	WhlT	60062	2809	13W-15N	A1
900	WhlT	60090	2809	13W-15N	A1
Apple Ln					
10	BlmT	60466	3595	3W-27S	C5
10	PKFT	60466	3595	3W-27S	B4
1000	LMBD	60148	3026	19W-0S	D6
1200	ELGN	60120	2855	32W-11N	D4
2000	WDRG	60517	3206	21W-8S	A2
16100	TYPK	60487	3424	10W-19S	B2
S Apple Ln					
12800	ALSP	60803	3276	5W-15S	B7
12800	ALSP	60803	3348	5W-15S	B1
W Apple Ln					
16500	WrnT	60031	2477	16W-35N	D7
Apple St					
900	HFET	60169	2859	23W-11N	A3
1100	SMBG	60169	2859	23W-12N	A2
1100	SMBG	60173	2859	23W-12N	A2
Applebee St					
100	BRTN	60010	2750	25W-20N	E2
Apple Blossom Ct					
1000	LKZH	60047	2698	24W-22N	C4
S Apple Blossom Ln					
26100	MONE	60449	3683	6W-31S	A6
Appleby Cir					
1200	MDLN	60060	2590	19W-28N	C5
Appleby Ct					
800	NPVL	60540	3142	25W-7S	A7
2300	WHTN	60187	3083	23W-3S	A6
Appleby Dr					
100	GLHT	60139	2968	24W-3N	D5
2200	WHTN	60187	3082	23W-3S	E5
2300	WHTN	60187	3083	23W-3S	A5
Appleby Ln					
4000	RNPK	60471	3594	4W-26S	D2
Appleby Rd					
100	IVNS	60067	2805	23W-15N	A2
1400	PLTN	60067	2805	22W-15N	A1
1700	IVNS	60067	2804	23W-15N	D2
Apple Creek Ln					
900	DSPN	60016	2863	12W-10N	B4
24100	PNFD	60586	3416	30W-19S	B4
Applecross Rd					
2100	IVNS	60010	2751	25W-16N	A7
Applegate Av					
800	WCHI	60185	3022	30W-1N	C2
900	DRGV	60516	3206	19W-8S	C1
Applegate Cir					
10	LKZH	60047	2698	24W-22N	C4
Apple Gate Ct					
7200	JLET	60586	3415	33W-20S	A5
Applegate Ct					
400	NPVL	60565	3203	27W-8S	D2
2900	NfdT	60025	2810	10W-13N	B6
W Applegate Ct					
200	RDLK	60073	2531	24W-32N	C4
Apple Gate Dr					
-	JLET	60586	3415	32W-21S	C7
Applegate Dr					
1300	NPVL	60565	3203	27W-8S	C2
Applegate Ln					
500	LKZH	60047	2698	24W-22N	C4
2900	NfdT	60025	2810	10W-13N	A6
Apple Grove Ln					
1500	WTMT	60559	3145	18W-7S	A6
Apple Hill Ct					
1100	ELGN	60120	2855	32W-12N	D1
Apple Hill Ct N					
2500	BFGV	60089	2701	16W-22N	D3
Apple Hill Ct S					
2200	BFGV	60089	2701	16W-22N	E4
Apple Hill Ln					
-	LNSH	60069	2701	16W-22N	E3
10	MTSN	60443	3505	7W-24S	C5
200	SMWD	60107	2857	28W-11N	B4
2100	BFGV	60089	2701	16W-22N	E3
2200	AURA	60506	3137	38W-7S	A7
N Apple Hill Ln					
22700	BFGV	60089	2701	16W-22N	E3
22700	LNSH	60069	2701	16W-23N	E3
22700	VrnT	60069	2701	16W-23N	E3
Applejack Rd					
10	RGMW	60008	2806	19W-14N	B3
E Apple Orchard Ln					
1300	VNHL	60061	2702	14W-23N	B2
1300	VNHL	60069	2702	14W-23N	B2
1300	VrnT	60069	2702	14W-23N	B2
W Apple Orchard Ln					
15100	VNHL	60069	2702	15W-23N	B1
15100	VrnT	60069	2702	15W-23N	A1
Apple River Dr					
300	NPVL	60565	3204	25W-10S	A6
Appleton Ct					
4900	JNBG	60050	2472	30W-36N	A3
Appleton Dr					
300	VNHL	60061	2647	17W-25N	C5
400	BTVA	60510	3078	34W-1S	D2
Appleton Ln					
-	DrrT	60014	2638	39W-26N	D3
-	LKWD	60014	2638	39W-26N	D3
300	LKVL	60046	2474	23W-36N	E3
1100	GNVA	60134	3020	33W-1N	E2
1100	GNVA	60174	3020	33W-2N	E2
1100	SCRL	60174	3020	33W-2N	E2
1200	SCRL	60134	3020	33W-2N	E2
Apple Tree Ct					
100	YKVL	60560	3333	42W-14S	C1
Appletree Ct					
10	LIHL	60156	2693	38W-22N	A3
200	BFGV	60089	2754	17W-20N	A1
600	DRFD	60015	2703	11W-20N	C7
800	BRLT	60103	2910	29W-6N	D7
800	NHBK	60062	2756	10W-17N	E4
N Apple Tree Ct					
900	PLTN	60067	2752	20W-17N	E5
Appletree Dr					
17100	CCHL	60478	3426	4W-20S	D5
17100	HLCT	60429	3426	4W-20S	D5
Apple Tree Ln					
600	GLNC	60022	2758	7W-17N	B4
700	HDPK	60035	2704	9W-23N	B1
900	WCHI	60185	3022	29W-0S	E7
900	WCHI	60185	3080	29W-0S	E1
1600	WnfT	60185	3080	29W-0S	E1
Appletree Ln					
200	WLMT	60091	2812	5W-13N	B7
500	DRFD	60015	2756	11W-20N	C1
600	DRFD	60015	2703	11W-20N	C7
800	GNVW	60025	2811	7W-13N	B5
1200	AURA	60506	3137	38W-5S	B4
1300	LYVL	60048	2647	15W-27N	E1
2600	NHBK	60062	2756	10W-17N	E4
7500	WLBK	60527	3207	17W-8S	C2
24200	PNFD	60585	3266	30W-14S	B6
E Appletree Ln					
10	ANHT	60004	2754	17W-16N	A7
S Appletree Ln					
1100	BRLT	60103	2910	29W-6N	D7
W Apple Tree Ln					
26500	CbaT	60010	2697	26W-22N	C4
W Appletree Ln					
10	ANHT	60004	2754	17W-16N	A7
700	BRLT	60103	2966	29W-6N	D1
800	BRLT	60103	2910	29W-6N	D7
Apple Tree Rd					
100	NtrT	60093	2811	5W-15N	E3
100	WNKA	60093	2811	5W-15N	E3
Appletree St					
6600	HRPK	60133	2911	27W-8N	D3
Apple Valley Dr					
900	BRLT	60103	2910	30W-6N	C6
1600	WCDA	60084	2588	25W-29N	B4
Apple Valley Rd					
800	HRVD	60033	2406	50W-39N	A5
1500	BGBK	60490	3267	27W-12S	C3
W Appleway Ct					
13800	HMGN	60491	3343	17W-17S	C5
Applewood Ct					
-	DRGV	60516	3144	18W-7S	E7
10	CRY	60013	2695	32W-23N	B2
300	BGBK	60440	3268	25W-12S	B2
2300	JLET	60586	3416	30W-20S	C3
3100	HDPK	60035	2704	10W-24N	A1
15800	WDWH	60083	2420	15W-39N	A4
N Applewood Ct					
8100	HRPK	60133	2857	26W-9N	E7
S Applewood Ct					
8000	HRPK	60133	2857	26W-9N	E7
W Applewood Ct					
16500	WrnT	60031	2477	16W-35N	D6
Applewood Dr					
-	WCDA	60084	2588	25W-29N	B4
-	WcnT	60084	2588	25W-29N	B4
300	BGBK	60440	3204	25W-11S	B7
300	BGBK	60440	3268	25W-12S	B2
12800	HTLY	60142	2744	42W-19N	E3
Applewood Ln					
100	BMDL	60108	2969	22W-4N	B3
500	ALGN	60102	2695	32W-20N	B7
900	ALGN	60102	2748	32W-20N	B1
2200	WDSK	60098	2582	39W-29N	C3
2400	DrrT	60098	2582	39W-29N	C4
4000	NHBK	60062	2756	12W-18N	B3
4100	MTSN	60443	3506	5W-25S	C7
16000	ODHL	60487	3424	11W-19S	A2
16000	ODPK	60462	3424	11W-19S	A1
16000	ODPK	60487	3424	11W-19S	A1
E Applewood Ln					
6600	SPGV	60050	2414	30W-38N	A7
6600	SPGV	60081	2414	30W-38N	A6
N Applewood Ln					
1500	SPGV	60081	2414	30W-38N	A6
W Applewood Ln					
-	BtnT	60050	2414	30W-38N	A7
-	SPGV	60050	2414	30W-38N	A7
6600	SPGV	60081	2414	30W-38N	A6
Appley Av					
100	LYVL	60048	2591	16W-29N	D4
Appling Ln					
300	BGBK	60440	3269	23W-11S	A1
Appollo Ct					
400	WHTN	60187	3082	24W-2S	D3
Appomattox Cir					
900	NPVL	60540	3203	27W-8S	B1
Appomattox Tr					
1200	CLSM	60188	2967	28W-4N	B3
Apricot Ct					
1400	MPPT	60056	2807	16W-14N	D3
Apricot St					
900	HFET	60169	2859	23W-11N	B3
1600	BGBK	60490	3267	26W-12S	D3
April Av					
200	VNHL	60061	2647	17W-25N	C5
6200	MHRY	60050	2470	35W-34N	B7
6200	MHRY	60050	2527	35W-34N	B1
April Ct					
300	NARA	60542	3078	36W-3S	A6
9200	MKNA	60448	3503	11W-23S	E3
April Ln					
100	NARA	60542	3078	35W-3S	A6
1400	WPHR	60096	2363	10W-41N	B7
1400	WPHR	60096	2422	10W-41N	B1
9200	MKNA	60448	3503	11W-23S	E3
Aptakisic Rd					
-	LGGV	60047	2700	18W-22N	E5
-	VrnT	60047	2700	18W-22N	E5
5100	BFGV	60047	2701	17W-22N	B5
5100	BFGV	60089	2701	17W-22N	B5
5100	LGGV	60047	2701	17W-22N	A5
5100	LGGV	60089	2701	17W-22N	B5
Aptakisic Rd CO-A44					
-	LGGV	60047	2700	18W-22N	E5
-	VrnT	60047	2700	18W-22N	E5
5100	BFGV	60047	2701	17W-22N	B5
5100	BFGV	60089	2701	17W-22N	B5
5100	LGGV	60047	2701	17W-22N	A5
5100	LGGV	60089	2701	17W-22N	B5
W Aptakisic Rd					
-	VrnT	60069	2702	14W-21N	B5
400	BFGV	60069	2701	17W-22N	C5
400	BFGV	60089	2701	17W-22N	C5
400	BFGV	60089	2702	15W-21N	A5
400	LNSH	60069	2702	15W-21N	A5
400	LNSH	60089	2702	15W-21N	A5
400	VrnT	60069	2701	17W-22N	B5
500	BFGV	60069	2702	15W-21N	A5
700	BFGV	60089	2754	16W-18N	C2
700	WLNG	60089	2754	16W-18N	C2
1200	BFGV	60047	2701	17W-22N	B5
1200	LGGV	60047	2701	17W-22N	B5
1200	LGGV	60089	2701	17W-22N	B5
15600	LNSH	60069	2701	17W-22N	B5
16100	VrnT	60089	2701	16W-22N	E5
W Aptakisic Rd CO-A44					
-	VrnT	60069	2702	14W-21N	B5
400	BFGV	60069	2701	17W-22N	C5
400	BFGV	60089	2701	17W-22N	C5
400	BFGV	60089	2702	15W-21N	A5
400	LNSH	60069	2702	15W-21N	A5
400	LNSH	60089	2702	15W-21N	A5
400	VrnT	60069	2701	17W-22N	B5
500	BFGV	60069	2702	15W-21N	A5
1200	BFGV	60047	2701	17W-22N	B5
1200	LGGV	60047	2701	17W-22N	B5
1200	LGGV	60089	2701	17W-22N	B5
15600	LNSH	60069	2701	17W-22N	B5
16100	VrnT	60089	2701	16W-22N	E5
Aqua Ct					
300	VNHL	60061	2647	17W-25N	B5
Aqualand Wy					
900	SCRL	60174	3021	33W-2N	B1
Aqueduct Dr					
10	DMND	60416	3941	33W-39S	B1
Aquinas Ct					
11100	ODPK	60467	3422	14W-19S	E2
Arabian Av					
1800	NPVL	60565	3204	24W-8S	E2
Arabian Ct					
10	SMWD	60107	2856	30W-10N	C5
700	RLKP	60030	2589	22W-30N	C1
700	WCDA	60084	2643	27W-26N	C2
Arabian Dr					
13400	HMGN	60491	3343	16W-18S	E7
Arabian Pkwy					
400	SYHW	60118	2799	36W-15N	E4
Arabian Spur					
1400	MchT	60051	2529	30W-33N	A3
Arabian Tr					
10100	BLVY	60098	2468	39W-34N	C7
10100	BLVY	60098	2525	39W-34N	D1
10100	GwdT	60098	2468	39W-34N	C7
10100	GwdT	60098	2525	39W-34N	D1
N Aralia Dr					
1700	MPPT	60056	2808	13W-15N	D2
1800	PTHT	60070	2808	13W-15N	D2
Arapaho Dr					
10	TNTN	60476	3428	0E-20S	E5
2000	WCHI	60185	2966	30W-3N	B6
Arapaho Pl					
7900	ODPK	60462	3346	9W-16S	C3
7900	OrlT	60462	3346	9W-16S	C3
Arapaho Tr					
500	LKVL	60046	2475	22W-38N	B1
S Arapaho Tr					
13800	HMGN	60491	3343	16W-16S	D3
Arapahoe Ct					
1200	NPVL	60540	3202	28W-8S	E2
Arapahoe Tr					
100	CLSM	60188	2968	25W-2N	A7
N Arapahoe Tr					
600	LKVL	60046	2474	23W-36N	E5
600	RLKH	60073	2474	23W-36N	E5
Arbeleda Ln					
2200	NHBK	60062	2810	10W-15N	A2
Arbon Ct					
100	LYWD	60411	3510	4E-25S	C7
200	CRTE	60417	3596	0E-28S	E6
Arbor Av					
10	SRGV	60554	3135	42W-7S	D7
100	WCHI	60185	3022	29W-1N	C3
300	WHTN	60187	3082	25W-1S	B1
600	WnfT	60185	3022	29W-1N	C3
1200	HDPK	60035	2704	9W-21N	B5
7400	BRRG	60527	3208	14W-8S	D1
W Arbor Blvd					
18700	WrnT	60030	2533	18W-32N	D5
18900	GYLK	60030	2533	18W-32N	D5
Arbor Cir					
-	LKMR	60051	2529	29W-32N	D4
1100	LNHT	60046	2475	21W-37N	D2
2200	DRGV	60515	3143	21W-4S	E1
Arbor Ct					
10	BFGV	60089	2754	17W-18N	B3
10	SMWD	60107	2856	30W-10N	C6
200	BGBK	60440	3269	23W-12S	A3
400	GNEN	60137	3025	22W-0S	B6
400	LYVL	60048	2591	16W-29N	D5
400	WNFD	60190	3023	26W-0N	E4
600	OSWG	60543	3262	39W-12S	E4
900	WHTN	60187	3082	25W-1S	B1
1000	ANHT	60005	2861	17W-11N	B2
1000	ANHT	60056	2861	17W-11N	B2
1000	MPPT	60005	2861	17W-11N	B2
1000	MPPT	60056	2861	17W-11N	B2
1100	LKBF	60044	2593	10W-29N	E4
1600	DRN	60561	3207	18W-8S	A1
1800	GRNE	60031	2477	15W-36N	E5
16500	PNFD	60586	3416	29W-19S	D4
N Arbor Ct					
38500	WDWH	60083	2420	14W-38N	C7
W Arbor Ct					
1600	PLTN	60067	2752	23W-17N	A5
Arbor Dr					
-	RGMW	60173	2806	21W-12N	A7
-	SMBG	60067	2806	21W-12N	A7
-	SMBG	60173	2805	22W-12N	C7
-	SMBG	60173	2806	21W-12N	A7
10	EMHT	60126	3027	16W-0S	E7
10	LKBF	60044	2593	10W-29N	E4
10	SMWD	60107	2856	30W-10N	C6
10	YkTp	60126	3027	16W-0S	E7
100	CLSM	60188	2968	25W-3N	B6
200	LKBF	60044	2594	10W-29N	A4
300	NPVL	60540	3141	27W-7S	B7
300	NpvT	60540	3141	27W-7S	B7
500	RLKP	60073	2532	22W-34N	B1
1100	RMVL	60446	3268	25W-14S	B6
1200	LMNT	60439	3342	19W-15S	D1
2600	MchT	60050	2528	31W-33N	C2
3000	MHRY	60050	2528	31W-33N	C2
4700	RGMW	60008	2806	21W-12N	A7
4700	RGMW	60008	2860	21W-12N	A1
4700	RGMW	60173	2860	21W-12N	A1
4700	SMBG	60008	2806	21W-12N	A7
4700	SMBG	60008	2860	21W-12N	A1
4700	SMBG	60173	2860	21W-12N	A1
7200	TYPK	60477	3424	9W-21S	E6
11700	ODPK	60467	3344	14W-18S	D6
S Arbor Dr					
-	PNFD	60544	3416	29W-19S	D2
12500	ALSP	60803	3276	4W-14S	D6
15900	PNFD	60586	3416	29W-19S	D3
Arbor Ln					
10	DndT	60102	2747	34W-19N	D2
10	DndT	60118	2747	34W-19N	D2
100	MltT	60137	3083	22W-3S	B6
200	BMDL	60108	2969	22W-4N	D3
400	WTMT	60559	3144	18W-7S	E6
400	WTMT	60559	3145	18W-7S	A6
400	WynT	60185	2966	30W-3N	B5
500	BtlT	60543	3262	39W-12S	E4
500	OSWG	60543	3262	39W-12S	E3
500	SEGN	60177	2908	35W-7N	B4
1000	GNVW	60025	2811	6W-13N	C6
1100	LKFT	60045	2703	12W-23N	B2
1400	NfdT	60062	2756	12W-17N	C6
1400	NHBK	60062	2756	12W-17N	C6
1500	ELGN	60123	2908	35W-9N	B1
1600	CTHL	60403	3418	25W-21S	B7
1600	CTHL	60403	3498	25W-21S	B1
1600	JLET	60435	3498	25W-21S	B1
2000	NHFD	60093	2811	6W-14N	C3
2800	AURA	60502	3079	33W-3S	A6
3200	PRGV	60012	2585	32W-27N	B7
5200	CTWD	60445	3347	6W-15S	E1
7200	JSTC	60458	3148	10W-8S	B7
9700	MKNA	60448	3503	12W-24S	D5
N Arbor Ln					
1100	PLTN	60067	2752	23W-17N	A5
1300	PLTN	60010	2752	23W-17N	A5
1300	PltT	60010	2752	23W-17N	A5
W Arbor Ln					
21200	ElaT	60047	2699	21W-24N	D1
21200	KLDR	60047	2699	21W-24N	D1
26200	CNHN	60410	3672	32W-30S	C5
26300	AxST	60447	3672	32W-30S	C5
26300	CNHN	60447	3672	32W-30S	C5
Arbor Rd					
300	ISLK	60042	2586	28W-28N	E7
7600	MchT	60097	2469	36W-35N	D6
7600	WRLK	60097	2469	36W-35N	D6
Arbor Sq					
-	SMBG	60173	2860	21W-12N	A1
Arbor St					
700	JLET	60432	3500	21W-23S	A3
W Arbor Ter					
16500	LKPT	60441	3342	20W-18S	B7
N Arbor Tr					
100	PKFT	60466	3595	2W-28S	C6
S Arbor Tr					
10	PKFT	60466	3595	2W-28S	C6
12200	PSHT	60463	3275	7W-14S	B6
12200	WthT	60463	3275	7W-14S	B6
Arbor Cove					
800	PLTN	60067	2752	22W-17N	B6
Arbor Creek Dr					
-	JLET	60586	3417	28W-20S	A4
16700	PnfT	60586	3416	29W-20S	E5
23000	PnfT	60586	3417	28W-20S	A4
Arbor Creek Rd					
10	CmpT	60175	2962	39W-3N	E6
Arbordale Ct					
10	ALGN	60102	2746	36W-19N	E2
Arbordale Dr					
12900	PNFD	60585	3338	29W-15S	D2
Arbordale Ln					
1700	ALGN	60102	2747	36W-19N	A2
E Arboretum Cir					
200	WHTN	60187	3082	24W-3S	D6
N Arboretum Cir					
400	WHTN	60187	3082	24W-3S	D6
600	MltT	60187	3082	24W-3S	D6
S Arboretum Cir					
300	WHTN	60187	3082	24W-3S	D6
W Arboretum Cir					
300	WHTN	60187	3082	24W-3S	D6
Arboretum Ct					
10	NBRN	60010	2698	24W-21N	B5
Arboretum Dr					
10	LMBD	60148	3084	20W-2S	B3
10	NBRN	60010	2698	24W-21N	B5
S Arboretum Dr					
14600	HMGN	60491	3343	17W-17S	D6
Arboretum Ln					
700	CmpT	60175	2961	42W-5N	D2
Arboretum Rd					
300	MltT	60137	3083	22W-2S	C4

STREET Block	City	ZIP	Map#	CGS	Grid
Arboretum Wy					
400	OSWG	60543	3263	37W-13S	D6
Arbor Falls Ct					
5700	JLET	60586	3416	31W-21S	A7
Arbor Falls Dr					
1800	JLET	60586	3416	31W-21S	A7
Arborfields Dr					
1800	JLET	60586	3416	31W-21S	A7
Arbor Gate Ct					
1900	JLET	60586	3415	31W-21S	E7
Arbor Gate Dr					
1800	JLET	60586	3416	31W-21S	A7
5600	JLET	60586	3415	31W-21S	E7
5600	PnfT	60586	3415	31W-21S	E7
5600	PnfT	60586	3416	31W-21S	A7
Arbor Gate Ln					
300	BFGV	60089	2701	17W-21N	C7
300	BFGV	60089	2754	17W-20N	A1
Arbor Glen Blvd					
-	HFET	60169	2805	23W-12N	A7
-	HFET	60195	2805	23W-12N	A7
-	HFET	60195	2859	23W-12N	A1
-	SMBG	60169	2805	23W-12N	A7
-	SMBG	60195	2804	23W-12N	E7
-	SMBG	60195	2805	23W-12N	A7
-	SMBG	60195	2859	23W-12N	A1
Arbor Glen Dr					
-	JLET	60586	3416	31W-21S	A7
Arbor Hill Ct					
300	NLNX	60451	3501	18W-24S	A5
Arbor Lakes Dr					
-	MNKA	60447	3672	34W-29S	A3
Arbor Ridge Dr					
100	MTGY	60538	3199	36W-9S	E5
11000	ODPK	60467	3344	13W-16S	E4
11000	ODPK	60467	3345	13W-16S	A4
11000	OrlT	60467	3344	13W-16S	E4
11000	OrlT	60467	3345	13W-16S	A4
Arbors Edge Ct					
10	BGBK	60490	3267	26W-13S	D5
Arborsedge Dr					
3000	JLET	60436	3497	27W-25S	C7
Arborside Dr					
1100	AURA	60502	3139	32W-5S	C4
Arborside Ln					
2500	AURA	60502	3139	32W-5S	B4
Arborview Blvd					
13600	PNFD	60585	3337	33W-16S	A3
Arborview Cir					
13500	PNFD	60585	3337	33W-16S	A3
Arbor View Dr					
4300	LSLE	60532	3143	22W-4S	B1
Arbor Villa Dr					
5600	PTBR	60010	2642	29W-26N	C3
Arborvitae Cir					
16000	CTHL	60403	3418	25W-19S	B2
Arbor Vitae Ln					
2000	HRPK	60133	2911	27W-9N	C1
Arbor Vitae Rd					
1200	DRFD	60015	2703	11W-21N	C7
Arborvitae Rd					
500	WNKA	60093	2812	4W-15N	B1
Arborwood Cir					
1500	RMVL	60446	3339	26W-17S	E5
Arborwood Ct					
10	RMVL	60446	3339	26W-17S	E5
Arbour Ct					
400	MDLN	60060	2590	18W-28N	E6
W Arbour Pl					
-	CHCG	60607	3033	1W-0N	D4
-	CHCG	60612	3033	1W-0N	D4
Arbour Walk Dr					
8900	FKFT	60423	3504	11W-25S	A7
9000	FKFT	60423	3592	11W-25S	A1
Arbury Ct					
10	BGBK	60440	3204	24W-11S	D7
10	WNVL	60555	3080	30W-2S	C4
700	RMVL	60446	3269	23W-14S	A6
W Arcade Dr					
25300	LkvT	60046	2474	25W-37N	B2
W Arcade Dr N					
25400	LkvT	60046	2474	25W-37N	A2
W Arcade Dr S					
25300	LkvT	60046	2474	25W-37N	A2
Arcade Pl					
10	LGNG	60525	3087	12W-4S	B7
W Arcade Pl					
-	CHCG	60602	3034		D5
100	CHCG	60603	3034		D5
100	CHCG	60606	3034	0W-0S	B5
1300	CHCG	60607	3033	1W-0S	D5
Arcadia Av					
100	RMVL	60446	3268	24W-14S	E7
17700	LNSG	60438	3429	3E-21S	E6
Arcadia Cir					
2500	NPVL	60540	3140	29W-7S	D7
Arcadia Ct					
-	PNFD	60586	3415	32W-19S	C3
10	BRRG	60527	3208	16W-10S	A6
100	BGBK	60440	3269	23W-11S	B2
200	VNHL	60061	2647	17W-25N	C5
2200	AURA	60503	3201	31W-10S	D6
Arcadia Dr					
6200	TYPK	60477	3425	7W-20S	B3
Arcadia Ln					
-	HNWD	60047	2644	24W-24N	C7
-	LKZH	60047	2644	24W-24N	C7
10	KdlT	60560	3332	44W-17S	E7
Arcadia Rd					
10	LbvT	60044	2592	13W-28N	E6
Arcadia St					
200	PKFT	60466	3595	2W-26S	D2
3400	SKOK	60203	2866	4W-11N	C3
3700	SKOK	60076	2866	4W-11N	C3
5100	SKOK	60077	2865	6W-11N	D3
5400	MNGV	60053	2865	6W-11N	D3
5400	SKOK	60053	2865	6W-11N	D3
7200	MNGV	60053	2864	9W-11N	D3
7800	NLES	60053	2864	9W-11N	B3
7800	NLES	60714	2864	9W-11N	B3
Arcadia Tr					
500	ROSL	60172	2913	22W-8N	B2
Arcadian Ct					
20400	OMFD	60461	3506	4W-24S	E6
Arcadian Dr					
20300	OMFD	60461	3506	4W-24S	E6
Arcadian Wy					
20500	OMFD	60461	3506	4W-24S	E6
Arcady Dr					
1000	LKFT	60045	2649	12W-24N	B7
Arch Ct					
100	JLET	60432	3499	23W-23S	A4
W Arch Dr					
28300	CbaT	60010	2696	28W-23N	E2
S Arch St					
2900	CHCG	60608	3091	1W-2S	D3

STREET Block	City	ZIP	Map#	CGS	Grid
Archbury Ln					
2300	PKRG	60068	2917	11W-8N	D1
Archel Hanson Ter					
5300	SKOK	60077	2865	6W-11N	D3
Archer Av					
-	JSTC	60458	3209	11W-9S	E2
-	JSTC	60480	3209	11W-9S	E2
-	LmnT	60439	3272	15W-12S	A1
-	LmnT	60480	3208	15W-11S	C7
-	LmnT	60480	3272	15W-12S	A1
-	PlsT	60480	3208	14W-11S	C7
500	WKGN	60085	2537	10W-33N	A3
600	AURA	60506	3199	36W-7S	E1
7200	CHCG	60501	3148	9W-5S	E3
7200	CHCG	60638	3148	9W-5S	E3
7200	SMMT	60501	3148	9W-5S	E3
8000	WLSP	60480	3209	13W-10S	A5
9000	PlsT	60480	3209	13W-10S	A5
13900	HmrT	60441	3342	20W-16S	B4
13900	HmrT	60491	3342	20W-16S	B4
14400	LktT	60441	3342	20W-17S	A5
14500	LKPT	60441	3342	21W-17S	A5
14700	LKPT	60441	3341	21W-17S	E6
14700	LktT	60441	3341	21W-17S	E6
Archer Av SR-171					
-	JSTC	60458	3209	11W-9S	E2
-	JSTC	60480	3209	11W-9S	E2
-	LmnT	60439	3272	15W-12S	A1
-	LmnT	60480	3208	15W-11S	C7
-	LmnT	60480	3272	15W-12S	A1
-	PlsT	60480	3208	14W-11S	C7
8000	WLSP	60480	3209	13W-10S	A5
9000	PlsT	60480	3209	13W-10S	A5
13900	HmrT	60441	3342	20W-16S	B4
13900	HmrT	60491	3342	20W-16S	B4
14400	LktT	60441	3342	20W-17S	A5
14500	LKPT	60441	3342	21W-17S	A5
14700	LKPT	60441	3341	21W-17S	E6
14700	LktT	60441	3341	21W-17S	E6
N Archer Av					
100	MDLN	60060	2590	18W-27N	D7
S Archer Av					
-	JSTC	60458	3209	11W-9S	E2
-	JSTC	60458	3210	11W-8S	A2
-	JSTC	60480	3209	11W-9S	E2
-	WLSP	60480	3209	11W-9S	E2
10	MDLN	60060	2646	18W-27N	D1
1900	CHCG	60616	3092	0W-2S	A2
2400	CHCG	60608	3092	0W-2S	A2
2500	CHCG	60608	3091	2W-3S	C4
3400	CHCG	60609	3091	2W-3S	B5
3700	CHCG	60632	3091	3W-3S	B5
4000	CHCG	60632	3090	3W-4S	E7
4600	CHCG	60632	3150	5W-5S	A2
5300	CHCG	60638	3150	5W-5S	A2
5400	CHCG	60638	3149	7W-5S	C3
10800	LMNT	60439	3272	16W-13S	A4
11300	LMNT	60439	3271	16W-13S	E5
12700	LMNT	60439	3343	18W-15S	A1
12900	LMNT	60439	3342	19W-16S	C3
13400	HMGN	60439	3342	19W-15S	D2
13400	HMGN	60491	3342	19W-15S	D2
13500	HMGN	60441	3342	19W-16S	D3
13500	HmrT	60441	3342	19W-16S	D3
13500	HmrT	60491	3342	19W-16S	D3
S Archer Av SR-83					
10800	LMNT	60439	3272	16W-12S	A3
S Archer Av SR-171					
-	JSTC	60458	3209	11W-9S	E2
-	JSTC	60458	3210	11W-8S	A2
-	JSTC	60480	3209	11W-9S	E2
-	WLSP	60480	3209	11W-9S	E2
10800	LMNT	60439	3272	16W-13S	A4
11300	LMNT	60439	3271	16W-13S	E5
12700	LMNT	60439	3343	18W-15S	A1
12900	LMNT	60439	3342	19W-16S	C3
13400	HMGN	60439	3342	19W-15S	D2
13400	HMGN	60491	3342	19W-15S	D2
13500	HMGN	60441	3342	19W-16S	D3
13500	HmrT	60441	3342	19W-16S	D3
13500	HmrT	60491	3342	19W-16S	D3
W Archer Av					
6400	CHCG	60638	3149	8W-5S	A3
6800	CHCG	60638	3148	9W-5S	D3
7100	CHCG	60501	3148	8W-5S	E3
7100	SMMT	60501	3148	8W-5S	E3
Archer Ln					
800	ELWD	60421	3675	25W-31S	C6
S Archer Rd					
5500	SMMT	60501	3148	10W-7S	B7
6300	BDPK	60501	3148	9W-7S	C5
6600	BDPK	60455	3148	9W-7S	C6
6700	BGVW	60455	3148	9W-7S	C6
6700	BGVW	60501	3148	9W-7S	C6
6800	BDPK	60458	3148	9W-7S	C6
6800	BGVW	60458	3148	9W-7S	C6
7000	JSTC	60458	3148	10W-7S	B7
7000	JSTC	60501	3148	10W-7S	B7
7300	JSTC	60458	3210	10W-8S	A1
S Archer Rd SR-171					
5500	SMMT	60501	3148	10W-7S	B7
6300	BDPK	60501	3148	9W-7S	C5
6600	BDPK	60455	3148	9W-7S	C6
6700	BGVW	60455	3148	9W-7S	C6
6700	BGVW	60501	3148	9W-7S	C6
6800	BDPK	60458	3148	9W-7S	C6
6800	BGVW	60458	3148	9W-7S	C6
7000	JSTC	60458	3148	10W-7S	B7
7000	JSTC	60501	3148	10W-7S	B7
7300	JSTC	60458	3210	10W-8S	A1
Arches Ct					
-	JLET	60586	3415	32W-20S	C5
Arches Dr					
2700	JLET	60586	3415	32W-20S	C5
Archibald St					
-	LtRT	60545	3259	47W-12S	D4
-	PLNO	60545	3259	47W-12S	D4
Arctic Ct					
13000	LMNT	60439	3343	16W-15S	D1
Arctic Ln					
13400	LMNT	60439	3343	16W-15S	D1
Ardaugh Av					
1900	CTHL	60403	3417	26W-21S	E7
Arden Av					
3300	BKFD	60513	3088	10W-3S	A5
3800	LYNS	60513	3088	10W-3S	A6
Arden Ct					
10	OKBK	60523	3085	18W-2S	A3
Arden Ln					
10	RDLK	60073	2589	23W-30N	A2
200	RDLK	60073	2588	23W-30N	E2
2100	FmtT	60073	2588	23W-30N	E1
2100	RDLK	60030	2588	23W-30N	E1
19900	FftT	60448	3502	14W-24S	E4
19900	MKNA	60448	3502	14W-24S	E4

STREET Block	City	ZIP	Map#	CGS	Grid
Arden Pl					
2700	JLET	60435	3497	27W-23S	C3
W Arden Pl					
1600	JLET	60435	3498	26W-23S	A3
2000	JLET	60435	3497	26W-23S	E3
Ardennes Ct					
600	WnfT	60190	3081	28W-1S	A2
Arden Shore Dr S					
200	LKBF	60044	2594	10W-29N	A4
Arden Shore Rd					
-	LKBF	60044	2593	10W-29N	E4
-	LKBF	60044	2594	10W-29N	A4
Arden Shore Rd N					
-	LKBF	60044	2594	10W-29N	A3
Ardglass Ct					
400	BGBK	60440	3205	22W-11S	D7
W Ardith St					
2800	JLET	60435	3417	27W-20S	B6
2800	PnfT	60431	3417	27W-20S	B6
2800	PnfT	60435	3417	27W-20S	B6
Ardley Ct					
100	NPVL	60565	3203	26W-10S	E6
Ardmore Av					
100	OKTR	60181	3085	17W-1S	A1
100	VLPK	60181	3085	17W-1S	A1
100	YkTp	60181	3085	17W-1S	B1
500	AddT	60101	2971	18W-2N	A7
500	AddT	60181	2971	18W-2N	A7
500	ADSN	60101	2971	18W-2N	A7
500	ADSN	60181	2971	17W-2N	A7
900	ITSC	60143	2914	20W-7N	A5
1500	GLHT	60139	2969	22W-2N	B7
2200	IVNS	60067	2804	24W-15N	D1
2400	HFET	60067	2804	24W-15N	D1
2400	HFET	60192	2804	24W-15N	D1
E Ardmore Av					
300	ROSL	60172	2913	23W-7N	B5
N Ardmore Av					
10	VLPK	60181	3027	18W-1N	A2
800	ADSN	60181	3027	17W-2N	B1
900	ADSN	60181	2971	18W-2N	A7
900	VLPK	60181	2971	18W-2N	A7
1100	ADSN	60101	2971	18W-2N	A7
1100	VLPK	60101	2971	18W-2N	A7
S Ardmore Av					
10	VLPK	60181	3027	17W-0N	A5
400	ADSN	60101	2971	17W-2N	A6
600	AddT	60101	2971	17W-2N	A7
600	ADSN	60101	2971	17W-2N	A7
600	ADSN	60181	2971	17W-2N	A7
700	ADSN	60101	2971	17W-2N	A7
700	VLPK	60101	2971	17W-2N	A7
1300	YkTp	60181	3027	17W-0S	A7
1600	OKTR	60181	3027	17W-1S	A7
1700	OKTR	60181	3085	18W-1S	A2
1700	VLPK	60181	3085	18W-1S	A2
1700	YkTp	60181	3085	18W-1S	A2
W Ardmore Av					
-	CHCG	60646	2920	4W-7N	B4
300	BmdT	60172	2912	23W-7N	E5
300	ROSL	60172	2912	23W-7N	E5
400	BmdT	60172	2913	23W-7N	A5
900	CHCG	60640	2921	1W-7N	E4
1200	CHCG	60660	2921	1W-7N	D4
1200	ITSC	60143	2914	21W-7N	A5
1300	ITSC	60143	2913	21W-7N	E5
2400	CHCG	60659	2921	3W-7N	A4
2600	CHCG	60659	2920	3W-7N	E4
5800	CHCG	60646	2919	7W-7N	B4
6300	CHCG	60631	2919	8W-7N	A4
6700	CHCG	60631	2918	8W-7N	E4
7700	CHCG	60068	2918	9W-7N	C4
7700	PKRG	60068	2918	9W-7N	C4
N Ardmore Cir					
4600	JNBG	60050	2471	30W-36N	E4
4600	JNBG	60050	2472	30W-36N	A4
W Ardmore Cir					
20800	LktT	60544	3340	26W-16S	A4
Ardmore Ct					
300	VNHL	60061	2647	17W-25N	C5
1100	SMBG	60193	2912	25W-9N	C1
S Ardmore Ct					
14000	LktT	60544	3340	26W-16S	A4
Ardmore Dr					
1100	NPVL	60540	3203	28W-8S	A1
1200	CRY	60013	2641	31W-24N	D6
1300	RLKB	60073	2475	23W-35N	A7
Ardmore Ln					
10	GNVW	60025	2811	6W-13N	D7
1700	WHTN	60187	3082	26W-1S	A1
1900	WHTN	60187	3081	27W-1S	D1
N Ardmore Ln					
38500	LkvT	60046	2416	24W-38N	D7
Ardmore Rd					
100	DSPN	60016	2862	14W-12N	C1
Ardmore St					
10	AddT	60106	2915	17W-7N	C5
Ardmore Ter					
600	LYVL	60048	2591	16W-28N	E6
E Ardmore Ter					
400	ADSN	60101	2971	18W-2N	A6
Ardrum					
-	NLNX	60451	3590	16W-25S	A1
Ardsley Rd					
600	WNKA	60093	2811	5W-16N	E1
Ardwick Dr					
1600	HFET	60169	2858	25W-12N	B1
E Ardyce Ln					
900	MPPT	60056	2808	14W-13N	C6
Area Dr					
600	ISLK	60051	2642	29W-27N	C1
600	NndT	60051	2642	29W-27N	C1
Arena Dr					
-	BlmT	60411	3509	2E-23S	C3
-	LYWD	60411	3509	2E-23S	C3
Argent Ln					
-	AURA	60504	3202	30W-8S	C1
Argo Ln					
1300	HmrT	60441	3420	21W-18S	A1
1300	LKPT	60441	3420	21W-18S	A1
1300	LktT	60441	3420	21W-18S	A1
Argonaut Pl					
400	NCHI	60088	2593	11W-30N	D1
Argonne Dr					
800	NCHI	60064	2537	10W-32N	A5
1000	NCHI	60064	2536	12W-31N	C6
10300	WDRG	60517	3270	20W-12S	C2
Argonne Ridge Rd					
200	DGvT	60527	3207	17W-10S	C5
Argonne Woods Dr					
10300	DGvT	60517	3270	19W-12S	C2
10300	WDRG	60517	3270	19W-12S	C2
Argyle Av					
10	BmdT	60172	2912	25W-6N	B7
10	JltT	60433	3500	21W-24S	A5
300	BMDL	60108	2912	25W-6N	B7

STREET Block	City	ZIP	Map#	CGS	Grid
Argyle Av					
600	BMDL	60172	2912	24W-6N	C7
600	FSMR	60422	3507	3W-22S	B2
600	HMWD	60430	3507	3W-22S	B1
18300	HMWD	60430	3427	3W-22S	B7
S Argyle Av					
300	EMHT	60126	3027	16W-0N	E4
Argyle Ln					
1600	NLNX	60451	3588	19W-27S	D4
1700	NLNX	60433	3588	19W-27S	D4
Argyle St					
200	BmdT	60148	3025	21W-2N	E1
400	BmdT	60148	2969	21W-2N	E7
500	MltT	60148	3025	21W-1N	E2
1000	BNVL	60106	2915	16W-6N	D6
W Argyle St					
1800	CHCG	60640	2921	2W-6N	B6
1900	CHCG	60625	2921	2W-6N	B6
3500	CHCG	60625	2920	4W-6N	B6
3900	CHCG	60630	2920	5W-6N	B6
6000	CHCG	60630	2919	7W-6N	B6
6300	CHCG	60656	2919	8W-6N	A6
6600	CHCG	60656	2918	8W-6N	E6
7200	HDHT	60656	2918	9W-6N	C6
7600	CHCG	60706	2918	9W-6N	C6
7600	HDHT	60706	2918	9W-6N	C6
7800	NRDG	60706	2918	9W-6N	B6
8500	NRDG	60656	2918	10W-6N	A6
8600	NRDG	60706	2917	10W-6N	E6
8700	CHCG	60706	2917	10W-6N	E6
Argyll Ln					
10	NPVL	60563	3140	30W-5S	C2
10	NpvT	60563	3140	30W-5S	B2
400	SMBG	60194	2858	24W-11N	C4
S Ari Ct					
300	ADSN	60101	2969	21W-3N	E6
300	BmdT	60101	2969	21W-3N	E6
300	BmdT	60148	2969	21W-3N	E6
Ari Dr E					
3500	GNVW	60025	2809	10W-15N	E3
Ari Dr W					
3700	GNVW	60025	2809	10W-15N	E3
Ari Ln					
3600	GNVW	60025	2809	10W-15N	E2
Ariana Dr					
200	BRLT	60103	2909	31W-8N	D3
Ariel Ct					
4300	NPVL	60564	3266	28W-12S	E3
Aris Ct					
15600	ODPK	60462	3346	11W-18S	A7
Aristocrat Dr					
300	BGBK	60440	3268	25W-12S	A3
300	BGBK	60490	3268	25W-12S	A3
Arizona Av					
-	WKGN	60087	2479	12W-36N	B4
-	WkgT	60087	2479	12W-36N	B4
3100	NCHI	60088	2593	11W-30N	C2
N Arizona Av					
300	GNWD	60425	3428	1W-22S	A7
300	GNWD	60425	3508	1W-22S	B1
S Arizona Av					
100	JLET	60433	3499	22W-24S	C5
Arizona Blvd					
10	HFET	60169	2859	23W-11N	B3
Arizona Ct					
17900	ODPK	60467	3423	12W-21S	C6
Arizona Tr					
8500	WLSP	60480	3208	14W-9S	E4
Arizona Pass					
600	EGVV	60007	2859	21W-9N	E7
700	EGVV	60007	2913	21W-9N	E1
Arkansas Ct					
17900	ODPK	60467	3423	12W-21S	C6
Arkansas Dr					
900	EGVV	60007	2913	22W-8N	D2
Arkansas Rd					
10	NCHI	60088	2593	12W-29N	C4
Arklow Pl					
1900	SMBG	60194	2858	26W-10N	A5
Arland Ct					
10	LIHL	60156	2692	38W-23N	D3
Arleen Ct					
2000	SMBG	60194	2858	26W-10N	A5
Arlene Av					
7500	WLBK	60527	3207	16W-8S	E1
S Arlene Av					
10	PLTN	60074	2806	19W-15N	D1
Arlene Ct					
100	WLNG	60090	2755	14W-17N	C5
Arlene Dr					
500	ADSN	60143	2970	19W-5N	D1
500	WDDL	60191	2970	19W-5N	D1
1800	AraT	60504	3138	35W-5S	C2
1800	AURA	60504	3138	35W-5S	C2
12000	HMGN	60491	3344	15W-18S	C7
Arlingdale Ct					
2500	RGMW	60067	2805	22W-14N	C5
Arlingdale Dr					
2400	RGMW	60067	2805	22W-14N	B4
5700	RGMW	60008	2805	21W-14N	C5
Arlington Av					
100	LSLE	60532	3142	24W-5S	D2
100	LSLE	60563	3142	24W-5S	D2
100	NPVL	60565	3204	25W-10S	B5
400	ELGN	60120	2855	33W-10N	B5
400	GNEN	60137	3025	22W-0S	B6
400	LslT	60540	3142	24W-5S	D3
400	WTMT	60559	3085	17W-4S	C6
500	DSPN	60016	2862	13W-11N	E3
800	LGNG	60525	3087	13W-4S	A7
2700	HDPK	60035	2704	9W-23N	B2
S Arlington Av					
100	EMHT	60126	3028	15W-1N	A3
Arlington Cir					
5200	HRPK	60133	2911	26W-6N	E6
Arlington Ct					
100	WNVL	60555	3080	30W-2S	C4
200	CLSM	60188	3024	24W-1N	E2
500	VNHL	60061	2647	16W-25N	C4
1000	RDLK	60073	2532	23W-32N	A6
1100	HRPK	60133	2912	26W-6N	A6
1300	GNVA	60134	3020	33W-1N	E2
3600	AURA	60504	3202	31W-8S	A2
10600	PlsT	60462	3345	13W-15S	B2
10600	PlsT	60464	3345	13W-15S	B2
10600	PlsT	60467	3345	13W-15S	B2
Arlington Dr					
-	BRLT	60103	2911	27W-7N	D5
-	BRLT	60133	2911	27W-7N	D5
-	CPVL	60110	2801	33W-16N	A1
-	CPVL	60118	2801	33W-16N	A1
-	EDND	60118	2801	33W-16N	A1
-	WLNG	60089	2754	16W-18N	D3
10	DMND	60416	3941	33W-39S	C2
10	RDLK	60073	2532	23W-32N	A5
10	RMVL	60446	3340	24W-15S	D1

STREET Block	City	ZIP	Map#	CGS	Grid
Arlington Dr					
10	RMVL	60446	3341	23W-15S	A1
100	PltT	60010	2751	24W-18N	C2
200	HRPK	60133	2911	27W-7N	D5
1600	WLNG	60090	2754	16W-18N	D4
4100	RNPK	60471	3594	5W-26S	C3
7500	BtnT	60081	2414	30W-39N	B5
7500	SPGV	60081	2414	30W-39N	B5
12100	HTLY	60142	2744	43W-19N	B2
17600	CCHL	60478	3426	4W-21S	D6
W Arlington Dr					
16000	LbvT	60048	2591	16W-30N	E2
Arlington Dr E					
5200	HRPK	60133	2912	26W-6N	A6
5500	BmdT	60133	2912	25W-6N	A6
Arlington Dr W					
1200	HRPK	60133	2911	26W-6N	E6
1200	HRPK	60133	2912	26W-6N	A6
Arlington Ln					
10	FXLK	60020	2473	28W-36N	A4
200	GYLK	60030	2475	21W-34N	D7
500	SEGN	60177	2908	35W-7N	B4
600	RLKB	60046	2475	21W-34N	D7
1400	GRNE	60031	2477	17W-35N	A5
1400	SMBG	60193	2858	25W-10N	B6
1700	GLHT	60139	2969	23W-3N	A6
10600	PlsT	60462	3345	13W-15S	A2
10600	PlsT	60467	3345	13W-15S	A2
17600	HLCT	60429	3427	3W-21S	A6
W Arlington Ln					
400	CteT	60417	3685	0W-32S	C7
Arlington Pkwy					
600	SYHW	60118	2799	36W-15N	E4
W Arlington Pl					
500	CHCG	60614	2978	0W-3N	A5
Arlington Rd					
-	FXLK	60020	2414	28W-39N	E5
-	FXLK	60020	2415	28W-39N	A5
10	FXLK	60020	2472	28W-36N	E4
10	FXLK	60020	2473	28W-36N	A4
300	ITSC	60143	2914	19W-6N	D6
700	RVSD	60546	3088	9W-2S	D4
N Arlington Rd					
100	IVNS	60010	2751	23W-16N	D7
Arlington St					
500	HFET	60169	2859	22W-11N	B4
1500	BGBK	60490	3267	26W-13S	D6
7800	TYPK	60477	3424	9W-19S	C2
Arlington Heights Rd					
100	ANHT	60004	2754	17W-18N	A2
100	ANHT	60089	2754	17W-18N	A2
100	BFGV	60089	2754	17W-18N	A2
300	BFGV	60089	2754	18W-18N	A3
N Arlington Heights Rd					
-	ANHT	60007	2861	18W-11N	A4
10	ANHT	60004	2807	17W-14N	A4
10	ANHT	60005	2807	17W-14N	A5
10	BFGV	60089	2754	18W-20N	A1
10	VrnT	60089	2754	18W-20N	A2
100	EGvT	60007	2861	18W-10N	A5
100	EGVV	60007	2861	18W-10N	A5
100	VrnT	60004	2754	17W-20N	A2
300	BFGV	60047	2754	18W-20N	A1
300	ITSC	60143	2914	19W-6N	D5
300	LGGV	60047	2754	18W-20N	A1
300	VrnT	60047	2754	18W-20N	A1
400	BFGV	60047	2701	18W-20N	A7
400	BFGV	60089	2701	17W-20N	A7
400	LGGV	60047	2701	18W-20N	A7
500	LGGV	60089	2701	17W-20N	A7
1200	AddT	60143	2914	19W-7N	D3
1200	EGVV	60007	2914	19W-7N	D3
2000	ANHT	60004	2754	17W-17N	A5
2900	BFGV	60004	2754	17W-17N	A4
3300	ANHT	60089	2754	17W-16N	A7
N Arlington Heights Rd CO-10					
1200	AddT	60143	2914	19W-7N	D3
1200	EGVV	60007	2914	19W-7N	D3
1200	ITSC	60143	2914	19W-7N	D3
N Arlington Heights Rd CO-V69					
10	BFGV	60089	2754	18W-20N	A2
10	VrnT	60089	2754	18W-20N	A2
100	ANHT	60004	2754	17W-20N	A2
100	VrnT	60004	2754	17W-20N	A2
300	BFGV	60047	2754	18W-20N	A1
300	LGGV	60047	2754	18W-20N	A1
300	VrnT	60047	2754	18W-20N	A1
400	BFGV	60047	2701	18W-20N	A7
400	BFGV	60089	2701	17W-20N	A7
400	LGGV	60047	2701	18W-20N	A7
400	LGGV	60089	2701	18W-20N	A7
S Arlington Heights Rd					
-	ANHT	60004	2807	17W-13N	A6
10	ANHT	60005	2807	17W-13N	A6
10	EGvT	60007	2860	18W-9N	E7
10	EGvT	60007	2861	18W-10N	A6
10	EGVV	60007	2860	18W-9N	E7
10	EGVV	60007	2861	18W-10N	A6
100	VrnT	60004	2754	17W-18N	A2
100	VrnT	60089	2754	17W-18N	A2
400	ANHT	60004	2754	17W-18N	A3
400	ANHT	60089	2754	17W-18N	A3
400	BFGV	60004	2754	17W-18N	A3
400	BFGV	60089	2754	17W-18N	A3
600	EGVV	60007	2914	19W-8N	D2
1200	ANHT	60005	2861	18W-11N	A3
1400	ITSC	60143	2914	19W-8N	D3
2400	ANHT	60007	2861	18W-11N	A3
2400	EGVV	60005	2861	18W-11N	A3
Arlon Rd					
800	AURA	60506	3137	36W-5S	D3
W Arlyd Rd					
16300	BFGV	60069	2701	16W-22N	D5
16300	VrnT	60069	2701	16W-22N	D5
Armbrust Av					
10	MltT	60187	3023	26W-0N	E4
10	MltT	60187	3024	26W-0N	A4
Armitage Av					
-	ADSN	60101	2970	21W-2N	A7
-	NHLK	60164	2972	13W-2N	D7
10	BmdT	60137	2969	23W-2N	A7
10	BmdT	60148	2970	21W-2N	A7
10	GLHT	60139	2968	23W-2N	E7
300	BmdT	60148	2969	21W-2N	E7
300	NHLK	60164	2973	13W-2N	A7
400	BmdT	60139	2969	23W-2N	A7
400	GLHT	60137	2969	23W-2N	A7
400	LydT	60160	2973	13W-2N	A7
400	LydT	60164	2973	13W-2N	A7
400	NHLK	60160	2973	13W-2N	A7
600	GLHT	60139	2969	22W-2N	C7
1300	MLPK	60160	2973	11W-2N	D7
1300	RVGV	60171	2973	11W-2N	E7
1700	FNPK	60131	2973	11W-2N	D7
2500	FNPK	60160	2973	12W-2N	B7
2500	MLPK	60131	2973	12W-2N	B7

STREET Block	City	ZIP	Map#	CGS	Grid
Armitage Av					
3200	MLPK	60164	2973	12W-2N	B7
9600	LydT	60131	2973	12W-2N	C7
E Armitage Av					
10	AddT	60101	2970	18W-2N	E7
10	ADSN	60101	2970	18W-2N	E7
10	ADSN	60101	2971	18W-2N	A7
10	ADSN	60181	2971	18W-2N	A7
10	VLPK	60101	2971	18W-2N	A7
10	VLPK	60181	2971	18W-2N	A7
200	EMHT	60126	2972	15W-2N	A7
W Armitage Av					
100	EMHT	60126	2971	16W-2N	D7
300	CHCG	60614	2978	0W-2N	A6
500	EMHT	60101	2971	17W-2N	C7
1400	CHCG	60614	2977	1W-2N	D6
1500	CHCG	60622	2977	1W-2N	D6
1900	CHCG	60647	2977	2W-2N	B6
2700	CHCG	60647	2976	4W-2N	D7
3900	CHCG	60639	2976	4W-2N	B7
4800	CHCG	60639	2975	6W-2N	E7
6600	CHCG	60707	2975	8W-2N	A7
6700	CHCG	60707	2974	9W-2N	C7
7100	EDPK	60707	2974	9W-2N	C7
Armitage Ct					
18000	HMWD	60430	3428	1W-21S	A7
W Armitage Ct					
1700	ADSN	60101	2970	20W-2N	A7
1700	ADSN	60148	2970	20W-2N	A7
1700	BmdT	60148	2970	20W-2N	A7
Armory Dr					
-	SHLD	60473	3428	0W-19S	C3
-	SHLD	60476	3428	0W-19S	C3
-	TNTN	60473	3428	0W-19S	C3
-	TNTN	60476	3428	0W-19S	C3
W Armory Dr					
100	SHLD	60473	3428	0W-19S	C3
100	TNTN	60473	3428	0W-19S	C3
100	TNTN	60476	3428	0W-19S	C3
500	HRVY	60426	3428	0W-19S	B3
500	SHLD	60426	3428	0W-19S	B3
Armory Pl					
1600	WKGN	60085	2479	11W-35N	E6
Armory Rd					
11400	BfdT	53147	2351	40W-43N	B4
11400	HbnT	53147	2351	40W-43N	B4
11400	HbnT	60034	2351	40W-43N	B4
Armour Blvd					
1100	MDLN	60060	2647	18W-25N	A4
Armour Cir					
900	LKFT	60045	2649	12W-26N	C3
Armour Ct					
3700	WDRG	60517	3143	23W-7S	A7
22300	TroT	60404	3584	30W-27S	C4
Armour Dr					
900	LKBF	60044	2593	11W-29N	E4
N Armour St					
400	CHCG	60607	3033	1W-0N	D3
400	CHCG	60622	3033	1W-0N	D3
Armsby Rd					
-	HbnT	60034	2350		E4
-	LinT	60034	2350		E4
100	LinT	53147	2350		E3
W Armstrong Av					
5200	CHCG	60630	2919	6W-7N	C4
5200	CHCG	60646	2919	6W-7N	C4
Armstrong Ct					
1400	EGVV	60007	2913	21W-8N	E2
6700	WDRG	60517	3143	22W-7S	C7
Armstrong Ct N					
600	BFGV	60089	2754	15W-20N	E1
Armstrong Dr					
100	BFGV	60089	2754	16W-20N	D2
200	WLNG	60089	2754	16W-20N	D2
700	BFGV	60089	2755	15W-20N	A2
Armstrong Ln					
-	BbyT	60134	3018	39W-0N	E5
10	GnvT	60134	3018	39W-0N	E6
200	GnvT	60134	3019	38W-0N	A6
900	NLNX	60451	3589	18W-25S	A1
1400	EGVV	60007	2913	21W-8N	E2
25000	PNFD	60585	3265	31W-13S	E5
Armstrong Ln S					
900	GnvT	60134	3019	38W-0N	A5
Armstrong St					
800	ALGN	60102	2694	34W-21N	C6
Armwood Ln					
1800	MDLN	60060	2590	20W-28N	A6
Army Trail Blvd					
300	AddT	60101	2970	20W-3N	A5
300	ADSN	60101	2970	20W-3N	A5
500	BmdT	60101	2970	20W-3N	A5
W Army Trail Blvd					
200	ADSN	60101	2970	20W-3N	B5
300	AddT	60101	2970	19W-3N	B5
Army Trail Rd					
-	ADSN	60101	2969	21W-3N	E4
10	AddT	60101	2970	20W-3N	A5
10	ADSN	60101	2970	21W-3N	A4
10	BMDL	60101	2969	22W-4N	D4
10	BmdT	60101	2969	22W-4N	D4
10	BmdT	60101	2970	21W-3N	A5
10	BRLT	60103	2966	30W-5N	A2
10	BRLT	60185	2966	29W-4N	E3
10	SchT	60174	2964	35W-5N	C2
10	WYNE	60174	2964	34W-5N	D2
10	WYNE	60184	2964	34W-5N	D2
10	WYNE	60184	2966	30W-5N	A2
10	WynT	60103	2966	29W-4N	E3
10	WynT	60184	2966	30W-5N	A2
10	WynT	60185	2966	29W-4N	E3
100	BMDL	60108	2969	22W-4N	B4
100	BmdT	60108	2969	22W-4N	C4
100	WYNE	60184	2965	32W-5N	C2
200	WYNE	60103	2966	30W-5N	B2
200	WYNE	60185	2965	31W-5N	E2
200	WYNE	60185	2966	31W-5N	A2
200	WynT	60184	2965	31W-5N	E2
300	BMDL	60139	2969	22W-4N	B4
300	BmdT	60139	2969	22W-4N	C4
300	BRLT	60103	2967	28W-4N	A3
300	CLSM	60103	2967	28W-4N	A3
300	CLSM	60188	2967	28W-4N	A3
300	SCRL	60174	2964	34W-5N	D2
300	SCRL	60184	2964	34W-5N	D2
400	GLHT	60139	2969	22W-4N	B4
400	WynT	60103	2967	28W-4N	A3
400	WynT	60185	2967	28W-4N	A3
500	BRLT	60184	2966	30W-5N	A2
500	BRLT	60185	2967	28W-4N	A3
500	GLHT	60108	2969	22W-4N	B4
Army Trail Rd CO-11					
-	ADSN	60101	2969	21W-3N	E4
-	BmdT	60101	2969	21W-3N	E4
10	AddT	60101	2970	20W-3N	A5
10	ADSN	60101	2970	21W-3N	A4
Army Trail Rd CO-11					
10	BMDL	60101	2969	22W-4N	D4
10	BmdT	60101	2970	21W-3N	A5
10	BRLT	60103	2966	30W-5N	A2
10	BRLT	60185	2966	29W-4N	E3
10	WynT	60103	2966	29W-4N	E3
10	WynT	60185	2966	29W-4N	E3
100	BMDL	60108	2969	22W-4N	B4
100	BmdT	60108	2969	22W-4N	C4
200	WYNE	60103	2966	30W-5N	B2
200	WYNE	60184	2966	30W-5N	A2
300	BMDL	60139	2969	22W-4N	B4
300	BmdT	60139	2969	22W-4N	C4
300	BRLT	60103	2967	28W-4N	A3
300	CLSM	60103	2967	28W-4N	A3
300	CLSM	60188	2967	28W-4N	A3
300	WynT	60184	2966	30W-5N	A2
400	GLHT	60139	2969	22W-4N	B4
400	WynT	60103	2967	28W-4N	A3
400	WynT	60185	2967	28W-4N	A3
500	BRLT	60184	2966	30W-5N	A2
500	BRLT	60185	2967	28W-4N	A3
500	GLHT	60108	2969	22W-4N	B4
Army Trail Rd CO-20					
-	WYNE	60184	2965	33W-5N	B2
E Army Trail Rd					
10	GLHT	60139	2969	23W-4N	A4
100	BMDL	60108	2968	23W-4N	E4
100	BMDL	60139	2968	23W-4N	E4
100	GLHT	60108	2968	23W-4N	E4
100	GLHT	60139	2968	23W-4N	E4
300	BMDL	60108	2969	23W-4N	B4
300	BMDL	60139	2969	23W-4N	B4
300	GLHT	60108	2969	23W-4N	B4
E Army Trail Rd CO-11					
10	GLHT	60139	2969	23W-4N	A4
100	BMDL	60108	2968	23W-4N	E4
100	BMDL	60139	2968	23W-4N	E4
100	GLHT	60108	2968	23W-4N	E4
100	GLHT	60139	2968	23W-4N	E4
300	BMDL	60108	2969	23W-4N	B4
300	BMDL	60139	2969	23W-4N	B4
300	GLHT	60108	2969	23W-4N	B4
W Army Trail Rd					
100	BMDL	60108	2968	26W-4N	A3
100	BMDL	60139	2968	23W-4N	E4
100	GLHT	60108	2968	23W-4N	E4
100	GLHT	60139	2968	23W-4N	E4
200	BmdT	60108	2968	25W-4N	A3
200	BmdT	60188	2968	25W-4N	A3
200	CLSM	60108	2968	26W-4N	A3
200	CLSM	60188	2968	26W-4N	A3
400	BMDL	60108	2967	26W-4N	E3
400	BMDL	60133	2968	25W-4N	B3
400	BmdT	60108	2967	26W-4N	E3
400	BmdT	60133	2968	25W-4N	B3
400	BmdT	60188	2967	26W-4N	E3
400	CLSM	60108	2967	26W-4N	E3
400	CLSM	60188	2967	26W-4N	E3
500	HRPK	60108	2967	26W-4N	E3
500	HRPK	60133	2967	27W-4N	B3
500	HRPK	60188	2967	26W-4N	E3
700	CLSM	60133	2967	27W-4N	B3
1300	BRLT	60103	2967	28W-4N	B3
1300	BRLT	60188	2967	28W-4N	B3
1300	CLSM	60103	2967	28W-4N	B3
1300	CLSM	60188	2967	28W-4N	B3
1300	HRPK	60103	2967	28W-4N	B3
W Army Trail Rd CO-11					
100	BMDL	60108	2968	26W-4N	A3
100	BMDL	60139	2968	23W-4N	E4
100	GLHT	60108	2968	23W-4N	E4
100	GLHT	60139	2968	23W-4N	E4
200	BmdT	60108	2968	25W-4N	A3
200	BmdT	60188	2968	25W-4N	A3
200	CLSM	60108	2968	26W-4N	A3
200	CLSM	60188	2968	26W-4N	A3
400	BMDL	60108	2967	26W-4N	E3
400	BMDL	60133	2968	25W-4N	B3
400	BmdT	60108	2967	26W-4N	E3
400	BmdT	60133	2968	25W-4N	B3
400	BmdT	60188	2967	26W-4N	E3
400	CLSM	60108	2967	26W-4N	E3
400	CLSM	60188	2967	26W-4N	E3
500	HRPK	60108	2967	26W-4N	E3
500	HRPK	60133	2967	27W-4N	B3
500	HRPK	60188	2967	26W-4N	E3
700	CLSM	60133	2967	27W-4N	B3
1300	BRLT	60103	2967	28W-4N	B3
1300	BRLT	60188	2967	28W-4N	B3
1300	CLSM	60103	2967	28W-4N	B3
1300	HRPK	60103	2967	28W-4N	B3
Arnett St					
-	FDHT	60411	3509	1E-24S	B6
Arnold Av					
400	RMVL	60446	3340	24W-15S	D3
400	SMWD	60107	2911	28W-9N	A1
600	AURA	60506	3199	36W-8S	D2
900	MltT	60137	3025	23W-1N	A3
Arnold Ct					
800	DSPN	60016	2862	15W-10N	A4
Arnold Dr					
6300	WDRG	60517	3143	22W-7S	B6
Arnold Ln					
3100	NHBK	60062	2756	11W-18N	D3
Arnold Pl					
-	EVTN	60202	2867	1W-9N	C6
4000	OKLN	60453	3276	5W-12S	C2
Arnold St					
1000	CHHT	60411	3508	0W-25S	C7
1400	CHHT	60411	3596	0W-25S	C1
E Arnold St					
700	SDWH	60548	3258	51W-14S	A7
N Arnold St					
700	PNFD	60544	3338	30W-17S	C7
W Arnold St					
8400	RVGV	60171	2974	10W-3N	A5
Aron Ct					
200	BRLT	60103	2911	28W-7N	A5
Aronomink Cir					
1800	ELGN	60123	2854	36W-9N	A7
1900	ELGN	60123	2853	36W-9N	E7
Arquilla Cir					
20000	OMFD	60461	3506	4W-24S	D5
Arquilla Ct					
300	BMDL	60108	2969	22W-4N	D3
300	WKGN	60087	2480	10W-36N	A3
Arquilla Dr					
100	ALGN	60102	2694	35W-21N	B6
2300	LslT	60515	3143	21W-6S	E4
4900	RNPK	60471	3594	6W-27S	A4
5300	RNPK	60471	3593	6W-27S	E4
E Arquilla Dr					
10	CHHT	60411	3508	1W-24S	A4
N Arquilla Dr					
200	CHHT	60411	3508	1W-24S	A4
300	CHHT	60411	3507	1W-24S	E5
W Arquilla Dr					
300	GNWD	60425	3508	0W-22S	B1
500	GNWD	60425	3428	0W-22S	B7
7600	PSHT	60463	3346	9W-15S	D2
9200	MKNA	60448	3503	11W-22S	E1
Arquilla Ln					
1200	FSMR	60422	3507	3W-23S	B3
Arquilla Pl					
-	NLNX	60451	3501	17W-24S	D6
S Arran Dr					
19600	FftT	60423	3504	9W-23S	E4
W Arran Dr					
7400	FftT	60423	3504	9W-23S	E3
Arrington Cir					
1700	NCHI	60064	2536	12W-32N	C6
Arrington Dr					
1600	NCHI	60064	2536	11W-32N	C6
Arrington Wy					
2400	NCHI	60064	2536	11W-32N	D6
Arron Ct					
200	VNHL	60061	2647	17W-25N	C5
Arrow Ct					
400	LslT	60540	3142	24W-6S	D4
Arrow Ln					
2000	RVWD	60015	2703	12W-21N	B6
8000	DRN	60561	3207	17W-9S	C3
Arrow St					
2300	CPVL	60110	2748	32W-18N	C4
Arrow Tr					
400	WLNG	60090	2754	16W-17N	C5
Arrow Glen Ct					
100	MltT	60187	3081	26W-2S	E4
Arrowhead Ct					
-	HPSR	60140	2743	45W-19N	B2
10	PKFT	60466	3595	2W-26S	D2
100	BGBK	60440	3269	23W-11S	B1
100	PNFD	60544	3416	31W-18S	A1
2000	GNVA	60134	3019	36W-0N	D6
6300	IHPK	60525	3146	14W-7S	D5
6700	LGGV	60047	2646	19W-25N	C6
13600	ODPK	60462	3346	10W-16S	B2
S Arrowhead Ct					
300	RDLK	60073	2531	24W-32N	C4
Arrow Head Dr					
17200	LKPT	60441	3420	20W-20S	B5
Arrowhead Dr					
-	HmrT	60441	3420	19W-21S	D6
-	NLNX	60441	3420	19W-21S	D6
10	ALGN	60102	2694	33W-21N	E6
10	TNTN	60476	3428	0E-20S	E4
100	HPSR	60140	2743	45W-19N	B2
100	HshT	60140	2743	45W-19N	B2
100	MNKA	60447	3583	33W-28S	B7
200	MltT	60187	3081	26W-2S	E3
200	SRWD	60404	3496	30W-23S	B5
400	CmpT	60119	2961	42W-4N	C4
400	CmpT	60175	2961	42W-4N	C4
400	GLBT	60136	2799	38W-16N	B2
500	YKVL	60560	3333	42W-14S	D1
600	ELGN	60120	2855	32W-12N	B2
600	MltT	60555	3081	26W-2S	E4
800	ELWD	60421	3675	25W-31S	C5
900	DYR	46311	3598		E3
2200	AURA	60564	3202	30W-10S	C5
2200	NPVL	60564	3202	30W-10S	C5
9500	HYHL	60465	3210	10W-11S	A6
9500	PSHL	60465	3210	10W-11S	A6
N Arrowhead Dr					
900	PLTN	60074	2753	20W-17N	A5
25500	ElaT	60060	2646	19W-26N	C4
25500	LGGV	60060	2646	19W-25N	D5
25700	FmtT	60060	2646	19W-26N	C4
W Arrowhead Dr					
19000	ElaT	60060	2646	19W-25N	D5
19000	LGGV	60060	2646	19W-25N	D5
Arrowhead Ln					
100	BGBK	60440	3205	23W-11S	B7
100	NBRN	60010	2644	25W-24N	A7
100	NBRN	60010	2698	25W-24N	A1
100	NBRN	60451	3502	15W-25S	C7
100	NlxT	60451	3502	15W-25S	C7
500	CLLK	60012	2640	35W-27N	B1
700	SCRL	60174	2965	33W-3N	A5
8200	ODPK	60462	3346	10W-16S	B3
8200	OrlT	60462	3346	10W-16S	B3
N Arrowhead Ln					
24800	LKBN	60010	2644	25W-24N	A6
24800	NBRN	60010	2644	25W-24N	A6
Arrowhead Pl					
100	BGBK	60440	3269	23W-11S	B1
Arrowhead St					
200	PKFT	60466	3595	2W-26S	D2
400	NARA	60542	3078	35W-3S	B6
E Arrowhead St					
200	NARA	60542	3078	35W-4S	B7
N Arrowhead St					
300	NARA	60542	3078	35W-3S	B7
W Arrowhead St					
200	NARA	60542	3078	35W-3S	B7
Arrowhead Tr					
100	CLSM	60188	2967	26W-3N	E6
100	CLSM	60188	2968	26W-2N	A7
100	CLSM	60188	3024	26W-2N	A1
11200	IHPK	60525	3208	14W-8S	D1
Arrowhead Trc					
5000	OKFT	60452	3426	6W-20S	A5
17200	BmnT	60452	3426	6W-20S	A5
17200	BmnT	60477	3426	6W-20S	A5
17200	OKFT	60452	3425	6W-20S	E5
Arrowhead Farm Dr					
8300	BRRG	60527	3208	14W-9S	C3
Arrowmaker Pass					
400	ElgT	60124	2853	38W-9N	A7
400	ElgT	60124	2907	38W-9N	A1
Arrowwood Ct					
10	SMWD	60107	2857	26W-11N	E4
200	SMBG	60193	2859	21W-10N	D6
600	LNHT	60046	2476	19W-36N	C3
1100	AURA	60504	3201	32W-9S	C4
Arrowwood Dr					
10	HNWD	60047	2644	23W-24N	D6
2900	OSWG	60543	3262	39W-12S	E3
Arrow Wood Ln					
1400	DRGV	60515	3084	20W-3S	B6
Arrowwood Ln					
100	NHBK	60062	2755	13W-18N	E2
200	NHBK	60062	2756	13W-18N	A3
2600	RGMW	60008	2805	21W-14N	C5
3700	HFET	60192	2804	25W-14N	A3
Arrowwood Tr					
2800	RVWD	60015	2702	13W-20N	D7
Arrowwood Wy					
1700	GRNE	60048	2534	17W-31N	C6
Arroyo Av					
19800	LYWD	60411	3510	3E-23S	A4
Arroyo Ct					
15400	OKFT	60452	3347	7W-18S	C7
Arroyo Dr					
15200	OKFT	60452	3347	7W-18S	C7
15700	OKFT	60452	3425	7W-18S	C1
15800	BmnT	60477	3425	7W-18S	C1
Arroyo St					
-	RNPK	60443	3593	7W-27S	C4
Arsenal Rd					
-	CnhT	60421	3674	27W-30S	C5
-	RMVL	60446	3340	25W-15S	C2
S Arsenal Rd					
-	FrnT	60481	3853	26W-37S	E3
-	WMTN	60481	3853	26W-37S	E3
W Arsenal Rd					
-	FrnT	60481	3853	26W-37S	E3
-	WMTN	60481	3853	26W-37S	E3
Artaius Pkwy					
1500	LYVL	60048	2647	16W-27N	E1
1500	VNHL	60061	2647	16W-27N	E1
S Artaius Pkwy					
1500	LYVL	60048	2647	16W-27N	E2
1500	VNHL	60061	2647	16W-27N	E2
Artell Av					
-	MRGO	60152	2634	49W-26N	C2
Artell St					
400	MRGO	60152	2634	49W-26N	C2
Artesian Av					
-	MKHM	60428	3427	3W-19S	C3
11900	BLID	60406	3277	3W-14S	B6
11900	BLID	60655	3277	3W-14S	B6
11900	CHCG	60655	3277	3W-14S	B6
13100	BLID	60406	3349	3W-15S	B1
14900	HRVY	60426	3349	3W-17S	C6
15900	BmnT	60428	3427	3W-19S	B2
16700	HLCT	60429	3427	3W-20S	C4
N Artesian Av					
400	CHCG	60612	3033	3W-0N	A3
1200	CHCG	60622	3033	3W-1N	A1
1500	CHCG	60647	3033	3W-1N	A1
2400	CHCG	60647	2977	3W-3N	A5
3600	CHCG	60618	2977	3W-4N	A2
4400	CHCG	60618	2921	3W-5N	A7
5400	CHCG	60625	2921	3W-6N	A5
5500	CHCG	60659	2921	3W-6N	A5
6300	CHCG	60645	2921	3W-7N	A3
7400	CHCG	60645	2867	3W-9N	A7
S Artesian Av					
300	CHCG	60612	3033	3W-0S	A6
2500	CHCG	60608	3091	3W-2S	B2
3500	CHCG	60632	3091	3W-3S	B5
5400	CHCG	60629	3151	3W-5S	B2
5400	CHCG	60632	3151	3W-5S	B3
7400	CHCG	60652	3151	3W-8S	B7
7600	CHCG	60652	3213	3W-8S	B1
9800	CHCG	60655	3213	3W-11S	B7
9800	CHCG	60805	3213	3W-11S	B7
9800	ENGN	60805	3213	3W-11S	B7
10200	CHCG	60655	3277	3W-12S	B1
11800	BLID	60406	3277	3W-13S	B5
11800	BLID	60655	3277	3W-13S	B5
Artesian Pk					
34200	LKBF	60044	2593	11W-28N	D5
Artesian Rd					
2900	NPVL	60564	3202	29W-10S	C5
Artesian St					
12800	LMNT	60439	3272	16W-13S	A4
W Arthington St					
-	CHCG	60607	3034		D6
1000	CHCG	60607	3033	1W-0S	E6
2400	CHCG	60612	3033	3W-0S	A6
2800	CHCG	60612	3032	4W-0S	D6
3100	CHCG	60624	3032	4W-0S	D6
4600	CHCG	60644	3032	5W-0S	A6
4800	CHCG	60644	3031	6W-0S	E6
5900	CHCG	60304	3031	7W-0S	B6
5900	OKPK	60304	3031	7W-0S	B6
Arthur Av					
10	AddT	60101	2971	17W-4N	A4
10	CNHL	60514	3145	17W-5S	C2
10	ROSL	60172	2913	23W-8N	A3
100	ADSN	60101	2971	17W-4N	A4
100	FXLK	60020	2473	28W-37N	A2
100	SEGN	60177	2908	34W-9N	D1
200	ROSL	60172	2912	23W-8N	E3
700	EGVV	60007	2915	17W-8N	B3
700	LYVL	60048	2591	16W-28N	C7
1000	BKLY	60163	3028	14W-0N	C3
2000	JLET	60432	3499	22W-21S	C1
2000	LktT	60432	3499	22W-21S	C1
2000	LktT	60441	3499	22W-21S	C1
2200	EGvT	60007	2915	16W-8N	D3
2200	LktT	60441	3419	22W-21S	C7
3100	BKFD	60513	3087	11W-3S	D5
3100	LGPK	60513	3087	11W-3S	D5
3100	LGPK	60525	3087	11W-3S	D5
4500	BKFD	60513	3147	11W-4S	D1
4600	MCCK	60513	3147	11W-4S	D1
4600	MCCK	60525	3147	11W-4S	D1
N Arthur Av					
1000	JLET	60432	3499	22W-22S	C2
1400	JLET	60432	3499	22W-22S	C1
1400	LktT	60441	3499	22W-22S	C1
S Arthur Av					
-	ANHT	60004	2807	17W-13N	C5
-	ANHT	60005	2807	17W-13N	C5
400	MPPT	60056	2807	16W-13N	C6
W Arthur Av					
1600	CHCG	60626	2921	2W-8N	C2
2000	CHCG	60645	2921	3W-8N	A2
2600	CHCG	60645	2920	3W-8N	E2
3100	LNWD	60645	2920	3W-8N	D2
3300	LNWD	60712	2920	4W-8N	C2
4700	LNWD	60712	2919	5W-8N	E2
7100	CHCG	60631	2918	8W-8N	D2
Arthur Ct					
10	CRTE	60417	3597	1E-28S	A6
10	DRFD	60015	2756	11W-20N	D2
10	HNWD	60047	2645	21W-24N	D6
10	SMWD	60107	2856	29W-10N	E6
200	AddT	60106	2971	16W-3N	D4
200	BNVL	60106	2971	16W-3N	D4
3000	WKGN	60085	2536	12W-33N	B1
5300	GRNE	60031	2478	15W-35N	A6
14400	DLTN	60419	3350	0E-16S	D4
17900	ODPK	60467	3423	13W-21S	B6
Arthur Dr					
-	MONE	60449	3683	6W-31S	B5
100	WDSK	60098	2524	42W-31N	B7
500	CRY	60013	2695	31W-23N	D1
600	LMBD	60148	3026	18W-0S	E6
800	ELGN	60120	2855	32W-12N	C2
1900	WKGN	60087	2479	11W-38N	D1
9700	AlqT	60102	2695	32W-22N	B4
17900	ODPK	60467	3423	13W-21S	B7
Arthur Rd					
1200	NPVL	60540	3142	25W-7S	A6
1800	WCHI	60185	3021	31W-2N	D1
1800	WynT	60185	3021	31W-2N	D1
3400	CRTE	60417	3597	0E-28S	A6
Arthur St					
10	CHCG	60068	2918	10W-8N	B2
10	CHCG	60631	2918	10W-8N	B2
10	PKRG	60068	2918	10W-8N	B2
1200	CTCY	60409	3430	3E-19S	A1
2000	PKRG	60068	2917	11W-8N	D2
9100	GfnT	60014	2639	38W-25N	A4
W Arthur St					
100	EMHT	60126	3027	16W-1N	E2
Arthur Ter					
3600	MKHM	60428	3426	4W-19S	D2
Arthur Wy					
800	AURA	60505	3138	34W-6S	D5
Arthur Compton Ct					
300	WNVL	60555	3080	29W-2S	E3
Arthurs Pass					
2100	NLNX	60451	3588	19W-27S	E4
Arthur Terrace Ct					
3900	MKHM	60428	3426	4W-19S	D2
Artona Dr					
6900	JLET	60586	3495	32W-21S	C1
Art Schultz Dr					
2800	JLET	60586	3415	32W-20S	D4
Arts Cir Dr					
-	EVTN	60201	2867	2W-11N	C2
Aryshire Ct					
4300	NPVL	60564	3266	29W-12S	D3
Asbury					
-	RGMW	60008	2806	20W-13N	A5
Asbury Av					
100	CHCG	60202	2867	3W-9N	A6
100	CHCG	60645	2867	3W-9N	A6
100	EVTN	60202	2867	3W-9N	A6
300	BNHL	60021	2696	29W-22N	B3
400	FRGV	60021	2696	30W-22N	B3
1100	WNKA	60093	2758	6W-16N	D7
1200	EVTN	60201	2867	3W-11N	A3
2500	EVTN	60201	2813	3W-12N	A7
2700	EVTN	60091	2813	2W-13N	A7
2700	WLMT	60091	2813	2W-13N	A7
Asbury Cir					
7700	HRPK	60133	2857	26W-9N	E7
Asbury Ct					
10	LIHL	60156	2692	38W-22N	D3
500	FRGV	60021	2696	30W-22N	B3
600	ANTH	60002	2357	24W-42N	D6
900	WNKA	60093	2758	6W-16N	D7
1200	ELGN	60120	2801	32W-12N	D7
7200	LGGV	60047	2646	18W-25N	D5
7600	SPGV	60081	2413	30W-39N	E5
S Asbury Ct					
10	LKFT	60045	2649	13W-25N	A4
Asbury Dr					
-	SPGV	60081	2413	30W-39N	E5
200	RDLK	60073	2531	23W-32N	E5
400	AURA	60502	3139	32W-7S	D7
700	GLHT	60139	2969	22W-2N	D7
800	BFGV	60089	2702	15W-21N	A6
2600	AURA	60504	3201	32W-8S	C1
2700	AURA	60502	3201	32W-8S	C1
Asbury Ln					
10	CRY	60013	2695	32W-23N	C1
400	HFET	60169	2859	22W-11N	B4
400	HFET	60194	2859	23W-11N	B4
400	SMBG	60194	2859	23W-11N	B4
700	GLHT	60139	2969	22W-2N	D7
800	SMBG	60193	2859	23W-9N	A7
800	SMBG	60193	2913	23W-9N	A1
Asbury Rd					
2200	NHBK	60062	2757	10W-16N	A7
Asbury Cir Dr					
1800	JLET	60435	3498	26W-22S	A3
Ascot Cir					
10	SMBG	60194	2859	23W-10N	B5
Ascot Ct					
-	JLET	60431	3495	33W-22S	B1
200	LKBF	60044	2593	11W-29N	E5
500	LKZH	60047	2699	22W-21N	A5
700	HFET	60169	2858	24W-11N	D3
700	LYVL	60048	2647	16W-27N	E1
1300	RLKP	60030	2589	22W-30N	C1
1700	WHTN	60187	3083	23W-3S	A5
3500	ISLK	60042	2586	30W-28N	B6
3800	LSLE	60532	3082	24W-3S	D6
4400	RNPK	60471	3594	5W-26S	C3
8800	ODPK	60462	3424	11W-18S	A1
24000	WldT	60564	3266	30W-12S	C3
S Ascot Ct					
25600	CNHN	60410	3672	33W-31S	C5
Ascot Dr					
-	PKRG	60068	2917	11W-8N	D1
900	CLLK	60014	2639	37W-24N	C7
900	CLLK	60014	2693	37W-23N	C1
900	ELGN	60123	2908	35W-9N	B1
900	ELGN	60177	2908	35W-9N	B1
900	SEGN	60177	2908	35W-9N	B1
Ascot Ln					
-	SEGN	60177	2907	37W-7N	C5
10	AURA	60504	3201	32W-7S	D1
10	BNHL	60010	2696	30W-21N	A6
10	WLBK	60527	3145	16W-6S	D5
10	WNVL	60555	3080	29W-2S	C3
300	RMVL	60446	3340	24W-16S	E5
400	OKBK	60523	3084	18W-3S	E5
500	SMWD	60107	2856	29W-11N	D4
600	HnrT	60107	2856	29W-11N	D4
600	HnrT	60120	2856	29W-11N	D4
2100	SPGV	60081	2354	31W-42N	E6
21400	FKFT	60423	3592	11W-25S	A1
Ascot Pl					
19700	MKNA	60448	3503	12W-23S	D4
W Ascot Pl					
1500	ADSN	60101	2970	20W-5N	A1
Ascot Rd					
2300	NHBK	60062	2810	8W-16N	D1
Ascot St					
-	JLET	60431	3495	33W-22S	B1
Ascot Wy					
1100	BRLT	60103	2966	30W-5N	C1
Ash Av					
100	WDSK	60098	2524	41W-32N	C5
1200	BNVL	60106	2915	17W-7N	C3
1200	EGVV	60007	2915	17W-7N	C3
9400	FftT	60448	3503	11W-23S	E3
N Ash Av					
100	WDDL	60191	2971	17W-5N	C1
200	WDDL	60191	2915	17W-5N	C7
400	AddT	60191	2915	17W-5N	C7
S Ash Av					
4300	HMND	46327	3352		E4

STREET Block	City	ZIP	Map#	CGS	Grid
Ash Ct					
10	BGBK	60490	3267	26W-12S	E2
10	SMWD	60107	2857	27W-10N	C6
200	WNFD	60190	3023	27W-0S	D6
500	SMBG	60193	2858	24W-9N	D7
1400	CLSM	60188	2967	28W-4N	A4
1900	AURA	60506	3137	38W-5S	B4
12800	HTLY	60142	2744	42W-19N	D3
13300	PSHT	60463	3347	7W-15S	B2
W Ash Ct					
12300	BHPK	60099	2421	12W-40N	C4
Ash Dr					
10	ODHL	60013	2641	31W-26N	D4
100	BGBK	60490	3267	26W-12S	E2
1000	ELGN	60120	2855	32W-11N	D4
18700	WrnT	60031	2476	18W-36N	E4
18700	WrnT	60046	2476	18W-36N	E4
W Ash Dr					
1100	MPPT	60056	2861	16W-11N	D3
18600	WrnT	60031	2476	18W-36N	E4
18600	WrnT	60046	2476	18W-36N	E4
Ash Ln					
10	LynT	60458	3209	11W-8S	E1
300	GNEN	60137	3083	23W-1S	A2
600	WLNG	60090	2754	16W-17N	D5
800	NHBK	60062	2757	10W-17N	A4
8900	HYHL	60457	3209	11W-10S	E5
16400	LKPT	60441	3420	20W-19S	B3
20100	LYWD	60411	3509	3E-23S	E4
28300	WmTp	60481	3761	32W-34S	C5
S Ash Pl					
-	HPSR	60140	2795	46W-16N	E2
Ash Rd					
200	LKZH	60047	2698	24W-23N	B2
600	HFET	60169	2859	23W-11N	B4
600	SMBG	60194	2859	23W-11N	B4
1100	SMBG	60169	2859	23W-12N	B2
1100	SMBG	60173	2859	23W-12N	B2
Ash St					
10	BlmT	60466	3595	2W-26S	C2
10	CPVL	60110	2748	32W-18N	C6
10	CTSD	60525	3147	12W-6S	C4
10	FKFT	60423	3591	12W-26S	E2
10	LKZH	60047	2698	23W-23N	E2
10	PKFT	60466	3595	2W-26S	C2
100	NLNX	60451	3501	17W-24S	C5
200	CLLK	60014	2639	35W-25N	E4
200	CLLK	60014	2640	35W-25N	A4
300	EGVV	60007	2915	18W-8N	A2
500	LYVL	60048	2591	16W-28N	D6
600	ALGN	60102	2694	33W-21N	D6
600	ROSL	60172	2913	22W-7N	C5
700	FSMR	60422	3506	4W-22S	E2
700	HLCT	60422	3506	4W-22S	E2
700	HLCT	60429	3506	4W-22S	E2
700	WNKA	60093	2812	5W-15N	A2
900	SCRL	60174	3020	35W-2N	B1
1100	BCHR	60401	3774	0W-36S	D7
1100	LIHL	60156	2694	35W-22N	A4
1100	WNKA	60093	2811	5W-15N	E2
1400	HHLL	60051	2586	30W-29N	A3
1600	DSPN	60018	2862	13W-9N	E7
1700	NHFD	60093	2811	7W-15N	C2
1800	WKGN	60087	2480	10W-36N	A5
2400	CHHT	60411	3596	1W-26S	A2
2400	SCHT	60411	3596	1W-26S	A2
7500	MchT	60097	2469	36W-36N	D4
14500	ODPK	60462	3345	11W-17S	E5
14500	OrlT	60462	3345	11W-17S	E5
17600	TYPK	60487	3423	11W-21S	E6
20700	VrnT	60015	2702	14W-20N	B7
21600	LkvT	60046	2417	21W-38N	D6
E Ash St					
10	LMBD	60148	3026	19W-0N	C4
N Ash St					
-	WKGN	60087	2480	10W-35N	A5
200	WKGN	60085	2537	10W-34N	A1
1600	WKGN	60085	2480	10W-35N	A5
27900	WcnT	60084	2587	25W-27N	E7
35700	GrtT	60041	2474	25W-35N	A5
42300	AntT	60002	2356	26W-42N	D6
S Ash St					
10	PLTN	60067	2805	21W-15N	C1
100	PltT	60067	2805	21W-15N	C1
W Ash St					
10	LMBD	60148	3026	20W-0N	B4
10	PNFD	60544	3338	29W-17S	D5
10	PnfT	60544	3338	29W-17S	D5
19600	JknT	60421	3675	24W-30S	E3
Ashbel Av					
10	NHLK	60164	3028	14W-1N	C1
N Ashbel Av					
10	HLSD	60162	3028	14W-0S	C6
10	PvsT	60162	3028	14W-0S	C6
1200	BKLY	60163	3028	14W-0N	C4
Ashborne Dr					
14700	HMGN	60491	3343	17W-17S	B6
Ashbrook Cir					
900	BGBK	60440	3268	25W-12S	B2
Ashbrook Ct					
10	GYLK	60030	2475	21W-35N	E5
200	AURA	60502	3139	32W-7S	C7
Ashbrook Dr					
1100	MDLN	60060	2646	19W-27N	B1
Ashbrook Ln					
-	JLET	60586	3415	33W-21S	B6
400	SEGN	60177	2908	34W-7N	C4
2200	GYLK	60030	2475	20W-35N	E6
11000	IHPK	60525	3146	13W-6S	E5
19200	MKNA	60448	3502	15W-23S	C3
Ashbrook Pl					
5400	DRGV	60515	3143	21W-5S	E3
Ashbrooke Ct					
600	SCRL	60175	2963	36W-5N	E2
Ashbrooke Rd					
1900	RMVL	60446	3339	27W-18S	B7
1900	RMVL	60446	3417	27W-18S	C1
1900	RMVL	60446	3339	27W-18S	B7
Ashburn Ct					
10	SMBG	60193	2857	27W-10N	D5
1600	WHTN	60187	3082	25W-2S	B3
Ashburn Ln					
500	WynT	60185	2966	29W-4N	D3
Ashburton Ct					
1900	ALGN	60102	2747	35W-20N	A1
Ashburton Ln					
100	PTON	60468	3860	9W-37S	D3
Ashbury Av					
900	DRGV	60516	3206	19W-8S	D1
N Ashbury Av					
100	BGBK	60440	3269	22W-11S	C1
800	BGBK	60440	3205	22W-9S	C4
1100	BGBK	60517	3205	22W-9S	C4
1100	WDRG	60517	3205	22W-9S	C4
S Ashbury Av					
100	BGBK	60440	3269	22W-12S	D2
Ashbury Cir					
100	PKRG	60068	2863	11W-9N	C7
Ashbury Ct					
10	BGBK	60440	3205	22W-10S	C6
200	ROSL	60172	2912	25W-7N	C4
400	LMNT	60439	3342	19W-15S	E1
1000	GNVA	60134	3020	36W-0N	A5
11400	MKNA	60448	3590	14W-26S	E2
E Ashbury Ct					
2200	ANHT	60004	2807	16W-15N	D2
W Ashbury Ct					
1800	IVNS	60067	2804	23W-14N	E4
1800	IVNS	60067	2805	23W-14N	A4
Ashbury Dr					
400	DGvT	60521	3146	15W-6S	A4
400	HNDL	60521	3146	16W-6S	A4
1200	LMNT	60439	3270	19W-14S	D7
1200	LMNT	60439	3342	18W-15S	E1
3000	NPVL	60564	3203	28W-11S	A7
Ashbury Ln					
10	BNHL	60010	2748	30W-20N	E2
400	LMNT	60439	3342	19W-15S	E1
1100	LYVL	60048	2592	15W-28N	A6
1600	RMVL	60446	3339	26W-17S	D6
W Ashbury Ln					
1800	IVNS	60067	2804	23W-14N	E4
1800	IVNS	60195	2804	23W-14N	E5
1800	PltT	60195	2804	23W-14N	E5
1900	IVNS	60067	2805	23W-14N	A4
Ashbury Ln E					
100	ROSL	60172	2912	25W-7N	C4
Ashbury Ln W					
200	ROSL	60172	2912	25W-7N	B4
Ashby Ct					
300	GNVA	60134	3019	37W-1N	C3
Ashby Ln					
100	YkTp	60181	3085	18W-1S	A1
2100	JLET	60586	3415	33W-21S	A6
2300	NasT	60586	3415	33W-21S	A6
Ashby St					
2400	AURA	60506	3198	39W-7S	E1
N Ashby Wy					
10	BNVL	60106	2971	16W-5N	E1
Ashcott Ln					
4200	JLET	60586	3496	29W-21S	D1
Ashcroft Ct					
10	ALGN	60102	2747	36W-19N	A3
10	BGBK	60490	3267	27W-11S	D1
10	FRGV	60021	2696	30W-22N	B4
200	OSWG	60543	3263	36W-13S	D6
Ashcroft Dr					
100	BGBK	60490	3267	27W-11S	D2
Ashcroft Ln					
10	SMBG	60193	2859	22W-10N	B6
200	OSWG	60543	3263	37W-13S	D6
Ashe Rd					
10	BtlT	60545	3196	44W-10S	D6
10	SgrT	60545	3196	44W-10S	D6
10	SgrT	60554	3196	44W-10S	D6
500	SgrT	60511	3196	44W-10S	D6
Ashely Ln					
-	PLNO	60545	3260	45W-14S	C7
-	PLNO	60545	3332	45W-14S	C1
Asheville Ct					
100	VNHL	60061	2647	16W-25N	C5
Ashfield Ct					
100	BMDL	60108	2968	24W-5N	D2
Ashfield Rd					
800	NPVL	60540	3142	25W-7S	B7
Ashford Av					
10700	FKFT	60423	3591	13W-26S	B3
Ashford Cir					
300	BRLT	60103	2967	28W-5N	B3
1700	ANHT	60004	2754	16W-17N	C5
1700	WLNG	60090	2754	16W-17N	C5
20400	MKNA	60448	3502	14W-24S	D6
Ashford Ct					
10	BFGV	60089	2754	17W-17N	B5
10	LNSH	60069	2702	15W-23N	A2
10	SBTN	60010	2804	25W-15N	A3
1500	WHTN	60187	3082	23W-1S	E2
4300	JLET	60586	3416	29W-21S	D7
6400	LSLE	60532	3142	24W-6S	D5
14200	ODPK	60467	3345	13W-16S	A4
15900	TYPK	60477	3424	9W-19S	D1
28500	GNOK	60044	2593	13W-28N	A6
Ashford Dr					
-	LKFT	60044	2593	13W-28N	A6
-	ShdT	60044	2593	13W-28N	A6
4600	MTSN	60443	3506	5W-24S	B5
13300	GNOK	60044	2592	13W-28N	E6
13300	GNOK	60044	2593	13W-28N	A6
14700	LMNT	60439	3343	18W-15S	A1
Ashford Ln					
100	WTMT	60559	3145	17W-6S	B5
300	GYLK	60030	2533	19W-32N	B5
1200	JLET	60431	3496	29W-22S	D2
1400	AURA	60502	3139	32W-5S	D3
1500	BCHR	60401	3774	0W-35S	C7
1700	CLLK	60014	2693	36W-22N	D3
2200	SEGN	60177	2907	37W-7N	C6
4700	JLET	60586	3496	29W-22S	D2
W Ashford Ln					
500	ANHT	60004	2753	18W-18N	E2
500	ANHT	60004	2754	17W-20N	A2
Ashford St					
-	MhtT	60442	3677	20W-31S	C5
Ash Fork Tr					
400	CRY	60013	2641	32W-24N	B7
Ashgate Cross					
26800	PNFD	60585	3337	33W-15S	A3
Ashgate Wy					
-	NasT	60543	3337	33W-16S	A4
-	PNFD	60585	3337	33W-16S	A4
Ash Grove Ln					
300	OSWG	60543	3262	39W-12S	E2
300	OSWG	60543	3263	39W-12S	A2
Ashington Cir					
10	LKBF	60044	2593	11W-29N	E5
Ashington Ct					
1900	NlxT	60451	3502	16W-24S	A5
Ashington Ln					
11900	FftT	60423	3590	15W-27S	D5
11900	FKFT	60423	3590	15W-27S	D5
11900	NlxT	60423	3590	15W-27S	D5
11900	NlxT	60451	3590	15W-27S	D5
Ashkirk Ct					
10	IVNS	60010	2803	25W-16N	E1
Ashland Av					
-	CRTE	60417	3684	1W-29S	E1
-	CteT	60417	3684	1W-29S	E1
-	DXMR	60426	3349	2W-16S	D3
-	FSMR	60411	3507	1W-23S	E3
-	FSMR	60422	3507	1W-23S	E3
-	RVDL	60827	3349	2W-16S	D3
10	AURA	60505	3199	36W-9S	E3
10	AURA	60506	3199	36W-8S	E3
10	DSPN	60016	2862	14W-10N	C4
10	FTPK	60130	3030	9W-0N	C5
10	MTGY	60505	3199	36W-9S	E3
10	MTGY	60506	3199	36W-8S	E3
10	MTGY	60538	3199	36W-9S	E3
10	RVFT	60130	3030	9W-0N	C5
100	AURA	60538	3199	36W-9S	E3
100	CHCG	60202	2867	3W-9N	A6
100	CHCG	60645	2867	3W-9N	A6
200	AURA	60505	3200	36W-8S	A3
200	HDPK	60035	2704	9W-23N	C1
200	HIWD	60040	2704	9W-23N	C1
300	CHHT	60411	3507	1W-24S	E5
400	ELGN	60123	2854	33W-10N	E6
500	EDND	60118	2801	33W-16N	B1
700	WLMT	60091	2812	3W-14N	D5
800	RVFT	60305	3030	9W-1N	C3
1100	EVTN	60202	2867	3W-10N	A4
1300	DSPN	60016	2863	13W-10N	A4
1400	CHHT	60411	3595	1W-25S	E1
1500	EDPK	60707	3030	9W-1N	C1
1500	RVFT	60707	3030	9W-1N	C1
1600	KLWH	60043	2812	4W-14N	C4
2200	RGMW	60008	2806	20W-14N	A4
2300	EVTN	60201	2867	3W-12N	A1
2400	EVTN	60201	2813	3W-12N	A7
2600	EVTN	60091	2813	3W-13N	A7
2600	WLMT	60091	2813	3W-13N	A7
2600	WLMT	60201	2813	3W-13N	A7
3300	BlmT	60466	3595	1W-27S	E5
3300	BlmT	60475	3595	1W-27S	E5
3300	CteT	60475	3595	1W-27S	E5
3500	CteT	60417	3595	1W-28S	E6
3500	STGR	60475	3595	1W-28S	E6
9100	FNPK	60131	2973	11W-3N	D4
12900	BLID	60406	3277	2W-15S	D7
12900	BLID	60827	3277	1W-15S	D7
12900	CTPK	60406	3277	1W-15S	D7
12900	CTPK	60406	3349	2W-15S	D1
12900	CTPK	60827	3277	1W-15S	D7
12900	CTPK	60827	3349	1W-15S	D1
13200	BLID	60406	3349	1W-15S	D1
13200	ClmT	60827	3349	1W-15S	D1
14300	HRVY	60426	3349	1W-17S	E5
14300	ThtT	60426	3349	1W-17S	E5
15600	HRVY	60426	3427	2W-19S	E1
16000	MKHM	60426	3427	1W-19S	E2
16100	MKHM	60428	3427	2W-19S	E3
16500	HLCT	60428	3427	1W-19S	E3
16500	HLCT	60429	3427	1W-19S	E3
16500	HRVY	60428	3427	1W-19S	E3
16500	HRVY	60429	3427	1W-19S	E3
17100	EHZC	60429	3427	1W-21S	E6
17400	HMWD	60429	3427	1W-20S	E5
18100	HMWD	60430	3427	1W-21S	E7
18500	HMWD	60430	3507	1W-22S	E2
18800	BlmT	60430	3507	1W-22S	E2
20200	BlmT	60411	3595	1W-27S	E5
20200	SCHT	60411	3595	1W-27S	E5
20700	SCHT	60466	3595	1W-27S	E5
N Ashland Av					
10	CHCG	60607	3033	1W-0N	D4
10	CHCG	60612	3033	1W-0N	D4
10	LGNG	60525	3087	12W-4S	B6
10	PLTN	60074	2806	20W-16N	A1
200	LGPK	60525	3087	12W-3S	B6
300	CHCG	60622	3033	2W-1N	C1
300	PKRG	60068	2864	10W-9N	B7
1200	PLTN	60074	2753	20W-17N	A5
1600	CHCG	60622	2977	1W-2N	C7
1900	CHCG	60614	2977	2W-2N	C6
2600	CHCG	60657	2977	1W-3N	C4
3500	CHCG	60613	2977	1W-3N	C5
4400	CHCG	60613	2921	1W-5N	C7
4400	CHCG	60640	2921	1W-6N	C6
6400	CHCG	60626	2921	1W-8N	C2
6400	CHCG	60660	2921	2W-8N	C2
7600	CHCG	60626	2867	2W-9N	C6
9200	NLES	60714	2864	10W-11N	B3
S Ashland Av					
-	BLID	60406	3349	1W-15S	D1
-	CTPK	60406	3349	1W-15S	D1
-	CTPK	60827	3349	1W-15S	D1
10	CHCG	60607	3033	1W-0S	D6
10	CHCG	60612	3033	1W-0S	D6
10	LGNG	60525	3087	12W-4S	B7
10	PLTN	60074	2806	20W-15N	A1
300	LGNG	60525	3147	12W-5S	B2
1200	CHCG	60608	3033	1W-1S	D7
1300	PKRG	60068	2918	10W-7N	B3
1600	CHCG	60608	3091	2W-1S	D1
1900	CHCG	60631	2918	10W-7N	B4
1900	PKRG	60631	2918	10W-7N	B4
3400	CHCG	60609	3091	2W-4S	D7
4700	CHCG	60609	3151	2W-8S	D7
5500	CHCG	60636	3151	1W-6S	D3
5500	CTSD	60525	3147	12W-6S	B3
7500	CHCG	60620	3213	2W-8S	D1
9400	CHCG	60643	3213	1W-10S	D6
10900	CHCG	60643	3277	2W-12S	D2
11800	CTPK	60643	3277	1W-13S	D5
12200	CTPK	60827	3277	1W-14S	D7
12800	BLID	60406	3277	1W-15S	D7
12800	BLID	60827	3277	1W-15S	D7
12800	CTPK	60406	3277	1W-15S	D7
13300	ClmT	60827	3349	1W-16S	D2
13300	RVDL	60827	3349	1W-16S	D2
13300	ThtT	60827	3349	1W-16S	D2
13800	DXMR	60426	3349	1W-16S	D3
23600	CteT	60417	3595	1W-28S	E7
23600	CteT	60475	3595	1W-28S	E7
23600	STGR	60475	3595	1W-28S	E7
24000	CteT	60417	3684	2W-29S	E1
W Ashland Av					
100	AURA	60506	3199	36W-8S	E3
100	AURA	60538	3199	36W-8S	E3
100	MTGY	60506	3199	36W-8S	E3
100	MTGY	60538	3199	36W-8S	E3
27400	AntT	60081	2415	27W-38N	B7
N Ashland Blvd					
6800	CHCG	60626	2921	1W-8N	C1
7200	CHCG	60626	2867	1W-9N	C7
Ashland Ct					
200	BFGV	60089	2754	17W-20N	A1
200	VNHL	60061	2647	17W-25N	C5
E Ashland Ct					
1000	AURA	60505	3200	36W-9S	A3
N Ashland Dr					
100	MHRY	60050	2527	34W-31N	D6
W Ashland Dr					
5000	MHRY	60050	2527	34W-32N	D5
Ashland Ln					
1300	WLMT	60091	2812	4W-14N	D4
S Ashland Ln					
300	LKFT	60045	2648	13W-25N	E5
Ashland Pl					
400	HDPK	60035	2758	7W-20N	B1
Ashland St					
10	OSWG	60543	3263	37W-12S	C4
300	HFET	60169	2859	22W-11N	B4
600	EDND	60118	2801	33W-16N	B1
Ashlawn Av					
10	OSWG	60543	3263	37W-11S	C1
10	OswT	60538	3263	37W-11S	D1
10	OswT	60543	3263	37W-11S	C1
Ashlawn Dr					
1000	LKFT	60045	2649	12W-26N	B2
Ashley Cir					
-	JLET	60431	3496	29W-22S	C2
5100	LSLE	60563	3142	24W-5S	C3
5100	LslT	60563	3142	24W-5S	C3
N Ashley Cir					
28000	GNOK	60048	2592	14W-28N	D7
28000	LbvT	60048	2592	14W-28N	D7
Ashley Ct					
-	LKPT	60441	3419	21W-19S	E2
10	CRTE	60417	3685	1W-29S	B2
200	OSWG	60543	3264	36W-11S	A1
200	ROSL	60172	2912	24W-7N	C5
300	OKBK	60523	3085	17W-3S	C5
600	JltT	60433	3499	23W-24S	B7
700	HFET	60169	2858	24W-12N	D1
900	WTMT	60559	3145	18W-6S	A5
1500	WDSK	60098	2524	40W-32N	E5
1600	DRN	60561	3207	18W-9S	A3
2100	LslT	60515	3143	21W-5S	E3
3200	LGGV	60047	2700	19W-21N	C6
3800	RGMW	60008	2806	20W-14N	A5
9400	FKFT	60423	3503	11W-25S	E6
10000	HTLY	60142	2692	38W-22N	D4
14400	ODPK	60462	3346	10W-17S	B4
15400	MHTN	60442	3677	19W-30S	E3
S Ashley Ct					
1200	VNHL	60061	2702	15W-23N	A2
16700	HMGN	60491	3422	15W-20S	B4
Ashley Ct N					
1000	LKPT	60441	3419	21W-19S	E2
Ashley Ct S					
1000	LKPT	60441	3419	21W-19S	E2
Ashley Dr					
-	JLET	60431	3496	29W-22S	D2
-	JLET	60586	3496	29W-22S	D2
300	NLNX	60451	3501	18W-24S	B4
400	MltT	60137	3083	23W-2S	A4
3300	MaiT	60025	2810	10W-12N	A7
3400	MaiT	60025	2809	10W-12N	E7
4400	MHRY	60050	2527	33W-33N	E4
8300	ODPK	60462	3346	10W-17S	B4
38800	LkvT	60046	2416	25W-38N	B6
38900	AntT	60046	2416	25W-38N	B6
N Ashley Dr					
32900	WrnT	60030	2534	17W-33N	C4
Ashley Ln					
200	WYNE	60184	2909	33W-6N	A6
600	SMBG	60194	2858	25W-11N	B4
900	LKFT	60045	2650	9W-25N	B5
1000	LYVL	60048	2591	17W-29N	B3
1100	IVNS	60010	2803	25W-15N	E1
1100	SBTN	60010	2803	25W-15N	E1
8200	TYPK	60477	3424	10W-19S	C1
N Ashley Ln					
1200	ADSN	60101	2970	20W-5N	B2
1700	WKGN	60085	2479	12W-35N	B5
Ashley Rd					
1700	HFET	60169	2858	24W-12N	D1
1900	HFET	60169	2804	24W-12N	D7
7500	KdlT	60560	3334	41W-17S	B7
Ashley St					
10100	HTLY	60142	2692	39W-22N	C4
Ashley Wy					
100	BMDL	60108	2912	24W-5N	D7
100	BMDL	60108	2968	24W-5N	D1
200	MTGY	60543	3263	38W-11S	B1
Ashley Oaks Ln					
10	FSMR	60422	3507	2W-23S	D3
Ashley Woods Dr					
-	PvsT	60154	3086	14W-2S	D3
2600	WSTR	60154	3086	14W-2S	D3
Ashling Ct					
2800	SMBG	60193	2857	27W-10N	C6
Ashlyn Ln					
1100	ANTH	60002	2359	20W-41N	A7
Ashridge Ln					
-	UYPK	60417	3684	3W-30S	C3
-	UYPK	60466	3684	3W-30S	C3
Ashton Av					
700	RMVL	60446	3340	24W-16S	C4
Ashton Ct					
10	SEGN	60177	2908	35W-7N	C5
400	SMBG	60193	2859	23W-10N	A6
1000	SMWD	60107	2910	30W-9N	C1
1300	AURA	60504	3201	32W-9S	C4
1400	WLNG	60090	2754	15W-18N	E3
1600	WHTN	60187	3024	23W-0N	E4
1600	WHTN	60187	3025	23W-0N	A4
2800	WSTR	60154	3086	13W-2S	E4
14800	LKPT	60441	3421	18W-20S	A4
Ashton Dr					
-	WLSP	60527	3208	15W-10S	C5
10	BRRG	60527	3208	15W-10S	C5
W Ashton Dr					
-	PNFD	60586	3415	31W-20S	D4
Ashton Ln					
-	CLLK	60014	2640	34W-25N	D4
-	HMGN	60441	3421	18W-20S	A4
-	HMGN	60491	3421	18W-20S	A4
600	SEGN	60177	2907	37W-7N	C5
1200	NPVL	60540	3203	28W-8S	A1
10900	ODPK	60467	3345	13W-16S	A4
14800	LKPT	60441	3421	18W-20S	A4
Ashtonlee Ct					
2700	NPVL	60565	3203	26W-10S	D6
Ashwood Ct					
10	SgrT	60506	3136	40W-5S	A4
300	VNHL	60061	2647	17W-25N	B6
400	LNHT	60046	2476	19W-36N	C3
400	SMBG	60193	2858	24W-10N	E6
N Ashwood Ct					
1200	ADSN	60101	2970	19W-5N	C2
Ashwood Dr					
200	SMBG	60193	2858	24W-9N	E7
1400	ELGN	60123	2907	36W-8N	E3
2200	JLET	60586	3416	30W-21S	B6
8000	GwdT	60097	2469	37W-34N	C7
8000	MchT	60097	2469	37W-34N	C7
17100	ODPK	60467	3422	14W-20S	D4
Ashwood Ln					
1800	AURA	60506	3137	38W-5S	B4
5300	GRNE	60031	2478	15W-36N	A4
Ashwood Rd					
-	WldT	60564	3266	31W-12S	A3
Ashwood Park Ct					
4000	WldT	60564	3266	31W-12S	A2
Ashworth Ln					
-	YKVL	60560	3333	42W-17S	D6
Aspen Av					
5400	LslT	60515	3143	21W-6S	E4
Aspen Cir					
100	GLBT	60136	2799	38W-14N	B5
E Aspen Cir					
10	HNVL	60030	2532	22W-33N	C2
Aspen Ct					
10	BFGV	60089	2701	17W-20N	A7
10	LMNT	60439	3270	20W-14S	C6
10	SMWD	60107	2857	27W-10N	C6
100	NARA	60542	3078	35W-4S	A7
100	SMBG	60194	2858	25W-10N	B5
200	BGBK	60440	3269	23W-11S	B1
300	CLSM	60188	2968	26W-4N	A4
300	WNFD	60190	3023	27W-0N	C5
400	NPVL	60540	3203	27W-8S	C1
600	ANTH	60002	2357	24W-42N	D5
600	BRLT	60103	2910	29W-9N	D1
1000	LKZH	60047	2698	24W-22N	C3
1300	ELGN	60120	2855	31W-11N	E4
2700	NHBK	60025	2809	11W-15N	D2
2800	AURA	60504	3201	31W-8S	D1
3200	JLET	60431	3497	28W-23S	B4
5700	DrrT	60014	2638	38W-26N	E3
6800	SPGV	60081	2414	30W-38N	B6
15800	OKFT	60452	3347	8W-18S	B7
18500	WrnT	60030	2533	18W-34N	E1
18800	WrnT	60046	2476	18W-36N	D3
19200	MKNA	60448	3502	15W-23S	C3
20700	VrnT	60015	2702	14W-20N	B7
20700	VrnT	60015	2755	15W-20N	B2
W Aspen Ct					
900	PltT	60067	2752	22W-17N	C4
900	PltT	60074	2752	22W-17N	C4
16600	HmrT	60441	3420	20W-18S	B1
16600	LKPT	60441	3420	20W-18S	B1
20800	LktT	60544	3340	26W-16S	A4
Aspen Dr					
-	BGBK	60440	3205	23W-11S	B7
10	SMBG	60194	2858	25W-10N	B5
10	VNHL	60061	2647	17W-25N	B5
100	NLNX	60451	3501	17W-24S	C5
200	BCHR	60401	3864	0W-36S	D1
200	BGBK	60440	3269	23W-11S	B1
200	NlxT	60451	3501	17W-24S	C5
400	DYR	46311	3598		D3
500	LMBD	60148	3084	20W-1S	A1
600	BFGV	60089	2701	17W-21N	A7
600	RMVL	60446	3340	25W-15S	C1
1600	LKFT	60045	2703	12W-23N	C1
1800	HRPK	60133	2911	27W-8N	D3
2000	WDSK	60098	2582	39W-29N	C3
2100	JNBG	60050	2471	31W-35N	D6
9200	MaiT	60016	2863	11W-11N	D3
19100	ElaT	60060	2646	19W-25N	C4
N Aspen Dr					
1700	MPPT	60056	2808	13W-15N	E2
S Aspen Dr					
10300	PSHL	60465	3274	10W-12S	A1
Aspen Ln					
10	BDWD	60481	3942	30W-40S	B4
10	CPVL	60110	2748	32W-18N	C5
10	GLNC	60022	2758	6W-18N	D3
100	AURA	60504	3201	32W-8S	D1
100	HDPK	60035	2757	8W-20N	E1
1200	EGVV	60007	2915	18W-8N	A3
1200	YKVL	60560	3260	44W-14S	D7
1700	JltT	60433	3587	21W-26S	E3
1700	JltT	60433	3588	21W-26S	A3
1900	GLHT	60139	2969	23W-3N	B5
5900	DrrT	60014	2638	38W-26N	E3
6000	MTSN	60443	3505	7W-24S	B6
6700	DRN	60559	3145	18W-7S	A6
6700	WTMT	60559	3145	18W-7S	A7
8200	TYPK	60477	3424	10W-19S	B2
9200	MaiT	60016	2863	11W-11N	D3
10500	DGvT	60439	3270	19W-12S	D2
10500	DGvT	60517	3270	19W-12S	D2
10500	WDRG	60517	3270	19W-12S	D2
12000	HMGN	60491	3422	15W-20S	C3
W Aspen Ln					
21000	LktT	60544	3339	26W-16S	E4
21000	LktT	60544	3340	25W-16S	B4
Aspen Rd					
200	WDDL	60191	2971	17W-4N	B2
1900	ALGN	60102	2695	32W-20N	B7
2800	NHBK	60062	2756	11W-16N	E7
6700	LSLE	60532	3142	24W-7S	C7
Aspen St					
500	FKFT	60423	3503	12W-25S	D7
600	FftT	60423	3503	12W-25S	D7
900	HFET	60169	2859	22W-11N	B3
3700	FSMR	60422	3506	4W-22S	D2
14500	ODPK	60462	3346	11W-17S	A5
Aspen Wy					
100	DRFD	60015	2756	11W-20N	C2
500	ANTH	60002	2357	24W-42N	D5
N Aspen Wy					
1200	ADSN	60101	2970	20W-5N	B2
Aspen Colony St					
10	FXLK	60020	2414	28W-38N	D7
Aspen Pointe Dr					
200	VNHL	60061	2647	17W-25N	B4
Assell Av					
900	AURA	60505	3138	35W-6S	C5
Assembly Ct					
10	BGBK	60440	3205	22W-10S	C6
Assembly Dr					
400	BGBK	60440	3205	22W-10S	D6
E Aster Av					
800	PLTN	60074	2753	19W-18N	B3
Aster Cir					
2100	LYWD	60411	3509	2E-24S	D5
Aster Ct					
300	AURA	60504	3139	31W-7S	E7
300	MNKA	60447	3672	33W-29S	B2
300	RMVL	60446	3339	26W-17S	D7
400	LNHT	60046	2476	19W-37N	C2
600	LSLE	60532	3143	22W-5S	C3
800	NARA	60542	3078	34W-3S	C5
900	LIHL	60156	2693	37W-22N	B4
1000	MDLN	60060	2590	19W-28N	B5
1300	BTVA	60510	3078	33W-1S	E2
1900	JNBG	60050	2471	30W-37N	E2
2200	NPVL	60565	3204	24W-10S	D5
22500	FKFT	60423	3591	13W-27S	A4
N Aster Ct					
2200	RLKB	60073	2475	23W-36N	A4
34300	GrtT	60073	2531	25W-34N	A1

Chicago 7-County Street Index

STREET Block City ZIP Map# CGS Grid

W Aster Ct
24200 PNFD 60585 3338 30W-15S B3
Aster Dr
- HDPK 60035 2704 10W-22N A4
10 SMBG 60173 2859 21W-10N E5
100 SMBG 60193 2859 21W-10N E6
300 MNKA 60447 3672 33W-29S A2
600 GRNE 60031 2477 18W-34N A7
1500 RMVL 60446 3339 26W-17S D6
1800 YKVL 60560 3333 43W-16S B5
2300 CTHL 60403 3417 27W-21S D6
15800 LKPT 60441 3420 19W-20S D4
22300 FKFT 60423 3591 13W-27S A4
Aster Ln
- HMGN 60491 3343 16W-17S D5
100 HFET 60169 2859 23W-11N B2
100 MTSN 60443 3593 7W-26S C2
400 BRLT 60103 2911 27W-7N C6
900 WCHI 60185 3022 29W-2N D1
1400 BGBK 60490 3267 26W-12S E3
1400 BGBK 60490 3268 26W-12S A3
2800 DRN 60561 3206 20W-9S C4
8200 TYPK 60477 3424 10W-21S B5
N Aster Pl
2100 RLKB 60073 2475 23W-36N A4
Aster St
10 DYR 46311 3598 C1
15300 ODPK 60462 3346 9W-18S E7
15300 OrlT 60462 3346 9W-18S E7
Aster Tr
1400 WDSK 60098 2582 40W-28N A5
Aston Ct
- HMGN 60491 3344 15W-17S B6
Aston Dr
2100 WDRG 60517 3206 21W-9S A3
Aston Wy
14600 LKPT 60441 3421 18W-19S B3
Astony Ct
5700 HNDL 60521 3146 15W-6S B4
Astor Av
- YkTp 60148 3084 18W-1S E2
- YkTp 60181 3084 18W-1S E2
1700 OKTR 60181 3084 18W-1S E2
7000 HRPK 60133 2911 27W-9N C1
Astor Ct
- WCHI 60185 3022 29W-2N D1
10 LNSH 60045 2702 14W-23N C2
200 VLPK 60181 3027 17W-0N B4
2500 GNVW 60025 2809 10W-15N E2
4900 LGGV 60047 2700 19W-23N C1
Astor Ln
- BmdT 60148 2969 21W-2N E7
- BmdT 60148 2970 21W-2N A7
600 WLNG 60090 2755 13W-17N D5
2900 MTGY 60538 3198 40W-10S B6
5400 ANHT 60005 2860 19W-12N D2
5400 ANHT 60008 2860 19W-12N D2
5400 RGMW 60008 2860 19W-12N D2
Astor Pl
10 MltT 60187 3024 26W-0N A5
200 NHBK 60062 2758 7W-16N B7
200 NHFD 60062 2758 7W-16N B7
200 NHFD 60093 2758 7W-16N B7
600 GRNE 60031 2535 14W-33N C3
1100 GLNC 60022 2758 7W-18N B4
W Astor Pl
5200 MONE 60449 3683 6W-31S A5
Astor St
1600 BNHM 60633 3351 2E-16S D4
1600 CTCY 60409 3351 2E-16S D4
1600 CTCY 60633 3351 2E-16S D4
2200 SLVL 60411 3509 2E-25S D7
N Astor St
1200 CHCG 60611 3034 0E-1N C1
1400 CHCG 60610 3034 0E-1N C1
1500 CHCG 60610 2978 D7
1500 CHCG 60614 2978 D7
26600 AntT 60002 2415 26W-38N D7
Astoria Ct
10 EMHT 60126 3027 16W-0S D6
200 BRTN 60010 2750 25W-17N E5
500 VNHL 60061 2647 16W-25N C5
S Astoria Ct
14000 LktT 60544 3340 25W-16S B4
Astoria Pl
- EMHT 60126 3027 16W-0S D7
Astoria Wy
10 PKRG 60068 2863 11W-9N C7
W AT&T Center Dr
2000 HFET 60192 2804 25W-13N A6
Atchison Dr
400 RtdT 60140 2798 40W-15N B3
Athena Ct
- OMFD 60461 3507 3W-24S A5
10 TYPK 60477 3505 8W-23S B3
600 SMBG 60193 2858 24W-9N D6
Athens Ct
10 VNHL 60061 2647 16W-25N C5
Athens Rd
2400 BlmT 60411 3507 3W-25S C7
2400 OMFD 60461 3507 3W-25S B7
S Atherton Ct
- BMDL 60108 2969 23W-5N B1
Athletic Av
16500 MDLN 60060 2590 19W-29N C4
Athletic Field Ln
- HDPK 60035 2704 9W-22N C5
Atkinson Cir
7300 JLET 60586 3415 33W-21S B7
Atkinson Dr
- SRGV 60554 3136 40W-7S B6
Atkinson Rd
- LbvT 60064 2592 13W-29N E4
1000 LbvT 60044 2593 13W-29N A4
1000 LKBF 60044 2593 12W-29N A4
1000 NCHI 60044 2593 13W-29N A4
1000 ShdT 60044 2593 12W-29N A4
1100 GNOK 60044 2593 13W-29N A4
1100 NCHI 60064 2593 13W-29N A4
1200 GNOK 60048 2592 14W-29N C4
1200 LbvT 60048 2592 14W-29N C4
2200 LbvT 60044 2592 14W-29N C4
13100 GNOK 60044 2592 13W-29N E4
13100 NCHI 60044 2592 13W-29N E4
13100 NCHI 60064 2592 13W-29N E4
N Atkinson Rd
- AvnT 60030 2533 20W-34N B1
33000 GYLK 60030 2533 20W-33N B3
S Atkinson Rd
10 GYLK 60030 2533 20W-32N B4
100 AvnT 60030 2533 20W-32N B4
Atlanta Ct
800 NPVL 60540 3141 27W-7S B7
Atlantic Av
- SMWD 60107 2857 26W-11N E4
- WkgT 60085 2479 12W-35N A5
800 HFET 60169 2857 26W-11N E3
800 HFET 60194 2857 26W-11N E3
2200 LydT 60164 2973 12W-2N C6
2300 FNPK 60131 2973 12W-2N C6
2300 LydT 60131 2973 12W-2N C6
3400 GRNE 60031 2479 13W-35N A5
3400 WkgT 60031 2479 13W-35N A5
3700 GRNE 60031 2478 13W-35N E5
4100 SRPK 60176 2973 12W-5N C1
14600 DLTN 60419 3350 0W-17S B5
14600 DLTN 60827 3350 0W-17S B5
14600 RVDL 60827 3350 0W-17S B5
S Atlantic Av
14300 RVDL 60827 3350 0W-16S C4
14500 DLTN 60419 3350 0W-17S C4
14500 DLTN 60827 3350 0W-16S C4
W Atlantic Av
500 WKGN 60085 2480 10W-35N A5
2600 WKGN 60085 2479 12W-35N C5
12900 WkgT 60085 2479 12W-35N A5
Atlantic Dr
200 VNHL 60061 2647 17W-25N B5
900 WCHI 60185 3022 30W-2N B2
1200 WynT 60185 3022 30W-2N B1
13300 HMGN 60491 3343 16W-17S E5
Atlantic Ln
400 EGVV 60007 2859 22W-9N D7
Atlantic Rd
2100 NCHI 60088 2593 11W-29N D4
Atlantic St
3300 FNPK 60131 2973 12W-4N C4
S Atlantic St
13600 RVDL 60827 3350 0W-16S C2
Atlas Ln
1200 NPVL 60540 3203 26W-8S D2
Atrium Dr
500 VNHL 60061 2647 17W-25N C4
S Atrium Wy
10 EMHT 60126 3027 16W-0S D6
Atten Dr
2400 MltT 60187 3081 26W-2S D3
2400 WHTN 60187 3081 26W-2S D3
Attenborough Ct
300 GYLK 60030 2533 19W-33N C3
Attenborough Wy
400 GYLK 60030 2533 19W-33N B3
Atteridge Rd
10 LKFT 60045 2649 10W-27N E2
10 LKFT 60045 2650 10W-27N A1
Attica Rd
3400 OMFD 60461 3506 4W-24S E6
Attleboro Ct
100 WNVL 60555 3080 30W-2S C4
1100 SMBG 60193 2912 24W-8N C2
Attleboro Ln
- BRLT 60107 2856 29W-9N D7
- SMWD 60107 2856 29W-9N D7
Attleboro on Auburn
10 RGMW 60008 2806 19W-14N C3
W Attrill St
2600 CHCG 60647 2977 3W-2N A6
Atule St
4000 NCHI 60088 2593 11W-30N D2
E Atwater Av
400 EMHT 60126 3028 15W-1N B3
Atwater Ct
5100 LSLE 60563 3142 24W-5S C3
5100 LslT 60563 3142 24W-5S C3
Atwater Dr
- MDLN 60060 2590 19W-27N B7
Atwater Pkwy
10 FXLK 60020 2473 27W-36N B3
Atwell St
100 ElgT 60124 2853 38W-11N A5
Atwood Av
2000 BKLY 60162 3028 14W-0S C5
2000 BKLY 60163 3028 14W-0S C5
2000 HLSD 60162 3028 14W-0S C5
Atwood Cir
1700 LslT 60565 3204 24W-9S E3
1700 NPVL 60565 3204 24W-9S E3
Atwood Ct
10900 ODPK 60467 3345 13W-16S A3
E Atwood Ct
400 EMHT 60126 3028 15W-0N B5
Aubrey Ct
- ALGN 60118 2746 37W-19N C2
2400 WCHI 60185 2965 32W-4N C4
Aubrey Ln
- ALGN 60118 2746 37W-19N C2
Aubrey Ter
5500 DGvT 60516 3144 20W-6S A4
5500 DRGV 60515 3144 20W-6S A4
5500 DRGV 60516 3144 20W-6S A4
Aubrieta Ct
15400 ODPK 60462 3346 9W-18S E7
15400 OrlT 60462 3346 9W-18S E7
Aubrieta Ln
15300 ODPK 60462 3346 9W-18S E7
Auburn
10 RGMW 60008 2806 20W-13N A5
Auburn Av
200 WNKA 60093 2811 5W-15N E2
300 OSWG 60543 3264 35W-12S B2
900 HDPK 60035 2704 10W-23N B2
1300 NPVL 60565 3204 24W-9S D3
S Auburn Av
12700 PSHT 60463 3275 8W-15S A7
Auburn Cir
600 SMBG 60193 2858 25W-9N B7
Auburn Ct
10 VNHL 60061 2647 17W-25N C5
200 SCRL 60174 2964 36W-3N A6
400 NLNX 60451 3500 20W-24S B5
600 CLLK 60014 2693 36W-23N D2
800 HDPK 60035 2704 9W-23N B2
9200 ODPK 60462 3345 11W-16S E3
10400 HTLY 60142 2692 39W-21N C6
Auburn Dr
10 GLHT 60139 2968 24W-3N E5
500 ISLK 60042 2586 29W-28N C5
Auburn Ln
10 AlqT 60010 2695 31W-20N C7
10 BNHL 60010 2695 31W-20N C7
500 SMBG 60193 2858 25W-9N B7
900 BRLT 60103 2910 30W-7N C4
1000 BFGV 60089 2754 17W-20N A1
1100 VrnT 60089 2754 17W-20N A1
1400 GRNE 60031 2477 17W-35N B6
2300 NHBK 60062 2809 11W-15N E1
8200 FftT 60423 3504 10W-24S C5
N Auburn Ln
600 LkvT 60046 2418 20W-39N A5
600 LNHT 60046 2418 20W-39N A5
W Auburn Ln
400 CteT 60417 3685 0W-32S C7
Auburn Rd
800 WNKA 60093 2758 5W-16N E7
Auburn Hills Ln
- AddT 60101 2970 21W-3N A5
- ADSN 60101 2970 21W-3N A5
- BmdT 60101 2970 21W-3N A5
Auburn Lakes Dr
1600 SRWD 60404 3495 31W-24S E6
Auburn Ridge Dr
17000 LKPT 60441 3419 22W-20S D5
W Auburn Woods Ct
400 PLTN 60067 2752 21W-17N D6
N Auburn Woods Dr
800 PLTN 60067 2752 21W-17N D6
Aucutt Rd
100 MTGY 60538 3199 37W-9S B4
2000 MTGY 60538 3198 39W-9S E4
Audobn Wy
- LNSH 60069 2702 14W-22N B5
Audobon Wy
- LNSH 60069 2702 14W-21N B5
- VrnT 60069 2702 14W-21N B5
Audra Cir
1800 AURA 60504 3201 33W-9S A3
Audrey Av
600 AraT 60505 3138 34W-5S C3
600 AURA 60505 3138 34W-5S C3
800 BlmT 60411 3510 4E-25S B7
2700 BHPK 60087 2479 12W-37N C3
2700 WKGN 60087 2479 12W-37N C3
2900 NPVL 60540 3202 29W-8S C1
5700 OswT 60560 3334 40W-15S C3
7600 KdlT 60560 3334 40W-15S C3
W Audrey Av
800 JLET 60436 3498 25W-24S C6
12600 BHPK 60087 2479 12W-37N B3
Audrey Ct
400 DYR 46311 3510 D6
S Audrey Ct
200 MPPT 60056 2861 17W-12N B1
Audrey Ln
200 CPVL 60110 2747 34W-17N E7
500 WLNG 60090 2755 15W-17N A5
2500 NHBK 60062 2809 11W-15N C1
4300 BRLT 60103 2967 27W-5N C2
4300 HRPK 60103 2967 27W-5N C2
4300 HRPK 60133 2967 27W-5N C2
S Audrey Ln
10 ANHT 60005 2807 17W-12N C7
10 MPPT 60056 2807 17W-12N C7
100 MPPT 60056 2861 17W-12N B1
Audubon Av
6700 WDRG 60517 3143 21W-7S E7
Audubon Ct
400 CmpT 60175 2961 42W-5N D2
600 MltT 60148 3083 21W-2S E4
700 AURA 60506 3198 39W-8S E2
Audubon Dr
2000 GLHT 60139 2968 23W-4N E4
2000 GLHT 60139 2969 23W-4N A4
Audubon Ln
800 AURA 60506 3198 39W-8S E2
1600 BKBN 60015 2703 12W-22N C4
Audubon Pl
500 HDPK 60035 2704 9W-24N C1
Audubon Rd
200 MltT 60148 3083 21W-2S E4
300 RVSD 60546 3088 9W-2S D4
300 SMWD 60107 2857 28W-10N B5
Audubon St
600 HFET 60169 2859 22W-11N C4
700 SMBG 60169 2859 22W-11N C3
700 SMBG 60173 2859 22W-11N C3
Augsburg St
- GrtT 60041 2474 25W-35N A7
August Ln
10 CRY 60013 2695 33W-23N A1
W August Ln
1600 LKMR 60051 2529 30W-34N A1
1600 MchT 60051 2529 30W-34N A1
1900 MchT 60051 2528 30W-34N E1
24600 ElaT 60047 2644 24W-25N C4
25700 NBRN 60010 2644 24W-25N C4
August St
1300 CTHL 60403 3498 25W-21S B1
Augusta
- NLNX 60442 3589 17W-27S C4
Augusta Av
- WCHI 60185 3022 29W-0S C6
- WnfT 60185 3022 29W-0S D6
900 ELGN 60120 2855 33W-12N A1
Augusta Blvd
- BGBK 60490 3267 27W-12S C3
4800 MONE 60449 3683 6W-31S A5
W Augusta Blvd
1200 CHCG 60622 3033 1W-1N E2
2800 CHCG 60622 3032 5W-1N A2
3000 CHCG 60651 3032 3W-1N D2
4700 CHCG 60651 3031 7W-1N C2
5900 OKPK 60302 3031 7W-1N B2
Augusta Ct
- LIHL 60156 2693 37W-21N C5
- PNFD 60585 3337 32W-15S C2
- WldT 60585 3337 32W-15S C2
10 GLHT 60139 2968 23W-4N E4
100 PSHT 60463 3275 7W-14S B5
500 WNFD 60190 3023 26W-1N E2
500 WNFD 60190 3024 26W-1N A2
Augusta Dr
10 DRFD 60015 2757 10W-20N B1
10 GLBT 60136 2799 38W-14N B5
10 SMWD 60107 2856 29W-10N D5
10 VNHL 60061 2647 17W-25N C5
100 MHRY 60050 2527 34W-32N D5
100 PSHT 60463 3275 8W-15S B7
100 PSHT 60463 3347 8W-15S B1
100 RLKP 60073 2532 23W-33N A2
200 WynT 60185 2966 30W-4N C4
700 NARA 60542 3078 35W-3S C5
900 CLLK 60014 2693 37W-24N C1
1600 NPVL 60563 3140 30W-5S B2
1600 NpvT 60563 3140 30W-5S B2
20100 OMFD 60461 3507 3W-24S C5
N Augusta Dr
2500 WKGN 60083 2478 14W-37N C2
Augusta Ln
100 PSHT 60463 3347 8W-15S B1
300 LslT 60540 3143 23W-7S A7
1600 SRWD 60404 3583 31W-25S E1
14700 HMGN 60491 3343 17W-17S C6
18600 HLCT 60429 3506 4W-22S E1
Augusta Rd
100 MTGY 60543 3263 38W-11S B1
Augusta St
10 CHCG 60651 3031 7W-1N B2
10 OKPK 60302 3031 7W-1N B2
100 GYLK 60030 2532 21W-33N D3
200 MYWD 60153 3030 10W-1N A2
600 MYWD 60153 3029 11W-1N D2
700 OKPK 60302 3030 8W-1N E2
800 MLPK 60160 3029 10W-1N E2
800 MYWD 60160 3029 10W-1N E2
1100 RVFT 60302 3030 8W-1N D2
1100 RVFT 60305 3030 9W-1N C2
Augusta Wy
1400 SPGV 60081 2355 30W-43N A4
1700 BtnT 60071 2355 30W-43N A4
1700 BtnT 60081 2355 30W-43N A4
2400 AURA 60506 3136 39W-5S E3
2500 HDPK 60035 2704 9W-23N C3
Augusta Green
- VNHL 60061 2647 16W-27N D1
N Augustana Av
34700 GrtT 60041 2474 25W-34N A7
Augustana Ct
- GrtT 60041 2474 25W-34N A7
2200 NPVL 60565 3204 24W-10S C5
Augustana Dr
1000 NPVL 60565 3204 25W-10S C5
W August Zupec Dr
13900 WDWH 60083 2420 13W-39N D5
Aulwurm Dr
- ClmT 60827 3349 1W-15S D1
13300 BLID 60406 3349 2W-15S C1
13300 ClmT 60406 3349 2W-15S C1
N Aurelia Ct
600 PLTN 60067 2752 21W-16N D7
Aurora Av
10 NPVL 60540 3141 28W-7S A6
600 AURA 60505 3138 35W-6S C6
700 SchT 60174 2908 35W-6N B6
900 AURA 60504 3138 35W-6S B4
900 AURA 60506 3138 35W-6S B4
1000 NpvT 60540 3141 27W-7S B6
1100 AURA 60542 3138 35W-6S B4
1300 NPVL 60540 3140 29W-7S D7
2900 AURA 60504 3140 29W-7S C7
2900 NPVL 60504 3140 29W-7S C7
3300 LIHL 60156 2692 39W-23N C2
Aurora Av SR-25
700 AURA 60505 3138 35W-6S C5
900 AURA 60504 3138 35W-6S B4
900 AURA 60506 3138 35W-6S B4
1100 AURA 60542 3138 35W-6S B4
Aurora Ct
400 VNHL 60061 2647 16W-25N C5
Aurora Rd
- AURA 60504 3138 35W-6S B4
1100 AURA 60506 3138 35W-6S B4
N Aurora Rd
10 NPVL 60563 3140 30W-6S B4
10 NpvT 60563 3140 30W-6S B4
200 AURA 60502 3139 31W-6S E4
200 AURA 60563 3139 31W-6S E4
200 NPVL 60563 3139 31W-6S E4
200 NpvT 60563 3139 31W-6S E4
400 NpvT 60502 3139 31W-6S E4
1500 NPVL 60540 3140 29W-6S D4
1500 NpvT 60540 3140 29W-6S D4
N Aurora St
100 WCHI 60185 3022 30W-0N B4
S Aurora St
100 WCHI 60185 3022 30W-0N B4
Aurora Wy
200 WNVL 60555 3080 29W-3S D6
400 WHTN 60187 3024 25W-0S B7
800 WHTN 60187 3082 25W-1S B1
Aurora Av Ln
1200 AURA 60504 3138 35W-5S B4
Aurora Market Pl
- AURA 60504 3202 30W-8S C2
- AURA 60540 3202 30W-8S C2
- NPVL 60540 3202 30W-8S C2
Austen Ct
10300 MKNA 60448 3503 12W-23S C4
Austgen Pl
500 DYR 46311 3598 D5
3100 SjnT 46311 3598 D5
Austin Av
10 CPVL 60110 2748 33W-18N B5
400 GNVA 60134 3020 34W-1N D3
500 PKRG 60068 2864 10W-9N A6
500 WDSK 60098 2581 41W-30N C1
600 AraT 60505 3138 34W-6S E5
1300 AURA 60505 3138 34W-5S E4
1500 CRTE 60417 3685 0W-30S C3
1500 CteT 60417 3685 0W-30S C3
7600 BRBK 60459 3211 7W-8S C2
7600 SKOK 60077 2865 7W-9N B6
7800 MNGV 60053 2865 7W-10N B5
7800 SKOK 60053 2865 7W-9N B6
8700 OKLN 60453 3211 7W-10S C5
8700 OKLN 60459 3211 7W-10S C5
10300 CHRG 60415 3275 7W-12S C1
10300 OKLN 60415 3275 7W-12S C1
10300 OKLN 60453 3275 7W-12S C1
11000 ALSP 60482 3275 7W-12S C3
11000 CHRG 60482 3275 7W-12S C3
16300 BmnT 60477 3425 7W-19S C2
E Austin Av
200 LYVL 60048 2591 16W-28N E6
N Austin Av
1700 CHCG 60639 2975 7W-2N B7
2700 CHCG 60634 2975 7W-3N B5
4300 CHCG 60630 2975 7W-5N B1
4400 CHCG 60630 2919 7W-5N B7
5400 CHCG 60646 2919 7W-7N B4
6900 NLES 60714 2919 7W-8N C1
S Austin Av
4700 StkT 60638 3149 7W-5S C5
4900 CHCG 60638 3149 7W-7S C5
6400 BDPK 60638 3149 7W-7S C5
11500 ALSP 60482 3275 7W-13S C4
12200 WhtT 60463 3275 7W-14S C6
12200 WhtT 60803 3275 7W-14S C6
12700 PSHT 60463 3275 7W-15S C7
12700 ALSP 60803 3275 7W-15S C7
W Austin Av
100 LYVL 60048 2591 16W-28N D6
N Austin Blvd
10 CHCG 60302 3031 7W-0N B4
10 CHCG 60644 3031 7W-0N B5
10 OKPK 60302 3031 7W-0N B4
10 OKPK 60304 3031 7W-0N B5
400 CHCG 60651 3031 7W-0N B4
700 OKPK 60302 3031 7W-0N B4
1000 CHCG 60651 3031 7W-1N B1
1500 CHCG 60639 3031 7W-1N B1
1500 OKPK 60639 3031 7W-1N B1
1500 OKPK 60651 3031 7W-1N B1
1600 CHCG 60639 2975 7W-2N B7
S Austin Blvd
10 CHCG 60644 3031 7W-1S C7
10 OKPK 60302 3031 7W-0S B5
10 OKPK 60304 3031 7W-1S C7
200 OKPK 60644 3031 7W-1S C7
600 CHCG 60304 3031 7W-1S C7
1000 CCRO 60304 3031 7W-0S B7
1000 CCRO 60644 3031 7W-0S B7
1000 CCRO 60804 3031 7W-0S B7
1500 CCRO 60804 3089 7W-3S C5
3800 SKNY 60402 3089 7W-3S C6
Austin Cir
1600 JLET 60432 3499 21W-23S E4
1600 JltT 60432 3499 21W-23S E4
Austin Ct
100 VNHL 60061 2647 16W-25N C5
300 KdlT 60560 3334 40W-15S B3
300 OswT 60560 3334 40W-15S B3
1700 WHTN 60187 3082 24W-2S D3
3200 NPVL 60564 3203 28W-11S A7
5400 MchT 60072 2470 34W-37N D2
5400 RGWD 60072 2470 34W-37N D2
Austin Dr
200 SRWD 60404 3495 31W-24S E6
14900 LKPT 60441 3420 18W-20S E4
14900 LKPT 60441 3421 18W-20S A4
Austin Ln
200 SMBG 60195 2859 23W-12N A2
17000 ODPK 60467 3423 13W-20S B4
W Austin Ln
1000 PLTN 60067 2805 22W-15N B2
Austin St
400 DRGV 60515 3144 19W-5S D2
1000 EVTN 60202 2867 2W-9N A6
3100 NPVL 60564 3203 28W-11S A7
N Austin St
34800 WKGN 60085 2479 12W-33N B7
34800 WkgT 60085 2479 12W-33N B7
W Austrian Ct
14000 HMGN 60491 3421 17W-19S C3
Austrian Dr
10 RMVL 60446 3269 23W-14S A7
S Austrian Pine St
1900 LKPT 60441 3419 22W-20S D4
1900 LktT 60441 3419 22W-20S D4
Authority Dr
10 DRGV 60515 3143 21W-4S D1
10 DRGV 60532 3143 21W-4S D1
10 LSLE 60532 3143 21W-4S D1
10 LslT 60515 3143 21W-4S D1
Auto Ct
- MTSN 60443 3505 6W-25S E7
5500 MTSN 60443 3593 6W-25S E1
Autobahn Dr E
11500 PSPK 60464 3274 9W-13S C4
Autobahn Dr N
8000 PSPK 60464 3274 10W-13S C4
Autobahn Dr S
8000 PSPK 60464 3274 10W-13S C4
Autobahn Dr W
11500 PSPK 60464 3274 10W-13S C4
Automall Dr
13900 HTLY 60142 2744 41W-17N E6
Automatic Electric Dr
- NHLK 60164 2972 14W-2N D7
W Autullo Dr
7600 WRTH 60482 3274 9W-12S D2
S Autullo St
10800 WRTH 60482 3274 9W-12S D2
Autumn Av
1600 SMBG 60193 2912 25W-8N B3
Autumn Blvd
500 LKMR 60051 2530 28W-32N A5
N Autumn Cir
600 LNHT 60046 2418 20W-39N A5
Autumn Ct
100 BFGV 60089 2701 16W-21N C7
500 ELGN 60123 2853 36W-12N E2
500 RDLK 60073 2530 26W-34N E2
Autumn Dr
600 ROSL 60172 2912 24W-6N D6
700 BGBK 60490 3268 26W-13S A5
800 ANTH 60002 2358 22W-42N B6
1000 CLLK 60014 2639 37W-24N B7
1200 WDSK 60098 2581 41W-30N D2
2900 WDRG 60517 3205 22W-9S D4
16900 TYPK 60477 3425 7W-20S C4
22300 FKFT 60423 3591 13W-27S A4
N Autumn Dr
1600 JLET 60431 3497 28W-21S B1
1600 PnfT 60431 3497 28W-21S B1
W Autumn Dr
2400 RDLK 60073 2530 26W-34N E2
Autumn Hl
800 WDND 60118 2800 34W-15N D4
Autumn Ln
10 SMWD 60107 2856 29W-9N D7
200 MPPT 60056 2808 14W-13N B6
200 VNHL 60061 2647 17W-25N C5
900 AURA 60505 3138 34W-5S D4
2900 DYR 46311 3598 D4
9600 GwdT 60098 2525 38W-33N D3
W Autumn Rd
1400 PLTN 60067 2752 22W-17N A5
1400 PltT 60067 2752 22W-17N A5
N Autumn Rdg
- CbaT 60013 2642 28W-24N E6
Autumn St
- MRGO 60152 2634 49W-26N C3
Autumn Tr
10 BNHL 60010 2748 32W-19N D3
W Autumn Tr
1300 ADSN 60101 2970 20W-5N B1
Autumn Wy
5200 JNBG 60050 2472 30W-37N B2
Autumncrest Ct
1500 CLLK 60014 2693 36W-23N C2
Autumncrest Dr
1500 CLLK 60014 2693 37W-23N C2
Autumn Fields Blvd
- JLET 60586 3415 33W-20S A6
- NasT 60586 3415 33W-20S A6
Autumn Glen Dr
10 HRVD 60033 2406 50W-39N B4
100 CmgT 60033 2406 50W-39N B4
Autumn Grove Cir
2300 AURA 60504 3201 32W-9S C3
Autumn Grove Ct
2500 AURA 60504 3201 32W-9S C4
Autumn Lake Dr
3000 AURA 60504 3139 31W-7S D7
3000 AURA 60504 3201 32W-8S C2
Autumn Mist Ct
200 NARA 60542 3137 38W-4S A2
Autumn Ridge Dr
100 MTGY 60538 3199 36W-10S E5

STREET Block	City	ZIP	Map#	CGS	Grid
Autumn Ridge Dr					
6100	JLET	60586	3415	31W-21S	E6
11200	ODPK	60467	3422	14W-21S	E7
Autumn Trails Ct					
-	SRWD	60404	3496	30W-22S	B2
Autumn Valley Ln					
11100	FKFT	60423	3591	13W-25S	A1
Autumnwind Ct					
300	BGBK	60440	3269	22W-13S	D4
Autumn Wind Ln					
1700	AURA	60504	3201	33W-9S	A3
Autumn Woods Ct					
1700	RMVL	60446	3339	27W-17S	D6
Autumn Woods Ln					
600	BbyT	60119	3017	43W-0S	A7
600	BbyT	60119	3075	43W-0S	A1
1700	RMVL	60446	3339	27W-17S	D5
Auvergne Av					
4600	LSLE	60532	3143	22W-4S	C1
Auvergne Pl					
500	RVFT	60305	3030	10W-0N	B4
N Auxplaines St					
2700	RVGV	60171	2974	10W-3N	A5
Aux Sable Dr					
-	AxST	60447	3672	33W-28S	B1
100	MNKA	60447	3672	33W-28S	B1
Ava St					
400	HDPK	60035	2705	7W-21N	A7
Avalon Av					
600	RMVL	60446	3340	24W-16S	D3
2200	JLET	60435	3497	26W-22S	E3
2900	TroT	60435	3497	27W-23S	C3
6000	OKFT	60452	3347	7W-18S	C6
14200	DLTN	60419	3351	1E-16S	B4
15600	SHLD	60473	3351	1E-18S	B7
15900	SHLD	60473	3429	1E-18S	B1
S Avalon Av					
300	GNWD	60425	3509	1E-23S	B3
7600	CHCG	60619	3215	1E-9S	A2
9500	CHCG	60628	3215	1E-11S	A6
W Avalon Av					
1600	JLET	60435	3498	26W-23S	A3
Avalon Ct					
10	CLLK	60013	2641	32W-24N	A7
10	CRY	60013	2641	32W-24N	A7
100	ROSL	60172	2912	25W-7N	C4
1200	WHTN	60187	3082	25W-2S	A3
1500	SCRL	60174	2963	36W-2N	E7
1700	GLHT	60139	2969	23W-3N	A6
2000	GNVW	60062	2809	12W-14N	B3
2300	AURA	60503	3201	32W-10S	B6
2900	ELGN	60124	2853	37W-11N	C3
14000	ODPK	60462	3346	10W-16S	B3
Avalon Ct N					
2100	BFGV	60089	2701	16W-22N	D4
Avalon Ct S					
2200	BFGV	60089	2701	16W-22N	D4
Avalon Dr					
500	DYR	46311	3598		D1
1800	WLNG	60090	2808	14W-15N	B2
2100	BFGV	60089	2701	16W-22N	D4
2900	ELGN	60124	2853	37W-11N	C3
Avalon Ln					
-	BGBK	60440	3268	25W-12S	C2
1000	LYVL	60048	2591	16W-29N	D3
2600	MTGY	60538	3198	40W-10S	C6
5300	LIHL	60156	2692	39W-23N	C2
Avard Rd					
100	WynT	60185	2966	30W-4N	B4
200	WYNE	60184	2966	30W-4N	B4
200	WynT	60184	2966	30W-4N	B4
Avard St					
-	WCHI	60185	3022	30W-0N	B4
Avati Ln					
1500	AURA	60505	3139	33W-5S	A3
Avebury Ct					
400	ROSL	60172	2912	24W-6N	D5
Avebury Ln					
400	ROSL	60172	2912	24W-6N	D6
Avena Cir					
300	NPVL	60565	3203	26W-10S	D5
Avena Ct					
400	NPVL	60565	3203	27W-10S	D6
Avenel Dr					
16400	ODPK	60467	3422	14W-19S	E3
Avenida Del Este St					
9800	ODPK	60462	3345	12W-17S	D6
Avenida Del Norte St					
9800	ODPK	60462	3345	12W-17S	C6
Avenue E					
2800	GNVW	60025	2810	10W-14N	A3
S Avenue A					
10600	CHCG	60617	3280	4E-12S	C1
10600	HMND	46320	3280	4E-12S	C1
11100	CHCG	46320	3280	4E-12S	C3
Avenue B					
2900	GNVW	60025	2810	10W-14N	A4
S Avenue B					
10500	CHCG	60617	3280	4E-11S	C1
Avenue Barbizon					
10	YkTp	60523	3084	19W-2S	D4
Avenue C					
2900	GNVW	60025	2810	10W-14N	A4
S Avenue C					
10600	CHCG	60617	3280	4E-12S	C2
Avenue Chappelle					
800	DndT	60118	2800	34W-14N	D5
Avenue Chateaux E					
-	DRGV	60523	3084	18W-2S	E4
-	OKBK	60523	3084	18W-2S	E4
500	YkTp	60523	3084	18W-2S	E4
Avenue Chateaux N					
10	YkTp	60523	3084	19W-2S	D4
Avenue Cherbourg					
700	YkTp	60523	3084	19W-2S	D4
Avenue D					
2900	GNVW	60025	2810	10W-14N	A4
S Avenue D					
10600	CHCG	60617	3280	4E-12S	C1
S Avenue E					
10800	CHCG	60617	3280	4E-12S	C2
S Avenue F					
10300	CHCG	60617	3216	4E-11S	C7
10300	CHCG	60617	3280	4E-11S	C1
S Avenue G					
9700	CHCG	60617	3216	4E-11S	C6
10300	CHCG	60617	3280	4E-11S	C1
Avenue G Dr					
-	CHCG	60617	3216	4E-11S	C7
-	HMND	46320	3216	4E-11S	C7
S Avenue H					
9700	CHCG	60617	3216	4E-10S	B6
10300	CHCG	60617	3280	4E-12S	B3
S Avenue J					
9600	CHCG	60617	3216	4E-10S	B6
10300	CHCG	60617	3280	4E-11S	B1
S Avenue K					
13300	CHCG	60633	3352	4E-15S	B1
S Avenue L					
9500	CHCG	60617	3216	4E-10S	B5
10300	CHCG	60617	3280	4E-12S	B3
13200	CHCG	60633	3352	4E-15S	B1
Avenue la Tour					
10	YkTp	60523	3084	19W-2S	D4
Avenue la Tours					
-	DRGV	60515	3084	19W-2S	D4
-	DRGV	60523	3084	19W-2S	D4
600	YkTp	60523	3084	19W-2S	D4
Avenue Lorie					
700	OKBK	60523	3084	18W-2S	E4
700	YkTp	60523	3084	18W-2S	E4
S Avenue M					
9500	CHCG	60617	3216	4E-10S	B5
10300	CHCG	60617	3280	4E-11S	B1
13000	CHCG	60633	3280	4E-15S	B7
13100	CHCG	60633	3352	4E-15S	B1
S Avenue N					
9500	CHCG	60617	3216	4E-10S	B5
10300	CHCG	60617	3280	4E-11S	B1
13000	CHCG	60633	3280	4E-15S	B7
13100	CHCG	60633	3352	4E-15S	B1
Avenue Normandy E					
10	YkTp	60523	3084	19W-2S	E4
Avenue Normandy N					
10	YkTp	60523	3084	19W-2S	D4
Avenue Normandy S					
10	YkTp	60523	3084	19W-2S	D4
Avenue Normandy W					
600	YkTp	60523	3084	19W-2S	D4
S Avenue O					
8900	CHCG	60617	3216	4E-10S	B4
10300	CHCG	60617	3280	3E-13S	B4
11800	CHCG	60633	3280	3E-13S	B5
13100	CHCG	60633	3352	3E-15S	B1
13600	BNHM	60633	3352	3E-15S	B2
Avenue Orleans					
100	YkTp	60523	3084	19W-2S	D4
Avenue Royal					
100	YkTp	60523	3084	19W-2S	D4
Avenue Vendome					
500	YkTp	60523	3084	18W-2S	E4
Averill Cir					
1300	GNVA	60134	3020	33W-1N	E3
1300	GNVA	60134	3021	33W-1N	A3
1500	GnvT	60134	3021	33W-1N	A3
Averill Ct					
10	NBRN	60010	2644	24W-25N	C5
Averill Dr					
1000	BTVA	60510	3077	36W-2S	E3
Averill Rd					
600	GNVA	60134	3021	33W-1N	A3
600	GnvT	60134	3021	33W-1N	A3
1900	WCHI	60185	3021	33W-1N	B3
Avers Av					
8400	SKOK	60076	2866	4W-10N	C4
9200	SKOK	60203	2866	4W-11N	C2
9500	EVTN	60201	2866	4W-11N	C2
14400	MDLN	60445	3348	4W-17S	D5
15500	MDLN	60428	3348	4W-18S	D7
18700	FSMR	60422	3506	4W-22S	D2
19000	RchT	60430	3506	4W-22S	D2
N Avers Av					
400	CHCG	60624	3032	4W-0N	C3
700	CHCG	60651	3032	4W-0N	C3
1500	CHCG	60647	3032	4W-1N	C1
2000	CHCG	60647	2976	4W-2N	C6
4000	CHCG	60618	2976	4W-5N	C1
4300	CHCG	60625	2976	4W-5N	C1
4400	CHCG	60625	2920	4W-5N	C7
6100	CHCG	60659	2920	4W-7N	C3
6300	CHCG	60712	2920	4W-7N	C3
6900	LNWD	60712	2920	4W-8N	C1
S Avers Av					
1200	CHCG	60623	3032	4W-1S	C7
1200	CHCG	60624	3032	4W-1S	C7
2200	CHCG	60623	3090	4W-2S	C2
4500	CHCG	60632	3090	4W-4S	C7
5100	CHCG	60632	3150	4W-5S	C2
7100	CHCG	60629	3150	4W-8S	C7
9100	CHCG	60805	3212	4W-11S	C6
9100	ENGN	60805	3212	4W-11S	C6
9800	CHCG	60655	3212	4W-11S	C7
10300	CHCG	60655	3276	4W-12S	C1
11900	ALSP	60803	3276	4W-14S	C5
11900	WthT	60803	3276	4W-14S	C5
13400	CTWD	60472	3348	4W-15S	D2
13400	RBBN	60472	3348	4W-15S	D2
S Avers Ct					
12000	ALSP	60803	3276	4W-14S	D5
Avery Av					
1200	WHTN	60187	3024	23W-0S	E6
Avery Ct					
700	GRNE	60031	2534	16W-33N	E3
N Avery Ct					
10	PLTN	60067	2805	22W-16N	C1
10	PltT	60067	2805	22W-16N	C1
Avery Pl					
5200	OKLN	60453	3211	6W-10S	D4
W Avery St					
300	EMHT	60126	3027	16W-0S	D7
Aviara Ct					
3100	NPVL	60564	3202	30W-10S	B6
Aviary Ln					
300	BGBK	60490	3267	26W-12S	E4
Aviation Av					
1900	WynT	60185	2965	32W-2N	B7
W Aviation Dr					
2900	BHPK	60087	2421	12W-38N	B7
2900	WKGN	60087	2421	12W-38N	B7
Aviator Ln					
2600	GNVW	60025	2810	9W-14N	B4
Aviemore Ln					
20900	FftT	60423	3504	9W-25S	E7
Avignon Ct					
1400	HDPK	60035	2704	8W-21N	D6
W Avilon Av					
400	RDLK	60073	2531	23W-33N	E2
Avilon Ct					
300	RDLK	60073	2531	23W-33N	D2
Avon Av					
-	BGVW	60455	3210	9W-10S	D6
100	NfdT	60093	2811	7W-15N	B3
100	NHFD	60093	2811	7W-15N	C3
7000	CHRG	60415	3210	8W-11S	E6
7000	OKLN	60415	3210	8W-11S	E6
7000	OKLN	60453	3210	8W-11S	E6
S Avon Av					
11100	ALSP	60803	3275	6W-13S	E3
11300	ALSP	60803	3276	6W-13S	A4
Avon Ct					
600	ELBN	60119	3017	43W-0N	B5
600	LslT	60540	3142	24W-6S	C4
600	VNHL	60061	2647	17W-25N	C4
700	WNVL	60555	3080	30W-1S	C3
800	GNEN	60137	3024	23W-1N	E3
800	WHTN	60187	3024	23W-1N	E3
1300	NPVL	60564	3267	28W-11S	A1
1300	SMBG	60193	2912	25W-8N	B2
10600	PSHL	60465	3274	10W-12S	A2
E Avon Ct					
1600	ANHT	60004	2807	16W-15N	C1
N Avon Ct					
500	OSWG	60543	3200	35W-10S	A6
S Avon Ct					
600	OSWG	60543	3200	35W-10S	A7
W Avon Ct					
18100	WrnT	60030	2534	18W-33N	A3
Avon Dr					
700	WNVL	60555	3080	30W-1S	C3
1800	HFET	60192	2855	31W-12N	E1
N Avon Dr					
37000	GrtT	60046	2474	25W-37N	A3
37000	LkvT	60046	2474	25W-37N	A3
Avon Ln					
-	NHBK	60062	2757	9W-18N	B2
10	SBTN	60010	2804	24W-14N	C3
17300	TYPK	60487	3424	10W-20S	A5
E Avon Ln					
1700	ANHT	60004	2807	16W-15N	C1
Avon Rd					
10	DRFD	60015	2757	9W-18N	B2
10	EGVV	60007	2914	19W-8N	D1
10	NHBK	60062	2757	9W-18N	B2
100	NfdT	60062	2757	9W-18N	B2
N Avon Rd					
100	EMHT	60126	3028	15W-1N	A2
Avon St					
400	AURA	60505	3200	35W-8S	B1
Avondale Av					
-	PKRG	60068	2918	9W-8N	B1
2300	PKRG	60068	2863	11W-9N	D6
N Avondale Av					
-	CHCG	60614	2977	2W-2N	C6
2600	CHCG	60647	2977	3W-3N	A5
3500	CHCG	60618	2976	4W-4N	C3
3800	CHCG	60641	2976	4W-4N	C2
5100	CHCG	60630	2919	7W-6N	C6
5600	CHCG	60631	2919	8W-7N	A4
5600	CHCG	60646	2919	7W-7N	A4
6700	CHCG	60631	2918	9W-8N	C2
6700	PKRG	60068	2918	9W-8N	C2
6700	PKRG	60631	2918	9W-8N	C2
Avondale Ct					
10	WNVL	60555	3080	30W-2S	C3
100	BGBK	60440	3269	23W-11S	B2
3300	JLET	60451	3500	19W-22S	D2
W Avondale Dr					
200	PLTN	60067	2752	21W-17N	D4
Avondale Ln					
10	YkTp	60148	3084	20W-2S	A3
500	HFET	60169	2859	22W-11N	B3
600	AURA	60504	3201	31W-8S	D2
2000	WLMT	60091	2812	4W-13N	B7
3300	JLET	60451	3500	19W-22S	D2
Avonelle Dr					
200	CHHT	60411	3508	1W-24S	A4
N Ayer St					
10	HRVD	60033	2406	50W-38N	B7
S Ayer St					
100	HRVD	60033	2406	50W-38N	A7
500	DhmT	60033	2406	50W-38N	A7
Ayers St					
700	BGBK	60440	3204	24W-10S	D5
Aylesbury Av					
4700	MTSN	60443	3506	5W-24S	B6
Aylesbury Ln					
2500	DRN	60561	3206	19W-8S	C2
Aynsley Dr					
1000	LKFT	60045	2649	12W-27N	B1
Ayr Ln					
3600	CRTE	60417	3597	0E-28S	A7
Ayre Ct					
3600	CRTE	60417	3597	0E-28S	A7
Ayre Dr					
6600	MHRY	60050	2527	35W-31N	A6
Ayres Dr					
-	AURA	60506	3136	40W-7S	B6
E Ayres St					
10	HNDL	60521	3086	15W-4S	B7
W Ayres St					
10	HNDL	60521	3086	15W-4S	A7
Ayrshire Ct					
11000	WDSK	60098	2582	40W-30N	B1
Ayrshire Ln					
300	IVNS	60067	2751	23W-16N	E7
Ayshire Ct					
800	FKFT	60423	3592	9W-26S	E3
W Azalea Av					
4500	MONE	60449	3683	5W-31S	C4
Azalea Cir					
100	RMVL	60446	3339	26W-17S	E6
100	SMWD	60107	2857	27W-10N	C5
Azalea Ct					
600	NPVL	60540	3140	29W-7S	D7
2100	RDLK	60073	2531	25W-33N	A2
5500	RGMW	60008	2860	19W-12N	D1
Azalea Dr					
10	SMBG	60173	2859	21W-10N	E5
1000	MNSR	46321	3510		E2
4300	LSLE	60532	3142	24W-4S	D1
Azalea Ln					
400	HFET	60169	2859	23W-11N	B2
E Azalea Ln					
1100	PLTN	60074	2753	19W-18N	C3
W Azalea Ln					
1800	MPPT	60056	2808	13W-14N	E4
W Azalea Pl					
1700	MPPT	60056	2808	13W-14N	D4
Azalea Rd					
100	FftT	60423	3592	11W-26S	A2
100	FKFT	60423	3592	11W-26S	A1
Aztec Cir					
1500	NPVL	60563	3141	26W-5S	D2
Aztec Ct					
10	BrnT	60010	2802	28W-14N	E4
Aztec Dr					
400	CLSM	60188	2967	26W-3N	E6
Aztec Ln					
10	RtdT	60142	2745	40W-18N	C4
E Aztec Ln					
1700	MPPT	60056	2808	13W-15N	E2
Aztec St					
24400	LkvT	60046	2416	24W-39N	C5
Azure Cir					
11700	FKFT	60423	3590	14W-27S	E5
Azure Dr					
11700	FKFT	60423	3590	14W-27S	D5
11700	GGnT	60423	3590	14W-27S	D5
Azure Cove					
3000	AURA	60503	3201	31W-10S	D5
B					
B Ct					
9700	MKNA	60448	3503	12W-23S	D4
B Rd					
-	BtvT	60510	3079	33W-1S	B2
-	WnfT	60510	3079	33W-1S	B2
B St					
-	HDPK	60037	2704	9W-23N	D1
-	HIWD	60037	2704	9W-23N	D1
-	MrnT	60037	2704	9W-24N	D1
10	NCHI	60088	2594	10W-30N	A2
N B St					
42200	ANTH	60002	2357	24W-42N	B6
42200	AntT	60002	2357	24W-42N	B6
W B St					
-	MYWD	60153	3030	10W-1S	A7
-	PvsT	60141	3030	10W-1S	A7
-	PvsT	60153	3030	10W-1S	A7
Babb Av					
7800	SKOK	60077	2865	6W-9N	D6
N Babbit Av					
900	ADSN	60101	2970	19W-4N	D3
E Babcock Av					
900	ADSN	60101	2971	17W-2N	B6
W Babcock Av					
500	EMHT	60126	2971	17W-2N	C6
600	EMHT	60101	2971	17W-2N	C6
Babcock Ct					
1100	MDLN	60060	2590	19W-27N	B7
Babcock Dr					
-	BTVA	60510	3078	34W-2S	C5
-	BtvT	60510	3078	34W-2S	C5
E Babcock Dr					
800	PLTN	60074	2753	19W-16N	B7
N Babcock Dr					
100	PLTN	60074	2753	19W-16N	B7
100	PLTN	60074	2806	19W-16N	B1
Babetta Av					
600	PKRG	60068	2863	11W-9N	D7
Babette Ct					
5500	BmnT	60477	3425	6W-19S	D2
5500	OKFT	60452	3425	6W-19S	D2
5500	OKFT	60477	3425	6W-19S	D2
Babs Tr					
21200	RlyT	60152	2634	50W-25N	B5
Babson Ln					
10	SchT	60175	2963	37W-4N	C5
Babst Ct					
2100	LSLE	60532	3142	24W-6S	E5
Baccarrat Ct					
1100	JLET	60431	3496	29W-22S	C2
Bacchus Ln					
-	BtnT	60081	2355	30W-43N	A4
Bach Ct					
-	WDSK	60098	2524	40W-33N	E3
100	WHTN	60187	3082	24W-2S	C4
Bach St					
800	NHBK	60062	2757	10W-17N	A4
W Bachman Rd					
26000	GrtT	60041	2473	26W-37N	E2
N Back Bay Ct					
36100	WrnT	60031	2477	17W-36N	C4
Back Bay Dr					
10	SBTN	60010	2803	26W-14N	C3
Backbay Rd					
7400	MchT	60097	2469	36W-36N	D3
7400	WRLK	60097	2469	36W-36N	D3
Bacon Rd					
30900	FmtT	60030	2588	23W-30N	E2
30900	FmtT	60073	2588	23W-30N	E2
30900	RDLK	60030	2588	23W-30N	E2
30900	RDLK	60073	2588	23W-30N	E2
N Bacon Rd					
31500	FmtT	60030	2531	23W-32N	D5
31500	RDLK	60073	2531	23W-32N	D5
31600	AvnT	60030	2531	23W-32N	D5
32000	AvnT	60073	2531	23W-32N	D5
Badger Ct					
200	CmpT	60175	2961	43W-6N	B1
300	OSWG	60543	3263	38W-12S	B2
Badger Ln					
-	HMGN	60491	3344	16W-18S	A7
400	OSWG	60543	3263	38W-12S	B2
15400	HMGN	60491	3422	16W-18S	A1
Badger Rd					
3400	EGvT	60005	2861	16W-10N	D6
3400	MPPT	60005	2861	16W-10N	D6
Badger St					
1200	YKVL	60560	3333	42W-16S	C4
Badin Av					
800	OSWG	60543	3264	35W-12S	C2
Baert Ln					
100	CmpT	60175	2962	39W-3N	E5
Baffin Rd					
1400	GNVW	60025	2810	8W-13N	E6
Bagley St					
-	WDSK	60098	2524	41W-31N	C6
E Bagley St					
100	WDSK	60098	2524	41W-31N	D6
W Bagpipe Ct					
23000	ElaT	60047	2645	23W-25N	A5
23000	HNWD	60047	2645	23W-25N	A5
Bahama Ct					
600	SMBG	60193	2858	24W-9N	D7
Bahama Ln					
500	SMBG	60193	2858	24W-9N	D7
Bahia Ct					
-	FKFT	60423	3590	14W-28S	E6
-	FKFT	60423	3591	14W-28S	A6
Bahr Rd					
10	PltT	60140	2851	42W-12N	D2
Bailey Ct					
300	MRGO	60152	2634	49W-26N	B3
Bailey Dr					
500	BTVA	60510	3078	34W-2S	C3
500	BtvT	60510	3078	34W-2S	C3
800	SRWD	60404	3496	29W-22S	D3
Bailey Ln					
-	ElaT	60047	2644	24W-24N	C7
-	HNWD	60047	2644	24W-24N	C7
-	HPSR	60140	2796	46W-15N	A3
-	LKZH	60047	2644	24W-24N	C7
-	NBRN	60047	2644	24W-24N	C7
Bailey Rd					
10	PKFT	60466	3595	2W-26S	C2
7800	DRN	60561	3207	18W-9S	A4
E Bailey Rd					
10	NPVL	60565	3204	25W-9S	A3
500	LslT	60565	3204	25W-9S	B3
W Bailey Rd					
10	NPVL	60565	3203	26W-8S	E3
10	NPVL	60565	3204	26W-9S	A3
500	NpvT	60565	3203	26W-8S	D3
1000	NPVL	60564	3203	27W-8S	B2
1000	NpvT	60564	3203	27W-8S	B2
Bailey St					
-	LtRT	60545	3332	45W-14S	B1
-	PLNO	60545	3260	45W-13S	B7
-	PLNO	60545	3332	45W-14S	B1
Baileys Crossing Dr					
1200	LMNT	60439	3271	17W-14S	B7
Baimbridge Dr					
7500	DRGV	60516	3207	18W-8S	A2
7500	DRN	60516	3207	18W-8S	A2
Bainbridge Blvd					
2300	WCHI	60185	2965	32W-4N	C4
Bainbridge Ct					
2500	AURA	60506	3136	39W-6S	E6
Bainbridge Dr					
900	NPVL	60563	3140	29W-5S	D3
E Bairstow Av					
9800	BHPK	60087	2480	9W-37N	C2
W Bairstow Av					
10000	BHPK	60087	2480	10W-37N	B2
12900	BHPK	60087	2479	12W-37N	A2
12900	WrnT	60087	2479	12W-37N	A2
W Bairstow St					
-	BHPK	60087	2479	12W-37N	B2
Baje Industrial Dr					
100	AURA	60505	3200	35W-7S	A1
Bajt Ln					
200	JLET	60432	3499	21W-23S	E4
200	JltT	60432	3499	21W-23S	E4
Baker Av					
800	DndT	60118	2801	32W-14N	C5
17500	CCHL	60478	3426	5W-21S	C6
18500	CCHL	60478	3506	5W-22S	C1
18900	CCHL	60477	3506	5W-22S	C2
18900	RchT	60477	3506	5W-22S	C2
S Baker Av					
10	JLET	60433	3499	23W-24S	B5
8300	CHCG	60617	3216	3E-9S	A3
S Baker Av US-41					
8400	CHCG	60617	3216	3E-9S	A3
Baker Cir					
10	RMVL	60446	3341	23W-16S	A4
Baker Ct					
100	NPVL	60565	3203	26W-10S	E6
800	GNEN	60137	3083	21W-1S	D1
7600	DRN	60561	3207	17W-8S	C2
17800	CCHL	60478	3426	5W-21S	C6
Baker Dr					
300	BbyT	60134	3018	39W-0N	E5
300	BmdT	60143	2913	21W-6N	E6
500	ITSC	60143	2913	21W-6N	E6
N Baker Dr					
1000	ITSC	60143	2913	21W-7N	E4
1000	ITSC	60143	2914	21W-7N	A4
S Baker Dr					
400	BmdT	60143	2913	21W-6N	E6
400	ITSC	60143	2913	21W-6N	E6
Baker Ln					
10	NPVL	60565	3203	26W-10S	E6
10	NPVL	60565	3204	26W-10S	A6
200	SchT	60175	2963	37W-5N	D2
N Baker Ln					
29300	FmtT	60060	2588	24W-29N	C4
Baker Pl					
1500	DRGV	60516	3206	20W-8S	B1
Baker Rd					
10	GNOK	60044	2592	13W-28N	E5
10	GNOK	60045	2592	13W-28N	E5
W Baker Rd					
12000	GGnT	60423	3590	15W-28S	C7
12000	MhtT	60423	3590	15W-28S	C7
12000	MhtT	60442	3590	16W-28S	A7
12800	MhtT	60442	3589	18W-28S	B7
13600	MHTN	60442	3589	18W-28S	B7
15200	MhtT	60442	3588	19W-28S	E7
Baker St					
2100	AURA	60506	3137	38W-6S	A5
N Baker St					
600	ITSC	60143	2913	21W-7N	E5
Baker Ter					
12000	GwdT	60098	2524	41W-33N	E2
Baker Hill Ct					
8300	SchT	60175	2963	37W-6N	D1
Baker Hill Dr					
-	GNEN	60137	3025	21W-0S	D7
Bakers Ct					
-	LKMR	60051	2529	29W-32N	D4
Bakers Dr					
100	LKMR	60051	2529	29W-32N	D4
Bakersmill Dr					
700	BGBK	60440	3268	24W-12S	D2
Bakewell Ln					
600	NPVL	60565	3204	25W-8S	B3
Bakley St					
11000	HTLY	60142	2692	40W-21N	A7
Balaton Dr					
-	LKPT	60441	3419	21W-20S	E4
Balbo Dr					
-	LynT	60525	3147	13W-7S	B5
10	CTSD	60525	3147	13W-7S	B5
E Balbo Dr					
10	CHCG	60605	3034	0E-0S	C6
Balboa Ct					
600	SMBG	60193	2858	24W-9N	D7
N Balboa Dr					
39000	LkvT	60046	2416	24W-39N	C6
Balboa Ln					
7100	FXLK	60020	2415	28W-39N	A6
Balboa Ter E					
700	BRLT	60103	2911	28W-7N	B4
Balboa Ter W					
700	BRLT	60103	2911	28W-7N	A4
Bald Eagle Ct					
400	GYLK	60030	2533	20W-32N	A5
Bald Eagle Ln					
100	BCHR	60401	3864	0E-36S	E1
Bald Eagle Rd					
40200	AntT	60002	2416	23W-40N	E3
W Bald Eagle Rd					
25500	LkvT	60046	2474	25W-37N	A2
Balder Dr					
8300	AlqT	60013	2696	29W-23N	C1
Balder St					
8200	AlqT	60013	2696	29W-23N	C1
Bald Knob Pt					
500	JNBG	60051	2472	29W-35N	C5
Bald Knob Rd					
500	JNBG	60051	2472	29W-35N	C5
Baldwin Av					
10	WKGN	60085	2536	12W-33N	C1
500	WKGN	60085	2479	12W-33N	C7

STREET Block City ZIP Map# CGS Grid

Baldwin Av
700 WkgT 60085 2479 12W-35N C7
N Baldwin Av
1700 WKGN 60085 2479 12W-35N C5
1700 WkgT 60085 2479 12W-35N C5
S Baldwin Av
10 CLLK 60014 2639 36W-25N C4
7400 CHCG 60649 3153 2E-8S C7
Baldwin Ct
10 LIHL 60156 2692 38W-23N D2
1400 NPVL 60565 3203 27W-8S C2
1500 WLNG 60090 2754 16W-18N D4
2000 GLHT 60139 2969 23W-3N A4
2100 HRPK 60133 2967 27W-5N C1
2400 AURA 60503 3201 32W-10S C5
2400 SMBG 60193 2857 26W-10N E6
N Baldwin Ct
1300 PLTN 60074 2753 19W-17N C4
Baldwin Dr
1400 NPVL 60565 3203 27W-8S C2
Baldwin Ln
- FmtT 60060 2588 24W-28N C6
- FmtT 60084 2588 24W-28N C6
1200 WCDA 60084 2588 24W-28N C6
2000 HRPK 60133 2967 27W-5N C1
2900 LIHL 60156 2692 38W-23N D3
E Baldwin Ln
1200 PLTN 60074 2753 19W-17N C4
N Baldwin Ln
- PLTN 60074 2753 19W-17N C4
S Baldwin Ln
700 RMVL 60446 3417 26W-18S E2
700 RMVL 60446 3418 26W-18S A2
S Baldwin Pl
- HPSR 60140 2795 46W-16N E2
Baldwin Rd
400 NndT 60050 2585 31W-30N D3
700 HDPK 60035 2705 7W-21N B7
1300 IVNS 60067 2752 22W-16N A6
1300 PLTN 60067 2752 22W-16N A6
1600 IVNS 60067 2751 23W-16N E6
2100 IVNS 60010 2751 23W-16N D6
E Baldwin Rd
400 PLTN 60067 2753 20W-16N A7
400 PLTN 60074 2753 20W-16N A7
N Baldwin Rd
1600 PLTN 60074 2753 19W-18N C3
Baldwin Tr
8000 HYHL 60457 3210 10W-10S C5
Baldwin Wy
1800 BGBK 60490 3267 27W-12S B3
N Baldwin Wy
2200 PLTN 60074 2753 19W-18N C2
2200 PltT 60074 2753 19W-18N C2
Balkan Dr
400 CmpT 60175 2962 39W-3N D6
Ball Av
10 CPVL 60110 2748 32W-17N C7
Ball St
200 ELGN 60123 2854 34W-11N D4
Ballantrae Dr
600 NHBK 60062 2757 8W-18N E4
Ballantrae Pl
1100 MDLN 60060 2647 17W-27N A2
Ballantrae Wy
3700 FSMR 60422 3506 4W-23S D4
3900 RchT 60443 3506 4W-23S D3
Ballard Ct
8500 TYPK 60487 3424 10W-21S B6
Ballard Dr
400 ALGN 60102 2695 32W-20N A7
8600 TYPK 60487 3424 10W-21S B6
28000 LbvT 60045 2592 13W-28N E7
28000 LbvT 60048 2592 13W-28N E7
Ballard Rd
- PltT 60124 2852 39W-10N E6
1600 MaiT 60068 2863 11W-11N E3
1600 PKRG 60068 2863 11W-11N E3
1700 MaiT 60016 2863 11W-11N E3
1700 PKRG 60016 2863 11W-11N E3
9100 CLLK 60014 2639 38W-25N A4
9100 GfnT 60014 2639 38W-25N A4
9400 GfnT 60014 2638 40W-25N B4
9400 LKWD 60014 2638 40W-25N B4
10100 LKWD 60098 2638 40W-25N B4
10100 LKWD 60142 2638 40W-25N B4
10400 GfnT 60098 2638 40W-25N B4
10400 GfnT 60142 2638 40W-25N B4
E Ballard Rd
2200 DSPN 60016 2863 12W-11N C3
2500 MaiT 60016 2863 12W-11N C3
W Ballard Rd
8100 NLES 60714 2864 10W-11N A3
8500 MaiT 60016 2864 10W-11N A3
8500 MaiT 60714 2864 10W-11N A3
8700 MaiT 60714 2863 10W-11N E3
8700 NLES 60714 2863 10W-11N E3
9000 MaiT 60016 2863 11W-11N D3
9000 MaiT 60068 2863 11W-11N D3
9000 PKRG 60016 2863 11W-11N D3
9000 PKRG 60068 2863 11W-11N D3
9700 DSPN 60016 2863 12W-11N B3
Ballentine St
1600 WKGN 60087 2479 11W-37N D3
Ballina Ln
1600 BLVY 60050 2584 35W-30N A2
1600 NndT 60012 2584 35W-30N A2
Ballinary Ct
11700 ODPK 60467 3422 14W-21S D6
Ballou Ct
10 BGBK 60440 3204 24W-10S E5
Bally Rd
400 MHRY 60050 2528 31W-31N D7
Balm Ct
300 WDDL 60191 2915 17W-6N C6
Balmoral Av
- CHCG 60018 2917 12W-6N B5
- CHCG 60666 2917 12W-6N B5
10 NHFD 60093 2811 7W-14N B3
600 WSTR 60154 3029 12W-0S B6
1200 CTCY 60409 3430 3E-19S A1
1400 WSTR 60154 3087 12W-1S B1
2000 GNVW 60025 2811 7W-14N A3
9600 RSMT 60018 2917 12W-6N B5
W Balmoral Av
1000 CHCG 60640 2921 2W-6N B5
2400 CHCG 60625 2921 3W-6N A5
2600 CHCG 60625 2920 3W-6N E5
5400 CHCG 60630 2919 6W-6N C5
6300 CHCG 60656 2919 8W-6N A5
6800 CHCG 60656 2918 8W-6N E5
7900 LydT 60656 2918 10W-6N B5
7900 NpkT 60656 2918 10W-6N B5
Balmoral Cir
600 LslT 60540 3142 26W-7S A6
600 NPVL 60540 3142 26W-7S A6

STREET Block City ZIP Map# CGS Grid

Balmoral Cir
1600 IVNS 60067 2805 22W-14N A3
Balmoral Cres
2800 FSMR 60422 3507 3W-23S A3
Balmoral Ct
200 GLHT 60139 2969 23W-3N A5
500 RLKP 60030 2589 22W-30N B1
800 EDND 60118 2801 32W-16N C2
1300 AURA 60502 3078 33W-3S E6
3900 RGMW 60008 2806 19W-14N C3
8700 LynT 60527 3208 14W-10S C4
S Balmoral Ct
- LKFT 60045 2648 13W-25N E6
Balmoral Dr
10 DMND 60416 3941 33W-39S B2
100 BGBK 60440 3269 22W-11S C1
300 BRLT 60103 2911 28W-6N B6
300 MDLN 60060 2646 19W-27N C2
800 EDND 60118 2801 32W-16N C2
1500 IVNS 60067 2805 22W-14N A3
1500 PLTN 60067 2805 22W-14N A3
4400 RNPK 60443 3594 5W-26S B3
4400 RNPK 60471 3594 5W-26S B3
11200 HTLY 60142 2692 40W-22N A5
25200 SRWD 60404 3583 31W-25S E1
S Balmoral Dr
22900 FftT 60423 3591 13W-27S B5
23000 GGnT 60423 3591 13W-27S B5
Balmoral Gln
1300 FSMR 60422 3507 3W-23S A3
Balmoral Ln
- MTGY 60506 3198 40W-9S B4
200 BRTN 60010 2751 24W-18N D2
200 PltT 60010 2751 24W-18N D2
500 IVNS 60067 2805 22W-14N A3
800 CmpT 60175 2906 40W-6N B6
800 NHBK 60062 2810 9W-15N B1
1000 ELGN 60103 2856 31W-9N A7
17600 HLCT 60429 3427 3W-21S A6
S Balmoral Woods Dr
26700 CteT 60417 3685 0W-32S D7
26800 CteT 60417 3774 0W-32S D1
Balsam Av
10 LKVL 60046 2475 23W-37N A2
Balsam Cir
5300 GRNE 60031 2478 14W-35N B5
Balsam Ct
100 LKVL 60046 2475 22W-37N A2
300 SMBG 60193 2858 24W-10N E6
6200 LGGV 60047 2700 18W-24N D1
8200 FXLK 60020 2415 28W-39N A5
8200 FXLK 60081 2415 28W-39N A5
9900 FftT 60448 3503 12W-24S D4
9900 MKNA 60448 3503 12W-24S D4
Balsam Dr
300 MltT 60137 3083 22W-3S B5
7800 MchT 60097 2469 36W-34N C7
8000 GwdT 60097 2469 37W-34N C7
8000 WRLK 60097 2469 37W-34N C7
Balsam Ln
- DSPN 60018 2917 12W-8N B2
900 BRLT 60103 2910 29W-6N E6
E Balsam Ln
400 PLTN 60074 2753 20W-17N A5
S Balsam Ln
13800 LktT 60544 3339 26W-16S E4
Balsam Rd
1700 HDPK 60035 2757 9W-20N C1
Balsum Ln
20400 CTHL 60403 3418 25W-19S B3
20400 LktT 60403 3418 25W-19S B3
Baltic Cir
13200 LMNT 60439 3343 17W-15S C2
Baltimore Av
600 WTMT 60559 3085 16W-4S D7
S Baltimore Av
3900 HMND 46327 3352 E3
8300 CHCG 60617 3215 3E-9S E2
8400 CHCG 60617 3216 3E-9S A3
12900 CHCG 60633 3280 3E-15S A7
13100 CHCG 60633 3352 3E-15S A1
Baltimore Dr
1700 EGVV 60007 2913 22W-9N C1
W Baltimore Dr
200 VNHL 60061 2647 17W-26N B2
E Baltimore St
100 WMTN 60481 3853 27W-38S E6
E Baltimore St SR-53
100 WMTN 60481 3853 27W-38S E6
W Baltimore St
200 WMTN 60481 3853 28W-38S C7
W Baltimore St SR-53
200 WMTN 60481 3853 28W-38S C7
Balton Ct
800 NPVL 60563 3140 29W-5S E4
Baltrusol Ct
200 YKVL 60560 3333 42W-17S C6
Baltusro Dr
- MONE 60449 3683 6W-31S A5
Baltusrol Dr
800 ELGN 60123 2853 36W-9N E7
900 ELGN 60123 2907 36W-9N E1
8800 ODPK 60462 3424 11W-18S A1
E Baltusrol Dr
100 VNHL 60061 2647 16W-26N D2
Baltusrol Ln
300 LslT 60540 3143 23W-7S A7
Baltz Ct
1500 JLET 60431 3495 32W-22S C1
Baltz Dr
1400 JLET 60431 3495 32W-22S D1
Baltz Rd
26300 SwdT 60447 3495 32W-24S C5
26300 TroT 60404 3495 32W-24S C5
Bamberg Ct
1200 HRPK 60133 2911 26W-7N E5
Bamboo Ln
5200 WldT 60564 3266 31W-13S A5
Banbridge Ct
9400 PlsT 60462 3345 11W-15S D2
Banburry Rd
1800 DRGV 60516 3144 20W-6S A5
Banbury
- BFGV 60089 2701 17W-21N B6
Banbury Av
200 EGVV 60007 2914 19W-8N C2
1400 SCRL 60174 2964 34W-3N D7
1400 SCRL 60174 3020 34W-2N D1
1900 YKVL 60560 3333 42W-16S D5
Banbury Cir
1100 NPVL 60540 3142 25W-7S A6
Banbury Ct
10 LIHL 60156 2692 38W-23N D2
10 SMWD 60107 2856 29W-9N D7
600 ROSL 60172 2913 23W-6N B6
900 SMBG 60194 2858 26W-11N A3

STREET Block City ZIP Map# CGS Grid

Banbury Ct
1000 BGBK 60440 3205 21W-9S E4
1000 SCRL 60174 3020 34W-2N D1
N Banbury Ct
36100 WrnT 60031 2477 18W-36N A5
Banbury Dr
800 GYLK 60030 2533 20W-33N B3
W Banbury Dr
18000 WrnT 60031 2477 18W-36N A4
Banbury Ln
200 GYLK 60030 2533 20W-33N B3
1100 NlxT 60451 3500 19W-24S E5
1500 ELGN 60123 2907 36W-8N E3
2900 LIHL 60156 2692 38W-23N D2
Banbury Pl
9700 MNSR 46321 3510 C3
Banbury Rd
100 MDLN 60060 2590 19W-29N D5
100 NARA 60510 3078 35W-3S B5
100 NARA 60542 3078 35W-3S B5
800 BTVA 60510 3078 35W-3S B7
800 BtvT 60510 3078 35W-3S B7
1400 IVNS 60067 2751 23W-17N E5
1400 IVNS 60067 2752 23W-17N A6
S Banbury Rd
400 ANHT 60005 2807 17W-13N B6
Banbury Ter
400 ROSL 60172 2913 23W-6N B6
Banbury Wy
600 BGBK 60440 3205 21W-9S E4
Bancroft Ct
400 MltT 60137 3083 23W-2S A4
S Baneberry Cir
15300 LKPT 60441 3342 20W-18S B7
Baneberry Ln
10 RVWD 60015 2702 14W-21N C7
Banford Cir
3200 LIHL 60156 2692 38W-23N E2
Banford Ct
10 LIHL 60156 2692 38W-23N E2
Banford Rd
11000 GwdT 60098 2525 40W-32N A5
11000 WDSK 60098 2525 40W-32N A5
Bangert Ct
2500 NPVL 60564 3266 29W-12S D2
W Bangor Ct
20800 LktT 60544 3340 26W-16S A5
Bangor Dr
8500 TYPK 60477 3504 10W-23S B3
Bangor Ln
1400 AURA 60504 3201 31W-9S D4
1800 EGVV 60007 2913 22W-9N C1
Bangs St
100 WCDA 60084 2643 26W-27N E2
400 AURA 60505 3200 35W-8S C3
1000 AraT 60505 3200 35W-9S C3
1200 AraT 60538 3200 35W-9S C4
1200 MTGY 60538 3200 35W-9S C4
Bank Dr
- LydT 60164 2973 12W-2N C6
- MLPK 60160 2973 12W-2N C6
- MLPK 60164 2973 12W-2N C6
300 MHRY 60050 2528 32W-31N A6
1200 SMBG 60173 2859 21W-11N D3
Bank Ln
10 BFGV 60089 2754 16W-20N C1
500 HIWD 60040 2704 9W-23N D2
1100 WKGN 60099 2421 10W-38N E6
1100 WKGN 60099 2422 10W-38N A6
1400 GNVA 60134 3020 33W-1N E3
1400 GNVA 60134 3021 33W-1N A3
1400 GNVA 60185 3021 33W-1N A3
1400 GnvT 60185 3021 33W-1N A3
N Bank Ln
500 LKFT 60045 2650 10W-26N A3
Bankfield Ct
900 NPVL 60540 3142 25W-7S C7
Banks
- NLNX 60451 3588 19W-26S D3
Banks Dr
1800 ELGN 60123 2800 36W-13N A7
Banks St
7200 JSTC 60458 3147 11W-8S E7
7200 JSTC 60458 3209 11W-8S E1
E Banks St
10 CHCG 60610 3034 0E-1N C1
Bankview Dr
10 FKFT 60423 3503 12W-25S D6
500 FftT 60423 3503 12W-25S D6
3400 JLET 60431 3497 28W-23S A4
3400 TroT 60431 3497 28W-23S A4
Bann St
25200 MHTN 60442 3677 19W-30S E4
Bannister Ct
6400 LSLE 60532 3142 23W-7S E6
Bannister Dr
1300 NPVL 60565 3203 27W-8S C2
Bannister Ln
2200 AURA 60504 3201 33W-9S B4
Bannock Ct
100 EDND 60118 2801 32W-16N C2
1400 BRLT 60103 2967 28W-5N B1
Bannock Rd
800 EDND 60118 2801 32W-16N C2
Bannockburn
2100 IVNS 60067 2804 23W-14N D3
Bannockburn Cir
7100 LKWD 60014 2639 37W-24N A6
Bannockburn Ct
10 BKBN 60015 2703 11W-22N D4
Bannockburn Dr
- GfnT 60142 2692 39W-23N D1
- LKWD 60014 2692 39W-23N D1
- LKWD 60142 2692 39W-23N D1
Bantry Blvd
- MKNA 60448 3504 10W-23S B3
- MKNA 60477 3504 10W-23S B3
8600 TYPK 60477 3504 10W-23S B3
Bantry Dr
24400 SRWD 60404 3584 30W-25S B1
Banyan Dr
400 NHBK 60062 2756 11W-18N C3
800 EGVV 60007 2914 18W-8N E1
Banyan Tree Ln
400 BFGV 60089 2701 17W-22N C3
Banyon Ct
1100 NPVL 60540 3141 28W-7S B7
S Banyon Ct
15300 LKPT 60441 3342 20W-18S A7
Banyon Ln
500 LGNG 60525 3147 13W-5S A1
Barat Ct
700 LKFT 60045 2650 10W-25N B5
Barb Av
3400 PKCY 60085 2536 13W-33N A3

STREET Block City ZIP Map# CGS Grid

Barbara Av
800 SEGN 60177 2908 35W-8N B2
6200 TYPK 60477 3425 7W-20S B3
Barbara Ct
300 MRGO 60152 2634 50W-25N A4
300 RlyT 60152 2634 50W-25N A4
600 BMDL 60157 2913 22W-6N B7
900 RLKP 60073 2532 23W-33N A3
1200 CRTE 60417 3685 0W-29S C1
1200 NPVL 60540 3203 27W-8S C2
18900 LNSG 60438 3510 4E-22S B1
W Barbara Ct
21400 KLDR 60047 2699 21W-21N D6
Barbara Dr
3100 GNVW 60025 2810 10W-15N A3
7200 WRLK 60097 2469 36W-37N E2
Barbara Ln
- MTGY 60538 3200 35W-9S A5
100 NLNX 60451 3501 18W-23S B4
100 NlxT 60451 3501 18W-23S B4
100 STGR 60475 3596 1W-28S A6
100 STGR 60475 3595 1W-28S E6
200 STGR 60475 3595 1W-28S B7
600 LKMR 60051 2529 29W-31N C6
600 NndT 60051 2529 29W-31N C6
1100 WCDA 60084 2588 25W-28N A6
1100 WcnT 60084 2588 25W-28N A6
1200 CHHT 60411 3507 2W-25S D7
16900 TYPK 60477 3425 7W-20S C4
W Barbara Ln
7800 FftT 60423 3504 9W-24S D4
Barbara St
900 LIHL 60156 2694 34W-22N C4
Barbara Ann Dr
- SCRL 60175 2963 37W-3N D7
Barbara Jean Ln
100 JLET 60436 3497 27W-24S D5
Barbary Ln
400 WDSK 60098 2581 41W-30N D2
2400 GNVW 60025 2809 11W-15N E2
2400 GNVW 60062 2809 11W-15N E2
Barber Ct
1100 WDND 60118 2800 35W-16N B1
2800 JLET 60435 3497 27W-23S C3
Barber Ln
600 JLET 60435 3497 27W-23S C3
9600 GNWD 60098 2468 38W-36N E4
N Barber Ln
800 JLET 60435 3497 27W-22S C2
800 TroT 60435 3497 27W-22S C2
Barber St
300 WCHI 60185 3022 29W-0N C5
W Barber St
- CHCG 60607 3034 0W-1S A7
- CHCG 60608 3034 0W-1S A7
Barberry Av
400 DYR 46311 3510 D6
E Barberry Cir
400 YKVL 60560 3333 43W-16S B4
W Barberry Cir
500 YKVL 60560 3333 43W-16S B4
Barberry Ct
1000 ELGN 60120 2855 32W-12N D2
1100 DRGV 60515 3084 19W-3S C6
2900 AURA 60502 3079 32W-3S C7
3800 HFET 60192 2804 25W-14N A3
11600 HTLY 60142 2745 39W-20N D1
E Barberry Ct
2300 ANHT 60004 2807 16W-15N C2
N Barberry Ct
34300 GrtT 60073 2530 25W-34N E1
Barberry Dr
10 CLLK 60014 2639 37W-25N A4
10 HNWD 60047 2645 22W-24N B6
Barberry Ln
10 CmpT 60175 2905 41W-6N E7
600 WLNG 60090 2754 16W-17N D5
700 LKFT 60045 2650 10W-27N B1
900 RLKB 60073 2474 24W-34N C7
900 RLKB 60073 2531 24W-34N C1
1300 GRNE 60031 2478 14W-35N D5
1300 WrnT 60031 2478 14W-35N D5
1500 AvnT 60073 2474 24W-35N C6
1500 RLKH 60073 2474 24W-35N C6
4200 ZION 60099 2421 12W-41N B2
8900 HYHL 60457 3209 11W-10S E4
8900 HYHL 60457 3210 11W-10S A4
9000 MaiT 60016 2863 11W-11N D2
9100 PlsT 60457 3209 11W-10S E4
9100 PlsT 60480 3209 11W-10S E4
11500 HTLY 60142 2745 39W-20N D1
E Barberry Ln
900 MPPT 60056 2808 14W-14N C4
1100 PLTN 60074 2753 19W-18N C3
N Barberry Ln
1600 MPPT 60056 2808 14W-14N C4
35700 GRNE 60031 2478 14W-35N D5
35700 WrnT 60031 2478 14W-35N D5
Barberry Rd
100 HDPK 60035 2757 8W-20N D2
500 HDPK 60035 2704 9W-21N C7
1800 NHBK 60062 2756 11W-16N E7
N Barberry Rd
34200 GrtT 60073 2530 26W-34N D1
Barberry Tr
600 FRGV 60021 2696 29W-23N B2
Barberry Wy
- JLET 60586 3495 33W-22S A1
900 JLET 60447 3495 33W-22S A1
Barbers Corner Rd
100 BGBK 60440 3205 22W-11S B7
Barbhill Dr
10 SchT 60175 2907 38W-7N A5
Barbra Ct
500 UYPK 60466 3684 3W-29S C2
Barbs Wy
10900 ODPK 60467 3423 13W-20S A4
Barclay Blvd
100 LNSH 60069 2702 15W-22N A3
500 BFGV 60089 2702 15W-21N A7
500 LNSH 60089 2702 15W-21N A5
Barclay Cir
900 LKFT 60045 2649 12W-27N C1
1200 IVNS 60010 2751 24W-17N C4
Barclay Ct
10 OswT 60538 3263 37W-11S D1
900 BTVA 60510 3078 34W-1S D3
3800 LSLE 60532 3082 24W-3S D7
5500 CNHL 60514 3145 16W-6S D3
5500 DGvT 60514 3145 16W-6S D3
5600 LGGV 60047 2701 17W-23N A2
6500 DRGV 60516 3144 20W-7S A6
E Barclay Ct
400 EMHT 60126 3028 14W-0S C6
Barclay Dr
200 GLHT 60139 2969 23W-4N A3
500 BGBK 60440 3204 24W-11S D7

STREET Block City ZIP Map# CGS Grid

Barclay Dr
700 BGBK 60440 3268 24W-11S C1
Barclay Ln
1300 DRFD 60015 2703 11W-21N D6
3000 WLMT 60091 2811 6W-13N E6
Barclay Pl
400 MltT 60137 3083 23W-2S A4
Barclay Rd
10 AURA 60563 3080 30W-4S C7
10 WNVL 60563 3080 30W-4S C7
7700 DRN 60561 3206 19W-8S D2
Barcliffe Ln
100 SMBG 60194 2858 24W-10N D5
Barcoo Bnd
2600 NLNX 60451 3589 19W-27S A5
Barcroft Ct
10 SEGN 60177 2908 36W-8N A2
1100 NPVL 60540 3204 25W-7S C1
5100 HFET 60010 2751 24W-16N B7
Barcroft Dr
5100 HFET 60010 2751 24W-16N B7
5100 IVNS 60010 2751 24W-16N B7
Bard Rd
1200 CLLK 60014 2639 38W-24N A7
1200 GfnT 60014 2639 38W-24N A7
1200 LKWD 60014 2639 37W-24N B6
Bardmour Ln
400 WNFD 60190 3023 26W-1N E2
Bards Av
1100 NPVL 60564 3203 28W-11S A7
Bardsey Dr
10 SMBG 60194 2858 25W-10N C5
Bardwell Ln
8500 CLLK 60014 2639 37W-24N A7
8500 LKWD 60014 2639 37W-24N A7
Bardwell St
500 AURA 60505 3200 35W-9S B4
Bardwick Ct
5000 HFET 60010 2751 24W-16N B7
Barger Ct
2200 WHTN 60187 3081 26W-2S D4
Bar Harbor Ct
- PGGV 60140 2797 42W-15N D4
2500 NPVL 60564 3202 29W-10S D6
Barharbor Ct
10 LIHL 60156 2693 38W-22N A4
Barharbor Dr
4200 LIHL 60156 2693 38W-22N A4
4400 LIHL 60156 2692 38W-22N E4
Bar Harbor Ter
1200 NHBK 60062 2756 10W-17N E5
Bar Harbour Ct
2800 AURA 60504 3201 31W-9S D4
Bar Harbour Rd
10 SMBG 60173 2859 21W-10N D5
10 SMBG 60193 2859 21W-10N D5
1300 AURA 60504 3201 31W-9S D4
Baring Ridge Dr
- JLET 60586 3415 32W-21S D7
- JLET 60586 3495 31W-22S D1
Bark Ct
700 LKBN 60010 2642 28W-24N E7
700 LKBN 60010 2696 28W-24N E1
Barkdoll Rd
2200 NPVL 60565 3204 25W-10S B6
Barkei Dr
1600 BTVA 60510 3078 34W-2S D5
Barkei Ln
100 LslT 60563 3082 25W-4S A7
100 NPVL 60563 3082 25W-4S A7
Barker Av
4700 RGMW 60008 2806 20W-12N B7
4700 RGMW 60008 2860 19W-12N B1
Barker St
- LYWD 60411 3510 4E-24S B6
Barkley Av
- WNVL 60563 3080 30W-3S C6
10 WNVL 60555 3080 30W-3S C5
Barkley Ct
6000 MHRY 60050 2527 34W-32N B5
N Barkley Ct
21900 KLDR 60047 2699 22W-21N B5
Barko Pkwy
10 RtdT 60142 2745 40W-19N C3
Barkridge Ct
2300 LSLE 60532 3142 24W-5S D3
Barkston Dr
1200 AURA 60502 3139 33W-6S B4
Barkston Ln
- AraT 60502 3139 33W-6S B4
- AURA 60502 3139 33W-6S B4
Barkwood Ct
3100 HDPK 60035 2704 10W-23N A1
Bark Wood Rd
2500 SMBG 60173 2805 21W-13N D6
Barley Av
10 NPVL 60563 3141 26W-5S D3
Barley Ct
2600 AURA 60502 3079 32W-4S C7
Barleycorn Ct
8900 ODPK 60462 3346 11W-18S A7
Barlina Rd
500 CLLK 60014 2639 37W-24N C7
1300 LKWD 60014 2639 37W-24N B7
Barlow Dr
400 CmpT 60175 2961 41W-3N E5
400 CmpT 60175 2962 41W-3N A5
Barlow Ln
1100 MDLN 60060 2590 19W-27N B7
Barnaby Dr
300 OSWG 60543 3264 35W-11S B2
400 OSWG 60543 3200 35W-11S B7
Barnaby Pl
700 WLNG 60090 2755 15W-18N A3
Barnard Dr
10300 CHRG 60415 3275 8W-12S B1
Barnard Ln
10 HDPK 60035 2758 7W-20N A2
10 NtrT 60062 2758 7W-20N A2
Barnard Mill Rd
4800 RGWD 60072 2470 34W-36N B3
5400 MchT 60072 2470 34W-36N C3
6300 MchT 60097 2470 35W-37N A3
6300 RGWD 60097 2470 35W-37N A2
6700 MchT 60097 2469 35W-37N E2
6700 RGWD 60097 2469 35W-37N E2
7100 WRLK 60097 2469 36W-37N E2
7200 RcmT 60097 2469 36W-37N E1
Barnes Av
- WCHI 60185 3022 30W-0N B6
- WnfT 60185 3022 30W-0N B6
10 WNFD 60190 3023 26W-0N D5
500 WnfT 60185 3023 28W-0N A6
Barnes Dr
500 WMTN 60481 3943 27W-39S C1

Chicago 7-County Street Index

STREET Block	City	ZIP	Map#	CGS	Grid
Barnes Ln					
3200	NPVL	60564	3202	28W-11S	E7
3200	NPVL	60564	3266	28W-11S	E1
Barnes Rd					
100	ELGN	60124	2853	37W-11N	C4
400	AURA	60506	3198	39W-8S	D2
400	MTGY	60506	3198	39W-8S	D2
400	SgrT	60506	3198	39W-8S	D2
N Barnes Rd					
-	AURA	60506	3136	39W-6S	D6
S Barnes Rd					
100	AURA	60506	3136	39W-7S	D7
100	SgrT	60506	3136	39W-7S	D7
300	SgrT	60506	3198	39W-7S	D1
Barneswood Dr					
1000	DRGV	60515	3084	20W-3S	B6
Barnett Ln					
1700	BRLT	60103	2909	31W-8N	E3
Barney Ct					
2700	MchT	60051	2528	31W-32N	D4
2700	MHRY	60051	2528	31W-32N	D4
N Barney Dr					
10	JLET	60435	3497	27W-23S	D5
10	JLET	60436	3497	27W-24S	D5
Barnhart Ct					
1200	ZION	60099	2422	10W-41N	B2
Barnhart St					
2300	WCHI	60185	2965	32W-4N	C5
Barnhill Dr					
900	MDLN	60060	2590	20W-28N	A6
Barn Owl Dr					
-	HPSR	60140	2795	47W-15N	D4
21300	RchT	60443	3593	8W-25S	C1
Barn Owl Ln					
2400	ELGN	60124	2853	36W-10N	D6
Barnsdale Rd					
1100	LGPK	60525	3087	12W-2S	C4
Barnside Cir					
200	GNVA	60134	3019	37W-1N	C3
Barnside Ct					
800	CmpT	60175	2906	39W-6N	D7
Barnside Rd					
900	NLNX	60451	3589	17W-25S	D1
900	NlxT	60451	3589	17W-25S	D1
Barnsley Pl					
400	NHBK	60062	2758	8W-17N	A5
Barnstable Ct					
3000	AURA	60504	3201	31W-8S	D2
Barn Swallow Ct					
6300	GRNE	60031	2534	16W-33N	C2
Barnswallow Ct					
10	AURA	60506	3137	38W-7S	A6
Barn Swallow Dr					
200	WDSK	60098	2525	40W-32N	A5
400	LNHT	60046	2476	19W-37N	B2
S Barn Swallow Ln					
200	VNHL	60061	2647	16W-24N	C7
W Barnswallow Ln					
23700	FmtT	60060	2644	23W-27N	D2
23700	FmtT	60084	2644	23W-27N	D2
Barnswallow Rd					
10	LKFT	60045	2649	10W-25N	E6
Barn Swallow Wy					
500	ELGN	60123	2853	36W-12N	E2
Barnwall Ct					
5100	LSLE	60532	3142	24W-5S	D3
W Barnwall Dr					
1300	AddT	60101	2970	20W-3N	B5
1300	ADSN	60101	2970	20W-3N	B5
Barnwood Ct					
400	RDLK	60073	2531	24W-33N	C2
4800	MHRY	60050	2527	33W-31N	D6
Barnwood Dr					
5400	GRNE	60031	2478	15W-36N	A5
Barnwood Tr					
200	MHRY	60050	2527	33W-31N	D6
Barolo Dr					
24800	PNFD	60586	3416	31W-19S	A3
Baron Ct					
1400	BRLT	60103	2967	28W-5N	B1
Baron Dr					
200	BtnT	60081	2414	29W-38N	D6
2100	HLCT	60429	3427	2W-20S	C4
Baron Ln					
200	RtdT	60142	2745	40W-18N	C4
Baron Rd					
19300	MKNA	60448	3502	14W-23S	D3
Baron St					
8800	WDRG	60517	3206	20W-10S	B5
Baronet Ct					
10	LIHL	60156	2692	39W-21N	D5
E Baronet Ln					
-	ANHT	60004	2806	19W-15N	C2
1300	PLTN	60074	2806	19W-15N	C2
Barons Ct					
5100	GRNE	60031	2478	15W-36N	A4
Barr Av					
-	BDWD	60408	3942	31W-41S	B5
Barr Ct					
5700	HRPK	60133	2911	26W-7N	E5
W Barr Rd					
8900	PtnT	60468	3860	11W-36S	A2
Barr St					
100	BDWD	60408	3942	31W-41S	B5
Barra Ln					
100	IVNS	60067	2752	22W-16N	B7
Barr Creek Ct					
-	RLKB	60073	2474	24W-34N	C7
Barr Creek Ln					
4500	NPVL	60564	3266	29W-12S	D3
Barr Elm Av					
10	JltT	60433	3499	21W-24S	E5
Barrett Ct					
1700	NCHI	60064	2536	11W-32N	D6
Barrett Dr					
2200	ALGN	60102	2747	36W-18N	A4
2300	NCHI	60064	2536	11W-32N	D6
Barrett Ln					
100	SMBG	60193	2859	23W-9N	A7
Barrett St					
100	DGvT	60439	3206	20W-11S	C7
100	LktT	60441	3419	23W-21S	B7
100	WDRG	60439	3206	20W-11S	C7
400	ELGN	60120	2855	33W-11N	A4
6300	DRGV	60516	3144	20W-7S	C6
Barreville Rd					
1300	MHRY	60050	2585	32W-30N	B1
1300	NndT	60050	2585	32W-30N	B1
1700	PRGV	60050	2585	32W-29N	B3
2600	PRGV	60012	2585	32W-27N	B7
4300	PRGV	60012	2641	32W-27N	B1
4900	CLLK	60012	2641	32W-27N	B1
4900	PRGV	60014	2641	32W-27N	B1
Barrington					
-	BGBK	60490	3267	27W-13S	C4
Barrington Av					
500	CPVL	60118	2801	33W-16N	B2
500	DndT	60118	2801	33W-16N	B2
600	CPVL	60110	2801	33W-16N	B2
600	EDND	60110	2801	33W-16N	B2
600	EDND	60118	2801	33W-16N	B2
Barrington Av SR-68					
500	CPVL	60110	2801	33W-16N	B2
500	DndT	60118	2801	33W-16N	B2
500	EDND	60110	2801	33W-16N	B2
500	EDND	60118	2801	33W-16N	B2
Barrington Ct					
10	LIHL	60156	2693	37W-22N	A4
500	UYPK	60466	3684	3W-30S	C3
1500	ALGN	60102	2694	35W-21N	B6
1900	AURA	60503	3201	32W-10S	D6
7000	WDRG	60517	3144	21W-8S	A7
W Barrington Ct					
20800	LktT	60544	3340	26W-16S	A5
Barrington Dr E					
-	WldT	60503	3201	32W-10S	C7
2500	AURA	60503	3201	32W-10S	C7
Barrington Dr W					
-	AURA	60503	3201	32W-10S	B6
W Barrington Ln					
20800	LktT	60544	3340	26W-16S	A5
Barrington Rd					
-	HFET	60010	2803	27W-12N	D7
-	HFET	60192	2803	26W-13N	D7
200	WCDA	60084	2643	26W-26N	E2
400	WcnT	60084	2643	26W-26N	E2
700	HFET	60169	2857	27W-12N	D1
700	HFET	60194	2857	27W-11N	D3
700	SMWD	60107	2857	27W-11N	D4
1900	HFET	60169	2803	27W-12N	D7
6100	HRPK	60133	2911	27W-8N	D3
7600	HRPK	60107	2911	27W-9N	D1
7600	SMWD	60107	2911	27W-9N	D1
7600	SMWD	60133	2911	27W-9N	D1
N Barrington Rd					
10	BrnT	60010	2803	25W-15N	E3
10	SBTN	60010	2803	26W-14N	E4
10	SMBG	60107	2857	27W-11N	D5
10	SMBG	60194	2857	27W-11N	D5
10	SMWD	60107	2857	27W-11N	D4
200	HFET	60169	2857	27W-11N	D4
25900	CbaT	60084	2643	26W-26N	D4
25900	TRLK	60010	2643	26W-26N	D4
25900	TRLK	60084	2643	26W-26N	D4
25900	WcnT	60084	2643	26W-26N	D3
26300	WCDA	60084	2643	26W-26N	D3
N Barrington Rd SR-59					
25900	CbaT	60084	2643	26W-26N	D4
25900	TRLK	60010	2643	26W-26N	D4
25900	TRLK	60084	2643	26W-26N	D4
25900	WcnT	60084	2643	26W-26N	D3
26300	WCDA	60084	2643	26W-26N	D3
S Barrington Rd					
10	HFET	60192	2803	25W-13N	E6
10	SBTN	60010	2803	25W-13N	E5
10	SMBG	60193	2857	27W-10N	D6
10	SMBG	60194	2857	27W-10N	D6
100	BNHL	60010	2750	25W-16N	E7
100	BRTN	60010	2750	25W-16N	E7
100	IVNS	60010	2750	25W-17N	E5
300	BNHL	60010	2803	26W-15N	E1
300	BrnT	60010	2803	26W-15N	E1
300	HRPK	60133	2857	26W-10N	D7
300	IVNS	60010	2803	26W-15N	E1
300	SMBG	60133	2857	26W-10N	D7
300	SMWD	60107	2857	26W-10N	D6
300	SMWD	60133	2857	26W-10N	D7
300	SMWD	60193	2857	26W-10N	D6
600	SMBG	60107	2857	26W-10N	D6
900	BrnT	60010	2750	25W-16N	E7
1000	HRPK	60107	2911	27W-9N	D1
1000	HRPK	60133	2911	27W-9N	D1
1000	SMWD	60107	2911	27W-9N	D1
1000	SMWD	60133	2911	27W-9N	D1
3000	HFET	60010	2803	25W-13N	E5
3000	SBTN	60192	2803	25W-13N	E5
Barrington Bourne Rd					
10	BNHL	60010	2748	31W-20N	E1
Barrington Commons Ct					
100	BRTN	60010	2750	27W-20N	C1
100	BRTN	60010	2751	25W-20N	A1
Barrington Hills Rd					
10	BNHL	60010	2749	28W-18N	E2
Barrington Point Rd					
800	BRTN	60010	2751	25W-18N	B2
N Barrington Woods Rd					
2200	PLTN	60074	2752	21W-18N	D2
2300	DRPK	60074	2752	21W-18N	D2
2300	PltT	60074	2752	21W-18N	D2
Barron Blvd					
-	AvnT	60030	2533	20W-32N	A5
-	AvnT	60048	2533	20W-32N	A5
-	GYLK	60048	2533	20W-32N	A5
10	GYLK	60030	2533	20W-33N	A3
Barron Blvd SR-83					
-	AvnT	60030	2533	20W-32N	A5
-	AvnT	60048	2533	20W-32N	A5
-	GYLK	60048	2533	20W-32N	A5
10	GYLK	60030	2533	20W-33N	A3
N Barron Blvd					
34200	AvnT	60030	2533	20W-34N	A1
34200	GYLK	60030	2533	20W-34N	A1
N Barron Blvd SR-83					
34200	AvnT	60030	2533	20W-34N	A1
34200	GYLK	60030	2533	20W-34N	A1
Barron Dr					
1800	CHCG	60617	3216	4E-10S	C5
Barron St					
100	BNVL	60106	2971	16W-4N	E2
Barrow Ct					
1000	UYPK	60466	3684	3W-30S	B3
Barrow Dr					
10	CLLK	60014	2640	35W-24N	A7
Barrow Ln					
12700	PNFD	60585	3339	28W-15S	A1
Barrow Rd					
25400	MhtT	60442	3677	19W-31S	D5
Barrow on Duxbury					
10	RGMW	60008	2805	22W-13N	B7
Barry Av					
10	MltT	60187	3023	26W-0N	E4
10	MltT	60188	3023	26W-0N	E4
100	LktT	60441	3419	23W-21S	B7
7400	BtnT	60081	2414	29W-39N	C6
10800	FNPK	60131	2972	13W-3N	D4
10800	LydT	60131	2972	13W-3N	D4
10800	LydT	60164	2972	14W-3N	D4
W Barry Av					
200	AddT	60101	2970	19W-4N	D3
200	ADSN	60101	2970	19W-4N	D3
600	CHCG	60657	2978	0W-3N	A4
W Barry Av					
800	CHCG	60657	2977	2W-3N	B4
2600	CHCG	60618	2977	3W-3N	A4
2700	CHCG	60618	2976	3W-3N	E4
3900	CHCG	60641	2976	5W-3N	B4
4700	CHCG	60641	2975	7W-3N	C4
5500	CHCG	60634	2975	8W-3N	A4
7000	CHCG	60634	2974	9W-3N	C4
7100	CHCG	60707	2974	9W-3N	C4
7500	EDPK	60707	2974	9W-3N	C4
7900	EDPK	60171	2974	9W-3N	B4
Barry Ln					
500	CRTE	60417	3685	0W-30S	B3
700	WTMT	60559	3145	18W-6S	A4
1100	SLVL	60411	3509	2E-25S	D7
1600	GNVW	60025	2809	11W-14N	D4
4100	OKFT	60452	3426	5W-19S	C2
Barry Pl					
2800	NCHI	60088	2594	10W-30N	A1
Barry Rd					
100	NCHI	60088	2594	10W-30N	A1
600	NCHI	60088	2593	10W-30N	E1
S Barry Rd					
500	ElgT	60177	2909	33W-8N	A2
500	SEGN	60177	2909	33W-8N	A2
Barry St					
7000	RSMT	60018	2916	13W-8N	E1
7100	DSPN	60018	2916	13W-8N	E1
Barrymore Ct					
2000	HRPK	60133	2911	27W-6N	D6
Barrymore Dr					
1500	DRN	60561	3207	18W-9S	A3
Barrypoint Rd					
100	RVSD	60546	3088	10W-3S	B6
Barryscourt					
1000	LKFT	60045	2649	12W-25N	B5
N Barsumian Dr					
25100	TRLK	60010	2643	27W-25N	C5
Bartel Rd					
1000	JLET	60433	3588	21W-25S	A1
1000	JltT	60433	3500	21W-25S	A7
1000	JltT	60433	3588	21W-25S	A1
Bartels Rd					
5500	BmdT	60133	2912	25W-7N	A5
5500	HRPK	60133	2912	25W-7N	A5
Bartelt Pl					
200	BbyT	60134	3018	39W-0N	E5
Bartelt Rd					
100	BbyT	60134	3018	39W-0N	E5
Barth Dr					
2200	NPVL	60565	3204	25W-10S	A5
N Barthelme Av					
800	JLET	60435	3498	25W-22S	B2
Barthelone Av					
1600	CTHL	60403	3418	25W-21S	B7
1600	CTHL	60403	3498	25W-21S	B1
1600	CTHL	60435	3498	25W-21S	B1
1600	JLET	60403	3498	25W-21S	B1
1600	JLET	60435	3498	25W-21S	B1
Bartholdi Ct					
1000	CLSM	60188	2968	25W-4N	B4
Barth Pond Ln					
21200	LktT	60403	3417	26W-19S	E3
Bartleson St					
200	JLET	60433	3499	23W-24S	A6
Bartlett Av					
700	ANTH	60002	2358	23W-42N	A6
9000	BKFD	60513	3087	11W-2S	E4
9100	BKFD	60525	3087	11W-2S	D4
9100	LGPK	60525	3087	11W-2S	D4
E Bartlett Av					
-	BRLT	60103	2910	29W-8N	D3
-	BRLT	60103	2911	28W-8N	A3
N Bartlett Av					
700	PNFD	60544	3338	29W-17S	C7
W Bartlett Av					
100	BRLT	60103	2910	29W-8N	E3
Bartlett Ct					
2900	NPVL	60564	3202	29W-10S	C6
N Bartlett Ln					
39900	WDWH	60083	2420	13W-40N	E4
Bartlett Pl					
200	ELGN	60120	2855	33W-10N	A5
Bartlett Plz					
10	BRLT	60103	2910	29W-8N	E4
10	BRLT	60103	2911	28W-8N	A3
Bartlett Rd					
-	BNHL	60010	2803	28W-16N	A1
-	HFET	60010	2803	28W-12N	A7
-	HFET	60010	2857	28W-12N	A1
-	HFET	60107	2857	28W-11N	A4
-	SMWD	60107	2857	28W-11N	A4
10	BrnT	60010	2803	28W-13N	A5
10	SBTN	60010	2803	28W-13N	A5
N Bartlett Rd					
-	HFET	60010	2857	28W-11N	A4
-	HFET	60107	2857	28W-11N	A4
10	SMWD	60107	2857	28W-11N	A4
S Bartlett Rd					
-	BRLT	60120	2910	29W-9N	E1
10	SMWD	60107	2857	28W-10N	A6
200	WynT	60103	2910	28W-7N	E5
400	BRLT	60103	2910	29W-7N	E6
400	BRLT	60103	2966	29W-5N	E1
400	WynT	60103	2966	29W-5N	E1
500	SMWD	60107	2856	28W-9N	E7
1100	SMWD	60107	2910	29W-9N	E1
2000	BRLT	60107	2910	29W-9N	E1
S Bartlett Rd CO-6					
200	WynT	60103	2910	28W-7N	E5
400	BRLT	60103	2910	29W-7N	E6
400	BRLT	60103	2966	29W-5N	E1
400	WynT	60103	2966	29W-5N	E1
W Bartlett Rd					
10	BRLT	60103	2909	32W-8N	D3
10	BRLT	60103	2910	30W-8N	B3
10	BRLT	60120	2909	32W-8N	D3
10	ELGN	60103	2910	31W-8N	A3
10	ELGN	60120	2909	31W-8N	E3
10	HnrT	60103	2909	31W-8N	E3
10	HnrT	60103	2910	30W-8N	A3
10	HnrT	60120	2909	32W-8N	D3
200	ELGN	60103	2909	31W-8N	E3
2100	SEGN	60103	2909	33W-8N	B3
2100	SEGN	60120	2909	33W-8N	B3
2100	SEGN	60177	2909	33W-8N	B3
W Bartlett Rd CO-61					
2100	BRLT	60103	2909	33W-8N	B3
2100	BRLT	60120	2909	33W-8N	B3
2100	HnrT	60120	2909	33W-8N	B3
2100	SEGN	60103	2909	33W-8N	B3
2100	SEGN	60120	2909	33W-8N	B3
2100	SEGN	60177	2909	33W-8N	B3
Bartlett Ter					
800	LYVL	60048	2591	16W-29N	D4
Bartlett Pointe Dr					
-	BRLT	60103	2909	32W-8N	C2
-	HnrT	60103	2909	32W-8N	C2
-	HnrT	60120	2909	32W-8N	C2
Bartmouth Ct					
-	BRRG	60527	3146	15W-7S	B6
Barton Av					
100	CHCG	60202	2867	2W-9N	A6
100	CHCG	60645	2867	2W-9N	A6
200	EVTN	60202	2867	2W-9N	A6
12000	HTLY	60142	2744	42W-20N	A1
Barton Cir					
100	SMBG	60194	2859	23W-10N	B5
Barton Ct					
300	BRLT	60103	2967	28W-5N	B1
1000	GNVW	60025	2811	7W-13N	A7
Barton Dr					
-	LMNT	60439	3271	18W-14S	B6
200	SchT	60175	2908	36W-6N	A7
300	SchT	60175	2907	36W-6N	E7
700	CTSD	60525	3147	12W-6S	B4
700	LynT	60525	3147	12W-6S	B4
800	OSWG	60543	3264	35W-12S	C2
Barton Ln					
-	HNDL	60521	3146	14W-6S	C4
600	CLLK	60014	2693	36W-23N	D1
900	PTON	60468	3861	8W-37S	B2
1000	WllT	60468	3861	8W-37S	B2
16400	OKFT	60452	3426	5W-19S	C2
E Barton Ln					
700	PTON	60468	3861	8W-37S	B2
Barton Pl					
300	CLSM	60188	2967	27W-2N	D7
N Barton Tr					
10	BTVA	60510	3077	37W-1S	D1
10	GnvT	60510	3077	37W-1S	D1
S Barton Tr					
10	BTVA	60510	3077	37W-1S	D2
Barton Creek Ct					
10	LIHL	60156	2693	37W-22N	C5
Barton Creek Dr					
500	LIHL	60156	2693	36W-22N	C4
Bartram Rd					
-	NARA	60510	3076	38W-3S	E6
100	RVSD	60546	3088	9W-3S	C4
400	NRIV	60546	3088	9W-2S	C3
2000	NARA	60542	3076	39W-3S	E5
2000	NARA	60542	3077	38W-3S	A6
Bartson Ln					
1600	AraT	60502	3139	33W-6S	A5
1600	AraT	60505	3139	33W-6S	A5
Baseline Rd					
900	BtlT	60512	3196	44W-9S	D5
900	BtlT	60545	3196	44W-9S	D5
900	SgrT	60545	3196	44W-9S	D5
900	SgrT	60554	3196	44W-9S	D5
4700	MTGY	60538	3199	38W-10S	A5
4700	MTGY	60543	3199	38W-10S	A5
4800	AraT	60538	3199	38W-9S	B5
10000	BtlT	60512	3197	42W-9S	C5
10000	SgrT	60506	3197	42W-9S	C5
10000	SgrT	60554	3197	42W-9S	C5
26300	CnhT	60421	3674	27W-31S	D6
26300	CnhT	60421	3763	28W-33S	C4
26300	ELWD	60421	3674	27W-31S	D6
26300	ELWD	60421	3763	28W-33S	C4
Basham Av					
14000	HmrT	60441	3342	20W-16S	B4
Basil Av					
400	ShdT	60044	2593	12W-28N	B5
Basil Ct					
16500	LKPT	60441	3420	20W-21S	B6
Basil Dr					
16600	LKPT	60441	3420	20W-21S	B7
Basin Dr					
1100	LKPT	60441	3341	21W-18S	E7
1200	LKPT	60441	3342	21W-18S	A7
Baskin Dr					
800	JLET	60404	3496	29W-22S	D3
800	JLET	60431	3496	29W-22S	D3
800	SRWD	60404	3496	29W-22S	D3
Baskin Rd					
1500	MDLN	60060	2647	17W-25N	A4
Bass St					
100	SRWD	60404	3496	30W-24S	C5
300	WsIT	60481	3943	27W-40S	D3
Bassett Av					
100	NCHI	60088	2593	10W-30N	E2
100	NCHI	60088	2594	10W-30N	A2
Bassett Dr					
1200	JLET	60431	3495	32W-22S	C2
Bassford Av					
10	LGNG	60525	3087	13W-4S	A6
100	LGPK	60525	3087	13W-4S	A6
Bass Lake Rd					
22500	PNFD	60544	3339	28W-16S	A4
Bassler Dr					
100	ISLK	60042	2586	29W-28N	D6
Basswood Cir					
1400	GNVW	60025	2810	8W-14N	D5
26800	PNFD	60585	3337	33W-15S	A3
Basswood Ct					
10	BtlT	60512	3262	40W-11S	C1
100	EGVV	60007	2861	17W-9N	A6
300	BRLT	60103	2967	28W-5N	B1
300	CLSM	60188	2968	26W-4N	A4
1000	BTVA	60510	3078	36W-2S	A4
1200	ELGN	60120	2855	32W-11N	D4
1500	GNVW	60025	2810	8W-14N	D5
S Basswood Ct					
100	RDLK	60073	2531	24W-32N	C4
Basswood Dr					
10	VNHL	60061	2647	17W-25N	B6
100	EGVV	60007	2861	17W-9N	A7
200	NARA	60542	3077	37W-4S	D7
200	NPVL	60540	3203	26W-8S	D2
300	NHBK	60062	2755	13W-18N	E3
300	NHBK	60062	2756	13W-18N	A3
300	WhlT	60062	2756	13W-18N	A3
1400	BGBK	60490	3267	26W-13S	E5
4400	LSLE	60532	3143	22W-4S	B1
8000	GwdT	60097	2526	37W-34N	C1
8000	MchT	60097	2526	37W-34N	C1
8900	TYPK	60487	3424	11W-22S	A7
9100	TYPK	60487	3423	11W-21S	E7
Basswood Ln					
800	FKFT	60423	3503	13W-24S	B6
1800	GLHT	60139	2969	23W-3N	A5
E Basswood Ln					
1800	MPPT	60056	2808	13W-14N	D4
N Basswood Ln					
1200	MPPT	60056	2808	13W-14N	D4
W Basswood Ln					
21300	LktT	60544	3339	26W-16S	E4
Basswood Rd					
1200	HFET	60169	2859	22W-12N	C2
Basswood Rd					
1200	SMBG	60169	2859	22W-12N	C2
1200	SMBG	60173	2859	22W-12N	C2
8100	ODPK	60462	3346	10W-17S	C5
8100	OrlT	60462	3346	10W-17S	C5
E Basswood Rd					
2200	JLET	60432	3500	21W-22S	A2
S Basswood Rd					
100	LKFT	60045	2649	11W-25N	D5
25700	CNHN	60410	3672	33W-31S	A5
25800	AxST	60410	3672	33W-31S	A6
Basswood St					
800	HFET	60169	2859	22W-11N	C3
1100	SMBG	60169	2859	22W-11N	C2
1100	SMBG	60173	2859	22W-12N	C2
Basswood Wy					
-	PNFD	60585	3337	33W-16S	A3
Bastian Dr					
200	SRGV	60554	3135	43W-7S	B6
Bataan Dr					
-	FTPK	60130	3030	10W-0S	A6
-	FTPK	60153	3030	10W-0S	A6
-	MYWD	60153	3030	10W-0S	A6
1300	BDVW	60153	3029	11W-0S	E6
1300	BDVW	60155	3029	11W-0S	E6
1300	MYWD	60153	3029	11W-0S	D6
1300	MYWD	60155	3029	11W-0S	E6
Bataan St					
1700	JLET	60435	3417	27W-21S	C7
1700	JLET	60435	3497	27W-21S	C1
Batavia Av					
500	AURA	60506	3138	35W-7S	B6
N Batavia Av					
10	BTVA	60510	3078	35W-0S	B1
500	BTVA	60510	3020	35W-0S	B7
600	BTVA	60134	3020	35W-0S	B7
600	GNVA	60134	3020	35W-0S	B7
N Batavia Av SR-31					
10	BTVA	60510	3078	35W-0S	B1
500	BTVA	60510	3020	35W-0S	B7
600	BTVA	60134	3020	35W-0S	B7
600	GNVA	60134	3020	35W-0S	B7
S Batavia Av					
10	BTVA	60510	3078	35W-2S	A4
200	BtvT	60510	3077	36W-3S	E6
200	BtvT	60510	3078	36W-3S	A6
200	BtvT	60539	3077	36W-3S	E6
200	BtvT	60539	3078	36W-3S	A6
200	BtvT	60542	3077	36W-3S	E6
600	GNVA	60134	3020	35W-0N	B6
S Batavia Av SR-31					
10	BTVA	60510	3078	35W-2S	A4
200	BtvT	60510	3077	36W-3S	E6
200	BtvT	60510	3078	36W-3S	A6
200	BtvT	60539	3077	36W-3S	E6
200	BtvT	60539	3078	36W-3S	A6
200	BtvT	60542	3077	36W-3S	E6
600	GNVA	60134	3020	35W-0N	B6
Batavia Ct					
1300	BRLT	60103	2967	27W-5N	B1
Batavia Ln					
200	HFET	60169	2859	23W-11N	B4
Batavia Rd					
-	BtvT	60510	3079	33W-1S	B1
-	WnfT	60510	3079	31W-1S	D2
10	WNVL	60555	3080	29W-2S	D5
100	WnfT	60510	3080	30W-2S	B4
300	WNVL	60555	3081	28W-3S	A5
Batavia Rd (Private)					
-	WnfT	60510	3079	31W-1S	E2
-	WnfT	60510	3080	30W-2S	A3
Bateman Cir N					
300	BNHL	60010	2749	30W-18N	A3
Bateman Cir S					
300	BNHL	60010	2749	30W-18N	A3
Bateman Rd					
-	BNHL	60010	2801	30W-15N	E2
-	BNHL	60010	2802	30W-15N	A1
10	BNHL	60010	2749	30W-16N	A7
Bateman St					
7200	DRGV	60516	3206	20W-8S	C1
Bates Ct					
-	OrlT	60467	3422	14W-19S	C3
1500	SMBG	60193	2912	25W-9N	B1
Bates Ln					
1400	SMBG	60193	2912	25W-9N	B1
Bates Pl					
1900	DRGV	60516	3144	20W-7S	A6
Bates Rd					
1500	JltT	60433	3587	23W-25S	B1
Bates St					
100	WHTN	60187	3023	26W-0S	D7
Bath & Tennis Dr					
-	OKBK	60523	3085	16W-2S	E4
-	OKBK	60523	3086	15W-2S	A4
Bath & Tennis Club Rd					
10	LKBF	60044	2593	11W-28N	E7
Batley St					
3300	ElgT	60124	2853	38W-11N	A5
Batson Ct					
100	NLNX	60451	3501	18W-24S	B6
Battershall Dr					
32800	GYLK	60030	2534	18W-32N	A4
32800	WrnT	60030	2534	18W-32N	A4
Bauer Ct					
-	NARA	60506	3076	39W-3S	C6
-	NARA	60542	3076	39W-3S	C6
1000	SDWH	60548	3258	51W-14S	A7
Bauer Dr					
-	RLKB	60073	2474	23W-35N	E5
Bauer Rd					
-	BtvT	60506	3076	39W-3S	E7
300	NPVL	60563	3141	27W-5S	C2
300	NpvT	60563	3141	27W-5S	C2
2500	NARA	60542	3076	39W-3S	D6
2600	NARA	60506	3076	39W-3S	D6
E Bauer Rd					
10	NPVL	60563	3141	26W-5S	E3
600	LslT	60563	3141	26W-5S	E3
900	LslT	60563	3142	26W-5S	A3
900	NPVL	60563	3142	26W-5S	A3
N Bauer Rd					
100	MHRY	60050	2528	32W-32N	B5
W Bauer Rd					
10	NpvT	60563	3141	27W-5S	D2
500	NPVL	60563	3141	27W-5S	B2
1200	WNVL	60555	3141	28W-4S	A2
1200	WNVL	60563	3141	28W-4S	A2
E Bauer St					
800	HMND	46320	3352		E7
Bauman Ct					
200	WnfT	60185	3022	29W-0S	E7
300	WDDL	60191	2914	18W-7N	E4
300	WDDL	60191	2915	18W-7N	A4
Bauman St					
600	MRGO	60152	2634	49W-25N	C4

Chicago 7-County Street Index

STREET Block	City	ZIP	Map#	CGS	Grid
Baumann Tr					
300	BtlT	60543	3198	39W-10S	D7
300	OSWG	60543	3198	39W-10S	D7
Baumgartner St					
9600	HTLY	60142	2691	41W-22N	E4
Bavarian Ct					
5700	HRPK	60133	2911	26W-7N	E4
Bavarian Ln					
1000	DRN	60561	3145	17W-7S	B7
Baxter Ct					
700	LKVL	60046	2417	22W-39N	C4
2200	ELGN	60123	2908	36W-9N	A2
W Baxter Ct					
-	OswT	60543	3265	32W-14S	B7
-	PNFD	60585	3265	32W-14S	B7
Baxter Ln					
500	HFET	60169	2858	24W-11N	D3
1300	LKVL	60046	2417	22W-39N	C4
Baxter Pkwy					
10	RVWD	60015	2756	12W-20N	A1
10	WdfT	60015	2756	12W-20N	B1
Bay Ct					
800	BRLT	60103	2911	28W-7N	B4
1200	WTMT	60559	3144	18W-7S	E5
1600	NPVL	60565	3204	26W-9S	A3
2700	NLNX	60451	3502	15W-25S	C7
N Bay Ct					
200	LKBN	60010	2643	26W-24N	D6
3200	CHCG	60618	2977	3W-4N	A3
Bay Dr					
-	EGVV	60007	2914	19W-7N	C3
10	ITSC	60143	2914	19W-7N	C3
Bay Ln					
10	FXLK	60020	2473	28W-36N	A5
Bay Pl					
1200	GRNE	60031	2479	12W-35N	A6
1200	GRNE	60085	2479	12W-35N	A6
1200	WkgT	60031	2479	13W-35N	A6
1200	WkgT	60085	2479	13W-35N	A6
Bay Rd					
10	FXLK	60020	2472	28W-36N	E4
10	FXLK	60020	2473	27W-35N	B5
900	JNBG	60051	2529	29W-34N	B1
900	LKMR	60051	2529	29W-34N	B1
900	MchT	60051	2529	29W-34N	B1
1100	JNBG	60051	2472	30W-35N	A7
1100	LKMR	60051	2472	30W-35N	A7
3100	NndT	60012	2584	34W-28N	D5
3100	PRGV	60012	2584	34W-28N	D5
Bay Rd CO-A26					
900	JNBG	60051	2529	29W-34N	B1
900	LKMR	60051	2529	29W-34N	B1
900	MchT	60051	2529	29W-34N	B1
1100	JNBG	60051	2472	30W-35N	A7
1100	LKMR	60051	2472	30W-35N	A7
E Bay Rd					
100	GrtT	60051	2529	29W-34N	D1
100	MchT	60051	2529	29W-34N	D1
300	LKMR	60051	2529	29W-34N	C1
E Bay Rd CO-A26					
100	GrtT	60051	2529	29W-34N	D1
100	MchT	60051	2529	29W-34N	D1
300	LKMR	60051	2529	29W-34N	C1
N Bay Rd					
10	PSHT	60463	3274	9W-13S	C4
10	PSHT	60465	3274	9W-13S	C4
S Bay Rd					
10	PSHT	60463	3274	9W-13S	C4
10	PSHT	60465	3274	9W-13S	C4
W Bay Rd					
10	PSHT	60463	3274	9W-13S	C4
10	PSHT	60465	3274	9W-13S	C4
Bay Rdg					
-	JLET	60586	3415	31W-21S	E7
Bay St					
200	WDDL	60191	2914	18W-5N	E7
Bayberry Ct					
10	SMWD	60107	2857	27W-10N	C6
100	GLHT	60139	3025	22W-1N	B2
200	WCHI	60185	3022	30W-1N	B2
1600	WKGN	60048	2535	14W-32N	C6
2600	JLET	60435	3497	27W-21S	D1
5300	RGMW	60008	2860	19W-12N	C1
12600	PlsT	60464	3273	13W-14S	B7
15200	ODPK	60462	3346	10W-18S	B7
28800	LKMR	60051	2529	28W-32N	D5
W Bayberry Ct					
26200	CNHN	60410	3672	32W-31S	C7
Bay Berry Dr					
700	CRY	60013	2695	32W-22N	A3
Bayberry Dr					
300	ALGN	60102	2694	34W-21N	C6
400	BtlT	60543	3263	39W-12S	A3
400	OSWG	60543	3262	39W-12S	E3
400	OSWG	60543	3263	39W-12S	A3
700	BRLT	60103	2910	29W-8N	D3
1200	JLET	60435	3498	26W-22S	A2
2900	BFGV	60089	2701	17W-23N	B2
3400	NHBK	60062	2756	11W-18N	C3
S Bayberry Dr					
26000	CNHN	60410	3672	32W-31S	C7
Bayberry Ln					
10	CLLK	60014	2639	37W-25N	B4
400	MltT	60187	3082	25W-1S	C2
400	WHTN	60187	3082	25W-1S	C2
1300	DRFD	60015	2703	11W-20N	C7
2000	HFET	60169	2858	25W-12N	B1
2300	ElaT	60047	2753	19W-20N	B1
2300	LGGV	60047	2753	19W-20N	B1
7200	DRN	60561	3207	18W-8S	A1
9200	TYPK	60487	3423	11W-21S	E6
N Bayberry Ln					
400	LslT	60563	3141	26W-5S	E3
400	NPVL	60563	3141	26W-5S	E3
S Bayberry Ln					
13200	DPgT	60544	3340	26W-15S	A2
Baybrook Ct					
10	OKBK	60523	3085	18W-2S	A3
1800	NPVL	60564	3266	28W-12S	E3
N Baybrook Ct					
1200	ADSN	60101	2970	19W-4N	C2
Baybrook Dr					
10	CTSD	60525	3147	13W-7S	B6
3600	AURA	60504	3202	30W-9S	A3
3900	AURA	60564	3202	31W-9S	A3
S Baybrook Dr					
10	PLTN	60074	2806	19W-15N	C1
Baybrook Ln					
10	OKBK	60523	3084	18W-2S	E4
10	OKBK	60523	3085	18W-2S	A4
1000	CLSM	60188	2967	27W-4N	C4
1700	NPVL	60564	3266	28W-12S	E3
1700	NPVL	60564	3267	28W-12S	A3
Baybury Dr					
100	ELWD	60421	3675	25W-31S	C5
Baybury Rd					
7300	DGvT	60516	3206	19W-8S	D1
7300	DRGV	60516	3206	19W-8S	D1
N Baycliff Dr					
2800	MchT	60050	2471	31W-34N	D7
Bay Colony Dr					
200	NPVL	60565	3203	26W-8S	D2
9400	DSPN	60016	2863	11W-11N	C2
9400	MaiT	60016	2863	11W-11N	C2
Bay Creek Ln					
-	PNFD	60586	3416	30W-19S	B3
W Bayer Dr					
600	PLTN	60067	2752	21W-17N	C5
600	PltT	60067	2752	21W-17N	C5
Bayfield Ct					
-	TYPK	60477	3504	9W-23S	E3
Bayfield Dr					
-	TYPK	60477	3504	9W-23S	D3
1900	AURA	60503	3201	31W-10S	D6
Bayhead Ct					
4300	AURA	60504	3202	30W-8S	B2
Bayhill Av					
900	NPVL	60565	3204	25W-8S	B2
Bay Hill Ct					
600	RVWD	60015	2703	12W-20N	A7
21800	FmtT	60060	2589	21W-28N	C6
Bayhill Ct					
2400	AURA	60503	3201	32W-11S	D7
8100	ODPK	60462	3346	10W-18S	C7
10700	HTLY	60142	2692	39W-21N	C5
Bayhill Dr					
1400	NLNX	60451	3500	19W-24S	E6
Bayhill Ln					
900	SRWD	60404	3496	31W-25S	A7
900	SRWD	60404	3584	31W-25S	A1
Bayles Dr					
700	RMVL	60446	3418	26W-18S	A2
Baylor Ct					
1300	NPVL	60565	3204	24W-9S	C4
Bay Meadow Ln					
2800	LKMR	60051	2472	30W-34N	A7
Bay Meadows Dr					
1300	BRLT	60103	2966	29W-5N	C1
1300	WynT	60103	2966	29W-5N	C1
N Baynard Rd					
200	ADSN	60101	2970	19W-3N	C5
Bay Oaks Dr					
1400	JNBG	60051	2472	30W-34N	B7
1400	LKMR	60051	2472	30W-34N	A7
2100	LKMR	60051	2529	30W-34N	A1
Bayonne Av					
-	BHPK	60087	2479	13W-38N	A1
-	GNOK	60044	2593	13W-28N	A5
-	LKFT	60044	2593	13W-28N	A5
-	NptT	60087	2479	13W-38N	A1
-	WrnT	60087	2479	13W-38N	A1
200	ShdT	60044	2593	13W-29N	A5
7900	WRLK	60097	2469	36W-36N	C3
40100	BHPK	60099	2421	12W-40N	A4
40100	WDWH	60099	2421	12W-40N	A4
N Bayonne Av					
36900	WkgT	60087	2479	13W-36N	A3
36900	WrnT	60087	2479	13W-36N	A3
37500	BHPK	60087	2479	13W-37N	A2
38500	BHPK	60087	2421	13W-38N	A7
38500	WKGN	60083	2421	13W-38N	A7
38500	WKGN	60087	2421	13W-38N	A7
38700	BHPK	60083	2421	12W-38N	A6
38700	WDWH	60083	2421	12W-38N	A6
Bayou Ct					
11000	HTLY	60142	2745	39W-20N	B1
E Bayou Ct					
700	FXLK	60041	2530	26W-34N	D1
W Bayou Ct					
600	FXLK	60041	2530	26W-34N	D1
Bayou Dr					
-	LKMR	60041	2530	27W-32N	A5
Bayport Ln					
8600	AlqT	60013	2696	29W-23N	D2
S Bayport Ln					
1300	RDLK	60073	2531	23W-31N	E7
Bay Reef Dr					
10	SBTN	60010	2803	27W-13N	C5
Bay Rum Ct					
10	BRRG	60527	3208	15W-9S	A4
Bays Pl					
200	LKBN	60010	2643	26W-25N	C4
200	LKBN	60084	2643	26W-25N	C4
200	TRLK	60010	2643	26W-25N	C4
Bay Scott Cir					
-	NpvT	60564	3202	28W-8S	E2
1900	NPVL	60540	3202	28W-8S	E2
1900	NPVL	60564	3202	28W-8S	E2
Bay Shore Dr					
600	PGGV	60140	2797	41W-14N	E5
600	PGGV	60140	2798	41W-14N	A5
Bayshore Dr					
200	ShdT	60044	2593	11W-29N	D4
300	NCHI	60088	2593	11W-29N	D4
300	ShdT	60088	2593	11W-29N	D4
700	ANTH	60002	2357	24W-41N	D7
900	SMBG	60194	2858	24W-11N	D3
N Bay Shore Dr					
37100	LkvT	60046	2474	25W-37N	A2
Bayshore Rd					
37300	LkvT	60046	2474	25W-37N	A2
Bayside Cir					
4400	HFET	60192	2804	24W-15N	B2
Bayside Ct					
700	WLNG	60090	2754	16W-17N	D6
2300	LSLE	60532	3142	24W-5S	D3
4100	ZION	60099	2421	12W-41N	C1
E Bayside Ct					
1500	HFET	60192	2804	24W-15N	B2
W Bayside Ct					
1600	HFET	60192	2804	25W-15N	A2
Bayside Dr					
-	CLSM	60133	2967	27W-4N	B3
-	CLSM	60188	2967	27W-4N	B3
200	PLTN	60074	2753	19W-17N	D5
200	PltT	60074	2753	19W-17N	C5
1400	WLNG	60004	2754	16W-17N	D6
1400	WLNG	60090	2754	16W-17N	D6
2300	HRPK	60133	2967	27W-4N	B3
N Bayside Dr					
41200	AntT	60002	2416	25W-41N	A1
Bayside Ln					
1000	SRWD	60404	3496	30W-22S	A3
1400	WLNG	60090	2754	16W-17N	D6
Bayside Rd					
1000	ELGN	60123	2800	34W-13N	E7
1000	ELGN	60123	2854	34W-13N	E1
Bayswater Cir					
-	GRNE	60031	2478	15W-37N	A3
Baythorne Dr					
1100	FSMR	60422	3507	3W-23S	A3
3100	RchT	60430	3507	3W-23S	A3
Bay Tree Cir					
300	VNHL	60061	2647	16W-26N	D3
Baytree Cir					
-	SRWD	60404	3583	31W-25S	E2
Bay Tree Ct					
400	VNHL	60061	2647	16W-26N	D3
Baytree Ct					
-	SRWD	60404	3583	31W-25S	E2
Baytree Dr					
-	BRLT	60120	2910	29W-9N	C2
800	BRLT	60103	2910	29W-9N	D2
1500	RMVL	60446	3339	26W-17S	E6
Bayview Av					
400	NPVL	60565	3203	27W-9S	D4
Bayview Ct					
100	CRTE	60417	3596	0W-28S	C6
100	WNVL	60555	3080	29W-3S	C5
200	BMDL	60108	2969	22W-4N	B3
500	MchT	60051	2472	29W-34N	C7
1100	FRGV	60021	2696	30W-22N	A3
2700	ALGN	60102	2693	36W-21N	D6
Bay View Dr					
4300	NndT	60014	2586	30W-27N	A7
4800	RNPK	60471	3594	6W-26S	A2
41200	AntT	60002	2417	22W-41N	B1
Bayview Dr					
900	RLKB	60073	2474	23W-34N	E7
900	RLKB	60073	2531	23W-34N	E1
1400	LKZH	60047	2699	22W-21N	B6
W Bayview Dr					
23500	AntT	60002	2416	24W-41N	D1
24300	ANTH	60002	2416	24W-41N	D1
25700	GrtT	60041	2474	25W-35N	A6
27500	FXLK	60041	2473	27W-35N	B7
27500	GrtT	60041	2473	27W-34N	B7
Bay View Ln					
10	GYLK	60030	2475	20W-34N	E7
Bayview Ln					
1300	JNBG	60050	2472	30W-35N	A5
1900	AURA	60506	3137	38W-5S	B3
N Bayview Ln					
800	GrtT	60050	2472	28W-35N	D6
800	GrtT	60051	2472	28W-35N	D6
800	MchT	60050	2472	28W-35N	D6
2500	LKMR	60051	2529	29W-34N	C1
2500	MchT	60051	2529	29W-34N	C1
2800	MchT	60051	2472	29W-34N	C7
Bayview Pt					
300	SMBG	60194	2859	22W-10N	C4
Bay View Rd					
-	FRGV	60021	2696	30W-22N	A3
1100	FRGV	60021	2695	30W-22N	E3
Bayview Rd					
100	ELGN	60123	2801	33W-13N	A7
100	ELGN	60123	2854	34W-13N	E1
100	ELGN	60123	2855	33W-13N	A1
7900	WRLK	60097	2469	36W-36N	C3
Bayview St					
-	NndT	60042	2642	29W-27N	D1
-	WcnT	60042	2642	29W-27N	D1
Bay View Beach Rd					
-	NndT	60014	2585	30W-27N	E7
-	PRGV	60014	2585	30W-27N	E7
Baywood Ln					
13100	HMGN	60491	3343	16W-17S	E5
Bazan Rd					
-	BtlT	60560	3261	41W-13S	E4
Bazz Dr					
6400	JLET	60586	3415	32W-20S	C4
Beach Av					
10	LGNG	60525	3087	12W-4S	C6
300	LGPK	60525	3087	12W-3S	C6
W Beach Av					
1600	CHCG	60622	3033	2W-1N	C1
3200	CHCG	60622	3032	4W-1N	D1
3200	CHCG	60651	3032	4W-1N	D1
5200	MchT	60050	2527	34W-34N	D1
24700	LkvT	60046	2416	24W-39N	B5
Beach Ct					
100	SEGN	60177	2908	34W-9N	D2
Beach Dr					
100	ALGN	60102	2747	34W-20N	D1
500	AlqT	60102	2747	34W-20N	C1
2100	AlqT	60021	2695	31W-22N	E3
2100	FRGV	60021	2695	31W-22N	E3
2400	AlqT	60102	2695	31W-22N	D4
7300	MchT	60097	2469	36W-35N	D5
N Beach Dr					
24100	CbaT	60013	2642	28W-24N	D7
W Beach Dr					
600	ADSN	60101	2970	19W-4N	D2
3000	MHRY	60050	2528	32W-31N	C7
3100	NndT	60050	2528	32W-31N	C7
24900	AntT	60002	2357	24W-43N	B4
Beach Ln					
3500	NfdT	60062	2756	12W-16N	C7
W Beach Ln					
40200	AntT	60002	2417	22W-40N	B3
Beach Pl					
700	MDLN	60060	2590	19W-28N	C6
5000	MHRY	60050	2527	34W-33N	D2
W Beach Pl					
10000	BHPK	60087	2422	10W-38N	B7
Beach Rd					
-	BHPK	60087	2422	9W-38N	B7
-	BtnT	60087	2422	9W-38N	B7
-	NndT	60050	2586	30W-29N	A4
-	TNLK	53181	2354		D1
10	GLNC	60022	2758	6W-18N	D4
1300	MchT	60051	2529	29W-32N	C6
1600	MHRY	60050	2527	34W-33N	D2
7600	MchT	60097	2469	36W-35N	D6
W Beach Rd					
1100	WKGN	60087	2421	11W-38N	E7
1100	WKGN	60099	2421	10W-38N	E7
1500	BHPK	60099	2421	11W-38N	E7
10000	BHPK	60087	2422	10W-38N	A7
10000	BHPK	60099	2422	10W-38N	A7
10800	WKGN	60099	2422	10W-38N	A7
12500	BHPK	60087	2421	12W-38N	B7
12600	WDWH	60083	2421	12W-38N	B7
12600	WKGN	60083	2421	12W-38N	B7
Beach St					
100	JLET	60436	3498	24W-24S	E5
200	AURA	60505	3138	34W-7S	C7
1300	NndT	60014	2586	30W-27N	A7
1300	NndT	60014	2642	30W-27N	A1
1500	BTVA	60510	3078	35W-2S	C4
1800	BDVW	60155	3029	12W-0S	C6
E Beach St					
200	EMHT	60126	3027	17W-1N	B2
200	VLPK	60126	3027	17W-1N	B2
200	VLPK	60181	3027	17W-1N	B2
W Beach St					
26300	AntT	60002	2356	26W-42N	D6
Beachcomber Dr					
1100	SMBG	60193	2912	24W-9N	D1
W Beach Grove Rd					
23500	AntT	60002	2416	25W-41N	B2
Beach Park Av					
-	AntT	60002	2417	22W-40N	B3
Beach Park Dr					
-	BHPK	60099	2422	9W-38N	B7
S Beach Park Dr					
-	BHPK	60099	2422	9W-38N	D7
N Beachside Rd					
2100	MchT	60050	2527	34W-34N	D1
2100	MHRY	60050	2527	34W-33N	D2
Beach View Dr					
2700	MCLK	60050	2470	33W-34N	E7
Beachview Dr					
-	PGGV	60140	2797	42W-15N	C4
10	RLKB	60073	2475	23W-34N	A7
100	RLKB	60073	2474	23W-34N	E7
W Beachview Dr					
41900	AntT	60002	2356	26W-41N	E7
Beachview Ln					
100	NBRN	60010	2698	25W-23N	A1
Beachview Rd					
-	PGGV	60140	2797	42W-15N	C4
Beachview Ter					
14600	DLTN	60419	3350	0E-17S	E5
14900	DLTN	60473	3350	0E-17S	E5
14900	SHLD	60419	3350	0E-17S	E5
14900	SHLD	60473	3350	0E-17S	E5
N Beachway					
24600	CbaT	60013	2642	28W-24N	E6
Beach Way Dr					
100	ALGN	60102	2695	33W-21N	A6
Beachway St					
5900	NndT	60013	2642	29W-26N	B3
Beachwood Ct					
-	ANTH	60002	2357	25W-41N	B7
Beach Wy Dr					
100	FRGV	60021	2696	30W-23N	A3
Beacon Av					
-	GfnT	60142	2745	39W-20N	D1
10	RMVL	60446	3268	23W-14S	E7
10	RMVL	60446	3269	23W-14S	A7
11400	HTLY	60142	2692	39W-20N	D7
11400	HTLY	60142	2745	39W-20N	D1
14300	ODPK	60462	3345	12W-17S	D5
N Beacon Av					
10	LGNG	60525	3087	12W-4S	C6
Beacon Blvd					
200	CHHT	60411	3595	2W-26S	C2
1900	CHHT	60466	3595	2W-26S	C1
1900	PKFT	60466	3595	2W-26S	C1
Beacon Ct					
10	BFGV	60089	2754	17W-17N	B5
1900	CHHT	60411	3595	2W-26S	D2
4400	HFET	60192	2804	25W-15N	B2
8900	ODHL	60487	3424	11W-19S	A3
Beacon Dr					
500	LKBN	60010	2696	28W-23N	E1
600	LKBN	60010	2643	28W-24N	A7
600	LKBN	60010	2697	28W-24N	A1
700	CbaT	60010	2643	28W-24N	A7
800	SMBG	60193	2858	24W-9N	D7
800	SMBG	60193	2912	24W-9N	D1
7900	PSHT	60463	3274	10W-13S	C5
Beacon Ln					
1300	BRLT	60103	2967	28W-5N	B1
8900	ODHL	60487	3424	11W-19S	A3
S Beacon Ln					
400	RDLK	60073	2531	23W-32N	E4
Beacon Pl					
-	CRTE	60417	3685	0E-29S	E1
200	MNSR	46321	3430		D6
Beacon St					
-	NCHI	60088	2593	12W-30N	B2
-	SYHW	60118	2800	34W-15N	D4
-	WDND	60118	2800	34W-15N	D4
100	BtnT	60081	2414	29W-39N	D5
2900	NCHI	60044	2593	12W-30N	B2
2900	NCHI	60064	2593	12W-30N	B2
2900	ShdT	60044	2593	12W-30N	B2
2900	ShdT	60064	2593	12W-30N	B2
7300	FXLK	60081	2414	29W-39N	D5
N Beacon St					
4400	CHCG	60613	2921	1W-5N	D7
4400	CHCG	60640	2921	1W-5N	D7
Beacon Bay					
10	LKMR	60051	2529	28W-33N	E3
Beacon Hill Dr					
10	BrnT	60010	2803	28W-15N	A2
10	SBTN	60010	2803	27W-15N	A2
N Beacon Hill Dr					
5100	MchT	60050	2472	29W-37N	B2
5200	JNBG	60050	2472	29W-37N	B2
Beaconridge Dr					
100	BGBK	60440	3269	22W-12S	B3
Beaconsfield Av					
500	NPVL	60565	3203	27W-10S	B5
Beaconsfield Ct					
-	LNSH	60069	2702	15W-23N	A3
10	LNSH	60069	2701	15W-23N	E3
Beagle Club Rd					
-	BvlT	60407	4030	32W-43S	C3
-	GDLY	60407	4030	32W-43S	C3
-	RedT	60407	4030	32W-43S	C3
Bealer Cir					
100	BbyT	60134	3018	39W-0S	D7
Beall St					
8400	SjnT	46311	3598		E7
9000	SjnT	46311	3687		E2
S Beall St					
5500	HMND	46320	3352		E7
Bear Claw Ct					
5500	HFET	60192	2856	30W-12N	B3
Bear Claw Ln					
22600	FKFT	60423	3592	9W-27S	E4
Bear Creek Ct					
4200	AURA	60564	3202	30W-9S	B4
Beardsley St					
100	CLLK	60014	2640	34W-26N	B3
Bear Flag Dr					
1400	HRPK	60133	2911	26W-7N	E4
Bear Island Av					
10800	ODPK	60467	3423	13W-19S	A2
Bear Paw Ct					
1000	CLSM	60188	2967	27W-3N	C6
Beatrice Av					
100	SCRL	60174	3020	34W-2N	C1
Beatrice Ln					
1100	LMNT	60439	3271	18W-13S	B4
Beattie St					
500	ELWD	60421	3675	25W-31S	B7
Beau Ct					
600	DSPN	60016	2862	15W-10N	A4
Beau Dr					
200	DSPN	60016	2862	15W-11N	A4
200	MPPT	60016	2862	15W-11N	A4
200	MPPT	60056	2862	15W-11N	A4
1200	PKRG	60068	2864	10W-10N	A5
Beau Bien Blvd					
100	LSLE	60532	3142	24W-5S	D2
100	LSLE	60563	3142	24W-5S	D3
100	LslT	60563	3142	24W-5S	D3
400	LslT	60540	3142	24W-5S	C3
Beau Bien Blvd W					
4700	LSLE	60532	3142	24W-5S	C2
Beau Bien Ct					
4600	LSLE	60532	3142	24W-5S	C2
Beaubien Ct					
10	LKZH	60047	2698	23W-23N	E1
N Beaubien Ct					
100	CHCG	60601	3034	0E-0N	C4
100	CHCG	60603	3034	0E-0N	C4
Beau Bien Ln E					
4700	LSLE	60532	3142	24W-5S	D2
Beau Brummel Ct					
1000	SYHW	60118	2800	36W-15N	A3
Beau Brummel Dr					
1000	SYHW	60118	2800	36W-15N	A3
Beaudin Blvd					
-	WDRG	60440	3270	21W-12S	A3
-	WDRG	60517	3270	21W-12S	A3
10400	BGBK	60440	3269	21W-12S	E2
10400	BGBK	60517	3269	21W-12S	E2
10400	WDRG	60440	3269	21W-12S	E2
10400	WDRG	60517	3269	21W-12S	E2
Beau Meade Rd					
10	OSWG	60543	3263	36W-11S	E1
Beau Monde Blvd					
2300	LSLE	60532	3142	24W-4S	D1
Beau Monde Dr					
4400	LSLE	60532	3142	24W-4S	D1
Beau Monde Ln					
2300	LSLE	60532	3142	24W-4S	D1
Beau Monde Ter					
2300	LSLE	60532	3142	24W-4S	D1
Beaumont Cir					
1300	BRLT	60103	2967	28W-5N	B1
Beaumont Ct					
200	BRLT	60103	2967	28W-5N	A1
2100	AURA	60502	3139	32W-7S	B7
2100	AURA	60502	3201	32W-7S	B1
Beaumont Dr					
800	NPVL	60540	3140	29W-7S	C7
800	NPVL	60540	3202	29W-7S	C1
Beaumont Ln					
10	LMBD	60148	3084	20W-2S	A3
10	YkTp	60148	3084	20W-2S	A3
200	PltT	60010	2751	23W-18N	E3
Beaumont Pl					
1900	NHBK	60062	2757	9W-16N	B7
Beauport Dr					
2300	NPVL	60564	3202	29W-10S	D5
Beaupre Ct					
1400	HDPK	60035	2704	8W-21N	D7
Beau Ridge Ct					
700	AURA	60506	3137	36W-5S	E3
Beau Ridge Dr					
700	AURA	60506	3137	36W-5S	E3
Beauteau St					
100	LKZH	60047	2698	23W-23N	E3
Beauwick Dr					
100	OswT	60538	3199	36W-10S	E6
Beaver Cross					
100	OSWG	60543	3263	38W-11S	A2
Beaver Ct					
400	OSWG	60543	3263	38W-11S	A2
600	NPVL	60563	3140	28W-6S	E4
800	CmpT	60175	2961	43W-5N	B1
S Beaver Ct					
13600	HMGN	60491	3343	16W-16S	E3
Beaver Dr					
400	SMWD	60107	2857	28W-10N	B6
700	NPVL	60563	3140	28W-5S	E4
Beaver Ln					
300	CmpT	60175	2961	43W-5N	B1
900	GNVW	60025	2811	6W-13N	C6
Beaver Rd					
600	GNVW	60025	2811	6W-13N	C7
7600	MchT	60097	2469	36W-35N	D6
7600	WRLK	60097	2469	36W-35N	D6
Beaver St					
100	YKVL	60560	3333	43W-16S	C4
Beaver Creek Ct					
10	BGBK	60490	3267	26W-11S	D2
19300	MKNA	60448	3502	15W-23S	C3
Beaver Creek Dr					
100	BGBK	60490	3267	26W-11S	D1
N Beaver Creek Dr					
2100	VNHL	60061	2591	17W-27N	C7
2100	VNHL	60061	2647	17W-27N	C1
Beaver Creek Ln					
19200	MKNA	60448	3502	15W-23S	C3
Beaver Dam Ln					
14000	HTLY	60140	2744	43W-19N	A2
14000	HTLY	60142	2744	43W-19N	A2
Beaver Dam Rd					
6200	MTSN	60443	3505	7W-24S	C6
W Beaver Den Tr					
-	HMGN	60491	3422	15W-19S	A2
W Beaver Lake Dr					
12800	HMGN	60491	3344	16W-16S	A3
12800	HmrT	60491	3344	16W-16S	A3
13000	HMGN	60491	3343	16W-16S	E3
Beaver Pond Ct					
9200	LKWD	60014	2639	38W-24N	A6
Beaver Pond Dr					
900	MRGO	60152	2634	49W-27N	C1
Beaver Pond Pl					
900	MRGO	60152	2634	49W-27N	C1
Beaver Pond Rd					
1600	IVNS	60067	2805	23W-15N	A1
Beaver Run Dr					
3900	KLDR	60047	2699	21W-22N	E5
3900	LGGV	60047	2699	20W-22N	E5
3900	LGGV	60047	2700	20W-22N	A4
Beck Av					
100	SEGN	60177	2908	34W-9N	D1
Beck Ln					
4400	MchT	60072	2470	33W-36N	E4
4400	RGWD	60072	2470	33W-36N	E4
S Beck Pl					
8700	HMTN	60456	3212	5W-10S	B4
Beck Rd					
5900	CmgT	60033	2405	53W-37N	A7
5900	DhmT	60033	2405	53W-37N	A7
5900	DhmT	60033	2463	53W-37N	A1
E Beck Rd					
2300	LNHT	60046	2418	20W-38N	B7

Block	City	ZIP	Map#	CGS	Grid
N Beck Rd					
10	LNHT	60046	2476	19W-38N	B1
600	LNHT	60046	2418	20W-39N	B4
800	LkvT	60046	2418	20W-39N	B4
39500	AntT	60002	2418	20W-39N	B4
39500	AntT	60046	2418	20W-39N	B4
S Beck Rd					
10	LNHT	60046	2476	20W-37N	B1
Becker Av					
1400	BTVA	60510	3078	33W-2S	E4
Becker Ct					
1700	CLLK	60014	2693	36W-22N	E3
Becker Ln					
900	AraT	60505	3138	33W-6S	E4
900	AURA	60505	3138	33W-6S	E4
Becker Rd					
800	GNVW	60025	2811	7W-14N	B4
E Becker St					
600	HMND	46320	3352		E7
Becker Ter					
18600	CCHL	60478	3506	6W-22S	A1
Becket Av					
2900	WSTR	60154	3086	13W-2S	E4
3000	PvsT	60558	3086	13W-2S	E4
3000	WSTR	60558	3086	13W-2S	E4
Becket Ct					
10100	MKNA	60448	3503	12W-23S	C3
Becket Ln					
3500	NPVL	60564	3266	28W-11S	E1
3500	NPVL	60564	3267	28W-11S	A1
Beckett Cir					
1300	SMBG	60173	2859	22W-10N	D5
Beckett Ln					
1300	SMBG	60173	2859	21W-10N	E5
Beckett Crossing Dr					
400	MDLN	60060	2646	20W-26N	B2
900	FmtT	60060	2646	20W-26N	B2
Becking Av					
300	WDSK	60098	2524	42W-31N	C7
Beckman Ln					
1200	BTVA	60510	3078	34W-2S	E4
1200	BtvT	60510	3078	34W-2S	E4
Beckman Tr					
10	ElgT	60124	2907	38W-9N	B1
100	ElgT	60124	2853	38W-9N	B7
Beckwith Ct					
1800	JLET	60586	3416	29W-21S	D7
2800	NHBK	60062	2756	11W-17N	E5
Beckwith Ln					
3400	CRTE	60417	3597	0E-28S	A6
3400	STGR	60475	3597	0E-28S	A6
Beckwith Rd					
6400	MNGV	60053	2865	7W-11N	A2
6700	MNGV	60053	2864	8W-11N	D2
7900	NLES	60053	2864	8W-11N	D2
7900	NLES	60714	2864	8W-11N	D2
Beckwith St					
200	AURA	60505	3139	33W-7S	A7
400	AraT	60505	3139	33W-7S	A6
500	AraT	60504	3139	33W-7S	A6
Becky Av					
300	WMTN	60481	3943	27W-39S	C2
Becky Ct					
14800	OKFT	60452	3348	6W-17S	A5
Becky Lee Trc					
11600	HTLY	60142	2745	40W-20N	A1
Bede Cir					
500	NARA	60542	3078	35W-3S	C6
Bede Ct					
100	NARA	60542	3078	35W-3S	C6
Bedford Av					
10	SRGV	60554	3135	42W-7S	D7
Bedford Ct					
10	ALGN	60102	2694	35W-21N	A6
10	HNWD	60047	2699	21W-23N	C2
10	LNSH	60069	2702	13W-21N	D5
200	WNVL	60555	3080	30W-2S	B3
300	PKCY	60085	2535	13W-34N	E2
400	NPVL	60540	3142	25W-7S	B6
800	SMBG	60193	2912	24W-9N	D1
900	BFGV	60089	2701	18W-21N	A7
1000	ELGN	60120	2855	32W-12N	C2
1900	WHTN	60187	3082	25W-2S	B4
5700	HRPK	60133	2911	26W-7N	E5
Bedford Dr					
10	VNHL	60061	2647	16W-25N	C5
600	CLLK	60014	2639	36W-24N	D7
1000	BmdT	60188	2967	26W-4N	E4
1000	CLSM	60188	2967	26W-4N	E4
5000	JLET	60586	3416	30W-21S	C7
9200	WDRG	60517	3206	20W-11S	B7
9600	HTLY	60142	2692	38W-22N	D4
9700	HTLY	60156	2692	38W-22N	D4
W Bedford Dr					
1100	PLTN	60067	2805	22W-15N	B2
Bedford Ln					
200	BMDL	60108	2969	22W-4N	C3
200	WNVL	60555	3080	30W-2S	B3
300	BGBK	60440	3205	22W-11S	C7
300	BGBK	60440	3269	22W-11S	C1
500	DSPN	60016	2862	14W-11N	C3
600	WNFD	60190	3023	27W-0N	C4
800	LYVL	60048	2591	17W-28N	B7
2300	DRN	60561	3206	19W-8S	D2
4100	AURA	60564	3202	30W-9S	B4
9200	ODPK	60462	3345	11W-18S	E7
17000	TYPK	60477	3424	9W-20S	D4
19500	MKNA	60448	3503	12W-23S	C3
N Bedford Ln					
10	GNVA	60134	3019	36W-1N	E3
S Bedford Ln					
10	GNVA	60134	3019	38W-1N	B3
Bedford Rd					
10	MDLN	60060	2647	17W-27N	A1
1600	HFET	60169	2858	24W-12N	D1
Bedford St					
-	WSTR	60154	3086	13W-2S	E4
-	WSTR	60154	3087	13W-2S	A4
-	WSTR	60525	3087	13W-2S	A4
Bedfordshire Dr					
-	LGGV	60047	2647	18W-24N	A7
-	LGGV	60047	2701	18W-23N	A1
Bedlington Cir					
23800	DRPK	60010	2698	23W-21N	D5
Bedlington Dr					
1500	IVNS	60010	2751	24W-17N	D5
Bednarcik Ct					
10	OSWG	60543	3263	37W-12S	D3
Bee Ct					
200	CRY	60013	2695	31W-23N	C2
Beebe Ct					
400	SMWD	60107	2911	28W-9N	A1
Beebe Dr					
-	NPVL	60540	3202	29W-8S	C2
-	NPVL	60564	3202	29W-8S	C2
-	NpvT	60564	3202	29W-8S	C2
Beech Av					
-	WLMT	60091	2811	6W-13N	D6
10	WKGN	60087	2480	10W-36N	B4
6000	DrrT	60014	2638	38W-26N	E3
6000	GfnT	60014	2638	38W-25N	E4
9800	LKWD	60014	2638	38W-26N	E3
E Beech Av					
10	WDSK	60098	2524	41W-32N	D5
W Beech Av					
200	WDSK	60098	2524	41W-32N	C5
Beech Ct					
300	CLSM	60188	2968	26W-4N	A4
300	NPVL	60540	3141	28W-6S	A6
300	WynT	60185	2966	29W-3N	D5
W Beech Ct					
300	SMBG	60193	2859	23W-10N	A6
Beech Dr					
10	ElaT	60047	2698	24W-23N	B3
10	LKZH	60047	2698	24W-23N	B3
200	GNVW	60025	2811	6W-13N	C6
300	WLNG	60090	2755	13W-17N	E5
800	BGBK	60440	3268	24W-12S	C3
800	ELGN	60120	2856	31W-10N	A6
E Beech Dr					
10	SMBG	60193	2859	23W-10N	B6
W Beech Dr					
10	SMBG	60193	2859	22W-9N	C7
200	SMBG	60193	2858	23W-10N	E6
Beech Ln					
500	NLNX	60451	3501	18W-25S	A7
1100	HDPK	60035	2705	7W-21N	A6
6500	GRNE	60048	2534	16W-32N	C5
N Beech Rd					
1700	MPPT	60056	2808	13W-15N	E2
Beech St					
-	ISLK	60042	2586	28W-28N	D7
-	WcnT	60042	2586	28W-28N	D7
100	HDPK	60035	2705	7W-21N	A6
200	WLSP	60480	3209	12W-9S	B4
300	PlsT	60480	3209	12W-9S	C4
1500	SPGV	60081	2414	30W-38N	A6
3600	FSMR	60422	3506	4W-22S	D2
14500	ODPK	60462	3345	11W-17S	E5
N Beech St					
27500	WcnT	60042	2586	28W-27N	E7
27500	WcnT	60042	2642	28W-27N	E1
27800	ISLK	60042	2586	28W-27N	E7
Beechcraft Dr					
100	NLNX	60451	3501	18W-25S	A7
Beechcraft Ln					
-	CLLK	60012	2640	34W-26N	C2
Beecher Av					
500	WNFD	60190	3023	27W-0S	B6
700	WnfT	60190	3023	27W-0S	B6
1400	WHTN	60187	3024	25W-0S	A6
Beecher Rd					
-	BtlT	60512	3260	44W-11S	E2
2000	BtlT	60545	3260	44W-12S	E4
2000	BtlT	60560	3260	44W-12S	E4
2000	YKVL	60545	3260	44W-12S	E4
2000	YKVL	60560	3260	44W-12S	E4
E Beecher Rd					
1000	BtlT	60512	3197	43W-10S	A7
1000	BtlT	60512	3260	44W-11S	E1
1000	BtlT	60512	3261	43W-11S	A1
1000	BtlT	60545	3260	44W-11S	E1
1000	BtlT	60545	3261	43W-11S	A1
W Beecher Rd					
1000	BtlT	60512	3196	44W-10S	E7
1000	BtlT	60512	3260	44W-11S	E1
1000	BtlT	60545	3196	44W-10S	E7
1000	BtlT	60545	3260	44W-11S	E1
4900	WllT	60468	3861	7W-36S	C2
6500	PTON	60468	3861	7W-36S	C2
6900	PtnT	60468	3861	8W-37S	A2
Beecher St					
100	WNFD	60190	3023	27W-0S	C6
W Beecher St					
200	YKVL	60560	3333	43W-15S	B3
Beechmont Ct					
10	SMBG	60193	2857	27W-10N	C5
Beechnut Av					
600	WKGN	60085	2536	12W-33N	B4
Beechnut Dr					
10	SBTN	60010	2803	27W-15N	B2
1700	HHLL	60051	2586	30W-29N	A3
19300	FftT	60448	3503	11W-23S	E3
19300	MKNA	60448	3503	11W-23S	E3
Beechnut Ln					
7000	DRN	60561	3145	17W-8S	B7
7100	DRN	60561	3207	17W-8S	B1
Beechnut Rd					
1800	NfdT	60062	2757	10W-18N	B3
2000	DRFD	60062	2757	10W-18N	B3
8700	HYHL	60457	3209	11W-10S	E4
9000	HYHL	60480	3209	11W-10S	E4
9000	PlsT	60480	3209	11W-10S	E4
Beechtree Ln					
800	BRLT	60103	2910	29W-6N	D7
Beechwood Av					
1800	GRNE	60031	2478	15W-36N	A5
1900	KLWH	60043	2812	4W-14N	C4
1900	WLMT	60091	2812	4W-14N	C4
N Beechwood Av					
38500	AntT	60081	2415	28W-38N	A7
38500	FXLK	60020	2415	28W-38N	A7
Beechwood Ct					
-	DRGV	60516	3144	18W-7S	E6
-	LKPT	60432	3420	20W-21S	B7
300	WHTN	60187	3082	25W-2S	A4
1200	SMBG	60193	2859	21W-10N	D5
21100	FmtT	60060	2645	21W-27N	D1
21100	MDLN	60060	2645	21W-27N	D1
E Beechwood Ct					
10	BFGV	60089	2754	17W-18N	B3
W Beechwood Ct					
10	BFGV	60089	2754	17W-18N	A3
Beechwood Dr					
100	MNKA	60447	3583	33W-28S	C7
200	MNKA	60447	3672	33W-28S	C1
300	RMVL	60446	3269	23W-14S	A6
400	WTMT	60559	3144	18W-6S	E5
500	RDLK	60073	2532	23W-34N	A2
500	RLKP	60073	2532	23W-34N	A2
S Beechwood Dr					
1000	MPPT	60056	2861	16W-11N	D3
Beechwood Ln					
-	LNHT	60046	2476	19W-37N	C2
300	MltT	60137	3083	22W-2S	B4
1400	GRNE	60031	2478	15W-36N	A5
Beechwood Rd					
500	BFGV	60089	2754	17W-18N	A3
600	LKZH	60047	2699	22W-22N	A4
1000	ANHT	60004	2754	18W-18N	A3
1000	BFGV	60004	2754	18W-18N	A3
5900	MTSN	60443	3505	7W-24S	C5
E Beechwood Rd					
2200	JLET	60432	3500	21W-22S	A2
Beed Av					
-	ELBN	60119	3017	42W-0N	C5
Beeline Dr					
100	BNVL	60106	2915	16W-6N	E6
100	CHCG	60106	2915	16W-6N	E6
Beels Ct					
1600	BTVA	60510	3078	34W-2S	E4
Beethoven Ct					
100	WHTN	60187	3082	24W-2S	C4
Beggs Ln					
600	MRGO	60152	2634	50W-26N	A2
Begonia Ct					
15400	ODPK	60462	3346	9W-18S	E7
Begonia Dr					
10	MTSN	60443	3593	7W-26S	C2
Behan Rd					
1100	NndT	60014	2642	30W-27N	A1
1300	NndT	60014	2641	31W-27N	E1
2300	PRGV	60014	2641	31W-27N	D1
Behles Wy					
100	WYNE	60184	2965	33W-5N	B1
Behm Dr					
300	GYLK	60030	2532	21W-33N	D3
Behrens St					
800	YKVL	60560	3333	42W-15S	D2
Behrns Dr					
2900	LydT	60164	2972	14W-3N	C4
Behrs Cir Dr E					
500	WNVL	60555	3081	28W-3S	A6
Behrs Cir Dr S					
300	WNVL	60555	3081	28W-3S	A6
Behrs Cir Dr W					
500	WNVL	60555	3081	28W-3S	A6
Beinlich Ct					
1000	GLNC	60022	2758	7W-18N	B4
Beinoris Dr					
100	WDDL	60191	2915	17W-6N	B5
Beiriger Dr					
10	DYR	46311	3598		C4
Beisner Rd					
800	EGvT	60007	2914	19W-9N	B1
800	EGVV	60007	2914	19W-8N	B1
Beith Rd					
10	CmpT	60119	2961	43W-3N	B6
10	CmpT	60119	2962	41W-3N	A7
10	CmpT	60119	3018	41W-2N	A2
10	CmpT	60151	2961	43W-3N	B6
Belair Ct					
100	DGvT	60561	3207	18W-8S	A1
600	CLSM	60188	2968	25W-3N	A6
Bel Air Dr					
300	GNVW	60025	2864	9W-12N	C1
400	GNVW	60025	2810	9W-12N	C7
Belair Dr					
800	DRN	60561	3207	17W-8S	B1
Bel Aire Ct					
10	BRRG	60527	3208	15W-10S	B5
Belaire Ct					
10	BFGV	60089	2754	17W-18N	B3
900	NPVL	60563	3141	27W-5S	B3
E Bel Aire Dr					
2600	ANHT	60004	2807	16W-14N	D5
W Bel Aire Ln					
600	MPPT	60056	2861	16W-11N	E3
Belaire Rd					
100	BFGV	60089	2754	17W-18N	B3
N Bel Aire Ter					
500	PLTN	60074	2753	20W-16N	B6
Belcourt Ln					
1700	BRLT	60103	2856	31W-9N	A7
1700	ELGN	60103	2856	31W-9N	A7
Belden Av					
10	BmdT	60148	2970	21W-2N	A6
200	BmdT	60137	2969	23W-2N	A7
200	BmdT	60139	2969	23W-2N	A7
200	BmdT	60148	2969	21W-2N	E7
200	GLHT	60137	2969	23W-2N	A7
200	GLHT	60139	2969	23W-2N	A7
1000	ADSN	60181	2971	18W-2N	A7
1000	VLPK	60181	2971	18W-2N	A7
5100	DRGV	60515	3144	19W-5S	D2
9100	FNPK	60131	2973	11W-2N	D6
9600	FNPK	60164	2973	12W-2N	C6
9600	LydT	60164	2973	12W-2N	C6
E Belden Av					
100	EMHT	60126	2971	16W-3N	E6
100	EMHT	60126	2972	15W-2N	A6
300	AddT	60126	2972	15W-2N	A6
W Belden Av					
-	FNPK	60171	2973	11W-2N	D6
-	RVGV	60171	2973	11W-2N	E6
100	VLPK	60181	2971	18W-2N	A7
300	CHCG	60614	2978	0W-2N	A6
400	ADSN	60101	2970	19W-2N	D7
400	EMHT	60126	2971	17W-2N	C6
500	EMHT	60101	2971	17W-2N	C6
700	AddT	60101	2970	19W-2N	C7
800	CHCG	60614	2977	1W-2N	D6
2400	CHCG	60647	2977	3W-2N	A6
2800	CHCG	60647	2976	3W-2N	E6
3900	CHCG	60639	2976	4W-2N	B6
6400	CHCG	60639	2975	8W-2N	A6
6400	CHCG	60707	2975	8W-2N	A6
7200	CHCG	60707	2974	9W-2N	D6
7200	EDPK	60707	2974	9W-2N	C6
8600	RVGV	60171	2974	10W-2N	A6
27600	AntT	60081	2415	27W-38N	A7
Belden Dr					
500	DYR	46311	3598		D1
Belden Pl					
200	MNSR	46321	3430		D6
N Belden St					
1200	MHRY	60050	2585	32W-30N	A1
S Belden St					
1300	MHRY	60050	2585	32W-30N	A1
W Belden St					
4000	CHCG	60639	2976	5W-2N	B6
4000	CHCG	60647	2976	5W-2N	B6
4700	CHCG	60639	2975	6W-2N	D6
Belden Wy					
1000	JLET	60435	3497	26W-22S	E2
Beldon Ct					
2000	JLET	60586	3415	33W-21S	B7
Belfast Ter					
500	CRTE	60417	3596	0E-28S	E6
500	CRTE	60417	3597	0E-28S	A6
Belfield Rd					
-	CLLK	60014	2693	37W-23N	B1
-	GfnT	60014	2693	37W-23N	B1
8600	LKWD	60014	2693	37W-23N	A1
Belford Ln					
10	RGMW	60008	2805	23W-12N	B7
Believers Wy					
900	MTSN	60443	3505	6W-25S	E7
900	MTSN	60443	3506	6W-25S	A7
Belinder Ln					
-	RGMW	60008	2805	21W-13N	C6
600	SMBG	60008	2805	21W-13N	C5
800	SMBG	60173	2805	21W-13N	C6
Bell Av					
800	LGNG	60525	3087	13W-4S	A6
1400	LbvT	60048	2591	17W-30N	B2
1400	WNSP	60525	3087	13W-4S	A6
1400	WNSP	60558	3087	13W-4S	A6
1700	LYVL	60048	2591	17W-30N	B2
N Bell Av					
300	CHCG	60612	3033	2W-0N	B4
1300	CHCG	60622	3033	2W-1N	B1
1500	CHCG	60647	3033	2W-1N	B1
2100	CHCG	60647	2977	2W-2N	B6
3300	CHCG	60618	2977	2W-4N	B3
5300	CHCG	60625	2921	2W-6N	B5
6200	CHCG	60659	2921	2W-7N	B3
6800	CHCG	60645	2921	2W-8N	B1
7500	CHCG	60202	2867	2W-9N	B7
7500	CHCG	60645	2867	2W-9N	B7
7500	EVTN	60202	2867	2W-9N	B7
S Bell Av					
100	CHCG	60612	3033	2W-0S	B5
1300	CHCG	60608	3033	2W-1S	B7
2200	CHCG	60608	3091	2W-2S	B2
4000	CHCG	60609	3091	2W-4S	B6
6300	CHCG	60636	3151	2W-7S	B5
8900	CHCG	60620	3213	2W-11S	B6
9500	CHCG	60643	3213	2W-11S	B6
11500	CHCG	60643	3277	2W-13S	C4
11800	BLID	60406	3277	2W-13S	C5
11800	BLID	60643	3277	2W-13S	C5
Bell Ct					
100	OSWG	60543	3263	37W-12S	D4
Bell Dr					
-	AlqT	60013	2696	30W-23N	A1
100	CRY	60013	2695	30W-23N	E1
100	CRY	60013	2696	30W-23N	A1
400	DSPN	60016	2862	15W-11N	A3
400	LslT	60565	3204	25W-8S	B2
400	NPVL	60565	3204	25W-8S	B2
1700	HRPK	60133	2967	27W-5N	D1
Bell Ln					
800	WNKA	60093	2758	6W-16N	E7
4400	HRPK	60133	2967	27W-5N	D2
Bell Rd					
-	LMNT	60439	3272	16W-12S	A3
-	LmnT	60480	3272	15W-12S	A2
100	SwdT	60447	3583	33W-25S	A1
100	TroT	60404	3583	33W-25S	C1
12700	LmnT	60439	3344	16W-15S	A2
13100	HMGN	60491	3344	15W-15S	A2
13100	HmrT	60491	3344	15W-15S	A2
N Bell Rd					
-	CNHN	60410	3672	33W-30S	C4
9900	AxST	60447	3672	33W-30S	C4
9900	CnhT	60410	3672	32W-30S	C3
9900	MNKA	60447	3672	32W-29S	C3
24800	AxST	60410	3672	32W-30S	C3
24800	CNHN	60447	3672	33W-30S	C4
24800	MNKA	60410	3672	32W-30S	C4
S Bell Rd					
-	AxST	60447	3672	32W-31S	C6
-	CNHN	60410	3672	32W-31S	C6
-	CNHN	60447	3672	32W-31S	C6
13500	HMGN	60491	3344	16W-16S	A3
13500	HmrT	60491	3344	16W-16S	A3
13500	LMNT	60439	3344	15W-16S	A3
15900	HMGN	60491	3422	15W-20S	B3
Bella Ct					
3000	LSLE	60563	3142	25W-5S	C3
3000	LslT	60563	3142	25W-5S	C3
Bella Ln					
12500	LMNT	60439	3271	17W-14S	C7
Bellagio Cir					
18400	TYPK	60477	3425	8W-22S	A7
18400	TYPK	60477	3505	8W-22S	A1
Bellair Ln					
1900	WDSK	60098	2524	41W-32N	D4
Bellair St					
10	DXMR	60426	3349	1W-17S	E4
10	HRVY	60426	3349	1W-17S	E4
Bellaire Av					
300	DSPN	60016	2863	12W-11N	C3
300	MaiT	60016	2863	12W-11N	C3
Bellaire Ct					
2300	DSPN	60016	2863	12W-11N	B2
Bellaire Rd					
5100	OKFT	60452	3425	6W-20S	E3
5100	OKFT	60452	3426	6W-20S	A3
Bellar Ct					
400	NARA	60542	3078	35W-3S	B6
E Bellarmine Dr					
400	JLET	60436	3498	26W-24S	A6
W Bellarmine Dr					
400	JLET	60436	3498	26W-24S	A6
Bellarny Rd					
-	CCHL	60478	3506	6W-22S	A1
Bellavista Pkwy					
28500	NPVL	60563	3081	27W-4S	B7
28500	WNVL	60555	3081	27W-4S	B7
28500	WNVL	60563	3081	27W-4S	B7
Belle Av					
10	ELGN	60123	2854	34W-12N	D1
100	HDPK	60035	2705	8W-22N	A4
900	JLET	60432	3499	22W-22S	C3
900	JltT	60432	3499	22W-22S	C3
E Belle Av					
900	JLET	60432	3499	22W-22S	C2
900	JltT	60432	3499	22W-22S	C2
N Belle Av					
1000	JLET	60432	3499	22W-22S	C2
S Belle Av					
10	PLTN	60074	2806	19W-15N	C1
Belle Ct					
300	GYLK	60030	2532	21W-32N	D4
500	HRVY	60426	3350	0W-18S	B7
600	PHNX	60426	3350	0W-18S	B7
Belle Dr					
10	NHLK	60164	2972	13W-2N	E7
300	MLPK	60160	2973	13W-2N	A7
300	MLPK	60164	2973	13W-2N	A7
300	NHLK	60164	2973	13W-2N	A7
Belle Ln					
10	SEGN	60177	2908	34W-9N	D2
2800	SMBG	60193	2857	27W-10N	D6
S Belle Ln					
23000	CNHN	60410	3584	29W-27S	E6
Belle St					
17000	OKFT	60452	3425	6W-20S	E4
Belleaire Dr					
3800	DRGV	60515	3084	20W-4S	B6
Belleaire Ln					
3900	DRGV	60515	3084	20W-4S	B7
Belleau Dr					
10	WnfT	60190	3081	28W-1S	B1
Belleau Woods Ct					
1400	WHTN	60187	3081	26W-1S	D2
3000	JLET	60435	3417	27W-21S	C6
Belleau Woods Dr					
2100	WHTN	60187	3081	26W-1S	D2
2100	WnfT	60187	3081	26W-1S	D2
2800	JLET	60435	3417	27W-21S	C6
Bellechase Cir					
10	SMBG	60173	2859	21W-10N	D4
Bellechase Dr					
1500	NlxT	60451	3589	17W-26S	D3
Belle Foret Dr					
300	LKBF	60044	2593	11W-29N	C4
N Belle Foret Dr					
-	NptT	60083	2420	14W-40N	C3
-	WDWH	60083	2420	14W-40N	C3
N Bellefort Pl					
8500	NLES	60714	2864	8W-10N	E4
Belleforte Av					
8800	NLES	60714	2864	8W-11N	E3
9100	MNGV	60053	2864	8W-11N	E3
Belleforte Av N					
1200	CHCG	60302	3030	8W-1N	E1
1200	CHCG	60707	3030	8W-2N	E1
1200	OKPK	60302	3030	8W-1N	E1
Belle Haven Dr					
1300	GYLK	60030	2475	20W-34N	E7
1300	GYLK	60030	2532	21W-34N	D1
Belle Isle Ln					
800	VNHL	60061	2647	18W-25N	A6
Belle Plaine Av					
-	CHCG	60631	2918	10W-8N	A2
-	PKRG	60631	2918	10W-8N	A2
-	SRPK	60176	2973	12W-5N	C2
10	PKRG	60068	2918	10W-8N	A2
1400	PKRG	60068	2917	11W-8N	E2
10200	FNPK	60131	2973	12W-5N	A2
10200	SRPK	60131	2973	12W-5N	A2
N Belle Plaine Av					
37000	BHPK	60031	2479	13W-37N	A3
37000	BHPK	60087	2479	13W-37N	A3
37000	WrnT	60031	2479	13W-37N	A3
37000	WrnT	60087	2479	13W-37N	A3
W Belle Plaine Av					
800	CHCG	60613	2977	1W-5N	E1
2000	CHCG	60618	2977	3W-5N	A1
2800	CHCG	60618	2976	4W-5N	C1
4600	CHCG	60641	2976	5W-5N	A1
5600	CHCG	60641	2975	7W-5N	C1
6200	CHCG	60634	2975	7W-5N	B1
7300	NRDG	60706	2974	9W-5N	C1
7700	NRDG	60634	2974	9W-5N	C1
8200	CHCG	60634	2974	10W-5N	A1
Belleplaine Dr					
16400	MKHM	60428	3426	4W-19S	E3
N Belle Plaine Rd					
36700	WKGN	60087	2479	13W-36N	A3
36700	WrnT	60087	2479	13W-36N	A3
Belle Plaine St					
300	GRNE	60031	2536	13W-34N	A1
500	GRNE	60031	2479	13W-34N	A7
Beller Ct					
8500	DRN	60561	3206	20W-9S	B4
Beller Dr					
-	DGvT	60516	3206	20W-9S	C4
-	DGvT	60561	3206	20W-9S	C4
2800	DRN	60561	3206	20W-9S	A4
8300	DRN	60517	3206	20W-9S	A4
8300	WDRG	60517	3206	20W-9S	A4
Beller Rd					
1800	WDRG	60517	3206	20W-9S	A3
8200	DGvT	60516	3206	20W-9S	A3
8200	DRN	60517	3206	20W-9S	A3
8200	DRN	60561	3206	20W-9S	A3
8200	WDRG	60516	3206	20W-9S	A3
Belle Rive Ct					
7800	TYPK	60477	3424	9W-20S	D5
Belleview Av					
900	JLET	60436	3498	26W-25S	A7
900	RKDL	60436	3498	26W-25S	A7
1600	WSTR	60154	3087	13W-1S	A2
Belleview Ln					
100	BTVA	60510	3078	35W-2S	C4
Bellevue Av					
700	ELGN	60120	2855	33W-12N	A1
7900	BtnT	60081	2414	30W-39N	A4
7900	SPGV	60081	2414	30W-39N	A4
Bellevue Cir					
700	OSWG	60543	3200	34W-11S	C7
Bellevue Dr					
100	RLKP	60073	2532	22W-33N	B3
Belle Vue Ln					
200	SRGV	60554	3135	42W-6S	D4
Bellevue Pl					
500	HDPK	60035	2705	7W-20N	A7
2200	NHBK	60062	2757	10W-16N	A7
E Bellevue Pl					
10	CHCG	60610	3034	0E-1N	C2
10	CHCG	60611	3034	0E-1N	C2
Bellflower Cir					
1700	GRNE	60048	2534	17W-32N	C6
Bellflower Ln					
700	BGBK	60440	3268	24W-12S	C3
1400	JLET	60447	3495	33W-22S	A1
11200	HTLY	60142	2691	41W-20N	D7
Bellingham Ct					
2300	AURA	60503	3201	33W-10S	B7
Bellingham Dr					
200	BRTN	60010	2751	24W-18N	C2
Bellingham Ln					
200	BRLT	60103	2910	30W-8N	C3
200	HnrT	60103	2910	30W-8N	C3
2200	AURA	60503	3201	32W-10S	B6
Bellingrath Ct					
800	NPVL	60563	3141	26W-6S	E4
E Bello Cir					
1300	LKPT	60441	3420	21W-20S	A4
1300	LktT	60441	3420	21W-20S	A4
S Bello Dr					
1400	LKPT	60441	3420	21W-20S	A4
Bell Oak Ln					
10	LMNT	60439	3272	15W-14S	A5
Bellview Av					
400	WCHI	60185	3022	29W-1N	C3
Bellview Ct					
2200	GRNE	60031	2478	15W-36N	A4
Bellwood Av					
-	WSTR	60154	3029	12W-0S	B6
10	BLWD	60104	3029	12W-0S	B5
400	HLSD	60162	3029	13W-0N	A5
2700	LydT	60164	2972	13W-3N	E5
2800	FNPK	60131	2972	13W-3N	E5

Chicago 7-County Street Index

STREET Block	City	ZIP	Map#	CGS	Grid
Bellwood Av					
2800	FNPK	60164	2972	13W-3N	E5
Bellwood Dr					
10	BNHL	60010	2750	28W-20N	A2
Bellwood Ln					
3300	GNVW	60025	2810	10W-14N	A5
3400	GNVW	60025	2809	10W-14N	E5
Belmar Ct					
10	BFGV	60089	2701	17W-21N	B6
Belmar Ln					
800	BFGV	60089	2701	17W-21N	A6
Belmont Av					
100	LKVL	60046	2475	22W-37N	A1
300	AddT	60106	2971	17W-4N	B4
1600	JLET	60432	3499	21W-23S	E3
1600	JltT	60432	3499	21W-23S	E3
2000	JLET	60432	3500	21W-23S	A3
10500	FNPK	60131	2972	13W-4N	E4
10500	FNPK	60131	2973	13W-4N	A4
10700	FNPK	60164	2972	13W-3N	E4
10800	LydT	60164	2972	13W-4N	E4
11000	LydT	60131	2972	13W-4N	D4
E Belmont Av					
400	AddT	60101	2971	17W-3N	B4
400	ADSN	60101	2971	17W-3N	B4
700	AddT	60106	2971	17W-3N	B4
800	AddT	60106	2972	15W-3N	B4
800	AddT	60126	2972	15W-3N	B4
800	BNVL	60106	2972	15W-3N	B4
800	FNPK	60131	2972	15W-3N	B4
N Belmont Av					
10	ANHT	60004	2807	17W-14N	B3
10	ELGN	60123	2854	36W-11N	A4
S Belmont Av					
10	ANHT	60004	2807	17W-14N	B5
10	ELGN	60123	2854	36W-11N	A5
100	ANHT	60005	2807	17W-13N	B5
700	ElgT	60123	2854	36W-10N	A5
1200	ANHT	60005	2861	17W-12N	B1
W Belmont Av					
10	BNVL	60106	2971	16W-4N	E4
300	CHCG	60657	2978	0W-4N	A3
700	CHCG	60657	2977	2W-4N	C3
1900	CHCG	60618	2977	2W-4N	B3
2700	CHCG	60618	2976	5W-4N	A4
3900	CHCG	60641	2976	4W-4N	B4
4700	CHCG	60641	2975	7W-4N	A4
5500	CHCG	60634	2975	6W-4N	C4
6700	CHCG	60634	2974	10W-4N	B4
7100	CHCG	60707	2974	10W-4N	B4
7500	EDPK	60707	2974	9W-4N	C4
7900	EDPK	60171	2974	9W-3N	B4
8000	RVGV	60171	2974	10W-3N	B4
8000	RVGV	60634	2974	10W-3N	B4
8700	CHCG	60634	2973	11W-4N	D4
8700	RVGV	60171	2973	11W-4N	D4
8700	RVGV	60634	2973	11W-4N	D4
9000	FNPK	60171	2973	11W-3N	E4
9000	RVGV	60131	2973	11W-3N	E4
9800	FNPK	60131	2973	12W-4N	A4
Belmont Ct					
300	RLKP	60030	2589	22W-30N	B1
700	ANTH	60002	2357	24W-42N	C6
700	RMVL	60446	3340	24W-15S	D2
1000	SMBG	60193	2912	24W-8N	C2
2000	ELGN	60123	2854	36W-10N	A6
5400	WKGN	60048	2535	15W-31N	A7
N Belmont Ct					
1600	ANHT	60004	2807	17W-15N	B1
Belmont Dr					
10	DMND	60416	3941	33W-39S	B2
10	RMVL	60446	3340	24W-16S	D3
10	RMVL	60446	3341	23W-15S	A2
200	RLKP	60030	2589	22W-30N	B1
1700	GNOK	60048	2592	14W-30N	C3
E Belmont Dr					
10	RMVL	60446	3341	23W-15S	A2
S Belmont Dr					
11300	PNFD	60585	3266	30W-13S	C5
Belmont Ln					
400	BRLT	60103	2967	28W-5N	B1
500	CLSM	60188	3024	24W-1N	D3
500	WHTN	60187	3024	24W-1N	D3
S Belmont Ln					
700	ANHT	60005	2807	17W-13N	A7
Belmont Pkwy					
500	SYHW	60118	2799	36W-15N	E4
Belmont Pl					
100	AddT	60101	2970	20W-3N	A4
100	ADSN	60101	2970	20W-3N	A4
200	MNSR	46321	3430		D6
Belmont Rd					
4400	DRGV	60515	3143	21W-4S	E1
5200	LslT	60515	3143	21W-6S	E5
5500	LslT	60516	3143	21W-6S	E4
5600	DRGV	60516	3143	21W-6S	E4
22000	RNPK	60471	3594	5W-26S	B3
Belmont Rd CO-2					
4400	DRGV	60515	3143	21W-4S	E1
5200	LslT	60515	3143	21W-5S	E3
5600	DRGV	60516	3143	21W-6S	E4
5600	LslT	60516	3143	21W-6S	E4
Belmont St					
300	ELGN	60123	2854	36W-10N	A6
300	ElgT	60123	2854	36W-10N	A6
Belmont Harbor Dr					
-	CHCG	60613	2978	0W-4N	A2
Belmora Park Blvd					
38800	LKVL	60046	2416	23W-38N	E6
38800	LkvT	60046	2416	23W-38N	E6
Beloit Av					
400	FTPK	60130	3030	9W-0S	D5
7100	BGVW	60455	3148	9W-8S	D7
7300	BGVW	60455	3210	9W-8S	D1
S Beloit Av					
10800	WRTH	60482	3274	9W-12S	D2
Beloit Ct					
1800	NPVL	60565	3204	24W-9S	D3
Beloit Dr					
1700	NPVL	60565	3204	24W-9S	D3
Belom Ln					
21500	SRWD	60404	3584	30W-26S	B2
21500	TroT	60404	3584	30W-26S	B2
Belot Ln					
700	NLNX	60451	3590	15W-25S	C1
Belson Ln					
4200	AlqT	60014	2641	33W-25N	A4
S Belt Cir Dr					
6700	BDPK	60638	3148	8W-7S	E6
Belter Ct					
1800	GNVA	60134	3019	36W-0S	E6
1800	GnvT	60134	3019	36W-0S	E7
Belter Dr					
1000	WHTN	60187	3082	23W-2S	E3
Belvedere Blvd					
700	BGBK	60490	3267	26W-13S	D5
Belvedere Ln					
400	AURA	60502	3139	31W-7S	E7
400	AURA	60504	3139	31W-7S	E7
400	NpvT	60502	3139	31W-7S	E7
400	NpvT	60504	3139	31W-7S	E7
Belvidere Av					
100	FTPK	60130	3030	9W-0N	D4
Belvidere Pk					
-	WKGN	60085	2536	11W-33N	D3
Belvidere Rd					
-	AvnT	60030	2531	24W-32N	B5
-	AvnT	60073	2531	24W-32N	B5
-	GRNE	60031	2535	14W-33N	D3
-	GrtT	60030	2531	24W-32N	B5
-	GrtT	60073	2530	28W-31N	A6
-	GrtT	60073	2531	24W-32N	B5
-	LKMR	60041	2530	27W-31N	A6
-	LKMR	60051	2529	28W-31N	D6
-	LKMR	60051	2530	28W-31N	A6
-	LKMR	60073	2530	27W-31N	B6
-	PKCY	60085	2535	13W-33N	E3
-	RDLK	60073	2531	24W-32N	B5
-	VOLO	60051	2530	27W-31N	A6
-	VOLO	60073	2530	28W-31N	A6
-	VOLO	60073	2531	25W-32N	A6
-	WcnT	60051	2529	28W-31N	D6
-	WcnT	60051	2530	28W-31N	A6
-	WcnT	60073	2530	27W-31N	A6
-	WKGN	60031	2535	14W-33N	D3
2900	PKCY	60085	2536	12W-33N	B3
2900	WKGN	60085	2536	12W-33N	B3
3800	WKGN	60085	2535	13W-33N	E4
Belvidere Rd SR-120					
-	AvnT	60030	2531	24W-32N	B5
-	AvnT	60073	2531	24W-32N	B5
-	GRNE	60031	2535	14W-33N	D3
-	GrtT	60030	2531	24W-32N	B5
-	GrtT	60073	2530	28W-31N	A6
-	GrtT	60073	2531	24W-32N	B5
-	LKMR	60041	2530	27W-31N	A6
-	LKMR	60051	2529	28W-31N	D6
-	LKMR	60051	2530	28W-31N	A6
-	LKMR	60073	2530	27W-31N	B6
-	PKCY	60085	2535	13W-33N	E3
-	RDLK	60073	2531	24W-32N	B5
-	VOLO	60051	2530	27W-31N	A6
-	VOLO	60073	2530	28W-31N	A6
-	VOLO	60073	2531	25W-32N	A6
-	WcnT	60051	2529	28W-31N	D6
-	WcnT	60051	2530	28W-31N	A6
-	WcnT	60073	2530	27W-31N	A6
-	WKGN	60031	2535	14W-33N	D3
2900	PKCY	60085	2536	12W-33N	B3
2900	WKGN	60085	2536	12W-33N	B3
3800	WKGN	60085	2535	13W-33N	E3
E Belvidere Rd					
10	GYLK	60030	2532	20W-32N	E4
10	HNVL	60030	2532	22W-33N	C4
400	GYLK	60030	2533	19W-32N	C4
700	AvnT	60030	2533	19W-32N	C4
E Belvidere Rd SR-120					
10	GYLK	60030	2532	21W-32N	E4
10	HNVL	60030	2532	22W-33N	C4
400	GYLK	60030	2533	19W-32N	C4
700	AvnT	60030	2533	19W-32N	C4
W Belvidere Rd					
-	GRNE	60031	2534	15W-33N	E4
-	GRNE	60048	2534	15W-33N	E4
-	WrnT	60031	2534	15W-33N	E4
-	WrnT	60048	2534	17W-32N	B4
-	WrnT	60048	2535	15W-33N	B4
10	HNVL	60030	2532	22W-33N	A4
10	HNVL	60073	2532	22W-33N	A4
100	RDLK	60073	2532	23W-32N	A4
100	RLKP	60030	2532	23W-32N	A4
100	RLKP	60073	2532	23W-32N	A4
200	GYLK	60030	2532	21W-32N	E4
300	AvnT	60030	2532	21W-32N	D4
700	AvnT	60030	2531	23W-32N	D4
700	AvnT	60073	2531	24W-32N	D4
700	RDLK	60073	2531	23W-32N	E4
1800	AvnT	60030	2533	18W-32N	D4
1800	GYLK	60030	2533	18W-32N	E4
2000	WrnT	60030	2533	18W-32N	E4
4200	GRNE	60031	2535	14W-33N	D3
4200	WKGN	60031	2535	14W-33N	D3
4200	WKGN	60085	2535	14W-33N	D3
4400	WrnT	60031	2535	15W-33N	A4
18000	GYLK	60030	2534	18W-32N	A4
18000	WrnT	60030	2534	18W-32N	A4
W Belvidere Rd SR-120					
-	GRNE	60031	2534	15W-33N	E4
-	GRNE	60048	2534	15W-33N	E4
-	WrnT	60031	2534	15W-33N	E4
-	WrnT	60048	2534	17W-32N	B4
-	WrnT	60048	2535	15W-33N	B4
10	GYLK	60030	2532	21W-32N	E4
10	HNVL	60030	2532	22W-33N	A4
10	HNVL	60073	2532	22W-33N	A4
100	RDLK	60073	2532	23W-32N	A4
100	RLKP	60030	2532	23W-32N	A4
100	RLKP	60073	2532	23W-32N	A4
300	AvnT	60030	2532	21W-32N	D4
700	AvnT	60030	2531	23W-32N	D4
700	AvnT	60073	2531	24W-32N	D4
700	RDLK	60073	2531	23W-32N	E4
1800	AvnT	60030	2533	18W-32N	D4
1800	GYLK	60030	2533	18W-32N	E4
2000	WrnT	60030	2533	18W-32N	E4
4200	GRNE	60031	2535	14W-33N	D3
4200	WKGN	60031	2535	14W-33N	D3
4200	WKGN	60085	2535	14W-33N	D3
4400	WrnT	60031	2535	15W-33N	A4
18000	GYLK	60030	2534	18W-32N	A4
18000	WrnT	60030	2534	18W-32N	A4
Belvidere St					
100	WKGN	60085	2537	10W-33N	A2
1000	WKGN	60085	2536	11W-33N	C3
Belvidere St SR-120					
100	WKGN	60085	2537	10W-33N	B2
2600	WKGN	60085	2536	11W-33N	C3
Belvidere Line Dr					
2000	ELGN	60123	2854	36W-12N	A1
E Bemes Rd					
300	CteT	60417	3685	0E-32S	E6
500	CteT	60417	3686	1E-32S	B7
2100	CteT	60417	3687	3E-32S	A7
3300	HnrT	46311	3687	3E-32S	A7
Bemis Rd					
500	LMBD	60137	3083	21W-1S	D2
500	LMBD	60148	3083	21W-1S	D2
500	MltT	60137	3083	21W-1S	D2
Ben Ct					
1400	WPHR	60096	2363	10W-41N	B7
N Ben St					
500	PLNO	60545	3259	47W-13S	C6
S Ben St					
10	PLNO	60545	3259	47W-14S	C7
800	LtRT	60545	3259	47W-14S	C7
Benbrook Av					
2900	NndT	60050	2585	30W-29N	E5
S Benck Dr					
12300	ALSP	60803	3276	4W-14S	D6
W Benck Dr					
3600	ALSP	60803	3276	4W-14S	D6
E Bend Dr					
3000	AlqT	60102	2695	32W-22N	C4
Bender Ln					
600	WnfT	60185	3080	29W-1S	E3
Bender Rd					
-	DSPN	60016	2863	12W-11N	C3
10	PKFT	60466	3595	2W-26S	C3
Bender St					
-	SDWH	60548	3258	51W-14S	A7
-	SdwT	60548	3258	51W-14S	A7
Bending Ct					
600	DSPN	60016	2808	13W-13N	D6
Bending Ln					
700	PltT	60124	2852	40W-9N	B7
Bending Creek Rd					
32700	LKMR	60051	2529	28W-32N	D4
E Bending Creek Tr					
2800	CteT	60417	3687	3E-30S	A3
Bending Oaks Ct					
5300	DGvT	60515	3144	20W-5S	A3
5300	DRGV	60515	3144	20W-5S	A3
Bending Oaks Pl					
5400	DGvT	60515	3144	20W-5S	A3
5400	DRGV	60515	3144	20W-5S	A3
Benedetti Dr					
800	NPVL	60563	3141	27W-5S	C4
Benedict Av					
10	JLET	60436	3497	26W-24S	E5
Benedictine Pkwy					
5800	LSLE	60532	3142	24W-6S	D5
5800	LSLE	60540	3142	24W-6S	D5
5800	LslT	60540	3142	24W-6S	D5
W Benes Rd					
26600	AntT	60002	2415	26W-38N	D7
Benet Ln					
23000	JLET	60586	3416	28W-20S	E5
23000	PnfT	60586	3416	29W-20S	E5
Bengson Ct					
500	RLKP	60073	2532	23W-33N	A3
Benham Ct					
200	SCRL	60174	2964	36W-3N	A6
Benham Dr					
1300	JLET	60431	3495	32W-22S	C2
Benich Ln					
6500	JLET	60586	3415	32W-20S	D5
Beninford Ln					
900	WTMT	60559	3145	17W-6S	B5
Bening Dr					
2100	WDRG	60517	3206	21W-9S	A3
N Benjamin Av					
35600	GrtT	60041	2473	25W-35N	E5
W Benjamin Av					
900	AntT	60081	2414	28W-38N	E7
900	FXLK	60020	2414	28W-38N	E7
900	FXLK	60081	2414	28W-38N	E7
1100	BtnT	60081	2414	28W-38N	E7
Benjamin Ct					
10	BlmT	60411	3510	3E-25S	A7
Benjamin Dr					
-	SRWD	60404	3584	30W-25S	B1
2600	MchT	60097	2526	36W-34N	D1
2700	MchT	60097	2469	36W-34N	D7
Benjamin Pl					
2000	HMND	46394	3280		E5
Benjamin Rd					
-	VNHL	60061	2648	15W-24N	A6
-	VrnT	60061	2648	15W-24N	A6
Benjamin Franklin Ct					
400	AURA	60504	3140	29W-6S	D5
Ben Levin Dr					
200	HMND	46324	3430		D3
Bennacott Ln					
400	BRRG	60527	3208	15W-9S	B4
Bennet Av					
17100	SHLD	60473	3429	2E-20S	C3
Bennett Av					
-	SKOK	60076	2866	4W-10N	D5
400	JLET	60433	3499	23W-24S	B6
500	JltT	60433	3499	23W-24S	B6
2400	EVTN	60201	2866	4W-12N	D1
2500	EVTN	60201	2812	4W-12N	D7
2700	EVTN	60091	2812	3W-13N	D7
2700	WLMT	60091	2812	3W-13N	D7
4100	GRNE	60031	2535	14W-34N	D1
8800	SKOK	60203	2866	4W-11N	D3
S Bennett Av					
400	PLTN	60067	2805	21W-15N	D3
7100	CHCG	60649	3153	2E-8S	C7
7600	CHCG	60649	3215	2E-9S	C2
7800	CHCG	60617	3215	2E-9S	C2
Bennett Ct N					
-	OSWG	60543	3265	33W-11S	A1
Bennett Ct S					
-	OSWG	60543	3265	33W-11S	A2
Bennett Dr					
-	NARA	60506	3076	39W-3S	E7
-	NARA	60510	3076	39W-3S	E7
-	PSHL	60465	3274	10W-12S	B3
-	SgrT	60506	3076	39W-3S	E7
400	NARA	60542	3076	39W-3S	E7
600	ELGN	60120	2855	32W-12N	C2
3000	NPVL	60564	3203	28W-11S	A7
Bennett Ln					
-	FXLK	60020	2473	28W-37N	A3
200	DSPN	60016	2862	15W-11N	A3
Bennett Pl					
1800	DSPN	60018	2863	12W-9N	B6
3000	AURA	60502	3139	31W-5S	E3
3000	AURA	60563	3139	31W-5S	D3
Bennett Rd					
-	MTWA	60048	2648	14W-26N	C4
-	VrnT	60045	2648	14W-26N	C4
-	VrnT	60048	2648	14W-26N	C4
300	EGvT	60007	2861	18W-10N	A5
300	EGVV	60007	2861	18W-10N	A5
N Bennett St					
10	GNVA	60134	3020	34W-1N	C3
800	SCRL	60134	3020	34W-1N	C3
800	SCRL	60174	3020	34W-1N	C3
N Bennett St SR-25					
10	GNVA	60134	3020	34W-1N	C3
800	SCRL	60134	3020	34W-1N	C3
800	SCRL	60174	3020	34W-1N	C3
S Bennett St					
10	GNVA	60134	3020	34W-1N	C4
S Bennett St SR-25					
10	GNVA	60134	3020	34W-1N	C3
Bennington Ct					
10	LMNT	60439	3271	18W-14S	A7
1300	GNVW	60025	2810	9W-13N	B5
1900	ELGN	60123	2854	36W-10N	A6
2300	NPVL	60565	3203	27W-10S	C6
7600	BLVY	60098	2526	36W-32N	C5
7600	MchT	60098	2526	36W-32N	C5
Bennington Dr					
-	CLSM	60133	2967	27W-4N	C3
-	CLSM	60188	2967	27W-4N	C3
-	HRPK	60133	2967	27W-4N	C3
800	CLLK	60014	2639	36W-24N	C7
800	CLLK	60014	2693	36W-23N	C1
6900	GRNE	60031	2477	17W-35N	B7
9600	HTLY	60142	2692	39W-22N	D4
Bennington Ln					
100	BRLT	60103	2909	31W-8N	D2
100	ELGN	60120	2909	31W-8N	D2
2400	MHRY	60050	2527	34W-34N	B1
Benny Av					
500	WKGN	60085	2536	11W-33N	E3
Benoy Ct					
8900	LKWD	60014	2639	37W-24N	A7
Benridge Ct					
800	MDLN	60060	2590	20W-28N	A6
Bensley Av					
-	LNSG	60438	3429	2E-20S	D4
200	BNHM	60409	3351	2E-17S	D5
200	BNHM	60633	3351	2E-17S	D5
200	CTCY	60409	3351	2E-17S	D5
20200	LYWD	60411	3509	2E-24S	D5
S Bensley Av					
-	CHCG	60633	3351	2E-16S	D2
9500	CHCG	60617	3215	3E-11S	D6
10300	CHCG	60617	3279	2E-11S	D1
14000	BNHM	60633	3351	2E-16S	D3
14500	BNHM	60409	3351	2E-16S	D4
14500	CTCY	60409	3351	2E-16S	D4
Benson Av					
1600	EVTN	60201	2867	2W-11N	B2
S Benson Av					
100	PNFD	60544	3416	29W-18S	D1
Benson Ct					
800	NARA	60542	3077	38W-3S	B6
1500	BTVA	60510	3078	34W-2S	E4
Benson Dr					
-	BRLT	60103	2967	28W-5N	A2
Benson Ln					
700	GNOK	60048	2592	14W-29N	B4
Benson Rd					
800	GNOK	60048	2592	14W-29N	B4
S Benson St					
3100	CHCG	60608	3091	1W-3S	D4
Bent Av					
200	SCRL	60174	2964	35W-3N	B6
Bent St					
600	ELGN	60120	2855	33W-10N	B5
Bent Creek Ct					
100	RGMW	60067	2805	21W-13N	D5
200	SMBG	60067	2805	21W-13N	D5
200	SMBG	60173	2805	21W-13N	D5
1300	NPVL	60565	3204	24W-8S	E2
Bent Creek Rdg					
10	DRFD	60015	2757	9W-20N	B1
500	DRFD	60015	2704	9W-20N	B7
Bentgrass Av					
5200	RNPK	60471	3594	6W-27S	A5
5300	RNPK	60471	3593	6W-27S	E5
Bent Grass Dr					
15100	LKPT	60441	3420	20W-20S	C5
Bent Grass Ln					
-	WDSK	60098	2582	39W-30N	C2
Bentley Av					
5500	CNHL	60514	3145	17W-6S	C4
5500	DGvT	60514	3145	17W-6S	C4
5700	WLBK	60514	3145	17W-6S	C5
5800	WLBK	60527	3145	17W-7S	C6
5900	WTMT	60527	3145	17W-6S	C5
6700	DRN	60527	3145	17W-7S	C7
6700	DRN	60561	3145	17W-7S	C7
7200	DRN	60561	3207	17W-8S	C1
Bentley Ct					
10	DRFD	60015	2756	11W-20N	E2
500	DRGV	60516	3144	19W-7S	D7
1900	GLHT	60139	2969	23W-3N	A5
2600	LSLE	60532	3142	24W-7S	C6
Bentley Dr					
6900	GRNE	60031	2477	17W-35N	B6
W Bentley Dr					
23300	JLET	60586	3416	29W-21S	E7
23300	PnfT	60586	3416	29W-21S	E7
Bentley Ln					
100	SMBG	60193	2859	23W-9N	A7
1000	BRLT	60103	2910	29W-6N	E6
8600	SPGV	60081	2414	29W-40N	C2
W Bentley Ln					
2200	RDLK	60073	2530	25W-33N	E2
2200	RDLK	60073	2531	25W-33N	B2
Bentley Pl					
300	BFGV	60089	2701	16W-21N	D7
Bentley Rd					
2600	HDPK	60035	2703	10W-23N	E3
E Bentley Rd					
700	NLNX	60451	3589	17W-25S	D1
900	NlxT	60451	3589	17W-25S	D1
S Bentley Rd					
900	NLNX	60451	3589	17W-25S	D1
Bent Oak Tr					
1300	AURA	60506	3137	37W-5S	D4
Benton Av					
100	SCHT	60411	3596	1W-27S	A4
400	LGNG	60525	3147	12W-4S	C1
5100	DRGV	60515	3144	19W-5S	D3
5300	DRGV	60516	3144	19W-5S	D3
E Benton Av					
10	NPVL	60540	3141	26W-6S	E5
1000	NPVL	60540	3142	26W-6S	A5
W Benton Av					
10	NPVL	60540	3141	27W-6S	C5
E Benton Blvd					
-	CHCG	60601	3034	0E-0N	D4
Benton Ct					
10	ALGN	60102	2692	38W-21N	E6
10	ALGN	60102	2693	38W-21N	A6
700	LKVL	60046	2417	22W-39N	C4
S Benton Ct					
700	EMHT	60126	3028	15W-0N	A5
W Benton Dr					
7200	FftT	60423	3505	9W-23S	A4
7200	RchT	60423	3505	9W-23S	A4
7300	FftT	60423	3504	9W-23S	E4
Benton Ln					
100	BMDL	60108	2968	24W-5N	C2
600	BbyT	60134	3018	39W-0N	D6
E Benton Pl					
10	CHCG	60601	3034	0E-0N	C4
Benton Rd					
400	LKVL	60046	2417	22W-39N	B4
Benton St					
700	EMHT	60126	3028	15W-0N	B5
1300	CRTE	60417	3685	1W-29S	B2
2400	PltT	60067	2805	20W-13N	E5
2400	RGMW	60008	2805	20W-13N	E5
2400	RGMW	60067	2805	20W-13N	E5
E Benton St					
10	OSWG	60543	3263	37W-13S	C4
100	JLET	60432	3499	23W-23S	A4
1000	AURA	60504	3200	34W-8S	D1
1000	AURA	60505	3200	34W-8S	D1
N Benton St					
10	PLTN	60067	2805	20W-16N	E1
100	PLTN	60067	2752	20W-16N	E7
100	WDSK	60098	2524	41W-31N	D7
S Benton St					
100	PLTN	60067	2805	20W-15N	E2
100	WDSK	60098	2524	41W-31N	D7
W Benton St					
10	AURA	60505	3138	35W-7S	A7
10	AURA	60506	3138	36W-7S	A7
10	JLET	60432	3498	24W-23S	E4
10	OSWG	60543	3263	37W-12S	C4
Bent Ridge Ln					
600	BRTN	60010	2698	25W-20N	B7
600	ELGN	60120	2855	32W-12N	D2
Bentson St					
500	BtIT	60543	3263	39W-12S	A3
500	OSWG	60543	3263	39W-12S	A3
Bent Tree Ct					
10	BGBK	60440	3205	22W-9S	C4
10	HNWD	60047	2644	24W-25N	C4
200	NLNX	60451	3500	19W-24S	E6
500	OSWG	60543	3263	36W-11S	E1
1000	ELGN	60120	2855	32W-12N	C1
Bent Tree Dr					
-	BTVA	60134	3019	36W-0S	D6
-	BTVA	60510	3019	36W-0S	D6
1800	GNVA	60134	3019	36W-0N	D5
Bent Tree Ln					
100	NLNX	60451	3500	19W-24S	E6
100	SMBG	60195	2859	23W-12N	A2
Bentwood Dr					
-	BlmT	60411	3510	4E-24S	B6
-	LYWD	60411	3510	4E-24S	B6
12200	HMGN	60491	3422	15W-20S	B4
Bentwood Ln					
6300	WLBK	60527	3146	15W-7S	A6
Benzie Cir					
1500	RMVL	60446	3417	26W-18S	E1
Benzie Ct					
-	RMVL	60446	3417	26W-18S	E1
Berdnick St					
3600	RGMW	60008	2806	20W-15N	A2
N Bereman Rd					
10	OswT	60538	3199	37W-10S	D6
S Bereman Rd					
10	OswT	60538	3199	37W-10S	D6
W Berenice Av					
1800	CHCG	60613	2977	2W-4N	B2
2400	CHCG	60618	2977	3W-4N	A2
4700	CHCG	60641	2975	6W-4N	D2
4700	CHCG	60641	2976	5W-4N	A2
5500	CHCG	60634	2975	7W-4N	B2
6700	CHCG	60634	2974	8W-4N	E2
Berens St					
10	DYR	46311	3598		C3
Beresford Dr					
3600	DrrT	60098	2583	37W-28N	B6
Berg Dr					
1400	DLTN	60419	3351	1E-18S	B7
1400	SHLD	60419	3351	1E-18S	B7
1400	SHLD	60473	3351	1E-18S	B7
Berg St					
10	ALGN	60102	2694	34W-21N	C6
Bergamot Ct					
5600	NPVL	60564	3266	29W-13S	C5
Bergamot Ln					
5500	NPVL	60564	3266	29W-13S	C5
N Bergen St					
34900	GrtT	60041	2474	25W-34N	A7
E Bergera Rd					
-	BDWD	60408	3942	31W-41S	B4
W Bergera Rd					
300	BDWD	60408	3941	32W-41S	D4
300	BDWD	60408	3942	31W-41S	A4
Bergeren Ct					
2800	NndT	60012	2584	35W-29N	A4
Berglund Pl					
600	NHBK	60062	2757	8W-17N	E5
Bergman Ct					
10	FTPK	60130	3030	9W-0N	D4
Bergman Dr					
300	BRKT	60511	3196	45W-8S	C2
Bergman Rd					
3000	NndT	60051	2586	30W-29N	B5
Bergstrom St					
3700	JLET	60431	3497	28W-22S	A2
3800	JLET	60431	3496	29W-22S	D3
Beringer Ct					
7600	GRNE	60031	2476	18W-35N	E6
Berk Ln					
10	CRTE	60417	3596	0W-28S	D6
Berkeley Av					
600	WNKA	60093	2811	5W-15N	E1
900	FDHT	60411	3509	1E-25S	A6
1400	FDHT	60411	3597	1E-25S	A1
S Berkeley Av					
4100	CHCG	60653	3092	1E-4S	E6
5200	CHCG	60615	3152	1E-5S	E2
Berkeley Ct					
1200	SRWD	60404	3496	31W-24S	A6
8800	ODPK	60462	3346	11W-16S	A4
Berkeley Dr					
200	BGBK	60440	3268	24W-11S	C1
Berkeley Rd					
500	BRWN	60402	3088	9W-2S	D3
500	BRWN	60546	3088	9W-2S	D3
500	RVSD	60546	3088	9W-2S	D3
2100	HDPK	60035	2704	10W-22N	A5
Berkenshire Ln					
1100	EGVV	60007	2914	19W-8N	C3
1300	ITSC	60143	2914	19W-8N	C3
Berkhansted Ct					
8300	ODPK	60462	3346	10W-16S	B3
Berkley Av					
10	JltT	60433	3500	21W-24S	A5
S Berkley Av					
100	EMHT	60126	3027	16W-1N	D3
Berkley Ct					
600	SMBG	60194	2859	22W-10N	C5
1300	BFGV	60089	2701	16W-21N	C6
1600	DRFD	60015	2703	12W-21N	C5
1600	WdfT	60015	2703	12W-21N	C5

STREET Block City ZIP Map# CGS Grid
Berkley Ct
2100 NPVL 60565 3203 26W-9S E5
25800 WcnT 60084 2587 26W-28N D7
Berkley Dr
- HFET 60169 2859 23W-11N B3
500 DYR 46311 3510 D7
600 RMVL 60446 3340 25W-15S B1
E Berkley Dr
10 ANHT 60004 2754 17W-17N A6
S Berkley Dr
100 RDLK 60073 2531 25W-33N A3
W Berkley Dr
10 ANHT 60004 2754 18W-17N A6
400 ANHT 60004 2753 18W-17N E6
Berkley Ln
1000 LMNT 60439 3270 18W-14S E7
1000 LMNT 60439 3271 18W-14S A6
E Berkley Ln
10 HFET 60169 2859 23W-11N A3
W Berkley Ln
100 HFET 60169 2858 23W-11N E3
100 HFET 60169 2859 23W-11N A3
Berkley Pl
300 SMWD 60107 2857 28W-10N B6
Berkley Rd
1100 LKZH 60047 2699 22W-22N C3
Berkley St
900 CPVL 60110 2748 33W-17N B6
1600 ELGN 60123 2854 35W-10N A6
Berkshire Av
400 RMVL 60446 3340 24W-15S D3
E Berkshire Av
400 LMBD 60148 3026 19W-1N D2
700 VLPK 60181 3026 19W-1N D2
W Berkshire Av
10 LMBD 60148 3026 20W-1N B2
Berkshire Cir
- LGGV 60047 2647 18W-24N A7
2000 CPVL 60110 2801 32W-16N D1
Berkshire Ct
- RGMW 60008 2806 19W-12N C7
10 BRRG 60527 3208 15W-9S B2
10 GRNE 60031 2535 14W-34N C1
10 SBTN 60010 2803 27W-13N B5
10 SEGN 60177 2908 35W-7N C5
10 SMWD 60107 2856 29W-9N D7
100 GLHT 60139 2968 24W-3N D6
300 DGvT 60516 3206 19W-9S D4
300 DSPN 60016 2808 14W-12N C7
300 SRGV 60554 3135 41W-6S E5
400 WYNE 60184 2966 30W-4N A4
500 SMBG 60193 2859 22W-9N B6
600 OSWG 60543 3264 35W-11S B1
1000 ELGN 60120 2855 32W-10N D5
2500 WKGN 60087 2478 14W-36N D3
2500 WrnT 60031 2478 14W-36N D3
2500 WrnT 60087 2478 14W-36N D3
4000 CPVL 60110 2801 32W-16N D1
6400 LSLE 60532 3142 24W-7S C6
7800 HRPK 60133 2858 26W-9N A7
Berkshire Dr
10 CLLK 60014 2640 35W-24N B7
10 WLNG 60090 2754 16W-18N E4
200 CLLK 60014 2639 36W-24N E6
200 LKVL 60046 2475 22W-37N C1
800 MTSN 60443 3505 7W-25S C7
2600 GNVA 60134 3019 37W-0N C6
2800 MKHM 60428 3427 3W-19S A2
7700 HRPK 60133 2858 26W-9N A7
12500 MKNA 60448 3502 15W-24S B4
S Berkshire Dr
300 LKFT 60045 2648 13W-25N E5
Berkshire Ln
10 BRRG 60527 3208 15W-9S B2
10 LNSH 60069 2702 13W-22N E3
10 VrnT 60069 2702 13W-23N E2
200 SRGV 60554 3135 41W-6S E5
300 DSPN 60016 2808 14W-12N D7
600 SMBG 60193 2859 22W-9N C6
700 CLSM 60188 2967 27W-2N D7
900 PGGV 60140 2797 41W-14N E5
1000 LKZH 60010 2698 24W-21N D5
1200 ElaT 60010 2698 24W-21N C6
1200 GYLK 60030 2532 21W-34N D1
9800 HTLY 60142 2692 40W-22N B4
E Berkshire Ln
100 MPPT 60056 2862 15W-12N A2
N Berkshire Ln
10 RDLK 60073 2531 25W-33N A3
W Berkshire Ln
10 MPPT 60056 2862 15W-12N A2
Berkshire Pl
800 CRTE 60417 3596 0W-28S C6
1900 WHTN 60187 3082 25W-2S A4
Berkshire Rd
600 WCHI 60185 3022 28W-1N E2
600 WnfT 60185 3022 28W-1N E2
600 WnfT 60185 3023 28W-1N A2
Berkshire St
- CHCG 60651 3031 7W-1N B1
400 OKPK 60302 3031 8W-1N A1
800 OKPK 60302 3030 8W-1N E2
1100 OKPK 60305 3030 8W-1N D1
1600 GLHT 60139 2968 24W-3N D6
7400 RVFT 60305 3030 9W-1N C1
10800 WSTR 60154 3086 13W-2S E2
Berkshire Ter
300 ROSL 60172 2913 23W-6N B6
Berlex Cir
- FDHT 60411 3509 1E-25S A7
N Berlin Av
600 JLET 60435 3498 24W-22S D1
W Berlin Av
400 JLET 60435 3498 24W-22S D1
Berltsum Ln
1300 WDSK 60098 2582 40W-30N B1
Berman Rd
2600 NARA 60542 3076 39W-3S D7
Bermuda Colony St
10 FXLK 60020 2414 28W-38N D6
Bermuda Dunes Pl
800 NHBK 60062 2756 12W-17N C4
Bern Ct
100 ElaT 60047 2698 23W-23N E1
100 LKZH 60047 2698 23W-23N E1
2600 WDRG 60517 3205 21W-9S E3
Bernadette Ln
400 BTVA 60510 3078 36W-2S A3
Bernadine St
17400 LNSG 60438 3430 4E-20S C4
18700 LNSG 60438 3510 4E-22S C1
Bernard Ct
10 BFGV 60089 2754 17W-18N A3
34700 LKZH 60047 2699 21W-22N C3
Bernard Dr
- ODPK 60467 3422 14W-21S E6
Bernard Dr
10 BFGV 60089 2754 17W-18N B3
10 WLNG 60090 2754 16W-18N D3
1000 ANHT 60004 2754 18W-18N A3
1000 ANHT 60089 2754 18W-18N A3
1000 BFGV 60004 2754 18W-18N A3
17700 ODPK 60467 3423 13W-21S A6
W Bernard Dr
1300 ADSN 60101 2970 20W-2N B6
Bernard Pl
2700 EVTN 60201 2812 4W-13N B7
2700 WLMT 60091 2812 4W-13N B7
N Bernard St
2400 CHCG 60647 2976 4W-3N D5
3600 CHCG 60618 2976 4W-4N D2
4300 CHCG 60625 2976 4W-5N D1
5000 CHCG 60625 2920 4W-6N D5
5500 CHCG 60659 2920 4W-6N D5
Bernard Wy
- JLET 60447 3495 33W-22S B2
Bernay Ct
10 ODHL 60013 2641 30W-26N E3
Bernay Dr
3600 NHBK 60062 2756 12W-18N C3
Bernay Ln
- BFGV 60089 2754 17W-20N A1
1600 BFGV 60047 2754 18W-20N A1
1600 LGGV 60047 2754 18W-20N A1
3800 HFET 60192 2804 24W-14N B3
Berner Dr
100 ELGN 60120 2855 31W-12N E2
100 HnrT 60120 2855 31W-12N E2
400 HFET 60120 2855 31W-12N E2
400 HFET 60192 2855 31W-12N E2
Berner Rd
10 HshT 60140 2796 45W-14N D5
Bernette Ct
1000 NPVL 60540 3141 26W-6S E5
W Bernhard Rd
16800 JknT 60421 3587 22W-28S C7
16800 JknT 60421 3588 21W-28S A7
16800 JknT 60442 3588 21W-28S A7
16800 JLET 60421 3587 22W-28S C7
16800 JLET 60421 3588 21W-28S A7
16800 MhtT 60442 3588 21W-28S A7
Bernice Av
- GLHT 60137 2969 23W-2N B7
10 BmdT 60137 3025 23W-2N B1
10 NHLK 60164 2972 13W-2N E7
300 MLPK 60160 2973 13W-2N A7
300 NHLK 60160 2973 13W-2N A7
300 NHLK 60164 2973 13W-2N A7
400 BmdT 60137 2969 23W-2N B7
500 BmdT 60139 2969 23W-2N B7
500 GLHT 60139 2969 23W-2N B7
2500 LNSG 60438 3429 3E-20S E4
2500 LNSG 60438 3430 4E-20S B4
9300 SRPK 60176 2973 11W-4N D2
11600 HTLY 60142 2692 40W-21N A5
Bernice Ct
400 WLNG 60090 2755 15W-17N A5
N Bernice Ct
200 RDLK 60073 2531 23W-34N E1
S Bernice Ct
200 RDLK 60073 2531 23W-34N E1
Bernice Dr
100 BNVL 60106 2971 16W-3N E4
100 SchT 60175 2963 38W-3N B7
N Bernice Dr
36800 LkvT 60046 2475 22W-36N C3
W Bernice Dr
10400 PlsT 60462 3345 13W-15S B2
10500 PlsT 60464 3345 13W-15S B1
Bernice Rd
- MNSR 46321 3430 4E-20S C4
- MNSR 60438 3430 4E-20S C4
1800 LNSG 60438 3429 2E-20S E4
1800 LNSG 60473 3429 2E-20S E4
1800 SHLD 60473 3429 2E-20S E4
2600 LNSG 60438 3430 4E-20S C4
N Bernice St
26700 WcnT 60084 2642 28W-26N E2
N Bernice Ter
39100 BHPK 60099 2421 11W-39N E6
Bernie Ct
500 LslT 60565 3204 25W-8S A2
500 NPVL 60565 3204 25W-8S A2
Bernina Ct
10 LYWD 60411 3598 4E-25S C1
Bernyce Dr
500 LIHL 60156 2694 35W-21N B5
Berriedale Dr
500 CRY 60013 2695 31W-23N D2
Berron Ln
100 BNHL 60010 2748 30W-16N E7
100 BNHL 60010 2749 30W-16N A7
Berrong Av
42500 BtnT 60096 2363 10W-42N A6
42500 WPHR 60096 2363 10W-42N A6
Berrong Ct
42600 BtnT 60096 2363 10W-42N A6
Berry Av
500 GYLK 60030 2533 20W-33N A2
Berry Ct
100 NPVL 60540 3141 28W-7S A6
100 NpvT 60540 3141 28W-7S A6
2100 SMBG 60194 2858 26W-11N A4
2400 WKGN 60085 2479 11W-35N C6
3100 NndT 60012 2584 35W-28N A5
Berry Dr
- CHCG 60616 3092 0E-2S C2
300 NPVL 60540 3141 28W-6S A6
400 NpvT 60540 3141 28W-7S A6
Berry Ln
1100 FSMR 60422 3507 3W-23S B3
1800 DSPN 60018 2863 12W-10N B5
Berry Pkwy
10 PKRG 60068 2918 9W-8N B1
E Berry Rd
400 BRTN 60010 2751 25W-20N A1
Berry Rdg
600 JLET 60431 3497 28W-24S B6
Berry St
100 PKFT 60466 3595 3W-25S B1
900 ELBN 60119 3017 43W-0N A5
2400 JLET 60435 3417 27W-20S D5
2400 LktT 60403 3417 27W-20S D5
2400 PnfT 60403 3417 27W-20S D5
2400 PnfT 60435 3417 27W-20S D5
Berrybrook Ct
19600 TYPK 60477 3504 10W-23S B4
Berry Path Tr
900 MTSN 60443 3505 7W-25S C7
Berrywood Ln
- BtlT 60543 3262 40W-12S C2
300 OSWG 60543 3262 40W-12S C2
Berrywood Ln
6500 DRGV 60516 3144 19W-7S D6
Berseem Ct
10 OKBK 60523 3085 18W-2S A3
Berta Dr
1400 CTHL 60403 3418 25W-21S B6
S Berta Rd
100 DMND 60416 3941 34W-41S A4
400 BvlT 60416 3941 34W-41S A4
1100 BvlT 60407 3941 33W-41S A6
2000 BvlT 60407 4030 34W-43S A1
N Berta St
- DMND 60416 3941 33W-39S C2
- FlxT 60416 3941 33W-39S C2
Berteau Av
10000 SRPK 60176 2973 12W-5N B1
E Berteau Av
400 EMHT 60126 3028 15W-2N B1
N Berteau Av
100 BRLT 60103 2911 28W-8N A3
100 EMHT 60126 3028 15W-1N B2
S Berteau Av
100 BRLT 60103 2911 28W-8N A3
W Berteau Av
1400 CHCG 60613 2977 2W-5N B1
1900 CHCG 60618 2977 3W-5N A1
2800 CHCG 60618 2976 3W-5N E1
3900 CHCG 60641 2976 5W-5N B1
4800 CHCG 60641 2975 7W-5N C1
5500 CHCG 60634 2975 8W-5N A1
7300 NRDG 60706 2974 9W-5N C1
7700 NRDG 60634 2974 9W-5N C1
8200 CHCG 60634 2974 10W-5N A1
N Bertha Ln
22000 CbaT 60010 2697 26W-22N E4
22200 NBRN 60010 2697 26W-22N E4
Bertino Dr
- DMND 60416 3941 33W-40S B4
Bertling Ln
100 WNKA 60093 2812 4W-15N C3
Bertoldo Rd
10 PKFT 60466 3595 2W-26S C3
Bertram Ln
1900 HDPK 60035 2757 9W-20N C2
Bertram Rd
- BtlT 60512 3197 41W-9S E5
- SgrT 60506 3197 41W-9S E5
Bertrand Ln
3800 BHPK 60087 2422 10W-38N A7
3800 WKGN 60099 2422 10W-38N A7
4200 WKGN 60099 2421 10W-39N E6
Berwick
2100 IVNS 60067 2804 23W-14N D3
N Berwick Blvd
200 WKGN 60085 2536 11W-34N D1
1600 WKGN 60085 2479 11W-35N D5
1800 WKGN 60087 2479 11W-35N D5
Berwick Ct
10 LNSH 60069 2703 13W-22N A4
400 SMBG 60193 2859 23W-9N A6
1600 FSMR 60422 3506 4W-23S D4
8900 LKWD 60014 2639 37W-24N A7
Berwick Dr
200 AURA 60506 3136 38W-7S E7
200 AURA 60506 3198 38W-7S E1
N Berwick Ln
33800 WrnT 60031 2534 17W-33N B2
Berwick Pl
600 ROSL 60172 2912 25W-6N C6
Berwyn Av
700 NCHI 60044 2593 12W-30N B2
700 NCHI 60064 2593 12W-30N B2
700 ShdT 60044 2593 12W-30N B2
700 ShdT 60064 2593 12W-30N B2
W Berwyn Av
900 CHCG 60640 2921 1W-6N E5
1900 CHCG 60625 2921 3W-6N A5
2600 CHCG 60625 2920 3W-6N E5
4300 CHCG 60630 2920 5W-6N A5
4800 CHCG 60630 2919 6W-6N E5
6600 CHCG 60656 2918 8W-6N E5
6600 CHCG 60656 2919 8W-6N A5
7800 NpkT 60656 2918 9W-6N B5
8400 NRDG 60656 2918 10W-6N A6
8400 NRDG 60706 2918 10W-6N A6
8600 CHCG 60656 2917 10W-6N E6
Berwyn Ct
2000 JNBG 60050 2471 30W-36N E3
Berwyn St
1200 BtnT 60081 2414 30W-40N A4
9700 RSMT 60018 2917 12W-6N B6
Beryl Ln
- AvnT 60073 2531 25W-32N B5
- RDLK 60073 2531 25W-32N B5
Besley Pl
300 WKGN 60085 2537 10W-33N A2
N Besly Ct
1800 CHCG 60622 2977 1W-2N D7
Bessie Coleman Dr
500 CHCG 60666 2917 13W-7N A5
Best Dr
- CHCG 60637 3152 0E-6S D4
E Best Dr
1300 ANHT 60004 2754 17W-17N C5
Best Pl
2000 AURA 60506 3137 38W-6S A6
Besty Ross Pl
1100 BGBK 60490 3267 27W-14S B7
Beta Dr
10 SgrT 60506 3136 40W-5S B3
10 SRGV 60506 3136 40W-5S B3
Beth Ct
600 GRNE 60031 2534 16W-33N E3
16000 OKFT 60452 3425 6W-19S E1
17900 HMWD 60430 3427 3W-21S B6
20300 RlyT 60152 2634 49W-25N C5
Beth Dr
10800 ODPK 60467 3423 13W-21S A5
15600 HMGN 60441 3342 19W-17S D6
15600 HmrT 60441 3342 19W-17S D6
Beth Ln
2900 NPVL 60564 3202 29W-10S D7
Bethany Dr
500 SRWD 60404 3496 30W-23S B3
Bethany Ln
8500 TYPK 60487 3424 10W-20S B4
Bethel Av
700 BGBK 60490 3267 26W-13S D6
10400 HTLY 60142 2692 39W-20N C7
10400 HTLY 60142 2745 39W-20N C1
Bethel Blvd
2700 ZION 60099 2422 10W-40N A4
N Bethel Dr
400 JLET 60435 3497 27W-23S D3
700 TroT 60435 3497 27W-23S D3
Bethel Ln
10 SMBG 60194 2859 23W-10N A5
Bethel on Asbury
10 RGMW 60008 2806 19W-15N B3
Bethesda Blvd
1900 ZION 60099 2422 10W-40N B2
Bethlehem Av
- ZION 60099 2421 11W-41N E1
Bethlehem Av SR-173
- ZION 60099 2421 11W-41N D1
Bethlehem Rd
- AURA 60504 3140 30W-7S B6
Betsy Ct
10 RLKP 60030 2589 22W-30N B1
Betsy Ross Ct
400 AURA 60504 3140 29W-6S D5
Bette Ln
1000 GNVW 60025 2809 11W-13N D6
Bettenhausen Dr
18000 TYPK 60487 3424 10W-21S B7
Betty Av
200 PKCY 60085 2536 13W-33N A2
Betty Ct
100 BRLT 60103 2911 28W-8N A3
10400 RSMT 60018 2917 13W-8N A1
Betty Dr
100 IVNS 60010 2751 23W-17N D4
900 BFGV 60089 2754 16W-17N C4
900 LKZH 60047 2698 24W-23N B2
900 WhlT 60004 2754 16W-17N C4
1200 JLET 60586 3496 31W-22S A2
N Betty Dr
3100 ANHT 60004 2754 16W-17N C5
3100 WhlT 60004 2754 16W-17N C4
3200 BFGV 60089 2754 16W-17N C4
Betty Ln
- NlxT 60448 3501 17W-22S D1
500 SHLD 60473 3428 0E-19S E2
600 AraT 60505 3138 34W-6S D5
600 AURA 60505 3138 34W-6S D5
13900 BLID 60406 3349 3W-16S A3
W Betty Ln
10 NasT 60544 3337 33W-18S A7
W Betty Ter
8400 MaiT 60714 2864 10W-10N A4
8500 NLES 60714 2864 10W-10N A4
Betty Ann Ln
15300 OKFT 60452 3347 6W-18S D7
Betula St
600 JLET 60436 3498 25W-25S B7
700 RKDL 60436 3498 25W-24S B7
N Beulah Av
2900 RVGV 60171 2973 11W-3N E4
Beulah Ln
800 ELGN 60120 2855 32W-10N C5
E Bevan Dr
400 JLET 60435 3497 26W-23S E4
W Bevan Dr
400 JLET 60435 3497 26W-23S E3
Beverley Ln
100 WLSP 60480 3209 11W-9S D2
Beverly Av
- EMHT 60126 3027 16W-0S D7
400 AddT 60101 2971 17W-2N B6
16400 TYPK 60477 3425 7W-19S C3
N Beverly Av
100 WHTN 60187 3023 26W-0S E7
400 VLPK 60181 3027 17W-1N B2
36400 WrnT 60031 2476 18W-36N E4
S Beverly Av
100 WHTN 60187 3023 26W-0S E7
500 MltT 60187 3081 27W-1S C1
500 WHTN 60187 3081 27W-1S C1
600 AddT 60101 2971 17W-2N B7
600 ADSN 60101 2971 17W-2N B7
9100 CHCG 60620 3213 2W-10S D5
9500 CHCG 60643 3213 1W-11S D7
10700 CHCG 60643 3277 1W-12S E2
Beverly Blvd
100 NLNX 60451 3501 18W-23S B3
100 NlxT 60451 3501 18W-23S B3
13100 HTLY 60142 2744 43W-18N B4
W Beverly Cir
1500 HRPK 60133 2911 26W-7N E5
Beverly Cir E
5800 HRPK 60133 2911 26W-7N E5
Beverly Ct
100 SMWD 60107 2910 29W-9N E1
200 SMBG 60193 2858 23W-9N E7
1000 LMBD 60148 3083 21W-1S E2
1000 LMBD 60148 3084 21W-1S A2
1500 AURA 60502 3079 33W-4S A7
1600 HRPK 60133 2911 26W-7N D5
Beverly Dr
- AraT 60502 3139 33W-4S A1
- AURA 60502 3139 33W-4S A1
300 WLMT 60091 2812 5W-13N A7
900 WLNG 60090 2754 15W-18N E4
900 WLNG 60090 2755 15W-18N B3
1100 LKVL 60046 2474 23W-36N E3
1200 LKVL 60046 2475 23W-36N A4
1200 RLKB 60073 2474 24W-35N C6
1500 RLKH 60073 2474 24W-35N C7
1700 ANHT 60004 2807 17W-15N B2
2500 AURA 60502 3079 33W-4S A7
10000 SKOK 60076 2812 5W-12N A7
10000 WLMT 60076 2812 5W-12N A7
S Beverly Dr
26700 GGnT 60449 3682 9W-32S A7
26700 MonT 60449 3682 9W-32S A7
Beverly Dr E
- HRPK 60133 2911 26W-7N E5
Beverly Ln
200 GNVW 60025 2811 6W-13N C6
1300 SMWD 60107 2910 29W-9N E1
1900 BFGV 60089 2701 17W-22N B4
8600 ODPK 60462 3346 10W-15S A1
8700 PlsT 60462 3346 10W-15S A1
N Beverly Ln
1500 ANHT 60004 2807 17W-15N B2
S Beverly Ln
10 ANHT 60004 2807 17W-14N B5
300 ANHT 60005 2807 17W-13N B7
300 MPPT 60056 2861 17W-12N C1
22600 FftT 60423 3591 13W-27S B5
Beverly Pl
10 LNSG 60438 3430 C5
10 MNSR 46321 3430 D5
400 LKFT 60045 2650 9W-24N B7
800 DRFD 60015 2704 10W-21N A7
1100 HDPK 60035 2650 10W-24N B7
1600 HDPK 60035 2704 9W-22N D5
Beverly Rd
100 BRTN 60010 2751 24W-20N B1
100 HnrT 60120 2802 30W-13N A6
100 HnrT 60120 2856 30W-12N A1
Beverly Rd
100 HnrT 60192 2802 30W-13N A6
100 HnrT 60192 2856 30W-12N A1
200 HFET 60192 2802 30W-13N A6
2900 HFET 60118 2802 30W-13N A5
Beverly St
10 WHTN 60187 3023 26W-0S E6
400 MltT 60187 3023 26W-0N E4
Beverly Tr
- ELGN 60120 2855 32W-11N C5
Beverly Wy
7500 BtnT 60081 2414 30W-39N B5
7600 SPGV 60081 2414 30W-39N B5
W Beverly Glen Pkwy
1600 CHCG 60643 3213 2W-11S D7
Beverly Griffin Dr
- RMVL 60446 3340 24W-15S D2
Bevier Pl
100 AURA 60505 3200 35W-8S B2
Bexley Ct
10 NBRN 60010 2644 25W-24N A7
Bianco Dr
300 EGVV 60007 2915 18W-9N A1
Bianco Ter
2300 GNVW 60025 2864 9W-12N C1
9800 MaiT 60016 2863 11W-12N D1
S Bianco Villa Dr
1300 LKPT 60441 3342 21W-17S A6
Biarritz Ct
100 BMDL 60108 2968 24W-5N D1
Bible Baptist Dr
- BHPK 60087 2421 12W-39N B6
Bibury Ln
1200 IVNS 60010 2803 25W-15N E1
Bicek Ct
4400 HFET 60192 2804 24W-15N B1
Bicek Dr
1500 HFET 60192 2804 24W-15N B1
Bicentennial Ct
25100 PNFD 60544 3337 31W-17S E6
Bicentennial Dr
2200 CTHL 60403 3497 26W-22S D1
2200 CTHL 60435 3497 26W-22S E1
Bidwell Dr
900 GRNE 60031 2534 16W-33N D4
Bielby Ln
7900 LynT 60525 3208 13W-9S E2
7900 WLSP 60525 3208 13W-9S E2
N Bierman Av
10 LMBD 60148 3026 18W-1N E3
10 LMBD 60181 3026 18W-1N E3
300 VLPK 60181 3026 18W-1N E2
Biermann Ct
600 MPPT 60056 2808 14W-13N B5
Biesterfield Rd
10 EGVV 60007 2914 21W-8N A2
1300 EGVV 60007 2913 21W-9N D1
1500 EGVV 60193 2913 21W-9N D1
Biesterfield Rd SR-53
1000 EGVV 60007 2914 21W-8N A2
Big Axe Rd
10 ElgT 60124 2907 38W-8N A4
10 ElgT 60175 2907 38W-8N A4
Big Bear Ct
6400 IHPK 60525 3146 14W-7S D6
Big Bear Dr
6400 IHPK 60525 3146 14W-7S E5
Big Bear Tr
800 CRY 60013 2641 32W-24N B7
800 CRY 60013 2695 32W-24N C1
Big Bend Dr
1800 DSPN 60016 2863 12W-11N B2
Big Buck Tr
7800 FKFT 60423 3592 9W-27S D4
Big Cloud Pass
400 LIHL 60156 2693 36W-21N D5
Big Eagle Tr
900 CLSM 60188 2967 27W-3N C5
Bigelow Av
12100 HBRN 60034 2350 41W-42N E6
Bigelow Rd
10 PKFT 60466 3595 2W-26S C3
Big Foot Ln
1000 NPVL 60563 3141 27W-5S B3
Big Hollow Rd
28600 GrtT 60041 2472 28W-34N E7
28600 GrtT 60051 2472 28W-34N E7
28700 GrtT 60051 2529 28W-34N D1
28800 MchT 60051 2529 28W-34N D1
W Big Hollow Rd
- GrtT 60041 2474 25W-34N A7
- RDLK 60073 2474 25W-34N B7
27200 FXLK 60041 2473 27W-34N B7
27700 GrtT 60041 2473 28W-34N A7
28300 GrtT 60041 2472 28W-34N E7
28500 GrtT 60051 2472 28W-34N E7
W Big Hollow Rd SR-134
- GrtT 60041 2474 25W-34N A7
- RDLK 60073 2474 25W-34N B7
27200 FXLK 60041 2473 27W-34N B7
27200 GrtT 60041 2473 26W-34N D7
Bighorn Ct
10 BmT 60010 2802 28W-14N E4
Big Horn Dr
10 MltT 60187 3082 25W-2S A3
E Big Horn Dr
10 HNVL 60030 2532 21W-33N C2
W Big Horn Dr
10 HNVL 60030 2532 22W-33N B2
12800 HTLY 60142 2691 41W-20N C7
Bighorn Rd
500 NPVL 60563 3081 26W-4S E7
Big Horn Tr
1200 CLSM 60188 2967 28W-4N B4
1400 CLSM 60185 2967 28W-4N B4
1400 WynT 60185 2967 28W-4N B4
1400 WynT 60188 2967 28W-4N B4
Big Musky Cir Ln
- BDWD 60481 3942 30W-40S C2
- RedT 60481 3942 30W-40S C2
Big Oak Cir
1800 NHBK 60062 2757 9W-17N B4
Big Oak Ct
1500 LKFT 60045 2703 12W-23N A2
W Big Oak Dr
24400 LkvT 60046 2474 24W-37N C1
Big Oak Ln
10 RVWD 60015 2703 12W-21N A7
1900 NHBK 60062 2757 10W-17N B4
Big Oak Tr
1300 AURA 60506 3137 37W-5S C4
Big Oaks Ct
10 SMWD 60107 2857 28W-10N A5
Big Oaks Rd
10 SMWD 60107 2856 28W-10N E5
10 SMWD 60107 2857 28W-10N A5

STREET Block	City	ZIP	Map#	CGS	Grid
Big Oaks Rd					
10	TVLY	60013	2695	32W-23N	C2
2300	DRPK	60074	2752	21W-18N	D2
2300	PLTN	60074	2752	21W-18N	D2
2300	PltT	60074	2752	21W-18N	D2
W Big Oaks Rd					
17800	WrnT	60030	2534	18W-33N	A4
Big Peninsula Rd					
100	ELGN	60123	2801	33W-14N	B6
200	ELGN	60123	2800	33W-13N	E7
Big Rail Dr					
300	NPVL	60540	3141	27W-6S	D5
Big Rock Av					
600	LtRT	60545	3259	47W-13S	D5
600	PLNO	60545	3259	47W-13S	D5
S Big Run Dr					
-	GGnT	60423	3591	13W-27S	B5
22900	FftT	60423	3591	13W-27S	B5
Big Run Ln					
13300	DPgT	60441	3342	21W-15S	A2
13800	HMGN	60491	3343	17W-17S	C6
Big Sable Pt					
8800	FKFT	60423	3504	11W-24S	A5
Big Sky Tr					
600	CRY	60013	2695	32W-24N	C1
Big Sur Pkwy					
1200	ALGN	60102	2748	32W-20N	B1
Big Terra Ln					
200	GRNE	60031	2534	16W-34N	D2
Big Timber Ct					
10	ELGN	60123	2854	34W-12N	D1
Big Timber Dr					
600	JLET	60431	3497	27W-23S	B3
600	JLET	60435	3497	27W-23S	B3
Big Timber Rd					
10	DndT	60124	2799	37W-14N	D7
10	ELGN	60124	2799	37W-14N	D6
10	ElgT	60124	2799	36W-13N	D7
10	GLBT	60124	2799	36W-13N	D7
10	GLBT	60136	2799	36W-13N	D7
10	HPSR	60140	2743	46W-18N	A5
10	HshT	60140	2743	46W-18N	A5
10	HshT	60140	2744	43W-17N	A6
10	RtdT	60124	2799	36W-13N	D7
10	RtdT	60136	2798	39W-15N	D4
10	RtdT	60136	2798	38W-14N	C6
10	RtdT	60140	2744	43W-17N	A6
10	RtdT	60140	2797	42W-16N	D1
10	RtdT	60140	2798	39W-15N	D4
10	RtdT	60142	2744	42W-17N	C7
10	RtdT	60142	2797	43W-16N	B1
200	DndT	60136	2799	37W-14N	C6
200	GLBT	60124	2798	39W-14N	E5
200	GLBT	60136	2798	39W-14N	E5
200	RtdT	60124	2798	39W-14N	E5
300	ELGN	60123	2799	36W-13N	E7
300	ELGN	60123	2800	36W-13N	A7
500	ELGN	60123	2854	36W-13N	A1
500	RtdT	60136	2797	41W-16N	E1
800	ElgT	60123	2799	36W-13N	E7
Big Timber Rd CO-21					
10	DndT	60124	2799	37W-14N	D7
10	ELGN	60124	2799	37W-14N	D6
10	ElgT	60124	2799	36W-13N	D7
10	GLBT	60124	2799	36W-13N	D7
10	GLBT	60136	2799	36W-13N	D7
10	HPSR	60140	2743	46W-18N	A5
10	HshT	60140	2743	46W-18N	A5
10	HshT	60140	2744	43W-17N	A6
10	RtdT	60124	2799	36W-13N	D7
10	RtdT	60136	2798	39W-15N	D4
10	RtdT	60136	2799	38W-14N	C6
10	RtdT	60140	2744	43W-17N	A6
10	RtdT	60140	2797	42W-16N	D1
10	RtdT	60140	2798	39W-15N	D4
10	RtdT	60142	2744	42W-17N	C7
10	RtdT	60142	2797	43W-16N	B1
200	DndT	60136	2799	37W-14N	C6
200	GLBT	60124	2798	39W-14N	E5
200	GLBT	60136	2798	39W-14N	E5
200	RtdT	60124	2798	39W-14N	E5
300	ELGN	60123	2799	36W-13N	E7
300	ELGN	60123	2800	36W-13N	A7
500	ELGN	60123	2854	36W-13N	A1
500	RtdT	60136	2797	41W-16N	E1
800	ElgT	60123	2799	36W-13N	E7
Big Timber Camp					
1500	RtdT	60123	2799	38W-14N	B6
1500	RtdT	60124	2799	38W-14N	B6
Big Tree Ln					
3100	WLMT	60091	2811	6W-13N	D7
Big Woods Dr					
400	BTVA	60510	3077	37W-1S	C2
400	BtvT	60510	3077	37W-1S	C2
Big Woods Rd					
-	AURA	60502	3079	32W-4S	C7
Bilarda Ct					
1400	GNVA	60134	3020	36W-1N	A4
Bill Ct					
2300	NPVL	60565	3204	24W-10S	C5
N Bill St					
10	PLNO	60545	3259	47W-13S	C6
S Bill St					
10	PLNO	60545	3259	47W-14S	C7
Bill Aldis Av					
10	CPVL	60110	2747	34W-17N	E7
Bill Barth Dr					
-	SCRL	60174	2964	35W-4N	B4
Billie Limacher Ln					
2700	JLET	60586	3415	32W-20S	D5
S Billings Ct					
100	BMDL	60108	2969	23W-5N	B1
Billings St					
300	ELGN	60123	2854	34W-10N	E5
Bills Ln					
-	HGKN	60525	3147	12W-7S	D5
Billybob Dr					
-	NARA	60506	3137	38W-4S	A1
Billy Burns Rd					
900	WYNE	60184	2965	32W-5N	C1
Billy Casper Ln					
10	MDLN	60445	3348	6W-17S	A4
Biloba St					
8800	ODPK	60462	3346	11W-17S	A5
Biloxie Ct					
700	CLSM	60188	2967	27W-2N	C7
Bilstone Dr					
-	LYWD	60411	3509	2E-23S	D4
Bilter Rd					
-	AURA	60502	3079	31W-4S	D7
900	AURA	60502	3138	34W-4S	D1
900	NARA	60502	3138	34W-4S	D1
900	NARA	60542	3138	34W-4S	D1
1400	AraT	60502	3139	33W-4S	A1
1700	AraT	60504	3139	33W-4S	A1
1700	AURA	60504	3139	33W-4S	A1
Bilter Rd					
1900	NpvT	60502	3139	33W-4S	B1
1900	NpvT	60504	3139	33W-4S	B1
2200	AURA	60502	3139	33W-4S	B1
Biltmore Cir					
2400	AURA	60503	3201	32W-11S	C7
2400	AURA	60503	3265	32W-11S	C1
Biltmore Ct					
10	LIHL	60156	2693	36W-21N	D5
800	NPVL	60563	3141	26W-6S	E4
800	NPVL	60563	3142	26W-5S	A4
900	RMVL	60446	3340	25W-16S	C4
Biltmore Dr					
200	NBRN	60010	2698	25W-23N	A2
600	BRLT	60103	2856	31W-9N	A7
600	BRLT	60103	2910	31W-9N	A1
600	ELGN	60103	2856	31W-9N	A7
8500	ODPK	60462	3424	10W-18S	B1
Biltmore Ln					
10600	HTLY	60142	2692	39W-21N	C5
Biltmore Rd					
3900	DRGV	60515	3084	18W-4S	E6
3900	YkTp	60515	3084	18W-4S	E6
Biltmore St					
2800	JLET	60435	3417	27W-20S	B6
2800	PnfT	60431	3417	27W-20S	B6
2800	PnfT	60435	3417	27W-20S	B6
Bimini Ln					
2600	NLNX	60451	3590	15W-25S	C1
Binder Rd					
7100	DRGV	60516	3206	20W-8S	A1
Binder St					
-	AraT	60504	3200	34W-9S	D3
500	AURA	60505	3200	35W-8S	B3
1300	AURA	60504	3200	34W-8S	E3
Binford Dr					
7900	ODPK	60462	3346	10W-16S	C3
Bingham Cir					
100	MDLN	60060	2590	20W-27N	B7
Bingham Ct					
200	MDLN	60060	2590	20W-27N	B7
800	GRNE	60031	2534	16W-33N	C4
N Bingham St					
2000	CHCG	60647	2977	3W-2N	A6
Binnie Rd					
10	CPVL	60110	2746	37W-17N	C7
10	CPVL	60118	2746	37W-17N	C7
10	DndT	60110	2746	37W-17N	C7
10	DndT	60118	2746	36W-17N	E7
10	RtdT	60118	2746	38W-17N	C7
10	WDND	60110	2746	37W-17N	C7
10	WDND	60118	2746	37W-17N	C7
400	DndT	60118	2747	36W-17N	A7
400	WDND	60118	2747	36W-17N	A7
600	GLBT	60118	2746	38W-17N	A7
600	GLBT	60136	2746	38W-17N	A7
Binnie Lakes Tr					
100	RtdT	60118	2746	38W-17N	B7
Bio-Logic Plz					
10	MDLN	60060	2646	18W-26N	E2
Birch					
-	RMVL	60446	3340	25W-15S	B1
Birch Av					
10	MltT	60187	3024	26W-0N	A5
10	ShdT	60044	2593	12W-28N	B5
10	WKGN	60087	2480	10W-36N	B4
800	DRGV	60515	3144	19W-5S	C1
1400	HRPK	60133	2911	26W-8N	E2
9000	MNGV	60053	2864	8W-11N	E3
9200	MKNA	60448	3503	11W-23S	E3
9200	MKNA	60448	3504	11W-23S	A3
9400	FftT	60448	3503	11W-23S	E3
18000	CCHL	60478	3426	5W-21S	C7
18900	CCHL	60478	3506	5W-22S	C2
N Birch Av					
-	BHPK	60087	2479	12W-37N	B2
29400	ShdT	60044	2593	12W-29N	B4
29500	LKBF	60044	2593	12W-29N	B4
Birch Ct					
10	MDLN	60060	2646	18W-26N	E2
200	LKFT	60045	2649	11W-25N	D5
300	ROSL	60172	2913	22W-6N	B6
900	DRFD	60015	2703	11W-21N	E6
13600	LMNT	60439	3343	17W-15S	B2
16000	ODHL	60487	3424	11W-19S	A1
22900	PnfT	60586	3416	28W-20S	E4
E Birch Ct					
10	KdlT	60560	3333	43W-16S	A3
W Birch Ct					
10	KdlT	60560	3333	44W-16S	A3
6400	MONE	60449	3682	8W-32S	C7
Birch Dr					
200	SRWD	60404	3496	30W-23S	C4
300	WHTN	60187	3024	25W-0S	A6
600	BCHR	60401	3864	0W-36S	C2
1100	ELGN	60120	2855	32W-11N	D4
1600	BKLY	60162	3028	14W-0N	C4
1600	BKLY	60163	3028	14W-0N	C4
1600	HLSD	60162	3028	14W-0N	C4
1600	HLSD	60163	3028	14W-0N	C4
4200	GRNE	60031	2535	14W-34N	D2
4200	ZION	60099	2421	12W-41N	B2
7300	MchT	60097	2469	36W-36N	D4
E Birch Dr					
400	GNWD	60425	3508	0E-22S	E2
500	GNWD	60425	3509	0E-22S	A2
S Birch Dr					
1100	MPPT	60056	2861	16W-11N	D3
W Birch Dr					
2400	RDLK	60073	2530	26W-34N	E1
Birch Ln					
10	BDWD	60481	3942	30W-40S	C4
10	RedT	60481	3942	30W-40S	C4
100	ODHL	60103	2641	31W-26N	D3
100	SCRL	60175	2963	37W-3N	C6
600	FRGV	60021	2696	29W-23N	B2
600	OMFD	60461	3507	3W-24S	B6
800	CHHT	60411	3507	1W-24S	E6
1000	RMVL	60446	3340	25W-15S	B1
1100	LynT	60458	3209	11W-8S	D2
1100	WNSP	60558	3146	14W-6S	D3
1400	SEGN	60177	2908	36W-8N	A2
1500	PKRG	60068	2863	11W-10N	E5
1800	AURA	60506	3137	38W-5S	B4
1900	MHRY	60050	2528	32W-33N	C2
2200	ANHT	60005	2860	19W-12N	D1
2200	RGMW	60005	2860	19W-12N	D1
2200	RGMW	60008	2806	19W-12N	C7
2200	RGMW	60008	2860	19W-12N	C1
8900	HYHL	60457	3209	11W-10S	E5
N Birch Ln					
34200	WrnT	60031	2534	17W-34N	B1
W Birch Ln					
14600	WDWH	60083	2478	14W-38N	C1
Birch Pl					
1700	RGMW	60008	2860	21W-12N	A1
Birch Pl					
1700	SMBG	60008	2860	21W-12N	A1
1700	SMBG	60173	2860	21W-12N	A1
Birch Rd					
300	WDSK	60098	2524	41W-32N	D4
500	GwdT	60098	2524	41W-32N	D5
600	GLNC	60022	2758	7W-17N	C5
700	LKBF	60044	2594	10W-28N	A5
1000	HMWD	60430	3428	1W-22S	A7
1200	HMWD	60430	3508	1W-22S	A1
1300	HMWD	60430	3427	1W-22S	E7
1600	NHBK	60062	2756	10W-16N	E7
15300	MKHM	60426	3348	4W-18S	D7
15300	MKHM	60428	3348	4W-18S	D7
Birch St					
10	CPVL	60110	2748	32W-18N	C5
10	CTSD	60525	3147	12W-6S	C4
10	HGKN	60525	3147	12W-6S	C4
10	PKFT	60466	3595	2W-26S	C3
100	WNFD	60190	3023	27W-0N	C5
100	WNKA	60093	2812	5W-15N	A3
400	BTVA	60510	3078	36W-0S	A1
500	ITSC	60143	2914	20W-6N	B5
600	ALGN	60102	2694	33W-21N	E6
600	PKCY	60085	2536	12W-33N	B3
600	SRGV	60554	3135	42W-4S	D2
600	WKGN	60085	2536	12W-33N	B3
1100	LIHL	60156	2694	35W-22N	A4
1500	HHLL	60051	2586	30W-29N	A3
1700	DSPN	60018	2863	12W-9N	B7
2100	DSPN	60018	2917	12W-9N	B1
2300	LktT	60435	3417	26W-20S	D6
2300	PnfT	60435	3417	26W-20S	D6
3400	FNPK	60131	2973	11W-4N	D3
7000	BGVW	60455	3210	8W-10S	E5
7400	AlqT	60014	2640	33W-24N	D7
8400	FXLK	60020	2415	28W-39N	A5
8400	FXLK	60081	2415	28W-39N	A5
9100	ODPK	60462	3345	11W-17S	E5
20700	VrnT	60015	2702	14W-20N	B7
E Birch St					
10	ELBN	60119	3017	43W-2N	A2
W Birch St					
21500	LkvT	60046	2417	21W-38N	D6
Birch Tr					
10	WLNG	60090	2754	16W-17N	E4
Birchbark Ct					
13600	ODPK	60462	3346	10W-16S	B2
Birch Bark Dr					
5200	HFET	60192	2802	30W-12N	C7
Birchbark Tr					
1000	CLSM	60188	2967	27W-3N	C5
1400	WynT	60185	2967	28W-3N	A6
1400	WynT	60188	2967	28W-3N	A6
Birchbrook Ct					
600	MltT	60137	3083	22W-1S	D2
Birchcreek Ct					
11900	OrlT	60467	3344	14W-17S	C6
W Birchdale Av					
7900	EDPK	60171	2974	9W-3N	B5
7900	EDPK	60707	2974	10W-3N	B5
Birchdale Ct					
10	CmpT	60175	2962	39W-4N	E3
Birchdale Dr					
1000	ELGN	60123	2854	35W-10N	C6
S Birchdale Dr					
14400	HMGN	60491	3343	17W-17S	D5
Birchdale Ln					
1100	AURA	60504	3202	30W-9S	A3
Birch Hollow Dr					
500	ANTH	60002	2358	21W-42N	C7
Birch Lakes Dr					
10	HNWD	60047	2645	22W-25N	B6
Birch Tree Ct					
-	EMHT	60126	3027	16W-0S	E7
Birchwood Av					
10	DRFD	60015	2756	11W-20N	C2
300	EGVV	60007	2914	19W-7N	D3
300	EGVV	60007	2915	18W-8N	A1
600	DSPN	60018	2862	14W-9N	D7
1900	DSPN	60018	2863	12W-9N	B7
2300	WLMT	60091	2812	5W-13N	B6
2700	WLMT	60091	2811	5W-13N	E6
3800	SKOK	60076	2866	4W-9N	B7
5300	SKOK	60077	2865	6W-9N	D7
E Birchwood Av					
10	HNDL	60521	3086	15W-4S	A6
S Birchwood Av					
2400	HHLL	60051	2586	30W-29N	B3
2500	NndT	60051	2586	30W-29N	B4
W Birchwood Av					
10	HNDL	60521	3086	15W-4S	A6
300	PLTN	60067	2752	21W-17N	D4
1300	CHCG	60626	2867	1W-9N	C7
2400	CHCG	60645	2867	3W-9N	A7
2700	CHCG	60645	2866	3W-9N	E7
3100	CHCG	60076	2866	3W-9N	D7
3100	SKOK	60076	2866	3W-9N	D7
6800	NLES	60714	2864	8W-9N	E7
7200	CHCG	60631	2864	9W-9N	C7
7200	CHCG	60714	2864	9W-9N	C7
Birchwood Ct					
10	GfnT	60156	2693	38W-23N	A1
10	OswT	60538	3199	36W-10S	D7
10	SgrT	60506	3136	40W-5S	A3
10	SMWD	60107	2857	28W-12N	B2
300	VNHL	60061	2647	17W-25N	B6
400	DGvT	60527	3145	17W-7S	C5
400	WTMT	60527	3145	17W-7S	C5
700	NARA	60542	3137	37W-4S	C1
700	WLBK	60527	3145	16W-8S	E7
2200	GNVW	60025	2864	9W-12N	C1
2800	WLMT	60091	2811	5W-14N	E5
W Birchwood Ct					
14300	HMGN	60491	3343	16W-17S	E6
Birchwood Ct N					
2300	BFGV	60089	2701	17W-22N	B3
Birchwood Ct S					
2100	BFGV	60089	2701	17W-22N	B4
Birchwood Dr					
-	BtlT	60560	3333	41W-15S	E2
-	GwdT	60097	2469	37W-34N	C7
-	YKVL	60560	3333	41W-15S	E2
10	PlsT	60464	3273	13W-14S	B7
100	BRTN	60010	2751	24W-20N	C2
100	WNVL	60555	3080	29W-3S	D6
200	DRPK	60010	2751	24W-20N	C2
200	MltT	60137	3083	22W-3S	B5
200	RLKB	60073	2474	23W-36N	E5
300	ANTH	60002	2357	23W-43N	E4
300	ANTH	60002	2358	23W-43N	A4
400	NARA	60542	3077	37W-4S	D7
600	BGBK	60490	3267	26W-13S	E4
900	PGGV	60140	2797	42W-15N	E4
1400	GRNE	60031	2478	15W-35N	B6
2800	WRLK	60097	2469	37W-34N	C7
Birchwood Dr					
3200	HLCT	60429	3427	3W-20S	A4
3300	HLCT	60429	3426	4W-20S	E4
3400	WKGN	60085	2536	13W-31N	A6
8800	ODHL	60487	3424	11W-19S	A2
N Birchwood Dr					
10	NPVL	60540	3141	28W-6S	A5
S Birchwood Dr					
10	NPVL	60540	3141	28W-6S	A5
W Birchwood Dr					
200	RMVL	60446	3269	23W-14S	A7
13600	HMGN	60491	3343	17W-17S	D5
Birchwood Ln					
-	GfnT	60156	2693	38W-23N	A1
200	BMDL	60108	2969	22W-4N	B3
1100	HDPK	60035	2704	9W-22N	C4
2100	BFGV	60089	2701	17W-22N	B4
2200	NHFD	60093	2811	7W-15N	A2
2300	JLET	60435	3497	26W-22S	D2
2400	WLMT	60091	2812	5W-13N	A6
2600	BKBN	60015	2703	11W-23N	D3
2600	WdfT	60015	2703	11W-23N	D2
N Birchwood Ln					
2000	ANHT	60004	2807	16W-16N	D1
S Birchwood Ln					
20700	FftT	60423	3504	9W-25S	D6
W Birchwood Ln					
15500	LbvT	60048	2592	15W-30N	A2
Birchwood Pkwy					
2200	WDRG	60517	3205	21W-9S	E3
Birchwood Pl					
1800	DRGV	60515	3083	21W-2S	E4
1800	DRGV	60515	3084	21W-3S	A4
Birchwood Rd					
10	DRFD	60015	2757	10W-18N	B2
10	NfdT	60062	2757	10W-18N	B2
100	DndT	60110	2748	33W-18N	A6
200	HNDL	60521	3086	15W-4S	A6
700	FKFT	60423	3503	12W-24S	C6
800	AraT	60505	3138	34W-6S	E5
800	AURA	60505	3138	34W-6S	E5
1000	HNDL	60521	3085	16W-4S	E6
1000	OKBK	60521	3085	16W-4S	E6
1000	OKBK	60523	3085	16W-4S	E6
3600	PKFT	60466	3594	4W-26S	D3
3600	RNPK	60471	3594	4W-26S	D3
Birchwoode Ct					
7000	TYPK	60477	3425	8W-19S	A2
Bird Ln					
2200	BTVA	60510	3077	37W-1S	C3
Bird St					
500	ELGN	60123	2854	34W-12N	D3
Birdie Dr					
12600	HTLY	60142	2744	42W-19N	D3
Birdsall St					
2400	BLID	60406	3277	3W-14S	A6
Birds Bridge Rd					
22800	TroT	60404	3584	30W-27S	B6
22800	TroT	60447	3584	30W-28S	B6
24300	CnhT	60447	3584	30W-28S	B6
Birdseye Ct					
13200	PNFD	60585	3337	32W-15S	D2
Birdsong Ct					
600	LslT	60540	3142	24W-6S	C4
2300	SMBG	60194	2857	26W-11N	E3
Birginal Dr					
700	BNVL	60106	2915	16W-6N	D5
Birkdale Ct					
10	LIHL	60156	2692	38W-21N	D5
400	WNFD	60190	3023	26W-1N	D2
1100	NPVL	60563	3141	27W-5S	B3
Birkdale Rd					
300	LKBF	60044	2593	11W-28N	D6
Birkett Av					
800	HMND	46327	3352		E4
Birkey Av					
300	CTHL	60403	3418	24W-21S	D6
S Birkhoff Av					
8300	CHCG	60620	3214	0W-9S	A3
W Birks Av					
1200	LGNG	60525	3147	13W-5S	A1
1200	LynT	60525	3147	13W-5S	A1
Birkshire Dr					
3500	MchT	60050	2471	32W-37N	B2
Birmingham Av					
100	CHHT	60411	3596	0W-26S	B2
Birmingham Ct					
100	ROSL	60172	2912	25W-7N	C4
1500	CLLK	60014	2693	36W-22N	C3
W Birmingham Ct					
5000	BHPK	60083	2421	13W-39N	A5
5000	BHPK	60099	2421	13W-39N	A5
Birmingham Dr					
1500	AURA	60502	3139	32W-5S	B3
Birmingham Ln					
-	SMBG	60193	2859	21W-9N	D7
1500	CLLK	60014	2693	36W-22N	C3
Birmingham Pl					
-	JLET	60586	3415	32W-21S	D7
-	JLET	60586	3495	32W-21S	D1
10	VNHL	60061	2647	16W-25N	C6
Birmingham St					
6000	CHRG	60415	3275	7W-12S	B1
Birnam Tr					
200	DGvT	60527	3207	17W-10S	C5
W Biros Ln					
200	RDLK	60073	2531	23W-31N	E7
Bisbee Dr					
2900	JLET	60432	3500	20W-22S	C2
Biscay Ct					
1100	AURA	60502	3139	32W-6S	B4
Biscayne Ct					
200	BMDL	60108	2912	25W-6N	B7
Biscayne Dr					
1200	EGVV	60007	2914	19W-8N	C3
Biscayne Rd					
3400	MHRY	60050	2585	32W-30N	B1
Biscayne St					
200	BMDL	60108	2912	25W-6N	B7
200	BMDL	60172	2912	25W-6N	B7
200	BmdT	60172	2912	25W-6N	B7
Bishop Av					
900	AURA	60506	3199	36W-8S	D2
Bishop Ct					
300	BRLT	60103	2967	28W-5N	B1
300	IVNS	60010	2751	25W-16N	A6
800	SMBG	60194	2858	25W-11N	A3
1500	MPPT	60056	2808	14W-13N	C5
39500	LkvT	60046	2416	24W-39N	C4
W Bishop Ct					
1000	PLTN	60067	2805	22W-15N	B3
Bishop Rd					
17700	TYPK	60487	3424	10W-21S	B6
Bishop St					
700	WCHI	60185	3022	29W-0S	D6
800	AURA	60506	3199	36W-8S	E2
Bishop St					
1000	ANTH	60002	2357	23W-41N	E7
N Bishop St					
10	CHCG	60607	3033	1W-0N	D4
800	CHCG	60622	3033	1W-1N	D2
S Bishop St					
800	CHCG	60607	3033	1W-0S	D6
1800	CHCG	60608	3091	1W-1S	D1
4600	CHCG	60609	3091	1W-4S	D7
4700	CHCG	60609	3151	1W-5S	D1
5500	CHCG	60636	3151	1W-7S	D5
7500	CHCG	60620	3213	1W-8S	D1
9400	CHCG	60643	3213	1W-11S	D6
10800	CHCG	60643	3277	1W-13S	D3
12200	CHCG	60643	3277	1W-14S	E6
12200	CTPK	60827	3277	1W-14S	E6
Bishop Ford Memorial Expwy					
-	BlmT	-	3429	1E-21S	B7
-	BlmT	-	3509	1E-22S	B2
-	BlmT	-	3597	1E-26S	C3
-	CHCG	-	3214	0E-11S	D7
-	CHCG	-	3215	1E-11S	A7
-	CHCG	-	3278	0E-14S	E5
-	CHCG	-	3279	1E-13S	A3
-	CHCG	-	3351	1E-15S	B1
-	CTCY	-	3351	1E-17S	C4
-	DLTN	-	3351	1E-18S	B7
-	FDHT	-	3509	1E-24S	C6
-	GNWD	-	3509	1E-23S	B3
-	LYWD	-	3509	1E-23S	B4
-	SHLD	-	3351	1E-18S	B7
-	SHLD	-	3429	1E-21S	B7
-	SLVL	60411	3597	1E-26S	C3
-	ThtT	-	3429	1E-20S	B5
Bishop Ford Mem Expwy I-94					
-	CHCG	-	3214	0E-11S	D7
-	CHCG	-	3215	1E-11S	A7
-	CHCG	-	3278	0E-14S	E5
-	CHCG	-	3279	1E-14S	A6
-	CHCG	-	3351	1E-15S	B1
-	CTCY	-	3351	2E-16S	C3
-	DLTN	-	3351	1E-18S	B7
-	SHLD	-	3351	1E-18S	B7
-	SHLD	-	3429	1E-20S	B3
Bishop Ford Mem Expwy SR-394					
-	BlmT	-	3429	1E-21S	B7
-	BlmT	-	3509	1E-22S	B2
-	BlmT	-	3597	1E-26S	C3
-	FDHT	-	3509	2E-25S	C7
-	GNWD	-	3509	1E-22S	B2
-	LYWD	-	3509	1E-23S	B4
-	SHLD	-	3429	1E-21S	B7
-	SLVL	60411	3597	1E-26S	C3
-	ThtT	-	3429	1E-20S	B4
Bishop Quarter Ln					
100	OKPK	60301	3031	8W-0N	A4
100	OKPK	60302	3031	8W-0N	A4
Bishops Wy					
1700	MDLN	60060	2590	20W-28N	A6
Bishops Gate					
500	NLNX	60451	3502	15W-25S	B7
700	NLNX	60451	3590	16W-26S	A2
Bismark Ct					
700	EGVV	60007	2913	21W-8N	D2
Bismark St					
7700	RvsT	60546	3088	9W-3S	C6
Bison Ln					
1200	HFET	60192	2856	31W-12N	A2
1900	JNBG	60050	2471	30W-37N	E1
Bison Rd					
500	OSWG	60543	3263	39W-11S	A1
Bison Tr					
1200	CLSM	60188	2967	28W-3N	B5
Bisque Dr					
800	BNHL	60010	2697	27W-20N	C7
Bissel St					
10	JLET	60432	3499	22W-23S	C4
10	JltT	60432	3499	22W-23S	C4
E Bissell Dr					
800	PLTN	60074	2753	19W-16N	B7
N Bissell Dr					
100	PLTN	60074	2753	19W-16N	B7
Bissell Rd					
100	AdnT	60034	2349		E3
100	LinT	53147	2349		E3
N Bissell St					
1600	CHCG	60614	2977	1W-2N	E7
Bitternut Ln					
4100	GRNE	60031	2478	14W-36N	D4
Bitterroot Dr					
6900	JLET	60586	3495	32W-21S	C1
Bitter Spring Ct					
-	ALGN	60102	2746	36W-18N	E4
Bittersweet Av					
700	NCHI	60044	2593	12W-30N	B2
2400	HHLL	60051	2586	30W-29N	B3
2500	NndT	60051	2586	30W-29N	B4
Bittersweet Ct					
-	DSPN	60018	2863	13W-9N	A6
10	WDRG	60517	3143	21W-7S	E6
300	SMBG	60193	2858	23W-10N	E6
2200	AURA	60506	3137	38W-6S	A5
Bittersweet Dr					
100	FmtT	60060	2645	21W-26N	E3
800	NHBK	60062	2757	9W-17N	C4
1000	BRLT	60103	2911	28W-6N	B6
1000	WynT	60103	2911	28W-6N	B6
1100	PLNO	60545	3259	48W-13S	B5
7300	GRNE	60031	2477	18W-35N	A7
7400	GRNE	60031	2476	18W-35N	E7
Bittersweet Ln					
-	SRWD	60404	3496	31W-22S	A3
100	SMWD	60107	2856	30W-10N	C6
400	ElgT	60124	2907	38W-8N	A3
600	NlxT	60451	3501	16W-24S	E6
700	HNDL	60521	3146	14W-5S	C2
13200	HTLY	60142	2744	42W-20N	C1
E Bittersweet Ln					
1800	MPPT	60056	2808	13W-14N	D4
Bittersweet Pl					
-	BtnT	60081	2414	29W-38N	C6
N Bittersweet Pl					
38300	AntT	60081	2415	27W-38N	B7
W Bittersweet Pl					
600	CHCG	60613	2977	1W-5N	E1
600	CHCG	60613	2978		A1
6500	CHCG	60634	2975	8W-5N	A1
Bittersweet Rd					
500	SchT	60175	2963	37W-3N	D6
500	SCRL	60175	2963	37W-3N	D6
Bittersweet Tr					
500	CLLK	60014	2640	34W-26N	C3
26400	FmtT	60060	2645	22W-26N	B3
26400	HNWD	60060	2645	22W-26N	B3
Bixtone Pth					
10	ElaT	60047	2644	24W-25N	D5

STREET Block	City	ZIP	Map#	CGS	Grid
Bixtone Pth					
10	HNWD	60047	2644	24W-25N	D4
Bjork Dr					
1000	NlxT	60451	3500	19W-23S	E4
Black Dr					
-	CHCG	60636	3151	1W-7S	E5
Black Rd					
-	JLET	60447	3495	33W-22S	A3
1800	JLET	60435	3498	26W-23S	A3
2000	JLET	60435	3497	26W-22S	E3
2300	TroT	60435	3497	27W-22S	D3
3100	JLET	60431	3497	28W-22S	A3
3900	JLET	60431	3496	28W-22S	E3
W Black Rd					
-	SwdT	60447	3495	33W-23S	C3
200	SRWD	60404	3496	31W-23S	A3
800	JLET	60435	3498	25W-22S	B3
3900	JLET	60404	3496	29W-23S	E3
3900	JLET	60431	3496	29W-23S	E3
23400	SRWD	60431	3496	29W-23S	E3
24600	TroT	60404	3496	30W-22S	A3
24900	SRWD	60404	3495	31W-22S	E3
24900	TroT	60404	3495	31W-22S	D3
25900	JLET	60447	3495	32W-23S	C3
Blackberry					
-	NLNX	60442	3589	17W-27S	C4
Blackberry Ct					
10	SgrT	60506	3135	41W-5S	D4
100	YKVL	60560	3261	43W-13S	B6
800	GRNE	60031	2476	18W-34N	E7
900	LIHL	60156	2693	37W-22N	C4
1300	LYVL	60048	2591	17W-30N	B2
1500	NPVL	60565	3204	24W-10S	D5
W Blackberry Ct					
10	SMWD	60107	2856	30W-10N	C5
Blackberry Dr					
100	BGBK	60440	3268	24W-12S	D2
400	BLVY	60098	2525	38W-31N	E6
1800	GNVA	60134	3019	36W-1N	D2
1800	SCRL	60134	3019	36W-1N	D2
1800	SCRL	60174	3019	36W-1N	D2
3700	LIHL	60156	2693	37W-22N	B4
Blackberry Ln					
1900	HFET	60169	2857	26W-12N	E1
7600	WLBK	60527	3207	17W-8S	D2
E Blackberry Ln					
200	YKVL	60560	3261	43W-13S	C6
S Blackberry Ln					
25400	CNHN	60410	3672	31W-31S	E5
25400	CnhT	60410	3672	31W-31S	E5
W Blackberry Ln					
100	YKVL	60560	3261	43W-13S	B6
Blackberry Rd					
1600	MTGY	60506	3198	39W-9S	E5
1700	MTGY	60538	3198	39W-9S	E5
Blackberry Tr					
10	AURA	60506	3136	39W-7S	D7
Blackberry Wy					
500	GnvT	60134	3019	38W-0N	A4
Blackberry Creek Dr					
1200	ELBN	60119	3017	43W-0N	B6
Blackberry Hill Rd					
500	BbyT	60119	3075	43W-1S	B2
Blackberry Ridge Dr					
500	AURA	60506	3136	39W-6S	D5
2200	JLET	60586	3415	31W-21S	E6
Blackburn Av					
400	DRGV	60516	3206	19W-8S	D1
400	DRN	60561	3206	19W-8S	E1
7000	DRGV	60516	3144	19W-8S	D7
7300	DRN	60516	3206	19W-8S	D1
Blackburn Cir					
1000	LYVL	60048	2591	17W-29N	B4
Blackburn Ct					
500	DRGV	60516	3206	19W-8S	D1
1200	NPVL	60540	3142	25W-7S	A6
2200	AURA	60503	3265	32W-11S	B1
12400	MKNA	60448	3502	15W-24S	B4
12400	MKNA	60451	3502	15W-24S	B4
Blackburn Dr					
900	GYLK	60030	2533	19W-33N	B2
1600	MDLN	60060	2590	20W-27N	A7
11600	ODPK	60467	3344	14W-16S	D4
E Blackburn Dr					
900	IVNS	60067	2751	23W-17N	E5
W Blackburn Dr					
900	IVNS	60067	2751	23W-17N	D5
Blackburn Pl					
6700	DRGV	60516	3144	19W-7S	D7
Blackburn St					
700	GRNE	60031	2478	13W-35N	E7
1400	WHTN	60187	3082	23W-1S	E2
Black Cherry Cir					
3200	CPVL	60110	2747	35W-17N	C6
Black Cherry Ln					
800	RLKH	60073	2474	24W-36N	C4
900	LkvT	60041	2474	24W-36N	C4
900	RLKH	60041	2474	24W-36N	C4
Blackcherry Ln					
10	MltT	60137	3083	23W-3S	A5
W Black Cherry Ln					
24300	LkvT	60041	2474	24W-36N	C4
24300	RLKH	60041	2474	24W-36N	C4
24300	RLKH	60073	2474	24W-36N	C4
Black Diamond Ct					
10	LIHL	60156	2693	37W-21N	C5
Black Duck Ln					
200	BmdT	60108	2967	26W-5N	E2
Blackfoot Ct					
500	WLNG	60090	2754	16W-17N	D5
Blackfoot Dr					
300	BGBK	60490	3267	26W-12S	E3
300	BGBK	60490	3268	26W-12S	A3
16600	LKPT	60441	3420	20W-19S	C3
S Blackfoot Dr					
16700	LKPT	60441	3420	20W-20S	B4
W Black Forest Ct					
12000	HMGN	60491	3422	15W-18S	C1
S Black Forest Ln					
11600	PSPK	60464	3274	10W-13S	C5
Black Forest Tr					
12100	HMGN	60491	3422	15W-18S	C1
Black Fox Ln					
13000	LMNT	60439	3343	17W-15S	D1
Black Friars Rd					
15300	ODPK	60462	3346	11W-18S	A7
Blackhawk Av					
400	CPVL	60110	2748	32W-18N	D5
1100	NndT	60051	2585	31W-30N	D1
W Blackhawk Av					
26000	GrtT	60041	2473	26W-35N	E6
Blackhawk Blvd					
-	WnfT	60510	3080	30W-1S	A3
N Blackhawk Cir					
1300	SEGN	60177	2908	36W-8N	A2

STREET Block	City	ZIP	Map#	CGS	Grid
S Blackhawk Cir					
500	SEGN	60177	2908	36W-8N	A2
Blackhawk Ct					
100	WDDL	60191	2915	18W-7N	A4
1100	SMBG	60193	2913	22W-9N	C1
3100	SCRL	60174	2965	33W-3N	A5
11600	FftT	60448	3502	14W-23S	D4
11600	MKNA	60448	3502	14W-23S	D4
Blackhawk Dr					
-	MrnT	60037	2704	9W-24N	D1
10	MltT	60187	3081	26W-2S	E4
10	MltT	60187	3082	26W-2S	A3
10	MonT	60466	3595	3W-28S	B5
10	PKFT	60466	3595	4W-27S	A5
10	SmbT	60193	2913	23W-8N	A2
10	TNTN	60476	3428	0E-20S	E4
100	MNKA	60447	3583	33W-28S	B7
200	CLSM	60188	2968	25W-2N	B7
200	CLSM	60188	3024	25W-2N	B1
200	CNHL	60514	3145	17W-5S	B2
200	CNHL	60559	3145	17W-5S	B2
200	PKFT	60466	3594	4W-27S	E4
200	SchT	60177	2908	35W-7N	B6
200	WTMT	60559	3145	17W-5S	B2
300	BTVA	60510	3077	36W-0S	E1
500	ALGN	60102	2694	35W-21N	B5
500	ALGN	60156	2694	35W-21N	B5
500	BTVA	60510	3019	36W-0S	E7
500	LIHL	60102	2694	35W-21N	B5
500	LIHL	60156	2694	35W-21N	B5
500	WTMT	60559	3085	17W-4S	B7
600	BTVA	60510	3020	36W-0S	A7
700	RedT	60408	3941	32W-40S	D4
700	UYPK	60466	3684	3W-31S	B4
800	ELGN	60120	2855	32W-12N	C1
800	ROSL	60172	2913	22W-8N	B2
800	ROSL	60193	2913	22W-8N	B2
800	SmbT	60172	2913	22W-8N	B2
1000	UYPK	60449	3684	3W-30S	B4
1200	ELGN	60120	2801	32W-12N	C7
1400	MPPT	60056	2861	16W-12N	C2
1700	WCHI	60185	3021	31W-2N	D2
1700	WynT	60185	3021	31W-2N	D2
3600	RGMW	60008	2806	20W-15N	B2
7200	TYPK	60477	3504	9W-23S	E3
S Blackhawk Dr					
24300	CNHN	60410	3672	32W-29S	D3
W Blackhawk Dr					
-	HmrT	60441	3420	20W-20S	C5
16000	LKPT	60441	3420	20W-20S	C5
17800	WrnT	60030	2534	17W-33N	A3
Blackhawk Ln					
500	BGBK	60440	3268	24W-11S	D1
800	RVWD	60015	2702	13W-21N	E7
1300	BRLT	60103	2967	28W-6N	A1
4300	LGGV	60047	2700	19W-22N	C3
4400	LSLE	60532	3142	24W-4S	D1
13900	ODPK	60462	3346	9W-16S	C3
25600	LKBN	60010	2644	25W-24N	A6
25600	NBRN	60010	2644	25W-24N	A6
S Blackhawk Pkwy					
19100	MKNA	60448	3504	10W-23S	B3
Blackhawk Pl					
200	BGBK	60440	3268	24W-11S	E1
Blackhawk Rd					
10	ElaT	60047	2646	20W-25N	A5
10	ElaT	60060	2646	20W-25N	A5
10	GLNC	60022	2758	7W-20N	C2
10	HDPK	60035	2758	7W-20N	B2
10	HNWD	60047	2646	20W-25N	A5
200	RVSD	60546	3088	9W-3S	D5
300	BRWN	60402	3088	9W-3S	D5
300	RVSD	60402	3088	9W-3S	D5
2500	WLMT	60091	2812	5W-14N	A5
2800	WLMT	60091	2811	5W-14N	E5
4800	LtRT	60545	3332	46W-14S	A1
Blackhawk St					
10	AURA	60506	3138	36W-7S	A6
400	JLET	60432	3499	21W-23S	E4
400	JltT	60432	3499	21W-23S	E3
W Blackhawk St					
400	CHCG	60610	3034	0W-1N	A1
800	CHCG	60610	3033	1W-1N	E1
800	CHCG	60622	3033	1W-1N	E1
Blackhawk Ter					
200	BNVL	60106	2915	16W-5N	D7
Blackhawk Tr					
100	AlqT	60102	2695	32W-21N	A5
300	TNLK	53181	2354		B2
1500	WLNG	60090	2754	16W-17N	D5
3100	SCRL	60174	2965	33W-4N	A5
6200	IHPK	60525	3146	14W-7S	D6
N Blackhawk Tr					
30700	FmtT	60030	2588	24W-30N	C1
41200	WDWH	60083	2421	13W-41N	A1
41400	WDWH	60099	2421	13W-41N	A1
Blackhawk Springs Dr					
10	LtRT	60545	3332	46W-15S	A2
Blackheath Ln					
1300	RVWD	60015	2703	12W-21N	B6
Black Hill Dr					
100	HnrT	60107	2856	30W-9N	B7
Black Hill Ridge Dr					
1800	JLET	60586	3415	31W-21S	D7
S Blackman Av					
10	JLET	60435	3498	24W-24S	D5
10	JLET	60436	3498	24W-24S	D5
Blackman Ct					
2600	GNVA	60134	3019	37W-0N	C6
Blackman Rd					
2600	GNVA	60134	3019	37W-0N	C6
E Blackman St					
100	HRVD	60033	2406	50W-38N	B6
W Blackman St					
100	HRVD	60033	2406	50W-38N	A6
Blackman Ter					
700	ANTH	60002	2357	23W-42N	D6
Black Oak Av					
18300	TYPK	60487	3424	10W-22S	B7
N Black Oak Av					
40500	AntT	60002	2416	24W-40N	C2
Black Oak Ct					
10	BGBK	60490	3267	26W-11S	E2
1900	SCRL	60174	2965	33W-4N	A4
2200	LSLE	60532	3142	24W-6S	D5
Black Oak Dr					
1000	DRGV	60515	3084	19W-3S	C6
1800	MchT	60050	2526	36W-33N	D2
4200	LSLE	60532	3082	23W-4S	E7
Black Oak Rd					
-	HtdT	60033	2464	48W-34N	E7
Black Oak Tr					
1300	AURA	60506	3137	36W-5S	D3
12100	HTLY	60142	2744	42W-19N	D2
Black Partridge					
-	LmnT	60439	3270	20W-13S	A4

STREET Block	City	ZIP	Map#	CGS	Grid
Black Partridge Ln					
4400	LSLE	60532	3142	24W-4S	C1
Black Partridge Rd					
700	NndT	60051	2528	31W-31N	D7
1000	NndT	60051	2585	31W-30N	D1
Black Pine Tr					
12100	HMGN	60491	3422	15W-18S	C1
Blacksmith Ct					
28800	LKMR	60051	2529	28W-32N	D5
Blacksmith Dr					
2100	WHTN	60187	3083	23W-3S	A5
2200	MltT	60137	3083	23W-3S	A5
Blacksmith Ln					
1000	LMNT	60439	3271	18W-13S	A5
Blacksmith St					
28700	LKMR	60051	2529	28W-32N	E5
Black Stallion Ct					
1100	NPVL	60540	3204	24W-8S	D1
Black Stallion Dr					
1100	NPVL	60540	3204	24W-8S	D1
Blackstone Av					
-	GRNE	60031	2536	13W-34N	A1
-	LNSG	60438	3429	1E-21S	B7
-	ThtT	60438	3429	1E-21S	B7
300	WLSP	60480	3209	12W-9S	D2
3600	MKHM	60428	3426	4W-19S	D2
3800	GRNE	60031	2535	14W-34N	D1
5500	CTSD	60525	3147	13W-6S	A3
6200	LynT	60525	3147	13W-7S	B5
7100	JSTC	60458	3147	11W-8S	E7
7100	JSTC	60458	3148	11W-8S	A7
7200	JSTC	60458	3209	11W-8S	E1
14200	DLTN	60419	3351	1E-16S	B4
19900	BlmT	60411	3509	1E-23S	B3
19900	LYWD	60411	3509	1E-23S	B3
20200	MTSN	60443	3506	5W-24S	C5
20200	OMFD	60461	3506	5W-24S	C5
S Blackstone Av					
100	LGNG	60525	3087	13W-4S	A7
200	GNWD	60425	3509	1E-23S	B3
200	LGNG	60525	3147	13W-4S	A1
500	LynT	60525	3147	13W-5S	A1
4900	CHCG	60615	3153	1E-5S	A2
5500	CHCG	60637	3153	1E-6S	A3
7100	CHCG	60619	3153	1E-8S	B7
7500	CHCG	60619	3215	1E-8S	B1
Blackstone Ct					
500	LKVL	60046	2417	22W-39N	B5
600	AURA	60504	3202	30W-8S	A2
600	LslT	60540	3142	24W-6S	C4
Blackstone Dr					
3800	AURA	60504	3202	30W-8S	A2
6500	DRGV	60516	3144	19W-7S	D6
Blackstone Ln					
13100	PNFD	60585	3338	30W-15S	A2
Blackstone Pl					
500	HDPK	60035	2758	7W-20N	B1
E Blackstone Pl					
400	OKTR	60181	3027	17W-0S	C7
400	VLPK	60181	3027	17W-0S	C7
W Blackstone Pl					
25500	LkvT	60046	2474	25W-37N	A2
Blackstone St					
100	TNTN	60476	3428	0E-21S	E6
Black Swan Ct					
2000	DRN	60561	3206	19W-10S	E4
W Blackthorn Ct					
200	RDLK	60073	2531	23W-33N	E4
Blackthorn Dr					
200	BFGV	60089	2701	16W-23N	C3
500	CLLK	60014	2640	33W-26N	D3
1400	GNVW	60025	2810	8W-14N	D5
1400	JLET	60586	3496	29W-22S	D1
Blackthorn Ln					
1000	NHBK	60062	2757	10W-17N	A5
1100	DRFD	60015	2703	10W-21N	E6
W Blackthorn Ln					
10	LKFT	60045	2649	11W-25N	E5
Blackthorn Rd					
200	RchT	60443	3593	8W-26S	B1
600	WNKA	60093	2812	5W-16N	A1
1000	RVWD	60015	2755	13W-20N	D1
Blackthorne Ln					
200	LslT	60540	3204	24W-8S	D1
200	WNVL	60555	3080	29W-3S	D5
S Blackthorne Rd					
24900	MHTN	60442	3677	19W-30S	E3
Blackthorne Ridge Dr					
-	FftT	60448	3502	15W-23S	C2
12000	MKNA	60448	3502	15W-23S	C2
Black Twig Cir					
10	LKZH	60047	2699	22W-22N	A4
Black Twig Rd					
10	RGMW	60008	2806	20W-13N	A6
N Black Velvet Ln					
37000	WrnT	60083	2477	17W-37N	B3
N Black Walnut					
24800	CbaT	60013	2642	28W-24N	D6
Black Walnut Ct					
700	SRGV	60554	3135	41W-5S	E3
700	SRGV	60554	3136	41W-5S	A3
1500	NPVL	60565	3204	24W-10S	D6
Black Walnut Dr					
800	SRGV	60554	3136	41W-4S	A2
900	SgrT	60554	3136	41W-4S	A2
Black Walnut Ln					
2900	SCRL	60174	2965	33W-4N	B4
Black Walnut Tr					
10	PlsT	60464	3273	11W-14S	D7
10	PSPK	60464	3273	11W-14S	D7
5600	LGGV	60047	2700	18W-23N	E1
5600	LGGV	60047	2701	18W-23N	A1
Blackwater Ct					
15900	TYPK	60477	3424	9W-19S	C1
Blackwater Dr					
3200	JLET	60431	3417	28W-21S	B6
Blackwell Ln					
1600	AURA	60504	3201	33W-9S	B5
Black Willow Dr					
10	CmpT	60175	2962	39W-5N	E3
Black Wolf Ct					
10	ALGN	60102	2746	37W-20N	C1
W Blackwolf Rd					
1200	RDLK	60073	2531	24W-34N	C1
Bladon Rd					
1300	SMBG	60195	2858	24W-12N	D2
Blaine Av					
6200	HMND	46320	3430		D2
6200	HMND	46324	3430		D2
S Blaine Av					
-	POSN	60469	3349	3W-16S	B3
5800	HMND	46320	3352		D7
5800	HMND	46320	3430		D1
14800	POSN	60426	3349	3W-17S	B5
Blaine Ct					
700	SMBG	60173	2805	21W-13N	C6

STREET Block	City	ZIP	Map#	CGS	Grid
Blaine Ct E					
3200	AURA	60504	3201	31W-8S	E2
Blaine Ct W					
3200	AURA	60504	3201	31W-8S	E2
Blaine Pl					
6400	BtnT	60081	2414	29W-38N	D7
Blaine St					
10	HNDL	60521	3146	15W-5S	B2
300	BTVA	60510	3078	35W-1S	A3
300	YKVL	60560	3333	43W-15S	B3
E Blaine St					
500	HRVD	60033	2406	49W-38N	B6
W Blaine St					
200	PTON	60468	3860	9W-37S	E3
300	HRVD	60033	2406	50W-38N	A6
Blair Ct					
500	LslT	60532	3143	22W-6S	C4
Blair Ln					
100	IVNS	60067	2752	22W-16N	A7
200	BTVA	60510	3078	36W-1S	A2
300	BGBK	60440	3269	23W-11S	A1
400	BGBK	60440	3268	23W-11S	E1
1200	HFET	60169	2858	25W-12N	C2
2100	GLHT	60139	2969	23W-4N	B4
7200	FXLK	60020	2415	28W-39N	A5
16400	OKFT	60452	3426	5W-19S	C2
Blair St					
10	WnfT	60185	3022	29W-0N	D5
100	WCHI	60185	3022	29W-0N	D5
200	WNFD	60190	3023	26W-0N	E5
500	PKFT	60466	3594	4W-25S	E1
500	PKFT	60466	3595	3W-26S	A2
E Blair St					
500	WnfT	60185	3022	29W-0N	D5
600	WCHI	60185	3022	29W-0N	D5
S Blair St					
-	PNFD	60585	3265	32W-14S	C7
W Blair St					
100	WCHI	60185	3022	30W-0N	C5
400	WnfT	60185	3022	30W-0N	B5
Blake Ct					
600	CLSM	60188	2967	28W-3N	B6
N Blake Dr					
100	GDLY	60407	4030	32W-43S	D2
Blake Ln					
4000	GNVW	60062	2809	11W-15N	D2
4100	GNVW	60025	2809	11W-15N	D2
Blake Rd					
-	MchT	60050	2528	32W-34N	B1
-	MHRY	60050	2528	32W-34N	B1
Blake St					
-	PLNO	60545	3332	45W-14S	B1
S Blake St					
3600	CHCG	60609	3091	2W-3S	B5
Blakely Ct					
25700	PNFD	60585	3337	32W-15S	D3
Blakely Dr					
-	PNFD	60544	3337	32W-15S	D3
13200	PNFD	60585	3337	32W-15S	D2
24800	PNFD	60585	3338	31W-15S	A2
Blakely Ln					
2500	NPVL	60540	3202	29W-8S	D1
Blakely Pkwy					
400	WcnT	60010	2644	25W-26N	A4
400	WcnT	60084	2644	25W-26N	A4
W Blakely Pkwy					
25400	WcnT	60010	2644	25W-26N	A4
25400	WcnT	60084	2644	25W-26N	A4
Blakely St					
300	WCHI	60185	3022	29W-0N	D5
300	WDSK	60098	2581	42W-30N	C2
Blakewood Cir					
600	WnfT	60185	3081	28W-1S	A3
600	WnfT	60187	3081	28W-1S	A3
600	WnfT	60190	3081	28W-1S	A3
Blanc Ct					
1600	GRNE	60031	2477	18W-35N	A5
Blanchan Av					
1100	LGPK	60513	3087	11W-2S	D4
1100	LGPK	60525	3087	11W-2S	D4
1500	PvsT	60525	3087	11W-2S	D4
3500	BKFD	60513	3087	11W-3S	D6
4500	BKFD	60513	3147	11W-4S	D1
4600	BKFD	60525	3147	11W-4S	D1
4600	MCCK	60525	3147	11W-4S	D1
Blanchard Cir					
10	SBTN	60010	2803	26W-13N	D5
10	WHTN	60187	3082	24W-2S	C4
E Blanchard Cir					
8000	GLkT	60450	3761	33W-33S	A3
N Blanchard Ct					
1400	WHTN	60187	3024	23W-0N	E5
Blanchard Ln					
2900	WCHI	60185	2965	32W-4N	B4
Blanchard Rd					
-	BHPK	60087	2480	10W-37N	B3
-	WkgT	60087	2479	11W-36N	E3
-	WkgT	60087	2480	10W-37N	B3
600	WKGN	60087	2480	10W-37N	A3
1700	WKGN	60087	2479	11W-37N	D3
2800	BHPK	60087	2479	12W-37N	C3
W Blanchard Rd					
12300	BHPK	60087	2479	12W-36N	C3
12300	WKGN	60087	2479	12W-36N	C3
12300	WkgT	60087	2479	12W-36N	C3
12900	WrnT	60087	2479	13W-37N	A3
13100	WrnT	60031	2479	13W-37N	A3
13300	WKGN	60031	2478	13W-37N	E3
13300	WKGN	60087	2478	13W-37N	E3
13300	WrnT	60031	2478	13W-37N	E3
13300	WrnT	60087	2478	13W-37N	E3
Blanchard St					
200	HRVD	60033	2406	50W-38N	A7
1000	DRGV	60516	3144	20W-6S	B4
2100	LslT	60516	3144	21W-6S	A4
N Blanchard St					
400	WHTN	60187	3024	23W-0S	E6
S Blanchard St					
100	WHTN	60187	3024	23W-0S	E7
800	WHTN	60187	3082	23W-1S	E2
Blanche Ct					
10	CbaT	60010	2698	25W-22N	A4
10	NBRN	60010	2698	25W-22N	A4
Blandford Av					
800	JLET	60451	3500	19W-22S	D2
3500	NLNX	60451	3500	19W-22S	E2
Blandford Ct					
1500	SMBG	60173	2859	21W-10N	E4
3000	JLET	60451	3500	19W-22S	C2
Blaney Dr					
700	DYR	46311	3598		E4
2800	SjnT	46311	3598		E4
Blarne					
-	NLNX	60451	3590	16W-25S	A1
Blarney Dr					
4600	MTSN	60443	3506	5W-24S	B5

STREET Block	City	ZIP	Map#	CGS	Grid
Blarney Ln					
28300	LKBN	60010	2696	28W-22N	E3
Blarney Rd					
8000	TYPK	60477	3424	10W-21S	C6
Blarney Stone Ln					
2900	AlqT	60013	2641	31W-25N	C4
Blaze Tr					
900	WLNG	60090	2754	15W-16N	E6
900	WLNG	60090	2755	15W-16N	A6
Blazer Av					
7600	JSTC	60458	3209	11W-8S	E2
Blazer St					
7500	JSTC	60458	3209	11W-8S	E1
Blazing Star Ct					
-	GNVA	60134	3019	37W-0N	B5
-	LKVL	60046	2474	23W-37N	D2
24300	PNFD	60585	3338	30W-14S	B1
Blazingstar Ct					
3000	NPVL	60564	3202	30W-11S	A7
Blazing Star Dr					
-	LKVL	60046	2474	23W-37N	D2
-	LkvT	60046	2474	23W-37N	D2
200	MNKA	60447	3672	33W-29S	B3
Blazingstar Ln					
-	JLET	60447	3495	33W-22S	A2
Blazing Star Rd					
800	GYLK	60030	2533	19W-31N	C6
Blazing Star Tr					
700	CRY	60013	2641	32W-24N	B7
E Blecke Av					
10	ADSN	60101	2970	18W-2N	E7
10	ADSN	60101	2971	18W-2N	A7
Blenheim Ct					
10	MltT	60137	3083	23W-2S	A4
Blenheim Dr					
800	SMBG	60195	2858	24W-12N	D2
Bliss Ct					
2900	JLET	60586	3415	32W-20S	C5
Bliss Dr					
100	OKBK	60523	3086	15W-1S	B2
Bliss Rd					
10	BbyT	60506	3076	40W-2S	B4
10	BbyT	60510	3076	41W-2S	A5
10	BbyT	60554	3076	40W-2S	B4
10	SgrT	60554	3135	41W-5S	D3
10	SRGV	60506	3135	42W-6S	D4
10	SRGV	60554	3135	41W-5S	D3
100	SgrT	60506	3075	41W-4S	E7
100	SgrT	60506	3135	41W-5S	D3
100	SgrT	60554	3075	41W-4S	E7
300	BbyT	60506	3075	41W-4S	E7
300	BbyT	60554	3075	41W-4S	E7
500	BbyT	60119	3076	41W-2S	A5
Bliss Rd CO-78					
10	BbyT	60506	3076	40W-2S	B4
10	BbyT	60510	3076	41W-2S	A5
10	BbyT	60554	3076	40W-2S	B4
10	SgrT	60554	3135	41W-5S	D3
10	SRGV	60506	3135	42W-6S	D4
10	SRGV	60554	3135	41W-5S	D3
100	SgrT	60506	3075	41W-4S	E7
100	SgrT	60506	3135	41W-5S	D3
100	SgrT	60554	3075	41W-4S	E7
300	BbyT	60506	3075	41W-4S	E7
300	BbyT	60554	3075	41W-4S	E7
500	BbyT	60119	3076	41W-2S	A5
W Bliss St					
800	CHCG	60622	3033	1W-1N	E2
Blitsch Pl					
3800	JNBG	60050	2471	31W-35N	D5
Blivin St					
-	BtnT	60081	2414	30W-40N	A3
-	SPGV	60081	2414	30W-40N	A3
7600	SPGV	60081	2413	30W-39N	E4
Blivin St CO-V43					
-	BtnT	60081	2414	30W-40N	A3
-	SPGV	60081	2414	30W-40N	A3
7600	SPGV	60081	2413	30W-39N	E4
Block Ct					
8000	TYPK	60477	3504	10W-23S	C4
Block Ln					
-	BtnT	60099	2362	11W-43N	D4
-	WPHR	60099	2362	11W-43N	D4
Block Rd					
7400	KdlT	60560	3334	40W-17S	C7
Block St					
700	BCHR	60401	3864	0W-37S	C2
Blodgett Av					
-	DGvT	60516	3206	19W-9S	D4
10	CNHL	60514	3145	17W-5S	C2
5100	DRGV	60515	3144	19W-5S	D3
5900	DRGV	60516	3144	19W-6S	D5
E Blodgett Av					
10	LKBF	60044	2593	10W-29N	E5
100	LKBF	60044	2594	10W-29N	A5
W Blodgett Av					
100	LKBF	60044	2593	11W-29N	E5
700	ShdT	60044	2593	12W-29N	B5
Blodgett Ct					
400	NPVL	60565	3203	27W-10S	C6
Blodgett Rd					
-	AxST	60450	3761	32W-33S	C4
-	AxST	60481	3761	32W-33S	C4
-	CNHN	60481	3761	32W-33S	C4
-	CnhT	60481	3761	32W-33S	E4
-	WmTp	60481	3761	32W-33S	E4
17700	HmrT	60448	3421	17W-21S	C7
17700	HmrT	60491	3421	17W-21S	C7
17700	NlxT	60448	3421	17W-21S	C7
17700	NlxT	60448	3501	17W-22S	C1
Bloner Pkwy					
1000	AlqT	60021	2696	30W-22N	A4
1000	FRGV	60021	2696	30W-22N	A4
W Bloners Dr					
28600	CbaT	60013	2642	28W-24N	D7
28800	AlqT	60013	2642	28W-24N	D7
Bloom St					
10	HDPK	60035	2704	8W-23N	D2
Bloomfield Cir					
300	BMDL	60108	2968	24W-5N	C1
500	GNVA	60134	3019	36W-1N	D2
Bloomfield Cir E					
300	OSWG	60543	3263	36W-13S	E5
Bloomfield Cir W					
-	OSWG	60543	3263	36W-13S	D5
Bloomfield Ct					
-	OSWG	60543	3263	36W-13S	E5
300	VNHL	60061	2647	18W-25N	A5
3100	AURA	60504	3201	31W-8S	D2
W Bloomfield Ct					
700	PLTN	60067	2805	21W-14N	C4
Bloomfield Dr					
-	DrrT	60098	2581	41W-28N	C5
-	WDSK	60098	2581	41W-28N	C5
400	BGBK	60440	3268	23W-12S	E3
1100	BRLT	60107	2856	29W-9N	D7

Block	City	ZIP	Map#	CGS	Grid
Bloomfield Dr					
1100	SMWD	60107	2856	29W-9N	D7
2600	LSLE	60532	3142	24W-7S	D6
2800	JLET	60436	3497	27W-25S	C7
10400	PlsT	60464	3345	13W-15S	B1
11800	HTLY	60142	2744	42W-20N	A1
W Bloomfield Dr					
20900	LktT	60544	3340	26W-16S	A5
Bloomfield Ln					
-	BMDL	60108	2968	24W-5N	C2
300	GNEN	60137	3083	23W-1S	A2
700	AURA	60504	3201	31W-8S	D2
Bloomfield Pkwy					
200	BMDL	60108	2968	24W-5N	C2
Bloomingbank Rd					
10	RVSD	60546	3088	10W-3S	B6
Bloomingdale Av					
1600	MLPK	60160	2973	11W-2N	D7
3300	MLPK	60160	3029	12W-2N	B1
W Bloomingdale Av					
1500	CHCG	60622	2977	2W-2N	C7
2300	CHCG	60647	2977	3W-2N	A7
2800	CHCG	60647	2976	3W-2N	E7
4200	CHCG	60639	2976	5W-2N	B7
4800	CHCG	60639	2975	6W-2N	D7
6300	CHCG	60707	2975	8W-2N	A7
6700	CHCG	60707	2974	9W-2N	C7
7100	EDPK	60707	2974	9W-2N	C7
7900	EDPK	60171	2974	9W-2N	B7
Bloomingdale Ct					
100	GLHT	60139	2969	23W-3N	B6
Bloomingdale Rd					
10	GNEN	60137	3025	23W-1N	A3
10	GNEN	60187	3025	23W-1N	A3
10	WHTN	60187	3025	23W-1N	A3
100	MltT	60137	3025	23W-1N	A3
100	MltT	60188	3025	23W-1N	A3
300	GLHT	60137	3025	23W-2N	A1
300	GLHT	60139	3025	23W-2N	A1
300	MltT	60139	3025	23W-1N	A2
1200	BmdT	60137	3025	23W-2N	A1
1200	BmdT	60139	3025	23W-2N	A1
1200	BmdT	60188	3025	23W-2N	A1
1400	BmdT	60137	2969	23W-2N	A7
1400	BmdT	60139	2969	23W-2N	A7
1400	GLHT	60137	2969	23W-2N	A7
1400	GLHT	60139	2969	23W-3N	A5
2100	BMDL	60108	2969	23W-4N	A3
2100	BMDL	60139	2969	23W-4N	A3
2100	GLHT	60108	2969	23W-4N	A3
Bloomingdale Rd CO-4					
10	GNEN	60137	3025	23W-1N	A3
10	GNEN	60187	3025	23W-1N	A3
10	WHTN	60187	3025	23W-1N	A3
100	MltT	60137	3025	23W-1N	A3
100	MltT	60188	3025	23W-1N	A3
300	GLHT	60137	3025	23W-2N	A1
300	GLHT	60139	3025	23W-2N	A1
300	MltT	60139	3025	23W-1N	A2
1200	BmdT	60137	3025	23W-2N	A1
1200	BmdT	60139	3025	23W-2N	A1
1200	BmdT	60188	3025	23W-2N	A1
1400	BmdT	60137	2969	23W-2N	A7
1400	BmdT	60139	2969	23W-2N	A7
1400	GLHT	60137	2969	23W-2N	A7
1400	GLHT	60139	2969	23W-3N	A6
2100	BMDL	60108	2969	23W-4N	A3
2100	BMDL	60139	2969	23W-4N	A3
2100	GLHT	60108	2969	23W-4N	A3
E Bloomingdale Rd					
100	ITSC	60143	2914	19W-6N	C6
N Bloomingdale Rd					
100	BMDL	60108	2913	23W-5N	A7
100	BMDL	60108	2969	23W-5N	A1
200	BMDL	60172	2913	23W-6N	A6
N Bloomingdale Rd CO-4					
100	BMDL	60108	2913	23W-5N	A7
100	BMDL	60108	2969	23W-5N	A1
200	BMDL	60172	2913	23W-6N	A6
S Bloomingdale Rd					
-	GLHT	60139	2969	23W-4N	A3
100	BMDL	60108	2969	23W-5N	A2
200	BMDL	60139	2969	23W-4N	A3
S Bloomingdale Rd CO-4					
-	GLHT	60139	2969	23W-4N	A3
100	BMDL	60108	2969	23W-5N	A2
200	BMDL	60139	2969	23W-4N	A3
W Bloomingdale Rd					
100	ITSC	60143	2914	20W-6N	B7
600	ADSN	60143	2914	20W-5N	B7
1100	ADSN	60143	2970	20W-5N	A1
1100	ITSC	60143	2970	20W-5N	A1
N Bloomington Av					
3900	ANHT	60004	2753	19W-18N	C2
3900	PltT	60004	2753	19W-18N	C2
4000	ElaT	60004	2753	19W-18N	C2
4000	ElaT	60047	2753	19W-18N	C2
Bloomsbury Ct					
10	ALGN	60102	2747	35W-19N	B3
2100	AURA	60502	3139	33W-5S	B4
2100	AURA	60505	3139	33W-5S	B4
Bloomsbury Ln					
-	MTSN	60443	3594	6W-25S	A1
Blossom					
300	LKMR	60051	2529	28W-32N	E5
300	LKMR	60051	2530	28W-32N	A5
Blossom Av					
-	WDSK	60098	2581	41W-28N	C6
Blossom Ct					
10	SBTN	60010	2803	27W-13N	C6
200	BFGV	60089	2754	17W-20N	A1
700	NPVL	60540	3140	29W-7S	C7
700	OSWG	60543	3263	38W-13S	B6
1700	HDPK	60035	2757	9W-20N	C1
4800	WKGN	60087	2478	14W-37N	B1
S Blossom Dr					
12800	ALSP	60803	3276	5W-15S	B7
12800	ALSP	60803	3348	5W-15S	B1
W Blossom Dr					
4400	ALSP	60803	3276	5W-15S	C7
Blossom Ln					
10	GLF	60029	2865	8W-12N	A1
800	OSWG	60543	3263	38W-13S	B6
800	PTHT	60070	2809	13W-15N	A2
1900	AURA	60503	3201	32W-10S	C5
8500	TYPK	60487	3424	10W-19S	B2
W Blossom Ln					
20900	DPgT	60544	3340	26W-15S	A2
S Blossom Row					
1900	HMND	46394	3280		D5
Blossom St					
1400	NndT	60014	2586	30W-28N	A6
1800	NndT	60012	2586	30W-28N	A6
2300	LktT	60435	3417	27W-20S	D5
2300	PnfT	60435	3417	27W-20S	D5
12000	WKGN	60087	2479	12W-37N	C1
Blossom St					
12400	BHPK	60087	2479	12W-37N	B1
Blossom Ridge Dr					
1800	BGBK	60490	3267	27W-12S	C3
Blouin Dr					
1000	DLTN	60419	3351	1E-18S	A7
1100	SHLD	60419	3351	1E-18S	A7
1100	SHLD	60473	3351	1E-18S	A7
Blue Ct					
6000	AlqT	60014	2641	32W-26N	B3
6000	NndT	60014	2641	32W-26N	B3
N Blue Ct					
3600	NndT	60014	2641	32W-26N	B3
S Blue Ct					
6100	AlqT	60014	2641	32W-25N	B4
6100	NndT	60014	2641	32W-25N	B4
Blue Ash Dr					
200	BFGV	60089	2701	17W-23N	B2
Blue Aster Dr					
900	RMVL	60446	3340	25W-15S	C1
Blue Bayou Dr					
11700	HTLY	60142	2745	39W-20N	B1
Blue Bell Ct					
1700	NPVL	60565	3204	24W-10S	D6
25500	PNFD	60585	3337	31W-15S	D2
Bluebell Ct					
500	LSLE	60532	3143	22W-5S	C3
2500	RLKB	60073	2475	22W-36N	B3
Bluebell Dr					
2200	AURA	60506	3137	38W-6S	A5
Blue Bell Ln					
25400	PNFD	60585	3337	31W-15S	D2
Bluebell Ln					
700	PGGV	60140	2797	41W-15N	E4
700	PGGV	60140	2798	41W-15N	A4
1300	BTVA	60510	3078	33W-1S	E2
2400	ELGN	60124	2853	37W-9N	D7
S Bluebell Ln					
-	MONE	60449	3683	5W-31S	C5
Blueberry Hl					
-	KdlT	60560	3334	41W-17S	A5
Blueberry Ln					
100	RLKB	60073	2475	22W-36N	A3
1900	AURA	60506	3137	38W-6S	A5
Blueberry Rd					
100	LYVL	60048	2591	17W-28N	B5
Blue Bill Ct					
200	BmdT	60108	2967	26W-5N	E2
Bluebill Ln					
600	GNCY	53128	2353		B2
Bluebill Lake Ct					
21200	LktT	60403	3417	26W-19S	E4
Bluebird Av					
4200	ZION	60099	2362	12W-42N	B6
Bluebird Ct					
10	HNWD	60047	2645	21W-26N	C3
10	SMWD	60107	2856	29W-9N	E7
10	SMWD	60107	2910	29W-9N	E1
4900	NndT	60012	2640	35W-27N	A1
E Bluebird Ct					
4300	GRNE	60031	2535	14W-34N	D1
Bluebird Dr					
400	BGBK	60440	3268	24W-12S	E4
400	BGBK	60440	3269	23W-12S	A4
8800	TYPK	60487	3424	11W-21S	A7
Blue Bird Ln					
21700	FKFT	60423	3591	13W-26S	A2
21800	FftT	60423	3591	13W-26S	A2
Bluebird Ln					
10	NPVL	60565	3203	26W-8S	E2
10	NPVL	60565	3204	26W-8S	A2
400	VrnT	60015	2755	15W-20N	A1
1000	ROSL	60172	2912	24W-7N	C4
2000	KdlT	60560	3333	41W-16S	E5
2100	RGMW	60008	2806	19W-14N	C4
Bluebird St					
800	VrnT	60015	2755	15W-20N	A1
Blue Blossom Ln					
-	JLET	60431	3495	33W-22S	A1
-	JLET	60447	3495	33W-22S	A1
Bluebonnet Ct					
700	AURA	60505	3138	34W-5S	C3
Bluebonnet Dr					
500	AURA	60504	3138	35W-5S	C3
500	AURA	60505	3138	35W-5S	C3
Blue Bonnet Ln					
500	WDSK	60098	2581	41W-30N	D2
E Bluebonnet Ln					
300	HFET	60169	2859	22W-11N	B3
500	HFET	60173	2859	22W-11N	C3
500	SMBG	60173	2859	22W-11N	C3
N Bluebonnet Ln					
1000	HFET	60169	2859	23W-11N	B2
Blue Devil Dr					
10	PTON	60468	3860	9W-37S	E4
Bluefin Dr					
26000	WmTp	60481	3761	32W-34S	D5
Bluefin Ln					
28400	WmTp	60481	3761	32W-34S	D5
Blue Flag Av					
6900	WDRG	60517	3143	22W-7S	D7
Blue Flag Ct					
10	WDRG	60517	3143	21W-7S	D7
Bluegill Cir					
10	BDWD	60481	3942	30W-40S	D2
10	RedT	60481	3942	30W-40S	D2
Blue Grass Ct					
10	OKBK	60523	3085	18W-3S	A6
400	NPVL	60563	3141	26W-5S	E3
Bluegrass Ct					
1900	SCRL	60174	2964	34W-4N	D4
2700	RLKP	60030	2532	22W-31N	B7
N Blue Grass Ct					
2200	RLKB	60073	2474	23W-36N	E4
Blue Grass Dr					
12900	LMNT	60439	3342	20W-15S	B1
27700	CNHN	60410	3672	33W-30S	A5
27700	MNKA	60447	3672	33W-30S	A5
Bluegrass Dr					
-	MTGY	60506	3198	39W-9S	E5
300	WHTN	60187	3082	24W-2S	D3
Bluegrass Ln					
-	PLNO	60545	3259	46W-13S	E5
-	PLNO	60545	3260	46W-13S	A5
400	GNVA	60134	3019	37W-1N	C3
1200	AURA	60502	3078	34W-3S	E6
1500	JLET	60586	3496	29W-22S	E1
Bluegrass Pkwy					
-	OswT	60543	3264	35W-12S	A3
200	OSWG	60543	3264	35W-11S	C2
Bluegrass Tr					
5900	MHRY	60050	2527	34W-32N	B4
Blue Heron Blvd					
29800	BCHR	60401	3864	0E-36S	D1
Blue Heron Cir					
400	BRLT	60103	2909	32W-9N	C1
Blue Heron Cir					
1100	ANTH	60002	2358	21W-41N	E7
1300	ANTH	60002	2417	21W-41N	E1
3500	RLKP	60030	2532	22W-31N	C7
3800	CPVL	60110	2747	35W-17N	B6
Blue Heron Ct					
100	RDLK	60073	2531	25W-33N	A2
200	CmpT	60175	2962	40W-5N	C2
Blue Heron Dr					
-	BFGV	60089	2701	17W-23N	C2
-	OSWG	60543	3263	37W-14S	C7
1400	CLLK	60014	2693	37W-23N	C2
5800	LGGV	60047	2701	17W-23N	C2
10600	ODPK	60467	3423	13W-20S	B4
13100	PlsT	60467	3344	13W-15S	E1
Blue Heron Wy					
300	BRLT	60103	2909	32W-8N	D2
1100	ROSL	60172	2912	24W-7N	C4
Blue Heron Cove					
13100	PNFD	60585	3339	28W-15S	A2
Blue Hill Ter					
1200	NHBK	60062	2756	10W-17N	E5
Blue Iris Ct					
4300	ISLK	60042	2586	28W-27N	E7
Blue Iris Ct N					
24800	PNFD	60585	3266	31W-14S	A7
Blue Iris Ct S					
25000	PNFD	60585	3337	31W-14S	E1
Blue Iris Ln					
12300	PNFD	60585	3266	31W-14S	A7
12500	PNFD	60585	3337	31W-14S	E1
S Blue Island Av					
1200	CHCG	60607	3033	1W-1S	E7
1200	CHCG	60608	3033	1W-1S	D7
1600	CHCG	60608	3091	1W-1S	D1
Blue Island Dr					
1700	NndT	60012	2586	30W-28N	A6
1700	NndT	60014	2586	30W-28N	A6
Blue Island-Riverdale Rd					
-	RVDL	60827	3350	1W-15S	B2
Bluejay Cir					
700	EGVV	60007	2913	22W-8N	C2
Blue Jay Ct					
10	WDRG	60517	3143	21W-7S	E7
200	MltT	60188	3023	26W-1N	E3
400	MPPT	60056	2808	15W-13N	A6
3300	DrrT	60098	2583	37W-28N	A5
Blue Jay Dr					
-	ODPK	60467	3423	13W-20S	A4
100	BlmT	60411	3509	3E-25S	E7
Blue Jay Ln					
10	HNWD	60047	2645	22W-26N	C4
Bluejay Ln					
1200	JLET	60586	3496	29W-22S	D2
3500	NPVL	60564	3266	30W-11S	A2
Blue Jay Rd					
-	HRVD	60033	2464	50W-36N	B3
4600	DhmT	60033	2464	50W-36N	B3
Blue Jay Rdg					
-	BCHR	60401	3864	0E-36S	E1
Bluejay Tr					
2300	ELGN	60123	2853	36W-12N	E2
Blue Jay Wy					
10	DYR	46311	3510		C5
E Blue Lake Cir					
600	CmpT	60175	2962	40W-4N	B4
N Blue Lake Cir					
500	CmpT	60175	2962	40W-4N	B4
W Blue Lake Cir					
600	CmpT	60175	2962	40W-4N	B4
Blue Larkspur Ln					
200	CmpT	60119	2961	43W-4N	B4
1100	NPVL	60540	3142	25W-7S	A7
Blue Mesa Tr					
200	CRY	60013	2695	32W-23N	B1
Bluemont Ct					
2300	NPVL	60565	3204	25W-10S	A5
Bluemont Dr					
-	SRWD	60404	3584	30W-25S	B1
-	TroT	60404	3584	30W-25S	B1
Blue Mound Dr					
700	CLLK	60014	2639	37W-24N	C7
Blue Pine Dr					
-	BLVY	60050	2584	35W-30N	B2
1800	NndT	60012	2584	35W-30N	B2
Blueridge Av					
8400	HYHL	60457	3209	11W-9S	E4
Blue Ridge Ct					
400	OSWG	60543	3200	34W-11S	D7
500	ELGN	60123	2853	36W-12N	E3
3500	CPVL	60110	2747	36W-18N	B5
3600	AURA	60504	3202	31W-9S	A3
Blue Ridge Dr					
10	GLHT	60139	2968	24W-3N	E5
300	OSWG	60543	3264	34W-11S	E1
400	OSWG	60543	3200	34W-11S	E7
700	HnrT	60107	2856	30W-9N	B7
700	SMWD	60107	2856	30W-10N	C6
1800	JLET	60586	3415	31W-21S	D7
3300	CPVL	60110	2747	36W-18N	B5
Blue Ridge Pkwy					
1000	ALGN	60102	2695	32W-20N	B7
1000	ALGN	60102	2748	32W-20N	B1
Blue Sky Ln					
6400	RchT	60443	3593	8W-25S	B1
Blue Springs Dr					
500	FXLK	60041	2473	26W-34N	C7
600	FXLK	60041	2530	26W-34N	D1
Blue Spruce Ct					
300	LKVL	60046	2475	22W-37N	B2
800	LNHT	60046	2476	19W-37N	C3
2400	AURA	60502	3079	32W-3S	C6
8200	TYPK	60477	3424	10W-19S	C2
Bluespruce Ct					
6200	LGGV	60047	2646	18W-24N	D7
N Blue Spruce Ct					
38800	WDWH	60083	2420	14W-38N	C6
S Blue Spruce Ct					
14300	ODPK	60462	3346	11W-17S	A4
Blue Spruce Ln					
600	MDLN	60060	2590	19W-28N	C6
2200	AURA	60502	3079	32W-4S	C7
Bluestar Av					
-	JLET	60447	3495	33W-22S	A3
Bluestem Cir					
1800	AURA	60504	3201	33W-8S	A2
4000	ZION	60099	2362	12W-41N	B7
Blue Stem Ct					
10	SMWD	60107	2856	29W-10N	D6
24800	TRLK	60010	2643	26W-24N	C6
Bluestem Ct					
200	SchT	60175	2907	38W-7N	B5
1500	MNKA	60447	3672	33W-30S	A4
3000	NPVL	60565	3203	27W-11S	C7
3000	WldT	60565	3203	27W-10S	C7
Blue Stem Dr					
-	SRWD	60404	3495	31W-24S	E7
Bluestem Dr					
-	GNVA	60134	3019	37W-0N	B5
700	BGBK	60440	3205	21W-10S	E5
Bluestem Ln					
500	GYLK	60030	2533	19W-32N	D5
600	ALGN	60102	2693	37W-20N	B7
600	HPSR	60140	2795	47W-15N	D3
900	BTVA	60510	3078	34W-2S	E3
1400	MNKA	60447	3672	33W-30S	A4
1500	GNVW	60025	2810	9W-14N	D5
Bluestem Pkwy					
2000	LYWD	60411	3509	2E-24S	D5
N Bluestem Rd					
34000	GrtT	60073	2531	25W-34N	A1
W Bluestem Rd					
25500	GrtT	60073	2531	25W-34N	A1
Blue Stern Ct					
6400	LGGV	60047	2646	18W-24N	E7
Bluestone Dr					
-	SCRL	60174	2964	35W-2N	B7
Bluestone Bay Dr					
600	NLNX	60451	3502	15W-25S	C7
600	NlxT	60451	3502	15W-25S	C7
700	NLNX	60451	3590	15W-25S	B1
Bluewater Cir					
2700	NPVL	60564	3202	29W-10S	D6
Bluewater Dr					
2500	WCDA	60084	2588	24W-29N	B3
E Bluewater Ln					
100	VNHL	60061	2647	16W-26N	C3
S Blue Water Pkwy					
-	PNFD	60585	3265	32W-14S	B7
-	PNFD	60585	3337	32W-14S	B1
Bluff Av					
10	LGNG	60525	3087	12W-4S	C7
100	GYLK	60030	2532	21W-32N	D4
300	LGNG	60525	3147	12W-4S	C1
Bluff Ct					
10	TVLY	60013	2695	31W-22N	D3
200	LKBN	60010	2643	26W-24N	C7
200	WKGN	60085	2537	10W-34N	A2
400	LslT	60540	3142	24W-5S	D3
600	SMWD	60107	2856	29W-10N	D5
1900	RDLK	60073	2531	25W-33N	A2
Bluff Dr					
600	SchT	60175	2964	35W-5N	B2
17200	WrnT	60030	2534	17W-33N	B3
N Bluff Dr					
40300	AntT	60002	2416	25W-40N	B3
Bluff Dr N					
200	SchT	60175	2964	35W-5N	B2
Bluff Dr S					
100	SchT	60175	2964	35W-5N	B3
Bluff Ln					
-	AntT	60002	2416	25W-40N	A3
600	LslT	60540	3142	24W-5S	D3
W Bluff Ln					
25300	AntT	60002	2416	25W-40N	A3
28800	CbaT	60010	2696	28W-23N	D3
Bluff Rd					
-	AlqT	60102	2695	32W-22N	B4
-	DGvT	60439	3271	18W-11S	A1
10	TVLY	60013	2695	31W-22N	C3
100	DGvT	60439	3207	17W-11S	B7
100	DGvT	60527	3207	16W-11S	D7
600	DGvT	60439	3270	19W-12S	C3
600	LKBF	60044	2594	10W-28N	B5
600	LMNT	60439	3270	19W-12S	C3
900	GLNC	60022	2758	6W-18N	C4
1200	RMVL	60441	3269	22W-13S	C5
1200	RMVL	60446	3269	22W-13S	C5
16900	DPgT	60441	3269	21W-13S	D5
16900	DPgT	60441	3270	21W-13S	A4
16900	DPgT	60517	3269	21W-13S	D5
16900	DPgT	60517	3270	21W-13S	A4
W Bluff Rd					
10	DGvT	60439	3270	20W-13S	B4
10	DPgT	60441	3270	20W-13S	B4
10	DPgT	60517	3270	20W-13S	B4
10	LmnT	60439	3270	20W-13S	B4
Bluff St					
10	AURA	60505	3200	36W-8S	A2
200	LKPT	60441	3419	22W-18S	D1
200	LktT	60441	3419	22W-18S	D1
300	WNKA	60093	2758	6W-16N	D7
500	CLSM	60188	2968	25W-3N	A6
500	WKGN	60085	2537	10W-34N	A2
600	GLNC	60022	2758	6W-17N	C4
N Bluff St					
10	JLET	60436	3498	24W-24S	E5
300	JLET	60435	3498	24W-23S	E4
27900	WcnT	60084	2587	25W-27N	E7
W Bluff St					
25300	CNHN	60410	3672	31W-30S	E4
Bluff City Blvd					
700	ELGN	60120	2855	32W-10N	D6
Bluff City Blvd SR-25					
500	ELGN	60120	2855	33W-10N	A6
N Bluff Lake Rd					
40100	AntT	60002	2416	25W-40N	A3
40400	AntT	60002	2415	25W-40N	E2
Bluffs Edge Dr					
200	LKFT	60045	2650	9W-25N	C5
300	MchT	60051	2529	29W-33N	D3
Blujay Dr					
-	YKVL	60560	3333	41W-14S	E1
Blume Dr					
1400	ELGN	60124	2907	37W-8N	C2
1400	ElgT	60124	2907	37W-8N	C2
W Blyth Ct					
14400	GNOK	60048	2592	14W-30N	C1
Blyth Wy					
19500	MKNA	60448	3503	12W-23S	C3
Blythe Ct					
2000	IVNS	60010	2751	24W-16N	B6
Blythe Rd					
300	RVSD	60546	3088	9W-3S	D4
Boa Tr					
1100	CLSM	60188	2967	28W-4N	B4
Boal Pkwy					
700	WNKA	60093	2758	6W-16N	D7
700	WNKA	60093	2811	6W-16N	D1
E Boarder St					
2500	DMND	60416	3941	33W-40S	C2
Boardman Cir					
400	BGBK	60440	3204	24W-10S	D5
Boardman Ct					
100	LKBF	60044	2593	11W-28N	E7
Boardman St					
1600	WKGN	60087	2479	11W-37N	D3
Boardwalk					
-	ODHL	60487	3423	11W-19S	E2
Boardwalk Blvd					
2500	HFET	60169	2857	26W-11N	D3
Boardwalk Blvd					
2500	HFET	60194	2857	26W-11N	D3
S Boardwalk Ct					
800	PLTN	60067	2805	21W-14N	D3
W Boardwalk Dr					
100	PLTN	60067	2805	21W-14N	D3
Boardwalk Ln					
-	ODHL	60462	3423	11W-19S	E1
-	ODHL	60487	3423	11W-19S	E1
-	ODPK	60462	3423	11W-19S	E1
9400	ODPK	60467	3423	11W-19S	D2
Boardwalk Pl					
10	PKRG	60068	2863	11W-9N	D7
100	EGVV	60007	2914	19W-8N	D1
S Boardwalk Pl					
22700	CNHN	60410	3584	29W-27S	E5
Boardwalk Ter					
9100	ODHL	60487	3423	11W-19S	E2
Boardwalk Bay					
400	BDWD	60408	3942	30W-41S	B5
400	RedT	60481	3942	30W-41S	B5
Boat Ln					
10	MTGY	60543	3263	37W-11S	B1
Boathouse Rd					
-	PGGV	60140	2798	41W-14N	B5
Bobbi Ln					
-	MaiT	60016	2863	11W-11N	D3
-	PKRG	60016	2863	11W-11N	D3
-	PKRG	60068	2863	11W-11N	D3
Bob Blair Rd					
500	MNKA	60447	3583	34W-28S	A7
Bobby Dr					
-	BNVL	60106	2971	16W-3N	E4
Bobby Ln					
10	BDWD	60408	3942	31W-42S	B6
400	MDLN	60060	2590	19W-28N	C7
3900	SRPK	60176	2973	11W-4N	D2
S Bobby Ln					
100	MPPT	60056	2807	16W-12N	D7
100	MPPT	60056	2861	16W-12N	D1
Bobby Ann Ct					
-	ROSL	60172	2912	25W-6N	B6
Bobby Jones Ln					
6300	WDRG	60517	3143	23W-7S	A6
Bobby Locke Dr					
5100	MDLN	60445	3347	6W-16S	E3
Bobcat Ct					
400	OSWG	60543	3263	38W-11S	A2
Bob Ofarrell Ln					
1100	WKGN	60099	2421	10W-38N	E7
1100	WKGN	60099	2422	10W-38N	A7
Bobolink Cir					
1500	WDSK	60098	2582	39W-30N	C2
Bobolink Ct					
8300	ODPK	60462	3346	10W-18S	B6
Bobolink Dr					
-	NPVL	60563	3141	28W-5S	B2
10	GYLK	60030	2533	19W-33N	C4
300	BMDL	60108	2968	24W-4N	D3
300	BMDL	60139	2968	24W-4N	D3
300	GLHT	60139	2968	24W-4N	D3
500	HNDL	60521	3086	14W-4S	C6
500	WNFD	60190	3023	26W-1N	E2
4100	LGGV	60047	2700	18W-21N	E5
E Bobolink Dr					
10	CTSD	60525	3147	12W-5S	C3
Bobolink Ln					
1000	DRN	60561	3207	17W-9S	B3
1900	LbvT	60048	2590	18W-30N	E1
2000	LbvT	60048	2533	18W-31N	E7
2000	LbvT	60048	2591	18W-31N	A1
2600	NHBK	60062	2756	10W-16N	E6
3300	RGMW	60008	2806	20W-13N	B6
Bob-O-Link Rd					
-	SPGV	60081	2413	31W-39N	C5
Bob O Link Rd					
600	DRGV	60148	3083	21W-2S	E4
600	DRGV	60515	3083	21W-2S	E4
600	MltT	60148	3083	21W-2S	E4
Bobolink Rd					
-	DRGV	60148	3083	21W-2S	E4
-	DRGV	60515	3083	21W-2S	E4
-	MltT	60148	3083	21W-2S	E4
700	HDPK	60035	2704	8W-21N	D6
2800	FSMR	60422	3507	3W-23S	A3
8000	ODPK	60462	3346	10W-18S	C6
N Bobolink Rd					
400	MPPT	60056	2807	15W-14N	E4
W Bobolink Rd					
400	MPPT	60056	2807	16W-14N	E4
600	ANHT	60004	2807	16W-14N	E4
600	ANHT	60056	2807	16W-14N	E4
Bobolink Ter					
4200	SKOK	60076	2866	5W-10N	A4
4700	SKOK	60076	2865	5W-10N	E4
4700	SKOK	60077	2865	6W-10N	E4
N Bobolink Tr					
34300	WrnT	60030	2533	18W-34N	E1
Bob White Cir					
16300	ODPK	60467	3423	12W-19S	D2
Bobwhite Ct					
100	BMDL	60108	2968	23W-4N	E3
3700	PltT	60008	2806	20W-13N	B6
3700	PltT	60067	2806	20W-13N	B6
3700	RGMW	60008	2806	20W-13N	B6
Bob White Ln					
600	NLNX	60451	3589	18W-27S	A4
12300	PNFD	60585	3266	30W-14S	C7
12400	PNFD	60585	3338	30W-14S	C1
Bobwhite Ln					
200	BMDL	60108	2968	23W-4N	E3
2600	WCHI	60185	2966	29W-3N	D5
3600	RGMW	60008	2806	20W-13N	B6
21000	DRPK	60010	2698	23W-21N	E6
Boca Rio Dr					
6100	OKFT	60452	3347	7W-18S	B7
15100	BmnT	60452	3347	7W-18S	B7
Bock Rd					
17700	LNSG	60438	3429	2E-21S	D6
17700	ThtT	60438	3429	2E-21S	D6
18500	BlmT	60411	3429	2E-21S	D7
18500	BlmT	60438	3429	2E-21S	D7
Bockman Rd					
19000	MngT	60152	2578	48W-29N	E3
19000	SenT	60152	2578	48W-29N	E3
Boddington Ln					
2500	NPVL	60564	3202	29W-9S	C4
W Bode Cir					
-	HFET	60169	2858	24W-11N	D4
-	HFET	60194	2858	24W-11N	D3
700	SMBG	60169	2858	24W-11N	D4
700	SMBG	60194	2858	24W-11N	D4
Bode Rd					
-	HnrT	60120	2856	31W-11N	A4
10	HFET	60010	2856	29W-11N	E3
10	HFET	60010	2857	28W-11N	A3

STREET Block City ZIP Map# CGS Grid

Bode Rd
10 HFET 60107 2856 29W-11N E3
10 HFET 60107 2857 28W-11N A3
10 HFET 60169 2859 23W-11N A3
10 HnrT 60010 2856 29W-11N E3
10 HnrT 60107 2856 29W-11N E3
10 SMWD 60010 2856 29W-11N E3
10 SMWD 60107 2856 29W-11N E3
10 SMWD 60107 2857 28W-11N A3
100 HFET 60120 2856 29W-11N E3
100 HFET 60169 2858 24W-11N D3
300 ELGN 60120 2855 31W-11N E4
300 HnrT 60120 2855 32W-11N C4
800 HFET 60194 2858 24W-11N D3
800 SMBG 60169 2858 24W-11N D3
800 SMBG 60194 2858 24W-11N D3
2300 HFET 60194 2857 26W-11N E4
2300 SMBG 60194 2857 26W-11N E4
2300 SMWD 60194 2857 26W-11N E4
2400 HFET 60169 2857 26W-11N E4
E Bode Rd
\- HFET 60169 2857 27W-11N D4
\- SMWD 60010 2857 27W-11N D4
10 HFET 60010 2857 27W-11N D4
10 HFET 60107 2857 28W-11N A4
10 SMWD 60107 2857 27W-11N D4
Bode St
10000 AURA 60503 3265 31W-11S D2
10000 AURA 60585 3265 31W-11S D2
10000 WldT 60585 3265 31W-11S D2
Bodega Dr
200 RMVL 60446 3340 25W-16S C3
S Bodin St
200 HNDL 60521 3145 16W-5S E2
5800 DGvT 60521 3145 16W-6S E4
W Bodine Dr
25200 BDWD 60408 3942 31W-40S A4
Bodio Pl
100 JLET 60432 3499 23W-23S B4
Boeger Av
1200 HLSD 60162 3028 13W-1S E7
1200 WSTR 60154 3028 13W-1S E7
1200 WSTR 60162 3028 13W-1S E7
1400 WSTR 60154 3086 13W-2S E3
Boeger Ct
11000 WSTR 60154 3086 13W-1S E2
W Boeger Dr
100 ANHT 60004 2754 17W-17N A4
100 ANHT 60089 2754 17W-17N A4
100 BFGV 60089 2754 17W-17N A4
Boehme St
2000 LKPT 60441 3419 22W-20S B5
Boeing Dr
200 NLNX 60451 3501 18W-25S A7
Boerderij Wy
2700 DrrT 60098 2582 38W-29N E4
2900 DrrT 60098 2583 38W-29N A5
W Boesch Pl
26100 FXLK 60041 2473 26W-36N E3
26100 GrtT 60041 2473 26W-36N E3
N Bogdan Ln
2200 JLET 60432 3500 21W-22S A2
S Bogdan Ln
2200 JLET 60432 3500 21W-22S A2
W Bogey Ln
1000 PLTN 60067 2805 22W-14N B4
Bogie Ln
\- FXLK 60081 2414 29W-39N D6
Bohannon Cir
700 OSWG 60543 3264 34W-11S C1
Bohemian Rd
2500 RedT 60481 3942 30W-42S D7
Bohland Av
10 BLWD 60104 3029 12W-0N B5
Bohlander Av
\- BKLY 60104 3028 13W-0N E4
\- BLWD 60104 3028 13W-0N E4
5400 BKLY 60163 3028 14W-0N D4
Bohlmann Pkwy
22500 RNPK 60443 3593 7W-27S D4
22500 RNPK 60471 3593 7W-27S D4
Bohr Av
1300 MTGY 60538 3199 37W-9S B5
Bokelman Av
100 ROSL 60172 2913 23W-7N A4
Boland Dr
10 BrnT 60010 2803 27W-14N A4
Bolcum Rd
10 CmpT 60175 2962 39W-5N D3
10 SchT 60175 2963 38W-6N A1
800 CmpT 60175 2963 38W-6N A1
Boles Lp
100 MrnT 60037 2704 8W-24N D1
100 MrnT 60040 2704 8W-24N D1
Bolger Ct
5100 MHRY 60050 2584 33W-30N D1
Bolingbrook Dr
\- BGBK 60440 3269 22W-13S B5
\- RMVL 60446 3269 22W-13S B5
Bolingbrook Dr SR-53
\- BGBK 60440 3269 22W-13S B5
\- RMVL 60446 3269 22W-13S B5
N Bolingbrook Dr
\- LslT 60565 3205 22W-10S B6
100 BGBK 60440 3269 22W-11S B1
300 BGBK 60440 3205 22W-10S B6
600 DPgT 60440 3205 22W-10S B5
N Bolingbrook Dr SR-53
\- LslT 60565 3205 22W-10S B6
100 BGBK 60440 3269 22W-11S B1
300 BGBK 60440 3205 22W-10S B6
600 DPgT 60440 3205 22W-10S B5
S Bolingbrook Dr
\- RMVL 60446 3269 23W-13S B5
500 BGBK 60440 3269 23W-13S B4
S Bolingbrook Dr SR-53
\- RMVL 60446 3269 23W-13S B5
500 BGBK 60440 3269 23W-13S B4
Bolleana Ct
1800 HFET 60192 2804 25W-14N A3
Bolles Av
10 WnfT 60185 3022 29W-0N E5
100 WNFD 60190 3023 27W-0N C5
400 WnfT 60185 3023 28W-0N A5
400 WnfT 60190 3023 28W-0N A5
Bolling Av
1600 JNBG 60051 2472 30W-35N A6
1800 JNBG 60051 2471 30W-35N E6
Bolson Dr
1400 DRGV 60516 3144 20W-7S B6
Bolton Ct
\- OSWG 60543 3263 36W-12S E3
N Bolton Pl
38000 AntT 60002 2415 26W-38N D7
38000 AntT 60002 2473 26W-38N D1
Bolton Wy
700 HRPK 60133 2912 25W-9N A1
Bolz Rd
10 BNHL 60110 2748 33W-19N B4
10 CPVL 60110 2748 33W-19N B4
200 DndT 60110 2748 33W-19N B4
800 CPVL 60102 2748 33W-18N A4
800 DndT 60102 2748 33W-18N A4
Bolzano Ct
10 LYWD 60411 3598 4E-25S C1
W Bombay Wy
900 PLTN 60067 2752 22W-16N B7
900 PltT 60067 2752 22W-16N B7
N Bon Aire Dr
700 PLTN 60074 2753 20W-16N B6
Bonaire Rd
13400 HTLY 60142 2744 42W-20N B1
Bonaparte Av
\- NCHI 60088 2593 12W-30N B2
700 NCHI 60044 2593 12W-30N B2
700 ShdT 60044 2593 12W-30N B2
S Bonaparte St
2900 CHCG 60608 3091 1W-2S D3
Bonaventure Dr
1000 EGVV 60007 2914 20W-8N A3
1500 NPVL 60563 3141 28W-5S A2
Bonaventure Dr W
600 OSWG 60543 3264 35W-11S C1
Bonbury Ln
14000 ODPK 60462 3346 10W-16S C4
Boncosky Rd
100 DndT 60118 2800 35W-14N B5
100 SYHW 60118 2800 35W-14N D5
100 WDND 60118 2800 35W-14N B5
S Bond Av
8400 CHCG 60617 3216 3E-9S A3
Bond Cir
2800 NPVL 60563 3140 29W-5S C3
Bond Dr
\- LMNT 60439 3270 20W-14S B7
100 BTVA 60510 3078 35W-2S C4
100 BtvT 60510 3078 35W-2S C4
700 AntT 60002 2356 26W-41N D7
Bond St
\- BDVW 60154 3087 12W-1S B1
\- BDVW 60155 3087 12W-1S B1
\- WSTR 60154 3087 12W-1S B1
10 EGvT 60007 2861 17W-10N B5
10 EGVV 60007 2861 17W-10N B5
400 LNSH 60069 2701 16W-22N E4
500 GNCY 53128 2353 A3
500 VrnT 60069 2701 16W-22N E5
1200 NPVL 60563 3140 29W-5S C3
1200 NpvT 60563 3140 29W-5S C3
2300 MonT 60449 3682 7W-30S D3
2300 MonT 60449 3683 6W-30S A3
2300 MonT 60466 3682 7W-30S D3
2300 UYPK 60449 3682 7W-30S D3
2300 UYPK 60449 3683 6W-30S A3
2300 UYPK 60466 3682 7W-30S D3
Bonded Pkwy
600 SMBG 60107 2857 27W-10N D6
600 SMBG 60193 2857 27W-10N D7
600 SMWD 60107 2857 27W-10N D7
Boneset Ct
700 NPVL 60540 3140 29W-7S D7
Boneset Dr
1000 CLLK 60014 2639 37W-24N B6
Bonfield Av
200 SchT 60174 2908 35W-6N C7
S Bonfield St
2700 CHCG 60608 3091 1W-2S D3
W Bong Rd
6800 MonT 60449 3682 8W-30S B3
Bong St
5100 MchT 60097 2469 36W-37N E2
N Bonham Ct
40200 AntT 60002 2417 22W-40N B3
Bonhill Dr
3900 PltT 60004 2753 19W-18N C2
Bonita Av
700 EGVV 60007 2914 18W-9N E1
700 EGVV 60007 2915 18W-9N A1
W Bonita Av
1400 MPPT 60056 2861 16W-12N C1
Bonita Ct
2600 LSLE 60532 3142 24W-4S C1
Bonita Dr
1000 PKRG 60068 2918 10W-7N A3
1200 PKRG 60068 2917 10W-7N E3
Bonita Ln
900 MHRY 60050 2528 32W-31N B7
1000 MHRY 60050 2585 32W-30N B1
Bonnell Ct
26100 CNHN 60481 3761 32W-33S C3
26100 CnhT 60481 3761 32W-33S C3
Bonnema Av
1300 NPVL 60565 3204 24W-10S C5
Bonnema Ct
1200 NPVL 60565 3204 24W-10S C5
Bonner Av
1000 AURA 60505 3138 34W-7S D7
Bonner Dr
4600 MHRY 60050 2527 33W-33N E3
Bonner Ln
200 LNHT 60046 2476 19W-37N B1
2100 SPGV 60081 2413 31W-41N E1
9600 SPGV 60081 2354 31W-41N E7
E Bonner Rd
600 WCDA 60084 2588 24W-28N C6
600 WcnT 60084 2588 25W-28N A6
1100 FmtT 60060 2588 24W-28N C6
1100 WCDA 60060 2588 24W-28N C6
1200 FmtT 60084 2588 24W-28N C6
E Bonner Rd CO-A36
600 WCDA 60084 2588 24W-28N C6
600 WcnT 60084 2588 25W-28N A6
1100 FmtT 60060 2588 24W-28N C6
1100 WCDA 60060 2588 24W-28N C6
1200 FmtT 60084 2588 24W-28N C6
W Bonner Rd
600 WCDA 60084 2587 26W-28N E6
600 WcnT 60084 2587 26W-28N E6
27000 WcnT 60051 2587 27W-28N A6
W Bonner Rd CO-A36
600 WCDA 60084 2587 26W-28N E6
600 WcnT 60084 2587 26W-28N E6
27000 WcnT 60051 2587 27W-28N A6
Bonness Av
11100 MKNA 60448 3503 13W-23S A4
Bonnie Av
1000 PKRG 60068 2918 10W-7N A3
Bonnie Ct
10 LIHL 60156 2694 34W-22N C4
100 TNTN 60476 3428 0W-20S D5
400 SchT 60175 2963 38W-4N A5
500 NpvT 60563 3140 30W-5S B3
7200 WDRG 60517 3205 21W-8S E1
Bonnie Dr
300 LKPT 60441 3420 21W-18S A1
300 LktT 60441 3420 21W-18S A1
800 SchT 60175 2963 38W-3N A5
7100 GfnT 60014 2638 39W-24N D6
7100 GfnT 60142 2638 39W-24N D6
7100 LKWD 60014 2638 39W-24N D6
Bonnie Ln
10 CNHL 60514 3145 16W-5S D2
10 KdlT 60560 3333 42W-17S C6
300 EGvT 60007 2861 17W-9N B7
300 EGVV 60007 2861 17W-9N B7
300 SchT 60175 2963 38W-3N A6
400 RtdT 60124 2799 39W-14N A6
500 IVNS 60067 2752 22W-16N B7
900 GNCY 53128 2352 E4
1800 HFET 60169 2858 25W-12N A2
N Bonnie Ln
400 PtnT 60468 3860 10W-37S C4
400 PTON 60468 3860 10W-37S C4
24200 ElaT 60047 2645 21W-24N D7
24200 HNWD 60047 2645 21W-24N D7
W Bonnie Ln
800 PTON 60468 3860 10W-37S D4
Bonnie St
10 SchT 60174 3021 33W-2N B1
10 SchT 60185 3021 33W-2N B1
10 WynT 60185 3021 33W-2N B1
Bonnie Tr
5400 OKFT 60452 3425 6W-20S E4
Bonnie Tr E
17000 OKFT 60452 3425 6W-20S E4
Bonnie Tr W
17000 OKFT 60452 3425 6W-20S E4
Bonnie Bay Dr
5000 RcmT 60071 2353 33W-41N D7
5000 RcmT 60071 2412 34W-41N D1
Bonnie Brae Av
200 GYLK 60030 2532 20W-33N E2
200 ITSC 60143 2914 19W-5N D7
300 GYLK 60030 2533 20W-33N A2
E Bonnie Brae Av
100 WhlT 60056 2808 13W-13N E5
N Bonnie Brae Av
100 EMHT 60126 3027 17W-1N C1
Bonnie Brae Cres
2900 FSMR 60422 3507 3W-23S A4
Bonnie Brae Ct
700 BGBK 60440 3205 22W-10S C5
700 DPgT 60440 3205 22W-10S C5
Bonnie Brae Dr
800 DRGV 60516 3144 19W-7S C6
S Bonnie Brae Dr
1200 MHRY 60050 2585 32W-30N C1
Bonnie Brae Ln
100 DGvT 60527 3207 16W-9S D3
800 BGBK 60440 3205 22W-10S C5
Bonnie Brae Pl
1400 RVFT 60305 3030 9W-1N D1
1500 EDPK 60707 3030 9W-1N D1
1500 RVFT 60707 3030 9W-1N D1
Bonnie Brae Rd
10 HNDL 60521 3086 16W-4S A7
500 HNDL 60521 3085 16W-4S E7
10800 GfnT 60142 2691 41W-21N E6
10800 HTLY 60142 2691 41W-21N E6
N Bonnie Brae Rd
\- OMCK 60083 2476 18W-37N E3
37000 WrnT 60046 2476 18W-37N E3
Bonniebrook Av
400 MDLN 60060 2590 19W-28N C6
Bonnie Brook Dr
800 PTHT 60070 2808 14W-15N C2
Bonnie Brook Ln
900 RDLK 60073 2531 24W-34N C1
900 RLKB 60073 2531 24W-34N C1
E Bonnie Brook Ln
2400 WKGN 60087 2479 11W-37N D3
N Bonnie Brook Ln
1900 WKGN 60087 2479 11W-37N D2
2600 BHPK 60087 2479 11W-37N D2
S Bonnie Brook Ln
2200 WKGN 60087 2479 11W-36N C4
W Bonnie Brook Ln
2700 WKGN 60087 2479 11W-37N C3
12000 BHPK 60087 2479 12W-37N B2
Bonnie Dundee Rd
400 CPVL 60110 2801 33W-16N B1
400 CPVL 60118 2801 33W-16N B1
400 EDND 60118 2801 33W-16N B1
500 EDND 60110 2801 33W-16N B1
Bonnieglen
\- NLNX 60451 3590 15W-26S B3
Bonnie Glen Ln
1300 GNVW 60025 2811 8W-13N A5
Bonnieglen Pl
10600 ODPK 60462 3345 13W-18S B7
Bonnie Ridge Rd
7500 LKWD 60014 2638 38W-24N E7
Bonnieville St
\- LKPT 60441 3419 21W-20S D4
Bonny Glen Gates
\- IVNS 60067 2804 23W-14N E3
W Bonnyrigg Ct
23000 ElaT 60047 2645 23W-25N A5
Bon Terre Rd
700 NLNX 60451 3501 17W-25S D7
700 NLNX 60451 3589 17W-25S D1
Book Ct
1000 NPVL 60540 3203 28W-8S A1
Book Rd
10 NPVL 60564 3202 29W-10S E5
10 NPVL 60564 3266 29W-11S E1
10 NpvT 60564 3202 29W-10S E5
10 WldT 60564 3202 29W-10S E5
10 WldT 60564 3266 29W-11S E1
200 NPVL 60540 3202 29W-9S E5
1100 NPVL 60540 3203 28W-8S A1
S Book Rd
11500 NPVL 60564 3266 29W-13S E5
11500 WldT 60564 3266 29W-14S E7
11600 WldT 60585 3266 29W-14S E7
11900 PNFD 60585 3266 29W-14S E7
12400 PNFD 60585 3338 29W-14S E1
12400 WldT 60585 3338 29W-14S E1
Boomer Ln
2500 YKVL 60512 3261 42W-13S C5
2500 YKVL 60560 3261 42W-13S C5
3100 BtlT 60560 3261 42W-13S C5
Boone Ct
2900 JLET 60435 3417 27W-19S C3
Boone Dr
800 CLSM 60188 2968 25W-3N A5
Boone Creek Cir
1900 MchT 60050 2528 33W-33N A2
1900 MHRY 60050 2528 33W-33N A2
Boone Creek Ct
800 NndT 60050 2526 36W-31N E7
900 BLVY 60050 2583 36W-30N D1
900 NndT 60050 2583 36W-30N D1
Booth Ct
300 ELGN 60120 2855 33W-10N A5
Booth St
500 GNCY 53128 2353 A3
Boothbay Ln
3100 AURA 60504 3201 31W-9S D4
Booth Tarkington St
200 CmpT 60175 2962 40W-4N C4
Borde Ct
1300 LbvT 60048 2592 15W-29N B3
Bordeaux Ct
10 ODHL 60013 2641 30W-26N E3
10 ODHL 60013 2642 30W-26N A3
700 EGVV 60007 2914 19W-9N C1
700 IVNS 60010 2751 24W-17N B6
1400 HDPK 60035 2704 8W-21N D7
1900 WLNG 60090 2808 14W-15N C2
3500 HLCT 60429 3426 4W-21S E7
3900 NHBK 60062 2756 12W-18N B3
Bordeaux Ct E
600 BFGV 60089 2701 17W-21N B5
Bordeaux Ct W
600 BFGV 60089 2701 17W-21N B5
Bordeaux Dr
600 NHBK 60062 2756 12W-18N B4
3700 HFET 60192 2804 24W-14N C3
4100 NfdT 60062 2756 12W-18N A4
4700 GfnT 60156 2692 38W-22N E4
4700 LIHL 60156 2692 38W-22N E4
4800 HTLY 60142 2692 38W-22N E4
4800 HTLY 60156 2692 38W-22N D4
Bordeaux Ln
1600 LGGV 60047 2700 18W-20N E7
1600 LGGV 60047 2753 18W-20N E1
1600 LGGV 60089 2753 18W-20N E1
1600 VrnT 60089 2753 18W-20N E1
2500 NPVL 60540 3140 29W-7S D7
Bordeaux Pl
2700 LSLE 60532 3142 24W-4S C1
Borden Av
200 CRY 60013 2695 31W-23N D1
Borden Cir
1300 ELGN 60120 2855 31W-11N E3
Borden Ct
10 ROSL 60172 2912 24W-7N C5
1200 ELGN 60120 2855 32W-11N D3
Borden Dr
900 ROSL 60172 2912 24W-7N C5
1300 ELGN 60120 2855 31W-11N E3
Borden St
400 WDSK 60098 2524 42W-31N B7
1200 MHRY 60050 2528 32W-33N A3
11900 HTLY 60142 2691 40W-21N E6
N Border Dr
400 JLET 60435 3498 26W-23S A4
Border Ln
200 LKBN 60010 2697 26W-23N E1
200 NBRN 60010 2697 26W-23N D1
Border Rd
\- CbaT 60010 2697 25W-21N E6
3100 GNVA 60134 3019 37W-1N C3
W Borders Dr
1200 PLTN 60067 2805 22W-15N A2
1300 IVNS 60067 2805 22W-15N B2
Boren Av
10 WCDA 60084 2643 26W-26N E2
Borhart
11700 HTLY 60142 2744 42W-20N A1
Borio Dr
\- CTHL 60441 3418 25W-19S B4
16000 CTHL 60403 3418 25W-19S B3
16000 LktT 60403 3418 25W-19S B3
16400 LktT 60441 3418 25W-19S B3
Borkshire Ln
2700 AURA 60502 3079 32W-3S B7
Borman Ct
900 EGVV 60007 2913 21W-8N E2
Borman Dr
600 NLNX 60451 3589 18W-25S A1
Borman Expwy
\- HMND - 3430 C5
\- LNSG - 3430 C4
\- MNSR - 3430 C5
Borman Expwy I-80
\- HMND - 3430 C5
\- LNSG - 3430 C5
\- MNSR - 3430 C5
Borman Expwy I-94
\- HMND - 3430 C5
\- LNSG - 3430 C5
\- MNSR - 3430 C4
Borman Expwy US-6
\- HMND - 3430 C5
\- LNSG - 3430 C5
\- MNSR - 3430 C4
Borman Expwy US-41
\- HMND - 3430 E5
Borman Pl
1700 DRGV 60516 3206 20W-8S A1
Bormet Dr
8100 TYPK 60477 3424 10W-19S C2
Bormet Rd
9400 MKNA 60448 3503 11W-23S E2
N Boro Ln
1400 MPPT 60056 2808 13W-14N E3
Borough Ct
1100 WHTN 60187 3082 23W-1S E2
N Borre Dr
31500 LKMR 60051 2529 28W-31N E6
Borris Cir
100 SMWD 60107 2857 28W-11N B4
Borthwick Ln
100 IVNS 60067 2752 22W-18N B4
Bos Dr
17700 ODPK 60467 3423 13W-21S A6
N Boschome Cir
21100 KLDR 60047 2699 21W-21N D6
S Boschome Cir
21200 KLDR 60047 2699 21W-21N D6
Boschome Dr
21400 KLDR 60047 2699 21W-21N D6
Bosi Ct
10 BGBK 60490 3268 26W-12S A3
Bosi Dr
15100 HmrT 60491 3420 18W-19S E2
Boston Av
1200 JLET 60435 3498 25W-22S B1
Boston Cir
1000 SMBG 60193 2913 22W-7N D4
Boston Ct
200 SEGN 60177 2908 35W-8N C4
1400 BRLT 60103 2967 28W-5N B1
Boston Hbr
1000 SMBG 60193 2913 22W-9N B1
Boston Rd
7300 MchT 60097 2469 36W-37N D3
N Boston St
200 CHHT 60411 3595 2W-26S E1
W Boston St
1800 CHHT 60411 3595 2W-26S D1
Boswell Ln
1200 NPVL 60564 3203 28W-11S A7
1200 NPVL 60564 3267 28W-11S A1
N Bosworth Av
1400 CHCG 60622 3033 1W-1N D1
1600 CHCG 60622 2977 1W-2N D7
2600 CHCG 60614 2977 1W-3N D5
2600 CHCG 60657 2977 1W-3N D5
3500 CHCG 60613 2977 1W-4N D3
6400 CHCG 60626 2921 1W-8N C2
6400 CHCG 60660 2921 1W-8N C2
7600 CHCG 60626 2867 1W-9N C6
Bosworth Dr
10 GLHT 60139 2968 23W-4N E4
Bosworth Ln
900 EGVV 60007 2915 18W-8N A2
1800 NHFD 60093 2811 7W-15N B2
Bosworthfield Rd
\- CbaT 60010 2698 25W-20N A7
900 BRTN 60010 2698 25W-20N A7
Bothwell Cir
1000 BGBK 60440 3268 25W-11S B1
Bothwell Ct
1000 BGBK 60440 3268 25W-11S B1
Bothwell Ln
1000 BGBK 60440 3268 25W-11S B1
N Bothwell St
10 PLTN 60067 2805 22W-14N B4
100 PLTN 60067 2752 21W-16N E7
S Bothwell St
10 PLTN 60067 2805 21W-15N E1
Botsford Pl
2100 HFET 60169 2858 26W-12N A1
Botterman Rd
15300 CrlT 60142 2743 44W-20N C1
N Bough Ct
35200 GRNE 60031 2478 15W-35N A6
E Boughton Rd
100 BGBK 60440 3205 21W-10S E6
1900 BGBK 60440 3206 21W-10S A5
1900 WDRG 60440 3206 21W-10S A5
1900 WDRG 60517 3206 21W-10S A5
W Boughton Rd
100 BGBK 60440 3205 23W-11S B7
400 BGBK 60440 3204 23W-11S E7
700 BGBK 60440 3268 25W-11S A1
1200 BGBK 60490 3268 25W-11S A1
21600 BGBK 60490 3267 27W-12S C2
22300 WldT 60490 3267 27W-12S B3
22300 WldT 60564 3267 27W-12S B3
Boula Av
14300 HmrT 60441 3342 20W-17S A5
S Boulder Av
10 JLET 60432 3499 22W-24S C5
10 JLET 60433 3499 22W-24S C5
10 JltT 60432 3499 22W-24S C5
Boulder Ct
100 FKFT 60423 3503 12W-25S D7
100 GLBT 60136 2799 38W-15N A4
1300 WDSK 60098 2582 40W-30N B1
2300 NPVL 60565 3203 27W-10S B6
2300 WldT 60565 3203 27W-10S B6
4000 AURA 60504 3202 30W-8S B2
4000 AURA 60564 3202 30W-8S B2
4000 NpvT 60564 3202 30W-8S B2
8000 LGGV 60060 2646 20W-26N A4
18900 HMWD 60430 3508 1W-22S B2
S Boulder Ct
8100 LGGV 60060 2646 20W-25N A4
W Boulder Ct
10 PSHL 60465 3274 10W-12S B3
Boulder Dr
\- ALGN 60102 2693 37W-21N C6
\- BNHL 60110 2748 33W-19N B3
\- CPVL 60110 2748 33W-19N B3
\- LIHL 60102 2693 37W-21N C6
10 GLBT 60136 2799 38W-14N A5
10 LIHL 60156 2693 37W-21N B5
300 GLHT 60139 2969 23W-3N B5
1700 DRN 60516 3206 18W-9S E3
1700 DRN 60561 3206 18W-9S E3
E Boulder Dr
1800 MPPT 60056 2808 13W-14N D5
S Boulder Dr
14300 HMGN 60491 3343 17W-17S D5
W Boulder Dr
20800 LktT 60544 3340 26W-16S A5
Boulder Ln
1400 WDSK 60098 2582 40W-30N B1
4800 HFET 60010 2751 24W-16N C7
4800 HFET 60010 2804 24W-16N C1
4800 HFET 60192 2804 24W-16N C1
Boulder Rd
\- CNHN 60481 3761 32W-33S C4
2300 DYR 46311 3598 E3
Boulder Bluff Ct
\- ALGN 60102 2747 35W-18N B4
Boulder Bluff Ln
1400 ALGN 60102 2747 35W-18N B4
Boulder Hill Pass
10 MTGY 60538 3199 37W-10S C6
10 OswT 60538 3199 37W-10S C6
200 OswT 60538 3263 36W-11S D2
300 OSWG 60543 3263 36W-11S E1
Boulder Ridge Ct
10 BGBK 60490 3267 26W-11S D2
19100 MKNA 60448 3502 15W-22S C2
Boulder Ridge Dr
1500 BGBK 60490 3267 26W-11S E1
19100 MKNA 60448 3502 15W-23S C3
Boulders Dr
4900 GRNE 60031 2478 15W-36N B5
S Boulevard Wy
2400 CHCG 60623 3090 3W-2S E2
W Boulevard de John
24200 WldT 60564 3266 30W-12S B2
Boulevard View Av
\- GRNE 60031 2479 13W-35N A7
N Boulevard View Av
36000 WKGN 60087 2479 13W-36N A3
36000 WrnT 60087 2479 13W-36N A3
38500 WDWH 60083 2421 13W-38N A7
Boulton Blvd
13600 GNOK 60045 2648 13W-27N D1
13600 MTWA 60045 2648 13W-27N D1

STREET Block	City	ZIP	Map#	CGS	Grid
Boundary Rd					
5900	DGvT	60516	3144	20W-6S	B5
Boundary Hill Rd					
400	LslT	60517	3205	22W-8S	C2
400	LslT	60540	3205	22W-8S	C2
400	LslT	60565	3205	22W-8S	C2
400	WDRG	60517	3205	22W-8S	C2
400	WDRG	60565	3205	22W-8S	C2
Bourbon Ln					
400	NPVL	60565	3204	25W-9S	A4
Bourbon Pkwy					
1500	SMBG	60193	2857	27W-10N	D6
1500	SMWD	60107	2857	27W-10N	D6
1500	SMWD	60193	2857	27W-10N	D6
Bourn St					
500	HRVD	60033	2406	49W-38N	B5
Bourne Ln					
100	BMDL	60108	2969	23W-5N	B2
1000	SMBG	60193	2858	24W-9N	C7
Bourtzos Av					
500	BRkT	60511	3196	45W-8S	C2
Bouterse St					
2100	PKRG	60068	2863	11W-9N	D6
Bouy Bay					
10	LKMR	60051	2529	28W-33N	E3
Bovidae Cir					
500	NPVL	60565	3203	27W-8S	C3
Bow Ln					
10	BNHL	60010	2696	30W-20N	A7
Bow Tr					
1500	WLNG	60090	2754	16W-17N	D5
Bowdish St					
-	ELBN	60119	3017	42W-0N	C5
Bowditch Av					
800	AURA	60506	3199	36W-8S	D2
E Bowen Av					
400	CHCG	60653	3092	0E-4S	D6
Bowen Ct					
400	ELGN	60120	2855	33W-10N	B5
Bowen Dr					
400	MNSR	46321	3510		D4
E Bowen Dr					
-	CHCG	60615	3152	0E-5S	D2
Bowen Pl					
100	JLET	60433	3499	23W-24S	A6
E Bowen St					
10	FKFT	60423	3591	11W-25S	E1
W Bowen St					
10	FKFT	60423	3591	12W-25S	D1
Bower Ct					
25400	PNFD	60585	3337	31W-15S	D2
Bower Ln					
400	OSWG	60543	3263	36W-12S	E3
400	OSWG	60543	3264	36W-12S	A3
Bowes Rd					
10	ELGN	60123	2908	36W-9N	A1
10	ELGN	60177	2908	36W-9N	A1
10	ElgT	60124	2907	37W-9N	D1
10	PltT	60124	2852	40W-10N	B7
10	PltT	60124	2906	39W-9N	D1
10	SEGN	60123	2908	36W-9N	A1
10	SEGN	60177	2908	36W-9N	A1
400	ELGN	60123	2907	38W-9N	A1
400	ELGN	60124	2907	36W-9N	E1
400	ElgT	60123	2907	36W-9N	E1
500	ElgT	60123	2908	35W-9N	B1
500	ElgT	60177	2908	35W-9N	A1
700	PltT	60124	2907	39W-9N	A1
1000	ELGN	60123	2854	35W-9N	C7
1000	ELGN	60177	2854	35W-9N	C7
1000	SEGN	60177	2854	35W-9N	C7
Bowes Rd CO-17					
10	ELGN	60123	2908	36W-9N	A1
10	ELGN	60177	2908	36W-9N	A1
10	ElgT	60124	2907	37W-9N	D1
10	PltT	60124	2852	40W-10N	B7
10	PltT	60124	2906	39W-9N	D1
10	SEGN	60123	2908	36W-9N	A1
10	SEGN	60177	2908	36W-9N	A1
400	ELGN	60123	2907	38W-9N	A1
400	ELGN	60124	2907	36W-9N	E1
400	ElgT	60123	2907	36W-9N	E1
500	ElgT	60123	2908	35W-9N	B1
500	ElgT	60177	2908	35W-9N	A1
700	PltT	60124	2907	39W-9N	A1
Bowes Bend Dr					
10	PltT	60124	2852	41W-9N	A7
500	PltT	60124	2906	41W-9N	A1
N Bowgren Cir					
700	CmpT	60119	2961	41W-2N	E7
800	CmpT	60119	3017	41W-2N	E1
S Bowgren Cir					
600	CmpT	60119	3017	41W-2N	E1
700	CmpT	60119	2961	41W-2N	E7
Bowgren Dr					
-	CmpT	60119	3017	41W-2N	E1
Bowie Ct					
200	BGBK	60440	3268	23W-12S	E2
3700	JLET	60435	3417	27W-19S	C3
Bowie Dr					
900	CLSM	60188	2968	25W-3N	A5
Bowie Ln					
-	MNKA	60447	3672	33W-30S	B3
W Bowler St					
2100	CHCG	60612	3033	2W-0S	B6
Bowles Rd					
-	AntT	60002	2416	24W-41N	C1
1100	ANTH	60002	2357	25W-41N	B7
1100	ANTH	60002	2416	24W-41N	C1
Bowling Av					
-	BHPK	60099	2421	12W-39N	C5
12100	WKGN	60087	2421	12W-39N	C6
39100	BHPK	60087	2421	12W-39N	C6
Bowling Green Ct					
600	NPVL	60563	3141	27W-5S	C3
Bowling Green Dr					
800	GNWD	60425	3508	1W-22S	A2
800	HMWD	60425	3508	1W-22S	A2
800	HMWD	60430	3508	1W-22S	A2
1500	LKFT	60045	2649	13W-24N	A7
1800	LKFT	60045	2648	13W-24N	E7
Bowman Ct					
100	BGBK	60440	3205	22W-11S	B7
Bowman Dr					
1600	AURA	60506	3137	38W-5S	A3
Bowman St					
10	MTSN	60443	3506	6W-24S	A5
200	SCRL	60174	3020	35W-2N	B1
N Bowmanville Av					
5300	CHCG	60625	2921	2W-6N	B5
5400	CHCG	60640	2921	2W-6N	B5
Bowstring Ct					
1300	CLSM	60188	2967	28W-4N	B3
Box Canyon					
2400	NLNX	60451	3588	19W-27S	E4
Box Car Av					
200	NPVL	60540	3141	27W-6S	C5
Boxelder Ct					
10	BGBK	60490	3267	26W-12S	D2
W Box Elder Ln					
200	MltT	60187	3023	26W-0N	E4
Box Elder St					
400	FKFT	60423	3503	12W-25S	C7
Boxelder St					
100	BGBK	60490	3267	26W-12S	D3
Boxford Ct					
2200	AURA	60503	3201	32W-10S	B6
Boxford Ln					
2300	AURA	60503	3201	32W-10S	B7
Boxwood Ct					
10	SMWD	60107	2857	26W-11N	E4
1000	WLNG	60090	2754	15W-18N	E3
1100	CLLK	60014	2693	37W-23N	C1
12500	HTLY	60142	2744	42W-19N	D2
W Boxwood Ct					
300	RDLK	60073	2531	23W-32N	E4
Boxwood Dr					
100	HNWD	60047	2644	23W-25N	D6
500	SMBG	60193	2858	24W-9N	D7
800	CLLK	60014	2639	37W-24N	C7
800	MNSR	46321	3510		E5
1000	CLLK	60014	2693	37W-23N	C1
2600	ELGN	60124	2853	37W-11N	D4
N Boxwood Dr					
1100	MPPT	60056	2808	15W-14N	B4
S Boxwood Dr					
900	MPPT	60056	2808	15W-14N	B5
Boxwood Ln					
-	JLET	60586	3415	33W-20S	A6
-	NasT	60586	3415	33W-20S	A6
10	CmpT	60175	2961	41W-6N	E1
10	CRY	60013	2695	32W-23N	C1
700	BFGV	60089	2754	17W-17N	B5
2300	AURA	60502	3079	32W-3S	C7
Boxwood St					
200	BGBK	60490	3267	26W-12S	D3
Boyce Ln					
10400	BHPK	60087	2480	10W-38N	A1
Boyce Rd					
700	SRGV	60554	3136	40W-5S	B3
S Boyd Av					
200	EMHT	60126	3028	15W-1N	B3
Boyd Ct					
800	BTVA	60510	3078	34W-2S	D4
Boyd Dr					
-	BbyT	60134	3018	39W-0N	E5
-	GnvT	60134	3018	39W-0N	E5
Boyer Ct					
11100	MKNA	60448	3503	13W-24S	A5
Boyer Ln					
-	PLNO	60545	3260	45W-13S	B5
Boyer Rd					
-	CPVL	60118	2746	37W-18N	D4
10	ALGN	60118	2746	37W-19N	D4
10	DndT	60118	2746	37W-19N	D3
900	ALGN	60102	2746	37W-19N	D4
S Boyer St					
11200	LmnT	60439	3271	17W-13S	B4
W Boyington Ln					
7000	MonT	60449	3682	8W-30S	A4
N Boyle Ter					
3000	RVGV	60171	2974	10W-3N	B4
3100	CHCG	60634	2974	10W-3N	B4
3100	RVGV	60634	2974	10W-3N	B4
Boyne Ct					
11800	ODPK	60467	3422	14W-21S	D5
N Boynton Dr					
100	PLTN	60074	2753	19W-16N	B7
100	PLTN	60074	2806	20W-15N	A2
Braberry Ln					
3400	PRGV	60012	2584	33W-28N	E5
Bracken Ln					
400	NHFD	60093	2811	7W-15N	A2
W Brackenridge Dr					
12300	MKNA	60448	3502	15W-23S	B3
12300	NlxT	60448	3502	15W-23S	B3
Brackley Ln					
10	SBTN	60010	2804	25W-15N	A1
Brackman Av					
200	CRTE	60417	3685	0W-30S	C3
Brad Ct					
400	LslT	60565	3204	25W-8S	A2
400	NPVL	60565	3204	25W-8S	A2
Brad Dr					
700	NLNX	60451	3589	18W-27S	A5
Bradbury Cir					
-	AURA	60504	3139	31W-7S	E7
1000	CLSM	60188	2968	26W-4N	A4
Bradbury Ct					
10	FRGV	60021	2696	30W-22N	B4
Bradbury Ln					
300	BRLT	60103	2911	28W-8N	A4
500	GNVA	60134	3019	36W-1N	E2
Braddock Dr					
100	MLPK	60160	3030	10W-1N	A2
2500	NPVL	60565	3204	25W-10S	B6
Braden Wy					
-	MNSR	46321	3510		E1
Bradfield Ct					
1000	UYPK	60466	3684	3W-30S	B3
Bradford Cir					
200	BTVA	60510	3077	36W-1S	E1
200	BTVA	60510	3078	36W-1S	A1
400	EGVV	60007	2860	19W-9N	C7
Bradford Ct					
-	LKVL	60046	2475	22W-38N	C1
10	LKBF	60044	2593	11W-29N	E5
100	OSWG	60543	3263	37W-14S	C6
300	LktT	60441	3499	23W-21S	B1
900	SMBG	60193	2858	24W-9N	D7
1000	ELGN	60120	2855	32W-12N	D1
3600	CPVL	60110	2746	36W-18N	E5
3600	CPVL	60110	2747	36W-18N	A5
7300	GRNE	60031	2477	18W-34N	A7
14100	GNOK	60048	2592	14W-30N	D2
24200	PNFD	60585	3338	30W-15S	B1
E Bradford Ct					
700	ANHT	60004	2754	17W-16N	B6
S Bradford Ct					
100	LKFT	60045	2649	13W-25N	A4
W Bradford Ct					
6600	MONE	60449	3682	8W-32S	B7
Bradford Dr					
2400	AURA	60506	3136	39W-7S	E7
20900	MKNA	60448	3502	14W-25S	E7
E Bradford Dr					
1000	WHTN	60187	3082	24W-3S	E5
N Bradford Dr					
2600	ANHT	60004	2754	17W-16N	B6
S Bradford Dr					
2100	WHTN	60187	3082	23W-3S	E5
Bradford Ln					
-	CLLK	60156	2693	36W-22N	D4
-	LIHL	60156	2693	36W-22N	D4
-	NpvT	60563	3140	30W-5S	C4
-	RDLK	60073	2531	23W-32N	E4
-	RDLK	60073	2532	23W-32N	A4
-	WDND	60118	2800	36W-16N	A2
10	MDLN	60060	2646	19W-27N	B1
10	OKBK	60523	3086	15W-2S	B3
900	SMBG	60193	2858	24W-9N	C7
1200	ANTH	60002	2359	20W-41N	A7
1700	CLLK	60014	2693	36W-22N	D3
2000	AURA	60506	3137	38W-6S	A5
9300	ODPK	60462	3423	11W-18S	D1
12700	PNFD	60585	3338	30W-15S	B1
Bradford Pkwy					
600	WYNE	60184	2966	30W-4N	A3
600	WYNE	60185	2966	30W-4N	A3
Bradford Pl					
10	CRTE	60417	3596	0W-28S	C7
Bradford Rd					
10	JltT	60433	3587	23W-26S	A2
10	JltT	60436	3587	23W-26S	A2
300	JLET	60433	3587	23W-26S	A2
Bradford Place Dr					
300	BGBK	60440	3268	25W-12S	A4
300	BGBK	60490	3268	25W-12S	A4
Bradley Av					
600	MTSN	60443	3505	6W-25S	E7
Bradley Cir					
300	SCRL	60174	2964	36W-3N	A6
1200	ELGN	60120	2801	32W-12N	D7
Bradley Ct					
200	BMDL	60108	2969	22W-4N	B3
200	DSPN	60016	2862	15W-11N	B3
1300	SPGV	60081	2414	30W-39N	A5
1400	DRGV	60516	3144	20W-7S	B6
1500	NPVL	60565	3204	24W-8S	C2
11200	ODPK	60467	3422	14W-21S	E6
11200	OrlT	60467	3422	14W-21S	E6
E Bradley Ct					
900	PLTN	60074	2753	19W-18N	B3
S Bradley Ct					
5700	HRPK	60133	2911	26W-7N	E5
W Bradley Ct					
3600	MHRY	60050	2528	32W-33N	B2
Bradley Ct N					
5900	HRPK	60133	2911	26W-7N	E5
Bradley Dr					
1800	MTGY	60538	3198	38W-9S	E5
2300	JLET	60586	3415	33W-21S	B6
6300	WDRG	60517	3143	22W-7S	B6
6900	GRNE	60031	2477	17W-35N	B5
N Bradley Dr					
200	CHHT	60411	3507	2W-24S	E4
Bradley Ln					
-	LMBD	60148	3026	19W-0S	D6
10	HFET	60169	2859	23W-11N	A4
1200	EGVV	60007	2914	21W-8N	A2
Bradley Lp					
3400	HDPK	60035	2650	9W-24N	D7
Bradley Pl					
2300	EVTN	60202	2866	3W-10N	D4
W Bradley Pl					
800	CHCG	60613	2977	1W-4N	E2
1900	CHCG	60618	2977	2W-4N	B2
Bradley Rd					
400	BFGV	60089	2754	17W-18N	B4
N Bradley Rd					
-	GNOK	60044	2592	14W-28N	D6
200	LbvT	60045	2648	13W-26N	D3
200	MTWA	60045	2648	13W-26N	D3
800	LbvT	60048	2648	14W-27N	D2
800	MTWA	60048	2648	14W-27N	D2
27500	GNOK	60045	2648	14W-27N	D2
27500	GNOK	60048	2648	14W-27N	D2
27700	GNOK	60045	2592	14W-28N	D6
27700	GNOK	60048	2592	14W-28N	D6
27700	LbvT	60048	2592	14W-28N	D6
27900	LbvT	60045	2592	13W-27N	D7
E Bradley St					
10	DSPN	60016	2862	14W-11N	C3
W Bradley St					
10	DSPN	60016	2862	15W-11N	B3
Bradoc St					
800	CHHT	60411	3507	2W-24S	D6
Bradrock Dr					
10	DSPN	60018	2862	14W-9N	C6
Brads Wy					
14800	HMGN	60441	3342	19W-17S	D6
14800	HmrT	60441	3342	19W-17S	D6
E Bradshire Ct					
2300	ANHT	60004	2807	16W-15N	C2
Bradwell Cir					
2000	IVNS	60010	2750	25W-16N	E7
Bradwell Ln					
1200	MDLN	60060	2647	17W-27N	A1
Bradwell Rd					
100	HFET	60010	2751	24W-16N	C7
100	IVNS	60010	2750	25W-16N	E7
100	IVNS	60010	2751	25W-16N	A7
2000	IVNS	60067	2751	23W-16N	E7
Brae Ct					
7100	GRNE	60031	2477	17W-34N	A7
Braeborn Ct					
1400	WLNG	60090	2754	16W-18N	D3
Braeburn Av					
1100	FSMR	60422	3507	3W-23S	C3
Braeburn Cir					
200	SgrT	60506	3135	41W-5S	E4
Brae Burn Ct					
1500	RVWD	60015	2703	12W-22N	A5
Braeburn Ct					
-	WDSK	60098	2581	41W-28N	C5
Braeburn Dr					
-	WCDA	60084	2588	25W-29N	B4
-	WcnT	60084	2588	25W-29N	B3
10	OswT	60538	3199	36W-10S	E6
10	PKFT	60466	3595	3W-28S	B6
100	OswT	60538	3200	36W-10S	A6
1100	ELGN	60123	2800	35W-13N	B7
Braeburn Ln					
10	BNHL	60010	2695	30W-20N	E7
10	BNHL	60010	2696	30W-20N	A7
100	HDPK	60035	2758	7W-20N	C1
8000	ODPK	60462	3346	10W-18S	C7
Braeburn Rd					
10	BNHL	60010	2696	30W-21N	A5
10	EDND	60118	2801	33W-16N	B2
600	EDND	60118	2801	33W-16N	B2
600	IVNS	60067	2751	23W-16N	B6
900	MDLN	60060	2590	19W-28N	C6
9700	AlqT	60010	2696	30W-21N	A5
9700	AlqT	60021	2696	30W-21N	A5
Braeburn Wy					
-	WDSK	60098	2581	41W-28N	D5
Braeloch Ct					
7800	ODPK	60462	3346	9W-18S	C7
28600	GNOK	60044	2593	13W-28N	A6
W Brae Loch Rd					
-	WrnT	60030	2533	19W-33N	C3
900	GYLK	60030	2533	19W-33N	C3
19500	AvnT	60030	2533	19W-33N	D3
Braeman Ct					
800	LYVL	60048	2647	15W-27N	E1
Braemar Av					
400	NPVL	60563	3141	26W-5S	E2
Braemar Cir					
7100	LKWD	60014	2638	38W-24N	E6
Braemar Ct					
10	LKZH	60010	2698	24W-21N	D5
200	BGBK	60440	3269	22W-12S	C2
Braemar Dr					
10	EGVV	60007	2914	19W-8N	D3
Braemar Gln					
200	BGBK	60440	3269	22W-12S	C2
Braemar Ln					
500	DRPK	60010	2698	24W-21N	C5
500	LKZH	60010	2698	24W-21N	C5
W Braemar Ln					
7300	FftT	60423	3504	9W-23S	E4
Braemar Pkwy					
-	GfnT	60142	2692	39W-21N	C6
-	GfnT	60156	2692	39W-21N	C6
10600	HTLY	60142	2692	39W-21N	C6
Braemar Rd					
700	FSMR	60422	3507	3W-22S	A2
Braemar St					
800	MDLN	60060	2590	19W-28N	D6
Braemoor Dr					
1000	DRGV	60515	3084	19W-3S	C5
Braemore Dr					
2900	WCHI	60185	2965	32W-4N	C4
Braemore Ln					
-	YKVL	60560	3333	42W-17S	E6
W Braemore Close					
14100	GNOK	60048	2535	14W-31N	D7
Braeside					
-	BRTN	60010	2751	25W-18N	B2
W Braeside Dr					
300	ANHT	60004	2753	18W-17N	E6
300	ANHT	60004	2754	18W-17N	A6
Braeside Ln					
1600	NHBK	60062	2757	8W-16N	E6
Braeside Pl					
700	BRTN	60010	2751	25W-18N	B2
Braeside Rd					
300	HDPK	60035	2758	7W-20N	C2
W Braewick Rd					
17700	WrnT	60031	2477	17W-36N	B5
Braewood Dr					
600	ALGN	60102	2747	35W-19N	C2
1400	DndT	60102	2747	35W-19N	C2
1400	DndT	60118	2747	35W-19N	C2
Braga Dr					
2400	BDVW	60155	3087	11W-1S	C1
Bragg Ct					
300	BRLT	60103	2911	28W-7N	B5
Bragg St					
200	BRLT	60103	2911	28W-7N	B5
Brahms Cir					
100	WHTN	60187	3082	24W-2S	C4
Brahms Ct					
100	GLHT	60139	2968	23W-4N	E4
1400	BRLT	60103	2967	28W-5N	B1
Brahms Ln					
2700	WDSK	60098	2524	41W-33N	E3
N Brainard Av					
10	LGNG	60525	3087	13W-4S	B7
200	LGPK	60525	3087	13W-3S	B5
900	WSTR	60525	3087	12W-3S	B5
S Brainard Av					
10	LGNG	60525	3087	12W-4S	B7
300	LGNG	60525	3147	13W-5S	B3
500	LynT	60525	3147	12W-5S	B1
5400	CTSD	60525	3147	13W-7S	B6
13000	CHCG	60633	3279	3E-15S	E7
13100	CHCG	60633	3351	3E-15S	E1
13300	CHCG	60633	3352	3E-15S	A1
13700	BNHM	60633	3352	4E-16S	B3
13800	HMND	46327	3352	4E-16S	C4
E Brainard Ct					
100	HRVD	60033	2406	49W-38N	D5
N Brainard St					
10	NPVL	60540	3141	26W-6S	D5
500	NPVL	60563	3141	26W-6S	D4
S Brainard St					
10	NPVL	60540	3141	26W-6S	D6
W Brainard St					
100	HRVD	60033	2406	49W-39N	D5
Brainerd Av					
100	LYVL	60048	2591	16W-29N	D5
S Braintree Ct					
100	SMBG	60193	2858	25W-10N	C6
N Braintree Dr					
10	SMBG	60193	2858	25W-10N	C5
10	SMBG	60194	2858	25W-11N	C4
500	HFET	60169	2858	25W-11N	C4
500	HFET	60194	2858	25W-11N	C4
S Braintree Dr					
10	SMBG	60193	2858	25W-9N	C7
10	SMBG	60194	2858	25W-10N	C6
800	SMBG	60193	2912	25W-9N	C1
Braintree Ln					
100	BMDL	60108	2969	23W-5N	A2
600	BRLT	60103	2910	30W-7N	C5
Brair Cove					
800	PLTN	60067	2752	22W-17N	B5
Bramanti Tr					
3200	SCHT	60475	3596	0W-27S	C4
3200	STGR	60475	3596	0W-27S	C4
Bramble Av					
1100	BGBK	60490	3268	25W-12S	B4
Bramble Ct					
300	SMBG	60193	2858	23W-10N	E6
1100	BGBK	60490	3268	25W-12S	B3
13000	HMGN	60491	3422	16W-18S	A1
Bramble Dr					
21300	FKFT	60423	3592	11W-25S	A1
Bramble Ln					
200	DRPK	60010	2699	22W-20N	B7
300	SMBG	60193	2858	24W-10N	E6
Bramblebush Ct					
10	WDRG	60517	3144	20W-7S	B6
S Bramble Hill Rd					
22500	TroT	60404	3584	30W-27S	B5
Bramblewood Dr					
-	SJHN	46373	3687		E1
-	SJnT	46311	3687		E1
15500	OKFT	60452	3347	8W-18S	A7
Bramer Av					
10	CPVL	60118	2800	34W-16N	E2
10	EDND	60118	2800	34W-16N	E2
300	CPVL	60110	2800	34W-16N	E1
Bramlett Dr					
18100	OrlT	60487	3423	11W-21S	E7
Bramlette Ct					
11800	HMGN	60491	3344	14W-17S	C6
11800	ODPK	60467	3344	14W-17S	C6
11800	OrlT	60467	3344	14W-17S	C6
Brampton Ct					
300	LNSH	60045	2702	13W-23N	D1
1000	UYPK	60466	3684	3W-30S	C3
Brampton Ln					
-	VrnT	60045	2702	14W-23N	C1
200	LNSH	60045	2702	13W-23N	D1
200	LNSH	60069	2702	14W-23N	C2
200	VrnT	60069	2702	14W-23N	C2
W Brampton Ln					
300	ANHT	60004	2754	18W-18N	A2
500	ANHT	60004	2753	18W-18N	E2
Brancaster Dr					
24000	WldT	60564	3266	30W-12S	C3
Branch Av					
10	WNVL	60555	3080	30W-2S	C3
700	WnfT	60555	3080	29W-2S	C3
W Branch Ct					
2400	NPVL	60565	3203	26W-10S	E6
Branch Rd					
1000	GRNE	60031	2477	15W-35N	E6
N Branch Rd					
1200	WLMT	60091	2811	6W-14N	D4
Branchaw Blvd					
100	NLNX	60451	3501	18W-23S	B3
100	NlxT	60451	3501	18W-23S	B3
Branchwood Cir					
1300	NPVL	60563	3140	28W-5S	E4
Branchwood Ct					
300	SMBG	60193	2858	23W-10N	E6
Branchwood Dr					
10	SMBG	60193	2858	24W-10N	E6
10	SMBG	60194	2858	24W-10N	E6
Brand Ln					
800	DRFD	60015	2704	10W-21N	B7
Brandau Ct					
8400	TYPK	60487	3424	10W-21S	B6
Brandau Dr					
18000	TYPK	60487	3424	10W-21S	B7
Brandeis Ct					
1700	NPVL	60565	3204	24W-9S	D3
Branden Ct					
1300	BRLT	60103	2967	28W-6N	B1
Branden Ln					
1300	BRLT	60103	2967	28W-5N	B1
E Brandenberg Rd					
26700	GrtT	60041	2530	26W-34N	C2
W Brandenberg Rd					
-	VOLO	60041	2530	27W-34N	B2
27000	GrtT	60041	2530	27W-34N	A2
28000	GrtT	60041	2529	28W-33N	E2
28000	LKMR	60041	2529	28W-33N	E2
28000	LKMR	60051	2529	28W-33N	E2
E Brandenberry Ct					
2400	ANHT	60004	2807	16W-15N	D3
2400	PTHT	60004	2807	16W-15N	D3
2400	WhlT	60004	2807	16W-15N	D3
Brandess Dr					
3100	GNVW	60025	2810	10W-15N	A3
Branding Av					
1400	DRGV	60515	3084	20W-2S	B4
Brandon Av					
10	GNEN	60137	3025	22W-0S	B7
S Brandon Av					
7900	CHCG	60649	3216	3E-9S	A2
8900	CHCG	60617	3216	3E-10S	A4
13000	CHCG	60633	3280	3E-15S	A7
13100	CHCG	60633	3352	3E-15S	A1
Brandon Blvd					
200	BtvT	60539	3077	36W-3S	E5
600	WNFD	60190	3023	27W-0N	D4
Brandon Ct					
-	NARA	60542	3077	38W-3S	A6
100	BGBK	60440	3268	23W-11S	E1
100	OSWG	60543	3199	36W-11S	E7
1900	GLHT	60139	2969	23W-3N	A5
W Brandon Ct					
100	PLTN	60067	2752	21W-17N	E6
Brandon Dr					
1400	WHTN	60187	3082	24W-1S	D2
N Brandon Dr					
10	GLHT	60139	2968	23W-3N	E4
100	GLHT	60139	2969	23W-3N	A5
S Brandon Dr					
1900	GLHT	60139	2969	23W-3N	A5
Brandon Pl					
700	WLNG	60090	2755	15W-18N	A3
Brandon Rd					
-	JltT	60436	3498	25W-25S	C7
10	GNVW	60025	2811	7W-14N	A3
10	NHFD	60093	2811	7W-14N	A3
10	RKDL	60436	3498	25W-25S	C7
1000	JltT	60436	3586	25W-27S	D4
1700	JLET	60436	3586	25W-26S	D3
2000	GNVW	60093	2811	7W-14N	A3
2400	JltT	60421	3586	24W-27S	D5
8900	DRN	60561	3206	19W-10S	D5
S Brandon Rd					
22500	JknT	60421	3586	24W-28S	D7
22500	JLET	60436	3586	24W-27S	D5
22500	JltT	60421	3586	24W-28S	D7
22500	JltT	60436	3586	24W-28S	D7
23500	JknT	60421	3675	24W-28S	D1
23900	ELWD	60421	3675	25W-29S	C2
23900	JLET	60421	3675	25W-29S	C2
W Brandon Rd					
21100	KLDR	60047	2699	21W-21N	D6
Brandt Av					
9500	OKLN	60453	3211	6W-11S	E6
9700	OKLN	60453	3212	6W-11S	A7
Brandt Dr					
200	HPSR	60140	2795	46W-16N	E2
700	LIHL	60156	2694	34W-22N	C5
900	DndT	60118	2801	32W-14N	C6
900	DndT	60120	2801	32W-14N	C6
900	ELGN	60118	2801	32W-14N	C6
900	ELGN	60120	2801	32W-14N	C6
900	HnrT	60120	2801	32W-14N	C6
Brandt Rd					
-	BRTN	60010	2697	26W-21N	D7
26000	CbaT	60010	2697	26W-21N	D7
Brandy Cir					
1400	NPVL	60540	3204	24W-8S	C1
Brandy Dr					
400	CLLK	60014	2639	36W-24N	E6
Brandy Pkwy					
1500	SMBG	60193	2857	27W-10N	D7
1500	SMWD	60107	2857	27W-10N	D7

STREET / Block City ZIP Map# CGS Grid

Brandy Pkwy
1500 SMWD 60193 2857 27W-10N D7
Brandywine Ln
100 EGVV 60007 2914 19W-8N D2
Brandywine Cir
1100 ALGN 60102 2747 35W-19N B2
1200 BTVA 60510 3078 36W-2S A4
Brandywine Ct
10 SEGN 60177 2908 35W-8N B3
100 LslT 60540 3142 25W-6S B4
100 VNHL 60061 2647 17W-26N B3
Brandywine Dr
700 ROSL 60172 2912 24W-6N D5
Brandywine Rd
10 SBTN 60010 2803 27W-14N A3
1200 LYVL 60048 2591 17W-28N A6
Brandywyn Ct
1100 BFGV 60089 2701 17W-21N B6
Brandywyn Ct N
1500 BFGV 60089 2701 17W-21N B5
Brandywyn Ln
2100 BFGV 60089 2701 16W-22N D4
2100 VrnT 60089 2701 17W-22N C4
Branford Av
10 BTVA 60510 3078 34W-1S D2
Branford Ln
\- BbyT 60134 3018 39W-0S E7
1500 NPVL 60564 3266 28W-11S E2
1500 NPVL 60564 3267 28W-11S A2
E Brannick Rd
7600 MNKA 60447 3672 34W-29S A2
Brannock Ln
\- TYPK 60477 3504 10W-23S B3
Brannon Ct
\- SRWD 60404 3495 31W-23S E4
Brannon Ln
\- BbyT 60134 3018 39W-0S E7
Brannon Trc
\- SRWD 60404 3495 31W-23S E4
Branpton Ln
3000 DYR 46311 3598 D4
Branson Dr
\- BTVA 60134 3019 37W-0S C7
\- GnvT 60134 3019 37W-0S C7
700 BTVA 60510 3019 37W-0S C7
Brantley Pl
400 WHTN 60187 3024 25W-0S C7
Brantwood Av
10 EGVV 60007 2914 19W-8N D2
W Brantwood Av
10 EGVV 60007 2914 19W-9N D1
Brantwood Ct
600 EGVV 60007 2914 19W-9N D1
Brantwood Pl
800 EGVV 60007 2914 18W-8N E1
N Brashares Dr
200 ADSN 60101 2970 19W-3N C5
Brassel St
100 LktT 60441 3419 22W-21S C6
Brassfield Av
900 RMVL 60446 3340 25W-15S C1
Brassie Av
1000 FSMR 60422 3507 3W-23S B4
Brassie Ct
10 WDRG 60517 3143 23W-7S B7
400 UYPK 60417 3684 2W-30S D3
15700 ODPK 60462 3424 10W-18S C1
29000 FmtT 60060 2589 21W-28N C5
Brassie Dr
2700 GNVW 60025 2810 9W-13N B6
15200 ODPK 60462 3346 10W-18S C7
15600 ODPK 60462 3424 9W-18S C1
Brassie Ln
400 UYPK 60417 3684 2W-30S C4
Brave Ct
1200 CLSM 60188 2967 28W-4N B4
Braver Ct
1300 WLNG 60090 2754 16W-18N D3
Bravery Ct
\- SRWD 60404 3496 31W-24S A5
Bravo Ct
300 BRLT 60103 2967 28W-5N B1
Braxton Ct
200 GYLK 60030 2533 19W-33N C3
6300 GRNE 60031 2534 16W-33N D3
Braxton Ln
\- AURA 60504 3201 31W-7S E1
10 AURA 60504 3139 31W-7S E7
W Braxton Ln
21000 LktT 60544 3339 26W-16S E3
Braxton Rd
1400 LYVL 60048 2591 17W-30N A2
Braxton Wy
100 GYLK 60030 2533 19W-33N C3
W Bray Ct
1400 ANHT 60005 2860 19W-12N D1
E Braymore Cir
1300 AURA 60564 3201 31W-9S E4
W Braymore Cir
1300 AURA 60564 3201 31W-9S E4
Braymore Cir S
1300 AURA 60564 3201 31W-9S E4
Braymore Ct
100 IVNS 60010 2750 25W-16N E7
Braymore Dr
900 GYLK 60030 2533 19W-33N B3
N Braymore Dr
1800 IVNS 60010 2750 25W-16N E6
1800 IVNS 60010 2751 25W-16N A6
S Braymore Dr
1600 IVNS 60010 2750 25W-16N E6
1600 IVNS 60010 2751 25W-16N A6
Brayton Av
13100 WthT 60406 3349 3W-15S A1
Brayton Pl
2100 JLET 60586 3415 33W-21S B7
E Brayton St
10 CHCG 60628 3278 0W-14S C6
W Brayton St
10 CHCG 60628 3278 0W-14S C6
Breakenridge Farm
10 OKBK 60523 3085 16W-3S E6
Breakers Dr
3600 FSMR 60422 3506 4W-24S D4
3600 OMFD 60461 3506 4W-24S D4
Breakers Pt
600 SMBG 60194 2859 22W-10N C4
Breakwater Wy
7900 PSHT 60463 3274 9W-13S C4
Breanne Ln
13800 HMGN 60491 3421 17W-19S C2
Breasted Av
1700 DRGV 60516 3144 20W-6S A5
Breaton Wy
\- LKWD 60014 2692 39W-23N D1

Brechin Tr
2700 ELGN 60124 2853 37W-12N C1
Breckenridge Av
1000 LKFT 60045 2649 11W-24N D7
Breckenridge Blvd
18200 FftT 60448 3422 14W-21S D7
18200 ODPK 60467 3422 14W-21S D7
Breckenridge Cir
2700 AURA 60504 3201 32W-7S D1
Breckenridge Ct
100 GLBT 60136 2799 38W-15N A4
2500 AURA 60504 3201 32W-8S C2
8100 BLVY 60098 2526 37W-32N C5
Brecken Ridge Dr
1000 SRWD 60404 3496 30W-22S B2
Breckenridge Dr
10 AURA 60504 3201 32W-8S C2
100 GLBT 60136 2799 38W-15N B4
1900 JLET 60586 3415 32W-21S D7
8000 LGGV 60060 2645 20W-26N E4
8000 LGGV 60060 2646 20W-26N A4
8400 PSHL 60465 3274 10W-12S B1
19600 MKNA 60448 3502 15W-23S C4
19600 NlxT 60448 3502 15W-23S C3
19800 NlxT 60451 3502 15W-23S C4
N Breckenridge Dr
20000 ElaT 60047 2644 23W-24N E7
20000 ElaT 60047 2698 23W-24N E1
20000 HNWD 60047 2644 23W-24N E7
Breckenridge Ln
2600 NPVL 60565 3203 27W-10S B7
2800 NPVL 60564 3203 27W-10S B7
Breckenridge Rd
6600 LSLE 60532 3142 24W-7S C7
Breen Rd
\- JLET 60421 3675 24W-29S D3
Breen St
1500 JltT 60436 3586 24W-25S E2
W Breen St
7100 NLES 60714 2864 9W-10N D4
Brees Wy Ln
1400 NHBK 60062 2757 9W-17N C6
Breeze Dr
700 LKVL 60046 2475 23W-36N A3
800 LKVL 60046 2474 23W-36N E3
S Breeze Dr
200 LKVL 60046 2474 23W-36N E3
200 LKVL 60046 2475 23W-36N A3
Breeze Wy
1400 BGBK 60490 3267 26W-12S E4
Breezeland Ct
6000 CPVL 60110 2747 36W-18N A5
Breezeland Rd
5700 CPVL 60110 2747 36W-17N A6
Breezewood Ter
2200 HRPK 60133 2911 27W-8N C3
Breezy Ln
700 NndT 60051 2586 29W-29N C4
Breezy Pt
\- ElgT 60124 2853 37W-9N D7
Breezy Lawn Rd
1500 BtnT 60081 2355 30W-42N A5
1500 SPGV 60081 2355 30W-42N A5
Breezy Point Ln
100 FXLK 60020 2473 27W-37N A2
Bregenz Ct
100 LYWD 60411 3598 4E-25S C1
Breitwieser Ln
3400 NPVL 60564 3202 30W-11S B7
3400 NPVL 60564 3266 30W-11S B1
Brementowne Dr
6800 BmnT 60477 3425 8W-19S A2
6800 TYPK 60477 3425 8W-19S A2
Brementowne Rd
6800 TYPK 60477 3425 8W-19S A2
Bremer Ct
\- CteT 60417 3687 4E-29S B2
600 GNEN 60137 3025 22W-0S C6
Bremer St
500 WMTN 60481 3853 27W-38S D6
Bremer Tr
\- CteT 60417 3687 4E-29S B2
Bremerton Ct
3200 AURA 60504 3201 31W-8S E2
Bremerton Ln
3200 AURA 60504 3201 31W-8S E2
Brendan St
20000 FKFT 60423 3503 11W-24S E4
20100 FKFT 60423 3504 11W-24S A5
Brenden Ln
16400 OKFT 60452 3426 5W-19S B2
Brendon Ct
100 ROSL 60172 2912 25W-7N B4
Brendon Dr
800 SMBG 60194 2857 26W-11N E3
S Brennan Av
9500 CHCG 60617 3215 2E-11S D6
Brennan Hwy
15300 MKHM 60426 3348 4W-18S E7
15300 MKHM 60428 3348 4W-18S E7
15400 MKHM 60428 3426 4W-18S D1
Brenner Ct
10 LYWD 60411 3598 4E-25S C1
200 CRTE 60417 3596 0E-28S E6
S Brenner Ct
10300 WldT 60564 3266 30W-12S B2
Brent Ct
2200 SMBG 60194 2857 26W-11N E5
Brent Rd
1100 NHBK 60062 2810 8W-15N D1
Brenta Ct
100 LYWD 60411 3598 4E-25S C1
Brentford Dr
1600 NPVL 60563 3141 26W-5S E2
Brenton Ct
2800 JLET 60431 3417 28W-20S A5
2800 JLET 60586 3417 28W-20S A5
Brenton Dr
3800 JLET 60431 3417 28W-20S A5
Brentwood Av
2200 MTGY 60538 3199 38W-9S A5
2300 MTGY 60538 3198 39W-9S E5
14400 ODPK 60462 3345 11W-17S E4
Brentwood Cir
1000 BFGV 60089 2754 17W-17N C4
5200 LGGV 60047 2701 17W-22N A5
Brentwood Ct
\- BNVL 60106 2972 15W-4N B3
200 BMDL 60108 2969 22W-4N B4
400 ROSL 60172 2912 24W-6N E6
500 WynT 60103 2966 29W-5N D1
700 ALGN 60102 2694 34W-20N C7
700 GNEN 60137 3083 22W-1S C1
800 SMBG 60193 2858 24W-9N D7
800 WCHI 60185 3022 30W-0S B6
1100 GNVA 60134 3020 34W-1N E3

Brentwood Ct
1100 HRPK 60133 2911 26W-9N E1
1200 FSMR 60422 3507 3W-22S A2
2000 WHTN 60187 3083 23W-2S A4
2900 WDRG 60517 3205 22W-9S C3
S Brentwood Ct
16700 HMGN 60491 3422 15W-20S B3
W Brentwood Ct
20800 LktT 60544 3340 25W-16S B4
Brentwood Dr
10 GLBT 60136 2799 38W-14N B5
10 GLNC 60022 2758 6W-18N D3
200 CHHT 60411 3507 1W-23S E4
300 DSPN 60016 2862 15W-11N B3
700 BNVL 60106 2972 15W-4N B4
800 CRY 60013 2642 30W-24N A7
800 JLET 60435 3497 26W-22S E3
800 WCHI 60185 3022 30W-0S B6
900 RLKB 60073 2531 24W-34N D1
1000 RLKB 60073 2474 24W-35N D7
1500 RLKH 60073 2474 24W-35N D7
1600 MDLN 60060 2590 20W-27N A7
5700 HFET 60192 2856 31W-12N A2
N Brentwood Dr
500 CLLK 60014 2639 36W-24N D7
S Brentwood Dr
600 CLLK 60014 2639 36W-24N D7
W Brentwood Dr
100 PltT 60074 2752 21W-18N D2
Brentwood Ln
1000 WHTN 60187 3082 23W-2S E4
1500 WHTN 60187 3083 23W-2S A4
1700 NndT 60050 2585 31W-30N D2
4100 WKGN 60087 2478 14W-36N D4
7300 GRNE 60031 2534 18W-34N A1
7500 WmT 60031 2534 18W-34N A1
N Brentwood Ln
800 MPPT 60056 2808 14W-14N B4
W Brentwood Ln
21500 LkvT 60046 2417 21W-39N C5
21600 LKVL 60046 2417 22W-39N C5
Brentwood Ln E
1800 WHTN 60187 3083 23W-2S A4
Brentwood Pl
300 DRGV 60515 3084 18W-4S E6
900 GNVA 60134 3020 34W-1N E3
1100 JLET 60435 3497 26W-22S E2
Brentwood Rd
2100 NHBK 60062 2757 10W-16N A6
Brentwood Tr
10 ELGN 60120 2855 31W-11N E4
1300 BGBK 60490 3339 28W-15S A1
Brenwood Dr
10 LslT 60540 3204 23W-8S E1
Brestal Ct
1600 NPVL 60565 3204 25W-9S B3
Bret Dr
6200 OKFT 60452 3425 7W-18S B1
Bretman St
\- BNVL 60106 2972 15W-5N A1
Breton Av
\- BtvT 60510 3077 38W-3S A5
\- NARA 60542 3077 38W-3S A5
Breton Ct
10 BTVA 60510 3078 36W-1S A2
Breton Rd
21300 FKFT 60423 3592 10W-25S B1
Breton Lakes Dr
800 WLBK 60527 3145 16W-7S E6
6300 DGvT 60527 3145 16W-7S E6
Bretons Dr
\- LKVL 60046 2475 22W-37N C1
W Bretons Dr
3100 MHRY 60050 2528 32W-32N B6
Brett Cir
200 WCDA 60084 2644 25W-27N B1
Brett Ct
100 MHTN 60442 3678 18W-31S B5
E Brett Ct
200 ANHT 60005 2861 17W-12N A1
Brett Dr
\- NLNX 60451 3589 18W-27S A5
100 MHTN 60442 3678 18W-31S B4
19100 MKNA 60448 3503 13W-23S B3
Brett Ln
3800 GNVW 60025 2809 11W-14N D3
Brett St
24900 PNFD 60544 3337 31W-16S E4
24900 PNFD 60544 3338 31W-16S A3
Bretz Dr
4400 RNPK 60471 3594 5W-27S B4
17700 HMWD 60430 3428 0W-21S B6
17700 HMWD 60476 3428 0W-21S B6
17700 TNTN 60430 3428 0W-21S B6
17700 TNTN 60476 3428 0W-21S B6
Brewer Ct
1000 WDND 60118 2800 35W-16N C1
Brewer Ln
2600 WDRG 60517 3205 21W-9S D4
Brewer Rd
3100 DRN 60561 3206 20W-9S A4
Brewster Av
\- BKFD 60513 3087 12W-3S C6
\- BKFD 60525 3087 12W-3S C6
\- LGNG 60513 3087 12W-3S C6
\- LGPK 60525 3087 12W-3S C6
10 LGPK 60525 3087 12W-3S B6
S Brewster Av
200 LMBD 60148 3026 20W-0N B5
Brewster Ct
100 BMDL 60108 2969 23W-5N A2
Brewster Ln
10 LGNG 60525 3087 12W-3S C6
100 LGPK 60525 3087 12W-4S C6
500 SMBG 60193 2858 25W-9N C7
800 BRLT 60103 2910 30W-7N C5
Brewster Creek Blvd
\- BRLT 60120 2910 31W-7N A4
1400 BRLT 60120 2909 31W-7N E5
1400 WynT 60184 2909 31W-7N E5
Brewster Creek Cir
10 WYNE 60184 2909 33W-6N A6
Brian Av
600 SMBG 60194 2858 26W-11N A4
Brian Cir
1200 LYVL 60048 2590 18W-29N E3
Brian Ct
10 ALGN 60102 2694 34W-21N B6
200 GNVA 60134 3019 36W-1N D3
200 MHTN 60442 3678 18W-31S A5
800 GRNE 60031 2534 16W-33N E3
1400 MNKA 60447 3672 34W-30S A3
2800 MTGY 60538 3198 40W-10S C5
22500 RNPK 60471 3594 5W-27S C5
Brian Ct E
\- ANTH 60002 2359 20W-41N A7

Brian Ct W
\- ANTH 60002 2359 20W-41N B7
Brian Dr
10 GLHT 60139 2968 24W-3N E5
800 CTHL 60403 3418 25W-21S C7
2300 NHBK 60062 2810 10W-15N A2
2400 NHBK 60062 2809 10W-15N E2
Brian Ln
200 PTHT 60070 2808 14W-15N B2
2800 BtlT 60538 3198 40W-10S B5
2800 MTGY 60538 3198 40W-10S B5
W Brian Ln
200 BDWD 60408 3942 31W-40S B4
200 RedT 60408 3942 31W-40S B4
S Brian Pl
12800 PlsT 60464 3273 12W-15S C7
12800 PlsT 60464 3345 12W-15S C1
Brianne Ct
\- RNPK 60443 3593 7W-26S C3
Brianne Ln
15500 OKFT 60452 3347 8W-18S B7
Briar Av
400 GRNE 60031 2536 13W-34N A1
400 LYVL 60048 2591 16W-28N E6
500 GRNE 60031 2479 13W-34N A7
17600 HMWD 60430 3427 2W-21S D6
Briar Ct
\- PKRG 60016 2863 11W-11N D4
\- PKRG 60068 2863 11W-11N D4
1300 DSPN 60018 2862 13W-9N E6
1300 DSPN 60018 2863 12W-9N A7
2200 HFET 60169 2857 26W-12N E1
8800 MaiT 60016 2863 11W-11N D4
W Briar Ct
7700 FftT 60423 3504 9W-24S D5
Briar Dr
\- SKOK 60077 2811 6W-13N E7
\- SKOK 60091 2811 6W-13N E7
\- SPGV 60081 2413 31W-39N C5
200 WLMT 60091 2811 6W-13N D7
17100 TYPK 60487 3423 11W-20S E5
Briar Ln
\- HFET 60169 2857 26W-12N E1
\- HFET 60169 2858 25W-12N B1
10 GLNC 60022 2758 6W-17N D6
10 GNVA 60134 3020 34W-1N D4
100 NARA 60542 3078 36W-3S A7
100 NpvT 60563 3140 30W-5S B3
200 HDPK 60035 2757 9W-20N C2
200 LNHT 60046 2476 20W-37N B2
300 LKBF 60044 2594 10W-28N A6
400 LKFT 60045 2650 10W-25N A5
400 MNSR 46321 3430 D7
500 NHFD 60093 2811 7W-15N B2
500 WNKA 60093 2812 4W-15N C1
600 AddT 60106 2971 16W-4N D3
600 AddT 60191 2971 16W-4N D3
600 BNVL 60106 2971 16W-4N D3
1200 RLKB 60073 2475 23W-34N A7
3600 HLCT 60429 3506 4W-22S D1
7400 HRPK 60133 2911 27W-9N D1
13900 PNFD 60544 3337 31W-16S E4
15100 OKFT 60452 3347 7W-18S D7
S Briar Ln
300 AddT 60106 2971 16W-4N D2
300 AddT 60191 2971 16W-4N D2
300 BNVL 60106 2971 16W-4N D2
13000 PSHT 60463 3347 8W-15S A1
13000 WthT 60463 3347 8W-15S A1
25900 MONE 60449 3682 6W-31S E5
Briar Pl
100 PltT 60010 2751 24W-18N C2
300 ITSC 60143 2914 19W-6N D6
E Briar Pl
900 ANHT 60004 2807 17W-16N B1
W Briar Pl
600 CHCG 60657 2978 0W-3N A4
700 CHCG 60657 2977 3W-4N A2
Briar Rd
\- GNVW 60025 2864 8W-12N E1
\- GNVW 60029 2864 8W-12N E1
10 GLF 60029 2864 8W-12N E1
10 GLF 60029 2865 8W-12N A1
300 ISLK 60042 2586 28W-28N E6
600 WCDA 60084 2587 26W-28N C7
6300 WLBK 60527 3146 15W-7S B5
N Briar Rd
38100 AntT 60081 2415 27W-38N B7
Briar St
10 GNEN 60137 3025 21W-0S E7
10 GNEN 60148 3025 21W-0S E7
10 MltT 60137 3025 21W-0S E7
10 MltT 60148 3025 21W-0S E7
Briar Tr
2500 SMBG 60173 2805 21W-13N D6
Briarbranch Ter
200 RchT 60443 3593 8W-26S B2
Briarbrook Dr
1000 WHTN 60187 3082 23W-2S E4
Briarcliff Ct
10 LIHL 60156 2692 38W-23N E3
100 MTGY 60538 3199 36W-10S E6
100 RMVL 60446 3339 27W-17S D6
600 MltT 60148 3083 21W-2S E4
600 MltT 60148 3084 21W-2S A4
6400 LSLE 60532 3142 24W-7S D6
Briarcliff Dr
1400 NlxT 60451 3589 16W-26S E3
1500 NlxT 60451 3590 16W-26S A3
7600 JLET 60586 3415 33W-20S A6
Briarcliff Ln
\- MTGY 60538 3199 36W-9S E5
400 BRLT 60103 2911 27W-7N C5
500 HFET 60169 2858 24W-12N E2
2700 LIHL 60156 2692 38W-22N E3
Briarcliff Rd
10 DRGV 60148 3083 21W-2S E4
10 DRGV 60515 3083 21W-2S E4
10 MltT 60148 3083 21W-2S E4
10 OswT 60538 3199 37W-10S D6
1300 MTGY 60538 3199 36W-9S E5
E Briarcliff Rd
100 BGBK 60440 3269 22W-11S C2
W Briarcliff Rd
100 BGBK 60440 3269 23W-12S A2
400 BGBK 60440 3268 24W-11S D2
1300 BGBK 60490 3268 26W-12S A2
1400 BGBK 60490 3267 26W-12S E2
Briarcliffe Blvd
1000 WHTN 60187 3082 23W-2S E4
Briarcliffe Dr
12300 LMNT 60439 3270 20W-14S A7
Briarcliffe Ln
1200 HDPK 60035 2704 10W-23N A2
Briar Cove
1400 WHTN 60187 3081 26W-1S E2

Briar Cove
1400 WHTN 60187 3082 26W-1S A2
Briar Creek Dr
10 HNWD 60047 2645 22W-26N C3
Briarcrest Ln
1600 NLNX 60451 3588 19W-26S E3
5200 LGGV 60047 2701 18W-22N A4
Briarfield Ln
5300 LIHL 60156 2692 38W-21N E6
Briarford Ln
2400 GNVW 60062 2809 11W-15N D2
Briargate Av
\- BlmT 60411 3508 0W-24S C5
\- CHHT 60411 3508 1W-24S A5
1200 JLET 60435 3498 25W-22S B2
Briargate Cir
10 SgrT 60506 3135 41W-5S E3
Briargate Ct
2700 WCHI 60185 2965 32W-4N B4
Briargate Dr
200 GYLK 60030 2532 20W-33N E3
300 GYLK 60030 2533 20W-33N A2
400 SEGN 60177 2907 37W-7N D5
1000 DRFD 60015 2704 10W-21N B6
1000 DRFD 60035 2704 10W-21N B6
1000 HDPK 60035 2704 10W-21N B6
6500 DRGV 60516 3144 19W-7S D6
13000 HTLY 60142 2744 43W-19N B4
16700 CCHL 60478 3426 4W-20S D3
16700 MKHM 60428 3426 4W-20S D3
Briargate Ln
300 DRPK 60010 2699 22W-20N B7
300 DRPK 60010 2752 22W-20N B1
Briargate Rd
10 CRY 60013 2695 31W-23N C2
200 TVLY 60013 2695 31W-23N C2
Briargate Ter
10 BmdT 60157 2913 21W-7N E5
300 HNDL 60521 3086 15W-4S A6
Briarheath Dr
1600 AURA 60505 3139 33W-6S A4
Briarheath Ln
100 NPVL 60565 3203 26W-9S E5
Briarhill Ct
2200 NPVL 60565 3203 27W-10S C5
Briar Hill Dr
2000 SMBG 60194 2858 26W-11N A3
2100 SMBG 60194 2857 26W-11N E3
Briarhill Dr
2200 NPVL 60565 3203 27W-10S C5
Briarhill Ln
400 GNVW 60025 2810 9W-12N C7
N Briar Hill Ln
600 AddT 60101 2970 19W-4N D4
600 ADSN 60101 2970 19W-4N D4
W Briar Patch Ln
13100 LMNT 60439 3343 16W-15S E2
13100 LMNT 60439 3344 15W-15S A2
Briarpoint Ct
300 LKZH 60047 2699 22W-22N B4
Briar Ridge Ct
100 LKVL 60046 2475 22W-37N B2
Briarridge Ct
2000 JLET 60586 3416 31W-21S A7
Briar Ridge Ln
10 LKVL 60046 2475 22W-37N A2
Briartree Ln
5000 BDPK 60638 3211 6W-8S E1
5000 BRBK 60459 3211 6W-8S E1
5000 BRBK 60638 3211 6W-8S E1
Briarwood Av
\- SMWD 60107 2911 27W-9N C1
\- SMWD 60133 2911 27W-9N C1
100 CPVL 60110 2801 33W-17N A1
100 CPVL 60118 2801 33W-17N A1
100 OKBK 60523 3085 17W-2S C3
600 RMVL 60446 3340 24W-16S C3
1700 HRPK 60133 2911 27W-9N C1
Briarwood Cir
\- OKBK 60523 3085 17W-2S C3
10 CLLK 60014 2639 38W-25N A4
10 DrrT 60014 2639 38W-25N A4
Briar Wood Ct
300 GRNE 60031 2535 14W-33N C2
Briarwood Ct
10 IHPK 60525 3146 13W-7S E5
10 SMBG 60193 2858 24W-10N E6
100 ELGN 60120 2855 32W-11N D3
100 MTSN 60443 3505 6W-24S E5
400 VNHL 60061 2647 16W-24N E6
600 ANTH 60002 2357 24W-42N D5
600 ELWD 60421 3675 25W-31S C6
2500 AURA 60506 3136 39W-6S E5
2700 WDRG 60517 3205 21W-9S D3
11700 BRRG 60527 3208 14W-9S C2
Briarwood Dr
10 CLLK 60014 2639 38W-26N A3
10 GfnT 60014 2639 38W-25N A4
10 GLBT 60136 2799 38W-14N B5
10 WNVL 60555 3080 29W-3S D5
400 WLNG 60090 2754 15W-17N E6
500 BRRG 60527 3208 15W-9S A4
500 DYR 46311 3510 E5
700 LynT 60458 3209 11W-8S D2
1300 NPVL 60540 3141 28W-7S A6
1400 NPVL 60540 3140 28W-7S E6
1700 JNBG 60050 2472 30W-37N A1
4800 CLLK 60012 2639 38W-26N A2
4800 CLLK 60098 2639 38W-26N A2
4800 DrrT 60012 2639 38W-27N A1
4800 DrrT 60014 2639 38W-26N A3
4800 DrrT 60098 2639 38W-26N A2
E Briarwood Dr
10 SMWD 60107 2856 30W-10N C6
10 SMWD 60107 2857 28W-9N A7
S Briarwood Dr E
2800 MPPT 60005 2861 17W-10N C5
S Briarwood Dr W
2700 ANHT 60005 2861 17W-10N B5
2700 ANHT 60056 2861 17W-10N B4
2700 MPPT 60005 2861 17W-10N B4
2700 MPPT 60056 2861 17W-10N B4
W Briarwood Dr
10 SMWD 60107 2856 30W-10N C6
13600 HMGN 60491 3343 16W-17S E6
Briarwood Ln
10 IHPK 60525 3146 14W-6S D5
10 IHPK 60525 3147 13W-7S A6
10 LNSH 60045 2702 13W-23N D1
10 OKBK 60523 3085 17W-2S C4
10 PltT 60067 2805 20W-13N E6
10 SMBG 60067 2805 20W-13N E6
10 SMBG 60173 2805 20W-13N E6
200 PltT 60067 2806 20W-13N A6
300 ALGN 60102 2694 35W-21N B6
300 BMDL 60108 2969 22W-4N C3

STREET Block	City	ZIP	Map#	CGS	Grid
Briarwood Ln					
500	EGVV	60007	2861	18W-10N	A6
600	OSWG	60543	3263	37W-13S	C5
600	ROSL	60172	2912	24W-6N	C6
1000	NHBK	60062	2757	10W-17N	A6
1200	LYVL	60048	2647	16W-27N	D1
2600	MaiT	60025	2864	9W-12N	B1
8800	ODPK	60462	3346	11W-15S	A2
9100	HYHL	60457	3209	11W-10S	E5
11500	BRRG	60527	3208	14W-9S	D2
20700	FftT	60448	3503	13W-25S	A6
Briarwood Lp					
100	OKBK	60523	3085	17W-2S	C3
Briarwood Pl					
400	HDPK	60035	2758	7W-20N	B1
Briarwood Sq					
10	IHPK	60525	3147	12W-7S	B6
Briarwood St					
100	ELGN	60120	2855	32W-11N	D3
Briarwood Central					
-	OKBK	60523	3085	17W-2S	C3
Briarwood North Dr					
100	OKBK	60523	3085	17W-2S	C3
Briarwood Pass					
200	OKBK	60523	3085	16W-2S	D3
Briarwood South Dr					
10	OKBK	60523	3085	17W-2S	C4
Brice Av					
200	MDLN	60060	2590	18W-27N	E7
N Brice Ct					
1900	PLTN	60074	2753	19W-18N	C3
Bricher Rd					
10	GNVA	60134	3019	37W-2N	C2
10	GNVA	60174	3019	37W-2N	C2
10	SCRL	60134	3019	37W-2N	C2
10	SCRL	60174	3019	37W-2N	C2
100	SchT	60134	3019	37W-2N	C2
600	GnvT	60134	3019	37W-2N	B2
600	GnvT	60175	3019	37W-2N	B2
600	SchT	60175	3019	37W-2N	B2
600	SCRL	60175	3019	37W-2N	B2
Brickhouse Av					
-	NHLK	60164	3028	14W-1N	D1
Bricknock Pl					
-	CRTE	60417	3685	0E-29S	E1
Brickstone Dr					
8100	FftT	60423	3504	10W-24S	C6
Brickton Pl					
100	CHCG	60631	2918	9W-7N	B4
100	PKRG	60068	2918	9W-7N	B4
100	PKRG	60631	2918	9W-7N	B4
Brickton Reau					
400	PKRG	60068	2917	11W-8N	D2
Brickvale Dr					
2300	EGVV	60007	2915	16W-7N	D3
Brickyard Ct					
-	JLET	60421	3586	24W-28S	E7
-	JLET	60421	3675	24W-28S	E1
Brickyard Dr					
-	JknT	60421	3675	24W-29S	E1
-	JLET	60421	3586	24W-28S	E7
-	JLET	60421	3587	24W-28S	A7
-	JLET	60421	3675	24W-29S	E1
Bridalwood Ln					
17400	TYPK	60487	3424	11W-20S	A5
Briden Dr					
800	MRGO	60152	2634	50W-26N	A2
Bridge Ct					
1200	BRLT	60103	2967	28W-6N	A1
Bridge Ln					
200	TRLK	60010	2643	26W-25N	C5
2600	DrrT	60098	2582	39W-28N	B5
Bridge Rd					
-	LMNT	60439	3270	20W-14S	C6
S Bridge Rd					
-	JknT	60421	3586	24W-28S	E7
-	JLET	60421	3586	24W-28S	E7
23900	JknT	60421	3675	24W-29S	E2
23900	JLET	60421	3675	24W-29S	E2
Bridge St					
-	EVTN	60201	2866	3W-12N	E1
-	LYWD	60411	3510	4E-25S	B7
100	WHTN	60187	3024	25W-0S	B7
100	WMTN	60481	3853	27W-38S	C7
800	BlmT	60411	3510	4E-25S	B7
5200	MchT	60050	2472	29W-37N	D2
Bridge St SR-53					
100	WMTN	60481	3853	27W-38S	C7
N Bridge St					
100	YKVL	60560	3333	42W-14S	C1
900	YKVL	60560	3261	42W-12S	C4
1200	BtlT	60560	3261	42W-13S	C5
2400	YKVL	60512	3261	42W-12S	C4
2600	BtlT	60512	3261	42W-12S	C4
N Bridge St SR-47					
100	YKVL	60560	3333	42W-14S	C1
900	YKVL	60560	3261	42W-12S	C4
1200	BtlT	60560	3261	42W-13S	C5
2400	YKVL	60512	3261	42W-12S	C4
2600	BtlT	60512	3261	42W-12S	C4
S Bridge St					
100	YKVL	60560	3333	42W-17S	C6
1300	KdlT	60560	3333	42W-17S	D6
S Bridge St SR-47					
100	YKVL	60560	3333	42W-17S	C6
1300	KdlT	60560	3333	42W-17S	C6
W Bridge St					
100	JLET	60432	3498	24W-23S	E4
400	JLET	60435	3498	24W-23S	D3
25400	CNHN	60410	3672	32W-30S	E5
Bridgedale Ct					
1500	CLLK	60014	2693	36W-23N	D2
Bridgedale Rd					
1300	CLLK	60014	2693	36W-23N	D2
Bridgeham St					
3000	ElgT	60124	2853	37W-11N	B5
Bridgehampton Dr					
1200	JLET	60586	3496	30W-22S	B2
Bridgeman Ln					
500	RMVL	60446	3417	26W-18S	E1
Bridgeport Dr					
-	SmbT	60193	2913	22W-8N	C2
1200	SMBG	60193	2913	22W-8N	C2
N Bridgeport Dr					
1400	MPPT	60056	2807	15W-14N	E3
Bridgeport Ln					
1400	AURA	60504	3201	32W-9S	D4
N Bridgeport Ln					
10	GNVA	60134	3019	36W-1N	E3
S Bridgeport Ln					
10	GNVA	60134	3019	38W-1N	B3
Bridgeport Pl					
600	WLNG	60090	2755	15W-18N	A3
N Bridgeport Ter					
600	LNHT	60046	2418	19W-39N	B6
Bridgestone Ct					
500	IVNS	60010	2750	26W-17N	E6
500	IVNS	60010	2751	25W-17N	A5
Bridget Ct					
100	BNVL	60106	2971	16W-3N	E4
6000	BRRG	60527	3146	15W-7S	C7
Bridget Pl					
500	WLNG	60090	2755	15W-17N	A5
Bridgeview Cir					
300	GNVA	60134	3019	37W-1N	C4
Bridgeview Ct					
700	WLNG	60090	2754	16W-17N	D6
W Bridgeview Ct					
500	PLTN	60067	2805	21W-16N	C1
Bridgeview Dr					
10	OSWG	60543	3200	34W-10S	D6
Bridgeview Ln					
1100	LKFT	60045	2649	12W-24N	B7
Bridgeview Pt					
600	SMBG	60194	2859	22W-10N	C4
Bridgeview Rd					
-	ELGN	60123	2800	35W-14N	B6
N Bridgeview St					
10	PLTN	60067	2805	21W-16N	C1
Bridgewater Ct					
100	NPVL	60565	3204	26W-9S	A5
27600	LKBN	60010	2643	27W-24N	B7
27600	LKBN	60010	2697	27W-24N	B1
Bridgewater Dr					
2400	WDSK	60098	2581	40W-29N	E4
2400	WDSK	60098	2582	40W-29N	A5
Bridgewater Ln					
10	MDLN	60060	2646	19W-27N	B1
200	BMDL	60108	2969	23W-4N	A3
1300	LGGV	60047	2700	18W-21N	E6
Bridgeway Ct					
400	OKBK	60523	3085	17W-3S	B5
Bridgewood Dr					
10	ANTH	60002	2358	23W-43N	A4
10	SlmT	53104	2358	23W-43N	A5
Bridgton on Asbury					
10	RGMW	60008	2806	19W-15N	B2
Bridle Cir					
2400	RLKB	60073	2475	21W-36N	D4
Bridle Ct					
10	BRRG	60527	3208	15W-10S	B5
500	LKMR	60051	2529	29W-32N	D4
600	CmpT	60175	2961	42W-5N	C2
600	LYVL	60048	2591	16W-27N	E7
1800	SCRL	60174	2964	34W-4N	D5
2400	RLKB	60073	2475	21W-36N	D4
S Bridle Ct					
14600	HMGN	60491	3344	15W-17S	B5
W Bridle Ct					
17500	WrnT	60031	2534	17W-34N	B1
Bridle Ln					
10	BKBN	60015	2703	12W-23N	B2
200	SMBG	60173	2859	21W-10N	E4
300	LKFT	60045	2649	11W-25N	D6
600	AlqT	60013	2642	29W-24N	B6
600	CRY	60013	2642	29W-24N	B6
600	WHTN	60187	3024	24W-0N	D4
700	MltT	60187	3024	24W-0N	D4
1500	BRLT	60103	2966	30W-5N	B2
N Bridle Ln					
34300	WrnT	60031	2534	17W-34N	B1
Bridle Pth					
10	FmtT	60084	2644	23W-26N	D4
10	HNWD	60047	2644	23W-26N	D4
S Bridle Pth					
25600	CNHN	60410	3672	33W-31S	B5
W Bridle Ter					
1400	ADSN	60101	2970	20W-5N	B2
Bridle Tr					
400	WLNG	60090	2755	15W-16N	B7
N Bridle Tr					
22600	KLDR	60047	2699	21W-22N	D3
Bridle Creek Dr					
10	CmpT	60175	2962	41W-4N	A5
S Bridle Creek Dr					
10	CmpT	60175	2962	40W-3N	B5
Bridlegate Ln					
800	NHFD	60093	2758	7W-16N	B7
Bridle Path					
-	LMNT	60439	3272	15W-13S	B4
Bridle Path Cir					
200	OKBK	60523	3085	18W-3S	A6
Bridle Path Ct					
200	FRGV	60021	2696	28W-22N	E3
10600	WldT	60564	3266	29W-12S	C3
Bridle Path Dr					
6400	RchT	60443	3593	8W-25S	B1
Bridlepath Dr					
10	LNHT	60046	2418	19W-38N	C7
10	LNHT	60046	2476	19W-38N	C1
S Bridle Path Dr					
23600	MhtT	60442	3590	15W-28S	B7
Bridle Path Ln					
100	FRGV	60010	2696	28W-22N	D3
100	FRGV	60021	2696	28W-22N	D3
Bridle Path Wy					
-	RLKP	60030	2532	21W-31N	C7
-	RLKP	60030	2589	21W-31N	C1
Bridle Post Dr					
1500	AURA	60506	3137	37W-6S	B4
Bridlespur Dr					
-	NPVL	60540	3142	25W-6S	C5
400	LslT	60540	3142	25W-6S	C5
N Bridle Trail Rd					
24000	VrnT	60045	2702	14W-24N	C1
W Bridle Trail Rd					
17000	GRNE	60031	2477	17W-36N	C4
17000	WrnT	60031	2477	17W-36N	C4
17100	WrnT	60083	2477	17W-36N	C4
E Bridleway Ct					
2800	CPVL	60110	2747	36W-18N	A6
W Bridleway Ct					
2900	CPVL	60110	2746	36W-18N	E5
2900	CPVL	60110	2747	35W-17N	B7
N Bridlewood Av					
36000	GRNE	60031	2477	17W-36N	A4
36000	WrnT	60031	2477	17W-36N	A4
Bridlewood Cir					
100	LIHL	60156	2692	38W-21N	E6
Bridlewood Ct					
200	SMBG	60173	2859	21W-10N	E4
5100	LGGV	60047	2701	17W-21N	A5
Bridlewood Dr					
1900	HFET	60192	2802	30W-12N	C7
1900	HFET	60192	2856	30W-12N	B1
Bridlewood Ln					
10	NHBK	60062	2757	8W-17N	D6
10	NHFD	60093	2811	7W-14N	B3
2600	NndT	60012	2584	35W-29N	B4
5100	LGGV	60047	2701	17W-21N	A5
Bridlewood Rd					
10	NHBK	60062	2757	8W-17N	E6
Bridlewood Tr					
10	BrnT	60010	2803	26W-14N	D3
10	SBTN	60010	2803	26W-14N	D3
Brier Ct					
200	ISLK	60042	2586	28W-28N	D6
Brier St					
10	KLWH	60043	2812	4W-14N	C3
10	KLWH	60093	2812	4W-14N	C3
10	WNKA	60093	2812	4W-14N	C4
600	WNKA	60043	2812	4W-14N	C4
W Brier Ter					
23500	ANTH	60002	2416	23W-41N	E1
23500	AntT	60002	2416	23W-41N	E1
Brierfield Ct					
10	LKBF	60044	2593	11W-29N	E5
Briergate Dr					
1000	NPVL	60563	3141	28W-5S	B3
Brier Glen Dr					
1900	JLET	60586	3416	30W-21S	B7
Brierhill Dr					
10	RLKP	60073	2532	22W-33N	A3
3400	ISLK	60042	2586	28W-28N	D6
Brier Hill Rd					
10	HPSR	60140	2796	44W-14N	E6
10	HshT	60140	2743	44W-18N	E5
10	HshT	60140	2796	44W-16N	E2
300	HTLY	60140	2743	44W-19N	E2
300	PltT	60140	2796	44W-13N	E7
900	CrlT	60140	2743	44W-19N	E2
900	CrlT	60142	2743	44W-19N	E2
Brierhill Rd					
400	DRFD	60015	2704	10W-20N	A7
400	DRFD	60015	2757	10W-20N	B1
Brier Hill Rd US-20					
10	HshT	60140	2743	44W-17N	E7
400	HshT	60140	2796	44W-16N	E2
Brierwood Dr					
10	CmpT	60175	2906	41W-6N	A7
10	CmpT	60175	2962	41W-6N	A1
Brierwood Ln					
10	HNWD	60047	2644	24W-24N	D7
10	LKZH	60047	2644	24W-24N	D7
10	LKZH	60047	2698	24W-24N	D1
10	PltT	60124	2905	43W-8N	B4
Brigade Ln					
25000	PNFD	60544	3337	31W-17S	E5
25000	PNFD	60544	3338	31W-17S	A5
Brigadoon Dr					
4000	ZION	60099	2362	12W-42N	C7
Brigantine Ct					
4600	HFET	60192	2804	24W-15N	B1
Brigantine Dr					
800	NLNX	60451	3590	15W-25S	C1
Brigantine Ln					
10	TDLK	60030	2533	18W-34N	D1
4500	HFET	60192	2804	24W-15N	B1
4600	SBTN	60010	2804	24W-15N	B1
Briggs Av					
300	NndT	60012	2586	30W-28N	A5
300	NndT	60050	2586	30W-28N	A5
Briggs Ct					
1700	LSLE	60532	3142	23W-6S	E5
Briggs St					
400	WNVL	60555	3080	30W-3S	B6
400	WNVL	60563	3080	30W-3S	B6
500	AURA	60563	3080	30W-3S	B6
N Briggs St					
10	JltT	60432	3499	22W-23S	D3
10	JltT	60433	3499	21W-23S	E4
100	JLET	60432	3499	22W-23S	D3
S Briggs St					
10	JLET	60433	3499	22W-24S	E5
10	JltT	60433	3499	22W-25S	E7
1200	JLET	60433	3587	21W-25S	E1
1200	JltT	60433	3587	21W-25S	E1
1400	LKPT	60441	3419	22W-21S	D7
1500	LkrT	60441	3419	22W-21S	D7
17500	LKPT	60432	3419	22W-21S	D7
17500	LkrT	60432	3419	22W-21S	D7
18000	JLET	60432	3499	21W-22S	E1
18000	JltT	60432	3499	21W-22S	E1
18000	LkrT	60432	3499	21W-22S	E1
Brigham Ct					
700	GNVA	60134	3020	36W-0N	A4
Brigham Ln					
1600	CLLK	60014	2693	36W-22N	C3
Brigham Tr					
10100	HBRN	60034	2350	41W-42N	E7
Brigham Wy					
800	GNVA	60134	3020	36W-0N	A5
Bright St					
3000	FNPK	60131	2973	13W-3N	A4
Bright Oaks Cir					
10	CRY	60013	2641	31W-24N	C7
Brighton Av					
-	WKGN	60085	2537	10W-33N	B4
Brighton Cir					
700	PTBR	60010	2642	29W-26N	C3
1500	AURA	60506	3137	38W-5S	B3
N Brighton Cir W					
900	CLLK	60012	2585	33W-27N	A7
Brighton Ct					
-	HMGN	60491	3344	15W-16S	B3
-	MKNA	60451	3502	15W-24S	B5
-	NlxT	60451	3502	15W-24S	B5
10	FRGV	60021	2696	29W-22N	B4
10	HNWD	60047	2646	20W-24N	A7
200	WNVL	60555	3080	30W-2S	B3
300	CRTE	60417	3685	0W-29S	C1
400	BMDL	60108	2968	25W-4N	A3
500	ELGN	60123	2853	36W-10N	E7
600	BRLT	60103	2910	29W-6N	E7
1000	SMBG	60193	2912	24W-9N	C1
1600	NHBK	60062	2756	10W-16N	E6
2700	GNVA	60134	3019	37W-0N	C5
2800	WSTR	60154	3086	13W-2S	E4
4400	GRNE	60031	2535	14W-34N	B1
6300	LSLE	60532	3142	24W-6S	C5
7000	WDRG	60517	3144	20W-7S	B6
8200	ODPK	60462	3346	10W-16S	C4
S Brighton Ct					
400	PLTN	60067	2805	22W-15N	B2
Brighton Dr					
-	PGGV	60140	2797	41W-14N	E5
100	WHTN	60187	3082	25W-2S	B4
400	BMDL	60108	2968	25W-4N	A3
400	BmdT	60108	2968	25W-4N	A3
400	BmdT	60133	2968	25W-4N	A3
700	SgrT	60554	3135	41W-5S	E3
700	SRGV	60554	3135	41W-5S	E3
1000	CLSM	60188	2967	27W-4N	D4
1600	MDLN	60060	2590	20W-27N	A7
Brighton Ln					
-	CPVL	60118	2746	38W-18N	C5
Brighton Ln					
10	OKBK	60523	3086	15W-2S	B3
200	BGBK	60440	3268	25W-11S	B1
300	CRTE	60417	3685	0W-29S	C1
400	DndT	60124	2799	38W-14N	C5
400	DYR	46311	3598		D4
400	GLBT	60124	2799	38W-14N	C5
400	GLBT	60136	2799	38W-14N	C5
700	LGNG	60525	3147	13W-5S	A2
1300	RLKB	60046	2475	21W-35N	D6
1600	JLET	60586	3416	30W-21S	C7
1600	JLET	60586	3496	30W-21S	C1
1900	HFET	60169	2804	26W-12N	A7
1900	HFET	60169	2858	25W-12N	B1
5000	RNPK	60471	3594	4W-26S	D3
5600	AlqT	60102	2747	34W-20N	C1
6000	GfnT	60014	2638	38W-25N	D4
6000	LKWD	60014	2638	38W-26N	D4
10300	HTLY	60142	2692	39W-22N	C4
12300	WldT	60585	3266	29W-14S	D7
E Brighton Ln					
900	CLLK	60012	2584	33W-27N	E7
900	CLLK	60012	2585	33W-27N	A7
900	NndT	60012	2584	33W-27N	E7
S Brighton Ln					
500	PLTN	60067	2805	22W-15N	B2
Brighton Pl					
10	BRRG	60527	3146	14W-7S	C6
600	WLNG	60090	2755	15W-18N	A3
3600	MHRY	60050	2585	32W-30N	B1
N Brighton Pl					
1900	ANHT	60004	2807	17W-16N	B1
2700	ANHT	60004	2754	17W-17N	C6
S Brighton Pl					
100	ANHT	60004	2807	17W-13N	B5
3900	CHCG	60632	3091	3W-4S	A6
W Brighton Pl					
100	MPPT	60056	2807	15W-14N	E3
100	MPPT	60056	2808	15W-14N	A3
Brighton Rd					
200	EGVV	60007	2914	19W-8N	C2
E Brighton Rd					
1100	LslT	60563	3142	25W-5S	A3
1100	NPVL	60563	3142	25W-5S	A3
Brighton St					
1100	GNEN	60137	3025	21W-0S	E7
1100	GNEN	60137	3026	21W-0S	A7
1900	DRGV	60516	3144	20W-7S	A6
Brighton Wy					
10	OswT	60538	3199	37W-11S	D7
Brighton Bay					
200	ROSL	60172	2912	25W-7N	B5
Brighton Farm Rd					
-	AntT	60002	2359	19W-42N	D5
Bright Ridge Rd					
10	SMBG	60193	2859	22W-10N	B5
10	SMBG	60194	2859	22W-10N	B5
Brightwater Dr					
6900	AntT	60081	2415	27W-38N	A6
6900	FXLK	60081	2415	27W-39N	A6
E Brightway Rd					
19900	MKNA	60448	3502	14W-24S	E5
N Brightway Rd					
11400	MKNA	60448	3502	14W-24S	D5
S Brightway Rd					
11400	MKNA	60448	3502	14W-24S	D5
11700	FftT	60451	3502	14W-24S	D5
11700	MKNA	60451	3502	14W-24S	D5
W Brightway Rd					
20100	MKNA	60448	3502	14W-24S	D5
Brightwood Pl					
1600	AURA	60506	3137	38W-7S	B7
Brigitte Ct					
16500	ODHL	60487	3424	11W-19S	A3
Brigitte Ter					
11100	ODPK	60467	3344	14W-16S	E4
Brimfield Dr					
700	PltT	60124	2906	40W-8N	C2
Brimstone Rd					
1900	PnfT	60544	3339	27W-18S	C7
1900	RMVL	60446	3339	27W-18S	C7
1900	RMVL	60544	3339	27W-18S	C7
Brinckman Wy					
-	ELGN	60123	2853	37W-12N	D1
-	ELGN	60124	2853	37W-12N	D1
Brindle Ct					
2800	NHBK	60062	2756	11W-17N	E4
Brindlewood Ct					
10	ALGN	60102	2747	35W-20N	A1
700	ElgT	60124	2799	38W-13N	A7
Brindlewood Dr					
2100	JLET	60586	3416	30W-21S	B7
Brindlewood Ln					
300	ElgT	60124	2799	38W-13N	A7
700	PltT	60124	2799	38W-13N	A7
2000	ALGN	60102	2746	35W-20N	E1
2000	ALGN	60102	2747	35W-20N	A1
Brink Dr					
100	JLET	60435	3497	27W-23S	C5
Brink St					
10	CLLK	60014	2640	35W-26N	B3
600	WDSK	60098	2581	41W-30N	E1
E Brink St					
100	HRVD	60033	2406	50W-37N	B7
19600	AdnT	60033	2406	48W-38N	E7
19600	CmgT	60033	2406	49W-38N	C7
19600	DhmT	60033	2406	49W-38N	C7
19600	HtdT	60033	2406	48W-38N	E7
W Brink St					
100	DhmT	60033	2406	50W-38N	A7
100	HRVD	60033	2406	50W-37N	A7
800	DhmT	60033	2405	51W-38N	E7
800	HRVD	60033	2405	51W-38N	E7
W Brink St SR-173					
100	DhmT	60033	2406	50W-38N	A7
100	HRVD	60033	2406	50W-37N	A7
800	DhmT	60033	2405	51W-38N	E7
800	HRVD	60033	2405	51W-38N	E7
Brinker Rd					
10	BNHL	60010	2750	27W-17N	A4
Brinmore Ct					
2300	NPVL	60540	3202	29W-8S	D1
Brisbane Dr					
100	AlqT	60013	2642	29W-24N	D7
100	CbaT	60013	2642	29W-24N	D7
2700	LIHL	60156	2692	38W-23N	D3
Brisbane Rd					
10	NLNX	60451	3502	16W-24S	A6
10	NlxT	60451	3502	16W-24S	A6
Bristlecone Ct					
1100	DRN	60561	3145	17W-7S	B6
1800	NPVL	60565	3204	25W-9S	B4
Bristle Cone Dr					
-	CLLK	60012	2640	33W-27N	E1
Bristlecone Dr					
13700	LkrT	60544	3339	26W-16S	E3
S Bristlecone Ln					
13800	LkrT	60544	3339	26W-16S	E4
Bristol					
9100	HTLY	60142	2692	40W-22N	B3
Bristol Av					
-	PNFD	60585	3338	30W-15S	B1
10	RMVL	60446	3340	23W-15S	E1
10	RMVL	60446	3341	23W-15S	A1
600	WSTR	60154	3029	12W-1S	C7
600	YKVL	60560	3333	42W-14S	C1
1400	WSTR	60154	3087	12W-1S	C1
Bristol Bnd					
11100	ODPK	60467	3423	13W-21S	A6
Bristol Cir					
1900	CPVL	60110	2801	32W-16N	D1
Bristol Ct					
-	RGMW	60008	2806	19W-12N	C7
10	BRRG	60527	3208	15W-9S	A2
10	BtlT	60543	3262	40W-13S	C4
10	GRNE	60031	2535	14W-34N	D1
10	LKBF	60044	2593	11W-29N	E5
10	LNSH	60069	2702	13W-22N	E4
10	SchT	60175	2907	36W-7N	E6
200	BGBK	60440	3268	24W-12S	C3
200	DRFD	60015	2756	11W-20N	E2
200	SRGV	60554	3135	42W-7S	D7
900	PGGV	60140	2797	41W-14N	E5
1000	SMWD	60107	2910	29W-9N	E1
1000	WHTN	60187	3082	23W-3S	E5
1100	GLHT	60139	3024	23W-1N	E2
1200	HRPK	60133	2911	26W-9N	E1
1200	SRWD	60404	3496	31W-24S	A6
1300	ROSL	60172	2912	25W-7N	B5
2400	AURA	60504	3201	32W-9S	C5
2800	LNHT	60046	2418	19W-38N	C7
2800	WDND	60118	2800	36W-16N	A3
4100	NHBK	60062	2756	12W-17N	A4
5000	CPVL	60110	2801	32W-16N	D1
7200	GGnT	60449	3682	9W-31S	A4
7600	WDRG	60517	3206	20W-8S	A2
10300	MKNA	60448	3503	12W-23S	C4
21300	FKFT	60423	3592	11W-25S	B1
N Bristol Ct					
10	MDLN	60060	2647	17W-27N	A1
1900	NPVL	60565	3203	26W-9S	D4
S Bristol Ct					
10	MDLN	60060	2647	17W-27N	A1
400	PLTN	60067	2805	22W-15N	B2
600	LKFT	60045	2648	14W-25N	C6
2000	NPVL	60565	3203	26W-9S	D4
W Bristol Ct					
300	BMDL	60108	2968	25W-5N	C1
Bristol Dr					
300	CLLK	60014	2639	35W-24N	E6
300	CLSM	60188	2967	26W-3N	D7
600	BRTN	60010	2751	25W-18N	A2
700	ALGN	60102	2694	35W-20N	A7
800	DRFD	60015	2756	11W-20N	E1
2700	LSLE	60532	3142	24W-6S	C5
2700	LSLE	60540	3142	24W-6S	C5
2700	NPVL	60540	3142	24W-6S	C5
N Bristol Dr					
100	BMDL	60108	2968	25W-5N	C1
Bristol Ln					
-	LYWD	60411	3509	2E-24S	D4
10	WNVL	60555	3080	29W-2S	C3
100	EGvT	60007	2915	18W-7N	A3
100	WDDL	60191	2915	18W-7N	A3
300	FRGV	60021	2696	29W-22N	B4
400	GYLK	60030	2533	20W-33N	B3
400	SMBG	60194	2858	24W-11N	D4
500	EGVV	60007	2914	19W-8N	B2
800	NLNX	60451	3590	15W-25S	C1
1100	BFGV	60089	2701	18W-21N	A6
1200	BFGV	60089	2700	18W-21N	E6
1300	BFGV	60047	2700	18W-21N	E6
1300	LGGV	60047	2700	18W-21N	E6
1900	CPVL	60110	2801	32W-16N	D1
7500	HRPK	60133	2911	26W-9N	E1
7700	TYPK	60477	3424	9W-19S	D3
9300	HTLY	60142	2692	40W-22N	B3
20700	OMFD	60461	3507	3W-25S	A7
S Bristol Ln					
200	ANHT	60005	2807	17W-13N	B6
25600	GGnT	60449	3682	9W-31S	A5
Bristol Rd					
-	BtlT	60002	2359		B4
10	NHFD	60093	2811	7W-15N	B3
400	SchT	60175	2907	36W-6N	E6
700	JltT	60433	3587	23W-26S	A2
700	JltT	60436	3586	24W-26S	E2
700	JltT	60436	3587	23W-26S	A2
3200	WKGN	60087	2479	11W-37N	D1
10700	BtlT	53104	2359		A1
11900	BtlT	53142	2359		B3
12400	AntT	60002	2359		B4
Bristol Rd US-45					
-	BtlT	60002	2359		B4
10700	BtlT	53104	2359		A1
11900	BtlT	53142	2359		B3
12400	AntT	60002	2359		B4
Bristol St					
200	NHFD	60093	2811	7W-15N	B3
600	PGGV	60140	2797	41W-14N	E5
N Bristol St					
200	NHFD	60093	2811	7W-15N	B2
Bristol Wk					
1700	HFET	60169	2858	25W-12N	B1
Bristol Wy					
200	BGBK	60440	3268	24W-12S	C2
300	CRY	60013	2642	30W-24N	A7
Bristol Bay					
1200	ELGN	60123	2907	36W-9N	E2
Bristol Park Dr N					
7800	TYPK	60477	3424	9W-21S	D5
Bristol Park Dr S					
7700	TYPK	60477	3424	9W-21S	D6
Bristol Ridge Rd					
10	BtlT	60512	3261	41W-12S	E3
10	BtlT	60512	3262	40W-13S	B4
10	YKVL	60512	3261	41W-12S	E3
2600	BtlT	60543	3262	40W-13S	B4
2600	BtlT	60560	3262	40W-13S	B4
Bristol Trail Rd					
900	LKZH	60047	2699	22W-22N	C4
1400	KLDR	60047	2699	21W-22N	C4
Britannia Dr					
1700	DndT	60124	2799	37W-14N	D6
1700	ELGN	60124	2799	37W-14N	D6
Britta Av					
3500	FNPK	60131	2973	11W-4N	C3
Britta Ln					
800	GNVA	60134	3020	34W-1N	E3
900	BTVA	60510	3020	36W-0S	A7
Brittain Av					
300	GYLK	60030	2532	21W-32N	E5

STREET Block	City	ZIP	Map#	CGS	Grid
Brittania Wy					
1400	ROSL	60172	2912	25W-7N	B4
Brittany Av					
-	LslT	60540	3204	25W-8S	C1
-	NPVL	60540	3204	25W-8S	C1
10600	HTLY	60142	2692	40W-21N	B6
Brittany Bnd					
900	LIHL	60156	2692	38W-22N	E4
Brittany Cir					
100	HPSR	60140	2795	47W-15N	E4
Brittany Ct					
10	BGBK	60440	3268	25W-11S	C2
10	SEGN	60177	2908	35W-9N	B1
300	GNVA	60134	3019	36W-1N	E3
900	CmpT	60175	2906	39W-7N	E4
900	CmpT	60175	2907	39W-7N	A4
900	ElgT	60175	2907	39W-7N	A4
900	PlfT	60175	2907	39W-7N	A4
900	SchT	60175	2907	39W-7N	A4
1300	AURA	60504	3201	32W-9S	C4
1500	DRN	60561	3207	18W-8S	A1
1500	WHTN	60187	3082	24W-1S	E2
1600	LGGV	60047	2701	18W-20N	A7
1600	WLNG	60090	2754	16W-18N	D4
2100	GLHT	60139	2968	24W-4N	E4
2200	SMBG	60194	2857	26W-11N	E4
2200	SMBG	60194	2858	26W-11N	A4
2800	SCRL	60175	2964	36W-4N	A3
4000	NHBK	60062	2756	12W-18N	B4
6100	GRNE	60031	2534	16W-34N	D1
7600	FKFT	60423	3504	9W-25S	E7
11600	SPGV	60081	2355	30W-43N	A4
E Brittany Ct					
200	ANHT	60004	2754	17W-17N	A6
Brittany Dr					
-	AlqT	60013	2642	30W-25N	A4
10	AlqT	60013	2641	30W-26N	E3
10	NLNX	60451	3500	19W-24S	D6
10	NlxT	60451	3500	19W-24S	D6
10	NndT	60013	2641	30W-26N	E3
10	ODHL	60013	2641	30W-26N	E3
10	ODHL	60013	2642	30W-25N	A4
100	SMWD	60107	2856	29W-10N	E7
2500	JLET	60441	3417	27W-19S	D3
3400	JLET	60435	3417	27W-19S	D3
4400	LSLE	60532	3142	24W-4S	C1
4400	LslT	60532	3142	24W-4S	C1
4400	LslT	60563	3142	24W-4S	C1
5300	MchT	60050	2527	34W-33N	C2
5300	MHRY	60050	2527	34W-33N	C2
10600	PlsT	60462	3345	13W-15S	A1
13200	PlsT	60467	3345	13W-15S	B2
21200	FKFT	60423	3504	9W-25S	E7
21200	FKFT	60423	3592	9W-25S	E1
E Brittany Dr					
10	ANHT	60004	2754	17W-17N	A6
W Brittany Dr					
400	ANHT	60004	2753	18W-17N	E5
400	ANHT	60004	2754	18W-17N	A5
Brittany Ln					
10	LNSH	60069	2702	13W-23N	D3
400	DYR	46311	3598		D4
400	LNHT	60046	2418	20W-38N	A6
1400	HFET	60192	2804	24W-14N	B3
1600	BFGV	60047	2701	18W-20N	A7
1600	BFGV	60089	2701	18W-20N	A7
1600	LGGV	60047	2701	18W-20N	A7
1600	LGGV	60089	2701	18W-20N	A7
18000	LNSG	60438	3429	2E-21S	C6
18100	ThtT	60438	3429	2E-21S	C6
E Brittany Ln					
10	HNVL	60030	2532	22W-33N	C3
N Brittany Ln					
10	GLHT	60139	2968	24W-4N	E4
10	HNVL	60030	2532	21W-33N	C3
W Brittany Ln					
2100	GLHT	60139	2968	24W-4N	E4
Brittany Rd					
900	HDPK	60035	2704	8W-21N	D6
900	LKZH	60047	2699	22W-22N	B4
3800	NHBK	60062	2756	12W-18N	B4
Brittany Sq					
600	GYLK	60030	2533	20W-33N	A2
Brittany St					
24400	PnfT	60586	3416	30W-19S	B2
Brittany Tr					
-	HnrT	60120	2855	31W-11N	E4
100	ELGN	60120	2855	31W-11N	E3
Brittany Wy					
600	ISLK	60042	2586	29W-28N	C5
Britten St					
1200	WDRG	60517	3206	20W-9S	B3
Brittney Ln					
6000	TYPK	60477	3425	7W-20S	C3
Britton Dr					
-	MchT	60081	2472	29W-37N	D1
Brixham Ln					
1400	JNBG	60051	2472	30W-35N	A6
Brixham Pl					
10	SMBG	60194	2858	25W-10N	B5
Brixton Ct					
10	ALGN	60102	2693	37W-21N	A6
6200	JLET	60586	3415	31W-21S	D7
Brnot Av					
2600	WKGN	60087	2479	12W-36N	C3
Broad Av					
-	CHCG	60613	2977	1W-5N	D1
S Broad St					
2900	CHCG	60608	3091	1W-2S	D3
W Broad St					
3300	MHRY	60050	2528	32W-33N	B3
Broadland Dr					
-	PGGV	60140	2797	42W-15N	D4
W Broadland Ln					
1500	LKFT	60045	2649	13W-25N	A5
Broadlawn Dr					
1200	JLET	60586	3496	30W-22S	B2
Broadleys Ct					
10	BKBN	60015	2703	12W-23N	C2
Broadmeadow Rd					
1100	WNKA	60093	2811	5W-15N	E3
Broadmoor Av					
10	LNSG	60438	3430		C6
10	MNSR	46321	3430		C6
Broadmoor Cir					
3900	AURA	60564	3202	30W-9S	B4
Broadmoor Ct					
3900	AURA	60564	3202	30W-9S	B5
N Broadmoor Ct					
1500	PLTN	60067	2752	21W-18N	D3
W Broadmoor Ct					
200	PLTN	60067	2752	21W-18N	D3
Broadmoor Dr					
8400	PSHL	60465	3274	10W-12S	B1
Broadmoor Ln					
200	BRLT	60103	2911	28W-8N	A4
N Broadmoor Ln					
1900	VNHL	60061	2647	17W-27N	C1
Broadmoor Pl					
1000	DRFD	60015	2703	11W-21N	D6
Broadsmoor Dr					
-	BGBK	60490	3339	28W-14S	B1
Broadsmore Dr					
-	DndT	60118	2746	36W-18N	E4
500	LKFT	60045	2649	11W-25N	D6
1800	ALGN	60102	2747	36W-18N	A4
2100	ALGN	60102	2746	36W-18N	E4
W Broadsmore Ln					
1800	GrtT	60073	2531	25W-33N	B3
1800	RDLK	60073	2531	25W-33N	A3
Broadview Av					
-	BLWD	60104	3028	13W-0N	E5
-	BLWD	60162	3028	13W-0N	E5
-	WnfT	60185	3022	29W-0N	E5
400	HDPK	60035	2758	7W-20N	A1
400	HLSD	60162	3028	13W-0N	E5
500	AddT	60101	2970	20W-3N	A5
600	HDPK	60035	2705	7W-20N	A7
N Broadview Av					
10	LMBD	60148	3026	20W-0N	A3
700	AddT	60148	3026	20W-1N	A1
W Broadview Av					
1200	CteT	60417	3596	1W-29S	A7
1200	CteT	60417	3685	1W-29S	A1
1400	CteT	60417	3684	1W-29S	E1
Broadview Ct					
7600	SPGV	60081	2413	31W-39N	E5
Broadview Village Sq					
-	NRIV	60155	3087	11W-1S	E2
-	NRIV	60546	3087	11W-1S	E2
700	BDVW	60155	3087	11W-1S	E1
Broadway					
300	SchT	60174	2963	36W-3N	E6
300	SCRL	60174	2963	36W-3N	E6
N Broadway					
700	AURA	60505	3138	35W-6S	B5
N Broadway SR-25					
10	AURA	60505	3138	35W-7S	B7
S Broadway					
10	AURA	60505	3138	35W-7S	B7
10	AURA	60505	3200	36W-8S	A2
700	AURA	60505	3199	36W-8S	E3
800	AURA	60505	3199	36W-8S	E3
800	MTGY	60505	3199	36W-8S	E3
800	MTGY	60538	3199	36W-8S	E3
S Broadway SR-25					
10	AURA	60505	3138	35W-7S	B7
10	AURA	60505	3200	36W-8S	A2
700	AURA	60505	3199	36W-8S	E3
800	AURA	60505	3199	36W-8S	E3
800	MTGY	60505	3199	36W-8S	E3
800	MTGY	60538	3199	36W-8S	E3
Broadway Av					
-	CteT	60417	3774	1W-33S	B1
10	CHHT	60411	3508	1W-24S	A6
100	EVTN	60201	2812	3W-13N	E7
100	WLMT	60091	2812	3W-13N	E7
100	WLMT	60201	2812	3W-13N	E7
700	NCHI	60064	2537	10W-31N	A6
800	NCHI	60064	2536	11W-31N	E7
800	WDSK	60098	2524	40W-31N	E6
9100	BKFD	60513	3087	11W-3S	E5
14700	HRVY	60426	3350	1W-17S	A6
E Broadway Av					
900	BtnT	60096	2362	10W-42N	E7
900	WPHR	60096	2362	10W-42N	E7
N Broadway Av					
10	PKRG	60068	2917	11W-8N	D2
600	PKRG	60068	2863	11W-9N	E7
1000	LMBD	60148	3026	18W-0N	E4
1100	LMBD	60181	3026	18W-0N	E4
1100	VLPK	60181	3026	18W-0N	E4
38700	AntT	60002	2415	26W-38N	E6
S Broadway Av					
900	PKRG	60068	2917	11W-8N	E2
W Broadway Av					
900	BtnT	60096	2362	11W-42N	E7
900	WPHR	60096	2362	11W-42N	E7
Broadway Ct					
800	LKZH	60047	2699	21W-22N	C5
1500	WLNG	60090	2754	16W-18N	D3
Broadway Ln					
2200	SMBG	60194	2857	26W-10N	E5
Broadway Rd					
6700	RcmT	60071	2352	36W-42N	E5
6700	RcmT	60071	2353	35W-42N	A5
S Broadway Rd					
1000	AURA	60505	3199	36W-8S	E3
1000	MTGY	60505	3199	36W-8S	E3
1000	MTGY	60538	3199	36W-9S	E4
S Broadway Rd CO-29					
1300	MTGY	60538	3199	36W-9S	E5
S Broadway Rd SR-25					
1000	AURA	60505	3199	36W-8S	E3
1000	MTGY	60505	3199	36W-8S	E3
1000	MTGY	60538	3199	36W-9S	E4
Broadway St					
10	MLPK	60160	3029	11W-0N	D3
10	MYWD	60153	3029	11W-0N	D3
100	LYVL	60048	2591	16W-29N	E5
400	CLLK	60014	2639	36W-25N	E5
700	LKWD	60014	2639	36W-25N	D5
1300	BLID	60406	3349	3W-15S	B1
1900	MLPK	60160	2973	11W-2N	D7
2000	FNPK	60131	2973	11W-2N	D7
2000	MLPK	60131	2973	11W-2N	D7
2100	CTHL	60403	3418	24W-21S	E6
2100	CTHL	60435	3418	24W-21S	E6
2100	CTHL	60441	3418	24W-20S	E6
2100	LktT	60435	3418	24W-21S	E6
2800	RBBN	60406	3349	3W-15S	A1
5500	RHMD	60071	2353	35W-42N	B6
5800	RcmT	60071	2353	35W-42N	B6
15700	LktT	60441	3419	23W-19S	A2
15700	RMVL	60441	3419	23W-18S	A1
16200	CTHL	60441	3419	23W-19S	A2
17000	LktT	60441	3418	24W-20S	E6
Broadway St SR-7					
2100	CTHL	60403	3418	24W-21S	E6
2100	CTHL	60435	3418	24W-21S	E6
2100	CTHL	60441	3418	24W-20S	E6
2100	LktT	60435	3418	24W-21S	E6
15800	LktT	60441	3419	23W-19S	A2
15800	RMVL	60441	3419	23W-19S	A2
16200	CTHL	60441	3419	23W-19S	A2
17000	LktT	60441	3418	24W-20S	E6
Broadway St SR-53					
2100	CTHL	60403	3418	24W-21S	E6
2100	CTHL	60435	3418	24W-21S	E6
2100	CTHL	60441	3418	24W-20S	E6
2100	LktT	60435	3418	24W-21S	E6
15700	LktT	60441	3419	23W-19S	A2
15700	RMVL	60441	3419	23W-18S	A1
16200	CTHL	60441	3419	23W-19S	A2
Broadway St SR-53					
17000	LktT	60441	3418	24W-20S	E6
N Broadway St					
10	DSPN	60016	2862	14W-12N	D2
10	JLET	60435	3498	24W-23S	E3
10	JLET	60436	3498	24W-24S	E5
1600	CTHL	60403	3498	24W-22S	E1
1600	CTHL	60435	3498	24W-22S	E1
1600	LktT	60435	3498	24W-21S	E1
1700	CTHL	60403	3418	24W-21S	E7
1700	CTHL	60435	3418	24W-21S	E7
1800	LktT	60435	3418	24W-21S	E7
2000	CTHL	60441	3418	24W-21S	E6
2800	CHCG	60614	2978	0W-3N	A4
2800	CHCG	60657	2978	0W-3N	A4
3500	CHCG	60613	2978	0W-4N	A3
3700	CHCG	60613	2977	1W-5N	E1
4400	CHCG	60613	2921	1W-5N	E7
4400	CHCG	60640	2921	1W-5N	D7
5500	CHCG	60660	2921	1W-7N	D3
6300	CHCG	60626	2921	1W-7N	D3
N Broadway St SR-7					
1600	CTHL	60403	3498	24W-22S	E1
1600	CTHL	60435	3498	24W-22S	E1
1600	JLET	60435	3498	24W-21S	E1
1600	LktT	60435	3498	24W-21S	E1
1700	CTHL	60403	3418	24W-21S	E7
1700	CTHL	60435	3418	24W-21S	E7
1800	LktT	60435	3418	24W-21S	E7
2000	CTHL	60441	3418	24W-21S	E6
N Broadway St SR-53					
700	JLET	60435	3498	24W-23S	E3
1600	CTHL	60403	3498	24W-22S	E1
1600	CTHL	60435	3498	24W-22S	E1
1600	LktT	60435	3498	24W-21S	E1
1700	CTHL	60403	3418	24W-21S	E7
1700	CTHL	60435	3418	24W-21S	E7
1800	LktT	60435	3418	24W-21S	E7
2000	CTHL	60441	3418	24W-21S	E6
N Broadway St US-14					
5200	CHCG	60640	2921	1W-6N	D5
5500	CHCG	60660	2921	1W-6N	D4
S Broadway St					
10	JLET	60435	3498	24W-24S	D7
10	JLET	60436	3498	24W-24S	D7
600	MHRY	60050	2528	32W-31N	C7
600	NndT	60050	2528	32W-31N	C7
900	MHRY	60050	2585	32W-30N	C1
W Broadway St					
100	FXLK	60050	2472	29W-37N	D2
100	GrtT	60050	2472	29W-37N	D2
100	MchT	60050	2472	29W-37N	D2
800	JNBG	60050	2472	29W-37N	B2
Broch Wy					
1800	MTGY	60538	3198	40W-9S	B5
Brock Ct					
10	OSWG	60543	3263	36W-11S	D1
Brockfield Ct					
6900	LGGV	60047	2646	18W-25N	D5
Brockhurst Ct					
1000	UYPK	60466	3684	3W-30S	B3
W Brockman Av					
16400	BFGV	60069	2701	16W-23N	D3
16400	VrnT	60069	2701	16W-23N	D3
16600	BFGV	60089	2701	16W-23N	D3
Brocks End Ct					
900	NPVL	60540	3203	28W-8S	A1
Brockton Cir					
2300	NPVL	60565	3203	27W-10S	C6
Brockton Ct					
1100	AURA	60504	3201	31W-9S	D4
E Brockton Ct					
2400	ANHT	60004	2807	16W-15N	C1
N Brockton Ct					
8100	HRPK	60133	2857	26W-9N	E7
S Brockton Ct					
8000	HRPK	60133	2857	26W-9N	E7
W Brockton Ct					
20800	LktT	60544	3340	26W-16S	A5
Brockton Ln					
500	SMBG	60193	2858	25W-9N	B7
1900	GLHT	60139	2968	24W-3N	D5
9200	MaiT	60016	2863	11W-12N	D1
16400	OKFT	60452	3426	5W-19S	B2
Brockway St					
1800	JLET	60431	3417	28W-21S	A7
2100	PLTN	60067	2805	21W-14N	E4
2700	RGMW	60008	2805	21W-13N	E5
2700	RGMW	60067	2805	21W-13N	E5
N Brockway St					
10	PLTN	60067	2805	21W-16N	E1
100	PLTN	60067	2752	21W-16N	E7
S Brockway St					
10	PLTN	60067	2805	21W-15N	E1
1100	RGMW	60067	2805	21W-14N	E4
Brockway Pond Ct					
1800	JLET	60431	3417	28W-21S	A7
Brockwood Rd					
700	NLNX	60451	3501	17W-24S	D6
700	NLNX	60451	3589	16W-25S	E1
Brock Wy Dr					
10	OSWG	60543	3263	37W-11S	D1
Brodhead Dr					
-	AURA	60504	3140	30W-7S	B6
Brodick Ln					
10	IVNS	60067	2752	22W-17N	B4
Brodie Ct					
300	NPVL	60540	3142	25W-7S	B6
W Brodie Dr					
25700	GrtT	60041	2473	25W-36N	E3
25700	GrtT	60041	2474	25W-36N	A3
W Brodman Av					
8400	CHCG	60656	2974	10W-5N	A1
8400	CHCG	60706	2974	10W-5N	A1
8400	NRDG	60706	2974	10W-5N	A1
8500	CHCG	60656	2973	11W-5N	E1
Brody Ln					
-	GwdT	60098	2524	41W-33N	E2
N Broecker Av					
42200	BtnT	60099	2362	11W-42N	D6
Broken Arrow Dr					
-	LktT	60441	3420	20W-20S	B5
16300	LKPT	60441	3420	20W-20S	B5
N Broken Bow Pass					
25500	CbaT	60010	2643	26W-25N	E4
Broken Sound Pkwy					
-	VNHL	60061	2647	16W-27N	D1
Broker Av					
200	ITSC	60143	2914	19W-6N	D7
200	WDDL	60143	2914	19W-6N	D7
400	WDDL	60191	2914	19W-6N	D7
Broker Rd					
10	BmdT	60157	2913	22W-6N	C7
200	BMDL	60108	2913	22W-6N	B7
400	BMDL	60157	2913	22W-6N	C7
Brom Ct					
-	NPVL	60540	3141	27W-7S	D7
10	SYHW	60118	2800	35W-15N	D4
Brom Dr					
700	NPVL	60540	3141	27W-7S	C7
Bromley Ct					
1100	AURA	60502	3139	31W-6S	E4
1800	SMBG	60194	2858	25W-11N	A3
N Bromley Dr					
200	MHRY	60050	2527	33W-32N	D5
W Bromley Dr					
4900	MHRY	60050	2527	33W-32N	D5
Bromley Ln					
3100	AURA	60502	3139	31W-6S	E5
Bromley Pl					
800	NHBK	60062	2810	8W-16N	D1
Bromley St					
8200	ODPK	60462	3346	10W-17S	B5
Brompton Av					
700	NCHI	60044	2593	12W-30N	B3
W Brompton Av					
700	CHCG	60657	2977	1W-4N	E3
700	CHCG	60657	2978	0W-4N	A3
Brompton Cir					
800	BGBK	60440	3204	25W-11S	C7
800	BGBK	60440	3268	25W-11S	C1
Brompton Ct					
10	BGBK	60440	3204	25W-11S	C7
200	OSWG	60543	3200	35W-10S	A6
800	CLSM	60188	3024	24W-1N	E2
1600	CLLK	60014	2693	36W-22N	D3
19100	MKNA	60448	3503	12W-23S	C2
Brompton Dr					
100	SRGV	60554	3135	42W-6S	D5
7700	DRN	60561	3206	19W-8S	D2
Brompton Ln					
-	CLLK	60014	2693	36W-23N	D3
-	GRNE	60031	2478	15W-37N	A3
700	BGBK	60440	3204	24W-11S	C7
Brompton Rd					
1600	CLLK	60014	2693	36W-22N	D3
Bronk Cor					
4300	JLET	60586	3416	29W-21S	D7
Bronk Rd					
-	JLET	60586	3496	29W-22S	D1
800	JLET	60404	3496	29W-22S	D3
800	JLET	60431	3496	29W-22S	D2
800	SRWD	60404	3496	29W-22S	D3
800	SRWD	60431	3496	29W-22S	D3
N Bronk Rd					
-	JLET	60586	3416	29W-21S	D6
S Bronk Rd					
-	PnfT	60586	3416	29W-21S	D7
2000	JLET	60586	3416	29W-21S	D7
18000	JLET	60586	3496	29W-22S	D1
18000	PnfT	60586	3496	29W-22S	D1
18100	TroT	60586	3496	29W-21S	D1
18300	JLET	60431	3496	29W-22S	D1
Bronson Av					
100	NCHI	60088	2594	10W-31N	A1
Bronson Ln					
700	HDPK	60035	2705	7W-20N	B7
Bronte Ct					
3700	NPVL	60564	3267	28W-11S	A2
Bronx Av					
8700	SKOK	60077	2865	6W-10N	E4
10000	SKOK	60077	2811	6W-12N	E7
10000	WLMT	60077	2811	6W-12N	E7
10000	WLMT	60091	2811	6W-12N	E7
Bronx Pl					
-	SKOK	60077	2865	6W-11N	E2
Brook Av					
14300	ODPK	60462	3345	12W-17S	C4
19800	LYWD	60411	3509	3E-23S	E4
22000	RNPK	60471	3594	6W-26S	B3
Brook Cir					
400	NBRN	60010	2698	25W-22N	B4
Brook Ct					
-	OSWG	60543	3263	36W-13S	D4
10	LNHT	60046	2476	20W-38N	B1
10	WDRG	60517	3144	21W-7S	A7
100	BGBK	60440	3269	23W-11S	B1
600	MltT	60137	3083	21W-1S	D2
1400	AURA	60504	3201	32W-9S	C4
2800	JLET	60431	3417	28W-20S	A5
Brook Dr					
400	CLLK	60014	2639	36W-24N	E6
1400	DRGV	60515	3084	20W-2S	B4
7600	MchT	60097	2469	36W-35N	D5
E Brook Dr					
500	ANHT	60005	2861	17W-11N	B4
Brook Ln					
-	BGVW	60455	3210	10W-9S	C2
-	BGVW	60458	3210	10W-9S	C2
-	JSTC	60458	3210	10W-9S	C2
10	LNHT	60046	2418	20W-38N	B7
10	LNHT	60046	2476	20W-37N	B1
10	PSHT	60463	3274	10W-14S	C6
10	PSPK	60463	3274	10W-14S	C6
10	PSPK	60464	3274	10W-14S	C6
100	PTHT	60070	2808	15W-14N	A3
100	VNHL	60061	2647	16W-26N	C3
400	GNVW	60025	2811	6W-13N	C5
700	SMWD	60107	2857	28W-11N	B4
1200	DRGV	60515	3144	20W-5S	C3
1200	NPVL	60540	3141	28W-6S	A3
1400	AURA	60504	3201	32W-9S	C4
Brook Pl					
-	HNDL	60521	3086	16W-4S	A6
Brook Rd					
100	PTHT	60070	2808	15W-14N	A4
3200	HDPK	60035	2704	9W-24N	C1
Brook St					
10	CPVL	60110	2747	34W-17N	E7
100	ALGN	60102	2694	33W-21N	E6
200	ELGN	60120	2854	34W-12N	E2
1300	SCRL	60174	2963	36W-3N	E7
Brookbank Dr					
3800	HRPK	60133	2967	27W-4N	C3
Brook Bank Ln					
5500	LGGV	60047	2701	17W-22N	B3
Brookbank Rd					
5100	DRGV	60515	3144	20W-5S	B2
5500	DRGV	60516	3144	20W-6S	C4
7300	DRN	60561	3207	16W-8S	D1
7500	DRN	60527	3207	16W-8S	D2
7900	DGvT	60527	3207	16W-9S	D2
7900	WLBK	60527	3207	16W-9S	D3
Brookbank St					
6900	DRN	60561	3145	16W-7S	D7
Brookbridge Rd					
100	TVLY	60013	2695	32W-22N	C3
Brook Crossing Ct					
1200	NPVL	60564	3203	28W-10S	A6
11200	ODPK	60467	3422	14W-20S	E5
Brook Crossing Dr					
11300	ODPK	60467	3422	14W-20S	E5
Brook Crossing Ln					
17300	ODPK	60467	3422	14W-20S	E5
Brookdale Ct					
2000	PltT	60067	2805	20W-13N	E6
11800	ODPK	60467	3422	14W-20S	D5
W Brookdale Ct					
20800	LktT	60544	3340	25W-16S	B5
Brookdale Dr					
-	BMDL	60101	2969	22W-4N	C4
300	BMDL	60108	2969	22W-4N	C4
300	BmdT	60108	2969	22W-4N	C4
1000	CPVL	60110	2748	33W-17N	B7
1100	DndT	60110	2748	33W-17N	B7
7400	DRN	60561	3207	17W-8S	C1
N Brookdale Dr					
600	SMBG	60194	2858	25W-11N	B4
Brookdale Ln					
10	PltT	60173	2805	20W-13N	E6
10	SMBG	60173	2805	20W-13N	E6
100	PltT	60067	2805	20W-13N	E6
200	PltT	60067	2806	20W-13N	A6
N Brookdale Ln					
200	PltT	60067	2805	20W-13N	E6
200	PltT	60067	2806	20W-13N	A6
S Brookdale Ln					
200	PltT	60067	2806	20W-13N	A6
Brookdale Rd					
1300	NPVL	60563	3140	29W-5S	D4
1900	NpvT	60563	3140	29W-5S	C3
2700	GNVW	60025	2809	11W-15N	D2
2700	GNVW	60062	2809	11W-15N	D2
2700	NHBK	60062	2809	11W-15N	D2
3200	NHBK	60025	2809	11W-15N	D2
W Brooke Av					
2800	WKGN	60087	2479	12W-36N	B4
12500	WkgT	60087	2479	12W-36N	B4
18500	WrnT	60030	2533	18W-32N	E5
Brooke Ct					
-	FKFT	60423	3590	14W-26S	D3
Brooke Ln					
10	SBTN	60010	2803	27W-15N	A2
W Brookedge Dr					
100	HPSR	60140	2795	47W-15N	E3
Brookfield Av					
8400	BKFD	60513	3088	10W-3S	A6
8400	BKFD	60546	3088	10W-3S	A6
8400	RVSD	60546	3088	10W-3S	A6
8700	BKFD	60513	3087	11W-3S	E6
E Brookfield Av					
100	WhlT	60056	2808	13W-13N	E5
Brookfield Cir					
17700	ODPK	60467	3422	14W-21S	D6
19500	TYPK	60477	3504	10W-23S	B4
Brookfield Ct					
700	LKZH	60047	2699	22W-22N	B5
1700	AURA	60503	3201	32W-10S	C5
S Brookfield Ct					
25700	CNHN	60410	3672	32W-31S	D6
Brookfield Dr					
1400	JLET	60586	3496	30W-22S	B1
Brookfield Ln					
10	GNVA	60134	3019	36W-1N	E3
W Brookfield Ln					
25200	CNHN	60410	3672	32W-31S	C6
W Brookfield St					
300	LMBD	60148	3026	20W-1N	A3
Brook Forest Av					
-	JLET	60404	3496	30W-22S	C2
-	PnfT	60586	3496	30W-21S	C1
100	SRWD	60404	3496	30W-23S	C5
100	SRWD	60431	3496	29W-23S	C5
900	JLET	60431	3496	30W-22S	C2
1100	JLET	60586	3496	30W-22S	C2
Brook Forest Av SR-59					
-	JLET	60404	3496	30W-22S	C2
-	PnfT	60586	3496	30W-21S	C1
100	SRWD	60404	3496	30W-23S	C5
100	SRWD	60431	3496	29W-23S	C5
900	JLET	60431	3496	30W-22S	C2
1100	JLET	60586	3496	30W-22S	C2
Brook Forest Ln					
400	NBRN	60010	2698	25W-22N	B4
Brookgate Dr					
17200	ODPK	60467	3422	14W-20S	D5
Brookhaven Av					
7600	DRN	60561	3207	17W-8S	B2
Brookhaven Cir					
10	SBTN	60010	2803	27W-15N	B1
300	SRGV	60554	3197	42W-7S	D1
500	BRkT	60554	3197	42W-7S	D1
Brookhaven Ct					
100	SRGV	60554	3197	42W-7S	D1
Brookhaven Dr					
200	EGVV	60007	2914	18W-8N	E2
8200	FKFT	60423	3592	10W-27S	C4
N Brookhaven Dr					
30500	GNOK	60048	2592	14W-30N	D1
Brookhaven Ln					
400	CmpT	60175	2906	39W-6N	E7
Brookhaven Rd					
4300	GRNE	60031	2535	14W-34N	C1
Brookhaven Tr					
200	PGGV	60140	2798	41W-14N	A5
Brook Hill Ct					
11800	ODPK	60467	3422	14W-21S	D6
Brookhill Ct					
200	SMBG	60193	2859	23W-9N	B7
Brook Hill Dr					
11200	ODPK	60467	3422	14W-20S	E4
11200	OrlT	60467	3422	14W-20S	E4
Brookhill Dr					
10	NHFD	60093	2758	7W-16N	B7
4500	LGGV	60047	2700	19W-23N	D2
S Brook Hill Ln					
10	VNHL	60061	2647	16W-24N	D6
Brookhill Rd					
100	LbvT	60048	2591	17W-30N	B1
Brookhurst Ln					
10	AddT	60191	2971	17W-5N	B2
10	WDDL	60191	2971	17W-5N	B2
Brooking Ct					
600	LKVL	60046	2417	22W-39N	C5
Brooklands Ln					
13100	PNFD	60585	3338	30W-15S	B3
Brooklea Ct					
300	NPVL	60565	3204	25W-9S	A4
Brookline Ct					
1200	NPVL	60563	3142	25W-6S	B4
6000	LSLE	60532	3142	23W-6S	E5
W Brookline Ct					
400	PLTN	60067	2805	21W-14N	D4
Brookline Ln					
800	PKRG	60068	2864	10W-9N	B6

STREET Block	City	ZIP	Map#	CGS	Grid
Brookline St					
500	CHHT	60411	3595	2W-26S	C2
700	SEGN	60177	2908	35W-8N	C3
S Brooklodge Ln					
10600	PSHL	60465	3274	9W-12S	C2
Brooklyn Dr					
600	AURA	60502	3139	32W-7S	C7
Brookmeade Dr					
3200	RGMW	60008	2806	20W-12N	B7
Brookmont Ln					
300	NBRN	60010	2698	25W-23N	B2
Brook Park Ln					
10	PKFT	60466	3595	2W-28S	D6
Brookpoint Ct					
8400	TYPK	60477	3504	10W-23S	B3
Brookridge Ct					
10500	FKFT	60423	3503	13W-25S	A7
10500	FKFT	60423	3591	13W-25S	B1
Brookridge Dr					
-	PNFD	60586	3415	31W-20S	E5
-	PnfT	60586	3415	31W-20S	E5
2400	JLET	60586	3415	31W-20S	E6
10400	FKFT	60423	3591	13W-25S	B1
19500	TYPK	60477	3504	10W-23S	B3
Brookridge Rd					
400	DGvT	60516	3206	19W-9S	C4
400	DRN	60516	3206	19W-9S	C4
700	DRN	60561	3206	19W-10S	C4
Brookridge Creek Dr					
10400	FKFT	60423	3591	13W-25S	B1
N Brooks Av					
300	JLET	60435	3498	24W-23S	D4
Brooks Ln					
10400	CHRG	60415	3275	8W-12S	A2
10400	WRTH	60415	3275	8W-12S	A2
10400	WRTH	60482	3275	8W-12S	A2
N Brooks St					
26500	WcnT	60084	2643	28W-26N	A2
Brooksedge Av					
3400	NPVL	60564	3266	30W-11S	B1
W Brooks Farm Rd					
-	RDLK	60073	2531	25W-34N	A1
25500	GrtT	60073	2531	25W-34N	A1
25800	GrtT	60073	2530	25W-34N	E1
25900	RDLK	60073	2530	25W-34N	E1
Brookshire Ct					
10	AURA	60502	3201	32W-8S	B1
100	NPVL	60540	3140	29W-6S	E5
Brookshire Dr					
11500	ODPK	60467	3422	14W-20S	D5
11900	HMGN	60491	3422	14W-20S	D5
N Brookshire Dr					
5000	MchT	60050	2471	32W-36N	B3
Brookshire Ln					
10	AURA	60502	3201	32W-8S	B1
Brookshire Estates Ct					
2100	JLET	60586	3416	30W-21S	B7
Brookshire Estates Dr					
2100	JLET	60586	3416	30W-21S	B7
Brookshore Ct					
-	PNFD	60544	3415	31W-18S	E2
400	SRWD	60404	3496	30W-24S	B5
Brookshore Dr					
15600	PNFD	60544	3415	31W-18S	E1
15600	PnfT	60544	3415	31W-18S	E1
N Brookshore Dr					
100	SRWD	60404	3496	30W-23S	C4
S Brookshore Dr					
100	SRWD	60404	3496	30W-24S	C5
Brookside Av					
-	WkgT	60031	2536	12W-33N	A1
300	ALGN	60102	2693	36W-21N	D6
1100	WKGN	60085	2536	11W-34N	E1
Brookside Blvd					
20800	OMFD	60461	3507	4W-25S	A7
Brookside Cir					
300	WHTN	60187	3024	24W-0N	C4
Brookside Ct					
-	BGBK	60440	3269	23W-12S	B3
100	LbvT	60048	2591	17W-30N	C1
100	WNVL	60555	3080	30W-3S	C5
900	MRGO	60152	2634	49W-25N	C4
1000	HRPK	60133	2911	26W-9N	E1
2200	AURA	60502	3139	33W-5S	B4
3700	RLKP	60030	2532	22W-31N	C7
9100	ODPK	60462	3423	11W-18S	E1
9100	ODPK	60462	3424	11W-18S	A1
S Brookside Ct					
24000	CteT	60417	3598	3E-29S	A7
24000	CteT	60417	3687	3E-29S	A1
W Brookside Ct					
8100	PSPK	60464	3274	10W-14S	B6
27000	LKBN	60010	2697	27W-22N	B4
Brookside Dr					
10	ELGN	60123	2853	37W-11N	D3
10	ElgT	60123	2853	37W-11N	D3
10	ElgT	60124	2853	37W-11N	D3
10	GLHT	60139	2968	24W-3N	D5
10	LMNT	60439	3272	15W-13S	B4
10	ROSL	60172	2912	24W-7N	E4
300	WLMT	60091	2812	5W-13N	A7
400	WTMT	60559	3144	18W-6S	E5
500	DRGV	60516	3144	18W-6S	E5
500	NBRN	60010	2697	26W-23N	E1
500	WTMT	60516	3144	18W-6S	E5
600	WNFD	60190	3023	27W-0S	B6
800	BRLT	60103	2911	28W-7N	A5
1200	SEGN	60177	2907	37W-7N	C5
1400	HFET	60169	2858	26W-12N	A2
7400	HRPK	60133	2911	26W-9N	E1
N Brookside Dr					
36000	GRNE	60031	2477	17W-36N	B4
36000	WrnT	60031	2477	17W-36N	B5
S Brookside Dr					
11600	PSPK	60464	3274	10W-13S	C5
W Brookside Dr					
8100	PSPK	60464	3274	10W-14S	B6
Brookside Ln					
10	BtlT	60512	3262	40W-11S	B1
200	WLBK	60527	3145	16W-6S	D5
300	GLNC	60022	2758	6W-16N	D7
600	FKFT	60423	3591	12W-25S	C1
800	DRFD	60015	2756	11W-20N	D1
1200	DRGV	60515	3084	20W-3S	B6
1300	NHBK	60062	2757	10W-17N	A5
1700	LGGV	60047	2753	18W-20N	D1
1800	HFET	60169	2858	25W-12N	A2
2200	AURA	60502	3139	32W-5S	B4
2600	SMBG	60173	2805	21W-13N	C6
Brookside Rd					
10	PKFT	60466	3595	3W-28S	B6
200	NBRN	60010	2698	25W-23N	A1
W Brookside St					
800	PLTN	60067	2805	22W-15N	C1
800	PltT	60067	2805	22W-15N	C1
Brookside Wy					
3000	WRLK	60097	2468	38W-35N	E6
NW Brookside Wy					
22300	LKBN	60010	2697	27W-22N	C4
W Brookside Wy					
22200	LKBN	60010	2697	27W-22N	C4
Brookside Glen Ct					
19300	TYPK	60477	3504	10W-23S	C3
Brookside Glen Dr					
7600	TYPK	60477	3504	10W-23S	C3
8700	FftT	60448	3504	10W-23S	C3
8700	MKNA	60448	3504	10W-23S	C3
8700	TYPK	60448	3504	10W-23S	C3
Brookside West Dr					
600	CmpT	60119	2961	42W-4N	E4
600	CmpT	60175	2961	42W-4N	D3
Brookston Dr					
10	SMBG	60193	2859	21W-10N	D5
200	SMBG	60173	2859	21W-10N	D5
Brook Stone Ct					
-	FKFT	60423	3592	10W-27S	B4
Brookstone Ct					
10	SMWD	60107	2856	29W-10N	E7
1800	RMVL	60446	3339	27W-17S	C5
2500	AURA	60502	3139	32W-5S	C3
Brookstone Dr					
-	MHTN	60442	3677	19W-30S	E4
10	SMWD	60107	2856	29W-10N	E6
1000	CLSM	60188	2967	27W-3N	B5
Brookstone Ln					
-	BGBK	60490	3267	28W-14S	A7
-	BGBK	60490	3339	27W-15S	B1
Brookstone Pl					
6000	GRNE	60031	2534	16W-33N	D3
Brookstone Rd					
600	GYLK	60030	2532	21W-33N	D3
Brookton on Auburn					
10	RGMW	60008	2806	19W-14N	B3
Brookvale Dr					
700	WLNG	60090	2754	15W-18N	E3
Brookvale Ter					
700	GLNC	60022	2758	6W-16N	C7
Brookview Ct					
10	DGvT	60527	3146	15W-6S	A4
1600	AURA	60502	3139	32W-5S	C3
Brookview Dr					
23100	BlmT	60466	3595	2W-28S	C6
23100	CteT	60475	3595	2W-28S	C6
Brookview Ln					
-	BGBK	60440	3269	23W-12S	B3
11600	OrlT	60467	3344	14W-17S	D4
S Brookview Ln					
1700	RGMW	60067	2805	21W-13N	D5
Brookway Dr					
2200	GNVA	60134	3019	36W-1N	D3
Brookwood Av					
1700	DRGV	60516	3144	20W-7S	A6
22300	SLVL	60411	3598	3E-27S	A4
Brookwood Cir					
1400	ALGN	60102	2694	34W-21N	B6
Brookwood Ct					
10	ANHT	60004	2754	17W-16N	A7
10	ELGN	60123	2800	36W-14N	B7
100	VNHL	60061	2647	16W-24N	E6
2000	SEGN	60177	2907	37W-7N	D6
2200	JLET	60435	3497	26W-22S	E2
2300	AURA	60502	3139	32W-6S	B5
17400	ODPK	60467	3422	14W-21S	D5
Brookwood Dr					
200	SchT	60174	2964	35W-5N	B2
200	SCRL	60174	2964	35W-5N	B2
300	OMFD	60461	3507	3W-24S	B6
1700	FSMR	60422	3507	3W-23S	B4
1700	WCHI	60185	3080	29W-1S	C1
1700	WnfT	60185	3080	29W-1S	C1
2000	SEGN	60177	2907	37W-7N	C6
6000	OKFT	60452	3425	7W-18S	C1
11500	ODPK	60467	3422	14W-20S	D5
12900	HTLY	60142	2744	41W-20N	C1
20900	PKFT	60466	3507	3W-25S	B7
22100	BlmT	60411	3598	3E-26S	A3
22100	SLVL	60411	3598	3E-26S	A3
E Brookwood Dr					
1200	ANHT	60004	2754	17W-16N	C7
S Brookwood Dr					
-	WDDL	60191	2970	18W-5N	E1
W Brookwood Dr					
10	ANHT	60004	2754	17W-16N	A6
Brookwood Ln					
-	BGBK	60440	3268	25W-11S	B1
E Brookwood Ln					
100	BGBK	60440	3268	25W-11S	B1
W Brookwood Ln					
100	BGBK	60440	3268	25W-11S	B1
Brookwood Pl					
100	WDDL	60191	2970	18W-5N	E1
Brookwood Rd					
1700	LSLE	60532	3142	23W-6S	E5
Brookwood St					
10	BNVL	60106	2915	16W-5N	E7
Brookwood Ter					
300	ROSL	60172	2913	23W-6N	B6
Brookwood Tr					
300	MHRY	60050	2527	34W-31N	C7
400	NndT	60050	2527	34W-31N	C7
Brookwood Ter 1					
300	OMFD	60461	3507	3W-24S	B6
Brookwood Ter 2					
400	OMFD	60461	3507	3W-24S	B6
Brookwood Ter 3					
500	OMFD	60461	3507	3W-24S	C6
Brookwood Ter 4					
500	OMFD	60461	3507	3W-24S	B6
Brookwood Ter 5					
600	OMFD	60461	3507	3W-24S	B6
Brookwood Ter 6					
700	OMFD	60461	3507	3W-24S	B6
Brookwood Wy Dr					
2600	RGMW	60008	2806	20W-14N	A5
N Broomsedge Rd					
34100	GrtT	60073	2531	25W-34N	A1
Brophy Av					
1200	PKRG	60068	2918	10W-7N	A3
1800	CHCG	60631	2918	10W-7N	A4
1800	PKRG	60631	2918	10W-7N	A4
Brorson Ln					
1400	JNBG	60050	2472	30W-36N	A3
1400	MchT	60050	2472	30W-36N	A3
Brorson St					
24500	AvnT	60073	2474	24W-35N	C6
24500	RLKB	60073	2474	24W-35N	C6
Brosam Dr					
5700	JLET	60586	3496	31W-22S	A2
W Bross Av					
2200	CHCG	60608	3091	2W-3S	B4
Brossman St					
2900	NPVL	60564	3202	28W-11S	E7
Brouch Ln					
1000	AraT	60505	3138	34W-6S	D4
1000	AURA	60505	3138	34W-6S	D4
Brougham Dr					
10	WLNG	60090	2754	16W-18N	D3
10	WLNG	60090	2755	15W-18N	A2
Brougham Ln					
700	OKBK	60523	3084	18W-3S	E6
Brower Dr					
900	ROSL	60172	2912	24W-7N	C5
N Browe School Rd					
38500	OMCK	60083	2419	16W-39N	D6
Brown Av					
-	AntT	60002	2358	22W-41N	B7
-	AntT	60002	2417	22W-41N	B1
100	FTPK	60130	3030	9W-0N	C4
700	EVTN	60202	2866	3W-10N	E5
1200	JltT	60432	3499	22W-23S	D4
1400	JLET	60432	3499	22W-23S	D4
2100	EVTN	60201	2866	3W-12N	E1
7500	RVFT	60130	3030	9W-0N	C4
7500	RVFT	60305	3030	9W-0N	C4
S Brown Av					
1300	HMND	46394	3280		E4
W Brown Av					
26300	AntT	60002	2415	26W-38N	D6
Brown Cir					
500	EGVV	60007	2913	21W-9N	D1
N Brown Cir					
4100	GRNE	60031	2478	14W-35N	D7
S Brown Cir					
4100	GRNE	60031	2478	14W-35N	D7
Brown Ct					
800	BTVA	60510	3078	36W-2S	A3
800	SMBG	60193	2912	25W-9N	C1
2200	NPVL	60565	3204	24W-10S	C5
Brown Dr					
8800	FKFT	60423	3592	11W-25S	A1
11800	LMNT	60439	3270	20W-14S	C6
Brown Ln					
8700	TYPK	60487	3424	11W-21S	A6
24000	PNFD	60586	3416	30W-19S	B3
Brown Rd					
10	CmpT	60175	2962	41W-5N	A2
Brown Rd CO-81					
800	CmpT	60175	2962	40W-5N	B2
W Brown Rd					
16800	JknT	60421	3677	21W-31S	A6
16800	JknT	60442	3677	21W-31S	A6
16800	MhtT	60421	3677	21W-31S	A6
16800	MhtT	60442	3677	21W-31S	A6
26200	FmtT	60084	2644	25W-26N	B3
26200	WcnT	60084	2644	25W-26N	B3
Brown St					
-	FDHT	60411	3509	1E-24S	B6
200	WnfT	60185	3022	29W-0N	D5
300	WCDA	60084	2643	26W-27N	D1
300	WCHI	60185	3022	29W-0N	D5
500	WDSK	60098	2581	41W-30N	D1
1000	WCDA	60084	2587	26W-28N	D6
1200	DSPN	60016	2862	13W-11N	E3
1300	DSPN	60016	2863	13W-11N	A3
2600	LKPT	60441	3419	22W-20S	C5
2600	LktT	60441	3419	22W-20S	C5
5100	SKOK	60077	2865	6W-10N	D5
26500	AntT	60002	2415	26W-38N	D6
E Brown St					
100	HRVD	60033	2406	50W-38N	B6
100	WCHI	60185	3022	29W-0N	D5
500	WnfT	60185	3022	29W-0N	D5
N Brown St					
1700	MHRY	60050	2528	32W-33N	B2
W Brown St					
10	LMBD	60148	3026	20W-1N	B2
100	HRVD	60033	2406	50W-38N	A6
100	WCHI	60185	3022	30W-0N	C5
200	WnfT	60185	3022	30W-0N	B5
1400	ANHT	60004	2806	18W-14N	D3
Brown Deer Dr					
900	WTMT	60559	3085	18W-3S	B6
Brown Derby Rd					
-	HMWD	60430	3428	0W-21S	B5
-	HMWD	60476	3428	0W-21S	B6
-	TNTN	60476	3428	0W-21S	B6
Browne Ct					
1100	WKGN	60099	2421	11W-39N	E6
Brownell St					
200	ThtT	60476	3428	0E-21S	E6
200	TNTN	60476	3428	0E-21S	E6
Browning Av					
10	WDND	60118	2801	33W-15N	A3
100	WKGN	60085	2537	10W-33N	B3
E Browning Av					
500	CHCG	60653	3092	0E-3S	D5
Browning Ct					
200	WHTN	60187	3082	24W-1S	C2
800	VNHL	60061	2647	16W-25N	D3
1900	HDPK	60035	2703	10W-23N	E3
Browning Dr					
17200	ODPK	60467	3423	13W-20S	B5
Browning Ln					
900	LKZH	60047	2699	22W-22N	B3
Browns Ct					
-	AraT	60504	3200	33W-8S	E2
S Brownstone Av					
1400	ANHT	60005	2861	17W-11N	C4
1400	ANHT	60056	2861	17W-11N	C4
1400	MPPT	60005	2861	17W-11N	C4
1400	MPPT	60056	2861	17W-11N	C4
Brownstone Dr					
-	SCRL	60174	2964	35W-3N	C6
Brownstone Pl					
-	SMBG	60193	2912	25W-8N	B2
W Brownstone Wy					
4300	WKGN	60085	2535	14W-32N	D5
Brownville Rd					
200	HDPK	60035	2758	7W-20N	C2
Bruce Av					
100	AddT	60101	2971	17W-3N	B6
600	FSMR	60422	3507	3W-22S	B2
600	HMWD	60430	3507	3W-22S	B1
Bruce Cir					
17300	HMGN	60491	3421	18W-20S	A5
17400	HmrT	60491	3421	18W-20S	A5
Bruce Cir N					
10	HNWD	60047	2644	23W-24N	E7
Bruce Cir S					
10	HNWD	60047	2644	23W-24N	D7
Bruce Ct					
10	LktT	60441	3419	22W-20S	D6
900	LbvT	60048	2592	15W-29N	B4
18700	NlxT	60448	3502	15W-22S	C1
Bruce Dr					
-	HPSR	60140	2796	46W-15N	A3
Bruce Dr					
900	ELGN	60120	2855	32W-11N	C4
4800	RNPK	60471	3594	6W-27S	B5
4800	UYPK	60471	3594	6W-27S	B5
W Bruce Dr					
8400	MaiT	60714	2864	10W-10N	A5
8400	NLES	60714	2864	10W-10N	A5
8700	NLES	60714	2863	10W-10N	E5
Bruce Ln					
10	NpvT	60563	3140	30W-5S	B3
N Bruce Ln					
700	GNWD	60425	3428	0W-21S	B7
E Bruce Rd					
12400	HMGN	60491	3422	15W-21S	B5
W Bruce Rd					
100	LktT	60441	3419	22W-20S	C6
600	LKPT	60441	3419	22W-20S	C6
1100	HmrT	60441	3420	21W-20S	A6
1100	LKPT	60441	3420	21W-20S	A6
1100	LktT	60441	3420	21W-21S	A6
13700	HmrT	60491	3421	17W-20S	D5
14800	HMGN	60441	3421	18W-20S	A5
14800	HMGN	60491	3421	18W-20S	A5
14900	HMGN	60491	3420	21W-20S	A6
E Bruce St					
600	JLET	60432	3499	23W-22S	B2
N Bruce St					
100	BCVL	60407	4030	33W-44S	B4
W Bruce St					
600	JLET	60432	3499	23W-22S	B2
Bruce Robert Ln					
800	HPSR	60140	2795	46W-15N	E3
Brucewood Ct					
10	BFGV	60089	2754	16W-18N	C2
Brucewood Dr					
200	BFGV	60089	2754	16W-18N	C3
Bruell St					
100	YKVL	60560	3333	42W-15S	D2
300	BtlT	60560	3333	42W-15S	D2
Brumley Dr					
2400	FSMR	60422	3507	3W-22S	B1
3600	FSMR	60422	3506	4W-22S	D1
3600	HLCT	60422	3506	4W-22S	D1
3600	HLCT	60429	3506	4W-22S	D1
Brummel Dr					
1200	EGVV	60007	2861	17W-9N	C7
1800	EGvT	60007	2861	16W-9N	D7
Brummel Pl					
2200	EVTN	60202	2866	3W-9N	D6
Brummel St					
900	EVTN	60202	2867	2W-9N	A6
1700	EVTN	60202	2866	3W-9N	E6
3800	SKOK	60076	2866	4W-9N	B6
4600	SKOK	60076	2865	5W-9N	E6
4900	SKOK	60077	2865	6W-9N	D6
Brundige Dr					
900	BbyT	60119	3018	39W-0N	E4
900	BbyT	60134	3018	39W-0N	E4
Brundige Rd					
-	BbyT	60134	3018	39W-1N	E3
10	BbyT	60119	3018	39W-1N	E3
10	CmpT	60119	3018	39W-2N	E2
10	SCRL	60119	3018	39W-2N	E1
10	SCRL	60175	3018	39W-2N	E1
Bruner Pl					
400	HNDL	60521	3085	16W-4S	E7
N Bruner St					
10	HNDL	60521	3145	16W-4S	E1
400	HNDL	60521	3085	16W-4S	E7
S Bruner St					
10	HNDL	60521	3145	16W-5S	E2
5500	DGvT	60521	3145	16W-6S	E3
Brunette Dr					
1400	DRGV	60516	3144	20W-7S	B6
Bruning Dr					
1900	WslT	60481	3943	27W-40S	D3
Bruning Dr W					
-	ITSC	60143	2913	21W-7N	D4
1800	ITSC	60157	2913	21W-7N	D4
Bruno Ct					
800	NPVL	60563	3140	29W-6S	D4
W Bruns Rd					
5700	MONE	60449	3682	8W-31S	C6
5700	MonT	60449	3682	8W-31S	C6
6800	GGnT	60449	3682	8W-32S	A6
12800	MhtT	60442	3678	17W-31S	D6
Brunschon Ln					
-	HTLY	60142	2691	40W-22N	E4
Brunswick Cir					
900	SMBG	60193	2913	23W-9N	B1
2400	WDRG	60517	3143	21W-7S	E7
Brunswick Ct					
300	SMWD	60107	2857	28W-9N	A7
300	SMWD	60107	2911	28W-9N	A1
1300	ELGN	60120	2801	32W-12N	D7
1300	NPVL	60540	3142	25W-7S	B7
2600	LSLE	60532	3142	25W-7S	C6
Brunswick Dr					
200	BFGV	60089	2754	16W-20N	D1
2000	JLET	60586	3415	31W-21S	D7
Brunswick Hbr					
1000	SMBG	60193	2913	23W-9N	B1
Brunswick Ln					
10	LNSH	60069	2702	13W-22N	E4
1100	AURA	60504	3201	32W-9S	D4
Brunswick Rd					
7700	DRN	60516	3206	19W-8S	E2
7700	DRN	60561	3206	19W-8S	E2
E Brunswick St					
10	HMND	46327	3352		C4
Brush Rd					
2500	SMBG	60173	2805	21W-13N	D6
Brush Hill Cir					
1300	NPVL	60540	3140	28W-6S	E5
1300	NPVL	60540	3141	28W-6S	A5
2400	JLET	60432	3500	21W-22S	A2
Brush Hill Ln					
800	LKZH	60047	2699	22W-22N	B3
1700	GNVW	60025	2810	8W-15N	E2
Brush Hill Rd					
-	EMHT	60126	3027	16W-0S	E7
-	EMHT	60126	3028	15W-0S	A7
7500	BRRG	60527	3208	15W-8S	A1
7500	DGvT	60527	3208	15W-8S	A1
7500	WLBK	60527	3208	15W-8S	A1
E Brush Hill Rd					
-	EMHT	60126	3028	15W-0S	A7
Brush Lake Ct					
21200	LktT	60403	3417	26W-19S	E3
Brush Lake Dr					
21200	LktT	60403	3417	26W-19S	E3
Brushwood Dr					
10	RchT	60443	3593	8W-26S	B1
Brushwood Ln					
8100	TYPK	60477	3504	10W-23S	C3
17100	ODPK	60467	3422	14W-20S	D5
Brushwood Ln					
19300	TYPK	60448	3504	10W-23S	C3
Bryan Av					
700	EMHT	60126	3027	16W-0S	E6
1100	JLET	60435	3498	25W-22S	C3
Bryan Ct					
1500	AURA	60504	3201	32W-9S	C5
Bryan Dr					
300	CRY	60013	2642	30W-24N	A7
Bryan Pl					
4500	DRGV	60515	3144	19W-4S	C1
S Bryan St					
500	EMHT	60126	3027	16W-0N	E5
Bryan Tr					
400	NlxT	60451	3502	15W-24S	C5
1000	FftT	60448	3502	15W-24S	C5
1000	NlxT	60448	3502	15W-24S	C5
Bryant Av					
-	PLTN	60067	2805	21W-14N	D4
10	GNEN	60137	3025	22W-0S	D7
600	BRTN	60010	2750	25W-20N	E1
700	BRTN	60010	2697	25W-20N	E7
700	WNKA	60093	2759	5W-16N	B7
700	WNKA	60093	2812	5W-16N	B1
2300	EVTN	60201	2867	2W-12N	A1
2600	EVTN	60201	2813	2W-13N	A7
17300	HLCT	60429	3427	3W-20S	A5
Bryant Av SR-53					
10	GNEN	60137	3025	22W-0S	D7
W Bryant Av					
10	PLTN	60067	2805	21W-14N	D4
10	RGMW	60008	2805	21W-14N	E4
Bryant Ct					
10	CLLK	60014	2640	35W-26N	B3
19300	MKNA	60448	3503	13W-23S	A3
Bryant Pl					
200	VNHL	60061	2647	17W-26N	B3
Bryant Rd					
10800	MKNA	60448	3503	13W-23S	A3
11100	MKNA	60448	3502	14W-23S	E4
Bryant St					
1000	AURA	60506	3137	37W-5S	C3
Bryant Wy					
200	BGBK	60440	3268	24W-11S	D1
Bryce Ct					
300	BRLT	60103	2910	29W-8N	E2
Bryce Pl					
1200	DRGV	60515	3084	20W-3S	B5
Bryce Tr					
500	ROSL	60172	2913	22W-8N	B3
Brynhaven Ct					
500	EGVV	60007	2861	18W-10N	A6
Brynhaven St					
500	EGVV	60007	2861	18W-10N	A6
Bryn Mawr Av					
-	CHCG	60018	2917	12W-6N	B6
-	CHCG	60666	2917	12W-6N	B6
-	ITSC	60143	2914	20W-6N	B5
-	RSMT	60018	2917	12W-6N	B6
-	SRPK	60176	2917	12W-6N	B6
-	SRPK	60666	2917	12W-6N	B6
-	WDDL	60191	2915	17W-6N	C5
10	AddT	60106	2915	17W-6N	C5
10	BNVL	60106	2915	16W-7N	D5
400	BmdT	60172	2913	23W-6N	A5
400	ROSL	60172	2913	23W-6N	A5
500	BmdT	60172	2912	23W-6N	E5
500	PKCY	60085	2535	13W-33N	E3
600	BRLT	60103	2910	29W-6N	D6
600	ROSL	60172	2912	23W-7N	E5
600	WKGN	60085	2535	13W-33N	E3
E Bryn Mawr Av					
100	ITSC	60143	2914	19W-6N	C5
800	ROSL	60172	2913	22W-6N	C5
W Bryn Mawr Av					
10	BmdT	60172	2913	23W-6N	A5
10	ROSL	60172	2913	23W-6N	A5
100	ITSC	60143	2914	20W-6N	B5
500	BmdT	60172	2912	24W-6N	D6
500	ROSL	60172	2912	24W-6N	C6
900	CHCG	60640	2921	1W-7N	D4
900	CHCG	60660	2921	1W-7N	E4
1500	ITSC	60143	2913	21W-6N	E5
2400	CHCG	60625	2921	3W-7N	A4
2400	CHCG	60659	2921	3W-7N	A4
2700	CHCG	60625	2920	5W-7N	B5
2700	CHCG	60659	2920	5W-7N	A5
3900	CHCG	60630	2920	5W-7N	A5
3900	CHCG	60646	2920	5W-7N	A5
4800	CHCG	60646	2919	6W-6N	E5
5400	CHCG	60630	2919	7W-7N	C4
6300	CHCG	60631	2919	8W-7N	A4
6300	CHCG	60656	2919	8W-7N	A4
6600	CHCG	60631	2918	8W-7N	D4
6600	CHCG	60656	2918	8W-7N	D4
7800	NpkT	60631	2918	9W-7N	B5
7900	LydT	60656	2918	9W-6N	B5
7900	NpkT	60656	2918	9W-6N	B5
8000	LydT	60631	2918	10W-6N	A5
8000	MaiT	60631	2918	10W-6N	A5
8600	CHCG	60631	2917	10W-7N	E5
8600	CHCG	60656	2917	10W-7N	E5
Bryn Mawr Ct					
600	SMBG	60194	2857	28W-12N	B2
2000	JNBG	60050	2471	30W-36N	E3
Bryn Mawr Dr					
2000	AraT	60506	3199	38W-8S	B3
Bryn Mawr Ln					
-	CLLK	60098	2638	39W-26N	B2
Bryn Mawr Wy					
11400	FftT	60423	3590	14W-26S	E2
11400	MKNA	60448	3590	14W-26S	E2
Brynn Dr					
-	MhtT	60442	3678	18W-31S	B4
100	MHTN	60442	3678	18W-31S	B5
Buccaneer Dr					
900	GNVW	60025	2810	10W-14N	A3
900	SMBG	60173	2805	21W-13N	C5
Buchanan Ct					
400	VNHL	60061	2647	17W-26N	B4
Buchanan Dr					
-	ALGN	60102	2747	36W-19N	B3
7000	GRNE	60031	2477	17W-35N	B5
Buchanan Ln					
10	SMWD	60107	2856	29W-10N	E5
Buchanan Rd					
3600	JNBG	60050	2471	32W-35N	B5
Buchanan St					
10	EGvT	60018	2862	15W-9N	A7
S Buchanan St					
400	WMTN	60481	3853	27W-39S	D7
800	WMTN	60481	3943	27W-39S	D1
Bucher Rd					
-	MTGY	60543	3263	38W-11S	B1
Buck Av					
-	WKGN	60087	2479	11W-36N	D5

Chicago 7-County Street Index

STREET Block	City	ZIP	Map#	CGS	Grid
Buck Av					
10	WKGN	60087	2480	10W-36N	B5
3400	JLET	60431	3497	28W-22S	A2
3800	JLET	60431	3496	29W-22S	D3
Buck Ct					
200	CmpT	60175	2905	43W-6N	B7
5700	WTMT	60559	3144	18W-6S	E4
36700	WrnT	60046	2476	18W-36N	D3
Buck Dr					
300	HNVL	60030	2532	21W-33N	C3
10400	ODPK	60467	3423	13W-20S	B4
10800	HTLY	60142	2692	40W-21N	A6
Buck Pth					
16700	LKPT	60441	3342	20W-17S	A6
16700	LktT	60441	3342	20W-17S	A6
Buck Tr					
7900	BRRG	60527	3208	14W-9S	C2
Buckboard Ct					
10	BGBK	60490	3268	26W-13S	A4
Buckboard Dr					
10	WLNG	60090	2755	15W-18N	A2
400	WLNG	60090	2754	15W-18N	E2
600	NLNX	60451	3501	17W-23S	D3
600	NlxT	60451	3501	17W-23S	D3
3500	ALGN	60102	2693	37W-20N	C7
Buckboard Rd					
500	BGBK	60490	3268	26W-13S	A4
Buckeridge Ct					
1800	GRNE	60031	2477	16W-36N	D4
Buckeye Ct					
21100	LktT	60544	3340	26W-16S	A3
W Buckeye Ct					
15300	LKPT	60441	3342	20W-18S	B7
Buckeye Dr					
400	NPVL	60540	3203	27W-8S	D2
400	WLNG	60090	2755	13W-17N	D5
600	HFET	60169	2859	23W-11N	A4
Buckeye Ln					
500	BGBK	60440	3268	24W-11S	E1
N Buckeye Rd					
20500	DRPK	60010	2751	23W-20N	E1
20500	ElaT	60010	2698	23W-20N	E7
20500	ElaT	60010	2751	23W-20N	E1
W Buckeye Rd					
23300	DRPK	60010	2698	23W-21N	E7
23300	ElaT	60010	2698	23W-21N	E7
Buckeye St					
600	ELGN	60123	2854	34W-12N	D2
Buckhorn Dr					
3700	NndT	60012	2584	35W-28N	B6
Buckhorn Ln					
100	NARA	60542	3137	37W-4S	C1
Bucki Ln					
8500	WLSP	60480	3208	13W-9S	E4
Buckingham Av					
1600	WSTR	60154	3087	13W-1S	A2
3000	LGPK	60525	3087	13W-2S	A4
3000	WSTR	60525	3087	13W-2S	A4
Buckingham Cir					
300	ELGN	60120	2855	32W-11N	C4
2300	WDRG	60517	3143	21W-7S	E7
Buckingham Ct					
10	DRFD	60015	2756	11W-20N	E2
10	LKZH	60047	2699	22W-22N	B4
100	EGVV	60007	2914	19W-8N	D3
100	OSWG	60543	3200	35W-10S	A6
200	GYLK	60030	2533	19W-33N	B3
200	SMBG	60193	2859	22W-10N	C6
700	CLSM	60188	2967	27W-4N	D5
700	HFET	60169	2858	24W-11N	C3
700	WHTN	60187	3082	25W-2S	B4
800	CLLK	60014	2639	35W-24N	E7
800	MDLN	60060	2590	20W-28N	A6
1100	WLNG	60090	2754	16W-18N	D3
1200	SRWD	60404	3496	31W-24S	A6
5700	RGMW	60008	2805	21W-13N	C5
5700	RGMW	60067	2805	21W-13N	C5
8400	WLSP	60480	3209	13W-9S	A3
9100	HTLY	60142	2692	40W-23N	B3
S Buckingham Ct					
600	LKFT	60045	2648	14W-25N	C6
Buckingham Dr					
10	RDLK	60073	2532	23W-32N	A4
10	RLKP	60030	2532	23W-32N	A4
10	RLKP	60073	2532	23W-32N	A4
10	SgrT	60506	3136	41W-6S	A4
100	GYLK	60030	2533	19W-33N	B3
200	ALGN	60102	2694	35W-21N	A6
200	BRLT	60103	2911	28W-6N	A6
300	CLLK	60014	2639	36W-24N	E7
1000	CLSM	60188	2967	27W-4N	D5
1900	WHTN	60187	3082	25W-2S	B4
2700	LSLE	60532	3142	24W-6S	C5
2800	NPVL	60540	3142	24W-6S	C5
4300	GRNE	60031	2535	14W-34N	D2
11100	ODPK	60467	3422	14W-21S	D7
11100	ODPK	60467	3423	13W-21S	A7
19500	MKNA	60448	3502	14W-23S	D4
E Buckingham Dr					
1000	NPVL	60563	3142	25W-5S	A3
N Buckingham Dr					
100	SgrT	60506	3136	40W-5S	B3
100	SRGV	60506	3136	40W-5S	B3
Buckingham Ln					
10	BFGV	60089	2754	16W-20N	D1
10	YkTp	60181	3085	18W-1S	A1
200	YkTp	60148	3085	18W-1S	A1
Buckingham Pl					
10	LNSH	60069	2702	13W-22N	D3
300	SRWD	60404	3496	31W-24S	A5
400	DRGV	60516	3144	19W-7S	D7
400	DRN	60516	3144	19W-7S	D7
400	DRN	60561	3144	19W-7S	D7
400	LYVL	60048	2591	16W-28N	E6
W Buckingham Pl					
600	CHCG	60657	2977	1W-4N	E3
600	CHCG	60657	2978	0W-4N	A3
Buckingham Rd					
-	BHPK	60087	2479	11W-37N	D1
-	WKGN	60087	2479	11W-37N	D1
100	MltT	60137	3083	22W-1S	C2
400	MDLN	60060	2590	20W-28N	A7
Buckingham Wy					
500	BGBK	60440	3205	21W-9S	D4
Buckingham Glen Cir					
1500	NfdT	60025	2810	10W-14N	A5
Buckingham Place Dr					
9000	MaiT	60016	2863	11W-11N	E3
9000	MaiT	60714	2863	10W-11N	E3
9000	NLES	60714	2863	10W-11N	E3
Buckland Dr					
2600	AURA	60503	3265	33W-11S	B1
Buckland Ln					
2500	NHBK	60062	2757	10W-18N	A3
Buckley Ct					
500	UYPK	60466	3684	3W-30S	C3
2000	NPVL	60565	3203	26W-9S	D4
Buckley Rd					
-	AvnT	60030	2533	20W-32N	B5
-	AvnT	60048	2533	20W-32N	B5
-	FmtT	60048	2533	19W-31N	B6
-	FmtT	60048	2590	19W-31N	D1
-	GNOK	60044	2592	13W-30N	E1
-	GYLK	60030	2533	20W-32N	B5
-	GYLK	60048	2533	20W-32N	B5
-	LbvT	60044	2592	13W-30N	D1
-	LbvT	60044	2593	13W-30N	A1
-	LbvT	60048	2590	18W-30N	D1
-	LbvT	60064	2592	13W-30N	E1
-	LYVL	60048	2590	19W-31N	D1
-	NCHI	60044	2592	13W-30N	E1
-	ShdT	60088	2593	12W-30N	B2
-	ShdT	60064	2593	12W-30N	B2
10	LbvT	60048	2591	16W-30N	D2
10	LYVL	60048	2591	16W-30N	D2
1500	NCHI	60088	2593	11W-30N	E2
2000	NCHI	60064	2593	12W-30N	B2
2100	GNOK	60048	2592	13W-30N	E1
3400	ShdT	60044	2593	12W-30N	B2
3400	ShdT	60064	2593	12W-30N	B2
3500	NCHI	60044	2593	12W-30N	A2
4400	LSLE	60532	3143	22W-4S	B1
8800	HMTN	60456	3212	5W-10S	A4
Buckley Rd SR-137					
-	AvnT	60030	2533	20W-32N	B5
-	AvnT	60048	2533	20W-32N	B5
-	FmtT	60048	2533	19W-31N	B6
-	FmtT	60048	2590	19W-31N	D1
-	GNOK	60044	2592	13W-30N	E1
-	GYLK	60030	2533	20W-32N	B5
-	GYLK	60048	2533	20W-32N	B5
-	LbvT	60044	2592	13W-30N	D1
-	LbvT	60044	2593	13W-30N	A1
-	LbvT	60048	2590	18W-30N	D1
-	LbvT	60064	2592	13W-30N	E1
-	LYVL	60048	2590	19W-31N	D1
-	NCHI	60044	2592	13W-30N	E1
-	ShdT	60088	2593	12W-30N	B2
10	LbvT	60048	2591	16W-30N	D2
10	LYVL	60048	2591	16W-30N	D2
1500	NCHI	60088	2593	11W-30N	E2
2000	NCHI	60064	2593	12W-30N	B2
2100	GNOK	60048	2592	13W-30N	E1
3400	ShdT	60044	2593	12W-30N	B2
3400	ShdT	60064	2593	12W-30N	B2
3500	NCHI	60044	2593	12W-30N	A2
N Buckley Rd					
10	BNHL	60010	2696	28W-21N	E6
100	CbaT	60010	2696	28W-21N	E6
W Buckley Rd					
1100	LbvT	60048	2592	15W-30N	A2
14400	GNOK	60048	2592	14W-30N	C2
15700	LbvT	60048	2591	16W-30N	E2
W Buckley Rd SR-137					
1100	LbvT	60048	2592	15W-30N	A2
14400	GNOK	60048	2592	14W-30N	C2
15700	LbvT	60048	2591	16W-30N	E2
Buckminster Ct					
200	LKBF	60044	2593	11W-29N	D5
Bucknel Ct					
100	GNVW	60025	2810	10W-15N	B2
Bucknell Ct					
1700	NPVL	60565	3204	24W-9S	C3
Buckner Ct					
14100	LktT	60544	3340	26W-16S	A4
Buckner Pond Wy					
16400	LktT	60403	3417	26W-19S	E3
Buckskin					
10	LMNT	60439	3272	15W-13S	B5
Buckskin Ct					
700	CmpT	60175	2962	39W-5N	D2
Buckskin Dr					
-	OswT	60543	3263	37W-14S	D7
700	OSWG	60543	3263	37W-14S	D7
Buckskin Ln					
10	HnrT	60107	2856	30W-10N	C5
10	SMWD	60107	2856	30W-10N	C5
100	HnrT	60120	2856	30W-10N	C5
600	CPVL	60110	2748	33W-17N	B7
1000	CLSM	60188	2967	27W-3N	C6
2900	RLKP	60030	2589	22W-31N	C1
Buckskin Tr					
400	CmpT	60175	2962	39W-5N	D2
Bucksport Ln					
-	BCHR	60401	3774	0W-35S	D6
Bucktail Dr					
300	OSWG	60543	3262	39W-11S	E2
Bucktail Ln					
1900	SRGV	60554	3134	44W-7S	D7
Buckthorn Cir					
300	NHBK	60062	2756	13W-18N	A3
Buckthorn Ct					
10	WNVL	60555	3080	30W-2S	C4
400	BFGV	60089	2754	16W-20N	D1
500	YKVL	60560	3333	43W-16S	B4
18300	TYPK	60487	3424	10W-22S	A7
20200	FmtT	60060	2646	20W-26N	A3
Buckthorn Dr					
100	NARA	60542	3137	37W-4S	C1
1500	HFET	60192	2804	24W-15N	B2
2200	ALGN	60102	2695	32W-20N	C7
E Buckthorn Dr					
1800	MPPT	60056	2808	13W-15N	E3
Buckthorn Ln					
-	RDLK	60073	2531	23W-33N	E4
300	ELGN	60120	2855	31W-11N	E3
3600	DRGV	60515	3084	20W-3S	B6
S Buckthorn Ln					
13500	DPgT	60544	3339	26W-15S	D3
13500	LktT	60544	3339	26W-15S	D3
Buckthorn Rd					
10	SBTN	60010	2803	26W-14N	D4
Buckthorn Ter					
600	BFGV	60089	2754	15W-20N	E1
Buckthorne Ln					
200	HLSD	60162	3028	13W-0S	E5
Bud Ct					
300	MltT	60187	3023	26W-0N	E4
S Bud Ct					
23000	CNHN	60410	3584	29W-27S	D6
Budd Rd					
12400	FoxT	60560	3332	45W-17S	B7
N Budd St					
2400	RVGV	60171	2974	10W-3N	A5
Budingen Ln					
8400	TYPK	60477	3424	10W-20S	B5
8400	TYPK	60487	3424	10W-20S	B5
S Budler Rd					
-	PnfT	60544	3417	27W-18S	C1
-	RMVL	60446	3417	27W-18S	C1
13400	WldT	60544	3339	27W-15S	C3
14200	PnfT	60446	3339	27W-16S	C5
14200	PnfT	60544	3339	27W-16S	C5
14200	RMVL	60446	3339	27W-17S	C6
14200	RMVL	60544	3339	27W-16S	C5
Budlong Rd					
-	OswT	60543	3262	39W-13S	E5
Buege Ln					
-	WLSP	60480	3208	14W-9S	D3
N Buell Av					
200	AURA	60506	3137	37W-6S	C6
S Buell Av					
10	AURA	60506	3137	37W-7S	C7
200	AURA	60506	3199	37W-7S	C1
W Buell Av					
400	JLET	60435	3498	25W-23S	C4
Buell Ct					
1200	JLET	60435	3498	25W-23S	B4
9900	OKLN	60453	3211	6W-11S	D7
10100	OKLN	60453	3275	6W-11S	D1
N Buell Ct					
100	AURA	60506	3137	37W-7S	C6
Buell Dr					
-	NPVL	60540	3140	28W-7S	E7
Buell Rd					
10	OswT	60543	3262	39W-13S	E5
10	OswT	60560	3262	39W-13S	E5
W Buell St					
25200	CNHN	60410	3672	31W-30S	E4
Buena Av					
-	FXLK	60081	2414	29W-39N	D4
7100	BtnT	60081	2414	29W-39N	D6
25000	LkvT	60046	2416	25W-38N	B7
W Buena Av					
600	CHCG	60613	2977	1W-5N	E1
600	CHCG	60613	2978	0W-5N	A1
Buena Rd					
400	LKFT	60045	2649	11W-25N	E6
1100	LKFT	60035	2649	10W-24N	E7
3300	HDPK	60035	2650	10W-24N	A7
3300	LKFT	60035	2650	10W-24N	A7
3300	LKFT	60045	2650	10W-24N	A7
Buena Ter					
-	ANTH	60002	2357	23W-41N	E7
Buena Vista Av					
1600	CHHT	60411	3596	1W-25S	A1
Buena Vista Blvd					
-	RNPK	60443	3593	7W-27S	C4
Buena Vista Cir					
1600	CHHT	60411	3596	1W-26S	A1
Buena Vista Ct					
800	RLKB	60073	2474	24W-34N	D7
Buena Vista Dr					
100	GNEN	60137	3083	23W-1S	A2
100	MltT	60137	3083	22W-1S	C2
300	GNEN	60187	3083	23W-1S	A2
300	WHTN	60187	3083	23W-1S	A2
1300	WHTN	60187	3082	23W-1S	E2
5700	CLLK	60014	2639	37W-26N	B3
5700	DrrT	60014	2639	37W-26N	B3
N Buesching Rd					
10	LKZH	60047	2699	23W-23N	A3
S Buesching Rd					
10	LKZH	60047	2699	23W-22N	A3
W Buesching Rd					
22300	LKZH	60047	2699	23W-22N	A4
Buffalo Av					
300	CTCY	60409	3352	3E-17S	A5
1300	CTCY	60409	3430	3E-19S	A2
S Buffalo Av					
8200	CHCG	60617	3216	4E-9S	A3
10600	CHCG	60617	3280	3E-12S	A3
13000	CHCG	60633	3280	3E-15S	A7
13100	CHCG	60633	3352	3E-15S	A1
Buffalo Cir					
700	CLSM	60188	2967	27W-3N	C6
Buffalo Dr					
-	PltT	60124	2852	39W-10N	E6
700	MNKA	60447	3583	33W-28S	C6
Buffalo St					
1200	JLET	60433	3587	22W-25S	C1
1200	JltT	60433	3587	22W-25S	C1
Buffalo Tr					
400	WLNG	60090	2754	16W-17N	D5
1100	BTVA	60510	3078	34W-2S	D5
1100	BtvT	60510	3078	34W-2S	D5
Buffalo Creek Dr					
800	LKZH	60047	2699	22W-22N	B5
N Buffalo Grove Rd					
-	ANHT	60090	2754	16W-17N	C6
-	VrnT	60069	2701	16W-23N	D2
-	VrnT	60089	2701	17W-22N	C4
-	WLNG	60090	2754	16W-17N	C5
600	BFGV	60089	2701	16W-23N	D2
1600	BFGV	60069	2701	17W-21N	C5
2700	ANHT	60004	2754	16W-17N	C6
3300	BFGV	60089	2754	16W-17N	C6
3300	WhlT	60004	2754	16W-17N	C6
3500	WhlT	60089	2754	16W-17N	C6
16600	BFGV	60061	2701	16W-23N	D1
16600	VNHL	60061	2701	16W-23N	D2
23700	VNHL	60069	2701	16W-23N	D1
23700	VrnT	60061	2701	16W-23N	D1
N Buffalo Grove Rd CO-W14					
-	VrnT	60089	2701	17W-22N	C4
10	BFGV	60089	2754	17W-20N	C1
600	BFGV	60089	2701	17W-21N	C5
1600	BFGV	60069	2701	17W-21N	C5
1600	VrnT	60069	2701	17W-22N	C5
S Buffalo Grove Rd					
-	WhlT	60004	2754	16W-17N	C4
10	BFGV	60089	2754	16W-18N	D4
10	WLNG	60089	2754	16W-18N	C2
100	WLNG	60090	2754	16W-18N	D3
800	WhlT	60089	2754	16W-17N	C4
N Buffalo Run St					
20700	KLDR	60047	2699	21W-20N	D7
Bugle Ct					
900	RLKB	60073	2475	21W-36N	C4
Bugle Ln					
900	RLKB	60073	2475	21W-36N	D4
Buhl Rd					
4400	NndT	60014	2585	31W-27N	E7
4400	PRGV	60014	2585	31W-27N	E7
4500	NndT	60014	2641	31W-27N	E1
4500	PRGV	60014	2641	31W-27N	E1
Builders Ct					
3700	LitT	53147	2349		E1
Bulger Av					
16700	HLCT	60428	3427	2W-20S	C4
16700	HLCT	60429	3427	2W-20S	C4
16700	MKHM	60428	3427	2W-20S	C4
Bulger Ct					
-	WNVL	60555	3141	27W-4S	C2
Buli Ln					
200	BGBK	60490	3267	26W-12S	E3
200	BGBK	60490	3268	26W-12S	A2
Bull Creek Ct					
38400	BHPK	60087	2422	10W-38N	A7
38400	BHPK	60099	2422	10W-38N	A7
Bull Creek Dr					
-	LYVL	60048	2590	18W-30N	E2
1200	LbvT	60048	2591	18W-30N	A1
1300	LbvT	60048	2590	18W-30N	E1
Bulldog Dr					
7600	SMMT	60501	3148	9W-6S	C3
S Bulletin Ct					
5100	HMND	46320	3352		D6
Bullfrog Rd					
-	SYHW	60118	2800	35W-15N	C3
Bullock Dr					
100	HDPK	60037	2704	8W-23N	E2
Bull Ridge Dr					
1700	McHT	60050	2526	36W-33N	D2
W Bull Ridge Dr					
12800	HTLY	60142	2744	41W-20N	C1
Bull Run Ct					
600	NPVL	60540	3203	27W-8S	C1
Bull Run Dr					
-	RMVL	60446	3341	23W-15S	A2
2600	AURA	60503	3265	32W-11S	B1
Bull Run Tr					
8000	DrrT	60098	2583	37W-29N	B3
Bull Valley Dr					
1100	WDSK	60098	2582	39W-30N	C2
Bull Valley Rd					
-	BLVY	60098	2582	39W-31N	B1
-	WDSK	60098	2582	39W-30N	B1
3000	NndT	60050	2528	32W-31N	B7
4000	MHRY	60050	2528	33W-31N	A7
4200	MHRY	60050	2527	34W-31N	B7
4600	NndT	60050	2527	34W-31N	B7
6100	BLVY	60050	2526	36W-31N	D7
6100	NndT	60050	2526	35W-31N	E7
7400	BLVY	60098	2526	38W-31N	A7
9300	BLVY	60098	2525	38W-31N	D7
10000	DrrT	60098	2525	39W-31N	B7
Bull Valley Rd CO-A32					
4000	MHRY	60050	2528	33W-31N	A7
4000	NndT	60050	2528	32W-31N	A7
4200	MHRY	60050	2527	33W-31N	E7
4600	NndT	60050	2527	33W-31N	E7
Bulrush Dr					
1600	HFET	60169	2858	25W-11N	B3
Bumble Bee Dr					
9200	MaiT	60016	2863	11W-11N	D3
Bundleflower Ct					
5300	NPVL	60564	3266	29W-13S	C5
Bundoran Ct					
13200	PlsT	60462	3345	11W-15S	E1
Bundoran Dr					
9200	PlsT	60462	3345	11W-15S	E1
Bunescu Ct					
1500	BFGV	60089	2700	18W-21N	E7
Bunescu Ln					
1500	BFGV	60089	2700	18W-21N	E7
Bunker Av					
1300	FSMR	60422	3507	3W-23S	B3
Bunker Cir					
2000	NPVL	60563	3140	30W-5S	B2
2000	NpvT	60563	3140	30W-5S	B2
Bunker Ct					
700	RVWD	60015	2703	13W-20N	A7
1600	GNVA	60134	3020	36W-0N	A6
E Bunker Ct					
400	VNHL	60061	2647	16W-25N	D5
Bunker Dr					
8000	ODPK	60462	3346	10W-18S	C6
Bunker Ln					
1300	CPVL	60110	2801	33W-17N	C1
4000	WLMT	60091	2811	7W-14N	B5
8800	CLLK	60014	2639	37W-26N	A3
8800	DrrT	60014	2639	37W-26N	A3
Bunker Rd					
100	BbyT	60119	3018	40W-0S	B6
600	BbyT	60119	3076	41W-1S	A2
600	BbyT	60510	3076	41W-1S	A2
7300	DRN	60561	3207	17W-8S	C1
Bunker Rd CO-16					
100	BbyT	60119	3018	40W-0S	B6
600	BbyT	60119	3076	41W-1S	A2
600	BbyT	60510	3076	41W-1S	A2
Bunker St					
500	WDSK	60098	2581	41W-30N	D2
1900	CHHT	60411	3595	2W-26S	D2
Bunker Ter					
200	BmdT	60143	2969	21W-5N	E1
Bunker Hill Av					
10	SEGN	60177	2908	35W-8N	B3
Bunker Hill Cir					
300	AURA	60504	3140	30W-7S	A7
6700	DRGV	60516	3144	20W-7S	A7
Bunker Hill Ct					
10	ALGN	60102	2693	37W-20N	B7
500	MDLN	60060	2646	19W-27N	C2
600	NPVL	60540	3203	27W-8S	C1
1100	WHTN	60187	3082	23W-2S	E3
Bunker Hill Dr					
200	BGBK	60440	3268	24W-12S	E2
1600	JLET	60435	3497	27W-21S	C1
2500	ALGN	60102	2693	37W-20N	B7
4300	ALGN	60102	2692	38W-21N	E6
Bunning Dr					
400	DRGV	60516	3144	19W-6S	D4
400	WTMT	60516	3144	19W-6S	D4
Bunny Av					
5600	McHT	60050	2472	29W-37N	C1
Bunratty Dr					
-	LKPT	60441	3342	21W-17S	A6
Bunratty Ln					
4200	JLET	60586	3416	29W-21S	E7
Bunting Cir					
10	BGBK	60440	3205	21W-10S	D5
Bunting Ct					
200	VrnT	60015	2755	14W-20N	B1
700	WCHI	60185	2966	29W-3N	D5
Bunting Ln					
10	NPVL	60565	3203	26W-8S	E2
10	NPVL	60565	3204	26W-8S	A2
200	BMDL	60108	2969	23W-4N	A3
W Bunting Ln					
600	ANHT	60004	2807	16W-14N	E4
600	MPPT	60004	2807	16W-14N	E4
600	MPPT	60056	2807	16W-14N	E4
Buoy Ct					
100	LKBN	60010	2643	28W-24N	A7
100	LKBN	60010	2697	28W-24N	A1
Bur Ln					
5800	NndT	60014	2641	32W-26N	C3
6000	AlqT	60014	2641	32W-26N	B4
Burbank Av					
200	WDSK	60098	2581	41W-30N	D2
Burbank St					
2400	JLET	60435	3417	27W-20S	D5
2400	LktT	60403	3417	27W-20S	D5
2400	PnfT	60403	3417	27W-20S	D5
2400	PnfT	60435	3417	27W-20S	D5
E Burbank St					
100	HRVD	60033	2406	50W-38N	B6
W Burbank St					
100	HRVD	60033	2406	50W-38N	A6
Burberry Cir					
10	SMBG	60173	2859	22W-10N	C6
Burberry Ln					
1400	SMBG	60173	2859	21W-10N	E5
Burch Dr					
16200	LKPT	60441	3420	20W-19S	B3
Burchell Av					
200	HIWD	60040	2704	9W-23N	C2
700	HDPK	60035	2704	9W-23N	C2
Bur Dent Dr					
10	CLLK	60014	2640	35W-26N	A3
Burdett Av					
400	BmdT	60137	3025	23W-2N	A1
400	BmdT	60148	3025	21W-2N	E1
400	BmdT	60188	3024	23W-2N	E1
400	BmdT	60188	3025	23W-2N	A1
700	GLHT	60139	3024	23W-2N	E1
700	GLHT	60188	3024	23W-2N	E1
Burdette Av					
200	BmdT	60188	3023	26W-2N	E1
600	BmdT	60139	3025	22W-2N	C1
600	GLHT	60139	3025	22W-2N	C1
Burdette Ct					
1200	GLHT	60139	3025	22W-2N	D1
Burdick Rd					
24800	PNFD	60585	3338	31W-15S	A3
Burdick St					
300	LYVL	60048	2591	16W-28N	C6
Burger Av					
1300	JLET	60433	3587	22W-25S	D1
1300	JltT	60433	3587	22W-25S	D1
Burgess Cir					
800	BFGV	60089	2701	18W-20N	A7
Burgess Ct					
600	SMBG	60194	2857	28W-12N	B1
Burgess Dr					
10	GLHT	60139	2968	23W-4N	E4
900	ElgT	60124	2853	38W-10N	B5
5100	JLET	60586	3416	30W-21S	B7
Burgess Pl					
3400	DRN	60561	3206	20W-9S	A4
Burgess Rd					
10	GNVA	60134	3020	36W-1N	A4
Burgess Hill Rd					
600	NPVL	60565	3203	27W-8S	B2
Burgett Rd					
9400	HbnT	60034	2351	38W-43N	E5
9400	HbnT	60034	2352	38W-43N	A5
9400	HbnT	60071	2352	38W-43N	A5
W Burgett Rd					
7200	HbnT	60034	2352	37W-43N	C5
7200	HbnT	60071	2352	37W-43N	C5
7200	RcmT	60071	2352	37W-43N	C5
N Burgoyne Rd					
1000	ANHT	60004	2806	18W-15N	E2
W Burgoyne Rd					
1200	ANHT	60004	2806	18W-15N	D2
Burgundy Ct					
600	EGVV	60007	2860	19W-9N	C7
600	OSWG	60543	3262	39W-11S	D1
Burgundy Dr					
16000	PNFD	60586	3416	30W-19S	C3
21300	FKFT	60423	3592	11W-25S	A1
Burgundy Ln					
1100	AURA	60505	3138	34W-6S	D4
2400	NHBK	60062	2810	10W-15N	A1
18000	HLCT	60429	3426	4W-21S	E6
Burgundy Pkwy					
1500	SMBG	60193	2857	27W-10N	D6
1500	SMWD	60107	2857	27W-10N	D6
1500	SMWD	60193	2857	27W-10N	D6
Burgundy Pl					
4400	LSLE	60532	3142	24W-4S	C1
Burham Ln					
-	OSWG	60543	3263	36W-12S	E4
Burham St					
11100	HTLY	60142	2744	42W-20N	B1
E Buried Oak Dr					
3100	CteT	60417	3598	4E-29S	B7
Burk Av					
500	WNVL	60555	3080	28W-3S	E6
Burke Ct					
200	SMBG	60193	2859	22W-10N	C6
1000	NPVL	60563	3140	30W-5S	B3
2800	WDRG	60517	3143	22W-7S	D7
9900	FftT	60448	3503	12W-24S	D4
9900	MKNA	60448	3503	12W-24S	D4
Burke Dr					
300	CLSM	60188	2967	26W-4N	E4
300	CLSM	60188	2968	25W-4N	B4
400	JltT	60433	3499	21W-24S	E6
2000	WPHR	60096	2363	10W-41N	B7
N Burke Dr					
1900	ANHT	60004	2807	17W-16N	B1
2000	ANHT	60004	2754	17W-16N	B7
Burke Ln					
-	BTVA	60510	3078	34W-3S	D5
1200	SEGN	60177	2908	36W-9N	A2
1500	ELGN	60123	2908	36W-9N	A2
1500	ELGN	60177	2908	36W-9N	A2
Burkhardt Ct					
300	FTPK	60130	3030	9W-0N	D5
W Burkhardt Dr					
2800	CHCG	60623	3032	3W-1S	E7
Burkhart Dr					
10	OswT	60543	3264	35W-12S	B3
W Burkhart Ln					
26800	FXLK	60041	2530	26W-34N	C1
26800	GrtT	60041	2530	26W-34N	C1
26800	VOLO	60041	2530	26W-34N	C1
W Burkitt Pl					
700	ANHT	60004	2753	18W-18N	E2
Burl Ct					
20600	JLET	60433	3500	20W-24S	B6
20600	NlxT	60433	3500	20W-24S	B6
Burleigh Ln					
100	IVNS	60067	2752	22W-18N	B4
S Burley Av					
-	CHCG	60617	3280	3E-12S	A3
8200	CHCG	60617	3216	4E-9S	A3
12300	CHCG	60633	3280	3E-14S	A6
13100	CHCG	60633	3352	3E-15S	A1
S Burley Av US-41					
8500	CHCG	60617	3216	4E-9S	A3
Burling Rd					
10	RVSD	60546	3088	9W-3S	C5

Block	City	ZIP	Map#	CGS	Grid
N Burling St					
1300	CHCG	60610	3034	0W-1N	A1
2400	CHCG	60614	2978	0W-3N	A5
2800	CHCG	60657	2978	0W-3N	A4
Burlington Av					
-	DRGV	60559	3144	18W-5S	E2
-	WTMT	60559	3144	18W-5S	E2
10	CNHL	60514	3145	16W-5S	D2
10	CNHL	60521	3145	16W-5S	D2
10	LGNG	60525	3087	13W-4S	A7
10	LslT	60563	3141	26W-5S	E3
10	WNSP	60525	3087	13W-4S	A7
10	WNSP	60558	3086	13W-4S	E7
10	WNSP	60558	3087	13W-4S	A7
300	DRGV	60515	3144	18W-5S	E2
300	LSLE	60515	3142	24W-5S	C3
300	LslT	60563	3142	24W-5S	C3
400	NPVL	60563	3142	25W-5S	B3
500	WTMT	60559	3145	17W-5S	B2
900	LSLE	60532	3143	23W-5S	A2
1000	WNSP	60558	3146	14W-4S	D1
1600	LSLE	60532	3142	23W-5S	E2
2200	DRGV	60515	3143	21W-5S	D2
2400	LslT	60515	3143	21W-5S	E2
2700	LSLE	60515	3143	21W-5S	D2
8800	BKFD	60513	3088	11W-3S	A6
8900	BKFD	60513	3087	11W-4S	D6
E Burlington Av					
10	LGNG	60525	3087	12W-4S	C7
10	WTMT	60559	3145	17W-5S	B2
200	CNHL	60514	3145	17W-5S	B2
W Burlington Av					
10	LGNG	60525	3087	12W-4S	B7
10	WTMT	60559	3145	18W-5S	A2
300	DRGV	60515	3145	18W-5S	A2
300	WTMT	60515	3145	18W-5S	A2
400	DRGV	60515	3144	18W-5S	E2
400	DRGV	60559	3144	18W-5S	E2
400	WTMT	60515	3144	18W-5S	E2
400	WTMT	60559	3144	18W-5S	E2
Burlington Ln					
-	UNON	60180	2635	46W-24N	C6
Burlington Rd					
10	CmpT	60124	2905	43W-7N	B5
10	CmpT	60151	2905	43W-7N	B5
10	CmpT	60175	2905	41W-6N	E6
10	CmpT	60175	2962	40W-5N	B2
10	PltT	60124	2905	41W-6N	E6
10	PltT	60151	2905	41W-6N	E6
100	BrlT	60140	2795	48W-13N	A7
100	CmpT	60175	2906	41W-6N	A7
100	HshT	60140	2795	48W-13N	A7
400	PltT	60140	2905	41W-6N	E6
Burlington Rd CO-2					
10	CmpT	60124	2905	43W-7N	B5
10	CmpT	60151	2905	43W-7N	B5
10	CmpT	60175	2905	41W-6N	E6
10	CmpT	60175	2962	40W-5N	B2
10	PltT	60124	2905	41W-6N	E6
10	PltT	60151	2905	41W-6N	E6
100	CmpT	60175	2906	41W-6N	A7
400	PltT	60140	2905	41W-6N	E6
Burlington Rd CO-46					
100	BrlT	60140	2795	48W-13N	A7
100	HshT	60140	2795	48W-13N	A7
N Burlington Rd					
11300	RcmT	60071	2353	34W-43N	C4
11300	RHMD	60071	2353	34W-43N	C4
11400	RdlT	53181	2353	34W-43N	C4
11400	TNLK	53128	2353	34W-43N	C4
11400	TNLK	53181	2353	34W-43N	C4
11400	TNLK	60071	2353	34W-43N	C4
N Burlington Rd CO-V33					
11300	RcmT	60071	2353	34W-43N	C4
11300	RHMD	60071	2353	34W-43N	C4
11400	RdlT	53181	2353	34W-43N	C4
11400	TNLK	53128	2353	34W-43N	C4
11400	TNLK	53181	2353	34W-43N	C4
11400	TNLK	60071	2353	34W-43N	C4
E Burlington St					
10	RVSD	60546	3088	9W-3S	D5
300	BRWN	60402	3088	9W-3S	D5
300	BRWN	60546	3088	9W-3S	D5
W Burlington St					
100	BKFD	60513	3088	10W-3S	B5
100	BKFD	60546	3088	10W-3S	B5
100	RVSD	60546	3088	10W-3S	B5
Burlwood Ct					
400	RchT	60443	3593	8W-26S	B2
Burman Dr					
4600	AlqT	60014	2640	33W-25N	D4
4800	CLLK	60014	2640	33W-25N	D4
Burn Rdg					
-	ElgT	60123	2799	38W-14N	A6
-	RtdT	60123	2799	38W-13N	A7
-	RtdT	60124	2799	38W-14N	A6
Burnell Ct					
1800	BTVA	60510	3078	34W-3S	D5
Burnet Rd					
24600	HNWD	60047	2645	22W-24N	C7
Burnett Av					
-	BtnT	60099	2422	8W-41N	E2
-	ZION	60099	2422	8W-41N	E2
10	LKVL	60046	2475	23W-37N	A1
Burnett Dr					
1300	AURA	60502	3139	31W-5S	E3
E Burnett Rd					
100	ISLK	60042	2586	28W-28N	E5
200	WcnT	60042	2586	28W-29N	E5
800	ISLK	60042	2587	28W-29N	A5
800	WcnT	60042	2587	28W-29N	A5
W Burnett Rd					
-	NndT	60051	2586	29W-29N	C5
100	ISLK	60042	2586	29W-29N	C5
300	NndT	60042	2586	29W-29N	D5
Burnette Dr					
10	ANTH	60002	2358	23W-42N	A6
Burnham Av					
100	BNHM	60409	3352	3E-18S	B7
100	BNHM	60633	3352	3E-18S	B7
100	CTCY	60409	3352	3E-17S	B6
900	CTCY	60409	3430	4E-21S	B6
1500	LNSG	60438	3430	4E-19S	B3
18700	LNSG	60438	3510	3E-24S	B6
19300	LNSG	60411	3510	4E-22S	B2
19400	LYWD	60411	3510	4E-23S	B2
20300	BlmT	60411	3510	4E-24S	B5
21100	BlmT	60411	3598	3E-27S	B5
22300	SLVL	60411	3598	3E-27S	B5
22900	CteT	60417	3598	3E-27S	B5
S Burnham Av					
-	BNHM	60409	3352	4E-16S	B4
-	CTCY	60409	3352	4E-16S	B4
7800	CHCG	60617	3215	3E-8S	E1
7900	CHCG	60649	3215	3E-9S	E2
13800	BNHM	60633	3352	4E-16S	B4

Block	City	ZIP	Map#	CGS	Grid
S Burnham Av					
13800	CHCG	60633	3352	3E-16S	B2
Burnham Ct					
800	AURA	60502	3139	32W-6S	C5
900	GNVW	60025	2810	9W-13N	B6
1100	MDLN	60060	2646	19W-27N	B1
2000	ALGN	60102	2746	35W-20N	E1
2000	ALGN	60102	2747	35W-20N	A1
10600	WldT	60564	3266	30W-12S	A3
Burnham Dr					
-	HFET	60010	2804	24W-15N	B1
500	UYPK	60466	3684	3W-29S	B2
4500	HFET	60192	2804	24W-15N	B1
Burnham Ln					
700	BTVA	60510	3078	34W-2S	D4
E Burnham Ln					
10	BbyT	60134	3076	39W-1S	E1
W Burnham Ln					
10	BbyT	60134	3076	39W-0S	E1
Burnham Pl					
100	EVTN	60202	2867	2W-10N	C4
2000	WHTN	60187	3082	25W-2S	B4
Burnham St					
1100	CLSM	60188	2968	25W-4N	A4
5100	LSLE	60563	3142	25W-5S	C3
5100	LslT	60563	3142	25W-5S	C3
Burnidge Ct					
300	SEGN	60177	2908	34W-9N	E1
Burning Tr					
10	MltT	60187	3082	26W-2S	A4
700	CLSM	60188	2967	27W-3N	C5
1500	WHTN	60187	3082	26W-1S	A2
Burning Bush					
-	AntT	60002	2358		D4
-	BtlT	53104	2358		D4
-	BtlT	60002	2358		D4
S Burning Bush Ct					
13800	HMGN	60491	3343	16W-16S	E3
Burning Bush Dr					
500	YKVL	60560	3333	43W-16S	A4
Burning Bush Ln					
-	PTHT	60070	2808	13W-15N	E1
1500	HFET	60192	2804	24W-15N	B2
N Burning Bush Ln					
800	MPPT	60056	2808	13W-14N	E5
800	WhlT	60056	2808	13W-13N	E5
1800	PTHT	60056	2808	13W-15N	E2
1800	PTHT	60070	2808	13W-15N	E2
Burning Bush Tr					
10	CLLK	60012	2640	35W-27N	B2
10	NndT	60012	2640	35W-27N	B1
Burning Oak Dr					
200	DndT	60118	2747	36W-17N	A7
200	WDND	60118	2747	36W-17N	A7
Burning Oak Tr					
10	BNHL	60010	2695	30W-22N	E4
10	BNHL	60010	2696	30W-22N	A4
1500	AlqT	60010	2696	30W-22N	A5
Burning Trail Ct					
1600	WHTN	60187	3082	25W-1S	A2
Burning Tree Cir					
6500	MHRY	60050	2526	35W-32N	E4
6500	MHRY	60050	2527	35W-32N	A4
Burning Tree Ct					
1500	LSLE	60532	3082	23W-4S	E7
1500	LSLE	60532	3083	22W-4S	B7
E Burning Tree Ct					
1600	ANHT	60004	2754	16W-17N	C5
1600	WLNG	60090	2754	16W-17N	C5
N Burning Tree Ct					
21700	KLDR	60047	2699	22W-21N	B5
Burning Tree Dr					
7100	MHRY	60050	2526	36W-32N	D4
7500	MchT	60050	2526	36W-32N	D4
7500	MchT	60098	2526	36W-32N	D4
Burning Tree Ln					
10	DRFD	60015	2756	11W-20N	D2
500	NPVL	60563	3141	27W-5S	B3
E Burning Tree Ln					
400	ANHT	60004	2754	17W-17N	B5
W Burning Tree Ln					
400	ANHT	60004	2753	18W-17N	E5
Burning Tree Rd					
10	RGMW	60008	2806	20W-13N	A6
Burnley Cir					
400	SMBG	60193	2859	22W-10N	B6
Burnley Dr					
11600	ODPK	60467	3344	14W-16S	D4
S Burno Dr					
400	PLTN	60067	2805	21W-15N	D2
Burns Av					
600	FSMR	60422	3507	3W-22S	B2
600	HMWD	60430	3507	3W-22S	B2
1600	WSTR	60154	3086	13W-1S	E1
Burns Dr					
1300	ELGN	60120	2855	31W-10N	D6
Burns St					
-	PLNO	60545	3259	47W-12S	D4
500	CLSM	60188	3024	24W-1N	D2
500	MltT	60188	3024	24W-1N	D2
S Burnside Av					
9100	CHCG	60619	3214	0E-10S	D5
Burnside Cir					
200	BRLT	60103	2911	28W-7N	A5
Burnside Ct					
-	NLNX	60451	3501	17W-24S	D5
100	VNHL	60061	2647	17W-26N	C4
700	AURA	60504	3201	31W-8S	E2
19900	OMFD	60461	3506	4W-24S	D4
Burnside Wy					
2500	WKGN	60087	2480	10W-36N	B4
2500	WkgT	60087	2480	10W-36N	B3
S Burnside Station Dr					
18700	MKNA	60448	3503	11W-22S	E2
Burnt Ember Ct					
10	BFGV	60089	2754	17W-20N	A1
Burnt Ember Ln					
300	BFGV	60089	2701	17W-21N	C7
300	BFGV	60089	2754	17W-20N	A1
Bur Oak Ct					
900	CLLK	60014	2641	32W-24N	A6
Burr Av					
700	WNKA	60093	2811	5W-16N	E1
700	WNKA	60093	2812	5W-16N	A1
800	WNKA	60093	2759	5W-16N	A7
Burr Ct					
-	BtlT	60560	3262	40W-13S	C4
Burr Rd					
10	SchT	60175	2907	38W-6N	B7
10	SchT	60175	2963	38W-5N	A2
900	SchT	60177	2907	38W-6N	B7
900	SEGN	60177	2907	38W-6N	B7
Burr St					
200	MchT	60050	2472	29W-37N	D2
1000	LIHL	60156	2694	35W-22N	B4
2500	BtlT	60560	3262	40W-13S	C5

Block	City	ZIP	Map#	CGS	Grid
Burr Hollow Dr					
19500	AntT	60002	2359	19W-41N	C7
Burridge Ct					
900	LYVL	60048	2591	17W-28N	C5
Burris Av					
700	ShdT	60044	2593	12W-29N	A4
3000	WKGN	60087	2479	12W-36N	B4
Burris Ct					
10	PSHT	60463	3275	8W-14S	B6
Burr Oak Av					
200	DRFD	60015	2756	11W-20N	D1
2000	BLID	60406	3277	3W-14S	B7
2000	BLID	60827	3277	3W-14S	B7
2000	CTPK	60406	3277	3W-14S	B7
2000	CTPK	60827	3277	3W-14S	B7
2200	FTPK	60130	3088	9W-2S	C2
2200	NRIV	60546	3088	9W-2S	C2
2500	RVSD	60546	3088	9W-2S	C2
3000	ALSP	60406	3276	4W-15S	D7
3000	BLID	60406	3276	4W-15S	D7
3300	WthT	60406	3276	4W-15S	E7
3500	ALSP	60803	3276	4W-15S	D7
5800	BKLY	60163	3028	14W-0N	C4
W Burr Oak Av					
1600	CTPK	60827	3277	2W-15S	C7
1700	BLID	60406	3277	2W-14S	D7
1700	CTPK	60406	3277	2W-15S	C7
1900	BLID	60827	3277	2W-14S	C7
Burr Oak Av E					
-	ELGN	60120	2855	32W-10N	C7
Burr Oak Av S					
-	ELGN	60120	2855	32W-10N	C7
Burr Oak Cir					
300	CRY	60013	2642	30W-24N	A7
1400	AURA	60506	3137	37W-5S	C3
Burr Oak Ct					
-	SMWD	60107	2856	30W-9N	C7
10	LKZH	60047	2699	22W-22N	B3
100	DRFD	60015	2756	11W-20N	D2
400	NPVL	60540	3141	28W-7S	A6
900	OKBK	60523	3086	15W-1S	B1
1300	MchT	60050	2526	36W-33N	C3
1400	HNDL	60521	3086	15W-3S	B5
1500	WHTN	60187	3081	26W-1S	C2
2000	RDLK	60073	2531	25W-33N	A2
13100	PSHT	60463	3347	7W-15S	B1
Burr Oak Dr					
10	CLLK	60014	2639	37W-25N	B4
10	LKZH	60047	2699	22W-22N	A3
100	MltT	60137	3083	22W-3S	C5
400	OSWG	60543	3262	39W-12S	E2
400	OSWG	60543	3263	39W-12S	A3
700	WTMT	60559	3085	17W-4S	B7
1300	GNVW	60025	2811	8W-14N	A3
1400	GNVW	60025	2810	8W-14N	E3
1600	GRNE	60048	2534	16W-32N	C6
3200	WKGN	60087	2478	14W-37N	C1
3300	WDWH	60083	2478	14W-37N	C1
3300	WKGN	60083	2478	14W-37N	C1
7600	MchT	60050	2526	36W-33N	D3
7600	MHRY	60050	2526	36W-33N	D3
16900	HMGN	60491	3422	15W-20S	B4
E Burr Oak Dr					
100	ANHT	60004	2754	17W-17N	B5
1300	MPPT	60056	2808	13W-14N	E4
1700	WLNG	60090	2754	17W-17N	C5
W Burr Oak Dr					
10	ANHT	60004	2754	17W-17N	A5
500	ANHT	60004	2753	18W-17N	E5
Burr Oak Dr E					
1900	GNVW	60025	2811	8W-14N	A4
Burr Oak Dr W					
1900	GNVW	60025	2810	8W-14N	E3
Burr Oak Ln					
10	DGvT	60527	3207	17W-10S	D5
10	SMBG	60193	2859	23W-10N	B6
200	SchT	60175	2907	38W-6N	A7
700	DndT	60118	2747	35W-18N	B4
700	PTHT	60070	2808	14W-14N	C3
700	UYPK	60466	3684	3W-29S	B2
1200	BRTN	60010	2751	24W-20N	B1
1800	LNHT	60046	2476	20W-37N	A1
1900	GLHT	60139	2969	23W-3N	A5
3300	ISLK	60042	2586	28W-28N	E6
3300	ISLK	60042	2587	28W-28N	A5
3300	ISLK	60051	2587	28W-28N	A5
7100	CTSD	60525	3147	12W-8S	B7
11400	BRRG	60527	3208	14W-8S	D2
17300	HLCT	60429	3426	4W-20S	E5
20000	MKNA	60448	3502	14W-24S	E5
N Burr Oak Ln					
38300	WDWH	60083	2420	14W-38N	D7
W Burr Oak Ln					
14300	WDWH	60083	2420	14W-38N	D6
21200	ElaT	60047	2699	21W-24N	D1
21200	KLDR	60047	2699	21W-24N	D1
Burr Oak Pl					
500	HNDL	60521	3086	15W-3S	B5
Burr Oak Rd					
-	LslT	60532	3142	23W-6S	E4
-	WnfT	60185	3023	28W-2N	B2
700	WynT	60185	3023	28W-1N	B2
1200	LKFT	60045	2649	10W-27N	E1
1400	HNDL	60521	3086	15W-3S	B5
1600	HMWD	60430	3427	2W-21S	D6
2300	NHFD	60093	2811	8W-15N	A2
5300	LSLE	60532	3142	23W-5S	E3
15300	FoxT	60545	3331	48W-15S	A2
15300	FoxT	60560	3331	48W-15S	A2
15300	LtRT	60545	3330	49W-15S	E2
15300	LtRT	60545	3331	48W-15S	A2
15300	LtRT	60560	3331	48W-15S	A2
Burr Oak St					
2100	HRPK	60133	2911	27W-8N	C3
Burr Oak Tr					
10	RVWD	60015	2702	13W-21N	E6
Burr Oaks Ct					
10	BGBK	60440	3205	22W-10S	D5
6300	FXLK	60020	2414	28W-39N	E5
W Burr Oaks Dr					
3200	JLET	60431	3497	28W-23S	B4
3200	JLET	60435	3497	28W-23S	B4
3200	TroT	60435	3497	28W-23S	B4
Burr Oaks Ln					
1900	HDPK	60035	2757	9W-20N	C1
Burrows Rd					
-	DhmT	60033	2464	49W-37N	C2
-	HRVD	60033	2464	49W-37N	C2
Burr Ridge Clb					
200	BRRG	60527	3146	15W-6S	C5
Burr Ridge Ct					
2500	WDRG	60517	3205	21W-9S	D3
Burr Ridge Dr					
1700	HFET	60192	2804	25W-14N	A4
S Burr Ridge Dr					
21900	TroT	60404	3584	30W-26S	B3

Block	City	ZIP	Map#	CGS	Grid
Burr Ridge Pkwy					
10	BRRG	60527	3208	14W-8S	C1
1000	BRRG	60527	3146	15W-7S	B7
Burry Ct					
1100	CTHL	60403	3418	25W-21S	C7
N Burry St					
1200	JLET	60435	3498	25W-22S	C1
1500	CTHL	60403	3498	25W-22S	C1
Burry Cir Dr					
1600	JLET	60435	3498	25W-21S	C1
1700	CTHL	60403	3418	25W-21S	C7
1900	CTHL	60403	3498	25W-21S	C1
Burshire Ct					
1800	JLET	60586	3415	33W-20S	A5
Burshire Dr					
1700	JLET	60586	3415	33W-21S	A7
1700	JLET	60586	3495	33W-21S	A1
Burside Ln					
200	SchT	60175	2907	38W-6N	B7
Burson St					
-	LtRT	60545	3259	47W-12S	D4
-	PLNO	60545	3259	47W-13S	D4
Burtis Av					
10	HDPK	60035	2704	9W-23N	D3
10	HIWD	60040	2704	9W-23N	D3
Burton Av					
-	AntT	60081	2414	28W-38N	D7
-	AntT	60081	2472	28W-38N	D1
-	GrtT	60081	2472	28W-37N	D1
10	CRY	60013	2695	31W-23N	E1
10	WKGN	60085	2536	11W-34N	D1
400	HDPK	60035	2758	7W-20N	B1
800	HDPK	60035	2705	7W-21N	A7
17000	LKPT	60441	3419	21W-20S	E5
17000	LKPT	60441	3420	21W-20S	A5
Burton Ct					
1500	AURA	60505	3139	33W-5S	A3
11500	WSTR	60154	3086	14W-2S	C3
E Burton Ct					
600	HMND	46394	3280		E5
W Burton Ct					
14200	GNOK	60048	2592	14W-31N	D1
Burton Dr					
200	BRLT	60103	2909	32W-8N	D4
500	LKFT	60045	2649	12W-26N	C2
700	BTVA	60510	3019	36W-0S	E7
11400	WSTR	60154	3086	14W-2S	D3
Burton Ln					
1800	PKRG	60068	2863	11W-10N	E4
E Burton Pl					
10	CHCG	60610	3034	0E-1N	C1
S Burton Pl					
100	ANHT	60005	2807	17W-13N	B5
W Burton Pl					
100	CHCG	60610	3034	0W-1N	B1
Burton Rd					
8300	WRLK	60097	2469	37W-35N	B5
Burton St					
200	GYLK	60030	2532	21W-33N	E3
Burton Ter					
900	GNVW	60025	2811	7W-14N	A5
Burton Tr					
3600	NndT	60012	2586	30W-28N	A6
3600	NndT	60014	2586	30W-28N	A6
E Burville Rd					
100	CteT	60417	3685	0E-30S	E3
100	CteT	60417	3686	1E-30S	B3
2000	CteT	60417	3687	3E-30S	A3
3200	SjnT	46311	3687	4E-30S	B2
W Burville Rd					
100	CRTE	60417	3685	0W-30S	C3
100	CteT	60417	3685	0W-30S	C3
Burwood Dr					
3500	WKGN	60085	2535	13W-32N	E6
3500	WKGN	60085	2536	13W-32N	A6
3500	WrnT	60085	2535	13W-32N	E6
Burwood Rd					
5300	NndT	60013	2641	31W-26N	D3
5300	ODHL	60013	2641	31W-26N	D3
Bury Ct					
10	SgrT	60506	3136	40W-5S	B3
Busch Pkwy					
900	BFGV	60089	2702	15W-21N	A5
1500	RVWD	60015	2702	14W-21N	B6
Busch Rd					
10	MltT	60137	3025	22W-1N	C2
Bush Blvd					
-	BGBK	60490	3339	27W-14S	C1
-	BGBK	60544	3339	27W-14S	C1
Bush Ct					
1600	LYVL	60048	2590	18W-30N	E2
W Bush Ct					
6000	MONE	60449	3682	7W-31S	D5
E Bush Dr					
100	ELWD	60421	3675	25W-31S	C7
100	JknT	60421	3675	25W-31S	B7
Bush Pl					
6400	DRGV	60516	3144	20W-7S	A6
S Bush Rd					
24800	ELWD	60421	3675	25W-30S	D3
24800	JknT	60421	3675	25W-30S	D3
24800	JLET	60421	3675	25W-30S	D3
Bush St					
600	JLET	60433	3499	23W-24S	A6
600	JltT	60433	3499	23W-24S	A6
800	LSLE	60532	3143	22W-4S	B1
Bush Tr					
2700	MHRY	60051	2528	31W-33N	D2
Bushrun Ct					
600	LKZH	60047	2699	22W-21N	B6
Bushthorn Dr					
100	ELWD	60421	3675	25W-31S	B6
Bushwood Dr					
2400	AURA	60506	3136	39W-5S	E3
2400	ELGN	60124	2799	37W-15N	E3
Business Pkwy					
5300	RGWD	60072	2470	34W-36N	D5
Business Center Dr					
-	BGBK	60440	3268	24W-13S	C4
E Business Center Dr					
400	MPPT	60056	2808	14W-13N	B6
W Business Center Dr					
13800	GNOK	60045	2592	13W-28N	D6
13800	GNOK	60048	2592	13W-28N	D6
13800	LbvT	60045	2592	13W-28N	D6
13800	LbvT	60048	2592	13W-28N	D6
E Busse Av					
-	DSPN	60016	2808	15W-12N	B7
10	MPPT	60056	2808	15W-12N	B7
N Busse Av					
5000	CHCG	60656	2918	8W-6N	E6
W Busse Av					
10	MPPT	60056	2808	15W-12N	A7
300	MPPT	60056	2807	16W-12N	E7
Busse Hwy					
10	PKRG	60068	2918	10W-9N	A1

Block	City	ZIP	Map#	CGS	Grid
Busse Hwy					
200	PKRG	60068	2864	10W-9N	A7
500	PKRG	60068	2863	10W-9N	E7
1700	DSPN	60016	2863	12W-10N	C5
Busse Ln					
-	LkvT	60046	2474	25W-37N	A2
Busse Rd					
10	EGVV	60007	2861	16W-9N	C7
10	MPPT	60005	2861	17W-10N	C6
10	MPPT	60056	2861	17W-10N	C6
600	EGvT	60007	2861	17W-9N	C7
900	EGVV	60007	2915	17W-8N	C3
1000	BNVL	60106	2915	16W-7N	C4
Busse Rd SR-83					
200	EGVV	60007	2861	16W-9N	C7
600	EGvT	60007	2861	17W-9N	C7
900	EGVV	60007	2915	17W-8N	C3
1000	BNVL	60106	2915	16W-7N	C4
S Busse Rd					
10	ANHT	60056	2807	16W-12N	C7
10	MPPT	60056	2807	16W-12N	C7
200	MPPT	60056	2861	16W-10N	C5
1700	EGvT	60056	2861	16W-10N	C5
2100	MPPT	60005	2861	16W-10N	C5
2200	EGVV	60007	2861	17W-10N	C6
Bussey Ct					
800	SMWD	60107	2911	27W-9N	C1
Bussey Dr					
22800	JLET	60586	3417	28W-19S	A4
22800	PNFD	60586	3417	28W-19S	A4
22800	PnfT	60586	3417	28W-19S	A4
23000	PNFD	60586	3416	28W-19S	E4
Butera Ln					
10	SBTN	60010	2803	26W-14N	C4
Butler Av					
3200	CHHT	60411	3596	0W-27S	B4
3200	SCHT	60411	3596	0W-27S	B4
3200	STGR	60411	3596	0W-27S	B4
3200	STGR	60475	3596	0W-27S	B4
Butler Ct					
10	ALGN	60102	2747	36W-18N	A4
1700	NPVL	60565	3204	24W-9S	C3
8800	ODPK	60462	3424	10W-18S	A1
N Butler Ct					
1400	VNHL	60061	2647	17W-26N	B2
S Butler Ct					
14100	LktT	60544	3340	26W-16S	A4
26900	CteT	60417	3774	0W-32S	D1
Butler Dr					
200	BRLT	60103	2909	32W-8N	C4
200	LKFT	60045	2649	10W-25N	E5
900	CLLK	60014	2639	37W-24N	B7
S Butler Dr					
-	CHCG	60628	3279	1E-14S	A6
12400	CHCG	60633	3279	1E-14S	A6
Butler Ln					
-	LkvT	60046	2417	21W-39N	E5
-	LNHT	60046	2417	21W-39N	E5
5700	LGGV	60047	2701	17W-23N	A2
S Butler Ln					
22600	FftT	60423	3591	13W-27S	B5
Butler Pl					
500	PKRG	60068	2918	10W-8N	B1
Butler St					
-	BlmT	60411	3509	1E-24S	B6
-	FDHT	60411	3509	1E-24S	B6
-	OSWG	60560	3334	39W-15S	E1
1600	CHHT	60411	3596	0W-25S	C1
2500	BlmT	60411	3596	0W-26S	C2
Butler Wk					
3300	AURA	60564	3201	31W-9S	E5
Butler Bay Ct					
1000	ELGN	60120	2855	32W-12N	D1
N Butrick St					
10	WKGN	60085	2536	11W-34N	E1
500	WKGN	60085	2479	11W-35N	E7
2600	WKGN	60087	2479	11W-37N	E3
S Butrick St					
10	WKGN	60085	2536	11W-34N	E2
Butte Ct					
10	NPVL	60540	3142	26W-6S	A5
Butte Ln					
200	CPVL	60110	2748	33W-17N	B6
Butter Creek Ct					
-	HFET	60169	2858	23W-11N	E3
Buttercup Ct					
2300	AURA	60506	3137	38W-6S	A5
13000	HMGN	60491	3344	16W-18S	A7
N Buttercup Ct					
100	PNFD	60544	3415	31W-18S	E1
Buttercup Ln					
10	YkTp	60181	3085	17W-1S	B1
100	MTSN	60443	3593	7W-26S	C2
100	SjnT	46311	3598		D5
300	OKTR	60181	3085	17W-1S	B1
400	SMBG	60173	2859	21W-10N	E4
1100	BRLT	60103	2910	29W-6N	D7
2300	CTHL	60403	3417	27W-21S	D6
5500	GRNE	60031	2535	15W-33N	A2
24800	MHTN	60442	3677	19W-30S	E3
Buttercup Pl					
500	SMBG	60173	2859	21W-11N	E3
Buttercup Bank					
100	BRRG	60527	3146	14W-6S	C5
Butterfield Cir					
1800	FSMR	60422	3507	3W-23S	B4
1800	FSMR	60461	3507	3W-23S	B4
1800	RchT	60461	3507	3W-23S	B4
Butterfield Cir E					
900	SRWD	60404	3496	29W-25S	D7
900	SRWD	60404	3584	31W-25S	A1
Butterfield Cir W					
900	SRWD	60404	3496	31W-25S	A7
900	SRWD	60404	3584	31W-25S	A1
Butterfield Ct					
100	LKZH	60047	2698	24W-23N	D2
100	RGMW	60008	2805	22W-13N	B5
400	HFET	60067	2804	23W-14N	E4
800	SRWD	60404	3496	31W-25S	A7
Butterfield Dr					
200	BMDL	60108	2968	24W-4N	C3
600	ALGN	60102	2694	34W-20N	C7
16700	CCHL	60478	3426	4W-20S	D3
16700	MKHM	60428	3426	4W-20S	D3
W Butterfield Dr					
10600	FftT	60423	3591	13W-27S	B5
Butterfield Ln					
300	LYVL	60048	2591	17W-28N	B5
1200	ZION	60099	2362	12W-41N	B7
1300	BtnT	60099	2421	12W-41N	B1
1300	ZION	60099	2421	12W-41N	B1
1700	FSMR	60422	3507	2W-23S	C4
1700	OMFD	60422	3507	2W-23S	C4
1700	OMFD	60461	3507	2W-23S	C4
8600	ODPK	60462	3346	11W-15S	A2

Block	City	ZIP	Map#	CGS	Grid
S Butterfield Ln					
900	RDLK	60073	2531	23W-32N	E6
W Butterfield Ln					
400	RDLK	60073	2531	23W-32N	E5
Butterfield Pkwy					
21200	MTSN	60443	3594	4W-25S	D1
Butterfield Rd					
-	GwdT	60098	2524	41W-32N	E5
-	LMBD	60515	3084	19W-2S	C4
-	WDSK	60098	2524	41W-32N	E5
-	WnfT	60563	3080	30W-3S	B6
-	YkTp	60515	3084	19W-2S	C4
10	AURA	60502	3079	32W-3S	B6
10	AURA	60510	3079	33W-3S	B6
10	BtvT	60502	3079	33W-3S	B6
10	DRGV	60137	3083	22W-2S	D4
10	DRGV	60515	3083	21W-2S	D4
10	LKZH	60047	2698	24W-23N	C2
10	MltT	60137	3083	22W-2S	C4
10	MltT	60187	3082	24W-3S	E5
10	MltT	60515	3083	22W-2S	D4
10	MltT	60555	3082	25W-3S	A5
10	OKTR	60181	3085	18W-1S	A2
10	WHTN	60187	3081	27W-2S	B4
10	WHTN	60187	3082	25W-3S	A5
10	WHTN	60187	3083	23W-2S	A4
10	WHTN	60555	3082	25W-3S	B5
10	WnfT	60185	3081	28W-2S	B4
10	WnfT	60510	3079	31W-3S	E6
10	WnfT	60555	3081	27W-2S	B4
10	WNVL	60555	3080	30W-3S	B6
10	WNVL	60555	3081	28W-2S	B4
10	WNVL	60563	3080	30W-3S	B6
100	AraT	60510	3078	35W-4S	C7
100	AraT	60542	3078	35W-4S	C7
100	INCK	60061	2647	17W-25N	B6
100	MDLN	60060	2647	17W-25N	B5
100	MDLN	60061	2647	17W-25N	B6
100	MltT	60187	3081	27W-2S	B4
100	MltT	60187	3083	23W-2S	A4
100	MltT	60555	3081	27W-2S	B4
100	NARA	60510	3078	35W-4S	C7
100	NARA	60542	3078	35W-4S	C7
100	VNHL	60060	2647	17W-25N	B6
100	VNHL	60061	2647	17W-25N	B6
100	WNVL	60185	3081	28W-2S	A5
100	YkTp	60181	3085	18W-1S	A2
200	WHTN	60137	3083	23W-2S	A4
300	AURA	60563	3080	30W-3S	B6
300	WnfT	60510	3080	30W-3S	B6
300	WnfT	60555	3080	30W-3S	B6
500	DRGV	60148	3083	21W-2S	D4
500	LMBD	60148	3084	19W-2S	D3
500	MltT	60148	3083	21W-2S	D4
500	OKBK	60181	3085	18W-2S	A2
500	OKBK	60523	3085	17W-1S	B2
500	OKTR	60523	3085	17W-1S	B2
500	WHTN	60555	3081	27W-2S	B4
500	WnfT	60187	3081	27W-2S	B4
500	YkTp	60148	3084	19W-2S	D3
500	YkTp	60523	3084	19W-2S	D3
600	AraT	60502	3078	34W-4S	C7
600	AURA	60502	3078	35W-4S	C7
600	AURA	60510	3078	34W-3S	C7
600	NARA	60502	3078	34W-4S	C7
700	AURA	60502	3080	31W-3S	A6
700	AURA	60510	3080	31W-3S	A6
700	OKBK	60148	3084	19W-2S	D3
700	OKBK	60523	3084	19W-2S	D3
700	WnfT	60502	3080	31W-3S	A6
800	DRGV	60148	3084	21W-2S	A4
800	DRGV	60515	3084	20W-2S	B4
800	MltT	60148	3084	21W-2S	A4
800	MltT	60515	3084	21W-2S	A4
1500	FSMR	60422	3507	3W-23S	B4
2700	YkTp	60523	3085	18W-2S	A3
3300	BLWD	60104	3029	12W-0N	A4
3900	BLWD	60162	3029	12W-0N	A4
3900	HLSD	60162	3029	12W-0N	A4
4100	HLSD	60104	3029	13W-0N	A4
4300	BLWD	60104	3028	14W-0S	D5
4300	BLWD	60162	3028	14W-0S	D5
4300	HLSD	60162	3028	14W-0S	D5
5200	BKLY	60163	3028	14W-0S	C5
5200	HLSD	60163	3028	14W-0S	C5
5900	BKLY	60162	3028	14W-0S	C5
5900	EMHT	60162	3028	14W-0S	C6
6000	EMHT	60126	3028	14W-0S	B6
22300	RNPK	60471	3594	5W-27S	C4
Butterfield Rd CO-W11					
100	INCK	60061	2647	17W-25N	B6
100	MDLN	60060	2647	17W-25N	B6
100	MDLN	60061	2647	17W-25N	B6
100	VNHL	60060	2647	17W-25N	B6
100	VNHL	60061	2647	17W-25N	B6
Butterfield Rd SR-56					
-	WnfT	60563	3080	30W-3S	B6
10	AURA	60502	3079	32W-3S	B6
10	AURA	60510	3079	33W-3S	B6
10	BtvT	60502	3079	33W-3S	B6
10	DRGV	60137	3083	22W-2S	D4
10	DRGV	60515	3083	21W-2S	D4
10	MltT	60137	3083	22W-2S	C4
10	MltT	60187	3082	24W-3S	E5
10	MltT	60515	3083	22W-2S	D4
10	MltT	60555	3082	25W-3S	A5
10	OKTR	60181	3085	18W-1S	A2
10	WHTN	60187	3081	27W-2S	B4
10	WHTN	60187	3082	25W-3S	A5
10	WHTN	60187	3083	23W-2S	A4
10	WHTN	60555	3082	25W-3S	B5
10	WnfT	60185	3081	28W-2S	B4
10	WnfT	60510	3079	31W-3S	E6
10	WnfT	60555	3081	27W-2S	B4
10	WNVL	60555	3080	30W-3S	B6
10	WNVL	60555	3081	28W-2S	B4
100	AraT	60510	3078	35W-4S	C7
100	AraT	60542	3078	35W-4S	C7
100	MltT	60187	3081	27W-2S	B4
100	MltT	60187	3083	23W-2S	A4
100	MltT	60555	3081	27W-2S	B4
100	NARA	60510	3078	35W-4S	C7
100	NARA	60542	3078	35W-4S	C7
100	WNVL	60185	3081	28W-2S	A5
100	WNVL	60563	3080	30W-3S	B6
100	YkTp	60181	3085	18W-1S	A2
200	WHTN	60137	3083	23W-2S	A4
300	AURA	60563	3080	30W-3S	B6
400	WnfT	60555	3080	29W-3S	D6
500	DRGV	60148	3083	21W-2S	D4
500	LMBD	60148	3084	19W-2S	D3
500	MltT	60148	3083	21W-2S	D4
500	OKBK	60181	3085	18W-2S	A2
500	OKBK	60523	3085	17W-1S	B2
500	OKTR	60523	3085	17W-1S	B2
500	WHTN	60555	3081	27W-2S	B4

Block	City	ZIP	Map#	CGS	Grid
Butterfield Rd SR-56					
500	WnfT	60187	3081	27W-2S	B4
500	YkTp	60148	3084	19W-2S	D3
500	YkTp	60523	3084	19W-2S	D3
600	AraT	60502	3078	34W-4S	C7
600	AURA	60502	3078	35W-4S	C7
600	AURA	60510	3078	34W-3S	C7
600	NARA	60502	3078	34W-4S	C7
700	AURA	60502	3080	31W-3S	A6
700	AURA	60510	3080	31W-3S	A6
700	OKBK	60148	3084	19W-2S	D3
700	OKBK	60523	3084	19W-2S	D3
700	WnfT	60502	3080	31W-3S	A6
700	WnfT	60510	3080	30W-3S	A6
800	DRGV	60148	3084	21W-2S	A4
800	DRGV	60515	3084	20W-2S	B4
800	MltT	60148	3084	21W-2S	A4
800	MltT	60515	3084	21W-2S	A4
1000	LMBD	60515	3084	19W-2S	C4
2700	YkTp	60523	3085	18W-2S	A3
4000	BLWD	60104	3029	13W-0N	A4
4000	HLSD	60162	3029	13W-0N	A4
4100	HLSD	60104	3029	13W-0N	A4
4200	BLWD	60162	3029	13W-0N	A5
4300	BLWD	60104	3028	14W-0S	D5
4300	BLWD	60162	3028	14W-0S	D5
4300	HLSD	60162	3028	14W-0S	D5
5200	BKLY	60163	3028	14W-0S	C5
5200	HLSD	60163	3028	14W-0S	C5
5900	BKLY	60162	3028	14W-0S	C5
5900	EMHT	60162	3028	14W-0S	C6
6000	EMHT	60126	3028	14W-0S	B6
E Butterfield Rd					
-	LMBD	60148	3084	19W-2S	D3
100	EMHT	60126	3028	15W-0S	A6
500	BKLY	60162	3028	15W-0S	A6
500	BKLY	60163	3028	15W-0S	A6
500	EMHT	60162	3028	15W-0S	A6
E Butterfield Rd SR-56					
-	LMBD	60148	3084	19W-2S	D3
100	EMHT	60126	3028	15W-0S	A6
500	BKLY	60162	3028	15W-0S	A6
500	BKLY	60163	3028	15W-0S	A6
500	EMHT	60162	3028	15W-0S	A6
N Butterfield Rd					
100	LYVL	60048	2591	17W-29N	A4
500	MDLN	60060	2591	17W-29N	A4
600	LYVL	60060	2591	17W-29N	A4
1300	LbvT	60048	2591	17W-30N	A3
N Butterfield Rd CO-W11					
100	LYVL	60048	2591	17W-29N	A4
500	MDLN	60060	2591	17W-29N	A4
600	LYVL	60060	2591	17W-29N	A4
1300	LbvT	60048	2591	17W-30N	A3
S Butterfield Rd					
-	LbvT	60060	2591	17W-28N	B7
-	LbvT	60061	2591	17W-27N	B7
-	MDLN	60060	2591	17W-27N	B7
-	MDLN	60061	2591	17W-27N	B7
-	VNHL	60061	2591	17W-28N	B7
100	LYVL	60048	2591	17W-28N	B6
400	MDLN	60060	2647	17W-25N	B4
400	MDLN	60061	2647	17W-25N	B4
400	VNHL	60061	2647	17W-25N	B4
900	VNHL	60060	2647	17W-26N	A3
S Butterfield Rd CO-W11					
-	LbvT	60060	2591	17W-28N	B7
-	LbvT	60061	2591	17W-27N	B7
-	MDLN	60060	2591	17W-27N	B7
-	MDLN	60061	2591	17W-27N	B7
-	VNHL	60061	2591	17W-28N	B7
100	LYVL	60048	2591	17W-28N	B6
400	MDLN	60060	2647	17W-25N	B4
400	MDLN	60061	2647	17W-25N	B4
400	VNHL	60061	2647	17W-25N	B4
900	VNHL	60060	2647	17W-26N	A3
W Butterfield Rd					
-	EMHT	60181	3027	16W-1S	D7
-	OKTR	60181	3027	16W-1S	D7
100	EMHT	60126	3027	16W-0S	E7
W Butterfield Rd SR-56					
-	EMHT	60181	3027	16W-1S	D7
-	OKTR	60181	3027	16W-1S	D7
100	EMHT	60126	3027	16W-0S	D7
Butterfly Ct					
29600	LKBF	60044	2593	12W-29N	B4
Butterfly Dr					
-	NPVL	60563	3080	29W-4S	C7
Butterfly Ln					
2200	GNVW	60025	2810	9W-15N	C3
Butterfly Rd					
400	BGBK	60490	3268	26W-12S	A4
Buttermilk Ct					
4400	NPVL	60564	3266	29W-12S	D3
Buttermilk Ln					
1200	BTVA	60510	3077	36W-2S	E4
Butternut Av					
400	WDDL	60191	2971	17W-4N	C2
N Butternut Cir					
900	FKFT	60423	3503	13W-25S	B7
S Butternut Cir					
900	FKFT	60423	3503	13W-25S	B7
Butternut Ct					
100	RLKB	60073	2475	22W-36N	A4
800	FKFT	60423	3503	13W-25S	B7
800	ROSL	60172	2913	23W-6N	A7
1800	GRNE	60031	2478	15W-36N	A5
7600	WDRG	60517	3205	22W-8S	D2
18000	ODPK	60467	3423	12W-21S	C7
S Butternut Ct					
13500	LktT	60544	3339	27W-16S	D4
13500	PnfT	60544	3339	27W-16S	D4
Butternut Dr					
10	NPVL	60540	3141	26W-7S	D7
10	NPVL	60540	3203	26W-7S	D1
100	BGBK	60440	3268	24W-12S	D2
300	BFGV	60089	2701	17W-23N	C2
300	WDDL	60191	2971	17W-5N	C2
700	NARA	60542	3077	37W-3S	C7
9100	CLLK	60014	2639	38W-26N	A4
9100	DrrT	60014	2639	38W-26N	A4
9200	GfnT	60014	2639	38W-26N	A4
9400	DrrT	60014	2638	38W-26N	E3
9800	LKWD	60014	2638	38W-26N	E3
Butternut Ln					
10	MltT	60137	3083	22W-3S	B5
10	WnfT	60502	3079	32W-3S	D6
200	SMWD	60107	2857	27W-10N	C6
300	WNVL	60555	3080	29W-3S	D5
700	ELGN	60123	2854	36W-12N	A2
800	MPPT	60056	2807	16W-14N	D3
900	NHBK	60062	2757	10W-17N	A5
1000	WhlT	60004	2807	16W-14N	D3
W Butternut Ln					
1300	ANHT	60005	2806	18W-14N	D4
4400	WKGN	60085	2535	14W-32N	C5

Block	City	ZIP	Map#	CGS	Grid
Butternut Rd					
200	BNHL	60010	2749	28W-18N	E2
200	BNHL	60010	2750	28W-18N	A3
17500	HLCT	60429	3427	3W-21S	B5
Butternut Tr					
300	FKFT	60423	3503	13W-25S	B7
500	FftT	60423	3503	13W-25S	B7
Butte View Dr					
200	BGBK	60490	3267	26W-12S	E3
200	BGBK	60490	3268	26W-12S	A2
Buttitta Dr					
1500	HRPK	60133	2857	27W-9N	D7
1500	SMWD	60107	2857	27W-9N	D7
1500	SMWD	60133	2857	27W-9N	D7
Button Rd					
-	BfdT	53147	2351	39W-43N	D4
-	BfdT	60034	2351	39W-43N	D4
10100	HbnT	60034	2351	39W-43N	D4
Buttonwood Cir					
500	NPVL	60540	3141	28W-7S	A7
500	NpvT	60540	3141	28W-7S	A7
800	NPVL	60540	3203	28W-7S	A1
1600	SMBG	60173	2859	21W-10N	E6
Buttonwood Ct					
10	IHPK	60525	3146	14W-6S	D4
600	LslT	60540	3142	24W-5S	C3
800	MRGO	60152	2634	49W-27N	C1
Buttonwood Dr					
1100	WTMT	60559	3144	18W-6S	E5
Buttonwood Ln					
700	MRGO	60152	2634	49W-26N	C2
1100	NHBK	60062	2757	8W-17N	D5
1300	GNVW	60025	2810	9W-13N	D5
Buttonwood Wk					
2900	HLCT	60429	3427	3W-21S	A6
Buxton Ct					
10	LNSH	60045	2702	13W-23N	D2
1500	WLNG	60090	2754	16W-17N	D6
Byerley Dr					
-	LktT	60441	3341	21W-17S	E5
Byman Ln					
1900	VNHL	60061	2647	16W-27N	D1
Byrd Ct					
100	CNHL	60514	3145	16W-5S	D2
Byrd Rd					
500	RVSD	60546	3088	9W-2S	D3
Byrne Dr					
9400	AlqT	60021	2695	31W-22N	E4
W Byrne Dr					
2300	AlqT	60021	2695	31W-22N	D4
Byron Av					
-	AddT	60106	2971	17W-4N	B3
-	ADSN	60106	2971	17W-4N	B3
10	BMDL	60101	2969	22W-4N	D3
10	BMDL	60108	2969	22W-4N	D3
10	BmdT	60101	2969	22W-4N	D3
300	BmdT	60108	2969	22W-4N	D3
600	AddT	60101	2970	19W-4N	C3
600	ADSN	60101	2970	19W-4N	C3
Byron Av CO-24					
10	BMDL	60101	2969	22W-4N	D3
10	BMDL	60108	2969	22W-4N	D3
10	BmdT	60101	2969	22W-4N	D3
700	BmdT	60108	2969	22W-4N	D3
W Byron Av					
10	ADSN	60101	2970	18W-4N	E3
1000	AddT	60101	2970	19W-4N	C3
Byron Ct					
10	HNWD	60047	2645	22W-25N	C5
400	WHTN	60187	3024	23W-0S	E7
600	DRFD	60015	2704	10W-20N	A7
700	OMFD	60461	3506	4W-25S	D6
900	NPVL	60540	3204	25W-8S	B1
10700	BLVY	60098	2525	39W-31N	C7
10700	BLVY	60098	2582	39W-31N	C1
S Byron Ct					
700	MPPT	60056	2862	15W-11N	A2
Byron Dr					
16300	ODHL	60462	3424	11W-19S	A2
16300	ODHL	60487	3424	11W-19S	A2
16300	ODPK	60462	3424	11W-19S	A2
Byron Ln					
1000	ELGN	60123	2854	35W-13N	B1
2000	HDPK	60035	2703	10W-22N	E4
Byron St					
400	WMTN	60481	3853	27W-38S	D7
6000	RSMT	60018	2917	12W-7N	B4
9300	SRPK	60176	2973	11W-4N	C2
W Byron St					
1000	CHCG	60613	2977	1W-4N	E2
1900	CHCG	60618	2977	3W-4N	A2
2800	CHCG	60618	2976	4W-4N	D2
4100	CHCG	60641	2976	5W-4N	A2
5500	CHCG	60634	2975	7W-4N	B2
5500	CHCG	60641	2975	7W-4N	C2
6800	CHCG	60634	2974	9W-4N	D2
Byrum Blvd					
2400	JLET	60431	3417	28W-20S	A6
2400	PnfT	60431	3417	28W-20S	A6
Byzar Av					
-	MKNA	60448	3502	15W-23S	C4

C

Block	City	ZIP	Map#	CGS	Grid
C Ct					
9900	MKNA	60448	3503	12W-23S	D4
C Ln					
-	AntT	60002	2357	25W-42N	B5
C Rd					
-	WnfT	60510	3079	32W-1S	C2
C St					
-	HIWD	60037	2704	9W-23N	D1
-	MrnT	60037	2704	9W-23N	D1
200	NCHI	60088	2594	10W-30N	A2
W C St					
-	MYWD	60153	3030	10W-1S	A7
-	PvsT	60141	3030	10W-1S	A7
-	PvsT	60153	3030	10W-1S	A7
S Cabernet Ct					
10	BRRG	60527	3146	15W-7S	C5
Cabernet Ln					
24100	PNFD	60586	3416	30W-19S	B3
Cable Ct					
400	SMBG	60193	2858	25W-9N	A7
Cable Pl					
10	NCHI	60064	2593	11W-31N	E1
10	NCHI	60088	2593	11W-31N	E1
Cabot Dr					
-	LSLE	60532	3142	24W-4S	D1
2200	LSLE	60532	3082	24W-4S	D7
Cabot Ln					
1300	SMBG	60193	2858	25W-9N	B7
1600	GNVW	60025	2810	10W-14N	A4
W Cabrini St					
600	CHCG	60607	3034	0W-0S	A6
1000	CHCG	60607	3033	1W-0S	E6

Block	City	ZIP	Map#	CGS	Grid
Cabriolet Ct					
1900	NPVL	60565	3203	27W-9S	D4
Ca Crest Dr					
500	SRWD	60404	3496	30W-23S	B4
Cactus Ct					
2400	JLET	60586	3415	32W-20S	C6
Cactus Dr					
1600	NPVL	60563	3141	26W-4S	D1
Cactus Tr					
1100	CLSM	60188	2967	28W-3N	B6
Cadbury Cir					
2500	LIHL	60156	2692	38W-22N	D3
Caddy Av					
100	CPVL	60110	2748	32W-17N	C7
Caddy Ct					
9000	ODPK	60462	3345	11W-17S	E5
9000	ODPK	60462	3346	11W-17S	A5
Caddy Ln					
2500	JLET	60435	3497	27W-23S	D4
Caddy St					
2400	FSMR	60422	3507	3W-23S	B3
Cadella Cir					
3800	AURA	60564	3202	30W-9S	A4
Cadence Dr					
13300	HTLY	60142	2744	43W-19N	B3
Cades Ct					
500	BGBK	60440	3205	22W-10S	D6
Cadet Ct					
1500	WHTN	60187	3082	25W-1S	A2
Cadillac Cir					
-	RMVL	60446	3417	26W-18S	E1
S Cadillac Cir					
600	RMVL	60446	3417	26W-18S	E1
W Cadillac Cir					
1500	RMVL	60446	3417	26W-18S	E1
Cadillac Dr					
600	WHTN	60187	3024	24W-0N	D5
S Cadwell Av					
400	EMHT	60126	3028	15W-0S	B6
800	BKLY	60162	3028	15W-0S	B6
800	BKLY	60163	3028	15W-0S	B6
800	EMHT	60162	3028	15W-0S	B6
1000	PvsT	60126	3028	14W-0S	B7
1000	YkTp	60126	3028	14W-0S	B7
N Cady Dr					
100	PLTN	60074	2753	19W-16N	B7
100	PLTN	60074	2806	19W-16N	B1
Caesar Dr					
400	BNHL	60010	2750	27W-18N	B3
N Cagwin Av					
10	JLET	60435	3498	24W-23S	D5
10	JLET	60436	3498	24W-23S	D5
S Cagwin Av					
10	JLET	60435	3498	24W-24S	D5
10	JLET	60436	3498	24W-24S	D5
Cagwin Dr					
16300	LKPT	60441	3420	20W-21S	B6
16700	LktT	60441	3420	20W-21S	A6
Cahill Dr					
1000	LKFT	60045	2649	12W-27N	B1
Cahill Rd					
10	TVLY	60013	2695	31W-22N	D3
400	SMWD	60107	2856	29W-10N	E5
W Cahill Ter					
7800	CHCG	60634	2974	9W-4N	B3
Cahills Wy					
23800	PNFD	60586	3416	29W-19S	C3
Caine Ct					
3800	NPVL	60564	3267	28W-12S	A2
Caine Dr					
3400	NPVL	60564	3267	28W-11S	A2
W Caine Rd					
24700	LkvT	60041	2474	25W-36N	B4
25000	GrtT	60041	2474	25W-36N	B4
Cairns Ct					
100	WDSK	60098	2524	42W-31N	B6
Cairo Ct					
700	MDLN	60060	2590	19W-28N	C6
Caitlin Ct					
700	GYLK	60030	2533	19W-34N	D2
6800	WLBK	60527	3146	16W-7S	A7
S Caitlin Ct					
17100	PnfT	60586	3416	30W-20S	B5
Caladonia Dr					
9400	TYPK	60487	3423	11W-20S	E4
Calais Cir					
600	HDPK	60035	2704	8W-21N	D7
600	HDPK	60035	2757	8W-20N	D1
Calais Ct					
10	ODHL	60013	2641	30W-26N	E3
Calais Dr					
-	HDPK	60035	2757	9W-20N	D1
-	HDPK	60035	2704	8W-21N	D7
Calamos Ct					
2000	NPVL	60563	3140	29W-4S	C1
Calamus Ln					
1300	GYLK	60030	2533	19W-32N	C6
Calchester on Auburn					
10	RGMW	60008	2806	19W-14N	C3
Calcutta Ln					
1300	NPVL	60563	3141	28W-5S	B2
N Calder Ln					
39100	BHPK	60083	2421	13W-39N	A6
E Calduto Cir					
500	VLPK	60181	3027	17W-0S	C6
Caldwell Av					
300	CHHT	60411	3508	1W-24S	A5
7900	MNGV	60053	2864	8W-10N	E4
7900	NLES	60714	2864	8W-10N	E4
Caldwell Av US-14					
7900	MNGV	60053	2864	8W-10N	E4
7900	NLES	60714	2864	8W-10N	E4
N Caldwell Av					
-	NLES	60053	2865	8W-9N	A7
5700	CHCG	60646	2920	5W-7N	A4
6000	CHCG	60646	2919	7W-8N	B2
6800	CHCG	60714	2919	7W-8N	B2
6800	NLES	60714	2919	7W-8N	B2
7200	CHCG	60646	2865	8W-9N	A7
7200	CHCG	60714	2865	8W-9N	A7
7200	NLES	60646	2865	8W-9N	A7
7200	NLES	60714	2865	8W-9N	A7
7900	MNGV	60053	2865	8W-9N	A7
7900	MNGV	60714	2865	8W-9N	A7
8000	MNGV	60053	2864	8W-10N	E5
8000	MNGV	60714	2864	8W-10N	E5
8000	NLES	60714	2864	8W-10N	E5
N Caldwell Av US-14					
-	NLES	60053	2865	8W-9N	A7
6000	CHCG	60646	2919	7W-8N	B2
6800	CHCG	60714	2919	7W-8N	B2
6800	NLES	60714	2919	7W-8N	B2
7200	CHCG	60646	2865	8W-9N	A7
7200	CHCG	60714	2865	8W-9N	A7
7200	NLES	60646	2865	8W-9N	A7
7200	NLES	60714	2865	8W-9N	A7

Block	City	ZIP	Map#	CGS	Grid
N Caldwell Av US-14					
7900	MNGV	60053	2865	8W-9N	A7
7900	MNGV	60714	2865	8W-9N	A7
8000	MNGV	60053	2864	8W-10N	E5
8000	MNGV	60714	2864	8W-10N	E5
8000	NLES	60714	2864	8W-10N	E5
Caldwell Dr					
9600	HTLY	60142	2692	40W-22N	B4
W Caldwell Dr					
200	RDLK	60073	2531	23W-31N	E7
Caldwell Ln					
1400	HFET	60169	2858	25W-12N	B2
2800	GNVA	60134	3019	37W-0N	C4
Caledonia					
-	NLNX	60442	3589	17W-27S	D4
Caledonia Av					
1100	ZION	60099	2422	9W-40N	B4
2100	JltT	60433	3500	21W-23S	A5
Caledonia Ct					
2200	NPVL	60564	3202	29W-10S	D5
Caledonia Ln					
1100	CLLK	60014	2693	37W-22N	B3
Caledonian Dr					
-	SRGV	60554	3135	42W-6S	B4
E Calendar Av					
400	LGNG	60525	3087	12W-4S	C6
700	BKFD	60513	3087	12W-4S	C6
700	BKFD	60525	3087	12W-4S	C6
W Calendar Av					
10	LGNG	60525	3087	12W-4S	B7
Calendula Ct					
100	RMVL	60446	3339	26W-17S	E6
Caletta Ter					
5700	OKFT	60452	3347	7W-17S	D5
Calgary Cir					
-	JLET	60421	3675	25W-29S	D1
Calgary Dr					
-	JLET	60421	3675	25W-29S	C1
Calhoun Av					
200	BNHM	60409	3351	2E-17S	E6
200	BNHM	60633	3351	2E-17S	E6
200	CTCY	60409	3351	2E-17S	E6
S Calhoun Av					
9500	CHCG	60617	3215	3E-11S	D6
10300	CHCG	60617	3279	2E-12S	D1
13400	CHCG	60633	3351	2E-15S	D1
13900	BNHM	60633	3351	2E-16S	D3
14500	BNHM	60409	3351	2E-16S	D4
14500	CTCY	60409	3351	2E-16S	D4
W Calhoun Av					
25900	AntT	60002	2415	26W-38N	E6
25900	LkvT	60002	2415	26W-38N	E6
W Calhoun Pl					
10	CHCG	60602	3034		D5
10	CHCG	60606	3034		D5
E Calhoun St					
100	WDSK	60098	2524	41W-31N	D7
N Calhoun St					
10	AURA	60504	3200	34W-7S	E1
10	AURA	60505	3200	34W-7S	E1
100	AURA	60505	3138	34W-7S	E7
S Calhoun St					
300	AraT	60504	3200	34W-8S	E2
W Calhoun St					
100	WDSK	60098	2524	41W-31N	E7
Cali Ct					
900	LYVL	60048	2647	15W-27N	E1
Calico Av					
1200	NPVL	60564	3203	28W-10S	A6
Calico Ct					
10	BGBK	60490	3268	26W-13S	A5
2500	JLET	60441	3417	27W-19S	D4
Calico Dr					
700	AURA	60506	3137	36W-5S	E3
Caliendo Cir					
2500	MTGY	60538	3198	40W-10S	D6
Caliente Ct					
700	LYVL	60048	2647	16W-27N	E1
California Av					
-	MKHM	60429	3427	3W-19S	B3
-	POSN	60406	3349	3W-16S	A3
10	CPVL	60110	2747	34W-17N	E7
300	AURA	60506	3138	36W-6S	A5
600	PLTN	60008	2805	20W-14N	E3
600	PLTN	60067	2805	20W-14N	E3
600	RGMW	60008	2805	20W-14N	E3
700	DLTN	60419	3351	0E-17S	A4
1000	AURA	60506	3137	37W-6S	C5
2000	JLET	60432	3499	22W-22S	C1
2000	LktT	60432	3499	22W-22S	C1
2000	LktT	60441	3499	22W-22S	C1
2100	LktT	60432	3419	22W-21S	C7
2100	LktT	60441	3419	22W-21S	C7
2300	NCHI	60088	2593	11W-29N	C4
3000	PltT	60067	2805	20W-13N	E6
3000	RGMW	60067	2805	20W-13N	E5
12300	BLID	60406	3277	3W-15S	A7
13000	BLID	60406	3349	3W-15S	A1
13000	WthT	60406	3349	3W-15S	A1
13700	BLID	60469	3349	3W-16S	A3
13700	POSN	60469	3349	3W-16S	A3
14800	BmnT	60426	3349	3W-17S	B6
14800	HRVY	60426	3349	3W-17S	B6
14800	POSN	60426	3349	3W-17S	B6
15000	MKHM	60426	3349	3W-17S	B6
15700	MKHM	60428	3427	3W-18S	B1
17000	HLCT	60429	3427	3W-20S	B5
18200	HMWD	60430	3427	3W-21S	B7
18400	HMWD	60430	3507	3W-22S	B1
N California Av					
10	CHCG	60612	3033	3W-0N	A4
10	MDLN	60060	2646	19W-27N	C1
100	MDLN	60060	2590	19W-27N	C7
700	CHCG	60612	3032	3W-0N	E3
700	CHCG	60622	3032	3W-1N	E2
1200	JLET	60432	3499	22W-22S	C1
1300	JltT	60432	3499	22W-22S	C1
1300	LktT	60432	3499	22W-22S	C1
1500	CHCG	60647	3032	3W-1N	E1
1600	CHCG	60647	2976	3W-2N	E7
2700	CHCG	60618	2976	3W-4N	E3
4400	CHCG	60618	2920	3W-5N	E7
4400	CHCG	60625	2920	3W-5N	E7
5500	CHCG	60659	2920	3W-6N	E5
6300	CHCG	60645	2920	3W-8N	E2
7200	CHCG	60645	2866	3W-9N	E7
7500	CHCG	60202	2866	3W-9N	E7
7500	EVTN	60202	2866	3W-9N	E7
S California Av					
10	CHCG	60612	3033	3W-0S	A6
10	MDLN	60060	2646	19W-27N	C1
1100	CHCG	60608	3033	3W-1S	A7
1100	CHCG	60623	3033	3W-1S	A7
1500	PltT	60067	2805	20W-13N	E5
1500	RGMW	60008	2805	20W-13N	E5
1600	CHCG	60608	3091	3W-2S	A2

Block	City	ZIP	Map#	CGS	Grid
S California Av					
1600	CHCG	60623	3091	3W-2S	A2
3300	CHCG	60632	3091	3W-4S	A7
4700	CHCG	60632	3151	3W-7S	A6
5400	CHCG	60629	3151	3W-8S	A7
7900	CHCG	60652	3213	3W-9S	A3
8700	CHCG	60805	3213	3W-10S	A4
8700	ENGN	60805	3213	3W-11S	A7
9800	CHCG	60655	3213	3W-11S	A7
9800	ENGN	60655	3213	3W-11S	A7
10200	CHCG	60655	3277	3W-12S	A1
10200	CHCG	60805	3277	3W-11S	A1
10200	ENGN	60655	3277	3W-11S	A1
10200	ENGN	60805	3277	3W-11S	A1
14400	BmnT	60406	3349	3W-17S	A4
14400	BmnT	60469	3349	3W-17S	A4
14500	POSN	60469	3349	3W-17S	A5
W California Av					
10200	BHPK	60099	2422	10W-39N	B6
S California Blvd					
2400	CHCG	60608	3091	3W-2S	A3
2400	CHCG	60623	3091	3W-2S	A2
California Ct					
800	AURA	60506	3137	37W-6S	D5
3100	RGMW	60008	2805	22W-13N	B6
10900	ODPK	60467	3423	13W-21S	A6
California St					
1500	EGVV	60007	2859	21W-9N	E7
13300	BLID	60406	3349	3W-15S	A2
W California Ter					
700	CHCG	60657	2977	3W-4N	A2
California Tr					
11800	OrlT	60467	3344	14W-16S	C3
Calistoga					
-	NLNX	60442	3589	17W-27S	C4
-	NLNX	60451	3589	17W-27S	C4
Calitonia Dr					
15200	MKHM	60428	3349	3W-18S	A7
S Calkey St					
10	DMND	60416	3941	33W-40S	C3
Calkins Dr					
10	SRGV	60554	3135	42W-7S	B7
Calla Dr					
300	MHTN	60442	3678	18W-31S	B5
1600	JLET	60435	3497	27W-21S	B1
1700	JLET	60435	3417	27W-21S	C7
N Callahan Rd					
1500	WCDA	60073	2587	26W-29N	C5
1500	WCDA	60084	2587	26W-28N	D5
1500	WcnT	60084	2587	26W-29N	E4
28800	WcnT	60073	2587	26W-29N	E4
30100	WcnT	60030	2587	26W-29N	E4
Callan Av					
100	CHCG	60202	2867	2W-9N	B6
100	CHCG	60626	2867	2W-9N	B6
100	EVTN	60202	2867	2W-9N	B6
Callan Dr					
9500	PlsT	60462	3345	11W-15S	D2
Callander Ct					
3900	WldT	60564	3266	30W-12S	A4
Callaway Ct					
1500	SRWD	60404	3496	29W-25S	D7
Callaway Dr N					
1200	SRWD	60404	3496	31W-25S	A7
1200	SRWD	60404	3584	31W-25S	A1
Callaway Dr W					
900	SRWD	60404	3496	31W-25S	A7
900	SRWD	60404	3584	31W-25S	A1
Callen Ln					
1200	DSPN	60016	2808	13W-13N	D5
E Callero Cir					
1000	MPPT	60056	2808	14W-13N	C6
Callero Ct					
600	ROSL	60172	2913	23W-6N	A6
N Callero Dr					
9200	NLES	60714	2864	10W-11N	B2
Callery Ct					
10	BGBK	60490	3268	25W-12S	A3
Callery Dr					
300	BGBK	60440	3268	25W-12S	A3
300	BGBK	60490	3268	25W-12S	A3
Callery Rd					
4100	WldT	60564	3265	31W-13S	E5
4100	WldT	60564	3266	31W-13S	A5
Callview Dr					
10	CTSD	60525	3147	13W-5S	A3
10	LGNG	60525	3147	13W-5S	A3
Callie Av					
8500	MNGV	60053	2865	7W-10N	B4
S Callie Dr					
-	PNFD	60586	3415	31W-20S	E5
Callista Dr					
8200	FKFT	60423	3592	10W-27S	C4
Callista St					
600	MHRY	60050	2528	33W-32N	A4
Calmer Dr					
2700	NlxT	60433	3500	20W-24S	C5
Cals Ct					
23100	CmgT	60033	2405	52W-39N	C5
Cal Sag Rd					
-	ALSP	60445	3275	6W-15S	E7
-	ALSP	60803	3275	6W-15S	E7
-	CTWD	60472	3348	5W-15S	B2
-	RBBN	60445	3348	5W-15S	B2
-	RBBN	60472	3348	5W-15S	B2
4400	CTWD	60445	3348	6W-15S	A1
5100	CTWD	60445	3275	6W-15S	E7
W Cal Sag Rd					
-	PlsT	60480	3273	12W-13S	D4
-	PSHT	60463	3275	7W-14S	B5
5400	ALSP	60445	3275	6W-14S	E7
5400	ALSP	60803	3275	7W-14S	C6
5400	CTWD	60445	3275	6W-14S	E7
5500	ALSP	60463	3275	7W-14S	C6
5500	WthT	60463	3275	6W-14S	D6
5500	WthT	60803	3275	7W-14S	C6
8000	PSHT	60463	3274	10W-13S	C5
8000	PSHT	60464	3274	10W-13S	C5
8000	PSPK	60464	3274	10W-13S	C5
8500	PlsT	60464	3274	11W-13S	A4
8600	PlsT	60464	3273	12W-13S	D4
W Cal Sag Rd SR-83					
-	PlsT	60480	3273	12W-13S	D4
-	PSHT	60463	3275	7W-14S	B5
5400	ALSP	60445	3275	6W-14S	E7
5400	ALSP	60803	3275	7W-14S	C6
5400	CTWD	60445	3275	6W-14S	E7
5500	ALSP	60463	3275	7W-14S	C6
5500	WthT	60463	3275	6W-14S	D6
5500	WthT	60803	3275	7W-14S	C6
8000	PSHT	60463	3274	10W-13S	C5
8000	PSHT	60464	3274	10W-13S	C5
8000	PSPK	60464	3274	10W-13S	C5
8500	PlsT	60464	3274	11W-13S	A4
8600	PlsT	60464	3273	12W-13S	D4
Calumet Av					
1300	DYR	46311	3510		E7
1300	DYR	46311	3598		E3
6200	HMND	46320	3430		E1
6200	HMND	46324	3430		E6
7800	MNSR	46321	3430		E5
8100	SjnT	46311	3598		E5
8200	SjnT	46373	3598		E5
8600	MNSR	46321	3510		E7
8900	SJHN	46373	3598		E7
9000	SJHN	46373	3687		E1
9300	SjnT	46311	3687		E2
10100	HnrT	46311	3687		E4
11300	HnrT	46303	3687		E7
14100	DLTN	60419	3350	0E-16S	D3
15400	SHLD	60473	3350	0E-18S	D7
Calumet Av US-41					
6200	HMND	46320	3430		E1
6200	HMND	46324	3430		E2
N Calumet Av					
900	AURA	60506	3137	37W-6S	C5
S Calumet Av					
10	AURA	60506	3137	37W-7S	C7
400	AraT	60506	3199	37W-8S	C2
400	AURA	60506	3199	37W-7S	C1
1000	HMND	46320	3280		E2
1100	HMND	46394	3280		E7
1800	CHCG	60616	3092	0E-1S	C1
2500	HMND	46327	3280		E7
3000	HMND	46320	3352		E1
3000	HMND	46327	3352		E7
3500	CHCG	60653	3092	0E-3S	D5
4600	CHCG	60615	3092	0E-4S	D7
4700	CHCG	60615	3152	0E-5S	D1
5600	CHCG	60637	3152	0E-7S	D5
5900	HMND	46320	3430		E1
6100	HMND	46324	3430		E1
7000	CHCG	60619	3152	0E-8S	D7
7500	CHCG	60619	3214	0E-10S	D4
9400	CHCG	60628	3214	0E-11S	D6
10300	CHCG	60628	3278	0E-12S	D2
13300	CHCG	60827	3350	0E-15S	D1
S Calumet Av US-41					
1400	HMND	46394	3280		E7
2100	HMND	46320	3280		E5
2500	HMND	46327	3280		E7
3000	HMND	46320	3352		E1
3000	HMND	46327	3352		E7
5900	HMND	46320	3430		E1
6100	HMND	46324	3430		E1
Calumet Av E					
10	WNVL	60555	3080	29W-3S	D5
Calumet Av W					
100	WNVL	60555	3080	30W-3S	B5
Calumet Blvd					
100	HRVY	60426	3350	1W-17S	A4
Calumet Ct					
200	BGBK	60440	3268	23W-12S	E2
Calumet Expwy					
-	CRTE	60417	3597	1E-28S	C6
-	CRTE	60417	3686	1E-29S	C1
-	CteT	60401	3774	0W-33S	C2
-	CteT	60417	3597	2E-27S	C5
-	CteT	60417	3685	0E-32S	D6
-	CteT	60417	3686	1E-29S	C1
-	CteT	60417	3774	0W-33S	C2
-	SLVL	60411	3597	1E-27S	C5
-	STGR	60411	3597	2E-27S	C4
-	STGR	60475	3597	1E-28S	C5
Calumet Expwy SR-394					
-	CRTE	60417	3597	1E-28S	C6
-	CRTE	60417	3686	1E-29S	C1
-	CteT	60401	3774	0W-33S	C2
-	CteT	60417	3597	2E-27S	C5
-	CteT	60417	3685	0E-32S	D6
-	CteT	60417	3686	1E-29S	C1
-	CteT	60417	3774	0W-33S	C2
-	SLVL	60411	3597	1E-27S	C5
-	STGR	60411	3597	2E-27S	C4
-	STGR	60475	3597	1E-28S	C5
Calumet St					
200	OSWG	60543	3263	37W-13S	C4
9300	SjnT	46311	3687		E2
Calumet Wy					
500	CTCY	60409	3352	4E-18S	B7
Calvary Ct					
2500	LGGV	60047	2753	19W-20N	C1
Calvary Ln					
2700	ZION	60099	2421	11W-40N	D4
Calvert Ct					
2200	NPVL	60565	3204	25W-9S	B5
Calvert Dr					
4600	RGMW	60008	2806	19W-12N	C7
4700	RGMW	60008	2860	19W-12N	C1
Calvin Av					
-	BKLY	60126	3028	15W-0S	B5
-	EMHT	60126	3028	15W-0S	B5
200	WnfT	60185	3022	28W-0N	E5
2000	BKLY	60162	3028	14W-0S	C6
2000	BKLY	60163	3028	15W-0S	B5
2000	EMHT	60162	3028	14W-0S	C6
Calvin Cir					
-	EVTN	60201	2866	4W-12N	C1
Calvin Ct					
100	WNFD	60190	3023	26W-0N	D5
300	MltT	60190	3023	26W-0N	D5
400	GRNE	60031	2535	14W-33N	C3
1300	NPVL	60540	3142	25W-7S	B7
1900	RVWD	60015	2702	13W-22N	E4
W Calvin Dr					
22000	AntT	60002	2417	22W-40N	C3
Calvin St					
-	LtRT	60545	3259	47W-12S	D4
-	PLNO	60545	3259	47W-12S	D4
Calwagner Av					
2200	LydT	60164	2973	12W-2N	C6
2400	FNPK	60131	2973	12W-3N	C6
2400	FNPK	60164	2973	12W-3N	C6
2400	LydT	60131	2973	12W-3N	C6
Calwagner St					
2600	FNPK	60131	2973	12W-3N	C5
Calypso Ln					
15500	ODPK	60462	3346	9W-18S	E7
W Camarga Ct					
200	VNHL	60061	2647	17W-26N	B2
Camargo Club Dr					
500	LIHL	60156	2693	36W-22N	C4
Camarie Ct					
300	NPVL	60540	3141	26W-6S	E4
300	NPVL	60540	3142	26W-6S	A4
Camberley Cir					
-	PvsT	60154	3086	14W-2S	C3
-	WSTR	60154	3086	14W-2S	D3
Camberley Ct					
10	HNDL	60521	3146	15W-5S	A3
1600	BRLT	60103	2967	28W-5N	B1
Camberwell Ct					
10	ALGN	60102	2693	38W-21N	A6
Cambia Dr					
300	SMBG	60193	2912	23W-8N	E1
1300	SMBG	60193	2913	23W-8N	A2
Cambourne Ln					
1600	SMBG	60194	2858	25W-10N	B5
Cambria Ct					
-	JLET	60431	3495	32W-22S	D1
1600	ALGN	60102	2747	36W-18N	A4
2000	GNVW	60062	2809	12W-14N	C3
3100	AURA	60503	3201	31W-10S	E5
10700	HTLY	60142	2692	39W-21N	B5
Cambria Dr					
-	BGVW	60455	3274	9W-11S	D1
-	JLET	60431	3495	32W-22S	D1
W Cambria Dr					
300	RDLK	60073	2531	23W-32N	E5
Cambria Ln					
1600	ALGN	60102	2747	36W-18N	B4
N Cambria Ln					
1100	LMBD	60148	3026	18W-0S	E6
S Cambria Ln					
1100	LMBD	60148	3026	18W-0S	E6
N Cambria St					
100	BCVL	60407	4030	33W-44S	B4
Cambrian Ct					
100	ROSL	60172	2912	25W-7N	C4
Cambridge Av					
10	SMWD	60107	2910	30W-9N	C1
10	SMWD	60107	2911	28W-9N	A1
600	MTSN	60443	3505	6W-25S	E6
1100	BlmT	60422	3507	2W-23S	D3
1100	BlmT	60430	3507	2W-23S	D3
1100	FSMR	60422	3507	2W-23S	D3
1100	FSMR	60430	3507	2W-23S	D3
1500	AURA	60506	3137	36W-5S	E2
1500	CHHT	60422	3507	2W-23S	D4
1500	OMFD	60422	3507	2W-23S	D4
1500	OMFD	60461	3507	2W-23S	D4
3800	PKCY	60085	2535	13W-33N	E2
N Cambridge Av					
800	CHCG	60610	3034	0W-1N	A2
2800	CHCG	60614	2978	0W-3N	A4
2800	CHCG	60657	2978	0W-3N	A4
S Cambridge Av					
500	EMHT	60126	3028	15W-0N	A4
N Cambridge Blvd					
-	WDWH	60083	2421	13W-39N	A6
39400	BHPK	60083	2421	13W-39N	A5
39600	BHPK	60099	2421	13W-39N	A5
Cambridge Cir					
500	DRFD	60015	2756	11W-20N	E1
4100	CCHL	60478	3426	5W-21S	C6
9700	MKNA	60448	3503	12W-23S	D4
13800	PNFD	60544	3339	28W-16S	B4
Cambridge Ct					
10	BFGV	60089	2754	16W-17N	D5
10	CRY	60013	2695	32W-23N	C1
10	FKFT	60423	3591	11W-25S	E1
10	GNVA	60134	3019	36W-1N	D3
100	BMDL	60108	2969	23W-5N	A2
100	FftT	60423	3591	11W-25S	E1
100	SCRL	60174	3020	34W-2N	E1
200	CmpT	60175	2962	39W-5N	E2
200	MltT	60137	3083	23W-2S	A4
200	OSWG	60543	3263	37W-14S	C6
700	DGvT	60516	3206	19W-9S	D3
800	WMTN	60481	3943	27W-39S	E1
1000	DYR	46311	3510		D6
1100	HDPK	60035	2704	10W-23N	B2
1200	SRWD	60404	3496	31W-24S	A6
1900	PLTN	60074	2753	19W-18N	C3
7800	BLVY	60098	2526	36W-32N	C4
7800	MchT	60098	2526	36W-32N	C4
16000	MKHM	60428	3427	3W-19S	B2
E Cambridge Ct					
10	GYLK	60030	2533	19W-33N	C3
N Cambridge Ct					
200	GYLK	60030	2533	19W-33N	C3
1900	PLTN	60074	2753	19W-20N	C2
S Cambridge Ct					
9700	PSHL	60465	3210	10W-11S	A7
W Cambridge Ct					
900	GYLK	60030	2533	19W-33N	B3
Cambridge Dr					
-	BTVA	60134	3019	37W-0S	B7
-	GnvT	60134	3019	37W-0S	B7
-	HTLY	60142	2692	38W-22N	D4
-	HTLY	60156	2692	38W-22N	D5
-	LIHL	60156	2692	38W-22N	D5
-	TRLK	60010	2643	26W-25N	D4
10	GYLK	60030	2533	19W-34N	B2
10	HNWD	60047	2645	20W-25N	E6
10	OKBK	60523	3085	17W-2S	C4
400	WynT	60185	2966	29W-4N	D3
500	SMBG	60193	2858	25W-9N	C7
700	BRRG	60527	3208	15W-9S	A3
700	BTVA	60510	3019	37W-0S	B7
800	BFGV	60089	2754	16W-17N	D5
800	BFGV	60090	2754	16W-17N	D5
800	WLNG	60090	2754	16W-17N	D5
900	EGVV	60007	2861	16W-9N	D7
900	EGVV	60007	2915	17W-9N	C1
900	LYVL	60048	2591	16W-28N	E7
1600	ELGN	60123	2800	36W-13N	D4
1700	SCRL	60174	3020	34W-2N	E1
1800	CPVL	60110	2748	32W-18N	D6
2000	SCRL	60174	3021	33W-2N	A1
2300	NHBK	60062	2809	11W-15N	D1
2400	AURA	60506	3136	39W-7S	E6
4000	CCHL	60478	3426	5W-21S	C6
5000	MHRY	60050	2527	34W-32N	D5
7900	ODPK	60462	3346	10W-16S	C4
9800	MKNA	60448	3503	12W-23S	C4
13400	LMNT	60439	3271	17W-14S	D6
16100	MKHM	60428	3427	3W-19S	B2
21500	KLDR	60047	2699	22W-21N	B5
N Cambridge Dr					
10	GNVA	60134	3019	36W-1N	D3
400	PLTN	60067	2752	22W-16N	C7
S Cambridge Dr					
10	GNVA	60134	3019	36W-1N	D4
25900	CteT	60417	3687	3E-31S	A6
W Cambridge Dr					
22100	KLDR	60047	2699	22W-21N	B5
Cambridge Ln					
10	GLHT	60139	3024	23W-2N	E1
10	GLHT	60139	3025	23W-2N	A1
10	LNSH	60069	2702	14W-22N	C4
10	RVWD	60015	2702	14W-22N	D4
100	BMDL	60108	2969	23W-5N	A2
300	SRWD	60404	3496	30W-24S	A7
500	LKBF	60044	2594	10W-28N	A7
600	HFET	60169	2858	24W-12N	D2
700	SMBG	60169	2858	24W-12N	D2
700	SMBG	60195	2858	24W-12N	D2
800	CLLK	60014	2639	35W-24N	E7
900	WLMT	60091	2812	4W-14N	C5
1000	DYR	46311	3510		D7
1800	MTGY	60538	3198	40W-9S	B5
1800	NLNX	60451	3590	16W-25S	A1
1800	WHTN	60187	3082	23W-2S	E4
2300	WDRG	60517	3143	21W-7S	E7
2800	OMFD	60461	3507	3W-25S	A7
Cambridge Pkwy					
-	FXLK	60041	2473	26W-34N	C7
-	GrtT	60041	2473	26W-34N	C7
Cambridge Pl					
800	WLNG	60090	2755	15W-18N	A3
17100	ODHL	60487	3423	11W-20S	E5
17100	TYPK	60487	3423	11W-20S	E5
Cambridge Rd					
700	SEGN	60177	2908	35W-8N	C3
2500	AURA	60506	3136	39W-7S	E6
6400	WLBK	60527	3146	15W-7S	A6
6900	DRGV	60516	3144	20W-8S	A7
6900	DRGV	60517	3144	20W-8S	A7
7000	WDRG	60517	3144	20W-8S	A7
7100	DRGV	60516	3206	21W-8S	A1
7100	DRGV	60517	3206	21W-8S	A1
7100	WDRG	60516	3206	21W-8S	A1
7100	WDRG	60517	3206	21W-8S	A1
7400	MchT	60097	2469	36W-36N	D3
7500	DRN	60516	3206	19W-8S	C2
7500	DRN	60561	3206	19W-8S	C2
W Cambridge Rd					
14900	FmtT	60060	2590	19W-29N	C3
14900	MDLN	60060	2590	19W-29N	C3
N Cambridge Row					
800	ADSN	60101	2970	21W-4N	A3
Cambridge St					
100	DSPN	60016	2862	14W-12N	C1
500	DSPN	60016	2808	14W-13N	B6
1900	CHHT	60411	3595	2W-26S	E2
7100	BGVW	60455	3210	8W-10S	E5
10100	WSTR	60154	3029	12W-1S	B7
10200	PvsT	60162	3029	12W-1S	A7
10200	WSTR	60162	3029	12W-1S	A7
W Cambridge St					
1300	ANHT	60004	2753	18W-16N	D7
Cambridge Wy					
400	BGBK	60440	3205	22W-9S	D4
600	BGBK	60517	3205	22W-9S	D4
600	WDRG	60517	3205	22W-9S	D4
5500	BmdT	60133	2912	25W-6N	A6
5500	BmdT	60172	2912	25W-6N	A6
5500	HRPK	60133	2912	25W-6N	A6
Cambridge Lakes Dr					
-	PGGV	60140	2797	41W-15N	E4
Camdan Rd					
14100	HMGN	60491	3344	15W-16S	B4
Camden Av					
400	RMVL	60446	3340	23W-15S	E2
Camden Cir					
400	OSWG	60543	3263	37W-14S	C6
Camden Ct					
10	CRY	60013	2695	32W-23N	B1
10	LIHL	60156	2692	38W-23N	E2
10	PTBR	60010	2642	29W-26N	C3
100	LNSH	60069	2703	12W-22N	B3
100	SMBG	60194	2857	26W-10N	E5
200	NPVL	60540	3142	25W-6S	B6
200	CRTE	60417	3596	0W-28S	C6
400	BMDL	60108	2968	25W-5N	A2
1400	GRNE	60031	2477	17W-35N	B6
1700	GNVW	60025	2810	8W-15N	E2
2800	WCHI	60185	2965	32W-4N	C4
13900	ODPK	60462	3346	10W-16S	C4
Camden Ln					
-	BCHR	60401	3774	0W-35S	D6
-	BGVW	60455	3274	9W-11S	D1
600	PTBR	60010	2642	29W-26N	C3
800	AURA	60504	3201	31W-9S	E3
800	NHFD	60093	2758	7W-16N	B7
2000	HRPK	60133	2967	27W-5N	C1
E Camden Ln					
200	RLKB	60073	2475	22W-36N	B5
N Camden Ln					
800	SEGN	60177	2908	35W-7N	B4
2100	RLKB	60073	2475	22W-36N	B5
W Camden Ln					
400	SEGN	60177	2908	35W-7N	B4
Camden Pl					
200	VNHL	60061	2647	17W-24N	B7
1500	WHTN	60187	3082	24W-1S	C2
6800	DRGV	60516	3144	20W-7S	A7
Camden Rd					
6800	DRGV	60516	3144	20W-7S	A7
7100	DRGV	60516	3206	20W-8S	B1
Camden Bay					
2300	ELGN	60123	2907	36W-9N	E2
18900	MKNA	60448	3503	13W-22S	B2
Camden Cove					
400	WPHR	60096	2363	10W-43N	A5
Camder Dr					
400	DGvT	60516	3206	20W-10S	B6
400	DGvT	60517	3206	20W-10S	B6
400	WDRG	60517	3206	20W-10S	B6
Camdon Cir					
500	BRLT	60103	2911	28W-7N	A4
Camel Rd					
1300	AraT	60504	3138	34W-5S	C4
Camel Bend Ct					
200	SMBG	60194	2857	27W-10N	D5
Camelia Dr					
7300	HRPK	60133	2911	27W-9N	C1
Camelia Ln					
8400	ODPK	60462	3346	10W-18S	B7
Camellia Ct					
10	SMWD	60107	2856	30W-10N	B5
2000	NPVL	60565	3204	25W-9S	B5
7600	MchT	60097	2469	36W-37N	D1
Camellia Dr					
900	MNSR	46321	3510		E2
Camellia Ln					
1600	SMBG	60173	2859	21W-11N	E4
1700	SMBG	60173	2860	20W-10N	A5
Camellia Pl					
1000	FRGV	60021	2696	28W-22N	D3
Camelot Av					
11900	MKNA	60448	3502	14W-23S	D3
Camelot Cir					
4300	NPVL	60564	3266	28W-12S	E3
Camelot Ct					
100	BGBK	60440	3205	23W-10S	A7
100	BGBK	60440	3269	22W-11S	B1
800	CLLK	60014	2639	36W-24N	C7
13800	OrlT	60467	3344	14W-16S	D3
E Camelot Ct					
1300	ANHT	60004	2754	17W-16N	C7
S Camelot Ct					
700	LKFT	60045	2648	13W-25N	E6
22300	TroT	60404	3584	30W-27S	C4
Camelot Dr					
10	OKBK	60523	3085	17W-2S	C4
600	BRRG	60527	3208	15W-9S	A4
800	CLLK	60014	2639	36W-24N	C7
Camelot Ln					
100	LYVL	60048	2592	15W-28N	A5
200	CLSM	60188	2968	25W-3N	A6
200	LbvT	60048	2592	15W-28N	A5
1100	LMNT	60439	3271	18W-14S	B6
1500	HFET	60010	2751	24W-16N	B7
2000	LYWD	60411	3509	2E-24S	D5
11600	OrlT	60467	3344	14W-16S	D3
Camelot Pl					
900	CLLK	60014	2639	36W-24N	C7
W Camelot Rd					
24100	TroT	60404	3584	30W-27S	C4
Camelot St					
10500	PvsT	60154	3087	13W-1S	A1
10500	PvsT	60162	3087	13W-1S	A1
10500	WSTR	60154	3087	13W-1S	A1
10500	WSTR	60162	3087	13W-1S	A1
Camelot Wy					
100	BGBK	60440	3205	22W-11S	B7
100	BGBK	60440	3269	22W-11S	B1
Cameno Pl					
9800	ODPK	60462	3345	12W-18S	D6
Cameron Av					
200	LktT	60441	3419	23W-20S	B6
S Cameron Av					
3800	HMND	46327	3352		D3
Cameron Ct					
1400	HFET	60010	2751	24W-16N	B7
2700	DRN	60561	3206	19W-9S	C3
5900	NndT	60014	2641	32W-26N	C3
W Cameron Ct					
-	PNFD	60585	3265	32W-14S	B7
Cameron Dr					
600	ANTH	60002	2357	24W-42N	B5
Cameron Ln					
9300	MNGV	60053	2864	9W-11N	D2
Cameron Pkwy					
11200	ODPK	60467	3422	14W-21S	E6
Cameron Wy					
400	ANHT	60004	2753	18W-18N	E3
400	BFGV	60004	2753	18W-18N	E3
400	BFGV	60089	2753	18W-18N	E3
Camille Av					
1000	DRFD	60015	2703	11W-21N	D6
Cammeron Ct					
10	AURA	60504	3201	31W-8S	D1
Camp Alphonse					
4000	PltT	60010	2752	22W-17N	A4
4000	PltT	60067	2752	22W-17N	A4
4000	PltT	60074	2752	22W-17N	A4
Campbell Av					
-	MKHM	60428	3427	3W-19S	B3
500	WHTN	60187	3024	24W-0S	D7
700	CHHT	60411	3507	1W-25S	E7
700	CTCY	60409	3352	3E-18S	A7
900	WHTN	60187	3082	24W-1S	D1
1100	DSPN	60016	2862	13W-9N	D6
1400	CHHT	60411	3595	1W-26S	E1
1700	DSPN	60016	2863	12W-10N	B5
3200	SCHT	60411	3595	1W-27S	E4
9500	OKLN	60453	3211	6W-11S	D6
14900	HRVY	60426	3349	3W-17S	B6
15500	HRVY	60426	3427	3W-18S	B1
15700	MKHM	60426	3427	3W-18S	C1
15900	BmnT	60428	3427	3W-19S	B2
N Campbell Av					
10	GNWD	60425	3508	0E-22S	D2
400	CHCG	60612	3033	3W-0N	A3
700	CHCG	60622	3033	3W-0N	A3
1500	CHCG	60647	3033	3W-1N	A1
2700	CHCG	60647	2977	3W-3N	A4
3600	CHCG	60618	2977	3W-4N	A2
4400	CHCG	60618	2921	3W-5N	A7
4400	CHCG	60625	2921	3W-5N	A7
5500	CHCG	60659	2921	3W-6N	A5
6300	CHCG	60645	2921	3W-7N	A3
7200	CHCG	60645	2867	3W-9N	A7
S Campbell Av					
10	GNWD	60425	3508	0E-23S	D3
1200	CHCG	60608	3033	3W-1S	A7
1200	CHCG	60612	3033	3W-1S	A7
3700	CHCG	60632	3091	3W-4S	B6
4700	CHCG	60632	3151	3W-5S	A1
5600	CHCG	60629	3151	3W-7S	B5
7500	CHCG	60652	3213	3W-8S	B1
9400	ENGN	60805	3213	3W-11S	B6
9800	CHCG	60655	3213	3W-11S	B7
9800	CHCG	60805	3213	3W-11S	B7
10300	CHCG	60655	3277	3W-13S	B3
11800	BLID	60406	3277	3W-13S	B5
11800	BLID	60655	3277	3W-13S	B5
14300	POSN	60469	3349	3W-17S	B4
Campbell Ct					
200	GNVA	60134	3020	35W-1N	B4
500	WHTN	60187	3082	24W-1S	D1
700	WDND	60118	2800	35W-16N	C2
900	BTVA	60510	3078	34W-1S	D2
1000	LKBF	60044	2593	11W-29N	E4
1000	ShdT	60044	2593	11W-29N	E4
9800	LKWD	60014	2638	38W-25N	E4
W Campbell Ct					
600	ANHT	60005	2806	18W-14N	E5
Campbell Dr					
10	GLHT	60139	2968	24W-3N	E5
100	BGBK	60440	3268	25W-11S	B1
400	NpvT	60563	3140	30W-5S	B3
500	NPVL	60563	3140	30W-5S	B3
800	WCHI	60185	3022	29W-1N	E2
900	GRNE	60031	2534	16W-33N	D4
Campbell Ln					
1200	HFET	60169	2858	25W-12N	C2

STREET Block	City	ZIP	Map#	CGS	Grid
Campbell Ln					
25800	PNFD	60585	3337	32W-15S	C2
W Campbell Ln					
4300	WKGN	60048	2535	14W-31N	D6
W Campbell Pl					
-	CHCG	60610	3034		D2
Campbell St					
200	HRVD	60033	2406	50W-38N	A7
700	GNVA	60134	3020	35W-1N	B3
2000	ANHT	60005	2806	19W-14N	D5
2000	RGMW	60005	2806	19W-14N	D5
2000	RGMW	60008	2806	19W-14N	B4
12800	LMNT	60439	3272	16W-13S	A4
E Campbell St					
10	ANHT	60005	2807	17W-14N	A5
1100	ANHT	60004	2807	17W-14N	C5
W Campbell St					
10	ANHT	60005	2807	18W-14N	A5
400	ANHT	60005	2806	18W-14N	D5
400	JLET	60435	3498	25W-23S	B4
1500	RGMW	60005	2806	18W-14N	D5
1500	RGMW	60008	2806	18W-14N	D5
2500	JLET	60435	3497	27W-23S	C4
W Campbell Park Dr					
2200	CHCG	60612	3033	2W-0S	B6
Camp Dan Beard					
5300	WhlT	60062	2755	13W-18N	E2
Camp Dean Rd					
10	BRkT	60511	3196	46W-8S	B1
200	BRkT	60511	3134	46W-7S	B7
Campden Ln					
2500	NHBK	60062	2757	10W-18N	A4
Camp Flint Dr					
200	DndT	60118	2801	34W-15N	A4
Campground Rd					
1100	DSPN	60016	2863	12W-10N	A4
Camphill Cir					
1900	IVNS	60067	2804	23W-15N	E1
Camp Horner Rd					
33900	GrtT	60041	2530	26W-34N	D2
33900	RDLK	60073	2530	26W-34N	D2
Campion Dr					
-	HPSR	60140	2795	47W-16N	D1
N Campion Rd					
34000	GrtT	60041	2530	28W-34N	A2
Camp Logan Rd					
-	ZION	60099	2422	9W-41N	D1
E Camp McDonald Rd					
10	MPPT	60056	2808	13W-15N	D3
10	MPPT	60070	2808	13W-15N	D3
10	PTHT	60056	2808	13W-15N	D3
10	PTHT	60070	2808	13W-15N	D3
900	WLNG	60070	2808	14W-15N	C3
900	WLNG	60090	2808	14W-15N	C3
1000	PTHT	60090	2808	14W-15N	D3
W Camp McDonald Rd					
10	MPPT	60056	2808	15W-15N	A3
10	MPPT	60070	2808	15W-15N	A3
10	PTHT	60056	2808	15W-15N	A3
10	PTHT	60070	2808	15W-15N	A3
100	MPPT	60056	2807	16W-14N	D3
100	PTHT	60056	2807	15W-15N	E3
100	PTHT	60070	2807	16W-14N	D3
400	ANHT	60004	2807	16W-14N	D3
400	WhlT	60004	2807	16W-14N	D3
Camp Moffett					
-	NCHI	60088	2593	11W-30N	D2
Campton Ct					
300	LYLK	60175	2961	43W-5N	B2
Campton Crossings Dr					
10	CmpT	60175	2962	40W-4N	C4
Campton Forpre Tr					
500	CmpT	60175	2961	41W-4N	E4
Campton Hills Dr					
10	CmpT	60119	2961	42W-4N	C5
10	CmpT	60119	2962	41W-3N	A6
10	CmpT	60175	2962	40W-3N	C7
10	SCRL	60175	2962	39W-3N	E7
10	SCRL	60175	2963	38W-3N	A7
100	SchT	60175	2963	38W-3N	A7
400	CmpT	60175	2961	41W-3N	E6
Campton Meadows Rd					
700	CmpT	60119	2962	40W-3N	B6
Campton Oaks Dr					
200	CmpT	60175	2962	40W-5N	C2
Campton Ridge Dr					
700	CmpT	60175	2961	41W-5N	E1
Campton Trail Rd					
10	CmpT	60175	2962	41W-5N	A2
Campton Woods Dr					
10	CmpT	60119	2962	40W-3N	B7
300	CmpT	60175	2962	40W-3N	B7
Campus Av					
-	RchT	60443	3506	5W-25S	B7
700	MTSN	60443	3506	5W-25S	B7
Campus Cir					
10	LKFT	60045	2650	9W-26N	B3
300	WKGN	60085	2536	12W-33N	C1
Campus Dr					
300	ELGN	60120	2855	31W-10N	D5
700	MDLN	60060	2647	17W-26N	A2
700	VNHL	60061	2647	17W-26N	A2
2700	JLET	60435	3497	27W-22S	C2
4100	AURA	60504	3140	30W-6S	A5
N Campus Dr					
2200	EVTN	60201	2867	2W-12N	C1
S Campus Dr					
1900	EVTN	60201	2867	2W-11N	C2
W Campus Dr					
200	ANHT	60004	2753	18W-17N	E5
200	ANHT	60004	2754	18W-17N	A5
S Campus Pkwy					
1400	CHCG	60608	3034		E7
S Canal Rd					
23000	CNHN	60410	3584	31W-28S	A7
23000	CNHN	60436	3584	31W-28S	A7
23000	CnhT	60410	3584	31W-28S	A7
23000	CnhT	60447	3584	31W-28S	A7
23000	TroT	60410	3584	31W-28S	A7
24600	CNHN	60410	3672	31W-29S	E1
Canal Rd N					
24700	CNHN	60447	3584	31W-28S	A6
24700	CnhT	60447	3584	30W-27S	B6
24700	TroT	60404	3584	30W-27S	B5
24700	TroT	60447	3584	30W-27S	B6
25200	CnhT	60447	3583	31W-27S	E6
25200	TroT	60447	3583	31W-27S	E6
25600	MNKA	60447	3583	32W-28S	C7
Canal St					
100	WMTN	60481	3853	27W-38S	C6
200	LMNT	60439	3270	19W-13S	D5
500	LKPT	60441	3419	22W-19S	C2
1700	LktT	60441	3419	23W-21S	B6
1800	BLID	60406	3349	2W-15S	C1
16700	SHLD	60473	3428	0W-20S	C4
16700	SHLD	60476	3428	0W-20S	C4
Canal St					
16700	TNTN	60473	3428	0W-20S	C4
16700	TNTN	60476	3428	0W-20S	C4
N Canal St					
10	CHCG	60606	3034	0W-0N	A4
10	CHCG	60661	3034	0W-0N	A4
300	CHCG	60610	3034	0W-0N	A4
S Canal St					
-	CHCG	60606	3034	0W-0S	A5
-	CHCG	60609	3092	0W-4S	B7
10	CHCG	60661	3034	0W-0S	A5
300	CHCG	60607	3034	0W-0S	A6
1500	CHCG	60616	3034	0W-1S	A7
1600	CHCG	60616	3092	0W-2S	A2
16600	SHLD	60473	3428	0W-19S	C3
24900	CNHN	60410	3672	31W-30S	E4
Canal Bank Rd					
-	FTVW	60402	3089	7W-4S	C7
-	SKNY	60804	3089	7W-4S	C7
6600	FTVW	60402	3148	8W-5S	E2
6600	FTVW	60402	3149	8W-5S	A1
7100	FTVW	60534	3148	8W-5S	E2
7100	SMMT	60534	3148	8W-5S	E2
7300	LYNS	60534	3148	9W-5S	E2
7300	SMMT	60501	3148	9W-5S	D2
7300	SMMT	60525	3148	9W-5S	D2
15100	DGvT	60439	3270	19W-13S	D4
15100	DGvT	60527	3270	19W-13S	D4
15100	LmnT	60439	3270	19W-13S	D4
15100	LMNT	60439	3271	18W-12S	A3
15100	LMNT	60527	3270	19W-13S	D4
15100	LMNT	60527	3271	18W-12S	A3
S Canal Bank Rd					
-	SMMT	60534	3148	9W-5S	D2
7400	SMMT	60501	3148	9W-5S	D2
7400	SMMT	60525	3148	9W-5S	D2
S Canalport Av					
1700	CHCG	60616	3092	0W-1S	A1
2000	CHCG	60608	3091	1W-1S	E1
2000	CHCG	60608	3092	0W-1S	A1
Canary Av					
1000	KdlT	60560	3333	41W-16S	E5
1000	KdlT	60560	3334	41W-16S	A5
Canary Ct					
10	LslT	60540	3142	25W-5S	B3
Canary Dr					
-	BlmT	60411	3509	3E-25S	E7
Canary Ln					
6400	HGKN	60525	3147	11W-7S	E5
Canary Rd					
100	MltT	60148	3083	21W-2S	E4
Canary Grass Ln					
8400	FXLK	60081	2415	27W-39N	A5
N Canavan Ct					
9800	NLES	60714	2864	10W-12N	A1
Canbury Ct					
1500	WLNG	60090	2754	16W-18N	D4
Candeur Dr					
3700	NPVL	60564	3267	28W-11S	B1
Candice Ct					
23800	CteT	60417	3597	2E-28S	E7
Candida Rd					
1000	ELGN	60123	2801	33W-13N	A7
Candleberry Ct					
300	YKVL	60560	3333	42W-16S	C5
Candleberry Ln					
1700	KdlT	60560	3333	42W-16S	D5
1700	YKVL	60560	3333	42W-16S	D5
2100	AURA	60506	3137	38W-6S	A5
Candlegate Cir					
100	RchT	60443	3593	8W-26S	B1
Candlelight Ct					
300	BGBK	60440	3269	23W-12S	A2
Candlelight Dr					
-	MTGY	60538	3198	41W-9S	A5
-	SgrT	60538	3198	41W-9S	A5
10	SLVL	60411	3597	2E-25S	D1
Candlelight Dr E					
8500	WLSP	60480	3208	13W-9S	E4
Candlelight Dr W					
8500	WLSP	60480	3208	13W-9S	E4
Candlelight Ln					
-	BtlT	53104	2358		E4
1700	AURA	60504	3201	33W-9S	A3
Candlelyte Ct					
300	ROSL	60172	2912	24W-8N	E3
Candlenut Dr					
1100	NPVL	60540	3141	28W-6S	A5
E Candlenut Ln					
1100	PLTN	60074	2753	19W-18N	C2
Candleridge Ct					
700	BRLT	60103	2911	28W-8N	B4
S Candlestick Wy					
1200	WKGN	60085	2535	14W-32N	D5
Candlewick Ct					
10	NARA	60542	3077	37W-3S	C5
10	NARA	60542	3137	36W-4S	D1
Candlewood Ct					
10	CRY	60013	2642	30W-24N	A7
400	ALGN	60102	2694	34W-20N	C7
1200	AURA	60502	3139	31W-5S	E4
1400	WLNG	60004	2754	16W-17N	D6
1400	WLNG	60090	2754	16W-17N	D6
2300	JLET	60586	3416	30W-21S	B6
3000	FSMR	60422	3507	3W-23S	A2
3700	DRGV	60515	3084	19W-3S	C6
5300	LSLE	60532	3142	24W-5S	D3
Candlewood Dr					
10	NBRN	60010	2644	24W-25N	B5
1000	DRGV	60515	3084	20W-3S	B6
1300	CLLK	60014	2693	36W-23N	D2
2200	JLET	60586	3416	30W-21S	B6
Candlewood Ln					
-	LKPT	60441	3419	21W-20S	E5
10	NBRN	60010	2644	24W-25N	C5
300	WNVL	60555	3080	29W-3S	D5
400	WnfT	60555	3080	29W-3S	D5
1300	HFET	60169	2858	25W-11N	B2
Candlewood Rd					
1000	ELGN	60123	2801	33W-13N	A7
Candlewood Tr					
300	CRY	60013	2642	30W-24N	A7
Candlewood Hill Rd					
1200	NHBK	60062	2756	10W-17N	E5
S Candota Av					
100	MPPT	60056	2807	16W-12N	E7
200	MPPT	60056	2861	16W-12N	E1
Cane Garden Cir					
200	AURA	60504	3139	31W-6S	E5
N Canfield Av					
2100	CHCG	60068	2918	9W-7N	B4
2100	CHCG	60631	2918	9W-7N	B4
2100	PKRG	60068	2918	9W-7N	B4
2100	PKRG	60631	2918	9W-7N	B4
4400	CHCG	60634	2974	9W-5N	B1
4400	NRDG	60706	2918	10W-5N	B7
N Canfield Av					
4400	NRDG	60706	2974	9W-5N	B1
5100	CHCG	60656	2918	10W-5N	B7
5100	CHCG	60706	2918	10W-5N	B7
5100	NRDG	60656	2918	10W-5N	B7
5200	NpkT	60656	2918	9W-6N	B5
5500	NpkT	60631	2918	9W-7N	B5
Canfield Ct					
2500	NPVL	60564	3266	29W-12S	D4
S Canford Cliffs Dr					
1400	MPPT	60056	2861	17W-11N	C4
Canham St					
-	PLNO	60545	3259	48W-13S	B5
Canidae Ct					
200	SCRL	60174	2964	34W-4N	E4
Cannes Ct					
3400	HLCT	60429	3426	4W-21S	E7
W Cannock Chase					
24400	TroT	60404	3584	30W-26S	B4
Cannon Ct					
1200	BTVA	60510	3077	36W-2S	E4
1200	BTVA	60539	3077	36W-2S	E4
1200	BtvT	60539	3077	36W-2S	E4
1600	WHTN	60187	3082	24W-1S	E2
1800	SMBG	60193	2858	25W-9N	A7
Cannon Dr					
-	CHCG	60614	2978	0W-2N	B7
400	GNVA	60134	3019	37W-1N	C2
N Cannon Dr					
-	CHCG	60657	2978	0W-3N	A4
1800	CHCG	60614	2978	0W-2N	B6
S Cannon Dr					
2300	EGvT	60005	2861	16W-10N	E6
2300	MPPT	60005	2861	16W-10N	E6
2300	MPPT	60056	2861	16W-10N	E6
Cannon Ln					
-	FDHT	60411	3509	1E-24S	B6
S Cannonade Ct					
13700	HMGN	60491	3344	15W-16S	C3
Cannon Ball Dr					
-	GYLK	60030	2532	21W-32N	E5
Cannonball Tr					
200	YKVL	60560	3261	42W-13S	C5
3100	BtlT	60560	3261	42W-13S	D5
3100	YKVL	60512	3261	42W-13S	C5
N Cannonball Tr					
10	BtlT	60512	3261	41W-11S	E2
10	YKVL	60512	3261	41W-12S	E3
1600	BtlT	60512	3262	41W-11S	A1
S Cannonball Tr					
10	BtlT	60512	3261	42W-12S	D4
10	YKVL	60512	3261	42W-12S	D4
2900	YKVL	60560	3261	42W-13S	D4
Canon Rd					
11800	ODPK	60467	3422	14W-19S	D3
11800	OrlT	60467	3422	14W-19S	C3
Canonero Dr					
800	NPVL	60540	3142	25W-7S	A7
1000	NPVL	60540	3204	26W-8S	A1
Canopy Dr					
700	LslT	60540	3141	26W-7S	E7
700	RDLK	60073	2531	24W-34N	C1
Cantal Ct					
10	WLNG	60090	2808	14W-15N	C1
Canter Ln					
1400	BRLT	60103	2910	30W-6N	B7
1400	BRLT	60103	2966	30W-6N	B1
Canterbury Dr					
8400	BRRG	60527	3208	15W-9S	A4
Canterbury Ln					
10	OKBK	60523	3086	15W-3S	B5
Canterbury Cir					
1200	LYVL	60048	2591	17W-28N	A6
Canterbury Ct					
-	GRNE	60031	2477	16W-36N	E5
10	CmpT	60175	2906	40W-7N	C6
10	LIHL	60156	2693	36W-21N	C5
10	PSHT	60463	3274	9W-13S	D5
10	SMWD	60107	2857	28W-11N	B5
10	WLMT	60091	2813	2W-13N	B6
100	BMDL	60108	2969	23W-5N	A2
100	LslT	60540	3142	25W-6S	B4
100	OSWG	60543	3200	35W-10S	B6
200	NLNX	60451	3501	18W-24S	B5
300	HNDL	60521	3086	15W-4S	A7
300	MltT	60137	3083	22W-2S	C4
1100	ELGN	60120	2855	32W-10N	D5
1500	DRN	60561	3207	18W-8S	A2
1600	JLET	60586	3496	30W-21S	B1
1600	WCHI	60185	3022	29W-0S	E7
1600	WCHI	60185	3080	29W-1S	E1
1600	WnfT	60185	3080	29W-1S	E1
2700	SBTN	60010	2804	24W-14N	C3
3800	RNPK	60471	3594	4W-27S	D4
4300	SCRL	60174	2965	33W-5N	B3
25000	PNFD	60585	3337	31W-14S	E1
S Canterbury Ct					
10	LKFT	60045	2649	13W-25N	A4
W Canterbury Ct					
1500	ANHT	60004	2753	18W-16N	D6
Canterbury Dr					
100	MHRY	60050	2527	34W-32N	D5
100	WynT	60185	2966	29W-4N	E4
400	CLSM	60188	2967	26W-4N	E4
600	HRPK	60133	2912	25W-9N	A1
700	CLLK	60014	2640	35W-24N	A7
900	SMBG	60195	2858	24W-12N	D2
2500	NHBK	60062	2809	10W-16N	E1
2500	NHBK	60062	2810	10W-16N	A1
10900	MKNA	60448	3503	13W-22S	A1
12400	PNFD	60585	3266	31W-14S	A7
12500	PNFD	60585	3338	31W-14S	A1
12600	PNFD	60585	3337	31W-14S	D1
E Canterbury Dr					
1400	ANHT	60004	2754	16W-16N	C6
W Canterbury Dr					
10	ANHT	60004	2754	18W-16N	A6
Canterbury Ln					
-	MDLN	60061	2647	17W-25N	B5
-	OKTR	60181	3085	17W-1S	B1
-	PGGV	60140	2797	41W-14N	E5
-	VLPK	60181	3085	18W-1S	A1
-	VNHL	60060	2647	17W-25N	B5
-	VNHL	60061	2647	17W-25N	B5
-	YkTp	60148	3085	18W-1S	A1
-	YkTp	60181	3085	18W-1S	A1
10	BGBK	60440	3269	23W-12S	A3
10	HNWD	60047	2646	20W-24N	A7
300	IVNS	60010	2751	23W-17N	D6
300	IVNS	60067	2751	23W-16N	D6
800	ISLK	60042	2586	28W-28N	E7
1200	GNVW	60025	2811	7W-14N	A5
1400	INCK	60060	2647	17W-25N	B5
1400	MDLN	60060	2647	17W-25N	B5
2100	LSLE	60532	3082	24W-4S	D7
2100	LslT	60532	3082	24W-4S	D7
Canterbury Ln					
6000	HFET	60192	2855	31W-12N	E1
6100	ELGN	60120	2855	31W-12N	E1
6200	WLBK	60527	3145	16W-6S	D5
7200	GGnT	60449	3682	9W-31S	A5
7200	MonT	60449	3682	9W-31S	A5
8000	WDRG	60517	3205	22W-9S	D3
15500	ODPK	60462	3346	10W-18S	C7
E Canterbury Ln					
10	BFGV	60089	2701	16W-21N	D6
10	NHFD	60093	2811	7W-14N	B3
N Canterbury Ln					
1700	PLTN	60074	2753	18W-18N	D3
2200	RLKB	60073	2475	22W-36N	B4
W Canterbury Ln					
10	NHFD	60093	2811	7W-14N	A3
Canterbury Ln W					
10	BFGV	60089	2701	16W-21N	D7
Canterbury Pl					
-	CCHL	60478	3506	6W-22S	A2
2000	WHTN	60187	3082	25W-2S	B4
7300	DRGV	60516	3206	19W-8S	D1
7400	DRN	60516	3206	19W-8S	D1
Canterbury Rd					
10	AURA	60506	3136	39W-7S	E6
10	LNSH	60069	2702	13W-22N	E4
Canterbury St					
-	HLSD	60154	3086	13W-1S	D1
-	HLSD	60162	3086	13W-1S	D1
1600	JLET	60586	3496	30W-21S	C1
9800	BDVW	60154	3087	12W-1S	B1
9800	BDVW	60155	3087	12W-1S	B1
9800	WSTR	60154	3087	13W-1S	A1
10700	PvsT	60154	3086	13W-1S	E1
10700	PvsT	60162	3086	13W-1S	E1
10700	WSTR	60154	3086	13W-1S	E1
10700	WSTR	60162	3086	13W-1S	E1
S Canterbury St					
20700	SRWD	60404	3496	30W-25S	C7
20700	TroT	60404	3496	30W-25S	C7
20900	SRWD	60404	3584	30W-25S	C1
20900	TroT	60404	3584	30W-25S	C1
Canterbury Tr					
10	RMVL	60446	3339	27W-17S	D5
400	ROSL	60172	2913	22W-8N	C3
E Canterbury Tr					
1200	PLTN	60074	2753	18W-18N	D3
N Canterbury Tr					
1700	PLTN	60074	2753	18W-18N	D3
Canterbury Wy					
200	RLKP	60030	2589	22W-30N	B1
S Canterbury Wy					
16300	LKPT	60441	3421	17W-19S	C3
Cantibury Ct					
4700	LGGV	60047	2700	18W-23N	E2
Cantigny Ct					
1200	NARA	60542	3078	35W-3S	C5
1300	NPVL	60565	3204	25W-8S	B2
Cantigny Dr					
10	WnfT	60190	3081	28W-1S	B1
N Cantigny Dr					
10	WnfT	60190	3081	28W-1S	B1
S Cantigny Dr					
200	WnfT	60190	3081	28W-1S	A2
W Cantigny Dr					
10	WnfT	60190	3081	28W-1S	A1
Cantigny Ln					
13800	HMGN	60491	3343	17W-17S	C6
Cantigny Rd					
10700	CTSD	60525	3147	13W-7S	A7
10800	CTSD	60525	3146	13W-7S	E7
Cantigny Wy					
1400	WHTN	60187	3081	26W-1S	D2
Canton Ct					
-	OSWG	60543	3263	36W-13S	E4
Canton Dr					
-	OSWG	60543	3263	36W-12S	E4
Canton Ln					
100	SMWD	60107	2856	29W-11N	D4
Cantore Dr					
2800	NPVL	60564	3202	30W-10S	C7
2800	WldT	60564	3202	30W-10S	C7
S Canvasback Ct					
14400	HMGN	60491	3344	15W-17S	C5
Canvasback Ln					
10	BmdT	60108	2967	26W-5N	E2
W Canvasback St					
10	BGVW	60455	3210	9W-9S	D3
Canyon Ct					
-	LKMR	60051	2530	28W-32N	A5
10	ALGN	60102	2746	37W-20N	C1
10	BtlT	60543	3262	40W-13S	B5
10	BtlT	60560	3262	40W-13S	B5
1400	BGBK	60490	3268	26W-12S	A2
2600	AURA	60503	3265	32W-11S	D1
7600	GRNE	60031	2476	18W-35N	E6
Canyon Dr					
500	RMVL	60446	3417	27W-18S	C1
500	RMVL	60544	3417	27W-18S	C1
2500	JLET	60586	3415	32W-20S	C5
2600	AURA	60503	3265	32W-11S	D1
N Canyon Dr					
100	BGBK	60490	3267	26W-11S	E2
200	BGBK	60490	3268	26W-11S	A1
S Canyon Dr					
100	BGBK	60490	3267	26W-12S	E2
100	BGBK	60490	3268	26W-12S	A2
Canyon Ln					
600	ELGN	60123	2853	36W-12N	E2
600	ELGN	60123	2854	36W-12N	A2
Canyon Tr					
200	CLSM	60188	2968	26W-3N	A5
300	CLSM	60188	2967	26W-3N	E5
Canyon Creek Ct					
-	AURA	60503	3201	33W-10S	A6
25500	CbaT	60010	2643	26W-25N	E4
Canyon Creek Dr					
-	AURA	60503	3201	33W-10S	A6
-	OswT	60503	3201	33W-10S	A6
Canyon Run Rd					
700	NPVL	60565	3204	25W-9S	B4
Canyon View Ct					
1100	JLET	60432	3500	20W-22S	B2
Canyon View Ln					
1100	JLET	60432	3500	20W-22S	B2
Cap Ct					
18800	CCHL	60478	3506	6W-22S	B2
Cape Av					
400	WynT	60185	2967	28W-3N	A7
600	WynT	60185	2966	29W-3N	C6
Cape Ct					
-	SMBG	60193	2858	25W-9N	B7
Cape Ln					
600	SMBG	60193	2858	25W-9N	B7
Cape Rd					
10	LslT	60540	3142	25W-6S	B4
Cape Wy					
200	GNVA	60134	3019	36W-1N	E4
Cape Breton Ct					
1600	HFET	60192	2804	25W-15N	B2
Cape Cod Ct					
6400	LSLE	60532	3142	25W-7S	C6
Cape Cod Ln					
-	LKMR	60041	2530	28W-32N	A6
-	LKMR	60051	2530	28W-32N	A6
-	PGGV	60140	2797	42W-15N	C4
10600	HTLY	60142	2745	39W-20N	C1
Cape Cove Cir					
6600	NndT	60012	2584	35W-27N	A7
6600	NndT	60012	2640	35W-27N	A1
Capella Ct					
10	LIHL	60156	2693	36W-22N	E5
Capes Dr					
100	ELBN	60119	3017	44W-2N	A2
N Capillo Av					
37000	LkvT	60046	2475	20W-37N	E2
Capista Dr					
100	SRWD	60404	3496	30W-22S	C2
13500	PNFD	60544	3338	29W-16S	D4
Capistrano Ct					
10	NpvT	60563	3140	30W-5S	C4
Capistrano Ln					
10400	ODPK	60467	3423	13W-21S	B5
10400	OrlT	60467	3423	13W-21S	B5
Capistrano Ter					
900	BRLT	60103	2911	28W-7N	B5
Capital Ct					
200	SRWD	60404	3496	31W-24S	A5
1800	SMBG	60193	2858	25W-9N	A7
Capital Dr					
300	SRWD	60404	3496	31W-24S	A6
400	LKZH	60047	2699	22W-23N	C2
14300	PNFD	60544	3337	31W-17S	E6
Capital Ln					
300	GRNE	60031	2534	17W-34N	A1
10500	HTLY	60142	2692	39W-21N	B6
Capital St					
-	ELGN	60124	2799	37W-14N	E6
Capitol Av					
2500	AURA	60503	3201	32W-10S	C7
Capitol Dr					
200	BGBK	60440	3269	21W-11S	E1
200	SRGV	60554	3135	42W-6S	D4
300	SgrT	60554	3135	42W-6S	D4
1000	WLNG	60090	2808	14W-16N	C1
7200	DRN	60561	3207	16W-8S	E1
9000	MaiT	60016	2863	11W-11N	E3
9000	MaiT	60068	2863	11W-11N	E3
9000	PKRG	60068	2863	11W-11N	E3
N Capitol Dr					
7100	LNWD	60076	2920	4W-8N	C1
7100	LNWD	60712	2920	4W-8N	C1
7100	SKOK	60076	2920	4W-8N	C1
W Capitol Dr					
1200	ADSN	60101	2970	20W-3N	B6
Capitol St					
3300	SKOK	60076	2866	4W-10N	D4
Cappaella St					
-	WDSK	60098	2581	41W-28N	C6
Cappel Ln					
21600	FKFT	60423	3591	12W-26S	C2
Cappelletti Dr					
3000	SCHT	60411	3596	1W-27S	A3
W Capri Av					
2000	JLET	60436	3497	26W-24S	E6
Capri Ct					
600	RDLK	60073	2531	23W-33N	D2
2900	AURA	60503	3201	31W-10S	D6
3700	NfdT	60025	2809	11W-13N	E7
3800	NPVL	60564	3267	27W-11S	B2
Capri Dr					
200	RDLK	60073	2531	23W-33N	D2
1700	AURA	60503	3201	32W-10S	D5
E Capri Dr					
800	PLTN	60074	2753	19W-18N	B4
N Capri Dr					
1800	PLTN	60074	2753	19W-18N	C3
Capri Ln					
1300	DYR	46311	3510		D7
1600	DYR	46311	3598		D1
1900	SMBG	60193	2858	25W-9N	A7
5000	RNPK	60471	3594	6W-26S	A2
5600	MNGV	60053	2865	7W-11N	C2
Capri Ter					
100	WLNG	60090	2755	14W-18N	C3
1100	MHRY	60050	2585	32W-30N	C1
Caprice Dr					
800	SRWD	60404	3496	30W-24S	B6
Capstan Dr					
4400	HFET	60192	2804	25W-15N	A2
Captain Hook Cove					
100	LKMR	60051	2529	28W-33N	D3
Captains Dr					
9600	AlqT	60102	2695	32W-22N	C4
Captains Ln					
1000	WLNG	60090	2754	15W-17N	E5
Captain's Cove					
10	LKMR	60051	2529	28W-33N	E3
Captiva Dr					
-	AURA	60504	3201	33W-9S	A5
Captons Ln					
8300	DRN	60561	3207	17W-9S	B4
Capulet Cir					
10	PltT	60124	2852	39W-10N	D5
Capulet Ct					
10	PltT	60124	2852	39W-11N	D5
Capulina Av					
5800	MNGV	60053	2865	8W-10N	A4
Cara Dr					
1900	CTHL	60403	3417	26W-21S	E7
Cara Ln					
-	OKBK	60523	3084	18W-3S	E5
Caraway Ct					
-	MKNA	60448	3503	13W-22S	B2
600	NPVL	60540	3140	29W-7S	D7
16300	LKPT	60441	3420	20W-21S	B6
Carberry Cir					
1100	IVNS	60067	2751	24W-17N	C5
Carboy Rd					
1600	EGvT	60005	2861	16W-10N	E5
1600	EGvT	60056	2861	16W-10N	E5
1600	MPPT	60005	2861	16W-10N	E5
1600	MPPT	60056	2861	16W-10N	E5
W Carboy Rd					
500	EGvT	60005	2861	16W-10N	E5
500	EGvT	60056	2861	16W-10N	E5
500	MPPT	60056	2861	16W-10N	E5
Cardiff Cir					
1900	CPVL	60110	2748	32W-18N	C5
Cardiff Ct					
-	HMGN	60491	3344	15W-16S	B4
10	ALGN	60102	2694	35W-21N	A6

Block	City	ZIP	Map#	CGS	Grid
Cardiff Ct					
900	SMBG	60194	2858	25W-11N	B3
Cardiff Dr					
200	ALGN	60102	2694	35W-21N	A6
900	CLLK	60014	2640	35W-24N	B7
900	CLLK	60014	2694	35W-23N	B1
900	CLLK	60156	2694	35W-23N	B1
Cardiff Rd					
800	NPVL	60565	3203	27W-8S	B2
Cardigan Ct					
700	NPVL	60565	3203	27W-8S	C2
Cardigan Pl					
-	HFET	60169	2804	26W-12N	A7
1900	HFET	60169	2858	26W-12N	A1
Cardinal Av					
500	OSWG	60543	3264	35W-11S	B2
500	OswT	60543	3264	35W-11S	B2
1400	MLPK	60160	3029	13W-1N	A2
N Cardinal Av					
200	ADSN	60101	2971	17W-3N	B4
500	AddT	60106	2971	17W-4N	B4
500	ADSN	60106	2971	17W-3N	B4
Cardinal Cir					
9100	ODHL	60487	3423	11W-19S	E2
Cardinal Ct					
-	DRPK	60010	2698	23W-21N	E6
10	SMWD	60107	2856	29W-9N	D7
10	WDRG	60517	3143	21W-7S	E7
100	DYR	46311	3510		C6
100	ISLK	60042	2586	29W-29N	D4
300	NARA	60542	3137	37W-4S	C1
400	MDLN	60060	2646	19W-27N	C1
600	GYLK	60030	2533	20W-33N	A3
700	LslT	60540	3142	24W-5S	C3
1000	BTVA	60510	3078	33W-2S	E3
1500	LNHT	60046	2417	21W-38N	E7
1700	WLNG	60090	2754	16W-18N	D3
1800	FSMR	60422	3507	3W-23S	A4
2100	GRNE	60031	2478	15W-36N	A4
2200	SMBG	60194	2857	26W-12N	B2
2200	SMBG	60194	2858	26W-11N	A4
20700	FKFT	60423	3503	11W-25S	E6
24200	FmtT	60060	2588	24W-28N	C7
N Cardinal Ct					
1100	PLTN	60074	2753	19W-17N	B5
S Cardinal Ct					
1800	WKGN	60048	2535	14W-31N	D6
W Cardinal Ct					
4900	MONE	60449	3683	6W-31S	B6
Cardinal Dr					
-	BlmT	60411	3509	3E-25S	E7
-	FmtT	60047	2645	21W-26N	C3
-	LKZH	60047	2699	22W-21N	A5
-	MchT	60097	2469	36W-37N	D1
-	SRGV	60554	3135	43W-5S	A4
10	OswT	60560	3334	40W-15S	B2
100	BMDL	60108	2968	23W-4N	E4
100	HNWD	60047	2645	21W-26N	C3
400	BRLT	60103	2910	31W-9N	A1
400	GLHT	60108	2968	23W-4N	E4
400	GLHT	60139	2968	23W-4N	E4
1000	ZION	60099	2362	12W-42N	B6
1100	AlqT	60102	2747	35W-19N	C2
1200	ALGN	60102	2747	35W-19N	C2
2000	NLNX	60451	3589	18W-27S	B4
2000	NlxT	60451	3589	18W-27S	B4
2100	RGMW	60008	2806	19W-13N	B5
2600	HnrT	60120	2856	31W-11N	A4
6400	HGKN	60525	3147	11W-7S	E6
16700	ODPK	60467	3423	13W-20S	B3
N Cardinal Dr					
1000	PLTN	60074	2753	19W-17N	C5
Cardinal Ln					
-	HDPK	60035	2704	10W-23N	A3
10	CPVL	60110	2748	32W-17N	D6
10	ROSL	60172	2912	24W-7N	C4
300	BGBK	60490	3267	26W-12S	E3
700	EGVV	60007	2913	22W-8N	D2
800	JLET	60432	3499	22W-22S	C1
1100	NPVL	60540	3203	26W-8S	E1
2400	WLMT	60091	2812	5W-13N	A5
3300	DrrT	60098	2583	38W-28N	A5
3300	SPGV	60081	2354	32W-42N	B5
18000	TYPK	60487	3424	11W-21S	A7
21200	DhmT	60033	2464	50W-36N	B3
E Cardinal Ln					
1000	MPPT	60056	2808	14W-13N	C6
W Cardinal Ln					
22200	RLKB	60073	2532	22W-34N	C1
Cardinal Pl					
300	MDLN	60060	2646	19W-27N	C1
300	SRWD	60404	3496	30W-23S	B5
Cardinal St					
200	AddT	60101	2971	17W-3N	B6
Cardinal Wy					
-	HPSR	60140	2795	47W-16N	D1
200	ISLK	60042	2586	28W-29N	D4
200	WcnT	60042	2586	28W-29N	D4
1800	LGGV	60047	2753	18W-20N	E1
Cardinal Cove					
-	ElgT	60124	2853	37W-9N	D7
Cardinal Creek Blvd					
-	BCHR	60401	3774	0E-36S	D7
-	BCHR	60401	3864	0E-36S	E1
-	WshT	60401	3864	0E-36S	E2
Cardinal Lake Dr					
10800	FftT	60423	3591	13W-26S	A2
10800	FKFT	60423	3591	13W-26S	A2
Cardington Wy					
3200	JNBG	60051	2472	30W-35N	A6
Carefree Av					
8800	ODPK	60462	3346	11W-16S	A2
W Carefree Dr					
13600	HMGN	60491	3343	17W-17S	D6
Caren Ct					
10	SEGN	60177	2908	35W-9N	B2
1400	BFGV	60089	2701	17W-21N	B5
Caren Dr					
400	BFGV	60089	2701	17W-21N	B5
W Carey Av					
8600	RVGV	60171	2973	11W-3N	D6
8600	RVGV	60171	2974	10W-3N	A5
Carey Cir					
300	MltT	60137	3083	21W-2S	D4
Carey Ct					
300	BMDL	60108	2969	22W-4N	D3
300	CHHT	60411	3507	2W-24S	D5
Carey Dr					
-	ROSL	60172	2913	23W-8N	B3
-	SmbT	60172	2913	23W-8N	B3
1100	MHRY	60050	2585	32W-30N	B1
Carey Ln					
10	SMWD	60107	2857	28W-11N	A4
Carey St					
-	PLNO	60545	3260	45W-13S	C6
1600	JltT	60433	3499	21W-25S	E7
N Carey St					
-	BvlT	60407	4030	33W-44S	B3
400	BCVL	60407	4030	33W-44S	B3
Carey Wy					
100	BRLT	60103	2909	31W-8N	E3
Cargill Dr					
2000	NHBK	60062	2757	10W-16N	A7
Cariann Ln					
1300	GNVW	60025	2811	6W-13N	C5
1300	WLMT	60091	2811	6W-13N	C5
E Carib Ln					
1700	MPPT	60056	2808	13W-14N	D3
Caribou Cross					
-	NHBK	60015	2756	13W-18N	A2
-	RVWD	60015	2756	13W-18N	A2
-	RVWD	60062	2756	13W-18N	A2
10	NHBK	60062	2755	13W-20N	E2
10	NHBK	60062	2756	13W-18N	A2
Caribou Ct					
10	BGBK	60490	3267	26W-12S	D2
4100	JLET	60431	3496	29W-23S	E4
Caribou Dr					
10	HNVL	60030	2532	21W-33N	D3
Caribou Ln					
1200	HFET	60192	2856	31W-12N	A2
10800	ODPK	60467	3423	13W-20S	A5
Caribou Tr					
500	CmpT	60175	2962	39W-5N	D2
1200	CLSM	60188	2967	28W-4N	B4
Caridnal Ct					
-	NHBK	60062	2756	12W-18N	A3
Carillon Dr					
-	AvnT	60030	2475	20W-35N	E6
-	AvnT	60030	2476	20W-35N	A6
-	AvnT	60046	2475	20W-35N	E5
1900	GYLK	60030	2476	20W-35N	A6
2200	GYLK	60030	2475	20W-35N	E5
N Carillon Dr					
-	DPgT	60544	3340	26W-15S	A2
-	LktT	60544	3339	26W-16S	D3
-	RMVL	60446	3340	26W-15S	A2
-	RMVL	60544	3340	26W-15S	A2
21500	DPgT	60544	3339	26W-15S	D3
S Carillon Dr					
-	LktT	60441	3340	25W-16S	A4
-	RMVL	60441	3340	25W-16S	A4
21100	LktT	60544	3339	26W-16S	E3
21100	LktT	60544	3340	26W-16S	A4
Carillon Lakes Dr					
-	LktT	60446	3417	26W-19S	E2
-	RMVL	60446	3417	26W-19S	E2
21300	LktT	60403	3417	26W-19S	E2
Carl Av					
-	BRTN	60010	2750	26W-20N	E1
800	ELGN	60120	2855	32W-11N	C3
N Carl Av					
500	BRTN	60010	2750	26W-20N	E1
Carl Blvd					
2600	EGVV	60007	2915	17W-7N	B4
2600	WDDL	60191	2915	17W-7N	B4
Carl Ct					
10	LIHL	60156	2694	34W-21N	C5
200	RLKB	60073	2474	23W-35N	E6
200	RLKB	60073	2475	23W-35N	A6
500	PTHT	60070	2808	15W-15N	A1
N Carl Ct					
2300	MchT	60051	2528	30W-34N	E1
Carl Dr					
1700	RLKB	60073	2474	23W-35N	E5
1800	RLKB	60073	2475	23W-35N	A5
4300	LSLE	60532	3142	23W-4S	E1
Carl Rd					
-	MONE	60449	3682	7W-32S	E6
Carl St					
10600	HTLY	60142	2692	40W-21N	B6
Carla Dr					
100	SEGN	60177	2908	35W-8N	C2
500	SRWD	60404	3496	30W-23S	C4
Carlborg Ct					
22200	RNPK	60471	3594	6W-26S	A3
Carleah St					
8800	MaiT	60016	2863	11W-11N	D4
8800	PKRG	60016	2863	11W-11N	D4
8800	PKRG	60068	2863	11W-11N	D4
Carlemont Dr					
1500	CLLK	60014	2693	36W-22N	E3
Carleton Av					
400	GNEN	60137	3025	22W-0N	D5
1300	NPVL	60565	3204	24W-9S	C5
Carleton Cir					
10	IVNS	60010	2750	25W-16N	E7
1300	NPVL	60565	3204	24W-9S	C4
Carleton Ct					
10	IVNS	60010	2751	25W-16N	A7
Carleton Dr					
7500	BtnT	60081	2414	30W-39N	B5
7600	SPGV	60081	2414	30W-39N	B5
Carleton Rd					
2000	HFET	60169	2804	24W-12N	E7
Carletta Rd					
10	PltT	60124	2905	43W-9N	B1
Carley Ct					
10	LMNT	60439	3271	18W-13S	A5
Carling Rd					
2000	HFET	60169	2804	24W-12N	D7
Carlino Dr					
100	BRLT	60103	2909	31W-8N	E3
Carlisle Av					
10	NfdT	60062	2757	9W-20N	B2
100	WTMT	60559	3145	18W-6S	A5
300	DRFD	60015	2757	9W-20N	B1
400	DRFD	60015	2704	10W-20N	B7
600	DRFD	60015	2757	9W-19N	B1
1100	EGVV	60007	2914	19W-8N	D3
1300	ITSC	60007	2914	19W-8N	D3
1300	ITSC	60143	2914	19W-8N	D3
Carlisle Ct					
100	CRY	60013	2695	32W-23N	C2
200	OSWG	60543	3263	37W-14S	B6
500	GNEN	60137	3083	22W-1S	B2
600	SRGV	60554	3135	41W-5S	E2
1800	SMBG	60194	2858	25W-11N	A3
1900	DRN	60561	3206	18W-10S	E5
3600	PRGV	60012	2641	32W-27N	B1
8200	HRPK	60133	2857	26W-9N	E7
8400	BRRG	60527	3208	15W-9S	A4
N Carlisle Ct					
300	RDLK	60073	2530	25W-33N	E2
S Carlisle Ct					
13100	DPgT	60544	3339	26W-15S	E2
Carlisle Dr					
-	BbyT	60506	3076	40W-3S	C6
-	HRPK	60193	2857	26W-9N	E7
-	NARA	60506	3076	40W-3S	C6
-	SMBG	60193	2857	26W-9N	E7
10	OKBK	60523	3085	17W-2S	C4
700	WDSK	60098	2524	42W-32N	C5
1300	BRTN	60010	2751	24W-17N	C4
1300	IVNS	60010	2751	24W-17N	C4
3800	PRGV	60012	2585	32W-27N	B7
4300	PRGV	60012	2641	32W-27N	B1
7800	HRPK	60133	2858	26W-9N	A7
8000	HRPK	60133	2857	26W-9N	E7
Carlisle Ln					
-	CPVL	60118	2746	37W-18N	C5
300	LNSH	60045	2702	14W-23N	D2
9000	ODPK	60462	3346	11W-17S	A5
9900	LKWD	60014	2638	38W-26N	D3
S Carlisle Ln					
13200	DPgT	60544	3339	26W-15S	E2
Carlisle Pl					
1200	DRFD	60015	2704	10W-21N	A6
Carlisle Rd					
10	ElaT	60047	2646	20W-25N	A6
10	HNWD	60047	2645	20W-24N	E7
10	HNWD	60047	2646	20W-25N	A6
400	BTVA	60510	3078	36W-2S	A3
Carlisle St					
-	WSTR	60154	3086	13W-2S	E4
-	WSTR	60154	3087	13W-2S	A4
-	WSTR	60525	3087	13W-2S	A4
1300	ALGN	60102	2746	35W-20N	E2
2000	ALGN	60102	2747	35W-20N	A2
Carlisle on Duxbury					
10	RGMW	60008	2805	22W-13N	B7
Carlislie Ln					
17000	LKPT	60441	3420	21W-20S	A5
17100	LKPT	60441	3419	21W-20S	E5
Carl Lee Rd					
300	SchT	60174	2908	34W-6N	D7
Carlow Cir					
16100	MhtT	60442	3677	20W-31S	C5
Carlow Dr					
800	DSPN	60016	2808	13W-13N	D7
900	BGBK	60446	3268	26W-14S	A6
900	BGBK	60490	3268	26W-14S	A6
900	RMVL	60446	3268	26W-14S	A6
2200	DGvT	60516	3206	19W-10S	D5
2200	DGvT	60561	3206	19W-10S	D5
2200	DRN	60561	3206	19W-10S	D5
Carl P Cassata Sr Ln					
6800	HDHT	60706	2918	8W-5N	E7
6900	NRDG	60706	2918	8W-5N	E7
S Carls Dr					
9500	WldT	60503	3201	31W-11S	D7
9500	WldT	60503	3265	31W-11S	D1
9500	WldT	60585	3201	31W-11S	D7
9500	WldT	60585	3265	31W-11S	D1
Carl Sandburg Rd					
10	CmpT	60175	2962	40W-4N	C5
Carl Sands Dr					
300	CRY	60013	2696	30W-24N	A1
Carlsbad					
1900	NPVL	60563	3081	26W-4S	E7
1900	NPVL	60563	3141	26W-4S	E1
Carlsbad Cir					
2600	AURA	60503	3265	32W-11S	D1
Carlsbad Ct					
800	ELGN	60123	2907	36W-9N	E1
Carlsbad Dr					
6100	TYPK	60477	3425	7W-20S	B3
Carlsbad Tr					
400	ROSL	60172	2913	22W-8N	B3
Carlson Ct					
500	BTVA	60510	3078	34W-1S	D2
900	NPVL	60563	3141	27W-5S	B4
1400	NARA	60542	3077	37W-3S	B6
Carlson Dr					
1300	SMWD	60107	2911	28W-9N	B1
2000	NHBK	60062	2757	9W-16N	B7
2000	NHBK	60062	2810	9W-16N	B1
Carlson Ln					
1700	WHTN	60187	3024	24W-0N	D4
Carlton Av					
1300	WHTN	60187	3024	25W-0N	B5
Carlton Ct					
10	EMHT	60126	3027	16W-0S	D7
100	SMBG	60193	2858	24W-10N	D6
300	GNCY	53128	2353		B3
300	SEGN	60177	2909	33W-9N	B1
400	OSWG	60543	3263	38W-13S	B6
1500	NLNX	60451	3588	19W-27S	D4
3000	WSTR	60154	3086	13W-2S	E4
Carlton Dr					
-	JLET	60586	3415	32W-21S	D7
200	CLSM	60188	3024	24W-1N	C2
300	BMDL	60108	2969	22W-4N	C3
600	ELGN	60120	2855	32W-12N	C2
2400	WDRG	60517	3143	21W-7S	E7
2400	WDRG	60517	3205	21W-8S	D1
Carlton Ln					
900	SMBG	60193	2858	24W-10N	C6
S Carlton Ln					
14700	HMGN	60491	3344	15W-17S	A5
Carlton Pl					
-	BFGV	60089	2701	17W-21N	A7
-	LGGV	60089	2701	17W-21N	A7
Carlton Rd					
7700	DRN	60561	3206	19W-8S	D2
Carlton St					
21300	LktT	60403	3417	26W-20S	D5
21500	PnfT	60403	3417	26W-20S	D5
21500	PnfT	60435	3417	26W-20S	D5
N Carlton St					
500	WHTN	60187	3024	25W-0S	B6
S Carlton St					
200	WHTN	60187	3024	25W-0S	B7
Carlton Ihde Dr					
-	PSHL	60465	3274	10W-12S	B3
Carlton Mews Ct					
200	SRGV	60554	3135	41W-6S	D5
Carly St					
-	FftT	60448	3503	12W-22S	C2
-	MKNA	60448	3503	12W-22S	C2
Carlyle Cir					
800	LKBF	60044	2593	11W-29N	E5
Carlyle Ct					
10	LslT	60540	3142	24W-6S	D4
100	ELGN	60120	2855	31W-11N	E3
200	OSWG	60543	3263	37W-14S	B6
600	LKVL	60046	2417	22W-39N	C5
700	NHBK	60062	2756	12W-18N	C4
2200	BFGV	60089	2701	16W-22N	D4
3000	JLET	60451	3500	19W-22S	D2
17300	TYPK	60487	3423	11W-20S	E5
N Carlyle Ct					
1100	ANHT	60004	2807	17W-15N	C3
Carlyle Dr					
-	NlxT	60451	3500	19W-22S	D2
600	JLET	60451	3500	19W-22S	D2
Carlyle Ln					
10	BFGV	60089	2701	16W-22N	D4
500	BGBK	60440	3268	24W-12S	E2
N Carlyle Ln					
900	ANHT	60004	2807	17W-14N	C3
N Carlyle Pl					
1900	ANHT	60004	2807	17W-16N	C1
S Carlyle Pl					
300	ANHT	60004	2807	16W-13N	C5
Carlyle Rd					
1400	NPVL	60564	3267	28W-11S	A1
1500	NPVL	60564	3266	28W-11S	E1
1600	WldT	60564	3266	28W-11S	E1
Carlyle Ter					
900	HDPK	60035	2704	8W-21N	E7
Carlysle Dr					
500	CNHL	60514	3145	16W-6S	D4
500	DGvT	60514	3145	16W-6S	D4
Carman Av					
-	BFGV	60089	2754	15W-20N	E1
-	VrnT	60069	2754	15W-20N	E1
-	VrnT	60089	2754	15W-20N	E1
400	BFGV	60089	2755	15W-20N	A1
Carmel Blvd					
1800	ZION	60099	2422	10W-39N	A5
2300	ZION	60099	2421	11W-39N	E5
Carmel Ct					
1100	NPVL	60540	3141	28W-6S	B5
1600	HFET	60169	2858	25W-12N	B2
9000	SPGV	60081	2413	31W-41N	C2
Carmel Dr					
2900	FSMR	60422	3507	3W-22S	A1
5500	HRPK	60133	2912	26W-6N	A6
6100	JLET	60586	3415	31W-20S	D6
N Carmel Dr					
900	PLTN	60074	2753	20W-17N	A5
Carmel Ln					
10	BRBK	60459	3211	7W-8S	C1
400	BGBK	60440	3268	23W-12S	E2
1400	CRY	60013	2641	31W-25N	D6
Carmel Pkwy					
10	MDLN	60060	2591	18W-28N	A6
N Carmela Ct					
400	ADSN	60101	2970	20W-4N	B3
Carmelhead Ln					
200	SMBG	60193	2859	23W-10N	B6
Carmella Dr					
10	CLLK	60012	2640	35W-26N	A2
Carmella Ln					
800	ELGN	60120	2855	32W-10N	C5
Carmen Av					
2900	NndT	60050	2586	30W-29N	A5
W Carmen Av					
1400	CHCG	60640	2921	2W-6N	C6
2400	CHCG	60625	2921	3W-6N	A6
3400	CHCG	60625	2920	4W-6N	C6
4100	CHCG	60630	2920	5W-6N	A6
5600	CHCG	60630	2919	7W-6N	B6
6300	CHCG	60656	2919	7W-6N	A6
6600	CHCG	60656	2918	8W-6N	E6
7200	CHCG	60706	2918	9W-6N	C6
7200	HDHT	60706	2918	9W-6N	C6
7700	NRDG	60706	2918	9W-6N	C6
8600	NRDG	60706	2917	10W-6N	E6
8700	CHCG	60706	2917	10W-6N	E6
Carmen Ct					
2400	LNHT	60046	2476	19W-37N	B1
Carmen Dr					
1500	EGVV	60007	2916	15W-8N	A2
W Carmichael Dr					
7600	PSHT	60463	3274	9W-14S	D6
Carn Av					
-	TYPK	60448	3504	11W-23S	A3
-	TYPK	60477	3504	11W-23S	A3
8800	MKNA	60448	3504	11W-23S	A3
N Carnaby					
8100	HRPK	60133	2857	26W-9N	E7
S Carnaby					
8000	HRPK	60133	2857	26W-9N	E7
Carnaby Ct					
800	SMBG	60194	2858	25W-11N	A3
Carnaby Pl					
10	MNSR	46321	3510		C4
W Carnahan Av					
11000	BHPK	60099	2421	11W-38N	E6
11100	WKGN	60087	2421	11W-38N	E6
Carnation Ct					
200	WKGN	60085	2537	10W-34N	A2
600	OSWG	60543	3263	37W-13S	B6
1800	AURA	60506	3137	38W-5S	B3
Carnation Dr					
600	OSWG	60543	3263	38W-13S	B6
2200	CTHL	60403	3417	27W-21S	D6
Carnation Ln					
200	HFET	60169	2859	23W-11N	B3
700	MTSN	60443	3506	5W-25S	C6
Carnation St					
10	DYR	46311	3598		C1
3400	FNPK	60131	2973	13W-4N	A2
Carnegie Ct					
1600	NPVL	60565	3204	24W-9S	C4
Carnegie St					
900	RGMW	60008	2806	20W-15N	A3
Carney Av					
700	WKGN	60085	2536	11W-33N	D4
Carney Ct					
900	ANTH	60002	2358	23W-42N	A6
Carney Ln					
600	BbyT	60134	3018	39W-0N	D6
Carnoustie Ct					
800	ELGN	60123	2854	36W-9N	A7
Carnoustie Dr					
8800	ODPK	60462	3346	11W-18S	A7
Carnoustie Ln					
10	IVNS	60067	2804	23W-15N	D1
Carol Av					
700	ELGN	60123	2854	35W-12N	B2
700	WDSK	60098	2524	42W-31N	B6
800	MHRY	60050	2528	31W-33N	C7
1000	WLNG	60090	2755	14W-16N	C6
5800	MNGV	60053	2865	7W-10N	B4
15900	HRVY	60426	3428	0W-19S	B1
15900	HRVY	60473	3428	0W-19S	B1
15900	SHLD	60426	3428	0W-19S	B1
15900	SHLD	60473	3428	0W-19S	B1
21700	SLVL	60411	3597	2E-26S	C2
W Carol Av					
6900	NLES	60714	2864	8W-10N	E4
Carol Cir					
3300	ISLK	60042	2586	28W-28N	E5
Carol Ct					
10	BGBK	60440	3268	25W-11S	C1
10	CRTE	60417	3597	1E-28S	A6
200	STGR	60475	3595	1W-28S	E6
200	STGR	60475	3596	1W-28S	A6
300	HDPK	60035	2758	7W-20N	C2
800	CLSM	60188	2968	24W-3N	C5
1200	JNBG	60051	2472	30W-35N	B5
1400	PLTN	60074	2753	19W-17N	D4
1400	PltT	60074	2753	19W-17N	D4
1500	NHBK	60062	2757	9W-17N	C6
1700	DRFD	60015	2703	12W-21N	C6
10400	RSMT	60018	2917	13W-8N	A1
15100	ODPK	60462	3346	10W-18S	B6
W Carol Ct					
7100	NLES	60714	2864	8W-10N	D4
Carol Dr					
500	CmpT	60175	2961	42W-4N	C3
2800	JLET	60432	3500	20W-22S	C2
W Carol Dr					
600	CmpT	60175	2961	42W-5N	C3
Carol Ln					
100	BGBK	60440	3268	25W-11S	C1
100	GYLK	60030	2532	20W-33N	E2
800	CRTE	60417	3597	1E-28S	A6
1100	GLNC	60022	2758	6W-18N	C3
1200	DRFD	60015	2703	12W-21N	C6
1300	DSPN	60018	2862	13W-10N	D5
1300	NPVL	60565	3203	26W-8S	D2
1300	WdfT	60015	2703	12W-21N	C6
1600	SLVL	60411	3597	2E-26S	C2
3300	BHPK	60099	2421	11W-39N	E5
3300	ZION	60099	2421	11W-39N	E5
3400	GNVW	60062	2809	12W-14N	B4
5100	GRNE	60031	2478	15W-35N	B6
9000	SPGV	60081	2414	30W-40N	B2
N Carol Ln					
500	RDLK	60073	2531	23W-34N	D2
36800	LkvT	60046	2475	21W-36N	E3
39200	BHPK	60099	2421	11W-39N	E5
39200	ZION	60099	2421	11W-39N	E5
S Carol Ln					
300	BDWD	60408	3942	31W-42S	B6
400	MPPT	60056	2861	17W-12N	C1
W Carol Ln					
300	EMHT	60126	2971	16W-3N	D5
6200	PSHT	60463	3275	7W-14S	B6
26800	GrtT	60041	2530	26W-34N	C1
Carol Pl					
1300	MTGY	60538	3200	34W-9S	C4
Carol Rd					
300	NlxT	60451	3501	18W-23S	A3
Carol St					
1000	DRGV	60516	3144	19W-7S	C6
1200	NLES	60714	2864	10W-10N	A4
1200	PKRG	60068	2864	10W-10N	A4
1200	PKRG	60714	2864	10W-10N	A4
1300	PKRG	60068	2863	10W-10N	E4
1500	DRGV	60515	3084	20W-4S	A7
3600	SKOK	60076	2866	4W-10N	C4
4800	SKOK	60076	2865	6W-10N	E4
4800	SKOK	60077	2865	6W-10N	E4
W Carol St					
7300	NLES	60714	2864	9W-10N	D4
8500	PKRG	60068	2864	10W-10N	A4
8500	PKRG	60714	2864	10W-10N	A4
Carol Ann Dr					
10	SMWD	60107	2857	28W-11N	A4
Carol Ann Ln					
4500	RNPK	60471	3594	5W-27S	C4
Carol Belle Tr					
5500	OKFT	60452	3347	6W-18S	D7
Carol Crest Ct					
1100	SYHW	60118	2800	35W-15N	C3
Carol Crest Dr					
1200	SYHW	60118	2800	35W-15N	C3
Carole St					
-	SRGV	60554	3136	40W-7S	B7
Carolian Dr					
400	LKZH	60047	2699	22W-22N	A3
Carolina Av					
4300	NndT	60014	2586	30W-27N	A7
4500	NndT	60014	2642	30W-27N	A1
Carolina Ct					
1400	SMBG	60193	2912	25W-8N	A2
Carolina Dr					
900	WCHI	60185	3022	30W-2N	B2
1600	EGVV	60007	2913	21W-8N	D2
1600	SLVL	60411	3597	2E-27S	C4
Carolina Ln					
9200	ODPK	60462	3345	11W-16S	E3
Carolina St					
200	BGBK	60490	3267	26W-12S	D3
Caroline Av					
-	BCHR	60401	3864	0W-36S	D1
900	JltT	60433	3587	22W-26S	C2
1400	HMND	46394	3280		D4
4900	WNSP	60558	3146	13W-5S	E2
N Caroline Av					
200	EMHT	60126	3028	15W-1N	B1
39000	WDWH	60083	2420	15W-39N	B6
Caroline Ct					
100	GNVA	60134	3020	34W-1N	D4
600	DRFD	60015	2703	10W-21N	E7
22000	FKFT	60423	3590	14W-26S	D3
Caroline Dr					
2700	HMWD	60430	3427	3W-21S	B6
3000	PnfT	60435	3417	27W-19S	C3
3200	JLET	60435	3417	27W-19S	C4
3300	JNBG	60051	2472	30W-35N	B6
Caroline Pl					
500	WKGN	60085	2537	10W-33N	A3
Caroline St					
600	MRGO	60152	2634	49W-26N	C3
N Caroline St					
10	CLLK	60014	2640	35W-26N	A3
S Caroline St					
10	CLLK	60014	2640	35W-25N	A4
Carollynn St					
1600	AraT	60502	3139	33W-4S	A1
1600	AURA	60502	3139	33W-4S	A1
Carolwood Ln					
8000	WDRG	60517	3205	22W-9S	C3
8100	BGBK	60440	3205	22W-9S	C4
8100	BGBK	60517	3205	22W-9S	C4
Carolyn Ct					
10	LKZH	60047	2698	23W-23N	E3
10	LKZH	60047	2699	23W-23N	A3
700	ELBN	60119	3017	43W-0N	B6
5100	OKFT	60452	3347	6W-18S	E6
10800	ODPK	60467	3345	13W-18S	A7
Carolyn Dr					
600	GNEN	60137	3025	22W-0N	C4
1800	AraT	60504	3138	35W-5S	C2
1800	AURA	60504	3138	35W-5S	C2
W Carolyn Dr					
900	PLTN	60067	2805	22W-15N	B2
Carolyn Ln					
800	PKRG	60068	2863	11W-9N	D6
5500	DGvT	60521	3146	16W-6S	A3
5500	HNDL	60521	3146	16W-6S	A3
S Carolyn Ln					
11700	ALSP	60803	3276	5W-13S	B4

Chicago 7-County Street Index

STREET Block City ZIP Map# CGS Grid

Carolyn Rd
2000 AURA 60506 3137 38W-7S A7
Caron Ct
600 SMBG 60193 2858 25W-9N A7
S Carondolet Av
12200 CHCG 60633 3278 3E-14S A6
13100 CHCG 60633 3352 3E-15S A1
Carousel Ct
- RLKP 60030 2589 21W-31N C1
1900 JLET 60435 3498 26W-22S A1
Carousel Dr
3900 GNVW 60062 2809 11W-15N E2
Carpathian Dr
- CLLK 60012 2641 33W-26N A2
- NndT 60014 2641 33W-26N A2
Carpenter Av
- OSWG 60560 3334 39W-15S E2
- WLNG 60090 2755 14W-17N B5
500 OKPK 60302 3030 8W-0S E5
500 OKPK 60304 3030 8W-0S E5
2100 JLET 60586 3415 33W-21S B6
2300 NasT 60586 3415 33W-21S B6
Carpenter Blvd
100 CPVL 60110 2800 34W-16N E1
100 CPVL 60118 2800 34W-16N E1
200 CPVL 60110 2747 34W-17N E7
Carpenter Ct
10 NARA 60542 3078 35W-4S B7
1000 EGVV 60007 2913 21W-8N E2
2700 WDRG 60517 3143 22W-7S D6
30900 WNVL 60555 3081 28W-3S B7
E Carpenter Dr
200 PLTN 60067 2752 20W-17N E6
200 PLTN 60067 2753 20W-17N A6
300 PLTN 60074 2753 20W-17N A6
1300 PltT 60074 2753 19W-17N C6
Carpenter Rd
- SKOK 60646 2919 6W-8N D1
10 DGvT 60439 3206 19W-11S C7
10 DRN 60439 3206 19W-11S C7
400 DGvT 60439 3270 19W-11S C1
7000 SKOK 60077 2919 6W-8N D1
Carpenter St
- BtlT 60560 3261 42W-13S C6
- YKVL 60560 3261 42W-13S C6
10 CPVL 60110 2747 34W-17N D7
10 DGvT 60439 3270 19W-12S C3
10 FKFT 60423 3591 12W-26S D1
10 LmnT 60439 3270 19W-12S C3
100 CLLK 60014 2639 36W-25N E4
600 CHHT 60411 3508 1W-24S A6
3300 BlmT 60475 3596 1W-28S A6
3300 STGR 60475 3596 1W-28S A6
5100 DRGV 60515 3144 19W-6S C4
5400 DRGV 60516 3144 19W-6S C4
10800 MKNA 60448 3503 13W-23S A3
18300 HMWD 60430 3428 1W-22S A7
18500 HMWD 60430 3508 1W-22S A1
N Carpenter St
10 CHCG 60607 3033 1W-0S E5
600 CHCG 60622 3033 1W-0N E3
S Carpenter St
700 CHCG 60607 3033 1W-0S E6
1800 CHCG 60608 3091 1W-1S E1
5000 CHCG 60609 3151 1W-5S E2
5500 CHCG 60621 3151 1W-8S E7
7500 CHCG 60620 3213 1W-10S E4
7500 CHCG 60621 3213 1W-8S E1
9600 CHCG 60643 3213 1W-11S E6
10200 CHCG 60643 3277 1W-12S E1
12200 CHCG 60643 3278 1W-14S A6
12200 CTPK 60643 3278 1W-14S A6
12700 CTPK 60827 3278 1W-15S A7
Carr Cir
- WHTN 60187 3081 26W-2S E4
Carr Ct
500 SMBG 60193 2858 25W-9N A7
1400 EGVV 60007 2913 21W-8N E2
1700 BTVA 60510 3078 35W-2S C5
Carr St
800 ELGN 60123 2854 35W-11N C5
4500 RGMW 60008 2806 19W-12N D7
4600 RGMW 60008 2860 19W-12N C1
Carrboro Ct
2300 NPVL 60565 3204 25W-10S A5
Carrel St
100 WNFD 60190 3023 27W-0N C5
Carriage Av
1200 LGNG 60525 3147 13W-5S A2
Carriage Ct
10 OKBK 60523 3085 18W-3S A6
200 BGBK 60490 3267 26W-11S E1
400 OSWG 60543 3263 37W-13S B5
600 CmpT 60175 2962 40W-3N B6
600 SMBG 60193 2913 22W-9N C1
900 RLKB 60046 2475 21W-35N C6
1000 NPVL 60540 3141 27W-6S B6
1600 GNOK 60048 2592 14W-30N C3
2600 AURA 60504 3201 32W-8S C1
W Carriage Ct
1800 ADSN 60101 2970 21W-4N A4
Carriage Dr
10 SLVL 60411 3597 2E-25S E1
100 CLSM 60188 3024 25W-2N A1
400 WCHI 60185 3022 29W-0S D7
400 WnfT 60185 3022 29W-0S D7
500 BTVA 60510 3078 36W-0S A1
700 BTVA 60134 3020 36W-0S A7
700 BTVA 60510 3020 36W-0S A7
700 GnvT 60134 3020 36W-0S A7
800 ALGN 60102 2747 33W-20N E2
4900 GRNE 60031 2478 15W-35N B6
7700 NndT 60012 2583 36W-27N D7
Carriage Ln
10 HIWD 60040 2704 9W-24N D1
10 JLET 60433 3587 23W-26S A3
10 JltT 60433 3587 23W-26S A3
10 LMNT 60439 3272 15W-14S A6
10 SLVL 60411 3597 2E-25S D1
1000 GYLK 60030 2533 19W-34N C1
1100 SMBG 60193 2913 22W-9N C1
1200 NHBK 60062 2757 9W-18N D3
1300 BGBK 60490 3268 26W-11S A1
1300 RLKB 60046 2475 21W-35N C7
1400 BGBK 60490 3267 26W-11S E1
1400 WTMT 60559 3145 18W-7S A6
2300 LNHT 60046 2418 20W-38N B7
2900 WKGN 60085 2536 12W-33N B1
8100 FXLK 60081 2414 29W-40N C3
8400 TYPK 60477 3424 10W-20S B5
8400 TYPK 60487 3424 10W-20S B5
12700 CTWD 60445 3275 7W-15S D7
12700 WthT 60445 3275 7W-15S D7
12700 WthT 60463 3275 7W-15S D7
18300 LNSG 60438 3429 2E-21S D7
18500 BlmT 60411 3429 2E-21S D7

Carriage Ln
18500 BlmT 60438 3429 2E-21S D7
E Carriage Ln
800 PLTN 60074 2753 19W-18N B2
1700 CteT 60417 3686 2E-32S D7
W Carriage Ln
300 BNVL 60106 2971 16W-5N E1
13600 MhtT 60442 3678 17W-29S D2
Carriage Pl
10 BRRG 60527 3146 14W-7S C6
3700 OMFD 60461 3506 4W-24S D4
Carriage Rd
10 NBRN 60010 2698 25W-22N A3
Carriage Tr
10 PSHT 60463 3274 9W-14S D6
100 BRTN 60010 2697 25W-20N E7
S Carriage Tr
200 MHRY 60050 2527 33W-31N D6
300 NndT 60050 2527 34W-31N D6
Carriage Wy
100 WLMT 60091 2811 5W-13N E7
200 BMDL 60108 2969 22W-4N C3
300 DRFD 60015 2757 9W-20N B1
400 SEGN 60177 2907 37W-7N D5
600 DRFD 60015 2704 9W-20N B7
800 ELGN 60120 2855 32W-12N C1
800 HDPK 60035 2704 9W-20N B7
1300 ROSL 60172 2912 25W-6N B6
2500 AURA 60504 3201 32W-8S C1
6200 OKFT 60452 3347 7W-17S B5
6600 LGGV 60047 2646 19W-24N C7
E Carriage Wy
10 HLCT 60429 3427 3W-21S A6
Carriage Greens Dr
8400 DRN 60561 3206 18W-9S E4
8600 DRN 60561 3207 18W-9S A4
8700 DRN 60439 3207 18W-10S A5
Carriage Hill Cir
200 LbvT 60048 2591 16W-30N D3
200 LYVL 60048 2591 16W-30N D3
Carriage Hill Ct
300 SRGV 60554 3135 43W-6S B4
600 ISLK 60042 2586 28W-28N E6
Carriage Hill Dr
200 AURA 60506 3137 38W-7S A7
600 GNVW 60025 2810 8W-13N E7
Carriage Hill Ln
600 SRGV 60554 3135 43W-6S B4
700 SgrT 60554 3135 43W-6S B4
Carriage Hill Rd
10 WLNG 60090 2755 15W-18N A2
100 WLNG 60090 2754 15W-18N E3
300 NPVL 60565 3204 25W-9S A4
700 ISLK 60042 2586 28W-29N E4
700 ISLK 60042 2587 28W-28N A6
1800 LSLE 60532 3142 24W-7S E6
Carriage House Ln
10 PlsT 60467 3345 13W-15S A2
Carriage Park Av
900 LKBF 60044 2593 12W-28N B6
900 LKBF 60045 2593 12W-28N B6
900 LKFT 60045 2593 12W-28N B6
Carriage Ridge Ln
400 LMNT 60439 3271 18W-13S A5
Carriage Station Pl
14300 LKPT 60441 3421 17W-19S B3
W Carriageway Cir
700 PLTN 60067 2805 21W-14N C3
S Carriageway Ct
700 PLTN 60067 2805 21W-15N D2
Carriageway Dr
500 BFGV 60089 2754 17W-17N B5
5000 RGMW 60008 2860 19W-12N C1
N Carriageway Dr
- BFGV 60004 2754 17W-17N B5
3400 ANHT 60004 2754 17W-17N B4
3400 BFGV 60089 2754 17W-18N B4
S Carriageway Ln
800 PLTN 60067 2805 21W-14N C3
Carriage Wy Ct
600 LslT 60540 3142 25W-7S B7
Carriage Wy Dr
100 BRRG 60527 3146 14W-7S C7
400 BRLT 60103 2966 29W-5N D2
400 WynT 60103 2966 29W-5N D1
Carriage Wy Ln
10 RtdT 60142 2745 41W-18N B5
Carrick Rd
400 MTSN 60443 3506 5W-24S B6
Carrick Wy
- TYPK 60477 3504 10W-23S B3
S Carrie Av
- JLET 60410 3585 28W-27S A5
22300 CNHN 60410 3585 28W-27S A4
Carrie Ct
- NlxT 60448 3501 16W-22S E2
300 NARA 60542 3078 35W-3S C6
3600 AlqT 60014 2641 32W-25N B4
W Carrie Ct
7800 FftT 60423 3504 9W-23S D4
Carrie Ollmann Ln
800 EGVV 60007 2914 19W-8N B1
Carrier Cir
1800 JLET 60586 3416 29W-21S D7
Carrington Ct
1800 NlxT 60451 3502 16W-24S A4
N Carrington Ct
3900 HLCT 60429 3426 4W-22S D7
18400 HLCT 60429 3506 4W-22S D1
Carrington Dr
- DndT 60118 2800 36W-16N B2
- ELGN 60118 2799 36W-16N E2
- ELGN 60124 2799 36W-16N E2
- WDND 60118 2799 36W-16N E2
2600 WDND 60118 2800 36W-16N B2
3100 NndT 60014 2641 32W-26N C3
3800 HLCT 60429 3426 4W-22S D7
3800 HLCT 60429 3506 4W-22S D1
3900 CCHL 60478 3506 4W-22S D1
16700 SHLD 60473 3429 2E-19S C3
18300 BmnT 60430 3426 4W-22S D7
Carrington Ln
- PnfT 60586 3496 29W-21S D1
2200 AURA 60504 3201 32W-8S B2
4200 JLET 60586 3496 29W-21S D1
Carrington Wy
2300 GNVW 60025 2809 11W-15N E3
2300 GNVW 60062 2809 11W-15N E3
Carrol Ct
900 SCRL 60174 2963 36W-3N E6
1500 DRN 60561 3207 18W-8S A1
Carrol Ln
10 CRY 60013 2695 32W-23N C1
1700 DRN 60561 3206 18W-8S E1
Carrol Rd
100 SCRL 60174 2963 36W-3N E6

Carrol Gate Rd
10 WHTN 60187 3082 25W-2S A3
600 MltT 60187 3082 25W-1S A2
W Carroll Av
1600 CHCG 60607 3033 2W-0N C4
1600 CHCG 60612 3033 2W-0N B4
1900 CHCG 60622 3033 2W-0N B4
2900 CHCG 60612 3032 4W-0N D4
3100 CHCG 60624 3032 4W-0N D4
4700 CHCG 60644 3032 5W-0N A4
Carroll Dr
12200 HMGN 60491 3422 15W-19S B2
Carroll Pkwy
2200 FSMR 60422 3507 2W-22S C2
N Carroll Pkwy
500 GNWD 60425 3428 0W-21S C7
Carroll Rd
700 LKFT 60045 2649 11W-27N C1
800 LKFT 60045 2593 12W-27N C7
Carroll Sq
600 EGvT 60007 2861 18W-10N A6
600 EGVV 60007 2861 18W-10N A6
E Carroll St
10 CTCY 60409 3352 C7
10 HMND 46320 3352 C7
Carroll Wy
200 BRLT 60103 2909 32W-8N C3
N Carrollton Ct
8100 HRPK 60133 2857 26W-9N E7
S Carrollton Ct
8000 HRPK 60133 2857 26W-9N E7
Carrollwood Rd
2500 NPVL 60540 3140 29W-7S D7
Carry Ln
- BFGV 60089 2754 17W-20N B1
Carse Av
15700 HRVY 60426 3428 1W-19S A1
N Carson Av
400 JLET 60435 3498 24W-23S D4
Carson Ct
200 CLSM 60188 2968 25W-3N A5
1400 HMWD 60430 3507 1W-22S E2
1800 SMBG 60193 2858 25W-9N A7
Carson Dr
1000 MLPK 60160 3029 12W-1N C2
1400 HMWD 60430 3507 1W-22S E2
18900 BlmT 60430 3507 1W-22S E2
W Carson Dr
25100 LkvT 60046 2474 25W-37N B2
Carswell Av
900 EGVV 60007 2915 18W-8N A2
Carswell Ct
900 EGVV 60007 2915 18W-8N A2
W Carter Av
200 WDDL 60191 2970 19W-5N D1
200 WDDL 60191 2971 18W-5N A1
Carter Ct
10 SEGN 60177 2907 37W-7N C4
200 NHBK 60062 2758 7W-16N A6
300 WDDL 60191 2970 18W-5N E1
1300 NCHI 60064 2536 11W-32N C5
1300 WKGN 60085 2536 11W-32N C5
W Carter Ct
6000 MONE 60449 3682 7W-31S D5
Carter St
300 LYVL 60048 2591 17W-28N C6
N Carter St
400 PLTN 60067 2752 21W-16N D7
600 GNCY 53128 2353 A2
900 BfdT 53128 2353 A2
N Carter St CO-B
700 GNCY 53128 2353 A2
900 BfdT 53128 2353 A2
N Carter St CO-U
- GNCY 53128 2353 A2
S Carter St
100 GNCY 53128 2353 A3
Carters Grove Ct
200 GYLK 60030 2533 20W-34N A2
Carthage Ct
300 BMDL 60108 2969 22W-4N B3
1600 NPVL 60565 3204 24W-9S D4
4500 NndT 60012 2640 33W-27N E1
Carthage Ln
10 HFET 60169 2859 23W-11N A3
Cartier Av
- TYPK 60477 3424 9W-21S D5
Cart Wright Tr
500 MHRY 60050 2527 34W-32N C5
Carver Av
2500 NCHI 60064 2536 11W-32N C5
S Carver Dr
- CHCG 60827 3279 1E-15S A7
- CHCG 60827 3351 1E-15S B1
Carver Ln
100 SMBG 60193 2858 25W-10N B6
100 SMBG 60194 2858 25W-10N B6
12400 GfnT 60142 2691 41W-20N D7
Carver Lake Ct
16300 LktT 60403 3417 26W-19S E3
N Carvis Dr
34700 WrnT 60046 2476 18W-34N E7
Cary Av
100 HDPK 60035 2705 7W-21N B7
9600 SRPK 60176 2973 12W-4N C2
Cary Plz
25800 WcnT 60084 2587 25W-28N E6
Cary Rd
900 ALGN 60102 2694 33W-21N E6
1000 AlqT 60102 2694 33W-21N E6
1000 AlqT 60102 2695 32W-22N B4
1700 ALGN 60013 2695 32W-22N B4
2000 CRY 60102 2695 32W-22N B4
2200 CRY 60013 2695 32W-22N B4
Cary Rd CO-V36
900 ALGN 60102 2694 33W-21N E6
1000 AlqT 60102 2694 33W-21N E6
1300 AlqT 60102 2695 32W-22N B4
1700 ALGN 60013 2695 32W-22N B4
2000 CRY 60102 2695 32W-22N B4
2200 CRY 60013 2695 32W-22N B4
Cary St
10 CRY 60013 2695 31W-23N E1
10 SchT 60177 2908 35W-7N C6
400 CRY 60013 2696 30W-23N A2
Cary-Algonquin Rd
- ALGN 60013 2695 32W-22N B3
- CRY 60102 2695 32W-22N B3
100 CRY 60013 2695 32W-22N B3
200 TVLY 60013 2695 32W-23N C2
400 CRY 60013 2641 31W-24N D7
Cary-Algonquin Rd CO-V36
- ALGN 60013 2695 32W-22N B3
- CRY 60102 2695 32W-22N B3
100 CRY 60013 2695 32W-22N B3
200 TVLY 60013 2695 32W-23N C2

Cary-Algonquin Rd CO-V36
400 CRY 60013 2641 31W-24N D7
N Caryl Av
100 NHLK 60164 2972 13W-2N E7
100 NHLK 60164 3028 13W-2N E1
1500 MLPK 60160 3028 13W-1N E2
S Caryl Av
100 NHLK 60164 3028 13W-1N E1
200 MLPK 60160 3028 13W-1N E2
Caryn Cir
700 SHLD 60473 3429 0E-19S A2
Caryn Ln
3000 WKGN 60085 2536 12W-33N B1
Caryn Ter
1100 NHBK 60062 2757 9W-17N D5
Cary Point Dr
300 CRY 60013 2696 30W-23N A2
Caryville Ln
100 SMBG 60193 2858 26W-10N A6
Cary Woods Cir
- AlqT 60013 2695 31W-23N E3
- CRY 60013 2695 31W-23N E2
Casa Ct
- PTHT 60070 2808 14W-15N B3
Casa Dr
1000 SMBG 60173 2859 22W-11N D4
Casa Solana Dr
800 WHTN 60187 3082 24W-2S E3
Cascade Av
700 RMVL 60446 3269 23W-14S A7
Cascade Cir
- DGvT 60527 3207 16W-10S E6
9200 BRRG 60527 3207 16W-10S E6
W Cascade Cir
2200 RDLK 60073 2530 25W-33N E3
2200 RDLK 60073 2531 25W-33N A3
Cascade Ct
- FmtT 60060 2588 24W-29N B3
- MRGO 60152 2634 49W-27N C1
- WCDA 60084 2588 24W-29N B3
10 SEGN 60177 2908 36W-9N A1
1500 NPVL 60565 3203 26W-9S D3
3300 JLET 60451 3500 19W-22S D2
7900 ODPK 60462 3346 9W-17S C4
N Cascade Ct
1200 LKFT 60045 2649 12W-24N B7
S Cascade Ct
1200 LKFT 60045 2649 12W-24N B7
1400 BRTN 60010 2750 25W-17N E5
W Cascade Ct
21200 LktT 60544 3339 26W-16S E5
Cascade Ct E
10 BRRG 60527 3207 16W-10S E6
Cascade Ct W
10 BRRG 60527 3207 16W-10S E6
Cascade Dr
- MRGO 60152 2634 49W-27N C1
10 IHPK 60525 3146 13W-7S E5
100 CLLK 60012 2639 35W-27N E1
100 CLLK 60012 2640 35W-26N A2
1000 AURA 60506 3137 38W-6S B4
5400 LSLE 60532 3142 24W-6S D4
N Cascade Dr
1800 VNHL 60061 2647 17W-27N B1
Cascade Ln
300 OSWG 60543 3263 36W-11S E2
300 OSWG 60543 3264 36W-11S A2
1300 PLTN 60074 2753 19W-18N C3
1400 BRTN 60010 2750 25W-17N E5
3300 JLET 60451 3500 19W-22S D2
Cascade Wy
- GRNE 60046 2476 18W-34N E7
- WrnT 60046 2476 18W-34N E7
7300 GRNE 60031 2477 18W-34N A7
7600 GRNE 60031 2476 18W-34N E7
Cascade Ridge Dr
1600 JLET 60586 3495 32W-21S D1
Cascara Ln
4400 LSLE 60532 3143 22W-4S C1
Casco Bay
300 WPHR 60096 2363 10W-43N A5
Case Ct
400 SMBG 60193 2858 25W-9N A7
2900 AURA 60503 3201 31W-10S D7
S Case Ct
- PNFD 60544 3338 30W-17S A7
Case Dr
700 ROSL 60172 2912 24W-7N D5
16500 LKPT 60441 3420 20W-19S C3
Case Ln
1100 ELGN 60120 2855 32W-11N D3
Case Pl
600 EVTN 60202 2867 2W-9N B6
W Case Rd
- WCDA 60073 2587 27W-29N B3
25000 WCDA 60084 2587 27W-29N B3
25000 WcnT 60051 2587 27W-29N A3
25000 WcnT 60073 2587 27W-29N B3
25000 WcnT 60084 2587 27W-29N B3
Case St
100 LslT 60563 3141 26W-5S E3
100 LslT 60563 3142 25W-4S A2
100 MTGY 60538 3199 37W-9S C5
100 NPVL 60563 3141 26W-5S E3
100 NPVL 60563 3142 25W-4S A2
700 EVTN 60202 2867 2W-9N B6
Casey Ct
500 AURA 60502 3139 32W-7S C7
900 SMBG 60173 2805 21W-13N C6
28400 LKBN 60010 2696 28W-22N E3
Casey Ln
700 HRVD 60033 2464 50W-37N A1
800 HPSR 60140 2795 46W-15N E3
S Casey Ln
14400 HMGN 60491 3343 17W-17S C5
W Casey Rd
- LYVL 60048 2533 19W-31N C7
17100 LbvT 60048 2534 18W-31N A7
17100 WKGN 60048 2534 16W-31N C7
17200 LbvT 60030 2534 17W-31N A7
18100 LbvT 60030 2533 18W-31N D7
19000 FmtT 60030 2533 19W-31N D7
19000 FmtT 60048 2533 19W-31N C7
19000 GYLK 60030 2533 19W-31N C7
19000 GYLK 60048 2533 19W-31N C7
19000 LbvT 60048 2533 19W-31N D7
Cash Rd
22500 CmgT 60033 2405 51W-39N D3
Cashel Ln
8700 TYPK 60477 3504 10W-23S B3
S Cashel Bay Rd
24900 MHTN 60442 3677 19W-30S E3
Cashew Dr
7400 ODPK 60462 3346 9W-18S D7
Cashlenan Dr
- MhtT 60442 3590 15W-27S C5

Cashlenan Dr
- MhtT 60451 3590 15W-27S C5
- NlxT 60451 3590 15W-27S C5
Cashmore Rd
3200 WDWH 60083 2478 14W-37N C1
3200 WKGN 60087 2478 14W-37N C1
N Cashmore Rd
38000 WDWH 60083 2478 14W-38N C1
38200 WDWH 60083 2420 14W-38N C7
Casimer Pulaski Dr
- WKGN 60064 2536 12W-32N A5
- WKGN 60085 2535 13W-32N E4
- WKGN 60085 2536 12W-32N A5
- WrnT 60085 2535 13W-32N E4
3100 NCHI 60064 2536 12W-32N A5
Casimer Pulaski Dr CO-A29
- WKGN 60064 2536 12W-32N A5
- WKGN 60085 2535 13W-32N E4
- WKGN 60085 2536 12W-32N A5
- WrnT 60085 2535 13W-32N E4
3100 NCHI 60064 2536 12W-32N A5
Casino Center Dr
- HMND 46320 3280 D2
900 LkeC 46320 3280 E3
Caspian Ln
- LKPT 60441 3419 21W-20S E5
Cass Av
- DGvT 60439 3207 17W-11S C7
- DGvT 60439 3271 17W-12S C2
- DGvT 60527 3207 17W-11S C7
1600 LYVL 60048 2591 17W-30N C2
N Cass Av
10 WTMT 60559 3145 18W-5S B2
500 WTMT 60559 3085 17W-4S B7
N Cass Av CO-15
600 WTMT 60559 3085 17W-4S B7
S Cass Av
- DGvT 60561 3207 17W-10S B5
- DRN 60561 3207 17W-10S B5
10 WTMT 60559 3145 18W-7S B6
700 DGvT 60561 3145 17W-7S B7
700 DRN 60561 3145 17W-7S B7
6600 DRN 60559 3145 17W-7S B6
6600 WTMT 60561 3145 17W-7S B6
9700 DGvT 60439 3207 17W-11S C6
9800 DGvT 60527 3207 17W-10S B5
S Cass Av CO-15
- DGvT 60439 3207 17W-10S B5
- DGvT 60527 3207 17W-10S B5
- DGvT 60561 3207 17W-10S B5
- DRN 60561 3207 17W-10S B5
400 WTMT 60559 3145 17W-6S B3
700 DGvT 60561 3145 17W-7S B7
700 DRN 60561 3145 17W-7S B7
6600 DRN 60559 3145 17W-7S B6
6600 WTMT 60561 3145 17W-7S B6
Cass Ct
1700 LYVL 60048 2591 17W-30N C2
S Cass Ct
3500 OKBK 60523 3085 18W-3S B5
3500 WTMT 60523 3085 18W-3S B5
3500 WTMT 60559 3085 18W-3S B5
Cass Ln
800 EGVV 60007 2914 21W-8N A2
Cass Ln E
1300 WTMT 60559 3145 18W-7S B6
Cass Ln W
1300 WTMT 60559 3145 18W-7S A6
Cass St
10 LMNT 60439 3270 19W-13S D5
100 BtnT 60081 2414 29W-39N D5
100 WDSK 60098 2524 41W-31N D7
300 CRTE 60417 3685 0W-29S C2
5200 OKLN 60453 3211 6W-10S E5
E Cass St
10 JLET 60432 3499 23W-23S A4
900 JltT 60432 3499 22W-23S C4
1800 JLET 60433 3499 21W-23S E4
1800 JltT 60433 3499 21W-23S E4
1900 JltT 60432 3500 20W-23S B4
1900 JltT 60433 3500 20W-23S B4
2000 NlxT 60433 3500 20W-23S B4
2000 NlxT 60433 3500 20W-23S B4
2500 JLET 60432 3500 20W-23S B4
E Cass St US-6
10 JLET 60432 3499 23W-23S A4
E Cass St US-30
10 JLET 60432 3499 23W-23S A4
800 JltT 60432 3499 23W-23S A4
1800 JLET 60433 3499 21W-23S E4
1800 JltT 60433 3499 21W-23S E4
1900 JltT 60432 3500 20W-23S B4
1900 JltT 60433 3500 20W-23S B4
2000 NlxT 60432 3500 20W-23S B4
2000 NlxT 60433 3500 20W-23S B4
2500 JLET 60432 3500 20W-23S B4
W Cass St
10 JLET 60432 3498 24W-23S E4
100 JLET 60435 3498 24W-23S E4
W Cass St US-6
10 JLET 60432 3498 24W-23S E4
W Cass St US-30
10 JLET 60432 3498 24W-23S E4
100 JLET 60435 3498 24W-23S E4
Cassandra Ln
600 UYPK 60466 3684 3W-29S C2
1600 LKMR 60051 2529 30W-33N B2
1600 MchT 60051 2529 30W-33N B2
Cassandra Tr
5000 RGWD 60072 2470 34W-37N B3
N Casseday Av
10 JLET 60432 3499 23W-23S B4
Casselberry N
10400 HTLY 60142 2692 39W-21N C6
Casselberry S
10400 HTLY 60142 2692 39W-21N C6
Cassidy Ln
300 ElgT 60124 2853 38W-10N A7
300 PltT 60124 2852 39W-10N E7
300 PltT 60124 2853 38W-10N A7
Cassie Dr
600 JLET 60435 3497 27W-23S C3
700 TroT 60435 3497 27W-23S C3
Cassin Rd
10 NPVL 60565 3204 25W-10S B5
Castaway Ct
1600 HFET 60010 2804 24W-16N B1
Castaway Ln
1600 HFET 60010 2804 25W-15N B1
1600 HFET 60192 2804 25W-15N B1
1600 SBTN 60010 2804 25W-15N B1
4800 HFET 60010 2751 24W-16N B7
5100 IVNS 60010 2751 24W-16N B7
Castbourne Ct
1600 WHTN 60187 3082 23W-1S E2
1600 WHTN 60187 3083 23W-1S A2

STREET Block	City	ZIP	Map#	CGS	Grid
Castello Av					
9600	FNPK	60131	2973	12W-2N	C6
9600	FNPK	60164	2973	12W-2N	C6
9600	LydT	60164	2973	12W-2N	C6
Castilian Cir					
2200	NHBK	60062	2810	10W-15N	A2
Castilian Ct					
1000	GNVW	60025	2809	11W-13N	D5
1000	NfdT	60025	2809	11W-13N	D5
Castilleja Ct					
700	NPVL	60540	3141	28W-7S	A7
Castillian Wy					
1500	MDLN	60060	2590	19W-29N	C4
Castine Wy					
1200	BCHR	60401	3774	0W-35S	D5
Castle Av					
10	DndT	60118	2801	32W-14N	C5
Castle Cir					
300	LGPK	60525	3087	12W-2S	C4
Castle Ct					
100	BRTN	60010	2751	24W-20N	C2
100	PltT	60010	2751	24W-20N	C2
400	MTSN	60443	3506	5W-24S	B6
500	BGBK	60440	3205	21W-11S	D7
1700	ELGN	60103	2856	31W-9N	A7
2100	WKGN	60087	2479	11W-37N	D1
3500	JLET	60431	3417	28W-21S	A7
3500	PnfT	60431	3417	28W-21S	A7
8600	LynT	60527	3208	14W-9S	C4
E Castle Ct					
800	PLTN	60074	2753	19W-18N	B2
Castle Dr					
-	BHPK	60087	2422	9W-38N	B7
-	BHPK	60099	2422	9W-38N	B7
-	OKBK	60523	3085	16W-1S	D1
-	OKTR	60181	3085	16W-1S	D1
-	OKTR	60523	3085	16W-1S	D1
700	BvlT	60407	3941	33W-42S	A7
700	CmpT	60175	2961	41W-5N	E2
1000	GNVW	60025	2809	11W-13N	E6
1200	PKRG	60068	2917	10W-7N	E3
1200	PKRG	60068	2918	10W-7N	A3
5100	BLWD	60104	3028	13W-0N	E3
8400	TYPK	60477	3424	10W-20S	B5
8400	TYPK	60487	3424	10W-21S	B5
W Castle Dr					
12000	NlxT	60448	3502	15W-22S	C1
Castle Ln					
2700	RGMW	60008	2805	21W-13N	C5
Castle Rd					
400	FXLK	60050	2472	28W-37N	D2
3200	DrrT	60098	2581	40W-28N	E5
3200	WDSK	60098	2581	40W-28N	E5
3400	DrrT	60098	2582	40W-28N	A6
3400	WDSK	60098	2582	40W-28N	A6
18700	HMWD	60430	3508	1W-22S	B2
N Castle Rd					
500	ADSN	60101	2970	20W-4N	A4
Castlebar Ct					
10	SEGN	60177	2908	35W-7N	B4
2100	HRPK	60133	2967	27W-5N	C2
E Castlebar Ct					
400	RLKB	60073	2475	22W-36N	B5
Castlebar Ln					
4400	HRPK	60133	2967	27W-5N	C2
15000	ODPK	60462	3346	11W-17S	A6
Castlebar Tr					
14100	WDSK	60098	2581	43W-30N	A1
Castleberry Dr					
8100	DrrT	60098	2583	37W-28N	B6
8100	NndT	60098	2583	37W-28N	B6
Castle Connor Dr					
3800	RNPK	60471	3594	4W-27S	D5
Castle Dargan Dr					
4800	CCHL	60478	3506	6W-22S	A1
Castlefield Ln					
-	CLLK	60014	2693	36W-22N	D3
N Castleford Ln					
1300	BHPK	60083	2420	13W-39N	E5
1300	BHPK	60083	2421	13W-39N	A5
Castlegate Ct					
10	VNHL	60061	2647	16W-25N	E5
800	LKFT	60045	2649	12W-26N	C2
W Castle Island Av					
8400	CHCG	60656	2918	10W-5N	A7
Castle Pines Cir					
1800	ELGN	60123	2854	36W-9N	A7
1900	ELGN	60123	2853	36W-10N	E7
Castle Pines Ct					
-	LIHL	60156	2693	37W-21N	C5
Castle Pines Ln					
400	RVWD	60015	2756	12W-20N	A1
2300	AURA	60503	3201	33W-10S	B7
Castlerea Ct					
10	CRY	60013	2641	31W-24N	D6
Castlerea Ln					
600	DSPN	60016	2808	13W-13N	D6
Castle Ridge Dr					
-	JLET	60586	3415	32W-21S	D7
Castle Rock Cir					
4100	AURA	60564	3202	30W-9S	B3
Castle Rock Ct					
700	WDND	60118	2800	36W-16N	A1
Castlerock Ct					
-	LKWD	60014	2692	39W-23N	D1
Castle Rock Dr					
12400	HTLY	60142	2744	43W-19N	B2
Castle Rock Ln					
10	BMDL	60108	2968	24W-5N	D1
Castleshire Dr					
900	WDSK	60098	2524	42W-31N	B7
Castleton Ct					
10	NBRN	60010	2644	25W-24N	B6
700	CLSM	60188	2967	27W-3N	D6
800	MDLN	60060	2590	20W-28N	A6
1000	RLKP	60030	2589	22W-30N	C1
Castleton Rd					
1400	LYVL	60048	2591	17W-30N	A2
Castleview Ct					
500	NBRN	60010	2697	25W-23N	E3
500	NBRN	60010	2698	25W-23N	A3
Castlewood Ct					
100	ROSL	60172	2912	25W-7N	A4
300	HFET	60067	2804	23W-14N	E4
900	GRNE	60031	2477	17W-35N	C7
1300	LMNT	60439	3271	17W-14S	B7
2700	AURA	60504	3201	32W-8S	D1
Castlewood Dr					
10	CPVL	60110	2748	33W-18N	A5
10	DndT	60110	2748	33W-18N	A5
600	HmrT	60107	2856	30W-10N	B6
600	SMWD	60107	2856	30W-10N	B6
1300	LMNT	60439	3271	18W-14S	B7
1400	WHTN	60187	3082	24W-1S	D2
Castlewood Ln					
300	BFGV	60089	2701	17W-21N	C7
300	BFGV	60089	2754	17W-20N	A1
300	BRLT	60103	2911	28W-6N	B6
300	DRFD	60015	2756	12W-20N	C1
600	DRFD	60015	2703	12W-20N	C7
E Castlewood Ln					
800	BRLT	60103	2911	28W-7N	B5
Castlewood Rd					
1900	DRFD	60015	2704	10W-21N	B6
1900	DRFD	60035	2704	10W-21N	B6
1900	HDPK	60035	2704	10W-21N	B6
W Castlewood Ter					
700	CHCG	60640	2921	1W-6N	E6
Castlewood Tr					
5800	MHRY	60050	2527	34W-32N	B5
Catalina Av					
6200	OKFT	60452	3347	7W-18S	B7
Catalina Ct					
600	LNHT	60046	2417	21W-39N	D5
15500	ODPK	60462	3346	9W-18S	E7
Catalina Dr					
1100	HRPK	60133	2912	26W-6N	A6
1300	HRPK	60133	2911	26W-6N	E6
15100	ODPK	60462	3346	9W-18S	E7
15100	OrlT	60462	3346	9W-18S	E7
S Catalina Dr					
100	RDLK	60073	2531	25W-33N	A3
Catalina Ln					
-	AraT	60504	3201	33W-9S	A5
-	AURA	60504	3200	33W-9S	E5
-	AURA	60504	3201	33W-9S	A5
Catalpa Av					
100	ITSC	60143	2914	20W-6N	B6
100	WDDL	60191	2971	17W-5N	B1
200	WDDL	60191	2915	17W-5N	B7
300	ROSL	60172	2913	23W-7N	B5
300	SchT	60174	2908	35W-6N	B7
400	AddT	60191	2915	17W-5N	B7
1400	WKGN	60085	2536	11W-34N	D2
7200	WDRG	60517	3205	21W-8S	D1
20100	LYWD	60411	3510	3E-23S	A4
W Catalpa Av					
1000	CHCG	60640	2921	2W-6N	C5
2400	CHCG	60625	2921	3W-6N	A5
2600	CHCG	60625	2920	3W-6N	E5
5300	CHCG	60630	2919	6W-6N	C5
6300	CHCG	60656	2919	8W-6N	A5
6600	CHCG	60656	2918	8W-6N	E5
7800	NpkT	60656	2918	9W-6N	B5
8600	CHCG	60656	2917	10W-6N	E5
Catalpa Ct					
-	BCHR	60401	3864	0W-36S	C5
10	BGBK	60490	3267	26W-12S	E2
10	WDRG	60517	3205	21W-8S	D1
200	ROSL	60172	2913	22W-7N	B5
1000	FKFT	60423	3503	13W-25S	B6
1400	SPGV	60081	2414	30W-38N	A6
8900	TYPK	60487	3424	11W-20S	A5
12100	PNFD	60585	3266	30W-14S	B7
20400	CTHL	60403	3418	25W-19S	B3
20400	LktT	60403	3418	25W-19S	B3
Catalpa Dr					
500	RDLK	60073	2532	23W-34N	A2
500	RLKP	60073	2532	23W-34N	A2
7600	MchT	60097	2469	36W-34N	D7
Catalpa Ln					
400	DLTN	60419	3350	0E-16S	E3
400	LYVL	60048	2647	16W-27N	C1
600	BRLT	60103	2910	29W-6N	C1
1000	NPVL	60540	3203	26W-8S	E1
11600	WDSK	60098	2582	40W-29N	A3
11900	WDSK	60098	2581	40W-29N	E3
W Catalpa Ln					
1700	MPPT	60056	2861	17W-11N	C3
Catalpa Pl					
200	WLMT	60091	2812	3W-13N	D6
W Catalpa Rd					
26500	AntT	60002	2356	26W-43N	D4
Catalpa St					
100	AddT	60106	2971	17W-4N	B4
100	ADSN	60101	2971	17W-4N	B4
100	ADSN	60106	2971	17W-4N	B4
800	BCHR	60401	3864	0W-36S	C1
1500	HHLL	60051	2586	30W-29N	A4
6800	HRPK	60133	2911	27W-8N	C3
20700	VmT	60015	2702	14W-20N	B7
E Catalpa St					
400	JLET	60432	3499	23W-23S	B4
700	ADSN	60101	2971	17W-3N	B5
N Catalpa St					
100	ADSN	60101	2971	17W-3N	B4
Catamaran Cir					
-	PGGV	60140	2798	41W-15N	B5
-	RtdT	60140	2798	41W-15N	A5
Catawba Ct					
10	HMGN	60491	3422	15W-19S	C3
Catawba Ln					
8000	HRPK	60133	2857	26W-9N	D7
W Catawba Ln					
13400	HMGN	60491	3343	16W-16S	E4
S Catawba Rd					
16500	HMGN	60491	3422	15W-19S	C3
Catbird Ln					
300	VmT	60015	2755	14W-20N	B1
Catclaw Ct					
5300	NPVL	60564	3266	29W-13S	D5
Cater Ln					
200	LbvT	60048	2591	17W-30N	C2
Caterpillar Dr					
-	MTGY	60538	3198	39W-10S	E6
-	MTGY	60538	3199	39W-10S	A6
-	MTGY	60543	3199	39W-10S	A6
10	JLET	60435	3497	27W-24S	D5
10	JLET	60436	3497	27W-24S	D5
Catfish Cir					
10	BDWD	60481	3942	30W-39S	D2
Catfish Dr					
26000	WmTp	60481	3761	32W-34S	D6
Cathedral Ct					
2200	GRNE	60031	2478	15W-36N	A4
Catherine					
-	JSTC	60458	3210	10W-9S	B2
Catherine Av					
1000	NPVL	60540	3142	25W-6S	A5
2200	TNLK	53181	2354		A2
N Catherine Av					
10	LGNG	60525	3087	12W-4S	B6
200	LGPK	60525	3087	12W-3S	B6
43300	AntT	60002	2357	25W-43N	A4
S Catherine Av					
10	LGNG	60525	3087	12W-4S	B7
300	LGNG	60525	3147	12W-5S	B3
5500	CTSD	60525	3147	12W-6S	B3
W Catherine Av					
7900	LydT	60656	2918	10W-6N	A5
7900	NpkT	60656	2918	10W-6N	A5
8400	CHCG	60656	2918	10W-6N	A5
8600	CHCG	60656	2917	10W-6N	E5
25000	AntT	60002	2357	25W-42N	B5
Catherine Ct					
-	WLNG	60090	2755	15W-17N	B5
10	CLLK	60014	2640	35W-25N	B4
200	OSWG	60543	3263	36W-11S	E1
500	WDDL	60191	2970	18W-5N	E2
800	GYLK	60030	2533	20W-33N	B2
1000	NPVL	60540	3141	26W-6S	E5
1000	NPVL	60540	3142	25W-6S	A5
13900	ODPK	60462	3345	11W-16S	E3
19900	FKFT	60423	3503	11W-24S	E4
W Catherine Ct					
24900	PnfT	60586	3416	31W-20S	A5
Catherine Dr					
900	DYR	46311	3598		E2
13900	ODPK	60462	3345	11W-16S	E3
W Catherine Dr					
24900	PnfT	60586	3415	31W-20S	E5
24900	PnfT	60586	3416	31W-20S	A5
25100	PNFD	60586	3415	31W-20S	E5
Catherine Ln					
-	KLDR	60047	2699	20W-22N	E3
100	MTGY	60538	3199	36W-9S	D5
19700	TYPK	60477	3504	11W-23S	A4
19800	MKNA	60448	3503	13W-23S	B4
Catherine St					
300	AraT	60505	3139	33W-7S	A6
300	AURA	60505	3139	33W-7S	A6
300	LMNT	60439	3270	19W-13S	E5
1000	JLET	60435	3498	25W-22S	B2
2200	NHBK	60062	2757	10W-17N	A5
N Catherine St					
10	JLET	60436	3498	25W-23S	C5
1200	JLET	60435	3498	25W-22S	B1
1500	CTHL	60403	3498	25W-22S	B1
34500	GrtT	60041	2473	25W-34N	E7
Catherine Ln Rd					
200	ELGN	60123	2854	34W-12N	E1
Cathryn Ct					
700	MltT	60188	3024	25W-1N	A3
Cathryn St					
10	FXLK	60020	2473	27W-37N	A2
W Cathy Dr					
1000	JLET	60431	3585	28W-25S	B1
Cathy Ln					
12900	PNFD	60585	3338	29W-15S	C2
13000	WldT	60585	3338	29W-15S	C2
N Cathy Ln					
100	MPPT	60056	2807	16W-13N	E7
S Cathy Ln					
700	MPPT	60056	2807	16W-12N	E7
W Cathy Ln					
800	MPPT	60056	2807	16W-12N	E7
Catino Ct					
600	ROSL	60172	2913	23W-6N	A6
N Catino Ct					
200	MPPT	60056	2808	14W-13N	C6
W Catino St					
600	ANHT	60005	2806	18W-13N	E6
W Catino Ter					
8100	NLES	60714	2864	10W-11N	B2
Catkins Wy					
400	AlqT	60013	2642	30W-24N	B6
400	CRY	60013	2642	30W-24N	B6
Catlin Sq					
-	BbyT	60134	3018	39W-0N	D6
Catlow Ct					
-	BRTN	60010	2750	27W-20N	C1
W Caton Av					
800	JLET	60435	3498	25W-23S	C3
Caton Cor					
2300	JLET	60586	3416	29W-21S	D6
W Caton St					
2100	CHCG	60647	2977	2W-2N	B7
Caton Crest Ct					
2400	CTHL	60403	3417	27W-21S	D6
Caton Crest Dr					
2300	CTHL	60403	3417	27W-21S	D6
2300	PnfT	60403	3417	27W-21S	D6
2300	PnfT	60435	3417	27W-21S	D6
Caton Farm Rd					
1700	CTHL	60403	3418	26W-20S	A6
1700	CTHL	60441	3418	26W-20S	A6
1900	CTHL	60403	3417	28W-20S	B6
1900	LktT	60403	3417	26W-20S	E6
1900	LktT	60403	3418	26W-20S	A6
2300	CTHL	60435	3417	28W-20S	A6
2300	LktT	60435	3417	28W-20S	A6
2300	PnfT	60435	3417	28W-20S	A6
2400	PnfT	60403	3417	27W-20S	D6
2500	JLET	60435	3417	27W-20S	C6
2900	JLET	60431	3417	27W-20S	B6
3000	PnfT	60431	3417	28W-20S	B6
W Caton Farm Rd					
-	JLET	60431	3416	30W-20S	C6
-	PnfT	60431	3416	30W-20S	C6
10	JLET	60586	3415	32W-21S	C6
10	NasT	60586	3415	32W-21S	C6
200	CTHL	60403	3418	24W-20S	D6
200	CTHL	60441	3418	24W-20S	D6
3500	JLET	60431	3417	28W-20S	A6
3500	PnfT	60431	3417	28W-20S	A6
4700	JLET	60586	3416	29W-20S	C6
23300	PnfT	60586	3416	30W-20S	C6
25000	PnfT	60586	3415	31W-20S	E6
25600	PNFD	60586	3415	32W-20S	D6
Caton Ridge Dr					
-	JLET	60431	3495	31W-21S	E1
1600	JLET	60586	3495	31W-21S	E1
1700	JLET	60586	3415	31W-21S	E7
Cat Schooner Ln					
10	TDLK	60030	2533	19W-34N	C1
Cattail Cir					
1800	AURA	60504	3201	33W-8S	A3
Cattail Ct					
10	HNWD	60047	2645	21W-25N	D6
2800	WCDA	60084	2588	25W-30N	A2
Cattail Dr					
-	BCHR	60401	3864	0E-36S	E2
W Cattail Ln					
23300	ElaT	60010	2698	23W-20N	E7
Cattail Run					
2100	GRNE	60031	2478	14W-36N	D4
2100	WrnT	60031	2478	14W-36N	D4
Cattleman Dr					
2100	NLNX	60451	3589	19W-27S	A4
Catulpa St					
19500	FftT	60448	3503	11W-23S	E4
19500	MKNA	60448	3503	11W-23S	E4
Caulfield Pt					
-	YKVL	60560	3333	42W-17S	E7
Caumet Av					
-	BNHM	60633	3352	3E-16S	A3
Cavalcade Cir					
600	NPVL	60540	3141	26W-7S	E7
600	NPVL	60540	3142	26W-7S	A7
Cavalcade Ct					
2700	AURA	60503	3201	32W-10S	D6
Cavalier Ct					
400	WDND	60118	2800	34W-15N	D3
1600	WHTN	60187	3082	24W-2S	D3
Cavalieri Ln					
400	LslT	60540	3142	24W-5S	D3
Cavalry Ct					
14700	PNFD	60544	3337	31W-17S	E6
Cavalry Dr					
200	BMDL	60108	2968	24W-4N	D4
200	BmdT	60108	2968	24W-4N	D4
Cavan Ln					
600	DSPN	60016	2862	15W-11N	A4
Cave Creek Ct					
4100	AURA	60564	3202	30W-9S	B4
W Cavecreek Ct					
13700	HMGN	60491	3343	17W-17S	D6
Cavell Av					
1100	HDPK	60035	2704	9W-21N	B6
Cavin Av					
100	PTPR	53158	2363	10W-43N	B4
100	WPHR	53158	2363	10W-43N	B4
100	WPHR	60096	2363	10W-43N	B4
Cavin Dr					
1700	NCHI	60088	2593	11W-30N	C2
Cawdor Ln					
100	IVNS	60067	2752	22W-16N	B7
Caxton Dr					
1700	WHTN	60187	3082	26W-1S	A1
Cayman Ct					
10	OswT	60538	3199	36W-11S	D7
1600	BRLT	60103	2967	27W-5N	B2
Cayman Dr					
10	OswT	60538	3199	36W-11S	D7
E Cayuga Av					
100	EMHT	60126	3027	16W-0N	E5
100	EMHT	60126	3028	15W-0N	A5
Cayuga Ct					
10	HNWD	60047	2646	19W-25N	B5
100	BMDL	60108	2968	25W-5N	B1
S Cayuga Ct					
17300	LKPT	60441	3420	20W-20S	B5
Cayuga Dr					
1000	NHBK	60062	2756	11W-17N	D5
E Cayuga Ln					
2000	MPPT	60056	2808	13W-15N	E3
Cayuga St					
400	JLET	60432	3499	21W-23S	E4
400	JltT	60432	3499	21W-23S	E3
N Cayuga Tr					
25400	LKBN	60010	2643	27W-25N	B5
W Cayuse Ct					
16300	LKPT	60441	3420	20W-20S	C4
Ceals Ct					
1400	NPVL	60565	3203	26W-9S	D3
Cebold Dr					
10	OSWG	60543	3263	37W-11S	D1
10	OswT	60538	3263	37W-11S	D1
10	OswT	60543	3263	37W-11S	C1
Cebula Ct					
10	BGBK	60440	3204	24W-10S	D5
Cecelia Av					
1300	JltT	60436	3586	24W-25S	D1
Cecelia Ct					
14300	HmrT	60491	3343	18W-18S	B7
14300	HmrT	60491	3421	17W-18S	B1
Cecelia St					
100	GYLK	60030	2532	21W-33N	E3
Cecily Dr					
1600	JLET	60435	3417	27W-21S	C7
1600	JLET	60435	3497	27W-21S	C1
S Cecily Dr					
16200	PnfT	60586	3416	29W-19S	E3
Cedar Av					
-	CHCG	60613	2977	1W-5N	D1
-	FXLK	60020	2473	27W-36N	C3
-	GRNE	60031	2478	15W-35N	A6
-	WrnT	60031	2478	15W-35N	A6
10	LKVL	60046	2417	22W-38N	A7
10	LKVL	60046	2475	22W-38N	A1
100	HDPK	60035	2705	7W-21N	A6
400	EMHT	60126	3028	15W-0S	B6
400	YkTp	60126	3028	15W-0S	B6
700	ELGN	60120	2855	33W-12N	A2
700	WKGN	60085	2536	11W-33N	C4
900	SCRL	60174	2964	35W-3N	C6
2000	HRPK	60133	2911	27W-8N	C2
2600	GNVA	60134	3019	37W-0N	C5
17700	CCHL	60478	3426	5W-21S	C6
18500	CCHL	60478	3506	5W-22S	C1
35400	AvnT	60073	2474	24W-35N	C6
N Cedar Av					
200	WDDL	60191	2971	17W-5N	B1
300	WDDL	60191	2915	17W-6N	B7
500	AddT	60191	2915	17W-6N	B6
3800	BHPK	60099	2421	11W-38N	E7
3800	WKGN	60087	2421	11W-38N	E7
3800	WKGN	60099	2421	11W-38N	E7
22600	RLKB	60073	2475	22W-34N	B7
S Cedar Av					
500	EMHT	60126	3028	15W-0N	B4
900	YkTp	60126	3028	15W-0S	B6
4400	HMND	46327	3352		E4
W Cedar Av					
21600	LkvT	60046	2417	21W-38N	D6
Cedar Cir					
-	BmnT	60426	3426	5W-19S	B1
100	SMWD	60107	2857	28W-10N	A6
Cedar Ct					
10	CTCY	60409	3351	2E-16S	C4
10	LMNT	60439	3270	20W-14S	C6
10	MltT	60190	3023	26W-0N	D5
10	SEGN	60177	2908	35W-7N	B4
10	VNHL	60061	2647	17W-26N	C3
10	WNVL	60555	3080	30W-1S	C2
100	SMBG	60193	2858	24W-10N	E6
300	CLSM	60188	2968	26W-4N	A4
300	SMWD	60107	2857	28W-10N	A5
500	MNSR	46321	3510		D1
600	RMVL	60446	3269	23W-14S	A6
1600	WPHR	60096	2363	9W-43N	C5
1800	DSPN	60018	2863	12W-9N	B6
2100	GNVW	60025	2864	9W-12N	D1
2200	NHBK	60062	2809	11W-16N	D1
5200	LSLE	60532	3142	24W-5S	D3
8600	FKFT	60423	3504	10W-25S	B6
17400	HMGN	60491	3421	18W-20S	A5
18800	CCHL	60478	3506	5W-22S	C2
E Cedar Ct					
10	KdlT	60560	3333	43W-16S	A4
W Cedar Ct					
10	KdlT	60560	3333	44W-16S	A4
6500	MONE	60449	3682	8W-32S	C7
Cedar Ct N					
400	BFGV	60089	2701	17W-22N	C4
Cedar Ct S					
400	BFGV	60089	2701	17W-22N	C4
Cedar Dr					
-	PNFD	60585	3337	33W-15S	A2
-	WldT	60564	3265	31W-12S	E4
10	CLLK	60014	2639	37W-25N	B4
10	NARA	60542	3137	36W-4S	D1
10	WLNG	60090	2754	15W-18N	E4
7400	MchT	60097	2469	36W-36N	D4
N Cedar Dr					
38600	LkvT	60046	2416	23W-38N	D6
W Cedar Dr					
22000	AntT	60002	2417	22W-40N	C3
22300	RLKB	60073	2532	22W-34N	B1
26600	AntT	60002	2356	26W-42N	D6
Cedar Ln					
-	AntT	60002	2417	22W-41N	B2
10	BDWD	60481	3942	30W-40S	B4
10	LNSH	60069	2702	14W-23N	D3
10	LynT	60458	3209	11W-8S	E1
10	WYNE	60184	2965	32W-5N	D2
100	AddT	60106	2971	17W-4N	B3
100	ADSN	60101	2971	17W-4N	B3
100	ADSN	60106	2971	17W-4N	B3
200	GLNC	60022	2758	6W-17N	D5
300	EGVV	60007	2915	18W-8N	A1
300	GNEN	60137	3083	23W-1S	A2
300	SRWD	60404	3496	30W-23S	C4
400	FKFT	60423	3503	13W-25S	C7
400	WLMT	60091	2812	4W-13N	B6
500	LMBD	60148	3026	18W-0N	E5
700	BRLT	60103	2910	29W-6N	D6
700	CHHT	60411	3507	1W-24S	E6
800	NHBK	60062	2757	10W-17N	A4
1000	DYR	46311	3510		C7
1600	SPGV	60081	2414	30W-39N	A6
6700	DRN	60559	3145	18W-7S	A6
6700	WTMT	60559	3145	18W-7S	A6
9200	PKRG	60068	2863	11W-11N	E3
9300	MaiT	60016	2863	11W-11N	E2
17500	TYPK	60477	3424	9W-21S	E5
28300	WmTp	60481	3761	32W-34S	C5
34400	AvnT	60073	2532	21W-34N	C1
E Cedar Ln					
600	MPPT	60056	2808	14W-14N	B4
2900	CteT	60417	3687	3E-30S	B2
N Cedar Ln					
10	GNWD	60425	3508	0E-22S	E1
23500	ElaT	60047	2698	23W-23N	E2
23500	LKZH	60047	2698	23W-23N	E2
S Cedar Ln					
10	GNWD	60425	3508	0E-22S	D2
12700	PSHT	60463	3274	9W-15S	D7
12700	PSHT	60463	3346	9W-15S	D1
W Cedar Ln					
900	ANHT	60005	2860	18W-12N	E1
8000	NLES	60714	2864	10W-10N	B5
Cedar Rd					
-	HMGN	60439	3343	18W-16S	B3
-	LMNT	60439	3343	18W-16S	B3
1600	HMWD	60430	3427	2W-21S	D6
3600	PKFT	60466	3594	4W-26S	D3
3600	PKFT	60471	3594	4W-26S	D3
3600	RNPK	60471	3594	4W-26S	D3
6400	OKFT	60452	3347	8W-18S	B6
7600	MchT	60097	2469	36W-35N	D5
7600	WRLK	60097	2469	36W-35N	D5
14300	HMGN	60491	3343	17W-17S	B5
16200	FKFT	60423	3591	12W-26S	C2
N Cedar Rd					
100	NLNX	60451	3501	18W-24S	C5
1300	NlxT	60451	3501	18W-22S	B1
1500	NLNX	60448	3501	17W-22S	B2
1500	NlxT	60448	3501	18W-22S	B1
2500	NLNX	60441	3501	18W-22S	B1
2500	NlxT	60441	3501	18W-22S	B1
S Cedar Rd					
10	NLNX	60451	3501	17W-25S	C7
700	NlxT	60451	3589	18W-26S	C3
900	NLNX	60451	3589	18W-25S	C1
13800	HMGN	60439	3343	18W-16S	B4
13800	HMGN	60491	3343	18W-16S	B4
15200	HmrT	60491	3343	18W-18S	A7
15600	HMGN	60491	3421	18W-20S	A5
15600	HmrT	60491	3421	18W-19S	A2
16300	LKPT	60441	3421	18W-20S	A5
16500	HMGN	60441	3421	18W-20S	A5
16500	HmrT	60441	3421	18W-19S	A3
16500	LKPT	60491	3421	18W-19S	A3
17800	NLNX	60441	3421	17W-21S	B7
17800	NLNX	60491	3421	17W-21S	B7
17800	NlxT	60441	3421	17W-22S	B7
17800	NlxT	60451	3421	17W-22S	B7
17800	NlxT	60491	3421	17W-21S	B7
22500	NLNX	60442	3589	17W-27S	C4
22500	NlxT	60442	3589	17W-27S	C4
22800	MhtT	60442	3589	17W-27S	C5
23500	MHTN	60442	3589	17W-28S	C7
23900	MHTN	60442	3678	18W-31S	C6
23900	MhtT	60442	3678	18W-31S	C6
26300	MhtT	60442	3767	18W-35S	C7
27800	WltT	60442	3767	18W-35S	C7
S Cedar Rd US-52					
27700	MhtT	60442	3767	18W-35S	C7
27800	WltT	60442	3767	18W-35S	C7
Cedar Rdg					
10	LKBN	60010	2643	26W-24N	E7
Cedar St					
-	FXLK	60081	2415	28W-39N	A5
-	LKZH	60047	2698	23W-22N	E4
-	LKZH	60047	2699	23W-22N	A4
10	CTSD	60525	3147	12W-6S	C5
10	PKFT	60466	3595	2W-27S	C4
100	AURA	60506	3138	35W-7S	A7
100	PKRG	60068	2864	10W-9N	B7
300	WNKA	60093	2812	4W-15N	B2
400	LIHL	60156	2694	35W-22N	B4
700	WLSP	60480	3209	12W-9S	C4
900	DRFD	60015	2703	11W-21N	D7
1100	GLHT	60137	3025	23W-1N	A2
1100	GLHT	60139	3025	23W-1N	A2
1100	MltT	60137	3025	23W-1N	A2
1400	PKRG	60068	2863	11W-9N	E7
1500	HHLL	60051	2586	30W-29N	A4
2000	DSPN	60018	2863	12W-9N	B7
2200	DSPN	60018	2917	12W-9N	B1
8300	ODPK	60462	3346	10W-16S	B2
8500	AntT	60081	2415	28W-39N	A5
8500	FXLK	60020	2415	28W-39N	A5
E Cedar St					
10	ANHT	60005	2861	18W-12N	A1
10	CHCG	60610	3034	0E-1N	C2

STREET Block	City	ZIP	Map#	CGS	Grid
E Cedar St					
10	CHCG	60611	3034	0E-1N	C2
N Cedar St					
10	PLTN	60067	2805	21W-16N	D1
100	PLTN	60067	2752	21W-16N	D7
S Cedar St					
10	PLTN	60067	2805	21W-14N	D3
100	PltT	60067	2805	21W-15N	D2
100	WDDL	60191	2971	17W-5N	B2
200	AddT	60191	2971	17W-5N	B2
W Cedar St					
200	ANHT	60005	2861	18W-12N	A1
300	SCRL	60174	2964	35W-3N	A7
400	ANHT	60005	2860	18W-12N	E1
2200	ANHT	60005	2806	19W-12N	C7
2200	RGMW	60005	2806	19W-12N	C7
2200	RGMW	60008	2806	19W-12N	C7
Cedar Ter					
800	DRFD	60015	2703	11W-21N	D7
3100	ISLK	60042	2586	29W-28N	D5
3100	NndT	60042	2586	29W-28N	D5
Cedarbend Dr					
100	RMVL	60446	3269	23W-14S	A7
S Cedarbend Dr					
13600	HMGN	60491	3343	17W-17S	D5
Cedar Breaks Ct					
2600	JLET	60586	3415	32W-20S	C5
Cedarbrook Rd					
100	NPVL	60565	3203	26W-9S	E4
Cedar Creek Ct					
10	PSHT	60463	3275	8W-14S	B5
24100	PNFD	60586	3416	30W-19S	C3
W Cedar Creek Ct					
13200	HMGN	60491	3343	16W-17S	E4
Cedar Creek Cto					
2700	WCDA	60084	2588	25W-30N	B2
Cedar Creek Dr					
900	LKZH	60047	2699	22W-22N	C3
3900	JNBG	60050	2472	30W-35N	A5
4000	JNBG	60050	2471	30W-36N	E4
Cedar Creek Ln					
24100	PNFD	60586	3416	30W-19S	B3
Cedar Crest Dr					
900	CLLK	60014	2639	37W-24N	B7
2000	HDPK	60035	2704	10W-21N	A5
Cedarcrest Dr					
400	SMWD	60107	2857	28W-10N	B6
N Cedar Crest Dr					
38700	AntT	60046	2416	25W-39N	B6
38700	LkvT	60046	2416	25W-39N	B6
S Cedarcrest Dr					
10	SMBG	60169	2858	24W-10N	E6
10	SMBG	60193	2858	24W-9N	E7
800	SMBG	60193	2912	24W-9N	E1
Cedarcrest Ln					
1100	BKBN	60015	2703	11W-22N	D5
W Cedar Crest Ln					
25200	LkvT	60046	2416	25W-38N	B6
Cedar Crest St					
400	RDLK	60073	2531	23W-33N	E2
Cedardale Pl					
700	AURA	60506	3137	36W-5S	E3
Cedardell St					
10	NndT	60042	2642	29W-27N	D1
10	NndT	60051	2642	29W-27N	D1
10	WcnT	60042	2642	29W-27N	D1
10	WcnT	60051	2642	29W-27N	D1
Cedarfield Dr					
100	BRLT	60103	2909	32W-8N	C3
Cedar Gate Cir					
10	SgrT	60506	3135	41W-5S	E4
Cedar Glade Dr					
2600	NPVL	60564	3202	29W-10S	C6
2900	WldT	60564	3202	29W-11S	C7
3000	NPVL	60564	3266	29W-11S	C1
3300	WldT	60564	3266	29W-11S	C1
Cedar Glen Ct					
-	LYVL	60048	2591	17W-30N	C2
Cedar Glen Dr					
10	PltT	60067	2806	19W-14N	C4
10	RGMW	60008	2806	19W-14N	C4
1600	LYVL	60048	2591	17W-30N	C2
14800	HMGN	60491	3421	18W-18S	A1
14800	HmrT	60491	3421	18W-18S	A1
S Cedar Glen Dr					
2300	ANHT	60005	2861	17W-11N	B4
2300	ANHT	60056	2861	17W-11N	B4
2300	MPPT	60056	2861	17W-11N	B4
2600	MPPT	60005	2861	17W-10N	B4
Cedar Glen Dr N					
2500	LYWD	60411	3509	3E-23S	E4
Cedar Grove Ct					
10	ALGN	60102	2746	37W-19N	D3
Cedar Hill Ln					
-	LslT	60517	3143	21W-7S	D6
N Cedar Lake Av					
700	LKVL	60046	2417	22W-38N	A6
Cedar Lake Dr					
-	RDLK	60073	2531	23W-31N	D7
Cedar Lake Ln					
24000	LkvT	60046	2416	24W-38N	D7
Cedar Lake Rd					
-	FmtT	60030	2531	23W-31N	D7
-	FmtT	60030	2588	23W-30N	D1
-	RDLK	60030	2588	23W-30N	D1
-	RDLK	60073	2531	23W-31N	D7
-	RDLK	60073	2588	23W-30N	D1
1900	RDLK	60073	2588	23W-30N	D1
N Cedar Lake Rd					
10	LKVL	60046	2474	23W-35N	E5
10	LkvT	60046	2474	23W-37N	E1
200	RDLK	60073	2531	23W-33N	E2
800	RLKB	60073	2531	23W-34N	E1
1000	RLKB	60073	2474	23W-34N	E7
1300	LKVL	60073	2474	23W-36N	E4
1300	RLKB	60046	2474	23W-36N	E4
N Cedar Lake Rd CO-V63					
10	LKVL	60046	2474	23W-35N	E5
10	LkvT	60046	2474	23W-37N	E1
200	RDLK	60073	2531	23W-33N	E2
800	RLKB	60073	2531	23W-34N	E1
1000	RLKB	60073	2474	23W-34N	E7
1300	LKVL	60073	2474	23W-36N	E4
1300	RLKB	60046	2474	23W-36N	E4
S Cedar Lake Rd					
10	RDLK	60073	2531	23W-32N	E4
400	AvnT	60030	2531	23W-32N	E4
400	AvnT	60073	2531	23W-32N	E4
N Cedar Lake Wy					
38900	LKVL	60046	2416	23W-38N	E6
38900	LkvT	60046	2416	23W-38N	E6
Cedar Lakes Ct					
2200	JLET	60586	3416	30W-20S	B4
Cedarledge Ct					
4800	CPVL	60110	2747	36W-18N	A5
Cedar Mound Rd					
100	RLKP	60073	2532	23W-33N	A4
Cedar Point Ct					
2200	ELGN	60123	2907	36W-8N	E2
Cedar Pointe Dr					
-	JLET	60586	3495	31W-21S	E1
Cedar Ridge Dr					
-	HmrT	60441	3421	18W-20S	A3
-	LKPT	60441	3420	19W-20S	E4
-	LKPT	60441	3421	18W-20S	A4
10	ALGN	60102	2694	35W-21N	A6
10	ALGN	60156	2694	35W-21N	A6
10	LIHL	60156	2694	35W-21N	A6
300	LKVL	60046	2474	23W-36N	E4
2200	JLET	60586	3415	31W-21S	D6
12400	HMGN	60491	3344	15W-17S	B6
Cedar Ridge Rd					
100	RNPK	60471	3594	4W-27S	D4
Cedar Run Dr					
600	WLNG	60090	2754	16W-18N	E2
Cedar Tree Ct					
300	HFET	60169	2858	23W-11N	E2
Cedar Valley Dr					
38700	LkvT	60046	2416	24W-38N	C6
Cedarwood Av					
100	BGBK	60440	3269	22W-12S	C2
E Cedarwood Cir					
1900	RLKH	60073	2474	23W-35N	E5
N Cedarwood Cir					
600	RLKH	60073	2474	23W-35N	D5
S Cedarwood Cir					
600	RLKH	60073	2474	23W-35N	D5
W Cedarwood Cir					
1900	RLKH	60073	2474	23W-35N	D5
Cedarwood Ct					
100	BGBK	60440	3269	22W-11S	C1
600	WLNG	60090	2754	16W-17N	D5
1000	EGVV	60007	2914	19W-8N	D2
1400	GRNE	60031	2478	15W-35N	A5
11200	FKFT	60423	3590	14W-26S	E3
11200	FKFT	60423	3591	13W-26S	A3
E Cedarwood Ct					
100	PLTN	60067	2753	20W-17N	A5
200	PLTN	60074	2753	20W-17N	A5
Cedarwood Dr					
-	ELWD	60421	3675	25W-31S	B5
-	FltT	60423	3591	13W-26S	A3
-	FKFT	60423	3591	13W-26S	A3
-	HmrT	60491	3421	18W-19S	A2
-	JknT	60421	3675	25W-31S	B5
100	ANTH	60002	2358	23W-43N	A4
100	CteT	60417	3596	1W-28S	A7
100	CteT	60475	3596	1W-28S	A7
100	STGR	60475	3596	1W-28S	A7
1200	CTHL	60403	3497	27W-22S	D2
1200	CTHL	60435	3497	27W-22S	D2
1200	JLET	60435	3497	27W-22S	D2
1200	TroT	60403	3497	27W-22S	D2
1200	TroT	60435	3497	27W-22S	D2
8800	ODHL	60487	3424	11W-19S	A2
8800	ODPK	60462	3424	11W-19S	A2
8800	ODPK	60487	3424	11W-19S	A2
Cedarwood Ln					
1200	GNVW	60025	2810	9W-13N	C5
1500	WLNG	60090	2754	16W-17N	D6
1600	ALGN	60102	2695	32W-20N	B7
4100	MTSN	60443	3506	5W-25S	C6
W Cedarwood Ln					
24800	LkvT	60041	2474	24W-36N	B4
25000	GrtT	60041	2474	25W-36N	B4
Celano Dr					
4600	WKGN	60048	2535	14W-32N	C5
Celebration Ct					
100	HNVL	60073	2532	22W-33N	B3
Celebration Dr					
-	NPVL	60563	3080	30W-4S	C7
-	NPVL	60563	3140	30W-4S	C1
-	WNVL	60563	3080	30W-4S	C7
Celebration Wy					
700	BGBK	60440	3204	24W-10S	D6
700	BGBK	60565	3204	24W-10S	D6
Celebrity Cir E					
1500	HRPK	60133	2911	26W-6N	E6
Celebrity Cir W					
1500	HRPK	60133	2911	26W-6N	D6
Celeste Ln					
3700	NPVL	60564	3267	28W-11S	B1
N Celia Av					
20500	BFGV	60069	2754	16W-20N	D1
20500	BFGV	60089	2754	16W-20N	D1
20500	VnvT	60069	2754	16W-20N	D1
Cellular Dr					
1400	ANHT	60004	2753	18W-17N	D4
Celtic Cir					
12600	MhtT	60442	3677	20W-31S	C5
Celtic Ct					
10600	MKNA	60448	3503	13W-23S	B3
Celtic Ash Ct					
700	NPVL	60540	3142	25W-7S	A7
Celtic Glen Dr					
2000	MPPT	60056	2808	13W-14N	E4
2000	WhlT	60025	2808	13W-14N	E4
2000	WhlT	60056	2808	13W-14N	E4
Cemetary Rd					
100	FKFT	60423	3503	11W-25S	E7
Cemetery Rd					
-	LNSH	60061	2702	15W-23N	A2
-	LNSH	60069	2702	15W-23N	A2
-	VNHL	60061	2702	15W-23N	A2
34700	RedT	60408	4031	31W-43S	B1
N Cemetery Rd					
1400	WmT	60031	2477	16W-35N	D6
34500	GRNE	60031	2534	16W-34N	D1
34500	WmT	60031	2534	16W-34N	D1
34700	GRNE	60031	2477	16W-35N	D7
S Cemetery Rd					
100	GRNE	60031	2534	16W-34N	D1
100	WmT	60031	2534	16W-34N	D1
30300	WshT	60401	3864	0W-37S	C3
Cenco Pkwy					
3300	FNPK	60131	2972	14W-4N	D4
Centenary Ct					
2400	NPVL	60565	3204	25W-10S	B5
Centennial Av					
10300	HTLY	60142	2692	39W-20N	C7
10400	HTLY	60142	2745	39W-20N	C1
Centennial Cir					
16000	TYPK	60477	3425	8W-19S	A1
Centennial Ct					
3100	HDPK	60035	2704	10W-23N	A1
4300	GRNE	60031	2478	14W-35N	D6
15600	ODPK	60462	3345	12W-18S	C7
15600	ODPK	60462	3423	12W-18S	C1
Centennial Dr					
-	WHTN	60187	3024	24W-0S	D6
600	HPSR	60140	2796	46W-15N	A3
800	HshT	60140	2796	46W-15N	A3
900	MPPT	60056	2808	14W-13N	B7
1500	JLET	60431	3585	28W-25S	A1
1600	ANTH	60002	2417	21W-40N	D2
6800	BmnT	60477	3425	8W-19S	A2
6800	TYPK	60477	3425	8W-19S	A2
15700	ODPK	60462	3423	12W-18S	C1
W Centennial Dr					
10	HNVL	60073	2532	22W-33N	B3
Centennial Ln					
3000	HDPK	60035	2704	10W-23N	A1
W Centennial Pl					
1700	ADSN	60101	2970	20W-4N	A3
Center					
-	RVDL	60827	3349	1W-16S	E2
Center Av					
-	CHCG	60419	3350	0E-16S	E2
-	CHCG	60827	3350	0E-16S	E2
10	WLNG	60090	2755	14W-17N	C4
100	AURA	60505	3200	35W-8S	B2
200	WnfT	60187	3081	27W-2S	D4
300	WHTN	60187	3081	27W-2S	D4
300	WHTN	60555	3081	27W-2S	D4
300	WnfT	60555	3081	27W-2S	D4
400	WNFD	60190	3023	27W-1N	D3
400	WnfT	60185	3023	27W-1N	D3
400	WnfT	60190	3023	27W-1N	D3
500	CLSM	60188	2968	24W-3N	C6
900	ELBN	60119	3017	43W-2N	A1
1200	CHHT	60411	3508	0W-25S	C7
1400	CHHT	60411	3596	0W-25S	B1
1400	WHTN	60187	3082	25W-1S	A1
2000	NHBK	60062	2757	10W-17N	B5
3900	LYNS	60534	3088	9W-4S	C7
4400	LSLE	60532	3143	23W-4S	B1
4500	LYNS	60534	3148	9W-4S	C1
4600	MCCK	60534	3148	9W-4S	C1
6600	HRPK	60133	2911	27W-8N	C2
10400	FNPK	60131	2973	13W-3N	A4
13900	DLTN	60419	3350	0E-16S	E3
14400	HRVY	60426	3350	1W-18S	A7
15900	HRVY	60426	3428	1W-20S	A5
16700	EHZC	60429	3428	1W-20S	A5
16700	HRVY	60429	3428	1W-20S	A5
17400	HMWD	60429	3428	1W-20S	A5
18100	HMWD	60430	3428	1W-21S	A7
18300	HMWD	60430	3508	1W-22S	A1
30300	LbvT	60048	2591	16W-30N	E2
E Center Av					
10	LKBF	60044	2593	11W-28N	E6
100	LKBF	60044	2594	10W-28N	A6
S Center Av					
5400	SMMT	60501	3148	9W-5S	D3
17500	EHZC	60429	3428	1W-21S	A6
17500	HMWD	60429	3428	1W-21S	A6
17500	HMWD	60430	3428	1W-21S	A6
W Center Av					
10	LKBF	60044	2593	11W-28N	E6
8300	RVGV	60171	2974	10W-3N	A5
8600	RVGV	60171	2973	11W-3N	D6
Center Brch					
10	GNVW	60093	2810	8W-15N	D3
Center Cir					
1900	DRN	60516	3206	18W-8S	E2
Center Ct					
10	BtlT	60543	3263	39W-12S	A4
100	HFET	60192	2805	23W-12N	A7
100	PltT	60195	2805	23W-12N	A7
100	SMBG	60192	2805	23W-12N	A7
100	SMBG	60195	2805	23W-12N	A7
800	SRWD	60404	3496	29W-23S	C3
1100	HMWD	60430	3508	1W-23S	A2
8600	AlqT	60021	2696	29W-23N	C2
8600	FRGV	60021	2696	29W-23N	C2
Center Dr					
-	CPVL	60110	2748	33W-17N	B7
-	CPVL	60118	2748	33W-17N	B7
-	EDND	60118	2748	33W-17N	B7
-	RtdT	60136	2799	38W-16N	B1
-	SMBG	60173	2805	22W-12N	D7
10	ALGN	60102	2747	34W-20N	D1
10	GLBT	60136	2799	38W-16N	B1
200	VNHL	60061	2647	16W-26N	D3
800	SchT	60177	2908	34W-7N	E4
1000	MRGO	60152	2634	49W-27N	D1
1000	SEGN	60177	2908	34W-7N	E4
1100	SenT	60152	2634	49W-27N	D1
1800	CPVL	60110	2801	33W-16N	B1
1800	CPVL	60118	2801	33W-16N	B1
1800	EDND	60110	2801	33W-16N	B1
1800	EDND	60118	2801	33W-16N	B1
2500	WDRG	60517	3205	21W-8S	D1
2600	WDRG	60517	3143	21W-7S	D7
7300	McHT	60097	2469	36W-36N	D4
11600	LMNT	60439	3271	18W-13S	B5
N Center Dr					
36600	WmT	60031	2476	18W-36N	E3
S Center Dr					
21700	NLNX	60451	3590	15W-26S	B2
21700	NlxT	60451	3590	15W-26S	B2
Center Ln					
-	WDSK	60098	2524	41W-31N	D7
400	RLKP	60073	2532	23W-33N	A3
1200	ANHT	60004	2807	16W-15N	D3
1200	PTHT	60004	2807	16W-15N	D3
N Center Ln					
32500	AvnT	60030	2531	24W-32N	C5
Center Pkwy					
100	YKVL	60560	3261	43W-13S	C6
Center Rd					
-	HnrT	60107	2856	29W-10N	E5
10	SMWD	60107	2856	29W-10N	E5
300	FKFT	60423	3591	12W-27S	E4
11100	PSHL	60465	3273	11W-13S	E3
S Center Rd					
22500	FltT	60423	3591	12W-27S	E5
22500	FKFT	60423	3591	12W-27S	E5
23000	GGnT	60423	3591	12W-28S	E7
W Center Rd					
300	PLTN	60074	2752	21W-18N	C2
300	PltT	60074	2752	21W-18N	C2
Center St					
-	AvnT	60030	2533	19W-33N	C4
-	BRTN	60010	2751	24W-20N	B1
-	GNVA	60134	3019	36W-1N	E2
-	GNWD	60098	2468	38W-36N	D4
-	HPSR	60140	2795	47W-16N	E2
-	RedT	60408	3942	31W-39S	A2
-	WcnT	60084	2642	28W-26N	E3
-	WmTp	60408	3942	31W-39S	A2
-	WmTp	60481	3942	31W-39S	A2
10	AddT	60106	2915	17W-6N	C6
10	ALGN	60102	2747	33W-20N	D1
10	BNVL	60106	2915	17W-6N	C6
10	CLLK	60014	2640	35W-26N	A3
10	FXLK	60041	2473	27W-36N	C4
10	GYLK	60030	2532	20W-33N	E4
10	HNDL	60521	3086	15W-4S	A7
10	PTBR	60010	2642	29W-26N	D4
10	WcnT	60010	2642	28W-26N	D3
100	FRGV	60021	2696	30W-22N	A3
100	WCHI	60185	3022	29W-0N	C4
300	GNEN	60137	3025	23W-0N	A5
300	GYLK	60030	2533	19W-33N	C4
300	HLSD	60162	3029	13W-0S	A7
300	PvsT	60162	3029	13W-0S	A7
300	WKGN	60085	2480	10W-35N	A7
400	WDSK	60098	2524	41W-31N	D7
600	EGvT	60007	2915	17W-8N	A3
700	BTVA	60510	3078	34W-1S	D2
700	DSPN	60016	2863	13W-10N	A6
1000	ELGN	60120	2854	33W-12N	E1
1100	DSPN	60018	2863	13W-10N	A6
1400	GNVA	60134	3020	36W-1N	A2
10000	HBRN	60034	2351	40W-41N	A7
19800	MKNA	60448	3503	13W-24S	A4
23800	CmgT	60033	2405	52W-38N	B7
Center St CO-A27					
-	AvnT	60030	2533	19W-33N	C4
500	GYLK	60030	2533	19W-33N	C4
Center St CO-V51					
-	GYLK	60030	2533	20W-33N	A3
E Center St					
10	GNWD	60425	3508	0E-22S	E2
100	ITSC	60143	2914	19W-6N	C6
100	YKVL	60560	3333	42W-15S	C1
500	BlmT	60425	3509	0E-22S	A2
500	BlmT	60476	3509	0E-22S	A2
500	GNWD	60425	3509	0E-22S	A2
700	SDWH	60548	3330	51W-14S	A1
N Center St					
10	BNVL	60106	2971	16W-5N	E1
10	JLET	60435	3498	24W-23S	E4
10	JLET	60436	3498	24W-23S	E5
10	NPVL	60540	3141	26W-6S	D5
10	PLNO	60545	3259	47W-13S	C5
10	SEGN	60177	2908	34W-8N	D3
100	BDWD	60408	3942	31W-40S	A3
200	PNFD	60544	3338	29W-17S	D7
400	NPVL	60563	3141	26W-6S	D4
600	MHRY	60050	2528	32W-32N	B4
600	RedT	60408	3942	31W-40S	A3
700	WmTp	60408	3942	31W-40S	A2
700	WmTp	60481	3942	31W-40S	A2
1600	CTHL	60403	3498	24W-21S	D1
1700	CTHL	60403	3418	24W-21S	D7
14700	LtRT	60545	3259	47W-13S	C5
42200	ANTH	60002	2358	22W-42N	B6
42200	AntT	60002	2358	22W-42N	B6
N Center St US-30					
100	JLET	60435	3498	24W-23S	E4
S Center St					
10	BNVL	60106	2971	16W-5N	E2
10	JLET	60435	3498	24W-24S	E5
10	JLET	60436	3498	24W-24S	E5
10	PLNO	60545	3259	47W-14S	D7
10	SEGN	60177	2908	34W-8N	D3
100	BDWD	60408	3942	31W-42S	A7
100	GDLY	60407	4030	32W-43S	D2
300	RedT	60408	3942	31W-42S	A7
300	RedT	60408	4031	31W-42S	A1
600	LtRT	60545	3259	47W-14S	D7
W Center St					
100	GNWD	60425	3508	0E-22S	D2
100	ITSC	60143	2914	20W-6N	B6
100	WDDL	60191	2915	18W-6N	A7
100	YKVL	60560	3333	43W-15S	B1
10000	BHPK	60087	2480	10W-38N	B1
12700	BHPK	60087	2479	12W-38N	B1
12700	WKGN	60087	2479	12W-38N	B1
Centerfield Ct					
1000	HDPK	60035	2704	9W-22N	C4
Centerpoint Ct					
5600	GRNE	60031	2477	16W-34N	E7
5600	GRNE	60031	2534	15W-34N	E1
Center Point Dr					
26400	ELWD	60421	3674	26W-32S	E7
26400	ELWD	60421	3763	26W-32S	E1
26400	JknT	60421	3674	26W-32S	E7
26400	JknT	60421	3763	26W-32S	E1
Centerway Ct					
-	GLNC	60022	2758	6W-17N	C5
Centerway Wk					
15900	TYPK	60477	3424	9W-19S	E1
Centoni Dr					
1100	LKZH	60047	2698	24W-23N	B2
Central Av					
-	ELGN	60120	2855	32W-10N	C7
-	RchT	60443	3593	6W-26S	E3
-	RchT	60471	3593	6W-26S	E3
-	RNPK	60471	3593	6W-26S	E3
-	RVFT	60305	3030	10W-0N	B4
10	AddT	60101	2971	17W-2N	B6
10	AddT	60106	2971	17W-4N	B4
10	ADSN	60101	2971	17W-2N	B6
10	ADSN	60106	2971	17W-4N	B4
10	AURA	60506	3137	37W-7S	B7
10	HDPK	60035	2705	8W-22N	A4
10	MTSN	60443	3505	6W-24S	E5
10	RchT	60477	3505	7W-22S	E2
10	RKDL	60436	3498	25W-25S	B7
10	ROSL	60172	2913	23W-7N	A4
100	DGvT	60527	3207	16W-9S	D4
100	LKVL	60046	2417	22W-38N	A7
100	LKVL	60046	2475	22W-38N	B1
100	ROSL	60172	2912	25W-7N	A4
200	AURA	60506	3199	37W-7S	B1
200	WLMT	60091	2813	3W-13N	A6
300	HDPK	60035	2704	8W-22N	E4
300	NHFD	60093	2811	7W-15N	C2
400	AddT	60191	2915	17W-6N	B6
400	ADSN	60191	2971	17W-4N	B4
400	WDDL	60191	2915	17W-6N	B5
400	WMTN	60481	3853	27W-37S	D4
400	WNVL	60555	3081	27W-3S	B6
500	AddT	60191	2971	17W-4N	B4
500	DGvT	60516	3206	19W-9S	C4
500	MonT	60449	3682	7W-29S	E2
500	UYPK	60449	3682	7W-29S	E2
500	WDDL	60106	2971	17W-4N	B4
500	WDDL	60191	2971	17W-4N	B4
600	HRPK	60133	2912	25W-7N	A4
600	JLET	60436	3498	25W-25S	B7
600	ROSL	60133	2912	25W-7N	A4
700	DGvT	60561	3206	19W-9S	C4
700	DRN	60561	3206	20W-9S	C4
700	WLMT	60091	2812	3W-13N	D6
800	DRFD	60015	2756	12W-20N	C1
800	MonT	60466	3682	7W-30S	E3
800	UYPK	60466	3682	7W-30S	E3
1100	BNVL	60007	2915	17W-7N	B3
1100	BNVL	60106	2915	17W-7N	B3
1200	EGVV	60007	2915	17W-7N	B3
1300	HRPK	60172	2912	25W-7N	B4
1600	NfdT	60062	2756	11W-16N	C7
1600	NHBK	60062	2756	11W-16N	C7
1700	DSPN	60018	2917	12W-8N	A2
2700	WKGN	60085	2536	12W-33N	B2
3000	WLMT	60091	2811	6W-13N	D6
3800	PvsT	60558	3086	14W-4S	D7
3800	WNSP	60558	3086	14W-4S	D7
4400	WNSP	60558	3146	14W-4S	D1
7100	BRRG	60527	3146	14W-8S	D7
7100	BRRG	60527	3208	14W-8S	D1
7100	IHPK	60525	3146	14W-8S	D7
7100	IHPK	60527	3146	14W-8S	D7
7200	OKPK	60301	3030	9W-0N	C4
7200	OKPK	60302	3030	9W-0N	C4
7200	OKPK	60305	3030	9W-0N	C4
7200	RVFT	60301	3030	9W-0N	C4
7300	FTPK	60130	3030	9W-0N	D4
7400	RVFT	60130	3030	9W-0N	C4
7500	BDPK	60459	3211	6W-8S	D1
7500	BDPK	60638	3211	6W-8S	D1
7500	BRBK	60459	3211	6W-10S	D4
7800	SKOK	60053	2865	6W-9N	C6
7800	SKOK	60077	2865	6W-9N	C6
8600	OKLN	60453	3211	6W-11S	D7
8600	OKLN	60459	3211	7W-9S	D4
8700	MNGV	60053	2865	7W-10N	C4
10200	OKLN	60453	3275	6W-12S	D2
10400	CHRG	60415	3275	6W-12S	D2
11000	ALSP	60453	3275	6W-12S	D3
11000	ALSP	60482	3275	6W-12S	D3
11000	CHRG	60453	3275	6W-12S	D3
11000	CHRG	60482	3275	6W-12S	D3
12700	ALSP	60445	3275	7W-15S	D7
12700	ALSP	60803	3275	7W-15S	D7
12700	CTWD	60445	3275	7W-15S	D7
12700	CTWD	60463	3275	7W-15S	D7
12700	CTWD	60803	3275	7W-15S	D7
12900	CTWD	60445	3347	7W-15S	D1
13000	WthT	60445	3347	6W-15S	D1
13000	WthT	60463	3347	6W-15S	D1
13900	BmnT	60445	3347	7W-17S	D5
14100	MDLN	60445	3347	7W-17S	D5
14500	BmnT	60452	3347	7W-17S	D4
14500	OKFT	60452	3347	7W-17S	D4
15700	OKFT	60452	3425	7W-18S	D1
15800	BmnT	60452	3425	7W-18S	D1
15800	BmnT	60477	3425	6W-21S	E6
15900	OKFT	60477	3425	7W-19S	D1
18100	RchT	60477	3425	6W-21S	E7
21100	MTSN	60443	3593	7W-26S	E2
21800	RNPK	60443	3593	6W-26S	E2
Central Av CO-A47					
400	HDPK	60035	2704	8W-22N	E4
E Central Av					
10	LMBD	60148	3026	19W-0S	C7
N Central Av					
10	CHCG	60644	3031	7W-0N	C3
100	WDDL	60191	2971	17W-5N	B1
400	AddT	60191	2915	17W-6N	B7
400	HIWD	60040	2704	9W-23N	C2
600	WDDL	60191	2915	17W-7N	B5
700	CHCG	60651	3031	7W-0N	C3
1500	CHCG	60639	3031	7W-1N	C1
1700	CHCG	60639	2975	6W-2N	C7
2700	CHCG	60634	2975	7W-2N	C7
2700	CHCG	60641	2975	7W-2N	C7
4300	CHCG	60630	2975	7W-5N	C1
4400	CHCG	60630	2919	7W-5N	C7
5500	CHCG	60646	2919	6W-6N	C5
6600	CHCG	60712	2919	6W-8N	D2
6600	LNWD	60646	2919	6W-8N	D2
6600	LNWD	60712	2919	6W-8N	D2
6900	CHCG	60077	2919	6W-8N	D2
7000	NLES	60077	2919	6W-8N	C1
7000	NLES	60714	2919	6W-8N	C1
7000	SKOK	60077	2919	6W-8N	C1
7000	SKOK	60646	2919	6W-8N	C1
7000	SKOK	60714	2919	6W-8N	C1
7200	NLES	60077	2865	7W-9N	C7
7200	NLES	60714	2865	7W-9N	C7
7200	SKOK	60077	2865	7W-9N	C7
S Central Av					
-	MONE	60449	3682	7W-30S	E4
-	StkT	60402	3089	6W-4S	D7
10	CHCG	60644	3031	7W-0S	C5
10	HIWD	60040	2704	9W-23N	C3
100	WDDL	60191	2971	17W-5N	B2
200	AddT	60106	2971	17W-5N	B2
200	AddT	60191	2971	17W-5N	B2
200	WDDL	60106	2971	17W-5N	B2
1100	CCRO	60644	3031	6W-0S	D7
1100	CCRO	60804	3031	6W-0S	D7
1500	CCRO	60804	3089	7W-1S	D1
3800	SKNY	60402	3089	6W-3S	D6
3800	SKNY	60804	3089	6W-3S	D6
4600	FTVW	60402	3089	6W-4S	D7
4600	FTVW	60638	3089	6W-4S	D7
4600	FTVW	60638	3149	6W-4S	D1
4600	StkT	60638	3089	6W-4S	D7
4600	StkT	60638	3149	6W-4S	D1
5000	CHCG	60638	3149	7W-5S	D2
7000	BDPK	60638	3149	7W-8S	D7
7300	BDPK	60459	3211	7W-8S	D1
7300	BDPK	60638	3211	7W-8S	D1
7300	BRBK	60459	3211	7W-8S	D1
11100	ALSP	60453	3275	7W-13S	D5
11100	ALSP	60482	3275	7W-13S	D5
11100	CHRG	60415	3275	7W-13S	D3
11100	CHRG	60453	3275	7W-13S	D3
11100	CHRG	60482	3275	7W-13S	D3
11100	OKLN	60453	3275	7W-13S	D5
11400	ALSP	60803	3275	7W-13S	D5
11400	OKLN	60803	3275	7W-13S	D5
12500	ALSP	60463	3275	7W-14S	D7
12500	WthT	60463	3275	7W-14S	D7
12500	WthT	60803	3275	7W-14S	D7
12600	ALSP	60445	3275	6W-14S	D7
12600	CTWD	60445	3275	6W-14S	D7
12600	CTWD	60463	3275	6W-14S	D7
12600	CTWD	60803	3275	6W-14S	D7
23200	MonT	60449	3593	7W-28S	E7
23200	RchT	60471	3593	7W-28S	E5
23200	UYPK	60449	3593	7W-28S	E7
24000	UYPK	60449	3682	6W-29S	E1
25300	MonT	60449	3682	6W-30S	E4
25300	UYPK	60466	3682	6W-30S	E4
W Central Av					
200	LMBD	60148	3026	20W-0S	B7
23500	LkvT	60046	2416	23W-38N	E6
E Central Blvd					
10	VLPK	60181	3027	17W-0N	B4
W Central Blvd					
10	VLPK	60181	3027	18W-0N	A4

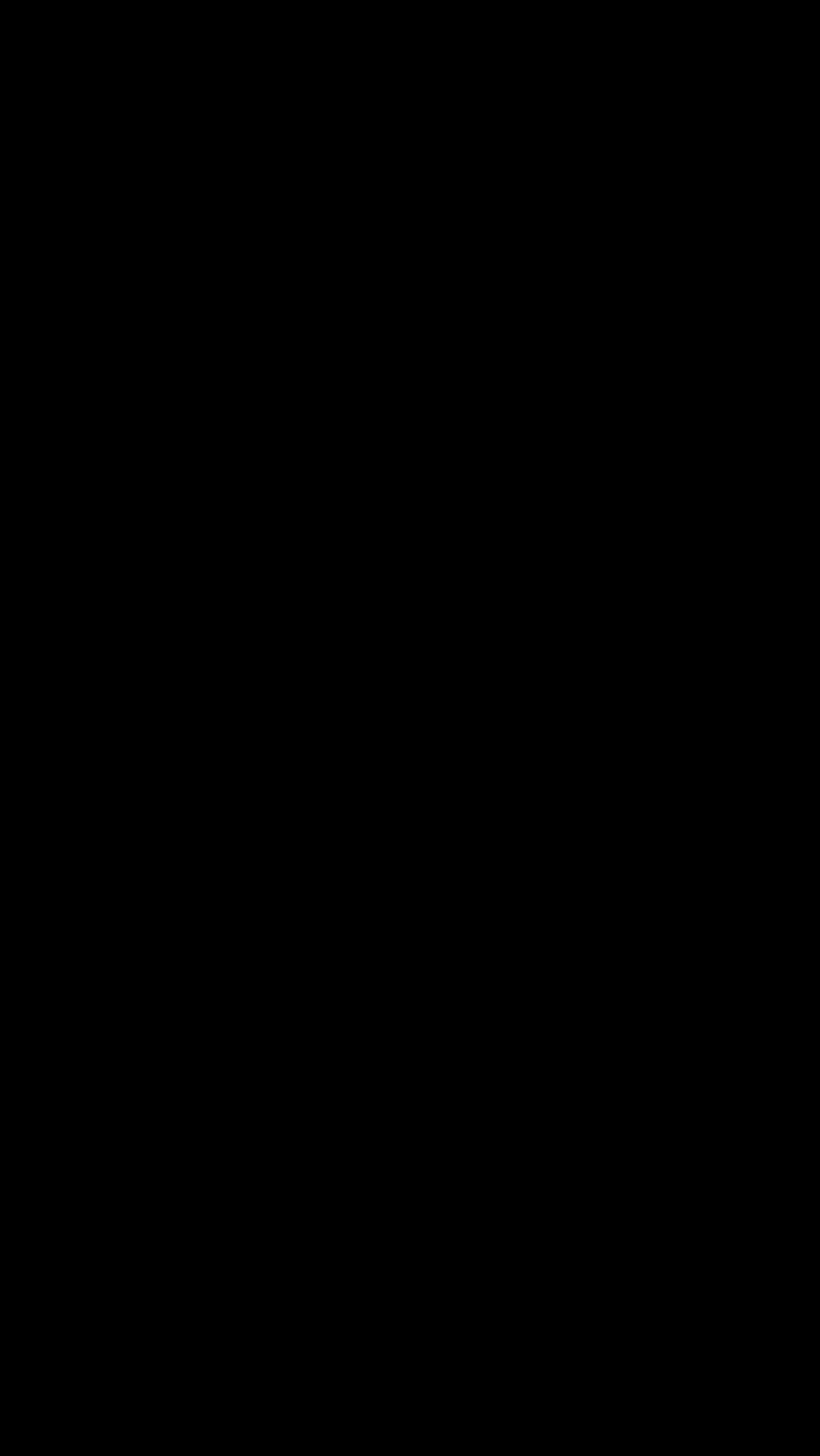

Chicago 7-County Street Index

STREET Block City ZIP Map# CGS Grid

W Central Blvd
300 LMBD 60148 3026 19W-0S D5
300 LMBD 60181 3026 19W-0S D5
300 VLPK 60181 3026 19W-0S D5
Central Ct
400 AddT 60101 2970 20W-3N A5
800 HDPK 60035 2704 8W-22N D5
3100 GNVW 60025 2810 10W-12N A7
3100 NfdT 60025 2810 10W-12N A7
14500 OKFT 60452 3347 6W-17S D5
Central Dr
- DGvT 60439 3207 17W-11S C6
10 BtlT 60560 3334 41W-14S A1
300 PltT 60124 2852 39W-11N E5
2500 BDVW 60155 3087 11W-1S D1
2500 FSMR 60422 3507 3W-22S B2
2500 PnfT 60435 3417 27W-20S C5
2600 JLET 60435 3417 27W-20S C5
Central Pkwy
200 GwdT 60098 2524 41W-32N E4
1400 GNVW 60025 2810 8W-12N E7
3400 WDSK 60098 2524 41W-32N E4
Central Rd
10 AddT 60101 2970 20W-5N A2
10 AddT 60143 2970 20W-5N A2
100 NLNX 60451 3501 18W-25S B7
400 ADSN 60143 2970 20W-5N A1
600 ELGN 60123 2854 34W-10N E6
800 GLF 60025 2811 7W-13N B7
800 GNVW 60025 2811 8W-12N A7
1700 GNVW 60025 2810 9W-13N B7
E Central Rd
- ANHT 60056 2807 17W-12N C7
- MaiT 60025 2810 10W-13N A7
- MPPT 60005 2807 17W-12N C7
10 ANHT 60005 2807 17W-13N B7
200 MPPT 60056 2808 14W-13N C7
400 DSPN 60016 2808 14W-13N C7
400 DSPN 60056 2808 14W-13N C7
800 MaiT 60016 2808 13W-13N D7
800 WhlT 60016 2808 13W-13N D7
1200 MPPT 60016 2808 14W-13N C7
1500 DSPN 60016 2809 12W-13N B7
1500 MPPT 60056 2807 17W-12N C7
1500 NfdT 60016 2809 12W-13N A7
3100 GNVW 60025 2810 10W-13N A7
3100 NfdT 60025 2810 10W-13N A7
3500 MaiT 60025 2809 10W-13N E7
3500 NfdT 60025 2809 10W-13N E7
3600 MaiT 60016 2809 12W-13N A7
9500 GNVW 60016 2809 11W-13N C7
9500 GNVW 60025 2809 11W-13N C7
W Central Rd
10 HFET 60192 2803 25W-13N E7
10 MPPT 60056 2808 15W-13N A7
10 PltT 60195 2805 22W-13N A7
10 SBTN 60010 2803 25W-13N E7
10 SMBG 60195 2805 22W-13N A7
100 ANHT 60005 2807 18W-12N A7
100 HFET 60192 2805 22W-13N A7
100 SMBG 60192 2805 22W-13N A7
200 HFET 60192 2804 24W-13N B7
200 MPPT 60056 2807 16W-13N C7
200 SMBG 60192 2804 23W-13N E7
200 SMBG 60195 2804 23W-13N E7
500 ANHT 60005 2806 18W-12N E7
1500 ANHT 60056 2807 16W-13N C7
1600 ANHT 60008 2806 18W-13N D7
1600 RGMW 60008 2806 18W-13N E7
1700 MPPT 60005 2807 16W-13N C7
1800 RGMW 60005 2806 19W-13N D7
26200 GrtT 60041 2473 26W-36N D3
Central St
- SKOK 60076 2811 5W-13N E7
- SKOK 60076 2812 5W-12N B7
- SKOK 60077 2811 5W-13N E7
- SKOK 60201 2812 5W-12N B7
- WLMT 60076 2811 5W-13N E7
- WLMT 60091 2811 5W-13N E7
- WLMT 60091 2812 5W-12N B7
- WLMT 60201 2812 5W-12N B7
600 EVTN 60201 2813 2W-13N B7
1700 EVTN 60201 2812 3W-13N D7
1900 MHRY 60050 2527 33W-33N E2
3500 LNSG 60438 3430 4E-21S C6
5200 GNVW 60025 2811 6W-13N D7
5200 GNVW 60077 2811 6W-13N D7
5200 WLMT 60077 2811 6W-13N D7
Central Park Av
- PKFT 60466 3594 4W-27S E5
- RNPK 60466 3594 4W-27S E5
100 EVTN 60201 2812 4W-12N C7
100 WLMT 60091 2812 4W-13N C7
100 WLMT 60201 2812 4W-13N C7
700 FSMR 60422 3506 4W-23S E3
700 HLCT 60422 3506 4W-22S E2
700 HLCT 60429 3506 4W-22S E2
1000 RchT 60430 3506 4W-23S E3
1700 RchT 60422 3506 4W-23S E4
2100 EVTN 60201 2866 4W-11N C2
7200 SKOK 60076 2866 4W-9N C7
8800 SKOK 60203 2866 4W-11N C3
13300 RBBN 60472 3348 4W-16S D3
14500 MDLN 60445 3348 4W-17S D6
14800 MDLN 60426 3348 4W-17S D5
14800 MKHM 60426 3348 4W-17S D5
14800 MKHM 60445 3348 4W-17S D5
16500 MKHM 60428 3426 4W-20S E3
16900 HLCT 60429 3426 4W-20S E4
17500 CCHL 60478 3426 4W-21S E6
17500 HLCT 60478 3426 4W-21S E6
19800 OMFD 60461 3506 4W-23S E4
23100 MonT 60466 3594 4W-28S E6
23100 RNPK 60471 3594 4W-28S E6
N Central Park Av
400 CHCG 60624 3032 4W-0N C3
700 CHCG 60651 3032 4W-0N C3
1500 CHCG 60647 3032 4W-1N C1
1600 CHCG 60647 2976 4W-2N C6
3600 CHCG 60618 2976 4W-4N C2
4300 CHCG 60625 2976 4W-5N C1
4400 CHCG 60625 2920 4W-5N C7
5600 CHCG 60659 2920 4W-7N C3
6300 LNWD 60659 2920 4W-7N C3
6400 LNWD 60712 2920 4W-8N C2
S Central Park Av
- CHCG 60629 3150 4W-6S D3
- CHCG 60632 3150 4W-6S D3
10 CHCG 60624 3032 4W-1S D7
1100 CHCG 60623 3032 4W-1S D7
1600 CHCG 60623 3090 4W-2S D3
7500 CHCG 60652 3212 4W-9S D2
9100 CHCG 60805 3212 4W-10S D5
9100 ENGN 60805 3212 4W-10S D5
9900 CHCG 60655 3212 4W-11S D7
10200 CHCG 60655 3276 4W-13S D4

S Central Park Av
10200 CHCG 60805 3276 4W-11S D1
10200 ENGN 60805 3276 4W-11S D1
11600 MTPK 60655 3276 4W-13S D4
11600 WthT 60655 3276 4W-13S D4
11900 ALSP 60803 3276 4W-14S D5
11900 MTPK 60803 3276 4W-14S D5
12300 WthT 60803 3276 4W-14S D6
Central Park Blvd
10300 HTLY 60142 2692 39W-20N C7
Central Park Dr
700 RLKB 60073 2474 24W-34N C7
1200 BmdT 60188 2967 26W-4N E4
Central Park Pl
300 LktT 60441 3419 23W-21S B7
S Central Park Pl
500 VNHL 60061 2647 16W-24N D7
Central Park Rd
10 NPVL 60540 3141 26W-6S D5
Central Parkway Rd
500 GwdT 60098 2524 41W-32N D4
500 WDSK 60098 2524 41W-32N D4
Central Skokie Rd
200 LKBF 60044 2593 12W-29N C5
200 ShdT 60044 2593 12W-29N C5
Centre Av
- CHCG 60613 2977 1W-5N D1
Centre Dr
- HNVL 60073 2532 22W-33N B3
10 HNVL 60030 2532 22W-33N B3
Centre St
10 PKFT 60466 3595 3W-27S B4
Centre Cir Dr
1400 DRGV 60515 3084 20W-2S B3
Centrella St
3700 FNPK 60131 2972 13W-4N E2
3700 FNPK 60131 2973 13W-4N A3
3700 LydT 60131 2972 13W-4N E2
Centre Point Cir
1800 NPVL 60563 3141 26W-4S E1
1800 NPVL 60563 3142 26W-4S A1
Centurion Ln
1000 VNHL 60061 2647 17W-26N C3
S Centurion Ln
2700 NLNX 60451 3588 19W-27S D5
W Centurion Ln
1500 NLNX 60451 3588 19W-27S D5
Century Cir
11500 PNFD 60564 3266 31W-13S A5
11500 PNFD 60585 3266 31W-13S A5
Century Ct
10 LKZH 60047 2699 22W-22N B4
10 MTGY 60543 3263 37W-11S C2
100 SMBG 60193 2859 23W-10N A6
Century Dr
10 MTGY 60543 3263 37W-11S B2
10 ROSL 60172 2913 22W-7N C4
10 WLNG 60090 2755 14W-17N C6
100 WDDL 60191 2970 18W-5N E1
300 HPSR 60140 2796 46W-16N A2
Century Ln
1000 AURA 60505 3200 34W-7S D1
Century Rd
21400 MTSN 60443 3594 4W-25S E1
Century Farm Ln
600 NPVL 60563 3141 28W-5S B2
Century Oaks Dr
100 CbaT 60010 2697 26W-22N E4
100 NBRN 60010 2697 26W-22N E3
1100 ELGN 60123 2800 35W-13N B7
Century Point Ln
2200 BMDL 60108 2968 23W-4N E3
2200 GLHT 60139 2968 23W-4N E3
2200 GLHT 60139 2969 23W-4N A3
W Cerena Cir
- PNFD 60586 3415 31W-20S D4
Cerena Ct
3400 AURA 60504 3201 31W-8S E2
Ceresia Dr
700 CLLK 60014 2640 33W-26N D3
Ceriseto U
- DRFD 60015 2757 10W-20N A2
Cermak Av
- NptT 60099 2360 16W-42N E7
- WDWH 60099 2360 16W-42N D7
Cermak Ct
1600 NPVL 60563 3140 29W-5S E2
Cermak Rd
- OKBK 60523 3086 14W-1S B2
1100 ALGN 60102 2695 33W-21N A6
4200 AlqT 60102 2694 33W-21N E5
4200 AlqT 60102 2695 33W-21N A5
6200 BRWN 60402 3089 8W-2S A2
6200 CCRO 60402 3089 7W-1S B2
6200 CCRO 60804 3089 7W-1S B2
6800 BRWN 60402 3088 8W-1S E2
7100 BRWN 60130 3088 8W-1S D2
7100 BRWN 60546 3088 8W-1S D2
7100 NRIV 60130 3088 8W-1S D2
7100 NRIV 60546 3088 8W-1S D2
11300 HLSD 60154 3086 14W-1S C2
11300 HLSD 60162 3086 14W-1S C2
11300 PvsT 60154 3086 14W-1S C2
11300 PvsT 60162 3086 14W-1S C2
11300 WSTR 60154 3086 14W-1S C2
11300 WSTR 60162 3086 14W-1S C2
11600 PvsT 60523 3086 14W-1S C2
E Cermak Rd
10 CHCG 60616 3092 0E-1S C1
100 BDWD 60408 3942 31W-40S B4
200 RedT 60408 3942 31W-40S A4
200 RedT 60481 3942 31W-40S A4
W Cermak Rd
10 CHCG 60616 3092 0W-2S A2
100 BDWD 60408 3942 31W-40S A4
400 BDWD 60408 3941 32W-40S D4
400 RedT 60408 3941 32W-40S D4
700 CHCG 60608 3092 0W-1S A1
800 CHCG 60608 3091 3W-2S A2
900 BDVW 60141 3087 13W-1S A2
900 BDVW 60155 3087 11W-1S C2
900 NRIV 60141 3087 13W-1S A2
900 NRIV 60155 3087 13W-1S A2
900 NRIV 60546 3087 13W-1S A2
900 PvsT 60141 3087 13W-1S A2
2700 CHCG 60623 3091 3W-1S A2
3400 CHCG 60623 3090 5W-1S B2
4500 CCRO 60804 3090 5W-1S A2
4700 HLSD 60154 3086 13W-2S D2
4700 HLSD 60162 3086 13W-1S D2
4700 PvsT 60162 3086 13W-2S D2
4800 CCRO 60804 3089 7W-1S C2
6100 BRWN 60402 3089 7W-1S B2
6100 CCRO 60402 3089 7W-1S B2
7200 BRWN 60130 3088 10W-1S A2
7200 BRWN 60402 3088 10W-1S A2

W Cermak Rd
7200 BRWN 60546 3088 10W-1S A2
7200 NRIV 60130 3088 10W-1S A2
7200 NRIV 60546 3088 10W-1S A2
7300 FTPK 60130 3088 9W-1S D2
7300 FTPK 60546 3088 9W-1S D2
7900 FTPK 60141 3088 9W-1S B2
7900 PvsT 60141 3088 9W-1S B2
7900 PvsT 60546 3088 9W-1S B2
8000 NRIV 60141 3088 10W-1S B2
9800 BDVW 60154 3087 12W-1S C2
9800 PvsT 60154 3087 12W-2S C2
9800 PvsT 60155 3087 12W-2S C2
9800 WSTR 60154 3087 12W-1S C2
10100 PvsT 60525 3087 12W-1S B2
10700 WSTR 60154 3086 13W-1S E2
11200 PvsT 60154 3086 14W-1S D2
Cerman Dr
- NLNX 60451 3589 18W-25S A1
Cernan Ct
1000 EGVV 60007 2914 21W-8N A2
1100 EGVV 60007 2913 21W-8N E2
Cernan Dr
800 BLWD 60104 3029 12W-0S C6
Cerny Rd
600 WNVL 60555 3080 29W-2S D4
Cesario Ct
- WHTN 60187 3081 26W-1S E3
Cessna Ct
800 NLNX 60451 3501 18W-25S A7
Cessna Ln
8400 DGvT 60516 3206 19W-9S E4
Chablis Ln
16100 PNFD 60586 3416 30W-19S C3
Chaco Ct
10 BrnT 60010 2802 28W-14N E5
Chad Ct
2000 MTGY 60538 3198 40W-10S B5
Chad Ln
2100 MTGY 60538 3198 40W-10S B6
Chadbourn Dr
8800 ODPK 60462 3424 11W-19S A2
8900 ODHL 60462 3424 11W-19S A3
8900 ODHL 60487 3424 11W-19S A3
Chaddick Dr
100 WLNG 60090 2755 14W-16N C7
Chadsford Ct
400 CLSM 60188 2967 27W-2N D7
Chadwick Ct
10 LIHL 60156 2692 39W-23N D2
1000 AURA 60502 3139 32W-6S C4
21300 FKFT 60423 3592 11W-25S B1
N Chadwick Ct
23100 KLDR 60047 2699 21W-23N D2
Chadwick Dr
1000 GYLK 60030 2533 20W-34N B1
Chadwick Ln
1200 WDND 60118 2800 35W-16N B1
1300 WDND 60118 2747 35W-17N C7
2100 GLHT 60139 2969 23W-4N A3
3400 LIHL 60156 2692 39W-23N D2
Chadwick Wy
2000 MDLN 60060 2590 20W-29N A5
Chadwicke Cir
1700 NPVL 60540 3140 28W-7S E7
1700 NPVL 60540 3202 28W-7S E1
Chadwicke Ct
- CPVL 60118 2746 37W-18N C4
1700 NPVL 60540 3202 29W-8S D2
Chaffee Ct
1400 EGVV 60007 2914 21W-8N A3
Chaffee Ln
- NLNX 60451 3589 18W-25S A1
Chaffield Dr
500 CmpT 60175 2961 42W-4N D4
Chainolks State Pk
16900 AntT 60081 2414 28W-40N E2
16900 AntT 60081 2415 28W-40N A2
N Chalary Ct
300 PLTN 60067 2752 22W-16N C7
Chalen Ct
17000 LKPT 60441 3420 21W-20S A4
Chalet Ct
100 CRTE 60417 3596 0E-28S D6
Chalet Dr
10 AlqT 60014 2640 33W-25N E5
10 CLLK 60014 2640 33W-25N E5
1100 CLSM 60188 2967 26W-4N E4
1100 DGvT 60561 3207 17W-9S B2
1100 DRN 60561 3207 17W-9S B2
Chalet Ln
10 CRTE 60417 3596 0E-28S D6
Chalet Rd
1200 NPVL 60563 3141 28W-6S A4
Chalfont Dr
1300 SMBG 60194 2858 25W-11N B4
Chalk Hill Cir
- PNFD 60544 3338 31W-16S A5
Chalk Hill Ct
24900 PNFD 60544 3338 31W-16S A5
Chalk Hill Rd
14100 PNFD 60544 3338 31W-16S A5
Chalkstone Av
3000 ElgT 60124 2853 38W-11N B5
Challdon Ct
1000 NPVL 60540 3142 26W-7S A7
Challedon Ct
600 CmpT 60119 2961 43W-4N B4
Challen Ct
2300 WCHI 60185 2965 32W-4N C4
Challen Pl
5400 DRGV 60515 3143 21W-5S E3
5400 LslT 60515 3143 21W-5S E3
Challenge Dr
1100 BTVA 60510 3077 36W-2S E4
1100 BTVA 60510 3078 36W-2S A4
Challenger Ct
1700 WHTN 60187 3082 24W-2S C4
Challis Dr
3300 CteT 60417 3598 4E-29S C7
3300 SjnT 46311 3598 4E-29S C7
Chally Dr
10 KdlT 60560 3332 44W-16S D5
N Chalmers Ct
400 RMVL 60446 3340 25W-15S B2
W Chalmers Pl
800 CHCG 60614 2977 1W-2N E6
Chalmers St
200 GNVA 60134 3020 34W-0N C4
Chalmette Ct
1700 NPVL 60565 3204 25W-9S B4
Chambellan Ln
10 WYNE 60184 2965 32W-5N B1
W Chamberlain Dr
28500 CbaT 60010 2696 28W-23N E2

Chamberlain Ln
500 NPVL 60540 3140 28W-7S E7
Chamberlin Dr
- RMVL 60446 3268 25W-14S A7
Chambers Dr
- HFET 60192 2804 24W-16N B1
1300 RMVL 60446 3269 23W-14S B6
4900 HFET 60010 2751 24W-16N C7
4900 HFET 60010 2804 24W-16N B1
5000 IVNS 60010 2751 24W-16N C7
Chambery Ct
1900 WLNG 60090 2808 14W-15N C2
Chambord Ct
100 BMDL 60108 2968 24W-5N D1
Chambord Ln
3300 HLCT 60429 3426 4W-21S E6
Chambourd Dr
2300 BFGV 60089 2701 16W-22N E4
Chamomile Dr
21900 FKFT 60423 3590 14W-26S E3
Chamonieux Dr
10600 PSHL 60465 3274 10W-12S B2
Champagne Ct
1300 LslT 60563 3142 25W-5S A2
1300 NPVL 60563 3142 25W-5S A3
Champagne Ln
1400 ELGN 60123 2908 36W-9N A1
1400 ELGN 60177 2908 36W-9N A1
1400 SEGN 60177 2908 36W-9N A1
N Champaign Dr
40900 AntT 60002 2417 22W-40N B2
Champart St
3100 ZION 60099 2421 11W-41N D1
Champion Ct
11300 PNFD 60585 3266 30W-13S B5
Champion Ct W
11300 PNFD 60585 3266 30W-13S B5
Champion Dr
2100 RLKP 60030 2532 22W-31N B7
24200 PNFD 60585 3266 30W-13S A5
W Champion Dr
24000 NPVL 60564 3266 29W-13S C5
24000 NPVL 60585 3266 30W-13S C5
24600 PNFD 60585 3266 30W-13S A5
24700 PNFD 60564 3266 30W-13S A5
24700 WldT 60564 3266 30W-13S A5
Champion Rd
- NPVL 60585 3266 29W-13S C5
2500 NPVL 60564 3266 29W-13S C5
4000 PNFD 60564 3266 31W-13S A5
4000 PNFD 60585 3266 31W-13S A5
4000 WldT 60564 3266 31W-13S A5
4200 WldT 60564 3265 31W-13S E5
Champion St
9300 SPGV 60081 2413 31W-41N D1
Champion Forest Ct
1100 WHTN 60187 3024 25W-0N A5
1200 MltT 60187 3024 25W-0N A5
Champions Ct
28600 FmtT 60060 2589 21W-28N D5
Championship Pkwy N
- FmtT 60047 2645 22W-27N C2
- FmtT 60060 2645 21W-27N C2
10 HNWD 60047 2645 22W-27N C2
Champlain Av
7900 TYPK 60477 3424 9W-21S D6
14800 DLTN 60419 3350 0E-17S E6
S Champlain Av
200 BlmT 60425 3508 0E-23S E3
200 GNWD 60425 3508 0E-23S E3
4200 CHCG 60653 3092 0E-4S D7
4600 CHCG 60615 3092 0E-4S D7
4700 CHCG 60615 3152 0E-5S D1
6000 CHCG 60637 3152 0E-7S D6
7100 CHCG 60619 3152 0E-8S D7
7500 CHCG 60619 3214 0E-9S E2
9400 CHCG 60628 3214 0E-10S E5
10500 CHCG 60628 3278 0E-12S E2
Champlain Ct
- LKPT 60441 3419 21W-20S E5
Champlain Rd
10 SBTN 60010 2803 27W-14N A4
Champlain St
400 JLET 60436 3586 24W-25S E1
500 JltT 60436 3586 24W-25S D1
15400 DLTN 60419 3350 0E-18S E6
15400 SHLD 60419 3350 0E-18S E7
15400 SHLD 60473 3350 0E-18S E7
N Champlain St
2200 ANHT 60004 2753 18W-16N E7
Champlaine Av
600 WTMT 60559 3085 16W-4S D7
Champlaine Ct
600 WTMT 60559 3085 17W-4S D7
1200 SMBG 60193 2913 22W-8N C2
W Chanay St
2700 CHCG 60647 2977 2W-3N C5
Chancel Cir
800 GNEN 60137 3083 21W-1S D1
Chancel Ln
10 GNEN 60137 3083 21W-1S D1
Chancellor Av
- BtvT 60539 3077 36W-3S E5
Chancellor Ct
10 HNWD 60047 2645 22W-24N A6
100 GNCY 53128 2353 B3
800 NPVL 60540 3203 27W-7S B1
Chancellor Dr
10 ROSL 60172 2912 24W-7N D4
W Chancellor Dr
15800 HmrT 60441 3420 19W-19S C2
15800 HmrT 60491 3420 19W-19S C2
15800 LKPT 60491 3420 19W-19S C2
Chancellor St
1200 EVTN 60201 2813 2W-13N A7
1700 EVTN 60201 2812 3W-13N E7
Chancellors Av
100 BtvT 60539 3077 36W-3S E6
Chancery Ct
- CPVL 60118 2746 37W-18N C4
5500 LIHL 60156 2692 38W-21N D5
Chancery Ln
- CPVL 60118 2746 37W-18N C4
300 LKZH 60047 2699 23W-22N A3
900 CRY 60013 2695 32W-22N B3
Chancery Rd
5400 GRNE 60031 2478 15W-36N A3
5500 GRNE 60031 2477 16W-36N E3
Chancery Wy
5300 LIHL 60156 2692 38W-21N D5
Chandelle Dr
10 NPVL 60564 3202 29W-9S D4
10 NpvT 60564 3202 29W-9S D4
Chandler Av
500 GNVA 60134 3020 33W-1N E2
900 SCRL 60134 3020 33W-1N E2

Chandler Av
900 SCRL 60174 3020 33W-1N E2
1800 SCRL 60174 3021 33W-2N A1
S Chandler Av
100 EMHT 60126 3028 15W-1N A3
Chandler Ct
2300 AURA 60502 3139 32W-5S B3
S Chandler Ct
14200 LktT 60544 3339 26W-16S E5
Chandler Dr
100 MDLN 60060 2590 19W-28N D7
4100 HRPK 60133 2967 27W-5N D2
Chandler Ln
10 HFET 60169 2859 23W-11N A4
2100 GNVW 60025 2809 10W-15N E3
N Chandler Ln
- WKGN 60083 2478 14W-37N C1
Chandler Rd
600 GRNE 60031 2534 16W-33N E3
Chaney Av
200 CTHL 60403 3418 24W-21S D7
200 CTHL 60435 3418 24W-21S D7
200 LktT 60435 3418 24W-21S D7
W Chaney Av
10000 BHPK 60099 2422 10W-38N B7
W Chaney St
12500 BHPK 60087 2421 12W-38N B7
Chang Ct
2000 NPVL 60540 3202 29W-8S E1
Channahon Ct
7400 FXLK 60020 2415 28W-39N A5
Channahon Rd
- JltT 60436 3498 25W-25S C7
- RKDL 60436 3498 25W-25S C7
1200 JltT 60436 3586 25W-25S B1
1200 RKDL 60436 3586 26W-25S B1
1600 JLET 60436 3585 26W-25S E2
1600 JltT 60436 3585 26W-25S E2
3200 TroT 60436 3585 28W-26S B3
3400 JLET 60410 3585 28W-27S B4
Channahon Rd US-6
- JltT 60436 3498 25W-25S C7
- RKDL 60436 3498 25W-25S C7
1200 JltT 60436 3586 26W-25S B1
1200 RKDL 60436 3586 26W-25S B1
1600 JLET 60436 3585 26W-25S E2
1600 JltT 60436 3585 26W-25S E2
3200 TroT 60436 3585 28W-26S B3
3400 JLET 60410 3585 28W-27S B4
Channahon St
300 SRWD 60404 3496 29W-24S D5
300 SRWD 60431 3496 29W-24S D5
300 TroT 60431 3496 29W-24S D5
W Channel Av
25900 AntT 60002 2415 26W-40N E3
Channel Ct
800 PltT 60124 2852 40W-9N B7
Channel Dr
10 PTBR 60010 2642 29W-26N C3
200 ISLK 60042 2586 28W-28N D5
2100 AlqT 60021 2695 31W-22N E4
2100 FRGV 60021 2695 31W-22N E3
N Channel Dr
10 RLKB 60073 2475 23W-34N A7
200 RLKB 60073 2474 23W-34N E7
S Channel Dr
10 RLKB 60073 2475 23W-34N A7
100 RLKB 60073 2474 23W-34N E7
W Channel Dr
28500 GrtT 60041 2472 28W-34N E7
28500 GrtT 60051 2472 28W-34N E7
Channel Ln
- GrtT 60041 2473 26W-36N E4
300 FXLK 60041 2473 27W-35N C5
W Channel Ln
2400 NndT 60050 2585 31W-30N D2
Channel Rd
7200 CHCG 60076 2866 3W-9N D7
7200 SKOK 60076 2866 3W-9N D7
Channel Beach Av
1300 JNBG 60050 2472 30W-36N A4
1500 MchT 60050 2472 30W-36N A4
1800 JNBG 60050 2471 30W-36N E4
N Channel View Dr
39200 AntT 60002 2416 25W-39N A5
Channing Ct
200 ELGN 60120 2855 33W-11N A3
1600 MLPK 60160 3030 10W-1N A2
Channing Dr
100 HPSR 60140 2796 46W-15N A3
N Channing St
10 ELGN 60120 2855 33W-11N A4
S Channing St
10 ELGN 60120 2855 33W-11N A4
W Channon Dr
25300 CNHN 60410 3672 31W-29S E3
Chanora Ct
- HFET 60192 2804 25W-14N A3
Chanticleer Av
1200 BGBK 60490 3268 25W-12S A3
Chanticleer Ln
100 HNDL 60521 3146 15W-6S B4
Chantilly Blvd
1400 HDPK 60035 2704 8W-21N D7
Chantilly Cir
5500 LIHL 60156 2692 38W-21N D5
Chantilly Ct
300 LslT 60540 3143 23W-7S A7
300 WDRG 60517 3143 23W-7S A7
300 WDRG 60540 3143 23W-7S A7
400 WNFD 60190 3023 26W-1N D2
1400 HDPK 60035 2704 8W-21N D7
Chantilly Ln
10 HNWD 60047 2645 23W-24N A6
10 NARA 60542 3077 37W-3S C5
10 NARA 60542 3137 36W-4S D1
18000 HLCT 60429 3426 4W-21S E6
Chanwahon Rd
13900 HTLY 60142 2744 43W-19N A2
Chaparral Cir
200 ELGN 60120 2855 31W-11N E4
Chaparral Ct
300 ELGN 60120 2855 31W-11N E4
Chaparrel Dr
4200 WldT 60564 3266 31W-12S A3
Chapel Ct
1000 DRFD 60015 2703 11W-21N D5
1500 NHBK 60062 2757 9W-17N C5
Chapel Hl
5600 GRNE 60031 2477 15W-36N E4
5600 GRNE 60031 2478 15W-36N A4
Chapel Rd
2100 AlqT 60010 2695 31W-21N C6
2100 AlqT 60102 2695 31W-21N C6
2100 BNHL 60010 2695 31W-21N C6
2700 BNHL 60102 2695 32W-21N C6

STREET Block City ZIP Map# CGS Grid

N Chapel St
10 ELGN 60120 2855 33W-11N A4
10 WKGN 60085 2537 10W-34N A1
S Chapel St
10 ELGN 60120 2855 33W-11N A4
10 WKGN 60085 2537 10W-34N A2
Chapel Ct North Dr
900 GNEN 60137 3083 21W-1S E1
900 MltT 60137 3083 21W-1S D1
Chapel Ct South Dr
900 GNEN 60137 3083 21W-1S D1
900 MltT 60137 3083 21W-1S D1
Chapel Hill Ct
10 WTMT 60559 3145 17W-6S B4
Chapel Hill Dr
2600 HnrT 60120 2856 31W-11N A4
21500 DRPK 60010 2698 23W-21N D6
N Chapel Hill Dr
2600 ANHT 60004 2754 17W-16N B6
Chapel Hill Ln
400 NHFD 60093 2811 7W-15N B2
Chapel Hill Rd
- MchT 60051 2528 31W-32N D4
- MHRY 60051 2528 31W-32N D4
15500 ODPK 60462 3346 10W-18S B7
15600 ODPK 60462 3424 10W-18S B1
Chapel Hill Rd CO-V40
- MchT 60051 2528 31W-32N D4
- MHRY 60051 2528 31W-32N D4
N Chapel Hill Rd
1000 MchT 60051 2528 31W-34N E1
1000 MHRY 60051 2528 31W-34N E1
1500 LKMR 60051 2528 31W-34N E1
2700 MchT 60051 2471 30W-34N E7
2900 JNBG 60051 2471 31W-35N E6
3500 JNBG 60050 2471 31W-35N E6
N Chapel Hill Rd CO-A26
3100 JNBG 60051 2471 31W-35N E6
3500 JNBG 60050 2471 31W-35N E6
N Chapel Hill Rd CO-V40
1000 MchT 60051 2528 31W-34N E1
1000 MHRY 60051 2528 31W-34N E1
1500 LKMR 60051 2528 31W-34N E1
2700 MchT 60051 2471 30W-34N E7
2900 JNBG 60051 2471 31W-35N E6
3500 JNBG 60050 2471 31W-35N E6
Chapel Oaks Dr
100 BFGV 60089 2701 16W-23N C2
Chapin Wy
- OSWG 60543 3265 33W-11S A2
W Chaplin Av
10700 BHPK 60099 2422 10W-38N A7
10700 WKGN 60099 2422 10W-38N A7
Chaplin Ct
2000 HRPK 60133 2911 27W-6N D6
W Chaplin St
12500 BHPK 60087 2421 12W-38N B7
13100 WDWH 60083 2421 13W-38N A6
13300 WDWH 60083 2420 13W-38N E6
Chapman Ct
1400 GLHT 60139 2969 21W-2N D7
2400 RGMW 60008 2805 20W-14N E5
8100 DRN 60561 3207 18W-9S B3
Chapman Dr
- CRTE 60417 3597 1E-29S C7
1800 JLET 60586 3416 29W-21S C7
Chapman Ln
1300 DRN 60561 3207 18W-9S A3
Chapman Rd
- SRGV 60554 3136 40W-5S B2
Chapparal Ter
700 RchT 60443 3593 8W-26S B2
Chappel Av
200 CTCY 60409 3351 2E-17S C5
500 ThtT 60409 3351 2E-17S C6
500 ThtT 60473 3351 2E-17S C6
15800 ThtT 60473 3429 2E-18S C1
17800 LNSG 60438 3429 2E-21S C5
22100 SLVL 60411 3597 2E-26S D3
S Chappel Av
- CHCG 60409 3351 2E-15S C2
- CHCG 60633 3351 2E-15S C2
- CTCY 60409 3351 2E-16S C2
6700 CHCG 60649 3153 2E-7S C6
7500 CHCG 60649 3215 2E-9S C2
7800 CHCG 60617 3215 2E-9S C2
Chappel Ct
1200 GLHT 60139 3024 24W-2N E1
Chappel St
- MRGO 60152 2634 50W-26N B2
Char Ln
13900 BmnT 60445 3348 6W-16S A3
13900 CTWD 60445 3348 6W-16S A3
Chara Ct
400 BRLT 60103 2910 29W-9N D1
Charabanc Ln
10 WLNG 60090 2754 15W-18N E2
100 WLNG 60090 2755 15W-18N A2
Charal Ln
300 HDPK 60035 2758 7W-20N A1
Chard Ct
500 GYLK 60030 2533 20W-33N A3
N Chardon Ln
30000 FmtT 60030 2588 24W-30N C2
W Chardon Rd
22900 FmtT 60030 2589 22W-30N A2
22900 RLKP 60030 2589 22W-30N B2
23100 RDLK 60030 2589 23W-30N A2
23100 RDLK 60073 2589 23W-30N A2
23400 FmtT 60030 2588 23W-30N D2
23400 FmtT 60073 2588 23W-30N E2
23400 RDLK 60030 2588 23W-30N E2
23400 RDLK 60073 2588 23W-30N E2
24600 WCDA 60084 2588 24W-30N B2
24800 WcnT 60030 2588 25W-30N B2
Chardonnay Ln
500 CLLK 60014 2639 36W-24N E6
Charger Ct
1300 CLSM 60188 2967 28W-4N B4
Charing Cross Rd
10 CHHT 60411 3508 1W-24S A5
100 LMBD 60148 3026 19W-0S C6
300 EGVV 60007 2860 18W-9N E7
500 DGvT 60516 3206 20W-10S B6
500 DGvT 60517 3206 20W-10S B6
500 EGVV 60007 2914 18W-9N E1
500 WDRG 60516 3206 20W-10S B6
500 WDRG 60517 3206 20W-10S B6
1300 DRFD 60015 2756 11W-20N C1
Chariot Ct
100 WLNG 60090 2755 15W-18N A2
W Chariot Ct
1700 EGvT 60056 2861 17W-10N C5
1700 MPPT 60056 2861 17W-10N C5
Chariot Ln
2700 OMFD 60461 3507 3W-24S B6
Chariot Rd
10 WLNG 60090 2755 15W-18N A2
Charismatic Dr
700 OSWG 60543 3264 35W-12S C2
Charity Av
200 JLET 60433 3499 23W-25S A7
E Charity Av
100 JLET 60433 3499 23W-25S A7
100 JLET 60433 3587 23W-25S A1
Charity Ct
- ZION 60099 2421 12W-40N C4
Charity Ln
10 BtlT 60512 3261 41W-12S E2
Charlela Ln
900 EGVV 60007 2914 20W-8N A3
Charlemagne Av
3200 HLCT 60429 3426 4W-21S E7
3200 HLCT 60429 3427 4W-21S A7
Charlemagne Cir
10 ROSL 60172 2913 23W-6N A6
Charlemagne Dr
500 NHBK 60062 2756 12W-18N B4
N Charlemagne Dr
3800 HFET 60192 2804 24W-14N B3
Charlemagne Dr W
1500 HFET 60192 2804 25W-14N B3
Charlemagne Ln
3100 SCRL 60174 2965 33W-4N A5
Charlemaine Dr
3300 AURA 60504 3201 31W-9S E4
3300 AURA 60504 3202 31W-9S A4
Charlene Ln
1000 SMBG 60193 2858 24W-10N C6
Charles Av
800 GRNE 60031 2478 14W-35N D7
900 WPHR 60096 2363 10W-42N B6
1200 ALGN 60102 2748 34W-19N A3
1700 ALGN 60102 2747 34W-19N E3
10100 PSHL 60465 3274 10W-11S B1
N Charles Av
10 VLPK 60181 3027 17W-1N B3
S Charles Av
10 VLPK 60181 3027 17W-0N B3
W Charles Av
4100 GRNE 60031 2535 14W-34N D2
Charles Ct
10 BFGV 60089 2754 16W-17N D5
10 CRTE 60417 3597 1E-28S B6
10 VNHL 60061 2647 17W-24N A6
100 MTGY 60543 3263 38W-11S A1
300 WCHI 60185 3021 31W-0N E5
400 SEGN 60177 2908 35W-8N C2
500 DGvT 60516 3206 19W-9S D4
500 GLHT 60139 2969 22W-3N B6
1600 WLNG 60090 2808 14W-15N C1
3300 ISLK 60042 2586 29W-28N D5
W Charles Ct
700 ADSN 60101 2970 19W-4N D4
Charles Dr
- RVDL 60827 3349 1W-16S D2
300 ANTH 60002 2357 24W-43N C4
400 EGvT 60007 2860 19W-9N C7
400 EGVV 60007 2860 19W-9N C7
1500 GLHT 60139 2969 22W-2N B6
1600 WLNG 60090 2808 14W-15N C1
3700 NHBK 60062 2756 12W-17N B5
E Charles Dr
10 NHLK 60164 2972 13W-2N E7
S Charles Dr
300 PNFD 60544 3416 29W-18S C2
300 PnfT 60544 3416 29W-18S C2
Charles Ln
10 BDWD 60408 3942 31W-42S B6
100 RtdT 60142 2745 41W-18N A4
500 LMBD 60148 3026 20W-0N A5
500 MltT 60148 3026 20W-0N A5
500 YkTp 60148 3026 20W-0N A5
1800 AraT 60505 3138 33W-5S E2
1800 AURA 60505 3138 33W-5S E2
5800 OKFT 60452 3347 7W-18S D7
Charles Pl
200 WLMT 60091 2811 5W-13N E7
Charles Rd
10100 GwdT 60098 2525 39W-33N C2
11900 GwdT 60098 2524 41W-34N E1
Charles Rd CO-A28
10100 GwdT 60098 2525 39W-33N C2
11900 GwdT 60098 2524 41W-34N E1
Charles St
- WHTN 60187 3023 26W-0S D7
10 BtlT 60543 3262 40W-12S C4
10 CPVL 60110 2747 34W-17N E7
100 GNVA 60134 3020 36W-1N A3
200 CHHT 60411 3507 1W-23S E3
200 LslT 60563 3142 25W-5S A3
500 AURA 60506 3137 36W-7S E6
500 LKPT 60441 3419 22W-20S C4
600 NPVL 60563 3142 25W-5S A3
800 CRTE 60417 3597 1E-28S A6
1200 MchT 60051 2528 32W-33N C3
1200 MHRY 60051 2528 32W-33N C3
1900 WDSK 60098 2524 41W-32N D4
3000 LydT 60164 2972 13W-3N E4
3100 FNPK 60131 2972 13W-3N E4
3100 FNPK 60164 2972 13W-3N E4
4700 HLSD 60154 3086 13W-1S D1
4700 HLSD 60162 3086 13W-1S D1
4700 PvsT 60162 3086 13W-1S D1
4700 WSTR 60154 3086 13W-1S D1
4700 WSTR 60162 3086 13W-1S D1
10000 RHMD 60071 2353 34W-42N C6
10600 HTLY 60142 2692 40W-21N A6
21800 MTSN 60443 3594 4W-26S E2
E Charles St
10 PLNO 60545 3259 47W-14S D7
600 ANHT 60004 2807 17W-15N B1
N Charles St
10 NPVL 60540 3142 25W-6S A5
1000 LslT 60563 3142 25W-5S A3
1000 NPVL 60563 3142 25W-5S A3
S Charles St
10 NPVL 60540 3142 26W-6S A6
200 LslT 60540 3142 25W-7S A6
1000 NPVL 60540 3204 26W-7S A1
9400 CHCG 60643 3213 2W-10S D6
9500 CHCG 60620 3213 1W-11S D6
10300 CHCG 60643 3277 1W-12S D1
W Charles St
10 PLNO 60545 3259 47W-14S C7
Charles J Miller Rd
- NndT 60051 2528 32W-31N B7
3000 MHRY 60050 2528 32W-31N B7
3000 NndT 60050 2528 32W-31N B7
Charleston Av
200 RMVL 60446 3340 25W-16S C4
Charleston Cir
16700 LKPT 60441 3420 21W-20S A4
Charleston Ct
10 HNWD 60047 2700 20W-24N B1
200 SMBG 60193 2857 26W-10N E6
1400 GNVA 60134 3020 34W-0N E4
1600 MLPK 60160 3030 10W-1N A2
5800 HRPK 60133 2911 26W-7N D5
Charleston Dr
100 NLNX 60451 3589 18W-26S B1
400 NlxT 60451 3589 18W-26S B1
1000 SCRL 60174 3020 36W-2N A2
1100 SCRL 60174 3019 36W-2N E2
2000 AURA 60506 3137 38W-6S A5
2400 SMBG 60193 2857 26W-10N E6
6700 DRN 60561 3145 17W-7S C6
8400 BRRG 60527 3208 15W-9S A4
13900 ODPK 60462 3345 11W-16S E3
Charleston Ln
- GLBT 60136 2799 38W-16N B1
- RtdT 60136 2799 38W-16N B1
700 HFET 60192 2804 24W-14N D4
700 IVNS 60067 2804 24W-14N D4
1600 HLCT 60429 3427 2W-20S D4
Charleston Rd
10 HNDL 60521 3146 15W-6S B4
3400 BHPK 60087 2479 11W-38N D1
3400 WKGN 60087 2479 11W-38N D1
4000 MTSN 60443 3594 5W-26S C1
N Charleston Rd
38100 BHPK 60087 2479 11W-37N E2
38100 WKGN 60087 2479 11W-37N E2
Charleston St
1500 BTVA 60510 3077 36W-1S D1
6400 OKFT 60452 3347 8W-18S B7
W Charleston St
2000 CHCG 60614 2977 2W-2N B6
2000 CHCG 60647 2977 2W-2N B6
Charlestown Ct
10 BGBK 60440 3205 22W-10S C5
Charlestown Dr
- NPVL 60540 3142 26W-6S A5
400 BGBK 60440 3205 22W-10S D6
Charlestowne Dr
1000 WCHI 60185 3022 30W-2N C1
Charlestowne Ln
2600 NPVL 60564 3202 29W-10S C6
N Charlesworth Av
800 JLET 60432 3499 22W-22S B2
N Charleton Av
10 WLSP 60480 3209 12W-9S C3
S Charleton Av
100 WLSP 60480 3209 12W-9S C3
600 PlsT 60480 3209 12W-9S C4
Charleton Pl
10 OKBK 60523 3085 17W-2S B3
Charlie Ct
2700 GNVW 60025 2809 11W-15N D2
2700 GNVW 60062 2809 11W-15N D2
2700 NHBK 60062 2809 11W-15N D2
W Charlie St
24000 CnhT 60410 3584 30W-28S C7
Charlie Collins Cir
- SLVL 60411 3597 2E-26S C3
Charlotte Av
200 CLLK 60014 2639 37W-25N A5
200 GfnT 60014 2639 37W-25N A5
3000 MchT 60050 2528 32W-32N C4
3000 MHRY 60050 2528 32W-32N C4
W Charlotte Av
400 JLET 60435 3498 24W-23S D4
Charlotte Cir
10 EMHT 60126 3027 16W-0S D6
1500 AURA 60564 3201 31W-9S E5
Charlotte Ct
10 BGBK 60440 3205 22W-10S C6
10 CRY 60013 2695 31W-23N D1
200 ElgT 60124 2853 37W-12N C2
300 SMBG 60193 2857 26W-10N E6
600 NlxT 60451 3501 17W-25S D7
2100 WHTN 60187 3081 26W-2S E3
10600 PlsT 60462 3345 13W-15S A1
21600 SLVL 60411 3597 2E-26S C2
S Charlotte Ct
1600 LMBD 60148 3084 19W-1S C1
Charlotte Dr
14100 SenT 60098 2581 43W-28N A5
18000 LNSG 60438 3429 1E-21S C6
N Charlotte Dr
37500 WDWH 60031 2478 15W-37N A2
37500 WDWH 60083 2478 15W-37N A2
Charlotte Ln
200 BGBK 60440 3205 22W-10S C6
Charlotte Pl
100 CRY 60013 2695 31W-23N D1
Charlotte Rd
- MPPT 60005 2861 17W-10N C5
- MPPT 60056 2861 17W-10N C5
W Charlotte Rd
22800 JLET 60586 3417 28W-19S A3
22800 PNFD 60586 3417 28W-19S A3
22800 PnfT 60586 3417 28W-19S A3
Charlotte St
200 MDLN 60060 2590 18W-28N D6
1400 WMTN 60481 3853 27W-37S C4
N Charlotte St
400 PLTN 60067 2752 21W-16N E7
600 LMBD 60148 3026 19W-1N C2
S Charlotte St
10 LMBD 60148 3026 19W-0N C4
Charlton Ct
500 LKVL 60046 2475 22W-37N C2
Charlton Rd
700 LKVL 60046 2475 21W-37N C2
W Charmaine Rd
8000 NRDG 60706 2918 10W-6N B6
Charmel Dr
- AntT 60081 2414 28W-38N E7
- FXLK 60081 2414 28W-38N E7
Charmille Ln
200 WDDL 60191 2970 18W-5N E1
200 WDDL 60191 2971 18W-5N A1
Charmingfare Dr
2200 WDRG 60517 3205 21W-8S E2
Charminster Ct
10 ALGN 60102 2693 37W-20N A7
Charnbrook Dr
- JNBG 60051 2471 30W-35N E6
1300 JNBG 60051 2472 30W-35N A6
Charnswood Ct
16600 TYPK 60477 3425 8W-19S A3
Charnswood Dr
6800 TYPK 60477 3425 8W-19S A3
Charolotte Ln
600 OSWG 60543 3199 36W-11S E7
600 OSWG 60543 3200 35W-10S B7
Charrington Dr
8800 FKFT 60423 3592 11W-25S A1
9100 FftT 60423 3592 11W-25S A1
Charron Ln
2000 WKGN 60085 2536 11W-34N D2
Charter Dr
3000 AURA 60503 3201 31W-10S D5
N Charter Hall Dr
500 PLTN 60067 2752 21W-16N D6
Charter Oak Ct
2700 AURA 60502 3079 32W-4S B7
Charter Oak Dr
2500 AURA 60502 3079 33W-4S B7
2500 AURA 60502 3139 32W-4S B1
Charter Oaks Ct
1100 BRLT 60103 2910 30W-6N C7
Charter Oaks Dr
1100 BRLT 60103 2910 30W-6N C7
Charter One Av
- SCRL 60174 2965 32W-3N B5
- SCRL 60185 2965 32W-3N B5
- WynT 60185 2965 32W-3N B5
Charter Point Dr
2000 ANHT 60004 2807 16W-16N D1
2100 ANHT 60004 2754 16W-16N D7
Chartres Ct
17900 HLCT 60429 3426 4W-21S E6
Chartres Dr
1400 NHBK 60062 2756 11W-17N D6
Chartwell Ct
1200 SRWD 60404 3496 31W-24S A7
Chartwell Dr
100 WNFD 60190 3023 27W-0N D4
W Chartwell Dr
20700 KLDR 60047 2752 20W-20N E1
Chartwell Rd
1300 SMBG 60195 2858 24W-12N D2
Chartwell Trc
1200 SRWD 60404 3496 31W-24S A7
Chas Dr
2400 RGMW 60008 2805 20W-14N E4
Chase Av
10 YkTp 60148 3026 19W-1S D7
10 YkTp 60148 3084 19W-1S D1
600 EGVV 60007 2915 17W-9N B1
2000 DSPN 60018 2863 12W-9N B7
3600 SKOK 60076 2866 4W-9N C7
3700 LNWD 60076 2866 4W-9N C7
3700 LNWD 60712 2866 4W-9N C7
4900 DRGV 60515 3143 21W-5S E2
4900 LNWD 60712 2865 6W-9N E7
4900 SKOK 60712 2865 6W-9N E7
5000 SKOK 60077 2865 6W-9N D7
5500 LslT 60515 3143 21W-6S E3
5600 LslT 60516 3143 21W-6S E4
5700 DRGV 60516 3143 21W-6S E5
6200 WDRG 60516 3143 21W-6S E5
6200 WDRG 60517 3143 21W-7S E5
E Chase Av
400 JLET 60432 3499 23W-22S B3
N Chase Av
10 LMBD 60148 3026 18W-1N D3
100 BRLT 60103 2911 28W-8N A2
S Chase Av
- BRLT 60103 2911 28W-8N A3
300 LMBD 60148 3026 18W-0N D5
W Chase Av
1800 CHCG 60626 2867 2W-9N B7
2000 CHCG 60645 2867 2W-9N B7
2700 CHCG 60645 2866 3W-9N E7
3800 LNWD 60076 2866 4W-9N B7
3800 SKOK 60076 2866 4W-9N B7
4600 LNWD 60712 2866 5W-9N A7
4700 LNWD 60712 2865 6W-9N E7
4800 SKOK 60077 2865 6W-9N E7
4800 SKOK 60712 2865 6W-9N E7
7100 CHCG 60631 2864 9W-9N C7
7100 CHCG 60714 2864 9W-9N C7
7100 NLES 60714 2864 9W-9N C7
7700 CHCG 60068 2864 9W-9N C7
7700 PKRG 60068 2864 9W-9N C7
Chase Ct
- WNVL 60555 3081 27W-4S B7
10 LMBD 60148 3026 18W-0S D6
200 BGBK 60440 3269 23W-11S B1
300 SMWD 60107 2857 28W-10N B5
600 WHTN 60187 3024 24W-0S D6
900 GRNE 60031 2534 16W-33N D3
1400 BFGV 60089 2700 18W-21N E7
N Chase Ct
42100 AntT 60002 2356 26W-42N D6
Chase Dr
500 CNHL 60514 3145 16W-6S D4
Chase Ln
700 LMBD 60148 3026 19W-0S D6
1800 AURA 60502 3139 33W-6S A4
Chase St
500 PKFT 60466 3594 4W-25S E1
500 PKFT 60466 3595 4W-25S A1
1300 ALGN 60102 2748 32W-20N B1
N Chase St
100 WHTN 60187 3024 24W-0S D6
S Chase St
100 WHTN 60187 3024 24W-0S D7
1100 WHTN 60187 3082 24W-1S D1
Chase Ter
300 SMWD 60107 2857 28W-10N B6
Chase Tr
1000 NLNX 60451 3589 19W-27S A5
1100 NLNX 60451 3588 19W-27S E5
W Chasefield Cir
5400 MHRY 60050 2527 34W-32N C6
Chasefield Ln
800 CLLK 60014 2639 36W-24N D7
Chasemoor Dr
7600 BRRG 60527 3208 14W-8S D2
Chase Pointe Ct
1300 NPVL 60565 3204 24W-8S E1
Chasewood Ct
2500 AURA 60502 3139 32W-6S C5
Chasewood Dr
500 SEGN 60177 2907 37W-7N D6
1300 LKZH 60010 2699 23W-21N A6
1300 LKZH 60047 2699 23W-21N A6
2300 LslT 60515 3143 21W-6S E4
Chasse Cir
200 SCRL 60174 2964 34W-4N D4
Chasta Ln
- JLET 60421 3675 24W-29S D2
W Chastworth Ln
- LktT 60446 3339 26W-16S E5
- RMVL 60446 3339 26W-16S E5
21100 LktT 60544 3339 26W-16S E5
Chat Ct
1500 NPVL 60565 3203 26W-8S E3
Chatam Ln
- BLVY 60098 2525 38W-33N E3
10 RDLK 60073 2532 23W-32N A4
10 RLKP 60030 2532 23W-32N A4
10 RLKP 60073 2532 23W-32N A4
Chateau
5400 ANHT 60005 2860 19W-12N D1
5400 RGMW 60005 2860 19W-12N D1
5400 RGMW 60008 2860 19W-12N D1
Chateau Av
900 AURA 60505 3138 34W-6S D4
Chateau Ct
7900 ODPK 60462 3346 9W-17S C4
Chateau Dr
10 DndT 60118 2800 35W-14N C5
10 DYR 46311 3598 C4
200 BtnT 60081 2414 29W-38N D6
300 BFGV 60089 2754 17W-20N C1
5400 RGMW 60008 2860 19W-12N D1
Chateau Ln
100 DYR 46311 3598 D4
Chateau Pl
4400 LSLE 60532 3142 24W-4S C1
Chateau Bluff Dr
- SYHW 60118 2800 34W-15N D4
- WDND 60118 2800 34W-15N D4
Chateaugay Av
700 NPVL 60540 3142 25W-7S A7
Chateaugay Ct
300 CmpT 60119 2961 42W-4N C4
Chateaugay Dr
1300 SPGV 60081 2355 30W-41N A7
Chateaugay Ln
10 CmpT 60119 2961 43W-4N B4
Chateau West Dr
200 DndT 60118 2800 35W-14N C6
Chateaux Ct
500 OSWG 60543 3263 38W-13S B6
Chateaux Bourne Dr
500 BRTN 60010 2751 24W-18N C3
Chatelaine Ct
300 WLBK 60527 3145 17W-6S D5
Chatfield Cross
11700 HTLY 60142 2744 42W-20N A1
Chatfield Ct
100 HDPK 60037 2704 8W-23N D1
1500 ROSL 60172 2912 25W-7N B4
2400 AURA 60504 3201 32W-8S C2
Chatfield Ln
1900 LSLE 60532 3142 24W-7S E6
Chatfield Rd
500 NlxT 60451 3502 16W-24S A5
900 MKNA 60448 3502 16W-24S A5
900 MKNA 60451 3502 16W-24S A5
900 WNKA 60093 2759 5W-16N A7
1100 WNKA 60093 2758 5W-16N E7
Chatham Av
- YkTp 60181 3027 17W-2N B1
10 AddT 60101 2971 17W-3N B6
10 ADSN 60181 3027 17W-2N B1
10 VLPK 60181 3027 17W-2N B1
200 ADSN 60181 2971 17W-2N B7
600 ADSN 60101 2971 17W-2N B7
4200 GRNE 60031 2535 14W-33N D3
N Chatham Av
400 VLPK 60181 3027 17W-1N B2
S Chatham Av
500 EMHT 60126 3028 15W-0N A5
Chatham Cir
400 BFGV 60089 2754 17W-18N B3
600 ALGN 60102 2694 35W-20N A7
1700 DRFD 60015 2703 12W-21N B7
Chatham Ct
- WDRG 60517 3206 20W-10S A6
10 FRGV 60021 2696 29W-22N B4
10 SEGN 60177 2908 35W-7N B4
100 BMDL 60108 2969 23W-5N A2
200 ROSL 60172 2912 25W-7N B5
500 WynT 60185 2966 29W-4N E3
1200 LYVL 60048 2647 15W-27N E1
1500 SMBG 60193 2858 25W-10N B6
1900 NPVL 60565 3204 25W-9S A4
2500 GNVA 60134 3019 37W-0N C6
3700 JLET 60435 3417 27W-19S C3
Chatham Dr
- RMVL 60446 3339 27W-17S B6
800 CLSM 60188 2967 27W-3N D5
1200 LMNT 60439 3271 18W-14S A7
1900 WHTN 60187 3082 25W-2S C4
W Chatham Dr
- PNFD 60585 3337 32W-14S C1
- WldT 60585 3337 32W-14S C1
1000 PLTN 60067 2805 22W-15N B2
Chatham Ln
- WDND 60118 2800 36W-16N A3
10 OKBK 60523 3086 15W-2S B4
10 ROSL 60172 2912 25W-7N B5
1400 SMBG 60193 2858 25W-10N B6
2400 BLVY 60098 2525 38W-33N E3
2700 GwdT 60098 2525 38W-33N D3
3100 WDND 60118 2799 36W-15N E3
W Chatham Ln
4600 NndT 60012 2639 36W-27N D1
Chatham Pl
10 OswT 60538 3199 36W-10S E6
1000 VNHL 60061 2647 17W-27N C1
S Chatham Pl
400 ANHT 60004 2807 17W-13N C5
400 ANHT 60005 2807 17W-13N C5
Chatham Rd
- CbaT 60010 2697 25W-21N E6
500 GNVW 60025 2811 8W-13N A7
2400 AURA 60506 3136 39W-7S E6
3300 WKGN 60087 2479 11W-37N C1
W Chatham Rd
25500 CbaT 60010 2697 26W-21N E5
25500 CbaT 60010 2698 25W-21N A6
Chatham St
13100 BLID 60406 3349 2W-16S C2
13800 DXMR 60406 3349 2W-16S C3
Chatham Wy
- LkvT 60046 2476 18W-36N D4
18700 WrnT 60046 2476 18W-36N D4
Chatham Cove
400 WPHR 60096 2363 10W-43N A5
Chatsford Ct
1600 BRLT 60103 2967 28W-5N A2
Chatsworth Av
200 SRGV 60554 3135 41W-6S D5
Chatsworth Cir
100 SMBG 60194 2859 23W-10N B5
Chatsworth Ct
800 HFET 60169 2858 25W-11N C3
5800 HRPK 60133 2911 26W-7N D5
Chatsworth Ln
1200 HFET 60169 2858 25W-11N C3

STREET Block	City	ZIP	Map#	CGS	Grid
Chattanooga Ct					
900	NPVL	60540	3203	27W-8S	B1
Chattanooga Tr					
1200	CLSM	60188	2967	28W-4N	B4
Chaucer Ct					
-	ELGN	60120	2855	32W-11N	D5
100	WLBK	60527	3146	15W-7S	A6
300	MltT	60137	3083	22W-2S	C4
400	SMBG	60193	2858	24W-9N	E7
1700	NPVL	60565	3204	24W-10S	D5
1700	RMVL	60446	3339	27W-17S	D5
Chaucer Dr					
1700	RMVL	60446	3339	27W-17S	D5
5600	OKFT	60452	3347	7W-18S	D6
8300	WLSP	60480	3209	13W-9S	A4
10800	WLSP	60480	3208	13W-9S	E3
16700	ODPK	60467	3423	13W-20S	A3
Chaucer Ln					
10	SMWD	60107	2857	28W-11N	B4
900	HDPK	60035	2704	8W-21N	E7
2100	GLHT	60139	2969	23W-4N	A3
Chaucer St					
-	BDVW	60154	3087	12W-1S	B1
-	BDVW	60155	3087	12W-1S	B1
6400	WLBK	60527	3146	15W-7S	B6
9900	WSTR	60154	3087	12W-1S	B1
10200	PvsT	60162	3087	12W-1S	A1
10200	WSTR	60162	3087	12W-1S	A1
Chaucer Wy					
700	BFGV	60089	2701	17W-21N	B6
Chautauqua St					
1300	BTVA	60510	3078	36W-2S	A4
Chayes Ct					
2700	FSMR	60422	3507	3W-22S	B1
2700	HMWD	60422	3507	3W-22S	B1
2700	HMWD	60430	3507	3W-22S	B1
Chayes Park Dr					
2800	FSMR	60422	3507	3W-22S	A1
2800	HMWD	60422	3507	3W-22S	A1
2800	HMWD	60430	3507	3W-22S	A1
Che Che Pinqua St					
-	WnfT	60510	3080	30W-1S	A3
Checker Dr					
300	BFGV	60047	2754	17W-20N	A1
300	BFGV	60089	2754	17W-20N	A1
300	LGGV	60047	2754	17W-20N	A1
300	VrnT	60047	2754	17W-20N	A1
300	VrnT	60089	2754	17W-20N	A1
500	BFGV	60089	2701	17W-20N	B7
W Checker Rd					
1600	BFGV	60047	2754	18W-20N	A1
1600	BFGV	60089	2754	18W-20N	A1
1600	LGGV	60047	2754	18W-20N	A1
1600	LGGV	60089	2754	18W-20N	A1
1600	VrnT	60047	2754	18W-20N	A1
1600	VrnT	60089	2754	18W-20N	A1
1800	LGGV	60047	2753	18W-20N	E1
1800	LGGV	60089	2753	18W-20N	E1
1800	VrnT	60089	2753	18W-20N	E1
2300	ElaT	60047	2753	19W-20N	C1
Checkerberry Ct					
1200	LYVL	60048	2591	17W-30N	B2
Chedworth Ct					
2500	NHBK	60062	2756	10W-18N	E4
2500	NHBK	60062	2757	10W-18N	A3
Cheekwood Ct					
1000	EGVV	60007	2914	19W-8N	D2
Cheever Av					
200	GNVA	60134	3020	35W-0N	A4
Cheiftain Ct					
12700	LMNT	60439	3343	18W-15S	A1
Cheker Sq					
1900	EHZC	60429	3427	2W-20S	D5
1900	HLCT	60429	3427	2W-20S	D5
1900	HLCT	60430	3427	2W-20S	D5
Chellington Dr					
3100	JNBG	60051	2472	30W-35N	A6
Chelmsford Ct					
1600	BRLT	60103	2967	28W-5N	A2
Chelmsford Dr					
3200	SPGV	60081	2413	32W-39N	B5
Chelmsford Ln					
600	EGvT	60007	2860	19W-9N	D7
600	EGVV	60007	2860	19W-9N	D7
600	EGVV	60007	2914	19W-8N	C1
Chelmsford Pl					
1900	HFET	60169	2858	26W-12N	A1
Chelse Ct					
3800	JLET	60431	3497	28W-22S	A3
Chelsea Av					
10	SRGV	60554	3135	42W-7S	D7
4400	LSLE	60532	3143	22W-4S	B1
N Chelsea Av					
1400	PLTN	60067	2752	21W-18N	D4
Chelsea Cir					
200	LKVL	60046	2475	22W-37N	A1
200	WNFD	60190	3023	27W-0N	D4
2800	OMFD	60461	3507	3W-25S	A7
Chelsea Ct					
600	ELGN	60123	2853	37W-10N	D7
800	AURA	60504	3201	32W-9S	C3
900	NlxT	60451	3502	16W-25S	A7
1600	WHTN	60187	3081	26W-2S	E3
13800	HMGN	60491	3421	17W-19S	D3
Chelsea Dr					
-	HNWD	60047	2644	24W-24N	C7
600	ALGN	60102	2747	33W-20N	E1
800	WLNG	60090	2755	15W-18N	A3
1000	BRLT	60103	2910	29W-6N	E6
2500	WDRG	60517	3205	21W-9S	D3
14000	ODPK	60462	3346	10W-16S	C3
Chelsea Ln					
10	CRY	60013	2695	32W-23N	C1
900	AURA	60504	3201	32W-9S	D3
900	SMBG	60193	2912	24W-9N	D1
1000	BGBK	60440	3205	21W-9S	D4
1000	BGBK	60517	3205	21W-9S	D4
1000	WDRG	60517	3205	21W-9S	D4
1400	NPVL	60565	3204	24W-8S	C2
8300	WLSP	60480	3208	13W-9S	E3
24900	PNFD	60544	3337	31W-16S	E3
24900	PNFD	60544	3338	31W-16S	A3
Chelsea Pl					
9700	MKNA	60448	3503	12W-23S	D4
17400	CCHL	60478	3426	4W-20S	E5
W Chelsea Pl					
1600	CHCG	60643	3277	2W-12S	D2
Chelsea Rd					
2300	NHBK	60062	2810	8W-15N	E1
6800	TYPK	60477	3425	8W-19S	A2
Chelsea St					
10	BMDL	60108	2968	24W-5N	E1
800	NLNX	60451	3501	16W-25S	E7
800	NlxT	60451	3501	16W-25S	E7
800	NlxT	60451	3502	16W-25S	A7
Chelsea Cove					
400	ROSL	60172	2912	25W-6N	C5
Chelsea on Auburn					
10	RGMW	60008	2806	19W-15N	B3
Chelsey Ct					
-	FXLK	60081	2414	29W-39N	D4
700	GRNE	60031	2534	16W-33N	E2
Chelsey St					
2600	BFGV	60089	2701	16W-22N	D3
2600	VrnT	60089	2701	16W-22N	D3
Cheltenham Dr					
1200	GNEN	60137	3026	20W-0S	A7
1200	GNEN	60148	3026	20W-0S	A7
Cheltenham Pl					
1900	HFET	60169	2858	25W-12N	B1
1900	SMBG	60194	2858	26W-11N	A3
E Cheltenham Pl					
3000	CHCG	60617	3215	1E-9S	A3
3000	CHCG	60649	3215	1E-9S	A3
3000	CHCG	60649	3216	3E-8S	A1
Cheltenham Rd					
1000	EGVV	60007	2914	19W-8N	B3
Chelton Rd					
10	RMVL	60446	3340	24W-16S	E5
Chemes Ln					
-	BTVA	60510	3078	33W-3S	E5
Chemung Dr					
3700	GwdT	60097	2469	37W-35N	A5
3700	WRLK	60097	2469	37W-35N	A5
Chemung St					
23800	CmgT	60033	2405	52W-38N	A7
Chenault Ct					
10	BFGV	60089	2754	16W-18N	C4
Chenault Rd					
300	BFGV	60089	2754	17W-18N	C4
S Chennault Av					
24900	MonT	60449	3682	8W-30S	A3
Chepstow Ct					
1700	NPVL	60540	3202	28W-7S	E1
Cherbourg Ct					
10	WLNG	60090	2808	14W-15N	C1
Cherbourg Ct N					
600	BFGV	60089	2754	17W-20N	B1
Cherbourg Ct S					
500	BFGV	60089	2754	16W-20N	C1
Cherbourg Dr					
500	BFGV	60089	2754	17W-20N	B1
600	BFGV	60089	2701	16W-20N	C7
W Cheri Ct					
9600	GGnT	60423	3591	12W-28S	E6
Cheri Ln					
100	ANTH	60002	2357	23W-42N	E5
Cherice Dr					
400	WNVL	60555	3080	30W-2S	C4
Cherie Ct					
22200	RNPK	60471	3594	6W-26S	A3
Cheriton Cir					
1400	GYLK	60030	2475	20W-34N	E7
Cherokee Ct					
500	CLSM	60188	2967	26W-2N	E7
900	LKVL	60046	2474	24W-37N	D2
2000	CPVL	60110	2748	32W-18N	C4
N Cherokee Ct					
33500	WrnT	60030	2534	17W-33N	B3
Cherokee Dr					
200	BGBK	60440	3268	23W-12S	E3
900	DRN	60561	3207	17W-8S	B1
1900	WCHI	60185	2966	30W-3N	B6
3500	JNBG	60050	2471	32W-35N	B5
6400	IHPK	60525	3146	14W-7S	D6
N Cherokee Dr					
24800	LKBN	60010	2643	25W-24N	E6
Cherokee Ln					
2800	RVWD	60015	2702	13W-21N	E5
Cherokee Pl					
1000	LMNT	60439	3270	19W-14S	D7
Cherokee Rd					
10	LKZH	60047	2699	23W-22N	A3
10	VNHL	60061	2647	16W-25N	C5
100	ALGN	60102	2747	33W-20N	D1
100	AlqT	60102	2747	33W-20N	D1
200	LKFT	60045	2650	10W-25N	A6
500	HDPK	60035	2758	7W-20N	B2
900	WLMT	60091	2812	5W-14N	B5
1900	CPVL	60110	2748	32W-18N	C4
2000	BNHL	60110	2748	32W-18N	C4
2100	WKGN	60087	2479	11W-36N	D4
S Cherokee Rd					
8400	PSPK	60464	3274	10W-14S	B6
Cherokee Tr					
300	LIHL	60156	2694	34W-21N	B5
1300	RLKB	60073	2474	24W-35N	D7
1500	RLKH	60073	2474	24W-35N	D7
8100	TYPK	60477	3424	10W-21S	C5
S Cherokee Tr					
13900	HMGN	60491	3343	16W-16S	D4
W Cherokee Tr					
24200	FmtT	60030	2588	24W-31N	C1
25600	CNHN	60410	3672	32W-30S	D3
Cherry Av					
-	ELGN	60120	2855	32W-10N	C6
-	RVGV	60171	2973	11W-3N	D5
-	RVGV	60131	2973	11W-3N	D5
600	LKFT	60045	2650	10W-26N	B4
2000	HRPK	60133	2911	27W-8N	C2
8900	MNGV	60053	2865	8W-11N	A3
9100	FNPK	60131	2973	11W-3N	D5
N Cherry Av					
1100	CHCG	60622	3033	1W-1N	E2
S Cherry Av					
3100	NndT	60051	2586	29W-28N	B5
3200	ISLK	60042	2586	29W-28N	B5
3200	ISLK	60051	2586	29W-28N	B5
W Cherry Av					
6800	NLES	60714	2918	8W-8N	E1
8800	RVGV	60171	2973	11W-3N	E5
8900	FNPK	60131	2973	11W-3N	E5
8900	RVGV	60131	2973	11W-3N	E5
26500	AntT	60002	2356	26W-42N	D5
Cherry Cir					
500	MaiT	60025	2809	11W-12N	E7
900	BRLT	60103	2911	27W-7N	C5
E Cherry Cir					
700	ITSC	60143	2914	19W-7N	C5
Cherry Ct					
100	WDSK	60098	2524	41W-32N	D5
200	BGBK	60440	3205	23W-11S	A7
300	MaiT	60025	2863	10W-12N	E1
400	ROSL	60172	2913	22W-7N	B4
700	ITSC	60143	2914	19W-7N	C5
800	SMBG	60194	2858	25W-11N	B3
1700	LKVL	60046	2417	22W-40N	B3
1700	WHTN	60187	3024	24W-0N	D4
4300	HFET	60192	2804	25W-15N	B2
7600	MchT	60097	2469	36W-37N	D1
7600	RcmT	60097	2469	36W-37N	D1
S Cherry Ct					
11200	PSHL	60465	3274	10W-13S	C3
Cherry Dr					
800	SMBG	60194	2858	25W-11N	B3
1300	BTVA	60510	3078	33W-2S	E4
2400	MchT	60097	2526	36W-34N	C1
2700	MchT	60097	2469	36W-34N	C7
N Cherry Dr					
10	BtlT	60543	3263	38W-12S	A3
500	GNWD	60425	3428	0W-22S	C7
S Cherry Dr					
10	BtlT	60543	3263	38W-12S	A4
Cherry Ln					
-	PGGV	60140	2797	42W-15N	D4
-	WmTp	60481	3761	32W-34S	C5
10	GnvT	60134	3020	34W-0N	E5
10	GnvT	60134	3021	33W-0N	A5
100	FXLK	60041	2473	27W-35N	B6
100	GrtT	60041	2473	27W-35N	B6
200	SCHT	60411	3596	1W-27S	A3
300	MaiT	60025	2863	10W-12N	E1
400	MaiT	60025	2809	11W-12N	E7
400	MltT	60137	3025	22W-1N	B3
500	GNEN	60137	3025	22W-1N	B3
500	NfdT	60025	2809	11W-12N	E7
800	TNTN	60476	3428	0E-21S	E6
900	LMBD	60148	3026	19W-0S	D6
1000	BCHR	60401	3864	0W-36S	D1
1000	HDPK	60035	2704	9W-22N	C4
1100	BCHR	60401	3774	0W-36S	D7
1400	NndT	60014	2586	30W-27N	A7
1900	NHBK	60062	2757	10W-17N	A5
2100	LSLE	60532	3142	24W-4S	D1
2600	NHBK	60062	2756	11W-17N	D5
8400	ODPK	60462	3346	10W-16S	B2
15300	MKHM	60426	3348	4W-18S	E7
15300	MKHM	60428	3348	4W-18S	E7
15800	OKFT	60452	3347	8W-18S	B7
18800	LNSG	60438	3510	3E-22S	A1
E Cherry Ln					
700	ANHT	60004	2754	17W-16N	B7
2800	CteT	60417	3687	3E-30S	A2
N Cherry Ln					
6800	LNWD	60712	2920	4W-8N	C1
S Cherry Ln					
26000	MONE	60449	3682	6W-31S	E6
W Cherry Ln					
23300	ElaT	60047	2698	23W-23N	E2
23300	LKZH	60047	2698	23W-23N	E2
Cherry Pkwy					
10100	SKOK	60076	2811	5W-12N	E7
Cherry St					
-	CHCG	60631	2864	9W-9N	C7
-	NHFD	60093	2811	7W-15N	C2
-	NtrT	60093	2811	6W-15N	C2
-	PKRG	60631	2864	9W-9N	C7
-	WMTN	60481	3853	28W-39S	B7
10	ELGN	60120	2854	34W-12N	E3
10	PKFT	60466	3595	3W-27S	B4
10	ROSL	60172	2913	22W-7N	B4
100	CRY	60013	2695	30W-23N	E1
200	ELGN	60120	2855	33W-12N	A3
200	PKRG	60068	2864	10W-9N	B7
200	SEGN	60177	2908	34W-8N	D3
300	AddT	60106	2971	17W-4N	C3
400	ADSN	60106	2971	17W-4N	C3
400	HMND	46324	3430		D3
400	WNKA	60093	2812	4W-15N	B2
600	SRGV	60554	3135	42W-4S	D2
1000	DRFD	60015	2703	11W-21N	C6
1100	LIHL	60156	2694	35W-22N	B4
1100	WNKA	60093	2811	5W-15N	E2
1400	PKRG	60068	2863	10W-9N	E7
1800	WHTN	60187	3024	24W-0N	D4
15400	DLTN	60419	3350	0E-18S	E6
15400	SHLD	60473	3350	0E-18S	E6
19300	FftT	60448	3504	11W-23S	A4
19300	MKNA	60448	3504	11W-23S	A4
N Cherry St					
700	ITSC	60143	2914	19W-7N	C5
S Cherry St					
100	ITSC	60143	2914	19W-6N	C7
400	JLET	60436	3498	24W-24S	D6
500	ADSN	60143	2914	19W-5N	C7
500	EMHT	60126	3028	15W-0N	A4
25400	CNHN	60410	3672	31W-30S	E5
S Cherry Blossom Blvd					
-	PNFD	60543	3265	33W-14S	B7
-	PNFD	60543	3337	33W-14S	B1
-	PNFD	60585	3337	33W-14S	B1
Cherry Blossom Ct					
800	WCHI	60185	3022	30W-1N	B2
Cherry Blossom Ln					
800	NPVL	60540	3141	27W-7S	D7
N Cherry Cove Ct					
2500	RLKB	60073	2475	22W-36N	B4
E Cherry Cove Ln					
200	RLKB	60073	2475	22W-36N	B4
N Cherry Cove Ln					
2500	RLKB	60073	2475	22W-36N	B3
Cherry Creek Av					
8500	TYPK	60487	3424	10W-20S	B4
Cherry Creek Cir					
-	NlxT	60433	3588	20W-26S	B3
Cherry Creek Ct					
-	JLET	60433	3588	20W-26S	B2
16500	NlxT	60433	3588	20W-26S	B2
Cherry Creek Dr					
700	GYLK	60030	2533	20W-34N	B1
18300	HMWD	60430	3427	3W-22S	B7
18300	HMWD	60430	3507	3W-22S	B1
Cherry Creek Ln					
400	PTHT	60070	2754	16W-16N	E6
Cherry Hill Av					
8400	TYPK	60477	3424	10W-20S	B3
8400	TYPK	60487	3424	10W-19S	B2
16300	ODPK	60462	3424	10W-19S	B2
16300	ODPK	60487	3424	10W-19S	B2
Cherry Hill Cir					
10	HNWD	60047	2646	19W-24N	B7
Cherry Hill Ct					
400	SMBG	60193	2859	23W-9N	A6
Cherryhill Ct					
2900	MHRY	60050	2470	34W-34N	B7
Cherry Hill Dr					
100	CbaT	60010	2697	26W-22N	D4
100	NBRN	60010	2697	26W-22N	D4
3600	FSMR	60422	3506	4W-22S	D2
E Cherry Hill Dr					
400	AddT	60101	2971	17W-2N	B6
400	ADSN	60101	2971	17W-2N	B6
N Cherry Hill Dr					
1900	ANHT	60004	2807	16W-16N	C1
2100	ANHT	60004	2754	16W-16N	C7
Cherry Hill Ln					
12100	HTLY	60142	2744	42W-19N	E3
Cherry Hill Rd					
-	JknT	60421	3588	21W-27S	B5
-	JknT	60442	3588	21W-27S	B5
-	JltT	60421	3588	21W-27S	B5
-	JltT	60432	3500	20W-23S	B4
-	MhtT	60421	3588	21W-27S	B5
-	MhtT	60442	3588	21W-27S	B5
-	NlxT	60421	3588	21W-27S	B5
-	NlxT	60432	3500	20W-23S	B4
-	NlxT	60442	3588	21W-27S	B5
10	JltT	60433	3500	21W-25S	B7
10	NLNX	60433	3500	20W-24S	B5
10	NLNX	60451	3500	21W-25S	B7
10	NlxT	60433	3500	21W-25S	B7
100	NlxT	60451	3500	21W-25S	B7
400	DYR	46311	3598		D3
700	JLET	60433	3500	21W-25S	B7
1200	JLET	60433	3588	21W-26S	B2
1200	JltT	60433	3588	20W-25S	B1
1500	NlxT	60433	3588	21W-26S	B2
S Cherry Hill Rd					
23100	JknT	60421	3588	20W-28S	B7
23100	JknT	60442	3588	20W-28S	B7
23100	JltT	60421	3588	20W-28S	B7
23100	MhtT	60421	3588	20W-28S	B7
23100	NlxT	60421	3588	20W-28S	B7
23100	NlxT	60442	3588	20W-28S	B7
23500	JLET	60421	3588	21W-28S	B7
23500	JLET	60442	3588	21W-28S	B7
23900	JknT	60421	3677	20W-31S	B6
23900	JLET	60421	3677	21W-29S	B2
23900	JLET	60442	3677	21W-29S	B2
23900	MhtT	60421	3677	20W-31S	B6
23900	MhtT	60442	3677	20W-31S	B6
25900	JknT	60442	3677	20W-31S	B6
26300	JknT	60421	3766	20W-32S	B1
26300	JknT	60442	3766	20W-32S	B1
26300	MhtT	60421	3766	20W-32S	B1
26300	MhtT	60442	3766	20W-32S	B1
Cherry Hills Ct					
15500	ODPK	60462	3346	10W-18S	A7
Cherry Hills Ln					
900	NPVL	60563	3141	28W-5S	B3
Cherry Ridge Dr					
2200	JLET	60586	3415	31W-21S	E6
Cherry Stone Pl					
8500	TYPK	60487	3424	10W-19S	B2
Cherrytree Av					
6700	WDRG	60517	3143	21W-7S	D6
Cherry Tree Ct					
3800	JLET	60435	3417	27W-19S	D2
Cherrytree Ct					
10	WDRG	60517	3143	21W-7S	D7
N Cherry Tree Ct					
10	NARA	60542	3077	37W-3S	C5
10	NARA	60542	3137	37W-4S	D1
S Cherry Tree Ct					
10	NARA	60542	3137	36W-4S	E1
Cherrytree Dr					
2400	AURA	60506	3136	39W-7S	E6
Cherry Tree Ln					
900	GLNC	60022	2758	7W-17N	B5
3700	JLET	60435	3417	27W-19S	D2
4400	WKGN	60083	2478	14W-37N	C1
7600	WLBK	60527	3207	17W-8S	D2
Cherry Vail Wy					
7900	DrrT	60098	2583	36W-28N	C6
7900	NndT	60098	2583	36W-28N	C6
Cherry Valley Rd					
300	VNHL	60061	2647	18W-24N	A6
N Cherry Valley Rd					
600	BLVY	60050	2526	36W-31N	D7
1000	BLVY	60050	2583	36W-30N	D1
1000	BLVY	60098	2583	36W-30N	D1
1000	NndT	60050	2583	36W-30N	D1
S Cherry Valley Rd					
1600	BLVY	60050	2583	36W-29N	C3
1600	BLVY	60098	2583	36W-29N	C3
1600	NndT	60050	2583	36W-29N	C3
2300	DrrT	60098	2583	37W-28N	C6
2300	NndT	60098	2583	37W-28N	C6
3700	DrrT	60012	2583	37W-28N	C7
3700	NndT	60012	2583	37W-27N	C7
Cherrywood Av					
200	PLTN	60067	2752	21W-18N	D3
Cherrywood Cir					
2000	NPVL	60565	3203	26W-9S	E4
Cherrywood Ct					
10	IHPK	60525	3146	14W-6S	D5
100	RMVL	60446	3339	26W-18S	E7
300	VNHL	60061	2647	16W-24N	E7
1300	ALGN	60102	2694	34W-20N	B7
1900	JLET	60435	3498	26W-22S	A1
2100	GRNE	60031	2478	15W-36N	A4
6400	FXLK	60020	2414	28W-39N	E5
15400	ODPK	60462	3346	10W-18S	B7
Cherrywood Dr					
10	PlsT	60464	3273	13W-14S	A6
10	SMBG	60193	2859	23W-10N	A5
500	NARA	60542	3077	37W-4S	D7
500	WLNG	60090	2754	15W-17N	E6
S Cherrywood Dr					
1100	MPPT	60056	2861	17W-11N	C3
Cherrywood Ln					
10	LNSH	60015	2702	13W-22N	D4
10	LNSH	60069	2702	13W-22N	D4
10	RVWD	60015	2702	13W-22N	D4
10	RVWD	60069	2702	13W-22N	D4
100	MltT	60137	3083	22W-3S	C5
100	RMVL	60446	3339	27W-17S	D5
700	WLBK	60527	3207	16W-8S	E1
900	WCHI	60185	3022	29W-2N	D1
1400	NLNX	60451	3588	19W-26S	E3
1700	LNHT	60046	2417	21W-38N	D7
1700	LNHT	60046	2475	21W-37N	D1
1700	LNHT	60046	2476	19W-38N	B1
7100	SPGV	60081	2414	30W-38N	A6
17700	HMWD	60430	3427	3W-21S	B6
W Cherrywood Ln					
15200	LbvT	60048	2592	15W-30N	A2
16500	WDWH	60083	2419	16W-40N	D2
Cherrywood Pl					
2700	HLCT	60429	3427	3W-21S	B5
Cherrywood Rd					
100	BFGV	60089	2754	17W-18N	B2
Chertsey Ct					
8200	ODPK	60462	3346	10W-17S	B4
Cherveny Pl					
1200	WMTN	60481	3943	26W-39S	E1
Cheryl Ct					
100	RtdT	60142	2745	41W-18N	B5
3800	AURA	60504	3202	30W-8S	A3
Cheryl Ln					
-	ELGN	60123	2801	33W-14N	B6
10800	ODPK	60467	3423	13W-21S	A5
W Cheryl Ln					
200	PLTN	60067	2805	21W-15N	D2
Chesapeak Ln					
300	OSWG	60543	3264	34W-11S	D2
300	OswT	60543	3264	34W-12S	D2
Chesapeake Blvd					
800	GYLK	60030	2532	20W-34N	E1
800	GYLK	60030	2533	20W-34N	A2
Chesapeake Ct					
200	VNHL	60061	2647	17W-26N	B3
1100	BRLT	60103	2910	29W-6N	E7
4000	HFET	60192	2804	24W-15N	B3
6800	GRNE	60031	2477	17W-35N	B6
Chesapeake Dr					
-	MHRY	60050	2527	34W-33N	C2
600	BGBK	60440	3269	21W-11S	E1
1500	HFET	60192	2804	24W-15N	B3
4100	AURA	60504	3202	30W-8S	B1
5600	MchT	60050	2527	34W-33N	C2
11600	PNFD	60585	3266	30W-13S	B5
N Chesapeake Dr					
23100	KLDR	60047	2699	21W-23N	D2
23200	LKBN	60010	2697	26W-23N	C2
Chesapeake Ln					
300	BMDL	60108	2912	25W-6N	A7
1700	SMBG	60193	2912	25W-8N	A2
2600	NHBK	60062	2756	10W-17N	E6
N Chesapeake Ln					
1100	PLTN	60074	2753	19W-17N	C6
E Chesapeake Pl					
-	PvsT	60558	3086	14W-2S	D4
-	WSTR	60154	3086	14W-2S	D4
-	WSTR	60558	3086	14W-2S	D4
Chesapeake Rd					
600	SCRL	60175	2963	36W-5N	E2
600	SCRL	60175	2964	36W-5N	A2
3600	SchT	60175	2963	36W-5N	E2
Chesapeake Tr					
800	RLKH	60073	2474	24W-36N	D5
Chesapeake Wy					
-	GNVA	60134	3020	33W-1N	E3
-	GNVA	60134	3021	33W-2N	A2
Chesapeake Bay					
100	WPHR	60096	2363	10W-43N	A4
2300	ELGN	60123	2907	36W-9N	E1
Chesham Ct					
1200	WDRG	60517	3206	20W-9S	B3
Cheshire Av					
1100	NPVL	60540	3142	25W-7S	A6
Cheshire Ct					
-	OSWG	60543	3263	36W-12S	E4
200	BGBK	60440	3205	22W-11S	C7
500	YKVL	60560	3261	42W-13S	D5
1900	WHTN	60187	3083	23W-2S	A4
8300	DrrT	60098	2583	37W-28N	B6
22500	DRPK	60010	2752	22W-20N	B2
W Cheshire Ct					
12400	HMGN	60491	3344	15W-17S	B4
Cheshire Dr					
1900	HFET	60192	2802	30W-12N	C7
2200	AURA	60502	3139	32W-7S	B7
2200	AURA	60502	3201	32W-8S	B1
2200	AURA	60505	3139	33W-7S	B7
2400	AURA	60504	3201	32W-8S	C1
Cheshire Ln					
1800	WHTN	60187	3083	23W-2S	A4
Cheshire Rd					
5100	GRNE	60031	2478	15W-35N	B6
Chesire Ct					
2600	WDND	60118	2800	36W-16N	B2
Chesney Dr					
-	SRGV	60554	3135	42W-6S	C5
W Chesney Dr					
25300	LkvT	60046	2474	25W-37N	A1
Chesnut Ct					
-	ELGN	60120	2855	31W-11N	E4
Chesnut St					
-	ELGN	60120	2855	31W-11N	E4
-	HnrT	60120	2855	31W-11N	E4
Chessington Dr					
2700	NlxT	60451	3590	16W-27S	A5
2900	MhtT	60451	3590	16W-27S	A5
Chesson Ct					
1000	FrnT	60481	3943	26W-39S	E1
1000	WMTN	60481	3943	26W-39S	E1
Chesson St					
-	LYWD	60411	3510	4E-24S	B6
Chester Av					
600	ELGN	60120	2855	33W-12N	B2
6500	HGKN	60525	3147	11W-7S	D6
N Chester Av					
10	PKRG	60068	2918	8W-8N	D1
4400	CHCG	60634	2974	10W-5N	A1
4400	CHCG	60656	2974	10W-5N	A1
4800	CHCG	60706	2918	10W-6N	A6
5000	NRDG	60706	2918	10W-6N	A6
5300	CHCG	60656	2918	10W-6N	A5
5500	CHCG	60631	2918	10W-6N	A5
8100	PKRG	60068	2864	10W-10N	A5
8100	PKRG	60714	2864	10W-10N	A5
9000	MaiT	60714	2864	10W-11N	A3
9000	NLES	60714	2864	10W-11N	A3
S Chester Av					
10	PKRG	60068	2918	10W-7N	A3
E Chester Ct					
500	AURA	60504	3201	31W-8S	D2
W Chester Ct					
500	AURA	60504	3201	32W-8S	D2
Chester Dr					
3800	GNVW	60025	2809	11W-15N	D2
4100	GNVW	60062	2809	11W-15N	D2
Chester Ln					
200	MPPT	60056	2808	15W-14N	A4
200	PTHT	60056	2808	15W-14N	A4
200	PTHT	60070	2808	15W-14N	A4
1200	EGVV	60007	2914	21W-8N	A1
Chesterfield Av					
10	GNEN	60137	3025	23W-0S	A6
10	WHTN	60137	3025	23W-0S	A6
600	NPVL	60540	3142	25W-7S	B7
Chesterfield Ct					
10	BRRG	60527	3208	15W-9S	B2
200	OSWG	60543	3263	36W-12S	E2
200	SMBG	60193	2857	27W-10N	D6
1000	MHRY	60050	2527	33W-32N	E4
W Chesterfield Ct					
800	PLTN	60067	2752	21W-16N	D6
Chesterfield Dr					
100	OSWG	60543	3263	36W-11S	E2
4700	MHRY	60050	2527	33W-33N	D3
S Chesterfield Dr					
1500	ANHT	60005	2861	18W-12N	A2
1700	ANHT	60005	2860	19W-12N	D2
Chesterfield Ln					
300	NARA	60542	3138	35W-4S	B1
300	VNHL	60061	2647	17W-24N	B7

STREET Block	City	ZIP	Map#	CGS	Grid
Chesterfield Ln					
400	NARA	60542	3078	35W-4S	B7
400	SEGN	60177	2908	35W-7N	C4
500	LKZH	60010	2698	24W-21N	C6
1100	AvnT	60030	2532	21W-34N	D1
1100	GYLK	60030	2532	21W-34N	D1
1900	AURA	60503	3201	33W-10S	A6
15700	ODPK	60462	3423	11W-18S	E1
Chesterfield Rd					
7100	NndT	60012	2583	36W-27N	D7
Chesterton Ct					
7900	WDRG	60517	3206	21W-9S	A3
Chesterton Dr					
100	VOLO	60041	2530	27W-33N	C3
8000	WDRG	60517	3206	21W-9S	A3
Chestnut					
10	LMNT	60439	3272	15W-14S	A6
Chestnut Av					
10	CNHL	60514	3145	16W-5S	D2
10	WTMT	60559	3085	17W-4S	B6
200	SCHT	60411	3595	2W-27S	D3
200	SCHT	60411	3596	1W-27S	A4
200	SCRL	60174	2964	35W-3N	B6
300	WDSK	60098	2581	41W-30N	D1
1300	KLWH	60043	2812	3W-14N	D4
1300	WLMT	60043	2812	3W-14N	D4
1700	GNVW	60025	2810	9W-14N	C4
1900	WLMT	60091	2812	4W-14N	B4
7700	WDRG	60517	3205	21W-8S	E2
9000	FNPK	60131	2973	12W-3N	A5
9000	FNPK	60171	2973	11W-3N	C5
9000	RVGV	60171	2973	11W-3N	C5
17500	CCHL	60478	3426	5W-21S	C6
18600	CCHL	60478	3506	5W-22S	C2
N Chestnut Av					
10	ANHT	60005	2807	18W-14N	A5
1600	ANHT	60004	2806	18W-15N	E1
1900	ANHT	60004	2807	18W-16N	A1
2300	ANHT	60004	2754	18W-16N	A7
S Chestnut Av					
500	ANHT	60005	2807	18W-13N	A7
600	PKCY	60085	2536	13W-33N	A3
1200	ANHT	60005	2861	18W-12N	A1
W Chestnut Av					
8900	FNPK	60131	2973	11W-3N	E5
8900	FNPK	60171	2973	11W-3N	E5
8900	RVGV	60171	2973	11W-3N	E5
Chestnut Cir					
10	LNHT	60046	2418	20W-38N	A7
10	LNHT	60046	2476	19W-38N	B1
300	WPHR	60096	2363	9W-43N	C5
1300	YKVL	60560	3260	44W-14S	E7
W Chestnut Cir					
15300	LKPT	60441	3342	20W-18S	B7
Chestnut Cross					
1300	LMNT	60439	3270	19W-14S	D7
1300	LMNT	60439	3342	18W-15S	E1
Chestnut Ct					
-	LYWD	60411	3510	3E-23S	A4
-	MKNA	60448	3503	13W-22S	B1
10	CRY	60013	2695	32W-23N	C1
10	CTCY	60409	3429	2E-18S	D1
10	PKFT	60466	3595	2W-27S	C4
300	WNVL	60555	3080	29W-3S	D6
400	SMBG	60193	2858	25W-9N	C7
500	WCDA	60084	2643	26W-26N	C2
600	ALGN	60102	2694	34W-20N	C7
700	BRLT	60103	2910	29W-9N	D1
700	MRGO	60152	2634	49W-27N	C1
800	WNKA	60093	2812	5W-15N	A2
1400	YKVL	60560	3260	44W-14S	E7
3300	HLCT	60429	3426	4W-20S	E4
5900	DrrT	60014	2638	38W-26N	E4
5900	DrrT	60014	2639	38W-26N	A3
7300	WDRG	60517	3205	21W-8S	D1
8200	FftT	60423	3504	10W-24S	C5
14000	HMGN	60491	3344	15W-16S	C4
N Chestnut Ct					
10	HNWD	60047	2699	21W-23N	C1
S Chestnut Ct					
10	GNWD	60425	3508	0E-22S	E2
10	HNWD	60047	2699	21W-23N	C2
W Chestnut Ct					
10	FKFT	60423	3591	11W-26S	E1
Chestnut Ct E					
10	BFGV	60089	2701	16W-22N	D4
Chestnut Ct W					
10	BFGV	60089	2701	16W-22N	D3
Chestnut Dr					
-	PGGV	60140	2797	42W-14N	D5
-	RtdT	60140	2797	42W-14N	D5
100	WLNG	60090	2754	15W-18N	E4
400	NARA	60542	3078	35W-3S	B7
500	OSWG	60543	3263	37W-14S	C7
600	CLSM	60188	2967	26W-3N	D6
800	DRN	60561	3145	17W-7S	C7
1300	RLKB	60073	2474	23W-35N	D7
3200	FSMR	60422	3507	4W-23S	A3
3200	MHRY	60050	2528	32W-33N	C2
3400	HLCT	60429	3426	4W-20S	E4
6000	DrrT	60014	2638	38W-25N	E4
6000	GfnT	60014	2638	38W-25N	E4
7600	ODPK	60462	3346	9W-18S	D7
8100	PSHL	60465	3274	10W-13S	B4
8900	TYPK	60487	3424	11W-20S	A5
9000	HYHL	60457	3209	11W-9S	E4
9100	HYHL	60480	3209	11W-9S	E4
9100	LynT	60480	3209	11W-9S	E4
E Chestnut Dr					
100	SMWD	60107	2857	28W-10N	A5
2400	MchT	60097	2469	36W-34N	C7
2400	MchT	60097	2526	36W-34N	C1
S Chestnut Dr					
100	SMWD	60107	2857	28W-10N	A5
1400	MPPT	60056	2861	16W-11N	D4
2400	MchT	60097	2526	36W-34N	C1
18700	TroT	60404	3495	32W-22S	D2
W Chestnut Dr					
7600	MchT	60097	2469	36W-37N	C2
Chestnut Ln					
10	WNFD	60190	3023	27W-1N	D3
100	BGBK	60490	3267	26W-12S	D3
100	FKFT	60423	3591	11W-26S	E2
100	WnfT	60185	3023	27W-1N	D3
100	WnfT	60190	3023	27W-1N	D3
500	BCHR	60401	3864	0W-36S	C1
500	DRN	60561	3145	17W-7S	C7
500	PTON	60468	3861	8W-37S	B3
600	GLNC	60022	2758	7W-17N	B5
700	MRGO	60152	2634	49W-27N	C1
1200	YKVL	60560	3260	44W-14S	E7
1700	HFET	60192	2804	25W-14N	B3
8300	AlqT	60013	2696	29W-23N	C1
13600	HTLY	60142	2744	42W-20N	B1
14000	HMGN	60491	3344	15W-16S	C4
15100	BmnT	60452	3347	8W-18S	B6
Chestnut Ln					
15100	OKFT	60452	3347	8W-18S	B6
N Chestnut Ln					
10	GNWD	60425	3508	0E-22S	E1
S Chestnut Ln					
100	GNWD	60425	3508	0E-22S	E2
24600	CteT	60417	3687	3E-30S	B2
W Chestnut Ln					
17300	WrnT	60031	2534	17W-34N	B1
21400	LktT	60544	3339	26W-16S	D4
27400	BCHR	60401	3864	0W-36S	C1
27400	CteT	60401	3774	1W-33S	B2
Chestnut Rd					
10	DRFD	60062	2757	10W-18N	B2
10	NfdT	60062	2757	10W-18N	A2
2000	HMWD	60430	3427	2W-21S	C6
S Chestnut Rd					
25800	MONE	60449	3682	6W-31S	E5
25800	MONE	60449	3683	6W-31S	A5
Chestnut Rdg					
400	FXLK	60081	2414	29W-40N	C3
500	MNKA	60447	3672	34W-30S	A4
Chestnut St					
-	BRTN	60010	2751	25W-20N	A2
-	WKGN	60087	2480	10W-35N	A5
-	WMTN	60481	3853	28W-38S	B7
100	HNDL	60521	3146	15W-5S	A1
100	PKFT	60466	3595	2W-27S	C4
100	WNKA	60093	2812	5W-15N	B3
200	ANTH	60002	2357	23W-41N	E7
300	BTVA	60510	3078	34W-1S	C2
300	MDLN	60060	2646	18W-27N	E2
500	HNDL	60521	3145	16W-5S	E1
500	WKGN	60085	2480	10W-35N	A7
600	DRFD	60015	2703	11W-20N	E7
700	LMNT	60439	3270	19W-14S	D6
800	WNSP	60558	3086	14W-4S	D7
1400	HnrT	60120	2855	31W-11N	E4
2200	NHBK	60062	2757	10W-17N	A5
2400	JLET	60435	3417	27W-20S	D5
2400	LktT	60403	3417	27W-20S	D5
2400	LktT	60435	3417	27W-20S	D5
2400	PnfT	60435	3417	27W-20S	D5
6400	MNGV	60053	2865	8W-10N	A4
6800	HRPK	60133	2911	27W-8N	B2
7000	HRPK	60107	2911	27W-8N	B2
7000	SMWD	60107	2911	27W-8N	B2
7000	SMWD	60133	2911	27W-8N	B2
E Chestnut St					
10	CHCG	60610	3034	0E-1N	C2
10	CHCG	60611	3034	0E-1N	C2
200	BRTN	60010	2751	25W-20N	A2
N Chestnut St					
10	AURA	60506	3138	36W-7S	A7
100	AddT	60101	2971	18W-4N	A4
100	ADSN	60101	2971	18W-4N	A4
400	PLTN	60067	2752	21W-16N	D7
37500	BHPK	60087	2480	10W-37N	A2
42200	AntT	60002	2356	26W-42N	D6
S Chestnut St					
-	DSPN	60018	2917	13W-8N	A1
10	AURA	60506	3138	36W-7S	A7
1900	DSPN	60018	2863	13W-9N	A7
7100	RSMT	60018	2917	13W-8N	A1
W Chestnut St					
10	CHCG	60610	3034	0W-1N	B2
10	CHCG	60611	3034	0W-1N	B2
900	CHCG	60622	3033	1W-1N	E2
Chestnut Ter					
10	BFGV	60089	2701	16W-22N	C4
10	VrnT	60089	2701	16W-22N	C4
Chestnut Tr					
9300	OrlT	60487	3423	11W-21S	E7
9300	TYPK	60487	3423	11W-21S	E7
Chestnut Grove Dr					
1900	JLET	60586	3416	30W-21S	A7
Chestnut Hill Ct					
-	SRGV	60554	3135	42W-4S	D2
Chestnut Hill Ln					
-	SRGV	60554	3135	42W-4S	D2
Chestnut Hill Rd					
1600	JLET	60586	3416	30W-21S	C7
1600	JLET	60586	3496	30W-21S	C1
Chestnut Hills Cir					
100	BRRG	60527	3146	15W-8S	A7
100	BRRG	60527	3208	15W-8S	B1
Chestnut Hills Dr					
7200	BRRG	60527	3146	15W-8S	B7
7200	BRRG	60527	3208	15W-8S	B1
Chestnut Pointe Dr					
3000	JLET	60432	3500	19W-22S	C2
3000	JLET	60451	3500	19W-22S	D2
Chestnut Ridge Dr					
1300	NPVL	60540	3141	28W-6S	A5
1400	NPVL	60540	3140	29W-6S	D5
Chestnut Ridge Rd					
22000	KLDR	60047	2699	22W-21N	C6
W Chestnut Ridge Rd					
22100	KLDR	60047	2699	22W-21N	B6
Cheswick Ct					
10	SMBG	60194	2857	26W-10N	E5
1300	WLNG	60090	2754	16W-18N	D4
N Cheswick Ct					
2100	RLKB	60073	2475	22W-36N	B5
Cheswick Dr					
900	GRNE	60031	2477	18W-35N	A6
14000	ODPK	60462	3346	10W-16S	B4
Cheswick Ln					
1400	LKZH	60047	2699	21W-21N	C5
1900	AURA	60503	3201	33W-10S	B6
Chetwood Ct					
1400	MDLN	60060	2590	20W-27N	B7
Chetwood Dr					
1000	CLSM	60188	2967	27W-4N	D4
9700	HTLY	60142	2692	38W-22N	D4
Cheval Dr					
10	HNDL	60521	3085	16W-4S	E7
10	HNDL	60523	3085	16W-4S	E7
10	OKBK	60523	3085	16W-4S	E7
Cheviot Ct					
100	ROSL	60172	2912	25W-7N	B4
Cheviot Dr					
1900	IVNS	60010	2751	24W-16N	C6
Cheviot Rd					
300	BRLT	60103	2910	30W-8N	C3
300	HnrT	60103	2910	30W-8N	C3
Cheviot on Duxbury					
10	RGMW	60008	2805	22W-13N	B6
Chevy Chase Ct					
7300	FXLK	60020	2415	28W-39N	A5
Chevy Chase Dr					
2400	JLET	60435	3417	27W-20S	B5
2400	PnfT	60435	3417	27W-20S	B5
2600	JLET	60431	3417	27W-20S	C5
E Chevy Chase Dr					
10	BFGV	60090	2755	14W-20N	C2
N Chevy Chase Rd					
-	FmtT	60047	2645	21W-26N	C2
-	HNWD	60047	2645	21W-26N	C2
26800	FmtT	60060	2645	21W-27N	E1
27800	FmtT	60060	2589	20W-27N	E7
27800	MDLN	60060	2589	20W-27N	E7
27800	MDLN	60060	2645	21W-27N	E1
E Chewink Ct					
100	PLTN	60067	2752	20W-16N	E6
Chewton Gln					
1000	NHBK	60062	2757	8W-17N	D6
Cheyenne Av					
600	AURA	60506	3137	37W-6S	D6
Cheyenne Ct					
10	PltT	60124	2798	39W-13N	E7
100	BGBK	60440	3268	24W-11S	D1
700	ELGN	60123	2853	36W-12N	E1
17000	LKPT	60441	3420	20W-20S	C4
W Cheyenne Ct					
17800	WrnT	60030	2534	17W-33N	A3
Cheyenne Dr					
500	LIHL	60156	2694	35W-21N	B5
2700	NPVL	60565	3203	27W-10S	B7
2800	WldT	60565	3203	27W-10S	B7
S Cheyenne Dr					
12000	PSHT	60463	3275	8W-14S	A6
Cheyenne Ln					
700	ELGN	60123	2853	36W-12N	E1
800	NLNX	60451	3501	16W-25S	E7
Cheyenne Rd					
-	WkgT	60087	2479	12W-36N	A5
3400	WkgT	60031	2479	13W-36N	A5
3600	GRNE	60031	2479	13W-36N	A5
3700	GRNE	60031	2478	13W-36N	E5
W Cheyenne Rd					
2500	WKGN	60087	2479	12W-36N	C5
12700	WkgT	60087	2479	12W-36N	A5
12800	WkgT	60031	2479	12W-36N	A5
Cheyenne St					
600	RLKH	60073	2474	23W-36N	D4
Cheyenne Tr					
400	CLSM	60188	2967	26W-3N	E6
Chianti Tr					
2500	RVWD	60015	2755	13W-20N	E1
Chicago					
-	DSPN	60016	2863	12W-11N	A3
Chicago Av					
-	CNHL	60521	3145	17W-4S	C1
-	HNDL	60521	3145	17W-4S	C1
10	CHCG	60644	3031	8W-1N	A3
10	CHCG	60651	3031	8W-1N	A3
10	CNHL	60514	3145	17W-4S	C1
10	MYWD	60153	3030	10W-1N	A3
10	OKPK	60302	3031	8W-1N	A3
10	RVFT	60153	3030	10W-1N	A3
10	RVFT	60305	3030	10W-1N	B3
100	CHCG	60202	2867	2W-9N	C6
100	CHCG	60626	2867	2W-9N	C6
100	EVTN	60202	2867	2W-9N	B6
100	EVTN	60626	2867	2W-9N	C6
200	DRGV	60515	3144	20W-4S	A1
400	CNHL	60559	3145	17W-4S	C1
400	WNFD	60190	3023	28W-0S	B6
400	WTMT	60514	3145	17W-4S	C1
400	WTMT	60559	3145	17W-4S	C1
500	HDPK	60035	2704	8W-23N	D3
500	HDPK	60040	2704	8W-23N	D3
500	HIWD	60035	2704	8W-23N	D3
500	HIWD	60040	2704	8W-23N	D3
500	LSLE	60532	3143	22W-5S	C2
700	MYWD	60153	3029	11W-1N	E3
700	OKPK	60302	3030	10W-1N	B3
800	MLPK	60160	3029	10W-1N	E3
800	MYWD	60160	3029	10W-1N	E3
1100	OKPK	60305	3030	10W-1N	B3
1200	EVTN	60201	2867	2W-11N	B3
2100	DRGV	60515	3143	21W-4S	E1
5800	BKLY	60163	3028	14W-1N	C3
8600	CLLK	60014	2639	37W-24N	B6
8600	GfnT	60014	2639	37W-24N	B6
16700	LNSG	60438	3430	3E-20S	A4
18600	LNSG	60438	3510	3E-22S	A1
E Chicago Av					
10	CHCG	60610	3034	0E-1N	C2
10	CHCG	60611	3034	0E-0N	C2
10	NPVL	60540	3141	26W-6S	E5
10	WTMT	60559	3145	17W-4S	B1
100	CNHL	60514	3145	17W-4S	B1
100	CNHL	60559	3145	17W-4S	B1
100	HMND	46327	3352		D4
100	HNDL	60521	3146	15W-5S	B1
100	WTMT	60514	3145	17W-4S	B1
600	WNSP	60558	3146	14W-4S	C1
1000	NPVL	60540	3142	25W-6S	B5
1100	LsIT	60540	3142	25W-6S	B5
E Chicago Av CO-17					
800	NPVL	60540	3141	26W-6S	E5
1000	NPVL	60540	3142	25W-6S	B5
1100	LsIT	60540	3142	25W-6S	B5
N Chicago Av					
-	ELWD	60421	3675	25W-31S	B7
-	JknT	60421	3675	25W-31S	B7
400	MDLN	60060	2590	18W-28N	D7
600	ANHT	60005	2806	18W-14N	D4
1500	ANHT	60004	2806	18W-15N	D2
38000	WDWH	60083	2420	15W-38N	B7
38000	WDWH	60083	2478	15W-38N	B1
38000	WKGN	60083	2478	15W-38N	B1
38000	WKGN	60087	2478	15W-38N	B1
S Chicago Av					
10	MDLN	60060	2646	18W-27N	E1
6700	CHCG	60637	3152	0E-7S	E6
7000	CHCG	60619	3152	0E-7S	E6
7300	CHCG	60619	3153	1E-8S	A7
7500	CHCG	60619	3215	3E-10S	E4
7800	CHCG	60649	3215	1E-8S	B1
7900	CHCG	60617	3215	2E-9S	B2
9200	CHCG	60617	3216	3E-10S	A5
W Chicago Av					
10	CHCG	60610	3034	0W-1N	A2
10	CHCG	60611	3034	0W-1N	A2
10	DRGV	60515	3145	18W-4S	A1
10	HNDL	60521	3146	15W-4S	A1
10	NPVL	60540	3141	27W-6S	D6
10	WTMT	60559	3145	18W-5S	A1
100	DRGV	60515	3144	18W-4S	E1
500	HNDL	60521	3145	16W-5S	E1
600	CHCG	60622	3034	0W-1N	A2
800	CHCG	60622	3033	1W-0N	D3
800	CNHL	60514	3145	16W-4S	E1
800	CNHL	60521	3145	16W-4S	E1
1900	CHCG	60612	3033	2W-1N	C3
2700	CHCG	60612	3032	4W-1N	C3
2700	CHCG	60622	3032	4W-1N	C3
3100	CHCG	60624	3032	3W-1N	D3
3100	CHCG	60651	3032	3W-1N	D3
W Chicago Av					
4500	CHCG	60644	3032	5W-1N	A3
4800	CHCG	60644	3031	6W-1N	E3
4800	CHCG	60651	3031	6W-1N	E3
5900	OKPK	60302	3031	7W-1N	B3
10100	BHPK	60099	2422	10W-39N	B6
24200	GrtT	60041	2474	25W-34N	B7
E Chicago Ct					
10	ELGN	60120	2855	33W-11N	B4
Chicago Pl					
3100	SCHT	60411	3596	1W-27S	A4
Chicago Rd					
-	SHLD	60473	3428	0E-20S	E4
10	OSWG	60543	3263	37W-12S	C3
100	CHHT	60411	3508	1W-23S	A4
300	ThtT	60476	3428	0E-21S	E5
300	TNTN	60476	3428	0E-20S	E5
400	BlmT	60430	3507	1W-23S	E3
400	CHHT	60411	3507	1W-23S	E3
400	CHHT	60430	3507	1W-23S	E3
400	HMWD	60430	3507	1W-23S	E3
900	SHLD	60476	3428	0E-20S	E5
1500	CHHT	60411	3596	1W-27S	B3
2500	SCHT	60411	3596	1W-26S	A2
3000	SCHT	60475	3596	1W-27S	B4
3000	STGR	60475	3596	1W-27S	B4
3700	CRTE	60417	3596	1W-28S	B7
3700	CRTE	60475	3596	1W-28S	B7
14100	DLTN	60419	3350	0E-17S	E5
15100	SHLD	60419	3350	0E-17S	E6
15300	SHLD	60473	3350	0E-17S	E6
Chicago Rd SR-1					
1100	CHHT	60411	3508	1W-25S	A7
1500	CHHT	60411	3596	1W-26S	B3
2500	SCHT	60411	3596	1W-26S	A2
3000	SCHT	60475	3596	1W-27S	B4
3000	STGR	60475	3596	1W-27S	B4
3700	CRTE	60417	3596	1W-28S	B7
3700	CRTE	60475	3596	1W-28S	B7
Chicago Rd US-34					
10	OSWG	60543	3263	37W-12S	C3
Chicago Skwy					
-	CHCG	-	3152	0E-8S	E6
-	CHCG	-	3153	1E-8S	A7
-	CHCG	-	3215	3E-10S	E4
-	CHCG	-	3216	3E-10S	A6
-	CHCG	-	3280	4E-11S	C1
-	HMND	-	3280	4E-11S	C1
Chicago Skwy I-90					
-	CHCG	-	3152	0E-7S	D6
-	CHCG	-	3153	1E-8S	A7
-	CHCG	-	3215	3E-10S	E4
-	CHCG	-	3216	3E-10S	A6
-	CHCG	-	3280	4E-11S	C1
-	HMND	-	3280	4E-11S	C1
Chicago Skwy W					
-	CHCG	-	3152	0E-7S	D6
-	CHCG	-	3215	3E-10S	D4
Chicago Skwy W I-90					
-	CHCG	-	3152	0E-7S	D6
-	CHCG	-	3215	3E-10S	D4
Chicago St					
-	WMTN	60481	3853	27W-38S	C6
100	CRY	60013	2695	30W-23N	E2
100	CRY	60013	2696	30W-23N	A2
100	WCHI	60185	3022	29W-0N	C4
13000	BLID	60406	3277	2W-14S	C6
13000	BLID	60406	3349	2W-15S	C1
E Chicago St					
-	ELGN	60120	2855	31W-10N	E5
-	ELGN	60123	2854	34W-11N	E4
10	ELGN	60120	2854	34W-11N	E4
500	HMND	46327	3352		D4
1400	HnrT	60120	2855	31W-10N	E5
E Chicago St SR-19					
-	ELGN	60123	2854	34W-11N	E4
10	ELGN	60120	2854	34W-11N	E4
300	ELGN	60120	2855	31W-11N	D5
1400	HnrT	60120	2855	31W-10N	E5
E Chicago St SR-312					
800	HMND	46327	3352		E4
N Chicago St					
10	JLET	60432	3499	23W-23S	A4
100	ELWD	60421	3675	25W-32S	B7
400	JknT	60421	3675	25W-32S	B7
N Chicago St SR-53					
500	JLET	60432	3499	23W-23S	A3
S Chicago St					
-	JLET	60432	3499	23W-24S	A5
-	JLET	60436	3498	24W-24S	E5
10	JLET	60433	3499	23W-24S	A5
100	ELWD	60421	3675	25W-32S	B7
600	JLET	60436	3499	23W-25S	A7
600	JltT	60436	3499	23W-25S	A7
900	JLET	60433	3587	23W-25S	A1
900	JLET	60436	3587	24W-25S	A1
900	JltT	60433	3587	24W-25S	A1
900	JltT	60436	3587	24W-25S	A1
2400	JLET	60421	3587	23W-27S	A6
3000	JknT	60421	3587	23W-28S	A6
S Chicago St SR-53					
-	JLET	60432	3499	23W-24S	A5
-	JLET	60436	3498	24W-24S	E5
10	JLET	60433	3499	23W-24S	A5
600	JLET	60436	3499	23W-25S	A7
600	JltT	60436	3499	23W-25S	A7
900	JLET	60433	3587	23W-25S	A1
900	JLET	60436	3587	24W-25S	A1
900	JltT	60433	3587	24W-25S	A1
900	JltT	60436	3587	24W-28S	A6
2400	JLET	60421	3587	23W-27S	A6
3000	JknT	60421	3587	23W-28S	A6
S Chicago St US-6					
-	JLET	60432	3499	23W-24S	A5
-	JLET	60436	3498	24W-24S	E5
10	JLET	60433	3499	23W-24S	A5
10	JLET	60436	3499	23W-24S	A5
S Chicago St US-52					
-	JLET	60436	3498	24W-24S	E6
400	JLET	60433	3499	23W-24S	A6
600	JLET	60436	3499	23W-25S	A7
600	JltT	60436	3499	23W-25S	A7
W Chicago St					
10	PNFD	60544	3338	29W-18S	D7
100	ELGN	60123	2854	35W-11N	C4
W Chicago St SR-19					
100	ELGN	60123	2854	34W-11N	E4
S Chicago Beach Dr					
4800	CHCG	60615	3153	2E-5S	B1
S Chicago Bloomington Tr					
12900	HMGN	60491	3422	16W-20S	A5
13100	HMGN	60491	3421	17W-21S	C6
13900	HMGN	60448	3421	17W-21S	D6
13900	HmrT	60491	3421	17W-21S	D6
Chicagoland Cir					
3200	JLET	60431	3417	28W-19S	B3
Chicagoland Cir					
3200	PnfT	60435	3417	28W-19S	B3
Chicago Ridge Mall Dr					
-	CHRG	60415	3211	8W-11S	B6
-	CHRG	60453	3211	8W-11S	B7
-	OKLN	60453	3211	8W-11S	B6
300	OKLN	60415	3211	8W-11S	A6
Chicago Tube Dr					
900	RMVL	60441	3340	25W-17S	C6
900	RMVL	60446	3340	25W-17S	C6
Chichester on Asbury					
10	RGMW	60008	2806	19W-15N	B3
Chickadee Cir					
16300	ODPK	60467	3423	12W-19S	D2
Chickadee Ct					
2300	WCHI	60185	2966	29W-3N	E5
Chickaloon Dr					
6000	MchT	60050	2527	35W-33N	B3
6000	MHRY	60050	2527	35W-33N	A3
Chickamauga Ln					
1500	LGGV	60047	2700	18W-20N	E7
1500	LGGV	60047	2753	18W-20N	E1
Chickasaw Ct					
200	SchT	60175	2907	38W-7N	A6
Chickasaw Dr					
1500	NPVL	60563	3141	26W-5S	E2
S Chickasaw Tr					
14000	HMGN	60491	3343	16W-16S	D4
Chick Evans Ln					
6600	WDRG	60517	3143	23W-7S	A7
Chick Evans St					
300	BGBK	60490	3267	27W-12S	D3
Chickory Ct					
700	MltT	60187	3024	25W-0N	A4
Chickory Ridge Tr					
1100	CRY	60013	2641	32W-24N	B7
N Chicora Av					
6700	NLES	60714	2919	7W-8N	C2
6700	SKOK	60646	2919	7W-8N	C2
6900	CHCG	60646	2919	6W-8N	C1
Chicory Ct					
100	RGMW	60008	2805	21W-14N	D5
200	BFGV	60089	2754	16W-20N	D1
700	NPVL	60540	3141	28W-7S	A7
8400	DRN	60561	3206	20W-9S	C4
Chicory Ln					
10	BFGV	60089	2702	14W-21N	B6
10	RVWD	60015	2702	14W-21N	B6
200	BFGV	60089	2754	16W-20N	D2
1100	AURA	60564	3202	30W-9S	B4
E Chicory Ln					
900	RLKB	60046	2475	21W-35N	C5
Chicory Tr					
13900	HMGN	60491	3342	18W-16S	E4
14000	HmrT	60491	3342	18W-16S	E4
Chidester Av					
600	GNEN	60137	3025	22W-0N	C4
Chief Ct					
300	MNKA	60447	3672	32W-28S	D1
Chieftain Ln					
600	MltT	60187	3082	25W-2S	A3
N Childrens Plz					
2300	CHCG	60614	2978		C5
Childs Av					
5500	HNDL	60521	3146	15W-6S	B4
Childs Ct					
2000	WHTN	60187	3023	26W-0S	E7
Childs St					
-	WHTN	60187	3023	26W-0S	D7
10	WnfT	60185	3022	29W-0S	E7
10	WnfT	60185	3023	28W-0S	A7
10	WnfT	60190	3023	28W-0S	A7
100	WNFD	60190	3023	27W-0S	D7
400	WHTN	60187	3024	25W-0S	B7
Childs Dream St					
100	BtvT	60539	3077	36W-3S	D5
Chillem Dr					
10	BTVA	60510	3078	34W-2S	C3
10	BtvT	60510	3078	35W-2S	C3
900	BTVA	60510	3079	33W-2S	A3
900	BtvT	60510	3079	33W-2S	A3
Chillems Dr					
6700	BtnT	60081	2414	29W-38N	D6
W Chillems Dr					
-	BtnT	60081	2414	29W-38N	D6
Chillon Dr					
10	LYWD	60411	3598	4E-25S	C1
Chilmark Ln					
2100	SMBG	60193	2857	26W-10N	E6
2100	SMBG	60193	2858	26W-10N	A6
Chiltern Dr					
200	LKFT	60045	2649	11W-26N	C3
Chilton Ct					
-	FKFT	60423	3592	10W-27S	B5
Chilton Ln					
700	WLMT	60091	2811	5W-13N	E5
Chilvers Ct					
300	NPVL	60565	3204	25W-10S	A6
Chimney Rock					
800	IVNS	60067	2804	23W-14N	E4
Chimney Rock Ct					
14200	PNFD	60544	3337	31W-16S	E5
S China Pl					
2100	CHCG	60616	3092	0W-1S	B1
W Chinaberry Ct					
20800	DPgT	60544	3340	26W-15S	A2
Chinaberry Ln					
-	WldT	60564	3265	31W-12S	E2
4000	WldT	60564	3266	31W-12S	A3
Chinkapinoak Dr					
2000	MPPT	60056	2808	13W-14N	E4
2000	WhlT	60025	2808	13W-14N	E4
2000	WhlT	60056	2808	13W-14N	E4
S Chinook Dr					
17200	LKPT	60441	3420	20W-20S	B5
Chinook Rd					
2300	WKGN	60087	2479	11W-36N	C4
Chip Ct					
600	GRNE	60031	2534	16W-33N	E3
Chipewa Dr					
7100	MchT	60097	2469	36W-36N	D4
Chipili Dr					
200	NHBK	60062	2758	7W-17N	A6
Chipmunk Dr					
300	OSWG	60543	3263	38W-11S	A2
E Chippendale Dr					
300	BRLT	60103	2911	28W-7N	B5
S Chippendale Dr					
900	BRLT	60103	2911	27W-7N	C6
Chippendale Ln					
1800	GLHT	60139	2968	24W-3N	D5
Chippendale Rd					
1700	HFET	60169	2858	24W-12N	C1
1900	HFET	60169	2804	24W-12N	C7
Chipper Ct					
23200	PNFD	60544	3416	29W-19S	E2

Block	City	ZIP	Map#	CGS	Grid
S Chippewa Av					
13800	BNHM	60633	3352	3E-16S	A2
Chippewa Cir					
900	CPVL	60110	2748	32W-18N	C5
Chippewa Ct					
10	BRRG	60527	3208	14W-9S	C3
10	LKBN	60010	2643	26W-24N	C7
200	BGBK	60440	3268	23W-12S	E2
2400	LSLE	60532	3142	24W-4S	D2
5100	OKFT	60452	3426	6W-20S	A5
Chippewa Dr					
10	TNTN	60476	3428	0E-20S	E5
300	MNKA	60447	3583	33W-28S	B6
400	NPVL	60563	3141	26W-4S	E1
600	ELGN	60120	2855	32W-12N	C2
600	RLKH	60073	2474	23W-36N	D4
1900	MltT	60187	3081	26W-2S	E4
1900	WHTN	60187	3081	26W-2S	E4
6700	PSHT	60463	3275	8W-14S	A5
Chippewa Ln					
300	WCHI	60185	2966	30W-3N	B6
600	DRN	60561	3207	17W-8S	C2
900	WLMT	60091	2812	5W-14N	A5
Chippewa Rd					
500	CmgT	60033	2405	51W-38N	E6
500	HRVD	60033	2405	51W-38N	E6
1800	WKGN	60087	2479	11W-36N	C5
W Chippewa Rd					
17800	WmT	60030	2534	17W-33N	A3
Chippewa St					
1200	JLET	60433	3587	22W-25S	C1
1200	JltT	60433	3587	22W-25S	C1
Chippewa Tr					
-	SRGV	60554	3136	41W-7S	A6
300	LIHL	60156	2694	34W-21N	B5
400	CLSM	60188	2967	26W-3N	E6
1300	WLNG	60090	2754	16W-17N	D5
8000	TYPK	60477	3424	10W-21S	C5
S Chippewa Tr					
13500	HMGN	60491	3343	16W-16S	D3
Chippewa Pass					
10	PltT	60124	2852	41W-10N	A6
Chippewa Pathway					
1400	RVWD	60015	2702	13W-21N	E5
Chipping Campden Dr					
10	IVNS	60010	2804	25W-15N	A1
10	SBTN	60010	2804	25W-15N	A1
Chippingham Rd					
1800	WDRG	60517	3206	20W-9S	A2
Chipstone Dr					
1300	SEGN	60177	2908	34W-9N	D1
Chipwood Dr					
25500	CNHN	60410	3672	31W-29S	E2
25600	CNHN	60447	3672	31W-29S	E2
25600	CnhT	60410	3672	31W-29S	E2
25600	CnhT	60447	3672	31W-29S	E2
Chisholm Ct					
500	ROSL	60172	2913	22W-8N	C3
Chisholm Tr					
700	ROSL	60172	2913	22W-8N	C3
11800	OrlT	60467	3344	14W-16S	C2
Chisolm Tr					
10	ElgT	60124	2799	39W-13N	A7
10	PltT	60124	2798	39W-13N	E7
10	PltT	60124	2799	39W-13N	A7
Chiszar Dr					
-	NlxT	60451	3502	15W-24S	B5
12400	MKNA	60448	3502	15W-24S	B4
12400	MKNA	60451	3502	15W-24S	B5
Chittenden Ct					
2700	NPVL	60564	3202	29W-10S	C5
E Chivalry Ct					
1500	PLTN	60074	2806	19W-15N	D2
Choate Ct					
10	LNSH	60069	2701	16W-23N	E2
Choate Rd					
10	PKFT	60466	3595	2W-26S	C3
Choctaw Rd					
2200	WKGN	60087	2479	11W-36N	D5
S Choctaw Rd					
12900	PSHT	60463	3346	9W-15S	E1
W Choctaw Rd					
7300	PSHT	60463	3274	9W-15S	E7
W Choctaw Tr					
13000	HMGN	60491	3343	16W-16S	E2
13000	HMGN	60491	3344	16W-16S	A2
Chokeberry Dr					
4600	NPVL	60564	3266	29W-13S	D4
E Cholo Ln					
1900	MPPT	60056	2808	13W-14N	E4
Chopin Ct					
400	SMBG	60193	2858	24W-9N	E7
400	WHTN	60187	3082	25W-2S	C4
Chopin Ln					
2400	WDSK	60098	2524	41W-33N	E3
Chovan Dr					
800	JLET	60435	3497	27W-22S	D2
Chris Ct					
1700	WdfT	60015	2703	12W-21N	B5
Chris Ln					
4000	NndT	60014	2641	32W-26N	A3
S Chris Ln					
700	MPPT	60056	2861	17W-12N	B2
W Chris Larkin Ln					
27000	GrtT	60041	2473	27W-35N	C6
27100	FXLK	60041	2473	27W-35N	C6
Chrisman Dr					
200	SMWD	60107	2857	28W-11N	A5
Christa Ct					
900	EGVV	60007	2913	21W-8N	E1
S Christa Ct					
10700	PSHL	60465	3274	10W-12S	C2
Christa Dr					
5300	WldT	60564	3265	31W-13S	E4
N Christa Dr					
33400	GrtT	60041	2530	26W-33N	D2
Christeen Dr					
8100	JSTC	60458	3210	10W-9S	B3
Christian Ct					
10	OSWG	60543	3200	34W-10S	D7
Christian Ln					
2200	LSLE	60532	3142	24W-6S	D5
Christian Wy					
200	WDSK	60098	2524	41W-31N	D6
Christiana Av					
8200	SKOK	60076	2866	4W-10N	D5
N Christiana Av					
700	CHCG	60651	3032	4W-0N	D3
800	CHCG	60624	3032	4W-1N	D2
2800	CHCG	60647	2976	4W-3N	D5
3600	CHCG	60618	2976	4W-4N	D2
5100	CHCG	60625	2920	4W-6N	D5
5500	CHCG	60659	2920	4W-6N	D5
6400	LNWD	60659	2920	4W-8N	D3
6400	LNWD	60712	2920	4W-8N	D2
S Christiana Av					
1200	CHCG	60624	3032	4W-1S	D7
1400	CHCG	60623	3032	4W-1S	D7
1500	CHCG	60623	3090	4W-1S	D1
4300	CHCG	60632	3090	4W-4S	D7
5000	CHCG	60632	3150	4W-6S	D3
7100	CHCG	60629	3150	4W-8S	E7
7700	CHCG	60652	3212	4W-8S	E2
10300	CHCG	60655	3276	4W-12S	E1
10300	CHCG	60805	3276	4W-11S	E1
10300	ENGN	60805	3276	4W-11S	E1
Christiansen Av					
-	LkvT	60046	2417	21W-38N	D6
Christie Av					
8000	LYNS	60534	3088	10W-4S	B7
Christie Ct					
10	ALGN	60102	2746	37W-19N	D2
100	TNLK	53181	2354		D1
Christie Dr					
2600	ALGN	60102	2746	37W-19N	D2
Christie Ln					
100	TNLK	53181	2354		C1
Christina Cir					
10	WHTN	60187	3082	24W-2S	D3
Christina Ct					
-	RGWD	60072	2470	34W-36N	D3
200	BtvT	60510	3077	38W-2S	A4
9400	SPGV	60081	2413	31W-41N	D1
Christina Dr					
2600	LNSG	60438	3429	3E-21S	E7
2600	LNSG	60438	3430	3E-21S	A7
9000	HYHL	60457	3209	11W-10S	E5
9100	HYHL	60480	3209	11W-10S	E5
9100	PlsT	60480	3209	11W-10S	E5
18500	BlmT	60411	3430	3E-21S	A7
21100	MTSN	60443	3505	7W-25S	C7
21100	MTSN	60443	3593	7W-25S	C1
Christina Ln					
1300	NHBK	60062	2756	11W-17N	D6
1400	JLET	60435	3498	25W-22S	B1
1400	LKFT	60045	2703	11W-24N	D1
2200	GNVA	60134	3019	36W-0N	D5
13800	HMGN	60491	3343	18W-16S	A4
Christine Av					
3400	JLET	60431	3497	28W-25S	B7
3400	JLET	60431	3585	28W-25S	B1
5400	MchT	60050	2472	29W-37N	D2
Christine Ct					
200	STGR	60475	3595	1W-28S	E6
200	STGR	60475	3596	1W-28S	A6
1000	JLET	60431	3497	28W-25S	B7
1000	JLET	60431	3585	28W-25S	B1
4800	LGGV	60047	2700	18W-23N	E1
9100	ODPK	60462	3345	11W-16S	E4
18400	NlxT	60448	3421	17W-21S	D7
18400	NlxT	60448	3501	17W-22S	D1
S Christine Ct					
1200	VNHL	60061	2702	15W-23N	A2
Christine Dr					
600	LKMR	60051	2529	29W-31N	C7
600	NndT	60051	2529	29W-31N	C7
900	ANTH	60002	2359	20W-42N	A6
Christine Ln					
300	HNVL	60030	2532	21W-33N	C3
Christine Wy					
100	BGBK	60440	3268	24W-11S	C1
N Christmas l					
35400	GrtT	60041	2473	26W-35N	E6
Christopher Av					
17000	ODHL	60487	3424	11W-20S	A4
17000	TYPK	60487	3424	11W-20S	A4
Christopher Ct					
200	RLKB	60073	2474	23W-35N	E5
200	RLKB	60073	2475	23W-35N	A5
1200	ELGN	60120	2855	32W-12N	D2
1200	SYHW	60118	2800	35W-15N	C4
16900	TYPK	60477	3425	7W-20S	C4
E Christopher Ct					
1700	RMVL	60446	3339	27W-18S	D7
W Christopher Ct					
1700	RMVL	60446	3339	27W-18S	D7
Christopher Dr					
-	LMNT	60439	3342	20W-15S	B1
400	DGvT	60439	3270	19W-12S	C3
500	NBRN	60010	2698	24W-22N	B4
1700	DRFD	60015	2703	12W-20N	C7
5300	BmnT	60452	3425	6W-20S	E5
5300	BmnT	60477	3425	6W-20S	E5
5300	OKFT	60452	3425	6W-20S	E5
Christopher Ln					
-	JNBG	60050	2471	32W-34N	C7
600	CLSM	60188	2967	28W-3N	A6
600	WynT	60185	2967	28W-3N	A6
600	WynT	60188	2967	28W-3N	A6
Christopher St					
-	LtRT	60545	3332	46W-14S	B1
-	PLNO	60545	3332	46W-14S	B1
Christopher Wy					
-	RcmT	60071	2353	34W-42N	C5
-	RHMD	60071	2353	34W-42N	C5
10	FXLK	60020	2473	28W-36N	A4
Christ The King					
1300	MchT	60097	2469	36W-36N	E3
Christy Cir					
500	GYLK	60030	2532	21W-33N	D4
Christy Ln					
10	BtlT	60560	3261	41W-13S	E5
Chronicle Dr					
-	GNVA	60134	3019	37W-0N	D5
Chukar Ct					
-	RHMD	60071	2353	34W-42N	D5
Chukar Pl					
3000	DrrT	60098	2581	42W-28N	C6
Chukker Ct					
400	WLNG	60090	2755	15W-16N	B7
Church Av					
10	YkTp	60148	3026	18W-1S	E7
10	YkTp	60148	3084	18W-1S	E1
S Church Av					
1100	YkTp	60148	3026	18W-0S	E7
Church Blvd					
100	HRVD	60033	2406	50W-38N	B7
Church Ct					
10	FKFT	60423	3591	11W-26S	E2
400	BRLT	60103	2910	29W-8N	E3
6800	WDRG	60517	3143	22W-7S	C7
N Church Ct					
800	EMHT	60126	2971	16W-3N	D5
Church Dr					
3400	MchT	60097	2469	36W-35N	D6
15600	SHLD	60473	3350	0E-18S	E7
E Church Dr					
800	PLTN	60074	2753	19W-16N	B7
800	PLTN	60074	2806	20W-16N	B1
Church Ln					
-	LKBF	60044	2594	10W-28N	A6
15400	OKFT	60452	3347	8W-18S	A7
Church Rd					
-	KLWH	60043	2812	4W-14N	B3
-	NtrT	60043	2812	4W-14N	B3
-	WNKA	60043	2812	4W-14N	B3
10	NtrT	60093	2812	4W-14N	B3
10	WNKA	60093	2812	4W-15N	B3
200	AddT	60106	2971	16W-4N	D3
200	BFGV	60089	2754	17W-18N	C2
200	BNVL	60106	2971	16W-4N	D3
500	DndT	60118	2800	34W-14N	D6
500	DndT	60123	2800	34W-14N	D6
500	ELGN	60118	2800	34W-14N	D6
500	ELGN	60123	2800	34W-14N	D6
500	WDND	60118	2800	34W-14N	D6
800	AURA	60505	3138	34W-5S	D4
800	LKFT	60045	2650	10W-27N	A2
1100	AraT	60505	3138	34W-5S	D4
1300	AraT	60504	3138	34W-5S	D4
1500	AURA	60504	3138	34W-5S	D4
1900	AraT	60502	3138	34W-4S	D2
2000	AURA	60502	3138	34W-4S	D1
2600	AURA	60502	3078	34W-4S	E7
6200	HRPK	60133	2911	27W-7N	D4
9800	AlqT	60021	2695	30W-21N	E6
9800	BNHL	60010	2695	30W-21N	E6
9800	BNHL	60021	2695	30W-21N	E6
10300	AlqT	60010	2695	31W-21N	E5
14300	CrlT	60142	2691	42W-21N	A5
14300	CrlT	60180	2691	42W-21N	A5
E Church Rd					
10	BCHR	60401	3774	0E-35S	E7
10	WshT	60401	3774	0E-35S	E7
N Church Rd					
100	BNVL	60106	2971	16W-5N	E1
200	BNVL	60106	2915	16W-5N	E7
600	EMHT	60126	2971	16W-3N	D5
900	AddT	60106	2971	16W-3N	D5
900	EMHT	60106	2971	16W-3N	D5
S Church Rd					
-	EMHT	60106	2971	16W-3N	D5
-	EMHT	60126	2971	16W-3N	D5
700	AddT	60106	2971	16W-3N	D4
700	BNVL	60106	2971	16W-3N	D4
1000	MPPT	60056	2861	16W-11N	D3
W Church Rd					
10	BCHR	60401	3774	0W-35S	C7
600	WshT	60401	3774	1W-35S	A7
Church St					
10	LKZH	60047	2698	23W-23N	E3
10	WNFD	60190	3023	28W-0S	B6
100	BTVA	60510	3078	34W-0S	C1
100	FKFT	60423	3591	11W-26S	E2
100	NLNX	60451	3501	17W-24S	C6
200	CLLK	60014	2639	35W-25N	E4
200	CLLK	60014	2640	35W-25N	A4
200	WCHI	60185	3022	30W-0N	B5
200	YKVL	60560	3333	43W-15S	C2
300	ElaT	60047	2699	23W-23N	A2
300	EVTN	60201	2867	2W-11N	B3
300	LKZH	60047	2699	23W-23N	A2
1000	GNVW	60025	2810	8W-13N	E6
1100	NHBK	60062	2757	9W-17N	C5
1600	EVTN	60201	2866	3W-11N	E3
1700	JNBG	60050	2472	30W-35N	A5
1800	WslT	60481	3943	27W-40S	D3
1900	DYR	46311	3598		D2
1900	JNBG	60050	2471	31W-35N	E5
1900	MaiT	60016	2863	11W-11N	E3
1900	PKRG	60068	2863	11W-11N	E3
2500	SKOK	60203	2866	4W-11N	D2
3700	SKOK	60076	2866	5W-11N	B3
4700	SKOK	60076	2865	6W-11N	E2
4700	SKOK	60077	2865	5W-11N	E3
5500	MNGV	60053	2865	7W-11N	C2
5500	SKOK	60053	2865	6W-11N	E2
6600	HRPK	60133	2911	27W-8N	D3
6700	MNGV	60053	2864	9W-11N	D3
7800	NLES	60053	2864	9W-11N	B3
7800	NLES	60714	2864	9W-11N	B3
8500	DrrT	60012	2583	37W-27N	B7
10100	HBRN	60034	2351	40W-42N	A7
E Church St					
10	PLNO	60545	3259	47W-13S	D5
100	EMHT	60126	3027	16W-1N	E2
100	EMHT	60126	3028	15W-1N	A3
100	LYVL	60048	2591	16W-29N	E5
100	WDSK	60098	2524	41W-31N	D7
200	MNKA	60447	3583	33W-28S	B7
600	SDWH	60548	3330	51W-15S	A2
700	CnhT	60447	3583	33W-28S	B7
1000	SdwT	60548	3330	51W-15S	A2
1400	LtRT	60548	3330	51W-15S	A2
2300	DSPN	60016	2863	11W-11N	C3
2300	MaiT	60016	2863	11W-11N	C3
E Church St SR-120					
100	WDSK	60098	2524	41W-31N	D7
E Church St US-34					
600	SDWH	60548	3330	51W-15S	A2
1000	SdwT	60548	3330	51W-15S	A2
1400	LtRT	60548	3330	51W-15S	A2
N Church St					
10	ADSN	60101	2970	18W-3N	E5
1400	MHRY	60050	2528	32W-33N	B3
10300	HTLY	60142	2692	40W-21N	A6
23100	CbaT	60010	2696	28W-23N	E2
S Church St					
10	ADSN	60101	2970	18W-3N	E6
100	WCDA	60084	2643	26W-27N	E1
10300	CHCG	60643	3277	1W-12S	D1
11100	HTLY	60142	2692	40W-20N	A7
W Church St					
10	PLNO	60545	3259	48W-13S	C5
10	WDSK	60098	2524	41W-31N	D7
100	EMHT	60126	3027	16W-1N	E3
100	LYVL	60048	2591	16W-29N	D5
100	MNKA	60447	3583	33W-28S	B7
100	WCDA	60084	2643	26W-27N	E1
8000	MNGV	60053	2864	10W-11N	B3
8000	NLES	60053	2864	10W-11N	B3
8000	NLES	60714	2864	10W-11N	B3
8500	MaiT	60016	2864	10W-11N	A3
8500	MaiT	60714	2864	10W-11N	A3
8600	MaiT	60016	2863	10W-11N	E3
8700	MaiT	60068	2863	10W-11N	E3
8700	PKRG	60068	2863	10W-11N	E3
9300	DSPN	60016	2863	11W-11N	D3
W Church St SR-120					
10	WDSK	60098	2524	41W-31N	D7
W Church Ter					
8000	NLES	60714	2864	10W-11N	B3
Church Hill Ln					
3700	AlqT	60014	2641	33W-25N	A4
Churchhill St					
-	CHCG	60647	2977	2W-3N	B5
W Churchill Av					
8000	MNGV	60053	2864	10W-11N	B3
8000	MNGV	60714	2864	10W-11N	B3
8000	NLES	60053	2864	10W-11N	B3
8000	NLES	60714	2864	10W-11N	B3
Churchill Cir					
2100	WKGN	60048	2535	15W-31N	A7
N Churchill Cir					
9000	NLES	60714	2864	10W-11N	B3
Churchill Ct					
-	MDLN	60061	2647	17W-25N	B5
-	VNHL	60061	2647	17W-25N	B5
10	SEGN	60177	2908	36W-7N	A5
100	WynT	60185	2967	28W-3N	B6
200	LMBD	60148	3026	21W-1N	A3
200	MltT	60148	3026	21W-1N	A3
200	RLKB	60073	2475	22W-36N	D6
300	SYHW	60118	2800	36W-15N	A4
400	BTVA	60510	3078	34W-1S	D2
600	OSWG	60543	3263	38W-13S	B5
700	ANTH	60002	2357	25W-42N	B6
800	BRTN	60010	2697	25W-20N	E7
800	BRTN	60010	2698	25W-20N	A7
1200	BFGV	60089	2701	16W-21N	D6
1200	BRLT	60103	2910	30W-6N	B7
1400	INCK	60060	2647	17W-25N	A5
1400	MDLN	60060	2647	17W-25N	A5
1600	GNOK	60048	2592	14W-30N	C3
2000	HDPK	60035	2703	11W-22N	E4
2100	WKGN	60048	2535	15W-31N	A7
5700	LGGV	60047	2701	17W-23N	A2
6900	DRGV	60516	3144	19W-7S	E7
Churchill Dr					
-	PLNO	60545	3259	46W-13S	E5
-	PLNO	60545	3260	46W-13S	A5
10	DMND	60416	3941	33W-39S	B2
700	NLNX	60451	3589	18W-25S	A1
900	NPVL	60563	3140	29W-5S	C3
1000	BGBK	60440	3204	25W-11S	B7
1000	BGBK	60440	3268	25W-11S	B1
7400	HRPK	60133	2911	26W-9N	E1
10600	ODPK	60467	3423	13W-20S	A3
14100	HMGN	60491	3344	15W-16S	B3
E Churchill Dr					
1500	PLTN	60074	2753	19W-16N	D7
21900	RNPK	60471	3594	5W-26S	C3
S Churchill Dr					
4400	RNPK	60471	3594	5W-26S	B3
11300	PNFD	60585	3266	30W-13S	B5
Churchill Ln					
10	AURA	60504	3202	31W-8S	A1
10	MltT	60137	3083	22W-2S	D3
100	WYNE	60184	2965	32W-5N	D2
200	GRNE	60031	2534	16W-34N	D1
300	WmT	60031	2534	16W-34N	D1
600	OSWG	60543	3263	38W-13S	B5
1200	GYLK	60030	2532	21W-34N	C1
1300	GYLK	60030	2475	21W-34N	C7
1400	RLKB	60030	2475	21W-34N	C7
1700	GLHT	60139	2969	23W-3N	A5
2000	HDPK	60035	2703	11W-22N	E4
2000	HDPK	60035	2704	10W-22N	A5
5400	WKGN	60048	2535	15W-31N	A7
5600	WKGN	60048	2534	15W-31N	E7
Churchill Pl					
200	CNHL	60514	3145	16W-5S	D3
Churchill Rd					
-	FXLK	60081	2414	29W-39N	D4
-	SMBG	60194	2858	24W-12N	D2
10	WnfT	60190	3023	27W-0N	C4
300	MltT	60190	3023	26W-0N	D4
300	WNFD	60190	3023	26W-0N	D4
1200	BRLT	60103	2910	30W-6N	C7
1200	BRLT	60103	2966	30W-5N	A1
1200	ROSL	60172	2912	25W-7N	C5
1300	SMBG	60195	2858	24W-12N	D2
Churchill St					
-	MNGV	60053	2865	8W-11N	A3
200	NHFD	60093	2811	7W-15N	B3
7400	MNGV	60053	2864	9W-11N	C3
7700	MNGV	60714	2864	9W-11N	C3
7700	NLES	60053	2864	9W-11N	C3
7700	NLES	60714	2864	9W-11N	C3
W Churchill St					
2000	CHCG	60622	2977	2W-2N	B7
2000	CHCG	60647	2977	2W-2N	B7
Churchview Dr					
16500	ODPK	60467	3423	11W-19S	E3
Churn Rd					
10	MTSN	60443	3505	7W-24S	C4
Cibis Rd					
700	SchT	60175	2963	38W-3N	A5
Cicero Av					
-	ALSP	60803	3348	5W-15S	A1
-	CTWD	60803	3348	5W-15S	A1
13100	CTWD	60445	3348	6W-15S	A2
13900	BmnT	60445	3348	5W-16S	A3
14300	MDLN	60445	3348	5W-17S	A4
14700	MDLN	60452	3348	5W-17S	A5
14800	OKFT	60452	3348	5W-17S	A5
14900	OKFT	60445	3348	5W-17S	A6
15700	BmnT	60426	3426	6W-20S	A3
15700	BmnT	60452	3426	6W-20S	A3
15700	OKFT	60426	3426	5W-18S	A1
15700	OKFT	60452	3426	6W-20S	A3
16700	BmnT	60477	3426	6W-20S	A3
17000	BmnT	60478	3426	6W-20S	B4
17000	CCHL	60477	3426	6W-20S	B4
17000	CCHL	60478	3426	5W-21S	B7
18400	CCHL	60478	3506	6W-24S	B6
18800	CCHL	60477	3506	5W-22S	B2
18800	RchT	60477	3506	5W-22S	B2
19900	MTSN	60443	3506	6W-24S	B4
19900	RchT	60443	3506	6W-24S	B4
21100	MTSN	60443	3594	6W-26S	B2
21900	RNPK	60471	3594	6W-27S	B5
22700	UYPK	60471	3594	6W-27S	B5
22900	UYPK	60449	3594	6W-27S	B5
Cicero Av SR-50					
-	ALSP	60803	3348	5W-15S	A1
-	CTWD	60803	3348	5W-15S	A1
13100	CTWD	60445	3348	6W-15S	A2
13900	BmnT	60445	3348	5W-16S	A3
14300	MDLN	60445	3348	5W-17S	A4
14700	MDLN	60452	3348	5W-17S	A5
14800	OKFT	60452	3348	5W-17S	A5
14900	OKFT	60445	3348	5W-17S	A6
15700	BmnT	60426	3426	6W-20S	A3
15700	BmnT	60452	3426	6W-20S	A3
15700	OKFT	60426	3426	5W-18S	A1
15700	OKFT	60452	3426	6W-20S	A3
16700	BmnT	60477	3426	5W-20S	A3
17000	BmnT	60478	3426	6W-20S	B4
17000	CCHL	60477	3426	6W-20S	B4
17000	CCHL	60478	3426	6W-20S	B4
18400	CCHL	60478	3506	6W-24S	B6
18800	CCHL	60477	3506	5W-22S	B2
18800	RchT	60477	3506	5W-22S	B2
19900	MTSN	60443	3506	6W-24S	B4
19900	RchT	60443	3506	6W-24S	B4
21100	MTSN	60443	3594	6W-26S	B2
21900	RNPK	60471	3594	6W-27S	B5
22700	UYPK	60471	3594	6W-27S	B5
22900	UYPK	60449	3594	6W-27S	B5
Cicero Av SR-83					
-	ALSP	60803	3348	5W-15S	A1
-	CTWD	60803	3348	5W-15S	A1
13100	CTWD	60445	3348	6W-15S	A2
13900	BmnT	60445	3348	5W-16S	A3
14300	MDLN	60445	3348	5W-17S	A4
N Cicero Av					
10	CHCG	60644	3031	5W-0N	E5
700	CHCG	60651	3031	6W-1N	E3
1600	CHCG	60639	2975	5W-2N	E7
1600	CHCG	60639	3031	5W-1N	E1
2700	CHCG	60641	2975	6W-3N	E4
4300	CHCG	60630	2975	5W-5N	E1
4400	CHCG	60630	2919	6W-5N	E7
5600	CHCG	60646	2919	6W-7N	E4
6300	CHCG	60712	2919	6W-7N	E3
6300	LNWD	60712	2919	6W-7N	E4
7200	LNWD	60712	2865	5W-9N	E7
7300	SKOK	60077	2865	5W-9N	E7
7300	SKOK	60712	2865	5W-9N	E7
N Cicero Av SR-50					
10	CHCG	60644	3031	5W-0N	E5
700	CHCG	60651	3031	6W-1N	E3
1500	CHCG	60639	3031	5W-1N	E1
1600	CHCG	60639	2975	5W-2N	E7
2700	CHCG	60641	2975	6W-3N	E4
4300	CHCG	60630	2975	5W-5N	E1
4400	CHCG	60630	2919	6W-5N	E7
5600	CHCG	60646	2919	6W-7N	E4
6300	CHCG	60712	2919	6W-7N	E3
6300	LNWD	60712	2919	6W-7N	E4
7200	LNWD	60712	2865	5W-9N	E7
7300	SKOK	60077	2865	5W-9N	E7
7300	SKOK	60712	2865	5W-9N	E7
S Cicero Av					
-	CTWD	60445	3348	5W-15S	A1
-	CTWD	60803	3348	5W-15S	A1
-	MonT	60466	3683	6W-29S	B2
-	UYPK	60466	3683	6W-29S	B2
10	CHCG	60644	3031	6W-0S	E5
800	CHCG	60644	3032	5W-0S	A6
1000	CCRO	60804	3032	5W-0S	A7
1000	CHCG	60804	3032	5W-0S	A7
1500	CCRO	60804	3090	5W-4S	A6
3400	SKNY	60804	3090	5W-3S	A5
3700	CCRO	60632	3090	5W-3S	A6
3700	CHCG	60632	3090	5W-3S	A6
3700	CHCG	60804	3090	5W-3S	A6
4200	CHCG	60638	3090	6W-4S	A7
4600	CHCG	60632	3150	5W-5S	A2
4600	CHCG	60638	3150	5W-5S	A2
6100	CHCG	60629	3150	5W-7S	A6
6400	BDPK	60638	3150	5W-7S	A6
6700	BDPK	60629	3150	5W-7S	A7
7400	BDPK	60638	3212	5W-8S	A1
7400	BRBK	60459	3212	6W-9S	A3
7400	CHCG	60629	3212	5W-8S	A1
7400	CHCG	60638	3212	5W-8S	A1
7400	CHCG	60652	3212	6W-9S	A3
7700	CHCG	60459	3212	6W-9S	A3
8600	HMTN	60453	3212	6W-9S	A4
8600	HMTN	60456	3212	6W-9S	A4
8600	HMTN	60459	3212	6W-9S	A4
8600	HMTN	60652	3212	6W-9S	A4
8600	OKLN	60459	3212	6W-9S	A4
8900	OKLN	60456	3212	6W-10S	A4
9900	OKLN	60453	3212	6W-11S	A7
10200	OKLN	60453	3276	5W-12S	A1
11000	ALSP	60453	3276	5W-12S	A3
11000	ALSP	60655	3276	5W-12S	A3
11000	CHCG	60453	3276	5W-12S	A3
11000	CHCG	60655	3276	5W-12S	A3
11100	CHCG	60803	3276	5W-13S	A4
11600	ALSP	60803	3276	6W-13S	A4
13100	ALSP	60803	3348	5W-15S	A1
23100	MonT	60449	3594	6W-28S	B7
23100	RNPK	60471	3594	6W-28S	B7
23100	UYPK	60449	3594	6W-28S	B7
23100	UYPK	60471	3594	6W-28S	B7
24000	MonT	60449	3683	6W-29S	B1
S Cicero Av SR-50					
-	CTWD	60445	3348	5W-15S	A1
-	CTWD	60803	3348	5W-15S	A1
-	MonT	60466	3683	6W-29S	B2
-	UYPK	60466	3683	6W-29S	B2
10	CHCG	60644	3031	6W-0S	E5
800	CHCG	60644	3032	5W-0S	A6
1000	CCRO	60804	3032	5W-0S	A7
1000	CHCG	60804	3032	5W-0S	A7
1500	CCRO	60804	3090	5W-4S	A6
3400	SKNY	60804	3090	5W-3S	A5
3700	CCRO	60632	3090	5W-3S	A6
3700	CHCG	60632	3090	5W-3S	A6
3700	CHCG	60804	3090	5W-3S	A6
4200	CHCG	60638	3090	5W-4S	A7
4600	CHCG	60632	3150	5W-5S	A2
4600	CHCG	60638	3150	5W-5S	A2
6100	CHCG	60629	3150	5W-7S	A6
6400	BDPK	60638	3150	5W-7S	A6
6700	BDPK	60629	3150	5W-7S	A7
7400	BDPK	60638	3212	5W-8S	A1
7400	BRBK	60459	3212	6W-9S	A3
7400	CHCG	60629	3212	5W-8S	A1
7400	CHCG	60638	3212	5W-8S	A1
7400	CHCG	60652	3212	6W-9S	A3
7700	CHCG	60459	3212	6W-9S	A3
8600	HMTN	60453	3212	6W-9S	A4
8600	HMTN	60456	3212	6W-9S	A4
8600	HMTN	60459	3212	6W-9S	A4
8600	HMTN	60652	3212	6W-9S	A4
8600	OKLN	60453	3212	6W-9S	A4
8600	OKLN	60459	3212	6W-9S	A4
8900	OKLN	60456	3212	6W-10S	A4
10200	OKLN	60453	3276	5W-12S	A1
11000	ALSP	60453	3276	5W-12S	A3
11000	ALSP	60655	3276	5W-12S	A3
11000	ALSP	60803	3276	5W-12S	A3
11000	CHCG	60453	3276	5W-12S	A3
11000	CHCG	60655	3276	5W-12S	A3
11100	CHCG	60803	3276	5W-13S	A4
13100	ALSP	60803	3348	5W-15S	A1
23100	MonT	60449	3594	6W-28S	B7
23100	RNPK	60471	3594	6W-28S	B7
23100	UYPK	60449	3594	6W-28S	B7
23100	UYPK	60471	3594	6W-28S	B7
24000	MonT	60449	3683	6W-29S	B1

Street / Block	City	ZIP	Map#	CGS	Grid
S Cicero Av SR-83					
-	CTWD	60445	3348	5W-15S	A1
-	CTWD	60803	3348	5W-15S	A1
12700	ALSP	60803	3276	6W-15S	A7
13100	ALSP	60803	3348	5W-15S	A1
Cico Rd					
-	DPgT	60441	3269	21W-14S	E6
-	DPgT	60441	3270	21W-14S	A6
Cider Ct					
1000	LKZH	60047	2698	24W-22N	C4
Cider Ln					
800	PTHT	60070	2808	13W-15N	E2
Cider St					
100	BGBK	60490	3267	27W-12S	C3
Cider Grove Ct					
5500	JLET	60586	3416	31W-21S	A7
Cigrand Ct					
600	BtvT	60510	3077	37W-3S	C5
Cimarron Ct					
300	AURA	60504	3201	32W-8S	D2
1300	ELGN	60120	2855	31W-11N	E4
2400	NPVL	60565	3204	25W-10S	B6
Cimarron Dr					
10	CRY	60013	2695	32W-24N	C1
700	CRY	60013	2641	32W-24N	B7
1400	NLNX	60451	3588	19W-26S	E2
E Cimarron Dr					
300	AURA	60504	3201	32W-8S	D2
W Cimarron Dr					
300	AURA	60504	3201	32W-8S	D2
Cimarron Rd					
200	LMBD	60148	3026	21W-1N	A2
200	MltT	60148	3026	21W-1N	A2
Cimarron Rd W					
200	LMBD	60148	3026	21W-1N	A3
200	MltT	60148	3026	21W-1N	A3
W Cimarron Wy					
2100	ADSN	60101	2969	21W-4N	E4
Cimmaron Cir					
-	CLLK	60012	2640	33W-27N	E1
Cimmaron Ct					
1400	JNBG	60050	2472	30W-36N	A3
Cimmarron Dr					
700	CLSM	60188	2967	27W-3N	C6
Cinderford Ct					
100	OSWG	60543	3263	36W-12S	E2
Cinderford Dr					
100	OSWG	60543	3263	36W-11S	E2
Cinderford Pl					
100	OSWG	60543	3263	36W-11S	E2
Cindy Ct					
1400	JLET	60586	3496	30W-22S	B1
S Cindy Ct					
11300	WldT	60585	3265	32W-13S	C5
Cindy Ln					
-	EGVV	60007	2913	21W-8N	E2
100	WLNG	60090	2755	15W-17N	A5
1400	DSPN	60018	2862	14W-10N	D6
3700	GNVW	60025	2809	11W-13N	E6
3800	NfdT	60025	2809	11W-13N	E6
Cindy Jo Av					
10200	HTLY	60142	2692	40W-21N	A6
Cinema Dr E					
2100	HRPK	60133	2911	27W-6N	C7
Cinema Dr W					
2000	HRPK	60133	2911	27W-6N	C6
Cinema Ln					
11600	PNFD	60585	3266	30W-13S	A5
Cinnamon Cir					
13100	PNFD	60585	3337	31W-15S	D2
Cinnamon Ct					
300	BGBK	60440	3269	22W-13S	D4
400	BRLT	60103	2910	30W-8N	B2
1900	JLET	60435	3498	26W-22S	A1
17800	LKPT	60441	3420	20W-21S	B6
25500	PNFD	60585	3337	32W-15S	D2
Cinnamon Ln					
8200	AntT	60081	2415	27W-39N	A5
8200	FXLK	60081	2415	27W-39N	A5
Cinnamon Creek Dr					
-	PlsT	60465	3209	11W-11S	E6
-	PlsT	60480	3209	11W-11S	E6
10	PSHL	60465	3209	11W-11S	E6
Cinnamon Creek Ln					
-	HMGN	60491	3343	18W-18S	A7
Cinnamon Creek Rd					
14600	HMGN	60491	3343	18W-18S	A7
Circle Av					
10	WHTN	60187	3024	25W-0S	B6
100	BMDL	60108	2913	22W-6N	B7
100	BMDL	60108	2969	23W-5N	B2
100	BMDL	60157	2913	22W-6N	B7
100	BmdT	60108	2913	22W-6N	B7
100	BmdT	60157	2913	22W-6N	B7
100	FTPK	60130	3030	9W-1S	D7
200	LMBD	60148	3026	19W-0S	C6
300	ROSL	60172	2913	22W-6N	B7
400	DGvT	60527	3207	16W-9S	E4
400	WnfT	60185	3022	30W-0S	C7
1400	FTPK	60130	3088	9W-1S	D1
1400	GLHT	60139	2969	22W-2N	C7
1500	NRIV	60130	3088	9W-1S	D1
7200	OKPK	60130	3030	9W-0N	D4
7200	OKPK	60302	3030	9W-0N	D4
E Circle Av					
200	PTHT	60070	2807	15W-15N	E2
N Circle Av					
-	BMDL	60157	2913	22W-5N	B7
10	BMDL	60108	2969	22W-5N	B1
10	PTBR	60010	2642	29W-26N	D3
100	BMDL	60108	2913	22W-6N	B7
40000	AntT	60002	2416	25W-40N	A4
S Circle Av					
10	PTBR	60010	2642	29W-25N	C4
100	BMDL	60108	2969	22W-5N	B1
W Circle Av					
200	PTHT	60070	2807	15W-15N	E2
Circle Ct					
10	OswT	60538	3263	36W-11S	D1
200	SMBG	60193	2806	21W-12N	A7
400	DRFD	60015	2756	11W-20N	C1
1000	MRGO	60152	2634	50W-26N	B3
1400	EGVV	60007	2913	21W-9N	E1
1500	WKGN	60085	2480	10W-35N	B5
1900	CHHT	60411	3596	1W-26S	B1
4900	CTWD	60445	3348	6W-15S	A1
7000	BGVW	60455	3210	8W-10S	E4
10900	PSHL	60465	3274	10W-12S	C3
W Circle Ct					
1100	MchT	60050	2472	30W-36N	B4
18800	WrnT	60030	2533	18W-33N	D4
Circle Dr					
-	CstT	60481	3942	29W-41S	E5
-	DSPN	60016	2809	12W-12N	B7
-	DSPN	60016	2863	12W-12N	A1
-	ElaT	60047	2645	21W-24N	D7
Circle Dr					
-	NfdT	60016	2809	12W-12N	B7
-	RedT	60408	3942	30W-41S	D5
-	RedT	60481	3942	29W-41S	E5
-	SchT	60174	2908	34W-6N	D7
10	ALGN	60102	2747	34W-20N	D1
10	BFGV	60089	2754	17W-20N	C2
10	DRPK	60010	2751	23W-20N	E1
10	DRPK	60010	2752	23W-20N	A1
10	DXMR	60426	3349	2W-16S	D4
10	HNWD	60047	2645	21W-24N	D7
10	INCK	60061	2647	17W-24N	B6
100	ALGN	60102	2694	34W-20N	D7
200	CLLK	60014	2640	35W-24N	A6
200	LKBF	60044	2593	10W-28N	E6
500	CteT	60417	3684	3W-29S	C2
500	FXLK	60020	2473	28W-35N	A5
500	LYVL	60048	2591	16W-28N	D6
500	UYPK	60417	3684	3W-29S	C2
500	UYPK	60466	3684	3W-29S	C2
600	ROSL	60172	2913	22W-7N	C3
700	TRLK	60010	2643	26W-25N	C4
1400	HnrT	60120	2855	31W-11N	E4
2400	HLCT	60429	3427	3W-20S	B4
2700	MKHM	60428	3427	3W-19S	B2
5200	MchT	60050	2472	29W-37N	D2
5700	MchT	60097	2469	36W-37N	E1
5700	WRLK	60097	2469	36W-37N	E1
7800	BRRG	60527	3208	14W-8S	D2
8000	PSHL	60465	3274	10W-12S	C2
10000	RHMD	60071	2353	34W-41N	D7
10400	OKLN	60453	3275	7W-12S	D1
13500	OrlT	60462	3345	11W-16S	D2
13500	PlsT	60462	3345	11W-16S	D2
19400	FmtT	60060	2646	19W-26N	C3
25000	AntT	60002	2357	25W-42N	B6
E Circle Dr					
100	NLNX	60451	3502	15W-25S	C7
100	NlxT	60451	3502	15W-24S	C6
1900	NHFD	60093	2758	8W-16N	A7
4900	CTWD	60445	3348	6W-15S	A2
8300	TYPK	60477	3424	10W-20S	C4
N Circle Dr					
400	WMTN	60481	3853	27W-38S	D5
600	CmpT	60175	2961	41W-4N	E3
2200	PltT	60067	2806	20W-13N	A7
34300	AvnT	60073	2532	22W-34N	C1
34300	RLKP	60073	2532	22W-34N	C1
34400	RLKB	60073	2532	22W-34N	C1
41500	AntT	60002	2356	26W-41N	D7
NE Circle Dr					
10	JltT	60433	3500	21W-24S	A5
NW Circle Dr					
10	JltT	60433	3499	21W-24S	E5
10	JltT	60433	3500	21W-24S	A5
S Circle Dr					
-	MchT	60097	2469	36W-35N	D6
200	ADSN	60101	2970	19W-3N	D6
200	EGvT	60067	2806	20W-13N	A7
200	PltT	60067	2806	21W-12N	A7
200	SMBG	60067	2806	21W-12N	A7
400	WMTN	60481	3853	27W-38S	D5
1400	MPPT	60056	2861	16W-11N	D3
34000	AvnT	60030	2532	22W-34N	C2
34000	HNVL	60030	2532	22W-34N	C2
SE Circle Dr					
100	JltT	60433	3500	21W-24S	A5
SW Circle Dr					
100	JltT	60433	3499	21W-24S	E5
100	JltT	60433	3500	21W-24S	A5
W Circle Dr					
10	NLNX	60451	3502	15W-25S	C7
10	NlxT	60451	3502	15W-25S	C7
400	ADSN	60101	2970	19W-3N	D6
3400	BHPK	60099	2422	10W-39N	A6
3400	ZION	60099	2422	10W-39N	A5
4900	CTWD	60445	3348	6W-15S	A2
8300	TYPK	60477	3424	10W-20S	B4
Circle Dr E					
10	OswT	60538	3199	36W-11S	E7
100	OswT	60538	3263	36W-11S	E1
Circle Dr N					
100	ISLK	60042	2586	29W-28N	D5
Circle Dr S					
100	ISLK	60042	2586	29W-28N	D5
Circle Dr W					
10	OSWG	60543	3263	37W-11S	C1
10	OswT	60538	3199	37W-11S	C7
10	OswT	60538	3263	36W-11S	D1
10	OswT	60543	3263	37W-11S	C1
Circle Ln					
300	LKFT	60045	2650	9W-25N	C5
S Circle Ln					
1500	PltT	60067	2805	20W-14N	E5
S Circle Pkwy					
12700	PlsT	60464	3273	12W-15S	D7
12700	PlsT	60464	3345	12W-15S	D1
W Circle Pkwy					
9700	PlsT	60464	3273	12W-15S	C7
W Circle Pl					
5000	CTWD	60445	3347	6W-15S	E2
Circle Rd					
-	ELGN	60123	2854	34W-10N	E6
100	FRGV	60021	2696	30W-23N	B2
Circle St					
1800	DSPN	60018	2863	13W-9N	A6
2300	CTHL	60403	3417	26W-21S	E6
2300	LktT	60403	3417	26W-21S	E6
E Circle St					
100	LktT	60441	3419	21W-18S	E1
W Circle St					
100	LktT	60441	3419	21W-18S	D1
Circle Ter					
300	BmdT	60157	2913	21W-7N	E4
Circle Tr					
7400	MchT	60097	2469	36W-35N	D5
W Circle Dr Pkwy					
13200	CTWD	60445	3347	6W-15S	E1
13200	CTWD	60445	3348	6W-15S	A1
Circlegate Rd					
100	NLNX	60451	3589	17W-26S	C2
E Circle Hill Dr					
300	ANHT	60004	2754	17W-16N	B7
Circle Ridge Ct					
10	BRRG	60527	3208	15W-10S	A6
Circle Ridge Dr					
100	BRRG	60527	3208	15W-10S	A6
Circuit Ct					
200	LKVL	60046	2474	23W-36N	E4
Circuit Dr					
1700	RLKB	60073	2475	23W-35N	A6
Citadel Cir					
500	WTMT	60559	3085	17W-4S	C7
Citadel Ct					
700	DSPN	60016	2862	14W-11N	C4
E Citadel Ct					
1500	PLTN	60074	2806	19W-15N	C2
Citadel Dr					
-	JLET	60431	3497	27W-22S	B2
-	JLET	60435	3497	27W-22S	B2
600	WTMT	60559	3085	17W-4S	C7
700	NPVL	60565	3204	24W-9S	D3
Citation Cir					
10	WHTN	60187	3082	24W-2S	D3
Citation Ct					
100	PltT	60175	2906	39W-8N	E4
Citation Dr					
300	OSWG	60543	3264	35W-12S	B2
700	NPVL	60540	3142	25W-7S	A7
W Citation Dr					
12000	HMGN	60491	3344	15W-16S	C3
Citation Ln					
200	CmpT	60119	2961	43W-4N	B4
300	RLKP	60030	2589	22W-30N	C1
1200	HRPK	60133	2912	26W-6N	A6
Citizen Av					
800	ELBN	60119	3017	43W-0N	B5
N Cityfront Plaza Dr					
400	CHCG	60611	3034		E4
Civic Dr					
200	SMBG	60193	2858	25W-10N	C6
Civic Center Av					
-	MTGY	60506	3198	39W-9S	D5
Civic Center Dr					
700	NLES	60714	2864	8W-9N	E6
Civic Center Plz					
200	GLHT	60139	2969	23W-3N	A6
Claim St					
300	AURA	60505	3138	34W-7S	C7
Clair Ct					
10	ROSL	60172	2912	25W-7N	C4
Clair St					
700	ELGN	60123	2854	34W-12N	D3
Claire Av					
400	RMVL	60441	3340	25W-15S	B3
400	RMVL	60446	3340	25W-15S	A2
S Claire Blvd					
-	CTWD	60445	3348	4W-16S	D4
2900	BLID	60406	3349	3W-15S	A2
2900	RBBN	60406	3349	3W-15S	A2
2900	RBBN	60472	3349	3W-15S	A2
13500	RBBN	60406	3348	3W-16S	E2
13500	RBBN	60472	3348	4W-16S	D3
14200	CTWD	60472	3348	4W-16S	D4
Claire Ct					
100	BmdT	60188	3024	23W-2N	E1
2000	GNVW	60025	2810	9W-15N	D3
Claire Ln					
300	CRY	60013	2642	30W-24N	A7
400	PTHT	60070	2808	14W-15N	B2
16200	SHLD	60473	3428	0E-19S	E2
Claire St					
4800	AlqT	60014	2640	33W-24N	D7
4800	CLLK	60014	2640	33W-24N	D7
Clairemont Ct					
300	AURA	60504	3140	31W-7S	A7
Claire View Ct					
200	LKZH	60047	2698	23W-23N	E2
Clairmont Av					
10	JltT	60433	3500	21W-24S	A5
Clairmont Ct					
1400	VNHL	60061	2647	16W-26N	C2
9100	ODPK	60462	3346	11W-17S	A5
Clancy Dr					
-	DSPN	60016	2808	13W-13N	E6
9200	MaiT	60016	2863	11W-11N	E1
9200	NLES	60016	2863	11W-11N	E2
9200	NLES	60714	2863	11W-11N	E2
Clanyard Rd					
10	HshT	60140	2744	44W-19N	A2
10	HTLY	60140	2744	44W-19N	A2
10	HTLY	60142	2744	44W-19N	A2
100	HshT	60140	2743	44W-19N	E2
100	HTLY	60140	2743	44W-19N	E2
Clara Av					
1200	JLET	60435	3498	25W-22S	B2
2500	AURA	60502	3139	32W-5S	D3
N Clara Av					
1100	JLET	60435	3498	25W-22S	C2
41100	AntT	60002	2415	26W-41N	E1
Clara Ct					
10	ALGN	60102	2693	36W-21N	D6
1600	AURA	60502	3139	32W-5S	C3
W Clara Ct					
8300	NLES	60714	2864	10W-10N	A5
W Clara Dr					
8400	MaiT	60714	2864	10W-10N	A5
8400	NLES	60714	2864	10W-10N	A5
25800	GrtT	60041	2473	25W-36N	E4
25800	GrtT	60041	2474	25W-36N	A4
N Clara Pl					
100	EMHT	60126	3028	15W-1N	A2
Clara St					
100	WCHI	60185	3022	30W-0N	C4
2500	MchT	60050	2471	31W-34N	D7
W Clarage Ct					
24200	TroT	60404	3496	30W-25S	C7
Clare Av					
8800	MKNA	60448	3504	11W-23S	A3
8800	MKNA	60477	3504	11W-23S	A3
8800	TYPK	60477	3504	11W-23S	A3
Clare Cir					
24900	MHTN	60442	3677	19W-30S	E3
24900	MHTN	60442	3678	19W-30S	A3
Clare Ct					
1200	CLSM	60188	2967	26W-4N	E4
E Clare Ct					
10	PLTN	60067	2805	20W-14N	E3
N Clare Ct					
100	WDDL	60191	2970	18W-5N	E1
W Clare Ct					
400	WDDL	60191	2970	18W-5N	D1
Clare Dr					
300	BMDL	60108	2969	22W-5N	D2
19800	FftT	60477	3504	10W-23S	B4
19800	TYPK	60477	3504	10W-23S	B4
Clare Rd					
4600	JLET	60431	3496	29W-22S	D1
Claremont Av					
400	WCHI	60185	3022	29W-1N	D3
15400	HRVY	60426	3349	2W-18S	C7
15900	MKHM	60428	3427	2W-19S	C2
15900	ThtT	60428	3427	2W-19S	C2
N Claremont Av					
300	CHCG	60612	3033	2W-0N	B4
1200	CHCG	60622	3033	2W-1N	B1
1500	CHCG	60647	3033	2W-1N	B1
1600	CHCG	60647	2977	2W-2N	B7
4200	CHCG	60618	2977	2W-5N	A1
4500	CHCG	60625	2921	2W-5N	A7
6000	CHCG	60659	2921	2W-7N	A3
N Claremont Av					
6300	CHCG	60645	2921	2W-7N	A3
7500	CHCG	60202	2867	2W-9N	A7
7500	CHCG	60645	2867	2W-9N	A7
7500	EVTN	60202	2867	2W-9N	A7
S Claremont Av					
700	CHCG	60612	3033	2W-0S	B6
1300	CHCG	60608	3033	2W-1S	B7
2500	CHCG	60608	3091	2W-2S	B2
3400	CHCG	60609	3091	2W-3S	B5
5400	CHCG	60609	3151	2W-5S	B2
5600	CHCG	60636	3151	2W-6S	B3
7400	CHCG	60620	3213	2W-8S	B1
7400	CHCG	60636	3213	2W-8S	B1
9500	CHCG	60643	3213	2W-11S	B7
10300	CHCG	60643	3277	2W-12S	B1
Claremont Ct					
100	KdlT	60560	3333	42W-17S	C6
100	YKVL	60560	3333	42W-17S	C6
400	DRGV	60516	3144	19W-7S	E7
15400	HRVY	60426	3349	2W-18S	C7
Claremont Dr					
10	DGvT	60561	3145	18W-7S	A7
10	NPVL	60540	3141	28W-6S	B5
200	DRN	60561	3145	18W-7S	A7
400	DRGV	60516	3144	19W-8S	C7
400	DRN	60516	3144	19W-8S	E7
400	DRN	60561	3144	19W-8S	E7
7500	TYPK	60477	3424	9W-20S	D4
N Claremont Dr					
1000	PLTN	60074	2753	19W-17N	D5
1000	PltT	60074	2753	19W-17N	D5
Claremont Rd					
1800	HFET	60169	2858	24W-12N	D1
3700	JNBG	60050	2471	32W-35N	B5
W Claremont St					
200	EMHT	60126	3027	16W-1N	E3
Clarence Av					
-	CCHL	60478	3426	5W-21S	C7
500	OKPK	60302	3031	8W-0S	A5
500	OKPK	60304	3031	8W-0S	A6
1100	BRWN	60304	3031	8W-1S	A7
1100	BRWN	60402	3031	8W-1S	A7
1500	BRWN	60402	3089	8W-2S	A3
3900	SKNY	60402	3089	8W-4S	A6
N Clarence Av					
1600	ANHT	60004	2807	17W-15N	C1
W Clarence Av					
6500	CHCG	60631	2919	8W-7N	A3
7200	CHCG	60631	2918	9W-7N	D3
Clarence Dr					
5100	WldT	60564	3266	30W-13S	C4
Clarendon Av					
10	AddT	60148	3026	19W-2N	D1
4600	RNPK	60471	3594	5W-27S	B4
N Clarendon Av					
500	LMBD	60148	3026	19W-1N	D2
3900	CHCG	60613	2977	0W-5N	E1
4400	CHCG	60613	2921	1W-5N	E7
4400	CHCG	60640	2921	1W-5N	E7
S Clarendon Av					
400	ADSN	60101	2970	19W-2N	D7
Clarendon Ct					
400	CNHL	60514	3145	16W-6S	D4
400	DGvT	60514	3145	16W-6S	D4
800	AURA	60504	3201	33W-8S	A3
5900	HRPK	60133	2911	27W-7N	D4
7400	FXLK	60020	2415	28W-39N	A5
E Clarendon Ct					
600	ANHT	60004	2807	17W-15N	B3
E Clarendon Dr					
10	RLKB	60073	2475	22W-35N	B6
N Clarendon Dr					
900	RLKB	60073	2531	23W-34N	E1
1000	RLKB	60073	2474	23W-34N	E7
W Clarendon Dr					
10	RLKB	60073	2475	23W-35N	A7
200	RLKB	60073	2474	23W-34N	E7
400	GrtT	60041	2473	28W-35N	A6
Clarendon Ln					
200	BGBK	60440	3268	24W-11S	D1
600	AURA	60504	3201	33W-8S	B3
2800	WDRG	60517	3205	22W-9S	D3
W Clarendon Rd					
1000	ANHT	60004	2806	18W-15N	E3
12700	BHPK	60099	2421	12W-39N	B4
12800	BHPK	60083	2421	12W-39N	B4
Clarendon St					
800	HFET	60169	2859	23W-11N	A3
E Clarendon St					
10	PTHT	60070	2808	15W-15N	A3
1000	ANHT	60004	2807	17W-15N	B3
W Clarendon St					
200	ANHT	60004	2807	18W-15N	A3
400	PTHT	60070	2807	16W-15N	D3
500	ANHT	60004	2806	18W-15N	E3
Clarendon Hills Rd					
200	DGvT	60527	3207	16W-10S	D5
300	CNHL	60514	3145	16W-6S	D3
300	DGvT	60514	3145	16W-6S	D3
5700	WLBK	60514	3145	16W-6S	D4
5800	WLBK	60527	3145	17W-7S	D7
6500	DRN	60527	3145	16W-7S	D6
6600	DRN	60561	3145	17W-7S	D6
7200	DRN	60561	3207	16W-8S	D1
7400	DRN	60527	3207	17W-8S	D2
7400	WLBK	60527	3207	17W-8S	D2
Clarendon Springs Ct					
700	SMBG	60194	2858	25W-11N	B3
Claret Dr					
400	BFGV	60089	2754	17W-20N	C1
Clarewood Cir					
300	GYLK	60030	2533	19W-33N	B3
Clarewood Ln					
1900	MDLN	60060	2590	19W-29N	B3
7300	GRNE	60031	2477	18W-34N	A7
7300	GRNE	60031	2534	18W-34N	A1
Claria Dr					
10	ROSL	60172	2913	23W-7N	A4
100	ROSL	60172	2912	23W-7N	E4
N Clarice Av					
20500	BFGV	60069	2754	16W-20N	E1
20500	BFGV	60089	2754	16W-20N	E1
20500	VrnT	60069	2754	16W-20N	E1
20600	BFGV	60069	2701	16W-20N	E7
20600	BFGV	60089	2701	16W-20N	E7
20600	VrnT	60069	2701	16W-20N	E7
W Claridan Av					
25000	ANTH	60002	2357	25W-42N	B6
25000	AntT	60002	2357	25W-42N	B6
Claridge Cir					
200	BGBK	60440	3268	25W-12S	B3
600	HFET	60169	2858	24W-11N	C4
Claridge Ct					
10	BGBK	60440	3268	25W-12S	C2
10	SMWD	60107	2857	28W-12N	B2
Claridge Ct					
400	LKVL	60046	2475	21W-37N	D2
800	SMBG	60193	2859	23W-9N	B7
2000	NHBK	60062	2757	8W-16N	D7
7200	LGGV	60047	2646	18W-25N	D5
14300	ODPK	60462	3346	9W-17S	D4
W Claridge Ct					
1200	PLTN	60067	2752	22W-17N	B5
Claridge Dr					
-	BGVW	60455	3274	9W-11S	D1
1100	LYVL	60048	2591	17W-29N	B3
Claridge Ln					
2100	NHBK	60062	2757	8W-16N	D7
2100	NHBK	60062	2810	9W-15N	B1
2400	MTGY	60538	3198	40W-10S	C6
Claridge St					
10800	WSTR	60154	3086	13W-2S	E2
Clarington Wy					
10	NBRN	60010	2644	24W-25N	B6
Clarion Ct					
300	OSWG	60543	3263	37W-13S	B6
900	IVNS	60010	2804	25W-15N	A1
Clarissa Ct					
500	NPVL	60540	3204	26W-8S	A1
Clarissa Ln					
2800	AURA	60502	3079	33W-3S	B7
2800	BtvT	60502	3079	33W-3S	B7
Clark Av					
-	ELBN	60119	3017	42W-0N	C4
10	BtlT	60543	3263	39W-12S	A4
10	LIHL	60156	2693	35W-22N	E4
10	OSWG	60543	3263	39W-12S	A4
200	NCHI	60088	2594	10W-31N	A1
S Clark Av					
4300	HMND	46327	3352		C4
Clark Ct					
100	AURA	60505	3200	35W-8S	B1
Clark Dr					
100	SRWD	60404	3496	30W-24S	C5
900	GRNE	60031	2534	16W-33N	D3
4100	RNPK	60471	3594	5W-26S	C3
6300	WDRG	60517	3143	22W-7S	C6
N Clark Dr					
100	PLTN	60074	2806	20W-15N	A2
200	PLTN	60074	2753	19W-16N	B7
W Clark Dr					
3400	ENGN	60805	3212	4W-11S	D6
Clark Ln					
800	DSPN	60016	2862	15W-10N	B5
1100	DSPN	60018	2862	15W-10N	B5
11600	GfnT	60142	2744	41W-20N	D1
16300	TYPK	60477	3425	8W-19S	B2
Clark Rd					
100	AlqT	60010	2696	29W-23N	D2
100	BRKT	60511	3196	46W-9S	A5
100	BRKT	60545	3196	46W-9S	A5
100	LtRT	60545	3196	46W-9S	A5
1900	DYR	46311	3598		E2
N Clark Rd					
8600	RcmT	60071	2413	32W-40N	C3
8600	RcmT	60081	2413	32W-40N	C3
8600	SPGV	60071	2413	32W-40N	C3
8600	SPGV	60081	2413	32W-40N	C3
8900	RcmT	60071	2354	32W-41N	C7
8900	SPGV	60081	2354	32W-41N	C7
10500	RcmT	60081	2354	32W-41N	C7
10500	SPGV	60071	2354	32W-41N	C7
Clark St					
-	SHLD	60473	3350	0W-17S	C6
-	SHLD	60473	3428	0W-20S	C3
-	TNTN	60473	3428	0W-20S	C3
-	TNTN	60476	3428	0W-20S	C3
10	AURA	60505	3200	35W-7S	B1
100	MRGO	60152	2634	49W-26N	B2
600	ELGN	60123	2854	34W-12N	B2
700	EVTN	60201	2867	2W-11N	B2
1300	NARA	60542	3078	35W-3S	B5
1400	BTVA	60510	3078	35W-3S	B5
1400	BTVA	60542	3078	35W-3S	B5
14600	DLTN	60419	3350	0W-17S	C5
14600	DLTN	60827	3350	0W-17S	C5
14600	RVDL	60827	3350	0W-17S	C5
14900	HRVY	60426	3350	0W-17S	C5
17600	UNON	60180	2635	46W-25N	D4
E Clark St					
-	DMND	60416	3941	33W-39S	B2
10	GNWD	60425	3508	0E-22S	E2
10	PLNO	60545	3259	47W-13S	D6
N Clark St					
10	CHCG	60602	3034	0W-0N	B4
10	CHCG	60603	3034	0W-0N	B4
100	CHCG	60601	3034	0W-0N	B4
300	CHCG	60610	3034	0W-0N	B3
1000	JLET	60432	3499	22W-22S	D2
1000	JltT	60432	3499	22W-22S	D2
1600	CHCG	60610	2978	0W-2N	B7
1600	CHCG	60614	2978	0W-2N	B7
2700	CHCG	60657	2978	0W-3N	A4
3000	CHCG	60657	2977	0W-3N	E4
3500	CHCG	60613	2977	1W-5N	D1
4400	CHCG	60613	2921	1W-5N	D7
4400	CHCG	60640	2921	1W-5N	D7
5700	CHCG	60660	2921	2W-7N	C3
6300	CHCG	60626	2921	2W-7N	C3
7200	CHCG	60626	2867	2W-9N	C7
7500	CHCG	60202	2867	2W-9N	C6
7500	EVTN	60202	2867	2W-9N	C6
S Clark St					
10	CHCG	60602	3034	0W-0S	B5
10	CHCG	60603	3034	0W-0S	B5
100	CHCG	60604	3034	0W-0S	B5
300	CHCG	60605	3034	0W-0S	B6
1400	CHCG	60616	3034	0W-1S	B7
1600	CHCG	60616	3092	0W-1S	B1
13900	RVDL	60827	3350	0W-16S	C3
14500	DLTN	60419	3350	0W-17S	C4
14500	DLTN	60827	3350	0W-17S	C4
W Clark St					
10	PLNO	60545	3259	47W-13S	C6
23500	PNFD	60586	3416	29W-19S	D3
23500	PnfT	60586	3416	29W-19S	D3
25700	AntT	60002	2357	25W-42N	A6
Clarke Av					
500	WKGN	60085	2537	10W-33N	A2
N Clarke St					
2400	RVGV	60171	2973	11W-3N	E5
Clarkson Av					
1200	WKGN	60085	2536	11W-34N	E1
Clarkson Ct					
1500	NPVL	60565	3204	24W-9S	D3
Clary Sage Dr					
22100	FKFT	60423	3590	14W-26S	E3
Clason St					
-	LtRT	60545	3332	45W-14S	B1
-	PLNO	60545	3332	45W-14S	B1

STREET Block	City	ZIP	Map#	CGS	Grid
Classic Ct					
-	CbaT	60010	2696	28W-22N	D4
22300	LKBN	60010	2696	28W-22N	D4
Classic Ln					
20000	OMFD	60461	3506	4W-24S	D5
Classic Rd					
100	SMBG	60193	2913	23W-9N	A1
Classic St					
-	WKGN	60087	2480	10W-36N	B3
S Claude Av					
5500	HMND	46320	3352		E7
Claude Ct					
1100	CHHT	60411	3508	0W-25S	C7
E Claudia Av					
1100	JLET	60433	3499	22W-24S	C5
1100	JltT	60433	3499	22W-24S	C5
Clausen Av					
3800	PvsT	60525	3086	13W-4S	E7
3800	WNSP	60558	3086	13W-4S	E7
4400	WNSP	60558	3146	13W-4S	E1
Clauser Ln					
1300	WDRG	60517	3206	20W-10S	B6
Claussen Ct					
13900	DLTN	60419	3350	0E-16S	E2
Claussen Dr					
1200	WDSK	60098	2524	42W-31N	A7
Clavey Ct					
400	HDPK	60035	2757	8W-20N	D1
Clavey Ln					
-	GNVW	60025	2810	9W-12N	C7
400	HDPK	60035	2757	8W-20N	D1
1300	GRNE	60031	2476	18W-35N	E6
1300	WrnT	60046	2476	18W-35N	E6
Clavey Rd					
700	HDPK	60035	2758	8W-20N	A1
1000	HDPK	60035	2757	8W-20N	E1
Clavinia Av					
1600	DRFD	60015	2703	12W-20N	C7
1600	DRFD	60015	2756	12W-20N	C1
Clay Av					
10	HDPK	60037	2704	9W-23N	D2
10	HIWD	60037	2704	9W-23N	D2
10	HIWD	60040	2704	9W-23N	D2
Clay Ct					
10	OswT	60538	3199	37W-11S	D7
900	DRFD	60015	2703	11W-21N	D7
1600	MLPK	60160	3030	10W-1N	A2
1600	WDSK	60098	2524	41W-32N	D5
Clay St					
100	ALGN	60102	2694	33W-20N	D7
100	ALGN	60102	2747	33W-20N	D1
200	MTGY	60538	3199	37W-9S	D4
300	WDSK	60098	2524	41W-32N	D5
E Clay St					
200	JLET	60432	3499	23W-23S	A4
N Clay St					
100	HNDL	60521	3146	15W-4S	A1
400	HNDL	60521	3086	15W-4S	A7
S Clay St					
10	HNDL	60521	3146	15W-5S	A1
W Clay St					
10	JLET	60432	3498	24W-23S	E3
Claymont Ct					
600	ALGN	60102	2695	32W-20N	A7
Claymoor St					
300	HNDL	60521	3146	15W-6S	B4
Claymore Ln					
100	NpvT	60563	3140	30W-5S	B3
Clayton Av					
10	LKVL	60046	2417	21W-38N	C7
10	LKVL	60046	2475	21W-38N	C1
800	ELGN	60123	2854	35W-12N	B2
Clayton Cir					
700	SMBG	60194	2857	26W-11N	E4
Clayton Ct					
-	DSPN	60016	2862	15W-10N	A5
500	WDDL	60191	2915	18W-6N	A6
1100	GNVA	60134	3019	37W-0N	D5
7000	DRGV	60516	3144	19W-7S	D7
E Clayton Ct					
1600	ANHT	60004	2807	16W-15N	C2
N Clayton Ct					
22400	KLDR	60047	2699	20W-22N	E4
Clayton Ln					
500	DSPN	60016	2808	14W-12N	C7
500	DSPN	60056	2808	14W-12N	C7
500	MPPT	60056	2808	14W-12N	C7
Clayton Rd					
200	HLSD	60162	3028	13W-0S	E5
Clayton St					
300	WCHI	60185	3022	29W-0N	D5
E Clayton St					
10	WKGN	60085	2537	9W-34N	B1
W Clayton St					
100	WKGN	60085	2537	10W-34N	B1
1000	WKGN	60085	2536	10W-34N	E1
Clayton Marsh Dr					
1300	LIHL	60156	2693	35W-22N	E4
1500	AlqT	60156	2693	35W-22N	E3
Clear Dr					
1400	BGBK	60490	3267	26W-12S	E2
Clear Vw					
10	LMNT	60439	3272	15W-13S	B4
Clearbrook Ct					
200	SMBG	60193	2859	23W-9N	B7
2100	NPVL	60564	3202	29W-10S	D5
2200	WCDA	60084	2588	25W-29N	A3
S Clearbrook Dr					
2500	ANHT	60005	2861	17W-11N	B4
Clearbrook Ln					
200	BMDL	60108	2969	22W-4N	B3
Clearbrook St					
3900	MHRY	60050	2528	32W-33N	A3
Clearbrook Park Dr					
900	MDLN	60060	2646	18W-26N	E3
Clear Creek Cross					
18100	ODPK	60467	3422	14W-21S	E7
Clear Creek Ct					
2500	JLET	60586	3415	33W-20S	B6
Clear Creek Dr					
2500	JLET	60586	3415	32W-20S	C6
E Clear Creek Bay					
1700	PLTN	60074	2753	19W-18N	C3
Clearcroft Av					
800	BGBK	60490	3268	26W-13S	A6
Clearing Ct					
1900	NLNX	60451	3590	16W-26S	A3
1900	NlxT	60451	3590	16W-26S	A3
Clearmont Dr					
200	EGVV	60007	2914	18W-8N	E2
300	EGVV	60007	2915	18W-8N	A2
Clearmont Ln					
2100	LIHL	60142	2692	39W-22N	C3
Clear Sky Tr					
200	LIHL	60156	2693	36W-22N	D4
Clearview Av					
400	WCDA	60084	2588	25W-27N	B7
400	WCDA	60084	2644	24W-27N	B1
3600	GRNE	60031	2479	13W-35N	A5
W Clearview Av					
2600	WKGN	60085	2479	12W-35N	C5
12800	WkgT	60085	2479	12W-35N	B5
12900	WkgT	60031	2479	12W-35N	A5
S Clearview Cir					
300	RDLK	60073	2531	23W-32N	E4
Clearview Ct					
300	WPHR	60096	2362	11W-43N	D5
400	LKVL	60046	2417	22W-39N	B4
600	ALGN	60102	2694	34W-20N	C7
1200	BFGV	60089	2701	16W-21N	D6
3700	GRNE	60031	2478	13W-35N	E5
14300	ODPK	60462	3346	11W-17S	A4
E Clearview Ct					
400	RLKB	60073	2475	22W-36N	B4
Clearview Dr					
600	GNVW	60025	2810	10W-13N	B7
2800	JLET	60436	3497	27W-25S	C7
3100	WRLK	60097	2469	36W-35N	C7
4200	MHRY	60050	2527	33W-33N	E2
4200	MHRY	60050	2528	33W-33N	A2
8800	ODPK	60462	3346	11W-17S	A4
W Clearview Dr					
22500	ANTH	60002	2358	22W-42N	B7
22500	AntT	60002	2358	22W-42N	B7
Clearvue Ct					
9800	MKNA	60448	3503	12W-23S	D2
W Clear Water Cir					
1400	AvnT	60073	2531	24W-34N	C1
1400	RLKB	60073	2474	24W-34N	B7
1400	RLKB	60073	2531	25W-34N	B1
Clearwater Ct					
10	LKZH	60047	2699	22W-21N	B6
10	SMWD	60107	2856	29W-10N	E7
300	CLSM	60188	2968	25W-3N	A5
600	OSWG	60543	3263	38W-12S	B2
700	WLNG	60090	2754	16W-17N	D5
N Clearwater Ct					
1100	PLTN	60067	2752	22W-17N	A5
Clearwater Dr					
-	AURA	60504	3138	35W-5S	B3
-	NARA	60504	3138	35W-5S	B3
-	NasT	60586	3415	32W-20S	B4
-	PGGV	60140	2797	42W-15N	D4
-	YKVL	60560	3333	42W-14S	E1
400	AURA	60542	3138	35W-5S	B3
400	NARA	60542	3138	35W-5S	B3
1500	WLNG	60090	2754	16W-17N	D5
2000	DSPN	60018	2862	14W-9N	C7
2000	OKBK	60523	3086	15W-1S	A2
3100	JLET	60586	3415	32W-20S	C4
3900	KLDR	60047	2700	20W-22N	A5
3900	LGGV	60047	2699	20W-22N	E4
3900	LGGV	60047	2700	20W-22N	A5
31500	LKMR	60051	2529	28W-31N	E6
S Clearwater Dr					
-	PNFD	60586	3415	32W-19S	D3
Clearwater Ln					
300	SMBG	60194	2859	22W-10N	C4
500	OSWG	60543	3263	38W-12S	A2
1500	WLNG	60090	2754	16W-17N	D6
4100	NPVL	60564	3267	28W-12S	A3
4300	NPVL	60564	3266	28W-12S	E3
4600	WldT	60564	3266	28W-12S	E3
Clearwater Wy					
-	ELGN	60123	2853	36W-12N	E1
2000	ELGN	60123	2854	36W-12N	A1
Clearwater N St					
400	ROSL	60172	2912	24W-6N	E7
Clearwater South St					
500	ROSL	60172	2912	24W-6N	D7
Clearwater W St					
900	ROSL	60172	2912	24W-6N	D7
Clearwood Ct					
600	AURA	60504	3201	31W-8S	E2
Cleary Av					
1400	JLET	60435	3498	25W-22S	B1
3400	PnfT	60431	3497	28W-22S	A1
3500	JLET	60431	3497	28W-22S	A1
W Cleary Av					
800	JLET	60435	3498	25W-22S	C1
N Cleaver St					
1100	CHCG	60622	3033	1W-1N	D1
Cleaview Ct					
2800	JLET	60436	3497	27W-25S	C7
Cleavland Dr					
500	BGBK	60440	3204	24W-10S	D5
E Cleburne St					
200	BRLT	60103	2911	28W-7N	A5
S Cleburne St					
800	BRLT	60103	2911	28W-7N	B5
Cleek Ct					
29000	FmtT	60060	2589	21W-29N	C5
Clem Dr					
7200	GRNE	60031	2477	18W-35N	A5
Clematis Dr					
1200	SMBG	60193	2857	27W-10N	C6
1200	SMWD	60107	2857	27W-10N	C6
2000	ALGN	60102	2695	32W-20N	B7
Clemens Rd					
1600	DRN	60561	3206	18W-8S	E1
1600	DRN	60561	3207	18W-8S	A1
Clement St					
1500	CTHL	60403	3498	24W-21S	D1
1500	JLET	60435	3498	24W-22S	D1
1700	CTHL	60403	3418	24W-21S	D7
N Clement St					
800	JLET	60435	3498	24W-22S	D2
Clement Wy					
-	JLET	60586	3415	32W-21S	C7
Clementi Ct					
1900	AURA	60503	3201	33W-10S	B6
Clementi Ln					
1900	AURA	60503	3201	33W-10S	B6
Clement Lodge Rd					
500	MchT	60051	2528	31W-32N	D5
Clemson Dr					
1500	NPVL	60565	3204	24W-8S	C2
Clendenin Ln					
1400	RVWD	60015	2703	13W-22N	A5
Clennon Dr					
-	AxST	60447	3672	34W-29S	A1
-	MNKA	60447	3672	34W-29S	A1
Cleo Ct					
600	WLNG	60090	2754	16W-18N	D2
Cleveland Av					
10	CPVL	60110	2800	34W-16N	E1
10	CPVL	60110	2801	34W-16N	A1
10	CPVL	60118	2801	34W-16N	A1
10	EDND	60118	2801	34W-16N	A1
10	LKVL	60046	2475	23W-37N	A1
300	AURA	60506	3199	36W-7S	E1
300	LYVL	60048	2591	16W-28N	D6
400	BTVA	60510	3078	34W-1S	D2
400	ELGN	60120	2855	32W-10N	B5
900	PKRG	60068	2918	9W-8N	C3
1000	CTCY	60409	3352	3E-17S	A5
1100	BKFD	60513	3087	11W-3S	D6
1100	LGPK	60513	3087	11W-3S	D6
1100	LGPK	60525	3087	11W-3S	D6
1400	CTCY	60409	3351	2E-17S	D4
1500	PvsT	60525	3087	11W-2S	D4
1600	JLET	60432	3499	21W-22S	E3
1800	JltT	60432	3499	21W-22S	E3
13800	BLID	60406	3349	3W-16S	B3
13800	POSN	60469	3349	3W-16S	B3
25700	MONE	60449	3682	7W-31S	D5
E Cleveland Av					
400	JLET	60432	3499	23W-22S	B3
N Cleveland Av					
-	CHCG	60610	2978	0W-2N	A7
1300	CHCG	60610	3034	0W-1N	A1
1700	CHCG	60614	2978	0W-2N	A7
S Cleveland Av					
400	ANHT	60005	2807	17W-13N	C6
900	MPPT	60056	2807	17W-13N	C7
14000	POSN	60469	3349	3W-16S	B3
14900	BmnT	60426	3349	3W-17S	B5
14900	BmnT	60469	3349	3W-17S	B5
Cleveland Ct					
100	SMBG	60193	2859	23W-10N	A6
1000	VNHL	60061	2647	17W-26N	B3
W Cleveland Dr					
5100	MchT	60050	2527	34W-34N	C2
Cleveland Rd					
-	FftT	60448	3502	14W-24S	E6
700	HNDL	60521	3146	14W-5S	C3
3300	FftT	60448	3503	13W-24S	A6
Cleveland St					
10	CTCY	60409	3430		C2
200	CRY	60013	2696	30W-23N	A2
300	HMND	46324	3430		E2
600	AURA	60505	3138	34W-6S	C6
600	WNFD	60190	3023	27W-0S	C7
600	WNFD	60190	3081	27W-1S	C1
600	WnfT	60187	3081	27W-1S	C1
1000	EVTN	60202	2867	3W-10N	A5
1100	LKPT	60441	3419	21W-19S	D4
1200	WLMT	60091	2812	5W-14N	A4
1300	NtrT	60093	2812	5W-14N	A4
1900	EVTN	60202	2866	3W-10N	E5
3300	SKOK	60076	2866	4W-10N	D5
4700	SKOK	60076	2865	6W-10N	E5
5200	SKOK	60077	2865	6W-10N	D5
5300	MNGV	60077	2865	6W-10N	D5
5700	MNGV	60053	2865	7W-10N	B5
E Cleveland St					
1000	HMND	46320	3430		E2
W Cleveland St					
6800	MNGV	60053	2864	8W-10N	E5
6800	NLES	60714	2864	8W-10N	D5
Cleven Av					
1100	MPPT	60056	2807	16W-12N	D7
1100	MPPT	60056	2861	16W-12N	D1
Clifden Ct					
1300	WHTN	60187	3081	26W-1S	E1
Cliff Av					
100	LktT	60441	3419	23W-21S	B7
Cliff Ct					
300	LslT	60532	3143	22W-6S	C5
400	LslT	60540	3142	24W-5S	D4
900	CLSM	60188	2967	26W-3N	E5
N Cliff Ct					
2500	MchT	60051	2528	30W-34N	E1
Cliff Dr					
10	PltT	60124	2852	39W-11N	E4
Cliff St					
100	WLSP	60480	3209	12W-9S	B4
Clifford Av					
700	ELGN	60123	2854	34W-12N	D2
N Clifford Av					
5700	CHCG	60646	2919	6W-7N	E4
Clifford Ct					
10	ELGN	60123	2854	34W-12N	D2
N Clifford Ct					
800	PLNO	60545	3259	47W-13S	C5
Clifford Dr					
8500	DRN	60561	3206	20W-9S	B4
Clifford Rd					
600	MltT	60137	3083	21W-2S	D4
Clifford St					
1600	GLHT	60139	2968	23W-3N	E6
3400	EVTN	60201	2812	4W-13N	B7
Clifford Ter					
3700	SKOK	60076	2866	4W-10N	C4
Cliffside Ct					
1700	NPVL	60565	3204	25W-9S	B4
W Cliffside Dr					
21200	KLDR	60047	2699	21W-21N	D7
Cliffside Ln					
9200	ODPK	60462	3345	11W-18S	E7
Cliffside Cir Dr					
10	WLSP	60480	3209	12W-9S	B4
Cliff View Ln					
1000	CLSM	60188	2967	27W-3N	C5
Cliffwood Ln					
400	GRNE	60031	2476	18W-34N	E7
400	GRNE	60031	2533	18W-34N	E1
Clifton Av					
-	BCHR	60401	3774	0W-35S	D7
400	MltT	60137	3025	21W-0N	D4
400	RMVL	60446	3340	24W-15S	D2
800	GNEN	60137	3025	21W-0N	D4
1600	HDPK	60035	2704	9W-22N	D5
8800	MKNA	60448	3504	11W-23S	A4
N Clifton Av					
10	PKRG	60068	2864	10W-9N	A7
10	PKRG	60068	2918	8W-8N	D1
500	ELGN	60123	2854	35W-12N	C2
2000	CHCG	60614	2977	1W-2N	E6
3000	CHCG	60657	2977	1W-3N	D4
3700	CHCG	60613	2977	1W-4N	E2
4400	CHCG	60613	2921	1W-5N	D7
4500	CHCG	60640	2921	1W-5N	D7
4800	CHCG	60656	2918	10W-6N	A6
4800	CHCG	60706	2918	10W-6N	A6
4800	NRDG	60656	2918	10W-6N	A7
4800	NRDG	60706	2918	10W-6N	A6
8400	NLES	60714	2864	10W-10N	A4
S Clifton Av					
10	ELGN	60123	2854	35W-11N	C5
10	PKRG	60068	2918	10W-8N	A2
Clifton Ct					
10	SEGN	60177	2908	36W-9N	A2
400	SMBG	60193	2912	24W-9N	E1
2400	NPVL	60565	3204	25W-10S	A5
3000	AURA	60504	3201	31W-8S	D2
6200	JLET	60586	3415	31W-21S	D7
17700	TYPK	60487	3424	11W-21S	A6
Clifton Dr					
10	RLKP	60073	2532	22W-33N	A3
Clifton Ln					
100	BGBK	60440	3268	25W-11S	C1
8800	TYPK	60487	3424	11W-21S	A6
W Clifton Ln					
13900	HMGN	60491	3343	17W-17S	C5
Clifton Pl					
2200	HFET	60169	2857	26W-12N	E1
2200	HFET	60169	2858	25W-12N	C1
Clifton Wy					
8800	MKNA	60448	3504	11W-23S	A3
Clifton Park Av					
14400	MDLN	60445	3348	4W-17S	D5
14800	MDLN	60426	3348	4W-17S	D5
14800	MKHM	60426	3348	4W-17S	D6
15500	MKHM	60428	3348	4W-18S	D7
15500	MKHM	60428	3426	4W-18S	D1
S Clifton Park Av					
9800	ENGN	60805	3212	4W-11S	D7
10200	ENGN	60805	3276	4W-13S	C3
13400	RBBN	60472	3348	4W-15S	D2
Cline Av					
-	ELBN	60119	3017	42W-0N	C4
-	HMND	-	3280		E7
Cline Av SR-912					
-	HMND		3280		E7
Clinton Av					
-	HRVY	60426	3350	1W-17S	B6
-	OKPK	60301	3030	8W-0N	E4
100	OKPK	60302	3030	8W-0N	E5
500	OKPK	60304	3030	8W-0S	E5
1100	BRWN	60304	3030	8W-0S	E7
1200	BRWN	60402	3030	8W-1S	E7
1500	BRWN	60402	3088	8W-2S	E3
4300	SKNY	60402	3088	8W-4S	E7
4400	FTVW	60402	3088	8W-4S	E7
4500	FTVW	60402	3148	8W-4S	E1
16100	HRVY	60426	3428	0W-19S	C2
16100	SHLD	60426	3428	0W-19S	C2
N Clinton Av					
100	EMHT	60126	3028	15W-1N	B2
W Clinton Av					
24400	RLKH	60073	2474	24W-35N	C5
24500	AvnT	60073	2474	24W-35N	B5
25400	AntT	60002	2416	25W-40N	A4
Clinton Ct					
200	WHTN	60187	3024	25W-0S	A7
1600	MLPK	60160	3030	10W-1N	A2
W Clinton Ct					
1200	PLTN	60067	2805	22W-15N	B2
Clinton Pl					
400	FTPK	60130	3030	9W-0N	D4
600	EVTN	60201	2813	2W-13N	B7
1400	RVFT	60305	3030	9W-1N	D1
1500	EDPK	60707	3030	9W-1N	D1
1500	RVFT	60707	3030	9W-1N	D1
Clinton St					
10	NlxT	60451	3501	18W-23S	A4
100	PKRG	60068	2864	10W-9N	B7
200	MTGY	60538	3199	37W-9S	D4
500	LKPT	60441	3419	22W-19S	C2
600	WKGN	60085	2537	10W-33N	B3
12700	BLID	60406	3277	3W-15S	A7
14500	HRVY	60426	3350	1W-17S	B5
E Clinton St					
10	CTCY	60409	3352		C6
10	HMND	46320	3352		C6
10	JLET	60432	3499	23W-23S	A4
900	JltT	60432	3499	22W-23S	C4
N Clinton St					
10	CHCG	60661	3034	0W-0N	A4
300	CHCG	60610	3034	0W-0N	A4
1200	NLNX	60451	3500	18W-23S	E3
1200	NlxT	60451	3500	18W-23S	E3
2400	RVGV	60171	2974	10W-3N	B5
S Clinton St					
10	CHCG	60661	3034	0W-0S	A6
300	CHCG	60607	3034	0W-0S	A5
1800	CHCG	60616	3092	0W-1S	A1
W Clinton St					
10	JLET	60432	3498	24W-23S	E4
Clipper Ct					
10	TDLK	60030	2533	18W-34N	D1
2200	ELGN	60123	2908	35W-9N	C1
Clipper Dr					
-	RGMW	60008	2805	21W-13N	C6
-	SMBG	60008	2805	21W-13N	C6
-	SMBG	60173	2805	21W-13N	C6
3800	HRPK	60133	2967	26W-4N	D3
Clipper Cove					
2600	SMBG	60173	2805	21W-13N	C6
Clock Tower Plz					
10	ELGN	60120	2855	33W-10N	A5
Clohesey Dr					
600	BFGV	60089	2701	17W-20N	A7
Cloister Ct					
1600	OKBK	60523	3085	17W-3S	C5
1600	OKBK	60559	3085	17W-3S	C5
1600	WTMT	60559	3085	17W-3S	C5
9200	FKFT	60423	3503	11W-25S	E7
9200	FKFT	60423	3504	11W-25S	A7
Cloister Pl					
-	FKFT	60423	3503	11W-25S	E7
Clonard St					
-	MTSN	60443	3506	5W-24S	B5
Cloos Ct					
400	WNFD	60190	3023	27W-0N	D4
Cloud Ct					
500	SMBG	60193	2858	25W-9N	B7
Clove Ct					
10	SEGN	60177	2908	35W-7N	B4
1400	MPPT	60056	2807	16W-14N	D3
Clove Dr					
21900	FKFT	60423	3590	14W-26S	E3
Clover Av					
10	LKBF	60044	2593	12W-28N	B5
10	ShdT	60044	2593	12W-28N	B5
W Clover Av					
3600	MHRY	60050	2528	32W-32N	B5
Clover Cir					
-	MNKA	60447	3672	33W-29S	A2
10	SMWD	60107	2856	29W-10N	D6
600	HPSR	60140	2795	47W-15N	D3
Clover Ct					
10	ALGN	60102	2693	37W-20N	B7
100	BRLT	60103	2911	28W-7N	A5
100	HNVL	60073	2532	22W-33N	B3
300	GNVA	60134	3019	36W-1N	D3
600	NPVL	60540	3141	28W-7S	A6
600	NpvT	60540	3141	28W-7S	A6
700	LYLK	60175	2961	43W-5N	A6
700	YKVL	60560	3333	42W-16S	D5
800	GNVW	60025	2810	9W-13N	B7
1100	BTVA	60510	3078	34W-2S	E3
1600	RMVL	60446	3339	26W-17S	D5
1900	NHBK	60062	2756	11W-16N	D7
4800	JLET	60586	3416	30W-21S	C7
4900	LGGV	60047	2700	19W-23N	C1
6900	DRN	60561	3144	18W-7S	E7
N Clover Ct					
200	PNFD	60544	3337	31W-18S	E7
700	LNHT	60046	2418	20W-39N	A5
1300	ADSN	60101	2970	20W-5N	B1
Clover Dr					
-	SRGV	60554	3136	40W-7S	B7
10	CLLK	60014	2639	37W-26N	B3
10	DrrT	60014	2639	37W-26N	B4
400	ALGN	60102	2693	37W-20N	B7
1000	MNKA	60447	3672	33W-29S	A2
1500	IVNS	60067	2805	23W-15N	A3
1600	IVNS	60067	2804	23W-14N	E3
5200	LSLE	60532	3143	22W-5S	C3
5700	LslT	60532	3143	22W-6S	C4
N Clover Dr					
10	CLLK	60014	2639	37W-25N	B4
Clover Hl					
-	MchT	60050	2470	33W-34N	E7
-	MCLK	60050	2470	33W-34N	E7
Clover Ln					
-	HMGN	60491	3343	16W-17S	D5
-	MHRY	60051	2528	31W-32N	E4
10	DRPK	60010	2751	23W-20N	E2
400	LKFT	60045	2649	11W-26N	D3
500	BGBK	60440	3205	23W-10S	B6
500	RLKB	60073	2475	22W-35N	B6
600	SMBG	60193	2858	25W-9N	B7
600	UYPK	60449	3684	3W-30S	B4
600	UYPK	60466	3684	3W-30S	B4
700	GLNC	60022	2758	7W-17N	B5
800	PGGV	60140	2797	41W-15N	E4
1100	MchT	60051	2528	31W-33N	E4
1200	HFET	60192	2804	24W-15N	C1
2000	WDRG	60517	3206	20W-10S	A5
2100	GNVA	60134	3019	36W-1N	D3
2300	NHFD	60093	2810	8W-15N	E3
2300	NHFD	60093	2811	8W-15N	A3
3300	MTSN	60443	3594	4W-26S	E2
3400	ZION	60099	2422	10W-39N	A6
4800	JLET	60586	3416	30W-21S	C7
16500	TYPK	60487	3424	10W-19S	B3
W Clover Ln					
-	GNOK	60048	2592	15W-30N	B2
15200	LbvT	60048	2592	15W-30N	A2
Clover Mdws					
100	BRRG	60527	3146	14W-6S	C5
Clover Rd					
300	ISLK	60042	2586	28W-28N	E6
600	WCDA	60084	2587	26W-27N	C7
1800	NHBK	60062	2756	11W-16N	D7
2100	NHBK	60062	2809	11W-16N	D1
N Clover St					
4000	CHCG	60641	2976	5W-5N	A1
Clover Chase Cir					
100	WDSK	60098	2581	41W-30N	C2
Cloverdale Av					
1400	HDPK	60035	2704	10W-21N	B5
Cloverdale Ct					
10	ALGN	60102	2747	36W-19N	A3
10	BFGV	60089	2701	17W-21N	A7
600	LslT	60540	3142	24W-5S	C3
1900	SMBG	60194	2858	25W-10N	A5
Cloverdale Ln					
10	SMBG	60194	2858	26W-10N	A5
800	BGBK	60440	3268	24W-12S	C3
1900	ALGN	60102	2747	36W-19N	A2
Cloverdale Pl					
700	AURA	60506	3137	36W-5S	D3
Cloverdale Rd					
10	BMDL	60108	2912	25W-6N	A7
10	BmdT	60108	2912	25W-6N	A7
10	BmdT	60172	2912	25W-6N	A7
100	BmdT	60133	2912	25W-6N	A7
100	HRPK	60133	2912	25W-6N	A7
100	HRPK	60172	2912	25W-6N	A7
2300	NPVL	60564	3266	29W-12S	D2
Cloverfield Cir					
10	CmpT	60175	2907	38W-7N	A5
500	CmpT	60175	2906	39W-7N	E4
700	SchT	60175	2907	38W-7N	A5
Cloverfield Dr					
10	PltT	60124	2906	39W-8N	E4
10	PltT	60175	2906	39W-8N	E4
600	CmpT	60175	2907	39W-7N	A4
600	SchT	60175	2907	38W-7N	A4
800	CmpT	60175	2906	39W-7N	E4
Cloverfield Ln					
800	AURA	60504	3201	31W-8S	E3
Cloverfield Rd					
300	SchT	60175	2907	38W-7N	A4
Clover Hill Ct					
700	EGVV	60007	2914	20W-8N	B2
1000	ELGN	60120	2855	32W-12N	D1
Clover Hill Ln					
100	ElaT	60010	2698	24W-23N	B1
100	LKZH	60047	2698	24W-23N	C1
100	NBRN	60010	2698	24W-23N	B1
600	BbyT	60119	3075	42W-0S	C1
600	EGVV	60007	2914	19W-8N	B3
1000	ELGN	60120	2855	32W-12N	D1
N Clover Hill Ln					
-	LKZH	60047	2698	24W-23N	C1
-	NBRN	60010	2698	24W-23N	C1
Clover Hills Ct					
10	GnvT	60510	3077	38W-0S	B1
Cloverleaf Ct					
500	NPVL	60565	3203	26W-9S	D3
Cloverleaf Dr					
-	MRGO	60152	2634	49W-25N	C4
Cloverleaf Rd					
10	MTSN	60443	3505	7W-24S	D5
Cloverridge Dr					
200	LKPT	60441	3420	21W-19S	A2
Clover Ridge Ln					
-	ITSC	60143	2914	20W-7N	B5
Clovertree Ct					
2400	AURA	60506	3136	39W-6S	E5
Cloverview Dr					
8300	TYPK	60477	3424	10W-21S	C6
8300	TYPK	60487	3424	10W-21S	B6
Clovetree Ct					
700	NPVL	60540	3141	28W-7S	B7
Clow Creek Dr					
9900	WldT	60585	3265	31W-11S	E1
S Clow International Pkwy					
100	BGBK	60490	3268	25W-12S	A2
200	BGBK	60440	3268	25W-12S	A2

STREET Block City ZIP Map# CGS Grid

Club Cir
10 LKBN 60010 2643 26W-24N E7
900 GNVW 60025 2811 7W-13N A6
Club Ct
16400 LktT 60403 3417 26W-19S E3
Club Dr
1400 GLHT 60139 2968 24W-2N D7
3400 NPVL 60564 3202 30W-10S B5
Club Rd
- MchT 60051 2528 31W-34N D1
1000 BLVY 60098 2582 39W-30N B1
1000 WDSK 60098 2582 39W-30N B1
N Club Rd
2300 MchT 60051 2528 31W-34N E1
Club Ter
100 BmdT 60143 2970 21W-5N A1
100 ITSC 60143 2970 21W-5N A1
Club Cir Dr
14500 BmnT 60445 3347 8W-17S B5
14500 OKFT 60452 3347 8W-17S B5
Club House Av
2200 NPVL 60563 3140 30W-4S C2
2200 NpvT 60563 3140 30W-4S C2
Club House Cir
500 ROSL 60172 2913 22W-7N B3
Club House Ct
6000 GRNE 60031 2534 16W-33N D2
Clubhouse Ct
1400 GLHT 60139 2968 24W-2N D7
Club House Dr
- ODHL 60013 2642 30W-26N A4
300 BMDL 60108 2968 24W-5N C2
Clubhouse Dr
- NBRN 60010 2644 24W-24N C7
10 WLBK 60527 3145 16W-7S D6
100 LynT 60458 3209 11W-8S D2
500 SchT 60175 2963 38W-5N A1
1700 AURA 60504 3200 33W-10S E5
S Clubhouse Dr
200 PLTN 60074 2806 19W-15N B2
Club House Ln
- OSWG 60543 3262 39W-11S D2
Clubhouse Ln
- HFET 60169 2858 25W-12N B1
100 LKZH 60047 2698 24W-22N C3
2500 WKGN 60087 2480 10W-36N B3
3700 OMFD 60461 3506 4W-24S D4
Clubhouse St
200 BGBK 60490 3267 26W-12S D3
Club Lake Ct
1600 ANTH 60002 2417 20W-40N E2
Club Lake Dr
- ANTH 60002 2418 20W-40N A2
900 ANTH 60002 2417 21W-40N E2
Clublands Pkwy
- JLET 60447 3495 33W-21S A1
- JLET 60586 3415 33W-21S B7
- JLET 60586 3495 33W-21S A1
- NasT 60586 3415 33W-21S B6
Clubside Ct
10 DGvT 60527 3146 15W-6S A4
Clubside Dr
10 WLBK 60527 3145 16W-7S D6
Club Tree Dr
- BRLT 60103 2911 28W-9N A2
- SMWD 60103 2911 28W-9N A2
3000 SMWD 60107 2911 28W-9N A1
E Clubview Ct
400 ADSN 60101 2971 17W-4N B4
Cluverius Av
- NCHI 60064 2537 10W-31N A7
300 NCHI 60088 2537 10W-31N A7
N Clybourn Av
1200 CHCG 60610 3034 0W-1N A1
1600 CHCG 60614 2977 1W-2N E7
1600 CHCG 60622 2977 1W-2N E7
2700 CHCG 60618 2977 1W-2N D6
2700 CHCG 60647 2977 2W-3N B5
2700 CHCG 60657 2977 2W-3N B4
Clybourne St
1300 BTVA 60510 3077 36W-1S E1
Clyde Av
100 CHCG 60202 2867 2W-9N B6
100 CHCG 60626 2867 2W-9N B6
100 EVTN 60202 2867 2W-9N B6
200 CTCY 60409 3351 2E-17S C6
800 DRGV 60516 3144 19W-6S C5
4300 LYNS 60534 3088 10W-4S B7
4500 LYNS 60534 3148 10W-4S B1
4600 MCCK 60525 3148 10W-4S B1
4600 MCCK 60534 3148 10W-4S B1
15400 DLTN 60419 3351 2E-18S C7
15400 DLTN 60473 3351 2E-18S C7
15400 ThtT 60409 3351 2E-18S C7
15400 ThtT 60473 3351 2E-18S C7
16600 SHLD 60473 3429 2E-19S D3
17900 ThtT 60438 3429 2E-21S D7
18000 LNSG 60438 3429 2E-21S D7
18400 HMWD 60430 3507 3W-22S B1
18500 BlmT 60411 3429 2E-21S D7
18500 BlmT 60438 3429 2E-21S D7
21500 SLVL 60411 3597 2E-26S D2
N Clyde Av
10 PltT 60067 2805 22W-16N B1
100 PltT 60067 2752 22W-16N B7
200 PLTN 60067 2752 22W-16N B7
300 IVNS 60067 2752 22W-16N B7
17700 LNSG 60438 3429 2E-21S D5
17700 ThtT 60438 3429 2E-21S D5
S Clyde Av
- CHCG 60633 3351 2E-15S C2
- CTCY 60409 3351 2E-16S C2
10 PltT 60067 2805 22W-15N B1
6700 CHCG 60649 3153 2E-7S C6
7500 CHCG 60649 3215 2E-9S C2
9500 CHCG 60617 3215 2E-11S C6
Clyde Ct
100 SchT 60174 2908 35W-6N C7
100 SchT 60174 2964 35W-6N C1
12800 NlxT 60451 3590 16W-26S A1
Clyde Dr
1200 LslT 60540 3203 26W-8S E1
1200 NPVL 60540 3203 26W-8S E1
1300 NPVL 60565 3203 26W-9S E4
Clyde Pkwy
10 SchT 60174 2908 34W-6N C7
700 SchT 60174 2964 34W-6N C1
Clyde Rd
2400 HMWD 60430 3507 3W-22S C1
2500 HMWD 60430 3427 3W-22S B7
18400 FSMR 60422 3507 3W-22S B1
Clyde St
10 GLF 60029 2865 8W-12N A1
100 GNVW 60025 2865 8W-12N A1
100 GNVW 60029 2865 8W-12N A1
Clyde Ter
2300 HMWD 60430 3507 2W-22S C1
4800 MCCK 60525 3148 10W-5S B1
Clydesdale Ct
300 CmpT 60175 2906 40W-6N B7
Clydesdale Dr
1700 WHTN 60187 3083 23W-3S A5
Clydesdale Ln
14500 HMGN 60491 3344 15W-17S B5
Clynderven Rd
8300 BRRG 60527 3208 15W-9S A4
CO-1 Ferry Rd
200 WNVL 60555 3081 28W-4S A7
CO-1 Plainfield-Naperville Rd
100 NPVL 60564 3203 28W-9S B3
100 NPVL 60565 3203 28W-9S B3
100 NpvT 60564 3203 28W-9S B3
400 NpvT 60565 3203 27W-8S B3
CO-1 Raymond Dr
300 NPVL 60563 3140 29W-4S E1
CO-1 River Rd
10 NPVL 60563 3140 28W-5S E4
10 NPVL 60563 3141 28W-6S A4
10 WNVL 60555 3081 28W-3S A7
CO-2 Belmont Rd
4400 DRGV 60515 3143 21W-4S E1
5600 DRGV 60516 3143 21W-6S E4
5600 LslT 60515 3143 21W-6S E4
5600 LslT 60516 3143 21W-6S E4
CO-2 Burlington Rd
10 CmpT 60124 2905 43W-7N B5
10 CmpT 60151 2905 43W-7N B5
10 CmpT 60175 2905 41W-6N E6
10 CmpT 60175 2962 40W-6N B1
10 PltT 60124 2905 43W-7N C5
10 PltT 60151 2905 43W-7N C5
100 CmpT 60175 2906 41W-6N A7
400 PltT 60140 2905 43W-7N C5
CO-2 Finley Rd
- DRGV 60515 3143 21W-4S E1
10 DRGV 60515 3083 21W-4S E7
10 DRGV 60532 3083 21W-4S E7
10 LslT 60532 3083 21W-4S E7
10 LslT 60532 3084 21W-4S A7
3000 DRGV 60515 3084 20W-3S B5
CO-2 Hobson Rd
10 LslT 60517 3143 22W-7S C7
10 LslT 60540 3143 23W-7S B7
10 LslT 60540 3204 26W-8S A1
10 WDRG 60517 3143 23W-7S B7
100 NPVL 60540 3204 25W-8S C1
100 WDRG 60540 3143 23W-7S A7
400 LslT 60565 3204 25W-8S B1
400 NPVL 60565 3204 25W-8S B1
500 LslT 60540 3205 23W-7S A1
2200 DRGV 60516 3143 21W-6S E4
2200 LslT 60516 3143 21W-6S E4
CO-3 Allen Rd
10 HPSR 60140 2795 46W-16N E1
10 HPSR 60140 2796 45W-16N B1
100 HshT 60140 2796 45W-16N B1
CO-3 Ferry Rd
- WNVL 60555 3081 28W-4S A7
- WNVL 60555 3141 28W-4S A1
CO-3 River Rd
300 NPVL 60555 3140 28W-4S E1
300 NPVL 60563 3140 28W-4S E1
300 WNVL 60555 3140 28W-4S E1
300 WNVL 60563 3140 28W-4S E1
500 WNVL 60555 3141 28W-4S A1
CO-3 Warrenville Rd
10 LSLE 60532 3082 25W-4S B7
10 NPVL 60532 3082 25W-4S B7
10 NPVL 60563 3082 25W-4S B7
200 WNVL 60563 3081 27W-4S D7
300 WNVL 60555 3081 26W-4S E7
400 DRGV 60532 3143 22W-4S D1
400 LSLE 60532 3143 21W-4S D1
400 LslT 60532 3143 21W-4S D1
400 NPVL 60555 3081 26W-4S E7
400 NPVL 60563 3081 26W-4S E7
500 LslT 60563 3082 25W-4S B7
1400 LSLE 60532 3083 23W-4S A7
1400 LslT 60532 3083 23W-4S A7
1600 LslT 60532 3082 23W-4S E7
2100 LSLE 60532 3142 24W-4S D1
2200 DRGV 60515 3143 21W-4S E1
2600 LSLE 60515 3143 21W-4S D1
CO-3 E Warrenville Rd
1000 LslT 60563 3081 26W-4S E7
1000 NPVL 60563 3081 26W-4S E7
1000 NPVL 60563 3082 26W-4S A7
1100 LslT 60563 3082 25W-4S A7
CO-3 W Warrenville Rd
100 LslT 60563 3081 26W-4S D7
100 NPVL 60555 3081 27W-4S D7
100 NPVL 60563 3081 27W-4S D7
100 WNVL 60555 3081 27W-4S D7
100 WNVL 60563 3081 27W-4S D7
CO-4 Bloomingdale Rd
10 GNEN 60137 3025 23W-1N A3
10 GNEN 60187 3025 23W-1N A3
10 WHTN 60187 3025 23W-1N A3
100 MltT 60137 3025 23W-1N A3
100 MltT 60188 3025 23W-1N A3
300 GLHT 60137 3025 23W-2N A1
300 GLHT 60139 3025 23W-2N A1
300 MltT 60139 3025 23W-1N A2
1200 BmdT 60137 3025 23W-2N A1
1200 BmdT 60139 3025 23W-2N A1
1200 BmdT 60188 3025 23W-2N A1
1400 BmdT 60137 2969 23W-2N A7
1400 BmdT 60139 2969 23W-2N A7
1400 GLHT 60137 2969 23W-2N A7
1400 GLHT 60139 2969 23W-2N A7
2100 BMDL 60108 2969 23W-4N A3
2100 BMDL 60139 2969 23W-4N A3
2100 GLHT 60108 2969 23W-4N A3
CO-4 N Bloomingdale Rd
100 BMDL 60108 2913 23W-5N A7
100 BMDL 60108 2969 23W-4N A2
200 BMDL 60172 2913 23W-6N A6
CO-4 S Bloomingdale Rd
- GLHT 60139 2969 23W-4N A3
100 BMDL 60108 2969 23W-5N A1
200 BMDL 60139 2969 23W-4N A3
CO-4 Harter Rd
100 SgrT 60554 3134 44W-4S E1
300 SgrT 60554 3135 43W-4S A2
300 SRGV 60554 3134 43W-4S E2
300 SRGV 60554 3135 43W-4S A2
CO-4 Roselle Rd
300 BMDL 60108 2913 23W-6N A6
300 BMDL 60172 2913 23W-6N A6
300 ROSL 60108 2913 23W-6N A6
300 ROSL 60172 2913 23W-6N A6
CO-4 N Roselle Rd
300 ROSL 60172 2913 23W-7N A3
CO-4 S Roselle Rd
10 ROSL 60172 2913 23W-7N A5
700 BMDL 60108 2913 23W-6N A6
700 ROSL 60108 2913 23W-6N A6
CO-5 Glen Ellyn Rd
- GLHT 60137 3025 22W-1N C1
100 GLHT 60139 3025 22W-2N C1
300 BMDL 60108 2969 22W-3N C5
300 BMDL 60139 2969 22W-3N C5
300 GLHT 60139 2969 22W-3N C5
400 BmdT 60101 2969 22W-3N C6
400 BmdT 60139 2969 22W-3N C6
400 GLHT 60101 2969 22W-3N C6
1300 BmdT 60139 3025 22W-2N C1
CO-5 Main St
300 MltT 60137 3025 22W-1N C2
500 GLHT 60137 3025 22W-1N C2
500 GLHT 60139 3025 22W-1N C2
500 MltT 60139 3025 22W-1N C2
CO-5 N Main St
800 GNEN 60137 3025 22W-1N C3
800 MltT 60137 3025 22W-1N C3
CO-5 Park Blvd
10 MltT 60137 3083 22W-3S B5
200 GNEN 60137 3083 22W-2S C3
400 MltT 60532 3083 22W-3S B6
CO-5 S Park Blvd
400 GNEN 60137 3083 22W-1S C2
400 MltT 60137 3083 22W-1S C2
CO-5 Silver Glen Rd
10 CmpT 60124 2905 42W-7N E6
10 CmpT 60151 2905 41W-6N E6
10 CmpT 60175 2905 42W-7N D6
10 CmpT 60175 2906 40W-7N B6
10 SchT 60175 2907 38W-6N B6
10 SchT 60177 2907 38W-6N B6
10 SEGN 60177 2907 38W-6N B6
100 SchT 60175 2908 36W-6N A6
700 CmpT 60175 2907 38W-6N A6
700 SEGN 60175 2907 38W-6N B6
CO-6 S Bartlett Rd
200 WynT 60103 2910 28W-7N E5
400 BRLT 60103 2910 28W-6N E6
400 BRLT 60103 2966 28W-5N E1
400 WynT 60103 2966 28W-5N E1
CO-6 Galligan Rd
10 GLBT 60118 2746 39W-18N A4
10 GLBT 60136 2746 39W-17N A7
10 GLBT 60136 2799 39W-16N A1
10 RtdT 60118 2746 39W-17N A7
10 RtdT 60136 2746 39W-18N A4
10 RtdT 60142 2746 39W-18N A4
CO-7
- GNEN 60137 3025 22W-1N B3
CO-7 Damisch Rd
10 PGGV 60140 2798 40W-14N B6
10 RtdT 60140 2798 40W-14N B5
CO-7 Geneva Rd
500 GNEN 60137 3025 22W-1N C3
500 MltT 60137 3025 22W-1N C3
CO-7 Reinking Rd
10 PGGV 60140 2798 40W-14N B7
10 PltT 60140 2798 40W-13N B7
CO-7 St. Charles Rd
10 BmdT 60188 3023 26W-2N E2
10 BmdT 60188 3024 25W-1N A2
10 CLSM 60188 3023 26W-2N E2
10 CLSM 60188 3024 25W-1N A2
10 MltT 60188 3024 23W-1N E2
10 WynT 60188 3023 27W-2N D1
100 WynT 60185 3023 27W-2N C1
300 MltT 60188 3025 23W-1N A3
400 LMBD 60148 3025 21W-0N E3
400 MltT 60137 3025 21W-0N D3
400 MltT 60148 3025 21W-1N D3
400 GNEN 60137 3025 21W-0N D3
CO-7 W St. Charles Rd
600 LMBD 60148 3026 21W-0N A3
600 MltT 60148 3026 21W-0N A3
700 LMBD 60148 3025 21W-0N E3
700 MltT 60148 3025 21W-0N E3
CO-8 Elmhurst Rd
2300 EGvT 60007 2915 16W-7N E3
2300 EGVV 60007 2915 16W-7N E3
CO-8 Fabyan Pkwy
10 BbyT 60134 3018 39W-0S D7
10 BTVA 60134 3019 37W-0S C6
10 BTVA 60510 3019 37W-0S C6
10 GnvT 60134 3018 39W-0S E7
10 GnvT 60134 3019 37W-0S C7
100 BbyT 60119 3076 39W-0S D1
100 BbyT 60510 3076 40W-1S C2
100 GNVA 60134 3019 37W-0S D6
100 GnvT 60510 3019 37W-0S C7
300 BbyT 60119 3018 39W-0S D7
CO-8 E Fabyan Pkwy
- BTVA 60134 3020 35W-0S B6
10 BTVA 60510 3020 34W-0S E6
10 GNVA 60134 3020 35W-0S C6
10 GNVA 60510 3020 35W-0S C6
300 GnvT 60510 3020 34W-0S C6
1100 GnvT 60134 3020 34W-0S E6
1400 BTVA 60510 3021 33W-0N B6
1400 GnvT 60134 3021 33W-0S A6
1400 GnvT 60510 3021 33W-0N B6
1800 WCHI 60185 3021 33W-0N B6
CO-8 W Fabyan Pkwy
- GnvT 60510 3019 36W-0S D6
10 BTVA 60134 3020 35W-0S B7
10 BTVA 60510 3020 35W-0S B7
10 GNVA 60134 3020 35W-0S B7
10 GnvT 60134 3020 35W-0S A7
800 GnvT 60510 3020 36W-0S A7
1000 BTVA 60134 3019 36W-0S E7
1000 BTVA 60510 3019 36W-0S E7
1000 GNVA 60134 3019 36W-0S E7
1000 GnvT 60134 3019 36W-0S E7
CO-8 S Madison St
5400 DGvT 60521 3146 16W-6S A3
5400 HNDL 60521 3146 16W-7S A7
5800 DGvT 60527 3146 16W-6S A4
5900 BRRG 60527 3146 16W-6S A5
6300 WLBK 60527 3146 15W-7S A5
7200 DGvT 60527 3208 16W-8S A1
7200 WLBK 60527 3208 16W-8S A1
7600 BRRG 60527 3208 15W-8S A2
CO-8 York Rd
2700 OKBK 60523 3086 15W-3S B5
3600 HNDL 60521 3086 15W-3S B6
3700 OKBK 60521 3086 15W-3S B6
CO-8 N York Rd
200 BNVL 60106 2915 15W-5N E7
300 CHCG 60106 2915 15W-5N E7
800 EGVV 60007 2915 15W-7N E4
CO-8 N York Rd
800 EGVV 60106 2915 15W-7N E4
CO-9 Highland Av
2900 LMBD 60148 3084 19W-2S C4
2900 LMBD 60515 3084 19W-2S C4
2900 YkTp 60148 3084 19W-2S C4
2900 YkTp 60515 3084 19W-2S C4
3200 DRGV 60515 3084 19W-3S C6
CO-9 Kaneville Rd
1500 GNVA 60134 3020 36W-1N A3
1700 GNVA 60134 3019 36W-1N E4
CO-9 W Kaneville Rd
1100 GNVA 60134 3020 36W-1N A3
CO-9 Lemont Rd
10 DGvT 60439 3270 19W-12S C1
10 WDRG 60439 3270 19W-12S C3
10 WDRG 60517 3270 19W-12S C3
200 DGvT 60439 3206 19W-11S C7
200 DGvT 60517 3270 19W-12S C3
200 DRN 60439 3206 19W-11S C7
500 LMNT 60439 3270 19W-12S C3
700 DGvT 60516 3206 19W-11S C7
700 DGvT 60561 3206 19W-11S C7
700 DRN 60516 3206 19W-11S C7
700 DRN 60561 3206 19W-11S C7
7200 DRGV 60516 3206 19W-8S C1
7300 WDRG 60516 3206 19W-8S C1
7500 DRN 60517 3206 19W-8S C2
7500 WDRG 60517 3206 19W-8S C2
7500 WDRG 60561 3206 19W-8S C2
7600 DGvT 60517 3206 19W-8S C2
CO-9 Main St
10 DRGV 60516 3144 19W-6S C4
3900 DRGV 60515 3084 19W-4S C6
5500 DRGV 60515 3144 19W-6S C4
7100 DRGV 60516 3206 19W-8S C1
CO-10 N Arlington Heights Rd
1200 AddT 60143 2914 19W-7N D4
1200 EGVV 60007 2914 19W-7N D4
1200 ITSC 60143 2914 19W-7N D4
CO-10 Main St
10 BbyT 60119 3075 43W-1S A3
10 BbyT 60119 3076 41W-1S A2
10 BbyT 60134 3076 39W-1S E2
10 BbyT 60510 3076 41W-1S A2
10 BTVA 60510 3077 37W-1S C2
10 BtvT 60510 3077 37W-1S C2
200 BtvT 60134 3077 38W-1S A2
500 BtvT 60134 3076 38W-1S E2
500 BtvT 60510 3076 38W-1S E2
2000 BTVA 60539 3077 36W-1S D2
2000 BtvT 60539 3077 36W-1S D2
CO-10 N Prospect Av
- AddT 60191 2914 19W-7N D4
- ITSC 60191 2914 19W-7N D4
10 ITSC 60143 2914 19W-6N D5
300 AddT 60143 2914 18W-7N D5
CO-10 S Prospect Av
100 ITSC 60143 2914 18W-6N D6
200 WDDL 60143 2914 19W-6N D7
200 WDDL 60191 2914 19W-6N D7
CO-11 Army Trail Rd
- ADSN 60101 2969 21W-3N E4
10 AddT 60101 2970 20W-3N A5
10 ADSN 60101 2970 21W-3N A4
10 BMDL 60101 2969 22W-4N D4
10 BmdT 60101 2969 22W-4N D4
10 BmdT 60101 2970 21W-3N A5
10 BRLT 60103 2966 29W-5N D3
10 BRLT 60185 2966 29W-4N E3
10 WynT 60103 2966 29W-4N E3
10 WynT 60185 2966 29W-4N E3
100 BMDL 60108 2969 22W-4N B4
100 BmdT 60108 2969 22W-4N C4
200 WYNE 60103 2966 30W-5N B2
200 WYNE 60184 2966 29W-5N D3
300 BMDL 60139 2969 22W-4N B4
300 BmdT 60139 2969 22W-4N C4
300 BRLT 60103 2967 28W-4N A3
300 CLSM 60103 2967 28W-4N A3
300 CLSM 60188 2967 28W-4N A3
300 WynT 60184 2966 29W-5N D3
400 GLHT 60139 2969 22W-4N B4
400 WynT 60103 2967 28W-4N A3
400 WynT 60185 2967 28W-4N A3
500 BRLT 60184 2966 29W-5N D3
500 BRLT 60185 2967 28W-4N A3
500 GLHT 60108 2969 22W-4N B4
CO-11 E Army Trail Rd
10 GLHT 60139 2969 23W-4N B4
100 BMDL 60108 2968 23W-4N E4
100 BMDL 60139 2968 23W-4N E4
100 GLHT 60108 2968 23W-4N E4
100 GLHT 60139 2968 23W-4N E4
300 BMDL 60108 2969 23W-4N B4
300 BMDL 60139 2969 23W-4N B4
300 GLHT 60108 2969 23W-4N B4
CO-11 W Army Trail Rd
100 BMDL 60108 2968 24W-4N D4
100 BMDL 60139 2968 23W-4N E4
100 GLHT 60108 2968 24W-4N D4
100 GLHT 60139 2968 24W-4N D4
200 BmdT 60108 2968 25W-4N A3
200 BmdT 60188 2968 25W-4N A3
200 CLSM 60108 2968 25W-4N A3
200 CLSM 60188 2968 25W-4N A3
400 BMDL 60108 2967 26W-4N E3
400 BMDL 60133 2968 25W-4N B3
400 BmdT 60108 2967 26W-4N E3
400 BmdT 60133 2968 25W-4N B3
400 BmdT 60188 2967 26W-4N E3
400 CLSM 60108 2967 26W-4N E3
400 CLSM 60188 2967 26W-4N E3
500 HRPK 60108 2967 26W-4N E3
500 HRPK 60133 2967 28W-4N B3
500 HRPK 60188 2967 26W-4N E3
700 CLSM 60133 2967 28W-4N B3
1300 BRLT 60103 2967 28W-4N B3
1300 BRLT 60188 2967 28W-4N B3
1300 CLSM 60103 2967 28W-4N B3
1300 HRPK 60103 2967 28W-4N B3
CO-11 French Rd
10 BrlT 60140 2795 47W-14N C6
10 HPSR 60140 2795 47W-15N C4
10 HshT 60140 2795 47W-13N C7
CO-13 W Diehl Rd
- WNVL 60555 3141 28W-4S B1
CO-13 Ferry Rd
- WNVL 60555 3081 28W-4S B7
CO-13 Raymond Dr
900 NPVL 60563 3140 29W-5S E2
CO-13 River Rd
100 WNVL 60555 3081 28W-4S A7
CO-13 Winfield Rd
- NPVL 60555 3141 28W-4S B1
- NPVL 60563 3141 28W-4S B1
CO-13 Winfield Rd
10 WNFD 60190 3023 27W-0N C6
10 WnfT 60555 3081 28W-3S B6
100 WNFD 60190 3081 27W-1S C1
100 WnfT 60185 3081 28W-3S B6
100 WnfT 60187 3081 27W-1S B1
100 WnfT 60190 3081 27W-1S C1
300 WNFD 60185 3023 27W-0N C5
300 WnfT 60185 3023 27W-0N C5
300 WnfT 60190 3023 27W-0N C5
3600 WNVL 60555 3141 28W-4S B1
4200 WNVL 60555 3081 28W-1S B2
CO-14 N Eola Rd
10 NpvT 60502 3139 31W-7S D6
10 NpvT 60563 3139 31W-5S D2
100 AURA 60502 3079 31W-3S E7
100 AURA 60502 3139 31W-5S D3
100 AURA 60510 3079 31W-3S E7
100 AURA 60563 3139 31W-5S D3
100 WnfT 60510 3079 31W-3S E7
300 AURA 60504 3139 31W-7S D7
CO-15 N Cass Av
600 WTMT 60559 3085 17W-4S B7
CO-15 S Cass Av
- DGvT 60439 3207 17W-10S B5
- DGvT 60527 3207 17W-10S B5
200 DGvT 60561 3207 17W-8S B1
200 DRN 60561 3207 17W-10S B5
400 WTMT 60559 3145 18W-6S B4
700 DGvT 60561 3145 17W-7S B7
700 DRN 60561 3145 17W-7S B7
6600 DRN 60559 3145 17W-7S B6
6600 WTMT 60561 3145 17W-7S B6
CO-15 Deerpath Rd
10 AraT 60506 3077 38W-4S A7
10 BtvT 60506 3077 38W-4S A7
CO-15 Healy Rd
200 SgrT 60506 3075 41W-4S E7
200 SgrT 60506 3076 40W-4S B7
200 SgrT 60554 3075 41W-4S E7
CO-15 Midwest Rd
2200 OKBK 60181 3085 17W-2S B2
2200 OKBK 60523 3085 17W-2S B2
2300 YkTp 60523 3085 17W-2S B3
3400 OKBK 60559 3085 17W-3S B5
3500 WTMT 60523 3085 17W-3S B6
3500 WTMT 60559 3085 17W-3S B5
CO-15 Norris Rd
10 BbyT 60506 3076 40W-3S B7
10 SgrT 60506 3076 40W-4S B7
CO-15 Oak St
200 AraT 60506 3077 38W-4S A7
200 AraT 60542 3077 38W-4S A7
200 NARA 60542 3077 38W-4S A7
CO-15 Summit Av
10 OKTR 60181 3027 17W-1S B7
10 OKTR 60181 3085 17W-1S B2
10 VLPK 60181 3027 17W-1S B7
10 YkTp 60181 3085 17W-1S B2
400 OKBK 60523 3085 17W-1S B2
400 OKTR 60523 3085 17W-1S B2
500 OKBK 60181 3085 17W-1S B2
CO-15 Tanner Rd
- AraT 60506 3077 38W-4S B7
- BtvT 60506 3077 38W-4S B7
10 BbyT 60506 3076 40W-4S B7
10 NARA 60506 3076 40W-3S C7
200 AraT 60506 3076 38W-3S E7
200 BtvT 60506 3076 38W-3S E7
200 NARA 60542 3076 39W-3S E7
200 SgrT 60506 3076 39W-3S E7
CO-16 Bunker Rd
100 BbyT 60119 3018 40W-0N A5
600 BbyT 60119 3076 41W-1S A1
600 BbyT 60510 3076 41W-1S A1
CO-17
- PltT 60124 2852 41W-10N A7
CO-17 Bowes Rd
10 ELGN 60123 2908 36W-9N A1
10 ELGN 60177 2908 36W-9N A1
10 ElgT 60124 2907 37W-9N D1
10 PltT 60124 2852 41W-10N A7
10 PltT 60124 2906 39W-9N E1
10 SEGN 60123 2908 36W-9N A1
10 SEGN 60177 2908 36W-9N A1
400 ELGN 60123 2907 37W-9N D1
400 ELGN 60124 2907 36W-9N E1
400 ElgT 60123 2907 36W-9N E1
500 ElgT 60123 2908 35W-9N B1
500 ElgT 60177 2908 35W-9N A1
700 PltT 60124 2907 39W-9N A1
CO-17 E Chicago Av
800 NPVL 60540 3141 26W-6S E5
1000 NPVL 60540 3142 26W-6S A5
1100 LslT 60540 3142 25W-6S A5
CO-17 Maple Av
500 LSLE 60532 3142 23W-6S E4
500 LSLE 60532 3143 23W-5S A4
500 LSLE 60540 3142 24W-6S C4
500 LslT 60532 3143 22W-5S A4
500 LslT 60540 3142 24W-6S C4
500 NPVL 60532 3142 24W-6S C4
500 NPVL 60540 3142 24W-6S C4
1400 DRGV 60515 3144 20W-6S A4
1400 DRGV 60516 3144 20W-6S A4
1500 LslT 60532 3142 23W-6S E4
1700 DGvT 60515 3144 20W-6S A4
1700 DGvT 60516 3144 20W-6S A4
1900 LslT 60515 3144 20W-6S A4
1900 LslT 60516 3144 20W-6S A4
2200 LslT 60516 3143 21W-6S E4
2600 DRGV 60516 3143 21W-6S D4
2800 DRGV 60515 3143 22W-6S D4
2800 LslT 60515 3143 22W-6S D4
CO-17 Muirhead Rd
- PltT 60124 2852 40W-9N B7
CO-17 Plato Rd
400 PltT 60124 2851 41W-10N E6
400 PltT 60124 2852 41W-10N A6
CO-18 W Hawthorne Ln
1700 WCHI 60185 3021 31W-2N D2
1800 WnfT 60185 3021 31W-1N D2
CO-18 Kress Rd
10 WCHI 60185 3021 32W-0N D4
300 WnfT 60185 3021 31W-1N D3
CO-18 Powis Rd
100 WCHI 60185 2965 31W-3N E6
100 WynT 60185 2965 31W-3N E6
700 WCHI 60185 3021 31W-2N E1
1100 WynT 60185 3021 31W-2N E1
CO-19 Dunham Rd
- SchT 60103 2909 33W-7N B5
10 SchT 60174 2965 33W-4N A3
10 SchT 60184 2965 33W-4N A3
10 SCRL 60174 2964 34W-4N E5
10 SCRL 60174 2965 33W-4N A3

Chicago 7-County Street Index

Block	City	ZIP	Map#	CGS	Grid
CO-19 Dunham Rd					
10	SCRL	60184	2965	33W-4N	A3
10	WYNE	60120	2909	33W-7N	B6
10	WYNE	60174	2965	33W-4N	A3
10	WYNE	60184	2909	33W-6N	B7
10	WYNE	60184	2965	33W-6N	B1
200	BRLT	60120	2909	33W-7N	B5
200	SchT	60120	2909	33W-7N	B5
500	SchT	60174	2964	34W-4N	E5
CO-20 Army Trail Rd					
100	WYNE	60184	2965	33W-5N	B2
CO-20 E Grand Av					
10	BNVL	60106	2972	15W-3N	A5
10	EMHT	60106	2972	15W-3N	A5
10	EMHT	60126	2972	15W-3N	A5
100	AddT	60106	2972	15W-3N	A5
100	AddT	60126	2972	15W-3N	A5
100	FNPK	60131	2972	15W-3N	B5
100	FNPK	60164	2972	15W-3N	B5
100	LydT	60164	2972	15W-3N	B5
CO-20 W Grand Av					
10	BNVL	60106	2971	16W-3N	E5
10	EMHT	60106	2971	16W-3N	E5
10	EMHT	60126	2971	17W-3N	C5
300	AddT	60106	2971	16W-3N	D5
CO-21 Big Timber Rd					
10	DndT	60124	2799	37W-14N	D7
10	ELGN	60124	2799	37W-14N	D6
10	ElgT	60124	2799	36W-13N	D7
10	GLBT	60124	2799	36W-13N	E7
10	GLBT	60136	2799	36W-13N	E7
10	HPSR	60140	2743	46W-18N	A5
10	HshT	60140	2743	46W-18N	A5
10	HshT	60140	2744	43W-17N	B7
10	RtdT	60124	2799	36W-13N	E7
10	RtdT	60136	2798	39W-15N	D4
10	RtdT	60136	2799	38W-14N	C6
10	RtdT	60140	2744	43W-17N	B7
10	RtdT	60140	2797	42W-16N	E1
10	RtdT	60140	2798	39W-15N	D4
10	RtdT	60142	2744	42W-17N	C7
10	RtdT	60142	2797	43W-17N	C1
200	DndT	60136	2799	37W-14N	C6
200	GLBT	60124	2798	39W-14N	E5
200	GLBT	60136	2798	39W-14N	E5
200	RtdT	60124	2798	39W-14N	E5
300	ELGN	60123	2800	36W-13N	A7
500	ELGN	60123	2854	35W-12N	C1
500	RtdT	60136	2797	41W-16N	E1
800	ELGN	60123	2799	36W-13N	E7
800	ElgT	60123	2799	36W-13N	E7
CO-21 Fabyan Pkwy					
600	WCHI	60185	3021	32W-0S	D6
700	BTVA	60510	3021	32W-0N	B6
700	GnvT	60510	3021	32W-0N	B6
CO-21 Geneva Rd					
10	MltT	60187	3023	27W-1N	D3
10	MltT	60187	3024	25W-0N	C3
10	MltT	60188	3023	26W-1N	E3
10	MltT	60188	3024	25W-0N	C3
10	MltT	60190	3023	27W-1N	D3
10	WNFD	60187	3023	26W-1N	E3
10	WNFD	60188	3023	26W-1N	E3
10	WNFD	60190	3023	26W-1N	E4
10	WnfT	60185	3023	26W-1N	E4
10	WnfT	60187	3023	27W-1N	D3
10	WnfT	60190	3023	26W-1N	E4
100	WNFD	60185	3023	26W-1N	E4
200	GNEN	60137	3025	23W-1N	A3
200	GNEN	60187	3025	23W-1N	A3
200	WHTN	60187	3024	25W-1N	B3
200	WHTN	60187	3025	23W-1N	A3
300	MltT	60137	3025	23W-1N	A3
700	WCHI	60185	3022	28W-0N	E4
700	WnfT	60185	3022	28W-0N	E4
CO-21 E Geneva Rd					
100	CLSM	60188	3024	24W-0N	C3
100	GNEN	60137	3024	23W-0N	E3
100	GNEN	60137	3025	23W-1N	A3
100	GNEN	60187	3025	23W-1N	A3
100	GNEN	60188	3024	23W-1N	E3
100	MltT	60188	3024	23W-1N	E3
100	WHTN	60137	3024	23W-1N	E3
100	WHTN	60187	3024	23W-0N	E3
100	WHTN	60187	3025	23W-1N	A3
100	WHTN	60188	3024	23W-1N	E3
600	MltT	60187	3024	23W-0N	E3
CO-21 W Geneva Rd					
100	MltT	60187	3024	24W-0N	C3
100	MltT	60188	3024	24W-0N	C3
100	WHTN	60187	3024	24W-0N	C3
100	WHTN	60188	3024	24W-0N	C3
CO-22 N Addison Rd					
100	WDDL	60191	2970	18W-5N	E1
200	WDDL	60191	2914	18W-6N	E7
300	AddT	60101	2970	18W-4N	E4
300	ADSN	60101	2970	18W-4N	E3
800	ADSN	60191	2970	18W-4N	E3
CO-22 S Addison Rd					
-	ADSN	60101	2970	18W-4N	E3
100	WDDL	60191	2970	18W-5N	E2
200	ADSN	60191	2970	18W-5N	E2
CO-22 Plank Rd					
10	PltT	60124	2852	39W-12N	E3
10	PltT	60140	2851	41W-12N	E2
10	PltT	60140	2852	39W-12N	E3
700	ElgT	60124	2853	38W-12N	A3
700	PltT	60124	2853	38W-12N	A3
CO-23 Gary Av					
-	BMDL	60108	2968	25W-4N	B3
-	BMDL	60133	2968	25W-4N	B3
-	BMDL	60188	2968	25W-4N	B4
-	HRPK	60133	2912	25W-7N	B5
-	ROSL	60133	2912	25W-6N	B6
10	BMDL	60108	2912	25W-6N	B7
10	BMDL	60172	2912	25W-6N	B7
10	BmdT	60108	2912	25W-6N	B7
10	BmdT	60172	2912	25W-6N	B7
10	MltT	60187	3024	25W-1N	B3
10	MltT	60188	3024	25W-1N	B3
10	WHTN	60187	3024	25W-1N	B3
100	CLSM	60188	3024	25W-2N	B1
300	CLSM	60188	2968	25W-2N	B7
400	BMDL	60172	2968	25W-5N	B1
500	BmdT	60172	2968	25W-5N	B1
500	HRPK	60172	2912	25W-6N	B6
500	ROSL	60172	2912	25W-6N	B6
1100	CLSM	60133	2968	25W-4N	B4
CO-23 N Gary Av					
-	CLSM	60188	3024	25W-2N	B1
-	HRPK	60133	2912	25W-7N	B4
-	HRPK	60172	2912	25W-7N	B4
200	ROSL	60172	2912	25W-6N	B6
200	SMBG	60172	2912	25W-6N	B6
200	SMBG	60193	2912	25W-6N	B6
1500	MltT	60187	3024	25W-0N	B5
CO-23 N Gary Av					
1500	WHTN	60187	3024	25W-0N	B5
CO-23 S Gary Av					
100	BMDL	60108	2968	25W-3N	B5
100	BMDL	60172	2968	25W-3N	B5
200	BMDL	60133	2968	25W-4N	B3
CO-23 N Naper Blvd					
-	LslT	60563	3142	25W-4S	B2
1500	NPVL	60563	3142	25W-4S	B1
CO-23 Naperville Rd					
10	LSLE	60532	3082	25W-4S	B7
10	LSLE	60563	3082	25W-4S	B7
10	LslT	60563	3082	25W-4S	B7
10	MltT	60187	3082	24W-3S	C5
10	MltT	60563	3082	25W-3S	B7
10	NPVL	60532	3082	25W-4S	B7
10	NPVL	60563	3082	25W-4S	B7
10	WHTN	60187	3082	24W-3S	C5
100	LslT	60532	3082	25W-4S	B7
100	LslT	60563	3142	25W-4S	B1
400	LslT	60532	3142	25W-4S	B1
400	LSLE	60532	3142	25W-4S	B1
400	LSLE	60563	3142	25W-4S	B1
400	LslT	60563	3142	25W-4S	B1
400	NPVL	60532	3142	25W-4S	B1
400	NPVL	60563	3142	25W-4S	B1
CO-23 N Naperville Rd					
1600	LslT	60563	3142	25W-4S	B2
1600	NPVL	60563	3142	25W-4S	B2
CO-23 S Naperville Rd					
700	WHTN	60187	3082	24W-3S	C6
2000	MltT	60187	3082	24W-3S	C5
CO-24 Byron Av					
10	BMDL	60101	2969	22W-4N	D3
10	BMDL	60108	2969	22W-4N	D3
10	BmdT	60101	2969	22W-4N	D3
700	BmdT	60108	2969	21W-4N	D3
CO-24 Jericho Rd					
10	AURA	60506	3198	39W-8S	E2
10	BRkT	60511	3196	44W-9S	D3
10	MTGY	60506	3198	39W-8S	E2
10	SgrT	60506	3197	41W-9S	E4
10	SgrT	60506	3198	39W-8S	E2
10	SgrT	60511	3196	46W-9S	A4
10	SgrT	60554	3196	46W-9S	A4
10	SgrT	60554	3197	43W-9S	A4
2400	AraT	60506	3198	39W-8S	E2
2400	AraT	60538	3198	39W-8S	E2
2400	AURA	60538	3198	39W-8S	E2
2400	MTGY	60538	3198	39W-8S	E2
CO-24 Meacham Rd					
-	EGVV	60143	2913	21W-7N	D3
-	ITSC	60143	2913	21W-7N	D3
-	ITSC	60157	2913	21W-7N	D3
CO-24 Medinah Rd					
10	BMDL	60101	2969	21W-5N	D2
10	BMDL	60108	2969	21W-5N	D2
10	BMDL	60157	2913	22W-5N	D7
10	BmdT	60101	2969	21W-5N	D2
10	BmdT	60143	2913	22W-7N	D5
10	BmdT	60157	2913	22W-6N	D7
300	ITSC	60143	2913	22W-6N	D6
300	ITSC	60157	2913	22W-6N	D6
300	ROSL	60143	2913	22W-7N	D4
300	ROSL	60157	2913	22W-7N	D4
400	BMDL	60157	2969	21W-4N	D3
400	BmdT	60108	2969	21W-4N	D3
400	BmdT	60157	2969	21W-4N	D3
700	BMDL	60101	2913	21W-5N	D7
CO-24 Walter Dr					
100	BMDL	60101	2969	22W-4N	D3
100	BMDL	60108	2969	22W-4N	D3
100	BmdT	60101	2969	22W-4N	D4
CO-25 Fairview Av					
3800	DRGV	60515	3084	18W-3S	E6
3800	OKBK	60523	3084	18W-3S	E6
3800	YkTp	60515	3084	18W-3S	E6
3800	YkTp	60523	3084	18W-3S	E6
CO-25 Meyers Rd					
-	YkTp	60148	3084	18W-2S	E2
-	YkTp	60181	3084	18W-2S	E2
-	YkTp	60515	3084	18W-3S	E6
2700	OKBK	60523	3084	18W-2S	E4
2700	YkTp	60523	3084	18W-2S	E3
CO-25 S Meyers Rd					
1200	YkTp	60148	3026	18W-1S	E7
1300	YkTp	60148	3084	18W-1S	E1
1600	OKTR	60181	3084	18W-1S	E1
1600	YkTp	60181	3084	18W-1S	E1
2000	YkTp	60523	3084	18W-2S	E2
CO-26 Hughes Rd					
10	BbyT	60119	3017	43W-0N	A5
10	BbyT	60119	3018	41W-0S	A7
400	ELBN	60119	3017	43W-0N	A5
800	BbyT	60134	3018	39W-0S	E7
CO-26 Thorndale Av					
-	BNVL	60191	2915	17W-7N	C4
10	AddT	60143	2914	19W-7N	D4
10	AddT	60191	2914	19W-7N	D4
10	BNVL	60106	2915	16W-6N	E5
10	CHCG	60106	2915	16W-6N	E5
10	ITSC	60191	2914	19W-7N	D4
10	WDDL	60191	2915	18W-7N	A4
300	ITSC	60143	2914	18W-7N	E4
300	WDDL	60143	2914	18W-7N	E4
300	WDDL	60191	2914	18W-7N	E4
CO-26 E Thorndale Av					
10	WDDL	60191	2915	16W-7N	D5
100	EGVV	60007	2915	17W-7N	B4
300	EGVV	60191	2915	17W-7N	C4
500	BNVL	60106	2915	17W-7N	C4
500	BNVL	60191	2915	17W-7N	C4
500	EGVV	60106	2915	17W-7N	C4
CO-27 Highlake Rd					
10	WnfT	60185	3023	28W-0N	A5
10	WnfT	60190	3023	28W-0N	A5
500	WNFD	60190	3023	27W-0S	C6
700	WCHI	60185	3022	28W-0N	E5
700	WnfT	60185	3022	28W-0N	E5
CO-27 Jewell Rd					
10	MltT	60187	3023	26W-0N	E5
10	MltT	60187	3024	26W-0N	A5
10	MltT	60190	3023	26W-0N	E5
10	WNFD	60187	3023	26W-0N	E5
10	WNFD	60190	3023	26W-0N	E5
600	WHTN	60187	3024	25W-0N	A5
CO-27 Prince Crossing Rd					
300	WCHI	60185	3022	29W-0N	E4
300	WnfT	60185	3022	29W-0N	E4
CO-28 N Villa Av					
10	AddT	60101	2971	17W-3N	A5
400	ADSN	60101	2971	17W-3N	B5
800	VLPK	60181	3027	17W-2N	B1
900	VLPK	60101	2971	17W-2N	B7
900	VLPK	60181	2971	17W-2N	B7
CO-28 S Villa Av					
10	AddT	60101	2971	17W-2N	B7
10	ADSN	60101	2971	17W-2N	B7
CO-28 S Villa Av					
400	AddT	60181	2971	17W-2N	B7
400	ADSN	60181	2971	17W-2N	B7
400	VLPK	60101	2971	17W-2N	B7
CO-28 Wood Dale Rd					
-	AddT	60101	2971	17W-3N	A5
-	ADSN	60101	2971	17W-3N	A5
CO-28 N Wood Dale Rd					
-	EGvT	60007	2915	18W-7N	A4
-	EGVV	60007	2915	18W-7N	A4
-	WDDL	60007	2915	18W-7N	A4
10	AddT	60101	2971	17W-4N	B4
10	AddT	60191	2971	17W-4N	B2
10	ADSN	60101	2971	17W-4N	B2
10	ADSN	60191	2971	17W-5N	B2
10	WDDL	60191	2971	18W-5N	A1
100	AddT	60106	2971	17W-4N	B4
200	WDDL	60191	2915	18W-7N	A4
400	AddT	60191	2915	17W-6N	A6
500	ADSN	60106	2971	17W-4N	B3
1400	EGVV	60191	2915	18W-7N	A4
CO-29 S Broadway Rd					
1300	MTGY	60538	3199	36W-9S	E5
CO-29 Greenbrook Blvd					
10	BRLT	60103	2911	27W-7N	D6
10	BRLT	60133	2911	27W-7N	D6
10	HRPK	60133	2911	27W-7N	D6
1300	BmdT	60133	2911	26W-7N	E5
CO-29 E Mill St					
10	MTGY	60538	3199	36W-9S	D4
CO-29 Montgomery Rd					
100	MTGY	60538	3199	36W-9S	D5
200	MTGY	60538	3200	35W-9S	C4
300	AURA	60505	3200	35W-9S	A4
300	MTGY	60505	3200	35W-9S	C4
500	AraT	60505	3200	35W-9S	C4
500	AraT	60538	3200	35W-9S	C4
1400	AraT	60504	3200	34W-9S	E4
1400	AURA	60504	3200	34W-9S	E4
1400	MTGY	60504	3200	34W-9S	E4
CO-29 Stearns Rd					
10	BRLT	60103	2910	30W-7N	A5
10	BRLT	60120	2909	32W-7N	D5
10	BRLT	60120	2910	31W-7N	A5
10	BRLT	60184	2909	31W-7N	E5
10	SchT	60120	2909	32W-7N	D5
10	WynT	60120	2909	32W-7N	D5
10	WynT	60184	2909	31W-7N	E5
100	BRLT	60103	2911	28W-6N	B6
500	WynT	60103	2911	28W-6N	A6
CO-29 E Stearns Rd					
-	BRLT	60133	2911	27W-7N	D6
-	HRPK	60103	2911	27W-7N	C6
-	HRPK	60133	2911	27W-7N	C6
200	BRLT	60103	2911	27W-6N	B6
200	WynT	60103	2911	27W-6N	B6
CO-29 W Stearns Rd					
100	BRLT	60103	2910	30W-7N	B5
500	BRLT	60120	2910	30W-7N	A5
CO-30 Huntley Rd					
10	CPVL	60110	2746	39W-19N	A2
10	CPVL	60118	2746	39W-19N	A2
10	DndT	60110	2746	39W-19N	A2
10	DndT	60118	2746	39W-19N	A2
10	RtdT	60118	2746	39W-19N	A2
10	RtdT	60142	2746	39W-19N	A2
200	RtdT	60118	2745	39W-19N	E2
200	RtdT	60142	2745	39W-19N	E2
300	CPVL	60110	2747	36W-17N	A6
300	DndT	60118	2747	36W-17N	A7
300	WDND	60118	2747	36W-17N	A7
500	GfnT	60102	2745	39W-19N	E2
500	GfnT	60142	2745	39W-19N	E2
500	RtdT	60102	2745	39W-19N	E2
CO-30 W Main St					
200	CPVL	60110	2800	34W-16N	D1
200	CPVL	60118	2800	35W-16N	D1
200	WDND	60118	2800	35W-16N	D1
CO-31 87th St					
1600	DGvT	60516	3206	20W-10S	B4
1600	DGvT	60517	3206	20W-10S	B4
1600	DGvT	60561	3206	20W-10S	B4
1600	DRN	60561	3206	20W-10S	B4
1600	WDRG	60517	3206	20W-10S	B4
1600	WDRG	60561	3206	20W-10S	B4
2800	DRN	60516	3206	20W-10S	B4
3200	DRN	60517	3206	20W-10S	B4
CO-31 Lemont Rd					
700	DGvT	60516	3206	20W-9S	C4
700	DGvT	60561	3206	20W-9S	C4
700	DRN	60516	3206	20W-9S	C4
700	DRN	60561	3206	20W-9S	C4
8300	DGvT	60517	3206	20W-9S	C3
8300	DRN	60517	3206	20W-9S	C3
CO-31 Plainfield Rd					
-	DGvT	60517	3206	19W-9S	C3
-	DRN	60517	3206	19W-9S	C3
10	DRGV	60516	3206	19W-9S	D3
10	DRGV	60561	3206	19W-9S	D3
10	DRN	60516	3206	19W-9S	D3
10	DRN	60561	3206	19W-9S	D3
100	BRRG	60527	3146	15W-7S	B6
100	DRN	60527	3145	16W-7S	E7
100	DRN	60561	3145	16W-7S	E7
100	WLBK	60527	3145	16W-7S	E7
100	WLBK	60527	3146	15W-7S	B6
100	WLBK	60561	3145	16W-7S	E7
200	DGvT	60516	3206	18W-9S	E3
300	DRN	60561	3207	18W-8S	B2
400	DRN	60527	3207	17W-8S	D1
400	WLBK	60527	3207	17W-8S	D1
400	WLBK	60561	3207	17W-8S	D1
500	DGvT	60561	3206	19W-9S	C3
1500	DRGV	60516	3207	18W-8S	A2
1500	DRN	60516	3207	18W-8S	A2
1700	DRGV	60561	3207	18W-8S	A2
CO-32 Mill St					
-	NPVL	60555	3081	27W-4S	C7
-	NPVL	60563	3081	27W-4S	C7
-	WNVL	60555	3081	27W-4S	C7
-	WNVL	60563	3081	27W-4S	C7
10	NPVL	60563	3141	27W-4S	C1
10	WNVL	60555	3141	27W-4S	C1
10	WNVL	60563	3141	27W-4S	C1
CO-32 N Mill St					
900	NPVL	60563	3141	27W-5S	C3
1400	NpvT	60563	3141	27W-5S	C2
1900	WNVL	60555	3141	27W-4S	C1
1900	WNVL	60563	3141	27W-4S	C1
CO-32 Plato Rd					
10	PltT	60124	2851	43W-10N	A6
10	PltT	60140	2851	43W-10N	A6
400	PltT	60124	2852	41W-10N	A6
CO-32 Warrenville Rd					
-	NPVL	60555	3081	27W-4S	C7
-	NPVL	60563	3081	27W-4S	C7
CO-32 Warrenville Rd					
-	WNVL	60563	3081	27W-4S	C7
100	WNVL	60555	3081	27W-3S	B6
CO-33 75th St					
-	AURA	60504	3202	28W-8S	E2
-	AURA	60564	3202	30W-8S	B2
-	NPVL	60540	3203	28W-8S	A2
-	NPVL	60564	3203	27W-8S	B2
-	NPVL	60565	3203	28W-8S	A2
-	NpvT	60504	3202	30W-8S	B2
10	LslT	60540	3204	25W-8S	A2
10	LslT	60565	3204	24W-8S	E2
10	NPVL	60540	3204	25W-8S	C2
10	NPVL	60565	3204	25W-8S	A2
10	WLBK	60527	3207	16W-8S	E1
100	DRN	60527	3207	16W-8S	D1
100	DRN	60561	3207	16W-8S	E1
200	DRGV	60516	3206	19W-8S	E1
200	DRN	60516	3206	19W-8S	E1
400	DGvT	60516	3206	19W-8S	C1
400	DRGV	60561	3206	19W-8S	E1
400	DRN	60561	3206	19W-8S	E1
400	LslT	60565	3205	23W-8S	A2
400	NPVL	60540	3202	29W-8S	D2
400	NPVL	60564	3202	29W-8S	D2
400	NpvT	60564	3202	29W-8S	C2
400	WLBK	60561	3207	17W-8S	D1
500	LslT	60540	3205	22W-8S	B2
500	WDRG	60516	3206	19W-8S	C1
600	AURA	60540	3202	30W-8S	C2
600	NpvT	60564	3203	28W-8S	A2
1000	WDRG	60517	3206	20W-8S	C1
1500	DRGV	60516	3207	18W-8S	A1
1500	DRN	60516	3207	18W-8S	A1
2100	WDRG	60517	3205	23W-8S	A2
2900	LslT	60517	3205	22W-8S	D2
CO-33 Rippburger Rd					
700	PltT	60124	2851	41W-10N	E6
CO-33 Russell Rd					
10	PltT	60124	2852	41W-10N	A5
300	PltT	60124	2851	41W-10N	E5
CO-34 31st St					
500	DRGV	60515	3084	19W-2S	D4
500	DRGV	60523	3084	19W-2S	D4
500	OKBK	60523	3084	18W-2S	E4
500	YkTp	60515	3084	19W-2S	D4
500	YkTp	60523	3084	19W-2S	D4
CO-34 Oak Brook Rd					
100	OKBK	60523	3086	15W-3S	B4
100	PvsT	60523	3086	15W-2S	C4
800	OKBK	60523	3085	17W-3S	B4
2000	YkTp	60523	3085	17W-2S	B4
2800	OKBK	60523	3084	19W-3S	D4
3000	DRGV	60523	3084	18W-2S	E4
3000	YkTp	60523	3084	19W-3S	D4
CO-34 Randall Rd					
-	SCRL	60174	2963	36W-3N	D5
-	SCRL	60175	2963	36W-3N	D5
10	ALGN	60102	2746	36W-19N	E3
10	ALGN	60118	2746	36W-19N	E3
10	DndT	60102	2746	36W-19N	E3
10	DndT	60118	2746	37W-19N	E2
10	DndT	60118	2799	37W-16N	E1
10	ELGN	60118	2853	36W-9N	E7
10	ELGN	60123	2907	37W-6N	D7
10	ELGN	60124	2799	37W-16N	E2
10	ELGN	60124	2853	36W-9N	E7
10	ELGN	60124	2907	37W-6N	D7
10	ElgT	60123	2907	37W-6N	D7
10	ElgT	60124	2853	36W-9N	E7
10	ElgT	60124	2907	37W-6N	D7
10	SchT	60174	2963	37W-5N	D2
10	SchT	60175	2963	37W-5N	D2
10	WDND	60118	2746	37W-17N	E7
10	WDND	60118	2799	37W-16N	E1
100	SCRL	60134	3019	37W-2N	D1
100	SCRL	60174	3019	37W-2N	D1
100	SCRL	60175	3019	37W-2N	D1
200	GNVA	60134	3019	37W-2N	D1
200	SchT	60175	2907	37W-6N	D7
200	SEGN	60124	2907	36W-8N	D3
200	SEGN	60177	2907	37W-6N	D7
300	CPVL	60110	2746	37W-19N	E2
300	CPVL	60118	2746	36W-17N	E7
300	SEGN	60175	2907	36W-8N	D4
300	WDND	60110	2746	36W-17N	E7
900	GNVA	60174	3019	37W-2N	D1
2300	DndT	60110	2746	37W-19N	E2
CO-34 N Randall Rd					
-	BtvT	60510	3077	37W-3S	C6
-	BtvT	60539	3077	37W-3S	C6
-	BtvT	60542	3077	37W-3S	C6
-	DndT	60123	2799	37W-14N	E6
-	NARA	60506	3137	37W-4S	C2
-	NARA	60539	3077	37W-3S	C6
-	NARA	60542	3137	37W-4S	C1
10	AraT	60542	3077	37W-4S	C7
10	AURA	60506	3137	37W-4S	C1
10	BTVA	60510	3077	37W-1S	D1
10	DndT	60124	2799	37W-14N	E6
10	ELGN	60118	2799	37W-14N	E6
10	ELGN	60123	2799	37W-14N	E6
10	ELGN	60123	2853	37W-12N	D2
10	ELGN	60124	2799	37W-14N	E6
10	ElgT	60123	2799	36W-13N	E7
10	ElgT	60123	2853	37W-12N	D2
10	ElgT	60124	2799	36W-13N	E7
10	ElgT	60124	2853	37W-12N	D2
10	NARA	60542	3077	37W-4S	C7
10	SYHW	60118	2799	37W-14N	E6
10	WDND	60118	2799	37W-16N	E3
100	SCRL	60174	2963	37W-3N	D7
100	SCRL	60175	2963	37W-3N	D7
200	BTVA	60510	3019	37W-0S	D7
200	DndT	60118	2799	37W-16N	E2
200	SYHW	60124	2799	37W-15N	E4
300	SchT	60174	2963	36W-3N	D6
300	SchT	60175	2963	36W-3N	D6
400	GnvT	60134	3019	37W-0S	D7
400	GnvT	60510	3019	37W-0S	D7
500	BTVA	60134	3019	37W-0S	D7
500	ELGN	60124	2853	37W-12N	D2
500	GNVA	60134	3019	37W-0S	D7
1700	AURA	60542	3137	37W-5S	C2
CO-34 S Randall Rd					
-	BtvT	60542	3077	37W-3S	C6
-	NARA	60539	3077	37W-3S	C6
-	NARA	60542	3077	37W-3S	C6
10	BTVA	60510	3077	37W-2S	D4
10	BTVA	60539	3077	37W-2S	D4
10	BtvT	60539	3077	37W-2S	D4
10	SchT	60174	2963	36W-2N	D7
10	SchT	60175	2963	36W-2N	D7
10	SCRL	60174	2963	36W-2N	D7
10	SCRL	60175	2963	36W-2N	D7
100	ELGN	60123	2853	36W-11N	E5
CO-34 S Randall Rd					
100	ELGN	60124	2853	36W-11N	E5
200	BtvT	60510	3077	37W-2S	D4
300	SchT	60174	3019	36W-2N	D1
300	SchT	60175	3019	36W-2N	D1
300	SCRL	60174	3019	36W-2N	D1
300	SCRL	60175	3019	36W-2N	D1
1400	GNVA	60134	3019	36W-0N	D5
1500	ALGN	60102	2746	36W-19N	E2
1800	BTVA	60134	3019	37W-0S	D6
1800	BTVA	60510	3019	37W-0S	D6
1800	GnvT	60134	3019	37W-0S	D6
1800	GnvT	60510	3019	37W-0S	D6
CO-35 55th St					
-	CNHL	60521	3145	16W-6S	E3
-	DGvT	60521	3145	16W-6S	E3
-	DRGV	60515	3145	18W-5S	A3
-	DRGV	60559	3145	18W-5S	A3
-	HNDL	60521	3145	16W-6S	E3
-	WTMT	60559	3145	18W-5S	A3
100	CNHL	60514	3145	16W-5S	D3
100	DRGV	60515	3144	19W-6S	D3
100	DRGV	60516	3144	19W-6S	D3
100	DRGV	60559	3144	19W-6S	D3
100	WTMT	60559	3144	19W-6S	D3
200	DGvT	60514	3145	17W-5S	D3
CO-35 E 55th St					
10	HNDL	60521	3146	15W-6S	B3
10	WTMT	60559	3145	17W-5S	B3
300	CNHL	60514	3145	17W-5S	C3
300	WTMT	60514	3145	17W-5S	C3
CO-35 W 55th St					
-	CNHL	60514	3145	16W-6S	E3
-	CNHL	60521	3145	16W-6S	E3
10	HNDL	60521	3146	15W-5S	A3
10	WTMT	60559	3145	18W-5S	B3
300	DRGV	60515	3145	18W-5S	A3
300	DRGV	60559	3145	18W-5S	A3
300	WTMT	60515	3145	18W-5S	A3
500	DGvT	60521	3145	17W-6S	B3
500	HNDL	60521	3145	17W-6S	B3
CO-36 Allen Rd					
10	HPSR	60140	2795	47W-16N	E1
CO-36 Getty Rd					
-	CrlT	60140	2743	45W-20N	A1
-	CrlT	60142	2743	45W-20N	A1
-	HPSR	60140	2743	45W-20N	A1
-	HshT	60140	2743	45W-20N	A1
CO-36 Harmony Rd					
10	HPSR	60140	2795	47W-16N	D1
10	HshT	60140	2795	47W-16N	D1
CO-36 N Main St					
2200	CLSM	60188	3024	24W-1N	C3
2200	MltT	60188	3024	24W-1N	C3
2200	WHTN	60187	3024	24W-1N	C3
2200	WHTN	60188	3024	24W-1N	C3
CO-36 Schmale Rd					
-	BMDL	60188	2968	24W-4N	D4
-	CLSM	60108	2968	24W-4N	D4
10	BMDL	60108	2968	24W-4N	D4
10	BMDL	60139	2968	24W-4N	D4
10	GLHT	60108	2968	24W-4N	D4
10	GLHT	60139	2968	24W-4N	D4
100	CLSM	60188	2968	24W-3N	D6
100	CLSM	60188	3024	24W-2N	D1
100	GLHT	60188	2968	24W-3N	D6
400	CLSM	60139	3024	24W-2N	D1
400	GLHT	60139	3024	24W-2N	D1
400	GLHT	60188	3024	24W-2N	D1
1800	CLSM	60139	2968	24W-3N	D5
CO-36 N Schmale Rd					
100	CLSM	60139	3024	24W-2N	D1
100	CLSM	60188	3024	24W-2N	D1
100	GLHT	60139	3024	24W-2N	D1
100	GLHT	60188	3024	24W-2N	D1
CO-36 S Schmale Rd					
100	CLSM	60188	3024	24W-1N	C3
100	GLHT	60188	3024	24W-1N	D2
200	MltT	60188	3024	24W-1N	C3
400	WHTN	60188	3024	24W-1N	C3
CO-36 N State St					
100	HPSR	60140	2795	47W-15N	E3
CO-36 S State St					
100	HPSR	60140	2795	46W-16N	E2
CO-37 Crescent Blvd					
200	GNEN	60137	3025	21W-0N	E4
200	LMBD	60137	3025	21W-0N	E4
200	LMBD	60148	3025	21W-0N	E4
200	MltT	60137	3025	21W-0N	E4
CO-38 63rd St					
-	LslT	60517	3143	21W-7S	E5
10	DGvT	60527	3145	16W-6S	E5
10	DGvT	60527	3146	16W-6S	A5
10	WLBK	60527	3145	16W-6S	E5
10	WLBK	60527	3146	16W-6S	A5
400	DGvT	60559	3145	17W-6S	C5
400	WTMT	60527	3145	17W-6S	C5
400	WTMT	60559	3145	17W-6S	C5
800	DRGV	60516	3144	19W-6S	D5
1400	DGvT	60516	3144	20W-7S	B5
1900	LslT	60516	3144	20W-7S	A5
2100	DRGV	60516	3143	21W-7S	E5
2100	LslT	60516	3143	21W-7S	E5
2200	WDRG	60516	3143	21W-7S	E5
2200	WDRG	60517	3143	21W-7S	E5
CO-38 E 63rd St					
10	WTMT	60527	3145	17W-6S	B5
10	WTMT	60559	3145	17W-6S	B5
CO-38 W 63rd St					
10	WTMT	60559	3145	16W-7S	D5
400	DGvT	60516	3144	19W-6S	E5
400	DRGV	60516	3144	19W-6S	E5
400	WTMT	60516	3144	19W-6S	E5
400	WTMT	60559	3144	21W-7S	A5
CO-38 Hobson Rd					
-	LslT	60517	3143	21W-7S	D6
-	WDRG	60517	3143	21W-7S	D6
CO-40 College Rd					
-	LslT	60532	3142	24W-7S	C7
-	LslT	60540	3142	24W-7S	C7
-	LslT	60540	3204	24W-7S	C1
-	NPVL	60532	3142	24W-7S	C7
-	NPVL	60540	3142	24W-7S	C7
-	NPVL	60540	3204	24W-7S	C1
5600	LSLE	60532	3142	24W-6S	E4
CO-40 Getty Rd					
-	CrlT	60140	2743	45W-20N	A1
-	CrlT	60142	2743	45W-20N	A1
-	HPSR	60140	2743	45W-20N	A1
-	HshT	60140	2743	45W-20N	A1
CO-40 Penny Rd					
10	BNHL	60010	2801	32W-16N	E1
10	BNHL	60118	2801	32W-16N	E1
10	CPVL	60110	2801	32W-16N	E1
10	CPVL	60118	2801	32W-16N	E1
10	EDND	60110	2801	32W-16N	E1

STREET Block	City	ZIP	Map#	CGS	Grid
CO-40 Penny Rd					
10	EDND	60118	2801	32W-16N	E1
CO-40 Wehrli Rd					
100	LslT	60540	3204	24W-8S	C1
100	NPVL	60540	3204	24W-8S	C1
200	LslT	60565	3204	24W-8S	C2
CO-40 Yackley Av					
4300	LSLE	60532	3142	24W-7S	D6
CO-41 N 16000W Rd					
6700	EsxT	60481	4031	30W-46S	D7
6700	EsxT	60935	4031	30W-46S	D7
6700	RedT	60481	4031	30W-46S	D7
CO-41 Hobson Rd					
2200	DRGV	60516	3143	21W-6S	E4
2200	LslT	60516	3143	21W-6S	E4
CO-41 Keslinger Rd					
10	BbyT	60119	3017	42W-1N	D4
10	BbyT	60119	3018	39W-1N	E4
10	BbyT	60134	3018	39W-0N	E4
10	ELBN	60119	3017	42W-1N	D4
10	GNVA	60134	3019	38W-0N	A4
10	GnvT	60134	3019	38W-0N	A4
500	BbyT	60134	3019	38W-1N	A4
CO-43 County Farm Rd					
-	CLSM	60133	2967	27W-4N	D3
10	HRPK	60133	2911	27W-6N	D7
10	HRPK	60133	2967	27W-3N	D6
10	MltT	60187	3023	26W-0S	D6
10	MltT	60190	3023	26W-0N	D6
10	WHTN	60187	3023	26W-0S	D6
10	WNFD	60190	3023	26W-0N	D6
10	WnfT	60185	3023	27W-2N	D2
10	WynT	60133	2911	27W-6N	D7
10	WynT	60133	2967	27W-6N	D1
10	WynT	60185	3023	27W-2N	D1
100	WNFD	60185	3023	27W-1N	D3
100	WnfT	60190	3023	27W-1N	D3
300	CLSM	60185	2967	27W-2N	D7
300	CLSM	60188	2967	27W-2N	D7
300	WynT	60185	2967	27W-2N	D7
300	WynT	60188	2967	27W-2N	D7
500	BRLT	60103	2911	27W-7N	D5
500	BRLT	60133	2911	27W-7N	D5
500	HRPK	60103	2911	27W-7N	D5
CO-43 N County Farm Rd					
-	CLSM	60185	2967	27W-3N	D7
-	MltT	60187	3023	27W-1N	D3
-	MltT	60190	3023	27W-1N	D3
-	WynT	60185	2967	27W-3N	D7
-	WynT	60188	2967	27W-3N	D7
100	WHTN	60187	3023	27W-1N	D3
900	CLSM	60188	2967	27W-3N	D5
1200	CLSM	60133	2967	27W-4N	D3
1200	HRPK	60133	2967	27W-4N	D3
CO-43 S County Farm Rd					
100	WHTN	60187	3023	26W-0S	D7
400	WHTN	60187	3081	26W-0S	D1
CO-45 Allen Rd					
10	HshT	60140	2795	47W-16N	D1
500	HPSR	60140	2795	47W-16N	D1
CO-46 Burlington Rd					
100	BrlT	60140	2795	48W-13N	B7
100	HshT	60140	2795	48W-13N	B7
CO-46 Walker Rd					
10	BrlT	60140	2795	48W-14N	A6
10	HshT	60140	2795	49W-16N	A2
CO-47 Highland Av					
10	ELGN	60123	2853	37W-12N	D2
10	ELGN	60124	2853	37W-12N	D2
10	ElgT	60123	2853	37W-12N	D2
10	ElgT	60124	2853	38W-12N	B1
10	PltT	60124	2798	39W-13N	D7
10	PltT	60124	2852	39W-13N	E1
10	PltT	60124	2852	38W-12N	B1
10	RtdT	60124	2798	40W-14N	C6
200	RtdT	60140	2798	40W-14N	C6
CO-48 Scott Rd					
10	BRkT	60554	3134	44W-4S	D1
10	SgrT	60554	3134	44W-4S	D1
CO-50 Schick Rd					
100	HRPK	60133	2967	27W-5N	D2
400	BMDL	60108	2968	25W-5N	A2
400	BMDL	60172	2968	25W-5N	A2
400	BmdT	60108	2967	26W-5N	E2
400	BmdT	60133	2967	26W-5N	E2
400	BmdT	60172	2968	25W-5N	A2
500	BmdT	60108	2968	25W-5N	A2
500	BmdT	60133	2968	25W-5N	A2
500	WynT	60133	2967	26W-5N	D2
CO-51 Dittman Rd					
10	CmpT	60124	2905	42W-8N	D4
10	PltT	60124	2851	42W-10N	D6
10	PltT	60124	2905	42W-7N	D5
400	CmpT	60175	2905	42W-7N	D6
CO-51 Herrick Rd					
10	NPVL	60555	3081	27W-4S	D7
10	NPVL	60563	3081	27W-4S	D7
10	WnfT	60555	3081	27W-3S	D5
10	WNVL	60555	3081	27W-4S	D7
10	WNVL	60563	3081	27W-4S	D7
600	WHTN	60187	3081	27W-2S	D4
600	WnfT	60187	3081	27W-2S	D4
CO-53 Dean St					
10	CmpT	60175	2962	39W-4N	E5
800	CmpT	60175	2963	39W-4N	A4
800	SchT	60175	2963	39W-4N	A4
CO-53 W Diehl Rd					
-	NPVL	60563	3140	29W-4S	E1
27500	NpvT	60563	3141	27W-4S	C1
27500	WNVL	60563	3141	27W-4S	C1
28200	NPVL	60563	3141	28W-4S	A1
28200	WNVL	60555	3141	28W-4S	A1
CO-54 Collins Av					
-	ADSN	60101	2969	21W-3N	E6
-	BmdT	60101	2969	21W-3N	E6
-	BmdT	60148	2969	21W-3N	E6
CO-54 Swift Rd					
-	MltT	60148	3025	21W-1N	E1
10	ADSN	60101	2969	21W-2N	E7
10	BmdT	60101	2969	21W-2N	E7
10	BmdT	60148	2969	21W-2N	E7
10	BmdT	60148	3025	21W-2N	E1
CO-56 Woodward Av					
7500	WDRG	60517	3206	21W-9S	A4
8300	DRN	60517	3206	21W-9S	A4
8300	DRN	60561	3206	21W-9S	A4
CO-59 Tyrrell Rd					
10	GLBT	60136	2799	38W-15N	C5
10	RtdT	60136	2799	38W-16N	B3
200	RtdT	60118	2799	38W-16N	B2
500	DndT	60124	2799	38W-15N	C5
500	DndT	60136	2799	37W-14N	C6
500	GLBT	60124	2799	38W-15N	C5
CO-61 W Bartlett Rd					
2100	BRLT	60103	2909	33W-8N	B3
2100	BRLT	60120	2909	33W-8N	B3
2100	HnrT	60120	2909	33W-8N	B3
2100	SEGN	60103	2909	33W-8N	B3
2100	SEGN	60120	2909	33W-8N	B3
2100	SEGN	60177	2909	33W-8N	B3
CO-63 Freeman Rd					
10	HTLY	60142	2744	41W-18N	E5
10	RtdT	60136	2745	39W-17N	E6
10	RtdT	60142	2745	39W-17N	E6
100	GLBT	60118	2746	39W-17N	A6
100	GLBT	60136	2745	39W-17N	E6
100	GLBT	60136	2746	39W-17N	A6
100	GLBT	60142	2745	39W-17N	E6
100	GLBT	60142	2746	39W-17N	A6
100	RtdT	60118	2746	39W-17N	A6
100	RtdT	60136	2746	39W-17N	A6
100	RtdT	60142	2746	39W-17N	A6
400	HTLY	60142	2745	41W-18N	A6
CO-69 Empire Rd					
10	CmpT	60175	2961	43W-5N	A2
10	CmpT	60175	2962	41W-6N	A1
CO-71 Mooseheart Rd					
10	BtvT	60539	3077	37W-3S	D6
10	BtvT	60542	3077	37W-3S	D6
10	NARA	60542	3077	37W-3S	D6
200	BtvT	60510	3077	37W-3S	C6
200	NARA	60539	3077	37W-3S	D6
CO-74					
-	JLET	60433	3587	23W-26S	A4
-	JLET	60436	3587	23W-26S	A4
-	JltT	60433	3587	23W-26S	A4
-	JltT	60436	3587	23W-26S	A4
CO-77 N Farnsworth Av					
2300	AraT	60504	3138	34W-4S	E1
2300	AURA	60502	3138	34W-4S	E1
2300	AURA	60504	3138	34W-4S	E1
2600	AURA	60502	3078	33W-4S	E7
CO-77 Kirk Rd					
-	BTVA	60510	3020	33W-0S	E7
-	GnvT	60134	3020	33W-0S	E7
10	GNVA	60134	3021	33W-2N	A2
10	GnvT	60134	3021	33W-2N	A2
10	SCRL	60134	3021	33W-2N	A2
10	SCRL	60174	3021	33W-2N	A2
100	GNVA	60185	3021	33W-1N	A4
100	GnvT	60185	3021	33W-1N	A4
CO-77 N Kirk Rd					
-	SchT	60174	2965	33W-5N	A3
-	SchT	60184	2965	33W-5N	A3
-	SCRL	60174	2965	33W-3N	A5
10	BTVA	60510	3078	33W-1S	E1
600	BTVA	60510	3020	33W-0S	E7
1200	GnvT	60134	3020	33W-0S	E6
CO-77 S Kirk Rd					
-	AURA	60502	3078	33W-3S	E6
-	BTVA	60502	3078	33W-2S	E5
-	BtvT	60502	3078	33W-3S	E5
10	BTVA	60510	3078	33W-3S	E6
10	BtvT	60510	3078	33W-3S	E6
300	SCRL	60174	2965	33W-3N	A6
700	SCRL	60174	3021	33W-2N	A1
CO-78 Bliss Rd					
10	BbyT	60506	3076	40W-2S	B4
10	BbyT	60510	3076	40W-2S	B4
10	BbyT	60554	3076	40W-2S	B4
10	SgrT	60554	3135	41W-5S	D3
10	SRGV	60506	3135	42W-6S	D4
10	SRGV	60554	3135	41W-5S	D3
100	SgrT	60506	3075	41W-3S	E7
100	SgrT	60506	3135	41W-5S	D3
100	SgrT	60554	3075	41W-3S	E7
300	BbyT	60506	3075	41W-3S	E7
300	BbyT	60554	3075	41W-3S	E7
500	BbyT	60119	3076	40W-2S	B4
CO-80 Corron Rd					
10	CmpT	60175	2906	40W-6N	C7
10	CmpT	60175	2962	40W-6N	B1
10	PltT	60124	2906	40W-9N	C2
10	PltT	60175	2906	40W-8N	C4
CO-81					
200	CmpT	60175	2962	40W-4N	C3
CO-81 Brown Rd					
800	CmpT	60175	2962	40W-5N	B2
CO-81 Lafox Rd					
10	BbyT	60119	3018	40W-1N	B4
10	CmpT	60119	3018	40W-2N	B1
10	CmpT	60175	2962	40W-3N	C5
200	CmpT	60119	2962	40W-3N	B7
CO-81 Old Lafox Rd					
10	CmpT	60175	2962	40W-3N	B7
CO-83 Orchard Rd					
1100	AraT	60506	3198	39W-9S	E4
1100	AraT	60538	3198	39W-9S	E4
1100	AURA	60506	3198	39W-9S	E4
1100	AURA	60538	3198	39W-9S	E4
1100	MTGY	60506	3198	39W-9S	E4
1100	MTGY	60538	3198	39W-9S	E4
CO-84 Kaneville Rd					
10	GNVA	60134	3019	37W-0N	B6
10	GnvT	60134	3019	38W-0N	A6
CO-84 Peck Rd					
10	GNVA	60134	3019	38W-2N	B1
10	GnvT	60134	3019	38W-2N	B1
400	SCRL	60175	2963	38W-3N	B7
900	GnvT	60175	3019	37W-1N	B2
900	SchT	60175	3019	37W-1N	B2
900	SCRL	60175	3019	37W-1N	B2
CO-A1 W Russell Rd					
11900	BtnT	53158	2362	12W-43N	B4
11900	BtnT	60099	2362	12W-43N	B4
11900	PTPR	53158	2362	12W-43N	B4
12600	PTPR	60099	2362	12W-43N	B4
13000	NptT	53158	2362	13W-43N	A4
13000	NptT	60099	2362	13W-43N	A4
13400	NptT	60099	2361	15W-42N	A5
13400	PTPR	53158	2361	15W-42N	A5
13400	WDWH	53158	2361	15W-42N	A5
13400	WDWH	60099	2361	15W-42N	A5
13400	ZION	60099	2361	15W-42N	A5
13800	PTPR	60099	2361	15W-42N	A5
16100	NptT	60099	2360	16W-42N	E5
16100	WDWH	60099	2360	16W-42N	E5
CO-A2 128th St					
18100	AntT	60002	2359	20W-43N	A4
18100	BtlT	53104	2359	20W-43N	A4
18100	BtlT	53142	2359		B4
18100	BtlT	60002	2359	20W-43N	A4
18400	AntT	53104	2358	20W-43N	E4
18400	AntT	53104	2359	20W-43N	A4
18400	AntT	60002	2358	20W-43N	E4
18400	BtlT	53104	2358	20W-43N	E4
CO-A2 North Av					
10	ANTH	60002	2358	21W-43N	D4
10	AntT	60002	2358	22W-43N	B5
200	ANTH	60002	2357	23W-42N	E5
CO-A2 W North Av					
21400	ANTH	60002	2358	21W-43N	D4
21400	AntT	53104	2358	21W-43N	E4
21400	AntT	60002	2358	21W-43N	E4
21400	BtlT	53104	2358	21W-43N	E4
21400	BtlT	60002	2358	21W-43N	E4
CO-A4 9th St					
1900	WPHR	60096	2363	10W-42N	A6
3100	BtnT	60096	2363	10W-42N	A6
3400	BtnT	60096	2362	11W-42N	E6
3400	WPHR	60096	2362	11W-42N	E6
CO-A4 W 9th St					
11400	BtnT	60096	2362	11W-42N	D6
11400	WPHR	60096	2362	11W-42N	D6
11600	BtnT	60099	2362	12W-42N	C6
11600	WPHR	60099	2362	11W-42N	D6
11700	ZION	60099	2362	12W-42N	C6
CO-A6 21st St					
2700	ZION	60099	2421	11W-41N	E2
3600	BHPK	60099	2421	12W-41N	C2
4600	BtnT	60099	2421	12W-41N	B2
4800	WDWH	60099	2421	12W-41N	B2
CO-A6 W 21st St					
12800	BHPK	60099	2421	12W-41N	B2
12800	BtnT	60099	2421	12W-41N	B2
12800	WDWH	60083	2421	11W-40N	E2
12800	WDWH	60099	2421	12W-41N	A2
13200	ZION	60099	2421	11W-40N	E2
13400	BtnT	60083	2420	13W-40N	E2
13400	BtnT	60099	2420	13W-40N	E2
13400	WDWH	60083	2420	13W-40N	E2
13400	ZION	60099	2420	13W-41N	E2
13800	NptT	60083	2420	13W-40N	E2
CO-A7 Main St Rd					
100	BtnT	60081	2414	29W-39N	D5
100	FXLK	60081	2414	29W-39N	D5
CO-A7 N State Park Rd					
7000	BtnT	60081	2414	28W-39N	D6
7000	FXLK	60020	2414	28W-39N	D6
7000	FXLK	60081	2414	28W-39N	D6
CO-A8 33rd St					
1200	ZION	60099	2422	10W-39N	B5
2300	ZION	60099	2421	11W-39N	D5
2400	BHPK	60099	2421	11W-39N	D5
CO-A8 W 33rd St					
11500	BHPK	60099	2421	11W-39N	D5
11500	ZION	60099	2421	11W-39N	D5
12000	BHPK	60087	2421	12W-39N	C5
CO-A9 W Wadsworth Rd					
2200	BHPK	60087	2421	11W-38N	D6
2200	BHPK	60099	2421	13W-38N	A6
2200	WKGN	60087	2421	11W-39N	D6
2200	WKGN	60099	2421	13W-38N	A6
4000	NptT	60083	2420	13W-39N	E6
4000	WDWH	60083	2420	15W-38N	A6
10000	BHPK	60099	2422	10W-39N	A6
12600	BHPK	60083	2421	12W-39N	A6
12600	WDWH	60083	2421	12W-39N	A6
15800	NptT	60083	2419	16W-38N	D6
15800	WDWH	60083	2419	15W-39N	E6
16100	OMCK	60083	2419	16W-38N	D6
CO-A10 Grass Lake Rd					
2000	LkvT	60046	2418	20W-39N	A6
2000	LNHT	60046	2418	20W-39N	A6
CO-A10 W Grass Lake Rd					
100	FXLK	60020	2415	28W-38N	A6
100	FXLK	60081	2415	28W-38N	A6
600	FXLK	60020	2414	28W-38N	E6
19000	OMCK	60046	2418	19W-38N	D6
19000	OMCK	60083	2418	19W-38N	D6
20700	LkvT	60046	2417	22W-39N	B4
20700	LkvT	60046	2418	19W-38N	C6
20700	LNHT	60046	2417	22W-39N	B4
20700	LNHT	60046	2418	19W-38N	C6
21200	LkvT	60002	2417	21W-39N	D4
21600	LKVL	60002	2417	21W-39N	C4
21600	LKVL	60046	2417	21W-39N	C4
22700	AntT	60002	2417	22W-40N	A4
22700	AntT	60046	2417	22W-40N	A4
23300	AntT	60002	2416	25W-40N	B3
23300	LKVL	60002	2416	23W-40N	E3
25800	AntT	60002	2415	26W-38N	D6
27700	AntT	60081	2415	27W-38N	B6
29600	BtnT	60081	2414	28W-38N	E6
29600	FXLK	60081	2414	28W-38N	E6
CO-A11 W Gelden Rd					
20700	LkvT	60046	2417	21W-39N	D5
20700	LkvT	60046	2418	20W-39N	A5
20700	LNHT	60046	2417	21W-39N	E5
20700	LNHT	60046	2418	20W-39N	A5
21900	LKVL	60046	2417	22W-39N	C5
CO-A12 W Petite Lake Rd					
-	LKVL	60046	2417	23W-39N	A6
-	LkvT	60046	2417	23W-39N	A6
23400	LKVL	60046	2416	24W-38N	C6
23400	LkvT	60046	2416	24W-38N	C6
CO-A14 W Millburn Rd					
17500	OMCK	60083	2419	18W-38N	A7
18400	OMCK	60083	2418	18W-38N	E7
18600	LNHT	60046	2418	18W-38N	E7
18600	OMCK	60046	2418	18W-38N	E7
CO-A15 Oak Grove Rd					
19300	AdnT	60033	2406	49W-40N	D1
19900	CmgT	60033	2406	49W-40N	D1
CO-A15 W Yorkhouse Rd					
1200	BHPK	60087	2479	11W-37N	E2
1200	WKGN	60087	2479	11W-37N	E2
2500	WkgT	60087	2479	12W-37N	C2
3300	WKGN	60087	2478	13W-37N	E1
3300	WrnT	60087	2479	11W-37N	E2
3500	NptT	60083	2478	13W-37N	E1
10000	BHPK	60087	2480	10W-37N	A2
13900	NptT	60083	2478	14W-38N	D1
13900	WDWH	60087	2478	13W-38N	D1
13900	WKGN	60083	2478	14W-38N	D1
CO-A16 E Tryon Grove Rd					
5600	RcmT	60071	2412	34W-40N	C3
5600	RHMD	60071	2412	34W-40N	C3
CO-A17 Main St Rd					
200	BtnT	60081	2414	30W-39N	B4
200	FXLK	60081	2414	29W-39N	D5
500	BtnT	60081	2414	30W-39N	B4
1900	SPGV	60081	2413	30W-39N	E4
CO-A17 N State Park Rd					
-	MchT	60081	2472	29W-37N	D1
6100	AntT	60081	2472	29W-38N	D1
6100	BtnT	60081	2472	29W-38N	D1
6100	GrtT	60081	2472	29W-38N	D1
6500	AntT	60081	2414	29W-38N	D7
6500	BtnT	60081	2414	29W-38N	D7
6500	FXLK	60020	2414	29W-38N	D7
6500	FXLK	60081	2414	29W-38N	D7
CO-A18 W Engle Dr					
21100	LkvT	60046	2475	21W-36N	E3
CO-A18 W Genoa Av					
20600	LkvT	60046	2476	20W-37N	A3
20700	LkvT	60046	2475	21W-36N	D3
CO-A18 N Granada Blvd					
300	LkvT	60046	2476	20W-37N	A2
300	LNHT	60046	2476	20W-37N	A2
CO-A18 Monaville Rd					
10	LKVL	60046	2475	23W-36N	A3
10	LKVL	60073	2475	23W-36N	A3
10	RLKB	60073	2475	23W-36N	A3
200	LKVL	60046	2474	23W-36N	E3
400	LkvT	60046	2474	23W-36N	E3
CO-A18 E Monaville Rd					
10	LKVL	60046	2475	22W-36N	B3
10	LKVL	60073	2475	23W-36N	A3
10	LkvT	60046	2475	22W-36N	B3
10	LkvT	60073	2475	22W-36N	A3
10	RLKB	60046	2475	22W-36N	A3
10	RLKB	60073	2475	23W-36N	A3
CO-A18 W Monaville Rd					
22400	LkvT	60046	2475	22W-36N	B3
22400	RLKB	60046	2475	22W-36N	B3
22400	RLKB	60073	2475	22W-36N	B3
22500	LkvT	60073	2475	22W-36N	B3
22600	LKVL	60046	2475	22W-36N	B3
22600	LKVL	60073	2475	22W-36N	B3
23700	LKVL	60046	2474	24W-36N	D3
23700	LkvT	60046	2474	24W-36N	D3
24800	GrtT	60046	2474	25W-37N	B3
25400	GrtT	60041	2474	25W-37N	A3
25400	LkvT	60041	2474	25W-37N	A3
CO-A18 N Nathan Hale Dr					
36800	LkvT	60046	2475	21W-36N	E3
CO-A19 Golf Rd					
-	WKGN	60085	2480	10W-36N	A5
700	WKGN	60087	2480	10W-36N	A5
1100	WKGN	60087	2479	10W-36N	E4
CO-A19 W Greenwood Av					
300	WKGN	60085	2480	10W-36N	B5
300	WKGN	60087	2480	10W-36N	B5
CO-A19 Sunset Av					
1400	WKGN	60087	2479	11W-36N	E4
3500	GRNE	60031	2478	13W-36N	E4
3500	WKGN	60087	2478	13W-36N	E4
3800	WrnT	60031	2478	13W-36N	D4
3800	WrnT	60087	2478	13W-36N	D4
CO-A20 W Diggins St					
500	HRVD	60033	2406	50W-38N	A6
1000	CmgT	60033	2405	51W-38N	E6
1000	HRVD	60033	2405	51W-38N	E6
CO-A20 E Grand Av					
10	FXLK	60020	2473	28W-36N	A3
CO-A20 S Oak Grove Rd					
6100	CmgT	60033	2405	52W-38N	A7
CO-A20 Ramer Rd					
22800	CmgT	60033	2405	52W-38N	B7
22800	HRVD	60033	2405	51W-38N	D6
CO-A20 Rollins Rd					
10	FXLK	60020	2473	27W-36N	B5
400	FXLK	60041	2473	26W-35N	C5
600	GrtT	60041	2473	26W-35N	D5
CO-A20 E Rollins Rd					
10	RLKB	60073	2475	22W-35N	A6
700	RLKB	60046	2475	22W-35N	C6
900	GYLK	60046	2475	21W-35N	D5
CO-A20 N Rollins Rd					
-	GRNE	60031	2476	18W-35N	E5
-	WrnT	60031	2476	18W-35N	E5
-	WrnT	60046	2476	18W-35N	E5
CO-A20 W Rollins Rd					
-	GRNE	60031	2476	18W-35N	E5
10	RLKB	60073	2475	22W-35N	B6
200	RLKB	60073	2474	23W-35N	E6
500	RLKH	60073	2474	23W-35N	E6
1000	AvnT	60073	2474	23W-35N	E6
19000	AvnT	60046	2476	19W-35N	B5
19000	WrnT	60046	2476	19W-35N	D5
20500	AvnT	60046	2475	21W-35N	D5
20500	GYLK	60046	2475	21W-35N	D5
20500	GYLK	60030	2476	20W-35N	A5
20800	GYLK	60046	2475	21W-35N	E5
21300	RLKB	60046	2475	21W-35N	D5
24800	GrtT	60041	2474	23W-35N	E6
24800	GrtT	60073	2474	23W-35N	E6
25900	GrtT	60041	2473	26W-35N	D5
CO-A22 Airport Rd					
100	HRVD	60033	2464	50W-37N	A1
21600	DhmT	60033	2464	50W-37N	A1
22000	DhmT	60033	2463	51W-37N	D1
22000	HRVD	60033	2463	51W-37N	D1
CO-A22 McGuire Rd					
18700	HtdT	60033	2464	48W-37N	E2
20100	DhmT	60033	2464	48W-37N	E2
20100	HRVD	60033	2464	50W-37N	B1
CO-A22 Washington St					
3000	PKCY	60085	2536	12W-33N	B2
3000	WKGN	60085	2536	12W-33N	B2
3400	GRNE	60031	2536	13W-34N	A2
3400	GRNE	60085	2536	13W-34N	A2
3900	GRNE	60031	2535	14W-34N	C1
4300	WrnT	60031	2535	14W-34N	C1
6000	GRNE	60031	2534	16W-34N	D1
6000	WrnT	60031	2534	16W-34N	D1
13700	PKCY	60085	2535	14W-34N	C1
CO-A22 E Washington St					
10	RDLK	60073	2532	23W-34N	A2
10	RLKP	60073	2532	22W-34N	B2
400	HNVL	60030	2532	22W-34N	B2
400	HNVL	60073	2532	22W-34N	B2
CO-A22 W Washington St					
10	RDLK	60073	2532	23W-34N	A2
10	RLKP	60073	2532	23W-34N	A2
100	RDLK	60073	2531	23W-34N	E1
17000	GRNE	60031	2534	17W-34N	C1
17000	WrnT	60031	2534	17W-34N	C1
18200	WrnT	60030	2534	18W-34N	A1
18300	GRNE	60031	2533	18W-34N	E1
18300	WrnT	60030	2533	18W-34N	E1
18300	WrnT	60031	2533	18W-34N	E1
18500	GRNE	60030	2533	18W-34N	E1
18700	TDLK	60030	2533	18W-34N	E1
18900	GYLK	60030	2533	20W-34N	A1
18900	TDLK	60031	2533	18W-34N	D1
19400	AvnT	60030	2533	20W-34N	A1
20700	GYLK	60030	2532	21W-33N	D2
21600	AvnT	60030	2532	21W-33N	D2
21700	AvnT	60073	2532	21W-33N	D2
21700	HNVL	60030	2532	21W-33N	D2
CO-A24 Gages Lake Rd					
5400	GRNE	60031	2534	15W-33N	E2
5400	GRNE	60085	2535	15W-33N	A3
5400	WrnT	60031	2534	15W-33N	E2
5700	GRNE	60048	2534	16W-33N	D2
CO-A24 W Gages Lake Rd					
17100	GRNE	60031	2534	16W-33N	C2
17100	GRNE	60048	2534	16W-33N	C2
17100	WrnT	60030	2534	16W-33N	D2
17100	WrnT	60031	2534	16W-33N	C2
17100	WrnT	60048	2534	16W-33N	C2
18400	WrnT	60030	2533	18W-33N	E2
18700	GYLK	60030	2533	18W-34N	D2
18800	TDLK	60030	2533	18W-34N	D2
CO-A26 Bay Rd					
900	JNBG	60051	2529	30W-34N	B1
900	LKMR	60051	2529	30W-34N	B1
900	MchT	60051	2529	30W-34N	B1
1100	JNBG	60051	2472	30W-34N	B7
1100	LKMR	60051	2472	30W-34N	B7
CO-A26 E Bay Rd					
100	GrtT	60051	2529	29W-34N	D1
100	MchT	60051	2529	29W-34N	C1
300	LKMR	60051	2529	29W-34N	C1
CO-A26 N Chapel Hill Rd					
3100	JNBG	60051	2471	30W-35N	E7
3500	JNBG	60050	2471	31W-35N	E6
CO-A26 W Johnsburg Rd					
2300	JNBG	60050	2471	31W-35N	C6
CO-A27 Center St					
-	AvnT	60030	2533	19W-33N	B4
500	GYLK	60030	2533	19W-33N	B4
CO-A27 Flat Iron Rd					
5600	HRVD	60033	2463	51W-37N	D1
22800	CmgT	60033	2405	51W-37N	D7
22800	DhmT	60033	2405	51W-37N	D7
22800	HRVD	60033	2405	51W-37N	D7
23000	DhmT	60033	2463	52W-36N	B3
CO-A27 Streit Rd					
23500	DhmT	60033	2463	52W-36N	B4
CO-A28 Charles Rd					
10100	GwdT	60098	2525	40W-34N	B1
11900	GwdT	60098	2524	41W-34N	E1
CO-A29 14th St					
600	NCHI	60064	2537	10W-32N	A5
1000	NCHI	60064	2536	10W-32N	E5
1100	WKGN	60085	2536	10W-32N	E5
CO-A29 Casimer Pulaski Dr					
-	WKGN	60064	2536	12W-32N	C5
-	WKGN	60085	2535	13W-32N	E5
-	WKGN	60085	2536	12W-32N	C5
-	WrnT	60085	2535	13W-32N	E5
3100	NCHI	60064	2536	12W-32N	C5
CO-A31 ML King Jr Dr					
-	LbvT	60044	2535	13W-31N	E7
-	LbvT	60044	2536	12W-31N	B7
-	WKGN	60085	2535	13W-31N	E7
-	WKGN	60085	2536	12W-31N	B7
3100	NCHI	60064	2536	12W-31N	B7
3100	ShdT	60044	2536	12W-31N	B7
CO-A32 Bull Valley Rd					
4000	MHRY	60050	2528	33W-31N	A7
4000	NndT	60050	2528	32W-31N	A7
4200	MHRY	60050	2527	34W-31N	D7
4600	NndT	60050	2527	34W-31N	D7
CO-A33 W Jackson St					
200	WDSK	60098	2524	42W-31N	C7
CO-A33 Kishwaukee Valley Rd					
1100	WDSK	60098	2524	42W-31N	B7
13700	SenT	60098	2524	43W-31N	A7
CO-A33 W Peterson Rd					
-	LbvT	60048	2590	18W-30N	E2
-	LbvT	60048	2591	18W-30N	A2
-	LYVL	60048	2591	18W-30N	A2
1800	LYVL	60048	2590	18W-30N	E2
19200	FmtT	60048	2590	19W-30N	D2
19500	FmtT	60060	2590	19W-30N	C2
19800	FmtT	60030	2590	20W-30N	A2
19800	GYLK	60030	2590	20W-30N	A2
19800	GYLK	60048	2590	20W-30N	B2
19800	RLKP	60030	2590	20W-30N	A2
20700	FmtT	60030	2589	20W-30N	E2
20700	GYLK	60030	2589	20W-30N	E2
20700	RLKP	60030	2589	20W-30N	E2
21500	FmtT	60060	2589	21W-30N	D2
22000	RLKP	60060	2589	22W-30N	B2
CO-A34 W Winchester Rd					
-	LbvT	60048	2591	17W-29N	B3
-	LYVL	60060	2591	17W-29N	C3
-	MDLN	60048	2591	17W-29N	C3
-	MDLN	60060	2591	17W-29N	C3
100	LYVL	60048	2591	17W-29N	C3
1400	LYVL	60048	2590	20W-30N	B3
1400	LYVL	60060	2590	20W-30N	B3
1400	MDLN	60048	2590	18W-29N	E3
1400	MDLN	60060	2590	18W-29N	E3
19100	FmtT	60048	2590	20W-30N	B3
19100	FmtT	60060	2590	20W-30N	B3
20000	RLKP	60030	2590	20W-30N	A3
CO-A35 W South St					
100	WDSK	60098	2581	42W-30N	B1
1100	DrrT	60098	2581	42W-30N	B1
14000	SenT	60098	2581	43W-30N	A2
CO-A36 E Bonner Rd					
600	WCDA	60084	2588	25W-28N	B6
600	WcnT	60084	2588	25W-28N	B6
1100	FmtT	60060	2588	24W-28N	C6
1100	WCDA	60060	2588	24W-28N	C6
1200	FmtT	60084	2588	24W-28N	C6
CO-A36 W Bonner Rd					
600	WCDA	60084	2587	27W-28N	B6
600	WcnT	60084	2587	27W-28N	B6
27000	WcnT	60051	2587	27W-28N	A6
CO-A38 E Hawley St					
10	MDLN	60060	2590	20W-28N	A7
CO-A38 W Hawley St					
10	MDLN	60060	2590	19W-28N	D7
200	FmtT	60060	2589	22W-27N	B7
200	HNWD	60047	2589	22W-27N	B7
200	HNWD	60060	2589	22W-27N	B7
1800	FmtT	60060	2590	20W-27N	A7
20800	MDLN	60060	2589	21W-27N	E7
21700	FmtT	60047	2589	22W-27N	C7
21700	MDLN	60047	2589	22W-27N	C7
CO-A38 Ridgefield Rd					
8500	DrrT	60012	2583	37W-27N	B7
8600	CLLK	60012	2583	37W-27N	B7
8900	DrrT	60098	2583	38W-27N	A7
CO-A40 W Everett Rd					
1000	LKFT	60045	2649	12W-24N	B7
1800	LKFT	60045	2648	13W-24N	E7
1800	VrnT	60045	2648	14W-24N	D7
2100	MTWA	60045	2648	14W-24N	D7
3200	MTWA	60048	2648	14W-24N	D7
3400	VrnT	60048	2648	14W-24N	D7
CO-A42 Miller Rd					
300	NBRN	60010	2698	25W-23N	A1
500	LKBN	60010	2697	25W-24N	E1
500	LKBN	60010	2698	25W-24N	A1
500	NBRN	60010	2697	25W-24N	E1
24600	ElaT	60010	2698	25W-23N	A1
24600	ElaT	60047	2698	24W-24N	C1
24600	LKZH	60047	2698	24W-24N	C1

Block	City	ZIP	Map#	CGS	Grid
CO-A42 W Miller Rd					
500	LKBN	60010	2697	26W-24N	D1
500	NBRN	60010	2697	26W-24N	D1
CO-A42 W Union Rd					
-	UNON	60180	2635	47W-25N	B5
18700	CrlT	60152	2635	48W-25N	A4
18700	CrlT	60180	2635	47W-25N	B5
CO-A43 Duffy Ln					
-	BKBN	60015	2703	12W-22N	B4
2000	RVWD	60015	2703	12W-22N	A4
2600	RVWD	60015	2702	13W-22N	E4
2800	LNSH	60015	2702	13W-22N	E4
2800	LNSH	60069	2702	13W-22N	E4
CO-A44 Aptakisic Rd					
-	LGGV	60047	2700	18W-22N	E5
-	VrnT	60047	2700	18W-22N	E5
5100	BFGV	60047	2701	17W-22N	B5
5100	BFGV	60089	2701	17W-22N	B5
5100	LGGV	60047	2701	17W-21N	A5
5100	LGGV	60089	2701	17W-22N	B5
CO-A44 W Aptakisic Rd					
-	VrnT	60069	2702	14W-21N	B5
400	BFGV	60069	2701	17W-22N	C5
400	BFGV	60089	2701	17W-22N	C5
400	BFGV	60089	2702	15W-21N	A5
400	LNSH	60069	2702	15W-21N	A5
400	LNSH	60089	2702	15W-21N	A5
400	VrnT	60069	2701	17W-22N	C5
500	BFGV	60069	2702	15W-21N	A5
1200	BFGV	60047	2701	17W-22N	B5
1200	LGGV	60047	2701	17W-22N	B5
1200	LGGV	60089	2701	17W-22N	B5
15600	LNSH	60069	2701	15W-21N	E5
16100	VrnT	60089	2701	16W-22N	E5
CO-A44 E Coral Rd					
-	UNON	60180	2635	47W-24N	C6
18100	CrlT	60152	2635	47W-24N	A7
18100	CrlT	60180	2635	47W-24N	B6
CO-A44 W Coral Rd					
18800	CrlT	60152	2635	47W-24N	A7
18800	CrlT	60180	2635	47W-24N	A7
19200	CrlT	60152	2634	48W-24N	E7
19700	RlyT	60152	2634	49W-24N	B7
CO-A45 James R Rakow Rd					
-	AlqT	60014	2694	33W-23N	E1
-	CLLK	60156	2694	34W-23N	B1
-	LIHL	60156	2694	34W-23N	B1
1000	CLLK	60014	2694	34W-23N	C1
1000	LIHL	60014	2694	34W-23N	C1
CO-A46 Ackman Rd					
7700	CLLK	60014	2693	38W-23N	A2
7800	GfnT	60014	2693	38W-23N	A2
8100	GfnT	60156	2693	37W-23N	B2
8900	LKWD	60014	2693	37W-23N	B2
9300	GfnT	60014	2692	38W-23N	E2
9300	GfnT	60156	2692	38W-23N	E2
9300	LIHL	60156	2692	38W-23N	E2
9300	LKWD	60014	2692	38W-23N	E2
9300	LKWD	60156	2693	37W-23N	A2
CO-A46 Cuba Rd					
-	CbaT	60010	2698	24W-21N	B6
23500	DRPK	60010	2698	23W-21N	D6
23500	LKZH	60010	2698	23W-21N	E6
23500	LKZH	60047	2698	23W-21N	E6
23700	ElaT	60010	2698	25W-21N	A6
CO-A46 W Cuba Rd					
100	LKZH	60010	2699	23W-21N	A6
100	LKZH	60047	2699	23W-21N	A6
400	DRPK	60010	2698	23W-21N	E6
400	LKZH	60010	2698	23W-21N	E6
400	LKZH	60047	2698	23W-21N	E6
25200	CbaT	60010	2698	25W-21N	B6
CO-A47 Central Av					
400	HDPK	60035	2704	8W-22N	E4
CO-A47 Deerfield Pkwy					
-	BFGV	60089	2702	13W-20N	D7
-	RVWD	60015	2702	13W-20N	D7
400	BFGV	60089	2701	16W-21N	E6
400	VrnT	60089	2701	16W-21N	E6
CO-A47 Deerfield Rd					
1600	DRFD	60015	2703	12W-20N	B7
1700	WdfT	60015	2703	12W-20N	C7
2100	RVWD	60015	2703	12W-20N	B7
2300	RVWD	60015	2702	13W-21N	E7
3700	BFGV	60089	2702	14W-21N	B7
CO-A47 Harmony Rd					
11500	GfnT	60142	2691	42W-20N	B7
CO-A47 W Main Street Rd					
11900	HTLY	60142	2691	41W-21N	E7
12100	GfnT	60142	2691	41W-21N	E7
CO-A47 Marengo Rd					
13300	CrlT	60142	2691	43W-21N	A5
13300	GfnT	60142	2691	42W-21N	B6
14100	CrlT	60180	2691	43W-21N	A5
CO-A48 Algonquin Rd					
9100	ALGN	60102	2693	38W-21N	A6
9100	GfnT	60102	2693	38W-21N	A6
9400	ALGN	60102	2692	38W-21N	E6
9400	GfnT	60102	2692	38W-21N	E6
9400	LIHL	60156	2692	38W-21N	E6
10000	GfnT	60142	2692	39W-21N	C6
10000	GfnT	60156	2692	39W-21N	C6
10400	HTLY	60142	2692	40W-21N	A6
CO-A48 W Algonquin Rd					
1100	ALGN	60102	2694	35W-21N	B6
1100	ALGN	60156	2694	35W-21N	B6
1100	LIHL	60102	2694	34W-21N	C6
1100	LIHL	60156	2694	35W-21N	B6
1400	LIHL	60102	2693	35W-21N	E6
2500	ALGN	60102	2693	36W-21N	D6
2500	ALGN	60156	2693	36W-21N	D6
2500	LIHL	60156	2693	36W-21N	D6
3700	GfnT	60156	2693	36W-21N	D6
CO-A49 Harmony Rd					
13500	GfnT	60142	2691	42W-20N	B7
13500	HTLY	60142	2691	42W-20N	B7
13900	CrlT	60142	2691	43W-20N	A7
14600	CrlT	60142	2743	45W-20N	A1
CO-A49 Long Grove Rd					
10	DRPK	60010	2752	22W-20N	B1
100	BRTN	60010	2751	23W-20N	D1
100	DRPK	60010	2751	23W-20N	D1
100	ElaT	60010	2751	23W-20N	E1
500	DRPK	60074	2752	22W-20N	C1
CO-A49 W Long Grove Rd					
3400	ElaT	60047	2700	20W-20N	A7
3400	LGGV	60047	2700	20W-20N	A7
3500	KLDR	60047	2700	20W-20N	A7
20700	KLDR	60047	2699	20W-20N	E7
21400	ElaT	60074	2699	21W-20N	D7
21600	DRPK	60074	2752	21W-20N	D1
21600	ElaT	60074	2752	21W-20N	D1
21700	DRPK	60010	2752	21W-20N	C1
CO-A50 County Line Rd					
2000	ALGN	60102	2748	32W-20N	B2
2000	AlqT	60102	2748	32W-20N	B2

Block	City	ZIP	Map#	CGS	Grid
CO-A50 County Line Rd					
2200	BNHL	60010	2748	32W-20N	C2
2200	BNHL	60102	2748	32W-20N	C2
CO-A50 W County Line Rd					
10	BNHL	60010	2749	30W-18N	A2
100	ALGN	60102	2748	32W-19N	E2
100	BNHL	60010	2748	32W-19N	E2
100	BNHL	60102	2748	32W-19N	E2
300	AlqT	60010	2749	29W-20N	D2
CO-A50 E Lake Cook Rd					
100	BFGV	60089	2754	16W-20N	D2
100	WLNG	60089	2754	16W-20N	D2
1300	WLNG	60090	2754	16W-20N	D2
CO-A52					
-	HTLY	60142	2692	40W-20N	A7
CO-A52 Dundee Rd					
10	GfnT	60102	2745	38W-20N	D2
10	RtdT	60102	2745	38W-20N	D2
10	RtdT	60142	2745	38W-20N	D2
9700	GfnT	60156	2745	39W-20N	D1
10300	GfnT	60142	2745	39W-20N	C1
10300	HTLY	60142	2745	39W-20N	C1
10600	HTLY	60142	2692	39W-20N	C7
10700	GfnT	60142	2692	39W-20N	B7
CO-A52 E Main St					
11300	HTLY	60142	2692	40W-20N	A7
11800	HTLY	60142	2691	40W-21N	E7
Coach Dr					
-	DSPN	60018	2917	12W-8N	B2
1600	NPVL	60565	3204	25W-9S	A4
11400	MKNA	60448	3590	14W-25S	D1
Coach Ln					
-	HLCT	60429	3427	3W-21S	A6
1000	LMNT	60439	3271	18W-13S	A5
Coach Rd					
-	YKVL	60560	3333	42W-17S	D6
10	WLNG	60090	2755	15W-18N	A3
100	NHFD	60093	2811	7W-15N	A3
800	HMWD	60430	3508	1W-22S	A1
2300	ElaT	60047	2753	19W-20N	B1
2300	LGGV	60047	2700	19W-20N	C7
2300	LGGV	60047	2753	19W-20N	B1
E Coach Rd					
800	PLTN	60074	2753	19W-18N	B2
N Coach Rd					
2100	PLTN	60074	2753	20W-18N	B2
S Coach Rd					
12100	PSHT	60463	3274	9W-14S	D6
W Coach Rd					
7600	PSHT	60463	3274	9W-14S	D6
Coach & Surrey Ln					
2400	AURA	60506	3136	39W-7S	E7
2500	AURA	60506	3198	39W-7S	E1
Coachford Ct					
24600	SRWD	60404	3584	30W-25S	B1
Coach House Rd					
6400	LSLE	60532	3142	25W-7S	C6
Coachlight Ln					
6100	BtnT	60081	2472	29W-37N	B1
6100	GrtT	60081	2472	29W-37N	B1
6100	MchT	60081	2472	29W-37N	B1
Coach Light Rd					
6000	NndT	60012	2584	35W-29N	A3
6000	NndT	60050	2584	35W-29N	A3
Coachlite Tr					
100	CLSM	60188	3024	25W-2N	A1
Coachmaker Dr					
200	NHBK	60062	2757	8W-18N	D3
Coachmans Rd					
1600	DRN	60561	3207	18W-9S	A4
14000	HMGN	60491	3343	17W-17S	C5
Coachsurry					
2200	AURA	60506	3137	38W-7S	A7
2300	AURA	60506	3136	39W-7S	D7
Coachway Ln					
22400	RNPK	60471	3594	5W-27S	C4
Coachwood Tr					
6900	TYPK	60477	3425	8W-19S	A3
E Coady Dr					
-	CnhT	60447	3583	33W-28S	B6
100	MNKA	60447	3583	33W-28S	B6
W Coady Dr					
400	MNKA	60447	3583	33W-28S	B7
W Coal City Rd					
-	DMND	60408	3941	32W-39S	E2
-	DMND	60416	3941	32W-39S	E2
-	DMND	60481	3941	32W-39S	E2
400	BDWD	60408	3941	32W-39S	E2
400	BDWD	60481	3941	32W-39S	E2
400	RedT	60408	3941	32W-39S	E2
400	RedT	60408	3942	31W-39S	A2
400	WmTp	60408	3942	31W-39S	A2
400	WmTp	60481	3941	32W-39S	E2
400	WmTp	60481	3942	29W-39S	E2
23200	CstT	60481	3942	29W-39S	E2
23200	CstT	60481	3943	29W-40S	A2
23200	WMTN	60481	3942	29W-39S	E2
23200	WMTN	60481	3943	29W-40S	A2
23200	WmTp	60481	3943	29W-40S	A2
23500	RedT	60481	3942	29W-40S	D2
24000	BDWD	60408	3942	30W-39S	B2
24000	BDWD	60481	3942	30W-39S	D2
W Coal City Rd SR-113					
-	DMND	60408	3941	32W-39S	E2
-	DMND	60416	3941	32W-39S	E2
-	DMND	60481	3941	32W-39S	E2
500	BDWD	60408	3941	32W-39S	E2
500	BDWD	60481	3941	32W-39S	E2
500	RedT	60408	3941	32W-39S	E2
500	WmTp	60481	3941	32W-39S	E2
Coales Rd					
700	BlmT	60411	3508	0W-23S	B3
700	CHHT	60411	3508	0W-23S	B3
Coales St					
800	CHHT	60411	3508	1W-23S	B3
Coastal Dr					
2800	AURA	60503	3201	31W-10S	D5
S Coast Guard Dr					
6400	CHCG	60637	3153	2E-7S	C5
6400	CHCG	60649	3153	2E-7S	C5
S Coast Guard Dr US-41					
6400	CHCG	60637	3153	2E-7S	C5
6400	CHCG	60649	3153	2E-7S	C5
CO-B					
500	BfdT	53128	2353		A2
500	GNCY	53128	2353		A2
800	BfdT	53128	2352		A3
800	GNCY	53128	2352		E3
1600	BfdT	53128	2351		E2
1900	BfdT	53147	2351		A1
2300	LinT	53147	2351		A1
2700	LinT	53147	2350		E1
CO-B 304th Av					
11500	AntT	53179	2356		B3
11500	AntT	60002	2356		B3
11500	SlmT	53179	2356		B3

Block	City	ZIP	Map#	CGS	Grid
Cobb Cir					
200	BGBK	60440	3269	23W-11S	A1
Cobb Ct					
400	DGvT	60516	3206	20W-10S	B5
Cobb Dr					
400	DGvT	60516	3206	20W-10S	B5
400	WDRG	60517	3206	20W-10S	B5
Cobb St					
8700	HGKN	60525	3147	11W-7S	D6
Cobblebrook Ln					
1900	NPVL	60565	3204	24W-8S	E2
Cobble Creek Dr					
-	GRNE	60031	2534	16W-33N	E2
Cobble Hill Ct					
1000	HFET	60169	2858	24W-12N	C1
Cobbler Ct					
10	SEGN	60177	2908	35W-7N	B4
100	SRGV	60554	3197	42W-7S	D1
400	BRLT	60103	2967	28W-5N	B3
16300	TYPK	60487	3424	10W-19S	B2
E Cobbler Ct					
200	RLKB	60073	2475	22W-35N	B5
Cobbler Ln					
10	SMBG	60173	2859	22W-10N	C5
10	SMBG	60194	2859	22W-10N	C5
100	SRGV	60554	3197	42W-7S	D1
200	BFGV	60089	2701	16W-21N	D6
300	BFGV	60089	2754	16W-18N	D3
300	WLNG	60089	2754	16W-18N	D3
300	WLNG	60090	2754	16W-18N	D3
Cobblers Cross					
900	ELGN	60120	2855	32W-12N	D1
1200	ELGN	60120	2801	32W-12N	C7
5200	MHRY	60050	2527	34W-31N	D6
Cobblestone Cir					
200	HRVD	60033	2464	50W-37N	A1
600	MaiT	60016	2809	11W-13N	D7
600	NfdT	60016	2809	11W-13N	D7
600	NfdT	60025	2809	11W-13N	D7
Cobble Stone Ct					
7100	TYPK	60477	3425	8W-19S	A2
Cobblestone Ct					
10	BFGV	60089	2754	16W-20N	D1
10	PSHL	60465	3274	10W-12S	B3
100	OSWG	60543	3200	35W-10S	B6
100	TNLK	53181	2354		C2
200	SMBG	60173	2860	21W-10N	A4
300	LIHL	60156	2693	37W-21N	B5
600	ELGN	60120	2855	32W-12N	D2
900	SRWD	60404	3496	30W-23S	B5
1000	NHBK	60062	2757	8W-18N	D3
1200	NPVL	60564	3203	28W-10S	A7
1400	JNBG	60050	2472	30W-36N	A3
1900	RMVL	60446	3339	27W-18S	C7
4200	GRNE	60031	2535	14W-33N	D2
S Cobble Stone Ct					
20300	FftT	60423	3504	9W-24S	E6
Cobblestone Dr					
-	ALGN	60102	2748	33W-19N	B3
-	ALGN	60110	2748	33W-19N	B3
-	DndT	60102	2748	33W-19N	B3
-	DndT	60110	2748	33W-19N	B3
-	SCRL	60174	2964	35W-3N	C6
300	NPVL	60540	3141	27W-6S	B6
300	AURA	60506	3199	38W-7S	A1
1900	CPVL	60110	2748	33W-19N	B3
2600	PRGV	60012	2584	34W-29N	D4
2800	NndT	60012	2584	34W-29N	D5
W Cobblestone Dr					
10	CteT	60417	3774	0W-32S	D1
Cobblestone Ln					
10	MltT	60187	3024	25W-0N	A5
500	BFGV	60089	2701	15W-21N	E6
500	BFGV	60089	2754	16W-20N	D1
800	ELWD	60421	3675	25W-31S	B6
6600	LGGV	60047	2646	19W-24N	C7
S Cobblestone Ln					
25700	CNHN	60410	3672	32W-31S	C6
W Cobblestone Ln					
1700	MchT	60051	2528	30W-34N	E1
1700	MchT	60051	2529	30W-34N	A1
Cobblestone Rd					
1900	PnfT	60544	3339	27W-18S	C7
1900	RMVL	60446	3339	27W-18S	C7
1900	RMVL	60544	3339	27W-18S	C7
Cobblestone Tr					
5700	MHRY	60050	2527	34W-32N	C5
22400	FKFT	60423	3590	14W-27S	D4
Cobblestone Wy					
-	DrrT	60098	2582	40W-29N	A4
-	WDSK	60098	2582	40W-29N	A4
1100	WDSK	60098	2581	40W-29N	E4
Cobblestones Rd					
-	DYR	46311	3510		E5
-	MNSR	46321	3510		E5
Cobblewood Dr					
2400	NHBK	60062	2810	10W-15N	A2
2500	NHBK	60062	2809	10W-15N	E2
Cobblewood Ln					
10	HNWD	60047	2644	23W-25N	E5
CO-B N Carter St					
300	GNCY	53128	2353		A2
900	BfdT	53128	2353		A2
CO-B Franklin St					
300	GNCY	53128	2353		A2
CO-B Freeman St					
200	GNCY	53128	2353		A3
Coblestone Ln					
-	BRLT	60120	2909	31W-7N	D6
-	BRLT	60184	2909	32W-7N	D6
CO-B Main St					
700	GNCY	53128	2353		A3
800	BfdT	53128	2352		E3
800	GNCY	53128	2352		E3
CO-B Tuttle Rd					
11000	SlmT	53179	2356		B1
CO-B Twin Lakes Rd					
100	BfdT	53128	2353		B1
100	GNCY	53128	2353		B1
100	RdlT	53128	2353		B1
CO-B Wilmot Rd					
30000	SlmT	53179	2356		B1
CO-C 110th St					
34000	RdlT	53181	2354		E1
34000	RdlT	53181	2355		B1
34000	TNLK	53181	2354		E1
34000	TNLK	53181	2355		B1
CO-C 113th St					
30500	SlmT	53179	2356		A1
30500	SlmT	53192	2356		A1
CO-C 114th St					
30700	SlmT	53192	2356		A1
CO-C 116th St					
31600	RdlT	53181	2355		C2
31800	TNLK	53181	2355		C2
CO-C 336th Av					
11000	RdlT	53181	2355		B2

Block	City	ZIP	Map#	CGS	Grid
CO-C 336th Av					
11000	TNLK	53181	2355		B1
Cocalico Ct					
1500	NPVL	60563	3141	27W-5S	B2
CO-C Fox River Rd					
11300	SlmT	53192	2356		A1
Cochise Cir					
600	BGBK	60440	3268	24W-11S	D1
Cochise Ct					
10	OKBK	60523	3085	18W-2S	A3
300	CLSM	60188	2968	26W-2N	A7
400	CLSM	60188	2967	26W-2N	E7
Cochise Dr					
6500	IHPK	60525	3146	14W-7S	E6
Cochise Pl					
500	CLSM	60188	2967	26W-2N	E7
Cochise St					
700	HFET	60169	2859	23W-11N	A4
Cochran St					
100	MHTN	60442	3677	19W-31S	E5
1000	AURA	60506	3137	38W-6S	B4
2400	BLID	60406	3277	3W-14S	A6
W Cochrane Av					
800	JLET	60436	3498	25W-24S	C6
CO-C Wilmot Rd					
24300	SlmT	53179	2357		C1
27200	SlmT	53179	2356		D2
30800	SlmT	53192	2356		A1
31200	RdlT	53181	2355		E1
31200	RdlT	53192	2355		E1
CO-CJ Horton Rd					
13600	BtlT	53142	2360		B1
15200	BtlT	53142	2359		C2
17200	BtlT	53104	2359		B3
CO-CK 125th St					
32000	RdlT	53181	2355		C3
CO-CK 336th Av					
12500	RdlT	53181	2355		B3
12700	BtnT	60081	2355		B4
12700	RdlT	60081	2355		B4
CO-CK State Line Rd					
900	BtnT	60081	2355	30W-43N	A4
900	RdlT	53181	2355	30W-43N	A4
900	RdlT	60081	2355	29W-43N	B4
1000	SPGV	60081	2355	30W-43N	B4
1400	BtnT	60071	2355	30W-43N	A4
1600	BtnT	53181	2354	31W-43N	D4
1600	BtnT	60071	2354	31W-43N	D4
1600	RcmT	53181	2354	31W-43N	D4
1600	RcmT	60071	2354	31W-43N	D4
1600	RcmT	60081	2354	31W-43N	D4
1600	RdlT	53181	2354	31W-43N	D4
1600	RdlT	60071	2354	31W-43N	D4
1600	RdlT	60081	2354	31W-43N	D4
S Codo Dr					
15900	HmrT	60491	3420	18W-19S	E2
Codorus Rd					
10	OswT	60538	3199	37W-11S	D7
10	OswT	60538	3263	37W-11S	C1
Cody Ct					
10	DRFD	60015	2704	10W-20N	B7
100	RtdT	60124	2798	39W-14N	E6
300	NPVL	60540	3141	27W-6S	B6
2600	AURA	60503	3265	31W-11S	D1
Cody Ln					
10	DRFD	60015	2704	10W-20N	B7
600	UYPK	60466	3684	3W-29S	B2
Coe Rd					
200	CNHL	60514	3085	16W-4S	E7
200	CNHL	60514	3145	16W-4S	D1
200	WTMT	60514	3085	16W-4S	E7
200	WTMT	60559	3085	16W-4S	E7
CO-EM E Lakeshore Dr					
1700	TNLK	53181	2354		B4
3100	RcmT	60071	2354		B4
3100	TNLK	60071	2354		B4
Coey Ln					
8400	HYHL	60457	3210	10W-10S	B6
CO-EZ 39th Av					
10400	PTPR	53158	2362		D2
12600	BtnT	53158	2362		E4
12600	BtnT	60096	2362		E4
12600	BtnT	60099	2362		E4
Coffman Ln					
10	LtRT	60545	3259	48W-11S	B2
Cog Cir					
800	CLLK	60014	2640	33W-25N	E6
6900	AlqT	60014	2640	33W-25N	E6
CO-G Donin Dr					
2400	ANTH	60002	2357	23W-43N	E4
Cog Hill Ct					
10	LIHL	60156	2693	36W-22N	C4
Coghill Ct					
1400	NARA	60542	3078	35W-2S	B5
N Cog Hill Ct					
1300	VNHL	60061	2647	17W-26N	B2
S Cog Hill Dr					
22900	FftT	60423	3591	13W-27S	B5
Cog Hill Ln					
14800	HMGN	60491	3343	17W-17S	C6
Coghill Ln					
13700	ODPK	60462	3346	11W-16S	A3
Coghill St					
10	CTHL	60403	3417	27W-20S	D6
10	PnfT	60403	3417	27W-20S	D6
10	PnfT	60435	3417	27W-20S	D6
CO-H					
-	BfdT	53128	2353		B3
-	GNCY	53128	2353		A2
500	BfdT	53128	2352		E1
500	GNCY	53128	2352		E2
CO-H 88th Av					
10500	PTPR	53158	2361		D3
12200	NptT	60099	2361		D3
12200	PTPR	60099	2361		D3
Cohasset Ct					
700	GRNE	60031	2535	14W-33N	D3
Cohasset Rd					
100	LslT	60540	3142	25W-6S	B4
Cohen Ct					
-	DRFD	60015	2703	12W-21N	B7
CO-H Freeman St					
300	GNCY	53128	2353		A3
CO-H Walworth St					
100	GNCY	53128	2353		A3
CO-HM 116th St					
33600	RdlT	53181	2355		B2
33600	TNLK	53181	2355		B2
35000	RdlT	53181	2354		E2
35000	TNLK	53181	2354		E2
CO-HM 374th Av					
12600	RcmT	60081	2354		C4
12600	RdlT	53181	2354		C3
12600	RdlT	60081	2354		C4

Block	City	ZIP	Map#	CGS	Grid
CO-HM Wilmot Rd					
35600	RdlT	53181	2354		D2
35600	TNLK	53181	2354		D2
Coil Plus Dr					
14400	PNFD	60544	3338	30W-16S	B5
S Coirnne Cir					
-	PNFD	60586	3415	31W-20S	D5
CO-JF 119th St					
23800	SlmT	53179	2357		E2
CO-JF 260th Av					
-	SlmT	53179	2357		D2
CO-JI Hastings Ct					
32500	GRNE	60031	2477	16W-37N	E3
CO-KD 336th Av					
9800	RdlT	53181	2355		B1
9800	TNLK	53181	2355		B3
12700	BtnT	60081	2355		B4
12700	RdlT	60081	2355		B4
Cokes Rd					
1400	HMGN	60491	3342	19W-16S	C4
1400	HmrT	60441	3342	19W-16S	C4
1400	HmrT	60491	3342	19W-16S	C4
Colaric Ct					
1400	JLET	60431	3495	32W-22S	D1
Colaric Dr					
-	JLET	60431	3495	32W-22S	D1
Colbee Benton Rd					
1400	GYLK	60030	2533	19W-31N	C6
Colbert Rd					
2600	WKGN	60085	2536	12W-33N	C1
Colburn Av					
100	JltT	60433	3499	23W-25S	A7
200	JLET	60433	3499	23W-24S	A7
Colby Ct					
700	GRNE	60031	2534	16W-33N	E3
Colby Dr					
2100	NndT	60050	2585	31W-29N	E3
Colby Ln					
1400	SMBG	60193	2912	25W-9N	B1
Colby Rd					
-	GRNE	60031	2534	16W-33N	E3
-	WrnT	60031	2534	16W-33N	E3
Colby Commerce Dr					
-	BmdT	60172	2912	25W-6N	B6
-	HRPK	60133	2912	25W-6N	B6
-	HRPK	60172	2912	25W-6N	B6
-	ROSL	60133	2912	25W-6N	B6
-	ROSL	60172	2912	25W-6N	B6
Colby Point Rd					
2100	NndT	60050	2585	31W-29N	D3
Colchester Av					
1900	HFET	60192	2802	30W-12N	B7
Colchester Ct					
2100	HFET	60192	2802	30W-12N	B7
Colchester Dr					
500	OSWG	60543	3263	36W-13S	E5
Colcord Pl					
800	GNEN	60137	3025	21W-0N	D4
Coldren Dr					
10	PTHT	60070	2808	14W-15N	C3
200	WLNG	60090	2808	14W-15N	C3
Cold Spring Ct					
200	RGMW	60067	2805	21W-13N	D5
Cold Spring Rd					
100	BRTN	60010	2751	24W-20N	C2
Coldspring Rd					
1100	ELGN	60120	2855	32W-12N	D2
1200	CLSM	60188	2967	27W-4N	C3
N Coldspring Rd					
1900	ANHT	60004	2807	16W-16N	E1
2000	ANHT	60004	2754	16W-16N	E7
Coldspring St					
10	AURA	60506	3137	38W-7S	A7
Cold Springs Dr					
12300	HTLY	60142	2744	42W-19N	D3
Cold Springs Rd					
-	AlqT	60013	2695	32W-23N	C3
-	CRY	60013	2695	32W-23N	C3
-	TVLY	60013	2695	32W-23N	C3
N Cold Springs Rd					
10	BLVY	60098	2526	38W-32N	A5
10	GwdT	60098	2526	38W-32N	A5
S Cold Springs Rd					
10	BLVY	60098	2526	38W-31N	A6
10	GwdT	60098	2526	38W-31N	A6
Coldstream Cir					
10	LNSH	60069	2702	14W-22N	C4
S Coldwater Rd					
26300	ELWD	60421	3675	24W-32S	D7
26300	JknT	60421	3675	24W-32S	D7
Cole Av					
-	OSWG	60543	3263	38W-14S	B7
300	MltT	60187	3024	25W-0N	B4
400	WHTN	60187	3024	24W-0N	D4
E Cole Av					
100	WHTN	60187	3024	24W-0N	D4
W Cole Av					
200	WHTN	60187	3024	24W-0N	C4
Cole Ct					
-	PLNO	60545	3260	45W-13S	C6
400	SMBG	60193	2858	25W-9N	A7
500	GRNE	60031	2535	14W-33N	C3
7500	OswT	60560	3334	40W-15S	C3
Cole Dr					
400	SEGN	60177	2907	37W-7N	C4
Cole Ln					
2700	NLNX	60451	3589	18W-27S	B5
Coleen Ct					
2800	RGMW	60008	2806	20W-13N	A5
Coleman Dr					
300	ELGN	60120	2855	32W-10N	C5
16200	ODPK	60467	3423	13W-19S	A2
Coleman Ln					
400	CmpT	60175	2961	43W-5N	B2
W Coleman Pl					
5100	MONE	60449	3683	6W-31S	A5
Colerain St					
23100	PNFD	60544	3416	28W-19S	E2
23100	PnfT	60544	3416	28W-19S	E2
Coleridge Ct					
1200	WDRG	60517	3206	20W-10S	B5
S Coles Av					
7100	CHCG	60649	3153	3E-8S	D7
7500	CHCG	60649	3215	3E-8S	E1
7800	CHCG	60649	3216	3E-8S	A1
7900	CHCG	60617	3216	3E-9S	A2
Colette Ct					
8100	ODPK	60462	3346	10W-18S	C7
Colette Ln					
8500	HYHL	60457	3210	10W-10S	A4
Colfax Av					
400	CNHL	60514	3145	17W-5S	C3
400	CNHL	60559	3145	17W-5S	C3
400	WTMT	60559	3145	17W-5S	C3
2100	GNVW	60025	2864	9W-12N	D1

Chicago 7-County Street Index

STREET Block	City	ZIP	Map#	CGS	Grid
S Colfax Av					
500	EMHT	60126	3028	15W-0N	A5
7400	CHCG	60649	3153	3E-8S	D7
7500	CHCG	60649	3215	3E-9S	D2
7800	CHCG	60617	3215	3E-9S	D3
Colfax Ct					
1600	BRLT	60103	2967	27W-5N	B1
1600	NPVL	60563	3140	29W-5S	D3
Colfax Pl					
3300	EVTN	60201	2866	4W-12N	B1
3300	SKOK	60076	2866	4W-12N	B1
Colfax St					
400	AURA	60505	3138	34W-7S	D6
600	EVTN	60201	2867	2W-12N	B1
1800	EVTN	60201	2866	4W-12N	C1
4000	SKOK	60076	2866	5W-12N	B1
E Colfax St					
10	PLTN	60067	2752	21W-16N	D7
200	PLTN	60067	2753	20W-16N	A7
400	PLTN	60074	2753	20W-16N	A7
N Colfax St					
500	SDWH	60548	3330	51W-14S	A1
S Colfax St					
100	SDWH	60548	3330	51W-15S	A2
W Colfax St					
10	PLTN	60067	2752	22W-16N	C6
Colfax Ter					
2300	EVTN	60201	2867	3W-12N	A1
Colford Av					
10	WnfT	60185	3022	29W-0N	E4
400	WCHI	60185	3022	29W-0N	D4
Colgate Av					
3300	ZION	60099	2422	10W-39N	B5
Colgate Ct					
500	HFET	60169	2858	24W-12N	E2
1100	NPVL	60565	3204	25W-10S	C6
Colgate Ln					
5600	MTSN	60443	3505	7W-25S	D6
Colgate St					
1200	WLMT	60091	2812	5W-14N	B4
Colina Av					
5800	OKFT	60452	3347	7W-18S	D6
Colina Calle Ct					
100	AxST	60447	3672	32W-29S	C2
100	MNKA	60447	3672	32W-29S	C2
Collector Car Dr					
-	GNOK	60045	2592	14W-28N	D6
-	GNOK	60048	2592	14W-28N	D6
-	LbvT	60048	2592	14W-28N	D6
Colleen Ct					
1500	AURA	60505	3138	34W-5S	E3
S Colleen Ct					
21700	TroT	60404	3584	30W-26S	C2
W Colleen Ct					
25600	CNHN	60410	3672	32W-30S	D3
Colleen Dr					
500	LYWD	60411	3510	4E-25S	B7
700	CRY	60013	2641	30W-24N	E7
Colleen Ln					
1500	AURA	60505	3138	34W-5S	D3
College Av					
100	PTPR	53158	2363	10W-43N	B5
100	WPHR	53158	2363	10W-43N	B5
100	WPHR	60096	2363	10W-43N	B5
400	WHTN	60187	3024	24W-0S	D6
500	AURA	60505	3138	35W-7S	C7
800	MTSN	60443	3506	5W-25S	B7
1500	WHTN	60187	3025	23W-0S	A5
1800	GNEN	60137	3025	23W-0S	A5
1800	WHTN	60137	3025	23W-0S	A5
W College Blvd					
800	ADSN	60101	2969	21W-4N	E3
College Cross					
100	RGMW	60008	2805	22W-13N	C5
100	SMBG	60008	2805	21W-13N	C5
100	SMBG	60173	2805	21W-13N	C5
400	RGMW	60067	2805	22W-13N	C5
College Dr					
-	DSPN	60016	2863	12W-12N	A1
-	GYLK	60030	2533	19W-33N	C2
-	MaiT	60016	2863	12W-12N	A1
100	BMDL	60108	2969	22W-4N	B3
200	MPPT	60056	2808	15W-12N	A7
200	MPPT	60056	2862	15W-12N	A1
600	PltT	60173	2805	22W-13N	C6
600	SMBG	60173	2805	22W-13N	C6
2100	GLHT	60108	2969	23W-4N	B4
2100	GLHT	60139	2969	23W-4N	B4
E College Dr					
10	ANHT	60004	2754	17W-17N	A5
10	BFGV	60004	2754	17W-17N	A5
10	BFGV	60089	2754	17W-17N	A5
N College Dr					
1200	PNFD	60544	3338	29W-17S	D6
1200	PnfT	60544	3338	29W-17S	D6
W College Dr					
10	ANHT	60004	2754	17W-17N	A5
6300	PSHT	60463	3275	8W-14S	A5
6300	WthT	60463	3275	8W-14S	B5
7000	PSHT	60463	3274	8W-13S	E5
7900	PSHT	60464	3274	9W-13S	C5
7900	PSPK	60464	3274	9W-13S	C5
W College Dr SR-83					
6300	PSHT	60463	3275	8W-14S	A5
6300	WthT	60463	3275	8W-14S	B5
7000	PSHT	60463	3274	8W-13S	E5
7900	PSHT	60464	3274	9W-13S	C5
7900	PSPK	60464	3274	9W-13S	C5
College Ln S					
1300	WHTN	60187	3082	23W-2S	E4
1600	WHTN	60187	3083	23W-2S	A4
W College Pkwy					
800	CHCG	60608	3033	1W-1S	D7
800	CHCG	60608	3034		E7
College Pl					
700	HDPK	60035	2704	9W-24N	B1
College Rd					
-	GNEN	60137	3083	22W-2S	B3
-	LslT	60532	3142	24W-7S	C7
-	LslT	60540	3142	24W-7S	C7
-	MltT	60137	3083	22W-2S	B3
-	NPVL	60532	3142	24W-7S	C7
-	NPVL	60540	3142	24W-7S	C7
-	NPVL	60540	3204	24W-8S	C1
200	LslT	60540	3204	24W-8S	D2
300	LslT	60565	3204	24W-8S	D2
300	NPVL	60565	3204	24W-8S	D2
400	LKFT	60045	2650	10W-26N	A3
2200	LslT	60516	3143	21W-6S	D4
2700	DRGV	60516	3143	21W-6S	D4
5600	LSLE	60532	3142	24W-7S	C7
College Rd CO-40					
-	LslT	60532	3142	24W-7S	C7
-	LslT	60540	3142	24W-7S	C7
-	LslT	60540	3204	24W-8S	C1
-	NPVL	60532	3142	24W-7S	C7
College Rd CO-40					
-	NPVL	60540	3142	24W-7S	C7
-	NPVL	60540	3204	24W-8S	C1
5600	LSLE	60532	3142	24W-7S	C7
College St					
100	CLLK	60014	2640	35W-25N	A5
200	ELGN	60120	2855	33W-11N	A3
300	CLLK	60014	2639	35W-25N	E5
N College St					
100	BTVA	60510	3078	34W-1S	C1
S College St					
10	BTVA	60510	3078	34W-1S	C2
College Entrance 1					
-	CLLK	60012	2639	37W-27N	B1
-	DrrT	60012	2639	37W-27N	B1
College Green Dr					
1600	ELGN	60123	2854	36W-9N	A7
2000	ELGN	60123	2853	36W-9N	E7
2300	ELGN	60124	2853	36W-10N	D7
College Hill Cir					
2500	SMBG	60173	2805	22W-13N	C6
2600	RGMW	60008	2805	22W-13N	C6
2600	RGMW	60173	2805	22W-13N	C6
2600	SMBG	60008	2805	22W-13N	C6
Collegewood Ct					
2400	LSLE	60532	3142	24W-7S	D7
2400	LSLE	60540	3142	24W-7S	D7
2400	LslT	60532	3142	24W-7S	D7
2400	LslT	60540	3142	24W-7S	D7
Collen Ct					
100	LMBD	60148	3084	20W-1S	B1
Collen Dr					
10	LMBD	60148	3084	20W-1S	B1
10	YkTp	60148	3084	20W-1S	B1
Collett Ln					
2000	FSMR	60422	3507	2W-22S	C1
2000	HMWD	60430	3507	2W-22S	C1
Colley Dr					
400	SchT	60174	2908	34W-6N	D7
Collier Ct					
1200	WKGN	60085	2536	11W-32N	E5
6400	LGGV	60047	2646	18W-24N	E7
Collier Dr					
500	ANTH	60002	2357	24W-43N	D4
Colligan St					
25100	MHTN	60442	3677	19W-30S	E4
25100	MHTN	60442	3678	19W-30S	A4
Collin Cir					
300	BMDL	60108	2968	24W-5N	C2
Collin Dr					
19500	FftT	60423	3504	9W-23S	E4
Collingwood Ct					
10	BGBK	60440	3268	25W-11S	B1
1100	SRWD	60404	3496	30W-24S	B5
Collingwood Dr					
900	NPVL	60540	3142	25W-7S	C7
1100	NPVL	60540	3204	24W-8S	D1
E Collingwood Dr					
1200	LKPT	60441	3420	21W-18S	A1
Collingwood Ln					
1100	BGBK	60440	3268	25W-11S	B1
Collins Av					
-	ADSN	60101	2969	21W-3N	E6
-	ADSN	60148	2969	21W-3N	E6
-	ANTH	60002	2357	24W-43N	D4
-	BmdT	60101	2969	21W-3N	E6
-	BmdT	60148	2969	21W-3N	E6
1400	GNVW	60025	2810	10W-14N	A5
1400	NfdT	60025	2810	10W-14N	A5
7900	LYNS	60534	3088	10W-4S	C6
Collins Av CO-54					
-	ADSN	60101	2969	21W-3N	E6
-	BmdT	60101	2969	21W-3N	E6
-	BmdT	60148	2969	21W-3N	E6
Collins Cir					
1500	EGVV	60007	2914	21W-9N	A1
Collins Ct					
2300	BTVA	60510	3077	37W-1S	C2
2800	NPVL	60563	3140	29W-5S	C4
Collins Dr					
-	VNHL	60061	2647	17W-26N	C4
-	WDSK	60098	2524	42W-32N	C5
1100	ELBN	60119	3017	43W-2N	A1
1300	CLLK	60013	2641	32W-24N	A7
1300	CLLK	60013	2695	32W-24N	A1
1300	CRY	60013	2641	32W-24N	A7
1300	CRY	60013	2695	32W-24N	A1
S Collins Dr					
300	PNFD	60544	3416	29W-18S	D2
300	PNFD	60586	3416	29W-18S	D2
Collins Rd					
1400	OswT	60543	3264	36W-14S	A7
2700	OswT	60543	3263	37W-14S	C7
3800	OSWG	60543	3263	37W-14S	C7
18800	MngT	60152	2578	48W-30N	E2
20000	SenT	60152	2578	49W-30N	C2
Collins St					
1000	JLET	60432	3499	23W-22S	B1
1400	JLET	60441	3499	23W-21S	A1
1400	JltT	60432	3499	23W-22S	A1
1400	LktT	60432	3499	23W-21S	A1
1400	LktT	60441	3499	23W-21S	A1
2400	BLID	60406	3277	3W-14S	B6
Collins St SR-171					
1000	JLET	60432	3499	23W-22S	B1
1400	JLET	60441	3499	23W-21S	A1
1400	JltT	60432	3499	23W-22S	A1
1400	LktT	60432	3499	23W-21S	A1
1400	LktT	60441	3499	23W-21S	A1
N Collins St					
10	JLET	60432	3499	23W-23S	B3
10	SEGN	60177	2908	34W-8N	C2
N Collins St SR-171					
400	JLET	60432	3499	23W-23S	B4
N Collins St US-6					
10	JLET	60432	3499	23W-23S	A5
N Collins St US-30					
10	JLET	60432	3499	23W-23S	A5
S Collins St					
100	SEGN	60177	2908	34W-8N	C4
Coloma Ct N					
1500	WHTN	60187	3083	23W-1S	A2
Coloma Ct S					
1500	WHTN	60187	3083	23W-1S	A2
Coloma Pl					
1400	WHTN	60187	3082	23W-1S	E2
1600	WHTN	60187	3083	23W-1S	A2
Colomba Ct					
-	SCRL	60174	2964	34W-2N	E7
-	SCRL	60174	3020	34W-2N	E1
Colombia Dr					
-	LkvT	60046	2416	25W-38N	B7
Colonade Rd					
800	SRWD	60404	3496	30W-24S	B7
Colonel Bennett Ln					
600	CmpT	60175	2906	40W-6N	B7
Colonel Holcomb Dr					
6400	BLVY	60012	2584	35W-29N	A4
6400	NndT	60012	2584	35W-29N	A4
Colonial Av					
7200	AlqT	60014	2640	33W-24N	E6
7200	CLLK	60014	2640	33W-24N	E6
Colonial Cir					
300	GNVA	60134	3019	36W-1N	E3
Colonial Ct					
10	SMWD	60107	2856	29W-9N	E7
500	ALGN	60102	2747	33W-20N	E1
900	LKZH	60047	2698	24W-22N	C4
1000	NPVL	60540	3142	25W-6S	A5
S Colonial Ct					
17700	PnfT	60586	3415	32W-21S	D6
Colonial Dr					
-	NlxT	60432	3500	20W-22S	B2
800	WLNG	60090	2755	15W-18N	A3
1000	JLET	60432	3500	20W-22S	B2
2600	ELGN	60124	2853	37W-11N	C3
2600	ElgT	60124	2853	37W-11N	D4
4800	MONE	60449	3683	6W-31S	B5
E Colonial Dr					
100	VNHL	60061	2647	16W-27N	D1
Colonial Ln					
-	DSPN	60016	2862	15W-10N	A5
10	YkTp	60148	3084	20W-2S	A3
600	DSPN	60018	2862	15W-10N	A5
1600	NHFD	60093	2811	6W-15N	C3
Colonial Pkwy					
100	YKVL	60560	3333	43W-16S	C3
200	YkTp	60523	3084	19W-3S	D5
14500	PNFD	60544	3337	31W-17S	E7
W Colonial Pkwy					
1600	IVNS	60067	2805	22W-14N	A4
1600	PLTN	60067	2805	22W-14N	A4
Colonial Sq					
1300	MltT	60187	3082	25W-2S	A4
1300	WHTN	60187	3082	25W-2S	A4
Colonial St					
1900	AURA	60503	3201	32W-10S	C6
Colonnades Dr					
800	NHBK	60062	2757	8W-17N	E4
Colony Av					
500	LNHT	60046	2418	19W-39N	C6
Colony Ct					
10	OswT	60560	3334	40W-15S	C2
200	BMDL	60108	2969	22W-4N	B4
200	VNHL	60061	2647	17W-26N	B3
400	BGBK	60440	3269	22W-12S	B2
400	SRWD	60404	3496	30W-23S	B4
800	LNHT	60046	2418	19W-39N	C5
1100	SMWD	60107	2910	29W-9N	E1
1400	LMBD	60148	3084	20W-1S	B1
2400	NHBK	60062	2757	10W-17N	A6
3900	HFET	60192	2804	24W-14N	D3
4700	MHRY	60050	2527	33W-31N	E6
Colony Dr					
100	IVNS	60010	2751	25W-16N	A6
400	GNVA	60134	3019	37W-1N	B4
1000	CLLK	60014	2639	37W-24N	B7
1300	CRTE	60417	3685	1W-29S	A2
1400	CRTE	60417	3684	1W-29S	E2
N Colony Dr					
300	RLKP	60073	2532	23W-33N	A2
S Colony Dr					
2300	DSPN	60018	2861	16W-10N	E6
2300	MPPT	60018	2861	16W-10N	E6
2300	MPPT	60056	2861	16W-10N	E6
Colony Ln					
10	DRFD	60015	2757	10W-20N	B1
200	NLNX	60451	3589	18W-26S	B2
700	FKFT	60423	3592	9W-26S	E1
900	HFET	60192	2804	24W-14N	C3
1100	ROSL	60172	2912	24W-7N	C5
Colony Tr					
600	MHRY	60050	2526	36W-32N	E4
Colony Green Dr					
200	BMDL	60108	2969	22W-4N	B3
Colony Lake Dr					
800	SMBG	60194	2858	24W-11N	D3
Colorado Av					
-	FKFT	60423	3504	11W-25S	A6
10	FftT	60423	3503	12W-25S	C6
10	FKFT	60423	3503	12W-25S	C6
300	AURA	60506	3138	36W-6S	A5
900	AURA	60506	3137	37W-6S	C5
1200	JLET	60435	3498	25W-22S	B1
2100	ELGN	60123	2853	36W-12N	E2
2900	JLET	60431	3417	28W-20S	B4
3300	WKGN	60087	2479	12W-36N	B4
3300	WkgT	60087	2479	12W-36N	A4
E Colorado Av					
10	FftT	60423	3503	11W-25S	E6
10	FKFT	60423	3503	11W-25S	E6
W Colorado Av					
2100	NCHI	60088	2593	12W-30N	C2
Colorado Ct					
700	CLSM	60188	2967	27W-2N	D7
700	NPVL	60565	3203	27W-10S	B6
1100	AURA	60506	3137	37W-6S	C4
10900	ODPK	60467	3423	13W-21S	A6
Colorado Ln					
1500	EGVV	60007	2859	21W-9N	E7
Colson Dr					
10	CmpT	60175	2962	41W-5N	A2
Colt Dr					
300	CmpT	60119	3018	41W-2N	A1
13500	HMGN	60491	3343	16W-18S	D7
W Colt Dr					
13400	HMGN	60491	3343	16W-18S	E7
Colton Cir					
4200	NPVL	60564	3267	28W-12S	A3
Colton Ct					
2900	LSLE	60563	3142	24W-5S	C2
2900	LslT	60563	3142	24W-5S	C2
Colton Ln					
10	NHFD	60091	2811	6W-14N	E4
10	NHFD	60093	2811	6W-14N	E4
10	WLMT	60091	2811	6W-14N	E4
Colton Rd					
500	GYLK	60030	2533	19W-33N	B2
Colton St					
300	YKVL	60560	3333	42W-15S	C2
Colton Ridge Ct					
6300	JLET	60586	3415	31W-21S	D7
Columbia Av					
-	CteT	60417	3774	1W-32S	B1
-	FDHT	60411	3509	1E-24S	B6
10	CHCG	60068	2918	9W-8N	B2
10	CHCG	60631	2918	9W-8N	B2
10	FXLK	60020	2473	27W-36N	B3
10	PKRG	60068	2918	9W-8N	B2
400	LslT	60563	3141	26W-5S	E3
Columbia Av					
500	DSPN	60016	2862	14W-11N	C2
500	HNDL	60521	3146	14W-5S	C2
500	NPVL	60563	3141	26W-5S	E3
600	ELGN	60120	2855	33W-12N	B2
4800	LSLE	60532	3143	22W-5S	B2
8800	MNSR	46321	3510		E2
10200	DYR	46311	3510		D5
E Columbia Av					
100	EMHT	60126	3027	16W-2N	E1
100	EMHT	60126	3028	15W-2N	A1
W Columbia Av					
1000	CHCG	60626	2921	1W-8N	D1
3000	CHCG	60645	2921	2W-8N	B2
3300	LNWD	60712	2920	4W-8N	D2
7700	CHCG	60068	2918	9W-8N	C2
7700	CHCG	60631	2918	9W-8N	C2
7700	PKRG	60068	2918	9W-8N	C2
7700	PKRG	60631	2918	9W-8N	C2
Columbia Cir					
200	CRTE	60417	3596	0W-28S	C6
800	NARA	60542	3078	35W-3S	C6
1500	EGVV	60007	2913	21W-9N	E1
1600	BRLT	60103	2967	28W-5N	B1
Columbia Ct					
-	EGVV	60007	2913	21W-8N	E1
200	SMBG	60193	2857	26W-10N	E6
900	CLSM	60188	2968	25W-4N	B4
W Columbia Ct					
21000	ElaT	60047	2645	21W-25N	E6
Columbia Dr					
600	NLNX	60451	3502	16W-25S	A7
700	NLNX	60451	3590	16W-26S	A2
1400	EGVV	60007	2913	21W-9N	E1
1700	CHCG	60637	3153	2E-6S	B3
6700	BDPK	60455	3148	9W-7S	C6
6700	BDPK	60458	3148	9W-7S	C6
6700	BGVW	60455	3148	9W-7S	C6
6700	BGVW	60458	3148	9W-7S	C6
Columbia Ln					
-	RtdT	60118	2746	38W-17N	C7
-	RtdT	60118	2799	38W-16N	B1
-	RtdT	60136	2799	38W-16N	B1
800	DRN	60561	3145	17W-7S	C7
1400	BRTN	60010	2750	25W-17N	E5
1400	IVNS	60010	2750	25W-17N	E5
2400	MTGY	60538	3198	40W-10S	D6
Columbia St					
100	BTVA	60510	3078	35W-1S	C1
300	LslT	60540	3141	26W-7S	E7
300	LslT	60563	3141	26W-5S	E3
300	NPVL	60540	3141	26W-7S	E7
300	NPVL	60563	3141	26W-5S	E3
500	AURA	60505	3138	34W-7S	C7
900	CRTE	60417	3596	1W-28S	B7
900	CRTE	60417	3685	1W-29S	B2
900	CRTE	60475	3596	1W-28S	B7
900	CteT	60417	3596	1W-28S	B7
900	CteT	60475	3596	1W-28S	B7
900	STGR	60475	3596	1W-28S	B7
1400	FDHT	60411	3509	1E-24S	B6
E Columbia St					
300	JLET	60432	3499	23W-23S	B3
E Columbia St SR-53					
10	JLET	60432	3499	23W-23S	A3
N Columbia St					
10	NPVL	60540	3141	26W-6S	E5
300	NPVL	60563	3141	26W-6S	E4
1500	LslT	60563	3141	26W-5S	E3
S Columbia St					
10	NPVL	60540	3141	26W-6S	E6
700	LslT	60540	3141	26W-7S	E7
W Columbia Bay Dr					
25100	LkvT	60046	2416	25W-38N	B7
25100	LkvT	60046	2474	25W-37N	A1
N Columbia Bay Rd					
38300	LkvT	60046	2416	25W-38N	B7
W Columbia Bay Rd					
25000	LkvT	60046	2416	25W-38N	B7
Columbian Av N					
700	OKPK	60302	3031	8W-1N	A2
1200	CHCG	60707	3031	8W-1N	A1
Columbian Dr					
-	LNSG	60438	3430	3E-20S	A5
Columbine Av					
500	LslT	60532	3143	22W-6S	C4
6600	GfnT	60014	2639	38W-25N	A5
6700	LKWD	60014	2639	38W-25N	A5
N Columbine Av					
10	LMBD	60148	3026	21W-1N	A3
300	MltT	60148	3026	21W-1N	A2
N Columbine Av SR-53					
10	LMBD	60148	3026	21W-1N	A3
300	MltT	60148	3026	21W-1N	A2
S Columbine Av					
10	LMBD	60148	3026	21W-0S	A6
500	MltT	60148	3026	21W-0N	A5
500	YkTp	60148	3026	21W-0N	A5
1000	MltT	60148	3025	21W-0S	E7
1100	GNEN	60137	3025	21W-0S	E7
1100	GNEN	60148	3025	21W-0S	E7
1100	LMBD	60148	3025	21W-0S	E7
S Columbine Av SR-53					
10	LMBD	60148	3026	21W-0S	A6
500	MltT	60148	3026	21W-0N	A5
500	YkTp	60148	3026	21W-0N	A5
1000	MltT	60148	3025	21W-0S	E7
1100	GNEN	60137	3025	21W-0S	E7
1100	GNEN	60148	3025	21W-0S	E7
1100	LMBD	60148	3025	21W-0S	E7
Columbine Blvd					
-	HFET	60010	2802	28W-13N	E6
-	HnrT	60192	2802	29W-12N	D7
4800	HFET	60192	2802	29W-13N	D7
Columbine Cir					
400	SMBG	60173	2859	21W-11N	E4
1500	RMVL	60446	3339	26W-17S	E6
S Columbine Cir					
13300	PNFD	60585	3338	30W-15S	B3
Columbine Ct					
10	SMWD	60107	2856	30W-10N	C6
300	RMVL	60446	3339	26W-17S	E6
700	LKZH	60047	2699	23W-22N	A4
1700	YKVL	60560	3333	43W-16S	B5
34300	GrtT	60073	2531	25W-34N	A1
Columbine Dr					
-	ElgT	60124	2907	36W-9N	D1
200	CNHL	60514	3085	16W-4S	D7
300	SMBG	60173	2859	21W-10N	E4
700	ELGN	60124	2853	36W-9N	D7
800	ELGN	60124	2907	36W-9N	D1
1700	SMBG	60173	2860	20W-10N	A5
1800	YKVL	60560	3333	43W-16S	B5
2100	RDLK	60073	2531	25W-33N	A2
N Columbine Dr					
1300	MPPT	60056	2808	13W-14N	D3
Columbine Ln					
10	RVWD	60015	2702	14W-21N	C6
200	RMVL	60446	3339	26W-17S	E6
400	BGBK	60440	3268	23W-12S	E3
400	BGBK	60440	3269	23W-12S	A3
400	WCHI	60185	3022	29W-2N	D1
4500	MTSN	60443	3506	5W-24S	B6
Columbine East Rd					
700	SchT	60175	2907	38W-7N	A4
900	ElgT	60175	2907	38W-7N	A4
Columbine West Rd					
10	ElgT	60175	2907	38W-7N	A4
10	SchT	60175	2907	38W-7N	A4
N Columbus Av					
37200	LkvT	60046	2476	20W-37N	A2
37500	LNHT	60046	2476	20W-37N	A2
W Columbus Av					
2400	CHCG	60629	3151	3W-8S	B7
2400	CHCG	60629	3213	3W-8S	A1
2400	CHCG	60636	3151	3W-8S	B7
2400	CHCG	60652	3151	3W-8S	B7
2400	CHCG	60652	3213	3W-8S	A1
2900	CHCG	60652	3213	4W-9S	D3
4000	HMTN	60456	3212	5W-9S	C4
4000	HMTN	60652	3212	5W-9S	C4
Columbus Blvd					
3700	LYNS	60534	3088	9W-3S	C6
3700	RvsT	60534	3088	9W-3S	C6
3700	RvsT	60546	3088	9W-3S	C6
Columbus Ct					
10600	ODPK	60467	3423	13W-21S	B6
Columbus Dr					
800	MTGY	60543	3263	38W-11S	A1
800	OSWG	60543	3263	38W-11S	A1
1400	BGBK	60490	3267	26W-11S	E1
4800	OKLN	60453	3212	6W-10S	A5
4900	OKLN	60453	3211	6W-10S	E6
N Columbus Dr					
-	CHCG	60601	3034	0E-0N	C4
-	CHCG	60603	3034	0E-0N	C4
400	CHCG	60611	3034	0E-0N	C4
21000	CbaT	60010	2697	25W-21N	E7
21000	CbaT	60010	2698	25W-21N	A6
S Columbus Dr					
200	CHCG	60603	3034	0E-0S	C6
200	CHCG	60604	3034	0E-0S	C5
300	CHCG	60605	3034	0E-0S	C5
11100	WRTH	60482	3274	9W-13S	E3
Columbus Ln					
9000	MaiT	60016	2863	11W-11N	E3
9000	NlsT	60016	2863	11W-11N	E3
9000	PKRG	60068	2863	11W-11N	E3
Columbus Pkwy					
10	BFGV	60090	2755	14W-20N	C2
Columbus St					
600	LKMR	60051	2529	29W-31N	C6
600	NndT	60051	2529	29W-31N	C6
900	WLMT	60091	2812	4W-14N	C5
Colville Pl					
400	WKGN	60087	2480	10W-36N	A5
Colwyn Dr					
1300	SMBG	60194	2858	25W-11N	B4
Colwyn Ter					
500	DRFD	60015	2704	10W-21N	A6
600	DRFD	60015	2703	10W-21N	E6
S Comanche Ct					
17200	LKPT	60441	3420	20W-20S	C5
Comanche Dr					
1300	BGBK	60490	3267	26W-12S	E3
1300	BGBK	60490	3268	26W-12S	A3
S Comanche Dr					
12900	PSHT	60463	3346	9W-15S	E1
13000	PlsT	60463	3346	9W-15S	E1
Comanche Tr					
1900	RLKB	60073	2474	23W-35N	E5
Comandra Cir					
16800	HMGN	60491	3422	15W-20S	C4
CO-MB 152nd Av					
10400	BtlT	53142	2360		A4
11700	BtlT	60002	2360		B4
11700	NptT	60002	2360		A4
CO-MB Westminster Ln					
6800	GRNE	60031	2477	16W-36N	E3
Comet Dr					
200	BDWD	60408	3942	31W-42S	B7
200	RedT	60408	3942	31W-42S	B7
300	RedT	60408	4031	30W-42S	B1
1100	AURA	60505	3138	34W-5S	D3
Comfort Dr					
-	NPVL	60563	3080	29W-4S	D7
-	NPVL	60563	3140	29W-4S	D1
E Comfort Ln					
10	PLTN	60067	2752	20W-16N	E7
N Comfort Ln					
400	PLTN	60067	2752	20W-16N	E7
W Comfort St					
10	PLTN	60067	2752	21W-16N	E7
Comiskey Av					
-	BtvT	60542	3077	37W-3S	C6
-	NARA	60542	3077	37W-3S	C6
Comiskey Rd					
600	BRLT	60120	2909	32W-9N	C1
600	HnrT	60120	2909	32W-9N	C1
CO-ML 88th Av					
11600	PTPR	53158	2361		D2
CO-ML 116th St					
8000	PTPR	53158	2361		D2
CO-ML 122nd St					
-	BtlT	53142	2360		E3
8800	PTPR	53158	2361		B3
9100	PTPR	53158	2360		E3
CO-ML Springbrook Rd					
4800	PTPR	53158	2362		C1
6800	PTPR	53158	2361		E2
Commanche Ct					
500	CLSM	60188	2967	27W-2N	C7
2200	WKGN	60087	2479	11W-36N	D5
Commanche Ln					
400	CLSM	60188	2967	26W-3N	E6
Commanche Tr					
400	WLNG	60090	2754	16W-17N	D5
Commerce Ct					
800	BFGV	60089	2701	15W-21N	E7
4200	LSLE	60532	3142	24W-4S	C1
Commerce Dr					
-	DRGV	60515	3083	22W-4S	D7
-	WHTN	60187	3024	25W-0S	B7
10	GYLK	60030	2533	19W-32N	B4
10	SMBG	60173	2859	21W-12N	B1
10	SMBG	60195	2859	23W-12N	A1
200	CLLK	60014	2640	35W-26N	A3
200	CLSM	60188	2968	24W-2N	C7
700	OKBK	60523	3085	16W-1S	E2
800	SEGN	60177	2908	34W-9N	D1
1000	GNVA	60134	3020	34W-1N	E4
1000	LKZH	60047	2699	22W-23N	B1

STREET
Block City ZIP Map# CGS Grid

Commerce Dr
1000 WCHI 60185 3022 31W-0N A6
1000 WnfT 60185 3022 31W-0N A6
1200 CRTE 60417 3597 1E-28S B6
1400 ALGN 60102 2746 35W-20N E2
1500 DndT 60118 2800 34W-14N D6
1500 ELGN 60118 2800 34W-14N D6
1500 ELGN 60123 2800 34W-14N D6
1700 EGvT 60007 2861 16W-9N D6
1700 EGVV 60007 2861 16W-9N C6
1700 MTGY 60538 3199 37W-9S B4
2300 LYVL 60048 2590 19W-30N C3
2500 FmtT 60048 2590 19W-30N C3
2500 FmtT 60060 2590 19W-30N C3
3800 SCRL 60174 3021 33W-2N B1
3900 WynT 60185 3021 33W-2N B1
W Commerce Dr
26500 VOLO 60073 2530 26W-31N D7
Commerce Ln
1400 JLET 60431 3585 28W-25S A2
Commerce Pkwy
800 CPVL 60110 2747 35W-17N D6
Commerce Rd
10 MTGY 60543 3263 38W-11S A1
Commerce St
300 AURA 60504 3139 31W-7S E7
400 BRRG 60527 3146 15W-7S A7
700 LKPT 60441 3419 22W-19S C3
2900 FNPK 60131 2973 11W-3N D4
Commerce Center Dr
- MonT 60449 3683 6W-29S A2
Commercial Av
- MHRY 60050 2527 33W-33N D3
300 CTCY 60409 3352 3E-17S A5
2600 CHHT 60411 3596 1W-26S B2
2600 SCHT 60411 3596 1W-27S B4
3000 NHBK 60062 2756 11W-18N C3
3300 SCHT 60475 3596 1W-27S B4
3300 STGR 60475 3596 1W-27S B4
15200 HRVY 60426 3350 1W-18S A7
15600 HRVY 60426 3428 1W-19S A2
17700 LNSG 60438 3430 3E-21S A6
S Commercial Av
7900 CHCG 60617 3215 1E-9S A3
7900 CHCG 60649 3215 1E-9S A3
9200 CHCG 60617 3216 3E-11S A6
10300 CHCG 60617 3279 3E-11S E1
12800 CHCG 60633 3280 3E-14S A7
13200 CHCG 60633 3352 3E-15S A1
W Commercial Av
10 ADSN 60101 2970 18W-2N E7
27900 LKBN 60010 2697 28W-21N A5
28000 LKBN 60010 2696 28W-21N E5
Commercial Blvd
- RDLK 60073 2531 24W-34N C1
Commercial Dr
- MKNA 60448 3503 13W-23S B3
- WLNG 60090 2755 14W-17N B5
100 YKVL 60560 3261 43W-12S B3
21100 ElaT 60047 2645 21W-25N D4
21100 ElaT 60060 2645 21W-25N D4
Commercial Rd
6000 CLLK 60014 2640 35W-24N B6
Commercial St
- CmgT 60033 2405 51W-39N D3
- HRVD 60033 2405 51W-39N D4
10500 RHMD 60071 2353 34W-43N C4
E Commercial St
- BNVL 60106 2915 17W-6N B7
100 WDDL 60191 2915 17W-6N B7
W Commercial St
100 WDDL 60191 2915 18W-6N A7
400 PNFD 60544 3338 30W-18S C7
Commercial Wy
4200 GNVW 60025 2809 11W-13N D7
4200 NfdT 60025 2809 11W-13N D7
Commodore Ct
1500 SMBG 60193 2912 25W-8N B2
Commodore Ln
1500 SMBG 60193 2912 25W-8N B2
S Commodore Whalen Dr
- CHCG 60637 3153 2E-7S C5
- CHCG 60649 3153 2E-7S C5
Common Dr
- BGBK 60440 3269 22W-12S B3
Common Wy
- BFGV 60089 2754 17W-20N B1
Common Ridings Wy
2100 IVNS 60010 2751 25W-16N A7
Commons Cir
400 CNHL 60514 3145 17W-5S C3
Commons Ct
100 WLNG 60090 2755 13W-17N D4
S Commons Ct
400 DRFD 60015 2756 10W-20N E1
Commons Dr
- ALGN 60102 2746 37W-19N E2
- AURA 60504 3202 30W-8S B2
- AURA 60564 3202 30W-8S B2
- NpvT 60504 3202 30W-8S B2
- NpvT 60564 3202 30W-8S B2
10 PSPK 60464 3274 10W-14S C6
100 CHRG 60415 3211 8W-11S B7
100 GNVA 60134 3019 37W-1N D3
100 SCRL 60134 3019 37W-1N D3
200 OKLN 60415 3211 8W-11S B7
200 OKLN 60453 3211 8W-11S B7
600 SRWD 60404 3496 30W-23S B4
1100 SMBG 60173 2859 22W-11N D2
1400 WDSK 60098 2582 40W-29N A4
N Commons Dr
10 AURA 60504 3140 30W-7S B7
10 AURA 60504 3202 30W-7S A1
4600 CHCG 60656 2918 10W-5N A7
S Commons Dr
10 AURA 60504 3202 30W-8S B1
Commons Rd
- WNVL 60555 3141 28W-4S B2
- WNVL 60563 3141 28W-4S B2
600 NPVL 60563 3141 27W-5S C2
600 NpvT 60563 3141 27W-5S C2
E Commons Tr
300 VNHL 60061 2647 16W-27N D2
Commonwealth Av
700 WKGN 60085 2536 11W-33N E4
1900 NCHI 60064 2536 11W-31N E7
2300 NCHI 60064 2593 11W-31N E1
2400 JLET 60435 3417 27W-20S B5
2400 PnfT 60435 3417 27W-20S B5
4700 WNSP 60558 3146 14W-5S D2
7100 BRRG 60525 3146 15W-7S B7
7100 BRRG 60527 3146 15W-7S B7
7100 BRRG 60527 3208 14W-8S D1
7100 IHPK 60525 3146 15W-7S B7
7100 IHPK 60527 3146 15W-7S B7
N Commonwealth Av
200 ELGN 60123 2854 34W-11N C3
700 AURA 60506 3137 37W-6S D5
2300 CHCG 60614 2978 0W-2N B6
2800 CHCG 60657 2978 0W-3N B4
S Commonwealth Av
10 AURA 60506 3137 37W-7S D7
10 ELGN 60123 2854 34W-11N C5
200 AURA 60506 3199 37W-7S D1
400 AraT 60506 3199 37W-7S D1
Commonwealth Ct
900 BRTN 60010 2697 26W-21N E6
900 BRTN 60010 2698 25W-20N A7
900 CbaT 60010 2698 25W-20N A7
900 VNHL 60061 2647 16W-26N D3
1000 BGBK 60440 3268 25W-11S B1
Commonwealth Dr
100 BGBK 60440 3268 25W-11S B1
200 CLSM 60188 3024 25W-1N C2
300 CLLK 60014 2640 34W-25N B5
6900 BRRG 60527 3146 14W-7S D6
Commonwealth Ln
- EMHT 60126 3027 16W-0S D7
W Commonwealth Ln
300 EMHT 60126 3027 16W-0S D7
Communications Dr
- SMBG 60173 2805 21W-13N D7
Community Cir
1600 IVNS 60067 2805 23W-14N A4
1600 PltT 60067 2805 23W-14N A4
Community Dr
200 LGPK 60525 3087 12W-2S C4
900 MltT 60187 3081 26W-1S E1
900 WHTN 60187 3081 26W-1S E1
Community St
17500 LNSG 60438 3430 4E-20S B5
Community Wy
1500 IVNS 60067 2805 23W-14N A4
1500 PltT 60067 2805 23W-14N A4
Community Memorial Dr
1300 LGNG 60525 3147 13W-5S A2
1300 LynT 60525 3147 13W-5S A2
1300 WNSP 60525 3147 13W-5S A2
1300 WNSP 60558 3147 13W-5S A2
Como Av
17000 LKPT 60441 3419 21W-20S E5
Como Ct
6800 TYPK 60477 3425 8W-22S A7
Compass Ct
1100 NPVL 60540 3204 25W-8S B1
S Compass Ln
25900 MONE 60449 3683 6W-31S A5
Compass Pt
1000 ELGN 60123 2908 35W-8N A2
Compass Rd
2400 GNVW 60025 2810 9W-15N C3
2400 GNVW 60062 2810 9W-15N B3
Comprehensive Dr
2000 AURA 60505 3139 33W-5S A2
Compton Av
1100 ALGN 60102 2748 34W-19N A2
2500 HDPK 60035 2704 9W-23N C3
Compton Ct
10 ALGN 60102 2748 33W-19N B2
800 GRNE 60031 2534 16W-33N D4
4400 WPHR 60096 2362 11W-42N D5
14200 ODPK 60467 3344 14W-16S E4
Compton Dr
1400 ALGN 60102 2748 33W-19N A2
9600 HTLY 60142 2692 39W-22N D4
Compton Ln
- MDLN 60060 2590 20W-27N B7
10 PTHT 60070 2808 15W-14N A3
200 SMBG 60194 2858 25W-10N B5
W Compton Pt
1000 ADSN 60101 2970 19W-3N C4
Compton Rd
2800 AURA 60504 3201 31W-8S D2
8100 WDRG 60517 3206 20W-9S A3
Compubill Dr
9400 ODPK 60462 3345 11W-17S D5
E Comstock Av
100 ADSN 60101 2971 18W-2N A7
400 ADSN 60181 2971 17W-2N A7
600 VLPK 60101 2971 17W-2N B7
W Comstock Av
500 EMHT 60101 2971 17W-2N C7
500 EMHT 60126 2971 17W-2N C7
Comstock Ct
2200 NPVL 60564 3202 29W-10S D5
Comstock Dr
- ElgT 60124 2853 38W-10N A6
- PltT 60124 2853 38W-10N A6
Comstock Ln
800 DRN 60561 3207 17W-8S C2
2200 NPVL 60564 3202 29W-10S E5
Comstock Pl
400 HDPK 60035 2758 7W-20N B1
S Comstock St
10 JLET 60435 3498 24W-24S D5
10 JLET 60436 3498 24W-24S D5
Comstock on Asbury
10 RGMW 60008 2806 19W-14N B4
Conachie Ct
1000 VNHL 60061 2646 18W-25N E6
Conan Doyle Rd
1000 NPVL 60564 3267 28W-11S A1
1000 WldT 60564 3267 28W-11S B1
1000 WldT 60565 3267 28W-11S B1
1500 NPVL 60564 3266 28W-11S E1
1900 WldT 60564 3266 28W-11S E1
Conant Av
500 PnfT 60435 3417 27W-20S C5
Conant Ct
2700 GNVA 60134 3019 37W-0N C5
Concert Ln
100 NPVL 60540 3141 26W-6S D5
Concha Ct
15400 OKFT 60452 3347 7W-18S C7
Conco St
100 NARA 60542 3138 35W-4S A1
Concord Av
10 RMVL 60446 3340 23W-15S E2
10 SEGN 60177 2908 35W-8N C4
400 FRGV 60021 2696 29W-22N B3
500 RMVL 60446 3341 23W-15S A1
1400 PvsT 60154 3087 13W-1S A1
1400 PvsT 60162 3087 13W-1S A1
1400 WSTR 60154 3087 13W-1S A1
1400 WSTR 60162 3087 13W-1S A1
Concord Cir
900 MDLN 60060 2591 18W-27N A7
6600 NndT 60012 2584 35W-27N A7
7100 FXLK 60020 2414 28W-39N D5
Concord Ct
- BGVW 60455 3274 9W-11S D1
- WDWH 60083 2420 14W-39N C5
10 BtlT 60560 3261 42W-13S D5
10 SBTN 60010 2803 27W-14N A3
100 DYR 46311 3510 D7
100 WNVL 60555 3080 30W-2S C3
500 CHHT 60411 3595 2W-26S D1
600 ALGN 60102 2694 34W-20N C7
700 LNHT 60046 2418 19W-39N C5
900 CLSM 60139 3024 23W-1N E2
900 CLSM 60188 3024 23W-1N E2
1300 ELGN 60120 2855 31W-10N E6
1400 DRGV 60516 3144 20W-7S B7
1500 SCRL 60174 2964 34W-2N D6
2400 MTGY 60538 3198 39W-10S D7
3100 NHBK 60062 2756 11W-17N D5
3300 ISLK 60042 2586 30W-28N B5
3300 JLET 60441 3417 27W-19S D4
5800 HRPK 60133 2911 27W-7N D5
Concord Dr
- MTGY 60543 3198 39W-10S D7
- RDLK 60073 2531 23W-32N E4
- WDRG 60517 3144 20W-7S A7
10 OKBK 60523 3085 17W-2S C4
100 MLPK 60160 3030 10W-1N A2
200 GLHT 60139 2969 23W-3N A6
300 CHHT 60411 3595 2W-26S D1
400 SMWD 60107 2857 28W-10N B6
600 CLLK 60014 2693 36W-23N D1
900 BRLT 60103 2910 30W-6N C7
900 ISLK 60042 2586 30W-28N B5
1100 ELGN 60120 2855 32W-10N D6
1300 LKFT 60045 2649 12W-26N B3
1400 DRGV 60516 3144 20W-7S A7
1900 BtlT 60512 3198 41W-10S A6
1900 DRGV 60517 3144 20W-7S A7
1900 MHRY 60050 2585 33W-30N A2
1900 MTGY 60512 3198 40W-10S B7
1900 MTGY 60538 3198 40W-10S C7
2400 WDRG 60517 3143 21W-7S E7
2400 WDRG 60517 3205 21W-8S E1
4700 RcmT 60071 2412 33W-41N E1
8000 BLVY 60098 2526 37W-32N B5
8000 MchT 60098 2526 37W-32N B5
9100 ODPK 60462 3345 11W-16S E4
21300 FKFT 60423 3591 13W-25S B1
N Concord Dr
200 BLVY 60098 2526 36W-32N C5
200 MchT 60098 2526 36W-32N C5
S Concord Dr
- MTGY 60538 3198 39W-10S E6
100 BtlT 60543 3198 39W-10S D7
100 MTGY 60543 3198 39W-10S D7
100 OSWG 60543 3198 39W-10S D7
200 MTGY 60543 3262 39W-11S D1
200 OSWG 60543 3262 39W-11S D1
W Concord Dr
1400 ANHT 60004 2753 18W-16N D7
Concord Ln
- BGVW 60455 3274 9W-11S D1
- BmdT 60188 3024 23W-1N E1
- GLHT 60188 3024 23W-1N E1
- JSTC 60458 3209 11W-9S E3
- JSTC 60458 3210 11W-9S A3
- PSHL 60455 3274 9W-11S D1
- PSHL 60465 3274 9W-11S D1
- WNFD 60185 3023 27W-1N C3
- WnfT 60185 3023 27W-1N C3
10 CLSM 60139 3024 23W-1N E2
10 CLSM 60188 3024 23W-1N E2
100 BGBK 60440 3205 23W-10S B6
400 EGVV 60007 2859 22W-9N D7
400 NBRN 60010 2698 25W-23N B2
500 BRTN 60010 2751 25W-18N A3
500 DSPN 60016 2808 13W-12N D7
500 DSPN 60016 2862 13W-12N D1
700 HFET 60192 2804 23W-14N D3
700 LMBD 60148 3026 18W-0S E6
700 WNFD 60190 3023 27W-1N C3
1200 LYVL 60048 2592 15W-27N B7
1200 SMBG 60193 2858 25W-9N B7
2400 WLMT 60091 2812 5W-13N B6
4400 SKOK 60076 2866 5W-10N A5
4500 GNVW 60062 2809 12W-14N B3
5700 CNHL 60514 3145 16W-6S E4
10700 HTLY 60142 2692 39W-21N B5
N Concord Ln
- WKGN 60083 2478 14W-37N C2
6900 NLES 60714 2919 8W-8N A1
W Concord Ln
200 CHCG 60614 2978 0W-2N B7
2100 BmdT 60101 2969 21W-3N E6
2100 BmdT 60148 2969 21W-3N E6
14300 WDWH 60083 2420 14W-39N D5
Concord Pl
600 BRTN 60010 2751 25W-18N A3
700 DGvT 60561 3207 17W-9S B3
700 DRN 60561 3207 17W-9S B3
1400 DRGV 60516 3144 20W-7S B7
2600 HLCT 60429 3427 3W-20S B4
W Concord Pl
300 CHCG 60614 2978 0W-2N A7
900 CHCG 60614 2977 1W-2N E7
2000 CHCG 60622 2977 2W-2N B7
2000 CHCG 60647 2977 2W-2N B7
3700 CHCG 60647 2976 4W-2N C7
4800 CHCG 60639 2975 6W-2N E7
Concord Rd
100 LslT 60540 3142 25W-6S B5
300 NPVL 60540 3142 25W-6S B5
Concord Sq
200 GRNE 60031 2535 14W-33N C2
Concord St
10 YkTp 60126 3028 15W-0S B6
300 EMHT 60126 3028 15W-0S A6
600 AURA 60505 3200 36W-8S A2
1100 BTVA 60510 3078 35W-2S A4
Concord Tr
6700 NndT 60012 2584 35W-27N A7
Concord Wy
600 PTHT 60070 2808 14W-14N B4
W Concord Wy
600 PLTN 60067 2805 21W-14N C3
Concord Cove
800 HFET 60192 2804 23W-14N D3
Concorde Cir
1400 HDPK 60035 2704 9W-20N D7
N Concorde Ct
22100 KLDR 60047 2699 22W-20N C7
Concorde Dr
700 HDPK 60035 2704 9W-20N D7
Concorde Pl
4500 LSLE 60532 3142 25W-5S B2
Concordia Ct
4500 MDLN 60445 3348 5W-17S B6
Concordia Ln
- ANHT 60004 2806 18W-15N E3
- VrnT 60045 2648 14W-24N C7
1800 SMBG 60193 2858 25W-9N A7
W Concrete Dr
27500 LKMR 60041 2530 27W-32N A5
27500 LKMR 60073 2530 27W-32N A5
Condado Dr
5900 OKFT 60452 3347 7W-18S C6
Conde Ct
2000 BTVA 60510 3078 34W-3S E5
Conde St
100 WCHI 60185 3022 29W-0N D5
Condell Dr
700 LYVL 60048 2591 16W-28N D7
E Condit St
10 CTCY 60409 3352 C7
10 HMND 46320 3352 C7
Condor Cir
8300 LKWD 60014 2693 38W-23N A1
Condor Ct
10 HNWD 60047 2645 21W-24N D6
E Condor Ct
8700 AxST 60447 3672 33W-30S C3
8700 CnhT 60410 3672 33W-30S C3
Condor Ln
11700 CrlT 60142 2743 45W-20N A1
Coneflower Ct
600 RMVL 60446 3340 25W-15S C1
1100 MNKA 60447 3672 33W-29S A3
Coneflower Dr
- SRGV 60554 3136 41W-7S A6
300 MNKA 60447 3672 33W-29S A3
600 RMVL 60446 3340 25W-15S C1
5000 NPVL 60564 3266 29W-13S D5
Coneflower Ln
2300 ALGN 60102 2747 36W-18N A4
Coneflower Rd
1300 GYLK 60030 2533 19W-31N C6
Conestoga Rd
600 NPVL 60563 3141 27W-4S B2
600 NpvT 60563 3141 27W-5S C2
Conestoga Tr
400 CRY 60013 2641 32W-24N C7
W Conestoga Tr
3700 PRGV 60012 2585 32W-27N B7
Conesus Ct
10 HNWD 60047 2646 19W-25N B4
Confederation Dr
900 BRLT 60103 2910 30W-6N C7
Congdon Av
600 ELGN 60120 2855 32W-12N C1
Congress Av
2500 AURA 60503 3201 32W-10S C7
N Congress Cir
400 ROSL 60172 2912 24W-7N D4
S Congress Cir
500 ROSL 60172 2912 24W-7N D4
Congress Cir W
10 ROSL 60172 2912 24W-7N D4
Congress Ct
400 WDDL 60191 2914 18W-5N E7
7100 GRNE 60031 2534 17W-34N A1
Congress Dr
200 NLNX 60451 3589 18W-26S B2
900 BRLT 60103 2910 29W-6N C6
9100 MaiT 60016 2863 11W-11N D3
9300 DSPN 60016 2863 11W-11N D3
E Congress Dr
100 CHCG 60605 3034 0E-0S C5
Congress Ln
1400 FDHT 60411 3509 1E-25S B7
E Congress Pkwy
10 CHCG 60605 3034 0E-0S C5
200 CLLK 60014 2640 34W-25N C5
W Congress Pkwy
10 CHCG 60605 3034 0W-0S C5
100 CHCG 60607 3034 0W-0S B5
900 CHCG 60607 3033 2W-0S B5
1500 CHCG 60612 3033 2W-0S B5
2800 CHCG 60612 3032 3W-0S E5
3200 CHCG 60624 3032 5W-0S A5
4600 CHCG 60644 3032 5W-0S A5
4800 CHCG 60644 3031 6W-0S D6
Congress St
- MYWD 60153 3029 11W-0S E6
10 VLPK 60181 3027 17W-0S B6
300 MYWD 60153 3030 10W-0S A6
600 ELGN 60120 2855 33W-10N B5
2600 BLWD 60104 3029 12W-0S C6
3800 HLSD 60104 3029 12W-0S A6
3800 HLSD 60162 3029 12W-0S A6
E Congress St
500 EMHT 60126 3028 14W-0S B6
S Congress St
200 ADSN 60101 2971 17W-3N B6
W Congressional Ct
100 VNHL 60061 2647 17W-26N B2
Congressional Ln
700 RVWD 60015 2703 12W-20N A7
Congress Park Av
8800 BKFD 60513 3087 11W-4S E7
8800 BKFD 60513 3088 10W-4S B7
8800 BKFD 60534 3088 10W-4S B7
8800 LYNS 60534 3088 10W-4S B7
9500 BKFD 60525 3087 11W-4S D7
9500 LGNG 60525 3087 11W-4S D7
S Congress Plaza Dr
- CHCG 60604 3034 0E-0S C6
- CHCG 60605 3034 0E-0S C6
Congrove Dr
1800 AURA 60503 3201 33W-10S B5
Conifer Ct
700 MltT 60137 3083 22W-1S C2
2800 AURA 60502 3079 32W-3S C7
10900 ODPK 60467 3423 13W-20S A3
W Conifer Dr
21300 LktT 60544 3339 26W-16S D3
Conifer Ln
5100 GRNE 60031 2478 15W-36N A4
Conifer St
13000 PNFD 60585 3337 33W-15S A2
Coniston Ct
10 WNFD 60190 3023 27W-0N C5
Conkey St
400 HMND 46320 3430 D1
400 HMND 46324 3430 D1
E Conkey St
200 HMND 46320 3430 D1
200 HMND 46324 3430 D1
Conlee Dr
18000 HMGN 60491 3422 16W-21S A7
18300 NlxT 60448 3422 16W-22S A7
18300 NlxT 60448 3502 16W-22S A1
18300 NlxT 60491 3422 16W-22S A7
Conley Ct
- ELBN 60119 3017 43W-2N A1
E Conley Dr
200 ELBN 60119 3017 43W-2N A1
Conley Rd
10600 GfnT 60014 2638 39W-24N B7
10600 GfnT 60142 2638 39W-24N B7
10600 LKWD 60014 2638 39W-24N B7
Connacht St
10 LMNT 60439 3342 19W-15S C1
Connamara Ct
1200 WTMT 60559 3144 18W-7S E5
Connecticut Av
500 NPVL 60565 3203 27W-10S C6
1200 JLET 60435 3498 25W-22S B2
3000 NCHI 60088 2593 12W-30N B2
Connecticut Ct
18000 ODPK 60467 3423 13W-21S A7
Connecticut Tr
4100 NndT 60012 2584 35W-27N A7
6600 NndT 60012 2583 35W-27N E7
Connell St
10 RKDL 60436 3498 25W-25S B7
Connemara Ct
10600 MKNA 60448 3503 13W-23S B3
Connemera Dr
10 BNHL 60010 2802 30W-15N B1
Conners Rd
100 PltT 60124 2905 43W-9N B2
Connie Ct
1800 AraT 60505 3139 33W-5S A2
1800 AURA 60505 3139 33W-5S A2
W Connie Ct
9600 GGnT 60423 3591 12W-28S E5
Connie Dr
1900 CTHL 60403 3417 26W-21S E7
Connie Ln
1900 MPPT 60056 2861 17W-12N B1
Connolly Ln
2600 WDND 60118 2800 36W-16N A2
Connor Av
100 LktT 60441 3419 22W-20S C5
300 LKPT 60441 3419 22W-20S C5
Connor Ct
8000 LGGV 60060 2645 20W-25N E4
17000 TYPK 60477 3424 9W-20S E4
Connor Dr
8600 LGGV 60060 2645 20W-25N E4
Connor Ln
11800 HTLY 60142 2691 40W-22N E3
11800 HTLY 60142 2692 40W-22N A3
Connor St
1300 LKPT 60441 3419 22W-20S D4
N Conover Ct
100 YKVL 60560 3261 43W-13S B6
Conover Dr
- JLET 60421 3586 24W-28S D7
Conover Ln
400 BtlT 60560 3261 43W-14S B7
400 YKVL 60560 3261 43W-14S B7
Conquest Ct
1200 SRWD 60404 3496 31W-24S A6
Conrad Av
6500 HGKN 60525 3147 11W-7S D6
W Conrad Av
7200 NLES 60714 2864 9W-10N D4
Conrad Ct
1000 EGVV 60007 2913 21W-8N E2
2200 AURA 60503 3201 32W-10S B5
Conrad Ln
400 LKZH 60047 2699 21W-22N C4
800 NLNX 60451 3589 18W-25S A1
1000 SRWD 60404 3496 29W-25S D7
1000 SRWD 60404 3584 31W-25S A1
Conrad St
4800 SKOK 60076 2865 6W-10N E4
4800 SKOK 60077 2865 6W-10N E4
N Conrad St
100 PTON 60468 3860 9W-37S E3
300 PtnT 60468 3860 9W-37S E3
S Conrad St
100 PTON 60468 3860 9W-37S E3
N Conservatory Dr
200 CHCG 60624 3032 4W-0N C4
Conservatory Ln
400 AURA 60502 3139 31W-7S E7
500 NpvT 60504 3139 31W-7S E7
Considine Rd
600 GNVA 60134 3020 36W-0S A6
600 GnvT 60134 3020 36W-0S A6
Constance Av
1600 SLVL 60411 3597 2E-26S C2
17100 SHLD 60473 3429 2E-20S C3
S Constance Av
7100 CHCG 60649 3153 2E-8S B7
7900 CHCG 60617 3215 2E-9S C2
7900 CHCG 60649 3215 2E-9S C2
Constance Dr
100 NlxT 60451 3502 16W-24S A6
Constance Ln
10 NfdT 60062 2756 12W-18N B2
10 NHBK 60015 2756 12W-18N B2
10 WdfT 60015 2756 12W-18N B2
100 CHHT 60411 3507 1W-23S E4
200 NHBK 60062 2756 12W-18N B3
600 DRFD 60015 2703 12W-20N C7
S Constance Ln
100 CTSD 60525 3147 12W-6S B5
W Constance Ln
100 CTSD 60525 3147 12W-6S B5
100 LynT 60525 3147 12W-6S B5
Constellation Dr
1100 AURA 60505 3138 34W-5S D3
Constitution Av
5700 GRNE 60031 2477 16W-36N E4
N Constitution Av
800 ISLK 60042 2586 28W-29N E4
800 ISLK 60042 2587 27W-28N A7
S Constitution Av
800 ISLK 60042 2586 28W-29N E4
800 ISLK 60042 2587 27W-28N A7
Constitution Ct
10 VNHL 60061 2647 17W-26N C3
2000 AURA 60506 3137 38W-6S A6
2000 ELGN 60123 2853 36W-10N E7
2600 LkvT 60046 2418 19W-39N C5
2600 LNHT 60046 2418 19W-39N C5
9900 ODPK 60462 3423 12W-18S C1
25100 PNFD 60544 3337 31W-17S E6
Constitution Dr
- PvsT 60154 3086 14W-2S D3
- WSTR 60154 3086 14W-2S D3
100 BMDL 60108 2968 23W-5N E2
1500 GNVW 60025 2810 9W-14N C4
2600 LkvT 60046 2418 19W-39N C5
2600 LNHT 60046 2418 19W-39N C5

STREET Block City ZIP Map# CGS Grid

Constitution Dr
9900 ODPK 60462 3423 12W-18S C1
E Constitution Dr
500 PLTN 60074 2753 20W-18N A2
N Constitution Dr
10 AURA 60506 3137 38W-6S A6
S Constitution Dr
10 AURA 60506 3137 38W-7S A7
Constitution Rd
800 NlxT 60451 3589 16W-25S E1
800 NlxT 60451 3590 16W-25S A1
Constitution Wy
- BtlT 60543 3262 40W-12S B3
S Consumers Av
500 PLTN 60074 2806 19W-15N C3
Conte Pkwy
10 WCHI 60185 2966 31W-3N A7
10 WynT 60185 2966 31W-3N A7
W Conti Pkwy
10 EDPK 60707 2974 9W-3N C5
Continental Av
1800 NPVL 60563 3140 30W-6S B4
Continental Dr
- VNHL 60061 2647 16W-25N E5
10 WNVL 60555 3080 30W-2S C5
4100 WKGN 60031 2478 14W-36N D3
4100 WKGN 60087 2478 14W-36N D3
Continental Ln
100 SMBG 60194 2857 27W-11N D3
100 SMBG 60194 2858 26W-10N A5
Convent Ct
- FKFT 60423 3503 11W-25S E6
Convention Center Dr
- SMBG 60173 2805 21W-12N E7
- SMBG 60173 2859 21W-12N E1
18400 TYPK 60477 3425 8W-22S A7
18500 TYPK 60477 3505 8W-22S A1
Conventry Cir
- SRWD 60404 3583 31W-25S E1
N Converse Ln
34300 GrtT 60041 2530 26W-34N E1
34300 GrtT 60073 2530 26W-34N E1
34300 RDLK 60073 2530 26W-34N E1
N Converse Rd
27800 ISLK 60042 2586 28W-27N E7
27800 WcnT 60042 2586 28W-27N E7
42400 AntT 60002 2356 28W-42N A5
42400 FXLK 60002 2356 28W-42N A5
Conway Ct
10 GYLK 60030 2475 20W-35N E5
500 BRRG 60527 3208 15W-9S A4
6600 BmnT 60445 3347 8W-17S A5
N Conway Ct
10 SEGN 60177 2908 34W-7N D4
S Conway Ct
10 SEGN 60177 2908 34W-7N D5
Conway Ln
1900 AURA 60503 3201 33W-10S A6
Conway Rd
100 LKFT 60045 2649 12W-25N B6
Conway St
600 WDSK 60098 2524 42W-31N C7
Conway Bay
400 ROSL 60172 2913 22W-8N C3
N Conway Bay
1200 PLTN 60074 2753 18W-18N D4
Conway Farms Dr
- LKFT 60045 2648 13W-25N E6
- LKFT 60045 2649 13W-25N A5
- VrnT 60045 2649 13W-25N A5
CO-O 110th St
39500 RdlT 53128 2353 E1
39500 TNLK 53128 2353 E1
39500 TNLK 53181 2353 E1
40000 BfdT 53128 2353 E1
Cook Av
- ALSP 60453 3275 6W-12S E3
- ALSP 60803 3275 6W-12S E3
9900 OKLN 60453 3211 6W-11S E7
10100 OKLN 60453 3275 6W-11S E1
E Cook Av
10 LYVL 60048 2591 16W-29N D4
W Cook Av
100 LYVL 60048 2591 16W-29N D4
25700 AntT 60002 2357 25W-43N A4
25800 AntT 60002 2356 25W-43N E4
Cook Rd
2100 LtRT 60545 3258 50W-12S D4
Cook St
- LtRT 60545 3259 47W-14S C7
- PLNO 60545 3259 47W-14S C7
600 WCDA 60084 2587 26W-28N C7
N Cook St
10 PLNO 60545 3259 47W-13S C6
100 BDWD 60408 3941 32W-41S D5
100 BRTN 60010 2751 25W-20N A1
S Cook St
100 BDWD 60408 3941 32W-41S D6
100 BRTN 60010 2751 25W-18N A2
100 RedT 60408 3941 32W-41S D6
300 PLNO 60545 3259 47W-14S C7
900 BrnT 60010 2751 25W-17N A4
W Cook St
25700 WcnT 60084 2587 25W-28N E7
25700 WcnT 60084 2588 25W-28N A7
25900 WCDA 60084 2587 25W-28N E7
Cokane Av
500 ELGN 60120 2855 33W-10N B6
Cooke Ct
2000 WKGN 60085 2536 11W-33N D2
Cookson Av
3000 ElgT 60124 2853 38W-11N B4
Cool Creek Ct
800 WldT 60565 3203 27W-11S B7
2100 AURA 60503 3201 33W-10S B6
Cool Creek Dr
1800 SCRL 60174 2965 33W-4N A4
2200 AURA 60503 3201 33W-10S B6
Cooley Av
10 WNFD 60190 3023 27W-0S D6
300 MltT 60190 3023 26W-0S E6
Cooley Pl
1400 FSMR 60422 3507 3W-23S A3
Coolidge Av
- PLTN 60067 2752 22W-17N B5
- PltT 60067 2752 22W-17N B5
- PltT 60074 2752 22W-17N B5
10 WCHI 60185 3022 29W-1N E4
10 WnfT 60185 3022 29W-1N E4
100 LYVL 60048 2591 16W-28N D6
500 GNEN 60137 3083 22W-1S B1
1000 WHTN 60187 3082 23W-1S E1
1400 AURA 60505 3138 33W-7S E7
1500 BKLY 60163 3028 14W-0N C4
1600 AraT 60505 3139 33W-7S A7
1600 AURA 60505 3139 33W-7S A7
1600 WHTN 60187 3083 23W-1S A1
2000 MchT 60051 2471 31W-34N E7
N Coolidge Av
- BHPK 60087 2422 10W-38N B7
600 PLTN 60067 2752 22W-16N B6
38600 BHPK 60099 2422 10W-38N B7
S Coolidge Av
300 WCHI 60185 3022 29W-0N E5
W Coolidge Av
100 BRTN 60010 2750 25W-18N E2
Coolidge Ct
10 SMWD 60107 2856 29W-10N D6
Coolidge Pl
200 LYVL 60048 2591 16W-28N D6
200 OSWG 60543 3263 38W-12S A3
Coolidge St
10 CTCY 60409 3430 C3
10 EGvT 60018 2862 15W-9N A7
10 HMND 46324 3430 C3
3000 OKBK 60523 3086 15W-2S A4
N Coolidge St
38000 BHPK 60087 2480 10W-38N B1
Coolidge St N
300 BlmT 60411 3508 1W-23S A3
300 CHHT 60411 3508 1W-23S A3
300 HMWD 60430 3508 1W-23S A3
Coolidge St S
200 CHHT 60411 3508 1W-24S A6
Cool Springs Ct
3200 NPVL 60564 3202 30W-11S B7
Cool Stone Bnd
100 LlHL 60156 2693 36W-21N D5
Coombs Rd
10 ElgT 60124 2799 38W-13N A7
10 ElgT 60124 2853 39W-12N A2
10 PltT 60124 2853 39W-12N A2
10 RtdT 60124 2799 38W-14N A6
200 PltT 60124 2799 38W-13N A7
500 GLBT 60124 2799 38W-14N A6
500 GLBT 60136 2799 38W-14N A6
Cooney Dr
12100 GwdT 60098 2524 41W-33N D2
W Cooney Island Rd
26000 GrtT 60041 2473 26W-36N E4
Coonley Rd
300 RVSD 60546 3088 10W-3S B6
Co Op Ln
4700 HMTN 60453 3212 5W-10S A4
4700 HMTN 60456 3212 5W-10S A4
4700 OKLN 60453 3212 5W-10S A4
Cooper Av
100 ELGN 60120 2854 34W-12N E1
600 ELGN 60120 2855 33W-12N B1
14400 DXMR 60426 3349 2W-17S C6
14600 HRVY 60426 3349 2W-17S C6
Cooper Ct
10 HNWD 60047 2645 22W-25N B5
600 SMBG 60173 2859 22W-12N C2
900 BFGV 60089 2700 18W-21N E7
900 EGVV 60007 2913 21W-8N E1
1600 HRPK 60133 2911 26W-6N D6
2800 WDRG 60517 3143 22W-7S D7
Cooper Ct E
600 AURA 60504 3201 31W-8S D2
E Cooper Dr
800 PLTN 60074 2753 19W-17N B6
Cooper Ln
1800 ALGN 60102 2747 36W-18N A4
1800 HDPK 60035 2703 10W-23N E3
1800 HDPK 60035 2704 10W-22N A4
Cooper Pl
3700 CRTE 60417 3596 0W-28S D7
Cooper Rd
1300 HFET 60169 2858 24W-12N D2
13900 BLID 60406 3348 3W-16S E3
13900 BLID 60406 3349 3W-16S A3
13900 BLID 60472 3348 3W-16S E3
13900 BLID 60472 3349 3W-16S A3
13900 RBBN 60406 3349 3W-16S A3
13900 RBBN 60472 3348 3W-16S E3
13900 RBBN 60472 3349 3W-16S A3
14000 RBBN 60406 3348 3W-16S E3
23100 CstT 60481 4031 29W-44S E5
23100 RedT 60481 4031 29W-44S E5
N Cooper Rd
500 NLNX 60451 3501 17W-23S C4
600 NlxT 60451 3501 17W-23S C4
S Cooper Rd
100 NLNX 60451 3501 17W-25S C7
100 NlxT 60451 3501 17W-25S C7
600 NLNX 60451 3589 17W-25S C1
Cooper St
- PLNO 60545 3259 47W-13S C5
Coopers Grove Ct
3000 BLID 60406 3348 4W-17S E4
3000 BLID 60472 3348 4W-17S E4
3000 RBBN 60472 3348 4W-17S E4
CO-O Richmond Rd
1700 TNLK 53181 2353 E1
Copenhagen Ct
11600 BNVL 60106 2972 14W-4N C3
11600 FNPK 60131 2972 14W-4N B3
Copley Ct
- SMBG 60173 2859 23W-12N B1
Copley Ln
800 JLET 60431 3497 28W-25S B7
Copley St
2200 AURA 60506 3137 38W-6S A6
Copper Ct
10 BGBK 60440 3268 25W-11S C1
10 GLHT 60139 2968 24W-4N E4
23400 CTHL 60403 3418 26W-21S A6
Copper Dr
10 PnfT 60544 3338 29W-17S D5
Copper Canyon Tr
300 CRY 60013 2641 32W-24N C7
300 CRY 60013 2695 31W-24N C1
Copperfield Av
1200 JLET 60432 3499 22W-23S D3
1600 JltT 60432 3499 21W-23S E3
Copperfield Ct
1100 AURA 60504 3202 30W-9S B3
2600 NPVL 60565 3203 27W-10S D6
Copperfield Dr
10 ElaT 60047 2645 23W-24N A6
10 HNWD 60047 2645 23W-24N A6
2600 NPVL 60565 3203 27W-10S C7
Copperfield Ln
1000 SMBG 60193 2913 23W-9N A1
1700 CLLK 60014 2693 36W-22N D4
Coppergate Rd
8900 WDRG 60517 3206 20W-10S C6
Copper Leaf Dr
- CNHN 60410 3672 32W-30S E4
Copper Mountain Dr
100 GLBT 60136 2799 38W-15N A4
Copper Springs Ln
300 ElgT 60124 2853 38W-10N A7
Copperwood Dr
10 BFGV 60089 2701 16W-21N D5
Copperwood Ln
10 CmpT 60175 2961 42W-5N D2
CO-P Richmond Rd
1700 TNLK 53181 2353 E1
1800 RdlT 53128 2353 E1
1800 RdlT 53181 2353 E1
1800 TNLK 53128 2353 E1
12500 RcmT 60071 2353 D4
12500 RHMD 60071 2353 D4
12500 TNLK 60071 2353 D4
Copter Ln
15000 LktT 60441 3340 24W-17S E7
15000 RMVL 60441 3340 24W-17S E7
Coquille Cir
11700 FKFT 60423 3590 14W-27S D5
Coquille Dr
11600 FftT 60423 3590 14W-27S D5
11600 FKFT 60423 3590 14W-27S D5
CO-Q Winfield Rd
16800 BtlT 53104 2359 B1
Cora Av
100 FXLK 60020 2473 27W-37N B2
Cora Ct
100 TNTN 60476 3428 0E-20S D5
Cora St
1600 CTHL 60403 3498 24W-21S E1
1600 JLET 60435 3498 24W-21S E1
1700 CTHL 60403 3418 24W-21S E7
N Cora St
800 JLET 60435 3498 24W-22S E2
S Cora St
900 DSPN 60016 2863 13W-10N A5
1100 DSPN 60018 2863 13W-10N A5
Coral Av
600 BRLT 60103 2911 28W-7N B4
2000 AURA 60506 3137 38W-6S A4
2900 MchT 60051 2528 31W-32N C4
Coral Ct
200 BGBK 60440 3205 23W-11S A7
500 SMBG 60193 2858 25W-9N B7
600 LNHT 60046 2417 21W-39N D5
Coral Dr
- NPVL 60563 3140 29W-4S D2
500 DYR 46311 3598 D1
1100 LKPT 60441 3341 21W-18S E7
1100 LktT 60441 3341 21W-18S E7
W Coral Dr
8300 CHCG 60656 2918 10W-5N A7
8300 CHCG 60706 2918 10W-5N A7
8300 NRDG 60656 2918 10W-5N A7
8300 NRDG 60706 2918 10W-5N A7
Coral Ln
100 WLNG 60090 2754 16W-18N E4
Coral Pkwy
1400 NHBK 60062 2756 11W-17N C6
Coral Rd
8300 WRLK 60097 2469 37W-35N B6
8700 GwdT 60097 2469 37W-35N B6
E Coral Rd
16800 CrlT 60180 2635 46W-24N D6
17100 UNON 60180 2635 46W-24N D6
18100 CrlT 60152 2635 47W-24N A7
E Coral Rd CO-A44
- UNON 60180 2635 47W-24N C6
18100 CrlT 60152 2635 47W-24N A7
18100 CrlT 60180 2635 47W-24N B6
S Coral Rd
7800 CrlT 60152 2635 48W-24N A7
W Coral Rd
18800 CrlT 60152 2635 48W-24N A7
18800 CrlT 60180 2635 48W-24N A7
19200 CrlT 60152 2634 48W-24N E7
19700 RlyT 60152 2634 49W-24N C7
W Coral Rd CO-A44
18800 CrlT 60152 2635 48W-24N A7
18800 CrlT 60180 2635 48W-24N A7
19200 CrlT 60152 2634 48W-24N E7
19700 RlyT 60152 2634 49W-24N C7
E Coral St
11700 HTLY 60142 2692 40W-21N A7
11800 HTLY 60142 2691 41W-20N E7
Coralbell Ct
10 RMVL 60446 3340 26W-17S A5
Coral Bell Dr
1300 JLET 60435 3498 25W-22S B1
Coralberry Ct
1300 YKVL 60560 3333 43W-16S A3
Coralberry Ln
1400 DRGV 60515 3084 20W-3S B6
Coral Berry Pth
4200 GRNE 60031 2478 14W-36N D4
Coral Cove
2300 ELGN 60123 2907 36W-9N E1
Coral Oaks Ln
7600 RlyT 60152 2634 50W-24N A7
Coral Reef Ct
10 TDLK 60030 2533 19W-34N D1
200 RMVL 60446 3340 25W-16S C3
Coral Reef Wy
1300 LKZH 60047 2699 22W-21N A7
S Corbett St
2500 CHCG 60608 3091 1W-2S E2
N Corbin St
100 PNFD 60544 3416 29W-18S D1
200 PNFD 60544 3338 29W-18S C7
W Corcoran Pl
5500 CHCG 60644 3031 7W-0N C4
5900 CHCG 60302 3031 7W-0N B4
5900 OKPK 60302 3031 7W-0N B4
S Corcoran Rd
8700 HMTN 60456 3212 5W-10S B5
Corday Dr
800 NPVL 60540 3140 29W-7S E7
800 NPVL 60540 3202 29W-7S E1
Cordgrass Rd
2800 NPVL 60564 3266 29W-13S C5
Cord Grass Tr
1400 WDSK 60098 2582 40W-29N A5
Cordial Dr
400 DSPN 60018 2862 15W-10N A6
600 DSPN 60018 2861 16W-10N E5
600 MPPT 60056 2861 16W-10N D5
Cordoba Ct
9800 ODPK 60462 3345 12W-18S C6
Cordoba St
900 UYPK 60466 3684 3W-30S A2
Cordova Ct
900 WHTN 60187 3082 24W-2S E3
Cordova Rd
100 CPVL 60110 2748 33W-18N B5
Cordula Cir
1100 NPVL 60564 3267 28W-11S A1
Coreopsis Ct
100 RMVL 60446 3339 26W-17S E6
12600 PNFD 60585 3338 30W-14S B1
Corey Dr
10 SBTN 60010 2803 26W-13N D5
Corey Ln
800 PTHT 60070 2754 16W-16N D6
800 PTHT 60090 2754 16W-16N D6
800 WLNG 60090 2754 16W-16N D6
E Coreys Ct
200 VNHL 60061 2647 16W-27N D2
Coriander Ct
17800 LKPT 60441 3420 20W-21S B6
Coriander Ln
1000 FmtT 60060 2590 19W-29N B5
1000 MDLN 60060 2590 19W-29N B5
21000 FKFT 60423 3590 14W-26S E3
Corinne Rd
2000 AURA 60506 3137 38W-7S A7
Corinth Ct
10 TYPK 60477 3505 8W-23S C3
Corinth Dr
10 TYPK 60477 3505 8W-23S C3
Corinth Rd
2600 OMFD 60461 3507 3W-24S B6
Cork Av
8700 HYHL 60457 3210 11W-10S A6
8700 HYHL 60458 3210 10W-10S A4
8700 JSTC 60457 3210 10W-9S A4
8700 JSTC 60458 3210 10W-9S A4
9400 HYHL 60465 3210 10W-10S A6
9400 PSHL 60457 3210 10W-10S A6
9400 PSHL 60465 3210 10W-10S A6
S Cork Av
7100 JSTC 60458 3148 11W-8S A7
7300 JSTC 60458 3210 11W-8S A1
8500 HYHL 60457 3210 11W-9S A4
8500 HYHL 60458 3210 11W-9S A4
8500 JSTC 60457 3210 11W-9S A4
Cork Ln
6300 MHRY 60050 2527 35W-32N B5
Cork Rd
18100 TYPK 60477 3424 10W-21S C7
E Corktree Ln
1700 MPPT 60056 2808 13W-14N D4
Corktree Rd
4500 WldT 60564 3265 31W-12S E3
4500 WldT 60564 3266 31W-12S A3
Corley Ct
1300 ELGN 60120 2855 31W-11N D3
Corley Dr
1300 ELGN 60120 2855 31W-11N E3
S Corliss Av
10300 CHCG 60628 3278 1E-12S E1
13100 CHCG 60827 3278 0E-15S E7
13100 CHCG 60827 3350 0E-15S E1
Cormar Dr
900 LKZH 60047 2645 22W-24N B7
900 LKZH 60047 2699 22W-24N B1
Cormorant St
21500 LktT 60403 3417 26W-19S D3
Cormoy Ln
11800 ODPK 60467 3422 14W-21S D6
19300 TYPK 60477 3504 10W-23S B3
Corneils Rd
9000 BtlT 60512 3261 43W-11S B2
9000 YKVL 60512 3261 43W-11S B2
9000 YKVL 60545 3261 43W-11S B2
9000 YKVL 60560 3261 43W-11S B2
10200 BtlT 60545 3260 44W-11S D2
10200 BtlT 60545 3261 43W-12S A2
10200 BtlT 60560 3261 43W-11S B2
10200 YKVL 60545 3260 44W-11S D2
11400 LtRT 60545 3260 44W-12S D2
W Cornelia Av
500 CHCG 60657 2978 0W-4N A3
700 CHCG 60657 2977 1W-4N E3
1900 CHCG 60618 2977 2W-4N B3
2600 WKGN 60085 2536 12W-33N C1
4000 CHCG 60618 2976 5W-4N B3
4300 CHCG 60641 2976 5W-4N A3
4700 CHCG 60641 2975 5W-4N E3
5500 CHCG 60634 2975 8W-4N A3
8200 CHCG 60634 2974 10W-4N A3
N Cornelia St
400 JLET 60435 3498 25W-23S C3
Cornelius Av
1400 JLET 60433 3587 23W-25S B1
1400 JltT 60433 3587 23W-25S B1
Cornell Av
- MLPK 60165 3029 12W-2N B1
- SNPK 60165 3029 12W-2N B1
100 DSPN 60016 2862 14W-12N C1
200 CTCY 60409 3351 2E-17S C5
400 VLPK 60181 3027 17W-0S B7
400 YkTp 60181 3027 17W-0S B7
1000 ANHT 60004 2754 16W-16N D7
1000 PTHT 60004 2754 16W-16N D7
1000 PTHT 60070 2754 16W-16N D7
1000 WLNG 60004 2754 16W-16N D7
1000 WLNG 60090 2754 16W-16N D7
1100 PTHT 60090 2754 16W-16N D7
1900 MLPK 60160 3029 12W-2N B1
2000 LydT 60160 2973 12W-2N B7
2000 LydT 60164 2973 12W-2N B7
2000 MLPK 60160 2973 12W-2N B7
2200 MTGY 60506 3198 39W-8S E2
2200 MTGY 60538 3198 39W-8S E2
2200 MTGY 60538 3199 38W-8S A2
3800 PKCY 60085 2535 13W-33N E3
4400 GRNE 60031 2535 14W-33N C3
4500 DRGV 60515 3144 20W-4S A1
15100 CTCY 60419 3351 2E-17S C6
15100 DLTN 60409 3351 2E-17S C6
15100 DLTN 60419 3351 2E-17S C6
17000 SHLD 60473 3429 1E-20S B4
22100 SLVL 60411 3597 2E-27S C3
E Cornell Av
- BrnT 60010 2750 25W-17N E4
- BRTN 60010 2750 25W-17N E4
400 BrnT 60010 2751 25W-17N A4
400 BRTN 60010 2751 25W-17N A4
N Cornell Av
10 VLPK 60181 3027 17W-1N B3
S Cornell Av
- CHCG 60615 3093 1E-4S A7
- CHCG 60637 3153 2E-6S B3
- CHCG 60649 3153 2E-7S B6
- CHCG 60653 3093 1E-4S A7
300 VLPK 60181 3027 17W-0S B6
4800 CHCG 60615 3153 2E-5S B1
7500 CHCG 60649 3215 2E-8S B1
8100 CHCG 60617 3215 2E-9S B2
W Cornell Av
800 PLTN 60067 2752 22W-16N B7
1100 IVNS 60067 2752 22W-16N B7
1100 PltT 60067 2752 22W-16N B7
Cornell Cir
1600 HFET 60169 2858 26W-12N A2
Cornell Ct
- HMGN 60491 3344 15W-16S B3
- SRGV 60554 3136 40W-7S B6
10 GLHT 60139 2968 24W-4N E4
10 SEGN 60177 2908 35W-7N B4
100 GNVW 60025 2810 10W-15N A2
800 SRWD 60404 3496 30W-24S B7
1400 HFET 60169 2858 26W-12N A2
1400 PTHT 60070 2754 16W-16N D6
1400 WLNG 60090 2754 16W-16N D6
1500 LKFT 60045 2649 13W-26N A3
1700 NPVL 60565 3204 24W-8S D3
W Cornell Ct
3600 MHRY 60050 2528 32W-33N B2
Cornell Dr
10 LNSH 60069 2702 13W-23N D3
700 OSWG 60543 3200 35W-11S B7
1400 HFET 60169 2858 26W-12N A2
1800 NLNX 60451 3502 16W-25S A7
S Cornell Dr
- CHCG 60637 3153 2E-6S B4
- CHCG 60649 3153 2E-6S B4
Cornell Ln
300 ALGN 60102 2694 33W-20N E7
300 ELGN 60123 2853 36W-10N E6
800 SMBG 60193 2858 25W-9N C7
800 SMBG 60193 2912 25W-9N C1
1100 YKVL 60560 3261 43W-14S A7
S Cornell Ln
13000 PlsT 60464 3346 10W-15S C1
Cornell Pl
1500 HFET 60169 2858 26W-12N A2
Cornell Rd
1700 FSMR 60422 3507 2W-23S D4
3100 WKGN 60087 2479 11W-37N E2
3200 BHPK 60087 2479 11W-37N E2
N Cornell Rd
37800 BHPK 60087 2479 11W-38N E1
37800 WKGN 60087 2479 11W-38N E1
Cornell St
900 WLMT 60091 2812 4W-14N B5
N Cornell St
40500 BHPK 60099 2421 12W-40N B3
Cornell Ter
1400 HFET 60169 2858 26W-12N A2
Cornell Wy
5600 MTSN 60443 3505 7W-25S E7
Corners Dr
10 BRPK 60010 2699 22W-20N A7
Cornerstone Dr
- YKlT 60560 3333 43W-16S B4
- YKVL 60560 3333 43W-16S B4
4400 WPHR 60096 2362 11W-42N D6
N Cornerstone Dr
10 VOLO 60041 2530 27W-33N C3
S Cornerstone Dr
- VOLO 60041 2530 27W-33N C4
Cornerstone Pl
- SMBG 60193 2912 25W-8N B2
Cornerstone Rd
- BtvT 60539 3077 36W-3S E6
Cornfield Dr
800 MTSN 60443 3505 7W-25S C7
Cornfield Rd
700 MTSN 60443 3505 7W-24S C6
Cornflower Tr
3400 NHBK 60062 2809 11W-16N C1
Cornflower Wy
3300 SPGV 60081 2413 32W-39N B6
Cornhill Dr
- ODPK 60467 3344 14W-16S D4
E Corning Av
200 PTON 60468 3861 9W-37S A3
400 WlIT 60468 3861 9W-37S A3
W Corning Av
100 PTON 60468 3861 8W-37S B3
200 PTON 60468 3860 9W-37S E3
8700 PtnT 60468 3860 10W-37S B3
Corning Ct
5000 JLET 60586 3496 30W-22S C2
E Corning Rd
100 WshT 60401 3864 0E-37S E4
W Corning Rd
10 WshT 60401 3864 0W-37S C4
4900 WlIT 60468 3861 7W-37S C4
W Corning St
700 PtnT 60468 3860 10W-37S C3
700 PTON 60468 3860 10W-37S C3
Cornwall Av
200 SEGN 60177 2908 35W-8N C4
Cornwall Cir
200 MNSR 46321 3510 D4
700 SRGV 60554 3135 41W-5S E2
Cornwall Ct
10 CRTE 60417 3596 0W-28S D6
700 BGBK 60440 3205 22W-10S C5
Cornwall Dr
10 CRTE 60417 3596 0W-28S D6
400 LYLK 60175 2961 43W-5N B2
6800 JLET 60431 3495 32W-22S C2
Cornwall Ln
2800 GNVA 60134 3019 37W-1N C3
Cornwall Rd
200 LslT 60540 3142 25W-6S C4
300 NPVL 60540 3142 25W-6S C5
Cornwallis Ln
900 MNSR 46321 3510 E5
Corona Av
700 RMVL 60446 3268 24W-14S E7
Corona Ct
800 RLKB 60073 2474 24W-34N D7
1200 AURA 60505 3138 34W-5S E3
N Corona Dr
5700 RGMW 60008 2805 22W-13N C5
5700 RGMW 60067 2805 22W-13N C5
36600 LkvT 60046 2476 20W-36N A3
36900 LkvT 60046 2475 20W-36N E3
S Corona Dr
5700 RGMW 60008 2805 22W-13N C5
5700 RGMW 60067 2805 22W-13N C5
Corona Rd
2200 WKGN 60087 2480 10W-36N B4
Coronado Ct
800 ELGN 60123 2853 36W-9N E7
Coronado Dr
17500 ODPK 60467 3423 13W-21S B6
Coronado Vista
5700 CLLK 60014 2639 37W-26N A3
5700 DrrT 60014 2639 37W-26N A3

STREET Block City ZIP Map# CGS Grid

Coronet Ln
800 CTSD 60525 3147 13W-6S A4
800 LynT 60525 3147 13W-6S A4
Coronet Rd
10 MltT 60148 3083 21W-2S E4
10 MltT 60148 3084 21W-2S A4
500 GLF 60025 2811 7W-12N B7
500 GNVW 60025 2811 7W-12N B7
Corporate Blvd
900 AURA 60502 3138 34W-4S D2
1000 AraT 60504 3138 34W-4S E2
1000 AURA 60504 3138 34W-4S D2
Corporate Cir N
900 GYLK 60030 2533 19W-32N B4
Corporate Cir S
900 GYLK 60030 2533 19W-32N B4
Corporate Cross
- SMBG 60173 2860 21W-10N A4
Corporate Dr
- NHBK 60015 2756 13W-20N A2
- NHBK 60062 2756 13W-20N A2
- RVWD 60015 2755 13W-20N E2
- RVWD 60015 2756 13W-20N A2
- RVWD 60062 2756 13W-20N A2
- WdfT 60015 2756 13W-20N A2
100 ELGN 60123 2800 34W-14N E6
100 ELGN 60123 2801 34W-14N A6
1100 MHRY 60050 2584 33W-30N E1
3200 JLET 60431 3585 28W-25S B1
W Corporate Dr
2100 ADSN 60101 2969 21W-3N D5
Corporate Ln
2000 NPVL 60563 3080 29W-4S D7
2000 NPVL 60563 3140 29W-4S D1
Corporate Pkwy
- DndT 60118 2746 37W-19N C3
- RtdT 60118 2746 37W-19N C3
2600 ALGN 60102 2746 37W-19N D2
2600 ALGN 60118 2746 37W-19N D2
Corporate Grove Dr
700 BFGV 60089 2702 15W-21N A6
Corporate West Dr
2400 LSLE 60532 3142 24W-4S C1
2600 LSLE 60532 3082 25W-4S C7
Corporate Woods Pkwy
100 VNHL 60061 2701 16W-24N D1
300 VNHL 60061 2647 16W-24N D7
700 VNHL 60061 2648 15W-24N A7
1100 VrnT 60061 2648 15W-24N A7
Corporetum Dr
1400 LSLE 60532 3143 23W-4S A1
Corregidor St
1700 JLET 60435 3417 27W-21S C7
1700 JLET 60435 3497 27W-21S C1
Corri Ln
400 PLNO 60545 3259 47W-14S C7
500 LtRT 60545 3259 47W-14S C7
Corrie Ln
1300 NlxT 60451 3589 16W-26S E3
1400 NlxT 60451 3590 16W-26S A3
Corrigan St
1200 ELBN 60119 3017 43W-0N B5
Corrine Av
200 CLLK 60014 2639 37W-25N A5
Corrington Ct
200 SMWD 60107 2857 27W-11N C4
Corrinthia Ct
500 EGVV 60007 2915 18W-9N A1
Corrinthia Dr
400 EGVV 60007 2915 18W-9N A1
Corron Rd
10 CmpT 60175 2906 40W-7N C6
10 CmpT 60175 2962 40W-5N B1
10 PltT 60124 2906 40W-9N C2
10 PltT 60175 2906 40W-8N C4
500 PltT 60124 2852 40W-9N C7
Corron Rd CO-80
10 CmpT 60175 2906 40W-7N C6
10 CmpT 60175 2962 40W-5N B1
10 PltT 60124 2906 40W-9N C2
10 PltT 60175 2906 40W-8N C4
500 PltT 60124 2852 40W-9N C7
Corsair Ct
800 NLNX 60451 3501 18W-25S A7
Corsair Rd
9200 FKFT 60423 3591 11W-27S E5
9200 FKFT 60423 3592 11W-27S A5
Corsaire Ln
10 SMBG 60173 2859 21W-10N D4
Corso Dr
- ODPK 60467 3422 14W-19S E2
Corsswind Dr
5200 RNPK 60471 3593 6W-27S E5
5200 RNPK 60471 3594 6W-27S A5
Cortbridge Rd
800 IVNS 60067 2751 24W-17N D6
S Cortesi St
- VLPK 60181 3027 17W-0N B4
Cortez Ct
200 NPVL 60563 3141 26W-4S D1
W Cortez Dr
3100 CHCG 60622 3032 3W-1N E2
3100 CHCG 60651 3032 3W-1N E2
Cortez St
1200 MLPK 60160 3029 11W-1N D2
W Cortez St
- CHCG 60622 3033 1W-1N D2
2800 CHCG 60622 3032 3W-1N E2
3200 CHCG 60651 3032 4W-1N D2
4800 CHCG 60651 3031 6W-1N E2
Cortina Ct
1000 SRWD 60404 3496 30W-24S B7
Cortland Av
200 ADSN 60101 2970 20W-2N B7
200 ADSN 60148 2970 20W-2N B7
200 BmdT 60148 3025 21W-2N E1
200 LMBD 60148 2970 20W-2N B7
Cortland Cir
10 LKZH 60047 2698 24W-21N C5
Cortland Ct
100 GNEN 60137 3083 21W-1S D1
W Cortland Ct
1600 ADSN 60101 2970 20W-2N A7
1600 ADSN 60148 2970 20W-2N A7
Cortland Dr
500 LKZH 60047 2698 24W-22N C5
1300 NPVL 60565 3203 27W-8S D2
Cortland Ln
1200 WCDA 60084 2588 24W-28N C6
10700 HTLY 60142 2692 39W-21N B5
W Cortland Pkwy
7900 EDPK 60707 2974 9W-2N B7
W Cortland St
1200 CHCG 60614 2977 1W-2N D7
1400 CHCG 60622 2977 2W-2N C7
2000 CHCG 60647 2977 2W-2N B7
W Cortland St
2800 CHCG 60647 2976 3W-2N E7
3900 CHCG 60639 2976 5W-2N B7
4800 CHCG 60639 2975 6W-2N E7
6300 CHCG 60707 2975 8W-2N A7
6700 CHCG 60707 2974 8W-2N E7
7800 EDPK 60707 2974 9W-2N B7
Cortland Ter
1200 WCDA 60084 2588 24W-28N C6
Cortney Cir
900 CPVL 60110 2748 32W-18N D5
Cortney Dr
900 CPVL 60110 2748 32W-18N D5
Cory Av
100 WKGN 60085 2480 10W-34N A7
Cory Ln
5800 OKFT 60452 3425 7W-18S C1
Corydalis St
24200 PNFD 60585 3338 30W-14S B1
Cosman Rd
10 EGvT 60007 2860 19W-9N C7
10 EGVV 60007 2860 19W-9N C7
Cosman Wy
1900 ALGN 60102 2747 36W-19N A3
Cosmic Dr
2400 JLET 60431 3417 28W-20S B6
2400 PnfT 60431 3417 28W-20S B6
E Cossitt Av
10 LGNG 60525 3087 12W-4S C7
700 BKFD 60513 3087 12W-4S C7
700 LGNG 60513 3087 12W-4S C7
W Cossitt Av
10 LGNG 60525 3087 12W-4S B7
1400 WNSP 60525 3087 13W-4S A7
1400 WNSP 60558 3087 13W-4S A7
CO-T50 Lawrence Rd
6600 CmgT 60033 2405 51W-39N D5
6600 HRVD 60033 2405 51W-39N D5
CO-T50 Oak Grove Rd
22600 CmgT 60033 2405 51W-39N D3
22600 HRVD 60033 2405 51W-39N D3
CO-T55 Marengo Rd
4600 DhmT 60033 2464 50W-37N A2
5000 HRVD 60033 2464 50W-37N A2
CO-T58 Maple St
300 MRGO 60152 2634 49W-24N C7
6300 RlyT 60152 2634 49W-25N C4
CO-T59 Deerpass Rd
1100 MngT 60152 2578 49W-28N D6
1100 SenT 60152 2578 49W-28N D6
3500 MRGO 60152 2578 49W-28N D6
4700 MngT 60152 2634 49W-27N D1
4700 MRGO 60152 2634 49W-27N D1
4700 SenT 60152 2634 49W-27N D1
CO-T64 Millstream Rd
4700 SenT 60152 2635 47W-27N B1
4700 SenT 60180 2635 47W-27N B1
CO-T65 Jefferson St
17700 UNON 60180 2635 47W-24N C7
CO-T65 Main St
6000 UNON 60180 2635 46W-25N D4
CO-T65 N Union Rd
4700 SenT 60180 2635 46W-27N D1
5100 UNON 60180 2635 46W-26N D3
CO-T65 S Union Rd
6600 CrlT 60180 2635 47W-25N C5
6600 UNON 60180 2635 47W-25N C5
CO-T65 W Union Rd
- CrlT 60180 2635 46W-25N C4
- UNON 60180 2635 46W-25N C4
Cotherstone Pl
900 ANTH 60002 2357 24W-42N B5
W Cotswald Dr
23600 WldT 60585 3266 29W-14S D7
Cotswolds Ct
2500 NHBK 60062 2756 10W-18N E3
2500 NHBK 60062 2757 10W-18N A3
Cotswolds Wy
700 NHBK 60062 2756 10W-18N E4
700 NHBK 60062 2757 10W-18N A4
Cottage Av
200 GNEN 60137 3025 23W-0N A5
600 NPVL 60540 3141 27W-6S C5
E Cottage Av
10 CPVL 60110 2747 34W-17N E7
10 CPVL 60110 2800 35W-16N C1
W Cottage Av
18700 GRNE 60031 2476 18W-34N D7
18700 GRNE 60046 2476 18W-34N D7
18700 WrnT 60031 2476 18W-34N D7
18700 WrnT 60046 2476 18W-34N D7
Cottage Ct
17200 TYPK 60487 3424 10W-20S B4
Cottage Dr
7100 GfnT 60014 2639 37W-24N B6
Cottage Ln
10 MDLN 60445 3347 6W-17S E4
Cottage Pl
10 FXLK 60020 2473 27W-36N B3
W Cottage Pl
- CHCG 60607 3033 1W-0S D5
900 JLET 60436 3498 25W-24S C6
Cottage Rd
600 BTVA 60510 3078 34W-2S D3
24700 GLkT 60416 3761 32W-35S D7
24700 GLkT 60450 3761 32W-35S D7
24700 WmTp 60481 3761 32W-35S D7
N Cottage Rd
23500 ElaT 60047 2699 21W-23N D2
Cottage St
100 SRWD 60404 3496 29W-24S C6
100 SRWD 60431 3496 29W-24S C6
800 TroT 60404 3496 29W-24S C6
800 TroT 60431 3496 29W-24S C6
Cottage St SR-59
100 SRWD 60404 3496 29W-24S C6
100 SRWD 60431 3496 29W-24S C6
800 TroT 60404 3496 29W-24S C6
800 TroT 60431 3496 29W-24S C6
Cottage Cove
1100 ELGN 60123 2907 36W-9N E1
Cottage Grove Av
- BlmT 60425 3509 0E-25S A7
- CHHT 60425 3509 0E-25S A7
1000 CHHT 60411 3509 0E-25S A7
1000 FDHT 60411 3509 1E-25S A7
1400 CHHT 60411 3597 1E-25S A1
1400 FDHT 60411 3597 1E-25S A1
13800 CHCG 60827 3351 1E-16S A3
13800 DLTN 60419 3351 1E-16S A4
14900 DLTN 60473 3351 1E-17S A6
15600 SHLD 60419 3351 1E-18S A7
15600 SHLD 60473 3351 1E-18S A7
15900 SHLD 60473 3429 0E-19S A3
20400 BlmT 60411 3509 0E-25S A7
21500 BlmT 60411 3597 0E-26S A2
Cottage Grove Av
21500 SLVL 60411 3597 0E-26S A2
21900 SLVL 60411 3597 0E-26S A2
21900 STGR 60411 3597 0E-26S A2
21900 STGR 60475 3597 0E-26S A2
22300 SLVL 60475 3597 1E-27S A4
22500 BlmT 60475 3597 1E-27S A4
22900 CRTE 60417 3597 1E-27S B5
N Cottage Grove Av
- BlmT 60425 3429 1E-22S A7
- BlmT 60476 3429 1E-22S A7
- ThtT 60476 3429 1E-22S A7
10 BlmT 60425 3509 0E-22S A1
10 BlmT 60476 3509 0E-22S A1
10 GNWD 60425 3509 0E-22S A1
S Cottage Grove Av
10 BlmT 60425 3509 0E-23S A3
10 BlmT 60476 3509 0E-22S A2
10 GNWD 60425 3509 0E-22S A2
1400 CRTE 60417 3686 0E-30S A3
1400 CteT 60417 3686 1E-31S A6
2200 CHCG 60616 3092 0E-2S C2
3400 CHCG 60653 3092 1E-4S E7
4600 CHCG 60615 3092 1E-4S E7
4700 CHCG 60615 3152 0E-7S E5
5400 CHCG 60637 3152 1E-5S E2
7000 CHCG 60619 3152 1E-7S E6
7500 CHCG 60619 3214 0E-8S E1
9500 CHCG 60628 3214 0E-11S E7
10300 CHCG 60628 3278 0E-12S E2
12400 CHCG 60628 3279 0E-14S A7
20000 BlmT 60411 3509 1E-24S A5
20000 CHHT 60411 3509 1E-24S A5
20000 CHHT 60425 3509 1E-24S A5
S Cottage Hill Av
100 EMHT 60126 3027 16W-0N E4
Cottage Hill Ln
600 SchT 60174 2908 35W-6N B7
Cotter Ct
- LtRT 60545 3332 45W-14S B1
- PLNO 60545 3332 45W-14S B1
Cottie Dr
6900 JLET 60431 3495 32W-22S C1
Cottington Ct
500 SMBG 60194 2858 25W-11N B4
Cottington Dr
1600 SMBG 60194 2858 25W-11N A4
Cotton Creek Ct
2700 NPVL 60564 3202 30W-10S B6
Cottoneaster Av
300 OSWG 60543 3263 36W-14S E6
Cottoneaster Ct
400 OSWG 60543 3263 36W-13S E6
Cottonwood Cir
10 BTVA 60510 3078 34W-1S D2
500 BGBK 60440 3268 24W-11S E1
Cottonwood Ct
300 SMBG 60193 2858 24W-9N E7
400 WNVL 60555 3080 30W-2S B5
700 WLBK 60527 3145 16W-8S E7
1000 AvnT 60073 2531 24W-33N C2
1000 RDLK 60073 2531 24W-33N C2
1000 WLNG 60090 2754 16W-16N D7
1700 YKVL 60560 3260 44W-14S D7
2200 ELGN 60123 2907 36W-8N E2
3100 HDPK 60035 2704 10W-23N A1
3300 MHRY 60050 2528 32W-33N B2
3700 HLCT 60429 3426 4W-20S D5
4000 ISLK 60042 2586 28W-28N E6
5800 JNBG 60050 2471 30W-37N E1
8300 FXLK 60081 2415 28W-39N A5
9400 MaiT 60016 2863 11W-12N D1
15200 ODPK 60467 3344 14W-18S D6
17500 WrnT 60030 2534 17W-33N B3
23600 CnhT 60447 3583 32W-28S E7
23600 CnhT 60447 3672 32W-28S E1
Cottonwood Dr
- HnrT 60107 2856 30W-10N B6
- HnrT 60120 2856 30W-10N B6
- LKPT 60432 3420 20W-21S B7
- SMWD 60107 2856 30W-10N B6
- SMWD 60120 2856 30W-10N B6
10 WHTN 60187 3023 26W-0S E6
200 EGVV 60007 2861 17W-9N B7
200 MltT 60187 3023 26W-0N E5
300 NARA 60542 3077 36W-3S D7
600 DYR 46311 3598 E3
800 ELWD 60421 3675 25W-31S C6
1200 AURA 60506 3137 37W-6S C4
1500 GNVW 60025 2810 9W-14N C5
2200 ELGN 60123 2907 36W-8N E2
2200 ELGN 60123 2908 36W-8N A3
11100 PSHL 60465 3274 10W-13S B3
18300 TYPK 60487 3424 11W-22S A7
Cottonwood Ln
300 NPVL 60540 3141 28W-7S A6
400 SMBG 60193 2858 23W-9N E7
800 MRGO 60152 2634 49W-27N C1
900 BRLT 60103 2910 29W-6N E6
1100 MRGO 60152 2578 49W-27N C7
1300 CLLK 60014 2639 37W-26N A3
1300 DrrT 60014 2639 37W-26N A3
23700 CnhT 60447 3672 32W-28S E1
S Cottonwood Ln
13700 LktT 60544 3340 26W-16S A3
W Cottonwood Ln
900 MPPT 60056 2861 16W-11N D4
1300 ANHT 60005 2806 18W-14N D4
Cottonwood Pl
100 NLNX 60451 3500 19W-24S E6
Cottonwood Rd
10 DRFD 60015 2757 9W-18N B3
10 NfdT 60062 2757 9W-18N B3
100 BFGV 60089 2754 17W-18N B3
400 FKFT 60423 3503 12W-25S C7
E Cottonwood Rd
2200 JLET 60432 3500 21W-22S A2
Cottonwood Tr
200 CRY 60013 2695 32W-23N B1
300 CRY 60013 2641 32W-24N B7
1400 YKVL 60560 3260 44W-14S D7
N Cottonwood Tr
4200 HFET 60192 2804 25W-15N A2
W Cottonwood Tr
1700 HFET 60192 2804 25W-15N B2
E Cottonwood Wy
1000 PLTN 60074 2753 19W-17N C6
Cotuit Ct
100 SMBG 60193 2858 25W-10N C6
500 MltT 60137 3083 21W-1S D2
CO-U
500 BfdT 53128 2353 A1
500 GNCY 53128 2353 A2
CO-U 136th Av
10400 BtlT 53142 2360 C3
12600 BtlT 53142 2360 B4
12600 NptT 60002 2360 B4
CO-U N Carter St
- GNCY 53128 2353 A2
W Couch Pl
- CHCG 60601 3034 E4
200 CHCG 60606 3034 0W-0N B4
600 CHCG 60661 3034 0W-0N A4
700 CHCG 60607 3034 0W-0N A4
Cougar Dr
100 BGBK 60490 3267 26W-12S E2
Cougar Ln
800 OSWG 60543 3263 39W-11S A2
W Cougar St
10 CHCG 60623 3090 4W-3S C4
10 CHCG 60632 3090 4W-3S C4
Cougar Tr
1100 AlqT 60013 2642 30W-24N A6
E Cougar Tr
700 HFET 60169 2859 22W-11N C4
700 SMBG 60169 2859 22W-11N C4
700 SMBG 60173 2859 22W-11N C4
700 SMBG 60194 2859 22W-11N C4
Cougar Wy
- VNHL 60061 2647 16W-24N D6
- VrnT 60061 2647 16W-24N D6
Coulter Ln
400 CmpT 60175 2962 39W-3N D6
Coulter Rd
5100 OKFT 60452 3425 6W-20S E3
5100 OKFT 60452 3426 6W-20S A3
W Coulter St
2000 CHCG 60608 3091 2W-2S B2
Council Av
10 OswT 60503 3201 33W-11S A7
Council Ct
300 SmbT 60193 2913 23W-8N B2
600 CmpT 60119 2961 42W-4N C4
Council Tr
300 LIHL 60156 2694 34W-21N B5
E Council Tr
100 ANHT 60005 2861 17W-12N A2
100 MPPT 60056 2862 15W-12N A1
W Council Tr
10 MPPT 60056 2862 15W-12N A1
300 MPPT 60056 2861 16W-12N E2
Council Hill Rd
600 CPVL 60118 2801 33W-16N B1
600 EDND 60110 2801 33W-16N B1
600 EDND 60118 2801 33W-16N B1
S Countess Ln
25900 CteT 60417 3685 1W-31S B5
Count Fleet Ct
600 NPVL 60540 3142 26W-7S A7
Country Ct
10 DRFD 60015 2756 11W-20N D2
10 LMNT 60439 3271 18W-14S A6
100 BGBK 60440 3268 25W-11S B1
400 LslT 60540 3143 23W-7S A7
1000 CRTE 60417 3686 1E-30S B2
1300 LbvT 60048 2590 18W-30N E2
15800 ODPK 60462 3424 10W-18S A1
22400 NlxT 60451 3590 16W-27S A4
Country Dr
10 CTSD 60525 3147 12W-7S B6
10 LslT 60540 3142 24W-6S C4
1000 SRWD 60404 3496 30W-23S A4
1800 GYLK 60030 2533 18W-32N D4
1900 WrnT 60030 2533 18W-33N D4
2000 PLNO 60545 3259 48W-13S B4
E Country Dr
200 BRLT 60103 2911 28W-7N A5
S Country Dr
700 BRTN 60010 2750 26W-18N E3
800 BNHL 60010 2750 26W-18N E3
W Country Dr
200 BRLT 60103 2911 28W-7N A5
Country Ln
10 DRPK 60010 2699 22W-20N A7
10 DRPK 60010 2752 22W-20N A1
10 HDPK 60035 2757 9W-20N C2
10 NfdT 60093 2811 7W-16N A1
10 NHFD 60093 2811 7W-16N A1
10 ODPK 60467 3344 14W-17S D5
100 AlqT 60013 2642 29W-24N D6
100 CbaT 60013 2642 29W-24N D6
100 MaiT 60016 2809 12W-12N D7
200 ALGN 60102 2694 34W-21N C6
200 GLF 60029 2864 8W-12N E1
200 GNVW 60025 2864 8W-12N E1
200 GNVW 60029 2864 8W-12N E1
300 GNVW 60025 2810 8W-12N E7
400 CLLK 60012 2639 36W-27N E1
400 SMWD 60107 2857 28W-10N A6
500 BCHR 60401 3864 0W-36S C1
500 YkTp 60148 3084 19W-1S C1
600 GLNC 60022 2758 6W-16N C6
800 BFGV 60089 2754 17W-18N A2
1000 CRTE 60417 3686 1E-30S B2
1100 LMNT 60439 3271 18W-14S A6
1200 NHBK 60062 2757 9W-17N D6
1400 DRFD 60015 2756 11W-20N C2
2100 MchT 60051 2528 31W-33N D4
3000 WKGN 60087 2478 15W-37N B1
3100 WLMT 60091 2811 6W-14N E5
3300 ElaT 60047 2700 19W-22N C4
3300 LGGV 60047 2700 19W-22N C4
3300 WDWH 60083 2478 15W-37N B1
3300 WKGN 60083 2478 15W-37N B1
6100 SenT 60180 2635 46W-25N C4
6100 UNON 60180 2635 46W-25N C4
7500 DRN 60561 3207 17W-8S B2
10200 BHPK 60087 2480 10W-38N B1
17200 EHZC 60429 3427 2W-20S D5
18300 LNSG 60438 3429 2E-21S C7
18500 BlmT 60411 3429 2E-21S C7
18500 BlmT 60438 3429 2E-21S C7
E Country Ln
10 ANHT 60004 2754 17W-17N A4
10 BFGV 60089 2754 17W-17N A4
N Country Ln
43200 BtlT 53142 2360 16W-43N D4
43200 NptT 53142 2360 16W-43N D4
43200 NptT 60099 2360 16W-43N D4
S Country Ln
900 DSPN 60016 2862 15W-11N A3
900 MPPT 60016 2862 15W-11N A3
900 MPPT 60056 2862 15W-11N A2
22300 NLNX 60451 3590 16W-27S A3
22300 NlxT 60451 3590 16W-27S A4
24700 CRTE 60417 3686 1E-30S B2
W Country Ln
18500 WrnT 60030 2533 18W-32N E4
18600 GYLK 60030 2533 18W-32N E4
Country Ln E
600 ROSL 60172 2912 24W-6N D6
Country Ln N
600 ROSL 60172 2912 24W-6N D6
Country Ln S
700 ROSL 60172 2912 24W-6N D6
Country Pl
- OMCK 60046 2476 19W-38N D1
- OMCK 60083 2476 19W-38N D1
400 LNHT 60046 2476 19W-37N C2
800 LKFT 60045 2649 11W-24N C6
5000 WKGN 60087 2478 15W-37N B2
Country Rd
10 OswT 60560 3334 40W-15S D2
200 OSWG 60560 3334 39W-15S D2
Country Tr
4300 GRNE 60031 2535 14W-33N C2
Country Aire Dr
- MKHM 60426 3348 4W-18S E6
- MKHM 60428 3348 4W-18S E6
Country Brook Ln
300 HRVD 60033 2464 50W-37N A2
Country Club Av
3400 GRNE 60031 2479 13W-36N A4
3400 WkgT 60031 2479 12W-36N A4
3400 WrnT 60031 2479 13W-36N A4
3400 WrnT 60087 2479 13W-36N A4
3500 GRNE 60031 2478 13W-36N E4
7700 WKGN 60087 2479 12W-36N B4
7700 WkgT 60087 2479 12W-36N B4
Country Club Blvd
1600 NPVL 60563 3140 30W-5S B2
1600 NpvT 60563 3140 30W-5S B2
E Country Club Ct
10 PLTN 60067 2752 20W-17N E4
N Country Club Ct
13100 PSHT 60463 3346 9W-15S D1
S Country Club Ct
13200 PSHT 60463 3346 9W-15S D2
Country Club Dr
- LIHL 60156 2693 37W-21N C5
- MPPT 60056 2808 14W-14N B4
- PTHT 60056 2808 14W-14N B4
10 BMDL 60108 2968 24W-5N D1
10 CTSD 60525 3147 12W-6S C5
10 NHLK 60164 2972 13W-2N D7
10 PTHT 60070 2808 14W-14N B4
100 MchT 60050 2528 31W-32N C5
100 MHRY 60050 2528 31W-32N C5
100 NHLK 60164 3028 13W-2N E1
300 BNVL 60106 2915 16W-6N D7
400 NHLK 60160 3029 12W-2N A1
400 NHLK 60164 3029 12W-2N A1
500 ITSC 60143 2914 19W-7N D5
600 BRLT 60103 2966 29W-4N E3
600 WynT 60103 2966 29W-4N E3
600 WynT 60185 2966 29W-4N E3
800 LGNG 60525 3147 13W-5S A3
800 LYVL 60048 2591 15W-28N E7
800 LYVL 60048 2592 15W-27N A7
2000 WDRG 60517 3206 21W-8S A2
2400 OMFD 60461 3507 3W-24S B5
2600 RchT 60461 3507 3W-24S B5
17500 CCHL 60478 3426 4W-21S D6
17500 HLCT 60429 3426 4W-21S D6
17800 BmnT 60430 3426 4W-21S D6
17800 CCHL 60430 3426 4W-21S D6
Countryclub Dr
1700 LGGV 60047 2700 19W-20N D7
1700 LGGV 60047 2753 19W-20N D1
E Country Club Dr
10 NHLK 60164 2972 13W-2N D7
10 NHLK 60164 3028 13W-2N E1
N Country Club Dr
100 ADSN 60101 2970 19W-3N C5
400 AddT 60101 2970 19W-3N C4
S Country Club Dr
9300 ENGN 60805 3213 3W-10S A5
Country Club Ln
10 MltT 60187 3082 25W-2S B3
100 VNHL 60061 2647 17W-24N B7
400 GNEN 60137 3025 21W-0N D5
400 MltT 60137 3025 21W-0N D5
600 ITSC 60143 2914 19W-7N D5
800 NHBK 60062 2757 8W-16N E7
1000 SMBG 60193 2912 25W-9N B1
1100 SmbT 60193 2912 25W-9N B1
8000 NRIV 60546 3088 10W-2S B2
8400 ODPK 60462 3346 10W-17S B5
W Country Club Ln
7900 EDPK 60171 2974 9W-2N B7
7900 EDPK 60707 2974 9W-2N B7
Country Club Pl
100 GNVA 60134 3020 35W-1N A4
Country Club Rd
10 SchT 60174 2964 34W-4N D3
10 SchT 60184 2964 34W-4N D3
10 WYNE 60174 2964 34W-4N E3
10 WYNE 60184 2964 34W-4N E3
100 CHHT 60411 3507 2W-25S E7
100 CHHT 60411 3508 1W-25S A7
300 SCRL 60174 2964 34W-4N D3
400 CLLK 60014 2639 36W-24N C6
800 LKWD 60014 2639 36W-25N C6
900 LKZH 60047 2698 24W-23N B2
1000 ELGN 60123 2801 33W-13N A7
9100 BLVY 60098 2582 39W-30N C1
9100 DrrT 60098 2582 39W-30N C1
9100 DrrT 60098 2583 38W-30N A2
9500 WDSK 60098 2582 38W-30N D2
11900 DrrT 60098 2581 40W-31N E1
11900 WDSK 60098 2581 40W-31N E1
41400 AntT 60002 2415 26W-41N D1
41500 AntT 60002 2356 26W-41N D7
Country Club Rd CO-V25
9100 BLVY 60098 2582 39W-30N C1
9100 DrrT 60098 2582 39W-30N C1
9100 DrrT 60098 2583 38W-30N A2
S Country Club Rd
2100 DrrT 60098 2583 37W-28N A5
4000 DrrT 60012 2583 37W-27N B7
S Country Club Rd CO-V25
2100 DrrT 60098 2583 37W-28N A5
4000 DrrT 60012 2583 37W-27N B7
Country Club East
- CTSD 60525 3147 12W-6S C4
Country Club Hills Dr
- FXLK 60081 2414 29W-39N D6
Country Club West
- CTSD 60525 3147 12W-6S C4
Country Commons Rd
100 CRY 60013 2695 32W-23N C2
100 TVLY 60013 2695 32W-23N C2
Country Creek Dr
800 NLNX 60451 3589 18W-26S A2
Country Creek Wy
7300 DGvT 60516 3206 19W-8S D1
7300 DRGV 60516 3206 19W-8S D1
W Country Estates Rd
26500 CbaT 60010 2697 26W-21N C5

STREET Block	City	ZIP	Map#	CGS	Grid
Country Farm Dr					
1800	NPVL	60563	3140	30W-4S	B1
Countryfield Ln					
700	ELGN	60120	2855	31W-12N	E2
Country Glen Dr					
-	JLET	60431	3496	29W-22S	C2
-	JLET	60586	3496	29W-22S	C2
-	SRWD	60404	3496	29W-22S	C2
10	NpvT	60563	3140	30W-6S	A4
Country Glen Ln					
1000	CLSM	60188	2967	27W-4N	D4
Country Hill Av					
600	CLLK	60012	2639	36W-27N	E1
Country Hills Dr					
-	KdlT	60560	3333	42W-17S	E6
1800	YKVL	60560	3333	42W-17S	E6
Country Knoll Ct					
2100	ELGN	60123	2853	36W-11N	E4
2100	ElgT	60123	2853	36W-11N	E4
Country Knoll Ln					
1700	ELGN	60123	2854	36W-11N	A4
2000	ELGN	60123	2853	36W-11N	E3
2000	ElgT	60123	2853	36W-11N	E3
E Country Lake Rd					
2700	ANHT	60004	2754	16W-16N	E7
Country Lakes Dr					
100	NPVL	60563	3140	30W-5S	B2
100	NpvT	60563	3140	30W-5S	B2
Country Ln Ct					
400	WCDA	60084	2588	25W-27N	A7
W Country Ln Dr					
14500	WDWH	60083	2420	14W-38N	C7
Country Manor Ln					
10	PlsT	60462	3345	13W-15S	A1
10	PlsT	60467	3345	13W-15S	A1
Country Oak Ln					
300	IVNS	60067	2804	23W-15N	E2
Country Oaks Ct					
2600	AURA	60502	3139	32W-4S	B1
Country Oaks Dr					
-	JNBG	60050	2471	30W-36N	E3
10	BNHL	60010	2749	30W-20N	A2
1800	JLET	60586	3416	30W-21S	B7
Country Oaks Ln					
10	BNHL	60010	2748	30W-20N	E1
10	BNHL	60010	2749	30W-20N	A1
Country Pond Dr					
11600	MKNA	60448	3590	14W-25S	D1
N Country Ridge Ct					
400	LKZH	60047	2699	22W-22N	A4
S Country Ridge Ct					
400	LKZH	60047	2699	22W-22N	A4
Country Ridge Dr					
2200	JLET	60586	3415	31W-21S	E6
6400	OKFT	60452	3347	8W-18S	B7
Countryridge Dr					
500	WNVL	60555	3080	29W-2S	C4
Country Ridge Ln					
300	BMDL	60108	2969	22W-4N	C3
1100	BGBK	60440	3268	25W-11S	B1
Country Ridge Sq					
600	WDSK	60098	2581	41W-30N	D2
Country School Rd					
200	DndT	60118	2747	35W-18N	C5
Country Shire Ln					
8200	FXLK	60081	2414	29W-40N	D3
Countryside Av					
2200	MTGY	60538	3199	38W-9S	A5
2300	MTGY	60538	3198	39W-9S	E4
Countryside Cir					
2000	NPVL	60565	3203	26W-9S	E5
Countryside Ct					
10	BRRG	60527	3146	15W-7S	B5
10	WLBK	60527	3146	15W-7S	B5
900	GNVW	60025	2809	10W-13N	E6
900	NfdT	60025	2809	10W-13N	E6
20200	FftT	60423	3504	10W-24S	C6
N Countryside Ct					
100	BDWD	60408	3941	32W-41S	D6
25400	LKBN	60010	2643	27W-25N	B5
S Countryside Ct					
200	BDWD	60408	3941	32W-41S	D6
Countryside Ctr					
400	YKVL	60560	3261	42W-14S	C6
Countryside Dr					
-	SRWD	60404	3495	31W-24S	E7
100	ALGN	60102	2748	32W-20N	A1
300	ROSL	60172	2913	23W-7N	B4
600	WHTN	60187	3024	24W-0N	D4
700	BGBK	60490	3268	26W-13S	A5
900	HRPK	60133	2912	26W-8N	A2
1100	ELGN	60123	2800	35W-13N	C7
1200	ALGN	60102	2695	32W-20N	A7
1400	BFGV	60089	2753	18W-18N	E3
1800	LbvT	60048	2590	18W-30N	E2
3200	JNBG	60050	2471	31W-35N	E6
23900	CNHN	60410	3672	31W-29S	E2
N Countryside Dr					
25300	LKBN	60010	2643	27W-25N	B5
W Countryside Dr					
900	PLTN	60067	2752	22W-17N	B6
Countryside Hwy					
600	MDLN	60060	2646	18W-27N	E1
700	MDLN	60060	2590	18W-28N	E6
900	MDLN	60060	2591	17W-28N	A7
Countryside Ln					
200	LNHT	60046	2476	20W-37N	B1
900	CLSM	60188	2967	27W-4N	C4
1100	SEGN	60177	2907	37W-7N	C5
1400	LGGV	60047	2753	18W-20N	D1
1900	RLKB	60073	2474	23W-35N	E5
3500	GNVW	60025	2809	11W-13N	D6
3500	NfdT	60025	2809	11W-13N	D6
20300	FftT	60423	3504	10W-24S	D6
E Countryside Ln					
10	PTHT	60070	2808	15W-16N	A1
N Countryside Ln					
22000	CbaT	60010	2697	26W-22N	C4
E Countryside Pkwy					
-	BtlT	60560	3261	41W-14S	E7
100	YKVL	60560	3261	42W-14S	C6
W Countryside Pkwy					
100	YKVL	60560	3261	43W-14S	C7
Countryside Plz					
10	CTSD	60525	3147	12W-6S	B4
Countryside Lake Dr					
26300	FmtT	60047	2646	20W-26N	A3
26300	FmtT	60060	2646	20W-26N	A2
26300	LGGV	60047	2646	20W-26N	A3
26300	LGGV	60060	2646	20W-26N	A3
26800	FmtT	60060	2645	20W-26N	E2
Country Spring Dr					
-	MchT	60050	2471	31W-36N	E3
2300	JNBG	60050	2471	31W-36N	E3
Country Squire Ct					
10	PSHT	60463	3274	9W-14S	D5
Country Squire Dr					
1400	GNVA	60134	3020	36W-0N	A5
S Country Squire Rd					
10	PSHT	60463	3274	9W-14S	D5
Countrytrail Ct					
600	ISLK	60042	2586	28W-28N	E7
W Country Valley Dr					
21500	FmtT	60060	2645	21W-26N	D3
Countryview Blvd					
-	HTLY	60140	2744	43W-19N	A3
-	HTLY	60142	2744	43W-19N	B2
Countryview Dr					
10	OswT	60560	3334	40W-15S	B1
10	WldT	60564	3203	28W-10S	A5
10	WldT	60565	3203	28W-10S	A5
Country View Ln					
10	CmpT	60119	2961	42W-4N	D5
12400	HMGN	60491	3422	15W-19S	B1
E Country Walk Dr					
10	RLKB	60073	2475	23W-36N	A4
W Country Walk Dr					
10	RLKB	60073	2475	23W-36N	A4
200	RLKB	60073	2474	23W-36N	E4
300	LKVL	60046	2474	23W-36N	E4
300	RLKB	60046	2474	23W-36N	E4
Country Water Ct					
2200	ELGN	60123	2907	36W-8N	E2
Countrywood Dr					
900	ZION	60099	2362	12W-42N	B6
Country Woods Dr					
12000	HMGN	60491	3344	15W-18S	C7
12000	OrlT	60467	3344	15W-18S	C7
County Rd					
500	WMTN	60481	3853	27W-38S	D6
W County Rd					
20900	FrnT	60481	3853	26W-38S	E6
20900	WMTN	60481	3853	26W-38S	E6
N County St					
10	WKGN	60085	2537	10W-34N	B1
500	WKGN	60085	2480	10W-35N	B7
S County St					
10	WKGN	60085	2537	10W-34N	B2
County Fair Ct					
5100	MONE	60449	3683	6W-31S	A6
S County Fair Dr					
26000	MONE	60449	3683	6W-31S	B6
County Fairground					
600	GYLK	60030	2533	19W-33N	D4
County Farm Ct					
1400	WHTN	60187	3081	26W-1S	D2
County Farm Ln					
2300	SMBG	60194	2857	26W-10N	E5
County Farm Rd					
-	CLSM	60133	2967	27W-4N	D3
10	HRPK	60133	2911	27W-7N	D5
10	HRPK	60133	2967	27W-4N	D3
10	MltT	60187	3023	26W-0S	D6
10	MltT	60190	3023	27W-2N	D1
10	WHTN	60187	3023	26W-0S	D6
10	WNFD	60190	3023	27W-2N	D1
10	WnfT	60185	3023	27W-2N	D2
10	WnfT	60190	3023	27W-1N	D3
10	WynT	60133	2911	27W-6N	D7
10	WynT	60133	2967	27W-6N	D1
10	WynT	60185	3023	27W-2N	D2
100	WNFD	60185	3023	27W-1N	D3
100	WnfT	60190	3023	27W-1N	D3
300	CLSM	60185	2967	27W-2N	D7
300	CLSM	60188	2967	27W-2N	D7
300	WynT	60185	2967	27W-2N	D7
300	WynT	60188	2967	27W-2N	D7
500	BRLT	60103	2911	27W-7N	D5
500	BRLT	60133	2911	27W-7N	D5
500	HRPK	60103	2911	27W-7N	D5
23400	TroT	60431	3496	29W-24S	D7
County Farm Rd CO-43					
-	CLSM	60133	2967	27W-4N	D3
10	HRPK	60133	2911	27W-6N	D7
10	HRPK	60133	2967	27W-4N	D3
10	MltT	60187	3023	26W-0S	D6
10	MltT	60190	3023	27W-2N	D1
10	WHTN	60187	3023	26W-0S	D6
10	WNFD	60190	3023	27W-2N	D1
10	WnfT	60185	3023	27W-2N	D2
10	WynT	60133	2911	27W-6N	D7
10	WynT	60133	2967	27W-6N	D1
10	WynT	60185	3023	27W-2N	D2
100	WNFD	60185	3023	27W-1N	D3
100	WnfT	60190	3023	27W-1N	D3
300	CLSM	60185	2967	27W-2N	D7
300	CLSM	60188	2967	27W-2N	D7
300	WynT	60185	2967	27W-2N	D7
300	WynT	60188	2967	27W-2N	D7
500	BRLT	60103	2911	27W-7N	D5
500	BRLT	60133	2911	27W-7N	D5
500	HRPK	60103	2911	27W-7N	D5
N County Farm Rd					
-	CLSM	60185	2967	27W-3N	D7
-	MltT	60187	3023	26W-0S	D6
-	MltT	60190	3023	26W-0S	D6
-	WynT	60185	2967	27W-3N	D7
-	WynT	60188	2967	27W-3N	D7
100	WHTN	60187	3023	26W-0S	D6
900	CLSM	60188	2967	27W-3N	D6
1200	CLSM	60133	2967	27W-4N	D3
1200	HRPK	60133	2967	27W-4N	D3
N County Farm Rd CO-43					
-	CLSM	60185	2967	27W-3N	D7
-	MltT	60187	3023	26W-0S	D6
-	MltT	60190	3023	26W-0S	D6
-	WynT	60185	2967	27W-3N	D7
-	WynT	60188	2967	27W-3N	D7
100	WHTN	60187	3023	26W-0S	D6
900	CLSM	60188	2967	27W-3N	D6
1200	CLSM	60133	2967	27W-4N	D3
1200	HRPK	60133	2967	27W-4N	D3
S County Farm Rd					
-	WnfT	60187	3081	26W-1S	D2
100	WHTN	60187	3023	26W-0S	E7
1400	WHTN	60187	3081	26W-1S	D2
S County Farm Rd CO-43					
100	WHTN	60187	3023	26W-0S	E7
400	WHTN	60187	3081	26W-0S	D1
E County Lane Rd					
17000	AraT	60502	3139	32W-4S	B1
17000	AraT	60504	3139	33W-4S	B1
17000	NpvT	60502	3139	33W-4S	B1
17000	NpvT	60504	3139	33W-4S	B1
36200	AraT	60502	3079	32W-4S	B7
36200	AURA	60502	3079	32W-4S	B7
36200	NpvT	60502	3079	32W-4S	B7
County Line Ct					
500	HNDL	60521	3146	14W-5S	C1
County Line Ln					
6700	BRRG	60527	3146	14W-7S	C7
County Line Rd					
-	AlqT	60102	2747	35W-20N	B2
300	GLNC	60022	2758	6W-20N	C2
300	HDPK	60035	2758	7W-18N	B2
700	AraT	60502	3139	32W-7S	B6
700	AURA	60502	3139	32W-7S	B6
700	GLNC	60062	2758	7W-20N	B2
700	NtrT	60062	2758	7W-18N	B2
2000	ALGN	60102	2748	32W-20N	B2
2000	AlqT	60102	2748	32W-20N	B2
2200	BNHL	60010	2748	32W-20N	B2
2200	BNHL	60102	2748	32W-20N	B2
6900	ALGN	60102	2746	35W-20N	E2
6900	ALGN	60102	2747	35W-20N	A2
9300	FRGV	60010	2696	28W-22N	D4
9300	FRGV	60021	2696	28W-22N	D4
9300	LKBN	60010	2696	28W-22N	D4
9300	LKBN	60021	2696	28W-22N	D4
14400	CstT	60481	4031	29W-45S	E7
14400	EsxT	60481	4031	30W-46S	C7
14400	EsxT	60935	4031	30W-46S	C7
14400	RedT	60481	4031	30W-46S	C7
County Line Rd CO-A50					
2000	ALGN	60102	2748	32W-20N	B2
2000	AlqT	60102	2748	32W-20N	B2
2200	BNHL	60010	2748	32W-20N	B2
2200	BNHL	60102	2748	32W-20N	B2
N County Line Rd					
100	ALGN	60102	2746	36W-20N	D2
100	HNDL	60521	3146	15W-4S	C1
300	HNDL	60521	3086	15W-4S	C7
600	AddT	60126	2972	15W-3N	B6
600	EMHT	60126	2972	15W-3N	B6
600	EMHT	60126	3028	15W-2N	B1
600	EMHT	60164	2972	14W-2N	B7
600	NHLK	60164	2972	14W-2N	B7
600	NHLK	60164	3028	15W-2N	B1
700	LydT	60164	2972	15W-3N	B6
800	LynT	60521	3086	15W-4S	C7
800	LynT	60558	3086	15W-4S	C7
900	FNPK	60131	2972	15W-3N	B6
900	FNPK	60164	2972	15W-3N	B6
7500	ALGN	60118	2746	36W-20N	D2
S County Line Rd					
-	CLCY	60416	3941	32W-39S	C2
-	FlxT	60416	3941	32W-39S	C2
-	SwdT	60447	3495	33W-24S	C6
-	TroT	60404	3495	33W-24S	C6
10	HNDL	60521	3146	14W-7S	C6
400	DGvT	60527	3208	14W-10S	C5
400	WLSP	60480	3208	14W-10S	C5
400	WLSP	60527	3208	14W-10S	C5
2600	DMND	60416	3941	32W-39S	C2
5800	BRRG	60521	3146	15W-6S	C4
6000	BRRG	60527	3146	15W-6S	C4
6000	HNDL	60527	3146	15W-6S	C4
7400	BRRG	60527	3208	15W-8S	C2
8000	LynT	60527	3208	15W-8S	C2
8800	DGvT	60480	3208	14W-10S	C5
8800	LynT	60480	3208	14W-10S	C5
15600	NasT	60543	3337	33W-18S	B7
15600	NasT	60544	3337	33W-18S	B7
15600	NasT	60544	3415	33W-19S	B4
15600	PnfT	60543	3337	33W-18S	B7
15600	PnfT	60544	3337	33W-18S	B7
15600	PnfT	60544	3415	33W-19S	B4
16000	PNFD	60586	3415	32W-19S	B4
18300	JLET	60431	3495	32W-22S	C3
18300	JLET	60586	3495	32W-22S	C3
18600	JLET	60447	3495	32W-22S	C3
18700	JLET	60404	3495	32W-22S	C3
18700	TroT	60431	3495	32W-22S	C3
21400	SwdT	60447	3583	32W-26S	C3
21400	TroT	60404	3583	32W-26S	C3
21600	MNKA	60447	3583	32W-26S	C3
W County Line Rd					
10	BNHL	60010	2749	30W-20N	A2
100	ALGN	60102	2748	32W-19N	E2
100	BNHL	60010	2748	32W-19N	E2
100	BNHL	60102	2748	32W-19N	E2
300	AlqT	60010	2749	29W-20N	D2
W County Line Rd CO-A50					
10	BNHL	60010	2749	30W-20N	A2
100	ALGN	60102	2748	32W-19N	E2
100	BNHL	60010	2748	32W-19N	E2
100	BNHL	60102	2748	32W-19N	E2
300	AlqT	60010	2749	29W-20N	D2
County Meadows Ln					
-	GRNE	60031	2534	15W-33N	E2
-	WrnT	60031	2534	15W-33N	E2
Countrynell Av					
10	LydT	60164	2973	12W-2N	B6
Cour Caravelle					
10	PSHL	60465	3274	10W-13S	B3
Courcival Ln					
10	WYNE	60184	2965	32W-6N	C1
Cour D'Alene					
10	PSHL	60465	3274	10W-13S	B3
Cour Deauville					
10	PSHL	60465	3274	10W-13S	A4
Cour de la Reine					
10	PSHL	60465	3274	10W-13S	B4
Courier Av					
300	SchT	60174	2908	34W-6N	D7
Courier Ct					
1200	DRFD	60015	2703	11W-21N	D6
Cour la Salle					
10	PSHL	60465	3274	10W-13S	B3
Cour Leroux					
10	PSHL	60465	3274	10W-13S	B3
Cour Madeleine					
10	PSHL	60465	3274	10W-13S	B4
Cour Marquis					
10	PSHL	60465	3274	10W-13S	A4
Cour Masson					
10	PSHL	60465	3274	10W-13S	B3
Cour Michele					
10	PSHL	60465	3274	10W-13S	A4
Cour Monnet					
10	PSHL	60465	3274	10W-13S	B3
Cour Montreal					
10	PSHL	60465	3274	10W-13S	B3
Cour St. Tropez					
10	PSHL	60465	3274	10W-13S	B4
Course Dr					
100	LIHL	60156	2693	36W-21N	C6
W Course Dr					
2100	RVWD	60015	2703	13W-22N	A4
Court Av					
1000	HDPK	60035	2704	8W-21N	D6
Court Dr					
10	CTSD	60525	3147	13W-7S	B5
Court Pl					
10	NPVL	60540	3141	26W-6S	D5
W Court Pl					
-	CHCG	60606	3034	0W-0N	B4
10	CHCG	60602	3034	0W-0N	B4
600	CHCG	60661	3034	0W-0N	A4
700	CHCG	60607	3034	0W-0N	A4
Court St					
1700	MHRY	60050	2528	32W-33N	C2
N Court St					
1200	MHRY	60050	2528	32W-33N	B4
1600	MchT	60050	2528	32W-33N	C3
S Court St					
100	JLET	60433	3499	22W-24S	D5
100	JltT	60433	3499	22W-24S	D5
W Court St					
4700	MONE	60449	3683	6W-31S	A5
4700	MonT	60449	3683	5W-31S	C5
4700	UYPK	60449	3683	5W-31S	C5
5500	MONE	60449	3682	6W-31S	E5
Court Ter					
-	SHLD	60473	3428	0E-18S	E1
Court A					
1100	HRPK	60133	2912	26W-6N	A6
Courtaulds Dr					
1000	WDSK	60098	2582	40W-30N	A2
Court B					
1100	HRPK	60133	2912	26W-6N	A6
Court C					
1200	HRPK	60133	2912	26W-6N	A6
Court Connection					
13400	HMGN	60491	3421	16W-21S	E6
Court D					
1200	HRPK	60133	2911	26W-6N	D7
1200	HRPK	60133	2912	26W-6N	A6
Court E					
1200	HRPK	60133	2911	26W-6N	D6
1200	HRPK	60133	2912	26W-6N	A6
W Courte Dr					
8000	MaiT	60053	2864	10W-11N	B2
8000	MaiT	60714	2864	10W-11N	B2
8000	MNGV	60053	2864	10W-11N	B2
8000	NLES	60053	2864	10W-11N	B2
8000	NLES	60714	2864	10W-11N	B2
Courtenay Dr					
1800	WHTN	60187	3082	26W-1S	A1
Courtenay Ln					
100	SMBG	60193	2913	23W-9N	A1
Courtesy Ln					
400	DSPN	60018	2862	15W-10N	A6
1000	WLNG	60090	2755	13W-16N	D7
Court F					
5500	HRPK	60133	2912	26W-6N	A6
Court G					
1100	HRPK	60133	2912	26W-6N	A6
Court H					
1200	HRPK	60133	2912	26W-6N	A6
Court J					
1300	HRPK	60133	2911	26W-7N	E5
Court la Grov					
200	DRPK	60010	2752	22W-20N	C1
Courtland Av					
1500	PKRG	60068	2918	10W-7N	B4
2000	CHCG	60631	2918	10W-7N	B4
2000	PKRG	60631	2918	10W-7N	B4
N Courtland Av					
-	NRDG	60706	2918	10W-6N	B6
5300	CHCG	60656	2918	10W-6N	B6
5300	CHCG	60706	2918	10W-6N	B6
5300	LydT	60656	2918	10W-6N	B6
5600	CHCG	60631	2918	10W-7N	B5
5600	LydT	60631	2918	10W-6N	B5
5600	MaiT	60631	2918	10W-6N	B5
9200	NLES	60714	2864	10W-11N	B3
W Courtland Av					
7900	NRDG	60706	2918	10W-5N	B7
Courtland Cir					
600	WNSP	60558	3146	13W-5S	E2
4900	JLET	60586	3496	30W-22S	C2
Courtland Ct					
400	SMBG	60193	2858	24W-9N	D7
2300	AURA	60502	3139	32W-6S	B4
Courtland Dr					
200	SEGN	60177	2907	37W-8N	C3
1000	BFGV	60089	2701	17W-21N	A6
N Courtland Dr					
1500	ANHT	60004	2807	16W-15N	C2
Courtland Pl					
1000	AURA	60502	3139	32W-6S	B4
E Courtland St					
10	MDLN	60060	2646	18W-27N	D1
W Courtland St					
10	MDLN	60060	2646	19W-27N	C1
W Courtland Tr					
4800	MHRY	60050	2527	33W-31N	D6
Court Leona					
1300	HRPK	60133	2911	26W-6N	D6
Court Marguerite					
1300	HRPK	60133	2911	26W-7N	E5
Court Maria					
1300	HRPK	60133	2911	26W-6N	D6
Courtney Cir					
400	SRGV	60554	3135	42W-5S	D2
Courtney Dr					
1300	NPVL	60565	3203	27W-8S	B2
4600	LIHL	60156	2692	38W-23N	E2
6500	OKFT	60452	3347	8W-18S	B7
Courtney Ln					
10	CRY	60013	2641	30W-24N	E7
600	MRGO	60152	2634	49W-25N	B4
600	RlyT	60152	2634	49W-25N	B4
600	WNFD	60190	3023	27W-0N	D4
3100	SCHT	60411	3596	1W-27S	A4
S Courtney Rd					
11400	WldT	60585	3265	32W-13S	C5
Courtney St					
-	LtRT	60545	3260	46W-14S	A7
-	PLNO	60545	3260	46W-14S	A7
Court O					
1300	HRPK	60133	2911	26W-6N	E6
Court of Ash					
200	VNHL	60061	2647	17W-24N	A6
Court of Bayview					
10	NHBK	60062	2756	11W-17N	C4
Court of Birch					
700	VNHL	60061	2647	17W-24N	A7
Court of Bucks County					
10	LNSH	60069	2702	13W-23N	E2
Court of Connecticut River Vly					
10	LNSH	60069	2702	13W-23N	E2
Court of Elm					
300	VNHL	60061	2647	17W-24N	A7
Court of Fox River Vly					
10	LNSH	60069	2702	13W-23N	E2
Court of Harborside					
10	NHBK	60062	2756	11W-17N	C5
Court of Island Pt					
10	NHBK	60062	2756	11W-17N	D5
Court of Lagoon Vw					
10	NHBK	60062	2756	12W-17N	C5
Court of Mohawk Vly					
10	LNSH	60069	2702	13W-23N	E2
Court of Nantucket					
10	LNSH	60069	2702	13W-22N	E3
Court of Natchez					
10	LNSH	60069	2702	13W-23N	E2
Court of North Cor					
10	NHBK	60062	2756	11W-17N	D5
Court of Overlook Blf					
10	NHBK	60062	2756	12W-17N	C5
E Court of Shorewood					
200	VNHL	60061	2647	18W-24N	A6
S Court of Shorewood					
900	VNHL	60061	2647	18W-24N	A7
W Court of Shorewood					
200	VNHL	60061	2647	18W-24N	A7
Court of Spruce					
700	VNHL	60061	2647	17W-24N	A7
Court of Tidewater					
10	LNSH	60069	2702	13W-23N	E3
Court of Tyronwood					
10	NHBK	60062	2756	12W-17N	C5
Court of Wilmington					
10	LNSH	60069	2702	13W-23N	E3
Court of Wood Cr					
-	LNSH	60069	2702	13W-23N	E3
Court P					
1300	HRPK	60133	2911	26W-6N	E6
Court Q					
1300	HRPK	60133	2911	26W-6N	E6
Courtside Dr					
16500	LKPT	60441	3420	20W-19S	B3
Court Touraine					
500	DRPK	60010	2752	22W-20N	C2
Courtwright Ct					
7200	JLET	60586	3495	33W-21S	B1
Courtwright Dr					
1600	JLET	60586	3415	33W-21S	B7
1600	JLET	60586	3495	33W-21S	B1
Courtyard Cir					
2400	AURA	60506	3136	39W-6S	E4
Courtyard Dr					
-	OKTR	60181	3084	18W-1S	E2
600	SCRL	60174	2964	33W-3N	E5
Cour Versaille					
10	PSHL	60465	3274	10W-13S	B3
CO-V 116th St					
18200	BtlT	53104	2359		A2
18800	BtlT	53104	2358		B2
21600	SlmT	53104	2358		B2
CO-V 224th Av					
11000	SlmT	53104	2358		B1
CO-V12 Alden Rd					
9600	AdnT	60033	2349	45W-41N	A7
CO-V23 Lakewood Rd					
-	GfnT	60014	2692	38W-23N	E2
-	LKWD	60014	2692	38W-23N	E2
2400	LIHL	60156	2692	38W-21N	E5
9800	GfnT	60156	2692	38W-22N	E4
10300	GfnT	60102	2692	38W-21N	E6
CO-V24 Greenwood Rd					
1900	GwdT	60098	2525	39W-33N	D2
2100	BLVY	60098	2525	39W-34N	D1
2700	BLVY	60098	2468	39W-34N	D7
2700	GwdT	60097	2468	39W-35N	D6
2700	GwdT	60098	2468	39W-35N	D6
2700	WRLK	60097	2468	39W-35N	D6
2700	WRLK	60098	2468	39W-34N	D7
3100	GNWD	60097	2468	39W-35N	D6
3100	GNWD	60098	2468	39W-35N	D6
5800	GwdT	60097	2469	38W-37N	A1
5800	HbnT	60034	2469	38W-37N	A1
5800	HbnT	60097	2469	38W-37N	A1
9300	HbnT	60034	2352	38W-41N	A7
9300	HbnT	60071	2352	38W-41N	A7
CO-V25 Country Club Rd					
9100	DrrT	60098	2583	37W-29N	A4
CO-V25 S Country Club Rd					
2100	DrrT	60098	2583	37W-29N	A3
4000	DrrT	60012	2583	37W-27N	C7
CO-V25 N Fleming Rd					
10	GwdT	60098	2525	39W-32N	D5
CO-V25 S Fleming Rd					
10	DrrT	60098	2525	39W-32N	D5
10	GwdT	60098	2525	39W-32N	D6
200	BLVY	60098	2525	39W-32N	D5
900	BLVY	60098	2582	38W-30N	E1
900	DrrT	60098	2582	38W-30N	E1
CO-V25 Ridgefield Rd					
7800	CLLK	60012	2639	37W-27N	C1
7800	NndT	60012	2639	37W-27N	C1
8000	DrrT	60012	2639	37W-27N	C1
8100	CLLK	60012	2583	37W-27N	C7
8100	DrrT	60012	2583	37W-27N	C7
CO-V29 McHenry Av					
300	CLLK	60014	2639	36W-24N	E6
1000	CLLK	60014	2693	36W-23N	E1
CO-V29 Randall Rd					
8700	AlqT	60014	2693	36W-20N	E7
8700	CLLK	60014	2693	36W-20N	E7
9000	AlqT	60156	2693	36W-20N	E7
9100	CLLK	60156	2693	36W-20N	E7
9100	LIHL	60014	2693	36W-20N	E7
9100	LIHL	60156	2693	36W-20N	E7
CO-V29 N Randall Rd					
-	CLLK	60014	2693	36W-22N	E4
-	CLLK	60156	2693	36W-22N	E4
10	ALGN	60102	2693	36W-21N	E6
10	LIHL	60102	2693	36W-21N	E6
10	LIHL	60156	2693	36W-21N	E5
CO-V29 S Randall Rd					
10	ALGN	60102	2693	36W-21N	E6
10	LIHL	60102	2693	36W-21N	E6
10	LIHL	60156	2693	36W-21N	E6
11100	AlqT	60102	2746	36W-20N	E1
11900	ALGN	60102	2746	36W-20N	E1
CO-V30					
-	RcmT	60071	2352	35W-42N	E6
CO-V30 Keystone Rd					
10300	RcmT	60071	2352	36W-43N	E4
11300	GNCY	53128	2352	35W-43N	E4
11300	GNCY	60071	2352	35W-43N	E4
CO-V32 W Algonquin Rd					
400	ALGN	60102	2694	34W-21N	D6
1100	LIHL	60156	2694	34W-21N	C6
CO-V32 S Main St					
600	CLLK	60014	2640	35W-24N	B6
CO-V32 Pyott Rd					
100	ALGN	60102	2694	34W-21N	C6
100	LIHL	60156	2694	34W-23N	B2
800	CLLK	60014	2640	35W-24N	B7
800	CLLK	60156	2640	35W-24N	B7
800	LIHL	60156	2640	35W-24N	B7
8000	CLLK	60156	2694	35W-24N	B1

STREET Block	City	ZIP	Map#	CGS	Grid
CO-V33 N Burlington Rd					
11300	RcmT	60071	2353	34W-43N	D4
11300	RHMD	60071	2353	34W-43N	D4
11400	RdlT	53181	2353	34W-43N	D4
11400	TNLK	53128	2353	34W-43N	D4
11400	TNLK	53181	2353	34W-43N	D4
11400	TNLK	60071	2353	34W-43N	D4
CO-V33 Virginia Rd					
10	CLLK	60014	2640	35W-24N	A6
8000	CLLK	60014	2694	34W-23N	C2
8000	LIHL	60014	2694	34W-23N	C2
8200	CLLK	60156	2694	34W-23N	C1
8200	LIHL	60156	2694	34W-23N	C2
9200	ALGN	60013	2694	33W-22N	E3
9200	AlqT	60013	2694	33W-22N	E3
CO-V34 S Crystal Lake Rd					
200	MHRY	60050	2527	34W-31N	D6
300	NndT	60050	2527	34W-31N	D6
500	BLVY	60050	2584	34W-30N	C1
500	MHRY	60050	2584	34W-30N	C1
500	NndT	60050	2584	34W-30N	C1
2100	NndT	60012	2584	35W-29N	B3
2400	BLVY	60012	2584	35W-29N	B4
CO-V34 W Crystal Lake Rd					
4000	MHRY	60050	2528	33W-33N	A4
4300	MHRY	60050	2527	34W-31N	C7
CO-V34 Walkup Rd					
300	CLLK	60012	2640	35W-26N	A2
300	CLLK	60014	2640	35W-26N	B3
2600	BLVY	60012	2584	35W-29N	B4
2600	NndT	60012	2584	35W-27N	B7
4100	CLLK	60012	2584	35W-28N	B7
4400	NndT	60012	2640	35W-26N	A2
CO-V36 Cary Rd					
900	ALGN	60102	2694	33W-21N	E6
1000	AlqT	60102	2694	33W-21N	E6
1300	AlqT	60102	2695	33W-21N	A5
1700	ALGN	60013	2695	32W-22N	A4
2000	CRY	60102	2695	32W-22N	B4
2200	CRY	60013	2695	32W-22N	B3
CO-V36 Cary-Algonquin Rd					
-	ALGN	60013	2695	32W-22N	B3
-	CRY	60102	2695	32W-22N	B3
100	CRY	60013	2695	33W-21N	A5
200	TVLY	60013	2695	32W-23N	C2
400	CRY	60013	2641	31W-24N	C7
CO-V37 Lakeview Rd					
10500	RcmT	60071	2354	32W-43N	B4
10500	SPGV	60081	2354	32W-42N	B6
11500	TNLK	53181	2354	32W-43N	B4
11500	TNLK	60071	2354	32W-43N	B4
CO-V40 Chapel Hill Rd					
-	MchT	60051	2528	31W-32N	E4
-	MHRY	60051	2528	30W-32N	E4
CO-V40 N Chapel Hill Rd					
1000	MchT	60051	2528	31W-32N	E4
1000	MHRY	60051	2528	31W-32N	E4
1500	LKMR	60051	2528	31W-32N	E4
2700	MchT	60051	2471	30W-34N	E7
2900	JNBG	60051	2471	30W-34N	E7
3500	JNBG	60050	2471	31W-35N	E6
CO-V40 W Johnsburg Rd					
2300	JNBG	60050	2471	31W-35N	D6
CO-V40 Spring Grove Rd					
3600	JNBG	60050	2471	31W-37N	D1
4100	MchT	60050	2471	31W-37N	D1
5000	MchT	60081	2471	31W-37N	D1
5300	JNBG	60081	2471	31W-37N	D1
5600	RcmT	60050	2471	31W-37N	D1
5600	RcmT	60081	2471	31W-37N	D1
6100	RcmT	60050	2413	31W-38N	D7
6100	RcmT	60081	2413	31W-38N	D7
6300	SPGV	60081	2413	31W-38N	D7
CO-V40 Winn Rd					
7600	SPGV	60081	2413	31W-41N	D1
7800	RcmT	60081	2413	31W-41N	D1
9700	RcmT	60071	2354	31W-42N	D7
9700	SPGV	60071	2354	31W-42N	D7
9700	SPGV	60081	2354	31W-42N	D7
CO-V43 Blivin St					
-	BtnT	60081	2414	30W-40N	A3
-	SPGV	60081	2414	30W-40N	A3
7600	SPGV	60081	2413	31W-39N	E4
CO-V43 Richardson Rd					
8400	BtnT	60081	2414	30W-40N	A2
8400	SPGV	60081	2414	30W-40N	A2
9700	BtnT	60081	2355	30W-42N	A6
9700	SPGV	60081	2355	30W-42N	A6
CO-V44 Wilmot Rd					
7300	BtnT	60081	2414	30W-39N	B5
7600	SPGV	60081	2414	30W-39N	B5
7700	FXLK	60081	2414	29W-39N	B4
9500	FXLK	60081	2355	29W-42N	D6
10000	BtnT	60081	2355	29W-42N	D6
10900	AntT	60002	2355	29W-43N	D4
10900	FXLK	60002	2355	29W-43N	D4
CO-V45 N River Rd					
100	MchT	60051	2528	31W-31N	D7
100	NndT	60051	2528	31W-32N	D6
1000	MHRY	60051	2528	32W-33N	C4
CO-V45 S River Rd					
-	ISLK	60042	2586	29W-28N	C5
-	ISLK	60051	2586	29W-28N	C5
100	NndT	60051	2528	31W-31N	D6
900	NndT	60051	2585	30W-30N	E1
1500	HHLL	60051	2586	30W-30N	A2
1500	NndT	60051	2586	29W-28N	C5
3100	NndT	60042	2586	29W-29N	C5
CO-V45 Roberts Rd					
-	PTBR	60010	2642	28W-26N	D2
-	WcnT	60084	2642	28W-26N	D2
200	TRLK	60010	2643	26W-25N	D4
4000	ISLK	60042	2586	29W-27N	D7
4000	NndT	60042	2586	29W-27N	D7
4100	WcnT	60042	2586	29W-27N	D7
4600	NndT	60042	2642	29W-27N	D1
4600	NndT	60051	2642	29W-27N	D1
5000	WcnT	60010	2642	28W-26N	D2
27100	LKBN	60010	2643	27W-25N	C4
27700	CbaT	60010	2643	27W-25N	B4
CO-V45 W Roberts Rd					
28000	CbaT	60010	2643	26W-25N	C4
28000	LKBN	60010	2643	27W-25N	A4
28100	WcnT	60010	2643	26W-25N	C4
28300	PTBR	60010	2643	26W-25N	C4
28400	PTBR	60010	2642	28W-25N	E4
28400	WcnT	60010	2642	28W-25N	E4
28700	WcnT	60084	2642	28W-26N	E3
28800	PTBR	60084	2642	28W-26N	D3
29000	NndT	60042	2586	29W-27N	D7
29000	NndT	60042	2642	29W-27N	D1
29000	NndT	60051	2586	29W-27N	D7
29000	NndT	60051	2642	29W-27N	D1
29000	WcnT	60042	2586	29W-27N	D7
29400	ISLK	60042	2586	29W-27N	D7
29400	ISLK	60051	2586	29W-27N	D7
CO-V47 N Darrell Rd					
26600	PTBR	60010	2642	28W-26N	D3
26600	WcnT	60010	2642	28W-26N	D3
26600	WcnT	60084	2642	28W-26N	E3
26700	WcnT	60084	2643	28W-27N	A1
26900	ISLK	60042	2643	28W-27N	A1
26900	WcnT	60042	2643	28W-27N	A1
27300	ISLK	60084	2643	27W-27N	A1
27600	ISLK	60084	2587	28W-29N	A3
27600	WcnT	60084	2587	28W-29N	A3
27800	WcnT	60051	2587	27W-28N	A7
28300	ISLK	60042	2587	28W-28N	A5
28300	ISLK	60051	2587	27W-28N	A5
28300	WcnT	60042	2587	28W-28N	A5
30000	WcnT	60051	2586	28W-30N	E1
30800	LKMR	60051	2529	28W-31N	E7
30800	WcnT	60051	2529	28W-31N	E7
CO-V47 Rawson Bridge Rd					
-	PTBR	60010	2642	28W-26N	D3
-	WcnT	60010	2642	28W-26N	D3
-	WcnT	60084	2642	28W-26N	D3
CO-V49 Kelsey Rd					
200	LKBN	60010	2643	26W-24N	D6
200	TRLK	60010	2643	26W-24N	D6
CO-V49 N Kelsey Rd					
22000	CbaT	60010	2696	28W-22N	E4
22000	LKBN	60010	2696	28W-22N	E4
23500	LKBN	60010	2697	27W-23N	A1
23800	CbaT	60010	2697	27W-23N	A1
24100	CbaT	60010	2643	27W-24N	C7
24100	LKBN	60010	2643	27W-24N	B7
24300	TRLK	60010	2643	27W-24N	C7
CO-V50 River Rd					
100	LKBN	60010	2643	27W-24N	B6
CO-V51 Center St					
-	GYLK	60030	2533	20W-33N	A3
CO-V51 N Lake Av					
42000	AntT	60002	2356	26W-42N	D5
43400	AntT	53179	2356	26W-43N	D4
43400	SlmT	53179	2356	26W-43N	D4
CO-V57 Ela Rd					
-	ElaT	60010	2698	24W-21N	D6
400	LKZH	60047	2698	24W-22N	D4
800	DRPK	60010	2698	24W-22N	D5
800	LKZH	60010	2698	24W-22N	D5
CO-V57 N Ela Rd					
10	BRTN	60010	2751	24W-20N	D1
10	DRPK	60010	2751	24W-20N	D1
10	ElaT	60010	2751	24W-20N	D1
10	PltT	60010	2751	24W-20N	D1
100	DRPK	60010	2698	24W-20N	D7
CO-V58 Wilson Rd					
31600	GrtT	60030	2531	25W-31N	B6
31600	GrtT	60073	2531	25W-31N	B6
31600	RDLK	60073	2531	25W-31N	B6
31600	WcnT	60030	2531	25W-31N	B6
CO-V58 N Wilson Rd					
300	GrtT	60041	2530	26W-33N	E3
300	RDLK	60041	2530	26W-33N	E2
300	RDLK	60073	2530	26W-33N	E3
32500	GrtT	60030	2531	25W-32N	A5
32500	GrtT	60073	2531	25W-32N	A5
32500	RDLK	60073	2531	25W-32N	A5
32800	GrtT	60073	2530	26W-33N	E3
34600	GrtT	60041	2473	26W-34N	E7
CO-V60 Hainesville Rd					
1100	RLKB	60030	2475	22W-35N	C7
1100	RLKB	60073	2475	22W-35N	C7
CO-V60 N Hainesville Rd					
10	HNVL	60030	2532	22W-33N	C3
100	HNVL	60073	2532	22W-33N	C3
500	AvnT	60030	2532	22W-33N	C3
500	RLKP	60073	2532	22W-33N	C3
600	AvnT	60073	2532	22W-34N	C1
800	RLKB	60073	2532	22W-34N	C1
34600	RLKB	60073	2475	22W-34N	C7
CO-V61 N Fairfield Rd					
10	AvnT	60073	2531	24W-33N	C2
10	ElaT	60047	2645	22W-25N	B5
10	HNWD	60047	2645	22W-25N	B5
10	LKZH	60047	2645	22W-24N	B7
10	RDLK	60073	2531	24W-33N	C2
10	RLKB	60073	2531	24W-34N	C1
800	RLKB	60073	2531	24W-34N	C1
900	RLKB	60073	2474	24W-34N	C7
1200	AvnT	60073	2474	24W-35N	C7
1200	FmtT	60060	2588	24W-30N	C1
1200	WCDA	60060	2588	24W-30N	C1
1200	WCDA	60084	2588	24W-30N	C1
25700	HNWD	60060	2645	22W-25N	A4
25800	FmtT	60047	2645	22W-26N	A4
25800	FmtT	60060	2645	23W-26N	A3
25800	FmtT	60084	2645	23W-26N	A3
26400	FmtT	60060	2644	24W-27N	D1
26400	FmtT	60084	2644	24W-27N	D1
27200	FmtT	60084	2588	24W-27N	D7
29500	FmtT	60030	2588	24W-29N	D4
29500	WCDA	60030	2588	24W-29N	D4
31500	FmtT	60030	2531	24W-31N	C7
31600	AvnT	60030	2531	24W-32N	C6
32600	RDLK	60030	2531	24W-32N	C4
35400	RLKH	60073	2474	24W-35N	C6
35900	LkvT	60041	2474	24W-37N	C2
35900	LkvT	60073	2474	24W-35N	C5
36800	LKVL	60046	2474	24W-37N	C3
36800	LkvT	60046	2474	24W-36N	C3
38000	LkvT	60046	2416	24W-38N	D6
CO-V62 Quentin Rd					
21300	KLDR	60047	2699	21W-21N	C6
21600	LKZH	60047	2699	21W-21N	C5
CO-V62 N Quentin Rd					
20000	DRPK	60010	2752	22W-20N	C2
20000	DRPK	60074	2752	22W-20N	C2
20000	PltT	60010	2752	22W-20N	C2
20000	PltT	60074	2752	22W-20N	C2
20600	DRPK	60047	2752	22W-20N	C2
20600	DRPK	60074	2699	22W-20N	C7
20600	ElaT	60047	2699	21W-21N	C6
20600	KLDR	60047	2699	21W-21N	C6
20600	KLDR	60074	2752	22W-20N	C2
20800	ElaT	60074	2699	21W-21N	C6
20800	KLDR	60074	2699	21W-21N	C6
22000	LKZH	60047	2699	21W-23N	C2
23500	HNWD	60047	2699	21W-23N	C2
24200	ElaT	60047	2645	21W-24N	C7
24200	HNWD	60047	2645	21W-24N	C7
CO-V63 N Cedar Lake Rd					
10	LKVL	60046	2474	23W-37N	E2
10	LkvT	60046	2474	23W-37N	E1
200	RDLK	60073	2531	23W-34N	E1
800	RLKB	60073	2531	23W-34N	E1
1000	RLKB	60073	2474	23W-34N	E7
1300	LKVL	60073	2474	23W-36N	E4
1300	RLKB	60046	2474	23W-36N	E4
CO-V65 N Fremont Center Rd					
28000	FmtT	60060	2589	22W-28N	B5
28900	FmtT	60030	2589	22W-29N	B3
CO-V67 N Deep Lake Rd					
38200	LKVL	60046	2417	22W-39N	C6
38200	LKVL	60046	2475	21W-38N	D1
38200	LkvT	60046	2417	22W-39N	C6
38200	LNHT	60046	2417	21W-38N	D7
38200	LNHT	60046	2475	21W-38N	D1
40100	AntT	60002	2417	22W-40N	C4
40100	LKVL	60046	2417	22W-39N	C6
40100	LkvT	60002	2417	22W-39N	C6
40900	ANTH	60002	2417	22W-40N	C2
41700	ANTH	60002	2358	22W-42N	C6
41700	AntT	60002	2358	22W-42N	C6
43200	BtlT	53104	2358	22W-43N	C4
43200	BtlT	60002	2358	22W-43N	C4
CO-V68 N Alleghany Rd					
31000	FmtT	60030	2589	21W-30N	D1
31000	RLKP	60030	2589	21W-30N	D1
31200	FmtT	60030	2532	21W-31N	D7
31200	GYLK	60030	2532	21W-31N	D7
31200	RLKP	60030	2532	21W-31N	D7
31800	AvnT	60030	2532	21W-31N	D6
CO-V68 S Alleghany Rd					
200	AvnT	60030	2532	21W-32N	D6
200	GYLK	60030	2532	21W-32N	D6
CO-V69 N Arlington Heights Rd					
10	BFGV	60089	2754	18W-20N	A2
100	ANHT	60004	2754	17W-20N	A2
100	VrnT	60004	2754	17W-20N	A2
100	VrnT	60089	2754	17W-20N	A2
300	BFGV	60047	2754	17W-20N	A1
300	LGGV	60047	2754	17W-20N	A1
300	VrnT	60047	2754	18W-20N	A1
400	BFGV	60047	2701	18W-20N	A7
400	BFGV	60089	2701	18W-20N	A7
400	LGGV	60047	2701	18W-20N	A7
400	LGGV	60089	2701	18W-20N	A7
CO-V73 N Midlothian Rd					
700	FmtT	60060	2590	19W-28N	B5
700	MDLN	60060	2590	19W-28N	B5
2300	FmtT	60048	2590	19W-30N	C3
2300	LYVL	60048	2590	19W-30N	C3
2300	LYVL	60060	2590	19W-30N	C3
CO-V75 Diamond Lake Rd					
-	ElaT	60060	2646	19W-25N	D5
6300	LGGV	60047	2646	19W-24N	D7
6300	LGGV	60047	2700	19W-24N	D1
6300	LGGV	60060	2700	19W-24N	D1
6500	LGGV	60060	2646	19W-24N	D6
CO-V75 N Diamond Lake Rd					
6700	ElaT	60047	2646	19W-25N	D5
6700	ElaT	60060	2646	19W-25N	D6
6700	LGGV	60047	2646	19W-25N	D5
6700	LGGV	60060	2646	19W-25N	D5
6700	VrnT	60047	2646	19W-25N	D5
6700	VrnT	60060	2646	19W-25N	D6
25700	FmtT	60060	2646	19W-25N	D6
25700	LbvT	60060	2646	19W-25N	D6
CO-V76 N Gilmer Rd					
26500	FmtT	60047	2645	21W-26N	C3
26500	FmtT	60060	2645	21W-26N	C3
26500	HNWD	60047	2645	21W-26N	C2
26500	HNWD	60060	2645	21W-26N	D3
27100	MDLN	60060	2645	22W-27N	C1
27600	HNWD	60047	2589	22W-27N	B7
27600	HNWD	60060	2589	22W-27N	B7
27700	FmtT	60060	2589	23W-28N	A6
28100	FmtT	60060	2588	23W-29N	E5
29100	FmtT	60030	2588	24W-30N	B3
29500	WCDA	60030	2588	24W-30N	B3
29700	FmtT	60084	2588	24W-30N	B3
29700	WCDA	60060	2588	24W-30N	B3
29700	WCDA	60084	2588	24W-30N	B3
30800	WcnT	60030	2587	26W-30N	E2
30800	WcnT	60030	2588	25W-30N	A2
30800	WcnT	60073	2587	26W-30N	E2
30800	WcnT	60084	2587	26W-30N	E2
30800	WcnT	60084	2588	25W-30N	A2
31800	VOLO	60073	2587	26W-30N	D1
32600	VOLO	60073	2530	26W-31N	C7
33800	LKMR	60073	2530	26W-31N	C7
CO-V76 W Gilmer Rd					
100	ElaT	60047	2645	22W-27N	C1
100	ElaT	60060	2645	22W-27N	C1
100	HNWD	60047	2645	21W-25N	D4
100	HNWD	60060	2645	21W-25N	D4
18700	LGGV	60047	2700	18W-23N	D1
21300	LGGV	60047	2646	19W-24N	C7
22500	HNWD	60047	2646	20W-24N	B6
23300	ElaT	60047	2646	20W-24N	B6
26000	FmtT	60047	2645	21W-26N	D4
26000	FmtT	60060	2645	21W-26N	D4
CO-V77 Old McHenry Rd					
-	LGGV	60047	2700	20W-23N	B2
100	ElaT	60047	2645	21W-24N	D7
100	HNWD	60047	2645	21W-24N	D7
100	HNWD	60047	2699	20W-23N	E1
100	KLDR	60047	2645	21W-24N	D7
100	KLDR	60047	2699	20W-23N	E1
500	ElaT	60047	2700	20W-23N	A1
500	HNWD	60047	2700	20W-23N	A1
500	KLDR	60047	2700	20W-23N	A1
CO-V77 N Old McHenry Rd					
100	LGGV	60047	2700	18W-21N	D5
1100	BFGV	60047	2700	18W-21N	E6
1100	BFGV	60089	2700	18W-21N	E6
1100	LGGV	60089	2700	18W-21N	E6
3300	ElaT	60047	2700	18W-21N	D5
24500	ElaT	60047	2645	21W-24N	C7
24500	HNWD	60047	2645	22W-24N	B6
24900	LKZH	60047	2645	22W-24N	B6
25800	ElaT	60047	2644	23W-25N	D5
25800	HNWD	60047	2644	23W-24N	E6
Cove Av					
800	LKPT	60441	3341	21W-18S	E7
Cove Cir					
4400	JLET	60586	3416	29W-21S	D6
15700	PNFD	60586	3415	31W-18S	D2
Cove Ct					
10	BRRG	60527	3208	15W-9S	C4
500	LKBN	60010	2696	28W-23N	E1
700	BRLT	60103	2911	28W-7N	B4
900	WHTN	60187	3082	25W-1S	B1
1600	NPVL	60565	3204	26W-9S	A3
2300	AURA	60504	3201	32W-9S	C4
2300	ELGN	60123	2907	36W-9N	E2
3200	JNBG	60050	2471	31W-35N	D6
8100	TYPK	60477	3504	10W-23S	C3
13400	PSHT	60463	3347	7W-15S	C2
Cove Dr					
200	CHHT	60422	3507	2W-24S	D4
400	AlqT	60013	2642	29W-24N	C6
1000	PTHT	60070	2808	13W-15N	D2
1100	MPPT	60056	2808	13W-15N	D2
2200	HRPK	60133	2967	27W-5N	B2
E Cove Dr					
10	SBTN	60010	2803	26W-14N	C4
N Cove Dr					
800	PLTN	60067	2752	22W-17N	B6
S Cove Dr					
10	SBTN	60010	2803	26W-14N	C5
Cove Ln					
-	NfdT	60025	2809	11W-13N	D6
10	WnfT	60555	3081	27W-3S	D5
400	WLMT	60091	2812	5W-13N	A6
400	WTMT	60559	3145	18W-7S	A5
1800	GLHT	60139	2968	24W-3N	E5
4100	GNVW	60025	2809	11W-13N	D6
4400	HFET	60192	2804	25W-15N	B1
Cove Pt					
700	SMBG	60194	2859	22W-10N	C4
N Cove Rd					
33000	WrnT	60030	2533	18W-33N	E4
W Cove Wy					
25500	PNFD	60586	3415	31W-18S	D2
Cove Creek Ct					
6200	BRRG	60527	3146	15W-6S	B5
Covehill Ct					
200	SMBG	60194	2858	24W-10N	D5
Covell St					
10000	RHMD	60071	2353	34W-42N	C7
Covenant Ct					
4500	GRNE	60031	2535	14W-33N	C2
Covenant Ln					
-	LYWD	60411	3509	2E-24S	C5
Coventry Av					
100	BtnT	60081	2414	29W-38N	D6
100	FXLK	60020	2414	29W-38N	D6
100	FXLK	60081	2414	29W-38N	D6
Coventry Cir					
200	VNHL	60061	2647	16W-26N	C3
1100	GLHT	60139	3025	22W-1N	B2
Coventry Ct					
10	LKBF	60044	2593	11W-29N	E5
10	SEGN	60177	2908	35W-7N	B4
100	NPVL	60565	3203	26W-9S	E4
200	BMDL	60108	2969	22W-4N	C3
200	ELGN	60123	2854	36W-11N	A3
300	AURA	60504	3140	31W-7S	A7
300	CNHL	60514	3145	17W-6S	C3
400	GLHT	60139	3025	22W-1N	B2
500	BFGV	60089	2701	17W-22N	C5
500	CLLK	60014	2639	35W-25N	E6
500	OSWG	60543	3263	38W-12S	B2
600	MltT	60187	3024	25W-0N	A4
1200	ROSL	60172	2912	25W-7N	B5
1400	DRN	60561	3207	18W-8S	A1
2700	GNVA	60134	3019	37W-0N	C5
3300	HFET	60067	2804	23W-14N	E4
3300	JLET	60431	3497	28W-23S	B4
3600	HLCT	60429	3426	4W-20S	D5
6100	CPVL	60110	2747	36W-17N	A6
15200	ODPK	60462	3346	10W-18S	B7
W Coventry Ct					
27000	LKBN	60010	2643	27W-24N	C7
Coventry Ct S					
300	CLLK	60014	2639	35W-24N	E7
Coventry Dr					
10	MltT	60187	3024	25W-0N	A4
10	MltT	60188	3024	25W-0N	A4
700	LKFT	60045	2649	12W-25N	C6
7200	HRPK	60133	2912	26W-9N	A1
8700	WDRG	60517	3206	20W-10S	B5
N Coventry Dr					
7400	SPGV	60081	2413	32W-39N	B5
S Coventry Dr					
7200	SPGV	60081	2413	32W-39N	B5
Coventry Ln					
10	LNSH	60069	2702	14W-22N	D4
10	NBRN	60010	2644	25W-24N	B7
10	NBRN	60010	2698	25W-24N	A1
300	CRTE	60417	3596	0W-29S	C7
300	CRTE	60417	3685	0W-29S	C1
400	CLLK	60014	2639	35W-24N	E6
400	CLLK	60014	2640	35W-24N	A6
500	BFGV	60089	2701	17W-22N	B5
800	OKBK	60523	3085	16W-1S	E1
900	HDPK	60035	2704	9W-21N	B7
1000	CLLK	60014	2693	36W-23N	E1
1100	BGBK	60440	3268	25W-12S	B2
1100	BGBK	60490	3268	25W-12S	B3
1300	NHBK	60062	2756	11W-17N	D6
5100	GRNE	60031	2478	15W-35N	B6
7700	FftT	60423	3504	9W-25S	D7
7700	FKFT	60423	3504	9W-25S	D7
16400	CTHL	60403	3418	25W-19S	B3
16400	LktT	60403	3418	25W-19S	B3
17100	CCHL	60478	3426	5W-20S	D4
20400	LktT	60441	3418	25W-19S	B4
N Coventry Ln					
24000	LKBN	60010	2643	27W-24N	C7
S Coventry Ln					
16400	LKPT	60441	3420	18W-19S	E3
W Coventry Ln					
12800	HTLY	60142	2691	41W-20N	C7
24200	LKBN	60010	2643	27W-24N	C7
Coventry Pl					
700	WLNG	60090	2755	15W-18N	A3
1200	AURA	60506	3137	36W-5S	E4
W Coventry Pl					
200	MPPT	60056	2807	16W-14N	D3
Coventry Rd					
10	NHFD	60093	2811	7W-14N	A3
1400	SMBG	60195	2858	24W-12N	D2
1500	JLET	60451	3500	19W-23S	D3
1500	NLNX	60451	3500	19W-23S	D3
1900	JLET	60432	3500	19W-23S	C3
Coventry St					
600	MltT	60187	3024	25W-0N	A4
N Coventry Wy					
-	WrnT	60031	2535	14W-32N	C4
4600	WKGN	60085	2535	14W-32N	C4
Coventry Chase					
10	JLET	60431	3497	28W-24S	B6
Coventry Cove Ct					
10	LKVL	60046	2475	23W-37N	A2
Coventry Cove Ln					
10	LKVL	60046	2475	22W-37N	A2
Coventry Glen Dr					
1200	RDLK	60073	2531	24W-34N	C1
Coventry on Duxbury					
10	RGMW	60008	2805	22W-13N	B7
Covered Bridge Ct					
600	ELGN	60124	2853	37W-10N	D7
Covered Bridge Dr					
500	ELGN	60124	2853	36W-10N	D6
Covered Bridge Rd					
10	SBTN	60010	2803	26W-14N	D4
Covered Bridge Wy					
1400	JLET	60435	3497	27W-22S	C1
Covert Rd					
2200	GNVW	60025	2810	9W-12N	C7
Coveside Ln					
500	SMBG	60193	2912	24W-9N	E1
Covey Ct					
800	NlxT	60451	3590	15W-25S	B1
Covey St					
800	DndT	60118	2801	33W-14N	A5
Covington Cir					
700	CLLK	60014	2693	36W-23N	D1
Covington Ct					
10	ALGN	60102	2693	36W-21N	C6
10	BGBK	60490	3339	28W-15S	A1
100	OKBK	60523	3085	17W-3S	C5
100	WTMT	60523	3085	17W-3S	C5
100	WTMT	60559	3085	17W-3S	C5
200	NPVL	60565	3204	25W-10S	A5
1300	SCRL	60174	3019	36W-2N	E1
2200	JLET	60586	3415	33W-21S	B6
Covington Dr					
100	BMDL	60108	2968	25W-5N	A3
100	BMDL	60172	2968	25W-4N	A3
100	BmdT	60172	2968	25W-4N	A3
100	BRTN	60010	2697	25W-20N	E7
100	CbaT	60010	2697	25W-20N	E7
200	BRTN	60010	2698	25W-20N	A7
1000	LMNT	60439	3270	18W-14S	E7
1100	LMNT	60439	3271	18W-14S	A7
22500	DRPK	60010	2752	22W-20N	B1
W Covington Dr					
21000	LktT	60544	3340	25W-16S	B5
21100	LktT	60544	3339	26W-16S	E5
Covington Ln					
-	RLKB	60073	2475	22W-35N	B5
1300	LMNT	60439	3270	18W-14S	E7
2100	JLET	60586	3415	33W-21S	B7
3200	ALGN	60102	2693	36W-21N	C6
Covington Pl					
200	SMBG	60194	2858	25W-10N	C5
Covington Rd					
10	FXLK	60020	2472	28W-36N	E4
10	FXLK	60020	2473	27W-35N	B5
Covington Ter					
300	BFGV	60089	2754	17W-17N	C4
300	WhlT	60004	2754	17W-17N	C4
300	WhlT	60089	2754	17W-17N	C4
CO-W Fox River Rd					
-	AntT	60002	2355		D3
-	RdlT	60002	2355		D3
10200	SlmT	53105	2356		A1
10200	SlmT	53192	2356		A2
11700	RdlT	53181	2355		D3
11700	RdlT	53192	2355		E2
CO-W11 Butterfield Rd					
100	INCK	60061	2647	17W-25N	B6
100	MDLN	60060	2647	17W-25N	B6
100	MDLN	60061	2647	17W-25N	B6
100	VNHL	60060	2647	17W-25N	B6
100	VNHL	60061	2647	17W-25N	B6
CO-W11 N Butterfield Rd					
100	LYVL	60048	2591	17W-29N	B5
500	MDLN	60060	2591	17W-29N	B5
600	LYVL	60060	2591	17W-29N	B5
1300	LbvT	60048	2591	17W-30N	A3
CO-W11 S Butterfield Rd					
-	LbvT	60060	2591	17W-28N	B7
-	LbvT	60061	2591	17W-27N	B7
-	MDLN	60060	2591	17W-27N	B7
-	MDLN	60061	2591	17W-27N	B7
-	VNHL	60061	2591	17W-28N	B7
100	LYVL	60048	2591	17W-28N	B5
400	MDLN	60060	2647	17W-27N	B1
400	MDLN	60061	2647	17W-27N	B1
400	VNHL	60061	2647	17W-27N	B1
900	VNHL	60060	2647	17W-26N	A3
CO-W12 N Almond Rd					
-	WrnT	60030	2534	17W-34N	B1
34000	WrnT	60031	2534	17W-34N	B1
34300	GRNE	60031	2534	17W-34N	B1
CO-W14 N Buffalo Grove Rd					
-	VrnT	60089	2701	17W-22N	C4
10	BFGV	60089	2754	16W-20N	C1
600	BFGV	60089	2701	16W-20N	C7
1600	BFGV	60069	2701	17W-21N	C5
1600	VrnT	60069	2701	17W-22N	C5
CO-W15 N Hunt Club Rd					
1100	GRNE	60031	2477	17W-35N	C5
33000	GRNE	60031	2534	17W-33N	C3
33000	WrnT	60030	2534	17W-33N	C3
33000	WrnT	60031	2534	17W-33N	C3
33000	WrnT	60048	2534	17W-33N	C3
33200	GRNE	60030	2534	17W-33N	C3
33200	GRNE	60048	2534	17W-33N	C3
34500	WrnT	60031	2477	17W-34N	C7
36600	WrnT	60083	2477	17W-37N	C3
37200	OMCK	60083	2477	17W-34N	C7
38200	NptT	60083	2419	17W-38N	B7
38200	NptT	60083	2477	17W-34N	C7
38200	OMCK	60083	2419	17W-38N	B7
41600	NptT	60002	2360	17W-41N	B7
41600	NptT	60083	2360	17W-41N	B7
41600	OMCK	60083	2360	17W-42N	B7
43400	BtlT	53142	2360	17W-43N	B4
43400	NptT	53142	2360	17W-43N	B4
CO-W16 N Dilleys Rd					
1400	GRNE	60031	2478	15W-35N	A6
1400	WrnT	60031	2478	15W-35N	A6
1700	GRNE	60031	2477	15W-35N	E5
2000	WrnT	60031	2477	15W-36N	E4
2400	WDWH	60031	2477	16W-37N	E3
2700	WDWH	60083	2477	15W-36N	E4
37200	WrnT	60083	2477	15W-36N	E4
37900	NptT	60083	2419	16W-38N	E7
37900	NptT	60083	2477	15W-36N	E4
CO-W17 N Prairie Rd					
22000	BFGV	60069	2701	16W-22N	D4
22000	BFGV	60089	2701	16W-22N	D4
22000	VrnT	60069	2701	16W-22N	D4
22000	VrnT	60089	2701	16W-22N	D4
CO-W17 Weiland Rd					
100	BFGV	60089	2754	16W-20N	D1
100	WLNG	60089	2754	16W-20N	D2
300	BFGV	60069	2754	16W-20N	D1
300	VrnT	60069	2754	16W-20N	D1
300	VrnT	60089	2754	16W-20N	D1
800	BFGV	60089	2701	16W-20N	D7
1200	BFGV	60069	2701	16W-21N	E6
1600	VrnT	60069	2701	16W-21N	E6
1600	VrnT	60089	2701	16W-21N	E6
CO-W19 N St. Mary's Rd					
100	GNOK	60048	2592	15W-28N	B5
100	LYVL	60048	2592	15W-28N	B5
600	LbvT	60048	2592	15W-28N	B5
25000	MTWA	60045	2648	14W-24N	B6
25000	MTWA	60048	2648	15W-25N	B5
25000	VrnT	60045	2648	14W-24N	B6
25000	VrnT	60048	2648	14W-24N	B6
26100	LbvT	60048	2648	15W-26N	B2

STREET Block City ZIP Map# CGS Grid

CO-W19 N St. Mary's Rd
27500 MTWA 60048 2592 15W-27N B7
CO-W19 S St. Mary's Rd
200 GNOK 60048 2592 15W-28N B6
200 LbvT 60048 2592 15W-28N B6
200 LYVL 60048 2592 15W-28N B6
400 MTWA 60048 2592 15W-28N B6
CO-W20 N Oplaine Rd
10 GRNE 60031 2535 14W-34N C1
10 WrnT 60031 2535 14W-34N C1
400 GRNE 60031 2478 14W-34N C7
30900 GNOK 60048 2592 14W-30N C1
31000 GNOK 60048 2535 14W-31N C7
31500 WKGN 60048 2535 14W-31N C7
32300 WKGN 60085 2535 14W-32N C5
32300 WrnT 60048 2535 14W-32N C5
32300 WrnT 60085 2535 14W-32N C5
32800 WKGN 60031 2535 14W-33N C4
CO-W20 S Oplaine Rd
10 GRNE 60031 2535 14W-32N C6
10 WrnT 60031 2535 14W-34N C1
1000 WKGN 60031 2535 14W-33N C4
1000 WKGN 60085 2535 14W-33N C4
CO-W24 Riverwoods Rd
10 LNSH 60045 2702 14W-23N D2
10 LNSH 60069 2702 13W-21N E6
10 MTWA 60045 2648 13W-25N D5
10 RVWD 60015 2702 13W-22N D4
800 VrnT 60045 2648 14W-24N D6
1000 LNSH 60045 2648 14W-24N D7
1000 LNSH 60069 2648 14W-24N D7
2100 LNSH 60015 2702 14W-22N D4
2200 RVWD 60015 2703 12W-21N A7
3000 VrnT 60015 2702 13W-21N D6
CO-W24 Saunders Rd
10 NHBK 60015 2756 12W-20N A2
10 NHBK 60062 2756 12W-20N A2
10 RVWD 60015 2756 12W-20N A2
10 WdfT 60015 2756 12W-20N A2
400 DRFD 60015 2756 12W-20N A1
600 DRFD 60015 2703 12W-20N A7
600 RVWD 60015 2703 12W-20N A7
CO-W26 N Kilbourne Rd
39000 WDWH 60083 2420 14W-41N C1
39600 NptT 60083 2420 14W-41N C1
41000 NptT 60099 2420 14W-41N C1
41500 NptT 60099 2361 14W-42N C6
41500 WDWH 60099 2361 14W-41N C7
43300 PTPR 53158 2361 14W-42N C6
43300 PTPR 60099 2361 14W-42N C6
CO-W27 N Delaney Rd
43300 NptT 60099 2361 14W-43N D4
CO-W27 N Delany Rd
1100 GRNE 60031 2478 14W-36N D5
1400 WrnT 60031 2478 14W-36N D5
2100 WKGN 60087 2478 14W-36N D4
2100 WrnT 60087 2478 14W-36N D4
2200 WKGN 60031 2478 14W-36N D4
3000 WDWH 60083 2478 14W-37N D1
3000 WDWH 60087 2478 14W-37N D1
3000 WKGN 60083 2478 14W-37N D2
38000 WDWH 60083 2420 14W-38N D7
38000 WDWH 60087 2420 14W-38N D7
38000 WKGN 60083 2420 14W-38N D7
38000 WKGN 60087 2420 14W-38N D7
39900 NptT 60083 2420 14W-41N D1
41000 WDWH 60099 2420 14W-41N D1
CO-W29 Greenleaf Av
- WKGN 60085 2535 13W-33N D3
300 GRNE 60031 2535 13W-33N D2
300 PKCY 60085 2535 13W-33N D2
300 WrnT 60031 2535 13W-33N D2
CO-W29 S Greenleaf Av
10 GRNE 60031 2535 13W-33N D2
10 WrnT 60031 2535 13W-33N D2
200 PKCY 60085 2535 13W-34N D2
CO-W32 Kenosha Rd
1200 BtnT 60099 2362 11W-42N C7
1200 ZION 60099 2362 11W-42N C7
1500 BtnT 60099 2421 12W-41N C1
1500 ZION 60099 2421 12W-41N C1
1900 BHPK 60099 2421 12W-41N C2
CO-W32 N Kenosha Rd
400 BtnT 53158 2362 11W-43N D4
400 BtnT 60099 2362 11W-43N D5
400 PTPR 53158 2362 11W-43N D4
400 WPHR 60099 2362 11W-43N D5
800 ZION 60099 2362 11W-42N D6
40000 BHPK 60099 2421 12W-41N C1
40000 ZION 60099 2421 12W-40N B3
42800 WPHR 60096 2362 11W-43N D5
CO-W34 Lewis Av
- BtnT 60099 2421 11W-41N D1
- WPHR 60096 2421 11W-41N D1
400 BtnT 60096 2362 11W-42N D6
400 BtnT 60099 2362 11W-42N D6
400 WPHR 60096 2362 11W-42N D6
400 WPHR 60099 2362 11W-42N D6
1100 ZION 60096 2362 11W-42N D7
1100 ZION 60099 2362 11W-42N D7
1400 NCHI 60064 2536 11W-32N D5
1400 WKGN 60085 2536 11W-32N D5
1500 ZION 60099 2421 11W-41N D1
2300 NCHI 60064 2593 11W-31N D1
2300 NCHI 60088 2593 11W-31N D1
3100 BHPK 60099 2421 11W-39N D5
3400 WKGN 60087 2421 11W-39N D6
3400 WKGN 60099 2421 11W-39N D6
43300 BtnT 53158 2362 11W-43N E4
43300 PTPR 53158 2362 11W-43N E4
CO-W34 N Lewis Av
10 WKGN 60085 2536 11W-34N D1
500 WKGN 60085 2479 11W-34N D7
3200 BHPK 60087 2479 11W-37N D1
3200 WKGN 60087 2479 11W-37N D1
3700 WKGN 60087 2421 11W-38N D7
3800 BHPK 60087 2421 11W-38N D7
3800 BHPK 60099 2421 11W-38N D7
39200 WKGN 60099 2421 11W-39N D6
CO-W34 S Lewis Av
10 WKGN 60085 2536 11W-34N D2
1300 NCHI 60064 2536 11W-32N D5
CO-WG 128th St
- BtlT 53142 2360 16W-43N E4
- BtlT 60099 2360 16W-43N E4
- NptT 60099 2360 16W-43N E4
17900 AntT 60002 2359 18W-43N E4
17900 BtlT 53104 2359 18W-43N E4
17900 BtlT 53142 2359 18W-43N E4
CO-WG W State Line Rd
15200 BtlT 53142 2360 17W-43N B4
15200 BtlT 60002 2360 17W-43N B4
15200 NptT 60002 2360 17W-43N B4
16500 BtlT 60099 2360 16W-43N D4
16500 NptT 53142 2360 16W-43N D4
16500 NptT 60099 2360 16W-43N D4

CO-WG W State Line Rd
18500 AntT 60002 2359 19W-43N D4
18500 BtlT 53142 2359 19W-43N D4
18500 BtlT 60002 2359 18W-43N E4
18500 NptT 53142 2359 18W-43N D4
18500 NptT 60002 2359 18W-43N E4
19800 BtlT 53104 2359 B4
Cowing Ct
18300 HMWD 60430 3427 2W-22S D7
18400 HMWD 60430 3507 2W-22S D1
Cowing Ln
1900 CTHL 60403 3418 25W-21S C7
N Cowles Av
400 JLET 60435 3498 25W-23S C3
N Cowley Rd
10 RVSD 60546 3088 9W-3S C4
S Cowley Rd
10 RVSD 60546 3088 9W-3S C5
Cowlin St
7200 AlqT 60014 2640 33W-24N E6
7200 CLLK 60014 2640 33W-24N E6
Cowper Av
2300 EVTN 60201 2866 4W-12N C1
2500 EVTN 60201 2812 4W-12N C7
Cox Av
20400 FftT 60423 3505 8W-24S A5
20400 MTSN 60443 3505 8W-25S B6
20400 RchT 60443 3505 8W-25S B6
N Cox Dr
43400 AntT 60002 2357 25W-43N A4
Cox Ln
900 GnvT 60134 3076 39W-1S E1
900 GnvT 60134 3077 38W-1S A1
Coy Rd
- SdwT 60548 3258 51W-11S A2
Coyle Av
2600 EGVV 60007 2915 16W-8N E2
2600 EGVV 60007 2916 15W-8N A2
4900 LNWD 60077 2919 6W-8N D1
4900 LNWD 60712 2919 6W-8N D1
4900 SKOK 60077 2919 6W-8N D1
W Coyle Av
2400 CHCG 60645 2921 3W-8N A1
2600 CHCG 60645 2920 3W-8N E1
4800 LNWD 60077 2919 6W-8N E1
4800 LNWD 60712 2919 6W-8N E1
4800 SKOK 60077 2919 6W-8N E1
7200 CHCG 60631 2918 9W-8N D1
7200 CHCG 60714 2918 9W-8N D1
7200 NLES 60714 2918 9W-8N D1
Coyne Station Rd
9000 GfnT 60142 2691 42W-23N C2
9900 HTLY 60142 2691 41W-21N C7
Coyote Ct
200 OSWG 60543 3263 37W-12S B3
1200 HPSR 60140 2795 47W-15N D4
Coyote Tr
- NLNX 60451 3589 19W-27S A4
200 CRY 60013 2695 32W-23N C1
1000 NLNX 60451 3588 19W-27S E4
1200 HPSR 60140 2795 47W-15N E4
Coyote Ridge Ct
- JLET 60586 3495 32W-21S D1
Coyote Ridge Dr
- JLET 60586 3495 32W-21S D1
CO-Z 360th Av
- RdlT 53181 2354 D2
- TNLK 53181 2354 D1
CO-Z Wilmot Av
1600 TNLK 53181 2354 D1
Cozy Ln
1300 DYR 46311 3510 C7
1400 DYR 46311 3598 C1
Crab Apple Ct
1300 NPVL 60540 3141 28W-6S A5
Crabapple Ct
10 LIHL 60156 2693 37W-22N A4
200 JLET 60435 3497 27W-23S B4
800 WCHI 60185 3022 30W-1N C2
1300 BTVA 60510 3078 36W-2S A4
2300 AURA 60503 3201 32W-10S B6
Crabapple Dr
- PTHT 60070 2808 13W-15N E2
700 CLLK 60014 2639 37W-24N B7
900 PTHT 60070 2809 13W-15N A2
39700 LkvT 60002 2416 24W-39N B4
N Crabapple Dr
200 JLET 60435 3497 27W-23S B4
W Crabapple Dr
14500 WDWH 60083 2420 14W-38N C7
Crab Apple Ln
100 OKBK 60523 3027 16W-1S E7
100 OKBK 60523 3085 16W-1S E1
Crabapple Ln
10 BNHL 60010 2749 28W-18N E3
1000 SCRL 60174 2964 35W-3N C5
3700 WRLK 60097 2468 38W-35N E5
19500 FftT 60448 3503 11W-23S E3
Crabapple St
200 BGBK 60490 3267 26W-11S E1
Crab Apple Ter
2300 BFGV 60089 2701 16W-22N C4
Crab Orchard Dr
4400 HFET 60192 2804 24W-15N C1
Crabtree Av
2400 WDRG 60517 3205 21W-8S E2
2900 LslT 60517 3205 22W-8S C2
Crabtree Ct
600 LNHT 60046 2476 20W-37N B2
4200 GRNE 60031 2535 14W-33N D3
7700 WDRG 60517 3205 21W-8S E2
24300 PNFD 60585 3266 30W-14S B6
Crab Tree Dr
10 WTMT 60559 3145 18W-7S A6
Crabtree Dr
- DRGV 60516 3144 18W-7S E6
1500 CLLK 60014 2693 37W-22N C3
E Crabtree Dr
700 ANHT 60004 2754 16W-16N C7
N Crabtree Dr
1300 PLTN 60010 2752 23W-17N A4
1300 PLTN 60067 2752 23W-17N A4
1300 PltT 60010 2752 23W-17N A4
1300 PltT 60067 2752 23W-17N A4
Crab Tree Ln
700 BRLT 60103 2856 29W-9N C7
Crabtree Ln
200 GLF 60029 2865 8W-12N A1
200 GNVW 60025 2865 8W-12N A1
200 GNVW 60029 2865 8W-12N A1
200 VNHL 60061 2647 16W-25N C5
200 GNVW 60025 2811 7W-12N B7
300 WNVL 60555 3080 29W-3S D5
500 LKFT 60045 2650 10W-27N C1
800 CRY 60013 2642 30W-24N B7
900 DSPN 60016 2863 12W-10N B4

Crabtree Ln
900 PKRG 60068 2863 12W-10N B4
1000 ANTH 60002 2358 22W-42N C7
1000 LYVL 60048 2591 16W-27N C7
1200 SMBG 60193 2912 23W-8N E1
1500 BKBN 60015 2703 11W-21N C5
1500 DRFD 60015 2703 11W-21N C5
2100 NHBK 60062 2757 10W-17N A5
2200 ALGN 60102 2695 32W-20N C7
2700 NHBK 60062 2756 10W-17N E4
2900 WLMT 60091 2811 5W-13N E6
N Crabtree Ln
1100 MPPT 60056 2808 14W-14N B4
1200 PTHT 60056 2808 14W-14N B4
1200 PTHT 60070 2808 14W-14N B4
W Crabtree Ln
24800 LkvT 60041 2474 25W-36N B4
25000 GrtT 60041 2474 25W-36N B4
Crab Tree Rd
100 EDND 60118 2748 33W-17N B7
Cracow Av
4500 LYNS 60534 3148 10W-4S A1
4500 MCCK 60525 3148 10W-4S A1
4500 MCCK 60534 3148 10W-4S A1
W Craft Ct
28700 CbaT 60010 2696 28W-23N D2
Craftwell Dr
5100 RGWD 60072 2470 34W-37N D2
Craig Av
500 CRTE 60417 3685 1W-30S B3
Craig Ct
300 DRFD 60015 2756 12W-20N C1
300 STGR 60475 3595 1W-28S E6
400 MPPT 60005 2861 17W-12N B1
400 MPPT 60056 2861 17W-12N B1
18700 NlxT 60448 3502 15W-22S C1
Craig Dr
4700 WRLK 60097 2469 36W-36N C3
16400 OKFT 60452 3426 5W-19S B2
E Craig Dr
10 CHHT 60411 3508 1W-23S A3
2000 DSPN 60018 2917 12W-8N B2
S Craig Dr
2600 DSPN 60018 2917 12W-8N C2
W Craig Dr
3500 JLET 60431 3497 28W-25S B7
Craig Dr W
10 CHHT 60411 3508 0W-23S B4
100 CHHT 60411 3507 1W-23S E4
Craig Pl
300 HLSD 60162 3028 13W-0S E5
N Craig Pl
600 LMBD 60148 3026 19W-1N C2
800 ADSN 60101 2970 19W-4N D3
S Craig Pl
10 LMBD 60148 3026 19W-0N C4
Craig St
800 ALGN 60102 2694 34W-21N C6
Craig Ter
10 LKZH 60047 2698 24W-23N C1
Craigie Ln
100 IVNS 60067 2752 22W-16N B7
Crain St
800 EVTN 60202 2867 2W-10N B4
1200 PKRG 60068 2863 10W-10N E4
1200 PKRG 60068 2864 10W-10N A4
1700 EVTN 60202 2866 3W-10N E4
3300 SKOK 60076 2866 5W-10N B4
4700 SKOK 60076 2865 6W-10N E4
5000 SKOK 60077 2865 6W-10N D4
5400 MNGV 60077 2865 6W-10N D4
5400 SKOK 60053 2865 6W-10N D4
5600 MNGV 60053 2865 7W-10N C4
W Crain St
7200 NLES 60714 2864 9W-10N D4
7900 MaiT 60714 2864 9W-10N B4
8500 PKRG 60068 2864 10W-10N A4
8500 PKRG 60714 2864 10W-10N A4
Cramer Ct
800 WLBK 60527 3145 16W-7S E6
Cramer Ln
8300 DRN 60561 3206 20W-9S A4
Cranberry Ct
10 BGBK 60490 3267 26W-12S E2
10 HnrT 60120 2910 29W-9N D1
200 RDLK 60073 2531 23W-33N E3
2100 NPVL 60565 3204 25W-10S B5
8600 TYPK 60487 3424 10W-19S B3
15400 HMGN 60491 3344 16W-18S A7
N Cranberry Ct
200 JLET 60435 3497 27W-23S C4
Cranberry Ln
100 LKBN 60010 2643 27W-24N B6
500 CmpT 60175 2961 42W-5N C2
2400 AURA 60502 3079 32W-3S C7
N Cranberry St
100 BGBK 60490 3267 26W-11S D2
S Cranberry St
100 BGBK 60490 3267 26W-12S E3
N Cranberry Lake Dr
100 HNVL 60073 2532 22W-33N B3
Cranbrook Av
1400 SCRL 60174 2964 34W-2N D7
Cranbrook Cir
1200 AURA 60502 3139 32W-5S C4
Cranbrook Ct
1300 SMBG 60193 2912 24W-8N C2
Cranbrook Dr
10 DSPN 60016 2862 14W-12N B1
10 MPPT 60016 2862 14W-12N B1
10 MPPT 60056 2862 14W-12N B1
900 SMBG 60193 2912 24W-8N C2
1900 GNOK 60048 2592 14W-30N C2
Cranbrook Ln
500 RMVL 60446 3269 23W-14S A6
8700 BGVW 60453 3210 8W-10S E4
8700 BGVW 60455 3210 8W-10S E4
8700 BGVW 60459 3210 8W-10S E4
8700 BRBK 60459 3210 8W-10S E4
8700 OKLN 60453 3210 8W-10S E4
8700 OKLN 60459 3210 8W-10S E4
S Crandall Av
100 CLLK 60014 2639 36W-25N C4
W Crandall Av
6800 WRTH 60482 3275 8W-12S A3
6900 WRTH 60482 3274 8W-12S E3
Crandell Ct
100 SMBG 60193 2859 23W-9N A7
Crandell Ln
600 SMBG 60193 2859 23W-9N B7
Crandon Av
200 CTCY 60409 3351 2E-17S D5
S Crandon Av
- CHCG 60633 3351 2E-15S D2
- CTCY 60409 3351 2E-15S D2
6700 CHCG 60649 3153 2E-7S D6

S Crandon Av
7500 CHCG 60649 3215 2E-9S D2
7800 CHCG 60617 3215 2E-9S D3
10300 CHCG 60617 3279 2E-11S D1
E Crandon Ct
1500 CLLK 60014 2693 37W-23N B3
S Crandon Ct
100 BMDL 60108 2969 23W-5N B1
W Crandon Ct
1500 CLLK 60014 2693 37W-23N B2
Crandon Ln
1700 SMBG 60193 2858 25W-9N A7
Crandon Pl
1500 CLLK 60014 2693 37W-23N B2
Crane Av
300 MDLN 60060 2646 18W-26N D3
16700 HLCT 60428 3427 2W-20S C4
16700 HLCT 60429 3427 2W-20S C4
16700 MKHM 60428 3427 2W-20S C4
Crane Blvd
600 LYVL 60048 2591 17W-28N B6
Crane Ct
200 SYHW 60118 2800 36W-15N A3
2100 RGMW 60008 2806 19W-13N D6
2300 BTVA 60510 3077 37W-1S C1
2600 NPVL 60564 3266 29W-12S D2
Crane Dr
1100 SYHW 60118 2800 36W-15N A3
Crane Ln
400 SchT 60175 2963 37W-4N C4
Crane Rd
10 SchT 60174 2964 36W-4N A4
10 SchT 60175 2963 37W-5N C2
10 SCRL 60175 2964 36W-4N A4
100 SchT 60175 2907 37W-6N C6
100 SchT 60175 2964 35W-4N A4
100 SCRL 60174 2964 36W-4N A4
900 SchT 60177 2907 37W-6N C6
900 SEGN 60177 2907 37W-6N C6
Crane St
400 AraT 60505 3139 33W-7S A6
400 AURA 60505 3139 33W-7S A7
600 AraT 60504 3139 33W-7S A6
W Crane St
1400 ANHT 60004 2753 18W-18N D2
Cranesbill Dr
300 WCHI 60185 3022 29W-2N D1
W Crane View Ct
1300 RDLK 60073 2531 24W-34N C2
Cranfield Ln
19400 TYPK 60477 3504 10W-23S B3
Cranna Ct
11700 ODPK 60467 3422 14W-21S D6
Cranshire Ct
1600 DRFD 60015 2703 12W-21N C6
3500 HFET 60067 2804 23W-14N E4
Cranshire Ln
1800 NPVL 60565 3204 24W-9S E3
Cranston Av
3000 ElgT 60124 2853 37W-11N C4
Cranston Cir
2700 BtlT 60543 3262 40W-13S C4
2700 BtlT 60560 3262 40W-13S C4
Cranston Ct
100 GNEN 60137 3025 22W-0S B7
3100 WLMT 60091 2811 6W-14N E5
Cranston Rd
200 CmpT 60175 2906 39W-7N E6
700 CmpT 60175 2907 39W-7N A6
700 SchT 60175 2907 39W-7N A6
Crawford Av
2100 SKOK 60203 2866 5W-12N B2
2500 EVTN 60201 2812 4W-13N B7
2700 WLMT 60091 2812 4W-13N B7
2700 WLMT 60201 2812 4W-13N B7
7400 LNWD 60076 2866 4W-9N B7
7400 LNWD 60712 2866 4W-9N B7
7400 SKOK 60076 2866 5W-10N B5
9500 EVTN 60201 2866 5W-10N B5
9900 EVTN 60076 2866 5W-12N B1
19600 CCHL 60478 3506 5W-23S D4
19600 FSMR 60422 3506 5W-23S D4
19600 RchT 60443 3506 5W-23S D4
19800 MTSN 60443 3506 4W-25S D7
19800 OMFD 60461 3506 4W-25S D7
23100 MonT 60466 3594 5W-28S D6
23100 PKFT 60466 3594 5W-28S D7
23100 RNPK 60471 3594 5W-28S D7
23500 MonT 60417 3594 5W-28S D7
23500 UYPK 60466 3594 5W-28S D7
N Crawford Av
6400 CHCG 60646 2920 4W-8N B3
6400 CHCG 60659 2920 4W-8N B3
6400 CHCG 60712 2920 4W-8N B3
6700 LNWD 60712 2920 5W-8N B1
7200 LNWD 60076 2866 5W-9N B7
7300 LNWD 60076 2866 5W-9N B7
7300 SKOK 60076 2866 5W-9N B7
W Crawford Av
25000 ANTT 60002 2357 25W-42N B6
Crawford Ln
1500 HRPK 60133 2911 26W-6N E6
Crawford Pl
600 HDPK 60035 2705 7W-21N A7
Crawford Rd
10 PltT 60124 2906 40W-8N B2
10 PltT 60175 2906 40W-8N B4
700 PltT 60124 2852 40W-9N B7
N Crawford Rd
38800 NptT 60083 2418 18W-41N E1
38800 OMCK 60083 2418 18W-41N E2
40000 NptT 60002 2418 18W-41N E1
41700 NptT 60002 2359 18W-41N E7
41700 NptT 60083 2359 18W-41N E7
42500 BtlT 53142 2359 18W-41N E7
42500 BtlT 60002 2359 18W-41N E7
Crawford St
10 GNVA 60134 3020 35W-0N B4
E Crawford St
100 PTON 60468 3861 9W-37S A3
400 WlIT 60468 3861 9W-37S A3
W Crawford St
100 PTON 60468 3860 9W-37S E3
100 PTON 60468 3861 9W-37S A3
Crawling Stone Rd
10 BNHL 60010 2748 30W-18N E2
Crazy Horse Dr
3300 JLET 60451 3500 19W-23S D3
Cree Ct
500 MltT 60187 3081 26W-2S E4
Cree Ln
10 MltT 60187 3081 26W-2S E4
10 MltT 60187 3082 26W-2S A4
600 MltT 60555 3081 26W-2S E4
E Cree Ln
1700 MPPT 60056 2808 13W-14N D4

N Creed Av
- JLET 60432 3499 23W-23S B3
Creedence Av
- ZION 60099 2421 12W-40N C3
Creedence Dr
- ZION 60099 2421 12W-40N C3
Creek Av
1400 AraT 60505 3138 33W-5S E4
1400 AURA 60505 3138 33W-5S E4
Creek Ct
100 PTHT 60070 2808 15W-15N A1
200 LslT 60540 3143 23W-7S A7
N Creek Ct
33600 GrtT 60041 2530 26W-33N D2
W Creek Ct N
14800 HMGN 60491 3343 18W-17S A5
W Creek Ct S
14800 HMGN 60491 3343 18W-17S A5
Creek Dr
- ALSP 60803 3276 4W-14S D6
- OSWG 60543 3263 36W-13S E4
10 LslT 60540 3205 23W-8S A1
400 LslT 60540 3143 23W-7S A7
600 WDRG 60517 3143 23W-7S A7
600 WDRG 60540 3143 23W-7S A7
700 LslT 60517 3143 23W-7S A7
4800 WNSP 60558 3146 14W-5S D1
N Creek Dr
18300 TYPK 60477 3424 9W-22S E7
18500 TYPK 60477 3504 9W-22S E1
S Creek Dr
16000 MhtT 60442 3677 20W-29S D1
W Creek Dr
16000 MhtT 60442 3677 20W-29S C1
18300 TYPK 60477 3424 9W-22S E7
18300 TYPK 60477 3504 9W-22S E1
Creek Ln
1200 BTVA 60510 3077 36W-0S E1
2600 AlqT 60013 2641 31W-25N D4
Creek Rd
200 LtRT 60545 3258 49W-11S E1
1900 AlqT 60021 2695 30W-22N E4
1900 FRGV 60021 2695 30W-22N E4
1900 WKGN 60087 2479 11W-36N D5
2100 LtRT 60545 3259 48W-13S A5
3500 PLNO 60545 3259 48W-13S A5
W Creek Rd
9600 PlsT 60464 3345 12W-15S D1
9600 PSPK 60464 3345 12W-15S D1
Creek Bend Dr
700 BFGV 60061 2701 16W-23N C2
700 BFGV 60089 2701 16W-23N C2
700 VNHL 60061 2701 16W-23N C2
Creek Bend Ln
600 ANTH 60002 2357 24W-42N C5
Creek Bend Rd
2400 SMBG 60173 2805 21W-13N D6
Creek Crossing Ct
14600 OrlT 60467 3344 14W-17S D5
Creek Crossing Dr
11600 MKNA 60448 3502 14W-23S D3
11700 FftT 60448 3502 14W-23S D3
13900 ODPK 60467 3344 14W-17S D4
13900 OrlT 60467 3344 14W-17S D4
Creekmont Ct
16100 TYPK 60487 3424 10W-19S B2
Creeks Crossing Dr
- ALGN 60102 2747 36W-19N A3
- DndT 60102 2747 36W-19N A3
Creekside Av
16800 TYPK 60487 3424 10W-20S B4
Creekside Cir
- ALGN 60102 2747 36W-19N B3
10 ELGN 60123 2800 36W-14N A6
500 MNKA 60447 3672 34W-30S B3
600 GRNE 60031 2534 16W-33N E2
900 NPVL 60563 3141 27W-5S B4
Creekside Ct
10 NARA 60542 3137 37W-4S B1
10 SMWD 60107 2856 29W-10N E6
100 SCRL 60174 2964 36W-4N A5
200 LNHT 60046 2476 19W-37N D1
300 CmpT 60175 2961 43W-5N B2
400 DGvT 60527 3146 15W-7S A5
400 OSWG 60543 3263 37W-13S C5
400 WLBK 60527 3146 15W-7S A5
1000 PTHT 60070 2754 16W-16N D7
1000 WLNG 60090 2754 16W-16N D7
1300 ELGN 60123 2800 36W-14N A7
1300 NLNX 60451 3501 18W-23S A4
1300 NlxT 60451 3501 18W-23S A4
1800 DRN 60561 3206 18W-9S E4
2700 AURA 60502 3079 32W-4S D7
3300 WDRG 60517 3143 22W-6S E7
3600 WPHR 60096 2362 11W-41N E7
S Creekside Ct
13800 HMGN 60491 3343 16W-16S E3
24900 CteT 60417 3687 3E-30S B2
W Creekside Ct
5500 MHRY 60050 2527 34W-31N C6
Creekside Dr
- ANHT 60056 2807 15W-14N E4
- BmdT 60101 2969 22W-4N C4
- RGMW 60008 2806 20W-13N A6
- RMVL 60441 3340 26W-17S A6
10 SchT 60175 2963 38W-6N B1
100 BGBK 60440 3268 24W-12S D2
100 ELWD 60421 3675 25W-30S C5
100 PNFD 60544 3415 31W-18S E1
100 PNFD 60544 3416 31W-18S A1
100 PnfT 60544 3416 31W-18S A1
100 SchT 60175 2907 38W-6N B7
200 BbyT 60119 3075 43W-2S A4
300 BMDL 60108 2969 22W-4N C4
300 BmdT 60108 2969 22W-4N C4
300 VNHL 60061 2647 17W-25N B5
400 MDLN 60060 2647 17W-25N B5
400 MDLN 60061 2647 17W-25N B5
500 GNVA 60134 3020 35W-0N B4
700 MPPT 60056 2807 15W-14N E4
1000 WHTN 60187 3081 26W-1S E1
1000 WHTN 60187 3082 25W-1S A1
1300 RMVL 60544 3340 26W-17S A6
1400 HFET 60169 2858 25W-11N B2
2100 MltT 60187 3081 26W-1S E2
3000 JLET 60586 3415 32W-20S C4
5300 OKFT 60452 3347 6W-18S E7
6700 LGGV 60047 2646 19W-25N C5
9400 WRLK 60097 2468 38W-35N D7
9700 GwdT 60097 2468 39W-35N D7
9700 GwdT 60098 2468 39W-35N D7
11600 ODPK 60467 3344 14W-16S D4
S Creekside Dr
300 PLTN 60074 2806 19W-15N B2
W Creekside Dr
13000 HMGN 60491 3343 16W-16S E3

STREET Block City ZIP Map# CGS Grid

W Creekside Dr
13000 HMGN 60491 3344 16W-16S A3
21000 KLDR 60047 2699 21W-22N E3
Creek Side Ln
- WLSP 60527 3208 13W-8S E1
Creekside Ln
- DrrT 60098 2581 41W-28N C5
- MHRY 60050 2527 34W-33N D3
- WDSK 60098 2581 41W-28N C6
10 BNHL 60010 2802 28W-15N E2
300 ANTH 60002 2358 22W-42N B6
600 RLKP 60073 2532 23W-33N A3
1600 JNBG 60050 2472 30W-36N A3
8400 DGvT 60516 3206 18W-9S E4
8400 DRN 60516 3206 18W-9S E4
8400 DRN 60561 3206 18W-9S E4
19100 MKNA 60448 3502 14W-23S D3
Creekside Pth
14700 GNOK 60048 2535 14W-31N B7
14700 WKGN 60048 2535 14W-31N B7
Creekside Rd
- LGGV 60047 2646 19W-25N C6
6900 DRGV 60516 3144 19W-7S C7
N Creekside Tr
100 MHRY 60050 2527 34W-32N C5
S Creekside Tr
100 MHRY 60050 2527 34W-31N C6
Creekside Cove
1500 WHTN 60187 3081 26W-1S E2
Creekview Cir
11600 MKNA 60448 3502 14W-22S D1
Creekview Ct
11700 MKNA 60448 3502 14W-22S D1
Creek View Dr
1000 VNHL 60061 2701 16W-23N C2
1100 BFGV 60061 2701 16W-23N C2
1100 BFGV 60089 2701 16W-23N C2
Creekview Dr
- PNFD 60544 3415 31W-18S E2
- PNFD 60586 3415 31W-18S E2
100 PltT 60124 2906 41W-9N A2
14400 OrlT 60467 3344 14W-17S D5
14900 HMGN 60491 3342 18W-16S E3
14900 HMGN 60491 3343 18W-16S A3
Creek View Ln
500 SchT 60175 2963 38W-5N B1
Creekview Ln
800 LIHL 60156 2694 34W-22N B4
18700 FftT 60448 3502 14W-22S D2
18700 MKNA 60448 3502 14W-22S D2
Creek View Rd
2600 MTGY 60506 3198 39W-9S E5
Creekwood Ct
500 CLSM 60188 2967 27W-2N C7
500 PltT 60124 2906 40W-9N B1
500 WTMT 60559 3144 18W-6S E5
3600 DRGV 60515 3084 19W-3S C6
16100 HMGN 60491 3421 16W-19S E2
E Creekwood Ct
2500 CteT 60417 3686 3E-29S E1
2500 CteT 60417 3687 3E-29S A1
N Creekwood Ct
500 LKPT 60441 3420 21W-18S A1
Creekwood Dr
700 PltT 60124 2906 40W-9N B1
2100 MDLN 60060 2590 20W-29N A4
2300 FmtT 60060 2590 20W-29N A4
7900 BRRG 60527 3208 14W-9S E3
14300 OrlT 60467 3344 14W-17S C5
16000 HMGN 60491 3421 16W-19S E2
W Creekwood Dr
300 PLTN 60074 2752 21W-18N D2
Creel Dr
600 WDDL 60191 2915 17W-6N B5
Cregier Av
17000 SHLD 60473 3429 1E-20S C4
S Cregier Av
6700 CHCG 60649 3153 2E-7S B6
7500 CHCG 60649 3215 2E-8S B1
8300 CHCG 60617 3215 2E-10S B4
Crego Pl
400 GnvT 60134 3019 38W-0S A7
Creiger Av
18000 LNSG 60438 3429 2E-21S C7
Creighton Av
900 EGVV 60007 2914 19W-8N D2
1300 NPVL 60565 3204 24W-9S C3
Creighton Ln
400 SMBG 60193 2859 23W-9N B6
S Creme Rd
14300 HMGN 60491 3343 18W-17S B6
Cremin Ct
3300 AURA 60502 3139 31W-6S E4
Cremin Dr
10 LKVL 60046 2475 22W-37N C1
Cremin Ln
3200 AURA 60502 3139 31W-6S E4
N Cremona Av
37000 LkvT 60046 2476 20W-37N A2
Crenshaw Cir
1800 VNHL 60061 2647 16W-27N D1
Crenshaw Ct
10 BGBK 60490 3267 27W-12S C3
10 WldT 60490 3267 27W-12S C3
Crescent Av
3000 MHRY 60050 2528 32W-32N C4
3400 GRNE 60031 2479 13W-35N A6
3400 WkgT 60031 2479 13W-35N A6
3400 WkgT 60085 2479 13W-35N A6
16500 TYPK 60477 3424 9W-19S C3
19600 LYWD 60411 3509 3E-23S E3
E Crescent Av
100 EMHT 60126 3027 16W-1N E3
100 EMHT 60126 3028 15W-0N A5
N Crescent Av
10 PLTN 60067 2805 22W-16N C1
10 PltT 60067 2805 22W-16N C1
100 PLTN 60067 2752 22W-16N C7
4800 NRDG 60706 2918 10W-6N B7
5600 CHCG 60631 2918 10W-7N B5
5600 LydT 60631 2918 10W-7N B5
5600 MaiT 60631 2918 10W-7N B5
S Crescent Av
200 PLTN 60067 2805 22W-15N C2
200 PltT 60067 2805 22W-15N C2
300 PKRG 60068 2918 10W-8N B1
1900 CHCG 60631 2918 10W-7N B4
1900 PKRG 60631 2918 10W-7N B4
W Crescent Av
200 EMHT 60126 3027 16W-0N E4
800 PLTN 60067 2752 22W-16N C7
900 PKRG 60068 2918 10W-8N A1
1300 PKRG 60068 2917 10W-8N E1
2000 WKGN 60085 2479 11W-35N D6
3300 GRNE 60031 2479 12W-35N A6
3300 WkgT 60031 2479 12W-35N A6

STREET Block City ZIP Map# CGS Grid

W Crescent Av
3300 WkgT 60085 2479 12W-35N B6
Crescent Blvd
200 GNEN 60137 3025 22W-0N B5
200 LMBD 60137 3025 21W-0N D4
200 LMBD 60148 3025 21W-0N D4
200 MltT 60137 3025 21W-0N D4
400 LMBD 60148 3026 21W-0N A4
Crescent Blvd CO-37
200 GNEN 60137 3025 21W-0N E4
200 LMBD 60137 3025 21W-0N E4
200 LMBD 60148 3025 21W-0N E4
200 MltT 60137 3025 21W-0N E4
Crescent Ct
10 OswT 60538 3199 36W-10S E7
10 SMWD 60107 2856 29W-10N D6
400 WDSK 60098 2524 41W-31N D6
600 GNEN 60137 3025 22W-0N C5
700 BRLT 60103 2911 28W-8N B3
700 HRPK 60133 2912 26W-8N A3
1000 RLKB 60073 2474 24W-34N D7
1800 HDPK 60035 2705 7W-22N A5
1900 HFET 60169 2858 25W-12N A2
6500 OKLN 60453 3211 8W-10S A5
8400 WLSP 60480 3208 14W-9S D3
12900 CTWD 60445 3347 6W-15S E1
W Crescent Ct
900 PLTN 60067 2752 22W-16N B7
Crescent Dr
- ANTH 60002 2418 20W-40N A3
- BmnT 60426 3426 5W-19S B2
- FftT 60448 3503 13W-23S B2
10 DndT 60118 2747 35W-19N C3
10 FmtT 60060 2645 21W-26N D3
10 GLNC 60022 2758 6W-18N D4
10 HNWD 60047 2645 21W-26N D4
10 HNWD 60060 2645 21W-26N D4
10 MaiT 60025 2864 10W-12N B1
200 CHHT 60411 3507 1W-25S E6
300 LKBF 60044 2594 10W-28N A7
300 WLNG 60090 2755 14W-17N C5
600 DRGV 60516 3144 19W-7S D6
800 GNEN 60137 3025 21W-0N D4
1700 NndT 60012 2586 30W-28N A5
1700 NndT 60050 2586 30W-28N A5
2400 HLCT 60429 3427 3W-20S C3
2400 HMWD 60430 3427 3W-22S B7
3700 STGR 60475 3596 1W-28S A6
7900 WRLK 60097 2469 37W-36N C3
9100 FNPK 60131 2973 11W-4N D3
13500 OrlT 60462 3345 11W-16S E2
13500 PlsT 60462 3345 11W-16S E2
19100 MKNA 60448 3503 13W-23S B2
E Crescent Dr
600 ANHT 60005 2807 17W-12N B7
W Crescent Dr
21300 FmtT 60060 2645 21W-26N D4
Crescent Knl W
100 GNOK 60048 2592 14W-28N B5
Crescent Ln
- PNFD 60586 3415 31W-19S D2
10 CmpT 60175 2906 39W-6N E7
100 SMBG 60193 2857 27W-10N D6
1000 GLNC 60093 2759 5W-16N A6
1000 WNKA 60093 2759 5W-16N A6
1800 HFET 60169 2858 26W-12N A2
3400 GNVW 60025 2809 11W-14N B3
5300 OKFT 60452 3347 6W-18S E6
N Crescent Ln
2300 AURA 60504 3201 32W-9S C4
S Crescent Ln
2200 AURA 60504 3201 32W-9S B4
Crescent Pkwy
1000 AlqT 60021 2696 30W-22N A4
1000 FRGV 60021 2696 30W-22N A4
Crescent Pl
10 NLNX 60451 3500 20W-24S B5
10 NlxT 60433 3500 20W-24S B5
10 WLMT 60091 2812 3W-13N E6
300 GNVA 60134 3020 35W-0N B4
6400 HMND 46324 3430 E2
Crescent Rd
10 LKZH 60047 2698 24W-23N D1
100 FRGV 60021 2696 30W-23N B2
Crescent St
10 ELGN 60123 2854 34W-11N D4
400 WHTN 60187 3024 24W-0S D6
Crescent Ter
600 WCDA 60084 2587 26W-28N C7
Crescent Wy
700 HRPK 60133 2912 26W-9N A1
22500 RNPK 60471 3594 5W-27S C4
Crescent Green Dr
5200 OKFT 60452 3347 6W-18S E6
Crescent Green Ln
15100 OKFT 60452 3347 6W-18S E6
Crescent Knoll Dr E
100 GNOK 60048 2592 14W-28N C5
Crescent Lake Dr
1500 MTGY 60538 3199 37W-9S B4
16300 LktT 60403 3417 26W-19S E3
Crescent Oak Ln
2800 AURA 60502 3079 32W-3S B6
Crescenzo Ct
600 NLNX 60451 3501 18W-24S A6
Crescenzo Dr
2600 JLET 60436 3497 27W-24S D6
3000 SCHT 60411 3596 1W-27S A4
E Cresent Dr
- VLPK 60181 3027 17W-0N B4
Cress Creek Ct
500 CLLK 60014 2639 36W-24N E6
1400 NpvT 60563 3141 27W-5S C2
Cress Creek Dr
- WCHI 60185 3022 30W-0S B6
Cress Creek Ln
500 CLLK 60014 2639 36W-24N D7
Cress Creek Ter
500 CLLK 60014 2639 36W-24N C7
W Cressett Dr
7700 EDPK 60707 2974 9W-3N B5
7900 EDPK 60171 2974 9W-3N B5
Cressmoor Ct
8500 ODPK 60462 3346 10W-18S B7
Crest Av
- SmbT 60193 2912 25W-8N B2
100 EGVV 60007 2861 18W-9N A7
200 ADSN 60106 2971 17W-4N B3
200 EGvT 60007 2861 18W-9N A7
300 ADSN 60191 2971 17W-4N B3
300 BmdT 60157 2913 22W-7N C4
300 ROSL 60172 2913 22W-7N C4
400 AddT 60191 2971 17W-4N B3
400 EGvT 60007 2915 18W-9N A1
400 EGVV 60007 2915 18W-9N A1
500 AddT 60106 2971 16W-4N D3

STREET Block City ZIP Map# CGS Grid

Crest Av
500 BNVL 60106 2971 16W-4N D3
700 SMBG 60193 2912 25W-8N B2
E Crest Av
100 BNVL 60106 2972 15W-4N A3
N Crest Av
100 BRLT 60103 2911 28W-8N A3
S Crest Av
100 BRLT 60103 2911 28W-8N A3
W Crest Av
300 ITSC 60143 2913 21W-7N D4
300 ITSC 60157 2913 21W-7N D4
Crest Ct
10 WynT 60185 2967 27W-3N C7
200 BMDL 60108 2969 22W-5N B1
500 LKFT 60045 2650 10W-24N A7
600 MltT 60137 3083 21W-1S D2
1100 SMBG 60193 2913 23W-8N B1
4700 WKGN 60087 2478 14W-37N B1
4900 CCHL 60478 3506 6W-22S A1
8600 LyIT 60527 3208 14W-9S C4
Crest Dr
- PGGV 60140 2797 42W-14N D5
- RtdT 60140 2797 42W-14N D5
300 CRY 60013 2641 30W-24N E7
900 AlqT 60013 2641 30W-24N E7
Crest Ln
400 ANTH 60002 2357 23W-42N D6
600 LslT 60532 3143 22W-6S B5
1100 WNSP 60558 3146 14W-6S D4
Crest Rd
100 GNEN 60137 3025 22W-0S C7
1000 GNOK 60048 2592 14W-29N C4
6700 DRN 60561 3145 16W-8S E7
6700 WLBK 60527 3145 16W-8S E7
6700 WLBK 60561 3145 16W-7S E7
6900 DRN 60527 3145 16W-8S E7
7100 DRN 60561 3207 16W-8S E1
28200 WcnT 60051 2587 28W-28N A6
Crest St
400 WHTN 60187 3024 25W-0S B7
700 WHTN 60187 3082 25W-1S B1
1300 SMBG 60193 2913 23W-8N B2
1300 SmbT 60193 2913 23W-8N B2
W Crest St
1700 MchT 60051 2529 30W-32N A4
Crestbrook Ct
12800 CTWD 60445 3275 6W-15S E7
12800 CTWD 60445 3347 6W-15S E1
Crested Butte Ln
19600 MKNA 60448 3502 15W-23S B4
Crested Butte Tr
2600 JLET 60586 3416 30W-20S A5
Crestfield Av
800 LYVL 60048 2591 17W-28N B6
Crestfield Ct
2700 NPVL 60565 3203 26W-10S D6
Cresthaven Ln
1100 NPVL 60564 3267 28W-12S B2
N Cresthill Av
200 MchT 60051 2529 29W-32N B5
400 LKMR 60051 2529 29W-32N B5
Cresthill Ct
7400 FXLK 60020 2414 28W-39N E5
Crest Hill Dr
400 PTHT 60070 2754 16W-16N D7
25800 CbaT 60010 2697 25W-21N E5
Crestland Rd
10 INCK 60061 2647 17W-24N B6
10 VNHL 60061 2647 17W-24N B6
W Crestline Av
4100 CHCG 60652 3212 5W-9S B2
Crestline Dr
- ODPK 60467 3344 14W-16S D3
Creston Cir
10 AURA 60504 3201 31W-7S E1
W Creston Ct
21200 LktT 60544 3339 26W-16S E5
E Crestview Av
- EMHT 60126 2971 16W-2N E6
100 EMHT 60126 2972 15W-2N A6
Crestview Cir
1000 ELGN 60123 2800 35W-13N C7
1900 RMVL 60446 3339 27W-18S C7
Crest View Ct
100 MNKA 60447 3583 33W-28S C7
Crestview Ct
100 BRTN 60010 2751 24W-18N D3
100 PltT 60010 2751 24W-18N D3
600 LslT 60540 3142 24W-5S C3
13600 CTWD 60445 3348 6W-16S A3
17600 ODPK 60467 3422 14W-21S D6
21000 CbaT 60010 2698 25W-21N A7
Crestview Dr
10 DRFD 60015 2757 9W-20N B2
10 FXLK 60041 2473 27W-35N B5
200 WCDA 60084 2644 25W-27N B1
700 BGBK 60440 3204 24W-10S E6
700 BGBK 60565 3204 24W-10S E6
1000 ELGN 60123 2800 35W-13N C7
1000 LMNT 60439 3270 19W-14S E7
1100 BTVA 60510 3020 35W-0S A7
1200 BTVA 60510 3019 36W-0S E7
1800 JLET 60586 3415 33W-21S A7
2400 AURA 60502 3139 32W-6S C6
3600 LGGV 60047 2700 19W-22N C5
5700 WNSP 60558 3146 14W-6S D4
8100 WLSP 60480 3208 14W-9S D3
12600 HTLY 60142 2744 43W-19N B3
13900 HMGN 60491 3343 18W-16S A4
17600 ODPK 60467 3422 14W-21S D6
N Crestview Dr
- PLTN 60067 2752 20W-17N E5
800 PLTN 60067 2753 20W-17N A5
21000 CbaT 60010 2698 25W-21N A6
Crestview Ln
10 LKBN 60010 2697 27W-23N C2
10 VNHL 60061 2647 17W-26N C3
100 DYR 46311 3598 C5
2200 WLMT 60091 2812 4W-13N B6
Crestview Rd
300 AlqT 60021 2695 30W-22N E4
300 BNHL 60010 2695 30W-22N E4
300 BNHL 60021 2695 30W-22N E4
300 FRGV 60021 2695 30W-22N E4
10700 CTSD 60525 3147 13W-7S A6
10800 CTSD 60525 3146 13W-7S E6
Crestview Ter
10 BFGV 60089 2754 16W-18N C2
Crestville Ct
900 GRNE 60031 2479 13W-35N A7
N Crestwood Av
200 MchT 60051 2529 29W-32N B5
400 LKMR 60051 2529 29W-32N B5
Crest Wood Ct
100 HFET 60169 2859 23W-12N A1

STREET Block City ZIP Map# CGS Grid

Crest Wood Ct
100 SMBG 60195 2859 23W-12N A1
Crestwood Ct
10 OswT 60538 3199 36W-10S D7
300 ALGN 60102 2694 34W-21N B6
300 WDDL 60191 2971 17W-4N C2
900 SMWD 60107 2857 28W-9N A7
1000 BGBK 60440 3268 25W-11S B1
1000 EGVV 60007 2914 19W-8N D2
1300 NPVL 60540 3142 25W-7S B6
1400 AURA 60506 3137 37W-6S C5
5600 MTSN 60443 3505 7W-24S D5
13400 CTWD 60445 3347 6W-15S D2
Crestwood Dr
- CTHL 60403 3418 26W-21S A6
- SEGN 60177 2907 37W-7N D4
10 JLET 60432 3500 21W-23S A3
10 JltT 60432 3500 21W-23S A3
10 SMWD 60107 2857 28W-9N A7
100 EDND 60118 2801 33W-16N B2
300 CmpT 60175 2906 41W-6N A6
300 ROSL 60172 2913 23W-6N B6
400 DSPN 60016 2862 14W-11N C4
700 AURA 60506 3137 36W-5S E3
1100 NHBK 60062 2756 10W-17N E5
2000 PltT 60067 2806 20W-13N A6
2000 RGMW 60008 2806 20W-13N A6
3100 PKCY 60085 2536 12W-33N B3
3100 WKGN 60085 2536 12W-33N B3
3700 GNVW 60025 2809 11W-15N D3
3700 GNVW 60062 2809 11W-15N D3
4100 MHRY 60050 2528 33W-32N A4
4100 NfdT 60062 2809 11W-15N D3
5400 CTWD 60445 3347 6W-15S D2
E Crestwood Dr
600 ANHT 60004 2754 17W-16N B7
Crestwood Ln
- CPVL 60118 2746 38W-18N C5
- GNVW 60025 2809 10W-13N E5
- LMNT 60439 3271 18W-14S A6
- PltT 60067 2806 20W-13N A6
- RGMW 60008 2806 20W-13N A5
200 BMDL 60108 2969 22W-4N C3
1000 BGBK 60440 3268 25W-11S B1
2500 RVWD 60015 2703 13W-21N A6
2600 RVWD 60015 2702 13W-21N E6
3100 GNVW 60025 2810 10W-13N A5
10200 PvsT 60154 3087 12W-1S A2
10200 WSTR 60154 3087 12W-1S A2
S Crestwood Ln
300 MPPT 60056 2861 17W-12N C1
W Crestwood Ln
23100 ElaT 60047 2698 23W-23N E1
23100 ElaT 60047 2699 23W-23N A1
Crestwood Pt
- CPVL 60118 2746 38W-18N B5
Crestwood Rd
300 WDDL 60191 2971 17W-4N C2
5600 MTSN 60443 3505 7W-24S D5
Crestwood Vil
200 NHFD 60093 2811 6W-15N C3
Crete Blvd
300 CRTE 60417 3685 0W-30S B3
S Crete Ct
14100 LktT 60544 3339 26W-16S E4
14100 LktT 60544 3340 26W-16S A5
Crete Rd
3700 CRTE 60417 3597 0E-29S A7
3700 CRTE 60417 3685 0E-29S E1
3700 CteT 60417 3685 0E-29S E1
W Crete-Monee Rd
- CteT 60417 3684 3W-31S C5
- MonT 60417 3684 3W-31S C5
3200 MonT 60449 3683 4W-31S D5
3200 MonT 60449 3684 3W-31S B5
4000 UYPK 60449 3683 5W-31S D5
4200 MONE 60449 3683 5W-31S C5
S Cretewood Ln
23900 CteT 60417 3595 2W-29S E7
Creve Ct
10 OswT 60538 3199 37W-10S D7
Crewman Dr
100 GNVW 60025 2810 10W-14N A3
Crichton Ln
100 IVNS 60067 2752 22W-18N B3
Cricket Av
3400 JLET 60451 3500 19W-22S E2
3400 NLNX 60451 3500 19W-22S E2
W Cricket Ct
26300 CNHN 60410 3672 32W-31S C5
S Cricketwood Ct
14600 HMGN 60491 3343 17W-17S D5
S Cricketwood Dr
14600 HMGN 60491 3343 17W-17S D6
Crighton Av
10 ELGN 60123 2854 34W-11N D4
N Crilly Ct
1700 CHCG 60614 2978 C7
S Crilly Dr
- CHCG 60617 3216 4E-10S C6
Crimson Ct
10 LIHL 60156 2692 38W-23N E3
800 PTHT 60070 2809 13W-15N A1
1100 NPVL 60564 3203 28W-10S B6
2800 NHBK 60062 2756 11W-17N E4
4100 HFET 60192 2804 24W-15N B2
W Crimson Ct
21200 DPgT 60544 3339 26W-15S E2
Crimson Dr
500 CLLK 60014 2693 36W-23N D1
1000 WLNG 60090 2754 15W-16N E6
4100 HFET 60192 2804 24W-15N B2
15800 LKPT 60441 3420 19W-20S D4
Crimson Ln
1500 PLTN 60074 2753 19W-17N D4
1500 PltT 60074 2753 19W-17N D4
22300 FKFT 60423 3591 13W-27S A4
Cripple Creek Ct
10 SMBG 60194 2857 27W-10N D5
2700 NPVL 60564 3202 29W-10S C5
Cripple Creek Dr
7900 FmtT 60060 2645 20W-25N E4
7900 LGGV 60060 2645 20W-25N E4
Crisfield Dr
- AvnT 60030 2475 20W-34N E7
10 GYLK 60030 2475 20W-34N E7
Crispin Dr
600 ELGN 60123 2854 35W-9N B7
600 ElgT 60123 2854 35W-9N B7
700 ElgT 60123 2908 35W-9N B1
1100 ELGN 60123 2908 35W-9N B1
Criss Cir
300 EGVV 60007 2861 17W-10N B5
Crissey Av
- BTVA 60510 3020 35W-0S C6
- GNVA 60510 3020 35W-0S C6

STREET Block City ZIP Map# CGS Grid

Crissey Av
10 GNVA 60134 3020 34W-0N C4
Crissey Av SR-25
- BTVA 60510 3020 35W-0S C6
- GNVA 60510 3020 35W-0S C6
200 GNVA 60134 3020 35W-0N C4
W Crissy Av
10000 BHPK 60087 2422 10W-38N B7
10000 BHPK 60099 2422 10W-38N B7
Cristina Av
8300 ODPK 60462 3346 10W-16S B3
Cristopher Ct
- JNBG 60050 2471 32W-34N C7
Criswell Dr
200 JLET 60432 3499 21W-23S E4
200 JltT 60432 3499 21W-23S E4
Crocket Ln
15400 MKHM 60428 3349 3W-18S A7
E Crockett Av
900 ADSN 60101 2971 17W-2N B7
W Crockett Av
500 EMHT 60101 2971 17W-2N C7
500 EMHT 60126 2971 17W-2N C7
Crockett Ct
3600 JLET 60435 3417 27W-19S C3
3800 NndT 60014 2641 32W-26N A3
W Crocus Av
4600 MONE 60449 3683 5W-31S C4
Crocus Ln
10 MTSN 60443 3593 7W-26S C2
Croft Ln
- FKFT 60423 3503 12W-24S C6
1200 EVTN 60202 2867 2W-10N A4
Crofton Av N
1100 HDPK 60035 2704 8W-21N E6
Crofton Av S
600 HDPK 60035 2704 8W-20N E7
600 HDPK 60035 2757 8W-20N E1
Crofton Cir
2600 LIHL 60156 2692 38W-22N D3
Crofton Ct
10 CRY 60013 2695 32W-23N B1
10 LIHL 60156 2692 38W-22N D3
10 OSWG 60543 3263 36W-11S E1
700 SBTN 60010 2803 25W-15N E1
1000 HDPK 60035 2704 8W-21N E7
Crofton Dr
1700 ALGN 60102 2694 35W-20N A7
1700 ALGN 60102 2747 35W-20N A1
Crofton Ln
900 BFGV 60089 2754 17W-17N B4
N Crofton Ln
5300 BHPK 60083 2421 13W-39N A5
Crofton Rd
10 OSWG 60543 3263 36W-11S E1
Croftridge Ln
800 HDPK 60035 2704 8W-21N E6
Croftwood Ct
100 RGMW 60008 2805 21W-13N D5
Croghan Av
800 JLET 60436 3498 25W-24S C7
S Croissant Dr
13800 BNHM 60633 3351 2E-16S D3
Crompton Ct
10 FRGV 60021 2696 29W-22N B4
Crompton St
- WNKA 60093 2811 6W-15N D2
Cromwell Av
700 WSTR 60154 3029 12W-0S B7
8200 WDRG 60517 3206 20W-9S B3
Cromwell Cir
400 BRLT 60103 2967 28W-5N B3
400 BRLT 60133 2967 28W-5N B3
400 HRPK 60133 2967 28W-5N B3
Cromwell Ct
300 WTMT 60559 3145 18W-6S A5
400 LKZH 60047 2699 22W-21N A6
1300 VNHL 60061 2647 16W-26N D2
10100 MKNA 60448 3503 12W-23S C3
Cromwell Dr
- NCHI 60088 2593 11W-30N D2
1900 WHTN 60187 3082 25W-2S B4
2000 MltT 60187 3082 25W-3S B5
2000 MltT 60555 3082 25W-3S B5
2000 WHTN 60555 3082 25W-3S B5
Cromwell Ln
1200 NPVL 60564 3203 28W-11S A7
5500 OKFT 60452 3347 6W-17S D5
10000 MKNA 60448 3503 12W-23S C3
Cromwell Rd
10 PKFT 60466 3595 2W-27S C4
Cromwell St
1000 NARA 60542 3077 37W-3S B6
N Croname Rd
7300 NLES 60714 2865 7W-9N A7
Cronin Av
7500 JSTC 60458 3209 11W-8S E2
Cronin Blvd
- SRWD 60404 3495 31W-23S E4
Cronin Ct
1200 LMNT 60439 3271 18W-14S B7
Crooked Ln
10 CmpT 60175 2962 40W-6N B1
200 NBRN 60010 2697 26W-23N E2
Crooked Creek Ct
17900 ODPK 60467 3422 14W-21S E7
Crooked Creek Dr
- FftT 60423 3592 10W-27S C5
10 KdlT 60560 3333 42W-16S D5
10 YKVL 60560 3333 42W-16S D4
1300 BCHR 60401 3774 0W-35S D7
8100 FKFT 60423 3592 10W-27S C5
Crooked Creek Ln
300 NHFD 60093 2811 6W-15N C1
Crooked Creek Rd
2500 SMBG 60173 2805 21W-13N D6
Crooked Creek Tr
10 DRPK 60010 2752 22W-18N A2
10 PltT 60010 2752 22W-18N A2
N Crooked Lake Ln
- LkvT 60046 2417 21W-38N D7
200 LNHT 60046 2417 21W-38N D7
Crookedstick Ct
900 CLLK 60014 2641 33W-24N A6
W Crooked Stick Ct
500 VNHL 60061 2647 17W-26N B3
Crooked Tree Ct
200 NPVL 60565 3203 26W-10S E6
2000 MHRY 60050 2528 32W-33N B2
W Crooked Willow Ln
1200 PLTN 60067 2805 22W-14N B3
Cropland Dr
24000 PNFD 60544 3416 30W-18S B2
Crosby Ct
400 ELGN 60123 2854 34W-11N E4
1500 HRPK 60133 2911 26W-6N E6

Block	City	ZIP	Map#	CGS	Grid
N Crosby St					
900	CHCG	60610	3034	0W-1N	A2
Crosley Dr					
-	NCHI	60064	2594	10W-31N	A1
-	NCHI	60088	2594	10W-30N	A1
Cross Ct					
200	SRGV	60554	3135	42W-7S	D7
500	GRNE	60031	2535	14W-33N	C3
Cross Dr					
7300	MchT	60097	2469	36W-37N	D2
Cross Rd					
300	GRNE	60031	2535	14W-33N	C3
Cross St					
10	BtlT	60512	3261	41W-12S	E3
10	FXLK	60020	2473	28W-36N	A4
10	YKVL	60512	3261	41W-12S	E3
100	AURA	60506	3138	35W-7S	B6
100	AURA	60506	3200	36W-7S	A1
100	SRGV	60554	3135	42W-7S	D7
400	WMTN	60481	3853	27W-37S	D5
900	VLPK	60181	3027	17W-0S	B6
4400	DRGV	60515	3143	21W-5S	D2
4400	LslT	60515	3143	21W-5S	D2
11000	MKNA	60448	3503	13W-23S	A3
E Cross St					
10	SRGV	60554	3135	42W-7S	D7
500	WMTN	60481	3853	27W-37S	D5
N Cross St					
600	WHTN	60187	3024	24W-0S	C6
S Cross St					
300	WHTN	60187	3024	24W-0S	C7
W Cross St					
10	SRGV	60554	3135	42W-7S	C7
500	WMTN	60481	3853	27W-37S	D5
N Cross Tr					
100	MHRY	60050	2527	33W-32N	E5
S Cross Tr					
100	MHRY	60050	2527	33W-31N	E6
Cross Arm Dr					
400	GYLK	60030	2532	20W-32N	E5
400	GYLK	60030	2533	20W-32N	A6
Cross Creek Ct					
10	ElgT	60124	2907	38W-9N	A1
800	ROSL	60172	2913	22W-8N	C3
2600	AURA	60502	3079	32W-4S	C7
2700	JLET	60435	3497	27W-22S	C2
Cross Creek Dr N					
800	ROSL	60172	2913	22W-8N	C2
Cross Creek Ln					
100	LNHT	60046	2476	19W-37N	D1
Crosscreek Ln					
600	CmpT	60175	2962	39W-6N	D1
Cross Creek Pk W					
600	ROSL	60172	2913	22W-8N	C3
Cross Creek Sq					
-	CLLK	60014	2639	36W-24N	D7
Crossen Av					
10	EGVV	60007	2861	17W-9N	C7
Crossfield Ct					
1300	BFGV	60089	2701	16W-21N	D6
Crossing Ct					
-	PNFD	60586	3415	31W-18S	D2
500	RGMW	60008	2805	21W-13N	C5
1900	NPVL	60540	3202	29W-8S	E2
2000	LMBD	60148	3084	20W-1S	E2
Crossing Dr					
-	PNFD	60586	3415	32W-19S	D3
18300	TYPK	60487	3504	10W-22S	B1
Crossing Ln					
2000	NPVL	60540	3202	29W-8S	E1
Crossing Rd					
300	BGBK	60440	3269	22W-12S	C3
Crossing Wy					
700	SCRL	60174	2965	33W-3N	A5
Crossland Blvd					
6100	GRNE	60031	2534	16W-33N	D3
Crossland Ct					
800	GYLK	60030	2533	19W-33N	B2
Crossland Dr					
700	GYLK	60030	2533	19W-33N	B2
Crossman Cir					
-	PvsT	60141	3088	10W-1S	A1
Cross Meadow St					
300	MDLN	60060	2646	18W-27N	D2
Crossroad Dr					
1600	JLET	60431	3584	29W-26S	E2
E Crossroads Pkwy					
-	DPgT	60441	3269	22W-13S	C5
100	BGBK	60440	3269	22W-13S	B5
300	RMVL	60446	3269	22W-13S	C5
W Crossroads Pkwy					
200	BGBK	60440	3269	23W-13S	A5
400	BGBK	60440	3268	24W-13S	D6
700	BGBK	60446	3268	24W-14S	D6
700	RMVL	60446	3268	25W-14S	C7
1000	RMVL	60446	3340	25W-14S	B1
Crossroads of Commerce					
10	RGMW	60008	2806	20W-12N	B7
10	RGMW	60008	2860	20W-12N	B1
Cross Timber Rd					
10	BNHL	60010	2696	30W-21N	A6
Crossview Ct					
10	LIHL	60156	2692	38W-21N	D7
Crossview Ln					
5400	LIHL	60156	2692	38W-21N	D6
Cross Wicks Ct					
10	NBRN	60010	2644	24W-24N	B6
Crosswind Ct					
2100	JLET	60586	3415	33W-21S	A7
5900	JNBG	60050	2472	30W-37N	A1
Crosswind Dr					
1900	JLET	60586	3415	33W-21S	A7
5300	RNPK	60471	3593	6W-27S	E5
Crosswind Ln					
500	LNHT	60046	2417	21W-39N	D5
Croton Ct					
1300	AURA	60506	3137	38W-5S	B4
Crow Ln					
400	WLNG	60090	2754	16W-17N	D5
Crowe Av					
1400	DRFD	60015	2703	11W-21N	D5
1500	BKBN	60015	2703	11W-21N	D5
S Crowell St					
2700	CHCG	60608	3091	1W-2S	E3
Crowfoot Cir N					
1400	HFET	60169	2858	25W-11N	B3
Crowfoot Cir S					
1400	HFET	60169	2858	25W-11N	B3
Crowfoot Ct					
24300	PNFD	60585	3338	30W-14S	B1
Crowfoot Ln					
1400	MNKA	60447	3672	33W-30S	B4
25600	CNHN	60410	3672	32W-29S	D2
W Crowley Av					
10	JLET	60432	3498	24W-23S	E4
Crowley Rd					
18800	AdnT	60033	2406	48W-40N	E3
18800	HRVD	60033	2406	48W-40N	E3
20300	CmgT	60033	2406	49W-40N	C3
Crown Cir					
8400	WLSP	60480	3208	13W-9S	E3
Crown Ct					
-	DMND	60416	3941	34W-40S	A3
-	RLKP	60030	2532	21W-31N	C7
-	WCHI	60185	2965	31W-3N	E7
700	SMBG	60193	2859	23W-9N	A7
8600	LynT	60527	3208	14W-9S	C4
S Crown Ct					
300	PLTN	60074	2806	19W-15N	D2
Crown Dr					
1500	GNVW	60025	2809	11W-14N	E5
Crown Hl					
-	ELGN	60120	2855	32W-10N	C7
Crown Ln					
1400	GNVW	60025	2809	11W-14N	E5
6800	TYPK	60477	3425	8W-19S	A2
W Crown Ln					
600	PTON	60468	3860	9W-37S	D4
Crown Rd					
400	AddT	60126	2972	15W-3N	A5
500	AddT	60106	2972	15W-3N	A5
500	BNVL	60106	2972	15W-3N	A5
10400	FNPK	60131	2973	13W-3N	A5
21500	CbaT	60010	2697	26W-21N	D5
Crown St					
1300	AURA	60505	3200	34W-9S	D5
1300	MTGY	60505	3200	34W-9S	D5
1300	MTGY	60538	3200	34W-9S	D5
Crown Fox Ln					
1200	NLNX	60451	3501	17W-23S	D4
1200	NlxT	60451	3501	17W-23S	D4
Crown Point Ct					
500	BFGV	60089	2754	17W-20N	C1
Crown Point Dr					
500	BFGV	60089	2754	17W-20N	C1
600	BFGV	60089	2701	16W-21N	C6
Crown Point St					
2000	WDRG	60517	3144	21W-7S	A7
Crows Nest Ct					
10	TDLK	60030	2533	19W-34N	D1
Croyden Pl					
2300	NHBK	60062	2810	8W-16N	D1
Croyden Rd					
10	HNWD	60047	2645	20W-24N	E7
Croyden St					
100	MchT	60081	2472	29W-37N	D1
Croydon Ct					
100	OSWG	60543	3263	37W-14S	B6
1200	GNVA	60134	3020	36W-0N	A5
1200	WHTN	60187	3082	25W-1S	B2
Croydon Ln					
10	OKBK	60523	3086	15W-2S	B2
8900	ODPK	60462	3346	11W-18S	A7
Croydon on Duxbury					
10	RGMW	60008	2805	22W-13N	B6
Croyle Ct					
1100	SMBG	60193	2912	24W-8N	C2
Crozier Dr					
-	GYLK	60046	2475	21W-36N	D4
-	GYLK	60073	2475	21W-36N	D4
-	RLKB	60046	2475	21W-36N	D4
-	RLKB	60073	2475	21W-36N	D4
Cryder Ct					
-	BtlT	60543	3262	40W-12S	C4
-	BtlT	60560	3262	40W-12S	C4
Cryder Ln					
2300	JLET	60586	3416	29W-21S	D6
2300	PnfT	60586	3416	29W-21S	D6
Cryder Wy					
2800	BtlT	60543	3262	40W-12S	C4
2800	BtlT	60560	3262	40W-12S	C4
Crystal Av					
100	SEGN	60177	2908	34W-8N	D3
1100	DRGV	60516	3206	19W-8S	C1
1300	NPVL	60563	3140	29W-4S	D2
N Crystal Av					
600	ELGN	60123	2854	34W-12N	D2
W Crystal Av					
10	LMBD	60148	3026	20W-1N	B2
Crystal Cir					
2100	NndT	60012	2585	31W-28N	E6
2100	PRGV	60012	2585	31W-28N	E6
Crystal Ct					
100	STGR	60475	3596	1W-28S	A6
400	CLLK	60014	2639	37W-25N	B6
400	LKWD	60014	2639	37W-25N	B6
500	OSWG	60543	3200	33W-11S	E7
700	SRWD	60404	3496	30W-22S	B2
1000	GNVW	60025	2810	10W-13N	A6
1000	NfdT	60025	2810	10W-13N	A6
1300	NPVL	60563	3140	29W-5S	D2
2400	WDRG	60517	3205	21W-9S	E3
16800	TYPK	60477	3425	8W-20S	A3
W Crystal Ct					
4400	ALSP	60803	3276	5W-15S	B7
Crystal Ct N					
600	SMBG	60193	2859	22W-9N	B7
Crystal Ct S					
600	SMBG	60193	2859	22W-9N	B7
Crystal Dr					
500	SRWD	60404	3496	30W-22S	C2
2500	JLET	60435	3417	27W-20S	C5
2500	PnfT	60435	3417	27W-20S	C5
S Crystal Dr					
700	DMND	60416	3941	33W-40S	B4
1000	BvlT	60416	3941	33W-40S	B4
Crystal Ln					
100	BRLT	60103	2910	30W-8N	B3
100	HnrT	60103	2910	30W-8N	B3
200	CteT	60417	3596	1W-28S	A6
200	CteT	60475	3596	1W-28S	A6
200	STGR	60475	3596	1W-28S	A6
2400	PltT	60004	2753	19W-18N	C2
18000	LNSG	60438	3429	2E-21S	C6
18100	ThtT	60438	3429	2E-21S	C6
W Crystal Ln					
-	EGvT	60056	2861	17W-10N	C4
1700	MPPT	60056	2861	17W-10N	C4
Crystal Pl					
400	GRNE	60031	2476	18W-34N	E7
400	GRNE	60031	2533	18W-34N	E1
Crystal Rd					
2300	NHBK	60062	2810	8W-15N	D1
Crystal St					
10	CRY	60013	2695	31W-23N	D1
Crystal St US-14					
10	CRY	60013	2695	31W-23N	D1
E Crystal St					
400	MDLN	60060	2646	18W-27N	D1
S Crystal St					
10	ELGN	60123	2854	34W-11N	E4
W Crystal St					
100	MDLN	60060	2646	19W-27N	C1
2600	CHCG	60622	3033	3W-1N	A1
2700	CHCG	60622	3032	3W-1N	E1
3200	CHCG	60651	3032	4W-1N	D1
4800	CHCG	60651	3031	6W-1N	D2
Crystal Tr					
4700	MHRY	60050	2527	33W-31N	E6
Crystal Wy					
2100	NndT	60012	2585	31W-28N	D6
2100	PRGV	60012	2585	31W-28N	D6
N Crystal Beach Av					
10	CLLK	60014	2639	37W-25N	C4
Crystal Creek Dr					
8700	ODHL	60487	3424	10W-19S	A1
8700	ODPK	60487	3424	10W-19S	A1
10700	MKNA	60448	3503	13W-22S	A2
15900	HMGN	60491	3422	15W-19S	C2
16000	ODPK	60462	3424	10W-19S	A1
16000	TYPK	60462	3424	10W-19S	A1
16000	TYPK	60487	3424	10W-19S	A1
18700	FftT	60448	3503	13W-22S	A1
Crystal Creek Ln					
2400	ELGN	60124	2853	36W-10N	D6
Crystal Downs Ct					
10	LIHL	60156	2693	36W-22N	C4
Crystal Downs Dr					
-	HNWD	60047	2645	22W-26N	B4
-	HNWD	60060	2645	22W-26N	B4
E Crystal Lake Av					
10	CLLK	60014	2640	35W-26N	B4
500	AlqT	60014	2640	34W-26N	C4
500	NndT	60014	2640	34W-26N	C4
2900	AlqT	60013	2641	32W-26N	A4
2900	AlqT	60014	2641	32W-26N	A4
2900	NndT	60013	2641	32W-26N	A4
2900	NndT	60014	2641	32W-26N	A4
2900	ODHL	60013	2641	31W-26N	C4
W Crystal Lake Av					
10	CLLK	60014	2640	35W-26N	A4
200	CLLK	60014	2639	36W-26N	E4
Crystal Lake Ct					
13000	HMGN	60491	3422	16W-21S	A6
Crystal Lake Dr					
17400	HMGN	60491	3422	16W-21S	A6
S Crystal Lake Dr					
17900	HMGN	60491	3422	16W-21S	A7
Crystal Lake Rd					
10	ALGN	60102	2693	35W-21N	E6
10	LIHL	60102	2693	35W-21N	E6
10	LIHL	60156	2693	35W-21N	E6
700	AlqT	60013	2642	30W-25N	A5
700	CRY	60013	2642	30W-25N	A5
1100	LIHL	60156	2694	35W-22N	A4
1400	AlqT	60013	2641	31W-25N	D4
1400	CRY	60013	2641	30W-25N	E5
2800	NndT	60013	2641	31W-25N	D4
E Crystal Lake Rd					
700	AlqT	60013	2642	29W-25N	B5
1000	CRY	60013	2642	29W-25N	B5
S Crystal Lake Rd					
100	MHRY	60050	2527	34W-31N	C7
300	NndT	60050	2527	34W-31N	D6
500	BLVY	60050	2584	34W-30N	B1
500	MHRY	60050	2584	34W-30N	B1
500	NndT	60050	2584	34W-30N	B1
1600	NndT	60012	2584	35W-29N	B3
2400	BLVY	60012	2584	35W-29N	B4
S Crystal Lake Rd CO-V34					
100	MHRY	60050	2527	34W-31N	C7
300	NndT	60050	2527	34W-31N	D6
500	BLVY	60050	2584	34W-30N	B1
500	MHRY	60050	2584	34W-30N	B1
500	NndT	60050	2584	34W-30N	B1
2300	NndT	60012	2584	35W-29N	B3
2400	BLVY	60012	2584	35W-29N	B4
W Crystal Lake Rd					
4000	MHRY	60050	2528	33W-32N	A4
4300	MHRY	60050	2527	33W-32N	E5
W Crystal Lake Rd CO-V34					
4000	MHRY	60050	2528	33W-32N	A4
4300	MHRY	60050	2527	33W-32N	E5
Crystal Lake Wy					
19900	FftT	60423	3503	11W-24S	E5
19900	FftT	60448	3503	11W-24S	E5
19900	FKFT	60423	3503	11W-24S	E5
Crystal Meadow Ct					
10800	ODPK	60462	3345	13W-17S	A6
10800	ODPK	60467	3345	13W-17S	A6
Crystal Point Dr					
500	CLLK	60014	2640	34W-24N	B6
Crystal Ridge Ct					
10800	ODPK	60462	3345	13W-17S	A5
10800	ODPK	60467	3345	13W-17S	A5
Crystal Ridge Dr					
10	CLLK	60012	2640	35W-26N	A2
10	CLLK	60014	2640	35W-26N	B2
300	CLLK	60012	2639	35W-26N	E2
400	NndT	60012	2639	35W-26N	E2
W Crystal Rock Ct					
1500	RLKB	60073	2474	25W-34N	B7
Crystal Rock Rd					
3000	NPVL	60564	3202	30W-11S	B7
Crystal Shore Ct					
1200	CLSM	60188	2967	27W-4N	B5
Crystal Shore Dr					
1100	CLSM	60188	2967	27W-4N	B5
Crystal Springs Ct					
500	LKZH	60047	2699	22W-21N	A6
600	FXLK	60041	2473	26W-34N	C7
14900	ODPK	60467	3345	13W-17S	A6
Crystal Springs Ln					
10800	ODPK	60462	3345	13W-17S	A6
10800	ODPK	60467	3345	13W-17S	A6
Crystal Springs Rd					
6300	BLVY	60012	2584	35W-29N	A4
6300	NndT	60012	2584	35W-29N	A4
6800	BLVY	60012	2583	35W-29N	E4
6800	NndT	60012	2583	36W-29N	D4
7600	NndT	60098	2583	36W-29N	D3
7700	BLVY	60098	2583	36W-29N	C3
8100	DrrT	60098	2583	37W-29N	B3
Crystal Tree Ct					
1900	GNVA	60134	3019	36W-0N	D6
Crystal Tree Dr					
14400	ODPK	60462	3345	13W-17S	B5
Cuba Rd					
-	CbaT	60010	2698	24W-21N	B6
23500	DRPK	60010	2698	24W-21N	C6
23500	LKZH	60010	2698	23W-21N	E6
23500	LKZH	60047	2698	23W-21N	E6
23700	ElaT	60010	2698	24W-21N	C6
Cuba Rd CO-A46					
-	CbaT	60010	2698	24W-21N	B6
23500	DRPK	60010	2698	24W-21N	C6
23500	LKZH	60010	2698	23W-21N	E6
23500	LKZH	60047	2698	23W-21N	E6
23700	ElaT	60010	2698	24W-21N	C6
E Cuba Rd					
-	LKZH	60047	2699	21W-22N	D5
21100	KLDR	60047	2699	21W-22N	D5
21100	LGGV	60047	2699	21W-22N	E5
W Cuba Rd					
10	BNHL	60010	2697	27W-21N	A6
10	CbaT	60010	2697	26W-21N	C6
100	LKZH	60010	2699	22W-21N	A6
100	LKZH	60047	2699	22W-21N	B6
400	DRPK	60010	2698	23W-21N	E6
400	LKZH	60010	2698	23W-21N	E6
400	LKZH	60047	2698	23W-21N	E6
500	BNHL	60010	2696	28W-21N	E5
500	CbaT	60010	2696	28W-21N	E5
500	LKBN	60010	2696	28W-21N	E5
3100	ElaT	60047	2700	19W-22N	D5
3100	LGGV	60047	2700	20W-22N	A5
3700	KLDR	60047	2700	20W-22N	A5
20700	LGGV	60047	2699	20W-22N	E5
21700	KLDR	60047	2699	22W-21N	C6
25200	CbaT	60010	2698	25W-21N	A6
27000	LKBN	60010	2697	26W-21N	C6
W Cuba Rd CO-A46					
100	LKZH	60010	2699	22W-21N	A6
100	LKZH	60047	2699	22W-21N	A6
400	DRPK	60010	2698	23W-21N	E6
400	LKZH	60010	2698	23W-21N	E6
400	LKZH	60047	2698	23W-21N	E6
25200	CbaT	60010	2698	25W-21N	A6
Cuhlman Rd					
2200	LKMR	60051	2529	29W-33N	C2
2200	MchT	60051	2529	29W-33N	C2
Cul de Sac Dr					
10	WynT	60185	2966	29W-2N	C7
Culham Ct					
1300	WHTN	60187	3082	23W-3S	E5
Cullen Ct					
8700	FKFT	60423	3504	10W-24S	B6
Cullen Dr					
8500	FKFT	60423	3504	10W-24S	B6
Cullerton St					
3000	FNPK	60131	2972	13W-3N	E4
3000	FNPK	60164	2972	13W-3N	E5
3000	LydT	60164	2972	13W-3N	E5
E Cullerton St					
10	CHCG	60616	3092	0E-1S	C1
W Cullerton St					
500	CHCG	60616	3092	0W-1S	A1
800	CHCG	60608	3091	1W-1S	E1
800	CHCG	60608	3092		E2
3000	CHCG	60623	3090	3W-1S	E1
Culligan Pkwy					
10	NfdT	60062	2809	12W-16N	B1
Culloden St					
3700	FSMR	60422	3506	4W-23S	D4
W Cullom Av					
-	NRDG	60706	2974	8W-5N	D1
900	CHCG	60613	2977	1W-5N	E1
1900	CHCG	60618	2977	3W-5N	A1
2800	CHCG	60618	2976	4W-5N	C1
4000	CHCG	60641	2976	5W-5N	A1
4800	CHCG	60641	2975	7W-5N	C1
5500	CHCG	60634	2975	7W-5N	B1
6800	HDHT	60706	2974	8W-5N	E1
7700	CHCG	60634	2974	9W-5N	C1
7700	NRDG	60634	2974	9W-5N	C1
Cullom St					
-	FDHT	60411	3509	1E-24S	B6
-	SRPK	60176	2973	11W-5N	C1
Culpepper Dr					
1400	NPVL	60540	3142	24W-7S	C7
1400	NPVL	60540	3204	25W-7S	C1
1500	LslT	60540	3142	24W-7S	C7
Culver Ct					
2100	JLET	60586	3416	29W-21S	C7
Culver Ln					
1700	GNVW	60025	2810	8W-12N	D7
2800	WCHI	60185	2965	32W-4N	C4
Culver Rd					
10	OswT	60538	3263	37W-11S	D1
Culver St					
3300	EVTN	60201	2812	4W-12N	B7
5000	SKOK	60077	2811	6W-12N	E7
9500	MaiT	60016	2809	11W-12N	C7
W Culver St					
23100	PNFD	60544	3416	28W-19S	E2
23100	PnfT	60544	3416	28W-19S	E2
Culzean Ln					
10	IVNS	60067	2805	22W-16N	A1
Cumberland Av					
200	KLWH	60043	2812	4W-14N	C4
1400	NfdT	60062	2756	12W-17N	B6
1400	NHBK	60062	2756	12W-17N	B6
N Cumberland Av					
-	CHCG	60068	2918	10W-7N	A4
10	PKRG	60068	2864	10W-9N	A7
10	PKRG	60068	2918	8W-8N	D1
1000	NLES	60068	2864	10W-10N	A5
1000	NLES	60714	2864	10W-10N	A5
3200	RVGV	60171	2974	10W-4N	A4
3200	RVGV	60634	2974	10W-4N	A4
3700	CHCG	60634	2974	10W-5N	A2
4200	CHCG	60656	2974	10W-5N	A2
4200	CHCG	60706	2974	10W-5N	A2
4200	NRDG	60706	2974	10W-5N	A2
4500	CHCG	60656	2918	10W-6N	A5
4500	CHCG	60706	2918	10W-6N	A6
4500	NRDG	60706	2918	10W-6N	A6
4600	NRDG	60656	2918	10W-6N	A6
5500	CHCG	60631	2918	10W-6N	A5
8400	MaiT	60714	2864	10W-10N	A5
N Cumberland Av SR-171					
-	CHCG	60068	2918	10W-7N	A4
-	PKRG	60068	2918	10W-7N	A4
3200	RVGV	60171	2974	10W-4N	A4
3200	RVGV	60634	2974	10W-4N	A4
3700	CHCG	60634	2974	10W-5N	A2
4200	CHCG	60656	2974	10W-5N	A2
4200	CHCG	60706	2974	10W-5N	A2
4200	NRDG	60706	2974	10W-5N	A2
4500	CHCG	60656	2918	10W-6N	A6
4500	CHCG	60706	2918	10W-6N	A6
4500	NRDG	60706	2918	10W-6N	A6
4600	NRDG	60656	2918	10W-6N	A6
5500	CHCG	60631	2918	10W-6N	A5
S Cumberland Av					
10	PKRG	60068	2918	10W-8N	A2
1800	CHCG	60068	2918	10W-7N	A4
1800	CHCG	60631	2918	10W-7N	A4
Cumberland Cir					
2400	LGGV	60047	2700	19W-20N	C7
N Cumberland Cir					
1100	MHRY	60050	2527	33W-33N	E3
W Cumberland Cir					
4700	MHRY	60050	2527	33W-33N	E3
Cumberland Cir E					
1300	EGVV	60007	2914	19W-8N	D3
Cumberland Cir W					
1300	EGVV	60007	2914	19W-8N	C3
Cumberland Ct					
10	CRY	60013	2695	32W-23N	C1
200	GRNE	60031	2535	14W-34N	C1
800	NPVL	60565	3204	25W-10S	B5
900	BFGV	60089	2701	16W-21N	C5
900	CLSM	60188	2967	27W-3N	C5
900	ROSL	60172	2913	22W-8N	C3
1000	VNHL	60061	2647	17W-26N	C3
E Cumberland Ct					
24200	CteT	60417	3687	4E-29S	C1
Cumberland Dr					
10	LNSH	60069	2702	14W-22N	C3
10	SMBG	60194	2858	25W-10N	B5
1300	JLET	60431	3495	32W-21S	C1
1600	JLET	60586	3495	32W-21S	C1
1800	JLET	60586	3415	32W-21S	C7
7300	HRPK	60133	2911	26W-9N	E1
Cumberland Ln					
200	LKWD	60014	2639	36W-25N	C6
300	CLLK	60014	2639	36W-25N	C6
400	BGBK	60440	3268	24W-12S	E2
900	BFGV	60089	2701	16W-21N	D7
E Cumberland Ln					
3300	CteT	60417	3687	4E-29S	C1
Cumberland Pkwy					
1400	ALGN	60102	2695	32W-20N	A7
1400	ALGN	60102	2748	32W-20N	B1
N Cumberland Pkwy					
10	DSPN	60016	2862	14W-12N	C2
S Cumberland Pkwy					
10	DSPN	60016	2862	14W-11N	C2
Cumberland Rd					
1000	AURA	60504	3201	32W-9S	B5
Cumberland St					
600	HFET	60169	2859	23W-11N	A4
Cumberland Tr					
500	ELGN	60123	2854	36W-12N	A2
500	ROSL	60172	2913	22W-8N	C3
3200	OMFD	60461	3506	4W-24S	E5
3200	OMFD	60461	3507	3W-24S	A5
Cumberland Green Dr					
1700	SCRL	60174	3020	34W-2N	E2
1700	SCRL	60174	3021	33W-2N	A1
Cumberland Green Pkwy					
1900	SCRL	60174	3021	33W-2N	A1
Cumberland Trails					
-	DMND	60416	3941	33W-39S	A2
Cummings Av					
500	WKGN	60085	2537	10W-33N	A3
700	KLWH	60043	2812	4W-14N	C4
700	NtrT	60093	2812	4W-14N	C4
900	WKGN	60085	2536	11W-33N	E3
Cummings Dr					
100	BRLT	60103	2909	32W-8N	C3
Cummings Ln					
2000	FSMR	60422	3507	2W-22S	C2
Cummings St					
-	HTLY	60142	2691	40W-22N	E4
Cummins St					
-	PLNO	60545	3260	45W-14S	C7
-	YKVL	60545	3260	45W-14S	C7
Cumnock Rd					
300	IVNS	60067	2751	23W-16N	E7
700	MTSN	60443	3506	4W-25S	D6
700	OMFD	60461	3506	4W-25S	D6
Cumnor Av					
100	MltT	60137	3025	21W-0N	D5
400	GNEN	60137	3025	21W-0N	D4
600	BRTN	60010	2750	26W-20N	D1
700	BRTN	60010	2697	26W-20N	D7
700	CbaT	60010	2697	26W-20N	D7
N Cumnor Av					
20700	BRTN	60010	2697	26W-20N	D7
20700	CbaT	60010	2697	26W-20N	D7
Cumnor Ct					
400	DRFD	60015	2704	10W-21N	A6
Cumnor Rd					
10	DGvT	60516	3206	18W-9S	E3
10	DRGV	60515	3144	18W-5S	E2
10	DRGV	60559	3144	18W-5S	E2
10	DRN	60561	3206	18W-9S	E3
10	WTMT	60515	3144	18W-5S	E2
200	KLWH	60043	2812	4W-14N	C4
200	WLMT	60043	2812	3W-14N	D4
200	WLMT	60091	2812	3W-14N	D4
3800	DGvT	60515	3084	18W-4S	E7
3800	DRGV	60515	3084	18W-4S	E7
3800	OKBK	60523	3084	18W-4S	E7
3800	YkTp	60515	3084	18W-4S	E7
3800	YkTp	60523	3084	18W-4S	E7
4300	WTMT	60515	3084	18W-4S	E7
4300	WTMT	60559	3084	18W-4S	E7
5400	DRGV	60516	3144	18W-6S	E3
5900	WTMT	60516	3144	18W-6S	E5
5900	WTMT	60559	3144	18W-6S	E5
S Cumnor Rd					
1000	WTMT	60516	3144	18W-6S	E5
1000	WTMT	60559	3144	18W-6S	E5
Cunat Blvd					
100	RHMD	60071	2412	33W-40N	D3
Cunat Ct					
1300	LIHL	60156	2694	34W-22N	B4
Cuneo Dr					
7300	BtnT	60081	2414	29W-39N	D5
7300	FXLK	60081	2414	29W-39N	D5
Cunningham Cir					
1100	EGVV	60007	2913	21W-8N	E2
W Cunningham Ct					
17000	GRNE	60048	2534	17W-33N	C3
17000	WrnT	60048	2534	17W-33N	C3
Cunningham Dr					
100	BMDL	60108	2969	23W-4N	A3
200	PKFT	60466	3595	3W-26S	B3
700	ANTH	60002	2357	23W-42N	E6
1200	CTCY	60409	3429	3E-19S	E7
E Cunningham Dr					
10	PLTN	60067	2752	20W-17N	E5
100	PLTN	60067	2753	20W-17N	A5
200	PLTN	60074	2753	20W-17N	A5
W Cunningham Dr					
10	PLTN	60067	2752	21W-17N	D5
Cunningham Ln					
10	PKFT	60466	3595	3W-26S	B3
100	BMDL	60108	2969	23W-4N	A3
1600	CLLK	60014	2693	36W-22N	C3
Cupola Ct					
7100	AlqT	60013	2642	29W-24N	C6
Curling Pond Ct					
400	CmpT	60119	2962	40W-3N	B6
400	CmpT	60175	2962	40W-3N	B6

STREET Block	City	ZIP	Map#	CGS	Grid
Curling Pond Ct					
3400	NndT	60012	2583	35W-28N	E5
Curling Pond Rd					
300	WYNE	60184	2964	33W-5N	E2
300	WYNE	60184	2965	33W-5N	A2
Curran Ct					
2700	DRN	60561	3206	19W-9S	C3
Curran Pl					
900	ANTH	60002	2357	24W-42N	B5
Curran Rd					
500	RDLK	60073	2532	23W-32N	A5
N Curran Rd					
900	MchT	60050	2527	34W-33N	B3
900	MHRY	60050	2527	34W-33N	B3
32000	RDLK	60073	2531	23W-32N	E5
33100	RDLK	60073	2532	23W-32N	A4
S Curran Rd					
100	MchT	60050	2527	35W-32N	B5
100	MHRY	60050	2527	35W-31N	B6
100	NndT	60050	2527	35W-31N	B6
400	RDLK	60073	2532	23W-32N	A4
400	RLKP	60073	2532	23W-32N	A4
Currant Av					
8400	TYPK	60487	3424	10W-19S	B3
Currant Dr					
-	JLET	60431	3495	33W-22S	A1
-	JLET	60447	3495	33W-22S	A1
Current Ct					
10	PltT	60124	2852	41W-9N	A7
Curricle Rd					
10	WLNG	60090	2754	15W-20N	E2
10	WLNG	60090	2755	15W-18N	A2
Curry Ct					
200	AURA	60506	3138	35W-6S	A6
Curtins Ct					
12400	NlxT	60448	3502	15W-23S	B3
Curtis Av					
10	WNVL	60555	3080	28W-4S	E7
200	NPVL	60555	3140	28W-4S	E1
200	NPVL	60563	3140	28W-4S	E1
200	WNVL	60555	3140	28W-4S	E1
200	WNVL	60563	3140	28W-4S	E1
300	WNVL	60555	3081	28W-3S	A6
400	JLET	60435	3498	25W-22S	C2
W Curtis Av					
1100	JLET	60435	3498	25W-22S	B2
Curtis Ct					
200	BDWD	60408	3942	31W-41S	A5
Curtis Ln					
300	WldT	60564	3202	28W-10S	E6
5200	HRPK	60133	2911	27W-6N	C6
E Curtis Sq					
600	BbyT	60134	3018	39W-0N	E4
W Curtis Sq					
300	BbyT	60134	3018	39W-0N	E4
Curtis St					
-	DMND	60416	3941	33W-39S	C2
2800	DSPN	60018	2917	12W-8N	B2
Curtiss Av					
500	MltT	60190	3023	26W-0S	D6
Curtiss St					
800	DRGV	60515	3144	19W-5S	C3
1900	DRGV	60515	3143	21W-5S	D3
Curtmar Ct					
10	OswT	60538	3199	37W-10S	C7
Curve Ct					
5200	MchT	60050	2472	29W-37N	C2
Cushing Ln					
2400	AURA	60503	3201	33W-11S	B7
Custer Av					
100	CHCG	60202	2867	2W-9N	B6
100	CHCG	60626	2867	2W-9N	B6
100	CHCG	60645	2867	2W-9N	B6
1000	EVTN	60202	2867	2W-10N	B4
3900	BKFD	60513	3088	11W-4S	A7
3900	BKFD	60534	3088	11W-4S	A7
3900	LYNS	60513	3088	10W-4S	A6
3900	LYNS	60534	3088	11W-4S	A7
4500	BKFD	60513	3148	10W-4S	A1
4500	BKFD	60534	3148	10W-4S	A1
4500	LYNS	60513	3148	10W-4S	A1
4500	LYNS	60534	3148	10W-4S	A1
4500	MCCK	60513	3148	10W-4S	A1
4500	MCCK	60525	3148	10W-4S	A1
4500	MCCK	60534	3148	10W-4S	A1
Custer Ct					
500	WLNG	60090	2754	16W-17N	D5
7300	FXLK	60020	2415	28W-39N	A5
E Custer St					
10	LMNT	60439	3270	19W-14S	D6
W Custer St					
10	LMNT	60439	3270	19W-14S	C6
N Cutcheon Ter					
-	CHCG	60640	2921	1W-6N	E6
Cutler Ct					
-	BCHR	60401	3774	0W-35S	D5
Cutler St					
400	SCRL	60174	3020	35W-2N	A1
N Cutter Av					
1000	JLET	60432	3499	22W-22S	C1
1300	JltT	60432	3499	22W-22S	C1
1300	LktT	60432	3499	22W-22S	C1
Cutter Ln					
100	LKBN	60010	2642	28W-24N	E7
100	LKBN	60010	2643	28W-24N	A7
600	EGVV	60007	2913	22W-8N	D1
600	EGVV	60193	2913	22W-8N	D1
700	CbaT	60013	2642	28W-24N	E7
Cutters Run					
10	BrnT	60010	2803	27W-13N	A6
10	SBTN	60010	2803	27W-13N	A6
Cutters Mill Ct					
700	SMBG	60194	2858	25W-11N	B4
Cutters Mill Ln					
400	SMBG	60194	2858	25W-11N	B4
Cuttingham Ct					
2600	RGMW	60008	2806	19W-12N	C7
E Cuttriss St					
10	PKRG	60068	2864	9W-9N	C6
200	NLES	60714	2864	9W-9N	C6
200	PKRG	60714	2864	9W-9N	C6
W Cuttriss St					
200	PKRG	60068	2864	10W-9N	B6
Cutwood Ln					
900	CmpT	60175	2906	39W-6N	D6
Cuyahoga Dr					
900	BRLT	60103	2910	29W-6N	D6
Cuyahoga Ter					
100	WynT	60185	2966	29W-3N	D6
300	WynT	60103	2966	29W-5N	D2
Cuyler Av					
-	NHBK	60062	2758	7W-17N	A6
1200	BRWN	60304	3031	7W-1S	B7
1200	BRWN	60402	3031	7W-1S	B7
1200	OKPK	60304	3031	7W-1S	B7
1500	BRWN	60402	3089	7W-2S	B3
Cuyler Av					
3800	SKNY	60402	3089	7W-3S	B6
N Cuyler Av					
100	OKPK	60302	3031	7W-0N	B3
S Cuyler Av					
500	OKPK	60302	3031	7W-0S	B5
500	OKPK	60304	3031	7W-0S	B5
1100	BRWN	60304	3031	7W-0S	B7
1100	BRWN	60402	3031	7W-0S	B7
W Cuyler Av					
900	CHCG	60613	2977	1W-5N	E1
2000	CHCG	60618	2977	2W-5N	B1
3300	CHCG	60618	2976	4W-5N	D1
4600	CHCG	60641	2976	5W-5N	A1
4900	CHCG	60641	2975	6W-5N	E1
6200	CHCG	60634	2975	7W-5N	A1
Cuyler Av N					
800	OKPK	60302	3031	7W-1N	A2
Cyndi Ct					
1900	RGMW	60008	2806	18W-13N	D6
Cynthia Av					
1400	PKRG	60068	2863	10W-9N	E6
21500	SLVL	60411	3597	2E-26S	C2
Cynthia Ct					
100	WNVL	60555	3080	30W-3S	B5
16600	TYPK	60477	3424	10W-19S	B3
Cynthia Dr					
400	WNVL	60555	3080	30W-2S	B4
Cynthia Ln					
600	GLHT	60139	2969	22W-2N	C7
900	LIHL	60156	2694	34W-21N	C5
1400	HRPK	60133	2857	26W-9N	E7
13700	NlxT	60448	3421	17W-22S	D7
13700	NlxT	60448	3501	17W-22S	C1
Cypress Av					
10	FXLK	60020	2473	27W-36N	B4
500	BTVA	60510	3020	36W-0S	A7
500	BTVA	60510	3078	36W-0S	A1
1400	HRPK	60133	2911	26W-8N	D2
17500	CCHL	60478	3426	5W-21S	C6
18600	CCHL	60478	3506	5W-22S	D1
20100	LYWD	60411	3510	3E-23S	B4
Cypress Cir					
5300	GRNE	60031	2478	14W-35N	B5
S Cypress Cir					
16400	LKPT	60441	3342	20W-18S	B7
Cypress Ct					
10	LIHL	60156	2693	37W-21N	C5
10	PLTN	60067	2752	20W-17N	E4
200	WDDL	60191	2971	17W-5N	C2
400	SMBG	60193	2858	23W-9N	E6
800	JLET	60435	3497	26W-22S	D3
800	ROSL	60172	2913	23W-6N	B6
1500	HFET	60169	2858	25W-12N	B2
1500	HRPK	60133	2911	26W-8N	E2
2100	MTGY	60538	3198	40W-10S	C5
3000	BFGV	60089	2701	17W-23N	B2
3100	MHRY	60050	2528	32W-33N	C2
4000	CCHL	60478	3506	5W-23S	C2
4800	RNPK	60471	3594	6W-27S	A4
4900	BmnT	60452	3426	6W-20S	A4
4900	OKFT	60452	3426	6W-20S	A4
5000	HLSD	60162	3028	14W-0N	D4
5100	LSLE	60532	3142	24W-5S	D3
6700	NndT	60012	2640	35W-27N	A1
8900	ODPK	60462	3346	11W-17S	A6
9000	TYPK	60487	3424	11W-21S	A5
9300	MaiT	60016	2863	11W-12N	D1
W Cypress Ct					
21100	DPgT	60544	3339	26W-15S	E2
Cypress Dr					
-	BHPK	60099	2421	12W-40N	C3
-	LMNT	60439	3342	19W-15S	C2
-	ZION	60099	2421	12W-40N	C3
10	MltT	60137	3083	22W-3S	C5
100	BGBK	60440	3269	23W-12S	B2
100	SMWD	60107	2857	28W-10N	A5
500	NPVL	60540	3203	27W-8S	C1
900	AURA	60506	3137	38W-6S	B5
1200	WLNG	60090	2754	16W-18N	E3
3400	SPGV	60081	2354	32W-42N	B7
4800	HLSD	60162	3028	14W-0N	D4
7800	MchT	60097	2469	36W-37N	C2
19100	CCHL	60478	3506	5W-23S	D3
N Cypress Dr					
10	BtlT	60512	3198	40W-11S	B7
S Cypress Dr					
10	BtlT	60512	3198	40W-11S	B7
1000	MPPT	60056	2861	16W-11N	D3
W Cypress Dr					
900	ANHT	60005	2860	18W-12N	E1
Cypress Ln					
-	PNFD	60585	3337	33W-15S	A2
10	CTSD	60525	3147	12W-7S	B6
10	WNFD	60190	3023	27W-1N	D3
200	LYVL	60048	2591	16W-27N	D7
700	CLSM	60188	2967	28W-3N	B6
800	JLET	60435	3497	26W-22S	D2
1000	EGVV	60007	2914	18W-8N	E2
1000	CTHL	60403	3417	27W-21S	D6
1100	LynT	60458	3209	11W-8S	D2
1600	YKVL	60560	3260	44W-14S	D7
1900	NHBK	60062	2757	10W-16N	A7
N Cypress Ln					
10	NARA	60542	3077	37W-4S	D7
S Cypress Ln					
10	NARA	60542	3137	37W-4S	D1
12900	PSHT	60463	3346	9W-15S	D1
W Cypress Ln					
21100	DPgT	60544	3339	26W-15S	E2
N Cypress Pt					
2900	WKGN	60083	2478	14W-37N	C2
Cypress Rd					
26800	AxST	60410	3672	33W-31S	B6
26800	CNHN	60410	3672	33W-31S	B6
Cypress Sq					
10	ELGN	60123	2854	35W-12N	B2
Cypress St					
600	WKGN	60085	2537	10W-33N	A3
E Cypress St					
10	ANHT	60005	2807	17W-12N	B7
W Cypress St					
10	ANHT	60005	2807	18W-12N	A7
400	ANHT	60005	2806	18W-12N	E7
Cypress Bridge Rd					
500	LKZH	60047	2699	22W-21N	A6
Cypress Point Ct					
500	RVWD	60015	2756	12W-20N	B1
N Cypress Pointe Dr					
1500	VNHL	60061	2647	17W-27N	B2
Cyprus Cir					
400	LKVL	60046	2474	23W-36N	E4
Cyprus Rd					
15300	MKHM	60426	3348	4W-18S	E7
15300	MKHM	60428	3348	4W-18S	E7
S Cyril Av					
7100	CHCG	60649	3153	2E-8S	C7
Cyrus Dr					
-	SRGV	60554	3136	41W-7S	A6
Czacki St					
500	LMNT	60439	3270	19W-14S	E6
Czech Ter					
3900	BKFD	60513	3088	10W-4S	A6
3900	LYNS	60513	3088	10W-4S	A6
Czerkies Blvd					
-	JLET	60586	3495	33W-22S	B2
D					
D Ct					
9900	MKNA	60448	3503	12W-23S	D4
D Rd					
-	WnfT	60510	3079	32W-1S	C3
D St					
10	NCHI	60044	2594	10W-30N	A2
10	NCHI	60088	2594	10W-30N	A2
600	NCHI	60044	2593	10W-30N	E2
600	NCHI	60088	2593	10W-30N	E2
3200	HIWD	60037	2704	9W-23N	D1
3300	HIWD	60040	2704	9W-23N	D1
W D St					
-	MYWD	60153	3088	10W-1S	A1
-	PvsT	60141	3088	10W-1S	A1
-	PvsT	60153	3088	10W-1S	A1
Dacy St					
300	WDSK	60098	2524	42W-31N	C7
Dada Dr					
-	GRNE	60046	2476	18W-35N	D6
-	WrnT	60046	2476	18W-35N	D6
6500	GRNE	60031	2477	18W-35N	A6
7500	GRNE	60031	2476	18W-35N	E6
Dadeon St					
-	BDWD	60408	3942	31W-41S	B5
W Dady Ct					
18500	WrnT	60030	2533	18W-33N	E2
Dady Pl					
400	WKGN	60085	2537	10W-33N	A3
Daffodil Ct					
-	DYR	46311	3510		C5
-	LYWD	60411	3510		C5
1700	HDPK	60035	2704	10W-23N	A3
Daffodil Dr					
300	RMVL	60446	3339	26W-17S	D7
2200	CTHL	60403	3417	27W-21S	D6
Daffodil Ln					
300	MTSN	60443	3593	7W-26S	D2
S Daffodil Ln					
25600	MONE	60449	3683	5W-31S	C5
Daggets Ct					
4800	NPVL	60564	3266	29W-12S	E4
Daggett Av					
100	LKPT	60441	3419	22W-20S	C4
Dahlgren St					
-	NCHI	60088	2594	10W-31N	A1
Dahlia Ct					
100	RGMW	60008	2805	21W-13N	D5
1600	RMVL	60446	3339	26W-17S	D6
Dahlia Dr					
100	RMVL	60446	3339	26W-17S	D6
7300	HRPK	60133	2911	27W-9N	C1
E Dahlia Ln					
10	RLKB	60073	2475	22W-36N	A4
W Dahlia Ln					
10	RLKB	60073	2475	23W-36N	A4
Dahlstrom Ct					
500	BTVA	60510	3078	34W-2S	D3
Dahringer Rd					
10	WKGN	60085	2480	9W-35N	C7
Daiquiri Dr					
2600	RVWD	60015	2755	13W-20N	E1
Dairy Ln					
900	IVNS	60067	2751	23W-17N	E5
1200	CRTE	60417	3685	0W-29S	C2
1200	MDLN	60060	2590	19W-29N	D5
7400	LKWD	60014	2638	38W-24N	D7
Dairyherd Ln					
700	CmpT	60175	2906	39W-6N	D6
Dairyman Cir					
4300	NPVL	60564	3266	29W-12S	D3
Daisy Av					
2200	GNVW	60025	2810	9W-14N	C4
E Daisy Cir					
200	RMVL	60446	3339	26W-17S	E6
W Daisy Cir					
200	RMVL	60446	3339	26W-17S	E6
Daisy Ct					
-	DrrT	60098	2525	40W-31N	A7
1500	RMVL	60446	3339	26W-17S	E6
N Daisy Ct					
200	PNFD	60544	3337	31W-18S	E7
Daisy Ln					
-	BmdT	60172	2912	24W-6N	D6
-	ROSL	60172	2912	24W-6N	D6
500	RLKB	60073	2475	22W-35N	B6
1100	NPVL	60564	3203	28W-10S	B6
2500	CTHL	60403	3417	27W-21S	D6
4600	NndT	60012	2639	35W-27N	E1
Daisy Mdws					
100	BRRG	60527	3146	14W-6S	C5
Daisy St					
1600	AURA	60505	3139	33W-5S	A3
W Dakin St					
800	CHCG	60613	2977	1W-4N	E2
2500	CHCG	60618	2976	3W-4N	E2
2500	CHCG	60618	2977	3W-4N	A2
3900	CHCG	60641	2976	4W-4N	B2
5500	CHCG	60641	2975	7W-4N	C2
6400	CHCG	60634	2975	8W-4N	A2
6600	CHCG	60634	2974	8W-4N	E2
Dakota Cir					
900	NPVL	60563	3141	26W-4S	E2
900	NPVL	60563	3142	26W-4S	A2
Dakota Ct					
200	BGBK	60440	3268	23W-12S	E3
300	RLKB	60073	2474	23W-35N	E5
400	CLSM	60188	2967	27W-2N	C7
Dakota Dr					
-	SenT	60098	2581	43W-30N	A2
1000	WDSK	60098	2581	43W-30N	A2
1200	ELGN	60120	2801	32W-12N	C7
1300	BtlT	60560	3261	41W-14S	E7
1300	YKVL	60560	3261	41W-14S	E7
1600	EGVV	60007	2913	21W-8N	D2
5300	MchT	60072	2470	34W-37N	C2
5300	RGWD	60072	2470	34W-37N	C2
Dakota Ln					
7800	ODPK	60462	3346	9W-16S	C2
Dakota Rd					
2300	WKGN	60087	2479	11W-36N	C4
Dakota Rdg					
-	JNBG	60050	2472	30W-37N	A1
-	MchT	60050	2472	30W-37N	A1
1900	JNBG	60050	2471	31W-37N	E1
Dakota St					
500	CLLK	60012	2640	34W-26N	D2
Dakota Tr					
400	WLNG	60090	2754	16W-17N	D5
Dakota Fields Dr					
13300	HTLY	60142	2744	43W-19N	B2
Dakota Ridge Ct					
6300	JLET	60586	3415	31W-21S	D7
Dale Av					
-	WCHI	60185	3022	29W-0S	D6
-	WnfT	60185	3022	29W-0S	D6
200	ANHT	60004	2807	16W-15N	D2
200	PTHT	60004	2807	16W-15N	D2
200	PTHT	60070	2807	16W-15N	D2
1700	HDPK	60035	2705	8W-22N	A4
N Dale Av					
200	MPPT	60056	2807	16W-13N	D6
300	ANHT	60056	2807	16W-13N	D6
300	MHRY	60050	2528	32W-32N	B5
1100	PTHT	60004	2807	16W-15N	D3
1100	PTHT	60056	2807	16W-15N	D3
1100	PTHT	60070	2807	16W-15N	D3
1100	WhlT	60004	2807	16W-15N	D3
1800	ANHT	60004	2807	16W-15N	D1
38700	WDWH	60083	2421	13W-38N	A6
S Dale Av					
300	ANHT	60004	2807	16W-13N	D6
300	ANHT	60056	2807	16W-13N	D6
300	MPPT	60004	2807	16W-13N	D6
300	MPPT	60056	2807	16W-13N	D6
W Dale Av					
900	MchT	60051	2529	29W-32N	B5
Dale Cir					
1500	JLET	60586	3496	30W-22S	A1
Dale Ct					
600	AddT	60106	2971	17W-3N	C4
1800	SPGV	60081	2355	30W-41N	A7
Dale Dr					
1300	HnrT	60120	2855	31W-12N	E2
3400	CRTE	60417	3597	1E-28S	B6
W Dale Dr					
300	ADSN	60101	2970	18W-3N	E5
Dale Rd					
-	HMGN	60491	3422	15W-21S	B7
100	GLHT	60139	2969	23W-4N	A4
300	ADSN	60101	2970	18W-3N	E6
6700	DRN	60527	3145	16W-7S	D7
6700	DRN	60561	3145	16W-7S	D7
6700	WLBK	60527	3145	16W-7S	D7
6700	WLBK	60561	3145	16W-7S	D7
W Dale Rd					
1300	AddT	60101	2970	20W-4N	B4
1300	ADSN	60101	2970	20W-4N	B4
Dale St					
10	GNVW	60025	2811	6W-13N	D7
2400	DSPN	60018	2917	12W-8N	A1
Dalewood Av					
200	WDDL	60191	2914	18W-6N	E7
200	WDDL	60191	2970	19W-5N	C1
Dalewood Ct					
2100	JLET	60586	3416	29W-21S	E6
2200	WDRG	60517	3205	21W-8S	E2
Dalewood Dr					
4100	JLET	60586	3416	29W-21S	E6
Dalewood Ln					
500	HNDL	60521	3146	14W-5S	C2
Dalewood Pkwy					
2200	WDRG	60517	3205	21W-8S	E2
N Daley St					
10	DMND	60416	3941	33W-39S	C2
Dalhart Av					
400	RMVL	60446	3340	23W-15S	E1
Dallas Dr					
100	BRLT	60103	2909	32W-8N	D3
Dallas Pl					
1800	JltT	60433	3587	23W-26S	A2
E Dallas St					
200	WTMT	60559	3145	17W-5S	B3
W Dallas St					
-	DRGV	60515	3145	18W-5S	A3
-	WTMT	60515	3145	18W-5S	A3
10	WTMT	60559	3145	18W-5S	A3
W Dalphon Ct					
12300	HMGN	60491	3344	15W-16S	B4
Dalton Av					
200	MDLN	60060	2590	18W-28N	E7
Dalton Ct					
10	SBTN	60010	2803	26W-14N	C3
Dalton Dr					
400	RDLK	60073	2531	23W-31N	E6
9700	HTLY	60142	2692	38W-22N	D4
S Dalton Dr					
1300	RDLK	60073	2531	23W-31N	D7
Dalton Ln					
400	ROSL	60172	2912	24W-6N	D6
700	BGBK	60490	3267	26W-14S	E7
900	BGBK	60490	3268	26W-14S	A7
Dalton Pl					
600	NHBK	60062	2757	8W-17N	E5
Daly Av					
-	BtnT	60081	2414	29W-39N	D5
-	FXLK	60081	2414	29W-39N	D5
Daly Ln					
-	JLET	60586	3415	32W-21S	C7
Daly Rd					
1000	MltT	60187	3024	23W-0N	E4
1000	WHTN	60187	3024	23W-0N	E4
1400	WHTN	60187	3025	23W-0N	A4
Dam W					
10000	WhlT	60090	2755	13W-17N	E6
Damascus Av					
2800	ZION	60099	2422	9W-40N	C4
Damen Av					
16100	MKHM	60428	3427	2W-19S	D2
N Damen Av					
10	CHCG	60612	3033	2W-0N	C4
300	CHCG	60622	3033	2W-0N	C4
1500	CHCG	60647	3033	2W-1N	B1
1600	CHCG	60622	2977	2W-2N	B7
1600	CHCG	60647	2977	2W-2N	B7
1900	CHCG	60614	2977	2W-2N	B7
2600	CHCG	60618	2977	2W-2N	B7
2800	CHCG	60657	2977	2W-3N	B4
3500	CHCG	60613	2977	2W-2N	B7
4400	CHCG	60613	2921	2W-5N	B7
4400	CHCG	60618	2921	2W-5N	B7
4400	CHCG	60625	2921	2W-6N	B6
4400	CHCG	60640	2921	2W-6N	B6
6000	CHCG	60659	2921	2W-7N	B3
6000	CHCG	60660	2921	2W-7N	B3
6400	CHCG	60645	2921	2W-8N	B2
7000	CHCG	60626	2921	2W-8N	B1
7200	CHCG	60626	2867	2W-9N	B7
7200	CHCG	60645	2867	2W-9N	B7
7500	CHCG	60202	2867	2W-9N	B7
7500	EVTN	60202	2867	2W-9N	B7
S Damen Av					
10	CHCG	60612	3033	2W-0S	C5
1100	CHCG	60608	3033	2W-1S	C7
1400	CHCG	60608	3091	2W-4S	C7
4300	CHCG	60609	3091	2W-4S	C7
4300	CHCG	60609	3151	2W-5S	B1
5500	CHCG	60636	3151	2W-6S	C3
7500	CHCG	60620	3213	2W-9S	C3
9500	CHCG	60643	3213	2W-11S	C7
Damico Dr					
800	CHHT	60411	3507	2W-25S	D7
Damien Dr					
-	CbaT	60010	2697	28W-22N	A4
-	LKBN	60010	2696	28W-22N	E4
-	LKBN	60010	2697	28W-22N	A4
Damisch Rd					
10	PGGV	60140	2798	40W-14N	B6
10	RtdT	60140	2798	40W-14N	B6
Damisch Rd CO-7					
10	PGGV	60140	2798	40W-14N	B6
10	RtdT	60140	2798	40W-14N	B6
Damon St					
300	MRGO	60152	2634	49W-26N	B3
Dam Woods					
10000	WhlT	60062	2755	13W-17N	E4
10000	WhlT	60090	2755	13W-17N	E4
10000	WLNG	60062	2755	13W-17N	E4
10000	WLNG	60090	2755	13W-17N	E4
Dana Av					
2600	WKGN	60087	2479	12W-36N	C3
Dana Ct					
100	SMBG	60193	2913	23W-9N	A1
600	NPVL	60563	3141	27W-5S	C3
1000	ANTH	60002	2358	20W-41N	E7
4000	NHBK	60062	2756	12W-17N	B4
Dana Dr					
-	ELGN	60177	2854	34W-9N	E7
-	SEGN	60177	2854	34W-9N	E7
Dana Ln					
400	BNHL	60010	2750	27W-18N	B3
500	SMWD	60107	2857	28W-11N	B4
Dana Pt					
1700	ALGN	60102	2748	34W-19N	A3
Dana St					
23800	CmgT	60033	2405	52W-38N	A7
Dana Wy					
7800	BRRG	60527	3208	14W-8S	D2
Danada Ct					
1300	LSLE	60532	3082	25W-4S	B7
1300	LSLE	60563	3082	25W-4S	B7
1300	LslT	60563	3082	25W-4S	B7
1300	MltT	60563	3082	25W-3S	B7
1300	NPVL	60563	3082	25W-4S	B7
Danada Dr					
10	WHTN	60187	3082	24W-2S	C4
Danada Sq E					
10	MltT	60187	3082	24W-2S	D4
10	WHTN	60187	3082	24W-2S	C4
Danada Sq W					
10	MltT	60187	3082	24W-2S	C4
10	WHTN	60187	3082	24W-2S	C5
Danbury Cir					
5300	LIHL	60156	2692	39W-23N	C2
Danbury Ct					
10	LIHL	60156	2692	39W-23N	C2
10	SEGN	60177	2908	35W-8N	B3
400	SMBG	60193	2912	24W-9N	E1
2300	GNVA	60134	3019	36W-1N	D4
5200	LGGV	60047	2701	17W-22N	A4
14100	LktT	60544	3339	26W-16S	E4
S Danbury Ct					
100	LKFT	60045	2649	13W-25N	A4
Danbury Dr					
10	WNVL	60555	3080	30W-2S	C4
200	NPVL	60565	3203	26W-10S	D5
200	VNHL	60061	2647	17W-24N	B7
400	CLSM	60188	2967	26W-3N	E7
400	MltT	60137	3083	21W-2S	D4
500	OSWG	60543	3263	37W-14S	C6
2400	WDRG	60517	3143	21W-7S	E7
7700	DRN	60561	3206	19W-8S	D2
13900	LktT	60544	3339	26W-16S	E4
E Danbury Dr					
1000	CRY	60013	2641	32W-24N	B7
W Danbury Dr					
500	CRY	60013	2641	32W-24N	B7
Danbury Ln					
1300	DSPN	60018	2862	15W-10N	B6
8800	ODPK	60462	3346	11W-18S	A7
Danbury Pl					
2000	HFET	60169	2858	25W-12N	B1
Danbury Cove					
200	WPHR	60096	2363	10W-43N	A5
Danby Ct					
5900	HRPK	60133	2911	27W-7N	D5
Danby Dr					
700	MltT	60137	3083	21W-1S	D2
Danby St					
100	VLPK	60181	3085	18W-1S	A1
100	YkTp	60181	3085	18W-1S	A1
200	OKTR	60181	3085	18W-1S	A1
Dancer Ct					
1300	LYVL	60048	2590	18W-30N	E3
Dancer Dr					
-	AURA	60506	3136	39W-5S	D2
-	SgrT	60506	3136	39W-5S	D2
Dancer Ln					
-	OSWG	60543	3264	34W-11S	D2
Dancing Bear Ln					
1300	ELGN	60120	2855	31W-12N	E3
Dancing Water Ct					
300	CLSM	60188	2968	25W-3N	A5
Dandridge Ct					
800	ELGN	60120	2855	32W-12N	D2
Dane St					
700	WDSK	60098	2524	42W-31N	B7
Daneth Ct					
800	HDPK	60035	2704	8W-21N	E6
Danford Ln					
15700	ODPK	60462	3423	11W-18S	E1
Danford Wy					
2600	GNVA	60134	3019	37W-0N	C5
Danforth Ct					
5800	HRPK	60133	2911	27W-7N	D5
Danforth Dr					
900	BTVA	60510	3078	36W-2S	A3
Danhaven Ct					
2500	AURA	60502	3139	32W-6S	C5
Danhof Dr					
10	BGBK	60490	3339	28W-14S	B1
Dani Ln					
10600	ODPK	60462	3423	13W-18S	A1
Daniel Ct					
10	BlmT	60411	3510	3E-25S	A7
100	BRLT	60103	2911	28W-8N	B2
1000	LMBD	60148	3026	20W-0S	B7

STREET Block City ZIP Map# CGS Grid

Daniel Ct
1400 NHBK 60062 2756 12W-17N B6
Daniel Dr
100 BNVL 60106 2972 15W-3N A4
4600 AlqT 60014 2640 33W-25N D4
4800 CLLK 60014 2640 33W-25N D4
8000 BGVW 60455 3210 10W-9S C3
8000 BGVW 60458 3210 10W-9S C3
8000 JSTC 60458 3210 10W-9S C3
S Daniel Dr
13000 CHCG 60628 3278 0E-15S D7
13000 CHCG 60827 3278 0E-15S D7
13000 CHCG 60827 3350 0W-15S C1
Daniel Ln
1100 SDWH 60548 3258 51W-14S A7
9000 SPGV 60081 2414 30W-40N B2
11600 HTLY 60142 2745 40W-20N A1
Daniel St
- PLNO 60545 3259 47W-13S C5
300 WCDA 60084 2643 26W-27N D1
400 WCDA 60084 2587 26W-27N D7
Daniel Tr
11000 MKNA 60448 3503 13W-23S A3
Danielle Ct
- HLCT 60429 3427 3W-21S B5
700 SYHW 60118 2800 35W-15N C4
700 WldT 60565 3203 27W-11S C7
17000 OKFT 60452 3425 6W-20S E4
Danielle Ln
5700 OswT 60560 3334 40W-15S C3
Danielle Rd
300 MTSN 60443 3505 7W-24S C5
Daniel Lewis Dr
2100 NLNX 60451 3588 19W-27S D5
Daniels Av
10 ELGN 60120 2854 34W-12N E2
Daniels Ct
900 SMBG 60194 2858 24W-11N D3
N Daniels Ct
3000 ANHT 60004 2754 17W-17N B4
N Daniels Dr
10 BTVA 60510 3077 37W-1S D1
S Daniels Dr
10 BTVA 60510 3077 37W-1S C2
Daniels Ln
6200 OKFT 60452 3347 7W-17S C5
E Daniels Rd
10 PLTN 60067 2805 20W-15N E1
200 PLTN 60067 2806 20W-15N A1
W Daniels Rd
10 PLTN 60067 2805 21W-15N E1
400 PltT 60067 2805 21W-15N C1
Daniels St
100 WMTN 60481 3853 27W-38S E7
500 BGBK 60440 3204 24W-10S D5
N Daniels St
100 WMTN 60481 3853 27W-38S E6
Daniels Wy
200 GNVA 60134 3019 37W-1N C4
Danielson Ct
900 GRNE 60031 2477 17W-35N B7
Dan Ireland Ct
10 JLET 60435 3417 27W-19S B3
10 PnfT 60435 3417 27W-19S B3
Dan Ireland Dr
3000 JLET 60435 3417 27W-19S B2
3100 PnfT 60435 3417 27W-19S B2
3100 PnfT 60544 3417 27W-19S B2
Danlaur Ct
3300 NPVL 60564 3266 30W-11S B2
Danmar Tr
10 PSPK 60464 3272 14W-15S E7
10 PSPK 60464 3344 14W-15S E1
E Danne Rd
2800 CteT 60417 3687 4E-30S B4
3200 HnrT 46311 3687 4E-30S B4
Danneil Cir
8100 LGGV 60060 2646 20W-25N A4
Dannell Pl
100 BtnT 60081 2414 29W-39N D5
100 FXLK 60081 2414 29W-39N D5
Dannet Ct
1200 BFGV 60089 2701 17W-21N B6
Dannet Rd
700 BFGV 60089 2701 17W-21N B6
Danniel Ct
8100 LGGV 60060 2646 20W-25N A4
Danny Dr
500 SRWD 60404 3496 30W-23S C4
W Danny Ln
21200 LkvT 60046 2475 21W-36N D4
Dano
- JLET 60431 3495 33W-22S B1
- JLET 60586 3495 33W-22S B1
Dano St
- JLET 60431 3495 33W-22S B1
S Dan O'Connell Dr
15900 PNFD 60544 3416 29W-19S D2
15900 PNFD 60586 3416 29W-19S D3
16100 PnfT 60586 3416 29W-19S D3
Dan Patch Dr
15100 PNFD 60544 3338 30W-18S A7
15100 PNFD 60544 3416 30W-18S A1
N Dan Patch Ln
14300 GNOK 60048 2535 14W-31N C7
14300 WKGN 60048 2535 14W-31N C7
Dan Ryan Expwy
- CHCG - 3034 0W-1S A7
- CHCG - 3092 0W-2S A2
- CHCG - 3152 0W-7S C6
- CHCG - 3214 0W-11S A7
Dan Ryan Expwy I-57
- CHCG - 3214 1W-11S A7
Dan Ryan Expwy I-90
- CHCG - 3034 0W-1S A7
- CHCG - 3092 0W-2S A2
- CHCG - 3152 0W-6S B3
Dan Ryan Expwy I-94
- CHCG - 3034 0W-1S A7
- CHCG - 3092 0W-2S A2
- CHCG - 3152 0W-7S C6
- CHCG - 3214 0W-8S C1
Dan Ryan Expwy E
- CHCG - 3152 0W-7S C5
Dan Ryan Expwy E I-94
- CHCG - 3152 0W-7S C5
Dan Ryan Expwy W
- CHCG - 3152 0E-7S C6
Dan Ryan Expwy W I-94
- CHCG - 3152 0E-7S C6
Dansforth Dr
200 SMBG 60193 2858 24W-10N D6
Dansher Rd
5100 CTSD 60525 3147 12W-5S C2
S Dansher Rd
5200 CTSD 60525 3147 12W-5S C2

Dante Av
14200 DLTN 60419 3351 1E-16S B4
18200 ThtT 60438 3429 1E-21S B7
18500 LNSG 60438 3429 1E-21S B7
S Dante Av
- BlmT 60411 3509 1E-23S B3
- BlmT 60425 3509 1E-23S B3
200 GNWD 60425 3509 1E-23S B3
6800 CHCG 60637 3153 1E-7S B6
7300 CHCG 60619 3153 1E-8S B7
7500 CHCG 60619 3215 1E-8S A1
Dante Ct
- BNVL 60106 2972 15W-3N A4
100 SRWD 60404 3496 29W-24S D5
700 SMBG 60193 2858 23W-9N E7
Dante Dr
15600 SHLD 60473 3351 1E-18S B7
N Dante Dr
25100 ElaT 60047 2644 23W-25N E5
Danube Wy
10 OMFD 60461 3506 4W-25S D7
1800 BGBK 60490 3267 27W-12S C2
Danuta Ct
400 GNVA 60134 3019 36W-1N D2
Danvera Ln
1000 LKZH 60047 2645 22W-24N B7
Danvers Ct
1100 SMBG 60193 2912 24W-9N C1
Dara James St
400 DSPN 60016 2862 15W-11N B4
Darby Ct
300 CLLK 60014 2639 35W-24N E7
700 INCK 60061 2647 17W-25N A6
1500 BTVA 60510 3077 36W-1S D1
S Darby Ct
100 BMDL 60108 2969 23W-5N B1
Darby Ln
10 LNSH 60069 2702 14W-22N C4
1100 ROSL 60172 2912 24W-7N C5
W Darcy Av
600 JLET 60436 3498 24W-24S D5
Daren Dr
200 BlmT 60411 3598 4E-26S C1
200 LYWD 60411 3598 4E-26S C1
Darfler Ct
2600 AURA 60503 3201 32W-10S C6
Darien Ct
200 SYHW 60118 2799 36W-15N E3
200 SYHW 60118 2800 36W-15N A3
600 HFET 60169 2858 24W-11N C4
Darien Ln
200 SYHW 60118 2799 36W-15N E3
200 SYHW 60118 2800 36W-15N A3
7300 DRN 60561 3207 17W-8S B1
Darien Club Dr
1200 DRN 60559 3145 18W-7S B7
1200 DRN 60561 3145 18W-7S A7
1700 DRN 60561 3144 18W-7S E7
1900 DRGV 60516 3144 18W-7S E7
1900 DRN 60516 3144 18W-7S E7
Darien Lake Dr
1500 DRN 60561 3207 18W-8S A2
Darien Woods Ct
9000 DGvT 60439 3206 18W-10S E5
9000 DGvT 60561 3206 18W-10S E5
9000 DRN 60561 3206 18W-10S E5
Darin Dr
1100 LKPT 60441 3419 21W-19S E2
1100 LKPT 60441 3420 21W-19S A3
Darius Ln
900 NPVL 60565 3204 25W-9S C3
Dark Star Rd
1100 NPVL 60540 3142 25W-7S A7
S Darla Ct
900 WKGN 60085 2535 14W-33N C4
Darla Tr
19100 FftT 60448 3503 13W-23S A2
19100 MKNA 60448 3503 13W-23S A2
Darlene Ct
3600 AURA 60504 3202 31W-8S A2
4800 LGGV 60047 2700 18W-23N E2
5000 GRNE 60031 2478 15W-34N B7
Darlene Dr
4900 GRNE 60031 2478 15W-34N B7
Darlene Ln
400 GLHT 60139 3025 22W-2N B1
Darley Dr
- MTGY 60506 3198 40W-9S C4
- MTGY 60538 3198 40W-9S C4
1700 LSLE 60532 3142 23W-4S E1
1700 LslT 60532 3142 23W-4S E1
Darling Rd
500 BfdT 53128 2352 E1
900 BfdT 53128 2353 A2
900 GNCY 53128 2353 A2
Darling St
10 MltT 60187 3024 25W-0N C4
10 MltT 60188 3024 25W-0N C4
300 WHTN 60187 3024 25W-0N C4
N Darlington Cir
1200 HFET 60169 2858 25W-11N C3
W Darlington Cir
1300 HFET 60169 2858 25W-11N C3
Darlington Ct
1200 HFET 60169 2858 25W-11N C3
1300 ALGN 60102 2747 35W-20N A2
Darlington Dr
10 ElaT 60047 2646 20W-24N A7
10 HNWD 60047 2646 20W-24N A7
10 HNWD 60047 2699 20W-24N E1
10 KLDR 60047 2699 20W-24N E1
Darlington Ln
500 CLLK 60014 2640 35W-24N A6
1000 CLLK 60014 2694 34W-23N B1
Darlington Wy
- JLET 60421 3586 24W-28S E7
Darmstadt Rd
- BKLY 60162 3028 14W-0S C6
- BKLY 60163 3028 14W-0S C6
- HLSD 60162 3028 14W-0S C6
Darnell Dr
1200 MDLN 60060 2590 19W-29N B3
Darnell Ln
700 GRNE 60031 2534 16W-33N D3
Darnell St
1800 LYVL 60048 2591 17W-30N A1
Darrel Rd
- WcnT 60051 2529 28W-32N D6
500 LKMR 60051 2529 28W-32N D6
Darrell Cir
- PvsT 60141 3088 10W-1S A1
N Darrell Rd
26600 PTBR 60010 2642 28W-26N E3
26600 WcnT 60010 2642 28W-26N D3
26600 WcnT 60084 2642 28W-26N E3
26700 WcnT 60084 2643 28W-27N A2

N Darrell Rd
26900 ISLK 60042 2643 28W-27N A1
26900 WcnT 60042 2643 28W-27N A1
27300 ISLK 60084 2643 27W-27N A1
27600 ISLK 60084 2587 28W-30N A2
27600 WcnT 60084 2587 28W-30N A2
27800 WcnT 60051 2587 27W-28N A7
28300 ISLK 60042 2587 28W-28N A5
28300 ISLK 60051 2587 27W-28N A5
28300 WcnT 60042 2587 28W-28N A5
30000 WcnT 60051 2586 28W-30N E1
30800 LKMR 60051 2529 28W-31N D7
30800 WcnT 60051 2529 28W-31N D7
N Darrell Rd CO-V47
26600 PTBR 60010 2642 28W-26N E3
26600 WcnT 60010 2642 28W-26N D3
26600 WcnT 60084 2642 28W-26N E3
26700 WcnT 60084 2643 28W-27N A2
26900 ISLK 60042 2643 28W-27N A1
26900 WcnT 60042 2643 28W-27N A1
27300 ISLK 60084 2643 27W-27N A1
27600 ISLK 60084 2587 28W-30N A2
27600 WcnT 60084 2587 28W-30N A2
27800 WcnT 60051 2587 27W-28N A7
28300 ISLK 60042 2587 28W-28N A5
28300 ISLK 60051 2587 27W-28N A5
28300 WcnT 60042 2587 28W-28N A5
30000 WcnT 60051 2586 28W-30N E1
30800 LKMR 60051 2529 28W-31N D7
30800 WcnT 60051 2529 28W-31N D7
Darrow Av
1200 EVTN 60202 2866 3W-11N E3
1700 EVTN 60201 2866 3W-11N E2
N Darrow Dr
40100 AntT 60002 2417 22W-40N C3
Darrow Ln
2800 WKGN 60085 2536 12W-33N B2
E Darryl Dr
1800 WhlT 60004 2754 16W-17N C5
Darsha Rd
700 NLNX 60451 3589 16W-25S E1
Dartford Ct
1300 NPVL 60540 3142 25W-7S B7
Dartford Ln
10 SMBG 60194 2858 25W-10N B5
Dartmoor Av
300 RMVL 60446 3340 24W-16S E4
N Dartmoor Av
1500 PLTN 60067 2752 21W-18N D3
2000 JLET 60435 3497 26W-22S E2
W Dartmoor Av
200 PLTN 60067 2752 21W-17N D4
Dartmoor Ct
300 CLLK 60014 2693 35W-23N E1
1100 NPVL 60540 3204 25W-7S B1
Dartmoor Dr
- MHRY 60050 2528 32W-31N A6
10 CLLK 60014 2694 35W-23N A1
10 CLLK 60156 2694 35W-24N B1
100 RLKP 60073 2532 23W-33N A2
600 CLLK 60014 2639 36W-24N D7
800 CLLK 60014 2693 36W-24N C1
E Dartmoor Dr
100 CLLK 60014 2640 34W-24N C7
100 CLLK 60014 2694 34W-24N B1
S Dartmoor Dr
400 CLLK 60014 2640 34W-24N B7
W Dartmoor Dr
- MchT 60050 2527 34W-32N B5
4500 MHRY 60050 2527 33W-32N E5
17200 WrnT 60030 2534 17W-33N B4
Dartmoor Rd
- MchT 60050 2527 35W-32N A5
- MHRY 60050 2527 35W-32N A5
Dartmouth Av
800 MTSN 60443 3505 7W-25S E7
Dartmouth Ct
10 LNSH 60069 2701 16W-23N E2
10 SMWD 60107 2856 29W-9N D7
100 GNVA 60134 3019 36W-1N D3
100 GNVW 60025 2810 9W-15N B2
200 BMDL 60108 2969 22W-3N C4
800 BRLT 60103 2910 29W-6N E6
800 HRPK 60133 2858 26W-9N A7
1600 NPVL 60565 3204 24W-9S D3
Dartmouth Dr
300 ELGN 60123 2853 36W-10N E5
300 ElgT 60123 2853 36W-10N E5
700 ISLK 60042 2586 29W-28N B6
800 WHTN 60187 3082 25W-1S A1
1000 BRLT 60103 2910 29W-6N E6
Dartmouth Ln
10 ElaT 60047 2645 20W-25N E6
10 HNWD 60047 2645 20W-25N E6
400 SMBG 60193 2858 25W-9N B7
600 NLNX 60451 3502 16W-25S A7
700 BFGV 60089 2754 15W-20N E1
700 NLNX 60451 3590 16W-25S A1
1100 DRFD 60015 2756 11W-20N C1
2100 DRN 60561 3206 19W-8S D2
2800 OMFD 60461 3507 3W-25S A6
2800 WDND 60118 2800 36W-16N A3
8000 HRPK 60133 2858 26W-9N A7
W Dartmouth Ln
21000 ElaT 60047 2645 21W-25N E6
21000 HNWD 60047 2645 21W-25N E6
Dartmouth Pl
600 EVTN 60201 2867 2W-12N B1
3300 EVTN 60201 2866 4W-12N B1
3300 SKOK 60076 2866 4W-12N B1
Dartmouth Rd
1100 FSMR 60422 3507 2W-23S D3
8700 PSHL 60465 3274 10W-12S A2
Dartmouth St
1100 WLMT 60091 2812 5W-14N B5
1900 CHHT 60411 3595 1W-26S E2
Darty Dr
4800 CCHL 60478 3506 6W-22S A1
Darvin Dr
19100 MKNA 60448 3504 11W-23S A2
Darwin Ct
1600 WHTN 60187 3082 25W-1S B2
1600 WHTN 60187 3083 23W-1S A1
Darwin Ln
1400 WHTN 60187 3082 23W-1S E2
Darwin St
3100 NPVL 60564 3202 28W-11S E7
3100 NPVL 60564 3266 28W-11S E1
Daryl Ln
1100 NHBK 60062 2757 9W-17N D5
Dato Av
3000 HDPK 60035 2704 9W-23N B1
3400 HDPK 60035 2650 9W-24N C7
Dato Ct
100 SMWD 60107 2857 27W-11N C4

Dato Dr
10 SMWD 60107 2857 27W-11N C4
N Dato Ln
1000 WCDA 60084 2587 26W-28N D6
Daulton Ct
2800 BFGV 60089 2701 17W-23N C2
Daulton Dr
2800 BFGV 60089 2701 17W-23N C2
Dauntless Cir
300 GNVW 60025 2810 10W-15N A3
S Dauphin Av
8700 CHCG 60619 3214 1E-10S E4
10000 CHCG 60628 3214 0E-11S E7
10300 CHCG 60628 3278 0E-12S E1
Dauphin Dr
- JLET 60431 3495 32W-22S D2
Dauphine Av
600 NHBK 60062 2756 12W-18N B4
Dauphine Ct
10 ODHL 60013 2641 30W-26N E3
600 EGVV 60007 2914 19W-9N C1
600 NHBK 60062 2756 11W-18N C4
Davane Ln
6500 DGvT 60516 3144 19W-7S E6
6500 DRGV 60516 3144 19W-7S E6
Dave Ct
100 SMWD 60107 2857 28W-11N A4
Davenport Dr
2800 WCHI 60185 2965 32W-4N B5
Dave Pate Dr
- ROSL 60172 2912 24W-7N D4
Daves Ct
100 BRLT 60103 2909 31W-8N E3
Davey Ct
3100 AURA 60503 3201 31W-10S D6
Davey Dr
1100 BTVA 60510 3078 34W-2S D3
11600 HTLY 60142 2745 40W-20N A1
Davey Rd
2300 WDRG 60517 3269 21W-12S D4
2500 BGBK 60440 3269 22W-12S D4
2500 RMVL 60440 3269 22W-12S D4
2500 WDRG 60440 3269 22W-12S D4
17400 DGvT 60439 3270 20W-12S B2
17400 DGvT 60517 3270 20W-12S C2
17400 WDRG 60439 3270 20W-12S B2
17400 WDRG 60517 3270 20W-12S B2
David Av
1800 JltT 60433 3499 21W-25S E7
E David Av
400 JLET 60433 3499 23W-25S B7
David Ct
10 BlmT 60411 3510 3E-25S A6
100 BtlT 60543 3262 40W-12S C3
300 BDWD 60408 3942 31W-41S A5
300 BRLT 60103 2911 28W-8N A3
300 ISLK 60042 2586 29W-28N D5
5200 GRNE 60031 2478 14W-35N B5
5900 OKLN 60453 3211 7W-11S C6
N David Ct
35600 GrtT 60041 2474 25W-35N A5
David Dr
100 BCVL 60407 4030 34W-44S A4
100 BNVL 60106 2972 15W-3N A4
100 SMWD 60107 2857 27W-11N D4
300 ELGN 60120 2855 32W-10N C5
500 SRWD 60404 3496 30W-23S C4
800 ElgT 60123 2908 35W-9N A1
1100 EMHT 60106 2972 15W-3N A5
1100 EMHT 60126 2972 15W-3N A5
2000 DSPN 60018 2917 12W-8N B1
8300 WDRG 60517 3205 22W-9S C4
N David Dr
10 PLTN 60074 2753 19W-16N C7
10 PLTN 60074 2806 19W-16N C1
David Ln
100 HNWD 60047 2645 22W-25N C5
300 ROSL 60172 2913 23W-8N B3
300 SmbT 60172 2913 23W-8N B3
600 CLSM 60188 2967 26W-3N D6
900 EGVV 60007 2914 21W-8N A2
4500 AlqT 60014 2640 33W-25N E4
15400 OKFT 60452 3347 7W-18S C7
David Pl
8800 MaiT 60714 2863 11W-12N E2
8800 NLES 60016 2863 11W-12N E2
8800 NLES 60714 2863 11W-12N E2
8900 MaiT 60016 2863 11W-12N E1
David St
600 LIHL 60156 2694 34W-22N C4
900 ANTH 60002 2357 24W-42N D6
4800 MchT 60050 2472 29W-36N B3
David A Barry Dr
1200 SRWD 60404 3496 31W-24S A6
W Davids Ct
24400 WldT 60564 3266 30W-12S B2
Davids Ln
17900 ODPK 60467 3423 13W-21S B6
Davidson Ct
6400 GRNE 60031 2477 17W-35N C6
Davidson Dr
500 MNKA 60447 3583 33W-28S B6
700 CnhT 60447 3583 33W-28S B6
Davidson Rd
700 WldT 60564 3202 28W-10S E6
David T Doering Dr
- NCHI 60064 2536 11W-31N D6
Daviess Av
500 LKPT 60441 3419 22W-19S C3
Davinci Cir
400 BGBK 60440 3205 22W-11S C7
Da Vinci St
13100 LMNT 60439 3343 18W-15S A2
Davine Dr
1300 GLHT 60139 3025 22W-2N C1
1400 GLHT 60139 2969 22W-2N C7
Davis Av
600 JLET 60436 3498 25W-24S B7
600 RKDL 60436 3498 25W-25S B7
1100 DRFD 60015 2703 11W-21N D5
4000 RchT 60471 3594 5W-27S C5
9500 FNPK 60131 2973 11W-4N C3
S Davis Av
1200 HMND 46394 3280 E3
W Davis Av
1800 NndT 60050 2585 30W-29N E4
1800 NndT 60050 2586 30W-29N A4
Davis Cir
10 PLNO 60545 3259 47W-13S C6
Davis Ct
100 BGBK 60440 3269 23W-11S A2
100 RLKP 60073 2532 23W-33N A2
200 DSPN 60016 2862 14W-11N D2
200 WHTN 60187 3082 25W-2S A3
400 WDSK 60098 2581 41W-30N D1
2100 RGMW 60008 2805 20W-14N E4

Davis Ct
3000 HDPK 60037 2704 8W-23N E2
14200 DXMR 60406 3349 2W-17S C4
Davis Dr
10 BKLY 60163 3028 13W-0N E3
10 BLWD 60104 3028 13W-0N E3
10 BLWD 60163 3028 13W-0N E3
Davis Ln
100 CRY 60013 2695 30W-23N E1
200 BGBK 60440 3269 23W-11S A2
11800 HTLY 60142 2691 40W-22N E3
11800 HTLY 60142 2692 40W-22N E3
Davis Rd
300 BTVA 60510 3020 35W-0S C7
400 ELGN 60123 2800 35W-14N B6
1200 WDSK 60098 2581 41W-29N C3
1200 WDSK 60098 2582 40W-29N A3
11700 DrrT 60098 2581 41W-29N C3
13000 SenT 60098 2581 43W-30N A3
Davis St
200 EVTN 60201 2867 2W-11N B3
400 DRGV 60515 3144 19W-4S D1
500 PKFT 60466 3594 4W-25S E1
500 PKFT 60466 3595 4W-25S A1
600 MLPK 60160 3029 10W-1N E2
600 MLPK 60160 3030 10W-1N A2
1500 MaiT 60016 2863 11W-11N E3
1500 MaiT 60068 2863 11W-11N E3
1500 PKRG 60068 2863 11W-11N E3
1800 EVTN 60201 2866 3W-11N E3
2200 BLID 60406 3277 2W-14S C7
2300 NCHI 60064 2536 11W-31N E7
3300 SKOK 60203 2866 4W-11N D3
4000 SKOK 60076 2866 5W-11N B3
4700 SKOK 60076 2865 5W-11N E3
5100 SKOK 60077 2865 6W-11N D3
5400 SKOK 60053 2865 6W-11N D3
6600 MNGV 60053 2865 8W-11N A3
6700 MNGV 60053 2864 8W-11N E3
7800 NLES 60053 2864 9W-11N B3
7800 NLES 60714 2864 9W-11N B3
14300 DXMR 60406 3349 2W-17S C5
E Davis St
- ANHT 60004 2807 16W-13N C6
600 ANHT 60005 2807 17W-13N B5
W Davis St
10 ANHT 60005 2807 16W-13N C6
200 JLET 60436 3498 24W-24S E7
8000 MNGV 60053 2864 10W-11N B3
8000 NLES 60053 2864 10W-11N B3
8400 NLES 60714 2864 10W-11N A3
8600 MaiT 60016 2863 10W-11N E3
8600 MaiT 60016 2864 10W-11N A3
8600 MaiT 60714 2864 10W-11N A3
8700 MaiT 60068 2863 10W-11N E3
8700 PKRG 60068 2863 10W-11N E3
Davis Ter
600 GNEN 60137 3025 23W-0N B4
Davison St
900 JltT 60433 3499 21W-25S E7
1000 JltT 60433 3587 21W-25S E1
N Davisson St
2400 RVGV 60171 2974 10W-3N B5
N Davlin Ct
3000 CHCG 60618 2976 4W-3N C4
S Davol St
11200 CHCG 60643 3277 2W-13S D3
Davos Av
2700 WDRG 60517 3205 21W-9S D3
W Davy Ct
22800 JLET 60586 3417 28W-19S A4
22800 PnfT 60586 3417 28W-19S A4
Davy Ln
400 WMTN 60481 3853 28W-38S B6
400 WmTp 60481 3853 28W-38S B7
22000 CstT 60481 3943 27W-42S D6
Dawes Av
300 WHTN 60187 3082 24W-1S D1
500 GNEN 60137 3083 22W-1S C1
N Dawes Av
800 JLET 60435 3498 25W-22S C2
Dawes St
300 LYVL 60048 2591 17W-28N C5
1000 AURA 60506 3137 37W-5S D3
1100 LYVL 60048 2647 16W-27N C1
Dawn Av
400 GNEN 60137 3025 23W-0N A5
900 MltT 60137 3025 23W-1N A3
1300 MTGY 60538 3200 34W-9S D4
4600 CTSD 60525 3147 13W-7S A6
10300 NPVL 60564 3266 30W-12S B2
10300 WldT 60564 3266 30W-12S B2
Dawn Cir
500 GYLK 60030 2532 20W-33N E2
N Dawn Cir
38200 AntT 60081 2415 27W-38N B7
Dawn Ct
300 BMDL 60108 2969 22W-4N C3
500 DSPN 60016 2863 12W-11N C3
1500 LGGV 60047 2753 18W-20N D1
W Dawn Ct
17600 WrnT 60031 2534 17W-34N B1
Dawn Ln
10 CTCY 60409 3351 2E-16S C4
100 CHHT 60411 3507 1W-23S E4
1900 ZION 60099 2421 12W-41N B2
Dawn Pl
600 DRGV 60515 3144 19W-4S D1
Dawn Wy
100 NLNX 60451 3501 17W-25S C7
Dawngate Ct
4400 RGMW 60008 2806 20W-13N A5
Dawngate Ln
- RGMW 60067 2805 21W-13N E5
4400 RGMW 60008 2805 20W-13N E5
4400 RGMW 60008 2806 20W-13N A5
N Dawn Marie Dr
10 RDLK 60073 2531 25W-33N B3
S Dawn Marie Dr
10 RDLK 60073 2531 25W-33N B3
Dawnwood Ct
14300 HMGN 60491 3343 16W-17S D4
Dawson Av
19200 LktT 60441 3340 24W-17S E6
19200 RMVL 60441 3340 24W-17S E6
N Dawson Av
2800 CHCG 60618 2976 4W-3N D4
Dawson Ct
10 VNHL 60061 2646 18W-24N E6
2300 LNSH 60069 2703 12W-22N A4
2300 RVWD 60015 2703 13W-22N A4
2300 RVWD 60069 2703 13W-22N A4
Dawson Ln
1100 ALGN 60102 2693 35W-20N E7
1100 ALGN 60102 2746 35W-20N E1
2200 ALGN 60102 2694 35W-20N A7

STREET Block	City	ZIP	Map#	CGS	Grid
Dawson St					
10400	HTLY	60142	2692	39W-21N	C6
Day Ln					
10	CPVL	60110	2747	34W-17N	E6
Day St					
100	BMDL	60108	2969	23W-5N	A1
Daybreak Ct					
2400	ELGN	60123	2907	36W-8N	E4
Daybreak Dr					
1600	WKGN	60048	2534	15W-32N	E5
2100	AURA	60503	3201	32W-10S	B6
2100	LIHL	60142	2692	39W-22N	C3
5100	WKGN	60048	2535	15W-32N	A6
5100	WrnT	60048	2535	15W-32N	A6
Daybreak Ln					
600	CLSM	60188	2968	25W-3N	A6
1700	ZION	60099	2421	12W-41N	B2
7200	LGGV	60047	2646	18W-25N	E6
S Daybreak Ln					
900	RDLK	60073	2531	23W-32N	E5
W Daybreak Ln					
400	RDLK	60073	2531	23W-32N	E5
Daybreak Ter					
-	BFGV	60089	2701	16W-22N	D4
-	VrnT	60089	2701	16W-22N	D4
Daybreak Ridge Tr					
10	CRY	60013	2695	31W-23N	C1
Dayfield Ct					
23600	PNFD	60586	3416	29W-19S	D4
Dayfield Dr					
24000	PNFD	60586	3416	30W-19S	C4
Daylight Dr					
-	AURA	60503	3201	32W-10S	C7
Daylily Dr					
1500	RMVL	60446	3339	26W-17S	E6
N Days Ter					
7100	NLES	60714	2918	8W-8N	E1
Dayton Av					
300	WCHI	60185	3022	29W-0S	D7
Dayton Ct					
1100	BFGV	60089	2701	17W-21N	B6
E Dayton Ct					
700	GDLY	60407	4030	32W-43S	D2
700	RedT	60408	4030	32W-43S	D2
Dayton Rd					
1100	BFGV	60089	2701	17W-21N	B6
Dayton St					
1400	DSPN	60018	2862	15W-10N	A5
N Dayton St					
1400	CHCG	60622	3033	1W-1N	E1
1600	CHCG	60614	2977	1W-2N	E7
2700	CHCG	60657	2977	1W-3N	E5
4300	CHCG	60613	2921	1W-5N	E7
4300	CHCG	60613	2977	1W-5N	E1
4300	CHCG	60640	2921	1W-5N	E7
S Dayton St					
100	SDWH	60548	3330	51W-15S	A2
200	SdwT	60548	3330	51W-15S	A2
W Dayton St					
3900	MHRY	60050	2585	32W-30N	A1
Daytona Rd					
-	JknT	60421	3675	25W-29S	D2
-	JLET	60421	3675	25W-29S	D2
Daytona Wy					
-	PGGV	60140	2797	42W-15N	D4
Dayward Ct					
400	AURA	60505	3200	34W-8S	D2
S Deal Av					
22300	CNHN	60410	3585	28W-27S	A5
Deames St					
-	PLNO	60545	3260	45W-13S	C5
Dean Av					
700	HDPK	60035	2705	7W-20N	B7
1000	WLNG	60090	2755	14W-16N	C7
Dean Cir					
300	BGBK	60440	3205	23W-11S	A7
Dean Ct					
10	WYNE	60184	2966	30W-4N	C3
Dean Dr					
400	SEGN	60177	2908	35W-9N	C2
600	ELGN	60123	2908	35W-9N	C1
600	ELGN	60177	2908	35W-9N	C1
600	SEGN	60123	2908	35W-9N	C1
4000	OKLN	60453	3276	5W-12S	C3
6300	WDRG	60517	3143	22W-7S	B6
E Dean Dr					
1000	PLTN	60074	2753	19W-16N	B7
N Dean Dr					
100	PLTN	60074	2753	19W-16N	B7
100	PLTN	60074	2806	20W-15N	A2
Dean Ln					
-	CmpT	60175	2962	39W-4N	E4
Dean Pl					
-	MDLN	60060	2590	18W-27N	E7
Dean St					
10	CmpT	60175	2962	39W-4N	E4
10	SchT	60175	2963	38W-4N	A5
10	SCRL	60175	2963	36W-3N	D6
100	WDSK	60098	2524	41W-31N	D7
300	WDSK	60098	2581	41W-28N	C6
800	CmpT	60175	2963	38W-4N	A5
900	SCRL	60174	2963	36W-3N	D6
900	SCRL	60174	2964	36W-3N	A7
1800	SchT	60174	2963	36W-3N	D6
2000	DrrT	60098	2581	41W-27N	C7
11300	HTLY	60142	2692	40W-20N	A7
11400	HTLY	60142	2745	40W-20N	A1
11700	HTLY	60142	2744	40W-20N	E1
Dean St CO-53					
10	CmpT	60175	2962	39W-4N	E5
800	CmpT	60175	2963	38W-4N	A5
800	SchT	60175	2963	38W-4N	A5
N Dean St					
1300	CHCG	60622	3033	2W-1N	C1
Deana Ln					
5200	RchT	60471	3593	6W-27S	E5
5200	RNPK	60471	3593	6W-27S	E5
5200	RNPK	60471	3594	6W-27S	A5
Deane St					
-	DSPN	60016	2862	13W-10N	E5
-	DSPN	60018	2862	13W-10N	E5
1900	DSPN	60018	2863	13W-9N	A6
De Angelis Ct					
600	CHHT	60411	3507	1W-24S	E6
Deanna Dr					
400	BRLT	60103	2911	28W-7N	A4
Deanna Ln					
-	GLHT	60139	2969	22W-2N	C6
Deans Cove					
-	DGvT	60439	3270	20W-12S	C3
Dearborn Av					
1000	AURA	60505	3138	34W-7S	D6
1400	AraT	60504	3138	34W-7S	D6
1400	AraT	60505	3138	34W-7S	D6
1600	AraT	60504	3139	33W-7S	A6
1600	AraT	60505	3139	33W-7S	A6
S Dearborn Av					
4100	HMND	46327	3352		C3
Dearborn Cir					
-	AlqT	60013	2642	29W-25N	B4
-	NndT	60013	2642	29W-25N	B4
900	CLSM	60188	2968	25W-3N	A5
Dearborn Ct					
-	GNVA	60134	3021	33W-1N	B3
200	LKZH	60047	2698	23W-22N	E4
2900	NPVL	60563	3140	29W-5S	C3
2900	NpvT	60563	3140	29W-5S	C3
12900	HTLY	60142	2744	43W-19N	B4
18500	TYPK	60477	3505	8W-22S	B1
Dearborn Ln					
1000	VNHL	60061	2646	18W-25N	E5
Dearborn Pkwy					
5700	DRGV	60516	3144	19W-6S	D4
N Dearborn Pkwy					
1200	CHCG	60610	3034	0W-1N	B1
1500	CHCG	60610	2978		D7
1500	CHCG	60614	2978		D7
Dearborn St					
1600	CTHL	60403	3498	24W-21S	D1
1600	JLET	60435	3498	24W-21S	D1
1700	CTHL	60403	3418	24W-21S	D7
14600	DLTN	60419	3350	0W-17S	C5
14600	DLTN	60827	3350	0W-17S	C5
14600	RVDL	60827	3350	0W-17S	C5
15300	SHLD	60473	3350	0W-17S	D6
E Dearborn St					
10	PLNO	60545	3259	47W-14S	D6
N Dearborn St					
10	CHCG	60602	3034	0W-0N	B4
10	CHCG	60603	3034	0W-0N	B4
100	CHCG	60601	3034	0W-0N	B4
300	CHCG	60610	3034	0W-0N	B3
1200	JLET	60435	3498	24W-22S	D1
S Dearborn St					
10	CHCG	60602	3034	0W-0S	B5
10	CHCG	60603	3034	0W-0S	B5
100	CHCG	60604	3034	0W-0S	B5
300	CHCG	60605	3034	0W-0S	B6
1500	CHCG	60616	3034	0W-1S	B7
2300	CHCG	60616	3092	0W-2S	C2
3800	CHCG	60609	3092	0W-4S	C6
4700	CHCG	60609	3152	0W-5S	C1
13800	RVDL	60827	3350	0W-16S	C3
14500	DLTN	60419	3350	0W-17S	C4
14500	DLTN	60827	3350	0W-17S	C4
W Dearborn St					
10	PLNO	60545	3259	47W-14S	C7
Dearborn Tr					
13300	HTLY	60142	2744	43W-19N	B3
Dearlove Rd					
10200	GNVW	60016	2809	11W-13N	C7
10200	GNVW	60025	2809	11W-13N	D7
10200	MaiT	60016	2809	11W-13N	C7
10200	NfdT	60025	2809	11W-13N	C7
Debbie Ct					
2100	NPVL	60565	3204	25W-9S	B5
2600	PnfT	60435	3417	27W-20S	B5
E Debbie Dr					
10	MPPT	60056	2808	14W-13N	D7
Debbie Ln					
-	ODHL	60487	3423	11W-19S	E2
-	ODPK	60487	3423	11W-19S	E2
10	SMBG	60107	2857	27W-11N	D4
10	SMBG	60194	2857	27W-11N	D4
10	SMWD	60107	2857	27W-11N	D4
400	WMTN	60481	3943	27W-39S	D1
6600	RlyT	60152	2634	50W-25N	B5
9400	ODPK	60467	3423	11W-19S	E2
13700	NlxT	60448	3421	17W-22S	D7
15900	SHLD	60473	3351	1E-18S	A7
15900	SHLD	60473	3429	1E-18S	A1
Debden Dr					
800	ISLK	60042	2586	30W-28N	B6
Debill Ct					
10	VNHL	60061	2647	16W-24N	C6
Deblin Ln					
5100	OKLN	60453	3275	6W-12S	E3
De Boer Blvd					
-	WcnT	60084	2643	26W-26N	D2
Debolt Av					
4700	DRGV	60515	3144	19W-5S	D2
Debolt St					
-	LtRT	60545	3259	47W-12S	D3
-	PLNO	60545	3259	47W-12S	D3
Deborah Av					
600	ELGN	60123	2854	35W-12N	A2
2500	ZION	60099	2422	9W-40N	C4
2800	BtnT	60099	2422	9W-40N	C4
Deborah Cir					
1100	LYVL	60048	2591	18W-29N	A3
Deborah Ct					
600	SMBG	60193	2859	23W-9N	B7
23800	CteT	60417	3597	2E-28S	E7
Deborah Dr					
10	LMNT	60439	3270	20W-14S	C7
Deborah Ln					
-	BtnT	60081	2414	30W-40N	B2
100	WLNG	60090	2755	14W-18N	C4
500	LYWD	60411	3510	4E-25S	C7
2900	MchT	60051	2528	31W-33N	C3
9000	SPGV	60081	2414	30W-40N	B2
S Deborah Ln					
400	MPPT	60056	2861	17W-12N	C1
Deborah St					
600	GLBT	60136	2799	37W-15N	C3
Debra Av					
6100	TYPK	60477	3425	7W-20S	C4
Debra Ct					
10	SLVL	60411	3597	1E-27S	A4
3700	RGMW	60008	2806	20W-13N	A5
Debra Dr					
3100	ISLK	60042	2586	29W-28N	C5
15800	OKFT	60452	3425	6W-19S	E2
16100	BmnT	60477	3425	6W-19S	E2
16100	OKFT	60477	3425	6W-19S	E2
Debra Ln					
10	WLNG	60090	2755	14W-16N	C6
800	EGVW	60007	2914	21W-8N	A2
2500	GNVW	60025	2810	10W-15N	A2
2500	NHBK	60025	2810	10W-15N	A2
2500	NHBK	60062	2810	10W-15N	A2
2700	HMWD	60430	3427	3W-21S	B6
Debra Rd					
400	DSPN	60016	2862	15W-11N	A3
600	DSPN	60016	2861	16W-11N	E3
Debruyne St					
200	SCRL	60174	2963	36W-3N	E7
Decade Ct					
2500	ELGN	60124	2799	37W-13N	D7
S Decathalon Ln					
11500	PNFD	60585	3266	30W-13S	B5
Decatur Av					
10	NCHI	60088	2594	10W-30N	A1
600	SchT	60174	2908	34W-6N	D6
1200	LIHL	60156	2693	35W-22N	E4
Decatur St					
500	HFET	60169	2859	23W-11N	A4
Decker Dr					
10	AlqT	60013	2696	30W-23N	A1
10	CRY	60013	2696	30W-23N	A1
400	CRY	60013	2642	30W-24N	A7
Declaration Dr					
25100	PNFD	60544	3337	31W-17S	E5
Declaration Ln					
500	AURA	60502	3139	32W-7S	B7
De Cook Av					
2700	PKRG	60068	2863	11W-10N	C4
N De Cook Ct					
2300	PKRG	60068	2863	11W-10N	D4
S De Cook Ct					
2300	PKRG	60068	2863	11W-10N	D5
N Decorah Av					
34700	GrtT	60041	2474	25W-34N	A7
Dedham Ct					
100	WNVL	60555	3080	30W-2S	C3
Dedham Ln					
800	BRLT	60103	2910	30W-7N	C5
1500	SMBG	60193	2858	25W-9N	B7
S Dedlow Rd					
3200	NndT	60051	2586	30W-28N	B5
3300	ISLK	60042	2586	30W-28N	B5
3300	NndT	60042	2586	30W-28N	B5
Dee Ct					
300	BMDL	60108	2969	22W-4N	C4
8700	TYPK	60487	3424	10W-20S	B5
W Dee Dr					
1400	NndT	60051	2586	30W-28N	A5
Dee Ln					
400	ROSL	60172	2913	22W-7N	B4
Dee Rd					
-	MaiT	60714	2863	11W-12N	D1
100	DRPK	60074	2752	21W-18N	E2
100	NARA	60542	3078	35W-3S	A7
100	PltT	60074	2752	21W-18N	E2
8800	PKRG	60016	2863	11W-11N	D4
8800	PKRG	60068	2863	11W-11N	D4
9500	NLES	60016	2863	11W-11N	D2
9500	NLES	60714	2863	11W-11N	D2
10000	MaiT	60016	2809	11W-12N	D7
10000	MaiT	60016	2863	11W-12N	D1
10000	NfdT	60016	2809	11W-12N	D7
10000	NfdT	60025	2809	11W-12N	D7
N Dee Rd					
10	PKRG	60068	2917	11W-9N	D1
100	PKRG	60068	2863	11W-9N	D6
9600	MaiT	60016	2863	11W-12N	D1
9600	NLES	60016	2863	11W-12N	D1
9600	NLES	60714	2863	11W-12N	D1
S Dee Rd					
-	CHCG	60018	2917	10W-7N	E4
-	CHCG	60068	2917	10W-7N	E4
-	CHCG	60631	2917	10W-7N	E4
-	PKRG	60631	2917	10W-7N	E4
10	PKRG	60068	2917	11W-8N	D1
Deeke Ct					
10	ROSL	60172	2912	25W-7N	C5
Deep Haven Dr					
900	JltT	60432	3499	21W-22S	E2
N Deep Lake Rd					
38200	LKVL	60046	2417	21W-39N	C5
38200	LKVL	60046	2475	21W-38N	D1
38200	LkvT	60046	2417	21W-39N	C5
38200	LNHT	60046	2417	21W-38N	D7
38200	LNHT	60046	2475	21W-38N	D1
40100	AntT	60002	2417	22W-40N	C4
40100	LKVL	60002	2417	21W-39N	C5
40100	LkvT	60002	2417	21W-39N	C5
40900	ANTH	60002	2417	22W-40N	C2
41700	ANTH	60002	2358	22W-41N	C7
41700	AntT	60002	2358	22W-43N	C4
43200	BtlT	53104	2358	22W-43N	C4
43200	BtlT	60002	2358	22W-43N	C4
N Deep Lake Rd CO-V67					
38200	LKVL	60046	2417	21W-39N	C5
38200	LKVL	60046	2475	21W-38N	D1
38200	LkvT	60046	2417	21W-39N	C5
38200	LNHT	60046	2417	21W-38N	D7
38200	LNHT	60046	2475	21W-38N	D1
40100	AntT	60002	2417	22W-40N	C4
40100	LKVL	60002	2417	21W-39N	C5
40100	LkvT	60002	2417	21W-39N	C5
40900	ANTH	60002	2417	22W-40N	C2
41700	ANTH	60002	2358	22W-41N	C7
41700	AntT	60002	2358	22W-43N	C4
43200	BtlT	53104	2358	22W-43N	C4
43200	BtlT	60002	2358	22W-43N	C4
Deep Run Rd					
1300	NPVL	60540	3142	25W-7S	B6
1400	LSLE	60532	3142	25W-7S	C6
1400	NPVL	60532	3142	25W-7S	C6
Deep Spring Dr					
7600	MchT	60097	2469	36W-35N	D5
7600	WRLK	60097	2469	36W-35N	D5
Deep Water Ln					
2100	NPVL	60564	3202	29W-9S	D5
Deep Wood Ct					
700	EGVW	60007	2914	20W-8N	B3
Deepwood Ct					
100	BNHL	60010	2749	30W-18N	A4
400	LslT	60540	3204	26W-8S	A1
400	NPVL	60540	3204	26W-8S	A1
Deep Wood Dr					
3300	NndT	60012	2584	35W-28N	A5
Deep Wood Ln					
4800	RGMW	60008	2805	21W-13N	E5
4800	RGMW	60067	2805	21W-13N	D5
Deepwood Rd					
10	BNHL	60010	2748	30W-18N	E3
10	BNHL	60010	2749	30W-18N	A4
900	SCRL	60174	2964	35W-4N	B3
Deepwood Tr					
10	RVWD	60015	2702	13W-20N	E7
Deep Woods Ct					
800	GYLK	60030	2532	21W-33N	D2
1100	ELGN	60120	2801	32W-12N	C7
Deep Woods Dr					
1100	ELGN	60120	2801	32W-12N	C7
Deepwoods Dr					
500	MDLN	60060	2646	18W-26N	E2
Deer Av					
-	PLTN	60067	2752	22W-17N	A5
-	PltT	60067	2752	22W-17N	A5
-	PltT	60074	2752	22W-17N	A5
N Deer Av					
900	PLTN	60067	2752	22W-17N	A5
1100	PltT	60067	2752	22W-17N	A5
Deer Cross					
-	BCHR	60401	3864	0E-36S	E2
Deer Ct					
300	ANTH	60002	2358	22W-42N	B6
W Deer Ct					
1300	PLTN	60067	2752	22W-17N	A5
Deer Dr					
-	HmrT	60441	3420	19W-20S	E5
-	LKPT	60441	3420	19W-20S	E5
8100	GwdT	60097	2469	37W-34N	C7
8100	WRLK	60097	2469	37W-34N	C7
Deer Ln					
10	LMNT	60439	3342	19W-15S	C1
100	BRTN	60010	2751	23W-17N	D4
100	PltT	60010	2751	23W-17N	D4
200	SYHW	60118	2799	36W-15N	E3
6400	PSHT	60463	3275	8W-15S	B7
Deer Pth					
800	ANTH	60002	2358	22W-42N	C6
8000	JSTC	60458	3209	11W-9S	E3
W Deer Pth					
26400	CNHN	60410	3672	33W-31S	C6
Deer Run					
-	ELWD	60421	3675	26W-32S	B7
10	CLLK	60012	2640	35W-27N	B1
10	LNSH	60069	2702	13W-22N	D5
100	PltT	60010	2752	22W-18N	A2
500	AntT	60081	2414	28W-39N	E4
500	FXLK	60081	2414	28W-39N	D4
Deer St					
1100	YKVL	60560	3333	42W-16S	C4
3200	LslT	60517	3205	22W-8S	C2
3200	WDRG	60517	3205	22W-8S	C2
3300	WDRG	60565	3205	22W-8S	C2
Deer Tr					
200	LKBN	60010	2643	26W-24N	D7
900	RLKB	60073	2475	21W-36N	C4
3100	SPGV	60081	2413	32W-40N	C3
4500	NHBK	60062	2755	13W-18N	E2
4500	NHBK	60062	2756	13W-18N	A2
17200	ODPK	60467	3423	13W-20S	B5
Deerbrook Ln					
300	VNHL	60061	2646	18W-24N	E7
Deer Chase Av					
10400	ODPK	60467	3423	13W-20S	B4
10400	OrlT	60467	3423	13W-20S	B4
Deer Chase Ct					
20000	DRPK	60010	2751	23W-20N	D2
20000	PltT	60010	2751	23W-20N	D2
Deerchase Ct					
5900	JNBG	60050	2472	30W-37N	A1
Deer Chase Ln					
23600	WldT	60564	3266	29W-12S	C3
Deerchase Rd					
700	LKZH	60047	2699	22W-21N	B6
Deer Creek Ct					
10	LIHL	60156	2693	38W-22N	A3
24400	PNFD	60586	3416	30W-19S	B3
25100	CNHN	60410	3672	32W-30S	C4
Deer Creek Dr					
17100	ODPK	60467	3423	13W-20S	A4
17100	OrlT	60467	3423	13W-20S	A4
Deer Creek Ln					
1300	LIHL	60156	2693	38W-22N	A3
1400	BlmT	60411	3509	1E-25S	B7
1400	FDHT	60411	3509	1E-25S	B7
1400	FDHT	60411	3597	1E-25S	B1
1400	SLVL	60411	3509	1E-25S	B7
1400	SLVL	60411	3597	1E-25S	B1
5700	WTMT	60559	3144	18W-6S	E4
Deercreek Pkwy					
700	HDPK	60035	2757	8W-20N	D1
Deer Creek Rd					
1000	CPVL	60110	2748	33W-17N	A6
1000	DndT	60110	2748	33W-17N	A6
14000	WDWH	60083	2420	14W-39N	D5
Deercrest Dr					
-	ANTH	60002	2358	20W-41N	E7
-	ANTH	60002	2359	20W-42N	A7
-	ANTH	60002	2418	20W-41N	A1
-	AntT	60002	2418	20W-41N	A1
Deercrest Ln					
10	IHPK	60525	3146	14W-6S	D4
10	IHPK	60525	3147	12W-7S	B6
1900	NfdT	60062	2756	11W-16N	C7
Deercrest Sq					
10	IHPK	60525	3147	12W-7S	B6
Deer Crossing Ct					
300	HNVL	60030	2532	21W-33N	C2
Deere Ln					
1800	GLHT	60139	2968	24W-3N	E5
Deere Park Cir					
500	BRLT	60103	2910	29W-9N	E1
Deere Park Ct					
100	HDPK	60035	2758	6W-20N	C2
N Deere Park Dr E					
200	HDPK	60035	2758	6W-20N	C1
N Deere Park Dr W					
200	HDPK	60035	2758	6W-20N	C1
S Deere Park Dr					
-	GLNC	60022	2758	6W-20N	D2
10	HDPK	60035	2758	6W-20N	D2
Deere Park Ln					
1200	DRFD	60015	2703	11W-21N	E6
Deerfield Av					
7600	WDRG	60517	3205	21W-8S	E2
Deerfield Ct					
500	SMBG	60194	2857	26W-11N	E4
1300	HDPK	60035	2704	9W-21N	C5
1500	SCRL	60174	3020	34W-2N	D1
1800	HRPK	60133	2911	27W-7N	D5
15700	ODPK	60462	3424	10W-18S	C1
S Deerfield Ct					
20100	FftT	60423	3504	9W-24S	E5
Deerfield Dr					
10	HNWD	60047	2645	21W-25N	C4
300	BGBK	60440	3269	22W-12S	C2
400	OSWG	60543	3263	37W-14S	D6
500	SMWD	60107	2856	29W-10N	D5
2400	AURA	60506	3136	39W-6S	E5
Deerfield Ln					
10	WNVL	60555	3080	30W-2S	C3
1300	BRLT	60103	2966	30W-6N	B1
2600	RGMW	60008	2805	21W-13N	D5
Deerfield Pkwy					
-	RVWD	60015	2702	14W-21N	B7
100	BFGV	60089	2701	16W-21N	D6
400	BFGV	60089	2701	16W-21N	D6
400	VrnT	60089	2701	16W-21N	D6
800	BFGV	60089	2702	15W-20N	A7
Deerfield Pkwy CO-A47					
-	BFGV	60089	2702	14W-21N	B7
-	RVWD	60015	2702	14W-21N	B7
400	BFGV	60089	2701	16W-21N	D6
400	VrnT	60089	2701	16W-21N	D6
Deerfield Pl					
-	DRFD	60015	2703	10W-20N	E7
1100	HDPK	60035	2704	9W-21N	C6
Deerfield Rd					
10	DRFD	60015	2704	10W-21N	A7
10	DRFD	60035	2704	10W-21N	B7
10	HDPK	60015	2704	10W-21N	B7
600	DRFD	60015	2703	11W-21N	D7
700	HDPK	60035	2704	8W-21N	D5
1700	WdfT	60015	2703	12W-21N	C7
2100	RVWD	60015	2703	13W-21N	A7
3200	RVWD	60015	2702	13W-21N	D7
3700	BFGV	60089	2702	14W-21N	B7
Deerfield Rd CO-A47					
1600	DRFD	60015	2703	13W-21N	A7
1700	WdfT	60015	2703	12W-21N	C7
2100	RVWD	60015	2703	13W-21N	A7
2300	RVWD	60015	2702	13W-20N	D7
3700	BFGV	60089	2702	14W-21N	B7
Deerfield Wy					
300	GNVA	60134	3019	36W-1N	D4
Deerglen Ct					
1000	MltT	60137	3025	21W-1N	D2
Deer Glen Wy					
200	BMDL	60108	2969	22W-4N	C3
Deer Grove					
16700	PltT	60010	2751	23W-17N	E4
16700	PltT	60010	2752	22W-18N	A3
16700	PltT	60067	2751	23W-17N	E4
16700	PltT	60074	2752	22W-18N	A3
Deer Grove Ln					
100	PltT	60010	2752	22W-18N	A3
W Deer Haven Ct					
10	CRTE	60417	3596	0W-28S	D7
Deerhaven Dr					
-	CLLK	60156	2693	37W-22N	C4
-	LIHL	60156	2693	37W-22N	C4
200	MNKA	60447	3583	33W-28S	C7
200	MNKA	60447	3672	33W-28S	B1
1500	CLLK	60014	2693	37W-22N	C3
Deerhaven Tr					
600	CmpT	60175	2962	39W-5N	D1
Deer Hill Ct					
600	CPVL	60110	2748	33W-17N	A7
Deer Hollow Ln					
-	AxST	60447	3672	34W-31S	A6
Deering Ct					
800	WCHI	60185	3022	29W-1N	E2
Deering Ln					
300	BGBK	60440	3268	24W-11S	D1
Deering Bay Dr					
2500	NPVL	60564	3202	30W-11S	B7
3100	NPVL	60564	3266	30W-11S	B1
Deering Oaks Ln					
4800	NndT	60012	2640	33W-27N	D1
Deer Lake Ct					
-	ANTH	60002	2358	22W-42N	C6
-	AntT	60002	2358	22W-42N	C6
Deer Lake Dr					
200	HNVL	60030	2532	21W-33N	C2
20700	DRPK	60010	2698	23W-20N	E7
Deerlake Rd					
10	DRFD	60015	2756	10W-20N	E2
10	DRFD	60062	2756	10W-20N	E2
Deer Meadow Ln					
-	DRPK	60010	2698	23W-21N	E5
-	LKZH	60047	2698	23W-21N	E5
W Deer Meadow Ln					
12800	HTLY	60142	2744	41W-20N	D1
Deer Oaks Rd					
800	AraT	60506	3077	38W-3S	A7
800	BtvT	60506	3077	38W-3S	A7
N Deer Park Blvd					
-	DRPK	60074	2752	21W-20N	D1
-	KLDR	60047	2752	21W-20N	D1
-	KLDR	60074	2752	21W-20N	D1
-	PltT	60074	2752	21W-20N	D2
Deer Park Ct					
800	DRFD	60015	2703	11W-21N	E6
S Deer Park Dr					
12500	ALSP	60803	3276	4W-14S	D6
W Deer Park Dr					
3600	ALSP	60803	3276	4W-14S	D6
Deerpass Rd					
1100	MngT	60152	2578	49W-30N	D2
1100	SenT	60152	2578	49W-30N	D2
3500	MRGO	60152	2578	49W-27N	D7
4700	MngT	60152	2634	48W-27N	D1
4700	MRGO	60152	2634	48W-27N	D1
4700	SenT	60152	2634	48W-27N	D1
Deerpass Rd CO-T59					
1100	MngT	60152	2578	49W-30N	D2
1100	SenT	60152	2578	49W-30N	D2
3500	MRGO	60152	2578	49W-27N	D7
4700	MngT	60152	2634	48W-27N	D1
4700	MRGO	60152	2634	48W-27N	D1
4700	SenT	60152	2634	48W-27N	D1
Deerpath Cir					
1200	AURA	60506	3136	39W-5S	D4
1600	WPHR	60096	2363	9W-42N	C5
Deerpath Ct					
10	CRY	60013	2695	32W-23N	B3
200	SMBG	60193	2859	21W-10N	E6
300	WCDA	60084	2643	26W-26N	D3
500	DRFD	60015	2756	11W-20N	D1
800	HFET	60169	2858	24W-11N	C3
800	WHTN	60187	3082	25W-2S	B3
1000	WLNG	60090	2754	16W-18N	D3
1100	FXLK	60020	2414	28W-38N	E6
1200	BRLT	60103	2910	29W-6N	E7
1600	RLKB	60073	2474	23W-35N	D6
1600	RLKH	60073	2474	23W-35N	D6
1700	NPVL	60565	3204	25W-9S	B4
2900	CPVL	60118	2746	37W-18N	C5
6500	LSLE	60532	3142	24W-7S	E6
13300	HTLY	60142	2744	42W-18N	D4
Deer Path Dr					
-	LNHT	60046	2476	18W-37N	D3
-	WrnT	60046	2476	18W-37N	D3
200	BfdT	53128	2353		B1
200	GNCY	53128	2353		B1
16700	HMGN	60491	3422	15W-20S	C4
Deerpath Dr					
-	YKVL	60560	3333	41W-14S	E1
100	MNKA	60447	3583	33W-28S	C7
200	OSWG	60543	3263	38W-13S	B5
300	WPHR	60096	2363	9W-42N	C5
400	LNHT	60046	2476	19W-37N	B2
400	MchT	60050	2472	29W-37N	C1
400	SPGV	60050	2472	29W-37N	C1
600	DRFD	60015	2703	11W-20N	D7
600	LkvT	60046	2476	19W-37N	B3
2200	ELGN	60123	2907	36W-8N	E3
3000	JLET	60435	3497	27W-23S	C4
3100	JLET	60431	3497	27W-23S	B4
13500	ODPK	60462	3346	10W-16S	C2

STREET Block	City	ZIP	Map#	CGS	Grid
N Deerpath Dr					
10	VNHL	60061	2647	16W-25N	C5
37000	WrnT	60046	2476	18W-37N	E3
S Deerpath Dr					
10	VNHL	60061	2647	17W-24N	C6
Deer Path Ln					
800	ELWD	60421	3675	25W-31S	C6
Deer-Path Ln					
3200	SCHT	60411	3595	1W-27S	E4
Deer Path Ln					
22500	PNFD	60544	3339	28W-16S	A3
22600	PnfT	60544	3339	28W-16S	A4
Deerpath Ln					
-	DndT	60118	2746	37W-18N	D4
-	DSPN	60018	2917	12W-8N	B2
10	LGPK	60525	3087	12W-2S	B3
10	PSPK	60464	3274	10W-14S	B6
200	CPVL	60110	2748	33W-18N	B5
200	DndT	60110	2748	33W-18N	B5
400	DGvT	60439	3270	19W-12S	D2
800	HFET	60169	2858	24W-11N	C3
800	HshT	60140	2796	44W-14N	D5
2900	CPVL	60110	2746	37W-18N	D5
2900	CPVL	60118	2746	37W-18N	D5
5600	DRGV	60516	3144	18W-6S	E4
5600	DRGV	60559	3144	18W-6S	E4
5600	WTMT	60559	3144	18W-6S	E4
6600	HRPK	60133	2911	26W-8N	E3
8000	TYPK	60477	3504	10W-23S	C3
S Deerpath Ln					
11100	PSHL	60465	3274	11W-13S	A3
Deer Path Rd					
500	GNEN	60137	3025	22W-0N	C5
600	HRVD	60033	2406	49W-39N	C5
Deerpath Rd					
-	BGBK	60490	3339	28W-14S	A1
-	DRPK	60010	2698	23W-21N	E6
-	ElaT	60047	2698	23W-21N	E6
-	LKZH	60010	2698	23W-21N	E6
-	LKZH	60047	2698	23W-21N	E6
-	LKZH	60047	2699	22W-20N	A7
10	AddT	60106	2971	17W-5N	C2
10	AraT	60506	3077	38W-4S	A7
10	BtvT	60506	3077	38W-4S	A7
10	BtvT	60542	3077	38W-3S	A6
10	DRPK	60010	2752	22W-20N	A2
10	LIHL	60156	2694	35W-21N	A5
10	MTSN	60443	3505	7W-24S	D5
10	NARA	60542	3077	38W-3S	A6
10	PltT	60010	2752	22W-20N	A2
10	WDDL	60106	2971	17W-5N	C2
10	WDDL	60191	2971	17W-5N	C2
100	ALGN	60102	2695	32W-21N	A5
100	AURA	60506	3136	39W-5S	D3
100	SgrT	60506	3136	39W-5S	D3
200	AddT	60191	2971	17W-5N	C2
200	AlqT	60102	2695	32W-21N	A5
200	BTVA	60510	3077	37W-1S	C2
200	BtvT	60510	3077	37W-1S	C2
200	DRPK	60010	2699	23W-21N	A6
200	LKZH	60010	2699	22W-20N	A7
300	AraT	60506	3136	38W-4S	E1
300	NARA	60506	3136	38W-4S	E1
400	NARA	60506	3077	38W-3S	A6
600	EDND	60118	2801	33W-16N	B2
5100	OKFT	60452	3425	6W-20S	E4
5100	OKFT	60452	3426	6W-20S	A4
10400	BLVY	60098	2582	39W-30N	C1
10400	DrrT	60098	2582	39W-30N	C1
10400	WDSK	60098	2582	39W-30N	C1
20900	ElaT	60010	2699	23W-21N	A7
21100	FKFT	60423	3504	9W-25S	E7
21200	FKFT	60423	3592	9W-25S	E1
Deerpath Rd CO-15					
10	AraT	60506	3077	38W-4S	A7
10	BtvT	60506	3077	38W-4S	A7
E Deerpath Rd					
10	LKFT	60045	2649	10W-26N	E3
100	LKFT	60045	2650	10W-26N	A3
N Deerpath Rd					
-	BTVA	60510	3077	37W-1S	C2
-	BtvT	60510	3077	37W-1S	C2
-	GnvT	60510	3077	37W-1S	C2
S Deerpath Rd					
100	DRPK	60010	2752	22W-18N	A2
100	PltT	60010	2752	22W-18N	A2
W Deerpath Rd					
10	LKFT	60045	2649	11W-26N	D3
18500	WrnT	60030	2533	18W-33N	D4
18900	AvnT	60030	2533	18W-33N	D4
18900	GYLK	60030	2533	18W-33N	D4
Deerpath Sq					
300	LKFT	60045	2649	11W-26N	C3
Deer Path Tr					
10	BRRG	60527	3208	15W-9S	B3
10	LynT	60527	3208	15W-9S	C4
Deerpath Wy					
200	SchT	60175	2963	36W-5N	E2
Deer Point Dr					
10	HNVL	60030	2532	21W-33N	C4
10	HNWD	60047	2645	22W-25N	A6
10800	ODPK	60467	3423	13W-20S	A5
Deerpoint Dr					
-	SEGN	60177	2855	33W-9N	A7
-	SEGN	60177	2909	33W-9N	A1
10	MltT	60187	3023	26W-0N	E4
700	MltT	60187	3024	26W-0N	A4
2400	MTGY	60538	3198	40W-10S	C7
2500	BtlT	60512	3198	40W-10S	C7
2500	BtlT	60538	3198	40W-10S	C7
Deerpoint Ln					
-	KdlT	60560	3333	41W-16S	E5
Deer Ridge Dr					
16400	PNFD	60586	3416	29W-19S	D3
32700	WMTN	60481	3942	29W-40S	D3
W Deer Ridge Ln					
24100	ANTH	60002	2416	24W-41N	D1
24100	AntT	60002	2416	24W-41N	D1
Deer Ridge Rd					
32700	RedT	60408	3942	29W-40S	D2
32700	RedT	60481	3942	29W-40S	D2
32700	WMTN	60481	3942	29W-40S	D2
E Deer Run Ct					
1200	CteT	60417	3687	3E-29S	B1
Deer Run Dr					
-	JLET	60431	3496	29W-23S	E5
-	SRWD	60431	3496	29W-23S	E5
10	CmpT	60175	2962	40W-5N	C3
200	BDWD	60408	3942	31W-41S	B4
200	HNVL	60030	2532	21W-33N	C3
200	RedT	60481	3942	31W-41S	B4
500	NlxT	60451	3501	16W-24S	E4
500	NlxT	60451	3502	16W-24S	A5
1700	MTGY	60538	3199	36W-10S	E5
10700	ODPK	60467	3423	13W-20S	B4
16300	HmrT	60441	3420	20W-19S	B3
Deer Run Dr					
16300	LKPT	60441	3420	20W-19S	B3
Deerrun Dr					
700	DRFD	60015	2703	12W-20N	B7
700	WdfT	60015	2703	12W-20N	B7
N Deer Run Dr					
500	PLTN	60067	2752	21W-16N	C6
W Deer Run Dr					
11600	MKNA	60448	3502	14W-25S	D7
Deer Run Ln					
-	HnrT	60120	2855	31W-11N	E4
900	CmpT	60175	2962	40W-5N	D2
Deer Run Rd					
400	LKMR	60051	2529	29W-32N	D5
1500	GRNE	60031	2478	15W-35N	B5
Deer Run Tr					
900	SDWH	60548	3258	51W-14S	A6
1400	SdwT	60548	3258	51W-14S	A6
7500	MHRY	60050	2526	36W-32N	D5
S Deer Run Tr					
24300	CteT	60417	3687	3E-29S	B1
Deerskin Tr					
500	CLSM	60188	2967	26W-3N	E5
Deerslayer Dr					
500	CmpT	60119	2961	43W-4N	B4
Deer Trail Ct					
10	ODHL	60013	2641	31W-26N	E2
4500	NHBK	60062	2755	13W-20N	E2
Deer Trail Dr					
-	BtvT	60539	3077	37W-3S	D6
-	BtvT	60542	3077	37W-3S	D6
10	DYR	46311	3598		C4
36700	LkvT	60046	2476	18W-36N	D3
36700	LNHT	60046	2476	18W-36N	D3
36700	WrnT	60046	2476	18W-37N	D3
Deertrail Dr					
1000	ANTH	60002	2358	20W-42N	E6
Deer Trail Hl					
300	LKBN	60010	2643	26W-24N	E7
Deer Trail Ln					
-	DYR	46311	3598		D4
700	OKBK	60523	3085	16W-3S	D5
1200	LYVL	60048	2592	15W-28N	A7
Deer Trail Rd					
400	CHHT	60411	3507	2W-24S	D5
2800	SPGV	60081	2413	31W-40N	D2
Deer Valley Dr					
100	DRPK	60010	2752	22W-20N	B2
100	PltT	60010	2752	22W-20N	B2
100	PltT	60074	2752	22W-20N	B2
W Deervalley Dr					
13600	HMGN	60491	3343	17W-17S	D6
Deer Valley Ln					
-	HFET	60192	2856	30W-12N	B1
Deerview Dr					
200	HNVL	60030	2532	21W-33N	C3
17200	ODPK	60467	3423	13W-20S	B5
36800	WrnT	60046	2476	18W-36N	D3
Deerview Ln					
7900	BRRG	60527	3208	14W-9S	C2
Deerwood Ct					
1000	RDLK	60073	2531	24W-33N	C2
8200	BGBK	60440	3205	22W-9S	C3
8200	BGBK	60517	3205	22W-9S	C4
8200	WDRG	60517	3205	22W-9S	C4
9000	PSHL	60465	3209	11W-11S	E7
Deerwood Dr					
-	LKPT	60432	3420	20W-21S	B7
-	LKPT	60441	3420	20W-21S	B7
-	LktT	60432	3420	20W-21S	B7
600	SRWD	60404	3496	30W-23S	B5
3700	LGGV	60047	2700	20W-21N	A5
6300	NndT	60012	2584	35W-28N	A6
S Deerwood Dr					
12700	PSPK	60464	3274	9W-15S	D7
W Deerwood Dr					
7800	PSPK	60464	3274	9W-15S	C7
Deerwood Tr					
7100	MHRY	60050	2526	36W-32N	E5
7500	MchT	60050	2526	36W-32N	D5
7500	MchT	60098	2526	36W-32N	D5
Defoe Ct					
3700	NPVL	60564	3267	28W-11S	A2
Deforest Av					
1300	FDHT	60411	3509	1E-25S	B7
De Forest Ln					
1700	HRPK	60133	2967	27W-5N	C1
Degas Cir					
400	BGBK	60440	3205	22W-11S	C7
Degener Av					
1200	PvsT	60126	3028	14W-1S	C7
1200	PvsT	60126	3086	14W-1S	C1
1200	PvsT	60162	3028	14W-1S	C7
1300	PvsT	60162	3086	14W-1S	C1
Degroate Rd					
400	NLNX	60451	3500	19W-24S	E6
400	NlxT	60451	3500	19W-24S	E6
Dehne Rd					
2000	NHBK	60062	2757	10W-16N	A7
Deicke Dr					
10	GNEN	60137	3025	23W-0S	A7
Dejarld Dr					
6600	JLET	60586	3415	32W-20S	D6
De Jong Ln					
18200	LNSG	60438	3429	2E-21S	D7
W DeKalb St					
10	JLET	60436	3498	24W-24S	E5
Dekker St					
17800	LNSG	60438	3429	2E-21S	E6
W De Koven St					
500	CHCG	60607	3034	0W-0S	A6
Del Ct					
7800	DRN	60561	3207	17W-8S	C2
24200	ElaT	60047	2644	23W-24N	E7
N Delaby Rd					
37600	LkvT	60046	2474	25W-37N	A1
Delacourte Av					
700	BGBK	60490	3267	26W-13S	E6
Deland Ct					
8000	TYPK	60477	3424	10W-19S	C1
Delaney Dr					
3700	JLET	60435	3417	27W-19S	B3
6000	HFET	60192	2855	31W-12N	E1
6000	HnrT	60120	2855	31W-12N	E1
6000	HnrT	60192	2855	31W-12N	E1
Delaney Rd					
13300	HTLY	60142	2744	42W-20N	B1
N Delaney Rd					
41500	NptT	60099	2361	14W-42N	D5
41500	WDWH	60083	2420	14W-41N	D1
41500	WDWH	60099	2361	14W-42N	D5
41500	WDWH	60099	2420	14W-41N	D1
N Delaney Rd CO-W27					
43300	NptT	60099	2361	14W-43N	D4
W Delaney Rd					
1200	MhtT	60442	3589	17W-27S	C5
W Delaney Rd					
1200	MhtT	60451	3589	17W-27S	C5
1200	NlxT	60442	3589	17W-27S	C5
1200	NlxT	60451	3589	17W-27S	C5
1500	MhtT	60451	3590	16W-27S	A5
1500	NlxT	60442	3590	16W-27S	A5
1500	NlxT	60451	3590	16W-27S	A5
1800	MhtT	60442	3590	16W-27S	A5
12000	FftT	60423	3590	16W-27S	A5
12000	GGnT	60423	3590	16W-27S	A5
12000	MhtT	60423	3590	16W-27S	A5
12000	NlxT	60423	3590	16W-27S	A5
13600	NLNX	60442	3589	17W-28S	D5
14400	NLNX	60451	3589	18W-27S	B5
15200	MhtT	60442	3588	19W-27S	E5
15200	MhtT	60451	3588	19W-27S	E5
15200	NLNX	60451	3588	19W-27S	E5
15400	NLNX	60442	3588	19W-27S	E5
15400	NlxT	60451	3588	19W-27S	E5
15700	NlxT	60442	3588	20W-27S	C5
Delano St					
10	MltT	60187	3023	26W-0N	E4
10	MltT	60188	3023	26W-0N	E4
10	WNFD	60188	3023	26W-0N	E4
N Delany Rd					
10	GRNE	60031	2535	14W-34N	D1
700	GRNE	60031	2478	14W-36N	D4
1400	WrnT	60031	2478	14W-36N	D4
2100	WKGN	60087	2478	14W-37N	D1
2100	WrnT	60087	2478	14W-36N	D4
2200	WKGN	60031	2478	14W-37N	D1
3000	WDWH	60083	2478	14W-37N	D1
3000	WDWH	60087	2478	14W-37N	D1
3000	WKGN	60083	2478	14W-37N	D1
38000	WDWH	60083	2420	14W-38N	D7
38000	WDWH	60087	2420	14W-38N	D7
38000	WKGN	60083	2420	14W-38N	D7
38000	WKGN	60087	2420	14W-38N	D7
39900	NptT	60083	2420	14W-39N	D4
41000	WDWH	60099	2420	14W-41N	D1
N Delany Rd CO-W27					
1100	GRNE	60031	2478	14W-36N	D4
1400	WrnT	60031	2478	14W-36N	D4
2100	WKGN	60087	2478	14W-37N	D1
2100	WrnT	60087	2478	14W-36N	D4
2200	WKGN	60031	2478	14W-37N	D1
3000	WDWH	60083	2478	14W-37N	D1
3000	WDWH	60087	2478	14W-37N	D1
3000	WKGN	60083	2478	14W-37N	D1
38000	WDWH	60083	2420	14W-38N	D7
38000	WDWH	60087	2420	14W-38N	D7
38000	WKGN	60083	2420	14W-38N	D7
38000	WKGN	60087	2420	14W-38N	D7
39900	NptT	60083	2420	14W-39N	D4
41000	WDWH	60099	2420	14W-41N	D1
S Delany Rd					
10	GRNE	60031	2535	13W-34N	D2
100	PKCY	60085	2535	14W-34N	D2
N Delaplaine Rd					
10	RVSD	60546	3088	9W-3S	D4
S Delaplaine Rd					
10	RVSD	60546	3088	9W-3S	D5
Delasalle Av					
400	NPVL	60565	3203	27W-10S	C6
Delasalle Ct					
700	NPVL	60565	3203	27W-10S	B6
De la Salle Dr					
-	RMVL	60441	3418	24W-18S	E1
-	RMVL	60441	3419	23W-18S	A1
De la Salle Dr E					
-	RMVL	60441	3419	23W-18S	A1
De la Salle Dr W					
-	RMVL	60441	3418	23W-18S	E1
Delavan St					
-	LKPT	60441	3419	21W-20S	E5
Delaware Av					
2300	NCHI	60088	2593	12W-29N	C4
5600	GRNE	60031	2477	16W-36N	E5
Delaware Cir					
400	BGBK	60440	3205	23W-11S	A7
Delaware Ct					
10	SMBG	60193	2857	27W-10N	D6
300	CPVL	60110	2748	32W-18N	D5
1500	GNVA	60134	3021	33W-2N	A2
2700	LNHT	60046	2418	19W-39N	C5
4200	NPVL	60564	3267	28W-12S	A2
18000	ODPK	60467	3423	13W-21S	A7
Delaware Dr					
100	BGBK	60440	3269	23W-11S	A1
300	BGBK	60440	3205	23W-11S	A7
500	LIHL	60156	2694	34W-21N	B5
S Delaware Dr					
2200	MPPT	60056	2861	16W-10N	E6
W Delaware Dr					
16500	LKPT	60441	3420	20W-20S	B5
Delaware Ln					
600	EGVV	60007	2913	22W-9N	C1
2600	LNHT	60046	2418	19W-39N	C6
Delaware Pl					
600	JLET	60432	3499	23W-23S	B4
2100	JNBG	60051	2471	31W-35N	E6
E Delaware Pl					
10	CHCG	60610	3034	0E-1N	C2
10	CHCG	60611	3034	0E-1N	C2
W Delaware Pl					
10	CHCG	60611	3034	0W-1N	B2
500	CHCG	60610	3034	0W-1N	A2
Delaware Rd					
1700	WKGN	60087	2479	11W-36N	D5
7100	MchT	60097	2469	36W-36N	E3
Delaware St					
100	GfnT	60014	2638	38W-25N	E5
300	CPVL	60110	2748	32W-18N	D4
Delaware Tr					
500	CLSM	60188	2967	26W-3N	E5
1700	WLNG	60090	2754	16W-17N	C5
Delft Ct					
300	PTON	60468	3860	9W-37S	D3
Delft Ln					
-	PNFD	60586	3415	32W-19S	C3
E Delgado Dr					
500	PLTN	60074	2753	20W-17N	A5
Delia Av					
200	WCDA	60084	2644	25W-27N	B1
S Delia Av					
17300	JLET	60586	3415	31W-20S	D6
17300	PNFD	60586	3415	31W-20S	D6
Delia St					
300	BTVA	60510	3078	34W-1S	C1
Delicious Ct					
-	PTHT	60070	2808	13W-15N	E1
E Delite Inn Rd					
100	WshT	60401	3864	0E-39S	E7
W Delite Inn Rd					
100	WshT	60401	3864	0W-39S	D7
Delius Av					
700	AURA	60505	3138	34W-7S	C6
Delkir Ct					
500	NPVL	60565	3203	26W-9S	D4
Dell Av					
-	CHCG	60613	2977	1W-5N	D1
-	ELGN	60120	2855	32W-10N	D6
Dell Ct					
9000	HYHL	60457	3209	11W-9S	E4
N Dell Dr					
40100	AntT	60002	2417	22W-40N	C3
Dell Ln					
400	HDPK	60035	2758	7W-20N	C1
Dell Pl					
10	GLNC	60022	2758	5W-17N	E5
3000	GNVW	60025	2810	10W-13N	A6
Dell Rd					
800	NHBK	60062	2757	8W-17N	E4
1000	NHBK	60062	2758	8W-17N	A5
Della Av					
10	CLSM	60188	3024	25W-1N	B3
10	GfnT	60014	2638	38W-25N	E5
10	GfnT	60014	2639	38W-25N	A4
200	MltT	60188	3024	25W-1N	B3
Della Dr					
1400	HFET	60169	2858	25W-12N	B1
Della Ln					
100	OSWG	60543	3263	36W-12S	E3
Del Lago Dr					
400	SMBG	60173	2859	22W-11N	D4
Delles Rd					
300	WHTN	60187	3024	25W-0S	B7
600	MltT	60563	3082	25W-3S	B6
700	WHTN	60187	3082	25W-1S	B1
W Dellmar Av					
1200	JLET	60435	3498	25W-22S	B3
Dellmont Ct					
10	BFGV	60089	2701	16W-21N	D6
Dell Park Av					
100	LKPT	60441	3419	23W-20S	B5
100	LktT	60441	3419	23W-20S	B5
E Dells Wy					
10	HRVY	60426	3349	1W-17S	E6
100	HRVY	60426	3350	1W-17S	A6
W Dells Wy					
10	HRVY	60426	3349	2W-17S	C6
Dellshire Ln					
3600	MchT	60050	2471	32W-36N	B3
Dellwood Av					
100	LktT	60441	3419	23W-21S	B6
Dellwood Ct					
10	ALGN	60102	2746	37W-19N	D3
Del Mar Ct					
700	UYPK	60466	3684	4W-29S	A2
Delmar Ct					
500	EGVV	60007	2913	22W-9N	C1
Delmar Dr					
100	BGBK	60440	3269	23W-12S	B2
1400	NLNX	60451	3588	19W-26S	E2
N Del Mar Dr					
1100	PLTN	60067	2752	20W-17N	E5
Del Mar Ln					
300	RLKP	60030	2589	22W-30N	B1
Del Miller Ln					
6100	AlqT	60013	2642	30W-25N	B4
6100	NndT	60013	2642	30W-25N	B4
Delmonte Dr					
5500	HRPK	60133	2912	25W-6N	A6
Delnor Av					
200	SCRL	60174	2964	35W-3N	B5
Delnor Dr					
-	GNVA	60134	3019	37W-1N	D3
Delo Dr					
10	WCDA	60084	2643	26W-26N	E2
10	WcnT	60084	2643	26W-26N	E2
Del Ogier Dr					
1600	GNVW	60025	2811	7W-14N	B5
Delore Dr					
2200	MchT	60051	2528	31W-32N	D5
Delores Av					
-	BHPK	60087	2421	12W-38N	B6
Delphi Ct					
10	TYPK	60477	3505	8W-23S	B4
Delphi Dr					
-	OMFD	60461	3507	3W-24S	A5
Delphia Av					
700	EGVV	60007	2914	18W-9N	D1
700	EGVV	60007	2915	18W-9N	A1
9000	MaiT	60016	2864	10W-11N	A3
9000	MaiT	60714	2864	10W-11N	A3
9000	NLES	60714	2864	10W-11N	A3
9300	NLES	60016	2864	10W-11N	A3
N Delphia Av					
10	PKRG	60068	2918	8W-8N	D1
600	PKRG	60068	2864	10W-9N	A6
1100	NLES	60714	2864	10W-10N	A5
1100	PKRG	60714	2864	10W-10N	A6
4700	NRDG	60706	2918	10W-5N	A7
4800	CHCG	60706	2918	10W-6N	A7
4900	NRDG	60656	2918	10W-6N	A7
5200	CHCG	60656	2918	10W-6N	A5
5500	CHCG	60631	2918	10W-6N	A5
S Delphia Av					
10	PKRG	60068	2918	10W-8N	A3
Delphia Ct					
700	EGVV	60007	2915	18W-9N	A1
Del Prado Dr					
9000	PlsT	60465	3209	11W-11S	E6
9000	PlsT	60480	3209	11W-11S	E6
9000	PSHL	60465	3209	11W-11S	E6
Delray Dr					
-	AraT	60504	3201	33W-9S	A5
-	AURA	60504	3201	33W-9S	A5
Delrio Rd					
100	CPVL	60110	2748	33W-18N	B4
Delrose St					
1600	JLET	60435	3417	27W-21S	C7
1600	JLET	60435	3497	27W-21S	C1
Delta Av					
700	RMVL	60446	3269	23W-14S	A7
Delta Ct					
1100	ELGN	60123	2907	36W-9N	E1
Delta Dr					
-	AURA	60503	3201	31W-10S	D5
-	AURA	60504	3201	31W-10S	D5
1000	ELGN	60123	2907	36W-9N	E1
Delta Ln					
2300	EGVV	60007	2915	16W-7N	E3
Delta Pkwy					
10500	SRPK	60176	2973	13W-5N	A1
Delta Rd					
200	HDPK	60035	2758	7W-20N	C1
18700	HMWD	60430	3508	1W-22S	A2
Del Webb Blvd					
-	ElgT	60124	2853	37W-9N	C7
-	ElgT	60124	2907	37W-9N	C1
Del Webb Blvd					
-	SRWD	60404	3496	31W-24S	A6
-	TroT	60404	3496	31W-24S	A6
600	SRWD	60404	3495	31W-24S	E6
12800	HTLY	60142	2744	42W-18N	C4
Demaret Ct					
4000	WDRG	60517	3143	23W-7S	A6
Deming Pl					
-	BtnT	60081	2414	29W-38N	C6
100	WTMT	60559	3145	17W-6S	B5
300	DGvT	60527	3145	17W-6S	C5
300	DGvT	60559	3145	17W-6S	C5
300	WTMT	60527	3145	17W-6S	C5
W Deming Pl					
500	CHCG	60614	2978	0W-3N	A5
4400	CHCG	60639	2976	5W-3N	A5
4800	CHCG	60639	2975	6W-3N	D5
Demmond Ct					
1300	JLET	60432	3499	22W-22S	D1
Demmond St					
800	ELGN	60123	2854	35W-12N	C3
E Demmond St					
1100	JLET	60432	3499	22W-22S	C1
Dempsey Dr					
10	ELBN	60119	3017	43W-1N	A3
Dempsey Pl					
500	GNVA	60134	3019	36W-1N	E2
Dempster Av					
700	EGvT	60005	2861	16W-10N	D4
700	EGvT	60056	2861	16W-10N	D4
1500	MPPT	60056	2861	16W-10N	D4
1700	MPPT	60005	2861	17W-10N	C4
Dempster Ct					
-	PKRG	60068	2863	11W-11N	E4
Dempster St					
-	DSPN	60068	2863	12W-10N	C4
100	EVTN	60201	2867	3W-11N	A3
100	EVTN	60202	2867	3W-11N	A3
300	DSPN	60016	2861	16W-10N	E4
300	MPPT	60016	2861	16W-10N	E4
300	MPPT	60056	2861	16W-10N	E4
500	EGvT	60056	2861	16W-10N	E4
1200	NLES	60714	2863	11W-10N	D4
1200	PKRG	60068	2864	10W-10N	A4
1200	PKRG	60714	2863	11W-10N	D4
1200	PKRG	60714	2864	10W-10N	A4
1500	NLES	60068	2863	11W-11N	E4
1800	EVTN	60201	2866	5W-11N	B3
1800	EVTN	60202	2866	5W-11N	B3
2000	MaiT	60016	2863	12W-10N	C4
2000	PKRG	60016	2863	12W-10N	C4
2700	DSPN	60016	2863	11W-10N	C4
2700	PKRG	60068	2863	11W-10N	C4
3300	SKOK	60076	2866	5W-11N	B3
3300	SKOK	60203	2866	5W-11N	B3
4700	SKOK	60076	2865	5W-11N	E4
4700	SKOK	60077	2865	5W-11N	E4
5600	MNGV	60053	2865	8W-10N	A4
6700	MNGV	60053	2864	8W-11N	E3
7000	NLES	60053	2864	8W-11N	E4
7000	NLES	60714	2864	8W-11N	E4
Dempster St SR-58					
4800	SKOK	60076	2865	6W-11N	E4
4800	SKOK	60077	2865	6W-11N	E4
5600	MNGV	60053	2865	8W-10N	A4
6700	MNGV	60053	2864	8W-11N	E3
Dempster St US-14					
-	DSPN	60068	2863	12W-10N	C4
1200	NLES	60714	2863	11W-10N	D4
1200	PKRG	60068	2863	12W-10N	C4
1200	PKRG	60068	2864	10W-10N	A4
1200	PKRG	60714	2863	11W-10N	D4
1200	PKRG	60714	2864	10W-10N	A4
1500	NLES	60068	2863	11W-11N	E4
2000	MaiT	60016	2863	12W-10N	C4
2000	PKRG	60016	2863	12W-10N	C4
2300	DSPN	60016	2863	12W-10N	C4
6900	MNGV	60053	2864	8W-11N	E4
7000	NLES	60053	2864	8W-11N	E4
7000	NLES	60714	2864	8W-11N	E4
W Dempster St					
700	DSPN	60016	2862	15W-10N	A4
7000	MNGV	60053	2864	10W-11N	A4
7000	NLES	60053	2864	8W-11N	E4
7000	NLES	60714	2864	10W-11N	A4
7100	MNGV	60714	2864	8W-11N	D4
8500	PKRG	60068	2864	10W-10N	A4
8500	PKRG	60714	2864	10W-10N	A4
W Dempster St US-14					
7000	MNGV	60053	2864	10W-11N	A4
7000	NLES	60053	2864	8W-11N	E4
7000	NLES	60714	2864	10W-11N	A4
7100	MNGV	60714	2864	8W-11N	D4
8500	PKRG	60068	2864	10W-10N	A4
8500	PKRG	60714	2864	10W-10N	A4
Dena Av					
10	FXLK	60020	2473	27W-36N	A4
N Denal St					
5000	NRDG	60706	2918	10W-6N	A6
Denali					
400	NPVL	60563	3081	26W-4S	E7
Denali Ct					
-	BrnT	60010	2802	28W-14N	E5
800	BbyT	60119	3017	41W-1N	E4
Denali Ln					
600	CmpT	60119	3018	40W-2N	B2
Denali Rd					
10	BbyT	60119	3017	41W-1N	E4
N Denali Tr					
1400	MHRY	60050	2527	35W-33N	A3
Denali Ridge Dr					
6400	JLET	60586	3415	32W-21S	D7
Denberry Ct					
100	LKZH	60047	2698	23W-21N	E5
Denberry Dr					
200	LKZH	60047	2698	23W-21N	E5
300	ElaT	60047	2699	23W-21N	A5
300	LKZH	60047	2699	23W-21N	A5
N Deneen Ln					
200	MPPT	60056	2808	14W-13N	C6
Denell Ct					
10	CRTE	60417	3596	0W-28S	D6
Denell Dr					
-	HTLY	60142	2744	42W-20N	B1
10	CRTE	60417	3596	0W-28S	D6
Denham Dr					
10	OswT	60538	3200	36W-10S	A6
Denham Pl					
1000	SMBG	60194	2858	25W-11N	A3
Denice Ct					
4000	GNVW	60025	2809	11W-13N	D6
Denise Ct					
10	MTSN	60443	3505	7W-24S	C4
600	YKVL	60560	3261	43W-13S	B5
N Denise Ct					
500	ADSN	60101	2970	18W-4N	E4

STREET Block	City	ZIP	Map#	CGS	Grid
N Denise Dr					
1600	PLTN	60074	2753	20W-18N	A4
W Denise Dr					
200	RDLK	60073	2531	23W-31N	E7
200	RDLK	60073	2532	23W-31N	A7
Denise St					
12900	PNFD	60585	3338	29W-15S	D2
13000	WldT	60585	3338	29W-15S	D2
Denison Rd					
1700	NPVL	60565	3204	24W-9S	D3
Denker Ct					
500	CmpT	60175	2906	39W-6N	D6
Denker Ln					
600	CmpT	60175	2906	39W-6N	D7
Denker Rd					
10	CmpT	60175	2962	39W-6N	D1
100	CmpT	60175	2906	39W-6N	D7
Denley Av					
3700	FNPK	60131	2973	12W-4N	B3
3700	FNPK	60176	2973	12W-4N	B3
3700	SRPK	60131	2973	12W-4N	B3
3700	SRPK	60176	2973	12W-4N	B3
Dennis Av					
800	ALGN	60102	2694	34W-21N	C6
800	LIHL	60102	2694	34W-21N	C6
800	LIHL	60156	2694	34W-21N	C6
Dennis Blvd					
4200	JNBG	60050	2472	30W-36N	A4
4200	McHT	60050	2472	30W-36N	A4
Dennis Ct					
10	JLET	60433	3499	23W-24S	A6
10	JLET	60436	3499	23W-24S	A6
10	SMBG	60193	2858	25W-10N	C6
200	ELGN	60123	2854	35W-10N	B5
16000	OKFT	60452	3425	7W-19S	D1
Dennis Dr					
10	BNVL	60106	2972	15W-4N	A3
W Dennis Dr					
1700	MPPT	60056	2861	17W-10N	C5
Dennis Ln					
100	GLNC	60022	2758	6W-18N	D4
1100	HnrT	60107	2856	30W-10N	C7
1100	HnrT	60120	2856	30W-10N	C7
Dennis Pl					
1200	DSPN	60018	2862	13W-10N	D5
E Dennis Rd					
10	WLNG	60090	2755	15W-17N	A4
N Dennis Rd					
700	WLNG	60090	2755	15W-17N	A4
S Dennis Rd					
700	WLNG	60090	2755	15W-17N	A5
Dennison Dr					
10	GLHT	60139	2968	23W-4N	E4
Dennison Rd					
1600	HFET	60169	2858	24W-12N	E1
Denniston Ct					
400	WLNG	60090	2755	15W-17N	B5
Denny Av					
11000	MKNA	60448	3503	13W-23S	A4
Denny Ct					
4400	RGMW	60008	2806	20W-14N	A3
Denny Rd					
10	SgrT	60554	3136	40W-4S	A2
100	SRGV	60554	3136	41W-4S	A2
300	SgrT	60554	3135	41W-4S	E2
300	SRGV	60554	3135	41W-4S	E2
Denny St					
200	SchT	60174	3021	33W-2N	B1
Denoyer Tr					
200	WLNG	60090	2755	15W-18N	A3
Densmore Rd					
200	SgrT	60506	3136	40W-6S	C5
300	AURA	60506	3136	40W-6S	C6
N Denton Av					
1400	PLTN	60067	2752	21W-18N	D3
W Denton Av					
200	PLTN	60067	2752	21W-18N	D3
Denton Ct					
900	CLLK	60014	2640	35W-24N	B7
2200	SMBG	60194	2857	28W-12N	B1
2800	WSTR	60154	3086	13W-2S	E4
14000	LktT	60544	3339	26W-16S	E4
Denton Ln					
200	SEGN	60177	2907	37W-8N	C4
Denver Ct					
1200	NPVL	60540	3202	28W-8S	E2
Denver Dr					
100	BGBK	60440	3268	24W-11S	D2
200	DSPN	60018	2862	15W-10N	B6
1100	CPVL	60110	2748	33W-17N	C6
1400	MNKA	60447	3672	34W-30S	A3
S Denvir Av					
500	CHCG	60612	3033	3W-0S	A6
Depaul Ct					
300	DPgT	60441	3341	23W-15S	A2
300	MHRY	60050	2527	33W-32N	E5
1500	NPVL	60565	3204	24W-8S	D2
Depaul Dr					
300	ELGN	60123	2853	36W-10N	D6
Depaul Ln					
600	MTSN	60443	3506	6W-24S	A6
De Pinto					
-	BMDL	60172	2912	24W-6N	C7
Depot Dr					
2200	NCHI	60088	2593	12W-30N	C2
Depot Pl					
-	BmdT	60143	2913	21W-6N	E5
-	ITSC	60143	2913	21W-6N	E5
W Depot Pl					
-	BFGV	60089	2701	16W-21N	E5
16000	BFGV	60069	2701	16W-21N	E5
16000	VrnT	60069	2701	16W-21N	E5
Depot Rd					
700	GRNE	60031	2478	14W-35N	D6
1100	WrnT	60031	2478	14W-35N	D6
Depot St					
1000	GNVW	60025	2810	8W-13N	D6
17800	UNON	60180	2635	46W-25N	C4
E Depot St					
10	VNHL	60061	2647	16W-24N	C7
S Depot St					
10500	CHRG	60415	3274	8W-12S	E2
10500	CHRG	60482	3274	8W-12S	E2
10500	WRTH	60482	3274	8W-12S	E2
W Depot St					
10	ANTH	60002	2358	23W-42N	A6
400	ANTH	60002	2357	23W-42N	D6
22000	AntT	60002	2358	22W-42N	C6
Derby Ct					
10	LslT	60540	3204	24W-8S	E1
10	OKBK	60523	3084	18W-3S	E6
10	RLKP	60030	2589	22W-30N	B1
10	RtdT	60142	2745	41W-18N	B5
400	OSWG	60543	3263	38W-13S	B5
400	SMBG	60193	2859	23W-9N	A6
700	ANTH	60002	2357	24W-42N	B6
1500	NPVL	60563	3140	29W-5S	D3
2100	WHTN	60187	3083	23W-3S	A5
2600	ELGN	60124	2853	37W-11N	D4
3000	AURA	60502	3078	34W-3S	E6
9800	MKNA	60448	3503	12W-23S	D4
Derby Dr					
-	PLNO	60545	3259	46W-13S	E5
-	PLNO	60545	3260	46W-13S	A5
100	LslT	60540	3205	23W-8S	A1
1600	BTVA	60510	3078	35W-2S	C5
1700	NARA	60542	3078	35W-2S	C5
6700	GRNE	60031	2477	17W-35N	C5
25900	MONE	60449	3682	7W-31S	E5
S Derby Dr					
13900	HMGN	60491	3344	15W-16S	B3
Derby Ln					
-	RtdT	60142	2745	41W-18N	B5
10	FmtT	60047	2644	23W-26N	E4
10	FmtT	60084	2644	23W-26N	E4
10	HMGN	60491	3344	15W-16S	B4
10	HNWD	60047	2644	23W-26N	E4
10	OrlT	60467	3344	15W-16S	B4
100	RLKP	60030	2589	22W-30N	B1
300	CmpT	60175	2961	42W-4N	D4
1200	MDLN	60060	2647	17W-25N	A5
1500	BRLT	60103	2966	30W-5N	B2
4200	NndT	60012	2583	36W-27N	D7
9800	BDVW	60154	3029	12W-1S	C7
9800	BDVW	60155	3029	12W-1S	C7
9800	WSTR	60154	3029	12W-1S	C7
9900	MKNA	60448	3503	12W-23S	C4
S Derby Ln					
11500	PNFD	60585	3266	30W-13S	C5
W Derby Ln					
24000	PNFD	60585	3266	30W-13S	C6
Derby Rd					
-	LmnT	60439	3272	16W-12S	A1
-	LmnT	60480	3272	16W-12S	A1
400	WYNE	60184	2965	32W-5N	C2
12300	LMNT	60439	3271	17W-14S	C7
12700	LMNT	60439	3343	17W-15S	C2
13400	HMGN	60439	3343	17W-15S	C2
13400	HMGN	60491	3343	17W-15S	C2
Derby St					
1200	WLNG	60090	2755	15W-16N	A7
Derby Course					
600	SCRL	60174	2964	34W-3N	E5
Derby Glen Dr					
100	GNEN	60137	3024	23W-1N	E3
100	GNEN	60137	3025	23W-1N	A3
N Derbyshire Av					
800	ANHT	60004	2807	17W-14N	C3
Derbyshire Ct					
10	BGBK	60440	3205	22W-10S	C6
800	PTHT	60070	2807	15W-16N	E1
N Derbyshire Dr					
1100	ANHT	60004	2807	17W-15N	C3
Derbyshire Ln					
600	BGBK	60440	3205	22W-10S	C6
800	PTHT	60070	2807	15W-16N	E1
N Derbyshire Ln					
1900	ANHT	60004	2807	17W-16N	C1
S Derbyshire Ln					
10	ANHT	60004	2807	17W-13N	C5
Derek Wy					
19300	MKNA	60448	3503	13W-23S	A3
W Dering Ln					
24700	LkvT	60046	2416	25W-38N	B6
Deroo Lp					
700	HIWD	60040	2704	9W-24N	C1
N Derrough Av					
1100	NHLK	60164	2972	14W-3N	D5
2800	LydT	60164	2972	14W-3N	D5
3000	FNPK	60131	2972	14W-3N	D4
3000	FNPK	60164	2972	14W-3N	D4
Derry Ct					
600	SMBG	60193	2859	23W-9N	A7
Derry Ln					
1200	PGGV	60140	2797	41W-15N	E4
De Russey Rd					
500	BbyT	60119	3075	43W-2S	A4
Derwent Ln					
17400	TYPK	60487	3424	10W-20S	B5
W De Saible St					
200	CHCG	60609	3092	0W-3S	B5
Desert Dr					
-	NasT	60586	3415	32W-20S	C6
6700	JLET	60586	3415	32W-20S	C6
Deshannon Ct					
1000	BTVA	60510	3078	34W-2S	D4
Desiree Dr					
8300	TYPK	60477	3424	10W-19S	B3
8300	TYPK	60487	3424	10W-19S	B3
E Des Moines St					
10	WTMT	60559	3145	17W-5S	B3
300	CNHL	60514	3145	17W-5S	B3
300	CNHL	60559	3145	17W-5S	B3
W Des Moines St					
-	DRGV	60515	3145	18W-5S	A3
-	WTMT	60515	3145	18W-5S	A3
10	WTMT	60559	3145	18W-5S	A3
Desmond Dr					
200	SMBG	60193	2858	24W-9N	E7
500	WDSK	60098	2581	42W-30N	C2
Desota Ct					
3500	FNPK	60131	2973	12W-4N	C3
De Soto Av					
-	TYPK	60477	3424	9W-21S	D5
Des Plaines Av					
100	FTPK	60130	3030	9W-1S	C7
100	MYWD	60153	3030	10W-0N	A3
200	NRIV	60546	3088	9W-1S	C2
200	RVSD	60546	3088	10W-2S	B4
1500	FTPK	60130	3088	9W-1S	C2
1700	PKRG	60068	2917	11W-8N	E1
1800	PvsT	60130	3088	9W-1S	C1
2200	FTPK	60141	3088	9W-1S	C2
2200	FTPK	60546	3088	9W-1S	C2
2200	PvsT	60141	3088	9W-1S	C2
2200	PvsT	60546	3088	9W-1S	C2
Des Plaines Ct					
5600	GRNE	60031	2534	16W-33N	E2
5600	GRNE	60048	2534	16W-33N	E2
5600	WrnT	60031	2534	16W-33N	E2
5600	WrnT	60048	2534	16W-33N	E2
W Des Plaines Dr					
16000	LbvT	60048	2591	16W-30N	D2
Des Plaines Ln					
10	HFET	60169	2859	23W-11N	A4
Des Plaines St					
14400	HRVY	60426	3350	1W-17S	A5
Desplaines St					
2700	BLID	60406	3349	3W-15S	A2
N Des Plaines St					
10	JLET	60432	3498	24W-24S	D7
10	JLET	60436	3498	24W-24S	D7
400	PNFD	60544	3338	30W-18S	C7
N Desplaines St					
10	CHCG	60661	3034	0W-0N	A4
300	CHCG	60610	3034	0W-0N	A4
S Des Plaines St					
10	JLET	60432	3498	24W-23S	E5
10	JLET	60436	3498	24W-24S	E6
1600	JltT	60436	3586	24W-26S	E2
S Desplaines St					
10	CHCG	60661	3034	0W-0S	A5
300	CHCG	60607	3034	0W-0S	A6
1900	CHCG	60616	3092	0W-1S	A1
Des Plaines River Dr					
-	DPgT	60441	3269	21W-14S	E6
15100	DPgT	60439	3270	21W-13S	A5
15100	DPgT	60441	3270	21W-13S	A5
15100	LmnT	60439	3270	21W-13S	A5
Des Plaines River Rd					
3200	FNPK	60131	2973	11W-4N	E4
3200	RVGV	60131	2973	11W-4N	E4
3200	RVGV	60171	2973	11W-4N	E4
3500	SRPK	60131	2973	11W-4N	D3
3500	SRPK	60176	2973	11W-4N	D2
N Des Plaines River Rd					
-	DSPN	60016	2808	13W-13N	E6
-	WhlT	60056	2808	13W-13N	E6
2100	RVGV	60171	2974	10W-2N	A6
2400	RVGV	60171	2973	11W-3N	E5
3100	FNPK	60131	2973	11W-3N	E4
3100	RVGV	60131	2973	11W-3N	E4
N Des Plaines River Rd US-45					
-	DSPN	60016	2808	13W-13N	E6
-	WhlT	60056	2808	13W-13N	E6
Destiny Dr					
800	MTSN	60443	3505	7W-25S	D7
Detamble Av					
600	HDPK	60035	2705	8W-21N	A6
De Trevi					
-	BMDL	60172	2912	24W-6N	C7
-	BmdT	60172	2912	24W-6N	C7
Detroit St					
-	CTCY	60409	3430	4E-18S	B1
10	CRY	60013	2695	30W-23N	E2
10	CRY	60013	2696	30W-23N	A2
10	HMND	46320	3430	4E-18S	C1
E Detroit St					
10	CTCY	60409	3430		C1
10	HMND	46320	3430		D1
Dettmering St					
21100	MTSN	60443	3506	4W-24S	D6
21100	MTSN	60443	3594	4W-25S	E1
21100	OMFD	60461	3506	4W-24S	D6
Deveaux Ct					
-	SBTN	60010	2803	26W-15N	D3
Devereaux Wy					
-	SCRL	60174	3020	35W-2N	C1
S Deverell Ct					
1100	PLTN	60067	2805	21W-14N	D4
Deverell Dr					
10	NBRN	60010	2644	25W-24N	A7
Devereux Rd					
-	WDRG	60517	3206	20W-8S	B1
1600	DRGV	60516	3206	20W-8S	A1
7400	WDRG	60516	3206	20W-8S	A1
Deveron Cir					
300	CRY	60013	2695	31W-23N	D2
Deville Ln					
3500	SCRL	60175	2963	38W-3N	B6
Devlin Ct					
200	NPVL	60565	3203	26W-9S	D4
Devlin Rd					
-	BFGV	60089	2701	17W-21N	B6
10	FXLK	60020	2473	27W-36N	C4
10	FXLK	60041	2473	27W-36N	C4
Devoe Dr					
-	OSWG	60543	3265	33W-11S	A1
-	OswT	60543	3265	33W-11S	A1
Devon Av					
-	CHCG	60018	2917	11W-8N	D3
-	CHCG	60068	2917	11W-8N	D3
10	CHCG	60068	2918	10W-8N	A3
10	CHCG	60631	2918	10W-8N	A3
10	PKRG	60068	2918	10W-8N	A3
1400	PKRG	60068	2917	11W-8N	D3
4300	LSLE	60532	3142	23W-4S	E1
4300	LslT	60532	3142	23W-4S	E1
E Devon Av					
-	CHCG	60068	2917	11W-8N	D3
-	PKRG	60068	2917	11W-8N	D3
10	EGVV	60007	2914	19W-8N	D3
10	ITSC	60007	2914	19W-8N	D3
10	ITSC	60143	2914	19W-8N	D3
10	ROSL	60172	2913	23W-7N	A3
100	AddT	60007	2914	18W-8N	E3
100	AddT	60143	2914	18W-8N	E3
100	BRLT	60103	2910	28W-8N	E4
100	BRLT	60103	2911	28W-8N	A4
200	EGvT	60007	2914	19W-7N	D3
200	WDDL	60143	2914	18W-8N	E3
200	WDDL	60191	2914	19W-7N	D3
400	EGvT	60007	2915	18W-8N	A3
400	EGVV	60007	2915	18W-7N	A3
400	WDDL	60191	2915	18W-8N	A3
500	WDDL	60007	2915	18W-8N	A3
700	BmdT	60157	2913	22W-7N	C3
700	BmdT	60172	2913	22W-7N	C3
1000	WynT	60103	2911	28W-8N	A4
1100	BNVL	60007	2915	17W-8N	B3
1100	BNVL	60106	2915	18W-7N	A3
1100	HRPK	60133	2911	28W-8N	A4
2000	DSPN	60018	2917	12W-8N	C3
2000	RSMT	60018	2917	12W-8N	C3
2100	EGVV	60106	2915	16W-8N	E3
2500	CHCG	60018	2917	11W-8N	C3
S Devon Av					
100	BRLT	60103	2910	29W-8N	D3
W Devon Av					
10	BRLT	60103	2910	29W-7N	E4
10	ROSL	60172	2913	23W-7N	A3
100	ROSL	60172	2912	23W-7N	E3
1000	EGVV	60007	2914	20W-7N	B3
1000	ITSC	60007	2914	20W-8N	A3
1000	ITSC	60143	2914	20W-7N	B3
1200	CHCG	60626	2921	2W-8N	A2
1200	CHCG	60660	2921	2W-8N	A2
1900	CHCG	60645	2921	2W-8N	B2
1900	CHCG	60659	2921	2W-8N	B2
2600	CHCG	60645	2920	4W-8N	D2
2600	CHCG	60659	2920	5W-8N	A3
3100	CHCG	60712	2920	3W-8N	D3
3100	LNWD	60659	2920	5W-8N	A3
3100	LNWD	60712	2920	5W-8N	A3
3900	CHCG	60646	2920	4W-8N	B3
4500	LNWD	60646	2920	5W-8N	A3
4700	CHCG	60646	2919	6W-8N	E2
4700	CHCG	60712	2919	5W-8N	E3
5000	LNWD	60646	2919	6W-8N	E3
5000	LNWD	60712	2919	6W-8N	E3
6300	CHCG	60631	2919	8W-8N	A3
6600	CHCG	60631	2918	9W-8N	C3
7700	CHCG	60068	2918	9W-8N	C3
7700	PKRG	60068	2918	9W-8N	C3
10000	RSMT	60018	2917	12W-8N	B3
Devon Ct					
10	BGBK	60440	3205	22W-10S	D5
10	BRRG	60527	3208	15W-10S	B4
300	GYLK	60030	2533	19W-33N	C3
1100	CLSM	60188	2967	27W-4N	D4
36500	GRNE	60031	2477	16W-36N	D4
36500	GRNE	60083	2477	16W-36N	D3
36500	WrnT	60083	2477	16W-36N	D3
W Devon Ct					
10100	RSMT	60018	2917	12W-7N	B3
Devon Dr					
200	BRRG	60527	3208	15W-10S	B5
500	DYR	46311	3598		D1
900	ANTH	60002	2359	20W-42N	A7
17600	CCHL	60478	3426	4W-21S	D6
N Devon Dr					
1700	GLHT	60139	2968	24W-3N	E6
W Devon Dr					
10	GLHT	60139	2968	24W-3N	E6
23600	CNHN	60410	3584	29W-27S	D6
Devon Ln					
10	NPVL	60540	3142	25W-6S	B5
400	BGBK	60440	3205	22W-10S	D5
600	RMVL	60446	3269	23W-13S	B6
11100	HTLY	60142	2692	40W-22N	B3
W Devon Ln					
2000	JNBG	60050	2471	30W-36N	E3
Devon Ridge Ct					
10	BRRG	60527	3208	15W-10S	A6
Devon Ridge Dr					
9100	BRRG	60527	3208	15W-10S	A6
9100	DGvT	60527	3208	15W-10S	A6
Devonshire Av					
900	NPVL	60540	3141	27W-7S	B6
Devonshire Cir					
-	LGGV	60047	2647	17W-24N	A7
10	ELGN	60123	2800	36W-14N	B6
Devonshire Ct					
10	RLKP	60030	2589	22W-30N	B1
200	SMBG	60173	2859	21W-10N	E5
400	BGBK	60440	3269	22W-12S	B3
600	MHRY	60050	2527	34W-32N	D4
1000	HDPK	60035	2704	9W-21N	C6
1000	NPVL	60540	3141	27W-7S	B6
1700	ELGN	60123	2800	36W-14N	A6
1700	LKFT	60045	2703	13W-23N	A1
2400	AURA	60502	3139	32W-4S	B1
4200	NHBK	60062	2756	12W-17N	A4
Devonshire Dr					
10	CRTE	60417	3596	0W-28S	C6
10	OKBK	60523	3085	17W-2S	B4
600	DSPN	60018	2862	15W-10N	A5
700	DSPN	60018	2861	16W-10N	E5
700	MPPT	60018	2861	16W-10N	D5
700	MPPT	60056	2861	16W-10N	D5
1200	JLET	60435	3497	26W-22S	E2
N Devonshire Dr					
5100	McHT	60050	2471	32W-37N	B3
5200	McHT	60081	2471	32W-37N	B3
Devonshire Ln					
-	SRWD	60404	3584	31W-25S	A1
10	KLWH	60043	2812	3W-14N	D3
10	LNSH	60069	2702	13W-23N	D3
300	PKCY	60085	2535	13W-33N	E2
500	CLLK	60014	2639	35W-24N	E6
500	CLLK	60014	2640	35W-24N	A6
500	WHTN	60187	3082	24W-1S	D2
600	MltT	60137	3083	23W-2S	A4
900	DYR	46311	3510		E5
1300	HFET	60169	2858	25W-12N	B2
1600	SRWD	60404	3583	31W-25S	E1
10300	HLSD	60162	3029	12W-0S	A7
10300	WSTR	60154	3029	12W-0S	A7
10300	WSTR	60162	3029	12W-0S	A7
15300	ODPK	60462	3345	11W-18S	E7
22900	FKFT	60423	3590	14W-27S	D5
Devonshire Ln S					
1700	LKFT	60045	2703	13W-23N	A1
Devonshire Ln W					
1600	LKFT	60045	2703	13W-24N	A1
Devonshire Rd					
100	TRLK	60010	2643	26W-25N	D5
1100	BFGV	60089	2701	17W-21N	B6
2000	WKGN	60087	2479	11W-37N	D1
11700	AlqT	60102	2747	34W-20N	B1
11900	ALGN	60102	2747	34W-20N	B1
Devonshire St					
-	BDVW	60155	3029	12W-0S	C7
-	WSTR	60155	3029	12W-0S	B7
9900	WSTR	60154	3029	12W-0S	B7
Devonswood Dr					
2100	JLET	60586	3416	30W-21S	B6
Devonwood Av					
10	RMVL	60446	3341	23W-15S	A1
Devonwood Ct					
1300	BFGV	60089	2701	16W-21N	D6
Dewalt Ct					
10	EMHT	60126	3027	16W-0S	D6
De War Ter					
-	CRTE	60417	3685	0E-29S	E1
-	CRTE	60417	3686	0E-29S	A1
Dewberry Ln					
9000	ODPK	60462	3345	11W-18S	E7
15500	ODPK	60462	3346	11W-18S	A7
De Weide Trc					
9300	DrrT	60098	2582	38W-28N	E5
Dewes Ln					
2500	NPVL	60564	3202	29W-10S	D6
Dewes St					
1700	GNVW	60025	2810	9W-13N	D6
23400	AntT	60002	2416	23W-40N	E4
23400	LKVL	60002	2416	23W-40N	E4
Dewey Av					
100	CHCG	60202	2867	3W-9N	A6
100	CHCG	60645	2867	3W-9N	A6
200	NHLK	60164	2972	13W-2N	E6
300	LydT	60164	2973	13W-2N	A6
300	NCHI	60088	2594	10W-31N	A1
300	NHLK	60164	2973	13W-2N	A6
500	EVTN	60202	2866	3W-10N	E5
1000	EVTN	60202	2867	3W-10N	A4
2000	EVTN	60201	2867	3W-11N	A2
3600	RNPK	60471	3594	4W-27S	D5
3900	RchT	60471	3594	4W-27S	D5
4100	UYPK	60471	3594	5W-27S	C5
19700	LYWD	60411	3509	2E-23S	E3
19900	BlmT	60411	3509	2E-23S	E4
S Dewey Av					
300	JLET	60436	3498	24W-24S	D6
Dewey Cir					
9700	FKFT	60423	3591	12W-25S	D1
Dewey Ln					
8800	HYHL	60457	3210	11W-10S	A4
Dewey Rd					
10	IVNS	60067	2805	23W-16N	A1
100	IVNS	60067	2752	23W-16N	A7
Dewey St					
-	AntT	60081	2414	28W-38N	E7
-	FXLK	60020	2414	28W-38N	E7
-	FXLK	60081	2414	28W-38N	E7
100	HRVD	60033	2406	50W-38N	B7
N Dewey St					
100	DMND	60416	3941	33W-39S	B2
37800	GrtT	60081	2472	28W-37N	E1
37900	AntT	60081	2472	28W-37N	E1
38000	AntT	60081	2414	28W-38N	E7
Dewhurst St					
2500	NPVL	60564	3203	28W-10S	A6
Dewig Ct					
600	NARA	60542	3078	35W-3S	C6
De Windt Rd					
100	NtrT	60093	2811	5W-15N	E3
100	WNKA	60093	2811	5W-15N	E3
100	WNKA	60093	2812	5W-15N	A3
DeWitt Dr					
100	MTSN	60443	3506	6W-24S	B6
DeWitt Ln					
5100	DRGV	60515	3144	20W-5S	B2
N DeWitt Pl					
800	CHCG	60611	3034	0E-1N	C2
N De Woody Rd					
-	WKGN	60099	2421	11W-38N	E7
37800	BHPK	60087	2479	11W-37N	E1
38300	BHPK	60087	2421	11W-38N	E7
38300	WKGN	60087	2421	11W-38N	E7
38300	WKGN	60087	2479	11W-37N	E1
De Woody St					
3200	BHPK	60087	2479	11W-37N	E2
3200	WKGN	60087	2479	11W-37N	E2
Dexter Av					
100	ELGN	60120	2854	34W-10N	C6
700	RMVL	60446	3269	23W-14S	A7
700	RMVL	60446	3341	23W-15S	A1
Dexter Ct					
100	ELGN	60120	2854	34W-11N	E3
9200	ODPK	60462	3345	11W-17S	E5
Dexter Ln					
1700	DSPN	60018	2862	13W-9N	E6
N Dexter Ln					
900	HFET	60169	2858	25W-11N	C3
W Dexter Ln					
1100	HFET	60169	2858	25W-11N	C3
Dexter Rd					
7100	DRGV	60516	3144	20W-7S	B7
7100	DRGV	60516	3206	20W-8S	B1
Dexter St					
-	LYWD	60411	3510	4E-24S	C6
Deyo Av					
3900	BKFD	60513	3087	11W-4S	D7
4500	BKFD	60513	3147	11W-4S	D1
4600	BKFD	60525	3147	11W-4S	D1
4600	MCCK	60525	3147	11W-4S	D1
D Hutchinson Av					
3200	JLET	60431	3417	28W-21S	B7
S Diagonal Rd					
25700	ELWD	60421	3675	26W-31S	B6
25700	JknT	60421	3675	26W-31S	B6
Diamando St					
400	CLLK	60012	2640	35W-26N	A2
Diamond Ct					
2600	WDRG	60517	3143	22W-7S	D6
4100	NPVL	60564	3267	28W-12S	A2
11600	FKFT	60423	3590	14W-27S	D4
16900	LKPT	60441	3420	21W-20S	A4
Diamond Dr					
-	JNBG	60050	2471	32W-34N	B7
-	McHT	60050	2471	32W-34N	B7
1300	HFET	60192	2804	24W-15N	B1
5200	OKFT	60452	3347	6W-18S	E7
Diamond Ln					
500	AlqT	60013	2696	29W-23N	C1
Diamondback Wy					
300	ALGN	60102	2748	33W-19N	A2
Diamond Creek Ln					
1700	AURA	60503	3201	33W-10S	A6
Diamond Head Ct					
1200	SRWD	60404	3496	29W-25S	D7
Diamond Head Dr					
200	DSPN	60018	2862	15W-10N	B5
Diamond Head Dr E					
800	SRWD	60404	3496	31W-25S	A7
Diamond Head Dr W					
800	SRWD	60404	3496	31W-25S	A7
Diamond Head Tr					
-	PGGV	60140	2797	42W-15N	C4
Diamond K Ln					
800	JLET	60433	3587	22W-25S	D1
800	JltT	60433	3587	22W-25S	D1
Diamond Lake Rd					
-	ElaT	60060	2646	19W-24N	D6
600	MDLN	60060	2646	18W-26N	D3
1200	LbvT	60060	2646	18W-26N	D3
6300	LGGV	60047	2646	19W-24N	D6
6300	LGGV	60047	2700	19W-23N	D1
6500	LGGV	60060	2646	19W-24N	D6
Diamond Lake Rd CO-V75					
-	ElaT	60060	2646	19W-24N	D6
6300	LGGV	60047	2646	19W-24N	D6
6300	LGGV	60047	2700	19W-23N	D1
6500	LGGV	60060	2646	19W-24N	D6
N Diamond Lake Rd					
6700	ElaT	60047	2646	19W-25N	D5
6700	ElaT	60060	2646	19W-25N	D4
6700	LGGV	60047	2646	19W-25N	D5
6700	LGGV	60060	2646	19W-25N	D5
6700	VrnT	60047	2646	19W-25N	D5
6700	VrnT	60060	2646	19W-25N	D4
25700	FmtT	60060	2646	19W-25N	D4
25700	LbvT	60060	2646	19W-25N	D4
26300	MDLN	60060	2646	18W-26N	D3
N Diamond Lake Rd CO-V75					
6700	ElaT	60047	2646	19W-25N	D5
6700	ElaT	60060	2646	19W-25N	D4
6700	LGGV	60047	2646	19W-25N	D5
6700	LGGV	60060	2646	19W-25N	D5
6700	VrnT	60047	2646	19W-25N	D5
6700	VrnT	60060	2646	19W-25N	D4
25700	FmtT	60060	2646	19W-25N	D4
25700	LbvT	60060	2646	19W-25N	D4
E Diamond Pointe Dr					
600	MDLN	60060	2646	19W-26N	D3

STREET Block	City	ZIP	Map#	CGS	Grid
S Diamond Pointe Dr					
600	MDLN	60060	2646	19W-26N	D3
Diana Av					
200	SRWD	60404	3496	29W-24S	D6
3200	PKCY	60085	2536	12W-33N	A2
W Diana Av					
24000	LkvT	60046	2416	24W-38N	D7
Diana Ct					
-	CPVL	60118	2746	37W-18N	C4
-	MKNA	60448	3590	14W-26S	E1
300	BNVL	60106	2972	15W-4N	A3
900	RLKB	60073	2474	24W-35N	D7
24900	PNFD	60544	3338	31W-16S	A3
25000	PNFD	60544	3337	31W-16S	E3
Diana Ln					
9300	HTLY	60142	2692	40W-22N	B3
Diane Av					
10	BmdT	60137	3025	23W-2N	A1
400	BmdT	60137	2969	23W-2N	A7
500	GLHT	60137	2969	23W-2N	A7
500	GLHT	60139	2969	23W-2N	A7
600	ELGN	60123	2854	35W-12N	B2
Diane Ct					
10	SEGN	60177	2908	35W-9N	B2
200	WDSK	60098	2524	41W-32N	C4
300	GNVA	60134	3019	37W-1N	C4
500	LKPT	60441	3419	22W-20S	D4
800	MRGO	60152	2634	49W-26N	C3
5200	OKFT	60452	3347	6W-18S	E6
Diane Dr					
100	SMWD	60107	2856	29W-10N	E6
300	BFGV	60089	2754	16W-18N	C3
2800	AURA	60504	3201	31W-9S	D5
3100	AURA	60503	3201	31W-9S	D5
E Diane Dr					
500	PLTN	60074	2753	20W-18N	B3
N Diane Dr					
1700	PLTN	60074	2753	20W-18N	A3
S Diane Dr					
12600	PSHT	60463	3274	9W-14S	D7
Diane Ln					
-	OswT	60585	3337	33W-16S	A3
-	PNFD	60585	3337	33W-16S	A3
200	BGBK	60440	3205	22W-10S	B6
300	CHHT	60411	3507	1W-23S	E3
800	NPVL	60540	3141	26W-7S	D7
1200	EGVV	60007	2914	21W-8N	A1
Diane Rd E					
-	EGvT	60005	2861	16W-9N	D6
-	MPPT	60005	2861	16W-9N	D6
S Diane Wy					
16000	MhtT	60442	3677	20W-29S	D1
W Diane Wy					
16000	MhtT	60442	3677	20W-29S	C1
Dianne Dr					
1600	JLET	60432	3499	21W-23S	E4
Dichtl Ct					
2000	NPVL	60565	3204	25W-9S	B4
Dickens Av					
10	BmdT	60137	2969	23W-2N	A7
300	BmdT	60148	2969	21W-2N	E7
300	GLHT	60137	2969	23W-2N	A7
600	GLHT	60139	2969	22W-2N	C7
1100	NPVL	60563	3142	25W-5S	A3
E Dickens Av					
200	NHLK	60164	2972	13W-2N	E7
300	LydT	60164	2973	13W-2N	A7
300	NHLK	60164	2973	13W-2N	A7
W Dickens Av					
300	CHCG	60614	2978	0W-2N	A6
800	CHCG	60614	2977	1W-2N	D6
2000	CHCG	60647	2977	2W-2N	B6
3200	CHCG	60647	2976	5W-2N	B6
3800	CHCG	60639	2976	5W-2N	B6
4700	CHCG	60639	2975	6W-2N	D6
6300	CHCG	60707	2975	8W-2N	A6
6800	CHCG	60707	2974	8W-2N	E6
7200	EDPK	60707	2974	9W-2N	C6
10100	LydT	60164	2973	13W-2N	A7
10300	NHLK	60164	2973	13W-2N	A7
Dickens Cir					
8000	DRN	60561	3207	18W-9S	A3
Dickens Ct					
2500	AURA	60503	3265	32W-11S	C1
Dickens Dr					
2400	AURA	60503	3265	32W-11S	C1
10400	MKNA	60448	3503	13W-22S	B2
Dickens Rd					
100	NHFD	60093	2811	7W-15N	B3
Dickens St					
-	HLSD	60154	3086	13W-1S	D1
-	PvsT	60126	3086	14W-1S	C1
-	PvsT	60162	3086	14W-1S	C1
200	NHFD	60093	2811	7W-15N	B3
1400	JltT	60432	3499	22W-23S	D4
9800	BDVW	60154	3029	12W-1S	B7
9800	BDVW	60155	3029	12W-1S	B7
9800	WSTR	60154	3029	12W-1S	B7
10200	PvsT	60162	3029	12W-1S	A7
10900	WSTR	60154	3086	13W-1S	D1
10900	WSTR	60162	3086	13W-1S	D1
Dickens Tr					
10	ELGN	60120	2855	31W-11N	E3
Dickens Wy					
1000	SMBG	60193	2913	23W-9N	A1
Dickens Bay					
18700	MKNA	60448	3503	13W-22S	B1
Dickey Av					
1900	NCHI	60064	2536	11W-31N	D7
2300	NCHI	60064	2593	11W-31N	D1
2300	NCHI	60088	2593	11W-31N	D1
Dickie Av					
600	ELGN	60120	2855	32W-10N	C6
N Dickinson Av					
4100	CHCG	60641	2975	6W-5N	E1
Dickinson Ct					
100	VNHL	60061	2647	17W-26N	C3
Dickinson Dr					
100	WHTN	60187	3082	24W-2S	C3
Dickinson St					
1600	WKGN	60087	2479	11W-37N	D3
Dick Kolze Ln					
-	PLTN	60067	2805	22W-14N	B5
Dickson Av					
1400	DRGV	60516	3144	20W-7S	B7
Dickson Ct					
200	YKVL	60560	3261	42W-13S	C6
Dickson Rd					
400	BtlT	60512	3198	41W-10S	A7
400	BtlT	60512	3262	41W-11S	A1
400	SgrT	60538	3198	41W-10S	A7
Didrikson Ln					
6800	WDRG	60517	3143	23W-7S	A7
Dieckman St					
800	WDSK	60098	2581	41W-29N	E4
Diego Ln					
10500	ODPK	60467	3423	13W-21S	B6
Diehl Rd					
10	NPVL	60563	3139	31W-4S	E2
10	NpvT	60563	3139	31W-4S	E2
500	AURA	60502	3139	31W-4S	E2
500	AURA	60563	3139	31W-4S	E2
500	NpvT	60502	3139	31W-4S	E2
1900	AraT	60505	3138	34W-5S	E2
2200	AraT	60502	3139	32W-5S	B2
2200	AraT	60505	3139	32W-5S	B2
2200	AURA	60505	3139	32W-5S	B2
E Diehl Rd					
10	NPVL	60563	3141	26W-4S	E1
1000	NPVL	60563	3142	25W-4S	A1
1200	LslT	60563	3142	25W-4S	B1
W Diehl Rd					
10	NPVL	60563	3141	27W-4S	D1
300	NpvT	60563	3141	27W-4S	C1
500	AURA	60502	3139	31W-4S	D2
500	AURA	60563	3139	31W-4S	D2
500	NpvT	60502	3139	31W-4S	D2
500	NpvT	60563	3139	31W-4S	D2
1400	NPVL	60563	3140	30W-4S	A2
1700	NpvT	60563	3140	30W-4S	C2
27500	WNVL	60555	3141	27W-4S	B1
27500	WNVL	60563	3141	27W-4S	C1
W Diehl Rd CO-13					
-	WNVL	60555	3141	27W-4S	B1
W Diehl Rd CO-53					
-	NPVL	60563	3140	30W-4S	A2
27500	NpvT	60563	3141	27W-4S	C1
27500	WNVL	60555	3141	27W-4S	C1
27500	WNVL	60563	3141	27W-4S	C1
28200	NPVL	60563	3141	28W-4S	A1
Diehl Farm Ln					
-	BtlT	60560	3260	44W-14S	E7
-	YKVL	60560	3260	44W-14S	E7
Diekman Ct					
15000	DLTN	60419	3351	1E-17S	B5
Diekman Rd					
9500	CrlT	60142	2691	43W-22N	A4
9500	GfnT	60142	2691	43W-22N	A4
W Diemer St					
24400	AntT	60002	2416	24W-40N	C2
Diens Dr					
400	WLNG	60090	2755	15W-18N	A3
Dierking Ter					
700	EGvT	60007	2861	16W-9N	D7
700	EGVV	60007	2861	16W-9N	D7
800	EGvT	60007	2915	16W-9N	D1
800	EGVV	60007	2915	16W-9N	D1
Dierks Dr					
100	WNSP	60558	3146	13W-5S	E2
100	WNSP	60558	3147	13W-5S	A2
Dierks St					
10	BNVL	60106	2972	15W-5N	A1
Dietrich Dr					
1500	TNLK	53181	2354		A2
Dietrich Rd					
10	HPSR	60140	2743	45W-19N	B3
10	HshT	60140	2743	44W-19N	D3
Dietz St					
300	MRGO	60152	2634	50W-26N	B3
Digby Dr					
2000	NLNX	60451	3588	19W-27S	D4
E Diggins St					
100	HRVD	60033	2406	49W-38N	B6
E Diggins St SR-173					
100	HRVD	60033	2406	50W-38N	B6
W Diggins St					
100	HRVD	60033	2406	50W-38N	A6
800	CmgT	60033	2405	51W-38N	E6
800	HRVD	60033	2405	51W-38N	E6
W Diggins St CO-A20					
500	HRVD	60033	2406	50W-38N	A6
1000	CmgT	60033	2405	51W-38N	E6
1000	HRVD	60033	2405	51W-38N	E6
Dighton Ln					
600	SMBG	60173	2859	22W-11N	C3
Dijon Ct					
100	BMDL	60108	2968	24W-5N	D1
Dikran Rd					
-	MKNA	60448	3502	15W-23S	C4
-	NlxT	60448	3502	15W-23S	C4
-	NlxT	60451	3502	15W-23S	C4
Dilber Bay					
18800	MKNA	60448	3503	13W-22S	B2
S Dilger Av					
10	WKGN	60085	2536	12W-33N	C3
Dillard Ct					
1900	WDSK	60098	2582	40W-30N	B2
N Dilleys Rd					
1000	GRNE	60031	2478	15W-35N	A5
1400	WrnT	60031	2478	15W-35N	A5
1700	GRNE	60031	2477	15W-35N	E5
2000	WrnT	60031	2477	16W-37N	E1
2400	WDWH	60031	2477	16W-37N	E3
2700	WDWH	60083	2477	16W-37N	E1
37200	WrnT	60031	2477	16W-37N	E1
37900	NptT	60083	2419	16W-39N	E5
37900	NptT	60083	2477	16W-37N	E1
39000	WDWH	60083	2419	16W-39N	E5
N Dilleys Rd CO-W16					
1400	GRNE	60031	2478	15W-35N	A5
1400	WrnT	60031	2478	15W-35N	A5
1700	GRNE	60031	2477	15W-35N	E5
2000	WrnT	60031	2477	16W-37N	E1
2400	WDWH	60031	2477	16W-37N	E3
2700	WDWH	60083	2477	16W-37N	E1
37200	WrnT	60031	2477	16W-37N	E1
37900	NptT	60083	2419	16W-38N	E7
37900	NptT	60083	2477	16W-37N	E7
N Dillman Av					
800	JLET	60432	3499	23W-22S	B3
Dillman Ct					
400	NPVL	60540	3142	25W-6S	A4
N Dillman St					
300	PNFD	60544	3338	29W-18S	C7
Dillner Pl					
700	DLTN	60419	3350	0E-17S	E5
Dillon Ct					
100	GLBT	60136	2799	38W-14N	A5
700	GYLK	60030	2533	20W-33N	B2
N Dillon Ct					
37100	WrnT	60046	2476	18W-37N	D2
Dillon Dr					
700	EGVV	60007	2915	17W-7N	C5
700	EGVV	60191	2915	17W-7N	C5
700	WDDL	60191	2915	17W-7N	C5
Dillon Ln					
200	YkTp	60181	3085	18W-1S	A1
Dillon St					
-	PLNO	60545	3260	45W-14S	C7
Dillonfield Dr					
10	CmpT	60119	3018	41W-2N	B2
E Dillons Ct					
100	VNHL	60061	2647	16W-27N	C2
Dilorenzo Dr					
200	NPVL	60565	3204	25W-10S	A5
Dimmeydale Dr					
600	DRFD	60015	2703	10W-21N	E5
W Dina Ct					
25100	PNFD	60586	3415	31W-20S	E5
25100	PnfT	60586	3415	31W-20S	E5
Dinah Ct					
300	BMDL	60157	2913	22W-6N	B7
Dinah Rd					
100	BMDL	60108	2913	22W-6N	B7
100	BmdT	60157	2913	22W-6N	B7
200	BMDL	60157	2913	22W-6N	B7
400	ROSL	60172	2913	22W-6N	B6
Dineff Rd					
10	LMNT	60439	3272	15W-13S	A4
Dinosaur Rd					
10	BDWD	60481	3942	30W-40S	B2
Dinsmore Rd					
1000	WNKA	60093	2812	5W-16N	A1
Di Paolo Ctr					
-	NfdT	60025	2809	11W-13N	D7
4300	GNVW	60025	2809	11W-13N	D7
Dipietro Ln					
-	DRFD	60015	2757	10W-20N	A2
Diplomat Ln					
1400	FDHT	60411	3509	1E-25S	B7
Dipper Ct					
1700	NPVL	60565	3203	26W-9S	E3
Dirksen Dr					
1000	VNHL	60061	2647	17W-26N	B3
Dirkshire Dr					
9200	DrrT	60098	2583	38W-29N	A4
Dirleton Ln					
10	IVNS	60067	2752	22W-17N	B4
Discovery Dr					
-	WCHI	60185	3021	32W-0N	C5
2300	SMBG	60194	2857	26W-11N	E3
2600	JLET	60586	3415	32W-20S	C6
Distinctive Dr					
11200	FftT	60467	3422	14W-22S	E7
18300	MKNA	60467	3422	14W-22S	E7
18300	ODPK	60467	3422	14W-22S	E7
W District Blvd					
4100	CHCG	60632	3090	5W-4S	B6
N District Dr					
600	ITSC	60143	2914	21W-6N	A5
Ditka Dr					
-	RVGV	60171	2973	10W-3N	E5
Dittman Rd					
10	CmpT	60124	2905	42W-8N	D4
10	PltT	60124	2851	42W-9N	E7
10	PltT	60124	2905	42W-7N	D5
400	CmpT	60175	2905	42W-7N	D6
Dittman Rd CO-51					
10	CmpT	60124	2905	42W-8N	D4
10	PltT	60124	2851	42W-9N	E7
10	PltT	60124	2905	42W-7N	D5
400	CmpT	60175	2905	42W-7N	D6
Dittmer Ln					
100	LNHT	60046	2417	21W-38N	E7
Diversey Av					
-	AddT	60101	2971	17W-3N	B5
-	ADSN	60101	2971	17W-3N	B5
10	NHLK	60164	2972	14W-3N	D5
200	AddT	60101	2970	20W-3N	A5
400	AddT	60126	2972	15W-3N	A5
400	CLSM	60188	2967	28W-3N	A6
400	WynT	60185	2967	28W-3N	A6
400	WynT	60188	2967	28W-3N	A6
500	BmdT	60101	2970	20W-3N	A5
500	EMHT	60126	2972	15W-3N	A5
10400	FNPK	60131	2973	13W-3N	A5
10400	LydT	60131	2973	13W-3N	A5
10600	LydT	60164	2972	13W-3N	E5
10600	LydT	60164	2973	13W-3N	A5
E Diversey Av					
10	ADSN	60101	2971	18W-3N	A5
100	AddT	60126	2972	15W-3N	A5
100	EMHT	60126	2971	16W-3N	E5
100	EMHT	60126	2972	15W-3N	A5
W Diversey Av					
10	LydT	60164	2972	13W-3N	E5
10	NHLK	60164	2972	13W-3N	D5
100	EMHT	60126	2971	16W-3N	E5
1300	AddT	60101	2970	20W-3N	B5
1300	ADSN	60101	2970	20W-3N	B5
2200	CHCG	60618	2977	2W-3N	B5
2200	CHCG	60647	2977	2W-3N	B5
2700	CHCG	60618	2976	5W-3N	A5
2700	CHCG	60647	2976	5W-3N	A5
3900	CHCG	60639	2976	4W-3N	B5
4100	CHCG	60641	2976	5W-3N	B5
4700	CHCG	60639	2975	7W-3N	B5
4700	CHCG	60641	2975	7W-3N	B5
5500	CHCG	60634	2975	6W-3N	C5
6300	CHCG	60707	2975	7W-3N	A5
6700	CHCG	60634	2974	8W-3N	E5
6700	CHCG	60707	2974	8W-3N	E5
7100	EDPK	60707	2974	9W-3N	D5
Diversey Pkwy					
200	WCHI	60185	2966	30W-3N	B6
200	WynT	60185	2966	30W-3N	B6
W Diversey Pkwy					
300	CHCG	60614	2978	0W-3N	A4
300	CHCG	60657	2978	0W-3N	A4
700	CHCG	60614	2977	2W-3N	B4
700	CHCG	60657	2977	2W-3N	B4
1900	CHCG	60618	2977	2W-3N	B4
1900	CHCG	60647	2977	2W-3N	B4
Divine Dr					
-	MTSN	60443	3505	7W-25S	D7
Division Ct					
10	LMNT	60439	3270	19W-14S	D6
1400	GNVA	60134	3020	34W-1N	D2
1400	GNVA	60174	3020	34W-1N	D2
1400	SCRL	60134	3020	34W-1N	D2
1400	SCRL	60174	3020	34W-1N	D2
Division Dr					
7500	SRGV	60554	3135	42W-6S	C5
N Division Dr					
300	SRGV	60554	3135	42W-6S	C5
Division St					
-	CHCG	60106	2916	15W-5N	B7
-	CHCG	60666	2916	15W-5N	B7
-	LMNT	60439	3270	19W-13S	E5
10	ALGN	60102	2747	33W-20N	D1
10	BNVL	60106	2972	14W-5N	C1
10	BNVL	60131	2972	14W-5N	C1
10	BtlT	60512	3261	41W-12S	E3
10	CHCG	60106	2972	14W-5N	C1
10	CHCG	60131	2972	14W-5N	C1
10	CHCG	60651	3031	8W-1N	A2
10	GNVA	60134	3020	34W-1N	E2
Division St					
10	OKPK	60302	3031	8W-1N	A2
10	SCRL	60134	3020	34W-1N	E2
10	SCRL	60174	3020	34W-1N	E2
100	ALGN	60102	2694	33W-20N	D7
100	ELGN	60120	2854	34W-10N	C6
100	MLPK	60160	3030	10W-1N	A2
100	WDDL	60191	2915	17W-5N	B7
200	CRTE	60417	3685	0W-29S	C2
200	ELGN	60120	2855	33W-11N	A4
200	GNVA	60174	3020	34W-1N	D2
200	SEGN	60177	2908	35W-8N	C2
700	WDSK	60098	2581	41W-30N	C2
800	LSLE	60532	3143	23W-5S	B2
800	MLPK	60160	3029	12W-1N	C2
800	NHBK	60062	2757	10W-17N	A4
800	OKPK	60302	3030	9W-1N	C2
1000	BlmT	60411	3507	2W-25S	D7
1000	CHHT	60411	3507	2W-25S	D7
1100	OKPK	60305	3030	9W-1N	C2
1100	RVFT	60305	3030	9W-1N	C2
1300	HDPK	60035	2704	9W-21N	C6
1500	CHHT	60411	3595	2W-26S	D2
1900	GNVA	60134	3021	33W-2N	A2
1900	GnvT	60134	3021	33W-2N	A2
1900	SCRL	60134	3021	33W-2N	A2
1900	SCRL	60174	3021	33W-2N	A2
2900	JLET	60435	3417	27W-20S	B4
2900	JLET	60441	3417	27W-19S	C4
2900	PnfT	60435	3417	27W-20S	B4
3100	JLET	60431	3417	27W-20S	B4
3700	SNPK	60160	3029	12W-1N	B2
4100	HLSD	60162	3029	13W-0S	A7
4300	NHLK	60164	3029	13W-1N	A2
4300	NHLK	60165	3029	13W-1N	A2
4300	SNPK	60165	3029	13W-1N	A2
4400	MLPK	60164	3029	13W-1N	A2
4500	MLPK	60165	3029	13W-1N	A2
4600	MLPK	60160	3028	13W-1N	E2
11900	BLID	60643	3277	2W-14S	C5
11900	CHCG	60643	3277	2W-14S	C5
11900	ClmT	60406	3277	2W-14S	C5
11900	ClmT	60643	3277	2W-14S	C5
12700	BLID	60406	3277	2W-15S	C7
13000	BLID	60406	3349	2W-15S	C2
13700	DXMR	60406	3349	2W-16S	C3
19500	MKNA	60448	3503	13W-23S	A3
E Division St					
10	CHCG	60610	3034	0E-1N	C1
10	CHCG	60611	3034	0E-1N	C1
10	LMNT	60439	3270	19W-14S	D6
10	MDLN	60060	2590	18W-27N	D7
10	VLPK	60181	3027	17W-1N	B3
100	BCVL	60407	4030	33W-43S	B3
100	BvlT	60407	4030	33W-43S	B3
100	ITSC	60143	2914	19W-6N	C6
100	LKPT	60441	3419	21W-19S	E4
300	EMHT	60126	3027	17W-1N	B3
300	GDLY	60407	4030	33W-43S	B3
300	VLPK	60126	3027	17W-1N	B3
700	LMBD	60148	3026	18W-0N	D4
800	BvlT	60416	3941	34W-39S	A2
800	CLCY	60416	3941	34W-39S	A2
1000	LMBD	60181	3026	18W-0N	E4
1000	VLPK	60181	3026	18W-0N	E4
1100	LKPT	60441	3420	21W-19S	A4
1100	LktT	60441	3420	21W-19S	A4
1300	HmrT	60441	3420	21W-19S	A4
2600	DMND	60416	3941	33W-39S	B2
2900	DMND	60408	3941	33W-39S	B2
2900	DMND	60481	3941	33W-39S	B2
E Division St SR-113					
800	BvlT	60416	3941	34W-39S	A2
800	CLCY	60416	3941	34W-39S	A2
2600	DMND	60416	3941	33W-39S	B2
2900	DMND	60408	3941	33W-39S	B2
2900	DMND	60481	3941	33W-39S	B2
N Division St					
100	BDWD	60408	3941	32W-40S	E3
100	HRVD	60033	2406	50W-39N	B4
500	PtnT	60468	3860	9W-37S	E2
500	PTON	60468	3860	9W-37S	E2
500	RedT	60408	3941	32W-40S	E3
1100	BDWD	60481	3941	31W-40S	E2
1100	WmTp	60481	3941	31W-40S	E2
1800	CmgT	60033	2406	50W-39N	B4
N Division St SR-113					
100	BDWD	60408	3941	32W-40S	E3
500	RedT	60408	3941	32W-40S	E3
1100	BDWD	60481	3941	31W-40S	E2
1100	WmTp	60481	3941	31W-40S	E2
N Division St SR-173					
100	HRVD	60033	2406	50W-38N	B7
N Division St US-14					
100	HRVD	60033	2406	50W-39N	B4
1800	CmgT	60033	2406	50W-39N	B4
S Division St					
-	PNFD	60586	3416	30W-19S	C3
100	BDWD	60408	3941	31W-42S	E6
100	HRVD	60033	2406	50W-38N	B7
300	BDWD	60407	3941	32W-42S	E7
300	HRVD	60033	2464	50W-37N	B2
300	RedT	60407	3941	32W-42S	E7
300	RedT	60408	3941	32W-42S	E7
400	PTON	60468	3860	9W-37S	E4
500	BRTN	60010	2751	25W-18N	A3
500	EMHT	60126	3028	15W-0N	A4
600	PtnT	60468	3860	9W-37S	E4
800	BrnT	60010	2751	25W-18N	A4
800	DhmT	60033	2464	50W-37N	B2
14300	POSN	60469	3349	3W-17S	B4
S Division St SR-59					
-	PNFD	60586	3416	30W-19S	C3
S Division St SR-173					
100	HRVD	60033	2406	50W-38N	B7
S Division St US-14					
100	HRVD	60033	2406	50W-38N	B7
300	HRVD	60033	2464	50W-37N	B2
800	DhmT	60033	2464	50W-37N	B2
W Division St					
-	CTHL	60441	3419	23W-19S	A4
10	CHCG	60610	3034	0W-1N	A1
10	CHCG	60611	3034	0W-1N	A1
10	JLET	60435	3498	24W-23S	E4
10	LMNT	60439	3270	19W-13S	C5
10	MDLN	60060	2590	19W-27N	C7
10	VLPK	60181	3027	18W-1N	B3
100	BCVL	60407	4030	34W-44S	A3
100	BvlT	60407	4030	34W-44S	A3
100	ITSC	60143	2914	20W-6N	B6
100	LKPT	60441	3419	23W-19S	B4
300	LktT	60441	3419	23W-19S	B4
300	VLPK	60181	3026	18W-1N	E3
500	LMBD	60148	3026	18W-1N	E3
500	LMBD	60181	3026	18W-1N	E3
700	CHCG	60610	3033	1W-1N	E1
W Division St					
700	CHCG	60622	3033	1W-1N	E1
2700	CHCG	60622	3032	5W-1N	A2
3100	CHCG	60651	3032	3W-1N	D2
4500	CHCG	60651	3031	7W-1N	C2
5900	OKPK	60302	3031	7W-1N	B2
19500	CTHL	60403	3418	24W-19S	E4
19500	CTHL	60441	3418	24W-19S	E4
19500	LktT	60403	3418	24W-19S	E4
19500	LktT	60441	3418	24W-19S	E4
21300	LktT	60403	3417	26W-19S	D4
21300	LktT	60435	3417	26W-19S	E4
21400	JLET	60403	3417	26W-19S	D4
21400	JLET	60435	3417	26W-19S	D4
21400	JLET	60441	3417	26W-19S	D4
21400	PnfT	60435	3417	26W-19S	D4
21600	PnfT	60441	3417	27W-19S	D4
Dixie Av					
3300	PKCY	60085	2536	13W-33N	A2
3300	WKGN	60085	2536	12W-33N	A3
Dixie Ct					
1400	SMBG	60193	2912	25W-8N	A2
W Dixie Dr					
5200	ALSP	60803	3275	6W-13S	E4
Dixie Hwy					
-	CteT	60417	3774	0W-33S	C2
100	CHHT	60411	3507	2W-24S	E4
100	FSMR	60422	3507	2W-22S	D2
700	CHHT	60411	3508	1W-24S	A6
1000	BlmT	60422	3507	2W-22S	D2
1000	BlmT	60430	3507	2W-22S	D2
14700	DXMR	60426	3349	2W-17S	C5
14700	HRVY	60426	3349	2W-17S	C6
14700	POSN	60426	3349	2W-17S	C5
14700	POSN	60469	3349	2W-17S	C5
15500	HRVY	60428	3349	2W-18S	C7
15600	HRVY	60426	3427	2W-19S	C1
15600	HRVY	60428	3427	2W-19S	C1
15600	MKHM	60428	3427	2W-19S	C1
15800	ThtT	60428	3427	2W-19S	C1
16000	ThtT	60426	3427	2W-19S	D2
16600	HLCT	60428	3427	2W-19S	D3
16600	HLCT	60429	3427	2W-20S	D4
17000	EHZC	60429	3427	2W-20S	D4
17100	HLCT	60430	3427	2W-22S	D7
17400	EHZC	60430	3427	2W-20S	D5
17400	HMWD	60430	3427	2W-20S	D5
18400	HMWD	60430	3507	2W-23S	D2
18600	HMWD	60422	3507	2W-23S	D3
19200	FSMR	60430	3507	2W-23S	D2
27500	CteT	60401	3774	0W-34S	C4
27600	WshT	60401	3774	0W-34S	C4
28600	BCHR	60401	3774	0W-35S	C6
Dixie Hwy SR-1					
-	CteT	60417	3774	0W-33S	C2
27500	CteT	60401	3774	0W-34S	C4
27600	WshT	60401	3774	0W-34S	C4
28600	BCHR	60401	3774	0W-35S	C6
S Dixie Hwy					
300	BCHR	60401	3864	0W-39S	C7
300	WshT	60401	3864	0W-37S	C4
1100	BCHR	60401	3774	0W-36S	C7
25300	CRTE	60417	3685	0W-31S	B5
25300	CteT	60417	3685	0W-32S	B7
26700	CteT	60417	3774	0W-33S	C1
26900	CteT	60401	3774	0W-33S	C2
S Dixie Hwy SR-1					
300	BCHR	60401	3864	0W-39S	C7
300	WshT	60401	3864	0W-37S	C4
1100	BCHR	60401	3774	0W-36S	C7
25300	CRTE	60417	3685	0W-31S	B5
25300	CteT	60417	3685	0W-32S	B7
26700	CteT	60417	3774	0W-33S	C1
26900	CteT	60401	3774	0W-33S	C2
Dixmoor Dr					
17500	HLCT	60430	3427	2W-21S	C5
17500	HMWD	60430	3427	2W-21S	C5
Dixmoor St					
400	CTHL	60435	3417	27W-20S	C6
400	PnfT	60435	3417	27W-20S	C6
Dixon Av					
700	ELGN	60120	2855	33W-10N	B7
N Dixon Av					
400	JLET	60435	3498	24W-23S	D4
Dixon Ct					
600	GRNE	60031	2534	16W-33N	E2
700	HFET	60192	2804	23W-15N	D2
8300	DRN	60561	3206	20W-9S	B4
Dixon Dr					
-	LKPT	60441	3421	18W-20S	A4
1700	LSLE	60532	3142	23W-6S	E5
4000	HFET	60192	2804	23W-15N	D2
N Dixon Dr					
10	BTVA	60510	3077	37W-1S	D1
S Dixon Dr					
10	BTVA	60510	3077	37W-1S	D2
Dixon Ln					
14700	HMGN	60491	3343	17W-17S	B6
Dixon St					
7200	FTPK	60130	3030	9W-0N	D4
7200	FTPK	60302	3030	9W-0N	D4
7200	OKPK	60302	3030	9W-0N	D4
7500	RVFT	60130	3030	9W-0N	C4
7500	RVFT	60305	3030	9W-0N	C4
Dixon Springs Ln					
-	HTLY	60142	2744	43W-19N	A2
Dixon Wy Dr					
13700	LMNT	60439	3343	17W-15S	D1
D Miller Dr					
700	GNVW	60025	2810	10W-14N	A3
Dobbins St					
-	PLNO	60545	3260	45W-14S	C7
Dobson Av					
15300	DLTN	60473	3351	1E-18S	A6
15400	SHLD	60473	3351	1E-18S	A7
15600	DLTN	60419	3351	1E-18S	A7
15900	SHLD	60473	3429	1E-18S	A1
S Dobson Av					
7100	CHCG	60619	3153	1E-8S	A7
7100	CHCG	60637	3153	1E-8S	A7
7500	CHCG	60619	3215	1E-9S	A2
9500	CHCG	60628	3215	1E-11S	A6
13300	CHCG	60827	3351	1E-15S	A1
Dobson Ct					
15300	SHLD	60473	3351	1E-17S	A6
16900	SHLD	60473	3429	1E-19S	A3
Dobson Ln					
-	BbyT	60134	3018	39W-0N	E5
-	GnvT	60134	3018	38W-0N	E5
-	GnvT	60134	3019	38W-0N	A5
7700	FoxT	60541	3331	48W-17S	A7
Dobson St					
900	EVTN	60202	2867	2W-9N	A6
1700	EVTN	60202	2866	3W-9N	E6
3800	SKOK	60076	2866	5W-9N	B6
4600	SKOK	60076	2865	5W-9N	E6

STREET Block City ZIP Map# CGS Grid
Dobson St
4800 SKOK 60077 2865 6W-9N D6
W Dobson St
6800 NLES 60714 2864 8W-9N D6
Dochester Pl
400 EMHT 60126 3027 16W-0S D7
Dock Dr
600 LKBN 60010 2696 28W-23N E1
Dockside Ct
1000 NPVL 60540 3141 27W-6S B6
Docs Ln
- PKCY 60085 2536 12W-33N A3
Dodd Av
100 NHLK 60164 3028 13W-1N D1
Dodge Av
100 CHCG 60202 2866 3W-9N E6
100 CHCG 60645 2866 3W-9N E6
100 EVTN 60202 2866 3W-9N E6
2200 EVTN 60201 2866 3W-12N E1
2200 WKGN 60085 2536 11W-33N C3
9700 FNPK 60131 2973 12W-4N C3
Dodge Ct
800 CLSM 60188 2968 25W-3N A5
Dodson Av
- ELBN 60119 3017 42W-0N C6
Dodson Ct
2000 BTVA 60510 3078 34W-3S E6
Dodson St
100 GNVA 60134 3020 34W-1N D3
W Dodson St
100 BtnT 60099 2362 11W-42N D7
11800 ZION 60099 2362 11W-42N D7
Doe Cir
700 WTMT 60559 3144 18W-6S E4
Doe Ct
4100 JLET 60431 3496 29W-23S E4
Doe Ln
400 LKMR 60051 2530 28W-32N A5
17200 ODPK 60467 3423 13W-20S A5
N Doe Rd
1100 PLTN 60067 2751 23W-17N E5
1300 PLTN 60010 2751 23W-17N E5
1300 PltT 60010 2751 23W-17N E5
Doe Tr
16700 LKPT 60441 3342 20W-17S A6
W Doede Ln
13300 HMGN 60491 3421 16W-20S E4
Dogleg Ln
600 BRLT 60103 2910 31W-9N A1
Dogwood Cir
40500 AntT 60002 2416 24W-40N C3
S Dogwood Cir
300 RDLK 60073 2531 24W-32N C4
Dogwood Ct
10 CTCY 60409 3429 2E-18S D1
10 LIHL 60156 2693 38W-22N A4
10 SMWD 60107 2857 26W-11N E4
200 LNHT 60046 2476 19W-37N C2
400 DRPK 60010 2752 22W-20N B2
500 JLET 60431 3497 28W-23S B4
500 NARA 60542 3077 37W-3S D6
500 SMBG 60193 2858 24W-9N E7
500 WNVL 60555 3080 30W-2S B5
900 RMVL 60446 3340 25W-16S C3
1000 LKZH 60047 2698 24W-22N B3
1200 ELGN 60120 2855 31W-11N D4
1700 HFET 60192 2804 25W-14N B4
5400 WldT 60564 3266 31W-13S A5
8600 TYPK 60487 3424 10W-22S B7
Dogwood Dr
10 BtlT 60512 3198 41W-11S B7
400 DYR 46311 3598 D3
700 BtvT 60542 3077 37W-3S C6
700 NARA 60542 3077 37W-3S C6
1500 CLLK 60014 2693 37W-22N B3
1700 HFET 60192 2804 25W-14N A3
2100 LSLE 60532 3142 24W-4S D1
2900 MchT 60097 2469 36W-34N D7
8800 ODPK 60462 3346 11W-17S A6
15300 HMGN 60491 3344 15W-18S C7
21600 MTSN 60443 3594 4W-26S E2
Dogwood Ln
- BDWD 60408 3942 30W-40S B4
- RedT 60408 3942 30W-40S B4
10 BDWD 60481 3942 30W-40S B4
300 VNHL 60061 2647 16W-24N E7
700 LIHL 60156 2693 37W-22N A4
900 SchT 60175 2907 38W-7N B4
1100 AURA 60504 3201 32W-9S B4
1200 BRLT 60103 2910 29W-6N D7
1200 CLSM 60188 2967 28W-3N B6
6200 GRNE 60048 2534 16W-32N D5
17700 HLCT 60429 3427 3W-21S A6
E Dogwood Ln
1300 MPPT 60056 2808 14W-14N C4
N Dogwood Ln
2100 PLTN 60074 2753 19W-18N C3
S Dogwood Ln
12200 PSHT 60463 3275 7W-14S C5
12200 WthT 60463 3275 7W-14S C5
Dogwood Rd
10 RGMW 60008 2806 20W-13N A6
Dogwood St
10 PKFT 60466 3595 2W-27S C4
200 BGBK 60490 3267 26W-11S D1
1000 VrnT 60015 2702 15W-20N B7
Dogwood Ter
300 BFGV 60069 2754 16W-20N D1
300 BFGV 60089 2754 16W-20N D1
300 VrnT 60069 2754 16W-20N D1
Dogwood Tr
500 EGVV 60007 2915 18W-8N A3
Doheny Dr
- ISLK 60042 2586 29W-27N D7
- NndT 60042 2586 29W-27N D7
Dokter Pl
13400 HMGN 60491 3421 16W-19S D2
Dolcetto Ln
1600 GRNE 60031 2477 18W-35N A5
Dolder Ln
800 SPGV 60081 2414 30W-40N B2
Dole Av
10 CLLK 60014 2639 36W-25N E4
10 CLLK 60014 2640 35W-25N A4
N Dole Av
100 CLLK 60014 2640 35W-26N A3
Dolfor Cove
8500 BRRG 60527 3208 15W-9S B4
Dolle Ln
300 CLLK 60014 2639 35W-25N E4
Dollinger Dr
- RMVL 60446 3417 27W-18S B1
- RMVL 60544 3339 27W-18S B7
500 RMVL 60544 3417 27W-18S B1
Dolly Dr
200 BRkT 60511 3134 46W-7S A7
Dolores Ct
1000 INCK 60061 2647 18W-25N A6
W Dolores Ct
26600 GrtT 60041 2530 26W-33N D2
Dolores Dr
100 BNVL 60106 2972 15W-4N A4
3900 JNBG 60050 2471 31W-35N E5
6200 OKFT 60452 3347 7W-18S B7
Dolores St
100 MTGY 60543 3263 38W-11S A1
Dolorosa Dr
17500 ODPK 60467 3423 13W-21S B6
Dolo Rosa Ln
1300 CLLK 60014 2639 37W-25N A4
W Dolph St
200 YKVL 60560 3333 43W-15S B3
Dolphin Av
20100 LYWD 60411 3510 3E-23S A4
Dolphin Ct
10 MTGY 60543 3263 38W-11S B1
Dolphin Lake Dr
18100 HMWD 60430 3427 3W-21S B7
Dolton Av
- CTCY 60409 3351 1E-16S C4
- CTCY 60419 3351 1E-16S C4
1300 DLTN 60419 3351 1E-16S B3
Dolton Ln
400 CLSM 60188 3024 24W-1N D3
Dolton Rd
- CTCY 60419 3351 2E-16S C4
- DLTN 60419 3351 2E-16S C4
1600 CTCY 60409 3351 2E-16S C4
W Domagalla St
13400 WltT 60442 3767 17W-34S E5
Domartin Pl
400 WnfT 60190 3081 28W-1S A2
Domenic Ct
400 BNVL 60131 2972 14W-4N C2
N Dominick St
2000 CHCG 60614 2977 1W-2N D6
W Dominion Ct
400 WDDL 60191 2970 18W-5N E2
Dominion Dr
- WDDL 60191 2970 18W-5N E2
700 CmpT 60175 2961 41W-5N E1
S Dominion Dr
300 WDDL 60191 2970 18W-4N E2
W Dominion Dr
300 WDDL 60191 2970 18W-4N E2
Dominion Ln
2800 LKMR 60051 2472 30W-34N B7
Dona Ct
700 WDSK 60098 2524 42W-31N B6
Donahue Dr
12000 HTLY 60142 2691 41W-22N E3
Donald Av
10 WnfT 60185 3022 29W-0N E5
400 WnfT 60185 3023 28W-0N A5
N Donald Av
10 ANHT 60004 2807 16W-14N D5
S Donald Av
10 ANHT 60004 2807 16W-13N D5
Donald Ct
10 EMHT 60126 3027 16W-0S D6
1000 NlxT 60451 3502 15W-23S C4
2500 MaiT 60025 2864 9W-12N C1
N Donald Ct
35300 GrtT 60041 2473 26W-35N D6
Donald Dr
11200 HTLY 60142 2692 40W-20N A7
N Donald Dr
40100 AntT 60002 2417 22W-40N C3
Donald Ter
200 MaiT 60025 2864 9W-12N C1
Donald S Powers Dr
- MNSR 46321 3510 E4
Donat Ct
1200 BTVA 60510 3077 36W-2S E4
Donata Ct
- LKZH 60047 2699 22W-23N B2
Donatus Dr
18000 LNSG 60438 3429 1E-21S C6
Don Carlos Ct
10 HRPK 60133 2967 27W-5N C2
Don Carlos Dr
10 HRPK 60133 2967 27W-5N C2
Doncaster Cir
22600 DRPK 60010 2752 22W-20N A1
Doncaster Ct
1800 WHTN 60187 3082 23W-2S E4
1800 WHTN 60187 3083 23W-2S A4
4700 LGGV 60047 2700 18W-23N D2
Doncaster Dr
2500 AURA 60504 3201 32W-8S C1
E Dondanville Rd
8200 BvlT 60407 4030 33W-45S B7
8200 EsxT 60935 4030 33W-45S B7
8200 GflT 60407 4030 33W-45S B7
8200 RedT 60407 4030 33W-45S B7
Donegal Ct
200 MHRY 60050 2527 35W-32N A5
1100 WDSK 60098 2581 43W-30N A1
1200 CLSM 60188 2967 26W-4N E4
W Donegal Ct
12100 NlxT 60451 3590 15W-27S C5
Donegal Dr
600 ElgT 60124 2853 37W-10N B7
1400 MNKA 60447 3672 34W-30S A4
2200 DGvT 60561 3206 19W-10S D5
2200 DRN 60561 3206 19W-10S D4
S Donegal Dr
24800 MHTN 60442 3677 19W-30S E3
W Donegal Dr
15400 MHTN 60442 3677 19W-30S E3
Donegal Ln
10 RGMW 60008 2806 20W-15N A3
1000 NHBK 60062 2756 11W-17N D5
1100 LKZH 60010 2698 24W-21N D5
6400 MHRY 60050 2527 35W-32N A5
W Donegal Ln
12000 NlxT 60451 3590 15W-27S C5
Donegal Wy
24900 PNFD 60585 3338 31W-15S A1
E Donegal Bay
1200 PLTN 60074 2753 18W-18N D3
Donelson Ct
800 NPVL 60563 3140 29W-5S C4
Donin Ct
300 ANTH 60002 2357 23W-43N E4
Donin Dr
300 ANTH 60002 2357 23W-43N D4
Donin Dr CO-G
2400 ANTH 60002 2357 23W-43N D4
Donlea Rd
200 BNHL 60010 2749 29W-18N B4
200 BNHL 60010 2750 28W-18N A2
Donmaur Dr
1900 CTHL 60403 3418 26W-21S A7
Donna Av
700 JLET 60435 3497 26W-23S E3
700 JLET 60435 3498 26W-23S A3
S Donna Av
22300 CNHN 60410 3585 28W-27S A4
Donna Ct
300 BRLT 60103 2911 28W-8N A3
600 SMBG 60193 2859 23W-9N B7
700 WLNG 60090 2755 14W-17N D6
Donna Ln
300 BMDL 60101 2969 22W-4N D3
300 BMDL 60108 2969 22W-4N D3
300 BmdT 60101 2969 22W-4N D3
1000 BNVL 60106 2971 16W-5N D2
10800 ODPK 60467 3423 13W-21S A6
Donna St
500 AraT 60505 3138 34W-5S C3
500 AURA 60505 3138 34W-5S C3
Donna Marie Dr
16000 HMGN 60491 3422 15W-19S B2
Donnelly Pl
300 VNHL 60061 2647 16W-24N D7
800 MHRY 60050 2528 32W-31N B7
900 MHRY 60050 2585 32W-30N B1
Donnie Ct
900 JLET 60435 3498 25W-22S C2
Donnington Dr
900 MTSN 60443 3505 7W-25S C7
Donny Hill Rd
10 BbyT 60119 3075 43W-1S B1
Donoho Av
800 BCHR 60401 3864 0W-36S D1
Donohoe Rd
15700 LMNT 60439 3270 19W-13S C5
E Donovan Av
100 WDSK 60098 2524 41W-31N D6
W Donovan Av
10 WDSK 60098 2524 42W-31N C6
E Donovan Ct
10 CRTE 60417 3597 1E-28S B6
N Donovan Ct
1600 MHRY 60050 2528 32W-33N A2
W Donovan Ct
10 CRTE 60417 3597 1E-28S B6
Donovan Dr
1300 CHHT 60411 3507 2W-25S D7
1400 CHHT 60411 3595 2W-25S D1
3400 CRTE 60417 3597 1E-28S B6
3400 STGR 60475 3597 1E-28S B5
N Donovan St
1700 MHRY 60050 2528 33W-33N A2
1800 MchT 60050 2528 33W-33N A2
Donovan Glen Ct
3100 NfdT 60062 2809 11W-16N D1
3100 NHBK 60062 2809 11W-16N D1
Don Powers Al
- MNSR 46321 3430 E6
Don Walden Rd
- RMVL 60441 3340 24W-18S E7
- RMVL 60441 3418 24W-18S E1
Donwood Dr
600 LslT 60540 3142 24W-7S E7
600 LslT 60540 3204 24W-8S E1
Donwood Dr E
400 LslT 60540 3142 24W-7S E7
Donwood Dr N
10 LslT 60540 3142 24W-7S E7
Donwood Dr S
100 LslT 60540 3142 24W-7S E7
Donwood Dr W
400 LslT 60540 3142 24W-7S D7
Donwood Trails Dr
400 LSLE 60517 3142 23W-7S E7
400 LSLE 60532 3142 23W-7S E7
400 LslT 60517 3142 23W-7S E7
400 LslT 60532 3142 23W-7S E7
400 LslT 60540 3142 23W-7S E7
400 WDRG 60517 3142 23W-7S E7
Doogan Av
11000 WLSP 60480 3208 13W-9S E4
Dooley Dr
- BbyT 60134 3018 39W-0N E5
Doolin St
10 LMNT 60439 3270 20W-14S C7
Doolittle Dr
3100 NHBK 60062 2756 11W-18N D3
S Doolittle Dr
24900 MonT 60449 3682 8W-30S B4
25300 GGnT 60449 3682 8W-30S A4
Doolittle Ln
1400 GYLK 60030 2475 21W-34N E7
1400 GYLK 60030 2532 21W-34N E1
S Doonaree Cir
13500 HMGN 60491 3343 17W-16S C3
Dooneen Av
7900 TYPK 60477 3424 9W-20S C5
N Dora Av
1200 JLET 60432 3499 22W-22S C1
Dora St
2300 LydT 60164 2973 12W-2N B6
2400 FNPK 60131 2973 12W-3N B6
3700 SRPK 60131 2973 12W-4N B3
3700 SRPK 60176 2973 12W-4N B3
N Dora St
- LydT 60160 2973 12W-2N B7
- MLPK 60160 2973 12W-2N B7
2100 LydT 60164 2973 12W-2N B6
Doral Ct
10 BRBK 60459 3211 7W-8S C1
10 LIHL 60156 2693 37W-21N C5
100 DRFD 60015 2757 10W-20N A2
200 EGVV 60007 2859 22W-9N D7
1800 PSHT 60463 3347 8W-15S B2
4900 JLET 60586 3416 30W-21S C7
W Doral Ct
200 PLTN 60067 2752 21W-17N D4
Doral Dr
10 HNWD 60047 2645 22W-26N B3
10 HNWD 60060 2645 22W-26N B3
200 WynT 60185 2966 30W-4N C4
800 MRGO 60152 2634 49W-25N C4
900 BRLT 60103 2910 29W-8N C2
6200 GRNE 60031 2534 16W-33N D2
10800 FftT 60423 3591 13W-27S A5
S Doral Dr
25700 MONE 60449 3683 6W-31S A5
W Doral Dr
10 GLHT 60139 3024 24W-2N D1
Doral Ln
500 NARA 60542 3078 35W-3S B6
8900 ODPK 60462 3346 11W-16S A2
13800 HMGN 60491 3343 17W-17S C5
Doral Ter
400 UYPK 60466 3684 2W-30S C2
Dorchester Av
500 MltT 60187 3024 25W-0N A4
1700 ALGN 60102 2747 36W-19N A2
3400 GRNE 60031 2536 13W-34N A1
4100 GRNE 60031 2535 14W-34N D1
10400 WSTR 60154 3087 13W-1S A2
10700 WSTR 60154 3086 14W-1S D2
14200 DLTN 60419 3351 1E-17S B5
18000 LNSG 60438 3429 1E-21S B6
18000 ThtT 60438 3429 1E-21S B6
N Dorchester Av
100 WHTN 60187 3024 25W-0S A7
S Dorchester Av
100 WHTN 60187 3024 25W-0S A7
200 GNWD 60425 3509 1E-23S B3
4700 CHCG 60615 3153 1E-5S A2
5500 CHCG 60637 3153 1E-7S A5
7000 CHCG 60619 3153 1E-8S A7
7500 CHCG 60619 3215 1E-8S A1
9500 CHCG 60628 3215 1E-11S A6
Dorchester Cir
- LGGV 60047 2647 18W-24N A7
Dorchester Ct
10 ALGN 60102 2747 36W-19N A2
10 BGBK 60440 3205 22W-10S D5
10 HNWD 60047 2699 21W-23N C1
10 SgrT 60506 3135 41W-5S E3
10 SgrT 60506 3136 41W-5S A4
10 SMWD 60107 2856 29W-9N D7
10 WKGN 60085 2536 11W-34N E1
200 OSWG 60543 3263 37W-13S B5
200 WNVL 60555 3080 30W-2S B3
600 MltT 60137 3083 21W-1S D2
600 NPVL 60565 3203 27W-10S B5
1700 MDLN 60060 2590 19W-29N B4
2200 ELGN 60123 2853 36W-9N E7
2200 SMBG 60194 2857 28W-12N B2
2200 SMBG 60194 2858 26W-11N A4
Dorchester Dr
700 BGBK 60440 3205 22W-10S D5
800 CLSM 60188 2967 27W-3N D5
1200 MDLN 60060 2590 20W-29N B4
Dorchester Ln
200 GYLK 60030 2533 19W-33N B3
300 EGVV 60007 2914 19W-8N C3
1000 BRLT 60103 2910 30W-6N C7
1200 HFET 60169 2858 25W-11N C3
7800 DRN 60561 3207 17W-9S C2
Dorchester Pl
3600 MHRY 60050 2528 32W-31N B7
S Dorchester Pl
16400 LKPT 60441 3421 18W-19S B3
Dorchester Rd
300 SchT 60175 2963 36W-5N E3
300 SCRL 60175 2963 36W-5N E3
300 SCRL 60175 2964 36W-5N A3
W Dorchester Rd
800 PLTN 60067 2805 22W-15N C2
800 PltT 60067 2805 22W-15N C2
Dorchester St
400 ROSL 60172 2912 24W-6N C6
Dordan Ct
600 GRNE 60031 2534 16W-33N E3
Doreen Dr
1200 DSPN 60016 2862 15W-10N B5
1200 DSPN 60018 2862 15W-10N B5
Dorham Ln
11000 WDSK 60098 2582 40W-30N B1
11100 BLVY 60098 2582 40W-30N B1
Dori Ln
13900 BmnT 60445 3348 6W-16S A3
13900 CTWD 60445 3348 6W-16S A3
Doria Ln
3500 OMFD 60461 3506 4W-24S E6
Doriann Dr
3000 NHBK 60062 2809 11W-15N D1
E Doric Cir
10700 PSHL 60465 3274 10W-12S C2
W Doric Cir
10700 PSHL 60465 3274 10W-12S C2
Dorie Ln
100 TNTN 60476 3428 0E-20S D5
Dorina Dr
2300 NHFD 60093 2810 8W-15N E3
2300 NHFD 60093 2811 8W-15N A3
Doris Av
10 CLSM 60188 3024 25W-1N C3
10 JLET 60433 3499 23W-25S A7
10 JLET 60436 3499 23W-25S A7
10 JltT 60436 3499 23W-25S A7
10 MltT 60187 3024 25W-1N B3
Doris Av US-52
10 JLET 60433 3499 23W-25S A7
10 JLET 60436 3499 23W-25S A7
10 JltT 60436 3499 23W-25S A7
Doris Ct
10400 RSMT 60018 2917 13W-8N A1
Doris Dr
500 MLPK 60160 3030 10W-1N A2
Doris Ln
- WnfT 60185 3022 29W-0N E5
100 CHHT 60411 3507 1W-23S E4
Dorman Dr
800 SMWD 60107 2857 28W-10N A7
Dormy Ln
800 BNHL 60010 2697 27W-20N C7
Dorncliff Ln
800 BFGV 60089 2701 17W-20N B7
800 BFGV 60089 2754 17W-20N B1
Dornell Dr
3200 SCHT 60411 3596 1W-27S A4
3300 SCHT 60475 3596 1W-27S A4
3300 STGR 60475 3596 1W-27S A4
N Dorothy Av
- ANHT 60004 2807 17W-15N B2
Dorothy Ct
- RDLK 60073 2531 23W-34N E1
100 ISLK 60042 2586 29W-28N D6
4800 WKGN 60087 2478 14W-37N B1
26600 CNHN 60410 3672 33W-31S B7
Dorothy Dr
400 DSPN 60016 2862 15W-10N A5
2500 AURA 60504 3201 32W-9S C5
E Dorothy Dr
1200 PLTN 60074 2806 19W-16N C1
S Dorothy Dr
24300 CteT 60417 3686 2E-29S D1
Dorothy Ln
600 RDLK 60073 2531 23W-34N E1
7300 TYPK 60477 3424 9W-20S E3
W Dorothy Ln
- ElaT 60047 2753 19W-20N B1
- LGGV 60047 2753 19W-20N B1
Dorothy Rd
- ANHT 60004 2807 17W-15N B1
3200 GNVW 60025 2810 10W-15N A3
Dorothy St
- BHPK 60087 2479 12W-37N A1
- WKGN 60087 2479 12W-37N A1
- WrnT 60087 2479 12W-37N A1
W Dorothy St
12200 WKGN 60087 2479 12W-37N C1
12500 BHPK 60087 2479 12W-37N B1
Dorr Dr
1100 SRGV 60554 3136 40W-5S B2
Dorr Rd
8300 WRLK 60097 2469 37W-35N B5
Dorset Av
- OSWG 60543 3263 36W-13S D6
500 GNEN 60137 3025 22W-0S B7
4500 LSLE 60532 3143 23W-4S A1
W Dorset Av
400 PLTN 60067 2805 21W-15N D2
400 PltT 60067 2805 21W-15N D2
Dorset Cir
700 WLNG 60090 2755 15W-18N A3
Dorset Ct
- OSWG 60543 3263 36W-13S D5
10 GNEN 60137 3025 22W-0S B7
10 HNWD 60047 2644 23W-25N E5
10 SEGN 60177 2908 35W-8N B4
300 PKCY 60085 2535 13W-33N E2
500 NPVL 60540 3142 25W-7S B6
600 WLNG 60090 2755 15W-18N A3
Dorset Dr
400 WslT 60481 3943 27W-40S C2
600 WHTN 60187 3082 25W-2S B5
900 NHBK 60062 2756 12W-17N B4
Dorset Ln
100 SMBG 60193 2859 23W-9N A6
Dorset Pl
400 GNEN 60137 3025 23W-0S B7
Dorset St
400 PTHT 60070 2807 16W-15N D2
Dorsetshire Dr
100 CRTE 60417 3596 0W-28S C7
100 STGR 60475 3596 0W-28S C6
Dorsett Ct
10 AURA 60504 3202 30W-8S A1
Dorsett Ln
2800 NLNX 60451 3500 20W-24S C5
Dorsey Ct
10 CmpT 60119 3018 40W-2N B2
Dorshire Ct
100 SMBG 60193 2857 27W-10N D6
Dorstep Ln
8000 ODPK 60462 3346 10W-17S C4
Dorval Dr
2000 NPVL 60565 3203 27W-9S D4
E Dory Cir
3700 HRPK 60133 2967 26W-4N E3
S Dory Cir
1300 HRPK 60133 2967 26W-4N E4
W Dory Cir
3700 HRPK 60133 2967 26W-4N E3
Dory Ln
8600 LynT 60480 3208 14W-9S D4
8600 WLSP 60480 3208 14W-9S E4
N Dot Pl
41600 AntT 60002 2356 26W-41N E7
Dot St
1800 MchT 60050 2527 34W-33N C2
1800 MHRY 60050 2527 34W-33N C2
S Doty Av
- CHCG 60617 3215 2E-11S B7
- CHCG 60633 3351 2E-15S C2
10300 CHCG 60617 3279 1E-12S A1
10400 CHCG 60628 3278 1E-13S E3
12000 CHCG 60628 3279 1E-14S A7
12000 CHCG 60633 3278 0E-13S E5
12000 CHCG 60827 3279 1E-14S A7
12100 CHCG 60633 3279 0E-14S A5
13000 CHCG 60827 3351 2E-15S C2
Doty Rd
3500 DrrT 60098 2582 39W-27N D7
3500 WDSK 60098 2582 39W-27N D7
4000 DrrT 60098 2638 39W-27N D1
E Doty St
10 CTCY 60409 3352 C7
10 HMND 46320 3352 C7
Double Eagle Dr
6300 WDRG 60517 3143 23W-7S B6
6800 LslT 60517 3143 22W-7S B7
6800 LslT 60540 3143 22W-7S B7
Doud Ct
21600 FKFT 60423 3591 12W-26S C2
Dougall Dr
2400 NlxT 60433 3500 20W-23S B4
Dougall Rd
2400 NlxT 60432 3500 20W-23S B4
2500 NlxT 60433 3500 20W-23S B5
Douglas Av
10 ELGN 60120 2854 34W-11N E3
100 LYVL 60048 2591 16W-28N D5
200 WKGN 60085 2480 10W-35N A6
300 CLLK 60014 2639 36W-25N E4
300 CTCY 60409 3352 4E-17S C6
800 AURA 60505 3200 36W-9S A4
900 FSMR 60422 3507 3W-23S B3
1100 MTGY 60505 3200 36W-9S A4
1100 MTGY 60538 3200 36W-9S A4
2000 DSPN 60018 2862 14W-9N D7
2200 DSPN 60018 2916 13W-9N D1
11100 HTLY 60142 2692 40W-21N B6
N Douglas Av
10 ANHT 60004 2807 17W-14N B4
10 ANHT 60005 2807 17W-13N B5
400 VLPK 60181 3027 17W-1N B2
600 ADSN 60101 2971 17W-2N B7
700 ADSN 60181 2971 17W-2N B7
2200 ANHT 60004 2754 17W-16N B7
40800 AntT 60002 2416 25W-40N A2
S Douglas Av
300 CHCG 60637 3153 1E-7S A5
400 ANHT 60056 2861 17W-12N B1
400 MPPT 60056 2861 17W-12N B1
1000 ANHT 60005 2807 17W-12N B7
1200 ANHT 60005 2861 17W-12N B1
1200 MPPT 60005 2861 17W-12N B1
W Douglas Av
10 NPVL 60540 3141 27W-6S C5
7200 CHCG 60501 3148 9W-5S D3
7200 CHCG 60638 3148 9W-5S D3
7200 SMMT 60501 3148 9W-5S D3
W Douglas Blvd
3000 CHCG 60623 3032 4W-1S D7
Douglas Ct
10 BlmT 60411 3510 3E-25S A7
10 HFET 60169 2859 23W-11N A4
400 MltT 60188 3023 26W-1N D3
1100 WKGN 60085 2480 10W-35N B6

STREET Block	City	ZIP	Map#	CGS	Grid
N Douglas Ct					
1600	ANHT	60004	2807	17W-15N	B1
W Douglas Ct					
7700	FftT	60423	3504	9W-24S	D5
13100	BHPK	60083	2421	13W-39N	A6
Douglas Dr					
10	SgrT	60506	3135	41W-5S	E3
10	SgrT	60554	3135	41W-5S	E3
300	BMDL	60108	2969	22W-4N	C3
400	LKFT	60045	2650	9W-25N	B5
4100	ZION	60099	2362	12W-42N	B6
23600	WldT	60585	3338	30W-15S	C2
23700	PNFD	60585	3338	29W-15S	D2
Douglas Ln					
1000	CRTE	60417	3596	0W-29S	C7
1000	CRTE	60417	3685	0W-29S	C1
N Douglas Ln					
37500	LkvT	60046	2475	21W-37N	E1
37500	LNHT	60046	2475	21W-37N	E1
W Douglas Ln					
21300	DPgT	60544	3339	26W-15S	D3
21300	LktT	60544	3339	26W-15S	D3
21400	PnfT	60544	3339	27W-16S	D3
W Douglas Pkwy					
15200	LKPT	60441	3342	20W-18S	A7
Douglas Rd					
100	OSWG	60538	3200	35W-10S	A6
100	OSWG	60543	3200	35W-10S	A6
100	OswT	60538	3200	35W-10S	A6
100	OswT	60543	3200	35W-10S	A6
400	WldT	60564	3202	28W-10S	E5
400	WldT	60564	3203	28W-10S	A5
600	NPVL	60564	3202	28W-10S	E5
900	BTVA	60510	3020	34W-0S	D7
1000	HnrT	60107	2856	30W-10N	C7
1000	HnrT	60120	2856	30W-10N	C7
1100	OSWG	60543	3264	35W-11S	B2
1300	MTGY	60538	3200	36W-9S	A5
2300	OswT	60543	3264	35W-13S	B5
3600	DRGV	60515	3084	19W-3S	D6
3600	YkTp	60515	3084	19W-3S	D6
4300	DRGV	60515	3144	19W-4S	D1
Douglas St					
-	BHPK	60087	2421	12W-38N	B7
-	WKGN	60087	2421	12W-38N	B7
300	OSWG	60543	3263	38W-13S	B4
300	PKFT	60466	3595	3W-25S	A1
400	PKFT	60466	3507	3W-25S	A7
1000	AURA	60506	3137	37W-5S	C3
E Douglas St					
10	HMND	46320	3352		D6
N Douglas St					
100	ELWD	60421	3675	25W-32S	C7
100	WDSK	60098	2524	41W-31N	D7
S Douglas St					
100	ELWD	60421	3675	25W-31S	C6
W Douglas St					
400	JLET	60435	3498	25W-23S	C3
2000	JLET	60435	3497	26W-23S	E3
N Douglas Ter					
36100	GRNE	60031	2477	18W-36N	A4
36400	WrnT	60031	2477	18W-36N	A4
Douglas Trc					
-	LKBF	60044	2593	11W-29N	E4
-	ShdT	60044	2593	11W-29N	E4
Douglass Wy					
200	BGBK	60440	3205	22W-10S	C6
Dougshire Ct					
10	BRRG	60527	3146	14W-6S	C4
Dove Av					
1500	MLPK	60160	3029	13W-1N	A2
6800	WDRG	60517	3143	21W-7S	E7
18700	FftT	60448	3503	14W-22S	A1
18700	MKNA	60448	3503	13W-22S	A1
Dove Ct					
10	SBTN	60010	2803	26W-15N	E3
600	GYLK	60030	2533	20W-33N	A2
1100	NPVL	60540	3203	26W-8S	E1
1300	ANTH	60002	2416	24W-41N	C1
2300	NLNX	60451	3589	18W-27S	A4
3100	RGMW	60008	2806	19W-13N	D5
4700	JLET	60586	3496	29W-22S	C1
S Dove Ct					
1300	MPPT	60056	2861	16W-11N	D3
W Dove Ln					
7300	FftT	60423	3504	9W-24S	E6
Dove St					
2300	RGMW	60008	2806	19W-13N	D5
Dove Wy					
1000	AlqT	60013	2642	30W-24N	B6
1000	CRY	60013	2642	30W-24N	B6
Dover Av					
10	LGNG	60525	3087	13W-4S	A6
10	RMVL	60446	3340	23W-15S	E2
10	RMVL	60446	3341	23W-15S	A2
200	LGPK	60525	3087	13W-3S	A6
N Dover Av					
10	LGNG	60525	3087	13W-4S	A7
Dover Cir					
100	LNSH	60045	2702	14W-23N	D2
200	IVNS	60067	2804	23W-15N	E2
500	FKFT	60423	3592	9W-26S	D2
800	CPVL	60110	2748	32W-18N	D5
Dover Ct					
-	PGGV	60140	2797	41W-14N	E5
10	ALGN	60102	2694	35W-21N	A6
10	SMWD	60107	2856	29W-11N	D4
200	BMDL	60108	2969	22W-4N	B4
200	SRGV	60554	3135	42W-7S	B7
500	BFGV	60089	2701	17W-22N	B4
500	ROSL	60172	2912	25W-6N	C6
600	ELGN	60120	2855	32W-10N	D6
700	CLLK	60014	2640	35W-24N	A7
1000	GRNE	60031	2477	17W-35N	C6
1000	LYVL	60048	2591	17W-28N	B7
1000	VNHL	60061	2647	16W-26N	D2
1100	BTVA	60510	3078	34W-2S	E3
1200	SRWD	60404	3496	31W-24S	A7
1600	HFET	60192	2804	24W-15N	B1
1600	WHTN	60187	3082	23W-2S	E3
1600	WHTN	60187	3083	23W-2S	A3
1800	SMBG	60193	2858	25W-9N	A7
2300	LNHT	60046	2476	20W-36N	B3
7000	WDRG	60517	3144	20W-7S	B6
9600	HTLY	60142	2692	40W-22N	A4
11000	ODPK	60467	3345	13W-18S	A7
11000	OrlT	60467	3345	13W-18S	A7
11100	ODPK	60467	3344	13W-18S	E7
11100	OrlT	60467	3344	13W-18S	E7
17600	TYPK	60487	3424	10W-21S	B6
20300	DRPK	60010	2752	22W-20N	B1
N Dover Ct					
1800	ANHT	60004	2807	16W-15N	C1
Dover Ct N					
400	YKVL	60560	3261	42W-13S	D5
Dover Ct S					
400	YKVL	60560	3261	42W-13S	D5
Dover Dr					
10	DSPN	60018	2862	15W-10N	A6
10	OKBK	60523	3086	15W-2S	B3
400	OSWG	60543	3263	37W-13S	C6
400	ROSL	60172	2912	25W-6N	C6
600	ELGN	60120	2855	32W-10N	D6
5600	LslT	60532	3143	22W-6S	C4
Dover Ln					
10	GLF	60029	2864	8W-12N	E1
200	DSPN	60018	2862	15W-10N	B6
1000	AURA	60504	3201	31W-9S	D3
1200	EGVV	60007	2914	19W-8N	C3
1500	NPVL	60565	3204	25W-8S	B3
2100	SCRL	60174	2964	34W-3N	E5
N Dover Ln					
1700	ANHT	60004	2807	16W-15N	C1
Dover Pl					
700	WLNG	60090	2755	15W-18N	A3
W Dover Pl					
100	MPPT	60056	2808	15W-14N	A3
Dover Rd					
200	LKFT	60045	2703	11W-23N	E1
2100	WKGN	60087	2479	11W-37N	C1
5600	OKFT	60452	3347	7W-18S	D7
Dover St					
-	BDVW	60154	3087	12W-1S	B2
-	BDVW	60155	3087	12W-1S	B2
-	WSTR	60154	3087	12W-1S	B2
800	PGGV	60140	2797	41W-14N	E5
7000	BGVW	60455	3210	8W-10S	E5
E Dover St					
500	JLET	60432	3499	23W-23S	B4
N Dover St					
4400	CHCG	60613	2921	1W-5N	D7
4400	CHCG	60640	2921	1W-5N	D7
Dover Wy					
700	SRWD	60404	3496	31W-25S	A7
Dovercliff Wy					
1000	CLLK	60014	2693	37W-23N	B1
Dover Hill Rd					
-	SCRL	60175	2963	36W-5N	E3
10	SchT	60175	2963	36W-5N	E3
Doverton Ln					
400	FRGV	60021	2696	29W-22N	B4
Dove Valley Ln					
1600	BCHR	60401	3774	0W-35S	D6
N Dovington Ct					
800	HFET	60169	2858	25W-11N	C3
N Dovington Dr					
800	HFET	60169	2858	25W-11N	C3
W Dovington Dr					
1000	HFET	60169	2858	25W-11N	C3
Dow Av					
700	GNVA	60134	3020	35W-0N	B5
N Dowagiac Av					
6600	CHCG	60646	2919	6W-8N	D2
6600	LNWD	60646	2919	6W-8N	D2
6600	LNWD	60712	2919	6W-8N	D2
6800	SKOK	60646	2919	6W-8N	D2
Dowdell Dr					
-	LMNT	60439	3270	20W-14S	B7
Dowdle St					
200	ALGN	60102	2694	34W-21N	C6
Dowell Rd					
30000	ISLK	60051	2586	28W-29N	D3
30000	NndT	60051	2586	28W-29N	D3
30000	WcnT	60051	2586	28W-30N	D3
W Dowell Rd					
100	ISLK	60042	2586	29W-29N	C3
100	ISLK	60051	2586	29W-29N	C3
100	NndT	60051	2586	29W-29N	C3
100	NndT	60042	2586	29W-29N	C4
Dowie Memorial Dr					
2400	ZION	60099	2422	10W-40N	A3
Downen Dr					
10	AURA	60502	3078	34W-4S	E7
E Downer Pl					
10	AURA	60505	3138	35W-7S	A7
10	AURA	60506	3138	35W-7S	A7
100	AURA	60505	3200	35W-8S	C1
W Downer Pl					
10	AURA	60505	3138	35W-7S	A7
10	AURA	60506	3138	36W-7S	A7
1000	AURA	60506	3137	38W-7S	B7
2300	AURA	60506	3136	39W-7S	E7
Downers Dr					
300	DGvT	60439	3206	20W-11S	B7
300	DGvT	60516	3206	20W-11S	B7
300	WDRG	60516	3206	20W-11S	B7
400	DGvT	60439	3270	20W-11S	B1
2900	DRGV	60515	3084	20W-2S	B4
4300	DRGV	60515	3144	20W-4S	B1
5800	DRGV	60516	3144	20W-6S	B4
5900	DGvT	60516	3144	20W-6S	B5
Downes Dr					
10	NCHI	60088	2594	10W-30N	A1
Downey Ct					
1800	HRPK	60133	2911	27W-7N	D5
Downey Rd					
2000	HMWD	60430	3507	2W-22S	C1
Downey St					
600	HFET	60169	2858	25W-11N	B4
600	SMBG	60194	2858	25W-11N	B4
Downing Av					
1600	WSTR	60154	3087	13W-1S	A2
3000	LGPK	60525	3087	13W-2S	A4
3000	WSTR	60525	3087	13W-2S	A4
Downing Cir					
-	GRNE	60031	2477	16W-36N	E3
Downing Cir US-45					
-	GRNE	60031	2477	16W-36N	E3
Downing Ct					
600	ELBN	60119	3017	43W-2N	A2
1200	WHTN	60187	3082	23W-3S	E5
1700	NPVL	60563	3140	29W-5S	D3
2700	AURA	60502	3139	32W-5S	C3
Downing Dr					
200	BMDL	60108	2969	22W-5N	B2
800	HFET	60169	2858	24W-12N	D2
800	SMBG	60169	2858	24W-12N	D2
800	SMBG	60195	2858	24W-12N	D2
1100	HFET	60192	2804	24W-15N	C1
Downing Pl					
700	GNVA	60134	3020	34W-1N	D2
E Downing Pl					
-	VNHL	60060	2647	17W-25N	A5
-	VNHL	60061	2647	17W-25N	A5
1400	INCK	60060	2647	17W-25N	B5
1400	MDLN	60060	2647	17W-25N	A5
Downing Rd					
10	ANHT	60004	2754	16W-17N	C5
10	BFGV	60089	2754	16W-17N	C5
200	RVSD	60546	3088	9W-2S	D4
600	LYVL	60048	2591	16W-27N	E7
Downing Sq					
800	LNSH	60069	2703	12W-22N	A3
Downing St					
500	ELBN	60119	3017	43W-2N	A1
600	NLNX	60451	3502	15W-25S	B7
700	NLNX	60451	3590	15W-25S	B1
800	NHBK	60062	2756	12W-17N	B4
1200	ROSL	60172	2912	25W-6N	C6
1900	LMBD	60148	3083	21W-1S	E2
S Downing St					
16300	LKPT	60441	3421	17W-19S	B3
Downs Dr					
1500	WCHI	60185	3021	31W-1N	E4
1600	BNHM	60633	3351	2E-16S	D4
1600	CTCY	60409	3351	2E-16S	D4
1600	CTCY	60633	3351	2E-16S	D4
Downs Pkwy					
1300	LYVL	60048	2647	16W-27N	D1
Doxbury Ct					
2900	NLNX	60451	3500	20W-24S	C6
Doxbury Ln					
100	NLNX	60451	3500	20W-24S	C6
Doyle Ct					
10800	ODPK	60462	3345	13W-16S	A4
10800	ODPK	60467	3345	13W-16S	A4
10800	OrlT	60467	3345	13W-16S	A4
Doyle Dr					
-	NHLK	60164	3028	14W-2N	D1
Doyle Rd					
-	FrnT	60481	3763	26W-34S	E6
-	FrnT	60481	3766	21W-34S	A6
-	WltT	60442	3766	21W-34S	B6
9300	FRGV	60021	2696	29W-22N	C4
W Doyle Rd					
14700	WltT	60442	3767	18W-34S	B6
15700	WltT	60442	3766	20W-34S	C6
Dozer Dr					
-	GLBT	60136	2799	38W-16N	B2
S Drackert St					
800	HMND	46320	3352		E7
Dracut Ln					
800	SMBG	60173	2859	22W-11N	C3
Drae Ct					
600	WLNG	60090	2754	16W-18N	E2
Dragonfly Dr					
100	BRRG	60527	3146	14W-6S	C4
Drake Av					
300	BGBK	60490	3268	25W-12S	B3
8300	SKOK	60076	2866	4W-10N	C5
9200	SKOK	60203	2866	4W-11N	C2
9400	EVTN	60201	2866	4W-11N	C2
9400	EVTN	60203	2866	4W-11N	C2
E Drake Av					
300	ADSN	60101	2971	18W-3N	A6
N Drake Av					
700	CHCG	60624	3032	4W-0N	D3
700	CHCG	60651	3032	4W-0N	D3
1600	CHCG	60647	3032	5W-1N	A1
2400	CHCG	60647	2976	4W-3N	C5
2900	CHCG	60618	2976	4W-3N	C4
4300	CHCG	60625	2976	4W-5N	C1
5000	CHCG	60625	2920	4W-6N	C6
5600	CHCG	60659	2920	4W-7N	C3
6400	LNWD	60659	2920	4W-8N	C3
6400	LNWD	60712	2920	4W-8N	C2
S Drake Av					
1400	CHCG	60623	3032	4W-1S	D7
1600	CHCG	60623	3090	4W-1S	D1
4300	CHCG	60632	3090	4W-4S	D7
4600	CHCG	60632	3150	4W-5S	D1
8500	CHCG	60652	3212	4W-9S	D3
10300	CHCG	60655	3276	4W-12S	D1
10300	CHCG	60805	3276	4W-12S	D1
10800	ENGN	60805	3276	4W-11S	D1
Drake Cir					
400	SMBG	60193	2913	22W-9N	B1
Drake Ct					
300	BGBK	60490	3268	25W-12S	B3
1700	HRPK	60133	2967	27W-5N	D2
1700	NPVL	60565	3204	24W-9S	C3
W Drake Ct					
3600	MHRY	60050	2528	32W-33N	B2
Drake Dr					
4200	NndT	60012	2641	33W-27N	A1
4300	NndT	60012	2640	33W-27N	E1
4500	CLLK	60012	2640	33W-27N	E1
W Drake Dr					
27600	CNHN	60410	3672	33W-30S	A4
27700	MNKA	60447	3672	33W-30S	A4
Drake Ln					
-	CRY	60013	2695	32W-23N	B2
100	BmdT	60108	2967	26W-5N	E2
100	BMDL	60108	2968	26W-5N	A2
100	DSPN	60016	2862	14W-12N	C1
5200	MTSN	60443	3506	6W-25S	A7
5300	MTSN	60443	3505	6W-25S	E7
Drake Rd					
900	GNVW	60025	2810	8W-13N	E6
900	GNVW	60025	2811	8W-13N	A6
W Drake Rd					
25500	CbaT	60010	2697	26W-21N	E5
25500	CbaT	60010	2698	25W-21N	A5
Drake St					
300	LYVL	60048	2591	17W-28N	C6
Drake Ter					
10	PTHT	60070	2755	15W-16N	A7
1100	WLNG	60070	2755	15W-16N	A7
1100	WLNG	60090	2755	15W-16N	A7
Dralle Rd					
2000	MonT	60449	3683	5W-30S	D3
2000	MonT	60466	3683	5W-30S	D3
2000	UYPK	60449	3683	5W-30S	D3
2000	UYPK	60466	3683	5W-30S	D3
W Dralle Rd					
-	MonT	60449	3683	5W-30S	C3
-	UYPK	60449	3683	5W-30S	C3
-	UYPK	60466	3683	5W-30S	C3
2600	MonT	60449	3682	7W-29S	E2
4800	MonT	60466	3682	6W-29S	B2
6100	MonT	60466	3682	8W-29S	B2
6100	UYPK	60449	3682	8W-29S	B2
6100	UYPK	60466	3682	8W-29S	B2
6700	GGnT	60423	3682	9W-29S	A2
6700	GGnT	60449	3682	9W-29S	A2
6700	MonT	60423	3682	9W-29S	A2
Draper Av					
-	JLET	60432	3499	22W-23S	C3
-	JltT	60432	3499	22W-23S	C3
N Draper Av					
700	JLET	60432	3499	22W-22S	C2
700	JltT	60432	3499	22W-22S	C2
N Draper Rd					
100	BLVY	60050	2526	36W-31N	E6
100	McHT	60050	2526	35W-32N	E5
100	MHRY	60050	2526	35W-32N	E5
200	McHT	60050	2527	35W-32N	A5
N Draper Rd					
200	MHRY	60050	2527	35W-32N	A5
S Draper Rd					
100	BLVY	60050	2526	36W-31N	E6
100	MHRY	60050	2526	36W-31N	E6
100	NndT	60050	2526	36W-31N	E6
W Draper St					
1200	CHCG	60614	2977	1W-3N	D5
Drauden Rd					
-	PNFD	60544	3415	31W-18S	D1
-	PNFD	60586	3415	31W-18S	D1
-	PnfT	60544	3337	31W-18S	D7
-	PnfT	60544	3415	31W-18S	D1
S Drauden Rd					
-	TroT	60586	3495	31W-21S	E1
16000	PNFD	60586	3415	31W-19S	E3
17000	PnfT	60586	3415	31W-21S	E7
17200	JLET	60586	3415	31W-21S	E7
17800	JLET	60586	3495	31W-21S	E1
17800	PnfT	60586	3495	31W-21S	E1
W Draves Rd					
14000	WltT	60442	3767	17W-34S	D5
Drawbridge Ln					
1200	LMNT	60439	3271	18W-14S	B7
Drayton Ct					
300	YKVL	60560	3333	42W-17S	D6
S Drecksler Rd					
30900	PtnT	60468	3861	9W-39S	A7
30900	PTON	60468	3861	9W-39S	A7
30900	WltT	60468	3861	9W-39S	A7
Drendel Ln					
10	NPVL	60565	3203	26W-9S	E4
Drendel Rd					
4500	DRGV	60515	3143	21W-5S	D2
4500	LslT	60515	3143	21W-5S	D2
13000	HTLY	60142	2744	42W-19N	C3
W Dresden Av					
200	PLTN	60067	2752	21W-18N	D3
Dresden Ct					
1100	HFET	60192	2804	24W-15N	C2
Dresden Dr					
1000	HFET	60192	2804	24W-15N	C2
N Dresden Rd					
-	CLCY	60416	3941	34W-39S	A1
-	FlxT	60416	3941	34W-39S	A1
3900	GlkT	60450	3761	34W-34S	A5
W Dressel Rd					
25500	AntT	60002	2416	25W-40N	A2
W Dresser Dr					
700	MPPT	60056	2807	16W-12N	D7
Drew Av					
100	DGvT	60527	3208	15W-9S	B2
7500	BRRG	60527	3208	15W-8S	C2
Drew Ct					
10500	MKNA	60448	3503	13W-23S	B4
N Drew Ct					
-	PLTN	60067	2805	22W-15N	B1
-	PltT	60067	2805	22W-15N	B1
Drew Ln					
100	WKGN	60085	2536	12W-33N	C1
W Drew Ln					
-	PLTN	60067	2805	22W-15N	B1
800	PltT	60067	2805	22W-15N	B1
Drew St					
3200	DRGV	60515	3084	20W-3S	B5
S Drew St					
10500	CHCG	60643	3277	2W-12S	D1
Drewsbury Ln					
300	RMVL	60446	3340	24W-16S	E4
Drexel Av					
-	AURA	60504	3140	30W-7S	B6
400	GLNC	60022	2758	6W-16N	D7
1000	FDHT	60411	3509	1E-25S	A7
1500	FDHT	60411	3597	1E-25S	A1
4200	GRNE	60031	2478	14W-35N	D7
14200	DLTN	60419	3351	1E-16S	A4
15100	SHLD	60473	3351	1E-17S	A6
15400	DLTN	60473	3351	1E-18S	A7
15900	SHLD	60473	3429	1E-18S	A1
N Drexel Av					
10	LGNG	60525	3087	13W-4S	A7
100	LGPK	60525	3087	13W-4S	A7
S Drexel Av					
-	CHCG	60615	3152	1E-5S	E2
300	GNWD	60425	3509	1E-23S	A3
7100	CHCG	60619	3152	1E-8S	E7
7100	CHCG	60637	3152	1E-8S	E7
7500	CHCG	60619	3214	1E-9S	E2
9700	CHCG	60628	3214	1E-11S	E6
N Drexel Blvd					
38200	AntT	60002	2415	26W-38N	E6
S Drexel Blvd					
3900	CHCG	60653	3092	1E-4S	E6
4600	CHCG	60615	3092	1E-4S	E7
4700	CHCG	60615	3152	1E-5S	E1
Drexel Ln					
200	GLNC	60022	2758	6W-16N	D7
E Drexel Sq					
800	CHCG	60615	3152	0E-5S	D2
Driftwood Av					
600	RMVL	60446	3340	24W-16S	C3
20100	LYWD	60411	3510	3E-23S	B4
N Driftwood Av					
1400	PLTN	60067	2752	21W-17N	D4
Driftwood Ct					
10	ALGN	60102	2747	36W-19N	A2
10	SMWD	60107	2857	26W-11N	E4
700	MonT	60466	3684	4W-29S	A2
700	UYPK	60466	3684	4W-29S	A2
1000	WLNG	60090	2754	16W-18N	D3
1100	EGVV	60007	2914	19W-8N	C2
1100	FSMR	60422	3507	3W-23S	A2
1500	CLLK	60014	2693	37W-23N	B3
1800	HFET	60192	2804	25W-15N	A1
5300	LSLE	60532	3142	24W-5S	E3
20600	FmtT	60060	2646	20W-26N	A2
W Driftwood Ct					
27000	LKBN	60010	2697	27W-22N	C4
Driftwood Dr					
2400	HHLL	60051	2586	30W-29N	B4
S Driftwood Dr					
20400	FftT	60423	3504	9W-24S	D6
Driftwood Ln					
-	PGGV	60140	2797	42W-15N	D4
200	BMDL	60108	2969	22W-4N	B3
200	SMBG	60193	2859	21W-10N	E6
300	AURA	60504	3140	29W-6S	D6
300	WLMT	60091	2813	2W-13N	A7
500	HRVD	60033	2464	50W-37N	A2
600	NHBK	60062	2757	8W-16N	E7
600	NHBK	60062	2758	8W-17N	A6
1100	BRLT	60103	2910	29W-6N	D7
1500	CLLK	60014	2693	37W-22N	B3
2200	HRPK	60133	2967	27W-5N	B3
3600	LGGV	60047	2700	19W-22N	B5
17500	HMGN	60491	3421	17W-21S	D6
S Driftwood Tr					
100	MHRY	60050	2527	34W-31N	D6
300	NndT	60050	2527	34W-31N	D6
Driscoll Ct					
800	HDPK	60035	2704	8W-21N	D5
Driscoll Ln					
100	WDDL	60191	2915	18W-7N	A3
Drive-In Ln					
4800	AlqT	60014	2640	33W-24N	D6
4800	CLLK	60014	2640	33W-24N	D6
N Driveway					
800	GNEN	60137	3083	21W-1S	D1
S Driveway					
10	GNEN	60137	3083	21W-1S	D1
W Driveway					
800	GNEN	60137	3083	21W-1S	D1
Driving Park Rd					
1600	WHTN	60187	3024	24W-0N	D4
2100	CLSM	60188	3024	24W-0N	D4
2100	WHTN	60188	3024	24W-0N	D4
Dr Korczak Ter					
9100	SKOK	60076	2866	4W-11N	C3
9100	SKOK	60203	2866	4W-11N	C3
S Dr Martin L King Jr Dr					
-	CHCG	60615	3092	0E-4S	D7
2200	CHCG	60616	3092	0E-2S	C2
3500	CHCG	60653	3092	0E-4S	D6
4700	CHCG	60615	3152	0E-5S	D1
5400	CHCG	60637	3152	0E-5S	D2
7000	CHCG	60619	3152	0E-7S	D6
7500	CHCG	60619	3214	0E-11S	D7
9400	CHCG	60628	3214	0E-11S	D7
10300	CHCG	60628	3278	0E-12S	D2
13000	CHCG	60827	3278	0E-15S	D7
13200	CHCG	60827	3350	0E-15S	D1
Drom Ct					
500	ANTH	60002	2357	23W-42N	E5
Dromery St					
-	PKCY	60085	2536	12W-33N	B3
-	WKGN	60085	2536	12W-33N	B3
Dromey St					
600	PKCY	60085	2536	12W-33N	B3
Drove Av					
1100	DRGV	60515	3084	20W-4S	B7
Drover Ct					
8300	DRN	60561	3206	20W-9S	B4
Drover Dr					
1200	LMNT	60439	3271	18W-14S	A6
Drover Ln					
500	DRN	60561	3206	20W-9S	A4
500	WDRG	60517	3206	20W-9S	A4
Drover St					
800	ELBN	60119	3017	43W-2N	B1
S Drovers Ln					
300	PLTN	60067	2805	22W-15N	B2
Drucker Ln					
2600	NndT	60051	2528	31W-31N	D7
Druid Hills Ct					
1400	NPVL	60563	3141	27W-5S	B2
Drumm Ct					
-	JLET	60586	3415	32W-21S	C6
Drummer Dr					
1800	SMBG	60173	2805	21W-12N	E7
E Drummond Av					
10	GLHT	60139	2968	23W-3N	E6
100	GLHT	60139	2969	23W-3N	A6
W Drummond Av					
10	GLHT	60139	2968	24W-3N	D6
Drummond Cir					
1400	IVNS	60010	2751	24W-17N	C6
Drummond Ct					
400	ROSL	60172	2912	25W-7N	B5
Drummond Dr					
9200	TYPK	60487	3423	11W-21S	E5
Drummond Pl					
10400	FNPK	60131	2973	13W-3N	A5
10400	FNPK	60164	2973	13W-3N	A5
10400	LydT	60131	2973	13W-3N	A5
10400	LydT	60164	2973	13W-3N	A5
10600	LydT	60164	2972	13W-3N	E5
W Drummond Pl					
500	CHCG	60614	2978	0W-3N	A5
1100	CHCG	60614	2977	1W-3N	E5
3400	CHCG	60647	2976	4W-3N	D5
4200	CHCG	60639	2976	5W-3N	A5
4800	CHCG	60639	2975	6W-3N	D5
Drummore Ln					
800	FKFT	60423	3592	9W-26S	E3
Drury Ct					
700	GRNE	60031	2534	16W-33N	E3
Drury Ln					
-	AURA	60502	3139	33W-6S	B4
-	CPVL	60118	2746	37W-18N	D5
10	OKTR	60181	3027	16W-1S	D7
10	OKTR	60181	3085	16W-1S	D1
200	MltT	60148	3083	21W-2S	E3
2200	NHFD	60093	2811	7W-15N	A2
5400	OKLN	60453	3211	6W-11S	D7
9800	BDVW	60154	3029	12W-1S	C7
9800	BDVW	60155	3029	12W-1S	C7
9800	WSTR	60154	3029	12W-1S	B7
E Drury Ln					
200	NBRN	60010	2698	25W-23N	A1
400	BRTN	60010	2751	25W-20N	A1
N Drury Ln					
1100	PTHT	60004	2807	16W-15N	C3
1700	ANHT	60004	2807	16W-15N	C1
2600	ANHT	60004	2754	16W-16N	C6
20700	AvnT	60030	2476	20W-35N	A6
20700	GYLK	60030	2476	20W-35N	A6
20800	GYLK	60030	2475	20W-35N	E7
35400	AvnT	60046	2476	20W-35N	A6
S Drury Ln					
100	ANHT	60004	2807	16W-13N	C5
N Dryden Av					
100	ANHT	60004	2807	17W-14N	B4
Dryden Ct					
10	ALGN	60102	2747	36W-19N	B2
1300	NPVL	60564	3267	28W-11S	A2
N Dryden Ct					
2800	ANHT	60004	2754	17W-17N	B5
Dryden Ln					
800	HDPK	60035	2704	8W-21N	E7
2000	JLET	60435	3497	26W-22S	E2
N Dryden Ln					
2200	ANHT	60004	2754	17W-16N	B7
N Dryden Pl					
10	ANHT	60004	2807	17W-14N	B4
2900	ANHT	60004	2754	17W-17N	B5
S Dryden Pl					
100	ANHT	60004	2807	17W-13N	B5
300	ANHT	60005	2807	17W-13N	B6
Dryden Rd					
800	GNVA	60134	3020	35W-0N	A5
Dryden St					
8800	WDRG	60517	3206	20W-10S	B5

STREET Block	City	ZIP	Map#	CGS	Grid
Drydock					
100	LKMR	60051	2529	28W-33N	E4
Duane Dr					
8000	FftT	60423	3504	10W-25S	C7
Duane St					
200	GNEN	60137	3025	23W-0N	A5
Duane Ter					
300	GNEN	60137	3025	22W-0N	C5
Dublin Ct					
10	SEGN	60177	2908	35W-8N	B3
100	SMBG	60194	2857	26W-10N	E5
300	CLSM	60188	2968	25W-4N	B4
1200	WDSK	60098	2581	43W-30N	A1
1600	IVNS	60067	2805	22W-15N	A3
2700	AlqT	60013	2641	31W-25N	D4
4400	HRPK	60133	2967	27W-5N	C2
14100	HMGN	60491	3343	17W-16S	C2
Dublin Dr					
600	MDLN	60060	2590	19W-28N	C6
1600	NPVL	60564	3267	28W-12S	A3
6300	AlqT	60013	2641	31W-25N	D4
S Dublin Dr					
13600	HMGN	60491	3343	17W-16S	C3
W Dublin Dr					
13600	HMGN	60491	3343	17W-16S	C3
Dublin Ln					
-	PNFD	60585	3265	32W-14S	D7
-	PNFD	60585	3337	32W-14S	D1
200	SEGN	60177	2908	35W-8N	B4
200	SMBG	60194	2857	26W-10N	E5
2000	HRPK	60133	2967	27W-5N	C1
Dublin Rd					
300	BMDL	60108	2969	22W-4N	D2
Dublin St					
8900	ODPK	60462	3346	11W-17S	A6
Dublin Wy					
22800	LKBN	60010	2696	28W-22N	E3
N Dubois Av					
10	ELGN	60123	2854	35W-11N	C4
S Dubois Av					
10	ELGN	60123	2854	35W-11N	C5
Dubois Blvd					
4000	BKFD	60513	3087	11W-4S	D7
4500	BKFD	60513	3147	11W-4S	D1
4600	BKFD	60525	3147	11W-4S	D1
4600	MCCK	60525	3147	11W-4S	D1
Dubois Cir					
200	BGBK	60440	3205	22W-10S	C6
Dubonet Dr					
400	RVWD	60015	2755	13W-20N	E1
Duchesne Dr					
10	DndT	60118	2800	35W-14N	D5
Duchess Av					
1500	NLNX	60451	3588	19W-27S	D5
11900	MKNA	60448	3502	14W-23S	D3
Duchess Ct					
-	PTHT	60070	2808	13W-15N	E1
3600	DRGV	60515	3084	20W-3S	B6
Duchess Ln					
25900	CteT	60417	3685	0W-31S	B5
W Duchess Ln					
100	HPSR	60140	2795	47W-15N	E3
Duck Ln					
400	WDDL	60191	2914	18W-5N	E7
W Duck Ln					
26100	AntT	60002	2356	26W-41N	E7
Duck Pond Ln					
400	NBRN	60010	2698	25W-22N	A3
S Duffy Av					
8700	HMTN	60456	3212	5W-10S	B4
Duffy Dr					
700	CLLK	60014	2694	33W-24N	D1
Duffy Ln					
-	BFGV	60089	2754	16W-20N	C2
10	SRGV	60511	3134	45W-7S	C6
10	SRGV	60554	3134	45W-7S	C6
1600	BKBN	60015	2703	12W-22N	C4
1900	RVWD	60015	2703	12W-22N	C4
2600	RVWD	60015	2702	13W-22N	D4
2800	LNSH	60015	2702	13W-22N	E4
2800	LNSH	60069	2702	13W-22N	D4
Duffy Ln CO-A43					
-	BKBN	60015	2703	12W-22N	B4
2000	RVWD	60015	2703	12W-22N	A4
2600	RVWD	60015	2702	13W-22N	D4
2800	LNSH	60015	2702	13W-22N	E4
2800	LNSH	60069	2702	13W-22N	D4
Dugan Rd					
10	BRkT	60511	3134	44W-8S	D2
10	BRkT	60554	3134	45W-5S	D3
10	BRkT	60554	3196	45W-7S	D1
10	SgrT	60511	3196	44W-8S	D2
10	SgrT	60554	3134	45W-5S	D3
10	SgrT	60554	3196	45W-7S	D1
200	SRGV	60554	3134	45W-7S	D7
N Dugan Rd					
10	SgrT	60554	3134	45W-6S	D6
10	SRGV	60554	3134	45W-6S	D6
Dugan St					
100	WKGN	60085	2537	10W-34N	B1
Dugdale Cir					
-	WKGN	60085	2536	11W-33N	E3
Dugdale Rd					
1400	NCHI	60064	2536	12W-31N	C7
1400	WKGN	60085	2536	12W-31N	C7
W Dugdale Rd					
1200	WKGN	60085	2536	11W-32N	D4
2400	NCHI	60064	2536	11W-32N	C5
W Duggald Av					
3200	WKGN	60085	2479	12W-35N	B7
3200	WkgT	60085	2479	12W-35N	B7
Dugout Tr					
800	CLSM	60188	2967	27W-3N	B5
Dukane Dr					
2400	SCRL	60174	2964	33W-3N	E7
2400	SCRL	60174	2965	33W-3N	A7
Duke Ct					
1200	NPVL	60565	3204	24W-9S	C4
Duke Dr					
200	BlmT	60411	3598	4E-25S	C1
200	LYWD	60411	3598	4E-25S	C1
1300	NPVL	60565	3204	24W-9S	C4
5300	MTSN	60443	3505	6W-25S	E7
Duke St					
8800	DGvT	60516	3206	20W-10S	B5
8800	WDRG	60517	3206	20W-10S	B5
Dukes Cir					
10	LNSH	60069	2702	13W-22N	D4
Dukes Ct					
10	LNSH	60069	2702	13W-22N	E4
Dukes Ln					
10	LNSH	60069	2702	13W-22N	D4
Dukesberry Ln					
4800	HFET	60010	2804	24W-15N	B1
4900	HFET	60010	2751	24W-16N	B7
Dulles Rd					
10	DSPN	60016	2862	15W-11N	B3
600	DSPN	60016	2861	16W-11N	E3
600	MPPT	60016	2861	16W-11N	E3
600	MPPT	60056	2861	16W-11N	E3
Dumbarton Oaks Pl					
10	ELGN	60123	2854	35W-12N	B2
Dumfries Ct					
1500	IVNS	60067	2805	22W-15N	A3
Dumke Dr					
5200	OKLN	60453	3211	6W-10S	E6
Dumont Ln					
1700	SMBG	60194	2858	25W-11N	B3
Dumoulin Av					
4500	LSLE	60532	3143	23W-4S	A1
Duna Dr					
-	SRGV	60554	3136	41W-7S	A6
Dunamon Dr					
1200	BRLT	60103	2911	27W-7N	D5
1200	BRLT	60133	2911	27W-7N	D5
1200	HRPK	60133	2911	27W-7N	D5
S Dunbar Av					
9200	CHCG	60619	3214	0E-10S	D5
Dunbar Ct					
300	SMWD	60107	2911	28W-9N	A1
800	SMBG	60194	2858	25W-11N	B4
5000	JLET	60586	3416	30W-21S	C7
Dunbar Ln					
10	RGMW	60008	2806	20W-14N	A4
100	EDND	60118	2801	32W-16N	C2
Dunbar Rd					
300	WCDA	60084	2587	26W-27N	C7
300	WCDA	60084	2643	26W-27N	C1
500	MDLN	60060	2590	19W-29N	C5
900	FmtT	60060	2590	19W-29N	C5
1400	IVNS	60067	2752	23W-16N	A6
Dunbar St					
500	BCHR	60401	3864	1W-36S	B2
700	WshT	60401	3864	1W-36S	B2
1500	FSMR	60422	3506	4W-23S	D3
8600	WLSP	60480	3208	13W-9S	E4
Dunbar Ter					
500	CRTE	60417	3596	0E-28S	E7
500	CRTE	60417	3597	0E-28S	A6
Dunbarton Dr					
600	IVNS	60010	2750	25W-16N	E6
700	IVNS	60010	2751	25W-16N	A6
1100	AURA	60502	3139	31W-5S	D4
Dunbridge Ln					
900	RMVL	60446	3269	23W-14S	A6
Duncan Av					
500	DndT	60118	2801	33W-14N	A5
500	ELGN	60120	2801	33W-13N	B7
500	ElgT	60118	2801	33W-13N	B7
500	ElgT	60120	2801	33W-13N	B7
800	ELGN	60120	2855	33W-12N	A1
Duncan Ct					
4500	NPVL	60564	3266	29W-12S	E3
21200	LktT	60544	3339	26W-16S	E4
Duncan Dr					
700	AURA	60506	3137	37W-6S	B5
Duncan Ln					
-	PNFD	60586	3415	31W-19S	E3
2700	BTVA	60510	3077	37W-1S	C2
Duncan Pl					
1000	WDSK	60098	2582	40W-30N	B2
Duncan Rd					
15500	OKFT	60452	3347	7W-18S	D7
Duncan St					
10	PvsT	60126	3028	15W-0S	B7
500	YkTp	60126	3028	15W-0S	B7
W Duncan St					
100	JLET	60436	3498	24W-24S	E6
Dundee					
-	NLNX	60451	3590	15W-26S	C3
Dundee Av					
10	CPVL	60110	2801	33W-16N	C2
10	EDND	60110	2801	33W-16N	C2
10	EDND	60118	2801	33W-16N	C2
100	BRTN	60010	2750	25W-17N	E4
100	ELGN	60120	2854	33W-11N	E3
200	ELGN	60120	2855	33W-12N	A2
600	DndT	60118	2801	33W-14N	C6
600	FSMR	60422	3507	3W-22S	C1
600	HMWD	60430	3507	3W-22S	C1
800	BNHL	60010	2750	25W-18N	E4
1300	ELGN	60120	2801	33W-14N	C6
1500	DndT	60120	2801	33W-14N	C6
1500	ELGN	60118	2801	33W-14N	C6
17500	HLCT	60430	3427	3W-21S	C6
17500	HMWD	60430	3427	3W-21S	C6
Dundee Av SR-25					
10	CPVL	60110	2801	33W-16N	C2
10	EDND	60110	2801	33W-16N	C2
10	EDND	60118	2801	32W-16N	C3
600	DndT	60118	2801	33W-14N	C6
1100	ELGN	60120	2855	33W-12N	B1
1300	ELGN	60120	2801	33W-14N	C6
1500	DndT	60120	2801	33W-14N	C6
1500	ELGN	60118	2801	33W-14N	C6
Dundee Dr					
100	LktT	60441	3419	21W-18S	E2
1500	WHTN	60187	3082	23W-1S	E2
17200	LktT	60403	3417	26W-20S	E5
Dundee Ln					
10	BNHL	60010	2750	25W-17N	E5
10	BRTN	60010	2750	25W-17N	E5
Dundee Pkwy					
200	BFGV	60089	2754	17W-18N	C4
Dundee Pl					
9400	TYPK	60487	3423	11W-20S	E4
Dundee Rd					
-	BRTN	60010	2750	26W-17N	D5
-	CPVL	60110	2801	32W-16N	D1
-	CPVL	60118	2801	32W-16N	D1
-	EDND	60110	2801	30W-15N	E1
-	EDND	60118	2801	32W-16N	D1
-	GLNC	60062	2758	7W-17N	A4
-	IVNS	60010	2750	26W-17N	D5
-	NtrT	60062	2758	7W-17N	A4
-	PLTN	60067	2751	23W-17N	D5
-	PltT	60067	2751	23W-17N	D5
-	WhlT	60062	2755	13W-18N	E4
-	WhlT	60062	2756	12W-17N	A4
-	WhlT	60090	2755	13W-18N	E4
-	WhlT	60090	2756	12W-17N	A4
-	WLNG	60062	2755	13W-18N	E4
-	WLNG	60090	2755	13W-18N	E4
-	WLNG	60090	2756	12W-17N	A4
10	BNHL	60010	2750	26W-17N	D5
10	GfnT	60102	2745	38W-20N	D2
10	GfnT	60142	2745	39W-20N	D1
10	RtdT	60102	2745	38W-20N	D2
10	RtdT	60142	2745	38W-20N	D2
100	BNHL	60010	2801	30W-15N	E1
100	BNHL	60010	2802	29W-16N	C1
200	BNHL	60010	2749	28W-16N	E7
300	GLNC	60022	2758	7W-17N	A4
400	NHBK	60062	2758	8W-17N	A4
500	NHBK	60062	2757	8W-18N	D4
2000	IVNS	60010	2751	23W-17N	D5
2000	IVNS	60067	2751	23W-17N	D5
2000	PltT	60010	2751	23W-17N	D5
3900	NHBK	60062	2756	12W-18N	B4
4100	NfdT	60062	2756	12W-17N	A4
9700	GfnT	60156	2745	39W-20N	D1
9700	HTLY	60142	2745	39W-20N	D1
10600	HTLY	60142	2692	40W-20N	B7
10700	GfnT	60142	2692	39W-20N	B7
Dundee Rd CO-A52					
10	GfnT	60102	2745	38W-20N	D2
10	RtdT	60102	2745	38W-20N	D2
10	RtdT	60142	2745	38W-20N	D2
9700	GfnT	60156	2745	39W-20N	D1
10300	GfnT	60142	2745	39W-20N	C1
10300	HTLY	60142	2745	39W-20N	C1
10600	HTLY	60142	2692	40W-20N	B7
10700	GfnT	60142	2692	39W-20N	B7
Dundee Rd SR-68					
-	BRTN	60010	2750	26W-17N	D5
-	CPVL	60110	2801	32W-16N	D1
-	CPVL	60118	2801	32W-16N	D1
-	EDND	60110	2801	30W-15N	E1
-	EDND	60118	2801	32W-16N	D1
-	GLNC	60062	2758	7W-17N	A4
-	IVNS	60010	2750	26W-17N	D5
-	NtrT	60062	2758	7W-17N	A4
-	PLTN	60067	2751	23W-17N	D5
-	PltT	60067	2751	23W-17N	D5
-	WhlT	60062	2755	13W-18N	E4
-	WhlT	60062	2756	12W-17N	A4
-	WhlT	60090	2755	13W-18N	E4
-	WhlT	60090	2756	12W-17N	A4
-	WLNG	60062	2755	13W-18N	E4
-	WLNG	60090	2755	13W-18N	E4
-	WLNG	60090	2756	12W-17N	A4
10	BNHL	60010	2750	26W-17N	D5
100	BNHL	60010	2801	30W-15N	E1
100	BNHL	60010	2802	29W-16N	C1
200	BNHL	60010	2749	28W-16N	E7
400	NHBK	60062	2758	8W-17N	A4
500	NHBK	60062	2757	8W-18N	D4
2000	IVNS	60010	2751	23W-17N	D5
2000	IVNS	60067	2751	23W-17N	D5
2000	PltT	60010	2751	23W-17N	D5
2500	NHBK	60062	2756	11W-18N	C4
4100	NfdT	60062	2756	12W-17N	A4
E Dundee Rd					
-	BFGV	60004	2754	17W-18N	B4
-	PltT	60004	2753	19W-18N	D4
-	WhlT	60062	2755	14W-18N	C4
-	WLNG	60062	2755	14W-18N	C4
10	BRTN	60010	2750	25W-17N	E5
10	BRTN	60010	2751	25W-17N	A5
10	IVNS	60010	2750	25W-17N	E5
10	IVNS	60010	2751	24W-17N	B5
10	PLTN	60067	2752	20W-18N	E4
10	PLTN	60067	2753	20W-18N	A4
10	PLTN	60074	2752	20W-18N	E4
10	PLTN	60074	2753	19W-18N	C4
10	PltT	60074	2752	20W-18N	E4
10	PltT	60074	2753	20W-18N	A4
10	WLNG	60090	2755	14W-18N	C4
100	IVNS	60067	2751	23W-17N	D5
100	PltT	60067	2753	20W-18N	A4
300	BFGV	60090	2754	16W-18N	D4
600	ANHT	60004	2754	17W-18N	B4
600	BFGV	60089	2754	17W-18N	B4
1000	ANHT	60089	2754	17W-18N	A4
E Dundee Rd SR-53					
-	PltT	60004	2753	19W-18N	D4
900	PLTN	60074	2753	19W-18N	C4
1500	PltT	60074	2753	19W-18N	C4
E Dundee Rd SR-68					
-	BFGV	60004	2754	17W-18N	B4
-	PltT	60004	2753	19W-18N	D4
-	WhlT	60062	2755	14W-18N	C4
-	WLNG	60062	2755	14W-18N	C4
10	BRTN	60010	2750	25W-17N	E5
10	BRTN	60010	2751	25W-17N	A5
10	IVNS	60010	2750	25W-17N	E5
10	IVNS	60010	2751	24W-17N	B5
10	PLTN	60067	2752	20W-18N	E4
10	PLTN	60067	2753	20W-18N	A4
10	PLTN	60074	2752	20W-18N	E4
10	PLTN	60074	2753	19W-18N	C4
10	PltT	60074	2752	20W-18N	E4
10	PltT	60074	2753	20W-18N	A4
10	WLNG	60090	2755	14W-18N	C4
100	IVNS	60067	2751	23W-17N	D5
100	PltT	60067	2753	20W-18N	A4
300	BFGV	60090	2754	16W-18N	D4
600	ANHT	60004	2754	17W-18N	B4
600	BFGV	60089	2754	17W-18N	B4
1000	ANHT	60089	2754	17W-18N	A4
W Dundee Rd					
-	PltT	60004	2753	19W-18N	D4
-	PltT	60074	2753	19W-18N	D4
10	BFGV	60090	2754	16W-18N	D4
10	WLNG	60089	2754	16W-18N	D4
10	WLNG	60090	2755	15W-18N	A4
100	PLTN	60067	2752	21W-18N	D4
100	PltT	60074	2752	21W-18N	D4
400	ANHT	60004	2754	17W-17N	C4
500	PLTN	60074	2752	21W-17N	C4
700	ANHT	60004	2753	18W-18N	D4
700	BFGV	60089	2753	18W-18N	D4
700	PltT	60067	2752	21W-17N	C4
800	WLNG	60090	2754	15W-17N	E4
1200	ANHT	60089	2754	17W-18N	A4
1200	BFGV	60089	2754	18W-18N	A4
1200	PltT	60010	2752	22W-17N	A4
1500	PLTN	60010	2751	23W-17N	E4
1700	PLTN	60067	2751	23W-17N	E5
1700	PltT	60010	2751	23W-17N	E5
1800	PltT	60067	2751	23W-17N	E5
W Dundee Rd SR-53					
-	ANHT	60004	2753	19W-18N	D4
-	PltT	60004	2753	19W-18N	D4
-	PltT	60074	2753	19W-18N	D4
W Dundee Rd SR-68					
-	PltT	60004	2753	19W-18N	D4
-	PltT	60074	2753	19W-18N	D4
10	BFGV	60090	2754	16W-18N	D4
10	WLNG	60089	2754	16W-18N	D4
10	WLNG	60090	2755	15W-18N	A4
100	PLTN	60067	2752	21W-18N	D4
100	PltT	60074	2752	21W-18N	D4
400	ANHT	60004	2754	17W-17N	C4
400	BFGV	60089	2754	17W-17N	C4
500	PLTN	60074	2752	21W-17N	C4
700	ANHT	60004	2753	18W-18N	D4
700	BFGV	60089	2753	18W-18N	D4
700	PltT	60067	2752	21W-17N	C4
800	WLNG	60090	2754	15W-17N	E4
1200	ANHT	60089	2754	17W-18N	A4
1200	PltT	60010	2752	22W-17N	A4
1500	PLTN	60010	2752	23W-17N	A4
1700	PLTN	60010	2751	23W-17N	E5
1700	PLTN	60067	2751	23W-17N	E5
1700	PltT	60010	2751	23W-17N	E5
1800	PltT	60067	2751	23W-17N	E5
E Dundee Quarter Dr					
10	PLTN	60074	2753	19W-18N	C4
Dundee Rd Row					
4200	NfdT	60062	2756	12W-18N	A4
4200	NHBK	60062	2756	12W-18N	A4
Dundonald Rd					
2400	FSMR	60422	3507	3W-23S	B3
Dunes Pl					
-	AntT	60020	2414	28W-38N	E7
-	AntT	60081	2414	28W-38N	E7
-	FXLK	60020	2414	28W-38N	E7
Dune Sand Ct					
900	DYR	46311	3598		E3
Dunfries St					
1300	FSMR	60422	3506	4W-23S	E3
Dunham Cir					
800	WYNE	60184	2965	33W-5N	B1
Dunham Ct					
-	HMGN	60491	3344	15W-16S	B3
100	WYNE	60184	2965	33W-5N	B1
600	MRGO	60152	2634	49W-25N	C4
700	BGBK	60440	3205	21W-10S	E5
1300	GNVA	60134	3020	34W-1N	E4
Dunham Dr					
100	LslT	60540	3205	23W-8S	A1
400	DGvT	60516	3206	20W-10S	B6
400	DGvT	60517	3206	20W-10S	B6
400	WDRG	60516	3206	20W-10S	B6
400	WDRG	60517	3206	20W-10S	B6
800	WCHI	60185	3022	29W-1N	E2
900	WnfT	60185	3022	29W-1N	E2
Dunham Ln					
700	BGBK	60440	3205	21W-10S	E5
800	BFGV	60089	2701	17W-21N	B7
Dunham Pl					
10	SCRL	60174	2964	34W-4N	E5
Dunham Rd					
-	SchT	60103	2909	33W-7N	B5
-	WDRG	60516	3206	20W-8S	B2
10	PKFT	60466	3595	2W-27S	C4
10	SchT	60174	2965	33W-5N	A3
10	SchT	60184	2965	33W-5N	A2
10	SCRL	60174	2964	34W-3N	E5
10	SCRL	60174	2965	33W-5N	A2
10	SCRL	60184	2965	33W-5N	A2
10	WYNE	60120	2909	33W-7N	B6
10	WYNE	60174	2965	33W-5N	A2
10	WYNE	60184	2909	33W-7N	B5
10	WYNE	60184	2965	33W-5N	B1
100	DGvT	60439	3206	20W-11S	B7
200	BRLT	60120	2909	33W-7N	B5
200	SchT	60120	2909	33W-7N	B5
400	DGvT	60439	3270	20W-11S	B1
500	GRNE	60031	2534	16W-33N	E2
500	SchT	60174	2964	34W-3N	E5
5200	CrlT	60180	2635	47W-24N	B6
5200	SenT	60152	2635	47W-25N	B4
5200	SenT	60180	2635	47W-25N	B4
5500	DRGV	60515	3144	20W-6S	B5
5500	DRGV	60516	3144	20W-7S	B6
7100	DRGV	60516	3206	20W-8S	C1
7600	WDRG	60517	3206	20W-8S	B2
8100	DGvT	60517	3206	20W-9S	B3
8100	DRN	60517	3206	20W-9S	B3
8100	DRN	60561	3206	20W-9S	B3
Dunham Rd CO-19					
-	SchT	60103	2909	33W-7N	B5
10	SchT	60174	2965	33W-5N	A3
10	SchT	60184	2965	33W-5N	A2
10	SCRL	60174	2964	34W-3N	E5
10	SCRL	60174	2965	33W-5N	A2
10	SCRL	60184	2965	33W-5N	A2
10	WYNE	60120	2909	33W-7N	B6
10	WYNE	60174	2965	33W-5N	A2
10	WYNE	60184	2909	33W-7N	B5
10	WYNE	60184	2965	33W-5N	A1
200	BRLT	60120	2909	33W-7N	B5
200	SchT	60120	2909	33W-7N	B5
500	SchT	60174	2964	34W-3N	E5
Dunham Place Coms					
100	SCRL	60174	2964	34W-4N	E5
Dunham Trails Rd					
500	WYNE	60184	2965	33W-5N	B1
Dunham Woods Ct					
2500	SCRL	60174	2964	34W-4N	D3
Dunham Woods Rd					
2400	DhmT	60033	2464	49W-34N	D7
Dunheath Dr					
1300	IVNS	60010	2751	24W-17N	C4
Dunhill Cir					
1800	GNVW	60025	2810	8W-15N	D2
Dunhill Ct					
800	GRNE	60031	2534	16W-33N	D3
1600	NHBK	60062	2757	9W-16N	C6
N Dunhill Ct N					
2000	ANHT	60004	2807	17W-14N	C4
Dunhill Ct N					
1900	ANHT	60004	2807	17W-14N	B4
Dunhill Dr					
500	LKZH	60047	2698	23W-22N	E4
600	BFGV	60089	2701	16W-20N	C7
7900	LKWD	60014	2638	38W-24N	D7
9600	HTLY	60142	2692	39W-22N	D4
Dunhill Ln					
10	NBRN	60010	2644	24W-24N	C7
600	CLSM	60188	3024	24W-1N	D3
1900	AURA	60503	3200	33W-10S	E6
1900	AURA	60503	3201	33W-10S	A6
Dunhill Rd					
900	GYLK	60030	2533	19W-33N	B3
Dunlap Pl					
100	SMBG	60194	2858	25W-10N	A5
Dunlap Rd					
10	PKFT	60466	3595	2W-27S	C4
Dunlap St					
100	HRVD	60033	2406	50W-38N	A7
Dunlap Reef Dr					
8800	FKFT	60423	3504	11W-25S	A6
Dunlay Av					
100	MltT	60137	3083	23W-3S	A5
Dunlay Ct					
200	WDDL	60191	2971	17W-5N	B1
2400	WKGN	60085	2536	11W-34N	C1
Dunlay St					
400	AddT	60191	2971	17W-5N	C1
400	WDDL	60191	2971	17W-5N	C1
Dunleer Dr					
300	CRY	60013	2641	31W-24N	D6
1200	MDLN	60060	2590	19W-29N	D5
S Dunlieth Ct					
26700	CteT	60417	3685	0W-32S	C7
Dun Lo Dr					
1500	WhlT	60004	2754	16W-17N	C4
Dunlop Av					
800	FTPK	60130	3030	9W-0S	C7
Dunmore Ct					
10	BGBK	60440	3205	23W-10S	B6
Dunmore Dr					
-	TYPK	60477	3504	10W-23S	B3
2200	DRN	60561	3206	19W-10S	D5
9200	PlsT	60462	3345	11W-15S	E1
Dunmore Ln					
700	BRLT	60103	2911	28W-7N	B4
Dunmore Pl					
1900	HFET	60169	2804	25W-12N	A7
Dunmore St					
2000	JLET	60431	3417	28W-21S	B7
Dunmurry Dr					
9300	PlsT	60462	3345	11W-15S	E2
Dunn Ct					
1300	FXLK	60020	2415	28W-38N	A6
1300	FXLK	60081	2415	28W-38N	A6
Dunning Av					
100	WDND	60118	2801	34W-15N	A4
300	WDND	60118	2800	34W-15N	E4
Dunree Ct					
7800	TYPK	60477	3504	9W-23S	D3
Dunree Ln					
11800	ODPK	60467	3422	14W-21S	D6
Dunridge Cir					
200	EDND	60118	2801	33W-16N	B2
Dunridge Ct					
400	EDND	60118	2801	33W-16N	A2
Dunrobin Cir					
2600	AURA	60503	3201	32W-10S	C6
Dunrobin Rd					
1300	NPVL	60540	3142	25W-6S	B6
1400	LSLE	60532	3142	25W-7S	C6
1400	NPVL	60532	3142	25W-7S	C6
Dunroven Lakes Ct					
6100	CPVL	60110	2747	36W-18N	A6
Dunroven Lakes Rd					
6300	CPVL	60110	2747	36W-18N	A5
Dunrovin Dr					
100	BNHL	60010	2749	28W-20N	E1
Duns Ct					
900	FKFT	60423	3592	9W-26S	E3
900	FKFT	60423	3593	8W-26S	A2
Dunsford Ct					
1800	SMBG	60194	2858	25W-11N	A3
Dunsinane Ln					
10	BKBN	60015	2703	11W-23N	C3
E Dunslow Ln					
1300	LKPT	60441	3342	21W-18S	A7
Dunstan Ln					
2800	BFGV	60089	2701	17W-23N	C2
Dunstan Rd					
800	GNVA	60134	3020	35W-0N	A5
Dunsten Cir					
500	NHBK	60062	2756	10W-18N	E4
Dunteman Dr					
100	BMDL	60108	2969	23W-4N	A3
100	BMDL	60139	2969	23W-4N	A3
100	GLHT	60139	2969	23W-4N	A3
N Dunton Av					
10	ANHT	60004	2807	17W-14N	A4
10	ANHT	60005	2807	17W-14N	A5
2800	ANHT	60004	2754	17W-17N	A5
S Dunton Av					
1000	ANHT	60005	2807	18W-12N	A7
1200	ANHT	60005	2861	18W-12N	A1
Dunton Ct					
100	MDLN	60060	2590	20W-27N	B7
Duntrune Ln					
100	IVNS	60067	2752	22W-18N	B4
W Dunvegan Ct					
28800	AlqT	60013	2642	28W-24N	D7
28800	CbaT	60013	2642	28W-24N	D7
Dunwick Ct					
10	LKZH	60010	2698	24W-21N	D5
Dunwood Ct					
7300	FXLK	60020	2414	28W-39N	E5
N DuPage Av					
10	AddT	60101	2970	20W-4N	B4
10	ADSN	60101	2970	20W-4N	B4
100	EMHT	60126	3028	15W-2N	B1
800	LMBD	60148	2970	20W-2N	B7
800	LMBD	60148	3026	20W-2N	B1
DuPage Blvd					
600	GNEN	60137	3025	22W-0S	C7
DuPage Ct					
10	ELGN	60120	2854	34W-11N	E4
E DuPage Ct					
100	PNFD	60544	3338	29W-16S	D4
100	PnfT	60544	3338	29W-16S	D4
DuPage Dr					
-	SCRL	60185	2965	32W-2N	B7
-	WynT	60174	2965	32W-3N	B7
-	WynT	60185	2965	32W-2N	B7
-	WynT	60185	3021	32W-2N	B1
200	BGBK	60440	3268	24W-11S	E1
300	BGBK	60440	3204	24W-11S	E7
7000	LslT	60517	3143	22W-7S	C7
7000	LslT	60517	3205	22W-8S	C1
7000	LslT	60540	3205	22W-8S	C1
7000	WDRG	60517	3143	22W-7S	C7
S DuPage Dr					
24300	CNHN	60410	3672	32W-29S	D2
DuPage Pkwy					
-	AURA	60502	3139	32W-4S	B1
-	AURA	60510	3079	32W-3S	C6
-	WnfT	60510	3079	32W-3S	C6
2700	AURA	60502	3079	32W-3S	C7
DuPage St					
100	SRWD	60404	3496	30W-24S	C5
200	ELGN	60120	2854	34W-10N	C7
300	ELGN	60120	2855	33W-11N	A4
400	WnfT	60185	3023	28W-0N	A5
600	WnfT	60185	3022	28W-0N	E5
700	WCHI	60185	3022	28W-0N	E5
W DuPage Country Club Dr					
23600	PnfT	60586	3416	29W-20S	D5
Du Pahze St					
300	NPVL	60565	3203	27W-10S	D7
Dupee Pl					
100	EVTN	60091	2813	2W-13N	A7
100	EVTN	60201	2813	2W-13N	A7
100	WLMT	60091	2813	2W-13N	A7

STREET Block	City	ZIP	Map#	CGS	Grid
Dupont Av					
4800	PLTN	60067	2805	21W-14N	D4
4800	RGMW	60008	2805	21W-14N	E4
4800	RGMW	60067	2805	21W-14N	D4
Dupont Ct					
600	EGVV	60007	2913	22W-9N	C1
Dupont Dr					
4400	HRPK	60133	2967	27W-5N	D2
Duquesne Av					
1300	NPVL	60565	3204	24W-9S	C3
Duran Ct					
1000	JLET	60431	3496	29W-22S	D2
Durand Dr					
2200	LslT	60515	3143	21W-6S	E4
5500	LslT	60516	3143	21W-6S	E4
Durango Ct					
10	ElaT	60047	2645	22W-25N	B5
10	GLBT	60136	2799	39W-15N	A4
10	HNWD	60047	2645	22W-25N	B5
Durango Dr					
100	GLBT	60136	2799	38W-15N	A4
Durango Ln					
2400	NPVL	60564	3202	29W-10S	D7
Durango Rd					
10	OswT	60538	3199	36W-10S	D7
Durfee Rd					
300	MltT	60187	3081	26W-2S	D3
300	WHTN	60187	3081	26W-2S	D3
600	MltT	60187	3082	26W-2S	A3
600	WHTN	60187	3082	25W-2S	A3
Durham Ct					
-	MKNA	60448	3502	15W-23S	B4
10	BRRG	60527	3208	15W-9S	A3
10	LNSH	60045	2702	13W-23N	D2
200	NPVL	60540	3142	25W-6S	B5
500	HFET	60169	2858	24W-12N	E1
700	HRPK	60133	2858	26W-9N	A7
1100	SMBG	60193	2913	22W-9N	B1
1600	CLLK	60014	2693	36W-22N	C3
1600	DRN	60561	3207	18W-9S	A2
W Durham Ct					
1900	RDLK	60073	2531	25W-33N	A3
Durham Dr					
100	CRTE	60417	3596	0W-28S	C6
500	FKFT	60423	3592	9W-26S	E2
1000	WHTN	60187	3082	23W-3S	E6
1200	AURA	60506	3137	36W-5S	D4
1500	IVNS	60067	2805	23W-15N	A1
1700	IVNS	60067	2804	23W-15N	E1
9100	HTLY	60142	2692	40W-22N	B3
Durham Ln					
-	SMBG	60195	2858	24W-12N	E2
200	BMDL	60108	2969	22W-4N	C3
500	HFET	60169	2858	24W-12N	D1
700	GYLK	60030	2533	20W-33N	B3
1200	LMNT	60439	3270	18W-14S	E7
N Durham Ln					
10	RDLK	60073	2531	25W-33N	A3
Durkin Rd					
17800	TYPK	60487	3424	10W-21S	B6
Durness Ct					
1400	NPVL	60565	3203	27W-8S	B3
2400	CTHL	60403	3418	26W-20S	A6
Dursey Ln					
600	DSPN	60016	2808	13W-13N	D5
600	MPPT	60016	2808	13W-13N	D5
600	MPPT	60056	2808	13W-13N	D5
Durst Av					
-	WKGN	60087	2479	11W-36N	E4
Dusk Dr					
1700	ZION	60099	2421	12W-41N	B1
Dusty Tr					
11900	OrlT	60467	3344	14W-16S	C3
Dusty Trails					
-	DMND	60416	3941	33W-39S	A2
N Dutch Cir					
2800	MchT	60050	2471	31W-34N	C7
S Dutch Dr					
23100	GGnT	60423	3591	12W-28S	E6
Dutch American Wy					
1300	BCHR	60401	3774	0W-35S	C7
Dutch Barn St					
10200	HTLY	60142	2692	39W-20N	C7
Dutch Creek Ln					
3600	JNBG	60050	2471	31W-35N	D5
Dutch Mill Ct					
5700	HRPK	60133	2911	26W-7N	E5
Dutra Av					
20500	BlmT	60411	3507	2W-24S	C6
20500	CHHT	60411	3507	2W-24S	C6
Dutton Rd					
27000	CteT	60401	3774	0E-33S	E2
Duval Ct					
10	BGBK	60490	3267	27W-12S	D4
Duvall Dr					
700	WDSK	60098	2581	42W-30N	B1
Duvan Dr					
7200	TYPK	60477	3424	9W-21S	E5
Duvick Av					
400	LtRT	60548	3330	50W-14S	B1
400	SDWH	60548	3258	50W-14S	B7
400	SDWH	60548	3330	50W-14S	B1
Duxbury Ct					
-	SMWD	60107	2910	29W-9N	E1
100	BMDL	60108	2969	23W-5N	A2
900	SMBG	60193	2858	24W-9N	D7
Duxbury Dr					
10	NBRN	60010	2644	25W-24N	A6
Duxbury Ln					
10	CRY	60013	2695	32W-23N	B1
700	BRLT	60103	2910	29W-7N	D5
800	SMBG	60193	2858	24W-9N	C7
Duxbury St					
10	RGMW	60008	2805	20W-14N	E4
10	RGMW	60067	2805	20W-14N	E4
Dvorak Dr					
6000	CLLK	60012	2584	35W-27N	B7
6000	NndT	60012	2584	35W-27N	B7
S Dwight Av					
10	JLET	60435	3498	25W-24S	B5
10	JLET	60436	3498	25W-24S	B6
Dwight Ct					
500	ANTH	60002	2357	23W-42N	E5
8900	ODHL	60487	3424	11W-19S	A3
Dwight St					
300	ELGN	60120	2855	33W-10N	A6
N Dwyer Av					
10	ANHT	60005	2806	18W-14N	E4
S Dwyer Av					
10	ANHT	60005	2806	18W-13N	E5
Dwyer Ct					
-	WNKA	60093	2812	5W-15N	A2
Dwyer St					
-	HTLY	60142	2692	40W-20N	A7
E Dyer Blvd					
200	HMND	46320	3430		D1
Dyer Dr					
1700	BRLT	60103	2909	31W-8N	D3
Dylan Dr					
10	OSWG	60543	3200	34W-10S	D7
N Dymond Rd					
100	LYVL	60048	2591	17W-28N	B5
S Dymond Rd					
100	LYVL	60048	2591	17W-28N	C6
900	VNHL	60061	2591	17W-28N	C7
Dystrup Rd					
600	DGvT	60439	3270	19W-12S	C3
E					
E Ct					
10000	MKNA	60448	3503	12W-23S	C4
E St					
200	NCHI	60088	2594	10W-30N	A2
E E St					
10	BtnT	60099	2422	9W-41N	C1
W E St					
-	MYWD	60153	3088	10W-1S	A1
-	PvsT	60141	3088	10W-1S	A1
-	PvsT	60153	3088	10W-1S	A1
Eagle Av					
100	BmdT	60157	2913	21W-7N	E5
1500	MLPK	60160	3028	13W-1N	E2
Eagle Bnd					
-	HmrT	60441	3420	19W-21S	D6
-	NLNX	60441	3420	19W-21S	D6
Eagle Cir					
-	NLNX	60451	3589	16W-25S	E1
-	NlxT	60451	3589	16W-25S	E1
1800	NLNX	60451	3590	16W-25S	A1
Eagle Ct					
10	SMWD	60107	2856	29W-10N	C5
100	DYR	46311	3510		D5
200	BGBK	60440	3268	24W-11S	E1
200	BMDL	60108	2968	23W-4N	E3
500	CmpT	60175	2961	42W-5N	C2
500	RVWD	60015	2756	12W-20N	B1
500	SMBG	60194	2857	26W-11N	E4
600	SchT	60175	2963	38W-5N	A2
1200	BRLT	60103	2910	29W-6N	E7
1200	WHTN	60187	3082	25W-2S	B3
1400	GLHT	60139	2968	24W-2N	D7
4300	GRNE	60031	2535	14W-34N	D1
6700	TYPK	60477	3425	8W-21S	B7
N Eagle Ct					
36100	LkvT	60041	2474	24W-36N	C4
Eagle Dr					
-	BlmT	60411	3509	2E-25S	E7
-	FDHT	60411	3509	2E-25S	E7
400	EGvT	60007	2861	18W-9N	A7
400	EGvT	60007	2915	17W-8N	B1
400	EGVV	60007	2861	18W-9N	A7
400	EGVV	60007	2915	17W-8N	B1
600	BNVL	60106	2915	16W-6N	D7
700	AURA	60506	3137	37W-6S	D5
2600	JLET	60436	3497	27W-24S	C6
2700	JLET	60431	3497	27W-24S	C6
6700	TYPK	60477	3425	8W-21S	A7
25500	ElaT	60047	2646	19W-25N	D5
25500	ElaT	60060	2646	19W-25N	D5
25500	LGGV	60047	2646	19W-25N	D5
25500	LGGV	60060	2646	19W-25N	D5
25900	VrnT	60060	2646	19W-25N	D4
S Eagle Dr					
26000	MONE	60449	3683	6W-31S	B6
Eagle Ln					
200	BMDL	60108	2968	23W-4N	E3
3800	RGMW	60008	2806	19W-13N	C7
N Eagle Ln					
600	PLTN	60067	2752	20W-16N	E6
Eagle Rd					
1300	ELGN	60123	2854	35W-12N	A2
1400	ElgT	60123	2854	35W-12N	A2
Eagle Rdg					
8200	SPGV	60081	2413	31W-40N	D3
Eagle St					
200	NPVL	60563	3141	27W-5S	D2
200	NpvT	60563	3141	27W-5S	D2
500	CLLK	60014	2639	36W-25N	D4
8700	HGKN	60525	3147	11W-7S	E5
E Eagle St					
1200	JLET	60432	3499	22W-23S	D3
1300	JltT	60432	3499	22W-23S	D3
N Eagle St					
10	NPVL	60540	3141	27W-6S	C5
500	NPVL	60563	3141	27W-5S	D4
1400	NpvT	60563	3141	27W-5S	D4
S Eagle St					
10	NPVL	60540	3141	27W-6S	C5
Eagle Ter					
10	BmdT	60143	2970	21W-5N	A1
10	BmdT	60157	2913	21W-7N	E5
10	ITSC	60143	2970	21W-5N	A1
Eagle Trc					
18700	MKNA	60448	3502	14W-22S	E1
Eagle Wy					
3400	AntT	60002	2417	21W-39N	C4
3400	LKVL	60002	2417	21W-39N	C4
3400	LKVL	60046	2417	21W-39N	C4
N Eagle Wy					
2500	HFET	60192	2803	25W-13N	E6
Eagle Brook Dr					
1300	GNVA	60134	3020	36W-0N	A6
1700	GnvT	60134	3020	36W-0S	A6
Eagle Brook Ln					
500	WldT	60565	3203	27W-11S	C7
700	WldT	60565	3267	27W-11S	B1
Eagle Chase Ct					
24200	PNFD	60544	3338	30W-16S	B3
Eagle Chase Dr					
24200	PNFD	60544	3338	30W-16S	B4
Eagle Creek Dr					
200	RLKB	60073	2474	23W-35N	E5
200	RLKB	60073	2475	22W-35N	A5
Eagle Creek Rd					
800	ELWD	60421	3675	25W-31S	B6
Eagle Crest Dr					
1200	LMNT	60439	3342	19W-15S	C1
Eagle Feather Ct					
13600	PNFD	60544	3338	30W-16S	B3
Eagle Grove Ct					
1600	WLNG	60090	2754	16W-18N	D3
E Eagle Lake Rd					
10	WshT	60401	3774	0E-34S	E5
W Eagle Lake Rd					
10	BCHR	60401	3774	0W-34S	D5
10	WshT	60401	3774	1W-34S	A5
Eagle Nest Ct					
13500	PNFD	60544	3338	30W-16S	C3
Eagle Nest Dr					
3400	CRTE	60417	3597	1E-28S	C7
3400	STGR	60475	3597	1E-28S	C5
Eagle Perch Ct					
13600	PNFD	60544	3338	29W-16S	C3
Eagle Point Dr					
900	MHRY	60050	2526	35W-32N	E4
900	MTSN	60443	3505	7W-25S	C7
Eagle Point Rd					
10	FXLK	60020	2472	28W-36N	E5
10	FXLK	60020	2473	28W-36N	A4
100	GrtT	60041	2472	28W-35N	E5
100	GrtT	60051	2472	28W-35N	E5
Eagle Pointe Dr					
10	BNHL	60010	2801	30W-15N	E1
10	BNHL	60010	2802	30W-16N	A1
Eagle Ridge Ct					
200	WCHI	60185	2966	30W-3N	C6
13500	PNFD	60544	3338	30W-16S	C3
Eagle Ridge Dr					
10	HNWD	60047	2645	22W-27N	C2
1300	ANTH	60002	2417	21W-41N	D1
1500	AntT	60002	2417	21W-41N	D2
6200	GRNE	60031	2534	16W-33N	D3
10400	ODPK	60467	3423	13W-21S	B7
10400	ODPK	60487	3423	13W-21S	B7
10400	OrlT	60487	3423	13W-21S	B7
14700	HMGN	60491	3343	17W-17S	C6
16000	TYPK	60477	3424	10W-19S	C2
W Eagle Ridge Dr					
1900	WKGN	60087	2421	11W-38N	D7
Eagle Ridge Ln					
500	ALGN	60102	2694	34W-20N	C7
12600	HTLY	60142	2744	42W-19N	C3
Eagles Nest Ct					
600	SchT	60175	2907	38W-7N	A4
Eagles Nest Dr					
400	DRN	60527	3145	17W-7S	C6
400	WLBK	60527	3145	17W-7S	D6
Eagles Nest Rd					
23400	AntT	60002	2416	23W-40N	E3
Eagles Roost					
5100	RcmT	60071	2353	34W-43N	D5
5100	RHMD	60071	2353	34W-43N	D5
Eagle View Dr					
400	CLSM	60188	2968	25W-2N	B7
Eagle Vista Dr					
1400	NLNX	60451	3588	19W-26S	E2
Eaglewood Ct					
5200	JLET	60586	3416	30W-20S	C5
Eaglewood Tr					
5900	MHRY	60050	2527	34W-31N	B6
Eagon Ln					
1400	RDLK	60073	2531	23W-31N	E7
Eaker Pl					
300	DSPN	60016	2862	15W-10N	B5
Eakin Creek Ct					
13000	HTLY	60142	2744	43W-19N	C3
Ealing on Duxbury					
10	RGMW	60008	2805	22W-13N	B6
W Eames St					
22000	CNHN	60410	3585	28W-27S	A5
22000	JLET	60410	3585	28W-27S	A5
23000	CnhT	60410	3585	28W-27S	A5
23200	CNHN	60410	3584	29W-28S	D6
23200	CnhT	60410	3584	29W-28S	D6
23200	JLET	60410	3584	29W-28S	D6
25800	CnhT	60410	3672	32W-30S	D5
26100	AxST	60447	3672	32W-30S	C5
26100	CNHN	60410	3672	33W-30S	B5
26100	CNHN	60447	3672	33W-30S	C5
27100	AxST	60410	3672	33W-30S	B5
27100	MNKA	60447	3672	33W-30S	B5
W Eames St US-6					
22000	CNHN	60410	3585	28W-27S	A5
22000	JLET	60410	3585	28W-27S	A5
23000	CnhT	60410	3585	28W-27S	A5
23200	CNHN	60410	3584	29W-28S	D6
23200	CnhT	60410	3584	29W-28S	D6
23200	JLET	60410	3584	29W-28S	D6
25800	CnhT	60410	3672	32W-30S	D5
26100	AxST	60447	3672	32W-30S	C5
26100	CNHN	60410	3672	33W-30S	B5
26100	CNHN	60447	3672	33W-30S	C5
27100	AxST	60410	3672	33W-30S	B5
27100	MNKA	60447	3672	33W-30S	B5
W Eamon Ct					
15500	MHTN	60442	3677	19W-30S	E4
Earhart Ct					
21300	LktT	60544	3339	26W-16S	E5
Earl Av					
1200	DSPN	60016	2862	13W-10N	D5
1200	DSPN	60018	2862	13W-10N	D5
Earl Ct					
10	BGBK	60440	3269	21W-12S	E2
10	BGBK	60517	3269	21W-12S	E2
10	WDRG	60517	3269	21W-12S	E2
10	WDRG	60517	3270	21W-12S	A2
400	DGvT	60561	3207	17W-9S	B2
Earl Dr					
500	NHFD	60093	2811	7W-15N	B2
3400	JLET	60431	3417	28W-21S	B7
3400	PnfT	60431	3417	28W-21S	B7
Earl Ln					
400	SEGN	60177	2908	34W-7N	D4
Earl Rd					
100	SRWD	60404	3496	30W-24S	B6
Earl St					
100	LktT	60441	3419	21W-18S	E1
S Earl St					
10	JLET	60435	3498	25W-24S	B6
10	JLET	60436	3498	25W-24S	B6
Earls Ct					
300	DRFD	60015	2756	11W-20N	D1
9200	OrlT	60487	3423	11W-21S	E6
N Earls Ct					
1000	PLTN	60067	2752	23W-17N	A5
Earlston Rd					
500	KLWH	60043	2812	4W-14N	C4
3900	DRGV	60515	3084	19W-4S	D7
3900	YkTp	60515	3084	19W-4S	D7
W Early Av					
1200	CHCG	60660	2921	1W-7N	D4
Early St					
200	PKFT	60466	3595	3W-25S	B1
East Av					
-	BKFD	60513	3147	11W-5S	D1
-	BKFD	60525	3147	11W-5S	D1
-	LGNG	60513	3147	11W-5S	D1
10	PKRG	60068	2864	9W-9N	C7
10	RVSD	60546	3088	9W-3S	C5
10	SMWD	60107	2857	27W-10N	C5
300	CHCG	60631	2864	9W-9N	C7
300	LslT	60563	3142	25W-5S	A3
300	NPVL	60563	3142	25W-5S	A2
600	PKRG	60631	2864	9W-9N	C7
700	LGNG	60525	3147	12W-5S	D2
700	MCCK	60525	3147	12W-5S	D2
800	CTSD	60525	3147	11W-5S	D2
1000	HRPK	60133	2911	27W-8N	C2
1000	SMWD	60107	2911	27W-9N	C1
1000	SMWD	60133	2911	27W-9N	C1
1200	BRWN	60304	3031	8W-1S	A7
1200	BRWN	60402	3031	8W-1S	A7
1200	OKPK	60304	3031	8W-1S	A7
1500	BRWN	60402	3089	8W-3S	A5
1500	CRTE	60417	3685	0W-30S	C3
1500	CteT	60417	3685	0W-30S	C3
3800	SKNY	60402	3089	8W-3S	A6
5800	HGKN	60525	3147	11W-6S	D5
N East Av					
10	AURA	60505	3200	34W-8S	D1
10	ElgT	60177	2908	34W-8N	E3
10	SEGN	60177	2908	34W-8N	E3
100	AURA	60505	3138	34W-7S	D7
300	OKPK	60302	3031	8W-0N	A3
S East Av					
10	AURA	60505	3200	34W-8S	D2
10	SEGN	60177	2908	34W-8N	E3
100	OKPK	60302	3031	8W-0S	A5
400	OKPK	60304	3031	8W-0S	A6
1100	BRWN	60304	3031	8W-0S	A7
1100	BRWN	60402	3031	8W-0S	A7
W East Av					
25300	AntT	60002	2416	25W-41N	A1
East Av N					
500	OKPK	60302	3031	8W-1N	A2
1200	CHCG	60302	3031	8W-1N	A1
1200	CHCG	60707	3031	8W-1N	A1
East Blvd					
600	MchT	60051	2529	29W-32N	C5
East Ct					
600	SHLD	60473	3429	0E-18S	A1
E East Ct					
400	EMHT	60126	3028	15W-1N	B2
East Dr					
-	CLSM	60188	2968	24W-3N	D5
-	SchT	60177	2908	34W-7N	E4
-	SMBG	60173	2860	21W-11N	A2
-	WLNG	60090	2808	14W-16N	D1
10	NHLK	60164	2972	13W-2N	D7
10	NHLK	60164	3028	13W-2N	D1
100	WKGN	60085	2536	12W-33N	B1
200	CmpT	60175	2961	42W-4N	D4
3300	NndT	60012	2586	30W-28N	A5
3300	NndT	60050	2586	30W-28N	A5
4100	MchT	60097	2469	36W-36N	E4
4200	NndT	60012	2583	36W-27N	E7
4800	RNPK	60471	3594	6W-27S	B5
19500	FftT	60423	3504	9W-23S	E3
19500	TYPK	60423	3504	9W-23S	E3
19500	TYPK	60477	3504	9W-23S	E3
N East Dr					
1600	AURA	60505	3139	33W-7S	A7
23300	CbaT	60010	2696	28W-23N	E2
40200	AntT	60002	2416	24W-40N	B3
East Ln					
100	LKBN	60010	2697	27W-23N	C2
200	LKZH	60047	2698	23W-23N	D1
500	GnvT	60134	3021	33W-0N	A4
5100	MCLK	60050	2470	34W-34N	D7
N East Ln					
32500	AvnT	60030	2531	24W-32N	C5
East Rd					
100	GNEN	60137	3025	22W-0S	C7
300	ELGN	60123	2854	34W-10N	D6
1300	WPHR	60096	2363	9W-41N	C7
1400	WPHR	60096	2422	9W-41N	E1
11100	PSHL	60465	3273	11W-13S	E3
N East Rd					
23400	ElaT	60047	2699	21W-23N	D2
42000	ANTH	60002	2358	22W-42N	B7
42000	AntT	60002	2358	22W-42N	B7
East St					
-	CLLK	60014	2639	36W-25N	D4
-	GrtT	60081	2472	29W-37N	D1
-	LtRT	60545	3259	47W-13S	C5
-	MchT	60081	2472	29W-37N	D1
-	PLNO	60545	3259	47W-13S	C5
-	RcmT	60071	2413	32W-39N	A4
10	CLLK	60014	2640	34W-26N	C4
10	WNFD	60190	3023	27W-0S	D6
600	MchT	60050	2472	29W-36N	C3
600	WNFD	60190	3081	27W-0S	D1
700	LMNT	60439	3270	19W-14S	E6
700	WNFD	60187	3081	27W-1S	D1
700	WnfT	60187	3081	27W-1S	D1
1100	CRTE	60417	3685	0W-29S	C2
8000	SPGV	60081	2413	30W-39N	E4
8000	SPGV	60081	2414	30W-39N	A4
10100	RHMD	60071	2353	34W-41N	C7
N East St					
100	HPSR	60140	2795	47W-16N	E2
100	MRGO	60152	2634	49W-26N	C2
100	WMTN	60481	3853	27W-38S	D6
500	PLNO	60545	3259	47W-13S	D5
1300	MRGO	60152	2578	49W-27N	C7
S East St					
100	MRGO	60152	2634	49W-26N	C2
100	WMTN	60481	3853	27W-38S	D6
1000	WDSK	60098	2581	41W-30N	D2
1300	LKPT	60441	3419	22W-20S	D4
Eastbrook Ct					
1700	SLVL	60411	3597	2E-27S	C5
Eastbrook Dr					
-	FKFT	60423	3591	13W-26S	B3
22900	CteT	60417	3597	2E-27S	C5
22900	SLVL	60411	3597	2E-27S	C5
N East Brook Rd					
2400	EDPK	60707	2974	9W-3N	B6
Eastcanton Ct					
1300	DRFD	60015	2703	10W-21N	E6
Eastchester Ct					
5100	JLET	60586	3496	30W-22S	C1
Eastchester Rd					
600	WLNG	60090	2755	15W-17N	A6
N East Cir Av					
5700	CHCG	60631	2918	8W-7N	E4
S Eastcliff Dr					
22100	TroT	60404	3584	30W-26S	B4
East Course Dr					
1400	RVWD	60015	2703	12W-21N	B5
East End Av					
400	CTCY	60409	3351	2E-17S	C6
400	DLTN	60409	3351	2E-17S	C6
400	DLTN	60419	3351	2E-17S	C6
700	BKLY	60162	3028	14W-0N	C4
700	BKLY	60163	3028	14W-0N	C4
700	HLSD	60162	3028	14W-0N	C4
1400	CHHT	60411	3508	0W-25S	B7
1500	CHHT	60411	3596	0W-26S	B3
2500	BlmT	60411	3596	0W-26S	B3
2700	SCHT	60411	3596	0W-26S	B3
3200	STGR	60411	3596	0W-27S	B4
East End Av					
3200	STGR	60475	3596	0W-27S	B4
15400	DLTN	60473	3351	2E-18S	C6
N East End Av					
1600	RLKB	60073	2475	22W-35N	B6
30200	LbvT	60048	2591	15W-30N	E2
N Eastend Av					
36000	GrtT	60041	2473	26W-36N	D4
S East End Av					
4900	CHCG	60615	3153	2E-5S	B1
7100	CHCG	60649	3153	2E-8S	B7
7500	CHCG	60649	3215	2E-8S	B1
9300	CHCG	60617	3215	2E-10S	B5
Eastern Av					
10	AURA	60505	3139	33W-7S	A7
10	AURA	60505	3201	33W-7S	A1
10	CNHL	60514	3145	16W-5S	D2
10	MltT	60137	3025	22W-1N	D2
100	BLWD	60104	3029	12W-0N	B4
100	BNVL	60007	2915	16W-7N	D3
100	BNVL	60106	2915	16W-7N	D3
100	EGVV	60007	2915	16W-7N	D3
100	EGVV	60106	2915	16W-7N	D3
200	AraT	60505	3139	33W-7S	A7
200	BRTN	60010	2751	25W-18N	B2
500	DYR	46311	3510		E5
800	GNEN	60137	3025	22W-1N	D3
7000	IHPK	60525	3146	14W-7S	D7
23300	MHTN	60442	3589	19W-28S	A7
23300	MhtT	60442	3589	19W-28S	A7
23300	MhtT	60451	3589	19W-28S	A7
23300	NLNX	60451	3589	19W-28S	A7
N Eastern Av					
10	JLET	60432	3499	23W-23S	A3
10	JLET	60433	3499	23W-23S	A5
100	BRLT	60103	2910	28W-8N	E2
100	MHTN	60442	3678	19W-30S	A4
200	MhtT	60442	3678	19W-30S	A4
700	PNFD	60544	3338	29W-17S	D6
1900	MHRY	60050	2527	33W-33N	E2
S Eastern Av					
10	JLET	60432	3499	23W-24S	A5
10	JLET	60433	3499	23W-24S	A5
100	BRLT	60103	2910	28W-8N	E3
100	MHTN	60442	3678	19W-31S	A5
400	JLET	60436	3499	23W-24S	A6
23200	MhtT	60442	3678	19W-30S	A3
W Eastern Av					
800	MchT	60050	2472	29W-37N	C2
Eastfield Rd					
10	OswT	60538	3200	36W-10S	A7
Eastgate Av					
200	CHHT	60411	3508	0W-24S	B5
S Eastgate Av					
25900	MONE	60449	3683	6W-31S	A6
Eastgate Ct					
10	WDRG	60517	3143	21W-6S	E5
100	ALGN	60102	2694	33W-20N	E7
300	NLNX	60451	3589	17W-25S	C1
Eastgate Dr					
100	ALGN	60102	2694	33W-20N	E7
200	ALGN	60102	2747	33W-20N	E1
17400	CCHL	60478	3426	5W-20S	D5
Eastgate Ln					
1400	BRLT	60103	2966	30W-5N	B1
Eastgate Rd					
200	YkTp	60148	3084	19W-1S	C2
700	CLLK	60014	2640	35W-24N	B6
Eastgrove Rd					
300	RVSD	60546	3088	9W-3S	D4
Eastham Ct					
10	SMBG	60193	2858	25W-10N	C6
Eastham Ln					
1300	SMBG	60193	2858	25W-10N	B6
Eastings Wy					
-	BrnT	60010	2803	27W-15N	B1
10	SBTN	60010	2803	27W-15N	B1
N Eastings Wy					
34300	WrnT	60031	2534	17W-34N	C1
E Eastlake Dr					
100	LKMR	60051	2529	28W-32N	D5
S Eastlake Pkwy					
-	HMGN	60491	3421	18W-19S	B3
16500	LKPT	60441	3421	18W-19S	A3
N Eastlake Ter					
7500	CHCG	60626	2867	1W-9N	D7
N East Lake Shore Dr					
26300	WcnT	60010	2644	25W-26N	A3
26300	WcnT	60084	2644	25W-26N	A3
Eastland Ct					
300	NPVL	60565	3203	26W-9S	D5
N Eastland St					
700	AddT	60126	2972	15W-2N	B6
700	EMHT	60126	2972	15W-3N	B6
Eastline Dr					
2400	JLET	60431	3417	28W-20S	B6
2400	PnfT	60431	3417	28W-20S	B6
Eastman Ct					
500	MPPT	60056	2808	15W-13N	B6
E Eastman Ct					
2000	ANHT	60004	2807	16W-14N	D4
N Eastman Dr					
600	MPPT	60056	2808	15W-13N	B5
Eastman Ln					
1800	HRPK	60133	2967	27W-5N	C1
Eastman St					
3700	LinT	53147	2349		E1
E Eastman St					
1300	ANHT	60004	2807	17W-14N	C4
W Eastman St					
10	ANHT	60004	2807	17W-14N	A4
400	ANHT	60005	2806	18W-14N	E4
700	CHCG	60610	3034	0W-1N	A1
800	CHCG	60610	3033	1W-1N	E1
800	CHCG	60622	3033	1W-1N	E1
2100	RGMW	60008	2806	19W-14N	C4
N Eastmann St					
200	HRVD	60033	2406	50W-38N	B7
S Eastmann St					
200	HRVD	60033	2406	50W-38N	A7
500	DhmT	60033	2406	50W-38N	A7
N Eastmoor Av					
36400	LkvT	60041	2474	24W-36N	B3
36400	LkvT	60046	2474	24W-36N	B3
Eastmoor Ln					
1500	ALGN	60102	2747	36W-19N	B2
1500	DndT	60102	2747	36W-19N	B2
Easton Av					
-	BFGV	60069	2701	16W-23N	C3
-	BFGV	60089	2701	16W-23N	C3
-	VrnT	60069	2701	16W-23N	C3
100	WCHI	60185	3022	29W-0N	D4
100	WHTN	60185	3022	29W-0N	D4
400	GNVA	60134	3020	35W-0N	B5
Easton Ct					
800	GYLK	60030	2533	19W-33N	B2

STREET Block	City	ZIP	Map#	CGS	Grid
Easton Ct					
1600	BFGV	60089	2754	16W-18N	D4
1600	GRNE	60031	2477	18W-35N	A5
1600	WLNG	60089	2754	16W-18N	D4
1600	WLNG	60090	2754	16W-18N	D4
5800	HRPK	60133	2911	27W-7N	D5
W Easton Ct					
700	PLTN	60067	2805	21W-15N	C2
Easton Dr					
-	RtdT	60118	2746	38W-17N	C7
-	RtdT	60118	2799	38W-16N	C1
1100	CLSM	60188	2967	27W-4N	B4
Easton Ln					
-	EGVV	60007	2913	21W-8N	E1
500	RMVL	60446	3340	25W-15S	A2
Easton Pl					
100	BRRG	60527	3208	14W-8S	D2
3000	SCRL	60175	2964	36W-5N	A3
Eastport Av					
900	JltT	60432	3499	21W-22S	E2
Eastport Ct					
500	ISLK	60042	2586	29W-28N	C6
East Ridge Dr					
-	JLET	60586	3495	31W-21S	E1
N East River Rd					
10	DSPN	60016	2863	12W-12N	C1
10	MaiT	60016	2863	12W-12N	C1
400	MaiT	60016	2809	12W-12N	C7
500	NfdT	60016	2809	12W-12N	C7
4400	CHCG	60634	2917	10W-5N	E7
4400	CHCG	60656	2917	11W-6N	E7
4700	CHCG	60706	2917	10W-5N	E7
4700	NRDG	60656	2917	10W-5N	E7
4700	NRDG	60706	2917	10W-5N	E7
5500	CHCG	60631	2917	11W-6N	E7
5600	CHCG	60018	2917	11W-6N	E7
5700	CHCG	60068	2917	10W-7N	E4
5700	PKRG	60068	2917	10W-7N	E4
5700	PKRG	60631	2917	10W-7N	E4
Eastry Ln					
-	BlmT	60411	3509	2E-23S	D4
-	LYWD	60411	3509	2E-23S	D4
Eastshore Dr					
900	FXLK	60020	2415	28W-38N	A6
900	FXLK	60081	2415	28W-38N	A6
Eastside Av					
6800	WDRG	60517	3144	21W-7S	A7
East Side Dr					
100	GNVA	60134	3020	34W-1N	D3
300	GnvT	60134	3020	34W-1N	D3
800	GNVA	60174	3020	34W-1N	D3
800	SCRL	60134	3020	34W-1N	D3
800	SCRL	60174	3020	34W-1N	D3
Eastview					
-	ALSP	60803	3276	5W-13S	A4
-	CHCG	60655	3276	5W-13S	A4
-	CHCG	60803	3276	5W-13S	A4
Eastview Av					
-	BNVL	60106	2915	16W-5N	D7
100	BNVL	60106	2971	16W-5N	D1
100	CLLK	60014	2640	35W-25N	A5
300	MchT	60051	2529	29W-32N	C5
Eastview Ct					
600	SMBG	60194	2859	22W-10N	C5
Eastview Dr					
1300	WKGN	60085	2480	10W-35N	B6
2000	DSPN	60018	2862	13W-9N	E7
2200	DSPN	60018	2916	13W-9N	E1
2700	JLET	60432	3500	20W-22S	B2
S East View Pk					
5400	CHCG	60615	3153	2E-5S	B2
Eastview Rd					
300	BtvT	60542	3077	36W-3S	E7
300	NARA	60542	3077	36W-3S	E7
N Eastview Rd					
33000	WrnT	60030	2534	17W-33N	B4
Eastview St					
10	ElgT	60177	2908	34W-8N	E3
10	SEGN	60177	2908	34W-8N	E3
600	ELGN	60120	2855	33W-11N	B4
Eastview Ter					
100	LMBD	60148	3026	19W-0N	C5
Eastway Dr					
10	OSWG	60543	3263	37W-11S	C1
3100	ISLK	60042	2586	28W-28N	E6
3100	WcnT	60042	2586	28W-28N	E7
Eastwick Ln					
500	BRLT	60103	2910	29W-6N	E2
1800	AURA	60503	3201	33W-10S	A5
Eastwind Ct					
3800	NHBK	60062	2756	12W-17N	B5
Eastwind Dr					
700	NLNX	60451	3590	15W-25S	D1
22700	RNPK	60471	3594	6W-27S	A5
Eastwood Av					
10	PTBR	60010	2642	28W-25N	D4
10	WcnT	60010	2642	28W-25N	D4
100	CbaT	60010	2642	29W-26N	D4
1800	HDPK	60035	2704	10W-22N	B4
2400	EVTN	60201	2867	3W-12N	A1
2500	EVTN	60201	2813	3W-12N	A7
2700	WLMT	60091	2813	3W-13N	A7
2700	WLMT	60201	2813	3W-13N	A7
4200	GRNE	60031	2535	14W-33N	D3
9300	SRPK	60176	2917	11W-5N	C7
33200	WrnT	60030	2534	17W-33N	B3
N Eastwood Av					
100	MPPT	60056	2807	15W-13N	E6
W Eastwood Av					
2000	CHCG	60625	2921	2W-5N	B7
2000	CHCG	60640	2921	2W-5N	B7
2900	CHCG	60625	2920	4W-5N	D7
4000	CHCG	60630	2920	5W-5N	B7
5600	CHCG	60630	2919	7W-5N	B7
6300	HDHT	60630	2919	7W-5N	A7
6300	HDHT	60706	2919	7W-5N	A7
8200	NRDG	60706	2918	10W-5N	A7
14100	GRNE	60031	2535	14W-33N	C3
14100	WrnT	60031	2535	14W-33N	C3
Eastwood Ct					
10	CbaT	60010	2642	29W-25N	D4
10	PTBR	60010	2642	29W-25N	D4
400	WDSK	60098	2524	41W-31N	D7
1700	SMBG	60195	2859	23W-12N	A1
4800	WKGN	60087	2478	14W-37N	B1
5200	JLET	60586	3416	30W-20S	C5
9900	SRPK	60176	2917	12W-5N	B7
S Eastwood Ct					
26700	CNHN	60410	3761	32W-32S	D1
Eastwood Dr					
-	DGvT	60439	3207	18W-11S	A6
-	JNBG	60050	2470	33W-34N	E7
-	LYWD	60411	3509	2E-23S	D4
10	DRFD	60015	2757	10W-20N	B2
1500	AURA	60506	3137	36W-5S	D3
2700	MCLK	60050	2470	33W-34N	E7

STREET Block	City	ZIP	Map#	CGS	Grid
Eastwood Dr					
3100	MchT	60097	2469	36W-34N	E7
3100	WRLK	60097	2469	36W-34N	E7
10300	HTLY	60142	2692	39W-21N	B5
N Eastwood Dr					
10	WDSK	60098	2524	41W-31N	D7
1900	ANHT	60004	2807	17W-15N	B1
N Eastwood Dr SR-47					
10	WDSK	60098	2524	41W-31N	D7
S Eastwood Dr					
-	RDLK	60073	2531	23W-31N	D6
10	WDSK	60098	2524	41W-31N	E7
200	WDSK	60098	2581	40W-30N	E1
2800	DrrT	60098	2581	40W-29N	E5
10900	PSHL	60465	3274	9W-12S	D3
26700	CNHN	60410	3761	32W-32S	D1
S Eastwood Dr SR-47					
10	WDSK	60098	2524	41W-31N	E7
200	WDSK	60098	2581	40W-30N	E1
2800	DrrT	60098	2581	40W-29N	E5
Eastwood Ext					
-	DGvT	60439	3207	17W-11S	B7
Eastwood Ln					
100	PTBR	60010	2642	29W-25N	D4
700	BFGV	60089	2754	15W-20N	E1
800	GNVW	60025	2811	7W-13N	B6
1100	NHBK	60062	2757	9W-17N	D5
1200	MchT	60051	2528	31W-33N	E3
1500	MHRY	60051	2528	31W-33N	E3
8000	WDRG	60517	3205	22W-9S	C3
Eastwood Pl					
4100	PKCY	60085	2535	14W-33N	D3
Eastwood Rd					
900	GLNC	60022	2758	6W-18N	C4
W Eastwood Rd					
10500	BHPK	60087	2480	10W-37N	A1
11100	WKGN	60087	2479	11W-37N	E1
12500	BHPK	60087	2479	12W-37N	C1
Easy Cir					
4000	NPVL	60564	3266	29W-12S	C2
Easy Ct					
1300	GLHT	60139	3025	22W-2N	D1
Easy St					
100	CLSM	60188	3024	25W-1N	B2
400	DSPN	60016	2862	15W-11N	B3
500	BmdT	60139	3025	22W-2N	C1
500	DRN	60527	3145	17W-7S	C6
500	GLHT	60139	3025	22W-2N	C1
1400	ELGN	60123	2854	35W-11N	B4
N Easy St					
500	PLTN	60067	2752	21W-16N	D6
W Easy St					
24300	PnfT	60586	3416	30W-19S	B3
24800	PNFD	60586	3416	31W-19S	A3
Eaton Av					
300	RMVL	60446	3340	24W-16S	E3
19300	JknT	60421	3675	24W-29S	E1
Eaton Ct					
10	EMHT	60126	3027	16W-0N	E4
800	SMBG	60193	2859	23W-9N	B7
900	LKVL	60046	2475	21W-37N	D2
1200	HDPK	60035	2704	10W-23N	B2
1700	GNEN	60137	3083	23W-1S	A2
1700	GNEN	60187	3083	23W-1S	A2
1700	WHTN	60187	3083	23W-1S	A2
11000	WSTR	60154	3086	13W-2S	E4
S Eaton Ct					
600	LKFT	60045	2648	14W-25N	C6
W Eaton Ct					
1100	PLTN	60067	2805	22W-15N	B2
Eaton Dr					
1800	WDRG	60517	3206	20W-9S	A3
Eaton Ln					
800	LKVL	60046	2475	21W-37N	C2
Eaton Pl					
-	AntT	60081	2414	28W-39N	E5
-	FXLK	60081	2414	28W-39N	E5
Eaton St					
200	NHFD	60093	2811	7W-15N	B3
E Eaton St					
600	HMND	46320	3352		E7
Eaton Wy					
-	MDLN	60060	2647	17W-27N	A1
600	WynT	60185	2966	29W-4N	D3
Eau Claire Ct					
5100	GRNE	60031	2478	15W-35N	B5
Ebbtide Pt					
700	SMBG	60194	2859	22W-10N	C4
Ebenezer Av					
2700	ZION	60099	2422	9W-40N	C4
Eberhard Ln					
1800	JLET	60586	3416	29W-21S	D7
S Eberhardt St					
19100	BlmT	60425	3508	0E-23S	E3
19100	GNWD	60425	3508	0E-23S	E3
S Eberhart Av					
3100	CHCG	60616	3092	0E-3S	D4
6100	CHCG	60637	3152	0E-7S	D5
7000	CHCG	60619	3152	0E-8S	D7
7500	CHCG	60619	3214	0E-9S	D2
10000	CHCG	60628	3214	0E-11S	D7
10300	CHCG	60628	3278	0E-12S	D2
13000	CHCG	60827	3278	0E-15S	D7
13100	CHCG	60827	3350	0E-15S	D1
Eberhart St					
10	MHTN	60442	3677	19W-30S	D4
Eberly Av					
4000	BKFD	60513	3087	11W-4S	D7
4000	BKFD	60525	3087	11W-4S	D7
4000	LGNG	60525	3087	11W-4S	D7
4100	LGNG	60513	3087	11W-4S	D7
4500	BKFD	60513	3147	12W-4S	D1
4500	BKFD	60525	3147	12W-4S	D1
4500	LGNG	60525	3147	12W-4S	D1
4600	LGNG	60513	3147	11W-4S	D1
4600	MCCK	60525	3147	11W-4S	D1
Eberly Ct					
-	PLNO	60545	3260	45W-13S	B6
Ebert Dr					
-	AlqT	60013	2696	30W-23N	A2
-	CRY	60013	2696	30W-23N	A2
W Ebert Pl					
8500	NLES	60714	2864	10W-10N	A4
W Ebinger Dr					
6500	NLES	60714	2918	8W-8N	E1
6500	NLES	60714	2919	8W-8N	A1
Ebony Ct					
5400	GRNE	60031	2478	15W-35N	A5
Ebony Dr					
600	OSWG	60543	3264	34W-12S	C2
Echo Av					
700	RMVL	60446	3268	23W-14S	E7
700	RMVL	60446	3340	23W-14S	E1
Echo Ct					
10	ElaT	60047	2645	23W-24N	A7
10	HNWD	60047	2645	23W-24N	A7

STREET Block	City	ZIP	Map#	CGS	Grid
Echo Ct					
10	VNHL	60061	2647	17W-26N	C3
Echo Dr					
1300	NLNX	60451	3588	19W-27S	E5
Echo Hl					
10	LIHL	60156	2694	35W-21N	B5
Echo Ln					
300	AURA	60504	3201	31W-8S	E2
400	DGvT	60527	3207	16W-10S	D6
500	GNVW	60025	2811	6W-13N	C7
3200	NHBK	60062	2756	11W-16N	D6
6700	WTMT	60559	3145	18W-7S	B6
S Echo Ln					
500	PLTN	60067	2805	21W-15N	C2
W Echo Ln					
600	PLTN	60074	2752	21W-17N	C5
600	PltT	60067	2752	21W-17N	C5
Echo Rd					
-	AntT	60002	2416	25W-40N	A3
Echo Hill Rd					
10	AlqT	60013	2641	31W-26N	D3
10	ODHL	60013	2641	31W-26N	D4
N Echo Lake Rd					
23500	ElaT	60047	2699	23W-23N	A1
23500	LKZH	60047	2699	23W-23N	A1
23900	ElaT	60047	2645	23W-24N	A7
23900	HNWD	60047	2645	23W-24N	A7
Echo Valley Ln					
100	CmpT	60119	2962	41W-3N	A7
Echo Woods Dr					
10	ALGN	60102	2695	33W-21N	A6
Eci Ln					
-	NCHI	60064	2593	11W-31N	E1
Eclipse Dr					
200	CLSM	60188	2968	25W-3N	A6
Ed Bossert Dr					
10	LMNT	60439	3270	19W-13S	D5
Edbrooke Av					
14600	DLTN	60419	3350	0W-17S	D5
14600	DLTN	60827	3350	0W-17S	D5
14600	RVDL	60419	3350	0W-17S	D5
14600	RVDL	60827	3350	0W-17S	D5
14900	SHLD	60419	3350	0W-17S	D5
14900	SHLD	60473	3350	0W-17S	D5
S Edbrooke Av					
10500	CHCG	60628	3278	0E-12S	C2
13300	CHCG	60827	3350	0W-15S	D1
13800	RVDL	60827	3350	0W-16S	D3
14500	DLTN	60419	3350	0W-17S	D4
14500	DLTN	60827	3350	0W-17S	D4
14500	RVDL	60419	3350	0W-17S	D4
Eddie Rd					
500	MltT	60137	3083	22W-2S	C4
Eddy Ct					
900	WHTN	60187	3024	23W-0N	E5
Eddy Ln					
100	NHFD	60093	2811	7W-15N	B3
1300	LKZH	60010	2699	22W-21N	A6
1300	LKZH	60047	2699	22W-21N	A6
Eddy St					
200	CHHT	60411	3507	1W-23S	E3
W Eddy St					
1100	CHCG	60657	2977	1W-4N	D3
1900	CHCG	60618	2977	2W-4N	B3
3100	CHCG	60618	2976	3W-4N	E3
4000	CHCG	60641	2976	5W-4N	B3
4800	CHCG	60641	2975	7W-4N	C3
5500	CHCG	60634	2975	7W-4N	B3
Eddystone Cir					
900	NPVL	60565	3203	27W-8S	B2
Edelweiss Av					
500	ANTH	60002	2357	24W-41N	D7
Edelweiss Ct					
500	ANTH	60002	2357	24W-41N	D7
Edelweiss Dr					
600	LKZH	60047	2699	23W-22N	A4
8400	PSPK	60464	3274	10W-13S	C4
Eden Av					
9800	SRPK	60176	2973	12W-4N	B2
Eden Ct					
8900	LKWD	60014	2639	37W-24N	A7
Eden Dr					
800	SMBG	60195	2858	24W-12N	D1
Eden Ln					
10	JLET	60431	3497	28W-24S	B5
10	TroT	60431	3497	28W-24S	B5
W Eden Ln					
400	CteT	60417	3774	0W-33S	C1
Eden Rd					
10	EGVV	60007	2914	18W-8N	D2
Eden Oaks Ln					
10	BlmT	60422	3507	2W-23S	D3
10	BlmT	60430	3507	2W-23S	D3
10	FSMR	60422	3507	2W-23S	D3
Edens Expwy					
-	CHCG	-	2919	6W-7N	E4
-	CHCG	-	2920	5W-5N	A7
-	GLNC	-	2758	7W-16N	B7
-	GNVW	-	2811	6W-13N	D6
-	HDPK	-	2757	8W-18N	E2
-	LNWD	-	2919	6W-8N	E2
-	MNGV	-	2865	7W-10N	C5
-	NfdT	-	2757	8W-18N	E2
-	NfdT	-	2811	7W-15N	C1
-	NHBK	-	2757	8W-18N	E2
-	NHBK	-	2758	7W-17N	A5
-	NHFD	-	2758	7W-16N	B7
-	NHFD	-	2811	6W-14N	D4
-	NtrT	-	2758	7W-18N	A4
-	NtrT	-	2811	6W-14N	D4
-	SKOK	-	2811	6W-13N	E7
-	SKOK	-	2865	7W-10N	C5
-	SKOK	-	2919	6W-8N	E1
-	WLMT	-	2811	6W-14N	D4
Edens Expwy I-94					
-	CHCG	-	2919	6W-8N	E3
-	CHCG	-	2920	5W-5N	A7
-	GLNC	-	2758	7W-16N	B7
-	GNVW	-	2811	6W-13N	D6
-	LNWD	-	2919	6W-8N	E2
-	MNGV	-	2865	6W-10N	D4
-	NfdT	-	2811	7W-15N	C1
-	NHBK	-	2758	7W-18N	A4
-	NHFD	-	2758	7W-16N	B7
-	NHFD	-	2811	7W-16N	C1
-	NtrT	-	2758	7W-18N	A4
-	NtrT	-	2811	6W-14N	D4
-	SKOK	-	2811	6W-13N	E7
-	SKOK	-	2865	7W-10N	C5
-	SKOK	-	2919	6W-8N	E1
-	WLMT	-	2811	6W-13N	D6
Edens Expwy US-41					
-	GLNC	-	2758	7W-16N	B7
-	HDPK	-	2757	8W-18N	E2
-	NfdT	-	2757	8W-18N	E2
-	NfdT	-	2811	7W-15N	C1

STREET Block	City	ZIP	Map#	CGS	Grid
Edens Expwy US-41					
-	NHBK	-	2757	8W-18N	E2
-	NHBK	-	2758	7W-17N	A5
-	NHFD	-	2758	7W-16N	B7
-	NHFD	-	2811	6W-14N	D4
-	NtrT	-	2758	7W-18N	A4
-	NtrT	-	2811	6W-14N	D4
Edens Ln					
400	NHFD	60093	2811	7W-15N	B1
N Edens Pkwy					
5400	CHCG	60630	2919	6W-6N	E5
5400	CHCG	60646	2919	6W-6N	E5
Edens Expressway Spur					
-	DRFD	-	2756	12W-18N	B2
-	DRFD	-	2757	10W-18N	A3
-	NfdT	-	2756	12W-20N	B2
-	NfdT	-	2757	10W-18N	A3
-	NfdT	-	2758	8W-18N	A3
-	NHBK	-	2756	12W-18N	C2
-	NHBK	-	2757	9W-18N	C3
-	NHBK	-	2758	8W-18N	A3
-	WdfT	-	2756	12W-20N	B2
Edens Expressway Spur I-94					
-	DRFD	-	2756	12W-18N	B2
-	DRFD	-	2757	10W-18N	A3
-	NfdT	-	2756	12W-20N	B2
-	NfdT	-	2757	10W-18N	A3
-	NfdT	-	2758	8W-18N	A3
-	NHBK	-	2756	12W-18N	C2
-	NHBK	-	2757	10W-18N	A3
-	NHBK	-	2758	8W-18N	A3
-	WdfT	-	2756	12W-20N	B2
Edens Expressway Spur E					
-	NfdT	-	2756	12W-20N	B2
-	NfdT	-	2757	10W-18N	A3
-	NHBK	-	2757	8W-18N	E3
-	WdfT	-	2756	12W-20N	B2
Edens Expressway Spur E I-94					
-	NfdT	-	2756	12W-20N	B2
-	NfdT	-	2757	10W-18N	A3
-	NHBK	-	2757	8W-18N	E3
-	WdfT	-	2756	12W-20N	B2
Edens Expressway Spur W					
-	DRFD	-	2756	12W-20N	B1
-	NfdT	-	2757	10W-18N	A3
-	WdfT	-	2756	12W-20N	B1
Edens Expressway Spur W I-94					
-	DRFD	-	2756	12W-20N	B1
-	NfdT	-	2757	10W-18N	A3
-	WdfT	-	2756	12W-20N	B1
Edentenny Rd					
1500	NLNX	60451	3502	16W-25S	A7
Edenwood Dr					
500	BmdT	60172	2912	24W-6N	D6
500	ROSL	60172	2912	24W-6N	D6
W Edgar Av					
25000	AntT	60002	2357	25W-42N	B6
Edgar Ct					
1200	GLHT	60139	3024	24W-2N	E1
Edgar Ln					
18100	OrlT	60487	3423	11W-21S	E7
Edgar St					
3000	PltT	60067	2805	20W-13N	E5
3000	RGMW	60008	2805	20W-13N	E5
3000	RGMW	60067	2805	20W-13N	E5
S Edgar St					
1700	PltT	60067	2805	20W-13N	E5
1700	RGMW	60008	2805	20W-13N	E5
1700	RGMW	60067	2805	20W-13N	E5
Edgar Allen Poe Ln					
700	MDLN	60060	2646	18W-26N	E2
Edgcote Ln					
600	LKFT	60045	2649	11W-26N	C3
Edgebrook Ct					
10	ALGN	60102	2693	36W-21N	D6
100	IHPK	60525	3146	13W-6S	E5
300	OSWG	60543	3263	38W-12S	B3
500	CLSM	60188	2968	25W-3N	A7
3700	AURA	60504	3202	30W-8S	A3
Edgebrook Dr					
200	BMDL	60108	2969	22W-5N	B2
400	CLLK	60014	2639	36W-25N	D6
500	SRWD	60404	3496	30W-23S	C4
Edgebrook Ln					
800	GLNC	60022	2758	7W-17N	B4
900	NHBK	60062	2757	8W-16N	E7
7000	HRPK	60133	2911	26W-8N	E2
8000	TYPK	60477	3504	10W-23S	C3
11000	IHPK	60525	3146	13W-6S	E5
Edgebrook Rd					
100	WDDL	60191	2971	18W-5N	A1
200	WDDL	60191	2915	18W-5N	A7
Edgebrook Ter					
600	ELGN	60120	2855	32W-10N	C6
N Edgebrook Ter					
6700	CHCG	60646	2919	7W-8N	B2
Edgebrooke Dr					
2200	LSLE	60532	3082	24W-3S	D6
2200	MltT	60532	3082	24W-3S	D6
Edgecliff Dr					
100	HDPK	60035	2704	8W-23N	E2
Edgecreek Dr					
3000	JLET	60432	3500	19W-23S	C3
3000	JLET	60451	3500	19W-22S	D2
Edgefield Ln					
300	LKFT	60045	2648	13W-25N	E4
300	LKFT	60045	2649	13W-25N	A5
1400	HFET	60169	2858	25W-12N	B2
Edge Hill Av					
1200	JLET	60432	3499	22W-22S	C2
Edgehill Dr					
100	BGBK	60440	3269	23W-12S	A2
Edge Lake Dr					
5600	OKLN	60453	3275	7W-12S	D1
Edgelake Pt					
300	SMBG	60194	2859	23W-10N	A4
Edgelawn Ct					
1800	AURA	60506	3137	38W-6S	B6
E Edgelawn Dr					
600	PLNO	60545	3259	47W-13S	D5
N Edgelawn Dr					
10	AURA	60506	3137	37W-6S	B6
800	PLNO	60545	3259	47W-13S	C5
S Edgelawn Dr					
10	AURA	60506	3137	37W-7S	B7
300	AURA	60506	3199	37W-8S	B1
500	AraT	60506	3199	37W-8S	B1
Edgemere Ct					
900	EVTN	60202	2867	2W-10N	C4
Edgemere Rd					
700	BFGV	60089	2701	17W-22N	B4
N Edgemond Ln					
26100	CbaT	60010	2697	26W-22N	D4
Edgemont Ln					
500	HFET	60169	2858	24W-12N	D1
500	PKRG	60068	2864	10W-9N	A6

STREET Block	City	ZIP	Map#	CGS	Grid
Edgemont Ln					
700	SMBG	60169	2858	24W-12N	D1
700	SMBG	60195	2858	24W-12N	D1
3000	PKRG	60068	2863	11W-9N	C6
E Edgemont Ln					
10	PKRG	60068	2864	9W-9N	C6
Edgemont St					
10	MDLN	60060	2590	19W-28N	D6
Edger Lee Masters Ln					
300	CmpT	60175	2962	40W-3N	C6
Edgerton Dr					
1100	JLET	60435	3497	26W-22S	E2
1500	CTHL	60403	3497	26W-22S	E1
S Edgerton Dr					
800	JLET	60435	3497	26W-22S	E3
Edgeview					
-	NLNX	60442	3589	17W-27S	D4
Edgeview Ct					
-	DRPK	60010	2698	23W-20N	E7
23500	DRPK	60010	2751	23W-20N	E1
Edgeware Rd					
100	EGVV	60007	2860	18W-9N	E7
Edgewater					
-	NLNX	60442	3589	17W-27S	D4
700	ANTH	60002	2357	24W-42N	C6
25000	GrtT	60041	2473	27W-35N	A6
Edgewater Av					
4200	HLSD	60162	3029	13W-0S	A7
4300	HLSD	60162	3028	13W-0S	E7
W Edgewater Av					
1400	CHCG	60660	2921	1W-7N	C4
Edgewater Ct					
100	MTGY	60538	3199	36W-10S	E5
200	BMDL	60108	2969	23W-4N	B3
300	SRGV	60554	3197	42W-7S	D1
1000	RLKB	60073	2475	23W-34N	A7
5100	JLET	60586	3496	30W-22S	C1
13900	LktT	60544	3339	26W-16S	E4
14000	GNOK	60048	2592	14W-30N	D2
N Edgewater Ct					
1100	PLTN	60067	2752	23W-17N	A4
36100	WrnT	60031	2477	17W-36N	B5
Edgewater Dr					
-	CCHL	60429	3506	4W-22S	D1
-	CCHL	60478	3506	4W-22S	D1
-	RMVL	60446	3339	27W-17S	D5
100	CLLK	60014	2639	37W-25N	B4
200	BMDL	60108	2969	22W-4N	B3
200	BRLT	60103	2909	32W-8N	D4
500	MNKA	60447	3672	34W-29S	A2
800	NPVL	60540	3141	27W-7S	D7
1100	NPVL	60540	3203	26W-7S	E1
2400	ElgT	60124	2853	37W-9N	D7
3600	HLCT	60429	3506	4W-22S	D1
14000	LktT	60544	3339	26W-16S	E4
Edgewater Ln					
-	PLTN	60067	2752	22W-17N	A5
100	SRGV	60554	3197	42W-8S	D1
400	WCDA	60084	2588	24W-28N	C6
1100	ANTH	60002	2357	24W-41N	D7
1100	ANTH	60002	2416	24W-41N	D1
N Edgewater Ln					
800	SRWD	60404	3496	30W-22S	B3
35000	GrtT	60041	2473	27W-35N	A6
S Edgewater Ln					
-	SRWD	60404	3496	30W-23S	B3
12700	PlsT	60464	3273	12W-15S	D7
12700	PSPK	60464	3273	12W-15S	D7
W Edgewater Ln					
1400	PLTN	60067	2752	23W-17N	A5
Edgewater Pkwy					
700	WCDA	60084	2588	25W-28N	A7
Edgewater Rd					
8000	NRIV	60546	3088	10W-2S	B4
8000	RVSD	60546	3088	10W-2S	B4
Edgewater St					
6800	BtnT	60081	2414	29W-39N	C6
Edgewild Ct					
100	SCRL	60175	2964	35W-4N	A4
Edgewood Av					
-	ADSN	60101	2970	19W-4N	D3
-	BNVL	60007	2915	17W-7N	C4
-	BNVL	60106	2915	17W-7N	C4
-	VLPK	60148	3026	19W-2N	D1
10	AddT	60148	3026	19W-2N	D1
10	CLLK	60014	2639	37W-25N	B4
10	LMBD	60148	3026	19W-2N	D1
100	AURA	60505	3139	33W-7S	A7
100	AURA	60505	3201	33W-7S	A1
100	HPSR	60140	2795	47W-15N	D3
1200	CHHT	60411	3508	1W-25S	A6
1200	EGVV	60007	2915	17W-7N	C3
1400	CHHT	60411	3596	1W-25S	A1
1600	CHHT	60411	3595	1W-25S	E1
5300	LynT	60525	3147	13W-5S	A3
5500	CTSD	60525	3147	13W-6S	A4
5500	LGNG	60525	3147	13W-6S	A4
N Edgewood Av					
-	EGVV	60007	2915	17W-7N	C4
-	EGVV	60191	2915	17W-7N	C4
10	LGNG	60525	3087	13W-4S	A7
100	WDDL	60191	2971	17W-5N	C1
200	LMBD	60148	3026	19W-1N	D2
200	WDDL	60191	2915	17W-5N	C7
300	LGPK	60525	3087	13W-3S	A6
300	WDDL	60106	2915	17W-6N	C7
S Edgewood Av					
10	LMBD	60148	3026	19W-0N	D4
100	LGNG	60525	3087	13W-4S	A7
200	LGNG	60525	3147	13W-5S	A1
300	WDDL	60106	2971	17W-4N	C2
300	WDDL	60191	2971	17W-4N	C2
500	EMHT	60126	3028	15W-0N	B5
1100	YkTp	60148	3026	19W-0S	D7
W Edgewood Av					
21600	LkvT	60046	2417	21W-38N	D6
28500	CbaT	60013	2642	28W-24N	E7
Edgewood Ct					
-	CPVL	60118	2746	38W-18N	B5
-	DRFD	60015	2756	11W-20N	D2
100	RGMW	60008	2805	21W-13N	D5
200	MltT	60137	3083	23W-2S	A4
200	RDLK	60073	2531	23W-31N	E6
300	MNKA	60447	3672	32W-29S	C1
800	HDPK	60035	2704	9W-20N	C7
800	SRGV	60554	3136	41W-5S	A2
1000	LMNT	60439	3270	19W-14S	C7
1500	BRLT	60103	2966	30W-5N	C2
1700	ALGN	60102	2747	35W-20N	A1
2300	MchT	60051	2528	31W-33N	E3
6300	OKFT	60452	3347	8W-17S	B6
7900	WDRG	60517	3205	22W-9S	D3
8900	TYPK	60487	3424	11W-21S	A5
20000	MKNA	60448	3502	14W-24S	E5
Edgewood Dr					
-	DGvT	60561	3206	20W-9S	B3

STREET Block	City	ZIP	Map#	CGS	Grid
Edgewood Dr					
-	DRN	60561	3206	20W-9S	B3
-	LGPK	60525	3087	13W-3S	A4
-	WDRG	60561	3206	20W-9S	B3
-	WSTR	60525	3087	13W-3S	A4
10	SMWD	60107	2857	28W-9N	A7
200	AlqT	60102	2747	34W-20N	C1
200	ANTH	60002	2357	23W-43N	E4
200	MNKA	60447	3672	32W-28S	C1
200	WLNG	60090	2755	14W-18N	D3
400	ANTH	60002	2358	23W-43N	A4
500	MNKA	60447	3583	32W-28S	C7
700	GNEN	60137	3025	22W-0N	D5
800	SRGV	60554	3135	41W-5S	E2
800	SRGV	60554	3136	41W-5S	A2
1200	CTCY	60409	3430	4E-19S	B1
1900	ALGN	60102	2747	35W-20N	A2
1900	WDSK	60098	2581	41W-29N	E3
2700	DYR	46311	3598		E4
2800	SjnT	46311	3598		E4
3100	WRLK	60097	2469	36W-35N	D7
8200	DGvT	60516	3206	20W-9S	B3
8200	WDRG	60516	3206	20W-9S	B3
8200	WDRG	60517	3206	20W-9S	B3
11400	MKNA	60448	3502	14W-24S	E5
15300	ODPK	60462	3346	10W-18S	B7
16400	PNFD	60586	3417	28W-19S	A3
35200	WrnT	60031	2477	16W-35N	D7
N Edgewood Dr					
36100	WrnT	60031	2477	18W-36N	A4
W Edgewood Dr					
900	MchT	60050	2472	30W-36N	B3
12000	HMGN	60491	3344	15W-17S	C6
12000	ODPK	60467	3344	15W-17S	C6
15300	LKPT	60441	3342	20W-18S	B7
Edgewood Ln					
-	CPVL	60118	2746	38W-18N	C5
200	PltT	60067	2805	20W-13N	E6
200	PltT	60067	2806	19W-14N	C3
400	NHFD	60093	2811	8W-15N	A2
500	EGVV	60007	2861	18W-9N	A6
800	GNVW	60025	2811	7W-13N	B7
1300	NHBK	60062	2757	8W-17N	D5
1300	WNKA	60093	2758	6W-16N	D7
1700	LGGV	60047	2753	18W-20N	D1
2600	RVWD	60015	2702	13W-22N	E5
N Edgewood Ln					
1400	MchT	60051	2528	31W-33N	E3
S Edgewood Ln					
500	LGNG	60525	3147	13W-5S	A2
500	LynT	60525	3147	13W-5S	A2
600	MPPT	60056	2861	16W-12N	D2
W Edgewood Ln					
2200	MchT	60051	2528	31W-33N	E3
Edgewood Pkwy					
2800	WDRG	60517	3205	22W-9S	C3
Edgewood Pl					
-	NBRN	60010	2698	24W-23N	B1
400	RVFT	60305	3030	10W-0N	B4
Edgewood Rd					
10	VNHL	60061	2647	16W-25N	C5
600	PltT	60124	2905	43W-8N	B3
700	HDPK	60035	2705	8W-21N	A7
1000	LKFT	60045	2650	10W-27N	A1
1400	LKFT	60045	2594	10W-27N	A7
1500	HDPK	60035	2704	9W-20N	C7
1800	BHPK	60087	2479	11W-38N	D1
1800	DRFD	60015	2704	9W-20N	C7
1800	WKGN	60087	2479	11W-38N	D1
4600	NndT	60012	2584	34W-29N	B5
4600	NndT	60050	2584	34W-29N	B5
4600	PRGV	60012	2584	34W-29N	B5
4600	PRGV	60050	2584	34W-29N	B5
6900	SPGV	60081	2413	32W-38N	B6
26500	AntT	60002	2356	26W-43N	D5
W Edgewood Rd					
500	LMBD	60148	3026	20W-0S	A7
500	MltT	60148	3026	21W-0S	A7
500	YkTp	60148	3026	20W-0S	A7
600	MltT	60148	3025	21W-0S	E7
6700	PSHT	60463	3275	8W-15S	A7
7000	PSHT	60463	3274	8W-15S	E7
10700	BHPK	60087	2480	10W-38N	A1
11000	BHPK	60087	2479	11W-37N	E1
11300	WKGN	60087	2479	11W-38N	D1
Edgewood St					
-	ELGN	60123	2853	36W-10N	E5
N Edgewood St					
38500	LkvT	60046	2417	21W-38N	C7
W Edgewood St					
6000	CCRO	60804	3089	7W-3S	B4
Edgewood Wk					
200	WnfT	60185	3080	29W-1S	C2
700	WnfT	60555	3080	29W-1S	C2
700	WNVL	60555	3080	29W-1S	C2
Edgington St					
2400	FNPK	60131	2973	11W-3N	C5
N Edie Ln					
100	JLET	60435	3497	27W-23S	D5
Edina Blvd					
2100	ZION	60099	2422	9W-39N	C4
Edinburg Ct					
1200	WHTN	60187	3082	23W-1S	E2
26400	CNHN	60410	3672	33W-32S	A7
Edinburg Ln					
4400	HRPK	60133	2967	27W-5N	C2
Edinburgh Ct					
200	NPVL	60540	3142	25W-6S	B6
700	IVNS	60010	2751	24W-16N	C7
1000	JLET	60431	3496	29W-22S	D2
1600	AURA	60504	3201	32W-9S	B4
9000	LKWD	60014	2639	38W-24N	A6
14600	HMGN	60491	3343	18W-17S	A6
N Edinburgh Ct					
800	RDLK	60073	2531	24W-34N	C1
Edinburgh Dr					
300	LKPT	60441	3420	21W-18S	A1
300	LktT	60441	3420	21W-18S	A1
1600	BRLT	60103	2855	31W-9N	E7
1600	BRLT	60103	2856	31W-9N	A7
13300	PSHT	60464	3346	10W-15S	C2
Edinburgh Ln					
400	WDND	60118	2800	35W-16N	C1
500	PTHT	60070	2808	14W-14N	B3
2100	AURA	60504	3201	33W-9S	A5
11200	HTLY	60142	2692	40W-22N	A3
S Edinburgh Ln					
19700	FftT	60423	3504	9W-23S	E4
Edinburgh Ln N					
1600	AURA	60504	3201	32W-9S	B4
Edinburgh Ln S					
1600	AURA	60504	3201	33W-9S	B5
Edingburgh Ct					
200	BGBK	60440	3205	22W-10S	B5
Edington Ct					
1100	CLSM	60188	2967	26W-4N	D4
Edington Ln					
500	GRNE	60031	2534	16W-33N	E3
1100	CLSM	60188	2967	26W-4N	D4
1100	MDLN	60060	2590	19W-27N	B7
Edison Av					
400	AURA	60505	3138	35W-6S	C4
2800	BLID	60406	3277	3W-15S	A7
3300	BLID	60406	3276	4W-15S	E7
3300	WthT	60406	3276	4W-15S	E7
5300	OKLN	60453	3211	7W-11S	D7
N Edison Av					
10	ELGN	60123	2854	35W-11N	C4
S Edison Av					
10	ELGN	60123	2854	35W-11N	C5
Edison Cir					
1600	HRPK	60133	2911	27W-7N	D5
Edison Ct					
10	FXLK	60020	2473	27W-37N	B2
10	WKGN	60085	2536	10W-34N	E1
Edison Dr					
200	NlxT	60451	3589	18W-26S	B2
Edison Ln					
21200	LktT	60544	3339	26W-16S	E4
25000	PNFD	60585	3265	31W-13S	E6
Edison Pl					
3600	RGMW	60008	2806	20W-15N	B2
Edison Rd					
10	JltT	60433	3587	23W-26S	A2
Edison St					
400	GNVA	60134	3020	35W-1N	B2
Edith Dr					
1600	JLET	60432	3499	21W-23S	E4
Edith Ln					
1700	AURA	60504	3201	33W-8S	A2
W Edmaire St					
1700	CHCG	60643	3277	2W-13S	C3
Edmer Av					
1100	OKPK	60302	3031	7W-1N	A1
Edmond Dr					
400	DYR	46311	3598		D1
Edmonds Av					
800	NLNX	60451	3501	17W-24S	C4
800	NlxT	60451	3501	17W-24S	C4
Edmund M Burke Rd					
3000	OMFD	60461	3507	4W-24S	A5
3300	OMFD	60461	3506	4W-24S	E5
W Edmunds St					
5400	CHCG	60630	2919	6W-6N	C6
Edna Av					
2300	PKRG	60068	2863	11W-10N	D6
Edna Ferber Cove					
300	CmpT	60175	2962	39W-4N	D4
S Edson Av					
200	LMBD	60148	3026	20W-0N	A5
W Edson Pl					
300	LMBD	60148	3026	20W-0S	B7
S Edson St					
2200	LMBD	60148	3084	20W-2S	B3
Edward Av					
4900	DRGV	60515	3143	21W-5S	E2
11600	HTLY	60142	2692	40W-21N	A5
N Edward Av					
36500	LkvT	60046	2475	21W-36N	D4
W Edward Av					
26200	GrtT	60041	2473	26W-34N	D7
Edward Ct					
400	DSPN	60016	2863	11W-11N	C3
W Edward Ct					
1700	MchT	60051	2529	30W-34N	A2
Edward Dr					
600	RMVL	60446	3418	26W-18S	A1
1400	NndT	60014	2586	30W-27N	A7
3400	CRTE	60417	3597	1E-28S	B6
5700	OKFT	60452	3347	7W-18S	C7
22500	RNPK	60471	3594	4W-27S	D4
E Edward Dr					
800	GNVW	60025	2810	10W-14N	A3
Edward Ln					
10	HNWD	60047	2646	20W-24N	A7
25100	TRLK	60010	2643	26W-25N	D5
Edward Pkwy					
18900	NlxT	60448	3501	16W-22S	E2
Edward Rd					
600	NPVL	60540	3142	25W-7S	A6
900	PTHT	60070	2808	14W-14N	C3
Edward St					
-	ALGN	60102	2694	33W-21N	D6
-	PLNO	60545	3260	46W-14S	B7
100	JLET	60436	3498	24W-25S	E7
800	WLNG	60090	2755	15W-17N	A5
1000	WLNG	60090	2754	15W-17N	E5
2700	BLID	60406	3349	3W-15S	A1
3000	MngT	60152	2578	50W-28N	A5
E Edward St					
200	LMBD	60148	3026	19W-0S	C7
1100	YkTp	60148	3026	18W-0S	E7
N Edward St					
10	MPPT	60056	2808	14W-13N	B7
S Edward St					
10	MPPT	60056	2808	15W-12N	B7
200	MPPT	60056	2862	15W-12N	B1
W Edward St					
10	LMBD	60148	3026	20W-0S	B7
400	GNEN	60137	3026	20W-0S	A7
400	GNEN	60148	3026	20W-0S	A7
Edward Cul de Sac St					
10	PTHT	60070	2808	14W-14N	D3
Edwards Av					
-	EDND	60118	2801	33W-16N	A1
10	NHLK	60164	2972	13W-2N	E7
10	NHLK	60164	3028	13W-2N	E1
10	NHLK	60164	3029	12W-2N	A1
10	WDND	60118	2801	33W-15N	A3
300	WDND	60118	2800	34W-15N	E3
900	CPVL	60118	2801	33W-16N	A1
1100	SCRL	60174	3020	34W-2N	D1
17000	CCHL	60478	3426	5W-21S	C7
E Edwards Av					
200	CPVL	60110	2800	34W-16N	E1
200	CPVL	60118	2800	34W-16N	E1
400	CPVL	60118	2801	34W-16N	A1
Edwards Ct					
6100	CPVL	60110	2747	36W-17N	A6
W Edwards Ct					
11800	BtnT	60099	2362	11W-42N	D7
11800	ZION	60099	2362	11W-42N	D7
Edwards Dr					
-	LMNT	60439	3342	20W-15S	B1
10	BmdT	60101	2969	21W-4N	D4
1000	BTVA	60510	3078	34W-2S	D4
Edwards Pl					
1000	WCDA	60084	2588	25W-28N	B6
Edwards Rd					
9500	AlqT	60021	2695	31W-22N	E4
9800	BNHL	60021	2695	31W-22N	E4
W Edwards Rd					
16800	NptT	60002	2360	17W-42N	A6
16800	NptT	60083	2360	17W-42N	B6
16800	OMCK	60083	2360	17W-42N	B6
16800	WDWH	60099	2360	16W-42N	D6
17500	OMCK	60002	2360	17W-42N	B6
18500	AntT	60002	2359	18W-42N	E6
18500	NptT	60002	2359	18W-42N	E6
Edwards St					
700	WKGN	60085	2480	10W-34N	A7
900	AURA	60505	3138	34W-6S	D6
900	WKGN	60085	2479	10W-35N	E7
Edythe St					
10	BtlT	60543	3262	40W-12S	C3
Eern Av					
-	MHTN	60442	3589	19W-29S	A7
-	MHTN	60442	3678	19W-29S	A2
-	MhtT	60442	3589	19W-29S	A7
-	MhtT	60442	3678	19W-29S	A2
Effie St					
-	PLNO	60545	3259	47W-12S	D4
Effingham Ct					
2800	SMBG	60193	2857	27W-10N	D6
Egan Ct					
100	SMWD	60107	2857	27W-11N	C4
Egan Dr					
10	SMWD	60107	2857	27W-11N	C4
Egandale Av					
4900	MCCK	60525	3148	10W-5S	B2
Egandale Rd					
2200	HDPK	60035	2705	8W-23N	A3
Egerton Ct					
1900	WDRG	60517	3206	20W-9S	A3
Egerton Dr					
1900	WDRG	60517	3206	21W-9S	A3
W Eggerding Dr					
500	ADSN	60101	2970	19W-4N	D3
Eggert Ln					
9100	SJHN	46373	3687		E1
Egg Harbour Ct					
10	SMBG	60173	2859	21W-10N	E5
Eggleston Av					
-	BlmT	60411	3508	0W-24S	C5
-	CHHT	60411	3508	0W-24S	C5
S Eggleston Av					
5900	CHCG	60621	3152	0W-6S	B4
7500	CHCG	60620	3214	0W-8S	B1
7500	CHCG	60621	3214	0W-8S	B1
9500	CHCG	60628	3214	0W-11S	B6
10400	CHCG	60628	3278	0W-12S	B2
13700	RVDL	60827	3350	0W-15S	B2
14500	HRVY	60426	3350	0W-16S	B4
14500	HRVY	60827	3350	0W-16S	B4
W Eggleston Av					
100	EMHT	60126	3027	16W-0N	E4
Egidi Dr					
200	WLNG	60090	2755	14W-18N	B4
W Egidi Ln					
16600	LbvT	60048	2534	16W-31N	C6
16600	WKGN	60048	2534	16W-31N	C6
S Egret Ct					
1900	WKGN	60048	2535	14W-31N	D6
Egret Dr					
21500	LktT	60403	3417	26W-19S	D3
S Egyptian Tr					
25200	MONE	60449	3682	7W-31S	E5
26500	MonT	60449	3682	7W-32S	E7
29700	WltT	60468	3861	7W-37S	E4
Eich Dr					
-	JLET	60431	3495	32W-22S	D2
21500	JLET	60435	3417	26W-19S	D3
21500	JLET	60441	3417	26W-19S	D3
21500	LktT	60403	3417	26W-19S	D3
Eichler Dr					
500	WDND	60118	2800	34W-15N	E3
Eicklemann Dr					
-	ITSC	60143	2914	20W-6N	B6
Eider Ct					
22800	PNFD	60585	3339	28W-15S	A2
Eider Dr					
22900	PNFD	60585	3338	28W-15S	E2
22900	PNFD	60585	3339	28W-15S	A2
Eileen Ct					
9200	ODPK	60462	3345	11W-16S	E2
Eileen St					
-	FlxT	60416	3941	34W-39S	A1
-	PLNO	60545	3260	45W-14S	B7
10	CLCY	60416	3941	34W-39S	A2
Eineke Blvd					
-	ALGN	60102	2746	36W-20N	D1
Eineke Ct					
10	ALGN	60102	2746	36W-20N	D1
N Eire St					
600	BDWD	60408	3942	31W-40S	A4
E Eisenhower Av					
600	PLTN	60074	2753	20W-16N	B7
Eisenhower Cir					
4200	HFET	60192	2804	24W-15N	D2
Eisenhower Ct					
1100	VNHL	60061	2647	17W-27N	C2
E Eisenhower Ct					
200	PLTN	60074	2753	20W-16N	B7
Eisenhower Dr					
10	OSWG	60543	3263	38W-12S	A3
400	MRGO	60152	2634	50W-26N	A3
2400	DSPN	60018	2917	12W-8N	B1
5200	MchT	60097	2469	36W-37N	E2
Eisenhower Expwy					
-	AddT	-	2971	18W-3N	A4
-	ADSN	-	2914	20W-5N	A7
-	ADSN	-	2970	19W-5N	C2
-	ADSN	-	2971	16W-3N	D5
-	BDVW	-	3029	11W-0S	C6
-	BKLY	-	3028	14W-0S	C5
-	BLWD	-	3029	11W-0S	D6
-	CHCG	-	3031	6W-0S	D6
-	CHCG	-	3032	5W-0S	A6
-	CHCG	-	3033	3W-0S	A5
-	CHCG	-	3034	0W-0S	A5
-	EMHT	-	2971	17W-3N	C5
-	EMHT	-	2972	15W-2N	A7
-	EMHT	-	3028	14W-1N	B2
-	FTPK	-	3030	10W-0S	B6
-	HLSD	-	3028	13W-0S	E6
-	HLSD	-	3029	12W-0S	A6
-	ITSC	-	2914	20W-5N	A7
-	MYWD	-	3029	11W-0S	D6
-	MYWD	-	3030	10W-0S	A6
-	NHLK	-	3028	15W-1N	B1
-	OKPK	-	3030	10W-0S	B6
-	OKPK	-	3031	7W-0S	B6
-	PvsT	-	3028	14W-0S	C6
-	WDDL	-	2970	19W-5N	C2
-	WSTR	-	3029	12W-0S	C6
Eisenhower Expwy I-290					
-	AddT	-	2971	18W-3N	A4
-	ADSN	-	2914	20W-5N	A7
-	ADSN	-	2970	19W-5N	C2
-	ADSN	-	2971	16W-3N	D5
-	BDVW	-	3029	11W-0S	C6
-	BKLY	-	3028	15W-1N	B3
-	BLWD	-	3029	11W-0S	D6
-	CHCG	-	3031	6W-0S	D6
-	CHCG	-	3032	5W-0S	B6
-	CHCG	-	3033	1W-0S	E5
-	CHCG	-	3034	0W-0S	A5
-	EMHT	-	2971	17W-3N	C5
-	EMHT	-	2972	15W-2N	A7
-	EMHT	-	3028	14W-1N	B2
-	FTPK	-	3030	10W-0S	B6
-	HLSD	-	3028	14W-0S	C5
-	HLSD	-	3029	12W-0S	A6
-	ITSC	-	2914	20W-5N	A7
-	MYWD	-	3029	11W-0S	D6
-	MYWD	-	3030	10W-0S	B6
-	NHLK	-	3028	15W-1N	B1
-	OKPK	-	3030	10W-0S	B6
-	OKPK	-	3031	8W-0S	A6
-	PvsT	-	3028	14W-0S	C6
-	WDDL	-	2970	19W-5N	C2
-	WSTR	-	3029	12W-0S	C6
Eisenhower Expwy US-20					
-	EMHT	-	2971	16W-2N	E7
-	EMHT	-	2972	15W-2N	A7
-	EMHT	-	3028	15W-2N	A1
Eisenhower Ln					
-	BGBK	60490	3339	27W-14S	C1
-	LSLE	60532	3143	23W-5S	A3
1600	LSLE	60532	3142	23W-6S	E4
Eisenhower Ln N					
10	LMBD	60148	3084	20W-2S	B3
Eisenhower Ln S					
10	LMBD	60148	3084	20W-2S	B3
Eisenhower Rd					
300	OKTR	60181	3085	17W-1S	B2
Eisenhower St					
10	EGvT	60018	2862	15W-9N	A7
Eklund Av					
400	GNVA	60134	3020	35W-1N	B2
Ekman Dr					
500	BTVA	60510	3078	34W-3S	D5
900	AURA	60510	3078	34W-3S	D5
Ela Rd					
-	ElaT	60010	2698	24W-21N	D6
10	IVNS	60067	2804	23W-16N	E1
100	IVNS	60010	2751	23W-17N	D6
100	IVNS	60067	2751	23W-17N	D5
400	LKZH	60047	2698	24W-21N	D5
800	DRPK	60010	2698	24W-22N	D5
800	LKZH	60010	2698	24W-22N	D5
1700	HFET	60067	2804	23W-13N	E6
1700	HFET	60192	2804	23W-13N	E6
1700	HFET	60195	2804	23W-13N	E6
1700	PltT	60067	2804	23W-13N	E6
1700	PltT	60192	2804	23W-13N	E6
1700	PltT	60195	2804	23W-13N	E6
Ela Rd CO-V57					
-	ElaT	60010	2698	24W-21N	D6
400	LKZH	60047	2698	24W-21N	D5
800	DRPK	60010	2698	24W-22N	D5
800	LKZH	60010	2698	24W-22N	D5
N Ela Rd					
10	BRTN	60010	2751	23W-20N	D1
10	DRPK	60010	2751	23W-20N	D1
10	ElaT	60010	2751	24W-20N	D1
10	PltT	60010	2751	23W-20N	D1
100	DRPK	60010	2698	24W-20N	D7
N Ela Rd CO-V57					
10	BRTN	60010	2751	23W-20N	D1
10	DRPK	60010	2751	23W-20N	D1
10	ElaT	60010	2751	24W-20N	D1
10	PltT	60010	2751	23W-20N	D1
100	DRPK	60010	2698	24W-20N	D7
S Ela Rd					
-	BRTN	60010	2751	24W-18N	D3
-	DRPK	60010	2751	24W-18N	D3
10	IVNS	60067	2804	23W-14N	E3
100	PltT	60010	2751	24W-18N	D3
800	HFET	60067	2804	23W-14N	E4
800	HFET	60192	2804	23W-14N	E4
Ela St					
10	BRTN	60010	2751	25W-20N	A2
Elaine Av					
3400	PKCY	60085	2536	13W-33N	A2
E Elaine Cir					
10	PTHT	60070	2808	14W-15N	C3
W Elaine Cir					
10	PTHT	60070	2808	14W-15N	B3
Elaine Ct					
1100	FSMR	60422	3507	3W-23S	A2
Elaine Dr					
3100	SenT	60098	2581	43W-28N	A6
S Elaine Dr					
12700	PNFD	60585	3337	32W-15S	C2
12700	WldT	60585	3337	32W-15S	C2
N Elaine Pl					
3400	CHCG	60657	2978	0W-4N	A3
Elaine Ter					
400	LKMR	60051	2529	29W-32N	C5
Elam Dr					
25400	MhtT	60442	3677	19W-30S	D4
Elayne Ct					
2700	MPPT	60005	2861	17W-10N	C4
Elbridge Av					
-	PSPK	60464	3274	10W-13S	B4
N Elbridge Av					
3000	CHCG	60618	2976	4W-3N	C4
El Cameno Real Dr					
9900	ODPK	60462	3345	12W-18S	C6
El Camino Ct					
9800	ODPK	60462	3345	12W-18S	D6
El Camino Ln					
9800	ODPK	60462	3345	12W-18S	D6
El Camino Ter					
15200	ODPK	60462	3345	12W-18S	D7
El Cid Ln					
2300	NHBK	60062	2810	10W-15N	A1
Eldamain Rd					
700	BtlT	60545	3196	44W-10S	D7
700	BtlT	60545	3260	45W-12S	D4
700	LtRT	60545	3260	45W-12S	D4
2000	PLNO	60545	3260	44W-14S	D7
3100	YKVL	60545	3260	44W-14S	D7
4000	BtlT	60545	3332	44W-14S	D1
4300	LtRT	60545	3332	44W-14S	D1
Elden Dr					
300	CRY	60013	2695	31W-23N	E1
400	CRY	60013	2641	31W-24N	E7
Elder Av					
100	CHHT	60411	3507	1W-25S	E7
100	CHHT	60411	3508	1W-25S	A7
300	SchT	60174	2964	35W-6N	B1
W Elder Av					
900	MchT	60050	2472	29W-36N	B4
Elder Ct					
400	MaiT	60025	2809	10W-12N	E7
700	GLNC	60022	2758	7W-17N	B5
1200	WLNG	60090	2754	16W-18N	E2
3100	NHBK	60062	2756	11W-16N	D6
6900	BGVW	60455	3210	8W-10S	E5
6900	BGVW	60455	3211	8W-10S	A5
15500	HMGN	60491	3343	16W-18S	E7
15500	HMGN	60491	3421	16W-18S	E1
N Elder Ct					
21300	KLDR	60047	2699	22W-21N	B6
Elder Dr					
200	RLKP	60073	2532	22W-33N	A2
1300	AURA	60506	3137	38W-5S	B4
3800	ISLK	60042	2586	28W-28N	D6
Elder Ln					
10	OKTR	60181	3085	17W-1S	C1
100	HDPK	60035	2758	6W-20N	C1
200	FRGV	60021	2696	30W-22N	A3
400	MaiT	60025	2809	11W-12N	E7
500	NfdT	60025	2809	11W-12N	E7
600	DRFD	60015	2703	10W-21N	E7
600	WNKA	60093	2812	4W-15N	B3
1600	NHFD	60093	2811	6W-15N	C3
2900	HHLL	60051	2586	30W-29N	A4
3300	FNPK	60131	2973	12W-4N	B3
3600	FNPK	60176	2973	12W-4N	B3
3600	SRPK	60176	2973	12W-4N	B3
N Elder Ln					
10	LGNG	60525	3087	13W-4S	A7
S Elder Ln					
1200	WKGN	60085	2535	14W-32N	D5
25800	MONE	60449	3682	6W-31S	E5
Elder Rd					
800	GNWD	60425	3428	1W-21S	B7
800	HMWD	60430	3428	1W-21S	B7
1300	HMWD	60430	3427	1W-21S	E7
Elderberry Cir					
900	NPVL	60563	3141	27W-6S	B4
Elderberry Ct					
700	LIHL	60156	2693	37W-22N	B4
Elderberry Dr					
1500	LYVL	60048	2591	17W-30N	B3
Elderberry Ln					
-	OrlT	60467	3423	13W-20S	B3
100	HNWD	60047	2644	23W-24N	D6
400	HnrT	60107	2910	29W-9N	D1
400	HnrT	60120	2910	29W-9N	D1
1600	LKVL	60046	2417	22W-40N	B3
10400	ODPK	60467	3423	13W-20S	B3
E Elderberry Ln					
600	MPPT	60056	2808	14W-14N	B5
Elderwood Ct					
6300	OKFT	60452	3347	7W-17S	B5
Eldon Pl					
500	DRGV	60516	3144	19W-6S	D4
W Eldor Av					
21500	AvnT	60030	2532	21W-34N	D2
El Dorado Ct					
10	LIHL	60156	2693	36W-21N	C5
100	MNKA	60447	3672	32W-29S	C2
Eldorado Ct					
2000	GNVA	60134	3019	36W-0N	E6
2400	NPVL	60564	3202	29W-10S	D6
Eldorado Dr					
1800	GNVA	60134	3019	36W-0N	D5
2000	CTHL	60403	3418	26W-21S	A6
6400	MNGV	60053	2865	8W-11N	A2
Eldorado Ln					
2500	NPVL	60564	3202	29W-10S	D6
Eldorado St					
800	WNKA	60093	2759	5W-16N	A7
800	WNKA	60093	2812		B1
S Eleanor Av					
10000	PSHL	60465	3210	10W-11S	B7
10000	PSHL	60465	3274	10W-11S	B1
Eleanor Ct					
22600	KLDR	60047	2699	20W-22N	E4
Eleanor Dr					
100	PTHT	60070	2755	15W-16N	A6
100	WLNG	60070	2755	15W-16N	A6
100	WLNG	60090	2755	15W-16N	A6
4500	LGGV	60047	2700	19W-23N	C2
Eleanor Ln					
200	GNVA	60134	3019	37W-1N	C4
10800	OrlT	60467	3423	13W-20S	A4
W Eleanor Ln					
21000	KLDR	60047	2699	21W-22N	E4
Eleanor Pl					
10	DGvT	60527	3207	16W-9S	E2
10	WLBK	60527	3207	16W-8S	E2
6900	DRN	60561	3145	16W-7S	D7
7200	DRN	60561	3207	16W-8S	D1
E Eleanor St					
-	ThtT	60476	3428	0E-21S	E5
100	TNTN	60476	3428	0E-21S	D5
S Eleanor St					
2500	CHCG	60608	3091	1W-2S	D3
W Eleanor St					
100	TNTN	60476	3428	0E-21S	D5
Eleanore Ct					
3700	RGMW	60008	2806	20W-13N	A5
Electric Av					
700	MltT	60187	3024	26W-0N	A5
5100	BKLY	60163	3028	14W-0N	C4
5100	HLSD	60162	3028	14W-0N	D4
5100	HLSD	60163	3028	14W-0N	C4
6000	EMHT	60126	3028	14W-0N	C4
Eletson Dr					
500	CLLK	60014	2639	36W-24N	E7
Elevator Rd					
13600	MhtT	60442	3767	17W-33S	C3
13600	WltT	60442	3767	17W-33S	C3
Elfering Ln					
900	ANTH	60002	2417	21W-41N	E1
Elfstrom Tr					
100	BtvT	60510	3077	37W-3S	C5
Elgiloy Dr					
10	HPSR	60140	2743	46W-19N	B2
Elgin Av					
10	DndT	60118	2801	33W-15N	A4
10	RMVL	60446	3340	23W-15S	E2
10	RMVL	60446	3341	23W-15S	A2
300	EDND	60118	2801	33W-15N	A4
600	FTPK	60130	3030	9W-0S	D5
700	ELGN	60120	2855	33W-10N	A7
700	SchT	60174	2908	35W-6N	B6
1200	JLET	60432	3499	22W-23S	D3
1200	JltT	60432	3499	22W-23S	D3
1400	FTPK	60130	3088	9W-1S	D1
1500	NRIV	60130	3088	9W-1S	D1

STREET Block City ZIP Map# CGS Grid

E Elgin Av
1000 JLET 60432 3499 22W-23S C3
1000 JltT 60432 3499 22W-23S C3
Elgin Ln
1300 SMBG 60194 2858 25W-10N C5
3300 SKOK 60203 2866 4W-11N D2
Elgin Rd
700 EVTN 60201 2867 2W-11N B2
1600 BNHL 60110 2748 33W-19N C3
1600 CPVL 60110 2748 33W-19N C3
1900 DndT 60110 2748 32W-19N C2
2100 ALGN 60102 2748 32W-19N C2
2100 ALGN 60110 2748 32W-19N C2
2100 BNHL 60010 2748 32W-19N C2
2100 BNHL 60102 2748 32W-19N C2
2800 EVTN 60201 2866 4W-11N D2
2800 EVTN 60203 2866 4W-11N D2
2800 SKOK 60203 2866 4W-11N D2
Elgin Rd SR-25
1600 BNHL 60110 2748 33W-19N C3
1600 CPVL 60110 2748 33W-19N C3
1900 DndT 60110 2748 32W-19N C2
2100 ALGN 60102 2748 32W-19N C2
2100 ALGN 60110 2748 32W-19N C2
2100 BNHL 60010 2748 32W-19N C2
2100 BNHL 60102 2748 32W-19N C2
Elgin St
10 SchT 60177 2908 35W-7N C6
10 SEGN 60177 2908 35W-7N C6
Elgin O'Hare Expwy
- AddT 60143 2914 21W-7N A4
- EGVV - 2913 21W-7N E3
- HRPK - 2912 26W-7N A4
- ITSC - 2913 21W-7N E3
- ITSC 60143 2914 21W-7N A4
- ROSL - 2913 23W-8N A3
- SMBG - 2912 26W-7N A4
- SmbT - 2912 23W-8N E2
- SmbT - 2913 21W-7N E3
Elgin O'Hare Expwy E
- HRPK - 2911 26W-7N E4
- HRPK - 2912 26W-7N A4
El Greco St
14900 LMNT 60439 3343 18W-15S A2
Eli Ln
- PltT 60124 2852 40W-11N B4
S Elias Ct
2900 CHCG 60608 3091 1W-2S E3
Eliasek Ct
100 SMWD 60107 2857 27W-11N C4
Elim Av
1900 ZION 60099 2422 9W-40N C2
N Elime Rd
40600 AntT 60002 2415 25W-40N E2
40600 AntT 60002 2416 25W-40N A3
Elinor Av
5400 LslT 60515 3143 21W-6S E4
5400 LslT 60516 3143 21W-6S E4
5700 LslT 60517 3143 21W-6S E4
5700 WDRG 60517 3143 21W-6S E4
Elinor Pl
1400 EVTN 60201 2867 3W-11N A3
Eliot Ln
100 OKTR 60181 3085 17W-1S B1
100 YkTp 60181 3085 17W-1S B1
3300 NPVL 60564 3266 28W-11S E1
3300 NPVL 60564 3267 28W-11S A1
Eliot Tr
1300 ELGN 60120 2855 31W-11N E3
Elise Blvd
11800 FKFT 60423 3590 14W-26S D3
22200 FftT 60423 3590 15W-27S D3
22200 FKFT 60451 3590 14W-26S D3
22200 NlxT 60451 3590 14W-26S D3
Elisha Av
2100 ZION 60099 2422 10W-39N B5
Elite Av
400 WCHI 60185 3022 29W-1N D3
Elite Dr
- GNCY 53128 2352 E2
Elizabeth Av
500 WNVL 60555 3081 27W-3S B6
900 NPVL 60540 3141 26W-6S E6
900 NPVL 60540 3142 26W-6S A6
1400 WKGN 60085 2536 11W-32N E6
1700 BtnT 60099 2422 9W-41N C1
1700 ZION 60099 2422 9W-39N C5
1800 NCHI 60064 2536 11W-31N E7
8100 ODPK 60462 3346 10W-16S C3
10600 HTLY 60142 2692 40W-21N B6
N Elizabeth Av
20500 BFGV 60069 2754 15W-20N E1
20500 BFGV 60089 2754 15W-20N E1
20500 VrnT 60069 2754 15W-20N E1
20700 VrnT 60069 2701 15W-20N E7
S Elizabeth Av
10 PLTN 60074 2806 19W-15N C1
Elizabeth Ct
- RMVL 60446 3340 25W-15S B1
10 LIHL 60156 2694 34W-22N C5
10 LMBD 60148 3026 20W-0N B5
10 OKPK 60302 3030 8W-0N E3
100 BRLT 60103 2911 28W-8N A3
100 WDDL 60191 2971 17W-5N B2
200 BMDL 60157 2913 22W-6N C7
900 WLNG 60090 2754 16W-16N D6
1100 CTHL 60403 3497 26W-22S D2
1100 CTHL 60435 3497 26W-22S D2
1100 TroT 60435 3497 26W-22S D2
1400 HFET 60169 2858 24W-12N E2
1800 DRFD 60015 2703 12W-21N B6
4900 BmnT 60452 3426 6W-20S A4
4900 BmnT 60477 3426 6W-20S A4
4900 OKFT 60452 3426 6W-20S A4
N Elizabeth Ct
36400 LkvT 60046 2475 21W-36N D4
36400 RLKB 60046 2475 21W-36N D4
36400 RLKB 60073 2475 21W-36N D4
S Elizabeth Ct
100 PLTN 60074 2806 19W-15N C1
W Elizabeth Ct
25300 PNFD 60585 3337 32W-14S B1
Elizabeth Dr
- BRLT 60103 2856 30W-9N B7
- BRLT 60107 2856 30W-9N B7
- WDDL 60191 2971 18W-5N A2
- WDSK 60098 2581 41W-28N D6
10 EGvT 60005 2861 16W-9N E6
300 WDDL 60191 2970 18W-5N E2
400 DGvT 60516 3206 20W-10S B6
400 DGvT 60517 3206 20W-10S B6
400 WDRG 60517 3206 20W-10S B6
900 HnrT 60107 2856 30W-9N B7
1400 GLHT 60139 2968 23W-2N E7
2200 BDVW 60155 3087 11W-2S D2
N Elizabeth Dr
2000 ANHT 60004 2753 18W-16N E7
2000 ANHT 60004 2806 20W-15N A2
36500 LkvT 60046 2475 21W-36N D4
36500 RLKB 60073 2475 21W-36N D4
S Elizabeth Dr
- PNFD 60543 3337 32W-14S B1
12700 PNFD 60585 3337 32W-15S B2
12700 WldT 60585 3337 32W-15S B2
W Elizabeth Dr
10 ADSN 60101 2970 18W-4N E4
Elizabeth Ln
10 CbaT 60010 2697 25W-21N E6
10 DRGV 60516 3207 18W-8S A1
10 DRN 60516 3207 18W-8S A1
10 DRN 60561 3207 18W-8S A1
10 PSPK 60464 3273 13W-14S A7
100 DRGV 60516 3206 18W-8S E1
100 GNCY 53128 2353 B3
400 DSPN 60018 2862 15W-10N A5
800 HPSR 60140 2795 46W-15N E3
1300 GNVW 60025 2811 8W-13N A6
1400 GNVW 60025 2810 8W-13N E6
1800 AraT 60505 3138 33W-5S E2
1800 AURA 60505 3138 33W-5S E2
2800 TNLK 53181 2353 E3
9300 SPGV 60081 2414 29W-41N C1
9500 FXLK 60081 2414 29W-41N C1
13700 NlxT 60448 3501 17W-22S D1
20700 FftT 60423 3504 9W-25S E7
20700 FKFT 60423 3504 9W-25S E7
N Elizabeth Ln
21000 CbaT 60010 2697 25W-21N E6
S Elizabeth Ln
1500 RDLK 60073 2531 23W-31N E7
14300 HMGN 60491 3343 17W-17S C5
Elizabeth Pl
300 GNVA 60134 3020 35W-0N B5
5300 RGMW 60008 2860 19W-12N C1
Elizabeth St
10 CTCY 60409 3430 4E-18S C1
10 HMND 46320 3430 4E-18S C1
100 WMTN 60481 3853 27W-39S D7
300 AddT 60101 2970 20W-3N A5
300 ADSN 60101 2970 20W-3N A5
400 BTVA 60510 3078 34W-1S C1
500 ANTH 60002 2357 24W-42N D6
600 EMHT 60126 3027 17W-1N C1
600 SEGN 60177 2908 34W-8N E3
700 WCHI 60185 3022 29W-0S D6
800 BlmT 60411 3510 4E-25S C7
800 ELGN 60120 2855 33W-10N B7
1200 CRTE 60417 3685 0W-29S B1
3000 MngT 60152 2578 50W-28N A5
10200 PvsT 60162 3087 12W-1S A1
10200 WSTR 60154 3087 12W-1S A1
10200 WSTR 60162 3087 12W-1S A1
E Elizabeth St
10 CTCY 60409 3430 C1
10 HMND 46320 3430 C1
N Elizabeth St
10 CHCG 60607 3033 1W-0N D4
200 LMBD 60148 3026 20W-1N B2
800 CHCG 60622 3033 1W-1N D2
800 JLET 60435 3498 24W-22S E2
S Elizabeth St
100 LMBD 60148 3026 20W-0N B5
1300 LMBD 60148 3084 20W-1S B1
1800 YkTp 60148 3084 20W-1S B2
4700 CHCG 60609 3151 1W-5S E1
5500 CHCG 60636 3151 1W-6S E4
7900 CHCG 60620 3213 1W-10S E4
10000 CHCG 60643 3213 1W-11S E7
10300 CHCG 60643 3277 1W-12S E1
12200 CTPK 60643 3277 1W-14S E6
12200 CTPK 60827 3277 1W-15S E7
W Elizabeth St
200 YKVL 60560 3333 43W-15S B3
8100 NLES 60714 2864 10W-11N B3
Elizabeth Tr
300 OKPK 60302 3030 8W-0N E3
Elk Blvd
300 DSPN 60016 2863 13W-11N A3
Elk Ct
800 WHTN 60187 3082 25W-2S B3
2300 SPGV 60081 2413 31W-40N E3
E Elk Ct
10 HNVL 60030 2532 22W-33N C2
Elk Dr
2300 SPGV 60081 2413 31W-40N D3
17300 ODPK 60467 3423 13W-20S A5
Elk St
200 MTGY 60543 3263 38W-11S B2
200 OSWG 60543 3263 38W-11S B2
Elk Tr
- MRGO 60152 2634 49W-25N C4
100 CLSM 60188 2968 25W-3N A5
1400 AlqT 60013 2642 30W-24N A6
E Elk Tr
100 CLSM 60188 2968 25W-3N B5
N Elk Grove Av
10 CHCG 60622 3033 2W-1N C1
E Elk Grove Blvd
200 EGVV 60007 2914 18W-8N E1
300 EGVV 60007 2915 18W-8N A1
W Elk Grove Blvd
500 EGvT 60007 2860 18W-9N D7
500 EGVV 60007 2860 18W-9N D7
500 EGVV 60007 2914 18W-9N E1
Elk Grove Town Ctr
- EGVV 60007 2914 19W-8N D1
Elkhorn Ct
200 BGBK 60440 3268 23W-12S E2
Ella Av
500 JLET 60433 3499 23W-25S B7
E Ella Av
400 JLET 60433 3499 23W-25S B7
Ella Ln
- ALGN 60118 2746 37W-19N C2
Elle Ct
10 SBTN 60010 2803 27W-15N A1
W Elle St
400 RMVL 60446 3340 25W-15S B2
Elleby Ct
- NARA 60506 3076 39W-4S C7
Ellen Av
1100 JltT 60433 3499 22W-24S C6
Ellen Ct
- GLHT 60139 3025 22W-2N B1
500 WDSK 60098 2524 40W-31N E7
5500 BmnT 60477 3425 6W-19S D2
5500 OKFT 60452 3425 6W-19S D2
5500 OKFT 60477 3425 6W-19S D2
Ellen Dr
10 BlmT 60411 3510 3E-25S A7
900 BFGV 60089 2754 16W-17N C4
Ellen Dr
900 WhlT 60004 2754 16W-17N C4
N Ellen Dr
3100 ANHT 60004 2754 16W-17N C5
3100 WhlT 60004 2754 16W-17N C4
3200 BFGV 60089 2754 16W-17N C4
S Ellen Dr
16400 PnfT 60586 3416 29W-19S E3
Ellen Ln
200 BTVA 60510 3077 36W-1S E2
20700 FftT 60423 3504 9W-25S E7
20700 FKFT 60423 3504 9W-25S E7
35000 GrtT 60041 2473 26W-35N E7
Ellen Rd
3600 NndT 60050 2528 32W-31N B7
N Ellen St
26700 WcnT 60084 2642 28W-26N E2
W Ellen St
1700 CHCG 60622 3033 2W-1N C1
Ellen Wy
800 LbvT 60048 2592 15W-29N A3
Ellendale Dr
1700 NHBK 60062 2756 10W-16N E7
Ellendale Rd
10 DRFD 60015 2757 10W-20N B2
10 NfdT 60062 2757 10W-20N B2
Ellington Av
3800 PvsT 60525 3086 13W-4S E7
3800 PvsT 60558 3086 13W-4S E7
3800 WNSP 60558 3086 13W-4S E7
5100 WNSP 60558 3146 13W-5S E2
Ellington Ct
600 FRGV 60021 2696 29W-23N B2
E Ellington Ct
10 SEGN 60177 2907 37W-8N C4
W Ellington Ct
10 SEGN 60177 2907 37W-8N C4
Ellington Dr
10 SMBG 60193 2858 25W-10N B5
10 SMBG 60194 2858 25W-10N C5
1600 AURA 60503 3201 32W-10S B5
1600 AURA 60504 3201 32W-10S B5
Ellinwood Av
1400 DSPN 60016 2863 13W-11N A4
Elliot Av
300 WCHI 60185 3022 30W-1N C3
Elliot Ct
600 SchT 60175 2963 38W-4N A5
1000 OMFD 60461 3506 4W-25S D7
Elliot Dr
1000 MNSR 46321 3510 E1
Elliot Ln
3000 HMWD 60430 3507 3W-22S A1
12400 GfnT 60142 2744 41W-20N D1
12400 HTLY 60142 2744 41W-20N D1
Elliot St
100 LKPT 60441 3419 21W-19S D2
100 LktT 60441 3419 21W-19S D2
Elliott Av
1000 AURA 60505 3200 36W-9S A4
1100 AURA 60538 3200 36W-9S A4
1100 MTGY 60505 3200 36W-9S A4
1100 MTGY 60538 3200 36W-9S A4
1200 PKRG 60068 2863 11W-10N C5
S Elliott Av
8100 CHCG 60617 3215 2E-9S C2
Elliott Ct
1700 PKRG 60068 2863 11W-10N C4
Elliott Dr
- TYPK 60477 3425 8W-21S A7
5200 HFET 60192 2856 30W-12N C1
Elliott St
500 BCHR 60401 3864 1W-36S B2
1500 PKRG 60068 2863 11W-10N C4
Ellis Av
- GRNE 60031 2479 13W-34N A7
10 MltT 60187 3024 25W-1N B3
10 MltT 60188 3024 25W-1N B3
300 WHTN 60187 3024 25W-0N B5
700 FDHT 60411 3509 1E-25S A6
900 WPHR 60096 2363 10W-42N B6
1400 FDHT 60411 3597 1E-25S A1
2900 WKGN 60085 2479 12W-33N B7
4200 GRNE 60031 2478 14W-34N D7
6800 LGGV 60047 2646 19W-25N C5
14200 DLTN 60419 3351 1E-16S A4
15300 DLTN 60473 3351 1E-18S A6
15400 SHLD 60473 3351 1E-18S A7
15900 SHLD 60473 3429 1E-18S A1
E Ellis Av
100 LYVL 60048 2591 16W-29N D4
N Ellis Av
100 WHTN 60187 3024 25W-0S B6
800 MltT 60187 3024 25W-0S B6
S Ellis Av
200 GNWD 60425 3509 1E-23S A3
2700 CHCG 60616 3092 0E-2S D3
3500 CHCG 60653 3092 1E-3S E5
4600 CHCG 60615 3092 1E-4S E7
5300 CHCG 60615 3152 1E-6S E3
7100 CHCG 60619 3152 1E-8S E7
7100 CHCG 60637 3152 1E-8S E7
7500 CHCG 60619 3214 1E-8S E1
9700 CHCG 60628 3215 1E-11S A6
11100 CHCG 60628 3278 0E-13S E3
13000 CHCG 60628 3279 1E-14S A7
13000 CHCG 60827 3279 1E-15S A7
13100 CHCG 60827 3351 1E-15S A1
W Ellis Av
200 LYVL 60048 2591 16W-29N C4
Ellis Ct
900 SHLD 60473 3429 1E-19S A2
2300 JLET 60433 3500 20W-25S C7
2300 NLNX 60433 3500 20W-25S C7
2300 NlxT 60433 3500 20W-25S C7
2300 NlxT 60451 3500 20W-25S C7
N Ellis Dr
31600 VOLO 60073 2530 26W-31N C6
Ellis Rd
100 LIHL 60156 2692 38W-21N E5
N Ellis St
1000 BNVL 60106 2915 16W-7N D3
1200 EGVV 60007 2915 16W-7N D4
S Ellis St
100 BNVL 60106 2971 16W-5N D1
400 AddT 60106 2971 16W-4N D1
W Ellis St
800 PLTN 60067 2805 22W-15N C2
800 PLTN 60067 2805 22W-15N C2
Ellis Johnson Ln
700 CmpT 60175 2962 40W-4N B4
Ellisville Ln
1400 SMBG 60193 2858 25W-10N B6
Ellithorp Ln
500 GnvT 60134 3019 38W-0S A7
S Ellna Ct
16300 PnfT 60586 3416 29W-19S D3
Ellridge Cir
400 HDPK 60035 2757 9W-20N C1
N Ellrie Ter
25000 ElaT 60047 2644 24W-25N D6
Ellsworth Av
100 AddT 60101 2971 17W-3N B6
400 ADSN 60101 2971 17W-2N B7
400 ADSN 60181 2971 17W-2N B7
400 VLPK 60101 2971 17W-2N B7
400 VLPK 60181 2971 17W-2N B7
500 AddT 60106 2971 17W-4N B3
600 VLPK 60181 3027 17W-1N B2
600 YkTp 60181 3027 17W-1N B2
N Ellsworth Av
500 ADSN 60101 2971 17W-2N B7
800 ADSN 60181 3027 17W-2N B1
800 VLPK 60181 3027 17W-2N B1
1000 ADSN 60101 2971 17W-2N B7
1000 VLPK 60101 2971 17W-2N B7
1000 VLPK 60181 2971 17W-2N B7
Ellsworth Ct
- BltT 60543 3262 40W-12S C3
Ellsworth Dr
- BltT 60543 3262 40W-12S C4
900 GYLK 60030 2533 20W-34N B2
Ellsworth St
100 CLLK 60014 2640 34W-26N B3
N Ellsworth St
10 NPVL 60540 3141 26W-6S D5
400 NPVL 60563 3141 26W-6S D4
S Ellsworth St
10 NPVL 60540 3141 26W-6S D5
Ellyn Av
500 GNEN 60137 3025 22W-0N C5
S Ellyn Av
100 GNEN 60137 3083 22W-1S C2
300 MltT 60137 3083 22W-1S C2
Ellyn Ct
10 GNEN 60137 3025 22W-0N C5
Ellynwood Dr
500 GNEN 60137 3025 21W-0N D5
Elm Av
- ELGN 60120 2855 32W-10N D6
- WDND 60110 2800 35W-16N D1
10 CPVL 60110 2800 35W-16N D1
10 CPVL 60118 2800 35W-16N D1
10 FXLK 60020 2473 27W-36N C4
10 HIWD 60040 2704 9W-23N D3
10 WDND 60118 2800 35W-16N D1
100 MDLN 60060 2646 18W-26N D3
100 NARA 60542 3077 36W-3S E7
200 NHLK 60164 3028 14W-1N D2
400 GNVA 60134 3020 34W-1N D7
1300 RLKB 60073 2475 22W-35N B6
1700 NHBK 60062 2757 9W-17N B6
2000 HRPK 60133 2911 27W-8N C3
2400 EVTN 60201 2812 3W-12N E7
2400 EVTN 60201 2866 3W-12N D1
3100 BKFD 60513 3087 11W-3S E4
3200 ISLK 60042 2586 28W-28N D5
4100 LYNS 60534 3088 9W-4S C7
4500 BKFD 60513 3147 11W-4S E1
4600 MCCK 60513 3147 11W-4S E1
4600 MCCK 60525 3147 11W-4S E1
7900 WDRG 60517 3205 22W-9S C3
8700 LynT 60480 3208 14W-10S D5
8700 WLSP 60480 3208 14W-10S D5
9200 MKNA 60448 3503 11W-23S E3
9200 MKNA 60448 3504 11W-23S A3
9300 FftT 60448 3503 11W-23S E3
E Elm Av
10 LGNG 60525 3087 12W-4S C7
10 ROSL 60172 2913 23W-7N A5
700 BKFD 60513 3087 12W-4S C7
700 BKFD 60525 3087 12W-4S C7
N Elm Av
100 EMHT 60126 3027 16W-1N E1
400 EMHT 60126 2971 16W-2N E7
W Elm Av
10 LGNG 60525 3087 12W-4S B7
10 ROSL 60172 2913 23W-7N A5
1400 WNSP 60525 3087 13W-4S A7
1400 WNSP 60558 3087 13W-4S A7
5800 BKLY 60163 3028 14W-0N C5
5800 HLSD 60162 3028 14W-0N C5
5800 HLSD 60163 3028 14W-0N C5
24900 AntT 60046 2416 24W-39N B4
24900 LkvT 60046 2416 24W-39N B4
Elm Cir
- GLF 60029 2865 8W-12N A1
9000 HYHL 60457 3209 11W-10S E4
E Elm Cir
700 ITSC 60143 2914 19W-7N C5
Elm Ct
- BmnT 60426 3426 5W-19S B1
- BRRG 60527 3146 15W-7S B6
10 BGBK 60440 3205 23W-10S A6
10 BGBK 60440 3269 23W-11S A1
10 CTCY 60409 3429 2E-18S D1
10 DGvT 60527 3207 17W-9S D3
100 ROSL 60172 2913 23W-7N A5
200 LYVL 60048 2591 16W-29N D5
200 NfdT 60062 2757 9W-18N B3
300 WynT 60185 2966 30W-3N B6
400 OKTR 60181 3085 17W-1S C1
600 SchT 60174 2908 34W-6N D7
900 NPVL 60540 3203 28W-8S A1
1200 GNVW 60025 2810 9W-13N D6
1800 SYHW 60118 2800 34W-15N D3
1800 WDND 60118 2800 34W-15N D3
1900 HRPK 60133 2911 27W-8N C3
3600 FSMR 60422 3506 4W-22S D2
9200 MKNA 60448 3503 11W-23S E3
13600 LMNT 60439 3343 17W-15S B2
16500 SHLD 60473 3428 0E-19S E2
E Elm Ct
300 GLNC 60022 2758 6W-18N C3
S Elm Ct
10 PSHT 60463 3346 9W-15S D1
W Elm Ct
300 GLNC 60022 2758 6W-18N C3
700 ITSC 60143 2914 19W-7N C5
1100 PLTN 60067 2805 21W-14N C3
Elm Dr
- BmnT 60426 3426 5W-19S B1
- CCHL 60478 3506 5W-23S C2
10 WnfT 60185 3023 28W-1N B2
300 WLNG 60090 2755 13W-17N D5
400 LYVL 60048 2591 16W-29N D4
1200 SMBG 60194 2858 25W-10N C5
1700 NLNX 60451 3501 18W-23S B3
1700 NlxT 60451 3501 18W-23S B3
8600 MaiT 60016 2863 10W-11N E2
8600 MaiT 60016 2864 10W-11N A2
Elm Dr
12000 BLID 60406 3277 3W-14S A5
16900 HLCT 60429 3426 4W-20S E4
28300 WmTp 60481 3761 32W-34S D5
N Elm Dr
800 NLNX 60451 3501 18W-24S B5
W Elm Dr
7900 NRDG 60706 2918 10W-5N B7
Elm Ln
10 HGKN 60525 3147 12W-7S C5
10 LynT 60458 3209 11W-8S E1
100 SMWD 60107 2857 28W-10N A6
700 WDSK 60098 2524 42W-31N C6
6000 MTSN 60443 3505 7W-24S C6
9400 GfnT 60014 2638 38W-25N E4
9500 LKWD 60014 2638 38W-25N E4
N Elm Ln
10 GNWD 60425 3508 0E-22S E2
2700 ANHT 60004 2754 17W-17N B6
S Elm Ln
10 GNWD 60425 3508 0E-22S E2
W Elm Ln
13700 WDWH 60083 2420 13W-38N E6
Elm Pl
- ODHL 60487 3424 11W-19S A2
10 LKZH 60047 2698 23W-22N D4
300 HDPK 60035 2704 8W-22N D4
300 OKTR 60181 3085 17W-1S C2
800 GLNC 60022 2758 7W-17N C4
Elm Rd
10 GNVA 60134 3021 33W-1N A4
10 GnvT 60134 3021 33W-1N A4
10 GnvT 60185 3021 33W-1N A4
100 BRTN 60010 2750 25W-20N E1
100 BRTN 60010 2751 25W-20N A1
100 WYNE 60184 2965 31W-5N D2
400 WCHI 60185 2965 32W-3N D6
400 WynT 60185 2965 32W-3N D6
500 BRTN 60010 2698 25W-20N A7
2000 HMWD 60430 3427 2W-21S D6
3600 PKFT 60466 3594 4W-26S E3
3600 RNPK 60471 3594 4W-26S E3
4200 GRNE 60031 2535 14W-34N C2
4300 WrnT 60031 2535 14W-34N C2
6600 NndT 60012 2584 35W-30N A2
13400 LbvT 60044 2592 13W-28N E6
N Elm Rd
24000 VrnT 60045 2702 14W-24N C1
24300 VrnT 60045 2648 14W-24N C7
24500 MTWA 60045 2648 14W-24N C7
S Elm Rd
23300 LNSH 60069 2702 14W-23N C2
23300 VrnT 60069 2702 14W-23N C2
23600 LNSH 60045 2702 14W-23N C1
Elm St
- FNPK 60131 2973 11W-4N E4
- FNPK 60171 2973 11W-4N E4
- FXLK 60020 2415 28W-39N A5
- FXLK 60081 2415 28W-39N A5
- MchT 60050 2527 34W-33N B2
- MHRY 60050 2527 34W-33N B2
- RHMD 60071 2353 34W-42N C5
- RVGV 60131 2973 11W-4N E4
- RVGV 60171 2973 11W-4N E4
10 CLLK 60014 2639 35W-25N E4
10 CLLK 60014 2640 35W-25N A4
10 CTSD 60525 3147 12W-6S C4
10 DRN 60527 3207 16W-8S D1
10 DRN 60561 3207 16W-8S D1
10 GNVW 60025 2864 9W-12N D1
10 GNVW 60053 2864 9W-12N D2
10 HNWD 60047 2645 20W-24N E7
10 HNWD 60047 2699 20W-24N E1
10 MNGV 60053 2864 9W-12N D2
10 MPPT 60056 2807 15W-15N E3
10 PKFT 60466 3595 3W-26S C3
10 PKRG 60068 2864 10W-9N A7
10 PTHT 60056 2807 15W-15N E3
10 PTHT 60070 2807 15W-15N E2
10 ROSL 60172 2913 23W-7N A5
100 ELGN 60123 2854 34W-11N E5
100 FKFT 60423 3503 12W-25S D7
100 FKFT 60423 3591 12W-25S D1
100 JLET 60433 3499 23W-25S A7
100 JLET 60436 3499 23W-25S A7
100 JltT 60433 3499 23W-25S A7
100 NLNX 60451 3501 17W-24S C6
200 BTVA 60510 3078 35W-1S A2
200 WLSP 60480 3209 12W-9S D3
300 DRFD 60015 2756 11W-20N E1
300 MRGO 60152 2634 49W-26N C3
400 DYR 46311 3598 D2
400 GNVW 60025 2810 9W-12N D7
500 HPSR 60140 2795 46W-15N E3
500 WNKA 60093 2812 4W-15N B2
600 ALGN 60102 2694 33W-21N E6
600 BCHR 60401 3864 0W-36S C2
600 DRFD 60015 2703 11W-20N E7
600 GNEN 60137 3025 22W-0N C4
600 RLKP 60073 2532 22W-34N B1
700 FSMR 60422 3506 4W-22S D3
700 HLCT 60422 3506 4W-22S E2
700 HLCT 60429 3506 4W-22S E2
800 SRGV 60554 3135 42W-4S D2
800 WNSP 60558 3146 14W-4S E1
900 NPVL 60540 3203 28W-8S A1
900 SCRL 60174 3020 35W-2N B1
1100 LIHL 60156 2694 35W-22N A4
1100 WNKA 60093 2811 5W-15N E2
1300 PKRG 60068 2863 11W-9N D7
1300 SPGV 60081 2414 30W-38N A6
1400 GNVA 60134 3020 35W-2N B2
1400 SCRL 60134 3020 35W-2N B2
3900 DRGV 60515 3084 19W-4S D7
3900 YkTp 60515 3084 19W-4S D7
4300 DRGV 60515 3144 19W-5S D2
4700 LSLE 60532 3143 22W-5S C2
4800 SKOK 60076 2865 6W-10N E4
4900 SKOK 60077 2865 6W-10N D4
5500 LslT 60532 3143 22W-6S C5
6100 UNON 60180 2635 46W-25N D4
6300 MNGV 60053 2865 8W-10N A4
6400 OKFT 60452 3347 8W-18S B6
7800 CmgT 60033 2405 51W-39N D4
8300 GwdT 60097 2469 37W-35N B6
12500 BLID 60406 3277 3W-15S B7
13500 ODPK 60462 3345 11W-16S E3
13500 OrlT 60462 3345 11W-16S E2
13500 PlsT 60462 3345 11W-16S E2
15400 DLTN 60419 3350 0E-18S E7
15400 SHLD 60473 3350 0E-18S E7
16800 SHLD 60473 3428 0E-19S E3
Elm St SR-120
- MchT 60050 2527 34W-33N B2
- MHRY 60050 2527 34W-33N B2

STREET Block	City	ZIP	Map#	CGS	Grid
E Elm St					
10	CHCG	60610	3034	0E-1N	C1
10	CHCG	60611	3034	0E-1N	C1
10	VLPK	60181	3027	17W-1N	B3
100	BDWD	60408	3942	31W-41S	A5
200	EMHT	60126	3027	17W-1N	B3
200	VLPK	60126	3027	17W-1N	B3
300	LMBD	60148	3026	19W-0N	C4
400	BtlT	60560	3333	42W-14S	D1
400	YKVL	60560	3333	42W-14S	D1
1000	WHTN	60187	3082	23W-1S	E1
1600	WHTN	60187	3083	23W-1S	A1
N Elm St					
10	HNDL	60521	3146	15W-4S	B1
10	PvsT	60162	3028	14W-0S	D6
100	SDWH	60548	3330	51W-14S	A1
200	HLSD	60162	3028	14W-0S	D5
200	MPPT	60056	2808	15W-13N	A6
300	HNDL	60521	3086	15W-4S	B7
700	ITSC	60143	2914	19W-7N	C5
700	SDWH	60548	3258	51W-14S	A7
1300	PLTN	60067	2753	20W-17N	A4
1500	PLTN	60074	2753	20W-17N	A4
1500	PltT	60067	2753	20W-17N	A4
1500	PltT	60074	2753	20W-17N	A4
2400	RVGV	60171	2973	11W-3N	E5
2600	RVGV	60131	2973	11W-3N	E5
2700	FNPK	60131	2973	11W-3N	E4
2800	FNPK	60171	2973	11W-3N	E4
26900	WcnT	60084	2642	28W-26N	E2
34700	FXLK	60041	2473	26W-34N	D7
34700	GrtT	60041	2473	26W-34N	D7
42200	AntT	60002	2356	26W-42N	D6
S Elm St					
10	HNDL	60521	3146	15W-5S	B2
10	MPPT	60056	2808	15W-12N	A7
100	HPSR	60140	2795	46W-16N	E2
100	NHLK	60164	3028	14W-1N	D1
100	PltT	60067	2805	21W-15N	C2
300	ITSC	60143	2914	19W-6N	C7
300	PLTN	60067	2805	21W-14N	C3
500	ADSN	60143	2914	19W-5N	C7
600	LktT	60441	3419	21W-18S	D1
600	MPPT	60056	2862	15W-12N	A2
900	DSPN	60016	2862	15W-11N	A3
900	MPPT	60016	2862	15W-11N	A3
1600	DSPN	60018	2863	13W-9N	A6
5200	NndT	60010	2642	29W-26N	D2
5200	NndT	60051	2642	29W-26N	D2
5800	BRRG	60521	3146	15W-6S	B4
7200	BRRG	60527	3146	15W-8S	B7
7200	BRRG	60527	3208	15W-8S	B1
12300	PSPK	60464	3273	11W-14S	E6
13900	HMGN	60491	3342	19W-16S	E4
14100	HmrT	60491	3342	19W-16S	E4
W Elm St					
10	CHCG	60611	3034	0W-1N	B2
10	DGvT	60527	3207	17W-9S	D3
10	VLPK	60181	3027	18W-1N	A3
100	ANHT	60004	2807	18W-14N	A3
100	WHTN	60187	3082	24W-1S	C1
300	VLPK	60181	3026	18W-1N	E3
400	CHCG	60610	3034	0W-1N	A2
500	ANHT	60004	2806	18W-14N	E3
500	LMBD	60148	3026	18W-1N	E3
500	LMBD	60181	3026	18W-1N	E3
1000	PLTN	60067	2752	22W-17N	B5
1500	HHLL	60051	2586	30W-29N	A4
3300	MchT	60051	2528	32W-33N	C3
3300	MHRY	60050	2528	32W-33N	B3
3300	MHRY	60051	2528	32W-33N	C3
4300	MHRY	60050	2527	34W-33N	C2
5200	MchT	60050	2527	34W-33N	C2
18000	WrnT	60030	2534	18W-32N	A4
21500	LkvT	60046	2417	21W-38N	D6
25400	GrtT	60041	2474	25W-34N	A7
W Elm St SR-31					
3600	MHRY	60050	2528	32W-33N	B3
W Elm St SR-120					
3300	MchT	60051	2528	32W-33N	C3
3300	MHRY	60050	2528	32W-33N	B3
3300	MHRY	60051	2528	32W-33N	C3
4300	MHRY	60050	2527	34W-33N	C2
5200	MchT	60050	2527	34W-33N	C2
Elm Ter					
4600	SKOK	60076	2866	5W-10N	A4
9600	MaiT	60016	2863	11W-12N	D2
Elma Av					
600	ELGN	60120	2801	33W-13N	B7
900	ELGN	60120	2855	32W-12N	C1
N Elma Av					
1000	ELGN	60120	2801	32W-12N	D7
Elm Cir Dr					
5000	OKLN	60453	3211	6W-11S	E7
9900	OKLN	60453	3212	6W-11S	A7
Elm Creek Ct					
10	EMHT	60126	3027	16W-0S	E7
Elm Creek Dr					
-	EMHT	60126	3027	16W-0S	E7
Elmcrest Av					
-	EMHT	60126	2972	15W-2N	A7
-	EMHT	60126	3028	15W-2N	A1
Elmcrest Dr					
-	WCDA	60084	2587	26W-28N	E7
-	WcnT	60084	2587	26W-28N	E7
Elmdale Av					
1600	GNVW	60025	2810	10W-14N	A4
1600	NfdT	60025	2810	10W-14N	A4
2400	BmnT	60428	3427	3W-19S	B2
W Elmdale Av					
1200	CHCG	60660	2921	1W-7N	C3
Elmdale Rd					
600	MaiT	60025	2810	10W-13N	A7
800	GNVW	60025	2810	10W-13N	A6
800	NfdT	60025	2810	10W-13N	A6
Elmer Ct					
400	ElgT	60124	2853	37W-12N	C2
Elmer St					
600	JltT	60433	3499	23W-24S	B7
Elm Gate Dr					
700	GNVW	60025	2810	9W-13N	C7
Elm Grove Dr					
500	ELGN	60123	2854	35W-10N	C6
W Elm Grove Dr					
25200	CbaT	60010	2698	25W-21N	A7
25200	DRPK	60010	2698	25W-21N	A7
W Elmgrove Dr					
7700	EDPK	60707	2974	9W-3N	B4
7900	EDPK	60171	2974	9W-3N	C4
Elmhurst Av					
10	CLLK	60014	2640	35W-26N	A4
E Elmhurst Av					
200	EMHT	60126	3028	15W-1N	A1
N Elmhurst Av					
10	MPPT	60056	2807	15W-13N	E6

STREET Block	City	ZIP	Map#	CGS	Grid
S Elmhurst Av					
100	MPPT	60056	2807	15W-12N	E7
200	MPPT	60056	2861	16W-12N	E1
Elmhurst Ln					
1300	SMBG	60194	2858	25W-11N	C4
Elmhurst Rd					
-	DSPN	60007	2861	16W-9N	E7
100	CLLK	60014	2640	35W-26N	A3
600	DSPN	60016	2861	16W-11N	E3
600	MPPT	60056	2861	16W-11N	E3
700	DSPN	60018	2861	16W-9N	E7
700	EGvT	60007	2861	16W-9N	E7
700	EGvT	60018	2861	16W-9N	E7
700	EGVV	60007	2861	15W-9N	E7
700	EGVV	60018	2861	15W-9N	E7
900	EGvT	60007	2915	15W-9N	E1
900	EGvT	60018	2915	15W-9N	E1
900	EGVV	60007	2915	16W-8N	E2
900	MPPT	60016	2861	16W-10N	E5
1700	CHCG	60007	2915	16W-8N	E2
1700	MPPT	60018	2861	15W-9N	E6
Elmhurst Rd CO-8					
2300	EGvT	60007	2915	15W-7N	E3
2300	EGVV	60007	2915	15W-7N	E3
Elmhurst Rd SR-83					
600	DSPN	60016	2861	16W-11N	E3
600	MPPT	60056	2861	16W-11N	E3
900	MPPT	60016	2861	16W-10N	E5
N Elmhurst Rd					
10	MPPT	60070	2808	15W-15N	A3
10	WLNG	60090	2755	15W-18N	A4
900	MPPT	60056	2808	15W-14N	A4
900	PTHT	60070	2755	15W-16N	A7
1000	PTHT	60090	2755	15W-16N	A7
1100	PTHT	60056	2808	15W-14N	A4
1100	PTHT	60070	2808	15W-14N	A4
N Elmhurst Rd SR-83					
10	MPPT	60070	2808	15W-15N	A3
10	PTHT	60070	2808	15W-15N	A1
10	WLNG	60090	2755	15W-18N	A4
900	MPPT	60056	2808	15W-14N	A4
900	PTHT	60070	2755	15W-16N	A7
1000	PTHT	60090	2755	15W-16N	A7
1100	PTHT	60056	2808	15W-14N	A4
S Elmhurst Rd					
10	MPPT	60056	2808	15W-14N	A4
10	MPPT	60070	2808	15W-14N	A4
10	PTHT	60056	2808	15W-14N	A4
10	PTHT	60070	2808	15W-14N	A4
10	WLNG	60090	2755	15W-17N	A5
400	MPPT	60056	2861	15W-12N	E2
900	DSPN	60016	2861	15W-11N	E3
900	PTHT	60090	2755	15W-17N	A6
1400	DSPN	60018	2861	16W-9N	E6
1400	MPPT	60018	2861	16W-9N	E6
1700	MPPT	60016	2861	15W-10N	E5
S Elmhurst Rd SR-83					
10	MPPT	60056	2808	15W-14N	A4
10	MPPT	60070	2808	15W-14N	A4
10	PTHT	60056	2808	15W-14N	A4
10	PTHT	60070	2808	15W-14N	A4
10	WLNG	60090	2755	15W-17N	A5
400	MPPT	60056	2861	15W-12N	E2
900	DSPN	60016	2861	15W-11N	E3
900	PTHT	60090	2755	15W-17N	A6
1400	DSPN	60018	2861	16W-9N	E6
1400	MPPT	60018	2861	16W-9N	E6
1700	MPPT	60016	2861	15W-10N	E5
Elmhurst St					
100	AddT	60191	2915	17W-6N	B6
100	WDDL	60191	2915	17W-6N	B6
1100	BNVL	60106	2915	16W-6N	D6
Elmira Av					
2100	DSPN	60018	2862	14W-9N	D7
2200	DSPN	60018	2916	14W-9N	D1
Elmira Ct					
5000	JLET	60586	3496	30W-22S	C2
N Elmkirk Pk					
2600	MchT	60051	2528	31W-32N	D6
Elmleaf Dr					
4300	MchT	60050	2472	30W-36N	B4
4500	JNBG	60050	2472	30W-36N	B4
Elm Ln Dr					
16800	TYPK	60477	3425	8W-20S	A4
E Elmo Ct					
700	GDLY	60407	4030	32W-43S	D1
700	RedT	60408	4030	32W-43S	D1
Elmo Rd					
-	ODHL	60013	2641	31W-26N	C3
Elmo St					
-	JLET	60432	3499	21W-23S	E4
-	JltT	60432	3499	21W-23S	E4
Elm Oak Rd					
2600	MchT	60051	2528	31W-32N	D5
Elmont Ct					
300	SMBG	60193	2859	22W-10N	C6
Elmore Av					
-	MNSR	46321	3430		E7
1700	DGvT	60515	3144	21W-5S	A3
1700	DRGV	60515	3144	21W-5S	A3
1900	DRGV	60515	3143	21W-5S	E3
1900	LslT	60515	3143	21W-5S	E3
1900	LslT	60515	3144	21W-5S	A3
Elmore Ct					
18100	TYPK	60487	3424	10W-21S	B7
Elmore St					
10	PKRG	60068	2864	9W-9N	B7
10	PKRG	60068	2918	9W-8N	B1
N Elmore St					
8000	NLES	60068	2864	9W-10N	B6
8000	NLES	60714	2864	9W-10N	B5
8000	PKRG	60068	2864	9W-10N	B6
8200	MaiT	60714	2864	9W-10N	B5
El Morro Ct					
5900	OKFT	60452	3347	7W-18S	C6
El Morro Ln					
5900	OKFT	60452	3347	7W-18S	C6
W Elm Park Av					
600	EMHT	60126	3027	17W-1N	C3
Elm Ridge Dr					
2200	NHBK	60062	2809	10W-15N	E1
2200	NHBK	60062	2810	10W-16N	A1
Elmridge Dr					
900	GLNC	60022	2758	7W-18N	C4
Elm Ridge Rd					
400	CPVL	60110	2748	33W-17N	A7
W Elms Ct Ln					
10	CteT	60417	3685	1W-32S	A7
1200	CteT	60417	3684	2W-32S	E7
Elmshire Dr					
3600	MchT	60050	2471	32W-36N	B3
Elmtree Ct					
100	SCRL	60174	2964	36W-4N	A4
Elm Tree Ln					
400	VNHL	60061	2647	16W-25N	C5

STREET Block	City	ZIP	Map#	CGS	Grid
S Elm Tree Ln					
100	EMHT	60126	3028	15W-1N	B3
Elm Tree Rd					
800	LKFT	60045	2650	10W-27N	B2
W Elm Tree Rd					
26000	AntT	60002	2415	26W-39N	E4
Elmwood Av					
10	AddT	60101	2971	17W-3N	B4
10	ADSN	60101	2971	17W-3N	B4
10	LGPK	60525	3087	12W-3S	B6
100	CHCG	60202	2867	2W-9N	B6
100	CHCG	60645	2867	2W-9N	B6
200	CLLK	60014	2639	37W-25N	A5
300	SchT	60174	2908	35W-6N	B7
400	EVTN	60202	2867	2W-10N	B5
400	JLET	60433	3499	23W-24S	B6
500	WLMT	60091	2813	3W-14N	A5
600	JltT	60433	3499	23W-24S	B6
1000	DRFD	60015	2703	11W-21N	D6
1000	GNVW	60025	2811	7W-14N	A5
1200	BRWN	60304	3031	8W-1S	A7
1200	BRWN	60402	3031	8W-1S	A7
1200	EVTN	60201	2867	2W-10N	B4
1200	OKPK	60304	3031	8W-1S	A7
1500	BRWN	60402	3089	8W-2S	A3
2300	WLMT	60091	2812	5W-14N	B5
3500	WLMT	60091	2811	6W-14N	D5
3900	SKNY	60402	3089	8W-4S	A7
5100	DRGV	60515	3144	19W-5S	D2
8000	SKOK	60077	2865	6W-10N	E5
21400	WslT	60481	3943	27W-41S	E6
E Elmwood Av					
100	WCHI	60185	3022	29W-1N	D3
N Elmwood Av					
10	PLTN	60074	2806	20W-16N	B1
10	WKGN	60085	2536	11W-34N	D1
100	OKPK	60302	3031	8W-0N	A3
100	WDDL	60191	2971	17W-5N	B1
200	FmtT	60060	2646	19W-26N	D3
200	LbvT	60060	2646	18W-26N	D3
300	WDDL	60191	2915	17W-6N	B7
400	AddT	60101	2971	17W-4N	B4
400	AddT	60191	2915	17W-6N	B7
400	ADSN	60101	2971	17W-4N	B4
900	WKGN	60085	2479	11W-35N	D6
1200	PLTN	60074	2753	20W-17N	B5
2600	WKGN	60087	2479	11W-37N	D3
26900	LbvT	60045	2648	14W-27N	D2
27200	LbvT	60048	2648	14W-27N	D2
27200	MTWA	60048	2648	14W-27N	D2
S Elmwood Av					
10	PLTN	60074	2806	20W-15N	B1
10	WKGN	60085	2536	11W-33N	D2
100	OKPK	60302	3031	8W-0N	A4
500	OKPK	60304	3031	8W-0S	A5
1100	BRWN	60304	3031	8W-0S	A7
1100	BRWN	60402	3031	8W-0S	A7
1300	NCHI	60064	2536	11W-32N	D5
W Elmwood Av					
100	WCHI	60185	3022	30W-1N	C3
25900	WCDA	60084	2587	25W-27N	E7
25900	WcnT	60084	2587	26W-27N	E7
26600	GrtT	60041	2473	26W-35N	D6
Elmwood Av N					
1000	OKPK	60302	3031	8W-1N	A1
1200	CHCG	60302	3031	8W-1N	A1
1200	CHCG	60707	3031	8W-1N	A1
E Elmwood Cir					
1900	ANHT	60004	2807	16W-16N	C1
Elmwood Ct					
-	BTVA	60510	3078	33W-2S	E3
-	BtvT	60510	3078	33W-2S	E3
10	IHPK	60525	3146	13W-7S	E5
10	MltT	60137	3083	23W-3S	B5
10	WNVL	60555	3080	30W-2S	C3
300	PltT	60067	2806	20W-13N	A7
4500	ALGN	60102	2694	33W-21N	E5
4500	AlqT	60102	2694	33W-21N	E5
11000	FftT	60448	3503	13W-24S	A6
12500	HTLY	60142	2744	42W-19N	D3
Elmwood Dr					
-	DndT	60118	2801	33W-14N	B5
10	HNWD	60047	2644	23W-24N	E7
10	IHPK	60525	3146	14W-6S	D4
10	NPVL	60540	3141	26W-7S	D7
10	NPVL	60540	3203	27W-8S	C1
10	OSWG	60543	3263	37W-12S	C3
200	MltT	60137	3083	22W-2S	C3
500	BFGV	60089	2754	17W-18N	B3
600	WHTN	60187	3082	25W-2S	A4
700	CPVL	60110	2748	33W-17N	A7
1600	HDPK	60035	2704	9W-22N	D5
1800	LNHT	60046	2418	20W-38N	A7
8000	GwdT	60097	2469	37W-34N	C7
8000	WRLK	60097	2469	37W-34N	C7
17800	TYPK	60487	3424	11W-21S	A6
E Elmwood Dr					
10	CHHT	60411	3508	1W-23S	A4
N Elmwood Dr					
10	AURA	60506	3137	36W-7S	D6
S Elmwood Dr					
10	AURA	60506	3137	37W-7S	D7
200	AURA	60506	3199	37W-7S	D1
500	AraT	60506	3199	37W-8S	D1
W Elmwood Dr					
100	CHHT	60411	3507	1W-23S	E4
100	CHHT	60411	3508	0W-23S	B4
9100	MaiT	60016	2863	11W-12N	D1
9100	NLES	60714	2863	11W-12N	D1
Elmwood Ln					
-	MONE	60449	3683	6W-31S	A5
-	MTSN	60443	3506	5W-25S	B7
10	LNSH	60069	2702	14W-23N	D3
200	ANTH	60002	2358	23W-43N	A5
200	SMBG	60193	2859	21W-10N	E6
300	BMDL	60108	2969	22W-3N	C5
700	WLNG	60090	2754	15W-18N	E2
900	EGVV	60007	2915	18W-8N	A2
2100	JltT	60433	3587	21W-26S	E3
N Elmwood Ln					
200	PltT	60067	2806	20W-13N	A7
200	SMBG	60067	2806	21W-12N	A7
S Elmwood Ln					
200	BRLT	60103	2910	30W-8N	C3
300	PltT	60067	2806	20W-13N	A7
300	SMBG	60067	2806	20W-13N	A7
W Elmwood Ln					
1000	BRLT	60103	2910	30W-8N	C3
Elmwood Pl					
200	HNDL	60521	3146	15W-6S	B3
1900	WdfT	60015	2703	11W-23N	D2
Elmwood Rd					
100	RMVL	60446	3269	23W-14S	A6
5000	OKFT	60452	3426	6W-20S	A4
5100	OKFT	60452	3425	6W-20S	E4

STREET Block	City	ZIP	Map#	CGS	Grid
Elmwood Sq					
10	IHPK	60525	3146	14W-6S	D5
Elmwood St					
-	WCHI	60185	3021	32W-1N	D3
10	MltT	60190	3023	26W-0S	E6
100	MltT	60187	3023	26W-0S	E6
100	WNFD	60187	3023	26W-0S	E6
100	WNFD	60190	3023	26W-0S	E6
1400	WMTN	60481	3853	27W-37S	D5
W Elmwood Ter					
100	EMHT	60126	3027	16W-1N	E3
Elodie Dr					
200	CmpT	60119	2962	40W-2N	B7
800	CmpT	60119	3018	40W-2N	B1
El Paso Ln					
100	CLSM	60188	2968	25W-2N	A7
Elrose Ct					
800	CTHL	60403	3418	25W-21S	C7
N Elroy Av					
100	BRLT	60103	2911	28W-8N	A2
S Elroy Av					
100	BRLT	60103	2911	28W-8N	A3
W Elsbury St					
17700	WrnT	60031	2477	17W-36N	A4
S Elsdon Av					
5400	CHCG	60632	3150	4W-5S	D2
Elsie Av					
100	CTHL	60403	3418	24W-21S	D7
100	CTHL	60435	3418	24W-21S	E7
100	LktT	60435	3418	24W-21S	E7
700	GRNE	60031	2478	15W-35N	A7
Elsie Dr					
500	MLPK	60160	3029	10W-1N	E1
500	MLPK	60160	3030	10W-1N	A1
S Elsie St					
24700	CNHN	60410	3672	31W-30S	E3
Elsinoor Dr					
10	LNSH	60069	2702	14W-22N	C3
Elsinoor Ln					
500	CLLK	60014	2640	35W-24N	A6
S Elsner Rd					
21200	FKFT	60423	3503	13W-25S	C7
21200	FKFT	60423	3591	12W-25S	C1
N Elston Av					
800	CHCG	60622	3033	1W-1N	D1
1600	CHCG	60622	2977	1W-2N	D7
1900	CHCG	60614	2977	1W-2N	C6
2300	CHCG	60647	2977	2W-2N	B5
2700	CHCG	60618	2977	1W-2N	D7
3100	CHCG	60618	2976	3W-4N	E3
4200	CHCG	60641	2976	4W-5N	B1
4300	CHCG	60630	2976	5W-5N	B1
4400	CHCG	60630	2920	5W-5N	A7
4900	CHCG	60630	2919	5W-6N	E6
5500	CHCG	60646	2919	6W-6N	E5
Elsworth Dr					
-	CHCG	60615	3152	0E-5S	D2
-	CHCG	60637	3152	0E-6S	D2
El Vista Av					
14700	OKFT	60452	3347	6W-17S	D6
Elwood Ct					
300	WTMT	60559	3144	18W-6S	E5
Elwood St					
-	LYWD	60411	3510	4E-24S	C6
10	FKFT	60423	3591	12W-25S	D1
1200	WMTN	60481	3853	27W-38S	D5
E Elwood St					
400	JLET	60432	3499	23W-23S	B3
W Elwood Manhattan Rd					
100	MHTN	60442	3677	20W-31S	B5
200	MhtT	60442	3677	19W-31S	E5
16200	JknT	60421	3677	20W-31S	B5
16200	MhtT	60421	3677	20W-31S	B5
Ely Ct					
1300	WLNG	60090	2754	16W-18N	E2
Ely St					
200	ELGN	60123	2854	34W-10N	E5
Elysees Ct					
3400	HLCT	60429	3426	4W-21S	E7
Elysian Dr					
10	TYPK	60477	3505	8W-23S	B3
Emanuel Av					
-	BHPK	60087	2421	12W-39N	B6
-	BHPK	60099	2421	12W-39N	B5
-	WKGN	60087	2421	12W-39N	B6
Embassy Ln					
1400	FDHT	60411	3509	1E-25S	B6
9000	MaiT	60016	2863	11W-11N	D3
9000	PKRG	60016	2863	11W-11N	D3
9000	PKRG	60068	2863	11W-11N	D3
Embassy Row					
2900	FSMR	60422	3507	3W-22S	A2
Embden Ln					
400	MltT	60187	3081	26W-2S	D4
400	WHTN	60187	3081	26W-2S	D4
500	WnfT	60187	3081	27W-2S	D4
700	MltT	60187	3082	25W-2S	A4
Ember Ln					
800	SPGV	60081	2414	29W-40N	B2
S Embers Ln					
2300	ANHT	60005	2861	17W-11N	B3
Emelia Ct					
2600	FSMR	60422	3507	3W-23S	B3
Emelia St					
100	CHHT	60411	3507	1W-24S	E4
100	CHHT	60411	3508	1W-24S	A4
Emerald Av					
400	CHHT	60411	3508	0W-24S	B5
800	GRNE	60031	2478	14W-35N	C7
3400	STGR	60475	3596	1W-28S	B6
3700	CteT	60417	3596	1W-28S	B7
3700	CteT	60475	3596	1W-28S	B7
3700	STGR	60417	3596	1W-28S	B7
10400	ODPK	60467	3423	13W-20S	B4
10400	OrlT	60467	3423	13W-20S	B4
15600	HRVY	60426	3428	0W-19S	B2
24800	PNFD	60585	3338	31W-15S	A1
24900	WldT	60585	3338	31W-15S	A1
N Emerald Av					
10	MDLN	60060	2646	19W-27N	C1
600	MDLN	60060	2590	19W-28N	C6
S Emerald Av					
10	MDLN	60060	2646	19W-27N	C1
2600	CHCG	60616	3092	0W-3S	A5
3400	CHCG	60609	3092	0W-4S	A6
5100	CHCG	60609	3152	0W-5S	A2
5500	CHCG	60621	3152	0W-6S	A3
7500	CHCG	60620	3214	0W-9S	A2
7500	CHCG	60621	3214	0W-8S	A1
9900	CHCG	60628	3214	0W-11S	A7
10300	CHCG	60628	3278	0W-13S	A3
13600	RVDL	60827	3350	1W-16S	A2
14500	HRVY	60426	3350	1W-16S	A4
14500	HRVY	60827	3350	1W-16S	A4
Emerald Ct					
-	PSHL	60465	3210	10W-11S	C7

STREET Block	City	ZIP	Map#	CGS	Grid
Emerald Ct					
300	BGBK	60440	3269	23W-12S	A3
800	WLBK	60527	3145	16W-7S	E5
2400	WDRG	60517	3205	21W-9S	E3
8900	HYHL	60457	3210	10W-10S	A5
14000	LktT	60544	3339	26W-16S	E4
19300	MKNA	60448	3503	12W-23S	C3
W Emerald Ct					
2600	NndT	60051	2528	31W-31N	D6
7700	FftT	60423	3504	9W-24S	E5
Emerald Dr					
10	SMWD	60107	2856	29W-10N	D5
800	NPVL	60540	3141	27W-7S	C7
800	NPVL	60540	3203	27W-8S	C1
800	PGGV	60140	2797	41W-15N	E4
1000	AURA	60506	3137	38W-6S	B4
1000	SMBG	60173	2859	22W-11N	D4
1200	LMNT	60439	3342	19W-15S	D1
N Emerald Dr					
100	MchT	60051	2528	31W-32N	D5
S Emerald Dr					
100	NndT	60051	2528	31W-31N	D6
Emerald Ln					
300	ALGN	60102	2748	33W-19N	B2
2400	LNHT	60046	2476	19W-36N	B3
2500	LkvT	60046	2476	19W-36N	C3
W Emerald Pkwy					
6300	MONE	60449	3682	7W-31S	C5
6300	MonT	60449	3682	7W-31S	C5
Emerald St					
-	DMND	60416	3941	34W-40S	A3
Emerald Wy					
-	MTSN	60443	3506	5W-24S	C5
N Emerald Bay					
1700	PLTN	60074	2753	18W-18N	D4
Emerald Green Dr					
300	WNVL	60555	3080	29W-2S	D4
Emerald Green Dr E					
300	WNVL	60555	3080	29W-2S	D4
Emerald Green Dr W					
300	WNVL	60555	3080	29W-2S	D4
Emerald Pointe Cir					
1700	JLET	60586	3495	31W-22S	E2
Emerald Pointe Dr					
5700	JLET	60586	3495	31W-21S	E1
5700	JLET	60586	3496	31W-21S	A1
N Emerald Shores Ct					
35000	GrtT	60041	2473	26W-35N	E6
Emerald Woods Ln					
1900	HDPK	60035	2704	10W-22N	A5
W Emerald Wy St N					
4300	ALSP	60803	3276	5W-14S	B7
W Emerald Wy St S					
4300	ALSP	60803	3276	5W-14S	B7
Emerson Av					
-	AntT	60002	2415	26W-38N	D6
300	GNEN	60137	3025	22W-1N	B3
500	MltT	60137	3025	22W-1N	C3
2000	LydT	60164	2973	12W-2N	C7
2000	MLPK	60160	2973	12W-2N	C7
2000	MLPK	60164	2973	12W-2N	C7
2300	FNPK	60131	2973	12W-2N	C7
3100	HLCT	60429	3427	3W-20S	A5
3700	RGMW	60008	2806	20W-14N	A4
4200	SRPK	60176	2973	12W-5N	B1
4800	PltT	60008	2805	21W-14N	E4
4800	PltT	60067	2805	21W-14N	E4
4800	RGMW	60008	2805	21W-14N	D4
4900	RGMW	60067	2805	21W-14N	D4
5100	PLTN	60008	2805	21W-14N	D4
5100	PLTN	60067	2805	21W-14N	D4
E Emerson Av					
1000	LMBD	60148	3026	18W-0N	E4
W Emerson Av					
10	PLTN	60008	2805	21W-14N	D4
10	PLTN	60067	2805	21W-14N	D4
10	RGMW	60008	2805	21W-14N	D4
10	RGMW	60067	2805	21W-14N	D4
Emerson Cir					
500	BGBK	60440	3268	24W-11S	E1
Emerson Ct					
200	BMDL	60108	2969	22W-3N	C5
700	WNFD	60190	3081	27W-0S	D1
1600	WHTN	60187	3082	24W-1S	C2
4400	SRPK	60176	2973	12W-5N	B1
13900	LktT	60544	3339	26W-16S	E4
S Emerson Ct					
900	MPPT	60056	2862	15W-11N	A2
Emerson Dr					
-	ODPK	60467	3423	11W-19S	E2
10	SMBG	60193	2858	25W-10N	B5
10	SMBG	60194	2858	25W-10N	A5
3800	SRPK	60176	2973	12W-4N	B2
7100	DRN	60561	3145	18W-8S	A7
7100	DRN	60561	3207	18W-8S	A1
Emerson Ln					
400	MDLN	60060	2646	18W-26N	E2
1200	LYVL	60048	2647	15W-27N	E1
1600	NPVL	60540	3140	29W-7S	D7
2300	NPVL	60540	3202	29W-8S	D1
N Emerson Ln					
400	HNVL	60030	2532	22W-33N	C2
Emerson Pl					
1100	VNHL	60061	2647	17W-27N	C1
1600	JltT	60433	3587	23W-26S	A2
Emerson St					
-	ANHT	60005	2861	18W-12N	A1
-	EVTN	60203	2866	3W-11N	E2
-	MNGV	60053	2865	6W-11N	D2
-	SKOK	60053	2865	6W-11N	D2
-	SKOK	60076	2865	6W-11N	E2
-	SKOK	60203	2866	3W-11N	E2
600	EVTN	60201	2867	3W-11N	A2
1800	EVTN	60201	2866	3W-11N	E2
3300	FNPK	60131	2973	12W-4N	B3
3600	SRPK	60131	2973	12W-4N	B3
3600	SRPK	60176	2973	12W-4N	B3
3900	SKOK	60076	2866	5W-11N	B2
5000	SKOK	60077	2865	6W-11N	E2
7200	MNGV	60053	2864	9W-11N	D2
E Emerson St					
100	ANHT	60005	2861	18W-12N	A1
2500	DSPN	60016	2863	11W-11N	C2
2500	MaiT	60016	2863	11W-11N	C2
N Emerson St					
10	MPPT	60056	2808	15W-13N	A6
6000	RSMT	60018	2917	12W-7N	B4
S Emerson St					
10	MPPT	60056	2808	15W-12N	A7
200	MPPT	60056	2862	15W-12N	A1
W Emerson St					
10	ANHT	60005	2861	18W-12N	A1
8600	MaiT	60016	2864	10W-11N	A2
8600	NLES	60016	2864	10W-11N	A2
8600	NLES	60714	2864	10W-11N	A2
8700	NLES	60016	2863	10W-11N	E2

STREET Block City ZIP Map# CGS Grid

W Emerson St
8900 MaiT 60016 2863 11W-11N D2
9300 DSPN 60016 2863 11W-11N D2
Emery Av
300 RMVL 60446 3340 24W-16S E3
Emery Ct
1800 SCRL 60174 3020 34W-2N E2
Emery Ln
3100 RBBN 60472 3348 4W-16S D4
N Emery Ln
400 EMHT 60126 2971 16W-2N D7
Emery St
700 RKDL 60436 3498 26W-24S A7
S Emery St
10 JLET 60435 3498 26W-24S A5
10 JLET 60436 3498 26W-24S A5
W Emery St
- JLET 60435 3498 26W-23S A4
Emil Ct
100 BRLT 60103 2911 28W-8N A3
Emil St
700 LMNT 60439 3270 19W-13S E5
Emile Ln
- FftT 60448 3423 13W-22S B7
- ODPK 60448 3423 13W-22S B7
10400 FftT 60467 3423 13W-22S B7
10400 ODPK 60467 3423 13W-22S B7
10400 OrlT 60487 3423 13W-22S B7
Emily Ct
10 BGBK 60490 3339 28W-15S B1
10 LMNT 60439 3342 19W-15S C2
300 KdlT 60560 3334 40W-16S B3
1900 WHTN 60187 3024 25W-0N C4
11600 SPGV 60081 2355 30W-43N A4
17900 TYPK 60477 3424 10W-21S C6
18600 HLCT 60429 3506 4W-22S E1
Emily Dr
- WldT 60490 3339 28W-15S B1
- WldT 60544 3339 28W-15S B1
2100 BGBK 60490 3339 28W-15S B1
Emily Ln
10 HmrT 60441 3342 19W-15S C2
10 LMNT 60439 3342 19W-15S C2
100 SchT 60174 2964 34W-6N C1
1600 AURA 60502 3079 33W-4S A7
2400 ElgT 60124 2907 37W-9N D2
2500 NlxT 60451 3502 15W-24S C5
3000 MchT 60051 2528 31W-33N C3
21900 FKFT 60423 3590 14W-26S D2
Emily Dickinson Ln
10 CmpT 60175 2962 40W-4N C5
Emlong St
2400 LktT 60403 3417 27W-20S D5
2400 LktT 60435 3417 27W-20S D5
2400 PnfT 60435 3417 27W-20S D4
Emma Cir
2600 AURA 60504 3201 32W-9S C5
2800 AURA 60503 3201 32W-9S D5
E Emma Ct
10 PLTN 60067 2805 20W-14N E3
Emma Ln
1700 AURA 60503 3201 32W-10S D5
1700 AURA 60504 3201 32W-10S D5
13900 MTWA 60045 2648 13W-26N D3
W Emma St
23500 CnhT 60410 3584 30W-28S C7
Emmaus Av
2100 ZION 60099 2422 10W-39N B5
N Emmaus Av
3300 BHPK 60099 2422 10W-39N B5
3300 ZION 60099 2422 10W-39N B5
Emmerson Av
200 ITSC 60143 2914 19W-6N D7
400 WDDL 60143 2914 19W-6N D7
400 WDDL 60191 2914 19W-6N D7
E Emmerson Ln
1400 MPPT 60056 2808 14W-13N C7
1500 DSPN 60016 2808 14W-13N C7
1500 DSPN 60056 2808 14W-13N C7
N Emmett St
2600 CHCG 60647 2976 4W-3N D5
W Emmett St
500 JLET 60435 3498 24W-24S D5
500 JLET 60436 3498 24W-24S D5
Emmons Ct
1100 LKFT 60045 2649 12W-27N B1
Emory Av
1100 NPVL 60565 3204 25W-10S C5
Emory Rd
- HFET 60169 2804 24W-12N E7
Empire Av
14600 DLTN 60419 3351 0E-17S A5
Empire Dr
100 MTGY 60543 3263 38W-11S A1
Empire Rd
10 CmpT 60175 2961 42W-5N D1
10 CmpT 60175 2962 41W-5N A1
Empire Rd CO-69
10 CmpT 60175 2961 42W-5N C1
10 CmpT 60175 2962 41W-5N A1
Empire Wy
600 RMVL 60446 3417 26W-18S E1
Emporia Ct
4100 NPVL 60564 3266 28W-12S E3
Empress Dr
- HMND 46320 3280 D2
2200 JLET 60436 3585 27W-26S C3
W Empress Ln
21500 LktT 60544 3339 26W-16S D3
21500 PnfT 60544 3339 26W-16S D3
Empress Rd
1900 JLET 60436 3585 28W-26S B2
1900 TroT 60436 3585 28W-26S B3
N Emroy Av
200 AddT 60126 2972 15W-3N A5
200 EMHT 60126 3028 15W-1N A1
600 EMHT 60126 2972 15W-2N A6
W Emvyale Ct
24400 PnfT 60586 3416 30W-20S B6
Enborn Dr
1300 JLET 60431 3495 32W-22S C2
Encina Dr
100 NPVL 60540 3141 28W-6S A5
1400 NPVL 60540 3140 28W-6S E5
Enclave Cir
100 BGBK 60440 3269 22W-11S B1
Enclave Ct
10 BRRG 60527 3208 15W-10S B5
Enclave Dr
- CRY 60013 2695 32W-23N A2
9000 BRRG 60527 3208 15W-10S B5
Enclave Ln
8000 TYPK 60477 3504 10W-23S C3
19300 TYPK 60448 3504 10W-23S C3
Enclave Wy
10 HNWD 60047 2700 20W-23N A1
E End Av
100 CLLK 60014 2639 37W-25N C4
3100 BHPK 60087 2479 11W-37N E2
3100 WKGN 60087 2479 11W-37N E2
W End Av
- BlmT 60411 3508 0W-24S C6
700 CHHT 60411 3508 0W-24S C6
W End Ct
100 OSWG 60543 3263 38W-13S B5
700 VNHL 60061 2647 17W-26N B4
E End Dr
10 GLBT 60136 2799 38W-16N B2
W End Dr
10 GLBT 60136 2799 38W-16N A2
W End Ln
13100 CTWD 60445 3347 6W-15S D1
W End Rd
600 ROSL 60172 2912 23W-6N E6
3900 DRGV 60515 3084 18W-4S E7
Enders Ln
- MltT 60188 3023 26W-1N E3
- WNFD 60188 3023 26W-1N E3
Endicott Cir
1800 CPVL 60110 2801 32W-17N D1
Endicott Ct
11200 ODPK 60467 3344 14W-16S E4
Endicott Rd
10 HIWD 60040 2704 9W-24N D1
Endwood Dr
- LGGV 60047 2647 17W-24N A7
- LGGV 60047 2701 17W-24N B1
6400 LGGV 60047 2646 18W-24N E7
Energy Dr
10 GNOK 60044 2592 13W-28N E5
10 LbvT 60045 2592 13W-28N E5
Enfield Av
3600 SKOK 60076 2866 5W-11N B3
4700 SKOK 60076 2865 5W-11N E3
5200 SKOK 60077 2865 6W-11N D3
7100 MNGV 60053 2864 8W-11N D3
Enfield Dr
800 NHBK 60062 2810 8W-16N D1
Enfield Ln
10 GYLK 60030 2475 20W-35N E6
10 GYLK 60030 2476 20W-35N A6
Engel Blvd
400 PKRG 60068 2917 11W-8N E2
Engels Pl
300 BtnT 60081 2414 29W-39N C5
Engemann Dr
- NPVL 60563 3080 29W-4S E7
W Enger Ln
8100 RVGV 60171 2974 10W-3N B4
Engle Ct
800 DLTN 60419 3351 1E-17S A5
W Engle Dr
21100 LkvT 60046 2475 21W-36N C3
W Engle Dr CO-A18
21100 LkvT 60046 2475 21W-36N C3
Engle Rd
2000 NPVL 60564 3266 29W-12S E4
W Engle Rd
4800 ALSP 60803 3276 6W-15S A7
Engle St
400 DLTN 60419 3350 0E-16S E4
Engles Pl
- BtnT 60081 2414 29W-39N C5
Englewood Av
10 BLWD 60104 3029 13W-0N A4
400 HLSD 60162 3029 13W-0N A5
1400 JLET 60432 3499 22W-21S C1
1500 JLET 60441 3499 22W-21S C1
1600 LktT 60441 3419 22W-21S C7
W Englewood Av
400 CHCG 60621 3152 0W-6S A4
N Englewood Ct
10 PltT 60067 2805 22W-15N B2
Englewood Rd
1000 HFET 60169 2858 24W-12N C1
English Cir
21400 FKFT 60423 3592 10W-25S B1
English Ct
1400 NPVL 60564 3203 28W-11S A7
English Dr
1700 GLHT 60139 2968 24W-3N D6
English Ln
200 WPHR 60096 2362 10W-43N E4
500 BtnT 60096 2363 10W-42N A6
500 WPHR 60096 2363 10W-42N A6
21300 FKFT 60423 3592 10W-25S B1
N English St
300 BDWD 60408 3941 32W-40S D4
300 RedT 60408 3941 32W-40S D4
S English St
100 BDWD 60408 3941 32W-41S D6
English Bay
10500 MKNA 60448 3503 13W-22S B1
English Oak Ln
- BtnT 60081 2413 30W-38N E6
- SPGV 60081 2413 30W-38N E6
- SPGV 60081 2414 30W-39N A5
1100 HnrT 60107 2856 30W-10N B5
1100 SMWD 60107 2856 30W-10N B5
English Oak Ter
400 BFGV 60089 2701 17W-22N C4
English Oaks Dr
700 CRY 60013 2695 32W-22N B3
English Prairie Rd
500 BtnT 60081 2355 30W-42N A7
500 FXLK 60081 2355 29W-41N C7
900 SPGV 60081 2355 30W-42N A7
2100 SPGV 60081 2354 31W-42N D7
2300 RcmT 60071 2354 31W-42N D7
2300 SPGV 60071 2354 31W-42N D7
Enid Ln
100 NHFD 60093 2811 7W-15N A3
Enid St
2400 JLET 60435 3417 27W-20S C6
2400 PnfT 60435 3417 27W-20S C6
N Enlund Dr
2200 PLTN 60074 2753 19W-18N C2
Ennerdale Av
- LKPT 60441 3419 21W-20S E4
Ennerdale Ln
100 WNFD 60190 3023 27W-0N B5
Ennis Ct
10 BGBK 60440 3205 22W-10S C5
10 CRY 60013 2641 31W-24N E6
Ennis Ln
300 BGBK 60440 3205 22W-10S C5
1700 WHTN 60187 3082 26W-1S A1
Enoch Av
2100 ZION 60099 2422 10W-40N B2
Enrico Fermi Ct
600 WNVL 60555 3080 29W-2S D4
Ensell Rd
900 LKZH 60047 2699 22W-23N C2
1200 ElaT 60047 2699 21W-23N C2
Ensenada Ct
100 CPVL 60110 2748 33W-18N B4
Ensenada Dr
100 CPVL 60110 2748 33W-18N B4
Enslen Dr
2700 DYR 46311 3598 E4
Enstrom Ct
- HTLY 60142 2691 41W-22N E3
Enstrom Ln
- HTLY 60142 2691 41W-22N E3
Enterprise Av
1800 NCHI 60088 2593 11W-30N D1
2100 BTVA 60510 3020 34W-0S E6
2100 GnvT 60134 3020 34W-0S E6
2100 GnvT 60510 3020 34W-0S E6
Enterprise Cir
- WCHI 60185 3021 32W-0S B6
Enterprise Ct
700 CHHT 60411 3507 2W-24S D6
700 NPVL 60563 3140 31W-5S A4
700 NpvT 60563 3140 31W-5S A4
1800 LYVL 60048 2590 19W-30N D1
3900 AURA 60504 3140 31W-6S A5
Enterprise Dr
- GNVW 60025 2810 9W-14N C4
- LktT 60403 3417 26W-20S E4
- PvsT 60154 3086 14W-2S D3
- SCRL 60174 3021 33W-2N A1
600 OKBK 60523 3085 16W-1S E2
600 OKBK 60523 3086 15W-1S A2
1200 RMVL 60446 3269 23W-14S A6
2200 PvsT 60162 3086 14W-2S D2
2200 WSTR 60154 3086 14W-2S D2
2200 WSTR 60162 3086 14W-2S D2
4300 JLET 60431 3496 29W-24S E5
4300 TroT 60431 3496 29W-24S E5
9400 MKNA 60448 3503 11W-23S E3
W Enterprise Dr
300 DSPN 60018 2861 16W-10N E6
300 MPPT 60056 2861 16W-10N E6
Enterprise Pkwy
400 ElaT 60047 2699 22W-23N A1
400 LKZH 60047 2699 22W-23N A1
Enterprise Rd
600 CHHT 60411 3507 2W-24S D6
Enterprise St
400 ELGN 60120 2855 33W-12N A2
500 AURA 60504 3140 31W-7S A6
Enterprise Park Av
3000 SCHT 60411 3596 1W-27S A4
3300 SCHT 60475 3596 1W-27S A4
3300 STGR 60475 3596 1W-27S A4
Entertainment Dr
- HGKN 60525 3147 12W-6S C5
Entrance Dr
800 ANHT 60005 2807 17W-12N B7
N Entrance Dr
25100 LkvT 60046 2474 25W-38N B1
Entrance Rd
- ELGN 60123 2801 33W-14N B6
S Entre Av
13800 BNHM 60633 3352 3E-16S B2
Entry Dr
1000 BNVL 60106 2971 16W-3N E4
1100 EMHT 60106 2971 16W-3N E5
1100 EMHT 60126 2971 16W-3N E5
Envee Dr
1400 BGBK 60490 3267 26W-11S E2
N Environ Cir
29600 LKBF 60044 2593 12W-29N A4
N Eola Rd
10 AURA 60502 3139 31W-7S D6
10 AURA 60563 3139 31W-5S D3
10 NpvT 60502 3139 31W-5S D2
100 AURA 60502 3079 31W-3S E7
100 AURA 60510 3079 31W-3S E7
100 NpvT 60563 3139 31W-5S D2
100 WnfT 60510 3079 31W-3S E7
200 AURA 60502 3201 31W-7S D1
200 AURA 60504 3139 31W-7S D7
200 AURA 60504 3201 31W-7S D1
N Eola Rd CO-14
10 AURA 60563 3139 31W-5S D4
10 NpvT 60563 3139 31W-5S D2
100 AURA 60502 3079 31W-3S E7
100 AURA 60502 3139 31W-4S D1
100 AURA 60510 3079 31W-3S E7
100 NpvT 60502 3139 31W-7S D6
100 WnfT 60510 3079 31W-3S E7
200 AURA 60504 3139 31W-7S D7
S Eola Rd
- AURA 60502 3201 31W-7S D1
- AURA 60585 3265 32W-11S C1
- WldT 60585 3265 32W-11S C2
500 AURA 60504 3201 32W-8S D2
2200 AURA 60503 3201 32W-11S C7
2200 WldT 60503 3201 32W-10S C6
9600 AURA 60503 3265 32W-11S C1
Eola Rd (Private)
- AURA 60502 3079 31W-3S E6
- AURA 60510 3079 31W-3S E6
- WnfT 60510 3079 31W-2S E4
Eon Ln
100 BDWD 60481 3942 30W-40S C2
100 RedT 60481 3942 30W-40S C2
Epping Pl
1700 SMBG 60194 2858 25W-10N B5
E Epson Ct
100 BMDL 60108 2969 23W-5N A1
Equestrian Cir
700 WnfT 60185 3081 28W-1S A3
700 WnfT 60190 3081 28W-1S A3
Equestrian Dr
500 WLNG 60090 2755 15W-16N A7
700 PTHT 60070 2755 15W-16N A7
W Equestrian Ln
25600 TroT 60404 3495 32W-22S D2
Equestrian Tr
15600 ODPK 60467 3345 13W-18S A7
15600 ODPK 60467 3422 14W-19S E1
15600 OrlT 60467 3345 13W-18S A7
15600 OrlT 60467 3422 14W-19S E1
Equestrian Wy
- RLKP 60030 2589 22W-30N C1
10 ElaT 60047 2644 23W-25N D5
10 HNWD 60047 2644 23W-25N D5
10 LMNT 60439 3272 15W-14S A6
Equity Dr
- SCRL 60174 3021 33W-2N A1
Era Dr
300 NHBK 60062 2756 12W-18N C3
Erb Farm Ct
1000 NPVL 60563 3141 28W-5S B2
Erb Farm Ln
900 NPVL 60563 3141 27W-5S B2
W Erhart Rd
22200 FmtT 60030 2589 22W-29N B3
22200 FmtT 60060 2589 22W-29N B3
22600 FmtT 60030 2588 23W-29N E4
22600 FmtT 60060 2588 23W-29N E4
Eric Av
200 MPPT 60056 2808 14W-13N B6
Eric Blvd
3200 PKCY 60085 2536 12W-33N A2
Eric Ct
200 BMDL 60108 2968 24W-5N D1
300 MPPT 60056 2808 14W-13N B6
500 LKZH 60047 2699 22W-22N C4
N Eric Dr
200 PLTN 60067 2752 21W-16N D7
Eric Ln
1200 LKZH 60047 2699 21W-22N C4
1500 LYVL 60048 2591 18W-29N A3
1700 LYVL 60048 2590 18W-29N E3
Eric Wy
500 BGBK 60440 3205 22W-10S B6
Erica Dr
900 FmtT 60084 2588 24W-28N B6
900 WCDA 60084 2588 24W-28N B6
Erick St
10 CLLK 60014 2640 34W-26N C3
10 NndT 60014 2640 34W-26N C3
100 CLLK 60012 2640 34W-26N C3
100 NndT 60012 2640 34W-26N C3
Ericka Dr
2200 BDVW 60155 3087 11W-2S D2
Ericksen Ln
22200 CstT 60481 3943 27W-41S D6
Erickson Ct
10 NARA 60542 3138 35W-4S C1
400 ELBN 60119 3017 43W-2N A2
18000 ODPK 60467 3423 12W-21S C7
Erickson Dr
2200 NPVL 60563 3080 29W-4S D7
Erie Av
- SPGV 60081 2355 30W-42N A5
N Erie Av
100 WHTN 60187 3023 26W-0S E7
S Erie Av
100 WHTN 60187 3023 26W-0S E7
400 MltT 60187 3023 26W-0S E7
5700 HMND 46320 3352 E7
6000 HMND 46320 3430 E1
Erie Cir
300 BMDL 60101 2969 21W-5N D1
300 BMDL 60108 2969 22W-5N D2
300 BmdT 60101 2969 21W-5N D1
Erie Ct
300 BMDL 60108 2969 22W-5N D2
700 CLSM 60188 2967 26W-3N E6
2300 NCHI 60088 2593 12W-30N B2
4000 HRPK 60133 2967 27W-5N D3
25000 CTHL 60403 3418 25W-19S B3
25000 LktT 60403 3418 25W-19S B3
Erie Dr
700 RMVL 60446 3340 24W-15S C2
Erie Ln
- LKPT 60441 3419 21W-20S E5
1900 HFET 60169 2804 25W-12N A7
1900 HFET 60169 2858 25W-12N A1
Erie St
- BDWD 60408 3942 31W-41S A4
- BLWD 60104 3029 12W-0N B3
10 CHCG 60644 3031 7W-0N B3
10 MYWD 60153 3030 10W-0N A3
10 OKPK 60302 3031 7W-0N B3
400 ELGN 60123 2853 36W-11N E5
400 ElgT 60123 2853 36W-11N E5
1000 OKPK 60302 3030 8W-0N D3
1100 RVFT 60302 3030 8W-0N D3
1100 RVFT 60305 3030 8W-0N D3
1700 ELGN 60123 2854 36W-11N A5
4600 BLWD 60104 3028 13W-0N E3
E Erie St
10 CHCG 60610 3034 0E-0N C3
10 CHCG 60611 3034 0E-0N C3
N Erie St
2400 RVGV 60171 2974 10W-3N B5
S Erie St
500 MltT 60187 3023 26W-0S E7
500 MltT 60187 3081 26W-1S E1
500 WHTN 60187 3023 26W-0S E7
500 WHTN 60187 3081 26W-1S E1
W Erie St
10 CHCG 60610 3034 0W-0N A3
10 CHCG 60611 3034 0W-0N B3
700 CHCG 60622 3034 0W-0N A3
1200 CHCG 60622 3033 2W-0N C3
1900 CHCG 60612 3033 3W-0N A3
3900 CHCG 60624 3032 4W-0N C3
4600 CHCG 60644 3032 5W-0N A3
4700 CHCG 60644 3031 6W-0N E3
5900 OKPK 60302 3031 7W-0N B3
Erika Ct
- LYWD 60411 3510 3E-23S A4
Erika Ln
- CPVL 60118 2746 37W-18N D5
Erin Ct
100 LMNT 60439 3270 19W-14S C7
3700 PRGV 60012 2641 32W-27N B1
S Erin Ct
14400 HMGN 60491 3343 16W-17S E5
Erin Dr
10 CRY 60013 2641 30W-24N E7
600 ElgT 60124 2853 37W-10N B7
S Erin Dr
13500 HMGN 60491 3343 17W-16S C3
W Erin Dr
8100 PSHL 60465 3210 10W-11S C7
W Erin Isl
26200 CNHN 60410 3672 32W-32S C7
Erin Ln
10 BRRG 60527 3146 14W-7S C5
200 NHBK 60062 2758 7W-16N A6
9200 ODPK 60462 3423 11W-18S D1
15600 ODPK 60462 3345 11W-18S E7
Erin Marie Ct
1900 AURA 60503 3201 32W-10S B6
Erins Glen Dr
1000 JLET 60431 3496 29W-22S D2
Ernest Av
10 FXLK 60020 2473 27W-37N B2
Ernest Ln
2000 JNBG 60050 2471 31W-35N E5
Ernesti Rd
12800 GfnT 60142 2691 42W-23N B3
Ernie Krueger Cir
2200 WKGN 60087 2479 13W-36N A4
S Ernie Krueger Dr
2100 WKGN 60087 2479 13W-36N A4
Ernst Ct
5200 WNSP 60558 3146 13W-5S E3
5200 WNSP 60558 3147 13W-5S A2
N Ernst Ct
900 CHCG 60611 3034 0E-1N C2
Ernst St
2400 LydT 60131 2973 12W-3N A6
2400 LydT 60164 2973 12W-3N A6
3500 FNPK 60131 2973 12W-4N A3
Eros Dr
- OMFD 60461 3507 3W-24S A5
Erskine Rd
2400 JltT 60433 3500 20W-23S B4
2400 NlxT 60433 3500 20W-23S B4
Escanaba Av
200 BNHM 60633 3351 3E-17S E4
200 CTCY 60409 3351 3E-17S E4
200 CTCY 60633 3351 3E-17S E4
17700 LNSG 60438 3429 3E-21S E6
18500 BlmT 60411 3429 3E-21S E7
S Escanaba Av
7800 CHCG 60617 3215 3E-9S E2
7800 CHCG 60649 3215 3E-9S E2
12600 CHCG 60633 3279 3E-14S E7
13100 CHCG 60633 3351 3E-15S E1
Escanaba Harbor Ct
- FKFT 60423 3504 11W-25S A7
Esch Rd
1600 TNLK 53181 2353 E3
1600 TNLK 53181 2354 A3
1900 RdlT 53181 2353 D3
Eshbach Ct
11900 ALGN 60102 2746 36W-20N D2
Eshcol Av
2100 ZION 60099 2422 10W-40N B2
Eskin Dr
1300 NfdT 60062 2756 12W-17N B5
1300 NHBK 60062 2756 12W-17N B6
Esla Ct
600 NPVL 60563 3140 29W-6S D4
Esmerelda Pl
800 ELGN 60120 2854 34W-12N E2
S Esmond St
10900 CHCG 60643 3277 2W-13S C3
Esplanade Dr
- ALGN 60102 2746 37W-19N E3
- ALGN 60118 2746 37W-19N E3
Esprit Ct
200 BMDL 60108 2968 24W-5N D1
Esquire Cir
4300 NPVL 60564 3267 28W-12S A3
4400 NPVL 60564 3266 28W-12S E3
Essel Ct E
1100 WHTN 60187 3082 23W-3S E5
Essel Ct W
1000 WHTN 60187 3082 24W-3S E5
Esselen Ct
400 CLSM 60188 2967 27W-2N D7
Essex Av
- NCHI 60064 2593 11W-31N D1
100 LslT 60540 3142 25W-6S B5
300 OSWG 60543 3200 33W-11S E7
300 OSWG 60543 3264 33W-11S E1
500 SchT 60174 2908 35W-6N B7
700 RMVL 60446 3268 23W-14S E7
700 RMVL 60446 3341 23W-14S A1
2000 NCHI 60088 2593 11W-31N D1
S Essex Av
7500 CHCG 60649 3153 3E-8S D7
7500 CHCG 60649 3215 3E-9S D3
8700 CHCG 60617 3215 3E-10S D4
Essex Cir
800 GYLK 60030 2533 19W-34N B2
Essex Ct
- DRFD 60015 2703 10W-21N E6
- GNVW 60025 2809 11W-13N D6
- NfdT 60025 2809 11W-13N D6
- SMBG 60193 2858 25W-10N A5
10 HNWD 60047 2646 20W-24N A7
10 SMBG 60194 2858 25W-10N A5
200 AURA 60504 3202 30W-8S A1
200 BGBK 60440 3268 24W-12S E3
300 BMDL 60108 2968 24W-5N C2
300 GNVA 60134 3019 36W-1N D4
300 WDDL 60191 2970 18W-5N E2
300 YKVL 60560 3261 42W-13S D5
400 SRGV 60554 3197 42W-8S D1
500 DRFD 60015 2704 10W-21N A6
700 GNEN 60137 3025 22W-0N C4
700 HRPK 60133 2858 26W-9N A7
900 MHRY 60050 2527 33W-32N E4
1100 BTVA 60510 3078 34W-2S E3
1700 SCRL 60174 2964 34W-3N D5
2000 SMWD 60107 2910 29W-9N E1
5700 HRPK 60133 2911 27W-7N D5
6100 WLBK 60527 3145 16W-6S D5
6200 WDRG 60517 3143 22W-6S B5
20400 CTHL 60403 3418 25W-19S B3
E Essex Ct
1200 RLKB 60073 2475 21W-36N D4
Essex Dr
- HFET 60192 2802 31W-12N A7
- HFET 60192 2856 31W-12N A1
- HMGN 60491 3344 15W-16S A3
- JLET 60435 3417 26W-19S D3
- LKPT 60441 3420 19W-20S D4
1000 OKTR 60181 3084 18W-1S E2
1000 YkTp 60181 3084 18W-1S E2
2500 NHBK 60062 2810 10W-15N A2
21500 LktT 60403 3417 26W-19S D3
W Essex Dr
22900 CNHN 60410 3584 29W-27S D6
Essex Ln
10 CRY 60013 2695 32W-23N B1
10 LNSH 60069 2702 14W-23N C3
10 WNVL 60555 3080 30W-2S C3
100 NLNX 60433 3500 20W-24S B5
100 NLNX 60451 3500 20W-24S B5
100 NlxT 60433 3500 20W-24S B5
200 NBRN 60010 2698 25W-23N B1
300 CLLK 60014 2639 36W-25N D6
300 LKWD 60014 2639 36W-25N D6
600 WNFD 60190 3023 27W-0N C4
N Essex Ln
2200 RLKB 60073 2475 21W-36N D4
W Essex Ln
13000 HTLY 60142 2744 42W-20N C1
Essex Pl
100 TRLK 60010 2643 26W-25N D5
200 WLMT 60091 2811 5W-13N E7
400 CLSM 60188 2967 26W-2N D7
1800 DRGV 60516 3144 20W-7S A7
W Essex Pl
900 ANHT 60004 2753 18W-16N E6

STREET Block City ZIP Map# CGS Grid

Essex Rd
10 EGVV 60007 2914 19W-8N D2
10 KLWH 60043 2812 4W-14N D4
10 WNKA 60093 2812 4W-14N D4
100 WHTN 60187 3081 27W-2S D3
100 WnfT 60187 3081 27W-2S D3
400 FRGV 60021 2696 30W-22N A4
600 GNEN 60137 3025 22W-0N C4
5500 LSLE 60532 3143 22W-6S B4
5500 LslT 60532 3143 22W-6S B4
5800 OKFT 60452 3347 7W-18S C7
6100 LslT 60517 3143 22W-6S B5
6100 WDRG 60517 3143 22W-6S B5
34300 CstT 60481 3942 30W-42S D7
34300 RedT 60408 3942 30W-42S D7
34300 RedT 60408 4031 30W-43S D1
34300 RedT 60481 3942 30W-42S D7
34300 RedT 60481 4031 30W-43S D1
36200 EsxT 60481 4031 29W-45S D7
36200 EsxT 60935 4031 29W-45S D7
Essex St
800 PTHT 60070 2808 15W-16N A1
1300 ALGN 60102 2694 34W-21N B6
10500 WSTR 60154 3087 13W-2S A3
Essex Wy
4800 RGMW 60008 2860 19W-12N C1
Essington Ct
4900 HFET 60010 2751 24W-16N B7
Essington Dr
10 RDLK 60073 2532 23W-32N A5
Essington Ln
600 BFGV 60089 2701 17W-20N B7
1000 RMVL 60446 3340 25W-15S B1
4900 HFET 60010 2751 24W-16N B7
Essington Rd
10 JLET 60431 3497 28W-23S B4
10 JLET 60435 3497 28W-23S B4
10 TroT 60431 3497 27W-23S B5
300 TroT 60435 3497 27W-23S B4
1700 JLET 60431 3417 27W-21S B7
2400 PnfT 60431 3417 27W-20S B6
2600 JLET 60435 3417 28W-20S B5
3200 PnfT 60435 3417 28W-19S B4
3600 PnfT 60544 3417 28W-19S B3
11100 BGBK 60490 3267 28W-13S B5
11100 BGBK 60585 3267 28W-13S B5
11100 PNFD 60490 3267 28W-13S B5
11100 PNFD 60585 3267 28W-13S B5
11100 WldT 60490 3267 28W-13S B5
11100 WldT 60585 3267 28W-13S B5
12400 BGBK 60490 3339 27W-14S B1
12400 WldT 60490 3339 27W-14S B1
12400 WldT 60544 3339 27W-14S B1
13000 BGBK 60544 3339 28W-15S B3
13000 BGBK 60585 3339 27W-15S B2
13000 PNFD 60544 3339 28W-15S B3
13000 PNFD 60585 3339 27W-15S B2
Esta Dr
600 PLNO 60545 3259 47W-14S D7
Estancia Ln
900 ALGN 60102 2746 37W-20N B1
Estate Cir
200 GRNE 60031 2534 16W-34N D2
1600 NPVL 60565 3204 24W-8S D2
Estate Ct
200 NHBK 60062 2756 12W-18N A3
Estate Dr
10 DRFD 60015 2756 10W-20N E2
10 GLNC 60022 2758 6W-18N D3
300 BFGV 60089 2754 17W-18N B3
Estate Ln
600 MDLN 60060 2590 19W-28N C5
1000 LKFT 60045 2649 12W-24N A7
1300 LKFT 60045 2703 13W-24N A1
1400 GNVW 60025 2809 10W-14N E5
6700 LGGV 60060 2646 19W-25N D5
W Estates Dr
1700 MPPT 60056 2861 17W-12N C1
Estelle Dr
10000 RSMT 60018 2917 12W-7N B3
Estes Av
400 SMBG 60193 2912 24W-8N D2
700 EGVV 60007 2915 16W-8N D1
700 GRNE 60031 2478 13W-35N E7
1000 LKFT 60045 2649 11W-24N D7
1900 DSPN 60018 2917 12W-8N B1
4900 LNWD 60077 2919 6W-8N E1
4900 LNWD 60712 2919 6W-8N E1
4900 SKOK 60077 2919 6W-8N D1
W Estes Av
1300 CHCG 60626 2921 2W-8N B1
1900 CHCG 60645 2921 2W-8N A1
2600 CHCG 60645 2920 3W-8N E1
4600 LNWD 60712 2920 5W-8N A1
4700 LNWD 60712 2919 5W-8N E1
6200 CHCG 60646 2919 7W-8N A1
6300 CHCG 60714 2919 8W-8N A1
6300 NLES 60714 2919 8W-8N A1
7300 CHCG 60631 2918 9W-8N C1
Estes Ct
900 SMBG 60193 2912 24W-8N D2
1100 NPVL 60540 3202 29W-8S D2
Estes St
10 WNVL 60555 3080 30W-3S B6
10 WNVL 60563 3080 30W-3S B6
300 GRNE 60031 2535 13W-34N E1
1000 GRNE 60031 2478 13W-35N E6
Esther Ct
11700 DrrT 60098 2525 40W-31N A7
Esther Dr
18000 ODPK 60467 3423 13W-21S B7
26700 LKBN 60010 2643 26W-25N C4
26700 LKBN 60084 2643 26W-25N C4
26700 TRLK 60010 2643 26W-25N C4
26700 WcnT 60010 2643 26W-25N C4
26700 WcnT 60084 2643 26W-25N C4
Esther Ln
700 CmpT 60175 2961 41W-6N E1
Esther St
10 CLLK 60014 2640 35W-25N B4
N Esther St
40300 AntT 60002 2415 26W-40N E3
Estinger Rd
4800 MTGY 60543 3263 37W-12S B3
4800 OSWG 60543 3263 37W-12S B3
Estling Ct
1200 AURA 60502 3139 31W-5S D4
Estonian Ln
- BFGV 60015 2702 14W-21N B6
- BFGV 60089 2702 14W-21N B6
14700 RVWD 60015 2702 14W-21N C6
14700 VrnT 60015 2702 14W-21N C6
Estuary Ct
1500 NPVL 60565 3203 26W-9S D3
Etchingham Dr
14400 LKPT 60441 3421 18W-19S B3
Eternity
- MTSN 60443 3505 7W-25S D7
Ethan Ln
7200 GGnT 60449 3682 9W-32S A7
7200 MonT 60449 3682 9W-32S A7
W Ethans Glen Dr
1500 PLTN 60067 2752 22W-17N A5
1700 PLTN 60067 2751 23W-17N E4
Ethel Av
5800 NndT 60014 2640 33W-26N E3
W Ethel Av
10 LMBD 60148 3026 20W-0S B6
400 YkTp 60148 3026 20W-0S A6
Ethel Ct
10400 RSMT 60018 2917 13W-8N A1
Ethel Ln
300 WDDL 60191 2971 17W-4N B2
Ethel St
10 WNFD 60190 3023 27W-1N D4
10 WnfT 60187 3023 27W-1N D4
10 WnfT 60190 3023 27W-1N D4
400 CLSM 60188 2967 27W-2N D7
400 WnfT 60185 3023 27W-1N D2
400 WynT 60185 2967 27W-2N D7
400 WynT 60185 3023 27W-2N D1
400 WynT 60188 2967 27W-2N D7
1000 ALGN 60102 2694 34W-21N C6
W Ethel St
700 PTON 60468 3860 10W-37S D4
Ethel Ter
3100 ISLK 60042 2586 29W-28N D5
Ethyl Ln
9200 TYPK 60487 3423 11W-22S E7
Eton Ct
10 SBTN 60010 2804 24W-14N C3
700 LYVL 60048 2591 15W-27N E7
1200 BFGV 60089 2754 16W-17N D5
Eton Dr
400 NBRN 60010 2698 25W-23N A1
500 NBRN 60010 2697 26W-23N E1
1700 HFET 60120 2855 31W-12N E1
1700 HFET 60192 2855 31W-12N E1
1700 HnrT 60120 2855 31W-12N E1
E Eton Dr
1300 ANHT 60004 2754 17W-17N C6
Eton Ln
1500 NPVL 60565 3204 25W-8S B2
Eton on Oxford
10 RGMW 60008 2805 22W-13N B6
Etowah Av
400 PTHT 60070 2807 16W-15N E2
Euclid Av
- GLHT 60137 3025 22W-1N B3
- GNEN 60137 3025 22W-1N B3
- MltT 60137 3025 22W-1N B3
10 OKTR 60181 3027 17W-1S B7
10 VLPK 60181 3027 17W-0S B7
10 YkTp 60181 3027 17W-0S B7
100 BMDL 60108 2969 22W-5N C2
100 GLNC 60022 2758 5W-16N E6
100 GNVA 60134 3020 34W-1N C3
100 PKRG 60068 2918 10W-8N B1
100 WNKA 60022 2758 5W-16N E6
100 WNKA 60093 2758 5W-16N E6
100 YkTp 60181 3085 17W-1S B1
200 AURA 60505 3200 36W-8S A3
200 BmdT 60137 2969 22W-2N B7
200 BmdT 60137 3025 22W-2N B1
200 BmdT 60139 3025 22W-2N B1
200 GLHT 60139 3025 22W-2N B1
200 WNKA 60093 2811 5W-15N E2
300 HIWD 60040 2704 9W-23N C1
400 GLHT 60139 2969 22W-2N B7
500 HDPK 60035 2704 9W-23N C1
1200 BRWN 60304 3031 8W-1S A7
1200 BRWN 60402 3031 8W-1S A7
1200 OKPK 60304 3031 8W-1S A7
1400 CHHT 60411 3508 1W-25S A7
1500 CHHT 60411 3596 1W-26S A2
2500 SCHT 60411 3596 1W-26S A2
3200 BlmT 60411 3596 1W-27S A4
3200 BlmT 60475 3596 1W-27S A4
3200 BRWN 60402 3089 8W-3S A5
3200 STGR 60411 3596 1W-27S A4
3200 STGR 60475 3596 1W-27S A4
3800 SKNY 60402 3089 8W-3S A6
6300 HMND 46324 3430 E2
7900 MNSR 46321 3430 E6
E Euclid Av
- MPPT 60056 2807 15W-14N E4
10 ANHT 60004 2807 16W-14N D4
10 MPPT 60056 2808 14W-14N C4
10 PTHT 60056 2808 15W-14N A4
10 PTHT 60070 2808 15W-14N A4
2000 WhlT 60025 2808 13W-14N E4
2000 WhlT 60056 2808 13W-14N E4
2400 ANHT 60056 2807 16W-14N D4
N Euclid Av
10 VLPK 60181 3027 17W-1N B3
100 OKPK 60301 3031 8W-0N A4
100 OKPK 60302 3031 8W-0N A3
S Euclid Av
10 VLPK 60181 3027 17W-0N B3
100 OKPK 60302 3031 8W-0N A5
500 EMHT 60126 3027 16W-0S E6
500 OKPK 60304 3031 8W-0S A5
600 EMHT 60126 3028 15W-0S A7
600 YkTp 60126 3028 15W-0S A7
1000 YkTp 60126 3027 15W-0S E6
1100 BRWN 60304 3031 8W-0S A7
1100 BRWN 60402 3031 8W-0S A7
6700 CHCG 60649 3153 2E-7S C6
7600 CHCG 60649 3215 2E-9S C2
7800 CHCG 60617 3215 2E-9S C2
W Euclid Av
- ANHT 60056 2807 15W-14N E4
- MPPT 60056 2807 15W-14N E4
- MPPT 60056 2808 15W-14N A4
- PTHT 60056 2808 15W-14N A4
- PTHT 60070 2808 15W-14N A4
10 ANHT 60004 2807 18W-14N A4
10 PLTN 60008 2805 21W-14N E4
10 PLTN 60067 2805 21W-14N E4
10 RGMW 60008 2805 21W-14N E4
10 RGMW 60067 2805 21W-14N E4
500 ANHT 60004 2806 18W-14N E4
700 ANHT 60005 2806 18W-14N E4
1100 IVNS 60067 2805 22W-14N A4
1600 ANHT 60008 2806 18W-14N D4
1600 RGMW 60005 2806 18W-14N D4
1600 RGMW 60008 2806 18W-14N D4
Euclid Av N
500 OKPK 60302 3031 8W-1N A3
800 OKPK 60302 3030 8W-1N E2
1200 CHCG 60302 3030 8W-1N E1
1200 CHCG 60707 3030 8W-1N E1
Euclid Ct
200 BMDL 60108 2969 22W-5N C2
500 HDPK 60035 2704 9W-23N C1
700 HIWD 60040 2704 9W-23N C1
1100 RNPK 60471 3594 4W-26S D2
1200 BFGV 60089 2701 16W-21N C6
Euclid Dr
3000 SCHT 60411 3596 1W-27S A4
W Euclid Dr
5400 MchT 60050 2527 34W-34N C1
Euclid Ln
1000 RNPK 60471 3594 4W-26S D2
S Euclid Pkwy
7400 CHCG 60649 3153 2E-8S C7
Euclid St
800 CTCY 60409 3352 3E-17S A6
Euclid Park Pl
2700 EVTN 60201 2813 2W-13N B7
N Eugene Av
20500 BFGV 60069 2754 16W-20N E1
20500 BFGV 60089 2754 16W-20N E1
20500 VrnT 60069 2754 16W-20N E1
20600 BFGV 60089 2701 16W-20N E7
20600 VrnT 60069 2701 16W-20N E7
Eugene Ct
400 CLLK 60014 2640 35W-25N A5
Eugene Ln
3100 AURA 60504 3201 31W-8S D2
Eugene Siegel Ct
16300 LktT 60403 3417 26W-19S E3
21100 LktT 60403 3418 26W-19S A3
Eugenia Dr
400 LslT 60540 3142 24W-5S C3
W Eugenia St
400 LMBD 60148 3026 20W-0N A4
W Eugenie St
100 CHCG 60614 2978 0W-2N A7
W Eugenie St SR-64
100 CHCG 60614 2978 0W-2N B7
Eula St
100 WMTN 60481 3853 27W-37S C5
100 WmTp 60481 3853 27W-37S C5
Eunice Av
800 JLET 60433 3587 22W-26S C2
800 JltT 60433 3587 22W-26S C2
E Eureka Av
10 LMNT 60439 3270 19W-14S D6
W Eureka Av
10 LMNT 60439 3270 19W-14S C6
E Eureka St
100 BDWD 60408 3942 31W-41S A6
W Eureka St
500 BDWD 60408 3941 32W-41S E6
Eustace St
1500 ThtT 60438 3429 1E-21S C7
Eva Av
3400 PKCY 60085 2536 13W-33N A2
W Eva Ln
1000 MPPT 60056 2861 16W-11N D3
Eva Ter
10 LKBF 60044 2593 11W-28N D5
Evan Ct
1600 RMVL 60446 3339 27W-18S D7
1600 RMVL 60446 3417 27W-18S D1
Evan Ln
800 LKVL 60046 2417 22W-39N C5
W Evan Ter
7800 FftT 60423 3504 9W-23S D4
Evans Av
10 NCHI 60088 2537 10W-31N A7
10 WHTN 60187 3024 26W-0S A6
100 AURA 60505 3200 36W-8S A2
400 MltT 60187 3024 26W-0N A4
14200 DLTN 60419 3351 0E-16S A3
15900 SHLD 60473 3351 0E-18S A7
15900 SHLD 60473 3429 0E-18S A1
16200 SHLD 60473 3428 0E-19S E1
S Evans Av
- CHCG 60628 3278 0E-15S E7
4300 CHCG 60653 3092 0E-4S E7
4600 CHCG 60615 3092 0E-4S E7
4700 CHCG 60615 3152 0E-5S E1
6100 CHCG 60637 3152 0E-7S E5
7200 CHCG 60619 3152 0E-8S E7
7500 CHCG 60619 3214 0E-9S E2
13000 CHCG 60827 3278 0E-15S E7
13400 CHCG 60827 3350 0E-15S E1
Evans Ct
300 SMWD 60107 2911 28W-9N A1
700 DLTN 60419 3351 0E-17S A5
1400 EGVV 60007 2914 21W-8N A3
16500 SHLD 60473 3428 0E-19S E2
17100 SHLD 60473 3429 0E-20S A3
Evans Dr
17000 SHLD 60473 3429 0E-20S A3
Evans Pl
7200 DRN 60561 3207 16W-8S D1
Evans Rd
1000 FSMR 60422 3507 2W-22S C2
W Evans St
200 PNFD 60544 3338 29W-17S C6
N Evanslawn Av
1700 AURA 60506 3137 37W-7S C6
S Evanslawn Av
10 AURA 60506 3137 37W-7S C7
200 AURA 60506 3199 37W-7S C1
Evanston Av
400 LKBF 60044 2594 10W-28N A6
N Evanston Av
10 ANHT 60004 2807 16W-14N D5
200 MPPT 60056 2807 16W-13N D6
S Evanston Av
10 ANHT 60004 2807 16W-13N D5
Evanston St
600 HFET 60169 2859 23W-11N A3
900 HFET 60195 2859 23W-11N A3
900 SMBG 60195 2859 23W-11N A3
Evanston Ter
900 LKZH 60047 2698 24W-23N C3
Evanswood Ln
600 SchT 60175 2963 38W-4N A4
Eveline St
38900 WDWH 60083 2420 15W-38N B6
Evelyn Rd
300 RVSD 60546 3088 9W-2S D4
Evelyn St
10 WNFD 60190 3023 27W-0S D6
10 WnfT 60190 3023 27W-0S D6
500 MltT 60190 3023 27W-0S D6
Evendale Rd
10400 HTLY 60142 2692 39W-21N C6
Evenhouse Av
- RSMT 60018 2917 11W-7N D4
Evening Lake Dr
400 CmpT 60124 2905 42W-7N D6
400 CmpT 60175 2905 42W-7N D6
Evening Song Ct
1900 SMBG 60194 2858 26W-11N A3
Evening Star Ct
300 BGBK 60440 3269 23W-12S A2
600 NARA 60542 3137 38W-4S A2
Evening Star Ln
1700 AURA 60504 3201 33W-9S A3
Evercrest Ct
2600 NPVL 60564 3202 30W-10S B6
Everdon Dr
16100 TYPK 60477 3424 9W-19S D2
W Everell Av
7200 CHCG 60631 2918 9W-7N D3
Everest Rd
10 MltT 60148 3084 21W-2S A4
100 MltT 60148 3083 21W-2S E4
Everett Av
400 CLLK 60014 2639 36W-25N E6
1200 DSPN 60018 2862 13W-9N E6
1400 DSPN 60018 2863 12W-9N A6
17000 SHLD 60473 3429 1E-20S B4
N Everett Av
35300 GrtT 60041 2474 25W-35N A6
S Everett Av
5400 CHCG 60615 3153 2E-5S B2
5400 CHCG 60637 3153 2E-6S B3
Everett Ct
100 WNVL 60555 3080 29W-2S C3
N Everett Dr
300 PLTN 60074 2753 19W-16N C7
Everett Ln
19000 MKNA 60448 3503 12W-24S D5
Everett Pl
- PKCY 60085 2535 14W-33N D3
Everett Rd
1800 BHPK 60087 2479 11W-38N D1
1800 WKGN 60087 2479 11W-38N D1
W Everett Rd
100 LKFT 60045 2649 11W-24N E7
1800 LKFT 60045 2648 13W-24N E6
1800 VrnT 60045 2648 13W-24N E6
2100 MTWA 60045 2648 13W-24N E6
3200 MTWA 60048 2648 14W-24N C6
3400 VrnT 60048 2648 14W-24N C6
W Everett Rd CO-A40
1000 LKFT 60045 2649 12W-24N A6
1800 LKFT 60045 2648 13W-24N E6
1800 VrnT 60045 2648 13W-24N E6
2100 MTWA 60045 2648 13W-24N E6
3200 MTWA 60048 2648 14W-24N C6
3400 VrnT 60048 2648 14W-24N C6
Everett St
2800 BLID 60406 3277 3W-15S A7
Everette Av
400 RMVL 60446 3340 24W-15S E2
Everett School Rd
1100 LKFT 60045 2649 12W-24N B7
Everglade Av
2700 WDRG 60517 3205 22W-9S C3
3200 LslT 60517 3205 22W-9S C3
3200 LslT 60565 3205 22W-9S C3
3200 WDRG 60565 3205 22W-9S C3
Everglades Rd
11700 HTLY 60142 2745 39W-20N B1
Evergreen Av
- BHPK 60087 2421 12W-39N C6
- BHPK 60087 2479 12W-37N C2
- BHPK 60099 2421 12W-39N C5
- CHCG 60613 2921 1W-5N D7
- CHCG 60613 2977 1W-5N D1
- WkgT 60087 2479 12W-37N C2
100 CteT 60475 3596 1W-28S A7
200 MNSR 46321 3430 C7
400 GLHT 60137 3025 23W-1N A2
400 GLHT 60139 3025 23W-1N A2
400 MltT 60137 3025 23W-1N A2
400 MltT 60139 3025 23W-1N A2
700 BmdT 60137 3025 23W-1N A2
700 BmdT 60139 3025 23W-1N A2
900 GNEN 60137 3025 23W-1N A3
1100 NPVL 60540 3141 28W-7S A6
1300 DSPN 60016 2862 13W-11N E3
1300 DSPN 60016 2863 13W-11N A3
1600 HRPK 60133 2911 27W-8N D2
2100 AlqT 60021 2695 31W-22N D4
42500 AntT 60002 2356 26W-43N D5
E Evergreen Av
100 DSPN 60016 2862 14W-11N C3
200 MPPT 60056 2808 15W-12N B7
900 DSPN 60016 2808 15W-12N B7
900 MPPT 60016 2808 15W-12N B7
N Evergreen Av
10 ADSN 60101 2970 19W-3N D5
100 ANHT 60005 2807 17W-14N A5
100 EMHT 60126 3027 16W-1N E2
200 WKGN 60085 2536 12W-33N C1
500 EMHT 60126 2971 16W-2N E7
1900 ANHT 60004 2807 17W-16N A1
2300 ANHT 60004 2754 17W-16N A7
2700 WKGN 60087 2479 12W-37N C3
37800 BHPK 60087 2479 12W-37N C1
39000 BHPK 60087 2421 12W-38N C6
S Evergreen Av
10 ADSN 60101 2970 19W-3N D6
10 ANHT 60005 2807 17W-13N A6
600 NCHI 60064 2536 12W-33N C4
600 WKGN 60064 2536 12W-33N C4
600 WKGN 60085 2536 12W-33N C4
1300 ANHT 60005 2861 18W-12N A1
W Evergreen Av
- MPPT 60056 2808 14W-13N B5
200 MPPT 60056 2807 16W-12N E7
400 CHCG 60610 3034 0W-1N A1
800 CHCG 60610 3033 1W-1N E1
1800 CHCG 60622 3033 2W-1N B1
2700 CHCG 60622 3032 5W-1N A1
3200 CHCG 60651 3032 4W-1N D1
6800 PSHT 60463 3275 8W-15S A7
Evergreen Cir
- BmnT 60426 3426 5W-19S B1
- GLHT 60137 3025 23W-1N A2
- MltT 60137 3025 23W-1N A2
- MltT 60139 3025 23W-1N A2
10 EGVV 60007 2861 18W-10N A5
200 GLBT 60136 2799 38W-15N B4
300 GLHT 60139 3025 23W-1N A2
1000 MTSN 60443 3506 4W-25S E7
1000 OMFD 60461 3506 4W-25S E7
2300 MHRY 60050 2528 32W-34N A1
2500 MchT 60050 2528 32W-34N A1
Evergreen Ct
10 DRFD 60015 2757 10W-18N A3
10 OSWG 60543 3263 37W-12S C3
10 PTBR 60010 2642 29W-26N D3
200 RLKB 60073 2474 23W-36N E5
200 RLKB 60073 2475 22W-35N A5
300 LYVL 60048 2591 16W-27N D7
300 SMBG 60193 2858 23W-10N E5
500 WKGN 60085 2479 12W-33N C7
600 ALGN 60102 2694 34W-20N C7
700 RMVL 60446 3340 24W-16S C4
1000 MDLN 60060 2590 20W-28N B5
1300 GNVW 60025 2811 8W-13N A5
1500 DRN 60561 3207 18W-9S A3
1700 LNHT 60046 2417 21W-39N E6
1700 LNHT 60046 2418 20W-39N A5
8300 FXLK 60020 2415 28W-39N A5
8300 FXLK 60081 2415 28W-39N A5
W Evergreen Ct
700 PLTN 60067 2805 21W-15N C3
Evergreen Dr
- BmnT 60426 3426 5W-19S B1
- VLPK 60181 3027 18W-0S A6
10 LMNT 60439 3270 20W-14S C6
10 SMWD 60107 2856 29W-9N D7
100 CmpT 60175 2962 41W-6N A1
100 FKFT 60423 3591 11W-26S E2
200 BTVA 60510 3078 36W-1S A2
200 INCK 60061 2647 17W-24N B7
200 VNHL 60061 2647 17W-24N B7
300 AURA 60506 3137 36W-5S E3
300 AURA 60542 3137 36W-5S E3
300 BGBK 60440 3269 22W-12S C2
300 NARA 60506 3137 36W-5S E3
300 NARA 60542 3137 36W-5S E3
1000 CLSM 60188 2967 27W-3N C6
1000 LKFT 60045 2649 12W-24N C7
1400 PLTN 60074 2753 19W-17N C5
3000 PnfT 60435 3417 27W-19S B4
3100 JLET 60431 3417 27W-19S B4
3100 JLET 60435 3417 27W-19S B4
4200 LslT 60532 3082 23W-4S E7
7300 ODPK 60462 3346 9W-18S E6
8800 GwdT 60097 2469 38W-35N A6
16300 TYPK 60477 3424 10W-19S C2
E Evergreen Dr
1200 PLTN 60074 2753 19W-17N C5
N Evergreen Dr
33400 WrnT 60030 2534 18W-33N A3
S Evergreen Dr
16300 HMGN 60491 3421 17W-19S C2
W Evergreen Dr
8100 FftT 60423 3504 10W-24S C4
Evergreen Ln
10 CPVL 60110 2748 32W-18N C5
100 NtrT 60093 2812 5W-15N A3
100 TNLK 53181 2354 D1
100 WNKA 60093 2812 5W-15N A3
200 BMDL 60108 2969 22W-4N C3
200 GLBT 60136 2799 38W-15N A4
500 MNSR 46321 3430 D7
600 HFET 60169 2858 24W-12N D1
700 BRLT 60103 2910 29W-6N D6
700 SMBG 60169 2858 24W-12N D1
700 SMBG 60195 2858 24W-12N D1
700 SRGV 60554 3135 41W-5S E2
1100 YKVL 60560 3260 44W-14S D7
1200 ELGN 60123 2907 36W-8N E2
1200 ELGN 60123 2908 36W-8N A2
1200 PGGV 60140 2797 42W-15N D4
1500 DRN 60561 3207 18W-9S A4
1700 PKRG 60068 2863 11W-10N D4
2000 RLKB 60073 2474 23W-35N E5
2400 WDRG 60517 3205 21W-8S E2
2800 AURA 60502 3079 32W-3S C7
4000 NfdT 60062 2756 12W-16N B7
11600 HTLY 60142 2744 42W-20N B1
S Evergreen Ln
26100 CNHN 60410 3672 32W-31S C7
W Evergreen Ln
300 EMHT 60126 2971 16W-3N D5
26300 CNHN 60410 3672 32W-32S C7
Evergreen Pkwy
100 CLLK 60014 2640 35W-26N A3
Evergreen Pl
10 LMNT 60439 3270 20W-14S C6
600 BFGV 60089 2754 17W-18N B3
Evergreen Rd
1200 HMWD 60430 3428 1W-22S A7
1300 HMWD 60430 3427 1W-22S E7
Evergreen St
10 EGVV 60007 2861 18W-10N A6
10 LKZH 60047 2698 23W-22N E4
100 OSWG 60543 3263 37W-12S D3
200 BNVL 60106 2972 15W-4N B2
1000 MDLN 60060 2590 20W-28N B5
1500 HHLL 60051 2586 30W-29N A4
1500 SCRL 60174 3019 36W-2N E1
34100 WslT 60481 3943 27W-41S E6
E Evergreen St
400 WHTN 60187 3024 24W-0S D7
1600 WHTN 60187 3025 23W-0S A7
1800 GNEN 60137 3025 23W-0S A7
1800 GNEN 60187 3025 23W-0S A7
W Evergreen St
200 WHTN 60187 3024 24W-0S C7
Evergreen Ter
1400 GNVW 60025 2811 8W-14N A5
16800 HMGN 60491 3422 15W-20S C4
N Evergreen Ter
1900 ANHT 60004 2807 16W-16N C1
Evergreen Wy
800 DRFD 60015 2704 10W-21N B7
800 HDPK 60015 2704 10W-21N B7
800 HDPK 60035 2704 10W-21N B7
Everington Ct
300 BGBK 60440 3205 22W-9S C4
Evernia Ct
800 GNVA 60134 3020 35W-1N B2
Evers Av
1200 HLSD 60162 3028 13W-1S E7
1200 WSTR 60154 3028 13W-1S E7
1200 WSTR 60154 3086 13W-1S E1
1200 WSTR 60162 3028 13W-1S E7
Evers St
14500 DLTN 60419 3350 0E-16S E4
15300 SHLD 60473 3350 0E-17S E6
Evert Ct
2100 NHBK 60062 2757 10W-16N A7
Everts Pl
200 HIWD 60040 2704 9W-23N D2
Everwood Ct
1200 AURA 60505 3139 33W-5S A4
Everwood Ln
1200 AraT 60502 3139 33W-5S A4
1200 AURA 60502 3139 33W-5S A4
1200 AURA 60505 3139 33W-5S A4
Everwood Rd
- LslT 60540 3204 24W-8S C1
Evolution Av
200 HIWD 60040 2704 9W-23N C3

Chicago 7-County Street Index

STREET Block	City	ZIP	Map#	CGS	Grid
Evon St					
13100	PNFD	60585	3338	30W-15S	C2
Ewell Av					
-	BNHM	60633	3352	3E-16S	A3
Ewell Ct					
200	BRLT	60103	2911	28W-7N	A6
Ewing Av					
2000	EVTN	60201	2866	4W-12N	D1
2600	EVTN	60201	2812	4W-13N	D7
2700	EVTN	60091	2812	4W-13N	D7
2700	WLMT	60091	2812	4W-13N	D7
2700	WLMT	60201	2812	4W-13N	D7
8800	SKOK	60076	2866	4W-11N	D3
8800	SKOK	60203	2866	4W-11N	D3
S Ewing Av					
9200	CHCG	60617	3216	4E-10S	B5
10300	CHCG	60617	3280	4E-13S	B5
11800	CHCG	60633	3280	4E-13S	B5
S Ewing Av US-12					
9500	CHCG	60617	3216	4E-10S	B5
S Ewing Av US-20					
9500	CHCG	60617	3216	4E-10S	B5
S Ewing Av US-41					
9200	CHCG	60617	3216	4E-10S	B5
E Ewing St					
800	JLET	60432	3499	22W-22S	C2
N Ewing St					
10	NPVL	60540	3141	27W-6S	C5
S Ewing St					
10	NPVL	60540	3141	27W-6S	C5
W Ewing St					
23600	PNFD	60586	3416	29W-19S	D3
23600	PnfT	60586	3416	29W-19S	D3
Excalibur Ct					
2000	LYWD	60411	3509	2E-24S	D5
Exchance Av					
-	BNHM	60633	3352	3E-16S	A3
Exchange Av					
200	BNHM	60633	3351	3E-17S	E5
200	CTCY	60409	3351	3E-17S	E6
200	CTCY	60633	3351	3E-17S	E5
3500	AURA	60504	3139	31W-7S	E6
3500	AURA	60504	3140	31W-7S	A6
9000	FNPK	60131	2973	11W-3N	D4
9000	RVGV	60131	2973	11W-3N	D4
9000	RVGV	60171	2973	11W-3N	D4
18200	LNSG	60438	3429	3E-21S	E7
S Exchange Av					
7100	CHCG	60649	3153	3E-8S	D7
7900	CHCG	60617	3215	3E-9S	E2
7900	CHCG	60649	3215	3E-9S	E2
12700	CHCG	60633	3279	3E-14S	E7
13100	CHCG	60633	3351	3E-15S	E1
W Exchange Av					
800	CHCG	60609	3092	0W-4S	A6
900	CHCG	60609	3091	1W-4S	E6
Exchange Blvd					
10	GLHT	60139	2968	23W-3N	E5
100	GLHT	60139	2969	23W-3N	A5
Exchange Ct					
500	AURA	60504	3140	30W-7S	A6
500	WLNG	60090	2755	14W-17N	B5
Exchange Dr					
200	CLLK	60014	2640	34W-25N	C4
E Exchange St					
10	CRTE	60417	3685	0E-29S	E2
10	CteT	60417	3685	0E-29S	E2
300	CteT	60417	3686	2E-30S	C2
500	CRTE	60417	3686	1E-29S	B2
2900	CteT	60417	3687	3E-30S	B3
3200	HnrT	46311	3687	4E-30S	C3
3200	SjnT	46311	3687	4E-30S	C3
W Exchange St					
10	CRTE	60417	3685	1W-29S	A2
10	CteT	60417	3685	0W-29S	D2
400	CteT	60417	3684	2W-29S	D2
800	CRTE	60417	3684	2W-29S	D2
2100	UYPK	60417	3684	2W-29S	D2
2200	UYPK	60466	3684	2W-29S	D2
Excy Dr					
300	AlqT	60021	2696	29W-23N	D2
300	FRGV	60021	2696	29W-23N	D2
Executive Cir					
1500	GNVW	60025	2809	10W-14N	E5
Executive Ct					
-	HFET	60010	2803	26W-13N	E5
-	HFET	60192	2803	26W-13N	E5
10	SBTN	60010	2803	26W-13N	E5
1000	WTMT	60559	3085	16W-3S	D6
W Executive Ct					
7900	CHCG	60634	2974	10W-5N	B1
7900	NRDG	60706	2974	10W-5N	B1
Executive Dr					
10	AURA	60504	3140	30W-7S	B7
10	AURA	60504	3202	30W-7S	B1
10	HNWD	60047	2645	22W-24N	C6
10	PSHL	60465	3274	9W-13S	D3
300	CLSM	60188	3024	24W-1N	C3
500	DGvT	60527	3208	16W-8S	A2
500	WLBK	60527	3208	16W-8S	A2
600	WLBK	60527	3207	16W-8S	E2
1500	DndT	60118	2800	35W-14N	D6
1500	ELGN	60118	2800	35W-14N	D6
1500	ELGN	60123	2800	35W-14N	D6
3000	MngT	60152	2578	49W-28N	D5
3200	JLET	60431	3497	28W-22S	B2
3200	JLET	60435	3497	28W-22S	B2
W Executive Dr					
2100	ADSN	60101	2969	21W-3N	E5
Executive Ln					
1400	GNVW	60025	2809	10W-14N	E5
Executive Pl					
1200	GNVA	60134	3020	33W-1N	E3
Executive Wy					
1000	DSPN	60018	2862	13W-10N	E6
Executive Wy Dr					
-	VNHL	60061	2647	16W-25N	E5
Exeter Ct					
-	AURA	60503	3201	31W-10S	D6
10	LNSH	60069	2701	15W-23N	E3
10	NPVL	60565	3204	26W-9S	A4
100	ROSL	60172	2912	25W-7N	C5
900	SMBG	60193	2912	23W-9N	E1
1200	WHTN	60187	3082	23W-1S	E2
1300	WLNG	60090	2754	16W-18N	D2
1400	HFET	60010	2751	24W-16N	B7
2900	WDND	60118	2800	36W-16N	A2
13900	ODPK	60467	3344	14W-16S	E3
Exeter Dr					
11200	ODPK	60467	3344	14W-16S	E4
Exeter Ln					
-	NfdT	60062	2756	12W-18N	A2
200	SRGV	60554	3135	41W-6S	D5
1400	SEGN	60177	2908	36W-8N	A3
4300	NHBK	60062	2756	12W-18N	A2

STREET Block	City	ZIP	Map#	CGS	Grid
Exeter Pl					
400	LKFT	60045	2649	12W-26N	B3
500	VNHL	60061	2647	16W-25N	C4
Exeter Rd					
10	MNSR	46321	3510		C4
W Exeter Rd					
20500	KLDR	60047	2700	20W-21N	A6
20600	KLDR	60047	2699	20W-21N	E6
Exeter on Oxford					
10	RGMW	60008	2805	22W-13N	B6
Exhibition Pl					
300	LktT	60441	3419	23W-21S	B7
Exit Rd					
-	ELGN	60123	2801	33W-13N	A7
Exmoor Av					
-	GNEN	60137	3083	22W-1S	C1
10	GNEN	60137	3025	22W-0S	C7
2200	HDPK	60035	2704	9W-22N	D3
N Exmoor Av					
500	BRTN	60010	2750	26W-20N	E1
700	BRTN	60010	2697	26W-20N	E7
700	CbaT	60010	2697	26W-20N	E7
Exmoor Ct					
10	HIWD	60040	2704	9W-23N	D3
100	DRFD	60015	2757	10W-20N	A2
500	CLLK	60014	2639	36W-24N	D6
2000	NPVL	60565	3204	25W-9S	B4
Exmoor Dr					
300	SMWD	60107	2857	28W-11N	A4
Exmoor Ln					
10	LNSH	60069	2702	13W-22N	D5
Exmoor Rd					
500	EGVV	60007	2914	19W-8N	C2
500	KLWH	60043	2812	4W-14N	C4
600	WNKA	60093	2812	4W-14N	C4
700	OMFD	60461	3506	4W-25S	D6
Exmoor Ter					
500	CLLK	60014	2639	36W-24N	D6
Exmoor Oaks Dr					
700	HDPK	60035	2704	9W-22N	D4
Exmore Dr					
1400	SMBG	60194	2858	25W-10N	B5
Exner Ct					
7300	DRN	60561	3207	18W-8S	A1
W Exner Ct					
800	PLTN	60067	2805	22W-15N	C3
Exner Rd					
6900	DRN	60561	3144	18W-8S	E7
6900	DRN	60561	3145	18W-7S	A7
7100	DRN	60561	3206	18W-8S	E1
7100	DRN	60561	3207	18W-8S	A1
7400	DRGV	60516	3207	18W-8S	A1
7400	DRN	60516	3207	18W-8S	A1
Exposition Av					
1400	AURA	60506	3137	37W-5S	D3
Express Center Dr					
-	CHCG	60666	2917	12W-5N	A7
-	CHCG	60666	2973	13W-5N	A1
-	SRPK	60176	2973	13W-5N	A1
Expressway Dr					
700	ITSC	60143	2914	20W-7N	B5
Exter Ct					
-	LktT	60441	3419	23W-21S	B7
Exton St					
7500	DRN	60561	3206	19W-8S	E2
N Ext To Barns					
38700	MltT	60187	3082	24W-3S	C6
Eynsford Dr					
8200	ODPK	60462	3346	10W-17S	B4
Eyre Cir					
15100	PNFD	60544	3338	30W-18S	B7
15100	PNFD	60544	3416	30W-18S	B1
Ezekiel Av					
1900	ZION	60099	2422	10W-41N	A2
Ezekiel Pl					
3200	ZION	60099	2422	10W-39N	A5
Ezra Av					
1900	ZION	60099	2422	10W-40N	A2

F

STREET Block	City	ZIP	Map#	CGS	Grid
F Ct					
10000	MKNA	60448	3503	12W-23S	C4
F St					
-	HDPK	60037	2704	8W-23N	D2
200	NCHI	60088	2594	10W-30N	A2
W F St					
-	MYWD	60153	3088	10W-1S	A1
-	PvsT	60141	3088	10W-1S	A1
-	PvsT	60153	3088	10W-1S	A1
Fabish Ct					
10	BFGV	60089	2701	16W-21N	D7
2400	SMBG	60193	2857	26W-10N	E6
E Fabish Dr					
10	BFGV	60089	2701	16W-21N	D7
W Fabish Dr					
10	BFGV	60089	2701	16W-20N	D7
Fabius St					
-	CLLK	60098	2638	40W-26N	B2
Fabyan Pkwy					
10	BbyT	60134	3018	39W-0S	D7
10	BTVA	60134	3019	37W-0S	C6
10	BTVA	60510	3019	37W-0S	C6
10	GnvT	60134	3018	38W-0S	E7
10	GnvT	60134	3019	38W-0S	A6
100	BbyT	60119	3076	40W-1S	C1
100	BbyT	60510	3076	40W-1S	C2
100	GNVA	60134	3019	37W-0S	D6
100	GnvT	60510	3019	37W-0S	C6
300	BbyT	60119	3018	39W-0S	D7
600	WCHI	60185	3021	31W-0N	E6
700	BTVA	60510	3021	32W-0N	B6
700	GnvT	60510	3021	32W-0N	B6
Fabyan Pkwy CO-8					
10	BbyT	60134	3018	39W-0S	D7
10	BTVA	60134	3019	37W-0S	C6
10	BTVA	60510	3019	37W-0S	C6
10	GnvT	60134	3018	38W-0S	E7
10	GnvT	60134	3019	38W-0S	A6
100	BbyT	60119	3076	40W-1S	C1
100	BbyT	60510	3076	40W-1S	C2
100	GNVA	60134	3019	37W-0S	D6
100	GnvT	60510	3019	37W-0S	C6
300	BbyT	60119	3018	39W-0S	D7
Fabyan Pkwy CO-21					
600	WCHI	60185	3021	31W-0N	E6
700	BTVA	60510	3021	32W-0N	B6
700	GnvT	60510	3021	32W-0N	B6
E Fabyan Pkwy					
-	BTVA	60134	3020	35W-0S	B6
10	BTVA	60510	3020	34W-0S	D6
10	GNVA	60134	3020	35W-0S	C6
10	GNVA	60510	3020	35W-0S	C6
100	BTVA	60510	3021	33W-0S	A6
100	GnvT	60134	3021	33W-0S	A6
100	GnvT	60510	3021	33W-0S	A6

STREET Block	City	ZIP	Map#	CGS	Grid
E Fabyan Pkwy					
300	GnvT	60510	3020	34W-0S	C6
1100	GnvT	60134	3020	34W-0S	D6
1800	WCHI	60185	3021	33W-0S	A6
E Fabyan Pkwy CO-8					
-	BTVA	60134	3020	35W-0S	B6
10	BTVA	60510	3020	34W-0S	D6
10	GNVA	60134	3020	35W-0S	C6
10	GNVA	60510	3020	35W-0S	C6
300	GnvT	60510	3020	34W-0S	C6
1100	GnvT	60134	3020	34W-0S	D6
1400	BTVA	60510	3021	33W-0S	A6
1400	GnvT	60134	3021	33W-0S	A6
1400	GnvT	60510	3021	33W-0S	A6
1800	WCHI	60185	3021	33W-0S	A6
W Fabyan Pkwy					
-	GnvT	60510	3019	36W-0S	D6
10	BTVA	60134	3020	35W-0S	A7
10	BTVA	60134	3020	36W-0S	A7
10	GNVA	60134	3020	36W-0S	A7
10	GnvT	60134	3020	36W-0S	A7
800	GnvT	60510	3020	36W-0S	A7
1000	BTVA	60134	3019	36W-0S	D6
1000	BTVA	60510	3019	36W-0S	D6
1000	GNVA	60134	3019	36W-0S	D6
1000	GnvT	60134	3019	36W-0S	D6
W Fabyan Pkwy CO-8					
-	GnvT	60510	3019	36W-0S	D6
10	BTVA	60134	3020	35W-0S	A7
10	BTVA	60134	3020	36W-0S	A7
10	GNVA	60134	3020	36W-0S	A7
10	GnvT	60134	3020	36W-0S	A7
800	GnvT	60510	3020	36W-0S	A7
1000	BTVA	60134	3019	36W-0S	D6
1000	BTVA	60510	3019	36W-0S	D6
1000	GNVA	60134	3019	36W-0S	D6
1000	GnvT	60134	3019	36W-0S	D6
Factory Rd					
6100	CLLK	60014	2640	35W-24N	B6
W Factory Rd					
10	ADSN	60101	2970	19W-2N	D7
500	AddT	60101	2970	19W-2N	C7
Factory St					
-	WCHI	60185	3022	30W-0N	C6
-	WnfT	60185	3022	30W-0N	C6
Factory Shops Blvd					
11800	HTLY	60142	2745	41W-17N	A6
11800	RtdT	60142	2745	41W-18N	A6
Faculty Cir					
10	LKFT	60045	2649	12W-26N	A4
Faculty Ln					
100	RMVL	60441	3341	23W-18S	A7
Fagan Ct					
1400	BTVA	60510	3077	36W-2S	E4
Fagan Rd					
1100	BTVA	60510	3077	36W-2S	E3
Fagan St					
100	DYR	46311	3598		D2
Fago Av					
-	BtnT	60099	2362	11W-43N	D5
300	WPHR	60096	2362	11W-43N	D5
300	WPHR	60099	2362	11W-43N	D5
N Fago Av					
42000	BtnT	60099	2362	11W-42N	D7
42000	ZION	60099	2362	11W-42N	D7
42200	WPHR	60096	2362	11W-42N	D7
42200	WPHR	60099	2362	11W-42N	D7
S Fair Av					
200	EMHT	60126	3028	15W-1N	B3
Fair Ln					
800	NHBK	60062	2757	10W-17N	A4
W Fair Ln					
15300	LbvT	60048	2592	15W-30N	A2
Fair St					
200	WDSK	60098	2581	41W-30N	E1
Fair Wy					
800	LbvT	60048	2592	15W-29N	B3
Fairbank Ct					
500	WCHI	60185	3022	30W-0N	B5
Fairbank Rd					
100	RVSD	60546	3088	9W-3S	C6
Fairbank St					
10	ADSN	60101	2970	20W-3N	B6
Fairbanks Av					
200	JltT	60432	3499	22W-23S	D4
300	JLET	60432	3499	22W-23S	D4
W Fairbanks Av					
10600	BHPK	60099	2422	10W-38N	A6
10700	WKGN	60099	2422	10W-38N	A6
Fairbanks Ct					
600	SMBG	60194	2859	22W-10N	C4
2500	NPVL	60540	3202	29W-8S	D1
24700	PNFD	60544	3416	31W-18S	A1
N Fairbanks Ct					
500	CHCG	60611	3034	0E-0N	C3
Fairbanks Pl					
200	MNSR	46321	3430		D5
Fairbluff Av					
10900	HTLY	60142	2692	39W-21N	C6
W Fairborn Ln					
400	RDLK	60073	2531	23W-31N	E7
Fairchild Av					
1100	JLET	60432	3499	22W-22S	D2
1100	JltT	60432	3499	22W-22S	C2
Fairchild Ct					
300	BMDL	60108	2969	22W-3N	C4
Fairchild Dr					
700	WMTN	60481	3853	27W-39S	E7
700	WMTN	60481	3943	27W-39S	E1
Fairchild Ln					
2300	WCHI	60185	2965	32W-4N	C5
Faircroft Rd					
100	BRLT	60103	2909	32W-8N	C3
Fair Elms Av					
4700	WNSP	60558	3146	14W-5S	D2
7100	BRRG	60527	3146	14W-8S	D7
7100	BRRG	60527	3208	14W-8S	D1
7100	IHPK	60525	3146	14W-8S	D7
7100	IHPK	60527	3146	14W-8S	D7
Faireno Ct					
1100	NPVL	60540	3142	25W-7S	A7
Faireno Dr					
10	CmpT	60119	2961	43W-4N	B4
Fairfax Av					
300	RMVL	60446	3340	24W-16S	D3
3800	RGMW	60008	2806	20W-14N	A5
E Fairfax Av					
10	PltT	60067	2805	20W-14N	E5
10	RGMW	60008	2805	20W-14N	E5
10	RGMW	60067	2805	20W-14N	E5
Fairfax Cir					
10	SgrT	60506	3135	41W-5S	E4
E Fairfax Cir					
1700	BRLT	60103	2967	28W-4N	B3
W Fairfax Cir					
1700	BRLT	60103	2967	28W-5N	B3

STREET Block	City	ZIP	Map#	CGS	Grid
Fairfax Ct					
10	BGBK	60490	3339	28W-15S	B1
10	SEGN	60177	2908	35W-8N	B4
10	WNVL	60555	3080	30W-1S	B2
800	BRTN	60010	2698	25W-20N	A7
900	ELGN	60120	2855	32W-12N	C1
6500	CPVL	60110	2747	36W-17N	A6
16500	TYPK	60477	3425	8W-19S	B3
Fairfax Ct E					
3500	AURA	60504	3202	31W-8S	A1
Fairfax Ct W					
3500	AURA	60504	3202	31W-8S	A2
Fairfax Dr					
200	MHRY	60050	2527	34W-31N	C6
400	LKVL	60046	2475	22W-37N	C2
500	NPVL	60540	3142	25W-7S	B6
4200	CLLK	60014	2641	33W-24N	A7
Fairfax Ln					
-	CLSM	60103	2967	28W-4N	B3
-	CLSM	60133	2967	28W-4N	B3
-	CLSM	60188	2967	28W-4N	B3
-	HRPK	60103	2967	28W-4N	B3
-	HRPK	60133	2967	28W-4N	B3
-	LKPT	60441	3419	21W-20S	E4
-	WynT	60103	2967	28W-5N	B2
10	LNSH	60069	2702	13W-22N	D5
10	VrnT	60015	2702	13W-22N	D5
300	GYLK	60030	2475	21W-34N	D7
1000	SEGN	60177	2908	35W-8N	B4
1300	BFGV	60089	2701	18W-21N	A6
1400	BFGV	60089	2700	18W-21N	E6
1500	BRLT	60103	2967	28W-5N	B2
1600	OKTR	60181	3084	18W-1S	E1
2400	LIHL	60156	2692	38W-22N	E3
Fairfax Rd					
10	FXLK	60020	2472	28W-36N	E4
10	FXLK	60020	2473	27W-35N	B5
1900	SCRL	60174	2964	34W-3N	D5
5600	OKFT	60452	3347	7W-18S	D7
Fairfax St					
4200	OKLN	60453	3276	5W-12S	B2
Fairfax Wy					
2400	YKVL	60560	3333	42W-17S	D6
2600	KdlT	60560	3333	42W-17S	D7
Fairfield Av					
-	KdlT	60560	3333	42W-17S	E6
-	YKVL	60560	3333	42W-17S	E6
10	AddT	60148	3026	19W-2N	D1
10	LMBD	60148	3026	19W-2N	D1
200	YkTp	60148	3084	19W-1S	D2
600	LMBD	60148	3084	19W-1S	D2
2900	DRGV	60515	3084	19W-2S	D4
2900	DRGV	60523	3084	19W-2S	D4
2900	YkTp	60515	3084	19W-2S	D4
2900	YkTp	60523	3084	19W-2S	D4
6400	BRWN	60402	3089	8W-3S	A4
14800	HRVY	60426	3349	3W-17S	B6
14800	POSN	60426	3349	3W-17S	B6
14800	POSN	60469	3349	3W-17S	B6
15000	MKHM	60426	3349	3W-17S	B6
20300	OMFD	60461	3506	4W-24S	E5
E Fairfield Av					
600	VLPK	60181	3027	17W-0N	C4
N Fairfield Av					
-	LydT	60160	2973	12W-2N	A7
-	MLPK	60160	2973	12W-2N	A7
200	CHCG	60612	3033	3W-0N	A4
400	LMBD	60148	3026	19W-1N	D2
800	CHCG	60622	3033	3W-1N	A2
1500	CHCG	60647	3033	3W-1N	A1
2200	LydT	60164	2973	12W-2N	A6
2300	FNPK	60131	2973	12W-2N	A6
2300	LydT	60131	2973	12W-2N	A6
2400	CHCG	60647	2977	3W-3N	A5
2900	CHCG	60618	2976	3W-3N	E4
2900	CHCG	60618	2977	3W-3N	A4
5600	CHCG	60625	2920	3W-6N	E5
5600	CHCG	60659	2920	3W-6N	E5
6300	CHCG	60645	2920	3W-7N	E3
7400	CHCG	60645	2866	3W-9N	E7
S Fairfield Av					
200	LMBD	60148	3026	19W-0N	D4
400	EMHT	60126	3027	16W-0S	D5
900	CHCG	60612	3033	3W-0S	A6
1000	CHCG	60608	3033	3W-1S	A7
1600	CHCG	60608	3091	3W-1S	A1
2800	LMBD	60148	3084	19W-2S	D4
4100	CHCG	60632	3091	3W-4S	A7
5000	CHCG	60632	3151	3W-6S	A3
5400	CHCG	60629	3151	3W-7S	A5
7900	CHCG	60652	3213	3W-9S	A2
9900	CHCG	60655	3213	3W-11S	A7
9900	CHCG	60805	3213	3W-11S	A7
9900	ENGN	60805	3213	3W-11S	A7
10600	CHCG	60655	3277	3W-12S	A2
Fairfield Cir					
600	EGVV	60007	2860	19W-9N	C7
1100	WKGN	60085	2479	11W-35N	E6
Fairfield Ct					
-	SMBG	60193	2859	23W-9N	A6
100	CLSM	60188	3024	23W-1N	E2
200	BMDL	60108	2969	23W-5N	B2
500	LMBD	60148	3084	19W-1S	D2
700	WTMT	60559	3145	17W-6S	C4
900	WKGN	60085	2480	10W-35N	A6
1000	WKGN	60085	2479	11W-35N	E6
1300	NPVL	60565	3204	24W-9S	C4
1300	WLNG	60090	2754	16W-18N	D3
W Fairfield Ct					
200	PLTN	60067	2752	21W-17N	D4
Fairfield Dr					
-	ELBN	60119	3017	42W-0N	C5
-	LGGV	60047	2700	18W-21N	E6
-	NlxT	60451	3500	19W-24S	E6
-	OSWG	60543	3263	36W-12S	E4
-	OSWG	60543	3264	36W-12S	A4
10	NLNX	60451	3500	19W-24S	E6
100	RMVL	60446	3339	27W-17S	C6
300	ISLK	60042	2586	28W-28N	E6
600	BRTN	60010	2751	24W-18N	C3
600	PltT	60010	2751	24W-18N	C3
2000	JLET	60586	3415	33W-21S	A7
6100	SenT	60180	2635	46W-25N	C4
6100	UNON	60180	2635	46W-25N	C4
15900	PNFD	60544	3416	29W-19S	D2
15900	PNFD	60586	3416	29W-19S	C4
Fairfield Ln					
10	CRY	60013	2695	32W-23N	B1
600	ALGN	60102	2694	35W-20N	B7
1500	HFET	60169	2858	25W-12N	C2
3000	AURA	60504	3201	31W-8S	D2
8400	FftT	60477	3504	10W-23S	B4
8700	TYPK	60477	3504	11W-23S	A4
8900	MKNA	60448	3504	11W-23S	A4
8900	TYPK	60448	3504	11W-23S	A4

STREET Block	City	ZIP	Map#	CGS	Grid
W Fairfield Ln					
17700	WrnT	60030	2534	17W-33N	A4
Fairfield Rd					
10	LNHT	60046	2475	20W-38N	E1
100	LNHT	60046	2417	20W-38N	E7
1100	GLNC	60022	2758	7W-18N	B4
1700	LNHT	60046	2476	20W-37N	A1
9600	HTLY	60142	2692	40W-22N	B4
N Fairfield Rd					
10	AvnT	60073	2531	24W-31N	C6
10	ElaT	60047	2645	22W-25N	B5
10	HNWD	60047	2645	22W-25N	B5
10	LKZH	60047	2645	22W-24N	B7
10	RDLK	60073	2531	24W-33N	C3
800	RLKB	60073	2531	24W-34N	C1
900	RLKB	60073	2474	24W-34N	C7
1200	AvnT	60073	2474	24W-35N	C7
1200	FmtT	60060	2588	24W-28N	C5
1200	WCDA	60060	2588	24W-28N	C5
1200	WCDA	60084	2588	24W-28N	C5
25700	HNWD	60060	2645	22W-26N	A4
25800	FmtT	60047	2645	22W-26N	A4
25800	FmtT	60060	2645	23W-26N	A3
25800	FmtT	60084	2645	23W-26N	A3
26400	FmtT	60060	2644	23W-27N	D1
26400	FmtT	60084	2644	23W-27N	D1
27200	FmtT	60084	2588	24W-27N	D7
29500	FmtT	60030	2588	24W-29N	D4
29500	WCDA	60030	2588	24W-29N	D4
31500	FmtT	60030	2531	24W-31N	C6
31600	AvnT	60030	2531	24W-31N	C6
32600	RDLK	60030	2531	24W-32N	C4
35400	RLKH	60073	2474	24W-35N	C6
35900	LkvT	60041	2474	24W-37N	D1
35900	LkvT	60073	2474	24W-35N	C5
36800	LKVL	60046	2474	24W-37N	C3
36800	LkvT	60046	2474	24W-36N	C3
38000	LkvT	60046	2416	24W-38N	D7
N Fairfield Rd CO-V61					
10	AvnT	60073	2531	24W-31N	C6
10	ElaT	60047	2645	22W-25N	B5
10	HNWD	60047	2645	22W-25N	B5
10	LKZH	60047	2645	22W-24N	B7
10	RDLK	60073	2531	24W-33N	C3
800	RLKB	60073	2531	24W-34N	C1
900	RLKB	60073	2474	24W-34N	C7
1200	AvnT	60073	2474	24W-35N	C7
1200	FmtT	60060	2588	24W-28N	C5
1200	WCDA	60060	2588	24W-28N	C5
1200	WCDA	60084	2588	24W-28N	C5
25700	HNWD	60060	2645	22W-26N	A4
25800	FmtT	60047	2645	22W-26N	A4
25800	FmtT	60060	2645	23W-26N	A3
25800	FmtT	60084	2645	23W-26N	A3
26400	FmtT	60060	2644	23W-27N	D1
26400	FmtT	60084	2644	23W-27N	D1
27200	FmtT	60084	2588	24W-27N	D7
29500	FmtT	60030	2588	24W-29N	D4
29500	WCDA	60030	2588	24W-29N	D4
31500	FmtT	60030	2531	24W-31N	C6
31600	AvnT	60030	2531	24W-31N	C6
32600	RDLK	60030	2531	24W-32N	C4
35400	RLKH	60073	2474	24W-35N	C6
35900	LkvT	60041	2474	24W-37N	D1
35900	LkvT	60073	2474	24W-35N	C5
36800	LKVL	60046	2474	24W-37N	C3
36800	LkvT	60046	2474	24W-36N	C3
38000	LkvT	60046	2416	24W-38N	D7
Fairfield St					
10600	WSTR	60154	3087	13W-2S	A3
W Fairfield Ter					
100	RLKB	60073	2474	23W-35N	E6
100	RLKB	60073	2475	23W-35N	A6
Fairfield Wy					
-	MTGY	60506	3198	40W-9S	B4
100	BMDL	60108	2969	23W-5N	B2
700	NARA	60542	3078	35W-3S	C5
2900	MTGY	60538	3198	40W-9S	A4
E Fairfield Wy					
100	BMDL	60108	2969	23W-5N	A2
Fairford Ln					
2500	NHBK	60062	2756	10W-18N	E4
2500	NHBK	60062	2757	10W-18N	A4
Fairgrounds Ct					
5100	MONE	60449	3683	6W-31S	A6
Fairhauser Ct					
2800	NPVL	60564	3266	29W-12S	C4
Fairhauser Rd					
2600	NPVL	60564	3266	29W-12S	C4
Fairhaven Ct					
10	GfnT	60156	2693	38W-23N	A2
1900	SMBG	60194	2858	26W-11N	A4
5400	DGvT	60515	3144	20W-6S	A4
5400	DGVT	60516	3144	20W-6S	A4
5400	DRGV	60515	3144	20W-6S	A4
Fairhaven Dr					
200	SCRL	60175	2963	37W-3N	C7
200	YKVL	60560	3261	42W-13S	D5
300	WPHR	60096	2363	10W-43N	A5
500	YKVL	60512	3261	42W-13S	D5
600	HRPK	60133	2912	25W-9N	A1
Fairhaven Ln					
400	MDLN	60060	2590	18W-28N	E7
1800	SMBG	60194	2858	25W-11N	A4
3000	GfnT	60156	2693	38W-23N	A2
Fairhill Rd					
400	LbvT	60048	2591	17W-30N	B2
Fairhills Dr					
-	DndT	60118	2800	34W-15N	D5
1000	WDND	60118	2800	34W-15N	D4
Fairhope Av					
700	GNVW	60025	2811	7W-14N	B3
700	NHFD	60025	2811	7W-14N	B3
700	NHFD	60093	2811	7W-14N	B3
S Fairlane Av					
100	EMHT	60126	3028	15W-1N	B2
Fairlane Ct					
100	BMDL	60108	2969	23W-5N	A2
1200	SMBG	60193	2912	25W-8N	B2
Fairlane Dr					
-	RtdT	60118	2799	38W-16N	C1
10	JLET	60435	3497	27W-23S	C4
10	JLET	60436	3497	27W-23S	C5
900	SMBG	60193	2912	25W-9N	B1
8800	BGVW	60455	3210	8W-10S	E5
8800	BGVW	60455	3211	8W-10S	A5
Fairlawn Av					
-	ELGN	60120	2855	32W-10N	C6
500	LYVL	60048	2591	17W-28N	B6
N Fairlawn Av					
10	MDLN	60060	2646	19W-27N	C1
400	MDLN	60060	2590	19W-28N	C7
Fairlawn Dr					
10	HNVL	60073	2532	22W-33N	B3
500	RLKP	60073	2532	22W-34N	B2
3300	MaiT	60025	2863	11W-12N	E1

STREET Block City ZIP Map# CGS Grid

Fairlawn Dr
3300 MaiT 60025 2864 10W-11N A2
N Fairlawn Dr
100 HNVL 60073 2532 22W-33N B3
200 RLKP 60073 2532 22W-33N B3
Fairlee Ct
400 SRGV 60554 3135 42W-5S D3
Fair Links Wy
600 GRNE 60031 2534 16W-33N D3
Fair Ln Dr
600 MNKA 60447 3583 34W-26S A4
600 SwdT 60447 3583 34W-26S A4
Fairmeadow Ln
100 LSLE 60532 3082 25W-3S B6
100 LSLE 60563 3082 25W-3S B6
100 MltT 60563 3082 25W-3S B6
Fair Meadow St
- BtvT 60510 3077 38W-3S A6
Fair Meadows Dr
- RMVL 60441 3340 25W-15S A3
500 RMVL 60446 3340 25W-15S A2
Fairmont Av
100 LktT 60441 3419 23W-21S B7
2800 AURA 60503 3201 31W-10S D6
3300 NPVL 60564 3202 30W-10S B7
Fairmont Ct
- DGvT 60516 3144 18W-7S E6
- WTMT 60516 3144 18W-7S E6
- WTMT 60559 3144 18W-7S E6
300 SCRL 60175 2963 37W-2N C7
800 DSPN 60018 2862 14W-10N D6
1200 ALGN 60102 2694 34W-20N B7
3700 AURA 60504 3202 30W-8S A1
9100 ODPK 60462 3345 11W-17S E6
9100 ODPK 60462 3346 11W-17S A6
Fairmont Dr
10 DMND 60416 3941 33W-39S B1
5900 WDRG 60517 3143 21W-6S D5
Fairmont Ln
400 RLKP 60030 2589 22W-30N C1
3300 NPVL 60564 3202 30W-10S B7
19200 MKNA 60448 3502 14W-23S D3
Fairmont Rd
1300 HFET 60169 2858 25W-12N C2
5400 WKGN 60048 2535 15W-31N A7
W Fairmont St
100 MPPT 60056 2807 15W-14N E3
Fairmount Av
- DRN 60561 3206 19W-8S D1
700 DRGV 60516 3144 19W-6S D4
1600 JLET 60432 3499 22W-21S C1
1600 LktT 60441 3419 22W-21S C7
1600 LktT 60441 3499 22W-21S C1
5100 DRGV 60515 3144 19W-6S D4
7200 DRGV 60516 3206 19W-8S D1
7400 DRN 60516 3206 19W-8S D1
7900 DGvT 60516 3206 19W-9S D3
N Fairmount Av
1200 JLET 60432 3499 22W-22S C1
Fairoak Ct
2000 NPVL 60565 3204 25W-9S B4
Fair Oak Ln
2600 MchT 60051 2528 31W-32N D5
Fairoak Rd
1700 NPVL 60565 3204 25W-9S B4
Fair Oaks Av
1100 CLLK 60014 2639 37W-25N A5
1100 GfnT 60014 2639 37W-25N A5
Fairoaks Av
900 DRFD 60015 2703 11W-21N D6
Fair Oaks Av N
500 OKPK 60302 3031 8W-1N A3
1200 CHCG 60302 3031 8W-1N A1
1200 CHCG 60707 3031 8W-1N A1
W Fair Oaks Cir
26300 AntT 60002 2356 26W-42N D6
Fairoaks Ct
- CCHL 60478 3426 6W-21S A6
W Fairoaks Ct
10 PLTN 60067 2805 21W-15N E2
Fair Oaks Dr
200 CmpT 60175 2906 40W-6N C7
200 CmpT 60175 2962 40W-6N B1
Fairoaks Dr
4900 CCHL 60478 3426 6W-21S A6
24500 RedT 60408 3942 30W-42S B7
Fair Oaks Rd
10 CLSM 60185 2967 28W-3N A6
10 CLSM 60188 2967 28W-3N A6
10 WynT 60185 2967 28W-3N A6
10 WynT 60188 2967 28W-3N A6
400 BRLT 60103 2967 28W-4N A3
400 CLSM 60103 2967 28W-4N A4
Fairport Dr
1300 GYLK 60030 2475 20W-34N E7
1300 GYLK 60030 2532 20W-34N E1
Fairview
- ELGN 60120 2855 32W-10N C7
Fairview Av
- AntT 60002 2415 27W-38N C6
- GNEN 60137 3025 21W-0S D7
- GNEN 60148 3025 21W-0S D7
- LKMR 60051 2529 29W-32N C5
- LMBD 60148 3025 21W-0S D7
- MchT 60051 2529 29W-32N C5
- MltT 60148 3025 21W-0S D7
10 DRFD 60015 2756 11W-20N D2
200 GNEN 60187 3025 23W-0S A7
200 WHTN 60187 3025 23W-0S A7
200 WNKA 60093 2812 4W-15N C3
300 WCHI 60185 3022 29W-1N C3
400 DRGV 60516 3144 19W-7S E7
400 DRN 60516 3144 19W-7S E7
400 DRN 60561 3144 19W-7S E7
400 YkTp 60148 3084 18W-1S E2
600 LMBD 60148 3084 18W-1S E2
600 LYVL 60048 2591 16W-28N D6
1000 LKFT 60045 2649 11W-24N E7
1000 WTMT 60516 3144 18W-6S E5
1000 WTMT 60559 3144 18W-6S E5
1100 DGvT 60516 3144 18W-6S E5
1300 CHHT 60411 3507 2W-25S D7
1400 CHHT 60411 3595 2W-25S D1
2100 AlqT 60021 2695 31W-22N D4
2100 JNBG 60050 2471 31W-35N E6
3000 SCHT 60411 3596 1W-27S A4
3300 SCHT 60475 3596 1W-27S A4
3300 STGR 60475 3596 1W-27S A4
3500 OKBK 60515 3084 19W-3S E6
3500 OKBK 60523 3084 19W-3S E6
3500 YkTp 60515 3084 19W-3S E6
3500 YkTp 60523 3084 19W-3S E6
3800 DRGV 60515 3084 19W-4S E7
4300 DRGV 60515 3144 19W-7S E7
5600 DRGV 60559 3144 18W-6S E4
6500 DRGV 60561 3144 19W-7S E6
6800 DGvT 60561 3144 19W-7S E7
7200 DRN 60516 3206 19W-8S E1
7400 DRGV 60516 3206 18W-8S E1
7400 DRGV 60561 3206 18W-8S E1
7400 DRN 60561 3206 18W-8S E1
8900 BKFD 60513 3087 11W-3S D6
9500 BKFD 60525 3087 11W-3S D6
9500 LGPK 60525 3087 11W-3S D6
12400 BLID 60406 3277 3W-14S A7
Fairview Av CO-25
3800 DRGV 60515 3084 19W-4S E7
3800 OKBK 60523 3084 19W-4S E7
3800 YkTp 60515 3084 19W-4S E7
3800 YkTp 60523 3084 19W-4S E7
Fairview Av SR-53
- GNEN 60137 3025 21W-0S D7
- GNEN 60148 3025 21W-0S D7
- LMBD 60148 3025 21W-0S D7
- MltT 60148 3025 21W-0S D7
N Fairview Av
100 MPPT 60056 2807 15W-13N E6
800 PKRG 60068 2864 10W-9N A6
900 NLES 60068 2864 10W-9N A6
900 NLES 60714 2864 10W-9N A6
1200 JLET 60432 3499 22W-22S C1
1400 LktT 60441 3499 22W-22S C1
2100 LktT 60441 3419 22W-21S C7
5500 CHCG 60631 2918 10W-7N A5
5500 CHCG 60656 2918 10W-6N A5
5500 LydT 60631 2918 10W-6N A5
5500 LydT 60656 2918 10W-6N A5
5500 MaiT 60631 2918 10W-7N A5
S Fairview Av
10 PKRG 60068 2918 10W-8N A1
100 EMHT 60126 3027 16W-1N D3
1000 LMBD 60148 3026 18W-0S E7
1800 CHCG 60631 2918 10W-7N A4
1800 PKRG 60631 2918 10W-7N A4
Fairview Cir
500 SMBG 60193 2858 24W-9N D7
W Fairview Cir
25200 LkvT 60046 2474 25W-37N B2
Fairview Ct
10 CNHL 60514 3145 16W-5S D2
100 GNVA 60134 3019 37W-1N C3
Fairview Dr
100 SCRL 60174 2963 36W-2N D7
100 SCRL 60174 3019 36W-2N D1
200 FmtT 60060 2646 19W-26N C2
200 MHTN 60442 3677 19W-30S D4
400 MhtT 60442 3677 19W-30S D4
500 AURA 60506 3137 36W-5S E3
500 NARA 60506 3137 36W-5S E3
500 NARA 60542 3137 36W-5S E3
19100 MDLN 60060 2646 19W-26N C2
22300 AntT 60002 2417 22W-40N B3
23100 DRPK 60010 2699 23W-20N A7
23200 DRPK 60010 2698 23W-20N E7
Fairview Ln
100 NHBK 60062 2756 12W-18N A3
100 SMWD 60107 2857 28W-9N A7
500 SMBG 60193 2858 24W-9N D7
600 SEGN 60177 2908 36W-9N A1
700 BRLT 60103 2910 29W-7N D4
1100 LGGV 60047 2700 18W-21N E6
2000 SHLD 60473 3429 2E-20S D4
2100 WDSK 60098 2582 39W-29N D3
4900 LNWD 60077 2919 6W-8N E1
4900 LNWD 60712 2919 6W-8N E1
5300 SKOK 60077 2919 6W-8N D1
N Fairview Ln
1300 MchT 60051 2528 31W-33N E3
37000 LkvT 60046 2474 25W-37N A2
W Fairview Ln
2200 MchT 60051 2528 31W-33N E3
Fairview Pkwy
10 RLKB 60073 2475 23W-35N A6
Fairview Rd
100 GLNC 60022 2758 5W-17N E5
800 HDPK 60035 2704 8W-21N E6
E Fairview St
10 ANHT 60005 2807 17W-13N A6
N Fairview St
40400 AntT 60002 2416 25W-40N A3
W Fairview St
- ANHT 60005 2806 18W-13N D6
10 ANHT 60005 2807 18W-13N A6
Fairview Ter
400 SchT 60174 2908 35W-6N B7
Fairview Park Av
300 CLLK 60014 2639 36W-26N E3
Fairway Av
400 MltT 60137 3025 21W-0N E5
Fairway Cir
900 LKBN 60010 2643 26W-24N C7
1400 GNVA 60134 3019 36W-0N E6
12300 BLID 60406 3277 3W-14S A6
Fairway Ct
200 PTHT 60070 2808 14W-14N C4
1600 GNVA 60134 3019 36W-0S E6
1900 HFET 60169 2804 25W-12N B7
1900 HFET 60169 2858 25W-12N B1
2000 SCRL 60174 2964 35W-4N C4
2900 GNVW 60025 2810 10W-13N B7
3500 CRTE 60417 3596 0W-28S D6
N Fairway Ct
900 PLTN 60067 2753 20W-17N A6
Fairway Dr
- GfnT 60014 2638 38W-25N E6
- GNVW 60025 2811 7W-14N C5
- LynT 60525 3208 13W-8S E2
- WLMT 60091 2811 7W-14N C5
10 GLHT 60139 2968 24W-2N D7
10 NPVL 60563 3140 30W-6S B4
10 NpvT 60563 3140 30W-5S B2
100 WLSP 60525 3208 13W-8S E2
200 BCHR 60401 3864 0W-36S D2
200 MPPT 60056 2808 14W-14N C4
200 PTHT 60056 2808 14W-14N C4
200 PTHT 60070 2808 14W-14N C4
300 BRLT 60103 2910 29W-9N D1
300 SchT 60175 2963 38W-5N A2
600 BNVL 60106 2915 16W-6N D6
600 GNVW 60025 2810 10W-13N B7
1000 FXLK 60020 2414 28W-39N E6
1100 LKFT 60045 2649 12W-24N A7
1200 LMNT 60439 3342 20W-15S B1
1500 LSLE 60532 3143 23W-6S A5
1500 LslT 60532 3143 23W-6S A5
2500 JLET 60435 3497 27W-23S D4
3400 CRTE 60417 3596 0W-28S D6
5400 CTWD 60445 3347 6W-15S D1
5400 WthT 60445 3347 6W-15S D1
5400 WthT 60463 3347 6W-15S D1
7000 LKWD 60014 2638 38W-24N D6
8800 ODPK 60462 3346 11W-17S A5
9100 ODPK 60462 3345 11W-17S E5
9200 MaiT 60016 2863 11W-12N D1
9200 NLES 60714 2863 11W-12N D1
39800 LkvT 60002 2416 24W-39N B4
N Fairway Dr
- VNHL 60061 2701 16W-24N D1
- VrnT 60069 2701 16W-24N D1
10 VNHL 60061 2647 16W-24N D7
800 PLTN 60067 2753 20W-17N A6
W Fairway Dr
3100 MchT 60050 2528 32W-32N B5
3100 MHRY 60050 2528 32W-32N B5
Fairway Ln
- CRTE 60417 3596 0E-29S E7
- CRTE 60417 3685 0E-29S E1
- CteT 60417 3685 0E-29S E1
100 WHTN 60187 3082 24W-1S C1
200 BmdT 60143 2913 21W-6N E6
200 BmdT 60143 2969 21W-5N E1
200 BmdT 60157 2913 21W-6N E6
200 CPVL 60110 2748 32W-17N C7
300 WTMT 60559 3145 18W-7S A6
400 ITSC 60143 2969 21W-5N E1
400 UYPK 60417 3684 2W-30S C4
400 UYPK 60466 3684 2W-30S C4
500 IVNS 60067 2751 23W-16N E6
500 IVNS 60067 2752 23W-16N A7
600 FKFT 60423 3592 10W-26S C2
1100 NHBK 60062 2757 8W-18N D3
1600 NPVL 60565 3204 25W-9S C3
2500 WKGN 60087 2480 10W-36N B3
5800 DrrT 60014 2639 37W-26N A3
10200 DrrT 60098 2525 39W-31N D7
Fairway Rd
10 CPVL 60110 2748 32W-17N C7
10 LKZH 60047 2698 24W-23N C3
Fairway Ter
4000 BmnT 60430 3426 4W-21S D7
4000 CCHL 60430 3426 4W-21S D7
4000 CCHL 60478 3426 5W-21S C7
Fairway View Dr
200 ALGN 60102 2693 36W-20N C7
200 LIHL 60156 2693 37W-21N C7
500 WLNG 60090 2754 16W-18N E3
Fairwind Ct
300 MTGY 60538 3199 37W-10S C5
Fairwind Dr
200 MTGY 60538 3199 37W-10S C5
200 MTGY 60538 3200 35W-10S A5
Fairwinds Ct
800 NPVL 60563 3141 26W-6S E4
Fairwood Ct
100 BGBK 60440 3269 23W-12S A2
1200 ELGN 60123 2854 35W-13N C1
S Fairwood Ct
20100 FftT 60423 3504 9W-24S E5
Fairwood Dr
100 BGBK 60440 3269 23W-12S A2
1100 ELGN 60123 2854 35W-13N C1
Fairwood Pl
1600 AURA 60506 3137 38W-7S B7
Faith Ct
200 BMDL 60108 2968 24W-5N E1
1900 LYWD 60411 3509 2E-24S D5
26500 GrtT 60041 2473 26W-35N D6
Faith Ln
800 BRLT 60103 2911 28W-7N A5
2200 AURA 60502 3079 32W-4S B7
Faith Pl
5200 MTSN 60443 3505 6W-24S E5
5200 MTSN 60443 3506 6W-24S A5
Faithorn Av
1500 CRTE 60417 3685 0W-30S C3
1500 CteT 60417 3685 0W-30S C3
Faiths Wy
10500 HTLY 60142 2692 39W-21N C5
Falcon Blvd
- AvnT 60073 2531 24W-34N C1
- RDLK 60073 2531 24W-34N C1
Falcon Ct
10 SBTN 60010 2803 26W-15N D3
100 BMDL 60108 2968 24W-4N E2
400 DRN 60527 3145 16W-6S E5
1100 WHTN 60187 3024 25W-0N A5
12800 LMNT 60439 3343 18W-15S A1
N Falcon Ct
3600 RGMW 60008 2806 20W-13N B5
S Falcon Ct
3500 RGMW 60008 2806 20W-13N B5
W Falcon Ct
3000 RGMW 60008 2806 20W-13N B5
4800 MONE 60449 3683 6W-31S B6
Falcon Dr
10 HNWD 60047 2645 22W-26N C3
100 BlmT 60411 3509 3E-25S E7
1500 WHTN 60187 3024 25W-0N B5
1600 MltT 60187 3024 25W-0N B5
2200 JLET 60586 3416 31W-21S A6
3800 NPVL 60564 3266 29W-12S C2
4100 WldT 60564 3266 29W-12S D2
12300 PNFD 60585 3266 30W-14S C7
E Falcon Dr
600 ANHT 60005 2861 17W-11N B3
600 ANHT 60056 2861 17W-11N B3
600 MPPT 60056 2861 17W-11N B3
N Falcon Dr
36100 GrtT 60041 2473 25W-36N E4
S Falcon Dr
1200 PLTN 60067 2805 22W-14N B4
1200 RGMW 60067 2805 22W-14N B4
1500 WKGN 60048 2535 14W-32N C5
Falcon Ln
- WHTN 60187 3024 25W-0N B4
600 CmpT 60175 2961 42W-4N C4
1400 HFET 60192 2856 30W-12N B2
2200 SPGV 60081 2354 31W-42N E6
Falcon Pl
10 WTMT 60559 3145 17W-7S B6
Falcon St
8700 HGKN 60525 3147 11W-7S E5
9800 RcmT 60071 2354 33W-41N A7
9800 RcmT 60071 2413 33W-41N A1
9900 RcmT 60071 2353 33W-41N E7
Falcon Tr
10 MltT 60188 3023 26W-1N E3
Falcon Greens Dr
9000 LKWD 60014 2693 37W-23N A1
Falcon Lakes Dr
10 SBTN 60010 2803 26W-14N E3
Falcon Ridge Ct
10 ALGN 60102 2694 35W-21N A6
Falcon Ridge Dr
9100 BGVW 60455 3210 9W-10S D5
Falconridge Wy
100 BGBK 60440 3205 22W-11S C7
Falcons Tr
10 ElgT 60124 2907 38W-7N A5
10 ElgT 60175 2907 38W-7N A5
10 SchT 60175 2907 38W-7N A5
W Falkirk Cir
26400 CbaT 60010 2697 26W-21N D6
Falkirk Ln
10 RGMW 60008 2805 20W-14N E4
W Falkirk Pl
400 PLTN 60074 2752 21W-18N D3
Falkirk Rd
10 HNWD 60047 2645 20W-24N E7
10 HNWD 60047 2646 20W-24N A7
Falkner Dr
3200 NPVL 60564 3267 28W-12S A2
Fall Cir
400 ROSL 60172 2912 24W-6N E7
Fall Ct
1300 WLNG 60090 2754 16W-18N D2
Fallbrook Ct
200 EDND 60118 2801 33W-15N B3
300 SMBG 60194 2857 27W-10N D5
W Fallbrook Ct
7600 FftT 60423 3504 9W-24S E5
Fall Brook Dr
2000 NPVL 60565 3204 25W-9S C4
Fallbrook Dr
10 GLHT 60139 2968 24W-4N E4
400 EDND 60118 2801 33W-15N B3
S Fallbrook Dr
1500 RDLK 60073 2531 23W-31N D7
1700 RDLK 60073 2588 23W-31N E1
Fallcreek Cir
10 OswT 60538 3200 36W-10S A6
Fallcreek Ct
1400 NPVL 60565 3203 26W-8S E3
Fallen Oak Tr
800 AURA 60506 3137 36W-5S D3
Falling Leaf Ln
1700 NHBK 60062 2757 9W-16N C6
Fallingwater Cir
20300 FftT 60423 3504 10W-24S B5
20300 FKFT 60423 3504 10W-24S B5
Falling Waters Blvd
- WrnT 60046 2476 19W-37N C3
2900 LNHT 60046 2476 19W-37N C3
Falling Waters Dr
2700 LNHT 60046 2476 19W-37N C2
2700 WrnT 60046 2476 19W-37N D2
Falling Waters Dr E
9100 BRRG 60527 3208 16W-10S A6
9400 DGvT 60527 3208 16W-10S A6
Falling Waters Dr W
- BRRG 60527 3207 16W-10S E5
- BRRG 60527 3208 16W-10S A6
- DGvT 60527 3208 16W-10S A5
Falling Waters Ln
2800 LNHT 60046 2476 19W-37N D2
Falling Waters Wy
500 LNHT 60046 2476 19W-37N D3
Fallon Ln
3700 JLET 60431 3497 28W-22S A2
Fallow Dr
13400 HTLY 60142 2744 43W-19N B2
Falls Cir
700 LKFT 60045 2649 10W-25N E6
Falls Ct
2500 JLET 60586 3415 32W-20S C6
Falls Ln
7200 MchT 60097 2469 36W-37N E2
7200 WRLK 60097 2469 36W-37N E2
Fallstone Dr
10 SMWD 60107 2857 28W-11N B4
100 LNSH 60045 2702 13W-23N D2
100 VrnT 60069 2702 13W-23N E2
Falls View Wy
- FKFT 60423 3590 14W-27S E4
Falmore Dr
700 BRLT 60103 2911 28W-7N B4
S Falmore Dr
1000 PLTN 60067 2805 22W-14N B4
Falmore Ln
500 BGBK 60440 3205 23W-10S B6
Falmouth Ct
2000 SMWD 60107 2910 30W-9N C1
Falmouth Ln
500 SMBG 60193 2858 25W-9N C7
Falmouth Wy
500 ROSL 60172 2912 25W-6N C6
Falmouth on Oxford
10 RGMW 60008 2805 22W-13N B6
Falson Ct
1400 WHTN 60187 3082 24W-1S D2
Fanad Ct
400 OSWG 60543 3263 38W-11S A2
Fanchon St
10 MltT 60188 3024 25W-1N B3
10 WHTN 60188 3024 25W-1N B3
200 CLSM 60188 3024 25W-1N B3
300 MltT 60187 3024 25W-0N B5
N Fanchon St
1400 MltT 60187 3024 25W-0N B5
1400 WHTN 60187 3024 25W-0N B5
Fane Ct
11900 ODPK 60467 3422 14W-20S D5
Fapp Cir
100 WHTN 60187 3023 26W-0S E7
100 WHTN 60187 3081 26W-1S E1
Faraday Rd
25100 MhtT 60442 3677 19W-30S D4
Fargo Av
600 EGVV 60007 2861 17W-9N B7
600 EGVV 60007 2915 17W-9N B1
1200 DSPN 60018 2862 13W-9N E7
1800 DSPN 60018 2863 12W-9N B7
1800 NndT 60050 2585 30W-29N E4
1800 NndT 60050 2586 30W-29N A4
3800 SKOK 60076 2866 4W-9N B7
5200 SKOK 60077 2865 6W-9N D7
W Fargo Av
1300 CHCG 60626 2867 1W-9N C7
2000 CHCG 60645 2867 2W-9N B7
2600 CHCG 60645 2866 3W-9N E7
3100 CHCG 60076 2866 3W-9N D7
3100 SKOK 60076 2866 3W-9N D7
3100 SKOK 60645 2866 3W-9N D7
6800 NLES 60714 2864 8W-9N E7
7600 CHCG 60631 2864 9W-9N C7
Fargo Blvd
500 GNVA 60134 3020 36W-0N A5
1500 GNVA 60134 3019 36W-0N E5
2700 GnvT 60134 3019 37W-0N C5
Fargo Cir
2600 GNVA 60134 3019 37W-0N C5
Far Hills Dr
200 BGBK 60440 3268 24W-12S E2
1500 BRLT 60103 2966 30W-5N C2
1600 WynT 60103 2966 30W-5N C2
Far Hills Rd
10 BNHL 60010 2748 32W-19N E3
Farina Ct
500 MDLN 60060 2646 19W-27N C2
Faringdon Dr
10 CLLK 60014 2640 35W-24N A7
Farington Ct
1400 NPVL 60563 3141 28W-5S A2
Farington Dr
5200 MHRY 60050 2527 34W-32N D5
Farington Ln
1400 AURA 60504 3201 32W-9S C4
Farley Dr
9500 HTLY 60142 2692 40W-22N A4
Farley Pl
700 DRGV 60515 3144 19W-5S D3
Farlin Ct
1000 LKFT 60045 2649 12W-27N B1
Farm Ct
200 OswT 60560 3334 40W-15S D2
Farm Dr
700 WCHI 60185 3022 29W-1N E2
Farm Rd
- BtvT 60542 3077 36W-3S D6
100 BtvT 60539 3077 36W-3S D6
1700 LKFT 60045 2648 13W-24N E7
1700 LKFT 60045 2649 13W-24N A7
W Farm St
10 CRTE 60417 3685 1W-30S B3
Farm Tr
400 WDSK 60098 2524 41W-32N C5
Farm Bridge Rd
400 LKZH 60047 2699 23W-22N A4
Farmbrook Ct
400 RMVL 60446 3269 23W-14S A6
Farmbrook Ln
5400 NndT 60014 2641 32W-26N B3
Farmcrest Ln
5500 LGGV 60047 2701 17W-22N B3
Farm Crest Ter
19000 CCHL 60478 3506 5W-22S D2
Farmgate Ct
300 GRNE 60031 2535 14W-33N C2
Farm Gate Dr
3200 NPVL 60564 3202 30W-11S A7
3200 NPVL 60564 3266 30W-11S A1
Farmgate Dr
100 SMBG 60193 2859 23W-9N A6
200 SMBG 60193 2858 23W-9N E6
Farm Gate Ln
100 BGBK 60440 3268 25W-11S B2
E Farmgate Ln
10 PLTN 60067 2752 20W-17N E5
10 PLTN 60067 2753 20W-17N A5
100 PLTN 60074 2753 20W-17N A5
Farmgate Rd
1300 BRLT 60103 2966 30W-5N B1
Farm Glen Ln
800 CLSM 60188 2967 27W-4N C4
Farmhill Av
8000 PSPK 60464 3274 10W-15S C7
Farmhill Cir
300 WCDA 60084 2587 26W-27N D7
300 WCDA 60084 2643 26W-27N D1
Farmhill Ct
300 ALGN 60102 2694 35W-21N B6
300 WCDA 60084 2643 26W-27N D1
400 LKVL 60046 2475 22W-36N B3
Farm Hill Dr
12500 HTLY 60142 2744 42W-18N D4
15800 ODPK 60462 3424 10W-18S A1
Farmhill Dr
200 ALGN 60102 2694 35W-21N B6
Farmhill Ln
- LkvT 60046 2475 22W-36N B3
- RLKB 60046 2475 22W-36N B3
- RLKB 60073 2475 22W-36N B3
800 LKVL 60046 2475 22W-36N B3
S Farmhill Ln
12700 PSPK 60464 3274 10W-15S C7
Farmhouse Rd
7800 FftT 60423 3504 9W-24S D6
Farmingdale Cir E
300 MDLN 60060 2647 16W-24N E6
300 MDLN 60061 2647 16W-24N E6
300 VNHL 60061 2647 16W-24N E6
Farmingdale Cir S
300 VNHL 60061 2647 16W-24N E6
Farmingdale Cir W
300 MDLN 60060 2647 17W-25N B5
300 MDLN 60061 2647 17W-25N B5
300 VNHL 60061 2647 17W-25N B5
Farmingdale Dr
7500 DRN 60561 3207 17W-8S C1
S Farmingdale Dr
16100 PnfT 60586 3416 30W-19S B3
16200 PNFD 60586 3416 30W-19S B3
Farmington Av
400 PnfT 60435 3417 27W-20S C6
4400 RNPK 60471 3594 5W-27S B4
Farmington Ct
10 LIHL 60156 2692 38W-22N E3
10 SEGN 60177 2908 36W-9N A1
100 RGMW 60008 2805 21W-14N D5
600 LKVL 60046 2475 22W-37N B1
1900 NPVL 60565 3203 26W-9S E4
5800 HRPK 60133 2911 27W-7N D5
Farmington Dr
10 BmT 60010 2803 25W-15N E2
10 SBTN 60010 2803 25W-15N E2
2800 LNHT 60046 2476 19W-38N C1
Farmington Ln
300 MDLN 60061 2647 17W-25N B5
300 VNHL 60061 2647 17W-25N B5
3900 JNBG 60050 2471 31W-36N C5
S Farmington Ln
19700 FftT 60423 3504 9W-23S E4
Farmington Rd
10 SBTN 60010 2803 25W-15N E2
2800 NHBK 60062 2809 11W-15N E1
Farmington Lakes Dr
2000 OSWG 60543 3200 35W-10S B7
Farmside Ct
10 BGBK 60490 3267 26W-13S D5
Farmside Dr
1700 CPVL 60110 2746 37W-17N D6
Farmside Ln
1500 BGBK 60490 3267 26W-13S E5
Farmsley Ct
5100 OKFT 60452 3426 6W-20S A4
Farmstead Ct
700 FKFT 60423 3503 13W-24S B6

STREET Block	City	ZIP	Map#	CGS	Grid
Farmstead Dr					
-	MHRY	60050	2526	35W-31N	E6
-	MHRY	60050	2527	35W-32N	A5
-	YKVL	60560	3261	42W-14S	D7
Farmstead Ln					
1300	BGBK	60490	3268	26W-13S	A5
7200	HRPK	60133	2912	25W-9N	A1
7200	SMBG	60133	2912	25W-9N	A2
7200	SMBG	60193	2912	25W-9N	A2
24000	PNFD	60544	3416	30W-18S	B2
Farmstead Rd					
3900	CPVL	60110	2747	35W-17N	B6
Farmstone Dr					
2000	BvlT	60416	3941	33W-40S	C4
2000	DMND	60416	3941	33W-40S	C4
Farm Trace Dr					
22900	RNPK	60471	3594	4W-27S	D5
23000	MonT	60466	3594	4W-27S	D5
N Farm View Cir					
25900	LKBN	60010	2643	27W-25N	C4
Farmview Ct					
500	UYPK	60466	3684	3W-30S	B4
16700	TYPK	60477	3424	10W-20S	B3
Farmview Dr					
8500	FKFT	60423	3592	10W-25S	B1
Farm View Ln					
700	RtdT	60140	2798	40W-15N	C3
Farm View Rd					
2400	NlxT	60451	3590	16W-27S	A4
2700	MhtT	60451	3590	16W-27S	A5
Farmview Rd					
100	CmpT	60119	2961	42W-4N	D5
500	UYPK	60466	3684	3W-30S	B4
600	UYPK	60449	3684	3W-30S	B4
W Farm View St					
13200	HMGN	60491	3343	16W-18S	E7
Farmwood Ct					
400	RDLK	60073	2531	24W-33N	C2
Farmwood Dr					
-	LGGV	60047	2646	19W-24N	D7
-	LGGV	60047	2700	19W-23N	D1
W Farmwood Dr					
1100	ADSN	60101	2970	20W-5N	B2
Farner Ct					
2900	RVWD	60015	2702	13W-22N	E4
Farnham Ct					
1900	SMBG	60194	2858	26W-11N	A3
5800	HRPK	60133	2911	26W-7N	D5
Farnham Dr					
-	LktT	60544	3339	26W-16S	D5
Farnham Ln					
400	WHTN	60187	3082	24W-1S	D2
E Farnham Ln					
100	WHTN	60187	3082	24W-1S	C2
W Farnham Ln					
100	WHTN	60187	3082	24W-1S	C2
Farnham Rd					
10	HDPK	60035	2703	11W-23N	E2
10	LKFT	60045	2703	11W-23N	E2
N Farnsworth Av					
10	AURA	60504	3200	33W-8S	E1
10	AURA	60505	3200	33W-7S	E1
100	AURA	60505	3138	34W-6S	E5
400	AraT	60505	3138	34W-6S	E5
500	AraT	60504	3138	34W-7S	E6
2300	AURA	60502	3138	34W-5S	E3
2300	AURA	60504	3138	34W-4S	E1
2600	AURA	60502	3078	33W-4S	E7
N Farnsworth Av CO-77					
2300	AraT	60504	3138	34W-4S	E1
2300	AURA	60502	3138	34W-5S	E3
2300	AURA	60504	3138	34W-4S	E1
2600	AURA	60502	3078	33W-4S	E7
S Farnsworth Av					
-	AURA	60503	3201	33W-10S	A5
-	AURA	60504	3201	33W-10S	A5
-	OswT	60503	3201	33W-10S	A6
10	AURA	60504	3200	33W-9S	E3
10	AURA	60505	3200	33W-8S	E1
400	AraT	60504	3200	34W-9S	E4
Farnsworth Cir					
-	WcnT	60010	2642	28W-26N	D3
400	PTBR	60010	2642	29W-26N	D3
Farnsworth Ct					
10	PTBR	60010	2642	29W-26N	D3
300	GNEN	60137	3083	23W-1S	A2
N Farnsworth Dr					
8100	NLES	60714	2864	10W-10N	B5
Farnsworth Ln					
1200	BFGV	60089	2700	18W-21N	E6
1900	NHBK	60062	2757	9W-16N	B6
2500	NHBK	60062	2756	10W-16N	E6
Farnsworth Rd					
-	AURA	60503	3201	33W-10S	A7
Farnum Av					
500	AURA	60505	3200	34W-8S	D2
Faro Ct					
10	OSWG	60543	3263	37W-12S	C4
Farquhar Av					
-	BLID	60406	3276	4W-14S	D7
Farragut Av					
-	NCHI	60088	2594	10W-30N	A1
500	NCHI	60064	2593	10W-31N	E1
500	NCHI	60088	2593	10W-31N	E1
700	RMVL	60446	3268	24W-14S	E7
W Farragut Av					
1800	CHCG	60640	2921	2W-6N	B5
2500	CHCG	60625	2921	3W-6N	A5
2700	CHCG	60625	2920	3W-6N	E5
5500	CHCG	60630	2919	6W-6N	C5
6900	CHCG	60656	2918	8W-6N	D5
8300	CHCG	60706	2918	10W-6N	A6
8300	NRDG	60656	2918	10W-6N	A6
8300	NRDG	60706	2918	10W-6N	A6
Farragut Ct					
1600	WHTN	60187	3082	25W-2S	B3
W Farragut Pl					
800	JLET	60435	3498	25W-23S	C4
Farragut St					
200	OMFD	60461	3507	3W-25S	B7
200	PKFT	60466	3507	3W-25S	B7
9700	CHCG	60018	2917	12W-6N	B6
Farrar Ct					
5200	DRGV	60515	3144	19W-5S	C3
S Farrar Dr					
1200	CHCG	60623	3032	3W-1S	E7
1500	CHCG	60623	3033	2W-1S	B7
1500	CHCG	60623	3090	3W-1S	E1
1500	CHCG	60623	3091	3W-1S	A1
Farrell Av					
1900	PKRG	60068	2863	11W-10N	D4
Farrell Dr					
7400	LKWD	60014	2639	37W-24N	A7
N Farrell Rd					
100	HmrT	60441	3420	21W-18S	A1
100	LKPT	60441	3420	21W-18S	A1
100	LktT	60441	3420	20W-18S	A1
700	LKPT	60441	3342	21W-18S	A7
900	LktT	60441	3342	20W-18S	A7
S Farrell Rd					
300	HmrT	60441	3420	21W-20S	A4
300	LKPT	60441	3420	21W-21S	A7
300	LktT	60441	3420	21W-20S	A4
14800	LKPT	60441	3342	20W-17S	A6
14800	LktT	60441	3342	20W-17S	A6
17800	LKPT	60432	3420	21W-21S	A7
17800	LktT	60432	3420	21W-21S	A7
18000	HmrT	60432	3420	20W-21S	A7
18000	HmrT	60432	3500	20W-22S	B1
18000	JltT	60432	3500	20W-22S	B1
18000	LktT	60432	3500	20W-22S	B1
18000	NlxT	60432	3500	20W-22S	B1
18300	LktT	60432	3500	21W-22S	A2
S Farrell St					
2600	CHCG	60608	3091	1W-2S	E2
Farrier Point Ln					
400	CmpT	60175	2962	39W-5N	E2
Farrington Cir					
10	LNSH	60069	2702	13W-24N	D1
Farrington Ct					
400	BFGV	60089	2701	17W-20N	B7
1500	AURA	60504	3201	32W-9S	C4
S Farrington Ct					
-	BMDL	60108	2969	23W-5N	A1
Farrington Dr					
400	LNSH	60069	2702	13W-24N	D1
400	VrnT	60045	2702	13W-24N	D1
500	BFGV	60089	2701	17W-20N	B7
700	BFGV	60089	2754	17W-20N	B1
Fars Cove					
8300	BRRG	60527	3208	15W-9S	C3
8300	DGvT	60527	3208	15W-9S	C3
Farthing Ln					
400	DSPN	60016	2862	15W-11N	B3
Farthingdale Ct					
21800	DRPK	60010	2698	23W-21N	E5
Far View Ct					
100	CmpT	60175	2962	41W-6N	A1
Farview Ct					
400	NARA	60542	3137	36W-4S	D1
Farview Dr					
300	NARA	60542	3137	36W-4S	E1
Far View Rd					
300	CmpT	60119	2962	41W-3N	A6
500	CmpT	60119	2961	41W-3N	E6
Farwell Av					
1600	DSPN	60018	2917	12W-8N	A2
4900	LNWD	60077	2919	6W-8N	E1
4900	LNWD	60712	2919	6W-8N	E1
4900	SKOK	60077	2919	6W-8N	D1
W Farwell Av					
1100	CHCG	60626	2921	2W-8N	B1
2400	CHCG	60645	2921	3W-8N	A1
2600	CHCG	60645	2920	3W-8N	E1
4700	LNWD	60712	2919	5W-8N	E1
7200	CHCG	60631	2918	9W-8N	D1
7200	CHCG	60714	2918	9W-8N	D1
7200	NLES	60714	2918	9W-8N	D1
Farwell Ct					
1000	GRNE	60031	2534	16W-33N	D4
Farwell Rd					
-	MTWA	60048	2648	14W-26N	C3
Farwell St					
10	MltT	60187	3024	25W-1N	B3
10	WHTN	60187	3024	25W-1N	B3
200	CLSM	60188	3024	25W-1N	B3
200	MltT	60188	3024	25W-1N	B3
Father Burns Dr					
10200	OKLN	60453	3275	6W-11S	E1
Faulkner Ct					
14100	LktT	60544	3339	27W-16S	B3
Faulkner Pl					
800	VNHL	60061	2647	17W-26N	C4
Faun Ln					
-	HnrT	60120	2856	31W-11N	A4
Faust Av					
-	JLET	60432	3499	22W-23S	C4
100	JltT	60432	3499	22W-23S	C4
Faversham Ct					
400	BGBK	60440	3205	22W-11S	D7
Fawell Blvd					
300	GNEN	60137	3083	22W-1S	B2
Fawell Ct					
600	WldT	60565	3267	27W-11S	C1
Fawn Ct					
10	BRRG	60527	3208	15W-9S	C4
500	CLSM	60188	2967	26W-3N	E5
600	SYHW	60118	2799	36W-15N	E3
1400	BGBK	60490	3267	26W-11S	E2
1400	BGBK	60490	3268	26W-11S	A2
4100	JLET	60431	3496	29W-23S	E5
5300	OKFT	60452	3347	6W-18S	E6
13400	ODPK	60462	3346	10W-15S	A2
Fawn Dr					
400	OSWG	60543	3263	38W-11S	A2
Fawn Grv					
3600	MchT	60097	2469	36W-35N	D5
Fawn Hllw					
1200	WDND	60118	2800	34W-15N	D4
Fawn Ln					
300	HNVL	60030	2532	21W-33N	C3
2800	SPGV	60081	2413	31W-40N	D3
3300	MchT	60097	2469	36W-35N	E6
E Fawn Ln					
400	PLTN	60074	2753	20W-18N	A2
Fawn Pth					
16700	LKPT	60441	3342	20W-17S	A6
16700	LktT	60441	3342	20W-17S	A6
Fawn Tr					
2900	PRGV	60012	2585	31W-28N	C6
8000	JSTC	60458	3209	11W-9S	E3
Fawn Creek Ln					
11000	ODPK	60467	3344	13W-18S	E7
11000	ODPK	60467	3345	13W-18S	A7
11100	OrlT	60467	3344	13W-18S	E7
15500	OrlT	60467	3345	13W-18S	A7
Fawn Lake Cir					
2300	NPVL	60564	3202	30W-10S	A5
W Fawn Lake Ct					
27400	CNHN	60410	3672	33W-30S	B4
Fawnlily Cir					
-	JLET	60431	3495	33W-22S	A1
-	JLET	60447	3495	33W-22S	A1
Fawn Ridge Ct					
900	YKVL	60560	3333	42W-16S	E5
Fawn Ridge Dr					
-	NndT	60013	2641	31W-26N	D2
10	ODHL	60013	2641	31W-26N	D2
Fawn Trail Ct					
2800	PRGV	60012	2585	31W-28N	C6
Fawn Trail Dr					
10800	ODPK	60467	3423	13W-20S	A5
Faxon Dr					
-	MTGY	60538	3198	41W-9S	A5
Faxon Rd					
10700	BtlT	60560	3261	43W-13S	A5
10700	YKVL	60560	3261	43W-13S	A5
10900	BtlT	60560	3260	44W-13S	E5
11600	BtlT	60545	3260	45W-13S	B5
11600	LtRT	60545	3260	46W-12S	A4
12000	PLNO	60545	3260	46W-12S	A4
Faxton Ln					
7200	JLET	60586	3415	33W-21S	B7
Fay Av					
10	WDND	60118	2801	33W-15N	A3
700	ADSN	60101	2971	17W-2N	C7
700	ADSN	60126	2971	17W-2N	C7
700	ADSN	60181	2971	17W-2N	B7
700	VLPK	60126	2971	17W-2N	C7
700	VLPK	60181	2971	17W-2N	C7
W Fay Av					
10	ADSN	60101	2970	18W-2N	E7
500	EMHT	60101	2971	17W-2N	C7
500	EMHT	60126	2971	17W-2N	C7
Fayette Ct					
100	MNKA	60447	3672	33W-30S	B4
Fayette Dr					
400	OSWG	60543	3264	35W-12S	B2
Fayette St					
100	BTVA	60510	3078	35W-0S	B1
500	HMND	46320	3352		D6
E Fayette St					
400	HMND	46320	3352		D6
Fayette Wk					
1700	HFET	60169	2858	25W-12N	B1
Fayetteville Av					
-	DndT	60118	2799	38W-16N	C1
-	RtdT	60118	2799	38W-16N	C1
Fays Ct					
300	SRGV	60554	3134	44W-7S	D7
Fays Ln					
1800	SRGV	60554	3134	44W-7S	E7
1900	BRKT	60554	3134	44W-7S	D7
Fears Dr					
-	MYWD	60153	3030	10W-1S	A7
-	PvsT	60141	3029	10W-1S	E7
-	PvsT	60141	3030	10W-1S	A7
-	PvsT	60153	3030	10W-1S	A7
Feather Ct					
300	CLSM	60188	2968	26W-3N	A5
13400	ODPK	60462	3346	11W-15S	A2
Feathercreek Rd					
5500	MTSN	60443	3505	6W-24S	E6
Featherock Dr					
400	AraT	60506	3199	38W-7S	A1
400	AURA	60506	3199	38W-7S	A1
Feather Sound Dr					
700	BGBK	60440	3205	21W-10S	D5
Featherstone Ct					
10	GfnT	60156	2693	38W-23N	A2
2300	SMBG	60194	2857	26W-10N	E5
Feature St					
-	BtnT	60096	2363	10W-43N	A5
-	WPHR	60096	2362	11W-43N	E5
-	WPHR	60096	2363	10W-43N	A5
Fechner Cir					
1400	NARA	60542	3077	37W-3S	B7
Federal Av					
-	AURA	60503	3201	32W-10S	C7
Federal Cir					
2300	LNHT	60046	2418	20W-39N	B5
25300	PNFD	60544	3337	31W-17S	E6
Federal Ct					
1900	JNBG	60050	2471	30W-35N	E5
1900	JNBG	60050	2472	30W-35N	A5
2400	LGGV	60047	2753	19W-20N	C1
2700	NndT	60012	2584	35W-29N	A4
9000	MaiT	60016	2863	11W-11N	D3
9000	MaiT	60068	2863	11W-11N	D3
9000	PKRG	60016	2863	11W-11N	E3
9000	PKRG	60068	2863	11W-11N	D3
Federal Dr					
400	CLLK	60014	2640	34W-25N	C5
2300	NRIV	60546	3088	9W-2S	D2
Federal Pkwy					
600	LNHT	60046	2418	20W-39N	B5
S Federal St					
300	CHCG	60604	3034	0W-0S	B5
500	CHCG	60605	3034	0W-0S	B6
3500	CHCG	60609	3092	0W-3S	C5
3500	CHCG	60616	3092	0W-3S	C5
4700	CHCG	60609	3152	0W-5S	C1
Federal Signal Dr					
2500	MonT	60449	3682	7W-29S	E1
2500	UYPK	60449	3682	7W-29S	E1
2500	UYPK	60466	3682	7W-29S	E1
Federation Pl					
400	ELGN	60123	2800	34W-13N	E7
Feece Dr					
10	BTVA	60510	3077	36W-1S	D2
10	BtvT	60510	3077	36W-1S	D2
10	BtvT	60539	3077	36W-1S	D2
Feehanville Rd					
800	MPPT	60056	2808	14W-13N	C6
1600	DSPN	60016	2808	14W-13N	D5
1600	MPPT	60016	2808	14W-13N	D5
Feeney Dr					
600	MNKA	60447	3672	33W-29S	A2
W Feeney Dr					
23200	PnfT	60586	3416	29W-19S	D3
23500	PNFD	60586	3416	29W-19S	D3
Feinberg Ct					
-	CRY	60013	2641	31W-24N	C7
Feinberg Dr					
-	CRY	60013	2641	31W-24N	C7
Feldner Ct					
100	PSHT	60463	3275	8W-15S	B7
Feldott Ln					
2000	NPVL	60540	3140	29W-7S	E7
Felicia Ct					
-	BMDL	60108	2969	22W-4N	D3
Fellemore Ln					
100	MTGY	60538	3199	36W-9S	D5
Fellows Ct					
100	EMHT	60126	3027	16W-1N	C3
Fellows Pl					
700	NCHI	60064	2537	10W-31N	A6
Fellows Rd					
10	GNCY	53128	2352		E4
10	GNCY	60071	2352		E4
10	RcmT	60071	2352		E4
500	BfdT	53128	2352		E3
Fellows St					
10	SCRL	60174	3020	35W-2N	B2
1200	SCRL	60174	3019	36W-2N	E1
N Fellowship Ln					
10	BtvT	60539	3077	36W-2S	E5
S Fellowship Ln					
-	BtvT	60542	3077	36W-3S	E6
100	BtvT	60539	3077	36W-3S	E6
Felsmith Rd					
10	HshT	60140	2743	46W-19N	B3
Felten St					
1600	AURA	60505	3139	33W-5S	A3
Feltes Ln					
2200	AraT	60542	3138	35W-4S	B1
2200	NARA	60542	3138	35W-4S	B1
Felton Rd					
800	AraT	60502	3139	33W-6S	A4
800	AURA	60502	3139	33W-6S	A4
800	AURA	60505	3139	33W-6S	A4
1100	AraT	60505	3139	33W-6S	A4
Fen Ln					
3000	WRLK	60097	2468	38W-35N	E6
Fencepost Ln					
500	CmpT	60175	2905	41W-7N	E5
500	CmpT	60175	2906	41W-7N	A5
Fence Rail Ct					
300	SchT	60175	2963	36W-5N	D2
Fencl Ln					
-	WSTR	60154	3028	13W-0S	E7
-	WSTR	60162	3028	13W-0S	E7
100	HLSD	60162	3028	13W-0S	E6
Fender Av					
100	LSLE	60532	3142	25W-4S	C1
100	LSLE	60563	3142	24W-5S	C3
100	LslT	60532	3142	25W-4S	C2
100	LslT	60563	3142	25W-4S	C2
Fender Rd					
1500	NPVL	60565	3204	25W-8S	C2
Fenimore Ln					
500	CmpT	60119	2961	43W-4N	A4
Fenimore Rd					
200	CLLK	60014	2640	33W-25N	D5
Fenmore Ct					
400	GNCY	53128	2353		B3
Fenmore Ln					
100	GNCY	53128	2353		B3
Fennel Ct					
700	SMBG	60193	2859	22W-9N	B7
Fennel Ln					
400	SMBG	60193	2859	22W-9N	B7
Fenton Av					
400	RMVL	60446	3340	24W-15S	E2
Fenton Ln					
300	WCHI	60185	3022	31W-0N	A5
1800	PKRG	60068	2863	11W-10N	E4
Fenton St					
900	AURA	60505	3138	34W-7S	E7
Fenview Cir					
700	ALGN	60102	2693	36W-20N	D7
Fenview Ct					
10	BGBK	60440	3205	21W-10S	D5
10	ODHL	60013	2641	31W-26N	D2
5300	LGGV	60047	2701	17W-22N	A4
11400	OrlT	60467	3344	14W-17S	E4
Fenview Dr					
21000	TRLK	60010	2643	27W-24N	C6
26800	LKBN	60010	2643	26W-24N	C6
Fenwick Ct					
1800	SMBG	60194	2858	25W-11N	B3
Fenwick Ln					
500	SEGN	60177	2908	35W-9N	B1
Fenwood Ct					
11500	OrlT	60467	3344	14W-17S	D5
Fenwood Ln					
200	HLSD	60162	3028	13W-0S	E5
Fenz Rd					
-	SMBG	60193	2912	25W-8N	B3
Ferdinand Av					
-	BGVW	60455	3210	9W-9S	D3
400	FTPK	60130	3030	9W-0S	D5
S Ferdinand Av					
7100	BGVW	60455	3148	9W-8S	D7
7300	BGVW	60455	3210	9W-8S	D1
W Ferdinand St					
1600	CHCG	60622	3033	2W-0N	B3
1900	CHCG	60612	3033	2W-0N	B3
4200	CHCG	60624	3032	5W-0N	B3
4700	CHCG	60644	3032	5W-0N	A3
4800	CHCG	60644	3031	6W-0N	E3
Fermi Ct					
300	SMBG	60193	2858	24W-10N	D6
Fern					
-	JSTC	60458	3210	10W-9S	C2
Fern Av					
-	GRNE	60085	2536	13W-34N	A2
-	PKCY	60085	2536	13W-34N	A2
900	SCRL	60174	3020	34W-2N	C1
2800	NHBK	60062	2756	11W-16N	E7
4000	LYNS	60534	3088	10W-4S	A7
5400	OKFT	60452	3347	6W-17S	E5
S Fern Av					
500	EMHT	60126	3028	15W-0N	B4
900	YkTp	60126	3028	15W-0S	B6
Fern Ct					
10	ISLK	60042	2586	29W-28N	D5
10	LKZH	60047	2699	22W-22N	C3
200	FXLK	60020	2473	27W-36N	C3
600	SMBG	60193	2859	23W-9N	B7
N Fern Ct					
1700	CHCG	60614	2978	0W-2N	A7
S Fern Ct					
600	EMHT	60126	3028	15W-0N	B5
W Fern Ct					
10	PLTN	60067	2805	21W-14N	E3
Fern Dr					
-	LKPT	60441	3420	19W-20S	C4
200	EGVV	60007	2914	18W-8N	E2
300	ISLK	60042	2586	28W-28N	E5
S Fern Dr					
1100	MPPT	60056	2861	16W-11N	D3
Fern Ln					
9300	MaiT	60016	2863	11W-11N	D2
Fern Rd					
-	ElaT	60047	2699	22W-22N	C3
10	LKZH	60047	2699	21W-22N	C3
E Fern Rd					
-	LKZH	60047	2699	22W-23N	C2
Fern St					
-	LNSG	60438	3429	2E-21S	D6
-	ThtT	60438	3429	2E-21S	D6
600	DGvT	60527	3207	16W-9S	D4
2100	CTHL	60403	3417	26W-21S	E7
W Fern St					
23500	PNFD	60586	3416	29W-19S	D2
23500	PnfT	60586	3416	29W-19S	D2
Fernald Av					
8500	MNGV	60053	2865	7W-10N	B4
N Fernandez Av					
1900	ANHT	60004	2753	18W-16N	E7
1900	ANHT	60004	2806	18W-16N	E1
S Fernandez Av					
100	ANHT	60005	2806	18W-13N	E5
1100	ANHT	60005	2860	18W-12N	E2
S Fernandez Ct					
1300	ANHT	60005	2860	18W-12N	E1
N Fernandez Pl					
1500	ANHT	60004	2806	18W-15N	E2
Ferncroft Ct					
1000	NPVL	60563	3141	28W-5S	A2
Ferndale Av					
100	RMVL	60446	3340	24W-16S	E4
1200	HDPK	60035	2704	9W-21N	B6
1600	NHBK	60062	2757	9W-17N	B4
N Ferndale Av					
300	EMHT	60126	3027	17W-2N	C1
Ferndale Ct					
10	LKZH	60047	2699	22W-22N	C4
200	PTHT	60070	2808	14W-14N	B3
300	SMBG	60193	2859	21W-9N	D6
400	BFGV	60089	2754	16W-20N	D1
1000	WLNG	60090	2754	15W-18N	E2
Ferndale Dr					
10	RLKB	60073	2475	23W-34N	A7
100	RLKB	60073	2474	23W-34N	E7
Ferndale Ln					
400	PTHT	60070	2808	14W-14N	B4
Ferndale Rd					
10	DRFD	60015	2757	9W-20N	B2
10	DRPK	60010	2752	23W-20N	A2
10	PltT	60010	2752	23W-20N	A2
300	GNVW	60025	2811	6W-13N	C6
Ferndale St					
500	GRNE	60031	2478	13W-34N	E7
Ferne Dr					
300	WLNG	60090	2755	13W-17N	D5
Fernilee Ct					
10	SgrT	60506	3136	41W-5S	A4
Fernleaf Dr					
1200	CLLK	60014	2693	36W-23N	D2
Fernview Ln					
36800	WrnT	60046	2476	18W-36N	D3
W Fernview Ln					
1700	HHLL	60051	2586	30W-30N	A2
1700	NndT	60051	2586	30W-30N	A2
2200	HHLL	60051	2585	30W-30N	E2
2200	NndT	60051	2585	30W-30N	E2
Fernwood Av					
900	JltT	60432	3499	22W-22S	D2
1000	JLET	60432	3499	21W-22S	D1
1000	LktT	60432	3499	21W-21S	D1
Fernwood Ct					
10	ALGN	60102	2747	36W-19N	A2
10	CRY	60013	2695	32W-22N	A3
10	RMVL	60446	3269	23W-14S	A7
10	SMWD	60107	2857	26W-11N	E4
10	VNHL	60061	2647	17W-25N	B6
300	WTMT	60559	3144	18W-6S	E5
1500	GRNE	60031	2478	14W-35N	B5
5600	MTSN	60443	3505	7W-24S	D4
8900	ODPK	60462	3346	11W-17S	A6
Fernwood Dr					
10	BGBK	60440	3269	23W-12S	A3
10	BNHL	60010	2748	30W-16N	E7
10	BNHL	60010	2801	30W-16N	E1
10	BNHL	60010	2802	30W-16N	A1
10	MaiT	60025	2864	9W-12N	C1
100	GNVW	60025	2864	9W-12N	C1
100	NPVL	60540	3203	27W-7S	C1
400	WTMT	60559	3144	18W-6S	E4
6500	LSLE	60532	3142	24W-7S	D6
N Fernwood Dr					
200	OSWG	60538	3200	35W-10S	B6
200	OSWG	60543	3200	35W-10S	B6
200	OswT	60538	3200	35W-10S	B6
200	OswT	60543	3200	35W-10S	B6
Fernwood Ln					
100	BMDL	60108	2968	24W-5N	C1
200	GNVW	60025	2864	9W-12N	C1
1700	ALGN	60102	2747	36W-19N	A2
S Fernwood Ln					
1800	NndT	60051	2585	31W-30N	E2
Fernwood Rd					
-	MTGY	60538	3199	36W-10S	D6
10	OswT	60538	3199	36W-10S	D6
200	OSWG	60543	3200	36W-10S	A6
200	OswT	60538	3200	36W-10S	A6
200	OswT	60543	3200	36W-10S	A6
Fernwood St					
200	HMND	46324	3430		D3
Fernwood Ter					
1400	NLNX	60451	3588	19W-26S	E2
1400	NLNX	60451	3589	19W-26S	A3
Ferrara Ct					
900	CRY	60013	2695	32W-23N	B2
Ferrari Ct					
300	BMDL	60157	2913	22W-6N	B6
Ferrari Dr					
1000	BNVL	60106	2971	16W-3N	E4
Ferret Cross					
700	OSWG	60543	3262	39W-11S	E1
700	OSWG	60543	3263	39W-11S	A2
Ferris Av					
8500	MNGV	60053	2865	7W-10N	A4
Ferris Pl					
100	RKDL	60436	3498	25W-25S	C7
400	JLET	60436	3498	26W-24S	A6
Ferris St					
-	JLET	60436	3498	25W-24S	C7
-	RKDL	60436	3498	25W-24S	C7
Ferro Dr					
-	NlxT	60433	3500	20W-24S	C6
-	NlxT	60451	3500	20W-24S	C6
1800	NLNX	60451	3500	19W-24S	D6
Ferry Rd					
-	AURA	60502	3079	31W-4S	E7
-	AURA	60502	3139	31W-4S	E1
-	WNVL	60555	3141	28W-4S	A1
10	NPVL	60563	3080	29W-4S	C7
10	WNVL	60563	3080	29W-4S	C7
100	AURA	60502	3080	30W-4S	B7
100	AURA	60563	3080	30W-4S	B7
100	NpvT	60502	3080	30W-4S	B7
100	NpvT	60563	3080	30W-4S	B7
27600	WNVL	60555	3081	27W-4S	B7
Ferry Rd CO-1					
200	WNVL	60555	3081	28W-4S	A7
Ferry Rd CO-3					
-	WNVL	60555	3141	28W-4S	A1
27600	WNVL	60555	3081	27W-4S	B7
Ferry Rd CO-13					
-	WNVL	60555	3081	28W-4S	B7
W Ferry Rd					
1300	NPVL	60563	3080	29W-4S	D7
1300	NPVL	60563	3140	29W-4S	D1

STREET Block	City	ZIP	Map#	CGS	Grid
W Ferry Rd					
1800	WNVL	60563	3080	29W-4S	D7
Ferry St					
1400	WKGN	60087	2479	11W-37N	E2
Ferryville Dr					
100	LIHL	60156	2692	38W-21N	D6
Ferson Ct					
200	LYLK	60175	2961	43W-5N	B3
Ferson Creek Rd					
-	SCRL	60174	2964	36W-4N	A5
10	SchT	60174	2963	36W-4N	E5
200	SchT	60174	2964	36W-3N	A5
Ferson Woods Dr					
10	SchT	60175	2963	38W-6N	B1
200	SchT	60175	2907	38W-6N	A7
Fescue Ct					
200	LKZH	60047	2699	23W-21N	A5
300	LYLK	60175	2961	43W-5N	A2
Fescue Dr					
1800	AURA	60504	3201	33W-8S	B2
24800	PNFD	60544	3338	31W-16S	A4
Fescue Rd					
2300	NPVL	60564	3266	29W-13S	D5
Fesseneva Ct					
4600	NPVL	60564	3266	29W-12S	D3
Fesseneva Ln					
4700	NPVL	60564	3266	29W-12S	C4
Fessler Av					
500	NPVL	60565	3203	27W-8S	C2
Fessler Dr					
100	BMDL	60108	2969	23W-5N	A1
Festival Ct					
1800	JLET	60435	3498	26W-22S	A2
N Fetz Av					
700	JLET	60435	3498	24W-23S	E3
W Fey Ln					
4400	ALSP	60803	3276	5W-13S	B5
Fiala Woods Ct					
200	NPVL	60565	3204	25W-10S	A6
Fiday Rd					
3200	JLET	60431	3417	28W-21S	B7
3200	JLET	60435	3417	28W-21S	B7
3300	PnfT	60431	3417	28W-21S	B7
W Fiday Rd					
3000	JLET	60431	3417	28W-21S	A7
3000	PnfT	60431	3417	28W-21S	A7
3100	JLET	60431	3416	28W-21S	E7
3100	PnfT	60431	3416	28W-21S	E7
Fiddlers Grn					
400	CPVL	60110	2800	35W-16N	C1
Fiddyment Dr					
1600	RMVL	60446	3339	27W-18S	D7
1700	RMVL	60446	3417	27W-18S	D1
Fidler Ct					
1500	AURA	60502	3079	33W-3S	A6
Field Av					
3100	BDVW	60155	3087	11W-2S	C2
N Field Blvd					
-	CHCG	60601	3034	0E-0N	D4
Field Ct					
-	GnvT	60134	3019	38W-0N	A4
500	DndT	60118	2747	36W-18N	B4
1200	NPVL	60540	3141	28W-6S	A6
1800	JLET	60586	3415	33W-21S	B7
6500	NndT	60012	2640	35W-27N	A1
N Field Ct					
10	LKFT	60045	2648	13W-26N	E4
10	LKFT	60045	2649	13W-26N	A4
Field Dr					
-	SMBG	60173	2860	21W-11N	A3
N Field Dr					
-	CHCG	60601	3034	0E-0N	D4
-	VrnT	60045	2648	13W-26N	E4
100	LKFT	60045	2648	13W-26N	E3
8100	NLES	60714	2864	10W-10N	B5
Field Ln					
300	SMWD	60107	2857	28W-10N	B5
W Field Pkwy					
21500	DRPK	60010	2752	21W-20N	C1
21500	DRPK	60074	2752	21W-20N	C1
N Field Rd					
23500	ElaT	60047	2699	21W-23N	D2
E Field St					
800	HMND	46320	3430		E1
800	HMND	46324	3430		E1
Fieldale Ln					
700	GYLK	60030	2533	19W-34N	D1
800	TDLK	60030	2533	19W-34N	D1
Fieldbrook Av					
2800	WCDA	60030	2588	25W-30N	B2
2800	WCDA	60084	2588	25W-30N	B2
Fieldbrook Dr					
-	PNFD	60544	3338	31W-16S	A5
25100	PNFD	60544	3337	31W-16S	E5
Field Crest Av					
8300	WLSP	60480	3208	14W-9S	E3
Fieldcrest Ct					
10	ALGN	60102	2694	35W-21N	A7
100	GYLK	60030	2475	20W-35N	E5
100	MNKA	60447	3583	32W-28S	C7
4500	JLET	60586	3416	29W-21S	D6
Fieldcrest Dr					
-	MKHM	60426	3426	5W-19S	C2
-	MKHM	60428	3426	5W-19S	C1
10	OSWG	60543	3263	37W-11S	D1
10	OswT	60538	3263	37W-11S	D1
10	SchT	60175	2964	36W-5N	A2
10	SCRL	60175	2964	36W-5N	A2
100	BRLT	60103	2909	32W-8N	B3
300	ALGN	60102	2694	35W-21N	B6
500	WCHI	60185	2966	29W-2N	D7
600	SEGN	60177	2908	35W-9N	A1
800	BGBK	60490	3268	26W-13S	A6
800	NPVL	60540	3202	29W-8S	D1
2100	MDLN	60060	2590	20W-29N	A5
2500	FmtT	60060	2589	20W-29N	E5
2500	MDLN	60060	2589	20W-29N	E5
4500	OKFT	60452	3426	5W-19S	B3
16200	BmnT	60426	3426	5W-19S	C2
16200	BmnT	60452	3426	5W-19S	C2
Fieldgate Dr					
100	SCRL	60174	2964	33W-3N	E6
S Fielding Av					
7700	CHCG	60620	3214	0W-8S	B1
Fielding Ct					
600	CmpT	60175	2906	39W-7N	E4
600	CmpT	60175	2907	39W-7N	A5
600	SchT	60175	2907	39W-7N	A5
Fielding Dr					
1500	GNVW	60025	2810	9W-14N	C4
W Fielding Ln					
300	RDLK	60073	2531	23W-32N	E4
Fielding Place Ct					
-	DRPK	60010	2751	23W-18N	D2
-	PltT	60010	2751	23W-18N	D2
Field Point Rd					
10	OswT	60538	3263	37W-11S	D1
Fields Dr					
300	KdlT	60560	3334	40W-15S	C2
5500	OswT	60560	3334	40W-15S	C2
Fields Ter					
-	WKGN	60087	2479	11W-36N	D3
Fieldside Dr					
900	MTSN	60443	3505	7W-25S	C7
Fieldside Ln					
1400	AraT	60542	3137	38W-4S	B1
1400	NARA	60542	3137	38W-4S	B1
Fieldside Ln E					
900	AURA	60504	3201	32W-8S	D3
Fieldside Ln W					
800	AURA	60504	3201	32W-9S	D3
Fieldstone Cir					
700	LKZH	60047	2699	22W-21N	A6
Fieldstone Ct					
-	IVNS	60010	2750	25W-17N	E6
100	LKVL	60046	2475	22W-36N	A3
300	BGBK	60440	3269	22W-13S	D4
300	NARA	60542	3137	38W-4S	A2
900	SchT	60175	2963	36W-4N	D3
900	SMBG	60194	2858	24W-11N	D3
1000	ELGN	60120	2855	32W-12N	D1
1100	BRLT	60103	2966	30W-5N	C1
1300	NPVL	60564	3203	28W-10S	A6
1700	RMVL	60446	3339	27W-17S	C5
1700	SRWD	60404	3495	31W-25S	E7
2000	JLET	60586	3415	31W-21S	E7
2600	AURA	60502	3079	32W-4S	C7
4200	GRNE	60031	2535	14W-33N	D2
27100	CbaT	60010	2643	27W-24N	C7
27100	LKBN	60010	2643	27W-24N	C7
S Fieldstone Ct					
300	RDLK	60073	2530	25W-33N	E4
300	RDLK	60073	2531	25W-32N	A4
25600	CNHN	60410	3672	32W-31S	C5
Fieldstone Dr					
-	WDSK	60098	2581	41W-29N	D4
-	WLBK	60527	3146	15W-7S	B6
10	LKVL	60046	2475	22W-36N	A3
1100	CLLK	60014	2693	37W-23N	C1
3100	GNVA	60134	3019	37W-1N	C2
4200	GRNE	60031	2535	14W-33N	D2
6700	BRRG	60527	3146	15W-7S	B6
13700	HTLY	60142	2744	43W-19N	B2
22600	FKFT	60423	3592	10W-27S	B4
Fieldstone Dr N					
1600	SRWD	60404	3495	31W-25S	E7
Fieldstone Dr S					
1600	SRWD	60404	3495	32W-25S	D7
1600	SRWD	60404	3583	31W-25S	E1
Fieldstone Ln					
-	SRWD	60404	3495	31W-25S	E7
-	SRWD	60404	3496	29W-25S	D7
400	HPSR	60140	2795	47W-15N	C3
400	HshT	60140	2795	47W-15N	C3
1100	BRLT	60103	2966	30W-5N	C1
Fieldstone Pl					
16300	LKPT	60441	3420	20W-19S	B3
S Fieldstone Pth					
25700	CNHN	60410	3672	32W-31S	C6
Fieldstone Rd					
10	RGMW	60008	2806	19W-14N	C4
Fieldstone Tr					
5700	MHRY	60050	2527	34W-32N	C5
Fieldstone Wy					
5300	JNBG	60050	2471	31W-37N	D2
Fieldview Ct					
15200	LKPT	60441	3342	20W-18S	B7
N Field View Dr					
36200	WrnT	60031	2477	17W-36N	B4
Fieldwood Dr					
1700	NHBK	60062	2757	10W-16N	A7
1800	NHBK	60062	2756	10W-16N	E7
S Fiene Dr					
800	ADSN	60101	2970	18W-2N	E7
Fiesta Dr					
900	UYPK	60466	3684	3W-30S	A2
2200	JLET	60432	3500	21W-23S	A3
2200	JltT	60432	3500	21W-23S	A3
Fife Ct					
700	IVNS	60010	2751	24W-16N	B6
Fifth Av					
-	HbnT	60034	2351	40W-41N	B7
Figard Ln					
500	DSPN	60016	2862	15W-11N	B3
Fighting Saints Ln					
-	SCRL	60174	2964	34W-3N	E5
Figura Dr					
7400	JSTC	60458	3209	11W-8S	E1
Filbert Dr					
100	SMWD	60107	2857	27W-10N	C6
Filip Rd					
10	ALGN	60102	2747	33W-20N	D1
Fillmore Av					
500	DYR	46311	3510		E5
500	MNSR	46321	3510		E5
Fillmore Ln					
10	SMWD	60107	2856	29W-10N	E6
Fillmore Rd					
3600	JNBG	60050	2471	32W-35N	B5
Fillmore St					
-	BDVW	60153	3029	11W-0S	E7
-	FTPK	60153	3030	10W-0S	A7
-	MYWD	60153	3029	11W-0S	D7
-	MYWD	60153	3030	10W-0S	A7
-	OKPK	60130	3030	9W-0S	D7
-	OKPK	60304	3030	9W-0S	D7
10	CHCG	60304	3031	7W-0S	B6
10	CHCG	60644	3031	7W-0S	B6
10	OKPK	60304	3031	8W-0S	A6
500	EMHT	60126	3028	15W-0S	A7
500	YkTp	60126	3028	15W-0S	A7
1700	BDVW	60155	3029	11W-0S	D7
7300	FTPK	60130	3030	9W-0S	D7
W Fillmore St					
1300	CHCG	60607	3033	1W-0S	D6
1800	CHCG	60612	3033	2W-0S	C6
2800	CHCG	60612	3032	4W-0S	D6
3100	CHCG	60624	3032	5W-0S	B6
5600	CHCG	60644	3031	7W-0S	C6
5900	CHCG	60304	3031	7W-0S	B6
5900	OKPK	60304	3031	7W-0S	B6
Filly Dr					
13500	HMGN	60491	3343	16W-18S	D7
Filly Ln					
600	RLKP	60030	2589	22W-30N	C1
1300	BRLT	60103	2966	30W-5N	C1
Filmore Av					
7400	HRPK	60133	2912	25W-9N	A2
Filweber Ct					
400	ANTH	60002	2357	23W-42N	D6
S Financial Pl					
300	CHCG	60604	3034	0W-0S	B5
400	CHCG	60605	3034	0W-0S	B6
800	CHCG	60607	3034	0W-0S	B6
Finbar Pl					
9300	OrlT	60487	3423	11W-21S	E6
Finborough Cir					
2000	NLNX	60451	3590	15W-25S	B1
2000	NlxT	60451	3590	15W-25S	B1
Finch Av					
15700	HRVY	60426	3428	1W-19S	A2
Finch Ct					
10	NPVL	60565	3203	26W-9S	E3
10	SMWD	60107	2856	30W-10N	C6
3600	RGMW	60008	2806	20W-13N	B5
4300	GRNE	60031	2478	14W-34N	D7
5900	LGGV	60047	2701	17W-23N	B1
13000	HMGN	60491	3344	16W-18S	A7
S Finch Ct					
1900	WKGN	60048	2535	14W-31N	C6
Finch Dr					
400	RDLK	60073	2531	25W-33N	A2
1400	JLET	60586	3496	29W-22S	D1
Finch St					
7600	SPGV	60081	2413	31W-39N	E5
Finch Tr					
700	MchT	60050	2472	29W-36N	C3
Fincharn Ln					
100	IVNS	60067	2752	22W-16N	A7
Finchley Ct					
1900	SMBG	60194	2858	26W-11N	A3
N Finley Av					
2200	FNPK	60171	2973	11W-2N	D6
2200	RVGV	60171	2973	11W-2N	D6
2300	FNPK	60131	2973	11W-2N	D6
S Finley Av					
13900	RBBN	60472	3348	4W-16S	E3
Finley Ct					
500	BTVA	60510	3078	34W-2S	D3
Finley Dr					
8900	HYHL	60457	3209	11W-9S	E4
8900	HYHL	60457	3210	11W-9S	A4
Finley Rd					
-	DRGV	60515	3143	21W-4S	E1
-	MrnT	60037	2704	9W-24N	D1
10	DRGV	60515	3083	21W-4S	E7
10	DRGV	60532	3083	21W-4S	E7
10	LslT	60532	3083	21W-4S	E7
10	LslT	60532	3084	21W-4S	A7
500	BbyT	60554	3075	43W-3S	A6
2400	DRGV	60148	3084	20W-2S	A3
2400	DRGV	60515	3084	20W-2S	A3
2400	LMBD	60148	3084	20W-2S	A3
2400	LMBD	60515	3084	20W-2S	A3
Finley Rd CO-2					
-	DRGV	60515	3143	21W-4S	E1
10	DRGV	60515	3083	21W-4S	E7
10	DRGV	60532	3083	21W-4S	E7
10	LslT	60532	3083	21W-4S	E7
10	LslT	60532	3084	21W-4S	A7
3000	DRGV	60515	3084	20W-2S	B4
S Finley Rd					
10	LMBD	60148	3026	20W-0S	A7
400	LMBD	60148	3084	20W-1S	A2
400	YkTp	60148	3084	20W-1S	A2
700	YkTp	60148	3026	20W-0S	A6
1000	GNEN	60137	3026	20W-0S	A7
1000	GNEN	60148	3026	20W-0S	A7
Finn Ct					
2400	JLET	60586	3416	29W-20S	D6
Finney St					
100	HRVD	60033	2406	50W-38N	B7
Finnie Rd					
7500	FoxT	60541	3330	49W-17S	E7
Finsbury Ln					
200	LGPK	60525	3087	12W-2S	C3
Finstad Dr					
100	LYVL	60048	2591	16W-30N	D2
Fintan Ct					
10600	MKNA	60448	3503	13W-23S	B3
Fiona Av					
19400	MKNA	60448	3503	13W-23S	B3
Fiore Dr					
1200	LKFT	60045	2649	12W-24N	B7
N Fiore Pkwy					
10	VNHL	60061	2647	18W-25N	A6
S Fiore Pkwy					
10	VNHL	60061	2647	18W-24N	A6
Fir Cir					
6600	NndT	60012	2640	35W-27N	A1
Fir Ct					
200	SMWD	60107	2857	27W-10N	C5
300	GNEN	60137	3083	23W-1S	A2
700	YKVL	60560	3333	43W-15S	A2
1300	NPVL	60540	3141	28W-6S	A6
2100	LKPT	60441	3419	22W-20S	D5
4000	HFET	60192	2804	24W-15N	B3
Fir Dr					
7800	MchT	60097	2469	36W-37N	D2
Fir Ln					
-	GNEN	60137	3083	23W-1S	A2
10	LynT	60458	3209	12W-8S	D1
28300	WmTp	60481	3761	32W-34S	D5
Fir St					
-	BCHR	60401	3864	0W-36S	D1
10	CPVL	60110	2748	32W-18N	C5
10	PKFT	60466	3595	3W-26S	B3
100	LIHL	60156	2694	35W-22N	A4
100	NLNX	60451	3501	17W-24S	C5
200	NlxT	60451	3501	17W-24S	C5
2200	GNVW	60025	2810	9W-13N	C6
8500	ODPK	60462	3346	10W-16S	B2
Fire Fox Ct					
1000	SCRL	60174	2965	33W-4N	A5
Firenze Dr					
200	CRY	60013	2695	32W-23N	B2
23000	FKFT	60423	3591	13W-27S	A5
23000	GGnT	60423	3591	13W-27S	A5
Fireside Ct					
1300	NPVL	60564	3203	28W-10S	A6
3800	JLET	60435	3417	27W-19S	C2
Fireside Dr					
6400	CHRG	60415	3275	8W-11S	B1
Firestone Ct					
10	NpvT	60563	3140	30W-5S	B2
N Firestone Ct					
4100	HFET	60192	2804	24W-15N	D2
Firestone Dr					
13300	ODPK	60462	3346	11W-15S	A2
25500	MONE	60449	3683	6W-31S	B5
N Firestone Dr					
3600	HFET	60192	2804	24W-14N	D3
W Firestone Dr					
800	HFET	60192	2804	24W-15N	D2
Firestone Ln					
1100	AURA	60502	3139	32W-6S	D4
N Firestone Ln					
3900	HFET	60192	2804	24W-14N	C3
Firethorn Ct					
10	BGBK	60490	3267	26W-11S	E1
10	LMNT	60439	3271	17W-15S	D7
10	LMNT	60439	3343	17W-15S	D1
Firethorn St					
1400	BGBK	60490	3267	26W-11S	E1
First Av					
-	HbnT	60034	2351	40W-41N	B7
First St					
-	PNFD	60586	3415	32W-19S	D3
100	WDSK	60098	2524	41W-31N	D7
1400	TNLK	53181	2354		A2
First Bank Plz					
-	LKZH	60047	2698	24W-22N	D4
Firth Ct					
500	FKFT	60423	3592	10W-26S	C2
7300	LKWD	60014	2639	38W-24N	A6
Firth Rd					
10	IVNS	60067	2804	23W-15N	E2
700	MDLN	60060	2590	19W-28N	C6
1600	IVNS	60067	2805	23W-15N	A2
Fischer Dr					
-	GLHT	60137	3025	23W-1N	A2
-	GLHT	60139	3025	23W-1N	A2
-	MltT	60137	3025	23W-1N	A2
N Fischer Dr					
900	ADSN	60101	2970	19W-4N	C2
33800	GrtT	60041	2530	26W-33N	C2
34000	VOLO	60041	2530	26W-33N	C2
Fischer St					
-	WHTN	60187	3024	24W-0S	D7
400	WNFD	60190	3023	27W-0S	C7
1100	WHTN	60187	3082	24W-1S	D1
W Fischer Farm Rd					
300	EMHT	60126	2971	16W-2N	D6
Fisher Av					
100	RKDL	60436	3498	25W-25S	C7
Fisher Dr					
100	AddT	60106	2971	17W-4N	C4
2100	NPVL	60563	3140	30W-4S	B2
2100	NpvT	60563	3140	30W-4S	B2
N Fisher Dr					
-	GNVA	60134	3019	37W-1N	C3
-	SchT	60134	3019	37W-1N	C2
-	SCRL	60134	3019	37W-1N	C2
S Fisher Dr					
-	GNVA	60134	3019	37W-1N	C4
-	GnvT	60134	3019	37W-1N	C4
Fisher Ln					
900	WNKA	60093	2759	5W-16N	A7
1000	GLNC	60093	2759	5W-16N	A7
Fisher Pl					
500	MNSR	46321	3510		D1
Fisher Rd					
-	NCHI	60088	2594	10W-30N	A1
30700	VOLO	60051	2530	28W-31N	A7
30700	WcnT	60051	2530	28W-31N	A7
30700	WcnT	60051	2586	28W-30N	E1
30700	WcnT	60051	2587	28W-30N	A1
Fisher St					
400	MNSR	46321	3510		D1
Fishermans Ter					
4100	LYNS	60534	3088	9W-4S	D7
4500	LYNS	60534	3148	9W-4S	D1
Fishhook Wy					
2300	WCDA	60084	2588	25W-29N	B3
Fishing Ln					
200	WDDL	60191	2970	18W-5N	E1
N Fish Lake Rd					
30700	WcnT	60030	2587	26W-30N	E1
30700	WcnT	60073	2587	26W-30N	E2
31000	VOLO	60030	2530	26W-31N	E7
31000	VOLO	60030	2587	26W-30N	E1
31000	VOLO	60073	2530	26W-31N	E7
31900	GrtT	60073	2530	26W-32N	E4
32900	GrtT	60041	2530	26W-33N	E4
Fishook Bay					
10	LKMR	60051	2529	28W-33N	E3
W Fisk Av					
800	JLET	60436	3498	25W-24S	C6
Fisk St					
15700	HRVY	60426	3428	1W-18S	A1
17100	EHZC	60429	3428	1W-20S	A5
17400	HMWD	60429	3428	1W-20S	A5
17400	HMWD	60430	3428	1W-20S	A5
Fiskeville Ln					
1100	SMBG	60193	2912	25W-9N	C1
Fitch Av					
4900	SKOK	60077	2919	6W-8N	D1
W Fitch Av					
2400	CHCG	60645	2921	3W-8N	A1
2600	CHCG	60645	2920	3W-8N	E1
3800	LNWD	60712	2920	4W-8N	B1
6300	CHCG	60646	2919	7W-8N	A1
7200	CHCG	60631	2918	9W-8N	D1
7200	CHCG	60714	2918	9W-8N	D1
7200	NLES	60714	2918	9W-8N	D1
Fitch Ct					
1800	BTVA	60510	3078	34W-3S	D5
Fitch Rd					
400	CHHT	60411	3507	2W-24S	D5
Fitchome St					
2200	AraT	60506	3198	39W-8S	D2
2200	AraT	60506	3199	38W-8S	A2
Fitzgerald Ln					
11100	GfnT	60142	2691	41W-20N	D7
11600	GfnT	60142	2744	41W-20N	D1
Fitzgerald Rd					
1800	WDRG	60516	3206	20W-8S	A1
1800	WDRG	60517	3206	20W-8S	A1
W Fitzhenry Ct					
700	GNWD	60425	3428	0W-21S	B7
Fitzhugh Turn					
-	YKVL	60560	3333	42W-17S	D7
Fitzpatrick Ct					
1600	JLET	60431	3497	28W-21S	B1
Fitzsimmons Dr					
10400	PlsT	60464	3345	13W-15S	B1
10500	PlsT	60462	3345	13W-15S	B1
Five Island Rd					
-	SchT	60174	2908	34W-6N	D7
Five Oaks Dr					
-	FftT	60423	3590	14W-28S	E5
-	FKFT	60423	3590	14W-28S	E5
Flag Ln					
-	SRWD	60404	3495	31W-24S	E7
Flag Day Dr					
1500	BTVA	60510	3078	34W-2S	E4
Flagg Ct					
300	HNDL	60521	3146	15W-4S	B1
Flagg Dr					
13100	PNFD	60585	3337	31W-15S	E2
13200	PNFD	60585	3338	31W-15S	A3
Flagg Ln					
700	WDSK	60098	2524	41W-31N	E6
Flagg St					
300	AURA	60505	3138	35W-7S	B7
Flagpole Ct					
10	ELGN	60124	2853	37W-11N	D5
Flagstaff Ct					
1900	GLHT	60139	2968	24W-3N	D5
Flagstaff Dr					
100	BGBK	60440	3268	24W-11S	E2
Flagstaff Ln					
10	HFET	60169	2859	23W-11N	A3
200	HFET	60169	2858	24W-11N	E3
1000	JLET	60432	3500	20W-22S	C2
1800	GLHT	60139	2968	24W-3N	D5
Flagstone Cir					
2600	NPVL	60564	3202	29W-9S	C4
Flagstone Ct					
2100	NARA	60542	3078	35W-3S	B6
Flagstone Dr					
1600	CLLK	60014	2693	37W-22N	B3
2200	CPVL	60110	2748	33W-19N	C3
Flagstone Ln					
1700	AURA	60502	3079	33W-3S	A6
Flagstone Pl					
-	SMBG	60193	2912	25W-8N	B2
Flagstone Turn					
-	NlxT	60451	3590	14W-27S	D4
11600	FKFT	60423	3590	14W-27S	D4
E Flake Dr					
1000	PLTN	60074	2753	19W-16N	B7
N Flake Dr					
100	PLTN	60074	2753	19W-16N	C7
Flambeau Ct					
600	RMVL	60446	3340	24W-15S	C1
Flambeau Dr					
2200	NPVL	60564	3203	28W-10S	A6
2200	NpvT	60564	3203	28W-10S	A6
2200	WldT	60564	3203	28W-10S	A6
S Flambeau Dr					
12000	PSHT	60463	3275	8W-14S	A6
Flame Ct					
600	CLSM	60188	3024	24W-1N	D2
Flame Dr					
200	CLSM	60188	3024	24W-1N	D2
Flamenco Ct					
10	NpvT	60563	3140	30W-5S	C3
Flamingo Cir					
8400	ODPK	60462	3346	10W-18S	B7
Flamingo Ct					
400	MltT	60148	3083	21W-2S	E4
Flamingo Dr					
-	HGKN	60525	3147	11W-7S	E5
10	ROSL	60172	2912	24W-7N	C4
8800	TYPK	60487	3424	11W-21S	A7
W Flamingo Dr					
1200	ROSL	60172	2912	25W-7N	C4
Flamingo Ln					
10	MltT	60148	3083	21W-2S	E3
W Flamingo Ln					
27500	AntT	60081	2415	27W-38N	C7
Flamingo Pkwy					
1200	LYVL	60048	2647	16W-27N	E1
Flamingo Ter					
8400	HYHL	60457	3210	10W-11S	B6
Flaming Oaks Ct					
700	WnfT	60185	3022	29W-0N	E4
Flanagan Cir					
400	MNKA	60447	3672	34W-29S	A1
Flanagan Dr					
500	MNKA	60447	3672	34W-29S	A2
Flanders Ct					
1100	AURA	60502	3139	32W-6S	B4
4700	JLET	60586	3416	29W-21S	C7
Flanders Ln					
400	GYLK	60030	2533	20W-33N	A3
N Flanders Ln					
100	WnfT	60190	3081	28W-1S	B1
S Flanders Ln					
-	PNFD	60544	3338	30W-17S	B7
W Flanders Ln					
100	WnfT	60190	3081	28W-1S	A1
W Flanders Rd					
4800	MchT	60050	2527	34W-34N	C1
4800	MCLK	60050	2470	33W-34N	D7
4800	MCLK	60050	2527	33W-34N	D1
5200	MHRY	60050	2527	34W-34N	C1
Flanigan Dr					
2900	LNSG	60438	3430	3E-20S	A4
Flannagan Ct					
17700	TYPK	60487	3424	10W-21S	A6
Flannigan Rd					
-	HPSR	60140	2743	45W-18N	C4
-	HshT	60140	2743	45W-18N	C4
Flat Iron Dr					
-	NPVL	60540	3202	28W-8S	E2
Flat Iron Rd					
5600	HRVD	60033	2463	51W-37N	D1
22800	CmgT	60033	2405	51W-38N	D7
22800	DhmT	60033	2405	51W-38N	D7
22800	HRVD	60033	2405	51W-38N	D7
23000	DhmT	60033	2463	52W-36N	B3
Flat Iron Rd CO-A27					
5600	HRVD	60033	2463	51W-37N	D1
22800	CmgT	60033	2405	51W-38N	D7
22800	DhmT	60033	2405	51W-38N	D7
22800	HRVD	60033	2405	51W-38N	D7
23000	DhmT	60033	2463	52W-36N	B3
Flat Rock Ct					
2300	NPVL	60564	3266	29W-12S	D3
Flat Rock Rd					
2400	DYR	46311	3598		E3
Flavin Rd					
-	PlsT	60480	3209	13W-10S	B6
-	PlsT	60480	3273	13W-12S	B2
-	WLSP	60480	3209	13W-10S	B6
Fleet Dr					
500	OSWG	60543	3264	35W-12S	C2
Fleet St					
10600	WSTR	60154	3086	13W-2S	E3
10600	WSTR	60154	3087	13W-2S	A3
Fleetwood Av					
300	BGBK	60440	3269	22W-12S	C2
Fleetwood Ct					
2200	NPVL	60565	3204	25W-10S	C6
Fleetwood Dr					
10	GLHT	60139	2968	24W-3N	D5
800	JLET	60432	3500	20W-22S	B2
1100	ELGN	60123	2854	35W-10N	A6
4000	FNPK	60131	2972	13W-5N	E2
Fleetwood Ln					
200	EGVV	60007	2861	17W-9N	B7
Fleetwood St					
10100	HTLY	60142	2692	39W-20N	C7
Fleming Av					
-	ZION	60099	2421	11W-41N	D2

STREET Block	City	ZIP	Map#	CGS	Grid
Fleming Dr					
10	WNFD	60190	3023	27W-0N	C5
E Fleming Dr N					
1400	ANHT	60004	2754	16W-17N	C5
E Fleming Dr S					
1400	ANHT	60004	2754	16W-17N	C5
Fleming Ln					
200	SMBG	60193	2858	23W-9N	E7
N Fleming Rd					
10	GwdT	60098	2525	39W-32N	D5
N Fleming Rd CO-V25					
10	GwdT	60098	2525	39W-32N	D5
S Fleming Rd					
10	DrrT	60098	2525	38W-31N	D6
10	GwdT	60098	2525	39W-32N	D6
200	BLVY	60098	2525	38W-31N	D6
900	BLVY	60098	2582	38W-30N	E1
900	DrrT	60098	2582	38W-30N	E1
S Fleming Rd CO-V25					
10	DrrT	60098	2525	38W-31N	D6
10	GwdT	60098	2525	39W-32N	D6
200	BLVY	60098	2525	38W-31N	D6
900	BLVY	60098	2582	38W-30N	E1
900	DrrT	60098	2582	38W-30N	E1
E Flentie Ln					
1400	ANHT	60004	2754	16W-17N	C5
1700	BFGV	60089	2754	16W-17N	C5
Fletcher Av					
10800	FNPK	60131	2972	13W-3N	E4
10800	FNPK	60164	2972	13W-3N	E4
10800	LydT	60164	2972	13W-3N	E4
N Fletcher Cir					
500	LKFT	60045	2649	12W-26N	B3
Fletcher Ct					
-	AURA	60506	3136	40W-6S	B6
Fletcher Dr					
10	DSPN	60016	2862	14W-11N	B2
100	WLNG	60090	2754	15W-17N	E5
100	WLNG	60090	2755	15W-17N	A4
4600	ELGN	60123	2853	37W-12N	D1
S Fletcher Dr					
800	WLNG	60090	2755	15W-17N	A5
900	WLNG	60090	2754	15W-17N	E5
Fletcher Ln					
-	AURA	60506	3136	40W-6S	C6
Fletcher Rd					
600	SchT	60174	2965	33W-5N	A3
600	SchT	60184	2964	33W-4N	E3
600	SchT	60184	2965	33W-5N	A3
600	SCRL	60174	2965	33W-5N	A3
600	SCRL	60184	2965	33W-5N	A3
600	WYNE	60184	2964	33W-4N	E3
600	WYNE	60184	2965	33W-5N	A3
W Fletcher St					
1800	CHCG	60657	2977	2W-3N	B4
2100	CHCG	60618	2977	2W-3N	B4
2800	CHCG	60618	2976	3W-3N	E4
4100	CHCG	60641	2976	5W-3N	B4
4800	CHCG	60641	2975	6W-3N	D4
6000	CHCG	60634	2975	7W-3N	B4
6900	CHCG	60634	2974	8W-3N	E4
7900	EDPK	60171	2974	9W-3N	B4
7900	EDPK	60707	2974	9W-3N	B4
Fleur-de-Lis Dr					
-	SCRL	60174	2964	34W-4N	E5
Flex Ct					
-	LKZH	60047	2699	22W-23N	C1
Flicker Ct					
10	NPVL	60565	3203	26W-9S	E4
Flicker Ln					
2100	RGMW	60008	2806	20W-14N	B5
Flinn Dr					
100	BTVA	60510	3078	35W-1S	B2
Flint Ct					
-	RMVL	60446	3417	26W-18S	E2
1000	AURA	60506	3137	37W-6S	D4
2300	DYR	46311	3598		E3
Flint Dr					
10	CbaT	60010	2697	27W-23N	B2
10	LKBN	60010	2697	27W-23N	B2
12000	HMGN	60491	3344	15W-17S	C5
12000	OrlT	60467	3344	15W-17S	C5
Flint Ln					
8600	ODPK	60462	3346	10W-15S	A2
W Flint Ln					
1400	RMVL	60446	3417	26W-18S	E2
Flint Tr					
300	CLSM	60188	2968	26W-3N	A5
400	CLSM	60188	2967	26W-3N	E5
700	CLLK	60012	2640	34W-27N	B1
700	NndT	60012	2640	34W-27N	B1
Flint Creek Dr					
23900	CbaT	60010	2697	27W-23N	A1
23900	LKBN	60010	2697	27W-23N	A1
24200	CbaT	60010	2643	27W-24N	A7
Flint Creek Ln					
800	YKVL	60560	3333	44W-15S	A3
Flint Creek Rd					
400	MltT	60187	3082	25W-2S	A3
400	WHTN	60187	3082	25W-2S	A3
Flintlock Ct					
300	OSWG	60543	3264	36W-11S	A1
Flintshire Dr					
1800	SMBG	60194	2858	25W-11N	A3
Flintstone Ct					
11700	FKFT	60423	3590	14W-27S	D4
Flintwood Ct					
900	RLKH	60073	2474	24W-35N	D5
Flock Av					
400	NPVL	60565	3203	26W-8S	D3
Flora Av					
-	GNVW	60025	2810	9W-12N	C7
100	MaiT	60025	2864	9W-12N	C1
200	GNVW	60025	2864	9W-12N	C1
Flora Dr					
400	ALGN	60102	2694	35W-20N	B7
1400	ElgT	60123	2908	35W-9N	A1
N Flora Pkwy					
100	ADSN	60101	2970	20W-3N	B5
Flora Pl					
300	HDPK	60035	2758	7W-20N	B1
Flora Fern Rd					
100	BDWD	60481	3942	30W-40S	C2
100	RedT	60481	3942	30W-40S	C2
Floral Av					
8000	SKOK	60077	2865	6W-10N	D5
W Floral Ct					
7700	FftT	60423	3504	9W-24S	E5
Floral Dr					
2800	NHBK	60062	2809	11W-16N	D1
3100	NfdT	60062	2809	11W-16N	D1
Floralwood Ct					
5300	JLET	60586	3416	30W-21S	B6
Florence Av					
-	LKZH	60047	2698	23W-22N	E4
100	CHCG	60202	2867	3W-9N	A6
Florence Av					
100	CHCG	60645	2867	3W-9N	A6
100	DGvT	60516	3206	18W-9S	E3
100	IVNS	60010	2751	23W-16N	D6
200	IVNS	60067	2751	23W-16N	D6
900	EVTN	60202	2867	3W-10N	A4
1100	WTMT	60559	3144	18W-6S	E5
1400	EVTN	60201	2867	3W-11N	A3
2900	WKGN	60085	2479	12W-33N	B7
3000	SCHT	60411	3596	0W-27S	B5
3000	STGR	60411	3596	0W-27S	B5
3000	STGR	60475	3596	0W-28S	B6
3800	DGvT	60515	3084	18W-3S	E6
3800	DRGV	60515	3084	18W-3S	E6
3800	OKBK	60515	3084	18W-3S	E6
3800	OKBK	60523	3084	18W-3S	E6
3800	YkTp	60515	3084	18W-3S	E6
4700	DRGV	60515	3144	18W-5S	E2
5400	DRGV	60516	3144	18W-5S	E3
7500	DRGV	60516	3206	18W-8S	E2
7500	DRN	60516	3206	18W-8S	E2
9700	SRPK	60176	2917	12W-6N	C6
E Florence Av					
400	JLET	60433	3499	23W-24S	B6
700	JltT	60433	3499	23W-24S	B6
N Florence Av					
20500	BFGV	60069	2754	15W-20N	E1
20500	BFGV	60089	2754	15W-20N	E1
20500	VrnT	60069	2754	15W-20N	E1
20800	VrnT	60069	2701	15W-20N	E7
W Florence Av					
25400	AntT	60002	2416	25W-40N	A2
Florence Blvd					
5600	MchT	60050	2470	34W-34N	C7
5600	MHRY	60050	2470	34W-34N	C7
Florence Ct					
-	WynT	60185	2967	28W-2N	A7
200	LYVL	60048	2591	16W-28N	D5
Florence Dr					
-	MchT	60050	2471	30W-36N	E4
600	PKRG	60068	2863	11W-9N	D6
4100	JNBG	60050	2471	30W-36N	E4
6000	HFET	60192	2855	31W-12N	D1
Florence Ln					
-	HDPK	60035	2705	8W-21N	A5
100	SchT	60174	2908	35W-6N	C7
100	SchT	60174	2964	35W-6N	C1
Florence Rd					
13100	NlxT	60448	3501	16W-22S	E2
13100	NlxT	60448	3502	16W-22S	A2
Florence St					
200	CLLK	60014	2639	36W-25N	E5
200	HMND	46324	3430		D2
1000	LMNT	60439	3270	19W-14S	D7
2200	BLID	60406	3277	2W-14S	B6
W Florence St					
700	MchT	60050	2472	29W-36N	B3
Florence Wy					
4100	NfdT	60025	2809	11W-13N	D7
Floresta Ln					
1300	CLLK	60014	2639	37W-25N	A4
Florian Dr					
300	DSPN	60016	2862	15W-10N	A4
23200	WMTN	60481	3853	29W-37S	A4
23200	WmTp	60481	3853	29W-37S	A4
Florida Av					
300	AURA	60506	3138	36W-6S	A5
400	AURA	60506	3137	36W-6S	E5
3400	GRNE	60031	2479	13W-36N	A5
3400	WkgT	60031	2479	12W-36N	A5
3400	WkgT	60087	2479	12W-36N	A5
3400	WrnT	60031	2479	12W-36N	A5
3700	GRNE	60031	2478	13W-36N	E5
3700	NCHI	60088	2593	12W-30N	C2
W Florida Av					
2600	WKGN	60087	2479	12W-36N	C5
12800	WkgT	60087	2479	12W-36N	A5
Florida Ct					
3700	NCHI	60088	2593	12W-30N	C2
18000	ODPK	60467	3423	13W-21S	A7
Florida Ln					
300	WNFD	60190	3023	27W-0S	C7
1000	EGVV	60007	2913	21W-8N	D3
Florimond Dr					
1000	ELGN	60123	2800	34W-13N	D7
1000	ELGN	60123	2854	34W-12N	D1
Florin Ct					
21700	FKFT	60423	3591	13W-26S	B2
Florina Ct					
100	WDDL	60191	2915	18W-6N	A6
Florine Ct					
300	CRY	60013	2641	31W-25N	D5
Florsheim Dr					
-	LYVL	60048	2648	15W-27N	A1
700	LYVL	60048	2647	16W-27N	E2
Flossmoor Av					
300	WKGN	60085	2536	11W-34N	C1
700	WKGN	60085	2479	11W-35N	C7
Flossmoor Ct					
600	NPVL	60563	3141	27W-5S	C2
Flossmoor Rd					
2000	BlmT	60422	3507	2W-22S	D2
2000	BlmT	60430	3507	2W-22S	D2
2000	FSMR	60422	3507	3W-22S	A2
3100	FSMR	60430	3507	3W-22S	A2
3200	RchT	60422	3507	4W-22S	A2
3200	RchT	60430	3507	4W-22S	A2
3300	RchT	60422	3506	4W-22S	E2
3300	RchT	60430	3506	4W-22S	E2
3400	FSMR	60422	3506	4W-22S	E2
3900	CCHL	60478	3506	6W-23S	A2
3900	FSMR	60430	3506	4W-22S	D2
4200	CCHL	60477	3506	4W-22S	D2
4200	RchT	60477	3506	6W-23S	A2
4800	RchT	60478	3506	6W-23S	A2
5400	RchT	60477	3505	7W-22S	D2
5600	TYPK	60477	3505	7W-22S	D2
Flossmoor St					
400	CTHL	60435	3417	27W-20S	C6
400	PnfT	60435	3417	27W-20S	C6
Flournoy St					
200	OKPK	60304	3031	7W-0S	B6
W Flournoy St					
1200	CHCG	60607	3033	1W-0S	D6
1600	CHCG	60612	3033	2W-0S	C6
2800	CHCG	60612	3032	4W-0S	C6
3100	CHCG	60624	3032	4W-0S	C6
4600	CHCG	60644	3032	5W-0S	A6
4800	CHCG	60644	3031	6W-0S	D6
N Flower Cir					
2000	ANHT	60004	2807	16W-16N	C1
Flower Ct					
2200	SMBG	60194	2857	26W-11N	E4
7400	HRPK	60133	2911	27W-9N	C1
Flower St					
1800	MHRY	60050	2527	33W-33N	E2
Flower St					
2400	JLET	60435	3417	27W-20S	D5
2400	LktT	60403	3417	27W-20S	D5
2400	PnfT	60403	3417	27W-20S	D5
2400	PnfT	60435	3417	27W-20S	D5
Flowerfield Ct					
10	LIHL	60156	2693	38W-22N	A3
1300	NPVL	60565	3204	24W-8S	E1
Flowermeadow Ct					
3600	JLET	60431	3497	28W-22S	A2
Flowermeadow St					
3600	JLET	60431	3497	28W-22S	A2
Flowers Av					
800	SMWD	60107	2911	27W-8N	C2
Flowerwood Ln					
12200	HTLY	60142	2744	43W-19N	B2
Floyd Ct					
7000	JLET	60586	3415	32W-21S	C6
N Floyd Ln					
100	CHHT	60411	3508	1W-23S	A4
S Floyd Ln					
100	CHHT	60411	3508	1W-23S	A4
Floyd Brown Ln					
1500	GLHT	60139	2969	22W-2N	D6
Fluid Power Dr					
500	GNVA	60134	3021	33W-1N	A3
500	GnvT	60134	3021	33W-1N	A3
Flyers Ln					
-	RMVL	60441	3419	23W-18S	A1
Flying Dutchman Ter					
500	SMBG	60193	2912	24W-9N	D1
Flynn Ct					
10	NARA	60542	3078	35W-4S	C7
W Flynn Creek Dr					
27100	CbaT	60010	2697	27W-21N	A6
27100	LKBN	60010	2697	27W-21N	A6
Foal Ln					
10	CmpT	60119	3018	41W-2N	A1
Foam Forms Pl					
10	WKGN	60085	2537	9W-34N	B1
Foley Dr					
-	SchT	60175	2907	36W-6N	E7
-	SCRL	60175	2907	36W-6N	E7
-	SCRL	60175	2908	36W-6N	A7
-	SCRL	60175	2964	36W-6N	A1
Foley Ln					
-	SCRL	60175	2907	36W-6N	E7
400	SchT	60175	2907	36W-6N	E7
Foley St					
100	BNVL	60106	2971	16W-5N	D1
Foli St					
-	PLNO	60545	3260	45W-14S	C7
Foliage Ln					
2200	DYR	46311	3598		E2
Folkers Dr					
-	FKFT	60423	3591	12W-25S	D1
Folkestone Wy					
22900	FKFT	60423	3590	14W-27S	D5
23000	GGnT	60423	3590	14W-27S	D5
Folkstone Ct					
1200	WHTN	60187	3082	25W-1S	B2
Folley Dr					
21100	LktT	60441	3417	26W-19S	E2
Foltz Dr					
1600	HFET	60169	2858	25W-12N	B1
Fonda Ln					
5300	HRPK	60133	2911	27W-6N	C6
Fontaine Ct					
10	BMDL	60108	2968	24W-5N	D1
Fontana Dr					
2400	GNVW	60025	2810	9W-12N	C7
Fontana Ln					
17100	LKPT	60441	3419	21W-20S	E4
Fontana Pl					
600	MDLN	60060	2590	19W-29N	C4
Fontana St					
-	JLET	60586	3415	32W-20S	C5
Football Dr					
1000	LKFT	60045	2648	13W-27N	E2
Foothill Ct					
1500	WHTN	60187	3082	25W-1S	A2
Foothill Dr					
1100	MltT	60187	3082	25W-1S	A2
1100	WHTN	60187	3082	25W-1S	A2
Foothill Rd					
2100	ELGN	60123	2853	36W-11N	E4
2100	ElgT	60123	2853	36W-11N	E4
Foran Ln					
1200	AURA	60506	3137	36W-5S	D4
Forbes Av					
2800	HFET	60192	2802	28W-13N	D6
Forbes Dr					
-	LSLE	60532	3082	24W-4S	C7
10	BbyT	60134	3018	39W-0S	E6
Forbes Rd					
-	NRIV	60546	3088	10W-3S	B5
-	RVSD	60546	3088	10W-3S	B5
Forbes Rd SR-171					
-	NRIV	60546	3088	10W-3S	B5
-	RVSD	60546	3088	10W-3S	B5
Ford Av					
600	ELGN	60120	2855	33W-13N	B1
S Ford Av					
2200	CHCG	60616	3092	0W-2S	A2
W Ford Av					
10000	BHPK	60087	2422	10W-38N	B7
10000	BHPK	60099	2422	10W-38N	B7
Ford Ct					
700	ELGN	60120	2855	32W-12N	B1
11800	PNFD	60585	3266	31W-13S	A6
W Ford Ct					
6000	MONE	60449	3682	7W-31S	D5
Ford Dr					
-	BbyT	60134	3018	39W-0N	E5
10	KdlT	60560	3332	44W-16S	E4
Ford Ln					
10	NPVL	60565	3203	26W-10S	E6
10	NPVL	60565	3204	26W-10S	A6
300	BRLT	60103	2910	29W-8N	D2
Ford Rd					
10	NLNX	60451	3589	18W-26S	B3
10	NlxT	60451	3589	18W-26S	B3
200	CNHN	60410	3672	32W-28S	E1
200	CNHN	60447	3672	32W-28S	E1
200	CnhT	60410	3583	31W-28S	E7
200	CnhT	60447	3672	32W-28S	E1
2600	NndT	60051	2528	31W-31N	D7
23200	TroT	60447	3583	32W-28S	E7
S Ford Rd					
11200	PlsT	60464	3272	14W-13S	D5
11200	PSPK	60464	3272	14W-14S	E5
11800	LMNT	60439	3272	14W-13S	D5
11800	PlsT	60439	3272	14W-13S	D5
W Ford Rd					
-	CNHN	60447	3672	32W-29S	E1
-	CnhT	60410	3672	32W-29S	E2
W Ford Rd					
-	CnhT	60447	3672	32W-29S	D1
23400	CNHN	60410	3672	31W-29S	E2
Ford St					
400	BbyT	60134	3018	39W-0N	E5
1200	GNVA	60134	3020	36W-1N	A3
N Ford St					
200	MRGO	60152	2634	50W-26N	B2
27900	WcnT	60084	2587	25W-27N	E7
S Ford St					
100	MRGO	60152	2634	50W-26N	B2
W Ford St					
12600	BHPK	60087	2421	12W-38N	B7
W Ford City Dr					
4000	CHCG	60652	3212	5W-8S	B1
Fordham Av					
400	AURA	60506	3137	37W-6S	D5
N Fordham Av					
700	AURA	60506	3137	37W-6S	D5
S Fordham Av					
10	AURA	60506	3137	37W-7S	D7
200	AURA	60506	3199	37W-7S	D1
Fordham Ct					
1500	NPVL	60565	3204	24W-9S	C3
7400	JLET	60586	3495	33W-21S	B1
Fordham Dr					
1200	GLHT	60139	3024	24W-2N	D1
7300	JLET	60586	3495	33W-21S	B1
Fordham Ln					
-	JLET	60586	3495	33W-21S	A1
Fordham Pl					
400	ROSL	60172	2912	24W-6N	D6
E Fordham St					
1500	BGBK	60490	3267	26W-13S	D5
W Fordham St					
1600	BGBK	60490	3267	27W-13S	D5
Fordham Wy Dr					
300	WTMT	60559	3145	17W-6S	B5
Fore Ct					
1200	WLNG	60090	2754	16W-18N	E2
E Foreman Dr					
-	CHCG	60617	3216	4E-10S	C5
W Foreman Dr					
11900	BtnT	60099	2362	12W-42N	C5
11900	WPHR	60096	2362	12W-42N	C5
11900	ZION	60099	2362	12W-42N	C5
Forest Av					
-	AntT	60002	2356	26W-41N	E7
-	AraT	60502	3139	33W-6S	A5
-	AURA	60502	3139	33W-6S	A5
10	FTPK	60130	3030	9W-0N	C5
10	FXLK	60020	2473	27W-37N	A2
10	LKZH	60047	2698	23W-23N	E3
10	ROSL	60172	2913	23W-6N	A6
10	RVFT	60130	3030	9W-0N	C5
10	RVSD	60546	3088	10W-3S	B5
100	GNEN	60137	3025	22W-0S	B7
100	OKPK	60301	3030	8W-0N	E3
100	OKPK	60302	3030	8W-0N	E3
100	WDSK	60098	2581	42W-30N	C1
100	WLSP	60480	3209	12W-9S	D3
200	MDLN	60060	2646	18W-26N	D2
200	OSWG	60543	3263	37W-13S	C4
200	ROSL	60172	2912	23W-6N	E6
200	RVFT	60305	3030	9W-0N	C4
300	SchT	60174	2908	35W-6N	B7
300	WCHI	60185	3022	29W-0N	D6
400	MltT	60137	3025	22W-1N	C2
400	WLMT	60091	2813	3W-14N	A5
500	GLHT	60137	3025	22W-1N	C2
600	ELGN	60120	2855	33W-11N	B4
600	LKFT	60045	2650	10W-26N	A2
600	PlsT	60480	3209	12W-9S	D4
600	WnfT	60185	3022	28W-0N	E6
700	GLHT	60139	3025	22W-1N	C2
700	GNVA	60134	3020	35W-0N	B5
700	WKGN	60085	2537	10W-33N	A2
700	WLMT	60091	2812	3W-14N	E5
800	DRFD	60015	2703	11W-21N	D6
900	EVTN	60202	2867	2W-10N	C4
900	GLNC	60022	2758	6W-18N	D3
1000	AraT	60505	3138	34W-6S	D3
1000	GNVW	60025	2811	7W-14N	A5
1100	AURA	60505	3138	34W-6S	E5
1200	EVTN	60201	2867	2W-11N	C3
1200	HDPK	60035	2705	8W-21N	A5
1300	CTCY	60409	3430	4E-19S	B2
1300	EDPK	60707	3030	9W-1N	C1
1300	RVFT	60707	3030	9W-1N	C1
2200	FTPK	60130	3088	9W-2S	C2
2200	FTPK	60546	3088	9W-2S	C2
2200	NRIV	60546	3088	9W-2S	C2
2200	RGMW	60008	2806	20W-14N	A4
3400	BKFD	60513	3087	11W-3S	E6
3500	WLMT	60091	2811	6W-14N	D5
3800	DRGV	60515	3084	19W-4S	C7
3800	PvsT	60558	3086	14W-4S	D6
3800	WNSP	60558	3086	14W-4S	D6
4300	DRGV	60515	3144	19W-4S	C1
4500	BKFD	60513	3147	11W-4S	E1
4500	MCCK	60513	3147	11W-4S	E1
4500	MCCK	60525	3147	11W-4S	E1
6900	HMND	46324	3430		C4
7500	MNSR	46321	3430		C5
13800	CHCG	60419	3350	0E-16S	D2
13800	CHCG	60827	3350	0E-16S	D2
13800	DLTN	60419	3350	0E-16S	D2
16700	OKFT	60452	3426	6W-20S	A3
16800	BmnT	60452	3426	6W-20S	A3
17000	BmnT	60477	3426	6W-20S	A4
17000	OKFT	60477	3426	6W-20S	A4
E Forest Av					
10	WCHI	60185	3022	29W-0N	C6
200	EMHT	60126	3028	15W-1N	A3
500	DSPN	60018	2862	14W-10N	C5
1000	WHTN	60187	3024	23W-0N	E5
1300	DSPN	60018	2863	13W-10N	A5
1700	WHTN	60187	3025	23W-0N	A5
N Forest Av					
10	PLTN	60074	2806	20W-16N	A1
100	PLTN	60074	2753	20W-16N	A7
200	BTVA	60510	3078	34W-1S	B3
200	HLSD	60162	3028	13W-0S	E5
400	MPPT	60056	2807	16W-13N	E6
600	ANHT	60004	2807	16W-13N	E6
600	ANHT	60056	2807	16W-13N	E6
600	MPPT	60004	2807	16W-13N	E5
700	BTVA	60510	3020	34W-0S	D7
1200	PltT	60067	2752	22W-17N	D5
2700	RVGV	60171	2974	10W-3N	A5
34700	GrtT	60041	2473	26W-34N	D7
36600	LkvT	60046	2476	20W-36N	A3
38500	AntT	60081	2415	27W-38N	B6
38500	FXLK	60081	2415	27W-38N	B7
39400	AntT	60002	2416	25W-39N	B5
S Forest Av					
10	NPVL	60540	3141	27W-6S	B5
10	PLTN	60074	2806	20W-15N	A1
100	HLSD	60162	3028	13W-0S	E7
100	ITSC	60143	2914	19W-6N	B6
200	BTVA	60510	3078	34W-1S	D2
9100	CHCG	60619	3214	0E-11S	D6
9400	CHCG	60628	3214	0E-11S	D6
10300	CHCG	60628	3278	0E-12S	D2
13400	CHCG	60827	3350	0E-15S	D1
19400	BlmT	60411	3508	0W-23S	C3
19400	GNWD	60411	3508	0W-23S	C3
19400	GNWD	60425	3508	0W-23S	C3
W Forest Av					
100	WHTN	60187	3024	24W-0N	C5
200	RDLK	60073	2531	23W-33N	E3
400	WCHI	60185	3022	30W-0N	B6
400	WnfT	60185	3022	30W-0N	B6
4400	WKGN	60085	2535	14W-33N	C4
14100	WrnT	60031	2535	14W-33N	D4
24400	AvnT	60073	2474	24W-35N	C6
26000	AntT	60002	2356	26W-41N	E7
Forest Av N					
1200	CHCG	60302	3030	8W-1N	E1
1200	CHCG	60707	3030	8W-1N	E1
1200	OKPK	60302	3030	8W-1N	E1
Forest Blvd					
10	PKFT	60466	3595	3W-26S	B3
Forest Cir					
500	ALGN	60102	2694	34W-21N	D6
Forest Ct					
10	BtlT	60543	3263	39W-12S	A4
200	ANTH	60002	2357	23W-43N	E4
300	BGBK	60440	3205	21W-11S	E7
400	SMBG	60193	2858	24W-10N	E5
800	BRLT	60103	2910	29W-6N	D6
1000	CLSM	60188	2967	27W-4N	C4
2200	LNSG	60438	3429	2E-21S	D7
2500	LNHT	60046	2476	19W-36N	B3
2600	WdfT	60015	2703	11W-23N	D2
3600	OMFD	60461	3506	4W-24S	D4
4900	OKFT	60452	3426	6W-20S	A3
15600	HmrT	60491	3420	19W-18S	C1
21700	MKNA	60448	3590	14W-26S	E2
N Forest Ct					
200	ADSN	60101	2971	17W-3N	B4
200	PLTN	60074	2753	20W-16N	A7
W Forest Ct					
26200	AntT	60002	2356	26W-41N	E7
Forest Dr					
-	BmnT	60426	3426	5W-19S	B1
-	OKFT	60426	3426	5W-19S	B1
-	OKFT	60452	3426	5W-19S	B1
-	TYPK	60477	3424	9W-21S	E6
200	AlqT	60014	2640	33W-25N	E5
200	CLLK	60014	2640	33W-25N	D5
200	DndT	60118	2747	35W-18N	C4
200	ISLK	60042	2586	28W-28N	D5
400	AURA	60502	3139	32W-7S	C7
400	NpvT	60502	3139	32W-7S	C7
500	BMDL	60108	2912	23W-6N	E7
500	BMDL	60108	2913	23W-6N	A7
500	BMDL	60172	2912	23W-6N	E7
500	BMDL	60172	2913	23W-6N	A7
500	BmdT	60108	2912	23W-6N	E7
500	BmdT	60172	2912	23W-6N	E7
500	ROSL	60172	2912	23W-6N	E7
500	ROSL	60172	2913	23W-6N	A7
800	SMWD	60107	2857	28W-9N	A7
900	ELGN	60123	2800	35W-13N	B7
1300	BCHR	60401	3864	0W-36S	D1
1400	GNVW	60025	2809	12W-14N	B5
2400	WDRG	60517	3205	21W-9S	D3
3400	MHRY	60050	2585	32W-30N	B1
3500	NndT	60050	2585	32W-30N	B1
6000	MNGV	60053	2865	7W-11N	B3
8400	HYHL	60457	3209	11W-9S	E3
14000	LbvT	60045	2648	14W-27N	C2
14000	MTWA	60045	2648	13W-27N	D2
37300	BHPK	60087	2480	9W-37N	B2
N Forest Dr					
200	AddT	60101	2971	17W-4N	B4
200	ADSN	60101	2971	17W-4N	B4
23900	ElaT	60047	2699	21W-24N	D1
24100	ElaT	60047	2645	21W-24N	D7
24200	HNWD	60047	2645	21W-24N	D7
33000	GYLK	60030	2533	18W-32N	E5
33500	WrnT	60030	2533	18W-33N	E3
43200	AntT	60002	2357	25W-43N	B4
S Forest Dr					
700	BRTN	60010	2750	26W-18N	D3
800	BNHL	60010	2750	26W-18N	D3
W Forest Dr					
24800	LkvT	60046	2416	25W-39N	B4
24900	AntT	60046	2416	25W-39N	B4
Forest Gln					
400	SchT	60175	2963	38W-4N	A4
5400	LGGV	60047	2701	18W-23N	A2
Forest Ln					
-	AntT	60002	2417	22W-40N	C2
-	JLET	60432	3500	19W-23S	D4
-	JLET	60451	3500	19W-23S	D4
10	CRY	60013	2641	31W-24N	C6
10	EGVV	60007	2861	18W-10N	A6
10	HFET	60010	2804	25W-14N	A3
10	HFET	60192	2804	25W-14N	A3
10	SBTN	60010	2804	25W-15N	A2
10	SBTN	60192	2804	25W-14N	A3
10	WnfT	60555	3080	29W-2S	E4
10	WNVL	60555	3080	29W-2S	E4
10	YkTp	60126	3028	15W-0S	B7
200	FmtT	60060	2646	19W-26N	C2
300	CmpT	60119	2962	41W-3N	A6
300	LYVL	60048	2591	16W-29N	C5
300	SMBG	60193	2858	23W-10N	E6
500	CTCY	60409	3430	4E-18S	B1
500	ThtT	60476	3428	0E-21S	E6
500	TNTN	60476	3428	0E-21S	E6
800	CLSM	60188	2967	27W-4N	C4
1000	LMNT	60439	3270	19W-14S	E7
2700	WKGN	60087	2479	11W-37N	D2
2800	LNSG	60438	3510	3E-22S	A1
8900	HYHL	60457	3209	11W-10S	E5
8900	HYHL	60457	3210	11W-10S	A5
10400	CHRG	60415	3275	8W-12S	B2
10600	CHRG	60482	3275	8W-12S	B2
10600	WRTH	60482	3275	8W-12S	B2
13300	DPgT	60441	3342	21W-15S	A2
14500	LKPT	60441	3342	21W-17S	A5
14500	LktT	60441	3342	21W-17S	A5
E Forest Ln					
10	PltT	60067	2805	20W-13N	E5
10	RGMW	60067	2805	21W-13N	E5
200	PltT	60067	2806	20W-13N	A5
N Forest Ln					
42400	AntT	60002	2356	27W-42N	A5

STREET Block	City	ZIP	Map#	CGS	Grid
W Forest Ln					
1600	CteT	60417	3595	2W-29S	E7
Forest Ln E					
9000	HYHL	60457	3209	11W-10S	E5
Forest Ln W					
9000	HYHL	60457	3209	11W-10S	E5
Forest Pl					
10	BFGV	60089	2754	16W-18N	C3
1300	CTCY	60409	3430	4E-19S	B2
1600	EVTN	60201	2867	2W-11N	C3
9500	MaiT	60016	2809	12W-12N	C7
Forest Rd					
300	HNDL	60521	3086	15W-4S	B7
300	HNDL	60521	3146	15W-4S	B1
600	GNVW	60025	2811	6W-13N	D7
700	LGPK	60525	3087	12W-3S	C5
Forest St					
10	CHHT	60411	3596	1W-26S	A2
100	NLNX	60451	3501	18W-24S	B5
100	WNKA	60093	2812	4W-15N	B3
300	OSWG	60543	3263	37W-13S	C5
300	WNFD	60190	3023	27W-0S	C7
600	WNFD	60190	3081	27W-0S	C1
600	WnfT	60187	3081	27W-0S	C1
9700	SjnT	46311	3687		C3
E Forest St					
100	MRGO	60152	2634	49W-26N	C3
N Forest St					
42100	AntT	60002	2358	22W-42N	B6
W Forest St					
700	MRGO	60152	2634	50W-26N	A3
Forest Tr					
10	OKBK	60523	3027	16W-1S	E7
10	OKBK	60523	3085	16W-1S	E1
300	SEGN	60177	2907	37W-8N	D4
900	SRGV	60554	3136	41W-4S	A2
5200	OKFT	60452	3425	6W-20S	E4
5400	LGGV	60047	2701	18W-23N	A2
Forest Vw					
-	MCLK	60050	2470	34W-34N	D7
Forest Wy					
500	BGBK	60440	3205	21W-11S	D7
Forest Cove Ct					
10	HnrT	60107	2856	29W-9N	E7
10	SMWD	60107	2856	29W-9N	E7
Forest Cove Dr					
1700	EGvT	60056	2861	17W-10N	C5
1700	MPPT	60056	2861	17W-10N	C5
S Forest Cove Dr					
100	RDLK	60073	2530	25W-33N	E4
W Forest Cove Dr					
2100	RDLK	60073	2530	26W-32N	E4
2100	RDLK	60073	2531	25W-32N	A4
Forest Cove Rd					
500	LKBF	60044	2594	10W-28N	A6
Forest Creek Ct					
3000	WldT	60565	3203	27W-11S	B7
Forest Creek Ln					
-	LbvT	60048	2591	17W-30N	B2
1900	LYVL	60048	2591	17W-30N	B2
2700	WldT	60565	3267	27W-11S	C1
2800	WldT	60565	3203	27W-11S	B7
Forestdale Ct					
1300	SMBG	60193	2858	25W-10N	C6
19500	MKNA	60448	3502	15W-23S	C3
Forestdale Pk					
10	CTCY	60409	3430	4E-18S	C1
Forest Edge Ct					
100	PSPK	60464	3272	14W-14S	E5
Forest Edge Dr					
100	PSPK	60464	3272	14W-14S	E6
600	VNHL	60061	2701	15W-23N	E1
600	VNHL	60061	2702	15W-23N	A1
25200	CNHN	60410	3672	32W-30S	D5
Forest Edge Ln					
600	DSPN	60016	2863	12W-11N	C3
4600	LGGV	60047	2700	19W-23N	D2
14800	OKFT	60452	3347	6W-17S	E5
N Forest Garden Rd					
27500	WcnT	60084	2587	27W-27N	C7
27500	WcnT	60084	2643	27W-27N	C1
Forest Gate Cir					
10	OKBK	60523	3085	16W-2S	D4
Forest Gate Rd					
1300	OKBK	60523	3085	16W-2S	D4
Forest Glen Av					
1600	HRPK	60133	2911	27W-8N	D2
N Forest Glen Av					
5200	CHCG	60630	2919	6W-6N	E5
5500	CHCG	60646	2919	6W-6N	E5
5800	CHCG	60646	2920	5W-7N	A3
S Forest Glen Blvd					
12300	PSPK	60464	3274	11W-14S	A6
W Forest Glen Blvd					
9000	PSPK	60464	3273	11W-14S	E6
9000	PSPK	60464	3274	11W-14S	A6
Forest Glen Ct					
800	BRLT	60103	2910	29W-8N	C3
9300	DRN	60439	3206	19W-10S	D6
Forest Glen Dr					
-	WNKA	60093	2758	6W-16N	E7
10	HNVL	60073	2532	22W-33N	B3
10	RLKP	60073	2532	22W-33N	B3
4200	HFET	60192	2804	25W-15N	A2
N Forest Glen Dr					
200	HNVL	60073	2532	22W-33N	B3
200	RLKP	60073	2532	22W-33N	B3
Forest Glen Dr E					
800	WNKA	60093	2758	5W-16N	E7
Forest Glen Dr N					
1200	WNKA	60093	2758	6W-16N	E7
Forest Glen Dr S					
1200	WNKA	60093	2758	6W-16N	E7
Forest Glen Dr W					
900	WNKA	60093	2758	6W-16N	E7
Forest Glen Ln					
600	CmpT	60175	2961	42W-5N	D2
700	OKBK	60523	3086	15W-1S	B1
Forest Glen Pkwy					
2500	WDRG	60517	3205	22W-8S	C2
3000	LslT	60517	3205	22W-8S	C2
Forest Glen Rd					
100	AddT	60191	2915	18W-6N	A6
100	WDDL	60191	2915	18W-6N	A6
Forest Glen St					
3700	LinT	53147	2349		E1
Forest Glen Tr					
2600	RVWD	60015	2702	13W-21N	E7
2600	RVWD	60015	2703	13W-21N	A7
Forest Grove Dr					
5400	JLET	60586	3416	30W-21S	B7
Forest Grove Ln					
3000	DRGV	60515	3084	19W-3S	C5
W Foresthill Ct					
7800	PSHT	60463	3346	9W-15S	D1
Forest Hill Dr					
10	MltT	60137	3083	22W-3S	B5
W Foresthill Ln					
7700	PSHT	60463	3346	9W-15S	D1
Forest Hill Rd					
500	LKFT	60045	2650	10W-25N	A6
7300	BRRG	60527	3208	14W-8S	D2
Forest Hill St					
1000	CTCY	60409	3430	4E-18S	B1
N Forest Hills Ct					
3000	WKGN	60083	2478	14W-37N	C2
Forest Hills Dr					
5600	CNHL	60514	3145	16W-6S	D3
Forest Hills Rd					
10	LKBF	60044	2593	11W-28N	E7
E Forest Knoll Dr					
-	PLTN	60074	2752	20W-18N	E3
200	PLTN	60074	2753	20W-18N	A3
Forest Knoll Rd					
200	GNOK	60044	2593	13W-29N	A5
200	LbvT	60044	2593	13W-29N	A5
N Forest Lake Ln					
29000	GNOK	60048	2592	14W-28N	C5
Forest Mews Dr					
500	OKBK	60523	3084	18W-3S	E6
500	OKBK	60523	3085	18W-3S	A6
Forest Oak Dr					
-	MchT	60050	2526	36W-32N	D5
-	MchT	60098	2526	36W-32N	D5
Forest Oak Ln					
-	SRWD	60404	3495	31W-25S	E7
Forest Park Dr					
2300	DYR	46311	3598		C3
Forest Park Ln					
10	HFET	60169	2859	23W-11N	A3
Forest Preserve					
-	PKRG	60068	2917	11W-8N	D2
W Forest Preserve Av					
6700	CHCG	60634	2974	10W-4N	A3
6700	CHCG	60706	2974	8W-5N	E1
6700	HDHT	60706	2974	8W-5N	E1
6800	HDHT	60634	2974	8W-5N	E1
6900	NRDG	60634	2974	8W-5N	D1
6900	NRDG	60706	2974	10W-4N	B3
8400	CHCG	60634	2973	10W-4N	E4
8600	RVGV	60171	2973	10W-4N	E4
8600	RVGV	60634	2973	10W-4N	E4
Forest Preserve Dr					
-	BRLT	60103	2966	30W-5N	A1
-	BRLT	60184	2966	30W-5N	A1
-	PvsT	60154	3087	12W-2S	B2
-	WDDL	60191	2971	18W-5N	A1
-	WSTR	60154	3087	12W-2S	B2
-	WynT	60184	2966	30W-5N	A1
200	LGPK	60525	3087	12W-2S	C3
300	WDDL	60191	2970	18W-5N	D1
2600	CHHT	60411	3596	1W-26S	A3
2600	SCHT	60411	3596	1W-26S	A3
2900	SCHT	60411	3595	1W-27S	E3
3000	BlmT	60466	3595	1W-27S	E4
3000	SCHT	60466	3595	2W-27S	E4
W Forest Preserve Dr					
500	ADSN	60143	2970	19W-5N	D1
500	WDDL	60191	2970	19W-5N	D1
6400	HDHT	60706	2919	8W-5N	A7
6600	CHCG	60634	2974	8W-5N	E2
6600	CHCG	60706	2974	8W-5N	E2
6600	HDHT	60706	2974	8W-5N	E2
6600	HDHT	60706	2975	7W-3N	B5
Forest Preserve Rd					
2200	BbyT	60119	3017	41W-0S	E7
N Forest Preserve Rd					
27000	FmtT	60084	2644	24W-27N	C1
Forest Ridge Dr					
-	AraT	60542	3077	38W-4S	B7
-	NARA	60542	3077	38W-4S	B7
3400	RcmT	60071	2354	32W-42N	B6
3400	SPGV	60081	2354	32W-42N	B6
13100	PSHT	60463	3347	7W-15S	B2
13400	BmnT	60445	3347	7W-15S	B2
13400	PSHT	60445	3347	7W-15S	B2
Forest Ridge Rd					
1500	SCRL	60174	2964	34W-3N	D5
Forest Trails Ct					
10	CmpT	60175	2961	42W-5N	D3
Forest View Av					
100	WDDL	60191	2915	18W-5N	A7
100	WDDL	60191	2971	18W-5N	A1
300	EGvT	60007	2861	18W-9N	A7
300	EGVV	60007	2861	18W-9N	A7
400	EGvT	60007	2915	17W-9N	B1
400	EGVV	60007	2915	17W-9N	B1
Forestview Av					
-	RVDL	60827	3350	0W-15S	B1
500	PKRG	60068	2863	11W-9N	D7
2600	BKFD	60513	3087	11W-2S	E3
N Forestview Av					
2400	RVGV	60171	2974	10W-3N	A5
4400	CHCG	60656	2917	10W-5N	E7
4400	CHCG	60656	2973	10W-5N	E1
W Forestview Av					
-	BKFD	60513	3087	10W-2S	E3
2400	NRIV	60546	3087	11W-2S	E3
2400	PvsT	60546	3087	11W-2S	E3
Forest View Av S					
300	WNVL	60555	3081	28W-4S	A7
600	WNVL	60555	3080	28W-4S	E7
Forestview Cir					
2400	AURA	60502	3201	32W-8S	C1
N Forest View Cir					
1200	PLTN	60067	2752	22W-17N	B4
Forest View Ct					
-	JLET	60431	3497	28W-24S	B7
1000	NPVL	60563	3140	28W-5S	E3
Forestview Ct					
100	AURA	60502	3201	32W-7S	B1
500	WNVL	60555	3080	29W-2S	D3
2800	CPVL	60110	2746	37W-17N	C6
8300	FKFT	60423	3592	10W-27S	C3
9800	MKNA	60448	3503	12W-24S	D5
13200	CTWD	60445	3347	6W-15S	E1
13600	HTLY	60142	2744	43W-19N	B3
S Forestview Ct					
24300	CteT	60417	3687	3E-29S	B1
Forest View Dr					
10	ElaT	60047	2645	21W-25N	C5
10	HNWD	60047	2645	21W-25N	C5
10	ShdT	60044	2593	11W-29N	D4
200	NlxT	60451	3502	15W-25S	C7
300	LKBF	60044	2593	11W-29N	D4
500	GNVA	60134	3020	35W-0N	B5
2800	CPVL	60110	2746	37W-18N	C5
2800	CPVL	60118	2746	37W-18N	C5
4200	NfdT	60062	2756	13W-18N	A3
4200	NHBK	60062	2756	13W-18N	A3
4400	WhlT	60062	2756	13W-18N	A3
Forest View Dr					
4700	NHBK	60062	2755	13W-18N	E3
4700	WhlT	60062	2755	13W-18N	E3
7800	OrlT	60462	3346	10W-17S	C6
8100	ODPK	60462	3346	10W-17S	C6
16700	TYPK	60477	3425	8W-20S	B4
Forestview Dr					
-	JLET	60436	3497	27W-24S	B7
10	HnrT	60120	2856	30W-11N	A4
200	WnfT	60555	3080	29W-2S	D3
200	WNVL	60555	3080	29W-2S	D3
300	ADSN	60106	2971	17W-4N	B4
600	AddT	60106	2971	16W-4N	D4
600	BNVL	60106	2971	16W-4N	C4
2300	CLLK	60014	2641	32W-24N	A6
3600	JLET	60431	3497	28W-24S	A7
6000	OKFT	60452	3347	8W-18S	B6
8200	FKFT	60423	3592	10W-27S	C3
9700	MKNA	60448	3503	12W-24S	D5
9900	FftT	60448	3503	12W-24S	D5
W Forest View Dr					
12000	HMGN	60491	3344	15W-16S	C2
12000	OrlT	60467	3344	15W-16S	C3
Forest View Ln					
5600	WKGN	60048	2534	15W-32N	E5
18600	LNSG	60438	3429	1E-22S	B7
18600	LNSG	60438	3509	1E-22S	B1
Forestview Ln					
-	SHLD	60473	3350	0W-17S	C5
1000	GNVW	60025	2811	7W-13N	A7
11900	PSPK	60464	3274	10W-14S	B5
13100	CTWD	60445	3347	6W-15S	E1
N Forestview Ln					
10	AURA	60502	3201	32W-8S	C1
S Forestview Ln					
10	AURA	60502	3201	32W-8S	B1
27500	CteT	60401	3774	0W-33S	C2
W Forest View Ln					
6700	NLES	60714	2918	8W-8N	E1
6700	NLES	60714	2919	8W-8N	A1
Forest View Rd					
400	LNHT	60046	2418	19W-38N	B6
5700	LSLE	60532	3143	23W-6S	A4
5700	LslT	60532	3142	23W-6S	E4
5700	LslT	60532	3143	23W-6S	A4
Forestview Rd					
100	BNVL	60106	2971	16W-4N	E4
2100	EVTN	60201	2866	4W-12N	D1
8800	SKOK	60076	2866	4W-11N	D3
9200	SKOK	60203	2866	4W-11N	D2
10700	CTSD	60525	3147	13W-7S	A6
N Forest View Rd					
40500	WDWH	60083	2421	13W-40N	A3
S Forestview Rd					
12800	PSHT	60463	3275	8W-15S	A7
12900	PSHT	60463	3347	8W-15S	A1
13000	WthT	60463	3347	8W-15S	A1
E Forestview Tr					
3000	CteT	60417	3687	3E-29S	B1
Forestview Wy					
-	PNFD	60585	3337	32W-15S	B2
800	ANTH	60002	2417	21W-40N	D2
Forestway Ct					
10	BFGV	60089	2754	17W-18N	A3
Forestway Dr					
-	GLNC	60093	2758	6W-16N	C7
-	NHFD	60093	2811	6W-16N	C1
-	NtrT	60093	2811	6W-16N	C1
-	WNKA	60093	2758	7W-17N	B5
-	WNKA	60093	2811	6W-16N	C1
10	DRFD	60015	2756	11W-20N	D2
200	NHBK	60062	2758	7W-17N	A6
400	BFGV	60089	2754	17W-18N	A3
800	GLNC	60022	2758	7W-17N	B5
17100	EHZC	60429	3427	2W-20S	D5
Forestway Ln					
300	WLNG	60090	2755	14W-18N	C4
Forestwood Ct					
-	RMVL	60446	3341	23W-15S	A1
Forestwood Dr					
10	RMVL	60446	3341	23W-15S	A1
600	RMVL	60446	3269	23W-14S	B7
2600	NndT	60051	2586	29W-29N	C4
Forest Wood Ln					
10	PKFT	60466	3595	2W-28S	D6
Forest Woods Dr					
11000	LynT	60480	3208	13W-9S	E4
11000	WLSP	60480	3208	13W-9S	E4
Forest Wy Cir					
4600	LGGV	60047	2700	19W-23N	D2
Forever Av					
1300	LYVL	60048	2590	18W-30N	E2
Forge Ln					
24600	PNFD	60585	3338	30W-15S	A3
Forgue Dr					
2600	NPVL	60564	3202	29W-10S	C6
N Fork Cir					
1900	ELGN	60123	2854	36W-12N	A3
S Fork Dr					
200	GRNE	60031	2534	16W-34N	D2
W Fork Dr					
1000	LKFT	60045	2648	13W-24N	E7
1300	LKFT	60045	2702	13W-24N	E1
Formoor Ln					
6200	GRNE	60031	2534	16W-33N	D4
N Forrest Av					
10	ANHT	60004	2807	16W-14N	C5
600	PTHT	60004	2807	16W-14N	D3
S Forrest Av					
10	ANHT	60004	2807	16W-13N	C6
500	ANHT	60005	2807	16W-13N	C6
Forrest Blvd					
1600	SCRL	60174	3020	34W-2N	D2
N Forrest Ln					
1800	ANHT	60004	2807	16W-15N	D1
2600	ANHT	60004	2754	16W-16N	C6
Forrestal Dr					
-	NCHI	60044	2593	11W-29N	C3
2500	NCHI	60088	2593	11W-29N	C3
Forrestal Village Quarters St					
10	NCHI	60088	2593	11W-30N	D2
W Forrester Dr					
-	PNFD	60585	3265	32W-14S	C7
-	WldT	60585	3265	32W-14S	C7
Forrest Fork Ct					
3900	LGGV	60047	2700	20W-22N	A4
Forrest View Dr					
-	TroT	60404	3584	31W-25S	A2
21200	SRWD	60404	3584	31W-25S	A2
S Forrestville Av					
4300	CHCG	60653	3092	0E-4S	D7
4700	CHCG	60615	3092	0E-4S	D7
4700	CHCG	60615	3152	0E-5S	D1
11200	CHCG	60628	3278	0E-13S	D3
13100	CHCG	60827	3278	0E-15S	E7
13100	CHCG	60827	3350	0E-15S	E1
Forster Av					
4800	SRPK	60176	2917	12W-6N	C6
5100	SRPK	60656	2917	12W-6N	C7
Forsyth Ln					
2300	AURA	60502	3079	32W-4S	C7
Forsythe Av					
500	CTCY	60409	3352	4E-17S	C6
S Forsythe Sq					
1900	HMND	46394	3280		D5
Forsythia Ct					
10	BGBK	60490	3267	26W-11S	E2
W Forsythia Ct					
20800	DPgT	60544	3340	26W-15S	A2
Forsythia Dr					
300	DRFD	60015	2756	12W-20N	B1
300	WdfT	60015	2756	12W-20N	B1
Forsythia Ln					
100	WYNE	60184	2966	30W-4N	B4
Forsythia St					
100	BGBK	60490	3267	26W-12S	E2
Fort St					
-	JLET	60432	3499	21W-23S	E4
Fort Beggs St					
500	PNFD	60544	3416	30W-18S	B1
500	PnfT	60544	3416	30W-18S	B1
Fort Dearborn Ct					
4000	HRPK	60133	2967	27W-5N	D2
Fort Hill Dr					
-	NPVL	60540	3202	29W-8S	D1
-	NPVL	60564	3202	29W-8S	D2
400	NPVL	60540	3140	29W-7S	D7
Fortress Dr					
1100	FXLK	60050	2472	28W-37N	D3
Fort Sheridan Av					
2700	HDPK	60035	2704	8W-23N	E2
2700	HDPK	60037	2704	8W-23N	E2
Fort Sumter Ct					
2600	AURA	60503	3265	33W-11S	B1
Fortuna Av					
1100	PKRG	60068	2863	11W-10N	D5
S Fortuna Av					
1100	PKRG	60068	2863	11W-10N	D5
Fortune Dr					
-	WKGN	60087	2421	12W-38N	B7
Fortune Bay Ct					
1300	HFET	60192	2804	24W-15N	C2
N Fortwood Ct					
10	PltT	60067	2805	22W-15N	B2
Forum Dr					
500	ROSL	60172	2913	22W-7N	B3
Forum Sq					
700	NfdT	60025	2809	11W-13N	D7
S Forums Ct					
1100	PTHT	60070	2755	15W-16N	A7
1100	PTHT	60090	2755	15W-16N	A7
1100	WLNG	60070	2755	15W-16N	A7
1100	WLNG	60090	2755	15W-16N	A7
E Fosket Dr					
1000	PLTN	60074	2806	20W-15N	A2
N Fosket Dr					
10	PLTN	60074	2806	19W-16N	C1
Foss Ct					
300	LKBF	60044	2594	10W-28N	A6
W Foss Rd					
6800	MonT	60449	3682	8W-30S	B3
7100	GGnT	60449	3682	8W-30S	A3
Fossil Dr					
200	FXLK	60041	2473	26W-36N	D4
Fossil Bay Ct					
200	BDWD	60481	3942	30W-40S	C3
200	RedT	60481	3942	30W-40S	C3
Fossil Cove Ct					
100	BDWD	60481	3942	30W-40S	C3
100	RedT	60481	3942	30W-40S	C3
Fossil Cove Ln					
-	BDWD	60481	3942	30W-40S	B3
-	RedT	60481	3942	30W-40S	B3
Fossil Cove Rd					
-	BDWD	60481	3942	30W-40S	C3
Fossil Creek Ct					
3800	AURA	60564	3202	30W-9S	A4
Fossil Lake Ct					
100	RedT	60481	3942	30W-40S	C3
Fossil Lake Rd					
-	BDWD	60481	3942	30W-40S	B3
-	RedT	60481	3942	30W-40S	C3
Fossil Point Ct					
200	BDWD	60481	3942	30W-40S	B3
Fossil Ridge Ct					
10	BDWD	60481	3942	30W-40S	B3
Fossil Ridge Rd					
-	BDWD	60481	3942	31W-40S	B3
Fossil Stone Rd					
2500	DYR	46311	3598		E2
Fossland Av					
-	BtnT	60099	2362	11W-43N	D5
-	WPHR	60096	2362	11W-43N	D5
-	WPHR	60099	2362	11W-43N	D5
N Fossland Av					
42200	BtnT	60099	2362	11W-42N	D7
42200	WPHR	60096	2362	11W-42N	D7
42200	WPHR	60099	2362	11W-42N	D7
42200	ZION	60099	2362	11W-42N	D7
Foss Park Av					
500	NCHI	60064	2537	10W-32N	A6
1900	NCHI	60088	2537	10W-31N	A6
Foster Av					
-	SRPK	60176	2917	12W-6N	C6
-	SRPK	60656	2917	12W-6N	C6
10	AddT	60106	2915	17W-6N	B6
10	BmdT	60157	2913	22W-6N	C6
10	BNVL	60106	2915	17W-6N	B6
10	WDDL	60106	2915	17W-6N	C6
10	WDDL	60191	2915	17W-6N	C6
100	AddT	60191	2915	17W-6N	B6
100	CHCG	60106	2915	16W-6N	E6
100	ROSL	60157	2913	22W-6N	C6
200	BmdT	60172	2912	25W-6N	B6
400	BMDL	60108	2913	23W-6N	C6
400	BMDL	60172	2912	25W-6N	B6
400	BmdT	60108	2912	25W-6N	B6
500	BRLT	60103	2910	29W-6N	D7
700	ShdT	60044	2593	12W-29N	A5
1100	LbvT	60044	2593	13W-29N	A5
2000	PTHT	60070	2808	14W-15N	C2
2000	WLNG	60070	2808	14W-15N	C2
2000	WLNG	60090	2808	14W-15N	C2
E Foster Av					
100	BMDL	60108	2913	23W-6N	A6
100	ROSL	60108	2913	23W-6N	A6
100	ROSL	60172	2913	23W-6N	A7
700	BmdT	60157	2913	22W-6N	B6
700	BmdT	60172	2913	22W-6N	C6
700	ROSL	60157	2913	23W-6N	B6
W Foster Av					
900	CHCG	60640	2921	2W-6N	B5
W Foster Av					
1900	CHCG	60625	2921	2W-6N	B5
2700	CHCG	60625	2920	3W-6N	D5
3900	CHCG	60630	2920	5W-6N	B6
4700	CHCG	60630	2919	6W-6N	D6
6300	CHCG	60656	2919	8W-6N	A6
6600	CHCG	60656	2918	8W-6N	E5
7200	CHCG	60706	2918	10W-6N	B6
7200	HDHT	60706	2918	10W-6N	B6
7200	HDHT	60706	2918	10W-6N	B6
7600	NRDG	60706	2918	9W-6N	C6
7800	NRDG	60656	2918	9W-6N	B6
8600	CHCG	60656	2917	11W-6N	E6
9400	SRPK	60656	2917	11W-6N	C6
9700	CHCG	60018	2917	12W-6N	B6
9700	SRPK	60018	2917	12W-6N	B6
9700	SRPK	60176	2917	12W-6N	B6
W Foster Av US-41					
900	CHCG	60640	2921	2W-6N	B5
1900	CHCG	60625	2921	2W-6N	B5
Foster Cir					
1400	ALGN	60102	2747	36W-19N	A3
Foster Ct					
2500	NPVL	60564	3266	29W-12S	D4
4700	JLET	60586	3416	29W-21S	C7
Foster Dr					
-	OSWG	60543	3265	33W-11S	A2
W Foster Dr					
-	CHCG	60640	2922	0W-6N	A5
W Foster Ln					
8000	MNGV	60053	2864	10W-11N	B2
8000	NLES	60053	2864	10W-11N	B2
8000	NLES	60714	2864	10W-11N	B2
Foster Pl					
7000	DRGV	60516	3144	19W-7S	C7
E Foster Pl					
100	LKFT	60045	2649	10W-25N	E5
100	LKFT	60045	2650	10W-25N	A5
W Foster Pl					
7100	CHCG	60656	2918	8W-6N	D6
7100	CHCG	60706	2918	8W-6N	D6
7100	HDHT	60656	2918	8W-6N	D6
7100	HDHT	60706	2918	8W-6N	D6
Foster Rd					
300	WCDA	60084	2644	25W-27N	B1
400	WCDA	60084	2588	25W-27N	B7
7000	DRGV	60516	3144	19W-7S	C7
10700	GfnT	60142	2638	40W-25N	B6
10700	LKWD	60142	2638	40W-25N	B6
Foster St					
10	BMDL	60108	2913	23W-6N	A6
10	BMDL	60172	2913	23W-6N	A6
10	ROSL	60108	2913	23W-6N	A6
10	ROSL	60172	2913	23W-6N	A6
1300	EVTN	60201	2867	3W-11N	A2
1700	EVTN	60201	2866	3W-11N	E2
3600	SKOK	60203	2866	4W-11N	C2
4200	SKOK	60076	2866	5W-11N	A2
4800	SKOK	60076	2865	6W-11N	E2
5200	SKOK	60077	2865	6W-11N	D2
5400	SKOK	60053	2865	6W-11N	D2
6600	MNGV	60053	2865	8W-11N	A2
7200	MNGV	60053	2864	9W-11N	D2
7900	NLES	60053	2864	9W-11N	B2
7900	NLES	60714	2864	9W-11N	B2
E Foster St					
200	ANHT	60005	2861	17W-12N	A2
Foster Wy					
300	BGBK	60440	3268	24W-11S	D1
Foster McGaw Dr					
3900	BHPK	60087	2421	12W-38N	C6
3900	WKGN	60087	2421	12W-38N	C6
Founder St					
-	ELBN	60119	3017	42W-0N	C5
Founders Cir					
14700	HMGN	60491	3344	16W-17S	A5
Founders Cross					
14800	HMGN	60491	3344	16W-17S	A6
Founders Dr					
-	NHBK	60062	2757	8W-16N	D7
-	NHBK	60062	2810	8W-16N	D1
Founders Wy					
20000	OMFD	60461	3506	4W-24S	D5
Founders Field Blvd					
-	HTLY	60142	2691	40W-22N	E4
Founders Pointe N					
10	BMDL	60108	2969	23W-5N	A2
Founders Pointe S					
100	BMDL	60108	2969	23W-5N	A2
Founders Pointe Dr					
-	BMDL	60108	2969	23W-5N	A2
Foundry St					
1400	SCRL	60174	2963	36W-3N	E6
Fountain Av					
3100	ElgT	60124	2853	38W-10N	B5
Fountain Dr					
-	WDRG	60517	3143	22W-7S	B7
Fountain Ln					
5000	MCLK	60050	2470	34W-34N	D7
Fountainbleau Dr					
3200	HLCT	60429	3426	4W-21S	E7
3200	HLCT	60429	3427	3W-21S	B6
18200	BmnT	60429	3426	4W-21S	E7
18200	BmnT	60430	3426	4W-21S	E7
Fountain Grass Cir					
100	BRLT	60103	2909	32W-8N	D3
Fountain Grass Ct					
2000	BRLT	60103	2909	32W-8N	C3
Fountain Green Dr					
1300	CLLK	60014	2693	36W-23N	D2
Fountainhead Dr					
10	WTMT	60559	3145	18W-6S	A4
Fountain Hill Dr					
11000	ODPK	60467	3423	13W-21S	A7
11100	ODPK	60467	3422	14W-21S	D7
Fountain Mist Ct					
18100	ODPK	60467	3423	12W-21S	C7
Fountain Pointe Cir					
9400	DRN	60439	3206	19W-10S	D6
Fountain Square Dr					
2300	OKBK	60148	3084	18W-2S	E3
2300	OKBK	60523	3084	18W-2S	E3
2300	YkTp	60148	3084	18W-2S	E3
2300	YkTp	60181	3084	18W-2S	E3
2300	YkTp	60523	3084	18W-2S	E3
Fountain Square Pl					
-	WKGN	60085	2535	13W-33N	E4
Fountain Valley Dr					
600	DndT	60118	2801	33W-14N	A5
Fountain View Dr					
-	CLSM	60133	2968	25W-4N	B4
-	CLSM	60188	2968	25W-4N	A4
800	DRFD	60015	2756	11W-20N	E1
E Fountainview Dr					
600	MDLN	60060	2646	18W-26N	E2

Block	City	ZIP	Map#	CGS	Grid
S Fountainview Dr					
27100	CteT	60417	3774	0W-33S	C1
E Fountainview Ln					
10	LMBD	60148	3084	19W-2S	C3
Four Lakes Av					
-	LslT	60532	3143	23W-6S	A5
1400	LSLE	60532	3143	23W-6S	A5
1800	LSLE	60532	3142	23W-6S	E5
1800	LslT	60532	3142	23W-6S	E5
Four Seasons Blvd					
-	AraT	60504	3200	33W-8S	E2
-	AURA	60504	3201	33W-8S	A2
-	GrtT	60041	2530	28W-33N	A4
-	LKMR	60041	2530	28W-33N	A4
-	LKMR	60051	2530	28W-32N	A4
700	AURA	60504	3200	33W-8S	E3
Four Seasons Ct					
10	BGBK	60440	3204	25W-11S	B7
10	EMHT	60126	3027	16W-0S	D6
Four Seasons Ln					
1000	BGBK	60440	3204	25W-11S	B7
Fourth Av					
-	HbnT	60034	2351	40W-41N	B7
Fourth St					
-	WMTN	60481	3853	28W-39S	B7
Four Winds Ln					
4400	NHBK	60062	2756	13W-18N	A2
Four Winds Wy					
300	CPVL	60110	2747	35W-17N	D6
3800	SKOK	60076	2866	4W-11N	B3
9100	SKOK	60203	2866	4W-11N	B3
Fouser Ct					
200	JLET	60433	3499	23W-24S	A6
Fowler Av					
900	EVTN	60202	2866	3W-10N	D4
1200	EVTN	60201	2866	3W-10N	D4
Fowler Cir					
30100	WNVL	60555	3081	28W-3S	B6
Fowler Dr					
-	GNVW	60025	2810	9W-13N	C5
Fox Av					
10	WDND	60118	2801	33W-15N	A4
700	GLHT	60139	2969	22W-2N	D7
W Fox Av					
25000	ANTH	60002	2357	25W-42N	B5
25000	AntT	60002	2357	25W-42N	B5
Fox Ct					
10	FoxT	60560	3332	45W-16S	C5
400	BMDL	60108	2968	25W-4N	A3
400	SCRL	60174	2964	35W-3N	C6
700	CLSM	60188	2967	27W-3N	C6
700	GLHT	60139	2969	22W-2N	D7
2900	PRGV	60012	2585	31W-28N	C6
5600	NndT	60012	2584	34W-27N	C7
9200	ODHL	60487	3423	11W-19S	E2
Fox Ct E					
10	BFGV	60089	2754	16W-20N	D1
Fox Ct W					
10	BFGV	60089	2754	16W-20N	D1
Fox Dr					
-	BmnT	60426	3426	5W-19S	B2
2400	AURA	60506	3136	39W-6S	E5
N Fox Dr					
40200	AntT	60002	2417	21W-40N	D3
Fox Gln					
-	FRGV	60010	2696	28W-22N	D3
-	FRGV	60021	2696	28W-22N	D3
Fox Hllw					
14600	LMNT	60439	3343	18W-15S	A2
Fox Ln					
-	PlsT	60464	3273	13W-14S	A6
-	PSPK	60464	3273	13W-14S	A6
-	RGMW	60008	2805	21W-13N	C5
-	RGMW	60067	2805	21W-13N	C5
-	SMBG	60008	2805	21W-13N	C5
-	SMBG	60067	2805	21W-13N	C5
-	SMBG	60173	2805	21W-13N	C5
10	WLNG	60090	2755	14W-16N	D7
10	WNKA	60093	2812	5W-14N	A3
300	WDSK	60098	2524	41W-32N	C5
1400	HNDL	60521	3086	15W-3S	B5
1800	ELGN	60123	2799	36W-14N	E6
1800	ELGN	60123	2800	36W-14N	A6
1800	ELGN	60124	2799	36W-14N	E6
2000	DSPN	60018	2917	12W-8N	B2
5000	GRNE	60031	2478	15W-35N	B6
6400	PSHT	60463	3275	8W-15S	B7
6400	WthT	60463	3275	8W-15S	B7
11300	BRRG	60527	3208	14W-9S	E2
13100	LMNT	60439	3343	18W-15S	A2
Fox Ln N					
10	PSPK	60464	3273	13W-14S	A6
Fox Ln S					
10	PSPK	60464	3273	13W-14S	A6
Fox Pth					
900	WDND	60118	2800	34W-15N	D4
Fox Rd					
10500	KdlT	60560	3333	44W-15S	A3
10500	YKVL	60560	3333	44W-15S	A3
11000	KdlT	60560	3332	44W-16S	E4
12600	FoxT	60560	3332	45W-16S	B4
13600	FoxT	60560	3331	47W-16S	D4
14000	FoxT	60545	3331	47W-16S	D4
Fox Run					
2100	WHTN	60187	3081	26W-1S	E2
6700	NndT	60012	2584	35W-29N	A4
6900	NndT	60012	2583	35W-29N	E4
Fox St					
100	AlqT	60013	2696	29W-23N	D1
100	CbaT	60013	2696	29W-23N	D1
500	JltT	60432	3499	21W-23S	E3
1600	NndT	60012	2586	30W-28N	A6
1600	NndT	60014	2586	30W-28N	A6
3200	WDRG	60517	3205	22W-8S	C2
E Fox St					
100	YKVL	60560	3333	42W-15S	C3
W Fox St					
100	YKVL	60560	3333	43W-15S	B3
500	KdlT	60560	3333	44W-15S	A3
28700	AlqT	60013	2696	28W-23N	D1
28700	CbaT	60013	2696	28W-23N	D1
Fox Tr					
-	ISLK	60042	2586	28W-28N	E5
10	LNSH	60069	2702	13W-22N	E5
100	FXLK	60041	2473	27W-35N	C6
1400	IVNS	60067	2805	22W-14N	A3
3900	NndT	60012	2584	34W-27N	C7
W Fox Tr					
-	AvnT	60073	2531	24W-34N	C1
500	RDLK	60073	2531	24W-34N	C1
24700	LkvT	60046	2474	24W-36N	B3
24900	GrtT	60046	2474	24W-36N	B3
26400	CNHN	60410	3672	33W-31S	C5
Foxanna Cir					
800	FRGV	60021	2696	29W-23N	C2
Fox Bend Cir					
10	BGBK	60440	3268	24W-12S	C3
Fox Bend Ct					
1600	NPVL	60563	3141	28W-5S	A2
Foxbend Ct					
15700	ODPK	60462	3424	10W-18S	C1
Foxbend Dr					
10	CmpT	60175	2905	41W-7N	E5
Fox Bluff Ct					
100	SchT	60175	2964	36W-5N	A3
Fox Bluff Dr					
100	SchT	60175	2964	36W-5N	A2
Fox Bluff Ln					
2200	SPGV	60081	2354	31W-41N	E7
2500	RcmT	60071	2354	31W-42N	D6
2500	SPGV	60071	2354	31W-42N	D6
9600	SPGV	60081	2413	31W-41N	E1
Foxboro Ct					
10	SMWD	60107	2856	29W-9N	D7
100	WNVL	60555	3080	30W-2S	C3
1000	SMBG	60193	2912	24W-9N	D1
1100	BRLT	60103	2910	30W-7N	C5
2500	NPVL	60564	3202	29W-10S	D6
Foxboro Dr					
400	WLNG	60090	2755	14W-17N	D5
3300	LslT	60517	3205	22W-9S	C4
3300	LslT	60565	3205	22W-9S	C4
3300	WDRG	60517	3205	22W-9S	C4
Fox Boro Ln					
10	GRNE	60031	2534	16W-34N	D1
Foxboro Ln					
1100	BRLT	60103	2910	30W-7N	B5
1100	SMBG	60193	2912	24W-8N	C2
2200	NPVL	60564	3202	29W-10S	D5
17600	HMGN	60491	3421	17W-21S	D6
Foxboro Tr					
4700	RcmT	60071	2353	33W-41N	E7
Foxborough Dr					
-	NlxT	60448	3502	15W-23S	C4
-	NlxT	60451	3502	15W-24S	B4
19700	MKNA	60448	3502	15W-24S	B4
19700	MKNA	60451	3502	15W-23S	B4
Foxborough Pl					
100	BRRG	60527	3208	14W-8S	D2
Foxborough Rd					
600	SchT	60175	2907	36W-6N	E7
Foxborough Tr					
300	BGBK	60440	3268	24W-12S	D3
Foxburrow Ln					
10	LMNT	60439	3343	17W-15S	D2
Fox Chase Blvd					
-	SCRL	60174	2964	34W-4N	D4
Fox Chase Cir					
900	SCRL	60174	2965	33W-4N	A5
2300	RLKB	60073	2475	22W-36N	C4
Fox Chase Ct					
200	OSWG	60543	3263	37W-11S	B2
900	SCRL	60174	2965	33W-4N	A5
1400	BRLT	60103	2966	30W-5N	C1
Fox Chase Dr					
800	RLKB	60073	2475	21W-36N	C4
3000	SCRL	60174	2965	33W-4N	A5
E Fox Chase Dr					
1100	RLKB	60073	2475	21W-36N	D4
1300	GYLK	60046	2475	21W-36N	D4
1300	GYLK	60073	2475	21W-36N	D4
N Fox Chase Dr					
2300	GYLK	60046	2475	21W-36N	E4
2300	RLKB	60073	2475	21W-36N	E4
Fox Chase Dr N					
200	OSWG	60543	3263	38W-11S	A2
Fox Chase Dr S					
100	OSWG	60543	3263	38W-12S	B3
Fox Chase Ln					
1000	SCRL	60174	2965	33W-4N	A5
Fox Chase Rd					
1300	BRLT	60103	2966	30W-5N	C1
22800	DRPK	60010	2752	22W-20N	A1
Fox Creek Ct					
24100	PNFD	60586	3416	30W-19S	C3
Fox Creek Dr					
500	CmpT	60175	2962	40W-4N	B4
4100	NndT	60012	2584	34W-27N	C7
4500	NndT	60012	2640	34W-27N	C1
Fox Creek Ln					
16300	PNFD	60586	3416	30W-19S	B3
Foxcroft Dr					
10	MltT	60137	3083	23W-2S	A4
1200	AURA	60506	3137	38W-5S	B4
Foxcroft Rd					
10	NPVL	60565	3203	26W-9S	E4
10	NPVL	60565	3204	26W-9S	A4
Foxcroft on Auburn					
10	RGMW	60008	2806	19W-14N	B3
Fox Crossing Av					
-	BtvT	60542	3077	36W-3S	D6
Foxdale Av					
600	WNKA	60093	2812	5W-16N	A1
800	WNKA	60093	2759	5W-16N	A7
Foxdale Ct					
600	ROSL	60172	2912	25W-6N	C6
N Foxdale Dr					
1200	AddT	60101	2970	20W-4N	B2
1200	ADSN	60101	2970	20W-5N	B2
W Foxdale Ln					
400	ANHT	60004	2753	18W-18N	E2
500	ANHT	60004	2754	18W-18N	A2
Foxfield Ct					
10	LIHL	60156	2692	39W-23N	B2
700	SCRL	60174	2965	33W-3N	A5
Foxfield Dr					
200	CmpT	60175	2961	42W-4N	D4
1700	JLET	60435	3417	27W-21S	C7
1700	JLET	60435	3497	27W-21S	C1
1800	AURA	60504	3200	33W-10S	E5
2700	SCRL	60174	2965	33W-3N	A5
2700	WCHI	60185	2965	33W-3N	B5
2700	WynT	60185	2965	33W-3N	B5
Foxfield Ln					
5700	LIHL	60156	2692	39W-23N	B2
Fox Field Rd					
2000	SCRL	60174	2964	34W-3N	E5
2700	SCRL	60174	2965	33W-3N	A5
Fox Fire Ct					
2200	GNVA	60134	3019	36W-0N	D5
Foxfire Dr					
10	BRBK	60459	3211	7W-8S	C1
10	LKZH	60047	2698	23W-21N	E5
6900	NndT	60012	2583	36W-28N	E6
S Foxfire Dr					
22600	FftT	60423	3591	13W-27S	B5
Foxford Dr					
200	AlqT	60013	2641	30W-25N	E5
200	CRY	60013	2641	30W-25N	E5
300	BFGV	60089	2701	17W-23N	C3
300	CRY	60013	2642	30W-25N	A5
S Foxford Dr					
-	MhtT	60442	3677	19W-30S	D3
24700	MHTN	60442	3677	19W-30S	E3
Foxford Ln					
-	AraT	60502	3139	33W-6S	B5
100	GNVA	60134	3020	35W-0N	B5
1300	LKPT	60441	3342	21W-18S	A7
19300	MKNA	60448	3504	11W-23S	A3
Foxford Rd					
500	BRLT	60103	2911	27W-7N	C5
Foxgate Ln					
5700	HNDL	60521	3146	15W-6S	A4
Fox Glade Ct					
1200	SCRL	60174	3020	35W-2N	B2
Fox Glen Cir					
10	KdlT	60560	3332	44W-16S	D4
Fox Glen Ct					
10	KdlT	60560	3332	44W-16S	E4
3000	SCRL	60174	2964	35W-5N	C2
Fox Glen Dr					
600	SchT	60174	2964	35W-5N	C2
600	SCRL	60174	2964	34W-5N	C2
1200	WYNE	60174	2964	35W-5N	C2
1200	WYNE	60184	2964	35W-5N	C2
N Fox Glen Dr					
9700	NLES	60714	2863	11W-12N	D1
Fox Glen Dr E					
10	KdlT	60560	3332	44W-16S	E4
Fox Glen Dr W					
10	KdlT	60560	3332	44W-16S	D4
Fox Glove Ct					
400	SchT	60175	2907	38W-7N	B5
1100	MNKA	60447	3672	33W-29S	A3
Foxglove Ct					
10	BGBK	60440	3268	23W-12S	E3
10	RMVL	60446	3340	26W-17S	A6
10	SMWD	60107	2856	30W-10N	C6
2400	ELGN	60124	2853	36W-9N	D7
Foxglove Dr					
700	ALGN	60102	2693	37W-20N	B7
1100	BTVA	60510	3078	34W-1S	E2
2100	NHBK	60062	2756	10W-16N	E7
3900	ZION	60099	2362	12W-41N	B7
Fox Glove Ln					
400	BRTN	60010	2751	24W-20N	D1
16100	WDWH	60083	2419	16W-40N	D3
16400	NptT	60083	2419	16W-40N	D3
Foxglove Ln					
1100	MRGO	60152	2578	49W-27N	C7
1100	MRGO	60152	2634	49W-27N	C1
1100	PLTN	60074	2753	19W-18N	C3
18700	MKNA	60448	3503	13W-22S	A1
Foxglove St					
2600	WDRG	60517	3143	21W-7S	D7
Foxgrove Dr					
-	SCRL	60175	2908	36W-6N	A7
-	SCRL	60175	2964	36W-6N	A1
Foxgrove Ln					
17100	TYPK	60487	3424	10W-20S	B4
Fox Harbor Rd					
200	TVLY	60013	2695	31W-22N	C3
Foxhead Ct					
200	BGBK	60440	3268	23W-12S	E3
Fox Hill Ct					
10	OswT	60560	3334	40W-14S	C1
900	LYLK	60175	2961	43W-5N	A2
1300	NARA	60542	3137	37W-4S	B1
Foxhill Ct					
100	NLNX	60451	3501	18W-24S	A6
2200	SCRL	60174	2964	34W-3N	D5
W Fox Hill Ct					
13100	LMNT	60439	3344	16W-15S	A2
Fox Hill Dr					
13100	LMNT	60439	3343	16W-15S	E1
13300	LMNT	60439	3344	16W-15S	A2
13400	HMGN	60491	3344	16W-15S	A2
36500	GRNE	60031	2477	16W-36N	D4
36500	GRNE	60083	2477	16W-36N	D4
36500	WrnT	60083	2477	16W-37N	D2
E Fox Hill Dr					
10	BFGV	60089	2754	16W-20N	D1
200	BFGV	60089	2701	16W-20N	D7
W Fox Hill Dr					
10	BFGV	60089	2701	16W-20N	C7
Fox Hill Ln					
1200	NARA	60542	3137	37W-4S	B1
Foxhill Pl					
1600	DRN	60561	3206	18W-9S	E4
1600	DRN	60561	3207	18W-9S	A4
Fox Hill Rd					
2800	AURA	60504	3201	31W-9S	D3
Foxhill Rd					
1400	NPVL	60563	3140	29W-5S	D3
Fox Hollow Dr					
21200	CbaT	60010	2697	26W-21N	D6
Foxhorn Ct					
1600	NPVL	60563	3141	26W-4S	E1
S Foxhound Ln					
17900	HMGN	60491	3422	16W-21S	A7
Fox Hound Tr					
1300	BCHR	60401	3774	0W-35S	D7
Fox Hunt Ct					
10	HNWD	60047	2644	24W-25N	C4
Fox Hunt Ln					
3200	SCRL	60174	2965	33W-4N	A5
Fox Hunt Rd					
10	BNHL	60010	2749	29W-20N	B1
Fox Hunt Tr					
10	ElaT	60047	2644	24W-25N	C4
10	HNWD	60047	2644	24W-25N	C4
100	BRTN	60010	2751	24W-20N	B1
700	DRFD	60015	2704	9W-20N	B7
Foxhunt Wy					
3800	FmtT	60030	2532	22W-31N	C7
3800	RLKP	60030	2532	22W-31N	C7
Foxhurst Rd					
10	FoxT	60541	3331	48W-17S	B7
N Fox I					
35000	GrtT	60041	2474	25W-35N	B7
Foxiana Ct					
10	OKBK	60523	3085	18W-2S	A3
Fox Knoll Ct					
2900	JNBG	60050	2471	31W-35N	C5
Fox Lake Rd					
5400	MchT	60050	2472	29W-37N	C2
6000	BtnT	60050	2472	29W-37N	C2
6000	BtnT	60081	2472	29W-37N	C2
N Fox Lake Rd					
32300	LKMR	60041	2530	27W-32N	B5
32300	LKMR	60073	2530	27W-32N	B6
32300	VOLO	60041	2530	27W-32N	B6
32300	VOLO	60073	2530	27W-32N	B6
Fox Meade Cir					
1700	MTGY	60538	3199	37W-10S	D5
Fox Meade Ct					
1700	MTGY	60538	3199	37W-10S	D5
Fox Meadow Cir					
2400	NHFD	60093	2810	8W-15N	E2
Fox Meadow Ct					
1800	GRNE	60031	2478	15W-36N	B5
2400	NHFD	60093	2810	8W-15N	D2
2400	NHFD	60093	2811	8W-15N	A2
Fox Meadow Dr					
-	NHFD	60093	2810	8W-15N	E2
Foxmeadow Dr					
2400	CTHL	60403	3417	27W-21S	D7
Fox Meadow Ln					
2400	NHFD	60093	2810	8W-15N	E2
2400	NHFD	60093	2811	8W-15N	A2
Fox Meadows Ct					
1300	SCRL	60174	2963	36W-3N	E6
Fox Mill Blvd					
10	CmpT	60175	2962	40W-4N	C5
Foxmoor Ct					
1600	MDLN	60060	2590	20W-27N	A7
Fox Moor Dr					
200	CmpT	60175	2961	43W-5N	B2
200	LYLK	60175	2961	43W-5N	B2
Foxmoor Dr					
-	MTGY	60506	3198	40W-9S	B4
-	MTGY	60538	3198	40W-9S	B4
Foxmoor Ln					
700	LKZH	60047	2699	22W-22N	B5
1400	ELGN	60123	2907	36W-8N	E3
1400	ELGN	60123	2908	36W-8N	A3
2200	AURA	60502	3079	32W-4S	B7
Foxmoor Rd					
100	FRGV	60021	2696	30W-22N	B4
Fox Path Ct					
1400	HFET	60192	2856	30W-12N	B2
Fox Path Ln					
1300	HFET	60192	2856	30W-12N	B2
Fox Pointe Cir					
2000	AURA	60504	3201	33W-9S	A4
Fox Pointe Dr					
2000	AURA	60504	3201	33W-9S	A4
Foxridge Ct					
1800	AURA	60502	3139	33W-6S	A4
1800	AURA	60505	3139	33W-6S	A4
3100	LslT	60517	3205	22W-8S	C2
3200	LslT	60565	3205	22W-8S	C2
3200	WDRG	60517	3205	22W-8S	C2
W Foxridge Ct					
-	DRPK	60010	2699	23W-21N	A7
-	LKZH	60010	2699	23W-21N	A7
Fox Ridge Dr					
500	FXLK	60020	2473	27W-35N	B5
500	GrtT	60020	2473	27W-35N	B5
1600	JLET	60586	3495	31W-21S	D1
Foxridge Ln					
1100	AURA	60502	3139	33W-6S	A4
Fox River Av					
700	SchT	60174	2908	34W-6N	D6
Fox River Dr					
10	DndT	60118	2801	34W-15N	A4
100	SchT	60174	2908	35W-6N	B7
1100	ALGN	60102	2747	33W-20N	D1
4400	LtRT	60545	3331	47W-16S	C4
5200	PLNO	60545	3331	47W-16S	C4
5900	FoxT	60545	3331	47W-15S	D3
5900	FoxT	60560	3331	47W-15S	D3
5900	LtRT	60560	3331	47W-15S	D3
N Fox River Dr					
24300	CbaT	60013	2643	28W-24N	A6
W Fox River Dr					
28500	CbaT	60010	2696	28W-23N	E2
Fox River Ln					
2600	NPVL	60565	3204	26W-10S	A6
Fox River Rd					
-	AntT	60002	2355		D4
-	RdlT	60002	2355		D4
10200	SlmT	53105	2356		A1
10200	SlmT	53192	2356		A2
11700	RdlT	53181	2355		D3
11700	RdlT	53192	2355		E2
Fox River Rd CO-C					
11300	SlmT	53192	2356		A1
Fox River Rd CO-W					
-	AntT	60002	2355		D4
-	RdlT	60002	2355		D4
10200	SlmT	53105	2356		A1
10200	SlmT	53192	2356		A2
11700	RdlT	53181	2355		D3
11700	RdlT	53192	2355		E2
W Fox River Rd					
27700	CbaT	60013	2643	28W-24N	A6
28400	CbaT	60013	2642	28W-24N	E7
28600	AlqT	60013	2642	28W-24N	D7
N Fox River St					
400	PNFD	60544	3338	30W-18S	C7
Fox Run Cir					
9300	FKFT	60423	3503	11W-25S	E6
Fox Run Ct					
9400	FKFT	60423	3503	11W-25S	E7
W Fox Run Ct					
12200	HTLY	60142	2744	42W-19N	D3
Fox Run Dr					
10	FoxT	60541	3331	48W-17S	A7
100	ELWD	60421	3675	25W-31S	B6
100	JknT	60421	3675	25W-31S	B6
200	NHBK	60062	2757	9W-18N	D3
700	GNVA	60134	3020	34W-0N	C4
1500	TNLK	53181	2353		E1
1500	TNLK	53181	2354		A1
1600	ANHT	60004	2754	16W-17N	C6
1800	EGVV	60007	2859	22W-9N	C6
Fox Run Ln					
-	AlqT	60102	2695	32W-20N	B7
400	HPSR	60140	2795	47W-15N	D3
600	ALGN	60102	2695	32W-20N	B7
6200	MTSN	60443	3505	7W-24S	C6
17400	LKPT	60441	3420	20W-20S	C5
40200	AntT	60002	2416	23W-40N	D3
Fox Run Rd					
200	GNOK	60048	2592	14W-29N	C4
Fox Sedge Tr					
1300	DrrT	60098	2582	40W-28N	A5
1300	WDSK	60098	2582	40W-28N	A5
Foxshire Ct					
10	SBTN	60010	2803	26W-14N	D3
Fox Shores Dr					
9600	AlqT	60102	2695	31W-22N	C4
Foxtail Cir					
600	CmpT	60175	2905	41W-7N	E6
Foxtail Ct					
1100	DRN	60561	3145	17W-7S	B6
2400	CTHL	60403	3417	27W-21S	D7
W Foxtail Ct					
20800	LktT	60544	3340	26W-16S	A3
Foxtail Dr					
1900	AURA	60504	3201	33W-8S	B2
21300	MKNA	60448	3590	14W-25S	E1
N Foxtail Dr					
22200	KLDR	60047	2699	21W-22N	D4
Fox Tail Ln					
10	RVWD	60015	2702	14W-21N	C7
100	LNHT	60046	2476	19W-37N	D1
Foxtail Ln					
200	OswT	60560	3334	40W-15S	D2
12300	HTLY	60142	2744	42W-18N	D4
13100	LMNT	60439	3344	16W-15S	A1
Foxtail Rd					
10	ElaT	60047	2645	21W-25N	D6
10	HNWD	60047	2645	21W-25N	D6
W Foxtail Rd					
25500	GrtT	60073	2531	25W-34N	A1
Fox Trail Ct					
-	WRLK	60097	2469	37W-36N	B4
400	OKBK	60523	3085	16W-3S	E5
800	LKFT	60045	2649	12W-24N	B6
1200	NPVL	60540	3204	24W-8S	D1
Fox Trail Dr					
300	BTVA	60510	3078	35W-2S	C5
400	BtvT	60510	3078	34W-2S	C4
9600	SPGV	60081	2414	30W-41N	A1
Fox Trail Ln					
400	OKBK	60523	3085	16W-3S	E5
22500	PNFD	60544	3339	28W-16S	A4
22500	PnfT	60544	3339	28W-16S	A4
Fox Trails Dr N					
-	AlqT	60013	2695	32W-23N	A2
500	CRY	60013	2695	32W-23N	A2
Fox Trails Dr S					
500	CRY	60013	2695	32W-23N	A3
Foxtree Av					
6600	WDRG	60517	3143	21W-7S	E6
Fox Valley Ct					
2200	AURA	60504	3201	32W-9S	B3
Fox Valley Dr					
1000	AURA	60504	3201	32W-9S	B3
Fox Valley Center Dr					
4000	AURA	60504	3140	30W-7S	B7
4000	AURA	60504	3202	30W-7S	B1
Fox View Dr					
900	JLET	60447	3495	33W-22S	B3
Foxview Highland Dr					
3200	MHRY	60050	2585	32W-30N	C1
Foxwick Ct					
500	PltT	60124	2852	40W-11N	B5
Fox Wilds Ct					
100	LYLK	60175	2961	43W-5N	A3
Fox Wilds Dr					
10	LYLK	60175	2961	44W-5N	A3
Foxwood Cir					
800	GNVA	60134	3020	34W-1N	E3
Foxwood Ct					
10	SchT	60175	2963	38W-6N	A1
300	LslT	60540	3205	23W-8S	A1
900	NLNX	60451	3589	18W-27S	A5
900	SMBG	60194	2858	24W-11N	D3
5300	JLET	60586	3416	30W-20S	C5
Foxwood Dr					
-	MhtT	60442	3589	18W-27S	A5
-	NLNX	60442	3589	18W-27S	A5
1600	NLNX	60451	3589	18W-26S	A3
26500	MonT	60449	3683	6W-32S	A7
N Foxwood Dr					
2000	NLNX	60451	3589	18W-27S	A4
Foxwood Ln					
10	CmpT	60175	2962	39W-5N	E1
10	LKBN	60010	2643	27W-24N	B7
10	SCRL	60174	2964	34W-4N	E5
100	PltT	60010	2752	23W-18N	A2
200	SchT	60175	2907	38W-6N	B7
200	SchT	60175	2963	38W-6N	B1
700	CmpT	60175	2963	39W-6N	A1
Foxwoods Ct					
11400	OKLN	60453	3275	6W-13S	D4
Foxwoods Dr					
5400	OKLN	60453	3275	6W-13S	D4
5400	OKLN	60803	3275	6W-13S	D4
5500	ALSP	60453	3275	6W-13S	D4
5500	ALSP	60482	3275	6W-13S	D4
11400	ALSP	60803	3275	6W-13S	D4
Foxworth Blvd					
500	LMBD	60148	3084	20W-1S	A2
1000	LMBD	60148	3083	21W-1S	E2
Foxworth Ct					
100	AURA	60502	3201	32W-8S	B2
Foxworth Ln					
-	WrnT	60031	2477	17W-35N	C6
6500	GRNE	60031	2477	17W-35N	C6
Framingham Ct					
600	GRNE	60031	2535	14W-33N	C3
Frances Av					
1000	HRPK	60133	2911	27W-9N	D1
1000	SMWD	60107	2857	27W-9N	D7
1000	SMWD	60107	2911	27W-9N	D1
1300	JNBG	60051	2472	30W-35N	A5
Frances Ct					
10	BFGV	60089	2754	16W-18N	C3
1000	LslT	60563	3142	25W-5S	B4
1000	NPVL	60563	3142	25W-5S	B4
W Frances Ct					
23500	CNHN	60410	3584	29W-27S	E6
24200	TroT	60404	3584	30W-25S	C1
Frances Ln					
10	CHHT	60411	3508	1W-23S	A3
10	PlsT	60467	3344	13W-15S	E1
10	PlsT	60467	3345	13W-15S	A1
200	BRTN	60010	2751	23W-18N	D2
200	PltT	60010	2751	23W-18N	D2
2800	BtlT	60538	3198	40W-10S	B5
2800	MTGY	60538	3198	40W-10S	B5
8900	ODPK	60462	3423	11W-18S	D1
8900	ODPK	60462	3424	11W-18S	A1
15500	ODPK	60462	3346	11W-18S	A7
Frances Pkwy					
900	PKRG	60068	2918	10W-7N	A3
1200	PKRG	60068	2917	10W-7N	E3
Frances St					
100	LKPT	60441	3419	23W-20S	B4
500	PHNX	60426	3350	0W-18S	B7
24300	PNFD	60585	3338	30W-15S	B3
S Frances Wy					
22900	CNHN	60410	3584	29W-27S	E6
Francesca Ct					
300	OSWG	60543	3263	36W-11S	E1
Franchesca Ct					
9900	ODPK	60462	3345	12W-18S	C6
Francine Av					
2200	JLET	60436	3497	26W-24S	E5
Francine Dr					
800	BRLT	60103	2911	28W-7N	A5
Francis Av					
10	CLLK	60014	2639	35W-25N	E4
10	FmtT	60060	2646	18W-26N	D4
10	LbvT	60060	2646	18W-26N	D4

Chicago 7-County Street Index

STREET Block	City	ZIP	Map#	CGS	Grid
Francis Av					
5800	CTSD	60525	3147	12W-6S	C4
N Francis Av					
36000	GrtT	60041	2473	26W-36N	E4
E Francis Cir					
3000	SCRL	60174	2965	33W-4N	A4
W Francis Cir					
1100	SCRL	60174	2965	33W-4N	A4
Francis Ct					
300	MHTN	60442	3678	18W-31S	A5
400	ZION	60099	2362	12W-42N	C7
9000	WDRG	60517	3206	20W-10S	A6
16400	ODPK	60467	3422	13W-19S	E3
Francis Dr					
-	GYLK	60046	2475	21W-36N	E5
-	RLKB	60046	2475	21W-36N	E5
-	RLKB	60073	2475	21W-36N	E5
S Francis Dr					
15200	PnfT	60544	3339	27W-18S	C7
15300	PnfT	60544	3417	27W-18S	C1
W Francis Dr					
1100	ANHT	60005	2806	18W-13N	D6
Francis Ln					
-	FKFT	60423	3503	11W-24S	E5
-	FKFT	60423	3504	11W-24S	A5
3300	JLET	60432	3500	19W-23S	D4
Francis Pl					
900	DYR	46311	3598		E4
W Francis Pl					
2600	CHCG	60647	2977	3W-2N	A6
2700	CHCG	60647	2976	3W-2N	E6
Francis Rd					
11500	FftT	60448	3502	14W-24S	E4
11500	MKNA	60448	3502	14W-24S	E4
11800	NlxT	60448	3502	14W-23S	D4
11800	NlxT	60451	3502	14W-23S	D4
E Francis Rd					
100	NLNX	60451	3501	16W-23S	E4
100	NlxT	60451	3501	16W-23S	E4
1000	NlxT	60448	3501	16W-23S	E4
1400	NlxT	60448	3502	16W-23S	A4
1400	NlxT	60451	3502	16W-23S	A4
W Francis Rd					
100	NLNX	60451	3501	18W-23S	B4
100	NlxT	60451	3501	18W-23S	B4
1000	JLET	60451	3500	19W-23S	D4
1000	NLNX	60451	3500	19W-23S	D4
1000	NlxT	60451	3500	19W-23S	D4
1400	JLET	60432	3500	19W-23S	D4
Francis St					
-	WCDA	60084	2643	26W-27N	D1
600	MRGO	60152	2634	49W-25N	C3
E Francis St					
100	TNTN	60476	3428	0E-21S	D6
400	JLET	60432	3499	23W-22S	B2
S Francis St					
200	BDWD	60408	3942	31W-42S	A6
Francis Bret Harte St					
300	CmpT	60175	2962	40W-3N	C6
Francisca Wy					
20600	FKFT	60423	3503	11W-24S	E6
Franciscan Dr					
1200	LMNT	60439	3271	18W-13S	B4
Franciscan Wy					
1900	WCHI	60185	2966	30W-3N	C6
Francisco Av					
12600	BLID	60406	3277	3W-14S	A7
13100	WthT	60406	3349	3W-15S	A1
13300	RBBN	60406	3349	3W-16S	A2
13900	BLID	60406	3349	3W-16S	A3
14300	BmnT	60406	3349	3W-17S	A4
18300	HMWD	60430	3427	3W-22S	A7
18400	HMWD	60430	3507	3W-22S	A1
N Francisco Av					
10	CHCG	60612	3032	3W-0N	E4
800	CHCG	60622	3032	3W-1N	E2
2400	CHCG	60647	2976	3W-3N	E5
3600	CHCG	60618	2976	3W-4N	E2
4400	CHCG	60618	2920	3W-5N	E7
4400	CHCG	60625	2920	3W-5N	E7
6000	CHCG	60659	2920	3W-7N	E3
6300	CHCG	60645	2920	3W-7N	E3
7300	CHCG	60645	2866	3W-9N	E7
7500	EVTN	60202	2866	3W-9N	E7
S Francisco Av					
10	CHCG	60612	3032	3W-0S	E5
1100	CHCG	60623	3032	3W-0S	E7
2400	CHCG	60623	3090	3W-2S	E2
3500	CHCG	60632	3090	3W-3S	E5
4600	CHCG	60632	3150	3W-5S	E1
5200	CHCG	60632	3151	3W-6S	A3
5400	CHCG	60629	3151	3W-7S	A5
7900	CHCG	60652	3213	3W-9S	A2
8600	CHCG	60805	3213	3W-9S	A4
8700	ENGN	60805	3213	3W-11S	A6
10200	CHCG	60655	3277	3W-12S	A1
10200	CHCG	60805	3277	3W-12S	A1
10200	ENGN	60805	3277	3W-12S	A1
14400	POSN	60469	3349	3W-17S	A5
14800	BmnT	60469	3349	3W-17S	A5
Francisco St					
4800	DRGV	60515	3143	21W-5S	D2
4800	LslT	60515	3143	21W-5S	D2
Francisco Ter					
100	OKPK	60301	3031	7W-0S	C6
100	OKPK	60302	3031	7W-0S	C6
Francis Ouimet Cir					
14000	MDLN	60445	3348	6W-16S	A3
Francis Scott Key Blvd					
-	BGBK	60490	3267	27W-14S	B7
-	PNFD	60490	3267	27W-14S	B7
Frank Av					
1500	VrnT	60015	2702	15W-20N	A7
W Frank Av					
200	JLET	60435	3498	24W-22S	E1
Frank Ct					
1700	GLHT	60139	2969	23W-3N	A6
N Frank Ct					
37600	GrtT	60081	2472	28W-37N	E1
Frank Dr					
-	JLET	60431	3496	29W-22S	D3
-	SRWD	60431	3496	29W-22S	D3
4800	SRWD	60404	3496	29W-22S	D3
6000	HFET	60192	2855	31W-12N	E1
Frank Ln					
1000	CteT	60401	3774	1W-33S	A2
10800	OrlT	60467	3423	13W-20S	A4
N Frank Pkwy					
4800	NRDG	60706	2918	9W-6N	B6
Frank Rd					
-	CLLK	60014	2693	37W-22N	B5
9900	ALGN	60102	2693	37W-21N	B6
9900	GfnT	60156	2693	37W-21N	B5
9900	LlHL	60102	2693	37W-21N	B6
9900	LlHL	60156	2693	37W-22N	B5
Frank St					
100	VLPK	60181	3027	17W-0S	B6
Franke Av					
10	CRY	60013	2695	31W-23N	E1
Frankfort Av					
-	OswT	60543	3264	35W-12S	B2
400	OSWG	60543	3264	35W-11S	B2
Frankfort Main					
10100	FKFT	60423	3591	12W-26S	C2
S Frankfort Square Rd					
-	FKFT	60423	3504	9W-25S	D7
19900	FftT	60423	3504	9W-25S	D7
W Frankfort Square Rd					
7600	FftT	60423	3504	9W-23S	D4
7900	TYPK	60423	3504	9W-23S	D4
7900	TYPK	60477	3504	9W-23S	D4
Frankie Ct					
500	PTHT	60070	2807	16W-15N	D2
Franklin Av					
10	FTPK	60130	3030	9W-0N	C5
10	RVFT	60130	3030	9W-0N	C5
100	AURA	60506	3137	36W-7S	E7
200	FKFT	60423	3591	12W-25S	C1
700	WPHR	60096	2363	9W-42N	C7
800	RVFT	60305	3030	9W-1N	C3
900	SEGN	60177	2908	35W-8N	B4
1000	CHHT	60411	3507	1W-25S	E7
1400	WPHR	60096	2422	9W-41N	C1
1500	EDPK	60707	3030	9W-1N	C1
1500	RVFT	60707	3030	9W-1N	C1
3800	PvsT	60558	3086	13W-4S	E7
3800	WNSP	60558	3086	13W-4S	E7
4400	WNSP	60558	3146	13W-5S	E1
5300	OKLN	60453	3211	6W-11S	D6
9300	FNPK	60131	2973	11W-3N	C4
10600	FNPK	60131	2972	13W-4N	E3
10600	LydT	60131	2972	13W-4N	E3
11500	BNVL	60131	2972	14W-4N	C2
E Franklin Av					
10	NPVL	60540	3141	26W-6S	D5
300	LGNG	60525	3087	12W-4S	C7
N Franklin Av					
600	PLTN	60067	2752	22W-16N	C6
35500	GrtT	60041	2474	25W-35N	A5
S Franklin Av					
5500	LynT	60525	3146	13W-6S	E3
W Franklin Av					
10	NPVL	60540	3141	27W-6S	C5
9200	FftT	60423	3592	11W-25S	A1
9200	FKFT	60423	3592	11W-25S	A1
9300	FftT	60423	3591	11W-25S	E1
9300	FKFT	60423	3591	11W-25S	E1
Franklin Blvd					
-	ELGN	60120	2855	33W-11N	B3
100	ELGN	60120	2854	34W-11N	E3
1300	FmtT	60060	2590	19W-29N	D3
1300	LYVL	60048	2590	19W-30N	D2
1300	LYVL	60060	2590	19W-29N	D3
1500	FmtT	60048	2590	19W-30N	D2
W Franklin Blvd					
-	CHCG	60612	3032	4W-0N	D3
3600	CHCG	60624	3032	4W-0N	C3
Franklin Cir					
21400	LktT	60544	3339	26W-16S	D4
21500	PnfT	60544	3339	26W-16S	D4
Franklin Ct					
10	BGBK	60440	3268	24W-11S	D2
10	SMWD	60107	2857	28W-11N	A4
1900	GRNE	60031	2477	15W-36N	E4
2600	LNHT	60046	2418	19W-39N	C5
3500	NndT	60014	2641	32W-26N	B3
4100	ZION	60099	2362	12W-42N	B6
5800	HRPK	60133	2911	26W-7N	D5
9000	ODPK	60462	3346	11W-17S	A5
14000	PnfT	60544	3339	27W-16S	D4
Franklin Dr					
400	SEGN	60177	2908	35W-8N	C4
900	BRLT	60103	2910	29W-6N	C6
1900	GNVW	60025	2809	11W-14N	C3
1900	GNVW	60062	2809	11W-14N	C4
22400	RNPK	60471	3594	5W-27S	B4
W Franklin Dr					
10	NHLK	60164	3028	14W-2N	D1
500	MPPT	60056	2861	16W-10N	E5
Franklin Ln					
400	EGVV	60007	2859	21W-9N	D7
400	EGVV	60007	2913	21W-9N	D1
600	LNHT	60046	2418	19W-39N	C5
700	SRWD	60404	3496	30W-24S	C6
1100	BFGV	60089	2700	18W-21N	E6
1100	BFGV	60089	2701	18W-21N	A6
24800	PNFD	60585	3266	31W-13S	A6
Franklin Pl					
1000	VNHL	60061	2647	17W-26N	B3
1900	HFET	60169	2858	25W-12N	A1
Franklin Pl E					
10	LKFT	60045	2649	10W-27N	E1
10	LKFT	60045	2650	10W-27N	A1
Franklin Rd					
100	GLNC	60022	2758	6W-18N	D3
Franklin St					
-	FNPK	60131	2973	11W-3N	E4
-	FNPK	60171	2973	11W-3N	D4
-	RVGV	60171	2973	11W-3N	D4
10	EGvT	60018	2862	15W-9N	A7
10	ELGN	60120	2854	34W-11N	E3
10	GNVA	60134	3020	35W-1N	C4
10	MltT	60187	3023	26W-1N	E3
10	MltT	60188	3023	26W-1N	E3
10	OSWG	60543	3263	37W-12S	C4
100	BMDL	60108	2968	24W-5N	E1
100	BMDL	60108	2969	23W-5N	A1
100	BRTN	60010	2750	27W-20N	C1
100	BRTN	60010	2751	25W-20N	A1
100	BTVA	60510	3078	35W-1S	C1
100	LKPT	60441	3419	22W-18S	D1
300	GNCY	53128	2353		A2
300	LktT	60441	3419	22W-18S	D1
400	DRGV	60515	3144	19W-5S	D2
500	HNDL	60521	3086	15W-4S	B7
600	WKGN	60085	2480	10W-34N	A7
700	WTMT	60559	3085	17W-4S	C7
900	BtnT	60099	2422	9W-41N	C1
900	WPHR	60096	2422	9W-41N	C1
1000	MDLN	60060	2590	20W-28N	A5
4000	ZION	60099	2362	12W-42N	C7
7200	FTPK	60130	3030	9W-0N	D4
7200	FTPK	60302	3030	9W-0N	D4
7200	OKPK	60302	3030	9W-0N	D4
7500	RVFT	60130	3030	9W-0N	C4
7500	RVFT	60305	3030	9W-0N	C4
7900	CmgT	60033	2405	51W-39N	D3
7900	HRVD	60033	2405	51W-39N	D3
Franklin St CO-B					
300	GNCY	53128	2353		A2
E Franklin St					
10	CLLK	60014	2640	35W-25N	B4
100	WHTN	60187	3024	24W-0S	D6
200	BRTN	60010	2751	25W-20N	A2
N Franklin St					
10	CHCG	60606	3034	0W-0N	B4
300	JLET	60432	3499	23W-23S	A4
400	CHCG	60610	3034	0W-0N	B3
S Franklin St					
10	CHCG	60606	3034	0W-0S	B5
300	CHCG	60607	3034	0W-0S	B5
W Franklin St					
10	CLLK	60014	2640	35W-25N	A4
100	WHTN	60187	3024	25W-0S	C6
Franklinville Rd					
-	DrrT	60098	2581	42W-30N	A2
-	WDSK	60098	2581	43W-30N	A2
Franklin Walsh St					
3700	LinT	53147	2349		E1
Frank Mraz Dr					
-	RVDL	60827	3350	1W-16S	A3
N Franks Av					
7000	NLES	60714	2918	8W-8N	E1
7100	NLES	60714	2864	8W-9N	E7
Franks Rd					
-	MRGO	60152	2634	48W-26N	D3
Frankstowne Ct					
3500	WldT	60565	3203	26W-11S	D7
3500	WldT	60565	3267	27W-11S	C1
Frankstowne Dr					
3400	WldT	60565	3203	27W-11S	C7
Frank Turk Dr					
2600	JLET	60586	3415	32W-20S	D4
Frank Wagner Av					
2300	BlmT	60411	3509	2E-25S	D7
2300	SLVL	60411	3509	2E-25S	D7
Fran Lin Pkwy					
800	MNSR	46321	3510		E2
Frans Ct					
3100	WPHR	60096	2363	10W-42N	A6
Fransean					
-	HGKN	60525	3147	11W-7S	D5
Fransican Wy					
-	WCHI	60185	2966	30W-3N	C6
Franson Ct					
1100	LKZH	60047	2645	22W-24N	B7
Franz Dr					
1000	LKFT	60045	2649	12W-24N	C7
N Franzen St					
300	BNVL	60106	2915	16W-6N	D7
S Franzen St					
100	BNVL	60106	2971	16W-5N	D1
W Fraser Rd					
24000	PNFD	60586	3416	30W-19S	B3
24300	PnfT	60586	3416	30W-19S	B3
Frazier Av					
500	ELGN	60123	2854	34W-12N	D2
Frazier Ct					
10	LtRT	60548	3258	50W-13S	C6
100	AURA	60506	3138	36W-7S	A7
200	AURA	60506	3200	36W-7S	A1
600	FXLK	60041	2473	27W-35N	B5
600	WHTN	60187	3082	25W-1S	B1
Frazier Rd					
15800	LtRT	60545	3258	49W-13S	E5
15800	LtRT	60545	3259	49W-13S	A5
17500	LtRT	60548	3258	50W-13S	C6
17600	SdwT	60548	3258	50W-13S	B6
Frazier St					
1600	WKGN	60087	2479	11W-37N	E2
Fred St					
18200	LNSG	60438	3429	3E-21S	E6
Frederick Av					
10	BLWD	60104	3029	12W-0N	A3
500	AURA	60505	3200	34W-8S	D2
500	SMWD	60107	2911	28W-9N	B1
7800	MNSR	46321	3430		D6
Frederick Ct					
10	SEGN	60177	2908	35W-9N	C1
200	HFET	60169	2858	23W-12N	E1
1200	ELGN	60120	2855	32W-12N	D1
W Frederick Ct					
25700	AntT	60002	2357	25W-42N	A6
Frederick Dr					
100	CHHT	60411	3507	1W-23S	E3
3600	OKBK	60523	3085	16W-3S	E6
3600	OKBK	60523	3086	16W-3S	A6
Frederick Ln					
200	HFET	60169	2858	24W-12N	E1
200	HFET	60169	2859	23W-12N	B1
1300	NPVL	60565	3203	26W-8S	D2
Frederick Pl					
200	WDDL	60191	2914	18W-5N	E7
200	WDDL	60191	2970	19W-5N	C1
Frederick Rd					
22300	CHHT	60411	3596	0E-27S	E4
22300	SCHT	60411	3596	0E-27S	E4
22300	SCHT	60475	3596	0E-27S	E4
22300	STGR	60475	3596	0E-27S	E4
Frederick St					
100	PNFD	60544	3416	29W-18S	D2
100	PNFD	60586	3416	29W-18S	C2
1600	CTHL	60403	3498	25W-21S	C1
1600	JLET	60435	3498	25W-21S	C1
E Frederick St					
1300	ANHT	60004	2807	17W-14N	C3
N Frederick St					
1200	JLET	60435	3498	25W-22S	C1
1500	CTHL	60403	3498	25W-22S	C1
S Frederick St					
15900	PNFD	60544	3416	29W-19S	C2
15900	PNFD	60586	3416	29W-19S	C2
Frederick Wy					
11500	HTLY	60142	2692	40W-20N	A7
11500	HTLY	60142	2745	40W-20N	A1
Fredericksburg Ct					
600	NPVL	60540	3203	27W-7S	C1
Fredericksburg Ln					
1800	AURA	60503	3201	33W-10S	A6
Frediani Ct					
1700	MPPT	60056	2807	17W-12N	C7
Fred Mohn Dr					
-	GNCY	53128	2352		E2
Fredonia St					
-	NlxT	60451	3589	17W-26S	C3
Fredric Ct					
2800	GNVW	60062	2809	11W-15N	D2
Fredrick Ct					
10	BlmT	60411	3510	3E-25S	A7
5200	GRNE	60031	2478	15W-35N	A6
Fredrick Rd					
500	GYLK	60030	2533	20W-33N	A2
Fredrickson Pl					
1200	HDPK	60035	2704	9W-21N	C5
Fredson Rd					
500	PKCY	60085	2536	13W-33N	A2
Freedom Ct					
400	GRNE	60031	2534	17W-34N	A1
1700	MPPT	60056	2808	13W-14N	D5
Freedom Dr					
-	SRWD	60404	3495	31W-24S	E6
-	SRWD	60404	3496	29W-24S	D7
N Freedom Dr					
2500	MchT	60050	2527	34W-34N	D1
2500	MCLK	60050	2527	34W-34N	D1
Freedom Pl					
-	BtlT	60512	3262	40W-12S	B3
-	BtlT	60543	3262	40W-12S	B3
Freedom Rd					
-	ELBN	60119	3017	43W-0N	B4
Freedom Wy					
-	LNHT	60046	2418	19W-39N	C6
15000	PNFD	60544	3337	31W-17S	E7
Freehauf St					
200	LMNT	60439	3270	19W-14S	D6
Freeland Av					
300	CTCY	60409	3352	4E-17S	B6
1200	CTCY	60409	3430	4E-19S	B2
Freeland Cir					
2600	NPVL	60564	3266	29W-12S	C3
Freeland Ct					
2500	NPVL	60564	3266	29W-12S	D3
Freeman Av					
400	SMWD	60107	2911	28W-9N	A1
Freeman Ct					
700	HFET	60067	2804	23W-15N	D2
700	HFET	60192	2804	23W-15N	D2
700	IVNS	60067	2804	23W-15N	D2
700	IVNS	60192	2804	23W-15N	D2
Freeman Ln					
10	BDWD	60408	3942	31W-42S	B7
Freeman Rd					
10	RtdT	60136	2745	41W-18N	A6
10	RtdT	60142	2745	41W-18N	A6
100	GLBT	60118	2746	39W-18N	A6
100	GLBT	60136	2745	41W-18N	A6
100	GLBT	60136	2746	39W-18N	A6
100	GLBT	60142	2745	41W-18N	A6
100	GLBT	60142	2746	39W-18N	A6
100	HFET	60192	2804	23W-15N	D2
100	IVNS	60067	2804	23W-15N	D2
100	RtdT	60118	2746	39W-18N	A6
100	RtdT	60136	2746	39W-18N	A6
100	RtdT	60142	2746	39W-18N	A6
400	HTLY	60142	2744	43W-18N	C5
400	RtdT	60142	2744	43W-18N	B5
500	HTLY	60140	2744	43W-18N	A4
700	HTLY	60142	2745	41W-18N	A6
10200	HbnT	60034	2350	41W-42N	E5
10200	HBRN	60034	2350	41W-42N	E5
10300	LinT	53147	2350	41W-42N	E5
10300	LinT	60034	2350	41W-42N	E5
Freeman Rd CO-63					
10	RtdT	60136	2745	41W-18N	A6
10	RtdT	60142	2745	41W-18N	A6
100	GLBT	60118	2746	39W-18N	A6
100	GLBT	60136	2745	41W-18N	A6
100	GLBT	60136	2746	39W-18N	A6
100	GLBT	60142	2745	41W-18N	A6
100	GLBT	60142	2746	39W-18N	A6
100	RtdT	60118	2746	39W-18N	A6
100	RtdT	60136	2746	39W-18N	A6
100	RtdT	60142	2746	39W-18N	A6
400	HTLY	60142	2745	41W-18N	A6
700	HTLY	60142	2744	41W-18N	E5
N Freeman Rd					
10	HFET	60192	2804	25W-14N	B5
10	SBTN	60010	2804	25W-14N	B5
10	SBTN	60192	2804	25W-14N	B5
Freeman St					
-	PLNO	60545	3259	48W-13S	B5
100	GNCY	53128	2353		A4
500	AraT	60504	3138	33W-7S	E6
500	AraT	60505	3138	33W-7S	E6
Freeman St CO-B					
200	GNCY	53128	2353		A3
Freeman St CO-H					
300	GNCY	53128	2353		A3
N Freeman St					
600	GNCY	53128	2353		A2
700	BfdT	53128	2353		A2
Freemont St					
400	YKVL	60560	3333	42W-14S	C1
Freeport Ct					
5100	JLET	60586	3496	30W-22S	C2
21500	LktT	60544	3339	26W-16S	D4
Freeport Dr					
200	BMDL	60108	2969	22W-5N	B2
Freesia Cir					
1600	HDPK	60035	2704	10W-22N	A4
Freesia Ct					
10	RMVL	60446	3340	26W-17S	A5
Freesia Dr					
10	RMVL	60446	3339	26W-16S	E5
10	RMVL	60446	3340	25W-17S	B5
Fremont Av					
200	RMVL	60446	3340	24W-16S	D3
E Fremont Av					
10	DSPN	60016	2862	14W-11N	C3
100	EMHT	60126	3027	16W-2N	E1
100	EMHT	60126	3028	15W-2N	A1
N Fremont Av					
30700	FmtT	60030	2589	23W-30N	A1
30700	FmtT	60073	2589	23W-30N	A1
30700	RDLK	60073	2589	23W-30N	A1
W Fremont Av					
100	EMHT	60126	2971	16W-2N	E7
300	EMHT	60126	3027	16W-2N	D1
Fremont Ct					
10	DSPN	60016	2862	15W-11N	B3
200	BMDL	60108	2969	22W-4N	C3
1700	HFET	60169	2858	24W-12N	E1
2800	SMBG	60193	2857	27W-10N	D6
E Fremont Ct					
2000	ANHT	60004	2807	16W-14N	C4
Fremont Ct E					
1000	BFGV	60089	2701	17W-21N	B5
Fremont Ct W					
1000	BFGV	60089	2700	18W-20N	E7
1000	BFGV	60089	2701	17W-21N	B5
Fremont Dr					
1300	HRPK	60133	2911	26W-7N	D4
Fremont Ln					
1900	JNBG	60050	2471	30W-35N	E5
1900	JNBG	60050	2472	30W-35N	A5
Fremont Rd					
1700	HFET	60169	2858	24W-12N	E1
Fremont St					
100	WCHI	60185	3022	30W-1N	C3
100	WDSK	60098	2581	41W-30N	D1
200	LMNT	60439	3270	19W-13S	D5
400	ELGN	60120	2855	33W-12N	A3
Fremont St					
900	BRLT	60103	2910	30W-6N	C6
E Fremont St					
10	ANHT	60004	2807	17W-14N	A4
N Fremont St					
10	NPVL	60540	3141	27W-6S	C5
100	PLTN	60067	2752	20W-16N	E7
1400	CHCG	60622	3033	1W-1N	E1
1700	CHCG	60614	2977	1W-2N	E7
3500	CHCG	60613	2977	1W-4N	E2
3500	CHCG	60657	2977	1W-4N	E3
S Fremont St					
10	NPVL	60540	3141	27W-6S	C5
100	PLTN	60067	2805	20W-15N	E1
W Fremont St					
100	ANHT	60004	2807	18W-14N	A4
1400	ANHT	60005	2806	18W-14N	D4
1700	ANHT	60008	2806	18W-14N	D4
1700	RGMW	60008	2806	18W-14N	D4
Fremont Wy					
-	BFGV	60089	2700	18W-21N	E6
-	BFGV	60089	2701	17W-21N	B5
-	LGGV	60089	2700	18W-21N	E6
1000	BFGV	60047	2700	18W-21N	E6
1000	LGGV	60047	2700	18W-21N	E6
N Fremont Center Rd					
28000	FmtT	60060	2589	22W-28N	B7
28900	FmtT	60030	2589	22W-29N	B3
N Fremont Center Rd CO-V65					
28000	FmtT	60060	2589	22W-28N	B7
28900	FmtT	60030	2589	22W-29N	B3
French Ct					
10	MDLN	60060	2647	18W-27N	A1
French Dr					
800	MDLN	60060	2646	18W-27N	E1
800	MDLN	60060	2647	18W-27N	A1
French Rd					
10	BrlT	60140	2795	47W-14N	C6
10	HPSR	60140	2795	47W-15N	C4
10	HshT	60140	2795	47W-14N	C5
9500	AdnT	60033	2350	43W-41N	A7
French Rd CO-11					
10	BrlT	60140	2795	47W-14N	C6
10	HPSR	60140	2795	47W-15N	C4
10	HshT	60140	2795	47W-14N	C5
French St					
100	BDWD	60408	3942	31W-41S	B6
French Wy					
700	MPPT	60056	2807	16W-13N	D6
Frenchmans Bend Dr					
1300	AURA	60564	3202	31W-9S	A4
Fresno Ct					
10	NPVL	60540	3141	28W-6S	A5
5800	HRPK	60133	2911	26W-7N	E5
Fresno Ln					
2400	JLET	60586	3415	31W-20S	E6
3000	HMWD	60430	3507	3W-22S	A1
18500	HMWD	60422	3507	3W-22S	A1
Fretheim Av					
25000	GrtT	60041	2474	25W-34N	B7
Freud Rd					
-	DGvT	60439	3207	18W-11S	B7
N Freund Av					
1400	MHRY	60050	2528	32W-33N	B3
W Freund Av					
3600	MHRY	60050	2528	32W-33N	B3
Friar Dr					
500	AraT	60504	3138	34W-5S	C2
600	AraT	60505	3138	34W-5S	C2
600	AURA	60504	3138	34W-5S	C2
Friar Ln					
1600	NPVL	60565	3204	24W-9S	E3
Friar Wy					
900	FKFT	60423	3504	11W-25S	A7
Friars Ct					
100	BGBK	60440	3205	22W-11S	B7
1500	WHTN	60187	3082	24W-1S	D2
N Friars Ct					
200	ADSN	60101	2970	19W-3N	C4
Friars Ln					
1700	MDLN	60060	2590	20W-28N	A7
Friar Tuck Av					
1500	HDPK	60035	2704	10W-22N	B4
Friar Tuck Ct					
10	LNSH	60069	2702	13W-23N	E3
Frieder Ct					
700	AURA	60504	3201	33W-8S	B3
Friedrich St					
1600	GLHT	60139	2968	24W-3N	D6
Frieh Dr					
-	RMVL	60441	3340	25W-15S	B3
-	RMVL	60446	3340	25W-15S	B3
N Frieh Dr					
400	RMVL	60446	3340	25W-15S	B2
N Friendly Av					
200	MchT	60051	2529	29W-32N	C5
W Friendly Av					
700	MchT	60051	2529	29W-32N	C5
Friendship Dr					
-	BRLT	60103	2911	28W-8N	B3
S Friendship Dr					
25600	MONE	60449	3682	7W-31S	D4
Friendship Ln					
300	WMTN	60481	3853	27W-38S	D6
Friendship Plz					
10	ADSN	60101	2970	18W-3N	E5
Friendship Sq					
100	RMVL	60446	3340	26W-17S	A6
Friendship Vil					
-	SMBG	60193	2858	23W-10N	E5
-	SMBG	60194	2858	23W-10N	E5
Friendship Village					
-	SMBG	60194	2858	23W-10N	E5
-	SMBG	60194	2859	23W-10N	A5
Fries Av					
-	DndT	60118	2801	33W-14N	A5
Frisco Ct					
200	BMDL	60108	2912	25W-6N	A7
Frisco Dr					
100	HRVD	60033	2464	50W-37N	B1
Frisco St					
200	BMDL	60108	2912	25W-6N	A7
200	BmdT	60172	2912	25W-6N	A7
Frits Ln					
-	GNVA	60134	3019	36W-1N	E4
Fritz					
-	RVDL	60827	3349	1W-16S	E2
Fritz Dr					
17500	LNSG	60438	3430	3E-20S	A5
Fritz Rd					
2100	DhmT	60033	2463	51W-35N	D6
W Fritz Rd					
-	PNFD	60586	3416	30W-19S	B4
-	PnfT	60586	3416	30W-19S	B4
Fritzer Ct					
-	JLET	60431	3495	32W-22S	D1

STREET Block	City	ZIP	Map#	CGS	Grid
Fritzer Dr					
-	JLET	60431	3495	32W-22S	D1
Fritzsche Rd					
200	LKMR	60051	2529	29W-31N	C7
200	NndT	60051	2529	29W-31N	C7
Frohling Rd					
14200	CrlT	60142	2691	43W-23N	A1
14200	GfnT	60142	2691	43W-23N	A1
Frolic Av					
-	BHPK	60087	2421	12W-39N	C6
-	BHPK	60099	2421	12W-39N	C6
N Frolic Av					
10	WKGN	60085	2536	12W-33N	B1
500	WKGN	60085	2479	12W-33N	B7
1400	WkgT	60085	2479	12W-35N	C6
2000	WKGN	60087	2479	12W-36N	C4
2000	WkgT	60087	2479	12W-36N	C4
37700	BHPK	60087	2479	12W-37N	C1
Front Av					
10300	FNPK	60131	2973	12W-4N	A3
S Front Av					
12100	CHCG	60628	3278	0E-14S	D5
Front St					
-	ALGN	60102	2694	33W-21N	D7
-	AlqT	60021	2696	29W-22N	C3
-	BNHL	60010	2696	29W-22N	C3
-	BNHL	60021	2696	29W-22N	C3
-	DGvT	60439	3207	17W-10S	C6
-	RHMD	60071	2353	34W-42N	C6
-	WLMT	60091	2811	6W-13N	D5
100	MHTN	60442	3677	19W-31S	E5
400	AURA	60505	3138	33W-7S	E6
500	LslT	60532	3143	22W-5S	C2
800	LSLE	60532	3143	23W-5S	B2
3400	MTSN	60443	3594	4W-25S	E1
3400	PKFT	60443	3594	4W-25S	E1
3400	PKFT	60466	3594	4W-25S	E1
10800	MKNA	60448	3503	13W-23S	A4
11200	FftT	60448	3502	14W-23S	E4
11200	MKNA	60448	3502	14W-23S	E4
E Front St					
100	HRVD	60033	2406	50W-38N	B7
100	WDDL	60191	2915	17W-5N	B7
100	WHTN	60187	3024	24W-0S	C7
N Front St					
100	BDWD	60408	3942	31W-41S	B5
100	MHRY	60050	2528	32W-32N	A5
200	RedT	60408	3942	31W-41S	B5
200	RedT	60481	3942	31W-41S	B5
N Front St SR-31					
100	MHRY	60050	2528	32W-32N	A5
N Front St SR-53					
100	BDWD	60408	3942	31W-41S	B5
200	RedT	60408	3942	31W-41S	B5
200	RedT	60481	3942	31W-41S	B5
S Front St					
100	BDWD	60408	3942	31W-42S	A6
100	MHRY	60050	2528	32W-31N	A6
300	RedT	60408	3942	31W-41S	B6
400	NndT	60050	2528	32W-31N	A7
700	RedT	60408	3941	31W-42S	E7
1000	MHRY	60050	2585	33W-30N	A1
1000	NndT	60050	2585	33W-30N	A1
S Front St SR-31					
100	MHRY	60050	2528	32W-31N	A6
400	NndT	60050	2528	32W-31N	A7
1000	MHRY	60050	2585	33W-30N	A1
1000	NndT	60050	2585	33W-30N	A1
S Front St SR-53					
100	BDWD	60408	3942	31W-42S	A6
300	RedT	60408	3942	31W-41S	B6
700	RedT	60408	3941	32W-42S	E7
W Front St					
100	HRVD	60033	2406	50W-38N	A7
100	WHTN	60187	3024	25W-0S	C7
Frontage					
-	HFET	60169	2858	24W-11N	E2
-	HFET	60195	2858	24W-11N	E2
-	SMBG	60195	2858	24W-11N	E2
Frontage Rd					
-	AddT	60101	2971	17W-3N	C5
-	AddT	60106	2971	17W-3N	C4
-	ADSN	60101	2971	17W-2N	C7
-	ADSN	60106	2971	17W-3N	C5
-	ADSN	60126	2971	17W-2N	C7
-	BGBK	60446	3268	26W-14S	A7
-	BGBK	60490	3268	26W-14S	A7
-	BGBK	60490	3340	26W-14S	A1
-	BGBK	60544	3268	26W-14S	A7
-	BlmT	60438	3429	1E-21S	B7
-	BlmT	60476	3429	1E-21S	B7
-	BLWD	60104	3029	12W-0S	A6
-	BNVL	60106	2971	17W-4N	C4
-	DGvT	60439	3270	20W-11S	B1
-	DPgT	60446	3268	26W-14S	A7
-	DPgT	60490	3268	26W-14S	A7
-	DPgT	60490	3340	26W-14S	A1
-	DPgT	60544	3268	26W-14S	A7
-	DPgT	60544	3340	26W-14S	A1
-	DRGV	60515	3084	20W-2S	B4
-	DRGV	60516	3206	18W-8S	E1
-	DRGV	60561	3206	18W-8S	E1
-	EMHT	60101	2971	17W-3N	C5
-	EMHT	60106	2971	17W-3N	C5
-	EMHT	60126	2971	17W-3N	C5
-	EMHT	60126	3027	17W-0N	C5
-	EMHT	60181	3027	17W-0S	C6
-	GrtT	60020	2473	27W-35N	B6
-	HLSD	60104	3029	13W-0S	A6
-	HLSD	60162	3028	13W-0S	E6
-	HMGN	60491	3421	17W-19S	D2
-	JLET	60431	3417	28W-19S	B4
-	JLET	60435	3417	28W-19S	B4
-	LktT	60441	3419	23W-19S	B2
-	LNSG	60438	3429	2E-20S	C5
-	MDLN	60445	3348	4W-17S	D4
-	NfdT	60062	2757	8W-18N	E3
-	NHBK	60062	2757	8W-18N	E3
-	NtrT	60093	2811	6W-14N	D4
-	OKBK	60181	3027	16W-1S	D7
-	OKBK	60523	3027	16W-1S	D7
-	OKBK	60523	3086	15W-1S	A1
-	OKTR	60181	3027	17W-0S	C7
-	PnfT	60435	3417	28W-19S	B4
-	PnfT	60446	3339	27W-17S	B7
-	RMVL	60441	3419	23W-19S	B2
-	RMVL	60446	3268	26W-14S	A7
-	RMVL	60446	3339	27W-17S	B7
-	RMVL	60490	3340	26W-14S	A1
-	RMVL	60544	3339	27W-17S	B7
-	RMVL	60544	3340	26W-14S	A1
-	SMBG	60193	2912	24W-8N	C2
-	SmbT	60193	2912	24W-8N	C2
-	SRPK	60176	2973	13W-5N	A1
-	ThtT	60438	3429	2E-20S	C5
-	ThtT	60476	3429	1E-21S	B7
Frontage Rd					
-	VLPK	60126	2971	17W-2N	C7
-	VLPK	60126	3027	17W-2N	C1
-	VLPK	60181	2971	17W-2N	C7
-	VLPK	60181	3027	17W-2N	C1
-	WDRG	60439	3270	20W-11S	B1
-	WDRG	60517	3270	20W-11S	B1
-	WNSP	60558	3146	14W-6S	D3
-	YkTp	60523	3028	15W-1S	B7
-	YkTp	60523	3086	15W-1S	A1
10	CNHL	60514	3145	16W-5S	D3
10	DGvT	60439	3206	20W-11S	C7
10	DGvT	60527	3207	16W-9S	E3
10	DRN	60439	3206	20W-11S	B7
10	GRNE	60031	2535	13W-34N	E2
10	PKCY	60085	2535	13W-34N	E2
10	SRGV	60554	3135	42W-7S	D6
10	WDRG	60439	3206	20W-11S	C7
10	WLBK	60527	3207	16W-9S	E3
100	DGvT	60561	3207	17W-9S	B4
100	DRN	60561	3207	17W-9S	B4
100	WDRG	60516	3206	20W-11S	B7
200	DGvT	60516	3206	20W-11S	B7
600	WCHI	60185	2966	29W-3N	D7
600	WynT	60185	2966	29W-3N	D7
700	LKVL	60046	2417	23W-38N	A6
1000	SMBG	60193	2858	24W-10N	C5
1000	SMBG	60194	2858	25W-10N	C5
1200	NHFD	60091	2811	6W-14N	D4
1200	NHFD	60093	2811	6W-14N	D4
1200	WLMT	60091	2811	6W-14N	D4
1200	WLMT	60093	2811	6W-14N	D4
2000	DSPN	60018	2863	13W-9N	A7
2200	DSPN	60018	2917	13W-9N	A1
4100	HLSD	60162	3029	13W-0S	A6
4300	OKFT	60452	3426	5W-19S	C3
4700	BmnT	60452	3426	5W-20S	A4
4700	BmnT	60477	3426	5W-20S	A4
7600	SKOK	60077	2865	6W-9N	C6
7700	MNGV	60053	2865	6W-9N	C6
8600	MNGV	60077	2865	6W-10N	C4
8600	SKOK	60053	2865	6W-10N	C4
9200	BGVW	60455	3210	8W-10S	E5
9200	OKLN	60453	3210	8W-10S	E5
9200	OKLN	60455	3210	8W-10S	E5
10000	SKOK	60077	2811	6W-12N	E7
10000	SKOK	60091	2811	6W-13N	E7
15500	PNFD	60544	3339	28W-17S	B6
15500	PnfT	60544	3339	28W-17S	B7
16100	BmnT	60426	3426	5W-19S	C2
16100	MKHM	60426	3426	5W-19S	C2
16100	MKHM	60428	3426	5W-19S	C2
32100	WmTp	60416	3942	31W-39S	A1
32100	WmTp	60481	3942	31W-39S	A1
32600	DMND	60408	3941	32W-39S	E2
32600	DMND	60416	3941	32W-39S	E2
32600	DMND	60481	3941	32W-39S	E2
32600	WmTp	60416	3941	32W-39S	E2
32600	WmTp	60481	3941	32W-39S	E2
35000	FXLK	60041	2473	27W-34N	B7
35000	GrtT	60041	2473	27W-34N	B7
42800	NptT	60099	2360	16W-42N	E6
42800	WDWH	60099	2360	16W-42N	E6
E Frontage Rd					
-	EGvT	60007	2860	20W-11N	A3
-	EGvT	60008	2860	20W-11N	A3
-	RGMW	60008	2860	20W-11N	A3
-	SMBG	60193	2912	25W-8N	B3
-	SmbT	60193	2912	25W-8N	B3
10	NHFD	60093	2811	6W-14N	D3
2900	RGMW	60008	2806	20W-13N	B6
3400	PltT	60067	2806	20W-13N	B6
3400	RGMW	60067	2806	20W-13N	B6
3500	PltT	60008	2806	20W-13N	B6
E Frontage Rd S					
-	JLET	60544	3417	27W-19S	B2
16200	JLET	60435	3417	27W-19S	B2
16200	PnfT	60431	3417	28W-19S	B3
16200	PnfT	60435	3417	27W-19S	B2
16200	PnfT	60544	3417	27W-19S	B2
N Frontage Rd					
-	IHPK	60525	3146	14W-7S	D5
-	LynT	60525	3146	14W-7S	D5
10	DRN	60561	3207	18W-10S	A5
200	BRRG	60527	3208	15W-8S	B1
300	DGvT	60527	3208	15W-8S	B1
300	DRN	60439	3207	18W-10S	A5
400	DGvT	60516	3206	19W-10S	D6
400	DGvT	60561	3206	19W-10S	D6
400	DRN	60516	3206	19W-10S	D6
500	DRN	60561	3206	19W-10S	D6
1200	PLTN	60074	2753	19W-17N	D4
1200	PltT	60074	2753	19W-17N	D4
6900	BRRG	60527	3146	14W-7S	D7
NE Frontage Rd					
-	JLET	60431	3416	28W-21S	E7
-	JLET	60431	3417	28W-21S	A6
-	PnfT	60431	3416	28W-21S	E7
-	PnfT	60431	3417	28W-21S	A6
10	JLET	60431	3496	29W-23S	E4
10	JLET	60431	3497	28W-22S	A3
10	SRWD	60431	3496	29W-23S	E4
10	TroT	60431	3496	29W-23S	E4
700	PnfT	60431	3496	28W-22S	E3
NW Frontage Rd					
-	JLET	60431	3416	29W-21S	E7
-	PnfT	60431	3416	29W-21S	E7
18000	JLET	60404	3496	29W-22S	E2
18000	JLET	60431	3496	29W-22S	E2
18000	PnfT	60431	3496	29W-22S	E2
19100	SRWD	60404	3496	29W-23S	D5
19100	SRWD	60431	3496	29W-23S	D5
19500	TroT	60431	3496	29W-23S	D5
S Frontage Rd					
-	BRRG	60525	3146	14W-8S	D7
-	BRRG	60527	3146	14W-8S	D7
-	BRRG	60527	3208	14W-8S	C1
-	HLSD	60162	3028	14W-0S	D6
-	IHPK	60525	3146	14W-8S	D7
-	IHPK	60527	3146	14W-8S	D7
-	RMVL	60446	3340	25W-14S	B1
10	DGvT	60439	3206	19W-10S	E5
10	DGvT	60561	3206	18W-10S	E5
10	DRN	60439	3206	19W-10S	E5
10	DRN	60561	3206	18W-10S	E5
10	GNWD	60425	3509	1E-23S	B3
200	DGvT	60561	3207	17W-9S	B4
200	DRN	60527	3207	17W-9S	C4
200	DRN	60561	3207	18W-10S	B5
400	BRRG	60527	3207	16W-9S	E4
400	DGvT	60527	3207	16W-9S	E4
400	WLBK	60527	3207	16W-9S	E4
500	DGvT	60439	3207	18W-10S	B5
500	DRN	60439	3207	18W-10S	B5
11800	BGBK	60440	3268	24W-14S	D6
11800	BGBK	60446	3268	25W-14S	C6
S Frontage Rd					
11800	DPgT	60446	3268	24W-14S	C6
11800	RMVL	60446	3268	25W-14S	C7
23000	CNHN	60410	3584	29W-28S	D7
S Frontage Rd W					
22500	CNHN	60436	3584	30W-27S	D6
22500	CNHN	60447	3584	30W-27S	D6
22700	TroT	60447	3584	30W-27S	C5
23000	TroT	60410	3584	30W-27S	D6
23500	CNHN	60410	3584	30W-28S	C7
23500	CnhT	60410	3584	30W-28S	C7
SE Frontage Rd					
-	SRWD	60431	3496	29W-24S	E5
2100	JLET	60436	3497	26W-24S	E7
2100	JLET	60436	3498	26W-24S	A7
2100	JltT	60436	3497	26W-24S	E7
2100	JltT	60436	3498	26W-24S	A7
2100	RKDL	60436	3498	26W-24S	A7
2100	TroT	60436	3497	26W-24S	E7
19900	JLET	60431	3496	29W-24S	E5
19900	TroT	60431	3496	29W-24S	E5
21200	TroT	60431	3496	29W-25S	D1
21200	TroT	60436	3584	29W-25S	D2
SW Frontage Rd					
-	CNHN	60404	3584	30W-26S	C4
10	SRWD	60404	3496	29W-24S	D5
10	TroT	60431	3496	29W-24S	D5
12800	BGBK	60490	3339	27W-15S	D2
12800	BGBK	60544	3339	27W-15S	D2
12800	DPgT	60490	3339	27W-15S	D2
12800	DPgT	60544	3339	27W-15S	D2
12800	RMVL	60490	3339	27W-15S	D2
12800	RMVL	60544	3339	27W-15S	D2
12800	WldT	60544	3339	27W-15S	D2
21200	SRWD	60431	3496	30W-25S	C7
21200	TroT	60404	3496	30W-25S	C7
21200	TroT	60404	3584	30W-25S	C2
21200	TroT	60431	3584	30W-25S	C2
21300	SRWD	60404	3584	30W-25S	C1
21300	SRWD	60431	3584	30W-25S	C2
21500	TroT	60436	3584	30W-26S	C2
W Frontage Rd					
-	ANHT	60004	2806	19W-15N	C2
-	JLET	60431	3417	28W-19S	A4
-	JLET	60544	3417	28W-19S	A3
-	JLET	60586	3416	28W-20S	E5
-	JLET	60586	3417	28W-20S	A4
-	NHFD	60091	2811	6W-14N	D4
-	PLTN	60004	2806	19W-15N	C2
-	PLTN	60074	2806	19W-15N	C2
-	PNFD	60586	3417	28W-19S	A4
-	PnfT	60586	3416	29W-20S	E6
-	PnfT	60586	3417	28W-20S	A4
-	SMBG	60173	2860	21W-11N	A3
-	WLMT	60091	2811	6W-14N	D4
10	NHFD	60093	2811	6W-14N	D3
10	NtrT	60093	2811	6W-14N	D3
600	NHFD	60093	2758	7W-16N	B7
800	GLNC	60062	2758	7W-16N	B7
1800	NHBK	60062	2758	7W-16N	B7
1800	RGMW	60008	2806	20W-13N	A6
1800	RGMW	60173	2806	21W-12N	A7
1800	SMBG	60008	2806	21W-12N	A7
1800	SMBG	60067	2806	21W-12N	A7
1800	SMBG	60173	2806	21W-12N	A7
1900	PltT	60067	2806	20W-13N	A7
2200	RGMW	60067	2806	20W-13N	A6
5400	MNGV	60053	2865	6W-11N	C2
5400	SKOK	60053	2865	6W-11N	C2
5400	SKOK	60077	2865	6W-11N	C2
23500	CNHN	60410	3584	30W-28S	C7
23500	CnhT	60410	3584	30W-28S	C7
W Frontage Rd S					
12400	NlxT	60448	3502	15W-22S	B2
Frontage Rd E					
-	SKOK	60077	2865	6W-9N	D7
Frontage Rd S					
-	PnfT	60446	3417	27W-18S	B2
-	PnfT	60544	3339	27W-18S	B7
-	RMVL	60446	3417	27W-18S	B2
-	RMVL	60544	3339	27W-18S	B7
-	RMVL	60544	3417	27W-18S	B2
15500	PnfT	60544	3417	27W-18S	B2
Frontage Rd W					
7300	SKOK	60077	2865	6W-9N	D7
W Frontage Ter					
8700	JSTC	60458	3210	11W-9S	A4
S Frontenac Av					
5900	CHCG	60621	3152	0W-6S	A4
Frontenac Ct					
3500	AURA	60504	3201	31W-8S	E1
Frontenac Dr					
900	DndT	60118	2800	35W-14N	C5
900	SYHW	60118	2800	35W-14N	C5
900	WDND	60118	2800	35W-14N	C5
W Frontenac Dr					
900	ANHT	60004	2753	18W-16N	E7
Frontenac Rd					
100	NPVL	60563	3139	31W-5S	E3
100	NPVL	60563	3140	31W-5S	A3
700	NpvT	60563	3140	31W-6S	A4
N Frontenac Rd					
-	AURA	60504	3140	31W-7S	A7
-	AURA	60504	3201	31W-7S	E1
300	AURA	60504	3139	31W-7S	E7
Frontenac St					
2800	NCHI	60064	2593	12W-30N	B2
2800	ShdT	60064	2593	12W-30N	B2
2900	NCHI	60044	2593	12W-30N	B2
S Frontenac St					
10	AURA	60504	3201	31W-9S	E3
10	AURA	60564	3201	31W-9S	E4
10	NpvT	60504	3201	31W-9S	E3
Frontier					
300	MNKA	60447	3672	33W-30S	C4
Frontier Ct					
22600	FKFT	60423	3592	9W-27S	E4
Frontier Dr					
200	ROSL	60172	2913	23W-7N	B5
Frontier Ln					
-	LktT	60403	3417	27W-19S	D3
-	LktT	60435	3417	27W-19S	D3
2600	JLET	60435	3417	27W-19S	D3
Frontier Wy					
100	BNVL	60106	2915	16W-7N	D4
Front Range Dr					
1100	SYHW	60118	2800	35W-15N	C3
Front Royal Ct					
1100	MHRY	60050	2527	33W-33N	E3
14000	LktT	60544	3339	27W-16S	D4
14000	PnfT	60544	3339	27W-16S	D4
Front Royal Dr					
800	MHRY	60050	2527	33W-32N	E4
4300	MHRY	60050	2528	33W-33N	A3
Fronza Pkwy					
-	EMHT	60126	3028	15W-0S	A7
Fronza Pkwy					
-	YkTp	60126	3028	15W-0S	A7
Frost Ct					
8300	WDRG	60517	3205	22W-9S	D4
21400	LktT	60544	3339	26W-16S	E4
Frost Dr					
-	MPPT	60056	2861	16W-11N	D3
2400	AURA	60503	3265	32W-11S	C1
2400	AURA	60585	3265	32W-11S	C1
Frost Ln					
1600	NPVL	60564	3202	28W-11S	E7
1600	NPVL	60564	3266	28W-11S	E1
Frost Pl					
400	LKFT	60045	2650	10W-26N	A3
Frost Rd					
2000	HFET	60192	2804	23W-13N	D6
2000	HFET	60195	2804	23W-13N	D6
2000	PltT	60192	2804	23W-13N	D6
2000	PltT	60195	2804	23W-13N	D6
Fruitwood Dr					
200	RLKB	60073	2474	23W-36N	E4
W Fry St					
1400	CHCG	60622	3033	1W-1N	D2
Fryendall Ct					
100	BbyT	60134	3018	39W-0S	E6
S Fryer St					
24900	CNHN	60410	3672	31W-30S	E4
Fulbright Ln					
10	SMBG	60193	2859	23W-10N	A5
10	SMBG	60194	2859	23W-10N	A5
Fulham Dr					
2000	NPVL	60564	3202	29W-9S	C5
Fullam Av					
200	NCHI	60088	2537	10W-31N	A7
Fulle St					
2100	RGMW	60008	2806	19W-13N	C7
Fuller Av					
10	OSWG	60543	3263	38W-13S	B4
N Fuller Av					
1200	JLET	60432	3499	22W-22S	C1
Fuller Ln					
100	KLWH	60043	2812	4W-15N	D3
100	WNKA	60093	2812	4W-15N	D3
200	BGBK	60440	3205	22W-10S	B6
Fuller Rd					
-	WrnT	60031	2478	15W-35N	B6
400	HNDL	60521	3086	15W-4S	B7
700	GRNE	60031	2478	15W-35N	B7
N Fuller Rd					
35700	GRNE	60031	2478	15W-36N	B5
35700	WrnT	60031	2478	15W-36N	B5
Fuller St					
-	HNDL	60521	3086	15W-4S	B7
800	JLET	60433	3499	22W-24S	C6
800	JltT	60433	3499	22W-24S	C6
W Fuller St					
1300	CHCG	60608	3091	1W-2S	D3
Fullerton Av					
200	BmdT	60148	2969	21W-3N	E6
300	AddT	60101	2971	17W-3N	B6
300	ADSN	60101	2971	17W-3N	A6
800	MNSR	46321	3430		E6
1600	FNPK	60131	2973	11W-3N	C6
9100	FNPK	60171	2973	11W-3N	C6
9100	RVGV	60171	2973	11W-3N	C6
9400	FNPK	60164	2973	11W-3N	C6
9400	LydT	60164	2973	11W-3N	C6
E Fullerton Av					
10	ADSN	60101	2970	18W-3N	E6
10	ADSN	60101	2971	18W-3N	A6
10	GLHT	60139	2968	23W-2N	E6
10	NHLK	60164	2972	13W-3N	E6
100	CLSM	60188	2968	25W-3N	C6
100	EMHT	60126	2972	15W-2N	A6
100	GLHT	60139	2969	23W-2N	A6
300	AddT	60126	2972	15W-2N	A6
300	LydT	60164	2972	13W-3N	E6
400	AddT	60101	2971	18W-3N	A6
500	GLHT	60188	2968	24W-2N	D6
W Fullerton Av					
-	NHLK	60164	2972	14W-3N	D6
10	ADSN	60101	2970	20W-3N	A6
10	GLHT	60139	2968	24W-3N	D6
100	CLSM	60188	2968	24W-2N	D6
100	GLHT	60188	2968	24W-2N	D6
200	EMHT	60126	2971	16W-3N	D6
400	AddT	60101	2970	19W-3N	D6
800	CHCG	60614	2977	2W-3N	C5
1800	ADSN	60101	2969	21W-2N	E6
1800	BmdT	60101	2969	21W-3N	E6
1800	BmdT	60148	2969	21W-3N	E6
1900	CHCG	60647	2977	2W-3N	B5
2700	CHCG	60647	2976	4W-3N	D6
3900	CHCG	60639	2976	4W-3N	B6
4700	CHCG	60639	2975	7W-3N	C6
6300	CHCG	60707	2975	7W-2N	A6
7200	CHCG	60707	2974	9W-2N	D6
7200	EDPK	60707	2974	9W-2N	B6
8000	EDPK	60171	2974	10W-3N	B6
8600	RVGV	60171	2973	11W-3N	E6
8600	RVGV	60171	2974	10W-3N	A6
9000	FNPK	60171	2973	11W-3N	D6
9000	RVGV	60131	2973	11W-3N	D6
9600	FNPK	60131	2973	12W-2N	A6
9600	FNPK	60164	2973	12W-2N	A6
9600	LydT	60164	2973	12W-2N	A6
9700	LydT	60131	2973	12W-2N	C6
10400	NHLK	60164	2973	13W-3N	A6
Fullerton Ct					
-	GLHT	60139	2969	22W-3N	C6
W Fullerton Pkwy					
300	CHCG	60614	2978	0W-2N	B5
Fulton Av					
-	BtnT	60099	2422	8W-40N	E3
-	WKGN	60085	2479	11W-36N	E5
-	WKGN	60087	2479	11W-36N	E5
-	ZION	60099	2422	8W-40N	E3
200	SCRL	60174	2964	35W-3N	B6
400	ADSN	60101	2971	17W-2N	B7
400	VLPK	60101	2971	17W-2N	B7
400	VLPK	60181	2971	17W-2N	B7
700	WPHR	60096	2363	9W-42N	C7
1500	WPHR	60096	2422	9W-41N	C1
N Fulton Av					
400	VLPK	60181	3027	17W-1N	B2
S Fulton Av					
10	WKGN	60085	2536	11W-33N	E3
W Fulton Blvd					
3200	CHCG	60612	3032	4W-0N	D4
3200	CHCG	60624	3032	4W-0N	D4
Fulton Ct					
1200	WKGN	60085	2536	11W-32N	E5
21500	LktT	60544	3339	26W-16S	D4
Fulton Dr					
1000	HnrT	60107	2856	29W-9N	E7
1000	HnrT	60107	2910	29W-9N	E1
Fulton Dr					
1000	SMWD	60107	2856	29W-9N	E7
1000	SMWD	60107	2910	29W-9N	E1
1100	HnrT	60120	2910	29W-9N	E1
1100	SMWD	60120	2910	29W-9N	E1
W Fulton Dr					
3600	CHCG	60624	3032	5W-0N	B4
Fulton Ln					
1700	HRPK	60133	2967	27W-5N	D2
Fulton St					
10	GNVA	60134	3020	35W-1N	B4
100	WMTN	60481	3853	27W-39S	D7
200	ELGN	60120	2854	33W-11N	E4
200	ELGN	60120	2855	33W-11N	A4
200	SEGN	60177	2908	34W-7N	D4
200	WCHI	60185	3022	29W-0N	C4
600	AURA	60505	3138	35W-7S	C7
700	AURA	60505	3200	34W-7S	C1
2100	BLID	60406	3349	2W-15S	C1
W Fulton St					
500	CHCG	60606	3034	0W-0N	A4
500	CHCG	60661	3034	0W-0N	A4
1200	CHCG	60607	3033	1W-0N	D4
1600	CHCG	60612	3033	3W-0N	A4
2800	CHCG	60612	3032	3W-0N	E4
3800	CHCG	60624	3032	4W-0N	C4
4500	CHCG	60644	3032	5W-0N	A4
5300	CHCG	60644	3031	6W-0N	D4
5900	CHCG	60302	3031	7W-0N	B4
5900	OKPK	60302	3031	7W-0N	B4
Fulton Ter					
16400	BmnT	60477	3425	7W-19S	C3
16600	TYPK	60477	3425	7W-19S	C3
W Fulton Market					
700	CHCG	60607	3034	0W-0N	A4
700	CHCG	60661	3034		E4
800	CHCG	60607	3033	1W-0N	E4
Fun Dr					
-	ODPK	60462	3345	12W-18S	C7
-	OrlT	60462	3345	12W-18S	C7
Funderburk Dr					
1400	WPHR	60096	2363	10W-41N	B7
2200	WPHR	60096	2422	10W-41N	B1
Funston Av					
400	HIWD	60040	2704	9W-23N	D2
Furlong Ct					
10	RLKP	60030	2589	22W-30N	B1
Furlong Dr					
100	ElaT	60047	2644	23W-25N	E4
100	HNWD	60047	2644	23W-25N	E4
800	LYVL	60048	2647	16W-27N	E1
1000	LYVL	60048	2591	16W-27N	E7
Furlong Ln					
300	FmtT	60030	2589	22W-30N	B1
300	RLKP	60030	2589	22W-30N	B1
Furman Dr					
1600	NPVL	60565	3204	24W-9S	C3
G					
G Ct					
10000	MKNA	60448	3503	12W-23S	C4
G St					
-	HDPK	60037	2704	8W-23N	D2
-	LKBF	60044	2593	10W-30N	E2
-	LKBF	60088	2593	10W-30N	E2
-	NCHI	60044	2594	10W-30N	A2
-	NCHI	60088	2593	10W-30N	E2
-	NCHI	60088	2594	10W-30N	A2
200	LKBF	60044	2594	10W-30N	A2
200	LKBF	60088	2594	10W-30N	A2
W G St					
-	MYWD	60141	3088	10W-1S	A1
-	MYWD	60153	3088	10W-1S	A1
-	PvsT	60141	3088	10W-1S	A1
-	PvsT	60153	3088	10W-1S	A1
Gable Ct					
1600	HRPK	60133	2911	26W-6N	D6
Gables Blvd					
-	MltT	60188	3024	25W-0N	B3
-	WHTN	60187	3024	25W-0N	B4
600	MltT	60187	3024	25W-0N	B4
N Gables Blvd					
100	WHTN	60187	3024	25W-0S	B7
S Gables Blvd					
100	WHTN	60187	3024	25W-0S	B7
700	WHTN	60187	3082	25W-1S	A1
1300	MltT	60187	3082	25W-1S	B1
W Gabreski Ln					
6900	MonT	60449	3682	8W-30S	A3
Gabriel Av					
1900	ZION	60099	2422	10W-39N	A5
N Gabriel Av					
3300	BHPK	60099	2422	10W-39N	A6
3300	ZION	60099	2422	10W-39N	A6
W Gabriel Ct					
22900	ElaT	60047	2699	23W-24N	A1
N Gabriel Dr					
23900	ElaT	60047	2699	22W-23N	A1
24000	ElaT	60047	2645	22W-24N	A7
Gabrielle Ln					
3600	AURA	60504	3140	31W-7S	A7
4000	NpvT	60504	3140	31W-7S	A7
10600	ODPK	60462	3423	13W-18S	A1
Gadwall Ct					
14400	HMGN	60491	3344	15W-17S	B5
Gadwom Dr					
-	LktT	60544	3339	26W-16S	D5
Gael Av					
2500	PnfT	60435	3417	27W-20S	C5
N Gael Dr					
800	JLET	60435	3497	27W-22S	D2
800	TroT	60435	3497	27W-22S	D2
1000	CTHL	60403	3497	27W-22S	D2
1000	CTHL	60435	3497	27W-22S	D2
1000	TroT	60403	3497	27W-22S	D2
Gaelic Ct					
10	IVNS	60010	2750	25W-16N	E7
Gaffield Pl					
800	EVTN	60201	2867	2W-12N	B1
Gaffrig Dr					
10	GYLK	60030	2533	20W-33N	B4
Gage Av					
-	FNPK	60131	2973	12W-4N	A4
3900	LYNS	60534	3088	9W-4S	C7
5600	RSMT	60018	2917	11W-7N	C5
11000	FNPK	60131	2972	13W-4N	D4
Gage Ct					
1200	JLET	60432	3499	22W-22S	D2
Gage Ln					
700	LKFT	60045	2649	12W-27N	C1
8100	AlqT	60013	2696	29W-23N	D1
Gage Rd					
100	RVSD	60546	3088	9W-3S	D5
Gage St					
-	LktT	60432	3419	22W-21S	D7

STREET Block	City	ZIP	Map#	CGS	Grid
Gage St					
-	LktT	60432	3499	22W-21S	D1
800	JltT	60432	3499	22W-22S	D2
1000	WNKA	60093	2758	5W-16N	E7
1000	WNKA	60093	2759	5W-16N	A7
1200	JLET	60432	3499	22W-22S	D2
6100	RSMT	60018	2917	11W-7N	C3
N Gage St					
1000	JLET	60432	3499	22W-22S	D2
1000	JltT	60432	3499	22W-22S	D2
N Gagemere Dr					
33700	WrnT	60030	2533	18W-33N	E3
N Gages Lake Dr					
33600	WrnT	60030	2533	18W-33N	E3
Gages Lake Rd					
5400	GRNE	60031	2534	16W-33N	D2
5400	GRNE	60031	2535	15W-33N	A3
5400	WrnT	60031	2534	16W-33N	D2
5700	GRNE	60048	2534	16W-33N	D2
Gages Lake Rd CO-A24					
5400	GRNE	60031	2534	16W-33N	D2
5400	GRNE	60031	2535	15W-33N	A3
5400	WrnT	60031	2534	16W-33N	D2
5700	GRNE	60048	2534	16W-33N	D2
W Gages Lake Rd					
17100	GRNE	60031	2534	16W-33N	C2
17100	GRNE	60048	2534	16W-33N	C2
17100	WrnT	60030	2534	17W-33N	B2
17100	WrnT	60031	2534	16W-33N	C2
17100	WrnT	60048	2534	16W-33N	C2
18400	WrnT	60030	2533	18W-34N	E2
18700	GYLK	60030	2533	18W-34N	D2
18800	TDLK	60030	2533	18W-34N	D2
W Gages Lake Rd CO-A24					
17100	GRNE	60031	2534	16W-33N	C2
17100	GRNE	60048	2534	16W-33N	C2
17100	WrnT	60030	2534	17W-33N	B2
17100	WrnT	60031	2534	16W-33N	C2
17100	WrnT	60048	2534	16W-33N	C2
18400	WrnT	60030	2533	18W-34N	E2
18700	GYLK	60030	2533	18W-34N	D2
18800	TDLK	60030	2533	18W-34N	D2
N Gagewood Ct					
33200	WrnT	60030	2534	17W-33N	C3
W Gagne Ln					
23500	PNFD	60586	3416	29W-20S	D5
23500	PnfT	60586	3416	29W-20S	D5
Gail Av					
10	NHLK	60164	3028	13W-1N	D1
5600	MONE	60449	3682	7W-30S	E4
5600	MonT	60449	3682	7W-30S	E4
5600	UYPK	60449	3682	7W-30S	E4
5600	UYPK	60466	3682	7W-30S	E4
7600	DRN	60561	3207	17W-8S	B2
Gail Ct					
10	BlmT	60411	3510	3E-25S	A7
10	CLLK	60014	2640	35W-25N	A5
10	LIHL	60156	2694	34W-21N	C5
N Gail Ct					
300	ANHT	60004	2807	16W-15N	D2
300	PTHT	60070	2807	16W-15N	D2
Gail Ct S					
200	ANHT	60004	2807	16W-15N	D2
200	PTHT	60004	2807	16W-15N	D2
200	PTHT	60070	2807	16W-15N	D2
Gail Dr					
1100	BFGV	60089	2701	17W-21N	B6
Gail Ln					
400	CHHT	60411	3507	2W-24S	D6
1100	SYHW	60118	2800	36W-15N	A3
14000	CTWD	60445	3347	6W-16S	E3
Gail St					
-	ANTH	60002	2357	23W-42N	E6
Gailine Av					
21500	SLVL	60411	3597	2E-26S	D2
Gainsboro Ct					
1400	WHTN	60187	3082	24W-1S	D2
Gainsboro Dr					
1500	WHTN	60187	3082	24W-1S	D2
Gainsborough Ct					
400	BGBK	60440	3269	22W-12S	B3
Gainsborough Dr					
300	RMVL	60446	3340	24W-16S	E4
Gainsborough Pl					
5700	OKFT	60452	3347	7W-18S	D6
E Gaisor Ct					
2100	CteT	60417	3686	2E-29S	E1
E Gaisor Dr					
2000	CteT	60417	3686	2E-29S	D2
S Galahad Dr					
22200	TroT	60404	3584	30W-27S	B4
Galahad Rd					
300	BGBK	60440	3205	22W-11S	D7
Galaway Dr					
-	MHRY	60050	2527	35W-31N	A6
Galbreath Dr					
10	WNVL	60555	3080	30W-2S	C4
Gale Av					
10	FTPK	60130	3030	9W-0N	B5
10	RVFT	60130	3030	9W-0N	B5
10	RVFT	60305	3030	9W-0N	B4
Gale Ln					
2300	ELGN	60123	2853	36W-10N	E6
Gale St					
100	AURA	60506	3200	36W-7S	A1
200	ELGN	60123	2853	36W-11N	E4
200	ElgT	60123	2853	36W-11N	E4
300	AURA	60506	3137	36W-7S	E7
300	AURA	60506	3199	36W-7S	B1
500	ELGN	60123	2854	36W-10N	A6
Gale St SR-31					
100	AURA	60506	3200	36W-7S	A1
W Gale St					
5300	CHCG	60630	2919	6W-6N	D6
N Galena Av					
3900	ANHT	60004	2753	19W-18N	D3
3900	PltT	60004	2753	19W-18N	D3
Galena Blvd					
300	AURA	60506	3136	40W-6S	B6
300	SRGV	60506	3136	40W-6S	B6
300	SRGV	60554	3136	40W-6S	B6
E Galena Blvd					
10	AURA	60505	3138	35W-7S	B7
10	AURA	60506	3138	35W-7S	B7
10	SRGV	60554	3135	41W-6S	E5
300	AURA	60505	3200	34W-8S	C1
300	SRGV	60506	3136	41W-6S	A6
300	SRGV	60554	3136	41W-6S	A6
400	SgrT	60554	3135	41W-6S	E5
900	AURA	60504	3200	34W-8S	C1
1400	AraT	60504	3200	33W-8S	E1
1400	AraT	60505	3200	33W-8S	E1
W Galena Blvd					
10	AURA	60505	3138	35W-7S	B7
10	AURA	60506	3136	39W-7S	E6
10	AURA	60506	3138	36W-7S	A7

STREET Block	City	ZIP	Map#	CGS	Grid
W Galena Blvd					
10	SgrT	60506	3136	39W-7S	E6
1800	AURA	60506	3137	38W-7S	A6
Galena Ct					
1200	NPVL	60564	3203	28W-10S	A5
1200	WldT	60564	3203	28W-10S	A5
N Galena Ct					
3800	ANHT	60004	2753	19W-18N	D3
Galena Dr					
3000	PnfT	60435	3417	27W-19S	B3
3100	JLET	60431	3417	27W-19S	B3
Galena Rd					
-	MTGY	60538	3199	39W-10S	A5
-	MTGY	60543	3199	39W-10S	A5
6100	MTGY	60538	3198	39W-10S	E6
6400	MTGY	60543	3198	40W-10S	D7
6700	BtlT	60512	3198	40W-10S	D7
6700	BtlT	60538	3198	39W-10S	D7
6700	BtlT	60543	3198	39W-10S	D7
6700	OSWG	60538	3198	39W-10S	D7
6700	OSWG	60543	3198	39W-10S	D7
7000	BtlT	60512	3262	41W-11S	A1
7700	BtlT	60543	3262	41W-11S	A1
8600	BtlT	60512	3197	43W-10S	A7
8600	BtlT	60512	3261	42W-11S	D1
8600	YKVL	60512	3197	42W-11S	C7
8600	YKVL	60512	3261	42W-11S	D1
11000	BtlT	60512	3196	44W-10S	E7
11000	BtlT	60545	3196	46W-10S	A6
12100	LtRT	60545	3196	46W-10S	A6
Galena St					
100	WCHI	60185	3022	29W-0N	C4
7600	LKWD	60014	2638	39W-24N	D6
N Galesburg Av					
3900	ANHT	60004	2753	19W-18N	D3
3900	PltT	60004	2753	19W-18N	D3
N Galesburg Ct					
3800	ANHT	60004	2753	19W-18N	D3
3800	PltT	60004	2753	19W-18N	D3
W Galeton Dr					
500	RDLK	60073	2531	23W-31N	E7
W Galeview Ln					
7600	FftT	60423	3504	9W-24S	D5
Galewood Dr					
100	BGBK	60440	3268	24W-12S	D2
Galilee Av					
-	BHPK	60099	2421	11W-39N	E5
1700	ZION	60099	2421	11W-39N	E5
Galitz St					
5100	SKOK	60077	2865	6W-9N	D6
5300	MNGV	60053	2865	6W-9N	D6
5300	MNGV	60077	2865	6W-9N	D6
Gall Ln					
100	NLNX	60451	3501	17W-24S	C5
Gallager Rd					
14400	MHTN	60442	3678	18W-31S	A6
14400	MhtT	60442	3678	18W-31S	A6
15000	MHTN	60442	3677	20W-31S	C6
15000	MhtT	60442	3677	20W-31S	C6
16000	JknT	60442	3677	20W-31S	B7
Gallagher Rd					
10	WKGN	60087	2480	10W-36N	B4
Gallant Ct					
1000	WHTN	60187	3024	25W-0N	B5
Gallatin Dr					
6900	JLET	60586	3415	32W-21S	C7
Gallek Rd					
9700	AlqT	60010	2695	31W-22N	D4
9700	AlqT	60021	2695	31W-22N	D4
9700	AlqT	60102	2695	31W-22N	D4
9700	BNHL	60010	2695	31W-22N	D4
9700	BNHL	60021	2695	31W-22N	D4
Galleon Ct					
10	TDLK	60030	2476	19W-34N	D7
10	TDLK	60030	2533	19W-34N	D1
Galleon Ln					
700	EGVV	60007	2913	22W-8N	D2
Galleon Wy					
400	DSPN	60016	2862	15W-11N	B3
Galleria Ct					
8500	SPGV	60081	2413	31W-40N	D2
Galligan Rd					
10	GLBT	60118	2746	39W-17N	A7
10	GLBT	60136	2746	39W-17N	A7
10	GLBT	60136	2799	38W-16N	A1
10	RtdT	60118	2746	39W-17N	A7
10	RtdT	60136	2746	39W-17N	A7
10	RtdT	60142	2746	39W-19N	A3
Galligan Rd CO-6					
10	GLBT	60118	2746	39W-17N	A7
10	GLBT	60136	2746	39W-17N	A7
10	GLBT	60136	2799	38W-16N	A1
10	RtdT	60118	2746	39W-17N	A7
10	RtdT	60136	2746	39W-17N	A7
10	RtdT	60142	2746	39W-19N	A3
Gallop Ct					
3300	RLKP	60030	2532	22W-31N	C7
Galloway Cir					
1700	IVNS	60010	2751	24W-16N	C6
Galloway Dr					
1100	WDSK	60098	2582	39W-30N	B1
1500	IVNS	60010	2751	24W-17N	C5
5200	HFET	60192	2802	30W-12N	C7
Galusha Rd					
10	WNVL	60555	3081	27W-3S	B6
100	WnfT	60555	3081	27W-3S	C6
Galvin Dr					
2200	ELGN	60124	2799	37W-15N	D3
2700	DndT	60118	2799	37W-15N	D3
2700	DndT	60124	2799	37W-15N	D3
Galvin Pkwy					
-	WDND	60118	2800	34W-16N	D2
100	HRVD	60033	2406	49W-38N	C7
Galvin Center Access					
-	SMBG	60173	2805	22W-12N	C7
Galway Av					
-	PNFD	60585	3265	32W-14S	D7
Galway Ct					
10	LMNT	60439	3272	16W-14S	A7
300	BMDL	60108	2969	22W-4N	D2
1100	NHBK	60062	2756	11W-17N	E5
1200	GNVA	60134	3020	36W-0N	A5
6900	DRN	60561	3144	18W-7S	E7
Galway Dr					
200	CRY	60013	2641	31W-24N	D6
700	PTHT	60070	2808	14W-15N	C2
1500	AURA	60505	3138	34W-5S	D3
4200	GfnT	60156	2693	38W-23N	A2
Galway Ln					
-	PGGV	60140	2797	41W-15N	E4
10	LMNT	60439	3272	16W-14S	A6
Galway Rd					
10	LMNT	60439	3272	16W-14S	A6
1000	JLET	60431	3496	29W-22S	D2
4700	JLET	60586	3496	29W-22S	D2

STREET Block	City	ZIP	Map#	CGS	Grid
Galway St					
200	GYLK	60030	2532	21W-33N	D2
Galway Bay					
19300	MKNA	60448	3503	13W-23S	B3
Gamay Ct					
7600	GRNE	60031	2476	18W-35N	E6
Gamay Dr					
-	PnfT	60586	3416	31W-19S	A3
16100	PNFD	60586	3416	31W-19S	A3
Gamble Dr					
500	LSLE	60532	3143	22W-5S	B3
Game Tr					
800	LKMR	60051	2529	28W-32N	E5
800	LKMR	60051	2530	28W-32N	A5
Game Farm Rd					
500	BtlT	60560	3333	43W-14S	B1
500	YKVL	60560	3333	43W-14S	B1
900	BtlT	60560	3261	43W-14S	B7
900	YKVL	60560	3261	43W-14S	B7
Gamon Rd					
800	WHTN	60187	3082	24W-1S	C2
Gander Ct					
1500	CLLK	60014	2693	37W-23N	A2
Gander Ln					
1300	CLLK	60014	2693	37W-23N	A3
Gannet Cir					
10	BGBK	60440	3205	21W-10S	D5
Gannet Ln					
500	BGBK	60440	3205	21W-10S	D5
2600	NLNX	60451	3502	15W-25S	C7
2600	NLNX	60451	3590	15W-25S	C1
Gannon Ct					
1000	HFET	60169	2858	24W-11N	C3
Gannon Dr					
800	HFET	60169	2858	24W-11N	C3
Gansett Pkwy					
3100	ElgT	60124	2853	38W-11N	A4
N Ganster Rd					
2700	BHPK	60087	2480	9W-37N	B3
Gant Cir					
10	SMWD	60107	2857	28W-11N	B4
Ganton Ct					
24500	WldT	60564	3266	30W-12S	A3
Garadice					
-	NLNX	60451	3590	16W-25S	A1
Garand Dr					
1600	DRFD	60015	2703	12W-21N	B6
S Garavogue Av					
14000	HMGN	60491	3344	15W-16S	C4
Garbo Ln					
5300	HRPK	60133	2911	27W-6N	C6
W Garcia Dr					
20700	LkvT	60046	2475	20W-37N	E3
20700	LkvT	60046	2476	20W-37N	A3
Garden Av					
10	BmdT	60172	2912	24W-6N	D7
10	BNVL	60106	2972	15W-5N	A1
10	ROSL	60172	2912	24W-6N	D7
200	BNVL	60106	2916	15W-5N	A7
600	BmdT	60172	2968	24W-5N	D1
800	GNVA	60134	3020	35W-0N	A6
1300	CHHT	60411	3507	1W-25S	E7
3800	WNSP	60558	3086	14W-4S	C7
E Garden Av					
10	PLTN	60067	2752	20W-17N	E4
300	PLTN	60067	2753	20W-17N	A4
300	PLTN	60074	2753	20W-17N	A4
N Garden Av					
10	ROSL	60172	2912	24W-7N	D4
400	EMHT	60101	2971	17W-2N	C7
400	EMHT	60126	2971	17W-2N	C7
S Garden Av					
10	ROSL	60172	2912	24W-7N	D5
W Garden Av					
10	PLTN	60067	2752	21W-17N	E4
Garden Cir					
200	HFET	60010	2857	27W-11N	C4
200	SMWD	60107	2857	27W-11N	B4
300	YKVL	60560	3333	43W-16S	B4
Garden Ct					
-	DRGV	60516	3144	18W-7S	E6
600	GNVW	60025	2810	9W-13N	D7
1200	NPVL	60540	3141	28W-7S	A6
1200	PTHT	60070	2754	15W-16N	E6
1300	BTVA	60510	3078	33W-2S	E4
1500	BFGV	60089	2702	15W-20N	A7
1500	MDLN	60060	2590	20W-29N	A4
1500	VrnT	60015	2702	15W-20N	A7
2400	PnfT	60435	3417	27W-20S	D5
5000	MCLK	60050	2527	33W-34N	E1
7300	RVFT	60305	3030	9W-0N	D4
7900	BGVW	60455	3148	9W-7S	C6
9800	SRPK	60176	2973	12W-4N	B2
S Garden Ct					
1400	PnfT	60544	3338	29W-17S	D5
W Garden Ct					
100	PLTN	60067	2752	21W-17N	E4
Garden Dr					
10	OswT	60538	3199	37W-10S	C7
100	BGBK	60440	3268	24W-12S	D2
300	WynT	60103	2966	29W-5N	D1
2700	LSLE	60532	3142	24W-7S	C7
Garden Ln					
-	FftT	60477	3505	9W-23S	A3
-	RchT	60423	3505	9W-23S	A3
100	PTHT	60070	2754	15W-16N	E6
800	WLNG	60090	2754	15W-16N	E6
800	WLNG	60090	2755	15W-16N	A6
2900	NndT	60012	2584	34W-29N	B5
6800	BGVW	60455	3148	9W-7S	C6
6800	BGVW	60458	3148	9W-7S	C6
7400	JSTC	60458	3209	11W-8S	E2
N Garden Ln					
23400	ElaT	60047	2699	21W-23N	D2
23400	KLDR	60047	2699	21W-23N	D2
Garden Pl					
1900	WKGN	60085	2479	11W-35N	D7
Garden Rd					
2000	AraT	60506	3199	38W-8S	A1
2200	AraT	60506	3198	38W-8S	E1
Garden St					
100	WCHI	60185	3022	29W-1N	D4
100	YKVL	60560	3333	43W-16S	B4
700	PKRG	60068	2918	10W-8N	A1
1300	PKRG	60068	2917	10W-8N	E1
2400	JLET	60435	3417	27W-20S	D5
2400	LktT	60403	3417	27W-20S	D5
2400	PnfT	60403	3417	27W-20S	D5
2500	PnfT	60435	3417	27W-20S	C5
3400	NfdT	60062	2756	11W-16N	C7
S Garden St					
1500	PltT	60067	2806	20W-13N	A5
1600	PltT	60008	2806	20W-13N	A5
1600	RGMW	60008	2806	20W-13N	A5
Garden Ter					
300	SRWD	60404	3496	30W-24S	C5

STREET Block	City	ZIP	Map#	CGS	Grid
Garden Ter					
2000	HFET	60169	2858	25W-12N	C1
E Garden Wk					
2600	ANHT	60004	2807	16W-14N	D5
Garden Wy					
-	SMBG	60194	2859	23W-10N	A5
200	BMDL	60108	2912	24W-5N	D7
200	BMDL	60108	2968	24W-5N	E1
Garden Crescent Ct					
10	ELGN	60123	2854	35W-12N	C2
Garden Crescent Dr					
10	ELGN	60123	2854	35W-12N	C2
Garden Grove Ct					
400	NARA	60542	3137	38W-4S	A2
Garden Hill Ln					
10	SCRL	60174	3020	34W-2N	E2
Gardenia Dr					
10	DYR	46311	3598		C1
Gardenia Ln					
300	BFGV	60089	2754	17W-20N	C1
600	BRLT	60103	2910	29W-6N	D7
E Gardenia Ln					
800	PLTN	60074	2753	19W-18N	B3
Garden Market St					
10	WNSP	60558	3146	13W-4S	E1
Garden Quarter Rd					
4400	MHRY	60050	2527	33W-32N	E4
Gardenside Ct					
1500	NPVL	60540	3202	28W-8S	E1
Garden View Ct					
15600	ODPK	60462	3346	9W-18S	E7
Gardenview Dr					
4200	NPVL	60564	3267	28W-12S	B2
Garden View Ln					
6200	MTSN	60443	3505	7W-25S	C6
Gardina Ln					
1300	CLLK	60014	2639	37W-25N	A4
1400	GfnT	60014	2639	37W-25N	A4
Gardiner Ct					
500	RMVL	60446	3269	23W-14S	A6
800	NARA	60542	3077	37W-3S	B6
Gardiner St					
3300	AURA	60505	3138	34W-6S	D6
Gardiner Glen Dr					
5100	JLET	60586	3496	30W-22S	B1
S Gardner					
-	PNFD	60544	3338	30W-17S	B7
Gardner Av					
20500	BlmT	60411	3507	2W-24S	C6
20700	CHHT	60411	3507	2W-25S	C7
Gardner Cir E					
1900	AURA	60503	3201	32W-10S	C6
Gardner Cir W					
2000	AURA	60503	3201	32W-10S	C6
Gardner Ct					
5700	HRPK	60133	2911	26W-7N	E5
Gardner Dr					
13700	HTLY	60142	2744	43W-19N	A2
Gardner Ln					
700	LKFT	60045	2650	10W-26N	B4
Gardner Rd					
200	AlqT	60021	2696	29W-23N	D3
200	FRGV	60021	2696	29W-22N	D3
600	BDVW	60154	3029	12W-1S	C7
600	BDVW	60155	3029	12W-1S	C7
600	WSTR	60154	3029	12W-1S	C7
600	WSTR	60155	3029	12W-1S	C7
700	FSMR	60422	3507	2W-22S	C2
1400	BDVW	60154	3087	12W-1S	C1
1400	BDVW	60155	3087	12W-1S	C1
1400	WSTR	60154	3087	12W-1S	C1
W Gardner Rd					
25100	WcnT	60084	2588	25W-28N	A5
Gardner St					
-	RcmT	60071	2413	33W-39N	A4
400	JLET	60433	3499	23W-24S	A7
500	JLET	60436	3499	23W-24S	A7
600	JltT	60433	3499	23W-24S	A6
600	JltT	60436	3499	23W-24S	A6
1100	JLET	60433	3587	23W-25S	A1
1100	JltT	60433	3587	23W-25S	A1
Gardner St US-52					
1000	JLET	60433	3499	23W-24S	A7
1000	JLET	60436	3499	23W-24S	A7
1100	JLET	60433	3587	23W-25S	A1
1100	JltT	60433	3587	23W-25S	A1
E Gardner St					
200	ELWD	60421	3675	25W-32S	C7
W Gardner St					
100	ELWD	60421	3675	25W-32S	B7
Gareth Ln					
200	SMBG	60193	2859	22W-10N	C6
Garfield Av					
-	LYVL	60048	2591	16W-28N	C6
10	LGPK	60525	3087	12W-3S	C4
200	FXLK	60041	2473	26W-35N	C5
200	NLNX	60451	3502	15W-25S	C7
200	NlxT	60451	3502	15W-25S	C7
300	AURA	60506	3138	36W-7S	A7
400	CTCY	60409	3352	4E-17S	C5
500	AURA	60506	3137	36W-7S	D7
700	BTVA	60510	3078	36W-1S	A3
800	LKBF	60044	2593	11W-28N	D5
800	LKPT	60441	3419	22W-19S	D4
1100	BKFD	60513	3087	12W-3S	C4
1100	BKFD	60525	3087	12W-3S	C4
1100	LYVL	60048	2647	16W-27N	D1
4700	LSLE	60532	3143	23W-5S	A2
6100	HMND	46324	3430		D2
8500	MNSR	46321	3430		D7
E Garfield Av					
10	PltT	60067	2805	20W-13N	E5
10	RGMW	60067	2805	20W-13N	E5
N Garfield Av					
10	HNDL	60521	3146	15W-4S	B1
10	MDLN	60060	2646	19W-27N	D1
100	MDLN	60060	2590	19W-27N	D7
300	HNDL	60521	3086	15W-4S	B7
S Garfield Av					
10	HNDL	60521	3146	15W-6S	B5
10	MDLN	60060	2646	19W-27N	D1
5800	BRRG	60521	3146	15W-6S	B4
6200	WLBK	60527	3146	15W-6S	B5
7200	BRRG	60527	3146	15W-8S	B7
7200	BRRG	60527	3208	15W-8S	B1
7600	HMND	46324	3430		D5
8100	DGvT	60527	3208	15W-9S	B3
SE Garfield Av					
300	MDLN	60060	2646	19W-27N	D2
SW Garfield Av					
300	MDLN	60060	2646	19W-27N	D2
500	FmtT	60060	2646	19W-27N	D2
W Garfield Av					
200	EMHT	60126	3027	16W-0N	E3
300	PTON	60468	3860	9W-37S	E4
700	PtnT	60468	3860	10W-37S	D4

STREET Block	City	ZIP	Map#	CGS	Grid
E Garfield Blvd					
-	CHCG	60637	3152	0E-5S	D2
10	CHCG	60609	3152	0E-5S	C2
10	CHCG	60615	3152	0E-5S	C2
10	CHCG	60621	3152	0E-6S	C3
N Garfield Blvd					
300	GYLK	60030	2533	20W-32N	A5
W Garfield Blvd					
-	CHCG	60629	3151	2W-5S	B3
-	CHCG	60632	3151	2W-5S	B3
10	CHCG	60609	3152	0W-5S	A2
10	CHCG	60615	3152	0W-5S	C2
10	CHCG	60621	3152	0W-5S	A2
10	CHCG	60637	3152	0W-5S	A2
900	CHCG	60609	3151	1W-5S	D3
900	CHCG	60621	3151	1W-6S	E3
1100	CHCG	60636	3151	1W-6S	E3
Garfield Ct					
900	CPVL	60110	2748	32W-17N	D7
8400	MNSR	46321	3430		D7
Garfield Dr					
900	CPVL	60110	2748	32W-17N	D7
Garfield Ln					
10	SMWD	60107	2856	29W-10N	E6
Garfield Rd					
10	CmpT	60175	2962	40W-2N	C7
900	CmpT	60119	3018	40W-2N	C1
900	CmpT	60175	3018	40W-2N	C1
3600	JNBG	60050	2471	32W-35N	B5
Garfield St					
10	CHCG	60304	3031	7W-0S	B6
10	CHCG	60644	3031	7W-0S	B6
10	GNVA	60134	3020	34W-1N	D3
10	HRVD	60033	2406	49W-38N	B7
10	JLET	60435	3498	24W-23S	D5
10	JLET	60436	3498	24W-23S	D5
10	OKPK	60304	3031	7W-0S	B6
10	OSWG	60543	3263	37W-12S	C3
100	BRTN	60010	2750	27W-20N	C1
400	WNFD	60190	3023	27W-0S	C7
800	OKPK	60304	3030	8W-0S	D6
1100	FTPK	60130	3030	8W-0S	D6
1100	FTPK	60304	3030	8W-0S	D6
N Garfield St					
900	LMBD	60148	2970	19W-2N	C7
900	LMBD	60148	3026	19W-2N	C1
S Garfield St					
1200	LMBD	60148	3026	19W-0S	C7
1200	LMBD	60148	3084	19W-1S	C1
1200	YkTp	60148	3026	19W-0S	C7
1200	YkTp	60148	3084	19W-1S	C1
Garfield Ter					
300	LMBD	60148	3026	19W-0N	C5
Garfield Ridge Ct					
10	WLBK	60527	3146	15W-7S	B6
Garland Av					
400	RMVL	60446	3340	24W-15S	E2
600	WNKA	60093	2812	4W-15N	B3
1800	HDPK	60035	2704	10W-21N	B6
Garland Ct					
100	GLHT	60139	2968	23W-4N	E4
100	GLHT	60139	2969	23W-4N	A4
500	LKZH	60047	2699	22W-21N	A6
1400	JLET	60432	3499	22W-22S	D1
N Garland Ct					
10	CHCG	60602	3034	0E-0N	C4
100	CHCG	60601	3034	0E-0N	C4
W Garland Ct					
7700	FftT	60423	3504	9W-24S	D5
Garland Ln					
1600	HRPK	60133	2911	26W-6N	D6
Garland Pl					
600	DSPN	60016	2863	12W-11N	B4
N Garland Rd					
28000	WCDA	60084	2587	26W-28N	E7
28100	WcnT	60084	2587	25W-28N	E6
28200	WCDA	60084	2588	25W-28N	A6
28200	WcnT	60084	2588	25W-29N	A4
Garlands Ln					
1000	BRTN	60010	2751	25W-20N	A1
Garlisch Dr					
10	EGVV	60007	2861	17W-10N	C5
Garman Rd					
10	PKFT	60466	3595	2W-27S	C4
Garnacha Dr					
-	GRNE	60031	2476	18W-35N	E5
Garner Av					
1000	WHTN	60187	3024	23W-0S	E6
Garnet Cir					
800	SMBG	60193	2913	23W-9N	B1
1400	HFET	60192	2804	24W-15N	B1
Garnet Ct					
900	NLNX	60451	3500	19W-24S	D6
1300	GRNE	60031	2478	14W-35N	B6
16500	ODHL	60467	3423	12W-19S	D3
16500	ODPK	60467	3423	12W-19S	D3
Garnet Dr					
300	NLNX	60451	3500	19W-24S	D6
1200	NHLK	60164	2972	14W-3N	C5
Garnett Av					
100	PTPR	53158	2363	10W-43N	B5
100	WPHR	53158	2363	10W-43N	B5
100	WPHR	60096	2363	10W-43N	B5
N Garnett Av					
-	BtnT	60099	2422	10W-41N	B2
-	ZION	60099	2422	10W-41N	B2
37500	BHPK	60087	2480	10W-37N	B2
39000	BHPK	60099	2422	10W-39N	B6
Garnett Pl					
1000	EVTN	60201	2867	2W-11N	A2
Garnette Ct					
3900	NPVL	60564	3267	28W-11S	B2
N Garnsey Av					
100	JLET	60432	3499	23W-23S	B4
W Garrett Ct					
7600	FftT	60423	3504	9W-23S	E4
Garrett Dr					
10900	ODPK	60467	3423	13W-21S	A5
Garrett Pl					
600	EVTN	60201	2867	2W-12N	C1
Garrett St					
900	WTMT	60559	3145	18W-6S	A5
N Garrick Av					
-	BHPK	60087	2479	12W-37N	B2
2400	WKGN	60087	2479	12W-36N	B3
35400	WkgT	60085	2479	12W-35N	B6
35600	WKGN	60085	2479	12W-35N	B5
36100	WkgT	60087	2479	12W-36N	B5
Garrison Av					
100	EVTN	60091	2813	2W-13N	B7
100	EVTN	60201	2813	2W-13N	B7
100	WDND	60118	2801	34W-15N	A3
100	WLMT	60091	2813	2W-13N	B7
Garrison Cir					
300	PTBR	60010	2642	29W-26N	D2

STREET Block	City	ZIP	Map#	CGS	Grid
Garrison Rd					
8300	WRLK	60097	2469	37W-35N	B5
Garth Ct					
2000	NPVL	60565	3203	26W-9S	D4
Garth Rd					
600	WLNG	60090	2755	15W-17N	A6
E Gartner Rd					
10	NPVL	60540	3141	26W-7S	E7
10	NPVL	60540	3203	26W-7S	D1
600	LslT	60540	3141	26W-7S	E7
900	NPVL	60540	3142	25W-7S	B7
W Gartner Rd					
-	NPVL	60565	3203	27W-8S	C2
10	NPVL	60540	3203	27W-8S	C2
N Garvey Ct					
200	CHCG	60601	3034		E4
Garvin St					
1000	JLET	60432	3499	22W-22S	C1
E Garvin St					
900	JLET	60432	3499	22W-22S	C1
E Garwood Av					
500	MPPT	60056	2808	15W-13N	A5
Gary Av					
-	BMDL	60133	2968	25W-4N	B3
-	BMDL	60188	2968	25W-4N	B4
-	HRPK	60172	2912	25W-7N	B5
-	ROSL	60133	2912	25W-7N	B5
-	ROSL	60172	2912	25W-7N	B5
-	RtdT	60142	2745	40W-19N	C4
10	BMDL	60108	2912	25W-6N	B7
10	BMDL	60172	2912	25W-6N	B7
10	BmdT	60108	2912	25W-6N	B7
10	BmdT	60172	2912	25W-6N	B7
10	MltT	60187	3024	25W-1N	B3
10	MltT	60188	3024	25W-1N	B3
10	WHTN	60187	3024	25W-1N	B3
100	CLSM	60188	3024	25W-2N	B1
200	CLSM	60188	2968	25W-2N	B7
400	BMDL	60108	2968	25W-5N	B1
400	BMDL	60172	2968	25W-5N	B1
500	BmdT	60172	2968	25W-5N	B1
500	HRPK	60133	2912	25W-6N	B7
700	AraT	60506	3199	38W-8S	A2
1100	CLSM	60133	2968	25W-4N	B4
1600	AraT	60505	3138	33W-5S	E3
1600	AURA	60505	3138	33W-5S	E3
Gary Av CO-23					
-	BMDL	60133	2968	25W-4N	B3
-	BMDL	60188	2968	25W-4N	B4
-	HRPK	60133	2912	25W-7N	B5
-	HRPK	60172	2912	25W-7N	B5
-	ROSL	60133	2912	25W-7N	B5
-	ROSL	60172	2912	25W-7N	B5
10	BMDL	60108	2912	25W-6N	B7
10	BMDL	60172	2912	25W-6N	B7
10	BmdT	60108	2912	25W-6N	B7
10	BmdT	60172	2912	25W-6N	B7
10	MltT	60187	3024	25W-1N	B3
10	MltT	60188	3024	25W-1N	B3
10	WHTN	60187	3024	25W-1N	B3
100	CLSM	60188	3024	25W-2N	B1
200	CLSM	60188	2968	25W-2N	B7
400	BMDL	60108	2968	25W-5N	B1
400	BMDL	60172	2968	25W-5N	B1
500	BmdT	60172	2968	25W-5N	B1
1100	CLSM	60133	2968	25W-4N	B4
N Gary Av					
-	CLSM	60188	3024	25W-2N	B1
-	HRPK	60133	2912	25W-7N	B4
-	HRPK	60172	2912	25W-7N	B4
100	MltT	60187	3024	25W-0S	C6
100	WHTN	60187	3024	25W-0S	C6
200	ROSL	60172	2912	25W-7N	B4
200	SMBG	60172	2912	25W-7N	B4
200	SMBG	60193	2912	25W-7N	B4
N Gary Av CO-23					
-	CLSM	60188	3024	25W-2N	B1
-	HRPK	60133	2912	25W-7N	B4
-	HRPK	60172	2912	25W-7N	B4
200	ROSL	60172	2912	25W-7N	B4
200	SMBG	60172	2912	25W-7N	B4
200	SMBG	60193	2912	25W-7N	B4
1500	MltT	60187	3024	25W-0N	B5
1500	WHTN	60187	3024	25W-0N	B5
S Gary Av					
100	BMDL	60108	2968	25W-5N	B2
100	BMDL	60172	2968	25W-5N	B2
200	BMDL	60133	2968	25W-4N	B3
S Gary Av CO-23					
100	BMDL	60108	2968	25W-5N	B2
100	BMDL	60172	2968	25W-5N	B2
200	BMDL	60133	2968	25W-4N	B3
Gary Ct					
10	CmpT	60175	2905	42W-7N	D6
700	WHTN	60187	3024	25W-0S	C6
1900	SMBG	60193	2912	25W-8N	A3
Gary Dr					
500	BGBK	60440	3269	21W-11S	D1
2800	FNPK	60131	2973	13W-3N	A5
2800	FNPK	60164	2973	13W-3N	A5
2800	LydT	60164	2973	13W-3N	A5
Gary Ln					
10	RtdT	60142	2745	40W-19N	C3
2000	GNVA	60134	3019	36W-0N	D4
Gary Ray Dr					
24000	JknT	60421	3675	24W-29S	E1
24000	JLET	60421	3675	24W-29S	E1
Garys Dr					
500	ANTH	60002	2358	23W-42N	A5
Garys Mill Rd					
10	WCHI	60185	3080	29W-0S	E1
10	WNFD	60190	3023	28W-0S	A7
10	WnfT	60185	3080	29W-0S	D1
10	WnfT	60190	3023	28W-0S	B7
500	WnfT	60190	3081	28W-0S	A1
600	WnfT	60190	3080	29W-0S	D1
Garywood Dr					
1400	BRRG	60527	3146	14W-6S	C5
Gasket Dr					
1300	BRLT	60103	2909	32W-8N	D2
1300	BRLT	60120	2909	32W-8N	D2
1300	ELGN	60120	2909	32W-8N	D2
Gaskin Dr					
20600	LkT	60441	3418	25W-18S	A1
20600	LkT	60446	3418	25W-18S	A1
20600	RMVL	60446	3418	25W-18S	A1
Gaslight Dr					
500	ALGN	60102	2747	35W-19N	C2
W Gaslight Square Dr					
3600	ALSP	60803	3276	4W-14S	D6
Gasoline Al					
700	BNVL	60106	2915	16W-6N	E5
Gast Rd					
10	HPSR	60140	2743	45W-18N	C5
10	HshT	60140	2743	45W-18N	C5
Gastes Ln					
14300	HMGN	60491	3343	18W-17S	B5
Gastville St					
10	AURA	60503	3201	33W-11S	A7
10	OSWG	60543	3201	33W-11S	A7
10	OswT	60503	3201	33W-11S	A7
10	OswT	60543	3201	33W-11S	A7
E Gate Rd					
-	CnhT	60410	3674	28W-28S	A1
S Gate Rd					
10	PltT	60124	2905	43W-9N	B1
Gates Av					
500	AURA	60505	3138	35W-6S	C5
700	BmdT	60143	2913	21W-6N	E5
Gates Ct					
24800	PNFD	60585	3266	31W-13S	A6
Gates Ln					
24800	PNFD	60585	3266	31W-13S	A6
24800	WldT	60585	3266	31W-13S	A6
24900	PNFD	60585	3265	31W-13S	E6
Gates Pl					
200	WNVL	60555	3081	28W-3S	A6
Gates St					
10	CLLK	60014	2640	35W-26N	B3
400	WCHI	60185	3022	29W-0S	D7
500	AURA	60505	3200	35W-8S	C3
1000	AraT	60505	3200	35W-9S	C4
1200	AURA	60505	3200	35W-9S	C4
1200	MTGY	60538	3200	35W-9S	C4
Gatesby Rd					
200	RVSD	60546	3088	9W-3S	C4
Gates Creek Dr					
100	OSWG	60543	3262	39W-12S	E2
Gateshead Av S					
-	EGVV	60007	2914	20W-8N	B2
Gateshead Dr					
300	NPVL	60565	3203	27W-10S	C6
1000	NPVL	60564	3203	28W-11S	A7
3200	NPVL	60564	3267	28W-11S	A1
Gateshead Ln N					
500	EGVV	60007	2914	19W-8N	C2
Gateshead Ln S					
500	EGVV	60007	2914	19W-8N	C2
Gateway Av					
-	JknT	60421	3675	25W-30S	C3
-	JLET	60421	3675	25W-30S	C3
Gateway Cir					
-	JLET	60421	3675	25W-30S	C3
-	RLKP	60030	2589	21W-31N	C1
W Gateway Cir					
25400	PNFD	60544	3337	31W-15S	D3
25400	PNFD	60585	3337	31W-15S	D3
Gateway Ct					
10	BGBK	60440	3269	23W-13S	A5
Gateway Dr					
-	ElgT	60123	2799	37W-13N	D7
700	BGBK	60440	3269	23W-13S	A5
1100	ELGN	60123	2799	37W-13N	D7
1100	ELGN	60124	2799	37W-13N	D7
1300	DndT	60124	2799	37W-13N	D7
E Gateway Dr					
400	TRLK	60010	2643	26W-25N	D5
N Gateway Dr					
-	MTSN	60443	3594	6W-26S	A2
W Gateway Dr					
10700	FftT	60423	3591	13W-27S	B5
Gateway Ln					
10	OKBK	60523	3086	15W-3S	B6
Gateway Rd					
10	BNVL	60106	2915	16W-5N	E7
N Gatewood Av					
1400	PLTN	60067	2752	21W-17N	D4
Gatewood Dr					
1800	GRNE	60031	2478	15W-36N	A5
Gatewood Ln					
200	BRLT	60103	2967	28W-5N	A2
300	GYLK	60030	2475	21W-34N	D7
3500	AURA	60504	3201	31W-8S	E1
3500	AURA	60504	3202	31W-8S	A1
8000	WDRG	60517	3205	22W-9S	C3
Gauger Av					
15900	HRVY	60426	3427	1W-19S	E2
16000	MKHM	60426	3427	1W-19S	E2
16000	MKHM	60428	3427	1W-19S	E2
Gavin Av					
600	RMVL	60446	3340	24W-16S	D4
Gavin Ct					
300	WCHI	60185	3022	30W-2N	B1
1100	LKFT	60045	2649	12W-25N	B5
W Gavin Ln					
4400	WKGN	60048	2535	14W-31N	C6
S Gawain Dr					
22100	TroT	60404	3584	30W-27S	B4
Gawne Ln					
10	BtlT	60560	3333	42W-15S	D2
10	YKVL	60560	3333	42W-15S	D2
N Gay Ct					
200	GNWD	60425	3508	0W-22S	B1
Gayle Ct					
100	SMWD	60107	2857	27W-11N	D4
600	WLNG	60090	2755	14W-17N	D5
2500	MaiT	60025	2864	9W-12N	C1
2500	NHBK	60062	2809	11W-15N	C1
11500	HTLY	60142	2692	40W-20N	A7
Gayle Dr					
4300	DrrT	60098	2581	42W-27N	C7
Gaylin Ct					
100	BNVL	60106	2971	16W-5N	E1
Gaylord Rd					
1600	CTHL	60403	3417	26W-21S	D7
1600	CTHL	60403	3497	27W-21S	D1
2200	LkT	60435	3417	26W-21S	D7
2200	PnfT	60435	3417	26W-21S	D7
2300	CTHL	60435	3417	26W-21S	D7
2300	LkT	60403	3417	26W-20S	D4
2300	PnfT	60403	3417	26W-20S	D4
15900	JLET	60403	3417	26W-19S	D2
15900	JLET	60435	3417	26W-20S	D4
15900	LkT	60446	3417	26W-19S	D2
15900	RMVL	60446	3417	26W-19S	D2
16300	JLET	60441	3417	26W-20S	D4
Gaylord St					
10	EGVV	60007	2861	18W-10N	A5
Gaynelle Rd					
6200	TYPK	60477	3425	7W-19S	B3
Gayton Ln					
400	SMBG	60193	2859	22W-9N	B7
Gazebo Ln					
200	LMBD	60148	3084	20W-2S	B3
Gear Dr					
-	NLNX	60451	3589	18W-25S	A1
-	NlxT	60451	3589	18W-25S	A1
10	NLNX	60451	3501	18W-25S	A7
Geddes Av					
100	PTPR	53158	2363	10W-43N	B5
100	WPHR	53158	2363	10W-43N	B5
Geddes Av					
100	WPHR	60096	2363	10W-43N	B5
Geddes Ct					
800	WPHR	60096	2363	10W-42N	B6
Gee Ct					
700	WLNG	60090	2754	16W-18N	D2
800	ELBN	60119	3017	43W-2N	A1
Gehrig Cir					
300	BGBK	60440	3269	23W-11S	A1
W Geier Rd					
18400	WrnT	60031	2476	18W-36N	E4
18700	WrnT	60046	2476	18W-36N	E4
Geise Rd					
-	BTVA	60502	3078	33W-2S	E4
-	BTVA	60502	3079	33W-2S	A4
-	BTVA	60510	3078	33W-2S	E4
-	BTVA	60510	3079	33W-2S	A4
-	BtvT	60502	3078	33W-2S	E4
-	BtvT	60502	3079	33W-2S	A4
-	BtvT	60510	3079	33W-2S	A4
Geissler St					
300	LKPT	60441	3420	21W-18S	A1
300	LkT	60441	3420	21W-18S	A1
N Gelden Ln					
600	LkvT	60046	2417	21W-39N	D6
600	LNHT	60046	2417	21W-39N	D6
W Gelden Rd					
20700	LkvT	60046	2417	21W-39N	E5
20700	LkvT	60046	2418	20W-39N	A5
20700	LNHT	60046	2417	21W-39N	E5
20700	LNHT	60046	2418	20W-39N	A5
21900	LKVL	60046	2417	22W-39N	C5
W Gelden Rd CO-A11					
20700	LkvT	60046	2417	21W-39N	E5
20700	LkvT	60046	2418	20W-39N	A5
20700	LNHT	60046	2417	21W-39N	E5
20700	LNHT	60046	2418	20W-39N	A5
21900	LKVL	60046	2417	22W-39N	C5
Gemini Ln					
2600	RVWD	60015	2755	13W-20N	E1
Genauldi Av					
1700	SMWD	60107	2911	28W-8N	B2
Gene Dr					
7600	MchT	60097	2469	36W-34N	D7
Gene Darfler Ct					
500	WldT	60565	3203	27W-11S	C7
General Ct					
14300	PNFD	60544	3338	31W-17S	A5
General Dr					
14300	PNFD	60544	3337	31W-17S	E5
14300	PNFD	60544	3338	31W-17S	A6
Generation Dr					
24600	PNFD	60585	3266	30W-13S	A5
Genesee Av					
10	ELGN	60123	2854	34W-12N	D1
Genesee Ct					
10	BGBK	60440	3205	23W-11S	A7
900	NPVL	60563	3140	30W-5S	A3
Genesee Dr					
500	NPVL	60563	3140	30W-5S	A4
500	NpvT	60563	3140	30W-5S	A4
N Genesee St					
10	WKGN	60085	2537	10W-34N	B1
500	WKGN	60085	2480	10W-34N	B7
26600	WcnT	60084	2643	28W-26N	A2
S Genesee St					
300	WKGN	60085	2537	10W-33N	B3
900	NCHI	60064	2537	10W-33N	B4
S Genesee St SR-137					
500	WKGN	60085	2537	10W-33N	B3
900	NCHI	60064	2537	10W-33N	B4
Geneva Av					
-	LKPT	60441	3419	21W-20S	E5
-	LkT	60441	3419	21W-20S	E6
10	BLWD	60104	3029	13W-0N	A4
300	MLPK	60160	2973	13W-2N	A7
300	MLPK	60164	2973	13W-2N	A7
300	NHLK	60160	2973	13W-2N	A7
300	NHLK	60164	2973	13W-2N	A7
400	HLSD	60162	3029	13W-0N	A5
400	LydT	60164	2973	13W-2N	A7
500	HLSD	60104	3029	13W-0N	A4
700	RMVL	60446	3268	24W-14S	E7
700	RMVL	60446	3340	24W-14S	E1
700	SchT	60174	2908	34W-6N	D6
N Geneva Av					
100	EMHT	60126	3028	15W-1N	B2
700	AddT	60126	2972	15W-2N	B6
700	EMHT	60126	2972	15W-2N	B6
Geneva Cir					
700	EGVV	60007	2913	21W-8N	D2
Geneva Ct					
-	IVNS	60010	2750	25W-16N	E7
10	CRTE	60417	3596	0E-28S	E6
10	LIHL	60156	2692	39W-23N	C3
300	SMBG	60193	2858	23W-9N	E7
600	INCK	60061	2647	17W-24N	A6
1300	BRLT	60103	2967	28W-5N	B1
2400	AURA	60503	3201	32W-10S	C6
N Geneva Ct					
800	EMHT	60126	2972	15W-3N	B6
Geneva Dr					
-	GNVA	60134	3021	33W-2N	A2
200	BlmT	60411	3598	4E-25S	C1
200	HRVY	60426	3428	1W-19S	A3
200	LYWD	60411	3598	4E-25S	C1
800	GNVA	60134	3020	34W-1N	E1
1600	WLNG	60090	2808	14W-15N	B1
2000	GnvT	60134	3021	33W-1N	A2
2000	WnfT	60185	3021	33W-1N	A2
6800	TYPK	60477	3505	8W-22S	A1
7700	GRNE	60031	2476	18W-34N	E7
7700	GRNE	60031	2533	18W-34N	E1
N Geneva Dr					
1300	PLTN	60074	2753	19W-17N	C5
1300	PltT	60074	2753	19W-17N	C5
Geneva Ln					
100	MchT	60051	2528	31W-32N	D6
100	NndT	60051	2528	31W-32N	D6
300	CRY	60013	2641	32W-24N	A7
1100	LKZH	60047	2698	24W-23N	B3
1300	BRLT	60103	2967	28W-5N	B1
2400	MTGY	60538	3198	40W-10S	D6
2900	LIHL	60142	2692	39W-22N	C3
2900	LIHL	60156	2692	39W-23N	C3
N Geneva Ln					
39300	BHPK	60099	2421	11W-39N	E5
39300	ZION	60099	2421	11W-39N	E5
Geneva Pl					
-	SKOK	60203	2866	4W-12N	C2
10	EVTN	60201	2866	4W-12N	C1
400	WHTN	60187	3024	24W-0N	D4
3600	MHRY	60050	2528	32W-31N	B7
Geneva Rd					
10	MltT	60187	3023	27W-1N	D3
10	MltT	60187	3024	25W-0N	A4
Geneva Rd					
10	MltT	60188	3023	26W-1N	E3
10	MltT	60188	3024	25W-0N	A4
10	MltT	60190	3023	27W-1N	D3
10	WCHI	60185	3022	29W-1N	E4
10	WNFD	60187	3023	26W-1N	E3
10	WNFD	60188	3023	26W-1N	E3
10	WNFD	60190	3023	28W-1N	A4
10	WnfT	60185	3022	29W-1N	E4
10	WnfT	60185	3023	28W-1N	A4
10	WnfT	60187	3023	27W-1N	D3
10	WnfT	60190	3023	28W-1N	A4
100	WNFD	60185	3023	28W-1N	A4
200	GNEN	60137	3025	23W-0N	A3
200	GNEN	60187	3025	23W-1N	A3
200	WHTN	60187	3024	25W-0N	A4
200	WHTN	60187	3025	23W-1N	A3
300	MltT	60137	3025	23W-0N	A3
600	SCRL	60174	2964	35W-2N	B7
600	SCRL	60174	3020	35W-2N	B1
1300	GNVA	60134	3020	35W-2N	C2
Geneva Rd CO-7					
500	GNEN	60137	3025	23W-0N	A3
500	MltT	60137	3025	23W-0N	A3
Geneva Rd CO-21					
10	MltT	60187	3023	27W-1N	D3
10	MltT	60187	3024	25W-0N	A4
10	MltT	60188	3023	26W-1N	E3
10	MltT	60188	3024	25W-0N	A4
10	MltT	60190	3023	27W-1N	D3
10	WNFD	60187	3023	26W-1N	E3
10	WNFD	60188	3023	26W-1N	E3
10	WNFD	60190	3023	28W-1N	A4
10	WnfT	60185	3023	28W-1N	A4
10	WnfT	60187	3023	27W-1N	D3
10	WnfT	60190	3023	28W-1N	A4
100	WNFD	60185	3023	28W-1N	A4
200	GNEN	60137	3025	23W-0N	A3
200	GNEN	60187	3025	23W-1N	A3
200	WHTN	60187	3024	25W-0N	A4
200	WHTN	60187	3025	23W-1N	A3
300	MltT	60137	3025	23W-0N	A3
700	WCHI	60185	3022	28W-1N	E4
700	WnfT	60185	3022	28W-1N	E4
Geneva Rd SR-31					
600	SCRL	60174	2964	35W-2N	B7
600	SCRL	60174	3020	35W-2N	B1
1300	GNVA	60134	3020	35W-2N	C2
E Geneva Rd					
100	CLSM	60188	3024	24W-1N	D3
100	GNEN	60137	3024	23W-1N	E3
100	GNEN	60137	3025	23W-0N	A3
100	GNEN	60187	3025	23W-0N	A3
100	GNEN	60188	3024	23W-1N	E3
100	MltT	60188	3024	23W-1N	E3
100	WHTN	60137	3024	23W-1N	E3
100	WHTN	60187	3024	24W-1N	D3
100	WHTN	60187	3025	23W-0N	A3
100	WHTN	60188	3024	23W-1N	E3
600	MltT	60187	3024	23W-0N	E3
E Geneva Rd CO-21					
100	CLSM	60188	3024	24W-1N	D3
100	GNEN	60137	3024	23W-1N	E3
100	GNEN	60137	3025	23W-0N	A3
100	GNEN	60187	3025	23W-0N	A3
100	GNEN	60188	3024	23W-1N	E3
100	MltT	60188	3024	23W-1N	E3
100	WHTN	60137	3024	23W-1N	E3
100	WHTN	60187	3024	24W-1N	D3
100	WHTN	60187	3025	23W-0N	A3
100	WHTN	60188	3024	23W-1N	E3
600	MltT	60187	3024	23W-0N	E3
W Geneva Rd					
100	MltT	60187	3024	24W-1N	C3
100	MltT	60188	3024	24W-1N	C3
100	WHTN	60187	3024	24W-1N	C3
100	WHTN	60188	3024	24W-1N	C3
W Geneva Rd CO-21					
100	MltT	60187	3024	24W-1N	C3
100	MltT	60188	3024	24W-1N	C3
100	WHTN	60187	3024	24W-1N	C3
100	WHTN	60188	3024	24W-1N	C3
Geneva St					
300	WDND	60118	2801	33W-15N	B3
400	WDND	60118	2800	34W-16N	E2
900	SRWD	60404	3496	30W-24S	B6
2000	JLET	60436	3586	24W-26S	D2
2000	JltT	60436	3586	24W-26S	D2
8000	WDRG	60517	3205	21W-9S	D3
E Geneva St					
100	WCHI	60185	3022	29W-0N	C4
N Geneva St					
10	ELGN	60120	2855	33W-11N	A4
S Geneva St					
10	ELGN	60120	2855	33W-11N	A4
W Geneva St					
100	WCHI	60185	3022	30W-0N	C4
Geneva Ter					
100	RLKB	60073	2474	23W-35N	E6
100	RLKB	60073	2475	23W-35N	A6
N Geneva Ter					
2200	CHCG	60614	2978	0W-3N	A5
Genevieve Dr					
700	SEGN	60177	2908	35W-9N	B1
9400	SjnT	46311	3687		E2
S Genoa Av					
8700	CHCG	60620	3214	1W-10S	A4
9300	CHCG	60620	3213	1W-11S	E6
9300	CHCG	60643	3213	1W-11S	E6
W Genoa Av					
20600	LkvT	60046	2476	20W-37N	A3
20800	LkvT	60046	2475	20W-37N	E3
W Genoa Av CO-A18					
20600	LkvT	60046	2476	20W-37N	A3
20800	LkvT	60046	2475	20W-37N	E3
Genoa Dr					
2700	NLNX	60451	3590	15W-25S	C1
W Gent Dr					
4100	WKGN	60031	2478	14W-37N	D2
4100	WKGN	60083	2478	14W-37N	D2
4100	WKGN	60087	2478	14W-37N	D2
Gentilly Dr					
10	OswT	60538	3199	36W-10S	E6
Gentle Breeze Ter					
500	CPVL	60110	2747	35W-17N	D6
Gentry Ct					
5700	LGGV	60047	2701	17W-23N	A2
Gentry Dr					
10	ElaT	60047	2645	23W-24N	A6
10	HNWD	60047	2645	23W-24N	A6
Gentry Ln					
16700	BmnT	60477	3425	7W-20S	D3
16700	TYPK	60477	3425	7W-20S	D3
Gentry Rd					
1200	HFET	60169	2858	24W-12N	E2
Gentry St					
200	OMFD	60461	3507	3W-25S	B7
200	PKFT	60461	3507	3W-25S	B7
200	PKFT	60466	3507	3W-25S	B7
Geo Brown Dr					
14200	ODPK	60462	3345	12W-16S	D4
Geoffrey Rd					
15100	OKFT	60452	3347	7W-18S	D6
George Av					
-	WKGN	60085	2537	10W-33N	B3
400	WCDA	60084	2587	26W-27N	D7
400	WCDA	60084	2643	26W-27N	D1
700	AURA	60505	3200	34W-8S	C2
2300	TroT	60435	3497	26W-22S	D2
2600	JLET	60435	3497	27W-22S	C2
W George Av					
2400	TroT	60435	3497	27W-22S	D2
2500	JLET	60435	3497	27W-22S	D2
George Ct					
400	GNVA	60134	3019	36W-1N	D2
500	ZION	60099	2362	12W-42N	C7
1700	GNVW	60025	2810	8W-12N	D7
2700	RGMW	60008	2806	19W-14N	C5
5200	GRNE	60031	2478	15W-35N	A5
N George Ct					
37000	LkvT	60046	2475	22W-37N	C3
S George Ct					
15900	PnfT	60586	3416	29W-19S	E3
George Dr					
10	MDLN	60060	2647	18W-27N	A1
16400	OKFT	60452	3426	5W-19S	B3
George Ln					
100	NPVL	60540	3142	25W-6S	A5
George Pl					
4100	SRPK	60176	2973	12W-5N	A2
George Rd					
10	WLNG	60090	2755	15W-17N	A4
George St					
-	RVGV	60171	2973	11W-2N	E7
10	BNVL	60106	2972	15W-4N	A3
10	GYLK	60030	2532	21W-33N	E4
100	WHTN	60187	3082	24W-1S	C2
200	STGR	60475	3596	0E-27S	E5
200	WCDA	60084	2587	26W-27N	D7
200	WCHI	60185	3022	30W-0N	B5
400	ELGN	60120	2855	33W-10N	B5
400	WDDL	60143	2914	18W-6N	D7
400	WDDL	60191	2914	18W-6N	E7
800	FNPK	60131	2972	15W-4N	A3
1000	BrnT	60010	2751	25W-18N	A4
1000	CTCY	60409	3351	3E-17S	E5
1000	CTCY	60409	3352	3E-17S	A5
1200	BRTN	60010	2751	25W-17N	A4
1600	DRGV	60516	3144	20W-6S	B4
1900	MLPK	60160	2973	11W-2N	E7
1900	MLPK	60160	3029	11W-2N	E1
2400	FNPK	60131	2973	12W-3N	B6
2400	LydT	60131	2973	12W-3N	B6
2400	LydT	60164	2973	12W-3N	B6
2800	TroT	60435	3497	27W-22S	C2
3000	WKGN	60085	2536	12W-33N	B1
3600	JLET	60435	3497	27W-22S	B2
5300	MNGV	60053	2865	6W-9N	D6
5300	MNGV	60077	2865	6W-9N	D6
5300	SKOK	60077	2865	6W-9N	D6
5700	RHMD	60071	2353	34W-42N	C6
E George St					
100	ITSC	60143	2914	19W-5N	C7
200	ANHT	60005	2807	17W-13N	B5
800	WDDL	60143	2914	19W-5N	C7
800	WDDL	60191	2914	19W-5N	C7
N George St					
1600	CHCG	60657	2977	2W-3N	C4
S George St					
10	MPPT	60056	2808	15W-12N	B7
200	MPPT	60056	2862	15W-12N	B1
W George St					
100	ITSC	60143	2914	19W-5N	C7
200	ANHT	60005	2807	18W-13N	A5
500	ANHT	60005	2806	18W-13N	E5
800	CHCG	60657	2977	1W-3N	D4
1800	CHCG	60618	2977	2W-3N	B4
2100	RGMW	60008	2806	19W-13N	C5
2800	CHCG	60618	2976	3W-3N	E4
3900	CHCG	60639	2976	5W-3N	E4
3900	CHCG	60641	2976	5W-3N	B4
4700	CHCG	60641	2975	7W-3N	C4
5500	CHCG	60634	2975	8W-3N	A4
6700	CHCG	60634	2974	8W-3N	E4
7100	CHCG	60707	2974	8W-3N	D4
7200	EDPK	60707	2974	9W-3N	C4
Georgean Ln					
800	SMBG	60193	2858	24W-10N	D6
Georgeann Ct					
600	MRGO	60152	2634	49W-26N	C3
Georgeanna St					
200	BtlT	60560	3261	43W-14S	C7
200	YKVL	60560	3261	43W-14S	C7
George Bell Dr					
-	GLHT	60139	2969	23W-4N	A4
George Bell Rd					
-	HDPK	60035	2650	9W-24N	C7
-	HDPK	60037	2650	9W-24N	C7
-	LKFT	60035	2650	9W-24N	C7
-	LKFT	60045	2650	9W-24N	B6
3600	LKFT	60037	2650	9W-24N	B6
George Brennan Hwy					
17000	BmnT	60452	3426	6W-20S	A5
17000	BmnT	60477	3426	6W-20S	A5
17000	OKFT	60452	3426	6W-20S	A5
17000	OKFT	60477	3426	6W-20S	A5
17200	CCHL	60452	3426	6W-20S	A5
17200	CCHL	60477	3426	6W-20S	A5
17300	BmnT	60477	3425	6W-21S	E5
George Bush Ct					
13700	HTLY	60142	2744	42W-18N	D5
George Michas Dr					
-	CTHL	60441	3418	24W-18S	D2
300	RMVL	60441	3418	24W-18S	D1
Georgetown Av					
200	RMVL	60446	3340	25W-16S	C3
Georgetown Cir					
2200	AURA	60503	3201	32W-10S	C7
3900	ALGN	60102	2693	37W-20N	A7
Georgetown Coms					
7200	FKFT	60423	3593	8W-25S	A1
7200	RchT	60443	3593	9W-25S	A1
Georgetown Ct					
10	ALGN	60102	2693	37W-20N	A7
300	BMDL	60108	2969	22W-4N	B4
1700	NPVL	60565	3204	24W-9S	D3
2300	AURA	60503	3201	32W-10S	C7
W Georgetown Ct					
21400	LkT	60544	3339	26W-16S	E5
Georgetown Dr					
-	SMBG	60133	2912	25W-8N	A2

STREET Block	City	ZIP	Map#	CGS	Grid
Georgetown Dr					
-	SMBG	60193	2912	25W-8N	B2
10	CRY	60013	2695	32W-23N	B1
300	CRY	60013	2641	32W-24N	B7
800	OSWG	60543	3264	35W-11S	C2
1300	BTVA	60510	3077	36W-1S	E2
1300	CLSM	60188	2967	28W-4N	B3
5400	MTSN	60443	3505	6W-25S	E7
13100	PlsT	60462	3345	13W-15S	A2
13100	PlsT	60464	3345	13W-15S	A2
13100	PlsT	60467	3345	13W-15S	A2
S Georgetown Dr					
14200	LktT	60544	3339	26W-16S	D5
14200	PnfT	60544	3339	27W-16S	C4
W Georgetown Dr					
21400	LktT	60544	3339	26W-16S	D5
Georgetown Ln					
1900	HFET	60169	2804	26W-12N	A7
1900	HFET	60169	2858	26W-12N	A1
2000	WKGN	60085	2479	11W-35N	D5
9400	LKWD	60014	2692	38W-23N	E1
Georgetown Rd					
21200	FKFT	60423	3592	9W-25S	E1
21200	FKFT	60423	3593	9W-25S	A1
Georgetown Sq					
300	ITSC	60143	2914	18W-6N	E7
300	WDDL	60143	2914	18W-6N	E7
300	WDDL	60191	2914	18W-6N	E7
9400	ODHL	60487	3423	11W-19S	D2
9400	ODPK	60467	3423	11W-19S	D2
Georgetown Wy					
-	VNHL	60069	2702	15W-23N	A1
1000	VNHL	60061	2702	15W-23N	A1
George Towne Ln					
800	BRTN	60010	2698	25W-20N	A7
900	CbaT	60010	2698	25W-20N	A7
George Washington Av					
-	JknT	60421	3763	26W-33S	E2
George Washington Dr					
24500	PNFD	60544	3338	30W-17S	A6
Georgia Ct					
1400	NPVL	60540	3140	28W-7S	E6
1800	SMBG	60193	2912	25W-8N	A2
18000	ODPK	60467	3423	13W-21S	A7
Georgia Dr					
1000	EGVV	60007	2913	21W-8N	D2
W Georgia Dr					
6900	MNGV	60053	2864	8W-10N	E4
6900	NLES	60714	2864	8W-10N	E4
Georgia Ln					
10300	OKLN	60453	3275	6W-12S	D1
Georgia Rd					
10	NCHI	60088	2593	12W-29N	C4
N Georgia St					
900	JLET	60435	3498	25W-22S	C3
Georgian Ct					
10	CLLK	60014	2640	35W-26N	A3
W Georgian Ct					
600	AddT	60101	2970	19W-3N	D6
600	ADSN	60101	2970	19W-3N	D6
Georgian Pl					
-	WDSK	60098	2581	41W-28N	D6
900	BRLT	60103	2910	29W-6N	E6
Georgiana Av					
8500	MNGV	60053	2865	7W-10N	B4
Georgia's Wy					
-	NLNX	60451	3501	16W-24S	E5
-	NLNX	60451	3502	16W-24S	A6
Georgina Ln					
3300	BLWD	60104	3029	12W-0N	A5
Georgine St					
-	GfnT	60014	2638	38W-25N	E4
Georgio Ln					
-	ODPK	60467	3423	13W-21S	B6
N Geraghty Av					
39000	BHPK	60099	2422	10W-39N	B6
N Geraghty St					
38000	BHPK	60087	2480	10W-38N	B1
38200	BHPK	60087	2422	10W-38N	B7
38400	BHPK	60099	2422	10W-38N	B7
Gerald Av					
800	SEGN	60177	2908	35W-9N	B2
1500	GLHT	60139	2969	22W-2N	B7
Geraldine Ct					
800	MRGO	60152	2634	49W-26N	C3
N Geraldine Ln					
2600	CbaT	60010	2642	28W-25N	D4
2600	PTBR	60010	2642	28W-26N	D3
2600	WcnT	60010	2642	28W-26N	D3
Geranium Ct					
1500	NPVL	60565	3204	24W-10S	D6
S Geranium Ln					
25800	MONE	60449	3683	5W-31S	C5
N Gerard Av					
400	VLPK	60181	3027	17W-1N	B2
Gerardi Ct					
-	BMDL	60108	2912	25W-6N	B7
-	BMDL	60172	2912	25W-6N	B7
-	BmdT	60172	2912	25W-6N	B7
Gerber					
-	BRLT	60103	2967	28W-5N	A2
Gerber Rd					
700	BRLT	60103	2967	28W-5N	A2
700	WynT	60103	2967	28W-5N	A2
700	WynT	60185	2967	28W-4N	A3
N Gerberding Av					
34600	GrtT	60041	2474	25W-34N	B7
Geri Av					
700	PLTN	60067	2752	21W-16N	C6
N Geri Ct					
400	PLTN	60067	2752	21W-16N	C6
Geri Ln					
300	DSPN	60016	2863	12W-11N	C3
Geringer Rd					
1100	ALGN	60102	2694	33W-21N	E6
1100	AlqT	60102	2694	33W-21N	E6
1100	AlqT	60102	2695	33W-21N	A5
Germaine Ln					
500	EGVV	60007	2861	18W-9N	A7
Germaine Pl					
10	SMBG	60173	2859	22W-10N	D5
500	EGVV	60007	2861	18W-9N	A7
German Church Rd					
10	DGvT	60527	3208	15W-9S	C3
10	LynT	60527	3208	15W-9S	C3
10800	WLSP	60480	3209	13W-9S	A3
10800	WLSP	60525	3209	13W-9S	A3
10900	WLSP	60480	3208	15W-9S	C3
10900	WLSP	60525	3208	15W-9S	C3
11400	BRRG	60527	3208	14W-9S	D3
W Germania Pl					
100	CHCG	60610	3034	0W-1N	B1
Geronimo St					
500	HFET	60169	2859	23W-11N	A4
W Gerri Ln					
200	ADSN	60101	3026	18W-2N	E1
Gerritsen Av					
8800	BKFD	60513	3088	10W-4S	B7
8800	LYNS	60513	3088	10W-4S	B7
8800	LYNS	60534	3088	10W-4S	B7
8900	BKFD	60513	3087	11W-4S	D7
9500	BKFD	60525	3087	11W-4S	D7
9500	LGNG	60525	3087	11W-4S	D7
Gerry Ct					
1200	WDSK	60098	2581	42W-30N	B2
Gerry Dr					
100	WDDL	60191	2915	18W-7N	A5
Gerry Ln					
5300	NndT	60014	2641	32W-26N	A2
Gerry St					
400	WDSK	60098	2581	42W-30N	C1
Gerry Steven Ct					
100	BNVL	60106	2971	16W-3N	E4
Gershwin Ct					
10	WHTN	60187	3082	24W-2S	C4
Gerson Dr					
8000	GwdT	60097	2469	37W-34N	C7
8000	WRLK	60097	2469	37W-34N	C7
Gerstung St					
10	PKFT	60466	3595	3W-26S	C2
Gerten Av					
600	AraT	60505	3138	34W-5S	C3
Gertrude St					
100	ELGN	60123	2854	34W-10N	D5
N Gerwal Av					
34000	AvnT	60030	2532	21W-34N	D2
Gerzevske Ln					
100	CLSM	60188	3024	25W-2N	C1
Getchell Av					
-	AvnT	60030	2532	21W-32N	D4
300	GYLK	60030	2532	21W-32N	D4
W Getson Av					
200	PNFD	60544	3416	29W-18S	D2
Gettler St					
2100	DYR	46311	3598		C2
9700	SjnT	46311	3687		C3
10000	HnrT	46311	3687		C3
Getty Av					
900	ELGN	60120	2855	32W-10N	C6
Getty Rd					
-	CrlT	60140	2743	45W-20N	A1
-	CrlT	60142	2743	45W-20N	A1
-	HPSR	60140	2743	45W-20N	A1
-	HshT	60140	2743	45W-20N	A1
Getty Rd CO-36					
-	CrlT	60140	2743	45W-20N	A1
-	CrlT	60142	2743	45W-20N	A1
-	HPSR	60140	2743	45W-20N	A1
-	HshT	60140	2743	45W-20N	A1
Getty Rd CO-40					
-	CrlT	60140	2743	45W-20N	A1
-	CrlT	60142	2743	45W-20N	A1
-	HPSR	60140	2743	45W-20N	A1
-	HshT	60140	2743	45W-20N	A1
Gettysburg Ct					
600	NPVL	60540	3203	27W-8S	C1
2700	LNHT	60046	2418	19W-39N	C5
14600	PNFD	60544	3337	31W-17S	E6
Gettysburg Dr					
200	BGBK	60440	3269	23W-11S	A1
2200	AURA	60506	3137	38W-6S	A6
4400	RGMW	60008	2805	20W-14N	E3
W Gettysburg Dr					
700	ANHT	60004	2753	18W-16N	E7
Gettysburg Rd					
1300	LGGV	60047	2700	18W-21N	E6
25200	PNFD	60544	3337	31W-17S	E6
Gettysburg St					
300	PKFT	60466	3595	4W-25S	A1
W Gettysburg St					
5400	CHCG	60630	2919	6W-6N	C6
Getzelman Dr					
1200	ELGN	60123	2854	35W-12N	B1
Getzelman Rd					
10	HPSR	60140	2795	47W-15N	E4
10	HshT	60140	2795	47W-15N	E4
100	BrlT	60140	2795	46W-14N	E6
Getzelman Ter					
1100	ALGN	60102	2695	33W-21N	A6
Gianna Dr					
10	BlmT	60430	3507	2W-23S	D3
10	FSMR	60422	3507	2W-23S	D3
10	FSMR	60430	3507	2W-23S	D3
Giant Oak Dr					
4300	NndT	60051	2586	30W-27N	B7
4300	NndT	60051	2642	29W-27N	B1
Giant Oaks Rd					
5800	GwdT	60097	2469	37W-37N	B1
5800	HbnT	60097	2469	37W-37N	B1
N Gibbons Av					
600	ANHT	60004	2807	16W-14N	C4
1000	PTHT	60004	2807	16W-14N	C4
S Gibbons Av					
10	ANHT	60004	2807	16W-13N	C5
400	ANHT	60005	2807	16W-13N	C6
Gibbons Ct					
10	SEGN	60177	2908	35W-9N	B2
Gibbons Dr					
600	NLNX	60451	3501	17W-23S	D4
600	NlxT	60451	3501	17W-23S	D4
Gibbs Dr					
10	SBTN	60010	2803	26W-13N	C6
Gibraltar Dr					
200	BGBK	60440	3269	22W-12S	C3
300	RMVL	60440	3269	22W-12S	D4
300	WDRG	60440	3269	22W-12S	D4
300	WDRG	60517	3269	22W-12S	D4
Gibson Dr					
1500	EGVV	60007	2859	21W-9N	D7
1700	EGVV	60007	2913	22W-9N	D1
Gibson Ln					
17100	SHLD	60473	3429	1E-20S	B3
Gibson Rd					
10	PKFT	60466	3595	3W-26S	B2
Gibson St					
400	MTSN	60443	3506	6W-24S	A5
Giddings Av					
5700	HNDL	60521	3146	15W-6S	B4
5800	HNDL	60527	3146	15W-6S	B4
7200	BRRG	60527	3146	15W-8S	B7
7200	BRRG	60527	3208	15W-8S	B1
Giddings St					
-	WDSK	60098	2581	41W-30N	E1
W Giddings St					
2000	CHCG	60640	2921	2W-5N	B7
2700	CHCG	60625	2920	3W-5N	E7
2700	CHCG	60625	2921	3W-5N	A7
5600	CHCG	60630	2919	7W-5N	B7
6200	HDHT	60630	2919	7W-5N	A7
6200	HDHT	60706	2919	7W-5N	A7
7700	HDHT	60706	2918	9W-5N	C7
7700	NRDG	60706	2918	9W-5N	C7
Giddington Ct					
1700	NlxT	60451	3502	16W-24S	A5
Gideon Av					
1700	BtnT	60099	2422	10W-41N	A1
1700	ZION	60099	2422	10W-39N	A5
Gideon Ct					
10	GNCY	53128	2353		A3
Gierz St					
300	DRGV	60515	3144	19W-5S	D1
Giese Rd					
100	BTVA	60510	3078	34W-2S	D4
100	BtvT	60510	3078	34W-2S	D4
1300	BTVA	60502	3078	34W-2S	D4
1300	BtvT	60502	3078	34W-2S	D4
Gieseke Dr					
6000	AlqT	60014	2641	32W-26N	C3
6000	NndT	60014	2641	32W-26N	C3
Gifford Ct					
10	MDLN	60060	2647	18W-27N	A1
1300	HRPK	60133	2911	26W-7N	E5
Gifford Pl					
200	ELGN	60120	2855	33W-11N	A5
2700	NLNX	60451	3500	20W-24S	B5
Gifford Rd					
800	ELGN	60120	2855	32W-9N	D7
900	BRLT	60120	2909	32W-9N	D2
900	ELGN	60120	2909	32W-9N	D2
1300	BRLT	60103	2909	32W-9N	D1
Gifford St					
400	GNCY	53128	2353		A2
N Gifford St					
10	ELGN	60120	2855	33W-11N	A3
S Gifford St					
10	ELGN	60120	2855	33W-11N	A4
Gigi Ln					
1700	DRN	60561	3206	18W-8S	E1
1900	DRGV	60516	3206	18W-8S	E1
1900	DRN	60516	3206	18W-8S	E1
Gilbert Av					
-	CLLK	60014	2639	37W-25N	A5
10	CNHL	60514	3145	17W-5S	C2
1100	DRGV	60515	3144	20W-5S	B2
1400	GfnT	60014	2639	37W-25N	A5
5200	LynT	60525	3147	13W-5S	A2
5200	WNSP	60525	3147	13W-5S	A2
5200	WNSP	60558	3147	13W-5S	A2
N Gilbert Av					
10	LGNG	60525	3087	13W-4S	A7
10	WNSP	60525	3087	13W-4S	A7
10	WNSP	60558	3087	13W-4S	A7
100	LGPK	60525	3087	13W-4S	A7
100	LGPK	60558	3087	13W-4S	A7
38600	BHPK	60099	2422	10W-38N	A6
Gilbert Ct					
3300	DRN	60561	3206	20W-9S	A4
3400	CRTE	60417	3597	1E-28S	B5
S Gilbert Ct					
8400	CHCG	60620	3214	0W-9S	A3
Gilbert Dr					
300	WDDL	60191	2970	18W-5N	E1
400	ADSN	60191	2970	18W-5N	D1
500	ADSN	60143	2970	19W-5N	D1
17500	LKPT	60441	3420	20W-21S	C6
E Gilbert Rd					
10	PLTN	60067	2805	20W-15N	E2
W Gilbert Rd					
500	PLTN	60067	2805	22W-15N	C2
N Gilbert St					
10	SEGN	60177	2908	34W-8N	D3
S Gilbert St					
10	SEGN	60177	2908	34W-7N	E4
700	SchT	60120	2909	33W-7N	A5
700	SchT	60177	2908	33W-7N	E4
700	SchT	60177	2909	33W-7N	A5
Gilbert Ter					
600	AraT	60506	3199	37W-8S	C2
Gilberto St					
1600	GLHT	60139	2968	24W-3N	D6
Gilboa Av					
1700	BtnT	60099	2422	10W-41N	A1
1700	ZION	60099	2422	10W-39N	A5
Gilcrest Ct					
2800	SMBG	60193	2857	27W-10N	D6
Gilda Ct					
-	OswT	60560	3334	40W-15S	C3
Gilead Av					
1700	ZION	60099	2422	10W-41N	A2
3100	ZION	60099	2421	10W-39N	E5
3300	BHPK	60099	2421	10W-39N	E5
S Giles Av					
3100	CHCG	60616	3092	0E-3S	C4
3300	CHCG	60653	3092	0E-3S	C4
Giles Ct					
400	BRLT	60103	2910	29W-8N	D3
Giles Dr					
9800	MKNA	60448	3503	12W-23S	D3
Gilgare Ln					
3700	HDPK	60035	2650	9W-24N	D7
3700	LKFT	60035	2650	9W-24N	D6
Gillenwater St					
-	BtvT	60510	3078	34W-3S	E5
1900	BTVA	60510	3078	34W-3S	E5
Gillett Av					
200	WKGN	60085	2480	10W-35N	A7
Gillett St					
-	SRGV	60554	3136	40W-7S	A6
Gillette Av					
700	AURA	60506	3137	36W-6S	E5
Gillian Rd					
38800	LkvT	60046	2416	24W-38N	C6
Gillian St					
1100	LMNT	60439	3270	19W-14S	E7
Gillick St					
-	PKRG	60068	2917	10W-8N	E2
10	CHCG	60631	2918	10W-8N	B2
10	PKRG	60068	2918	10W-8N	A2
10	PKRG	60631	2918	10W-8N	A2
Gillingham Ct					
10	ALGN	60102	2693	37W-21N	A7
Gillings Dr					
300	GRNE	60031	2535	14W-34N	C1
400	GRNE	60031	2478	14W-34N	D7
Gilman Av					
200	WLNG	60090	2755	14W-16N	B7
N Gilmer Rd					
26500	FmtT	60047	2645	22W-27N	C1
26500	FmtT	60060	2645	22W-27N	C1
26500	HNWD	60047	2645	22W-27N	C1
26500	HNWD	60060	2645	22W-27N	C1
27100	MDLN	60060	2645	22W-27N	C1
27600	HNWD	60047	2589	22W-28N	A6
27600	HNWD	60060	2589	22W-27N	B7
27700	FmtT	60060	2589	22W-28N	A6
28100	FmtT	60060	2588	23W-29N	D4
29100	FmtT	60030	2588	23W-29N	D4
29500	WCDA	60030	2588	24W-29N	D4
N Gilmer Rd					
29700	FmtT	60084	2588	24W-30N	C3
29700	WCDA	60060	2588	24W-29N	C3
29700	WCDA	60084	2588	25W-30N	A2
30800	WcnT	60030	2587	26W-30N	E2
30800	WcnT	60030	2588	25W-30N	A2
30800	WcnT	60073	2587	26W-30N	E2
30800	WcnT	60084	2587	26W-30N	E2
30800	WcnT	60084	2588	25W-30N	A2
31800	VOLO	60073	2587	26W-30N	D1
33800	LKMR	60073	2530	27W-31N	C7
35000	VOLO	60073	2530	27W-31N	B6
35000	WcnT	60073	2530	27W-31N	B6
N Gilmer Rd CO-V76					
26500	FmtT	60047	2645	22W-27N	C1
26500	FmtT	60060	2645	22W-27N	C1
26500	HNWD	60047	2645	22W-27N	C1
26500	HNWD	60060	2645	22W-27N	C1
27100	MDLN	60060	2645	22W-27N	C1
27600	HNWD	60047	2589	22W-28N	A6
27600	HNWD	60060	2589	22W-27N	B7
27700	FmtT	60060	2589	22W-28N	A6
28100	FmtT	60060	2588	23W-29N	D4
29100	FmtT	60030	2588	23W-29N	D4
29500	WCDA	60030	2588	24W-29N	D4
29700	FmtT	60084	2588	24W-30N	C3
29700	WCDA	60060	2588	24W-29N	C3
29700	WCDA	60084	2588	25W-30N	A2
30800	WcnT	60030	2587	26W-30N	E2
30800	WcnT	60030	2588	25W-30N	A2
30800	WcnT	60073	2587	26W-30N	E2
30800	WcnT	60084	2587	26W-30N	E2
30800	WcnT	60084	2588	25W-30N	A2
31800	VOLO	60073	2587	26W-30N	D1
32600	VOLO	60073	2530	27W-31N	C7
33800	LKMR	60073	2530	27W-31N	C7
W Gilmer Rd					
100	ElaT	60047	2645	21W-25N	D4
100	ElaT	60060	2645	21W-25N	D4
100	HNWD	60047	2645	21W-25N	D4
100	HNWD	60060	2645	21W-25N	D4
18700	LGGV	60047	2700	18W-23N	D1
21300	LGGV	60047	2646	19W-24N	C7
22500	HNWD	60047	2646	20W-25N	A6
23300	ElaT	60047	2646	20W-24N	B6
26000	FmtT	60047	2645	21W-26N	D4
26000	FmtT	60060	2645	21W-26N	D4
W Gilmer Rd CO-V76					
100	ElaT	60047	2645	21W-25N	D4
100	ElaT	60060	2645	21W-25N	D4
100	HNWD	60047	2645	21W-25N	D4
100	HNWD	60060	2645	21W-25N	D4
18700	LGGV	60047	2700	18W-23N	D1
21300	LGGV	60047	2646	19W-24N	C7
22500	HNWD	60047	2646	20W-25N	A6
23300	ElaT	60047	2646	20W-24N	B6
26000	FmtT	60047	2645	21W-26N	D4
26000	FmtT	60060	2645	21W-26N	D4
Gilmore Ct					
-	LKWD	60014	2692	38W-23N	D1
Gilmore Dr					
800	CmpT	60175	2905	41W-6N	E6
Gilmore Rd					
4500	OswT	60543	3264	33W-14S	E7
Gilmore St					
1000	AURA	60506	3137	37W-5S	C2
Gilpen Av					
1500	SEGN	60177	2854	34W-9N	D7
1500	SEGN	60177	2908	34W-9N	D1
Gilray Dr					
1300	JLET	60431	3495	32W-22S	C2
Gilson Ct					
4700	JLET	60586	3416	29W-21S	D7
Gina Dr					
300	NLNX	60451	3501	18W-25S	B6
N Ginger Cir					
2000	PLTN	60074	2753	19W-18N	C3
Ginger Ct					
-	SjnT	46311	3598		D6
10	RGMW	60008	2805	21W-14N	D5
Ginger Dr					
21400	FKFT	60423	3592	11W-25S	A1
Ginger Ln					
400	ELGN	60120	2855	31W-11N	E3
900	GNVA	60134	3019	37W-0N	D5
900	GnvT	60134	3019	37W-0N	D5
1300	NPVL	60565	3204	24W-10S	D5
1400	NLNX	60451	3588	19W-27S	D4
21200	FftT	60423	3592	11W-25S	A1
21200	FKFT	60423	3592	11W-25S	A1
Ginger Tr					
400	LKZH	60047	2699	22W-22N	A3
Gingerbrook Dr E					
-	DRGV	60515	3084	19W-2S	D4
-	DRGV	60523	3084	19W-2S	D4
700	YkTp	60523	3084	19W-3S	D5
Gingerbrook Dr N					
-	DRGV	60515	3084	19W-2S	D4
-	DRGV	60523	3084	19W-2S	D4
200	YkTp	60523	3084	19W-2S	D4
Gingerbrook Ln					
200	BRLT	60103	2911	28W-7N	A5
N Ginger Creek Dr					
1900	PLTN	60074	2753	19W-18N	C3
Ginger Creek Ln					
15100	ODPK	60467	3344	14W-18S	E7
Gingerwood Ln					
500	ElgT	60124	2907	38W-8N	A3
Ginger Woods Ct					
1400	PTHT	60070	2754	16W-16N	D6
1400	PTHT	60090	2754	16W-16N	D6
1400	WLNG	60090	2754	16W-16N	D6
Ginger Woods Dr					
2500	AURA	60502	3079	33W-3S	B7
Ginger Woods Pkwy					
1600	AraT	60502	3079	33W-4S	A7
2600	AURA	60502	3079	33W-3S	A7
Ginkgo Wy					
-	MltT	60532	3083	22W-3S	B6
Ginko Ct					
1600	MchT	60050	2526	36W-33N	C3
Ginko St					
100	BGBK	60490	3267	26W-12S	D2
Ginny Ln					
1200	WDSK	60098	2581	41W-30N	D3
Ginny Ln W					
700	YkTp	60523	3084	19W-2S	D4
Ginny E Ln					
100	YkTp	60523	3084	19W-2S	D4
Gino Ln					
10	HNWD	60047	2646	20W-24N	B7
Ginos Wy					
2300	FXLK	60020	2414	28W-39N	E5
Giordano Ct					
11100	HTLY	60142	2745	40W-20N	B1
Girard Av					
100	EVTN	60091	2813	2W-13N	B7
100	EVTN	60201	2813	2W-13N	B7
100	WLMT	60091	2813	2W-13N	B7
Girard Blvd					
10	JltT	60433	3587	23W-26S	A2
10	JltT	60436	3587	23W-26S	A2
Girot Ln					
-	BvlT	60416	3941	33W-40S	C3
-	DMND	60408	3941	33W-40S	C3
-	DMND	60416	3941	33W-40S	C3
N Gish Av					
38600	BHPK	60099	2422	10W-38N	A6
S Givins Ct					
8500	CHCG	60620	3214	0W-9S	A3
GK Ln					
10	BFGV	60089	2702	15W-21N	A5
10	LNSH	60069	2702	15W-21N	A5
10	LNSH	60089	2702	15W-21N	A5
Glacial Tr					
-	MchT	60072	2470	33W-37N	E1
-	RGWD	60072	2470	33W-37N	E1
Glacier Cir					
10	BrnT	60010	2802	28W-14N	E4
1500	CLLK	60014	2693	36W-23N	D2
Glacier Ct					
600	ROSL	60172	2913	22W-8N	C3
2100	ALGN	60102	2748	32W-20N	B1
3000	SCRL	60174	2965	33W-4N	A4
Glacier Dr					
-	WDSK	60098	2581	41W-29N	C4
400	HnrT	60107	2856	29W-11N	E4
400	SMWD	60107	2856	29W-11N	E4
Glacier Pkwy					
600	ALGN	60102	2695	32W-20N	B7
600	AlqT	60102	2695	32W-20N	B7
1100	ALGN	60102	2748	32W-20N	C1
Glacier Tr					
500	ROSL	60172	2913	22W-8N	B3
1500	CPVL	60110	2748	33W-19N	B3
Glacier Wy					
2800	WCDA	60084	2588	25W-30N	A2
2800	WcnT	60030	2588	25W-30N	A2
Glacier Park Av					
-	AURA	60504	3140	29W-6S	C5
-	AURA	60540	3140	29W-6S	C5
-	NPVL	60504	3140	29W-6S	C5
1900	NPVL	60540	3140	29W-6S	C5
Glacier Ridge Dr					
-	JLET	60586	3415	32W-21S	D7
9000	RcmT	60071	2412	33W-41N	E1
Glad Dr					
300	SchT	60175	2963	38W-3N	A6
Glad Ln					
-	HFET	60169	2858	24W-11N	E4
N Glade Av					
100	EMHT	60126	3027	17W-1N	C1
W Glade Dr					
25500	LkvT	60046	2474	25W-37N	A1
Glade Rd					
10	GLNC	60022	2758	6W-18N	D3
E Glade Rd					
10	PLTN	60067	2805	20W-15N	E2
W Glade Rd					
200	PLTN	60067	2805	21W-15N	D2
Gladiola Av					
7200	HRPK	60133	2911	27W-9N	C1
Gladiolus Dr					
200	RMVL	60446	3339	26W-17S	D6
Gladish Ln					
1200	GNVW	60025	2810	9W-13N	B6
Gladstone Av					
1200	WKGN	60085	2536	11W-33N	E2
3700	RvsT	60546	3088	9W-3S	C6
3800	LYNS	60534	3088	9W-3S	C6
3800	RvsT	60534	3088	9W-3S	C6
N Gladstone Av					
10	AURA	60506	3137	37W-7S	C6
S Gladstone Av					
10	AURA	60506	3137	37W-7S	C7
200	AURA	60506	3199	37W-7S	C1
400	AraT	60506	3199	37W-8S	C2
Gladstone Ct					
2100	GLHT	60139	2968	23W-4N	E4
2100	GLHT	60139	2969	23W-4N	A4
S Gladstone Ct					
14100	LktT	60544	3339	27W-16S	C3
Gladstone Dr					
-	LslT	60540	3205	23W-8S	A2
100	GLHT	60139	2969	23W-4N	A4
800	VNHL	60061	2647	16W-26N	D3
1900	WHTN	60187	3082	25W-2S	B4
2100	GLHT	60139	2968	24W-4N	E3
4200	GfnT	60156	2693	38W-23N	A2
7500	LslT	60565	3204	23W-8S	E2
7500	LslT	60565	3205	23W-8S	A2
Gladstone Ln					
300	ELGN	60120	2856	30W-11N	B5
400	ELGN	60120	2855	31W-10N	E5
Gladstone St					
-	BDVW	60155	3029	12W-0S	B6
-	WSTR	60155	3029	12W-0S	B6
10100	WSTR	60154	3029	12W-0S	B6
10300	HLSD	60154	3029	12W-0S	A6
10300	HLSD	60162	3029	12W-0S	A6
Gladville Av					
17700	HMWD	60430	3427	2W-21S	D6
18300	HMWD	60430	3507	2W-22S	D1
Gladys Av					
-	JLET	60421	3675	24W-29S	E1
100	FRGV	60021	2696	30W-22N	A3
3800	BLWD	60104	3029	12W-0S	A6
3800	HLSD	60104	3029	12W-0S	A6
3800	HLSD	60162	3029	12W-0S	A6
19900	JknT	60421	3675	24W-29S	E1
E Gladys Av					
100	EMHT	60126	2972	15W-2N	A7
200	ADSN	60101	2971	18W-2N	A7
W Gladys Av					
200	EMHT	60126	2971	16W-2N	D7
500	EMHT	60101	2971	17W-2N	C7
600	CHCG	60661	3034	0W-0S	A5
700	CHCG	60607	3034	0W-0S	A5
1300	CHCG	60607	3033	1W-0S	D5
2100	CHCG	60612	3033	2W-0S	B5
3800	CHCG	60624	3032	5W-0S	A5
4600	CHCG	60644	3032	5W-0S	A5
4700	CHCG	60644	3031	6W-0S	D5
Gladys Ct					
10	DRFD	60015	2757	9W-20N	B2
10	SEGN	60177	2908	35W-9N	C1
1100	WKGN	60099	2421	11W-39N	E6
Gladys Ln					
8100	HYHL	60457	3210	10W-11S	C7
8100	HYHL	60465	3210	10W-11S	B7
8100	PSHL	60465	3210	10W-11S	B7

Chicago 7-County Street Index

STREET
Block City ZIP Map# CGS Grid

Glamis Ln
100 IVNS 60067 2752 22W-16N A7
Glarus Ln
10 LYWD 60411 3510 4E-25S C7
10 LYWD 60411 3598 4E-25S B1
Glascow Ct
10 LIHL 60156 2692 38W-23N D2
Glasgow Ct
2100 HRPK 60133 2967 27W-5N C1
2700 SMBG 60194 2857 26W-10N D5
S Glasgow Dr
19700 FftT 60423 3504 9W-23S E4
Glasgow Ln
100 SMBG 60194 2857 26W-10N E5
600 PTHT 60070 2808 14W-14N B3
900 CLLK 60014 2693 37W-22N C3
Glasgow St
2500 PnfT 60435 3417 27W-20S C5
2700 JLET 60435 3417 27W-20S B5
2800 JLET 60431 3417 27W-20S B5
Glass Pointe Cir
5900 JLET 60586 3495 31W-22S E2
Glastonbury Ln
900 SMBG 60193 2912 24W-9N C1
Glastonbury St
10 MNSR 46321 3510 D3
E Glavin Ct
1000 PLTN 60074 2753 19W-18N B2
Gleason Av
800 AURA 60506 3199 36W-7S D1
Gleason Ct
- GwdT 60098 2524 41W-33N E2
Gleaston Dr
- LYWD 60411 3509 2E-23S D4
Glen Av
10 FXLK 60020 2473 27W-36N A3
10 YkTp 60148 3084 20W-2S A3
100 CLLK 60014 2640 34W-26N B3
100 WCHI 60185 3022 29W-0S C6
200 CLLK 60012 2640 34W-26N B3
400 LKBF 60044 2594 10W-28N A6
400 RMVL 60446 3340 24W-15S E1
1600 DRGV 60515 3144 20W-4S A1
Glen Blvd
- SCRL 60175 2963 37W-3N B6
Glen Cir
200 NBRN 60010 2697 25W-23N E1
N Glen Cir
1200 AURA 60506 3137 37W-6S C5
S Glen Cir
1300 AURA 60506 3137 37W-6S C5
Glen Ct
500 BMDL 60157 2913 22W-6N B6
500 YkTp 60148 3084 20W-2S A3
600 BmdT 60157 2913 21W-7N D5
700 GNVW 60025 2811 7W-13N A7
900 WKGN 60085 2536 10W-33N E3
1200 CLSM 60188 2967 27W-4N D4
Glen Dr
500 SRGV 60554 3197 42W-8S C1
1400 MHRY 60050 2527 33W-33N D3
18000 OrlT 60487 3423 11W-21S E7
N Glen Dr
33900 WrnT 60030 2533 18W-33N E2
S Glen Dr E
14300 HMGN 60491 3344 15W-17S C4
S Glen Dr W
14300 HMGN 60491 3344 15W-17S C4
W Glen Dr
3700 ALSP 60803 3276 4W-14S D6
Glen Dr N
10 WNVL 60555 3080 29W-3S E5
Glen Dr S
400 WNVL 60555 3080 29W-3S E7
Glen Ln
600 DRN 60561 3207 17W-9S C2
1100 HFET 60169 2858 25W-12N C1
Glen Pl
500 YkTp 60148 3084 20W-2S A3
Glen Rd
10 BmdT 60157 2913 21W-7N D5
100 HNWD 60047 2645 20W-24N E6
100 HNWD 60047 2646 20W-24N A6
200 DGvT 60439 3206 18W-10S E5
300 WynT 60185 3022 29W-2N D1
600 DGvT 60561 3206 18W-10S E5
600 DRN 60561 3206 18W-10S E5
S Glen Rd
11400 PlsT 60464 3272 14W-13S C5
Glen Rdg
500 CLLK 60014 2640 34W-26N D4
500 NndT 60014 2640 34W-26N D4
Glen St
100 GYLK 60030 2532 21W-32N D5
800 JLET 60432 3499 22W-22S C2
Glen Ter
18100 LNSG 60438 3429 3E-21S E6
Glen Wy
700 GRNE 60031 2534 16W-33N E3
Glen Arbor Ct
100 GNEN 60137 3025 23W-1N A3
Glenarye Dr
2700 LNHT 60046 2476 19W-37N C1
Glenayre Dr
800 GNVW 60025 2811 7W-13N A6
W Glenayre St
27600 FXLK 60041 2473 27W-35N B6
27600 GrtT 60041 2473 27W-35N B6
Glenbard Rd
400 GNEN 60137 3083 21W-1S D1
400 MltT 60137 3083 21W-1S D1
Glenbarr Ln
800 FKFT 60423 3592 9W-26S E3
W Glenbarr Ln
26200 CbaT 60010 2697 26W-21N D6
Glenberry Ln
8600 TYPK 60477 3504 10W-23S B3
Glenbriar Ct
1000 SCRL 60174 2964 34W-5N D3
Glenbriar Dr
2900 SCRL 60174 2964 34W-5N D2
Glenbrook Cir
10 GLBT 60136 2798 39W-14N E5
10 GLBT 60136 2799 39W-14N A5
11300 PNFD 60585 3266 30W-13S B5
Glenbrook Ct
100 IHPK 60525 3146 13W-6S E5
200 GLBT 60136 2799 39W-14N A5
6300 LSLE 60532 3142 25W-7S C6
24400 PNFD 60585 3266 30W-13S B5
Glenbrook Dr
10 PTHT 60070 2754 15W-16N E7
10 PTHT 60070 2755 15W-16N A7
10 WLNG 60090 2755 15W-16N A7
3200 NHBK 60062 2756 11W-17N D5
Glenbrook Ln
11000 IHPK 60525 3146 13W-6S E5
19400 TYPK 60477 3504 10W-23S C3
Glenbrook Ln E
6100 IHPK 60525 3146 13W-6S E5
Glenbrook Ln W
6100 IHPK 60525 3146 13W-6S E5
Glenbrook Pl
8100 TYPK 60477 3504 10W-23S C3
Glenbrook Rd
500 CLLK 60012 2640 33W-27N E1
Glenbrook Tr
5200 MHRY 60050 2527 34W-31N C6
5200 NndT 60050 2527 34W-31N C6
N Glenbrook Tr
100 MHRY 60050 2527 33W-32N E6
S Glenbrook Tr
100 MHRY 60050 2527 33W-31N E6
W Glenbrook Tr
4600 MHRY 60050 2527 33W-31N D6
4800 NndT 60050 2527 33W-31N D6
Glen Byrn Ct
300 SMBG 60194 2857 27W-10N D5
Glencoe Av
1200 HDPK 60035 2704 8W-21N E5
1200 HDPK 60035 2705 7W-21N B6
5000 MCCK 60525 3148 10W-5S A2
Glencoe Ct
10 NPVL 60565 3203 26W-10S D6
Glencoe Dr
800 GLNC 60022 2758 6W-18N D4
Glencoe Rd
- PltT 60067 2752 21W-17N C5
W Glencoe Rd
400 PLTN 60067 2805 21W-15N C1
700 PltT 60067 2805 21W-15N C1
Glencoe St
800 GNEN 60137 3025 23W-0N A4
800 GNEN 60187 3025 23W-1N A3
900 WHTN 60187 3025 23W-0N A5
E Glencoe St
300 PLTN 60067 2806 20W-15N A1
300 PLTN 60074 2806 20W-15N A1
Glencoe Ter
900 LKZH 60047 2698 24W-23N C2
Glencora St
- LtRT 60545 3259 47W-12S D4
- PLNO 60545 3259 47W-12S D4
Glencorse Cir
2100 JLET 60586 3416 30W-21S C7
Glen Cove Ln
600 PGGV 60140 2797 41W-14N E5
600 PGGV 60140 2798 41W-14N A5
Glen Crest Dr
600 MltT 60137 3083 21W-1S D2
Glencrest Dr
1000 IVNS 60010 2751 25W-17N B5
1100 BRTN 60010 2751 25W-17N B5
Glen Crest Ln
14800 HMGN 60491 3421 18W-18S A1
14800 HmrT 60491 3421 18W-18S A1
Glenda Ln
10 LtRT 60545 3259 48W-11S B1
Glendale Av
- CHCG 60613 2977 1W-5N D1
- CteT 60417 3774 1W-32S B1
10 HNDL 60521 3086 15W-3S A6
10 OKBK 60521 3086 15W-3S A6
10 OKBK 60523 3086 15W-3S A6
10 OSWG 60543 3263 37W-11S C2
10 OswT 60543 3263 37W-11S C2
300 HNDL 60523 3086 15W-3S A6
300 WNKA 60093 2811 5W-15N E2
300 WNKA 60093 2812 5W-15N A2
500 WHTN 60137 3025 23W-0S A6
500 WHTN 60187 3025 23W-0S A6
600 GNEN 60137 3025 23W-0S A6
1800 NHBK 60062 2757 10W-16N A7
E Glendale Av
10 HNDL 60521 3086 15W-3S A6
10 OKBK 60521 3086 15W-3S A6
10 OKBK 60523 3086 15W-3S A6
N Glendale Av
100 BRTN 60010 2751 25W-20N B2
S Glendale Av
100 BRTN 60010 2751 25W-18N B2
Glendale Blvd
10 HMND 46320 3430 C1
Glendale Ct
10 SMWD 60107 2857 27W-11N C4
2300 LNHT 60046 2476 20W-37N B3
Glendale Dr
100 BGBK 60440 3268 24W-11S C2
600 GNVW 60025 2811 7W-13N A7
600 PTHT 60070 2808 15W-15N A1
600 PTHT 60090 2808 15W-15N A1
600 WLNG 60090 2808 15W-15N A1
800 CLLK 60014 2639 36W-24N D7
4900 GRNE 60031 2478 15W-35N B6
Glen Dale Ln
15500 HMGN 60491 3421 18W-18S A1
15500 HmrT 60491 3421 18W-18S A1
Glendale Ln
200 GNVW 60025 2864 10W-12N A1
400 HFET 60169 2858 24W-11N E4
N Glendale Ln
9800 GNVW 60025 2864 10W-12N A1
9800 GNVW 60714 2864 10W-12N A1
9800 NLES 60714 2864 10W-12N A1
S Glendale Ln
600 MPPT 60056 2861 16W-12N D2
Glendale Pl
400 MDLN 60060 2590 18W-28N E6
Glendale Rd
- GNVW 60025 2810 10W-13N A6
10 BFGV 60089 2754 16W-18N C3
200 GNVW 60025 2864 10W-12N A1
200 GNVW 60714 2864 10W-12N A1
200 NLES 60714 2864 10W-12N A1
400 MaiT 60025 2810 10W-12N A7
400 ROSL 60172 2913 22W-6N C5
500 BmdT 60157 2913 22W-6N C6
500 ROSL 60157 2913 22W-6N C6
600 NfdT 60025 2810 10W-13N A7
700 BmdT 60172 2913 22W-6N C6
40000 BHPK 60099 2421 11W-40N D4
40200 ZION 60099 2421 11W-40N D4
E Glendale Rd
600 LYVL 60048 2591 15W-28N E6
W Glendale Rd
21600 ElaT 60047 2699 21W-24N C1
21600 HNWD 60047 2699 21W-24N C1
Glendale St
10 WLNG 60090 2755 14W-18N C4
900 BNVL 60106 2915 16W-5N D7
Glendale Ter
100 BMDL 60172 2913 23W-6N A7
100 BmdT 60108 2913 23W-6N B7
100 ROSL 60172 2913 23W-6N A7
300 BmdT 60157 2913 22W-6N C7
500 BmdT 60172 2912 23W-6N E7
500 ROSL 60172 2912 23W-6N E7
2300 HRPK 60133 2911 27W-8N B3
Glendale Tr
19400 TYPK 60477 3504 10W-23S B3
Glendell Av
1000 NCHI 60044 2593 11W-29N D3
1000 ShdT 60044 2593 11W-29N D3
Glendenning Pl
300 WKGN 60085 2480 10W-36N A5
300 WKGN 60087 2480 10W-36N A5
Glendenning Rd
300 KLWH 60043 2812 4W-14N C5
300 WLMT 60043 2812 4W-14N C5
300 WLMT 60091 2812 4W-14N C5
3600 YkTp 60515 3084 19W-4S D6
3800 DRGV 60515 3084 19W-3S D6
Glendower Ter
2700 ELGN 60124 2853 37W-12N C1
Gleneagle Cir
1800 ELGN 60123 2908 36W-9N A1
7300 LKWD 60014 2638 38W-24N E6
Glen Eagle Ct
13500 ODPK 60462 3346 11W-16S A2
Gleneagle Ct
1600 CPVL 60110 2746 37W-17N D6
1700 RMVL 60446 3339 27W-17S D5
Glen Eagle Dr
1000 AURA 60502 3139 32W-6S D5
Gleneagle Dr
1600 CPVL 60110 2746 37W-17N D6
1600 CPVL 60118 2746 37W-17N D7
1600 WDND 60118 2746 37W-17N D7
1700 RMVL 60446 3339 28W-17S B6
2000 JLET 60586 3416 30W-21S B7
2200 GNVA 60134 3019 37W-0N D6
S Glen Eagle Dr
22900 FftT 60423 3591 13W-27S B5
Gleneagle Ln
- BGBK 60440 3268 24W-13S E4
800 NHBK 60062 2757 8W-16N E7
Glen Eagles Ct
10 HNWD 60047 2645 22W-26N C2
500 IVNS 60067 2752 22W-16N B6
800 FKFT 60423 3592 9W-26S D2
3000 SCRL 60174 2964 34W-5N D2
Gleneagles Ct
2600 NPVL 60565 3203 27W-10S C6
Glen Eagles Dr
200 WNFD 60190 3023 26W-1N E2
2400 OMFD 60461 3507 3W-24S B5
Gleneagles Dr
2200 NPVL 60565 3203 27W-10S C6
2200 NpvT 60565 3203 27W-10S C6
Glen Eagles Ln
2200 RVWD 60015 2703 12W-20N A7
2200 RVWD 60015 2756 12W-20N A1
Gleneagles Ln
8800 DGvT 60516 3206 19W-10S E5
8800 DRN 60516 3206 19W-10S E5
8800 DRN 60561 3206 19W-10S E5
Glen Echo Rd
10 ELGN 60120 2855 31W-10N E5
10 HnrT 60120 2855 31W-11N E5
300 NPVL 60565 3204 25W-10S A5
Glen Ellyn Ln
- PLTN 60067 2752 21W-17N D6
Glen Ellyn Pl
500 GNEN 60137 3025 22W-0N C5
Glen Ellyn Rd
- GLHT 60137 3025 22W-1N C1
100 BMDL 60108 2969 22W-5N C2
100 GLHT 60139 3025 22W-2N C1
200 BmdT 60108 2969 22W-4N C4
300 BMDL 60139 2969 22W-4N C4
300 GLHT 60139 2969 22W-2N C7
400 BmdT 60101 2969 22W-3N C6
400 BmdT 60139 2969 22W-3N C6
400 GLHT 60101 2969 22W-3N C6
1300 BmdT 60139 3025 22W-2N C1
Glen Ellyn Rd CO-5
- GLHT 60137 3025 22W-1N C1
100 GLHT 60139 3025 22W-2N C1
300 BMDL 60108 2969 22W-4N C4
300 BMDL 60139 2969 22W-4N C4
300 GLHT 60139 2969 22W-2N C7
400 BmdT 60101 2969 22W-3N C6
400 BmdT 60139 2969 22W-3N C6
400 GLHT 60101 2969 22W-3N C6
1300 BmdT 60139 3025 22W-2N C1
Glen Entrance
13400 HMGN 60491 3421 16W-21S E6
Gleneyre Rd
8400 DRN 60561 3207 18W-9S A4
Glen Farm Ln
300 LKZH 60047 2699 22W-22N B4
Glen Flora Av
3400 GRNE 60031 2479 13W-35N A6
3400 GRNE 60085 2479 13W-35N A6
3400 WkgT 60085 2479 13W-35N A6
3800 GRNE 60031 2478 13W-35N E6
W Glen Flora Av
200 WKGN 60085 2480 10W-35N B6
900 WKGN 60085 2479 11W-35N E6
12800 WkgT 60085 2479 12W-35N A6
12900 GRNE 60031 2479 12W-35N A6
12900 GRNE 60085 2479 12W-35N A6
Glen Flora Dr
500 CLSM 60188 2968 25W-3N A6
Glenford Ct
1700 JLET 60586 3495 33W-21S B1
Glenford Dr
1700 JLET 60586 3495 33W-21S B1
2300 AURA 60502 3139 32W-6S C6
Glengarry Cir
20800 DRPK 60010 2698 23W-20N D7
Glengarry Ct
1600 ALGN 60102 2747 35W-20N A1
Glengarry Dr
100 BMDL 60108 2968 24W-5N C2
N Glengarry Dr
10 GNVA 60134 3020 33W-1N E3
S Glengarry Dr
10 GNVA 60134 3020 33W-1N E4
Glengarry Ln
10 SgrT 60506 3135 41W-5S E3
Glen Garry Rd
400 CRY 60013 2695 31W-23N D2
Glengary Ct
1300 WLNG 60090 2754 16W-18N D3
2300 SMBG 60194 2857 26W-10N E5
4100 HRPK 60133 2967 27W-5N C2
Glengary Dr
200 BGBK 60440 3269 23W-12S A2
1300 GLHT 60139 2969 21W-2N D7
1300 GLHT 60139 3025 23W-2N A1
Glengary Ln
1300 WLNG 60090 2754 16W-18N D3
Glengate Av
300 CHHT 60411 3508 0W-24S B5
E Glengate Av
10 CHHT 60411 3508 1W-24S A5
W Glengate Av
100 CHHT 60411 3508 1W-24S A5
200 CHHT 60411 3507 2W-24S E5
Glen Haven Ln
600 GNEN 60137 3083 22W-1S C2
600 MltT 60137 3083 22W-1S C2
Glen Hill Ct
10 GLHT 60139 3024 23W-2N E1
Glen Hill Dr
10 GLHT 60139 3024 23W-2N E1
10 GLHT 60139 3025 23W-2N A1
100 BmdT 60137 3025 23W-2N A1
100 GLHT 60137 3025 23W-2N A1
1400 GLHT 60139 2968 23W-2N E7
Glenhurst Ct
10 FRGV 60021 2696 30W-22N B4
10 WNVL 60555 3080 30W-2S C4
600 RMVL 60446 3269 23W-14S A6
Glenhurst Dr
18700 WrnT 60046 2476 18W-36N D4
Glenhurst Rd
22800 DRPK 60010 2752 22W-20N A1
Glenice Pkwy
200 FRGV 60021 2696 29W-22N B3
Glen Ivy Dr
600 ELGN 60120 2855 32W-10N D6
Glenlake Av
10 CHCG 60631 2918 9W-7N B3
10 PKRG 60068 2918 9W-7N B3
10 PKRG 60631 2918 9W-7N B3
1200 PKRG 60068 2917 10W-7N E4
9500 RSMT 60018 2917 11W-7N C3
E Glenlake Av
10 ROSL 60172 2913 23W-7N A4
W Glenlake Av
10 ROSL 60172 2913 23W-7N A4
100 ROSL 60172 2912 24W-7N E4
100 SMBG 60172 2912 24W-7N E4
1300 ITSC 60143 2913 21W-7N E4
1600 CHCG 60660 2921 2W-7N C3
2300 CHCG 60659 2921 3W-7N A3
2600 CHCG 60659 2920 3W-7N E3
4000 CHCG 60646 2920 5W-7N B3
4700 CHCG 60646 2919 5W-7N E3
7700 CHCG 60631 2918 9W-7N C3
7800 PKRG 60068 2918 9W-7N C3
7800 PKRG 60631 2918 9W-7N C3
Glen Lake Dr
100 BGBK 60440 3268 25W-11S C2
Glenlake Dr
- NfdT 60025 2809 11W-14N D4
- NfdT 60062 2809 11W-14N D4
800 CLSM 60188 2967 27W-4N C3
2000 GNVW 60025 2809 11W-14N D4
3300 GNVW 60025 2810 10W-14N A3
10800 ODPK 60467 3423 13W-18S A1
15500 ODPK 60467 3345 13W-18S A7
N Glen Lake Pl
38600 LkvT 60046 2416 23W-38N E6
Glen Lake Rd
1700 HFET 60169 2858 25W-12N C1
Glenlake St
9400 RSMT 60018 2917 11W-7N C3
Glen Leven Ct
200 SMBG 60194 2857 27W-10N D5
Glenlo Dr
4200 JLET 60586 3416 29W-21S D7
Glenmoor Ct
- MHRY 60050 2527 35W-31N A6
Glenmoor Dr
1800 WDND 60118 2800 35W-16N B1
2400 DndT 60118 2800 35W-16N B2
Glen Mor Dr
200 SRWD 60404 3496 31W-23S A4
Glenmora Dr
100 BRRG 60527 3208 15W-10S C5
Glenmora Ln
8900 BRRG 60527 3208 15W-10S C5
Glenmore Ct
800 ELGN 60124 2853 37W-12N D1
800 NPVL 60540 3142 25W-7S B7
1000 LKPT 60441 3342 21W-18S A7
1300 IVNS 60010 2751 24W-17N C5
Glenmore Dr
1700 GNOK 60048 2592 14W-30N D3
Glenmore Ln
900 ELGN 60124 2853 37W-12N C1
Glenmore Pl
400 ROSL 60172 2912 24W-6N C6
N Glenmore St
700 LKPT 60441 3342 21W-18S A7
Glenn Av
500 WLNG 60090 2755 14W-17N C6
W Glenn Av
3400 RBBN 60472 3348 4W-16S E3
Glenn Cir
11400 PNFD 60564 3265 31W-13S E5
11400 PNFD 60585 3265 31W-13S E5
11500 WldT 60564 3265 31W-13S E5
Glenn Ct
600 SMBG 60193 2859 23W-9N B7
6900 WDRG 60517 3143 22W-7S C7
Glenn Dr
400 BRRG 60527 3208 15W-10S A6
400 DGvT 60527 3208 15W-10S A6
500 NLNX 60451 3501 18W-25S A7
500 NLNX 60451 3589 18W-25S A1
1000 NCHI 60064 2536 10W-31N E6
1000 WKGN 60085 2536 10W-31N E6
N Glenn Dr
400 PLTN 60074 2753 19W-16N B6
W Glenn Ln
1200 MPPT 60056 2861 16W-11N D2
S Glenn Tr
1100 EGVV 60007 2913 21W-8N E2
W Glenn Tr
900 EGVV 60007 2913 21W-8N E2
Glennell Av
19500 MKNA 60448 3502 14W-23S D4
19700 FftT 60448 3502 14W-23S D4
Glen Oak Av
800 GNEN 60137 3025 21W-0N D5
800 MltT 60137 3025 21W-0N D5
18300 LNSG 60438 3429 3E-21S E7
Glen Oak Dr
800 SYHW 60118 2800 35W-15N B4
800 WNKA 60093 2759 5W-16N A7
1900 GNVW 60025 2811 7W-14N A4
1900 NHFD 60025 2811 7W-14N A4
2100 NHFD 60093 2811 7W-14N A4
Glen Oak Ln
1200 NHBK 60062 2757 9W-17N D5
Glenoak Ln
10 SchT 60175 2963 38W-5N B2
Glen Oak Rd
500 LMBD 60148 3026 21W-0N A4
8400 ODPK 60462 3346 10W-18S B7
Glen Oaks Ct
900 HPSR 60140 2796 45W-16N B1
900 HshT 60140 2743 45W-17N B7
900 HshT 60140 2796 45W-16N B1
2300 ALGN 60102 2748 32W-20N C1
16900 CCHL 60478 3426 4W-20S D4
Glen Oaks Dr
700 HPSR 60140 2796 45W-16N B1
700 HshT 60140 2796 45W-16N B1
16800 CCHL 60478 3426 4W-20S D4
Glen Oaks Ln
25100 SRWD 60404 3583 31W-25S E1
25100 SRWD 60404 3584 31W-25S A1
Glenoban Dr
100 NpvT 60563 3140 30W-5S C3
Glenoble Ct
10 OKBK 60523 3028 15W-1S B7
Glen Park Rd
10 DRGV 60515 3084 21W-2S A3
10 MltT 60137 3083 22W-2S C3
10 MltT 60148 3083 21W-2S A3
10 YkTp 60148 3084 21W-2S A3
100 MltT 60148 3083 21W-2S E3
200 GNEN 60137 3083 22W-2S C3
Glen Pointe Dr
- GLHT 60139 2969 23W-3N A5
Glenridge Ct
2000 JLET 60586 3415 31W-21S E7
Glenridge Dr
600 GNVW 60025 2811 7W-13N A7
Glen Ridge Ln
200 BMDL 60108 2969 22W-4N C3
Glenridge Ln
100 SMBG 60193 2857 26W-10N E6
Glenrise Av
- BmdT 60137 3025 22W-1N D1
- BmdT 60139 3025 22W-1N D1
- GLHT 60137 3025 22W-1N C2
- GLHT 60139 3025 22W-1N D1
1300 MltT 60137 3025 22W-1N C2
Glenrise Ct
100 MltT 60137 3025 22W-1N C3
Glen Rock Av
600 WKGN 60085 2537 10W-34N A2
800 WKGN 60085 2536 11W-33N E3
Glenrock Ln
1900 GLHT 60139 2969 23W-3N B5
Glenrose Ln
400 LIHL 60156 2692 38W-21N E7
S Glenroy Av
10700 CHCG 60643 3277 1W-12S E2
W Glenshire Dr
7500 FftT 60423 3504 9W-25S E7
7500 FKFT 60423 3504 9W-25S E7
Glenshire Rd
400 MaiT 60025 2810 10W-12N A7
400 NfdT 60025 2810 10W-12N A7
800 GNVW 60025 2810 10W-13N A7
Glenshire St
8600 TYPK 60477 3504 11W-23S A4
8700 MKNA 60448 3504 11W-23S A4
8700 TYPK 60448 3504 11W-23S A4
8900 FftT 60477 3504 11W-23S A4
9100 FftT 60448 3504 11W-23S A4
Glenside Cir
700 BGBK 60490 3267 26W-13S E5
Glenside Ct
900 HRPK 60133 2858 26W-9N A7
Glenside Dr
1300 BGBK 60490 3267 26W-13S E5
1300 BGBK 60490 3268 26W-13S A5
Glen Swilly Cir
18200 TYPK 60477 3425 8W-21S A7
Glen Valley Dr
10 MltT 60137 3083 22W-2S C3
200 GNEN 60137 3083 22W-2S C3
Glenview Av
500 AURA 60505 3138 34W-6S C4
500 HDPK 60035 2704 8W-22N D4
800 MDLN 60060 2590 19W-28N C6
1500 PKRG 60068 2863 11W-10N D5
5100 DRGV 60515 3144 21W-5S A3
5500 LslT 60515 3144 21W-6S A4
5500 LslT 60516 3144 21W-6S A4
N Glenview Av
10 LMBD 60148 3026 20W-0N A3
100 EMHT 60126 3027 17W-1N C1
400 EMHT 60126 2971 17W-2N C7
S Glenview Av
10 LMBD 60148 3026 20W-0N A4
Glen View Ct
15000 HmrT 60491 3420 18W-18S E1
15000 HmrT 60491 3421 18W-18S A1
Glenview Ct
10 BGBK 60490 3339 27W-15S B1
1300 RLKB 60073 2475 23W-35N A7
2200 SMBG 60194 2857 26W-11N E4
N Glenview Ct
900 PLTN 60067 2752 22W-17N C5
Glenview Dr
10 SchT 60175 2907 38W-6N A6
800 CmpT 60175 2907 38W-6N A6
6500 TYPK 60477 3425 8W-20S B4
11500 OrlT 60467 3344 14W-17S D4
Glenview Ln
10 LMNT 60439 3270 19W-14S E6
1300 BGBK 60490 3339 28W-15S E1
N Glenview Ln
300 PTON 60468 3860 9W-37S E3
Glenview Pl
100 FXLK 60020 2473 27W-36N B4
Glenview Rd
- WLMT 60091 2812 5W-13N A7
10 GNVW 60025 2811 7W-13N B7
10 GNVW 60091 2811 6W-13N D7
10 WLMT 60091 2811 6W-13N D7
1400 GNVW 60025 2810 9W-13N B6
2800 NfdT 60025 2810 9W-13N B6
3500 NfdT 60025 2809 10W-13N E6
3800 GNVW 60025 2809 11W-13N E6
Glen Vista Ln
20400 CTHL 60403 3418 25W-19S B2
20400 LktT 60403 3418 25W-19S B2

STREET Block City ZIP Map# CGS Grid

Glenway Dr
3000 GNVW 60062 2809 11W-15N D2
3100 GNVW 60025 2809 11W-15N D2
Glen Wood Av
10 GLNC 60093 2758 5W-16N E6
10 GLNC 60093 2759 5W-16N A6
Glenwood Av
100 WLSP 60480 3209 12W-9S B4
300 MchT 60051 2529 29W-32N C5
300 PlsT 60480 3209 12W-9S C4
400 GNEN 60137 3025 22W-0N B5
400 LKMR 60051 2529 29W-32N C5
500 ELGN 60120 2801 33W-13N B7
800 WKGN 60085 2479 11W-35N D7
1300 GNVW 60025 2811 8W-14N A4
1400 GNVW 60025 2810 8W-14N E4
N Glenwood Av
10 GNWD 60425 3508 0W-22S D1
4900 CHCG 60640 2921 1W-6N D6
5500 CHCG 60660 2921 1W-7N D3
6800 CHCG 60626 2921 1W-8N D1
7100 CHCG 60626 2867 1W-9N D7
W Glenwood Av
600 JLET 60435 3498 25W-23S B4
2000 JLET 60435 3497 26W-23S E4
3000 JLET 60431 3497 27W-23S B4
3000 TroT 60435 3497 27W-23S C4
Glenwood Cir
- SRGV 60506 3136 40W-5S B3
Glenwood Ct
10 BGBK 60490 3267 26W-13S E4
300 ALGN 60102 2694 34W-21N B6
2200 MchT 60051 2528 31W-33N E3
2700 NPVL 60564 3202 29W-10S D6
14900 HMGN 60491 3343 18W-18S A7
14900 HMGN 60491 3421 18W-18S A1
14900 HmrT 60491 3343 18W-18S A7
14900 HmrT 60491 3421 18W-18S A1
W Glenwood Ct
14000 GNOK 60048 2592 14W-30N D1
Glenwood Dr
- BMDL 60172 2968 25W-5N B1
10 RLKB 60073 2532 23W-34N A1
200 GnvT 60510 3077 38W-1S A2
200 RLKB 60073 2531 23W-34N E1
300 BMDL 60108 2968 25W-5N B1
500 SchT 60175 2907 36W-6N D7
12600 HTLY 60142 2744 43W-19N B3
Glenwood Ln
600 GNVW 60025 2810 10W-13N A7
600 LMBD 60148 3026 21W-1N A2
600 NfdT 60025 2810 10W-13N A7
1100 HFET 60010 2804 24W-16N C1
2200 MchT 60051 2528 31W-33N D3
6800 HRPK 60133 2912 26W-8N A2
14800 HMGN 60491 3343 18W-18S A7
14800 HMGN 60491 3421 18W-18S A1
14800 HmrT 60491 3343 18W-18S A7
14800 HmrT 60491 3421 18W-18S A1
S Glenwood Ln
600 LGNG 60525 3147 13W-5S A1
N Glenwood Pl
500 AURA 60506 3137 37W-6S C6
S Glenwood Pl
10 AURA 60506 3137 37W-7S C7
200 AURA 60506 3199 37W-8S C1
Glenwood Rd
100 GNWD 60425 3508 0W-23S C2
200 BlmT 60411 3508 0W-23S B4
200 CHHT 60411 3508 0W-23S B4
200 LKFT 60045 2650 10W-25N A6
19000 GNWD 60411 3508 0W-23S B3
19400 BlmT 60425 3508 0W-23S B3
19400 CHHT 60425 3508 0W-23S B3
E Glenwood Rd
800 GNVW 60025 2811 6W-13N D7
S Glenwood St
10 PLTN 60067 2806 20W-15N A1
Glenwood Tr
400 ELGN 60120 2801 33W-13N A7
Glenwood Dyer Rd
- GNWD 60425 3509 1E-23S B3
600 BlmT 60411 3509 2E-23S C4
600 LYWD 60411 3509 2E-23S C4
2400 BlmT 60411 3510 3E-24S A5
2400 LYWD 60411 3510 3E-24S A5
Glenwood Dyer Rd SR-83
2400 BlmT 60411 3510 3E-24S A5
2400 LYWD 60411 3509 3E-24S E5
2400 LYWD 60411 3510 3E-24S A5
E Glenwood Dyer Rd
100 BlmT 60425 3508 0E-23S E2
100 GNWD 60425 3508 0E-23S E2
400 BlmT 60425 3509 1E-23S A3
400 GNWD 60425 3509 1E-23S A3
800 BlmT 60411 3509 1E-23S B3
Glenwoodie St
10 PnfT 60435 3417 27W-20S C5
Glenwood Lansing Rd
800 BlmT 60411 3509 2E-22S C2
800 BlmT 60425 3509 1E-22S B2
800 GNWD 60411 3509 1E-22S B2
800 GNWD 60425 3509 1E-22S B2
1800 LYWD 60411 3509 2E-22S C2
2600 BlmT 60411 3510 3E-23S A2
2600 LNSG 60411 3510 4E-22S B2
2600 LNSG 60438 3510 4E-22S B2
2600 LYWD 60411 3510 3E-23S A2
3500 MNSR 46321 3510 4E-22S B2
E Glenwood Lansing Rd
- BlmT 60411 3509 1E-22S B2
- GNWD 60411 3509 1E-22S B2
200 BlmT 60425 3508 0E-22S E2
200 GNWD 60425 3508 0E-22S E2
600 BlmT 60425 3509 1E-22S A2
600 GNWD 60425 3509 1E-22S A2
E Glenwood Thornton Rd
18600 BlmT 60425 3508 0W-22S C1
18600 GNWD 60425 3508 0W-22S C1
Glenwoody Ct
8400 ODPK 60462 3346 11W-16S A2
Glenys Dr
400 LMNT 60439 3270 19W-14S E7
Gloria Av
400 WnfT 60185 3023 27W-1N D3
Gloria Cir
- EMHT 60126 3027 16W-0S D6
Gloria Ct
1500 AURA 60504 3201 32W-9S C5
2900 BtlT 60538 3198 40W-10S B6
2900 MTGY 60538 3198 40W-10S B6
3900 GNVW 60025 2809 11W-13N D6
Gloria Dr
1000 EGVV 60007 2913 21W-8N E3
E Gloria Dr
1200 PLTN 60074 2753 19W-16N D7
E Gloria Dr
1200 PLTN 60074 2806 19W-16N C1
Gloria Ln
400 OSWG 60543 3200 35W-11S A7
400 OSWG 60543 3264 36W-11S A1
3000 JLET 60435 3417 27W-19S B2
3800 PnfT 60435 3417 27W-19S B2
Gloria St
600 LKPT 60441 3419 21W-19S E2
Gloria Jean Dr
300 BNVL 60106 2972 15W-4N A3
Glory Ct
- SRWD 60404 3496 31W-24S A7
Glory Dr
- SRWD 60404 3496 31W-24S A6
Glos Av
2600 BLWD 60104 3029 12W-0N C4
Glos St
100 WYNE 60184 2965 32W-5N D2
Gloster Ct
700 GRNE 60031 2534 16W-33N D3
Gloucester Cir
1200 CLSM 60188 2967 27W-4N C4
Gloucester Cross
800 LKFT 60045 2649 12W-24N C6
Gloucester Ct
- IVNS 60010 2804 25W-15N A1
- SBTN 60010 2804 25W-15N A1
10 LNSH 60069 2702 14W-23N B3
1300 HFET 60192 2804 25W-15N A2
1700 WHTN 60187 3083 23W-2S A3
Gloucester Dr
- CRTE 60417 3596 0E-29S E7
- CRTE 60417 3685 0E-29S E1
700 EGVV 60007 2914 19W-8N C1
Gloucester Rd
1100 WDRG 60517 3206 20W-10S B6
Gloucester Wy N
200 DRGV 60515 3084 19W-3S D5
200 YkTp 60515 3084 19W-3S D5
200 YkTp 60523 3084 19W-3S D5
Gloucester Wy W
600 YkTp 60523 3084 19W-3S D5
Glouceston Ln
2200 NPVL 60564 3202 29W-10S D5
2200 WldT 60564 3202 29W-10S D5
Glouchester Cir
900 SMBG 60193 2913 22W-7N D4
Glouchester Hbr
1000 SMBG 60193 2913 23W-9N B1
Glover Dr
400 NARA 60542 3076 39W-3S E7
Glynn Rd
200 PLNO 60545 3259 47W-14S D7
Glynwood Ln
3600 HLCT 60429 3426 4W-20S D5
Godair Cir
- WLBK 60527 3146 16W-6S A5
10 DGvT 60527 3145 16W-6S E5
10 WLBK 60527 3145 16W-6S E5
700 DGvT 60527 3146 16W-6S A5
Godair Dr
- BRRG 60527 3146 16W-6S A5
10 DGvT 60527 3146 16W-6S A5
Goddard Ln
1700 HRPK 60133 2967 27W-5N D1
Godfrey Av
400 LktT 60441 3419 22W-21S C6
S Goebbert Rd
1900 ANHT 60005 2861 17W-11N B3
E Goebel Dr
10 LMBD 60148 3026 19W-1N C2
W Goebel Dr
10 LMBD 60148 3026 20W-1N B2
Goesel Dr
17900 TYPK 60487 3424 10W-21S B7
Goethe St
700 ELGN 60123 2854 34W-12N D2
E Goethe St
10 CHCG 60610 3034 0E-1N C1
W Goethe St
10 CHCG 60610 3034 0W-1N B1
N Gogol Av
34700 GrtT 60041 2472 28W-34N E7
34700 GrtT 60041 2473 28W-34N A7
Gold Cir
6100 HRPK 60133 2911 26W-7N E4
Gold St
200 PKFT 60466 3595 3W-27S A3
Gold Coast Ln
200 CTCY 60409 3430 4E-19S B2
Goldcrest Ct
10 BRLT 60107 2856 29W-9N D7
Golden Av
900 WDSK 60098 2581 42W-30N B2
1000 DrrT 60098 2581 42W-30N B2
Golden Dr
10 GLHT 60139 2968 24W-3N D5
100 CLSM 60188 2968 24W-3N D6
100 GLHT 60188 2968 24W-3N D6
N Golden Ln
1400 PnfT 60544 3338 29W-17S E5
Golden Spur
10 LMNT 60439 3272 15W-13S B5
Golden Bell Ct
1400 DRGV 60515 3084 20W-3S B6
Golden Eagle Cir
13500 PNFD 60544 3338 30W-16S B3
Golden Eagle Ct
40200 AntT 60002 2416 23W-40N E3
Golden Eagle Dr
- ALGN 60102 2693 36W-20N D7
- ALGN 60102 2746 36W-20N D1
- FftT 60467 3422 14W-22S E7
- MKNA 60467 3422 14W-22S E7
- ODPK 60467 3422 14W-22S E7
24200 PNFD 60544 3338 30W-16S B3
Goldeneye Ct
5800 LGGV 60047 2701 17W-23N B1
Goldeneye Ln
10 BmdT 60108 2968 26W-5N A2
Golden Fox Tr
- CNHN 60410 3672 33W-31S C6
Golden Gate Av
10600 HTLY 60142 2692 39W-21N B6
W Goldengate Ct
1700 ADSN 60101 2970 20W-4N A3
Golden Gate Dr
11600 FftT 60423 3590 14W-26S D2
11600 FftT 60448 3590 14W-26S E2
11600 MKNA 60448 3590 14W-26S E2
W Goldengate Dr
1400 ADSN 60101 2970 20W-4N A3
Golden Gate Ln
1800 NPVL 60563 3140 29W-6S D4
1800 NpvT 60540 3140 29W-6S C4
Golden Gate Ln
1800 NpvT 60563 3140 29W-6S C4
Golden Glow Ct
3000 NPVL 60564 3202 30W-11S A7
Golden Hawk Rd
5200 RcmT 60071 2353 34W-42N C5
5200 RHMD 60071 2353 34W-42N C5
Goldenhill St
100 BmdT 60133 2968 25W-4N B4
100 BmdT 60188 2968 25W-4N B4
100 CLSM 60133 2968 25W-4N B4
100 CLSM 60188 2968 25W-4N B4
Golden Larch Dr
10 NPVL 60540 3141 27W-7S D7
W Golden Meadow Ct
24100 PNFD 60585 3338 30W-15S C3
Golden Meadow Dr
13500 PNFD 60544 3338 30W-16S B3
13500 PNFD 60585 3338 30W-16S B3
S Golden Meadow Dr
13100 PNFD 60585 3338 30W-15S C3
13100 WldT 60585 3338 30W-15S C2
13400 PNFD 60544 3338 30W-15S C3
Golden Oak Cir
700 CLLK 60014 2640 33W-24N E7
Golden Oak Ct
8900 HYHL 60457 3209 11W-10S E5
Golden Oak Dr
1500 WDSK 60098 2582 40W-30N A2
S Golden Oak Dr
13700 HMGN 60491 3343 16W-17S E5
Golden Oak Ln
19800 MKNA 60448 3502 14W-24S D4
Golden Oaks Ln
500 CmpT 60175 2961 41W-4N E5
Golden Oaks Pkwy
1500 AURA 60506 3137 37W-5S C3
Golden Pheasant Dr
8800 TYPK 60487 3424 11W-21S A6
Golden Pond Ln
1800 WHTN 60187 3082 25W-2S B4
Golden Ridge Dr
1600 JLET 60586 3495 31W-21S D1
Golden Rod Av
600 RMVL 60446 3340 25W-15S B2
Goldenrod Cir
600 MTSN 60443 3506 5W-24S B6
Goldenrod Ct
700 CLLK 60014 2639 37W-24N B6
2300 AURA 60506 3137 38W-6S A5
N Goldenrod Ct
34300 GrtT 60073 2530 25W-34N E1
Golden Rod Dr
300 MNKA 60447 3672 33W-29S A2
Goldenrod Dr
- JLET 60447 3495 33W-22S A2
- SRGV 60554 3136 40W-7S B6
600 ALGN 60102 2693 37W-20N B7
600 BGBK 60440 3205 21W-10S E5
1300 BTVA 60510 3078 33W-1S E3
1300 NPVL 60540 3141 28W-7S A7
Golden Rod Ln
2000 JNBG 60050 2471 31W-37N E2
Goldenrod Ln
900 LKFT 60045 2703 12W-23N C1
1100 GYLK 60030 2533 19W-32N C5
1200 HFET 60192 2804 24W-15N C1
2200 GNVW 60025 2810 9W-15N B3
N Goldenrod Ln
40000 NptT 60083 2419 16W-40N E4
40000 WDWH 60083 2419 16W-40N E3
N Goldenrod Rd
34100 GrtT 60073 2530 26W-34N D1
Goldenrod Ter
1500 RLKB 60073 2474 23W-35N E6
Golden Rose Dr
8700 ODPK 60462 3424 10W-19S A1
Golden Sunset Dr
24200 PNFD 60585 3338 30W-15S B2
Golden Tree Ln
1600 JltT 60433 3587 23W-26S B2
Golden Valley Ct
10 ALGN 60102 2748 33W-19N A2
Golden Valley Ln
500 ALGN 60102 2748 33W-19N A2
Goldenwood Ct
200 AURA 60502 3139 32W-7S D7
Goldfield Ln
1200 JLET 60447 3495 33W-22S A2
Goldfinch Av
- KdlT 60560 3334 41W-17S A5
Gold Finch Cir
400 LNHT 60046 2476 19W-37N B2
Gold Finch Ct
10 HNWD 60047 2645 22W-26N C4
10 MltT 60188 3024 26W-1N A3
Goldfinch Ct
1000 ANTH 60002 2358 21W-42N E7
2700 CPVL 60110 2746 37W-18N C5
W Goldfinch Ct
21500 KLDR 60047 2699 21W-21N D5
Goldfinch Dr
3400 NPVL 60564 3266 30W-11S A1
Goldfinch Ln
600 NLNX 60451 3589 18W-27S A4
1000 ANTH 60002 2358 21W-41N E7
1200 ANTH 60002 2417 20W-41N E1
Goldfinch St
2300 WDRG 60517 3143 21W-7S E7
Gold Grove Pl
7100 DRN 60561 3144 18W-8S E7
7100 DRN 60561 3206 18W-8S E1
Goldhaber Ln
6500 JLET 60586 3415 32W-20S D4
Goldsboro Ln
- CLLK 60014 2693 37W-22N B3
Goldsmith Dr
- AURA 60563 3080 30W-4S B7
- NPVL 60563 3080 30W-4S B7
- WNVL 60563 3080 30W-4S B7
N Goldspring Ct
36200 WmT 60031 2477 17W-36N B4
Golf Av
- MchT 60051 2529 29W-32N C5
10 CNHL 60514 3145 16W-5S D2
400 MltT 60137 3025 21W-0N E5
1200 HDPK 60035 2704 9W-21N C6
3400 JLET 60451 3500 19W-22S E2
3500 NLNX 60451 3500 19W-22S E2
10000 RHMD 60071 2353 34W-41N D7
Golf Cir
1100 WHTN 60187 3082 25W-1S B1
Golf Ct
300 LYVL 60048 2591 16W-28N D7
700 LKBN 60010 2643 26W-24N D6
900 CTCY 60409 3352 4E-18S C7
Golf Ct
2100 GNVW 60025 2864 9W-12N D1
5000 MDLN 60445 3348 6W-17S A5
Golf Ctr
10 HFET 60169 2859 23W-11N A2
Golf Dr
- OKBK 60523 3086 15W-2S A3
1800 NPVL 60565 3204 25W-9S B4
W Golf Dr
7600 PSHT 60463 3346 9W-15S D1
Golf Ln
10 NtrT 60093 2812 4W-14N B3
10 WNKA 60093 2812 4W-15N B3
300 ALGN 60102 2695 32W-20N A7
300 ALGN 60102 2748 32W-20N A1
400 LKFT 60045 2649 11W-26N E3
600 LKBN 60010 2643 26W-24N D6
700 BNVL 60106 2915 16W-6N D6
800 WHTN 60187 3082 25W-1S B1
4200 LGGV 60047 2700 18W-22N E4
5900 DrrT 60014 2639 37W-26N A3
39800 LkvT 60002 2416 24W-39N C4
Golf Pl
- RGMW 60008 2860 19W-12N D2
Golf Rd
- ELGN 60120 2855 31W-12N E2
- EVTN 60203 2866 4W-11N D2
- HFET 60010 2856 29W-11N E3
- HFET 60010 2857 28W-12N A3
- HFET 60120 2856 31W-12N A2
- HnrT 60120 2855 31W-12N E2
- RGMW 60173 2860 20W-12N A2
- SKOK 60029 2865 8W-12N A1
- SKOK 60053 2865 8W-12N A1
- SMBG 60173 2860 20W-12N A2
- TVLY 60013 2695 31W-22N D3
- WKGN 60085 2480 10W-36N A5
500 CLLK 60014 2639 36W-25N D5
500 HFET 60192 2856 31W-12N A2
500 HnrT 60120 2856 31W-12N A2
500 HnrT 60192 2856 30W-11N B3
700 WKGN 60087 2480 10W-36N A5
1100 ANHT 60005 2860 19W-11N C2
1100 RGMW 60008 2860 19W-11N C2
1700 GNVW 60025 2864 9W-12N C2
1700 GNVW 60053 2864 9W-12N C2
1700 MNGV 60053 2864 9W-12N C2
1700 WKGN 60087 2479 11W-36N D4
2100 RGMW 60007 2860 19W-12N C2
2400 MaiT 60025 2864 9W-12N C2
2400 MaiT 60053 2864 9W-12N C2
2500 JLET 60432 3500 20W-22S C2
2500 MaiT 60714 2864 9W-12N B2
2500 NlxT 60432 3500 20W-22S C2
2800 EGvT 60007 2860 19W-12N C2
2800 EGvT 60008 2860 19W-12N B2
2900 JLET 60451 3500 20W-22S C2
3300 EVTN 60201 2866 4W-11N D2
3300 SKOK 60201 2866 4W-11N D2
3300 SKOK 60203 2866 4W-11N D2
3400 BKFD 60513 3088 10W-3S B5
3400 BKFD 60546 3088 10W-3S B5
3400 RVSD 60546 3088 10W-3S B5
4000 SKOK 60076 2866 5W-11N A2
4700 SKOK 60076 2865 5W-12N E2
4700 SKOK 60077 2865 8W-12N A1
6100 GLF 60029 2865 8W-12N A1
6100 GLF 60053 2865 8W-12N A1
6100 MNGV 60029 2865 7W-12N B2
6100 MNGV 60053 2865 8W-12N A1
6700 GLF 60025 2864 8W-12N E2
6700 GLF 60029 2864 8W-12N E2
6700 GLF 60053 2864 8W-12N E2
6800 MNGV 60025 2864 8W-12N E2
9200 MaiT 60016 2863 11W-12N C2
9200 NLES 60016 2863 11W-12N C2
9200 NLES 60714 2863 11W-12N C2
9500 DSPN 60016 2863 11W-12N C2
10500 ODPK 60462 3345 13W-17S A5
Golf Rd CO-A19
- WKGN 60085 2480 10W-36N A5
700 WKGN 60087 2480 10W-36N A5
1100 WKGN 60087 2479 11W-36N E4
Golf Rd SR-58
- ELGN 60120 2855 31W-12N E2
- HFET 60010 2856 29W-11N E3
- HFET 60010 2857 28W-12N A3
- HFET 60120 2856 31W-12N A2
- HnrT 60120 2855 31W-12N E2
- RGMW 60173 2860 20W-12N A2
- SMBG 60173 2860 20W-12N A2
500 HFET 60192 2856 31W-12N A2
500 HnrT 60120 2856 31W-12N A2
500 HnrT 60192 2856 30W-11N B3
1100 ANHT 60005 2860 19W-11N C2
1100 RGMW 60008 2860 19W-11N C2
1700 GNVW 60025 2864 9W-12N C2
1700 GNVW 60053 2864 9W-12N C2
1700 MNGV 60053 2864 9W-12N C2
2100 EGvT 60007 2860 19W-12N C2
2100 RGMW 60007 2860 19W-12N C2
2400 MaiT 60025 2864 9W-12N C2
2400 MaiT 60053 2864 9W-12N C2
2500 MaiT 60714 2864 9W-12N B2
2800 EGvT 60008 2860 19W-12N B2
6900 MNGV 60025 2864 8W-12N E2
9200 MaiT 60016 2863 11W-12N C2
9200 NLES 60016 2863 11W-12N C2
9200 NLES 60714 2863 11W-12N C2
9500 DSPN 60016 2863 11W-12N C2
E Golf Rd
10 ANHT 60005 2861 17W-11N A2
10 HFET 60169 2859 22W-12N C2
10 HFET 60173 2859 23W-12N A2
10 HFET 60195 2859 23W-12N A2
10 SMBG 60169 2859 22W-12N C2
10 SMBG 60173 2859 22W-12N C2
10 SMBG 60195 2859 23W-12N A2
500 DSPN 60016 2862 13W-12N D2
500 LYVL 60048 2591 16W-27N E7
600 MPPT 60005 2861 17W-11N B2
600 MPPT 60056 2861 17W-11N B2
1300 DSPN 60016 2863 12W-12N A2
1700 MaiT 60016 2863 12W-12N A2
1800 SMBG 60173 2860 21W-12N A2
2000 EGvT 60007 2860 21W-12N A2
2000 EGvT 60008 2860 21W-12N A2
2000 RGMW 60008 2860 21W-12N A2
2000 RGMW 60173 2860 20W-12N A2
E Golf Rd SR-58
10 ANHT 60005 2861 18W-11N A2
10 HFET 60169 2859 22W-12N C2
10 HFET 60173 2859 23W-12N A2
10 HFET 60195 2859 23W-12N A2
10 SMBG 60169 2859 22W-12N C2
10 SMBG 60173 2859 22W-12N C2
E Golf Rd SR-58
10 SMBG 60195 2859 23W-12N A2
500 DSPN 60016 2862 13W-12N D2
600 MPPT 60005 2861 17W-11N B2
600 MPPT 60056 2861 17W-11N B2
1300 DSPN 60016 2863 12W-12N A2
1700 MaiT 60016 2863 12W-12N A2
1800 SMBG 60173 2860 21W-12N A2
2000 EGvT 60007 2860 21W-12N A2
2000 EGvT 60008 2860 21W-12N A2
2000 RGMW 60008 2860 21W-12N A2
2000 RGMW 60173 2860 20W-12N A2
W Golf Rd
- HFET 60010 2857 27W-12N C3
10 ANHT 60005 2861 18W-12N A2
10 DSPN 60016 2862 15W-11N B3
10 HFET 60169 2859 23W-12N A2
10 HFET 60173 2859 23W-12N A2
10 HFET 60195 2859 23W-12N A2
10 MPPT 60016 2862 15W-11N B3
10 MPPT 60056 2862 15W-11N B3
10 SMBG 60169 2859 23W-12N A2
10 SMBG 60173 2859 23W-12N A2
10 SMBG 60195 2859 23W-12N A2
100 LYVL 60048 2591 16W-28N D7
200 SMBG 60195 2858 23W-12N E2
300 DSPN 60016 2861 16W-11N E3
300 DSPN 60056 2862 15W-11N B2
300 HFET 60169 2858 25W-12N C2
300 HFET 60195 2858 23W-12N E2
300 MPPT 60016 2861 16W-11N E3
500 ANHT 60005 2860 18W-11N E2
600 SMBG 60194 2858 24W-12N D2
700 RGMW 60008 2860 18W-12N E2
900 HFET 60194 2858 24W-12N D2
1600 SMBG 60169 2858 25W-12N B2
1900 MPPT 60056 2861 17W-11N C2
2000 MPPT 60005 2861 16W-11N E3
2100 HFET 60169 2857 28W-12N B3
2100 HFET 60194 2857 28W-12N B3
2100 SMBG 60194 2857 28W-12N B3
8000 MaiT 60025 2864 10W-12N A2
8000 MaiT 60053 2864 10W-12N A2
8000 MaiT 60714 2864 10W-12N A2
8000 MNGV 60053 2864 10W-12N A2
8000 NLES 60714 2864 10W-12N A2
8100 MaiT 60016 2864 10W-12N A2
8500 NLES 60016 2864 10W-12N A2
8600 MaiT 60016 2863 11W-12N E2
8700 MaiT 60714 2863 11W-12N E2
8700 NLES 60016 2863 11W-12N E2
8700 NLES 60714 2863 11W-12N E2
W Golf Rd SR-58
- HFET 60010 2857 27W-12N C3
10 ANHT 60005 2861 18W-12N A2
10 DSPN 60016 2862 15W-11N B3
10 HFET 60169 2859 23W-12N A2
10 HFET 60173 2859 23W-12N A2
10 HFET 60195 2859 23W-12N A2
10 MPPT 60016 2862 15W-11N B3
10 MPPT 60056 2862 15W-11N B3
10 SMBG 60169 2859 23W-12N A2
10 SMBG 60173 2859 23W-12N A2
10 SMBG 60195 2859 23W-12N A2
200 SMBG 60195 2858 23W-12N E2
300 DSPN 60016 2861 16W-11N E3
300 DSPN 60056 2862 15W-11N B2
300 HFET 60169 2858 25W-12N B2
300 HFET 60195 2858 23W-12N E2
300 MPPT 60016 2861 16W-11N E3
300 MPPT 60056 2861 16W-11N E3
300 SMBG 60169 2858 23W-12N E2
500 ANHT 60005 2860 18W-11N E2
600 SMBG 60194 2858 24W-12N D2
700 RGMW 60008 2860 18W-12N E2
900 HFET 60194 2858 24W-12N D2
2000 MPPT 60005 2861 16W-11N E3
2100 HFET 60169 2857 28W-12N B3
2100 HFET 60194 2857 28W-12N B3
2100 SMBG 60194 2857 28W-12N B3
8000 MaiT 60025 2864 10W-12N A2
8000 MaiT 60053 2864 10W-12N A2
8000 MaiT 60714 2864 10W-12N A2
8000 MNGV 60053 2864 10W-12N A2
8000 NLES 60714 2864 10W-12N A2
8100 MaiT 60016 2864 10W-12N A2
8500 NLES 60016 2864 10W-12N A2
8600 MaiT 60016 2863 11W-12N E2
8700 MaiT 60714 2863 11W-12N E2
8700 NLES 60016 2863 11W-12N E2
8700 NLES 60714 2863 11W-12N E2
Golf St
2700 PnfT 60435 3417 27W-20S C6
Golf Ter
100 WLMT 60091 2813 2W-13N A6
9600 MaiT 60016 2863 11W-12N E2
9600 MaiT 60714 2863 11W-12N E2
9600 NLES 60714 2863 11W-12N E2
E Golf Ter
10 ANHT 60005 2861 18W-12N A2
Golf Club Ln
600 FKFT 60423 3592 9W-26S D1
Golf Course Rd
- LIHL 60014 2693 36W-22N D4
- LIHL 60156 2693 36W-22N D4
800 CLLK 60014 2639 36W-24N D7
1000 CLLK 60014 2693 36W-23N C1
N Golf Cul de Sac St
800 DSPN 60016 2862 14W-12N D2
S Golf Cul de Sac St
800 DSPN 60016 2862 13W-12N D2
Golfers Ln
500 BRLT 60103 2910 31W-9N A1
E Golfhurst Av
800 MPPT 60056 2862 15W-11N B2
Golf Ln Dr
38000 WDWH 60083 2478 14W-38N C1
38000 WKGN 60083 2478 14W-38N C1
Golf Mill Ctr
100 MaiT 60016 2864 10W-11N A2
100 MaiT 60714 2864 10W-11N A2
100 NLES 60016 2864 10W-11N A2
100 NLES 60714 2864 10W-11N A2
Golfmoor Av
2900 WKGN 60087 2479 12W-36N B4
2900 WkgT 60087 2479 12W-36N B4
Golfmoor St
300 CTHL 60403 3417 27W-20S C6
300 PnfT 60435 3417 27W-20S C6
W Golfmoor St
12600 WKGN 60087 2479 12W-36N B4
12600 WkgT 60087 2479 12W-36N B4
Golf Ridge Cir
2400 NPVL 60563 3140 30W-5S A3
Golf Trail Ct
2400 AURA 60506 3136 39W-6S E4

Chicago 7-County Street Index

STREET Block	City	ZIP	Map#	CGS	Grid
Golfview Av					
17500	HLCT	60430	3427	2W-21S	C5
17500	HMWD	60430	3427	2W-21S	C5
18600	HMWD	60430	3507	2W-22S	C1
W Golfview Av					
25400	AntT	60002	2416	25W-40N	A4
Golf View Cir					
100	PTHT	60070	2808	14W-14N	C4
Golf View Ct					
10	BGBK	60440	3205	22W-10S	C7
Golfview Ct					
-	VNHL	60061	2647	16W-25N	D5
10	CPVL	60110	2748	32W-17N	D7
10	RLKB	60073	2475	23W-35N	A6
300	BMDL	60108	2969	22W-4N	D3
300	SchT	60175	2963	38W-5N	A1
1500	GLHT	60139	2968	24W-2N	D7
2000	WHTN	60187	3082	23W-2S	E4
2500	WKGN	60087	2480	10W-36N	B3
N Golfview Ct					
10	GLHT	60139	2968	24W-2N	E7
S Golfview Ct					
10	GLHT	60139	2968	24W-2N	E7
Golf View Dr					
-	LSLE	60532	3142	23W-7S	E6
400	CLLK	60014	2641	33W-24N	A6
1200	DGvT	60517	3206	20W-8S	B2
1200	WDRG	60517	3206	20W-8S	B2
1400	BRLT	60103	2910	30W-9N	A1
16000	HmrT	60441	3420	20W-20S	C5
16000	LKPT	60441	3420	20W-20S	C5
Golfview Dr					
-	HLCT	60430	3506	4W-22S	E1
-	HMWD	60429	3506	4W-22S	E1
-	HMWD	60430	3506	4W-22S	E1
10	GLHT	60139	2968	24W-2N	D7
10	NHLK	60164	2972	14W-2N	C7
100	CLSM	60188	2968	24W-2N	D7
100	GLHT	60188	2968	24W-2N	D7
400	MltT	60137	3083	21W-2S	D4
400	RLKB	60073	2474	24W-35N	D6
500	NBRN	60010	2697	26W-23N	E2
700	BmdT	60157	2913	22W-7N	C4
700	ROSL	60157	2913	22W-7N	C4
700	ROSL	60172	2913	22W-7N	C4
1600	DRN	60561	3206	18W-9S	E3
1600	DRN	60561	3207	18W-9S	A3
2300	JLET	60435	3417	27W-21S	C6
2300	PnfT	60435	3417	27W-21S	C6
2700	NPVL	60563	3140	31W-5S	A2
6000	GRNE	60031	2534	16W-33N	D3
6800	CTSD	60525	3146	13W-7S	E7
8400	ODPK	60462	3346	10W-17S	B5
8400	OrlT	60462	3346	10W-17S	B5
12500	HTLY	60142	2744	42W-19N	C3
18600	HLCT	60429	3506	4W-22S	E1
E Golfview Dr					
800	MPPT	60056	2862	15W-11N	B2
W Golfview Dr					
10	RLKB	60073	2475	23W-35N	A6
200	RLKB	60073	2474	23W-35N	E6
28600	AntT	60081	2414	28W-39N	D5
28600	FXLK	60081	2414	28W-39N	D5
28700	BtnT	60081	2414	28W-39N	D5
Golf View Ln					
10	FKFT	60423	3593	9W-26S	A2
10	RchT	60443	3593	9W-26S	A2
Golfview Ln					
10	CPVL	60110	2748	32W-17N	C7
10	CPVL	60110	2801	32W-16N	D1
10	LKBN	60010	2697	27W-23N	C3
100	EDND	60110	2801	32W-16N	D1
100	EDND	60118	2801	32W-16N	D1
1100	FSMR	60422	3507	2W-23S	C3
1100	GNVW	60025	2811	7W-13N	A6
S Golfview Ln					
12800	PSHT	60463	3275	8W-15S	B7
12800	PSHT	60463	3347	8W-15S	A1
W Golfview Ln					
6700	PSHT	60463	3347	8W-15S	A1
S Golfview Pl					
800	MPPT	60056	2862	15W-11N	B2
900	DSPN	60016	2862	15W-11N	B2
900	MPPT	60016	2862	15W-11N	B2
Golf View Rd					
-	BKFD	60513	3088	10W-2S	A4
-	BKFD	60546	3088	10W-2S	A4
-	SgrT	60506	3136	41W-6S	A4
10	SRGV	60506	3136	41W-6S	A4
3200	MHRY	60050	2528	32W-32N	C4
Golfview Rd					
10	LKZH	60047	2698	24W-23N	C1
900	GNVW	60025	2811	7W-13N	A6
Golfview St					
1200	AraT	60506	3199	37W-8S	C2
Golfview Ter					
-	WhlT	60089	2754	16W-17N	C4
10	BFGV	60089	2754	16W-18N	C3
10	WLNG	60089	2754	16W-18N	C3
10	WLNG	60090	2754	16W-18N	C3
800	WhlT	60004	2754	17W-17N	C4
3200	MHRY	60050	2528	32W-32N	C4
W Golfview Ter					
200	PLTN	60067	2752	21W-17N	D6
Gombis Dr					
-	HMGN	60491	3421	18W-21S	A6
-	HmrT	60491	3421	18W-21S	A6
Goneaway Ct					
1400	WHTN	60187	3082	25W-1S	A2
Goneaway Ln					
1600	WHTN	60187	3082	26W-1S	A2
Good Av					
200	DSPN	60016	2863	11W-11N	C3
200	MaiT	60016	2863	11W-11N	C3
1700	PKRG	60068	2863	11W-10N	C4
Good Ct					
200	DSPN	60016	2863	11W-11N	C2
Goodenow Av					
-	CteT	60417	3774	1W-32S	B1
E Goodenow Rd					
100	CteT	60401	3774	0E-33S	E2
W Goodenow Rd					
10	CteT	60401	3774	1W-33S	A2
500	CteT	60417	3774	1W-33S	A2
Goodhue Ln					
4700	JLET	60586	3416	30W-21S	C7
E Goodman Av					
10	LGNG	60525	3147	12W-4S	C1
W Goodman Av					
10	LGNG	60525	3147	13W-4S	A1
1400	WNSP	60525	3147	13W-4S	A1
1400	WNSP	60558	3147	13W-4S	A1
Goodman Ct					
700	BNHL	60010	2802	30W-15N	A2
700	BNHL	60118	2802	30W-15N	A2

STREET Block	City	ZIP	Map#	CGS	Grid
W Goodman St					
5600	CHCG	60630	2919	7W-6N	C6
Goodnow Blvd					
200	RDLK	60073	2531	23W-33N	E2
Goodrich Av					
100	GLHT	60139	3025	22W-2N	C1
500	MltT	60137	3025	22W-1N	C2
600	BmdT	60137	3025	22W-1N	C2
600	BmdT	60139	3025	22W-1N	C2
600	GLHT	60137	3025	22W-1N	C2
600	SchT	60174	2908	35W-6N	B6
E Goodrich Av					
2600	BNHM	60633	3351	3E-16S	E4
2700	BNHM	60633	3352	3E-16S	A4
W Goodrich Pl					
800	PLTN	60067	2752	22W-17N	B6
Goodridge Ter					
200	BmdT	60108	2912	23W-6N	E7
200	BmdT	60172	2912	23W-6N	E7
200	ROSL	60172	2912	23W-6N	E7
Good Speed Ln					
2300	SMBG	60194	2857	26W-11N	E3
Goodview Av					
1100	JNBG	60051	2472	30W-35N	B6
Goodwin Dr					
500	BGBK	60440	3205	22W-11S	C7
600	PKRG	60068	2863	11W-9N	C6
N Goodwin Dr					
1800	PLTN	60074	2753	19W-18N	C3
Goodwin Pl					
100	MDLN	60060	2590	18W-28N	D6
Goose Ln					
17000	LKPT	60441	3420	21W-20S	A4
Goose Lake Dr					
10	BNHL	60010	2750	27W-17N	A5
16200	LktT	60403	3417	26W-19S	E3
Gooseneck Ct					
400	DRN	60527	3145	17W-7S	C6
Gopher Ct					
300	CmpT	60175	2961	43W-6N	B1
Gordon Av					
200	RMVL	60446	3340	24W-16S	E3
200	RMVL	60446	3341	23W-16S	A3
400	CTCY	60409	3352	4E-17S	B6
1300	CTCY	60409	3430	4E-19S	B2
Gordon Ct					
200	ELGN	60123	2854	35W-10N	B5
400	WldT	60564	3203	28W-10S	A5
1900	DRN	60516	3206	18W-8S	E2
Gordon Dr					
500	CRTE	60417	3685	1W-30S	B3
2400	FSMR	60422	3507	3W-22S	B1
Gordon Ln					
100	ElgT	60177	2908	33W-8N	E3
100	SEGN	60177	2908	33W-8N	E3
1200	LMNT	60439	3342	20W-15S	C2
1300	HmrT	60441	3342	20W-15S	C2
N Gordon Pl					
700	JLET	60435	3498	25W-23S	B3
Gordon Rd					
-	BtlT	60512	3198	41W-10S	A7
-	BtlT	60538	3198	41W-10S	A7
-	MTGY	60506	3198	40W-9S	B5
-	MTGY	60538	3198	40W-9S	B5
200	AURA	60506	3136	40W-7S	B7
200	SRGV	60506	3136	40W-7S	B7
200	SRGV	60554	3136	40W-7S	B7
Gordon St					
-	NLNX	60451	3501	18W-23S	A4
10	EGVV	60007	2861	18W-10N	A5
1200	NlxT	60451	3501	18W-23S	A4
Gordon Ter					
400	NpvT	60563	3140	30W-5S	B3
600	UYPK	60466	3684	3W-29S	B2
800	WNKA	60093	2758	5W-16N	E7
1000	DRFD	60015	2756	11W-20N	C2
W Gordon Ter					
600	CHCG	60613	2977	1W-5N	E1
600	CHCG	60613	2978	0W-5N	A1
Gordon Johnston Dr					
100	HDPK	60037	2704	8W-23N	E2
Gore St					
10	BTVA	60510	3020	35W-0S	B7
Gorham Ct					
100	NARA	60542	3138	35W-4S	B1
N Gorham Ln					
15700	WDWH	60099	2361	15W-42N	A5
W Gorman Ct					
6600	MONE	60449	3682	8W-32S	B7
Gorman Dr					
100	RMVL	60446	3340	24W-16S	E4
S Gorman Tr					
26300	MONE	60449	3682	8W-32S	B7
26300	MonT	60449	3682	8W-32S	B7
Goshawk Ln					
300	VrnT	60015	2755	14W-20N	B1
Goss Av					
4000	SRPK	60176	2973	12W-5N	B2
Goss Ct					
1800	JLET	60586	3416	29W-21S	D7
Gosselin Cir					
800	BTVA	60510	3078	36W-2S	A4
N Gossell Rd					
25000	FmtT	60060	2588	24W-28N	C5
25000	FmtT	60084	2588	24W-28N	C5
25000	WCDA	60060	2588	24W-28N	C5
25000	WCDA	60084	2588	25W-29N	A3
29300	WcnT	60084	2588	25W-29N	A3
30400	WcnT	60030	2587	25W-30N	E2
30400	WcnT	60084	2587	25W-30N	E2
Gostlin St					
10	BNHM	60633	3352		C4
10	HMND	46327	3352		C4
Gostlin St SR-312					
10	BNHM	60633	3352		C4
10	HMND	46327	3352		C4
E Gostlin St					
300	HMND	46327	3352		E4
Gottschalk Av					
17800	HMWD	60430	3427	2W-21S	D7
18400	HMWD	60430	3507	2W-22S	D1
N Gougar Rd					
10	JLET	60432	3500	20W-22S	C1
10	JLET	60451	3500	20W-22S	C1
800	NlxT	60451	3500	20W-22S	C1
15900	HmrT	60441	3420	19W-19S	C2
15900	HmrT	60491	3420	19W-19S	C2
16100	LKPT	60441	3420	19W-20S	C5
17500	NLNX	60441	3420	19W-21S	C6
17700	HmrT	60432	3420	20W-21S	C7
17900	HmrT	60432	3500	19W-21S	C1
17900	HmrT	60441	3500	19W-21S	C1
17900	NLNX	60441	3500	20W-22S	C1
17900	NlxT	60432	3500	20W-22S	C1
17900	NlxT	60441	3500	19W-22S	C1
19100	NLNX	60451	3500	19W-23S	C3

STREET Block	City	ZIP	Map#	CGS	Grid
S Gougar Rd					
-	JLET	60432	3500	20W-25S	D7
-	JLET	60451	3500	19W-23S	C4
-	NlxT	60432	3500	20W-25S	D7
200	NLNX	60433	3500	20W-25S	D7
200	NLNX	60451	3500	19W-24S	D5
200	NlxT	60433	3500	19W-24S	D5
15100	HmrT	60441	3342	20W-18S	C7
15100	HmrT	60491	3342	20W-18S	C7
15100	LKPT	60441	3342	20W-18S	C7
15100	LKPT	60491	3342	20W-18S	C7
15300	HmrT	60491	3420	20W-18S	C1
15600	HmrT	60441	3420	19W-19S	C1
21300	NLNX	60433	3588	19W-26S	D3
21300	NLNX	60451	3588	19W-26S	D3
21300	NlxT	60433	3588	19W-26S	D3
21300	NlxT	60451	3500	20W-25S	D7
21300	NlxT	60451	3588	19W-26S	D3
24700	MHTN	60442	3677	20W-30S	D3
24700	MhtT	60442	3677	20W-32S	D7
26300	MHTN	60442	3766	20W-33S	D3
26300	MhtT	60442	3766	20W-33S	D3
28000	WltT	60442	3766	20W-35S	D7
Gould Av					
1200	JLET	60432	3499	22W-22S	D2
Gould Ct					
2100	JltT	60436	3497	26W-25S	E7
2100	RKDL	60436	3497	26W-25S	E7
2100	RKDL	60436	3585	26W-25S	E1
Gould Ctr					
10	EGvT	60007	2860	19W-12N	C2
10	EGvT	60008	2860	19W-12N	C2
10	RGMW	60008	2860	19W-12N	C2
Gould St					
500	BCHR	60401	3864	1W-36S	B2
700	WDSK	60098	2581	41W-30N	C1
E Gould St					
100	BCVL	60407	4030	33W-44S	A4
N Gould St					
300	GRNE	60031	2535	13W-34N	E1
400	GRNE	60031	2478	13W-34N	E7
W Gould St					
100	BCVL	60407	4030	34W-44S	A4
Gouwens Ln					
15500	DLTN	60419	3351	0E-18S	A7
15500	DLTN	60473	3351	0E-18S	A7
15500	SHLD	60473	3350	0E-18S	E7
15500	SHLD	60473	3351	0E-18S	A7
Government Ln					
25100	PNFD	60544	3337	31W-17S	E5
Governors Ct					
100	HNWD	60047	2645	22W-25N	A5
Governors Dr					
400	SMBG	60193	2858	23W-9N	E7
19900	FSMR	60422	3506	4W-24S	E5
19900	OMFD	60461	3506	4W-24S	E5
Governors Hwy					
800	FSMR	60422	3507	3W-22S	A2
2000	EHZC	60429	3427	2W-20S	D5
2000	EHZC	60430	3427	2W-20S	D5
17500	HLCT	60429	3427	3W-21S	B7
17500	HLCT	60430	3427	3W-21S	B7
17500	HMWD	60429	3427	3W-21S	B7
17500	HMWD	60430	3427	3W-21S	B7
18300	HMWD	60430	3507	3W-22S	A2
18400	HMWD	60422	3507	3W-22S	A2
19400	RchT	60422	3507	4W-23S	A3
19600	FSMR	60422	3506	4W-25S	D7
19600	RchT	60422	3506	4W-25S	D7
19800	OMFD	60461	3506	4W-23S	E4
21100	MTSN	60443	3506	5W-25S	D7
21100	OMFD	60461	3506	5W-25S	D7
21400	MTSN	60443	3594	5W-25S	D1
21800	RNPK	60443	3594	4W-26S	D2
21800	RNPK	60471	3594	5W-27S	D4
22500	RchT	60471	3594	5W-27S	D4
23100	UYPK	60449	3594	5W-27S	C5
23100	UYPK	60466	3594	5W-27S	C5
23300	MonT	60449	3594	5W-28S	B7
S Governors Hwy					
400	PTON	60468	3861	9W-37S	A4
24000	MonT	60449	3594	5W-29S	B7
24000	MonT	60449	3683	6W-29S	B1
24000	MonT	60466	3683	6W-29S	B1
24000	UYPK	60449	3594	5W-29S	B7
24000	UYPK	60449	3683	6W-29S	B1
24000	UYPK	60466	3683	6W-29S	B1
25100	UYPK	60449	3683	6W-30S	A3
25300	MONE	60449	3683	6W-30S	A4
25600	MONE	60449	3682	7W-32S	E7
26200	MonT	60449	3682	7W-32S	E7
29900	PtnT	60468	3861	9W-36S	A2
29900	WltT	60468	3861	8W-36S	A2
S Governors Hwy SR-50					
-	MonT	60466	3683	6W-29S	B2
-	UYPK	60466	3683	6W-29S	B2
400	PTON	60468	3861	9W-37S	A4
25100	MonT	60449	3683	6W-30S	A3
25100	UYPK	60449	3683	6W-30S	A3
25300	MONE	60449	3683	6W-30S	A4
25600	MONE	60449	3682	7W-32S	E7
26200	MonT	60449	3682	7W-32S	E7
29900	PtnT	60468	3861	9W-36S	A2
29900	WltT	60468	3861	8W-36S	A2
Governors Ln					
200	ELGN	60123	2854	36W-11N	A3
1800	HFET	60169	2858	25W-12N	A1
1900	HFET	60169	2857	26W-12N	E1
W Governors Pkwy					
-	CHCG	60624	3032	4W-0N	D4
Governors Tr					
200	YkTp	60523	3084	19W-2S	D4
Governors Wy					
100	HNWD	60047	2645	23W-25N	A5
W Go Wando Av					
600	MPPT	60056	2861	16W-12N	D1
Gowdey Rd					
1800	NPVL	60563	3140	29W-5S	C4
1900	NpvT	60563	3140	29W-5S	C4
Grace Av					
-	ZION	60099	2421	12W-40N	B3
10	NARA	60542	3077	36W-4S	E7
10	NARA	60542	3137	36W-4S	E1
500	MDLN	60060	2590	18W-28N	E7
1000	AURA	60506	3199	37W-8S	D2
N Grace Av					
10	PKRG	60068	2918	8W-8N	D1
900	PKRG	60068	2864	10W-9N	A6
8100	NLES	60714	2864	10W-10N	A5
S Grace Av					
100	EMHT	60126	3027	16W-1N	D3
1600	PKRG	60068	2918	10W-7N	A4
13900	RBBN	60472	3348	4W-16S	D4
Grace Ct					
10	BGBK	60440	3205	23W-10S	A6
100	AURA	60505	3138	35W-7S	C7

STREET Block	City	ZIP	Map#	CGS	Grid
Grace Ct					
100	AURA	60505	3200	35W-7S	C1
600	NLNX	60451	3502	15W-25S	C7
700	SMBG	60193	2858	24W-9N	D7
1000	MRGO	60152	2634	49W-25N	B4
1200	DRGV	60516	3144	20W-7S	B7
Grace Dr					
-	YKVL	60560	3333	42W-14S	E1
400	LIHL	60156	2694	34W-21N	C5
S Grace Dr					
1000	MPPT	60056	2861	16W-11N	D3
Grace Ln					
-	AntT	60002	2416	25W-40N	A3
100	BRTN	60010	2751	24W-18N	C3
100	CHHT	60411	3507	1W-23S	E4
100	FRGV	60021	2696	30W-22N	A3
100	PltT	60010	2751	24W-18N	C3
500	SMBG	60193	2858	24W-9N	D7
800	LKVL	60046	2474	24W-37N	D2
3800	GNVW	60025	2809	11W-14N	D5
S Grace Pl					
100	HPSR	60140	2796	46W-16N	A2
Grace Rd					
2700	NHBK	60062	2756	10W-17N	E5
8600	ODPK	60462	3346	10W-18S	A6
Grace St					
-	FXLK	60020	2473	28W-36N	A3
100	BNVL	60106	2972	15W-5N	A2
100	CteT	60417	3596	1W-28S	A7
100	CteT	60475	3596	1W-28S	A7
100	MRGO	60152	2634	49W-26N	C2
100	STGR	60475	3596	1W-28S	A7
800	ELGN	60120	2855	33W-10N	A6
1000	DSPN	60016	2862	13W-10N	E5
2400	TNLK	53181	2354		A2
4200	SRPK	60176	2973	11W-5N	C1
4500	SRPK	60176	2917	11W-5N	C7
N Grace St					
-	AddT	60101	3026	19W-2N	C1
10	LMBD	60148	3026	19W-1N	C2
900	AddT	60148	3026	19W-2N	C1
26900	WcnT	60084	2642	28W-26N	E2
S Grace St					
10	LMBD	60148	3026	19W-0S	C6
10	NARA	60542	3137	36W-4S	E1
400	AddT	60101	2970	19W-2N	C7
400	ADSN	60101	2970	19W-2N	C7
700	AddT	60148	2970	19W-2N	C7
900	AddT	60101	3026	19W-2N	C1
900	AddT	60148	3026	19W-2N	C1
1400	LMBD	60148	3084	19W-1S	D1
1400	YkTp	60148	3084	19W-1S	D1
W Grace St					
600	CHCG	60613	2978	0W-4N	A2
700	CHCG	60613	2977	1W-4N	D2
1900	CHCG	60618	2977	3W-4N	A2
2800	CHCG	60618	2976	4W-4N	C2
4000	CHCG	60641	2976	5W-4N	A2
5500	CHCG	60634	2975	7W-4N	B2
5500	CHCG	60641	2975	7W-4N	C2
6800	CHCG	60634	2974	9W-4N	D2
16600	LKPT	60441	3420	20W-19S	B3
Graceland Av					
-	CHCG	60613	2977	1W-5N	D1
200	DSPN	60016	2863	13W-11N	A4
700	DSPN	60016	2862	13W-10N	E4
Graceland Av US-12					
1000	DSPN	60016	2862	13W-10N	E4
Graceland Av US-45					
800	DSPN	60016	2862	13W-10N	E4
Graceland Ct					
12000	HMGN	60491	3344	15W-18S	C7
Graceland Dr					
15300	HMGN	60491	3344	15W-18S	C7
S Graceland Ln					
19900	FftT	60423	3504	9W-24S	D6
Graceland St					
100	DGvT	60516	3206	19W-9S	E3
Gracewood Dr					
1000	LYVL	60048	2591	17W-28N	B5
Graclyn Ct					
25800	CbaT	60010	2643	28W-25N	A4
Gracy Rd					
-	NndT	60012	2584	33W-29N	D3
-	PRGV	60012	2584	33W-29N	D3
-	PRGV	60050	2584	33W-29N	D3
W Gracy Rd					
3300	NndT	60050	2585	32W-29N	A4
3300	PRGV	60050	2584	33W-29N	E4
3300	PRGV	60050	2585	32W-29N	A4
Gracy St					
400	WDSK	60098	2524	41W-31N	D7
Grady Ct					
10	CmpT	60119	3018	41W-2N	A2
S Grady Ct					
2800	CHCG	60608	3091	1W-2S	D3
Grady Dr					
100	BGBK	60440	3268	25W-12S	B2
Graegin Pl					
800	DYR	46311	3598		E3
Graemere St					
200	NHFD	60093	2811	7W-15N	B3
Graf Rd					
7800	CmgT	60033	2405	51W-39N	C4
7800	HRVD	60033	2405	51W-39N	D4
W Graf Rd					
22900	CmgT	60033	2405	52W-40N	B3
Graff Av					
10000	RSMT	60018	2917	12W-7N	B3
Grafton Ct					
10	LKBF	60044	2593	11W-29N	E4
Grafton Ln					
3200	AURA	60502	3139	31W-5S	E4
Grafton Pl					
200	MTSN	60443	3506	5W-24S	B5
Grafton Farm Dr					
-	LIHL	60142	2692	39W-22N	B3
-	LIHL	60156	2692	39W-22N	B3
Graham Av					
1700	DRGV	60516	3206	20W-8S	A1
W Graham Av					
10	LMBD	60148	3026	20W-0S	B6
S Graham Ct					
14300	LktT	60544	3339	26W-16S	D5
W Graham Ct					
25900	GrtT	60041	2530	25W-34N	E1
Graham Dr					
10	RKDL	60436	3498	25W-25S	C7
Graham Rd					
600	NARA	60542	3078	35W-4S	C7
600	NARA	60542	3138	35W-4S	B1
Grainger Pkwy					
-	MTWA	60045	2648	14W-25N	D4
-	MTWA	60048	2648	14W-25N	D4
-	VrnT	60048	2648	14W-25N	D4
100	VrnT	60045	2648	14W-25N	C4

STREET Block	City	ZIP	Map#	CGS	Grid
W Gramercy Ln					
1000	ADSN	60101	2970	19W-3N	B5
Grammercy Park Ln					
200	YkTp	60148	3084	19W-1S	D1
N Granada Blvd					
300	LkvT	60046	2476	20W-37N	A2
300	LNHT	60046	2476	20W-37N	A2
N Granada Blvd CO-A18					
300	LkvT	60046	2476	20W-37N	A2
300	LNHT	60046	2476	20W-37N	A2
Granada Ct					
10	NpvT	60563	3140	30W-5S	C3
200	BGBK	60440	3205	23W-11S	A7
10600	PSHL	60465	3274	10W-12S	A2
Granada Ln					
7100	FXLK	60020	2415	27W-39N	B5
Granada Rd					
100	CPVL	60110	2748	33W-18N	B5
Granart Rd					
10	BRKT	60511	3134	46W-7S	A7
400	SRGV	60511	3134	45W-7S	C6
400	SRGV	60554	3134	45W-7S	C6
Granby Rd					
200	LKFT	60045	2650	10W-27N	A2
Grand Av					
-	GrtT	60041	2474	25W-37N	A3
-	LkvT	60041	2474	25W-37N	A3
-	LkvT	60046	2474	25W-37N	B2
10	RtdT	60124	2799	39W-14N	A5
10	WnfT	60187	3023	26W-0N	D4
10	WnfT	60190	3023	26W-0N	D4
100	AURA	60506	3138	35W-7S	A7
100	MltT	60187	3023	26W-0N	E4
200	CLLK	60014	2640	35W-25N	A5
200	RtdT	60124	2798	39W-14N	E5
200	WKGN	60085	2537	10W-34N	A1
600	ELGN	60120	2855	33W-12N	B3
700	GNEN	60137	3025	22W-0N	C4
900	WKGN	60085	2479	11W-35N	D7
900	WKGN	60085	2480	10W-34N	A7
1600	NndT	60014	2586	30W-28N	A6
3100	WkgT	60085	2479	12W-35N	B7
3300	GRNE	60031	2479	13W-35N	A7
3300	WKGN	60031	2479	12W-35N	A7
3600	MHRY	60050	2528	32W-33N	B3
3700	GRNE	60031	2478	13W-34N	D7
3800	PvsT	60558	3086	14W-4S	D7
3800	WNSP	60558	3086	14W-4S	D7
4400	WNSP	60558	3146	14W-5S	D2
4900	MCCK	60525	3148	10W-5S	B1
5100	DRGV	60515	3144	19W-5S	D3
5300	WrnT	60031	2478	15W-35N	A6
5700	DRGV	60516	3144	19W-6S	D4
5800	WrnT	60031	2477	17W-36N	C5
6000	GRNE	60031	2477	16W-35N	D5
7000	DRGV	60516	3206	19W-8S	D1
7600	GRNE	60031	2476	18W-35N	E5
7600	WrnT	60031	2476	18W-35N	E5
9800	FNPK	60131	2973	12W-3N	C5
10300	FNPK	60164	2973	11W-3N	C5
21600	WslT	60481	3943	27W-42S	E6
Grand Av SR-59					
-	GrtT	60041	2474	25W-37N	A3
-	LkvT	60041	2474	25W-37N	A3
-	LkvT	60046	2474	25W-37N	B2
Grand Av SR-132					
-	WKGN	60085	2537	10W-34N	B1
3300	GRNE	60031	2479	13W-35N	A7
3300	WKGN	60031	2479	12W-35N	A7
3300	WKGN	60085	2479	12W-35N	A7
3700	GRNE	60031	2478	13W-34N	D7
5300	WrnT	60031	2478	15W-35N	A6
5800	WrnT	60031	2477	17W-36N	C5
6000	GRNE	60031	2477	16W-35N	D5
7600	GRNE	60031	2476	18W-35N	E5
7600	WrnT	60031	2476	18W-35N	E5
E Grand Av					
10	BNVL	60106	2972	15W-3N	A5
10	CHCG	60610	3034	0E-0N	C3
10	CHCG	60611	3034	0E-0N	C3
10	EMHT	60106	2972	15W-3N	A5
10	EMHT	60126	2972	15W-3N	A5
10	FXLK	60020	2473	27W-36N	B3
10	LKVL	60046	2475	22W-38N	B1
100	AddT	60106	2972	15W-3N	B5
100	AddT	60126	2972	15W-3N	A5
100	FNPK	60131	2972	15W-3N	B5
100	FNPK	60164	2972	15W-3N	B5
100	LydT	60164	2972	15W-3N	B5
200	FXLK	60041	2473	27W-36N	C4
600	CokC	60611	3034	0E-0N	E3
1700	LkvT	60046	2475	20W-37N	E1
1700	LNHT	60046	2475	20W-37N	E1
1700	LNHT	60046	2476	20W-37N	B2
2000	LkvT	60046	2476	20W-37N	A2
E Grand Av CO-20					
10	BNVL	60106	2972	15W-3N	A5
10	EMHT	60106	2972	15W-3N	A5
10	EMHT	60126	2972	15W-3N	A5
100	AddT	60106	2972	15W-3N	A5
100	AddT	60126	2972	15W-3N	A5
100	FNPK	60131	2972	15W-3N	B5
100	FNPK	60164	2972	15W-3N	B5
100	LydT	60164	2972	15W-3N	B5
E Grand Av CO-A20					
10	FXLK	60020	2473	28W-36N	A3
E Grand Av SR-59					
500	FXLK	60020	2473	26W-36N	D4
500	FXLK	60041	2473	26W-36N	D4
E Grand Av SR-132					
10	LKVL	60046	2475	22W-38N	B1
1700	LkvT	60046	2475	20W-37N	E1
1700	LNHT	60046	2475	20W-37N	E1
1700	LNHT	60046	2476	20W-37N	B2
2000	LkvT	60046	2476	20W-37N	A2
N Grand Av					
40500	AntT	60002	2416	25W-40N	B2
W Grand Av					
-	AddT	60126	2972	14W-3N	B5
-	EMHT	60126	2972	14W-3N	B5
-	GrtT	60041	2474	25W-36N	A3
10	BNVL	60106	2971	16W-3N	E5
10	CHCG	60610	3034	0W-0N	A3
10	CHCG	60611	3034	0W-0N	A3
10	EMHT	60106	2971	16W-3N	D5
10	EMHT	60126	2971	16W-3N	C5
10	FXLK	60020	2472	28W-36N	E3
10	FXLK	60020	2473	28W-36N	A3
10	LKVL	60046	2475	23W-38N	A1
200	LKVL	60046	2474	24W-38N	C1
300	AddT	60106	2971	16W-3N	D5
400	LkvT	60046	2474	24W-38N	C1
700	CHCG	60622	3034	0W-0N	A3
800	CHCG	60622	3033	1W-0N	E3
1900	CHCG	60622	3033	2W-0N	C3
2800	CHCG	60612	3032	3W-0N	E3

Chicago 7-County Street Index

Block	City	ZIP	Map#	CGS	Grid
W Grand Av					
2800	CHCG	60622	3032	3W-1N	E2
3100	CHCG	60651	3032	3W-1N	E2
4300	CHCG	60639	3032	5W-1N	B1
4400	CHCG	60639	2976	5W-2N	A7
4700	CHCG	60639	2975	6W-2N	E7
6600	CHCG	60707	2975	8W-3N	A6
6700	CHCG	60707	2974	8W-3N	E6
7100	EDPK	60707	2974	8W-3N	E6
8000	EDPK	60171	2974	10W-3N	B5
8000	RVGV	60171	2974	9W-3N	B5
8600	RVGV	60171	2973	11W-3N	E5
8900	RVGV	60131	2973	11W-3N	E5
10400	FNPK	60131	2973	13W-3N	A5
10400	FNPK	60164	2973	13W-3N	A5
10400	LydT	60164	2973	13W-3N	A5
10500	LydT	60131	2973	13W-3N	A5
10700	FNPK	60131	2972	13W-3N	E5
10700	FNPK	60164	2972	13W-3N	E5
10700	LydT	60131	2972	13W-3N	E5
10700	LydT	60164	2972	13W-3N	E5
11200	NHLK	60164	2972	14W-3N	C5
18400	GRNE	60031	2476	18W-36N	E5
18400	WrnT	60031	2476	18W-36N	E5
18700	WrnT	60046	2476	19W-36N	C3
18900	LkvT	60046	2476	19W-36N	C3
19400	LNHT	60046	2476	18W-36N	D5
20800	LkvT	60046	2475	21W-37N	E1
20800	LNHT	60046	2475	21W-37N	E1
23000	LKZH	60047	2699	23W-22N	A4
23200	LKZH	60047	2698	23W-22N	E4
26000	GrtT	60041	2473	26W-36N	D4
26200	FXLK	60041	2473	26W-36N	D4
W Grand Av CO-20					
10	BNVL	60106	2971	16W-3N	E5
10	EMHT	60106	2971	16W-3N	C5
10	EMHT	60126	2971	16W-3N	C5
300	AddT	60106	2971	16W-3N	D5
W Grand Av SR-59					
-	GrtT	60041	2474	25W-36N	A3
26000	GrtT	60041	2473	26W-36N	D4
26200	FXLK	60041	2473	26W-36N	D4
26500	FXLK	60020	2473	26W-36N	D4
W Grand Av SR-132					
10	LKVL	60046	2475	23W-38N	A1
200	LKVL	60046	2474	24W-38N	C1
400	LkvT	60046	2474	24W-38N	C1
18400	GRNE	60031	2476	18W-36N	E5
18400	WrnT	60031	2476	18W-36N	E5
18700	WrnT	60046	2476	19W-36N	C3
18900	LkvT	60046	2476	19W-36N	C3
19400	LNHT	60046	2476	18W-36N	D5
20800	LkvT	60046	2475	21W-37N	E1
20800	LNHT	60046	2475	21W-37N	E1
Grand Blvd					
-	DPgT	60544	3340	25W-15S	A2
-	RMVL	60544	3340	25W-15S	A2
300	ELGN	60120	2855	32W-11N	C3
300	FmtT	60084	2644	24W-27N	B1
300	PKRG	60068	2864	10W-9N	B7
300	WCDA	60084	2644	24W-27N	B1
700	WCDA	60084	2588	25W-28N	B6
1000	AURA	60505	3200	34W-7S	D1
1200	RMVL	60446	3340	25W-15S	A2
3100	BKFD	60513	3087	11W-3S	D4
3100	BKFD	60525	3087	11W-3S	D4
3100	LGPK	60513	3087	11W-3S	D4
3100	LGPK	60525	3087	11W-3S	D4
N Grand Blvd					
37300	LkvT	60046	2474	25W-37N	A2
W Grand Blvd					
800	JLET	60436	3498	25W-24S	C5
1100	RMVL	60446	3340	25W-15S	B2
E Grand Cir					
2400	LkvT	60046	2476	19W-37N	B3
2400	LNHT	60046	2476	19W-37N	B3
Grand Ct					
7200	DRGV	60516	3206	19W-8S	E1
N Grand Ct					
8100	NLES	60714	2864	10W-10N	B5
Grand Dr					
100	AlqT	60013	2696	29W-23N	D2
100	CbaT	60013	2696	29W-23N	D2
2200	NHBK	60062	2809	11W-16N	D1
W Grand Dr					
18200	WrnT	60030	2534	18W-33N	A2
18300	WrnT	60030	2533	18W-33N	E2
Grand Pl					
400	AddT	60126	2972	15W-3N	A5
N Grand St					
8800	NLES	60714	2864	10W-11N	B3
Grand Canyon Av					
10500	HTLY	60142	2745	39W-20N	B1
Grand Canyon Dr					
300	BGBK	60440	3205	23W-11S	B7
Grand Canyon Pkwy					
800	HFET	60169	2858	23W-11N	E3
900	HFET	60169	2859	23W-11N	A2
900	HFET	60195	2859	23W-11N	A2
900	SMBG	60195	2859	23W-11N	A2
Grand Canyon St					
600	HFET	60169	2858	23W-11N	E4
Grand Central Ln					
10	SMBG	60193	2858	24W-10N	D6
10	SMBG	60194	2858	24W-10N	D5
Grand Cypress Ct					
1100	AURA	60502	3139	31W-6S	D4
Grand Duell Wy					
10	HRPK	60133	2967	27W-5N	C2
Grande Dr					
-	CnhT	60447	3672	32W-28S	C1
200	MNKA	60447	3672	33W-28S	C1
Grande Tr					
-	BtlT	60543	3262	40W-12S	C3
-	BtlT	60560	3262	40W-12S	C3
Grande Park Blvd					
-	PNFD	60543	3337	33W-15S	B3
-	PNFD	60585	3337	33W-15S	A3
Grande Pines Blvd					
12700	PNFD	60585	3337	33W-15S	B2
Grande Poplar Cir					
12900	PNFD	60585	3337	33W-15S	A1
Grande Poplar Ct					
26600	PNFD	60585	3337	33W-15S	B2
Grande Trail Ct					
-	BtlT	60560	3262	40W-12S	C4
Grandfield Dr					
-	SCRL	60175	2908	36W-6N	A7
-	SCRL	60175	2964	36W-6N	A1
Grandhaven Blvd					
-	LktT	60403	3417	26W-18S	E2
-	LktT	60446	3417	26W-18S	E2
-	RMVL	60446	3417	26W-18S	E2
Grand Haven Cir					
-	LktT	60441	3418	26W-18S	A1
-	LktT	60446	3418	26W-18S	A1
Grand Haven Cir					
-	RMVL	60446	3417	26W-18S	E1
-	RMVL	60446	3418	26W-18S	A1
Grand Haven Dr					
-	FKFT	60423	3504	11W-24S	A6
W Grandhaven Rd					
1400	RMVL	60446	3417	26W-18S	E2
Grand Highlands Dr					
1600	JLET	60586	3496	31W-21S	A1
Grand Lake Blvd					
200	WCHI	60185	3022	29W-1N	D3
200	WnfT	60185	3022	29W-1N	D3
E Grand Lake Blvd					
100	WCHI	60185	3022	29W-1N	C3
W Grand Lake Blvd					
100	WCHI	60185	3022	30W-1N	C3
Grand Lake Ct					
1100	NPVL	60540	3203	28W-8S	A2
Grandma's Ln					
10	SchT	60175	2963	37W-4N	D3
Grand Meadow Ln					
300	LKMR	60051	2529	29W-34N	C1
300	McHT	60051	2529	29W-34N	C1
Grand Mesa					
800	NLNX	60451	3589	19W-27S	A4
1000	NLNX	60451	3588	19W-27S	E4
Grand Monde Dr					
600	CmpT	60119	2962	40W-2N	B7
600	CmpT	60175	2962	40W-2N	B7
Grandmore Av					
3600	GRNE	60031	2479	13W-35N	A6
3700	GRNE	60031	2478	13W-35N	E6
W Grandmore Av					
12300	WKGN	60085	2479	12W-35N	B6
12700	WkgT	60085	2479	12W-35N	B6
Grand National Wy					
-	JknT	60421	3675	25W-29S	C2
-	JLET	60421	3675	25W-29S	C2
Grand Oak Ct					
1100	BRLT	60103	2910	30W-6N	C7
N Grand Oaks Ct					
36000	WrnT	60031	2476	18W-36N	E4
36000	WrnT	60046	2476	18W-36N	E5
Grand Pointe Blvd					
-	DndT	60118	2747	36W-17N	B7
1300	WDND	60118	2747	36W-17N	A7
Grandpointe Tr					
1800	AURA	60503	3201	33W-10S	A6
Grand Prairie Dr					
1300	NLNX	60451	3500	19W-24S	D6
2800	JLET	60431	3417	28W-20S	A4
S Grand Prairie Ln					
20300	FftT	60423	3504	9W-24S	E6
Grand Ridge Cir					
2700	AURA	60503	3201	32W-10S	D6
Grand Ridge Ct					
3600	JNBG	60051	2472	29W-35N	C5
Grand Ridge Rd					
200	SCRL	60175	2963	37W-2N	C7
Grandstand Pl					
1700	ELGN	60123	2854	36W-11N	A4
Grand Traverse Dr					
20300	FftT	60423	3504	11W-24S	A5
20300	FKFT	60423	3504	11W-24S	A6
Grandview					
-	NLNX	60451	3588	19W-26S	D3
-	NlxT	60451	3588	19W-26S	D3
Grandview Av					
100	GNEN	60137	3025	21W-0S	D6
900	LKPT	60441	3419	22W-19S	D3
2000	CTHL	60403	3417	26W-21S	E6
2300	LktT	60403	3417	26W-21S	E7
3600	GRNE	60031	2479	13W-35N	A7
3900	GRNE	60031	2478	14W-35N	D7
W Grandview Av					
3100	WKGN	60085	2479	12W-35N	B7
3100	WkgT	60085	2479	12W-35N	B7
Grand View Ct					
3600	SCRL	60175	2963	36W-5N	E2
3800	SchT	60175	2963	36W-5N	E2
Grandview Ct					
10	ALGN	60102	2694	34W-21N	B6
100	VOLO	60041	2530	27W-34N	C1
7300	CPVL	60110	2746	36W-18N	E5
Grand View Dr					
1500	JNBG	60050	2472	30W-36N	A4
1500	McHT	60050	2472	30W-36N	A4
1900	JNBG	60050	2471	30W-36N	E4
1900	McHT	60050	2471	30W-36N	E4
Grandview Dr					
-	CPVL	60110	2746	36W-18N	E5
-	CPVL	60110	2747	36W-18N	A5
-	CPVL	60118	2746	36W-18N	E5
-	DndT	60110	2747	36W-18N	A5
-	DndT	60118	2746	36W-18N	E5
-	DndT	60118	2747	36W-18N	A5
-	SHLD	60473	3350	0E-18S	D6
10	LKBN	60010	2643	25W-24N	E7
10	LKBN	60010	2644	25W-24N	A7
10	NBRN	60010	2643	25W-24N	E7
10	NBRN	60010	2644	25W-24N	A7
300	RLKP	60073	2532	22W-33N	B2
600	CLLK	60014	2640	33W-25N	D4
1000	NLNX	60451	3588	19W-26S	E3
1000	NLNX	60451	3589	19W-26S	A3
1400	AURA	60505	3200	33W-7S	E1
1500	AURA	60505	3201	33W-7S	A1
10500	PlsT	60464	3273	13W-14S	A7
15100	ODPK	60467	3344	14W-18S	D6
17600	HLCT	60429	3427	3W-21S	B6
W Grandview Dr					
2900	McHT	60050	2471	31W-34N	D7
Grandview Ln					
200	TNLK	53181	2354		C2
600	LKFT	60045	2650	10W-24N	B7
1100	HDPK	60035	2650	10W-24N	B7
8300	DGvT	60516	3206	20W-9S	B4
8300	DGvT	60561	3206	20W-9S	B4
8300	DRN	60561	3206	20W-9S	B4
8300	WDRG	60516	3206	20W-9S	B4
8300	WDRG	60517	3206	20W-9S	B4
8300	WDRG	60561	3206	20W-9S	B4
Grandview Pl					
100	LktT	60441	3419	23W-21S	B7
1800	MTGY	60538	3200	36W-10S	A6
2200	GNVW	60025	2810	9W-12N	C7
3000	DRN	60561	3206	20W-9S	B4
W Grandview St					
200	EMHT	60126	3027	16W-0N	E5
N Grandview Ter					
43200	AntT	60002	2357	25W-43N	B4
Grandville Av					
3400	GRNE	60031	2479	13W-35N	A6
3900	GRNE	60031	2478	13W-35N	D6
W Grandville Av					
2800	WKGN	60085	2479	12W-35N	B7
W Grandville Av					
2800	WkgT	60085	2479	12W-35N	B7
N Grandwood Dr					
36000	GRNE	60031	2476	18W-36N	E5
36000	WrnT	60031	2476	18W-36N	E5
37100	WrnT	60031	2477	18W-36N	A3
37300	OMCK	60031	2477	18W-36N	A3
Grandwood Lake Dr					
16400	LktT	60403	3417	26W-19S	E3
Grandys Ln					
-	FftT	60448	3503	11W-23S	E4
-	MKNA	60448	3503	11W-23S	E4
Grange Av					
2000	HDPK	60035	2704	10W-22N	B4
5400	OKFT	60452	3347	6W-17S	E5
Grange Ct					
10	EGVV	60007	2914	19W-8N	D2
600	WHTN	60187	3082	25W-2S	A3
Grange Dr					
10	EGVV	60007	2914	19W-8N	D2
17200	ODPK	60467	3422	14W-20S	C5
Granger					
3100	WynT	60103	2966	29W-5N	E1
Granger Rd					
900	BRLT	60103	2966	29W-5N	C1
900	WynT	60103	2966	29W-5N	C1
Granite Ct					
700	LIHL	60156	2693	37W-22N	B4
2600	PRGV	60012	2584	34W-29N	D4
3900	AURA	60504	3202	30W-8S	A2
Granite Dr					
7200	McHT	60097	2469	36W-37N	E1
7200	WRLK	60097	2469	36W-37N	E1
11000	MKNA	60448	3502	14W-23S	E3
11000	MKNA	60448	3503	13W-23S	A3
22600	FftT	60423	3590	14W-27S	D4
22600	FKFT	60423	3590	14W-27S	D4
W Granite St					
100	JLET	60435	3498	24W-22S	E3
Grant Av					
-	WDND	60118	2800	35W-16N	B1
10	LIHL	60156	2693	35W-22N	E4
100	FKFT	60423	3591	12W-25S	C1
100	GNVA	60134	3020	35W-1N	A3
200	CNHL	60514	3145	16W-5S	D3
200	FKFT	60423	3503	12W-25S	C7
500	JLET	60433	3499	23W-24S	B6
700	CHHT	60411	3508	1W-24S	D6
1300	MLPK	60160	3029	10W-1N	E2
2300	BLWD	60104	3029	12W-0N	C3
3600	PKFT	60466	3594	4W-27S	E4
3600	RNPK	60471	3594	4W-27S	E4
8800	BKFD	60513	3087	11W-3S	E5
9500	BKFD	60525	3087	11W-3S	D5
9500	LGPK	60525	3087	11W-3S	D5
16400	ODPK	60467	3423	13W-19S	A3
25500	GrtT	60041	2474	25W-36N	A3
E Grant Av					
700	JLET	60433	3499	23W-24S	B6
N Grant Av					
35000	TDLK	60046	2476	18W-35N	D7
35000	WrnT	60046	2476	18W-35N	D7
S Grant Av					
600	VLPK	60181	3027	17W-0N	B5
W Grant Av					
-	GRNE	60031	2476	18W-35N	D7
-	GRNE	60046	2476	18W-35N	D7
35100	TDLK	60046	2476	18W-35N	D7
35100	WrnT	60046	2476	18W-35N	D7
Grant Blvd					
-	CRTE	60417	3685	0E-29S	D1
Grant Cir					
600	HRPK	60133	2912	25W-9N	A1
Grant Ct					
300	LYVL	60048	2591	16W-29N	D5
600	BRRG	60527	3146	15W-6S	A4
1200	LGGV	60047	2700	18W-21N	D6
1500	HRPK	60133	2911	26W-6N	E6
7900	DRN	60561	3207	18W-9S	B3
25000	PNFD	60544	3337	31W-17S	E6
Grant Dr					
100	BGBK	60440	3269	23W-11S	A1
1200	CPVL	60110	2748	32W-17N	D7
E Grant Dr					
800	DSPN	60016	2862	13W-10N	D4
N Grant Dr					
10	ADSN	60101	2970	18W-3N	E5
S Grant Dr					
10	ADSN	60101	2970	18W-3N	E5
W Grant Dr					
800	DSPN	60016	2862	14W-10N	D4
E Grant Hwy					
100	MRGO	60152	2634	49W-26N	D3
11400	CrlT	60140	2743	45W-20N	A1
11400	CrlT	60142	2743	45W-20N	A1
11600	HPSR	60140	2743	45W-20N	A1
11600	HshT	60140	2743	45W-20N	A1
19200	CrlT	60152	2634	48W-25N	E4
19200	CrlT	60180	2634	48W-25N	E4
E Grant Hwy US-20					
100	MRGO	60152	2634	49W-26N	D3
11400	CrlT	60140	2743	45W-20N	A1
11400	CrlT	60142	2743	45W-20N	A1
11600	HPSR	60140	2743	45W-20N	A1
11600	HshT	60140	2743	45W-20N	A1
19200	CrlT	60152	2634	48W-25N	E4
19200	CrlT	60180	2634	48W-25N	E4
S Grant Hwy					
6500	CrlT	60152	2635	47W-24N	A6
6500	CrlT	60180	2635	47W-24N	A6
S Grant Hwy US-20					
6500	CrlT	60152	2635	47W-24N	A6
6500	CrlT	60180	2635	47W-24N	A6
W Grant Hwy					
100	MRGO	60152	2634	50W-26N	A2
W Grant Hwy US-20					
100	MRGO	60152	2634	50W-26N	A2
Grant Pl					
300	AURA	60505	3200	35W-8S	A2
300	PKRG	60068	2864	10W-9N	B7
1000	WCDA	60084	2588	25W-28N	B6
1100	VNHL	60061	2647	17W-26N	B3
1200	LGGV	60047	2700	18W-21N	D6
5800	McHT	60081	2472	29W-37N	D1
W Grant Pl					
400	CHCG	60614	2978	0W-2N	A6
Grant Rd					
900	LMNT	60439	3271	16W-12S	E2
900	LmnT	60439	3272	16W-12S	A2
1200	NHBK	60062	2757	8W-17N	D6
3600	JNBG	60050	2471	32W-35N	B6
Grant St					
-	CbaT	60010	2697	26W-21N	C6
10	CLLK	60014	2640	35W-26N	B3
10	OSWG	60543	3263	37W-12S	C3
100	EGvT	60018	2862	15W-9N	A7
Grant St					
100	HRVD	60033	2406	49W-38N	B7
200	DRGV	60515	3144	18W-4S	E1
200	DRGV	60559	3144	18W-4S	E1
200	PKFT	60466	3595	3W-25S	A1
300	LMNT	60439	3270	19W-13S	E5
500	ROSL	60172	2912	23W-8N	E3
500	SmbT	60172	2912	23W-8N	E3
600	WNFD	60190	3023	27W-0S	C7
600	WNFD	60190	3081	27W-0S	C1
600	WnfT	60187	3081	27W-0S	C1
800	BRLT	60103	2911	28W-7N	B5
1000	EVTN	60201	2867	3W-12N	A1
1100	WHTN	60187	3082	24W-1S	E1
1200	WLMT	60091	2812	5W-14N	A4
1300	NtrT	60093	2812	5W-14N	A4
1400	SmbT	60193	2912	23W-8N	E2
1800	EVTN	60201	2866	3W-12N	E1
2000	DRGV	60515	3143	21W-4S	E1
3000	OKBK	60523	3086	15W-2S	A4
3300	SKOK	60076	2866	5W-12N	B1
4000	OKLN	60453	3276	5W-12S	C2
7500	DGvT	60561	3145	18W-7S	B7
7600	DGvT	60561	3207	18W-8S	B1
14700	DLTN	60419	3350	0E-17S	E6
15600	SHLD	60473	3350	0E-18S	E7
17000	LNSG	60438	3430	4E-20S	B4
19100	LNSG	60438	3510	4E-22S	B2
N Grant St					
10	HNDL	60521	3146	15W-4S	A1
10	WTMT	60559	3145	18W-5S	A2
100	BRTN	60010	2750	26W-20N	E2
400	HNDL	60521	3086	15W-4S	A7
800	ADSN	60101	2970	18W-4N	E3
3900	DGvT	60559	3085	18W-4S	A7
3900	WTMT	60559	3085	18W-4S	A7
S Grant St					
-	AURA	60542	3138	35W-5S	A2
-	DGvT	60527	3208	15W-10S	A5
10	HNDL	60521	3146	15W-6S	A5
10	NARA	60542	3138	36W-4S	A1
10	WTMT	60559	3145	18W-5S	A3
100	JLET	60432	3499	23W-23S	B4
100	SDWH	60548	3330	51W-15S	A4
5800	BRRG	60521	3146	15W-6S	A4
6200	BRRG	60527	3146	15W-6S	A5
6200	WLBK	60527	3146	15W-6S	A5
7400	BRRG	60527	3208	15W-8S	B2
7500	DRN	60561	3207	18W-8S	B2
11400	RcmT	60071	2354	32W-43N	B4
11400	TNLK	53181	2354	32W-43N	B4
11400	TNLK	60071	2354	32W-43N	B4
W Grant St					
100	PLNO	60545	3259	47W-13S	C6
W Grant Vil					
200	HNDL	60521	3146	15W-6S	A4
Grantham Dr					
6900	JLET	60431	3495	32W-22S	C1
Grantham Ln					
-	SMBG	60193	2859	21W-9N	D6
1400	AURA	60503	3201	33W-10S	A6
Grantham Pl					
1800	HFET	60169	2858	26W-12N	A1
E Grantley Av					
100	EMHT	60126	3027	16W-1N	D2
100	EMHT	60126	3028	15W-2N	A1
W Grantley Av					
100	EMHT	60126	3027	16W-2N	E1
Grant Park Ct					
2500	CTHL	60403	3497	27W-22S	D2
Grants Tr					
16500	ODPK	60467	3423	13W-19S	A3
16500	OrlT	60467	3423	13W-19S	A3
Grant St Cto					
-	NARA	60542	3138	36W-4S	A1
Granville Av					
10	AddT	60143	2914	19W-7N	D5
10	BLWD	60104	3029	13W-0N	A5
10	CHCG	60068	2918	9W-7N	C3
10	CHCG	60631	2918	9W-7N	C3
10	ITSC	60143	2914	19W-7N	D5
300	PKRG	60068	2918	10W-7N	A3
500	HLSD	60104	3029	13W-0N	A5
500	HLSD	60162	3029	13W-0N	A5
1200	PKRG	60068	2917	10W-7N	E3
2700	LydT	60164	2973	13W-3N	A5
4900	DRGV	60515	3143	21W-5S	D2
4900	LslT	60515	3143	21W-5S	D2
9800	RSMT	60018	2917	12W-7N	B3
E Granville Av					
10	ROSL	60172	2913	23W-7N	B4
700	BmdT	60157	2913	22W-7N	C4
W Granville Av					
10	ROSL	60172	2913	23W-7N	A4
100	ROSL	60172	2912	23W-7N	E4
900	CHCG	60660	2921	2W-7N	B3
1900	CHCG	60659	2921	3W-7N	A3
3400	CHCG	60659	2920	4W-7N	C3
4000	CHCG	60646	2920	5W-7N	B3
Granville St					
900	MDLN	60060	2590	19W-28N	D6
Grape St					
2400	JLET	60435	3417	27W-20S	D5
2400	LktT	60403	3417	27W-20S	D5
2400	PnfT	60403	3417	27W-20S	D5
2400	PnfT	60435	3417	27W-20S	D5
W Grapevine Av					
26100	AntT	60002	2356	26W-42N	D5
Grape Vine Tr					
300	MTGY	60543	3198	39W-11S	D7
300	OSWG	60543	3198	39W-11S	D7
300	OSWG	60543	3262	39W-11S	D1
Graphics Ct					
-	TYPK	60477	3504	9W-22S	D1
Graphics Dr					
-	TYPK	60477	3504	9W-22S	D1
Grasmere Dr					
600	WNFD	60190	3023	27W-0N	B5
700	WnfT	60190	3023	27W-0N	B5
Grason St					
-	WTMT	60559	3145	18W-6S	A5
Grass Lake Dr					
2800	JLET	60435	3417	27W-19S	C3
W Grass Lake Dr					
27700	AntT	60081	2415	27W-39N	B6
27700	FXLK	60081	2415	27W-38N	A6
Grass Lake Rd					
2000	LkvT	60046	2418	20W-39N	A6
2000	LNHT	60046	2418	20W-39N	B6
Grass Lake Rd CO-A10					
2000	LkvT	60046	2418	20W-39N	A6
2000	LNHT	60046	2418	20W-39N	B6
W Grass Lake Rd					
100	FXLK	60020	2415	28W-38N	A6
100	FXLK	60081	2415	28W-38N	A6
600	FXLK	60020	2414	28W-38N	E6
W Grass Lake Rd					
19000	LNHT	60046	2418	19W-38N	C6
19000	OMCK	60046	2418	19W-38N	D6
19000	OMCK	60083	2418	19W-38N	D6
20700	LkvT	60046	2417	21W-39N	D4
20700	LkvT	60046	2418	20W-39N	A5
20700	LNHT	60046	2417	21W-39N	D4
21200	LkvT	60002	2417	21W-39N	D4
21600	LKVL	60002	2417	21W-39N	C4
21600	LKVL	60046	2417	21W-39N	C4
22700	AntT	60002	2417	22W-40N	A4
22700	AntT	60046	2417	22W-40N	A4
23300	AntT	60002	2416	24W-40N	C3
23300	LKVL	60002	2416	23W-40N	E3
25800	AntT	60002	2415	27W-38N	C6
27700	AntT	60081	2415	27W-38N	B6
29600	BtnT	60081	2414	28W-38N	E6
29600	FXLK	60081	2414	28W-38N	E6
W Grass Lake Rd CO-A10					
100	FXLK	60020	2415	28W-38N	A6
100	FXLK	60081	2415	28W-38N	A6
600	FXLK	60020	2414	28W-38N	E6
19000	LNHT	60046	2418	19W-38N	C6
19000	OMCK	60046	2418	19W-38N	D6
19000	OMCK	60083	2418	19W-38N	D6
20700	LkvT	60046	2417	21W-39N	D4
20700	LNHT	60046	2418	20W-39N	A5
20700	LNHT	60046	2417	21W-39N	D4
21200	LkvT	60002	2417	21W-39N	D4
21600	LKVL	60002	2417	21W-39N	C4
21600	LKVL	60046	2417	21W-39N	C4
22700	AntT	60002	2417	22W-40N	A4
22700	AntT	60046	2417	22W-40N	A4
23300	AntT	60002	2416	24W-40N	C3
23300	LKVL	60002	2416	23W-40N	E3
25800	AntT	60002	2415	27W-38N	C6
27700	AntT	60081	2415	27W-38N	B6
29600	BtnT	60081	2414	28W-38N	E6
29600	FXLK	60081	2414	28W-38N	E6
Grassland Dr					
-	FKFT	60423	3591	14W-28S	A6
-	GGnT	60423	3591	14W-28S	A6
Grassmere Ln					
6400	CPVL	60110	2747	36W-18N	A5
Grassmere Rd					
10	EGVV	60007	2914	19W-8N	D1
3300	NPVL	60564	3202	30W-11S	B7
3900	WldT	60564	3202	30W-11S	A7
Grassy Knoll Ct					
1800	RMVL	60446	3339	27W-17S	C5
Grassy Knoll Dr					
1800	RMVL	60446	3339	27W-17S	C5
S Gratten Av					
3000	CHCG	60608	3091	1W-2S	E3
N Gratton Rd					
38600	LkvT	60046	2417	22W-38N	C6
Graue Mill Ct					
2100	MHRY	60050	2528	32W-33N	A2
Graver Ct					
11100	WldT	60564	3266	30W-13S	B4
Graver Ln					
24200	WldT	60564	3266	30W-13S	B4
W Graves Av					
12000	WKGN	60087	2479	12W-37N	C2
12600	BHPK	60087	2479	12W-37N	B2
Gray Av					
300	MltT	60148	3083	21W-2S	E4
400	ELBN	60119	3017	43W-0N	A4
500	HDPK	60035	2705	8W-21N	A6
600	DRGV	60148	3083	21W-2S	E4
600	DRGV	60515	3083	21W-2S	E4
1000	AURA	60506	3199	37W-8S	D3
1000	MTGY	60506	3199	37W-8S	D3
Gray Ct					
300	GYLK	60030	2533	20W-33N	A3
600	WLNG	60090	2754	16W-18N	E2
2500	WKGN	60085	2536	12W-33N	C2
Gray Ln					
13400	LMNT	60439	3343	16W-15S	E1
19400	FftT	60423	3504	9W-23S	E3
19400	TYPK	60423	3504	9W-23S	E3
19400	TYPK	60477	3504	9W-23S	E3
Gray St					
10	GNVA	60134	3020	36W-1N	A2
10	GNVA	60174	3020	36W-1N	A2
10	SCRL	60134	3020	36W-1N	A2
10	SCRL	60174	3020	36W-1N	A2
1000	GNVA	60134	3019	36W-2N	E2
1000	SCRL	60134	3019	36W-2N	E2
1000	SCRL	60174	3019	36W-2N	E2
6100	BtnT	60081	2472	29W-38N	D1
6100	McHT	60081	2472	29W-38N	D1
N Gray Barn Ct					
23100	LKBN	60010	2696	28W-23N	E2
23100	LKBN	60010	2697	28W-23N	A3
Gray Barn Ln					
28000	LKBN	60010	2697	28W-23N	A2
28200	CbaT	60010	2696	28W-23N	E3
28200	LKBN	60010	2696	28W-23N	E3
Graycor Dr					
10	HLCT	60430	3427	3W-20S	B5
Grayfriars Ln					
300	IVNS	60067	2805	22W-15N	A2
Grayhawk Cir					
-	ALGN	60102	2746	37W-20N	B1
Grayhawk Ct					
10	ALGN	60102	2746	37W-20N	B1
3100	AURA	60503	3201	31W-10S	D6
Gray Hawk Dr					
-	MTSN	60443	3505	8W-25S	B7
6400	RchT	60443	3505	8W-25S	B7
21100	RchT	60443	3593	8W-25S	C1
Grayhawk Dr					
10	ALGN	60102	2746	37W-20N	B1
2100	AURA	60503	3201	31W-10S	E6
Grayling Ct					
4100	NCHI	60088	2593	12W-31N	C1
N Graylynn Dr					
200	WhlT	60056	2808	13W-13N	E6
Graymoor Ln					
10	BlmT	60422	3507	2W-24S	C4
10	BlmT	60461	3507	2W-24S	C4
10	FSMR	60422	3507	2W-24S	C4
10	OMFD	60422	3507	2W-24S	C4
10	OMFD	60461	3507	2W-24S	C5
Gray's Ct					
100	OSWG	60543	3264	36W-11S	A1
Gray's Dr					
200	OSWG	60543	3264	36W-11S	A2
Grayshire Ct					
1300	ELGN	60120	2801	32W-12N	D7
Grayshire Ln					
23200	LKBN	60010	2697	27W-23N	C2
Grays Reef Ct					
-	FKFT	60423	3504	11W-25S	A7

Chicago 7-County Street Index

STREET Block	City	ZIP	Map#	CGS	Grid
Gray Stone Ct					
-	FKFT	60423	3592	10W-27S	B4
Graystone Ct					
10	LslT	60565	3205	23W-8S	A2
10	NBRN	60010	2644	24W-24N	C7
Graystone Dr					
-	PnfT	60431	3417	28W-21S	B7
1400	AURA	60502	3139	32W-5S	B3
2000	JLET	60431	3417	28W-21S	A6
Graystone Ln					
10	NBRN	60010	2644	24W-24N	C6
Gray Wing Dr					
21500	LktT	60403	3417	26W-19S	D3
Graywood Dr					
500	LMBD	60148	3084	19W-1S	D2
500	YkTp	60148	3084	19W-1S	D2
Great America					
-	GRNE	60031	2478	15W-34N	A7
Great Bear					
-	GrtT	60051	2472	28W-34N	E7
Great Egret Dr					
-	BCHR	60401	3864	0E-36S	E1
10400	ODPK	60467	3423	13W-20S	B4
10400	OrlT	60467	3423	13W-20S	B4
Great Elm Ln					
700	HDPK	60035	2704	8W-21N	E6
Great Falls Dr					
1700	JLET	60586	3415	32W-21S	C7
1700	JLET	60586	3495	32W-21S	C1
Great Glen Ct					
700	IVNS	60010	2751	24W-16N	B6
Great Hill Rd					
3600	NndT	60012	2583	36W-28N	D6
Great Lakes Dr					
-	NCHI	60064	2593	12W-30N	C2
10	NCHI	60088	2593	12W-30N	C2
Great Meadow Dr					
2600	JLET	60432	3500	20W-22S	B2
Great Northern Tr					
-	UNON	60180	2635	46W-24N	D6
Great Oak Ct					
300	NPVL	60565	3204	25W-9S	A4
Great Oak Dr					
2400	LNHT	60046	2418	19W-38N	B7
Great Oak Ln					
2200	LNHT	60046	2418	20W-39N	B6
W Great Oaks Dr					
24400	CNHN	60410	3761	32W-32S	C1
Great Plaines Ct					
10800	HTLY	60142	2745	39W-20N	B1
Great Plaines Dr					
10400	HTLY	60142	2745	39W-20N	C1
Great Plains Av					
-	LKMR	60051	2530	28W-32N	A5
900	MTSN	60443	3505	7W-25S	C7
Great Plains Dr					
-	BGBK	60490	3267	27W-13S	C4
Great Ridge Dr					
1700	JLET	60586	3415	32W-21S	D7
1700	JLET	60586	3495	32W-21S	D1
Great Western Av					
100	MltT	60137	3025	23W-1N	A2
Greco Av					
2400	DSPN	60018	2917	12W-8N	A1
Greco Lane Ln					
-	SMBG	60193	2859	21W-9N	D6
Greeley Av					
2500	EVTN	60201	2812	5W-12N	B7
2500	SKOK	60076	2812	5W-12N	B7
2500	SKOK	60201	2812	5W-12N	B7
2500	WLMT	60091	2812	5W-12N	B7
2500	WLMT	60201	2812	5W-12N	B7
N Greeley St					
10	PLTN	60067	2805	21W-16N	E1
S Greeley St					
10	PLTN	60067	2805	21W-15N	D1
Greely Dr					
1100	JLET	60441	3500	19W-22S	D2
1100	JLET	60451	3500	19W-22S	D2
1100	NlxT	60441	3500	19W-22S	D2
Green Av					
-	BHPK	60087	2421	12W-38N	B7
-	BHPK	60087	2479	12W-37N	B1
-	WKGN	60087	2421	12W-38N	B7
-	WKGN	60087	2479	12W-37N	B1
10	LKFT	60044	2593	12W-28N	A6
10	ShdT	60044	2593	12W-28N	A5
N Green Av					
40100	BHPK	60099	2421	12W-40N	B4
Green Ct					
100	SMWD	60107	2857	27W-11N	D4
Green Dr					
6000	WDRG	60517	3143	22W-6S	D5
N Green Dr					
600	WLNG	60090	2755	15W-17N	A5
W Green Dr					
400	WLNG	60090	2755	15W-17N	A5
Green Ln					
100	CPVL	60110	2748	32W-17N	C6
2500	AlqT	60013	2641	31W-25N	D4
E Green Ln					
1400	MPPT	60056	2808	14W-13N	C7
Green Ln N					
1900	PLTN	60074	2753	19W-18N	C3
Green Ln S					
1800	PLTN	60074	2753	19W-18N	C3
Green Pl					
600	BbyT	60134	3018	39W-0N	D5
35500	WkgT	60085	2479	12W-35N	B6
36100	WkgT	60087	2479	12W-36N	B5
36400	WKGN	60087	2479	12W-36N	B5
Green Rd					
10	BbyT	60119	3075	42W-1S	C2
500	BbyT	60119	3017	42W-0S	C7
Green Rdg					
10	ELGN	60120	2855	32W-12N	C1
Green St					
-	MTSN	60443	3506	6W-24S	A6
200	MYWD	60153	3030	10W-0S	A5
200	PKFT	60466	3595	3W-27S	A3
400	BbyT	60119	3075	43W-2S	A4
700	MYWD	60153	3029	10W-0S	E5
1100	NlxT	60451	3501	18W-23S	A4
1200	NLNX	60451	3501	18W-23S	A4
1400	CHHT	60411	3508	0W-25S	C7
1400	CHHT	60411	3596	0W-25S	C1
2200	CTHL	60403	3417	26W-21S	E6
2300	LktT	60403	3417	26W-21S	E6
3000	SCHT	60411	3596	1W-28S	A6
3000	SCHT	60475	3596	1W-28S	A6
3000	STGR	60475	3596	1W-28S	A6
3700	CteT	60417	3596	1W-28S	A6
4300	RcmT	60071	2354	33W-41N	A7
4400	RcmT	60071	2353	33W-41N	E7
4400	RcmT	60071	2412	33W-41N	E1
9800	HbnT	60034	2351	40W-41N	B7

STREET Block	City	ZIP	Map#	CGS	Grid
Green St					
14400	HRVY	60426	3350	1W-17S	A5
14600	ODPK	60462	3345	11W-17S	E5
16500	HRVY	60426	3428	1W-19S	B3
26200	LbvT	60060	2646	18W-26N	D3
E Green St					
10	BNVL	60106	2972	15W-5N	B2
600	BNVL	60131	2972	15W-4N	B2
N Green St					
-	MchT	60050	2528	32W-33N	B2
10	CHCG	60607	3033	1W-0N	E4
10	CPVL	60110	2800	34W-17N	E1
100	CPVL	60110	2747	34W-17N	E7
100	MHRY	60050	2528	32W-32N	B5
300	CHCG	60622	3033	1W-0N	E4
S Green St					
-	CHCG	60643	3278	1W-13S	A4
10	CHCG	60607	3033	1W-0S	E5
10	CPVL	60110	2800	34W-16N	E1
100	MHRY	60050	2528	32W-31N	B7
600	NndT	60050	2528	32W-31N	B7
900	MHRY	60050	2585	32W-30N	B2
1100	NndT	60050	2585	32W-30N	B1
2600	CHCG	60608	3092	1W-2S	A3
5200	CHCG	60609	3152	1W-5S	A2
5500	CHCG	60621	3152	1W-6S	A4
7500	CHCG	60620	3214	1W-9S	A3
7500	CHCG	60621	3214	1W-8S	A1
9400	CHCG	60643	3214	1W-11S	A6
12200	CTPK	60827	3278	1W-14S	A6
12700	CTPK	60643	3278	1W-15S	A7
W Green St					
10	BNVL	60106	2971	16W-5N	D1
Green Acre Dr					
400	LbvT	60048	2591	17W-30N	B2
Greenacre Dr					
3700	NHBK	60062	2756	12W-17N	B5
Green Acres Dr					
100	NPVL	60540	3141	27W-7S	B7
100	NpvT	60540	3141	27W-7S	B7
Green Acres Ln					
1200	ELGN	60123	2800	35W-13N	C7
Greenacres Ln					
700	GNVW	60025	2811	7W-13N	B6
W Green Acres Ln					
1200	MPPT	60056	2861	16W-11N	D2
Greenbay Av					
300	CTCY	60409	3352	3E-17S	B6
1200	CTCY	60409	3430	3E-19S	B2
17000	LNSG	60438	3430	3E-20S	B4
18800	LNSG	60438	3510	3E-22S	B1
19500	LNSG	60411	3510	3E-23S	B2
S Green Bay Av					
8300	CHCG	60617	3216	4E-9S	B3
10300	CHCG	60617	3280	3E-12S	B3
13000	CHCG	60633	3280	3E-15S	B7
13000	CHCG	60633	3352	3E-15S	B1
13800	BNHM	60633	3352	3E-16S	B4
Greenbay Ct					
500	LKZH	60047	2699	22W-21N	B5
Greenbay Dr					
2200	HRPK	60133	2967	27W-4N	C3
Green Bay Pl					
2900	WKGN	60085	2536	12W-33N	B4
Green Bay Rd					
-	NCHI	60044	2593	11W-29N	D3
-	NCHI	60088	2593	11W-29N	D3
10	GLNC	60022	2758	6W-17N	D5
10	GLNC	60093	2758	5W-16N	E7
10	HDPK	60035	2704	8W-22N	E4
10	HDPK	60035	2758	7W-20N	A1
10	HIWD	60035	2704	9W-23N	D3
10	HIWD	60040	2704	8W-23N	D3
10	KLWH	60043	2812	4W-14N	C4
10	LKBF	60044	2593	11W-28N	D6
10	LKFT	60045	2593	11W-28N	E7
10	WNKA	60022	2758	5W-16N	E7
10	WNKA	60093	2758	5W-16N	E7
10	WNKA	60093	2812		C1
100	EVTN	60201	2812	3W-13N	E7
100	WLMT	60091	2812	4W-14N	D5
100	WLMT	60201	2812	3W-13N	E7
600	HDPK	60035	2705	8W-21N	A7
800	WNKA	60093	2759	5W-16N	A7
1000	NCHI	60064	2536	12W-31N	C6
1000	ShdT	60044	2593	11W-29N	D4
1000	ShdT	60088	2593	11W-29N	D4
1000	WKGN	60064	2536	12W-31N	C6
1000	WKGN	60085	2536	12W-31N	C6
1800	EVTN	60201	2867	3W-12N	A1
2400	NCHI	60064	2593	11W-30N	D3
10400	PTPR	53158	2362		A3
12600	NptT	53158	2362		A4
12600	NptT	60099	2362		A4
Green Bay Rd SR-31					
10400	PTPR	53158	2362		A3
12600	NptT	53158	2362		A4
12600	NptT	60099	2362		A4
Green Bay Rd SR-131					
600	LKBF	60044	2593	11W-28N	D5
1000	NCHI	60044	2593	11W-29N	D4
1000	NCHI	60064	2536	12W-31N	C6
1000	NCHI	60088	2593	11W-30N	D3
1000	ShdT	60044	2593	11W-29N	D4
1000	ShdT	60088	2593	11W-29N	D4
1000	WKGN	60064	2536	12W-31N	C6
1000	WKGN	60085	2536	12W-31N	C6
2400	NCHI	60064	2593	11W-30N	D3
N Green Bay Rd					
10	LKFT	60045	2650	10W-26N	A4
10	WKGN	60085	2536	12W-33N	B1
400	LKFT	60045	2649	11W-27N	E2
400	WKGN	60085	2479	12W-33N	B7
700	WkgT	60085	2479	12W-35N	B7
1400	LKBF	60044	2593	11W-27N	E7
1400	LKFT	60045	2593	11W-27N	E7
1400	WkgT	60031	2479	12W-35N	A6
2100	WKGN	60087	2479	12W-36N	A4
2100	WkgT	60087	2479	12W-36N	A4
36900	BHPK	60087	2479	12W-35N	A7
38300	BHPK	60087	2421	12W-38N	B7
38300	WKGN	60087	2421	12W-38N	B7
39000	BHPK	60083	2421	12W-39N	B6
39000	BHPK	60099	2421	12W-39N	B5
40800	BtnT	60099	2421	12W-40N	B2
40800	WDWH	60099	2421	12W-40N	B2
41000	ZION	60099	2421	12W-41N	B2
41700	ZION	60099	2362	13W-42N	A7
42000	BtnT	60099	2362	13W-42N	A7
42500	NptT	60099	2362	13W-42N	A7
43400	NptT	53158	2362	13W-43N	A4
43400	PTPR	53158	2362	13W-43N	A4
N Green Bay Rd SR-131					
10	WKGN	60085	2536	12W-33N	B1
400	WKGN	60085	2479	12W-33N	B7
700	WkgT	60085	2479	12W-35N	B7

STREET Block	City	ZIP	Map#	CGS	Grid
N Green Bay Rd SR-131					
1400	WkgT	60031	2479	12W-35N	A6
2100	WKGN	60087	2479	12W-36N	A4
2100	WkgT	60087	2479	12W-36N	A4
36900	BHPK	60087	2479	12W-35N	A7
38300	BHPK	60087	2421	12W-38N	B7
38300	WKGN	60087	2421	12W-38N	B7
39000	BHPK	60083	2421	12W-39N	B6
39000	BHPK	60099	2421	12W-39N	B5
40800	BtnT	60099	2421	12W-40N	B2
40800	WDWH	60099	2421	12W-40N	B2
41000	ZION	60099	2421	12W-41N	B2
41700	ZION	60099	2362	13W-42N	A7
42000	BtnT	60099	2362	13W-42N	A7
42500	NptT	60099	2362	13W-42N	A7
43400	NptT	53158	2362	13W-43N	A4
43400	PTPR	53158	2362	13W-43N	A4
S Green Bay Rd					
10	WKGN	60085	2536	12W-33N	B3
400	LKFT	60045	2650	10W-24N	A6
900	NCHI	60064	2536	12W-33N	B4
900	WKGN	60064	2536	12W-33N	B4
1100	HDPK	60035	2650	10W-24N	A7
1100	LKFT	60035	2650	10W-24N	A7
S Green Bay Rd SR-131					
10	WKGN	60085	2536	12W-33N	B3
900	NCHI	60064	2536	12W-33N	B4
900	WKGN	60064	2536	12W-33N	B4
Greenbelt					
28000	NCHI	60064	2536	12W-32N	B4
28000	WKGN	60085	2536	12W-32N	B4
Greenberg Ct					
24200	WldT	60564	3266	30W-13S	B4
E Greenbriar Av					
10	CHHT	60411	3508	1W-24S	A5
W Greenbriar Av					
100	CHHT	60411	3508	1W-24S	A5
Greenbriar Ct					
10	NPVL	60563	3141	26W-5S	D3
700	NARA	60542	3078	35W-3S	B5
4200	GRNE	60031	2535	14W-33N	D2
7900	BRRG	60527	3208	14W-9S	D2
N Greenbriar Ct					
26100	LKBN	60084	2643	27W-26N	C3
Greenbriar Dr					
-	BmdT	60143	2969	21W-5N	E1
-	BmdT	60157	2969	21W-5N	E1
-	MaiT	60016	2863	11W-12N	E1
-	MaiT	60025	2863	11W-12N	E1
10	DRFD	60015	2757	10W-20N	A2
10	GLBT	60136	2799	38W-14N	B5
100	ANTH	60002	2358	23W-42N	A5
100	NLNX	60451	3501	18W-24S	A6
300	CRTE	60417	3596	0E-28S	E6
400	GLHT	60139	3025	22W-1N	B2
1300	ADSN	60101	2969	21W-5N	D2
1300	BmdT	60101	2969	21W-5N	D2
1300	GNOK	60048	2592	14W-29N	C5
1300	LYVL	60048	2592	14W-29N	C5
1600	SMBG	60173	2859	21W-10N	E5
1600	SMBG	60173	2860	21W-10N	A5
3100	GNVW	60025	2810	10W-12N	A7
3200	MaiT	60025	2810	10W-12N	A7
3300	MaiT	60025	2809	10W-12N	E7
9400	HYHL	60457	3210	10W-10S	A6
N Greenbriar Dr					
1200	ADSN	60101	2969	21W-5N	D2
S Greenbriar Dr					
26700	MonT	60449	3683	6W-32S	A7
W Greenbriar Dr					
1400	MPPT	60056	2861	16W-12N	D2
Greenbriar Ln					
10	HNWD	60047	2646	19W-24N	B7
200	SMWD	60107	2856	29W-10N	E5
300	WNVL	60555	3080	29W-3S	D5
400	RVWD	60015	2755	13W-20N	D1
600	EGVV	60007	2913	22W-8N	C2
600	LKFT	60045	2650	10W-26N	B4
600	LNHT	60046	2476	20W-37N	B2
600	SmbT	60007	2913	22W-8N	C2
600	SmbT	60193	2913	22W-8N	C2
800	UYPK	60466	3684	3W-30S	A2
1000	NHBK	60062	2757	10W-17N	A6
1300	DRN	60561	3207	18W-9S	A2
1400	ROSL	60172	2913	22W-8N	C2
1400	SmbT	60172	2913	22W-8N	C2
4100	RNPK	60471	3594	5W-26S	C3
E Greenbriar Ln					
1100	PLTN	60074	2753	19W-18N	C3
Greenbriar Pl					
1500	AURA	60564	3202	30W-9S	B4
Green Briar Rd					
300	LslT	60540	3143	23W-7S	A7
Greenbriar Rd					
-	KdlT	60560	3333	43W-16S	B4
-	YKVL	60560	3333	43W-16S	B4
10	OswT	60538	3199	37W-10S	D6
300	GNEN	60137	3083	22W-1S	B2
Greenbriar St					
200	EGVV	60007	2860	18W-9N	E6
200	EGVV	60007	2861	18W-9N	A6
Greenbriar East Dr					
10	DRFD	60015	2757	9W-20N	B2
Green Bridge Ct					
2700	SMBG	60194	2857	26W-10N	E5
Green Bridge Ln					
400	PTHT	60070	2808	14W-14N	B4
2000	HRPK	60133	2967	27W-5N	C1
Greenbridge Ln					
7200	LGGV	60047	2646	18W-25N	E6
Green Brier Ct					
600	CLLK	60014	2639	36W-24N	D6
Greenbrier Ct					
10	LIHL	60156	2693	36W-21N	C5
W Greenbrier Ct					
1100	ANHT	60004	2806	18W-16N	E1
W Greenbrier Dr					
5000	MHRY	60050	2527	34W-32N	D6
Green Brier Ln					
500	CLLK	60014	2639	36W-24N	D6
Greenbrier Ln					
-	HTLY	60142	2744	42W-20N	C1
300	VNHL	60061	2647	17W-24N	B7
14700	HMGN	60491	3343	17W-17S	D6
Green Brier Ter					
700	CLLK	60014	2639	36W-24N	D6
Greenbrook Blvd					
10	BRLT	60103	2911	27W-7N	D6
10	BRLT	60133	2911	27W-7N	D6
1300	BmdT	60133	2911	27W-7N	D6
1300	HRPK	60133	2911	27W-7N	D6
Greenbrook Blvd CO-29					
10	BRLT	60103	2911	27W-7N	D6
10	BRLT	60133	2911	27W-7N	D6
1300	BmdT	60133	2911	27W-7N	D6
1300	HRPK	60133	2911	27W-7N	D6

STREET Block	City	ZIP	Map#	CGS	Grid
Greenbrook Ct					
10	WNVL	60555	3080	30W-2S	C3
1300	HRPK	60133	2911	26W-7N	E5
Greenbrook Dr					
2300	AURA	60502	3139	32W-5S	B3
Green Castle Ct					
700	WNDO	60118	2800	35W-16N	C2
Greencastle Ln					
9100	ODPK	60462	3345	11W-17S	E5
9100	ODPK	60462	3346	10W-17S	A6
Greencrest Dr					
300	BGBK	60440	3269	22W-11S	C1
Greendale Av					
900	NLES	60068	2864	10W-10N	A5
900	NLES	60714	2864	10W-10N	A5
1200	PKRG	60068	2864	10W-10N	A5
1200	PKRG	60714	2864	10W-10N	A5
1300	PKRG	60068	2863	11W-10N	E5
W Greendale Av					
8100	NLES	60068	2864	10W-10N	B6
8100	NLES	60714	2864	10W-10N	B5
8100	PKRG	60068	2864	10W-10N	B6
Greendale Rd					
600	MaiT	60025	2809	10W-13N	E7
600	NfdT	60025	2809	10W-13N	E7
600	NfdT	60025	2810	10W-13N	A7
Greene Ct					
200	WDDL	60191	2914	18W-5N	E7
1700	AURA	60506	3137	37W-7S	B6
Greene Ln					
22000	AntT	60002	2417	22W-40N	C2
Greene Rd					
-	BGBK	60440	3205	23W-10S	A6
10	LslT	60540	3205	23W-10S	A5
200	BGBK	60565	3205	23W-9S	A5
200	LslT	60565	3205	23W-10S	A5
600	LslT	60517	3143	23W-7S	A7
600	LslT	60540	3143	23W-7S	A7
600	WDRG	60517	3143	23W-7S	A6
6300	LslT	60517	3142	23W-7S	E7
6300	LslT	60540	3142	23W-7S	E7
6300	WDRG	60517	3142	23W-7S	E6
Greene Ridge Dr					
10	LslT	60565	3204	24W-9S	E3
10	NPVL	60565	3204	24W-9S	E3
Greenery Cir					
-	FXLK	60020	2415	28W-39N	A5
Green Feather Ln					
300	HnrT	60120	2856	30W-10N	B6
Greenfield Av					
200	GNEN	60137	3025	23W-0S	B6
200	GNEN	60187	3025	23W-0S	A6
200	WHTN	60187	3025	23W-0S	A6
800	JltT	60433	3499	22W-25S	C7
800	SEGN	60177	2908	35W-9N	B2
1100	WKGN	60085	2536	11W-32N	E6
1300	NCHI	60064	2536	11W-32N	E6
2200	NCHI	60064	2593	11W-31N	E1
2400	NCHI	60088	2593	11W-31N	E1
E Greenfield Av					
400	LMBD	60148	3026	19W-1N	C3
W Greenfield Av					
10	LMBD	60148	3026	20W-1N	B3
Greenfield Blvd					
22700	RNPK	60471	3593	6W-27S	E5
22900	RchT	60471	3593	6W-27S	E5
23000	UYPK	60449	3593	6W-27S	E5
Greenfield Cir					
300	GNVA	60134	3020	34W-1N	E3
Greenfield Ct					
-	GRNE	60031	2477	17W-35N	A5
10	HNWD	60047	2645	21W-25N	C5
600	BRLT	60103	2911	28W-8N	B4
900	MPPT	60056	2808	14W-14N	B5
1300	NPVL	60564	3203	28W-10S	A7
2400	AURA	60506	3137	38W-6S	A4
17600	ODPK	60467	3422	14W-21S	D6
23900	PNFD	60585	3338	29W-15S	C2
W Greenfield Ct					
14300	GNOK	60048	2592	14W-29N	C5
Greenfield Dr					
100	BMDL	60108	2968	24W-5N	C2
200	GNVW	60025	2864	9W-12N	C1
800	AURA	60506	3137	38W-6S	A5
2700	LSLE	60532	3142	24W-7S	C6
11700	ODPK	60467	3422	14W-21S	D5
12900	PNFD	60585	3338	29W-15S	C2
Greenfield Ln					
4100	CLLK	60014	2693	38W-22N	A3
4100	LIHL	60156	2693	38W-22N	A3
N Greenfield Ln					
900	MPPT	60056	2808	14W-14N	B4
S Greenfield Ln					
20100	FftT	60423	3504	9W-24S	D5
Greenfield Rd					
-	FNPK	60131	2973	12W-3N	B5
-	SgrT	60506	3135	41W-5S	E3
-	SgrT	60554	3135	41W-5S	E3
-	SRGV	60554	3135	41W-5S	E3
10	OswT	60538	3199	37W-10S	D6
200	SRWD	60404	3496	30W-23S	B4
400	PltT	60124	2852	41W-9N	A7
500	PltT	60124	2851	41W-9N	E7
1900	MTGY	60538	3199	38W-9S	A4
2000	HFET	60169	2804	25W-12N	C7
N Greenfield Rd					
100	CLLK	60014	2639	37W-25N	C4
Greenfield St					
-	OKPK	60302	3030	8W-1N	E1
10	CHCG	60651	3031	7W-1N	B1
10	OKPK	60302	3031	8W-1N	A1
1100	RVFT	60302	3030	8W-1N	D1
7800	RVFT	60305	3030	9W-1N	B1
Greenfield Turn					
600	YKVL	60560	3333	42W-16S	D5
Green Forest Rd					
21700	DRPK	60010	2698	24W-21N	C5
Green Garden Pl					
-	LKPT	60441	3419	23W-20S	B5
-	LKPT	60441	3499	23W-21S	B1
300	LktT	60441	3419	23W-21S	B7
Green Glade Wy					
-	WCDA	60084	2588	24W-29N	B3
Green Glen Ct					
1100	NlxT	60451	3501	16W-24S	E5
Greengold St					
2000	CTHL	60403	3417	26W-21S	E6
2300	CTHL	60435	3417	26W-21S	E6
2300	LktT	60403	3417	26W-21S	E6
2300	LktT	60435	3417	26W-21S	E6
Greenhaven Ln					
100	GRNE	60031	2535	14W-34N	C1
Green Heron Ln					
100	SgrT	60506	3135	41W-5S	E3
100	SgrT	60554	3135	41W-5S	E3

STREET Block	City	ZIP	Map#	CGS	Grid
Greenhill Ln					
400	SMBG	60193	2859	22W-10N	B6
Green Hills Ct					
10	SgrT	60506	3135	41W-5S	E3
Green House Dr					
12000	CHCG	60629	3150	4W-7S	D6
Greening Rd					
2400	NndT	60050	2585	31W-30N	D2
Green Knoll Av					
16800	ODPK	60467	3422	14W-20S	E4
Green Knoll Ln					
200	SMWD	60107	2857	26W-11N	E4
300	HFET	60169	2857	26W-11N	E4
Green Knolls Dr					
1100	BFGV	60089	2701	17W-21N	B6
Greenlake Dr					
1400	AURA	60502	3139	32W-5S	D3
Greenland Av					
14300	ODPK	60462	3345	12W-17S	C5
Green Lawn Av					
10	BNVL	60106	2972	15W-5N	A1
Greenlawn Av					
100	SchT	60174	2908	35W-7N	B6
Greenlawn St					
700	JLET	60433	3499	23W-24S	A7
700	JltT	60433	3499	23W-24S	A7
Greenleaf Av					
-	GNVW	60062	2809	12W-14N	B3
-	WKGN	60085	2535	13W-33N	E4
200	WLMT	60091	2813	2W-13N	A6
300	GRNE	60031	2535	13W-33N	E3
300	PKCY	60085	2535	13W-33N	E3
300	WrnT	60031	2535	13W-33N	E3
500	GLNC	60022	2758	6W-18N	D4
600	EGVV	60007	2915	17W-8N	B2
700	WLMT	60091	2812	3W-13N	E6
1500	LKFT	60045	2594	10W-27N	A7
1900	DSPN	60018	2917	12W-8N	B1
2600	EGVV	60007	2916	15W-8N	A1
3000	WLMT	60091	2811	6W-13N	E6
3400	ISLK	60042	2586	28W-28N	E6
Greenleaf Av CO-W29					
-	WKGN	60085	2535	13W-33N	D3
300	GRNE	60031	2535	13W-33N	E3
300	PKCY	60085	2535	13W-33N	E3
300	WrnT	60031	2535	13W-33N	E3
N Greenleaf Av					
10	GRNE	60031	2535	13W-34N	E1
700	GRNE	60031	2478	13W-35N	D7
35500	GrtT	60041	2474	25W-35N	A6
S Greenleaf Av					
10	GRNE	60031	2535	13W-34N	D2
10	WrnT	60031	2535	13W-34N	D2
200	PKCY	60085	2535	13W-34N	D2
S Greenleaf Av CO-W29					
10	GRNE	60031	2535	13W-34N	D2
10	WrnT	60031	2535	13W-34N	D2
200	PKCY	60085	2535	13W-34N	D2
W Greenleaf Av					
1200	CHCG	60626	2921	2W-8N	B1
1900	CHCG	60645	2921	2W-8N	A1
2600	CHCG	60645	2920	3W-8N	E1
4400	LNWD	60712	2920	5W-8N	A1
4800	LNWD	60077	2919	6W-8N	C1
4800	LNWD	60712	2919	6W-8N	C1
4800	SKOK	60077	2919	6W-8N	C1
5800	CHCG	60646	2919	7W-8N	B1
6300	CHCG	60714	2919	7W-8N	A1
6300	NLES	60714	2919	7W-8N	A1
7100	NLES	60714	2864	8W-10N	D4
7200	CHCG	60631	2918	9W-8N	D1
7200	CHCG	60714	2918	9W-8N	D1
7200	NLES	60714	2918	9W-8N	D1
Green Leaf Ct					
13200	PSHT	60463	3347	7W-15S	B2
Greenleaf Ct					
-	GRNE	60031	2535	14W-33N	D2
-	WTMT	60514	3145	17W-6S	C3
-	WTMT	60559	3145	17W-6S	C3
1500	BRLT	60103	2966	29W-5N	C2
2200	AURA	60506	3137	38W-6S	A5
3600	SPGV	60081	2413	32W-38N	B6
4000	PKCY	60085	2535	14W-33N	D2
18300	TYPK	60487	3424	11W-22S	A7
S Greenleaf Ct					
-	PLTN	60067	2805	21W-15N	C3
W Greenleaf Ct					
1800	RDLK	60073	2531	25W-33N	B4
Green Leaf Dr					
10	OKBK	60523	3085	16W-1S	E1
Greenleaf Dr					
300	VNHL	60061	2647	17W-26N	B3
400	MDLN	60060	2647	17W-26N	B3
400	MDLN	60061	2647	17W-26N	B3
900	JLET	60436	3497	27W-25S	C7
900	JLET	60436	3585	27W-25S	C1
3100	WRLK	60097	2469	36W-34N	D7
W Greenleaf Dr					
1800	RDLK	60073	2531	25W-33N	A3
Greenleaf Ln					
-	BtvT	60510	3079	33W-2S	A3
3600	BTVA	60502	3079	33W-2S	A4
3600	BTVA	60510	3079	33W-2S	A4
3600	BtvT	60502	3079	33W-2S	A4
3600	GNVW	60062	2809	12W-14N	B4
3600	NfdT	60062	2809	12W-14N	B4
W Greenleaf Pl					
28600	FXLK	60081	2414	28W-38N	E7
Greenleaf St					
100	EVTN	60202	2867	2W-10N	B4
1700	EVTN	60202	2866	3W-10N	E4
3300	SKOK	60076	2866	5W-10N	B4
4800	SKOK	60076	2865	6W-10N	E4
5300	SKOK	60077	2865	6W-10N	D4
6700	WDRG	60517	3143	21W-7S	E6
6700	WDRG	60517	3144	21W-7S	A7
N Greenleaf St					
-	GRNE	60031	2535	13W-34N	D1
W Greenleaf St					
7400	NLES	60714	2864	9W-10N	C4
7800	MaiT	60714	2864	9W-10N	B4
Greenleaf Tr					
13200	PSHT	60463	3347	7W-15S	B1
Greenlee Ct					
1400	NPVL	60540	3141	28W-7S	A7
Greenlee St					
700	MRGO	60152	2634	49W-26N	C2
Greenley St					
100	WDSK	60098	2581	41W-30N	D1
Green Manor Ct					
10800	ODPK	60462	3345	13W-17S	A5
10800	OrlT	60462	3345	13W-17S	A5
10800	OrlT	60467	3345	13W-17S	A5
Green Meadow Av					
12500	HTLY	60142	2744	43W-19N	B3

STREET Block	City	ZIP	Map#	CGS	Grid
Green Meadow Ct					
100	RGMW	60008	2805	21W-13N	D5
12500	HTLY	60142	2744	43W-19N	B2
Greenmeadow Ct					
700	CLLK	60014	2693	36W-23N	D2
Green Meadow Dr					
-	AddT	60101	2970	18W-4N	E4
10	ADSN	60101	2970	18W-4N	E4
10	GLHT	60139	2968	24W-3N	D5
N Greenmeadow Dr					
-	KLDR	60047	2699	21W-22N	D5
Green Meadow Ln					
500	GNVA	60134	3020	34W-1N	E2
500	GNVA	60134	3021	33W-1N	A2
1300	HRVD	60033	2405	50W-39N	E5
3000	AlqT	60013	2641	32W-25N	C4
3400	JLET	60431	3497	28W-23S	B3
3400	TroT	60431	3497	28W-23S	B3
S Green Meadow Ln					
20300	FftT	60423	3504	9W-24S	E6
N Green Meadows Blvd					
1100	SMWD	60107	2857	27W-11N	D4
S Green Meadows Blvd					
1600	SMWD	60107	2857	27W-11N	C5
W Green Meadows Blvd					
10	SMWD	60107	2857	27W-11N	C4
300	HFET	60010	2857	27W-11N	C4
Greenmeadows Dr					
10700	MKNA	60448	3503	13W-23S	B3
Green Meadows Ln					
200	HshT	60140	2743	46W-19N	A3
Green Meadows Pkwy					
19800	MKNA	60448	3503	13W-24S	B4
19900	FftT	60448	3503	13W-24S	B4
Green Mountain Ct					
700	BGBK	60440	3269	21W-11S	E1
Green Mountain Dr					
200	BGBK	60440	3269	21W-11S	E1
Green Oak Tr					
1300	AURA	60506	3137	36W-5S	D3
Green Oaks Ct					
1600	JLET	60586	3496	30W-21S	B1
Green Oaks Ct E					
400	ADSN	60101	2970	19W-4N	D4
Green Oaks Ct N					
500	ADSN	60101	2970	19W-4N	D4
Green Oaks Ct S					
400	AddT	60101	2970	19W-4N	D4
400	ADSN	60101	2970	19W-4N	D4
Green Oaks Dr					
10	CLLK	60014	2639	36W-26N	D4
Greenock					
2100	IVNS	60067	2804	23W-14N	D4
Greenpark Ct					
400	DRFD	60015	2756	11W-20N	C1
Green Pasture Rd					
10	ALGN	60102	2747	34W-20N	C1
10	AlqT	60102	2747	34W-20N	C1
Green Pastures Rd					
3400	CPVL	60110	2747	35W-18N	B5
Green Pheasant Ln					
1200	BTVA	60510	3077	36W-2S	E3
Greenridge Av					
1100	ALGN	60102	2747	34W-19N	E2
1100	ALGN	60102	2748	34W-19N	A2
Greenridge Rd					
900	BFGV	60089	2754	17W-17N	B4
N Green Ridge St					
700	ADSN	60101	2970	20W-4N	B3
Green River Ct					
400	SMBG	60194	2858	25W-11N	B4
Green River Dr					
1600	SMBG	60194	2858	25W-11N	B4
Greens Ct					
1400	GLHT	60139	2968	24W-2N	D7
2000	HFET	60169	2858	26W-12N	A2
Greensboro Ct					
200	EGVV	60007	2859	22W-9N	C7
900	NPVL	60540	3141	26W-6S	E5
S Greensboro Ct					
14100	PnfT	60544	3339	27W-16S	D5
Greensboro Dr					
1900	WHTN	60187	3082	25W-2S	B4
Greensburg Rd					
-	NRIV	60130	3088	9W-1S	C1
7600	FTPK	60130	3088	9W-1S	C1
7600	PvsT	60130	3088	9W-1S	C1
Greensfield Dr					
1100	NPVL	60563	3142	25W-6S	A4
Greenspoint Pkwy					
-	HFET	60010	2803	27W-12N	D7
2700	HFET	60169	2803	27W-12N	D7
Greens View Dr					
200	ALGN	60102	2693	36W-20N	C7
Greensward Wy					
400	RchT	60443	3593	8W-26S	B2
Green Trails Dr					
300	LslT	60540	3143	23W-7S	A7
400	WDRG	60517	3143	23W-7S	A7
400	WDRG	60540	3143	23W-7S	A7
500	LslT	60517	3142	23W-7S	E7
500	LslT	60540	3142	23W-7S	E7
500	WDRG	60517	3142	23W-7S	E7
600	LSLE	60517	3142	23W-7S	E7
600	LSLE	60532	3142	25W-7S	B6
600	LslT	60532	3142	23W-7S	E7
1200	JLET	60586	3496	30W-22S	B1
1200	SRWD	60404	3496	30W-22S	B2
1300	LSLE	60540	3142	25W-7S	B6
1300	NPVL	60532	3142	25W-7S	B6
1300	NPVL	60540	3142	25W-7S	B6
Greentree Av					
1000	DRFD	60015	2703	11W-21N	D6
Greentree Ct					
100	BGBK	60440	3269	22W-12S	B3
1200	LYVL	60048	2647	16W-27N	D1
Greentree Ln					
400	BGBK	60440	3269	22W-12S	B3
2300	LNHT	60046	2418	20W-38N	B7
Green Tree Pkwy					
100	LYVL	60048	2647	16W-27N	D1
Greentree Rd					
5000	OKFT	60452	3425	6W-20S	E4
5000	OKFT	60452	3426	6W-20S	A4
N Greentree Rd					
33200	WrnT	60030	2534	18W-33N	A3
33600	WrnT	60031	2534	18W-33N	A3
W Greentree Rd					
17700	WrnT	60030	2534	17W-33N	A4
Greenvale Rd					
10	VNHL	60061	2647	16W-25N	C5
500	LKFT	60045	2649	12W-26N	B3
Green Valley Ct					
2400	AURA	60503	3265	32W-11S	C1
7700	DRN	60561	3206	19W-8S	E2
E Green Valley Ct					
10	RLKB	60073	2475	22W-36N	A5
Green Valley Dr					
100	LMBD	60148	3026	20W-0N	B5
13900	ODPK	60467	3344	14W-16S	D4
14400	AdnT	60033	2349	43W-41N	E7
N Green Valley Dr					
10	NPVL	60540	3141	28W-6S	A5
S Green Valley Dr					
10	NPVL	60540	3141	28W-7S	A6
10600	PSHL	60465	3274	10W-12S	A2
Green Valley Dr W					
500	LMBD	60148	3026	20W-0N	B5
Green Valley Ln					
21800	FmtT	60060	2645	21W-27N	C1
N Green Valley Ln					
2100	RLKB	60073	2475	22W-36N	B5
Green Valley Rd					
2000	DRN	60561	3206	19W-8S	D2
Greenvalley St					
1100	BNVL	60106	2915	16W-6N	D7
Greenview Av					
-	CteT	60417	3774	0W-33S	B1
-	NLES	60714	2864	10W-10N	A5
-	PKRG	60068	2864	10W-10N	A5
-	PKRG	60714	2864	10W-10N	A5
10	WNVL	60555	3081	28W-3S	B6
500	DSPN	60016	2862	14W-11N	C4
600	PKCY	60085	2535	13W-33N	E3
600	WKGN	60085	2535	13W-33N	E3
600	WnfT	60555	3081	28W-3S	B6
8400	BKFD	60513	3088	10W-3S	A6
19700	MKNA	60448	3502	14W-23S	D4
N Greenview Av					
10	MDLN	60060	2646	19W-27N	C1
400	MDLN	60060	2590	19W-28N	D7
1200	CHCG	60622	3033	1W-1N	D1
2200	CHCG	60614	2977	1W-2N	D6
2600	CHCG	60657	2977	1W-3N	D5
3800	CHCG	60613	2977	1W-4N	D2
4400	CHCG	60613	2921	1W-5N	C7
4400	CHCG	60640	2921	1W-5N	C7
5800	CHCG	60660	2921	1W-7N	C3
6800	CHCG	60626	2921	1W-8N	C1
7200	CHCG	60626	2867	1W-9N	C7
S Greenview Av					
10	MDLN	60060	2646	19W-27N	C1
W Greenview Av					
25200	AntT	60002	2416	25W-39N	A4
Greenview Cir					
200	CTHL	60403	3417	27W-20S	D6
200	PnfT	60435	3417	27W-20S	C6
Greenview Ct					
100	NARA	60542	3137	38W-4S	A1
300	AlqT	60014	2640	33W-25N	E5
300	CLLK	60014	2640	33W-25N	E5
500	OSWG	60543	3263	38W-12S	A2
500	VNHL	60061	2647	16W-25N	D5
600	SchT	60175	2963	38W-5N	A4
1200	SMBG	60193	2913	23W-8N	B2
1400	SmbT	60193	2913	23W-8N	B2
Greenview Dr					
-	MltT	60137	3083	21W-1S	D2
200	AlqT	60014	2640	33W-25N	D5
200	CLLK	60014	2640	33W-25N	D5
300	PKCY	60085	2535	13W-33N	E3
500	WcnT	60084	2644	25W-26N	B2
800	AURA	60505	3138	34W-6S	D5
2000	DrrT	60098	2582	39W-29N	D3
2000	WDSK	60098	2582	39W-30N	C2
W Greenview Dr					
13200	WDWH	60083	2421	13W-40N	A3
13500	BtnT	60083	2420	13W-40N	E3
13500	WDWH	60083	2420	13W-40N	E3
Greenview Ln					
300	LKVL	60046	2474	23W-36N	E4
400	OSWG	60543	3263	38W-12S	A2
400	WLNG	60090	2755	15W-18N	A3
500	PltT	60124	2852	40W-10N	B5
Greenview Pl					
600	LKFT	60045	2650	10W-25N	B4
19500	TYPK	60477	3504	10W-23S	B3
Greenview Rd					
1900	NHBK	60062	2757	10W-16N	A7
2100	NHBK	60062	2810	10W-15N	A1
5300	NndT	60013	2641	31W-26N	D3
5300	ODHL	60013	2641	31W-26N	D3
5900	AlqT	60013	2641	31W-26N	D3
5900	LSLE	60532	3142	23W-6S	E5
5900	LslT	60532	3142	23W-6S	E5
14700	ODPK	60462	3345	13W-17S	A5
E Greenview Rd					
600	ITSC	60143	2914	19W-6N	D6
Greenview St					
700	GRNE	60031	2478	13W-35N	E7
Greenview Ter					
18000	CCHL	60478	3426	5W-21S	C7
Greenway Blvd					
-	TYPK	60448	3504	10W-23S	C3
-	TYPK	60477	3504	10W-23S	C3
Greenway Dr					
100	BMDL	60108	2969	23W-4N	B3
100	BMDL	60139	2969	23W-4N	A3
100	GLHT	60139	2969	23W-4N	A3
500	LKFT	60045	2648	13W-25N	E5
10100	HTLY	60142	2691	41W-20N	C7
16400	LMNT	60439	3342	20W-15S	B1
Greenway St					
100	PnfT	60435	3417	27W-20S	C5
Greenway Tr					
100	CLSM	60188	2968	25W-3N	A6
Greenwich Cir					
-	LGGV	60047	2647	17W-24N	B7
Greenwich Ct					
10	LKBF	60044	2593	11W-29N	E4
300	LslT	60540	3142	25W-6S	B4
4800	RGMW	60067	2805	21W-13N	E6
Greenwich Ln					
3300	ISLK	60042	2586	30W-28N	B5
N Greenwich Ln					
10	GNVA	60134	3019	36W-1N	E3
S Greenwich Ln					
10	GNVA	60134	3019	38W-1N	B3
Green Willow Ln					
4000	SCRL	60175	2964	35W-4N	B3
Greenwillow Ln					
1300	GNVW	60025	2810	8W-13N	D5
Greenwood					
-	ELGN	60120	2855	32W-9N	C7
Greenwood Av					
-	CHCG	60613	2977	1W-5N	D1
-	WkgT	60085	2479	12W-36N	A5
-	WkgT	60087	2479	12W-36N	A5
10	RMVL	60446	3341	23W-15S	A1
200	GLNC	60022	2758	6W-17N	D4
200	LKFT	60045	2650	10W-24N	A6
200	WNKA	60022	2758	6W-16N	D7
200	WNKA	60093	2758	6W-16N	D7
300	BMDL	60157	2913	22W-6N	C6
300	GYLK	60030	2532	21W-32N	D4
500	MDLN	60060	2590	18W-28N	E6
600	EDND	60118	2801	33W-16N	B1
700	BlmT	60411	3509	1E-24S	A6
700	FDHT	60411	3509	1E-24S	A6
800	CPVL	60110	2748	33W-17N	A7
900	DRFD	60015	2703	11W-21N	C6
1000	MYWD	60153	3030	10W-0S	B5
1400	FDHT	60411	3597	1E-25S	B1
1600	HRPK	60133	2911	27W-9N	D1
1600	KLWH	60043	2812	4W-14N	C5
1600	WLMT	60043	2812	4W-14N	C5
1900	KLWH	60091	2812	4W-14N	C5
2300	WLMT	60091	2812	5W-14N	B5
2400	HDPK	60035	2704	9W-23N	C2
3400	GRNE	60031	2479	13W-36N	A5
3400	WkgT	60031	2479	13W-36N	A5
3500	WLMT	60091	2811	6W-14N	D5
11800	GwdT	60098	2524	40W-32N	E6
11800	GwdT	60098	2525	40W-31N	A6
11800	WDSK	60098	2524	40W-32N	E6
11800	WDSK	60098	2525	40W-31N	A6
11900	BLID	60406	3277	3W-14S	B6
11900	BLID	60655	3277	3W-14S	B6
11900	CHCG	60655	3277	3W-14S	B6
13000	BLID	60406	3349	3W-15S	B1
16200	SHLD	60473	3429	1E-19S	A2
E Greenwood Av					
10	WKGN	60085	2480	10W-36N	B5
100	WDSK	60098	2524	41W-32N	D6
300	WKGN	60087	2480	9W-35N	C5
E Greenwood Av SR-137					
10	WKGN	60085	2480	10W-36N	B5
10	WKGN	60087	2480	10W-36N	B5
N Greenwood Av					
-	GNVW	60025	2810	10W-12N	A7
-	MaiT	60025	2810	10W-12N	A7
-	NfdT	60025	2810	10W-12N	A7
10	PKRG	60068	2864	10W-9N	A7
10	PKRG	60068	2918	10W-9N	A1
10	PLTN	60074	2806	20W-16N	B1
200	PLTN	60074	2753	20W-16N	B7
1000	NLES	60714	2864	10W-11N	A2
1000	PKRG	60714	2864	10W-10N	A5
2700	ANHT	60004	2753	18W-16N	D6
4800	CHCG	60656	2918	10W-6N	A7
4800	CHCG	60706	2918	10W-6N	A7
4800	NRDG	60706	2918	10W-6N	A7
8900	MaiT	60016	2864	10W-11N	A2
8900	MaiT	60714	2864	10W-11N	A2
9300	NLES	60016	2864	10W-11N	A2
9600	GNVW	60025	2864	10W-12N	A1
9600	MaiT	60025	2864	10W-12N	A1
9600	NLES	60025	2864	10W-12N	A1
S Greenwood Av					
10	PKRG	60068	2918	10W-8N	A2
10	PLTN	60074	2806	20W-15N	B1
200	GNWD	60425	3509	1E-23S	A3
4200	CHCG	60653	3093	1E-4S	A6
4600	CHCG	60615	3093	1E-4S	A7
4700	CHCG	60615	3153	1E-5S	A1
5100	CHCG	60615	3152	1E-5S	E2
5500	CHCG	60637	3152	1E-6S	E3
7100	CHCG	60619	3153	1E-8S	A7
7100	CHCG	60637	3153	1E-8S	A7
7600	CHCG	60619	3215	1E-8S	A1
9500	CHCG	60628	3215	1E-11S	A6
13000	CHCG	60827	3279	1E-15S	A7
13000	CHCG	60827	3351	1E-15S	A1
26300	CteT	60417	3686	1E-32S	B7
W Greenwood Av					
100	WDSK	60098	2524	41W-31N	C6
300	WKGN	60085	2480	10W-36N	A5
300	WKGN	60087	2480	10W-36N	A5
1100	WKGN	60087	2479	11W-36N	E5
1600	WKGN	60085	2479	11W-36N	D5
12900	WkgT	60031	2479	12W-36N	A5
12900	WkgT	60085	2479	12W-36N	A5
12900	WkgT	60087	2479	12W-36N	A5
27500	AntT	60081	2415	27W-38N	B7
28000	FXLK	60081	2415	28W-38N	A7
W Greenwood Av CO-A19					
300	WKGN	60085	2480	10W-35N	A5
300	WKGN	60087	2480	10W-35N	A5
Greenwood Cir					
700	NPVL	60563	3140	30W-5S	B4
1000	WDSK	60098	2524	41W-31N	D6
Greenwood Ct					
10	GNEN	60137	3025	22W-0S	B7
10	LslT	60540	3142	24W-6S	C4
800	BTVA	60510	3078	34W-1S	D2
800	CPVL	60110	2748	33W-17N	A7
800	ROSL	60172	2913	23W-6N	B6
1200	DRFD	60015	2703	11W-21N	E6
2100	SMWD	60107	2910	30W-9N	C1
2400	GNVW	60025	2810	10W-15N	A2
4400	ALGN	60102	2694	33W-21N	E5
4400	AlqT	60102	2694	33W-21N	E5
20700	OMFD	60461	3506	4W-25S	E6
E Greenwood Ct					
700	PLTN	60074	2753	20W-16N	B7
Greenwood Ct N					
10	BFGV	60089	2754	17W-18N	B3
Greenwood Ct S					
10	BFGV	60089	2754	17W-18N	B3
Greenwood Dr					
-	LkvT	60002	2417	20W-39N	E4
-	LkvT	60046	2417	20W-39N	E4
100	RLKP	60073	2532	23W-33N	A2
300	BGBK	60440	3269	22W-12S	C2
400	CbaT	60010	2644	25W-25N	B5
400	NBRN	60010	2644	25W-25N	B5
400	RDLK	60073	2532	23W-33N	A2
500	AURA	60506	3137	38W-6S	A6
700	WHTN	60187	3082	25W-1S	B1
800	LNHT	60046	2417	20W-39N	E4
3600	GwdT	60097	2469	37W-35N	B5
3600	WRLK	60097	2469	37W-35N	B5
9200	TYPK	60487	3423	11W-21S	E6
9400	MaiT	60016	2863	10W-11N	E2
9400	MaiT	60016	2864	10W-11N	A2
9400	NLES	60016	2863	10W-11N	E2
17800	OrlT	60487	3423	11W-21S	E6
20400	OMFD	60461	3506	4W-24S	E6
E Greenwood Dr					
600	MPPT	60056	2808	14W-14N	C4
N Greenwood Dr					
500	PLTN	60074	2753	20W-16N	B6
W Greenwood Dr					
21400	KLDR	60047	2699	21W-22N	D4
21600	LKZH	60047	2699	21W-22N	D4
Greenwood Ln					
200	HnrT	60120	2856	31W-10N	A6
800	CPVL	60110	2748	33W-17N	B7
800	CPVL	60110	2801	33W-17N	B1
800	CPVL	60118	2801	33W-17N	B1
800	EDND	60110	2801	33W-17N	B1
800	EDND	60118	2801	33W-17N	B1
2700	SchT	60174	2964	36W-4N	A4
2700	SCRL	60175	2964	36W-5N	A3
3700	SCRL	60175	2963	36W-5N	E2
Greenwood Pl					
300	OSWG	60543	3263	37W-13S	D6
5100	MCLK	60050	2470	34W-34N	D7
Greenwood Rd					
-	CTCY	60409	3429	2E-18S	C1
-	ThtT	60409	3429	2E-18S	C1
500	NHBK	60062	2756	10W-18N	E4
600	MaiT	60025	2810	10W-13N	A7
600	NfdT	60025	2810	10W-13N	A6
800	GNVW	60025	2810	10W-13N	A5
1900	GwdT	60098	2525	39W-34N	D2
2100	BLVY	60098	2525	39W-34N	D1
2300	NHBK	60062	2810	10W-15N	A1
2500	GNVW	60062	2810	10W-15N	A2
2500	NHBK	60025	2810	10W-15N	A2
2700	BLVY	60098	2468	39W-34N	D7
2700	GwdT	60097	2468	39W-34N	D7
2700	GwdT	60098	2468	39W-34N	D7
2700	WRLK	60097	2468	39W-34N	D7
2700	WRLK	60098	2468	39W-34N	D7
2800	HLCT	60429	3427	3W-21S	A6
3100	GNWD	60097	2468	38W-36N	E3
3100	GNWD	60098	2468	38W-36N	E3
5800	GwdT	60097	2469	38W-37N	A1
5800	HbnT	60034	2469	38W-37N	A1
5800	HbnT	60097	2469	38W-37N	A1
9300	HbnT	60034	2352	38W-41N	A7
9300	HbnT	60071	2352	38W-41N	A7
14300	DLTN	60419	3350	0E-16S	E4
14600	DLTN	60419	3351	1E-17S	B6
14900	SHLD	60419	3351	1E-17S	B6
14900	SHLD	60473	3351	1E-17S	B6
15900	ThtT	60409	3351	2E-18S	C7
15900	ThtT	60473	3351	2E-18S	C7
Greenwood Rd CO-V24					
1900	GwdT	60098	2525	39W-34N	D2
2100	BLVY	60098	2525	39W-34N	D2
2700	BLVY	60098	2468	39W-34N	D7
2700	GwdT	60097	2468	39W-34N	D7
2700	GwdT	60098	2468	39W-34N	D7
2700	WRLK	60097	2468	39W-34N	D7
2700	WRLK	60098	2468	39W-34N	D7
3100	GNWD	60097	2468	38W-36N	E3
3100	GNWD	60098	2468	38W-36N	E3
5800	GwdT	60097	2469	38W-37N	A1
5800	HbnT	60034	2469	38W-37N	A1
5800	HbnT	60097	2469	38W-37N	A1
9300	HbnT	60034	2352	38W-41N	A7
9300	HbnT	60071	2352	38W-41N	A7
Greenwood St					
-	MNGV	60053	2865	7W-11N	B3
100	EVTN	60201	2867	2W-11N	B3
800	JltT	60432	3499	22W-22S	D3
1900	EVTN	60201	2866	3W-11N	E3
3300	SKOK	60203	2866	4W-11N	C3
3500	SKOK	60076	2866	5W-11N	A3
4800	SKOK	60076	2865	6W-11N	E3
4800	SKOK	60077	2865	6W-11N	E3
5400	SKOK	60053	2865	6W-11N	D3
7100	MNGV	60053	2864	9W-11N	C3
7600	NLES	60053	2864	9W-11N	C3
7600	NLES	60714	2864	9W-11N	C3
34100	WslT	60481	3943	27W-41S	D5
Greenwood Ter					
-	CRTE	60417	3685	0E-29S	E1
-	CRTE	60417	3686	0E-29S	A1
-	CteT	60417	3685	0E-29S	E1
-	CteT	60417	3686	0E-29S	A1
W Greenwood Ter					
8000	EDPK	60171	2974	10W-3N	B5
8000	EDPK	60707	2974	10W-3N	B5
8000	RVGV	60171	2974	10W-3N	B5
Greenwood Center Ct					
20800	OMFD	60461	3506	4W-25S	E7
Gregg Ct					
200	SMWD	60107	2857	27W-11N	D4
Gregg Dr					
2900	MHRY	60050	2528	31W-31N	C7
Gregg Ln					
300	BFGV	60089	2754	16W-18N	C3
Gregg Rd					
600	NHBK	60062	2757	8W-17N	E4
W Gregg Rd					
14600	VrnT	60069	2702	14W-23N	C2
W Greggs Pkwy					
-	MDLN	60060	2647	17W-27N	B2
200	VNHL	60061	2647	16W-27N	D2
400	LYVL	60048	2647	16W-27N	E1
Greglawn Av					
200	PnfT	60435	3417	27W-20S	C6
Grego Ct					
300	PTHT	60070	2808	14W-15N	B3
Gregor Ln					
700	WLNG	60090	2755	15W-17N	A6
Gregory Av					
200	MNSR	46321	3430		D5
300	GLHT	60139	2969	22W-3N	B5
300	WLMT	60091	2813	3W-13N	A6
400	GLHT	60101	2969	22W-3N	B5
1200	WLMT	60091	2812	4W-13N	D7
3000	WLMT	60091	2811	5W-13N	E6
E Gregory Av					
100	DSPN	60016	2808	13W-13N	E6
100	WhlT	60056	2808	13W-13N	E6
Gregory Ct					
-	SRWD	60404	3496	30W-22S	C3
300	SMBG	60193	2912	23W-9N	E1
1000	EGVV	60007	2913	21W-8N	E3
1200	NPVL	60565	3203	27W-8S	C2
1400	INCK	60061	2647	17W-25N	A5
Gregory Dr					
10	BfdT	53128	2352		E3
10	GNCY	53128	2352		E3
400	CHHT	60411	3507	2W-25S	D7
3700	GNVW	60062	2809	12W-14N	B4
3700	NfdT	60062	2809	12W-14N	C4
4000	ZION	60099	2362	11W-42N	C6
Gregory Ln					
-	PLNO	60545	3260	45W-13S	B6
10	SBTN	60010	2803	26W-13N	D5
800	SMBG	60193	2858	24W-9N	C6
800	SMBG	60193	2912	23W-9N	E1
8600	MaiT	60016	2863	10W-12N	E1
8600	MaiT	60016	2864	10W-12N	A1
S Gregory Ln					
25900	CteT	60417	3685	1W-31S	B5
Gregory Pl					
900	SRGV	60554	3136	41W-4S	A2
1200	DRGV	60515	3084	20W-3S	B5
Gregory Rd					
600	BRRG	60521	3146	14W-6S	C4
600	BRRG	60527	3146	14W-6S	C4
Gregory St					
10	AURA	60504	3202	30W-8S	A2
100	AURA	60504	3140	30W-7S	A7
1200	JltT	60432	3499	22W-22S	D2
1300	JLET	60432	3499	22W-22S	D2
4600	JNBG	60050	2472	30W-36N	B3
4600	MchT	60050	2472	30W-36N	B3
11900	BLID	60406	3277	2W-14S	B6
11900	BLID	60643	3277	2W-14S	B6
11900	CHCG	60643	3277	2W-14S	B6
13000	BLID	60406	3349	2W-15S	B1
E Gregory St					
-	MPPT	60056	2808	14W-13N	C6
2000	ANHT	60004	2807	16W-13N	D6
2000	ANHT	60005	2807	16W-13N	C6
2500	ANHT	60056	2807	16W-13N	D6
2500	MPPT	60056	2807	16W-13N	D6
W Gregory St					
-	MPPT	60056	2808	15W-13N	A6
700	MPPT	60056	2807	16W-13N	E6
1000	ANHT	60004	2807	16W-13N	E6
1000	ANHT	60056	2807	16W-13N	E6
1400	CHCG	60640	2921	1W-6N	D5
2600	CHCG	60625	2920	3W-6N	E5
2600	CHCG	60625	2921	3W-6N	A5
4800	CHCG	60630	2919	6W-6N	E5
6300	CHCG	60656	2919	8W-6N	A5
7200	CHCG	60656	2918	9W-6N	D5
7400	CHCG	60631	2918	9W-6N	D5
7900	LydT	60656	2918	10W-6N	A5
7900	NpkT	60656	2918	10W-6N	A5
8600	CHCG	60656	2917	10W-6N	E5
Gregory M Sears Dr					
100	GLBT	60136	2799	38W-15N	A5
Greiving St					
200	DYR	46311	3598		D2
Gremley Av					
4000	SRPK	60176	2973	11W-5N	D2
Grenache Ct					
600	BRLT	60103	2911	28W-7N	A4
Grenadier Ct					
10	LNSH	60069	2702	13W-22N	D3
Greneda Dr					
1000	AURA	60506	3137	38W-6S	B4
Grenelefe Ln					
13900	HMGN	60491	3343	17W-17S	C6
Grengs Ln					
300	BbyT	60134	3018	38W-0S	E7
300	GnvT	60134	3018	38W-0S	E7
300	GnvT	60134	3019	38W-0S	A7
W Grennan Pl					
7000	NLES	60714	2864	8W-10N	D5
Grenoble Ct					
6600	LSLE	60532	3142	24W-7S	C7
Grenoble Dr					
18100	HLCT	60429	3426	4W-21S	E7
18200	HLCT	60430	3426	4W-21S	E7
18200	HMWD	60430	3426	4W-21S	E7
W Grenshaw St					
500	CHCG	60607	3034	0W-0S	A6
1300	CHCG	60607	3033	1W-0S	D6
2000	CHCG	60612	3033	2W-0S	B6
3600	CHCG	60624	3032	4W-0S	C7
N Gresham Av					
2900	CHCG	60618	2976	4W-3N	D4
Gresham Cir					
1900	WHTN	60187	3081	26W-1S	E1
1900	WHTN	60187	3082	26W-1S	A1
Gresham Ln E					
3200	AURA	60504	3201	31W-8S	E1
Gresham Ln W					
3100	AURA	60504	3201	31W-8S	D2
E Greshan Ct					
2400	ANHT	60004	2807	16W-15N	C2
Greta Av					
900	WDSK	60098	2581	42W-30N	B2
N Grethe Ct					
500	LKZH	60047	2699	21W-22N	C4
S Grethe Ct					
600	LKZH	60047	2699	21W-22N	C4
N Gretta Av					
10	WKGN	60085	2536	11W-34N	D1
S Gretta Av					
10	WKGN	60085	2536	11W-34N	D2
Grever Ct					
400	LKZH	60047	2699	23W-22N	A4
Grey Av					
100	CHCG	60645	2866	3W-9N	E6
700	EVTN	60202	2866	3W-10N	E5
1700	EVTN	60201	2866	3W-11N	E2
Grey Barn Rd					
10	SchT	60175	2963	37W-5N	C3
Grey Fox Ct					
100	HnrT	60107	2856	30W-10N	B6
100	SMWD	60107	2856	30W-10N	B6
Grey Fox Tr					
10600	NPVL	60564	3266	29W-12S	C3
10600	WldT	60564	3266	29W-12S	C3
Greyhawk Ct					
1600	JLET	60586	3415	31W-21S	E7
S Greyhawk Ct					
25200	CNHN	60410	3672	33W-30S	B4
Greyhawk Dr					
2000	JLET	60586	3415	31W-21S	E7
Grey Heron Ct					
2800	JNBG	60050	2471	31W-36N	C4
Greyshire Ct					
10	ALGN	60102	2747	36W-18N	A4
Greystem Cir					
2000	GRNE	60031	2478	14W-36N	D4
2100	WrnT	60031	2478	14W-36N	D4
Greystone Ct					
10	SMWD	60107	2857	26W-11N	E4
300	SMBG	60193	2859	21W-9N	D6
8200	LynT	60527	3208	14W-9S	C3
26100	CNHN	60481	3761	32W-33S	D3
26100	CnhT	60481	3761	32W-33S	D3
Greystone Dr					
-	HMGN	60491	3344	15W-16S	B4
1400	HmrT	60491	3344	15W-16S	B4
1400	GRNE	60031	2476	18W-35N	E6
E Greystone Dr					
1100	RLKB	60073	2475	21W-36N	D4
N Greystone Dr					
2300	RLKB	60073	2475	21W-36N	D4
S Greystone Dr					
14200	HMGN	60491	3344	15W-16S	B4
14200	HmrT	60491	3344	15W-16S	B4
Greystone Ln					
400	PTHT	60070	2808	14W-14N	B3

Block	City	ZIP	Map#	CGS	Grid
Greystone Ln					
500	BGBK	60440	3268	24W-12S	E4
500	WLNG	60090	2754	15W-18N	E3
600	LKZH	60047	2699	22W-22N	C4
Greystone Pl					
2100	HFET	60169	2858	26W-12N	A1
Greywall Ct					
7200	LGGV	60047	2646	18W-25N	E5
S Greywall Dr					
900	RDLK	60073	2531	23W-32N	E6
Greywall Ln					
10700	HTLY	60142	2692	39W-21N	B5
Grey Willow Rd					
1700	WHTN	60187	3024	24W-0N	D4
Greywood Dr					
-	SCRL	60175	2907	36W-6N	E7
-	SCRL	60175	2963	36W-6N	E1
Gridley Dr					
40500	AntT	60002	2416	23W-40N	D2
Griffen Dr					
-	MTGY	60506	3198	39W-10S	D5
-	MTGY	60538	3198	39W-10S	D5
Griffin Dr					
-	MTGY	60506	3198	39W-9S	D5
-	MTGY	60538	3198	39W-9S	D5
10	NHLK	60164	3028	14W-1N	D1
Griffin Ln					
500	CmpT	60175	2961	41W-4N	E4
Griffin Wy					
7700	WLBK	60527	3208	16W-8S	A2
Griffing Av					
200	WDSK	60098	2581	41W-30N	D1
Griffith Av					
-	BHPK	60099	2422	10W-38N	A7
-	ELBN	60119	3017	43W-0N	B5
-	WKGN	60099	2422	10W-38N	A7
600	AURA	60506	3199	36W-7S	E1
Griffith Ctr					
10	ALSP	60803	3275	7W-14S	D5
Griffith Ln					
-	CRTE	60417	3597	0E-29S	A7
-	CRTE	60417	3686	0E-29S	A1
Griffith Rd					
1000	LKFT	60045	2650	10W-27N	A1
Grill Dr					
13200	PNFD	60585	3337	31W-15S	E3
Grimes Av					
500	NPVL	60565	3203	27W-8S	C2
W Grimm Rd					
22900	ANTH	60002	2416	23W-41N	E1
22900	ANTH	60002	2417	23W-41N	A1
22900	AntT	60002	2416	23W-41N	E1
22900	AntT	60002	2417	23W-41N	A1
Grimsby on Oxford					
10	RGMW	60008	2805	22W-13N	B6
Grindel Dr					
-	ANHT	60005	2807	17W-12N	B7
-	MPPT	60056	2807	17W-12N	B7
Grinton Av					
200	JLET	60432	3499	22W-23S	C4
200	JltT	60432	3499	22W-23S	C4
W Grinton Dr					
23200	PnfT	60586	3416	29W-19S	E3
Grissom Ct					
300	HFET	60169	2858	23W-11N	E3
2800	WDRG	60517	3143	22W-7S	C7
Grissom Dr					
16900	TYPK	60477	3424	10W-20S	C4
E Grissom Dr					
1000	PLTN	60074	2753	19W-17N	B6
Grissom Ln					
100	HFET	60169	2858	23W-11N	E3
100	HFET	60169	2859	23W-11N	A3
Grissom Tr					
900	EGVV	60007	2914	21W-8N	A1
1100	EGVV	60007	2913	21W-8N	E2
S Griswold Av					
3100	NndT	60051	2586	29W-28N	C5
3200	ISLK	60042	2586	29W-28N	C5
3200	ISLK	60051	2586	29W-28N	C5
Griswold St					
300	ELGN	60123	2854	34W-10N	E5
Griswold Springs Rd					
15100	LtRT	60545	3331	48W-14S	A1
15700	LtRT	60545	3330	49W-15S	E1
16900	LtRT	60548	3330	50W-14S	C1
17100	SDWH	60548	3330	50W-14S	C1
17100	SdwT	60548	3330	50W-14S	C1
Groen Ct					
500	SMBG	60193	2859	22W-9N	C6
Groen Ln					
600	SMBG	60193	2859	22W-9N	C6
W Groh Ct					
1200	PLTN	60067	2805	22W-15N	B1
1200	PltT	60067	2805	22W-15N	B1
Gromer Rd					
10	HnrT	60107	2856	30W-10N	B6
10	HnrT	60120	2856	30W-10N	B6
10	SMWD	60107	2856	30W-10N	B6
10	SMWD	60120	2856	30W-10N	B6
Grommon Rd					
700	WldT	60564	3266	28W-11S	E2
1400	NPVL	60564	3266	28W-11S	E2
1400	NPVL	60564	3267	28W-11S	A2
Groot Dr					
-	EGVV	60007	2861	16W-9N	E7
E Gross St					
300	JLET	60432	3499	23W-22S	A2
Grosse Pointe Blvd					
-	LGGV	60047	2646	18W-25N	E5
-	VNHL	60047	2646	18W-25N	E5
-	VNHL	60061	2646	18W-25N	E5
-	VNHL	60061	2647	18W-25N	A5
Grosse Pointe Cir					
400	VNHL	60061	2647	18W-25N	A5
1800	HRPK	60133	2967	27W-5N	C3
Grosse Pointe Ct					
1800	HRPK	60133	2967	27W-5N	C3
Gross Point Rd					
-	NLES	60714	2865	7W-9N	B6
-	SKOK	60714	2865	7W-9N	B6
2500	EVTN	60201	2812	5W-12N	B7
2700	WLMT	60091	2812	5W-12N	B7
2700	WLMT	60201	2812	5W-12N	B7
7600	SKOK	60077	2865	7W-9N	C6
7800	MNGV	60053	2865	7W-9N	C6
7800	SKOK	60053	2865	7W-9N	C6
8300	MNGV	60077	2865	6W-10N	D5
9200	SKOK	60076	2865	6W-11N	E3
9400	SKOK	60076	2866	5W-11N	A2
9900	EVTN	60076	2866	5W-12N	B1
9900	EVTN	60201	2866	5W-12N	B1
W Gross Point Rd					
6000	NLES	60714	2865	7W-9N	A7
Grosvener Ct					
500	EGVV	60007	2860	18W-9N	E7
Grosvener Ln					
500	EGVV	60007	2860	18W-9N	E7
500	EGVV	60007	2914	18W-9N	E1
Grosvenor Cir					
1600	WHTN	60187	3082	25W-1S	A1
Grosvenor Ct					
300	BGBK	60440	3205	22W-9S	C4
Grosvenor Pl					
400	CHHT	60411	3508	1W-24S	A5
Groton Ct					
10	LNSH	60069	2701	16W-23N	E2
800	BRLT	60103	2910	30W-7N	B5
900	SMBG	60193	2912	24W-9N	C1
1600	WHTN	60187	3082	23W-1S	E2
1600	WHTN	60187	3083	23W-1S	A2
Groton Ln					
800	BRLT	60103	2910	30W-7N	B5
1300	WHTN	60187	3082	23W-1S	E2
Grotovsky Dr					
-	FftT	60448	3503	12W-22S	C2
-	MKNA	60448	3503	12W-22S	C2
Grotto Ct					
25400	PNFD	60585	3337	31W-15S	D2
Group Camp Rd					
3600	LslT	60565	3204	24W-9S	D4
6300	HtdT	60033	2464	48W-36N	E3
Grouse Ct					
700	VrnT	60015	2755	15W-20N	A1
2800	RGMW	60008	2806	19W-13N	C6
Grouse Ln					
400	VrnT	60015	2755	15W-20N	A1
2000	RGMW	60008	2806	19W-13N	C6
5400	RHMD	60071	2353	34W-42N	D5
Grouse Tr					
-	JNBG	60050	2471	31W-37N	D1
-	JNBG	60081	2471	31W-37N	D1
-	MchT	60081	2471	31W-37N	D1
Grouse Wy					
1500	CLLK	60014	2693	37W-22N	A3
Grove Av					
-	BRWN	60304	3030	8W-1S	E7
-	ELGN	60120	2855	32W-10N	C7
-	OKPK	60304	3030	8W-1S	E7
10	GNCY	53128	2353		A4
10	GNEN	60137	3025	21W-0S	D7
10	SchT	60174	2964	35W-5N	B3
10	SCRL	60174	2964	35W-5N	B3
100	DSPN	60016	2863	12W-11N	A3
100	FRGV	60021	2696	30W-22N	A3
200	WCHI	60185	3022	29W-1N	D3
200	WnfT	60185	3022	29W-1N	D3
300	AddT	60101	2970	19W-5N	B1
300	ADSN	60101	2970	20W-5N	B1
300	HIWD	60040	2704	9W-23N	C2
300	WDDL	60191	2915	18W-6N	A7
1200	BRWN	60402	3030	8W-1S	E7
1200	PKRG	60068	2918	9W-7N	B3
1400	WKGN	60085	2536	11W-32N	E6
1500	ADSN	60143	2970	20W-5N	A2
1500	HDPK	60035	2704	9W-21N	C7
1600	SMBG	60193	2912	25W-8N	A3
1800	NCHI	60064	2536	11W-31N	E7
3100	BRWN	60402	3088	8W-3S	E5
3400	GRNE	60031	2479	13W-35N	A6
3400	WkgT	60031	2479	13W-35N	A6
3400	WkgT	60085	2479	13W-35N	A6
3800	BKFD	60513	3088	11W-4S	A6
3800	GRNE	60031	2478	14W-35N	D6
3800	PvsT	60558	3086	14W-4S	D7
3900	SKNY	60402	3088	8W-4S	E6
4100	WNSP	60558	3086	14W-4S	D7
4400	FTVW	60402	3088	8W-4S	E7
4500	BKFD	60513	3148	11W-4S	A1
4500	FTVW	60402	3089	8W-4S	A7
4500	FTVW	60402	3149	8W-4S	A1
4500	MCCK	60513	3148	11W-4S	A1
4500	MCCK	60525	3148	11W-4S	A1
15900	OKFT	60452	3426	6W-19S	A1
E Grove Av					
100	HPSR	60140	2795	46W-16N	E2
300	HPSR	60140	2796	46W-16N	A2
N Grove Av					
100	OKPK	60301	3030	8W-0N	E3
100	OKPK	60302	3030	8W-0N	E3
200	ELGN	60120	2854	34W-12N	E3
1000	PLTN	60067	2752	22W-17N	B5
1100	PltT	60067	2752	22W-17N	B5
1300	PltT	60074	2752	22W-17N	B5
35500	AvnT	60041	2474	25W-35N	B5
35500	AvnT	60073	2474	25W-35N	B6
35500	GrtT	60041	2474	25W-35N	B6
35500	GrtT	60073	2474	25W-35N	B6
S Grove Av					
10	ELGN	60120	2854	34W-11N	E4
100	ELGN	60120	2855	33W-11N	A4
100	OKPK	60302	3030	8W-0N	E5
500	OKPK	60304	3030	8W-0S	E5
700	BRTN	60010	2751	25W-18N	A3
1100	BRWN	60304	3030	8W-0S	E7
1100	BRWN	60402	3030	8W-0S	E7
1200	BrnT	60010	2751	25W-17N	A5
1400	IVNS	60010	2751	25W-17N	A5
W Grove Av					
500	WKGN	60085	2480	10W-35N	A6
3300	GRNE	60031	2479	12W-35N	A6
3300	WkgT	60031	2479	12W-35N	A6
3300	WkgT	60085	2479	12W-35N	B6
3800	MHRY	60050	2528	32W-32N	A5
12500	WKGN	60085	2479	12W-35N	B6
Grove Av N					
500	OKPK	60302	3030	8W-1N	E3
1200	CHCG	60302	3030	8W-1N	E1
1200	CHCG	60707	3030	8W-1N	E1
Grove Ct					
10	ELGN	60120	2854	34W-10N	C7
100	BGBK	60440	3268	24W-12S	C2
100	LMNT	60439	3342	19W-15S	D1
400	BTVA	60510	3078	34W-2S	C4
1200	LKFT	60045	2703	12W-24N	B1
2200	LslT	60563	3082	25W-4S	B7
2200	NPVL	60563	3082	25W-4S	B7
6000	MNGV	60053	2865	7W-10N	B4
11800	MKNA	60448	3502	14W-24S	D4
Grove Dr					
-	ANHT	60005	2861	17W-11N	B2
-	ANHT	60056	2861	17W-11N	B2
-	TYPK	60477	3424	9W-21S	E6
600	ANHT	60004	2754	18W-18N	A4
600	BFGV	60089	2754	18W-18N	A4
600	EGVV	60007	2861	17W-9N	B7
1000	MPPT	60056	2861	17W-11N	C3
1400	RLKB	60073	2475	23W-35N	A6
1800	NHFD	60093	2811	7W-15N	C3
N Grove Dr					
21000	KLDR	60047	2699	21W-21N	E6
Grove Ln					
100	DRPK	60010	2751	23W-18N	E2
100	PltT	60010	2751	23W-18N	E2
300	MltT	60148	3025	21W-1N	E2
700	WNVL	60555	3080	29W-3S	D5
800	BGBK	60440	3268	24W-12S	C2
1900	AlqT	60013	2695	31W-22N	D3
1900	CRY	60013	2695	31W-22N	D3
2800	NfdT	60062	2809	12W-15N	B2
2900	TVLY	60013	2695	32W-22N	C3
Grove Pl					
100	WYNE	60184	2966	31W-5N	A2
100	WynT	60184	2966	31W-5N	A2
200	PTHT	60070	2808	15W-14N	A4
400	DRFD	60015	2756	11W-20N	E1
600	DRFD	60015	2703	11W-20N	E7
Grove Rd					
-	BtnT	60081	2414	29W-39N	C5
-	FXLK	60081	2414	29W-39N	C5
-	SPGV	60081	2414	29W-39N	C5
3600	OSWG	60543	3263	37W-13S	C5
4400	OswT	60543	3263	37W-13S	C6
5100	RGMW	60067	2805	21W-13N	D5
Grove St					
-	BCHR	60401	3864	0W-36S	C1
10	BtlT	60512	3261	41W-12S	D3
10	SRGV	60554	3135	42W-7S	C7
10	SRWD	60404	3496	30W-24S	C5
100	BDWD	60408	3942	31W-41S	B6
100	BNVL	60106	2971	16W-5N	E1
100	LKZH	60047	2698	23W-23N	E2
100	MDLN	60060	2646	18W-27N	D1
100	WDSK	60098	2524	41W-31N	D6
200	BmdT	60143	2913	21W-6N	E6
200	CLLK	60014	2639	35W-25N	E4
200	GLNC	60022	2758	6W-17N	C4
300	AURA	60505	3138	33W-7S	E7
400	ADSN	60101	2970	20W-5N	A2
400	ADSN	60143	2970	20W-5N	A2
500	BmdT	60143	2970	20W-5N	A2
600	PGGV	60140	2798	41W-14N	B7
600	PltT	60140	2798	40W-13N	B7
900	WNKA	60093	2758	6W-16N	D7
1000	DRGV	60515	3144	19W-5S	C3
1100	WDDL	60106	2971	16W-5N	C1
1100	WDDL	60191	2971	16W-5N	C1
1400	EVTN	60201	2867	3W-11N	A3
1600	AraT	60505	3139	33W-7S	A7
1600	AURA	60505	3139	33W-7S	A7
1700	EVTN	60201	2866	3W-11N	E3
1900	GNVW	60025	2810	9W-13N	D6
2400	BLID	60406	3349	3W-15S	B1
2900	NfdT	60025	2810	10W-13N	B6
3500	SKOK	60203	2866	4W-11N	C3
4000	SKOK	60076	2866	5W-11N	B3
4700	SKOK	60076	2865	5W-11N	E3
4700	SKOK	60077	2865	6W-11N	E3
5400	MNGV	60053	2865	6W-11N	D3
5400	SKOK	60053	2865	6W-11N	D3
11100	HTLY	60142	2692	40W-20N	A7
E Grove St					
10	ANHT	60005	2807	17W-13N	B5
10	LMBD	60148	3026	19W-0N	B3
1700	ANHT	60004	2807	16W-13N	D5
2500	ANHT	60056	2807	16W-13N	D5
2500	MPPT	60056	2807	16W-13N	D5
N Grove St					
10	CPVL	60110	2747	34W-17N	E7
10	CPVL	60110	2800	34W-17N	E1
2300	RVGV	60171	2973	10W-3N	E6
S Grove St					
10	CPVL	60110	2800	34W-16N	E1
2000	CHCG	60616	3092	0W-1S	B1
2600	CHCG	60608	3091	1W-2S	D3
W Grove St					
10	ANHT	60005	2807	17W-13N	A5
10	LMBD	60148	3026	20W-1N	B3
100	ITSC	60143	2914	19W-6N	C6
600	ANHT	60005	2806	18W-13N	D5
2000	RGMW	60005	2806	19W-13N	D5
2000	RGMW	60008	2806	19W-13N	D5
Grove Hill Ct					
100	BtvT	60510	3077	38W-1S	B3
Grove Hill Dr					
-	BtvT	60510	3077	38W-1S	B2
Groveland Av					
10	RVSD	60546	3088	10W-3S	B5
400	HDPK	60035	2758	7W-20N	B1
2900	NRIV	60546	3088	10W-2S	B4
W Groveland Av					
27600	AntT	60081	2415	27W-38N	B6
27600	FXLK	60081	2415	27W-38N	B6
E Groveland Pk					
600	CHCG	60616	3092	0E-3S	D4
Grovenor Dr					
100	SMBG	60193	2859	23W-9N	A7
S Grover Av					
3700	HMND	46327	3352		D2
S Grover Ct					
300	JLET	60433	3499	23W-24S	A6
W Grover St					
5600	CHCG	60630	2919	7W-6N	C6
Groveside Ln					
5400	RGMW	60008	2805	21W-13N	C5
Grovetown Dr					
2000	BRLT	60103	2909	32W-8N	C3
W Grovewood Ln					
7700	FftT	60423	3504	9W-24S	D5
Grow Ln					
10	SMWD	60107	2857	28W-10N	A5
Grumman Ct					
800	NLNX	60451	3501	18W-25S	A7
Grunewald St					
2400	BLID	60406	3277	3W-14S	A6
Guard Ranger Dr					
6900	OKBK	60523	3086	15W-3S	A5
21900	MltT	60187	3082	24W-3S	C6
25500	DRGV	60515	3083	22W-3S	D5
25500	MltT	60187	3083	22W-3S	D5
25500	MltT	60515	3083	22W-3S	D5
Guerin Rd					
700	GNOK	60048	2592	15W-31N	B1
700	LbvT	60048	2592	15W-31N	B1
700	WKGN	60048	2592	15W-31N	B1
W Guerin Rd					
15500	LbvT	60048	2592	15W-31N	A1
15500	WKGN	60048	2592	15W-31N	A1
15600	LbvT	60048	2591	15W-30N	E1
Guild Ln					
500	WYNE	60184	2965	32W-5N	D1
Guilford Coms					
7700	HRPK	60133	2912	26W-9N	A1
Guilford Rd					
10	OswT	60538	3199	37W-11S	D7
W Guinevere Ln					
24400	TroT	60404	3584	30W-27S	B4
Gulf Island Dr					
200	WLBK	60527	3145	16W-7S	D6
Gulf Keys Rd					
1100	HnrT	60107	2856	30W-9N	C7
1100	SMWD	60120	2856	30W-9N	C7
1200	SMWD	60107	2856	30W-9N	C7
Gulfstream Ct					
100	RLKP	60030	2589	22W-30N	A1
Gulf Stream Dr					
-	BRLT	60103	2966	30W-5N	C1
-	WynT	60103	2966	30W-5N	C1
Gulfstream Pkwy					
1200	LYVL	60048	2647	15W-27N	E1
Gulfstream Rd					
9200	FKFT	60423	3592	11W-27S	A4
9300	FKFT	60423	3591	11W-27S	E4
Gull Ct					
3900	RGMW	60008	2806	19W-13N	C7
S Gull Ct					
1000	PLTN	60067	2805	22W-14N	B3
Gullikson Dr					
6200	CHCG	60638	3148	8W-6S	E5
Gullo Av					
700	EGvT	60007	2861	17W-10N	B6
700	EGVV	60007	2861	17W-10N	B6
S Gullview Dr					
-	PtnT	60468	3860	10W-38S	C5
600	PTON	60468	3860	10W-38S	C5
Gum St					
100	NLNX	60451	3501	17W-24S	C6
Gundersen Dr					
300	CLSM	60188	3024	24W-1N	C3
300	MltT	60188	3024	24W-1N	C3
Gunderson Av					
500	OKPK	60302	3031	8W-0S	A5
500	OKPK	60304	3031	8W-0S	A5
1100	BRWN	60304	3031	8W-0S	A7
1200	BRWN	60402	3031	8W-1S	A7
1500	BRWN	60402	3089	8W-2S	A3
3900	SKNY	60402	3089	8W-4S	A7
Gunner Ct					
12400	HMGN	60491	3422	15W-19S	B3
Gunness Dr					
400	WnfT	60185	3022	30W-0S	C7
Gunnison Ct					
-	GLBT	60136	2799	38W-15N	A4
W Gunnison St					
1200	CHCG	60640	2921	1W-6N	D6
2400	CHCG	60625	2921	3W-6N	A6
2700	CHCG	60625	2920	3W-6N	E6
4400	CHCG	60630	2920	5W-6N	A6
4900	CHCG	60630	2919	6W-6N	E6
6300	HDHT	60630	2919	7W-6N	A6
6300	HDHT	60706	2919	7W-6N	A6
6600	HDHT	60706	2918	8W-6N	E7
7000	CHCG	60656	2918	8W-6N	E7
7000	CHCG	60706	2918	8W-6N	E7
7000	HDHT	60656	2918	8W-6N	E7
7800	NRDG	60706	2918	9W-6N	C7
Gunpowder Ln					
10	RtdT	60124	2798	39W-14N	E6
500	PltT	60124	2798	39W-13N	E7
Gunsmoke Ct					
1000	CLSM	60188	2967	27W-3N	C6
Gunston Av					
200	LslT	60540	3142	25W-6S	B4
W Gurnee Gln					
17000	GRNE	60031	2534	17W-34N	C1
17000	WrnT	60031	2534	17W-34N	C1
Gurnee Mills Cir E					
6000	GRNE	60031	2477	16W-35N	D5
Gurnee Mills Cir W					
6400	GRNE	60031	2477	16W-36N	C4
Gurney Av					
400	LKBF	60044	2594	10W-28N	A6
Gustafson St					
100	MHTN	60442	3677	19W-31S	E5
Gustave Av					
2200	LydT	60164	2973	12W-2N	C6
Gustave Ln					
2200	JLET	60586	3415	32W-21S	C6
Gustave St					
3200	FNPK	60131	2973	12W-4N	C4
Gustavus Ln					
800	SchT	60175	2963	37W-4N	B5
Gusto Dr					
1000	MTGY	60506	3199	38W-8S	A3
1000	MTGY	60538	3199	38W-8S	A3
Guth St					
-	EDND	60118	2801	33W-16N	B1
Guthrie Ct					
300	RtdT	60140	2798	40W-15N	C3
Guthrie Dr					
1500	IVNS	60010	2751	24W-17N	C5
Gyorr Av					
1900	SEGN	60177	2907	37W-8N	D3
Gypsum Cir					
2800	NPVL	60564	3202	29W-10S	C6
H					
H Ct					
10100	MKNA	60448	3503	12W-23S	C4
H St					
-	HDPK	60037	2704	8W-23N	D2
-	HIWD	60037	2704	8W-23N	D2
N H St					
40200	AntT	60002	2416	23W-40N	E3
Haag Ct					
1100	AURA	60504	3201	32W-9S	C3
Haar Ln					
1400	EGVV	60007	2913	21W-8N	E3
Haas Av					
3700	LYNS	60546	3088	9W-3S	D5
3800	LYNS	60534	3088	9W-3S	D6
3800	RVSD	60546	3088	9W-3S	D6
Haas Dr					
10700	PlsT	60464	3273	13W-14S	A7
Haas Rd					
17500	HMGN	60491	3422	16W-21S	A7
18100	NlxT	60448	3422	15W-22S	A7
18100	NlxT	60491	3422	15W-21S	A7
18300	NlxT	60448	3502	15W-22S	B1
Haase Av					
1200	HLSD	60154	3028	13W-1S	E7
1200	HLSD	60162	3028	13W-1S	E7
1200	PvsT	60162	3028	13W-1S	E7
1200	PvsT	60162	3086	13W-1S	E1
1200	WSTR	60154	3028	13W-1S	E7
1200	WSTR	60154	3086	13W-1S	E1
1200	WSTR	60162	3028	13W-1S	E7
1200	WSTR	60162	3086	13W-1S	E1
1400	PvsT	60154	3086	13W-1S	E1
Habberton Av					
1500	PKRG	60068	2863	11W-10N	E5
Haben Ln					
400	WLNG	60090	2755	15W-18N	A3
Haber Av					
2900	LydT	60164	2972	13W-3N	D4
3100	FNPK	60131	2972	13W-3N	D4
3100	FNPK	60164	2972	13W-3N	D4
Haber Ct					
200	CRY	60013	2695	32W-23N	C2
N Haber Ct					
400	NHLK	60164	2972	13W-2N	E7
Haber Rd					
-	AlqT	60013	2695	32W-23N	C2
200	CRY	60013	2695	32W-23N	C2
Habitat Ct					
6400	GRNE	60031	2534	16W-34N	C2
Hackberry Ct					
300	SMBG	60193	2858	24W-10N	D6
300	WDDL	60191	2971	17W-4N	C2
700	BRLT	60103	2910	29W-9N	D1
1200	ELGN	60120	2855	32W-11N	D4
1300	LYVL	60048	2591	17W-30N	B2
1400	NPVL	60540	3140	28W-6S	E6
S Hackberry Ct					
200	RDLK	60073	2531	23W-33N	E4
Hackberry Ct E					
600	BFGV	60089	2701	17W-22N	B4
Hackberry Ct W					
600	BFGV	60089	2701	17W-22N	B4
Hackberry Dr					
200	MltT	60137	3083	22W-3S	C4
200	SMWD	60107	2857	27W-10N	C6
E Hackberry Dr					
200	ANHT	60004	2754	17W-17N	B5
W Hackberry Dr					
300	ANHT	60004	2754	18W-17N	A5
500	ANHT	60004	2753	18W-17N	E5
Hackberry Ln					
10	GNVW	60025	2811	6W-13N	D7
600	ALGN	60102	2695	32W-20N	B7
1200	WNKA	60093	2811	6W-16N	E1
1700	LKFT	60045	2648	13W-24N	E7
1700	LKFT	60045	2649	13W-24N	A7
E Hackberry Ln					
600	MPPT	60056	2808	14W-14N	B5
Hackberry Rd					
-	DRFD	60015	2756	11W-20N	D1
400	FKFT	60423	3503	12W-25S	C7
N Hackberry Rd					
26200	FmtT	60060	2645	20W-26N	E3
Hacke Ln					
9500	FNPK	60131	2973	11W-4N	C3
N Hacker Av					
1000	JLET	60432	3499	23W-22S	B2
Hacker Dr					
2400	CTHL	60403	3417	26W-20S	D6
2400	CTHL	60435	3417	26W-20S	D6
2400	LktT	60435	3417	26W-20S	E6
2500	LktT	60403	3417	26W-20S	E6
Hacker St					
19800	MKNA	60448	3503	13W-23S	A4
Hackney Cir					
10	SBTN	60010	2803	27W-13N	A5
Hackney Dr					
1700	AURA	60502	3139	32W-5S	C3
1700	NpvT	60502	3139	32W-5S	C3
16100	ODPK	60467	3423	12W-19S	D2
Hackney Ln					
10	LNHT	60046	2418	19W-38N	C7
400	OSWG	60543	3263	37W-14S	D7
Haddam Pl					
1900	HFET	60169	2858	25W-12N	B1
Haddam Wy					
700	HRPK	60133	2912	25W-9N	A1
Haddassah Ct					
400	NPVL	60565	3203	27W-10S	D6
Haddassah Dr					
2600	NPVL	60565	3203	26W-10S	D6
Haddington Cir					
500	IVNS	60010	2803	25W-15N	E1
W Haddington Ct					
1200	PLTN	60067	2805	22W-15N	B2
E Haddock Pl					
-	CHCG	60601	3034	0E-0N	C4
W Haddock Pl					
200	CHCG	60601	3034		E4
200	CHCG	60606	3034	0W-0N	B4
W Haddon Av					
1800	CHCG	60622	3033	2W-1N	C2
2700	CHCG	60622	3032	3W-0N	E3
3200	CHCG	60651	3032	4W-1N	D2
4800	CHCG	60651	3031	6W-1N	E2
Haddon Cir					
300	VNHL	60061	2647	17W-24N	B7
300	VNHL	60061	2701	17W-24N	B1
Haddon Ct					
10	LIHL	60156	2692	38W-23N	E2
N Haddon Pl					
200	ADSN	60101	2970	19W-3N	B4
Haddon St					
1200	MLPK	60160	3029	11W-1N	D2
Haddow Av					
2200	DRGV	60515	3143	21W-5S	E2
2400	LslT	60515	3143	21W-5S	E2
N Haddow Av					
1500	ANHT	60004	2807	17W-15N	B2
2500	ANHT	60004	2754	17W-16N	B6
S Haddow Av					
1000	ANHT	60005	2807	17W-12N	B7
1200	ANHT	60005	2861	17W-12N	B1
N Haddow Ct					
1100	ANHT	60004	2807	17W-15N	B3
S Hadfield Dr					
12800	WldT	60585	3337	32W-15S	B2
Hadleigh Rd					
200	BGBK	60440	3269	22W-11S	C1
Hadley Cir					
1100	GRNE	60031	2477	17W-35N	A6
Hadley Ct					
400	BRLT	60103	2967	28W-5N	B2
1600	WLNG	60090	2754	16W-18N	D4
Hadley Dr					
1500	BTVA	60510	3077	36W-1S	E1
W Hadley Rd					
12200	HMGN	60491	3422	16W-20S	A5
Hadley Run Ln					
800	SMBG	60173	2859	22W-10N	C5
800	SMBG	60193	2859	22W-10N	C5
Hadrian Dr					
-	JLET	60431	3495	32W-22S	C2
Haegele Av					
2000	TNLK	53181	2354		A1
Haegers Bend Rd					
9700	AlqT	60102	2695	32W-22N	C4
9900	BNHL	60102	2695	32W-20N	C7
10100	AlqT	60010	2695	32W-21N	C5
10100	BNHL	60010	2695	32W-21N	C6

STREET Block City ZIP Map# CGS Grid

Haegers Bend Rd
11100 ALGN 60102 2695 31W-20N C7
11600 ALGN 60010 2748 32W-19N C2
11800 ALGN 60102 2748 32W-19N C2
11800 BNHL 60010 2748 32W-19N C2
11800 BNHL 60102 2748 32W-19N C2
12000 ALGN 60110 2748 32W-19N C2
12000 BNHL 60110 2748 32W-19N C2
Haerle Av
2300 TNLK 53181 2354 A2
W Hafenrichter Rd
- WldT 60564 3201 31W-10S E6
100 AURA 60503 3201 33W-10S A5
100 AURA 60504 3201 33W-10S A5
100 OswT 60503 3201 33W-10S A5
25000 AURA 60564 3201 31W-10S E6
25000 WldT 60503 3201 32W-10S D6
W Haft St
6300 CHCG 60631 2919 7W-7N A3
6300 CHCG 60646 2919 7W-7N A3
S Hagans Av
200 EMHT 60126 3027 16W-1N D3
Hagar Ct
1900 JLET 60586 3416 29W-21S D7
Hageman Pl
700 NPVL 60563 3142 25W-5S A4
Hagemann Dr
- BTVA 60510 3021 33W-0S A7
Hagen Ct
3800 WDRG 60517 3143 23W-7S A7
Hagen Ln
2000 FSMR 60422 3507 2W-22S C2
N Hager Av
100 BRTN 60010 2750 26W-20N D2
S Hager Av
100 BRTN 60010 2750 26W-18N D2
Hager Ln
300 GNVW 60025 2811 6W-13N C6
Haggard St
13400 HMGN 60491 3343 16W-18S D6
W Hague Ct
1200 JLET 60432 3499 22W-22S D2
E Hague Dr
10 ANTH 60002 2358 22W-42N A5
W Hague Dr
10 ANTH 60002 2358 23W-42N A5
Hague St
800 JLET 60432 3499 22W-22S D3
800 JltT 60432 3499 22W-22S D3
N Hague St
1200 JLET 60432 3499 22W-22S D1
Hahn Pl
900 WCHI 60185 3022 29W-0S D6
W Hahn St
100 EMHT 60126 3027 16W-1N E1
Hahndorf Rd
10 WCHI 60185 3022 29W-2N C1
10 WynT 60185 3022 29W-2N C1
Haider Av
2100 NPVL 60564 3266 29W-12S D3
W Haidi Ln
24000 LkvT 60046 2474 24W-37N D1
N Haig Ct
2100 PLTN 60074 2753 19W-18N B3
N Haig Point Ln
1500 VNHL 60061 2647 16W-26N D2
Hailshaw Ct
1200 WHTN 60187 3082 25W-1S B2
Haines Av
100 NLNX 60451 3501 18W-24S B6
100 NlxT 60451 3501 18W-24S B6
Haines Ct
1400 BTVA 60510 3019 36W-0S E7
Haines Dr
1500 BTVA 60510 3019 36W-0S E7
E Haines Dr
10 HNVL 60030 2532 22W-33N C3
W Haines St
800 CHCG 60622 3033 1W-1N E2
Hainesville Rd
1100 RLKB 60030 2475 22W-34N C7
1100 RLKB 60073 2475 22W-34N C7
Hainesville Rd CO-V60
1100 RLKB 60030 2475 22W-34N C7
1400 RLKB 60073 2475 22W-34N C7
N Hainesville Rd
10 HNVL 60030 2532 22W-34N C1
100 HNVL 60073 2532 22W-33N C3
500 AvnT 60030 2532 22W-34N C1
500 RLKP 60073 2532 22W-34N C1
600 AvnT 60073 2532 22W-34N C1
800 RLKB 60073 2532 22W-34N C1
34600 RLKB 60073 2475 22W-34N B7
N Hainesville Rd CO-V60
10 HNVL 60030 2532 22W-34N C1
100 HNVL 60073 2532 22W-33N C3
500 AvnT 60030 2532 22W-34N C1
500 RLKP 60073 2532 22W-34N C1
600 AvnT 60073 2532 22W-34N C1
800 RLKB 60073 2532 22W-34N C1
34600 RLKB 60073 2475 22W-34N B7
S Hainesville Rd
10 HNVL 60030 2532 22W-32N B4
Hainsworth Av
2200 FTPK 60130 3088 9W-2S C3
2200 NRIV 60546 3088 9W-2S C3
2500 RVSD 60546 3088 9W-2S C3
Haise Ct
1400 EGVV 60007 2913 21W-8N E3
Haise Ln
1400 EGVV 60007 2913 21W-8N E3
W Haladay Ln
300 BbyT 60134 3018 39W-0S E7
300 BbyT 60134 3076 39W-0S D1
Halbert Ln
700 IVNS 60010 2751 25W-16N A7
Halcyon Ln
400 NBRN 60010 2698 25W-23N B2
W Haldeman Av
800 JLET 60436 3498 25W-24S C6
Hale Av
- BRLT 60103 2911 28W-8N A2
300 RMVL 60446 3340 24W-16S E3
N Hale Av
100 BRLT 60103 2911 28W-8N A2
S Hale Av
100 BRLT 60103 2911 28W-8N A3
10300 CHCG 60643 3277 2W-12S C1
11800 BLID 60406 3277 2W-13S C5
11800 BLID 60643 3277 2W-13S C5
Hale Ct
10 GLHT 60139 2968 24W-3N E5
600 WLNG 60090 2754 16W-18N E2
Hale Dr
14900 ODPK 60462 3345 12W-17S C6
Hale Ln
3200 ISLK 60042 2586 30W-28N B6
3200 NndT 60042 2586 30W-28N B6
3200 NndT 60051 2586 30W-28N B6
Hale Rd
13300 LtRT 60545 3331 46W-14S E1
13300 LtRT 60545 3332 46W-14S A1
13800 PLNO 60545 3331 46W-14S E1
Hale St
200 MRGO 60152 2634 49W-26N B2
1300 MRGO 60152 2578 49W-27N B7
E Hale St
100 EMHT 60126 3028 15W-0S A6
N Hale St
10 PLNO 60545 3259 47W-13S D6
10 PLTN 60067 2805 20W-16N E1
100 PLTN 60067 2752 20W-16N E7
100 WHTN 60187 3024 24W-0S C6
S Hale St
10 PLNO 60545 3259 47W-14S D7
10 PLTN 60067 2805 20W-15N E2
200 ADSN 60101 2970 18W-3N E6
200 WHTN 60187 3024 24W-0S C7
700 LtRT 60545 3259 47W-14S D7
700 WHTN 60187 3082 24W-1S C1
1000 LtRT 60545 3331 47W-14S D1
1000 PLNO 60545 3331 47W-14S D1
Halesia Ct
7500 ODPK 60462 3346 9W-18S D7
Haley Ct
800 YKVL 60560 3333 42W-14S D1
11000 ODPK 60467 3423 13W-21S A7
Haley Dr
- JLET 60586 3415 32W-21S C6
Haley Rd
18700 NlxT 60448 3502 15W-22S B2
W Haley Rd
12800 MhtT 60442 3678 16W-31S E5
Haley Meadows Dr
600 RMVL 60446 3340 25W-15S C1
W Haleys Hill Ct
400 PLTN 60074 2752 21W-18N D3
Half Ln
100 ROSL 60172 2913 23W-8N A3
100 SmbT 60172 2913 23W-8N A3
Half Day Ln
1700 BKBN 60015 2703 12W-23N B2
Half Day Rd
10 LNSH 60045 2702 14W-23N C3
10 LNSH 60069 2702 14W-23N C3
10 VrnT 60069 2702 13W-23N D2
800 HDPK 60035 2703 11W-23N E3
800 HDPK 60035 2704 10W-23N A3
800 HIWD 60040 2704 9W-23N C3
800 WdfT 60015 2703 11W-23N D3
1100 BKBN 60015 2703 12W-23N C3
2200 VrnT 60015 2703 12W-23N C3
2300 LNSH 60069 2703 12W-23N A2
2300 VrnT 60069 2703 12W-23N A2
Half Day Rd SR-22
10 LNSH 60045 2702 14W-23N C3
10 LNSH 60069 2702 14W-23N C3
10 VrnT 60069 2702 13W-23N D2
800 HDPK 60035 2703 11W-23N E3
800 WdfT 60015 2703 11W-23N D3
1100 BKBN 60015 2703 12W-23N C3
1300 HDPK 60035 2704 10W-23N A3
2200 VrnT 60015 2703 12W-23N C3
2300 LNSH 60069 2703 12W-23N A2
2300 VrnT 60069 2703 12W-23N A2
W Half Day Rd
- LGGV 60089 2701 17W-23N B3
- VrnT 60089 2701 16W-22N D3
10 LNSH 60069 2702 15W-22N A3
100 BFGV 60069 2701 16W-22N C3
100 BFGV 60089 2701 16W-22N C3
100 VrnT 60069 2701 16W-22N C3
400 LNSH 60069 2701 15W-22N E3
5500 BFGV 60047 2701 17W-23N A3
5500 LGGV 60047 2701 17W-23N B3
14400 LNSH 60045 2702 14W-23N C2
14500 VrnT 60069 2702 15W-22N A3
W Half Day Rd SR-22
- LGGV 60089 2701 17W-23N B3
- VrnT 60089 2701 16W-22N D3
10 LNSH 60069 2702 15W-22N A3
100 BFGV 60069 2701 16W-22N C3
100 BFGV 60089 2701 16W-22N C3
100 VrnT 60069 2701 16W-22N C3
400 LNSH 60069 2701 15W-22N E3
5500 BFGV 60047 2701 17W-23N A3
5500 LGGV 60047 2701 17W-23N B3
14400 LNSH 60045 2702 14W-23N C2
14500 VrnT 60069 2702 15W-22N A3
Half Mile Tr
4600 NndT 60012 2584 33W-28N D6
4600 PRGV 60012 2584 33W-28N D6
Half Moon Cir
100 AURA 60504 3139 31W-6S E5
100 AURA 60504 3201 31W-7S E1
Half Moon Ct
500 OSWG 60543 3200 34W-11S E7
Half Moon Bay Ct
100 RMVL 60446 3340 25W-16S B4
Halfmoon Gate
- CLLK 60014 2693 36W-22N D4
- CLLK 60156 2693 36W-22N D4
1100 LIHL 60156 2693 36W-22N D4
Halfmoon Lake Wy
16400 LktT 60403 3417 26W-19S E3
Halien Ter
500 PKRG 60068 2863 11W-9N C7
Halifax Av
2900 WSTR 60154 3086 13W-2S E4
3000 PvsT 60154 3086 13W-2S E4
3000 PvsT 60558 3086 13W-2S E4
Halifax Ct
800 SMBG 60193 2912 24W-9N D1
4200 NPVL 60564 3266 28W-12S E3
Halifax Dr
1200 MDLN 60060 2590 19W-29N B4
W Halifax Dr
21700 PnfT 60544 3339 27W-16S D4
Halifax Rd
800 GRNE 60031 2534 16W-33N C4
800 WrnT 60048 2534 16W-33N C4
Halifax St
1900 LYVL 60048 2591 17W-30N A1
Haligus Rd
- HTLY 60142 2692 39W-20N C7
- RtdT 60142 2745 39W-20N C2
5600 CLLK 60014 2638 39W-26N C3
5600 CLLK 60098 2638 39W-26N C3
5600 DrrT 60014 2638 39W-26N C3
5600 DrrT 60098 2638 39W-26N C3
5800 GfnT 60014 2638 39W-26N C3
Haligus Rd
5800 GfnT 60098 2638 39W-26N C3
5800 LKWD 60098 2638 39W-26N C3
6100 LKWD 60014 2638 39W-24N D7
6100 LKWD 60142 2638 39W-26N C3
6400 GfnT 60142 2638 39W-24N D7
7600 GfnT 60014 2692 39W-23N D1
7600 GfnT 60142 2692 39W-23N D1
7600 LIHL 60142 2692 39W-23N D1
7600 LIHL 60156 2692 39W-23N D1
7600 LKWD 60014 2692 39W-23N D1
7600 LKWD 60142 2692 39W-23N D1
11700 HTLY 60142 2745 39W-20N C1
Halina Dr E
2400 GNVW 60025 2809 10W-15N E3
W Haling Rd
26000 AntT 60002 2415 26W-39N E4
Halkirk Cir
100 IVNS 60067 2805 22W-15N A1
Hall Ct
1300 BTVA 60510 3078 34W-2S E4
Hall Pl
1700 DRGV 60516 3206 20W-8S A1
Hall St
1100 SRGV 60554 3136 40W-5S B2
1600 DRGV 60516 3206 20W-8S B1
E Hall St
- SDWH 60548 3330 51W-15S A2
Halladay Ct
1400 BTVA 60510 3077 36W-2S E4
Halladay Dr
1100 BTVA 60510 3077 36W-2S E3
Hallberg Ln
1300 PKRG 60068 2863 10W-10N E4
1300 PKRG 60068 2864 10W-10N A4
Hallbraith Ct
10 NBRN 60010 2644 24W-25N B5
Haller Av
200 RMVL 60446 3340 24W-16S E3
200 RMVL 60446 3341 23W-16S A3
Hallick Dr
500 HFET 60010 2856 29W-11N E3
500 HFET 60107 2856 29W-11N E3
500 HnrT 60010 2856 29W-11N E3
500 HnrT 60107 2856 29W-11N E3
Halligan Cir
500 LKFT 60045 2649 12W-26N B2
Halligan Wy
10600 MKNA 60448 3503 13W-23S B2
Hallmark Ct
2000 CLSM 60188 3024 24W-0N D4
2000 WHTN 60187 3024 24W-0N D4
Hallmark Ln
400 BGBK 60440 3269 22W-12S B2
Halloran Ln
6000 HFET 60192 2855 31W-12N D1
Halloway St
4900 MTSN 60443 3506 6W-24S A5
E Halma Ln
1600 WDSK 60098 2582 40W-30N A2
W Halma Ln
1600 WDSK 60098 2582 40W-30N A2
Halpin Dr
100 DSPN 60016 2808 13W-13N E6
Halsey Ct
10 WDRG 60517 3143 22W-7S C6
Halsey Dr
2000 DSPN 60018 2917 12W-8N B2
3000 WDRG 60517 3143 22W-7S C6
Halsey Rd
200 OKTR 60181 3085 17W-1S C2
Halste Ln
- HDPK 60035 2704 8W-21N E6
Halstead Av
700 RMVL 60446 3340 24W-15S D2
Halsted Av
600 SchT 60174 2908 35W-6N B6
Halsted Blvd
3400 STGR 60475 3596 1W-28S B6
Halsted Ct
2200 AURA 60503 3201 33W-10S B5
Halsted Ln
1600 AURA 60503 3201 32W-10S B5
S Halsted Pkwy
6100 CHCG 60621 3152 0W-7S A5
Halsted St
- EHZC 60426 3428 0W-20S B4
- EHZC 60473 3428 0W-20S B4
3000 SCHT 60411 3596 1W-27S A5
3000 SCHT 60475 3596 1W-27S A5
3000 STGR 60475 3596 1W-27S A5
14300 HRVY 60426 3350 1W-17S A5
14300 RVDL 60827 3350 1W-17S A5
15000 PHNX 60426 3350 1W-18S B6
15600 HRVY 60426 3428 1W-19S B2
16900 SHLD 60426 3428 0W-20S B4
16900 SHLD 60473 3428 0W-20S B4
17100 EHZC 60429 3428 0W-20S B5
17300 EHZC 60430 3428 0W-20S B5
17300 HMWD 60429 3428 0W-20S B5
17300 HMWD 60430 3428 0W-20S B5
18000 GNWD 60425 3428 0W-21S B7
18000 HMWD 60425 3428 0W-21S B7
Halsted St SR-1
- EHZC 60426 3428 0W-20S B4
- EHZC 60473 3428 0W-20S B4
- PHNX 60426 3350 1W-18S B7
14300 HRVY 60426 3350 1W-17S A5
14300 HRVY 60827 3350 1W-17S A5
14300 RVDL 60827 3350 1W-17S A5
15600 HRVY 60426 3428 1W-19S B3
16900 SHLD 60426 3428 0W-20S B4
16900 SHLD 60473 3428 0W-20S B4
17100 EHZC 60429 3428 0W-20S B5
17300 EHZC 60430 3428 0W-20S B5
17300 HMWD 60429 3428 0W-20S B5
17300 HMWD 60430 3428 0W-20S B5
18000 GNWD 60425 3428 0W-21S B7
18000 HMWD 60425 3428 0W-21S B7
N Halsted St
10 CHCG 60607 3034 1W-0N A4
10 CHCG 60661 3034 1W-0N A4
300 CHCG 60610 3034 0W-0N A3
300 CHCG 60622 3034 0W-0N A3
900 CHCG 60610 3033 1W-1N E1
900 CHCG 60622 3033 1W-1N E1
1600 CHCG 60610 2977 0W-2N E7
1600 CHCG 60614 2977 0W-2N E7
1600 CHCG 60622 2977 0W-2N E7
2700 CHCG 60657 2977 0W-3N E4
3500 CHCG 60613 2977 1W-2N E7
S Halsted St
- RVDL 60827 3278 0W-15S A7
10 CHCG 60661 3034 1W-0S A5
100 CHHT 60411 3508 1W-25S B7
S Halsted St
1100 CHCG 60607 3034 1W-1S A7
1100 CHCG 60608 3034 1W-1S A7
1500 CHCG 60616 3034 0W-1S A7
1500 CHHT 60411 3596 1W-26S B1
1700 CHCG 60608 3092 0W-3S A5
1700 CHCG 60616 3092 0W-3S A5
2500 SCHT 60411 3596 1W-26S B2
3400 CHCG 60609 3092 0W-3S A4
4700 CHCG 60609 3152 1W-5S A1
5500 CHCG 60621 3152 0W-7S A6
7500 CHCG 60621 3214 0W-8S A1
8600 CHCG 60620 3214 1W-10S A5
9400 CHCG 60628 3214 1W-11S A7
9400 CHCG 60643 3214 1W-11S A7
10300 CHCG 60628 3278 1W-12S A1
10300 CHCG 60643 3278 1W-12S A1
12200 CHCG 60628 3278 1W-14S A6
12200 CTPK 60643 3278 1W-14S A6
12200 CTPK 60827 3278 1W-14S A6
13100 RVDL 60827 3350 1W-16S A4
14500 HRVY 60426 3350 1W-16S A4
14500 HRVY 60827 3350 1W-16S A4
18300 GNWD 60425 3428 0W-22S B7
18300 GNWD 60425 3508 1W-23S B3
18300 HMWD 60430 3428 0W-22S B7
18500 HMWD 60425 3508 1W-23S B3
18500 HMWD 60430 3508 1W-23S B3
19100 BlmT 60411 3508 1W-23S B3
19100 GNWD 60411 3508 1W-23S B3
S Halsted St SR-1
- RVDL 60827 3278 0W-15S A7
100 CHHT 60411 3508 1W-23S B4
9900 CHCG 60628 3214 1W-11S A7
9900 CHCG 60643 3214 1W-11S A7
10300 CHCG 60628 3278 1W-12S A1
10300 CHCG 60643 3278 1W-12S A1
12200 CTPK 60628 3278 1W-14S A6
12200 CTPK 60643 3278 1W-14S A6
12200 CTPK 60827 3278 1W-14S A6
13100 RVDL 60827 3350 1W-16S A4
14500 HRVY 60426 3350 1W-16S A4
14500 HRVY 60827 3350 1W-16S A4
18300 GNWD 60425 3428 0W-22S B7
18300 GNWD 60425 3508 1W-23S B3
18300 HMWD 60430 3428 0W-22S B7
18500 HMWD 60425 3508 1W-23S B3
18500 HMWD 60430 3508 1W-23S B3
19100 BlmT 60411 3508 1W-23S B3
19100 GNWD 60411 3508 1W-23S B3
Halts Pl
6100 CHCG 60631 2918 9W-7N C3
Haman Av
4200 HFET 60192 2804 24W-15N C2
4300 HFET 60067 2804 24W-15N C2
4300 IVNS 60067 2804 24W-15N C2
Haman Ct
4300 HFET 60192 2804 24W-15N C2
Haman Rd
10 HFET 60010 2804 24W-15N D1
10 HFET 60067 2804 24W-15N D1
10 HFET 60192 2804 24W-15N D1
10 IVNS 60067 2804 24W-15N D1
10 IVNS 60192 2804 24W-15N D1
N Haman Rd
100 IVNS 60010 2751 24W-16N D6
S Haman Rd
10 IVNS 60010 2751 24W-16N D7
200 HFET 60010 2751 24W-16N D7
S Hamann Ct
2000 HMND 46394 3280 E5
S Hamann Ct E
1900 HMND 46394 3280 D5
S Hamann Ct W
1900 HMND 46394 3280 D5
Hambletonian Dr
300 OKBK 60515 3084 18W-3S E6
300 OKBK 60523 3084 18W-3S E6
300 OKBK 60523 3085 17W-3S B6
300 YkTp 60515 3084 18W-3S E6
Hamelitz Ct
- GYLK 60030 2532 21W-32N E4
Hamelton Ct
4400 LGGV 60047 2700 18W-23N E3
Hamill Ln
10 CNHL 60514 3145 16W-5S D2
Hamilton Av
- DGvT 60527 3208 15W-9S B3
10 ELGN 60123 2854 34W-11N D3
100 FKFT 60423 3591 12W-25S C1
200 FKFT 60423 3503 12W-25S C7
500 WTMT 60559 3085 17W-4S C6
600 AURA 60505 3200 36W-8S A2
1200 HLSD 60162 3028 14W-1S C7
1200 PvsT 60126 3028 14W-1S C7
1200 PvsT 60126 3086 14W-1S C1
1200 PvsT 60162 3028 14W-1S C7
1200 PvsT 60162 3086 14W-1S C1
7200 BRRG 60527 3146 15W-8S B7
7200 BRRG 60527 3208 15W-8S B1
15900 MKHM 60428 3427 2W-19S C2
15900 ThtT 60428 3427 2W-19S C2
16200 TYPK 60477 3424 9W-19S D2
38200 AntT 60081 2415 27W-38N B7
N Hamilton Av
400 VLPK 60181 3027 17W-1N B2
2200 CHCG 60647 2977 2W-2N B6
3800 CHCG 60618 2977 2W-4N B2
4400 CHCG 60618 2921 2W-5N B7
4400 CHCG 60625 2921 2W-5N B7
6100 CHCG 60659 2921 2W-7N B3
6800 CHCG 60645 2921 2W-8N B1
7200 CHCG 60645 2867 2W-9N B7
S Hamilton Av
200 CHCG 60612 3033 2W-0S B5
1000 CHCG 60608 3033 2W-0S B7
1700 CHCG 60608 3091 2W-1S B1
3500 CHCG 60609 3091 2W-3S B5
5300 CHCG 60609 3151 2W-5S B2
5500 CHCG 60636 3151 2W-6S B3
7500 CHCG 60620 3213 2W-8S C1
9500 CHCG 60643 3213 2W-11S C6
10300 CHCG 60643 3277 2W-12S C1
Hamilton Ct
10 LKBF 60044 2593 11W-29N E4
100 WHTN 60187 3082 25W-2S A3
600 BRLT 60103 2910 30W-7N B5
700 SMBG 60194 2857 26W-11N E4
800 WTMT 60559 3085 17W-4S C7
1400 WKGN 60085 2536 11W-34N E1
1800 IVNS 60010 2751 25W-17N A6
9200 MaiT 60016 2863 11W-12N D1
9200 NLES 60714 2863 11W-12N D1
N Hamilton Ct
800 PLTN 60067 2752 21W-17N D6
Hamilton Dr
- PNFD 60585 3338 30W-15S B2
- WldT 60585 3338 30W-15S B2
400 WHTN 60187 3082 25W-2S A3
2100 CPVL 60110 2800 35W-16N C1
2100 CPVL 60118 2800 35W-16N B1
2100 WDND 60118 2800 35W-16N B1
2500 LNHT 60046 2418 19W-39N B5
5900 AlqT 60014 2641 32W-26N B4
5900 NndT 60014 2641 32W-26N A4
7000 GRNE 60031 2477 17W-35N B5
8500 MNGV 60053 2865 6W-10N C4
8500 SKOK 60053 2865 6W-10N C4
8500 SKOK 60077 2865 6W-10N C4
22400 RNPK 60471 3594 5W-27S C4
S Hamilton Dr
- CHCG 60620 3213 2W-9S C2
W Hamilton Dr
10 PLTN 60067 2752 21W-17N D6
6900 NLES 60714 2864 8W-10N E4
Hamilton Ln
10 OKBK 60523 3085 17W-2S C3
400 NARA 60542 3078 35W-4S B7
400 NARA 60542 3138 35W-4S B1
1100 DRFD 60015 2704 10W-21N A6
1100 LMBD 60148 3026 18W-0S E6
1200 NPVL 60540 3204 24W-8S C1
2200 DRN 60561 3206 19W-8S D2
W Hamilton Ln
300 PLTN 60067 2752 21W-17N D6
Hamilton Pkwy
1200 ITSC 60007 2914 21W-7N A3
1200 ITSC 60143 2913 21W-7N E3
1200 ITSC 60143 2914 21W-7N A3
Hamilton Pl
100 VNHL 60061 2647 17W-26N C3
2300 SMBG 60194 2857 26W-11N E4
Hamilton Rd
- UYPK 60466 3684 3W-30S A3
100 EGvT 60005 2861 16W-9N D6
900 UYPK 60466 3682 7W-30S D3
1200 MONE 60449 3682 7W-30S D4
1200 MONE 60466 3682 7W-30S D4
1200 MonT 60449 3682 7W-30S D4
1200 UYPK 60449 3682 7W-30S D4
W Hamilton Rd
3400 MonT 60449 3683 4W-30S E3
3400 MonT 60449 3684 4W-30S A3
3400 MonT 60466 3683 4W-30S E3
3400 MonT 60466 3684 4W-30S A3
3400 UYPK 60449 3684 4W-30S A3
3400 UYPK 60466 3684 4W-30S A3
Hamilton St
- SRWD 60404 3496 30W-22S B2
10 BNVL 60106 2972 15W-5N A1
100 CHCG 60106 2972 15W-5N A1
100 EVTN 60202 2867 2W-10N B4
400 WMTN 60481 3943 27W-40S C2
400 WslT 60481 3943 27W-40S C2
700 GNVA 60134 3020 35W-1N B3
N Hamilton St
100 LKPT 60441 3419 22W-18S D2
200 LktT 60441 3419 22W-18S D2
S Hamilton St
100 LKPT 60441 3419 22W-20S C4
Hamilton Wy
600 BTVA 60510 3019 37W-0S C7
Hamilton Wood
400 BlmT 60430 3507 1W-23S E3
400 CHHT 60411 3507 1W-23S E3
400 CHHT 60430 3507 1W-23S E3
500 CHHT 60422 3507 1W-23S E3
500 FSMR 60422 3507 1W-23S E3
500 FSMR 60430 3507 1W-23S E3
S Hamlet Av
11100 CHCG 60643 3277 1W-13S D3
Hamlet Cir
100 MTGY 60538 3200 36W-10S A5
Hamlet Rd
1000 NPVL 60564 3267 28W-11S A1
Hamlet St
100 BTVA 60510 3078 34W-1S D1
700 BTVA 60510 3020 34W-0S D7
Hamlin Av
800 FSMR 60422 3506 4W-23S D3
1000 RchT 60430 3506 4W-23S D3
7200 LNWD 60076 2866 4W-9N C7
7200 LNWD 60712 2866 4W-9N C7
7300 SKOK 60712 2866 4W-9N C7
7800 SKOK 60076 2866 4W-9N C6
9200 MaiT 60016 2863 11W-11N E3
9200 PKRG 60068 2863 11W-11N E3
9200 SKOK 60203 2866 4W-11N C2
9400 NLES 60016 2863 11W-11N E3
9400 NLES 60714 2863 11W-11N E3
9500 EVTN 60201 2866 4W-11N C2
14700 MDLN 60445 3348 4W-17S D6
15400 MDLN 60428 3348 4W-18S D7
15400 MKHM 60428 3348 4W-18S D7
15600 MKHM 60428 3426 4W-18S D1
16600 CCHL 60478 3426 4W-19S D3
N Hamlin Av
10 CHCG 60624 3032 4W-0N C5
10 PKRG 60068 2917 11W-9N E1
200 PKRG 60068 2863 11W-9N E7
1600 CHCG 60647 2976 4W-2N C7
1600 CHCG 60647 3032 4W-1N C1
1600 CHCG 60651 3032 4W-1N C1
2700 CHCG 60618 2976 4W-3N C5
4300 CHCG 60625 2976 4W-5N C1
4400 CHCG 60625 2920 4W-5N C7
6100 CHCG 60659 2920 4W-7N C3
6300 CHCG 60712 2920 4W-7N C3
6800 LNWD 60712 2920 4W-8N C1
7100 LNWD 60076 2920 4W-8N C1
7100 SKOK 60076 2920 4W-8N C1
9400 MaiT 60016 2863 11W-11N E2
9400 NLES 60016 2863 11W-11N E2
9400 NLES 60714 2863 11W-11N E2
S Hamlin Av
10 PKRG 60068 2917 11W-8N E1
1400 CHCG 60623 3032 4W-1S C7
1500 CHCG 60623 3090 4W-2S C3
4500 CHCG 60632 3090 4W-4S C7
4600 CHCG 60632 3150 4W-5S C1
5400 CHCG 60629 3150 4W-5S C7
7300 CHCG 60629 3212 4W-8S C1
7500 CHCG 60652 3212 4W-8S C1
9100 CHCG 60805 3212 4W-10S C5
9100 ENGN 60805 3212 4W-10S C5
9800 CHCG 60655 3212 4W-11S C7
10300 CHCG 60655 3276 4W-12S C2
11400 WthT 60655 3276 4W-13S D4
11400 WthT 60803 3276 4W-14S D5
11700 ALSP 60803 3276 4W-14S D5
13300 CTWD 60472 3348 4W-16S D2

STREET Block City ZIP Map# CGS Grid

S Hamlin Av
13300 RBBN 60472 3348 4W-16S D3
13300 WthT 60472 3348 4W-15S D2
S Hamlin Blvd
10 CHCG 60624 3032 4W-0S C5
Hamlin Ct
500 PKRG 60068 2917 11W-8N E2
S Hamlin Ct
4900 HMND 46320 3352 D5
12600 ALSP 60803 3276 4W-14S D7
13000 ALSP 60803 3348 4W-15S D1
Hamlin Ln
15100 PNFD 60544 3338 30W-18S B7
15100 PNFD 60544 3416 30W-18S B1
S Hamlin Ln
1700 RDLK 60030 2588 23W-31N E1
1700 RDLK 60073 2531 23W-31N E7
1700 RDLK 60073 2588 23W-31N E1
W Hamlin Ln
400 RDLK 60073 2531 23W-31N E7
Hamlin Rd
3600 JNBG 60050 2471 32W-35N B5
Hamlin St
400 PKFT 60466 3507 3W-25S A7
400 PKFT 60466 3595 3W-25S A1
800 EVTN 60201 2867 2W-11N B2
Hamman Wy
2600 AURA 60502 3139 32W-6S D4
Hammel Av
2100 AURA 60504 3201 33W-9S B5
Hammer Ln
500 NARA 60542 3078 35W-3S B6
Hammer Creek Ct
1500 NPVL 60563 3141 27W-5S C2
Hammerschmidt Av
600 LMBD 60148 3026 19W-0S C6
Hammersmith Ln
4300 GNVW 60025 2809 11W-14N C3
N Hammes Av
10 JLET 60435 3497 26W-23S E4
10 JLET 60436 3497 26W-24S E5
S Hammes Av
10 JLET 60435 3497 26W-24S E5
10 JLET 60436 3497 26W-24S E5
Hammond Av
300 ELGN 60120 2855 33W-9N A7
500 AURA 60506 3138 36W-6S A6
2400 BNHM 60633 3351 3E-16S E4
E Hammond Av
10 MDLN 60060 2590 18W-27N D7
2600 BNHM 60633 3351 3E-16S E4
2700 BNHM 60633 3352 3E-17S A4
W Hammond Av
10 MDLN 60060 2590 19W-27N D7
Hammond Dr
2000 SMBG 60173 2805 21W-13N C6
Hammond Ln
1400 FDHT 60411 3509 1E-24S B6
Hammond St
100 WCDA 60084 2644 25W-27N A1
N Hampden Ct
2600 CHCG 60614 2978 0W-3N A5
2700 CHCG 60657 2978 0W-3N A5
Hampdon Ct
200 BGBK 60440 3268 24W-12S D2
Hampshire Av
200 AURA 60505 3138 33W-7S E7
N Hampshire Av
100 EMHT 60126 3028 15W-1N B2
S Hampshire Av
400 EMHT 60126 3028 15W-0N B4
Hampshire Ct
10 BGBK 60440 3205 22W-10S C6
200 NLNX 60451 3501 18W-24S B5
200 NPVL 60565 3203 26W-9S E5
400 GYLK 60030 2533 20W-32N A5
1100 SMBG 60193 2913 22W-9N B1
1300 ROSL 60172 2912 25W-7N A4
6300 LSLE 60532 3142 24W-7S C6
N Hampshire Ct
100 BMDL 60108 2968 25W-5N C1
Hampshire Dr
600 HPSR 60140 2795 47W-15N D3
600 HshT 60140 2795 47W-15N C3
1600 EGVV 60007 2859 21W-9N D7
1600 EGVV 60007 2913 21W-9N D1
1800 HFET 60192 2855 31W-12N E1
W Hampshire Dr
300 BMDL 60108 2968 24W-5N C1
17800 WrnT 60031 2477 18W-36N A4
Hampshire Ln
- LKZH 60047 2698 24W-24N C1
- LYWD 60411 3509 2E-23S D4
200 BGBK 60440 3205 22W-10S C6
200 LKWD 60014 2639 37W-25N C5
400 CLLK 60014 2639 37W-25N C6
900 ELGN 60120 2855 32W-12N C1
3000 WKGN 60087 2478 15W-37N B2
4700 MchT 60050 2471 32W-36N B3
5200 MchT 60081 2471 32W-36N B3
24100 PNFD 60585 3338 30W-15S C2
N Hampshire Ln
37100 LkvT 60046 2474 25W-37N A2
W Hampshire Ln
300 BMDL 60108 2968 25W-5N C1
12500 HMGN 60491 3344 15W-17S B6
Hampshire Ln E
200 DGvT 60527 3207 17W-10S C5
Hampshire Ln W
200 DGvT 60527 3207 17W-10S C5
Hampshire Pkwy
800 CRTE 60417 3596 0W-28S D6
W Hampshire Pl
21500 FmtT 60060 2645 21W-26N D3
Hampson Ct
2600 ZION 60099 2421 11W-40N D4
Hampstead Ct
800 BRTN 60010 2697 25W-20N E7
Hampstead Ln
9000 WDRG 60517 3206 20W-10S B6
Hampsted Dr
- SgrT 60554 3135 42W-6S C4
- SRGV 60554 3135 42W-6S C4
Hampton Av
- NARA 60506 3076 39W-3S C6
100 WTMT 60559 3145 18W-6S A5
3800 PvsT 60558 3086 14W-4S D7
3800 WNSP 60558 3086 14W-4S D7
4300 WNSP 60558 3146 14W-4S D1
Hampton Blvd
- LbvT 60044 2593 13W-29N A3
100 NCHI 60044 2593 13W-29N A3
Hampton Cir
100 LslT 60540 3205 23W-8S A1
500 BRLT 60103 2911 28W-7N A4
600 ELGN 60120 2855 32W-10N D5
6800 GRNE 60031 2477 17W-35N B5
Hampton Ct
10 ALGN 60102 2747 35W-19N B2
10 BRRG 60527 3146 14W-7S C6
10 FSMR 60422 3507 4W-23S A3
10 FSMR 60430 3507 4W-23S A3
10 MDLN 60060 2591 17W-27N A7
10 RchT 60430 3507 4W-23S A3
10 RDLK 60073 2532 23W-32N A5
300 BMDL 60108 2969 22W-3N C4
300 CLLK 60012 2640 33W-26N D2
300 MltT 60148 3084 21W-2S A3
400 SchT 60175 2907 36W-7N D5
600 SRWD 60404 3496 31W-24S A6
900 CLSM 60188 2967 27W-3N D5
900 MHRY 60050 2527 33W-32N D4
1000 DRFD 60015 2703 12W-21N C6
1400 NPVL 60565 3204 25W-8S C2
1800 JLET 60586 3416 30W-21S B7
2100 SMWD 60107 2910 30W-9N C2
4100 GNVW 60025 2809 11W-15N D3
4100 GNVW 60062 2809 11W-15N D3
4100 NfdT 60062 2809 11W-15N D3
13200 PlsT 60462 3345 13W-15S A2
13200 PlsT 60467 3345 13W-15S A2
20100 FftT 60423 3504 9W-24S E5
W Hampton Ct
10 CRTE 60417 3685 0W-29S C1
13200 HTLY 60142 2744 43W-19N C2
Hampton Dr
10 OKBK 60523 3085 17W-2S B4
300 LKVL 60046 2475 22W-37N C2
400 WHTN 60187 3082 24W-2S C4
600 LkvT 60046 2475 22W-37N C2
600 WNVL 60555 3080 29W-2S C5
800 CLSM 60188 2967 27W-3N D5
900 RDLK 60073 2532 23W-32N A6
5700 LGGV 60047 2701 17W-23N A2
6000 CPVL 60110 2748 32W-17N D7
8100 WDRG 60517 3206 21W-9S A3
S Hampton Dr
1500 AURA 60506 3137 37W-6S C5
W Hampton Dr
100 RDLK 60073 2532 22W-32N A6
S Hampton Hbr
1000 SMBG 60193 2913 22W-9N B1
Hampton Ln
- YKVL 60560 3333 41W-16S E5
10 HNWD 60047 2700 20W-24N A1
10 MltT 60148 3084 21W-2S A3
10 YkTp 60148 3084 20W-2S A3
400 ROSL 60172 2912 25W-6N C6
1000 KdlT 60560 3333 41W-16S E5
1000 KdlT 60560 3334 41W-16S A5
1000 MDLN 60060 2647 17W-27N A1
1200 MDLN 60060 2591 17W-27N A7
1300 SMBG 60193 2858 25W-9N B7
2300 NHBK 60062 2809 11W-16N D1
Hampton Pk
900 BRTN 60010 2698 25W-20N A7
Hampton Pkwy
2700 EVTN 60091 2813 2W-13N A7
2700 EVTN 60201 2813 2W-13N A7
2700 WLMT 60091 2813 2W-13N A7
Hampton Pl
100 VNHL 60061 2647 17W-26N C3
300 HNDL 60521 3086 15W-4S B7
W Hampton Pl
1200 PLTN 60067 2805 22W-15N B1
Hampton Rd
- KLDR 60047 2699 21W-21N E5
10 OswT 60538 3199 37W-10S D6
200 SRGV 60554 3135 41W-6S E5
1800 HFET 60169 2858 24W-12N E1
1900 HFET 60169 2804 24W-12N E7
10600 PlsT 60462 3345 13W-15S A2
10600 PlsT 60467 3345 13W-15S A2
Hampton St
10 AlqT 60013 2695 32W-23N B1
10 CRY 60013 2695 32W-24N B1
400 CRY 60013 2641 32W-24N B7
Hampton Ter
400 LYVL 60048 2591 15W-28N E6
Hampton Course
600 WCHI 60185 3022 29W-1N E3
1300 SCRL 60174 2964 34W-4N C4
Hamptondale Rd
1100 WNKA 60093 2758 5W-16N E7
Hampton on Auburn
10 RGMW 60008 2806 19W-14N C3
Hamrick Av
300 RMVL 60446 3340 24W-16S D4
Hamshire Ct
600 OSWG 60543 3263 36W-12S E3
600 OSWG 60543 3264 36W-12S A3
Hamstead Ct
200 ROSL 60172 2912 25W-7N C5
W Hamstead Ct
1300 PLTN 60067 2805 22W-15N B2
Hanburg Ln
200 BGBK 60440 3268 25W-12S C2
Hanbury Ct
- BGVW 60455 3274 9W-11S D1
Hanbury Dr
200 LKZH 60047 2698 23W-22N E4
Hanbury Ln
1100 INCK 60061 2647 17W-25N A6
2400 MTGY 60538 3198 40W-10S C6
Hancock Av
- SchT 60177 2908 34W-7N D5
200 LKBF 60044 2593 11W-28N E5
300 SEGN 60177 2908 35W-7N C4
Hancock Ct
2300 NPVL 60564 3202 29W-10S D5
2700 LNHT 60046 2418 19W-38N C6
Hancock Dr
- HFET 60169 2858 25W-12N A1
- MchT 60097 2469 36W-36N D5
100 BMDL 60108 2968 23W-5N E2
200 NLNX 60451 3589 18W-26S B2
N Hancock Dr
2000 PLTN 60074 2753 20W-20N B1
Hancock Ln
5700 GRNE 60031 2477 16W-36N E4
Hancock St
1100 CLSM 60188 2968 25W-4N A4
10900 ODPK 60467 3423 13W-19S A3
11100 ODPK 60467 3422 14W-19S E3
Handel Ct
400 WHTN 60187 3082 24W-2S C4
Handel Ln
- WDSK 60098 2524 41W-33N E3
Handley Ct
700 LKZH 60047 2698 23W-22N E4
700 LKZH 60047 2699 23W-22N A4
800 MDLN 60060 2590 20W-28N A6
3000 LSLE 60563 3142 24W-5S C3
Handley Dr
- LslT 60563 3142 24W-5S C3
2900 LSLE 60563 3142 25W-5S C3
Handley Ln
2300 AURA 60502 3079 32W-3S C6
Haney Rd
15200 SHLD 60473 3350 0E-18S D6
S Hanford Ct
14200 PnfT 60544 3339 27W-16S C5
Hanford Ln
2500 AURA 60502 3139 32W-5S B3
Hanger Rd
10 RMVL 60441 3418 24W-18S D1
Hanging Fen Ct
2800 JNBG 60050 2471 31W-35N C5
W Hank Ct E
12600 HMGN 60491 3344 15W-17S B5
W Hank Ct W
12700 HMGN 60491 3344 15W-17S A5
Hankes Av
10 AURA 60505 3138 35W-6S C5
Hankes Rd
- SRGV 60554 3135 41W-5S D3
10 AURA 60506 3136 39W-6S D6
10 SgrT 60506 3136 40W-5S B4
300 SgrT 60506 3135 41W-5S E3
300 SRGV 60506 3135 41W-6S E4
300 SRGV 60506 3136 40W-5S B4
S Hankes Rd
10 AURA 60506 3136 39W-7S D7
Hank Hollow Dr
- KdlT 60560 3334 41W-17S A5
N Hanks Av
42100 BtnT 60099 2362 11W-42N D7
Hanlee Ct
1400 ELGN 60123 2854 35W-11N B4
Hanley Av
900 MHRY 60050 2528 32W-32N B4
1000 MHRY 60050 2527 33W-32N E4
Hanley Ct
1800 SMBG 60194 2858 25W-11N B3
Hanley Dr
700 ANTH 60002 2417 21W-41N D1
Hanley Ln
- HTLY 60142 2692 39W-22N C4
500 CLSM 60188 3024 24W-1N D3
500 WHTN 60187 3024 24W-1N D3
Hanlon Rd
200 GNOK 60048 2535 15W-31N B7
200 WKGN 60048 2535 15W-31N B7
200 WrnT 60048 2535 15W-32N B4
2200 GNOK 60048 2592 14W-31N B1
33000 WKGN 60031 2535 15W-32N B4
33000 WKGN 60085 2535 15W-32N B6
33000 WrnT 60031 2535 15W-32N B4
33000 WrnT 60085 2535 15W-32N B4
Hannaford Dr
- SgrT 60554 3135 42W-4S D2
- SRGV 60554 3135 42W-4S D2
Hannah Av
400 FTPK 60130 3030 9W-0S D5
1500 FTPK 60130 3088 9W-1S D1
Hannah Ct
- SEGN 60124 2907 38W-8N B3
1100 NPVL 60540 3202 29W-8S E1
Hannah Ln
- HNDL 60521 3146 14W-6S C3
Hannibal Cir
2400 JLET 60586 3416 29W-20S D6
4600 PnfT 60586 3416 29W-20S D6
W Hannibal Ct
21800 PnfT 60544 3339 27W-16S D5
Hannigan Dr
500 MNKA 60447 3672 34W-29S A2
Hanover Av
2100 JltT 60433 3500 21W-24S A5
10100 HTLY 60142 2692 39W-20N D7
Hanover Ct
- RGMW 60008 2860 19W-11N B2
10 BRRG 60527 3208 15W-10S B4
600 SMBG 60194 2859 23W-10N A5
700 OSWG 60543 3200 35W-10S B6
2200 NPVL 60565 3203 26W-10S D5
6400 LSLE 60532 3142 24W-7S C6
24600 PNFD 60585 3338 30W-15S A2
Hanover Dr
300 BGBK 60440 3269 22W-12S C2
1100 BTVA 60510 3078 34W-2S E4
4500 NndT 60012 2584 34W-27N C7
4500 NndT 60012 2640 34W-27N C1
7000 TYPK 60477 3424 9W-20S D4
Hanover Ln
10 SgrT 60506 3135 41W-5S E3
900 DYR 46311 3510 E6
1800 FSMR 60422 3507 2W-23S D3
Hanover Pl
- VNHL 60061 2647 16W-26N D2
W Hanover Pl
200 MPPT 60056 2807 15W-14N E3
Hanover St
300 HMND 46327 3352 D4
1200 WDRG 60517 3206 20W-9S B3
1500 CHHT 60411 3596 0W-25S C1
6900 HRPK 60133 2911 27W-8N D2
7100 BGVW 60455 3210 8W-10S E5
E Hanover St
100 HMND 46327 3352 D4
W Hanover St
7200 CHCG 60501 3148 9W-5S D3
7200 CHCG 60638 3148 9W-5S D3
7200 SMMT 60501 3148 9W-5S D3
N Hanover Hills Rd
21000 CbaT 60010 2698 25W-21N A5
21000 DRPK 60010 2698 25W-21N A5
Hans Brinker Ct
600 PTON 60468 3860 9W-37S D4
Hans Brinker Dr
300 PTON 60468 3860 9W-37S D4
Hanscom Ct
2300 SMBG 60193 2857 26W-10N E6
Hansel Rd
- AxST 60410 3672 32W-31S C6
- CNHN 60410 3672 33W-31S C6
E Hansel Rd
7400 AxST 60410 3672 34W-32S A7
7400 AxST 60450 3672 34W-32S A7
7400 CNHN 60410 3672 34W-32S A7
7400 CNHN 60447 3672 34W-32S A7
7400 CNHN 60450 3672 34W-32S A7
W Hansel Rd
25800 CNHN 60410 3672 32W-31S D5
25800 CnhT 60410 3672 32W-31S D5
Hansen Blvd
200 NARA 60506 3137 38W-4S A2
Hansen Ct
100 WDDL 60191 2915 18W-7N A5
Hansen Pl
700 PKRG 60068 2864 10W-9N A7
Hansen Rd
12100 HBRN 60034 2350 41W-42N E6
Hansford Av
2500 BTVA 60510 3019 37W-0S C7
Hanslik Ct
8900 WldT 60564 3201 31W-10S E6
Hansom Ct
200 WLNG 60090 2755 15W-18N A2
1900 NPVL 60565 3204 25W-9S B4
Hansom Dr
100 WLNG 60090 2755 15W-18N A2
Hanson Cir
10 RMVL 60446 3341 23W-16S A4
S Hanson Ct
25100 MonT 60449 3682 8W-30S A3
Hanson Rd
10 ALGN 60102 2694 35W-20N B7
10 LIHL 60102 2694 35W-20N B7
10 LIHL 60156 2694 35W-20N B7
10 LYLK 60151 2961 43W-5N A3
10 LYLK 60175 2961 43W-5N A3
11600 AlqT 60102 2747 34W-20N B1
11800 ALGN 60102 2747 34W-20N B1
Hanson St
800 BTVA 60510 3078 34W-1S D2
Hanssen Rd
5500 WDWH 60031 2478 15W-37N A2
5600 WDWH 60031 2477 16W-37N E2
5600 WDWH 60083 2477 16W-37N E2
5600 WrnT 60031 2477 16W-37N E2
Hapner Wy
3500 BTVA 60510 3077 37W-1S B2
Happ Rd
500 NHFD 60093 2811 7W-16N B1
800 NHFD 60093 2758 7W-16N B7
900 NHBK 60062 2758 7W-16N B7
900 NHFD 60062 2758 7W-16N B7
1000 NHBK 60093 2758 7W-16N B7
S Happ Rd
10 NHFD 60093 2811 6W-15N C3
10 NtrT 60093 2811 6W-14N C4
10 WLMT 60091 2811 6W-14N C4
W Happfield Dr
- ANHT 60089 2754 18W-18N A3
- BFGV 60089 2753 18W-18N E3
200 ANHT 60004 2754 18W-18N A3
200 BFGV 60004 2754 18W-18N A4
300 BFGV 60089 2754 18W-18N A3
800 ANHT 60004 2753 18W-18N E3
Happy Tr
10600 GwdT 60098 2525 39W-34N C1
Happy Hills Rd
100 CmpT 60175 2962 39W-3N E6
200 SCRL 60175 2962 39W-3N E7
Happy Hollow Rd
2400 GNVW 60025 2809 10W-15N E3
2400 GNVW 60025 2810 10W-15N A2
Happy Trails
- DMND 60416 3941 33W-39S A2
Hapsfield Ln
500 BFGV 60089 2754 17W-18N B4
Harasek St
600 LMNT 60439 3270 18W-14S E6
Har-Bar Cir
- WPHR 60096 2362 11W-42N E5
Har-Bar Dr
- WPHR 60096 2362 11W-42N E5
Harbor Av
1600 BNHM 60633 3351 2E-16S D4
1600 CTCY 60409 3351 2E-16S D4
1600 CTCY 60633 3351 2E-16S D4
S Harbor Av
9100 CHCG 60617 3216 4E-10S A5
Harbor Cir
4400 HFET 60192 2804 25W-15N B2
Harbor Ct
10 NPVL 60565 3204 26W-9S A3
10 VNHL 60061 2647 16W-25N D5
200 BMDL 60108 2969 22W-4N B3
1100 GLHT 60139 3024 23W-1N E2
2400 AURA 60504 3201 32W-9S C3
N Harbor Ct
- WmTp 60408 3942 31W-39S B2
- WmTp 60481 3942 31W-39S B2
300 BDWD 60408 3942 30W-40S C4
300 RedT 60408 3942 30W-40S C4
W Harbor Ct
7700 FftT 60423 3504 9W-24S E5
Harbor Dr
10 WLMT 60091 2813 2W-13N B6
100 MTGY 60543 3263 38W-11S B1
400 CPVL 60110 2800 35W-16N C1
400 WDND 60118 2800 35W-16N C1
1200 LKPT 60441 3341 21W-18S E7
2500 JLET 60431 3417 28W-20S B5
2500 JLET 60435 3417 28W-20S B5
7900 PSHT 60463 3274 9W-13S C4
14800 OKFT 60452 3347 7W-17S C5
E Harbor Dr
10 LKZH 60010 2699 22W-21N B6
10 LKZH 60047 2699 22W-21N B6
N Harbor Dr
100 CHCG 60601 3034 0E-0N D4
W Harbor Dr
100 LKZH 60047 2699 22W-21N A6
Harbor Ln
800 WPHR 60096 2363 10W-42N A6
2200 HRPK 60133 2967 27W-4N B3
2800 NHBK 60062 2756 11W-18N E4
5000 RNPK 60471 3594 6W-26S A3
Harbor Lndg
100 BDWD 60408 3942 30W-41S C4
100 RedT 60481 3942 30W-41S C4
N Harbor Pl
10 WKGN 60085 2537 9W-34N B1
S Harbor Pl
10 WKGN 60085 2537 10W-34N B2
Harbor Pt
1100 CLSM 60188 2967 27W-4N C3
Harbor Rd
100 LKBN 60010 2696 28W-23N E1
100 LKBN 60010 2697 28W-23N A1
7300 MchT 60097 2469 36W-37N E2
N Harbor Rd
21500 CbaT 60010 2697 27W-21N C5
22100 LKBN 60010 2697 27W-21N C5
Harbor St
10 GLNC 60022 2759 5W-17N A6
100 GLNC 60022 2758 5W-17N E6
Harbor Ter
400 BRLT 60103 2911 28W-7N B4
E Harbor Ter
500 BRLT 60103 2911 27W-7N C4
Harbor Ridge Dr
3200 ZION 60099 2362 11W-41N D7
N Harbor Ridge Dr
39800 AntT 60002 2416 24W-39N B4
39800 LkvT 60002 2416 25W-39N B4
40000 AntT 60046 2416 24W-40N C4
E Harbor Ridge Wy
2400 LNHT 60046 2418 19W-39N B5
Harborside Ct
3000 JLET 60586 3415 32W-20S C4
Harborside Dr
10 NHBK 60062 2756 11W-17N D5
Harborside Wy
- HNWD 60047 2645 22W-26N B2
Harbor Town Ct
900 GNVA 60134 3019 36W-0N E5
Harbor Town Dr
900 ELGN 60123 2908 36W-9N A1
15500 ODPK 60462 3346 9W-18S D7
15600 ODPK 60462 3424 9W-18S D1
Harbour Ct
1000 WLNG 60090 2754 16W-16N D6
1500 SMBG 60193 2912 25W-8N B2
Harbour Dr
1000 PTHT 60070 2754 16W-16N D6
1000 PTHT 60090 2754 16W-16N D6
1000 WLNG 60090 2754 16W-16N D6
1500 ANHT 60004 2754 16W-16N D7
1500 ANHT 60090 2754 16W-16N D7
Harbour Ln
22800 PNFD 60544 3339 28W-15S A3
22800 PNFD 60585 3339 28W-15S A3
Harbour Ter
100 EMHT 60126 3027 16W-1N E3
Harbour Towne Pl
1500 AURA 60564 3202 30W-9S B4
Harcourt Dr
1800 DGvT 60516 3206 20W-9S A3
1800 WDRG 60517 3206 21W-9S A3
Harcourt St
5200 BmnT 60452 3425 6W-20S E4
5200 OKFT 60452 3425 6W-20S E4
Harden St
300 ANTH 60002 2357 23W-41N D7
Hardin Av
500 AURA 60506 3137 36W-7S D7
Harding Av
10 CTCY 60409 3352 4E-17S B5
100 FRGV 60021 2696 29W-23N B2
100 LYVL 60048 2591 17W-28N B5
100 WKGN 60085 2480 10W-35N B5
200 GYLK 60030 2532 20W-32N E4
400 GNEN 60137 3083 22W-1S C1
1200 DSPN 60016 2862 13W-11N E3
1300 DSPN 60016 2863 13W-11N A3
1400 BKLY 60163 3028 14W-0N C4
1400 CTCY 60409 3351 2E-17S C5
1900 WKGN 60085 2479 11W-35N D5
3300 RcmT 60071 2354 32W-43N B4
8000 SKOK 60076 2866 4W-10N B5
9200 SKOK 60203 2866 4W-11N B2
9500 EVTN 60201 2866 4W-11N B2
14600 MDLN 60445 3348 4W-17S C5
18700 FSMR 60422 3506 4W-22S D2
18700 HLCT 60422 3506 4W-22S D2
18700 HLCT 60429 3506 4W-22S D2
19000 FSMR 60430 3506 4W-22S D2
20300 OMFD 60461 3507 3W-24S A5
E Harding Av
10 LGPK 60525 3087 12W-3S C5
1100 BKFD 60513 3087 12W-3S C5
1100 BKFD 60525 3087 12W-3S C5
N Harding Av
400 CHCG 60624 3032 4W-0N C3
700 CHCG 60651 3032 4W-0N C3
1500 CHCG 60647 3032 4W-1N C1
2300 CHCG 60647 2976 4W-2N B6
4000 CHCG 60618 2976 4W-5N B1
4100 CHCG 60641 2976 4W-5N B1
4300 CHCG 60625 2976 4W-5N B1
4400 CHCG 60625 2920 4W-5N B7
6000 CHCG 60659 2920 4W-7N B3
6700 LNWD 60712 2920 4W-8N B2
37500 LkvT 60046 2474 25W-37N A1
S Harding Av
1200 CHCG 60623 3032 4W-1S C7
1200 CHCG 60624 3032 4W-1S C7
1500 CHCG 60623 3090 4W-1S C1
4500 CHCG 60632 3090 4W-4S C7
4600 CHCG 60632 3150 4W-5S C1
7100 CHCG 60629 3150 4W-8S C7
9100 CHCG 60805 3212 4W-10S C5
9100 ENGN 60805 3212 4W-11S C6
10100 CHCG 60655 3212 4W-11S C7
10200 CHCG 60655 3276 4W-11S C1
11700 ALSP 60803 3276 4W-13S C5
11700 WthT 60803 3276 4W-13S C5
13300 CTWD 60472 3348 4W-15S C2
13300 RBBN 60472 3348 4W-15S C2
W Harding Av
10 LGPK 60525 3087 12W-3S B5
Harding Ct
100 GLHT 60139 2968 23W-4N E4
100 NARA 60542 3138 35W-4S C1
100 VNHL 60061 2647 17W-26N C4
Harding Dr
100 GLHT 60139 2969 23W-3N A4
Harding Ln
2400 DrrT 60098 2582 39W-28N B5
2400 WDSK 60098 2582 39W-28N B5
Harding Rd
10 MltT 60148 3026 21W-0S A6
10 YkTp 60148 3026 21W-0S A6
700 HNDL 60521 3146 14W-5S D3
1600 NHFD 60093 2811 6W-15N C3
E Harding Rd
- LMBD 60148 3026 19W-0S C6
W Harding Rd
10 LMBD 60148 3026 20W-0S B6
500 MltT 60148 3026 20W-0S A6
500 YkTp 60148 3026 20W-0S A6
Harding St
- OMFD 60461 3507 3W-25S B7
10 ELGN 60123 2854 33W-10N E5
10 ELGN 60123 2855 33W-10N A6
100 EGvT 60018 2862 15W-9N A7

STREET Block	City	ZIP	Map#	CGS	Grid
Harding St					
300	CPVL	60110	2801	32W-16N	D1
38500	BHPK	60087	2422	10W-38N	B7
38500	BHPK	60099	2422	10W-38N	B7
W Harding St					
200	EMHT	60126	3027	16W-0N	E5
Hardt Cir					
1200	BRLT	60120	2910	30W-7N	B5
Hardwick Ct					
10	SgrT	60506	3135	41W-5S	E4
Hardwood Ct					
4200	HRPK	60133	2967	27W-5N	C2
Hardwood Pth					
1900	RLKB	60046	2475	21W-35N	D5
Hardy Dr					
-	HRPK	60133	2911	26W-6N	D6
Harger Rd					
600	OKBK	60523	3085	16W-1S	E2
600	OKBK	60523	3086	15W-1S	A1
Harkison Blvd					
-	SgrT	60554	3136	40W-4S	B2
-	SRGV	60554	3136	40W-4S	B2
Harlan Av					
10	OswT	60503	3201	33W-11S	A7
1400	ELGN	60123	2854	35W-12N	B2
Harlan Ct					
1100	LKFT	60045	2649	11W-24N	D7
Harlan Ln					
1200	LKFT	60045	2649	11W-24N	E7
1400	LKFT	60045	2703	11W-24N	D1
Harlem Av					
-	CHCG	60402	3148	8W-5S	E2
-	CHCG	60501	3148	8W-5S	E2
-	CHCG	60638	3148	8W-5S	E2
-	FftT	60477	3504	9W-22S	E1
-	FftT	60477	3505	8W-23S	A2
-	FTVW	60501	3148	8W-5S	E2
-	SMMT	60501	3148	9W-5S	E2
-	SMMT	60534	3148	8W-5S	E2
-	TYPK	60477	3504	9W-22S	E1
10	GNVW	60025	2864	9W-11N	D3
10	GNVW	60053	2864	9W-11N	D3
10	MNGV	60053	2864	9W-11N	D3
400	GNVW	60025	2810	8W-13N	D7
1100	BRWN	60130	3030	8W-1S	D7
1100	BRWN	60304	3030	8W-1S	D7
1100	BRWN	60402	3030	8W-1S	D7
1100	FTPK	60130	3030	8W-1S	D7
1100	OKPK	60130	3030	8W-1S	D7
1100	OKPK	60304	3030	8W-1S	D7
1500	BRWN	60130	3088	8W-2S	E2
1500	BRWN	60402	3088	8W-2S	E2
1500	FTPK	60130	3088	8W-1S	D1
1500	NRIV	60130	3088	8W-2S	E2
2100	BRWN	60546	3088	9W-1S	D2
2100	NRIV	60546	3088	9W-1S	D2
2500	RVSD	60546	3088	9W-2S	D3
2800	RVSD	60402	3088	9W-2S	D3
3600	LYNS	60402	3088	8W-3S	E5
3600	LYNS	60534	3088	8W-3S	E5
3600	LYNS	60546	3088	8W-3S	E5
3800	SKNY	60402	3088	8W-3S	E6
4200	SKNY	60534	3088	8W-4S	E7
4400	FTVW	60402	3088	8W-4S	E7
4400	FTVW	60534	3088	8W-4S	E7
4500	FTVW	60402	3148	8W-5S	E1
4500	FTVW	60534	3148	8W-5S	E1
4500	LYNS	60534	3148	8W-5S	E1
8800	MNGV	60714	2864	8W-11N	D3
8800	NLES	60714	2864	8W-11N	D3
15900	ODPK	60462	3424	9W-19S	E1
15900	TYPK	60477	3424	9W-19S	E3
16300	OrlT	60477	3424	9W-19S	E2
18200	TYPK	60477	3425	8W-22S	A7
19300	TYPK	60477	3505	8W-22S	A2
Harlem Av SR-43					
-	CHCG	60402	3148	8W-5S	E2
-	CHCG	60501	3148	8W-5S	E2
-	CHCG	60638	3148	8W-5S	E2
-	FftT	60477	3505	8W-23S	A2
-	FTVW	60501	3148	8W-5S	E2
-	SMMT	60501	3148	8W-5S	E2
-	SMMT	60534	3148	9W-5S	E2
-	TYPK	60477	3505	8W-22S	A2
1100	BRWN	60130	3030	8W-1S	D7
1100	BRWN	60304	3030	8W-1S	D7
1100	BRWN	60402	3030	8W-1S	D7
1100	FTPK	60130	3030	8W-1S	D7
1100	OKPK	60130	3030	8W-1S	D7
1100	OKPK	60304	3030	8W-1S	D7
1500	BRWN	60130	3088	8W-2S	E2
1500	BRWN	60402	3088	8W-2S	E2
1500	FTPK	60130	3088	8W-1S	D1
1500	NRIV	60130	3088	8W-2S	E2
2100	BRWN	60546	3088	9W-1S	D2
2100	NRIV	60546	3088	9W-1S	D2
2500	RVSD	60546	3088	9W-2S	D3
2800	RVSD	60402	3088	9W-2S	D3
3600	LYNS	60402	3088	8W-3S	E5
3600	LYNS	60534	3088	8W-3S	E5
3600	LYNS	60546	3088	8W-3S	E5
3800	SKNY	60402	3088	8W-3S	E6
4200	SKNY	60534	3088	8W-4S	E7
4400	FTVW	60402	3088	8W-4S	E7
4400	FTVW	60534	3088	8W-4S	E7
4500	FTVW	60402	3148	8W-5S	E1
4500	FTVW	60534	3148	8W-5S	E1
4500	LYNS	60534	3148	8W-5S	E1
15900	ODPK	60462	3424	9W-19S	E1
15900	TYPK	60477	3424	9W-19S	E3
16300	OrlT	60477	3424	9W-19S	E2
18200	TYPK	60477	3425	8W-22S	A7
N Harlem Av					
10	FTPK	60130	3030	8W-0N	D4
10	FTPK	60302	3030	9W-0N	D5
10	FTPK	60304	3030	9W-0N	D5
10	OKPK	60130	3030	8W-0N	D4
10	OKPK	60302	3030	9W-1N	D3
10	OKPK	60304	3030	9W-0N	D5
100	PTON	60468	3861	9W-37S	A3
200	WllT	60468	3861	8W-37S	A3
300	PtnT	60468	3861	8W-37S	A2
400	OKPK	60301	3030	8W-0N	D4
400	OKPK	60305	3030	9W-1N	D3
400	RVFT	60301	3030	8W-0N	D4
400	RVFT	60302	3030	9W-1N	D3
400	RVFT	60305	3030	9W-1N	D3
1500	CHCG	60302	3030	8W-1N	D1
1500	CHCG	60707	3030	8W-1N	D1
1500	EDPK	60707	3030	8W-1N	D1
1500	RVFT	60707	3030	8W-1N	D1
1700	CHCG	60707	2974	8W-2N	D7
1700	EDPK	60707	2974	8W-2N	D7
2700	CHCG	60634	2974	9W-4N	D3
3900	NRDG	60634	2974	9W-2N	D7
3900	NRDG	60706	2974	9W-2N	D7

STREET Block	City	ZIP	Map#	CGS	Grid
N Harlem Av					
4400	HDHT	60706	2918	8W-5N	D7
4400	NRDG	60706	2918	8W-5N	D7
4700	CHCG	60656	2918	8W-6N	D7
4700	CHCG	60706	2918	8W-6N	D7
4700	HDHT	60656	2918	8W-6N	D7
5600	CHCG	60631	2918	9W-5N	D7
6500	CHCG	60714	2918	9W-5N	D7
6500	NLES	60714	2918	9W-5N	D7
7200	CHCG	60631	2864	8W-9N	D7
7200	CHCG	60714	2864	8W-9N	D7
7200	NLES	60714	2864	9W-9N	D7
7500	NLES	60631	2864	8W-9N	D7
8700	MNGV	60053	2864	8W-10N	D4
8700	MNGV	60714	2864	8W-10N	D4
N Harlem Av SR-43					
10	FTPK	60130	3030	8W-0N	D4
10	FTPK	60302	3030	9W-0N	D5
10	FTPK	60304	3030	9W-0N	D5
10	OKPK	60130	3030	8W-0N	D4
10	OKPK	60302	3030	9W-1N	D3
10	OKPK	60304	3030	9W-0N	D5
400	OKPK	60301	3030	8W-0N	D4
400	OKPK	60305	3030	9W-1N	D3
400	RVFT	60301	3030	8W-0N	D4
400	RVFT	60302	3030	9W-1N	D3
400	RVFT	60305	3030	9W-1N	D3
1500	CHCG	60302	3030	8W-1N	D1
1500	CHCG	60707	3030	8W-1N	D1
1500	EDPK	60707	3030	8W-1N	D1
1500	RVFT	60707	3030	8W-1N	D1
1700	CHCG	60707	2974	8W-2N	D7
1700	EDPK	60707	2974	8W-2N	D7
2700	CHCG	60634	2974	9W-4N	D3
3900	NRDG	60634	2974	9W-2N	D7
3900	NRDG	60706	2974	9W-2N	D7
4400	HDHT	60706	2918	8W-5N	D7
4400	NRDG	60706	2918	8W-5N	D7
4700	CHCG	60656	2918	8W-6N	D7
4700	CHCG	60706	2918	8W-6N	D7
4700	HDHT	60656	2918	8W-6N	D7
5600	CHCG	60631	2918	9W-5N	D7
6500	CHCG	60714	2918	9W-5N	D7
6500	NLES	60714	2918	9W-5N	D7
7200	CHCG	60631	2864	8W-9N	D7
7200	CHCG	60714	2864	8W-9N	D7
7200	NLES	60714	2864	9W-9N	D7
7500	NLES	60631	2864	8W-9N	D7
N Harlem Av SR-50					
100	PTON	60468	3861	9W-37S	A3
200	WllT	60468	3861	8W-37S	A3
300	PtnT	60468	3861	8W-37S	A2
S Harlem Av					
-	BGVW	60453	3210	8W-10S	E6
-	FKFT	60423	3505	8W-25S	A7
-	OKLN	60453	3210	8W-10S	E5
-	OKLN	60455	3210	8W-11S	E6
-	PlsT	60463	3346	9W-16S	E3
-	PSHT	60463	3346	9W-18S	E7
-	SMMT	60534	3148	9W-5S	E2
-	TYPK	60423	3505	8W-23S	A3
10	FTPK	60130	3030	9W-0S	D6
10	FTPK	60302	3030	9W-0S	D5
10	FTPK	60304	3030	9W-0S	D5
10	OKPK	60302	3030	9W-0S	D5
10	OKPK	60304	3030	9W-0S	D6
100	PTON	60468	3861	8W-37S	A4
700	OKPK	60130	3030	9W-0S	D6
5100	CHCG	60402	3148	8W-5S	E2
5100	FTVW	60402	3148	8W-5S	E2
5100	FTVW	60501	3148	8W-5S	E2
5400	CHCG	60501	3148	9W-6S	E3
5400	CHCG	60638	3148	9W-6S	E3
5400	SMMT	60501	3148	9W-6S	E3
6300	BDPK	60501	3148	8W-7S	E5
6400	BDPK	60638	3148	8W-7S	E5
6700	BGVW	60455	3148	9W-7S	E6
6700	BGVW	60501	3148	9W-7S	E6
6700	BGVW	60638	3148	9W-7S	E6
6800	BDPK	60455	3148	9W-7S	E7
7300	BDPK	60638	3210	8W-8S	E1
7300	BGVW	60455	3210	8W-11S	E7
7300	BGVW	60638	3210	8W-8S	E1
7700	BGVW	60459	3210	8W-8S	E2
7700	BRBK	60455	3210	8W-8S	E2
7700	BRBK	60459	3210	8W-8S	E2
9500	CHRG	60415	3210	8W-11S	E7
9500	CHRG	60455	3210	8W-11S	E7
9500	OKLN	60415	3210	8W-11S	E6
9600	BGVW	60415	3210	9W-11S	E7
10100	BGVW	60415	3274	8W-11S	E1
10100	BGVW	60455	3274	8W-11S	E1
10100	CHRG	60415	3274	9W-14S	E7
10100	PSHL	60415	3274	8W-11S	E1
10100	PSHL	60455	3274	8W-11S	E1
10100	PSHL	60465	3274	8W-11S	E1
10400	WRTH	60415	3274	9W-14S	E7
10400	WRTH	60482	3274	9W-14S	E7
10500	CHRG	60482	3274	9W-14S	E7
11600	PSHT	60463	3274	8W-13S	E5
11600	WRTH	60463	3274	8W-13S	E5
12900	WthT	60463	3346	9W-16S	E3
13500	BmnT	60445	3346	9W-18S	E7
13500	BmnT	60462	3346	9W-16S	E3
13500	WthT	60445	3346	9W-16S	E3
13500	WthT	60462	3346	9W-18S	E7
13700	OrlT	60462	3346	9W-17S	E5
14100	BmnT	60452	3346	9W-17S	E5
14100	OrlT	60445	3346	9W-17S	E5
14100	OrlT	60452	3346	9W-17S	E5
15100	ODPK	60462	3346	9W-18S	E6
15200	OKFT	60462	3346	9W-18S	E6
15700	ODPK	60462	3424	9W-18S	E1
15800	TYPK	60477	3424	9W-18S	E1
19300	FftT	60477	3505	9W-23S	A3
19300	RchT	60423	3505	9W-23S	A3
19300	TYPK	60477	3505	8W-23S	A3
19400	FftT	60423	3505	9W-23S	A4
19700	MTSN	60443	3505	9W-23S	A4
20600	RchT	60443	3505	9W-25S	A7
21500	FKFT	60423	3593	8W-26S	A2
21500	RchT	60443	3593	8W-26S	A2
22400	FKFT	60443	3593	8W-27S	A3
23100	FKFT	60449	3593	8W-28S	A7
23100	GGnT	60423	3593	8W-28S	A7
23100	GGnT	60449	3593	8W-28S	A7
23100	MonT	60449	3593	8W-28S	A7
23900	GGnT	60423	3682	9W-29S	A1
23900	GGnT	60449	3682	9W-30S	A3
23900	MonT	60423	3682	9W-29S	A2
23900	MonT	60449	3682	9W-30S	A3
29700	PtnT	60468	3861	9W-36S	A1
29700	WllT	60468	3861	9W-36S	A1
S Harlem Av SR-43					
-	BGVW	60453	3210	8W-10S	E6
-	FKFT	60423	3505	8W-25S	A7

STREET Block	City	ZIP	Map#	CGS	Grid
S Harlem Av SR-43					
-	OKLN	60415	3210	8W-11S	E6
-	OKLN	60453	3210	8W-10S	E5
-	OKLN	60455	3210	8W-11S	E6
-	PlsT	60463	3346	9W-16S	E3
-	SMMT	60534	3148	9W-5S	E2
-	TYPK	60423	3505	8W-23S	A3
10	FTPK	60130	3030	9W-0S	D6
10	FTPK	60302	3030	9W-0S	D5
10	FTPK	60304	3030	9W-0S	D5
10	OKPK	60302	3030	9W-0S	D5
10	OKPK	60304	3030	9W-0S	D6
700	OKPK	60130	3030	9W-0S	D6
5100	CHCG	60402	3148	8W-5S	E2
5100	FTVW	60402	3148	8W-5S	E2
5100	FTVW	60501	3148	8W-5S	E2
5400	CHCG	60501	3148	9W-6S	E3
5400	CHCG	60638	3148	9W-6S	E3
5400	SMMT	60501	3148	9W-6S	E3
6300	BDPK	60501	3148	8W-7S	E5
6300	BDPK	60638	3148	8W-7S	E5
6700	BGVW	60455	3148	9W-7S	E6
6700	BGVW	60501	3148	9W-7S	E6
6700	BGVW	60638	3148	9W-7S	E6
6800	BDPK	60455	3148	9W-7S	E7
7300	BDPK	60638	3210	8W-8S	E1
7300	BGVW	60455	3210	8W-11S	E7
7300	BGVW	60638	3210	8W-8S	E1
7700	BGVW	60459	3210	8W-8S	E2
7700	BRBK	60455	3210	8W-8S	E2
7700	BRBK	60459	3210	8W-8S	E2
9800	BGVW	60415	3210	8W-11S	E7
9800	CHRG	60415	3210	8W-11S	E7
9900	CHRG	60455	3210	8W-11S	E7
10100	BGVW	60415	3274	8W-11S	E1
10100	BGVW	60455	3274	8W-11S	E1
10100	CHRG	60415	3274	9W-14S	E7
10100	PSHL	60415	3274	8W-11S	E1
10100	PSHL	60455	3274	8W-11S	E1
10100	PSHL	60465	3274	8W-11S	E1
10400	WRTH	60415	3274	9W-14S	E7
10400	WRTH	60482	3274	9W-14S	E7
10500	CHRG	60482	3274	9W-14S	E7
11600	PSHT	60463	3274	8W-13S	E5
11600	WRTH	60463	3274	8W-13S	E5
12800	PSHT	60463	3346	9W-16S	E3
12900	WthT	60463	3346	9W-16S	E3
13500	BmnT	60445	3346	9W-18S	E7
13500	BmnT	60462	3346	9W-16S	E3
13500	WthT	60445	3346	9W-16S	E3
13500	WthT	60462	3346	9W-18S	E7
13700	OrlT	60462	3346	9W-17S	E5
14100	BmnT	60452	3346	9W-17S	E5
14100	OrlT	60445	3346	9W-17S	E5
14100	OrlT	60452	3346	9W-17S	E5
15100	ODPK	60462	3346	9W-18S	E6
15200	OKFT	60462	3346	9W-18S	E6
15700	ODPK	60462	3424	9W-18S	E1
15800	TYPK	60477	3424	9W-18S	E1
19300	FftT	60477	3505	9W-23S	A3
19300	RchT	60423	3505	9W-23S	A4
19300	TYPK	60477	3505	8W-23S	A3
19400	FftT	60423	3505	9W-23S	A4
19700	MTSN	60443	3505	9W-23S	A4
20600	RchT	60443	3505	9W-25S	A7
21500	FKFT	60423	3593	8W-26S	A2
21500	RchT	60443	3593	8W-26S	A2
22400	FKFT	60443	3593	8W-27S	A3
S Harlem Av SR-50					
100	PTON	60468	3861	8W-37S	A4
100	WllT	60468	3861	8W-37S	A4
W Harlem Av					
26300	AntT	60002	2415	26W-38N	D6
Harlem Ct					
-	OKPK	60301	3030	8W-0N	D3
-	OKPK	60302	3030	8W-0N	D3
Harlem Dr					
5200	SMMT	60501	3148	9W-5S	E2
Harley Rd					
10	CmpT	60119	3018	41W-2N	A1
400	BbyT	60119	3017	41W-1N	E4
400	BbyT	60119	3018	41W-1N	A2
Harleyford Rd					
1200	WDRG	60517	3206	20W-10S	B5
W Harloff Rd					
25900	AntT	60002	2415	25W-40N	E3
Harlow Av					
800	JltT	60433	3499	22W-25S	C7
Harlowe Ct					
600	NPVL	60565	3204	25W-8S	B2
Harlowe Ln					
400	NPVL	60565	3204	25W-9S	B3
Harlstone Dr					
2500	AURA	60502	3139	32W-7S	C6
Harmarc Pl					
5600	DRGV	60516	3144	18W-6S	E4
Harmess St					
800	CTCY	60409	3352	3E-17S	A6
Harmon Blvd					
700	HFET	60169	2858	25W-11N	B3
700	HFET	60194	2858	25W-11N	B3
700	SMBG	60169	2858	25W-11N	B3
700	SMBG	60194	2858	25W-11N	B3
Harmon Ct					
-	PNFD	60586	3415	31W-19S	E3
Harmon Ln					
16400	PNFD	60586	3415	31W-19S	E3
Harmoni Ln					
900	NlxT	60451	3502	16W-24S	A6
Harmony Ct					
-	ZION	60099	2421	12W-40N	C4
300	BGBK	60440	3269	22W-13S	D4
700	NARA	60542	3077	37W-3S	C6
700	NARA	60542	3137	37W-4S	C1
1200	LslT	60563	3142	25W-5S	A3
1400	ITSC	60143	2914	18W-6N	E6
N Harmony Ct					
39500	WDWH	60083	2420	14W-39N	C5
Harmony Dr					
-	ZION	60099	2421	12W-40N	C4
300	NARA	60542	3137	37W-4S	D1
400	WLNG	60090	2755	14W-17N	D5
900	MTGY	60538	3200	36W-9S	A4
1400	BRLT	60103	2967	28W-5N	A2
1400	WynT	60103	2967	28W-5N	A2
S Harmony Dr					
16100	PnfT	60586	3416	30W-19S	A3
Harmony Ln					
10	LktT	60544	3340	26W-17S	A5
10	RMVL	60446	3340	26W-17S	A5
200	EGVV	60007	2914	18W-8N	E2
500	LMBD	60148	3026	18W-0N	E5
500	LMBD	60181	3026	18W-0N	E5
500	VLPK	60181	3026	18W-0N	E5
600	GNVW	60025	2810	8W-13N	E7

STREET Block	City	ZIP	Map#	CGS	Grid
Harmony Rd					
10	HPSR	60140	2795	47W-16N	D1
10	HshT	60140	2795	47W-16N	D1
11500	GfnT	60142	2691	42W-20N	A7
13500	HTLY	60142	2691	42W-20N	B7
13900	CrlT	60142	2691	43W-20N	A7
14600	CrlT	60142	2743	44W-20N	D1
Harmony Rd CO-36					
10	HPSR	60140	2795	47W-16N	D1
10	HshT	60140	2795	47W-16N	D1
Harmony Rd CO-A47					
11500	GfnT	60142	2691	42W-20N	A7
Harmony Rd CO-A49					
13500	GfnT	60142	2691	42W-20N	B7
13500	HTLY	60142	2691	42W-20N	B7
13900	CrlT	60142	2691	43W-20N	A7
14600	CrlT	60142	2743	44W-20N	D1
Harms Av					
1000	LYVL	60048	2591	17W-28N	B6
Harms Ct					
700	WLNG	60090	2754	16W-18N	E2
Harms Rd					
-	SKOK	60053	2865	6W-11N	D3
10	GLF	60029	2865	7W-11N	C2
10	GLF	60053	2865	7W-11N	C2
10	MNGV	60053	2865	7W-11N	C2
10	SKOK	60029	2865	7W-12N	C1
500	GLF	60025	2811	7W-12N	C7
500	GNVW	60025	2811	7W-13N	C7
500	SKOK	60025	2811	7W-12N	C7
500	SKOK	60077	2811	7W-12N	C7
1300	WLMT	60091	2811	7W-13N	C7
2400	JLET	60441	3417	27W-19S	D3
3400	JLET	60435	3417	27W-19S	D2
8400	SKOK	60077	2865	6W-10N	D4
10000	GLF	60029	2811	7W-12N	C7
10000	GLF	60077	2811	7W-12N	C7
10000	SKOK	60029	2811	7W-12N	C7
Harmswood Ter					
5200	SKOK	60077	2865	6W-11N	D2
Harness Ln					
3200	RLKP	60030	2532	22W-31N	C7
Harnew Rd E					
9900	OKLN	60453	3212	6W-11S	A7
Harnew Rd S					
4800	OKLN	60453	3212	6W-11S	A7
4800	OKLN	60453	3276	6W-11S	A1
4900	OKLN	60453	3275	6W-11S	E1
Harnew Rd W					
9900	OKLN	60453	3211	6W-11S	E7
Harnish Dr					
1200	ALGN	60102	2694	35W-20N	A7
2300	ALGN	60102	2693	35W-20N	E7
2400	ALGN	60102	2746	35W-20N	E1
2400	AlqT	60102	2746	36W-20N	E1
Harold Av					
500	GLHT	60139	2969	22W-3N	B6
4800	SRPK	60176	2917	12W-6N	C6
N Harold Av					
100	NHLK	60164	2972	13W-2N	E7
100	NHLK	60164	3028	13W-2N	E1
800	LydT	60164	2972	13W-3N	E5
1500	MLPK	60160	3028	13W-1N	E2
1500	NHLK	60160	3028	13W-1N	E2
S Harold Av					
100	NHLK	60164	3028	13W-1N	E1
200	MLPK	60160	3028	13W-1N	E1
200	NHLK	60160	3028	13W-1N	E1
11900	PSHT	60463	3274	9W-14S	D6
Harold Ln					
-	LkvT	60046	2475	22W-36N	C4
N Harold Pl					
37900	AntT	60081	2472	28W-38N	E1
37900	GrtT	60081	2472	28W-37N	E1
38000	AntT	60081	2414	28W-38N	E7
Harold St					
-	ANHT	60004	2806	18W-16N	E1
300	CLLK	60014	2640	35W-25N	A5
16400	OKFT	60452	3426	5W-19S	B2
Harold H Hagbery Dr					
-	MNSR	46321	3510		E4
Harolds Cres					
2800	FSMR	60422	3507	3W-23S	A4
Harper Av					
-	TVLY	60013	2695	32W-23N	C2
800	CRY	60013	2695	32W-23N	C2
3200	BHPK	60087	2479	11W-37N	E2
3200	WKGN	60087	2479	11W-37N	E2
3400	GRNE	60031	2536	13W-34N	A1
3900	GRNE	60031	2535	14W-34N	D1
14400	DLTN	60419	3351	1E-16S	C4
18200	LNSG	60438	3429	1E-21S	C7
18200	ThtT	60438	3429	1E-21S	C7
22200	SLVL	60411	3597	1E-26S	C3
S Harper Av					
-	CHCG	60628	3215	1E-11S	B6
200	GNWD	60425	3509	1E-23S	B3
5100	CHCG	60615	3153	1E-5S	B2
6800	CHCG	60637	3153	1E-7S	B6
7000	CHCG	60619	3153	1E-7S	B6
7700	CHCG	60619	3215	1E-8S	B1
Harper Ct					
10	ALGN	60102	2694	34W-20N	C7
10	ALGN	60102	2747	34W-20N	C1
800	CRY	60013	2695	32W-23N	B2
5600	CHCG	60637	3153	1E-5S	B3
Harper Dr					
300	ALGN	60102	2694	34W-20N	C7
300	RtdT	60140	2798	40W-15N	C3
500	ALGN	60102	2747	34W-20N	C1
1000	AlqT	60102	2747	34W-20N	C1
Harper Ln					
100	LMNT	60439	3342	19W-15S	D1
1600	CLLK	60014	2693	37W-22N	B3
Harper Rd					
2000	DRN	60561	3206	19W-8S	E2
8400	TYPK	60477	3424	10W-21S	B6
8400	TYPK	60487	3424	10W-21S	B6
N Harper Rd					
37800	BHPK	60087	2479	11W-38N	E1
37800	WKGN	60087	2479	11W-37N	E1
Harper College Dr					
-	PLTN	60067	2805	22W-13N	B5
N Harrier Rd					
3600	WKGN	60087	2421	11W-38N	D7
3600	WKGN	60087	2479	11W-37N	D2
S Harriet Dr					
23000	CNHN	60410	3584	29W-27S	E6
E Harriet Ln					
800	BRTN	60010	2751	25W-18N	B2
S Harriet Ln					
2500	NndT	60051	2586	29W-29N	C4
Harriet St					
-	WNFD	60190	3023	26W-1N	E3
10	MltT	60187	3023	26W-1N	E3
10	MltT	60188	3023	26W-1N	E3

STREET Block	City	ZIP	Map#	CGS	Grid
E Harriet St					
100	TNTN	60476	3428	0E-21S	D6
W Harriet St					
100	TNTN	60476	3428	0E-21S	D6
Harriett Av					
900	AURA	60505	3200	34W-8S	D2
Harrington Ct					
10	HNWD	60047	2646	20W-24N	A7
W Harrington Ln					
4200	CHCG	60646	2920	5W-7N	A4
Harris Av					
10	CNHL	60514	3145	16W-5S	D3
E Harris Av					
10	LGNG	60525	3087	12W-4S	C7
W Harris Av					
10	LGNG	60525	3087	12W-4S	B7
Harris Ct					
500	BFGV	60089	2754	17W-20N	C1
Harris Dr					
-	NpvT	60502	3139	31W-5S	D3
500	BFGV	60089	2701	17W-20N	C7
500	BFGV	60089	2754	17W-20N	C1
800	BGBK	60440	3268	25W-12S	C3
1500	AURA	60502	3139	31W-5S	D3
3000	JLET	60431	3497	28W-21S	B1
3000	PnfT	60431	3496	29W-21S	E1
3000	PnfT	60431	3497	28W-21S	B1
3400	NHBK	60062	2756	11W-18N	C3
Harris Ln					
-	LtRT	60545	3260	45W-13S	B5
-	PLNO	60545	3260	45W-13S	B5
800	RMVL	60446	3269	23W-14S	A6
1600	NPVL	60565	3204	25W-9S	C3
Harris Rd					
-	GYLK	60048	2533	19W-31N	C7
200	GYLK	60030	2533	19W-32N	C5
1300	LYVL	60048	2590	19W-30N	C3
1300	LYVL	60060	2590	19W-30N	C3
1300	MDLN	60060	2590	19W-30N	C3
N Harris Rd					
30500	FmtT	60048	2590	19W-30N	C1
30500	LYVL	60048	2590	19W-30N	C1
31100	FmtT	60048	2533	19W-31N	C7
31100	LYVL	60048	2533	19W-31N	C7
31500	GYLK	60030	2533	19W-31N	C7
31500	GYLK	60048	2533	19W-31N	C7
Harrisburg Ct					
500	LNHT	60046	2418	19W-38N	C6
Harrison					
12300	BRTN	60010	2750	26W-20N	E2
Harrison Av					
10	MltT	60187	3023	26W-0N	E6
10	MltT	60187	3024	25W-0N	A6
100	MltT	60190	3023	26W-0N	E6
400	CTCY	60409	3352	4E-17S	B6
500	WNFD	60190	3023	26W-0S	D6
800	DYR	46311	3510		D7
1000	WCDA	60084	2588	25W-28N	B6
1100	BKFD	60513	3087	11W-3S	D5
1100	LGPK	60513	3087	11W-3S	D5
1100	LGPK	60525	3087	11W-3S	D5
1500	DYR	46311	3598		D1
1500	PvsT	60525	3087	11W-2S	D4
1600	MDLN	60060	2590	19W-29N	B4
6000	HMND	46320	3430		D1
6000	HMND	46324	3430		D5
7800	MNSR	46321	3430		D6
8700	MNSR	46321	3510		D1
12000	HBRN	60034	2350	41W-41N	E7
12000	HBRN	60034	2351	40W-41N	A7
E Harrison Av					
100	WHTN	60187	3024	24W-0N	D5
1500	WHTN	60187	3025	23W-0N	A5
N Harrison Av					
10	AURA	60506	3137	36W-7S	D6
10	PLTN	60067	2805	22W-16N	B1
10	PltT	60067	2805	22W-16N	B1
100	IVNS	60067	2752	22W-16N	B7
100	PLTN	60067	2752	22W-16N	B7
100	PltT	60067	2752	22W-16N	B7
1000	JLET	60432	3499	23W-22S	B2
28500	WcnT	60084	2588	25W-28N	B5
34000	AvnT	60073	2531	24W-34N	C2
34000	RDLK	60073	2531	24W-34N	C2
S Harrison Av					
-	PLTN	60067	2805	22W-15N	B1
10	AURA	60506	3137	36W-7S	D7
10	PltT	60067	2805	22W-15N	B1
200	AURA	60506	3199	36W-8S	E1
5900	HMND	46320	3352		D7
5900	HMND	46320	3430		D1
13900	BLID	60406	3349	3W-16S	A3
14700	BmnT	60469	3349	3W-17S	A5
14900	POSN	60469	3349	3W-17S	A5
W Harrison Av					
100	WHTN	60187	3024	24W-0N	C5
500	MltT	60187	3024	25W-0N	B6
12700	WKGN	60085	2479	12W-35N	B7
12700	WkgT	60085	2479	12W-35N	B7
Harrison Ct					
400	VNHL	60061	2647	17W-27N	C2
700	CRTE	60417	3685	1W-30S	A3
S Harrison Ct					
300	PLTN	60067	2805	22W-15N	B2
300	PltT	60067	2805	22W-15N	B2
Harrison Ln					
-	BbyT	60134	3076	39W-1S	E1
-	BGBK	60490	3267	27W-14S	D7
-	DPgT	60490	3267	27W-14S	D7
10	SMWD	60107	2856	29W-10N	E6
700	JNBG	60051	2472	29W-35N	C6
800	HFET	60192	2804	24W-15N	D3
Harrison Pl					
10	HNDL	60521	3146	15W-5S	A2
700	DYR	46311	3510		E6
2600	WKGN	60085	2479	12W-35N	C7
E Harrison Rd					
10	LMBD	60148	3026	19W-0S	C6
W Harrison Rd					
10	LMBD	60148	3026	20W-0S	A6
500	MltT	60148	3026	20W-0S	A6
Harrison St					
-	BLWD	60153	3029	11W-0S	D6
-	MYWD	60104	3029	11W-0S	D6
10	CHCG	60644	3031	7W-0S	B6
10	EMHT	60126	3028	15W-0S	B6
10	FTPK	60153	3030	10W-0S	A6
10	MYWD	60130	3030	10W-0S	A6
10	MYWD	60153	3030	10W-0S	A6
10	OKPK	60304	3031	8W-0S	A6
10	OKPK	60644	3031	7W-0S	B6
10	YkTp	60126	3028	15W-0S	B6
100	BRTN	60010	2750	25W-20N	E2
200	CPVL	60110	2801	32W-16N	D1
200	MTGY	60538	3199	37W-9S	C4
300	LYVL	60048	2591	16W-28N	D6

STREET Block	City	ZIP	Map#	CGS	Grid
Harrison St					
300	WCHI	60185	3022	30W-0N	B4
400	CTCY	60409	3352	4E-17S	B5
400	ELGN	60120	2855	32W-10N	B5
700	MYWD	60153	3029	11W-0S	E6
800	OKPK	60304	3030	8W-0S	E6
900	PKRG	60068	2918	9W-8N	B2
1000	BDVW	60153	3029	11W-0S	E6
1000	BDVW	60155	3029	11W-0S	E6
1000	MYWD	60155	3029	11W-0S	E6
1700	EVTN	60201	2813	3W-12N	A7
1700	GNVW	60025	2864	9W-12N	B1
1900	EVTN	60201	2812	3W-12N	E7
2600	BLWD	60104	3029	12W-0S	B6
2800	MaiT	60025	2864	10W-12N	A1
2900	EVTN	60201	2866	4W-12N	B1
2900	GNVW	60714	2864	10W-12N	B1
2900	NLES	60025	2864	10W-12N	B1
2900	NLES	60714	2864	10W-12N	B1
3300	EVTN	60076	2866	5W-12N	B1
3300	SKOK	60076	2866	4W-12N	B1
4100	HLSD	60154	3029	13W-0S	A6
4100	HLSD	60162	3028	14W-0S	C7
4100	HLSD	60162	3029	13W-0S	A6
4100	PvsT	60162	3028	14W-0S	C7
4100	WSTR	60154	3029	13W-0S	A6
5200	HLSD	60126	3028	14W-0S	C7
5200	PvsT	60126	3028	14W-0S	C7
7200	FTPK	60130	3030	9W-0S	D6
7200	FTPK	60304	3030	9W-0S	D6
7400	HRPK	60133	2912	26W-9N	A1
9300	MaiT	60016	2863	11W-12N	C1
13800	BLID	60406	3349	3W-16S	A3
13800	POSN	60469	3349	3W-16S	A3
34200	AvnT	60073	2531	24W-34N	C1
E Harrison St					
10	CHCG	60605	3034	0E-0S	C5
100	HRVD	60033	2406	50W-38N	B5
100	YkTp	60181	3027	17W-0S	B6
500	EMHT	60126	3028	14W-0S	B6
500	VLPK	60181	3027	17W-0S	C6
500	YkTp	60126	3028	14W-0S	B6
600	OKTR	60181	3027	17W-0S	C6
N Harrison St					
10	ALGN	60102	2694	33W-21N	E7
10	BTVA	60510	3078	35W-1S	A1
10	GNVA	60134	3020	34W-1N	D3
800	ALGN	60102	2695	32W-21N	A6
1600	AlqT	60102	2695	33W-21N	A6
S Harrison St					
10	ALGN	60102	2694	33W-20N	D7
10	BTVA	60510	3078	35W-1S	A2
100	GNVA	60134	3020	34W-0N	D4
100	OSWG	60543	3263	37W-12S	B4
W Harrison St					
10	CHCG	60605	3034	0W-0S	B6
100	CHCG	60607	3034	0W-0S	B5
100	EMHT	60126	3027	16W-0S	E6
100	HRVD	60033	2406	50W-38N	B5
800	CHCG	60607	3033	1W-0S	D5
1400	CHCG	60612	3033	3W-0S	A6
2800	CHCG	60612	3032	3W-0S	A6
3100	CHCG	60624	3032	4W-0S	C6
4500	CHCG	60644	3032	5W-0S	A6
4800	CHCG	60644	3031	6W-0S	D6
W Harrogate Rd					
1400	JLET	60435	3497	26W-22S	E1
Harrogate on Oxford					
10	RGMW	60008	2805	22W-13N	B7
10	RGMW	60067	2805	22W-13N	A7
Harrow Ct					
1700	WHTN	60187	3082	23W-2S	E3
N Harrow Ct					
800	ADSN	60101	2970	21W-4N	A3
Harrow Gate Dr					
1000	WDSK	60098	2582	39W-30N	B2
2100	IVNS	60010	2751	25W-16N	B7
2300	IVNS	60010	2804	25W-16N	B1
Harry Ct					
5200	NndT	60014	2641	33W-26N	A2
Harry Dr					
10800	HTLY	60142	2692	40W-21N	A6
Harry Caray Dr					
-	NHLK	60164	3028	14W-1N	D1
S Harry J Rogowski Dr					
11400	MTPK	60803	3276	3W-13S	E4
W Hart Av					
-	WKGN	60099	2422	10W-38N	A7
10700	BHPK	60099	2422	10W-38N	A7
N Hart Blvd					
100	HRVD	60033	2406	50W-38N	B7
S Hart Blvd					
100	HRVD	60033	2406	50W-38N	B7
Hart Dr					
2900	FNPK	60131	2972	13W-3N	E4
2900	FNPK	60131	2973	13W-3N	A4
18200	HMWD	60430	3428	1W-21S	A7
Hart Rd					
10	BNHL	60010	2697	26W-20N	C7
10	BRTN	60010	2697	26W-20N	C7
10	BTVA	60510	3078	34W-3S	C6
10	BTVA	60542	3078	34W-3S	C5
10	BtvT	60510	3078	34W-2S	C3
10	CbaT	60010	2697	26W-20N	C7
10	NARA	60510	3078	34W-2S	C5
10	NARA	60542	3078	34W-2S	C5
300	AURA	60510	3078	34W-3S	C6
300	BtvT	60542	3078	34W-3S	C6
400	AraT	60502	3078	34W-4S	C7
400	AraT	60510	3078	34W-3S	C7
400	AraT	60542	3078	34W-4S	C7
400	AURA	60502	3078	34W-4S	C7
400	NARA	60502	3078	34W-4S	C7
500	RDLK	60073	2531	23W-34N	E2
600	AvnT	60073	2531	23W-34N	E2
600	BNHL	60010	2750	26W-20N	D1
600	BRTN	60010	2750	26W-20N	D1
N Hart Rd					
20900	BRTN	60010	2697	26W-20N	C7
20900	CbaT	60010	2697	26W-21N	C6
W Hart Rd					
24200	AvnT	60073	2531	24W-34N	C2
24200	RDLK	60073	2531	24W-34N	C2
Hart St					
1800	DYR	46311	3598		D4
8000	SjnT	46311	3598		D5
N Hart St					
400	CHCG	60622	3033	2W-0N	C3
S Hart St					
-	PLTN	60067	2805	21W-16N	D1
W Hart St					
12500	WKGN	60087	2421	12W-38N	B7
12900	BHPK	60083	2421	12W-38N	A7
12900	BHPK	60087	2421	12W-38N	A7
12900	WDWH	60083	2421	13W-38N	A7
13400	WDWH	60083	2420	13W-38N	E7

STREET Block	City	ZIP	Map#	CGS	Grid
Harter Rd					
100	SgrT	60554	3134	44W-4S	E1
300	SgrT	60554	3135	43W-4S	A2
300	SRGV	60554	3134	43W-4S	E2
300	SRGV	60554	3135	43W-4S	A2
Harter Rd CO-4					
100	SgrT	60554	3134	44W-4S	E1
300	SgrT	60554	3135	43W-4S	A2
300	SRGV	60554	3134	43W-4S	E2
300	SRGV	60554	3135	43W-4S	A2
Hartfield Av					
-	YKVL	60560	3333	42W-17S	D5
Hartfield Dr					
700	NARA	60542	3078	35W-3S	C5
800	BTVA	60510	3078	34W-3S	C5
800	BTVA	60542	3078	34W-3S	C5
2400	MTGY	60538	3198	40W-10S	B7
2500	BtlT	60512	3198	40W-10S	B7
2500	BtlT	60538	3198	40W-10S	B7
Hartford Av					
500	AraT	60506	3199	37W-8S	D2
500	AURA	60506	3199	37W-8S	D2
Hartford Ct					
10	ALGN	60102	2694	35W-21N	A6
100	OSWG	60543	3200	35W-10S	A6
900	SMBG	60193	2913	23W-9N	A1
1600	HFET	60169	2858	24W-12N	D1
2300	NPVL	60565	3203	27W-10S	D5
10100	SRPK	60176	2973	12W-4N	B2
E Hartford Ct					
2500	ANHT	60004	2807	16W-15N	D2
Hartford Dr					
800	GRNE	60031	2477	17W-35N	B7
E Hartford Dr					
10	SMBG	60193	2913	23W-9N	B1
W Hartford Dr					
10	SMBG	60193	2913	23W-9N	A1
200	SMBG	60193	2858	23W-9N	E7
Hartford Ln					
-	BGBK	60440	3268	25W-12S	B3
-	DGvT	60516	3206	20W-9S	B3
-	WDRG	60517	3206	20W-9S	B3
700	BGBK	60440	3204	25W-11S	C7
900	EGVV	60007	2915	18W-8N	A2
1700	CLLK	60014	2693	36W-22N	D3
2100	GNVA	60134	3019	36W-1N	E3
Hartford Pl					
300	JltT	60433	3500	21W-24S	A5
Hartford Rd					
7300	DRGV	60516	3206	19W-8S	D1
Hartford St					
1300	GLHT	60139	2968	23W-2N	E7
1300	GLHT	60139	3024	23W-2N	E1
7100	BGVW	60455	3210	8W-10S	E4
Harth Ct					
6100	LSLE	60532	3142	23W-6S	E5
Hart Hills Rd					
10	BNHL	60010	2750	26W-18N	C2
Hartigan Rd					
2700	VOLO	60041	2530	27W-34N	C1
W Hartigan Rd					
27300	FXLK	60041	2530	27W-34N	B1
27300	VOLO	60041	2530	27W-34N	B1
27400	GrtT	60041	2530	27W-34N	B1
N Hartland Ct					
500	CHCG	60622	3033	2W-0N	C3
S Hartland Dr					
14000	PnfT	60544	3339	27W-16S	D4
Hartland Tr					
4700	MHRY	60050	2527	33W-31N	E6
Hartley Dr					
-	SMBG	60173	2859	21W-12N	E2
1600	ALGN	60102	2694	35W-20N	B7
1600	ALGN	60102	2747	35W-20N	A1
Hartman Ct					
300	SEGN	60177	2908	34W-9N	E2
Hartman Dr					
200	WldT	60564	3266	29W-11S	D1
14900	LktT	60441	3341	23W-18S	A7
15000	RMVL	60441	3341	23W-17S	A7
Hartmann Dr					
1200	SMBG	60193	2912	25W-9N	B1
1800	HRPK	60133	2912	25W-9N	A1
25400	CRTE	60417	3685	0W-30S	D4
25400	CteT	60417	3685	0W-30S	D4
Hartmann Ln					
500	WLMT	60091	2812	4W-13N	B6
N Hartong St					
600	PNFD	60544	3338	29W-18S	D7
Hartrey Av					
100	CHCG	60645	2866	3W-9N	E6
100	EVTN	60202	2866	3W-9N	E6
2100	EVTN	60201	2866	3W-12N	E1
2500	EVTN	60201	2812	3W-12N	E7
Harts Rd					
4100	RcmT	60072	2412	34W-38N	C7
4100	RcmT	60072	2413	33W-38N	A7
4100	RcmT	60081	2413	33W-38N	A7
4100	SPGV	60072	2413	33W-38N	A7
4100	SPGV	60081	2413	33W-38N	A7
5500	RcmT	60071	2412	34W-38N	C7
6000	RcmT	60097	2412	35W-38N	B7
W Harts Rd					
6600	NLES	60714	2865	8W-9N	A7
6600	NLES	60714	2918	8W-8N	E1
6600	NLES	60714	2919	8W-8N	A1
Hartsburg Ln					
1300	NARA	60542	3077	38W-3S	B6
W Harts Farm Rd					
22800	JLET	60544	3417	28W-19S	A3
22800	JLET	60586	3417	28W-19S	A3
22800	PnfT	60544	3417	28W-19S	A3
22800	PnfT	60586	3417	28W-19S	A3
Hartung Rd					
-	RGMW	60008	2805	21W-13N	C5
-	RGMW	60067	2805	21W-13N	C5
-	RGMW	60173	2805	21W-13N	D5
-	SMBG	60008	2805	21W-13N	C5
-	SMBG	60067	2805	21W-13N	C5
-	SMBG	60173	2805	21W-13N	C5
Hartway Ct					
200	MTGY	60538	3199	36W-9S	E4
Hartway Dr					
100	MTGY	60538	3199	36W-9S	E4
Hartwell Av					
600	ELGN	60120	2855	33W-12N	B1
S Hartwell Av					
6600	CHCG	60637	3152	0E-7S	C5
Hartwood Ct					
9200	ODPK	60462	3345	11W-16S	E3
Hartwood Dr					
900	SMWD	60107	2857	27W-9N	C7
900	SMWD	60107	2911	27W-9N	C1
Harty Ct					
10	PltT	60175	2906	39W-8N	E4

STREET Block	City	ZIP	Map#	CGS	Grid
Hartzell St					
2200	EVTN	60201	2812	3W-13N	D7
2900	WLMT	60091	2811	6W-13N	E7
Harvard Av					
10	DSPN	60016	2862	14W-12N	B1
10	MPPT	60016	2862	14W-12N	B1
10	MPPT	60056	2862	14W-12N	B1
100	BNHL	60010	2750	25W-18N	E4
100	BrnT	60010	2750	25W-18N	E4
100	NHLK	60164	3028	14W-1N	C1
200	BrnT	60010	2751	25W-18N	A4
600	BRTN	60010	2751	25W-18N	A4
1600	NPVL	60565	3204	24W-9S	D3
N Harvard Av					
-	NHLK	60164	3028	14W-2N	C1
10	ANHT	60005	2806	18W-14N	E4
800	AddT	60181	3027	18W-2N	A1
800	VLPK	60181	3027	18W-2N	A1
1500	ANHT	60004	2806	18W-15N	E2
4000	ANHT	60004	2753	18W-18N	E2
S Harvard Av					
10	VLPK	60181	3027	18W-0N	A4
100	ANHT	60005	2806	18W-13N	D5
200	ADSN	60101	2971	18W-3N	A6
700	ADSN	60181	2971	18W-2N	A7
700	VLPK	60101	2971	18W-2N	A7
700	VLPK	60181	2971	18W-2N	A7
800	AddT	60181	3027	18W-2N	A1
800	ADSN	60101	3027	18W-2N	A1
800	ADSN	60181	3027	18W-2N	A1
1300	ANHT	60005	2860	18W-12N	E1
6300	CHCG	60621	3152	0W-7S	B5
7500	CHCG	60620	3214	0W-8S	B1
7500	CHCG	60621	3214	0W-8S	B1
9500	CHCG	60628	3214	0W-11S	B6
10300	CHCG	60628	3278	0W-12S	B1
W Harvard Av					
19300	FmtT	60060	2590	19W-29N	C3
19300	MDLN	60060	2590	19W-29N	C3
Harvard Cir					
1000	SMBG	60193	2912	25W-9N	B1
4100	NndT	60012	2583	35W-27N	E7
E Harvard Cir					
200	SEGN	60177	2908	35W-8N	B3
N Harvard Cir					
1000	SEGN	60177	2908	35W-8N	B3
W Harvard Cir					
200	SEGN	60177	2908	35W-8N	B3
Harvard Ct					
-	GNVW	60062	2810	10W-15N	B2
10	SEGN	60177	2908	35W-8N	B3
100	GNVW	60025	2810	10W-15N	B2
300	SRWD	60404	3496	30W-24S	B6
400	BRLT	60103	2967	28W-5N	B2
500	LNHT	60046	2418	19W-38N	C6
800	HDPK	60035	2704	9W-22N	D4
800	ISLK	60042	2586	28W-27N	E7
900	RMVL	60446	3340	25W-16S	C3
1400	CLSM	60188	2967	28W-4N	A3
1600	LKFT	60045	2649	13W-26N	A2
S Harvard Ct					
700	PLTN	60067	2805	22W-15N	B3
Harvard Dr					
600	WNVL	60555	3080	30W-2S	C5
S Harvard Dr					
800	PLTN	60067	2805	22W-14N	B3
Harvard Ln					
10	HNWD	60047	2645	20W-25N	E6
200	BMDL	60108	2969	22W-4N	B4
200	BMDL	60139	2969	22W-4N	B4
200	BmdT	60108	2969	22W-4N	B4
200	GLHT	60108	2969	22W-4N	B4
200	GLHT	60139	2969	22W-4N	B4
400	BRLT	60103	2967	28W-5N	B2
500	HFET	60169	2858	24W-12N	E1
600	LYVL	60048	2591	16W-28N	E7
700	MTSN	60443	3505	6W-25S	E7
900	BFGV	60089	2754	16W-17N	D5
900	WLMT	60091	2812	4W-14N	B5
1400	SMBG	60193	2912	25W-9N	B1
1800	NLNX	60451	3590	16W-25S	A1
1800	NlxT	60451	3590	16W-25S	A1
2000	ELGN	60123	2853	36W-10N	E5
2000	ELGN	60123	2854	36W-10N	A5
3200	GfnT	60156	2692	38W-23N	E2
17700	CCHL	60429	3426	4W-21S	E6
17700	CCHL	60478	3426	4W-21S	E6
17700	HLCT	60478	3426	4W-21S	E6
Harvard Rd					
-	FSMR	60422	3507	2W-23S	D4
N Harvard Rd					
1200	ANHT	60004	2806	18W-15N	D2
Harvard St					
-	FTPK	60130	3030	10W-0S	A6
-	FTPK	60153	3030	10W-0S	A6
-	LktT	60432	3419	22W-21S	C7
-	LktT	60441	3419	22W-21S	C7
-	MYWD	60153	3030	10W-0S	A6
10	CHCG	60304	3031	7W-0S	B6
10	CHCG	60644	3031	7W-0S	B6
10	OKPK	60304	3031	8W-0S	A6
100	LktT	60441	3499	23W-21S	B1
600	WLMT	60091	2812	4W-13N	B6
2500	BDVW	60153	3029	12W-0S	C6
2500	BDVW	60155	3029	12W-0S	C6
2500	MYWD	60153	3029	12W-0S	C6
2500	MYWD	60155	3029	12W-0S	C6
7200	OKPK	60130	3030	9W-0S	C6
7200	OKPK	60304	3030	9W-0S	C6
E Harvard St					
10	PvsT	60126	3028	14W-0S	B7
10	YkTp	60126	3028	14W-0S	B7
500	EMHT	60126	3028	15W-0S	A7
W Harvard St					
7100	NLES	60714	2864	8W-9N	D6
Harvard Ter					
900	EVTN	60202	2867	2W-9N	A6
3800	SKOK	60076	2866	5W-9N	B6
5000	SKOK	60077	2865	6W-9N	D6
Harvard Hills Rd					
6600	CmgT	60033	2406	49W-39N	D4
6600	HRVD	60033	2406	49W-39N	D4
N Harve St					
10	PLNO	60545	3259	47W-13S	C6
S Harve St					
200	PLNO	60545	3259	47W-14S	C7
Harvell Dr					
1300	BTVA	60510	3077	36W-2S	E4
Harvest Av					
6700	WDRG	60517	3144	21W-7S	A7
Harvest Cir					
800	CLLK	60014	2639	37W-24N	B7
900	BFGV	60089	2701	16W-21N	C7
Harvest Cross					
100	ODPK	60467	3344	14W-17S	D5

STREET Block	City	ZIP	Map#	CGS	Grid
Harvest Ct					
-	ISLK	60042	2586	28W-28N	E6
10	BGBK	60490	3268	26W-13S	A5
100	VOLO	60041	2530	27W-34N	C1
100	WNVL	60555	3080	29W-3S	C5
200	AURA	60502	3201	32W-8S	B1
200	VNHL	60061	2647	16W-24N	E6
800	ANTH	60002	2358	22W-42N	B6
800	CmpT	60175	2961	42W-5N	D1
1000	WDSK	60098	2581	42W-30N	B2
1200	CLLK	60014	2639	37W-24N	B7
1200	NPVL	60564	3203	28W-10S	A6
3900	GNVW	60025	2809	11W-15N	D3
3900	GNVW	60062	2809	11W-15N	D3
11600	CrlT	60142	2743	44W-20N	C1
Harvest Dr					
10	SMWD	60107	2856	29W-9N	E7
100	DYR	46311	3598		D4
600	BGBK	60490	3268	26W-13S	A5
700	LKZH	60047	2699	22W-22N	B5
900	ANTH	60002	2358	22W-42N	B6
1100	SRWD	60404	3496	30W-23S	B5
1200	CTHL	60403	3418	25W-21S	B6
7800	FftT	60423	3504	10W-24S	C6
16400	LMNT	60439	3342	20W-15S	B1
Harvest Ln					
-	DRGV	60516	3144	18W-7S	E6
-	DYR	46311	3598		D5
-	SKOK	60076	2812	5W-12N	A7
200	CmpT	60175	2961	42W-5N	C2
300	SEGN	60177	2908	34W-8N	E3
400	ROSL	60172	2912	24W-6N	E7
700	MPPT	60056	2808	14W-13N	B6
1200	UYPK	60466	3684	3W-30S	C4
1500	WTMT	60559	3145	18W-7S	B6
1800	GLHT	60139	2968	24W-3N	D5
1800	JLET	60586	3416	29W-21S	D7
1800	PnfT	60586	3416	29W-21S	D7
2800	LNHT	60046	2476	19W-37N	C1
3800	GNVW	60025	2809	11W-15N	E3
3800	GNVW	60062	2809	11W-15N	E3
8500	DRN	60561	3206	20W-9S	B4
21400	RchT	60443	3593	8W-25S	B1
S Harvest Ln					
26100	CteT	60417	3684	2W-32S	E7
Harvest Pl					
800	ROSL	60172	2912	24W-6N	E7
2900	DRN	60561	3206	20W-9S	B4
Harvest Tr					
900	YKVL	60560	3333	42W-16S	E5
Harvester Ct					
400	WLNG	60090	2755	15W-17N	B5
Harvester Dr					
100	BRRG	60527	3146	15W-7S	A7
100	BRRG	60527	3208	14W-8S	C1
Harvester Rd					
1000	WCHI	60185	3021	31W-2N	E1
1000	WCHI	60185	3022	31W-2N	A1
1000	WnfT	60185	3022	31W-2N	A1
W Harvester St					
-	PNFD	60544	3338	30W-17S	A7
Harvest Gate					
10	LIHL	60156	2693	36W-21N	D5
400	ALGN	60102	2693	36W-21N	D6
400	LIHL	60102	2693	36W-21N	D6
W Harvest Glen Cir					
-	AlqT	60013	2642	28W-24N	D6
28300	CbaT	60013	2642	28W-24N	E6
Harvest Glen Ct					
10	HNWD	60047	2645	22W-24N	A7
Harvest Glen Rd					
-	CbaT	60013	2642	28W-24N	E7
Harvest Hill Ct					
11700	ODPK	60467	3422	14W-21S	D5
Harvest Hill Dr					
17400	ODPK	60467	3422	14W-20S	D5
N Harvest Hill Pl					
2200	RLKB	60073	2475	22W-36N	A4
Harvest Moon Ct					
500	NARA	60542	3137	38W-4S	A2
Harvest Ridge Rd					
3200	GNVA	60134	3019	37W-1N	C3
Harvest View Ln					
8600	TYPK	60477	3504	10W-23S	B3
Harvey Av					
10	GYLK	60030	2532	21W-33N	D3
100	WDDL	60191	2915	18W-5N	A7
100	WDDL	60191	2971	18W-5N	A1
1200	BRWN	60304	3031	7W-1S	B7
1200	BRWN	60402	3031	7W-1S	B7
1200	OKPK	60304	3031	7W-1S	B7
1500	BRWN	60402	3089	7W-2S	B3
3400	PKCY	60085	2536	13W-33N	A3
3800	PvsT	60525	3086	13W-4S	E7
3800	PvsT	60558	3086	13W-4S	E7
3800	SKNY	60402	3089	7W-3S	B6
3800	WNSP	60558	3086	13W-4S	E7
4400	WNSP	60558	3146	13W-4S	E1
5000	WNSP	60558	3147	13W-5S	A3
5400	LynT	60525	3147	13W-5S	A3
5700	LynT	60525	3146	13W-6S	E4
14500	HRVY	60426	3349	1W-17S	E5
S Harvey Av					
100	OKPK	60302	3031	7W-0N	B4
500	OKPK	60304	3031	7W-0S	B5
1100	BRWN	60304	3031	7W-0S	B7
1100	BRWN	60402	3031	7W-0S	B7
Harvey Av N					
1100	OKPK	60302	3031	7W-1N	B1
1200	CHCG	60639	3031	7W-1N	B1
1200	OKPK	60639	3031	7W-1N	B1
E Harvey Dr					
12500	NLNX	60451	3590	15W-26S	B2
12500	NlxT	60451	3590	15W-26S	B2
Harvey Ln					
-	GwdT	60098	2524	40W-32N	E4
Harvey Rd					
10	BmdT	60157	2913	22W-6N	C5
300	ROSL	60157	2913	22W-6N	C7
900	OSWG	60543	3201	33W-11S	A7
900	OSWG	60543	3265	33W-12S	A3
900	OswT	60503	3201	33W-11S	A7
900	OswT	60543	3201	33W-10S	A7
1200	OswT	60543	3265	33W-11S	A1
Harvey Sq					
600	BbyT	60134	3018	39W-0N	D5
Harvey St					
100	ELGN	60123	2854	34W-11N	D4
400	DSPN	60016	2862	14W-11N	C2
E Harvey Lake Dr					
400	VNHL	60061	2647	16W-26N	D3
Harwarden St					
200	GNEN	60137	3025	23W-0S	A6
200	WHTN	60187	3025	23W-0S	A6
1200	WHTN	60187	3024	23W-0S	E6
1600	GNEN	60187	3025	23W-0S	A6

STREET Block	City	ZIP	Map#	CGS	Grid
Harwarden St					
1600	WHTN	60137	3025	23W-0S	A6
Harwich Dr					
1100	CLSM	60188	2967	27W-4N	B3
Harwich Ln					
800	SMBG	60194	2858	24W-10N	D4
Harwick Ln					
3800	PKCY	60085	2535	13W-33N	E2
Harwinton Pl					
2100	HFET	60169	2857	26W-12N	E1
2100	HFET	60169	2858	25W-12N	B1
Harwood Av					
17700	HMWD	60430	3427	2W-22S	C7
18400	HMWD	60430	3507	2W-22S	C1
18600	FSMR	60422	3507	2W-22S	C1
18600	FSMR	60430	3507	2W-22S	C1
18600	HMWD	60422	3507	2W-22S	C1
Harwood Dr					
200	BGBK	60440	3269	23W-12S	A2
1100	GNOK	60048	2592	15W-31N	B1
Harwood St					
-	CHCG	60656	2918	8W-6N	E6
-	CHCG	60706	2918	8W-6N	E6
-	HDHT	60706	2918	8W-6N	E6
200	JLET	60432	3499	22W-23S	D4
200	JltT	60432	3499	22W-23S	D4
Haryan Wy					
-	GYLK	60030	2532	21W-33N	D2
Haskell St					
-	AntT	60081	2414	28W-38N	D7
N Haskins Av					
7700	CHCG	60626	2867	2W-9N	C6
Hassell Cir					
1200	HFET	60169	2804	25W-12N	C7
Hassell Ct					
1200	HFET	60169	2804	25W-12N	C7
Hassell Dr					
1300	HFET	60169	2804	25W-12N	C7
1300	HFET	60169	2858	25W-12N	C1
Hassell Pl					
1400	HFET	60169	2804	24W-13N	B7
Hassell Rd					
-	HFET	60169	2803	26W-12N	E7
-	HFET	60169	2804	26W-12N	A7
2300	HFET	60169	2857	26W-12N	E1
Hassert Blvd					
21000	BGBK	60440	3268	26W-12S	A4
21000	BGBK	60490	3268	26W-13S	A4
21100	BGBK	60490	3267	27W-12S	C4
21900	BGBK	60585	3267	27W-12S	C4
21900	WldT	60490	3267	27W-12S	C4
22000	WldT	60585	3267	27W-12S	B4
Hastings Av					
-	BtnT	60081	2414	29W-38N	D7
-	FXLK	60020	2414	29W-38N	D7
-	FXLK	60081	2414	29W-38N	D7
10	CLLK	60014	2639	35W-25N	E4
10	EGVV	60007	2914	19W-8N	D1
10	NfdT	60062	2758	7W-20N	A2
10	NtrT	60062	2758	7W-20N	A2
100	HDPK	60035	2758	7W-20N	A1
1800	DRGV	60516	3144	20W-7S	A6
2300	EVTN	60201	2866	4W-12N	C1
2500	EVTN	60201	2812	4W-12N	C7
Hastings Cir					
7200	FXLK	60020	2415	28W-39N	A5
Hastings Ct					
10	LIHL	60156	2692	38W-21N	D6
100	ROSL	60172	2912	25W-7N	B4
100	VNHL	60061	2647	17W-26N	C3
700	WLNG	60090	2755	15W-17N	A6
1900	SMBG	60194	2858	25W-11N	B3
3500	GRNE	60031	2477	16W-36N	E3
Hastings Ct CO-JI					
32500	GRNE	60031	2477	16W-36N	E3
Hastings Ct SR-50					
3500	GRNE	60031	2477	16W-36N	E3
S Hastings Ct					
14200	PnfT	60544	3339	27W-16S	D5
Hastings Dr					
10	CmpT	60175	2906	40W-6N	C6
1900	HFET	60169	2858	25W-12N	C1
2000	JLET	60586	3415	32W-21S	C7
7900	ODPK	60462	3346	9W-16S	D4
15100	DLTN	60419	3351	1E-17S	B6
Hastings Ln					
-	BFGV	60089	2754	15W-20N	E2
-	BFGV	60090	2754	15W-20N	E2
-	BFGV	60090	2755	15W-20N	A2
-	WLNG	60090	2755	15W-20N	A2
10	LNSH	60069	2703	13W-22N	A3
100	VrnT	60089	2755	15W-20N	A2
700	BFGV	60089	2755	15W-20N	A1
700	HRPK	60133	2858	26W-9N	A7
700	VrnT	60015	2755	15W-20N	A1
800	HRPK	60133	2857	26W-9N	E7
6300	LSLE	60532	3142	24W-7S	C6
9800	MKNA	60448	3503	12W-23S	D4
N Hastings Pl					
600	LNHT	60046	2418	20W-39N	A5
Hastings Rd					
400	LKFT	60045	2649	11W-26N	E3
600	WLNG	60090	2755	15W-17N	A6
1200	WDRG	60517	3206	20W-10S	B5
1300	DGvT	60516	3206	20W-10S	B5
1300	DGvT	60517	3206	20W-10S	B5
Hastings St					
700	ELGN	60120	2855	33W-10N	B6
700	PKRG	60068	2864	10W-9N	A7
1300	NPVL	60563	3140	29W-5S	D2
10800	WSTR	60154	3086	13W-2S	E2
W Hastings St					
1200	CHCG	60608	3033	1W-1S	D7
Hastings Mill Rd					
100	SMWD	60107	2857	28W-12N	B2
Hastings on Oxford					
10	RGMW	60008	2805	22W-13N	B7
10	RGMW	60067	2805	22W-13N	A7
Hatch Ln					
-	LSLE	60532	3083	22W-4S	C7
4300	LSLE	60532	3143	22W-4S	C1
Hatch Pl					
1600	DRGV	60516	3206	20W-8S	B1
Hatch St					
1800	DRGV	60516	3206	20W-8S	A1
Hatchery Rd					
2100	SPGV	60081	2413	31W-39N	E4
Hatfield Ct					
2500	ELGN	60123	2907	36W-8N	E3
Hatfield Ln					
1700	AURA	60503	3201	32W-10S	C5
1700	AURA	60504	3201	32W-10S	C5
2400	ELGN	60123	2907	36W-8N	E3
2400	SEGN	60177	2907	36W-8N	E4
Hathaway Av					
100	WnfT	60185	3023	28W-0N	A5

STREET Block	City	ZIP	Map#	CGS	Grid
Hathaway Cir					
500	LKFT	60045	2649	12W-26N	B3
1200	ELGN	60120	2855	32W-12N	D1
Hathaway Cres					
10	SgrT	60506	3136	41W-5S	A3
Hathaway Ct					
800	NARA	60542	3077	38W-3S	A6
Hathaway Ln					
6300	DRGV	60516	3144	20W-7S	A6
N Hathaway Ln					
-	BbyT	60134	3018	39W-0S	D6
S Hathaway Ln					
-	BbyT	60134	3018	39W-0S	D7
Hatherleigh Ct					
-	MPPT	60005	2861	17W-10N	C4
-	MPPT	60056	2861	17W-10N	C4
W Hatherleigh Ct					
1800	MPPT	60056	2861	17W-11N	C4
Hatherley Ct					
10	SgrT	60506	3136	41W-5S	A4
S Hatlen Av					
10	ANHT	60005	2807	17W-12N	C7
10	MPPT	60056	2807	17W-12N	C7
100	MPPT	60056	2861	17W-12N	C1
Hatlen Ct					
300	MPPT	60056	2861	17W-12N	C1
Hatte Gray Ct					
800	GNEN	60137	3024	23W-1N	E3
Hatte Gray Ln					
-	GNEN	60137	3024	23W-1N	E3
E Hattendorf Av					
10	ROSL	60172	2913	23W-7N	A4
W Hattendorf Av					
10	ROSL	60172	2913	23W-7N	A4
100	ROSL	60172	2912	24W-7N	E4
100	SMBG	60172	2912	24W-7N	E4
Hattie Av					
100	CPVL	60110	2800	34W-16N	E1
100	CPVL	60118	2800	34W-16N	E1
Hauby Ct					
1400	MNKA	60447	3672	33W-30S	B3
E Hauert St					
500	PTON	60468	3861	8W-37S	B3
900	WIIT	60468	3861	8W-37S	B3
N Hauge St					
35000	AvnT	60073	2474	24W-35N	C7
35000	RLKB	60073	2474	24W-35N	C7
Hauk Rd					
10	HPSR	60140	2743	46W-19N	B2
Hauser Ct					
200	NLNX	60451	3501	17W-24S	C5
N Haussen Ct					
3000	CHCG	60618	2976	4W-3N	C4
Havana Av					
6200	HMND	46320	3430		D1
6200	HMND	46324	3430		D1
Haven Av					
15900	ODHL	60487	3424	11W-19S	A2
15900	ODPK	60462	3424	11W-19S	A2
16200	ODHL	60487	3423	11W-20S	E3
E Haven Av					
100	NLNX	60451	3501	17W-25S	C6
W Haven Av					
-	NLNX	60433	3500	19W-24S	D6
100	NLNX	60451	3501	18W-24S	A6
700	NlxT	60451	3501	18W-24S	A6
900	NLNX	60451	3500	19W-25S	D7
900	NlxT	60451	3500	19W-25S	D7
Haven Ct					
3000	JLET	60435	3497	27W-23S	C3
9200	ODHL	60487	3423	11W-19S	E3
Haven Dr					
600	BRTN	60010	2751	24W-18N	C3
600	PltT	60010	2751	24W-18N	C3
N Haven Dr					
1500	PltT	60067	2752	21W-17N	C4
1500	PltT	60074	2752	21W-17N	C4
W Haven Dr					
300	ANHT	60005	2861	18W-12N	A1
900	ANHT	60005	2860	18W-12N	E1
Haven Ln					
700	JLET	60435	3497	27W-23S	C3
1800	GNOK	60048	2592	14W-30N	C2
2800	LNHT	60046	2418	19W-38N	D7
3000	OMCK	60083	2418	19W-38N	D7
N Haven Rd					
100	EMHT	60126	3028	15W-1N	A2
Haven St					
600	EVTN	60201	2867	2W-12N	B1
E Haven St					
300	ANHT	60005	2861	17W-12N	B1
400	ANHT	60056	2861	17W-12N	B1
400	MPPT	60056	2861	17W-12N	B1
W Haven St					
2100	MPPT	60056	2861	17W-12N	B1
Havenhill Dr					
1900	JLET	60586	3415	33W-21S	B7
Havens Ct					
400	DGvT	60516	3206	20W-10S	B5
400	DGvT	60517	3206	20W-10S	B5
400	WDRG	60517	3206	20W-10S	B5
1000	DRGV	60515	3084	19W-4S	C7
Havens Dr					
-	GwdT	60098	2524	40W-32N	E4
-	WDSK	60098	2524	40W-32N	E5
10	DGvT	60516	3206	20W-10S	B5
10	WDRG	60517	3206	20W-10S	B5
200	DGvT	60517	3206	20W-10S	B5
2500	WCHI	60185	2965	32W-4N	B4
8600	DRN	60561	3206	20W-10S	B5
8600	WDRG	60561	3206	20W-10S	B5
Havenshire Ct					
900	NPVL	60565	3203	28W-8S	A3
Havenshire Rd					
800	NPVL	60565	3203	27W-8S	B2
1600	AURA	60505	3139	33W-6S	A4
1700	AURA	60502	3139	33W-6S	A4
Havenwood Av					
400	HDPK	60035	2758	7W-20N	C2
Havenwood Ct					
100	RDLK	60073	2531	25W-33N	A3
300	LYVL	60048	2591	17W-28N	B6
3200	RGMW	60067	2805	21W-13N	D6
Havenwood Dr					
100	RDLK	60073	2531	25W-33N	A2
1000	LYVL	60048	2591	17W-28N	B6
Havenwood Ln					
900	LKFT	60045	2650	9W-25N	C4
Haverford Ct					
10	ALGN	60102	2747	36W-19N	A2
200	SMBG	60173	2859	21W-10N	E4
Haverford Dr					
1500	ALGN	60102	2747	36W-19N	A2
Haverford Wy					
5800	HFET	60192	2855	31W-12N	E1
5800	HFET	60192	2856	31W-12N	A1
Haverhill Cir					
1200	NPVL	60563	3142	25W-5S	A3
Haverhill Ct					
10	BGBK	60440	3205	22W-10S	D5
10	CRY	60013	2642	30W-25N	A5
400	SRGV	60554	3135	42W-5S	D2
E Haver Hill Ct					
300	ITSC	60143	2914	19W-7N	C5
E Haverhill Ct					
2500	ANHT	60004	2807	16W-15N	D2
Haverhill Dr					
1400	WHTN	60187	3082	24W-1S	D2
3000	AURA	60502	3139	31W-5S	D4
Haverhill Ln					
100	SMBG	60193	2858	26W-10N	A6
9900	HTLY	60142	2692	39W-22N	C5
14000	ODPK	60467	3344	14W-16S	E4
N Haverhill Ln					
500	SEGN	60177	2908	35W-7N	C4
S Haverhill Ln					
500	SEGN	60177	2908	35W-7N	C5
Haverhill on Auburn					
10	RGMW	60008	2806	19W-14N	B3
Haverman Ct					
10	ELGN	60120	2855	32W-10N	C5
Haversham Dr					
1300	AURA	60502	3139	31W-5S	E3
Haversham Ln					
10	NBRN	60010	2644	25W-24N	B7
10	NBRN	60010	2698	25W-24N	B1
Haverton Ct					
10	SMWD	60107	2857	28W-11N	A5
Haverton Dr					
2200	MDLN	60060	2590	20W-29N	A4
N Haverton Dr					
34200	WrnT	60031	2534	17W-34N	C1
Haverton Wy					
-	CbaT	60010	2697	25W-22N	E4
100	NBRN	60010	2697	25W-22N	E4
Haviland Ct					
4600	NPVL	60564	3266	29W-12S	C3
Haviland Dr					
10	JltT	60436	3587	24W-26S	A2
Hawaii Av					
2100	NCHI	60088	2593	11W-29N	D3
Hawaii Ct					
18000	ODPK	60467	3423	13W-21S	A7
Haweswood Ct					
3400	CRTE	60417	3596	0E-28S	D6
Haweswood Dr					
3400	CRTE	60417	3596	0E-28S	E6
3400	STGR	60475	3596	0E-28S	E6
Hawk Av					
1500	MLPK	60160	3029	13W-1N	A2
W Hawk Av					
1300	NndT	60051	2586	30W-29N	A5
Hawk Cir					
500	CmpT	60175	2961	42W-4N	C4
Hawk Ct					
200	SMBG	60193	2857	27W-10N	D6
400	DRN	60527	3145	17W-7S	D6
2000	RGMW	60008	2806	19W-13N	D6
17500	WrnT	60031	2534	17W-34N	B2
S Hawk Ct					
1900	WKGN	60048	2535	14W-31N	C6
Hawk Dr					
-	BRLT	60103	2966	29W-5N	D2
-	WynT	60103	2966	29W-5N	D2
100	PltT	60010	2751	24W-18N	D2
1400	BGBK	60490	3267	26W-12S	E3
Hawk Ln					
800	CLSM	60188	2967	27W-3N	B5
1800	EGVV	60007	2913	22W-8N	C2
2100	RGMW	60008	2806	19W-13N	C6
W Hawk Ln					
4900	MONE	60449	3683	6W-31S	B6
N Hawk St					
600	PLTN	60067	2752	20W-16N	E6
W Hawkes St					
1400	ANHT	60004	2753	18W-18N	D2
Hawkeye Dr					
200	CmpT	60119	2961	43W-4N	A4
Hawk Haven Rd					
15500	HMGN	60491	3342	19W-16S	D3
Hawk Hollow Dr					
-	BRLT	60103	2967	28W-5N	A2
Hawkins Av					
1700	DRGV	60516	3206	20W-8S	A1
Hawkins Cir					
10	WHTN	60187	3082	24W-2S	D4
Hawkins Ct					
1200	BRLT	60103	2910	29W-6N	E7
1300	SCRL	60174	2964	34W-4N	D4
Hawkins Ln					
10	SchT	60175	2963	38W-5N	B2
Hawkins St					
500	ELGN	60123	2854	34W-11N	D4
Hawkins Wy					
100	GNVA	60134	3019	37W-1N	C3
Hawknest Ln					
-	AURA	60503	3201	31W-10S	E6
Hawks Bill Ct					
12900	PNFD	60585	3337	32W-15S	C2
Hawks Bill Ln					
12700	PNFD	60585	3337	32W-15S	C2
Hawkshead Dr					
2800	MhtT	60442	3590	15W-27S	B5
2800	NlxT	60442	3590	15W-27S	B5
2800	NlxT	60451	3590	15W-27S	B5
Hawksley Ln					
1400	NARA	60542	3077	38W-3S	B7
Hawks Point Tr					
-	RcmT	60071	2354	33W-42N	A6
Hawkweed Dr					
-	NPVL	60564	3266	29W-13S	D6
Hawkweed Ln					
1100	LKFT	60045	2649	11W-27N	D1
Hawkwood Ct					
5100	CPVL	60110	2747	36W-18N	A5
Hawley Av					
10	WDND	60118	2801	34W-15N	A3
Hawley Ct					
10	GYLK	60030	2532	21W-33N	E3
400	NPVL	60565	3203	27W-10S	C6
500	MDLN	60060	2590	19W-27N	C7
Hawley Dr					
-	OSWG	60543	3265	33W-11S	A1
Hawley Ln					
100	GNVA	60134	3020	35W-0N	B5
11800	HTLY	60142	2691	40W-22N	E3
11800	HTLY	60142	2692	40W-22N	A3
Hawley St					
10	GYLK	60030	2532	20W-33N	E3
E Hawley St					
10	MDLN	60060	2590	18W-27N	E7
E Hawley St CO-A38					
10	MDLN	60060	2590	18W-27N	E7
W Hawley St					
10	MDLN	60060	2590	20W-28N	A7
200	FmtT	60060	2589	22W-27N	B7
200	HNWD	60047	2589	22W-27N	B7
200	HNWD	60060	2589	22W-27N	B7
1800	FmtT	60060	2590	20W-27N	A7
20800	MDLN	60060	2589	21W-27N	E7
21700	FmtT	60047	2589	22W-27N	C7
21700	MDLN	60047	2589	22W-27N	C7
W Hawley St CO-A38					
10	MDLN	60060	2590	20W-28N	A7
200	FmtT	60060	2589	22W-27N	B7
200	HNWD	60047	2589	22W-27N	B7
200	HNWD	60060	2589	22W-27N	B7
1800	FmtT	60060	2590	20W-27N	A7
20800	MDLN	60060	2589	21W-27N	E7
21700	FmtT	60047	2589	22W-27N	C7
21700	MDLN	60047	2589	22W-27N	C7
Hawley Woods Rd					
400	BNHL	60010	2750	27W-17N	C4
Hawthorn					
5100	LSLE	60532	3143	23W-5S	B3
Hawthorn Av					
10	GLNC	60022	2758	6W-17N	E5
Hawthorn Ct					
1400	HNDL	60521	3086	15W-3S	B5
3700	WKGN	60087	2478	13W-36N	E4
3700	WKGN	60087	2479	13W-36N	A4
Hawthorn Ctr					
-	VNHL	60061	2647	16W-26N	D4
Hawthorn Dr					
10	DMND	60416	3941	33W-39S	B1
10	HNWD	60047	2645	21W-24N	D7
10	KLDR	60047	2645	21W-24N	E7
200	TNLK	53181	2354		D1
700	SchT	60174	2963	36W-3N	E5
700	SCRL	60174	2963	36W-3N	D5
800	NPVL	60540	3141	26W-7S	D7
9000	HYHL	60457	3209	11W-10S	E5
14100	LMNT	60439	3343	17W-15S	B2
24500	AvnT	60073	2474	24W-35N	C5
W Hawthorn Dr					
900	ITSC	60143	2914	20W-6N	A7
Hawthorn Ln					
-	ANTH	60002	2357	24W-42N	D5
-	AntT	60002	2357	24W-42N	D5
-	PSPK	60464	3273	11W-14S	E5
100	HFET	60169	2859	23W-11N	B3
300	WLBK	60527	3207	17W-8S	C2
300	WNKA	60093	2812	4W-15N	C3
1000	BCHR	60401	3864	0W-36S	D1
2700	WLMT	60091	2812	5W-13N	A5
2900	WLMT	60091	2811	5W-13N	E5
7100	SPGV	60081	2414	30W-39N	A5
E Hawthorn Pkwy					
10	VNHL	60061	2647	16W-26N	C4
W Hawthorn Pkwy					
10	VNHL	60061	2647	17W-26N	B4
300	MDLN	60060	2647	17W-26N	B4
Hawthorn Pl					
-	LktT	60441	3419	23W-21S	B7
Hawthorne					
1700	SchT	60174	3021	32W-2N	C2
1700	SchT	60185	3021	32W-2N	C2
1700	WnfT	60185	3021	32W-2N	C2
1700	WynT	60185	3021	32W-2N	C2
Hawthorne Av					
-	FTPK	60130	3030	9W-0N	C4
-	RVFT	60130	3030	9W-0N	C4
-	RVFT	60305	3030	9W-0N	C4
10	AddT	60106	2915	17W-6N	C6
10	BNVL	60106	2915	17W-6N	C6
100	AddT	60191	2915	17W-6N	B6
100	WDDL	60191	2915	17W-6N	B6
300	AddT	60106	2971	16W-4N	D2
300	BNVL	60106	2971	16W-4N	D2
300	GRNE	60031	2536	13W-34N	A1
400	GRNE	60031	2479	13W-34N	A7
500	BmdT	60157	2913	22W-7N	C3
500	BRLT	60103	2910	29W-7N	D4
700	ROSL	60172	2913	22W-7N	C3
1600	WSTR	60154	3087	13W-1S	A2
2000	CTHL	60403	3418	24W-21S	E7
2000	HMWD	60430	3427	2W-21S	C6
4500	LYNS	60534	3148	10W-4S	B1
4600	MCCK	60525	3148	10W-4S	B1
4600	MCCK	60534	3148	10W-4S	B1
7100	WDRG	60517	3205	21W-8S	E1
9400	FftT	60448	3503	11W-23S	E3
N Hawthorne Av					
700	EMHT	60126	2971	16W-3N	D6
1900	LydT	60164	2973	12W-2N	B7
1900	MLPK	60160	2973	12W-2N	B7
1900	MLPK	60160	3029	12W-2N	B1
1900	MLPK	60164	2973	12W-2N	B7
1900	SNPK	60160	3029	12W-2N	B1
1900	SNPK	60165	3029	12W-2N	B1
2300	FNPK	60131	2973	12W-2N	B7
S Hawthorne Av					
100	EMHT	60126	3027	16W-1N	D3
W Hawthorne Av					
4800	BKLY	60162	3028	13W-0N	D4
4800	BKLY	60163	3028	13W-0N	D4
4800	HLSD	60162	3028	13W-0N	D4
5100	BKLY	60104	3028	13W-0N	E4
5100	BLWD	60104	3028	13W-0N	E4
5100	HLSD	60163	3028	14W-0N	C4
14100	LbvT	60045	2648	14W-27N	C2
7400	FftT	60423	3504	9W-25S	E6
25400	AntT	60002	2416	25W-39N	A5
Hawthorne Blvd					
-	MltT	60187	3024	25W-0N	B5
-	WHTN	60187	3024	25W-0N	B5
E Hawthorne Blvd					
100	MDLN	60060	2646	18W-27N	D1
1000	WHTN	60187	3024	23W-0N	E5
1700	WHTN	60187	3025	23W-0N	A5
1800	GNEN	60137	3025	23W-0N	A5
1800	WHTN	60137	3025	23W-0N	A5
S Hawthorne Blvd					
10	MDLN	60060	2646	18W-27N	E1
W Hawthorne Blvd					
100	MDLN	60060	2646	19W-27N	C1
600	WHTN	60187	3024	25W-0N	B5
Hawthorne Cir					
10	JltT	60433	3587	23W-25S	A2
600	LMBD	60148	3026	19W-0S	D6
700	PNFD	60544	3338	29W-17S	D7
W Hawthorne Cir					
300	MPPT	60056	2861	16W-10N	E4
Hawthorne Ct					
10	AURA	60506	3138	36W-7S	A7
10	BFGV	60089	2754	16W-18N	C3
10	CTCY	60409	3429	2E-18S	C1
200	SMBG	60193	2859	22W-9N	D6
200	SYHW	60118	2799	36W-15N	E3
300	ANTH	60002	2358	22W-42N	B6
300	CmpT	60175	2961	42W-5N	D2
500	YKVL	60560	3333	43W-16S	B4
600	CPVL	60110	2748	33W-17N	A7
700	BGBK	60440	3268	24W-12S	D2
1100	WLNG	60090	2754	16W-18N	D3
1400	NndT	60014	2586	30W-28N	A6
1600	NndT	60050	2585	31W-30N	D2
1700	RMVL	60446	3339	27W-17S	D6
1900	RLKP	60030	2532	22W-31N	B7
2000	PLNO	60545	3259	48W-12S	B4
E Hawthorne Ct					
10	LKBF	60044	2593	11W-28N	C6
10	LKBF	60044	2594	10W-28N	A7
S Hawthorne Ct N					
14500	HMGN	60491	3342	19W-17S	E5
S Hawthorne Ct S					
14700	HMGN	60491	3342	19W-17S	E6
W Hawthorne Ct					
300	LKBF	60044	2593	11W-28N	D6
Hawthorne Dr					
-	HLCT	60429	3427	2W-20S	D5
-	HLCT	60430	3427	2W-20S	D5
10	CTSD	60525	3147	13W-7S	B6
10	LNHT	60046	2476	20W-37N	A1
10	MonT	60466	3594	4W-28S	E6
10	NARA	60542	3137	36W-4S	D1
10	OSWG	60543	3263	36W-12S	D3
10	PKFT	60466	3594	4W-28S	E6
100	LNHT	60046	2418	20W-38N	A7
100	PltT	60010	2751	24W-18N	C2
600	FKFT	60423	3592	10W-26S	D2
800	CLLK	60014	2639	37W-24N	B7
1500	JltT	60433	3587	23W-25S	B1
6600	AlqT	60013	2641	31W-25N	E5
10100	ODPK	60462	3345	12W-17S	C6
17100	EHZC	60429	3427	2W-20S	D5
17500	CCHL	60478	3426	5W-21S	B6
E Hawthorne Dr					
10	RLKB	60073	2475	22W-35N	A6
N Hawthorne Dr					
36300	GrtT	60041	2474	25W-36N	A4
W Hawthorne Dr					
10	RLKB	60073	2475	23W-35N	A7
200	RLKB	60073	2474	23W-34N	E7
19500	FmtT	60060	2646	19W-26N	C2
19500	MDLN	60060	2646	19W-26N	C2
Hawthorne Ln					
-	SRWD	60404	3583	31W-25S	E1
-	WKGN	60087	2479	11W-37N	D2
10	BNHL	60010	2750	26W-17N	D4
10	FXLK	60020	2473	27W-36N	C4
10	MltT	60187	3082	25W-1S	C2
10	SMWD	60107	2857	28W-10N	B5
100	CHHT	60411	3507	1W-24S	E6
100	CHHT	60411	3508	1W-24S	A6
100	CPVL	60110	2748	33W-17N	B7
100	EDND	60110	2748	33W-17N	B7
100	EDND	60118	2748	33W-17N	B7
100	NLNX	60451	3501	17W-24S	C5
200	BMDL	60108	2969	22W-5N	B7
200	DSPN	60016	2863	12W-11N	B3
400	WHTN	60187	3082	25W-1S	C2
400	WNVL	60555	3080	29W-3S	D5
400	WynT	60185	3023	28W-2N	A2
500	CPVL	60110	2801	33W-16N	A1
500	CPVL	60118	2801	33W-16N	A1
600	WnfT	60185	3022	28W-2N	E2
600	WnfT	60185	3023	27W-1N	C2
600	WynT	60185	3022	28W-2N	E2
700	GNVA	60134	3020	35W-0N	B5
700	LbvT	60048	2592	15W-29N	A4
700	WCHI	60185	3022	28W-2N	E2
800	NHBK	60062	2756	10W-17N	E4
1100	EGVV	60007	2914	20W-8N	A2
1200	DRGV	60515	3144	20W-5S	E3
1200	HNDL	60521	3086	15W-3S	B5
1400	GNVW	60025	2811	7W-14N	A5
1500	HDPK	60035	2705	7W-22N	A5
1900	DRFD	60015	2756	12W-20N	B1
1900	RVWD	60015	2756	12W-20N	B1
1900	WdfT	60015	2756	12W-20N	B1
2000	EVTN	60201	2866	3W-11N	D2
2400	FSMR	60422	3507	3W-23S	B3
2900	DYR	46311	3598		C4
3000	HLCT	60429	3427	3W-21S	A5
4300	RGMW	60008	2806	20W-12N	B7
5600	DrrT	60014	2638	38W-26N	D3
5600	LKWD	60014	2638	38W-26N	D3
6800	HRPK	60133	2912	26W-8N	A2
9300	ODHL	60487	3423	11W-19S	E2
9300	ODPK	60467	3423	11W-19S	E2
21300	KLDR	60047	2699	22W-21N	C6
25100	AntT	60002	2416	25W-39N	B5
E Hawthorne Ln					
900	WCHI	60185	3022	29W-2N	D2
900	WnfT	60185	3022	29W-2N	D2
1000	WynT	60185	3022	29W-2N	E2
N Hawthorne Ln					
500	PTON	60468	3861	8W-37S	B3
500	WIIT	60468	3861	8W-37S	B3
W Hawthorne Ln					
10	WCHI	60185	3022	30W-2N	B2
10	WnfT	60185	3022	30W-2N	B2
900	WynT	60185	3022	30W-2N	A2
1300	WCHI	60185	3021	32W-1N	D2
1800	WnfT	60185	3021	32W-2N	D2
7400	FftT	60423	3504	9W-25S	E6
24000	AntT	60002	2416	24W-41N	D1
W Hawthorne Ln CO-18					
1700	WCHI	60185	3021	31W-2N	D2
1800	WnfT	60185	3021	31W-1N	D2
Hawthorne Pl					
10	MPPT	60056	2808	15W-14N	A4
10	PTHT	60070	2808	15W-14N	A4
900	LKFT	60045	2650	10W-27N	B2
1500	BKBN	60015	2703	11W-21N	D5
1500	DRFD	60015	2703	11W-21N	D5
1500	DRGV	60516	3207	18W-8S	A2
1500	DRN	60516	3207	18W-8S	A2
1500	DRN	60561	3207	18W-8S	A2
W Hawthorne Pl					
500	CHCG	60657	2978	0W-4N	A3
Hawthorne Rd					
10	ALGN	60102	2694	35W-21N	A6
10	BNHL	60010	2750	26W-17N	D4
10	BRTN	60010	2750	25W-18N	E3
10	LIHL	60156	2694	35W-21N	A5
200	GNOK	60048	2592	15W-28N	B5
200	LYVL	60048	2592	15W-29N	B5
300	BFGV	60089	2754	17W-18N	B3
500	FKFT	60423	3503	12W-25S	C7
5000	OKFT	60452	3425	6W-20S	E4
5000	OKFT	60452	3426	6W-20S	A4
5200	BmnT	60452	3425	6W-20S	E4
Hawthorne Rd SR-59					
10	BNHL	60010	2750	26W-17N	D4
10	BRTN	60010	2750	25W-18N	E3
Hawthorne Rdg					
1600	JLET	60586	3495	31W-21S	E1
Hawthorne Sq					
10	IHPK	60525	3146	13W-7S	E5
Hawthorne St					
-	PvsT	60126	3086	14W-1S	C1
-	PvsT	60162	3086	14W-1S	C1
-	PvsT	60523	3086	14W-1S	C1
100	ELGN	60123	2853	36W-11N	E5
200	ElgT	60123	2853	36W-11N	E4
200	GNEN	60137	3025	23W-0N	B5
200	WHTN	60137	3025	23W-0N	A4
200	WHTN	60187	3025	23W-0N	A4
3300	FNPK	60131	2973	12W-4N	B3
3600	FNPK	60176	2973	12W-4N	B3
3600	HtdT	60033	2464	48W-35N	E5
3600	SRPK	60176	2973	12W-4N	B3
E Hawthorne St					
10	ANHT	60004	2807	17W-14N	B4
N Hawthorne St					
6000	RSMT	60018	2917	12W-7N	B3
S Hawthorne St					
300	ELGN	60123	2853	36W-10N	E6
300	ElgT	60123	2853	36W-10N	E6
W Hawthorne St					
10	ANHT	60004	2807	18W-14N	A4
1600	ANHT	60005	2806	18W-14N	D4
Hawthorne Ter					
1700	DSPN	60016	2863	12W-11N	B3
S Hawthorne Tr					
26600	MonT	60449	3683	6W-32S	A7
Hawthorne Wy					
100	TVLY	60013	2695	32W-23N	C2
11600	GfnT	60142	2638	40W-25N	A5
22100	RNPK	60471	3594	5W-26S	B3
Hawthorn Grove Cir					
10	HNWD	60047	2646	20W-24N	A7
10	HNWD	60047	2700	20W-24N	A1
Hawthorn Grove Dr					
10	HNWD	60047	2646	20W-24N	B7
Hawthorn Hill Ln					
3100	CPVL	60110	2747	35W-17N	C6
Hawthorn Ridge Dr					
-	HNWD	60060	2645	22W-25N	B4
Hawthorn Village Coms					
200	VNHL	60061	2647	16W-26N	D4
HA Wyeth Sr Dr					
-	AURA	60505	3200	34W-9S	C3
Hay St					
100	PKFT	60466	3595	3W-25S	B1
Hayden Ct					
200	WMTN	60481	3853	27W-38S	C5
300	WHTN	60187	3082	24W-2S	C4
4600	MchT	60050	2472	29W-36N	B3
Hayden Dr					
700	MchT	60050	2472	30W-36N	B4
900	JNBG	60050	2472	30W-36N	B4
Hayden Ln					
5300	MchT	60072	2470	34W-37N	C2
5300	RGWD	60072	2470	34W-37N	C2
Haydn St					
2300	GwdT	60098	2524	40W-33N	E4
2300	WDSK	60098	2524	41W-33N	E3
Hayenga Ln					
7600	DRN	60561	3207	17W-8S	C2
Hayes Av					
10	LGNG	60525	3087	12W-4S	C7
10	NHLK	60164	2972	13W-3N	D6
200	RMVL	60446	3340	24W-16S	E3
200	RMVL	60446	3341	23W-16S	A3
700	LYVL	60048	2591	16W-28N	C7
W Hayes Av					
6600	CHCG	60631	2918	8W-8N	E2
6800	CHCG	60714	2918	8W-8N	E2
6800	NLES	60714	2918	8W-8N	E2
Hayes Av N					
1100	OKPK	60302	3031	7W-1N	B1
1200	CHCG	60302	3031	7W-1N	B1
1200	CHCG	60639	3031	7W-1N	B1
Hayes Ct					
700	HRVD	60033	2406	49W-38N	C6
1000	VNHL	60061	2647	17W-26N	B3
Hayes Dr					
-	CHCG	60637	3153	2E-7S	B4
-	CHCG	60649	3153	2E-6S	B4
Hayes Rd					
100	ALGN	60102	2747	34W-20N	D1
400	AlqT	60102	2747	34W-20N	C2
Hayes St					
600	RKDL	60436	3498	25W-24S	B7
3300	EVTN	60201	2866	4W-12N	B1
3300	SKOK	60076	2866	4W-12N	B1
N Hayes St					
100	HRVD	60033	2406	49W-38N	C7
W Hayford St					
3700	CHCG	60652	3212	4W-8S	C1
Hayle Ct					
700	NPVL	60540	3140	28W-7S	E7
Haylett Av					
500	WNVL	60555	3081	28W-3S	B6
W Hayley Ct					
2700	WKGN	60085	2536	12W-33N	C2
Hayloft Ln					
2400	ELGN	60124	2853	36W-10N	D6
N Haymond St					
2400	RVGV	60171	2974	10W-3N	B5
N Hayner Av					
42100	BtnT	60099	2362	11W-42N	D7
42200	WPHR	60099	2362	11W-42N	D7
S Haynes Ct					
2900	CHCG	60608	3091	1W-2S	E3
Haynes Dr					
200	AddT	60191	2915	17W-6N	B6
200	WDDL	60191	2915	17W-6N	B6
Hayrack Dr					
700	ALGN	60102	2693	37W-20N	C7
900	ALGN	60102	2746	37W-20N	C1
W Haystack Dr					
7400	FftT	60423	3504	9W-24S	E6
Hayward Av					
600	SMWD	60107	2911	28W-9N	B2
Hayward Ct					
10	LIHL	60156	2692	39W-23N	D2
6600	MHRY	60050	2527	35W-33N	A3
Hayward Ln					
5000	LIHL	60156	2692	39W-23N	D2
N Hayward St					
100	WDSK	60098	2524	41W-31N	C7
S Hayward St					
10	WDSK	60098	2524	41W-31N	E7
300	WDSK	60098	2581	41W-30N	C1

STREET Block	City	ZIP	Map#	CGS	Grid
Haywood Cir					
300	RDLK	60073	2531	24W-33N	D2
Haywood Dr					
1000	AvnT	60073	2531	24W-33N	C2
1000	RDLK	60073	2531	24W-33N	C2
Hazard Rd					
10	CPVL	60110	2748	32W-17N	C6
Hazel Av					
-	LGNG	60525	3087	12W-4S	C6
10	GLNC	60022	2758	6W-17N	D5
100	AURA	60505	3199	36W-8S	E2
100	AURA	60505	3200	36W-8S	A2
100	HDPK	60035	2705	8W-22N	A5
200	FXLK	60020	2473	27W-36N	C3
400	HDPK	60035	2704	8W-22N	E5
800	DRFD	60015	2703	11W-21N	D7
Hazel Ct					
-	WKGN	60085	2537	10W-34N	B2
100	ISLK	60042	2586	29W-28N	D5
600	ROSL	60172	2913	22W-6N	C6
1300	DSPN	60018	2862	13W-9N	E6
1300	DSPN	60018	2863	12W-9N	A7
1700	SYHW	60118	2800	35W-16N	C3
2300	NPVL	60565	3204	24W-10S	C5
10100	ODPK	60462	3345	12W-17S	C6
Hazel Dr					
300	SMBG	60193	2859	23W-9N	A7
400	ELGN	60123	2800	34W-13N	E7
Hazel Ln					
10	MltT	60187	3023	26W-0N	E5
700	MltT	60187	3024	26W-0N	A5
1500	WNKA	60093	2811	6W-16N	D1
3300	HLCT	60429	3426	4W-20S	E5
Hazel St					
-	WCHI	60185	3022	30W-0N	B5
-	WnfT	60185	3022	30W-0N	B5
6600	MNGV	60053	2865	8W-11N	A3
6700	MNGV	60053	2864	8W-11N	E3
E Hazel St					
100	WCHI	60185	3022	29W-0N	C5
N Hazel St					
4200	CHCG	60613	2977	1W-5N	E1
4400	CHCG	60613	2921	1W-5N	E7
4400	CHCG	60640	2921	1W-5N	E7
W Hazel St					
100	WCHI	60185	3022	30W-0N	C5
W Hazelcrest Dr					
400	PNFD	60544	3338	30W-16S	C4
N Hazelcrest Rd					
20000	ElaT	60074	2752	20W-20N	E1
20600	ElaT	60074	2753	20W-20N	A2
20600	PltT	60074	2753	20W-20N	A2
S Hazel Hill Dr					
1800	MPPT	60056	2861	17W-10N	C5
Hazelnut Cross					
1500	MDLN	60060	2590	19W-29N	B4
Hazel Nut Ct					
600	BRLT	60103	2910	29W-9N	D1
Hazelnut Dr					
10	SMWD	60107	2857	27W-10N	D7
Hazelnut Ln					
1700	AURA	60504	3201	33W-8S	A3
2500	RVWD	60015	2755	13W-20N	E1
W Hazelnut Ln					
21000	LktT	60544	3340	26W-16S	A3
N Hazeltime Dr					
-	VNHL	60061	2647	17W-27N	B1
2200	VNHL	60061	2591	17W-27N	B7
Hazeltine Wy					
300	YKVL	60560	3333	42W-16S	D5
N Hazelton Av					
100	WHTN	60187	3023	26W-0S	E7
S Hazelton Av					
100	WHTN	60187	3023	26W-0S	E7
600	MltT	60187	3081	27W-1S	C1
600	WHTN	60187	3081	27W-1S	C1
Hazelwood Ct					
10	LIHL	60156	2693	38W-22N	A3
400	CmpT	60175	2961	43W-5N	B2
400	LYLK	60175	2961	43W-5N	B2
1200	BTVA	60510	3019	36W-0S	E7
1400	GRNE	60031	2478	15W-35N	A5
Hazelwood Dr					
-	NLNX	60451	3589	17W-26S	D3
200	ANTH	60002	2357	23W-43N	E4
200	ANTH	60002	2358	22W-42N	B5
200	LNHT	60046	2417	20W-38N	E7
300	NPVL	60540	3141	27W-7S	C7
600	NlxT	60451	3589	17W-26S	D3
700	NHBK	60062	2756	11W-18N	E4
1700	LNHT	60046	2418	20W-38N	A7
2100	MchT	60050	2528	32W-34N	C2
2100	MHRY	60050	2528	32W-34N	C2
6000	NndT	60012	2584	35W-29N	B3
16700	PnfT	60586	3417	28W-20S	A4
16800	PnfT	60586	3416	29W-20S	E5
Hazelwood Ln					
300	MaiT	60025	2864	10W-12N	A1
400	MaiT	60025	2810	10W-12N	A7
Hazelwood Ter					
300	BFGV	60069	2754	16W-20N	E1
300	BFGV	60089	2754	16W-20N	E1
300	VrnT	60069	2754	16W-20N	E1
300	VrnT	60089	2754	16W-20N	E1
Hazelwood Tr					
10	LYLK	60175	2961	43W-5N	B2
500	CmpT	60175	2961	43W-5N	B2
Hazlewood Dr					
36100	LkvT	60041	2474	24W-36N	B4
Head Av					
16700	HLCT	60428	3427	2W-20S	C4
16700	HLCT	60429	3427	2W-20S	C4
16700	MKHM	60428	3427	2W-20S	C4
Headwater Cove					
10	SBTN	60010	2803	27W-14N	B4
Healthway Dr					
4000	AURA	60504	3202	30W-8S	B1
Healy Av					
200	ELGN	60120	2855	33W-11N	B5
200	RMVL	60446	3340	24W-16S	E4
200	RMVL	60446	3341	23W-16S	A4
Healy Rd					
-	EDND	60118	2801	30W-14N	E4
-	EDND	60118	2802	30W-14N	A3
-	HFET	60118	2801	30W-14N	E4
-	HFET	60118	2802	30W-14N	A3
10	BNHL	60010	2802	29W-15N	B1
10	BNHL	60118	2802	30W-14N	A3
200	SgrT	60506	3075	41W-3S	E7
200	SgrT	60506	3076	41W-3S	A7
200	SgrT	60554	3075	41W-3S	E7
Healy Rd CO-15					
200	SgrT	60506	3075	41W-3S	E7
200	SgrT	60506	3076	41W-4S	A7
200	SgrT	60554	3075	41W-3S	E7
Hearth Cir					
2000	LNSG	60438	3429	2E-21S	D7
Hearth Dr					
7500	HRPK	60133	2912	25W-9N	A1
Hearth Ln					
600	CLSM	60188	3024	24W-1N	D2
Hearthmoor Ct					
4400	LGGV	60047	2700	18W-22N	E4
Hearthside Ct					
1200	NPVL	60564	3203	28W-10S	A6
Hearthside Dr					
10	RchT	60443	3593	8W-25S	A1
200	BMDL	60108	2969	22W-4N	B3
23600	DRPK	60010	2698	23W-21N	D5
Hearthstone Ct					
800	AURA	60506	3137	37W-6S	B5
Hearthstone Dr					
100	BRLT	60103	2909	32W-8N	C3
Hearthstone Ln					
-	AraT	60542	3137	38W-4S	B1
Heartland Ct					
5600	CPVL	60110	2747	36W-18N	A5
Heartland Dr					
-	LKMR	60041	2530	28W-32N	A5
-	LKMR	60051	2530	28W-32N	A5
300	NLNX	60451	3501	18W-25S	A7
400	SRGV	60554	3135	43W-5S	B4
500	YKVL	60560	3261	42W-14S	E7
500	YKVL	60560	3333	42W-14S	D1
3100	GNVA	60134	3019	37W-1N	C3
3500	GnvT	60134	3019	37W-1N	B3
4500	RNPK	60471	3594	5W-27S	B5
Heartland Ln					
10800	HTLY	60142	2745	39W-20N	B1
N Heartland Pth					
2100	RLKB	60046	2475	21W-36N	C5
Heartland Gate					
1000	LIHL	60156	2693	36W-22N	E4
1100	CLLK	60014	2693	36W-22N	E4
1100	CLLK	60156	2693	36W-22N	E4
Heartland Park Ln					
900	ANTH	60002	2417	21W-40N	D2
W Heart O Lakes Blvd					
25700	AntT	60002	2415	26W-40N	E3
25700	AntT	60002	2416	25W-40N	A3
Heartstone Av					
-	YKVL	60560	3333	42W-17S	E5
Heartwood Ln					
900	LKZH	60047	2699	22W-22N	B4
S Heath Av					
1300	CHCG	60608	3033	2W-1S	B7
Heath Ct					
200	BRTN	60010	2751	24W-18N	C2
500	SMWD	60107	2911	28W-9N	B1
700	WTMT	60559	3145	17W-6S	B4
Heath Ln					
800	WTMT	60559	3145	17W-6S	B4
Heath Pl					
100	WTMT	60559	3145	17W-6S	B5
Heath Wy					
10	SBTN	60010	2803	26W-15N	D2
S Heathcliff Rd					
14700	HMGN	60491	3344	15W-17S	B6
Heather Av					
200	GYLK	60030	2532	20W-33N	E2
300	GYLK	60030	2533	20W-33N	A2
Heather Ct					
10	BGBK	60490	3267	27W-12S	C3
10	SMWD	60107	2857	27W-11N	B4
100	RGMW	60008	2805	21W-13N	D5
200	RMVL	60446	3339	26W-17S	E6
200	WNVL	60555	3080	30W-2S	B4
300	SMBG	60193	2859	21W-9N	E6
400	LNHT	60046	2476	19W-37N	C2
600	LslT	60540	3142	24W-5S	C3
800	ANTH	60002	2357	24W-42N	C5
1000	FRGV	60021	2696	29W-22N	C3
1500	WLNG	60090	2754	16W-17N	D6
1800	NHBK	60062	2756	11W-16N	E7
4200	ZION	60099	2362	12W-41N	B7
8300	TYPK	60477	3424	10W-21S	C5
8400	BRRG	60527	3208	15W-9S	B4
15100	ODPK	60462	3346	9W-18S	E6
18600	HMWD	60430	3507	1W-22S	E1
N Heather Ct					
1300	ADSN	60101	2970	19W-5N	C2
20800	KLDR	60047	2699	21W-20N	E7
S Heather Ct					
14300	HMGN	60491	3344	15W-17S	C4
W Heather Ct					
18600	WrnT	60030	2533	18W-34N	E2
24000	PNFD	60585	3338	30W-15S	C3
Heather Dr					
10	CLLK	60014	2639	37W-25N	A4
1400	AURA	60506	3137	38W-6S	B5
1600	ALGN	60102	2695	32W-21N	A5
1600	AlqT	60102	2695	32W-21N	B5
3300	MKHM	60428	3348	4W-18S	E6
5900	DrrT	60014	2639	37W-26N	A3
8500	BRRG	60527	3208	15W-9S	B4
Heather Knl					
5300	LGGV	60047	2700	18W-22N	E3
5300	LGGV	60047	2701	18W-22N	A3
Heather Ln					
10	ElaT	60047	2645	21W-24N	C7
10	HNWD	60047	2645	21W-24N	C7
10	OKBK	60523	3085	17W-2S	C4
10	SMWD	60107	2857	27W-11N	C4
100	WLMT	60091	2811	6W-13N	E7
200	WDDL	60191	2915	16W-6N	D6
200	WNFD	60190	3023	27W-0N	C4
400	CLSM	60188	2968	25W-2N	A7
400	DRPK	60010	2752	22W-20N	B1
400	DYR	46311	3598		D4
400	LKFT	60045	2650	10W-26N	A3
500	FKFT	60423	3592	9W-26S	D2
600	BRLT	60103	2910	29W-6N	D7
700	LYLK	60175	2961	43W-5N	A2
700	WNKA	60093	2811	6W-16N	D1
800	HFET	60169	2858	24W-12N	D1
800	WNKA	60093	2758	6W-16N	D7
1000	MNSR	46321	3510		E2
1100	GNEN	60137	3025	21W-0S	E7
1100	GNEN	60137	3026	21W-0S	A7
1100	IVNS	60067	2751	23W-17N	E5
1100	LKZH	60047	2699	22W-23N	C1
1200	GNVW	60025	2865	8W-12N	A1
1400	DSPN	60018	2862	13W-10N	D6
1600	DRN	60561	3206	18W-9S	E4
1600	DRN	60561	3207	18W-9S	A4
1700	HDPK	60035	2704	9W-21N	C7
1800	JLET	60431	3417	28W-21S	B7
1800	JLET	60431	3497	28W-21S	A1
1800	NHBK	60062	2756	11W-16N	E7
1800	PnfT	60431	3417	28W-21S	B7
1900	JNBG	60050	2471	31W-37N	E2
Heather Ln					
2800	MTGY	60538	3198	40W-10S	B6
2900	MTGY	60512	3198	40W-10S	B6
8200	TYPK	60477	3424	10W-21S	C5
8300	OrlT	60487	3424	10W-21S	B5
8300	TYPK	60487	3424	10W-21S	B5
N Heather Ln					
2100	PLTN	60074	2753	19W-18N	C2
S Heather Ln					
14300	HMGN	60491	3344	15W-17S	C5
14300	OrlT	60467	3344	15W-17S	C5
W Heather Ln					
1200	ANHT	60005	2806	18W-14N	D4
Heather Rd					
800	DRFD	60015	2704	10W-21N	B7
1200	HMWD	60430	3508	1W-22S	A1
1800	GNVA	60134	3020	36W-0S	A7
2000	BTVA	60510	3020	36W-0S	A7
2000	GnvT	60134	3020	36W-0S	A6
2000	GnvT	60510	3020	36W-0S	A7
2000	HMWD	60430	3507	2W-22S	C1
2400	FSMR	60422	3507	3W-22S	B1
2400	FSMR	60430	3507	3W-22S	B1
2700	HMWD	60422	3507	3W-22S	B1
Heather Rdg					
8200	FXLK	60081	2414	29W-40N	C3
Heather St					
1800	BGBK	60490	3267	27W-12S	C3
Heather Ter					
100	RLKB	60073	2475	22W-35N	B7
2000	NHFD	60093	2811	7W-15N	B2
Heather Tr					
7200	JSTC	60458	3148	10W-8S	B7
Heatherbrook Ct					
800	WHTN	60187	3082	25W-1S	B2
W Heatherbrook Tr					
5300	MonT	60449	3683	6W-32S	A7
Heathercliff Dr					
2200	GNOK	60048	2535	14W-31N	B7
2200	GNOK	60048	2592	14W-31N	B1
Heather Creek Dr					
16900	PnfT	60586	3416	29W-20S	E5
Heatherdale Ln					
11200	HTLY	60142	2691	41W-20N	C7
Heatherdown Wy					
700	BFGV	60089	2701	17W-21N	B6
Heatherfield Ct					
-	GNVW	60025	2811	6W-13N	C6
Heatherfield Dr					
100	ElgT	60124	2907	38W-8N	A3
Heatherfield Dr E					
10	ElgT	60124	2907	38W-8N	B3
Heatherfield Ln					
-	BtlT	60512	3261	42W-12S	D3
1000	GNVW	60025	2811	6W-13N	C6
Heather Glen					
-	NLNX	60451	3590	15W-26S	C3
-	NlxT	60451	3590	15W-26S	C3
Heather Glen Ct					
900	ANTH	60002	2416	24W-41N	C1
Heatherglen Ct					
15600	ODPK	60462	3345	13W-18S	A7
15600	ODPK	60462	3423	13W-18S	A1
Heather Glen Dr					
10	AURA	60504	3201	31W-7S	E1
100	AURA	60504	3139	31W-7S	E7
Heatherglen Dr					
15600	ODPK	60462	3423	13W-18S	A1
Heather Hill Cres					
1100	FSMR	60422	3507	3W-23S	D5
Heather Hill Ct					
3100	FSMR	60422	3507	3W-23S	A4
Heatherington Pl					
900	PltT	60124	2852	40W-9N	C7
E Heatherlea Dr					
100	PLTN	60067	2752	20W-17N	E5
W Heatherlea Dr					
10	PLTN	60067	2752	20W-17N	E5
Heathermead St					
400	RchT	60443	3593	8W-26S	B2
Heather Ridge Dr					
800	GRNE	60031	2534	16W-33N	E3
Heatherstone Av					
1700	MTGY	60538	3198	40W-9S	A4
Heatherstone Dr					
700	SMBG	60173	2859	22W-11N	C4
Heatherstone Ln					
2000	JLET	60586	3415	33W-21S	A7
Heatherton Ct					
1500	NPVL	60563	3141	28W-5S	A2
Heatherton Dr					
-	CteT	60417	3686	3E-31S	E6
800	NPVL	60563	3141	28W-5S	A3
Heatherwood Ct					
10	IHPK	60525	3146	14W-6S	D4
2900	SMBG	60194	2857	27W-10N	C5
14300	HMGN	60491	3343	16W-17S	D5
Heatherwood Dr					
400	OSWG	60543	3262	39W-12S	D3
2800	SMBG	60194	2857	27W-10N	D5
S Heatherwood Dr					
14300	HMGN	60491	3343	17W-17S	D4
Heatherwood Dr N					
-	OSWG	60543	3262	39W-11S	D2
Heatherwood Ln					
1100	AURA	60504	3201	31W-9S	E3
Heather Wy Ln					
1800	NLNX	60451	3588	19W-26S	E3
Heathgate Rd					
100	OswT	60538	3199	36W-10S	E6
100	OswT	60538	3200	36W-10S	A6
Heathrow Cir					
11400	ODPK	60467	3422	14W-20S	E4
Heathrow Ct					
10	LKBF	60044	2593	11W-29N	E4
400	BRRG	60527	3208	15W-8S	B2
1000	WHTN	60187	3082	23W-1S	E2
1100	AURA	60502	3139	33W-6S	B4
Heathrow Dr					
600	LNSH	60069	2701	16W-22N	E4
Heathrow Ln					
-	AURA	60502	3139	33W-6S	B4
900	NPVL	60540	3203	28W-8S	B1
W Heathwood Cir					
8900	MaiT	60016	2863	11W-12N	E1
8900	NLES	60016	2863	11W-12N	E1
8900	NLES	60714	2863	11W-12N	E1
W Heathwood Dr					
-	MaiT	60016	2863	11W-12N	D1
9000	NLES	60714	2863	11W-12N	D1
Heaton Ct					
10	SgrT	60506	3135	41W-5S	E4
Heaton Pk					
500	BtvT	60510	3077	37W-2S	B4
Heavens Gate					
-	CLLK	60014	2693	36W-22N	D4
Heavens Gate					
1000	LIHL	60156	2693	36W-22N	D4
N Hebbard St					
200	JLET	60432	3499	22W-23S	D4
200	JltT	60432	3499	22W-23S	D4
S Hebbard St					
100	JLET	60433	3499	22W-24S	D6
300	JltT	60433	3499	22W-24S	D5
Hebron Av					
1700	ZION	60099	2421	11W-40N	E3
Hebron Rd					
12400	HbnT	60034	2350	42W-42N	C6
12400	HBRN	60034	2350	42W-42N	C6
13600	AdnT	60033	2350	43W-42N	A6
13600	AdnT	60034	2350	43W-42N	A6
14100	AdnT	60033	2349	43W-42N	E6
Hecht Ct					
-	BRLT	60120	2909	31W-7N	E4
Hecht Dr					
1500	BRLT	60120	2909	31W-7N	E4
1500	BRLT	60120	2910	31W-7N	A4
Hecker Ct					
1100	ELGN	60120	2855	32W-11N	D3
Hecker Dr					
600	DndT	60118	2801	32W-14N	C5
600	ELGN	60120	2855	32W-11N	D3
Hector Ln					
3600	NPVL	60564	3266	30W-11S	B1
Hedg Ct					
1600	NPVL	60565	3204	25W-9S	B3
Hedge Ct					
100	GNEN	60137	3083	22W-1S	D1
W Hedge Pl					
2300	MchT	60051	2528	31W-34N	D1
Hedge Row					
2300	NHFD	60093	2810	8W-15N	E2
2300	NHFD	60093	2811	8W-15N	A2
Hedge Run					
200	HDPK	60035	2758	7W-20N	C1
W Hedge Apple Dr					
13000	HMGN	60491	3343	16W-16S	E2
13000	HMGN	60491	3344	16W-16S	A2
Hedge Row Ct					
4500	JLET	60586	3416	29W-21S	D6
Hedgerow Ct					
10	BGBK	60440	3268	24W-12S	D3
800	OSWG	60543	3263	37W-13S	C6
Hedge Row Dr					
2400	AURA	60502	3079	32W-3S	C6
2400	AURA	60510	3079	32W-3S	C6
2400	WnfT	60510	3079	32W-3S	C6
Hedgerow Dr					
200	BMDL	60108	2969	22W-4N	C3
1000	GYLK	60030	2533	19W-32N	B6
Hedgerow Ln					
700	BGBK	60440	3268	24W-12S	C3
700	OSWG	60543	3263	37W-13S	C6
3000	HMWD	60422	3507	3W-22S	A1
3000	HMWD	60430	3507	3W-22S	A1
Hedgewick Ct					
200	RchT	60443	3593	8W-26S	B2
Hedgewood Ct					
5300	LGGV	60047	2701	17W-22N	B4
17000	LKPT	60441	3419	22W-20S	C5
Hedgewood Dr					
7900	DRN	60561	3206	19W-9S	C3
17700	LKPT	60441	3419	22W-20S	D5
N Hedgewood Dr					
900	PLTN	60074	2753	20W-17N	B5
Hedgeworth Ct					
23600	DRPK	60010	2698	23W-21N	E5
S Heggs Rd					
9500	AURA	60503	3265	32W-11S	C2
9500	AURA	60585	3265	32W-12S	C3
9500	WldT	60585	3265	32W-12S	C3
9700	AURA	60543	3265	32W-12S	C3
9700	WldT	60543	3265	32W-12S	C3
12000	PNFD	60585	3265	32W-14S	C7
12000	PNFD	60585	3337	32W-15S	C2
12000	WldT	60585	3337	32W-15S	C2
13200	PNFD	60544	3337	32W-15S	C3
Heiden Av					
1500	CTHL	60403	3498	25W-22S	B1
1500	JLET	60435	3498	25W-22S	B1
1600	CTHL	60403	3418	25W-21S	B7
W Heiden Cir					
12900	LbvT	60044	2593	13W-30N	A2
12900	ShdT	60044	2593	13W-30N	A2
Heiden Dr					
-	LbvT	60044	2593	13W-30N	A3
Heidorn Av					
1200	HLSD	60162	3028	13W-1S	D7
1200	WSTR	60154	3028	13W-1S	D7
1200	WSTR	60162	3028	13W-1S	D7
1400	WSTR	60154	3086	13W-1S	D1
1600	HLSD	60162	3086	13W-1S	D1
1600	WSTR	60162	3086	13W-1S	D1
Heine Av					
200	ELGN	60123	2854	35W-11N	B3
Heine Ct					
100	SMWD	60107	2857	27W-11N	D4
Heine Dr					
100	SMWD	60107	2857	27W-11N	D4
Heinecke Dr					
12000	FftT	60448	3502	15W-23S	C3
12000	MKNA	60448	3502	15W-23S	C3
Heintz Dr					
500	SRWD	60404	3496	30W-22S	C2
Heinz Av					
12100	HTLY	60142	2691	41W-20N	E7
Heinz Dr					
1100	EDND	60118	2801	32W-15N	D4
3900	AURA	60504	3202	30W-8S	A3
Heisler Ct					
300	CLLK	60014	2639	35W-24N	E7
Hejka Rd					
-	DPgT	60441	3269	21W-13S	E4
-	DPgT	60517	3269	21W-13S	E4
Helen					
-	JSTC	60458	3210	10W-9S	B2
Helen Av					
800	SEGN	60177	2908	35W-8N	B2
1000	JLET	60433	3499	23W-25S	A7
1100	JLET	60433	3587	23W-25S	A1
1100	JltT	60433	3587	23W-25S	A1
Helen Ct					
10	SMWD	60107	2856	29W-9N	E7
400	DGvT	60516	3206	19W-9S	D4
1800	WHTN	60187	3082	24W-2S	C2
N Helen Ct					
34500	GrtT	60041	2473	27W-34N	B7
36400	LkvT	60046	2475	21W-36N	C4
36400	RLKB	60046	2475	21W-36N	C4
36400	RLKB	60073	2475	21W-36N	C4
Helen Dr					
400	NHBK	60062	2756	11W-18N	E4
Helen Dr					
500	BRLT	60103	2909	31W-8N	E2
900	MLPK	60160	3029	11W-1N	E2
1000	ALGN	60102	2748	33W-20N	A1
1100	AlqT	60102	2748	33W-20N	A1
1900	RMVL	60544	3417	27W-18S	B1
2000	PnfT	60446	3417	27W-18S	B1
2700	MaiT	60025	2864	10W-12N	B1
21800	PnfT	60544	3417	27W-18S	C1
21800	RMVL	60446	3417	27W-18S	C1
22300	SLVL	60411	3597	1E-27S	B4
N Helen Dr					
36500	LkvT	60046	2475	21W-36N	C3
Helen Ln					
1200	EGvT	60007	2914	21W-8N	A1
1200	EGVV	60007	2914	21W-8N	A1
9000	ODPK	60462	3346	11W-18S	A7
9100	ODPK	60462	3345	11W-18S	E7
14600	HMGN	60491	3343	18W-17S	B6
Helen St					
-	CLLK	60098	2638	40W-26N	B2
200	BmdT	60148	3025	21W-2N	E1
200	LMBD	60148	3025	21W-2N	E1
200	WCHI	60185	3022	29W-1N	D2
200	WnfT	60185	3022	29W-1N	D2
600	BmdT	60148	2969	21W-2N	E6
1100	PKRG	60068	2863	11W-10N	D5
Helena Av					
200	WCDA	60084	2587	26W-27N	D7
S Helena Av					
300	MPPT	60005	2861	17W-12N	B1
300	MPPT	60056	2861	17W-12N	B1
Helena Dr					
1200	WCHI	60185	3021	31W-0N	E5
1200	WCHI	60185	3022	31W-0N	A5
S Helena Dr					
11100	PSHL	60465	3273	11W-13S	E3
Helena Ln					
-	NptT	60083	2478	14W-38N	D1
-	WKGN	60083	2478	14W-38N	D1
N Helendale Rd					
35500	GrtT	60041	2473	26W-35N	E6
S Helene Av					
10300	NPVL	60564	3266	30W-12S	C2
10300	WldT	60564	3266	30W-12S	C2
Helene Ln					
1000	SMBG	60193	2858	24W-10N	C6
Helene St					
700	SRWD	60404	3496	29W-24S	D6
Helen Sandidge Ct					
16700	TYPK	60477	3425	7W-20S	C3
Helen's Wy Ct					
10	LslT	60565	3205	23W-8S	A2
Helfred Av					
3000	SCHT	60411	3595	1W-27S	E4
N Helgesen St					
700	PltT	60074	2752	21W-18N	C2
E Hellen Rd					
10	PLTN	60067	2805	20W-15N	E2
100	PLTN	60067	2806	20W-15N	A2
100	PLTN	60074	2806	20W-15N	A2
W Hellen Rd					
10	PLTN	60067	2805	21W-15N	D2
400	PltT	60067	2805	21W-15N	D2
Hellenic Dr					
20300	OMFD	60461	3507	4W-24S	A6
20400	OMFD	60461	3506	4W-24S	E6
Helles Av					
700	JLET	60436	3498	24W-24S	D5
Hellios Ct					
10	FXLK	60020	2473	27W-36N	C3
Helm Rd					
10	CPVL	60110	2748	32W-18N	D5
100	BNHL	60010	2748	32W-18N	D5
100	BNHL	60010	2749	30W-17N	A5
100	BNHL	60110	2748	32W-18N	D5
Hel-Mar Ln					
2400	JLET	60431	3417	28W-20S	A6
2400	PnfT	60431	3417	28W-20S	A6
Helmholz Av					
900	WKGN	60085	2536	10W-33N	E3
900	WKGN	60085	2537	10W-33N	A3
Helsted Av					
-	CteT	60401	3774	1W-33S	B1
-	CteT	60417	3774	1W-33S	B1
W Hemingway Cir					
14000	PnfT	60544	3339	27W-16S	D5
Hemingway Ct					
100	VNHL	60061	2647	16W-26N	C3
W Hemingway Ct					
21700	PnfT	60544	3339	27W-16S	D4
Hemingway Ln					
600	OKPK	60301	3031	7W-0S	C6
600	OKPK	60302	3031	7W-0S	C6
Hemlock Av					
200	RMVL	60446	3340	24W-16S	D3
N Hemlock Av					
100	WDDL	60191	2971	17W-5N	C1
200	WDDL	60191	2915	17W-5N	C7
400	AddT	60191	2915	17W-6N	C7
S Hemlock Av					
100	WDDL	60191	2971	17W-5N	C1
Hemlock Ct					
10	ELGN	60120	2855	32W-11N	D4
300	OSWG	60543	3263	36W-13S	E6
1700	GLHT	60139	2968	24W-3N	E6
9400	MaiT	60016	2863	11W-12N	D1
Hemlock Dr					
200	CmpT	60175	2962	39W-4N	E3
800	SYHW	60118	2800	35W-15N	D4
800	WDND	60118	2800	35W-15N	D3
1200	EGVV	60007	2915	18W-8N	A3
1700	GLHT	60139	2968	24W-3N	E6
1900	MchT	60050	2528	31W-33N	C2
7500	ODPK	60462	3346	9W-18S	D7
24300	PNFD	60585	3266	30W-14S	B7
Hemlock Ln					
-	OSWG	60543	3264	36W-13S	A6
10	HDPK	60035	2757	9W-20N	D2
200	LslT	60540	3204	24W-8S	D1
200	WCHI	60185	3022	30W-2N	B1
300	NPVL	60540	3203	27W-8S	C1
300	OSWG	60543	3263	36W-13S	E6
400	ROSL	60172	2912	24W-6N	E6
500	LslT	60540	3205	23W-8S	A1
500	LYVL	60048	2591	16W-27N	C7
700	CLSM	60188	2967	28W-3N	B6
700	LKPT	60441	3419	22W-20S	D6
1200	ELGN	60120	2855	32W-11N	D4
3100	NHBK	60062	2756	11W-16N	D6
8500	DRN	60561	3207	18W-9S	A4
N Hemlock Ln					
900	MPPT	60056	2808	14W-14N	C5
1200	PTHT	60056	2808	14W-14N	B4
1200	PTHT	60070	2808	14W-14N	B4

STREET Block	City	ZIP	Map#	CGS	Grid
Hemlock Pl					
1800	SMBG	60173	2860	21W-12N	A1
Hemlock Rd					
26800	CNHN	60410	3672	33W-31S	A6
Hemlock St					
10	PKFT	60466	3595	3W-27S	B4
100	BlmT	60466	3595	3W-27S	C4
900	DRFD	60015	2703	11W-21N	D7
2300	LktT	60403	3417	26W-20S	D5
2300	LktT	60435	3417	26W-20S	D5
2300	PnfT	60403	3417	26W-20S	D5
2300	PnfT	60435	3417	26W-20S	D5
6800	HRPK	60133	2911	27W-8N	C2
7000	SMWD	60107	2911	27W-8N	C2
7000	SMWD	60133	2911	27W-8N	C2
7400	AlqT	60014	2640	33W-24N	D7
8500	ODPK	60462	3346	10W-16S	B3
Hemlock Knoll Ter					
1400	NHBK	60062	2756	11W-17N	D6
Hemmer Rd					
11500	GfnT	60142	2691	42W-20N	C7
11500	HTLY	60142	2691	42W-20N	C7
11500	HTLY	60142	2744	42W-20N	C1
Hemmingsen Rd					
15600	CrlT	60180	2635	45W-25N	E5
Hemmingsen St					
-	PLNO	60545	3259	48W-13S	B5
Hempstead Av					
500	NPVL	60565	3203	27W-10S	C5
Hempstead Dr					
100	BMDL	60108	2969	23W-4N	A3
14100	ODPK	60462	3346	9W-16S	C4
Hempstead Ln					
300	BMDL	60108	2969	23W-4N	B3
Hempstead Pl					
100	NLNX	60433	3500	20W-24S	C5
100	NlxT	60433	3500	20W-24S	C5
Hemstead Rd					
100	MltT	60148	3083	21W-2S	E3
Hemstead St					
100	NCHI	60044	2593	13W-29N	A3
Hemstock Av					
1500	WHTN	60187	3081	26W-1S	E3
Hendee Av					
10300	BHPK	60087	2480	10W-37N	A2
N Hendee Ln					
1100	RLKB	60073	2475	22W-34N	B7
W Hendee Rd					
12000	WKGN	60087	2479	12W-37N	C2
12200	BHPK	60087	2479	12W-37N	B2
Hendee St					
300	ELGN	60123	2854	33W-10N	E5
300	ELGN	60123	2855	33W-10N	A6
N Henderson Av					
10	JLET	60432	3499	23W-23S	B4
10	JLET	60433	3499	23W-23S	B5
10	JltT	60432	3499	23W-23S	B5
Henderson Ln					
-	ODPK	60467	3344	14W-16S	D4
Henderson St					
100	BNVL	60106	2971	16W-5N	D2
W Henderson St					
1200	CHCG	60657	2977	1W-4N	D3
1900	CHCG	60618	2977	2W-4N	B3
3400	CHCG	60618	2976	4W-4N	C3
4100	CHCG	60641	2976	5W-4N	B3
4800	CHCG	60641	2975	7W-4N	C3
5500	CHCG	60634	2975	7W-4N	B3
7000	CHCG	60634	2974	8W-4N	E3
Hendricks Rd					
3100	RBBN	60472	3348	4W-16S	D3
S Hendricks Rd					
14100	RBBN	60472	3348	4W-16S	D3
Henke Dr					
8600	TYPK	60487	3424	10W-21S	B6
41500	BtnT	60099	2422	10W-41N	B1
41500	ZION	60099	2422	10W-41N	B1
Henke Pl					
2600	CHCG	60007	2916	15W-8N	A2
Henley Ct					
1600	WLNG	60090	2754	16W-18N	D4
Henley St					
1800	GNVW	60025	2810	9W-13N	D6
3300	NfdT	60025	2809	10W-13N	E6
3300	NfdT	60025	2810	10W-13N	A6
Henneberry Ln					
10	GLF	60025	2865	8W-12N	A1
10	GLF	60029	2865	8W-12N	A1
10	GNVW	60025	2865	8W-12N	A1
200	GNVW	60029	2865	8W-12N	A1
Hennepin Ct					
3800	JLET	60431	3417	28W-20S	A4
Hennepin Dr					
2600	JLET	60431	3417	27W-20S	B5
2600	JLET	60435	3417	27W-20S	B5
2600	JLET	60441	3417	27W-20S	C5
N Hennesey Pl					
300	JLET	60435	3497	27W-23S	D4
Hennessy Ct					
400	GLBT	60136	2799	38W-14N	B5
Hennig Dr					
6700	RlyT	60152	2634	50W-25N	A5
Hennig Rd					
-	RtdT	60140	2744	43W-18N	A5
-	RtdT	60142	2744	43W-18N	A5
300	HTLY	60140	2744	43W-18N	A5
300	HTLY	60142	2744	43W-18N	A5
Henning Ct					
600	NPVL	60540	3141	26W-7S	E7
6300	MNGV	60053	2865	8W-10N	A4
Henning Pl					
2100	JLET	60586	3415	33W-21S	B7
Henning Rd					
-	HshT	60140	2743	44W-18N	E5
-	HshT	60140	2744	44W-18N	A5
-	RtdT	60140	2744	44W-18N	A5
-	RtdT	60142	2744	44W-18N	A5
13000	LtRT	60545	3260	46W-11S	A2
Hennings Ct					
10	ANTH	60002	2357	24W-41N	D7
Hennning Ln					
2100	BtlT	60560	3262	40W-12S	B4
Henri Dr					
1200	WCDA	60084	2587	26W-28N	D6
Henrici Dr					
-	NHBK	60062	2757	8W-18N	E3
-	NHBK	60062	2758	8W-18N	A4
Henricksen Rd					
100	SchT	60175	2907	38W-6N	B6
Henrie Ct					
12100	HBRN	60034	2350	41W-42N	E7
Henrietta Av					
9400	BKFD	60513	3087	11W-3S	C5
9500	BKFD	60525	3087	11W-3S	C5
9500	LGPK	60525	3087	11W-3S	C5
Henry Av					
800	CTCY	60409	3351	3E-18S	E7
1200	DSPN	60016	2862	13W-10N	E5
1200	DSPN	60016	2863	13W-10N	A5
S Henry Av					
3700	HMND	46327	3352		E4
Henry Ct					
-	WHTN	60187	3081	26W-2S	E4
10	FXLK	60041	2473	26W-36N	D4
100	MTGY	60538	3199	36W-9S	E4
5300	GRNE	60031	2478	15W-35N	A5
18800	LNSG	60438	3510	4E-22S	B1
W Henry Ct					
2700	CHCG	60647	2976	3W-2N	E6
Henry Dr					
19000	MKNA	60448	3503	11W-23S	E2
Henry Ln					
3000	GfnT	60156	2693	38W-23N	A2
16600	TYPK	60477	3424	10W-19S	C3
W Henry Ln					
27100	CbaT	60010	2697	27W-22N	B4
27100	LKBN	60010	2697	27W-22N	B4
Henry Pl					
1400	WKGN	60085	2480	10W-35N	A6
Henry St					
100	ELGN	60120	2855	33W-11N	A4
100	MHTN	60442	3677	19W-31S	E5
200	DYR	46311	3598		D2
500	ANTH	60002	2357	24W-42N	D6
4300	OKFT	60452	3426	5W-19S	B2
8400	SjnT	46311	3598		E7
8700	ODPK	60462	3346	10W-18S	A6
9200	SjnT	46311	3687		E1
17000	LNSG	60438	3430	4E-20S	B3
18700	LNSG	60438	3510	4E-22S	B1
E Henry St					
-	MPPT	60056	2808	14W-13N	C7
10	ANHT	60004	2754	17W-17N	A5
600	JLET	60433	3499	23W-24S	B5
W Henry St					
-	MPPT	60056	2807	16W-13N	D7
-	MPPT	60056	2808	15W-13N	A7
10	ANHT	60004	2754	17W-17N	A5
Henry Ter					
700	MchT	60050	2472	29W-37N	C1
Henry Wy					
4200	NfdT	60062	2756	12W-18N	A4
Henry Wadsworth Longfellow Pl					
10	CmpT	60175	2962	39W-4N	D5
Henson Ct					
10	MTSN	60443	3506	6W-24S	A5
Henzada Av					
2500	MchT	60050	2528	31W-34N	D1
Herath Ln					
-	SRWD	60404	3496	30W-23S	B4
Herbert Av					
1000	BKLY	60163	3028	14W-1N	C3
Herbert Ct					
8900	ODHL	60487	3424	11W-19S	A3
W Herbert Ct					
4900	MONE	60449	3683	6W-31S	B5
Herbert Dr					
1900	WKGN	60087	2479	11W-38N	D1
Herbert Rd					
200	LKMR	60051	2529	29W-31N	C7
500	NndT	60051	2529	29W-31N	C7
N Herbert Rd					
10	RVSD	60546	3088	9W-3S	D4
S Herbert Rd					
10	RVSD	60546	3088	9W-3S	D5
Herbert St					
200	DGvT	60515	3084	18W-4S	E7
1000	DRGV	60515	3084	19W-4S	C7
W Herbert St					
5200	MONE	60449	3683	6W-31S	A5
Hercules Ct					
600	GNVW	60025	2810	10W-14N	A3
Hercules Ln					
1200	NPVL	60540	3203	26W-8S	E2
Hercules Rd					
11900	DrrT	60098	2581	41W-28N	D5
11900	WDSK	60098	2581	41W-28N	D5
Hereford Av					
100	CRTE	60417	3596	0W-28S	C5
Hereford Dr					
10	CRTE	60417	3596	0W-28S	D5
Heren Dr					
-	BNHL	60010	2749	28W-17N	E4
Heritage Blvd					
3100	MTSN	60443	3595	4W-26S	A1
N Heritage Cir					
1900	PLTN	60074	2753	20W-20N	B1
Heritage Ct					
100	GRNE	60031	2535	14W-34N	B1
200	BGBK	60490	3267	26W-11S	E1
200	WYNE	60184	2966	30W-5N	B2
500	SchT	60175	2907	38W-6N	B7
500	SCRL	60175	3019	37W-2N	C1
600	NPVL	60565	3204	25W-10S	B5
1400	LKFT	60045	2703	12W-24N	B1
2500	GNVA	60134	3019	37W-0N	C5
2500	GnvT	60134	3019	37W-0N	C5
5400	HRPK	60133	2911	26W-6N	E6
5500	WNSP	60558	3146	14W-6S	E3
7300	FKFT	60423	3592	9W-26S	E2
7500	SMMT	60501	3148	9W-5S	D3
Heritage Dr					
-	BFGV	60089	2701	17W-21N	A7
-	CTCY	60409	3430	3E-19S	B3
-	MngT	60152	2578	49W-28N	C5
10	LYWD	60411	3510		C6
10	BmdT	60172	2913	23W-6N	A6
100	CLLK	60014	2640	34W-24N	B6
100	MNKA	60447	3583	33W-28S	B7
100	PNFD	60544	3338	31W-17S	A7
100	PNFD	60544	3416	31W-18S	A1
200	AURA	60506	3137	38W-7S	A7
200	BtvT	60510	3077	37W-2S	B5
200	BtvT	60539	3077	37W-3S	D5
200	DYR	46311	3510		D6
200	ROSL	60172	2912	23W-6N	E6
300	WDDL	60191	2970	18W-5N	E1
500	HFET	60169	2858	24W-11N	D3
500	LNHT	60046	2418	19W-38N	C6
500	OSWG	60543	3200	35W-11S	B7
500	OSWG	60543	3264	35W-11S	B1
500	YKVL	60560	3333	42W-14S	D1
700	SMBG	60169	2858	24W-11N	D3
700	SMBG	60194	2858	24W-11N	D3
800	MPPT	60056	2808	13W-14N	D5
800	WhlT	60056	2808	13W-14N	D5
3600	NHBK	60062	2756	12W-17N	C5
11100	PSHL	60465	3274	11W-13S	A3
11900	LynT	60480	3208	14W-10S	A4
11900	LynT	60527	3208	14W-10S	C4
17200	SHLD	60473	3429	2E-20S	D4
19400	TYPK	60477	3504	10W-23S	C4
21900	FKFT	60423	3591	13W-26S	B3
N Heritage Dr					
1900	PLTN	60074	2753	19W-18N	C3
S Heritage Dr					
-	DMND	60416	3941	33W-40S	B4
100	MHRY	60050	2527	34W-31N	C6
17100	HMGN	60441	3421	18W-20S	A5
17100	HMGN	60491	3421	18W-20S	A5
17100	LKPT	60441	3421	18W-20S	A5
17100	LKPT	60491	3421	18W-20S	A5
W Heritage Dr					
800	ADSN	60101	2970	19W-3N	C5
2800	JLET	60431	3497	27W-23S	C5
2800	JLET	60435	3497	27W-23S	C5
2800	TroT	60431	3497	27W-23S	C5
Heritage Ln					
-	BRLT	60103	2966	30W-5N	B2
-	BRLT	60184	2966	30W-5N	B2
-	PLNO	60545	3259	47W-13S	C5
-	WYNE	60184	2966	30W-5N	B2
100	SMWD	60107	2856	29W-9N	E7
500	LKPT	60441	3419	22W-19S	D2
4400	LGGV	60047	2700	18W-22N	E3
6100	LSLE	60532	3142	24W-6S	E5
10400	HTLY	60142	2692	39W-20N	C7
11400	HTLY	60142	2745	39W-20N	C1
21200	DhmT	60033	2464	50W-36N	A3
21200	HRVD	60033	2464	50W-36N	A3
W Heritage Ln					
4800	WKGN	60083	2478	14W-37N	B2
4800	WKGN	60087	2478	14W-37N	B2
Heritage Pk					
-	JLET	60441	3417	27W-19S	D4
-	PnfT	60435	3417	27W-19S	D4
-	PnfT	60441	3417	27W-19S	D4
Heritage Pkwy					
-	DGvT	60517	3206	20W-11S	C7
-	WDRG	60516	3206	20W-11S	C7
-	WDRG	60517	3206	20W-11S	C7
200	RMVL	60446	3340	25W-16S	C3
9000	DGvT	60516	3206	20W-11S	B7
9000	DRN	60516	3206	20W-11S	B7
Heritage Pl					
-	BFGV	60089	2701	18W-21N	A7
Heritage Pth					
11300	BtnT	60071	2354	30W-43N	E4
11300	BtnT	60071	2355	30W-43N	A4
11300	BtnT	60081	2355	30W-43N	A4
Heritage St					
-	SCRL	60175	3019	37W-2N	B1
Heritage Tr					
-	CbaT	60010	2696	28W-23N	E3
-	HNVL	60073	2532	22W-33N	C3
10	HNVL	60030	2532	22W-33N	C3
Heritage Glen Ct					
900	BtvT	60510	3077	37W-2S	C5
Heritage Hill Dr					
1000	NPVL	60563	3141	28W-6S	B4
W Heritage Hills Ct					
3800	PRGV	60012	2585	32W-27N	A7
S Heritage Hills Rd					
-	PRGV	60012	2641	32W-27N	B1
4300	PRGV	60012	2585	32W-27N	B7
Heritage Lake Dr					
2400	JLET	60441	3417	27W-19S	C4
Heritage Lakes Dr					
1100	WHTN	60187	3082	24W-2S	E3
Heritage Meadows Dr					
11600	PNFD	60585	3266	30W-14S	B6
Heritage Oaks Cir					
-	ANTH	60002	2418	20W-40N	A3
3100	OKBK	60523	3084	18W-3S	E5
Heritage Oaks Ct					
3300	OKBK	60523	3084	18W-3S	E5
Heritage Oaks Dr					
-	ANTH	60002	2418	20W-40N	A3
-	NHBK	60062	2757	8W-17N	D6
-	PNFD	60585	3265	31W-14S	E6
10	SchT	60175	2907	38W-6N	B6
24800	PNFD	60585	3266	31W-14S	A7
Heritage Oaks Ln					
3000	OKBK	60523	3084	18W-3S	E5
W Heritage Oaks Rd					
28300	CbaT	60010	2696	28W-23N	E3
Heritage Pointe Ct					
1600	JLET	60586	3495	31W-22S	E2
1600	JLET	60586	3496	31W-21S	A1
Heritage Woods Dr					
100	WCHI	60185	2966	30W-2N	B7
Herkey Rd					
28800	GNOK	60044	2592	13W-28N	D5
28800	GNOK	60045	2592	13W-28N	D5
Herkimer St					
1300	JLET	60432	3499	23W-22S	A1
1400	JltT	60432	3499	23W-22S	A1
N Herkimer St					
10	JLET	60432	3499	23W-23S	A4
Herman Ct					
10	CRTE	60417	3685	0W-30S	C2
Herman St					
200	CRTE	60417	3685	0W-30S	C2
Herman Melville Ln					
600	CmpT	60175	2962	40W-3N	D6
W Hermann Av					
25600	AntT	60002	2415	26W-39N	E5
25600	AntT	60002	2416	25W-39N	A5
Hermans Ct					
-	JLET	60433	3499	22W-25S	D7
-	JltT	60433	3499	22W-25S	D7
Hermans Ln					
800	JLET	60433	3499	22W-25S	D7
800	JLET	60433	3587	22W-25S	D1
800	JltT	60433	3499	22W-25S	D7
800	JltT	60433	3587	22W-25S	D1
Herman Tonn Dr					
-	GNCY	53128	2352		E2
800	BfdT	53128	2352		D2
Hermes Av					
500	AURA	60505	3138	35W-6S	C5
1000	LMNT	60439	3270	19W-14S	C7
Hermes Dr					
-	OMFD	60461	3507	3W-24S	A5
W Hermione St					
6300	CHCG	60631	2919	8W-7N	A3
6300	CHCG	60646	2919	8W-7N	A3
Hermitage Av					
400	DRFD	60015	2704	10W-20N	A7
700	DRFD	60015	2703	10W-20N	E7
16100	MKHM	60428	3427	2W-19S	D3
16500	HLCT	60428	3427	2W-19S	D3
16500	HLCT	60429	3427	2W-19S	D3
16500	MKHM	60429	3427	2W-19S	D3
N Hermitage Av					
10	CHCG	60612	3033	2W-0N	C4
400	CHCG	60622	3033	2W-0N	C3
1600	CHCG	60622	2977	2W-2N	C7
1900	CHCG	60614	2977	2W-2N	C7
3500	CHCG	60657	2977	2W-4N	C3
4000	CHCG	60613	2977	2W-5N	C1
4400	CHCG	60613	2921	2W-5N	C7
4400	CHCG	60640	2921	2W-5N	C7
5600	CHCG	60660	2921	2W-7N	C4
6700	CHCG	60626	2921	2W-8N	C2
7500	CHCG	60202	2867	2W-9N	C7
7500	EVTN	60202	2867	2W-9N	C7
7700	CHCG	60626	2867	2W-9N	C6
S Hermitage Av					
600	CHCG	60612	3033	2W-0S	C6
1000	CHCG	60608	3033	2W-0S	C6
3400	CHCG	60608	3091	2W-3S	C5
3400	CHCG	60609	3091	2W-3S	C5
4700	CHCG	60609	3151	2W-5S	C2
5500	CHCG	60636	3151	2W-6S	C3
7500	CHCG	60620	3213	2W-10S	C5
Hermitage Cir					
1100	HFET	60169	2858	24W-12N	C1
Hermitage Dr					
700	AURA	60506	3137	38W-6S	A5
1500	NlxT	60451	3589	17W-26S	D3
Hermitage Ln					
1000	HFET	60169	2858	24W-12N	C1
Hermon Av					
1700	ZION	60099	2421	11W-40N	E3
Hermosa Av					
600	WcnT	60084	2644	25W-26N	B2
S Hermosa Av					
11100	CHCG	60643	3277	2W-13S	C3
Herndon St					
300	PKFT	60466	3595	3W-25S	B1
Heron Av					
1000	PTON	60468	3860	10W-38S	C5
1700	SMBG	60193	2912	25W-8N	A3
Heron Ct					
10	HNWD	60047	2646	20W-24N	A7
10	LIHL	60156	2692	38W-22N	E4
2200	RGMW	60008	2806	19W-14N	B4
4000	NPVL	60564	3266	29W-12S	D2
5200	JNBG	60050	2471	31W-37N	E2
Heron Dr					
400	LNHT	60046	2418	19W-38N	B6
1300	ANTH	60002	2416	24W-41N	C1
1400	AntT	60002	2416	24W-41N	D1
4400	LIHL	60156	2692	38W-22N	E4
4400	LIHL	60156	2693	38W-22N	A4
6100	OKFT	60452	3425	7W-18S	C1
11800	CrlT	60142	2743	45W-20N	B1
E Heron Dr					
10	PLTN	60067	2752	20W-16N	E6
Heron Ln					
10	BNHL	60010	2750	27W-17N	A4
2100	NLNX	60451	3589	18W-27S	A4
Heron St					
16200	LktT	60403	3417	26W-19S	D3
Heron Wy					
1000	WDSK	60098	2582	39W-30N	B2
1600	HFET	60192	2856	30W-12N	B1
N Herons Ct					
22800	KLDR	60047	2699	21W-22N	E3
Heron View Wy					
1800	RDLK	60073	2531	25W-33N	A2
Herr Dr					
900	NlxT	60451	3502	16W-24S	A6
Herren Ln					
10	OswT	60543	3262	39W-13S	E5
10	OswT	60560	3262	39W-13S	E5
Herrick Av					
9900	FNPK	60131	2973	12W-3N	B6
W Herrick Av					
-	RVGV	60171	2974	10W-3N	A6
8700	RVGV	60171	2973	11W-3N	E6
9000	FNPK	60131	2973	11W-3N	D6
9000	RVGV	60131	2973	11W-3N	D6
Herrick Dr					
300	MltT	60187	3024	25W-0N	A5
Herrick Rd					
10	NPVL	60555	3081	27W-4S	D7
10	NPVL	60563	3081	27W-4S	D7
10	RVSD	60546	3088	9W-3S	D5
10	WnfT	60555	3081	27W-3S	D5
10	WNVL	60555	3081	27W-4S	D7
10	WNVL	60563	3081	27W-4S	D7
300	BRWN	60402	3088	9W-3S	D4
300	RVSD	60402	3088	9W-3S	D4
600	WHTN	60187	3081	27W-2S	D4
600	WnfT	60187	3081	27W-2S	D4
Herrick Rd CO-51					
10	NPVL	60555	3081	27W-4S	D7
10	NPVL	60563	3081	27W-4S	D7
10	WnfT	60555	3081	27W-3S	D5
10	WNVL	60555	3081	27W-4S	D7
10	WNVL	60563	3081	27W-4S	D7
600	WHTN	60187	3081	27W-2S	D4
600	WnfT	60187	3081	27W-2S	D4
Herrick Hills Ct					
500	WnfT	60555	3081	27W-3S	D6
500	WNVL	60555	3081	27W-3S	D6
Herrington Blvd					
10	BbyT	60134	3018	39W-0N	E5
10	GnvT	60134	3018	39W-0N	E5
Herrington Dr					
-	BbyT	60119	3018	39W-0S	D7
500	BbyT	60134	3018	39W-0S	D6
Herrington Pl					
400	WDSK	60098	2581	42W-30N	C1
1100	GNVA	60134	3019	37W-0N	C5
Herrington Rd					
1100	GNVA	60134	3019	37W-0N	C5
1100	GnvT	60134	3019	37W-0N	C5
Herron Rd					
10	LKFT	60045	2649	11W-25N	E5
Hertel Ln					
1600	DRFD	60015	2703	12W-21N	C6
Herter Ln					
300	BtvT	60510	3077	37W-2S	B4
Hertford Ct					
1100	WHTN	60187	3082	25W-2S	B3
Hervey Av					
-	NCHI	60088	2536	11W-31N	E7
1400	NCHI	60064	2536	11W-32N	E5
1400	WKGN	60085	2536	11W-32N	E6
Hess Dr					
2200	CTHL	60403	3417	26W-21S	E7
N Hess Dr					
23700	CbaT	60013	2696	28W-23N	D1
Hess St					
8100	WLSP	60525	3208	13W-9S	E3
8200	WLSP	60480	3208	13W-9S	E3
N Hessing St					
2400	RVGV	60171	2974	10W-3N	B5
Hesterman Dr					
10	GLHT	60139	2968	24W-3N	D5
100	CLSM	60188	2968	24W-3N	D5
100	GLHT	60188	2968	24W-3N	D5
Hettinger Ln					
100	NARA	60542	3138	35W-4S	A1
Heustis St					
200	YKVL	60560	3333	42W-15S	C2
Hevern Dr					
400	WHTN	60187	3082	25W-2S	A3
Hewes Dr					
10	NBRN	60010	2698	25W-22N	B4
Hewes St					
1500	CRTE	60417	3685	0W-30S	C3
1500	CteT	60417	3685	0W-30S	C3
Hewitt Dr					
-	LNSH	60069	2702	13W-23N	E2
1000	DSPN	60016	2862	15W-10N	B5
1000	DSPN	60018	2862	15W-10N	B5
Heyer St					
-	AvnT	60073	2474	24W-35N	C7
-	RLKB	60073	2474	24W-35N	C7
Heywood Av					
400	AURA	60506	3199	36W-7S	D1
Hi Ct					
-	BRRG	60527	3208	15W-9S	B2
-	DGvT	60527	3208	15W-9S	B2
Hialeah Ct					
10	RLKP	60030	2589	22W-30N	B1
700	SYHW	60118	2800	36W-15N	A4
14000	HMGN	60491	3344	15W-16S	C4
Hialeah Ln					
200	FmtT	60030	2589	22W-30N	B1
200	RLKP	60030	2589	22W-30N	B1
1100	HRPK	60133	2911	26W-6N	E6
1100	HRPK	60133	2912	26W-6N	A6
N Hiawatha Av					
6000	CHCG	60646	2920	5W-7N	A3
6700	CHCG	60646	2919	7W-8N	B1
Hiawatha Blvd					
11000	MKNA	60448	3503	13W-23S	A4
Hiawatha Ct					
700	ELGN	60120	2855	32W-12N	B2
1300	HDPK	60035	2757	8W-20N	E2
S Hiawatha Ct					
700	MPPT	60056	2862	15W-11N	A2
13800	HMGN	60491	3343	16W-16S	E3
Hiawatha Dr					
10	CNHL	60514	3145	17W-5S	B2
100	CLSM	60188	2968	25W-3N	A6
200	BFGV	60089	2754	17W-18N	C3
200	LIHL	60156	2694	34W-21N	B5
500	ELGN	60120	2855	32W-12N	B3
700	MNKA	60447	3583	33W-28S	B6
6800	MchT	60097	2469	36W-36N	D3
6800	MchT	60097	2470	35W-36N	A3
W Hiawatha Dr					
13000	HMGN	60491	3343	16W-16S	E3
13000	HMGN	60491	3344	16W-16S	A3
Hiawatha Ln					
800	RVWD	60015	2702	13W-21N	E7
11200	IHPK	60525	3146	14W-6S	D5
Hiawatha Pkwy					
2200	WDRG	60517	3205	21W-9S	E3
Hiawatha Tr					
10	HDPK	60035	2757	8W-20N	E2
300	AddT	60191	2971	17W-5N	C1
300	WDDL	60191	2971	17W-5N	B1
1700	RLKH	60073	2474	24W-35N	D6
10100	ODPK	60462	3345	12W-18S	C6
E Hiawatha Tr					
100	MPPT	60056	2862	15W-12N	A2
N Hiawatha Tr					
34500	GrtT	60051	2529	28W-34N	D1
34600	GrtT	60051	2472	28W-34N	D7
W Hiawatha Tr					
10	MPPT	60056	2861	16W-12N	E2
10	MPPT	60056	2862	15W-12N	A2
Hibbard Rd					
10	NHFD	60093	2811	5W-14N	E4
10	NtrT	60091	2811	6W-14N	E4
10	NtrT	60093	2811	5W-14N	E4
10	WLMT	60091	2811	6W-13N	E6
10	WLMT	60093	2811	6W-14N	E4
10	WNKA	60093	2811	6W-15N	E2
800	WNKA	60093	2758	6W-16N	E7
Hibbard St					
1000	WDSK	60098	2581	41W-30N	D2
Hibiscus Cir					
100	MTSN	60443	3593	7W-26S	C2
Hibiscus Dr					
10100	ODPK	60462	3345	12W-17S	B6
Hibiscus Tr					
5700	CLLK	60012	2584	34W-27N	B7
5700	NndT	60012	2584	34W-27N	B7
Hickman Ln					
300	WDSK	60098	2524	40W-31N	E6
Hickok Av					
-	UYPK	60417	3684	3W-30S	C3
-	UYPK	60466	3684	3W-30S	B3
W Hickory Al					
26500	GrtT	60041	2473	26W-36N	D4
Hickory Av					
-	ANHT	60004	2754	17W-17N	B5
-	BFGV	60089	2754	17W-17N	B5
-	CPVL	60118	2747	35W-17N	B7
-	DndT	60118	2747	35W-17N	B7
-	GrtT	60041	2474	25W-34N	B7
10	AURA	60505	3200	34W-8S	D1
100	SMWD	60107	2857	28W-10N	A6
200	AddT	60106	2971	17W-4N	B3
200	RMVL	60446	3340	24W-16S	D3
400	ADSN	60106	2971	17W-4N	B3
8600	GfnT	60014	2639	37W-24N	B6
34300	WslT	60481	3943	27W-42S	E6
N Hickory Av					
100	BRLT	60103	2910	29W-8N	E2
1000	CHCG	60622	3033	1W-1N	E2
1100	ANHT	60004	2807	17W-15N	B2
1300	RLKB	60073	2475	22W-35N	A6
26100	FmtT	60060	2646	19W-26N	D3
34000	AvnT	60030	2532	22W-34N	C2
34000	HNVL	60030	2532	22W-34N	C2
39400	AntT	60002	2416	25W-39N	B5
S Hickory Av					
10	ANHT	60004	2807	17W-14N	B5
10	FXLK	60020	2473	27W-36N	B4
10	MDLN	60060	2646	18W-27N	E1
100	BRLT	60103	2910	29W-8N	E3
1200	MPPT	60005	2861	17W-12N	B1
W Hickory Av					
13500	HMGN	60491	3343	18W-16S	B3
13500	LMNT	60439	3343	18W-16S	A2
14200	HMGN	60439	3343	18W-16S	B3
18500	LbvT	60060	2646	18W-26N	E3
18500	MDLN	60060	2646	18W-26N	D3

STREET Block	City	ZIP	Map#	CGS Grid
W Hickory Av				
24400	AvnT	60073	2474 24W-35N	C6
24400	RLKB	60073	2474 24W-35N	C6
Hickory Ct				
10	BmdT	60157	2913 22W-6N	D7
10	BtvT	60510	3077 38W-3S	B5
10	CPVL	60110	2748 32W-18N	C5
10	CTCY	60409	3429 2E-18S	D1
10	KdlT	60560	3333 43W-16S	A4
10	PKFT	60466	3595 4W-25S	A1
200	LKBF	60044	2593 11W-28N	E6
200	NfdT	60062	2757 9W-18N	C3
300	SMBG	60193	2859 23W-10N	A6
600	NARA	60542	3078 35W-3S	B6
600	SchT	60174	2908 34W-6N	D7
700	SchT	60175	2907 36W-7N	E5
800	MRGO	60152	2634 49W-27N	C1
1300	DRGV	60515	3084 20W-3S	B5
1700	LNHT	60046	2417 20W-38N	E7
2100	GNVW	60025	2864 9W-12N	D1
2900	WDRG	60517	3205 22W-9S	D4
4500	LGGV	60047	2700 19W-23N	D2
12200	HTLY	60142	2744 42W-19N	C2
17000	ODHL	60487	3424 11W-20S	A4
18500	BlmT	60411	3429 2E-22S	E7
18500	LNSG	60411	3429 2E-22S	E7
18500	LNSG	60438	3429 2E-22S	E7
20500	FKFT	60423	3504 10W-24S	B6
25700	CnhT	60447	3672 32W-28S	D1
N Hickory Ct				
34500	GrtT	60041	2530 26W-34N	E1
36700	GrtT	60041	2474 25W-36N	A3
S Hickory Ct				
8400	WLSP	60480	3208 14W-9S	D4
24700	CteT	60417	3687 3E-30S	B2
W Hickory Ct				
20800	LktT	60544	3340 26W-16S	A3
Hickory Dr				
-	JNBG	60050	2470 34W-34N	D7
-	MchT	60050	2470 34W-34N	D7
10	CPVL	60110	2748 32W-18N	C5
10	LNHT	60046	2476 20W-38N	A1
10	OKBK	60523	3086 15W-1S	B1
100	CLLK	60014	2639 36W-26N	D3
100	LNHT	60046	2417 20W-38N	E7
100	LNHT	60046	2418 20W-38N	A7
400	WLNG	60090	2755 13W-17N	D5
500	BFGV	60089	2754 17W-18N	B2
1700	SYHW	60118	2800 35W-16N	C2
2300	DYR	46311	3598	E3
2800	MCLK	60050	2470 34W-34N	D7
6100	LSLE	60532	3142 24W-6S	C5
8800	ODHL	60487	3424 11W-20S	A4
10200	ODPK	60462	3345 12W-18S	C7
10200	ODPK	60467	3345 12W-18S	C7
19100	CCHL	60478	3506 5W-23S	C3
E Hickory Dr				
2700	GwdT	60097	2469 36W-34N	C7
2700	WRLK	60097	2469 36W-34N	C7
N Hickory Dr				
300	ITSC	60143	2914 20W-6N	B6
S Hickory Dr				
1400	MPPT	60056	2861 16W-11N	D3
W Hickory Dr				
7800	MchT	60097	2469 36W-37N	D2
11500	BHPK	60099	2421 11W-38N	D7
11500	WKGN	60099	2421 11W-38N	D7
Hickory Gln				
500	RchT	60443	3593 8W-26S	B2
Hickory Grv				
7300	MchT	60097	2469 36W-35N	D6
Hickory Ln				
-	SEGN	60177	2908 34W-8N	D4
10	ALGN	60102	2747 33W-20N	E1
10	ALGN	60102	2748 33W-20N	A1
10	BNHL	60010	2696 28W-21N	E6
10	BtlT	60543	3262 39W-12S	E4
10	BtlT	60560	3261 43W-13S	B6
10	BtvT	60510	3077 38W-3S	B5
10	CRY	60013	2641 32W-24N	C7
10	LNSH	60069	2702 14W-23N	D3
10	NHBK	60062	2757 8W-17N	D5
10	PvsT	60523	3086 14W-2S	D4
10	PvsT	60558	3086 14W-2S	D4
10	SchT	60120	2908 34W-6N	E6
10	SchT	60174	2908 34W-6N	E6
10	SchT	60177	2908 34W-6N	E6
10	WSTR	60523	3086 14W-2S	D4
10	WSTR	60558	3086 14W-2S	D4
10	YKVL	60560	3261 43W-13S	B6
100	SMBG	60193	2859 23W-10N	A6
200	ANTH	60002	2358 23W-43N	A4
200	LKBN	60010	2643 26W-24N	D7
200	NARA	60542	3077 38W-3S	B6
200	SMBG	60193	2858 24W-10N	B6
300	LynT	60458	3209 11W-8S	E2
400	MNSR	46321	3430	D7
500	WnfT	60185	3022 28W-1N	E2
500	WnfT	60185	3023 28W-1N	A2
700	CLSM	60188	2967 28W-3N	A6
700	MRGO	60152	2634 49W-27N	C1
700	WCHI	60185	3022 29W-1N	D2
900	DRN	60561	3207 17W-8S	B1
900	NPVL	60540	3203 26W-7S	D1
1000	EGVV	60007	2915 18W-8N	A2
1200	WDSK	60098	2581 42W-30N	B2
1500	WNKA	60093	2758 6W-16N	D7
1700	WHTN	60187	3024 26W-0S	A7
1800	GLHT	60139	2969 23W-3N	A5
2800	TNLK	53181	2353	E3
3300	HLCT	60429	3426 4W-20S	E5
4800	MchT	60050	2471 32W-36N	C3
4800	MchT	60081	2471 32W-36N	C3
5700	DrrT	60014	2639 38W-26N	A3
9000	HYHL	60457	3209 11W-10S	E5
15300	OKFT	60452	3347 8W-18S	B7
23600	CnhT	60447	3672 32W-28S	D1
27300	CteT	60401	3774 1W-33S	A2
E Hickory Ln				
2900	CteT	60417	3687 3E-30S	B2
N Hickory Ln				
10	GNWD	60425	3508 0E-22S	E2
400	PTON	60468	3861 8W-37S	B3
400	WlfT	60468	3861 8W-37S	B3
2500	ANHT	60004	2754 17W-16N	B6
25600	WCDA	60084	2588 25W-28N	A7
28100	WcnT	60084	2588 25W-28N	A6
34400	AvnT	60073	2532 21W-34N	D1
35200	AvnT	60073	2474 24W-35N	C6
41000	AntT	60002	2417 22W-41N	C2
S Hickory Ln				
13700	LktT	60544	3339 26W-16S	E4
W Hickory Ln				
2000	HFET	60192	2804 23W-13N	E6
2000	PltT	60192	2804 23W-13N	D6
2000	PltT	60195	2804 23W-13N	D6

STREET Block	City	ZIP	Map#	CGS Grid
W Hickory Ln				
12300	BHPK	60099	2421 12W-40N	C4
17200	WrnT	60030	2534 17W-33N	B3
23100	PNFD	60544	3416 28W-19S	E2
23100	PnfT	60544	3416 28W-19S	E2
25100	AntT	60002	2357 25W-43N	B4
26100	GrtT	60041	2473 26W-36N	D3
26300	FXLK	60041	2473 26W-36N	E3
Hickory Pl				
300	ELGN	60120	2855 33W-11N	A3
W Hickory Pl				
900	ADSN	60101	2970 19W-4N	C2
18500	WrnT	60030	2533 18W-32N	E4
Hickory Rd				
10	AlqT	60013	2641 31W-26N	E3
10	HNWD	60047	2645 21W-24N	E7
10	ODHL	60013	2641 31W-26N	E3
100	LIHL	60156	2694 35W-21N	A5
200	LKZH	60047	2698 24W-23N	B2
400	GwdT	60098	2524 41W-32N	E5
400	WDSK	60098	2524 41W-32N	E5
500	GNEN	60137	3025 21W-0N	D4
1100	HMWD	60430	3428 1W-21S	A7
2500	HMWD	60430	3427 3W-21S	B7
3000	HLCT	60429	3427 3W-21S	A7
3000	HLCT	60430	3427 3W-21S	A7
7600	MchT	60097	2469 36W-35N	D6
14500	HMGN	60491	3343 18W-15S	A2
14500	LMNT	60439	3343 18W-15S	A2
N Hickory Rd				
1700	FmtT	60060	2645 20W-26N	E3
1700	FmtT	60060	2646 20W-26N	A3
26100	LGGV	60060	2645 20W-26N	E3
W Hickory Rd				
10	LMBD	60148	3026 20W-0N	B5
14500	NptT	60099	2361 14W-42N	C6
E Hickory Rdg				
400	GNWD	60425	3509 0E-23S	A3
W Hickory Rdg				
27300	LKBN	60010	2643 27W-25N	B4
Hickory St				
-	NlxT	60448	3502 15W-22S	B1
-	RLKB	60073	2475 22W-34N	A7
-	TYPK	60477	3424 8W-21S	E5
10	CHHT	60411	3596 1W-25S	A1
10	CNHL	60514	3145 16W-4S	D1
10	GYLK	60030	2532 21W-33N	E3
100	FKFT	60423	3591 12W-26S	D2
100	NARA	60542	3078 35W-3S	B7
100	NLNX	60451	3501 18W-24S	B6
200	CHHT	60411	3595 2W-25S	D1
200	MTSN	60443	3594 4W-25S	E1
200	OSWG	60543	3263 37W-13S	B4
200	PKFT	60443	3594 4W-25S	E1
200	PKFT	60466	3594 4W-25S	E1
200	PKFT	60466	3595 4W-25S	A1
300	WKGN	60085	2537 10W-34N	A1
600	SRGV	60554	3135 42W-4S	D2
700	LMNT	60439	3270 19W-14S	D6
1000	WKGN	60085	2480 10W-35N	A6
1400	HHLL	60051	2586 30W-29N	A4
1600	HDPK	60035	2704 8W-22N	D5
1700	WKGN	60087	2480 10W-35N	A6
2300	DSPN	60018	2917 12W-9N	D4
6000	CmgT	60033	2405 52W-37N	B7
6000	DhmT	60033	2405 52W-37N	B7
6700	HRPK	60133	2911 27W-8N	C3
6800	TYPK	60477	3425 8W-21S	A5
7000	SMWD	60107	2911 27W-8N	C2
7000	SMWD	60133	2911 27W-8N	C3
9400	FftT	60448	3503 11W-23S	E3
18200	LNSG	60438	3429 2E-21S	D7
18500	BlmT	60411	3429 2E-21S	E7
18500	LNSG	60411	3429 2E-21S	E7
E Hickory St				
10	LMBD	60148	3026 19W-0N	C5
10	NLNX	60451	3501 18W-24S	B6
400	HNDL	60521	3146 15W-4S	B1
2000	CteT	60417	3686 2E-30S	D2
N Hickory St				
10	FKFT	60423	3591 12W-26S	D1
10	JLET	60436	3498 24W-24S	E5
100	BDWD	60408	3941 32W-41S	D5
300	RedT	60408	3941 32W-41S	D5
1100	FXLK	60020	2415 28W-39N	A5
1100	FXLK	60081	2415 28W-39N	A5
1200	JLET	60435	3498 24W-22S	E2
1500	CTHL	60403	3498 24W-21S	E1
1700	CTHL	60403	3418 24W-21S	E7
27500	WcnT	60042	2586 28W-27N	E7
27500	WcnT	60042	2642 28W-27N	E1
38700	LkvT	60046	2417 21W-38N	D6
39400	AntT	60081	2415 28W-39N	A5
S Hickory St				
10	JLET	60435	3498 24W-24S	E5
10	JLET	60436	3498 24W-24S	E5
10	PLTN	60067	2805 21W-15N	D1
100	BDWD	60408	3941 32W-41S	D6
100	PltT	60067	2805 21W-15N	D1
100	RedT	60408	3941 32W-41S	D6
200	GNWD	60425	3509 0E-23S	A2
W Hickory St				
10	HNDL	60521	3146 15W-4S	A1
300	LMBD	60148	3026 20W-0N	A5
500	HNDL	60521	3145 16W-4S	E1
25200	AntT	60002	2416 25W-41N	A1
28200	WcnT	60084	2643 28W-27N	A2
Hickory Ter				
100	ISLK	60042	2586 29W-28N	D5
4100	NndT	60014	2586 30W-27N	A7
N Hickory Ter				
1000	RLKB	60073	2475 22W-34N	B7
Hickory Tr				
1000	DRGV	60515	3084 19W-3S	C5
7300	MchT	60097	2469 36W-35N	D6
N Hickory Tr				
1200	ADSN	60101	2970 19W-5N	C2
W Hickory Tr				
700	MchT	60050	2472 29W-37N	C2
W Hickory Wk				
24400	TroT	60404	3584 30W-27S	B4
Hickory Creek Ct				
16600	PNFD	60586	3416 30W-19S	B4
S Hickory Creek Ct				
20700	FftT	60423	3505 8W-24S	A6
Hickory Creek Dr				
-	RNPK	60471	3594 5W-27S	B5
1100	NLNX	60451	3501 17W-23S	D4
1100	NlxT	60451	3501 17W-23S	D4
3200	JLET	60451	3500 19W-23S	D3
4700	UYPK	60471	3594 5W-27S	B5
9400	MKNA	60448	3503 11W-22S	E2
W Hickory Creek Dr				
-	MTSN	60443	3505 9W-25S	A6
7200	FftT	60423	3505 9W-25S	A6
7300	FftT	60423	3504 9W-25S	E7

STREET Block	City	ZIP	Map#	CGS Grid
S Hickory Creek Pl				
20700	FftT	60423	3505 9W-25S	A7
S Hickory Crest Ct				
9700	PSHL	60465	3209 11W-11S	E7
Hickory Grove Ct				
5500	JLET	60586	3416 31W-21S	A7
E Hickory Haven Dr				
200	GRNE	60031	2535 15W-33N	A2
W Hickory Haven Dr				
100	GRNE	60031	2535 15W-33N	A2
Hickory Hill Ct				
4300	JNBG	60050	2471 31W-36N	D4
Hickory Hill Dr				
700	VNHL	60061	2647 16W-24N	D7
N Hickory Hill Rd				
21700	KLDR	60047	2699 21W-21N	D5
Hickory Hills Dr				
4100	WKGN	60087	2478 14W-36N	D3
4100	WrnT	60031	2478 14W-36N	D3
4100	WrnT	60087	2478 14W-36N	D3
Hickory Hollow Dr				
200	DndT	60118	2800 36W-15N	A4
700	DndT	60118	2799 36W-15N	E4
Hickory Knoll Dr				
1600	DRFD	60015	2703 12W-21N	C5
1600	WdfT	60015	2703 12W-21N	B5
Hickory Knoll Ln				
400	WynT	60185	2966 29W-3N	D6
Hickorynut Dr				
4400	MchT	60050	2472 30W-36N	B4
Hickory Nut Wy				
10900	BtnT	60071	2355 30W-42N	A5
10900	BtnT	60081	2355 30W-42N	A5
Hickory Nut Grove Ln				
100	AlqT	60013	2642 29W-25N	B5
100	CbaT	60013	2642 29W-25N	B5
900	CRY	60013	2642 30W-25N	B5
Hickory Nut Grove Rd				
6000	AlqT	60013	2642 29W-24N	D7
6000	CbaT	60013	2642 29W-24N	D7
8000	CbaT	60013	2696 29W-23N	D2
8200	AlqT	60013	2696 29W-23N	D2
Hickory Oaks Ct				
10	BGBK	60490	3267 26W-11S	D1
Hickory Oaks Dr				
200	BGBK	60490	3267 26W-11S	D2
Hickory Park Ln				
1600	AURA	60504	3200 34W-9S	E3
1600	AURA	60504	3201 33W-8S	A3
Hickory Ridge Ct				
1000	FKFT	60423	3503 13W-25S	B7
Hickory Ridge Dr				
1300	MTGY	60538	3199 36W-9S	E4
Hickory Stick Ln				
19900	MKNA	60448	3502 14W-24S	E4
Hickory Trace Dr				
10	HYHL	60457	3210 10W-9S	A3
10	HYHL	60458	3210 10W-9S	A3
10	JSTC	60457	3210 10W-9S	A3
10	JSTC	60458	3210 10W-9S	A3
N Hickoryway Dr				
4400	JNBG	60050	2472 30W-36N	A4
4400	MchT	60050	2472 30W-36N	A4
4600	JNBG	60050	2471 30W-36N	E3
Hicks Dr				
700	ELBN	60119	3017 43W-1N	B2
N Hicks Pl				
200	PLTN	60067	2753 20W-16N	A7
200	PLTN	60074	2753 20W-16N	A7
Hicks Rd				
1400	PLTN	60008	2806 20W-14N	A4
1400	PLTN	60067	2806 20W-14N	A4
1400	RGMW	60008	2806 20W-14N	A4
1400	RGMW	60067	2806 20W-14N	A4
2700	ElaT	60047	2753 20W-20N	B1
2700	ElaT	60074	2753 20W-20N	A2
2700	LGGV	60047	2753 20W-20N	B1
2700	LGGV	60074	2753 20W-20N	A2
2700	PLTN	60074	2753 20W-20N	A2
20700	ElaT	60047	2700 20W-20N	B7
20700	LGGV	60047	2700 20W-20N	B7
Hicks Rd SR-53				
2700	ElaT	60047	2753 20W-20N	B1
2700	ElaT	60074	2753 20W-20N	A2
2700	LGGV	60047	2753 20W-20N	B1
2700	LGGV	60074	2753 20W-20N	A2
2700	PLTN	60074	2753 20W-20N	A2
20700	ElaT	60047	2700 20W-20N	B7
20700	LGGV	60047	2700 20W-20N	B7
N Hicks Rd				
500	PLTN	60067	2753 20W-17N	A5
500	PLTN	60074	2753 20W-17N	A5
1500	PltT	60067	2753 20W-18N	A4
1500	PltT	60074	2753 20W-18N	A4
2300	ElaT	60047	2753 20W-18N	A2
2300	ElaT	60074	2753 20W-18N	A2
2300	LGGV	60047	2753 20W-18N	A2
2300	LGGV	60074	2753 20W-18N	A2
N Hicks Rd SR-53				
2100	PLTN	60074	2753 20W-18N	A2
2300	ElaT	60047	2753 20W-18N	A2
2300	ElaT	60074	2753 20W-18N	A2
2300	LGGV	60047	2753 20W-18N	A2
2300	LGGV	60074	2753 20W-18N	A2
S Hicks Rd				
200	PLTN	60067	2806 20W-15N	A3
200	PLTN	60074	2806 20W-15N	A3
300	PLTN	60008	2806 20W-15N	A2
300	RGMW	60008	2806 20W-15N	A2
700	RGMW	60067	2806 20W-14N	A3
Hidden Ct				
1200	WHTN	60187	3082 25W-2S	A3
Hidden Ln				
9600	BLVY	60098	2525 38W-31N	D6
9600	DrrT	60098	2525 38W-31N	D6
Hidden Bay Ct				
1900	NPVL	60565	3204 25W-9S	B4
Hidden Brook Ct				
11700	ODPK	60467	3422 14W-20S	D5
Hidden Brook Dr				
10	NBRN	60010	2644 25W-24N	B6
Hiddenbrook Ln				
300	WLBK	60527	3146 15W-7S	A5
S Hidden Brook Tr				
1000	PLTN	60067	2805 22W-14N	A4
N Hidden Bunker Ct				
39900	AntT	60002	2416 25W-40N	B4
Hidden Creek Cir				
1700	PLTN	60074	2753 19W-18N	C3
Hidden Creek Ct				
2200	LSLE	60532	3082 24W-4S	D7
W Hidden Creek Ct				
1000	VNHL	60061	2646 18W-24N	E6
Hidden Creek Dr				
500	ANTH	60002	2358 21W-42N	C7
900	AntT	60002	2358 21W-42N	D6

STREET Block	City	ZIP	Map#	CGS Grid
Hiddencreek Ln				
-	AraT	60542	3077 38W-3S	B7
-	NARA	60542	3077 38W-3S	B7
100	NARA	60542	3137 37W-4S	B1
Hidden Creek Rd				
200	LKZH	60047	2699 22W-22N	C4
Hidden Glen Cir				
-	SCRL	60174	3020 34W-2N	D1
W Hidden Glen Dr				
2600	WKGN	60085	2536 12W-33N	C2
Hidden Glen Ln				
10	KdlT	60560	3333 42W-16S	D4
Hidden Green Cir				
-	BtnT	60081	2414 29W-39N	D6
-	FXLK	60081	2414 29W-39N	D5
Hidden Grove Cir				
1400	LSLE	60435	3497 27W-22S	C1
W Hidden Hill Ln				
900	PLTN	60067	2752 22W-16N	B7
900	PltT	60067	2752 22W-16N	B7
Hidden Hill Tr				
10	ElgT	60124	2853 37W-11N	C3
Hidden Hills Ct				
3900	LGGV	60047	2699 20W-22N	E5
Hidden Hills Tr				
10	RtdT	60118	2746 38W-17N	B6
Hidden Knoll Rd				
10	RtdT	60124	2798 39W-14N	E6
10	RtdT	60124	2799 39W-14N	A6
Hidden Lake Ct				
21300	LktT	60403	3417 26W-19S	E4
Hidden Lake Dr				
10	BRRG	60527	3208 15W-9S	C4
10	LynT	60527	3208 15W-9S	C4
900	BFGV	60089	2701 16W-21N	C7
Hidden Lake Ln				
-	RLKP	60030	2532 22W-31N	C7
-	RLKP	60030	2589 21W-31N	C1
Hidden Lake Rd				
700	NPVL	60565	3204 25W-9S	B4
S Hidden Lake Tr				
23100	BlmT	60411	3598 3E-28S	A6
23100	CteT	60417	3598 3E-28S	A6
Hidden Lakes Blvd				
-	BrnT	60010	2803 27W-15N	A1
-	SBTN	60010	2803 27W-15N	A1
Hidden Lakes Dr				
700	PltT	60124	2852 40W-10N	B5
Hidden Oak Ct				
6100	NndT	60012	2584 35W-28N	B5
Hidden Oak Dr				
6100	NndT	60012	2584 35W-28N	B5
Hidden Oaks Ct				
1700	JLET	60586	3496 30W-21S	B1
Hidden Oaks Dr				
100	PltT	60010	2751 23W-18N	E3
1300	AURA	60506	3137 37W-5S	D4
5400	JLET	60586	3416 30W-21S	B7
5400	JLET	60586	3496 30W-21S	B1
Hidden Oaks Ln W				
10	CbaT	60010	2698 25W-22N	A4
10	NBRN	60010	2698 25W-22N	A4
Hidden Oaks Rd				
400	CmpT	60175	2962 39W-4N	E4
Hidden Pines Dr				
10	DRPK	60010	2752 22W-20N	A2
Hidden Pond Cir				
100	AURA	60504	3139 31W-7S	E6
100	AURA	60504	3201 32W-8S	C2
Hidden Pond Ln				
200	NBRN	60010	2698 25W-23N	B1
N Hidden Prairie Ct				
500	PLTN	60067	2752 21W-16N	D6
Hidden Ridge Ln				
10	LktT	60441	3341 21W-16S	E3
10	RMVL	60441	3341 21W-16S	E3
1900	HDPK	60035	2704 10W-21N	A6
Hidden River Cir				
16400	PNFD	60586	3416 30W-19S	A3
Hidden River Dr				
16300	PNFD	60586	3416 30W-19S	A3
16300	PnfT	60586	3416 30W-19S	A3
Hidden Spring Dr				
1100	NPVL	60540	3141 28W-6S	A5
Hidden Springs Dr				
200	CmpT	60175	2961 42W-5N	D2
W Hidden Springs Tr				
13100	WDWH	60083	2421 13W-41N	A2
13300	WDWH	60083	2420 13W-41N	E2
13300	ZION	60099	2420 13W-41N	E2
N Hidden Trail Blvd				
2300	SPGV	60081	2413 31W-40N	E2
2500	RcmT	60081	2413 31W-40N	E2
S Hidden Trail Blvd				
2300	SPGV	60081	2413 31W-40N	E2
Hidden Trail Ct				
2200	SPGV	60081	2413 31W-40N	E2
Hidden Valley Cir				
16000	HMGN	60491	3421 16W-19S	E2
Hidden Valley Ct				
10	BGBK	60490	3267 26W-11S	D1
2800	CPVL	60110	2747 36W-17N	B6
16000	HMGN	60491	3421 16W-19S	E2
Hidden Valley Dr				
-	LslT	60565	3204 24W-9S	D5
1600	BGBK	60490	3267 26W-11S	D1
2000	NPVL	60565	3204 24W-9S	D4
13100	HMGN	60491	3421 16W-19S	E2
13100	HMGN	60491	3422 16W-19S	A2
21500	ElaT	60047	2699 21W-21N	C7
21500	ElaT	60074	2699 21W-21N	C7
21500	KLDR	60047	2699 21W-21N	C7
21500	KLDR	60074	2699 21W-21N	C7
W Hidden Valley Rd				
3400	LGGV	60047	2700 20W-21N	B6
Hidden Valley Tr				
-	HMGN	60491	3421 16W-19S	E1
Hidden Valley Cove				
11500	ODPK	60467	3422 14W-21S	D7
Hidden View Dr				
100	WTMT	60559	3145 17W-6S	B4
Hideaway Dr				
12000	HTLY	60142	2744 43W-19N	A2
Hideaway Ln				
8000	OswT	60560	3334 41W-15S	A1
9600	RcmT	60071	2353 34W-41N	D7
9600	RcmT	60071	2412 33W-41N	D1
W Higgins Av				
5400	CHCG	60630	2919 6W-6N	D6
6300	CHCG	60656	2919 6W-6N	C6
6600	CHCG	60656	2918 8W-6N	E5
7200	CHCG	60631	2918 8W-6N	E5
W Higgins Av SR-72				
7200	CHCG	60631	2918 8W-6N	E5
7200	CHCG	60656	2918 8W-6N	E5

STREET Block	City	ZIP	Map#	CGS Grid
Higgins Rd				
-	CHCG	60007	2916 15W-8N	A1
-	CHCG	60018	2916 15W-8N	A1
-	DndT	60118	2800 35W-16N	B2
-	DndT	60136	2799 37W-16N	C2
-	DSPN	60007	2916 15W-8N	A1
-	DSPN	60018	2916 15W-8N	A1
-	EGvT	60007	2860 18W-10N	E5
-	EGvT	60007	2861 18W-10N	A5
-	EGVV	60007	2861 18W-10N	A5
-	GLBT	60136	2799 39W-16N	A2
-	SYHW	60118	2800 35W-16N	B2
-	WDND	60118	2800 35W-16N	B2
10	GLBT	60136	2798 40W-16N	D2
10	HshT	60140	2743 46W-19N	A3
10	RtdT	60136	2798 40W-16N	D2
10	RtdT	60140	2798 40W-16N	C2
500	RtdT	60118	2799 38W-16N	B2
500	RtdT	60136	2799 38W-16N	B2
700	CHCG	60631	2918 10W-7N	A4
700	HPSR	60140	2743 45W-19N	B4
700	PKRG	60068	2918 10W-7N	A4
700	PKRG	60631	2918 10W-7N	A4
1500	CHCG	60018	2917 11W-7N	D4
1500	CHCG	60068	2917 11W-7N	D4
1500	CHCG	60631	2917 11W-7N	E4
1500	PKRG	60068	2917 11W-7N	D4
1500	PKRG	60631	2917 11W-7N	E4
2000	PKRG	60018	2917 11W-7N	D4
2500	DndT	60118	2799 38W-16N	B2
2500	DndT	60124	2799 37W-16N	D2
2500	ELGN	60118	2799 38W-16N	B2
2500	ELGN	60124	2799 38W-16N	B2
Higgins Rd SR-72				
-	DndT	60118	2800 35W-16N	B2
-	DndT	60136	2799 37W-16N	C2
-	EGvT	60007	2860 18W-10N	E5
-	EGvT	60007	2861 18W-10N	A5
-	EGVV	60007	2861 18W-10N	A5
-	GLBT	60136	2799 39W-16N	A2
-	SYHW	60118	2800 35W-16N	B2
-	WDND	60118	2800 35W-16N	B2
10	GLBT	60136	2798 40W-16N	D2
10	RtdT	60136	2798 40W-16N	D2
10	RtdT	60140	2798 40W-16N	C2
500	RtdT	60118	2799 38W-16N	B2
500	RtdT	60136	2799 38W-16N	B2
700	CHCG	60631	2918 10W-7N	A4
700	PKRG	60068	2918 10W-7N	A4
700	PKRG	60631	2918 10W-7N	A4
1500	CHCG	60018	2917 11W-7N	D4
1500	CHCG	60068	2917 11W-7N	D4
1500	CHCG	60631	2917 11W-7N	E4
1500	PKRG	60068	2917 11W-7N	D4
1500	PKRG	60631	2917 11W-7N	E4
2000	PKRG	60018	2917 11W-7N	D4
2500	DndT	60118	2799 38W-16N	B2
2500	DndT	60124	2799 37W-16N	D2
2500	ELGN	60118	2799 38W-16N	B2
2500	ELGN	60124	2799 38W-16N	B2
E Higgins Rd				
-	EGvT	60007	2860 18W-10N	E5
-	SMBG	60007	2860 20W-11N	A4
10	EGVV	60007	2861 17W-10N	B5
10	GLBT	60136	2799 38W-16N	A2
10	HFET	60169	2859 23W-11N	B3
600	HFET	60173	2859 22W-11N	C3
600	SMBG	60169	2859 22W-11N	C3
600	SMBG	60173	2859 21W-11N	D4
1700	SMBG	60173	2860 21W-11N	A4
1900	EGvT	60007	2861 16W-9N	D6
2400	EGVV	60007	2915 16W-9N	E1
2600	EGvT	60007	2915 16W-9N	E1
E Higgins Rd SR-72				
-	EGvT	60007	2860 18W-10N	E5
10	GLBT	60136	2799 38W-16N	A2
10	HFET	60169	2859 23W-11N	B3
600	HFET	60173	2859 22W-11N	C3
600	SMBG	60169	2859 22W-11N	C3
600	SMBG	60173	2859 21W-11N	D4
1700	SMBG	60173	2860 21W-11N	A4
1800	SMBG	60007	2860 20W-11N	A4
1900	EGvT	60007	2861 16W-9N	D6
1900	EGVV	60007	2861 16W-9N	D6
2400	EGVV	60007	2915 16W-9N	E1
2600	EGvT	60007	2915 16W-9N	E1
W Higgins Rd				
-	CHCG	60018	2916 13W-8N	E2
-	DSPN	60018	2916 13W-8N	E2
-	EDND	60118	2801 30W-14N	E4
-	HFET	60118	2801 30W-14N	E4
-	PKRG	60018	2917 11W-7N	D4
-	PKRG	60068	2917 11W-7N	D4
10	BrnT	60010	2803 27W-13N	A6
10	HFET	60169	2859 23W-11N	A3
10	HFET	60195	2859 23W-11N	A3
10	SBTN	60010	2803 27W-13N	B7
100	SMBG	60169	2859 23W-11N	A3
100	SMBG	60195	2859 23W-11N	A3
200	BrnT	60010	2802 28W-13N	E6
200	HFET	60010	2802 28W-13N	D5
200	HFET	60118	2802 28W-13N	D5
200	HFET	60192	2802 28W-13N	D5
200	HFET	60195	2858 23W-11N	E3
200	SBTN	60010	2802 28W-13N	E6
200	SMBG	60195	2858 24W-12N	D2
500	SMBG	60194	2858 24W-12N	D2
600	HFET	60169	2858 24W-12N	D2
600	SMBG	60169	2858 24W-12N	D2
1000	HFET	60194	2858 24W-12N	D2
1900	HFET	60169	2857 26W-12N	E1
2600	HFET	60010	2857 26W-12N	E1
2900	HFET	60010	2803 27W-12N	D7
3100	HFET	60169	2803 27W-12N	D7
7600	CHCG	60631	2918 10W-7N	B4
7700	PKRG	60068	2918 10W-7N	B4
7700	PKRG	60631	2918 10W-7N	B4
8300	CHCG	60068	2918 10W-7N	A4
8400	CHCG	60068	2917 10W-7N	E4
8400	CHCG	60631	2917 10W-7N	E4
8400	PKRG	60631	2917 10W-7N	E4
9300	CHCG	60018	2917 11W-7N	D4
9300	RSMT	60018	2917 12W-7N	D4
9300	RSMT	60068	2917 11W-7N	D4
9600	DSPN	60018	2917 12W-7N	C3
10200	CHCG	60666	2917 13W-8N	A2
10200	RSMT	60666	2917 12W-8N	A2
10700	CHCG	60666	2916 13W-8N	E2
10700	RSMT	60018	2916 13W-8N	E2
10700	RSMT	60666	2916 13W-8N	E2
W Higgins Rd SR-72				
-	CHCG	60018	2916 13W-8N	E2
-	DSPN	60018	2916 13W-8N	E2
-	EDND	60118	2801 30W-14N	E4
-	HFET	60118	2801 30W-14N	E4
-	PKRG	60018	2917 11W-7N	D4

Block	City	ZIP	Map#	CGS	Grid
W Higgins Rd SR-72					
10	BrnT	60010	2803	27W-13N	A6
10	HFET	60169	2859	23W-11N	A3
10	HFET	60195	2859	23W-11N	A3
10	SBTN	60010	2803	27W-13N	B6
100	SMBG	60169	2859	23W-11N	A3
100	SMBG	60195	2859	23W-11N	A3
200	BrnT	60010	2802	28W-13N	E6
200	HFET	60010	2802	28W-13N	E6
200	HFET	60118	2802	30W-14N	A5
200	HFET	60169	2858	25W-12N	B2
200	HFET	60192	2802	28W-13N	D5
200	HFET	60195	2858	23W-11N	E3
200	SBTN	60010	2802	28W-13N	E6
200	SMBG	60195	2858	24W-12N	D2
500	SMBG	60194	2858	24W-12N	D2
600	SMBG	60169	2858	24W-12N	D2
1000	HFET	60194	2858	24W-12N	D2
1900	HFET	60169	2857	26W-12N	E1
2600	HFET	60010	2857	26W-12N	E1
2600	HFET	60169	2803	27W-12N	D7
2900	HFET	60010	2803	27W-12N	D7
7600	CHCG	60631	2918	10W-7N	B4
7700	PKRG	60068	2918	10W-7N	B4
7700	PKRG	60631	2918	10W-7N	B4
8300	CHCG	60068	2918	10W-7N	A4
8400	CHCG	60018	2917	10W-7N	E4
8400	CHCG	60631	2917	10W-7N	E4
8400	PKRG	60068	2917	10W-7N	E4
8400	PKRG	60631	2917	10W-7N	E4
9300	CHCG	60068	2917	11W-7N	D4
9300	RSMT	60018	2917	12W-7N	C3
9300	RSMT	60068	2917	11W-7N	D4
9600	DSPN	60018	2917	12W-7N	C3
10200	CHCG	60666	2917	13W-8N	A2
10200	RSMT	60666	2917	12W-8N	A2
10700	CHCG	60666	2916	13W-8N	E2
10700	RSMT	60018	2916	13W-8N	E2
10700	RSMT	60666	2916	13W-8N	E2
Higginson Ln					
800	WNKA	60093	2812	5W-15N	A3
Higgins Quarters Dr					
1000	HFET	60169	2858	24W-11N	D3
1000	SMBG	60169	2858	24W-11N	D3
1000	SMBG	60194	2858	24W-11N	D3
E High Av					
100	HPSR	60140	2795	46W-15N	E3
High Ct					
500	WCDA	60084	2643	25W-26N	E2
High Rd					
10	CRY	60013	2695	31W-23N	D2
400	TVLY	60013	2695	31W-23N	D2
500	GNEN	60137	3025	22W-0S	B6
6700	DRN	60561	3145	16W-8S	D7
6700	WLBK	60527	3145	16W-7S	D7
6700	WLBK	60561	3145	16W-7S	D7
12900	DPgT	60441	3341	21W-15S	D2
12900	RMVL	60441	3341	21W-15S	D2
13500	LktT	60441	3341	22W-16S	D5
14500	LKPT	60441	3341	22W-16S	D4
N High Rd					
100	CRY	60013	2695	31W-23N	D1
W High Rd					
28500	GrtT	60041	2472	28W-35N	E6
High St					
-	CTPK	60827	3277	1W-15S	D7
10	HIWD	60040	2704	9W-23N	D3
10	WNKA	60093	2812	4W-14N	C3
100	WCHI	60185	3022	29W-0N	C4
200	AURA	60505	3138	35W-7S	C7
300	WCDA	60084	2643	26W-26N	D2
300	WCDA	60084	2644	25W-27N	A1
300	WcnT	60084	2644	25W-27N	A1
400	JltT	60432	3499	22W-23S	D4
500	GNVA	60134	3020	34W-1N	D2
500	JLET	60432	3499	22W-23S	D3
700	ELGN	60123	2854	34W-11N	C3
800	WLSP	60480	3209	12W-9S	C4
1800	AraT	60504	3138	34W-5S	C3
1800	AraT	60505	3138	34W-5S	C3
1800	BLID	60406	3277	2W-15S	C7
2000	BKLY	60126	3028	14W-0S	B5
2000	BKLY	60163	3028	14W-0S	B5
2000	EMHT	60126	3028	14W-0S	B5
2100	BKLY	60162	3028	14W-0S	B6
2100	EMHT	60162	3028	14W-0S	B6
E High St					
300	MDLN	60060	2646	18W-27N	E1
800	MDLN	60060	2647	18W-27N	A1
N High St					
38800	AntT	60002	2415	26W-38N	D6
W High St					
3700	MHRY	60050	2528	32W-32N	B5
25500	WCDA	60084	2644	25W-27N	A1
25500	WcnT	60084	2644	25W-27N	A1
Highbank Ct					
800	PltT	60124	2852	41W-9N	A7
High Bank Rd					
-	JLET	60421	3675	25W-30S	D3
High Bridge Ln					
4200	CHCG	60646	2920	5W-7N	A4
Highbridge Rd					
17000	CrlT	60180	2635	46W-26N	D3
17000	SenT	60180	2635	46W-26N	D3
17000	UNON	60180	2635	46W-26N	D3
Highbridge Tr					
200	MHRY	60050	2527	34W-31N	B6
Highbury Ct					
1000	ELGN	60120	2855	32W-11N	D4
Highbury Dr					
100	ELGN	60120	2855	32W-11N	C4
Highbury Ln					
500	GNVA	60134	3019	36W-1N	E2
1800	AURA	60502	3139	33W-5S	B4
1800	AURA	60505	3139	33W-5S	B4
Highbush Rd					
16800	ODPK	60467	3423	13W-20S	B4
High Chapparel Ct					
300	PltT	60124	2798	39W-13N	E7
Highcrest Dr					
400	WLMT	60091	2812	4W-13N	B6
8500	DRN	60561	3206	20W-9S	B4
Highfield Ct					
2200	AURA	60504	3201	32W-9S	B4
8000	TYPK	60477	3504	10W-23S	C3
N Highfield Dr					
18600	WrnT	60031	2476	18W-36N	E4
Highfield Dr W					
18700	LkvT	60046	2476	18W-36N	D4
18700	WrnT	60031	2476	18W-36N	D4
18700	WrnT	60046	2476	18W-36N	D4
Highfield Ln					
2200	AURA	60504	3201	32W-9S	B4
High Gate Ct					
8200	ODPK	60462	3346	10W-17S	B4
Highgate Ct					
10	SCRL	60174	2964	34W-4N	E4
600	WCHI	60185	3022	29W-1N	E3
1200	LYVL	60048	2591	17W-28N	B6
Highgate Ln					
900	GYLK	60030	2533	19W-32N	B5
Highgate Rd					
6800	CPVL	60110	2747	36W-18N	A5
Highgate Course					
10	SCRL	60174	2964	34W-4N	E4
High Gate Course					
800	GNEN	60137	3024	23W-1N	E3
S Highgoal Dr					
1200	WLNG	60090	2755	15W-16N	A7
W Highgoal Dr					
600	WLNG	60090	2755	15W-16N	A7
High Grove Blvd					
-	WLBK	60527	3146	15W-7S	A7
100	GLHT	60139	2969	22W-4N	B4
6800	BRRG	60527	3146	15W-7S	A7
High Grove Dr					
500	MNKA	60447	3672	34W-29S	A2
High Grove Ln					
1800	NPVL	60540	3140	29W-6S	C5
N High Grove Ln					
1900	PLTN	60074	2753	19W-18N	C3
High Hill Cir					
3500	CPVL	60110	2747	35W-17N	B6
High Holborn St					
100	LKFT	60045	2649	12W-26N	C4
Highknob Cir					
3700	NPVL	60564	3202	30W-11S	A7
High Knob Dr					
400	WHTN	60187	3082	25W-2S	A3
500	MltT	60187	3082	25W-2S	A3
Highknob Rd					
300	BGBK	60440	3268	24W-12S	C3
High Knoll Ct					
21500	KLDR	60047	2699	21W-21N	C6
Highlake					
-	WnfT	60185	3023	28W-0N	A4
Highlake Av					
600	WnfT	60185	3023	28W-0N	A4
Highlake Rd					
10	WnfT	60185	3023	28W-0N	B5
10	WnfT	60190	3023	28W-0N	A5
300	WNFD	60190	3023	27W-0S	C6
700	WCHI	60185	3022	29W-0N	E5
700	WnfT	60185	3022	29W-0N	E5
Highlake Rd CO-27					
10	WnfT	60185	3023	28W-0N	B5
10	WnfT	60190	3023	28W-0N	A5
300	WNFD	60190	3023	27W-0S	C6
700	WCHI	60185	3022	29W-0N	E5
700	WnfT	60185	3022	29W-0N	E5
Highland					
-	ELGN	60120	2855	32W-10N	C6
Highland Av					
-	BNHL	60102	2695	32W-21N	A7
-	CHCG	60613	2977	1W-5N	D1
-	WCHI	60185	3022	29W-1N	D3
-	WkgT	60087	2479	12W-36N	A5
-	WnfT	60185	3022	29W-1N	D3
10	ALGN	60102	2694	33W-20N	E7
10	ELGN	60123	2853	37W-12N	D2
10	ELGN	60124	2853	37W-12N	D2
10	ElgT	60123	2853	37W-12N	D2
10	ElgT	60124	2853	39W-13N	A1
10	FXLK	60020	2473	27W-36N	A3
10	PltT	60124	2798	39W-13N	D7
10	PltT	60124	2852	39W-13N	E1
10	PltT	60124	2853	39W-13N	A1
10	RtdT	60124	2798	40W-14N	C6
100	FmtT	60060	2645	21W-26N	E4
100	PGGV	60140	2798	41W-14N	B5
100	RtdT	60140	2798	40W-14N	C5
100	WLNG	60090	2755	14W-17N	C4
200	BfdT	53128	2353		A1
200	BmdT	60137	3025	22W-2N	B1
200	BmdT	60139	3025	22W-2N	B1
200	GLHT	60137	3025	22W-2N	B1
200	GLHT	60139	3025	22W-2N	B1
200	GNCY	53128	2353		B1
300	BmdT	60137	2969	22W-2N	C7
300	BmdT	60139	2969	22W-2N	C7
300	CLLK	60014	2639	36W-25N	D5
300	ELGN	60123	2854	36W-11N	A3
300	ElgT	60123	2854	36W-11N	A3
300	GLHT	60137	2969	22W-2N	C7
300	GLHT	60139	2969	22W-2N	B7
300	MltT	60139	3025	22W-1N	B2
300	NPVL	60540	3141	26W-6S	E6
300	WDSK	60098	2581	42W-30N	C1
400	ALGN	60102	2695	32W-21N	A7
400	WDND	60110	2800	34W-16N	E2
400	WDND	60118	2800	34W-16N	E2
500	ANTH	60002	2357	23W-42N	E5
500	CTWD	60445	3347	6W-15S	E1
700	TNTN	60476	3428	0E-20S	D4
800	GNEN	60137	3025	22W-0N	B3
900	AlqT	60102	2695	32W-21N	A7
900	MltT	60137	3025	22W-1N	B3
900	WCDA	60084	2644	25W-27N	B1
900	WKGN	60085	2480	10W-35N	A6
1000	LKFT	60045	2649	11W-24N	E7
1000	LKPT	60441	3419	21W-18S	E1
1000	LktT	60441	3419	21W-18S	E1
1100	LKPT	60441	3420	21W-18S	A1
1100	LktT	60441	3420	21W-18S	A1
1200	BRWN	60402	3031	7W-1S	B7
1200	WKGN	60085	2479	11W-35N	E6
1500	BRWN	60402	3089	7W-2S	B1
1500	WLMT	60091	2812	4W-13N	C6
1600	NHBK	60062	2756	11W-16N	C7
1700	CTHL	60403	3418	24W-21S	D7
1800	NfdT	60062	2756	11W-16N	C7
2600	EVTN	60201	2812	4W-13N	C7
2700	WLMT	60201	2812	4W-13N	C7
2900	DRGV	60515	3084	19W-3S	C6
2900	LMBD	60148	3084	19W-2S	C4
2900	LMBD	60515	3084	19W-2S	C4
2900	YkTp	60148	3084	19W-2S	C4
2900	YkTp	60515	3084	19W-2S	C4
3000	WLMT	60091	2811	5W-13N	E6
3400	GRNE	60031	2479	13W-36N	A5
3400	WkgT	60031	2479	13W-36N	A5
3700	GRNE	60031	2478	13W-36N	E5
3800	SKNY	60402	3089	7W-3S	B6
4300	DRGV	60515	3144	19W-5S	C2
4300	NndT	60014	2586	30W-27N	A7
4400	NndT	60014	2642	30W-27N	A1
7900	DGvT	60516	3206	19W-9S	C3
7900	DGvT	60561	3206	19W-9S	C2
7900	DRN	60561	3206	19W-9S	C2
12100	BLID	60406	3277	3W-14S	A6
14300	ODPK	60462	3345	12W-17S	C5
17100	HLCT	60429	3427	3W-20S	B5
Highland Av					
17500	BmnT	60477	3425	7W-21S	C6
17500	TYPK	60477	3425	7W-21S	C6
17700	HMWD	60430	3427	2W-21S	D6
18400	HMWD	60430	3507	2W-22S	D1
18800	BlmT	60430	3507	2W-22S	D2
Highland Av CO-9					
2900	DRGV	60515	3084	19W-3S	C6
2900	LMBD	60148	3084	19W-2S	C4
2900	LMBD	60515	3084	19W-2S	C4
2900	YkTp	60148	3084	19W-2S	C4
2900	YkTp	60515	3084	19W-2S	C4
Highland Av CO-47					
10	ELGN	60123	2853	37W-12N	D2
10	ELGN	60124	2853	37W-12N	D2
10	ElgT	60123	2853	37W-12N	D2
10	ElgT	60124	2853	39W-13N	A1
10	PltT	60124	2798	39W-13N	D7
10	PltT	60124	2852	39W-13N	E1
10	PltT	60124	2853	39W-13N	A1
10	RtdT	60124	2798	40W-14N	C5
200	RtdT	60140	2798	40W-14N	C5
E Highland Av					
10	ELGN	60120	2854	34W-11N	E4
10	ELGN	60123	2854	34W-11N	E4
10	VLPK	60181	3027	17W-0N	B4
200	ELGN	60120	2855	33W-11N	A4
200	HPSR	60140	2795	46W-15N	E3
300	HPSR	60140	2796	46W-15N	A3
400	MPPT	60056	2808	15W-13N	B5
N Highland Av					
-	ANHT	60005	2807	16W-13N	C6
-	VrnT	60004	2754	18W-18N	A2
-	VrnT	60089	2754	18W-18N	A2
10	AURA	60506	3137	36W-6S	E6
10	LMBD	60148	3026	18W-1N	E3
200	EMHT	60126	3027	16W-2N	D1
400	EMHT	60126	2971	16W-2N	D7
900	JLET	60435	3498	24W-22S	D2
1200	NARA	60506	3137	36W-5S	E3
1200	NARA	60542	3137	36W-5S	E3
1600	CTHL	60403	3498	24W-21S	D1
1900	ANHT	60004	2807	18W-16N	A1
3900	ANHT	60004	2754	18W-18N	A3
3900	BFGV	60089	2754	18W-18N	A3
S Highland Av					
-	YkTp	60148	3026	20W-0S	B7
10	ANHT	60005	2807	18W-13N	A7
10	AURA	60506	3137	36W-7S	E7
10	LMBD	60148	3026	18W-0N	E4
200	AURA	60506	3199	36W-7S	E1
500	OKPK	60302	3031	7W-0S	B5
500	OKPK	60304	3031	7W-0S	B5
600	BRTN	60010	2751	25W-18N	A3
1100	BRWN	60304	3031	7W-0S	B7
1100	BRWN	60402	3031	7W-0S	B7
1200	ANHT	60005	2861	18W-12N	A1
1200	LMBD	60148	3084	19W-2S	C3
1200	YkTp	60148	3084	19W-1S	C2
1500	ANHT	60005	2860	18W-12N	E2
25700	MonT	60449	3684	3W-32S	B6
25700	UYPK	60449	3684	3W-31S	B5
25700	UYPK	60466	3684	3W-31S	B5
W Highland Av					
10	VLPK	60181	3027	18W-0N	A4
100	ELGN	60123	2854	35W-11N	B3
1500	ElgT	60123	2854	35W-11N	B3
1600	CHCG	60660	2921	2W-7N	C3
2100	CHCG	60659	2921	2W-7N	B3
4300	CHCG	60646	2920	5W-7N	A3
6300	CHCG	60646	2919	7W-7N	A3
6500	CHCG	60631	2919	8W-7N	A3
7100	CHCG	60631	2918	8W-8N	D3
12500	WkgT	60085	2479	12W-36N	B5
12500	WkgT	60087	2479	12W-36N	B5
12700	WkgT	60031	2479	12W-36N	B5
25100	AntT	60002	2416	25W-39N	A5
Highland Blvd					
1200	HFET	60169	2858	24W-12N	E2
1200	SMBG	60169	2858	24W-12N	E2
1200	SMBG	60195	2858	24W-12N	E2
1700	HFET	60195	2858	24W-12N	D1
Highland Cir					
1100	WKGN	60085	2479	11W-35N	E6
2300	LNHT	60046	2476	19W-37N	B2
Highland Ct					
10	WDRG	60517	3205	21W-8S	D1
100	ISLK	60042	2586	29W-28N	D6
400	OSWG	60543	3263	37W-13S	B5
700	GYLK	60030	2532	21W-33N	E2
900	DRGV	60515	3144	19W-4S	C1
1000	ELGN	60123	2854	35W-11N	C3
1800	RMVL	60446	3417	27W-18S	C1
2300	SMBG	60194	2857	26W-10N	E5
3000	WPHR	60096	2363	10W-42N	A6
3400	NfdT	60025	2809	10W-13N	B4
5300	CTWD	60445	3347	6W-15S	E1
17300	HLCT	60429	3427	3W-20S	B5
S Highland Ct					
26400	CNHN	60410	3761	33W-32S	C1
Highland Dr					
-	ElaT	60047	2699	21W-23N	C2
-	HNWD	60047	2699	21W-23N	C1
-	PLTN	60067	2805	21W-14N	C4
-	SRWD	60404	3496	30W-23S	B3
-	TroT	60404	3496	30W-23S	A4
-	WLNG	60090	2754	15W-16N	E6
500	DndT	60118	2799	37W-16N	D2
500	ELGN	60118	2799	37W-16N	D2
500	ELGN	60124	2799	37W-16N	D2
700	MDLN	60060	2590	19W-28N	C6
1200	DSPN	60018	2862	13W-9N	E7
1200	PTHT	60070	2754	15W-16N	E6
1200	WLNG	60070	2754	15W-16N	E6
1300	DSPN	60018	2863	13W-9N	A7
2400	LNHT	60046	2476	19W-37N	B1
2400	RGMW	60067	2805	22W-14N	C4
2800	GNVW	60062	2809	11W-15N	E1
2800	NHBK	60062	2809	11W-15N	D1
2900	AlqT	60013	2641	32W-25N	C5
3300	ISLK	60042	2586	29W-28N	D5
4200	ZION	60099	2362	12W-41N	B7
8800	GwdT	60097	2469	38W-35N	A5
8800	WRLK	60097	2469	38W-35N	A5
11100	WldT	60564	3266	30W-13S	B4
11200	PNFD	60564	3266	30W-13S	B4
11200	PNFD	60585	3266	30W-13S	B4
E Highland Dr					
10	BtlT	60512	3262	40W-11S	C1
N Highland Dr					
800	CHHT	60411	3507	1W-24S	E6
5500	MchT	60050	2472	29W-37N	C2
S Highland Dr					
100	LKMR	60051	2529	29W-31N	D6
23500	MhtT	60442	3590	15W-28S	C7
W Highland Dr					
10	BtlT	60512	3262	40W-11S	B1
200	CHHT	60411	3507	1W-24S	E6
400	ELBN	60119	3017	43W-2N	A2
5300	MchT	60050	2527	34W-34N	C1
5500	PLTN	60067	2805	21W-14N	C4
5600	RGMW	60067	2805	21W-14N	C4
6600	PSHT	60463	3275	8W-15S	A7
21200	ElaT	60047	2699	21W-23N	D2
21200	KLDR	60047	2699	21W-23N	D2
21700	HNWD	60047	2699	21W-23N	D2
26200	CNHN	60410	3761	32W-32S	C2
Highland Dr S					
11300	PNFD	60585	3266	30W-13S	B5
Highland Ln					
900	NfdT	60025	2810	10W-13N	A6
1100	GNVW	60025	2809	10W-13N	E6
1200	GNVW	60025	2810	10W-13N	A5
5800	LKWD	60014	2638	38W-26N	D3
12700	HTLY	60142	2744	42W-19N	D3
Highland Pkwy					
3000	DRGV	60515	3084	19W-2S	C4
N Highland Pkwy					
1300	RLKB	60073	2475	22W-35N	A6
Highland Pl					
10	GLF	60029	2865	8W-12N	A1
400	HDPK	60035	2705	7W-21N	B7
600	HDPK	60035	2758	7W-20N	A1
3700	CCHL	60478	3426	4W-21S	D6
8100	MNSR	46321	3430		D6
Highland Rd					
10	DGvT	60527	3207	16W-9S	D4
10	GYLK	60030	2532	21W-33N	E2
10	IVNS	60067	2804	23W-16N	E1
100	IVNS	60067	2751	23W-16N	E7
200	MTSN	60443	3505	7W-24S	C6
300	GYLK	60030	2533	20W-33N	A2
500	HNDL	60521	3146	14W-4S	C1
800	FKFT	60423	3592	9W-26S	D2
2400	GNVA	60134	3019	37W-0N	D5
3200	NHBK	60062	2809	11W-15N	C1
4000	ZION	60099	2362	12W-42N	C7
S Highland Rd					
10500	CHRG	60415	3275	8W-12S	A2
10500	CHRG	60482	3275	8W-12S	A2
10500	WRTH	60482	3275	8W-12S	A2
W Highland Rd					
26700	CbaT	60010	2697	27W-21N	C6
Highland St					
10	CTCY	60409	3430	4E-18S	C1
10	HMND	46320	3430	4E-18S	C1
100	BMDL	60108	2913	22W-6N	C7
100	BMDL	60157	2913	22W-6N	C7
100	BmdT	60157	2913	22W-6N	C7
6600	HRPK	60133	2911	26W-8N	E3
E Highland St					
10	CTCY	60409	3430		C1
600	HMND	46320	3430		E1
W Highland St					
-	MPPT	60056	2807	15W-13N	E5
-	MPPT	60056	2808	15W-13N	A5
Highland Ter					
10	HNWD	60047	2645	21W-24N	C7
200	FmtT	60060	2646	19W-26N	C2
1700	GNVW	60025	2811	8W-14N	A4
W Highland Ter					
100	RLKB	60073	2475	23W-35N	A6
200	RLKB	60073	2474	23W-35N	E6
Highland Grove Ct N					
1000	BFGV	60089	2701	16W-21N	D7
Highland Grove Ct S					
10	BFGV	60089	2754	17W-20N	B1
Highland Grove Dr					
400	BFGV	60089	2754	16W-20N	C1
600	BFGV	60089	2701	16W-20N	D7
Highland Lake Dr					
-	LMBD	60148	3084	19W-2S	C3
Highland Park Dr					
1900	JLET	60432	3499	21W-23S	E4
1900	JLET	60432	3500	21W-23S	A4
1900	JltT	60432	3499	21W-23S	E4
2000	JltT	60432	3500	21W-23S	A4
Highlands					
1700	AlqT	60013	2642	29W-25N	C5
Highlands Dr					
-	ZION	60099	2421	12W-41N	C2
Highland Springs Dr					
-	ElgT	60123	2853	36W-12N	E3
-	JLET	60586	3496	31W-22S	A1
600	ELGN	60123	2853	36W-12N	E2
Highlands Woods Ct					
1700	JLET	60586	3496	31W-22S	A1
S Highlawn Av					
14100	RVDL	60827	3350	0W-16S	B3
Highline Rd					
5000	NndT	60012	2640	35W-27N	A2
Highlington Ct					
500	BCHR	60401	3864	0W-36S	D2
High Meadow Ct					
6500	LGGV	60047	2646	18W-24N	D7
Highmeadow Ct					
10	ALGN	60102	2747	36W-18N	B4
High Meadow Dr					
300	BLVY	60098	2526	38W-31N	A7
High Meadow Ln					
9200	BLVY	60098	2526	38W-31N	A6
Highmeadow Ln					
1600	ALGN	60102	2747	36W-18N	A4
High Meadow Rd					
500	CmpT	60175	2962	39W-4N	E4
2100	NPVL	60564	3266	29W-13S	C4
2700	WldT	60564	3266	29W-13S	C4
Highmoor Dr					
100	RLKP	60073	2532	22W-33N	A3
Highmoor Rd					
1000	LMBD	60148	3026	20W-0S	A7
1000	YkTp	60148	3026	20W-0S	A7
2200	HDPK	60035	2704	10W-22N	A3
High Pass Ln					
-	LslT	60563	3142	25W-5S	B3
High Plaine Dr					
1200	CLLK	60014	2639	37W-24N	B7
W Highplains Rd					
300	RDLK	60073	2531	23W-31N	E6
High Point Cir					
10	HNWD	60047	2645	22W-25N	B6
8300	DRN	60561	3207	17W-9S	C3
High Point Ct					
10	CmpT	60119	2961	41W-3N	E6
300	BGBK	60440	3269	22W-13S	D4
300	ROSL	60172	2913	22W-7N	B4
500	SchT	60175	2907	37W-6N	C7
1600	MTGY	60538	3199	36W-10S	E5
5400	LGGV	60047	2701	18W-23N	A2
Highpoint Ct					
700	SMBG	60193	2859	22W-9N	B7
High Point Dr					
10	HNWD	60047	2645	22W-25N	B6
300	LNHT	60046	2418	20W-38N	A7
1500	ELGN	60123	2800	34W-14N	E6
1500	ELGN	60123	2801	34W-14N	A6
1800	NPVL	60563	3142	25W-4S	A1
S Highpoint Dr					
200	RMVL	60446	3340	26W-17S	A6
200	RMVL	60544	3340	26W-17S	A6
W Highpoint Dr					
100	RMVL	60446	3340	26W-17S	A5
High Point Ln					
10	CmpT	60119	2961	41W-3N	E6
900	BRLT	60107	2856	29W-9N	D7
900	SMWD	60107	2856	29W-9N	D7
900	SMWD	60120	2856	29W-9N	C7
1200	NHBK	60062	2756	11W-17N	E5
N Highpoint Ln					
35700	GrtT	60041	2474	25W-35N	A5
E Highpoint Rd					
7200	KdlT	60560	3333	44W-17S	A7
N High Point Rd					
10	RDLK	60073	2531	24W-33N	B3
S High Point Rd					
10	RDLK	60073	2531	24W-33N	B3
W Highpoint Rd					
6800	FoxT	60560	3332	45W-16S	B4
25800	GrtT	60041	2473	25W-35N	E5
25800	GrtT	60041	2474	25W-35N	A5
High Point Tr					
100	DYR	46311	3598		D5
High Pointe Rdg					
200	ALGN	60102	2748	32W-20N	B1
Highpoint Park Ln					
19700	HFET	60169	2858	25W-12N	C1
High Rd Ct					
17500	LktT	60441	3341	22W-17S	D5
Highridge Av					
1400	WSTR	60154	3086	13W-1S	E1
High Ridge Ct					
800	DRN	60527	3145	17W-7S	C6
800	DRN	60561	3145	17W-7S	C6
High Ridge Dr					
-	AxST	60410	3672	34W-31S	A6
-	AxST	60447	3672	34W-31S	A6
800	WCHI	60185	3022	29W-1N	E3
W High Ridge Dr					
2000	RDLK	60073	2531	25W-33N	A4
20500	KLDR	60047	2700	20W-21N	A6
20600	KLDR	60047	2699	20W-21N	E6
High Ridge Ln					
10	RtdT	60140	2798	40W-15N	C3
High Ridge Pkwy					
2200	HLSD	60154	3086	13W-2S	E2
2200	HLSD	60162	3086	13W-2S	E2
2200	WSTR	60154	3086	13W-2S	E2
Highridge Pkwy					
1200	HLSD	60162	3028	13W-1S	E7
1200	WSTR	60154	3028	13W-1S	E7
1200	WSTR	60162	3028	13W-1S	E7
High Ridge Rd					
200	HLSD	60162	3028	13W-0N	D5
300	LMBD	60148	3026	19W-0S	C6
600	ROSL	60172	2913	22W-7N	C4
700	BmdT	60157	2913	22W-7N	C4
3500	CPVL	60110	2747	35W-18N	B5
Highridge Rd					
10	WLBK	60527	3145	16W-7S	D6
1000	LMBD	60148	3026	18W-0S	D6
1000	YkTp	60148	3026	18W-0S	D6
23000	CbaT	60010	2696	28W-23N	D3
23000	FRGV	60021	2696	28W-23N	D3
N High Ridge Rd					
23500	ElaT	60047	2698	23W-23N	E2
23500	LKZH	60047	2698	23W-23N	E2
23600	ElaT	60047	2699	23W-23N	A1
W Highridge Rd					
100	VLPK	60181	3027	18W-0S	A6
100	YkTp	60148	3027	18W-0S	A6
W High Ridge Tr					
13300	WDWH	60083	2420	13W-41N	E1
13300	WDWH	60083	2421	13W-41N	A1
13300	ZION	60099	2420	13W-41N	E1
High Ridge Pass					
800	CLSM	60188	2967	27W-3N	C5
High School Dr					
-	BKBN	60015	2703	11W-22N	D5
-	DRFD	60015	2703	11W-22N	D5
-	RDLK	60073	2531	23W-34N	E1
High Stone Wy					
8500	FKFT	60423	3592	10W-27S	B4
High Terrace Ln					
10	BKBN	60015	2703	12W-22N	C3
High Trail Dr					
3400	WDRG	60517	3143	22W-7S	B6
Highview Av					
10	FXLK	60020	2473	27W-36N	B4
600	AddT	60101	2970	19W-3N	D5
600	ADSN	60101	2970	19W-3N	D5
600	GNEN	60137	3025	22W-0S	C6
800	OMFD	60461	3506	4W-25S	D7
1800	MHRY	60050	2527	33W-33N	D2
16700	ODHL	60487	3423	11W-20S	E4
N Highview Av					
10	ADSN	60101	2970	18W-3N	D5
200	EMHT	60126	3027	16W-2N	D1
400	EMHT	60126	2971	16W-2N	D7
S Highview Av					
10	ADSN	60101	2970	18W-3N	D6
Highview Blvd					
700	AddT	60101	2970	19W-3N	D4
700	ADSN	60101	2970	19W-3N	D4
Highview Cir					
10	HNWD	60047	2645	20W-24N	E6
N Highview Cir					
10	HNWD	60047	2645	20W-24N	E6
S Highview Cir					
10	HNWD	60047	2645	20W-24N	E6
Highview Ct					
600	OSWG	60543	3263	38W-12S	A2
700	ANTH	60002	2357	24W-42N	C6
700	ELBN	60119	3017	43W-2N	A2
700	SchT	60175	2964	35W-5N	B3
W Highview Ct					
500	PNFD	60544	3416	30W-18S	C1
Highview Dr					
-	ANTH	60002	2357	24W-42N	C6
-	AntT	60002	2357	24W-42N	C6
10	KdlT	60560	3332	44W-17S	D6
100	LslT	60563	3142	25W-4S	B2
400	FRGV	60021	2696	29W-23N	B2
3600	NndT	60012	2586	30W-28N	A6
3700	NndT	60012	2585	30W-28N	E6
7800	MchT	60097	2526	37W-34N	C1
8000	GwdT	60097	2526	37W-34N	C1

Chicago 7-County Street Index

STREET Block	City	ZIP	Map#	CGS	Grid
N Highview Dr					
39400	AntT	60002	2415	25W-39N	E5
W Highview Dr					
700	ANTH	60002	2357	24W-42N	C6
700	AntT	60002	2357	24W-42N	C6
Highview Ln					
24400	AntT	60002	2357	25W-42N	A6
S Highview Ln					
19500	FftT	60423	3504	9W-23S	D3
Highview Rd					
12800	NLNX	60451	3590	16W-27S	A4
12800	NlxT	60451	3590	16W-27S	A4
28300	WcnT	60051	2587	28W-28N	A6
Highview St					
2300	SPGV	60081	2413	31W-39N	D4
Highview Ter					
600	LKFT	60045	2650	10W-25N	B4
Highwood Av					
-	HIWD	60035	2704	9W-23N	D2
10	HIWD	60040	2704	9W-23N	C2
300	HDPK	60035	2704	9W-23N	C2
Highwood Ct					
2300	AURA	60503	3201	32W-10S	B6
17100	ODPK	60467	3422	14W-20S	D4
Highwood Dr					
17100	ODPK	60467	3422	14W-20S	D5
S Highwood Dr					
11500	PSPK	60464	3274	10W-13S	B5
Highwood Ln					
4700	LIHL	60156	2692	38W-23N	D2
Highwood Rd					
1800	NndT	60051	2586	29W-29N	C4
2600	ISLK	60042	2586	29W-29N	C4
2600	ISLK	60051	2586	29W-29N	C4
N Highwood Rd					
21000	KLDR	60047	2699	22W-21N	C7
Highwoods Ct					
10	CmpT	60119	2962	41W-3N	A6
W Highwoods Dr					
24500	LkvT	60046	2416	24W-39N	B4
24900	AntT	60046	2416	24W-39N	B4
25100	AntT	60002	2416	25W-39N	A4
Higley Ct					
21600	FKFT	60423	3591	12W-26S	C2
Higley Ln					
21600	FKFT	60423	3591	12W-26S	C2
W Hilandale Ct					
21500	KLDR	60047	2699	21W-22N	C3
N Hilandale Ln					
22800	ElaT	60047	2699	21W-22N	D3
22800	KLDR	60047	2699	21W-22N	D3
Hilary Ln					
900	AlqT	60013	2642	30W-25N	B4
1100	HDPK	60035	2704	9W-22N	C5
Hilbrich Ct					
600	DYR	46311	3598		E4
600	SjnT	46311	3598		E4
Hilda Av					
36500	LkvT	60046	2475	21W-36N	D4
N Hilda Ln					
36800	LkvT	60046	2475	21W-36N	D3
Hildago Ct					
-	RNPK	60443	3593	7W-27S	C4
Hildago Dr					
-	RNPK	60443	3593	7W-27S	C4
Hilgers Ct					
2300	MDLN	60060	2646	18W-25N	E5
2300	VNHL	60060	2646	18W-25N	E5
N Hilgers Ct					
25500	MDLN	60060	2646	18W-25N	E5
25500	VNHL	60060	2646	18W-25N	E5
Hiline Av					
2800	NndT	60050	2585	30W-29N	E5
Hilkert Ct					
300	CLLK	60014	2639	35W-25N	E4
Hill Av					
-	LMBD	60148	3026	21W-0N	A4
-	MTGY	60503	3200	34W-9S	E4
-	MTGY	60504	3200	34W-9S	E4
-	OswT	60503	3200	34W-9S	E4
-	OswT	60543	3200	34W-9S	E4
10	AURA	60504	3200	34W-8S	D2
10	AURA	60505	3200	34W-8S	D2
100	AraT	60504	3200	34W-9S	E4
100	AraT	60505	3200	34W-9S	E3
100	AraT	60538	3200	34W-9S	E4
100	GNEN	60137	3025	23W-0S	A6
100	LMBD	60137	3025	21W-0N	E5
100	LMBD	60148	3025	21W-0N	E5
100	MltT	60137	3025	21W-0N	E5
100	MTGY	60505	3200	34W-9S	E4
100	NARA	60542	3078	35W-3S	A7
100	WHTN	60137	3025	23W-0S	A6
100	WHTN	60187	3025	23W-0S	A6
200	BRLT	60103	2911	28W-7N	A5
200	MTGY	60538	3200	34W-9S	E4
200	OswT	60504	3200	34W-9S	E4
200	OswT	60538	3200	34W-9S	E4
300	EMHT	60126	3028	15W-0N	A4
800	ELGN	60120	2855	33W-12N	A1
1300	WHTN	60187	3024	23W-0S	E6
N Hill Av					
26000	WcnT	60084	2644	25W-26N	A3
W Hill Av					
-	WKGN	60031	2535	14W-33N	C4
4400	WKGN	60085	2535	14W-33N	D4
4400	WrnT	60031	2535	14W-33N	D4
Hill Cir					
600	GNVW	60025	2811	7W-13N	A7
Hill Ct					
10	SchT	60177	2908	34W-7N	D4
10	SEGN	60177	2908	34W-7N	D4
100	WCHI	60185	3022	29W-2N	C1
100	WynT	60185	2966	29W-4N	E4
200	ISLK	60042	2586	28W-28N	E6
300	ANTH	60002	2357	23W-43N	E5
400	CNHL	60514	3145	17W-6S	C4
400	PTHT	60070	2808	15W-15N	A2
400	WCDA	60084	2588	25W-27N	B7
400	WCDA	60084	2644	25W-27N	B1
N Hill Ct					
34100	AvnT	60073	2531	24W-34N	C1
Hill Ct E					
300	BFGV	60089	2701	16W-20N	D7
Hill Ct W					
300	BFGV	60089	2701	16W-20N	D7
Hill Dr					
-	ALSP	60463	3275	7W-15S	D7
-	ALSP	60803	3275	7W-15S	D7
-	CTWD	60445	3275	7W-15S	D7
-	WhtT	60445	3275	7W-15S	D7
-	WhtT	60463	3275	7W-15S	D7
10	CLLK	60014	2640	35W-25N	B4
500	HFET	60169	2858	24W-11N	D3
700	SMBG	60169	2858	24W-11N	D3
700	SMBG	60194	2858	24W-11N	D3
Hill Dr					
4000	ZION	60099	2362	12W-41N	C7
7900	MchT	60097	2469	36W-37N	C2
N Hill Dr					
400	NBRN	60010	2698	25W-23N	A1
S Hill Dr					
-	ODHL	60467	3423	12W-19S	D3
-	OrlT	60467	3423	12W-19S	D3
W Hill Dr					
27600	AntT	60081	2415	27W-39N	B6
27800	FXLK	60081	2415	27W-39N	B6
Hill Ln					
2200	BTVA	60510	3077	37W-2S	C3
3100	WLMT	60091	2811	6W-13N	D6
Hill Rd					
10	FXLK	60020	2473	27W-36N	B4
100	WLBK	60527	3146	15W-7S	A6
400	DGvT	60439	3206	19W-11S	C7
400	DGvT	60439	3270	19W-11S	C1
600	WNKA	60093	2812	5W-15N	A3
900	NtrT	60093	2812	5W-15N	A3
1000	GNVA	60134	3020	34W-1N	E3
1100	NtrT	60093	2811	5W-14N	E3
1100	WNKA	60093	2811	5W-14N	E3
1200	NHFD	60093	2811	5W-14N	E3
1400	GNVA	60134	3021	33W-1N	A3
1400	GNVA	60185	3021	33W-1N	A3
1400	GnvT	60185	3021	33W-1N	A3
4300	RcmT	60071	2412	33W-41N	E1
4300	RcmT	60071	2413	33W-41N	A1
4300	RHMD	60071	2412	33W-41N	E1
7000	RlyT	60152	2634	49W-24N	D7
8000	FftT	60423	3504	10W-25S	C7
8300	FKFT	60423	3504	10W-25S	C7
25200	CnhT	60447	3583	31W-27S	E6
25200	TroT	60447	3583	31W-27S	E6
N Hill Rd					
100	MchT	60051	2529	30W-32N	A5
W Hill Rd					
600	DndT	60118	2747	35W-18N	C4
600	PLTN	60067	2752	21W-17N	C4
600	PLTN	60074	2752	21W-17N	C4
600	PltT	60067	2752	21W-17N	C4
Hill St					
-	CRTE	60417	3685	1W-30S	B3
10	BmdT	60172	2913	23W-7N	A5
10	ROSL	60172	2913	23W-7N	A5
100	CRY	60013	2695	30W-23N	E1
100	WLSP	60480	3209	12W-9S	C3
300	EDND	60118	2801	33W-16N	A2
300	WCDA	60084	2644	25W-27N	A1
400	DRGV	60515	3144	19W-5S	D3
400	WCDA	60084	2588	25W-27N	B7
500	HDPK	60035	2704	9W-24N	C1
600	WKGN	60085	2537	10W-33N	B3
800	JLET	60433	3499	22W-25S	C7
800	JltT	60433	3499	22W-25S	C7
3000	WLMT	60091	2811	5W-13N	E6
E Hill St					
10	VLPK	60181	3027	17W-1N	B2
10	YkTp	60181	3027	17W-1N	B2
100	WhlT	60056	2808	13W-13N	E6
300	YkTp	60126	3027	17W-1N	B2
400	MPPT	60056	2808	15W-13N	B6
500	BRTN	60010	2751	25W-18N	A3
N Hill St					
300	WDSK	60098	2524	42W-31N	C7
S Hill St					
100	WDSK	60098	2524	42W-31N	C7
100	WDSK	60098	2581	42W-31N	C1
W Hill St					
100	CHCG	60610	3034	0W-1N	A2
1300	PltT	60067	2752	22W-17N	B4
5700	MchT	60050	2527	34W-33N	C2
5700	MHRY	60050	2527	34W-33N	C2
Hill Ter					
500	WNKA	60093	2812	4W-15N	B3
S Hill Ter					
9900	PSHL	60465	3210	10W-11S	B7
Hillandale Ct					
100	NBRN	60010	2698	25W-22N	A4
Hillandale Dr					
100	BMDL	60108	2968	23W-5N	E2
400	BRLT	60103	2911	28W-7N	A4
800	ANTH	60002	2357	24W-42N	D6
N Hillandale Dr					
38500	AntT	60081	2415	27W-38N	B7
Hillandale Rd					
9600	RcmT	60071	2353	33W-41N	E7
9600	RcmT	60071	2412	33W-41N	E1
Hillandale St					
200	RDLK	60073	2531	23W-33N	E2
Hillard Dr					
-	ELGN	60120	2856	31W-10N	A7
Hillary Ct					
3100	JLET	60435	3417	28W-19S	B3
Hillary Ln					
15000	HMGN	60441	3342	19W-17S	D6
15000	HmrT	60441	3342	19W-17S	D6
15000	HmrT	60491	3342	19W-17S	D6
W Hillberry Ct					
800	LGNG	60525	3147	13W-5S	A2
Hillbrook Ln					
3000	AURA	60502	3079	33W-3S	A6
Hillburn Ct					
10	NBRN	60010	2644	25W-24N	A7
Hillburn Ln					
10	NBRN	60010	2644	25W-24N	A7
Hill Creek Ct					
17100	ODPK	60467	3422	14W-20S	E4
S Hillcreek Dr					
12600	PSPK	60464	3274	11W-14S	A7
Hill Crest Av					
700	PKCY	60085	2536	12W-33N	B3
Hillcrest Av					
-	AntT	60002	2356	26W-42N	D6
-	PKCY	60085	2536	12W-33N	B3
10	CHHT	60411	3508	0W-24S	B6
10	FXLK	60020	2473	27W-36N	B4
10	GNEN	60137	3025	23W-0S	B7
100	HNDL	60521	3146	14W-5S	C2
200	AddT	60101	2971	17W-3N	B4
200	ADSN	60101	2971	17W-3N	B4
200	HPSR	60140	2795	46W-15N	E3
200	YKVL	60560	3261	43W-14S	C7
300	HPSR	60140	2796	46W-15N	A3
400	BRTN	60010	2751	25W-18N	A3
500	SchT	60174	2908	35W-6N	B7
600	BmdT	60181	2913	21W-6N	E6
600	ITSC	60143	2913	21W-6N	E6
1000	HDPK	60035	2704	10W-21N	B6
1100	FRGV	60021	2695	30W-22N	E4
1100	FRGV	60021	2696	30W-22N	A3
1400	HRPK	60133	2911	26W-8N	E2
1400	NCHI	60064	2536	12W-32N	B5
5400	LslT	60515	3143	21W-6S	E4
Hillcrest Av					
5400	LslT	60516	3143	21W-6S	E4
8600	GfnT	60014	2639	37W-24N	B6
25600	AntT	60002	2416	25W-40N	A3
E Hillcrest Av					
100	AddT	60191	2915	17W-6N	B6
100	WDDL	60191	2915	17W-6N	B6
S Hillcrest Av					
500	EMHT	60126	3028	15W-0N	B5
600	FXLK	60020	2473	27W-35N	B6
600	FXLK	60041	2473	27W-35N	B6
600	GrtT	60020	2473	27W-35N	B6
900	YkTp	60126	3028	15W-0S	B6
W Hillcrest Av					
28500	CbaT	60013	2642	28W-24N	E7
Hillcrest Blvd					
10	HFET	60169	2859	23W-12N	A1
10	HFET	60195	2859	23W-12N	A1
10	SMBG	60173	2859	23W-12N	A1
10	SMBG	60195	2859	23W-12N	A1
300	HFET	60169	2858	24W-12N	D1
Hillcrest Cir					
9700	ODPK	60467	3423	12W-19S	D2
Hillcrest Ct					
10	OswT	60538	3199	37W-10S	C7
100	BRTN	60010	2751	24W-18N	C3
100	PltT	60010	2751	24W-18N	C3
500	HFET	60169	2858	24W-12N	E1
600	WDND	60118	2800	34W-16N	E2
1500	LMBD	60148	3084	20W-1S	B1
5900	DRGV	60516	3144	20W-6S	B5
8900	WDRG	60517	3206	20W-10S	C6
N Hillcrest Ct					
2200	RLKB	60073	2474	23W-36N	E4
Hill Crest Dr					
900	CLSM	60188	2967	27W-3N	C5
Hillcrest Dr					
-	SYHW	60118	2800	35W-16N	B3
-	WLNG	60090	2808	15W-15N	B2
10	ALGN	60102	2694	33W-21N	E6
10	BRRG	60527	3146	14W-7S	C6
10	ElaT	60047	2700	20W-23N	A1
10	HNWD	60047	2700	20W-23N	A1
10	SgrT	60506	3135	41W-5S	E3
100	BRTN	60010	2751	24W-18N	C3
100	HshT	60140	2743	46W-19N	A3
100	PltT	60010	2751	24W-18N	C3
400	PTHT	60070	2808	15W-15N	A2
500	BfdT	53128	2353		A1
500	BGBK	60440	3268	24W-13S	D4
500	SMBG	60193	2913	22W-8N	B2
500	SmbT	60193	2913	22W-8N	B2
600	LYVL	60048	2591	17W-29N	B4
700	RMVL	60446	3268	24W-14S	E7
700	WDND	60118	2800	35W-15N	D3
2500	DYR	46311	3598		D3
6800	DRGV	60516	3144	20W-7S	B7
6800	NndT	60012	2640	35W-27N	A1
6900	NndT	60012	2639	35W-27N	E1
8200	PlsT	60462	3346	10W-15S	B2
8200	PSHT	60462	3346	10W-15S	B2
8200	PSHT	60464	3346	10W-15S	B2
8500	ODPK	60462	3346	10W-15S	B2
11800	LMNT	60439	3271	18W-14S	B6
16300	TYPK	60477	3424	10W-19S	C3
16400	MKHM	60428	3426	4W-19S	E3
16600	HLCT	60428	3426	4W-19S	E3
16600	HLCT	60429	3426	4W-19S	E3
17600	CCHL	60478	3426	4W-21S	E6
E Hillcrest Dr					
5700	RHMD	60071	2353	34W-41N	C7
W Hillcrest Dr					
500	PNFD	60544	3338	30W-16S	C4
10500	PlsT	60464	3345	13W-15S	B2
23200	ElaT	60047	2698	23W-23N	E1
23200	ElaT	60047	2699	23W-23N	A2
23400	ElaT	60047	2700	20W-23N	A2
Hillcrest Ln					
100	BRLT	60103	2910	28W-8N	E3
100	BRLT	60103	2911	28W-8N	A3
200	CRTE	60417	3596	0W-28S	C6
300	LMBD	60148	3084	20W-1S	B1
500	LNHT	60046	2476	20W-37N	B2
600	DGvT	60439	3270	19W-12S	C3
700	CLLK	60014	2641	33W-24N	A6
1100	WDRG	60517	3206	20W-11S	A7
2800	NHBK	60062	2756	11W-17N	E6
5500	LslT	60532	3142	23W-6S	E4
8000	TYPK	60477	3424	10W-19S	C3
W Hillcrest Ln					
9000	PSPK	60464	3273	11W-14S	E6
9000	PSPK	60464	3274	11W-14S	A6
Hillcrest Pk					
1700	SYHW	60118	2800	35W-15N	D3
Hillcrest Pl					
3700	JNBG	60050	2471	31W-35N	D5
Hillcrest Rd					
-	DrrT	60098	2582	39W-29N	D3
-	WDSK	60098	2582	39W-29N	D4
10	AlqT	60013	2641	31W-25N	D4
10	ODHL	60013	2641	31W-25N	D4
600	WnfT	60185	3022	28W-1N	E2
600	WynT	60185	3022	28W-1N	E2
900	ELGN	60123	2800	34W-13N	C7
900	ELGN	60123	2854	35W-13N	C1
1000	GLNC	60022	2758	6W-18N	D3
1000	JLET	60433	3499	21W-24S	E5
1000	JltT	60433	3499	21W-24S	E5
1800	JltT	60432	3500	21W-23S	A4
1800	JltT	60433	3500	21W-23S	A4
3100	GNVA	60134	3019	37W-1N	C2
5600	DRGV	60516	3144	20W-6S	B4
14200	LMNT	60439	3271	17W-13S	B4
S Hillcrest Rd					
14300	HMGN	60491	3343	18W-17S	A5
30300	BCHR	60401	3864	0W-37S	D2
30300	WshT	60401	3864	0W-37S	D2
W Hillcrest Rd					
600	PltT	60074	2752	21W-18N	C2
Hillcrest Ter					
10	BmdT	60157	2913	22W-6N	C7
100	BMDL	60108	2913	23W-6N	B7
100	BMDL	60157	2913	23W-6N	B7
500	RLKP	60073	2532	22W-34N	B2
W Hilldale Av					
25200	AntT	60002	2416	25W-39N	A4
Hill Dale Dr					
35000	GrtT	60041	2473	27W-35N	B7
Hilldale Dr					
-	SCRL	60175	2907	36W-6N	E7
-	SCRL	60175	2963	36W-6N	E1
-	SCRL	60175	2964	36W-6N	A1
Hilldale Ln					
10	PTBR	60010	2642	29W-26N	C3
900	BFGV	60089	2701	16W-21N	D7
2100	GLHT	60139	2969	23W-4N	B4
Hilldale Pl					
200	LKFT	60045	2650	10W-25N	A6
Hilldale Rd					
10	FXLK	60020	2473	28W-36N	A4
Hiller Dr					
-	HmrT	60491	3421	17W-18S	B1
Hiller Ridge Rd					
2400	JNBG	60050	2471	31W-37N	D2
2500	JNBG	60081	2471	31W-37N	D2
2500	MchT	60081	2471	31W-37N	D2
N Hillfarm Ct					
23700	LKBN	60010	2697	27W-23N	C1
N Hillfarm Rd					
23600	LKBN	60010	2697	27W-23N	B1
Hillgate Rd					
19900	FftT	60448	3502	14W-24S	D5
19900	MKNA	60448	3502	14W-24S	D5
Hillgrove Av					
10	LGNG	60525	3087	13W-3S	A6
10	WNSP	60525	3087	13W-3S	A6
10	WNSP	60558	3086	14W-4S	D7
10	WNSP	60558	3087	13W-3S	A6
400	HNDL	60521	3146	15W-4S	B1
1100	WNSP	60558	3146	14W-4S	C1
E Hillgrove Av					
10	LGNG	60525	3087	12W-4S	C6
W Hillgrove Av					
10	LGNG	60525	3087	12W-4S	B7
1400	WNSP	60525	3087	13W-4S	A7
1400	WNSP	60558	3087	13W-4S	A7
Hill Grove Ct					
16100	WDWH	60083	2419	16W-39N	E4
Hillhurst Dr					
10	CRY	60013	2696	30W-23N	A1
300	CRY	60013	2642	30W-24N	A7
Hillman Ct					
10	WKGN	60085	2536	11W-34N	D1
Hill N Dale Ct					
200	GRNE	60031	2534	16W-34N	D2
S Hillock Av					
2500	CHCG	60608	3091	1W-2S	D3
Hills Av					
300	JLET	60432	3499	23W-22S	A1
1500	DSPN	60016	2863	13W-11N	A3
Hills & Dales Rd					
10	BNHL	60010	2750	27W-17N	B5
Hillsboro Blvd					
2400	AURA	60503	3201	32W-10S	C6
Hillsboro Ct					
2200	AURA	60503	3201	32W-10S	C6
2900	SCRL	60175	2963	37W-3N	C7
Hillsboro Dr					
1200	BTVA	60510	3078	33W-2S	E4
Hillsboro Ln					
2200	NPVL	60564	3202	29W-10S	D6
2400	MTGY	60538	3198	40W-10S	C7
2700	LIHL	60156	2692	38W-22N	E3
Hillsborough Ct					
1200	CLLK	60014	2693	36W-23N	D1
S Hillsdale Ct					
14200	PnfT	60544	3339	27W-16S	D5
S Hillsdale Ln					
14100	PnfT	60544	3339	27W-16S	C4
Hillsdale Rd					
100	JLET	60433	3499	22W-24S	D5
100	JltT	60433	3499	22W-24S	D5
10700	CTSD	60525	3147	13W-7S	A7
Hillshire Ct					
100	IVNS	60010	2751	25W-17N	A5
Hillshire Dr					
10	BRTN	60010	2751	25W-17N	A5
10	IVNS	60010	2751	25W-17N	A5
E Hillshire Dr					
4300	RcmT	60071	2353	33W-41N	E7
4300	RcmT	60071	2354	33W-41N	A7
W Hillshire Dr					
9600	RcmT	60071	2353	33W-41N	E7
Hillside Av					
-	BtnT	60099	2422	9W-41N	C2
-	ZION	60099	2422	9W-41N	C2
10	FXLK	60020	2473	27W-36N	A3
10	GYLK	60030	2532	21W-33N	E3
10	PTHT	60070	2808	15W-15N	A2
200	AURA	60505	3138	33W-7S	E7
200	WHTN	60137	3025	23W-0N	A5
500	ANTH	60002	2357	24W-41N	D7
500	AntT	60002	2357	24W-42N	D6
600	WcnT	60084	2644	25W-26N	B2
700	GNEN	60137	3025	22W-0N	D5
800	MltT	60137	3025	21W-0N	D5
1000	DRFD	60015	2703	11W-21N	D6
1000	NCHI	60044	2593	11W-29N	D3
1000	ShdT	60044	2593	11W-29N	D3
3000	WKGN	60085	2536	12W-33N	B2
15100	OKFT	60452	3347	7W-18S	C6
17100	HLCT	60429	3427	3W-20S	B5
17500	HMWD	60430	3427	2W-21S	C5
E Hillside Av					
100	BRTN	60010	2750	26W-18N	D2
100	BRTN	60010	2751	25W-18N	A3
N Hillside Av					
10	NHLK	60164	3028	14W-2N	D1
10	PvsT	60162	3028	14W-0S	D6
100	NHLK	60164	2972	14W-2N	D7
700	HLSD	60162	3028	14W-0N	D4
800	BKLY	60162	3028	14W-0N	D4
800	BKLY	60163	3028	14W-0N	D4
35500	AvnT	60073	2474	24W-35N	C6
39300	AntT	60002	2415	26W-39N	E5
S Hillside Av					
100	NHLK	60164	3028	14W-1N	D1
500	EMHT	60126	3027	16W-0N	D5
W Hillside Av					
100	BRTN	60010	2750	25W-18N	E3
300	EMHT	60126	3027	16W-0N	D3
25700	GrtT	60041	2474	25W-35N	A5
S Hillside Cir					
10	PSPK	60464	3274	10W-14S	B6
Hillside Ct					
10	FXLK	60020	2473	27W-37N	A2
200	LKZH	60047	2698	23W-22N	E4
200	WHTN	60187	3024	24W-0S	D7
300	SMBG	60193	2859	23W-9N	B7
400	SMWD	60107	2857	28W-10N	B5
500	BRTN	60010	2751	24W-18N	B3
600	BmdT	60157	2913	22W-6N	D5
600	ROSL	60157	2913	22W-6N	D6
700	ALGN	60102	2747	35W-19N	D2
900	BRLT	60103	2911	27W-7N	C5
1700	GRNE	60031	2477	17W-35N	A5
3000	DRN	60561	3206	20W-9S	B4
3300	WDRG	60517	3143	22W-7S	C7
3500	HFET	60192	2804	24W-14N	D4
4500	CLLK	60012	2640	34W-27N	B1
4500	NndT	60012	2584	34W-27N	B7
4500	NndT	60012	2640	34W-27N	B1
Hillside Ct					
16600	LKPT	60441	3342	20W-17S	B6
Hillside Dr					
-	DndT	60118	2801	33W-14N	B5
-	HRVD	60033	2406	50W-39N	B5
-	HYHL	60457	3210	10W-10S	A4
-	HYHL	60458	3210	10W-10S	A4
-	JSTC	60458	3210	10W-10S	A4
-	TYPK	60477	3504	9W-23S	E3
10	FXLK	60020	2473	27W-36N	A4
10	KdlT	60560	3332	44W-17S	D6
10	LKBN	60010	2696	28W-22N	E4
10	SchT	60175	2964	35W-6N	B1
100	BGBK	60440	3268	24W-11S	C1
200	ISLK	60042	2586	29W-28N	D5
300	ROSL	60172	2913	23W-7N	B4
300	SMWD	60107	2857	28W-10N	B5
400	DYR	46311	3598		D4
400	HDPK	60035	2758	7W-20N	A1
400	MDLN	60060	2646	19W-27N	C2
600	DGvT	60521	3145	16W-6S	E3
900	FmtT	60060	2646	19W-27N	C2
1100	NlxT	60451	3501	16W-23S	E4
3100	WRLK	60097	2469	36W-35N	C7
7200	SPGV	60081	2413	32W-39N	B5
14900	LKPT	60441	3342	20W-17S	B6
22100	RNPK	60471	3594	6W-26S	A3
31700	WcnT	60051	2529	28W-31N	D6
E Hillside Dr					
300	BNVL	60106	2916	15W-5N	A7
300	CHCG	60106	2916	15W-5N	A7
N Hillside Dr					
23300	CbaT	60010	2696	28W-23N	E2
37100	LkvT	60046	2474	25W-37N	A2
S Hillside Dr					
8400	PSPK	60464	3274	10W-14S	B7
W Hillside Dr					
-	WDDL	60191	2915	17W-6N	C7
100	RDLK	60073	2532	23W-34N	A1
300	BNVL	60106	2915	16W-6N	D7
5300	MchT	60050	2527	34W-34N	C1
24300	AvnT	60073	2474	24W-35N	C6
24300	RLKB	60073	2474	24W-35N	C6
Hillside Ln					
-	AntT	60002	2417	22W-41N	B1
10	FmtT	60060	2645	21W-26N	D4
100	DGvT	60527	3207	16W-10S	D5
300	EDND	60118	2801	33W-15N	A3
1000	MHRY	60051	2528	31W-32N	D4
1100	MchT	60051	2528	31W-33N	D3
1900	LSLE	60532	3142	23W-6S	E5
2600	EVTN	60201	2812	4W-13N	B7
2900	DRN	60561	3206	20W-9S	B4
11400	MKNA	60448	3502	14W-22S	D2
Hillside Pl					
300	NARA	60542	3077	36W-4S	E7
5700	TYPK	60477	3425	7W-20S	C3
Hillside Rd					
100	HbnT	53147	2350		B3
100	HbnT	60034	2350		B3
100	LinT	53147	2350	42W-43N	B4
300	NLNX	60451	3501	18W-24S	B6
300	NlxT	60451	3501	18W-24S	A6
400	JltT	60433	3587	23W-26S	B2
600	MaiT	60025	2809	10W-13N	E7
600	NfdT	60025	2809	10W-13N	E7
800	DrrT	60098	2524	42W-31N	A6
800	WDSK	60098	2524	42W-31N	A6
900	NHBK	60062	2757	9W-17N	C5
1100	ELGN	60123	2800	34W-13N	E7
3500	EVTN	60201	2812	4W-13N	B7
E Hillside Rd					
10	NPVL	60540	3141	26W-7S	D6
100	BRTN	60010	2751	23W-18N	E3
100	PltT	60010	2751	23W-18N	E3
200	PltT	60010	2752	23W-18N	A3
600	LslT	60540	3141	26W-7S	E6
1000	LslT	60540	3142	26W-7S	A6
1000	NPVL	60540	3142	26W-7S	A6
5100	NndT	60012	2584	34W-27N	C7
5400	NndT	60012	2640	34W-27N	C1
5700	CLLK	60012	2640	34W-27N	B1
S Hillside Rd					
21100	FftT	60423	3504	10W-25S	C7
21100	FftT	60423	3592	10W-25S	C1
W Hillside Rd					
10	NPVL	60540	3141	27W-7S	C6
6200	CLLK	60012	2640	35W-27N	A1
6200	NndT	60012	2640	35W-27N	A1
6900	NndT	60012	2639	35W-27N	E1
7200	NndT	60012	2583	36W-27N	E7
7700	NndT	60098	2583	36W-27N	C7
7900	DrrT	60012	2583	36W-27N	C7
Hillside St					
10	CPVL	60110	2800	34W-16N	E2
10	CPVL	60118	2800	34W-16N	E2
10	WDND	60110	2800	34W-16N	E2
10	WDND	60118	2800	34W-16N	E2
W Hillside St					
800	PLTN	60067	2805	22W-15N	C1
800	PltT	60067	2805	22W-15N	B1
Hillside Ter					
1800	AlqT	60013	2695	30W-22N	E3
1800	CRY	60013	2695	30W-22N	E3
Hillside Tr					
1900	AlqT	60013	2695	31W-22N	E3
1900	CRY	60013	2695	31W-22N	E3
Hill Side View Dr					
700	ALGN	60102	2747	34W-20N	D2
Hills Oak Ct					
2200	LSLE	60187	3082	24W-3S	D6
Hillstone Rd					
10	OswT	60538	3199	37W-10S	C6
Hilltop Av					
10	FXLK	60020	2472	28W-36N	E3
10	FXLK	60020	2473	28W-36N	A3
100	BRTN	60010	2751	24W-20N	B2
1200	BlmT	60411	3507	2W-25S	C7
1200	CHHT	60411	3507	2W-25S	C7
1500	CHHT	60411	3595	2W-25S	C1
1900	ZION	60099	2422	9W-41N	C2
16700	ODHL	60487	3424	11W-20S	A4
41400	BtnT	60099	2422	9W-41N	C2
N Hilltop Av					
38500	AntT	60002	2415	26W-38N	D7
Hilltop Blvd					
600	MHRY	60050	2528	32W-31N	C7
600	NndT	60050	2528	32W-31N	C7
1000	MHRY	60050	2585	32W-30N	C1
Hilltop Ct					
10	HNWD	60047	2700	19W-23N	B1
10	LMNT	60439	3270	18W-13S	E5
100	SYHW	60118	2800	36W-15N	A3
200	LKBN	60010	2643	26W-24N	D7
400	SMBG	60193	2858	24W-10N	E5
1800	NPVL	60565	3204	25W-9S	C4

STREET Block	City	ZIP	Map#	CGS Grid	
Hilltop Ct					
1900	WDSK	60098	2524	41W-32N	D4
15100	ODPK	60462	3345	12W-18S	B6
18300	TYPK	60487	3424	11W-22S	A7
Hilltop Dr					
-	HmrT	60448	3421	17W-21S	D7
10	ALGN	60102	2694	35W-21N	B5
10	LIHL	60102	2694	35W-21N	B5
10	LIHL	60156	2694	35W-21N	B5
10	SMBG	60193	2858	24W-10N	E6
10	SMBG	60194	2858	24W-10N	E6
100	MchT	60050	2472	29W-37N	D2
300	BtvT	60539	3077	36W-3S	E7
300	BtvT	60542	3077	36W-3S	E7
300	NARA	60542	3077	36W-3S	E7
300	SchT	60175	2963	38W-3N	A6
600	ITSC	60143	2913	21W-7N	E5
1000	LMNT	60439	3270	19W-13S	E5
1000	LMNT	60439	3271	18W-13S	A5
3100	WRLK	60097	2469	37W-34N	C7
4100	JNBG	60050	2472	30W-36N	A4
4400	MchT	60097	2469	36W-36N	D4
10200	ODPK	60462	3345	12W-18S	B6
N Hilltop Dr					
900	BmdT	60143	2913	21W-7N	E5
900	BmdT	60157	2913	21W-7N	E5
900	ITSC	60143	2913	21W-7N	E4
1000	ITSC	60157	2913	21W-7N	E4
4400	JNBG	60050	2472	30W-36N	A4
4400	MchT	60050	2472	30W-36N	A4
W Hilltop Dr					
10	CmpT	60175	2962	39W-3N	E6
10	CmpT	60175	2963	38W-3N	A6
25700	GrtT	60041	2473	25W-34N	E7
25700	GrtT	60041	2474	25W-34N	A7
Hilltop Ln					
100	SYHW	60118	2800	36W-15N	A4
800	GNCY	53128	2352		E3
1800	BKBN	60015	2703	12W-23N	B3
5500	WKGN	60048	2535	15W-32N	A5
9800	AlqT	60010	2695	30W-22N	E4
9800	AlqT	60021	2695	30W-22N	E4
9800	BNHL	60010	2695	30W-22N	E4
Hilltop Rd					
10	AlqT	60013	2641	31W-26N	E4
10	ElgT	60124	2853	37W-11N	D3
10	ODHL	60013	2641	31W-26N	E4
100	ELGN	60124	2853	37W-11N	D3
1700	HnrT	60120	2856	31W-11N	A3
2000	HFET	60169	2804	24W-12N	C7
4200	LGGV	60047	2700	18W-22N	E4
5200	LGGV	60047	2701	18W-22N	A4
8000	KdlT	60560	3334	40W-16S	B4
38600	AntT	60002	2415	26W-38N	D6
S Hilltop Rd					
25700	CteT	60417	3687	3E-31S	A5
Hilltop St					
200	WLSP	60480	3209	12W-9S	B4
N Hilltop Ter					
28300	FmtT	60047	2589	22W-28N	C6
28300	FmtT	60060	2589	22W-28N	C6
Hill Trail Dr					
4700	LSLE	60532	3142	24W-5S	C2
Hillview Av					
10	WCHI	60185	3022	29W-0N	D4
10	WnfT	60185	3022	29W-0N	D4
200	WnfT	60185	3023	28W-0N	A4
Hillview Ct					
-	HNWD	60047	2645	21W-25N	D4
-	HNWD	60060	2645	21W-25N	D4
10	KdlT	60560	3332	44W-17S	D6
400	LMNT	60439	3270	19W-14S	E6
600	WCHI	60185	3022	29W-0N	D5
25600	ElaT	60060	2645	21W-25N	D5
Hillview Dr					
10	LKBN	60010	2696	28W-22N	E4
10	WldT	60564	3203	28W-10S	A5
10	WldT	60565	3203	28W-10S	A5
300	GRNE	60031	2533	18W-34N	E1
300	WrnT	60030	2533	18W-34N	E1
300	WrnT	60031	2533	18W-34N	E1
400	GRNE	60031	2476	18W-34N	E7
800	LMNT	60439	3270	19W-14S	E7
2000	CHHT	60411	3595	2W-26S	C2
3700	NndT	60012	2585	31W-28N	D6
3700	PRGV	60012	2585	31W-28N	D6
9700	AlqT	60021	2695	30W-22N	E4
9800	BNHL	60010	2695	30W-22N	E4
9800	BNHL	60021	2695	30W-22N	E4
Hillview Rd					
1200	HMWD	60430	3508	1W-22S	A1
1300	HMWD	60430	3507	1W-22S	E1
Hillwick Ln					
200	SMBG	60193	2859	22W-10N	C6
Hillwood Av					
35300	GrtT	60041	2473	26W-35N	C6
Hillwood Cir					
900	RLKB	60073	2474	24W-34N	D7
Hillwood Pl					
100	AURA	60506	3137	38W-7S	B7
Hilly Ln					
10	LIHL	60156	2694	35W-21N	B5
100	DndT	60118	2799	37W-16N	E1
Hilly Wy					
6100	AlqT	60013	2641	31W-25N	D4
6100	ODHL	60013	2641	31W-25N	D4
E Hilton Av					
300	ADSN	60101	2971	18W-3N	A6
Hilton Dr					
-	ADSN	60101	2969	21W-4N	E4
-	BmdT	60101	2969	21W-4N	E4
300	GLHT	60139	2969	23W-4N	A3
9400	OKLN	60453	3212	5W-10S	A6
Hilton Ln					
200	EDND	60118	2801	33W-16N	B2
Hilton Pl					
100	ELGN	60120	2855	33W-11N	A4
Hilton St					
100	WLSP	60480	3209	12W-9S	D3
Hilton Head Ct					
1600	NPVL	60563	3140	30W-5S	A2
1600	NpvT	60563	3140	30W-5S	A2
Hilts Dr					
-	BbyT	60134	3018	39W-0N	E5
S Hi Lusi Av					
10	MPPT	60056	2807	16W-12N	E7
200	MPPT	60056	2861	16W-12N	E1
Hinckley St					
1000	AraT	60505	3200	35W-9S	B4
1000	AURA	60505	3200	35W-9S	B4
1300	MTGY	60505	3200	35W-9S	B4
1300	MTGY	60538	3200	35W-9S	B4
Hindsell Pl					
100	ELGN	60120	2855	33W-11N	A4
Hines Blvd					
-	MYWD	60153	3030	10W-1S	A7

STREET Block	City	ZIP	Map#	CGS Grid	
Hines Blvd					
-	PvsT	60141	3030	10W-1S	A7
-	PvsT	60141	3088	10W-1S	A1
-	PvsT	60153	3030	10W-1S	A7
Hines St					
100	NCHI	60088	2593	10W-30N	E2
Hingham Ct					
600	SMBG	60193	2858	24W-9N	D7
Hingham Ln					
100	BMDL	60108	2969	23W-5N	A2
500	SMBG	60193	2858	24W-9N	D7
Hinkle Ct					
700	SMBG	60193	2858	24W-10N	D6
Hinkle Ln					
10	SMBG	60193	2858	24W-10N	D6
Hinman Av					
1000	EVTN	60202	2867	2W-10N	B4
1200	EVTN	60201	2867	2W-10N	B4
Hinman St					
1100	AURA	60505	3200	35W-9S	B4
1300	AraT	60505	3200	35W-9S	B4
1300	MTGY	60505	3200	35W-9S	B4
1300	MTGY	60538	3200	35W-9S	B4
Hinricher Dr					
100	WLSP	60480	3209	12W-9S	B4
Hinsbrook Av					
1000	DRN	60561	3145	17W-7S	B7
Hinsdale Av					
4900	MCCK	60525	3148	10W-5S	A1
E Hinsdale Av					
10	HNDL	60521	3146	15W-5S	B2
W Hinsdale Av					
10	HNDL	60521	3146	15W-5S	A2
500	HNDL	60521	3145	16W-5S	E2
Hinsdale Oasis Rd					
-	BRRG	60521	3146	14W-6S	D4
-	HNDL	60521	3146	14W-6S	D4
Hinspeter Dr					
22400	FKFT	60423	3590	14W-27S	E4
22500	FKFT	60423	3591	13W-27S	A4
Hinswood Dr					
1000	DGvT	60561	3207	17W-9S	B3
1000	DRN	60561	3207	18W-9S	B3
Hinterlong Ct					
6100	LSLE	60532	3142	24W-6S	D5
Hinterlong Ln					
1500	NPVL	60563	3140	29W-6S	D4
Hintz Ln					
1500	WLNG	60090	2754	16W-17N	D6
E Hintz Rd					
10	WhlT	60090	2755	13W-16N	E6
10	WLNG	60090	2755	13W-17N	D6
200	ANHT	60004	2754	16W-17N	C6
1700	WLNG	60004	2754	16W-17N	D6
1700	WLNG	60090	2754	16W-17N	C6
2100	ANHT	60090	2754	16W-17N	D6
2300	PTHT	60070	2754	16W-17N	D6
2500	WLNG	60070	2754	16W-17N	E6
W Hintz Rd					
10	ANHT	60004	2754	18W-17N	A6
10	WLNG	60090	2755	14W-17N	B6
100	WLNG	60070	2754	15W-17N	E6
100	WLNG	60090	2754	15W-17N	E6
300	PTHT	60070	2754	15W-17N	E6
300	WLNG	60004	2754	15W-17N	E6
500	ANHT	60004	2753	18W-17N	E6
800	PTHT	60090	2755	14W-17N	B6
Hintze Ct					
2900	JLET	60435	3497	27W-22S	C2
Hintze Rd					
10	WslT	60481	3943	27W-41S	D4
S Hi Point Rd					
4400	NndT	60050	2584	33W-30N	E2
W Hippler Rd					
25900	CbaT	60010	2697	25W-21N	E7
Hiram Ct					
2200	WHTN	60187	3083	23W-3S	A5
Hiram Dr					
2200	WHTN	60187	3082	23W-3S	E5
2200	WHTN	60187	3083	23W-3S	A5
Hirsch Av					
300	CTCY	60409	3352	4E-17S	B6
E Hirsch Av					
100	NHLK	60164	3028	13W-1N	E1
200	MLPK	60160	3028	13W-1N	E1
200	MLPK	60164	3028	13W-1N	E1
300	MLPK	60160	3029	13W-1N	A1
300	MLPK	60164	3029	13W-1N	A1
300	NHLK	60164	3029	13W-1N	A1
400	NHLK	60165	3029	13W-1N	A1
400	SNPK	60165	3029	13W-1N	A1
W Hirsch Av					
3000	MLPK	60160	3029	12W-1N	B1
Hirsch Blvd					
900	CTCY	60409	3352	4E-18S	B7
900	CTCY	60409	3430	4E-18S	B1
W Hirsch Dr					
3100	CHCG	60622	3032	3W-1N	E1
3100	CHCG	60651	3032	3W-1N	E1
Hirsch St					
1200	CTCY	60409	3430	4E-19S	B3
4200	NHLK	60164	3029	13W-1N	A1
4200	NHLK	60165	3029	13W-1N	A1
4200	SNPK	60165	3029	13W-1N	A1
W Hirsch St					
2200	CHCG	60622	3033	3W-1N	A1
2700	CHCG	60622	3032	3W-1N	E1
3200	CHCG	60651	3032	4W-1N	C1
4800	CHCG	60651	3031	7W-1N	C1
5900	OKPK	60302	3031	7W-1N	B1
Hirsch Ter					
-	MLPK	60160	3028	13W-1N	E2
-	MLPK	60160	3029	13W-1N	A2
4600	NHLK	60160	3029	13W-1N	A2
4600	NHLK	60164	3029	13W-1N	A2
Hirschberg Av					
4200	SRPK	60176	2973	12W-5N	B1
4500	SRPK	60176	2917	12W-5N	B7
Hirschberg Ct					
4500	SRPK	60176	2973	11W-5N	D1
Hirst Ct					
300	LKBF	60044	2594	10W-28N	A6
Hise Ct					
300	SMWD	60107	2857	27W-11N	C4
Historical Ln					
-	LGGV	60047	2700	18W-21N	E6
Hitchcock Av					
500	DRGV	60532	3143	22W-5S	C3
500	LSLE	60532	3143	22W-5S	C3
500	LslT	60515	3143	22W-5S	C3
500	LslT	60532	3143	22W-5S	C3
1900	DRGV	60515	3143	21W-5S	E2
1900	DRGV	60515	3144	21W-5S	A2
2000	LSLE	60532	3142	24W-5S	E3
Hitching Post Ln					
100	RLKP	60030	2589	22W-30N	A1

STREET Block	City	ZIP	Map#	CGS Grid	
Hitching Post Ln					
2000	SMBG	60194	2858	26W-10N	A5
2200	SMBG	60194	2857	26W-10N	E5
Hithergreen Ct					
10	ALGN	60102	2693	37W-21N	A6
W Hoag Ct					
19300	FmtT	60060	2646	19W-26N	C3
Hobart Av					
1000	DRGV	60516	3144	19W-7S	C7
16700	ODHL	60487	3423	11W-20S	E4
S Hobart Av					
11900	PlsT	60464	3273	11W-14S	E5
11900	PSPK	60464	3273	11W-14S	E5
W Hobart Av					
-	CHCG	60631	2919	8W-7N	A4
6800	CHCG	60631	2918	8W-7N	E4
Hobart Ct					
10	SEGN	60177	2908	36W-9N	A1
Hobart Dr					
300	SEGN	60177	2908	36W-8N	A2
400	ElgT	60123	2908	35W-9N	A1
400	ElgT	60177	2908	35W-9N	A1
Hobbes Dr					
3500	NPVL	60564	3267	28W-11S	A1
W Hobbie St					
600	CHCG	60610	3034	0W-1N	A2
Hobble Brush Dr					
10	LKZH	60047	2699	22W-22N	B4
Hobble Bush Ln					
1000	ELGN	60120	2855	32W-12N	C1
S Hobble Bush Ln					
200	VNHL	60061	2647	16W-24N	C7
S Hobbs Av					
10	JLET	60433	3499	23W-24S	B5
Hobbs Dr					
800	JLET	60435	3498	25W-22S	C3
Hobbs Ln					
-	BtlT	60543	3262	40W-12S	C4
-	BtlT	60560	3262	40W-12S	C4
Hobby Av					
400	FKFT	60423	3503	12W-25S	C7
Hoberg Dr					
2600	JLET	60432	3500	20W-23S	C3
2600	JLET	60451	3500	20W-23S	C3
2600	NlxT	60451	3500	20W-23S	C3
N Hobson Av					
2000	CHCG	60614	2977	2W-3N	B5
Hobson Ct					
10	WDRG	60517	3143	22W-7S	C6
Hobson Dr					
900	BFGV	60089	2701	16W-21N	D7
Hobson Ln					
1800	AURA	60503	3201	33W-10S	B5
Hobson Rd					
10	LslT	60517	3143	23W-7S	A7
10	LslT	60540	3143	23W-7S	B7
10	LslT	60540	3204	24W-7S	D1
10	WDRG	60517	3143	23W-7S	A7
100	NPVL	60540	3204	25W-8S	C1
100	WDRG	60540	3143	23W-7S	A7
400	LslT	60565	3204	25W-8S	B1
400	NPVL	60565	3204	25W-8S	B1
500	LslT	60540	3205	23W-7S	A1
2200	DRGV	60516	3143	21W-6S	E5
2200	LslT	60516	3143	21W-6S	E5
2400	DRGV	60517	3143	21W-6S	E5
2500	WDRG	60516	3143	21W-6S	E5
Hobson Rd CO-2					
10	LslT	60517	3143	23W-7S	B7
10	LslT	60540	3143	23W-7S	B7
10	LslT	60540	3204	24W-7S	D1
10	WDRG	60517	3143	23W-7S	B7
100	NPVL	60540	3204	25W-8S	C1
100	WDRG	60540	3143	23W-7S	A7
400	LslT	60565	3204	25W-8S	B1
400	NPVL	60565	3204	25W-8S	B1
500	LslT	60540	3205	23W-7S	A1
2200	DRGV	60516	3143	21W-6S	E5
2200	LslT	60516	3143	21W-6S	E5
Hobson Rd CO-38					
-	LslT	60517	3143	23W-7S	A7
-	WDRG	60517	3143	23W-7S	A7
Hobson Rd CO-41					
2200	DRGV	60516	3143	21W-6S	E5
2200	LslT	60516	3143	21W-6S	E5
Hobson Gate Ct					
3900	LslT	60540	3143	23W-7S	A7
3900	WDRG	60517	3143	23W-7S	A7
3900	WDRG	60540	3143	23W-7S	A7
Hobson Hollow Dr					
1100	LslT	60540	3204	24W-8S	D1
1100	NPVL	60540	3204	24W-8S	D1
Hobson Mill Dr					
900	NPVL	60540	3204	26W-8S	A1
1000	LslT	60540	3203	26W-8S	E1
1000	LslT	60540	3204	26W-8S	A1
1000	NPVL	60540	3203	26W-8S	E1
Hobson Oaks Ct					
1200	NPVL	60540	3204	25W-8S	B1
Hobson Oaks Dr					
1200	NPVL	60540	3204	25W-8S	B1
Hobson Trails Dr					
600	LslT	60540	3142	23W-7S	E7
Hobson Valley Dr					
6700	LslT	60517	3143	22W-7S	B7
6700	LslT	60540	3143	22W-7S	B7
6700	WDRG	60517	3143	22W-7S	B7
Hoddam Ct					
2500	NPVL	60564	3266	29W-12S	D3
Hoddam Rd					
2600	NPVL	60564	3266	29W-12S	C3
Hodge Ln					
900	BTVA	60510	3078	34W-2S	D3
Hodges Rd					
10	OKTR	60181	3085	17W-1S	C2
Hodges St					
500	BCHR	60401	3864	0W-36S	C2
900	WshT	60401	3864	1W-36S	B2
Hodlmair Ct					
1400	EGVV	60007	2913	21W-8N	E3
Hodlmair Ln					
1300	EGVV	60007	2913	21W-8N	E2
N Hoeglund St					
38300	LkvT	60046	2416	25W-38N	B7
Hoeweed Ln					
800	CmpT	60175	2906	39W-6N	D6
S Hoey St					
2700	CHCG	60608	3091	1W-2S	E3
W Hoff Rd					
-	JknT	60421	3763	26W-32S	E2
14800	MHTN	60442	3767	18W-32S	A1
14800	MhtT	60442	3767	18W-32S	A1
15000	MHTN	60442	3766	19W-32S	D1
15000	MhtT	60442	3766	21W-32S	A2
16100	JknT	60421	3766	20W-32S	B2
16100	JknT	60442	3766	20W-32S	B2

STREET Block	City	ZIP	Map#	CGS Grid	
W Hoff Rd					
16100	MhtT	60421	3766	20W-32S	B2
Hoffman Av					
1400	PKRG	60068	2863	11W-10N	D5
Hoffman Blvd					
-	AURA	60503	3265	32W-11S	C1
-	AURA	60585	3265	32W-11S	D1
-	WldT	60585	3265	32W-11S	D1
Hoffman Ct					
3000	DYR	46311	3598		D5
Hoffman Ln					
800	RVWD	60015	2702	13W-21N	E7
Hoffman Pkwy					
-	DSPN	60016	2862	14W-10N	C4
Hoffman St					
-	BtlT	60545	3260	44W-13S	D5
-	LtRT	60545	3260	46W-13S	B6
-	PLNO	60545	3260	46W-13S	B6
2000	CTHL	60403	3418	24W-21S	D7
5200	SKOK	60077	2865	6W-10N	D5
E Hoffman St					
300	HMND	46327	3352		E5
Hoffman Ter					
-	MNGV	60053	2865	8W-11N	A2
Hoffner Dr					
900	GYLK	60030	2533	20W-33N	B4
Hogan Hl					
10	PltT	60124	2852	39W-9N	E7
300	PltT	60124	2906	39W-9N	E1
600	ElgT	60124	2853	38W-9N	A7
600	PltT	60124	2853	38W-9N	A7
W Hogan Ln					
-	WKGN	60083	2478	14W-37N	C2
Hogan St					
300	BGBK	60490	3267	26W-12S	D4
Hogarth Ln					
10	GLNC	60022	2758	6W-18N	E4
Hogbac Rd					
8500	GwdT	60098	2526	37W-33N	B3
Hoger Dr					
1000	MTSN	60443	3505	7W-25S	D7
Hohlfelder Rd					
1000	GLNC	60022	2758	7W-18N	B4
Hohman Av					
6300	HMND	46324	3430		D2
7400	HMND	46321	3430		D4
7400	MNSR	46321	3430		D7
8600	MNSR	46321	3510		D1
S Hohman Av					
3800	HMND	46327	3352		D4
4800	HMND	46320	3352		D5
5900	HMND	46320	3430		D1
6100	HMND	46324	3430		D1
Hohman St					
9600	SjnT	46311	3687		D2
Hojem Ln					
200	GYLK	60030	2532	21W-32N	D4
Holabird Cir					
10	HIWD	60040	2650	9W-24N	C7
Holabird Lp					
10	HDPK	60035	2650	9W-24N	C7
10	HDPK	60040	2650	9W-24N	C7
10	HIWD	60035	2650	9W-24N	C7
10	HIWD	60040	2650	9W-24N	C7
Holbek Dr					
700	ANTH	60002	2357	23W-42N	D6
Holbrook Av					
500	ELBN	60119	3017	43W-0N	A4
Holbrook Cir					
10	CHHT	60411	3507	1W-23S	E3
10	CHHT	60411	3508	1W-23S	A3
300	CHHT	60430	3508	1W-23S	A3
300	HMWD	60430	3508	1W-23S	A3
Holbrook Dr					
200	WLNG	60090	2808	14W-16N	B1
Holbrook Ln					
-	HFET	60169	2804	26W-12N	A7
1300	BTVA	60510	3019	36W-0S	E7
1900	HFET	60169	2858	25W-12N	B1
Holbrook Rd					
-	GNWD	60411	3508	1W-23S	A3
-	GNWD	60425	3508	1W-23S	A3
10	BlmT	60430	3507	2W-23S	D3
10	CHHT	60411	3507	1W-23S	E3
10	CHHT	60411	3508	1W-23S	A3
10	CHHT	60430	3507	1W-23S	E3
10	CHHT	60430	3508	1W-23S	A3
10	HMWD	60430	3507	1W-23S	E3
10	HMWD	60430	3508	1W-23S	A3
100	BlmT	60411	3507	1W-23S	E3
200	CHHT	60422	3507	1W-23S	E3
200	FSMR	60422	3507	2W-23S	D3
200	FSMR	60430	3507	2W-23S	D3
800	BlmT	60411	3508	1W-23S	A3
W Holbrook Rd					
600	BlmT	60411	3508	0W-23S	B3
600	GNWD	60411	3508	0W-23S	B3
600	GNWD	60425	3508	0W-23S	B3
600	HMWD	60430	3508	0W-23S	B3
W Holbrook St					
6200	CHCG	60646	2919	7W-7N	A3
NE Holcomb Dr					
600	MDLN	60060	2590	18W-28N	D6
NW Holcomb Dr					
700	MDLN	60060	2590	18W-28N	D6
Holden Av					
100	AURA	60506	3199	36W-8S	E3
200	AURA	60538	3199	36W-8S	E3
400	RMVL	60446	3340	24W-15S	E2
Holden Cir					
-	PKFT	60443	3594	4W-26S	E1
-	PKFT	60466	3594	4W-26S	E1
3000	MTSN	60443	3595	4W-26S	A2
3000	PKFT	60443	3595	4W-26S	A2
3000	PKFT	60466	3595	4W-26S	A2
3100	ElgT	60124	2853	38W-10N	B6
3300	MTSN	60443	3594	4W-26S	E1
Holden Ct					
800	LKFT	60045	2649	12W-25N	C5
N Holden Ct					
10	CHCG	60602	3034		D5
S Holden Ct					
500	CHCG	60605	3034	0E-0S	C6
Holden St					
3100	ElgT	60124	2853	38W-10N	B6
Holder Ln					
1700	NHFD	60093	2811	6W-15N	C3
Holdridge Av					
100	PTPR	53158	2363	10W-43N	B5
100	WPHR	53158	2363	10W-43N	B5
500	WPHR	60096	2363	10W-42N	B6
3300	BtnT	60099	2422	10W-41N	B1
N Holdridge Av					
38000	BHPK	60087	2480	10W-38N	B1
38300	BHPK	60087	2422	10W-38N	B7
39000	BHPK	60099	2422	10W-39N	B6

STREET Block	City	ZIP	Map#	CGS Grid	
N Holdridge Av					
39500	ZION	60099	2422	10W-39N	B6
Hole In the Wall Ct					
10	BDWD	60481	3942	30W-40S	B3
Hole In the Wall Rd					
-	BDWD	60481	3942	30W-40S	C3
100	BDWD	60408	3942	30W-40S	C3
100	RedT	60481	3942	30W-40S	C3
Holeman Av					
3200	CHHT	60411	3596	0W-27S	C4
3200	SCHT	60411	3596	0W-27S	C4
3200	SCHT	60475	3596	0W-27S	C4
3200	STGR	60411	3596	0W-27S	C4
3200	STGR	60475	3596	0W-27S	C4
3300	CRTE	60417	3596	0W-28S	C6
Holian Dr					
1300	SPGV	60081	2414	30W-39N	A5
2000	SPGV	60081	2413	30W-39N	E5
Holiday Ct					
15000	ODPK	60462	3345	12W-17S	C6
Holiday Dr					
800	AURA	60506	3137	36W-5S	D3
2400	HHLL	60051	2586	30W-29N	A4
S Holiday Dr					
12500	ALSP	60803	3275	6W-14S	E7
Holiday Ln					
100	HNVL	60073	2532	22W-33N	B3
700	DSPN	60016	2861	16W-10N	E4
700	DSPN	60016	2862	15W-10N	A5
700	MPPT	60016	2861	16W-10N	E4
700	MPPT	60056	2861	16W-10N	E4
Holiday Ter					
2300	LNSG	60438	3429	2E-20S	D5
Holiday Plaza Dr					
500	MTSN	60443	3506	6W-25S	A7
500	MTSN	60443	3594	6W-25S	A1
Holland Av					
16600	SHLD	60473	3428	0E-19S	D2
Holland Ct					
400	LKFT	60045	2649	11W-26N	D3
2400	AURA	60503	3201	32W-10S	C5
Holland Dr					
-	JknT	60421	3675	24W-28S	D1
-	JLET	60421	3675	24W-28S	D1
Holland Ln					
100	BbyT	60134	3018	39W-0N	D6
700	RMVL	60446	3417	26W-18S	E2
Holland Pl					
1400	DRGV	60515	3084	20W-3S	B5
Holland Rd					
18300	LNSG	60438	3429	2E-21S	C7
S Holland Rd					
8600	CHCG	60620	3214	0W-10S	B4
Holland Harbor Cir					
9000	FKFT	60423	3504	11W-25S	A7
Holland Harbor Dr					
20600	FKFT	60423	3504	11W-24S	A6
Hollenback Ct					
-	BtlT	60543	3262	40W-12S	C4
2800	NPVL	60565	3203	27W-10S	C7
Hollenbeck Dr					
-	LKPT	60441	3421	18W-19S	B3
Hollendale Villa					
1700	NHFD	60093	2811	6W-15N	C2
Hollett Dr					
-	CHCG	60629	3150	4W-7S	D6
Holli Ct					
1000	SMBG	60194	2858	24W-11N	C4
Hollingswood Av					
1000	NPVL	60564	3267	28W-11S	A1
Hollingswood Ct					
1000	NPVL	60564	3267	28W-11S	B1
Hollington Ln					
22500	DRPK	60010	2699	22W-20N	B7
N Hollis Av					
600	WKGN	60085	2479	12W-33N	B7
600	WkgT	60085	2479	12W-33N	B7
Hollis Cir					
3300	NPVL	60564	3266	30W-11S	A1
Hollister Ct					
2200	JLET	60586	3415	33W-21S	B7
Hollister Dr					
1300	BTVA	60510	3020	34W-0S	E7
1800	LYVL	60048	2647	15W-26N	E2
1800	VNHL	60048	2647	15W-26N	E2
1800	VNHL	60061	2647	15W-26N	E2
Holliston Ct					
900	SMBG	60193	2912	24W-9N	D1
Holliston on Asbury					
10	RGMW	60008	2806	19W-15N	B3
Hollow Gln					
800	JLET	60431	3497	28W-22S	A3
W Hollow St					
1600	MchT	60051	2529	30W-32N	A5
Hollow Wy					
100	FXLK	60041	2473	27W-35N	C6
Holloway Ct					
1900	AURA	60502	3139	33W-5S	A4
Holloway Dr					
500	RMVL	60446	3417	27W-18S	C1
Hollow Bend Ct					
2000	NPVL	60565	3204	24W-8S	E2
Hollow Hill Dr					
300	WCDA	60084	2587	26W-28N	D5
Hollows Rd					
16700	AlqT	60014	2641	32W-25N	B5
Hollowside Dr					
10	DndT	60118	2747	36W-18N	B4
100	ALGN	60110	2747	36W-18N	A4
100	ALGN	60118	2747	36W-18N	A4
100	CPVL	60110	2747	36W-18N	A4
100	DndT	60110	2747	36W-18N	A4
Hollow Tree Rd					
10600	ODPK	60462	3345	13W-17S	A5
Holly Av					
10	DGvT	60561	3145	18W-7S	A7
10	DRN	60561	3145	18W-7S	A7
100	DRN	60527	3145	16W-7S	D7
100	WLBK	60527	3145	16W-7S	D7
1500	DRN	60561	3144	18W-7S	E7
1600	NfdT	60062	2756	11W-16N	C7
1600	NHBK	60062	2756	11W-16N	C7
E Holly Av					
500	MPPT	60056	2808	15W-13N	B5
N Holly Av					
10	FXLK	60020	2473	27W-36N	B3
2000	CHCG	60614	2977	2W-2N	C6
2000	CHCG	60622	2977	2W-2N	C6
S Holly Av					
10	FXLK	60020	2473	27W-36N	A3
100	EMHT	60126	3028	15W-0N	B4
Holly Cir					
900	LKZH	60047	2644	24W-24N	C7
900	LKZH	60047	2698	24W-24N	C1
Holly Ct					
10	WLNG	60090	2754	16W-18N	E4

STREET Block City ZIP Map# CGS Grid

Holly Ct
400 VLPK 60181 3026 18W-1N E3
500 CmpT 60175 2905 41W-6N E7
500 SMWD 60107 2857 28W-10N B6
600 NARA 60542 3078 35W-3S B7
600 WynT 60185 2967 27W-3N B7
900 DRFD 60015 2703 11W-21N D7
900 NHBK 60062 2757 8W-17N E5
900 SYHW 60118 2800 35W-15N C3
1000 LKPT 60441 3419 21W-19S E3
1000 NfdT 60025 2810 10W-13N B6
1100 NPVL 60540 3203 27W-8S C1
1100 OKPK 60301 3030 8W-0N D3
1200 DRGV 60515 3084 20W-3S B5
1500 LGGV 60047 2700 18W-20N D7
2100 MchT 60051 2528 31W-33N E4
2200 NfdT 60062 2809 11W-16N D1
2200 NHBK 60062 2809 11W-16N D1
3800 CCHL 60478 3426 4W-20S D5
6300 LSLE 60532 3142 24W-6S D5
7300 RVFT 60305 3030 9W-0N D3
8200 PSHL 60465 3274 10W-13S B3
10000 ODPK 60462 3345 12W-17S C5
11900 LMNT 60439 3271 17W-14S D5
11900 PNFD 60585 3266 31W-14S A6
15300 OKFT 60452 3347 6W-18S E7
17700 TYPK 60487 3423 11W-21S E6
E Holly Ct
600 ADSN 60101 2971 17W-3N B4
700 MPPT 60056 2808 15W-13N B5
W Holly Ct
- LMBD 60148 3026 18W-1N E3
- LMBD 60181 3026 18W-1N E3
- VLPK 60181 3026 18W-1N E3
200 RDLK 60073 2531 23W-33N E4
300 GNWD 60425 3508 0W-22S B1
Holly Dr
10 CLLK 60014 2639 37W-25N B4
300 SMWD 60107 2857 28W-10N B6
700 BRLT 60103 2910 29W-8N D4
N Holly Dr
24800 CbaT 60013 2643 28W-24N A6
Holly Ln
- HFET 60169 2859 22W-11N B3
200 EGVV 60007 2860 18W-9N E7
200 EGVV 60007 2861 18W-9N A6
200 OSWG 60543 3262 39W-12S D2
1000 MNSR 46321 3510 E2
1100 ALGN 60102 2694 34W-21N C7
1100 DRFD 60015 2703 11W-21N D7
1300 WNKA 60093 2758 6W-16N E7
1800 BlmT 60422 3507 2W-23S C4
1800 BlmT 60461 3507 2W-23S C4
1800 FSMR 60422 3507 2W-23S C4
1800 OMFD 60461 3507 2W-23S C4
3600 RGMW 60008 2806 20W-13N A5
10000 MaiT 60016 2809 12W-12N C7
10000 MaiT 60016 2863 12W-12N C1
S Holly Ln
20100 FftT 60423 3504 9W-24S D5
Holly Rd
1800 HDPK 60035 2704 10W-22N A4
6200 GRNE 60048 2534 16W-32N D5
Holly St
10 PKFT 60466 3595 3W-26S B1
100 BGBK 60490 3267 26W-12S D3
400 ELGN 60123 2854 34W-11N D5
E Holly Wy
800 PLTN 60074 2753 19W-18N B3
N Holly Wy
1900 PLTN 60074 2753 19W-18N B3
Hollyberry Av
9000 MaiT 60016 2863 11W-11N D2
Hollyberry Dr
800 JLET 60435 3497 26W-22S E2
Hollybrook Ln
8400 TYPK 60477 3504 10W-23S B3
Hollycourt Ter
- ElaT 60047 2698 24W-24N C1
- LKZH 60047 2698 24W-24N C1
Hollycrest Av
1500 AURA 60506 3137 36W-5S E3
Hollydale Dr
2700 HMWD 60430 3427 3W-21S B6
Hollyhill Cir
1100 NlxT 60451 3500 19W-23S E4
Hollyhock Ct
10 LIHL 60156 2693 38W-22N A4
5200 GRNE 60031 2478 15W-35N A5
15100 ODPK 60462 3346 9W-18S D6
Holly Hock Ln
26300 GlkT 60450 3761 32W-34S C6
26300 WmTp 60481 3761 32W-34S C6
Holly Lynn Dr
200 AlqT 60013 2642 29W-24N C7
Holly Lynn Ln
3500 PnfT 60431 3416 28W-20S E5
3500 PnfT 60431 3417 28W-20S A5
3500 PnfT 60586 3416 28W-20S E5
Holly Ridge Dr
2200 JLET 60586 3415 31W-21S D6
Hollystone Ln
800 BFGV 60089 2701 17W-20N B7
Holly Towne Ct
1300 NPVL 60565 3204 24W-8S E1
Hollytree Ln
1500 CLLK 60014 2693 36W-23N D3
Hollywood Av
200 MNSR 46321 3430 C5
800 DSPN 60016 2862 13W-11N D3
800 ITSC 60143 2914 20W-7N A5
1300 GNVW 60025 2810 8W-14N E5
1300 GNVW 60025 2811 8W-14N A5
1700 HRPK 60133 2911 27W-9N C1
3300 BKFD 60513 3088 10W-3S A5
3800 BKFD 60534 3088 10W-3S A6
3800 LYNS 60534 3088 10W-3S A6
W Hollywood Av
900 CHCG 60640 2921 1W-7N E4
900 CHCG 60660 2921 1W-7N D4
2400 CHCG 60659 2921 3W-7N A4
3200 CHCG 60659 2920 4W-7N C4
4300 CHCG 60646 2920 5W-7N A4
Hollywood Blvd
100 SBTN 60010 2803 26W-13N D6
900 MHRY 60050 2528 32W-31N B7
900 MHRY 60050 2585 32W-30N B1
Hollywood Ct
100 WLMT 60091 2812 4W-13N B6
300 SEGN 60177 2908 34W-9N E1
700 HMND 46394 3280 D5
Hollywood Dr
4800 CCHL 60478 3426 6W-21S A6
8400 ODPK 60462 3346 10W-18S B6
Hollywood Ln
2500 JLET 60432 3500 20W-22S B2

Hollywood Ter
100 LKMR 60051 2529 29W-32N D6
S Holm Ct
14500 HMGN 60491 3344 15W-17S B5
E Holm Dr
800 JltT 60432 3499 21W-22S E2
W Holm Dr
12500 HMGN 60491 3344 15W-17S B5
N Holman Av
34700 GrtT 60041 2474 25W-34N B7
S Holmberg Ct
12000 ALSP 60803 3276 5W-14S C5
Holmes Av
- PSPK 60464 3274 10W-13S B4
10 ElaT 60047 2645 22W-25N B5
10 HNWD 60047 2645 22W-25N B5
200 CNHL 60514 3145 16W-6S D4
300 DGvT 60514 3145 16W-6S D4
800 DRFD 60015 2703 11W-21N C7
5700 WLBK 60514 3145 16W-6S D4
5800 WLBK 60527 3145 16W-6S D4
16900 HLCT 60429 3427 3W-20S A5
N Holmes Av
1000 JLET 60432 3499 22W-22S C2
S Holmes Av
11600 PlsT 60464 3274 10W-13S B5
11600 PSPK 60464 3274 10W-13S B5
Holmes Dr
13000 PlsT 60462 3345 13W-15S A1
13000 PlsT 60464 3345 13W-15S A1
Holmes Pl
100 MTGY 60538 3199 36W-9S E5
Holmes Rd
1300 ELGN 60123 2800 36W-14N B6
1500 ELGN 60123 2799 37W-14N E6
1500 ELGN 60124 2799 37W-14N E6
Holmes St
100 LMNT 60439 3270 19W-13S E5
Holmes Wy
10 SMBG 60193 2857 27W-10N D5
10 SMBG 60194 2857 27W-10N D6
Holste Rd
1800 NHBK 60062 2810 9W-15N B2
Holstein Ct
2300 NPVL 60564 3266 29W-12S D2
Holt Ln
2000 SEGN 60177 2907 37W-8N D3
Holt Rd
200 SwdT 60447 3583 33W-27S B5
200 TroT 60404 3583 33W-27S A5
600 MNKA 60447 3583 33W-27S B5
Holter Av
200 BTVA 60510 3077 36W-0S E1
Holtz Av
- ADSN 60101 2970 19W-4N C3
400 AddT 60101 2970 19W-4N C3
W Holtz Av
- AddT 60101 2970 20W-4N B3
1200 ADSN 60101 2970 20W-4N B3
Holy Ct
- ANTH 60002 2358 20W-41N E7
Holyoke Ct
200 WNVL 60555 3080 30W-2S B3
800 SMBG 60193 2858 24W-10N C6
800 SMBG 60193 2859 23W-10N A6
Holyoke Ln
100 VLPK 60181 3085 18W-1S A1
200 YkTp 60181 3085 18W-1S A1
300 OKTR 60181 3085 18W-1S A1
Holyoke on Auburn
10 RGMW 60008 2806 19W-14N C3
Homan Av
- ALSP 60406 3276 4W-14S E7
- RchT 60422 3506 4W-23S E2
- RchT 60430 3506 4W-23S E2
400 PKFT 60466 3507 4W-25S A7
500 MTSN 60443 3594 4W-25S E1
500 MTSN 60466 3594 4W-25S E1
500 PKFT 60443 3594 4W-25S E1
500 PKFT 60466 3506 4W-25S E7
500 PKFT 60466 3594 4W-25S E1
12600 BLID 60406 3276 4W-15S E7
12600 BLID 60803 3276 4W-14S E7
12800 ALSP 60803 3276 4W-15S E7
12800 ALSP 60803 3348 4W-15S E1
12800 WthT 60406 3276 4W-15S E7
12800 WthT 60406 3348 4W-15S E1
12800 WthT 60803 3276 4W-15S E7
12800 WthT 60803 3348 4W-15S E1
14300 MDLN 60445 3348 4W-17S E5
14800 MDLN 60426 3348 4W-17S E5
14800 MKHM 60426 3348 4W-18S E6
14800 MKHM 60445 3348 4W-17S E5
15500 MKHM 60428 3348 4W-18S E7
15500 MKHM 60428 3426 4W-19S E2
N Homan Av
10 CHCG 60624 3032 4W-0N D4
1100 CHCG 60651 3032 4W-1N D2
1500 CHCG 60647 3032 4W-1N D1
S Homan Av
10 CHCG 60624 3032 4W-1S D7
1100 CHCG 60623 3032 4W-1S D7
1500 CHCG 60623 3090 4W-1S D1
3600 CHCG 60632 3090 4W-3S D5
5000 CHCG 60632 3150 4W-6S D3
5400 CHCG 60629 3150 4W-7S D5
7500 CHCG 60652 3212 4W-9S D2
9100 ENGN 60805 3212 4W-11S D6
10200 CHCG 60655 3276 4W-13S E4
10200 CHCG 60805 3276 4W-11S D1
10200 ENGN 60805 3276 4W-11S D1
11400 CHCG 60803 3276 4W-13S E4
11400 MTPK 60655 3276 4W-13S E4
11400 MTPK 60803 3276 4W-13S E4
12300 ALSP 60803 3276 4W-14S E6
12300 WthT 60803 3276 4W-14S E6
12400 ALSP 60406 3276 4W-14S E6
12400 WthT 60406 3276 4W-14S E6
12500 BLID 60406 3276 4W-14S E6
12500 BLID 60803 3276 4W-14S E6
13300 RBBN 60472 3348 4W-16S E3
13300 WthT 60472 3348 4W-15S E2
Homan Cir
10 PKFT 60466 3594 4W-25S E1
Home Av
- BRTN 60010 2750 26W-20N E1
- VLPK 60181 3027 17W-0N C3
- WRTH 60482 3275 7W-13S B5
- WthT 60482 3275 7W-13S B5
10 WnfT 60555 3080 29W-3S C6
10 WNVL 60555 3080 29W-3S C6
100 OKPK 60302 3030 8W-0S E5
200 ITSC 60143 2914 19W-6N D7
500 ADSN 60143 2914 19W-5N D7
600 WKGN 60085 2537 10W-33N A2
700 EGVV 60007 2913 21W-9N E1

Home Av
900 OKPK 60304 3030 8W-0S E6
1100 BRWN 60304 3030 8W-0S E7
1100 BRWN 60402 3030 8W-1S E7
3100 BRWN 60402 3088 8W-3S E6
3900 SKNY 60402 3088 8W-4S E7
4400 FTVW 60402 3088 8W-4S E7
4400 MHRY 60050 2527 34W-33N D2
4500 FTVW 60402 3148 8W-4S E1
9200 MaiT 60016 2863 11W-11N E2
E Home Av
10 PLTN 60067 2752 20W-17N E4
100 PLTN 60067 2753 20W-17N A4
200 PLTN 60074 2753 20W-17N A4
N Home Av
10 PKRG 60068 2917 11W-9N E1
2100 PKRG 60068 2863 11W-11N E3
2200 MaiT 60016 2863 11W-11N E3
S Home Av
10 PKRG 60068 2917 11W-8N E1
23400 MonT 60449 3594 6W-29S B7
23400 MonT 60449 3683 6W-29S B1
23400 MonT 60466 3683 6W-29S B1
23400 UYPK 60449 3594 6W-29S B7
23400 UYPK 60466 3683 6W-29S B1
W Home Av
10 VLPK 60181 3027 18W-0N A3
6400 WRTH 60482 3275 8W-13S A4
6400 WthT 60482 3275 8W-13S B5
Home Cir
1500 EGVV 60007 2913 21W-9N E1
9300 MaiT 60016 2863 11W-11N E2
Home Ct
1100 SRWD 60404 3496 30W-23S B5
9300 MaiT 60016 2863 11W-11N E2
22500 FKFT 60423 3590 14W-27S E4
N Home Ct
1300 PLTN 60074 2753 20W-17N A4
Home Pl
1000 BGBK 60440 3268 25W-12S B2
Home St
800 JLET 60433 3587 22W-25S C1
800 JltT 60433 3587 22W-25S C1
2100 JLET 60433 3588 21W-25S A1
2100 JltT 60433 3588 21W-25S A1
E Home St
800 JLET 60433 3587 22W-25S C1
800 JltT 60433 3587 22W-25S C1
Home Ter
9200 MaiT 60016 2863 11W-11N E2
Homeland Rd
200 MTSN 60443 3506 5W-25S B7
600 RchT 60443 3506 5W-25S B7
Homer Av
300 RMVL 60446 3340 24W-16S D3
1000 AURA 60505 3200 36W-9S A4
1100 AURA 60538 3200 36W-9S A4
1100 MTGY 60538 3200 36W-9S A4
Homer Ct
1100 NPVL 60540 3202 28W-8S E1
Homer Dr
- BGBK 60440 3205 22W-11S B7
Homer St
400 ELGN 60123 2854 34W-10N E6
W Homer St
1500 CHCG 60622 2977 1W-2N D7
2000 CHCG 60647 2977 2W-2N B7
3100 CHCG 60647 2976 3W-2N D7
4500 CHCG 60639 2976 5W-2N A7
5100 CHCG 60639 2975 6W-2N D7
Homestead Av
- AURA 60506 3198 40W-8S C1
Homestead Ct
- AURA 60506 3198 39W-8S C1
- LKMR 60041 2530 28W-32N A5
- LKMR 60051 2530 28W-32N A5
500 ALGN 60102 2747 33W-20N E1
1700 PNFD 60544 3416 31W-18S A1
5500 CPVL 60110 2747 36W-17N A6
34000 WrnT 60031 2534 17W-34N A2
Homestead Dr
300 BGBK 60440 3205 21W-11S E7
300 BGBK 60440 3269 21W-11S E1
500 RtdT 60140 2798 40W-15N B4
800 YKVL 60560 3333 42W-14S E1
1100 YKVL 60560 3261 41W-14S E7
2500 NPVL 60564 3203 28W-10S B6
5400 CTWD 60445 3347 6W-15S D2
5500 WthT 60445 3347 6W-15S D2
5500 WthT 60463 3347 6W-15S D2
6700 MHRY 60050 2527 35W-32N A6
Homestead Ln
3200 GNVA 60134 3019 37W-1N C4
9100 BGVW 60455 3210 8W-10S E5
N Homestead Pl
500 JLET 60435 3497 27W-23S D3
Homestead Rd
1000 LGPK 60525 3087 12W-3S C4
N Homestead Rd
34000 WrnT 60031 2534 17W-34N B2
Homestead St
100 WDDL 60191 2971 18W-5N A1
W Homestead Tr
3700 PRGV 60012 2585 32W-27N B7
Hometown Dr
15900 PNFD 60544 3416 30W-19S B2
15900 PNFD 60586 3416 30W-19S B2
Hometown Ln
8700 HMTN 60456 3212 5W-10S A4
Homeward Gln
10 CmpT 60175 2906 39W-7N E6
Homeward Hill Dr
400 CmpT 60175 2906 39W-6N D7
Homewood Av
600 HDPK 60035 2704 8W-22N D4
17800 HMWD 60430 3427 2W-21S D7
18400 HMWD 60430 3507 2W-22S D1
S Homewood Av
10900 CHCG 60643 3277 2W-13S C3
Homewood Ct
200 CHHT 60411 3508 1W-24S A4
Homewood Dr
100 LYVL 60048 2591 16W-29N D4
200 BGBK 60440 3269 21W-11S E1
300 BGBK 60440 3205 21W-11S E7
Homewood Ln
800 NBRN 60010 2698 25W-23N A1
Honest Pleasure Dr
800 NPVL 60540 3142 26W-7S A7
1100 NPVL 60540 3203 26W-8S D2
W Honey Ct
300 RDLK 60073 2531 23W-32N E4
Honey Ln
- NBRN 60010 2698 25W-23N A2
10 NLNX 60451 3500 19W-24S E6
10 NlxT 60451 3500 19W-24S E6

Honey Ln
800 CRTE 60417 3597 1E-28S A6
6300 TYPK 60477 3425 7W-20S B3
W Honey Ln
21200 LkvT 60046 2475 21W-36N D3
Honeybear Ln
10 RMVL 60446 3269 23W-14S A7
Honeyberry Ct
10 NPVL 60540 3141 28W-6S A5
E Honey Hill Cir
700 WYNE 60184 2965 32W-4N C3
N Honey Hill Cir
10 WYNE 60184 2965 32W-4N C3
S Honey Hill Cir
10 WYNE 60184 2965 32W-4N B3
W Honey Hill Cir
700 WYNE 60184 2965 33W-4N B3
Honey Hill Dr
10 WYNE 60184 2965 32W-4N B3
100 WCDA 60084 2643 26W-27N E1
N Honey Hill Rd
1100 ADSN 60101 2970 19W-5N C2
Honey Lake Ct
200 NBRN 60010 2698 25W-22N A4
Honey Lake Rd
10 CbaT 60010 2698 25W-22N A4
10 NBRN 60010 2698 25W-22N A4
900 LKZH 60047 2698 24W-23N B3
1000 ElaT 60047 2698 24W-23N B3
Honey Locust
- CLLK 60012 2641 33W-27N A1
- NndT 60014 2641 33W-27N A1
Honey Locust Ct
800 BRLT 60103 2856 29W-9N D7
Honey Locust Dr
300 WLNG 60090 2755 13W-17N E5
1900 ALGN 60102 2695 32W-20N B7
3900 WldT 60564 3265 31W-12S E2
7200 JSTC 60458 3148 10W-7S B7
Honey Locust Ln
400 DRN 60561 3207 17W-8S C2
400 WLBK 60527 3207 17W-8S C2
W Honey Ridge Ct
22100 KLDR 60047 2699 22W-21N C5
Honeysuckle
300 ISLK 60042 2586 28W-28N E6
800 WCHI 60185 3022 30W-1N C2
Honey Suckle Ct
28800 LKMR 60051 2529 28W-32N D5
Honeysuckle Ct
10 BGBK 60490 3267 27W-13S C5
100 RGMW 60008 2805 21W-14N D5
2300 LNHT 60046 2476 20W-37N B3
8000 FXLK 60081 2415 27W-39N B6
W Honeysuckle Ct
100 RLKB 60073 2475 23W-36N A5
20800 DPgT 60544 3340 26W-15S A2
Honeysuckle Dr
- RMVL 60446 3339 26W-17S E6
10 CLLK 60014 2639 37W-25N B4
200 NHBK 60062 2755 13W-18N E3
600 NPVL 60540 3141 28W-7S A7
900 WLNG 60090 2755 15W-16N A7
13200 HTLY 60142 2744 42W-20N B1
E Honeysuckle Dr
10 RLKB 60073 2475 22W-36N A5
W Honeysuckle Dr
10 RLKB 60073 2475 23W-36N A5
Honeysuckle Ln
- JLET 60447 3495 33W-22S A2
300 WYNE 60184 2966 30W-4N B3
700 AURA 60506 3198 39W-8S E2
1100 BRLT 60103 2910 29W-6N E6
2400 RGMW 60008 2805 21W-14N D4
6100 GRNE 60031 2534 16W-34N D1
W Honeysuckle Rd
10 LKFT 60045 2649 11W-25N E5
Honeysuckle St
100 BGBK 60490 3267 26W-12S E3
Honeysuckle Rose Ln
- BRRG 60527 3207 16W-10S E6
400 DGvT 60527 3207 16W-10S D6
Honeytree Dr
200 RMVL 60446 3269 23W-14S A7
Honeywood Ct
2200 JLET 60586 3416 29W-21S D6
Honeywood Dr
1100 WTMT 60559 3144 18W-6S E5
Honing Rd
10 FXLK 60020 2473 27W-36N A4
S Honora Dr
17200 PnfT 60586 3416 30W-20S B6
17400 JLET 60586 3416 30W-20S B6
Honore Av
1900 NCHI 60064 2536 11W-31N D7
2300 NCHI 60064 2593 11W-31N D1
2300 NCHI 60088 2593 11W-31N D1
14100 DXMR 60426 3349 2W-16S D4
14600 HRVY 60426 3349 2W-17S D6
15600 HRVY 60426 3427 2W-18S D1
16100 MKHM 60428 3427 2W-19S D3
16500 HLCT 60428 3427 2W-19S D3
16500 HLCT 60429 3427 2W-19S D3
Honore St
- CHCG 60643 3277 2W-13S C5
- ClmT 60406 3277 2W-13S C5
- ClmT 60643 3277 2W-13S C5
12700 BLID 60406 3277 2W-15S D7
12700 CTPK 60827 3277 2W-15S D7
13000 BLID 60406 3349 2W-15S D1
N Honore St
1500 CHCG 60622 3033 2W-1N C1
1600 CHCG 60622 2977 2W-2N C7
2200 CHCG 60614 2977 2W-2N C6
2900 CHCG 60657 2977 2W-3N C4
4200 CHCG 60613 2977 2W-5N C1
5200 CHCG 60640 2921 2W-6N C5
6800 CHCG 60626 2921 2W-8N C1
7300 CHCG 60626 2867 2W-9N C7
S Honore St
100 CHCG 60612 3033 2W-0S C5
3500 CHCG 60608 3091 2W-3S C5
3500 CHCG 60609 3091 2W-3S C5
4600 CHCG 60609 3151 2W-5S C1
5500 CHCG 60636 3151 2W-7S C5
7500 CHCG 60620 3213 2W-9S C2
12300 CTPK 60827 3277 2W-14S D6
12600 BLID 60406 3277 2W-14S D7
Honors Ct
- SRWD 60404 3496 31W-24S A6
Honors Dr
100 SRWD 60404 3495 31W-24S E5
200 SRWD 60404 3496 31W-24S A5
Hood Av
3300 PKCY 60085 2536 12W-33N A3
3300 WKGN 60085 2536 12W-33N A3

Hood Av
17900 HMWD 60430 3427 1W-21S E7
18400 HMWD 60430 3507 1W-22S E1
W Hood Av
1800 CHCG 60660 2921 2W-7N B3
2000 CHCG 60659 2921 2W-7N B3
3000 CHCG 60659 2920 3W-7N D3
7700 CHCG 60631 2918 9W-7N C3
Hood Ct
200 BRLT 60103 2911 28W-7N A5
N Hook Cir
40800 AntT 60002 2417 22W-41N B2
Hook Dr
- GYLK 60046 2475 21W-35N D5
21700 RLKB 60046 2475 22W-35N B5
21700 RLKB 60073 2475 22W-35N B5
Hook Rd
100 CPVL 60110 2748 32W-17N C6
N Hooker St
1200 CHCG 60622 3033 1W-1N E1
Hooks Ct
- SHLD 60473 3428 0E-19S E3
Hooks Ln
1000 FXLK 60050 2472 28W-37N E2
Hoop Ct
1500 NLNX 60451 3588 19W-27S D5
Hoover Cir
700 OSWG 60543 3263 38W-12S A3
Hoover Ct
10 SMWD 60107 2856 29W-10N D6
1800 RGMW 60008 2805 20W-14N E4
S Hoover Ct
25800 MONE 60449 3682 7W-31S D5
Hoover Dr
200 WDDL 60191 2914 18W-5N E7
400 CPVL 60110 2748 32W-17N C7
700 CLSM 60188 2968 25W-3N A6
700 OSWG 60543 3263 38W-12S A3
Hoover Ln
- BTVA 60510 3078 36W-2S A3
Hoover St
- EGvT 60007 2861 15W-9N E7
- EGvT 60018 2861 16W-9N E7
- EGVV 60007 2861 15W-9N E7
400 EGvT 60018 2862 15W-9N A7
4300 RGMW 60008 2805 20W-14N E4
4300 RGMW 60008 2806 20W-14N A4
S Hoover St
25700 MONE 60449 3682 7W-31S D5
Hope Ct
300 ELGN 60123 2854 34W-11N E5
1900 LYWD 60411 3509 2E-24S D5
Hope Ln
400 MltT 60148 3083 21W-2S E4
400 MltT 60148 3084 21W-2S A4
2600 WKGN 60085 2479 12W-35N C5
Hope Pl
5200 MTSN 60443 3505 6W-24S E5
5200 MTSN 60443 3506 6W-24S A5
Hope St
10000 RSMT 60018 2917 12W-7N B3
Hopewell Ct
3000 AURA 60502 3139 31W-5S D3
N Hopewell Ct
22400 KLDR 60047 2699 21W-22N E4
Hopewell Dr
3000 AURA 60502 3139 31W-5S E4
Hopi Ct
100 NPVL 60563 3141 27W-5S D2
300 CLSM 60188 2968 25W-3N A5
Hopi Ln
600 ElgT 60124 2853 38W-9N A7
2700 CPVL 60110 2748 32W-18N C5
E Hopi Ln
1800 MPPT 60056 2808 13W-14N E5
2000 WhlT 60025 2808 13W-14N E5
2000 WhlT 60056 2808 13W-14N E5
Hopi Tr
1600 WLNG 60090 2754 16W-17N D5
Hopkins Av
10 AURA 60504 3200 34W-8S D1
10 AURA 60505 3200 34W-8S D1
3000 SCHT 60411 3596 0W-27S C5
3000 STGR 60411 3596 0W-27S C5
3000 STGR 60475 3596 0W-28S C6
3300 CRTE 60417 3596 0W-28S C6
3400 CRTE 60475 3596 0W-28S C6
Hopkins Ct
14900 ODPK 60462 3345 12W-17S C6
W Hopkins Pl
2000 CHCG 60620 3213 2W-10S B4
Hopkins Rd
7700 KdlT 60560 3334 39W-18S E7
Hopkins St
10200 HTLY 60142 2745 39W-20N D1
Hopman Dr
18200 TYPK 60487 3424 10W-21S B7
Hopps Rd
- ELGN 60123 2908 36W-8N A2
- SEGN 60177 2908 36W-8N A2
10 ELGN 60124 2907 37W-8N D2
10 ElgT 60124 2907 37W-8N D2
700 ELGN 60123 2907 38W-8N A2
700 ElgT 60123 2907 36W-8N E2
700 PftT 60124 2907 38W-8N A2
Horace Dr
500 ELGN 60120 2855 31W-10N E5
Horak Ln
700 GNCY 53128 2353 A3
Horatio Blvd
100 BFGV 60089 2754 16W-20N E1
400 BFGV 60069 2754 16W-20N E1
400 VrnT 60069 2754 16W-20N E1
600 BFGV 60089 2701 16W-20N E7
600 VrnT 60069 2701 16W-20N E7
20700 BFGV 60069 2701 16W-20N E7
Horeb Av
1700 ZION 60099 2421 11W-40N E3
Horizon Cir
100 CLSM 60188 2968 25W-3N B6
Horizon Ct
2000 ZION 60099 2421 12W-41N C2
2900 JLET 60435 3415 32W-20S C4
3800 NPVL 60564 3266 30W-11S A2
8400 FftT 60477 3504 10W-23S B4
8400 TYPK 60477 3504 10W-23S B4
N Horizon Ct
700 LNHT 60046 2418 20W-39N A5
Horizon Dr
400 BRLT 60103 2910 30W-9N C1
1000 BRLT 60120 2910 30W-9N C1
1300 JNBG 60050 2472 30W-37N A1
1300 MchT 60050 2472 30W-37N A1
Horizon Dr W
400 SCRL 60175 2963 37W-2N B7
400 SCRL 60175 3019 37W-2N B1

STREET Block City ZIP Map# CGS Grid

Horizon Ln
1300 NHBK 60062 2756 12W-17N C5
1600 AURA 60502 3079 33W-3S A6
Horizon Rdg
1000 LIHL 60156 2694 34W-22N B4
W Horizon Spur
23500 FmtT 60084 2644 23W-26N E3
Horizon Tr
- NLNX 60442 3589 18W-27S A5
- WLNG 60004 2754 16W-17N E5
- WLNG 60090 2754 16W-17N E5
2800 NLNX 60451 3589 18W-27S A5
Horn Rd
15100 ODPK 60462 3346 10W-18S B6
Hornbeam Ct
1000 FKFT 60423 3503 13W-25S B7
Hornblower
200 LKMR 60051 2529 28W-33N E3
Horncastle Ln
2100 NPVL 60564 3202 29W-9S C5
Horne St
10 SCRL 60174 3020 36W-2N A1
1100 SCRL 60174 3019 36W-2N E1
Horne Ter
800 DSPN 60016 2862 15W-10N B4
Horned Owl Ct
2300 ELGN 60123 2853 37W-12N D2
W Horner Av
2300 MonT 60449 3682 6W-30S E4
2300 MonT 60449 3683 6W-30S A4
2300 UYPK 60449 3682 6W-30S E4
2300 UYPK 60449 3683 6W-30S A4
2300 UYPK 60466 3682 6W-30S E4
N Horner Ln
- DSPN 60016 2808 14W-13N C7
- DSPN 60056 2808 14W-13N C7
100 MPPT 60056 2808 14W-13N C7
Horseshoe Cir
700 WCDA 60084 2643 27W-26N C3
Horseshoe Ct
10 SMWD 60107 2856 30W-10N C5
800 CLSM 60188 2967 27W-3N C5
1200 BRLT 60103 2966 30W-6N B1
2300 RLKP 60030 2532 22W-31N A7
7200 AlqT 60013 2642 29W-24N B6
7200 CRY 60013 2642 29W-24N B7
W Horseshoe Ct
1300 ADSN 60101 2970 20W-3N B5
Horseshoe Dr
- HRVD 60033 2406 50W-40N A2
10 BtvT 60510 3077 38W-2S B4
800 JLET 60435 3498 25W-22S C3
8400 TYPK 60487 3424 10W-19S B3
12500 NLNX 60451 3590 15W-26S B2
12500 NlxT 60451 3590 15W-26S B2
Horseshoe Ln
- MonT 60449 3684 3W-31S C4
- MonT 60466 3684 3W-31S C4
- UYPK 60466 3684 3W-31S C4
10 LMNT 60439 3272 15W-13S A4
1200 BRLT 60103 2910 30W-6N A7
1200 BRLT 60103 2966 30W-6N B1
3300 JLET 60432 3500 19W-23S D4
12400 MhtT 60442 3590 15W-28S B7
N Horseshoe Ln
34100 WrnT 60031 2534 17W-34N B2
W Horseshoe Ln
17400 WrnT 60031 2534 17W-34N B1
Horseshoe Tr
12600 HTLY 60142 2744 42W-19N E3
W Hortense Av
7400 CHCG 60631 2918 9W-7N C3
7700 PKRG 60068 2918 9W-7N C3
7700 PKRG 60631 2918 9W-7N C3
Horton Rd
13600 BtlT 53142 2360 B1
15200 BtlT 53142 2359 D2
17200 BtlT 53104 2359 B3
Horton Rd CO-CJ
13600 BtlT 53142 2360 B1
15200 BtlT 53142 2359 D2
17200 BtlT 53104 2359 B3
Hosler Dr
1100 BGBK 60446 3268 25W-14S C7
1100 RMVL 60446 3268 25W-14S C7
Hosmer Ln
1600 CTHL 60403 3498 25W-21S C1
1600 JLET 60435 3498 25W-21S C1
1700 CTHL 60403 3418 25W-21S C7
N Hosmer St
1200 JLET 60435 3498 25W-22S C1
1500 CTHL 60403 3498 25W-22S C1
Hospital Rd
- WNFD 60190 3023 27W-0N C6
Hotchkiss Ct
10 LNSH 60069 2701 16W-23N E2
Hotchkiss Dr
8500 FKFT 60423 3504 10W-24S B6
N Hotz Rd
- BFGV 60069 2701 15W-22N E3
10 LNSH 60069 2701 15W-23N E3
10 VrnT 60069 2701 15W-23N E3
Houbolt Dr
- JLET 60431 3497 28W-23S A5
- TroT 60431 3497 28W-23S A5
Houbolt Rd
100 JLET 60431 3497 28W-25S A7
100 TroT 60431 3497 28W-24S A5
1100 JLET 60431 3585 28W-25S B1
1400 JLET 60436 3585 28W-25S B2
Hough St
- LYVL 60048 2592 15W-28N A5
N Hough St
- NBRN 60010 2697 25W-21N E6
100 BRTN 60010 2750 25W-20N E1
700 BRTN 60010 2697 25W-20N E7
700 CbaT 60010 2697 25W-21N E6
N Hough St SR-59
- NBRN 60010 2697 25W-21N E6
100 BRTN 60010 2750 25W-20N E1
700 BRTN 60010 2697 25W-20N E7
700 CbaT 60010 2697 25W-21N E6
S Hough St
100 BRTN 60010 2750 25W-18N E3
800 BrnT 60010 2750 25W-18N E3
S Hough St SR-59
100 BRTN 60010 2750 25W-18N E3
Houghton Ct
100 WNFD 60190 3023 27W-1N C2
Houghton Ln
10 WNFD 60190 3023 27W-1N C2
Houlton Ct
800 SMBG 60193 2912 24W-9N E1
Houston Av
300 CTCY 60409 3352 3E-17S A5
900 ELGN 60120 2855 32W-10N C6
1700 JltT 60433 3587 23W-26S A2
N Houston Av
26700 WcnT 60084 2642 28W-26N E2
S Houston Av
8000 CHCG 60617 3216 3E-9S A2
12900 CHCG 60633 3280 3E-15S A7
13100 CHCG 60633 3352 3E-15S A1
Houston Ct
200 RDLK 60073 2531 24W-34N D1
Houston Dr
- FNPK 60131 2973 13W-3N A5
700 CPVL 60110 2748 33W-18N B5
Houston St
100 BTVA 60510 3078 35W-1S A1
500 LMNT 60439 3270 19W-14S E6
3000 FNPK 60131 2973 13W-3N A4
Hovland Ct
1700 EVTN 60201 2866 3W-11N E2
Howard Av
10 DSPN 60018 2862 13W-9N E7
10 EGvT 60018 2862 14W-9N B7
10 FXLK 60020 2473 27W-37N A2
10 PvsT 60162 3028 14W-0S C6
100 EDND 60118 2801 33W-15N B3
200 HLSD 60162 3028 14W-0S D5
300 AURA 60506 3137 36W-6S D6
500 ELGN 60124 2853 37W-11N D3
500 ElgT 60124 2853 37W-11N D3
1200 BKLY 60163 3028 14W-0N C3
1400 DSPN 60018 2863 13W-9N A7
2000 LslT 60515 3144 21W-5S A3
2100 LslT 60515 3143 21W-5S E3
3400 PKCY 60085 2536 13W-33N A2
3800 PvsT 60558 3086 13W-4S E7
3800 WNSP 60558 3086 13W-4S E7
4400 WNSP 60558 3146 13W-4S E1
5500 LynT 60525 3146 13W-6S E4
6500 IHPK 60525 3146 13W-7S E6
7900 LynT 60525 3208 13W-9S E2
7900 WLSP 60525 3208 13W-9S E3
N Howard Av
200 AddT 60126 2972 15W-3N A5
300 EMHT 60126 3028 15W-2N A1
600 EMHT 60126 2972 15W-2N A6
900 ADSN 60101 2970 19W-4N D3
S Howard Av
10 ROSL 60172 2913 23W-7N B5
5500 HMND 46320 3352 E7
Howard Cir
1200 WHTN 60187 3024 24W-0N D5
Howard Ct
- MaiT 60016 2863 11W-11N D4
- PKRG 60016 2863 11W-11N D4
- PKRG 60068 2863 11W-11N D4
10 BlmT 60411 3510 3E-25S A7
100 FXLK 60020 2473 27W-37N A2
600 EDND 60118 2801 33W-16N B2
1600 WHTN 60187 3024 24W-0N D4
S Howard Ct
24600 CNHN 60410 3672 32W-29S E3
Howard Dr
1000 SMBG 60193 2913 23W-9N A1
1100 WCHI 60185 3021 31W-2N D1
1100 WynT 60185 3021 31W-2N D1
Howard Sq
600 BbyT 60134 3018 39W-0N D5
Howard St
- BHPK 60087 2479 11W-38N D1
- WKGN 60087 2479 11W-38N D1
100 GNVA 60134 3020 34W-1N C3
300 EGvT 60007 2860 18W-9N E7
300 EGVV 60007 2860 18W-9N E7
600 JLET 60436 3498 25W-25S B7
600 RKDL 60436 3498 25W-25S B7
800 ElgT 60124 2853 37W-11N D3
800 SCRL 60174 3020 36W-2N A1
1000 EGVV 60007 2861 17W-9N C7
1100 SCRL 60174 3019 36W-2N E1
1200 EGvT 60007 2861 17W-9N C7
1800 WHTN 60187 3024 24W-0N D4
4700 JNBG 60050 2472 30W-36N B3
4700 MchT 60050 2472 30W-36N B3
5400 SKOK 60077 2865 6W-9N C7
5500 NLES 60077 2865 6W-9N C6
5500 NLES 60714 2865 6W-9N C6
N Howard St
500 HRVD 60033 2406 50W-38N A6
S Howard St
200 HRVD 60033 2406 50W-38N A7
300 PNFD 60544 3416 29W-18S D2
300 PNFD 60586 3416 29W-19S D3
15900 PnfT 60586 3416 29W-19S D3
W Howard St
1300 CHCG 60626 2867 1W-9N D6
1600 CHCG 60202 2867 2W-9N B6
1600 EVTN 60202 2867 2W-9N B6
1600 EVTN 60626 2867 2W-9N C6
1900 CHCG 60645 2867 2W-9N B6
2600 CHCG 60202 2866 5W-9N A7
2600 CHCG 60645 2866 5W-9N A7
2600 EVTN 60202 2866 5W-9N A7
3100 CHCG 60076 2866 3W-9N D7
3100 EVTN 60076 2866 3W-9N D7
3100 SKOK 60076 2866 3W-9N D7
4600 SKOK 60076 2865 5W-9N E7
5600 NLES 60077 2865 6W-9N C6
5600 NLES 60714 2865 6W-9N A6
5600 SKOK 60077 2865 7W-9N C6
5700 SKOK 60714 2865 7W-9N C6
6700 NLES 60714 2864 8W-9N E7
7100 CHCG 60631 2864 8W-9N D7
7100 CHCG 60714 2864 8W-9N D7
7100 NLES 60631 2864 8W-9N D7
7500 NLES 60068 2864 9W-9N C7
7500 PKRG 60068 2864 9W-9N C7
7500 PKRG 60631 2864 9W-9N C7
10000 BHPK 60087 2480 10W-38N B1
Howden Av
3000 TNLK 53181 2354 B3
Howdy Ln
1800 DRN 60561 3206 18W-8S E1
W Howdy Ln
4500 ALSP 60803 3276 5W-13S B4
Howe Av
17500 HLCT 60430 3427 2W-21S C5
17500 HMWD 60430 3427 2W-21S C5
Howe Ct
100 PltT 60010 2751 24W-18N C2
Howe Dr
7500 MchT 60097 2469 36W-37N D1
13500 OrlT 60462 3345 11W-16S D1
13500 PlsT 60462 3345 11W-16S D2
Howe Ln
1700 HRPK 60133 2967 27W-5N D1
Howe Rd
7500 MchT 60097 2469 37W-37N B1
7500 RcmT 60097 2469 37W-37N B1
7700 GwdT 60097 2469 37W-37N C1
Howe St
1200 BTVA 60510 3078 34W-3S E5
N Howe St
1100 CHCG 60610 3034 0W-1N A2
1800 CHCG 60614 2978 0W-2N A7
Howe Ter
- BRTN 60010 2751 24W-18N C2
100 PltT 60010 2751 24W-18N C2
Howell Dr
800 GNVA 60134 3020 34W-1N D2
800 GNVA 60174 3020 34W-1N D2
800 SCRL 60134 3020 34W-1N D2
1800 NLNX 60451 3590 16W-26S A3
1800 NlxT 60451 3590 16W-26S A3
Howell Pl
300 AURA 60505 3200 34W-8S C2
1000 AraT 60505 3200 34W-9S C4
1200 MTGY 60505 3200 34W-9S C4
1300 MTGY 60538 3200 34W-9S C4
W Howell Rd
2100 MchT 60051 2528 31W-34N E1
W Howland Av
2100 CHCG 60620 3213 2W-10S C4
Howland Dr
1200 JLET 60431 3495 32W-22S C1
Howliston Ct
900 JltT 60433 3587 22W-26S C2
Howliston St
1700 JltT 60433 3587 22W-26S C2
Hoxie Av
200 BNHM 60633 3351 2E-17S E5
200 CTCY 60409 3351 2E-17S E5
200 CTCY 60633 3351 2E-17S E5
200 ELGN 60123 2854 35W-11N B3
200 ElgT 60123 2854 35W-11N B3
S Hoxie Av
9600 CHCG 60617 3215 2E-11S D7
10300 CHCG 60617 3279 2E-12S D1
13400 CHCG 60633 3351 2E-15S E2
13900 BNHM 60633 3351 2E-16S E3
14500 CTCY 60409 3351 2E-16S E4
14500 CTCY 60633 3351 2E-16S E4
Hoy Av
100 WDSK 60098 2581 41W-30N C1
Hoy Rd
- WnfT 60185 3081 27W-2S B4
100 WHTN 60187 3081 27W-2S D4
100 WnfT 60555 3081 27W-2S C4
Hoyden Ct
800 SRGV 60554 3136 41W-5S A3
Hoyer Ct
300 NPVL 60565 3204 25W-10S A5
Hoyle Rd
700 MltT 60148 3025 21W-1N E2
Hoyles Av
500 AURA 60505 3200 35W-8S B2
Hoyne Av
13300 BLID 60406 3349 2W-15S C2
14200 DXMR 60426 3349 2W-16S C4
14600 HRVY 60426 3349 2W-17S C6
15600 HRVY 60426 3427 2W-18S C1
N Hoyne Av
200 CHCG 60612 3033 2W-0N B4
700 CHCG 60622 3033 2W-0N B3
1500 CHCG 60647 3033 2W-1N B1
1700 CHCG 60647 2977 2W-2N B7
2500 CHCG 60618 2977 2W-3N B5
5200 CHCG 60625 2921 2W-6N B5
6000 CHCG 60659 2921 2W-7N B3
6200 CHCG 60645 2921 2W-7N B3
7300 CHCG 60645 2867 2W-9N B7
7500 CHCG 60202 2867 2W-9N B7
7500 EVTN 60202 2867 2W-9N B7
S Hoyne Av
1200 CHCG 60608 3033 2W-1S B7
1200 CHCG 60612 3033 2W-1S B7
1700 CHCG 60608 3091 2W-2S B2
3400 CHCG 60609 3091 2W-3S B5
4700 CHCG 60609 3151 2W-5S B2
6200 CHCG 60636 3151 2W-8S C7
7500 CHCG 60620 3213 2W-8S C1
9500 CHCG 60643 3213 2W-11S C7
10200 CHCG 60643 3277 2W-12S C1
Hoyne St
12700 BLID 60406 3277 2W-15S C7
13000 BLID 60406 3349 2W-15S C1
Hoyt Av
700 AURA 60506 3137 36W-6S D6
Hoyt Dr
600 ELBN 60119 3017 43W-2N A1
Hoyt Ln
500 WNKA 60093 2812 4W-15N C2
Hoyt Pl
10 AURA 60506 3138 35W-7S A7
Hub Rd
200 WYNE 60184 2909 33W-6N A7
Hubbard Av
300 ELGN 60123 2854 35W-11N C3
1400 BTVA 60510 3020 33W-0S E7
1400 BTVA 60510 3021 33W-0S A7
1700 BtvT 60510 3021 33W-0S B7
Hubbard Cir
- LtRT 60545 3260 45W-13S B6
- PLNO 60545 3260 45W-13S B6
Hubbard Ct
100 WCDA 60084 2643 26W-27N D1
Hubbard Ln
200 CRTE 60417 3685 0W-30S C2
400 LKVL 60046 2417 22W-39N B4
6500 TYPK 60477 3425 8W-20S B3
Hubbard Pl
500 GnvT 60134 3019 38W-0S A7
1000 WNKA 60093 2759 5W-16N A7
Hubbard St
100 TNTN 60476 3428 0E-21S D6
900 WNKA 60093 2759 5W-16N A7
E Hubbard St
10 CHCG 60610 3034 0E-0N C3
10 CHCG 60611 3034 0W-0N C3
N Hubbard St
10 ALGN 60102 2694 33W-20N E7
S Hubbard St
10 ALGN 60102 2694 33W-20N E7
400 ALGN 60102 2747 33W-20N D1
W Hubbard St
10 CHCG 60611 3034 0W-0N C3
600 CHCG 60610 3034 0W-0N A3
700 CHCG 60622 3034 0W-0N A3
800 CHCG 60622 3033 2W-0N B3
1900 CHCG 60612 3033 2W-0N B3
4700 CHCG 60644 3032 5W-0N A3
4800 CHCG 60644 3031 6W-0N E3
Hubbard Wy
10 OswT 60538 3199 36W-10S E7
Hubbe Ct
- HTLY 60142 2692 40W-22N A3
Hubbell Ct
10 BNHL 60010 2750 25W-17N E4
Huber Ct
9400 ODPK 60467 3423 12W-19S D2
Huber Ln
400 GNVW 60025 2864 10W-11N A2
400 GNVW 60714 2864 10W-11N A2
400 NLES 60714 2864 10W-11N A2
700 GNVW 60025 2810 10W-13N A7
900 NfdT 60025 2810 10W-13N A6
N Huber Ln
9700 NLES 60714 2864 10W-12N A1
9900 GNVW 60025 2864 10W-12N A1
9900 GNVW 60714 2864 10W-12N A1
N Huber Ovl
9700 NLES 60714 2864 10W-12N B1
Huckins Dr
8500 FKFT 60423 3504 10W-24S B6
Huckleberry Ln
800 NHBK 60062 2756 10W-17N E4
900 GNVW 60025 2811 7W-14N A4
Hudson Av
400 CNHL 60514 3145 17W-5S C3
400 CNHL 60559 3145 17W-5S C3
400 WTMT 60559 3145 17W-5S C3
600 RMVL 60446 3340 24W-15S E1
700 BGBK 60440 3268 24W-14S E7
700 BGBK 60446 3268 24W-14S E7
700 RMVL 60440 3268 24W-14S E7
700 RMVL 60446 3268 24W-14S E7
N Hudson Av
1300 CHCG 60610 3034 0W-1N A1
1600 CHCG 60610 2978 0W-2N A7
2100 CHCG 60614 2978 0W-2N A6
3100 CHCG 60657 2978 0W-3N A4
W Hudson Av
26100 GrtT 60041 2473 26W-35N E5
Hudson Cir
2200 AURA 60502 3139 32W-7S B7
Hudson Ct
100 NPVL 60565 3204 26W-10S A5
100 ROSL 60172 2912 24W-7N E5
200 BGBK 60440 3268 23W-12S E2
600 EGVV 60007 2913 22W-9N D1
1000 BRLT 60103 2910 30W-7N C5
Hudson Dr
- MTGY 60543 3263 38W-11S A1
- OSWG 60543 3263 38W-11S A1
900 JLET 60447 3495 33W-22S D2
3900 HFET 60192 2804 24W-14N D3
Hudson Rd
700 GNVW 60025 2810 8W-13N E7
700 GNVW 60025 2811 8W-13N A7
Hudson St
10 DGvT 60561 3145 18W-8S A7
10 DGvT 60561 3207 18W-8S A1
10 DRN 60561 3145 18W-8S A7
10 DRN 60561 3207 18W-8S A1
500 HMND 46327 3352 D4
E Hudson St
800 HMND 46327 3352 E4
N Hudson St
10 WTMT 60559 3145 18W-5S A2
S Hudson St
10 WTMT 60559 3145 18W-5S A3
Hudson Tr
3200 OMFD 60461 3507 4W-24S A5
N Hudson Bay
1700 PLTN 60074 2753 18W-18N D3
Hudson Bluff Dr
500 ELGN 60123 2854 36W-12N A2
Huehl Rd
- DRFD 60015 2756 11W-18N C2
200 NHBK 60062 2756 11W-18N C4
E Huehn St
200 HMND 46327 3352 D4
Huemann Dr
2600 MchT 60050 2471 31W-34N D7
Huey Ct
1400 BTVA 60510 3078 34W-2S C4
N Huffman St
10 NPVL 60540 3141 26W-6S E5
S Huffman St
10 NPVL 60540 3141 26W-6S E5
Huggins Dr
- MKHM 60426 3426 4W-19S D2
- MKHM 60428 3426 4W-19S D2
E Hugh St
1500 DMND 60416 3941 33W-39S B2
N Hugh St
10 PLNO 60545 3259 47W-13S C6
S Hugh St
100 PLNO 60545 3259 47W-14S D7
Hughes Av
100 LktT 60441 3419 23W-20S B5
300 LKPT 60441 3419 23W-20S B5
1300 DRGV 60516 3206 20W-8S C1
Hughes Pl
600 BGBK 60440 3205 22W-10S B6
800 VNHL 60061 2647 16W-26N D3
Hughes Rd
10 BbyT 60119 3017 42W-0S D7
10 BbyT 60119 3018 39W-0S D7
400 ELBN 60119 3017 42W-0N C6
800 BbyT 60134 3018 39W-0S E7
Hughes Rd CO-26
10 BbyT 60119 3017 42W-0S D7
10 BbyT 60119 3018 39W-0S D7
400 ELBN 60119 3017 42W-0N B6
800 BbyT 60134 3018 39W-0S E7
Hughes St
22300 FKFT 60423 3590 14W-27S E4
22300 FKFT 60423 3591 14W-27S A4
Hughsdale St
3000 ElgT 60124 2853 37W-11N B4
Hugo Ct
400 VLPK 60181 3026 18W-1N E2
Huguelet Pl
8900 ODPK 60462 3346 11W-18S A6
Hull Av
1300 WSTR 60154 3029 12W-1S B7
1400 WSTR 60154 3087 12W-1S B1
2100 PvsT 60154 3087 12W-1S B2
2100 PvsT 60525 3087 12W-1S B2
Hull Ct
300 WKGN 60085 2480 10W-35N A7
1100 AURA 60504 3201 32W-9S B3
2100 NPVL 60565 3204 25W-9S B4
E Hull Dr
1100 WHTN 60187 3082 23W-3S E5
S Hull Dr
2100 WHTN 60187 3082 23W-3S E5
Hull Ln
900 CLLK 60014 2640 35W-24N A7
Hull St
3800 SKOK 60076 2866 4W-9N B6
4800 SKOK 60077 2865 6W-9N E6
Hull Ter
600 EVTN 60202 2867 2W-9N B6
Humber Ln
17300 TYPK 60487 3424 10W-21S B5
Humber Bridge Dr
21700 FftT 60423 3590 14W-26S D2
Humboldt Av
700 WNKA 60093 2812 5W-16N B1
N Humboldt Blvd
1600 CHCG 60647 2976 3W-2N E6
N Humboldt Dr
1000 CHCG 60622 3032 3W-1N E1
1500 CHCG 60647 3032 3W-1N E1
S Humboldt Dr
20700 FftT 60423 3504 9W-25S E7
Humbolt St
10300 HTLY 60142 2692 39W-20N D7
Humbraacht Cir
1200 BRLT 60120 2910 30W-7N B5
Humbracht Cir
- BRLT 60120 2910 30W-7N B4
Hummingbird Ct
10 SMWD 60107 2856 30W-10N C6
400 VrnT 60015 2755 14W-20N B1
1100 SRWD 60404 3496 30W-23S B4
24500 DRPK 60010 2698 24W-21N C5
W Hummingbird Ct
21500 KLDR 60047 2699 21W-21N D5
Hummingbird Dr
- BlmT 60411 3509 3E-25S E7
18000 TYPK 60487 3424 11W-21S A7
Hummingbird Ln
10 SMWD 60107 2856 30W-10N C6
300 BGBK 60440 3268 23W-12S E3
300 LNHT 60046 2476 19W-37N C2
500 VrnT 60015 2755 15W-20N B2
600 LslT 60540 3142 25W-5S C3
1000 PTON 60468 3860 10W-38S C5
1100 GYLK 60030 2533 19W-32N C4
11300 MKNA 60448 3502 14W-22S D1
11400 FftT 60448 3502 14W-22S D1
Hummingbird St
10 PltT 60140 2851 42W-12N C1
Hummingbird Wy
100 BRLT 60103 2910 28W-6N E6
Hummingbird Hill Dr
9700 ODPK 60467 3423 12W-19S D2
Humpfer St
200 HMND 46324 3430 D3
S Humphrey Av
100 OKPK 60302 3031 7W-0N B4
500 OKPK 60304 3031 7W-0S B5
1100 CCRO 60304 3031 7W-0S B7
1100 CCRO 60804 3031 7W-0S B7
Humphrey Av N
700 OKPK 60302 3031 7W-1N B2
1200 CHCG 60302 3031 7W-1N B1
1200 CHCG 60639 3031 7W-1N B1
Humphreys Ln
400 AURA 60504 3201 31W-8S D2
N Hundley St
600 HFET 60169 2858 25W-11N B4
W Hundley St
1400 HFET 60169 2858 25W-11N B4
Hundley Wy
1600 HFET 60169 2858 25W-11N B4
1600 HFET 60194 2858 25W-11N B4
1600 SMBG 60194 2858 25W-11N B4
N Hunt Av
35600 GrtT 60041 2473 26W-35N E5
S Hunt Av
5300 SMMT 60501 3148 9W-5S D3
W Hunt Av
2000 CHCG 60620 3213 2W-10S C4
Hunt Ct
10 MDLN 60060 2647 17W-26N A3
Hunt St
10 BtlT 60512 3261 42W-12S E3
Hunt Tr
10 LKBN 60010 2643 26W-24N E7
Huntcliff Ct
10 FRGV 60021 2696 29W-22N B4
Huntcliff Rd
1400 BRLT 60103 2910 30W-6N B7
1400 BRLT 60103 2966 30W-5N A1
Hunt Club Ct
1000 SCRL 60174 2964 34W-3N C6
3000 RLKP 60030 2589 21W-30N C1
23900 WldT 60564 3266 29W-12S C3
W Hunt Club Ct
12900 HMGN 60491 3422 16W-21S A6
Hunt Club Dr
- OSWG 60560 3334 39W-14S E1
- RtdT 60136 2745 39W-18N D5
- RtdT 60142 2745 39W-18N D5
10 OKBK 60523 3086 15W-2S B4
10 SCRL 60174 2964 34W-3N D6
20700 FKFT 60423 3503 11W-25S E6
S Hunt Club Dr
1000 MPPT 60056 2861 16W-11N E3
W Hunt Club Dr
17900 HMGN 60491 3422 16W-21S A7
Hunt Club Ln
10 OKBK 60523 3086 15W-2S B4
13700 PNFD 60544 3339 28W-16S A5
13800 PnfT 60544 3339 28W-16S A4
Hunt Club Rd
- RcmT 60071 2353 34W-42N D5
- RHMD 60071 2353 34W-42N D5
N Hunt Club Rd
1100 GRNE 60031 2477 17W-35N C6
33000 GRNE 60031 2534 17W-34N C2
33000 WrnT 60030 2534 16W-33N C4
33000 WrnT 60031 2534 17W-34N C2
33000 WrnT 60048 2534 17W-34N C2
33200 GRNE 60030 2534 17W-33N C3
33200 GRNE 60048 2534 17W-34N C2
34500 WrnT 60031 2477 17W-36N C7
36600 WrnT 60083 2477 17W-37N C3
37200 OMCK 60083 2477 17W-38N C1
38200 NptT 60083 2419 17W-38N B7
38200 NptT 60083 2477 17W-38N C1
38200 OMCK 60083 2419 17W-40N B3
41600 NptT 60002 2360 17W-43N B5
41600 NptT 60083 2360 17W-41N B7
41600 OMCK 60083 2360 17W-42N B7
43400 BtlT 53142 2360 17W-43N B4
43400 NptT 53142 2360 17W-43N B4
N Hunt Club Rd CO-W15
1100 GRNE 60031 2477 17W-35N C6
33000 GRNE 60031 2534 17W-34N C2

STREET Block	City	ZIP	Map#	CGS	Grid
N Hunt Club Rd CO-W15					
33000	WrnT	60030	2534	16W-33N	C4
33000	WrnT	60031	2534	17W-34N	C2
33000	WrnT	60048	2534	17W-34N	C2
33200	GRNE	60030	2534	17W-33N	C3
33200	GRNE	60048	2534	17W-33N	C3
34500	WrnT	60031	2477	17W-34N	C7
36600	WrnT	60083	2477	17W-37N	C3
37200	OMCK	60083	2477	17W-38N	C1
38200	NptT	60083	2419	17W-38N	B7
38200	NptT	60083	2477	17W-38N	C1
38200	OMCK	60083	2419	17W-40N	B3
41600	NptT	60002	2360	17W-43N	B5
41600	NptT	60083	2360	17W-41N	B7
41600	OMCK	60083	2360	17W-42N	B7
43400	BtlT	53142	2360	17W-43N	B4
43400	NptT	53142	2360	17W-43N	B4
Hunt Club Tr					
-	NptT	60083	2419	16W-40N	D2
-	WDWH	60083	2419	16W-40N	D2
S Hunter Av					
10	JLET	60435	3498	24W-24S	D5
10	JLET	60436	3498	24W-24S	D6
Hunter Cir					
1200	NPVL	60540	3204	25W-8S	C1
Hunter Ct					
10	BRRG	60527	3208	15W-10S	A4
10	OswT	60538	3199	36W-10S	E6
100	RLKP	60030	2589	22W-30N	A1
200	VNHL	60061	2647	18W-25N	A5
400	CmpT	60175	2961	42W-4N	D4
500	WLMT	60091	2812	4W-13N	B6
900	DRFD	60015	2703	11W-21N	D5
1500	GNVA	60134	3020	33W-1N	E2
9300	ODHL	60487	3423	11W-19S	E2
W Hunter Ct					
1200	ADSN	60101	2970	19W-4N	B2
Hunter Dr					
-	WLNG	60090	2754	16W-17N	D6
10	OswT	60538	3199	36W-10S	E6
10	ROSL	60172	2912	24W-7N	D5
300	CLSM	60188	2967	26W-4N	E4
300	CLSM	60188	2968	26W-4N	A4
600	OKBK	60523	3086	15W-1S	A2
700	BTVA	60510	3021	33W-0S	A7
700	BTVA	60510	3079	33W-0S	A1
1000	ELGN	60120	2855	32W-11N	D3
1200	SRWD	60404	3496	31W-24S	A6
1300	BRLT	60103	2966	30W-5N	B1
1600	SRWD	60404	3495	31W-24S	E6
5200	MHRY	60050	2527	34W-33N	D2
5600	RcmT	60071	2412	34W-41N	C1
5600	RHMD	60071	2412	34W-41N	C1
9200	ODHL	60487	3423	11W-19S	E2
9200	ODPK	60467	3423	11W-19S	E2
E Hunter Dr					
2200	ANHT	60004	2807	16W-16N	D1
S Hunter Dr					
20300	FftT	60423	3504	9W-24S	E6
Hunter Ln					
10	BtlT	60512	3261	42W-12S	D3
400	LKFT	60045	2649	11W-25N	D5
E Hunter Ln					
400	MNKA	60447	3672	33W-30S	C4
W Hunter Ln					
400	MNKA	60447	3672	33W-30S	C4
W Hunter Pth					
3200	MHRY	60050	2585	32W-30N	C1
Hunter Rd					
500	WLMT	60091	2812	5W-13N	B6
1000	GNVW	60025	2811	6W-13N	C6
1500	BmdT	60133	2967	26W-5N	D2
1500	HRPK	60133	2967	26W-5N	D2
Hunter St					
1000	LMBD	60148	3084	21W-1S	A2
1100	LMBD	60148	3083	21W-1S	E2
N Hunter St					
100	TNTN	60476	3428	0E-21S	D6
S Hunter St					
100	TNTN	60476	3428	0E-21S	D6
23500	CnhT	60410	3584	30W-28S	C7
Hunter Ter					
19400	NlxT	60448	3502	16W-23S	A3
19400	NlxT	60451	3502	16W-23S	A3
Hunter Tr					
300	PltT	60124	2852	40W-11N	B4
10100	HTLY	60142	2692	39W-21N	C5
16600	TYPK	60477	3425	8W-19S	A3
Hunterdon Ct					
200	SMBG	60194	2857	27W-10N	D5
Hunters Cir					
100	SMBG	60193	2859	23W-9N	A7
300	FRGV	60021	2696	30W-22N	B4
Hunters Ct					
2000	SPGV	60081	2354	31W-41N	E7
2000	SPGV	60081	2413	30W-41N	E1
Hunters Dr					
200	BCHR	60401	3774	0W-35S	D6
Hunters Ln					
10	CmpT	60175	2961	41W-5N	E3
800	LYVL	60048	2592	15W-27N	A7
1100	LKZH	60047	2698	24W-22N	B3
2300	RLKB	60073	2475	21W-36N	D4
24300	DRPK	60010	2698	24W-21N	C6
N Hunters Ln					
9600	SPGV	60081	2355	30W-41N	A7
9600	SPGV	60081	2414	30W-41N	A1
W Hunters Ln					
1700	SPGV	60081	2414	30W-41N	A1
1900	SPGV	60081	2354	31W-41N	E7
Hunters Pth					
10	LIHL	60156	2694	35W-21N	A5
600	MRGO	60152	2634	49W-25N	D4
6500	AlqT	60013	2641	31W-25N	D5
Hunters Rdg					
800	CmpT	60175	2961	41W-5N	E2
Hunters Rdg E					
1100	HFET	60192	2856	30W-12N	B2
Hunters Rdg W					
1100	HFET	60192	2856	30W-12N	B2
Hunters Tr					
1100	CLLK	60014	2693	37W-22N	B3
22600	FKFT	60423	3592	9W-27S	E4
Hunters Wy					
200	HNVL	60030	2532	21W-33N	C3
400	FRGV	60021	2696	30W-22N	A4
14900	LKPT	60441	3342	20W-17S	B6
Hunters Gate Rd					
300	SchT	60175	2963	36W-5N	E2
Hunters Glen Ct					
1600	WHTN	60187	3082	24W-1S	C2
Hunters Glen Dr					
100	WHTN	60187	3082	24W-1S	C2
Hunters Hill Dr					
10	CmpT	60175	2961	42W-4N	D3
400	CmpT	60175	2962	41W-5N	A3
Hunters Ridge Ct					
5500	HFET	60192	2856	30W-12N	B2
Hunters Ridge Dr					
-	BfdT	53128	2353		B2
800	GNCY	53128	2353		B2
Hunters Ridge Ln					
-	SRGV	60554	3135	42W-4S	C1
Hunter Trails Pkwy					
-	OKBK	60523	3085	16W-3S	D4
Hunter Woods Dr					
21100	FftT	60423	3504	9W-25S	D7
21100	FKFT	60423	3504	9W-25S	D7
21100	FKFT	60423	3592	9W-25S	D1
W Hunting Ct					
1100	PLTN	60067	2805	22W-15N	B2
W Hunting Dr					
1000	PLTN	60067	2805	22W-15N	B3
Hunting Tr					
100	BtvT	60510	3077	38W-2S	A4
Hunting Hound Ln					
1500	BRLT	60103	2966	30W-5N	B2
Huntington Blvd					
-	HFET	60169	2804	25W-12N	B7
-	SBTN	60010	2804	25W-13N	B6
-	SBTN	60192	2804	25W-13N	B6
600	WDND	60118	2799	36W-16N	E3
600	WDND	60118	2800	36W-16N	A2
1800	HFET	60169	2858	25W-12N	B1
3600	HFET	60192	2804	25W-14N	B4
4700	HFET	60010	2804	25W-15N	B1
4700	IVNS	60010	2804	25W-15N	B1
Huntington Cir					
-	LslT	60540	3142	24W-6S	C5
10	NPVL	60540	3142	24W-6S	C5
500	LKVL	60046	2475	21W-37N	C2
7700	HRPK	60133	2857	26W-9N	E7
17000	WrnT	60030	2534	17W-33N	C3
Huntington Ct					
10	BRRG	60527	3208	14W-8S	D2
10	MDLN	60060	2591	17W-27N	B7
10	MDLN	60060	2647	18W-27N	A2
100	MltT	60137	3083	21W-2S	D3
100	OSWG	60543	3200	35W-10S	A6
200	LGPK	60525	3087	12W-2S	B3
200	SRWD	60404	3496	30W-24S	B5
600	ALGN	60102	2694	34W-20N	C7
600	LslT	60540	3142	25W-6S	C5
700	LKZH	60047	2699	22W-22N	C4
1000	EGVV	60007	2914	20W-8N	A2
1100	CLSM	60188	2967	26W-4N	E4
1600	FSMR	60422	3507	2W-23S	E4
1700	WLNG	60090	2754	16W-18N	D3
8600	JSTC	60458	3210	10W-8S	A1
10000	ODPK	60462	3345	12W-17S	B6
15200	ODPK	60467	3345	12W-18S	C7
W Huntington Ct					
9200	MKNA	60448	3503	12W-22S	D1
Huntington Dr					
-	HFET	60107	2857	28W-11N	A4
10	ALGN	60102	2694	34W-20N	D7
10	ALGN	60102	2747	34W-20N	D1
10	WNVL	60555	3080	30W-1S	B2
200	SMWD	60107	2857	28W-11N	A4
600	CLSM	60188	2967	27W-4N	D4
700	AURA	60506	3137	36W-5S	E4
700	LKZH	60047	2699	22W-22N	C5
800	CLLK	60014	2639	36W-24N	D7
900	EGVV	60007	2914	20W-8N	A2
1100	MDLN	60061	2647	17W-27N	A1
1100	SRWD	60404	3496	30W-24S	A5
1100	VNHL	60061	2647	17W-27N	A1
1400	CTCY	60409	3429	2E-19S	D3
1400	GNVW	60025	2810	8W-14N	E5
1400	MDLN	60060	2591	17W-27N	B7
1400	MDLN	60060	2647	17W-27N	B1
1500	SHLD	60409	3429	2E-19S	D3
1500	SHLD	60473	3429	2E-20S	D3
N Huntington Dr					
-	MDLN	60060	2647	17W-27N	B1
-	MDLN	60061	2647	17W-27N	B1
-	VNHL	60061	2647	17W-27N	B1
100	MHRY	60050	2527	34W-32N	D5
2900	ANHT	60004	2754	17W-17N	C5
S Huntington Dr					
500	RDLK	60073	2531	23W-32N	E4
Huntington Dr N					
1100	ALGN	60102	2694	35W-21N	A6
1800	ALGN	60102	2693	35W-21N	E7
Huntington Ln					
-	BtlT	60512	3198	41W-10S	A7
10	BFGV	60089	2754	16W-18N	D4
10	BFGV	60090	2754	16W-18N	D4
10	WLNG	60090	2754	16W-18N	D4
600	SMBG	60193	2859	23W-9N	A7
1600	HDPK	60035	2704	9W-21N	B5
3100	NHBK	60062	2756	11W-16N	D6
3300	ISLK	60042	2586	30W-28N	A5
E Huntington Ln					
300	EMHT	60126	3028	15W-1N	B3
Huntington Pl					
100	MltT	60137	3083	21W-2S	D3
10200	ODPK	60462	3345	12W-17S	B6
Huntington Rd					
-	ADSN	60101	2970	20W-4N	A2
500	MltT	60137	3083	21W-2S	D3
1600	SCRL	60174	2964	34W-3N	D5
Huntington St					
100	NCHI	60044	2593	13W-29N	A3
W Huntington St					
6100	CHCG	60646	2919	7W-7N	A3
6300	CHCG	60631	2919	8W-7N	A3
Huntington Ter					
3400	CRTE	60417	3596	0W-28S	D6
3400	STGR	60475	3596	0W-28S	D6
Huntington Wy					
300	BGBK	60440	3205	22W-11S	D7
W Huntington Commons Rd					
500	DSPN	60016	2861	16W-11N	E3
500	MPPT	60016	2861	16W-11N	E4
500	MPPT	60056	2861	16W-11N	E4
Huntington Estates Dr					
5300	JLET	60586	3416	30W-20S	C5
Huntington Lakes Dr					
2300	WKGN	60048	2535	15W-31N	A7
Huntingwood Rd					
10	MTSN	60443	3505	7W-24S	D5
Huntleigh Ct					
1400	WHTN	60187	3082	24W-1S	D2
17900	CCHL	60478	3426	5W-21S	C6
Huntleigh Dr					
800	NPVL	60540	3142	25W-7S	B7
1000	NPVL	60540	3204	25W-7S	B1
1500	WHTN	60187	3082	24W-1S	D2
Huntleigh Rd					
10	PSPK	60464	3272	13W-14S	E7
12400	HMGN	60491	3344	15W-16S	B4
Huntleigh Rd					
12400	HmrT	60491	3344	15W-16S	B4
Huntley Ct					
10	CRTE	60417	3597	1E-28S	A6
Huntley Rd					
-	WDND	60110	2800	35W-16N	C1
10	CPVL	60110	2746	37W-18N	D5
10	CPVL	60118	2746	37W-18N	D5
10	DndT	60110	2746	37W-18N	D5
10	DndT	60118	2746	37W-18N	D5
10	RtdT	60118	2746	39W-19N	A2
10	RtdT	60142	2746	39W-19N	A2
200	RtdT	60118	2745	39W-19N	E2
200	RtdT	60142	2745	39W-19N	E2
300	CPVL	60110	2747	36W-17N	A6
300	DndT	60118	2747	36W-17N	A7
300	WDND	60118	2747	36W-17N	A7
500	GfnT	60102	2745	39W-19N	E2
500	GfnT	60142	2745	39W-19N	E2
500	RtdT	60102	2745	39W-19N	E2
700	CPVL	60110	2800	35W-17N	C1
700	CPVL	60118	2800	35W-17N	C1
700	WDND	60118	2800	35W-17N	C1
6600	LKWD	60014	2639	37W-24N	B7
6800	CLLK	60014	2639	37W-25N	B5
6900	GfnT	60014	2639	37W-25N	B6
7700	CLLK	60014	2693	37W-23N	B1
8100	LKWD	60014	2693	37W-23N	B1
8200	GfnT	60014	2693	37W-23N	B1
8200	GfnT	60156	2693	37W-23N	B2
Huntley Rd CO-30					
10	CPVL	60110	2746	37W-18N	D5
10	CPVL	60118	2746	37W-18N	D5
10	DndT	60110	2746	37W-18N	D5
10	DndT	60118	2746	37W-18N	D5
10	RtdT	60118	2746	39W-19N	A2
10	RtdT	60142	2746	39W-19N	A2
200	RtdT	60118	2745	39W-19N	E2
200	RtdT	60142	2745	39W-19N	E2
300	CPVL	60110	2747	36W-17N	A6
300	DndT	60118	2747	36W-17N	A7
300	WDND	60118	2747	36W-17N	A7
500	GfnT	60102	2745	39W-19N	E2
500	GfnT	60142	2745	39W-19N	E2
500	RtdT	60102	2745	39W-19N	E2
Huntley Ter					
500	CRTE	60417	3596	0E-28S	E6
3400	CRTE	60417	3597	0E-28S	A6
3400	STGR	60475	3597	0E-28S	A6
Huntley Woods Ct					
800	CRTE	60417	3597	0E-28S	A6
Huntley Woods Dr					
800	CRTE	60417	3597	1E-28S	A5
Huntly					
2100	IVNS	60067	2804	23W-14N	D4
Huntly Ct					
700	SMBG	60194	2857	26W-11N	E4
W Huntmaster Ln					
13100	LMNT	60439	3343	16W-15S	E2
13100	LMNT	60439	3344	16W-15S	A2
Huntsbridge Rd					
10	RchT	60443	3593	8W-26S	B2
Huntsman					
10	LMNT	60439	3272	15W-13S	B5
Huntsman Trails					
10	LtRT	60545	3258	50W-13S	C5
Huntsmoor Dr					
800	FKFT	60423	3592	9W-26S	D2
Hunt Wyck Ct					
1000	ELGN	60120	2855	32W-12N	D2
Huntwyck Ct					
200	SMBG	60173	2859	21W-11N	E3
Hurd Av					
2600	EVTN	60201	2812	4W-13N	D7
2700	WLMT	60091	2812	4W-13N	D7
2700	WLMT	60201	2812	4W-13N	D7
N Hurdale Ln					
23900	LKBN	60010	2697	28W-23N	A1
Hurlburt Ct					
100	LYVL	60048	2591	16W-29N	D5
W Hurlbut St					
6500	CHCG	60631	2919	8W-7N	A4
6600	CHCG	60631	2918	8W-7N	E4
Hurley Ln					
-	WHTN	60187	3082	25W-1S	A1
Hurlingham Ct					
10	WNVL	60555	3080	30W-2S	B5
Hurlingham Dr					
10	WNVL	60555	3080	30W-2S	C4
Huron Ct					
800	CLSM	60188	2968	25W-3N	A5
1000	ELGN	60120	2801	32W-12N	D7
S Huron Ct					
17200	LKPT	60441	3420	21W-20S	A5
Huron Dr					
100	BMDL	60108	2969	22W-5N	D2
600	RMVL	60446	3340	24W-15S	C1
800	ELGN	60120	2801	32W-12N	C7
1400	SPGV	60081	2355	30W-43N	A5
7100	MchT	60097	2469	36W-36N	E4
Huron St					
-	BKLY	60163	3028	14W-0N	C3
-	MLPK	60160	3029	10W-0N	E3
-	MYWD	60153	3029	10W-0N	E3
-	MYWD	60160	3029	10W-0N	E3
10	MYWD	60153	3030	10W-0N	A3
400	PKFT	60466	3595	4W-27S	A5
3500	NCHI	60088	2593	12W-30N	B2
16100	LktT	60403	3418	25W-19S	B3
E Huron St					
10	CHCG	60610	3034	0E-0N	C3
10	CHCG	60611	3034	0E-0N	C3
200	VNHL	60061	2647	16W-24N	D7
200	VNHL	60061	2701	16W-24N	D1
N Huron St					
2200	ANHT	60004	2753	18W-16N	E7
W Huron St					
10	CHCG	60610	3034	0W-0N	A3
10	CHCG	60611	3034	0W-0N	B3
800	CHCG	60622	3033	1W-0N	E3
1900	CHCG	60612	3033	3W-0N	A3
3100	CHCG	60612	3032	4W-0N	D3
3100	CHCG	60624	3032	4W-0N	C3
4600	CHCG	60644	3032	5W-0N	A3
4700	CHCG	60644	3031	7W-0N	C3
5900	OKPK	60302	3031	7W-0N	B3
Huron Ter					
2300	WKGN	60087	2479	11W-36N	D4
Huron Tr					
500	LIHL	60156	2694	34W-21N	C5
Huron Bay					
-	BHPK	60099	2422	9W-38N	D7
W Huron Hills Tr					
600	RLKH	60073	2474	23W-36N	D4
Husking Peg Ln					
2900	GNVA	60134	3019	37W-1N	C4
E Huston Rd					
7400	BCVL	60407	4030	33W-44S	A5
7400	BvlT	60407	4030	33W-44S	A5
8300	RedT	60407	4030	33W-44S	C5
Hutchings Av					
1100	GNVW	60025	2810	8W-13N	E6
N Hutchins Rd					
36000	GRNE	60031	2477	18W-36N	A4
36000	WrnT	60031	2477	18W-36N	A4
36500	OMCK	60031	2477	18W-36N	A3
36600	OMCK	60083	2477	18W-36N	A3
37400	LNHT	60046	2476	18W-37N	E2
37400	OMCK	60046	2476	18W-37N	E2
37400	OMCK	60083	2476	18W-37N	E2
Hutchins St					
100	WDSK	60098	2524	41W-31N	D7
W Hutchins St					
200	JLET	60435	3498	24W-22S	D2
Hutchinson Av					
20500	BlmT	60411	3507	2W-24S	C6
N Hutchinson St					
200	HRVD	60033	2406	49W-39N	D5
S Hutchinson St					
100	HRVD	60033	2406	50W-38N	A7
W Hutchinson St					
600	CHCG	60613	2977	1W-5N	E1
600	CHCG	60613	2978		A1
2000	CHCG	60618	2977	2W-5N	B1
3300	CHCG	60618	2976	4W-5N	D1
4400	CHCG	60641	2976	5W-5N	A1
4700	CHCG	60641	2975	6W-5N	D1
5500	CHCG	60634	2975	6W-5N	C1
Hutchison Rd					
-	BlmT	60430	3507	2W-22S	D2
700	FSMR	60422	3507	2W-22S	D2
Huttner Ct					
2000	HFET	60169	2858	26W-12N	A1
Hyacinth Ct					
10	LslT	60540	3142	24W-6S	D4
4800	JLET	60586	3416	30W-21S	C7
Hyacinth Dr					
600	DGvT	60527	3207	16W-10S	D6
10100	ODPK	60462	3345	12W-17S	C6
Hyacinth Ln					
100	DRFD	60015	2757	10W-20N	B2
300	MTSN	60443	3593	7W-26S	C2
Hyacinth Pl					
500	HDPK	60035	2650	9W-24N	B7
W Hyacinth St					
6200	CHCG	60646	2919	7W-7N	A3
6300	CHCG	60631	2919	8W-7N	A3
Hyacinth Ter					
3200	ISLK	60042	2586	29W-28N	D5
Hyacynth Ln					
900	BRLT	60103	2910	29W-6N	C7
Hyannis Cir					
1000	CLSM	60188	2967	27W-4N	B4
Hyannis Ct					
800	SMBG	60194	2858	24W-10N	D5
Hyatt Dr					
300	LYVL	60048	2591	16W-29N	D3
1300	WHTN	60187	3082	23W-3S	E5
Hybernia Dr					
1800	HDPK	60035	2704	10W-22N	A4
Hyde Ct					
2200	SMBG	60194	2857	28W-12N	B1
N Hyde Pk					
400	BbyT	60134	3076	39W-1S	D1
S Hyde Pk					
10	BbyT	60134	3076	39W-1S	E2
10	GnvT	60134	3076	39W-1S	E2
Hyde Park Av					
10	BLWD	60104	3029	13W-0N	A3
400	HLSD	60162	3029	13W-0N	A5
2100	WKGN	60085	2536	12W-33N	B1
2400	HHLL	60051	2586	30W-29N	B4
2400	NndT	60051	2586	30W-29N	B4
N Hyde Park Av					
2600	LydT	60164	2973	13W-3N	A6
S Hyde Park Av					
200	JLET	60436	3498	24W-24S	D6
W Hyde Park Av					
12900	GRNE	60031	2536	12W-33N	A1
12900	WKGN	60085	2536	12W-33N	A1
12900	WkgT	60031	2536	12W-33N	A1
12900	WkgT	60085	2536	12W-33N	A1
E Hyde Park Blvd					
800	CHCG	60615	3152	1E-5S	E1
1100	CHCG	60615	3153	1E-5S	A1
S Hyde Park Blvd					
5100	CHCG	60615	3153	2E-5S	B2
5400	CHCG	60637	3153	2E-6S	B3
Hyde Park Ln					
200	NPVL	60565	3204	25W-8S	B2
E Hydraulic Av					
100	YKVL	60560	3333	42W-15S	C2
W Hydraulic Av					
100	YKVL	60560	3333	43W-15S	B2
Hygate Dr					
1100	ROSL	60172	2912	24W-7N	C5
Hyland Pl					
10200	CHRG	60415	3275	8W-11S	B1
Hyles Blvd					
-	HMND	46320	3352		D7
Hyles Ct					
500	HMND	46320	3352		D7
Hypoint Dr					
400	DRPK	60010	2698	23W-21N	D6
S Hyslop Pl					
5900	HMND	46320	3430		D1
Hyte St					
-	PLNO	60545	3259	48W-13S	B5
Hythe Cir					
200	DrrT	60098	2526	36W-31N	C6
200	NndT	60098	2526	36W-31N	C6
Hywood Ln					
10	BGBK	60440	3205	23W-11S	A7
I					
I-55					
-	BCVL	-	4030	33W-43S	B2
-	BDWD	-	3941	33W-42S	C7
-	BGBK	-	3268	24W-13S	E5
-	BGBK	-	3269	23W-13S	A4
-	BGBK	-	3270	21W-11S	A1
-	BGBK	-	3339	28W-17S	B6
-	BRRG	-	3146	14W-8S	D7
-	BvlT	-	3941	33W-42S	C6
-	BvlT	-	4030	33W-43S	B2
-	CNHN	-	3584	30W-28S	D7
-	DGvT	-	3270	21W-11S	A1
-	DMND	-	3941	31W-39S	E2
-	DPgT	-	3268	24W-14S	C6
-	DPgT	-	3269	22W-12S	D2
-	DPgT	-	3270	21W-11S	A1
I-55					
-	GDLY	-	4030	33W-43S	B2
-	IHPK	-	3146	14W-8S	D7
-	JLET	-	3416	29W-21S	E6
-	JLET	-	3417	28W-18S	B1
-	JLET	-	3496	29W-24S	D6
-	PNFD	-	3339	27W-15S	D2
-	PNFD	-	3417	28W-18S	B1
-	PnfT	-	3339	27W-15S	D2
-	PnfT	-	3416	28W-21S	E7
-	PnfT	-	3417	28W-18S	B1
-	PnfT	-	3496	29W-24S	D6
-	RedT	-	3941	32W-39S	E2
-	RMVL	-	3268	25W-14S	B7
-	RMVL	-	3339	26W-15S	E2
-	RMVL	-	3340	26W-14S	A1
-	SRWD	-	3496	29W-23S	E3
-	TroT	-	3496	29W-23S	D5
-	TroT	-	3584	29W-26S	D2
-	WldT	-	3339	27W-15S	C3
-	WmTp	-	3941	31W-39S	E1
-	WmTp	-	3942	31W-39S	A1
I-55 Joliet Rd					
-	BGBK	-	3270	20W-11S	A1
-	BRRG	-	3146	14W-8S	D7
-	BRRG	-	3207	18W-10S	A4
-	BRRG	-	3208	15W-8S	B1
-	DGvT	-	3206	19W-10S	D5
-	DGvT	-	3207	16W-9S	D3
-	DGvT	-	3270	21W-11S	A1
-	DPgT	-	3270	20W-11S	A1
-	DRN	-	3206	20W-11S	B7
-	DRN	-	3207	18W-9S	B4
-	IHPK	-	3146	14W-7S	D7
-	WDRG	-	3206	20W-11S	C7
-	WDRG	-	3270	21W-11S	A1
-	WLBK	-	3207	18W-10S	A4
-	WLBK	-	3208	15W-8S	B1
I-55 Stevenson Expwy					
-	BDPK	-	3147	11W-7S	E6
-	BDPK	-	3148	10W-6S	A4
-	CHCG	-	3089	6W-4S	E6
-	CHCG	-	3090	5W-4S	A6
-	CHCG	-	3091	1W-2S	D3
-	CHCG	-	3092	0E-2S	C2
-	CTSD	-	3146	14W-8S	D7
-	CTSD	-	3147	12W-7S	C7
-	FTVW	-	3089	6W-4S	E7
-	FTVW	-	3148	10W-6S	B4
-	FTVW	-	3149	7W-5S	B1
-	HGKN	-	3147	13W-8S	A7
-	IHPK	-	3146	14W-8S	D7
-	SKNY	-	3089	6W-4S	E7
-	SMMT	-	3148	9W-5S	D2
-	StkT	-	3089	6W-4S	E7
I-57					
-	BLID	-	3277	2W-15S	D7
-	BLID	-	3349	3W-17S	B5
-	BmnT	-	3349	3W-17S	A6
-	BmnT	-	3425	6W-21S	E6
-	BmnT	-	3426	6W-21S	A7
-	BmnT	-	3426	5W-19S	B3
-	CCHL	-	3506	6W-22S	A1
-	CHCG	-	3213	1W-11S	E7
-	CHCG	-	3214	0W-11S	B6
-	CHCG	-	3277	1W-12S	D2
-	ClmT	-	3349	3W-17S	B5
-	CTPK	-	3277	2W-13S	D5
-	DXMR	-	3349	3W-17S	B5
-	MKHM	-	3348	4W-18S	E7
-	MKHM	-	3349	3W-17S	A6
-	MKHM	-	3426	5W-19S	D2
-	MONE	-	3682	7W-32S	D6
-	MonT	-	3593	7W-28S	E6
-	MonT	-	3682	7W-30S	D2
-	MTSN	-	3506	6W-23S	A4
-	MTSN	-	3594	6W-25S	A1
-	OKFT	-	3426	5W-19S	C2
-	POSN	-	3349	3W-17S	B6
-	PtnT	-	3860	11W-39S	B7
-	RchT	-	3426	6W-22S	A7
-	RchT	-	3506	6W-22S	A1
-	RchT	-	3593	7W-28S	D7
-	RNPK	-	3593	6W-26S	E3
-	RNPK	-	3594	6W-26S	A2
-	RVDL	-	3349	3W-17S	B5
-	UYPK	-	3593	7W-28S	D7
-	UYPK	-	3682	7W-29S	D2
I-57 Dan Ryan Expwy					
-	CHCG	-	3214	0W-11S	A7
I-80					
-	AxST	-	3583	34W-28S	A6
-	BmnT	-	3426	6W-21S	A6
-	FftT	-	3502	14W-22S	E1
-	FftT	-	3503	13W-22S	A1
-	JLET	-	3497	27W-24S	D7
-	JLET	-	3498	24W-24S	D6
-	JLET	-	3499	23W-24S	A6
-	JLET	-	3584	31W-26S	A3
-	JLET	-	3585	28W-25S	B1
-	JltT	-	3499	21W-24S	E6
-	JltT	-	3500	21W-24S	A6
-	MNKA	-	3583	33W-27S	C6
-	NLNX	-	3500	19W-24S	E5
-	NLNX	-	3501	17W-23S	D2
-	NlxT	-	3500	20W-24S	B6
-	NlxT	-	3501	17W-23S	D2
-	NlxT	-	3502	16W-22S	A2
-	ODPK	-	3502	14W-22S	E1
-	ODPK	-	3503	13W-22S	B1
-	RKDL	-	3498	25W-24S	B6
-	SwdT	-	3583	32W-27S	C6
-	TroT	-	3497	27W-24S	D7
-	TroT	-	3583	32W-27S	D5
-	TroT	-	3584	29W-26S	E3
I-80 Borman Expwy					
-	HMND	-	3430		D5
-	LNSG	-	3430		C5
-	MNSR	-	3430		D5
I-80 Kingery Expwy					
-	LNSG	-	3429	3E-20S	E4
-	LNSG	-	3430	3E-20S	B4
-	MNSR	-	3430	4E-20S	C4
-	ThtT	-	3429	2E-20S	C4
I-80 Moline Expwy					
-	BmnT	-	3425	7W-21S	D7
-	BmnT	-	3426	6W-21S	A6
-	CCHL	-	3426	4W-20S	E4
-	FftT	-	3503	11W-22S	E1
-	FftT	-	3504	9W-22S	D1
-	HLCT	-	3426	6W-21S	A6
-	HLCT	-	3427	3W-20S	A4
-	MKHM	-	3427	3W-20S	A4
-	MKNA	-	3503	12W-22S	D1
-	MKNA	-	3504	10W-22S	A1
-	ODPK	-	3503	12W-22S	D1

STREET Block	City	ZIP	Map#	CGS	Grid
I-80 Moline Expwy					
-	RchT	-	3425	7W-21S	D7
-	RchT	-	3505	7W-22S	C1
-	TYPK	-	3503	11W-22S	E1
-	TYPK	-	3504	9W-22S	E1
-	TYPK	-	3505	7W-22S	C1
I-80 Tri-State Tollway					
-	EHZC	-	3427	1W-20S	E4
-	EHZC	-	3428	0W-20S	C4
-	HLCT	-	3427	2W-20S	D4
-	LNSG	-	3429	2E-20S	C4
-	SHLD	-	3428	0E-20S	D4
-	SHLD	-	3429	0E-20S	A4
-	ThtT	-	3429	0E-20S	A4
-	TNTN	-	3428	0W-20S	C4
I-88 Ronald Reagan Mem Tollway					
-	AraT	-	3138	33W-4S	E2
-	AraT	-	3139	32W-4S	B2
-	AURA	-	3136	38W-5S	E2
-	AURA	-	3137	36W-5S	E2
-	AURA	-	3138	36W-5S	A2
-	AURA	-	3139	31W-4S	E1
-	BbyT	-	3075	42W-3S	B6
-	DRGV	-	3083	21W-4S	D7
-	DRGV	-	3084	21W-4S	A7
-	EMHT	-	3028	14W-0S	C6
-	HLSD	-	3028	14W-0S	C6
-	LMBD	-	3084	19W-2S	D4
-	LSLE	-	3083	23W-4S	A7
-	LSLE	-	3142	25W-4S	B1
-	LSLE	-	3143	23W-4S	A1
-	LslT	-	3083	21W-4S	D7
-	LslT	-	3084	21W-4S	A7
-	LslT	-	3142	23W-4S	E1
-	LslT	-	3143	23W-4S	A1
-	NARA	-	3137	38W-5S	A2
-	NARA	-	3138	35W-4S	B2
-	NPVL	-	3140	30W-4S	B1
-	NPVL	-	3141	28W-4S	B1
-	NPVL	-	3142	25W-4S	B1
-	NpvT	-	3139	32W-4S	B2
-	NpvT	-	3140	29W-4S	D1
-	OKBK	-	3028	15W-1S	B7
-	OKBK	-	3084	18W-2S	E3
-	OKBK	-	3085	18W-2S	A3
-	OKBK	-	3086	15W-1S	A1
-	PvsT	-	3028	14W-0S	C6
-	SgrT	-	3075	42W-4S	D7
-	SgrT	-	3135	41W-4S	D1
-	SgrT	-	3136	41W-4S	A1
-	SRGV	-	3135	41W-4S	D1
-	SRGV	-	3136	41W-4S	A1
-	WNVL	-	3141	27W-4S	D1
-	YkTp	-	3028	15W-0S	B7
-	YkTp	-	3084	20W-4S	A7
-	YkTp	-	3086	15W-1S	B1
I-90 Chicago Skwy					
-	CHCG	-	3152	0E-7S	E6
-	CHCG	-	3153	1E-8S	A7
-	CHCG	-	3215	3E-10S	E5
-	CHCG	-	3216	3E-10S	A6
-	CHCG	-	3280	4E-11S	C1
-	HMND	-	3280	4E-11S	C1
I-90 Chicago Skwy W					
-	CHCG	-	3152	0E-7S	D6
-	CHCG	-	3215	3E-10S	D4
I-90 Dan Ryan Expwy					
-	CHCG	-	3034	0W-0S	A5
-	CHCG	-	3092	0W-2S	B3
-	CHCG	-	3152	0W-5S	B1
I-90 Indiana East-West Toll Rd					
-	CHCG	-	3280		C1
-	HMND	-	3280		C1
-	HMND	-	3352		E4
I-90 Kennedy Expwy					
-	CHCG	-	2917	10W-7N	E4
-	CHCG	-	2918	8W-6N	E5
-	CHCG	-	2919	6W-6N	D6
-	CHCG	-	2920	5W-5N	A7
-	CHCG	-	2976	5W-5N	B1
-	CHCG	-	2977	3W-3N	A5
-	CHCG	-	3033	1W-0N	E3
-	CHCG	-	3034	0W-0S	A5
I-90 Kennedy Expwy E					
-	CHCG	-	2919	7W-6N	C6
I-90 Northwest Tollway					
-	ANHT	-	2860	18W-11N	E3
-	ANHT	-	2861	17W-10N	B4
-	CHCG	-	2916	13W-8N	E1
-	CHCG	-	2917	11W-7N	D4
-	DndT	-	2799	37W-15N	C4
-	DndT	-	2800	36W-14N	A6
-	DSPN	-	2861	16W-9N	E6
-	DSPN	-	2862	15W-9N	A7
-	DSPN	-	2916	13W-8N	E1
-	DSPN	-	2917	12W-8N	B2
-	EGvT	-	2860	18W-11N	D3
-	EGvT	-	2861	16W-10N	D6
-	EGvT	-	2862	15W-9N	A7
-	EGVV	-	2861	16W-10N	D6
-	ELGN	-	2799	36W-14N	E5
-	ELGN	-	2800	35W-14N	B6
-	ELGN	-	2801	32W-12N	C7
-	ElgT	-	2801	33W-13N	A7
-	GLBT	-	2798	39W-16N	D2
-	GLBT	-	2799	37W-15N	C4
-	HFET	-	2802	31W-12N	A7
-	HFET	-	2803	27W-12N	D7
-	HFET	-	2804	24W-12N	E7
-	HnrT	-	2801	32W-12N	C7
-	HnrT	-	2802	29W-12N	D7
-	HPSR	-	2743	46W-19N	A3
-	HshT	-	2743	44W-18N	E4
-	HshT	-	2744	43W-18N	A4
-	HTLY	-	2744	43W-18N	A4
-	HTLY	-	2745	41W-17N	A6
-	MPPT	-	2861	16W-10N	D6
-	RGMW	-	2859	21W-12N	E1
-	RGMW	-	2860	20W-12N	B1
-	RSMT	-	2916	13W-8N	E1
-	RSMT	-	2917	11W-7N	D4
-	RtdT	-	2744	43W-18N	A4
-	RtdT	-	2745	41W-17N	A7
-	RtdT	-	2798	39W-16N	D1
-	RtdT	-	2799	38W-15N	A3
-	SMBG	-	2804	24W-12N	E7
-	SMBG	-	2805	23W-12N	B7
-	SMBG	-	2859	21W-12N	D1
-	SmbT	-	2805	23W-12N	B7
-	SmbT	-	2859	21W-12N	D1
I-94					
-	BtlT	-	2360		D1
-	NptT	-	2360		D1
-	PTPR	-	2360		E1
I-94 Bishop Ford Mem Expwy					
-	CHCG	-	3214	0W-11S	C6
-	CHCG	-	3215	1E-11S	A7
-	CHCG	-	3278	0E-13S	E4
-	CHCG	-	3279	1E-14S	B7
-	CHCG	-	3351	1E-15S	B1
-	CTCY	-	3351	2E-16S	C3
-	DLTN	-	3351	2E-16S	C2
-	SHLD	-	3351	1E-18S	C7
-	SHLD	-	3429	1E-20S	B3
I-94 Borman Expwy					
-	HMND	-	3430		D5
-	LNSG	-	3430		C5
-	MNSR	-	3430		D5
I-94 Dan Ryan Expwy					
-	CHCG	-	3034	0W-1S	A7
-	CHCG	-	3092	0W-2S	B3
-	CHCG	-	3152	0W-7S	C6
-	CHCG	-	3214	0W-10S	C6
I-94 Dan Ryan Expwy E					
-	CHCG	-	3152	0W-7S	C5
I-94 Dan Ryan Expwy W					
-	CHCG	-	3152	0W-7S	C5
I-94 Edens Expwy					
-	CHCG	-	2919	6W-8N	E3
-	CHCG	-	2920	5W-5N	A7
-	GLNC	-	2758	7W-16N	B7
-	GNVW	-	2811	6W-13N	D6
-	LNWD	-	2919	6W-8N	E2
-	MNGV	-	2865	7W-10N	C5
-	NfdT	-	2811	7W-15N	C1
-	NHBK	-	2758	7W-18N	A4
-	NHFD	-	2758	7W-16N	B7
-	NHFD	-	2811	6W-14N	D4
-	NtrT	-	2758	7W-18N	A4
-	NtrT	-	2811	6W-14N	D4
-	SKOK	-	2811	6W-13N	E7
-	SKOK	-	2865	6W-12N	D1
-	SKOK	-	2919	6W-8N	E1
-	WLMT	-	2811	6W-14N	D4
I-94 Edens Expressway Spur					
-	DRFD	-	2756	11W-18N	E3
-	DRFD	-	2757	10W-18N	A3
-	NfdT	-	2756	12W-20N	B2
-	NfdT	-	2757	10W-18N	A3
-	NfdT	-	2758	7W-17N	B6
-	NHBK	-	2756	11W-18N	E3
-	NHBK	-	2757	8W-18N	E3
-	NHBK	-	2758	7W-17N	B6
-	WdfT	-	2756	12W-20N	B2
I-94 Edens Expressway Spur E					
-	NfdT	-	2756	12W-20N	B2
-	NfdT	-	2757	10W-18N	A3
-	NHBK	-	2757	8W-18N	E3
-	WdfT	-	2756	12W-20N	B2
I-94 Edens Expressway Spur W					
-	DRFD	-	2756	12W-20N	B1
-	NfdT	-	2757	10W-18N	A3
-	WdfT	-	2756	12W-20N	B1
I-94 Kennedy Expwy					
-	CHCG	-	2920	5W-5N	A7
-	CHCG	-	2976	4W-4N	B2
-	CHCG	-	2977	2W-2N	C6
-	CHCG	-	3033	1W-0N	E3
-	CHCG	-	3034	0W-0N	A4
I-94 Kingery Expwy					
-	LNSG	-	3429	3E-20S	E4
-	LNSG	-	3430	3E-20S	B4
-	MNSR	-	3430	4E-20S	C4
-	SHLD	-	3429	1E-18S	B1
-	ThtT	-	3429	1E-20S	B4
I-94 Tri-State Tollway					
-	BKBN	-	2703	12W-22N	A3
-	DRFD	-	2703	12W-21N	B5
-	DRFD	-	2756	12W-20N	B1
-	GNOK	-	2535	14W-31N	D7
-	GNOK	-	2592	14W-28N	C6
-	GNOK	-	2648	14W-27N	D1
-	GRNE	-	2477	16W-37N	E1
-	GRNE	-	2535	15W-34N	A2
-	LbvT	-	2535	14W-31N	D7
-	LbvT	-	2592	14W-28N	C6
-	LbvT	-	2648	13W-26N	E2
-	LKFT	-	2648	13W-24N	E6
-	LKFT	-	2702	13W-24N	E1
-	LKFT	-	2703	13W-23N	A2
-	LNSH	-	2703	12W-21N	B6
-	MTWA	-	2592	14W-28N	D7
-	MTWA	-	2648	13W-27N	D1
-	NptT	-	2360	16W-42N	E6
-	NptT	-	2419	17W-41N	C1
-	NptT	-	2477	16W-38N	E1
-	OMCK	-	2419	17W-41N	C1
-	OMCK	-	2477	16W-37N	E2
-	RVWD	-	2703	12W-22N	A3
-	VrnT	-	2648	13W-24N	E6
-	VrnT	-	2702	13W-23N	E1
-	VrnT	-	2703	12W-21N	B6
-	WdfT	-	2703	12W-22N	A3
-	WdfT	-	2756	12W-20N	B2
-	WDWH	-	2360	16W-42N	E6
-	WDWH	-	2419	16W-38N	E7
-	WDWH	-	2477	16W-37N	E1
-	WKGN	-	2535	14W-32N	C5
-	WrnT	-	2477	16W-37N	E1
-	WrnT	-	2478	15W-34N	A7
-	WrnT	-	2535	14W-32N	C5
I-190					
-	CHCG	-	2917	12W-6N	A5
-	CHCG	60666	2916	13W-6N	E5
-	RSMT	-	2917	11W-7N	E4
I-290					
-	ADSN	-	2914	20W-6N	B7
-	ADSN	-	2970	20W-5N	B1
-	EGvT	-	2860	20W-9N	A7
-	EGvT	-	2914	20W-8N	A1
-	EGVV	-	2914	20W-6N	B7
-	ITSC	-	2914	20W-8N	B3
-	RGMW	-	2860	20W-12N	A1
-	SMBG	-	2860	20W-9N	A7
I-290 Eisenhower Expwy					
-	AddT	-	2971	18W-3N	A4
-	ADSN	-	2914	20W-5N	A7
-	ADSN	-	2970	18W-4N	E3
-	ADSN	-	2971	16W-3N	D6
-	BDVW	-	3029	11W-0S	C6
-	BKLY	-	3028	14W-0S	C5
-	BLWD	-	3029	11W-0S	C6
-	CHCG	-	3031	7W-0S	C6
-	CHCG	-	3032	3W-0S	E5
-	CHCG	-	3033	1W-0S	E5
-	CHCG	-	3034	0W-0S	A5
-	EMHT	-	2971	17W-3N	C5
-	EMHT	-	2972	15W-2N	A7
-	EMHT	-	3028	15W-1N	B2
-	FTPK	-	3030	10W-0S	A6
-	HLSD	-	3028	13W-0S	E6
-	HLSD	-	3029	12W-0S	A6
-	ITSC	-	2914	20W-5N	A7
-	MYWD	-	3029	12W-0S	B6
-	MYWD	-	3030	10W-0S	B6
-	NHLK	-	3028	15W-1N	B1
-	OKPK	-	3030	10W-0S	A6
-	OKPK	-	3031	7W-0S	C6
-	PvsT	-	3028	14W-0S	C6
-	WDDL	-	2970	18W-4N	E3
-	WSTR	-	3029	12W-0S	C6
I-294 Kingery Expwy					
-	LNSG	-	3429	3E-20S	E4
-	LNSG	-	3430	3E-20S	A4
-	ThtT	-	3429	2E-20S	C4
I-294 Tri-State Tollway					
-	ALSP	-	3275	7W-14S	C5
-	ALSP	-	3276	5W-15S	A7
-	ALSP	-	3348	5W-15S	B1
-	BGVW	-	3210	9W-11S	E7
-	BKLY	-	3028	14W-1N	C3
-	BmnT	-	3348	4W-17S	E4
-	BmnT	-	3349	3W-17S	B6
-	BRRG	-	3146	14W-6S	D4
-	CHCG	-	2863	12W-9N	C7
-	CHCG	-	2917	12W-6N	B6
-	CHRG	-	3210	9W-11S	E7
-	CHRG	-	3274	8W-11S	E1
-	CHRG	-	3275	6W-14S	D6
-	CTSD	-	3146	13W-8S	E7
-	CTSD	-	3147	13W-8S	A7
-	CTSD	-	3209	13W-8S	A1
-	CTWD	-	3348	4W-17S	D4
-	DRFD	-	2756	12W-18N	B2
-	DSPN	-	2863	12W-10N	C4
-	DSPN	-	2917	12W-6N	B6
-	EHZC	-	3427	1W-20S	E4
-	EHZC	-	3428	0W-20S	C4
-	EMHT	-	3028	14W-0S	C6
-	FNPK	-	2972	14W-3N	B6
-	FNPK	-	2973	13W-4N	A3
-	GNVW	-	2809	11W-13N	C6
-	HGKN	-	3209	12W-8S	B1
-	HLCT	-	3427	3W-20S	C4
-	HLSD	-	3028	14W-0S	C6
-	HNDL	-	3086	14W-3S	C6
-	HNDL	-	3146	14W-6S	D4
-	HYHL	-	3210	10W-9S	B3
-	IHPK	-	3146	14W-7S	D6
-	JSTC	-	3209	11W-9S	E2
-	JSTC	-	3210	9W-9S	C4
-	LNSG	-	3429	2E-20S	C4
-	LydT	-	2972	14W-3N	B6
-	LydT	-	2973	13W-4N	A3
-	LynT	-	3086	14W-3S	C6
-	LynT	-	3146	14W-6S	D5
-	LynT	-	3147	13W-8S	A7
-	LynT	-	3209	12W-8S	D2
-	MaiT	-	2809	11W-13N	C7
-	MaiT	-	2863	12W-12N	C1
-	MDLN	-	3348	4W-16S	D4
-	MKHM	-	3349	3W-17S	A6
-	MKHM	-	3427	3W-19S	B2
-	NfdT	-	2756	13W-17N	A5
-	NfdT	-	2809	11W-13N	C6
-	NHBK	-	2756	12W-18N	B3
-	NHBK	-	2809	12W-16N	C1
-	NHLK	-	2972	14W-2N	B6
-	NHLK	-	3028	14W-2N	B1
-	OKBK	-	3086	15W-1S	B2
-	PKRG	-	2863	12W-10N	C5
-	POSN	-	3349	3W-17S	A4
-	PvsT	-	3028	14W-0S	C7
-	PvsT	-	3086	14W-1S	C1
-	RBBN	-	3348	5W-15S	B1
-	RSMT	-	2917	11W-7N	C3
-	SHLD	-	3428	0E-20S	D4
-	SHLD	-	3429	0E-20S	A4
-	SRPK	-	2917	12W-6N	C6
-	SRPK	-	2973	12W-4N	A3
-	ThtT	-	3429	0E-20S	A4
-	TNTN	-	3428	0E-20S	D4
-	WdfT	-	2756	13W-17N	A5
-	WhlT	-	2756	12W-18N	A4
-	WLNG	-	2756	12W-18N	A4
-	WLSP	-	3209	11W-9S	E2
-	WNSP	-	3086	14W-4S	C6
-	WNSP	-	3146	14W-7S	D6
-	WRTH	-	3275	6W-14S	D6
-	WthT	-	3275	7W-13S	C5
I-355					
-	ADSN	-	2914	20W-6N	B7
-	ADSN	-	2969	21W-4N	E3
-	ADSN	-	2970	20W-5N	A1
-	BmdT	-	2970	20W-5N	A1
-	ITSC	-	2914	20W-6N	B6
I-355 North-South Tollway					
-	ADSN	-	2969	21W-2N	E6
-	BGBK	-	3206	21W-10S	A6
-	BGBK	-	3270	20W-14S	B7
-	BmdT	-	2969	21W-3N	E6
-	BmdT	-	3025	21W-2N	E1
-	DPgT	-	3270	20W-14S	B7
-	DRGV	-	3083	21W-4S	D7
-	DRGV	-	3084	20W-2S	A3
-	DRGV	-	3143	22W-5S	C3
-	GNEN	-	3025	21W-0S	E7
-	HmrT	-	3342	20W-18S	C7
-	HmrT	-	3420	19W-21S	E7
-	LKPT	-	3342	20W-18S	C7
-	LKPT	-	3420	19W-21S	E7
-	LMBD	-	3025	21W-0S	E6
-	LMBD	-	3026	21W-0N	A5
-	LMBD	-	3083	21W-1S	E1
-	LMBD	-	3084	20W-2S	A3
-	LMNT	-	3270	20W-14S	B7
-	LMNT	-	3342	20W-18S	C7
-	LSLE	-	3083	21W-4S	E7
-	LSLE	-	3143	21W-7S	E6
-	LslT	-	3083	21W-4S	D7
-	LslT	-	3084	21W-4S	A7
-	LslT	-	3143	22W-6S	D4
-	MltT	-	3025	21W-0S	E7
-	MltT	-	3026	21W-0N	A4
-	MltT	-	3083	21W-1S	E1
-	NLNX	-	3420	19W-21S	E7
-	NLNX	-	3421	18W-22S	A7
-	NLNX	-	3501	18W-22S	A1
-	WDRG	-	3143	22W-6S	D5
-	WDRG	-	3205	21W-8S	E2
-	WDRG	-	3206	21W-9S	A3
-	WDRG	-	3270	20W-14S	B7
-	YkTp	-	3084	20W-1S	A2
Ian Ct					
26600	CNHN	60410	3672	33W-32S	B7
Ian Ln					
200	NLNX	60451	3501	17W-25S	D7
W Ibsen St					
7200	CHCG	60631	2918	9W-8N	D1
7200	CHCG	60714	2918	9W-8N	D1
7200	NLES	60714	2918	9W-8N	D1
Ice Cream Dr					
800	NARA	60506	3137	37W-4S	C2
800	NARA	60542	3137	37W-4S	C2
Ickenham Ln					
10	PltT	60124	2905	43W-8N	B4
Ida Av					
10	ANTH	60002	2357	23W-42N	E6
10	ANTH	60002	2358	23W-42N	A6
S Ida Ct					
500	EGvT	60056	2861	16W-10N	E4
500	MPPT	60056	2861	16W-11N	E4
Ida Dr					
2300	AlqT	60013	2641	31W-25N	D4
Ida Ln					
9200	MNGV	60053	2865	8W-11N	A2
N Ida Ln					
400	EMHT	60126	2971	16W-2N	D7
Ida Pl					
400	GLNC	60022	2758	6W-17N	E5
Ida Rd					
1700	HFET	60169	2858	24W-12N	E1
Ida St					
500	DSPN	60016	2863	13W-11N	A3
600	JLET	60436	3498	25W-24S	C6
Idabright Dr					
1200	JLET	60586	3496	30W-22S	A2
Idaho Ct					
3700	NCHI	60088	2593	12W-30N	C1
13900	PnfT	60544	3339	27W-16S	D4
18000	ODPK	60467	3423	13W-21S	A7
Idaho Pl					
1500	EGVV	60007	2913	21W-9N	E1
Idaho Rd					
2600	NPVL	60564	3202	29W-10S	C6
Idaho St					
-	NCHI	60088	2593	12W-30N	C2
800	CLSM	60188	2968	26W-3N	A5
Ideal					
-	MTSN	60443	3505	7W-25S	D7
Idlestone Ln					
10	SMBG	60194	2858	25W-10N	B5
N Idlewild Av					
10	MDLN	60060	2646	19W-27N	C1
400	MDLN	60060	2590	19W-28N	C7
Idle Wild Ct					
100	SMBG	60195	2859	23W-12N	A1
Idlewild Dr					
900	RLKB	60073	2531	23W-34N	E1
1000	RLKB	60073	2474	23W-34N	E7
13500	ODPK	60462	3345	11W-16S	E2
18000	CCHL	60478	3426	5W-21S	C7
N Idlewild Dr					
33500	WrnT	60030	2533	18W-33N	E3
Idlewild Ln					
1300	HMWD	60430	3507	2W-22S	D2
1500	BlmT	60430	3507	2W-22S	D2
1800	FSMR	60422	3507	2W-22S	D2
4400	HLSD	60162	3028	13W-0S	E5
Idlewood Dr					
300	BGBK	60440	3269	22W-12S	C2
Idlewood Ln					
2800	HDPK	60035	2704	10W-23N	B2
W Idlewood Ln					
15500	LbvT	60048	2592	15W-30N	A2
Ignace Ct					
12100	HMGN	60491	3422	15W-19S	C2
Ignatius St					
1400	JltT	60436	3586	24W-26S	D2
W IL-134					
25500	GrtT	60041	2474	25W-34N	A7
27300	FXLK	60041	2473	27W-34N	B7
27300	GrtT	60041	2473	27W-34N	B7
Ilene Dr					
3000	ISLK	60042	2586	29W-28N	C5
3000	NndT	60042	2586	29W-28N	C5
Iliad Dr					
10	RchT	60423	3505	8W-23S	B4
10	TYPK	60477	3505	8W-23S	B4
Illiamna Tr					
6600	MHRY	60050	2527	35W-33N	A3
Illi Indi Dr					
18400	LNSG	60438	3430	4E-21S	C7
Illini Ct					
-	KdlT	60560	3333	42W-15S	C3
-	YKVL	60560	3333	42W-15S	C3
Illini Dr					
100	MNKA	60447	3583	33W-28S	B7
300	CLSM	60188	2968	26W-3N	A7
300	YKVL	60560	3333	42W-15S	C3
400	CLSM	60188	2967	26W-3N	E7
1200	LKPT	60441	3419	21W-19S	E3
1200	LKPT	60441	3420	21W-19S	A3
1500	NlxT	60451	3590	16W-27S	A4
1500	PNFD	60544	3416	31W-18S	A1
1600	NLNX	60451	3590	16W-27S	A4
Illini Rd					
2600	WKGN	60087	2479	12W-36N	C5
Illinois Av					
-	BHPK	60083	2421	12W-39N	B5
-	BHPK	60087	2421	12W-39N	C5
-	BHPK	60099	2421	12W-39N	B5
10	SMBG	60193	2859	23W-10N	A6
100	SCRL	60174	2964	35W-3N	B7
200	ELGN	60120	2855	33W-11N	B5
300	BTVA	60510	3078	35W-1S	A1
3500	SCRL	60174	2965	33W-3N	A6
3800	SCRL	60185	2965	33W-3N	B6
5000	LSLE	60532	3142	24W-5S	E3
E Illinois Av					
10	AURA	60505	3138	35W-6S	B5
10	PLTN	60067	2805	20W-15N	E3
200	PLTN	60067	2806	20W-15N	A3
200	RGMW	60008	2805	20W-15N	E3
200	RGMW	60008	2806	20W-15N	A3
300	PLTN	60008	2806	20W-14N	A3
N Illinois Av					
200	GNWD	60425	3508	1W-22S	A1
200	GNWD	60430	3508	1W-22S	A1
200	HMWD	60425	3508	1W-22S	A1
200	HMWD	60430	3508	1W-22S	A1
200	VLPK	60181	3027	17W-1N	B3
500	GNWD	60425	3428	1W-22S	A7
500	HMWD	60425	3428	1W-22S	A7
500	HMWD	60430	3428	1W-22S	A7
900	ANHT	60005	2806	18W-14N	D3
1200	ANHT	60004	2806	18W-15N	D2
2100	ANHT	60004	2753	18W-16N	D7
S Illinois Av					
100	VLPK	60181	3027	17W-0N	B4
W Illinois Av					
10	AURA	60505	3138	35W-6S	B6
10	AURA	60506	3138	36W-6S	A5
10	PLTN	60067	2805	21W-15N	C3
500	AURA	60506	3137	36W-6S	E6
1300	IVNS	60067	2805	22W-14N	A3
2300	AURA	60506	3136	39W-6S	E5
10200	BHPK	60099	2422	10W-39N	B5
10200	ZION	60099	2422	10W-39N	B5
11500	BHPK	60099	2421	11W-39N	D5
Illinois Blvd					
10	HFET	60193	2858	24W-10N	E5
200	HFET	60169	2858	24W-10N	E5
600	HFET	60169	2859	23W-11N	A4
Illinois Ct					
-	SRWD	60404	3496	31W-24S	A6
10	PKFT	60466	3595	3W-25S	B1
200	ELGN	60120	2855	33W-11N	B4
10500	ODPK	60467	3423	13W-21S	A7
Illinois Dr					
-	SRWD	60404	3496	31W-24S	A6
S Illinois Dr					
200	ANHT	60005	2806	18W-13N	D5
W Illinois Dr					
12800	HTLY	60142	2744	42W-18N	C4
E Illinois Hwy					
10	NLNX	60451	3589	17W-25S	C1
10	NlxT	60451	3589	17W-25S	C1
W Illinois Hwy					
-	JLET	60433	3588	20W-25S	C1
-	NLNX	60433	3588	20W-25S	B1
-	NLNX	60451	3588	20W-25S	B1
-	NlxT	60433	3588	20W-25S	B1
-	NlxT	60451	3588	20W-25S	B1
100	NLNX	60451	3589	18W-25S	B1
100	NlxT	60451	3589	18W-25S	B1
Illinois Pkwy					
1300	ELGN	60123	2854	35W-12N	B2
Illinois Rd					
400	FKFT	60423	3503	12W-25S	C7
400	WLMT	60091	2812	5W-13N	A5
1600	NfdT	60062	2757	9W-16N	C6
2000	NHBK	60062	2757	10W-17N	A6
2500	NHBK	60062	2756	10W-17N	E6
2600	NtrT	60091	2812	5W-14N	A5
2600	NtrT	60093	2812	5W-14N	A4
2800	NtrT	60091	2811	5W-14N	E4
2800	NtrT	60093	2811	5W-14N	E4
2800	WLMT	60091	2811	6W-14N	D4
3000	WLMT	60093	2811	6W-14N	D4
3100	NHFD	60091	2811	6W-14N	D4
3400	NHFD	60093	2811	6W-14N	D4
E Illinois Rd					
100	LKFT	60045	2649	10W-26N	E3
100	LKFT	60045	2650	9W-26N	C4
Illinois St					
-	BrnT	60010	2751	25W-18N	A3
-	BRTN	60010	2751	25W-18N	A3
10	BlmT	60411	3598		C2
10	CHHT	60411	3596	1W-25S	B1
10	CPVL	60110	2800	34W-16N	E2
10	CPVL	60118	2800	34W-16N	E1
10	DYR	46311	3598		C2
10	EDND	60110	2800	34W-16N	E2
10	EDND	60118	2800	34W-16N	E2
10	ROSL	60172	2913	23W-8N	A3
10	SmbT	60172	2913	23W-8N	A3
100	BmT	60010	2750	25W-18N	E3
100	BRTN	60010	2750	25W-18N	E3
100	CHHT	60411	3595	3W-25S	C1
100	CLLK	60014	2640	34W-26N	B3
100	FRGV	60021	2696	29W-22N	B3
100	PKFT	60411	3595	3W-25S	C1
100	PKFT	60466	3595	4W-25S	A1
200	GNEN	60137	3025	23W-0S	A7
200	GNEN	60187	3025	23W-0S	A7
200	WHTN	60187	3025	23W-0S	A7
300	SchT	60174	2908	34W-6N	C7
400	CPVL	60118	2801	34W-16N	A1
400	EDND	60118	2801	34W-16N	A1
400	GNVA	60134	3020	35W-1N	B3
500	PKFT	60466	3594	4W-25S	E1
1400	SMBG	60193	2913	23W-8N	A2
1400	SmbT	60193	2913	23W-8N	A2
1600	DSPN	60018	2863	13W-9N	A6
2900	NCHI	60088	2593	11W-30N	E2
2900	ShdT	60088	2593	11W-30N	E2
3100	LNSG	60438	3430	3E-21S	B7
3700	NndT	60014	2586	30W-28N	A6
3700	ShdT	60044	2593	11W-29N	E3
3800	NCHI	60044	2593	11W-29N	E4
9600	HBRN	60034	2350	40W-41N	E7
E Illinois St					
10	CHCG	60610	3034	0E-0N	C3
10	CHCG	60611	3034	0E-0N	C3
100	LMNT	60439	3270	19W-13S	E5
100	WHTN	60187	3024	24W-0S	D7
1600	WHTN	60187	3025	23W-0S	A7
1800	GNEN	60137	3025	23W-0S	A7
1800	GNEN	60187	3025	23W-0S	A7
N Illinois St					
200	EMHT	60126	3028	15W-1N	A1
400	PNFD	60544	3338	30W-17S	C7
41500	BtnT	60099	2422	10W-41N	B1
S Illinois St					
100	JLET	60436	3498	24W-24S	D5
13700	RVDL	60827	3350	0W-15S	C2
14500	DLTN	60419	3350	0W-16S	B4
14500	DLTN	60827	3350	0W-16S	B4
W Illinois St					
10	CHCG	60610	3034	0W-0N	A3
10	CHCG	60611	3034	0W-0N	B3
10	SCRL	60174	2964	35W-2N	A7
100	WHTN	60187	3024	24W-0S	C7
Illinois Tr					
1000	DRFD	60015	2703	11W-21N	C6
Illinois Beach Park Rd					
-	BtnT	60099	2422	9W-39N	D6
Ill Prairie Pth					
-	BRLT	60103	2909	31W-8N	E3
-	BRLT	60103	2910	31W-8N	A2
-	ELGN	60103	2909	31W-8N	E3
Illusion Ct					
7100	JLET	60586	3415	32W-20S	C6
Imgrund Rd					
2500	NARA	60542	3076	39W-3S	E6
Imhoff Dr					
-	LIHL	60156	2694	34W-22N	C3
W Imlay St					
6500	CHCG	60631	2919	8W-8N	A2
6600	CHCG	60631	2918	8W-7N	D3
Immanuel Rd					
7700	KdlT	60560	3333	43W-17S	B7
Imperial Av					
1300	CTCY	60409	3430	3E-19S	A2

STREET Block	City	ZIP	Map#	CGS	Grid
Imperial Cir					
1600	NPVL	60563	3141	28W-5S	A2
Imperial Ct					
2800	AURA	60503	3265	32W-11S	C1
2900	FSMR	60422	3507	3W-22S	A2
22600	RNPK	60471	3593	6W-27S	E4
N Imperial Ct					
30200	FmtT	60030	2588	23W-30N	D2
W Imperial Ct					
10	PLTN	60067	2805	21W-15N	D2
1600	EGvT	60056	2861	16W-10N	D4
1600	MPPT	60056	2861	16W-10N	C4
Imperial Dr					
1500	GNVW	60025	2809	10W-14N	E4
2200	CTHL	60403	3418	26W-21S	A6
5200	RNPK	60471	3594	6W-27S	A3
5300	RNPK	60471	3593	6W-27S	E3
W Imperial Dr					
14500	LbvT	60048	2648	14W-26N	B2
14500	MTWA	60048	2648	14W-26N	B2
Imperial Ln					
-	BHPK	60087	2421	11W-38N	E7
-	BHPK	60087	2479	11W-38N	E1
11700	ODPK	60467	3422	14W-21S	D7
18200	FftT	60448	3422	14W-21S	D7
Imperial St					
10	CHCG	60068	2918	9W-8N	B2
10	CHCG	60631	2918	9W-8N	B2
10	PKRG	60068	2918	9W-8N	B2
Imperial Valley Tr					
2500	AURA	60503	3201	32W-11S	C7
2500	AURA	60503	3265	32W-11S	C1
Impressions Dr					
2700	LIHL	60156	2692	38W-22N	E3
Inca Blvd					
400	CLSM	60188	2967	26W-3N	E6
Inca Ct					
10	NPVL	60563	3141	26W-5S	D2
Independence					
23500	GrtT	60041	2473	26W-36N	D4
Independence Av					
10	JltT	60433	3500	21W-24S	A5
400	SEGN	60177	2908	35W-8N	C3
600	ELBN	60119	3017	42W-0N	C6
600	WTMT	60559	3085	17W-4S	D7
900	SCRL	60174	2964	34W-2N	D7
1000	SCRL	60174	3020	34W-2N	D1
1500	GNVW	60025	2810	9W-13N	B5
5600	OKFT	60452	3347	7W-18S	D7
Independence Blvd					
-	ISLK	60042	2586	28W-27N	E7
-	LNHT	60083	2418	19W-39N	D6
-	NLNX	60451	3500	19W-24S	E6
-	NLNX	60451	3501	18W-24S	A6
-	NlxT	60451	3500	19W-24S	E6
-	NlxT	60451	3501	18W-24S	A6
-	OMCK	60083	2418	19W-39N	D6
700	LkvT	60046	2418	19W-39N	C5
700	LNHT	60046	2418	19W-39N	C5
1000	YKVL	60560	3261	43W-14S	B7
N Independence Blvd					
10	LktT	60446	3341	23W-16S	A4
10	RMVL	60441	3341	23W-16S	A5
10	RMVL	60446	3341	23W-16S	A4
300	DPgT	60441	3341	23W-15S	A3
300	DPgT	60446	3341	23W-15S	A3
600	RMVL	60446	3269	23W-14S	A7
N Independence Blvd SR-53					
10	LktT	60446	3341	23W-16S	A4
10	RMVL	60441	3341	23W-16S	A5
10	RMVL	60446	3341	23W-16S	A4
300	DPgT	60441	3341	23W-15S	A3
300	DPgT	60446	3341	23W-15S	A3
600	RMVL	60446	3269	23W-14S	A7
S Independence Blvd					
500	CHCG	60624	3032	4W-0S	C6
1300	CHCG	60623	3032	4W-0S	D6
14200	LktT	60441	3341	23W-17S	A5
14200	RMVL	60441	3341	23W-17S	A5
14200	RMVL	60446	3341	23W-16S	A5
24300	CRTE	60417	3685	1W-29S	A2
S Independence Blvd SR-53					
14200	LktT	60441	3341	23W-17S	A5
14200	RMVL	60441	3341	23W-17S	A5
14200	RMVL	60446	3341	23W-16S	A5
Independence Ct					
700	YKVL	60560	3261	43W-14S	A7
1500	SCRL	60174	2964	34W-3N	D7
1700	MPPT	60056	2808	13W-14N	D4
1800	GRNE	60031	2477	16W-36N	D4
6000	MHRY	60050	2527	34W-32N	B5
14800	PNFD	60544	3338	31W-17S	A6
15700	OKFT	60452	3347	7W-18S	D7
E Independence Ct					
600	ANHT	60005	2861	17W-11N	B2
Independence Dr					
10	BTVA	60510	3077	36W-1S	D2
10	BtvT	60510	3077	36W-1S	D2
10	BtvT	60539	3077	36W-1S	D2
10	CHHT	60411	3596	1W-25S	A1
300	AURA	60506	3136	39W-6S	C5
300	AURA	60506	3137	38W-6S	A6
1000	BRLT	60103	2910	29W-6N	D7
8100	WLSP	60480	3208	14W-9S	D3
14400	PNFD	60544	3337	31W-17S	E6
14500	PNFD	60544	3338	31W-17S	A6
E Independence Dr					
600	PLTN	60074	2753	20W-18N	B2
Independence Ln					
200	BMDL	60108	2969	23W-5N	A2
400	BGBK	60440	3205	22W-11S	C7
Independence Wy					
14300	HMGN	60491	3344	15W-17S	B5
Indian Av					
1000	AURA	60505	3138	34W-7S	D6
1300	AraT	60505	3138	34W-7S	D6
1700	AraT	60505	3139	33W-7S	A6
1700	AURA	60505	3139	33W-7S	A6
Indian Ct					
100	LKBF	60044	2593	11W-28N	C6
100	LKBF	60044	2594	10W-28N	A7
300	MNKA	60447	3672	32W-28S	D1
S Indian Ct					
20200	FftT	60423	3504	10W-24S	C5
Indian Dr					
10	CNHL	60514	3145	17W-5S	C2
1100	ELGN	60120	2855	32W-12N	C1
Indian Ln					
-	LGGV	60047	2646	18W-25N	D5
-	LGGV	60060	2646	18W-25N	D5
100	DndT	60110	2748	33W-17N	A6
1400	CPVL	60110	2748	32W-18N	C4
7300	JSTC	60458	3209	11W-8S	E1
N Indian Ln					
33000	WrnT	60030	2533	18W-33N	D3
33300	AvnT	60030	2533	18W-33N	D3
35400	GrtT	60041	2473	26W-35N	E6
Indian Pt					
300	LKBN	60010	2643	26W-24N	D6
Indian Rd					
300	GNEN	60137	3025	21W-0S	E6
1000	GNVW	60025	2811	6W-13N	C6
2000	WKGN	60087	2479	12W-36N	C4
N Indian Rd					
6000	CHCG	60646	2919	7W-7N	B3
Indian Tr					
-	WTMT	60559	3085	18W-3S	A6
10	ALGN	60102	2694	35W-21N	A6
10	ALGN	60156	2694	35W-21N	A6
10	LIHL	60156	2694	35W-22N	A4
500	AvnT	60073	2532	22W-34N	C1
500	RLKP	60073	2532	22W-34N	B1
2600	NndT	60051	2528	31W-31N	D7
E Indian Tr					
100	AURA	60506	3138	35W-5S	B4
100	AURA	60542	3138	35W-5S	B4
200	AURA	60504	3138	35W-5S	B4
200	AURA	60505	3138	34W-5S	E4
500	AraT	60504	3138	34W-5S	C4
1400	AraT	60505	3138	33W-6S	E4
1400	AURA	60505	3139	33W-5S	B4
1700	AraT	60502	3139	33W-5S	B4
1700	AraT	60505	3139	33W-5S	B4
1700	AURA	60502	3139	33W-5S	B4
N Indian Tr					
35000	GrtT	60041	2472	28W-35N	E6
S Indian Tr					
24000	MhtT	60442	3590	15W-29S	B7
W Indian Tr					
-	LIHL	60156	2693	35W-22N	E4
-	SgrT	60506	3136	39W-5S	D4
2400	AURA	60506	3136	39W-5S	D4
Indian Wy					
600	BRTN	60010	2751	24W-20N	C1
700	BRTN	60010	2698	24W-20N	C7
700	DRPK	60010	2698	24W-20N	C7
700	SCRL	60174	2965	33W-4N	B5
Indiana Av					
-	BNHM	60633	3352	3E-16S	A3
10	LslT	60540	3204	24W-8S	D1
100	SCRL	60174	2964	35W-2N	B7
900	WKGN	60085	2479	11W-35N	D6
1300	BlmT	60411	3508	0E-25S	D7
1300	CHHT	60411	3508	0E-25S	D7
1900	LNSG	60438	3429	3E-21S	E6
1900	ThtT	60438	3429	3E-21S	E6
2600	LNSG	60438	3430	3E-21S	A6
4700	LSLE	60532	3142	24W-5S	D2
14600	DLTN	60419	3350	0E-17S	D5
14600	DLTN	60827	3350	0E-17S	D4
14600	RVDL	60419	3350	0E-17S	D4
14600	RVDL	60827	3350	0E-17S	D4
14900	SHLD	60419	3350	0W-17S	D5
14900	SHLD	60473	3350	0W-17S	D5
E Indiana Av					
10	BCHR	60401	3864	0E-37S	E2
10	WshT	60401	3864	0E-37S	E2
S Indiana Av					
1200	CHCG	60605	3034	0E-1S	C7
1500	CHCG	60616	3034	0E-1S	C7
1600	CHCG	60616	3092	0E-2S	C2
3400	CHCG	60653	3092	0E-3S	C4
4600	CHCG	60615	3092	0E-4S	C7
4700	CHCG	60615	3152	0E-5S	C1
5400	CHCG	60637	3152	0E-6S	C4
7000	CHCG	60619	3152	0E-8S	C7
7500	CHCG	60619	3214	0E-11S	C6
9400	CHCG	60628	3214	0E-11S	C6
10300	CHCG	60628	3278	0E-13S	D3
12900	RVDL	60628	3278	0W-14S	D7
12900	RVDL	60827	3278	0W-14S	D7
13000	CHCG	60827	3278	0W-15S	D7
13100	CHCG	60827	3350	0W-15S	D2
13400	RVDL	60827	3350	0W-16S	D4
13700	CHCG	60419	3350	0W-15S	D2
13700	DLTN	60419	3350	0W-16S	D4
13700	RVDL	60419	3350	0W-15S	D2
13900	DLTN	60827	3350	0W-16S	D4
W Indiana Av					
10	BCHR	60401	3864	1W-36S	A2
10	WshT	60401	3864	1W-36S	A2
Indiana Cir					
20900	OMFD	60461	3507	3W-25S	A7
Indiana Ct					
300	BMDL	60108	2969	22W-4N	B3
600	FKFT	60423	3503	12W-25S	C7
13200	HTLY	60142	2744	42W-18N	C4
17900	ODPK	60467	3423	12W-21S	C7
Indiana Ln					
700	EGVV	60007	2913	21W-8N	E2
Indiana Pkwy					
9700	MNSR	46321	3510		D3
Indiana St					
100	DYR	46311	3598		D2
100	OMFD	60461	3507	4W-25S	A7
100	PKFT	60466	3507	4W-25S	A7
100	PKFT	60466	3595	3W-25S	B1
700	WKGN	60085	2479	11W-35N	E7
900	NCHI	60088	2593	11W-30N	E3
1000	AURA	60506	3137	37W-5S	D2
3800	LKBF	60044	2593	11W-29N	E4
3800	NCHI	60044	2593	11W-29N	E4
E Indiana St					
300	WHTN	60187	3024	24W-0S	D7
800	HMND	46320	3352		E6
1600	WHTN	60187	3025	23W-0S	A7
1800	GNEN	60137	3025	23W-0S	A7
1800	GNEN	60187	3025	23W-0S	A7
N Indiana St					
200	AddT	60126	2972	15W-2N	A7
200	EMHT	60126	2972	15W-2N	A7
200	EMHT	60126	3028	15W-1N	A1
W Indiana St					
10	SCRL	60174	2964	35W-2N	A7
100	WHTN	60187	3024	24W-0S	C7
1000	GNWD	60425	3428	1W-22S	A7
1300	SCRL	60174	2963	36W-2N	E7
Indiana East-West Toll Rd					
-	CHCG	-	3280		C1
-	HMND	-	3280		C1
-	HMND	-	3352		E2
Indiana East-West Toll Rd I-90					
-	CHCG	-	3280		C1
-	HMND	-	3280		C1
-	HMND	-	3352		E2
Indianapolis Av					
200	DRGV	60515	3144	19W-4S	D1
2500	LslT	60515	3143	21W-4S	D1
S Indianapolis Av					
-	CHCG	60617	3280	4E-11S	C1
-	HMND	60617	3280	4E-11S	C1
10000	CHCG	60617	3216	4E-11S	B7
10600	HMND	46320	3280	4E-11S	C1
S Indianapolis Av US-12					
-	CHCG	60617	3280	4E-11S	C1
-	HMND	60617	3280	4E-11S	C1
10000	CHCG	60617	3216	4E-11S	B7
10600	HMND	46320	3280	4E-11S	C1
S Indianapolis Av US-20					
-	CHCG	60617	3280	4E-11S	C1
-	HMND	60617	3280	4E-11S	C1
10000	CHCG	60617	3216	4E-11S	B7
10600	HMND	46320	3280	4E-11S	C1
S Indianapolis Av US-41					
-	CHCG	60617	3280	4E-11S	C1
-	HMND	60617	3280	4E-11S	C1
10000	CHCG	60617	3216	4E-11S	B7
10600	HMND	46320	3280	4E-11S	C1
S Indianapolis Blvd					
1000	HMND	46320	3280		D3
1000	HMND	46394	3280		D3
10500	CHCG	60617	3280		C1
10500	HMND	60617	3280	4E-11S	C1
S Indianapolis Blvd US-12					
1000	HMND	46320	3280		D3
1000	HMND	46394	3280		D3
10500	CHCG	60617	3280		C1
10500	HMND	60617	3280	4E-11S	C1
S Indianapolis Blvd US-20					
1000	HMND	46320	3280		D3
1000	HMND	46394	3280		D3
10500	CHCG	60617	3280		C1
10500	HMND	60617	3280	4E-11S	C1
S Indianapolis Blvd US-41					
1000	HMND	46320	3280		D3
1000	HMND	46394	3280		D3
10500	CHCG	60617	3280		C1
10500	HMND	60617	3280	4E-11S	C1
Indian Boundary Ct					
25200	PNFD	60544	3415	31W-18S	E1
Indian Boundary Dr					
-	DGvT	60559	3085	18W-3S	A6
-	MLPK	60165	3029	12W-2N	C1
-	SNPK	60160	3029	12W-2N	C1
-	SNPK	60165	3029	12W-2N	C1
900	WTMT	60559	3085	18W-3S	A6
1900	MLPK	60160	2973	12W-2N	C7
1900	MLPK	60160	3029	12W-2N	C1
Indian Boundary Rd					
-	BGBK	60440	3204	25W-11S	B7
-	BGBK	60440	3268	25W-11S	C1
-	PNFD	60544	3415	31W-18S	E1
-	PnfT	60544	3415	31W-18S	E1
N Indian Boundary Rd					
2700	RVGV	60171	2973	10W-3N	E5
2800	RVGV	60171	2974	10W-3N	B5
Indian Boundary Line Rd					
10	PNFD	60544	3415	31W-18S	E1
10	PnfT	60544	3415	31W-18S	E1
100	PNFD	60544	3338	31W-18S	A7
200	PnfT	60544	3338	31W-18S	A7
S Indian Boundary Line Rd					
-	PNFD	60544	3415	32W-19S	C3
-	PNFD	60586	3415	32W-19S	C3
-	PnfT	60544	3415	32W-19S	C3
Indian Creek Ct					
100	INCK	60061	2647	17W-24N	B6
3100	BFGV	60089	2701	16W-23N	D2
Indian Creek Dr					
3100	BFGV	60069	2701	16W-23N	D2
3100	VrnT	60069	2701	16W-23N	D2
Indian Creek Rd					
4100	BtvT	60502	3079	33W-2S	A4
4100	BtvT	60510	3079	33W-2S	A4
N Indian Creek Rd					
23100	LNSH	60069	2702	15W-23N	A3
23100	VrnT	60069	2701	15W-23N	E2
23100	VrnT	60069	2702	15W-23N	A2
23200	LNSH	60069	2701	15W-23N	E2
W Indian Creek Rd					
-	ElaT	60047	2645	20W-25N	E5
6700	ElaT	60047	2646	19W-25N	C5
6700	ElaT	60060	2646	19W-25N	C5
6700	LGGV	60047	2646	19W-25N	D5
6700	LGGV	60060	2646	19W-25N	D5
20000	HNWD	60047	2646	19W-25N	C5
20500	ElaT	60060	2645	20W-25N	E5
20500	HNWD	60047	2645	20W-25N	E5
Indian Creek Tr					
26000	AxST	60410	3672	33W-31S	B7
26000	CNHN	60410	3672	33W-31S	B7
Indian Grass Ct					
1100	MNKA	60447	3672	33W-29S	B3
2500	NPVL	60564	3266	29W-13S	D5
24700	TRLK	60010	2643	26W-24N	C6
Indian Grass Ln					
1400	GYLK	60030	2533	19W-32N	C5
Indian Grass Rd					
2300	NPVL	60564	3266	29W-13S	D4
Indianhead Ct					
6300	IHPK	60525	3146	14W-7S	E5
Indian Head Ln					
2800	JLET	60435	3417	27W-19S	C3
Indianhead Tr					
6300	IHPK	60525	3146	14W-7S	E5
Indian Hill Av					
1400	HRPK	60133	2911	26W-8N	D3
Indian Hill Ct					
500	NPVL	60563	3141	27W-5S	C3
600	DRFD	60015	2703	11W-20N	C7
1400	HRPK	60133	2911	26W-8N	E3
Indian Hill Dr					
200	BFGV	60089	2754	17W-18N	A3
1200	BNVL	60106	2915	17W-7N	C4
1200	EGVV	60007	2915	17W-7N	C4
1200	SMBG	60193	2913	23W-8N	A2
1400	ROSL	60172	2913	23W-8N	A2
1400	ROSL	60193	2913	23W-8N	A2
1400	SmbT	60172	2913	23W-8N	A2
1400	SmbT	60193	2913	23W-8N	A2
1500	BNVL	60007	2915	17W-7N	C4
4000	CCHL	60478	3426	5W-20S	C5
S Indian Hill Dr					
1600	ROSL	60172	2913	23W-8N	A3
1600	ROSL	60193	2913	23W-8N	A3
1600	SmbT	60172	2913	23W-8N	A3
Indian Hill Ln					
1900	AURA	60503	3201	33W-10S	A7
Indian Hill Rd					
10	KLWH	60043	2812	4W-14N	B4
10	NtrT	60043	2812	4W-14N	B4
10	NtrT	60093	2812	4W-14N	B4
10	WLMT	60091	2812	5W-14N	A4
10	WNKA	60093	2812	4W-15N	B3
400	DRFD	60015	2756	11W-20N	C1
600	DRFD	60015	2703	11W-20N	C7
N Indian Hill Rd					
10	NtrT	60093	2812	5W-14N	A3
10	WNKA	60093	2812	4W-15N	B3
Indian Hill Tr					
10	CLLK	60012	2640	35W-27N	B1
10	NmdT	60012	2640	35W-27N	B1
Indian Hill Woods					
500	LslT	60563	3082	25W-4S	A7
500	NPVL	60563	3082	25W-4S	A7
Indian Joe Dr					
2800	BDVW	60154	3029	12W-0S	C6
2800	BDVW	60155	3029	12W-0S	C6
2800	WSTR	60154	3029	12W-0S	C6
2800	WSTR	60155	3029	12W-0S	C6
Indian Knoll Rd					
10	WnfT	60185	3023	28W-0N	A4
10	WynT	60185	3023	28W-2N	A2
400	WynT	60185	3022	28W-2N	E1
1600	NPVL	60565	3204	25W-9S	B3
Indian Knoll St					
-	WNFD	60190	3023	26W-1N	E3
10	WnfT	60190	3081	28W-1S	A1
Indian Knoll Tr					
200	WnfT	60185	3023	28W-0N	A5
Indian Mound Dr					
100	NlxT	60451	3502	15W-25S	C7
Indian Mound Rd					
10	SchT	60174	2964	36W-3N	A6
Indian Oaks Dr					
200	MNKA	60447	3583	33W-28S	B7
200	MNKA	60447	3672	33W-28S	B1
Indian Oaks Tr					
800	MRGO	60152	2634	50W-26N	A3
Indian Path Rd					
600	GYLK	60030	2533	19W-31N	D6
Indian Ridge Ct					
2500	GNVW	60025	2809	11W-15N	D2
Indian Ridge Dr					
500	ANTH	60002	2357	24W-42N	D5
2300	GNVW	60025	2809	11W-15N	C3
2500	GNVW	60062	2809	11W-15N	C2
W Indian Ridge Dr					
1600	MchT	60050	2472	30W-36N	A4
1900	MchT	60050	2471	30W-36N	E4
Indian Ridge Ln					
100	LKVL	60046	2475	22W-37N	B3
Indian Ridge Rd					
100	LbvT	60045	2648	14W-26N	D3
100	MTWA	60045	2648	14W-26N	D3
Indian Ridge Tr					
300	WCDA	60084	2643	26W-27N	D1
400	WCDA	60084	2587	26W-27N	D7
Indian Spring Ct					
2900	JLET	60435	3417	27W-19S	C3
Indian Spring Ln					
500	BFGV	60089	2701	17W-20N	B7
500	BFGV	60089	2754	17W-20N	B1
Indian Springs Dr					
100	LtRT	60548	3330	50W-14S	B1
Indian Trail Ct					
200	OKBK	60523	3085	16W-3S	D4
Indian Trail Dr					
10	WTMT	60559	3085	18W-3S	A6
500	PlsT	60464	3273	12W-14S	C7
1300	RVWD	60015	2702	13W-21N	E6
1600	NPVL	60565	3204	25W-9S	B3
Indian Trail Rd					
-	AURA	60542	3138	35W-5S	B4
-	NpvT	60502	3139	31W-6S	D4
100	OKBK	60523	3085	16W-3S	D5
300	AURA	60506	3137	37W-5S	B4
300	AURA	60506	3138	36W-5S	A4
500	ANTH	60002	2357	24W-42N	C5
500	WnfT	60190	3023	28W-0S	A7
1100	HNDL	60521	3086	15W-3S	B6
2900	AURA	60502	3139	32W-6S	C4
6000	GRNE	60031	2534	16W-34N	D1
8800	NBRN	60010	2644	25W-24N	A6
W Indian Trail Rd					
24500	ElaT	60010	2644	24W-24N	B7
24500	ElaT	60010	2698	24W-24N	B1
24500	NBRN	60010	2698	24W-24N	B1
24800	CbaT	60010	2644	25W-25N	A6
24800	LKBN	60010	2644	25W-25N	A6
24800	NBRN	60010	2644	25W-25N	A6
25000	CbaT	60010	2643	25W-25N	E5
25000	LKBN	60010	2643	25W-25N	E5
25000	TRLK	60010	2643	26W-25N	E5
Indian Tree Dr					
10	GLNC	60022	2758	7W-20N	B2
10	HDPK	60035	2758	7W-20N	B2
Indian Wells Cir					
700	ELGN	60123	2854	36W-9N	A7
Indian Wells Ln					
3600	NHBK	60062	2756	12W-17N	B4
Indianwood Blvd					
10	PKFT	60466	3595	3W-27S	B4
400	MonT	60466	3595	4W-28S	A6
Indianwood Dr					
-	VNHL	60061	2647	17W-26N	C3
10	TNTN	60476	3428	0E-20S	E4
400	CLSM	60188	2967	26W-2N	E7
Indianwood Ln					
100	IHPK	60525	3146	14W-6S	D5
100	LynT	60525	3146	14W-6S	D5
200	WCHI	60185	2966	30W-3N	B6
3200	JLET	60431	3497	28W-23S	B4
Indianwood Rd					
2900	WLMT	60091	2811	5W-14N	E5
Indian Woods Dr					
11100	BRRG	60525	3208	13W-8S	E1
11100	BRRG	60527	3208	13W-8S	E1
11100	IHPK	60525	3208	13W-8S	E1
Indie Ct					
18500	HLCT	60429	3506	4W-22S	D1
Indie Ln					
22300	SLVL	60411	3597	1E-27S	A4
22300	StGR	60411	3597	1E-27S	A4
Indigo Ct					
10	BGBK	60440	3205	21W-10S	E5
800	LKZH	60047	2699	22W-21N	B5
900	BmdT	60133	2912	25W-6N	A6
900	BmdT	60172	2912	25W-6N	A6
900	HRPK	60133	2912	25W-6N	A6
1900	JNBG	60050	2471	30W-37N	E2
24300	PNFD	60585	3338	30W-14S	B1
N Indigo Ct					
1700	MPPT	60056	2808	13W-14N	D3
Indigo Dr					
-	AURA	60503	3265	32W-11S	C2
-	AURA	60585	3265	32W-11S	C2
-	SgrT	60554	3135	43W-7S	A6
-	SRGV	60554	3135	43W-7S	A6
10	SjnT	46311	3598		C6
N Indigo Dr					
1300	MPPT	60056	2808	13W-14N	D4
Indigo Ln					
600	WDSK	60098	2581	41W-30N	D2
2300	GNVW	60025	2810	9W-14N	C5
Indi Illi Pkwy					
10	HMND	46324	3430		C3
6700	CTCY	60409	3430	4E-19S	C3
Industrial Av					
10	LKBN	60010	2696	28W-22N	E4
10	LKBN	60010	2697	28W-22N	A4
100	FXLK	60020	2473	27W-36N	A4
100	MNKA	60447	3672	34W-28S	A1
300	CLLK	60012	2640	34W-26N	C2
1900	ZION	60099	2421	11W-41N	D2
3600	ANHT	60005	2806	20W-15N	B3
3600	ANHT	60008	2806	20W-14N	A3
3600	RGMW	60008	2806	20W-14N	A3
3700	PLTN	60008	2806	20W-14N	A3
3700	PLTN	60067	2806	20W-14N	A3
Industrial Ct					
7600	SPGV	60081	2413	31W-39N	D5
Industrial Dr					
-	RVDL	60827	3350	1W-15S	A1
10	GLBT	60136	2799	39W-16N	A2
10	SCRL	60174	2964	34W-3N	E7
100	NPVL	60563	3140	30W-6S	B4
200	HPSR	60140	2796	46W-16N	A2
200	LNSH	60069	2701	15W-21N	E5
200	VrnT	60069	2701	15W-21N	E5
200	WCDA	60084	2587	26W-28N	D5
300	SEGN	60177	2908	34W-9N	C1
300	WCHI	60185	3021	31W-1N	E3
400	BNVL	60106	2915	16W-6N	D5
400	WnfT	60185	3021	31W-1N	E3
500	UYPK	60449	3682	7W-29S	D2
600	CRY	60013	2641	32W-24N	C7
600	CRY	60013	2695	31W-24N	C1
700	UYPK	60466	3682	7W-29S	E2
1200	LIHL	60156	2694	34W-22N	C3
1300	ITSC	60143	2914	18W-6N	E6
1400	MHRY	60050	2528	33W-33N	A3
1700	MTGY	60538	3199	37W-9S	B4
1800	LYVL	60048	2590	19W-30N	C1
7400	FTPK	60130	3088	9W-1S	C1
8500	JSTC	60458	3210	10W-9S	A3
9600	BGVW	60455	3210	9W-11S	D6
9600	BGVW	60457	3210	9W-11S	D6
9600	HYHL	60457	3210	9W-11S	D6
10300	HBRN	60034	2350	41W-42N	E6
N Industrial Dr					
600	EMHT	60126	2971	16W-3N	E5
900	BNVL	60106	2971	16W-3N	E5
900	EMHT	60106	2971	16W-3N	E5
NE Industrial Dr					
200	AraT	60505	3138	35W-5S	C3
200	AURA	60504	3138	35W-5S	C3
200	AURA	60505	3138	35W-5S	C3
S Industrial Dr E					
12300	WldT	60585	3266	29W-14S	C7
W Industrial Dr					
100	EMHT	60126	2971	16W-2N	E6
900	AURA	60506	3137	36W-5S	D3
5800	MONE	60449	3682	7W-31S	E6
5900	MonT	60449	3682	7W-31S	D6
W Industrial Dr N					
23800	PNFD	60585	3266	29W-14S	C7
23800	WldT	60585	3266	29W-14S	C7
W Industrial Dr S					
23800	PNFD	60585	3338	29W-14S	C1
23800	WldT	60585	3338	29W-14S	C1
Industrial Ln					
200	WhlT	60090	2755	13W-16N	E6
200	WLNG	60090	2755	13W-16N	D6
Industrial Rd					
10	CTCY	60409	3352		C5
10	HMND	46320	3352		C5
W Industrial Rd					
10	ADSN	60101	2970	18W-2N	E6
Industrial Heights Dr					
11900	WDSK	60098	2581	40W-29N	E3
11900	WDSK	60098	2582	40W-29N	A3
Industrial Park Dr					
16400	LmnT	60439	3270	19W-13S	C5
S Industrial Park Dr					
26400	ELWD	60421	3763	28W-33S	B3
Industry Av					
10	JLET	60435	3498	24W-22S	E1
10	JltT	60435	3498	24W-22S	E1
100	FKFT	60423	3591	11W-27S	E4
200	FftT	60423	3592	11W-27S	A4
200	FKFT	60423	3592	11W-27S	A4
Industry Dr					
1000	NLNX	60451	3589	17W-26S	D2
1000	NlxT	60451	3589	17W-26S	D2
W Ingalls Av					
10	JLET	60435	3498	24W-22S	D2
2000	JLET	60435	3497	26W-22S	E2
2300	CTHL	60403	3497	26W-22S	E2
2300	CTHL	60435	3497	26W-22S	E2
2300	TroT	60403	3497	26W-22S	E2
2500	TroT	60403	3497	26W-22S	E2
3200	JLET	60431	3497	27W-22S	B2
Ingalls Dr					
10	HRVY	60426	3349	2W-18S	D7
Ingalton Av					
-	WynT	60185	3022	29W-2N	C1
500	WnfT	60185	3022	29W-1N	D3
900	WCHI	60185	3022	29W-2N	C1
Ingemunson Dr					
2000	KdlT	60560	3333	41W-16S	E5
Ingersoll Ct					
2100	JLET	60586	3415	33W-21S	B7
Ingersoll Ln					
100	VLPK	60181	3085	18W-1S	A1
100	YkTp	60181	3085	18W-1S	A1
200	OKTR	60181	3085	18W-1S	A1
Ingersoll St					
15100	PNFD	60544	3338	30W-18S	A7
15100	PNFD	60544	3416	30W-18S	A1
Ingham Ln					
-	AURA	60506	3136	40W-6S	B6
-	SRGV	60554	3136	40W-6S	B6
Inglenook Ct					
21800	DRPK	60010	2698	23W-21N	E5
Inglenook Ln					
7300	GRNE	60031	2477	18W-35N	A5
21500	DRPK	60010	2698	23W-21N	E6
Ingleshire Ct					
10	OswT	60538	3199	36W-10S	E6
Ingleshire Rd					
10	OswT	60538	3199	36W-10S	E6
Ingleside Av					
100	AURA	60506	3137	37W-7S	D7
200	AURA	60506	3199	37W-7S	D1
14200	DLTN	60419	3351	1E-16S	A4

STREET Block City ZIP Map# CGS Grid

Ingleside Av
15200 SHLD 60473 3351 1E-17S A6
15400 DLTN 60473 3351 1E-18S A7
16300 SHLD 60473 3429 1E-19S A2
S Ingleside Av
200 GNWD 60425 3509 1E-23S A3
4700 CHCG 60615 3152 1E-5S E1
7100 CHCG 60619 3152 1E-8S E7
7100 CHCG 60637 3152 1E-8S E7
7500 CHCG 60619 3214 1E-8S E1
9700 CHCG 60628 3214 1E-11S E6
13100 CHCG 60827 3351 0E-15S A1
W Ingleside Av
26000 GrtT 60041 2473 26W-35N E6
Ingleside Ct
16900 SHLD 60473 3429 1E-20S A3
Ingleside Dr
300 BGBK 60440 3268 25W-12S B4
300 BGBK 60490 3268 25W-12S B4
N Ingleside Dr
35000 GrtT 60041 2473 26W-35N D7
Ingleside Pk
500 EVTN 60201 2813 2W-13N B7
Ingleside Pl
500 EVTN 60201 2813 2W-13N B7
3900 PKCY 60085 2535 13W-33N E3
W Ingleside Shore Rd
26300 GrtT 60041 2473 26W-36N D3
Inglewood Ln
1000 ELGN 60120 2855 32W-12N C2
Ingolsby Rd
22700 CnhT 60447 3583 32W-27S E6
22700 TroT 60404 3583 32W-27S E6
22700 TroT 60447 3583 32W-27S E6
S Ingolsby Rd
21900 SRWD 60404 3583 32W-26S E3
21900 TroT 60404 3583 32W-26S E3
Ingraham Av
300 CTCY 60409 3352 4E-17S C6
Ingram Dr
14500 NptT 60099 2361 14W-43N C4
Ingram Pl
800 DSPN 60016 2862 15W-10N B4
Ingram St
200 NHFD 60093 2811 7W-15N A3
Ingrid Ln
1600 CHHT 60411 3595 2W-25S C1
Inishowen Ct
500 OSWG 60543 3263 39W-11S A2
Inland Cir
700 NPVL 60563 3140 30W-6S B4
Inland Dr
400 WLNG 60090 2755 13W-17N D5
W Inland Dr
- ALSP 60803 3276 5W-15S B7
- ALSP 60803 3348 5W-15S B1
Inlet Dr
100 CPVL 60110 2800 35W-16N C1
100 WDND 60118 2800 35W-16N C1
Inlet Cove
100 CPVL 60110 2800 35W-16N C1
Inmans Wy
4800 RGWD 60072 2470 34W-36N C3
Inner Ct
100 NLNX 60451 3501 18W-23S B4
Inner Cir Dr
- DGvT 60439 3207 18W-11S A7
10 DSPN 60016 2862 15W-12N B2
100 MPPT 60056 2862 15W-12N B2
300 BGBK 60490 3268 26W-12S A3
S Inner Cir Dr
500 DSPN 60016 2862 13W-11N D2
500 MPPT 60056 2862 13W-11N D2
Innercircle Dr
1700 CTHL 60403 3418 25W-21S C7
1900 CTHL 60403 3498 25W-21S C1
Inner Ring Rd
- BtvT 60510 3079 33W-2S B4
- WnfT 60510 3079 33W-2S B4
Innesbrook Ct
- ALGN 60102 2746 37W-20N B2
Innetowne Ct
32600 LKMR 60051 2529 28W-32N D4
Innetowne Rd
32600 LKMR 60051 2529 28W-32N D4
Innisbrook Ct
2200 AURA 60504 3201 33W-8S B3
Innisbrook Dr
500 NpvT 60563 3140 30W-4S C2
Innisbrook Ln
14700 HMGN 60491 3343 17W-17S C5
Innishmor Ct
11700 ODPK 60467 3422 14W-21S D6
Innovation Dr
- WCHI 60185 3021 32W-0N B5
10 DSPN 60016 2862 14W-11N D3
Innsbrook Dr
100 HnrT 60107 2910 29W-9N E1
100 SMWD 60107 2910 29W-9N E1
15500 ODPK 60462 3346 9W-18S C7
15600 ODPK 60462 3424 9W-18S C1
Innsbruck Ct
600 LYVL 60048 2591 17W-29N B4
6700 LSLE 60532 3142 24W-7S C7
Innsbruck Ln
3400 CRTE 60417 3596 0E-28S E5
3400 STGR 60475 3596 0E-28S E5
Insignia Ct
10 HDPK 60035 2758 7W-20N B2
10 NtrT 60062 2758 7W-20N B2
8000 LGGV 60060 2645 20W-25N E4
S Insignia Ct
10 PLTN 60067 2805 20W-14N E3
W Institute Pl
200 CHCG 60610 3034 0W-1N A2
Interlachen Ln
400 WNFD 60190 3023 26W-1N E2
Interlaken Ct
800 LYVL 60048 2591 17W-29N B4
Interlaken Dr
700 LKZH 60047 2698 23W-24N E1
800 HNWD 60047 2698 23W-24N E1
Interlaken Ln
800 LYVL 60048 2591 17W-29N B4
Interlakin Dr
- LKPT 60441 3419 21W-20S E5
Interloch Ct
900 ALGN 60102 2747 35W-20N B1
Interlochen Ct
600 RVWD 60015 2703 12W-21N A6
W Interlochen Ct
8500 PSHL 60465 3274 10W-12S B1
S Interlochen Dr
10300 PSHL 60465 3274 10W-12S A1
Interlochen Ln
3400 NPVL 60564 3202 30W-10S B7

International Dr
- BtvT 60539 3077 36W-3S E5
- SCRL 60174 3021 32W-2N B1
2600 WynT 60185 3021 32W-2N B1
N International Dr
10 BtvT 60539 3077 36W-2S E5
10 BtvT 60539 3078 36W-3S A5
S International Dr
- BtvT 60539 3077 36W-3S E6
- BtvT 60542 3077 36W-3S E6
International St
1200 WLNG 60090 2754 16W-18N E2
International Wy
- JLET 60421 3675 24W-29S E1
Internationale Blvd
10 GLHT 60139 2968 23W-3N E5
10 GLHT 60139 2969 23W-3N A5
Internationale Pkwy
200 BGBK 60440 3269 22W-12S D2
300 WDRG 60440 3269 21W-12S D3
300 WDRG 60517 3269 21W-12S D3
1000 DGvT 60439 3270 19W-12S D2
1000 WDRG 60439 3270 19W-12S C2
1600 WDRG 60517 3270 20W-12S A2
2100 DGvT 60517 3270 21W-12S A3
2100 WDRG 60440 3270 21W-12S A3
Interocean Av
10 SCHT 60411 3596 1W-26S A2
W Interstate Rd
10 ADSN 60101 2970 18W-2N E7
Interurban Av
19300 BlmT 60411 3508 1W-23S B3
19300 HMWD 60430 3508 1W-23S B3
19400 CHHT 60411 3508 1W-23S B3
Intrepid St
1800 NCHI 60088 2593 11W-30N D1
Inverary Dr
7600 FftT 60423 3504 9W-25S E7
Inverdale Dr
400 IVNS 60010 2751 23W-16N D6
Inverleith Rd
900 LKFT 60045 2649 12W-26N B3
Inverness Av
2000 LslT 60515 3143 21W-5S E3
2400 DRGV 60515 3143 21W-5S D3
Inverness Cir
5000 JLET 60586 3416 30W-21S C6
Inverness Ct
10 LKBF 60044 2593 11W-29N E4
100 EGVV 60007 2859 22W-9N D7
300 MltT 60188 3023 26W-1N E3
300 WNFD 60190 3023 26W-1N E3
1300 ANTH 60002 2357 25W-41N B7
1500 NPVL 60563 3141 27W-5S C2
2300 AURA 60504 3201 32W-8S B2
9500 HTLY 60142 2692 40W-22N A4
20000 OMFD 60461 3507 3W-24S B5
N Inverness Ct
10 RDLK 60073 2531 25W-33N B3
Inverness Dr
100 AURA 60502 3201 32W-8S C2
300 AURA 60504 3201 32W-8S C2
300 CRY 60013 2642 30W-25N A5
400 GRNE 60031 2534 16W-33N D2
900 ANTH 60002 2357 25W-41N B7
900 ANTH 60002 2416 25W-41N B1
1200 ELGN 60120 2855 31W-10N D5
9300 HTLY 60142 2692 40W-22N B3
13500 ODPK 60462 3346 11W-16S A2
17100 ODHL 60487 3424 11W-20S A4
17100 TYPK 60487 3424 11W-20S A5
21600 PnfT 60544 3339 27W-16S D4
N Inverness Dr
2000 VNHL 60061 2647 17W-27N B1
Inverness Ln
- CRTE 60417 3686 0E-29S A1
- CteT 60417 3686 0E-29S A1
1000 ITSC 60143 2914 19W-7N D5
1200 AddT 60143 2914 19W-7N D5
2100 GNVW 60025 2810 10W-14N A3
3500 CRTE 60417 3596 0E-28S E6
3500 CRTE 60417 3597 0E-28S A6
W Inverness Ln
7400 FftT 60423 3504 9W-23S E4
Inverness Rd
600 LSLE 60532 3143 22W-5S B3
Inverness Tr
200 MHRY 60050 2527 34W-32N B5
Inverrary Dr
1400 NPVL 60563 3141 28W-5S A2
Inverrary Ln
100 VrnT 60015 2755 15W-20N B1
1200 PLTN 60074 2753 19W-18N C4
Inverray Rd
2100 IVNS 60067 2804 23W-15N D1
Inverway
10 IVNS 60067 2805 22W-16N A1
600 IVNS 60067 2752 23W-16N A6
700 IVNS 60067 2751 23W-16N E6
Inverway Ln
- LKWD 60014 2638 39W-25N D5
Inwood Dr
200 PTHT 60070 2808 14W-15N B2
200 PTHT 60090 2808 14W-15N B2
200 WLNG 60090 2808 14W-15N B2
W Inwood Dr
100 JLET 60435 3497 27W-23S D4
Inwood Ln
200 WNFD 60190 3023 26W-1N E2
S I-Oka Av
10 MPPT 60056 2807 16W-12N E7
200 MPPT 60056 2861 16W-12N E1
Iola Av
600 RMVL 60446 3340 24W-15S E1
N Iola Av
36500 GrtT 60041 2473 25W-36N E3
Iona Av
1700 NPVL 60565 3204 24W-9S D3
9700 FNPK 60131 2973 12W-4N C3
Iona Ct
1600 NPVL 60565 3204 24W-9S D3
Iona Ln
500 HRVD 60033 2463 51W-37N E1
Iona St
100 ALGN 60102 2695 32W-21N A5
100 AlqT 60102 2695 32W-21N A5
Ione Ct
1800 AURA 60503 3201 33W-10S B5
Ione Dr
10 SEGN 60177 2908 35W-8N A3
Ione Ln
1800 AURA 60503 3201 33W-10S B5
Ione St
13200 PNFD 60585 3338 30W-15S B3
Ionia Av
3400 OMFD 60461 3506 4W-24S E6

N Ionia Av
6000 CHCG 60646 2920 5W-7N A3
6400 CHCG 60712 2919 6W-8N D2
6400 LNWD 60646 2919 6W-8N D2
6400 LNWD 60712 2919 6W-8N D2
6700 NLES 60714 2919 6W-8N C2
6700 SKOK 60646 2919 6W-8N C2
6800 CHCG 60646 2919 7W-8N B1
6800 NLES 60646 2919 6W-8N C2
Iota Ct
1200 WLNG 60090 2754 16W-18N E2
Iowa Av
10 AddT 60101 3027 18W-2N A1
10 AddT 60181 3027 18W-2N A1
10 ADSN 60101 3027 18W-2N A1
10 ADSN 60181 3027 18W-2N A1
10 VLPK 60181 3027 18W-2N A1
200 JLET 60433 3499 23W-24S B5
500 SchT 60174 2908 34W-6N D6
900 AURA 60506 3138 36W-6S A4
N Iowa Av
10 ADSN 60101 2971 18W-3N A5
300 VLPK 60181 3027 18W-1N A2
S Iowa Av
10 ADSN 60101 2971 18W-3N A6
10 JLET 60432 3499 23W-24S B5
10 JLET 60433 3499 23W-24S B5
Iowa Ct
200 CLSM 60188 2968 25W-2N A7
300 FKFT 60423 3503 12W-25S D7
13200 HTLY 60142 2744 42W-18N C4
17900 ODPK 60467 3423 12W-21S C7
Iowa Dr
1600 EGVV 60007 2913 21W-8N D2
Iowa St
- MYWD 60153 3029 10W-1N E3
- MYWD 60153 3030 10W-1N A3
- MYWD 60160 3029 10W-1N E3
- NCHI 60088 2593 11W-30N E1
10 CHCG 60651 3031 7W-1N B2
10 OKPK 60302 3031 7W-1N B2
700 OKPK 60302 3030 8W-1N E3
1000 MLPK 60160 3029 11W-1N D3
7200 RVFT 60302 3030 9W-1N C2
7200 RVFT 60305 3030 9W-1N C2
S Iowa St
800 AddT 60181 3027 17W-1N B1
800 ADSN 60101 2971 18W-2N A7
800 ADSN 60101 3027 17W-1N B1
800 ADSN 60181 3027 17W-1N B1
900 AddT 60101 3027 18W-2N A1
W Iowa St
- GNWD 60430 3508 1W-22S A1
- HMWD 60430 3508 1W-22S A1
500 CHCG 60610 3034 0W-1N A2
1000 GNWD 60425 3508 1W-22S A1
1800 CHCG 60622 3033 3W-1N A2
3300 CHCG 60651 3032 5W-1N B2
4800 CHCG 60651 3031 7W-1N C2
5900 OKPK 60302 3031 7W-1N B2
Ipswich Ct
600 EGVV 60007 2860 19W-9N D7
600 EGVV 60007 2914 19W-9N D1
N Irene Av
3200 CHCG 60618 2976 3W-4N D3
Irene Dr
6000 HFET 60120 2855 31W-12N E1
6000 HFET 60192 2855 31W-12N E1
6000 HnrT 60120 2855 31W-12N E1
N Irene Dr
2300 DRPK 60074 2752 21W-18N E2
2300 PltT 60074 2752 21W-18N E2
Irene Ln
2000 GNOK 60048 2592 14W-29N D3
W Irene St
500 JLET 60436 3498 24W-24S D5
Irenes Courtyard
7000 TYPK 60477 3425 8W-19S A2
N Iride Dr
26700 FmtT 60060 2646 19W-26N C2
Iris Av
1300 CLSM 60188 2967 28W-3N A5
7200 HRPK 60133 2911 27W-9N D1
Iris Cir
10 RMVL 60446 3339 26W-17S E5
Iris Ct
- LKVL 60046 2474 23W-37N E3
100 OSWG 60543 3263 38W-13S B5
500 CLLK 60014 2639 37W-24N C6
3100 NHBK 60062 2756 11W-16N D7
S Iris Ct
25700 MONE 60449 3683 5W-31S B5
Iris Dr
200 SMWD 60107 2857 27W-10N C6
N Iris Dr
1800 PLTN 60074 2753 19W-18N B3
Iris Ln
300 CHHT 60411 3507 1W-23S E3
300 HDPK 60035 2758 7W-20N C1
800 NPVL 60540 3141 27W-7S C7
2400 DSPN 60018 2917 12W-8N B1
2500 CTHL 60403 3417 27W-21S D6
5800 LslT 60532 3143 22W-6S B4
W Iris Ln
4500 MONE 60449 3683 5W-31S C5
Iris Rd
100 DRN 60561 3145 16W-7S D6
Irish Ct
6900 DRN 60561 3144 18W-7S E7
Irish Indian Tr
1700 JLET 60436 3585 27W-26S D2
Irma Harvey Ln
6600 JLET 60586 3415 32W-20S D5
Irma Lee Cir
27800 GNOK 60045 2592 13W-27N D7
N Irma Lee Cir
27900 GNOK 60045 2592 13W-27N D7
Irmen Dr
500 ADSN 60143 2970 19W-5N D1
500 ADSN 60191 2970 19W-5N D1
500 WDDL 60191 2970 19W-5N D1
S Irmen Dr
400 AddT 60101 2970 19W-2N D6
400 ADSN 60101 2970 19W-2N D6
S Iron St
3200 CHCG 60608 3091 1W-3S D5
3200 CHCG 60609 3091 1W-3S D5
Ironbark Ct
200 BGBK 60440 3269 22W-12S C2
Ironbark Wy
200 BGBK 60440 3269 22W-12S C2
Iron Bridge Rd
- FftT 60423 3590 14W-26S D2
Irondale Ct
3300 JLET 60451 3500 19W-22S D2

Irondale Rd
2200 GNOK 60048 2535 15W-31N B7
2200 GNOK 60048 2592 15W-31N B1
Ironhawk Ct
300 CLSM 60188 2968 25W-3N A5
Iron Horse Ct
400 GYLK 60030 2533 20W-32N A5
Iron Liege Ct
1200 NPVL 60540 3142 25W-7S A7
Ironwood Av
- OSWG 60543 3263 36W-13S E6
900 DRN 60561 3145 17W-7S B7
W Ironwood Cir
13700 HMGN 60491 3343 17W-17S D5
Ironwood Ct
10 FftT 60423 3503 13W-24S B6
10 FKFT 60423 3503 13W-24S B6
10 LKZH 60047 2698 23W-22N D4
10 SMWD 60107 2857 28W-12N B2
100 BFGV 60089 2701 16W-22N C4
100 RGMW 60008 2805 21W-14N D5
100 VrnT 60089 2701 16W-22N C4
600 WLNG 60090 2754 16W-18N D3
700 CmpT 60175 2961 42W-5N C2
1100 ELGN 60120 2855 32W-12N D1
1200 SMBG 60193 2859 22W-10N D6
1300 AURA 60506 3137 38W-5S B4
2000 GRNE 60031 2478 15W-36N A4
3500 JLET 60435 3417 27W-19S D3
24800 PNFD 60585 3266 31W-14S A6
Ironwood Dr
- LKWD 60014 2638 38W-25N E4
200 BMDL 60108 2969 22W-5N C2
200 LNHT 60046 2476 19W-37N C1
200 MltT 60137 3083 22W-3S C5
400 DSPN 60016 2863 11W-11N D3
400 LslT 60540 3141 26W-7S E7
400 NPVL 60540 3141 26W-7S E7
600 EGVV 60007 2861 17W-9N A6
700 FftT 60423 3503 13W-24S B6
700 FKFT 60423 3503 13W-24S B6
1000 ELGN 60120 2855 32W-12N D1
1600 NPVL 60565 3204 25W-9S C3
2000 DrrT 60014 2638 38W-26N E4
16300 TYPK 60477 3424 10W-19S B3
23000 PnfT 60586 3416 28W-20S E4
23000 PnfT 60586 3417 28W-20S A4
E Ironwood Dr
1300 MPPT 60056 2808 14W-14N C5
N Ironwood Dr
600 ANHT 60004 2807 16W-14N D4
S Ironwood Dr
13700 LktT 60544 3339 26W-16S D4
Ironwood Ln
10 MltT 60187 3082 25W-2S A3
10 WHTN 60187 3082 25W-2S A3
1100 LSLE 60532 3143 23W-6S B5
9400 DSPN 60016 2863 11W-11N D2
9400 MaiT 60016 2863 11W-11N D2
N Ironwood Pl
900 MPPT 60056 2808 14W-14N C5
Iroquois Av
200 SCRL 60174 2964 35W-3N B6
400 NPVL 60563 3141 26W-5S D2
1000 NPVL 60563 3142 25W-5S A2
1200 LslT 60563 3142 25W-5S A2
Iroquois Ct
1200 BNVL 60106 2915 17W-7N C3
7900 WDRG 60517 3205 22W-8S D2
N Iroquois Ct
25100 LKBN 60010 2643 27W-25N B5
Iroquois Ct N
200 WNVL 60555 3080 29W-2S D4
Iroquois Ct S
200 WnfT 60555 3080 29W-2S D4
200 WNVL 60555 3080 29W-2S D4
Iroquois Ct W
500 WNVL 60555 3080 29W-2S D4
Iroquois Dr
10 CNHL 60514 3145 17W-5S B2
500 AURA 60506 3137 37W-6S C6
500 BTVA 60510 3019 36W-0S E7
900 ELGN 60120 2855 32W-12N C1
2300 GNVW 60025 2809 11W-15N C3
W Iroquois Dr
15900 LKPT 60441 3420 19W-20S C4
17700 WrnT 60030 2534 17W-33N B3
Iroquois Ln
1200 DRN 60561 3207 18W-9S B3
1300 BNVL 60106 2915 17W-7N C3
2200 RLKH 60073 2474 23W-36N D4
Iroquois Rd
200 HLSD 60162 3028 13W-0S D5
2600 WKGN 60087 2479 12W-36N C4
2600 WLMT 60091 2812 5W-14N A5
2900 WLMT 60091 2811 5W-14N E5
4700 AlqT 60102 2747 33W-20N D2
S Iroquois Rd
12400 PSPK 60464 3274 10W-14S B7
W Iroquois Rd
8400 PSPK 60464 3274 10W-14S B6
Iroquois St
100 PKFT 60466 3595 3W-27S A5
800 JLET 60433 3587 22W-25S C1
800 JlT 60433 3587 22W-25S C1
Iroquois Tr
100 WDDL 60191 2971 17W-5N B1
500 CLSM 60188 2967 27W-3N C6
34600 GrtT 60051 2472 28W-34N D7
W Iroquois Tr
13400 HMGN 60491 3343 16W-16S D3
Iroquois Trc
8000 TYPK 60477 3424 10W-21S C6
Irvine Ct
400 WLNG 60090 2754 16W-17N D5
Irvine Ln
2200 JLET 60586 3416 30W-21S C6
Irving Av
10 SchT 60174 2908 35W-6N B6
300 WDSK 60098 2524 41W-31N E7
900 WHTN 60187 3024 24W-0N D5
11900 BLID 60406 3277 2W-14S C6
11900 BLID 60643 3277 2W-14S C6
11900 CHCG 60643 3277 2W-14S C6
13100 BLID 60406 3349 2W-15S C1
14200 DLTN 60419 3350 0E-17S E6
14400 ODPK 60462 3345 12W-17S C5
15300 SHLD 60473 3350 0E-17S E6
15900 MKHM 60428 3427 2W-19S C2
15900 ThtT 60428 3427 2W-19S C2
N Irving Av
10 PvsT 60162 3028 14W-0S D4
700 HLSD 60162 3028 14W-0N D4
800 BKLY 60162 3028 14W-0N D4
1200 BKLY 60163 3028 14W-0N D3

S Irving Av
100 NHLK 60164 3028 14W-1N D1
Irving Blvd
200 CHHT 60411 3507 1W-25S E7
Irving Dr
1300 DRN 60561 3207 18W-9S A3
Irving Pkwy
1900 WKGN 60087 2479 11W-38N D1
Irving Pl
- WDRG 60517 3143 23W-7S B6
500 UYPK 60466 3684 3W-30S B3
Irving St
500 WHTN 60187 3024 24W-0S D6
E Irving St
- CNHL 60514 3145 17W-5S B2
10 WTMT 60559 3145 17W-5S B2
200 JLET 60432 3499 23W-23S B3
W Irving St
10 WTMT 60559 3145 18W-5S A2
Irving Park Rd
- CHCG 60176 2973 13W-5N A1
- CHCG 60634 2973 13W-5N A1
- CHCG 60666 2973 13W-5N A1
- ELGN 60120 2855 31W-11N E5
- FNPK 60131 2973 13W-5N A1
- HnrT 60120 2855 31W-11N E5
- ROSL 60157 2913 22W-7N C5
- ROSL 60172 2913 22W-7N C5
- SRPK 60666 2973 12W-5N A1
10 BmdT 60143 2913 22W-7N C5
10 BmdT 60143 2914 21W-6N A6
10 BmdT 60157 2913 22W-6N D5
10 HnrT 60107 2856 30W-10N C6
10 HnrT 60120 2856 31W-10N A5
10 ITSC 60143 2914 21W-6N A6
100 SMWD 60107 2856 30W-10N C6
100 SMWD 60120 2856 30W-10N C6
400 ITSC 60143 2913 21W-6N E6
800 HRPK 60133 2912 26W-9N A2
800 SMBG 60133 2912 26W-9N A2
1200 HRPK 60133 2911 27W-9N D1
1600 ELGN 60120 2856 31W-10N A5
1700 HRPK 60107 2911 27W-9N D1
1700 SMWD 60107 2911 27W-9N D1
1700 SMWD 60133 2911 27W-9N D1
10200 SRPK 60176 2973 12W-5N A1
Irving Park Rd SR-19
- CHCG 60176 2973 13W-5N A1
- CHCG 60634 2973 13W-5N A1
- CHCG 60666 2973 13W-5N A1
- ELGN 60120 2855 31W-11N E5
- FNPK 60131 2973 13W-5N A1
- HnrT 60120 2855 31W-11N E5
- ROSL 60157 2913 22W-7N C5
- ROSL 60172 2913 22W-7N C5
- SRPK 60666 2973 12W-5N A1
10 BmdT 60143 2913 22W-7N C5
10 BmdT 60143 2914 21W-6N A6
10 BmdT 60157 2913 22W-6N D5
10 HnrT 60107 2856 30W-10N C6
10 HnrT 60120 2856 31W-10N A5
10 ITSC 60143 2914 21W-6N A6
100 SMWD 60107 2856 30W-10N C6
100 SMWD 60120 2856 30W-10N C6
400 ITSC 60143 2913 21W-6N E6
800 HRPK 60133 2912 26W-9N A2
800 SMBG 60133 2912 26W-9N A2
1200 HRPK 60133 2911 27W-9N D1
1600 ELGN 60120 2856 31W-10N A5
1700 HRPK 60107 2911 27W-9N D1
1700 SMWD 60107 2911 27W-9N D1
1700 SMWD 60133 2911 27W-9N D1
9200 SRPK 60176 2973 11W-5N D2
E Irving Park Rd
10 BNVL 60106 2972 15W-5N A1
10 ROSL 60172 2913 23W-7N B4
10 SMWD 60107 2857 28W-9N A7
100 ITSC 60143 2914 19W-6N D6
100 WDDL 60191 2915 17W-5N B7
300 SMWD 60107 2911 27W-9N C1
400 BmdT 60157 2913 22W-7N C5
400 BNVL 60106 2915 17W-5N C7
400 CHCG 60106 2972 15W-5N A1
400 ROSL 60157 2913 22W-7N C5
900 BNVL 60131 2972 14W-5N B1
900 CHCG 60131 2972 14W-5N B1
900 HRPK 60107 2911 27W-9N C1
900 HRPK 60133 2911 27W-9N C1
900 SMWD 60133 2911 27W-9N C1
1100 WDDL 60143 2914 19W-6N D7
1200 WDDL 60191 2914 19W-6N D7
1300 ITSC 60191 2914 18W-6N E7
11500 CHCG 60666 2972 14W-5N C1
E Irving Park Rd SR-19
10 BNVL 60106 2972 15W-5N A1
10 ROSL 60172 2913 23W-7N B4
10 SMWD 60107 2857 28W-9N A7
100 ITSC 60143 2914 19W-6N D6
100 WDDL 60191 2915 17W-5N B7
300 SMWD 60107 2911 27W-9N C1
400 BmdT 60157 2913 22W-7N C5
400 BNVL 60106 2915 17W-5N C7
400 CHCG 60106 2972 15W-5N A1
400 ROSL 60157 2913 22W-7N C5
900 BNVL 60131 2972 14W-5N B1
900 CHCG 60131 2972 14W-5N B1
900 HRPK 60107 2911 27W-9N C1
900 HRPK 60133 2911 27W-9N C1
900 SMWD 60133 2911 27W-9N C1
1100 WDDL 60143 2914 19W-6N D7
1200 WDDL 60191 2914 19W-6N D7
1300 ITSC 60191 2914 18W-6N E7
11500 CHCG 60666 2972 14W-5N C1
W Irving Park Rd
- BNVL 60131 2972 14W-5N C1
- CHCG 60131 2972 13W-5N D2
- CHCG 60176 2973 10W-5N E2
- CHCG 60634 2973 10W-5N E2
- FNPK 60131 2972 13W-5N D2
- FNPK 60666 2972 13W-5N E2
10 BNVL 60106 2915 17W-5N C7
10 ROSL 60172 2913 23W-7N A4
10 SMWD 60107 2856 29W-10N D6
100 ROSL 60172 2912 23W-7N E4
100 SMBG 60172 2912 23W-7N E4
200 ITSC 60143 2914 20W-6N A6
200 WDDL 60191 2914 18W-6N E7
400 ITSC 60191 2914 18W-6N E7
400 SMBG 60193 2912 24W-8N D3
400 WDDL 60143 2914 18W-6N E7
600 CHCG 60613 2978 0W-5N A1
700 CHCG 60613 2977 2W-5N C1
700 HnrT 60107 2856 29W-10N D6
700 SmbT 60193 2912 24W-8N D3
900 HnrT 60120 2856 29W-10N D6
900 SMWD 60120 2856 29W-10N D6

STREET Block	City	ZIP	Map#	CGS	Grid
W Irving Park Rd					
1200	BmdT	60143	2914	20W-6N	A6
1300	WDDL	60191	2915	17W-5N	C7
1400	BmdT	60143	2913	21W-6N	E6
1400	ITSC	60143	2913	21W-6N	E6
1800	SMBG	60133	2912	25W-8N	B2
1900	CHCG	60618	2977	2W-5N	B1
1900	HRPK	60133	2912	25W-8N	B2
2700	CHCG	60618	2976	3W-5N	E1
3900	CHCG	60641	2976	5W-4N	A2
4600	CHCG	60641	2975	7W-5N	B2
5500	CHCG	60634	2975	6W-5N	C2
6600	CHCG	60634	2974	8W-5N	E2
7100	NRDG	60634	2974	8W-5N	D2
7100	NRDG	60706	2974	8W-5N	D2
7300	CHCG	60706	2974	9W-4N	D2
11000	CHCG	60666	2972	14W-5N	E2
11001	LydT	60131	2972	14W-5N	C2
W Irving Park Rd SR-19					
-	BNVL	60131	2972	14W-5N	C1
-	CHCG	60131	2972	13W-5N	D2
-	CHCG	60176	2973	10W-5N	E2
-	CHCG	60634	2973	10W-5N	E2
-	CHCG	60666	2972	13W-5N	D2
-	FNPK	60131	2972	13W-5N	D2
-	FNPK	60666	2972	13W-5N	E2
10	BNVL	60106	2915	17W-5N	C7
10	ROSL	60172	2913	23W-7N	A4
10	SMWD	60107	2856	29W-10N	D6
100	ROSL	60172	2912	23W-7N	E4
100	SMBG	60172	2912	23W-7N	E4
100	WDDL	60191	2915	18W-6N	A7
200	ITSC	60143	2914	20W-6N	A6
200	WDDL	60191	2914	18W-6N	E7
400	ITSC	60143	2914	18W-6N	E7
400	SMBG	60193	2912	24W-8N	D3
400	WDDL	60143	2914	18W-6N	E7
600	CHCG	60613	2978	0W-5N	A1
700	CHCG	60613	2977	2W-5N	C1
700	HnrT	60107	2856	29W-10N	D6
700	SmbT	60193	2912	24W-8N	D3
900	HnrT	60120	2856	29W-10N	D6
900	SMWD	60120	2856	29W-10N	D6
1200	BmdT	60143	2914	20W-6N	A6
1400	BmdT	60143	2913	21W-6N	E6
1400	ITSC	60143	2913	21W-6N	E6
1800	SMBG	60133	2912	25W-8N	B2
1900	CHCG	60618	2977	2W-5N	B1
1900	HRPK	60133	2912	25W-8N	B2
2700	CHCG	60618	2976	3W-5N	D1
3900	CHCG	60641	2976	5W-4N	A2
4600	CHCG	60641	2975	7W-5N	B2
5500	CHCG	60634	2975	6W-5N	C2
6600	CHCG	60634	2974	8W-5N	E2
7100	NRDG	60634	2974	8W-5N	D2
7100	NRDG	60706	2974	8W-5N	D2
7300	CHCG	60706	2974	9W-4N	D2
Irvington Ct					
500	BRLT	60103	2911	28W-7N	A4
500	WynT	60103	2911	28W-7N	A4
Irwin Av					
700	SchT	60174	2908	35W-6N	B6
1000	DSPN	60018	2862	13W-9N	E7
2300	PKRG	60068	2863	11W-9N	C7
Irwin Dr					
500	ElgT	60123	2908	35W-9N	A1
Irwinsale Dr					
-	JLET	60421	3675	24W-29S	D2
Isa Av					
10	CHHT	60411	3508	1W-25S	B7
Isa Dr					
400	WLNG	60090	2755	15W-17N	A5
Isabel Ct					
5400	JLET	60586	3496	30W-22S	B1
Isabel Dr					
1000	ALGN	60102	2694	34W-21N	C6
Isabel Ln					
-	SRWD	60404	3584	30W-25S	B1
Isabel St					
3800	SKOK	60076	2866	4W-10N	B5
Isabella St					
200	EVTN	60091	2813	2W-13N	A7
200	EVTN	60201	2813	3W-13N	A7
200	WLMT	60091	2813	3W-13N	A7
400	WLMT	60201	2813	3W-13N	A7
600	WLMT	60201	2812	3W-13N	E7
700	EVTN	60091	2812	3W-13N	E7
1000	EVTN	60201	2812	3W-13N	D7
3400	WLMT	60091	2812	4W-13N	B7
E Isabella St					
-	MPPT	60056	2808	15W-13N	A6
W Isabella St					
-	MPPT	60056	2808	15W-13N	A6
800	MPPT	60056	2807	15W-13N	E6
Isbell Dr					
-	SRGV	60554	3136	41W-7S	A7
W Isham Av					
7400	CHCG	60631	2918	9W-8N	C2
Isherwood Av					
2200	NCHI	60088	2537	10W-31N	A7
2200	NCHI	60088	2594	10W-31N	A1
Ishnala Dr					
1600	NPVL	60565	3204	25W-9S	B3
13500	ODPK	60462	3346	9W-16S	D2
W Ishnala Dr					
7200	PSHT	60463	3274	9W-15S	E7
7200	PSHT	60463	3346	9W-15S	D1
N Island Av					
10	BTVA	60510	3078	35W-1S	B1
33100	WrnT	60030	2533	18W-33N	E3
Island Cir					
3900	HRPK	60133	2967	26W-4N	D3
Island Ct					
-	SMBG	60193	2857	27W-10N	D6
800	DRFD	60015	2756	11W-20N	E1
900	BRLT	60103	2911	27W-7N	B4
1400	BtnT	60081	2414	30W-39N	A5
1900	WDSK	60098	2524	41W-32N	D5
Island Dr					
100	ISLK	60042	2586	29W-28N	D6
25100	PNFD	60544	3415	31W-18S	E2
W Island Dr					
24800	AntT	60002	2357	24W-43N	B4
Island Ln					
7700	WRLK	60097	2469	36W-36N	C3
7900	MchT	60097	2469	36W-36N	C3
Island Rd					
2100	DhmT	60033	2463	53W-35N	A6
5900	DhmT	60033	2405	53W-37N	A7
6000	CmgT	60033	2405	53W-37N	A7
Islandview Ct					
1600	HFET	60169	2858	26W-12N	A1
Island View Ln					
200	LKBN	60010	2643	26W-24N	D7
Islay Ln					
-	CRTE	60417	3685	0E-29S	E1
Islay Ln					
-	CteT	60417	3685	0E-29S	E1
3400	CRTE	60417	3596	0E-28S	E6
Isle Royal Cir					
13800	PnfT	60544	3339	27W-16S	D4
E Isle Royal Cir					
1200	PLTN	60074	2753	19W-18N	C3
Isle Royal Ct					
-	PGGV	60140	2797	42W-15N	D4
Isle Royal Dr					
1800	HRPK	60133	2967	27W-5N	C2
Isle Royal Bay					
500	ROSL	60172	2913	22W-8N	B3
Isleview Dr					
10	OSWG	60543	3263	37W-14S	C6
Isleworth Ct					
1400	AURA	60564	3202	31W-9S	A4
28600	GNOK	60044	2593	13W-28N	A6
Islington Ln					
200	SMBG	60193	2857	26W-10N	E6
W Isola Av					
20400	LkvT	60046	2476	20W-37N	A2
Issel Ct					
1400	BTVA	60510	3078	33W-2S	E4
N Itasca Rd					
200	AddT	60101	2970	20W-5N	B2
200	ADSN	60101	2970	20W-5N	B2
Itasca St					
300	WDDL	60191	2915	17W-6N	C6
400	BNVL	60106	2915	17W-6N	C6
1200	BNVL	60191	2915	17W-6N	C6
Ithaca Dr					
1500	LslT	60565	3204	24W-9S	D4
1500	NPVL	60565	3204	24W-9S	D4
Ithaca Rd					
3500	OMFD	60461	3506	4W-24S	E6
Ithica Ct					
10	TYPK	60477	3505	8W-23S	B4
Ithica Dr					
3400	OMFD	60461	3506	4W-24S	E5
Ivanhoe Av					
4300	LslT	60532	3143	22W-4S	C1
4400	LSLE	60532	3143	22W-4S	C1
9200	FNPK	60131	2973	11W-4N	D3
9200	FNPK	60176	2973	11W-4N	D3
9600	SRPK	60176	2973	12W-4N	B2
Ivanhoe Cir					
3700	SRPK	60176	2973	12W-4N	C3
Ivanhoe Ct					
3800	SRPK	60176	2973	12W-4N	B2
13800	PnfT	60544	3339	27W-16S	D4
W Ivanhoe Ct					
27000	FmtT	60084	2644	23W-27N	D2
S Ivanhoe Dr					
14300	RVDL	60827	3350	0W-16S	C4
Ivanhoe Ln					
10	AlqT	60013	2695	32W-23N	B1
10	CRY	60013	2695	32W-23N	B1
900	DYR	46311	3510		E5
N Ivanhoe Ln					
28600	FmtT	60060	2589	20W-28N	E5
W Ivanhoe Ln					
700	MPPT	60056	2861	16W-11N	E3
Ivanhoe Rd					
-	FmtT	60030	2533	20W-31N	A6
-	FmtT	60030	2590	20W-31N	B1
-	FmtT	60048	2533	20W-31N	A7
-	FmtT	60048	2590	20W-31N	B1
-	FmtT	60060	2589	20W-28N	E5
-	FmtT	60060	2590	20W-29N	A3
-	GYLK	60030	2590	20W-30N	B1
-	GYLK	60048	2590	20W-30N	B1
-	MDLN	60060	2589	20W-28N	E5
-	MDLN	60060	2590	20W-29N	A3
-	RLKP	60030	2590	20W-30N	A2
-	RLKP	60060	2590	20W-30N	A2
200	WcnT	60084	2644	25W-26N	A3
300	AvnT	60030	2533	20W-31N	A7
300	GYLK	60030	2533	20W-32N	A5
400	AvnT	60048	2533	20W-31N	A7
400	GYLK	60048	2533	20W-31N	A7
600	FmtT	60084	2644	25W-26N	A3
Ivanhoe Rd SR-83					
-	AvnT	60030	2533	20W-31N	A7
-	AvnT	60048	2533	20W-31N	A7
-	FmtT	60030	2533	20W-31N	A6
-	FmtT	60030	2590	20W-31N	B1
-	FmtT	60048	2533	20W-31N	A7
-	FmtT	60048	2590	20W-31N	B1
-	FmtT	60060	2589	20W-28N	E5
-	FmtT	60060	2590	20W-29N	A3
-	GYLK	60030	2533	20W-32N	A5
-	GYLK	60030	2590	20W-30N	B1
-	GYLK	60048	2533	20W-31N	A7
-	GYLK	60048	2590	20W-30N	B1
-	MDLN	60060	2589	20W-28N	E5
-	MDLN	60060	2590	20W-29N	A3
-	RLKP	60030	2590	20W-30N	A2
W Ivanhoe Rd					
-	WCDA	60084	2644	25W-26N	A3
23400	FmtT	60060	2644	23W-27N	E1
24000	FmtT	60084	2644	24W-26N	C2
25000	WcnT	60084	2644	24W-26N	C2
25700	WcnT	60084	2643	26W-26N	E3
26400	WCDA	60084	2643	26W-26N	D3
Ivanhoe Tr					
21700	PnfT	60544	3339	27W-16S	D4
Ivarene Ct					
600	CPVL	60110	2748	33W-17N	B7
Iverson Ln					
400	SMBG	60194	2858	25W-11N	B4
Ives Ct					
21700	PnfT	60544	3339	27W-16S	D4
Ivory Ln					
500	BRLT	60103	2909	31W-9N	E2
500	BRLT	60103	2910	31W-9N	A1
E Ivy Cir					
1800	LNHT	60046	2418	20W-39N	A5
Ivy Ct					
10	BGBK	60490	3267	27W-12S	C2
10	SEGN	60177	2908	35W-7N	B4
200	SMWD	60107	2857	27W-10N	C6
300	KLWH	60043	2812	4W-14N	C4
500	LKFT	60045	2650	10W-25N	B4
500	LKZH	60047	2699	22W-22N	A4
500	RLKB	60073	2475	22W-35N	B6
600	CmpT	60175	2905	41W-6N	E7
600	WLNG	60090	2754	16W-17N	D5
1100	BRLT	60103	2910	29W-6N	E7
1300	WTMT	60559	3144	18W-7S	E6
2000	SMBG	60194	2858	26W-10N	A5
4500	WPHR	60096	2362	11W-42N	D5
15000	HMGN	60491	3344	15W-17S	B6
W Ivy Ct					
7700	FftT	60423	3504	9W-24S	E4
Ivy Ct E					
1600	WHTN	60187	3082	23W-3S	E5
Ivy Ct E					
1600	WHTN	60187	3083	23W-3S	A5
Ivy Ct W					
1400	WHTN	60187	3082	23W-3S	E5
Ivy Dr					
4300	GNVW	60025	2809	11W-14N	C4
6100	LSLE	60532	3142	24W-6S	C5
Ivy Ln					
-	MTGY	60538	3198	41W-9S	A4
-	SgrT	60538	3198	41W-9S	A4
10	DGvT	60527	3207	16W-10S	D6
10	DYR	46311	3510		C7
10	MltT	60148	3083	21W-2S	E3
10	OKBK	60523	3085	17W-2S	B4
100	BGBK	60490	3267	27W-12S	C2
100	BMDL	60108	2969	22W-5N	C2
100	HDPK	60035	2758	6W-20N	C2
600	GLNC	60022	2758	6W-16N	C7
600	WNKA	60022	2758	6W-16N	D7
600	WNKA	60093	2758	6W-16N	C7
700	GLNC	60093	2758	6W-16N	C7
900	DRFD	60015	2703	11W-21N	E6
1200	ALGN	60010	2748	32W-20N	C1
1200	ALGN	60102	2748	32W-20N	C1
1200	BNHL	60010	2748	32W-20N	C1
1200	CLLK	60014	2639	37W-25N	A4
1300	NPVL	60563	3140	29W-5S	E3
1700	NHBK	60062	2756	11W-16N	D7
1800	AURA	60506	3137	38W-6S	B6
1900	GNVW	60025	2809	11W-14N	C4
3300	JNBG	60050	2471	31W-35N	D6
16800	LKPT	60441	3420	19W-20S	E4
E Ivy Ln					
200	ANHT	60004	2754	17W-16N	B7
1900	MPPT	60056	2808	13W-14N	E4
2000	WhlT	60025	2808	13W-14N	E4
2000	WhlT	60056	2808	13W-14N	E4
N Ivy Ln					
25000	ElaT	60047	2645	21W-25N	E6
25000	HNWD	60047	2645	21W-24N	E6
28300	LbvT	60048	2592	15W-28N	B6
33500	WrnT	60030	2534	17W-33N	B3
S Ivy Ln					
16400	PnfT	60586	3417	28W-19S	A3
26400	CNHN	60410	3672	32W-32S	C7
26400	CNHN	60410	3761	32W-32S	C1
W Ivy Ln					
300	ANHT	60004	2754	18W-16N	A7
Ivy Pl					
1600	JLET	60436	3498	26W-24S	A6
N Ivy Pl					
1900	PLTN	60074	2753	19W-18N	B3
S Ivy Pth					
20500	FftT	60423	3504	9W-24S	E6
Ivy Rd					
400	ISLK	60042	2586	28W-28N	E6
S Ivy St					
10	JLET	60435	3498	24W-24S	D5
10	JLET	60436	3498	24W-24S	D5
Ivy Wy					
1900	GNVW	60025	2809	11W-14N	C4
Ivy Hall Ln					
1000	BFGV	60089	2701	17W-21N	A7
Ivy Hill Ct					
1700	RMVL	60446	3339	27W-17S	D6
Ivy Log Ter					
600	RchT	60443	3593	8W-26S	B2
Ivy Ridge Dr					
-	HnrT	60120	2802	30W-12N	B7
-	HnrT	60192	2802	30W-12N	B7
2000	HFET	60192	2802	30W-12N	B7
Ivywild Ln					
3300	JLET	60451	3500	19W-22S	D2
J					
J Ct					
10200	MKNA	60448	3503	12W-23S	C4
Jacaranda Dr					
-	BRLT	60103	2967	28W-5N	A2
Jack Benny Dr					
10	WKGN	60087	2480	10W-36N	B5
Jack Dylan Dr					
100	HPSR	60140	2795	47W-15N	E4
Jack Frost Ln					
10	FXLK	60020	2473	28W-36N	A4
Jack London St					
10	CmpT	60175	2962	40W-4N	C4
Jackman Dr					
10	CLLK	60014	2640	35W-25N	A5
Jackman St					
200	HRVD	60033	2406	50W-38N	A7
Jack Pine Ct					
20500	FmtT	60060	2646	20W-26N	A3
Jackpine Ct					
10	BRRG	60527	3208	15W-9S	C2
10	DGvT	60527	3208	15W-9S	C2
N Jackpine Ct					
1200	PLTN	60067	2752	22W-17N	A5
1200	PltT	60067	2752	22W-17N	A5
Jack Pine Wy					
1800	LKPT	60441	3419	22W-20S	D4
Jack Rogers Ln					
6500	JLET	60586	3415	32W-20S	D6
Jackson Av					
10	SchT	60174	2908	35W-6N	B6
300	GLNC	60022	2758	6W-17N	D6
300	GLNC	60093	2758	5W-17N	E6
300	LYVL	60048	2591	16W-29N	D5
400	SCRL	60174	2964	35W-2N	C7
500	DYR	46311	3510		D6
500	RVFT	60305	3030	9W-0N	D3
700	CPVL	60110	2748	32W-17N	D7
700	SCRL	60174	3020	35W-2N	C1
1100	WCDA	60084	2588	25W-28N	A6
1100	WcnT	60084	2588	25W-28N	A6
1500	EDPK	60707	3030	9W-1N	C1
1500	RVFT	60707	3030	9W-1N	C1
2300	EVTN	60201	2867	3W-12N	A1
2500	EVTN	60201	2813	3W-12N	A7
2600	CHHT	60411	3596	1W-26S	B3
2600	SCHT	60411	3596	1W-27S	B4
3600	PKFT	60466	3594	4W-27S	E4
3600	RNPK	60471	3594	4W-27S	D4
6200	HMND	46324	3430		D3
7800	MNSR	46321	3430		D6
8800	BKFD	60513	3087	11W-3S	D4
8800	MNSR	46321	3510		D1
9500	BKFD	60525	3087	11W-3S	C4
9500	LGPK	60525	3087	11W-3S	C4
E Jackson Av					
100	HPSR	60140	2795	46W-16N	E2
300	HPSR	60140	2796	46W-16N	A2
900	LGPK	60525	3087	12W-3S	C5
1100	BKFD	60513	3087	12W-3S	C5
1100	BKFD	60525	3087	12W-3S	C5
N Jackson Av					
28500	WCDA	60084	2588	25W-28N	A6
28500	WcnT	60084	2588	25W-28N	A5
S Jackson Av					
5900	HMND	46320	3430		D1
W Jackson Av					
10	LGPK	60525	3087	12W-3S	B4
10	NPVL	60540	3141	27W-6S	C5
100	HPSR	60140	2795	47W-16N	E2
Jackson Blvd					
10	CHCG	60644	3031	7W-0S	B5
10	OKPK	60304	3031	8W-0S	A5
10	OKPK	60644	3031	7W-0S	B5
300	GYLK	60030	2533	20W-32N	A5
400	FTPK	60130	3030	9W-0S	D5
400	RVFT	60130	3030	9W-0S	C5
400	RVFT	60305	3030	9W-0S	C5
800	OKPK	60304	3030	8W-0S	E5
1100	FTPK	60304	3030	8W-0S	D5
E Jackson Blvd					
10	CHCG	60603	3034	0E-0S	C5
10	CHCG	60604	3034	0E-0S	C5
N Jackson Blvd					
300	HLSD	60162	3028	13W-0S	D5
W Jackson Blvd					
10	CHCG	60604	3034	0W-0S	A5
100	CHCG	60606	3034	0W-0S	B5
400	CHCG	60661	3034	0W-0S	A5
700	CHCG	60607	3034	0W-0S	A5
800	CHCG	60607	3033	1W-0S	E5
1500	CHCG	60612	3033	3W-0S	A5
2800	CHCG	60612	3032	5W-0S	A5
3100	CHCG	60624	3032	3W-0S	E5
4500	CHCG	60644	3032	5W-0S	A5
4800	CHCG	60644	3031	6W-0S	D5
5800	OKPK	60304	3031	7W-0S	B5
5800	OKPK	60644	3031	7W-0S	B5
Jackson Brch					
-	FKFT	60423	3590	14W-28S	E6
-	FKFT	60423	3591	14W-28S	A6
Jackson Cir					
900	EGVV	60007	2913	22W-8N	D2
Jackson Ct					
200	BRLT	60103	2911	28W-6N	A6
200	RtdT	60136	2799	38W-17N	B1
800	DYR	46311	3510		E6
900	VNHL	60061	2647	17W-27N	C2
1100	WKGN	60085	2536	11W-34N	E1
6100	WDRG	60517	3143	21W-6S	D5
8400	MNSR	46321	3430		D7
22500	RNPK	60471	3594	4W-27S	D4
36600	GrtT	60041	2474	25W-36N	A3
Jackson Dr					
200	ElgT	60124	2853	37W-12N	C2
2400	WDRG	60517	3143	22W-6S	D5
2700	PTHT	60070	2754	16W-17N	E6
2700	WLNG	60004	2754	16W-17N	E6
2700	WLNG	60090	2754	16W-17N	E6
5900	LslT	60516	3143	22W-6S	D5
5900	LslT	60517	3143	22W-6S	D5
N Jackson Dr					
39000	AntT	60081	2415	27W-39N	B5
39200	FXLK	60081	2415	27W-39N	B5
Jackson Ln					
-	PNFD	60586	3415	31W-19S	E2
10	SMWD	60107	2856	29W-10N	E6
100	BMDL	60108	2969	23W-5N	A2
Jackson Pl					
10	AURA	60505	3200	35W-8S	B1
10	OSWG	60543	3263	37W-12S	C3
900	DYR	46311	3510		E6
Jackson Rd					
10	CNHL	60514	3145	16W-5S	E2
N Jackson Rd					
200	CNHL	60514	3085	16W-4S	E7
200	CNHL	60514	3145	16W-4S	E1
Jackson St					
-	ClmT	60406	3349	1W-15S	E1
-	ClmT	60827	3349	1W-15S	E1
-	ClmT	60827	3350	1W-15S	A1
-	RGWD	60072	2470	34W-36N	D4
-	RVDL	60827	3349	1W-15S	E1
-	RVDL	60827	3350	1W-15S	A1
-	UNON	60180	2635	46W-25N	D5
10	AURA	60505	3200	35W-8S	B1
10	EDND	60118	2801	33W-16N	A2
10	PGGV	60140	2798	41W-13N	A7
100	ALGN	60102	2694	33W-20N	E7
100	EGvT	60018	2862	15W-9N	A7
100	GLBT	60136	2799	38W-16N	A1
100	WMTN	60481	3853	27W-38S	D6
200	BRLT	60103	2911	28W-6N	B6
200	YKVL	60560	3333	42W-14S	C1
300	PKFT	60466	3594	4W-25S	E1
300	WNVL	60555	3081	28W-3S	A6
400	BtlT	60560	3333	42W-14S	D1
600	HRPK	60133	2912	26W-8N	A3
700	LktT	60441	3341	22W-16S	D3
700	RMVL	60441	3341	22W-16S	D3
1000	NCHI	60064	2536	10W-32N	E6
1000	WKGN	60085	2536	10W-32N	E5
1100	AraT	60505	3200	35W-9S	B4
1200	MTGY	60505	3200	35W-9S	B4
1300	MTGY	60538	3200	35W-9S	B4
2900	BLWD	60104	3029	12W-0S	A5
3500	LNSG	60438	3430	4E-21S	C5
3800	BLWD	60162	3029	12W-0S	A5
3800	HLSD	60104	3029	12W-0S	A5
3800	HLSD	60162	3029	12W-0S	A5
14200	DLTN	60419	3350	0E-16S	D4
E Jackson St					
10	JLET	60432	3499	23W-23S	A4
10	OSWG	60543	3263	37W-12S	C4
10	VLPK	60181	3027	17W-0S	A6
100	EMHT	60126	3027	16W-0N	C5
100	MRGO	60152	2634	49W-26N	B2
200	EMHT	60126	3028	15W-0S	A6
300	WDSK	60098	2524	41W-31N	D7
1000	JltT	60432	3499	22W-23S	D4
1000	LMBD	60148	3026	18W-0S	E6
1000	LMBD	60181	3026	18W-0S	E6
1000	VLPK	60181	3026	18W-0S	E6
E Jackson St US-6					
400	JLET	60432	3499	23W-23S	B4
N Jackson St					
10	BTVA	60510	3078	35W-1S	A1
10	ELGN	60123	2854	34W-11N	D4
10	WKGN	60085	2536	10W-34N	E1
100	ELWD	60421	3675	25W-32S	B7
400	WKGN	60085	2480	10W-34N	A7
400	WKGN	60085	2537	9W-34N	C1
1900	WKGN	60087	2480	10W-36N	A4
S Jackson St					
10	ELGN	60123	2854	34W-11N	E4
100	ELWD	60421	3675	25W-32S	B7
100	WKGN	60085	2536	10W-33N	E3
S Jackson St					
200	DGvT	60521	3145	16W-6S	E4
200	DGvT	60527	3145	16W-6S	E4
200	DGvT	60527	3207	16W-10S	E6
200	HNDL	60521	3145	16W-5S	E3
300	BTVA	60510	3078	35W-1S	A2
600	BRRG	60527	3207	16W-10S	E6
900	NCHI	60064	2536	10W-33N	E4
W Jackson St					
-	JLET	60435	3498	24W-23S	E4
10	JLET	60432	3498	24W-23S	E4
10	OSWG	60543	3263	37W-12S	C3
10	VLPK	60181	3027	18W-0S	A6
100	EMHT	60126	3027	16W-0S	E6
200	WDSK	60098	2524	42W-31N	B7
300	LMBD	60148	3027	18W-0S	A6
W Jackson St CO-A33					
1000	WDSK	60098	2524	42W-31N	B7
W Jackson St SR-53					
10	JLET	60432	3498	24W-23S	E4
Jackson Branch Ct					
-	FKFT	60423	3591	14W-28S	A5
Jackson Branch Dr					
2000	NLNX	60451	3588	19W-27S	D4
Jaclay Ct					
100	SYHW	60118	2800	35W-15N	B3
Jacob Av					
300	JltT	60436	3586	24W-25S	E1
2900	MTGY	60512	3198	40W-10S	B6
2900	MTGY	60538	3198	40W-10S	B6
Jacob Ct					
10	BlmT	60411	3510	3E-25S	A7
900	WCHI	60185	3022	30W-2N	C2
24800	SRWD	60404	3496	30W-25S	B7
Jacob Dr					
-	FftT	60448	3503	13W-22S	B1
-	MKNA	60448	3503	13W-22S	B1
600	WNFD	60190	3023	27W-0N	D4
600	WnfT	60190	3023	27W-0N	D4
S Jacob Dr					
26500	CNHN	60410	3672	33W-32S	B7
26500	CNHN	60410	3761	33W-32S	B1
Jacob Ln					
10500	MKNA	60448	3503	13W-22S	B2
Jacob Fry Dr					
25200	PNFD	60585	3337	31W-15S	E2
Jacobs Ct					
-	BFGV	60089	2701	16W-21N	C6
800	DYR	46311	3598		E3
S Jacobs Ln					
26700	CteT	60417	3686	1E-32S	B7
Jacobsen Av					
10	GLHT	60139	2968	23W-2N	E7
100	BmdT	60137	2969	23W-2N	A7
100	GLHT	60137	2969	23W-2N	A7
100	GLHT	60139	2969	23W-2N	A7
Jacobson Dr					
1400	WKGN	60085	2536	11W-32N	E4
3700	WRLK	60097	2469	38W-35N	A6
3900	GNWD	60097	2469	38W-35N	A6
Jacqueline Ct					
10	LMNT	60439	3270	19W-14S	C7
Jacqueline Dr					
10	DRGV	60515	3144	20W-5S	B3
1100	CRTE	60417	3597	1E-28S	B6
9000	MaiT	60016	2863	11W-11N	E3
9000	MaiT	60714	2863	10W-11N	E3
9000	NLES	60714	2863	10W-11N	E3
Jacqueline Ln					
10	BNHL	60021	2696	29W-22N	B4
10	FRGV	60021	2696	29W-22N	B4
4100	NndT	60014	2641	33W-26N	A2
Jacquelyn Ct					
6000	TYPK	60477	3425	7W-20S	C3
Jacquelyn Dr					
10	BNVL	60106	2972	15W-4N	A4
Jacquelyn Ln					
2600	WKGN	60087	2479	12W-36N	C3
Jacquelynn Ct					
1000	MRGO	60152	2634	50W-25N	B4
1000	RlyT	60152	2634	50W-25N	B4
W Jacquie Av					
19100	LktT	60441	3340	24W-17S	E7
19100	LktT	60441	3341	23W-17S	A7
Jacqulyn Ln					
500	LKFT	60045	2649	11W-25N	D4
N Jade Av					
2500	ANHT	60004	2753	18W-16N	D6
Jade Ct					
-	LKPT	60441	3420	19W-20S	D4
Jade Ln					
4500	HFET	60192	2804	24W-15N	C1
S Jade Ln					
300	AvnT	60030	2531	25W-32N	B5
300	AvnT	60073	2531	25W-32N	B5
300	GrtT	60030	2531	25W-32N	B5
300	GrtT	60073	2531	25W-32N	B5
300	RDLK	60073	2531	25W-32N	B5
N Jaeger Lp					
1900	LSLE	60532	3142	24W-6S	E4
S Jaeger Lp					
1900	LSLE	60532	3142	24W-6S	E4
Jaguar Ct					
800	ElgT	60124	2853	37W-10N	B5
3900	JLET	60431	3496	29W-22S	D3
3900	JLET	60431	3497	28W-22S	A2
Jahns Dr					
1800	WHTN	60187	3082	24W-2S	D4
Jaime Ln					
1100	LYVL	60048	2591	18W-29N	A3
Jaipur Av					
800	NPVL	60540	3142	25W-7S	A7
Jake Ln					
200	HPSR	60140	2795	46W-15N	E3
300	HPSR	60140	2796	46W-15N	A3
Ja Lor Ct					
2400	WPHR	60096	2363	10W-42N	B6
Jamaica Colony St					
10	FXLK	60020	2414	28W-38N	D6
Jamatt Ct					
300	NPVL	60540	3142	25W-6S	A4
James					
-	BTVA	60510	3021	33W-0S	A7
James Av					
-	FNPK	60131	2973	13W-3N	A4
200	WCHI	60185	3022	29W-1N	D2
200	WnfT	60185	3022	29W-1N	D2
500	MDLN	60060	2590	18W-28N	E6
1000	WCDA	60084	2588	25W-28N	B6
3000	WPHR	60096	2363	10W-42N	A5
3100	BtnT	60096	2363	10W-42N	A5
N James Av					
34800	GrtT	60041	2474	25W-34N	B7
James Ct					
-	LKBF	60044	2593	11W-29N	D4
10	HNWD	60047	2645	20W-24N	E7

STREET Block	City	ZIP	Map#	CGS	Grid
James Ct					
10	HNWD	60047	2646	20W-24N	A7
10	MaiT	60025	2864	9W-12N	C1
200	BMDL	60157	2913	22W-6N	B7
400	ALGN	60102	2747	33W-20N	E1
400	BmdT	60137	3025	22W-2N	B1
400	GLHT	60137	3025	22W-2N	B1
400	GLHT	60139	3025	22W-2N	B1
600	MRGO	60152	2634	49W-25N	C4
800	WHTN	60187	3082	24W-1S	C1
800	WKGN	60085	2480	10W-35N	A7
1400	EGVV	60007	2913	21W-8N	E2
1400	LYVL	60048	2647	15W-27N	E1
1900	SMBG	60194	2858	25W-11N	A4
15100	HMGN	60491	3420	18W-21S	E6
N James Ct					
2300	ANHT	60004	2753	18W-16N	E7
36000	GrtT	60041	2473	26W-36N	D4
36400	LkvT	60046	2475	22W-36N	C4
36400	RLKB	60046	2475	22W-36N	C4
36400	RLKB	60073	2475	22W-36N	C4
S James Ct N					
1800	LKFT	60045	2703	12W-23N	C2
W James Ct S					
900	LKFT	60045	2703	12W-23N	C2
James Dr					
-	SKOK	60076	2866	5W-10N	A5
10	HNWD	60047	2700	20W-24N	A1
10	SchT	60174	2908	35W-6N	C7
10	WTMT	60559	3145	18W-6S	A4
100	BRLT	60103	2909	31W-8N	E2
2500	DYR	46311	3598		E3
5600	OKFT	60452	3347	7W-18S	D7
13900	CTWD	60445	3347	6W-16S	E3
N James Dr					
700	SchT	60174	2908	34W-6N	C7
36500	LkvT	60046	2475	21W-36N	C3
S James Dr					
700	SchT	60174	2908	34W-6N	C7
12100	ALSP	60803	3276	6W-14S	A5
W James Dr					
1500	EGvT	60056	2861	16W-10N	D5
1500	MPPT	60056	2861	16W-10N	D5
James Ln					
-	HPSR	60140	2796	46W-15N	B3
200	NPVL	60540	3142	25W-6S	A6
5200	CTWD	60445	3347	6W-16S	E3
14300	HmrT	60491	3421	17W-18S	B1
W James Ln					
7200	GGnT	60449	3682	9W-30S	A3
7200	MonT	60449	3682	9W-30S	A3
James Pl					
4400	MLPK	60160	2973	13W-2N	A7
4500	MLPK	60164	2973	13W-2N	A7
4500	NHLK	60160	2973	13W-2N	A7
4500	NHLK	60164	2973	13W-2N	A7
5200	OKLN	60453	3211	7W-10S	C6
26200	AntT	60002	2356	26W-41N	E7
James Rd					
100	BtnT	60081	2414	29W-41N	D1
100	FXLK	60081	2414	29W-41N	D1
100	SPGV	60081	2414	29W-41N	C1
28300	AntT	60081	2414	29W-41N	D1
James St					
-	LKFT	60045	2703	12W-23N	B2
10	GNVA	60134	3020	35W-1N	B4
10	WnfT	60185	3023	27W-1N	D2
100	BRTN	60010	2750	25W-20N	E1
100	MTGY	60538	3199	36W-9S	E3
200	BNVL	60106	2971	16W-3N	E4
200	BRTN	60010	2751	25W-20N	A1
400	CLLK	60014	2639	36W-25N	E5
800	SEGN	60177	2908	35W-9N	B1
900	WMTN	60481	3853	27W-38S	E6
2400	BLID	60406	3349	3W-15S	B1
3600	MHRY	60050	2528	32W-32N	B4
6000	BmnT	60477	3425	7W-19S	C2
6100	TYPK	60477	3425	7W-19S	C2
7300	FftT	60423	3504	9W-23S	E3
N James St					
10	PLNO	60545	3259	47W-13S	D6
10	PNFD	60544	3338	30W-18S	C7
10	PNFD	60544	3416	30W-18S	B1
10	PnfT	60544	3416	30W-18S	B1
S James St					
200	PLNO	60545	3259	47W-14S	D7
W James St					
600	VLPK	60181	3026	18W-1N	E2
2000	CHCG	60609	3151	2W-5S	C2
James Wy					
400	LslT	60540	3205	23W-8S	A1
1400	EGVV	60007	2913	21W-8N	E3
3400	JNBG	60050	2471	31W-35N	D6
E James Wy					
10	CRY	60013	2641	30W-24N	E7
W James Wy					
300	CRY	60013	2641	31W-24N	D7
James Frederick Cir					
-	LKVL	60046	2475	23W-37N	A2
W James J Davis Dr					
100	BtvT	60539	3077	36W-3S	D5
James Leigh Dr					
1900	AURA	60503	3201	33W-10S	B6
James Madison Cir					
-	CnhT	60421	3763	26W-33S	E2
-	JknT	60421	3763	26W-33S	E2
James Michener Dr					
10	CmpT	60175	2962	40W-4N	C4
Jameson Ct					
200	BGBK	60440	3269	22W-12S	C2
Jameson Wy					
900	WTMT	60559	3145	17W-6S	B5
James Pass					
1000	NLNX	60451	3588	19W-27S	E4
1000	NLNX	60451	3589	19W-27S	A4
James R Rakow Rd					
-	AlqT	60014	2694	33W-23N	E1
-	CLLK	60013	2694	33W-23N	E1
-	CLLK	60013	2695	33W-23N	A1
-	CLLK	60014	2693	35W-23N	E1
-	CLLK	60156	2694	35W-23N	B1
-	CRY	60013	2695	33W-23N	A1
-	LIHL	60014	2693	35W-23N	E1
-	LIHL	60156	2694	35W-23N	B1
1000	CLLK	60014	2694	33W-23N	E1
1000	LIHL	60014	2694	33W-23N	D1
James R Rakow Rd CO-A45					
-	AlqT	60014	2694	33W-23N	E1
-	CLLK	60156	2694	35W-23N	B1
-	LIHL	60156	2694	35W-23N	B1
1000	CLLK	60014	2694	33W-23N	E1
1000	LIHL	60014	2694	33W-23N	D1
Jamestown Av					
300	WTMT	60559	3085	17W-3S	C5
Jamestown Blvd					
-	GYLK	60030	2532	20W-34N	E1
Jamestown Cir					
1700	HFET	60169	2858	25W-12N	A1
Jamestown Ct					
10	GYLK	60030	2532	21W-34N	E1
200	RMVL	60446	3340	25W-16S	C4
300	AURA	60502	3139	32W-7S	C7
1100	SMBG	60193	2913	23W-8N	B2
3000	SMWD	60107	2911	28W-9N	A1
N Jamestown Dr					
1900	PLTN	60074	2753	19W-18N	B3
Jamestown Ln					
100	BGBK	60440	3269	22W-12S	B2
100	LNSH	60069	2702	15W-23N	A2
100	VNHL	60061	2702	15W-23N	A2
100	VNHL	60069	2702	15W-23N	A2
1800	ELGN	60123	2854	36W-11N	A4
2400	AURA	60502	3139	32W-7S	C7
Jamestown Rd					
-	HTLY	60142	2692	40W-22N	B4
W Jamestown Rd					
25700	PnfT	60586	3415	32W-21S	D6
Jamestown Tr					
700	YkTp	60523	3084	19W-3S	D5
Jamestowne Ct					
200	SYHW	60118	2799	36W-15N	E3
Jamestowne Ln					
10	YkTp	60181	3085	18W-1S	A1
Jamestowne Rd					
200	SYHW	60118	2800	36W-15N	A4
700	SYHW	60118	2799	36W-15N	E4
N Jamey Ln					
1000	ADSN	60101	2970	19W-4N	C3
Jamie Ct					
15900	OKFT	60452	3425	6W-19S	E1
18800	HMWD	60430	3508	1W-22S	A2
22700	RNPK	60471	3594	5W-27S	B5
Jamie Ln					
10	HNWD	60047	2646	20W-24N	A7
200	LKZH	60047	2698	23W-23N	E2
200	WCDA	60084	2587	26W-28N	D5
200	WcnT	60084	2587	26W-28N	D5
300	DGvT	60527	3207	16W-10S	D5
1100	HMWD	60430	3508	1W-22S	A2
1200	HMWD	60430	3507	1W-22S	E2
5400	OKFT	60452	3425	6W-19S	E1
Jamison Dr					
300	GLHT	60139	2969	23W-4N	B4
7600	FftT	60423	3504	9W-24S	D5
Jamison Ln					
500	HFET	60169	2804	24W-12N	D7
Jan St					
100	MHTN	60442	3678	18W-31S	A5
Janas Ct					
16900	LbvT	60048	2591	17W-30N	C1
Janas Dr					
13500	HMGN	60491	3342	19W-16S	D3
Janas Ln					
1200	LMNT	60439	3271	18W-14S	A6
E Janata Blvd					
10	LMBD	60148	3084	19W-2S	C3
Jandus Rd					
10	CRY	60013	2695	30W-23N	E2
200	CRY	60013	2696	30W-23N	A2
Jandus Cut Off Rd					
100	CRY	60013	2695	30W-23N	E2
100	CRY	60013	2696	30W-23N	A1
Jane Av					
100	LslT	60540	3142	25W-6S	B5
400	LMNT	60439	3271	18W-14S	B7
400	LMNT	60439	3343	18W-15S	B1
1100	NPVL	60540	3142	25W-6S	B5
E Jane Av					
1400	ANHT	60004	2807	16W-15N	C1
S Jane Cir					
13600	PnfT	60544	3339	27W-16S	D3
Jane Ct					
10	HNWD	60047	2645	20W-24N	E7
100	CNHL	60514	3145	16W-5S	D2
400	LMNT	60439	3271	18W-15S	B7
400	LMNT	60439	3343	18W-15S	B1
1300	JLET	60431	3497	28W-22S	B2
N Jane Dr					
10	ELGN	60123	2854	35W-11N	B4
S Jane Dr					
10	ELGN	60123	2854	35W-11N	B5
Jane Ln					
10	BNHL	60010	2696	29W-22N	B5
W Jane St					
10	GNWD	60425	3508	0E-22S	D2
Jane Wy					
8700	MNSR	46321	3510		D1
Jane Addams Dr					
-	PLTN	60074	2753	19W-16N	B6
Jane Addams Rd					
800	BGBK	60440	3268	25W-12S	C3
Janes Av					
5400	DRGV	60515	3143	21W-5S	E3
5400	LslT	60515	3143	21W-5S	E3
5700	LslT	60516	3143	21W-6S	E4
6000	DRGV	60516	3143	21W-6S	E5
6200	WDRG	60516	3143	21W-6S	E5
6300	DRGV	60517	3143	21W-7S	E7
6300	WDRG	60517	3143	21W-7S	E7
7100	WDRG	60517	3205	21W-8S	E2
8200	BGBK	60440	3205	21W-9S	E3
8200	BGBK	60517	3205	21W-9S	E3
8200	WDRG	60440	3205	21W-9S	E3
N Janes Av					
200	BGBK	60440	3269	21W-11S	E1
800	BGBK	60440	3205	21W-9S	E4
900	BGBK	60517	3205	21W-9S	E4
900	WDRG	60440	3205	21W-9S	E4
900	WDRG	60517	3205	21W-9S	E4
Janes Ct					
2300	WDRG	60517	3205	21W-8S	E2
Janes Lp					
100	HIWD	60040	2650	9W-24N	D7
100	HIWD	60040	2704	9W-24N	D1
Janeswood Dr					
2400	WDRG	60517	3143	21W-7S	D7
Janet Av					
10	DRN	60527	3207	16W-8S	E1
10	DRN	60561	3207	16W-8S	D1
10	WLBK	60527	3207	16W-8S	E1
100	SMWD	60107	2856	29W-10N	E6
19100	LktT	60441	3340	24W-17S	E6
19100	LktT	60441	3341	23W-17S	A6
Janet Ct					
100	FXLK	60020	2473	27W-37N	B2
100	WldT	60564	3266	29W-11S	E1
5400	OKFT	60452	3425	6W-19S	E2
N Janet Ct					
39500	AntT	60002	2415	25W-39N	E4
Janet Dr					
100	ISLK	60042	2586	29W-28N	D6
1300	WMTN	60481	3943	27W-39S	E2
2200	GNVW	60025	2810	10W-15N	A3
W Janet Dr					
100	BDWD	60408	3942	31W-42S	B6
Janet Ln					
-	GnvT	60134	3019	37W-0S	C7
6500	CHRG	60415	3211	8W-11S	A7
Janet Pl					
900	DYR	46311	3598		E4
Janet St					
1400	DRGV	60515	3084	20W-4S	A7
N Janette St					
42800	AntT	60002	2357	25W-42N	B5
Janice Av					
-	CteT	60417	3774	0W-33S	B1
700	LKPT	60441	3419	22W-20S	D4
1900	MLPK	60160	3029	13W-2N	A1
1900	MLPK	60164	3029	13W-2N	A1
2000	MLPK	60160	2973	13W-2N	A7
2000	NHLK	60160	2973	13W-2N	A7
2000	NHLK	60164	2973	13W-2N	A7
Janice Ct					
400	WLNG	60090	2808	15W-16N	B1
Janice Dr					
1100	SLVL	60411	3597	1E-27S	B3
10900	HTLY	60142	2691	41W-21N	E6
Janice Ln					
2200	BGBK	60490	3339	28W-15S	A1
2200	BGBK	60585	3339	28W-15S	A1
2200	PNFD	60585	3339	28W-15S	A1
S Janice Ln					
1300	RDLK	60073	2531	23W-31N	E6
W Janice Ln					
10	ADSN	60101	2970	18W-4N	E3
Janine Ct					
17000	ODPK	60467	3423	13W-20S	B4
Janine Ln					
400	SMBG	60193	2858	24W-9N	E7
Janis Ct					
100	AddT	60191	2971	17W-5N	C2
100	WDDL	60191	2971	17W-5N	C2
Janis Dr					
3800	RNPK	60471	3594	4W-27S	D5
Janke Dr					
1800	NHBK	60062	2757	9W-16N	B7
Jan Marie Ln					
800	ELGN	60120	2855	32W-11N	C5
Jann Ct					
10900	LynT	60525	3146	13W-6S	E5
10900	LynT	60525	3147	13W-6S	A5
Janny Rd					
-	GNVW	60025	2809	10W-15N	E3
Jansen Ln					
10	VNHL	60061	2646	18W-25N	E6
Jansen Farm Ct					
1100	ELGN	60123	2799	36W-13N	E7
1100	ELGN	60123	2853	36W-13N	E1
Jansen Farm Dr					
1100	ELGN	60123	2853	36W-13N	E1
1200	ELGN	60123	2799	36W-13N	E7
N Janssen Av					
2200	CHCG	60614	2977	1W-2N	D6
2700	CHCG	60657	2977	1W-3N	D5
3800	CHCG	60613	2977	1W-4N	D2
4900	CHCG	60640	2921	1W-6N	D6
Jaquays St					
400	LKPT	60441	3420	21W-19S	A2
Jardine					
-	MNKA	60447	3672	32W-29S	D2
Jared Dr					
1800	CTHL	60403	3418	26W-21S	A7
Jarlath Av					
600	DSPN	60018	2916	14W-9N	D1
Jarlath St					
5000	SKOK	60077	2865	6W-9N	D7
W Jarlath St					
2600	CHCG	60645	2867	3W-9N	A7
2700	CHCG	60645	2866	3W-9N	E7
3800	LNWD	60076	2866	4W-9N	C7
3800	LNWD	60712	2866	4W-9N	C7
3800	SKOK	60076	2866	4W-9N	C7
4800	LNWD	60712	2865	6W-9N	E7
7700	CHCG	60068	2864	9W-9N	C7
7700	CHCG	60631	2864	9W-9N	C7
7700	PKRG	60068	2864	9W-9N	C7
Jarvis Av					
400	DSPN	60018	2862	14W-9N	C7
1200	EGVV	60007	2861	17W-9N	C7
1900	DSPN	60018	2863	12W-9N	B7
3500	SKOK	60076	2866	4W-9N	C7
3700	LNWD	60076	2866	4W-9N	C7
3700	LNWD	60712	2866	4W-9N	C7
3700	SKOK	60712	2866	4W-9N	C7
4900	LNWD	60712	2865	6W-9N	E7
5100	SKOK	60077	2865	6W-9N	D7
W Jarvis Av					
1200	CHCG	60626	2867	2W-9N	C7
2000	CHCG	60645	2867	2W-9N	B7
2600	CHCG	60645	2866	3W-9N	E7
3100	SKOK	60076	2866	3W-9N	D7
4000	LNWD	60076	2866	5W-9N	B7
4000	LNWD	60712	2866	5W-9N	B7
4000	SKOK	60076	2866	5W-9N	B7
4500	SKOK	60712	2866	5W-9N	B7
4600	LNWD	60712	2865	6W-9N	E7
4600	SKOK	60077	2865	6W-9N	E7
4600	SKOK	60077	2866	5W-9N	B7
4600	SKOK	60712	2865	6W-9N	E7
5600	NLES	60077	2865	7W-9N	C7
5600	NLES	60714	2865	7W-9N	C7
6900	NLES	60714	2864	8W-9N	E7
7100	CHCG	60631	2864	9W-9N	D7
7100	CHCG	60714	2864	9W-9N	D7
E Jarvis Ct					
400	PLTN	60074	2753	20W-18N	A3
Jasmine Cir					
200	LNHT	60046	2476	19W-37N	C1
Jasmine Ct					
10	BGBK	60490	3267	27W-12S	C3
10	SMWD	60107	2856	30W-10N	B6
300	AURA	60504	3139	31W-6S	E5
1100	BRLT	60103	2910	29W-6N	D7
1200	NPVL	60540	3141	28W-7S	A7
1600	HDPK	60035	2704	10W-22N	A4
3200	NndT	60012	2584	35W-28N	B5
W Jasmine Ct					
18600	WrnT	60030	2533	18W-34N	E2
Jasmine Dr					
2000	CTHL	60403	3417	27W-21S	D6
7200	HRPK	60133	2911	27W-9N	D1
22100	FKFT	60423	3590	14W-26S	E3
Jasmine Ln					
10	RVWD	60015	2702	13W-21N	D7
2600	RGMW	60008	2805	21W-14N	D5
13200	HTLY	60142	2744	42W-20N	C1
S Jasmine Ln					
25600	MONE	60449	3683	5W-31S	B5
Jasmine Wy					
9100	FRGV	60021	2696	29W-22N	D3
Jason Ct					
-	WynT	60185	2967	28W-4N	A4
100	AURA	60502	3201	32W-7S	C1
200	BMDL	60108	2968	24W-5N	E1
400	SMBG	60173	2859	22W-11N	D4
700	DGvT	60527	3207	16W-10S	D5
Jason Dr					
2200	MTGY	60538	3198	40W-10S	C6
Jason Ln					
400	SMBG	60173	2859	22W-10N	D4
18000	LNSG	60438	3429	2E-21S	C6
N Jason Ln					
100	WDDL	60191	2970	18W-5N	E1
W Jason Ln					
400	WDDL	60191	2970	18W-5N	E1
Jaspen Ct					
1200	WLNG	60090	2754	16W-18N	E2
Jasper Av					
-	AntT	60002	2417	22W-40N	B4
-	AntT	60046	2417	22W-40N	B4
Jasper Ct					
1700	WHTN	60187	3083	23W-3S	A5
2500	GNVW	60062	2809	11W-15N	D1
2500	NHBK	60062	2809	11W-15N	D2
Jasper Dr					
1000	MchT	60050	2472	30W-36N	B3
1300	JNBG	60050	2472	30W-36N	B3
1400	WHTN	60187	3082	23W-3S	E5
1400	WHTN	60187	3083	23W-3S	A5
S Jasper Pl					
3600	CHCG	60609	3091	1W-3S	D5
W Jasper St					
700	JLET	60436	3498	25W-24S	C6
Jay Av					
1500	MLPK	60160	3028	13W-1N	E2
Jay Dr					
800	DRGV	60516	3144	19W-7S	D7
4200	ZION	60099	2362	12W-42N	B7
5600	NndT	60014	2641	32W-26N	A3
Jay Ln					
1600	SCRL	60174	3020	34W-2N	D1
2100	RGMW	60008	2806	19W-14N	C4
Jay St					
10	OSWG	60543	3263	37W-12S	C4
700	ELGN	60120	2855	33W-10N	A6
14000	SjnT	46311	3598		E4
Jayce Ct					
2000	CTHL	60403	3418	26W-21S	A7
Jaymia Ct					
10	LMNT	60439	3271	18W-13S	A5
Jayne St					
10	ALGN	60102	2747	34W-20N	D1
W Jayne St					
10	LMNT	60439	3270	19W-14S	C7
N Jean Av					
6700	CHCG	60646	2919	7W-8N	B2
S Jean Av					
21400	MTSN	60443	3594	4W-25S	D1
Jean Ct					
14800	OKFT	60452	3348	6W-17S	A5
22400	RNPK	60471	3594	4W-27S	D4
Jean Dr					
9600	HBRN	60034	2350	41W-41N	E7
Jean Ln					
16600	TYPK	60477	3425	8W-19S	A3
Jean Rd					
18800	FftT	60448	3502	14W-22S	D2
Jean St					
300	GLBT	60136	2799	37W-15N	C3
S Jean St					
400	PTON	60468	3860	10W-37S	D4
W Jean St					
4400	ALSP	60803	3276	5W-13S	B5
Jean Ter					
10	LKZH	60047	2698	24W-23N	C2
Jean Creek Dr					
13200	ODPK	60462	3346	11W-15S	A1
Jeanel Ln					
1500	AURA	60502	3139	32W-5S	D3
Jeanette Av					
1600	SCRL	60174	3020	34W-2N	E1
3100	WKGN	60085	2536	12W-33N	B3
3200	PKCY	60085	2536	12W-33N	B3
Jeanette Ct					
6400	BmnT	60477	3425	8W-21S	B6
6400	TYPK	60477	3425	8W-21S	B6
22300	FKFT	60423	3590	14W-27S	E4
N Jeanette Ct					
37600	GrtT	60081	2472	28W-37N	E1
Jeanette Pl					
100	MDLN	60060	2590	18W-28N	D6
Jeanie Ln					
8900	FKFT	60423	3504	11W-25S	A7
Jeanne Ct					
400	WDDL	60191	2970	18W-5N	E1
800	GYLK	60030	2533	19W-34N	D2
Jeanne Ln					
15500	HMGN	60491	3343	17W-18S	C7
15500	HmrT	60491	3343	17W-18S	C7
15500	HmrT	60491	3421	17W-18S	B1
Jeanne Ter					
300	WLNG	60090	2755	14W-17N	C5
Jeannette St					
800	DSPN	60016	2862	13W-10N	E4
1200	DSPN	60018	2862	13W-10N	E5
Jeans Rd					
10	DGvT	60527	3208	16W-11S	A7
10	DGvT	60527	3271	16W-11S	E1
200	DGvT	60527	3207	16W-11S	E7
Jefferey St					
4700	JNBG	60050	2472	30W-36N	B3
4700	MchT	60050	2472	30W-36N	B3
Jefferson Av					
10	ELGN	60120	2854	34W-12N	E2
300	GLNC	60022	2758	6W-17N	D6
600	CPVL	60110	2748	32W-17N	D7
600	ELGN	60120	2855	33W-12N	B2
600	SCRL	60174	2964	35W-2N	C7
1100	DRGV	60516	3144	20W-6S	B4
1400	DGvT	60516	3144	20W-6S	B4
1700	GNVW	60025	2810	8W-14N	E4
6200	HMND	46324	3430		E2
7800	MNSR	46321	3430		E6
8700	MNSR	46321	3510		E1
9300	BKFD	60513	3087	11W-3S	D5
9500	BKFD	60525	3087	11W-3S	C5
9500	LGPK	60525	3087	11W-3S	C5
14300	ODPK	60462	3345	12W-17S	D4
14300	PNFD	60544	3337	31W-17S	E5
E Jefferson Av					
100	HPSR	60140	2795	46W-16N	E2
300	HPSR	60140	2796	46W-16N	A2
300	NPVL	60540	3141	26W-6S	D5
1000	WHTN	60187	3024	23W-0S	E6
W Jefferson Av					
10	NPVL	60540	3141	28W-6S	A5
100	HPSR	60140	2795	47W-16N	E2
100	WHTN	60187	3024	25W-0S	C6
1400	NPVL	60540	3140	29W-6S	D6
1900	AURA	60504	3140	29W-6S	D6
1900	AURA	60540	3140	29W-6S	D6
Jefferson Ct					
-	FXLK	60041	2473	26W-35N	D5
10	SMWD	60107	2856	29W-10N	E5
10	WKGN	60085	2536	11W-34N	E1
300	VNHL	60061	2647	17W-26N	B3
400	WLNG	60090	2808	15W-16N	B1
700	WNFD	60190	3081	27W-1S	C1
8800	MNSR	46321	3510		E1
S Jefferson Ct					
700	BTVA	60510	3078	35W-1S	B3
W Jefferson Ct					
7700	FftT	60423	3504	9W-24S	D4
Jefferson Dr					
-	BGBK	60490	3267	27W-14S	C7
-	BGBK	60490	3339	27W-14S	C1
800	LNHT	60046	2418	20W-39N	B5
4400	RNPK	60471	3594	5W-27S	B4
W Jefferson Dr					
5600	WKGN	60048	2534	15W-31N	E7
Jefferson Ln					
10	AlqT	60013	2695	32W-23N	B1
10	CRY	60013	2695	32W-23N	B1
10	SMWD	60107	2856	29W-10N	E6
10	SMWD	60107	2857	28W-10N	A6
100	BMDL	60108	2968	23W-5N	E2
200	WDDL	60191	2970	18W-5N	E1
Jefferson Rd					
500	CLSM	60185	2967	27W-2N	C7
500	CLSM	60188	2967	27W-2N	C7
500	WynT	60185	2967	27W-2N	C7
500	WynT	60188	2967	27W-2N	C7
1300	HFET	60169	2858	24W-12N	E2
Jefferson Sq					
900	EGVV	60007	2914	18W-8N	E2
Jefferson St					
100	ALGN	60102	2694	33W-20N	D7
100	FXLK	60041	2473	26W-35N	D5
100	GNVA	60134	3020	34W-1N	D3
100	MTGY	60538	3199	37W-9S	C5
100	WMTN	60481	3853	27W-38S	D7
100	WNVL	60555	3081	28W-3S	B6
300	WNFD	60190	3023	27W-0S	C7
400	DLTN	60419	3350	0E-16S	D4
400	YKVL	60560	3333	43W-15S	C2
500	HNDL	60521	3086	15W-4S	B7
600	CRTE	60417	3685	1W-29S	A2
700	AURA	60505	3138	34W-6S	C5
1300	DSPN	60016	2863	12W-11N	B3
1300	LIHL	60156	2693	35W-22N	E3
1500	AlqT	60156	2693	35W-22N	E3
4700	HRPK	60133	2967	27W-5N	D1
14500	HRVY	60426	3350	1W-17S	B5
16200	HRVY	60426	3428	0W-19S	B2
16200	SHLD	60426	3428	0W-19S	B2
16200	SHLD	60473	3428	0W-19S	B2
17100	CrlT	60180	2635	46W-25N	E5
17100	UNON	60180	2635	47W-25N	C4
Jefferson St CO-T65					
17700	UNON	60180	2635	47W-25N	C4
E Jefferson St					
-	BNVL	60131	2972	15W-4N	B3
10	JLET	60432	3499	23W-23S	A5
10	OSWG	60543	3263	37W-12S	C4
100	BNVL	60106	2972	15W-4N	A3
E Jefferson St US-6					
10	JLET	60432	3499	23W-23S	A5
E Jefferson St US-30					
10	JLET	60432	3499	23W-23S	A5
N Jefferson St					
10	BTVA	60510	3078	35W-1S	B2
10	CHCG	60661	3034	0W-0N	A4
10	HRVD	60033	2406	50W-38N	B7
100	LKPT	60441	3419	22W-18S	D2
100	LktT	60441	3419	22W-18S	D2
100	WDSK	60098	2524	41W-31N	E7
400	CHCG	60610	3034	0W-0N	A4
S Jefferson St					
10	BTVA	60510	3078	35W-1S	B2
10	CHCG	60661	3034	0W-0S	A5
10	HRVD	60033	2406	50W-37N	B7
100	LKPT	60441	3419	22W-20S	C4
100	WDSK	60098	2524	41W-31N	E7
300	CHCG	60607	3034	0W-1S	A7
300	WDSK	60098	2581	41W-30N	D1
1600	CHCG	60616	3092	0W-1S	A1
W Jefferson St					
-	SwdT	60447	3495	32W-24S	C6
10	JLET	60432	3498	24W-23S	E5
10	OSWG	60543	3263	37W-12S	D4
100	SRWD	60404	3496	30W-23S	C5
100	SRWD	60431	3496	30W-23S	C5
200	JLET	60435	3498	25W-23S	C5
500	BNVL	60106	2971	16W-4N	E3
700	JLET	60436	3498	24W-23S	D5
800	AddT	60106	2971	16W-4N	D3
1200	TroT	60404	3496	31W-23S	A5
1800	JLET	60435	3497	27W-23S	C5
1800	JLET	60436	3497	27W-23S	C5
2800	JLET	60431	3497	27W-23S	C5
3200	TroT	60431	3497	28W-23S	B5
3700	JLET	60431	3496	30W-23S	C5
3700	TroT	60431	3496	30W-23S	C5
24200	SRWD	60404	3495	31W-23S	E5
24200	TroT	60404	3495	32W-24S	D5
W Jefferson St US-30					
10	JLET	60432	3498	24W-23S	E5
200	JLET	60435	3498	25W-23S	C5
W Jefferson St US-52					
-	SwdT	60447	3495	32W-24S	C6
100	SRWD	60404	3496	30W-23S	C5
100	SRWD	60431	3496	30W-23S	C5
800	JLET	60435	3498	25W-23S	D5
800	JLET	60436	3498	25W-23S	D5
1200	TroT	60404	3496	31W-23S	A5
1800	JLET	60435	3497	27W-23S	C5
1800	JLET	60436	3497	27W-23S	C5
2800	JLET	60431	3497	27W-23S	C5
3200	TroT	60431	3497	28W-23S	B5
3700	JLET	60431	3496	30W-23S	C5
3700	TroT	60431	3496	30W-23S	C5
24200	SRWD	60404	3495	31W-23S	E5
24200	TroT	60404	3495	32W-24S	D5
Jeffery Av					
300	CTCY	60409	3351	2E-17S	C5
400	DLTN	60419	3351	2E-17S	C6
600	DLTN	60409	3351	2E-17S	C6

STREET Block	City	ZIP	Map#	CGS	Grid
Jeffery Av					
600	ThtT	60409	3351	2E-17S	C6
600	ThtT	60419	3351	2E-17S	C6
600	ThtT	60473	3351	2E-17S	C6
4100	GRNE	60031	2535	14W-34N	D2
21500	SLVL	60411	3597	2E-26S	C2
S Jeffery Av					
-	CHCG	60409	3351	2E-15S	C2
-	CHCG	60633	3351	2E-15S	C1
-	CHCG	60827	3351	2E-15S	C2
-	CTCY	60409	3351	2E-16S	C2
9400	CHCG	60617	3215	2E-11S	C6
S Jeffery Blvd					
6700	CHCG	60649	3153	2E-8S	C7
7500	CHCG	60649	3215	2E-9S	C3
7800	CHCG	60617	3215	2E-8S	C1
Jeffery Ct					
900	SMBG	60193	2858	24W-10N	D6
1000	LMBD	60148	3026	20W-0S	B7
1400	HMWD	60430	3507	1W-22S	E1
Jeffery Ct N					
1100	NHBK	60062	2757	9W-17N	C5
Jeffery Ct S					
1200	NHBK	60062	2757	9W-17N	D5
Jeffery Ct W					
1100	NHBK	60062	2757	9W-17N	C5
Jeffery Dr					
1200	HMWD	60430	3507	1W-22S	E1
1200	HMWD	60430	3508	1W-22S	A1
S Jeffery Dr					
-	CHCG	60637	3153	2E-7S	C5
-	CHCG	60649	3153	2E-7S	C5
Jeffery Ln					
10	DSPN	60018	2862	15W-10N	B6
10	LtRT	60545	3259	48W-11S	B2
100	SMBG	60193	2858	24W-10N	D6
1400	NHBK	60062	2757	9W-17N	C5
Jeffery St					
200	NHFD	60093	2811	7W-15N	A2
Jeffrey Av					
500	GYLK	60030	2532	21W-33N	D3
900	JltT	60432	3499	22W-22S	D2
1600	GLHT	60139	2969	23W-3N	A6
17000	SHLD	60473	3429	2E-20S	C3
E Jeffrey Av					
200	WLNG	60090	2755	13W-17N	D5
W Jeffrey Av					
10	WLNG	60090	2755	14W-17N	C5
Jeffrey Ct					
700	WHTN	60187	3082	25W-2S	B3
900	SCRL	60174	2964	34W-3N	D5
2000	ELGN	60123	2800	36W-13N	A7
9100	SPGV	60081	2414	30W-41N	A1
E Jeffrey Dr					
1500	MPPT	60056	2808	14W-13N	D6
S Jeffrey Dr					
1300	ADSN	60101	2970	20W-2N	B7
1400	AddT	60101	2970	20W-2N	B7
21200	MTSN	60443	3594	4W-25S	D1
W Jeffrey Dr					
3000	JLET	60435	3497	27W-23S	C4
3100	JLET	60431	3497	27W-23S	C4
Jeffrey Ln					
100	BGBK	60440	3205	22W-10S	B6
300	WLNG	60090	2755	14W-17N	B5
2000	ELGN	60123	2800	36W-13N	A7
Jeffreys Pl					
200	HIWD	60040	2704	9W-23N	D2
Jen Av					
3400	PKCY	60085	2536	13W-33N	A3
Jenel Ct					
16300	LKPT	60441	3420	20W-19S	A3
Jenice Ct					
300	WCHI	60185	3022	29W-0N	E5
Jenkins Ct					
800	WLNG	60090	2755	15W-17N	A4
Jenkinson Ct					
2200	WKGN	60085	2536	11W-34N	D1
Jenkisson Av					
700	ShdT	60044	2593	12W-28N	A5
Jenks St					
1600	EVTN	60201	2813	3W-13N	A7
1700	EVTN	60201	2812	3W-13N	E7
Jenlor Ct					
300	WynT	60185	2965	31W-4N	D4
Jenna Cir					
2600	MTGY	60538	3198	40W-10S	D5
Jenna Ct					
-	MltT	60137	3083	21W-1S	D2
-	SEGN	60177	2908	35W-9N	A1
2700	MTGY	60538	3198	40W-10S	C5
Jenna Dr					
500	SEGN	60177	2908	35W-9N	A1
4500	GNVW	60025	2809	12W-14N	C5
4500	NfdT	60025	2809	12W-14N	C5
Jenna Ln					
26300	CbaT	60010	2643	26W-25N	D4
Jennerstown Dr					
-	JknT	60421	3675	24W-29S	D2
-	JLET	60421	3675	24W-29S	D2
Jennie Dr					
1200	NLNX	60451	3588	19W-27S	E5
Jennifer Av					
6100	TYPK	60477	3425	7W-20S	C3
Jennifer Cir					
500	LbvT	60060	2646	18W-26N	E3
Jennifer Ct					
-	BNHL	60010	2750	27W-17N	B6
-	GRNE	60031	2535	13W-34N	E1
400	WDDL	60191	2970	18W-5N	E1
700	LKFT	60045	2649	12W-24N	C7
700	NlxT	60451	3502	15W-24S	C5
800	ALGN	60102	2748	33W-20N	A1
900	SRGV	60554	3136	41W-4S	A2
1100	LKPT	60441	3419	21W-19S	E2
3400	STGR	60475	3596	1W-28S	A5
5500	OswT	60560	3334	40W-15S	C2
N Jennifer Ct					
800	ANHT	60004	2807	17W-15N	B2
Jennifer Dr					
500	BlmT	60411	3510	4E-25S	B7
900	BTVA	60510	3078	34W-2S	D3
17500	ODPK	60467	3423	13W-21S	A6
Jennifer Ln					
-	JNBG	60050	2471	32W-34N	C7
10	CTCY	60409	3351	2E-16S	C4
300	ROSL	60172	2913	23W-8N	B3
300	SmbT	60172	2913	23W-8N	B3
400	GYLK	60030	2532	21W-33N	D3
1000	BGBK	60440	3268	25W-11S	B2
1200	BGBK	60490	3268	25W-11S	A1
1600	MHRY	60050	2528	32W-33N	A2
1800	HFET	60169	2858	25W-12N	A2
3400	CRTE	60417	3597	1E-28S	B6
4000	PltT	60004	2753	19W-18N	C2
31500	LKMR	60051	2529	28W-31N	E6
W Jennifer Ln					
200	PLTN	60067	2752	21W-16N	D6
Jennifer St					
11800	FftT	60423	3590	14W-26S	D3
11800	FKFT	60423	3590	14W-26S	D3
W Jennings Ct					
21700	PnfT	60544	3339	27W-16S	D4
Jennings Dr					
400	CLLK	60156	2694	35W-24N	B1
400	LIHL	60156	2694	35W-24N	B1
Jenny Ln					
700	AraT	60506	3199	38W-8S	A2
15500	ODPK	60467	3345	13W-18S	A7
Jenny Jae Ln					
2700	NndT	60012	2584	34W-29N	D5
Jensen Av					
-	BtnT	60099	2362	11W-43N	D5
-	WPHR	60096	2362	11W-42N	D5
-	WPHR	60099	2362	11W-42N	D5
N Jensen Av					
24600	CbaT	60013	2643	28W-24N	A6
Jensen Blvd					
7400	HRPK	60133	2911	27W-9N	D1
Jensen Ct					
600	WKGN	60085	2537	10W-33N	A3
Jensen Dr					
1000	LKFT	60045	2649	12W-27N	B1
1600	CHCG	60644	3031	7W-0S	C5
N Jensen Ln					
31000	LbvT	60048	2592	15W-31N	A1
31000	WKGN	60048	2592	15W-31N	A1
31100	LbvT	60048	2535	15W-31N	A7
31100	WKGN	60048	2535	15W-31N	A7
W Jensen St					
24200	TroT	60404	3496	30W-25S	B7
24800	SRWD	60404	3496	30W-25S	B7
Jens Jensen Ln					
200	CmpT	60175	2961	42W-5N	C2
Jenyglenn Dr					
11400	FftT	60448	3502	14W-22S	E1
11400	MKNA	60448	3502	14W-22S	E1
Jerald Dr					
1000	JLET	60431	3585	28W-25S	B1
Jerele Av					
1400	BKLY	60104	3028	13W-0N	E4
1400	BKLY	60163	3028	13W-0N	E4
1400	BLWD	60104	3028	13W-0N	E4
1400	BLWD	60163	3028	13W-0N	E4
Jeremy Ln					
900	LYVL	60048	2591	17W-29N	B4
17100	ODPK	60462	3424	10W-20S	B4
17100	ODPK	60487	3424	10W-20S	B4
17100	TYPK	60487	3424	10W-20S	B4
Jeremy Ranch Ct					
3500	AURA	60564	3201	31W-9S	E4
3500	AURA	60564	3202	31W-9S	A4
Jeri Ln					
800	WCHI	60185	3022	29W-0N	E5
900	WnfT	60185	3022	29W-0N	E5
Jericho Cir					
1400	AraT	60506	3199	37W-8S	C2
1400	AURA	60506	3199	37W-8S	C2
Jericho Ln					
10	BTVA	60510	3077	36W-1S	E1
Jericho Rd					
10	AURA	60506	3198	39W-8S	E3
10	BRKT	60511	3196	44W-9S	D3
10	MTGY	60506	3198	39W-8S	E3
10	SgrT	60506	3197	41W-9S	E4
10	SgrT	60506	3198	39W-8S	E3
10	SgrT	60511	3196	46W-9S	A4
10	SgrT	60554	3196	46W-9S	A4
10	SgrT	60554	3197	43W-9S	A4
900	AURA	60506	3199	38W-8S	A2
1000	AraT	60506	3199	37W-8S	D2
2000	MTGY	60506	3199	38W-8S	A2
2200	AraT	60506	3198	39W-8S	E2
2200	AraT	60538	3198	39W-8S	E2
2200	AraT	60538	3199	38W-8S	A2
2200	MTGY	60538	3199	38W-8S	A2
2300	AURA	60538	3198	38W-8S	E2
2300	MTGY	60538	3198	38W-8S	E2
Jericho Rd CO-24					
10	AURA	60506	3198	39W-8S	E3
10	BRKT	60511	3196	44W-9S	D3
10	MTGY	60506	3198	39W-8S	E3
10	SgrT	60506	3197	41W-9S	E4
10	SgrT	60506	3198	39W-8S	E3
10	SgrT	60511	3196	46W-9S	A4
10	SgrT	60554	3196	46W-9S	A4
10	SgrT	60554	3197	43W-9S	A3
2400	AraT	60506	3198	39W-8S	E2
2400	AraT	60538	3198	39W-8S	E2
2400	AURA	60538	3198	39W-8S	E2
2400	MTGY	60538	3198	39W-8S	E2
Jerome Av					
-	WHTN	60187	3024	25W-0N	B4
10	MltT	60187	3023	26W-0N	E4
400	MltT	60187	3024	25W-0N	B4
3800	SKOK	60076	2866	4W-9N	B7
E Jerome Av					
600	JLET	60432	3499	23W-23S	B4
Jerome Ct					
1200	ANTH	60002	2359	20W-41N	A7
Jerome Dr					
500	NHLK	60164	2972	14W-2N	D6
Jerome Ln					
100	BGBK	60440	3205	22W-10S	B6
Jerome Pl					
300	WLNG	60090	2755	13W-17N	D5
Jerome St					
4600	SKOK	60076	2866	5W-9N	A7
4800	SKOK	60077	2865	6W-9N	E7
W Jerome St					
2500	CHCG	60645	2867	3W-9N	A7
2600	CHCG	60645	2866	3W-9N	E7
3100	CHCG	60076	2866	3W-9N	D7
3100	SKOK	60076	2866	3W-9N	D7
7700	CHCG	60631	2864	9W-9N	C7
Jerrie Ln					
2900	GNVW	60025	2810	10W-12N	B7
E Jerry Dr					
10	MPPT	60056	2808	14W-13N	D7
N Jersey Av					
5600	CHCG	60625	2920	3W-7N	D4
5600	CHCG	60659	2920	4W-7N	D4
W Jersey Av					
500	JLET	60435	3498	24W-23S	D4
25000	ANTH	60002	2357	25W-42N	B5
25000	AntT	60002	2357	25W-42N	B5
Jersey Ct					
1500	BFGV	60089	2701	16W-21N	D5
4000	NPVL	60564	3266	29W-12S	D2
S Jersey Ct					
13600	PnfT	60544	3339	27W-16S	D3
Jersey Ln					
500	EGVV	60007	2913	21W-9N	D1
Jerusha Av					
10	ELGN	60123	2854	34W-12N	D1
Jervey Ln					
100	BRLT	60103	2910	29W-7N	E4
Jessamine					
-	HPSR	60140	2795	47W-16N	D1
Jessamine Dr					
900	OSWG	60543	3264	35W-11S	C2
Jessen St					
100	PTON	60468	3861	9W-37S	A4
Jessica Ct					
10	HNWD	60047	2645	22W-27N	B1
200	NARA	60542	3078	35W-3S	B6
1900	WHTN	60187	3024	25W-0N	C4
2100	NPVL	60540	3202	29W-8S	D2
5700	RGMW	60008	2805	21W-13N	C5
25100	LkvT	60046	2416	25W-38N	B6
Jessica Dr					
200	WDDL	60191	2915	16W-6N	D6
900	FmtT	60084	2588	24W-28N	B6
1100	WCDA	60084	2588	24W-28N	B6
5300	BmnT	60452	3425	6W-20S	E4
5300	OKFT	60452	3425	6W-20S	E4
5500	BmnT	60477	3425	7W-20S	D4
5500	OKFT	60477	3425	7W-20S	D4
Jessica Ln					
300	BRLT	60103	2910	29W-8N	E2
1100	LYVL	60048	2591	18W-29N	A3
1900	NHBK	60062	2756	11W-16N	D7
2500	RGMW	60067	2805	21W-13N	D6
2500	RGMW	60173	2805	21W-13N	D6
2500	SMBG	60173	2805	21W-13N	D6
8200	TYPK	60477	3424	10W-19S	C3
S Jessica Ln					
19900	FftT	60423	3504	9W-24S	D4
Jessie Av					
5100	HMND	46320	3352		E6
Jessie Rd					
600	LIHL	60156	2694	34W-21N	C5
Jessie St					
10	JltT	60433	3499	21W-24S	E5
200	MHTN	60442	3677	19W-31S	D5
200	MHTN	60442	3678	19W-31S	A5
W Jessup St					
25300	CNHN	60410	3672	31W-30S	E5
Jester Ln					
1900	ALGN	60102	2694	35W-20N	A7
Jeter Ct					
-	BtlT	60543	3262	40W-12S	B3
Jeter Rd					
100	BRKT	60511	3196	45W-10S	B5
200	LtRT	60545	3196	45W-10S	B5
Jeter St					
-	BtlT	60543	3262	40W-12S	B3
Jethro Av					
1700	ZION	60099	2421	11W-40N	E3
Jethro Ct					
2800	ZION	60099	2421	11W-41N	E1
Jewel Av					
200	SCRL	60174	3020	34W-2N	D1
Jewel Ct					
1500	PLTN	60074	2806	19W-15N	D2
S Jewel Ct					
300	PLTN	60074	2806	19W-15N	C2
Jewel Dr					
-	MLPK	60160	2973	11W-2N	D7
-	MLPK	60160	3029	11W-2N	D1
4000	JNBG	60050	2472	30W-36N	A5
Jewel Ln					
-	HGKN	60525	3147	11W-7S	D5
1400	WMTN	60481	3853	28W-37S	A5
1400	WmTp	60481	3853	28W-37S	A5
Jewelflower Ct					
7800	JLET	60447	3495	33W-22S	A2
Jewelflower Ln					
1000	JLET	60447	3495	33W-22S	A2
Jewell Ct					
-	WNFD	60190	3023	27W-0S	C6
Jewell Rd					
10	MltT	60187	3023	26W-0N	D5
10	MltT	60187	3024	26W-0N	A5
10	MltT	60190	3023	27W-0N	D5
10	WNFD	60187	3023	26W-0N	E5
10	WNFD	60190	3023	27W-0N	D6
600	WHTN	60187	3024	25W-0N	A5
Jewell Rd CO-27					
10	MltT	60187	3023	26W-0N	D5
10	MltT	60187	3024	26W-0N	A5
10	MltT	60190	3023	26W-0N	E5
10	WNFD	60187	3023	26W-0N	E5
10	WNFD	60190	3023	26W-0N	E5
600	WHTN	60187	3024	25W-0N	A5
Jewett St					
100	ELGN	60123	2854	34W-10N	D5
100	RKDL	60436	3498	25W-25S	B7
800	WDSK	60098	2524	41W-31N	C6
Jewett Park Dr					
800	DRFD	60015	2703	11W-21N	E7
JFK Blvd					
10	EGVV	60007	2914	19W-8N	D2
N JF Kennedy Dr					
200	ADSN	60101	2970	18W-3N	E4
JFK Memorial Dr					
-	EDND	60118	2801	33W-16N	C1
200	CPVL	60110	2748	32W-17N	C7
200	EDND	60110	2748	33W-17N	C7
800	CPVL	60110	2801	33W-16N	C1
800	EDND	60110	2801	33W-16N	C1
JFK Memorial Dr SR-25					
-	EDND	60118	2801	33W-16N	C1
10	CPVL	60110	2748	33W-17N	C7
200	EDND	60110	2748	33W-17N	C7
800	CPVL	60110	2801	33W-16N	C1
800	EDND	60110	2801	33W-16N	C1
J Henry Wilson					
-	BtvT	60510	3078	36W-3S	A6
-	BtvT	60539	3077	36W-3S	E5
-	BtvT	60539	3078	36W-3S	A5
Jill Ct					
400	AddT	60126	2972	15W-3N	A5
400	EMHT	60126	2972	15W-3N	A5
500	DSPN	60018	2862	15W-10N	A5
1400	HMWD	60430	3507	1W-22S	E2
1400	RGMW	60008	2805	20W-14N	E3
1500	GLHT	60139	2969	22W-2N	C6
Jill Ln					
100	SMWD	60107	2857	27W-11N	D4
500	BGBK	60440	3205	22W-10S	C7
9200	SRPK	60176	2973	11W-5N	D2
Jill St					
-	FNPK	60131	2973	13W-3N	A5
Jill Ter					
1200	HMWD	60430	3507	1W-22S	E2
1200	HMWD	60430	3508	1W-22S	A2
Jillann Dr					
6200	OKFT	60452	3425	7W-18S	C1
Jillian Ct					
-	RNPK	60471	3594	5W-26S	C3
10900	ODPK	60467	3345	13W-18S	A7
10900	OrlT	60467	3345	13W-18S	A7
Jillian Rd					
10800	ODPK	60467	3345	13W-18S	A7
15300	ODPK	60462	3345	13W-18S	A7
Jill Peak Dr					
1100	SYHW	60118	2800	35W-15N	C4
Jim					
1300	NlxT	60451	3502	15W-25S	C7
Jim Dhamer Dr					
12600	HTLY	60142	2744	42W-18N	D5
Jimmick Ln					
-	ODPK	60467	3423	13W-20S	B4
Jingle Bell Ln					
100	AURA	60506	3137	36W-7S	E7
W Jl Smith Ln					
7000	MonT	60449	3682	8W-30S	A3
W Jo Ln					
1300	ANHT	60004	2806	18W-15N	D2
S Joalyce Ct					
11800	ALSP	60803	3276	5W-13S	B5
S Joalyce Dr					
11500	ALSP	60803	3276	5W-13S	A4
11500	CHCG	60655	3276	5W-13S	A4
11500	CHCG	60803	3276	5W-13S	A4
Joan Av					
11600	HTLY	60142	2692	40W-21N	A5
Joan Ct					
100	SchT	60175	2963	38W-3N	B6
300	BRLT	60103	2911	28W-8N	A3
400	GLBT	60136	2799	38W-15N	C3
700	ELGN	60120	2855	32W-10N	B6
900	NPVL	60540	3202	29W-8S	E1
Joan Dr					
100	LKZH	60047	2698	24W-23N	D1
100	PltT	60010	2751	23W-18N	D3
100	SchT	60175	2963	38W-3N	B7
E Joan Dr					
1200	PLTN	60074	2753	19W-16N	C7
Joan St					
-	HTLY	60142	2692	40W-21N	A5
800	ALGN	60102	2694	34W-21N	C6
Joan Marie Dr					
12000	HMGN	60491	3344	15W-18S	C7
Jo Ann Ct					
500	LKPT	60441	3419	22W-20S	D4
Jo Ann Dr					
3000	JLET	60431	3417	28W-21S	A7
3000	PnfT	60431	3417	28W-21S	A7
3100	PnfT	60431	3416	28W-21S	E7
Joann Dr					
700	WMTN	60481	3943	27W-39S	E1
Joann Ln					
3400	LslT	60517	3205	22W-9S	C4
3400	LslT	60565	3205	22W-9S	C4
3400	WDRG	60517	3205	22W-9S	C4
15800	OKFT	60452	3425	7W-18S	C1
W Jo Ann Ln					
200	ADSN	60101	2970	20W-4N	A3
Joanna Av					
1700	ZION	60099	2421	11W-41N	E1
Joanna Ct					
200	ANTH	60002	2357	23W-42N	E5
Joanne Dr					
3800	GNVW	60025	2809	11W-15N	D2
3900	GNVW	60062	2809	11W-15N	D2
Joanne Ln					
700	HRVD	60033	2464	50W-37N	A1
900	HRVD	60033	2463	51W-37N	E1
Jobe Av					
1500	SCRL	60174	3020	34W-2N	D1
W Jobev Ln					
4200	ALSP	60803	3276	5W-13S	C5
Jocare Dr					
9200	JSTC	60458	3209	11W-8S	E1
Jocelyn Pl					
300	HDPK	60035	2704	9W-23N	C2
300	HIWD	60040	2704	9W-23N	C2
Jockey Ct					
-	RLKP	60030	2589	22W-30N	B1
Jodan Dr					
-	ALSP	60453	3275	6W-12S	E3
-	ALSP	60803	3275	6W-12S	E3
10900	OKLN	60453	3275	6W-12S	E3
Jodave Av					
16800	HLCT	60429	3427	2W-20S	D4
17000	EHZC	60429	3427	2W-20S	D4
Jodee Dr					
2600	JLET	60435	3497	27W-24S	C5
2600	JLET	60435	3497	27W-24S	D5
Jodi Ct					
10	DYR	46311	3510		C7
1200	BRLT	60103	2910	30W-8N	B3
Jodi Ln					
100	BRLT	60103	2910	30W-8N	B3
S Jodi Rd					
19000	MKNA	60448	3503	11W-22S	E2
Jodi Ter					
18900	HMWD	60430	3508	1W-22S	A2
Jody Ct					
4100	RGMW	60008	2806	20W-13N	A5
W Jody Ct					
2100	MPPT	60056	2861	17W-12N	B1
Jody Ln					
600	HFET	60169	2858	24W-11N	C4
6000	BmnT	60477	3425	7W-19S	C2
6100	TYPK	60477	3425	7W-19S	C2
8800	MaiT	60016	2863	11W-12N	E1
W Jody Ln					
14200	WDWH	60083	2420	14W-39N	D5
Joe Ct					
-	HRVD	60033	2464	50W-37N	B1
800	LynT	60458	3209	11W-8S	E1
Joe Adler Dr					
2400	JLET	60586	3415	32W-20S	D6
Joe Favero Dr					
-	WKGN	60085	2480	10W-36N	B5
-	WKGN	60087	2480	10W-36N	B5
Joe Fullan Ct					
-	OKBK	60523	3086	15W-2S	A4
Joel Ct					
200	GLHT	60139	3025	22W-1N	B2
Joel Dr					
1000	AURA	60505	3138	34W-5S	D3
Joel Ln					
700	BFGV	60089	2701	16W-20N	E7
Joe Orr Ct					
10	CRTE	60417	3685	0W-29S	C2
Joe Orr Rd					
300	CRTE	60417	3685	0W-29S	C1
E Joe Orr Rd					
-	CHHT	60411	3507	2W-24S	C5
-	OMFD	60461	3507	2W-24S	C5
10	CHHT	60411	3508	0W-24S	B5
300	BlmT	60411	3508	0W-24S	C5
900	BlmT	60411	3509	0E-24S	A5
900	CHHT	60411	3509	0E-24S	A5
1100	FDHT	60411	3509	1E-24S	B5
1100	LYWD	60411	3509	2E-24S	C5
W Joe Orr Rd					
10	CHHT	60411	3507	2W-24S	D5
10	CHHT	60411	3508	1W-24S	A5
500	CHHT	60461	3507	2W-24S	D5
500	OMFD	60461	3507	2W-24S	D5
Joe Willie Ct					
4000	NPVL	60564	3266	29W-12S	D2
Joe Willie Dr					
4100	NPVL	60564	3266	29W-12S	D3
Joey Ct					
1000	NlxT	60451	3502	15W-23S	C4
Joey Dr					
10	EGvT	60007	2861	17W-10N	B5
10	EGVV	60007	2861	17W-10N	B5
N Joey Dr					
-	NLES	60714	2864	10W-11N	B3
Johanna Av					
9600	FNPK	60131	2973	12W-3N	C5
Johanna Dr					
10	LtRT	60545	3330	49W-15S	D2
W Johanna Dr					
8400	MaiT	60714	2864	10W-10N	A4
8400	NLES	60714	2864	10W-10N	A4
W Johanna Ter					
1600	ANHT	60005	2806	18W-14N	D5
Johelia Dr					
300	ANTH	60002	2357	23W-43N	D4
Johelia Ln					
400	ANTH	60002	2357	23W-43N	D4
John Av					
200	MchT	60050	2472	29W-37N	D2
17700	CCHL	60478	3426	5W-21S	B6
18400	CCHL	60478	3506	5W-22S	B1
18900	CCHL	60477	3506	5W-22S	B2
18900	RchT	60477	3506	5W-22S	B2
John Ct					
400	BMDL	60157	2913	22W-6N	C6
500	SMBG	60193	2859	23W-9N	B7
600	LynT	60458	3209	11W-8S	D2
700	ElaT	60047	2699	23W-23N	A1
700	LKZH	60047	2699	23W-23N	A1
2300	LKMR	60051	2529	30W-34N	A1
2300	MchT	60051	2529	30W-34N	A1
16300	LktT	60441	3418	25W-19S	B3
John Dr					
10	HNWD	60047	2646	20W-24N	A7
10	HNWD	60047	2700	20W-24N	A1
200	BRLT	60103	2911	28W-7N	A4
300	ELGN	60120	2855	32W-10N	C5
1100	HFET	60169	2858	24W-11N	C3
John St					
-	RcmT	60081	2413	32W-39N	B4
10	CLLK	60014	2640	34W-25N	C4
10	NARA	60542	3137	36W-4S	E1
10	NARA	60542	3138	36W-4S	A1
100	NLNX	60451	3501	18W-24S	B5
200	BRKT	60511	3196	45W-8S	C2
500	BNVL	60106	2972	15W-4N	B3
800	LMNT	60439	3270	19W-14S	D6
900	AddT	60106	2972	15W-4N	B4
900	AddT	60126	2972	15W-4N	B4
1000	YKVL	60560	3261	43W-14S	B7
1200	YKVL	60560	3260	44W-14S	D7
1600	GLHT	60139	2968	24W-3N	D6
2700	BLID	60406	3349	3W-15S	A1
3500	STGR	60475	3595	1W-28S	E6
3900	RcmT	60071	2413	32W-39N	A4
6400	GfnT	60014	2639	38W-25N	A4
E John St					
900	WslT	60481	3943	27W-40S	E2
N John St					
600	MHRY	60050	2528	32W-32N	C4
W John St					
10	PLNO	60545	3259	47W-13S	C6
700	JLET	60435	3498	25W-23S	C5
800	MHRY	60050	2528	32W-32N	B4
800	YKVL	60560	3261	43W-14S	A7
John St W					
10	AURA	60504	3201	32W-9S	B5
John Adams Dr					
-	JknT	60421	3763	26W-33S	E2
24400	PNFD	60544	3338	30W-17S	B6
Johnathon Rd					
10	LKZH	60047	2698	24W-23N	D2
John Bardeen Dr					
300	WNVL	60555	3080	29W-2S	D4
John Bourg Dr					
2500	JLET	60586	3415	32W-20S	D6
John Burge Ln					
-	DYR	46311	3598		C2
John Charles Dr					
18000	ODPK	60467	3423	13W-21S	B7
John David					
-	LMNT	60439	3342	20W-15S	B1
John Friend Dr					
900	NPVL	60540	3202	29W-8S	D1
John Greenleaf Whittier Pl					
800	CmpT	60175	2962	40W-3N	C5
John Hancock Ct					
400	AURA	60504	3140	29W-6S	D5
John Hancock Dr					
-	BGBK	60490	3267	27W-14S	B7
John Humphrey Dr					
14200	ODPK	60462	3345	11W-17S	D5
14200	OrlT	60462	3345	11W-17S	D5
John Kirkham Dr					
19100	LktT	60441	3340	24W-17S	E6
19100	LktT	60441	3341	23W-17S	A6
John Lee Ct					
21700	TroT	60404	3584	30W-26S	C2
John M Boor Dr					
10	GLBT	60136	2798	39W-15N	E4
10	GLBT	60136	2799	39W-15N	A4
10	RtdT	60124	2798	39W-15N	E4
400	RtdT	60136	2799	38W-15N	A4
N John Mogg Rd					
32800	GYLK	60030	2533	18W-32N	E4
32800	WrnT	60030	2533	18W-33N	E4
Johnor Av					
400	SCRL	60174	2964	35W-4N	B5
John Paul Jones Ln					
2000	BGBK	60490	3267	27W-14S	B7
John Rolfe Dr					
2300	SMBG	60194	2857	26W-11N	E3
Johns Ct					
2000	GNVW	60025	2810	9W-14N	D3
Johns Dr					
1800	GNVW	60025	2810	9W-14N	D3

Chicago 7-County Street Index

STREET Block City ZIP Map# CGS Grid

Johns Ln
10 AraT 60505 3138 34W-6S D6
Johnsburg Ct
2300 NPVL 60564 3202 29W-10S C5
Johnsburg Rd
6600 BtnT 60081 2414 30W-38N B6
6600 SPGV 60050 2414 30W-38N B7
6600 SPGV 60081 2414 30W-38N B6
N Johnsburg Rd
- BtnT 60050 2414 30W-38N B7
- BtnT 60081 2414 30W-38N B7
- BtnT 60081 2472 30W-36N B3
- SPGV 60050 2414 30W-38N B7
- SPGV 60081 2414 30W-38N B7
2000 JNBG 60050 2471 30W-35N E5
3700 JNBG 60050 2472 30W-35N A5
4100 MchT 60050 2472 30W-36N B3
5700 BtnT 60050 2472 30W-36N B3
5700 SPGV 60050 2472 30W-36N B3
5700 SPGV 60081 2472 30W-36N B3
W Johnsburg Rd
2100 JNBG 60050 2471 31W-35N D6
W Johnsburg Rd CO-A26
2300 JNBG 60050 2471 31W-35N D6
W Johnsburg Rd CO-V40
2300 JNBG 60050 2471 31W-35N D6
Johnsbury Ct
3200 AURA 60504 3201 31W-9S E5
Johnsbury Ln
3100 AURA 60504 3201 31W-9S D5
John's Circle Dr
- BfdT 53128 2352 E2
Johns Manville Av
- WKGN 60085 2479 12W-35N A5
12800 WkgT 60085 2479 12W-35N A5
12900 WkgT 60031 2479 12W-35N A5
W Johns Manville Pl
- WKGN 60085 2479 11W-35N E5
600 WKGN 60085 2480 10W-35N A5
Johns Manville Rd
3400 GRNE 60031 2479 13W-35N A5
3400 WkgT 60031 2479 12W-35N A5
3400 WkgT 60085 2479 12W-35N A5
12800 GRNE 60031 2478 13W-35N E5
John Smith Dr
2300 HFET 60194 2857 26W-11N E3
2300 SMBG 60194 2857 26W-11N E3
John Snow Av
- BRTN 60010 2751 25W-18N B2
Johnson Av
100 LYVL 60048 2591 16W-29N D4
200 FKFT 60423 3591 12W-25S C1
300 CTCY 60409 3352 3E-17S A5
400 FKFT 60423 3503 12W-25S C7
3800 PvsT 60558 3086 13W-4S E7
3800 WNSP 60558 3086 13W-4S E7
3900 NndT 60014 2586 30W-28N A7
4400 WNSP 60558 3146 13W-5S E1
S Johnson Av
3800 HMND 46327 3352 D5
Johnson Ct
10 NARA 60542 3138 35W-4S C1
W Johnson Ct
6800 MonT 60449 3682 8W-30S B3
Johnson Dr
- VrnT 60062 2755 15W-20N B1
- VrnT 60089 2755 15W-20N B1
1000 BFGV 60089 2755 15W-20N B1
1000 BFGV 60090 2755 15W-20N B1
E Johnson Dr
900 LslT 60540 3142 25W-7S B7
900 NPVL 60540 3142 25W-7S B7
1100 NPVL 60540 3204 25W-8S B1
1200 LslT 60565 3204 25W-8S B1
1200 NPVL 60565 3204 25W-8S B1
Johnson Ln
1100 BTVA 60510 3078 36W-1S A3
Johnson Rd
- BHPK 60099 2421 11W-39N D6
10 CmpT 60175 2962 39W-4N E5
10 CmpT 60175 2963 39W-4N A5
10 SchT 60175 2963 39W-4N A5
1200 NasT 60543 3337 33W-16S A5
1200 PNFD 60543 3337 33W-16S A5
9600 HbnT 60034 2350 42W-42N B7
W Johnson Rd
10300 CHCG 60666 2917 13W-8N A2
10500 CHCG 60666 2916 13W-8N E2
Johnson St
10 EDND 60118 2801 33W-16N A3
200 HPSR 60140 2796 46W-16N A2
200 YKVL 60560 3333 42W-15S D2
400 MRGO 60152 2634 50W-26N A3
900 FRGV 60021 2696 29W-23N C2
1400 LKPT 60441 3419 22W-20S D4
17300 CrlT 60180 2635 46W-25N E4
17300 UNON 60180 2635 46W-25N D4
N Johnson St
100 HRVD 60033 2406 49W-38N D6
100 WDSK 60098 2524 41W-31N D7
S Johnson St
100 HRVD 60033 2406 50W-38N A7
100 WDSK 60098 2524 41W-31N D7
W Johnson St
100 PLTN 60067 2805 21W-15N D1
Johnson Woods Dr
10 BTVA 60510 3078 34W-1S D2
Johnston Dr
900 AraT 60506 3199 38W-8S A3
Johnston Ln
12400 HMGN 60491 3422 15W-19S B2
Johnston Rd
8500 BRRG 60527 3208 14W-10S C4
8500 LynT 60527 3208 14W-10S C4
8700 LynT 60480 3208 14W-10S C4
Johnstone Dr
1300 BTVA 60510 3078 34W-2S E4
Johnstown Ct
1500 WHTN 60187 3082 24W-1S E2
Johnstown Ln
800 WHTN 60187 3082 24W-1S D2
Johnstown Rd
10 ElgT 60124 2853 37W-11N C5
Johnsway Dr
200 CmpT 60175 2906 39W-7N E4
Jolee Ct
24600 PNFD 60544 3416 30W-18S A1
Joliet Av
3900 LYNS 60534 3088 9W-4S C7
3900 RvsT 60534 3088 9W-4S C6
3900 RvsT 60546 3088 9W-4S C6
4500 LYNS 60534 3148 10W-5S C1
4600 MCCK 60534 3148 10W-4S C1
4700 MCCK 60525 3148 10W-5S C1
Joliet Dr N
7800 TYPK 60477 3424 9W-21S D5
Joliet Dr S
7700 TYPK 60477 3424 9W-21S D6
Joliet Hwy
- NLNX 60451 3502 15W-25S C7
- NlxT 60451 3502 15W-25S C7
E Joliet Hwy
100 NLNX 60451 3501 17W-25S C7
100 NlxT 60451 3501 17W-25S C7
900 NLNX 60451 3502 16W-25S A7
900 NlxT 60451 3502 16W-25S A7
W Joliet Hwy
100 NLNX 60451 3501 18W-25S B7
100 NlxT 60451 3501 18W-25S B7
Joliet Rd
- BGBK - 3270 20W-11S A1
- BRRG - 3207 16W-9S D3
- BRRG - 3208 15W-8S A2
- DGvT - 3206 20W-11S C7
- DGvT - 3207 17W-9S C4
- DGvT - 3270 20W-11S A1
- DPgT - 3270 20W-11S A1
- DRN - 3206 19W-10S D6
- DRN - 3207 17W-9S B4
- IHPK - 3146 14W-8S C7
- RMVL 60440 3269 22W-12S D4
- WDRG - 3206 20W-11S C7
- WDRG - 3270 20W-11S A1
- WDRG 60517 3269 22W-13S D4
- WLBK - 3207 16W-9S D3
- WLBK - 3208 15W-8S A2
10 BGBK 60440 3269 21W-12S D3
10 WDRG 60440 3269 21W-12S D3
200 DGvT 60527 3207 17W-9S D3
400 DGvT 60527 3208 15W-8S A2
800 CTSD 60525 3147 13W-7S A6
800 LynT 60525 3147 13W-7S B5
1100 RMVL 60446 3269 22W-14S B6
1200 DPgT 60441 3269 22W-13S C5
1700 RMVL 60441 3269 22W-13S C5
4300 LYNS 60534 3088 9W-4S C7
6100 HGKN 60525 3147 11W-6S D4
6500 IHPK 60525 3147 13W-7S A6
6600 CTSD 60525 3146 13W-7S E6
6900 BRRG 60525 3146 14W-7S D7
7000 BRRG 60527 3146 15W-7S C7
7200 LYNS 60402 3088 9W-4S E6
7200 SKNY 60402 3088 9W-4S E6
7900 LYNS 60534 3148 10W-5S B2
7900 MCCK 60525 3148 10W-5S A2
7900 MCCK 60534 3148 10W-5S B2
9000 MCCK 60525 3147 11W-6S D4
29200 WltT 60442 3767 17W-35S E7
Joliet Rd I-55
- BGBK - 3270 20W-11S A1
- BRRG - 3146 14W-8S D7
- BRRG - 3207 16W-9S D3
- BRRG - 3208 15W-8S A2
- DGvT - 3206 19W-10S D5
- DGvT - 3207 17W-9S C3
- DGvT - 3270 20W-11S A1
- DPgT - 3270 20W-11S A1
- DRN - 3206 20W-11S C7
- DRN - 3207 18W-9S A4
- IHPK - 3146 14W-8S C7
- WDRG - 3206 20W-11S C7
- WDRG - 3270 20W-11S A1
- WLBK - 3207 16W-9S D3
- WLBK - 3208 15W-8S A2
S Joliet Rd
10 PNFD 60544 3416 29W-18S D1
200 PNFD 60544 3338 29W-18S C7
300 PNFD 60586 3416 29W-18S E2
400 PtnT 60468 3860 9W-36S E2
400 PTON 60468 3860 9W-36S E2
S Joliet Rd US-30
10 PNFD 60544 3416 29W-18S D1
200 PNFD 60544 3338 29W-18S C7
300 PNFD 60586 3416 29W-18S E2
W Joliet Rd
13000 WltT 60442 3767 16W-35S E7
W Joliet Rd US-52
13000 WltT 60442 3767 16W-35S E7
Joliet St
10 BlmT 60411 3598 C2
10 DYR 46311 3598 E2
10 WCHI 60185 3080 30W-0S C1
10 WnfT 60185 3080 30W-0S C1
200 DXMR 60426 3349 2W-17S C5
200 WCHI 60185 3022 30W-0S C6
300 LMNT 60439 3270 19W-13S D5
1100 WnfT 60185 3022 29W-0S C7
2200 POSN 60426 3349 2W-17S C5
2200 POSN 60469 3349 2W-17S C5
Joliet St US-30
10 BlmT 60411 3598 C2
10 DYR 46311 3598 E2
N Joliet St
10 JLET 60432 3498 24W-23S E5
10 JLET 60436 3498 24W-23S E5
700 WMTN 60481 3853 27W-38S D5
S Joliet St
10 JLET 60432 3498 24W-24S E5
10 JLET 60436 3498 24W-24S E5
100 WMTN 60481 3853 27W-38S D7
800 JltT 60436 3498 24W-25S E7
800 WMTN 60481 3943 27W-39S D1
1600 JltT 60436 3586 24W-26S E2
W Joliet St
25300 CNHN 60410 3672 31W-30S E4
Jolley Av
2800 WKGN 60085 2536 12W-33N B2
Jo Mar Ct
1700 AraT 60505 3138 34W-5S D3
Jomar Ct
10900 MKNA 60448 3503 13W-23S A3
Jon Ct
300 DSPN 60016 2862 15W-11N A3
Jon Ln
500 DSPN 60016 2808 14W-12N C7
500 DSPN 60016 2862 14W-12N C1
500 MPPT 60056 2808 14W-12N C7
Jon Rd
15700 OKFT 60452 3425 7W-18S B1
Jonamac Av
10200 HTLY 60142 2745 39W-20N D1
Jonathan Ct
100 GNEN 60137 3083 21W-1S D2
100 MltT 60137 3083 21W-1S D2
Jonathan Dr
600 RDLK 60073 2588 23W-30N D1
1100 IVNS 60010 2803 25W-15N E1
1100 SBTN 60010 2803 25W-15N E2
8100 HYHL 60457 3210 10W-10S B5
N Jonathan Dr
400 PLTN 60074 2753 19W-16N C7
Jonathan Ln
300 BtvT 60510 3077 38W-2S A3
18900 HMWD 60430 3508 1W-22S A2
E Jonathan Ln
23700 CteT 60417 3597 3E-29S E7
23700 CteT 60417 3598 3E-28S A7
Jonathan Rd
2600 NndT 60050 2585 31W-30N D2
Jonathan Wy
200 BGBK 60490 3267 27W-12S C3
Jonathan Knolls Ln
39700 WDWH 60083 2419 16W-39N E4
39700 WDWH 60083 2420 15W-39N A4
39900 NptT 60083 2420 15W-39N A4
Jonathan Simpson Dr
3600 JLET 60431 3497 28W-22S A1
3800 JLET 60431 3496 29W-22S D2
Jonathon Ct
800 PTHT 60070 2809 13W-15N A2
1200 WCDA 60084 2588 24W-28N B6
W Jonathon Dr
22700 CNHN 60410 3584 29W-27S E5
Jonathon Ln
- WDSK 60098 2581 41W-28N C5
Jonathon Rd
16700 WrnT 60031 2477 16W-35N C6
W Jones Av
1500 NndT 60051 2586 30W-29N A5
Jones Ct
13300 PNFD 60585 3337 31W-15S E3
15000 OKFT 60452 3348 6W-17S A6
Jones Dr
- WKGN 60085 2536 11W-32N C5
100 BRLT 60103 2909 31W-8N E2
2500 NCHI 60064 2536 11W-32N D5
Jones Rd
- CmgT 60033 2405 51W-39N D4
- HFET 60169 2804 24W-12N D7
- HFET 60195 2858 24W-12N D1
- HRVD 60033 2405 51W-39N D4
- SRGV 60554 3136 41W-7S A7
400 JLET 60447 3495 33W-23S A4
400 SwdT 60447 3495 33W-23S A4
400 TroT 60404 3495 33W-23S A4
1200 HFET 60169 2858 24W-12N D1
1200 SMBG 60169 2858 24W-12N D1
1200 SMBG 60195 2858 24W-12N D1
Jones St
1600 GLHT 60139 2968 23W-3N E6
E Jones St
300 PLNO 60545 3259 47W-14S D6
N Jones St
2500 CHCG 60647 2977 2W-3N B5
W Jones St
10 PLNO 60545 3259 47W-14S C7
900 LtRT 60545 3259 48W-14S C7
1500 JLET 60435 3498 26W-23S A4
Jones Point Rd
1500 GYLK 60030 2533 19W-32N D5
1500 WrnT 60030 2533 19W-32N D5
S Jonesport Cir
13600 PnfT 60544 3339 27W-15S C2
W Jonesport Ct
13800 PnfT 60544 3339 27W-16S C4
Jonester Ct
1400 NPVL 60563 3141 26W-5S E3
Jono Dr
2800 AURA 60504 3201 32W-9S D4
Jonquil Av
600 LSLE 60532 3143 22W-5S C3
E Jonquil Cir
1400 ANHT 60004 2754 16W-16N C7
Jonquil Ct
100 RGMW 60008 2805 22W-13N B5
300 AURA 60504 3139 31W-7S E7
2300 NPVL 60540 3140 29W-7S D7
W Jonquil Ct
10 SMWD 60107 2856 30W-10N C5
Jonquil Dr
- MchT 60097 2469 36W-37N D1
- RMVL 60446 3339 26W-17S E6
Jonquil Ln
2500 WDRG 60517 3205 21W-8S D2
S Jonquil Ln
4500 MONE 60449 3683 5W-31S C5
20100 FKFT 60423 3504 9W-24S D5
Jonquil Ter
400 DRFD 60015 2756 11W-20N D1
700 DRFD 60015 2703 11W-20N D7
7100 HRPK 60133 2911 27W-9N D2
E Jonquil Ter
1600 ANHT 60004 2754 16W-16N C7
1600 ANHT 60004 2807 16W-16N C1
W Jonquil Ter
1400 CHCG 60626 2867 1W-9N C6
6800 NLES 60714 2864 8W-9N E6
7500 PKRG 60068 2864 9W-9N C6
7500 PKRG 60714 2864 9W-9N C6
Joplin Cir
1600 EGVV 60007 2913 21W-8N D2
W Joplin Ct
21700 PnfT 60544 3339 27W-16S D4
Joppa Av
1600 ZION 60099 2421 11W-40N E3
Jordan Av
600 RMVL 60446 3340 24W-15S E1
900 BDWD 60408 3941 32W-41S D4
Jordan Cir
2100 ELGN 60123 2853 36W-12N E2
Jordan Ct
900 WTMT 60559 3145 18W-6S A4
2100 ELGN 60123 2853 36W-12N E1
5600 MHRY 60050 2527 34W-32N B5
Jordan Ln
500 ISLK 60042 2586 29W-29N C4
500 ISLK 60051 2586 29W-29N C4
500 NndT 60051 2586 29W-29N C4
2100 ELGN 60123 2853 36W-12N E1
13500 PNFD 60544 3338 31W-16S A3
17400 HmrT 60441 3420 20W-20S C5
17400 LKPT 60441 3420 20W-20S C5
22000 RNPK 60471 3594 5W-26S C3
Jordan Ter
2000 BFGV 60089 2701 16W-22N D4
2000 VrnT 60089 2701 16W-22N D4
Jordan Wy
500 BGBK 60440 3205 22W-10S B6
Joren Tr
300 ANTH 60002 2357 23W-43N D4
Jorgenson Ct
800 RLKP 60073 2532 23W-33N A3
Jorie Blvd
700 OKBK 60523 3085 16W-2S D4
Jorie Ct
2300 CTHL 60403 3417 27W-21S D6
2300 CTHL 60435 3417 27W-21S D6
Jorstad Dr
- NARA 60506 3076 39W-3S D6
Josef Dr
16000 HMGN 60491 3422 15W-19S B2
Joseph Av
2600 DSPN 60018 2917 12W-8N B2
S Joseph Av
22300 CNHN 60410 3585 28W-27S A5
W Joseph Av
400 PNFD 60544 3338 30W-16S C4
Joseph Cir
1100 JNBG 60050 2472 30W-37N B2
Joseph Ct
- BFGV 60089 2701 16W-21N D5
- VrnT 60069 2701 16W-21N D5
10 LIHL 60156 2694 34W-22N C4
100 BRLT 60103 2909 31W-8N E3
400 BMDL 60157 2913 22W-6N C6
400 OSWG 60543 3199 38W-10S A7
400 OSWG 60543 3263 36W-11S E1
1700 ELGN 60123 2854 36W-11N A4
Joseph Dr
300 SEGN 60123 2908 36W-8N A4
300 SEGN 60177 2908 36W-8N A4
4000 WKGN 60031 2478 13W-37N D3
4000 WrnT 60031 2478 13W-37N D3
Joseph Ln
10 GLHT 60139 2968 23W-2N E7
100 NPVL 60563 3141 27W-5S D2
100 NpvT 60563 3141 27W-5S D2
N Joseph Ln
1300 ADSN 60101 2970 19W-5N C2
Joseph St
10 SchT 60177 2908 35W-7N B6
200 WDSK 60098 2524 41W-32N C4
600 LIHL 60156 2694 34W-22N C4
Josephine Av
100 SEGN 60177 2908 34W-9N D1
Josephine Ct
2300 RGMW 60008 2805 21W-14N D4
2300 RGMW 60067 2805 21W-14N D4
S Josephine Ct
10 DSPN 60016 2862 15W-11N B2
Josephine Dr
- MKNA 60448 3502 14W-22S D2
11700 FftT 60448 3502 14W-22S D2
11800 NlxT 60448 3502 15W-22S C1
Josephine St
8600 MaiT 60016 2863 10W-12N E1
Joseph J Schwab Rd
- DSPN 60016 2863 12W-10N B5
Joshel Ct
1400 GNVA 60134 3020 33W-1N E2
Joshua Ct
- BNHL 60010 2802 28W-13N E5
600 NPVL 60540 3141 28W-7S A7
5300 GRNE 60031 2478 15W-35N A5
Joshua Dr
200 HNWD 60047 2645 22W-27N B1
22300 SLVL 60411 3597 1E-27S C4
22500 FKFT 60423 3592 10W-27S C4
Joshua Ln
2500 NHBK 60062 2809 11W-15N D1
Joshua Tree
300 HRVD 60033 2406 49W-38N C7
Josilyn Ct
1800 LYVL 60048 2590 18W-30N E2
Joslyn Dr
10 ELGN 60120 2855 32W-11N C3
S Jourdan Ct
1900 CHCG 60608 3092 1W-1S A1
Journal Pl
900 DRFD 60015 2703 11W-21N E7
Jovanna Dr
17400 HLCT 60430 3427 3W-20S C5
17400 HMWD 60430 3427 3W-20S C5
Joy Av
3400 GRNE 60085 2536 13W-34N A2
3400 PKCY 60085 2536 13W-34N A2
Joy Ct
- BRRG 60527 3208 15W-10S C5
200 SRGV 60554 3135 42W-7S D7
600 MRGO 60152 2634 49W-25N B4
1000 ANTH 60002 2358 20W-41N E7
Joy Dr
100 BGBK 60440 3205 22W-11S B7
Joy Ln
- LYWD 60411 3509 2E-24S D5
500 SYHW 60118 2799 36W-15N E3
500 SYHW 60118 2800 36W-15N A3
600 ELGN 60124 2799 37W-15N E3
600 SYHW 60124 2799 37W-15N E3
1600 GNVW 60025 2809 11W-14N E4
Joy Rd
10 WnfT 60185 3022 30W-0S C7
Joy St
10 SRGV 60554 3135 42W-7S D7
Joyce Av
10 AddT 60148 3026 19W-2N D1
600 LMBD 60148 3026 19W-1N D2
700 VLPK 60148 3026 19W-1N D1
800 LydT 60164 2972 13W-3N E5
1300 GLHT 60139 2969 22W-2N D7
1600 JNBG 60050 2472 30W-36N A4
1600 MchT 60050 2472 30W-36N A4
E Joyce Av
1200 PLTN 60074 2806 19W-15N C1
N Joyce Av
38700 BHPK 60099 2422 10W-38N A7
Joyce Cir
16200 SHLD 60473 3428 0E-19S E1
Joyce Ct
10 ALGN 60102 2747 36W-18N A4
10 CRTE 60417 3685 1W-30S A2
10 GNEN 60137 3025 22W-0S B7
400 SHLD 60473 3428 0E-19S E1
700 WHTN 60187 3082 25W-2S B3
4900 MHRY 60050 2527 33W-32N D6
W Joyce Ct
21600 PnfT 60544 3339 27W-16S D4
Joyce Dr
1400 DSPN 60018 2862 15W-10N A5
1400 FSMR 60422 3506 4W-23S E3
1400 RchT 60430 3506 4W-23S E3
Joyce Ln
10 SMWD 60107 2856 29W-10N E6
100 CHHT 60411 3508 1W-23S A4
100 LKZH 60047 2698 24W-23N D2
800 ELGN 60120 2855 32W-11N C4
2100 NPVL 60564 3202 29W-10S D7
2100 WldT 60564 3202 29W-10S D7
4600 MHRY 60050 2527 33W-32N E6
11200 WLSP 60480 3208 14W-9S E3
N Joyce Ln
10 ADSN 60101 2971 18W-3N A5
W Joyce Ln
6200 CHCG 60634 2975 7W-5N B1
E Joyce Pl
100 PKRG 60068 2864 9W-9N C6
Joyce Rd
- JltT 60436 3497 27W-25S D7
- RKDL 60436 3497 27W-25S D7
- RKDL 60436 3585 27W-25S D1
- TroT 60436 3497 27W-25S D7
- TroT 60436 3585 27W-25S D1
S Joyce Rd
10 JLET 60435 3497 26W-24S D6
10 JLET 60436 3497 26W-24S D5
Joyce St
10 GNCY 53128 2352 E3
14100 SjnT 46311 3598 E4
Joyce C Ln
1600 AURA 60506 3137 38W-5S B3
Joyce Kilmer Ct
400 CmpT 60175 2962 40W-3N C6
J Pankow Dr
1600 GNVA 60134 3020 36W-1N A4
Juanita Dr
400 WldT 60564 3202 28W-10S E6
400 WldT 60564 3203 28W-10S A6
11700 ODPK 60467 3422 14W-19S D2
11700 OrlT 60467 3422 14W-19S D2
Juanita Ln
- BtlT 60512 3198 41W-11S A7
Juanita Vista
5800 DrrT 60014 2639 37W-26N A3
Jubilant Ct
3600 NPVL 60564 3267 28W-11S A1
N Jubilee Ct
200 HNVL 60030 2532 22W-33N B3
200 HNVL 60073 2532 22W-33N B3
Judd Av
4300 SRPK 60176 2973 12W-5N B1
Judd Ln
400 BTVA 60510 3078 34W-2S C4
400 BtvT 60510 3078 34W-2S C4
Judd St
2000 DRGV 60516 3206 19W-8S E2
2000 DRGV 60561 3206 19W-8S E2
2000 DRN 60561 3206 19W-8S E2
E Judd St
100 WDSK 60098 2524 41W-31N D7
W Judd St
200 WDSK 60098 2524 42W-31N C7
Judge Av
200 WKGN 60085 2536 11W-34N E1
900 WKGN 60085 2479 11W-35N E6
Judge Ct
400 JLET 60433 3587 23W-25S B1
400 JltT 60433 3587 23W-25S B1
9400 SPGV 60081 2413 31W-41N C1
Judge Pl
1300 WKGN 60085 2479 11W-35N E6
Judith Cir
300 OSWG 60543 3199 36W-11S E7
Judith Ct
10 BlmT 60411 3510 3E-25S A7
100 BRLT 60103 2911 28W-8N A3
200 CLSM 60185 2967 28W-4N A4
200 CLSM 60188 2967 28W-4N A4
200 WynT 60185 2967 28W-4N A4
500 WPHR 60096 2363 10W-42N A5
W Judith Ct
21800 PnfT 60544 3339 27W-16S C3
Judith Dr
400 ISLK 60042 2586 28W-28N E5
22800 PNFD 60586 3417 28W-19S A4
22800 PnfT 60586 3417 28W-19S A4
23000 PnfT 60586 3416 28W-19S E4
Judith Ln
10 CHHT 60411 3508 1W-23S A3
100 BlmT 60411 3508 1W-23S A3
E Judith Ann Dr
10 MPPT 60056 2808 15W-13N A5
Judson Av
600 HDPK 60035 2705 7W-21N A7
600 HDPK 60035 2758 8W-20N A1
1000 EVTN 60202 2867 2W-10N C4
1200 EVTN 60201 2867 2W-10N C4
Judson St
10 OSWG 60543 3263 37W-12S B4
100 BNVL 60106 2971 16W-4N E2
Judy Ct
600 ELGN 60123 2854 34W-12N C2
3600 JLET 60431 3497 28W-22S A2
5300 OKFT 60452 3425 6W-20S E4
Judy Dr
800 WMTN 60481 3943 27W-39S E1
1000 EGVV 60007 2913 21W-8N E3
W Judy Dr
18500 WrnT 60031 2476 18W-36N E3
Judy Ln
- HPSR 60140 2796 46W-15N A3
200 SMWD 60107 2857 27W-11N D4
3100 MHRY 60050 2528 32W-32N C4
3300 PKCY 60085 2536 12W-33N A3
3300 WKGN 60085 2536 12W-33N A3
Juel Cir
10 HNWD 60047 2645 21W-24N E7
Juel Dr
10 HNWD 60047 2645 20W-24N E7
10 HNWD 60047 2646 20W-24N A7
Juhlin Dr
18700 HMWD 60430 3507 1W-22S E2
Julep Av
200 OSWG 60543 3264 35W-12S A3
Jules Rd
200 IVNS 60067 2751 23W-16N E7
E Jules St
700 ANHT 60004 2807 17W-15N B2
1000 PTHT 60004 2807 17W-15N B2
Juli Ct
10 SEGN 60177 2908 35W-9N B2
600 SMBG 60193 2859 23W-9N A7
Juli Dr
400 SMBG 60193 2859 23W-9N A7
500 SEGN 60177 2908 35W-9N B2
600 NLNX 60451 3501 17W-23S D4
600 NlxT 60451 3501 17W-23S C4
W Julia Av
800 JLET 60433 3499 22W-24S C5
Julia Ct
1000 GLNC 60022 2758 7W-18N B4
1000 WCDA 60084 2588 25W-28N A6
N Julia Ct
41000 AntT 60002 2416 23W-41N E2
W Julia Ct
2700 CHCG 60647 2977 3W-2N A6
Julia Dr
400 RMVL 60446 3340 25W-15S A3
9300 SjnT 46311 3687 E2

STREET Block	City	ZIP	Map#	CGS	Grid
E Julia Dr					
200	VLPK	60181	3027	17W-0S	B6
S Julia Dr					
1100	VLPK	60181	3027	17W-0S	B6
Julia Ln					
1100	PLNO	60545	3259	48W-12S	B4
Julia St					
200	LMNT	60439	3270	19W-13S	E5
Julia Wy					
1800	LKMR	60051	2529	30W-33N	A2
1900	LKMR	60051	2528	30W-33N	E2
2000	MchT	60051	2528	30W-33N	E2
Julian Av					
10	ELGN	60120	2854	34W-12N	E2
Julian Ct					
900	LslT	60540	3141	26W-7S	E7
900	NPVL	60540	3141	26W-7S	E7
Julian St					
200	WKGN	60085	2537	10W-34N	A1
N Julian St					
10	NPVL	60540	3141	26W-6S	E5
200	TNTN	60476	3428	0E-20S	D5
S Julian St					
10	NPVL	60540	3141	26W-7S	E6
100	TNTN	60476	3428	0W-21S	D6
500	LslT	60540	3141	26W-7S	E6
W Julian St					
1600	CHCG	60622	3033	2W-1N	C1
N Julian Ter					
2600	RVGV	60171	2973	10W-3N	E5
Juliann Dr					
100	WDDL	60191	2970	18W-5N	E1
Julianna Ln					
-	BMDL	60101	2969	22W-4N	D3
-	BMDL	60108	2969	22W-4N	D3
-	BmdT	60101	2969	22W-4N	D3
Julianne Ct					
100	MHTN	60442	3678	18W-31S	A4
Julianne Dr					
100	MHTN	60442	3678	18W-31S	A5
Juliano Ct					
-	BNHL	60010	2749	30W-16N	A7
Julias Courtyard					
16000	TYPK	60477	3425	8W-19S	A2
W Julie Av					
200	PNFD	60544	3416	29W-18S	C1
Julie Ct					
600	JLET	60451	3500	19W-23S	D3
25800	WldT	60585	3265	32W-13S	C6
Julie Dr					
200	IVNS	60010	2751	24W-17N	D4
1900	EGVV	60007	2913	22W-9N	C1
1900	SMBG	60007	2913	22W-9N	C1
1900	SMBG	60193	2913	22W-9N	C1
Julie Ln					
-	BtlT	60512	3198	41W-11S	A7
10	MaiT	60025	2864	9W-12N	C1
10	MaiT	60053	2864	9W-12N	C2
10	MNGV	60053	2864	9W-12N	C2
10	RVWD	60015	2703	13W-22N	A4
10	VNHL	60061	2647	18W-25N	A6
200	HPSR	60140	2795	46W-15N	E3
300	HPSR	60140	2796	46W-15N	A3
1000	CRTE	60417	3597	1E-28S	B7
W Julie Ln					
17600	WrnT	60031	2534	17W-34N	B2
Julie Rd					
100	BGBK	60440	3205	22W-10S	B6
Julie St					
1900	GwdT	60098	2524	41W-32N	E4
1900	WDSK	60098	2524	41W-32N	E5
Julie Ann Ln					
800	ELGN	60120	2855	32W-10N	C5
Julies Wy					
-	ODPK	60462	3423	13W-18S	B1
15500	ODPK	60462	3345	13W-18S	B7
Juliet Av					
10	DPgT	60441	3341	23W-15S	A2
10	DPgT	60446	3341	23W-15S	A2
10	RMVL	60446	3341	23W-15S	A2
Juliet Ct					
100	CNHL	60514	3145	16W-5S	D1
Juliet Dr					
10	PltT	60124	2852	39W-11N	D5
Juliet Ln					
1400	LYVL	60048	2590	18W-30N	E2
1700	LYVL	60048	2591	18W-30N	A3
E Juliette St					
100	TNTN	60476	3428	0E-21S	D6
W Juliette St					
100	TNTN	60476	3428	0E-21S	D6
Juli Lyn Ct					
1400	NHBK	60062	2756	12W-17N	A6
Juli Lyn Ln					
1400	NHBK	60062	2756	12W-17N	A6
Julius Ct					
10	KdlT	60560	3333	43W-17S	B7
W Junction Dr					
21800	PnfT	60544	3339	27W-16S	C4
June Av					
3400	PKCY	60085	2536	13W-34N	A2
June Ln					
100	LMBD	60148	3084	20W-1S	B1
N June St					
2400	JLET	60435	3417	27W-20S	B6
2400	PnfT	60435	3417	27W-20S	B6
June Ter					
400	BRTN	60010	2751	25W-20N	A2
700	LKZH	60047	2698	23W-22N	E4
N June Ter					
10	LKFT	60045	2650	10W-26N	A4
S June Ter					
10	LKFT	60045	2650	10W-25N	A4
W Juneau Ct					
21800	PnfT	60544	3339	27W-15S	C3
W Juneau Dr					
21700	PnfT	60544	3339	27W-16S	D4
Juneberry Av					
6800	WDRG	60517	3143	21W-7S	D7
Juneberry Ln					
13100	HTLY	60142	2744	43W-19N	C2
Juneberry Rd					
300	RVWD	60015	2755	13W-20N	D1
500	RVWD	60015	2702	14W-20N	D7
4000	WldT	60564	3265	31W-13S	E4
4000	WldT	60564	3266	31W-13S	A4
Junebreeze Ln					
3500	WldT	60564	3266	30W-11S	C1
3600	NPVL	60564	3266	30W-11S	C1
Juneway Av					
700	VrnT	60015	2702	15W-20N	A7
700	VrnT	60015	2755	15W-20N	A1
34300	WldT	60481	3943	27W-42S	E6
Juneway Ct					
18000	CCHL	60478	3426	5W-21S	C7
Juneway Ter					
10	LKZH	60047	2698	24W-23N	D1
1200	RLKB	60073	2474	23W-35N	E7
11300	ShdT	60044	2593	11W-29N	D3
11400	NCHI	60044	2593	11W-29N	D3
W Juneway Ter					
1600	CHCG	60626	2867	2W-9N	C6
1800	CHCG	60202	2867	2W-9N	C6
1800	EVTN	60202	2867	2W-9N	C6
1800	EVTN	60626	2867	2W-9N	C6
Jungels Av					
400	AURA	60505	3138	34W-6S	C5
N Junie Ct					
800	JLET	60435	3498	25W-22S	B3
Junior Av					
10	GYLK	60030	2532	20W-32N	E4
Junior Pl					
1500	ELGN	60123	2854	35W-12N	B2
Junior Ter					
1700	DSPN	60016	2863	12W-11N	B3
N Junior Ter					
600	EMHT	60126	2971	17W-3N	C6
W Junior Ter					
600	CHCG	60613	2977	0W-5N	E1
600	CHCG	60613	2978		A1
Juniper Av					
-	ELGN	60120	2855	32W-10N	C7
3400	JLET	60431	3497	28W-22S	A1
3400	PnfT	60431	3497	28W-22S	B1
3800	JLET	60431	3496	29W-22S	D2
20100	LYWD	60411	3510	3E-23S	A4
Juniper Cir					
200	SMWD	60107	2857	27W-10N	C5
200	ALGN	60102	2694	34W-21N	D6
Juniper Ct					
-	LYWD	60411	3510	3E-23S	B3
10	BFGV	60089	2754	17W-18N	B2
10	LIHL	60156	2693	37W-22N	B5
10	SMWD	60107	2857	27W-10N	C5
10	WNVL	60555	3080	30W-1S	C2
100	LKVL	60046	2475	22W-37N	A2
300	CLSM	60188	2968	26W-3N	A5
500	CmpT	60175	2905	41W-6N	E7
800	DRFD	60015	2703	11W-21N	D7
2900	AURA	60502	3079	32W-3S	C7
8200	PSHL	60465	3274	10W-13S	B3
8800	ODPK	60462	3346	11W-17S	A6
8800	TYPK	60487	3424	11W-20S	A5
23500	DRPK	60010	2698	23W-20N	E7
25400	PNFD	60585	3337	31W-15S	D2
W Juniper Ct					
200	FftT	60423	3504	9W-24S	E6
14400	WDWH	60083	2420	14W-38N	C6
21400	LktT	60544	3339	27W-16S	D3
21400	PnfT	60544	3339	27W-16S	D3
Juniper Dr					
10	BmdT	60157	2913	22W-7N	C4
10	NARA	60542	3137	37W-4S	C1
10	ROSL	60157	2913	22W-7N	C4
100	NARA	60542	3077	37W-3S	D7
200	AddT	60191	2971	17W-5N	B2
200	WDDL	60191	2971	17W-5N	B2
500	NPVL	60540	3203	27W-8S	C1
600	LKMR	60051	2529	28W-32N	E5
700	LKMR	60051	2530	28W-32N	A5
E Juniper Dr					
400	PLTN	60067	2753	20W-17N	A5
400	PLTN	60074	2753	20W-17N	A5
1100	MPPT	60056	2808	14W-14N	C4
S Juniper Dr					
10	NARA	60542	3137	37W-4S	D1
Juniper Ln					
100	BMDL	60108	2969	22W-5N	C2
100	MltT	60137	3083	22W-3S	B6
200	BGBK	60440	3205	23W-11S	A7
300	SEGN	60177	2908	35W-8N	B4
400	SMBG	60193	2858	24W-9N	E6
600	BRLT	60103	2910	29W-6N	E6
600	CLLK	60014	2640	33W-25N	D5
600	LIHL	60156	2693	37W-22N	B4
800	NHBK	60062	2757	10W-17N	B4
900	DRN	60561	3207	17W-8S	B2
12000	HMGN	60491	3422	15W-20S	C4
19100	MKNA	60448	3502	15W-23S	C3
20700	ElaT	60010	2698	23W-20N	E7
20800	DRPK	60010	2698	23W-20N	E7
E Juniper Ln					
1100	MPPT	60056	2808	14W-14N	C5
N Juniper Ln					
2000	ANHT	60004	2754	18W-16N	A7
2000	ANHT	60004	2807	17W-14N	C4
W Juniper Ln					
21300	DPgT	60544	3339	26W-16S	D3
21300	LktT	60544	3339	26W-16S	D3
Juniper Pkwy					
300	LYVL	60048	2591	16W-27N	C7
Juniper Rd					
10	RGMW	60008	2806	19W-15N	C3
300	ISLK	60042	2586	28W-28N	E6
600	GNVW	60025	2811	6W-13N	D7
Juniper St					
-	OSWG	60543	3263	36W-13S	E6
100	WKGN	60085	2537	10W-34N	A2
200	PKFT	60466	3595	3W-26S	B3
6800	HRPK	60133	2911	27W-8N	D3
E Juniper St					
800	JLET	60432	3499	22W-22S	C1
N Juniper St					
35200	GRNE	60031	2478	15W-35N	A6
35200	WrnT	60031	2478	15W-35N	A6
Juniper Ter					
200	RLKB	60073	2474	23W-35N	E6
200	RLKB	60073	2475	23W-35N	A6
Juniper Wy					
10	LKVL	60046	2475	22W-37N	A2
Juniper Tree Ct					
300	HFET	60169	2858	24W-11N	E3
Jupiter Ct					
1000	NPVL	60540	3142	26W-6S	A5
21700	FmtT	60060	2589	21W-28N	C6
Juricic Dr					
2500	CTHL	60403	3417	27W-21S	D7
Justamere Rd					
3200	BGBK	60440	3205	22W-9S	C4
3200	LslT	60440	3205	22W-9S	C4
Justen Ln					
-	MchT	60072	2470	33W-36N	E4
-	RGWD	60072	2470	33W-36N	E4
-	RGWD	60072	2471	33W-36N	A3
S Justen Rd					
2300	NndT	60050	2585	31W-29N	D4
2300	PRGV	60012	2585	31W-29N	D4
2300	PRGV	60050	2585	31W-29N	D4
W Justen Rd					
2800	NndT	60050	2585	31W-29N	C3
2800	PRGV	60050	2585	31W-29N	C3
Justice					
-	MTSN	60443	3505	7W-25S	D7
Justice Ct					
1400	SRWD	60404	3496	31W-24S	A6
Justin Ct					
1400	NPVL	60540	3204	24W-8S	C1
3900	WRLK	60097	2469	38W-35N	A5
8000	TYPK	60477	3424	10W-19S	C2
N Justin Ct					
1300	ADSN	60101	2970	20W-5N	B1
S Justin Dr					
26700	CNHN	60410	3761	33W-32S	C1
Justina St					
200	HNDL	60521	3146	14W-4S	C1
300	HNDL	60521	3086	14W-4S	C7
Justine Av					
400	BGBK	60440	3205	22W-11S	D7
Justine St					
14500	HRVY	60426	3349	1W-17S	E5
16100	MKHM	60428	3427	1W-19S	E2
N Justine St					
200	CHCG	60607	3033	1W-0N	D4
S Justine St					
3300	CHCG	60608	3091	1W-3S	D4
4500	CHCG	60609	3091	1W-4S	D7
4700	CHCG	60609	3151	1W-5S	D1
5500	CHCG	60636	3151	1W-6S	D3
7900	CHCG	60620	3213	1W-9S	D2
9400	CHCG	60643	3213	1W-10S	D6
11500	CHCG	60643	3277	1W-13S	D4
12200	CTPK	60827	3277	1W-15S	D7
E Justins Ct					
200	VNHL	60061	2647	16W-27N	C1
K					
K Ct					
10200	MKNA	60448	3503	12W-23S	C4
Kacie Ct					
-	DRN	60527	3145	17W-7S	B6
-	DRN	60561	3145	17W-7S	B6
-	WTMT	60527	3145	17W-7S	B6
Kaelin Rd					
10	WYNE	60184	2966	30W-5N	B3
10	WynT	60185	2966	30W-4N	B5
200	WynT	60184	2966	30W-4N	B5
Kaelynn Ct					
10	SEGN	60177	2908	35W-9N	C1
Kaffel Ct					
10	FKFT	60423	3591	12W-25S	D1
E Kahler Rd					
100	WMTN	60481	3943	27W-39S	E1
900	FrnT	60481	3943	27W-39S	E1
W Kahler Rd					
21400	FrnT	60481	3943	26W-39S	E1
21400	WMTN	60481	3943	26W-39S	E1
Kahler Jr Dr					
2100	DYR	46311	3598		D3
Kaimi Ct					
1600	NPVL	60563	3141	26W-5S	E2
Kaimy Ct					
1500	AURA	60504	3201	32W-9S	C5
Kaindl Dr					
-	HLCT	60429	3427	3W-20S	B4
S Kainer Av					
100	BRTN	60010	2751	25W-18N	B2
Kairy St					
300	ANTH	60002	2357	23W-43N	E4
Kaiser Ct					
700	WldT	60565	3267	27W-11S	C1
W Kaiser Rd					
14500	NptT	60083	2420	14W-40N	C3
14500	WDWH	60083	2420	14W-40N	C3
Kaitlin Ct					
21200	MTSN	60443	3593	7W-25S	C1
Kaitlins Wy					
-	NBRN	60010	2698	25W-21N	B5
Kajer Ln					
1200	LKFT	60045	2649	12W-24N	B7
Kakos Ct					
600	ZION	60099	2362	12W-41N	C7
Kalamazoo Cir					
800	VNHL	60061	2647	18W-25N	A5
Kalamazoo Ct					
900	CLSM	60188	2968	26W-3N	A5
S Kalamazoo Ct					
13500	PnfT	60544	3339	27W-16S	C3
Kalamazoo Dr					
2200	NPVL	60565	3204	26W-10S	A6
Kalarama Dr					
100	NlxT	60451	3501	17W-23S	C4
Kaleigh Ct					
10	SBTN	60010	2803	27W-15N	A1
Kallien Av					
1300	NPVL	60540	3142	25W-6S	B5
Kallien Ct					
1300	NPVL	60540	3142	25W-6S	B5
Kalsow Ln					
-	HTLY	60142	2691	40W-22N	E3
-	HTLY	60142	2692	40W-22N	A3
Kalvelage Dr					
2700	BlmT	60411	3597	3E-26S	E2
2700	SLVL	60411	3597	3E-26S	E2
Kama Av					
2600	MchT	60050	2528	31W-34N	C1
2900	JNBG	60050	2528	32W-34N	C1
2900	MHRY	60050	2528	32W-34N	C1
Kame Ct					
200	LslT	60563	3142	25W-4S	B1
Kame Tr					
-	RGWD	60072	2470	33W-37N	D1
W Kamerling Av					
4000	CHCG	60651	3032	5W-1N	B1
4800	CHCG	60651	3031	6W-1N	E1
Kamiah Ct					
500	CLSM	60188	2967	26W-3N	D6
Kammes Ct					
400	WCHI	60185	3022	29W-0N	D5
400	WnfT	60185	3022	29W-0N	D5
Kammes Dr					
200	LSLE	60532	3142	24W-7S	D7
200	LslT	60532	3142	24W-7S	D7
200	LslT	60540	3142	24W-7S	D7
Kammes Dr E					
-	WynT	60188	3023	27W-2N	D1
Kammes Dr W					
-	WynT	60188	3023	27W-2N	D1
Kamp Ct					
17100	TYPK	60487	3424	10W-20S	B4
Kamp Dr					
-	NHBK	60062	2810	8W-16N	D1
Kanan Ct					
-	OKBK	60523	3085	17W-3S	B5
Kanawha Av					
13800	CHCG	60419	3350	0E-16S	E3
13800	CHCG	60827	3350	0E-16S	E3
13800	DLTN	60419	3350	0E-16S	E3
Kandahar Ct					
1800	WHTN	60187	3082	25W-2S	A3
Kane Av					
10	HGKN	60525	3147	11W-7S	D6
400	ELGN	60123	2854	35W-12N	B2
600	SchT	60174	2908	35W-6N	B6
N Kane Av					
26700	WcnT	60084	2642	28W-26N	E2
W Kane Av					
3600	MHRY	60050	2528	32W-32N	A4
Kane Ct					
10	WLBK	60527	3145	16W-7S	E6
Kane Ln					
-	BtvT	60510	3077	37W-2S	C3
2300	BTVA	60510	3077	37W-2S	C3
Kane St					
10	GNVA	60134	3020	34W-0N	D4
10	SEGN	60177	2908	34W-8N	D2
100	BDWD	60408	3942	31W-41S	A5
600	WDND	60118	2800	34W-16N	E2
700	AURA	60505	3138	34W-7S	C7
1100	AURA	60505	3200	34W-7S	D1
E Kane St					
600	HMND	46320	3352		E7
Kaneville Ct					
200	GNVA	60134	3019	37W-0N	D5
200	GnvT	60134	3019	37W-0N	D5
Kaneville Rd					
10	GnvT	60134	3019	38W-0S	A6
1500	GNVA	60134	3020	36W-1N	A4
1700	GNVA	60134	3019	36W-1N	E4
Kaneville Rd CO-9					
1500	GNVA	60134	3020	36W-1N	A4
1700	GNVA	60134	3019	36W-1N	E4
Kaneville Rd CO-84					
10	GNVA	60134	3019	38W-0S	A6
10	GnvT	60134	3019	38W-0S	A6
E Kaneville Rd					
2400	GNVA	60134	3019	36W-1N	D4
W Kaneville Rd					
1100	GNVA	60134	3020	36W-1N	A3
W Kaneville Rd CO-9					
1100	GNVA	60134	3020	36W-1N	A3
Kankakee Av					
-	BNHM	60633	3352	3E-16S	A3
S Kankakee Rd					
4000	BvlT	60407	4030	33W-46S	C7
4000	GDLY	60407	4030	33W-44S	C4
4000	RedT	60407	4030	33W-46S	C7
6900	EsxT	60935	4030	33W-46S	C7
6900	GflT	60407	4030	33W-46S	C7
N Kankakee St					
-	BDWD	60408	3941	32W-42S	C6
-	RedT	60408	3941	32W-42S	C7
100	WMTN	60481	3853	27W-38S	D5
200	BvlT	60407	4030	33W-43S	C2
200	GDLY	60407	4030	33W-43S	C2
600	BvlT	60407	3941	32W-42S	C7
600	GDLY	60407	3941	32W-42S	C7
600	RedT	60407	3941	32W-42S	C7
1500	WmTp	60481	3853	27W-37S	C4
S Kankakee St					
100	GDLY	60407	4030	33W-43S	C2
100	WMTN	60481	3853	27W-38S	D7
400	BvlT	60407	4030	32W-43S	C3
400	RedT	60407	4030	32W-43S	C3
800	WMTN	60481	3943	27W-39S	D1
23000	MhtT	60442	3589	17W-28S	E6
23000	NlxT	60442	3589	17W-28S	E6
23900	MhtT	60442	3678	16W-30S	E4
26300	MhtT	60442	3767	16W-33S	E3
27100	WltT	60442	3767	16W-33S	E3
E Kankakee River Dr					
300	WMTN	60481	3853	27W-37S	D5
W Kankakee River Dr					
22300	WMTN	60481	3853	28W-37S	B4
22300	WmTp	60481	3853	28W-37S	B4
Kanlow Dr					
5500	NPVL	60564	3266	29W-13S	C5
Kansas Ct					
17900	ODPK	60467	3423	12W-21S	C7
Kansas St					
10	FKFT	60423	3591	12W-26S	D1
10	GNVA	60134	3020	34W-0N	D4
800	CLSM	60188	2968	26W-3N	A5
2600	NCHI	60088	2593	11W-31N	E1
E Kansas St					
100	BbyT	60119	3017	43W-1N	A3
100	ELBN	60119	3017	43W-1N	A3
Kanst Dr					
-	CHCG	60629	3151	3W-7S	A6
Kao St					
100	NndT	60051	2642	29W-27N	D1
Kaplan Ct					
700	LMBD	60148	3026	19W-1N	D2
Kara Ct					
16700	OKFT	60452	3426	6W-20S	A3
Kara Ln					
-	RNPK	60471	3593	6W-27S	E4
Kara St					
-	RNPK	60471	3593	7W-27S	E4
-	RNPK	60471	3594	6W-27S	A4
Karban Rd					
200	OKTR	60181	3085	17W-1S	C2
N Karelia Rd					
34900	WrnT	60031	2477	16W-35N	D7
Karen Av					
200	RMVL	60446	3340	24W-16S	E3
200	RMVL	60446	3341	23W-16S	A3
Karen Cir					
100	BGBK	60440	3269	21W-11S	E1
Karen Ct					
10	HNWD	60047	2646	19W-24N	B7
100	RtdT	60142	2745	41W-18N	B5
600	CRTE	60417	3685	1W-30S	A3
1500	AURA	60504	3201	32W-9S	C5
3200	JLET	60431	3585	28W-25S	B1
N Karen Ct					
37800	GrtT	60081	2472	28W-37N	E1
41000	AntT	60002	2416	23W-41N	D2
Karen Dr					
-	HPSR	60140	2796	46W-15N	B3
200	DndT	60118	2747	35W-19N	D4
1300	WDND	60118	2747	36W-17N	B7
1300	WDND	60118	2800	36W-17N	B1
11000	ODPK	60467	3422	13W-19S	E2
11000	ODPK	60467	3423	13W-19S	A2
S Karen Dr					
1000	JLET	60431	3585	28W-25S	B1
W Karen Dr					
11400	WldT	60585	3265	32W-13S	C5
26000	WldT	60543	3265	32W-13S	C5
26300	WcnT	60084	2643	26W-26N	D3
Karen Ln					
800	NLNX	60451	3501	16W-25S	E7
2700	GNVW	60025	2810	10W-12N	B7
N Karen Ln					
1900	RLKB	60073	2475	23W-35N	A5
W Karen Ln					
10	RLKB	60073	2475	23W-35N	A5
700	PLTN	60067	2752	21W-16N	C6
18500	WrnT	60031	2476	18W-36N	E4
Karen Springs Dr					
16600	LKPT	60441	3420	20W-19S	A3
Karey Ct					
500	WLMT	60091	2812	5W-13N	A6
W Karl Av					
23000	CNHN	60410	3585	28W-27S	A4
Karl Ct					
1200	WCDA	60084	2587	26W-28N	E6
1200	WcnT	60084	2587	26W-28N	E6
Karlens Wy					
1400	JNBG	60050	2472	30W-37N	A2
1400	MchT	60050	2472	30W-37N	A2
Karli Ln					
17500	ODPK	60467	3422	14W-21S	E5
Karli Jean Ct					
8200	FKFT	60423	3592	10W-27S	C5
Karl Madsen Dr					
-	SCRL	60175	3019	38W-2N	B1
Karlov Av					
7400	LNWD	60076	2866	5W-9N	B7
7400	LNWD	60712	2866	5W-9N	B7
9600	SKOK	60076	2866	5W-12N	B1
9900	EVTN	60076	2866	5W-12N	B1
9900	EVTN	60201	2866	5W-12N	B1
14100	CTWD	60445	3348	5W-17S	C5
14200	MDLN	60445	3348	5W-16S	C4
22100	RNPK	60471	3594	5W-27S	D4
N Karlov Av					
10	CHCG	60624	3032	5W-0N	B4
800	CHCG	60651	3032	5W-1N	B2
1500	CHCG	60639	3032	5W-1N	B1
2700	CHCG	60639	2976	5W-3N	B5
2900	CHCG	60641	2976	5W-3N	B4
4500	CHCG	60630	2920	5W-5N	B7
6100	CHCG	60646	2920	5W-7N	B3
6300	CHCG	60712	2920	5W-7N	B3
6800	LNWD	60712	2920	5W-8N	B1
7200	LNWD	60712	2866	5W-9N	B7
7300	LNWD	60076	2866	5W-9N	B7
7300	SKOK	60076	2866	5W-9N	B7
S Karlov Av					
10	CHCG	60624	3032	5W-0S	B5
1100	CHCG	60623	3032	5W-1S	B7
1500	CHCG	60623	3090	5W-1S	B1
3900	CHCG	60632	3090	5W-4S	B6
4600	CHCG	60632	3150	5W-5S	B1
5400	CHCG	60629	3150	5W-7S	C5
7700	CHCG	60652	3212	5W-8S	C1
8600	HMTN	60456	3212	5W-9S	C4
8600	HMTN	60652	3212	5W-9S	C4
9100	OKLN	60453	3212	5W-10S	C5
10200	OKLN	60453	3276	5W-12S	C1
11500	ALSP	60655	3276	5W-13S	C4
11500	ALSP	60803	3276	5W-13S	C4
11500	CHCG	60655	3276	5W-13S	C4
13300	RBBN	60472	3348	5W-15S	C2
Karlskoga St					
200	WHTN	60187	3024	24W-0S	C6
Karner Dr					
1000	JLET	60433	3588	21W-25S	A1
1000	JltT	60433	3500	21W-25S	A7
1000	JltT	60433	3588	21W-25S	A1
Karns Rd					
10	LSLE	60532	3142	25W-5S	C2
10	LSLE	60563	3142	25W-5S	C2
10	LslT	60532	3142	25W-5S	C2
10	LslT	60563	3142	25W-5S	C2
S Karswell Ct					
-	BMDL	60108	2969	23W-5N	A1
Karyn Ct					
1200	SYHW	60118	2800	35W-15N	C4
Karyn Dr					
1300	SYHW	60118	2800	35W-15N	C4
Karyn Ln					
1200	GYLK	60030	2533	19W-32N	C5
Kasey Ct					
3300	JLET	60441	3417	27W-19S	D4
Kashmiri Av					
2600	MchT	60050	2528	31W-34N	D1
Kask Ln					
800	MltT	60187	3082	24W-2S	E4
800	WHTN	60187	3082	24W-2S	E5
Kaskaskia Av					
1300	ELGN	60123	2854	35W-12N	B2
Kaskaskia Ct					
2200	NPVL	60565	3204	26W-10S	A5
N Kaspar Av					
10	ANHT	60005	2806	18W-14N	E4
1500	ANHT	60004	2806	18W-15N	E1
S Kaspar Av					
100	ANHT	60005	2806	18W-13N	E5
1200	ANHT	60005	2860	18W-12N	E1
Kasper Av					
-	GfnT	60014	2638	38W-25N	E5
9300	GfnT	60014	2639	38W-25N	A5
Kasser Ct					
200	DndT	60110	2748	33W-18N	A5
N Kasson Av					
4400	CHCG	60630	2920	5W-5N	B7
Kasson St					
8000	CmgT	60033	2405	51W-40N	D3
8000	HRVD	60033	2405	51W-40N	D3
Kasten Dr					
1400	DLTN	60419	3351	1E-16S	B4
Kasting Ln					
900	MDLN	60060	2590	20W-28N	A5
Kate Dr					
-	YKVL	60560	3333	42W-14S	E1
Kate St					
700	ELGN	60123	2854	34W-10N	D5
Kateland Wy					
600	SEGN	60177	2907	37W-7N	C5
Kates Rd					
-	DRFD	60015	2756	10W-20N	E1
300	DRFD	60015	2757	10W-20N	A1
Kathe Ln					
3000	WKGN	60085	2536	12W-33N	B1
Katherine					
1200	JltT	60433	3499	22W-24S	D7
Katherine Ct					
10	BFGV	60089	2754	17W-18N	A3
Katherine Dr					
300	HNVL	60030	2532	21W-33N	C3
Katherine Ln					
800	HPSR	60140	2796	46W-15N	A3
N Katherine Ln					
600	ADSN	60101	2969	21W-4N	E3

Block	City	ZIP	Map#	CGS	Grid
Katherine St					
500	LKPT	60441	3419	21W-19S	D2
600	SCRL	60174	3019	36W-2N	E1
700	LktT	60441	3419	21W-19S	D2
Katherine Wy					
2700	EGVV	60007	2915	17W-7N	C4
Katherine's Cross					
11200	DPgT	60517	3269	21W-13S	E4
11200	WDRG	60517	3269	21W-13S	E4
W Kathey Ct					
23300	CNHN	60410	3584	29W-27S	E5
S Kathey Dr					
22700	CNHN	60410	3584	29W-27S	E5
Kathi Dr					
-	HPSR	60140	2796	46W-15N	B3
Kathleen					
-	NLNX	60451	3590	16W-25S	A1
Kathleen Av					
10600	HTLY	60142	2692	40W-21N	A6
Kathleen Cir					
2000	MTGY	60538	3198	39W-10S	D5
Kathleen Ct					
300	NBRN	60010	2698	25W-23N	B1
900	WDSK	60098	2581	42W-30N	B1
1200	ANTH	60002	2418	20W-41N	A1
2100	MTGY	60538	3198	39W-10S	D5
3000	HMWD	60430	3507	3W-22S	A1
4800	LGGV	60047	2700	18W-23N	E2
5200	OKFT	60452	3425	6W-20S	E4
10800	PSHL	60465	3274	10W-12S	C2
S Kathleen Ct					
12000	ALSP	60803	3276	4W-14S	C5
Kathleen Dr					
100	ELGN	60123	2854	35W-10N	B5
500	RMVL	60446	3417	27W-18S	D1
1200	ANTH	60002	2359	20W-41N	A7
1200	ANTH	60002	2418	20W-41N	A1
E Kathleen Dr					
10	DSPN	60016	2862	14W-11N	C4
100	PKRG	60068	2864	9W-9N	C6
W Kathleen Dr					
10	DSPN	60016	2862	15W-11N	B4
100	PKRG	60068	2864	9W-9N	B6
700	DSPN	60016	2861	16W-11N	E4
700	MPPT	60016	2861	16W-11N	E4
700	MPPT	60056	2861	16W-11N	E4
800	PLTN	60067	2805	22W-15N	C2
Kathleen Ln					
100	CHHT	60411	3508	1W-23S	A4
2800	FSMR	60422	3507	3W-23S	A4
4200	OKLN	60453	3276	5W-12S	B2
8600	TYPK	60487	3424	10W-20S	B4
Kathleen St					
400	GLBT	60136	2799	38W-15N	C3
Kathleen Wy					
1400	EGVV	60007	2913	21W-8N	E3
1400	EGVV	60007	2914	21W-8N	A3
Kathlyn Pl					
200	JLET	60436	3497	26W-24S	E6
W Kathryn Av					
16000	MhtT	60442	3677	20W-29S	C1
Kathryn Ct					
600	GNOK	60048	2592	14W-29N	B4
700	ANTH	60002	2417	21W-41N	D2
8100	BRRG	60527	3208	15W-9S	B3
W Kathryn Dr					
25800	AntT	60002	2415	25W-39N	E5
25800	AntT	60002	2416	25W-39N	A4
Kathryn Ln					
200	NARA	60542	3077	38W-4S	B7
1200	LKFT	60045	2649	11W-24N	C7
1200	LKFT	60045	2703	11W-24N	C1
5600	MTSN	60443	3505	7W-24S	D5
Kathy Ct					
700	NPVL	60540	3141	28W-7S	A7
1500	AURA	60504	3201	32W-9S	C5
8900	ODPK	60462	3346	11W-16S	A4
10100	MaiT	60016	2809	11W-12N	D7
10100	NfdT	60016	2809	11W-12N	D7
10100	NfdT	60025	2809	11W-12N	D7
S Kathy Ct					
10300	BGVW	60455	3274	9W-12S	D1
10300	PSHL	60455	3274	9W-12S	D1
10300	PSHL	60465	3274	9W-12S	D1
Kathy Ln					
10	ElaT	60047	2645	22W-25N	C5
10	HNWD	60047	2645	22W-25N	B5
500	BRLT	60103	2910	29W-8N	D2
600	SMBG	60173	2859	22W-11N	D3
W Kathy Ln					
8800	MaiT	60016	2863	11W-11N	E2
8800	MaiT	60714	2863	11W-11N	E2
8800	NLES	60016	2863	11W-11N	E2
8800	NLES	60714	2863	11W-11N	E2
21900	ElaT	60047	2645	21W-25N	C5
21900	HNWD	60047	2645	21W-25N	C5
Katie Cir					
1500	ELGN	60123	2854	35W-11N	B4
Katie Ct					
1900	JLET	60435	3417	27W-21S	C7
2500	AURA	60502	3079	32W-4S	B7
8200	FKFT	60423	3592	10W-27S	C5
17500	WrnT	60031	2534	17W-34N	B1
Katie Ln					
-	PLTN	60074	2806	19W-15N	C3
500	BRkT	60511	3134	46W-7S	A7
8200	FKFT	60423	3592	10W-27S	C5
S Katie Ln					
200	MHRY	60050	2528	32W-31N	C6
Katie Rd					
10	LMNT	60439	3342	19W-15S	D2
Katmai Tr					
6200	MHRY	60050	2527	35W-33N	B3
Katrina Ln					
10	SYHW	60118	2800	35W-15N	C4
Katrine					
-	LslT	60516	3143	21W-6S	D4
Katrine Av					
5500	DRGV	60515	3143	21W-6S	D4
5500	LslT	60515	3143	21W-6S	D4
5500	LslT	60516	3143	21W-6S	D4
S Katy Ct					
13600	PnfT	60544	3339	27W-16S	D3
Katy Ln					
8100	ODPK	60462	3346	10W-17S	C4
Kauai King Ct					
1000	NPVL	60540	3142	25W-7S	C7
Kaup Ln					
11600	OrlT	60467	3344	14W-16S	D3
Kautz					
-	SCRL	60174	2965	32W-3N	B5
-	SCRL	60185	2965	32W-3N	B5
-	WCHI	60185	2965	32W-3N	B5
-	WynT	60185	2965	32W-3N	B5
Kautz Rd					
-	AURA	60502	3079	32W-3S	B6
-	AURA	60502	3139	32W-7S	B7
-	AURA	60505	3139	32W-7S	B7
-	AURA	60510	3079	32W-3S	B6
-	BtvT	60502	3079	33W-3S	B5
-	BtvT	60510	3079	33W-3S	B5
-	GnvT	60185	3021	32W-0N	B4
-	WnfT	60510	3079	32W-3S	B6
10	AURA	60502	3201	33W-9S	B3
10	AURA	60505	3201	33W-9S	B3
10	SchT	60174	3021	32W-2N	B2
10	SchT	60185	3021	32W-2N	B2
10	SCRL	60174	2965	33W-3N	B7
10	SCRL	60185	2965	32W-3N	B6
10	WynT	60185	3021	33W-1N	B2
100	GNVA	60134	3021	32W-1N	B4
100	GnvT	60134	3021	32W-1N	B3
100	WCHI	60185	3021	33W-1N	B3
200	SCRL	60174	3021	33W-1N	B2
200	WnfT	60185	3021	32W-1N	B3
300	WynT	60174	2965	32W-3N	B6
300	WynT	60185	2965	32W-3N	B6
600	GnvT	60174	3021	32W-2N	B2
1500	AURA	60504	3201	33W-9S	B5
1700	AURA	60503	3201	32W-9S	B5
Kavalier Ct					
400	SMBG	60194	2857	26W-11N	E5
400	SMWD	60107	2857	26W-11N	E4
S Kay Av					
800	ADSN	60101	2970	19W-2N	D7
900	ADSN	60101	3026	19W-2N	D1
W Kay Av					
400	ADSN	60101	3026	19W-2N	D1
Kay Ct					
10	LIHL	60156	2694	34W-22N	D4
1700	SYHW	60118	2800	35W-15N	C3
S Kay Ct					
17400	PnfT	60586	3415	31W-20S	E6
Kay Dr					
-	JLET	60586	3415	31W-20S	E6
-	PnfT	60586	3415	31W-20S	E6
S Kay Dr					
17200	PnfT	60586	3416	31W-20S	A5
W Kay Dr					
25000	PnfT	60586	3415	31W-20S	E6
25000	PnfT	60586	3416	31W-20S	A6
25100	JLET	60586	3415	31W-20S	E6
Kay Rd					
1600	WHTN	60187	3025	23W-0N	A4
Kay St					
-	CLLK	60098	2638	39W-26N	B2
100	MHTN	60442	3678	18W-31S	A5
S Kay St					
800	PLNO	60545	3259	47W-14S	C7
900	LtRT	60545	3259	47W-14S	C7
W Kay St					
8300	NLES	60714	2864	10W-12N	A1
Kaye Ln					
200	DGvT	60527	3207	16W-10S	D5
Kayjay Dr					
3000	NHBK	60062	2809	11W-15N	D1
Kayla Ct					
-	ALGN	60118	2746	37W-19N	C2
Kayla Dr					
-	ALGN	60118	2746	37W-19N	C2
-	RtdT	60118	2746	37W-19N	C2
Kayla Ln					
4200	NfdT	60062	2756	12W-18N	A4
W Kayla Ln					
1600	WKGN	60087	2479	11W-36N	E3
Kaylee St					
24600	SRWD	60404	3496	30W-25S	B7
Kaylins Wy					
5200	MchT	60072	2470	34W-36N	C3
5200	RGWD	60072	2470	34W-36N	C3
Kaywood Ln					
1400	GNVW	60025	2811	7W-14N	B5
Kazimour Rd					
10	LKBN	60010	2643	27W-25N	A5
10	PTBR	60010	2643	27W-25N	A5
W Kazmer Rd					
14500	NptT	60083	2420	14W-40N	C3
14500	WDWH	60083	2420	14W-40N	C3
Kazwell St					
100	WLSP	60480	3209	12W-9S	C3
Kealsy Ln					
2200	AURA	60503	3201	33W-10S	B6
S Kean Av					
8000	JSTC	60458	3209	11W-9S	E3
8000	JSTC	60480	3209	11W-9S	E3
8000	WLSP	60458	3209	11W-9S	E3
8000	WLSP	60480	3209	11W-9S	E3
8200	HYHL	60457	3209	11W-11S	E7
8200	HYHL	60458	3209	11W-9S	E3
8200	LynT	60480	3209	11W-10S	E6
8300	HYHL	60480	3209	11W-9S	E3
8500	LynT	60457	3209	11W-10S	E6
8500	PlsT	60457	3209	11W-10S	E6
8500	PlsT	60480	3209	11W-11S	E7
9400	PlsT	60465	3209	11W-11S	E7
9400	PSHL	60457	3209	11W-11S	E7
9400	PSHL	60465	3209	11W-11S	E7
10000	PlsT	60465	3273	11W-12S	E1
10000	PlsT	60480	3273	11W-12S	E1
10000	PSHL	60465	3273	11W-12S	E1
S Kean Rd					
-	PSPK	60464	3273	11W-13S	E5
11200	PlsT	60464	3273	11W-13S	E5
Kearney Rd					
100	DGvT	60516	3206	18W-9S	E4
300	DGvT	60439	3206	19W-11S	E7
300	DRN	60516	3206	18W-9S	E4
400	DGvT	60439	3270	19W-11S	E1
9000	DGvT	60561	3206	19W-10S	E6
9000	DRN	60439	3206	19W-10S	E6
9000	DRN	60561	3206	19W-10S	E6
N Kearns Dr					
-	PNFD	60544	3338	29W-17S	D6
1200	PnfT	60544	3338	29W-17S	D6
Kearns St					
10	SchT	60177	2908	35W-7N	B6
S Kearsage Av					
700	EMHT	60126	3028	15W-0S	A5
N Kearsarge Av					
2900	CHCG	60641	2976	5W-3N	B4
Keating Av					
9000	SKOK	60076	2865	5W-11N	E3
14300	CTWD	60445	3348	5W-17S	A5
14300	MDLN	60445	3348	5W-17S	A5
N Keating Av					
1400	CHCG	60651	3032	5W-1N	A1
1500	CHCG	60639	3032	5W-1N	A1
2200	CHCG	60639	2975	5W-2N	E6
2200	CHCG	60639	2976	5W-2N	A6
2800	CHCG	60641	2975	5W-3N	E4
5000	CHCG	60630	2919	5W-6N	E6
6200	CHCG	60646	2919	5W-7N	E3
6300	LNWD	60646	2919	5W-7N	E3
6300	LNWD	60712	2919	5W-8N	E2
7200	LNWD	60712	2865	5W-9N	E7
S Keating Av					
-	HMTN	60456	3212	5W-10S	A5
-	OKLN	60456	3212	5W-10S	A5
4200	CHCG	60632	3090	5W-4S	A7
4600	CHCG	60632	3150	5W-5S	A1
6000	CHCG	60629	3150	5W-7S	A5
7700	CHCG	60652	3212	5W-8S	A1
8600	HMTN	60652	3212	5W-9S	A4
9100	OKLN	60453	3212	5W-10S	A5
10300	OKLN	60453	3276	5W-12S	A1
11000	CHCG	60453	3276	5W-12S	A3
11000	CHCG	60655	3276	5W-12S	A3
Keating Dr					
-	HTLY	60142	2691	40W-22N	E3
-	HTLY	60142	2692	40W-22N	A3
2200	AURA	60503	3201	33W-10S	B5
2200	AURA	60504	3201	33W-10S	A5
W Keating Dr					
1100	ANHT	60005	2806	18W-13N	D6
Keating St					
1600	GLHT	60139	2968	23W-3N	E6
Keats Av					
1300	NPVL	60564	3267	28W-11S	A1
1400	NPVL	60564	3266	28W-11S	E1
Keats Ct					
-	BLVY	60098	2525	39W-31N	C7
700	SMBG	60193	2858	24W-9N	E7
1900	HDPK	60035	2703	10W-22N	E3
Keats Ln					
1800	HDPK	60035	2703	10W-22N	E3
1800	HDPK	60035	2704	10W-22N	A4
Keck Av					
100	AURA	60505	3199	36W-9S	E3
100	AURA	60538	3199	36W-9S	E3
100	MTGY	60538	3199	36W-9S	E3
200	AURA	60505	3200	36W-9S	A3
Kedeka Rd					
200	SgrT	60506	3135	41W-5S	D3
200	SgrT	60554	3135	42W-5S	C3
200	SRGV	60554	3135	42W-5S	D3
Kedron Av					
1500	ZION	60099	2422	10W-41N	B2
Kedron Blvd					
1700	ZION	60099	2422	10W-41N	A2
Kedvale Av					
7400	LNWD	60076	2866	5W-9N	B7
7400	LNWD	60712	2866	5W-9N	B7
9100	OKLN	60453	3212	5W-10S	B5
9600	SKOK	60076	2866	5W-12N	B1
10200	OKLN	60453	3276	5W-12S	C1
14300	CTWD	60445	3348	5W-17S	C5
14300	MDLN	60445	3348	5W-17S	C5
16300	BmnT	60426	3426	5W-19S	C3
16300	OKFT	60452	3426	5W-19S	C3
16400	MKHM	60426	3426	5W-19S	C3
N Kedvale Av					
800	CHCG	60624	3032	5W-1N	B3
1400	CHCG	60651	3032	5W-1N	B1
1500	CHCG	60639	3032	5W-1N	B1
1600	CHCG	60639	2976	5W-2N	B6
4000	CHCG	60641	2976	5W-5N	B1
4300	CHCG	60630	2976	5W-5N	B1
4700	CHCG	60630	2920	5W-6N	B6
5600	CHCG	60646	2920	5W-6N	B5
6300	CHCG	60712	2920	5W-7N	B3
6300	LNWD	60712	2920	5W-7N	B3
7200	LNWD	60712	2866	5W-9N	B7
7300	LNWD	60076	2866	5W-9N	B7
7300	SKOK	60076	2866	5W-9N	B7
S Kedvale Av					
600	CHCG	60624	3032	5W-0S	B6
1200	CHCG	60623	3032	5W-1S	B7
2200	CHCG	60623	3090	5W-2S	B2
4300	CHCG	60632	3090	5W-4S	B7
5400	CHCG	60629	3150	5W-6S	B3
5400	CHCG	60632	3150	5W-6S	B3
8200	CHCG	60652	3212	5W-9S	C3
8600	HMTN	60456	3212	5W-9S	C4
8600	HMTN	60652	3212	5W-9S	C4
11500	ALSP	60655	3276	5W-13S	C4
11500	CHCG	60655	3276	5W-13S	C4
11900	ALSP	60803	3276	5W-14S	C5
13300	RBBN	60472	3348	5W-15S	C2
13800	CTWD	60445	3348	5W-16S	C3
13800	RBBN	60445	3348	5W-16S	C3
W Kedvale Av					
4700	CHCG	60630	2920	5W-5N	B7
Kedvale Ct					
200	BGBK	60440	3268	24W-11S	E1
Kedzie Av					
10	EVTN	60202	2867	2W-10N	C5
700	FSMR	60422	3507	4W-22S	A2
700	HMWD	60430	3507	3W-22S	A1
700	MonT	60466	3684	3W-29S	A2
700	UYPK	60466	3684	3W-29S	A2
800	RchT	60422	3507	4W-22S	A2
1100	FSMR	60430	3507	3W-22S	A2
12700	ALSP	60406	3276	4W-15S	E7
12700	BLID	60406	3276	4W-15S	E7
12700	WthT	60406	3276	4W-15S	E7
12900	WthT	60406	3348	4W-15S	E1
13200	WthT	60472	3348	3W-15S	E1
13300	RBBN	60472	3348	3W-15S	E1
14100	BLID	60406	3348	3W-16S	E4
14100	RBBN	60406	3348	4W-16S	E4
14200	MDLN	60406	3348	4W-16S	E4
14200	RBBN	60445	3348	4W-16S	E4
14300	BmnT	60406	3348	3W-17S	E4
14300	BmnT	60469	3348	3W-17S	E4
14300	MDLN	60469	3348	3W-17S	E4
14900	MDLN	60445	3348	3W-18S	E6
14900	MKHM	60426	3348	3W-18S	E6
14900	MKHM	60428	3348	3W-18S	E6
14900	MKHM	60445	3348	3W-18S	E6
14900	MKHM	60469	3348	3W-18S	E6
14900	POSN	60445	3348	3W-18S	E6
14900	POSN	60469	3348	3W-18S	E6
15300	MKHM	60428	3349	4W-18S	A7
15500	MKHM	60428	3427	4W-22S	A7
16600	HLCT	60428	3427	4W-19S	A3
16600	HLCT	60429	3427	4W-19S	A3
18000	HLCT	60430	3427	4W-21S	A7
18000	HMWD	60429	3427	4W-21S	A7
18000	HMWD	60430	3427	4W-21S	A7
18500	HMWD	60422	3507	3W-22S	A1
19200	RchT	60430	3507	3W-23S	A3
19800	FSMR	60461	3507	3W-23S	A4
19800	OMFD	60461	3507	3W-23S	A4
N Kedzie Av					
10	CHCG	60612	3032	4W-0N	E5
10	CHCG	60624	3032	4W-0N	E5
700	CHCG	60622	3032	4W-0N	D3
700	CHCG	60651	3032	4W-0N	D3
1500	CHCG	60647	3032	4W-1N	D1
1600	CHCG	60647	2976	4W-2N	D7
2700	CHCG	60618	2976	3W-4N	D2
4400	CHCG	60618	2920	3W-5N	D7
4400	CHCG	60625	2920	3W-6N	D6
5500	CHCG	60659	2920	3W-6N	D6
6200	CHCG	60645	2920	4W-8N	D1
6200	CHCG	60712	2920	3W-7N	D3
6200	LNWD	60659	2920	3W-7N	D3
6200	LNWD	60712	2920	4W-8N	D2
6400	LNWD	60645	2920	4W-8N	D2
6900	LNWD	60076	2920	4W-8N	D2
6900	SKOK	60076	2920	4W-8N	D2
6900	SKOK	60645	2920	4W-8N	D2
7200	CHCG	60645	2866	3W-9N	D7
7200	SKOK	60076	2866	3W-9N	D7
7200	SKOK	60645	2866	3W-9N	D7
7400	CHCG	60076	2866	3W-9N	D7
7500	CHCG	60202	2866	3W-9N	D7
7500	EVTN	60076	2866	3W-9N	D7
7500	EVTN	60202	2866	3W-9N	D7
S Kedzie Av					
10	CHCG	60612	3032	4W-1S	E7
10	CHCG	60624	3032	4W-1S	E7
1100	CHCG	60623	3032	4W-0S	E7
1600	CHCG	60623	3090	4W-4S	E7
3500	CHCG	60632	3090	4W-4S	E7
4600	CHCG	60632	3150	4W-8S	E7
5400	CHCG	60629	3150	4W-8S	E7
7300	CHCG	60629	3212	4W-8S	D1
7500	CHCG	60652	3212	3W-9S	E2
8500	ENGN	60652	3212	3W-9S	E4
8500	ENGN	60805	3212	4W-11S	E7
10200	CHCG	60655	3276	4W-12S	E2
10200	CHCG	60805	3276	3W-11S	E1
10200	ENGN	60805	3276	3W-11S	E1
11400	MTPK	60655	3276	4W-13S	E3
11400	MTPK	60803	3276	4W-13S	E3
11800	CHCG	60655	3276	4W-13S	E5
11800	WthT	60803	3276	4W-13S	E5
12200	ALSP	60803	3276	3W-14S	E6
12500	ALSP	60406	3276	3W-14S	E7
12500	BLID	60406	3276	3W-14S	E7
13500	RBBN	60472	3348	3W-16S	E3
14500	MDLN	60445	3348	4W-17S	E5
14500	POSN	60445	3348	4W-17S	E5
14500	POSN	60469	3348	4W-17S	E5
14800	MKHM	60426	3348	3W-17S	E5
14800	MKHM	60428	3348	3W-17S	E5
14800	MKHM	60445	3348	3W-17S	E5
14800	MKHM	60469	3348	3W-17S	E5
W Kedzie St					
7000	NLES	60714	2864	8W-10N	D5
N Keebie Ct					
1200	ADSN	60101	2970	19W-5N	D2
S Keefe Av					
6800	CHCG	60637	3152	0E-7S	D6
Keefe Pl					
-	FXLK	60081	2414	28W-39N	D5
Keel Ct					
4700	LSLE	60532	3142	25W-5S	C2
4700	LslT	60532	3142	25W-5S	C2
Keele Cir					
1500	CPVL	60110	2748	32W-18N	C5
Keele Dr					
1400	CPVL	60110	2748	32W-18N	D5
Keeler Av					
7400	LNWD	60076	2866	5W-9N	B7
7400	LNWD	60712	2866	5W-9N	B7
7800	SKOK	60076	2866	5W-9N	B6
13500	CTWD	60445	3348	5W-16S	C3
13500	CTWD	60472	3348	5W-16S	C3
13500	RBBN	60445	3348	5W-16S	C3
13500	RBBN	60472	3348	5W-16S	C3
14200	MDLN	60445	3348	5W-17S	C6
15000	BmnT	60426	3348	5W-17S	C6
15000	MDLN	60426	3348	5W-17S	C6
18600	CCHL	60478	3506	5W-22S	C1
20900	MTSN	60443	3506	5W-25S	C7
21200	MTSN	60443	3594	5W-25S	C1
N Keeler Av					
100	CHCG	60624	3032	5W-0N	B4
800	CHCG	60651	3032	5W-1N	B2
1500	CHCG	60651	3032	5W-1N	B1
1600	CHCG	60639	2976	5W-2N	B6
3200	CHCG	60641	2976	5W-4N	B2
4300	CHCG	60630	2976	5W-5N	B1
4700	CHCG	60630	2920	5W-6N	B6
6000	CHCG	60646	2920	5W-7N	B3
6300	CHCG	60712	2920	5W-7N	B3
6900	LNWD	60712	2920	5W-8N	B1
7200	LNWD	60712	2866	5W-9N	B7
7300	LNWD	60076	2866	5W-9N	B7
7300	SKOK	60076	2866	5W-9N	B7
S Keeler Av					
-	CHCG	60652	3212	5W-10S	B4
-	HMTN	60652	3212	5W-10S	B4
10	CHCG	60624	3032	5W-1S	B7
1100	CHCG	60623	3032	5W-1S	B7
1500	CHCG	60623	3090	5W-2S	B4
3900	CHCG	60632	3090	5W-4S	B6
4600	CHCG	60632	3150	5W-5S	B3
5400	CHCG	60629	3150	5W-7S	B6
8700	HMTN	60456	3212	5W-10S	B4
9100	OKLN	60453	3212	5W-11S	B7
10700	OKLN	60453	3276	5W-12S	C2
11000	OKLN	60655	3276	5W-12S	C3
11500	ALSP	60655	3276	5W-13S	C4
11500	CHCG	60655	3276	5W-13S	C4
11900	ALSP	60803	3276	5W-14S	C5
Keeley Ln					
-	WmTp	60408	3942	30W-39S	C1
-	WmTp	60481	3942	30W-39S	C1
31600	WMTN	60481	3853	29W-38S	A7
31600	WmTp	60481	3853	29W-38S	A7
S Keeley St					
2800	CHCG	60608	3091	1W-2S	E3
Keels Ct					
2200	ELGN	60123	2908	36W-9N	A1
Keenan Ln					
900	BCHR	60401	3864	0W-36S	D1
3400	GNVW	60025	2809	10W-15N	E3
3400	GNVW	60025	2810	10W-15N	A3
3700	GNVW	60062	2809	10W-15N	E3
Keene Av					
700	OSWG	60543	3264	35W-12S	B2
2900	NndT	60050	2585	30W-29N	E5
N Keene Av					
6200	CHCG	60646	2919	5W-7N	E3
6200	CHCG	60646	2920	5W-7N	A3
Keene Ln					
5200	HRPK	60133	2911	26W-6N	E6
Keenehand Ct					
4400	RNPK	60471	3594	5W-26S	B3
Keeneland Ct					
10	GYLK	60030	2532	21W-34N	E1
Keeney Av					
3200	STGR	60475	3596	0W-27S	C5
Keeney Ct					
5900	MNGV	60053	2865	7W-10N	B5
Keeney Rd					
10	BMDL	60108	2912	25W-6N	B7
10	BmdT	60108	2912	25W-6N	B7
10	BmdT	60172	2912	25W-6N	B7
400	ROSL	60172	2912	25W-6N	B7
Keeney St					
100	EVTN	60202	2867	2W-10N	B5
1900	EVTN	60202	2866	3W-10N	E5
3800	SKOK	60076	2866	5W-10N	A5
4700	SKOK	60076	2865	5W-10N	E5
5300	MNGV	60077	2865	6W-10N	D5
5300	SKOK	60077	2865	6W-10N	D5
5700	MNGV	60053	2865	7W-10N	C5
W Keeney St					
6800	MNGV	60053	2864	8W-10N	E5
6800	NLES	60714	2864	8W-10N	E5
Keenland Dr					
1300	BRLT	60103	2966	29W-5N	D1
Keep Av					
600	ELGN	60120	2855	33W-12N	B1
Keepataw Ct					
10	LMNT	60439	3270	19W-14S	E6
Keepataw Dr					
400	LMNT	60439	3270	19W-14S	E6
Keepataw Ln					
10	LMNT	60439	3270	19W-14S	E7
Kees Ln					
10	LtRT	60545	3330	49W-15S	D2
Kehm Blvd					
3300	PKCY	60085	2536	13W-33N	A3
Kehoe Blvd					
100	CLSM	60188	2968	25W-2N	B7
400	CLSM	60188	3024	24W-2N	C1
400	GLHT	60139	3024	24W-2N	C1
400	GLHT	60188	3024	24W-2N	C1
Kehoe Dr					
800	SCRL	60174	3020	36W-2N	A1
Keierleber Rd					
-	OswT	60543	3264	35W-12S	B3
Keil Rd					
10	WCHI	60185	2965	32W-3N	D6
10	WynT	60185	2965	32W-3N	D6
Keil St					
300	WYNE	60184	2965	32W-5N	D2
Keilman St					
100	DYR	46311	3598		D2
Keim Blvd					
-	PNFD	60544	3416	30W-18S	C1
Keim Cir					
1400	GNVA	60134	3019	36W-0N	E5
1400	GNVA	60134	3020	36W-0N	A5
Keim Ct					
1000	GNVA	60134	3019	36W-0N	E5
1500	SCRL	60174	2964	34W-4N	D4
1900	NPVL	60565	3204	25W-9S	C4
Keim Dr					
300	MltT	60187	3081	26W-2S	E4
300	WHTN	60187	3081	26W-2S	E4
2000	AURA	60503	3201	33W-10S	B6
2000	NPVL	60565	3204	25W-9S	C5
Keim Rd					
2200	NPVL	60565	3204	25W-10S	C6
4200	LSLE	60532	3082	23W-4S	E7
Keim Tr					
1000	SCRL	60174	2964	34W-4N	D5
1100	BRLT	60103	2910	29W-6N	E7
Keith Av					
-	WkgT	60085	2479	12W-35N	A5
300	CLLK	60014	2640	35W-25N	A5
2400	JLET	60435	3417	27W-20S	D4
2400	PnfT	60435	3417	27W-20S	D4
3400	GRNE	60031	2479	13W-35N	A5
3400	WkgT	60031	2479	13W-35N	A5
3700	GRNE	60031	2478	13W-35N	E5
3700	WrnT	60031	2478	13W-35N	E5
E Keith Av					
100	WKGN	60085	2480	10W-35N	B5
W Keith Av					
-	WkgT	60085	2479	12W-35N	C5
300	WKGN	60085	2480	10W-35N	A5
1100	WKGN	60085	2479	11W-35N	E5
12800	WkgT	60031	2479	12W-35N	B5
Keith Ct					
2300	RGMW	60008	2805	20W-14N	E4
Keith Dr					
5000	RNPK	60471	3594	6W-27S	A4
E Keith Dr					
3900	RcmT	60071	2413	32W-40N	A2
N Keith Dr					
28100	LbvT	60045	2592	13W-28N	D7
Keith Ln					
10	LKFT	60045	2650	9W-25N	B5
Keith Allen Dr					
23900	JknT	60421	3675	24W-29S	E1
23900	JLET	60421	3675	24W-29S	E1
Keithland Ct					
100	NLNX	60451	3501	17W-24S	C5
Kelberg Av					
1700	HFET	60192	2855	31W-12N	E1
Kelburn Rd					
300	DRFD	60015	2756	10W-20N	E1
300	DRFD	60015	2757	10W-20N	A1
Kellar Ct					
-	BbyT	60119	3018	39W-0S	D7
-	BbyT	60134	3018	39W-0S	D7
Kellar Pl					
10	SCRL	60174	3020	35W-2N	B1
Kellar Sq					
-	BbyT	60134	3018	39W-0S	D6
Kelle Ct					
1200	WHTN	60187	3082	23W-3S	E5
Keller Av					
10	WKGN	60085	2536	11W-33N	C2
Keller Ct					
10	BGBK	60440	3204	24W-10S	D5
Keller Dr					
400	PKCY	60085	2535	13W-33N	E2
3600	PKCY	60085	2536	13W-33N	A2
6000	BRRG	60527	3146	15W-6S	A5
Keller Ln					
3200	WldT	60565	3203	27W-11S	C7
Keller Pkwy					
700	WKGN	60085	2536	11W-33N	C3
Keller St					
-	LtRT	60545	3260	45W-13S	C5
-	PLNO	60545	3260	45W-13S	C5
300	LSLE	60563	3142	24W-5S	C2
300	LslT	60563	3142	24W-5S	C2

STREET Block	City	ZIP	Map#	CGS	Grid
Keller St					
4900	LSLE	60532	3142	24W-5S	C2
4900	LslT	60532	3142	24W-5S	C2
Kelley Ct					
1900	LYVL	60048	2590	18W-30N	D2
Kelley Dr					
1700	HFET	60192	2856	30W-12N	C1
Kelley Rd					
10	HPSR	60140	2743	46W-17N	A7
10	HshT	60140	2743	46W-17N	A7
N Kelley Rd					
38700	AntT	60081	2415	27W-38N	B6
38700	FXLK	60081	2415	27W-38N	B6
Kelli Ann Cir					
-	LKVL	60046	2474	23W-37N	E2
Kelling Ln					
300	GLNC	60022	2758	7W-18N	C3
Kellog					
10	CLLK	60014	2639	36W-25N	E4
Kellogg Av					
1800	WKGN	60085	2479	11W-36N	D5
1800	WKGN	60087	2479	11W-36N	D5
Kellogg Ct					
-	BtnT	60099	2422	9W-41N	C1
-	WPHR	60096	2422	9W-41N	C1
Kellogg Pl					
100	WHTN	60187	3024	23W-0S	E6
Kellogg St					
2400	CTHL	60403	3417	27W-20S	D6
2400	PnfT	60403	3417	27W-20S	D6
2400	PnfT	60435	3417	27W-20S	D6
2500	JLET	60435	3417	27W-20S	D6
Kells Dr					
8700	HYHL	60457	3210	10W-10S	A6
Kelltowne Ct					
3200	WldT	60565	3203	27W-11S	C7
Kelly Av					
400	YKVL	60560	3333	44W-15S	A3
500	GYLK	60030	2532	21W-33N	D3
1600	CTHL	60403	3498	24W-21S	D1
1600	JLET	60435	3498	24W-21S	D1
1700	CTHL	60403	3418	24W-21S	D7
N Kelly Av					
800	JLET	60435	3498	24W-22S	D2
Kelly Ct					
-	MltT	60187	3023	26W-0N	E4
-	MltT	60190	3023	26W-0N	E4
-	ROSL	60172	2912	24W-6N	D6
-	WNFD	60187	3023	26W-0N	E4
-	WNFD	60190	3023	26W-0N	E4
500	LMBD	60148	3026	18W-0N	E5
1300	BTVA	60510	3078	33W-2S	E5
1800	DRN	60559	3144	18W-7S	E7
1800	DRN	60561	3144	18W-7S	E7
3000	AURA	60504	3201	31W-9S	D5
5300	CPVL	60110	2747	36W-18N	A5
8300	WDRG	60517	3205	21W-9S	E4
9200	ODHL	60487	3423	11W-19S	E2
25800	WldT	60543	3265	32W-13S	C6
25800	WldT	60585	3265	32W-13S	C6
N Kelly Ct					
400	RMVL	60446	3340	25W-15S	B3
Kelly Dr					
-	NARA	60506	3076	39W-3S	D6
-	NARA	60542	3076	39W-3S	D6
800	CLSM	60188	2967	27W-4N	D4
2500	WDRG	60517	3205	21W-9S	E4
2900	ElgT	60124	2853	37W-10N	C7
Kelly Ln					
300	CLLK	60012	2640	33W-26N	E2
2600	HDPK	60035	2703	11W-23N	E2
33200	GrtT	60041	2530	27W-33N	C3
33200	VOLO	60041	2530	27W-33N	C3
Kelly Pl					
7200	DRGV	60516	3206	20W-8S	B1
Kelly Rd					
-	NptT	60083	2419	17W-40N	C4
-	OMCK	60083	2419	17W-40N	C4
4600	ISLK	60042	2642	29W-27N	C1
4600	ISLK	60051	2642	29W-27N	C1
4600	NndT	60042	2642	29W-27N	C1
4600	NndT	60051	2642	29W-27N	C1
27400	CnhT	60481	3761	32W-34S	E5
27400	WmTp	60481	3761	32W-34S	E6
W Kelly Rd					
-	NptT	60046	2418	19W-39N	E4
4700	LkvT	60046	2418	19W-40N	C4
15800	NptT	60083	2419	16W-40N	E4
15800	NptT	60083	2420	15W-40N	A4
15800	WDWH	60083	2419	15W-39N	E4
15800	WDWH	60083	2420	15W-40N	A4
17300	OMCK	60083	2419	17W-40N	B4
17500	OMCK	60083	2418	18W-40N	E4
19000	AntT	60046	2418	19W-40N	D4
19000	OMCK	60046	2418	19W-40N	D4
Kelly St					
10	EGVV	60007	2861	18W-10N	A5
2200	PNFD	60544	3338	30W-16S	C4
W Kelly St					
1200	ANHT	60004	2753	18W-16N	D6
W Kelly Ann Dr					
800	PLTN	60067	2805	22W-15N	C2
Kelly Ann Ln					
21600	TroT	60404	3584	30W-26S	C3
N Kelly Cain Ct					
2100	RLKB	60046	2475	21W-36N	C5
Kelly Farm Dr					
-	BRLT	60103	2967	28W-4N	A3
N Kelsey Av					
23000	CbaT	60010	2696	28W-23N	D2
Kelsey Ct					
10	SEGN	60177	2908	35W-7N	C4
W Kelsey Ct					
28400	CbaT	60010	2696	28W-23N	E2
Kelsey Ln					
17500	ODPK	60467	3422	14W-21S	D6
17500	OrlT	60467	3422	14W-21S	D6
Kelsey Pt					
28500	LKBN	60010	2696	28W-22N	E4
Kelsey Rd					
200	LKBN	60010	2643	26W-24N	C6
200	TRLK	60010	2643	26W-24N	C6
Kelsey Rd CO-V49					
200	LKBN	60010	2643	26W-24N	C6
200	TRLK	60010	2643	26W-24N	C6
N Kelsey Rd					
22000	CbaT	60010	2696	28W-22N	E4
22000	LKBN	60010	2696	28W-22N	E4
23500	LKBN	60010	2697	28W-23N	A1
23800	CbaT	60010	2697	28W-23N	A1
24100	CbaT	60010	2643	26W-24N	D6
24100	LKBN	60010	2643	27W-24N	B7
24300	TRLK	60010	2643	26W-24N	D6
N Kelsey Rd CO-V49					
22000	CbaT	60010	2696	28W-22N	E4
22000	LKBN	60010	2696	28W-22N	E4
23500	LKBN	60010	2697	28W-23N	A1
23800	CbaT	60010	2697	28W-23N	A1
24100	CbaT	60010	2643	26W-24N	D6
24100	LKBN	60010	2643	27W-24N	B7
24300	TRLK	60010	2643	26W-24N	D6
N Kelso Av					
4600	CHCG	60630	2920	5W-5N	B7
Kelso Glen Ct					
700	IVNS	60010	2751	23W-16N	D6
700	IVNS	60067	2751	23W-16N	D6
Kelvin Ln					
9400	SRPK	60176	2917	11W-6N	C7
Kemah Ct					
700	SMBG	60193	2858	24W-10N	D6
Kemah Ln					
200	SMBG	60193	2858	24W-10N	D6
Kemble Av					
1400	NCHI	60064	2536	11W-32N	D6
1400	WKGN	60085	2536	11W-32N	D6
2300	NCHI	60064	2593	12W-31N	C1
2300	NCHI	60088	2593	12W-31N	C1
Kemman Av					
-	BDVW	60155	3087	11W-2S	D3
-	BDVW	60525	3087	11W-2S	D3
-	PvsT	60155	3087	11W-2S	D3
100	BKFD	60513	3087	12W-3S	C4
100	BKFD	60525	3087	12W-3S	C4
100	LGNG	60513	3087	12W-3S	C4
100	LGNG	60525	3087	12W-3S	C4
100	LGPK	60525	3087	12W-3S	C4
1000	LGPK	60513	3087	11W-3S	C4
1500	PvsT	60525	3087	11W-2S	D3
Kemman Rd					
6600	GwdT	60034	2468	39W-38N	B1
6600	GwdT	60098	2468	39W-38N	B1
6600	HbnT	60034	2468	39W-38N	B1
9600	HbnT	60034	2351	40W-41N	B7
Kemmerer Ln					
2100	BGBK	60490	3339	28W-15S	B1
Kemper Dr					
-	ElaT	60047	2700	20W-23N	A2
-	HNWD	60047	2700	20W-23N	A1
-	KLDR	60047	2699	20W-23N	E3
-	KLDR	60047	2700	20W-23N	A1
10	ElaT	60047	2699	20W-23N	E3
1600	NPVL	60563	3140	30W-5S	A2
1600	NpvT	60563	3140	30W-5S	A2
15500	ODPK	60462	3346	11W-18S	A7
Kemper Ln					
10800	FftT	60423	3591	13W-27S	A5
W Kemper Pl					
600	CHCG	60614	2978	0W-2N	A6
Kempton Dr					
10	RMVL	60446	3340	24W-16S	E5
1300	LYVL	60048	2647	15W-27N	E1
1300	LYVL	60048	2648	15W-27N	A1
Kempton St					
-	JLET	60431	3495	33W-22S	B1
Ken Rd					
24000	DhmT	60033	2405	53W-37N	A7
Kenard Ct					
100	BDWD	60408	3941	32W-41S	E5
N Kenard St					
100	BDWD	60408	3941	32W-41S	E5
S Kenard St					
100	BDWD	60408	3941	32W-41S	E6
100	RedT	60408	3941	32W-41S	E6
N Kendal Ct					
1500	ANHT	60004	2807	16W-15N	C2
Kendal Rd					
10	EGVV	60007	2914	19W-8N	D2
Kendale Ln					
1700	GNVW	60025	2810	8W-14N	E4
Kendall Av					
500	EMHT	60126	3028	15W-0S	A6
500	YkTp	60126	3028	15W-0S	A6
W Kendall Av					
-	BtnT	60081	2472	28W-38N	D1
-	MchT	60081	2472	28W-38N	D1
28500	AntT	60081	2472	28W-37N	E1
28500	GrtT	60081	2472	28W-37N	E1
Kendall Cross					
-	JNBG	60050	2471	32W-34N	C7
-	JNBG	60050	2528	32W-34N	C1
Kendall Ct					
-	BFGV	60089	2701	16W-21N	C6
-	LYWD	60411	3509	2E-23S	D3
100	BMDL	60108	2969	23W-4N	B3
600	SMBG	60194	2857	28W-12N	B2
E Kendall Dr					
10	YKVL	60560	3261	42W-13S	C6
S Kendall Dr					
13600	PnfT	60544	3339	27W-16S	C3
W Kendall Dr					
100	YKVL	60560	3261	43W-13S	B6
Kendall Ln					
8600	ODPK	60462	3346	10W-18S	B7
Kendall Rd					
10	PltT	60124	2851	43W-10N	C7
10	PltT	60124	2905	43W-8N	C3
Kendall St					
800	GNVA	60134	3020	35W-0N	B5
900	ELBN	60119	3017	43W-0N	A5
10100	AlqT	60102	2695	33W-21N	A5
10200	AlqT	60102	2694	33W-21N	E5
N Kendall St					
10	AURA	60504	3200	34W-7S	E1
10	AURA	60505	3200	34W-7S	E1
100	AURA	60505	3138	34W-7S	E7
S Kendall St					
10	AraT	60504	3200	34W-8S	E2
10	AURA	60504	3200	34W-8S	E2
10	AURA	60505	3200	34W-8S	E2
W Kendall Ter					
1000	ADSN	60101	2970	19W-3N	C4
Kendall on Oxford					
10	RGMW	60008	2805	22W-13N	B6
Kendall Point Dr					
-	OSWG	60543	3264	34W-11S	C1
10	OSWG	60543	3200	34W-10S	C7
Kendall Ridge Blvd					
-	JLET	60431	3495	33W-21S	B1
-	NasT	60586	3495	33W-21S	B1
1700	JLET	60586	3495	33W-21S	B1
1800	JLET	60586	3415	33W-21S	B7
Kendallwood Ct					
600	CLLK	60014	2639	36W-24N	D7
Kendallwood Dr					
900	CLLK	60014	2639	36W-24N	D7
Kendler Ct					
700	LKFT	60045	2650	9W-25N	B6
Kendon Ct					
-	HMGN	60491	3344	15W-17S	B5
Kendrick Ct					
200	SMBG	60194	2858	24W-10N	C5
Kendridge Ct					
600	AURA	60502	3139	32W-7S	C6
Kendridge Ln					
2500	AURA	60502	3139	32W-7S	D6
Kendron Blvd					
2400	BtnT	60099	2422	9W-41N	C1
2400	ZION	60099	2422	9W-41N	C1
Kenicott Ln					
7300	JLET	60586	3495	33W-21S	B1
Kenilwood Ct					
1300	RVWD	60015	2702	13W-21N	E5
Kenilwood Ln					
1300	RVWD	60015	2702	13W-21N	E6
Kenilworth Av					
-	KLWH	60091	2812	4W-14N	C5
-	WLMT	60043	2812	4W-14N	C5
10	EGVV	60007	2914	19W-8N	D3
10	GNEN	60137	3025	23W-0S	A7
10	KLWH	60043	2812	4W-14N	C5
10	LktT	60446	3339	26W-17S	E5
10	LktT	60544	3339	26W-17S	E5
10	RMVL	60446	3339	26W-17S	E5
400	MltT	60137	3083	23W-2S	A4
500	EDND	60118	2801	33W-16N	A1
500	GNEN	60137	3083	23W-1S	A2
500	WHTN	60187	3024	24W-0S	D6
600	SEGN	60177	2908	35W-9N	C2
900	JLET	60435	3498	25W-22S	B2
900	MltT	60137	3025	23W-1N	A3
1200	BRWN	60304	3030	8W-1S	E7
1200	BRWN	60402	3030	8W-1S	E7
1200	OKPK	60304	3030	8W-1S	E7
1500	BRWN	60402	3088	8W-1S	E1
1900	WLMT	60091	2812	4W-14N	B4
2400	HHLL	60051	2586	30W-29N	B3
2600	NtrT	60093	2812	5W-14N	A4
2600	WLMT	60093	2812	5W-14N	A4
4300	SKNY	60402	3088	8W-4S	E7
4400	FTVW	60402	3088	8W-4S	E7
4500	FTVW	60402	3148	8W-4S	E1
E Kenilworth Av					
10	VLPK	60181	3027	17W-0N	B4
300	PTHT	60070	2808	15W-15N	B1
300	PTHT	60090	2808	15W-15N	B1
300	WLNG	60090	2808	15W-15N	B1
1000	LMBD	60148	3026	18W-0N	E4
1100	LMBD	60181	3026	18W-0N	E4
1100	VLPK	60181	3026	18W-0N	E4
1200	PLTN	60074	2806	19W-15N	C1
N Kenilworth Av					
10	MPPT	60056	2807	16W-13N	D7
100	OKPK	60301	3030	8W-0N	E3
100	OKPK	60302	3030	8W-0N	E3
300	EMHT	60126	3028	15W-2N	A1
500	EMHT	60126	2972	15W-2N	A6
S Kenilworth Av					
100	EMHT	60126	3028	15W-0N	A4
100	MPPT	60056	2807	16W-12N	D7
100	MPPT	60056	2861	16W-12N	D1
100	OKPK	60302	3030	8W-0N	E5
200	GNEN	60137	3025	23W-0S	A6
400	OKPK	60304	3030	8W-0S	E5
1100	BRWN	60304	3030	8W-0S	E7
1100	BRWN	60402	3030	8W-0S	E7
2500	NndT	60051	2586	30W-29N	B4
W Kenilworth Av					
10	PTHT	60070	2807	15W-15N	E2
10	PTHT	60070	2808	15W-15N	A1
10	VLPK	60181	3027	18W-0N	A4
300	LMBD	60148	3026	18W-0N	E3
300	PLTN	60067	2805	22W-15N	B1
300	VLPK	60181	3026	18W-0N	E3
400	PltT	60067	2805	22W-15N	B1
1300	IVNS	60067	2805	22W-15N	A1
Kenilworth Av N					
900	OKPK	60302	3030	8W-1N	E2
1200	CHCG	60302	3030	8W-1N	E1
1200	CHCG	60707	3030	8W-1N	E1
Kenilworth Cir					
900	NPVL	60540	3142	25W-7S	B7
900	NPVL	60540	3204	25W-7S	B1
1900	HFET	60169	2804	25W-12N	B7
1900	HFET	60169	2858	25W-12N	B1
Kenilworth Ct					
10	CRY	60013	2642	30W-25N	A5
10	LMBD	60148	3026	18W-0N	E3
10	RMVL	60446	3339	26W-17S	E5
200	GNEN	60137	3025	23W-0N	A4
400	DSPN	60016	2862	14W-11N	C4
500	GYLK	60030	2533	20W-33N	A3
600	GYLK	60030	2532	20W-33N	E2
Kenilworth Dr					
200	BGBK	60440	3269	22W-11S	C1
400	SMBG	60193	2859	22W-10N	B6
1000	WLNG	60090	2754	16W-18N	E3
1300	CTCY	60409	3430	4E-19S	C3
4600	RGMW	60008	2806	19W-12N	C7
4600	RGMW	60008	2860	19W-11N	B2
Kenilworth Ln					
-	MTGY	60538	3198	41W-9S	A5
1300	GNVW	60025	2811	8W-14N	A4
1400	GNVW	60025	2810	8W-14N	E4
Kenilworth Pl					
800	AURA	60506	3199	36W-7S	D1
E Kenilworth Rd					
500	PLTN	60067	2806	20W-15N	A1
500	PLTN	60074	2806	20W-15N	A1
Kenilworth St					
900	RLKB	60073	2532	23W-34N	A1
1000	RLKB	60073	2475	23W-34N	A7
Kenilworth Ter					
600	KLWH	60043	2812	4W-14N	C4
600	WLMT	60091	2812	4W-14N	C4
900	LKZH	60047	2698	24W-23N	C2
Kenloch Av					
100	LYVL	60048	2591	17W-28N	B5
Kenmar Ct					
100	BbyT	60119	3017	43W-0S	A6
Kenmar Dr					
10	BbyT	60119	3017	43W-0S	A6
10	ELBN	60119	3017	43W-0S	B7
Kenmar Ln					
10	BbyT	60119	3017	43W-0S	B6
Kenmare Ct					
600	DSPN	60016	2808	13W-13N	D6
Kenmare Dr					
600	DSPN	60016	2808	13W-13N	D6
1000	BRRG	60527	3146	15W-7S	B6
20900	SRWD	60404	3584	30W-25S	B1
Kenmore Av					
-	AraT	60504	3138	34W-5S	C3
-	AURA	60504	3138	34W-5S	C3
10	JltT	60433	3500	21W-24S	A5
400	DRFD	60015	2756	11W-20N	C1
800	AURA	60505	3138	34W-6S	C5
1200	JLET	60435	3498	25W-22S	B2
1600	AraT	60505	3138	34W-5S	C3
N Kenmore Av					
500	ADSN	60101	2970	21W-4N	A4
2000	CHCG	60614	2977	1W-2N	E6
2700	CHCG	60657	2977	1W-3N	E5
3700	CHCG	60613	2977	1W-4N	E2
4200	CHCG	60613	2921	1W-5N	E7
4500	CHCG	60640	2921	1W-5N	E7
5500	CHCG	60660	2921	1W-6N	E5
6300	CHCG	60626	2921	1W-7N	E4
S Kenmore Av					
100	EMHT	60126	3028	15W-1N	A3
Kenmore Cir					
15200	MHTN	60442	3678	19W-30S	A3
15300	MHTN	60442	3677	19W-30S	E3
Kenmore Ct					
2400	SMBG	60193	2857	26W-10N	E6
Kenmore Dr					
200	BGBK	60440	3269	22W-12S	C2
Kenmore Ln					
100	FmtT	60060	2646	19W-26N	C3
N Kenmore Rd					
38500	AntT	60002	2415	26W-38N	E6
Kenmore St					
500	BmdT	60148	2970	21W-2N	A7
1300	RLKB	60073	2475	22W-35N	B6
7600	LMBD	60148	3026	21W-1N	A1
7600	MltT	60148	3026	21W-1N	A2
Kennard St					
600	WKGN	60085	2537	10W-33N	B3
Kennebec Ln					
900	NPVL	60563	3141	26W-5S	E2
1000	NPVL	60563	3142	26W-5S	A2
Kennebunk Ct					
100	GLHT	60139	3025	22W-1N	B2
Kennedy Av					
1500	BTVA	60510	3077	36W-0S	E1
Kennedy Cir					
24400	PNFD	60544	3338	30W-16S	B4
Kennedy Ct					
-	BGBK	60490	3339	27W-14S	D1
3100	MTGY	60538	3198	41W-9S	A5
9000	ODPK	60462	3346	11W-17S	A6
9300	MNSR	46321	3510		D2
15400	MhtT	60442	3677	19W-31S	E5
24500	PNFD	60544	3338	30W-16S	B4
W Kennedy Ct					
6000	MONE	60449	3682	7W-31S	D5
Kennedy Dr					
-	AntT	60002	2357	24W-43N	C4
-	JLET	60404	3495	33W-22S	C3
-	JLET	60447	3495	33W-22S	B3
-	PLTN	60074	2753	19W-18N	C4
-	TroT	60404	3495	33W-22S	C3
10	CmgT	60033	2406	49W-38N	C7
10	HRVD	60033	2406	49W-38N	C7
300	ANTH	60002	2357	24W-43N	C4
1600	BTVA	60510	3077	36W-0S	E1
1600	NCHI	60064	2536	11W-32N	C5
1900	MchT	60050	2528	31W-33N	C2
3100	MTGY	60538	3198	41W-9S	A5
8900	MaiT	60016	2863	11W-11N	D3
E Kennedy Dr					
1300	SMWD	60107	2857	27W-11N	D4
N Kennedy Dr					
10	CPVL	60110	2748	33W-18N	C5
100	BNHL	60110	2748	33W-18N	C5
1200	SMWD	60107	2857	27W-11N	D4
N Kennedy Dr SR-25					
10	CPVL	60110	2748	33W-18N	C5
100	BNHL	60110	2748	33W-18N	C5
W Kennedy Dr					
100	SMWD	60107	2857	27W-11N	D4
14100	WKGN	60031	2535	14W-33N	D3
14100	WrnT	60031	2535	14W-33N	D3
Kennedy Expwy					
-	CHCG	-	2917	10W-7N	E4
-	CHCG	-	2918	8W-6N	E5
-	CHCG	-	2919	8W-6N	A5
-	CHCG	-	2920	5W-5N	A7
-	CHCG	-	2976	4W-4N	C2
-	CHCG	-	2977	2W-2N	C7
-	CHCG	-	3033	1W-0N	E3
-	CHCG	-	3034	0W-0S	A5
Kennedy Expwy I-90					
-	CHCG	-	2917	10W-7N	E4
-	CHCG	-	2918	8W-6N	E5
-	CHCG	-	2919	7W-6N	C5
-	CHCG	-	2920	5W-5N	A7
-	CHCG	-	2976	5W-5N	A1
-	CHCG	-	2977	2W-2N	C7
-	CHCG	-	3033	1W-1N	D1
-	CHCG	-	3034	0W-0N	A4
Kennedy Expwy I-94					
-	CHCG	-	2976	4W-4N	C2
-	CHCG	-	2977	2W-2N	C6
-	CHCG	-	3033	1W-1N	D1
-	CHCG	-	3034	0W-0N	A4
Kennedy Expwy E					
-	CHCG	-	2919	6W-6N	D6
Kennedy Expwy E I-90					
-	CHCG	-	2919	6W-6N	D6
Kennedy Ln					
-	HNDL	60521	3146	15W-6S	A4
1000	FDHT	60411	3509	1E-25S	B7
Kennedy Pl					
400	VNHL	60061	2647	17W-26N	B3
Kennedy Rd					
1600	BtlT	60512	3262	40W-11S	B1
1600	BtlT	60543	3262	40W-11S	B1
2300	BtlT	60560	3262	41W-12S	B4
8200	BtlT	60560	3261	41W-13S	E5
8900	YKVL	60560	3261	42W-13S	E5
W Kennedy Rd					
-	LbvT	60045	2648	13W-26N	E4
-	VrnT	60045	2649	13W-26N	A4
100	BDWD	60408	3942	31W-42S	A6
400	BDWD	60408	3941	32W-41S	E6
600	RedT	60408	3941	32W-41S	E6
700	LKFT	60045	2649	12W-26N	B4
1800	LKFT	60045	2648	13W-26N	E4
1800	VrnT	60045	2648	13W-25N	E4
4800	WltT	60468	3861	9W-38S	A6
6400	PtnT	60468	3861	9W-38S	A6
7200	PtnT	60468	3860	10W-38S	C6
W Kennedy Rd SR-60					
-	LbvT	60045	2648	13W-26N	E4
-	VrnT	60045	2649	13W-25N	A4
700	LKFT	60045	2649	12W-26N	B4
1800	LKFT	60045	2648	13W-26N	E4
1800	VrnT	60045	2648	13W-25N	E4
Kennedy St					
-	FNPK	60131	2973	11W-3N	E4
-	FNPK	60171	2973	11W-3N	D4
-	RVGV	60131	2973	11W-3N	D4
-	RVGV	60171	2973	11W-3N	D4
100	EGvT	60018	2862	15W-9N	A7
400	MRGO	60152	2634	50W-26N	A3
Kennemer Ct					
24500	WldT	60564	3266	30W-12S	B4
Kennesaw Ct					
1000	NPVL	60540	3203	27W-8S	B1
Kenneth Av					
10	PTHT	60070	2808	15W-16N	A1
7400	LNWD	60076	2866	5W-9N	A7
7400	LNWD	60712	2866	5W-9N	A7
9000	SKOK	60076	2866	5W-11N	A3
11700	HTLY	60142	2692	40W-21N	A5
14300	CTWD	60445	3348	5W-17S	B4
14300	MDLN	60445	3348	5W-17S	B4
N Kenneth Av					
200	CHCG	60624	3032	5W-0N	A4
1900	CHCG	60639	2976	5W-2N	A7
2800	CHCG	60641	2976	5W-3N	A4
4300	CHCG	60630	2976	5W-5N	A1
4800	CHCG	60630	2920	5W-6N	A6
5800	CHCG	60646	2920	5W-7N	A4
6800	LNWD	60712	2920	5W-8N	A1
7200	LNWD	60712	2866	5W-9N	A7
7300	LNWD	60076	2866	5W-9N	A7
7300	SKOK	60076	2866	5W-9N	A7
S Kenneth Av					
700	CHCG	60624	3032	5W-0S	A6
1400	CHCG	60623	3032	5W-1S	A7
1500	CHCG	60623	3090	5W-1S	A1
4700	CHCG	60632	3150	5W-5S	B1
5400	CHCG	60629	3150	5W-7S	B6
7700	CHCG	60652	3212	5W-8S	B2
8700	HMTN	60456	3212	5W-10S	B4
9500	OKLN	60453	3212	5W-11S	B6
10200	OKLN	60453	3276	5W-12S	B1
10800	CHCG	60453	3276	5W-12S	B3
10800	CHCG	60655	3276	5W-12S	B3
11500	ALSP	60803	3276	5W-13S	B4
Kenneth Cir					
10	ELGN	60120	2855	32W-12N	D2
Kenneth Ct					
14100	CTWD	60445	3348	5W-16S	B3
N Kenneth Ct					
300	GNWD	60425	3428	0W-22S	B7
300	GNWD	60425	3508	0W-22S	B1
S Kenneth Ct					
-	CHCG	60652	3212	5W-9S	B2
Kenneth Dr					
4800	AlqT	60014	2640	33W-25N	D4
8800	MaiT	60016	2863	11W-12N	E1
N Kenneth Dr					
35400	AvnT	60046	2476	20W-35N	A6
W Kenneth Dr					
1600	EGvT	60056	2861	16W-10N	D5
1600	MPPT	60056	2861	16W-10N	D5
Kenneth Ter					
8800	SKOK	60076	2866	5W-11N	A3
Kennett Ln					
1500	LKFT	60045	2649	12W-24N	A7
N Kennicott Av					
-	BFGV	60089	2753	18W-18N	E3
400	ANHT	60005	2806	18W-14N	E4
600	ANHT	60004	2806	18W-14N	E3
2700	ANHT	60004	2753	18W-17N	E5
4500	CHCG	60630	2920	5W-5N	B7
S Kennicott Av					
100	ANHT	60005	2806	18W-13N	E6
Kennicott Ct					
1700	ANHT	60004	2806	18W-15N	E1
1700	JLET	60586	3495	33W-21S	B1
1900	DSPN	60018	2863	12W-9N	B6
Kennicott Dr					
1100	LKFT	60045	2649	12W-27N	B1
N Kennicott Dr					
1900	ANHT	60004	2806	18W-16N	E1
2000	ANHT	60004	2753	18W-16N	E7
S Kennicott Dr					
1500	ANHT	60005	2860	18W-12N	E2
1600	ANHT	60008	2860	18W-12N	E2
1600	RGMW	60008	2860	18W-12N	E2
Kennicott Ln					
1700	JLET	60586	3495	33W-21S	B1
4100	GNVW	60025	2809	11W-14N	C5
Kennicott Pl					
800	MPPT	60056	2861	17W-11N	C2
Kennilworth Av					
10100	AlqT	60102	2694	33W-21N	E5
Kennington Ter					
700	LKFT	60045	2649	11W-26N	C3
N Kennison Av					
5000	CHCG	60630	2920	5W-6N	A6
Kennsington E					
900	DYR	46311	3510		E6
Kennsington Ln					
1600	CLLK	60014	2693	36W-22N	D3
N Kenosha Av					
3100	CHCG	60641	2976	5W-3N	B4
Kenosha Rd					
1200	BtnT	60099	2362	11W-41N	C7
1200	ZION	60099	2362	11W-41N	C7
1400	BtnT	60099	2421	12W-41N	C1
1400	ZION	60099	2421	12W-41N	C1
1900	BHPK	60099	2421	12W-41N	C2
Kenosha Rd CO-W32					
1200	BtnT	60099	2362	11W-41N	C7
1200	ZION	60099	2362	11W-41N	C7
1400	BtnT	60099	2421	12W-41N	C1
1400	ZION	60099	2421	12W-41N	C1
1900	BHPK	60099	2421	12W-41N	C2
N Kenosha Rd					
400	BtnT	53158	2362	11W-43N	D4
400	BtnT	60099	2362	11W-42N	D5
400	PTPR	53158	2362	11W-43N	D4
400	WPHR	60099	2362	11W-42N	D5
800	ZION	60099	2362	11W-42N	D6
40000	BHPK	60099	2421	12W-40N	B3
40000	ZION	60099	2421	12W-40N	B3
42800	WPHR	60096	2362	11W-42N	D5
N Kenosha Rd CO-W32					
400	BtnT	53158	2362	11W-43N	D4
400	BtnT	60099	2362	11W-42N	D5
400	PTPR	53158	2362	11W-43N	D4
400	WPHR	60099	2362	11W-42N	D5
800	ZION	60099	2362	11W-42N	D6
40000	BHPK	60099	2421	12W-40N	B3
40000	ZION	60099	2421	12W-40N	B3
42800	WPHR	60096	2362	11W-42N	D5
Kenosha St					
5300	RcmT	60071	2353	34W-42N	D6
5300	RHMD	60071	2353	34W-42N	B6
Kenosha St SR-173					
5300	RcmT	60071	2353	34W-42N	D6
5300	RHMD	60071	2353	34W-42N	B6

STREET Block	City	ZIP	Map#	CGS	Grid
Ken Peddy Ct					
1300	BTVA	60510	3077	36W-2S	E4
Kensey Ln					
900	PLNO	60545	3259	46W-13S	E5
900	PLNO	60545	3260	46W-13S	A5
Kensington Av					
1600	WSTR	60154	3086	13W-1S	E1
2200	WSTR	60154	3087	13W-2S	A2
3000	LGPK	60525	3087	13W-2S	A4
16100	TYPK	60477	3424	9W-19S	D2
E Kensington Av					
100	CHCG	60628	3278	0E-13S	D4
N Kensington Av					
10	LGNG	60525	3087	12W-4S	B7
200	LGPK	60525	3087	12W-3S	B5
S Kensington Av					
10	LGNG	60525	3087	12W-4S	B7
1100	CTSD	60525	3147	12W-5S	B3
1100	LGNG	60525	3147	12W-5S	B3
Kensington Cir					
10	WHTN	60187	3082	24W-2S	D4
Kensington Ct					
-	JLET	60431	3495	33W-21S	B1
10	ALGN	60102	2747	36W-19N	B2
10	HNWD	60047	2646	20W-24N	B6
10	SMWD	60107	2856	29W-11N	E4
100	SCRL	60175	2964	35W-4N	A3
200	GRNE	60031	2535	14W-34N	C1
300	BMDL	60108	2968	24W-4N	C3
400	NPVL	60563	3141	27W-5S	C3
400	NpvT	60563	3141	27W-5S	C3
500	NlxT	60451	3502	16W-24S	A5
500	ROSL	60172	2912	25W-6N	C6
1800	AURA	60506	3137	38W-7S	B7
2200	OKBK	60523	3085	16W-2S	D3
S Kensington Ct					
300	PLTN	60067	2805	22W-15N	B2
W Kensington Ct					
14200	LKPT	60441	3421	17W-19S	B3
27000	LKBN	60010	2697	27W-24N	C1
Kensington Dr					
10	LNSH	60069	2702	14W-22N	D4
10	NBRN	60010	2644	25W-24N	B6
10	VrnT	60015	2702	14W-22N	D4
10	WNVL	60555	3080	30W-2S	C3
300	OSWG	60543	3200	35W-10S	B6
300	SMWD	60107	2856	29W-11N	D4
400	MHRY	60050	2527	33W-32N	D4
900	NHBK	60062	2810	8W-16N	D1
1100	MDLN	60060	2590	19W-30N	B3
1500	ALGN	60102	2747	36W-19N	B2
2100	SMBG	60194	2858	26W-11N	A3
2200	SMBG	60194	2857	26W-11N	E3
11700	HTLY	60142	2744	42W-20N	C1
12900	PNFD	60585	3338	30W-15S	B2
19700	MKNA	60448	3502	14W-23S	D4
S Kensington Dr					
16400	HMGN	60491	3421	17W-19S	D3
Kensington Ln					
1900	HFET	60169	2804	24W-13N	B7
1900	HFET	60169	2858	25W-12N	A1
3100	ZION	60099	2362	11W-41N	D7
7600	HRPK	60133	2911	26W-9N	E1
8100	HRPK	60133	2857	26W-9N	E7
8100	SMBG	60193	2857	26W-9N	E7
S Kensington Ln					
-	MonT	60449	3682	9W-31S	A5
25600	GGnT	60449	3682	9W-31S	A5
Kensington Lp					
10	ELGN	60123	2854	35W-12N	C2
Kensington Pl					
-	CLSM	60188	3024	26W-2N	A1
500	AURA	60506	3137	37W-7S	C7
6500	DRGV	60516	3144	20W-7S	A6
Kensington Rd					
10	MltT	60148	3084	21W-2S	A3
100	MltT	60148	3083	21W-2S	E3
500	MltT	60137	3083	21W-2S	D3
1200	OKBK	60523	3085	16W-2S	D3
E Kensington Rd					
100	MPPT	60056	2808	13W-13N	D5
600	ANHT	60004	2807	16W-14N	C5
600	ANHT	60005	2807	16W-14N	C5
1400	WhlT	60056	2808	13W-13N	D5
1900	WhlT	60025	2808	13W-13N	E5
2400	MPPT	60056	2807	16W-14N	D5
W Kensington Rd					
200	MPPT	60056	2808	15W-13N	A5
300	MPPT	60056	2807	15W-13N	E5
600	ANHT	60004	2807	15W-13N	E5
600	ANHT	60056	2807	15W-13N	E5
600	MPPT	60004	2807	15W-14N	E5
Kensington St					
1100	SRWD	60404	3496	30W-24S	B6
Kensington Wy					
600	BGBK	60440	3205	21W-9S	D4
9000	ODPK	60462	3345	11W-18S	E6
9000	ODPK	60462	3346	11W-18S	A6
Kensington Estates Ct					
2000	JLET	60586	3416	30W-20S	C5
Kensington on Oxford					
10	RGMW	60008	2805	22W-13N	B6
Kenston Ct					
100	GNVA	60134	3020	35W-1N	B4
Kent Av					
10	CLLK	60014	2640	34W-25N	C4
300	EGvT	60007	2861	17W-9N	B6
300	EGVV	60007	2861	17W-9N	B6
300	RMVL	60446	3340	24W-16S	D3
1000	HDPK	60035	2704	9W-23N	B2
1000	PKRG	60068	2918	10W-7N	A3
S Kent Av					
700	EMHT	60126	3028	15W-0S	A6
W Kent Av					
700	CteT	60417	3685	1W-31S	B5
Kent Cir					
800	BRLT	60103	2910	29W-7N	D5
Kent Ct					
10	LNSH	60069	2703	13W-22N	A4
10	WLBK	60527	3145	16W-7S	E6
300	NPVL	60540	3142	25W-7S	A6
400	OSWG	60543	3200	35W-10S	A7
400	SMBG	60193	2858	24W-9N	E7
700	HRPK	60133	2858	26W-9N	A7
1000	BGBK	60440	3205	21W-9S	E4
1000	WHTN	60187	3082	23W-2S	E4
6300	LSLE	60532	3142	24W-6S	C6
21600	FKFT	60423	3591	12W-26S	C2
Kent Ln					
1300	BFGV	60089	2701	17W-21N	B6
1400	ELGN	60120	2855	31W-11N	E3
Kent Pl					
3600	CRTE	60417	3596	0E-28S	E6
Kent Rd					
10	WNKA	60093	2758	5W-16N	E7
100	MltT	60137	3083	21W-2S	D3
300	RVSD	60546	3088	9W-2S	D4
700	KLWH	60043	2812	4W-14N	C4
700	NtrT	60043	2812	4W-14N	C4
700	NtrT	60093	2812	4W-14N	C4
1700	HFET	60169	2858	24W-12N	E1
N Kent Rd					
100	MchT	60051	2529	30W-32N	A5
S Kent Rd					
22900	CNHN	60410	3584	29W-27S	D6
Kent St					
100	WCDA	60084	2643	25W-26N	E2
200	MRGO	60152	2634	50W-26N	B3
9800	BDVW	60154	3087	12W-1S	C1
9800	BDVW	60155	3087	12W-1S	C1
9800	WSTR	60154	3087	12W-1S	B1
Kent Tr					
12100	MKNA	60448	3502	15W-23S	C3
Kentland Ct					
10	RMVL	60446	3339	27W-17S	B5
Kentland Dr					
10	RMVL	60446	3339	27W-17S	B5
Kenton Av					
7400	LNWD	60076	2866	5W-9N	A7
7400	LNWD	60712	2866	5W-9N	A7
9600	SKOK	60076	2866	5W-12N	A1
13500	CTWD	60445	3348	5W-16S	B2
14100	MDLN	60445	3348	5W-17S	B6
15000	MDLN	60452	3348	5W-17S	B6
15000	OKFT	60452	3348	5W-17S	B6
15200	OKFT	60445	3348	5W-18S	B6
15300	BmnT	60445	3348	5W-18S	B7
15300	BmnT	60452	3348	5W-18S	B7
N Kenton Av					
100	CHCG	60624	3032	5W-0N	A4
600	CHCG	60644	3032	5W-0N	A3
700	CHCG	60651	3032	5W-0N	A3
1600	CHCG	60639	2976	5W-2N	A7
1600	CHCG	60639	3032	5W-1N	A1
2700	CHCG	60641	2976	5W-3N	A5
5100	CHCG	60630	2920	5W-6N	A6
5600	CHCG	60646	2920	5W-7N	A4
6400	CHCG	60712	2920	5W-8N	A3
6400	LNWD	60646	2920	5W-8N	A3
7000	LNWD	60712	2920	5W-8N	A1
S Kenton Av					
-	HMTN	60652	3212	5W-10S	A4
10	CHCG	60624	3032	5W-0S	A5
10	CHCG	60644	3032	5W-0S	A5
5700	CHCG	60629	3150	5W-6S	A3
7700	CHCG	60652	3212	5W-8S	A2
8700	HMTN	60456	3212	5W-10S	A4
9100	OKLN	60456	3212	5W-10S	A5
10100	OKLN	60453	3212	5W-11S	A7
10200	OKLN	60453	3276	5W-12S	A2
11000	CHCG	60453	3276	5W-12S	B3
11000	CHCG	60655	3276	5W-12S	B3
11500	ALSP	60803	3276	5W-13S	B4
W Kenton Ct					
7700	FftT	60423	3504	9W-24S	E4
Kenton Ln					
1900	GNOK	60048	2592	14W-30N	D3
Kenton Rd					
800	DRFD	60015	2704	10W-21N	A7
Kentshire Cir					
2900	NPVL	60564	3202	29W-9S	C5
3300	AURA	60504	3139	31W-7S	E7
Kentshire Ct					
2800	NPVL	60564	3202	29W-9S	C4
Kentshire Dr					
-	YKVL	60560	3333	42W-17S	D7
Kentuck Ct					
2300	NPVL	60564	3266	29W-12S	D4
Kentucky Av					
14500	HRVY	60426	3350	1W-17S	A5
N Kentucky Av					
4800	CHCG	60630	2920	5W-6N	A6
Kentucky Ct					
10	PKFT	60466	3595	3W-25S	B1
2100	WHTN	60187	3083	23W-3S	A5
2600	NCHI	60088	2593	11W-29N	C3
10600	ODPK	60467	3423	13W-21S	B7
Kentucky Ln					
900	EGVV	60007	2913	22W-8N	D2
E Kentucky Rd					
100	WshT	60401	3864	0E-39S	E6
W Kentucky Rd					
100	WshT	60401	3864	0W-38S	D6
Kentucky St					
200	PKFT	60466	3595	3W-25S	B1
Kentwood Ct					
1000	DYR	46311	3510		C6
8400	DRN	60561	3206	18W-9S	E4
Kentwood Dr					
1000	DYR	46311	3510		C6
W Kentwood Dr					
21700	PnfT	60544	3339	27W-16S	C3
E Ken-View Dr					
500	WMTN	60481	3853	27W-38S	D5
Kenwood Av					
10	WynT	60185	2966	30W-4N	B5
200	WYNE	60184	2966	30W-4N	B5
200	WYNE	60185	2966	30W-4N	B5
300	PnfT	60435	3417	27W-20S	C6
400	CLSM	60188	2967	28W-3N	A6
400	WCHI	60185	3022	30W-0N	B6
400	WynT	60185	2967	28W-3N	B6
400	WynT	60188	2967	28W-3N	A6
500	LYVL	60048	2591	15W-28N	E6
3400	GRNE	60031	2536	13W-34N	A1
4000	GRNE	60031	2535	14W-34N	D1
14200	DLTN	60419	3351	1E-16S	B4
15600	SHLD	60473	3351	1E-18S	B7
16400	SHLD	60473	3429	1E-19S	B2
S Kenwood Av					
4800	CHCG	60615	3153	1E-5S	A1
5400	CHCG	60637	3153	1E-6S	A3
7300	CHCG	60619	3153	1E-8S	A7
7500	CHCG	60619	3215	1E-8S	A1
Kenwood Ct					
1200	SHLD	60473	3429	1E-19S	B2
Kenwood Dr					
10	RLKP	60073	2532	22W-33N	A2
16200	SHLD	60473	3429	1E-19S	B1
Kenwood Rd					
1500	HFET	60169	2858	25W-12N	B2
Kenwood St					
10	CTCY	60409	3430		D1
10	HMND	46324	3430		E1
800	HMND	46320	3430		E1
E Kenwood St					
900	HMND	46320	3430		E1
900	HMND	46324	3430		E1
Kenyon Av					
400	RMVL	60446	3340	24W-15S	E2
Kenyon Ct					
2200	AURA	60502	3139	32W-5S	B4
Kenyon Dr					
1500	NPVL	60565	3204	24W-9S	D3
Kenyon Ln					
2300	AURA	60502	3139	32W-6S	B4
Kenyon Rd					
300	BRLT	60120	2909	33W-8N	A2
300	BRLT	60177	2909	33W-8N	A2
300	ElgT	60177	2909	33W-8N	A2
800	ElgT	60177	2908	33W-8N	E2
800	SEGN	60177	2908	33W-8N	E2
800	SEGN	60177	2909	33W-8N	A2
Kenyon St					
800	DRGV	60516	3144	19W-6S	C4
W Kenyon St					
23100	PNFD	60544	3416	28W-19S	E2
23100	PnfT	60544	3416	28W-19S	E2
E Kenz Ct					
600	LKVL	60046	2475	22W-37N	C1
N Keokuk Av					
4400	CHCG	60630	2920	5W-5N	B7
Keokuk Rd					
6300	IHPK	60525	3146	14W-7S	D5
N Keota Av					
6600	CHCG	60646	2919	7W-8N	C2
Keough St					
1200	LMNT	60439	3271	18W-14S	A7
Keppler Dr					
800	MRGO	60152	2634	50W-26N	A3
W Kepwick Ln					
21200	KLDR	60047	2699	21W-20N	D7
N Kerbs Av					
5600	CHCG	60646	2919	5W-7N	E4
5700	CHCG	60646	2920	5W-7N	A4
N Kercheval Av					
5700	CHCG	60646	2919	5W-7N	E4
5700	CHCG	60646	2920	5W-7N	A4
S Kerfoot Av					
8300	CHCG	60620	3214	0W-9S	A3
Keri Ln					
10	BRRG	60527	3208	15W-10S	A6
Kerim Ct					
1000	MRGO	60152	2634	49W-25N	C4
Kern St					
200	BDWD	60408	3942	31W-41S	B5
Kerr St					
13300	PNFD	60585	3337	32W-15S	C3
13400	PNFD	60544	3337	32W-15S	C3
Kerri Ct					
400	SMBG	60173	2859	21W-11N	E4
Kerriell Ct					
3600	NPVL	60564	3266	30W-11S	A2
Kerry Av					
17000	ODPK	60467	3423	13W-20S	B4
Kerry Ct					
-	WNFD	60190	3023	27W-0S	C6
300	CLSM	60188	2967	26W-4N	E3
400	PTHT	60070	2754	16W-16N	D6
600	GLBT	60136	2799	38W-15N	C4
10900	MKNA	60448	3503	13W-23S	A2
Kerry Ln					
10	WLNG	60090	2755	14W-16N	C6
100	WCDA	60084	2587	26W-28N	D6
100	WcnT	60084	2587	26W-28N	D6
300	DRFD	60015	2757	10W-20N	B1
700	WMTN	60481	3943	28W-39S	C1
1000	JLET	60431	3496	29W-22S	D2
2300	DRN	60561	3206	19W-10S	D5
S Kerry Ln					
13500	HMGN	60491	3343	17W-16S	D3
W Kerry Ln					
1800	NndT	60050	2585	30W-29N	E4
1800	NndT	60050	2586	30W-29N	A4
Kerry Wy					
10	PlsT	60464	3346	10W-15S	C1
300	GYLK	60030	2533	19W-32N	C5
E Kerry Brook Ln					
200	ANHT	60004	2754	17W-17N	A6
Kerry Winde Dr					
2300	NLNX	60451	3588	19W-27S	D4
N Kerwin Dr					
36700	GrtT	60041	2474	25W-36N	A3
Kerwin Ln					
-	GrtT	60041	2474	25W-36N	A3
S Kerwood St					
10	PLTN	60067	2806	20W-15N	A1
Keslinger Rd					
10	BbyT	60119	3017	42W-1N	D4
10	BbyT	60119	3018	39W-1N	E4
10	BbyT	60134	3018	40W-1N	C4
10	ELBN	60119	3017	42W-1N	D4
10	GNVA	60134	3019	37W-0N	C4
10	GnvT	60134	3019	38W-1N	B4
500	BbyT	60134	3019	38W-1N	A4
Keslinger Rd CO-41					
10	BbyT	60119	3017	42W-1N	D4
10	BbyT	60119	3018	39W-1N	E4
10	BbyT	60134	3018	40W-1N	C4
10	ELBN	60119	3017	42W-1N	D4
10	GNVA	60134	3019	37W-0N	C4
10	GnvT	60134	3019	38W-1N	B4
500	BbyT	60134	3019	38W-1N	A4
Kestral Dr					
3400	NPVL	60564	3266	30W-11S	B2
Kestrel Av					
18700	FftT	60448	3503	13W-22S	A1
18700	MKNA	60448	3503	13W-22S	A1
N Kestrel Av					
3600	WKGN	60087	2421	11W-38N	D7
3600	WKGN	60087	2479	11W-38N	D1
Kestrel Ln					
300	LNHT	60046	2476	19W-37N	C2
N Keswick Cir					
300	RDLK	60073	2531	25W-33N	B2
Keswick Ct					
10	LNSH	60069	2703	13W-22N	A4
N Keswick Ct					
300	RDLK	60073	2531	25W-33N	A2
Keswick Dr					
1100	FmtT	60060	2646	19W-27N	B1
1100	MDLN	60060	2646	19W-27N	B1
1300	WDRG	60517	3206	20W-11S	B7
Keswick Ln					
10	LslT	60540	3142	25W-6S	C5
10	NPVL	60540	3142	25W-6S	C5
400	CLSM	60188	3024	24W-1N	D3
W Keswick Pl					
15000	LKPT	60441	3421	18W-19S	A3
Keswick Rd					
10	EGVV	60007	2914	19W-8N	D1
Keswick St					
10	VNHL	60061	2647	16W-25N	C6
Ketch Ct					
3100	AURA	60503	3201	31W-10S	E6
Ketchum Rd					
10	HPSR	60140	2743	45W-17N	D7
10	HshT	60140	2743	45W-17N	D7
10	HshT	60140	2796	45W-16N	D1
Ketten Ct					
100	NPVL	60563	3141	27W-4S	D2
Ketten Dr					
100	NPVL	60563	3141	26W-4S	D2
W Kettering Ct					
21900	PnfT	60544	3339	27W-16S	C4
Kettering Dr					
4400	LGGV	60047	2700	18W-23N	E3
Kettering Ln					
-	GrtT	60041	2473	27W-35N	A6
10	LMNT	60439	3270	19W-14S	D6
Kettering Rd					
1300	MDLN	60060	2590	20W-28N	B5
2000	HFET	60169	2858	25W-12N	B1
Kettering on Oxford					
10	RGMW	60008	2805	22W-13N	B6
Ketterling Ct					
10	NBRN	60010	2644	25W-24N	B7
Kettle Av					
-	NARA	60542	3077	37W-3S	C7
Kettle Ct					
-	ISLK	60042	2586	28W-28N	E6
-	ISLK	60042	2587	28W-28N	A5
-	ISLK	60051	2587	28W-28N	A5
2000	LNSG	60438	3429	2E-21S	D7
Kettlehook Ct					
900	CmpT	60175	2961	42W-5N	D1
Kettlehook Dr					
2600	ELGN	60124	2853	37W-11N	D4
Keuka Ct					
10	HNWD	60047	2646	19W-25N	B4
Keuka St					
-	JltT	60433	3587	23W-26S	A2
10	JltT	60436	3586	24W-26S	E2
10	JltT	60436	3587	23W-26S	B3
Kevin Av					
10	LKVL	60046	2475	23W-37N	A1
1700	ELGN	60123	2854	36W-12N	A1
19200	MKNA	60448	3503	12W-23S	C3
E Kevin Cir					
1000	PLTN	60074	2753	19W-18N	B2
Kevin Ct					
500	CmpT	60175	2906	39W-6N	D6
10300	MKNA	60448	3503	12W-23S	C4
Kevin Dr					
1700	MTGY	60538	3199	38W-9S	A5
N Kevin Dr					
400	ADSN	60101	2970	19W-4N	D4
S Kevin Dr					
25600	CNHN	60410	3672	32W-31S	E5
Kevin Ln					
100	MTGY	60543	3263	38W-11S	A1
400	GYLK	60030	2532	21W-33N	D3
600	UYPK	60466	3684	3W-29S	B1
2600	RGMW	60008	2805	21W-13N	C5
19500	MKNA	60448	3503	12W-23S	C4
Kevin Wy					
400	MTSN	60443	3505	7W-24S	D5
Kevington Dr					
1100	ANTH	60002	2359	20W-42N	A6
Kevin Morris Ct					
1300	SMWD	60107	2857	27W-11N	D4
Kevyn Ln					
300	BNVL	60106	2915	16W-6N	D7
N Kewanee Av					
4700	CHCG	60630	2920	5W-5N	B7
Kewanee Ln					
3100	NPVL	60564	3266	30W-11S	B1
3100	WldT	60564	3266	30W-11S	B1
Kewaunee Ct					
400	PTHT	60070	2807	16W-15N	E2
W Kewaunee Dr					
17700	WrnT	60030	2534	17W-33N	A2
Key Ct					
100	JLET	60435	3497	27W-23S	D5
E Keyes Av					
100	HPSR	60140	2795	46W-16N	E2
300	HPSR	60140	2796	46W-16N	A2
Key Largo Dr					
100	RMVL	60446	3340	25W-16S	B4
600	FXLK	60041	2473	26W-34N	D7
Keystone Av					
10	FTPK	60130	3030	9W-0N	B5
10	FXLK	60020	2473	27W-36N	A3
10	RVFT	60130	3030	9W-0N	B5
100	FRGV	60021	2695	31W-22N	E3
800	NHBK	60062	2757	9W-17N	B5
1300	RVFT	60305	3030	9W-1N	B1
2200	FTPK	60130	3088	9W-2S	C2
2200	FTPK	60546	3088	9W-2S	C2
2200	NRIV	60546	3088	9W-2S	C2
2500	RVSD	60546	3088	9W-2S	C3
7400	LNWD	60076	2866	5W-9N	B7
7400	LNWD	60712	2866	5W-9N	B7
9700	SKOK	60076	2866	5W-12N	B1
9900	EVTN	60076	2866	5W-12N	B1
9900	EVTN	60201	2866	5W-12N	B1
14300	CTWD	60445	3348	5W-17S	C4
14500	MDLN	60445	3348	5W-17S	C5
19900	MTSN	60443	3506	5W-24S	C5
19900	RchT	60443	3506	5W-24S	C5
N Keystone Av					
200	CHCG	60624	3032	5W-0N	B4
800	CHCG	60651	3032	5W-1N	B2
1500	CHCG	60639	3032	5W-1N	B1
1600	CHCG	60639	2976	5W-2N	B6
4000	CHCG	60641	2976	5W-5N	B1
4400	CHCG	60630	2920	5W-6N	B6
6100	CHCG	60646	2920	5W-7N	B3
6300	CHCG	60712	2920	5W-7N	B3
6300	LNWD	60712	2920	5W-7N	B3
7200	LNWD	60712	2866	5W-9N	B7
7300	LNWD	60076	2866	5W-9N	B7
7300	SKOK	60076	2866	5W-9N	B7
S Keystone Av					
13500	RBBN	60472	3348	5W-16S	C2
13700	CTWD	60472	3348	5W-16S	C3
Keystone Ct					
10	BGBK	60440	3205	22W-10S	C6
300	GLNC	60022	2759		A5
1400	ELGN	60120	2855	31W-10N	E5
2300	NPVL	60565	3203	27W-10S	C6
5100	RGMW	60008	2860	19W-12N	C1
5400	JLET	60586	3416	30W-20S	B5
Keystone Dr					
600	BGBK	60440	3205	22W-10S	D6
3300	SPGV	60071	2413	32W-40N	C3
3300	SPGV	60081	2413	32W-40N	C3
Keystone Ln					
700	VNHL	60061	2647	17W-25N	B4
Keystone Pl					
-	HRPK	60133	2912	25W-8N	A2
-	SMBG	60133	2912	25W-8N	A2
-	SMBG	60193	2912	25W-8N	A2
Keystone Rd					
2800	NHBK	60062	2756	11W-17N	D6
7800	ODPK	60462	3346	9W-18S	D7
10300	RcmT	60071	2352	36W-43N	E5
11300	GNCY	53128	2352	36W-43N	E5
11300	GNCY	60071	2352	36W-43N	E5
Keystone Rd CO-V30					
10300	RcmT	60071	2352	36W-43N	E5
11300	GNCY	53128	2352	36W-43N	E5
11300	GNCY	60071	2352	36W-43N	E5
Keywest Dr					
1100	LKPT	60441	3341	21W-18S	E7
1200	LKPT	60441	3342	21W-18S	A7
Khater Dr					
-	MNKA	60447	3583	34W-26S	A4
-	SwdT	60447	3583	34W-26S	A4
Kickapoo Av					
400	BTVA	60510	3078	34W-1S	C3
Kickapoo Ct					
11600	FftT	60448	3502	14W-23S	D4
11600	MKNA	60448	3502	14W-23S	D4
Kickapoo Dr					
19300	TYPK	60477	3504	9W-23S	E3
19400	FftT	60423	3504	9W-23S	E3
19400	TYPK	60423	3504	9W-23S	E3
S Kickapoo Tr					
13500	HMGN	60491	3343	16W-16S	E3
N Kidd Dr					
43100	AntT	60002	2357	25W-43N	B4
N Kidder St					
10	PLNO	60545	3259	47W-13S	C6
Kidwell Dr					
2300	WCHI	60185	2965	32W-4N	C4
Kidwell Rd					
7100	DRGV	60516	3206	20W-8S	C1
Kiefer Dr					
1700	ZION	60099	2421	12W-41N	C1
Kielion Dr					
1300	BTVA	60510	3078	33W-2S	E5
Kiep Av					
600	JLET	60436	3498	24W-24S	E7
Kiess Dr					
3800	GNVW	60025	2809	11W-15N	D3
Kiest Av					
1800	NHBK	60062	2757	9W-17N	C5
Kilbery Av					
-	NARA	60542	3077	37W-3S	B7
Kilbery St					
-	NARA	60542	3077	37W-3S	C6
Kilbourn Av					
7400	LNWD	60076	2866	5W-9N	A7
7400	LNWD	60712	2866	5W-9N	A7
9200	SKOK	60076	2866	5W-11N	A2
14200	CTWD	60445	3348	5W-17S	B5
14200	MDLN	60445	3348	5W-17S	B5
15200	BmnT	60445	3348	5W-18S	B6
15200	OKFT	60445	3348	5W-18S	B6
16300	OKFT	60452	3426	5W-19S	C3
16600	CCHL	60452	3426	5W-19S	C3
16600	CCHL	60478	3426	5W-19S	C3
N Kilbourn Av					
10	CHCG	60624	3032	5W-0N	A4
600	CHCG	60644	3032	5W-0N	A3
800	CHCG	60651	3032	5W-1N	A2
1600	CHCG	60639	2976	5W-2N	A7
1600	CHCG	60639	3032	5W-1N	A1
2700	CHCG	60641	2976	5W-3N	A5
4400	CHCG	60630	2920	5W-5N	A7
5600	CHCG	60646	2920	5W-7N	A4
6400	CHCG	60712	2920	5W-8N	A3
7100	LNWD	60712	2920	5W-8N	A1
7300	LNWD	60076	2866	5W-9N	A7
7300	LNWD	60712	2866	5W-9N	A7
7300	SKOK	60076	2866	5W-9N	A7
S Kilbourn Av					
10	CHCG	60624	3032	5W-0S	A5
1100	CHCG	60623	3032	5W-1S	A7
1500	CHCG	60623	3090	5W-1S	A1
4700	CHCG	60632	3150	5W-5S	A2
5400	CHCG	60629	3150	5W-7S	B6
7700	CHCG	60652	3212	5W-9S	B2
8600	HMTN	60652	3212	5W-9S	B4
8700	HMTN	60456	3212	5W-10S	A4
10100	OKLN	60453	3212	5W-11S	B7
10200	OKLN	60453	3276	5W-12S	B1
10800	CHCG	60453	3276	5W-12S	B3
10800	CHCG	60655	3276	5W-12S	B3
11500	ALSP	60803	3276	5W-13S	B4
Kilbourn Rd					
-	WrnT	60031	2478	14W-35N	C6
900	GRNE	60031	2478	14W-35N	C6
N Kilbourne Rd					
39000	WDWH	60083	2420	14W-40N	C3
39600	NptT	60083	2420	14W-40N	C3
41000	NptT	60099	2420	14W-40N	C3
41500	NptT	60099	2361	14W-42N	C7
41500	WDWH	60099	2361	14W-41N	C7
43300	PTPR	53158	2361	14W-41N	C7
43300	PTPR	60099	2361	14W-41N	C7
N Kilbourne Rd CO-W26					
39000	WDWH	60083	2420	14W-40N	C3
39600	NptT	60083	2420	14W-40N	C3
41000	NptT	60099	2420	14W-40N	C3
41500	NptT	60099	2361	14W-41N	C7
41500	WDWH	60099	2361	14W-41N	C7
43300	PTPR	53158	2361	14W-41N	C7
43300	PTPR	60099	2361	14W-41N	C7
Kilburn Ct					
900	GYLK	60030	2533	20W-33N	A4
Kilburne Ln					
2800	NPVL	60564	3202	29W-10S	C6
Kilchurn Ln					
100	IVNS	60067	2752	22W-16N	B7
Kildare Av					
-	LbvT	60048	2591	17W-30N	B2
-	LYVL	60048	2591	17W-30N	B2
10	JltT	60433	3500	21W-24S	A5
7400	LNWD	60076	2866	5W-9N	A7
7400	LNWD	60712	2866	5W-9N	A7
9000	SKOK	60076	2866	5W-11N	B2
13500	CTWD	60472	3348	5W-16S	B2
13500	RBBN	60472	3348	5W-16S	B2
13900	CTWD	60445	3348	5W-16S	B3
14600	MDLN	60445	3348	5W-17S	C6
21100	MTSN	60443	3506	5W-25S	C7
21100	MTSN	60443	3594	5W-25S	C1
N Kildare Av					
10	CHCG	60624	3032	5W-0N	B4
800	CHCG	60651	3032	5W-1N	B2
1500	CHCG	60639	3032	5W-1N	B1

STREET Block	City	ZIP	Map#	CGS	Grid
N Kildare Av					
1600	CHCG	60639	2976	5W-2N	B7
4100	CHCG	60641	2976	5W-5N	A1
4300	CHCG	60630	2976	5W-5N	A1
5300	CHCG	60630	2920	5W-6N	A5
6100	CHCG	60646	2920	5W-7N	A3
6300	CHCG	60712	2920	5W-7N	A3
6800	LNWD	60712	2920	5W-8N	A1
7200	LNWD	60712	2866	5W-9N	B7
7300	LNWD	60076	2866	5W-9N	B7
7300	SKOK	60076	2866	5W-9N	B7
S Kildare Av					
600	CHCG	60624	3032	5W-1S	B7
1100	CHCG	60623	3032	5W-1S	B7
1500	CHCG	60623	3090	5W-1S	B1
4000	CHCG	60632	3090	5W-4S	B7
4700	CHCG	60632	3150	5W-6S	B3
5400	CHCG	60629	3150	5W-7S	B6
8500	CHCG	60652	3212	5W-9S	B4
8600	HMTN	60652	3212	5W-9S	B4
8700	HMTN	60456	3212	5W-10S	B4
9500	OKLN	60453	3212	5W-11S	B6
10200	OKLN	60453	3276	5W-12S	B1
11500	ALSP	60803	3276	5W-13S	B4
13300	RBBN	60472	3348	5W-15S	B2
13400	CTWD	60445	3348	5W-15S	B2
13400	CTWD	60472	3348	5W-15S	B2
Kildare Ct					
10	CRY	60013	2641	31W-24N	D6
10	DRFD	60015	2757	10W-20N	B1
300	CLSM	60188	2968	26W-4N	A4
4300	MTSN	60443	3594	5W-25S	C1
16600	TYPK	60477	3424	9W-19S	E3
Kildare Dr					
-	PNFD	60585	3337	32W-14S	C1
Kildare Ln					
10	DRFD	60015	2757	9W-20N	B1
Kildare Rd					
500	LbvT	60048	2591	17W-30N	B2
Kildare St					
400	GLBT	60136	2799	38W-15N	C4
Kildeer Ct					
10	WDRG	60517	3143	21W-7S	E7
Kildeer Dr					
200	WDSK	60098	2525	40W-32N	A5
500	BGBK	60440	3205	21W-10S	D6
1300	RLKB	60073	2474	24W-35N	D6
1500	RLKH	60073	2474	24W-35N	D7
Kildeer Ln					
300	VrnT	60015	2755	14W-20N	B1
400	CmpT	60119	2961	43W-4N	A4
2000	JNBG	60050	2471	31W-37N	E2
Kildeer St					
2300	WDRG	60517	3143	21W-7S	E7
Kildere Ct					
300	GYLK	60030	2532	21W-33N	D3
Kiley Dr					
11000	HTLY	60142	2692	40W-21N	B6
Kiley Ln					
11500	ODPK	60467	3422	14W-21S	D5
Kilheeney Dr					
500	MNKA	60447	3672	34W-29S	A1
Kilkenny Av					
19700	TYPK	60477	3504	11W-23S	A4
19800	FftT	60477	3504	11W-23S	A4
Kilkenny Ct					
-	PNFD	60585	3265	32W-14S	D7
400	CLSM	60188	2967	26W-4N	E4
500	GLBT	60136	2799	38W-15N	B4
1700	WDSK	60098	2582	40W-29N	A3
3500	AlqT	60014	2641	32W-25N	B4
Kilkenny Dr					
-	WldT	60585	3265	32W-14S	D7
8900	DRN	60561	3206	19W-10S	D5
12300	PNFD	60585	3265	32W-14S	D7
12300	PNFD	60585	3337	32W-14S	D1
S Kilkenny Dr					
800	WHTN	60187	3082	25W-1S	A1
3400	AlqT	60014	2641	32W-25N	B4
6100	NndT	60014	2641	32W-25N	B4
W Kilkenny Dr					
1600	WHTN	60187	3082	26W-1S	A1
Killarney Ct					
200	GYLK	60030	2532	21W-33N	D2
700	SMBG	60193	2859	23W-10N	A6
3600	RGMW	60008	2806	18W-13N	D6
8000	TYPK	60477	3424	10W-21S	C7
24500	WldT	60564	3266	30W-12S	B3
S Killarney Ct					
700	EMHT	60126	3028	15W-0N	B5
Killarney Dr					
2700	AlqT	60013	2641	31W-25N	C5
Killarney Ln					
800	BbyT	60119	3018	41W-1N	A2
1700	NHBK	60062	2758	7W-16N	A7
2100	JLET	60431	3417	28W-21S	B6
Killarney Pass Cir					
400	MDLN	60060	2590	19W-28N	C5
Killdeer Ct					
5900	LGGV	60047	2701	17W-23N	B1
Killdeer Dr					
1300	NPVL	60565	3204	26W-8S	A2
1700	NPVL	60565	3203	26W-9S	E4
Killdeer Ln					
3000	SCRL	60175	2964	35W-4N	A3
Killdeer Rd					
300	BMDL	60108	2968	24W-4N	D3
S Killeen Ct					
13600	PnfT	60544	3339	27W-16S	D3
Killey Ln					
300	GnvT	60134	3019	38W-0N	A4
Killian Ct					
-	WNKA	60093	2812	5W-15N	B1
Kilpatrick Av					
-	SKOK	60076	2865	5W-9N	E6
200	WLMT	60091	2811	5W-13N	E7
9100	HMTN	60453	3212	5W-10S	A5
9100	HMTN	60456	3212	5W-10S	A5
9100	OKLN	60453	3212	5W-10S	A5
9100	OKLN	60456	3212	5W-10S	A5
9100	SKOK	60076	2866	5W-11N	A3
10300	OKLN	60453	3276	5W-12S	A3
11000	CHCG	60453	3276	5W-12S	A3
11000	CHCG	60655	3276	5W-12S	A3
13900	CTWD	60445	3348	5W-17S	A4
14100	MDLN	60445	3348	5W-17S	B5
15100	OKFT	60445	3348	5W-18S	B7
15100	OKFT	60452	3348	5W-18S	B7
16700	BmnT	60452	3426	5W-20S	B3
16700	BmnT	60477	3426	5W-20S	B3
16700	OKFT	60452	3426	5W-20S	B3
16700	OKFT	60477	3426	5W-20S	B3
N Kilpatrick Av					
600	CHCG	60644	3032	5W-0N	A3
700	CHCG	60651	3032	5W-0N	A3
1500	CHCG	60639	3032	5W-1N	A1

STREET Block	City	ZIP	Map#	CGS	Grid
N Kilpatrick Av					
1900	CHCG	60639	2976	5W-2N	A7
2700	CHCG	60641	2976	5W-3N	A5
4000	CHCG	60641	2975	5W-5N	E1
4800	CHCG	60630	2919	6W-7N	D4
4900	CHCG	60630	2920	5W-6N	A6
5800	CHCG	60646	2919	5W-7N	E4
6100	CHCG	60646	2920	5W-7N	A3
6300	LNWD	60646	2919	5W-7N	E3
6300	LNWD	60712	2919	5W-8N	E2
7200	LNWD	60712	2865	5W-9N	E7
S Kilpatrick Av					
10	CHCG	60644	3032	5W-0S	A5
4200	CHCG	60632	3090	5W-4S	A7
5400	CHCG	60629	3150	5W-6S	A3
5400	CHCG	60632	3150	5W-6S	A3
5400	CHCG	60638	3150	5W-6S	A3
7700	CHCG	60652	3212	5W-8S	A1
8600	CHCG	60456	3212	5W-9S	A4
8600	HMTN	60456	3212	5W-9S	A4
8600	HMTN	60652	3212	5W-9S	A4
Kilpatrick Ln					
8700	HMTN	60456	3212	5W-10S	A4
8700	HMTN	60652	3212	5W-10S	A4
Kilrea Dr					
9300	PlsT	60462	3345	11W-15S	E2
Kilrenny					
800	IVNS	60067	2804	23W-14N	D3
W Kim Av					
1700	MPPT	60056	2861	17W-12N	C1
Kim Ct					
500	GRNE	60031	2535	14W-33N	D3
Kim Ln					
400	CmpT	60175	2906	39W-6N	E7
Kim Pl					
1000	LMNT	60439	3270	19W-14S	D7
Kimball Av					
200	WCDA	60084	2643	25W-27N	E1
300	WCDA	60084	2644	25W-27N	A1
500	WcnT	60084	2644	25W-27N	A1
6500	HGKN	60525	3147	11W-7S	D6
8200	SKOK	60076	2866	4W-10N	D5
8700	SKOK	60203	2866	4W-10N	D4
18400	HMWD	60430	3506	4W-22S	E1
E Kimball Av					
10	WDSK	60098	2581	41W-30N	D2
N Kimball Av					
1600	CHCG	60647	2976	4W-3N	D5
2700	CHCG	60618	2976	4W-3N	D5
4300	CHCG	60625	2976	4W-5N	D1
4400	CHCG	60625	2920	4W-5N	D7
5500	CHCG	60659	2920	4W-7N	D3
6400	LNWD	60659	2920	4W-8N	D3
6400	LNWD	60712	2920	4W-8N	D2
W Kimball Av					
400	WDSK	60098	2581	42W-30N	C2
600	PLTN	60067	2805	21W-15N	C2
Kimball Ct					
1200	LslT	60540	3203	26W-7S	E1
1200	NPVL	60540	3203	26W-7S	E1
2700	WDRG	60517	3143	22W-7S	D7
Kimball Ln					
4900	CPVL	60110	2747	36W-18N	A4
Kimball Pl					
5200	OKLN	60453	3211	6W-10S	D4
Kimball Rd					
400	WNFD	60190	3023	27W-0N	D4
700	HDPK	60035	2704	8W-21N	D5
Kimball St					
10	ELGN	60120	2854	34W-11N	E3
10	ELGN	60123	2854	34W-11N	E3
300	ELGN	60120	2855	33W-11N	A3
Kimball Hill Dr					
4800	RGMW	60008	2860	19W-11N	B3
Kimballwood Ln					
700	HDPK	60035	2704	8W-21N	E6
Kimbark Av					
14200	DLTN	60419	3351	1E-17S	B5
15600	SHLD	60473	3351	1E-18S	B7
16400	SHLD	60473	3429	1E-19S	B2
S Kimbark Av					
4700	CHCG	60615	3153	1E-5S	A1
7000	CHCG	60619	3153	1E-7S	A6
7000	CHCG	60637	3153	1E-7S	A6
7500	CHCG	60619	3215	1E-8S	A1
Kimbark Ct					
16700	SHLD	60473	3429	1E-19S	B2
Kimbark Rd					
10	RVSD	60546	3088	10W-3S	B5
W Kimbell Av					
200	EMHT	60126	2971	16W-2N	E7
Kimber Dr					
100	NLNX	60451	3501	18W-24S	B5
E Kimber Ln					
800	ANHT	60005	2861	17W-11N	B4
W Kimber Ln					
8200	PSPK	60464	3274	10W-13S	B4
Kimberley Cir					
10	OKBK	60523	3085	17W-2S	B3
Kimberley Ln					
10	OKBK	60523	3085	17W-2S	B3
10	YkTp	60523	3085	17W-2S	B3
600	SMWD	60107	2856	29W-10N	D5
Kimberly Av					
-	PltT	60067	2805	22W-14N	A5
-	PltT	60195	2805	22W-14N	A5
1600	ELGN	60123	2854	35W-12N	A2
E Kimberly Av					
10	PltT	60067	2805	20W-13N	E5
10	RGMW	60008	2805	20W-13N	E5
10	RGMW	60067	2805	20W-13N	E5
N Kimberly Av					
5000	CHCG	60630	2919	6W-7N	D4
5000	CHCG	60630	2920	5W-6N	A6
Kimberly Ct					
10	DRFD	60015	2756	11W-20N	C2
300	AURA	60504	3139	31W-6S	E5
1900	DRN	60561	3206	19W-10S	E4
4500	LGGV	60047	2700	19W-23N	C2
4800	OKFT	60452	3426	6W-20S	A3
8400	BRRG	60527	3208	15W-9S	A4
S Kimberly Ct					
25100	GGnT	60449	3682	9W-30S	A3
Kimberly Dr					
100	EDND	60118	2801	33W-16N	C2
300	CLSM	60188	2968	25W-3N	C6
1600	SMBG	60173	2859	21W-11N	E4
1600	SMBG	60173	2860	21W-11N	A3
5600	JLET	60586	3496	31W-22S	A1
6000	BmnT	60477	3425	7W-19S	B2
6100	TYPK	60477	3425	7W-19S	C3
Kimberly Ln					
100	LKFT	60045	2649	11W-24N	E7
100	LKFT	60045	2703	11W-24N	E1
600	MTGY	60538	3200	34W-9S	D4
800	CLLK	60014	2639	37W-24N	B7
900	ANTH	60002	2359	20W-42N	A7

STREET Block	City	ZIP	Map#	CGS	Grid
Kimberly Ln					
900	WPHR	60096	2363	10W-42N	B6
1600	RMVL	60446	3339	26W-18S	D7
10800	ODPK	60467	3423	13W-21S	A5
S Kimberly Ln					
26400	CNHN	60410	3761	33W-32S	B1
Kimberly Rd					
100	NBRN	60010	2698	25W-23N	B1
Kimberly Tr					
11000	MKNA	60448	3503	13W-23S	A2
Kimberly Wy					
800	LslT	60532	3143	23W-6S	B5
1000	LSLE	60532	3143	23W-6S	B4
Kimberry Ct					
100	RGMW	60008	2805	21W-14N	D4
Kimberwick Ln					
200	LslT	60540	3205	23W-8S	A1
36600	WrnT	60083	2477	16W-36N	D3
Kimer Ct					
500	CLLK	60012	2639	35W-27N	E1
Kimmel Ct					
9300	OrlT	60487	3423	11W-21S	E6
9300	TYPK	60487	3423	11W-21S	E6
Kimmer Ct					
1200	LKFT	60045	2649	12W-24N	B7
Kimmey Ln					
9500	FNPK	60131	2973	11W-4N	C3
Kin Ct					
500	WLMT	60091	2811	5W-13N	E6
Kincaid Ct					
10	DSPN	60016	2862	15W-10N	B4
6800	WDRG	60517	3143	22W-7S	D7
Kincaid Dr					
100	LKZH	60047	2698	23W-23N	E3
2700	WDRG	60517	3143	22W-7S	D7
Kincaid St					
500	HDPK	60035	2758	7W-20N	B1
600	HDPK	60035	2705	7W-20N	B7
Kindberg Ct					
800	ELBN	60119	3017	43W-0N	B4
Kindling Ct					
6300	LSLE	60532	3142	24W-7S	E6
10500	PlsT	60464	3345	13W-15S	B1
Kindrat Ln					
-	HMGN	60441	3342	19W-16S	D4
-	HMGN	60491	3342	19W-16S	D4
Kine Cir					
-	TNLK	53181	2353		E3
King Av					
100	DndT	60118	2801	33W-16N	B2
100	EDND	60118	2801	33W-15N	B3
7200	MchT	60097	2469	36W-37N	E2
9000	FNPK	60131	2973	11W-4N	D3
11200	FNPK	60131	2972	14W-4N	D4
King Cir					
1200	SHLD	60473	3351	1E-18S	B7
King Ct					
100	WLNG	60090	2755	15W-17N	A4
600	EDND	60118	2801	33W-15N	B3
6600	WDRG	60517	3143	22W-7S	D6
14800	GNOK	60048	2592	14W-30N	B2
King Dr					
10	SMWD	60107	2857	27W-9N	C7
10	SMWD	60107	2911	27W-9N	C1
1200	SHLD	60419	3351	1E-18S	B6
1200	SHLD	60473	3351	1E-18S	B6
1500	BKLY	60163	3028	14W-0N	C4
14800	GNOK	60048	2592	14W-30N	B2
King Ln					
500	DSPN	60016	2862	15W-10N	A4
King Rd					
-	BNHL	60010	2802	30W-15N	A2
-	BNHL	60118	2802	30W-15N	A2
13400	HMGN	60439	3343	18W-15S	A2
13400	HMGN	60491	3343	18W-15S	A2
13400	LMNT	60439	3343	18W-15S	A2
S King Rd					
13700	HMGN	60491	3343	18W-16S	A4
King St					
-	WDSK	60098	2581	41W-30N	E1
10	EGvT	60007	2861	17W-10N	B5
10	EGVV	60007	2861	17W-10N	B5
200	CLLK	60014	2639	36W-25N	E5
200	YKVL	60560	3333	43W-15S	C2
11000	FNPK	60131	2972	13W-4N	D3
King Alford Ct					
3100	SCRL	60174	2965	33W-4N	B4
3100	WYNE	60174	2965	33W-4N	B4
King Arthur Ct					
10	HnrT	60120	2856	31W-10N	A6
10	NHLK	60164	2972	14W-3N	C6
300	BGBK	60440	3205	21W-11S	D7
5500	DRGV	60515	3145	18W-6S	A4
5500	DRGV	60559	3145	18W-6S	A4
5500	WTMT	60559	3145	18W-6S	A4
20500	LYWD	60411	3509	2E-24S	E5
N King Arthur Ct					
1100	PLTN	60067	2752	21W-17N	E4
W King Arthur Ct					
10	PLTN	60067	2752	21W-17N	D5
King Arthur Dr					
-	NHLK	60164	2972	14W-3N	C6
20500	LYWD	60411	3509	2E-24S	E5
King Arthur Ln					
-	BHPK	60087	2422	9W-38N	C7
King Arthur Wy					
400	BGBK	60440	3205	21W-11S	D7
Kingbird Ct					
10	SBTN	60010	2803	26W-14N	D3
3000	NPVL	60564	3202	30W-11S	B7
Kingbird Ln					
3000	NPVL	60564	3202	30W-11S	B7
3000	NPVL	60564	3266	30W-11S	B1
N King Charles Ct					
1000	PLTN	60067	2752	21W-17N	E4
King Charles Ln					
3700	SCRL	60174	2965	33W-4N	B5
King Edward Av					
700	SCRL	60174	2965	33W-4N	B4
King Edward Blvd					
-	BHPK	60087	2422	9W-38N	C7
N King Edward Ct					
1300	PLTN	60067	2752	21W-17N	E4
1500	PltT	60074	2752	21W-17N	E4
Kingery Ct					
10	AddT	60101	2971	17W-3N	C6
10	ADSN	60101	2971	17W-3N	C6
Kingery Expwy					
-	LNSG	-	3429	2E-20S	C4
-	LNSG	-	3430	3E-20S	A4
-	MNSR	-	3430	4E-20S	C4
-	SHLD	-	3429	1E-20S	B4
-	ThtT	-	3429	2E-20S	C4
600	HNDL	60521	3085	16W-4S	D6
600	HNDL	60559	3085	16W-4S	D6
600	OKBK	60523	3085	16W-3S	D6

STREET Block	City	ZIP	Map#	CGS	Grid
Kingery Expwy					
600	OKBK	60559	3085	16W-3S	D6
600	WTMT	60559	3085	16W-3S	D6
900	WTMT	60523	3085	16W-3S	D6
Kingery Expwy I-80					
-	LNSG	-	3429	2E-20S	C4
-	LNSG	-	3430	3E-20S	A4
-	MNSR	-	3430	4E-20S	C4
-	ThtT	-	3429	2E-20S	C4
Kingery Expwy I-94					
-	LNSG	-	3429	3E-20S	E4
-	LNSG	-	3430	3E-20S	A4
-	MNSR	-	3430	4E-20S	C4
-	SHLD	-	3429	1E-20S	B4
-	ThtT	-	3429	1E-20S	B4
Kingery Expwy I-294					
-	LNSG	-	3429	2E-20S	C4
-	LNSG	-	3430	3E-20S	A4
-	ThtT	-	3429	2E-20S	C4
Kingery Expwy SR-83					
600	HNDL	60521	3085	16W-4S	D6
600	HNDL	60559	3085	16W-4S	D6
600	OKBK	60523	3085	16W-3S	D6
600	OKBK	60559	3085	16W-3S	D6
600	WTMT	60559	3085	16W-3S	D6
900	WTMT	60523	3085	16W-3S	D6
Kingery Expwy SR-394					
-	SHLD	-	3429	1E-20S	B3
Kingery Expwy US-6					
-	LNSG	-	3429	3E-20S	E4
-	LNSG	-	3430	3E-20S	A4
-	MNSR	-	3430	4E-20S	C4
Kingery Hwy					
-	AddT	60101	2971	17W-3N	C5
-	AddT	60106	2971	17W-4N	C3
-	AddT	60191	2971	17W-4N	C2
-	ADSN	60101	2971	17W-3N	C4
-	ADSN	60106	2971	17W-3N	C4
-	ADSN	60126	2971	17W-2N	C7
-	BNVL	60007	2915	16W-7N	C4
-	BNVL	60106	2971	17W-5N	C1
-	BNVL	60191	2971	16W-5N	C1
-	CNHL	60514	3085	16W-4S	E7
-	CNHL	60514	3145	16W-5S	E1
-	CNHL	60521	3085	16W-4S	E7
-	CNHL	60521	3145	16W-5S	E2
-	CNHL	60527	3145	16W-6S	E4
-	DGvT	60439	3271	16W-11S	E1
-	DGvT	60514	3145	16W-6S	E4
-	DGvT	60521	3145	16W-6S	E4
-	DGvT	60527	3271	16W-11S	E1
-	EGVV	60007	2915	16W-7N	D4
-	EMHT	60101	2971	17W-3N	C6
-	EMHT	60126	2971	17W-2N	C7
-	EMHT	60126	3027	17W-1N	C2
-	EMHT	60181	3027	17W-0S	C7
-	HNDL	60521	3085	16W-4S	E7
-	HNDL	60521	3145	16W-5S	E2
-	HNDL	60559	3085	16W-4S	D7
-	LmnT	60439	3271	16W-11S	E1
-	LmnT	60439	3272	16W-12S	A2
-	OKBK	60181	3085	16W-1S	D1
-	OKBK	60521	3085	16W-3S	D6
-	OKBK	60523	3085	16W-1S	D1
-	OKBK	60559	3085	16W-3S	D5
-	OKTR	60126	3027	17W-0S	C7
-	OKTR	60181	3027	17W-0S	C7
-	OKTR	60181	3085	16W-1S	D1
-	OKTR	60523	3085	16W-3S	D6
-	VLPK	60126	2971	17W-2N	C7
-	VLPK	60126	3027	17W-0N	C3
-	VLPK	60181	3027	17W-0S	C5
-	WDDL	60106	2971	16W-5N	C1
-	WDDL	60191	2971	17W-2N	C7
-	WTMT	60514	3085	16W-4S	E7
-	WTMT	60521	3085	16W-4S	E7
-	WTMT	60523	3085	16W-3S	D5
-	WTMT	60559	3085	16W-3S	D5
10	DGvT	60527	3207	16W-10S	E6
400	BNVL	60106	2915	16W-7N	D4
400	BRRG	60527	3207	16W-9S	E4
6200	WLBK	60527	3145	16W-6S	E5
6300	DGvT	60527	3145	16W-6S	E5
6700	DRN	60527	3145	16W-7S	E6
6700	DRN	60561	3145	16W-7S	E6
6700	WLBK	60561	3145	16W-7S	E6
7100	DRN	60527	3207	16W-8S	E1
7100	WLBK	60527	3207	16W-10S	E5
7200	DRN	60561	3207	16W-8S	E1
Kingery Hwy SR-83					
-	AddT	60101	2971	17W-3N	C5
-	AddT	60106	2971	17W-4N	C3
-	AddT	60191	2971	17W-4N	C2
-	ADSN	60101	2971	17W-3N	C4
-	ADSN	60106	2971	17W-3N	C4
-	ADSN	60126	2971	17W-2N	C7
-	BNVL	60007	2915	16W-7N	C4
-	BNVL	60106	2971	17W-5N	C1
-	BNVL	60191	2971	16W-5N	C1
-	CNHL	60514	3085	16W-4S	E7
-	CNHL	60514	3145	16W-5S	E2
-	CNHL	60521	3085	16W-4S	E7
-	CNHL	60521	3145	16W-5S	E2
-	CNHL	60527	3145	16W-6S	E4
-	DGvT	60439	3271	16W-11S	E1
-	DGvT	60514	3145	16W-6S	E4
-	DGvT	60521	3145	16W-6S	E4
-	DGvT	60527	3271	16W-11S	E1
-	EGVV	60007	2915	16W-7N	D4
-	EMHT	60101	2971	17W-3N	C6
-	EMHT	60126	2971	17W-2N	C7
-	EMHT	60126	3027	17W-1N	C2
-	EMHT	60181	3027	17W-0S	C7
-	HNDL	60521	3085	16W-3S	D6
-	HNDL	60521	3145	16W-5S	E2
-	HNDL	60559	3085	16W-3S	D6
-	LmnT	60439	3271	16W-11S	E1
-	LmnT	60439	3272	16W-12S	A1
-	OKBK	60181	3085	16W-1S	D1
-	OKBK	60521	3085	16W-3S	D6
-	OKBK	60523	3085	16W-1S	D1
-	OKBK	60559	3085	16W-3S	D6
-	OKTR	60126	3027	17W-0S	C7
-	OKTR	60181	3027	17W-0S	C7
-	OKTR	60181	3085	16W-1S	D1
-	OKTR	60523	3085	16W-3S	D6
-	VLPK	60126	2971	17W-2N	C7
-	VLPK	60126	3027	17W-0N	C3
-	VLPK	60181	3027	17W-0S	C5
-	WDDL	60106	2971	16W-5N	C1
-	WDDL	60191	2971	17W-2N	C7
-	WTMT	60514	3085	16W-4S	E7
-	WTMT	60521	3085	16W-4S	E7
-	WTMT	60523	3085	16W-3S	D5
-	WTMT	60559	3085	16W-3S	D5
10	DGvT	60527	3207	16W-10S	E6

STREET Block	City	ZIP	Map#	CGS	Grid
Kingery Hwy SR-83					
400	BNVL	60106	2915	16W-7N	D4
400	BRRG	60527	3207	16W-9S	E4
6200	DGvT	60527	3145	16W-6S	E5
6200	WLBK	60527	3145	16W-6S	E5
6600	DRN	60561	3145	16W-7S	E6
6700	DRN	60527	3145	16W-7S	E6
6700	WLBK	60561	3145	16W-7S	E6
7100	WLBK	60527	3207	16W-10S	E5
7200	DRN	60527	3207	16W-8S	E1
7200	DRN	60561	3207	16W-8S	E1
S Kingery Hwy					
7700	WLBK	60527	3207	16W-8S	E2
S Kingery Hwy SR-83					
7600	WLBK	60527	3207	16W-8S	E2
Kingery Quarter					
10	DGvT	60527	3207	16W-10S	D6
Kingery Quarter Rdg					
-	DGvT	60527	3207	16W-10S	E5
Kingfisher Ct					
100	CmpT	60175	2962	40W-5N	C2
3200	RGMW	60008	2806	19W-13N	C6
Kingfisher Ln					
2100	RGMW	60008	2806	19W-13N	C6
2300	NLNX	60451	3589	18W-27S	A4
Kingfisher Ln E					
3200	RGMW	60008	2806	19W-13N	C6
Kingfisher Rd					
400	BRLT	60103	2909	32W-9N	D2
N King George Ct					
1300	PLTN	60067	2752	21W-17N	E4
W King George Ct					
10	PLTN	60067	2752	21W-17N	E4
King George Dr					
-	BHPK	60087	2422	9W-38N	C7
King George Ln					
3700	SCRL	60174	2965	33W-4N	B5
W King Henry Ct					
10	PLTN	60067	2752	21W-17N	D5
King Henry Ln					
700	SCRL	60174	2965	33W-4N	B5
King James Av					
900	SCRL	60174	2965	33W-4N	B5
King James Ct					
3800	SCRL	60174	2965	33W-4N	B4
Kinglet Ct					
10	NPVL	60565	3203	26W-9S	E3
10	NPVL	60565	3204	26W-9S	A3
Kingman Ct					
1200	ELGN	60123	2800	36W-13N	A7
Kingman Dr					
1800	ELGN	60123	2800	36W-13N	A7
Kingman Ln					
10	HFET	60169	2859	23W-11N	A4
10	SMBG	60169	2859	23W-11N	A4
10	SMBG	60194	2859	23W-11N	A4
200	HFET	60169	2858	24W-11N	E4
King Muir Rd					
100	LKFT	60045	2649	12W-26N	C4
King Richard Cir					
1600	SCRL	60174	2965	33W-4N	B4
King Richard Ct					
3800	SCRL	60174	2965	33W-4N	B4
King Richard Dr					
-	BHPK	60087	2422	9W-38N	C7
King Richards Ct					
800	DRFD	60015	2703	12W-21N	C7
Kings Cir					
1200	WCHI	60185	3022	30W-2N	C1
Kings Cross					
1200	WCHI	60185	3022	30W-2N	C1
Kings Ct					
-	WSTR	60154	3086	13W-2S	D3
10	MltT	60137	3083	23W-3S	A6
200	DGvT	60561	3207	17W-9S	B3
200	LGPK	60525	3087	12W-2S	B3
1200	WCHI	60185	3022	30W-2N	C1
1400	NPVL	60563	3140	29W-5S	E3
2200	GNVA	60134	3019	36W-0S	E6
4800	RNPK	60471	3594	6W-27S	A4
S Kings Ct					
22400	TroT	60404	3584	30W-27S	B4
Kings Ln					
900	GNVW	60025	2811	7W-14N	A3
Kings Rd					
100	CPVL	60110	2748	33W-18N	A5
100	DndT	60110	2748	33W-18N	A5
400	FXLK	60020	2473	28W-35N	A5
18700	HMWD	60430	3508	1W-22S	B1
S Kings Rd					
-	BGBK	60585	3267	27W-13S	D5
2000	BGBK	60490	3267	26W-12S	D3
3300	BlmT	60466	3595	2W-28S	E7
3300	BlmT	60475	3595	2W-28S	E7
3300	CteT	60475	3595	2W-28S	E7
3300	STGR	60475	3595	2W-28S	E7
3500	CteT	60417	3595	2W-28S	E6
3500	STGR	60417	3595	2W-28S	E6
12000	DPgT	60490	3267	26W-14S	D7
24000	CRTE	60417	3684	2W-29S	E1
24000	CteT	60417	3684	2W-29S	D2
24500	UYPK	60417	3684	2W-29S	D2
Kings Row					
100	BRTN	60010	2751	24W-18N	D2
E Kings Row					
800	PLTN	60074	2753	19W-18N	B2
Kings Wy					
200	MchT	60051	2529	29W-33N	D3
Kings Wy N					
4500	GRNE	60031	2535	14W-33N	C2
Kings Wy W					
4800	GRNE	60031	2535	14W-33N	B2
Kingsborough Cove					
10	IVNS	60010	2750	25W-16N	E7
Kingsbridge Cir					
100	NPVL	60540	3142	25W-6S	A5
Kingsbridge Dr					
500	CLSM	60188	2967	26W-4N	D4
6200	AlqT	60013	2642	30W-25N	B4
Kingsbridge Rd					
200	EGVV	60007	2914	19W-8N	C2
Kingsbridge Wy					
700	BFGV	60089	2701	17W-21N	B6
Kingsbrook Ct					
-	WHTN	60187	3024	24W-0N	C4
Kingsbrook Dr					
16400	CTHL	60403	3418	25W-19S	B4
20400	LktT	60403	3418	25W-19S	B4
20400	LktT	60441	3418	25W-19S	B4
Kingsbrooke Cross					
400	BGBK	60440	3268	24W-12S	D4
Kingsbrooke Ct					
10	BGBK	60440	3268	24W-12S	D3
Kingsbury Av					
400	AURA	60505	3200	35W-8S	B1

STREET Block	City	ZIP	Map#	CGS	Grid
Kingsbury Ct					
10	OKBK	60523	3085	17W-2S	C3
200	WDRG	60517	3206	20W-10S	B6
600	ALGN	60102	2695	33W-20N	A7
600	BTVA	60510	3078	34W-1S	E2
1400	GRNE	60031	2477	17W-35N	B5
11200	HTLY	60142	2692	40W-22N	A4
S Kingsbury Ct					
9700	PSHL	60465	3210	10W-11S	A7
W Kingsbury Ct					
700	ANHT	60004	2753	18W-16N	E6
Kingsbury Dr					
-	HRPK	60133	2911	26W-9N	E1
300	SMBG	60193	2857	26W-9N	E7
7700	HRPK	60133	2857	26W-9N	E7
8200	HRPK	60193	2857	26W-10N	E7
W Kingsbury Dr					
300	ANHT	60004	2754	18W-16N	A6
500	ANHT	60004	2753	18W-16N	E6
Kingsbury Rd					
9700	HTLY	60142	2692	40W-22N	A4
N Kingsbury St					
-	CHCG	60610	3033	1W-1N	E1
400	CHCG	60606	3034	0W-0N	B3
900	CHCG	60610	3034	0W-1N	A2
1200	CHCG	60622	3033	1W-1N	E1
1600	CHCG	60614	2977	1W-2N	D7
1600	CHCG	60622	2977	1W-2N	E7
Kingsbury Estates Dr					
2000	JLET	60586	3416	30W-21S	B7
Kings Canyon Dr					
900	HnrT	60107	2856	30W-9N	B7
Kings Cove					
300	LslT	60532	3143	23W-6S	B4
Kings Cross Dr					
10	LNSH	60069	2702	13W-22N	D3
N Kingsdale Av					
5700	CHCG	60646	2919	5W-7N	E4
5800	CHCG	60646	2920	5W-7N	A4
Kingsdale Rd					
1000	HFET	60169	2858	25W-11N	B3
Kings Gate Ln					
1700	CLLK	60014	2693	37W-22N	B4
1800	LIHL	60014	2693	37W-22N	B4
1800	LIHL	60156	2693	37W-22N	B4
Kingshill Cir					
4100	AURA	60564	3202	30W-9S	B4
Kings Lair Dr					
3300	SPGV	60081	2413	32W-39N	B5
Kingsland Dr					
500	BTVA	60510	3020	34W-0S	E6
500	BTVA	60510	3078	34W-0S	D1
1300	GnvT	60510	3020	34W-0S	E6
Kingsley Ct					
-	ELGN	60120	2855	32W-11N	C4
Kingsley Dr					
1800	SMBG	60194	2858	25W-11N	A4
2400	NPVL	60565	3203	26W-10S	E6
W Kingsley Dr					
500	ANHT	60004	2754	18W-18N	A3
1100	ANHT	60004	2753	18W-18N	E3
Kingsley Ln					
1100	AURA	60505	3139	33W-6S	A4
Kingsman Ct					
-	SRGV	60554	3135	41W-5S	E3
Kings Mill Ct					
200	SMBG	60193	2859	23W-10N	B5
Kingsmill Ct					
-	ALGN	60102	2746	37W-20N	B1
2000	YKVL	60560	3333	42W-17S	C5
Kings Mill Dr					
10	CmpT	60175	2962	40W-5N	B1
Kingsmill Dr					
1000	ALGN	60102	2746	37W-20N	B2
Kingsmill Ln					
500	PTHT	60070	2808	14W-14N	C4
Kingsmill St					
2100	YKVL	60560	3333	42W-17S	D6
Kings Point Ct					
1100	NPVL	60563	3141	28W-5S	A3
3200	ISLK	60042	2586	30W-28N	B5
Kingspoint Dr E					
800	ADSN	60101	2970	21W-4N	A3
Kingspoint Dr N					
1800	ADSN	60101	2970	21W-4N	A3
Kingspoint Dr S					
1800	ADSN	60101	2970	21W-4N	A3
Kingspoint Dr W					
800	ADSN	60101	2969	21W-4N	E3
800	ADSN	60101	2970	21W-4N	A3
Kingsport Ct					
10	SEGN	60177	2908	36W-8N	A2
300	CLLK	60012	2639	36W-26N	E2
1400	NHBK	60062	2756	11W-17N	D6
Kingsport Dr					
10	SEGN	60177	2908	36W-8N	A3
100	SMBG	60193	2913	23W-9N	B1
200	SMBG	60193	2859	23W-9N	B7
300	GRNE	60031	2533	18W-34N	E1
300	GRNE	60031	2534	18W-34N	A1
300	WrnT	60030	2533	18W-34N	E1
300	WrnT	60031	2533	18W-34N	E1
400	GRNE	60031	2477	18W-34N	A7
1000	WLNG	60090	2754	15W-17N	E5
1100	WLNG	60004	2754	15W-17N	E5
Kingsport Rd					
16100	ODPK	60467	3423	13W-19S	A2
Kingston Av					
1300	AURA	60505	3200	34W-9S	C4
1300	MTGY	60505	3200	34W-9S	C4
1300	MTGY	60538	3200	34W-9S	C4
4400	LSLE	60532	3143	22W-4S	B1
5500	LslT	60532	3143	22W-5S	B4
S Kingston Av					
7300	CHCG	60649	3153	3E-8S	D7
7500	CHCG	60649	3215	3E-9S	D2
7800	CHCG	60617	3215	3E-10S	D4
Kingston Blvd					
500	FXLK	60050	2472	28W-37N	D2
700	GrtT	60050	2472	28W-37N	D2
Kingston Cir					
1700	CPVL	60110	2748	32W-17N	D7
1700	CPVL	60110	2801	32W-17N	D1
Kingston Ct					
-	SMWD	60107	2911	28W-8N	A2
10	CmpT	60175	2906	41W-7N	A6
400	MPPT	60056	2808	14W-13N	C6
500	ROSL	60172	2912	24W-6N	C6
1000	GLHT	60139	3024	23W-1N	E2
1000	VNHL	60061	2647	16W-26N	D2
1400	DSPN	60018	2862	13W-10N	D5
1400	SMBG	60193	2858	25W-9N	B7
3000	SMWD	60107	2910	30W-9N	C2
6900	TYPK	60477	3425	8W-19S	A2
S Kingston Ct					
20100	FftT	60423	3504	9W-24S	D5

STREET Block	City	ZIP	Map#	CGS	Grid
W Kingston Ct					
16400	VrnT	60069	2701	16W-23N	D2
Kingston Dr					
10	OKBK	60523	3085	17W-2S	B3
100	NLNX	60433	3500	20W-24S	C6
100	NLNX	60451	3500	20W-24S	C6
100	NlxT	60433	3500	20W-24S	C6
400	NlxT	60451	3500	20W-24S	C5
400	RMVL	60446	3340	24W-15S	E1
500	GNVA	60134	3020	34W-1N	E2
900	WHTN	60187	3025	23W-0N	A5
2200	WHTN	60187	3082	23W-3S	E5
2600	ISLK	60042	2586	28W-29N	D5
2900	BFGV	60089	2701	17W-23N	C2
5000	HFET	60010	2751	24W-16N	B7
5100	IVNS	60010	2751	24W-16N	B7
N Kingston Dr					
100	AddT	60101	2970	19W-3N	C5
100	ADSN	60101	2970	19W-3N	C5
W Kingston Dr					
7700	FftT	60423	3504	9W-24S	D5
Kingston Ln					
100	BMDL	60108	2969	22W-5N	B2
700	CLLK	60014	2639	35W-24N	E7
700	CLLK	60014	2640	35W-24N	A7
800	BRLT	60103	2910	29W-7N	D5
1200	SMBG	60193	2858	25W-9N	B7
9000	ODPK	60462	3346	11W-18S	A6
Kingston Pl					
-	ALGN	60102	2747	35W-19N	B2
-	AlqT	60102	2747	35W-19N	B2
-	MchT	60050	2472	29W-37N	D2
100	CHHT	60411	3507	1W-24S	E5
100	CHHT	60411	3508	1W-24S	A5
700	FXLK	60050	2472	28W-37N	D2
700	GrtT	60050	2472	29W-37N	D2
Kingston Rd					
100	BGBK	60440	3269	22W-12S	D2
2000	WKGN	60087	2479	11W-37N	D2
2500	NHBK	60062	2809	10W-16N	E1
2500	NHBK	60062	2810	10W-16N	A1
6800	TYPK	60477	3425	8W-19S	A2
N Kingston Row					
23500	VrnT	60069	2701	16W-23N	D2
Kingston St					
10800	WSTR	60154	3086	13W-2S	E3
24600	PNFD	60544	3416	30W-18S	A1
Kingston Ter					
300	DRFD	60015	2704	10W-21N	A7
Kingston Wy					
21500	MKNA	60448	3590	14W-26S	E2
Kingston Place Rd					
11800	ALGN	60102	2747	34W-20N	B1
11800	AlqT	60102	2747	34W-20N	B1
Kings Walk Dr					
4500	PLTN	60008	2805	20W-14N	E4
4500	PLTN	60067	2805	20W-14N	E4
4500	RGMW	60008	2805	20W-14N	E4
Kingsway Av					
2500	NLNX	60451	3588	19W-27S	D5
2900	NLNX	60442	3588	19W-27S	E5
N Kingsway Ct					
700	AraT	60506	3199	38W-8S	B2
N Kingsway Dr					
100	AURA	60506	3137	38W-7S	A7
300	AURA	60506	3199	38W-8S	B1
400	AraT	60506	3199	38W-8S	B1
Kingsway Dr S					
1800	AraT	60506	3199	38W-8S	B2
1800	AURA	60506	3199	38W-8S	B2
Kingsway St					
400	MDLN	60060	2590	20W-28N	A7
Kingswood Ct					
10	RVWD	60015	2703	13W-21N	A6
100	NPVL	60565	3203	26W-9S	E4
300	WLBK	60527	3146	15W-7S	A6
400	WYNE	60184	2966	30W-4N	B4
3300	JLET	60431	3497	28W-23S	B6
Kingswood Dr					
300	NARA	60542	3137	36W-4S	E1
700	CmpT	60175	2961	42W-5N	D2
6700	BRRG	60527	3146	15W-7S	A6
6700	WLBK	60527	3146	15W-7S	A6
11400	ODPK	60467	3344	14W-16S	D3
Kingswood Ln					
200	WLNG	60090	2755	14W-18N	D3
Kings Wy Dr					
-	BHPK	60087	2422	9W-38N	B7
King William Ct					
3700	SCRL	60174	2965	33W-4N	B4
King William St					
10	EDND	60118	2801	34W-16N	A2
Kingwood Ln					
1000	LKZH	60047	2699	22W-22N	B4
Kinkaid Ct					
400	DSPN	60016	2862	15W-10N	A4
W Kinley Blvd					
3000	MHRY	60050	2528	32W-31N	C7
Kinmonth Dr					
1000	JLET	60433	3588	21W-25S	A1
1000	JltT	60433	3500	21W-25S	A7
1000	JltT	60433	3588	21W-25S	A1
Kinne Cir					
1100	BTVA	60510	3077	36W-2S	E4
Kinne Rd					
3200	RBBN	60472	3348	4W-16S	D4
Kinnear Cove					
600	IVNS	60010	2803	25W-15N	E2
600	SBTN	60010	2803	25W-15N	E2
Kinross St					
1400	FSMR	60422	3506	4W-23S	D3
Kinsale Dr					
9000	MKNA	60448	3504	11W-23S	A4
9000	TYPK	60448	3504	11W-23S	A4
9000	TYPK	60477	3504	11W-23S	A4
Kinsel St					
200	LtRT	60545	3259	48W-14S	B7
200	PLNO	60545	3259	48W-14S	B7
W Kinsey Av					
1100	JLET	60436	3498	25W-24S	B7
1300	RKDL	60436	3498	25W-24S	B6
Kinsie Ct					
1100	NPVL	60540	3204	26W-8S	A1
W Kinsley Ct					
21900	PnfT	60544	3339	27W-16S	C4
N Kinsley Ln					
5300	BHPK	60083	2421	13W-39N	A5
Kinsley Pl					
7600	MNSR	46321	3430		D5
Kinston Ct					
800	NPVL	60540	3203	27W-7S	B1
Kinvara Av					
8900	MKNA	60448	3504	11W-23S	A3
S Kinvarra Dr					
12500	PlsT	60464	3273	12W-14S	C7
12500	PSPK	60464	3273	12W-14S	C7

STREET Block	City	ZIP	Map#	CGS	Grid
Kinzie Ln					
12400	GfnT	60142	2744	41W-20N	D1
N Kinzie Pl					
500	TNTN	60476	3428	0E-20S	D5
E Kinzie St					
10	CHCG	60610	3034	0E-0N	C3
10	CHCG	60611	3034		E4
N Kinzie St					
100	TNTN	60476	3428	0E-21S	D5
S Kinzie St					
100	TNTN	60476	3428	0E-21S	D6
W Kinzie St					
10	CHCG	60610	3034	0W-0N	A4
10	CHCG	60611	3034	0W-0N	C3
100	CHCG	60606	3034	0W-0N	A4
400	CHCG	60661	3034	0W-0N	A3
700	CHCG	60622	3034	0W-0N	A3
800	CHCG	60622	3033	1W-0N	D3
1400	CHCG	60607	3033	2W-0N	C3
1400	CHCG	60612	3033	2W-0N	B3
4000	CHCG	60624	3032	5W-0N	B4
4600	CHCG	60644	3032	5W-0N	A4
4800	CHCG	60644	3031	6W-0N	D4
N Kinzua Av					
6700	CHCG	60646	2919	6W-8N	C2
N Kiona Av					
4600	CHCG	60630	2920	5W-5N	B7
Kiowa Cir					
400	NPVL	60565	3204	25W-9S	B3
Kiowa Ct					
200	MltT	60187	3081	26W-2S	E3
S Kiowa Ct					
13700	HMGN	60491	3343	16W-16S	D3
Kiowa Dr					
400	MltT	60187	3081	26W-2S	E4
Kiowa Ln					
200	MltT	60187	3081	26W-2S	E4
E Kiowa Ln					
1900	MPPT	60056	2808	13W-14N	E4
W Kiowa Ln					
7200	PSHT	60463	3274	9W-14S	D6
7200	PSHT	60463	3346	9W-15S	E1
Kiowa Tr					
400	WLNG	60090	2754	16W-17N	D5
Kip Pl					
1000	LMNT	60439	3270	19W-14S	E7
Kipling Ct					
400	WHTN	60187	3024	23W-0S	E7
700	ROSL	60172	2913	22W-6N	B6
2000	HDPK	60035	2703	10W-22N	E4
W Kipling Ct					
24400	TroT	60404	3584	30W-26S	B4
Kipling Ln					
2000	HDPK	60035	2703	10W-22N	E4
Kipling Pl					
700	DRFD	60015	2704	10W-20N	A7
Kipling St					
10200	PvsT	60162	3029	12W-1S	A7
10200	WSTR	60154	3029	12W-1S	A7
10200	WSTR	60162	3029	12W-1S	A7
N Kirby Av					
5800	CHCG	60646	2920	5W-7N	A4
Kirby Ct					
1600	NPVL	60563	3140	29W-5S	D2
Kirby Dr					
8400	TYPK	60487	3424	10W-21S	B7
W Kirchhoff Rd					
100	ANHT	60005	2807	18W-13N	A7
500	ANHT	60005	2806	18W-13N	E6
1700	ANHT	60008	2806	18W-13N	E6
1700	RGMW	60008	2806	18W-13N	E6
Kirchoff Rd					
2000	ANHT	60005	2806	19W-13N	D6
2000	ANHT	60008	2806	19W-13N	D6
2000	RGMW	60008	2806	19W-13N	B5
4300	RGMW	60008	2805	20W-14N	E4
4500	RGMW	60067	2805	20W-14N	E4
Kirk Av					
400	EMHT	60126	3028	15W-0S	A7
400	YkTp	60126	3028	15W-0S	A7
500	ELGN	60120	2855	32W-10N	C6
S Kirk Av					
800	EMHT	60126	3028	15W-0S	A6
Kirk Ct					
3700	CCHL	60478	3426	4W-21S	D6
W Kirk Dr					
7500	NLES	60068	2864	9W-9N	C6
7500	NLES	60714	2864	9W-9N	C6
7500	PKRG	60068	2864	9W-9N	C6
Kirk Ln					
10000	LKWD	60014	2638	39W-24N	D6
Kirk Pl					
500	NpvT	60563	3140	30W-5S	B3
Kirk Rd					
-	BTVA	60510	3020	33W-0N	E6
-	GnvT	60134	3020	33W-0N	E6
10	GNVA	60134	3021	33W-0N	A4
10	GnvT	60134	3021	33W-1N	A3
10	SCRL	60134	3021	33W-2N	A2
10	SCRL	60174	3021	33W-2N	A2
100	GNVA	60185	3021	33W-0N	A4
100	GnvT	60185	3021	33W-0N	A4
Kirk Rd CO-77					
-	BTVA	60510	3020	33W-0N	E6
-	GnvT	60134	3020	33W-0N	E6
10	GNVA	60134	3021	33W-0N	A4
10	GnvT	60134	3021	33W-1N	A3
10	SCRL	60134	3021	33W-2N	A2
10	SCRL	60174	3021	33W-2N	A2
100	GNVA	60185	3021	33W-0N	A4
100	GnvT	60185	3021	33W-0N	A4
N Kirk Rd					
-	SchT	60174	2965	33W-5N	A3
-	SchT	60184	2965	33W-5N	A3
-	SCRL	60174	2965	33W-4N	A4
10	BTVA	60510	3078	33W-1S	E1
600	BTVA	60510	3020	33W-0S	E7
1200	GnvT	60134	3020	33W-0S	E7
N Kirk Rd CO-77					
-	SchT	60174	2965	33W-5N	A3
-	SchT	60184	2965	33W-5N	A3
-	SCRL	60174	2965	33W-4N	A4
10	BTVA	60510	3078	33W-1S	E1
600	BTVA	60510	3020	33W-0S	E7
1200	GnvT	60134	3020	33W-0S	E7
S Kirk Rd					
-	AURA	60502	3078	33W-3S	E6
-	BTVA	60502	3078	33W-2S	E5
-	BtvT	60502	3078	33W-2S	E4
-	BtvT	60510	3078	33W-2S	E4
10	BTVA	60510	3078	33W-2S	E3
10	BtvT	60510	3078	33W-2S	E3
300	SCRL	60174	2965	33W-3N	A7
700	SCRL	60174	3021	33W-2N	A1
S Kirk Rd CO-77					
-	AURA	60502	3078	33W-3S	E6
-	BTVA	60502	3078	33W-2S	E5

STREET Block	City	ZIP	Map#	CGS	Grid
S Kirk Rd CO-77					
-	BtvT	60502	3078	33W-2S	E4
10	BTVA	60510	3078	33W-2S	E3
10	BtvT	60510	3078	33W-2S	E3
300	SCRL	60174	2965	33W-3N	A7
700	SCRL	60174	3021	33W-2N	A1
Kirk St					
1100	EGVV	60007	2915	17W-7N	C4
1300	EVTN	60202	2867	3W-9N	A6
1700	EVTN	60202	2866	3W-9N	E6
3800	SKOK	60076	2866	4W-9N	B6
4800	SKOK	60077	2865	6W-9N	E6
5400	MNGV	60077	2865	6W-9N	D6
6100	MNGV	60053	2865	8W-9N	A6
W Kirk St					
7000	NLES	60714	2864	9W-9N	D6
Kirkcaldy Ct					
8000	PSHT	60464	3346	10W-15S	C2
Kirkhill Ln					
900	LKFT	60045	2649	12W-27N	C1
S Kirkland Av					
2200	CHCG	60623	3090	5W-2S	B2
7900	CHCG	60652	3212	5W-9S	B2
Kirkland Cir					
10	OSWG	60543	3200	34W-10S	D7
Kirkland Dr					
200	ALGN	60102	2694	35W-20N	A7
200	ELGN	60123	2854	34W-10N	E6
13600	HTLY	60142	2744	42W-20N	B1
Kirkland Ln					
10	YkTp	60181	3085	17W-1S	B1
200	YkTp	60148	3085	18W-1S	A1
600	OKTR	60181	3085	17W-1S	B1
Kirkland Rd					
600	ELGN	60123	2854	34W-10N	E6
N Kirkley Dr					
20600	KLDR	60047	2699	21W-20N	D7
Kirkstone Wy					
10100	MKNA	60448	3503	13W-23S	B3
10200	FftT	60448	3503	12W-23S	C4
Kirkwall Ct					
1400	IVNS	60010	2751	24W-17N	C5
W Kirkwall Ct					
14200	GNOK	60048	2592	14W-31N	D1
Kirkwall Ln					
500	SMBG	60193	2859	22W-10N	B6
Kirkwood Av					
-	DrrT	60098	2581	41W-28N	D6
-	WDSK	60098	2581	41W-28N	D6
100	PTPR	53158	2363	10W-43N	B5
100	WPHR	53158	2363	10W-43N	B5
100	WPHR	60096	2363	10W-43N	B5
N Kirkwood Av					
6000	CHCG	60646	2920	5W-7N	A3
6300	CHCG	60712	2920	5W-7N	A3
6300	LNWD	60712	2920	5W-7N	A3
Kirkwood Cir					
300	BGBK	60440	3205	23W-11S	A7
Kirkwood Ct					
6500	LSLE	60532	3142	24W-7S	D6
Kirkwood Dr					
900	IVNS	60067	2751	24W-17N	D5
1500	GNVA	60134	3020	33W-1N	E3
1500	GNVA	60134	3021	33W-1N	A3
Kirkwood Ln					
200	AURA	60504	3140	30W-7S	A7
Kirkwood Cove					
300	BRRG	60527	3208	15W-9S	B3
Kirman Av					
200	RMVL	60446	3341	23W-16S	A3
Kirschoff St					
6200	RSMT	60018	2917	12W-7N	B3
N Kirschoff St					
2000	LydT	60160	2973	12W-2N	B7
2000	LydT	60164	2973	12W-2N	B7
2000	MLPK	60160	2973	12W-2N	B7
W Kishwaukee Ln					
12700	HTLY	60142	2744	41W-20N	D1
Kishwaukee St					
-	SenT	60152	2634	48W-27N	E1
600	MRGO	60152	2634	49W-27N	C1
Kishwaukee Valley Rd					
1100	WDSK	60098	2524	42W-31N	B7
13700	SenT	60098	2524	43W-31N	A7
Kishwaukee Valley Rd CO-A33					
1100	WDSK	60098	2524	42W-31N	B7
13700	SenT	60098	2524	43W-31N	A7
Kit Ln					
13700	LMNT	60439	3343	17W-15S	C1
Kit Carson Dr					
6000	HRPK	60133	2911	26W-7N	E4
Kitchner St					
-	BDVW	60155	3029	12W-0S	B6
-	WSTR	60154	3029	12W-0S	B6
-	WSTR	60155	3029	12W-0S	B6
Kite Ct					
10	BGBK	60490	3267	27W-12S	D3
Kitson Cir					
1700	IVNS	60067	2751	23W-16N	E7
1700	IVNS	60067	2804	23W-16N	E1
Kitson Dr					
10	SBTN	60010	2803	26W-13N	C5
E Kitson Dr					
1000	PLTN	60074	2806	19W-16N	B1
N Kitson Dr					
10	PLTN	60074	2753	19W-17N	B5
10	PLTN	60074	2806	19W-16N	C1
Kittery on Auburn					
10	RGMW	60008	2806	19W-14N	B4
Kittridge Dr					
2000	WDND	60118	2800	35W-16N	B1
2400	DndT	60118	2800	35W-16N	B1
Kitty Av					
6600	CHRG	60415	3211	8W-11S	A7
10100	CHRG	60415	3275	8W-11S	A1
Kitty Ln					
8700	HYHL	60457	3210	10W-10S	A6
S Kittyhawk Ct					
13600	PnfT	60544	3339	27W-16S	C3
Kitty Hawk Dr					
200	RDLK	60073	2531	24W-34N	D1
Kittyhawk Ln					
1400	GNVW	60025	2810	10W-14N	A5
Kiwi Ct					
-	OSWG	60543	3263	39W-11S	A2
600	PltT	60140	2851	42W-12N	C1
Klafter Ct					
1200	SMWD	60107	2857	27W-11N	C4
Klaman St					
500	HRVD	60033	2406	49W-38N	B7
Klasen Rd					
3800	ALGN	60013	2694	33W-22N	E4
3800	ALGN	60013	2695	33W-22N	A4
3800	ALGN	60102	2694	33W-22N	E4
3800	AlqT	60013	2694	33W-22N	E4
3800	AlqT	60102	2695	33W-22N	A4

STREET Block	City	ZIP	Map#	CGS	Grid
Klasen Rd					
3800	CRY	60102	2695	33W-22N	A4
4400	AlqT	60102	2694	33W-22N	E4
4500	LIHL	60013	2694	33W-22N	E4
4500	LIHL	60102	2694	33W-22N	E4
4500	LIHL	60156	2694	33W-22N	E4
Klatt St					
-	PLNO	60545	3260	45W-14S	C7
Klehm Ct					
5100	SKOK	60077	2865	6W-10N	D5
Klein Av					
1200	DRGV	60516	3144	20W-8S	C7
1300	AURA	60505	3138	34W-6S	C5
Klein Dr					
1200	SMWD	60107	2857	27W-11N	C4
Klein Rd					
10	WCHI	60185	2966	29W-3N	E7
10	WynT	60185	2966	29W-4N	E3
600	BRLT	60103	2966	29W-4N	E3
600	WynT	60103	2966	29W-4N	E3
Klein Creek Ct					
100	CLSM	60188	2968	25W-3N	B5
Klein Creek Dr					
10	WNFD	60190	3023	26W-1N	E2
10	WNFD	60190	3024	26W-1N	A2
S Klemme Rd					
24200	CteT	60417	3687	3E-31S	A5
N Klick St					
100	HPSR	60140	2795	47W-16N	D2
S Klick St					
400	HPSR	60140	2795	47W-15N	D3
Klimm Av					
18300	HMWD	60430	3427	2W-22S	C7
18400	HMWD	60430	3507	2W-22S	C1
Kline Cir					
30800	WNVL	60555	3081	28W-3S	A7
Kline Ct					
1300	BTVA	60510	3078	33W-2S	E4
Kline CK Farm Rd					
21900	WnfT	60185	3023	27W-1N	C2
Klingenberg Ln					
-	BRTN	60010	2751	25W-18N	A2
Klinger Ln					
6500	JLET	60586	3415	32W-20S	D4
W Klondike Av					
26300	AntT	60002	2415	26W-38N	D6
Kluth Ct					
11600	MKNA	60448	3502	14W-24S	D5
Kluth Dr					
11200	FftT	60448	3502	14W-24S	E5
11200	MKNA	60448	3502	14W-24S	E5
Knaack Blvd					
-	CLLK	60012	2640	34W-26N	D3
-	CLLK	60014	2640	34W-26N	D3
-	NndT	60014	2640	34W-26N	D3
Knapp Ct					
1800	WHTN	60187	3082	24W-2S	E3
Knapp Dr					
1600	CTHL	60403	3418	25W-21S	A7
1600	CTHL	60403	3498	26W-21S	A1
1600	JLET	60435	3498	25W-21S	B1
W Knapp St					
25400	CNHN	60410	3672	31W-30S	E3
Knell Rd					
800	MTGY	60538	3199	37W-9S	C4
Knickerbocker Rd					
9600	AdnT	60033	2349	45W-41N	A7
10600	LinT	53147	2349	45W-41N	A7
10600	LinT	60033	2349	45W-41N	A7
Knight Av					
-	WKGN	60085	2536	12W-33N	A3
600	PKCY	60085	2536	12W-33N	A3
1500	NLNX	60451	3588	19W-27S	D5
8800	MaiT	60068	2863	10W-11N	E3
9000	MaiT	60016	2863	10W-11N	E3
9300	NLES	60016	2863	10W-11N	E3
N Knight Av					
10	PKRG	60068	2863	10W-9N	E7
10	PKRG	60068	2917	10W-9N	E1
1100	PKRG	60714	2863	10W-10N	E5
4800	CHCG	60656	2917	10W-6N	E7
4800	CHCG	60706	2917	10W-6N	E7
5000	NRDG	60706	2917	10W-6N	E6
8200	NLES	60714	2863	10W-10N	E5
9300	NLES	60016	2863	11W-11N	E2
S Knight Av					
300	PKRG	60068	2917	10W-8N	E3
Knight Ct					
300	BGBK	60440	3205	22W-11S	D7
1100	PTBR	60010	2642	28W-26N	D2
Knight St					
3800	GNVW	60025	2809	11W-14N	E5
Knight Bridge Ct					
-	MTSN	60443	3594	6W-25S	A1
Knightbridge Ct					
-	MNSR	46321	3510		D5
Knightbridge Pl					
-	MNSR	46321	3510		C5
Knight Hill Ct					
10	BFGV	60089	2754	17W-20N	A1
Knighton Pl					
-	EMHT	60126	3028	15W-0S	A6
E Knights Rd					
500	SDWH	60548	3258	51W-14S	A7
Knights Bridge Ct					
400	OSWG	60543	3264	36W-11S	A1
Knightsbridge Ct					
10	MDLN	60060	2647	17W-27N	B1
800	LKFT	60045	2649	12W-24N	C6
900	SMBG	60195	2858	24W-12N	C1
3700	AURA	60504	3202	30W-8S	A1
Knights Bridge Dr					
800	ISLK	60042	2586	29W-28N	B7
1800	MPPT	60056	2861	17W-11N	C4
Knightsbridge Dr					
10	MDLN	60060	2647	17W-27N	A1
Knightsbridge Ln					
800	HFET	60169	2858	24W-12N	D1
800	SMBG	60169	2858	24W-12N	D1
800	SMBG	60195	2858	24W-12N	D1
8900	ODPK	60462	3346	11W-18S	A6
Knightsbridge Pkwy					
300	LNSH	60069	2702	15W-22N	A4
Knobb Hill Ct					
100	GRNE	60031	2534	16W-34N	D1
Knobb Hill Rd					
100	GRNE	60031	2534	16W-34N	D1
E Knob Hill Dr					
200	ANHT	60004	2754	17W-16N	B7
Knob Hill Rd					
2500	JNBG	60050	2471	31W-35N	D6
Knoch Knolls Rd					
100	NPVL	60565	3203	27W-10S	C7
200	DPgT	60565	3203	27W-10S	C7
400	WldT	60565	3203	27W-10S	D7

STREET Block City ZIP Map# CGS Grid

Knockderry Ln
100 IVNS 60067 2752 22W-17N B4
Knoebel Dr
10 DGvT 60439 3270 19W-12S C3
Knoll Av
1900 MHRY 60050 2527 33W-33N D2
Knoll Ct
10 SBTN 60010 2804 25W-15N A2
500 WNFD 60190 3023 26W-0N D5
2800 LGGV 60047 2700 20W-20N A7
22600 NlxT 60451 3590 16W-27S A4
Knoll Dr
900 NPVL 60565 3204 25W-9S B3
2800 LGGV 60047 2700 20W-20N A7
Knoll Ln
700 HFET 60169 2858 24W-11N D3
1000 WLMT 60091 2812 4W-14N B5
Knoll Rd
25200 PNFD 60544 3337 31W-16S E4
Knoll St
100 WHTN 60187 3023 26W-0S D7
Knoll Creek Dr
300 SchT 60175 2963 37W-4N C4
Knoll Crest Dr
400 BRLT 60103 2910 31W-9N A1
Knoll Ln Ct
6100 WLBK 60527 3145 16W-6S D5
Knoll Ridge Rd
10 RGMW 60008 2806 20W-13N A6
Knolls Ct
25400 LkvT 60046 2474 25W-37N A2
Knollside Rd
900 NLNX 60451 3589 17W-25S D1
900 NlxT 60451 3589 17W-25S D1
Knoll Valley Dr
6100 WLBK 60527 3145 16W-6S D5
Knollview Ct
200 CmpT 60119 2962 40W-3N B7
Knoll Wick Rd
6100 WLBK 60527 3145 16W-6S D5
Knollwood Av
- DndT 60118 2801 33W-15N C4
- EDND 60118 2801 33W-15N B4
Knollwood Cir
100 RchT 60443 3593 8W-26S B1
1200 CLLK 60014 2693 36W-23N C1
1200 LKFT 60045 2593 12W-28N B6
2200 SMBG 60194 2857 28W-12N B2
3200 GNVA 60134 3019 37W-1N C3
Knoll Wood Ct
6100 WLBK 60527 3145 16W-6S D5
Knollwood Ct
10 OswT 60538 3199 37W-10S D6
100 OKBK 60523 3028 15W-1S B7
100 WDDL 60191 2971 16W-5N D2
100 BGBK 60440 3269 23W-12S A2
300 PltT 60067 2806 20W-13N A6
2300 SMBG 60194 2857 26W-10N E5
6300 LSLE 60532 3142 24W-7S C6
W Knollwood Ct
17600 WrnT 60030 2534 17W-32N B4
21700 PnfT 60544 3339 27W-15S D3
Knollwood Dr
- LKZH 60047 2698 24W-22N C3
- RLKP 60073 2532 22W-34N B1
- SMBG 60194 2857 26W-11N E3
10 CmpT 60175 2961 42W-6N E1
10 FSMR 60422 3507 2W-23S D3
10 OswT 60538 3199 37W-10S D6
100 CmpT 60175 2905 42W-6N E7
100 CteT 60417 3596 1W-28S A7
100 STGR 60417 3596 1W-28S A7
100 STGR 60475 3596 1W-28S A7
200 BMDL 60108 2968 25W-4N B3
400 CbaT 60010 2644 25W-25N A5
400 WDDL 60191 2971 17W-5N C1
500 MltT 60187 3024 25W-0N A4
600 CRY 60013 2695 33W-23N A3
600 MltT 60188 3024 25W-0N A4
900 BFGV 60089 2701 17W-21N A5
1100 CLSM 60188 2967 27W-4N C4
2200 ELGN 60123 2853 36W-11N E4
2900 MCLK 60050 2470 34W-34N D7
6300 OKFT 60452 3347 7W-17S B5
N Knollwood Dr
10 SMBG 60193 2857 26W-10N E6
10 SMBG 60194 2857 26W-10N E5
100 WHTN 60187 3024 25W-0S A7
1000 HFET 60169 2857 26W-11N E3
1000 HFET 60194 2857 26W-11N E3
1000 PLTN 60067 2752 22W-17N B5
1400 PltT 60067 2752 22W-17N B5
1400 PltT 60074 2752 22W-17N B5
34900 GrtT 60041 2473 26W-34N D7
S Knollwood Dr
10 SMBG 60193 2857 26W-10N E6
10 SMBG 60194 2857 26W-10N E6
400 WHTN 60187 3024 25W-0S A7
W Knollwood Dr
8200 PSPK 60464 3274 10W-14S B6
21700 PnfT 60544 3339 27W-16S C3
Knollwood Dr S
400 FXLK 60041 2473 27W-35N C5
Knollwood Ln
- NfdT 60025 2809 10W-13N E6
100 GLNC 60022 2758 6W-18N D3
100 YkTp 60181 3085 18W-1S A1
200 VNHL 60061 2647 16W-25N C5
200 YkTp 60148 3085 18W-1S A1
900 WCHI 60185 3022 29W-2N E2
1000 BRLT 60103 2910 30W-8N C3
1500 HDPK 60035 2705 7W-21N A5
2800 GNVW 60025 2810 9W-13N B6
2800 NfdT 60025 2810 10W-13N A6
3200 HMWD 60430 3506 4W-22S E1
3200 HMWD 60430 3507 4W-22S A1
3700 GNVW 60025 2809 11W-13N E6
8400 ODPK 60462 3346 10W-18S B7
Knollwood Pl
10 NLNX 60451 3500 20W-24S B5
10 NlxT 60433 3500 20W-24S B5
10 NlxT 60451 3500 20W-24S B5
2600 HLCT 60429 3427 3W-21S B6
2600 HLCT 60430 3427 3W-21S B6
Knoll Wood Rd
- DGvT 60527 3145 16W-6S D5
6000 WLBK 60527 3145 16W-6S D5
Knollwood Rd
200 FXLK 60041 2473 27W-35N C5
800 DRFD 60015 2704 10W-21N A7
1700 LKBF 60045 2593 12W-28N B6
1700 LKFT 60045 2593 12W-28N B6
1900 LKBF 60044 2593 12W-28N B6
1900 LKFT 60044 2593 12W-28N B6
Knollwood Wy
1300 RVWD 60015 2702 13W-21N E6
Knoll Wy Dr
6100 WLBK 60527 3145 16W-6S D5
Knottingham Cir
7900 DRGV 60516 3207 18W-9S A3
7900 DRN 60516 3207 18W-9S A3
7900 DRN 60561 3207 18W-9S A3
Knottingham Ct
1200 SMBG 60193 2913 22W-8N C1
Knottingham Dr
- EGVV 60007 2913 22W-8N C1
- SMBG 60007 2913 22W-8N C1
800 SMBG 60193 2913 22W-8N C1
1300 GRNE 60031 2477 17W-35N B5
Knottingham Ln
7500 DRGV 60516 3207 18W-8S A2
7500 DRN 60516 3207 18W-8S A2
7800 DRN 60561 3207 18W-8S A2
Knotty Pine Ct
7700 WDRG 60517 3205 21W-8S E2
Knotty Pine Dr
1400 ELGN 60123 2907 36W-8N D3
Knowles Rd
- WrnT 60046 2476 18W-35N D6
900 GRNE 60031 2476 18W-35N D6
N Knowles Rd
35800 GRNE 60031 2476 18W-35N D6
35800 WrnT 60031 2476 18W-35N D6
35800 WrnT 60046 2476 18W-35N D6
Knowlton Dr
2200 WDND 60118 2800 35W-16N B1
Knox Av
600 WLMT 60091 2811 5W-13N E6
9600 SKOK 60076 2866 5W-12N A1
14300 CTWD 60445 3348 5W-17S B5
14300 MDLN 60445 3348 5W-17S B5
15300 OKFT 60452 3348 5W-18S B6
N Knox Av
2200 CHCG 60639 2976 5W-2N A6
4100 CHCG 60641 2976 5W-5N A1
4400 CHCG 60630 2920 5W-5N A7
5900 CHCG 60646 2919 5W-7N E4
5900 CHCG 60646 2920 5W-7N A3
6300 CHCG 60712 2920 5W-7N A3
6400 CHCG 60646 2920 5W-8N A3
6400 LNWD 60646 2920 5W-8N A3
6400 LNWD 60712 2920 5W-8N A2
S Knox Av
4200 CHCG 60632 3090 5W-4S A7
4600 CHCG 60632 3150 5W-5S A2
5900 CHCG 60629 3150 5W-6S A5
8300 CHCG 60652 3212 5W-9S A3
8600 HMTN 60652 3212 5W-9S A4
9000 HMTN 60456 3212 5W-10S A5
9000 OKLN 60456 3212 5W-10S A5
9200 OKLN 60453 3212 5W-10S A5
10300 OKLN 60453 3276 5W-12S A1
11500 ALSP 60803 3276 5W-13S B4
Knox Cir
10 EVTN 60201 2866 4W-12N C1
Knox Ct
200 IVNS 60010 2750 25W-16N E7
200 IVNS 60010 2751 25W-16N A7
1700 NPVL 60565 3204 24W-8S D2
S Knox Ct
10100 OKLN 60453 3212 5W-11S A7
Knox Ln
900 BTVA 60510 3078 34W-1S D3
N Knox Pl
500 JLET 60435 3498 25W-23S C3
Knox St
- PnfT 60544 3339 27W-16S C3
E Knox St
500 PLTN 60074 2753 20W-17N A5
Knoxboro Ln
200 PltT 60010 2751 23W-18N E2
Knoxbury Ct
200 GRNE 60031 2535 14W-34N B1
500 ELGN 60123 2853 36W-10N E7
Knox Park Rd
200 LKZH 60047 2699 22W-22N C4
S Knyghtwood Dr
22300 TroT 60404 3584 30W-27S B4
Koala Ct
2900 WMTN 60481 3853 28W-39S C7
Koca Dr
25300 BDWD 60408 3942 31W-40S A3
Koch Ct
9700 ODPK 60467 3423 12W-19S D2
Koclanis Av
200 HLSD 60162 3028 14W-0S D5
Koda Dr
1500 MngT 60152 2578 50W-30N A2
Koehler Dr
1900 DSPN 60018 2862 13W-9N E7
8500 TYPK 60487 3424 10W-21S B7
Koehling Rd
1700 NfdT 60062 2757 9W-18N B3
Koepke Rd
2700 NHBK 60062 2756 11W-16N E6
Koerner Dr
400 WslT 60481 3943 27W-40S C2
Koerper Ct
500 WLMT 60091 2812 5W-13N A6
Kohl Av
100 BtnT 60081 2414 29W-38N D6
100 FXLK 60020 2414 29W-38N D6
100 FXLK 60081 2414 29W-38N D6
100 LKBF 60044 2593 11W-29N D4
100 ShdT 60044 2593 11W-29N D4
Kohley Rd
500 LslT 60532 3143 22W-6S B4
1100 LSLE 60532 3143 23W-6S B4
S Kohlwood Dr
20000 FftT 60448 3503 13W-24S B5
20000 MKNA 60448 3503 13W-24S B5
W Kokopelli Ct
11700 MKNA 60448 3502 14W-25S D7
Kolberg Ct
- OKTR 60181 3027 17W-0S C6
E Kolberg Ct
400 VLPK 60181 3027 17W-0S C7
400 YkTp 60181 3027 17W-0S B7
Kolin Av
- ALSP 60803 3276 5W-15S B7
14300 CTWD 60445 3348 5W-17S B4
14300 MDLN 60445 3348 5W-17S B4
N Kolin Av
800 CHCG 60624 3032 5W-1N B2
800 CHCG 60651 3032 5W-1N B2
S Kolin Av
1200 CHCG 60623 3032 5W-1S B7
1200 CHCG 60624 3032 5W-1S B7
1500 CHCG 60623 3090 5W-1S B1
4500 CHCG 60632 3090 5W-4S B7
4700 CHCG 60632 3150 5W-5S B2
5900 CHCG 60629 3150 5W-7S B6
8300 CHCG 60652 3212 5W-9S B3
S Kolin Av
8600 HMTN 60652 3212 5W-9S B4
8700 HMTN 60456 3212 5W-10S B4
9500 OKLN 60453 3212 5W-11S B6
10200 OKLN 60453 3276 5W-12S B1
11500 ALSP 60655 3276 5W-13S B4
11500 ALSP 60803 3276 5W-13S B4
11500 CHCG 60655 3276 5W-13S B4
13300 RBBN 60472 3348 5W-15S B2
13400 CTWD 60445 3348 5W-15S B2
13400 CTWD 60472 3348 5W-15S B2
Kolmar Av
7400 LNWD 60076 2866 5W-9N A7
7400 LNWD 60712 2866 5W-9N A7
9200 SKOK 60076 2866 5W-11N A2
13400 CTWD 60445 3348 5W-16S B2
14300 MDLN 60445 3348 5W-17S B5
N Kolmar Av
200 CHCG 60624 3032 5W-0N A4
1600 CHCG 60639 3032 5W-1N A1
1600 CHCG 60651 3032 5W-1N A1
2000 CHCG 60639 2976 5W-2N A6
2800 CHCG 60641 2976 5W-3N A4
4900 CHCG 60630 2920 5W-6N A6
5800 CHCG 60646 2920 5W-7N A4
6300 CHCG 60712 2920 5W-7N A3
6300 LNWD 60712 2920 5W-7N A3
7300 LNWD 60076 2866 5W-9N A7
7300 LNWD 60712 2866 5W-9N A7
7300 SKOK 60076 2866 5W-9N A7
S Kolmar Av
- CHCG 60623 3032 5W-1S A7
- CHCG 60623 3090 5W-1S A1
600 CHCG 60644 3032 5W-0S A6
1000 CHCG 60624 3032 5W-0S A7
4400 CHCG 60632 3090 5W-4S A7
4400 CHCG 60632 3150 5W-5S A1
5500 CHCG 60629 3150 5W-6S A4
8500 CHCG 60652 3212 5W-9S B4
8600 HMTN 60652 3212 5W-9S B4
8700 HMTN 60456 3212 5W-10S A4
9100 OKLN 60453 3212 5W-10S A5
9100 OKLN 60456 3212 5W-10S A5
10300 OKLN 60453 3276 5W-12S B2
11500 ALSP 60803 3276 5W-13S B4
Kolmar Ln
- CTWD 60445 3348 5W-16S B3
Koloff Ct
10 WDRG 60517 3143 22W-7S C7
Kolpin Dr
1200 DSPN 60016 2862 15W-10N A5
1200 DSPN 60018 2862 15W-10N A5
Kolze Av
4100 SRPK 60176 2973 11W-5N C1
4700 SRPK 60176 2917 11W-5N C7
E Komar Ln
1200 RLKB 60073 2475 21W-36N D4
S Komensky Av
1200 CHCG 60623 3032 5W-1S B7
1200 CHCG 60624 3032 5W-1S B7
1500 CHCG 60623 3090 5W-1S B1
4300 CHCG 60632 3090 5W-4S C7
5400 CHCG 60629 3150 5W-6S C3
5400 CHCG 60632 3150 5W-6S C3
7700 CHCG 60652 3212 5W-8S C1
8600 HMTN 60652 3212 5W-9S C4
8800 HMTN 60456 3212 5W-10S C4
9100 OKLN 60453 3212 5W-10S C5
9100 OKLN 60456 3212 5W-10S C5
10200 OKLN 60453 3276 5W-12S C1
11500 ALSP 60655 3276 5W-13S C5
11500 ALSP 60803 3276 5W-13S C5
11500 CHCG 60655 3276 5W-13S C5
13300 RBBN 60472 3348 5W-15S C2
Konen Av
300 AURA 60504 3138 35W-5S C2
400 AraT 60504 3138 35W-5S C2
500 AraT 60505 3138 34W-5S C2
500 AURA 60505 3138 35W-5S C2
N Konen Av
38500 AntT 60081 2415 27W-38N A7
Konrad Av
4000 LYNS 60534 3088 10W-4S A7
Konrad Ct
- PLNO 60545 3260 45W-13S C5
Koppie Dr
10 GLBT 60136 2746 39W-17N A7
Koppie Rd
- GLBT 60118 2746 38W-17N A7
- GLBT 60136 2746 38W-17N A7
Kopping Ln
9100 HYHL 60457 3209 11W-10S E5
9100 HYHL 60480 3209 11W-10S E5
9100 PlsT 60480 3209 11W-10S E5
Kora Ln
- ISLK 60042 2586 29W-28N C5
Korbel Dr
7300 GRNE 60031 2477 18W-35N A5
7500 GRNE 60031 2476 18W-35N E5
Korrel Av
2800 BLWD 60104 3029 12W-0N C4
Kortney Ln
30900 FmtT 60030 2588 23W-31N E1
30900 RDLK 60030 2588 23W-31N E1
30900 RDLK 60073 2588 23W-31N E1
S Kortney Ln
1800 RDLK 60030 2588 23W-31N E1
1800 RDLK 60073 2588 23W-31N E1
Kosan Cir
200 SMWD 60107 2857 27W-11N C4
N Kosciuszko Rd
2500 MchT 60050 2527 34W-34N D1
2500 MCLK 60050 2527 34W-34N D1
Koshare Cir
800 ElgT 60124 2853 38W-9N A7
Koshare Tr
500 ElgT 60124 2853 38W-9N A7
500 ElgT 60124 2907 38W-9N A1
Kossuth St
200 SEGN 60177 2908 34W-8N C2
500 GNCY 53128 2353 A3
Koster Ct
1200 GNVA 60134 3020 33W-1N E2
Kostner Av
- ALSP 60803 3276 5W-15S B7
700 MTSN 60443 3506 5W-25S C6
7400 LNWD 60076 2866 5W-9N A7
7400 LNWD 60712 2866 5W-9N A7
9000 SKOK 60076 2866 5W-11N A3
13500 CTWD 60445 3348 5W-17S B4
13500 CTWD 60472 3348 5W-16S B3
13500 RBBN 60472 3348 5W-16S B3
14200 MDLN 60445 3348 5W-17S B6
15200 BmnT 60426 3348 5W-18S B6
15200 BmnT 60445 3348 5W-18S B6
15200 OKFT 60445 3348 5W-18S B6
Kostner Av
17900 CCHL 60478 3426 5W-21S C7
22100 RNPK 60471 3594 5W-26S C3
N Kostner Av
10 CHCG 60624 3032 5W-0N A4
800 CHCG 60651 3032 5W-1N A2
1500 CHCG 60639 3032 5W-1N A1
1600 CHCG 60639 2976 5W-2N A7
3700 CHCG 60641 2976 5W-5N A1
4300 CHCG 60630 2976 5W-5N A1
4700 CHCG 60630 2920 5W-6N A6
6100 CHCG 60646 2920 5W-7N A3
6300 CHCG 60712 2920 5W-7N A3
6500 LNWD 60712 2920 5W-8N A2
7200 LNWD 60712 2866 5W-9N A7
7300 LNWD 60076 2866 5W-9N A7
7300 SKOK 60076 2866 5W-9N A7
S Kostner Av
- CHCG 60655 3276 5W-12S B3
- HMTN 60652 3212 5W-10S B4
10 CHCG 60624 3032 5W-1S B7
1100 CHCG 60623 3032 5W-1S B7
1500 CHCG 60623 3090 5W-2S B4
3500 CHCG 60632 3090 5W-3S A5
4700 CHCG 60632 3150 5W-6S B3
5400 CHCG 60629 3150 5W-7S B6
7300 CHCG 60629 3212 5W-8S B1
7300 CHCG 60652 3212 5W-8S B1
8700 HMTN 60456 3212 5W-10S B4
9000 OKLN 60456 3212 5W-10S B5
9300 OKLN 60453 3212 5W-11S B7
10200 OKLN 60453 3276 5W-12S B1
11000 CHCG 60453 3276 5W-12S B3
11900 ALSP 60803 3276 5W-15S B7
13300 CTWD 60445 3348 5W-15S B2
13300 RBBN 60445 3348 5W-15S B2
13300 RBBN 60472 3348 5W-15S B2
Kostner Ter
8800 SKOK 60076 2866 5W-11N A3
Kotlin Rd
14700 LMNT 60439 3271 18W-13S A4
Kott St
2600 BLID 60406 3349 3W-15S B1
Kouba Dr
5800 BKLY 60163 3028 14W-0N C4
5800 HLSD 60162 3028 14W-0N C4
5800 HLSD 60163 3028 14W-0N C4
Kraft Ct
10 GNVW 60025 2864 8W-12N E1
E Krage Dr
900 AddT 60101 2971 17W-2N B6
900 ADSN 60101 2971 17W-2N B6
Krakar Av
200 JLET 60432 3499 22W-23S D4
200 JltT 60432 3499 22W-23S D4
Kramer Av
- VLPK 60148 3026 19W-1N D1
10 AddT 60101 3026 19W-2N D1
10 AddT 60148 3026 19W-2N D1
10 ADSN 60101 3026 19W-2N D1
10 ADSN 60148 3026 19W-2N D1
900 ELGN 60120 2855 32W-10N C6
N Kramer Av
600 LMBD 60148 3026 19W-1N D1
600 VLPK 60148 3026 19W-1N D1
Kramer Ct
600 BTVA 60510 3078 34W-1S D2
Kramer Ln
900 SDWH 60548 3258 51W-14S A7
Kraml Dr
- DGvT 60527 3208 15W-9S A4
100 BRRG 60527 3208 15W-9S A4
Krause Av
400 SMWD 60107 2911 28W-9N B1
Krause Dr
- BFGV 60089 2702 15W-20N A7
- VrnT 60015 2702 15W-20N A7
Krause Ln
200 WLNG 60090 2755 14W-18N D3
S Kreiter Av
9300 CHCG 60617 3216 4E-10S B5
Kreitzburg St
9800 SjnT 46311 3687 D3
9900 HnrT 46311 3687 D3
Krenn Av
3200 HDPK 60035 2704 9W-24N B1
3400 HDPK 60035 2650 9W-24N C7
3500 LKFT 60045 2650 9W-24N C7
Krenz Av
300 CRY 60013 2695 31W-23N D1
Kresmery Ln
- BNHL 60010 2696 29W-22N C5
Kress Rd
10 WCHI 60185 3021 32W-1N D3
300 WnfT 60185 3021 32W-1N D3
700 WCHI 60185 3022 31W-0N A4
Kress Rd CO-18
10 WCHI 60185 3021 32W-1N D3
300 WnfT 60185 3021 32W-1N D3
Kresswood Dr
300 WCHI 60185 3080 29W-1S C1
400 MHRY 60050 2527 33W-31N E7
1700 WnfT 60185 3080 29W-0S D1
Kreutzer Rd
- GfnT 60142 2691 41W-20N D7
- HTLY 60142 2691 41W-20N D7
10 RtdT 60142 2745 41W-19N B2
400 HTLY 60142 2745 41W-19N A2
500 HTLY 60142 2744 41W-19N E2
500 RtdT 60142 2744 41W-19N E2
10300 GfnT 60102 2745 40W-19N D2
10300 GfnT 60142 2745 40W-19N D2
10300 RtdT 60102 2745 40W-19N D2
N Krings Ln
800 JLET 60435 3498 26W-22S A3
Kris Dr
10 NLNX 60451 3500 19W-24S E6
10 NlxT 60451 3500 19W-24S E6
900 NLNX 60451 3501 18W-24S A6
900 NlxT 60451 3501 18W-24S A6
Kris Tr
9600 PlsT 60462 3345 12W-15S D2
Kris Howard Dr
- PLTN 60067 2805 22W-14N A5
E Krista Ct
900 PLTN 60074 2806 19W-15N B1
S Krista Ln
100 PLTN 60074 2806 19W-15N B1
Kristan Av
1400 NCHI 60064 2536 11W-32N D6
1400 WKGN 60085 2536 11W-32N D6
2300 NCHI 60088 2536 11W-31N D7
Kristen Ct
- PLNO 60545 3260 45W-13S C6
600 NLNX 60451 3502 15W-25S C7
Kristen St
- PLNO 60545 3260 45W-13S C6
Kristen Tr
3100 NndT 60012 2584 33W-28N D5
S Kristi Dr
11300 WldT 60543 3265 32W-13S C5
11300 WldT 60585 3265 32W-13S C5
Kristin Cir
10 SMBG 60173 2859 23W-12N A1
10 SMBG 60195 2859 23W-12N A1
Kristin Ct
700 GRNE 60031 2534 16W-33N E3
700 WTMT 60559 3145 17W-6S C4
1000 BTVA 60510 3078 34W-2S D3
Kristin Dr
10 ElgT 60124 2907 38W-8N B3
10 SMBG 60173 2859 23W-12N A1
10 SMBG 60195 2859 23W-12N A1
1100 LYVL 60048 2591 17W-29N A3
Kristin Ln
700 WMTN 60481 3853 28W-39S B7
700 WMTN 60481 3943 28W-39S B1
Kristin St
400 DGvT 60514 3145 17W-6S C4
400 DGvT 60559 3145 17W-6S C4
400 WTMT 60559 3145 17W-6S C4
Kristina Ln
500 RDLK 60030 2588 23W-30N D1
500 RDLK 60073 2588 23W-30N D1
Kristine Dr
100 MTGY 60543 3263 38W-11S A1
Kristine Ln
22900 RNPK 60471 3594 4W-27S D5
Kristine Tr
19100 MKNA 60448 3503 13W-23S A3
Kristo Ln
8000 ODPK 60462 3346 10W-17S C4
Kristoff Ct
23100 PNFD 60544 3416 29W-19S E2
Kristoffer Ct
11700 OrlT 60467 3344 14W-16S D2
Kristoffer Ln
11700 OrlT 60467 3344 14W-16S D2
Kristy Ln
600 WLNG 60090 2755 15W-17N A6
W Kristy Ln
28600 AlqT 60013 2642 28W-24N D7
28600 CbaT 60013 2642 28W-24N D7
Kriwiel Dr
300 TNLK 53181 2354 C2
Kroc Dr
10 OKBK 60523 3085 16W-2S E4
Krohn Ct
900 BbyT 60119 3018 40W-1N B2
Kroll Ct
1500 NLNX 60451 3588 19W-27S D5
S Kroll Dr
12600 ALSP 60803 3276 6W-14S A7
Kromray Rd
300 LMNT 60439 3271 18W-14S A6
Kroner Ln
2000 HMWD 60430 3427 2W-21S C7
Kronmeyer Av
300 JLET 60432 3499 23W-22S A1
Kropp Ct
17100 ODPK 60467 3422 14W-20S E4
Krotiak Rd
10 PKFT 60466 3595 3W-26S B2
Krowka Dr
1800 DSPN 60018 2917 12W-8N B1
W Kruckenberg Rd
21700 ElaT 60047 2645 21W-25N C5
21700 HNWD 60047 2645 21W-25N C5
Krueger Ct
4500 LGGV 60047 2700 19W-23N C3
W Krueger Ct
19400 FmtT 60060 2646 19W-26N C3
19400 LGGV 60047 2646 19W-26N C3
N Krueger Rd
23000 LGGV 60047 2700 19W-23N C2
S Krueger Rd
- ElaT 60047 2699 21W-22N E4
21000 KLDR 60047 2699 21W-22N E4
21000 LGGV 60047 2699 21W-22N E5
Krueger St
2300 BLID 60406 3277 2W-14S B6
N Kruger Av
4800 CHCG 60630 2919 5W-6N E6
4800 CHCG 60630 2920 5W-6N A5
Kruger Rd
24900 HNWD 60047 2645 22W-25N C6
Kruk St
600 LMNT 60439 3270 18W-14S E6
Krunfus Dr
8900 CmgT 60033 2406 49W-40N C2
Krystal Ct
400 NLNX 60451 3501 16W-25S E7
Krystal Ln
800 NLNX 60451 3501 16W-25S E7
Krysten Ct
1800 GLHT 60139 2968 24W-3N D5
Kubek Rd
1300 NPVL 60564 3203 28W-10S A5
1300 WldT 60564 3203 28W-10S A5
Kublank St
- ALGN 60102 2747 36W-19N B3
Kudu Ct
2000 WHTN 60187 3023 26W-0S E7
Kudu Dr
2100 AURA 60503 3201 33W-10S A6
S Kuersten Rd
- MONE 60449 3683 5W-31S C6
- UYPK 60449 3683 5W-31S C6
26300 MonT 60449 3683 5W-31S C6
Kufrin Wy
1000 YkTp 60148 3026 18W-0S E7
Kuhn Rd
- BMDL 60108 2967 26W-4N E4
- BmdT 60108 2967 26W-4N E4
- BmdT 60188 3023 26W-2N E1
200 BmdT 60188 2967 26W-4N E4
200 CLSM 60188 2967 26W-2N E7
200 CLSM 60188 3023 26W-2N E1
E Kuhn Rd
4100 RcmT 60071 2412 33W-40N E3
4100 RcmT 60071 2413 33W-40N A3
4100 RHMD 60071 2412 33W-40N E3
4100 RHMD 60071 2413 33W-40N A3
N Kuhn Rd
100 BmdT 60188 3023 26W-2N E1
100 CLSM 60188 3023 26W-2N E1
Kummer Ct
1600 GNVA 60134 3020 36W-0N A5
Kungs Wy
400 JLET 60435 3497 27W-23S D3

STREET Block	City	ZIP	Map#	CGS	Grid
Kunkel Ln					
-	MTGY	60538	3199	36W-9S	E5
Kurns Rd					
-	BbyT	60510	3076	39W-3S	E5
-	NARA	60510	3076	39W-3S	E5
Kurt Ct					
10	LIHL	60156	2694	34W-22N	C4
300	CmpT	60175	2962	39W-3N	E6
S Kurt Ln					
23700	CteT	60417	3597	3E-28S	E7
W Kurt Rd					
23000	CNHN	60410	3584	29W-27S	D6
Kurtis Ln					
1200	LKFT	60045	2649	12W-24N	C7
1200	LKFT	60045	2703	12W-24N	C1
W Kuse Rd					
9600	GGnT	60423	3591	12W-28S	D6
Kyla Ct					
2100	MTGY	60538	3198	39W-10S	D5
Kyle Ct					
10	WLBK	60527	3145	16W-7S	E6
1200	WCDA	60084	2587	26W-28N	D5
N Kyle Ct					
25600	ElaT	60047	2645	22W-25N	A4
S Kyle Ct					
22700	ElaT	60047	2645	22W-25N	B5
S Kyle Dr					
200	WKGN	60085	2536	12W-33N	C2
Kylemore Ct					
1000	LKPT	60441	3342	21W-18S	A7
1100	DSPN	60016	2808	13W-13N	D6
1100	JLET	60431	3496	29W-22S	D2
9200	OrlT	60487	3423	11W-21S	E6
Kylemore Dr					
600	DSPN	60016	2808	13W-13N	D6
600	DSPN	60056	2808	13W-13N	D6
600	MPPT	60016	2808	13W-13N	D6
600	MPPT	60056	2808	13W-13N	D6
1100	LKZH	60047	2699	23W-21N	A6
Kylemore Ln					
19300	MKNA	60448	3504	11W-23S	A3
Kyra Ln					
3100	ElgT	60124	2853	38W-10N	A6
L					
L Ct					
10200	MKNA	60448	3503	12W-23S	C4
N L St					
-	AntT	60002	2417	23W-40N	A2
40700	ANTH	60002	2416	23W-40N	E2
40700	AntT	60002	2416	23W-40N	E2
Labrecque Dr					
2400	JLET	60586	3415	32W-20S	D6
Laburnum Ct					
3500	NHBK	60062	2756	11W-18N	C4
Laburnum Dr					
400	NHBK	60062	2756	12W-18N	C4
Laburnum Rd					
1400	HFET	60192	2804	24W-14N	B3
Lac du Beatrice Dr					
700	DndT	60118	2800	34W-14N	D5
Lace					
-	CHCG	60646	2919	5W-7N	E4
Lacebark Ct					
10	BGBK	60490	3267	26W-12S	E3
1100	DRN	60561	3145	18W-7S	A7
Lacey Av					
10	LslT	60532	3142	25W-4S	C1
10	LslT	60563	3142	25W-4S	B1
1300	LSLE	60532	3143	23W-4S	A1
2000	LSLE	60532	3142	24W-4S	E1
N Lacey Av					
5700	CHCG	60646	2919	6W-7N	E4
Lacey Rd					
3000	DRGV	60515	3084	21W-2S	A4
Laci Ct					
1300	INCK	60061	2647	17W-25N	A5
Lacoma Dr					
1200	LKPT	60441	3420	21W-19S	A2
Laconia Ln					
400	SMBG	60193	2912	24W-9N	E1
3000	AURA	60504	3201	31W-9S	E4
La Costa Av					
900	BRLT	60103	2910	29W-8N	C2
La Costa Ct					
10	LIHL	60156	2693	36W-21N	C5
2400	AURA	60503	3201	32W-10S	C7
Lacosta Ct					
800	ELGN	60123	2854	36W-9N	A7
La Costa Ln					
10800	FftT	60423	3591	13W-27S	A5
La Croix Ln					
23000	PNFD	60544	3338	28W-15S	E3
23000	PNFD	60585	3338	28W-15S	E3
La Crosse Av					
7800	BRBK	60459	3212	6W-8S	A2
8800	SKOK	60077	2865	6W-11N	E3
10000	SKOK	60077	2811	6W-12N	E7
10000	WLMT	60077	2811	6W-12N	E7
10000	WLMT	60091	2811	6W-12N	E7
15100	OKFT	60452	3348	6W-18S	A6
Lacrosse Av					
600	WLMT	60091	2811	6W-13N	D5
9500	OKLN	60453	3212	6W-11S	A6
10300	OKLN	60453	3276	6W-12S	A1
N La Crosse Av					
100	CHCG	60644	3031	6W-0N	E4
2200	CHCG	60639	2975	6W-2N	E6
4400	CHCG	60630	2975	6W-5N	E1
4400	CHCG	60641	2975	6W-5N	E1
5400	CHCG	60630	2919	6W-6N	E5
6200	CHCG	60646	2919	6W-7N	E3
6300	CHCG	60712	2919	6W-7N	E3
6300	LNWD	60712	2919	6W-7N	E3
S La Crosse Av					
4500	CHCG	60638	3090	6W-4S	A7
4600	CHCG	60638	3150	6W-5S	A1
6400	BDPK	60638	3150	6W-7S	A5
11700	ALSP	60803	3276	6W-13S	A5
Lacrosse Ct					
-	WLMT	60091	2811	6W-13N	D5
La Crosse Dr					
-	HmrT	60441	3420	19W-21S	E7
-	NLNX	60441	3420	19W-21S	E7
Lacrosse Dr					
300	BGBK	60440	3268	23W-11S	E1
Lacrosse Ln					
3300	NPVL	60564	3266	29W-11S	C1
3300	WldT	60564	3266	29W-11S	C1
Lacrosse St					
10	ALGN	60102	2695	32W-21N	A5
900	CLSM	60188	2968	26W-3N	A5
Lacy Av					
400	SMWD	60107	2911	28W-9N	B1
Ladd Ln					
5200	HRPK	60133	2911	27W-6N	C6
W Ladd St					
300	ANHT	60004	2754	18W-16N	A7
600	ANHT	60004	2753	18W-16N	E7
Lady Bar Av					
13700	HMGN	60491	3344	15W-16S	B3
W Lady Bar Av					
13800	HMGN	60491	3344	15W-16S	B3
W Lady Bar Ln					
12100	HMGN	60491	3344	15W-16S	B3
Lady Bird Ln					
9300	DSPN	60016	2863	11W-11N	D2
9300	MaiT	60016	2863	11W-11N	D2
Lady Marion Dr					
200	HnrT	60120	2856	31W-10N	A6
Lady Pointe Dr					
-	GNVA	60134	3019	37W-1N	B2
-	GnvT	60134	3019	37W-1N	B2
-	SchT	60134	3019	37W-1N	B2
Ladysmith Rd					
500	BRLT	60103	2911	27W-7N	C5
S Lafayette Av					
5500	CHCG	60609	3152	0W-6S	C3
6000	CHCG	60621	3152	0W-6S	C4
7500	CHCG	60620	3214	0W-11S	C6
7500	CHCG	60621	3214	0W-8S	C1
9400	CHCG	60628	3214	0W-11S	C6
10500	CHCG	60628	3278	0W-12S	C1
Lafayette Dr					
100	BGBK	60440	3269	23W-11S	A1
1000	SEGN	60177	2908	35W-8N	B3
Lafayette Ln					
200	HFET	60169	2804	24W-12N	E7
200	HFET	60169	2805	23W-12N	A7
200	HFET	60195	2805	23W-12N	A7
200	SMBG	60195	2805	23W-12N	A7
La Fayette Pl					
700	WTMT	60559	3085	17W-4S	C7
Lafayette Pl					
800	VNHL	60061	2647	17W-27N	C2
Lafayette Rd					
10	RVSD	60546	3088	9W-3S	D5
Lafayette St					
100	WMTN	60481	3853	27W-38S	D7
200	WDDL	60191	2914	19W-5N	C7
200	WDDL	60191	2970	18W-5N	E1
600	AURA	60505	3200	35W-9S	A3
1100	MTGY	60505	3200	35W-9S	A4
1200	MTGY	60538	3200	35W-9S	A4
3300	ElgT	60124	2853	38W-11N	A5
N Lafayette St					
2300	ANHT	60004	2753	18W-16N	E7
W Lafayette St					
10	JLET	60436	3498	24W-24S	E5
200	JLET	60435	3498	24W-24S	E5
Lafleur Ln					
3900	HFET	60192	2804	24W-14N	B3
Laflin Av					
16100	MKHM	60428	3427	1W-19S	E2
17100	EHZC	60429	3427	1W-20S	E4
17100	HRVY	60429	3427	1W-20S	E4
17400	HMWD	60429	3427	1W-20S	E5
17400	HMWD	60430	3427	1W-20S	E5
Laflin Ct					
600	CHCG	60607	3033	1W-0S	D6
S Laflin Pl					
3600	CHCG	60609	3091	1W-3S	D5
Laflin St					
-	CTPK	60827	3277	1W-15S	D7
N Laflin St					
200	CHCG	60607	3033	1W-0N	D4
S Laflin St					
10	CHCG	60607	3033	1W-0S	D5
1200	CHCG	60608	3033	1W-1S	D7
1500	CHCG	60608	3091	1W-2S	D2
4500	CHCG	60609	3091	1W-4S	D7
4700	CHCG	60609	3151	1W-6S	D4
5500	CHCG	60636	3151	1W-7S	D6
8500	CHCG	60620	3213	1W-10S	D5
9400	CHCG	60643	3213	1W-10S	D6
11200	CHCG	60643	3277	1W-13S	D3
12200	CHCG	60827	3277	1W-14S	D6
12200	CTPK	60643	3277	1W-14S	D6
12200	CTPK	60827	3277	1W-15S	D7
La Fontaine Ln					
3800	GNVW	60025	2809	11W-14N	D4
Laforge Ln					
-	GfnT	60014	2638	38W-25N	D4
-	LKWD	60014	2638	38W-25N	D4
Lafox Rd					
10	BbyT	60119	3018	40W-1N	B4
10	CmpT	60119	3018	40W-1N	B2
200	CmpT	60119	2962	40W-3N	B7
600	CmpT	60175	2962	40W-5N	B2
Lafox Rd CO-81					
10	BbyT	60119	3018	40W-1N	B4
10	CmpT	60119	3018	40W-1N	B2
10	CmpT	60175	2962	40W-4N	C5
200	CmpT	60119	2962	40W-3N	B7
N La Fox St					
10	SEGN	60177	2908	34W-9N	D1
1500	ELGN	60123	2854	34W-9N	E7
1500	ELGN	60177	2854	34W-9N	E7
1500	ELGN	60177	2908	34W-9N	D1
1500	SEGN	60123	2854	34W-9N	E7
1500	SEGN	60177	2854	34W-9N	E7
N La Fox St SR-31					
10	SEGN	60177	2908	34W-9N	D1
1500	ELGN	60123	2854	34W-9N	E7
1500	ELGN	60177	2854	34W-9N	E7
1500	ELGN	60177	2908	34W-9N	D1
1500	SEGN	60123	2854	34W-9N	E7
1500	SEGN	60177	2854	34W-9N	E7
S La Fox St					
10	SEGN	60177	2908	34W-8N	D4
400	SchT	60177	2908	34W-7N	D4
S La Fox St SR-31					
10	SEGN	60177	2908	34W-8N	D4
400	SchT	60177	2908	34W-7N	D4
La Fox River Dr					
100	ALGN	60102	2694	33W-20N	D7
400	ALGN	60102	2747	33W-20N	D1
Lageschulte St					
100	BRTN	60010	2750	26W-18N	E2
Lago Ln					
13700	ODPK	60462	3346	9W-16S	C2
N Lagoon Ct					
42300	AntT	60002	2357	25W-42N	A6
Lagoon Dr					
10	ElaT	60047	2645	21W-24N	D7
10	HNWD	60047	2645	21W-24N	D7
100	NHFD	60093	2811	6W-15N	D3
300	NtrT	60093	2811	6W-15N	D3
2200	AlqT	60021	2695	31W-22N	E4
N Lagoon Dr					
24600	CbaT	60013	2643	28W-24N	A6
Lagoon Ln					
-	NtrT	60093	2811	6W-15N	D2
-	WNKA	60093	2811	6W-15N	D2
10	NHFD	60093	2811	6W-14N	D3
Lagoon Rd					
10	FXLK	60020	2472	28W-36N	E4
10	FXLK	60020	2473	28W-36N	A4
Lagoon Ter					
500	RLKB	60073	2474	23W-35N	D6
Lago Vista Blvd					
-	LKPT	60441	3419	21W-20S	E4
-	LktT	60441	3420	21W-20S	A4
16800	LKPT	60441	3420	21W-20S	A4
La Grande Av					
6000	OKFT	60452	3347	7W-18S	C7
La Grande Ct					
6100	OKFT	60452	3347	7W-18S	C7
La Grange Rd					
-	LynT	60458	3209	11W-8S	D2
-	LynT	60480	3209	11W-10S	D5
-	LynT	60525	3209	11W-8S	D2
-	MKNA	60448	3423	12W-22S	D7
-	PlsT	60480	3209	11W-10S	D5
-	PlsT	60480	3273	12W-12S	D2
-	WLSP	60458	3209	11W-9S	D2
-	WLSP	60480	3209	11W-8S	D2
-	WLSP	60525	3209	12W-8S	D2
16700	ODHL	60467	3423	12W-22S	D7
16700	ODHL	60487	3423	12W-22S	D7
16700	ODPK	60467	3423	12W-22S	D7
16700	ODPK	60487	3423	12W-22S	D7
16700	OrlT	60467	3423	12W-22S	D7
16700	OrlT	60487	3423	12W-22S	D7
17500	TYPK	60487	3423	11W-21S	D5
18200	FftT	60448	3423	12W-21S	D7
18200	ODPK	60448	3423	12W-21S	D7
18200	TYPK	60448	3423	12W-21S	D7
19100	MKNA	60448	3503	12W-22S	D1
19200	FftT	60448	3503	12W-22S	D1
19800	FKFT	60423	3503	11W-23S	E4
19800	FKFT	60448	3503	11W-23S	E4
19800	MKNA	60423	3503	11W-23S	E4
La Grange Rd US-12					
-	LynT	60458	3209	11W-8S	D2
-	LynT	60480	3209	11W-10S	D5
-	LynT	60525	3209	11W-8S	D2
-	PlsT	60480	3209	11W-10S	D5
-	WLSP	60458	3209	11W-9S	D2
-	WLSP	60480	3209	11W-8S	D2
-	WLSP	60525	3209	12W-8S	D1
La Grange Rd US-20					
-	LynT	60458	3209	11W-8S	D2
-	LynT	60480	3209	11W-10S	D5
-	LynT	60525	3209	11W-8S	D2
-	PlsT	60480	3209	11W-10S	D5
-	WLSP	60458	3209	11W-9S	D2
-	WLSP	60480	3209	11W-8S	D2
-	WLSP	60525	3209	12W-8S	D2
La Grange Rd US-45					
-	LynT	60458	3209	11W-8S	D2
-	LynT	60480	3209	11W-10S	D5
-	LynT	60525	3209	11W-8S	D2
-	MKNA	60448	3423	12W-22S	D7
-	PlsT	60480	3209	11W-10S	D5
-	PlsT	60480	3273	12W-12S	D2
-	WLSP	60458	3209	11W-9S	D2
-	WLSP	60480	3209	11W-8S	D2
-	WLSP	60525	3209	12W-8S	D2
16700	ODHL	60467	3423	12W-22S	D7
16700	ODHL	60487	3423	12W-22S	D7
16700	ODPK	60467	3423	12W-22S	D7
16700	ODPK	60487	3423	12W-22S	D7
16700	OrlT	60467	3423	12W-22S	D7
16700	OrlT	60487	3423	12W-22S	D7
16900	TYPK	60487	3423	11W-20S	D4
18200	FftT	60448	3423	12W-21S	D7
18200	ODPK	60448	3423	12W-21S	D7
18200	TYPK	60448	3423	12W-21S	D7
19100	MKNA	60448	3503	12W-22S	D1
19200	FftT	60448	3503	12W-22S	D1
19800	FKFT	60423	3503	11W-23S	E4
19800	FKFT	60448	3503	11W-23S	E4
19800	MKNA	60423	3503	11W-23S	E4
N La Grange Rd					
-	PvsT	60154	3087	12W-3S	B5
-	WSTR	60154	3087	12W-3S	B5
10	LGNG	60525	3087	12W-4S	C6
100	FKFT	60423	3503	11W-25S	E7
100	LGPK	60525	3087	12W-4S	C6
600	FftT	60423	3503	11W-25S	E6
1000	PvsT	60525	3087	12W-3S	B5
N La Grange Rd US-12					
-	PvsT	60154	3087	12W-3S	B5
-	WSTR	60154	3087	12W-3S	B5
10	LGNG	60525	3087	12W-4S	C6
100	LGPK	60525	3087	12W-4S	C6
1000	PvsT	60525	3087	12W-3S	B5
N La Grange Rd US-20					
-	PvsT	60154	3087	12W-3S	B5
-	WSTR	60154	3087	12W-3S	B5
10	LGNG	60525	3087	12W-4S	C6
100	LGPK	60525	3087	12W-4S	C6
1000	PvsT	60525	3087	12W-3S	B5
N La Grange Rd US-45					
-	PvsT	60154	3087	12W-3S	B5
-	WSTR	60154	3087	12W-3S	B5
10	LGNG	60525	3087	12W-4S	C6
100	FKFT	60423	3503	11W-25S	E7
100	LGPK	60525	3087	12W-4S	C6
600	FftT	60423	3503	11W-25S	E6
1000	PvsT	60525	3087	12W-3S	B5
S La Grange Rd					
-	CTSD	60525	3147	12W-8S	C7
-	HGKN	60525	3147	12W-8S	C7
-	HGKN	60525	3209	12W-8S	C1
-	PlsT	60480	3273	12W-13S	D4
10	LGNG	60525	3087	12W-4S	C7
200	FKFT	60423	3591	12W-26S	C2
300	LGNG	60525	3147	12W-7S	C7
5200	CTSD	60525	3147	12W-5S	C3
7600	WLSP	60525	3209	12W-8S	C1
11800	PlsT	60464	3273	12W-14S	D7
11800	PSPK	60464	3273	12W-14S	D7
12700	PSPK	60464	3345	12W-18S	D7
13000	PlsT	60462	3345	11W-15S	D1
13000	PSPK	60462	3345	11W-15S	D1
13400	OrlT	60462	3345	11W-15S	D2
13500	ODPK	60462	3345	11W-16S	D2
15700	ODPK	60462	3423	12W-18S	D1
15800	ODPK	60467	3423	12W-19S	D2
16600	ODHL	60467	3423	12W-19S	D3
16600	ODHL	60487	3423	12W-19S	D3
16600	ODPK	60467	3423	12W-19S	D3
16600	ODPK	60487	3423	12W-19S	D3
16600	OrlT	60467	3423	12W-19S	D3
16600	OrlT	60487	3423	12W-19S	D3
S La Grange Rd					
20000	FKFT	60423	3503	12W-24S	E6
20000	FKFT	60448	3503	12W-24S	E6
20600	FftT	60423	3503	12W-24S	E6
21800	FftT	60423	3591	14W-28S	A7
22900	GGnT	60423	3591	13W-27S	A5
S La Grange Rd US-12					
-	CTSD	60525	3147	12W-8S	C7
-	HGKN	60525	3209	12W-8S	C1
-	WLSP	60525	3209	12W-8S	C1
10	LGNG	60525	3087	12W-4S	C7
300	LGNG	60525	3147	12W-7S	C7
6000	HGKN	60525	3147	12W-6S	C5
S La Grange Rd US-20					
-	HGKN	60525	3147	12W-8S	C7
-	HGKN	60525	3209	12W-8S	C1
-	WLSP	60525	3209	12W-8S	C1
10	LGNG	60525	3087	12W-4S	C7
300	LGNG	60525	3147	12W-7S	C7
5200	CTSD	60525	3147	12W-5S	C3
S La Grange Rd US-45					
-	HGKN	60525	3147	12W-8S	C7
-	HGKN	60525	3209	12W-8S	C1
-	PlsT	60480	3273	12W-13S	D4
-	WLSP	60525	3209	12W-8S	C1
10	LGNG	60525	3087	12W-4S	C7
200	FKFT	60423	3591	12W-26S	C2
300	LGNG	60525	3147	12W-7S	C7
5200	CTSD	60525	3147	12W-5S	C3
11800	PlsT	60464	3273	12W-14S	D7
11800	PSPK	60464	3273	12W-14S	D7
12700	PSPK	60464	3345	12W-18S	D7
13000	PlsT	60462	3345	11W-15S	D1
13000	PSPK	60462	3345	11W-15S	D1
13400	OrlT	60462	3345	11W-15S	D2
13500	ODPK	60462	3345	11W-16S	D2
15700	ODPK	60462	3423	12W-18S	D1
15800	ODPK	60467	3423	12W-19S	D2
16600	ODHL	60467	3423	12W-19S	D3
16600	ODHL	60487	3423	12W-19S	D3
16600	ODPK	60487	3423	12W-19S	D3
16600	OrlT	60467	3423	12W-19S	D3
16600	OrlT	60487	3423	12W-19S	D3
20000	FKFT	60423	3503	12W-24S	E6
20000	FKFT	60448	3503	12W-24S	E6
20600	FftT	60423	3503	12W-24S	E6
21800	FftT	60423	3591	14W-28S	A7
22900	GGnT	60423	3591	13W-27S	A5
Laguna Ct					
300	CLSM	60188	2968	26W-3N	A5
1000	RMVL	60446	3340	25W-16S	B3
1300	HRPK	60133	2911	26W-7N	E5
1500	WLNG	60090	2754	16W-17N	D5
N Laguna Ct					
1200	PLTN	60067	2752	22W-17N	C4
W Laguna Ct					
21900	PnfT	60544	3339	27W-16S	C4
Laguna Dr					
800	NndT	60051	2528	31W-31N	D7
Laguna Ln					
7800	ODPK	60462	3346	10W-16S	C3
7800	OrlT	60462	3346	10W-16S	C3
17000	LKPT	60441	3420	21W-20S	A4
Laguna Rd					
700	CLLK	60014	2693	36W-23N	D2
La Haigh Rd					
17900	HMWD	60430	3427	1W-21S	E6
Lahard Rd					
1200	NLNX	60451	3589	16W-25S	E1
1400	NLNX	60451	3590	16W-25S	A1
Lahinch Ct					
1100	DYR	46311	3510		E7
2800	AURA	60503	3265	31W-11S	D1
Lahinch Dr					
10	LMNT	60439	3343	17W-15S	B1
2600	AURA	60503	3265	31W-11S	D1
13200	PlsT	60462	3345	11W-15S	E2
Lahon Av					
22300	CHHT	60411	3596	0E-27S	E4
22300	SCHT	60411	3596	0E-27S	E4
22300	SCHT	60475	3596	0E-27S	E4
22300	STGR	60411	3596	0E-27S	E4
22300	STGR	60475	3596	0E-27S	E4
Lahon Rd					
22700	STGR	60475	3596	0E-27S	D5
22800	CRTE	60417	3596	0E-27S	D5
Lahon St					
-	PKRG	60068	2864	9W-9N	B6
1400	PKRG	60068	2863	10W-9N	E6
E Lahon St					
10	PKRG	60068	2864	9W-9N	C6
200	NLES	60068	2864	9W-9N	C6
200	NLES	60714	2864	9W-9N	C6
N Laird St					
10	NPVL	60540	3141	27W-6S	C5
S Laird St					
10	NPVL	60540	3141	27W-6S	C5
La Jolla Ct					
2700	AURA	60503	3201	32W-11S	D7
La Jolla Ter					
900	BRLT	60103	2911	28W-7N	B5
Lajunta Ct					
-	MKNA	60448	3502	15W-23S	C4
Lake					
-	ELGN	60120	2855	32W-10N	C6
Lake Av					
-	AntT	60002	2417	22W-40N	B4
-	AntT	60046	2417	22W-40N	B3
-	CHCG	60613	2977	1W-5N	D1
-	ELGN	60120	2855	32W-9N	C7
200	LKVL	60046	2417	22W-38N	B7
200	PKRG	60068	2918	9W-8N	B1
200	WDSK	60098	2581	41W-30N	D1
200	WLMT	60091	2813	3W-14N	A5
300	WCDA	60084	2644	25W-27N	A1
400	DRGV	60515	3084	19W-4S	D7
600	LKWD	60014	2639	37W-25N	C5
700	WLMT	60091	2812	3W-14N	D5
1000	WDSK	60098	2582	40W-30N	A3
1500	MchT	60051	2528	31W-33N	C3
1500	MHRY	60051	2528	31W-33N	C3
1900	HDPK	60035	2705	7W-22N	A4
2000	DrrT	60098	2582	40W-29N	A4
2200	CLLK	60014	2639	37W-25N	B5
2800	WLMT	60091	2811	6W-13N	D5
3500	GNVW	60025	2811	6W-13N	D5
E Lake Av					
-	NfdT	60025	2810	10W-13N	A5
200	GNVW	60025	2811	7W-14N	B5
200	WLMT	60091	2811	6W-13N	C5
500	WLMT	60025	2811	7W-14N	B5
700	GNVW	60091	2811	7W-14N	B5
1500	GNVW	60025	2810	9W-13N	C5
3800	GNVW	60025	2809	11W-14N	E5
N Lake Av					
10	FXLK	60020	2473	27W-36N	C3
N Lake Av					
39200	LkvT	60046	2416	24W-39N	B5
42000	AntT	60002	2356	26W-43N	D4
43400	AntT	53179	2356	26W-43N	D4
43400	SlmT	53179	2356	26W-43N	D4
N Lake Av CO-V51					
42000	AntT	60002	2356	26W-43N	D4
43400	AntT	53179	2356	26W-43N	D4
43400	SlmT	53179	2356	26W-43N	D4
S Lake Av					
10	FXLK	60020	2473	27W-36N	B4
10	TDLK	60030	2476	19W-35N	C7
1300	HMND	46320	3280		E3
1300	HMND	46394	3280		E5
S Lake Av N					
10	TDLK	60030	2476	19W-35N	C6
W Lake Av					
-	GNVW	60062	2809	12W-14N	B4
-	WhlT	60025	2809	12W-14N	A4
2400	GNVW	60025	2810	10W-14N	B4
3000	NfdT	60025	2810	10W-14N	A4
3400	GNVW	60025	2809	10W-14N	E4
4100	NfdT	60025	2809	12W-14N	A4
4100	NfdT	60062	2809	11W-14N	D4
21500	LkvT	60046	2417	21W-38N	D6
24500	AvnT	60073	2474	24W-35N	C6
25100	GrtT	60041	2474	25W-35N	B7
26000	AntT	60002	2415	26W-39N	E5
Lake Av E					
41700	NfdT	60025	2809	12W-14N	A4
Lake Blvd					
-	BFGV	60090	2754	16W-17N	D4
-	WLNG	60090	2754	16W-17N	D4
10	BFGV	60089	2754	16W-17N	D4
N Lake Blvd					
40200	AntT	60002	2416	25W-40N	B3
Lake Cir					
-	BtvT	60539	3077	36W-2S	E4
Lake Ct					
100	ANTH	60002	2357	23W-43N	E4
100	CLLK	60014	2639	36W-25N	D4
400	OSWG	60543	3263	38W-12S	B3
400	WKGN	60085	2537	10W-34N	A2
500	WCDA	60084	2588	25W-27N	A7
700	BTVA	60510	3020	34W-0S	D7
700	NLNX	60451	3501	17W-25S	D7
4100	ZION	60099	2421	12W-41N	C2
4900	CCHL	60478	3506	6W-22S	A2
N Lake Ct					
2500	JLET	60441	3417	27W-19S	D4
39300	AntT	60002	2416	25W-39N	B5
S Lake Ct					
900	WTMT	60559	3145	18W-6S	A5
W Lake Ct					
20600	LkvT	60046	2476	20W-36N	A3
Lake Dr					
-	LKMR	60051	2529	29W-32N	D5
-	PLTN	60067	2805	22W-14N	B5
-	PNFD	60586	3415	32W-19S	D3
10	ALGN	60102	2694	35W-21N	A6
10	ALGN	60156	2694	35W-21N	A6
10	DGvT	60527	3207	16W-9S	E2
10	LIHL	60156	2694	35W-21N	A5
10	PNFD	60544	3338	29W-16S	E3
10	PNFD	60585	3338	29W-16S	E3
10	PnfT	60544	3338	29W-16S	E4
10	PnfT	60585	3338	29W-16S	E3
10	WTMT	60559	3145	18W-7S	A6
100	OMFD	60461	3507	3W-24S	A5
400	WLBK	60527	3207	16W-9S	D2
500	WnfT	60185	3023	28W-0N	A4
1700	FSMR	60422	3507	3W-23S	B4
15700	OKFT	60452	3347	7W-18S	D7
15700	OKFT	60452	3425	7W-18S	D1
E Lake Dr					
5500	LSLE	60532	3143	23W-6S	A4
5500	LslT	60532	3143	23W-6S	A4
N Lake Dr					
27900	WcnT	60084	2588	25W-28N	A6
28100	WcnT	60084	2587	25W-28N	E6
35600	GrtT	60041	2474	25W-35N	B5
40400	AntT	60002	2417	22W-40N	B3
41500	AntT	60002	2357	25W-42N	B5
S Lake Dr					
400	WnfT	60185	3023	28W-0N	A5
2700	HHLL	60051	2586	30W-29N	A4
W Lake Dr					
100	CLSM	60139	3024	24W-2N	D1
100	CLSM	60188	3024	24W-2N	D1
100	GLHT	60139	3024	24W-2N	D1
21700	AvnT	60030	2532	21W-34N	C1
21700	AvnT	60073	2532	22W-34N	C1
21700	GYLK	60030	2532	21W-34N	C1
21900	RLKB	60073	2532	22W-34N	C1
22100	RLKP	60073	2532	22W-34N	C1
Lake Dr S					
-	ALGN	60156	2694	35W-21N	A6
-	LIHL	60156	2694	35W-21N	A6
100	ALGN	60102	2694	35W-21N	A6
Lake Ln					
10	FXLK	60020	2472	28W-36N	E4
100	ODHL	60013	2641	31W-26N	D3
W Lake Pkwy					
25100	WcnT	60084	2588	25W-28N	B6
Lake Rd					
500	GNEN	60137	3025	22W-0N	C5
600	LKFT	60045	2650	9W-27N	B1
700	NLNX	60451	3501	17W-25S	E7
700	NLNX	60451	3589	17W-25S	E1
700	NlxT	60451	3589	17W-25S	C7
1400	LKFT	60045	2594	10W-27N	B7
N Lake Rd					
300	LKMR	60051	2529	29W-32N	C5
300	LMBD	60148	3084	19W-1S	C2
33900	WrnT	60030	2533	18W-33N	E2
W Lake Rd					
26500	AntT	60002	2415	26W-39N	D6
Lake St					
-	AntT	60002	2357	25W-42N	A6
-	AntT	60002	2415	26W-38N	C6
-	BRLT	60103	2856	31W-9N	A7
-	BRLT	60120	2856	31W-9N	A7
-	BRTN	60010	2751	25W-18N	A2
-	CLLK	60014	2639	36W-25N	C4
-	ELGN	-	2855	32W-10N	D6
-	ELGN	60103	2856	31W-9N	A7
-	ELGN	60120	2856	31W-9N	A7
-	HnrT	60120	2856	31W-9N	A7
-	PnfT	60544	3339	27W-16S	D5
10	BmdT	60101	2969	21W-5N	D1
10	BmdT	60172	2912	25W-6N	B6
10	CHCG	60302	3031	7W-0N	B4
10	CHCG	60644	3031	7W-0N	B4
10	LKZH	60047	2698	23W-22N	E3
10	MYWD	60153	3030	10W-0N	B4
10	OKPK	60302	3031	8W-0N	A4

STREET Block	City	ZIP	Map#	CGS	Grid
Lake St					
10	ROSL	60172	2912	25W-6N	C6
10	RVFT	60305	3030	10W-0N	A4
10	WKGN	60085	2537	10W-34N	B2
100	ADSN	60101	2969	21W-5N	E2
100	BMDL	60101	2969	22W-5N	C1
100	BMDL	60108	2969	22W-5N	C1
100	BmdT	60143	2969	21W-5N	E2
100	ELGN	60120	2854	33W-11N	E4
100	LYVL	60048	2591	17W-29N	A4
100	WNKA	60093	2758	6W-16N	E7
200	AddT	60101	2970	20W-5N	A2
200	AddT	60143	2970	20W-5N	A2
200	ADSN	60101	2970	20W-5N	A2
200	ADSN	60143	2970	20W-5N	A2
200	BmdT	60133	2911	26W-7N	E5
200	EVTN	60201	2867	2W-11N	C3
300	AddT	60101	2971	17W-3N	B5
300	ADSN	60101	2971	17W-3N	B5
300	ANTH	60002	2357	23W-42N	D6
300	BTVA	60510	3020	35W-0S	C7
300	GLNC	60022	2758	6W-17N	E6
300	HRPK	60133	2912	25W-6N	B6
300	HRPK	60172	2912	25W-6N	B6
400	BmdT	60133	2912	25W-6N	B6
400	BmdT	60157	2969	21W-5N	E1
400	WCDA	60084	2588	25W-27N	A7
400	WCDA	60084	2644	25W-27N	A1
500	BmdT	60101	2970	20W-5N	A2
500	BmdT	60143	2970	20W-5N	A2
600	BMDL	60108	2912	24W-6N	D7
600	BMDL	60172	2912	24W-6N	D7
600	OKPK	60301	3031	8W-0N	A4
700	MYWD	60153	3029	11W-0N	E3
800	MLPK	60160	3029	10W-0N	E3
800	MYWD	60160	3029	10W-0N	E3
800	OKPK	60301	3030	8W-0N	B4
1000	MDLN	60060	2590	19W-28N	D5
1100	RVFT	60301	3030	8W-0N	D4
1200	DYR	46311	3510		C7
1200	FmtT	60048	2590	19W-29N	D4
1200	FmtT	60060	2590	19W-29N	D4
1200	LYVL	60048	2590	18W-29N	D4
1200	MDLN	60048	2590	19W-29N	D4
1400	MDLN	60060	2591	17W-29N	A4
1500	DYR	46311	3598		C1
1500	HRPK	60133	2911	26W-7N	E4
1700	EVTN	60201	2866	3W-11N	E3
3300	SKOK	60203	2866	4W-11N	D3
3400	LNSG	60438	3430	4E-21S	C6
3700	MNSR	46321	3430	4E-21S	C6
5500	MNGV	60053	2865	7W-11N	C3
5500	SKOK	60053	2865	6W-11N	D3
5500	SKOK	60077	2865	6W-11N	D3
7200	MNGV	60053	2864	9W-11N	D3
7800	NLES	60053	2864	9W-11N	B3
7800	NLES	60714	2864	9W-11N	B3
8000	WLSP	60480	3209	12W-9S	C2
Lake St SR-59					
300	ANTH	60002	2357	23W-42N	D6
Lake St US-20					
-	AddT	60101	2971	17W-3N	B5
-	BRLT	60103	2856	31W-9N	A7
-	BRLT	60120	2856	31W-9N	A7
-	ELGN	-	2855	32W-10N	D6
-	ELGN	60103	2856	31W-9N	A7
-	ELGN	60120	2856	31W-9N	A7
-	HnrT	60120	2856	31W-9N	A7
10	BmdT	60101	2970	21W-5N	A2
10	BmdT	60172	2912	25W-6N	B6
10	ROSL	60172	2912	25W-6N	C6
100	ADSN	60101	2969	21W-5N	E2
100	BMDL	60101	2969	22W-5N	C1
100	BMDL	60108	2969	22W-5N	C1
100	BmdT	60101	2969	21W-5N	E2
100	BmdT	60143	2969	21W-5N	E2
200	AddT	60101	2970	20W-5N	A2
200	AddT	60143	2970	20W-5N	A2
200	ADSN	60101	2970	20W-5N	A2
200	ADSN	60143	2970	20W-5N	A2
200	BmdT	60133	2911	26W-7N	E5
300	HRPK	60133	2912	25W-6N	B6
300	HRPK	60172	2912	25W-6N	B6
400	BmdT	60133	2912	25W-6N	B6
400	BmdT	60157	2969	21W-5N	E1
500	BmdT	60143	2970	20W-5N	A2
600	BMDL	60108	2912	24W-6N	D7
600	BMDL	60172	2912	24W-6N	D7
1500	HRPK	60133	2911	26W-7N	E4
Lake St US-45					
1000	MDLN	60060	2590	19W-28N	D5
1200	FmtT	60048	2590	19W-29N	D4
1200	FmtT	60060	2590	19W-29N	D4
1200	LYVL	60048	2590	18W-29N	D4
1200	MDLN	60048	2590	19W-29N	D4
E Lake St					
10	ADSN	60101	2971	17W-3N	B5
10	CHCG	60601	3034	0E-0N	C4
10	MLPK	60160	3028	13W-1N	E2
10	NHLK	60164	3028	13W-1N	D2
100	BMDL	60108	2969	23W-5N	B1
100	BRLT	60103	2910	28W-9N	E2
100	BRLT	60103	2911	28W-8N	A2
100	BRLT	60107	2910	28W-9N	E1
100	BRTN	60010	2750	26W-18N	D2
100	BRTN	60010	2751	25W-18N	A2
100	EMHT	60126	2971	16W-2N	D7
100	EMHT	60126	2972	15W-2N	A7
100	EMHT	60126	3028	15W-2N	A1
100	SMWD	60103	2910	28W-9N	E2
100	SMWD	60103	2911	28W-8N	A2
100	SMWD	60107	2910	28W-9N	E2
100	SMWD	60107	2911	28W-8N	A2
200	AddT	60101	2971	17W-3N	A5
200	BRLT	60107	2911	28W-8N	A2
300	EMHT	60101	2971	17W-3N	C6
400	RLKB	60073	2475	22W-34N	B7
400	WDSK	60098	2581	41W-30N	D1
500	HRPK	60133	2911	28W-8N	B2
800	AURA	60506	3199	36W-8S	D2
1000	BmdT	60133	2911	26W-7N	E5
1000	BmdT	60133	2912	25W-7N	A5
1000	HRPK	60133	2912	25W-7N	A5
E Lake St US-20					
10	ADSN	60101	2971	17W-3N	B5
10	MLPK	60160	3028	13W-1N	E2
10	NHLK	60164	3028	13W-1N	D2
100	BMDL	60108	2969	23W-5N	B1
100	BRLT	60103	2910	28W-9N	E2
100	BRLT	60103	2911	28W-8N	A2
100	BRLT	60107	2910	28W-9N	E1
100	SMWD	60103	2910	28W-9N	E2
100	SMWD	60103	2911	28W-8N	A2
100	SMWD	60107	2910	28W-9N	E2
100	SMWD	60107	2911	28W-8N	A2
200	AddT	60101	2971	17W-3N	A5
E Lake St US-20					
200	BRLT	60107	2911	28W-9N	A2
300	EMHT	60101	2971	17W-3N	C6
300	EMHT	60126	2971	17W-3N	C6
500	HRPK	60133	2911	28W-8N	B2
1000	BmdT	60133	2911	26W-7N	E5
1000	BmdT	60133	2912	25W-7N	A5
1000	HRPK	60133	2912	25W-7N	A5
N Lake St					
-	WrnT	60046	2476	18W-34N	D7
10	AURA	60506	3138	35W-6S	B5
10	GYLK	60030	2532	21W-33N	E3
10	MDLN	60060	2646	19W-27N	D1
900	MDLN	60060	2590	19W-28N	D6
1200	FmtT	60048	2590	19W-28N	D6
1200	FmtT	60060	2590	19W-28N	D6
1200	LYVL	60048	2590	19W-28N	D6
1200	MDLN	60048	2590	19W-28N	D6
1300	AURA	60542	3138	35W-6S	B5
1300	NARA	60542	3138	35W-6S	B5
1500	AvnT	60030	2475	21W-34N	E7
1500	GYLK	60030	2475	21W-34N	E7
5200	MchT	60050	2472	29W-37N	C2
36600	GrtT	60041	2473	26W-36N	B6
38700	AntT	60002	2415	27W-38N	C6
N Lake St SR-31					
10	AURA	60506	3138	35W-6S	B5
1300	AURA	60542	3138	35W-6S	B5
1300	NARA	60542	3138	35W-6S	B5
N Lake St US-45					
10	MDLN	60060	2646	19W-27N	D1
900	MDLN	60060	2590	19W-28N	D6
1200	FmtT	60048	2590	19W-28N	D6
1200	FmtT	60060	2590	19W-28N	D6
1200	LYVL	60048	2590	19W-28N	D6
1200	MDLN	60048	2590	19W-28N	D6
S Lake St					
10	AURA	60506	3138	36W-7S	A7
10	GYLK	60030	2532	20W-32N	E5
10	MDLN	60060	2646	18W-27N	D2
100	MTGY	60538	3199	37W-10S	B6
100	MTGY	60543	3199	37W-10S	B6
200	AURA	60506	3200	36W-7S	A1
300	AURA	60506	3199	36W-8S	E1
1000	LbvT	60060	2646	18W-26N	E3
1000	MTGY	60506	3199	37W-8S	D3
1100	AraT	60506	3199	37W-8S	D3
S Lake St SR-31					
10	AURA	60506	3138	36W-7S	A7
10	MTGY	60538	3199	37W-9S	C4
100	MTGY	60543	3199	37W-10S	B6
200	AURA	60506	3200	36W-7S	A1
300	AURA	60506	3199	36W-8S	E1
1000	MTGY	60506	3199	37W-8S	D3
1100	AraT	60506	3199	37W-8S	D3
S Lake St US-45					
10	MDLN	60060	2646	18W-27N	D2
1000	LbvT	60060	2646	18W-26N	E3
W Lake St					
-	AddT	60101	2971	17W-3N	C6
-	EMHT	60101	2971	17W-3N	C6
-	EMHT	60126	3028	14W-2N	C1
-	NHLK	60164	3028	14W-2N	C1
-	SMWD	60120	2910	30W-9N	C1
10	CHCG	60601	3034	0W-0N	A4
100	AddT	60101	2970	20W-4N	B3
100	ADSN	60101	2970	20W-4N	B3
100	BMDL	60108	2968	23W-5N	E1
100	BMDL	60108	2969	23W-5N	A1
100	BmdT	60108	2968	23W-5N	E1
100	BRTN	60010	2750	25W-18N	E2
100	CHCG	60606	3034	0W-0N	B4
200	BMDL	60108	2912	24W-6N	D7
200	BMDL	60172	2912	24W-6N	D7
200	BmdT	60108	2912	24W-5N	E7
200	ROSL	60108	2912	24W-6N	D7
200	ROSL	60172	2912	24W-6N	D7
300	EMHT	60126	2971	16W-2N	D6
400	CHCG	60661	3034	0W-0N	A4
500	BRLT	60103	2910	29W-9N	E1
500	BRLT	60107	2910	29W-9N	E1
500	BRLT	60120	2910	29W-9N	D1
500	HnrT	60103	2910	29W-9N	D1
500	HnrT	60120	2910	29W-9N	D1
500	SMWD	60107	2910	29W-9N	E1
600	BRLT	60103	2911	28W-8N	B3
600	HRPK	60103	2911	28W-8N	B3
600	HRPK	60133	2911	28W-8N	B3
600	SMWD	60107	2911	28W-8N	B3
700	CHCG	60607	3034	0W-0N	A4
800	CHCG	60607	3033	2W-0N	B4
900	MLPK	60160	3029	11W-1N	C3
900	MYWD	60153	3029	10W-0N	E3
900	MYWD	60160	3029	10W-0N	E3
1100	BRLT	60103	2856	30W-9N	B7
1100	BRLT	60107	2856	30W-9N	B7
1100	HnrT	60107	2856	30W-9N	B7
1100	SMWD	60107	2856	30W-9N	C7
1200	BRLT	60120	2856	30W-9N	B7
1400	BRLT	60120	2856	30W-9N	B7
1500	CHCG	60612	3033	1W-0N	D4
2200	BRLT	60133	2911	27W-8N	C3
2800	CHCG	60612	3032	3W-0N	E4
3100	CHCG	60624	3032	3W-0N	E4
3100	MchT	60051	2528	32W-33N	C3
3600	MLPK	60165	3029	12W-1N	B2
3600	SNPK	60160	3029	12W-1N	B2
3600	SNPK	60165	3029	12W-1N	B2
4500	CHCG	60644	3032	3W-0N	E4
4600	MLPK	60160	3028	13W-1N	E2
5500	CHCG	60644	3031	6W-0N	C4
5900	CHCG	60302	3031	7W-0N	B4
5900	OKPK	60302	3031	7W-0N	B4
8000	MNGV	60053	2864	10W-11N	B3
8000	NLES	60053	2864	10W-11N	B3
8000	NLES	60714	2864	10W-11N	B3
25700	WcnT	60084	2587	26W-28N	D7
25700	WcnT	60084	2588	25W-27N	A7
26300	AntT	60002	2356	26W-42N	D6
W Lake St US-20					
-	EMHT	60101	2971	17W-3N	C6
-	SMWD	60120	2910	30W-9N	C1
10	ADSN	60101	2970	20W-4N	B3
10	NHLK	60164	3028	14W-1N	C1
100	AddT	60101	2970	20W-4N	B3
100	BMDL	60108	2968	23W-5N	E1
100	BMDL	60108	2969	23W-5N	A1
100	BmdT	60108	2968	23W-5N	E1
200	BMDL	60108	2912	24W-6N	D7
200	BMDL	60172	2912	24W-6N	D7
200	BmdT	60108	2912	24W-5N	E7
200	ROSL	60108	2912	24W-6N	D7
200	ROSL	60172	2912	24W-6N	D7
300	AddT	60101	2971	17W-3N	A5
300	EMHT	60126	2971	16W-2N	D6
500	BRLT	60103	2910	29W-9N	E1
W Lake St US-20					
500	BRLT	60107	2910	29W-9N	E1
500	BRLT	60120	2910	29W-9N	D1
500	HnrT	60103	2910	29W-9N	D1
500	HnrT	60120	2910	29W-9N	D1
500	SMWD	60107	2910	29W-9N	E1
600	BRLT	60103	2911	28W-8N	B3
600	HRPK	60103	2911	28W-8N	B3
600	HRPK	60133	2911	28W-8N	B3
600	SMWD	60107	2911	28W-8N	B3
1100	BRLT	60103	2856	30W-9N	B7
1100	BRLT	60107	2856	30W-9N	B7
1100	HnrT	60107	2856	30W-9N	B7
1100	SMWD	60107	2856	30W-9N	C7
1400	BRLT	60120	2856	30W-9N	B7
1400	HnrT	60120	2856	30W-9N	B7
2200	BRLT	60133	2911	27W-8N	C3
4100	MLPK	60160	3029	13W-1N	A2
4100	MLPK	60165	3029	13W-1N	A2
4100	SNPK	60160	3029	13W-1N	A2
4100	SNPK	60165	3029	13W-1N	A2
4600	MLPK	60160	3028	13W-1N	E2
Lake Ter					
1000	ELGN	60123	2800	34W-13N	E7
1000	ELGN	60123	2854	34W-13N	E1
N Lake Ter					
1900	NfdT	60025	2810	10W-14N	A4
3000	GNVW	60025	2810	10W-14N	A4
S Lake Ter					
400	MDLN	60060	2646	19W-27N	D2
Lake Adalyn Dr					
10	SBTN	60010	2803	26W-13N	C6
N Lake Arlington Dr					
-	PTHT	60070	2754	16W-16N	E7
1900	ANHT	60004	2807	16W-16N	D1
2100	ANHT	60004	2754	16W-16N	E7
Lake Barrington Shrs					
-	LKBN	60010	2643	27W-24N	B7
Lake Bluff Dr					
5800	BmnT	60477	3425	7W-20S	C3
5800	TYPK	60477	3425	7W-20S	C4
N Lake Bluff Dr					
40500	AntT	60002	2417	22W-40N	C3
Lake Bluff Ln					
-	PGGV	60140	2797	42W-15N	C4
Lake Breeze Ct					
600	LKVL	60046	2475	22W-37N	C1
Lakebreeze Ct					
10	LKZH	60047	2698	24W-23N	C2
Lakebrook Ct					
11300	ODPK	60467	3422	14W-20S	E5
Lakebrook Dr					
17200	ODPK	60467	3422	14W-20S	E5
Lake Charles Dr					
1600	VNHL	60061	2647	16W-27N	C1
Lake Charlotte Ct					
500	SchT	60175	2963	38W-3N	A7
Lake Churchill Dr					
2000	RLKP	60030	2532	22W-31N	B7
Lakecliffe Dr					
1700	WHTN	60187	3082	23W-2S	E3
1700	WHTN	60187	3083	23W-2S	A3
Lake Cook Rd					
-	AlqT	60010	2749	28W-20N	D2
-	ANHT	60004	2753	19W-20N	D2
-	BNHL	60010	2749	28W-20N	D2
-	BNHL	60010	2750	27W-20N	A2
-	BRTN	60010	2750	25W-20N	E2
-	ElaT	60004	2753	19W-20N	C2
-	ElaT	60047	2753	20W-20N	A2
-	ElaT	60074	2753	20W-20N	A2
-	LGGV	60047	2753	20W-20N	A2
-	LGGV	60074	2753	19W-20N	B2
-	PLTN	60074	2753	20W-20N	A2
-	PltT	60004	2753	19W-20N	C2
-	PltT	60074	2753	20W-20N	A2
-	VrnT	60004	2753	19W-20N	D2
-	VrnT	60047	2753	19W-20N	D2
-	VrnT	60089	2753	18W-20N	D2
-	VrnT	60090	2755	14W-20N	D2
-	WhlT	60090	2755	14W-20N	D2
100	DRFD	60062	2757	10W-20N	A2
500	DRFD	60015	2757	10W-18N	A3
600	DRFD	60062	2756	10W-20N	E2
700	NHBK	60062	2756	10W-20N	E2
900	DRFD	60015	2756	11W-20N	D2
1000	HDPK	60035	2758	8W-18N	A2
1000	NfdT	60062	2758	8W-18N	A2
1000	NtrT	60062	2758	7W-20N	A2
1200	NfdT	60062	2757	8W-20N	E2
1300	HDPK	60035	2757	9W-20N	B2
1300	NHBK	60062	2757	9W-20N	B2
1400	NHBK	60035	2757	9W-20N	C2
1600	HDPK	60035	2757	9W-20N	C2
1900	NfdT	60015	2756	12W-20N	A2
1900	NfdT	60062	2756	12W-20N	A2
1900	NHBK	60015	2756	12W-18N	B2
1900	WdfT	60015	2756	12W-20N	A2
2200	RVWD	60015	2756	12W-18N	A2
2400	RVWD	60062	2756	13W-20N	A2
2700	RVWD	60015	2755	13W-20N	E2
2700	RVWD	60062	2755	13W-20N	E2
2700	VrnT	60015	2755	13W-20N	E2
2700	VrnT	60062	2755	13W-20N	E2
2700	WhlT	60062	2755	13W-20N	E2
4400	NHBK	60062	2755	13W-20N	E2
22000	DRPK	60010	2752	22W-20N	D2
22000	PltT	60010	2752	22W-20N	A2
22000	PltT	60074	2752	22W-20N	C2
23200	DRPK	60010	2751	23W-20N	E2
23200	ElaT	60010	2751	23W-20N	E2
23200	PltT	60010	2751	23W-20N	E2
23900	BRTN	60010	2751	23W-20N	D2
E Lake Cook Rd					
-	VrnT	60062	2755	14W-20N	D2
-	VrnT	60090	2755	14W-20N	D2
-	WhlT	60062	2755	14W-20N	D2
-	WhlT	60090	2755	14W-20N	C2
10	BFGV	60089	2754	16W-20N	D2
100	DRPK	60074	2752	20W-20N	E2
100	ElaT	60074	2752	20W-20N	E2
100	PltT	60074	2752	20W-20N	E2
100	WLNG	60089	2754	16W-20N	D2
200	BFGV	60089	2755	15W-20N	A2
200	BFGV	60090	2755	15W-20N	A2
200	WLNG	60090	2755	15W-20N	A2
1000	BFGV	60090	2754	16W-20N	D2
1000	WLNG	60090	2754	16W-20N	D2
E Lake Cook Rd CO-A50					
10	BFGV	60089	2754	16W-18N	C2
100	WLNG	60089	2754	16W-20N	D2
1300	WLNG	60090	2754	16W-20N	D2
W Lake Cook Rd					
-	ANHT	60004	2753	18W-20N	E2
-	VrnT	60004	2753	18W-20N	E2
-	VrnT	60047	2753	18W-20N	E2
W Lake Cook Rd					
-	VrnT	60089	2753	18W-20N	E2
10	BFGV	60089	2754	17W-18N	B2
100	DRPK	60074	2752	21W-20N	D2
100	PltT	60074	2752	21W-20N	D2
500	DRPK	60010	2752	21W-20N	C2
500	PltT	60010	2752	21W-20N	C2
1100	ANHT	60004	2754	17W-20N	A2
1100	VrnT	60004	2754	17W-20N	A2
1100	VrnT	60089	2754	17W-20N	A2
Lake Cornish Ct					
10	ALGN	60102	2748	33W-19N	A3
Lake Cornish Wy					
500	ALGN	60102	2748	33W-19N	A2
Lake Crest Av					
37500	BHPK	60087	2479	10W-37N	E2
Lake Dawnwood Dr					
4600	JNBG	60050	2472	30W-36N	A3
5000	MchT	60050	2472	30W-36N	A3
Lake Dr Ct					
10	ALGN	60102	2694	35W-21N	A6
Lake Edge Ct					
1300	HFET	60192	2804	24W-15N	C2
Lake Eleanor Ct					
100	WYNE	60185	2966	31W-4N	A5
Lake Eleanor Dr					
100	WYNE	60185	2966	31W-4N	A4
1600	DRFD	60015	2703	12W-21N	C6
W Lake Fairfield Ln					
24300	FmtT	60060	2588	24W-29N	C5
24300	WCDA	60060	2588	24W-29N	C5
24500	FmtT	60084	2588	24W-29N	C5
24500	WCDA	60084	2588	24W-29N	C5
Lakefield Dr					
11200	ODPK	60467	3422	14W-20S	E4
Lake Forrest Ln					
24800	SRWD	60404	3584	31W-25S	A1
Lake Front Dr					
-	BtnT	60099	2422	8W-40N	E3
-	ZION	60099	2422	8W-40N	E3
Lake Gillian Ct					
10	ALGN	60102	2748	32W-20N	B2
Lake Gillian Wy					
200	ALGN	60102	2748	33W-19N	B2
Lakegreen Dr					
21400	FmtT	60060	2589	21W-27N	D7
Lake Grove Dr					
2000	JLET	60586	3416	30W-21S	A7
Lakehill Ln					
100	CRTE	60417	3596	0W-28S	C6
Lake Hills Ct					
15700	ODPK	60462	3424	10W-18S	B1
Lake Hinsdale Dr					
-	DRN	60561	3145	16W-7S	D6
-	WLBK	60561	3145	16W-7S	D6
10	WLBK	60527	3145	16W-7S	D6
Lakehurst Dr					
1000	WKGN	60085	2535	13W-32N	E4
Lakehurst Rd					
200	WKGN	60085	2535	13W-32N	E4
Lake Julian Ln					
-	AlqT	60013	2696	30W-23N	A1
-	CRY	60013	2696	30W-23N	A1
Lake Katherine Dr					
11800	PSHT	60463	3274	9W-13S	D5
Lake Knoll Dr					
3300	NHBK	60062	2756	11W-16N	D7
3400	NfdT	60062	2756	11W-16N	C7
Lakeland Av					
400	FXLK	60020	2473	28W-35N	A5
400	GrtT	60041	2473	28W-36N	A5
1500	MHRY	60050	2527	33W-33N	E3
Lakeland Ct					
200	SMBG	60173	2859	22W-10N	C5
1000	WLNG	60090	2754	16W-16N	D7
Lakeland Dr					
100	PlsT	60464	3273	12W-14S	B7
500	LKBF	60044	2594	10W-28N	A6
600	SMBG	60194	2859	22W-10N	C5
700	SMBG	60173	2859	22W-10N	C5
N Lakeland Dr					
-	WcnT	60084	2643	26W-26N	C3
26000	LKBN	60084	2643	26W-26N	C3
Lakeland Ln					
-	PGGV	60140	2797	42W-15N	D4
Lakeland Plz					
10	FXLK	60020	2473	27W-36N	A3
W Lakeland Tr					
21900	PnfT	60544	3339	27W-16S	C4
Lakelawn Blvd					
300	AURA	60506	3138	36W-6S	A4
300	AURA	60506	3137	36W-6S	E4
Lake Lawn Ct					
200	JLET	60435	3498	25W-23S	B4
Lake Lawn Ln					
15100	ODPK	60467	3344	14W-18S	E7
E Lake Louise Dr					
1400	PLTN	60074	2753	19W-16N	C7
Lake Lynwood Dr					
19400	BlmT	60411	3509	3E-23S	E3
19400	LYWD	60411	3509	3E-23S	E3
19700	LYWD	60411	3510	3E-23S	A3
W Lake Manor Dr					
600	ADSN	60101	2970	19W-3N	D6
Lake Marian Rd					
10	CPVL	60110	2748	34W-17N	A6
10	DndT	60110	2748	34W-17N	A6
Lake Mary Dr					
-	BGBK	60544	3339	28W-15S	B2
-	PNFD	60544	3339	28W-15S	B2
13100	PNFD	60585	3339	28W-15S	B3
N Lake Matthews Tr					
34800	GrtT	60041	2472	28W-35N	E6
Lakemont Ct					
300	BMDL	60108	2968	24W-4N	C3
Lake Park Av					
3800	PKCY	60085	2535	13W-33N	E3
4100	GRNE	60031	2535	14W-34N	D1
S Lake Park Av					
2900	CHCG	60616	3092	0E-2S	D3
3500	CHCG	60653	3092	1E-4S	E6
4200	CHCG	60653	3093	1E-4S	A7
4600	CHCG	60615	3093	1E-4S	A7
4700	CHCG	60615	3153	1E-5S	A1
5400	CHCG	60637	3153	1E-5S	B2
W Lake Park Av					
22500	RLKB	60073	2475	22W-34N	A7
Lake Park Ct					
2800	LYWD	60411	3510	3E-23S	A2
Lake Park Dr					
2700	LYWD	60411	3510	3E-23S	A2
W Lake Park Dr					
200	ADSN	60101	2970	19W-3N	D6
Lakepark Ln					
6100	WLBK	60527	3145	16W-6S	E5
Lake Placid Ln					
2900	NHBK	60062	2756	11W-17N	D5
Lake Plaza Rd					
1000	ELGN	60123	2800	34W-13N	E7
Lake Plumleigh Ct					
10	ALGN	60102	2748	33W-19N	B2
Lake Plumleigh Wy					
300	ALGN	60102	2748	33W-19N	B2
Lake Point Cir					
4600	LGGV	60047	2700	19W-23N	D1
Lakepoint Ct					
22400	CNHN	60410	3584	29W-27S	D5
Lake Point Dr					
10	ROSL	60172	2913	22W-7N	C4
Lakepoint Dr					
13200	PNFD	60585	3338	28W-15S	E2
23600	CNHN	60410	3584	29W-27S	D4
Lake Pointe Ct					
1600	JLET	60586	3496	31W-21S	A1
Lake Pointe Dr					
1600	JLET	60586	3495	31W-22S	E2
5700	JLET	60586	3496	31W-21S	A1
Lake Ridge Ct					
10	BRRG	60527	3208	15W-9S	B3
800	AURA	60502	3139	32W-6S	C5
Lakeridge Ct					
10	SEGN	60177	2907	37W-7N	C5
600	NPVL	60563	3140	29W-6S	D4
900	SRGV	60554	3136	41W-4S	A2
6700	LGGV	60047	2646	19W-25N	C5
W Lakeridge Ct					
20500	KLDR	60047	2699	20W-21N	E5
20500	KLDR	60047	2700	20W-21N	A5
20700	LGGV	60047	2699	20W-21N	E5
Lake Ridge Dr					
2100	GLHT	60139	2969	23W-4N	A3
8100	BRRG	60527	3208	15W-9S	A3
8700	DGvT	60516	3206	19W-10S	E5
8700	DRN	60516	3206	19W-10S	E5
8700	DRN	60561	3206	19W-10S	E5
Lakeridge Dr					
500	SEGN	60177	2907	37W-7N	C5
2400	JLET	60441	3417	27W-19S	D3
6700	ElaT	60047	2646	19W-25N	C5
6700	ElaT	60060	2646	19W-25N	C5
6700	LGGV	60047	2646	19W-25N	C5
6700	LGGV	60060	2646	19W-25N	C5
E Lake Ridge Dr					
100	GLHT	60139	2969	23W-4N	A3
S Lakeridge Dr					
14000	PnfT	60544	3339	27W-16S	C4
W Lakeridge Dr					
26700	LKBN	60010	2697	26W-23N	C2
Lake Ridge Rd					
14300	ODPK	60462	3345	13W-17S	B5
Lake Ridge Club Ct					
10	BRRG	60527	3208	15W-9S	A3
Lake Ridge Club Dr					
10	BRRG	60527	3208	15W-9S	A2
Lake Run Ct					
-	NARA	60506	3076	39W-3S	C7
Lake Run Ln					
-	NARA	60506	3076	39W-4S	D7
Lake St. Clair Dr					
21400	LktT	60403	3417	26W-19S	D3
N Lakes Center Blvd					
39500	AntT	60002	2416	25W-39N	A5
Lakeshore					
10	ROSL	60172	2913	22W-7N	C4
Lake Shore Blvd					
300	WCDA	60084	2644	25W-27N	B1
400	WCDA	60084	2588	25W-27N	B7
1000	EVTN	60202	2867	2W-10N	C4
1200	EVTN	60201	2867	2W-11N	C3
N Lake Shore Cir					
2100	ANHT	60004	2754	16W-16N	D7
Lake Shore Ct					
1400	BRTN	60010	2751	24W-20N	C1
1800	RMVL	60446	3339	27W-17S	C6
Lakeshore Ct					
2300	AURA	60504	3201	32W-9S	B3
W Lake Shore Ct					
25700	WcnT	60084	2644	24W-26N	B3
Lake Shore Dr					
-	BHPK	60099	2422	9W-38N	B7
-	BTVA	60510	3077	36W-2S	E4
-	BTVA	60539	3077	36W-2S	E4
-	CRTE	60417	3596	0E-28S	D7
-	CRTE	60417	3685	0E-29S	D1
-	GrtT	60041	2472	28W-35N	E6
-	MchT	60050	2470	33W-34N	E7
10	AlqT	60013	2641	31W-26N	D4
10	CPVL	60110	2748	33W-18N	A5
10	DndT	60110	2748	33W-18N	A5
10	NndT	60013	2641	31W-26N	D4
10	ODHL	60013	2641	31W-26N	D4
10	WLBK	60527	3145	16W-7S	E6
100	CLLK	60014	2639	36W-25N	D5
100	LNHT	60046	2418	20W-38N	B7
200	BtvT	60539	3077	36W-2S	E4
400	EDND	60118	2801	33W-16N	B1
600	WCDA	60084	2588	25W-28N	B6
1200	CLSM	60188	2967	27W-4N	C4
1200	LSLE	60532	3143	23W-6S	A5
1800	RMVL	60446	3339	27W-17S	C6
2400	WDSK	60098	2582	39W-28N	C5
2500	LYWD	60411	3509	3E-23S	E3
2700	JLET	60431	3417	28W-20S	A5
4500	MCLK	60050	2470	33W-34N	E7
4500	MCLK	60050	2527	33W-34N	E1
11500	ODPK	60467	3422	14W-21S	D7
19400	BlmT	60411	3509	3E-23S	E3
37000	GrtT	60041	2474	25W-37N	A3
37000	LkvT	60041	2474	25W-37N	A3
37000	LkvT	60046	2474	25W-37N	A2
Lakeshore Dr					
-	OSWG	60543	3263	36W-13S	D4
-	UYPK	60449	3594	6W-27S	B5
10	BDWD	60481	3942	30W-40S	B4
10	RedT	60408	3942	30W-40S	B3
10	RedT	60481	3942	30W-40S	B4
4900	RNPK	60471	3594	6W-27S	A4
10200	PTPR	53158	2363		D1
13100	PNFD	60585	3338	29W-15S	E3
13100	PnfT	60544	3338	29W-15S	E3
13100	PnfT	60585	3338	29W-15S	E3
E Lake Shore Dr					
-	CHCG	60616	3092	1E-3S	E4
10	RLKP	60073	2532	22W-34N	B1
100	CHCG	60611	3034	0E-1N	C2
100	TRLK	60010	2643	26W-25N	D5
400	CbaT	60010	2644	25W-25N	B4
400	WcnT	60010	2644	25W-26N	B3
400	WcnT	60084	2644	25W-26N	A3
2600	GwdT	60097	2469	37W-34N	C7
3300	MchT	60097	2469	36W-35N	D6

STREET Block	City	ZIP	Map#	CGS	Grid
E Lake Shore Dr					
5200	WRLK	60097	2469	36W-37N	D2
E Lakeshore Dr					
1700	TNLK	53181	2354		B3
3100	RcmT	60071	2354		B4
3100	TNLK	60071	2354		B4
E Lakeshore Dr CO-EM					
1700	TNLK	53181	2354		B3
3100	RcmT	60071	2354		B4
3100	TNLK	60071	2354		B4
N Lake Shore Dr					
-	CHCG	-	2922	0W-5N	A7
-	CHCG	-	2978	0W-3N	B5
-	CHCG	-	3034	0E-0N	D4
-	CHCG	60640	2921	1W-7N	E4
-	CHCG	60660	2921	1W-7N	E4
-	CokC	-	3034	0E-0N	D4
100	MDLN	60060	2646	18W-27N	D2
100	TRLK	60010	2643	26W-25N	C5
400	PLTN	60067	2752	22W-16N	B6
900	RDLK	60073	2532	23W-34N	A1
900	RLKB	60073	2532	23W-34N	A1
1000	RLKB	60073	2475	23W-35N	A7
1100	CHCG	60610	3034	0E-1N	C1
1600	WDSK	60098	2582	39W-29N	C5
3200	CHCG	60657	2978	0W-4N	A2
3500	CHCG	60613	2978	0W-4N	A2
33500	WrnT	60030	2534	18W-33N	A3
33600	WrnT	60030	2533	18W-33N	E2
34500	TDLK	60046	2533	18W-34N	D1
34500	WrnT	60046	2533	18W-34N	D1
34600	WrnT	60046	2476	18W-34N	D7
37500	LkvT	60046	2474	25W-37N	A2
38500	AntT	60081	2415	28W-38N	A6
38500	FXLK	60081	2415	28W-38N	A6
40200	AntT	60002	2416	25W-40N	B3
N Lake Shore Dr US-41					
-	CHCG	-	2921	1W-6N	E6
-	CHCG	-	2922	0W-5N	A7
-	CHCG	-	2978	0W-5N	A1
-	CHCG	-	3034	0E-0N	D4
-	CokC	-	3034	0E-0N	D4
N Lake Shore Dr W					
-	CHCG	60614	2978	0W-3N	A4
2800	CHCG	60657	2978	0W-3N	A4
S Lake Shore Dr					
-	CHCG	-	3092	0E-2S	D3
-	CHCG	-	3093	1E-4S	A6
-	CHCG	-	3153	2E-5S	B1
-	CokC	60637	3153	2E-6S	C3
10	CHCG	60601	3034	0E-0S	D5
10	CHCG	60603	3034	0E-0S	D5
100	CHCG	60604	3034	0E-0S	D5
200	MDLN	60060	2646	18W-27N	D2
300	CHCG	60605	3034	0E-0S	D5
1500	CHCG	60616	3034	0E-1S	D7
5300	CHCG	60637	3153	2E-6S	C3
6000	AlqT	60013	2641	31W-25N	D4
6000	NndT	60013	2641	31W-25N	D4
S Lakeshore Dr					
100	LKMR	60051	2529	29W-31N	D6
6700	WTMT	60559	3145	18W-7S	A7
S Lake Shore Dr US-41					
-	CHCG	-	3092	0E-2S	D3
-	CHCG	-	3093	1E-4S	A6
-	CHCG	-	3153	2E-5S	B1
-	CokC	60637	3153	2E-6S	C3
10	CHCG	60601	3034	0E-0S	D5
10	CHCG	60603	3034	0E-0S	D5
100	CHCG	60604	3034	0E-0S	D5
300	CHCG	60605	3034	0E-0S	D5
1400	CHCG	60616	3034	0E-1S	D7
5300	CHCG	60637	3153	2E-6S	C3
W Lake Shore Dr					
10	CbaT	60010	2644	25W-25N	A4
10	WcnT	60010	2644	25W-26N	A4
10	WcnT	60084	2644	25W-26N	A4
100	TRLK	60010	2643	26W-25N	C5
200	ODHL	60013	2641	31W-26N	D3
900	RLKB	60073	2474	24W-35N	D6
900	RLKH	60073	2474	24W-35N	D6
1600	WDSK	60098	2582	40W-29N	B4
3300	GwdT	60097	2469	37W-35N	C6
5000	WRLK	60097	2469	36W-36N	D3
5100	MchT	60097	2469	36W-37N	D2
5300	NndT	60013	2641	31W-26N	D3
22800	AntT	60002	2417	23W-40N	A2
23000	ANTH	60002	2416	23W-40N	E2
23000	AntT	60002	2416	23W-40N	E2
24000	AvnT	60073	2474	24W-35N	D6
24800	AvnT	60041	2474	24W-35N	B6
24800	GrtT	60041	2474	25W-35N	A5
25000	CbaT	60010	2698	25W-21N	A6
25000	DRPK	60010	2698	25W-21N	A6
27500	AntT	60081	2415	27W-38N	A7
34400	AvnT	60073	2532	22W-34N	C1
Lake Shore Dr N					
300	BRTN	60010	2751	24W-20N	C1
Lake Shore Dr S					
1300	BRTN	60010	2751	24W-20N	C1
Lakeshore Ln					
200	BMDL	60108	2969	22W-4N	B2
Lake Shore Rd					
35200	GrtT	60041	2472	28W-35N	E6
Lakeshore Wy					
2800	TNLK	53181	2354		A3
Lake Shore Dr Ct					
19600	LYWD	60411	3509	3E-23S	E3
Lakeside Av					
400	CLLK	60014	2639	36W-25N	D5
1600	NCHI	60064	2537	10W-32N	A6
3200	NfdT	60062	2756	11W-16N	D7
3200	NHBK	60062	2756	11W-16N	C7
14600	DLTN	60419	3350	0E-17S	D5
Lake Side Cir					
2700	JLET	60431	3417	28W-20S	A5
Lakeside Ct					
10	KdlT	60560	3332	44W-17S	D6
10	SBTN	60010	2803	27W-15N	B2
100	NBRN	60010	2644	24W-25N	B5
200	SCRL	60174	2965	33W-3N	A6
800	PltT	60124	2852	40W-10N	B5
1100	AURA	60504	3201	32W-9S	C3
1100	NPVL	60564	3203	28W-10S	A7
2800	EVTN	60201	2813	2W-13N	B6
3200	JNBG	60050	2470	34W-35N	D6
S Lakeside Ct					
10	PNFD	60544	3338	29W-18S	C7
500	RDLK	60073	2531	25W-32N	A4
24000	CteT	60417	3598	4E-29S	B7
24000	CteT	60417	3687	4E-29S	B1
W Lakeside Ct					
7200	FftT	60423	3504	9W-23S	E3
Lake Side Dr					
10	WldT	60564	3202	29W-10S	D6
Lakeside Dr					
10	SBTN	60010	2803	27W-15N	A2
100	SCRL	60174	2964	33W-3N	E6
100	SCRL	60174	2965	33W-3N	A6
200	VNHL	60061	2647	18W-24N	A7
300	BGBK	60440	3205	21W-11S	E7
300	BGBK	60440	3269	21W-11S	E1
300	ROSL	60172	2913	23W-7N	A4
400	MltT	60137	3083	22W-2S	B4
600	DGvT	60521	3145	16W-6S	E4
700	GRNE	60031	2477	16W-35N	D7
700	WHTN	60187	3024	25W-0S	B7
800	BRLT	60103	2911	27W-7N	C4
800	DGvT	60516	3206	19W-9S	D4
900	WCHI	60185	3022	30W-2N	C1
1000	BKBN	60015	2703	12W-23N	A3
1100	NlxT	60448	3501	16W-23S	E4
1100	NlxT	60451	3501	16W-23S	E4
1200	RMVL	60446	3269	23W-13S	A6
1900	MTGY	60538	3199	36W-10S	E5
1900	MTGY	60538	3200	36W-10S	A5
2200	AURA	60504	3201	32W-9S	B3
4000	HRPK	60133	2967	27W-5N	B3
5500	LslT	60532	3142	23W-6S	E4
7800	FftT	60423	3504	9W-23S	D3
7800	FftT	60477	3504	9W-23S	D3
7800	TYPK	60477	3504	9W-23S	D3
10900	ODPK	60467	3423	13W-18S	A1
15500	ODPK	60467	3345	13W-18S	A7
16200	LKPT	60441	3420	20W-19S	B3
E Lakeside Dr					
200	VNHL	60061	2647	17W-24N	A6
N Lakeside Dr					
-	LktT	60446	3340	26W-16S	A5
-	RMVL	60446	3340	26W-16S	A5
10	LktT	60544	3340	26W-16S	A5
700	VNHL	60061	2647	17W-24N	A6
1000	PltT	60067	2752	21W-17N	C5
23700	ElaT	60047	2699	21W-24N	D1
24100	ElaT	60047	2645	21W-24N	D7
24100	HNWD	60047	2645	21W-24N	D7
34000	AvnT	60030	2532	21W-34N	D1
34000	GYLK	60030	2532	21W-34N	D1
34600	GrtT	60041	2473	26W-34N	D7
43100	AntT	60002	2357	25W-43N	B4
S Lakeside Dr					
1400	WKGN	60085	2536	12W-31N	A6
2100	LbvT	60044	2536	13W-31N	A7
2100	ShdT	60044	2536	13W-31N	A7
3600	WKGN	60085	2535	13W-32N	E5
3700	WrnT	60085	2535	13W-32N	E5
W Lakeside Dr					
600	PltT	60067	2752	21W-17N	C5
700	PLTN	60067	2752	21W-17N	C6
7300	FftT	60423	3504	9W-23S	D3
7700	FftT	60477	3504	9W-23S	D3
Lakeside Ln					
10	CbaT	60010	2644	24W-25N	B5
10	FXLK	60020	2473	27W-36N	B3
10	NBRN	60010	2644	24W-25N	B5
1100	CLSM	60188	2967	27W-4N	C4
Lakeside Pl					
10	GLNC	60022	2758	6W-20N	C2
10	HDPK	60035	2758	6W-20N	C2
5900	TYPK	60477	3425	7W-20S	C3
N Lakeside Pl					
38000	AntT	60002	2415	26W-38N	D7
38000	AntT	60002	2473	26W-38N	D1
W Lakeside Pl					
700	CHCG	60640	2921	1W-5N	E7
N Lakeside Plz					
1900	HFET	60169	2804	24W-12N	D7
1900	HFET	60169	2858	24W-12N	D1
W Lakeside Plz					
800	HFET	60169	2804	24W-12N	D7
Lakeside Rd					
10	FXLK	60020	2473	27W-37N	B2
Lakeside Ter					
300	GLNC	60022	2758	5W-17N	E5
300	GLNC	60022	2759	5W-17N	A5
S Lakeside Ter					
34100	WslT	60481	3943	27W-42S	E6
S Lakeside Tr					
24000	CteT	60417	3598	4E-29S	B7
24000	CteT	60417	3687	4E-29S	B1
Lakeside Cir Dr					
600	WLNG	60090	2754	16W-17N	D6
Lakeside Manor Rd					
400	HDPK	60035	2758	6W-20N	C1
Lakestone Ln					
800	AURA	60504	3202	30W-9S	A3
Lake Superior Dr					
900	MTSN	60443	3506	6W-25S	A7
Lake Trail Dr					
500	PlsT	60464	3273	12W-14S	B7
4600	LSLE	60532	3142	24W-5S	C2
4800	LSLE	60563	3142	24W-5S	C2
Lake Valley Dr					
4600	LSLE	60532	3142	24W-4S	C2
4700	LslT	60532	3142	25W-5S	C2
4700	LslT	60563	3142	25W-5S	C2
Lake View					
-	LMNT	60439	3272	15W-13S	B5
Lakeview					
-	NLNX	60442	3589	17W-27S	D4
Lake View Av					
400	HDPK	60035	2704	9W-23N	D2
400	HDPK	60037	2704	8W-23N	D2
400	HDPK	60040	2704	9W-23N	D2
400	HIWD	60037	2704	8W-23N	D2
400	HIWD	60040	2704	8W-23N	D2
Lakeview Av					
10	FXLK	60020	2473	27W-37N	B2
100	WCDA	60084	2643	26W-26N	D2
100	WCDA	60084	2644	25W-27N	A2
100	WcnT	60084	2644	25W-27N	A2
100	WKGN	60085	2537		B3
1100	CLLK	60014	2639	37W-24N	B6
1100	GfnT	60014	2639	37W-24N	B6
1200	JLET	60436	3498	25W-24S	B7
1200	RKDL	60436	3498	25W-24S	B7
N Lakeview Av					
2400	CHCG	60614	2978	0W-3N	A5
2700	CHCG	60657	2978	0W-3N	A4
38700	AntT	60002	2415	26W-38N	E6
38700	LkvT	60002	2415	25W-38N	E6
39000	AntT	60002	2416	25W-40N	A3
41300	BtnT	60099	2422	9W-41N	C1
41300	ZION	60099	2422	9W-41N	C1
W Lakeview Av					
19000	FmtT	60060	2646	19W-26N	C3
20500	LkvT	60046	2476	20W-36N	A4
22700	RLKB	60073	2475	22W-34N	A7
22900	AntT	60002	2417	23W-40N	A2
25500	WcnT	60084	2644	25W-27N	A2
25600	WCDA	60084	2644	25W-27N	A2
W Lakeview Av					
26000	GrtT	60041	2473	26W-35N	E6
Lakeview Cir					
300	BGBK	60440	3205	23W-11S	B7
400	EGVV	60007	2860	19W-9N	C7
27800	WcnT	60051	2587	28W-28N	A7
27800	WcnT	60084	2587	28W-28N	A7
E Lakeview Cir					
400	SchT	60175	2963	38W-5N	B2
N Lakeview Cir					
400	SchT	60175	2963	38W-5N	A2
27700	WcnT	60084	2587	28W-27N	A7
27800	WcnT	60051	2587	28W-27N	A7
28500	WcnT	60084	2642	28W-26N	E2
W Lakeview Cir					
300	SchT	60175	2963	38W-5N	A2
Lakeview Cir E					
18400	TYPK	60477	3425	8W-22S	B7
Lakeview Cir W					
18400	TYPK	60477	3425	8W-22S	B7
Lake View Ct					
300	DRFD	60015	2756	11W-20N	E1
500	BRLT	60103	2910	29W-7N	E4
2400	AURA	60506	3198	39W-7S	E1
34700	GrtT	60051	2472	28W-34N	E7
34800	GrtT	60041	2472	28W-34N	E7
Lakeview Ct					
10	WLBK	60527	3145	16W-7S	E6
10	WynT	60185	2967	28W-3N	B7
100	BMDL	60108	2969	23W-4N	B2
100	WNVL	60555	3080	29W-3S	C5
200	CRTE	60417	3596	0W-28S	C6
300	BFGV	60089	2754	17W-20N	B1
400	MPPT	60056	2808	14W-13N	C6
400	OSWG	60543	3263	37W-13S	C5
500	ROSL	60172	2913	22W-7N	B4
600	WynT	60185	2966	30W-3N	B5
2000	NPVL	60565	3204	25W-9S	B4
3900	LGGV	60047	2699	20W-22N	E4
6700	WDRG	60517	3143	22W-7S	B7
12300	OrlT	60467	3344	14W-16S	C3
21200	OrlT	60423	3504	11W-25S	A7
21200	FKFT	60423	3592	11W-25S	A1
N Lakeview Ct					
1200	PLTN	60067	2752	22W-17N	C5
33300	WrnT	60030	2533	18W-33N	E3
40400	AntT	60002	2417	22W-40N	B3
W Lake View Ct					
12300	HMGN	60491	3344	15W-16S	B2
W Lakeview Ct					
1200	RMVL	60446	3268	25W-14S	B6
7900	PSHT	60463	3346	9W-15S	C1
10000	PlsT	60464	3345	12W-15S	C1
21200	FmtT	60060	2645	21W-26N	D3
Lake View Dr					
100	AURA	60506	3136	39W-7S	E7
100	AURA	60506	3198	39W-7S	E1
Lakeview Dr					
-	ANHT	60090	2754	16W-17N	D6
-	JLET	60403	3417	27W-19S	D4
-	JLET	60441	3417	27W-19S	D4
-	LktT	60403	3417	27W-19S	D4
-	RMVL	60490	3268	25W-14S	B6
-	SRWD	60404	3495	31W-23S	E5
-	TroT	60404	3495	31W-23S	E5
10	BtlT	60560	3261	41W-13S	E5
10	MDLN	60060	2646	19W-27N	C2
10	WNVL	60555	3080	30W-3S	C5
100	BMDL	60108	2969	22W-5N	C1
100	WldT	60564	3203	28W-10S	A6
200	BFGV	60089	2754	17W-20N	C1
200	GNVA	60134	3019	37W-1N	C3
300	LKMR	60051	2529	29W-32N	C5
500	MltT	60187	3081	26W-2S	D4
500	OSWG	60543	3263	37W-13S	C5
500	WHTN	60187	3081	26W-2S	D4
600	MltT	60555	3081	26W-2S	D4
600	WHTN	60555	3081	26W-2S	D4
600	WLNG	60090	2754	16W-17N	C5
1200	BGBK	60446	3268	25W-14S	A7
1200	BGBK	60490	3268	25W-14S	A7
1200	DPgT	60446	3268	25W-14S	A7
1200	DPgT	60490	3268	25W-14S	A7
1200	DPgT	60544	3268	25W-14S	A7
1200	RMVL	60446	3268	25W-14S	A7
1400	DRN	60561	3207	18W-9S	A3
1700	ANHT	60004	2754	16W-17N	C5
1700	DGvT	60516	3206	18W-9S	E3
1700	DRN	60516	3206	18W-9S	E3
1700	DRN	60561	3206	18W-9S	E3
2400	MchT	60097	2526	36W-34N	C1
3500	ALGN	60102	2693	37W-20N	B7
3500	GwdT	60097	2469	37W-35N	C6
3500	HLCT	60429	3426	4W-22S	E7
3500	HLCT	60429	3506	4W-22S	E1
3500	HLCT	60430	3426	4W-22S	E7
3500	HMWD	60430	3426	4W-22S	E7
3500	WRLK	60097	2469	37W-35N	C6
3600	ISLK	60042	2586	29W-28N	D6
4000	BmnT	60430	3426	4W-21S	D6
4000	CCHL	60430	3426	4W-21S	D6
4000	CCHL	60478	3426	5W-21S	C6
7900	DRGV	60516	3206	18W-9S	E3
7900	DRGV	60561	3206	18W-9S	E3
9200	ODPK	60462	3345	11W-17S	E5
14700	ODPK	60462	3346	11W-17S	A5
15400	MHTN	60442	3677	19W-30S	E3
15400	MHTN	60442	3678	19W-30S	A3
22500	RLKB	60073	2475	22W-34N	B7
23200	LKBN	60010	2697	27W-23N	B2
23900	CNHN	60410	3672	32W-29S	E1
23900	CNHN	60447	3672	32W-29S	E1
23900	CnhT	60447	3672	32W-29S	D1
25500	LkvT	60046	2474	25W-37N	A3
N Lakeview Dr					
700	RDLK	60073	2532	23W-34N	A1
1200	PLTN	60067	2752	22W-17N	B5
1200	PltT	60067	2752	22W-17N	C5
27100	LKBN	60084	2643	27W-26N	C3
42100	AntT	60002	2358	22W-42N	B6
S Lakeview Dr					
16300	HmrT	60441	3420	20W-19S	B3
16300	LKPT	60441	3420	20W-19S	B3
26700	LKBN	60084	2643	27W-26N	C3
26700	WcnT	60084	2643	27W-26N	C3
W Lake View Dr					
12000	HMGN	60491	3344	15W-16S	B2
12000	OrlT	60467	3344	15W-16S	B2
12400	HMGN	60491	3344	15W-16S	B2
W Lakeview Dr					
24700	LkvT	60046	2416	24W-39N	B5
Lakeview Ln					
-	BRRG	60527	3208	16W-9S	A4
-	DGvT	60527	3208	16W-9S	A4
10	BNHL	60010	2750	26W-17N	D5
100	BMDL	60108	2969	23W-4N	B3
Lakeview Ln					
500	HFET	60169	2858	24W-11N	D4
6500	MONE	60449	3682	8W-31S	B6
21100	FKFT	60423	3504	11W-25S	A7
Lakeview Pkwy					
10	CbaT	60010	2644	25W-25N	B4
10	VNHL	60061	2647	16W-25N	D6
W Lakeview Pkwy					
21100	FmtT	60060	2645	21W-27N	E1
21200	MDLN	60060	2645	21W-27N	E1
Lakeview Pl					
10	LKZH	60047	2698	23W-23N	E3
200	LKBN	60010	2697	26W-23N	E1
200	NBRN	60010	2697	26W-23N	E1
W Lake View Pl					
12300	HMGN	60491	3344	15W-16S	B2
Lakeview Pt					
700	SMBG	60194	2859	22W-10N	C4
Lake View Rd					
10	HNWD	60047	2700	20W-23N	B1
Lakeview Rd					
-	BHPK	60099	2422	9W-38N	C7
1000	ELGN	60123	2800	33W-13N	E7
1000	ELGN	60123	2854	34W-12N	D1
6000	AlqT	60013	2641	31W-26N	D4
6000	NndT	60013	2641	31W-26N	D3
6000	ODHL	60013	2641	31W-26N	D3
10500	RcmT	60071	2354	32W-42N	B5
10500	SPGV	60081	2354	32W-42N	B6
11500	TNLK	53181	2354	32W-42N	B5
11500	TNLK	60071	2354	32W-42N	B5
Lakeview Rd CO-V37					
10500	RcmT	60071	2354	32W-42N	B5
10500	SPGV	60081	2354	32W-42N	B6
11500	TNLK	53181	2354	32W-42N	B5
11500	TNLK	60071	2354	32W-42N	B5
Lakeview St					
-	MchT	60050	2471	30W-36N	E4
1300	JNBG	60050	2472	30W-36N	A4
1600	MchT	60050	2472	30W-36N	A4
1800	JNBG	60050	2471	30W-36N	E4
19800	AvnT	60030	2476	19W-35N	B7
Lakeview Ter					
10	HDPK	60035	2758	6W-20N	C1
500	GNEN	60137	3025	22W-0S	C6
1700	WKGN	60048	2535	15W-32N	A6
7800	FftT	60423	3504	9W-23S	D3
7800	FftT	60477	3504	9W-23S	D3
7800	TYPK	60477	3504	9W-23S	D3
N Lakeview Ter					
41400	AntT	60002	2416	23W-41N	E1
41600	ANTH	60002	2357	23W-41N	E7
41600	AntT	60002	2357	23W-41N	E7
W Lakeview Ter					
7600	FftT	60423	3504	9W-23S	D3
7700	FftT	60477	3504	9W-23S	D3
18300	WrnT	60031	2477	18W-36N	A4
Lakeview Tr					
12000	OrlT	60467	3344	15W-18S	C7
12300	HMGN	60491	3344	15W-18S	B7
12300	HMGN	60491	3422	15W-18S	C1
Lakeview Wy					
19700	MKNA	60448	3503	12W-23S	D4
Lakeview Estates Blvd					
22800	FKFT	60423	3592	10W-27S	C5
23000	GGnT	60423	3592	10W-27S	C5
Lake Villa Av					
16100	TYPK	60477	3424	9W-19S	E2
Lakeville Rd					
4600	LinT	53147	2349		A2
4600	LinT	53184	2349		A2
Lake Vista					
-	LKVL	60046	2475	22W-37N	C1
W Lake Vista Av					
23600	AntT	60002	2416	23W-41N	D1
Lake Vista Ln					
3300	GwdT	60097	2469	37W-35N	B6
3500	WRLK	60097	2469	37W-35N	B6
N Lake Vista Ter					
37600	GrtT	60081	2472	28W-37N	E1
Lakeway Dr					
6400	MONE	60449	3682	8W-31S	C5
Lake Wood					
16600	FmtT	60084	2644	24W-27N	C2
Lakewood Av					
10	CLLK	60014	2639	37W-25N	B4
10	FXLK	60020	2473	27W-37N	B2
300	WKGN	60085	2536	12W-33N	B1
400	WkgT	60085	2536	12W-33N	B1
1700	MHRY	60050	2527	34W-33N	D2
19800	LYWD	60411	3509	3E-23S	E4
N Lakewood Av					
600	LKVL	60046	2416	23W-38N	E6
600	LkvT	60046	2416	23W-38N	E6
2600	CHCG	60614	2977	1W-3N	D5
2700	CHCG	60657	2977	1W-3N	D5
3900	CHCG	60613	2977	1W-4N	D2
5200	CHCG	60640	2921	1W-6N	D5
6100	CHCG	60660	2921	1W-7N	D3
6600	CHCG	60626	2921	1W-8N	D1
34700	WKGN	60085	2479	12W-33N	B7
34700	WkgT	60085	2479	12W-33N	B7
S Lakewood Av					
200	NHLK	60164	3028	13W-1N	D2
11900	PlsT	60464	3273	11W-14S	E5
11900	PSPK	60464	3273	11W-14S	E5
Lakewood Blvd					
-	HFET	60010	2803	25W-13N	E6
-	SBTN	60010	2803	25W-13N	E6
200	PKFT	60466	3595	3W-26S	A3
500	PKFT	60466	3594	4W-26S	E3
1700	HFET	60192	2804	25W-13N	A6
2000	HFET	60192	2803	25W-13N	E6
Lakewood Cir					
10	SCRL	60174	2964	36W-4N	A5
100	BRRG	60527	3208	15W-9S	B4
1000	CLSM	60188	2967	27W-4N	C3
1000	NPVL	60540	3202	29W-8S	D1
Lakewood Ct					
10	BGBK	60440	3268	25W-11S	B1
10	PKFT	60466	3595	4W-27S	A3
100	BMDL	60108	2968	23W-5N	E1
200	AURA	60506	3200	34W-8S	C3
200	WYNE	60184	2966	30W-4N	B4
600	OKBK	60523	3086	15W-1S	B1
900	BRTN	60010	2751	24W-18N	B2
3300	GNVW	60025	2810	10W-13N	A5
N Lakewood Ct					
10	SEGN	60177	2908	35W-7N	B4
S Lakewood Ct					
10	SEGN	60177	2908	35W-7N	A5
Lakewood Dr					
-	HmrT	60441	3420	20W-20S	B5
-	LKPT	60441	3420	20W-20S	B5
10	ANTH	53179	2357	23W-43N	E4
10	ANTH	60002	2357	23W-43N	E4
Lakewood Dr					
10	BbyT	60554	3075	43W-3S	A7
10	BKBN	60015	2703	12W-23N	B2
10	DGvT	60527	3207	16W-10S	D4
10	GLNC	60022	2758	6W-18N	E4
10	LslT	60540	3142	24W-6S	C4
10	ODHL	60013	2641	31W-26N	E3
10	SlmT	53179	2357	23W-43N	E4
10	WynT	60185	2966	29W-3N	D7
300	SgrT	60554	3075	43W-4S	B7
800	LKFT	60045	2649	12W-24N	A6
900	BRLT	60103	2910	29W-6N	D6
900	BRTN	60010	2751	24W-18N	B2
1400	JLET	60431	3497	28W-22S	B1
1800	WslT	60481	3943	27W-40S	D4
2300	DYR	46311	3598		C3
3300	PRGV	60012	2584	33W-28N	E5
6200	LSLE	60532	3142	24W-6S	D5
6400	AlqT	60013	2641	32W-25N	D5
16700	BmnT	60477	3425	7W-20S	D3
16700	TYPK	60477	3425	7W-20S	D3
Lake Wood Ln					
4100	ZION	60099	2421	12W-41N	C2
Lakewood Ln					
10	MltT	60187	3082	25W-2S	A3
14300	OrlT	60467	3344	14W-17S	D5
N Lakewood Ln					
22700	ElaT	60047	2699	22W-23N	A1
22700	LKZH	60047	2699	22W-23N	A1
23000	ElaT	60047	2698	23W-23N	E1
23000	LKZH	60047	2698	23W-23N	E1
S Lakewood Ln					
23200	ElaT	60047	2698	23W-23N	E1
23200	ElaT	60047	2699	23W-23N	A1
Lakewood Pkwy					
1500	RLKB	60073	2475	23W-35N	A6
Lakewood Pl					
10	HDPK	60035	2758	6W-20N	C1
700	AURA	60506	3137	36W-7S	D7
Lakewood Plz					
10	CPVL	60110	2748	33W-17N	C7
Lakewood Pth					
16300	HMGN	60491	3421	17W-19S	D2
Lakewood Rd					
-	BHPK	60099	2422	9W-38N	C7
-	MchT	60050	2528	33W-34N	A1
1000	ELGN	60123	2801	33W-13N	A7
1000	ELGN	60123	2855	33W-13N	A1
2400	LIHL	60156	2692	38W-22N	E3
4100	MHRY	60050	2527	33W-34N	E2
4100	MHRY	60050	2528	33W-34N	A1
8000	GfnT	60014	2692	38W-24N	E1
8000	LKWD	60014	2692	38W-23N	E1
8800	GfnT	60156	2692	38W-23N	E2
9800	GfnT	60014	2638	39W-24N	D7
9800	LKWD	60014	2638	39W-24N	D7
10100	GfnT	60142	2638	39W-24N	D7
10300	GfnT	60102	2692	38W-21N	E6
Lakewood Rd CO-V23					
-	GfnT	60014	2692	38W-23N	E2
-	LKWD	60014	2692	38W-23N	E2
2400	LIHL	60156	2692	38W-22N	E3
9800	GfnT	60156	2692	38W-22N	E4
10300	GfnT	60102	2692	38W-21N	E6
N Lakewood Ter					
300	RDLK	60073	2531	23W-33N	E2
Lakewood Creek Dr					
2700	MTGY	60506	3198	40W-10S	C5
2700	MTGY	60538	3198	40W-10S	C6
Lakewood Falls Dr					
-	LktT	60544	3339	26W-16S	E4
-	LktT	60544	3340	26W-16S	A4
-	PnfT	60544	3339	27W-16S	D4
-	RMVL	60441	3340	25W-16S	A4
-	RMVL	60544	3340	25W-16S	A4
Lakewood Farms Dr					
500	BGBK	60490	3268	26W-13S	A4
Lakewood Prairie Blvd					
-	JLET	60447	3495	33W-22S	A2
Lakewoods Ln					
-	SRWD	60404	3496	30W-25S	B7
-	SRWD	60404	3584	30W-25S	B1
S Lakewoods Ln					
21300	SRWD	60404	3584	30W-25S	B2
Lakewood Spring Dr					
-	LtRT	60545	3260	45W-13S	C6
-	PLNO	60545	3260	45W-13S	C6
Lake Zurich Dr					
10	LKZH	60047	2698	24W-22N	C3
Lake Zurich Rd					
400	BRTN	60010	2751	25W-20N	A1
600	BRTN	60010	2698	25W-20N	A7
900	CbaT	60010	2698	25W-20N	A7
900	DRPK	60010	2698	25W-20N	A7
N Lake Zurich Rd					
21000	BRTN	60010	2698	25W-21N	A7
21000	CbaT	60010	2698	25W-21N	A6
21000	DRPK	60010	2698	25W-21N	A6
Lakin Av					
-	ELBN	60119	3017	42W-0N	B5
Lalique Ct					
4600	JLET	60431	3496	29W-22S	E2
La Londe Av					
10	AddT	60148	3026	19W-2N	D1
10	LMBD	60148	3026	19W-2N	D1
N La Londe Av					
200	LMBD	60148	3026	19W-1N	D3
S La Londe Av					
10	ADSN	60101	2970	19W-3N	C6
500	LMBD	60148	3026	19W-0S	C6
N Lama Ln					
1300	MPPT	60056	2808	13W-14N	E3
Lamb Ct					
1300	DRGV	60516	3144	20W-7S	B7
Lamb Dr					
4800	OKLN	60453	3276	6W-11S	A1
4900	OKLN	60453	3275	6W-11S	E1
Lamb Ln					
1100	GRNE	60031	2477	17W-35N	C6
Lamb Rd					
300	GwdT	60098	2524	42W-33N	B2
300	HtdT	60098	2524	42W-33N	B2
300	WDSK	60098	2524	42W-33N	B2
Lambert Av					
200	SchT	60174	2964	35W-5N	B3
200	SCRL	60174	2964	35W-5N	B3
E Lambert Av					
1300	JLET	60432	3499	22W-23S	D3
1300	JltT	60432	3499	22W-23S	D3
Lambert Dr					
10	SMBG	60193	2859	23W-10N	B5
10	SMBG	60194	2859	23W-10N	B6
2400	AURA	60503	3201	33W-11S	B7
2400	AURA	60503	3265	33W-11S	B1
2400	OswT	60503	3201	33W-11S	B7

STREET Block	City	ZIP	Map#	CGS	Grid
N Lambert Dr					
40100	AntT	60002	2416	23W-40N	E3
40100	LKVL	60002	2416	23W-40N	E3
Lambert Ln					
-	ELGN	60120	2856	31W-9N	A7
500	BRLT	60103	2909	31W-9N	E1
500	BRLT	60120	2909	31W-9N	E1
600	BRLT	60103	2856	31W-9N	A7
700	ELGN	60103	2856	31W-9N	A7
Lambert Rd					
-	MltT	60187	3083	23W-2S	A4
-	WHTN	60187	3083	23W-2S	A4
10	GNEN	60137	3083	23W-1S	A2
300	MltT	60137	3083	23W-2S	A4
N Lambert Rd					
10	GNEN	60137	3025	23W-0S	A7
S Lambert Rd					
10	GNEN	60137	3083	23W-1S	A1
Lambert Tree Av					
300	HDPK	60035	2758	7W-20N	B1
Lambeth Ct					
10	OKBK	60523	3085	17W-2S	C4
Lambeth Ln					
600	JLET	60451	3500	19W-23S	D3
600	NLNX	60451	3500	19W-23S	D3
Lambrecht Rd					
900	FKFT	60423	3591	11W-27S	E4
W Lambs Ln					
14000	GNOK	60048	2592	14W-28N	D6
14000	LbvT	60045	2592	14W-28N	D6
14000	LbvT	60048	2592	14W-28N	D6
Lambs Farm					
-	GNOK	60048	2592	14W-28N	D6
Lamon Av					
600	WLMT	60091	2811	6W-13N	E6
7800	BRBK	60459	3212	6W-9S	A3
8600	OKLN	60453	3212	6W-9S	A4
8600	OKLN	60459	3212	6W-9S	A4
9500	SKOK	60077	2865	6W-11N	E2
10000	SKOK	60077	2811	6W-12N	E7
10000	WLMT	60077	2811	6W-12N	E7
10300	OKLN	60453	3276	6W-12S	A2
13500	CTWD	60445	3348	6W-16S	A3
13800	BmnT	60445	3348	6W-16S	A3
14300	MDLN	60445	3348	6W-17S	A5
14900	OKFT	60452	3348	6W-17S	A6
15700	OKFT	60452	3426	6W-18S	A1
N Lamon Av					
400	CHCG	60644	3031	6W-0N	E3
700	CHCG	60651	3031	6W-0N	E3
1600	CHCG	60639	3031	6W-1N	E1
2000	CHCG	60639	2975	6W-2N	E6
2700	CHCG	60641	2975	6W-3N	E5
4300	CHCG	60630	2975	6W-5N	E1
5400	CHCG	60630	2919	6W-6N	E5
5400	CHCG	60646	2919	6W-6N	E5
6800	LNWD	60077	2919	6W-8N	E1
6800	LNWD	60712	2919	6W-8N	E1
6800	SKOK	60077	2919	6W-8N	E1
7200	LNWD	60077	2865	6W-9N	E7
7200	LNWD	60712	2865	6W-9N	E7
7200	SKOK	60077	2865	6W-9N	E7
7200	SKOK	60712	2865	6W-9N	E7
S Lamon Av					
-	CHCG	60644	3031	6W-0S	E6
4300	CHCG	60638	3089	6W-4S	E7
4300	CHCG	60638	3090	6W-4S	A7
4600	CHCG	60638	3149	6W-5S	E1
6300	CHCG	60638	3150	6W-7S	A5
6400	BDPK	60638	3150	6W-7S	A5
11200	ALSP	60803	3276	6W-13S	A4
Lamon Ct					
14400	MDLN	60445	3348	6W-17S	A4
Lamond Av					
2600	LslT	60517	3143	21W-7S	D6
2600	WDRG	60517	3143	21W-7S	D6
Lamont Ct					
100	ElgT	60124	2853	37W-11N	C5
800	NPVL	60540	3202	29W-7S	D1
Lamont Pkwy					
100	BRLT	60103	2910	29W-7N	E4
W Lamont Rd					
500	EMHT	60126	2971	17W-3N	C5
Lamont Ter					
400	BFGV	60089	2701	17W-21N	C6
Lamorak Ct					
300	SMBG	60193	2859	22W-9N	C6
Lamorak Dr					
600	SMBG	60193	2859	22W-10N	C6
Lamphere Rd					
-	NndT	60051	2642	29W-27N	D1
28700	WcnT	60042	2642	29W-27N	D1
28900	NndT	60042	2642	28W-27N	D1
Lamplighter Ln					
-	BtlT	53104	2358		E4
Lampton Ln					
1000	DRFD	60015	2704	10W-21N	B6
Lampwick Ct					
400	NPVL	60563	3141	26W-4S	E2
S Lams Ct					
700	MPPT	60056	2807	16W-12N	E7
Lamson Dr					
800	WNKA	60093	2759	5W-16N	A7
Lanark Ln					
1000	IVNS	60067	2751	24W-17N	D5
W Lanark Ln					
800	PLTN	60067	2805	22W-15N	C2
Lanark St					
1400	FSMR	60422	3506	4W-23S	D3
Lancashire Ct					
1800	SMBG	60194	2858	25W-11N	A3
12200	MKNA	60448	3502	15W-23S	C4
Lancaster Av					
200	ANHT	60004	2807	16W-15N	D2
200	PTHT	60004	2807	16W-15N	D2
200	PTHT	60070	2807	16W-15N	D2
900	DRGV	60516	3144	19W-7S	D6
1000	EGVV	60007	2914	19W-8N	D2
1300	SCRL	60174	2964	34W-2N	D7
N Lancaster Av					
800	AURA	60506	3137	36W-6S	E5
S Lancaster Av					
10	AURA	60506	3137	36W-7S	E7
100	MPPT	60056	2807	16W-12N	D7
200	MPPT	60056	2861	16W-12N	D1
Lancaster Cir					
10	GRNE	60031	2535	14W-34N	B1
2100	NPVL	60565	3203	26W-9S	E4
2100	NPVL	60565	3204	25W-9S	A3
N Lancaster Cir					
-	ElgT	60177	2908	35W-8N	B4
900	SEGN	60177	2908	35W-8N	B4
S Lancaster Cir					
-	SchT	60175	2908	35W-7N	B4
-	SchT	60177	2908	35W-7N	B4
-	SEGN	60175	2908	35W-7N	B4
S Lancaster Cir					
900	SEGN	60177	2908	35W-7N	B5
Lancaster Ct					
10	ALGN	60102	2747	35W-19N	B4
10	BRRG	60527	3208	15W-9S	B3
100	LKBF	60044	2593	11W-29N	E4
100	VNHL	60061	2647	17W-26N	C3
400	IVNS	60010	2751	24W-17N	C5
700	CLLK	60014	2639	35W-24N	E6
1000	HFET	60169	2804	24W-12N	C7
1100	HFET	60169	2858	25W-12N	C1
1400	GYLK	60030	2475	21W-34N	D7
1900	NPVL	60565	3203	26W-9S	E4
23800	DRPK	60010	2698	23W-21N	D5
W Lancaster Ct					
12000	HMGN	60491	3344	15W-16S	C4
Lancaster Dr					
-	PnfT	60544	3339	27W-17S	B5
-	RMVL	60446	3339	27W-17S	B5
-	RMVL	60544	3339	27W-17S	B5
-	RtdT	60140	2798	41W-15N	A4
200	CLLK	60014	2639	35W-24N	E7
200	CLLK	60014	2640	35W-24N	A7
600	PGGV	60140	2797	41W-15N	E4
600	PGGV	60140	2798	41W-15N	A4
600	WNFD	60190	3023	27W-0N	C4
2700	MKHM	60428	3427	3W-19S	B2
2700	NLNX	60433	3500	20W-24S	D5
2700	NlxT	60433	3500	20W-24S	C5
5600	OKFT	60452	3347	7W-18S	D7
10000	MKNA	60448	3503	12W-23S	C3
N Lancaster Dr					
100	BGBK	60440	3268	23W-11S	E1
S Lancaster Dr					
100	BGBK	60440	3268	23W-12S	E2
100	BGBK	60440	3269	23W-12S	A2
Lancaster Ln					
10	DSPN	60018	2862	15W-10N	B6
10	LNSH	60069	2702	14W-22N	D4
700	GNVA	60134	3020	34W-1N	E2
900	DYR	46311	3510		E5
900	LKZH	60047	2698	24W-24N	D1
1300	ALGN	60102	2747	35W-19N	B3
1300	WDRG	60517	3206	20W-10S	B6
1900	WHTN	60187	3082	23W-2S	E4
15400	ODPK	60462	3346	11W-18S	A7
N Lancaster Ln					
2300	RLKB	60073	2475	22W-36N	C4
2600	LkvT	60046	2475	22W-36N	C4
S Lancaster Ln					
1400	WKGN	60048	2535	14W-32N	C5
Lancaster Pl					
900	DRGV	60516	3144	19W-7S	D6
Lancaster Rd					
100	SchT	60175	2907	36W-7N	E6
N Lancaster Rd					
-	ELGN	60123	2907	36W-8N	E4
-	SEGN	60123	2907	36W-8N	E4
-	SEGN	60123	2908	36W-8N	A4
-	SEGN	60177	2907	36W-8N	E4
-	SEGN	60177	2908	36W-8N	A4
Lancaster St					
10400	HTLY	60142	2745	39W-20N	C1
10500	HTLY	60142	2692	39W-20N	C7
10900	WSTR	60154	3086	13W-2S	E3
N Lancaster St					
10	MPPT	60056	2807	16W-13N	D7
Lancaster Wy					
1900	NHBK	60062	2757	9W-16N	B7
Lancastor Ct					
10	SMWD	60107	2856	29W-9N	E7
Lance Av					
-	ELBN	60119	3017	42W-0N	C5
Lance Ct					
1300	CLSM	60188	2967	28W-3N	A5
Lance Dr					
200	DSPN	60016	2862	15W-11N	A4
Lance Ln					
1200	CLSM	60188	2967	28W-3N	B5
Lancelot Av					
1500	HDPK	60035	2704	10W-22N	B5
Lancelot Ct					
300	BGBK	60440	3205	22W-11S	C7
Lancelot Ln					
10	HNWD	60047	2645	21W-24N	C6
S Lancelot Ln					
200	ANHT	60004	2806	19W-15N	D2
200	PLTN	60074	2806	19W-15N	D2
W Lancelot Ln					
24400	TroT	60404	3584	30W-27S	B4
Lancelot Wy					
300	BGBK	60440	3205	22W-11S	C7
300	BGBK	60440	3269	22W-11S	C1
Lancer Ct					
10	SEGN	60177	2908	35W-7N	B4
800	SRWD	60404	3496	30W-23S	C4
Lancer Ln					
800	AvnT	60030	2533	19W-33N	D3
800	GYLK	60030	2533	19W-34N	C2
Lancer Ln N					
-	GYLK	60030	2533	19W-34N	C1
N Lancers Dr					
400	ADSN	60101	2970	20W-4N	A4
N Landau Av					
400	JLET	60432	3499	23W-23S	B3
W Landau Ct					
-	KLDR	60047	2699	21W-22N	E5
Landau Ln					
200	WLNG	60090	2755	15W-18N	A2
W Landau Ln					
20200	FmtT	60060	2590	20W-28N	A6
Landau Rd					
500	UYPK	60417	3684	3W-30S	C3
500	UYPK	60466	3684	3W-30S	C3
Landcaster Cir					
500	ELGN	60123	2853	36W-10N	E7
5700	MHRY	60050	2527	34W-32N	C4
N Landcaster Ct					
1700	ANHT	60004	2807	16W-15N	C1
N Landen Dr					
2400	LydT	60164	2972	13W-3N	E5
2400	NHLK	60164	2972	13W-3N	E6
2600	FNPK	60131	2972	13W-3N	E5
2600	FNPK	60164	2972	13W-3N	E5
Landen Ln					
700	LKVL	60046	2417	22W-39N	C6
N Landers Av					
6000	CHCG	60646	2919	6W-7N	E3
Landers Dr					
5100	HFET	60192	2856	30W-12N	C1
Landfield Rd					
200	BTVA	60510	3077	36W-0S	E1
Landgraf Ln					
-	SgrT	60506	3198	39W-8S	D3
1100	MTGY	60506	3198	39W-9S	D3
Landing Dr					
4100	AURA	60504	3202	30W-8S	B2
Landing Rd					
900	NPVL	60540	3141	27W-6S	B6
Landings Ct					
1900	JLET	60431	3417	28W-21S	A7
4000	MchT	60050	2528	33W-34N	A1
4000	MHRY	60050	2528	33W-34N	A1
Landings Dr					
10700	ODPK	60467	3423	13W-20S	A4
10700	OrlT	60467	3423	13W-20S	A4
Landings Ln					
-	DSPN	60016	2863	11W-11N	D3
-	MaiT	60016	2863	11W-11N	D3
14800	OKFT	60452	3347	7W-17S	B6
Landings Rd					
3600	JLET	60431	3417	28W-21S	A7
3800	JLET	60431	3416	28W-21S	E7
Landis Ln					
200	DRFD	60015	2704	10W-21N	A6
Landl Rd					
-	NndT	60051	2529	29W-31N	B6
Landl Park Rd					
900	NndT	60051	2529	29W-31N	B6
Landmark					
10	NHFD	60093	2811	6W-15N	C3
Landmark Dr					
300	YKVL	60560	3261	42W-14S	C7
Landmark Ln					
20500	DRPK	60010	2752	22W-20N	B1
20600	DRPK	60010	2699	22W-20N	B7
Landmark Rd					
1500	AURA	60506	3137	37W-5S	D3
Landmark Vil					
-	CHCG	60657	2977	2W-3N	C4
Landmark Wy					
-	ANTH	60002	2416	24W-41N	D1
-	AntT	60002	2416	24W-41N	D1
Landmeier Rd					
100	EGVV	60007	2860	18W-9N	E7
300	EGvT	60007	2860	18W-9N	E7
300	EGvT	60007	2861	18W-9N	A7
1100	EGVV	60007	2915	17W-9N	C1
1800	EGvT	60007	2915	16W-9N	D1
2400	EGVV	60007	2861	16W-9N	E7
2500	EGvT	60018	2861	16W-9N	E7
Landon Av					
700	WPHR	60096	2363	9W-42N	C6
1400	WPHR	60096	2422	9W-41N	C1
Landon Cir					
-	MltT	60187	3082	25W-2S	A4
-	WHTN	60187	3082	25W-2S	A4
Landon Dr					
10	NPVL	60555	3080	29W-3S	D7
10	NPVL	60563	3080	29W-3S	D7
10	WNVL	60555	3080	29W-3S	D7
Landon Ln					
-	BKBN	60015	2703	11W-22N	E3
-	HDPK	60035	2703	11W-22N	E3
-	WdfT	60015	2703	11W-22N	E3
Landore Dr					
3100	NPVL	60564	3202	28W-11S	E7
3100	NPVL	60564	3203	28W-11S	A7
3200	NPVL	60564	3266	28W-11S	E1
Landover Pkwy					
10	HNWD	60047	2645	22W-24N	B6
Landreth Ct					
1700	AURA	60504	3200	34W-9S	E5
Landreth Ln					
400	NHFD	60093	2758	8W-16N	A7
Lands Ct					
1800	NndT	60012	2585	30W-28N	E6
Landsdown Av					
3200	NPVL	60564	3266	30W-11S	A2
3900	WldT	60564	3266	30W-11S	A1
Lands End					
9900	MNSR	46321	3510		D4
Landsend Ct					
3400	ISLK	60042	2586	28W-28N	D5
Landsfield Av					
10	DGvT	60516	3206	19W-9S	D2
Landsfield Ct					
200	DGvT	60516	3206	19W-9S	D3
Landsfield Pl					
200	DGvT	60516	3206	19W-9S	D3
Landshire Ct					
300	OSWG	60543	3263	36W-11S	E2
Landwehr Rd					
600	NHBK	60062	2756	11W-16N	D6
1800	GNVW	60025	2809	11W-14N	D4
1800	NfdT	60025	2809	11W-14N	D4
1800	NfdT	60062	2809	11W-14N	D4
2100	NfdT	60062	2756	11W-16N	D7
2100	NHBK	60062	2809	11W-14N	D3
2500	NHBK	60025	2809	11W-14N	D3
2600	GNVW	60062	2809	11W-14N	D3
Lane Ct					
6400	WLBK	60527	3145	16W-7S	E6
W Lane Ct					
22500	RLKB	60073	2475	22W-34N	B7
Lane Dr					
16500	LKPT	60441	3420	20W-19S	B3
E Lane Dr					
500	VLPK	60181	3027	17W-0S	C6
Lane Pl					
5300	DRGV	60515	3144	19W-5S	C3
Lane Rd					
400	WCHI	60185	3022	30W-1N	B2
400	WnfT	60185	3022	30W-1N	B2
Lane Lorraine St					
800	LKFT	60045	2649	12W-26N	C2
W Laneville Dr					
25800	GrtT	60041	2473	25W-35N	E5
25800	GrtT	60041	2474	25W-35N	A5
Lanfear Dr					
16300	LKPT	60441	3420	20W-21S	B6
Lanford Ln					
200	PTHT	60070	2808	15W-14N	A3
Lang Dr					
1500	BGBK	60490	3267	26W-12S	E2
Lang Rd					
-	RcmT	60071	2354	32W-42N	C6
-	SPGV	60081	2354	32W-42N	C6
Langdon Pl					
2200	HFET	60169	2857	26W-12N	E1
2200	HFET	60169	2858	25W-12N	C1
Lange Av					
900	BCHR	60401	3864	0W-36S	D1
Lange Ct					
500	LYVL	60048	2591	16W-29N	D4
Lange Rd					
100	BfdT	53128	2352	38W-43N	A4
100	HbnT	53128	2352	38W-43N	A4
100	HbnT	60034	2352	38W-43N	A4
100	HbnT	60071	2352	38W-43N	A4
Lange St					
500	MDLN	60060	2590	18W-27N	E7
900	MDLN	60060	2591	18W-28N	A7
18000	LNSG	60438	3430	4E-21S	C6
19200	LNSG	60438	3510	4E-22S	C2
Langford Ct					
10	BGBK	60440	3205	22W-10S	D5
1300	WHTN	60187	3082	23W-3S	E5
Langford Dr					
400	BGBK	60440	3205	22W-10S	C5
2900	GNVA	60134	3019	37W-1N	C2
Langford Ln					
2100	WHTN	60187	3082	23W-3S	E5
Langley Av					
14800	DLTN	60419	3350	0E-17S	E5
15500	SHLD	60473	3350	0E-18S	E7
16600	SHLD	60473	3429	0E-19S	A2
16800	SHLD	60473	3428	0E-19S	E3
S Langley Av					
3800	CHCG	60653	3092	0E-3S	D5
4600	CHCG	60615	3092	0E-4S	E7
4700	CHCG	60615	3152	0E-5S	E1
6000	CHCG	60637	3152	0E-7S	E6
7100	CHCG	60619	3152	0E-8S	E7
7500	CHCG	60619	3214	0E-9S	E3
9400	CHCG	60628	3214	0E-10S	E5
10500	CHCG	60628	3278	0E-12S	E2
13100	CHCG	60827	3278	0E-15S	E7
13100	CHCG	60827	3350	0E-15S	E1
Langley Cir					
1000	NPVL	60563	3140	29W-5S	D3
2700	GNVW	60025	2810	9W-13N	B5
Langley Ct					
400	SMBG	60193	2859	23W-9N	B6
800	GYLK	60030	2533	20W-33N	B3
5000	OKFT	60452	3426	6W-20S	A4
6500	WDRG	60517	3143	21W-7S	D6
27500	WcnT	60042	2642	28W-27N	D1
Langley Dr					
300	SMBG	60193	2859	23W-9N	B6
Langley St					
1900	NCHI	60088	2593	11W-31N	D1
Langoon Cir					
2000	JLET	60586	3415	33W-21S	B7
Langsford Ln					
6400	JLET	60586	3415	32W-20S	C5
6400	PNFD	60586	3415	32W-20S	C5
Langston Cir					
2900	SCRL	60175	3019	37W-2N	C1
Langston Ln					
-	CPVL	60118	2746	37W-18N	C4
Langston St					
900	FDHT	60411	3509	1E-24S	B6
Langton Ct					
200	BMDL	60108	2969	23W-4N	A2
Langton Dr					
100	BMDL	60108	2969	23W-4N	A3
Langton Ln					
200	BMDL	60108	2969	23W-4N	A3
Langtry Ct					
900	ELGN	60120	2855	32W-11N	C5
N Lannom Ln					
36300	GrtT	60041	2474	25W-36N	A4
Lansbrook Dr					
1200	SEGN	60177	2907	37W-7N	C5
Lansburgh Ct					
2300	AURA	60502	3139	32W-6S	B5
2300	NpvT	60502	3139	32W-6S	B5
Lansbury Cir					
5300	LIHL	60156	2692	38W-21N	E6
Lansbury Ct					
10	LIHL	60156	2692	38W-21N	E6
Lansdale St					
2600	AURA	60503	3201	32W-10S	C7
10400	HTLY	60142	2692	39W-20N	C7
N Lansing Av					
5700	CHCG	60646	2919	6W-7N	D4
Lansing Ct					
800	VNHL	60061	2647	18W-25N	A5
Lansing St					
10	HNDL	60521	3086	15W-4S	A7
Lantern Cir					
1400	NPVL	60540	3142	24W-7S	C7
1400	NPVL	60540	3204	24W-7S	C1
Lantern Ln					
1200	NlxT	60451	3502	16W-23S	A4
1500	JltT	60433	3587	23W-25S	B2
Lantry Ct					
100	CmpT	60119	3018	40W-2N	B2
Lanyon Dr					
1700	BRLT	60103	2909	31W-8N	D3
Lapalm Ct					
5300	OKFT	60452	3347	6W-17S	E6
Lapalm Dr					
5400	OKFT	60452	3347	7W-17S	D6
La Palma Ct					
1600	WHTN	60187	3082	24W-2S	D3
La Paz Ct					
15700	OKFT	60452	3347	7W-18S	C7
15700	OKFT	60452	3425	7W-18S	C1
La Paz Dr					
6000	OKFT	60452	3347	7W-18S	C7
Lapier St					
100	GLNC	60022	2758	5W-17N	E6
La Porte Av					
500	NHLK	60164	2972	13W-2N	D6
800	LydT	60164	2972	13W-3N	D5
3100	FNPK	60131	2972	13W-3N	D5
3100	LydT	60131	2972	13W-3N	D5
Laporte Av					
600	WLMT	60091	2811	6W-13N	D6
7800	BRBK	60459	3211	6W-8S	E2
8300	BRBK	60459	3212	6W-9S	A3
8600	OKLN	60453	3212	6W-9S	A4
8600	OKLN	60459	3212	6W-9S	A4
10300	OKLN	60453	3276	6W-12S	A1
14500	MDLN	60445	3348	6W-17S	A5
15100	OKFT	60452	3348	6W-18S	A6
N Laporte Av					
100	CHCG	60644	3031	6W-0N	E4
2000	CHCG	60639	2975	6W-2N	E6
4400	CHCG	60630	2975	6W-5N	E1
4400	CHCG	60641	2975	6W-5N	E1
5200	CHCG	60630	2919	6W-6N	E5
5400	CHCG	60646	2919	6W-6N	E5
6600	LNWD	60712	2919	6W-8N	E2
6700	LNWD	60077	2919	6W-8N	E2
6700	SKOK	60077	2919	6W-8N	E2
S Laporte Av					
4500	CHCG	60638	3089	6W-4S	E7
4700	CHCG	60638	3149	6W-5S	E2
6400	BDPK	60638	3149	6W-7S	E5
11600	ALSP	60803	3276	6W-13S	A4
La Porte Ct					
6700	BGVW	60455	3148	9W-7S	C6
S La Porte Ct					
300	ADSN	60101	2971	18W-3N	A5
E La Porte Dr					
200	ADSN	60101	2971	18W-3N	A5
Laporte Rd					
-	FftT	60477	3504	11W-23S	A4
-	FKFT	60423	3504	11W-23S	A4
W La Porte Rd					
-	FftT	60423	3504	11W-24S	A4
-	FftT	60448	3504	11W-24S	A4
-	FftT	60477	3504	11W-24S	A4
-	FKFT	60423	3504	11W-24S	A4
9400	FftT	60423	3503	11W-23S	E4
9400	FftT	60448	3503	11W-23S	E4
9400	FKFT	60423	3503	11W-23S	E4
9400	FKFT	60448	3503	12W-23S	D4
9400	MKNA	60423	3503	12W-23S	D4
9400	MKNA	60448	3503	12W-23S	D4
11200	FftT	60448	3502	14W-24S	E4
11200	MKNA	60448	3502	14W-24S	E4
Laporte Meadows Ct					
20000	FKFT	60423	3504	11W-24S	A5
Laporte Meadows Dr					
19900	FKFT	60423	3504	11W-24S	A4
Lapp Ln					
3200	NPVL	60564	3266	30W-11S	A1
3400	WldT	60564	3266	30W-11S	A1
La Quienta Dr					
4900	MONE	60449	3683	6W-31S	B5
La Quinta Ct					
10	LIHL	60156	2693	36W-21N	C5
Laramie Av					
-	CCRO	60804	3089	6W-4S	E6
-	SKNY	60804	3089	6W-4S	E6
500	WLMT	60091	2811	6W-13N	D6
600	GNVW	60025	2811	6W-13N	D7
6800	SKOK	60077	2919	6W-8N	D1
7500	BDPK	60459	3211	6W-8S	E1
7500	BDPK	60638	3211	6W-8S	E1
7500	BRBK	60459	3211	6W-9S	E3
7500	BRBK	60638	3211	6W-8S	E1
7500	SKOK	60077	2865	6W-9N	D6
8600	OKLN	60453	3211	6W-9S	E4
8600	OKLN	60459	3211	6W-9S	E4
10300	OKLN	60453	3275	6W-12S	E1
14700	MDLN	60445	3347	6W-17S	E6
14700	MDLN	60452	3347	6W-17S	E6
14700	OKFT	60452	3347	6W-18S	E7
15700	OKFT	60452	3425	6W-19S	E1
16700	BmnT	60452	3425	6W-20S	E4
16700	BmnT	60477	3425	6W-20S	E4
N Laramie Av					
10	CHCG	60644	3031	6W-0N	D5
700	CHCG	60651	3031	6W-1N	D1
1500	CHCG	60639	3031	6W-1N	D1
1600	CHCG	60639	2975	6W-2N	D7
2700	CHCG	60641	2975	6W-3N	D5
4300	CHCG	60630	2975	6W-5N	D1
4800	CHCG	60630	2919	6W-6N	D6
S Laramie Av					
-	FTVW	60402	3089	6W-4S	E7
-	StkT	60402	3089	6W-4S	E7
10	CHCG	60644	3031	6W-0S	D7
700	CCRO	60644	3031	6W-0S	E7
700	CCRO	60804	3031	6W-0S	E7
1500	CCRO	60804	3089	6W-1S	E1
3400	SKNY	60804	3089	6W-3S	E5
4500	CHCG	60638	3089	6W-4S	E7
4500	FTVW	60638	3089	6W-4S	E7
4600	CHCG	60638	3149	6W-5S	E2
4600	FTVW	60638	3149	6W-4S	E1
4700	StkT	60638	3149	6W-5S	E1
6500	BDPK	60638	3149	6W-7S	E5
11100	ALSP	60453	3275	6W-13S	E3
11100	ALSP	60803	3275	6W-13S	E3
11100	OKLN	60453	3275	6W-13S	E3
Laramie Blvd					
13300	CTWD	60445	3347	6W-15S	E2
13800	BmnT	60445	3347	6W-16S	E3
14000	MDLN	60445	3347	6W-16S	E3
Laramie Ct					
5200	OKFT	60452	3347	6W-18S	E6
E Laramie Ct					
14000	CTWD	60445	3347	6W-16S	E3
14000	MDLN	60445	3347	6W-16S	E3
W Laramie Ct					
14000	CTWD	60445	3347	6W-16S	E3
14000	MDLN	60445	3347	6W-16S	E3
Laramie Ln					
-	SKOK	60077	2865	6W-12N	D1
19000	CCHL	60478	3506	6W-22S	A2
Laramie Rd					
18600	CCHL	60478	3506	6W-22S	A1
Laramie St					
10	MDLN	60060	2590	19W-28N	D6
Laramie Tr					
100	BMDL	60108	2968	25W-5N	B1
100	BmdT	60108	2968	25W-5N	B1
E Laraway Rd					
-	NLNX	60442	3589	17W-27S	D3
-	NLNX	60451	3589	17W-27S	D3
-	NlxT	60442	3589	17W-26S	D3
-	NlxT	60451	3589	17W-26S	D3
10	JLET	60433	3587	22W-26S	C4
10	JLET	60436	3587	23W-26S	A4
10	JltT	60433	3587	22W-26S	C4
100	FKFT	60423	3591	11W-26S	E3
200	FftT	60423	3592	11W-26S	A3
200	FKFT	60423	3592	11W-26S	A3
1900	JltT	60421	3588	21W-26S	A4
1900	JltT	60433	3588	21W-27S	A4
2100	NlxT	60433	3588	21W-26S	B4
2400	NLNX	60433	3588	20W-27S	C3
2700	NLNX	60451	3588	20W-26S	B3
2800	NlxT	60451	3588	20W-26S	B3
12400	NLNX	60451	3590	16W-26S	A3
12400	NlxT	60451	3590	16W-26S	A3
W Laraway Rd					
-	NlxT	60451	3588	19W-27S	E3
10	NLNX	60442	3589	18W-26S	C3
10	NLNX	60451	3589	17W-26S	C3
10	NlxT	60442	3589	18W-26S	C3
10	NlxT	60451	3589	17W-26S	C3
100	JLET	60436	3586	24W-26S	E4
100	JLET	60436	3587	23W-26S	A4
100	JltT	60436	3586	26W-26S	E4
100	JltT	60436	3587	23W-26S	A4
500	FftT	60423	3592	10W-26S	C3
500	FKFT	60423	3592	10W-26S	C3
1000	NLNX	60451	3588	19W-26S	D3
7200	FKFT	60423	3593	9W-26S	A3
7200	FKFT	60443	3593	9W-26S	A3
7200	RchT	60443	3593	9W-26S	A3
9600	FftT	60423	3591	12W-26S	D3
9600	FKFT	60423	3591	12W-26S	D3
11000	FftT	60423	3590	15W-26S	C3

STREET Block City ZIP Map# CGS Grid

W Laraway Rd
11000 FKFT 60423 3590 15W-26S C3
11800 FKFT 60451 3590 15W-26S C3
11800 NlxT 60451 3590 15W-26S C3
12000 NLNX 60451 3590 15W-26S C3
20000 JltT 60421 3586 26W-26S A4
20800 JltT 60421 3585 26W-26S E4
Larch Av
4600 GNVW 60025 2809 12W-14N B4
E Larch Av
4500 GNVW 60025 2809 12W-14N C4
N Larch Av
100 EMHT 60126 3027 16W-1N E1
800 EMHT 60126 2971 16W-3N E5
Larch Ct
10 SMBG 60193 2857 27W-10N D5
W Larch Ct
21400 LktT 60544 3339 26W-16S E4
Larch Dr
600 CLSM 60188 2967 26W-3N D5
9300 MNSR 46321 3510 E2
N Larch Dr
1500 MPPT 60056 2808 13W-15N D3
W Larch Dr
21400 LktT 60544 3339 26W-16S D4
Larch Ln
300 GNEN 60137 3083 23W-1S A2
2300 HRPK 60133 2911 27W-8N B3
Larch Rd
10 FKFT 60423 3592 11W-26S A2
Larch A Ct
200 FKFT 60423 3592 11W-26S A2
Larch B Ct
100 FKFT 60423 3592 11W-26S A2
W Larchmont Av
1800 CHCG 60613 2977 2W-4N B2
Larchmont Ct
300 NPVL 60565 3203 26W-9S D5
900 AURA 60504 3201 32W-8S C3
Larchmont Dr
1200 EGVV 60007 2915 18W-8N A3
1300 BFGV 60089 2701 17W-21N A6
Larchmont Ln
100 BMDL 60108 2968 23W-5N E2
400 VNHL 60061 2647 16W-25N C5
800 LKFT 60045 2649 12W-26N C2
2400 AURA 60504 3201 32W-9S C3
2400 NpvT 60504 3201 32W-9S C3
Larchmont Rd
1900 HFET 60169 2804 23W-12N E7
1900 SMBG 60169 2804 23W-12N E7
1900 SMBG 60195 2804 23W-12N E7
Larchmont Wy
100 BGBK 60440 3268 24W-12S D2
Larchwood Ln
200 NARA 60542 3077 36W-4S E7
7200 WDRG 60517 3205 21W-8S D1
Laredo Tr
10 BMDL 60108 2968 25W-5N C1
10 BmdT 60108 2968 25W-5N C1
La Reina Ct
9900 ODPK 60462 3345 12W-17S C6
La Reina Real St
9900 ODPK 60462 3345 12W-17S C6
Largemouth Ln
- BDWD 60481 3942 30W-40S D2
- RedT 60481 3942 30W-40S D2
- WmTp 60481 3942 30W-40S D2
Largo Ct
1800 SMBG 60194 2858 25W-11N A3
S Largo Ct
14000 PnfT 60544 3339 27W-16S C4
Lariat Ct
10 LMNT 60439 3272 15W-13S A4
Larium Ln
400 CLLK 60012 2640 35W-27N A1
400 NndT 60012 2640 35W-26N A2
Lark Av
1500 MLPK 60160 3028 13W-1N E2
Lark Ct
2900 RGMW 60008 2806 19W-14N C4
Lark Ln
1000 SRWD 60404 3496 30W-23S B5
1400 NPVL 60565 3203 26W-8S E2
Lark St
500 GNVA 60134 3019 37W-0N D4
W Lark St
900 PTON 60468 3860 10W-37S D4
Larkdale Ct
1500 LNHT 60046 2417 21W-38N E7
Larkdale Dr
1700 NHBK 60062 2756 10W-16N E7
1900 GNVW 60025 2810 9W-13N D7
W Larkdale Ln
400 MPPT 60056 2807 15W-14N E5
600 ANHT 60004 2807 15W-14N E5
600 MPPT 60004 2807 15W-14N E5
Larkdale Rd
10 DRFD 60015 2757 10W-20N B2
Larkdale Row
200 WCDA 60084 2643 26W-27N C1
200 WcnT 60084 2643 26W-27N C1
400 WCDA 60084 2587 26W-27N C7
1000 WcnT 60084 2587 26W-28N C6
Larkdale East Rd
10 DRFD 60015 2757 9W-20N B2
Larkin Av
800 ELGN 60123 2854 35W-11N C4
2000 ELGN 60123 2853 36W-11N E4
2100 ElgT 60123 2853 36W-11N E4
N Larkin Av
10 JLET 60435 3498 26W-22S A2
10 JLET 60436 3498 26W-23S A5
1200 JLET 60403 3498 26W-22S A1
1600 CTHL 60403 3498 26W-21S A1
1800 CTHL 60403 3418 26W-21S A7
N Larkin Av SR-7
10 JLET 60435 3498 26W-22S A2
10 JLET 60436 3498 26W-23S A5
1200 JLET 60403 3498 26W-22S A1
S Larkin Av
- JltT 60436 3586 26W-25S A1
10 JLET 60435 3498 26W-25S A7
10 JLET 60436 3498 26W-25S A7
600 JltT 60436 3498 26W-24S A7
600 RKDL 60436 3498 26W-24S A7
1200 RKDL 60436 3586 26W-25S A1
S Larkin Av SR-7
- JltT 60436 3586 26W-25S A1
10 JLET 60435 3498 26W-25S A7
10 JLET 60436 3498 26W-25S A7
600 JltT 60436 3498 26W-24S A7
600 RKDL 60436 3498 26W-24S A7
1200 RKDL 60436 3586 26W-25S A1
Larkin Dr
200 WLNG 60090 2755 14W-16N C7
Larkin Ln
3500 MHRY 60050 2528 32W-31N B6
17600 CCHL 60478 3426 5W-21S B6
W Larkin Ln
25700 GrtT 60041 2474 25W-35N A7
25900 GrtT 60041 2473 26W-34N E7
Larkins Ln
500 NBRN 60010 2698 24W-22N B4
Larkspur Ct
10 LlHL 60156 2693 37W-22N A4
500 NPVL 60563 3141 26W-4S E1
900 LKFT 60045 2703 12W-23N C1
1000 PGGV 60140 2798 41W-15N A4
1200 PGGV 60140 2797 41W-15N E4
1400 RMVL 60446 3339 26W-17S E5
2200 AURA 60506 3137 38W-6S A5
17500 HMGN 60491 3421 16W-21S E6
18400 WrnT 60030 2533 18W-34N E2
N Larkspur Ct
34100 GrtT 60073 2530 25W-34N E1
Larkspur Dr
- HmrT 60448 3421 17W-21S D7
200 HDPK 60035 2757 8W-20N E1
400 BGBK 60440 3268 23W-12S E4
400 BGBK 60440 3269 23W-13S A4
1700 JLET 60586 3416 30W-21S B7
1700 JLET 60586 3496 30W-21S B1
3100 NndT 60012 2584 34W-28N B5
13500 HMGN 60491 3421 17W-21S D6
13700 HMGN 60448 3421 17W-21S D6
Larkspur Ln
- JNBG 60050 2471 32W-35N C5
10 CNHL 60514 3085 16W-4S D7
300 RDLK 60073 2531 25W-33N A2
600 MTSN 60443 3506 5W-24S B6
1000 DRN 60561 3145 17W-7S B7
1100 BTVA 60510 3078 34W-2S E4
1400 BtvT 60510 3078 34W-2S E4
2700 HLCT 60429 3427 3W-21S B5
4000 LlHL 60156 2693 37W-22N A4
4400 GfnT 60156 2693 38W-22N A4
5200 LSLE 60532 3143 22W-5S B3
6800 WDRG 60517 3143 21W-7S E6
12400 PNFD 60585 3266 30W-14S B7
12400 PNFD 60585 3338 30W-14S B1
15100 ODPK 60462 3346 9W-18S D6
15100 OrlT 60462 3346 9W-18S D6
17700 HMWD 60430 3427 3W-21S B6
E Larkspur Ln
10 BtlT 60512 3198 40W-11S B7
10 BtlT 60512 3262 40W-11S B1
N Larkspur Ln
1300 PLTN 60074 2753 20W-17N B5
W Larkspur Ln
10 BtlT 60512 3198 41W-11S B7
10 BtlT 60512 3262 40W-11S B1
10 SMWD 60107 2856 30W-10N C5
Larkspur St
1000 PGGV 60140 2797 41W-15N E4
1000 PGGV 60140 2798 41W-15N A4
N Larned Av
5200 CHCG 60630 2919 6W-6N D5
Larrabee Dr
2900 GNVA 60134 3019 37W-1N C4
Larrabee Ln
1200 NHBK 60062 2757 9W-17N D5
N Larrabee St
600 CHCG 60610 3034 0W-0N A3
1600 CHCG 60610 2978 0W-2N A7
1600 CHCG 60614 2978 0W-2N A7
Larraway Dr
1100 BFGV 60089 2701 17W-21N C6
Larry Ln
1500 GLHT 60139 2969 22W-2N C7
Larry St
7800 SjnT 46311 3598 E4
Larsdotter Ln
200 GNVA 60134 3019 37W-1N C3
Larsen Av
700 SMWD 60107 2911 28W-9N B1
Larsen Cir
10 RMVL 60446 3341 23W-16S A3
Larsen Ct
1400 NPVL 60563 3142 25W-5S B4
Larsen Ln
1400 LslT 60563 3142 25W-5S B3
1400 NPVL 60563 3142 25W-5S B3
Larson Av
1600 SCRL 60174 3020 34W-2N E1
Larson Ln
500 ROSL 60172 2913 23W-8N B3
500 SmbT 60172 2913 23W-8N B3
700 BNVL 60106 2915 16W-6N E5
700 SmbT 60193 2913 23W-8N B3
E Larson St
200 LtRT 60545 3259 47W-14S D7
200 PLNO 60545 3259 47W-14S D7
Larue St
100 PKFT 60466 3595 3W-25S B1
Lasalle Av
- TYPK 60477 3424 9W-21S D6
N Lasalle Blvd
300 CHCG 60610 3034 0W-1N B2
La Salle Ct
10 LktT 60441 3419 23W-21S B7
10 LktT 60441 3499 23W-21S B1
3400 FNPK 60131 2973 12W-4N C3
Lasalle Ct
10 SMWD 60107 2856 29W-9N E7
500 BFGV 60089 2701 17W-21N B5
N Lasalle Dr
1600 CHCG 60610 2978 0W-2N B7
1600 CHCG 60614 2978 0W-2N B7
N Lasalle Dr SR-64
1600 CHCG 60610 2978 0W-2N B7
1600 CHCG 60614 2978 0W-2N B7
W La Salle Dr
- CHCG 60614 2978 0W-2N B7
W La Salle Dr SR-64
- CHCG 60614 2978 0W-2N B7
Lasalle Ln
400 BFGV 60089 2701 17W-21N C5
12400 GfnT 60142 2691 41W-20N D7
La Salle Pl
500 ELGN 60123 2854 35W-12N B2
500 HDPK 60035 2704 8W-22N E5
Lasalle Rd
100 HnrT 60107 2856 29W-9N E7
100 SMWD 60107 2856 29W-9N E7
La Salle St
- DSPN 60016 2861 16W-10N E4
- MPPT 60016 2861 16W-10N E4
- MPPT 60056 2861 16W-10N E4
- SHLD 60473 3428 0W-20S C4
- TNTN 60473 3428 0W-20S C4
- TNTN 60476 3428 0W-20S C4
La Salle St
500 DSPN 60016 2862 14W-11N C3
1600 NPVL 60563 3140 29W-5S C2
1600 NpvT 60563 3140 29W-5S C2
14600 DLTN 60419 3350 0W-17S C5
14600 DLTN 60827 3350 0W-17S C5
14600 RVDL 60827 3350 0W-17S C5
14900 HRVY 60426 3350 0W-17S C5
15400 SHLD 60473 3350 0W-18S C7
E Lasalle St
100 VNHL 60061 2647 16W-24N D7
N Lasalle St
- CHCG 60610 3034 0W-0N B4
10 AURA 60505 3138 35W-7S B7
10 CHCG 60602 3034 0W-0N B4
10 CHCG 60603 3034 0W-0N B4
100 CHCG 60601 3034 0W-0N B4
S La Salle St
13800 RVDL 60827 3350 0W-16S C2
14500 DLTN 60419 3350 0W-17S C4
14500 DLTN 60827 3350 0W-17S C4
S Lasalle St
10 AURA 60505 3138 35W-7S C6
10 AURA 60505 3200 35W-8S A2
10 CHCG 60602 3034 0W-0S B5
10 CHCG 60603 3034 0W-0S B5
100 CHCG 60604 3034 0W-0S B5
600 CHCG 60605 3034 0W-0S B6
2600 CHCG 60616 3092 0W-2S B3
3400 CHCG 60609 3092 0W-3S B4
5500 CHCG 60609 3152 0W-6S B4
5500 CHCG 60621 3152 0W-6S B4
9100 CHCG 60620 3214 0W-10S C5
9800 CHCG 60628 3214 0W-11S C7
10200 CHCG 60628 3278 0W-12S C1
W Lasalle St
10 ANHT 60004 2807 18W-16N A1
N Las Casas Av
5600 CHCG 60646 2919 6W-7N E4
Las Flores Ln
15100 OKFT 60452 3347 7W-18S C7
Las Robles Ct
15200 OKFT 60452 3347 7W-18S B6
Las Robles St
15200 OKFT 60452 3347 7W-18S B6
Lasser Dr
1200 JLET 60586 3496 30W-22S B1
Lasso Ln
100 CmpT 60175 2962 41W-3N A5
N Latham Av
5400 CHCG 60630 2919 6W-6N E5
W Latham Ct
25400 PNFD 60585 3337 31W-15S D3
N Latham St
100 SDWH 60548 3330 51W-14S A1
800 SDWH 60548 3258 51W-14S A7
1300 SdwT 60548 3258 51W-14S A7
S Latham St
10 SDWH 60548 3330 51W-15S A2
Latham Tr
12000 HTLY 60142 2744 43W-19N B2
Lathem St
100 BTVA 60510 3078 35W-0S B1
1400 BTVA 60510 3079 33W-0S A1
Lathrop Av
10 FTPK 60130 3030 9W-0N C5
10 RVFT 60130 3030 9W-0N C5
10 RVFT 60305 3030 9W-0N C5
1500 EDPK 60707 3030 9W-1N C1
1500 RVFT 60707 3030 9W-1N C1
2200 FTPK 60130 3088 9W-2S C2
2200 FTPK 60546 3088 9W-2S C2
2200 NRIV 60546 3088 9W-2S C2
15500 HRVY 60426 3350 1W-18S A7
15500 HRVY 60426 3428 1W-20S A4
16200 HRVY 60428 3427 1W-19S E2
16200 MKHM 60428 3427 1W-19S E2
16700 HRVY 60429 3428 1W-20S A4
17100 EHZC 60429 3428 1W-20S A5
17300 EHZC 60430 3428 1W-20S A5
17300 HMWD 60429 3428 1W-20S A5
17300 HMWD 60430 3428 1W-20S A5
W Lathrop Ct
21900 PnfT 60544 3339 27W-16S C5
Lathrop Dr
4300 GNWD 60098 2468 38W-36N E4
4400 GNWD 60097 2468 38W-36N E4
Lathrop Ln
10 DndT 60118 2747 35W-19N C3
200 YkTp 60148 3085 18W-1S A1
200 YkTp 60181 3085 18W-1S A1
Latimer Ln
700 FSMR 60422 3507 2W-22S D2
Latonia Ct
22500 RNPK 60471 3594 5W-27S B4
Latonia Ln
22200 RNPK 60471 3594 5W-27S B5
22800 UYPK 60471 3594 5W-27S B5
Latoria Ln
2900 FNPK 60131 2973 13W-3N A5
2900 FNPK 60164 2973 13W-3N A5
2900 LydT 60131 2973 13W-3N A5
2900 LydT 60164 2973 13W-3N A5
Latour Ct
3900 HFET 60192 2804 24W-14N C3
Latrobe Av
- CTWD 60445 3347 6W-16S E2
100 NHFD 60093 2811 6W-15N D2
300 NtrT 60093 2811 6W-15N D2
6800 SKOK 60077 2919 6W-8N D1
7500 BDPK 60638 3211 6W-8S E1
7500 BRBK 60638 3211 6W-9S E3
7500 BRBK 60459 3211 6W-8S E1
8600 OKLN 60453 3211 6W-9S E4
8600 OKLN 60459 3211 6W-9S E4
9200 SKOK 60077 2865 6W-11N D2
15600 OKFT 60452 3347 6W-18S E7
15900 OKFT 60452 3425 6W-19S E1
N Latrobe Av
600 CHCG 60644 3031 6W-0N D3
700 CHCG 60651 3031 6W-0N D3
1600 CHCG 60639 3031 6W-2N D1
1900 CHCG 60639 2975 6W-2N D7
3200 CHCG 60630 2919 6W-6N D5
S Latrobe Av
4700 FTVW 60638 3149 6W-5S E1
4700 StkT 60638 3149 6W-5S E1
5000 CHCG 60638 3149 6W-5S E2
6400 BDPK 60638 3149 6W-7S E5
12300 ALSP 60803 3275 6W-14S E6
Lattice Dr
200 OSWG 60543 3263 38W-13S B5
Lauder Ln
400 IVNS 60067 2804 23W-15N D2
Lauderdale Ct
2600 MchT 60051 2472 29W-34N D7
Lauderdale Ct
2600 MchT 60051 2529 29W-34N D1
W Lauffer Rd
12500 HMGN 60491 3422 16W-20S A5
Laughing Water Tr
28700 GrtT 60051 2472 28W-35N D7
Laughry Ln
10 PSPK 60464 3273 12W-15S D7
Laughton Av
- OSWG 60560 3334 39W-14S E1
Laura Av
200 SRWD 60404 3496 29W-24S D6
Laura Ct
10 SEGN 60177 2908 36W-9N A1
400 NPVL 60563 3141 27W-5S C3
W Laura Dr
10 AddT 60101 2970 18W-2N E7
10 ADSN 60101 2970 18W-2N E7
Laura Ln
10 SgrT 60506 3135 41W-5S E3
10 SgrT 60554 3135 41W-5S E3
100 CHHT 60411 3507 1W-23S E4
100 NLNX 60451 3501 18W-23S B2
100 NlxT 60451 3501 18W-23S B2
100 TNTN 60476 3428 0E-20S D5
900 SLVL 60411 3597 1E-27S B3
900 STGR 60411 3597 1E-27S B3
1200 DGvT 60439 3270 20W-12S C2
1200 GNOK 60044 2592 13W-28N E5
1200 GNOK 60044 2593 13W-28N A5
1200 LbvT 60044 2592 13W-28N E5
1900 DSPN 60018 2917 12W-8N B1
6100 TYPK 60477 3425 7W-20S C3
11200 FKFT 60423 3590 14W-27S E4
11200 FKFT 60423 3591 14W-27S A4
16400 OKFT 60452 3426 5W-19S C2
S Laura Ln
600 DMND 60416 3941 33W-40S B4
1000 BvlT 60416 3941 33W-40S B4
24300 CteT 60417 3686 2E-29S D1
W Laura St
24000 CNHN 60410 3584 30W-28S C7
24000 CnhT 60410 3584 30W-28S C7
Laura Ingalls Wilder Rd
300 CmpT 60175 2962 40W-3N C6
E Laura Ingalls Wilder Rd
500 CmpT 60175 2962 40W-3N C6
W Laura Ingalls Wilder Rd
700 CmpT 60175 2962 40W-3N C5
Laura Kriss Ct
1200 JLET 60586 3496 30W-22S B2
Laurel Av
10 HDPK 60035 2705 8W-22N A4
100 WLMT 60091 2813 2W-13N B6
200 DSPN 60016 2862 13W-11N E3
300 HDPK 60035 2704 8W-22N D5
300 LYVL 60048 2591 16W-29N C4
300 RDLK 60073 2531 23W-33N E3
400 RMVL 60446 3340 24W-15S D2
400 WDSK 60098 2581 41W-30N D2
400 WMTN 60481 3853 27W-39S D7
600 WCDA 60084 2587 26W-28N C6
700 WLMT 60091 2812 3W-13N E6
1000 DRFD 60015 2756 11W-20N D2
1000 WNKA 60093 2759 5W-16N A7
1100 WNKA 60093 2758 6W-16N D7
1100 WNKA 60093 2811 5W-16N E1
1400 WKGN 60085 2536 11W-34N E2
1500 WdfT 60015 2756 11W-20N C2
1800 EVTN 60201 2866 3W-11N E2
2000 HRPK 60133 2911 27W-8N C2
2100 HRPK 60107 2911 27W-9N C2
2100 SMWD 60107 2911 27W-9N C2
3600 CCHL 60429 3426 4W-20S D4
3600 CCHL 60478 3426 4W-20S D4
3600 HLCT 60429 3426 4W-20S D4
4600 GNVW 60025 2809 12W-14N B5
5400 LynT 60525 3146 13W-6S E4
6200 IHPK 60525 3147 13W-7S A5
6200 LynT 60525 3147 13W-7S A5
16600 LKFT 60045 2649 11W-27N D1
E Laurel Av
10 LKFT 60045 2649 10W-27N E1
10 LKFT 60045 2650 10W-27N B1
300 EMHT 60126 3028 15W-0N B3
N Laurel Av
35600 GrtT 60041 2473 26W-35N E6
W Laurel Av
10 LKFT 60045 2649 11W-27N E1
21900 LKVL 60046 2417 21W-39N C6
21900 LkvT 60046 2417 21W-39N C6
26000 WcnT 60084 2643 26W-26N D3
Laurel Ct
10 CRTE 60417 3685 0W-30S C2
10 KdlT 60560 3333 43W-17S B7
10 SEGN 60177 2908 35W-7N B4
10 WNVL 60555 3080 30W-1S C2
100 ELGN 60120 2855 33W-11N A4
100 WLNG 60090 2755 15W-17N A4
300 SMWD 60107 2857 28W-10N A6
500 RLKB 60073 2474 23W-35N E6
1100 CLSM 60188 2967 27W-3N B6
1200 DRGV 60515 3084 20W-3S B6
1500 SYHW 60118 2800 35W-16N C2
2500 DYR 46311 3598 E3
2700 WDRG 60517 3205 21W-9S D3
W Laurel Ct
26000 CbaT 60084 2643 26W-26N E4
26000 WcnT 60084 2643 26W-26N E4
Laurel Dr
10 BmdT 60157 2913 22W-5N D7
10 LNHT 60046 2476 20W-37N B1
300 NARA 60542 3078 35W-3S D5
400 WldT 60564 3203 28W-10S A5
500 WldT 60564 3202 28W-10S E5
600 DYR 46311 3598 E3
800 CmpT 60175 2905 41W-6N E7
1000 AURA 60506 3137 38W-6S A4
4700 RNPK 60471 3594 5W-26S B3
16100 ODPK 60462 3424 10W-19S B1
20500 DRPK 60010 2752 23W-20N A1
20600 DRPK 60010 2699 23W-20N A7
N Laurel Dr
1700 MPPT 60056 2808 13W-15N D2
1700 PLTN 60074 2753 19W-18N B3
W Laurel Dr
7700 FftT 60423 3504 9W-24S D5
13000 LbvT 60045 2592 13W-28N D7
13900 LbvT 60048 2592 13W-28N D7
Laurel Ln
- WKGN 60087 2479 11W-36N D3
200 BMDL 60108 2969 22W-4N B3
200 WCHI 60185 2966 30W-2N B7
300 SMWD 60107 2857 28W-10N A6
700 CRY 60013 2695 32W-22N A3
1000 NPVL 60540 3203 26W-8S D1
Laurel Ln
1100 GRNE 60031 2476 18W-35N D6
1300 SMBG 60193 2913 23W-8N A2
1300 SmbT 60193 2913 23W-8N A2
1600 DRN 60561 3207 18W-9S A4
2500 WLMT 60091 2812 5W-13N A6
3200 HLCT 60429 3426 4W-20S E4
3200 HLCT 60429 3427 4W-20S A4
3600 CCHL 60429 3426 4W-20S D5
3600 CCHL 60478 3426 4W-20S D5
5900 WLBK 60527 3145 16W-6S E5
12200 HTLY 60142 2744 42W-19N D2
15100 HmrT 60441 3421 18W-20S A4
15100 LKPT 60441 3420 18W-20S E4
15100 LKPT 60441 3421 18W-20S A4
N Laurel Ln
28000 LbvT 60045 2592 13W-28N E7
W Laurel Ln
- ISLK 60042 2586 29W-27N D7
- ISLK 60051 2586 29W-27N D7
- NndT 60042 2586 29W-27N D7
21000 KLDR 60047 2699 21W-22N E4
27700 WcnT 60042 2586 28W-27N D7
Laurel Rd
800 NHBK 60062 2757 9W-17N B4
Laurel St
10 BTVA 60510 3078 35W-1S C2
10 JLET 60435 3498 24W-23S D5
10 JLET 60436 3498 24W-23S D5
100 WMTN 60481 3853 27W-39S D7
200 EGvT 60007 2914 18W-9N E1
200 EGVV 60007 2914 18W-9N D1
300 EGvT 60007 2915 18W-9N A1
300 EGVV 60007 2915 18W-9N A1
400 ELGN 60120 2855 33W-11N B4
Laurel Ter
600 GYLK 60030 2533 20W-33N A2
Laurel Tr
10 WLNG 60090 2754 16W-17N E4
Laurel Bay
700 NLNX 60451 3590 15W-25S C1
Laurel Glen Ct
13000 PSHT 60463 3347 7W-15S B1
Laurel Hill Dr
11000 ODPK 60467 3423 13W-20S A4
11100 ODPK 60467 3422 13W-20S E4
11100 OrlT 60467 3422 13W-20S E4
Laureli Cir
1100 NPVL 60540 3141 28W-6S A5
Laurel Oak Ct
10 BRRG 60527 3208 15W-10S B5
16200 CTHL 60403 3418 25W-19S B3
Laurel Oak Dr
16000 CTHL 60403 3418 25W-19S B3
Laurel Oaks Dr
1300 BRLT 60107 2856 30W-9N C7
1300 SMWD 60107 2856 30W-9N C7
1300 SMWD 60120 2856 30W-9N C7
Laurelton St
100 NCHI 60044 2593 12W-29N B3
Laurel Valley Ct
10 LlHL 60156 2693 36W-22N C4
N Laurel Valley Dr
2000 VNHL 60061 2647 17W-27N C1
Lauren Ct
900 WTMT 60559 3145 18W-6S B5
4000 MHRY 60050 2528 32W-33N A3
7000 GRNE 60031 2477 17W-34N B7
Lauren Dr
- JLET 60586 3416 31W-21S A6
W Lauren Dr
26400 CNHN 60410 3761 32W-32S C1
Lauren Ln
- AURA 60504 3201 33W-9S A3
300 BFGV 60089 2754 16W-18N C3
400 ISLK 60042 2586 29W-28N C5
400 NndT 60042 2586 29W-28N C5
N Lauren Ln
9800 NLES 60714 2864 10W-12N B1
Lauretta Pl
2700 HDPK 60035 2704 8W-23N D2
2700 HDPK 60037 2704 8W-23N D2
Laurette Ct
500 SMBG 60193 2859 22W-9N B7
S Laurie Av
11900 PlsT 60464 3274 10W-14S A5
11900 PSPK 60464 3274 10W-14S A5
Laurie Cir
100 BGBK 60440 3269 21W-11S E1
Laurie Ct
10 LKVL 60046 2475 23W-37N A1
500 GYLK 60030 2532 21W-33N D2
1100 BRRG 60521 3146 14W-6S C4
Laurie Dr
200 LKPT 60441 3420 21W-18S A1
200 LktT 60441 3419 21W-18S E1
200 LktT 60441 3420 21W-18S A1
Laurie Ln
100 MTGY 60543 3263 38W-11S B1
500 NHFD 60093 2811 7W-15N B1
600 BRLT 60103 2909 31W-8N E2
1000 BRRG 60521 3146 14W-6S C3
1000 HNDL 60521 3146 14W-6S C3
1000 HRPK 60133 2857 26W-9N E7
1300 BRRG 60527 3146 14W-6S C4
1500 SMWD 60107 2857 26W-9N D7
1500 SMWD 60133 2857 26W-9N D7
4400 AlqT 60014 2640 33W-25N E4
Laurie Rd
3700 LtRT 60545 3258 49W-13S E6
15800 LtRT 60545 3259 48W-14S A6
Laurie K Smith Dr
10 LtRT 60545 3259 48W-11S B1
N Laurine Dr
21200 CbaT 60010 2697 25W-21N E6
Laursen Ct
1000 ANTH 60002 2357 23W-42N E6
N Lavender Cir
34000 WrnT 60030 2533 18W-34N E2
Lavender Ct
5500 RGMW 60008 2860 19W-12N D2
Lavender Dr
1500 RMVL 60446 3339 26W-17S E7
Lavender Ln
11200 FKFT 60423 3590 14W-26S E3
11200 FKFT 60423 3591 13W-26S A3
Laverange Av
- MDLN 60445 3348 6W-17S A4
Laverggone St
- GfnT 60014 2638 38W-25N E5
Lavergne Av
- BmnT 60478 3426 6W-21S A7
- CCHL 60478 3426 6W-21S A7
400 WLMT 60091 2811 6W-13N D6
4300 NndT 60014 2586 30W-27N A7
4500 NndT 60014 2642 30W-27N A1

STREET Block	City	ZIP	Map#	CGS	Grid
Lavergne Av					
6800	LNWD	60077	2919	6W-8N	E2
6800	LNWD	60712	2919	6W-8N	E2
6800	SKOK	60077	2919	6W-8N	E1
7600	BRBK	60459	3211	6W-8S	E2
8600	OKLN	60453	3211	6W-9S	E4
8600	OKLN	60459	3211	6W-9S	E4
9200	SKOK	60077	2865	6W-11N	E7
10000	SKOK	60077	2811	6W-12N	E7
10000	WLMT	60077	2811	6W-12N	E7
10300	OKLN	60453	3275	6W-12S	E1
11000	ALSP	60453	3276	6W-12S	A3
11000	ALSP	60803	3276	6W-12S	A3
11000	OKLN	60453	3276	6W-12S	A3
13500	CTWD	60445	3348	6W-16S	A3
13800	BmnT	60445	3348	6W-16S	A3
14500	MDLN	60445	3348	6W-17S	A5
14500	MDLN	60452	3348	6W-17S	A5
14900	OKFT	60452	3348	6W-17S	A6
15700	OKFT	60452	3426	6W-18S	A1
18100	RchT	60478	3426	6W-21S	A7
N Lavergne Av					
10	CHCG	60644	3031	6W-0N	E4
10	NHLK	60164	3028	14W-2N	D1
500	NHLK	60164	2972	14W-2N	D6
700	CHCG	60651	3031	6W-0N	E3
1500	CHCG	60639	3031	6W-1N	E1
2000	CHCG	60639	2975	6W-2N	E6
4300	CHCG	60630	2975	6W-5N	E1
4300	CHCG	60641	2975	6W-5N	E1
4700	CHCG	60630	2919	6W-6N	E6
S Lavergne Av					
10	CHCG	60644	3031	6W-0S	E6
200	NHLK	60164	3028	14W-1N	D2
4400	CHCG	60638	3089	6W-4S	E7
6500	BDPK	60638	3149	6W-7S	E6
6500	CHCG	60638	3149	6W-7S	E6
11500	ALSP	60803	3276	6W-13S	A5
S Lavergne Dr					
1100	MPPT	60056	2861	17W-11N	C3
Lavergne Ln					
700	WnfT	60185	3080	28W-1S	E3
Lavergne St					
24200	PNFD	60585	3338	30W-15S	B2
Laverne Av					
1200	PKRG	60068	2864	10W-9N	A6
1300	PKRG	60068	2863	11W-9N	E6
N Laverne Av					
200	HLSD	60162	3028	14W-0S	D5
Laverne Ln					
400	BRTN	60010	2750	26W-20N	D1
7100	TYPK	60477	3425	8W-19S	A3
Laverne St					
200	ELBN	60119	3017	43W-2N	A2
Lavida Blvd					
10	JLET	60435	3417	27W-20S	C5
100	PnfT	60435	3417	27W-20S	C5
Lavigne Ln					
2000	NHBK	60062	2756	11W-16N	D7
Lavina Ct					
600	BGBK	60440	3204	24W-10S	D5
Lavina Dr					
500	BGBK	60440	3204	24W-10S	D5
N Lavinia Ln					
500	JLET	60435	3498	26W-23S	A3
La Vista Dr					
-	FmtT	60060	2589	21W-27N	D7
-	MDLN	60060	2589	21W-27N	D7
27300	FmtT	60060	2645	21W-27N	C1
27300	HNWD	60047	2645	21W-27N	C1
27300	HNWD	60060	2645	21W-27N	C1
27300	MDLN	60047	2645	21W-27N	C1
27300	MDLN	60060	2645	21W-27N	C1
27400	FmtT	60047	2645	21W-27N	C1
Lavoie Av					
500	ELGN	60120	2855	33W-10N	B5
Lawerence Rd					
1800	HRPK	60133	2967	27W-5N	C1
1800	WynT	60133	2967	27W-5N	C1
S Lawford Ct					
100	BMDL	60108	2969	23W-5N	A1
Lawhorn Ln					
-	WmTp	60481	3943	28W-39S	B1
32000	WmTp	60481	3853	28W-39S	B7
Lawler Av					
-	BmdT	60148	2970	21W-2N	A7
10	GNEN	60137	3025	21W-0S	D7
10	GNEN	60148	3025	21W-0S	D7
10	MltT	60148	3025	21W-0S	D7
10	MltT	60148	3083	21W-1S	E1
400	WLMT	60091	2811	6W-13N	D6
7600	BRBK	60459	3211	6W-8S	E1
8500	OKLN	60453	3211	6W-9S	E4
8500	OKLN	60459	3211	6W-9S	E4
9200	SKOK	60077	2865	6W-11N	E2
10300	OKLN	60453	3275	6W-12S	E2
13500	CTWD	60445	3348	6W-16S	A2
13700	BmnT	60445	3348	6W-16S	A3
N Lawler Av					
400	CHCG	60644	3031	6W-0N	E3
500	ADSN	60101	2969	21W-4N	E4
800	CHCG	60651	3031	6W-1N	E2
1500	CHCG	60639	3031	6W-1N	E1
2000	CHCG	60639	2975	6W-2N	E6
4000	CHCG	60641	2975	6W-5N	E1
4600	CHCG	60630	2919	6W-5N	E7
5400	CHCG	60646	2919	6W-6N	E5
S Lawler Av					
4400	CHCG	60638	3089	6W-4S	E7
5000	CHCG	60638	3149	6W-5S	E2
11100	ALSP	60453	3276	6W-13S	A3
11100	ALSP	60803	3276	6W-13S	A3
11100	OKLN	60453	3276	6W-13S	A3
11500	ALSP	60803	3275	6W-13S	E4
W Lawler Av					
7400	NLES	60714	2864	9W-9N	C6
Lawler Ct					
200	MltT	60148	3083	21W-2S	E3
Lawler Ln					
200	MltT	60148	3083	21W-2S	E3
Lawn Av					
3800	PvsT	60558	3086	14W-4S	D6
3800	WNSP	60558	3086	14W-4S	D6
4400	WNSP	60558	3146	14W-4S	D1
6200	HGKN	60525	3147	12W-7S	D5
W Lawn Av					
4400	WKGN	60085	2535	14W-33N	D4
14100	WrnT	60031	2535	14W-33N	D4
Lawn Cir					
900	WNSP	60558	3146	14W-6S	D4
Lawn Ct					
100	BFGV	60089	2701	16W-21N	D6
400	WKGN	60085	2537	10W-34N	A1
900	WNSP	60558	3146	14W-6S	D4
1300	MHRY	60050	2527	33W-33N	E3
1400	GYLK	60030	2532	21W-34N	D1
Lawn Ct					
2500	SMBG	60193	2857	26W-10N	E7
Lawn Dr					
5600	WNSP	60558	3146	14W-6S	D4
Lawn Ln					
300	DSPN	60016	2862	15W-11N	A3
Lawn Ter					
300	RDLK	60073	2531	23W-33N	E2
Lawndale					
-	ELGN	60120	2855	32W-10N	C6
Lawndale Av					
-	SKOK	60203	2866	4W-11N	C3
200	AURA	60506	3138	36W-6S	A5
400	WDSK	60098	2581	41W-30N	D1
2300	EVTN	60201	2866	4W-12N	C1
2600	EVTN	60201	2812	4W-13N	C7
2700	WLMT	60091	2812	4W-13N	C7
2700	WLMT	60201	2812	4W-13N	C7
4100	LYNS	60534	3088	10W-4S	B7
4500	LYNS	60534	3148	10W-5S	B1
4600	MCCK	60525	3148	10W-5S	B1
4600	MCCK	60534	3148	10W-5S	B1
5100	SMMT	60525	3148	10W-5S	B2
8000	SKOK	60076	2866	4W-10N	C5
14700	MDLN	60445	3348	4W-17S	D6
15400	MKHM	60428	3348	4W-18S	D7
16000	MKHM	60428	3426	4W-19S	D3
16600	CCHL	60429	3426	4W-19S	D3
16600	CCHL	60478	3426	4W-19S	D3
17900	BmnT	60430	3426	4W-21S	D7
17900	HLCT	60429	3426	4W-21S	D7
22400	RNPK	60471	3594	4W-27S	E5
N Lawndale Av					
400	CHCG	60624	3032	4W-0N	C3
1500	CHCG	60647	3032	4W-1N	C1
1500	CHCG	60651	3032	4W-1N	C1
1600	CHCG	60647	2976	4W-2N	C6
4100	CHCG	60618	2976	4W-5N	C1
4300	CHCG	60625	2976	4W-5N	C1
4400	CHCG	60625	2920	4W-5N	C7
6000	CHCG	60659	2920	4W-7N	C3
6300	LNWD	60659	2920	4W-7N	C3
7000	LNWD	60076	2920	4W-8N	C1
7000	LNWD	60712	2920	4W-8N	C1
7000	SKOK	60076	2920	4W-8N	C1
S Lawndale Av					
100	EMHT	60126	3028	15W-1N	A3
600	CHCG	60624	3032	4W-0S	C6
1200	CHCG	60623	3032	4W-1S	C7
1500	CHCG	60623	3090	4W-3S	C4
4700	CHCG	60632	3150	4W-6S	D3
5400	CHCG	60629	3150	4W-8S	D7
7500	CHCG	60652	3212	4W-8S	D1
8600	CHCG	60805	3212	4W-9S	D4
9200	ENGN	60805	3212	4W-11S	D6
9800	CHCG	60655	3212	4W-11S	D7
11500	CHCG	60655	3276	4W-13S	D4
11500	WthT	60655	3276	4W-13S	D4
11500	WthT	60803	3276	4W-13S	D4
12000	ALSP	60803	3276	4W-14S	D5
13300	RBBN	60472	3348	4W-16S	D3
W Lawndale Av					
7600	SMMT	60501	3148	9W-5S	C3
Lawndale Blvd					
10	FKFT	60423	3591	11W-25S	E1
Lawndale Ct					
10	FKFT	60423	3591	11W-25S	E1
Lawndale Dr					
10	MNSR	46321	3430		C7
1800	ALGN	60102	2747	36W-19N	B3
Lawndale St					
10	CTCY	60409	3430		C3
10	HMND	46324	3430	4E-19S	C3
100	EVTN	60201	2812	4W-13N	C7
100	WLMT	60091	2812	4W-13N	C7
100	WLMT	60201	2812	4W-13N	C7
Lawnmeadow Ln					
1100	NpvT	60540	3141	28W-7S	A6
1200	NPVL	60540	3141	28W-7S	A6
Lawnware Dr					
6100	MNGV	60053	2865	7W-10N	B5
Lawrence Av					
-	CHCG	60656	2917	11W-6N	D7
-	CTHL	60403	3498	24W-22S	D1
-	ELGN	60120	2854	34W-11N	E3
10	BmdT	60108	2912	25W-6N	A7
10	BmdT	60172	2912	25W-6N	A7
10	FXLK	60020	2473	27W-37N	A2
100	BMDL	60108	2912	23W-5N	E7
100	BMDL	60108	2913	23W-5N	A7
100	ELGN	60123	2854	35W-11N	C3
100	WDSK	60098	2581	41W-30N	D1
300	BMDL	60172	2912	25W-6N	A7
400	CHHT	60411	3595	2W-26S	D2
400	GNEN	60137	3025	23W-0N	A5
400	GYLK	60030	2533	20W-33N	A2
400	ROSL	60172	2913	22W-7N	B4
500	GRNE	60031	2479	12W-33N	A7
500	WkgT	60085	2479	12W-33N	A7
600	WKGN	60031	2479	12W-33N	A7
600	WKGN	60085	2479	12W-33N	A7
700	BmdT	60157	2913	22W-7N	B4
1000	LKFT	60045	2649	12W-24N	B7
1400	JLET	60435	3498	24W-22S	D1
1400	LKPT	60441	3419	22W-20S	C4
1500	ElgT	60123	2854	35W-11N	B3
2300	LktT	60441	3419	22W-20S	C5
3200	SCHT	60411	3596	1W-27S	A4
9400	SRPK	60176	2917	11W-6N	D7
E Lawrence Av					
800	WCHI	60185	3022	29W-0N	E5
W Lawrence Av					
-	CHCG	60640	2922	0W-6N	A6
-	SRPK	60176	2917	11W-6N	D7
700	CHCG	60640	2921	3W-6N	A6
1900	CHCG	60625	2921	2W-6N	B6
2700	CHCG	60625	2920	4W-6N	C7
3900	CHCG	60630	2920	4W-6N	B7
4600	CHCG	60630	2919	7W-6N	C7
6200	CHCG	60630	2919	7W-6N	A7
6200	HDHT	60630	2919	7W-6N	A7
6200	HDHT	60706	2919	7W-6N	A7
7200	HDHT	60706	2918	9W-6N	C7
7500	NRDG	60706	2918	9W-6N	C7
8300	NRDG	60656	2918	10W-6N	A7
8400	CHCG	60656	2918	10W-6N	A7
8400	CHCG	60706	2918	10W-6N	A7
8600	CHCG	60656	2917	11W-5N	E7
8600	CHCG	60706	2917	11W-5N	E7
8600	NRDG	60706	2917	11W-5N	E7
8700	NRDG	60656	2917	10W-6N	E7
Lawrence Cres					
1300	FSMR	60422	3507	3W-23S	B3
Lawrence Ct					
300	BmdT	60157	2913	21W-7N	D4
1300	AURA	60504	3201	32W-9S	D4
9400	SRPK	60176	2917	11W-5N	C7
Lawrence Ct					
10100	OKLN	60453	3211	6W-11S	D7
10100	OKLN	60453	3275	6W-11S	D1
15200	ODPK	60462	3346	10W-18S	B6
N Lawrence Ct					
36400	LkvT	60046	2475	21W-36N	C4
36400	RLKB	60046	2475	21W-36N	C4
36400	RLKB	60073	2475	21W-36N	C4
Lawrence Dr					
-	LKZH	60047	2698	24W-22N	C4
1100	MDLN	60060	2646	18W-26N	D3
3300	NPVL	60564	3266	28W-11S	E2
3400	WldT	60564	3266	28W-11S	E2
N Lawrence Dr					
36800	LkvT	60046	2475	21W-36N	C3
Lawrence Ln					
10	MTSN	60443	3506	6W-24S	A5
1400	NHBK	60062	2757	8W-17N	E6
1700	HDPK	60035	2757	9W-20N	D2
2500	HMWD	60430	3427	3W-21S	B6
3400	GNVW	60062	2809	12W-14N	B4
W Lawrence Ln					
2100	ANHT	60005	2861	17W-12N	B1
2100	ANHT	60056	2861	17W-12N	B1
2100	MPPT	60056	2861	17W-12N	B1
Lawrence Pkwy					
-	MHRY	60050	2528	33W-31N	A7
Lawrence Rd					
-	HRVD	60033	2405	51W-38N	D7
6600	CmgT	60033	2405	51W-38N	D6
Lawrence Rd CO-T50					
6600	HRVD	60033	2405	51W-38N	D6
8000	CmgT	60033	2405	51W-40N	C1
Lawrence St					
2800	NCHI	60088	2594	10W-30N	A1
E Lawrence St					
1900	CHHT	60411	3595	2W-26S	D2
S Lawrence St					
16100	PnfT	60544	3416	28W-19S	E3
W Lawrence St					
1900	CHHT	60411	3595	2W-26S	D2
Lawrence-Wilson Dr					
-	CHCG	60640	2922	0W-6N	A6
Lawson Blvd					
1200	GRNE	60031	2478	15W-35N	A6
2100	GRNE	60031	2477	16W-36N	E5
W Lawson Dr					
24000	CNHN	60410	3584	30W-28S	C6
24000	CNHN	60436	3584	30W-28S	C6
24000	CnhT	60410	3584	30W-28S	C6
Lawson Ln					
10	DXMR	60426	3349	2W-16S	D4
Lawson Rd					
-	AntT	60002	2356	28W-42N	A5
-	FXLK	60002	2356	28W-42N	A5
1900	SMBG	60194	2858	25W-11N	A4
3600	GNVW	60025	2809	10W-15N	E2
3600	GNVW	60062	2809	10W-15N	E2
Lawton Av					
300	JLET	60436	3498	24W-25S	E7
9500	OKLN	60453	3211	6W-11S	D6
Lawton Ln					
100	BGBK	60440	3269	22W-12S	D2
Lawton Rd					
10	RVSD	60546	3088	9W-3S	D5
300	BRWN	60402	3088	9W-3S	D5
300	RVSD	60402	3088	9W-3S	D5
Layne Ct					
1000	SRWD	60404	3496	30W-23S	B4
Lazy Ln					
6500	MONE	60449	3682	8W-31S	C5
W Lazy Acre Rd					
18600	OMCK	60083	2476	18W-37N	E3
18600	WrnT	60046	2476	18W-37N	E3
Lazy Hollow Ct					
1300	NPVL	60565	3204	24W-8S	E2
Lea Dr					
300	GnvT	60134	3019	38W-0N	A5
Lea Ln					
1300	KLDR	60047	2699	21W-22N	C4
1300	LKZH	60047	2699	21W-22N	C4
Lea Rd					
10	DRPK	60010	2752	23W-20N	A1
Leabrook Ct					
1800	NPVL	60565	3204	25W-9S	B4
Leabrook Ln					
1500	WHTN	60187	3081	26W-1S	E2
1500	WHTN	60187	3082	26W-1S	A2
Leabrook Cove					
1500	WHTN	60187	3081	26W-1S	E2
Leach Av					
100	JLET	60432	3499	22W-23S	D4
100	JltT	60432	3499	22W-23S	D4
Leach Dr					
2500	NPVL	60564	3203	28W-10S	A6
S Leach Dr					
15900	HmrT	60491	3420	18W-19S	E2
W Leach Dr					
23200	PnfT	60586	3416	29W-19S	E3
N Leader Av					
5900	CHCG	60646	2919	6W-7N	D4
Leadville Ct					
-	GLBT	60136	2799	38W-14N	A5
Leadville Ln					
10	GLBT	60136	2799	38W-14N	A5
Leaf Ct					
700	BRLT	60103	2910	29W-6N	D6
Leah Dr					
900	AlqT	60013	2642	30W-25N	B5
Leah Ln					
300	DrrT	60098	2581	40W-30N	E1
300	WDSK	60098	2581	40W-30N	E1
600	WDSK	60098	2582	40W-30N	A1
Leahy Cir					
400	DSPN	60016	2862	15W-11N	B3
Leahy Cir E					
500	DSPN	60016	2862	15W-11N	B4
Leahy Rd					
100	OKTR	60181	3085	17W-1S	C1
Leamington Av					
500	GNVW	60025	2811	6W-13N	D6
500	WLMT	60091	2811	6W-13N	D6
7600	BRBK	60459	3211	6W-8S	E2
8500	OKLN	60453	3211	6W-9S	E4
8500	OKLN	60459	3211	6W-9S	E4
N Leamington Av					
100	CHCG	60644	3031	6W-0N	E4
700	CHCG	60651	3031	6W-0N	E3
1500	CHCG	60639	3031	6W-1N	D1
2000	CHCG	60639	2975	6W-2N	D6
4000	CHCG	60641	2975	6W-5N	D1
5200	CHCG	60630	2919	6W-6N	D5
S Leamington Av					
10	CHCG	60644	3031	6W-0S	E5
4400	CHCG	60638	3089	6W-4S	E7
4600	CHCG	60638	3149	6W-5S	E1
S Leamington Av					
7100	BDPK	60638	3149	6W-8S	E7
11100	ALSP	60453	3275	6W-13S	E3
11100	ALSP	60803	3275	6W-13S	E3
11100	OKLN	60453	3275	6W-13S	E3
Leamington Ct					
400	NPVL	60565	3204	25W-9S	A4
Leamington Dr					
-	BmnT	60445	3347	6W-16S	E4
-	MDLN	60445	3347	6W-16S	E4
E Leamington Dr					
13900	BmnT	60445	3347	6W-16S	E3
W Leamington Dr					
13900	BmnT	60445	3347	6W-16S	E3
13900	CTWD	60445	3347	6W-16S	E3
Leamington St					
9400	SKOK	60077	2865	6W-11N	E2
Leana Av					
1200	JltT	60433	3499	22W-24S	C6
Leanne Ct					
2700	GNVW	60025	2809	11W-15N	D2
2800	GNVW	60062	2809	11W-15N	D2
13900	NlxT	60448	3501	17W-22S	C1
Leanne Ln					
18300	NlxT	60448	3501	17W-22S	D1
Lear Ct					
400	SMBG	60194	2857	26W-11N	E4
400	SMWD	60107	2857	26W-11N	E4
Lear Ln					
800	NLNX	60451	3501	18W-25S	A7
Lear St					
5100	MchT	60097	2469	36W-37N	E2
Leask Ln					
100	LslT	60532	3082	24W-4S	D7
200	LSLE	60532	3082	24W-4S	D7
300	MltT	60187	3082	24W-3S	D6
300	WHTN	60187	3082	24W-3S	D6
500	LSLE	60187	3082	24W-3S	D6
500	WHTN	60532	3082	24W-3S	D6
600	MltT	60532	3082	24W-3S	D6
Leather Leaf Ct					
3600	HFET	60192	2804	25W-14N	A4
Leather Leaf Ln					
3600	HFET	60192	2804	25W-14N	A4
N Leavenworth Av					
5500	CHCG	60630	2919	6W-6N	D5
Leavitt Av					
1000	FSMR	60422	3507	3W-23S	B2
14100	DXMR	60406	3349	2W-17S	C4
14300	DXMR	60426	3349	2W-17S	C5
14600	HRVY	60426	3349	2W-17S	C6
15900	MKHM	60428	3427	2W-19S	C1
15900	ThtT	60428	3427	2W-19S	C1
N Leavitt Av					
3000	CHCG	60618	2977	2W-3N	B4
N Leavitt St					
10	CHCG	60612	3033	2W-0N	B4
700	CHCG	60622	3033	2W-0N	B3
1500	CHCG	60647	3033	2W-1N	B1
1600	CHCG	60647	2977	2W-2N	B7
2600	CHCG	60618	2977	2W-3N	B4
4400	CHCG	60625	2921	2W-5N	B7
6100	CHCG	60659	2921	2W-7N	B3
6300	CHCG	60645	2921	2W-7N	B3
S Leavitt St					
-	CHCG	60609	3151	2W-5S	B1
10	CHCG	60612	3033	2W-0S	B6
1200	CHCG	60608	3033	2W-1S	B7
1700	CHCG	60608	3091	2W-2S	B3
3400	CHCG	60609	3091	2W-3S	B5
8800	CHCG	60620	3213	2W-11S	B6
9400	CHCG	60643	3213	2W-11S	B6
10200	CHCG	60643	3277	2W-12S	C1
Leaward					
10	LKMR	60051	2529	28W-33N	E4
Leawood Ct					
1100	JLET	60431	3585	28W-25S	B1
1200	ELGN	60120	2855	32W-11N	D3
1300	NPVL	60564	3203	28W-10S	A7
2800	WDRG	60517	3205	22W-9S	D3
Leawood Dr					
10	ROSL	60172	2912	24W-7N	D5
800	JLET	60431	3497	28W-25S	B7
900	JLET	60431	3585	28W-25S	B1
1000	ELGN	60120	2855	32W-11N	D3
Leawood Ln					
8000	WDRG	60517	3205	22W-9S	C3
8100	BGBK	60440	3205	22W-9S	D4
8100	BGBK	60517	3205	22W-9S	D4
Lebanon Av					
3000	ZION	60099	2421	11W-39N	E5
3200	BHPK	60099	2421	11W-39N	D5
Lebanon St					
600	AURA	60505	3200	35W-9S	A3
1100	MTGY	60505	3200	35W-9S	A4
1100	MTGY	60538	3200	35W-9S	A4
Lebaron Ct					
-	BbyT	60134	3018	39W-0N	E5
2600	GNVA	60134	3019	37W-0N	C5
Le Baron St					
10	PKCY	60085	2536	12W-33N	B1
10	WKGN	60085	2536	12W-33N	B1
Lechner Dr					
-	CrlT	60180	2635	46W-25N	E5
Lechner Ln					
2300	DSPN	60016	2863	12W-11N	C3
2300	MaiT	60016	2863	12W-11N	C3
Leiconi Ct					
1200	GNVA	60134	3020	34W-1N	E3
Leckrone Dr					
2400	JLET	60586	3415	32W-20S	D6
Le Claire Av					
6800	LNWD	60077	2919	6W-8N	D2
6800	LNWD	60712	2919	6W-8N	D2
6800	SKOK	60077	2919	6W-8N	D1
9400	SKOK	60077	2865	6W-11N	E2
13300	CTWD	60445	3347	6W-16S	E3
13700	BmnT	60445	3347	6W-16S	E3
14700	MDLN	60452	3348	6W-17S	A5
14800	OKFT	60452	3348	6W-18S	A7
15700	OKFT	60452	3426	6W-19S	A1
16900	BmnT	60452	3426	6W-20S	A4
16900	BmnT	60477	3426	6W-20S	A4
17000	OKFT	60477	3426	6W-20S	A4
18300	BmnT	60478	3426	6W-22S	A7
18300	CCHL	60478	3506	6W-22S	A1
18300	RchT	60478	3426	6W-22S	A7
18300	RchT	60478	3506	6W-22S	A1
Leclaire Av					
-	WLMT	60025	2811	6W-13N	D6
300	GNVW	60025	2811	6W-13N	D6
300	GNVW	60091	2811	6W-13N	D7
300	WLMT	60091	2811	6W-13N	D6
8300	BRBK	60459	3211	6W-9S	E3
8500	OKLN	60453	3211	6W-9S	E4
8500	OKLN	60459	3211	6W-9S	E4
Leclaire Av					
10500	OKLN	60453	3275	6W-12S	E2
13900	BmnT	60445	3348	6W-16S	A3
13900	CTWD	60445	3348	6W-16S	A3
N Leclaire Av					
10	CHCG	60644	3031	6W-0N	E4
700	CHCG	60651	3031	6W-0N	E3
1600	CHCG	60639	3031	6W-2N	E1
2000	CHCG	60639	2975	6W-2N	E6
2700	CHCG	60641	2975	6W-3N	E5
4800	CHCG	60630	2919	6W-6N	E6
S Leclaire Av					
4400	CHCG	60638	3089	6W-4S	E7
6300	CHCG	60638	3149	6W-7S	E5
6700	BDPK	60638	3149	6W-7S	E6
11100	ALSP	60453	3275	6W-13S	E3
11100	ALSP	60803	3275	6W-13S	E3
11100	OKLN	60453	3275	6W-13S	E3
Ledgestone Ct					
2800	NPVL	60564	3202	29W-10S	C7
Ledgestone Wy					
22300	FKFT	60423	3590	14W-27S	D4
Ledochowski St					
500	LMNT	60439	3270	19W-14S	E6
Lee Av					
10	LIHL	60156	2693	35W-22N	E4
1200	MLPK	60160	3029	10W-1N	E2
2800	WKGN	60085	2479	12W-35N	C6
3400	WkgT	60031	2479	13W-35N	A6
3400	WkgT	60085	2479	13W-35N	A6
3500	GRNE	60031	2479	13W-35N	A6
3700	RNPK	60471	3594	4W-27S	D4
4000	DRGV	60515	3084	20W-4S	A7
4200	GRNE	60031	2478	14W-35N	D6
5600	DGvT	60515	3144	20W-6S	A4
5600	DGvT	60516	3144	20W-6S	A4
5600	DRGV	60515	3144	20W-6S	A4
16400	ODPK	60467	3423	13W-19S	A3
N Lee Av					
38000	AntT	60081	2414	28W-38N	E7
38000	AntT	60081	2472	28W-38N	D1
38000	GrtT	60081	2472	28W-38N	D1
W Lee Av					
12600	WKGN	60085	2479	12W-35N	B6
12900	GRNE	60031	2479	12W-35N	A6
12900	WkgT	60031	2479	12W-35N	A6
12900	WkgT	60085	2479	12W-35N	A6
N Lee Blvd					
-	BKLY	60162	3028	13W-0N	D4
600	HLSD	60162	3028	13W-0N	D4
700	HLSD	60163	3028	13W-0N	D4
1400	BKLY	60163	3028	13W-0N	D4
W Lee Cir					
18300	WrnT	60031	2477	18W-36N	A4
Lee Ct					
-	SKOK	60077	2865	6W-10N	D4
-	WNFD	60190	3023	27W-0S	C6
10	GNWD	60425	3508	1W-22S	A1
10	HMWD	60430	3508	1W-22S	A1
300	CLLK	60014	2639	35W-24N	E6
800	SMWD	60107	2911	27W-9N	C1
900	BFGV	60089	2700	18W-20N	E7
4700	RNPK	60471	3594	5W-26S	B3
E Lee Ct					
23100	PNFD	60544	3416	28W-19S	E2
23100	PnfT	60544	3416	28W-19S	E2
N Lee Ct					
1700	PLTN	60074	2753	20W-18N	A4
Lee Dr					
300	CLLK	60014	2639	36W-24N	E6
W Lee Dr					
22200	AntT	60002	2417	22W-40N	C3
Lee Ln					
-	EGvT	60007	2861	16W-9N	D7
-	EGVV	60007	2861	16W-9N	D7
100	BGBK	60440	3269	23W-11S	A1
1400	BtnT	60081	2414	30W-40N	A3
W Lee Ln					
16200	VrnT	60069	2701	16W-23N	D2
S Lee Pkwy					
1800	CHCG	60616	3092	0W-1S	B1
W Lee Pl					
2000	CHCG	60612	3033	2W-0N	B3
2000	CHCG	60622	3033	2W-0N	B3
Lee Rd					
10	HDPK	60035	2757	9W-18N	D2
10	NHBK	60062	2757	9W-18N	D3
10	WnfT	60185	3022	31W-1N	A2
200	WCHI	60185	3022	29W-1N	D2
S Lee Rd					
11500	ALSP	60803	3276	5W-13S	A4
Lee St					
-	BRLT	60103	2911	28W-7N	A6
-	SRWD	60404	3584	30W-25S	B1
-	WynT	60103	2911	28W-7N	A6
100	MHTN	60442	3678	18W-31S	A5
200	EVTN	60202	2867	2W-10N	C4
200	PKFT	60466	3595	3W-25S	A1
500	GNEN	60137	3025	22W-0N	C5
700	EGVV	60007	2861	17W-10N	B5
1100	WLNG	60090	2754	15W-17N	E5
1700	DSPN	60018	2862	13W-9N	E7
1700	EVTN	60202	2866	3W-10N	E4
2200	DSPN	60018	2916	13W-9N	E1
2500	DRGV	60516	3143	21W-6S	E5
2500	WDRG	60516	3143	21W-6S	E5
2500	WDRG	60517	3143	21W-6S	D5
2900	FNPK	60131	2972	13W-3N	E5
2900	FNPK	60164	2972	13W-3N	E5
2900	LydT	60131	2972	13W-3N	E5
2900	LydT	60164	2972	13W-3N	E5
3300	SKOK	60076	2866	5W-10N	B4
4800	SKOK	60076	2865	6W-10N	E4
4900	SKOK	60077	2865	6W-10N	D4
5600	MNGV	60053	2865	7W-10N	C4
16700	ODPK	60467	3423	13W-20S	A3
18600	CCHL	60478	3506	5W-22S	B1
E Lee St					
10	PLNO	60545	3259	47W-13S	D6
N Lee St					
200	MPPT	60056	2808	13W-13N	E6
200	WhlT	60056	2808	13W-13N	E6
W Lee St					
10	PLNO	60545	3259	47W-13S	C6
3700	MHRY	60050	2528	32W-32N	B5
7200	NLES	60714	2864	9W-10N	D4
7800	MaiT	60714	2864	9W-10N	C4
Lee Ann Ln					
100	WDSK	60098	2581	41W-30N	C2
Leech Rd					
8000	CrlT	60180	2635	45W-24N	E7
Leeds Ct					
10	LNSH	60045	2702	13W-23N	D2
200	LKBF	60044	2593	11W-29N	D5
300	NPVL	60565	3204	25W-9S	A4
1300	WHTN	60187	3082	23W-3S	E5

Block	City	ZIP	Map#	CGS	Grid
Leeds Ct					
1700	MDLN	60060	2647	17W-25N	B4
Leeds Dr					
200	BNHL	60010	2749	28W-18N	E3
Leeds Ln					
1200	EGVV	60007	2914	19W-8N	C3
Leeds Rd					
5800	HFET	60192	2855	31W-12N	E1
5800	HFET	60192	2856	31W-12N	A1
Leeds Pass					
400	SMBG	60194	2858	25W-11N	C4
Leesburg Ct					
600	NPVL	60540	3142	25W-7S	B7
N Leeside St					
5100	MchT	60050	2472	29W-37N	C2
N Leesley Ct					
30800	LbvT	60048	2590	18W-30N	D1
Leesley Rd					
700	RVSD	60546	3088	9W-2S	D4
Leetrim Ct					
19400	MKNA	60448	3503	13W-23S	B3
Leeward Ct					
1400	GYLK	60030	2532	21W-34N	D1
Leeward Ln					
-	PGGV	60140	2798	41W-14N	A5
2000	HRPK	60133	2967	27W-4N	C3
Le Fevre Ln					
-	PLTN	60067	2752	21W-16N	D6
Legacy Blvd					
-	SCRL	60174	3021	33W-2N	A1
Legacy Ct					
-	RLKP	60030	2589	22W-30N	A1
Legacy Dr					
800	SEGN	60177	2907	37W-7N	C6
2300	AURA	60502	3139	32W-5S	B3
3300	JLET	60435	3417	27W-19S	C3
3300	JLET	60441	3417	27W-19S	C3
11500	PNFD	60585	3266	30W-13S	A5
Legacy Rdg					
900	ALGN	60102	2746	37W-20N	B1
Legacy Pointe Blvd					
-	JLET	60586	3415	32W-21S	C6
-	JLET	60586	3495	32W-22S	D1
-	TroT	60404	3495	32W-22S	D2
1500	JLET	60431	3495	32W-22S	C2
Legacy Pointe Ct					
-	JLET	60431	3495	32W-22S	C2
Legacy Pointe Dr					
-	JLET	60586	3415	32W-21S	C7
Legend Ct					
4200	AURA	60564	3202	30W-9S	B5
Legend Ln					
-	HFET	60169	2858	25W-12N	A2
-	MchT	60050	2527	35W-32N	B5
400	MHRY	60050	2527	35W-32N	B5
8200	ODPK	60462	3346	10W-16S	B2
Legends Ct					
2300	RVWD	60015	2756	13W-20N	A1
Legends Dr					
-	MltT	60555	3081	26W-2S	E4
600	CLSM	60188	2968	25W-3N	A6
1900	MltT	60187	3081	26W-2S	E4
1900	WHTN	60187	3081	26W-2S	E4
Legends Ln					
-	BNVL	60106	2972	15W-4N	B4
N Legett Av					
5900	CHCG	60646	2919	6W-7N	E3
Legion Ct					
500	WCDA	60084	2644	25W-26N	A2
500	WcnT	60084	2644	25W-26N	A2
S Legion Ct					
16000	PnfT	60586	3416	30W-19S	A2
Legion Dr					
200	ALGN	60102	2694	34W-20N	D7
900	CTCY	60409	3352	4E-18S	C7
900	CTCY	60409	3430	4E-18S	C1
Legion Ln					
10	BtvT	60539	3077	36W-2S	E5
Legion Rd					
9800	KdlT	60560	3333	43W-17S	C7
9800	YKVL	60560	3333	42W-17S	C6
11000	KdlT	60560	3332	44W-17S	E7
Legion St					
10	MYWD	60153	3030	10W-0S	A5
700	MYWD	60153	3029	10W-0S	E5
Legion Lake Ct					
21200	LktT	60403	3417	26W-19S	E4
Legrande Av					
900	AURA	60506	3137	37W-6S	D5
Le Grande Blvd					
10	AURA	60506	3137	37W-7S	C7
200	AURA	60506	3199	37W-7S	D1
400	AraT	60506	3199	37W-7S	C1
Lehigh Av					
-	MNGV	60077	2865	7W-9N	B6
-	NLES	60077	2865	7W-9N	B6
-	NLES	60714	2865	7W-9N	B6
-	SKOK	60077	2865	7W-9N	B6
1000	GNVW	60025	2810	9W-14N	D5
2600	GNVW	60062	2810	9W-15N	B2
2700	NHBK	60062	2810	9W-15N	B2
8800	MNGV	60053	2865	8W-11N	A3
N Lehigh Av					
6100	CHCG	60646	2919	7W-8N	C1
7000	NLES	60714	2919	7W-8N	C1
7200	CHCG	60646	2865	7W-9N	C7
7200	CHCG	60714	2865	7W-9N	C7
7200	NLES	60714	2865	7W-9N	B7
7600	NLES	60077	2865	7W-9N	B7
7600	SKOK	60077	2865	7W-9N	B7
7900	MNGV	60053	2865	7W-9N	B7
7900	MNGV	60077	2865	7W-9N	B7
Lehigh Cir					
900	NPVL	60565	3204	25W-10S	C6
Lehigh Ct					
10	ALGN	60102	2695	32W-21N	A6
S Lehigh Dr					
14100	PnfT	60544	3339	27W-16S	C4
Lehigh Ln					
200	BMDL	60108	2968	23W-5N	E2
700	BFGV	60089	2754	17W-17N	B5
Lehigh St					
13300	HTLY	60142	2744	42W-20N	B1
Lehman Av					
500	JLET	60433	3499	23W-24S	B6
500	JltT	60433	3499	23W-24S	B6
Lehman Cross					
-	BtlT	60543	3262	40W-12S	C2
Lehman Dr					
-	ELGN	60120	2855	31W-10N	E5
2300	WCHI	60185	2965	32W-4N	C4
2600	WynT	60185	2965	32W-4N	B5
Lehman St					
1700	ALGN	60102	2695	33W-21N	A6
W Lehmann Blvd					
25200	LkvT	60046	2474	25W-37N	A1
N Lehmann Ct					
2600	CHCG	60614	2978	0W-3N	A5
2700	CHCG	60657	2978	0W-3N	A4
Lehmer St					
7200	FTPK	60130	3030	9W-0S	D5
Lehnertz Av					
700	AURA	60505	3138	34W-6S	D5
N Leibert St					
26700	WcnT	60084	2642	28W-26N	E2
Leicester Ct					
300	BGBK	60440	3205	22W-11S	D7
1100	WHTN	60187	3082	23W-1S	E2
Leicester Rd					
10	MNSR	46321	3510		C3
200	KLWH	60043	2812	3W-14N	D4
700	EGVV	60007	2914	19W-9N	C1
Leigh Ct					
-	FKFT	60423	3590	14W-26S	D2
Leigh St					
700	AraT	60506	3199	38W-8S	A2
Leighlin Ln					
-	MhtT	60442	3677	20W-31S	D5
Leighlinbridge Rd					
-	MhtT	60442	3677	20W-30S	D4
Leighton Rd					
1200	MDLN	60060	2647	17W-26N	A3
1200	MDLN	60061	2647	17W-26N	A3
1200	VNHL	60060	2647	17W-26N	A3
1200	VNHL	60061	2647	17W-26N	A3
Leighton Tower					
1400	MDLN	60060	2647	17W-26N	A4
Leila Dr					
18700	FftT	60448	3502	14W-22S	D2
Leims Rd					
10	PKFT	60466	3595	3W-27S	B4
Leinster Dr					
1200	LMNT	60439	3342	19W-15S	C1
W Leisure Av					
-	AntT	60081	2415	28W-39N	A5
-	FXLK	60020	2415	28W-39N	A5
-	FXLK	60081	2415	28W-39N	A5
Leisure Dr					
100	FXLK	60020	2473	27W-37N	B1
Leisure Ln					
10	OswT	60543	3264	35W-14S	B7
Leisure St					
200	BtlT	60560	3261	43W-14S	C7
200	YKVL	60560	3261	43W-14S	C7
E Leisure Village Av					
7300	FXLK	60020	2414	28W-39N	E6
7500	FXLK	60020	2415	27W-39N	B5
Leitch Av					
200	LGNG	60525	3087	13W-4S	A7
200	LGNG	60525	3147	13W-4S	A1
5500	CTSD	60525	3147	13W-6S	A4
5500	LynT	60525	3147	13W-6S	A4
S Leitch Av					
-	LGNG	60525	3087	13W-4S	A7
Leith Av					
300	WKGN	60085	2536	11W-34N	D1
400	WKGN	60085	2479	11W-34N	D7
Leith Ct					
900	ELGN	60124	2853	37W-10N	D5
Leith Wy					
200	CRY	60013	2695	31W-23N	D2
Le Jardin Ct					
10	BFGV	60089	2754	16W-20N	E2
Le Jeune Av					
100	LKPT	60441	3419	21W-19S	E2
100	LktT	60441	3419	21W-19S	E2
Lektorich Ln					
2700	JLET	60586	3415	32W-20S	D5
Lela Ct					
1000	SMBG	60193	2858	24W-10N	C6
Lela Ln					
10	SMBG	60193	2858	24W-10N	C6
300	BRLT	60103	2910	29W-8N	D2
Leland Av					
-	HDHT	60706	2918	9W-5N	C7
-	NRDG	60706	2918	9W-5N	C7
1700	EVTN	60201	2866	3W-11N	D2
4000	LYNS	60534	3088	10W-4S	B6
9800	SRPK	60176	2917	12W-5N	B7
W Leland Av					
700	CHCG	60640	2921	1W-5N	E7
1900	CHCG	60625	2921	2W-5N	B7
2800	CHCG	60625	2920	3W-5N	D7
4100	CHCG	60630	2920	5W-5N	A7
5600	CHCG	60630	2919	7W-5N	C7
6800	HDHT	60706	2918	8W-5N	E7
8200	NRDG	60706	2918	10W-5N	A7
8400	CHCG	60656	2918	10W-5N	A7
8400	NRDG	60656	2918	10W-5N	A7
8600	CHCG	60656	2917	10W-5N	E7
11000	BHPK	60099	2421	11W-38N	E6
26000	AntT	60002	2415	26W-38N	E6
26000	LkvT	60002	2415	26W-38N	E6
Leland Ct					
100	BNVL	60106	2915	16W-6N	E7
600	LKFT	60045	2649	12W-25N	B6
Leland Ct N					
800	ElgT	60124	2853	38W-9N	B7
Leland Ct S					
800	ElgT	60124	2853	38W-9N	A7
Leland Ln					
-	HTLY	60142	2692	39W-20N	D7
11600	HTLY	60142	2745	39W-20N	D1
Lem Dr					
200	RDLK	60073	2531	24W-34N	D1
N Le Mai Av					
6200	CHCG	60646	2919	6W-7N	D3
6400	LNWD	60646	2919	6W-8N	D2
6500	LNWD	60712	2919	6W-8N	E2
6700	LNWD	60077	2919	6W-8N	E2
6700	LNWD	60077	2919	6W-8N	E2
Lemans Dr					
10	WLNG	60090	2808	14W-15N	B2
Lemar Av					
1800	EVTN	60201	2866	3W-11N	E2
Lembcke Rd					
19500	HtdT	60033	2464	48W-35N	E6
19700	DhmT	60033	2464	50W-35N	B6
Lemon Ln					
5200	HRPK	60133	2911	27W-6N	C7
N Lemon Rd					
28500	FmtT	60060	2590	20W-28N	A5
28500	MDLN	60060	2590	20W-28N	A5
N Lemont Av					
6100	CHCG	60646	2919	5W-7N	E3
6200	CHCG	60646	2920	5W-7N	A3
6300	CHCG	60712	2920	5W-7N	A3
6300	LNWD	60646	2920	5W-7N	A3
6300	LNWD	60712	2920	5W-7N	A3
Lemont Rd					
-	HmrT	60441	3342	19W-17S	D5
-	LMNT	60439	3270	19W-13S	D4
10	DGvT	60439	3270	19W-12S	C1
10	WDRG	60439	3270	19W-12S	D3
10	WDRG	60517	3270	19W-12S	D3
200	DGvT	60439	3206	19W-11S	C7
200	DGvT	60517	3270	19W-12S	D3
200	DRN	60439	3206	19W-11S	C7
700	DGvT	60516	3206	20W-9S	C4
700	DGvT	60561	3206	20W-9S	C4
700	DRN	60516	3206	20W-9S	C4
700	DRN	60561	3206	20W-9S	C4
7200	DRGV	60516	3206	20W-8S	C2
7300	WDRG	60516	3206	20W-8S	C2
7500	DRN	60517	3206	19W-8S	C2
7500	WDRG	60517	3206	19W-8S	C2
7500	WDRG	60561	3206	19W-8S	C2
7600	DGvT	60517	3206	19W-8S	C2
13500	HMGN	60439	3342	19W-16S	D3
13500	HMGN	60491	3342	19W-17S	D5
13500	LMNT	60439	3342	19W-16S	D3
13900	HMGN	60441	3342	19W-16S	D4
14400	HmrT	60491	3342	19W-17S	D5
Lemont Rd CO-9					
10	DGvT	60439	3270	19W-12S	C1
10	WDRG	60439	3270	19W-12S	D3
10	WDRG	60517	3270	19W-12S	D3
200	DGvT	60439	3206	19W-11S	C7
200	DGvT	60517	3270	19W-12S	D3
200	DRN	60439	3206	19W-11S	C7
500	LMNT	60439	3270	19W-12S	C3
700	DGvT	60516	3206	20W-9S	C4
700	DGvT	60561	3206	20W-9S	C4
700	DRN	60516	3206	20W-9S	C4
700	DRN	60561	3206	20W-9S	C4
7200	DRGV	60516	3206	20W-8S	C2
7300	WDRG	60516	3206	20W-8S	C2
7500	DRN	60517	3206	19W-8S	C2
7500	WDRG	60517	3206	19W-8S	C2
7500	WDRG	60561	3206	19W-8S	C2
7600	DGvT	60517	3206	19W-8S	C2
Lemont Rd CO-31					
700	DGvT	60516	3206	20W-9S	C4
700	DGvT	60561	3206	20W-9S	C4
700	DRN	60516	3206	20W-9S	C4
700	DRN	60561	3206	20W-9S	C4
8300	DGvT	60517	3206	20W-9S	C3
8300	DRN	60517	3206	20W-9S	C3
Lemont St					
100	LMNT	60439	3270	19W-13S	D5
Lemorr Av					
1100	JLET	60435	3498	25W-22S	B2
N Lemorr Av					
900	JLET	60435	3498	25W-22S	B3
W Lemorr Av					
1400	JLET	60435	3498	25W-22S	B2
Lemoyne Av					
400	RMVL	60446	3340	25W-15S	A2
500	LMBD	60148	3026	19W-1N	D1
E Le Moyne Av					
10	LMBD	60148	3026	19W-1N	C1
W Le Moyne Av					
-	NHLK	60164	3029	13W-1N	A1
-	NHLK	60165	3029	13W-1N	A1
10	LMBD	60148	3026	20W-1N	B1
3200	SNPK	60165	3029	12W-1N	A1
Le Moyne Ct					
-	MLPK	60160	3029	11W-1N	D1
W Le Moyne Dr					
2800	CHCG	60622	3032	3W-1N	E1
Le Moyne Pkwy					
-	OKPK	60302	3030	8W-1N	E1
-	OKPK	60305	3030	8W-1N	D1
-	RVFT	60305	3030	8W-1N	D1
10	CHCG	60651	3031	7W-1N	B1
10	OKPK	60302	3031	8W-1N	A1
Le Moyne St					
7200	OKPK	60302	3030	9W-1N	C1
7200	OKPK	60305	3030	9W-1N	C1
7200	RVFT	60305	3030	9W-1N	C1
E Le Moyne St					
10	NHLK	60164	3028	13W-1N	D1
300	NHLK	60164	3029	13W-1N	A1
400	NHLK	60165	3029	13W-1N	A1
400	SNPK	60165	3029	13W-1N	A1
W Le Moyne St					
1400	MLPK	60160	3029	11W-1N	D1
1600	CHCG	60622	3033	2W-1N	C1
2700	CHCG	60622	3032	5W-1N	A1
3200	CHCG	60651	3032	5W-1N	B1
4800	CHCG	60651	3031	7W-1N	C1
5900	OKPK	60302	3031	7W-1N	B1
Leness Ln					
1900	CTHL	60403	3418	26W-21S	A7
Lengl Dr					
10	SMBG	60193	2859	23W-10N	A6
Lenham Rd					
24400	PNFD	60585	3338	30W-15S	B3
Lenhertz Av					
1100	AURA	60505	3138	34W-6S	D5
Lenhertz Cir					
1100	AURA	60505	3138	34W-6S	E5
Lenhi Ct					
6800	JLET	60586	3415	32W-21S	C6
Lennan Brook Ln					
17900	ODPK	60467	3422	14W-21S	C6
Lennon Ct					
20500	FKFT	60423	3504	10W-24S	B6
Lennon Dr					
20500	FKFT	60423	3504	10W-24S	B6
Lennox Ct					
4600	JLET	60431	3496	29W-22S	D2
Lennox Rd					
200	WnfT	60187	3081	27W-2S	C3
Lennoxshire Dr					
1200	ELGN	60123	2800	35W-13N	B7
N Lenora St					
42800	AntT	60002	2357	25W-42N	B5
Lenore Ln					
-	ALGN	60102	2746	36W-20N	D1
18300	OrlT	60487	3423	11W-22S	E7
18300	TYPK	60487	3423	11W-22S	E7
N Lenore St					
700	ADSN	60101	2970	18W-4N	E3
Lenox Av					
600	WKGN	60085	2537	10W-33N	A4
700	BGBK	60490	3267	26W-13S	E6
900	NCHI	60064	2537	10W-33N	A4
N Lenox Av					
6100	CHCG	60646	2919	6W-7N	E3
6300	LNWD	60646	2919	6W-7N	D3
6300	LNWD	60712	2919	6W-7N	D3
Lenox Cir					
3700	MTGY	60538	3198	40W-10S	C7
Lenox Ct					
10	LMNT	60439	3270	18W-13S	E5
10	LMNT	60439	3271	17W-13S	B5
10	SEGN	60177	2908	35W-7N	B5
100	CLSM	60188	3024	23W-1N	E2
100	SMBG	60193	2857	26W-10N	E6
200	AvnT	60030	2475	21W-34N	D7
200	GYLK	60030	2475	21W-34N	D7
400	MTGY	60543	3263	37W-11S	B2
400	OSWG	60543	3263	37W-11S	B2
1400	WLNG	60090	2754	16W-18N	D4
1500	BRLT	60103	2967	28W-5N	B2
6000	LslT	60532	3143	22W-6S	B5
7200	LGGV	60047	2646	18W-25N	E5
7300	GRNE	60031	2477	18W-35N	A5
10200	HTLY	60142	2692	39W-21N	B5
N Lenox Ct					
2300	RLKB	60073	2475	22W-36N	C4
Lenox Dr					
400	MTGY	60543	3263	38W-11S	B2
400	OSWG	60543	3263	38W-11S	B2
Lenox Ln					
-	LMNT	60439	3271	18W-13S	A5
200	MDLN	60060	2591	18W-27N	A7
7100	MTGY	60538	3198	40W-10S	C7
9400	LKWD	60014	2692	38W-23N	E2
E Lenox Ln					
600	PLTN	60074	2753	20W-17N	B5
Lenox Rd					
700	GNVW	60025	2811	7W-13N	A7
700	MltT	60137	3025	22W-0N	C4
900	GNEN	60137	3025	22W-1N	C3
5500	LSLE	60532	3143	23W-6S	B4
5500	LslT	60532	3143	23W-5S	B4
Lenox St					
100	NLNX	60451	3501	17W-23S	C3
100	NlxT	60451	3501	17W-23S	C3
1000	LMNT	60439	3271	17W-13S	B5
N Lenox St					
100	BCVL	60407	4030	34W-44S	A4
400	BvlT	60407	4030	34W-44S	A4
S Lenox St					
100	BCVL	60407	4030	34W-44S	A4
Lenox St W					
400	OKPK	60302	3031	8W-1N	A1
Lenschow Rd					
10	BrlT	60140	2795	47W-14N	D6
10	HshT	60140	2795	47W-14N	D6
300	BrlT	60140	2796	46W-14N	A6
300	HshT	60140	2796	46W-14N	A6
Lentfer Ct					
10800	ODPK	60467	3423	13W-19S	A2
Lenwood Ct					
800	AraT	60506	3199	36W-8S	D1
800	AURA	60506	3199	36W-8S	D1
N Lenwood Dr					
2300	DRPK	60074	2752	21W-18N	D2
2300	PltT	60074	2752	21W-18N	D2
Lenz Rd					
10	PltT	60124	2906	41W-9N	A2
400	PltT	60124	2905	41W-9N	E2
Lenzi Av					
6000	HGKN	60525	3147	11W-6S	D4
6000	MCCK	60525	3147	11W-6S	D4
S Leo Ct					
1200	PLTN	60067	2805	22W-14N	C4
Leola Dr					
13800	GNOK	60044	2592	13W-28N	D5
Leola Ln					
400	SchT	60175	2963	37W-5N	D2
Leominster Av					
3400	PnfT	60431	3497	28W-22S	A1
3800	PnfT	60431	3496	29W-22S	E1
Leominster Ct					
200	WNVL	60555	3080	30W-2S	B3
Leon Dr					
500	TRLK	60010	2643	26W-25N	D4
E Leon Ln					
10	PTHT	60070	2808	14W-15N	B3
W Leon Ln					
10	PTHT	60070	2808	14W-15N	B3
Leon Pl					
1200	EVTN	60201	2867	2W-11N	A2
Leona					
-	JSTC	60458	3210	10W-9S	B2
N Leona Av					
6200	CHCG	60646	2919	6W-7N	D3
Leona Dr					
12100	WldT	60585	3266	29W-14S	D7
Leona St					
2600	FNPK	60131	2973	12W-3N	C5
W Leona Ter					
1300	ANHT	60005	2806	18W-13N	D5
Leonard Av					
5800	DRGV	60516	3143	21W-6S	E5
5800	LslT	60516	3143	21W-6S	E5
6200	DRGV	60516	3143	21W-6S	E5
6200	WDRG	60517	3143	21W-6S	E5
N Leonard Av					
1600	MHRY	60050	2528	32W-33N	B2
5500	CHCG	60630	2919	6W-7N	D5
5700	CHCG	60646	2919	7W-7N	C4
Leonard Dr					
600	DGvT	60527	3207	17W-9S	C4
600	DGvT	60561	3207	17W-9S	C4
600	DRN	60561	3207	17W-9S	C4
600	GRNE	60031	2534	16W-33N	D4
1200	JLET	60586	3496	31W-22S	A2
1200	SMBG	60193	2912	24W-8N	E1
1200	SmbT	60193	2912	23W-8N	E1
1200	SRWD	60404	3496	31W-22S	A2
6700	DRN	60527	3145	17W-7S	C7
6700	DRN	60561	3145	17W-7S	C7
13900	CTWD	60445	3348	5W-16S	A3
N Leonard Dr					
4800	CHCG	60656	2917	10W-6N	E6
4800	CHCG	60706	2917	10W-6N	E7
4800	NRDG	60706	2917	10W-6N	E6
5100	NRDG	60656	2917	10W-6N	E6
Leonard Ln					
-	NARA	60506	3076	39W-3S	D6
400	BRRG	60527	3208	15W-9S	B4
S Leonard Ln					
200	ANHT	60005	2807	16W-13N	C7
200	MPPT	60005	2807	16W-13N	C7
200	MPPT	60005	2861	17W-12N	B1
300	MPPT	60056	2861	17W-12N	B1
Leonard Pkwy					
600	CLLK	60014	2639	36W-25N	D4
Leonard Pl					
1100	EVTN	60201	2867	2W-12N	A1
N Leonard Rd					
34500	GrtT	60041	2472	28W-34N	E7
34800	GrtT	60041	2473	28W-34N	A7
S Leonard Rd					
10	PLTN	60074	2806	19W-15N	B1
W Leonard Rd					
800	PLTN	60067	2805	22W-15N	C1
800	PltT	60067	2805	22W-15N	C1
Leonard St					
10	ELGN	60123	2854	34W-11N	D4
10	MltT	60190	3023	26W-0N	E5
100	WNFD	60190	3023	26W-0N	E5
200	CHHT	60411	3507	1W-23S	E3
400	PKRG	60068	2864	10W-9N	A7
Leonard Wood W					
900	HDPK	60035	2650	9W-24N	C7
900	HDPK	60040	2650	9W-24N	C7
900	HIWD	60035	2650	9W-24N	C7
900	HIWD	60040	2650	9W-24N	C7
Leonard Wood Dr E					
3600	HDPK	60035	2650	9W-24N	D7
Leonard Wood Dr N					
-	HDPK	60040	2650	9W-24N	C7
10	HDPK	60035	2650	9W-24N	C7
100	LKFT	60035	2650	9W-24N	C7
Leonard Wood Dr S					
-	HIWD	60035	2650	9W-24N	C7
10	HDPK	60035	2650	9W-24N	C7
Leon Cook Dr					
-	HGKN	60525	3147	11W-8S	D7
W Leonora Ln					
7900	EDPK	60707	2974	9W-2N	B7
7900	EDPK	60707	3030	9W-2N	B1
Leo Singer Ln					
1100	WKGN	60099	2421	10W-38N	E6
N Leoti Av					
6400	CHCG	60646	2919	6W-8N	C2
Le Parc Cir					
200	BFGV	60089	2754	15W-20N	E2
Le Provence Cir					
400	NPVL	60540	3204	26W-8S	A1
Lerose Dr					
300	CHHT	60411	3508	1W-23S	A3
N Leroy Av					
6200	CHCG	60646	2919	6W-7N	D3
6400	LNWD	60646	2919	6W-8N	E2
6400	LNWD	60712	2919	6W-8N	E2
6700	LNWD	60077	2919	6W-8N	E2
6700	SKOK	60077	2919	6W-8N	E2
Leslee Ln					
200	HDPK	60035	2758	7W-20N	B1
Lesley Ln					
10	CLLK	60014	2640	34W-25N	B4
Lesli Ln					
24200	PNFD	60585	3266	30W-13S	B6
Leslie Av					
1300	RLKB	60073	2475	22W-35N	B7
N Leslie Av					
1600	RLKB	60073	2475	22W-35N	B6
Leslie Ct					
400	MaiT	60016	2809	12W-12N	C7
600	CLSM	60188	2967	28W-3N	A6
600	CmpT	60175	2961	43W-5N	A2
1300	GLHT	60139	3025	22W-2N	C1
Leslie Dr					
8800	ODHL	60462	3424	11W-19S	A3
8800	ODHL	60487	3424	11W-19S	A3
8800	ODPK	60462	3424	11W-19S	A3
W Leslie Dr					
26000	CNHN	60410	3761	32W-32S	C1
Leslie Ln					
10	LtRT	60545	3331	48W-14S	A1
100	BGBK	60440	3205	22W-10S	B6
200	BMDL	60108	2968	23W-5N	E2
300	WLNG	60090	2755	14W-17N	C5
600	GLHT	60139	3025	22W-2N	C1
600	SMBG	60194	2858	26W-11N	A4
700	FKFT	60423	3503	12W-24S	C6
1300	GLHT	60139	2969	22W-2N	C7
2400	HRPK	60133	2911	28W-8N	B3
5400	OKFT	60452	3425	6W-19S	D1
5500	BmnT	60452	3425	6W-19S	D1
5500	BmnT	60477	3425	6W-19S	D1
10300	CHRG	60415	3275	8W-12S	A1
N Leslie Ln					
10	PLTN	60067	2805	21W-16N	D1
8800	MaiT	60016	2863	11W-12N	E1
8800	MaiT	60714	2863	11W-12N	E1
8800	NLES	60714	2863	11W-12N	E1
S Leslie Ln					
1000	VLPK	60181	3027	18W-0S	A6
1200	DSPN	60016	2862	15W-10N	A5
1200	DSPN	60018	2862	15W-10N	A5
W Leslie Ln					
10	VLPK	60181	3027	18W-0S	A6
Leslie Ann Dr					
16300	BmnT	60477	3425	7W-19S	C3
16300	TYPK	60477	3425	7W-19S	C3
Lessenden Pl					
200	ELGN	60120	2855	33W-10N	A5
Lesser Av					
9800	FNPK	60131	2973	12W-4N	B3
N Lessing St					
800	CHCG	60622	3033	1W-1N	E2
N Lester Av					
4900	CHCG	60630	2919	6W-6N	C6
Lester Ln					
7700	DRN	60561	3207	18W-8S	B2
N Lester Ln					
40600	WDWH	60083	2420	13W-40N	E3
40700	BtnT	60083	2420	13W-40N	E3
Lester Rd					
10	PKFT	60466	3595	3W-27S	B4
Lester St					
-	WCHI	60185	3022	30W-0N	B6
-	WnfT	60185	3022	30W-0N	B6
400	WnfT	60185	3023	28W-0N	A5
400	WnfT	60190	3023	28W-0N	A5
E Lester St					
300	WCHI	60185	3022	29W-0N	D5
500	WnfT	60185	3022	29W-0N	D5
W Lester St					
100	WCHI	60185	3022	30W-0N	C5
Letterkenny Dr					
8900	TYPK	60477	3504	11W-23S	A4
Leupold Ln					
6600	JLET	60586	3415	32W-20S	D6
Levato Ln					
1400	MNKA	60447	3672	33W-30S	A4
Leven Av					
2700	NlxT	60451	3590	15W-27S	C5
2800	MhtT	60442	3590	15W-27S	C5
2800	MhtT	60451	3590	15W-27S	C5
Leverenz Rd					
400	WldT	60564	3202	28W-10S	E6
400	WldT	60564	3203	28W-10S	A6
800	NPVL	60565	3203	28W-10S	A6
900	NPVL	60564	3203	28W-10S	A6
2100	NPVL	60564	3202	29W-10S	C6
Leverett St					
300	TNTN	60476	3428	0E-21S	E6

STREET Block	City	ZIP	Map#	CGS	Grid
Levi Baxter St					
1500	GYLK	60030	2533	19W-31N	D6
Levine Ct					
500	ELGN	60120	2855	33W-11N	B4
W Levi Waite Rd					
26000	GrtT	60041	2530	26W-33N	E4
26000	GrtT	60073	2530	26W-33N	E4
26000	RDLK	60073	2530	26W-33N	E4
Lew St					
-	LtRT	60545	3259	47W-12S	D4
-	PLNO	60545	3259	47W-11S	D2
N Lew St					
10	PLNO	60545	3259	47W-13S	D6
S Lew St					
10	PLNO	60545	3259	47W-13S	D6
Lewe Ct					
2500	NRIV	60546	3088	10W-2S	B3
Lewis Av					
-	BtnT	60099	2421	11W-41N	D1
-	WPHR	60096	2421	11W-41N	D1
100	WCDA	60084	2643	26W-27N	D1
400	BtnT	60096	2362	11W-42N	D6
400	BtnT	60099	2362	11W-42N	D6
400	WPHR	60096	2362	11W-42N	D6
400	WPHR	60099	2362	11W-42N	D6
400	YkTp	60148	3084	19W-1S	D2
1100	ZION	60096	2362	11W-42N	D7
1100	ZION	60099	2362	11W-42N	D7
1400	NCHI	60064	2536	11W-31N	D7
1400	WKGN	60085	2536	11W-31N	D7
1500	ZION	60099	2421	11W-41N	D1
2300	NCHI	60064	2593	11W-30N	D1
2300	NCHI	60088	2593	11W-30N	D1
3100	BHPK	60099	2421	11W-39N	D5
3400	WKGN	60087	2421	11W-39N	D6
3400	WKGN	60099	2421	11W-39N	D6
43300	BtnT	53158	2362	11W-43N	E4
43300	PTPR	53158	2362	11W-43N	E4
Lewis Av CO-W34					
-	BtnT	60099	2421	11W-41N	D1
-	WPHR	60096	2421	11W-41N	D1
400	BtnT	60096	2362	11W-42N	D6
400	BtnT	60099	2362	11W-42N	D6
400	WPHR	60096	2362	11W-42N	D6
400	WPHR	60099	2362	11W-42N	D6
1100	ZION	60096	2362	11W-42N	D7
1100	ZION	60099	2362	11W-42N	D7
1400	NCHI	60064	2536	11W-31N	D7
1400	WKGN	60085	2536	11W-31N	D7
1500	ZION	60099	2421	11W-41N	D1
2300	NCHI	60064	2593	11W-30N	D1
2300	NCHI	60088	2593	11W-30N	D1
3100	BHPK	60099	2421	11W-39N	D5
3400	WKGN	60087	2421	11W-39N	D6
3400	WKGN	60099	2421	11W-39N	D6
43300	BtnT	53158	2362	11W-43N	E4
43300	PTPR	53158	2362	11W-43N	E4
N Lewis Av					
10	WKGN	60085	2536	11W-34N	D1
200	LMBD	60148	3026	19W-1N	D3
500	WKGN	60085	2479	11W-34N	D7
1700	WKGN	60087	2479	11W-35N	D7
3200	BHPK	60087	2479	11W-37N	D1
3700	WKGN	60087	2421	11W-38N	D7
3800	BHPK	60087	2421	11W-38N	D7
3800	BHPK	60099	2421	11W-38N	D7
39200	WKGN	60099	2421	11W-38N	D7
N Lewis Av CO-W34					
10	WKGN	60085	2536	11W-34N	D1
500	WKGN	60085	2479	11W-34N	D7
3200	BHPK	60087	2479	11W-37N	D1
3200	WKGN	60087	2479	11W-37N	D1
3700	WKGN	60087	2421	11W-38N	D7
3800	BHPK	60087	2421	11W-38N	D7
3800	BHPK	60099	2421	11W-38N	D7
39200	WKGN	60099	2421	11W-38N	D7
S Lewis Av					
10	LMBD	60148	3026	19W-0N	D4
10	WKGN	60085	2536	11W-33N	D4
1300	NCHI	60064	2536	11W-32N	D5
S Lewis Av CO-W34					
10	WKGN	60085	2536	11W-33N	D4
1300	NCHI	60064	2536	11W-32N	D5
Lewis Ct					
100	SCRL	60174	2964	36W-3N	A6
100	SMBG	60193	2859	23W-10N	A6
Lewis Dr					
-	LYWD	60411	3509	2E-23S	D3
200	WDDL	60191	2914	18W-7N	E3
200	WDDL	60191	2915	18W-7N	A3
15000	LkfT	60441	3340	24W-17S	E7
15000	RMVL	60441	3340	24W-17S	E7
Lewis Ln					
100	WHTN	60187	3082	24W-2S	C3
1800	NLNX	60451	3500	19W-23S	D3
1900	HDPK	60035	2757	9W-20N	C2
3900	JNBG	60051	2472	29W-35N	C5
Lewis Pl					
900	GNVA	60134	3019	37W-0N	C5
1800	WKGN	60085	2479	11W-35N	D7
Lewis Rd					
400	GNVA	60134	3019	37W-0N	C4
400	GnvT	60134	3019	37W-0N	B4
Lewis St					
-	OSWG	60543	3262	39W-12S	D3
10	BtlT	60543	3262	40W-12S	C3
2400	BLID	60406	3277	3W-14S	B6
3000	STGR	60475	3596	0W-27S	C4
3400	CRTE	60417	3596	0W-28S	C5
E Lewis St					
400	HMND	46320	3430		D1
Lewis Ter					
4400	SKOK	60076	2866	5W-11N	A2
Lewisburg Ln					
-	AURA	60504	3140	30W-7S	B6
Lewis Clark Dr					
6900	JLET	60586	3415	32W-21S	C6
Lewis Isle Ln					
500	PTHT	60070	2808	14W-14N	B3
Lewood Dr					
16300	PNFD	60586	3416	30W-19S	B3
16300	PnfT	60586	3416	30W-19S	B3
S Lewood Dr					
15900	PNFD	60544	3416	30W-18S	B2
15900	PNFD	60586	3416	30W-18S	B2
15900	PnfT	60586	3416	30W-19S	B2
Lexington Av					
10	SEGN	60177	2908	35W-8N	C3
200	FRGV	60021	2696	29W-22N	B3
600	ROSL	60172	2913	22W-6N	B6
700	SCRL	60174	2964	34W-2N	D7
700	YkTp	60126	3028	15W-0S	A6
1000	FDHT	60411	3509	1E-25S	B7
1400	FDHT	60411	3597	1E-25S	B1
1900	NCHI	60088	2593	11W-30N	D1
9500	BKFD	60513	3087	11W-3S	D4
9500	BKFD	60525	3087	11W-3S	C4
9500	LGPK	60525	3087	11W-3S	C4
14500	HRVY	60426	3349	1W-17S	E5
15600	HRVY	60426	3427	1W-18S	E1
18500	HMWD	60430	3507	2W-22S	C1
Lexington Cir					
800	HRPK	60133	2912	26W-9N	A1
1500	SMBG	60173	2859	21W-10N	E4
8600	ODPK	60462	3346	10W-18S	B6
E Lexington Cir					
10	BtlT	60560	3261	42W-13S	D5
10	YKVL	60560	3261	42W-13S	D5
W Lexington Cir					
10	BtlT	60560	3261	42W-13S	C5
10	YKVL	60560	3261	42W-13S	C5
Lexington Ct					
-	JLET	60431	3495	33W-22S	B1
10	SMWD	60107	2857	26W-11N	E4
10	WNVL	60555	3080	30W-2S	C3
200	AvnT	60030	2475	21W-34N	E7
200	GYLK	60030	2475	21W-34N	D7
200	SMBG	60173	2859	21W-10N	E4
600	MDLN	60060	2590	20W-28N	B6
700	NHBK	60062	2757	8W-17N	E4
700	NLNX	60451	3589	18W-25S	A1
700	WMTN	60481	3853	27W-39S	E7
6900	TYPK	60477	3425	8W-19S	A2
10600	FKFT	60423	3591	13W-25S	B1
27500	WcnT	60042	2642	28W-27N	D1
Lexington Dr					
10	DYR	46311	3510		C7
10	VNHL	60061	2647	16W-25N	C5
100	BFGV	60089	2754	15W-18N	E2
100	BGBK	60440	3269	23W-11S	A1
200	SMBG	60173	2859	21W-11N	E4
300	RMVL	60446	3340	24W-16S	E5
400	BFGV	60069	2754	15W-20N	E1
400	LKFT	60045	2649	12W-26N	B3
400	VrnT	60069	2754	15W-20N	E1
500	GNVA	60134	3020	34W-1N	E2
500	WLNG	60090	2754	15W-18N	E2
600	CHHT	60411	3507	2W-24S	C6
800	BFGV	60090	2754	15W-18N	E2
1000	BRLT	60103	2910	30W-6N	C7
1200	ALGN	60102	2694	34W-20N	B7
1200	ALGN	60102	2747	34W-20N	B1
1600	MTGY	60538	3199	37W-10S	C5
1600	MTGY	60538	3200	36W-10S	A5
2300	LGGV	60047	2700	19W-20N	C7
2400	LGGV	60047	2753	19W-20N	C1
2700	HLCT	60429	3427	3W-20S	A5
3500	HFET	60192	2804	24W-14N	D4
N Lexington Dr					
700	RLKB	60073	2475	22W-36N	C4
1900	PLTN	60074	2753	20W-20N	B2
S Lexington Dr					
2200	EGvT	60005	2861	16W-10N	E6
2200	MPPT	60005	2861	16W-10N	E6
2200	MPPT	60056	2861	16W-10N	E6
15900	PNFD	60586	3416	29W-19S	D3
W Lexington Dr					
1300	ANHT	60004	2753	18W-16N	D7
Lexington Ln					
-	AvnT	60030	2475	21W-34N	D7
-	CPVL	60118	2746	38W-18N	C5
-	GYLK	60030	2475	21W-34N	D7
200	GYLK	60030	2532	21W-34N	D1
800	ISLK	60042	2586	29W-28N	B5
900	BTVA	60510	3078	34W-2S	D3
1400	DRGV	60516	3144	20W-7S	B6
2300	NPVL	60540	3202	29W-8S	D1
2800	HDPK	60035	2704	10W-23N	A2
3000	GNVW	60025	2810	10W-15N	B1
3000	GNVW	60062	2810	10W-15N	B1
7100	FXLK	60020	2414	28W-39N	E5
10400	FKFT	60423	3591	13W-25S	B1
N Lexington Ln					
6700	CHCG	60646	2919	7W-8N	A1
6700	CHCG	60714	2919	7W-8N	A1
6700	NLES	60714	2919	7W-8N	A1
W Lexington Ln					
20500	KLDR	60047	2699	20W-21N	E6
20500	KLDR	60047	2700	20W-21N	A6
Lexington Ln E					
1100	LKZH	60047	2699	22W-21N	A5
Lexington Ln W					
1000	LKZH	60010	2699	22W-21N	A6
1000	LKZH	60047	2699	22W-21N	B6
Lexington Rd					
-	LSLE	60532	3142	24W-7S	D6
10	SBTN	60010	2803	27W-14N	B4
400	NLNX	60451	3589	18W-25S	A1
400	NlxT	60451	3589	18W-25S	A1
1400	GNOK	60048	2592	14W-30N	B3
1400	LbvT	60048	2592	14W-30N	B3
Lexington Sq E					
500	GRNE	60031	2535	14W-33N	C3
Lexington Sq W					
600	GRNE	60031	2535	14W-33N	C3
Lexington St					
-	FTPK	60130	3030	10W-0S	A6
-	FTPK	60153	3030	10W-0S	A6
200	EMHT	60126	3028	15W-0S	B6
200	YkTp	60126	3028	15W-0S	B6
400	MYWD	60153	3030	10W-0S	A6
500	PvsT	60126	3028	15W-0S	B6
600	OKPK	60304	3031	8W-0S	A6
700	MYWD	60153	3029	12W-0S	C6
800	OKPK	60304	3030	8W-0S	E6
900	WHTN	60187	3024	24W-0N	D5
1200	BDVW	60155	3029	12W-0S	C6
1200	MYWD	60155	3029	11W-0S	C6
1600	BDVW	60153	3029	11W-0S	D6
7200	OKPK	60130	3030	9W-0S	C6
W Lexington St					
500	CHCG	60607	3034	0W-0S	A6
1400	CHCG	60607	3033	1W-0S	D6
2400	CHCG	60612	3033	3W-0S	A6
2800	CHCG	60612	3032	4W-0S	D6
3100	CHCG	60624	3032	4W-0S	C6
4500	CHCG	60644	3032	5W-0S	A6
4800	CHCG	60644	3031	6W-0S	E6
Lexington Tr					
6700	NndT	60012	2583	35W-27N	E7
6700	NndT	60012	2584	35W-27N	A7
Lexy Ln					
800	HPSR	60140	2796	46W-15N	A3
N Leyden Av					
2200	RVGV	60171	2973	11W-3N	E6
S Leyden Av					
13700	CHCG	60419	3350	0E-15S	D2
13700	CHCG	60827	3350	0E-15S	D2
13700	DLTN	60419	3350	0E-15S	D2
13700	RVDL	60827	3350	0E-15S	D2
Leyden Ct					
3500	FNPK	60131	2973	11W-4N	C3
Leyden Ln					
700	WLMT	60091	2811	5W-13N	E5
Leyland Ln					
2600	AURA	60504	3201	32W-9S	C4
2600	NpvT	60504	3201	32W-9S	C4
N Leyte Ct					
27500	WcnT	60042	2642	28W-27N	E1
Leytonstone Dr					
1600	WHTN	60187	3082	25W-2S	B3
Lezlie Ln					
5300	GRNE	60031	2478	15W-35N	A6
Liam Ct					
5500	CPVL	60110	2746	36W-18N	E4
5500	CPVL	60110	2747	36W-18N	A4
N Liano Av					
5200	CHCG	60630	2919	6W-6N	D5
Liatris Dr					
8800	FKFT	60423	3504	11W-24S	A4
Libby St					
-	MNKA	60447	3672	34W-29S	A3
Liberty Av					
100	CLLK	60014	2640	34W-24N	B6
200	FRGV	60021	2696	30W-22N	A3
400	SEGN	60177	2908	34W-8N	C3
700	SCRL	60174	2964	34W-2N	D7
1100	CRY	60013	2641	31W-24N	D6
W Liberty Av					
10500	BHPK	60099	2422	10W-39N	A6
10700	WKGN	60099	2422	10W-38N	A6
23200	LkvT	60046	2416	23W-38N	E6
23200	LkvT	60046	2417	23W-38N	A6
Liberty Blvd					
3800	DGvT	60559	3085	18W-4S	A7
3800	OKBK	60523	3085	18W-4S	A7
3800	YkTp	60559	3085	18W-4S	A7
4000	WTMT	60559	3085	18W-4S	A7
Liberty Cir					
9700	ODHL	60467	3423	12W-19S	D3
16600	OrlT	60467	3423	12W-19S	D3
Liberty Ct					
10	BGBK	60440	3205	22W-10S	D5
10	CRY	60013	2641	31W-24N	D6
400	SMBG	60194	2857	26W-11N	E4
400	SMWD	60107	2857	26W-11N	E4
1400	SCRL	60174	2964	34W-2N	D7
1700	MPPT	60056	2808	13W-14N	D5
1800	EGVV	60007	2859	22W-9N	D7
15700	ODPK	60462	3423	12W-18S	C1
W Liberty Ct					
10300	BHPK	60099	2422	10W-38N	A6
Liberty Dr					
-	BbyT	60119	3017	43W-0N	B4
10	LMNT	60439	3272	16W-13S	A5
200	PKFT	60466	3595	3W-27S	B3
400	BGBK	60440	3205	22W-10S	D5
700	LYVL	60048	2591	15W-29N	E5
700	LYVL	60048	2592	15W-29N	A5
800	ELBN	60119	3017	43W-0N	B5
1000	NPVL	60540	3142	24W-7S	C7
1000	NPVL	60540	3204	24W-7S	C1
1400	GLHT	60139	2969	22W-2N	D6
E Liberty Dr					
300	WHTN	60187	3024	24W-0S	D7
1700	WHTN	60187	3025	23W-0S	A7
1800	GNEN	60137	3025	23W-0S	A7
1800	GNEN	60187	3025	23W-0S	A7
N Liberty Dr					
10	BrnT	60010	2803	27W-14N	A4
10	SBTN	60010	2803	27W-14N	A4
S Liberty Dr					
10	BrnT	60010	2803	27W-14N	A4
10	SBTN	60010	2803	27W-14N	A4
W Liberty Dr					
1200	WHTN	60187	3024	25W-0S	A7
25200	CNHN	60410	3672	31W-29S	E2
25200	CnhT	60410	3672	31W-29S	E2
Liberty Ln					
300	WDSK	60098	2581	41W-30N	D2
700	LMBD	60148	3026	18W-0S	E6
1000	NLNX	60451	3589	18W-26S	B2
1900	GRNE	60031	2477	16W-36N	E4
2900	LNHT	60046	2418	19W-38N	C6
3600	GNVW	60025	2809	10W-13N	E6
5800	MTSN	60443	3505	7W-25S	D7
11600	PNFD	60585	3266	30W-13S	A5
Liberty Pl					
1900	HFET	60169	2858	25W-12N	A1
N Liberty Rd					
31200	LbvT	60030	2533	18W-31N	D7
Liberty Sq					
5800	OKFT	60452	3347	7W-18S	C7
Liberty St					
-	CRTE	60417	3684	1W-29S	E1
10	WDND	60118	2801	34W-15N	A3
10	WnfT	60190	3023	28W-0S	B6
100	WKGN	60085	2537	10W-33N	B2
100	WNFD	60190	3023	27W-0S	C6
200	YKVL	60560	3333	42W-15S	C2
300	AURA	60505	3138	33W-7S	E7
400	WDND	60118	2800	34W-15N	E3
1200	CRTE	60417	3685	1W-29S	A1
1600	AraT	60505	3139	33W-7S	A7
1600	AURA	60505	3139	33W-7S	A7
1600	HRPK	60133	2911	27W-7N	D4
2100	AraT	60502	3139	33W-7S	B6
2100	AURA	60502	3139	32W-7S	C6
2200	NpvT	60502	3139	32W-7S	C6
3400	AURA	60504	3139	31W-7S	E6
3500	NpvT	60504	3139	31W-7S	E6
3600	AURA	60504	3140	30W-7S	A6
5600	RHMD	60071	2353	34W-42N	C6
E Liberty St					
100	BRTN	60010	2750	27W-20N	C1
100	BRTN	60010	2751	25W-20N	A1
100	WCDA	60084	2643	25W-27N	E1
200	JLET	60432	3499	23W-23S	B3
300	WCDA	60084	2644	25W-27N	A1
1000	FmtT	60084	2644	24W-27N	B1
1000	WcnT	60084	2644	25W-27N	B1
E Liberty St SR-176					
100	WCDA	60084	2643	25W-27N	E1
300	WCDA	60084	2644	25W-27N	A1
1000	FmtT	60084	2644	24W-27N	B1
1000	WcnT	60084	2644	25W-27N	B1
N Liberty St					
-	JLET	60432	3499	23W-23S	A3
10	ELGN	60120	2855	33W-12N	B2
40100	AntT	60002	2417	23W-40N	A3
N Liberty St SR-25					
10	ELGN	60120	2855	33W-12N	B2
S Liberty St					
10	ELGN	60120	2855	33W-10N	B7
S Liberty St SR-25					
10	ELGN	60120	2855	33W-10N	B6
W Liberty St					
-	CHCG	60607	3034	0W-1S	A7
-	CHCG	60608	3034	0W-1S	A7
-	FmtT	60060	2644	24W-27N	D1
-	FmtT	60084	2644	24W-27N	D1
-	ISLK	60042	2587	28W-27N	A7
-	ISLK	60042	2643	28W-27N	A1
-	ISLK	60084	2587	28W-27N	A7
-	ISLK	60084	2643	27W-27N	A1
-	WcnT	60042	2587	28W-27N	A7
-	WcnT	60042	2643	28W-27N	A1
-	WcnT	60084	2587	28W-27N	A7
100	BRTN	60010	2750	25W-20N	E1
100	WCDA	60084	2643	27W-27N	C1
600	WcnT	60084	2643	26W-27N	D1
W Liberty St SR-176					
-	FmtT	60060	2644	24W-27N	D1
-	FmtT	60084	2644	24W-27N	D1
-	ISLK	60042	2587	28W-27N	A7
-	ISLK	60084	2643	28W-27N	A1
-	ISLK	60084	2587	28W-27N	A7
-	ISLK	60084	2643	27W-27N	A1
-	WcnT	60042	2587	28W-27N	A7
-	WcnT	60084	2643	28W-27N	A1
-	WcnT	60084	2587	28W-27N	A7
100	WCDA	60084	2643	27W-27N	C1
600	WcnT	60084	2643	26W-27N	D1
Liberty Bell Ct					
800	LYVL	60048	2591	15W-28N	E7
Liberty Bell Ln					
700	LYVL	60048	2591	16W-28N	E7
Liberty Grove Blvd					
-	PNFD	60544	3338	31W-17S	A6
-	PnfT	60544	3337	31W-17S	E6
-	PnfT	60544	3338	31W-17S	A6
25100	PNFD	60544	3337	31W-17S	E6
Liberty Grove Dr					
8600	WLSP	60480	3208	13W-9S	E4
10800	WLSP	60480	3209	13W-9S	A4
Liberty Lakes Blvd					
-	WcnT	60084	2588	25W-29N	A3
2700	WCDA	60084	2588	25W-29N	A3
Liberty Park Ct					
1200	CTHL	60403	3497	27W-22S	D2
Library Ln					
-	SRPK	60176	2973	11W-5N	C1
10	GYLK	60030	2533	20W-33N	A3
300	SMWD	60107	2911	28W-9N	A1
Library Pl					
600	EVTN	60201	2867	2W-11N	B2
Library Rd					
-	RGMW	60008	2806	19W-13N	B5
Lichfield Dr					
4900	HFET	60010	2751	24W-16N	C7
Lido Ter E					
600	BRLT	60103	2911	28W-7N	B4
Lido Ter W					
600	BRLT	60103	2911	28W-7N	A4
Lido Tr					
200	BRLT	60103	2911	28W-7N	A4
N Lieb Av					
5200	CHCG	60630	2919	6W-6N	D5
Lies Rd					
10	CLSM	60188	2967	26W-3N	E5
100	BmdT	60188	2967	26W-4N	E5
100	BmdT	60188	2968	26W-4N	A5
100	CLSM	60188	2968	26W-4N	A5
100	WynT	60185	2966	30W-4N	B5
1400	CLSM	60185	2967	28W-4N	A5
1400	WynT	60185	2967	28W-4N	A5
1400	WynT	60188	2967	28W-4N	A5
E Lies Rd					
200	CLSM	60188	2968	25W-3N	C5
400	CLSM	60139	2968	24W-3N	D5
400	GLHT	60139	2968	24W-3N	D5
400	GLHT	60188	2968	24W-3N	D5
Light Rd					
10	MTGY	60543	3263	38W-11S	B1
N Lightfoot Av					
6600	CHCG	60646	2919	7W-8N	B2
Lighthouse Ct					
2700	LYWD	60411	3510	3E-23S	A3
Lighthouse Dr					
-	PGGV	60140	2797	42W-15N	D4
1000	SMBG	60193	2912	24W-9N	D1
1500	NPVL	60565	3204	25W-8S	A2
Lighthouse Ln					
-	BDWD	60408	3942	30W-40S	C4
-	PGGV	60140	2797	42W-15N	D4
-	RedT	60481	3942	30W-40S	C4
10	TDLK	60030	2476	19W-34N	D7
11700	PSHT	60463	3274	9W-13S	C5
Lightning Ct					
3200	JLET	60432	3500	19W-23S	D3
3200	JLET	60451	3500	19W-23S	C3
Lightning Tr					
1100	CLSM	60188	2967	27W-3N	C6
Lilac Av					
10	FXLK	60020	2473	27W-36N	A4
100	SchT	60174	2964	35W-5N	C3
4400	GNVW	60025	2809	12W-14N	C4
W Lilac Av					
4600	MONE	60449	3683	5W-31S	B4
Lilac Ct					
10	SEGN	60177	2908	35W-7N	B5
100	RGMW	60008	2805	21W-14N	D5
500	RLKB	60073	2475	22W-35N	C7
800	CLSM	60188	2967	28W-3N	B5
1000	LYVL	60048	2591	16W-27N	D7
1700	AURA	60506	3137	37W-6S	B6
1900	SMBG	60193	2912	25W-8N	A3
15100	ODPK	60462	3346	9W-18S	D6
20100	FKFT	60423	3503	11W-24S	E5
34000	AvnT	60030	2532	22W-34N	C2
34000	HNVL	60030	2532	22W-34N	C2
Lilac Dr					
10	DYR	46311	3510		C7
200	RMVL	60446	3339	26W-17S	E6
300	BCHR	60401	3864	0W-36S	D1
600	ALGN	60102	2695	32W-20N	B7
1400	CLLK	60014	2693	37W-22N	B3
5500	MchT	60097	2469	36W-37N	E2
5500	WRLK	60097	2469	36W-37N	E2
E Lilac Dr					
900	PLTN	60074	2753	19W-18N	B4
N Lilac Dr					
26200	LbvT	60060	2646	18W-26N	D3
Lilac Ln					
-	HRVD	60033	2405	51W-39N	E4
-	WLMT	60091	2811	6W-13N	D7
10	GLF	60029	2864	8W-12N	E1
10	LMBD	60148	3026	20W-0N	B5
10	SchT	60175	2907	38W-7N	B5
100	BFGV	60089	2754	16W-20N	E2
100	NARA	60542	3078	35W-3S	A7
100	WLNG	60090	2755	14W-17N	C4
300	AlqT	60013	2696	29W-23N	C1
300	ELGN	60123	2854	35W-10N	B5
300	MTSN	60443	3593	7W-26S	D2
400	EGVV	60007	2915	18W-9N	A1
400	WDDL	60191	2971	17W-5N	C2
600	DGvT	60527	3207	16W-10S	E6
800	JLET	60435	3497	26W-22S	E3
800	NPVL	60540	3141	27W-7S	C7
800	NPVL	60540	3203	27W-8S	C1
900	HDPK	60035	2704	9W-21N	B7
1200	CLSM	60188	2967	28W-3N	B5
1300	ADSN	60101	2970	20W-5N	B2
1800	AURA	60506	3137	38W-6S	A6
2900	NHBK	60062	2756	11W-16N	D7
8300	TYPK	60477	3424	10W-21S	B5
11900	HTLY	60142	2744	42W-20N	B1
16900	LKPT	60441	3420	19W-20S	C4
Lilac Pl					
1000	PLTN	60074	2753	19W-18N	C4
N Lilac Pl					
40500	AntT	60002	2416	24W-40N	C3
Lilac St					
10	BGBK	60490	3267	26W-11S	D2
2400	HHLL	60051	2586	30W-29N	A3
E Lilac St					
200	ELBN	60119	3017	43W-2N	A2
E Lilac Ter					
1600	ANHT	60004	2807	16W-16N	C1
Lilac Wy					
600	LMBD	60148	3026	18W-0S	D6
Lilas Ct					
200	NLNX	60451	3501	17W-23S	C4
200	NlxT	60451	3501	17W-23S	C4
Lill Av					
100	CLLK	60014	2640	35W-25N	A5
W Lill Av					
800	CHCG	60614	2977	1W-3N	E5
W Lill Ct					
7200	NLES	60714	2864	9W-10N	D4
S Lill St					
400	BRTN	60010	2750	25W-18N	E3
Lillian Av					
-	ANHT	60004	2807	17W-15N	B1
E Lillian Av					
1400	ANHT	60004	2807	16W-15N	C1
W Lillian Av					
10	ANHT	60004	2807	17W-15N	A1
1500	ANHT	60004	2806	18W-15N	D1
Lillian Ct					
200	GNVA	60134	3019	37W-1N	D3
600	NPVL	60564	3266	29W-11S	E2
600	WldT	60564	3266	29W-11S	E2
Lillian Ln					
10	BtlT	60560	3261	41W-13S	E4
300	DSPN	60016	2861	15W-11N	E3
1100	SDWH	60548	3258	51W-14S	A7
1100	WCHI	60185	3022	29W-2N	C1
E Lillian Ln					
1700	ANHT	60004	2807	16W-15N	C1
Lillian Pl					
200	BRLT	60103	2909	31W-8N	E4
W Lillian Pl					
22500	AntT	60002	2358	22W-41N	B7
Lillian St					
1100	ELGN	60123	2854	35W-10N	B5
N Lillian St					
600	MHRY	60050	2528	33W-32N	A4
800	MHRY	60050	2527	33W-32N	E4
W Lillian St					
4000	MHRY	60050	2528	32W-32N	A5
Lillibet Ter					
8600	MNGV	60053	2865	7W-10N	C4
Lillie St					
600	ELGN	60120	2855	33W-11N	B3
Lilly Ct					
1300	GYLK	60030	2532	21W-34N	D1
1700	HDPK	60035	2704	10W-22N	A4
E Lilly Ct					
900	PLTN	60074	2753	19W-18N	B3
E Lilly Ln					
800	PLTN	60074	2753	19W-18N	B3
Lilly St					
10	PltT	60124	2906	41W-9N	A2
Lilly Pad Ln					
22600	FKFT	60423	3592	9W-27S	E4
Lily Av					
700	MchT	60051	2529	29W-32N	C5
Lily Ct					
-	NndT	60014	2586	30W-28N	A6
10	BGBK	60440	3268	25W-12S	B2
600	SMBG	60193	2858	23W-9N	E7
19900	FKFT	60423	3504	11W-24S	A4
Lily Ln					
300	LKMR	60051	2529	29W-32N	D5
500	FRGV	60021	2696	29W-22N	C3
700	RMVL	60446	3340	24W-14S	E1
1200	CLSM	60188	2967	28W-3N	B5
1900	RDLK	60073	2531	25W-33N	A2
2300	GNVW	60025	2810	9W-15N	C3
3400	SjnT	46311	3598		D6
12400	PNFD	60585	3266	30W-14S	B7
12400	PNFD	60585	3338	30W-14S	C1
Lily St					
1600	AURA	60505	3139	33W-5S	A3
Lily Cache Ln					
100	BGBK	60440	3269	23W-12S	A3
400	BGBK	60440	3268	25W-12S	A3
1100	BGBK	60490	3268	26W-12S	A3
S Lily Cache Rd					
-	PnfT	60544	3416	28W-19S	E3
16200	PNFD	60586	3416	28W-19S	E3
16200	PnfT	60586	3416	29W-20S	E4
Lily Field Ln					
1000	BGBK	60440	3268	25W-12S	B2
Lily Lake Ct					
21100	LktT	60403	3417	26W-19S	E3
21100	LktT	60403	3418	26W-19S	A3
Lily Lake Ln					
21200	LktT	60403	3417	26W-19S	E3
26500	CNHN	60410	3761	32W-32S	C1
Lily Lake Pkwy					
200	LKMR	60051	2529	29W-31N	D6
N Lily Lake Rd					
100	MchT	60051	2529	29W-32N	C5
400	LKMR	60051	2529	29W-32N	C5
S Lily Lake Rd					
100	MchT	60051	2529	29W-31N	C7
100	NndT	60051	2529	29W-31N	C7
300	LKMR	60051	2529	29W-31N	C6
900	NndT	60051	2586	29W-30N	C2
Lily Pond Ln					
2000	SEGN	60177	2907	37W-8N	D4
Lily Pond Rd					
2200	DrrT	60098	2582	38W-29N	E4
2200	WDSK	60098	2582	38W-29N	E4

Chicago 7-County Street Index

STREET Block	City	ZIP	Map#	CGS Grid	
Lilywoods Wy					
-	PNFD	60585	3337	32W-15S	C2
Limar Ln					
1400	GNVW	60025	2809	10W-14N	E5
N Limb Ct					
35200	GRNE	60031	2478	15W-35N	A6
Limberi Ln					
300	CmpT	60175	2962	39W-3N	D6
W Lime St					
100	JLET	60435	3498	24W-23S	E3
Limerick Ct					
1800	DRN	60561	3144	18W-7S	E7
Limerick Dr					
500	ElgT	60124	2853	37W-10N	C7
1500	AURA	60505	3138	34W-5S	D3
2600	AlqT	60013	2641	31W-25N	D5
Limerick Ln					
-	PNFD	60585	3265	32W-14S	D7
-	RtdT	60124	2798	40W-14N	C6
600	SMBG	60193	2859	23W-9N	A7
800	MchT	60050	2527	35W-32N	B4
800	MHRY	60050	2527	35W-32N	B4
Limestone Ct					
22600	FKFT	60423	3590	14W-27S	D4
Limestone Dr					
-	SCRL	60174	2964	35W-2N	B7
500	BTVA	60510	3077	37W-1S	C2
500	BtvT	60510	3077	37W-1S	C2
Limestone Ln					
2000	CPVL	60110	2748	33W-19N	C3
Lincoln Av					
-	LMBD	60148	3026	20W-1N	A3
-	LSLE	60532	3083	23W-4S	A7
-	LslT	60532	3083	23W-4S	A7
10	BNVL	60106	2972	15W-5N	A1
10	EDND	60118	2800	34W-16N	E1
10	EDND	60118	2801	34W-16N	A2
10	ELGN	60120	2854	34W-12N	E2
10	RDLK	60073	2531	23W-33N	E3
10	RVSD	60546	3088	10W-3S	B5
100	FRGV	60021	2696	30W-23N	B2
200	DRGV	60515	3144	18W-4S	E1
200	WDND	60118	2801	34W-16N	A2
300	GLNC	60022	2758	6W-17N	C5
300	GYLK	60030	2533	20W-32N	A5
300	WDND	60118	2800	34W-16N	E2
300	WDSK	60098	2524	42W-31N	C7
400	CPVL	60110	2800	34W-16N	E2
400	CPVL	60118	2800	34W-16N	E2
400	FXLK	60041	2473	26W-35N	C5
400	WCHI	60185	3022	30W-0N	B5
500	AvnT	60030	2533	20W-32N	A5
500	WNFD	60190	3023	27W-0S	C7
600	CTCY	60409	3352	4E-17S	B6
600	ELGN	60120	2855	33W-12N	B2
600	LKBF	60044	2593	11W-28N	E5
700	GNEN	60137	3025	22W-0N	D4
700	WNKA	60093	2812	5W-16N	A1
800	WNKA	60093	2759	5W-16N	A7
900	CTCY	60409	3430	4E-18S	B1
1100	FRGV	60021	2695	30W-22N	E4
1100	SMWD	60107	2911	27W-9N	C1
1100	WCDA	60084	2588	25W-28N	B6
1100	WcnT	60084	2588	25W-28N	B6
1200	AlqT	60021	2695	30W-22N	E4
1200	CHHT	60411	3508	0W-25S	C7
1200	CRTE	60417	3685	1W-29S	B2
1700	CTHL	60403	3418	26W-21S	A6
1700	HMND	46394	3280		E4
1800	NHBK	60062	2757	9W-17N	B5
2400	LGGV	60047	2753	19W-20N	C1
2500	ElaT	60047	2753	19W-20N	C1
2500	LGGV	60047	2700	19W-20N	C7
2500	NRIV	60546	3088	10W-2S	B3
3700	MchT	60051	2529	30W-33N	B3
3700	MHRY	60050	2528	32W-33N	B3
3700	RcmT	60071	2354	32W-43N	B4
4300	LSLE	60532	3143	23W-5S	A2
4300	RGMW	60008	2806	20W-14N	A3
4400	RGMW	60008	2805	20W-14N	E4
5400	MNGV	60053	2865	7W-10N	B4
5400	MNGV	60077	2865	6W-10N	D4
7400	LNWD	60076	2866	5W-9N	A7
7400	LNWD	60712	2866	5W-9N	A7
7400	SKOK	60076	2866	5W-9N	A7
7400	SKOK	60712	2866	5W-9N	A7
7500	SKOK	60076	2865	5W-9N	E7
7500	SKOK	60077	2865	6W-9N	E6
8800	BKFD	60513	3087	11W-3S	D5
9500	BKFD	60525	3087	11W-3S	D5
9500	LGPK	60525	3087	11W-3S	D5
11100	HTLY	60142	2691	40W-20N	E7
13800	CHCG	60419	3350	0E-16S	D2
13800	CHCG	60827	3350	0E-16S	D2
13800	DLTN	60419	3350	0E-16S	D2
14100	DXMR	60426	3349	2W-17S	D4
14300	DLTN	60419	3351	1E-17S	A4
14400	HRVY	60426	3349	2W-18S	D7
15000	CTCY	60409	3351	1E-17S	C5
15000	DLTN	60409	3351	1E-17S	C5
15600	HRVY	60426	3427	2W-19S	D2
16000	HRVY	60428	3427	2W-19S	D2
16000	MKHM	60426	3427	2W-19S	D2
16000	MKHM	60428	3427	2W-19S	D2
17500	HLCT	60430	3427	3W-21S	B6
17500	HMWD	60430	3427	3W-21S	B6
Lincoln Av SR-53					
-	LSLE	60532	3083	23W-4S	A7
-	LslT	60532	3083	23W-4S	A7
4300	LSLE	60532	3143	23W-5S	A2
Lincoln Av US-41					
7400	LNWD	60076	2866	5W-9N	A7
7400	LNWD	60712	2866	5W-9N	A7
7400	SKOK	60076	2866	5W-9N	A7
7400	SKOK	60712	2866	5W-9N	A7
7500	SKOK	60076	2865	5W-9N	E7
7500	SKOK	60077	2865	5W-9N	E7
E Lincoln Av					
10	GLHT	60139	2968	23W-3N	E6
10	GLHT	60139	2969	23W-3N	A6
100	BRTN	60010	2750	26W-18N	D2
100	BRTN	60010	2751	25W-18N	A2
100	LYVL	60048	2591	16W-28N	E6
100	WHTN	60187	3024	24W-0S	C6
300	LGNG	60525	3087	12W-4S	C7
500	DSPN	60018	2862	14W-10N	C6
700	BKFD	60513	3087	12W-4S	C7
700	LGNG	60513	3087	12W-4S	C7
1300	DSPN	60018	2863	13W-10N	A6
N Lincoln Av					
-	ADSN	60101	3026	18W-1N	D1
-	ADSN	60148	3026	18W-1N	D1
-	ADSN	60181	3026	18W-1N	D1
10	ADSN	60101	2970	18W-3N	E5
10	AURA	60505	3200	34W-8S	D3
10	CPVL	60110	2747	34W-17N	D7
10	CPVL	60110	2800	34W-16N	D1
10	MDLN	60060	2646	19W-27N	D1
10	PKRG	60068	2863	10W-9N	E7
10	PKRG	60068	2917	11W-8N	D2
100	MDLN	60060	2590	19W-27N	D7
400	VLPK	60181	3026	18W-1N	D2
600	AURA	60505	3138	35W-6S	C5
600	GNVA	60134	3020	35W-1N	B2
700	SCRL	60134	3020	35W-1N	B2
700	SCRL	60174	3020	35W-1N	B2
700	VLPK	60148	3026	18W-1N	D1
1100	NLES	60714	2863	10W-10N	E5
1100	PKRG	60714	2863	10W-10N	E5
1800	CHCG	60614	2978	0W-2N	A6
2300	CHCG	60614	2977	0W-2N	E5
2600	CHCG	60657	2977	1W-3N	D4
3500	CHCG	60613	2977	2W-4N	C2
3900	CHCG	60618	2977	2W-4N	B2
4400	CHCG	60618	2921	2W-5N	B7
4400	CHCG	60625	2921	2W-5N	A7
5500	CHCG	60659	2921	3W-6N	A5
5600	CHCG	60659	2920	3W-7N	E4
6300	LNWD	60659	2920	4W-7N	C3
6300	LNWD	60712	2920	5W-8N	B1
7200	LNWD	60076	2866	5W-9N	A7
7200	LNWD	60712	2866	5W-9N	A7
7200	SKOK	60076	2866	5W-9N	A7
7200	SKOK	60712	2866	5W-9N	A7
9000	MaiT	60016	2863	10W-11N	E3
9300	NLES	60016	2863	10W-11N	E3
34700	WrnT	60046	2476	18W-34N	D7
38000	BHPK	60087	2480	10W-38N	A1
38500	AntT	60081	2415	27W-38N	B7
41000	AntT	60002	2417	22W-41N	B1
N Lincoln Av US-41					
5200	CHCG	60625	2921	3W-6N	A5
5500	CHCG	60659	2921	3W-6N	A5
5600	CHCG	60659	2920	3W-7N	E4
6300	LNWD	60659	2920	4W-7N	C3
6300	LNWD	60712	2920	5W-8N	B1
7200	LNWD	60076	2866	5W-9N	A7
7200	LNWD	60712	2866	5W-9N	A7
7200	SKOK	60076	2866	5W-9N	A7
7200	SKOK	60712	2866	5W-9N	A7
S Lincoln Av					
10	ADSN	60101	2970	18W-3N	E5
10	AURA	60505	3200	35W-8S	A2
10	CPVL	60110	2800	34W-16N	E1
10	CPVL	60118	2800	34W-16N	E1
10	GNVA	60134	3020	35W-1N	A3
10	MDLN	60060	2646	19W-27N	D1
10	PKRG	60068	2917	10W-8N	E2
10	WDND	60110	2800	34W-16N	E1
10	WDND	60118	2800	34W-16N	E1
200	WKGN	60085	2537	10W-33N	A4
800	AURA	60505	3199	36W-9S	E3
900	AURA	60538	3199	36W-9S	E3
900	MTGY	60505	3199	36W-9S	E3
900	MTGY	60538	3199	36W-9S	E3
900	NCHI	60064	2537	10W-33N	A4
2000	LMBD	60148	3084	20W-1S	B2
W Lincoln Av					
100	BRTN	60010	2750	25W-18N	E2
100	LYVL	60048	2591	16W-28N	D5
100	WHTN	60187	3024	25W-0S	B6
7600	SMMT	60501	3148	9W-5S	D3
Lincoln Av S					
1000	HDPK	60035	2705	7W-21N	A6
Lincoln Av W					
400	HDPK	60035	2705	8W-21N	A6
500	HDPK	60035	2704	8W-21N	E6
Lincoln Blvd					
4500	RNPK	60471	3594	5W-27S	B4
Lincoln Cir					
-	SRWD	60404	3495	31W-24S	E6
-	SRWD	60404	3496	31W-24S	A6
Lincoln Ct					
10	LMBD	60148	3026	20W-0N	B5
10	SEGN	60177	2908	35W-7N	B4
200	WDDL	60191	2914	19W-5N	D7
300	BMDL	60108	2969	22W-4N	C4
1200	SMWD	60107	2911	27W-9N	B1
1300	AURA	60506	3137	37W-6S	C5
4300	RGMW	60008	2805	20W-14N	E3
7400	FTPK	60130	3030	9W-0N	D4
9000	ODPK	60462	3346	11W-17S	A6
N Lincoln Ct					
1500	ANHT	60004	2807	17W-15N	B2
S Lincoln Ct					
25800	MONE	60449	3682	7W-31S	E5
W Lincoln Ct					
300	ADSN	60101	2970	18W-4N	E4
26400	GrtT	60041	2473	26W-36N	D3
Lincoln Ctr					
10	OKTR	60181	3085	18W-1S	A2
Lincoln Dr					
-	CRTE	60417	3685	0E-29S	D1
200	BRLT	60103	2911	28W-7N	A5
200	GLNC	60022	2758	6W-18N	D4
400	HFET	60169	2859	23W-11N	A4
400	HFET	60194	2859	23W-11N	A4
400	SchT	60175	2963	38W-3N	A6
400	SMBG	60194	2859	23W-11N	A4
8600	LYNS	60534	3088	10W-4S	A7
15200	MKHM	60428	3349	3W-18S	A7
N Lincoln Dr					
9100	MaiT	60016	2863	11W-11N	D3
W Lincoln Dr					
25100	LkvT	60046	2474	25W-37N	B3
41000	AntT	60002	2417	22W-41N	B2
Lincoln Hwy					
-	CHHT	60411	3507	3W-25S	C7
-	JLET	60431	3417	28W-19S	B4
-	JLET	60432	3500	20W-23S	C4
-	JLET	60435	3417	28W-19S	B4
-	NLNX	60433	3500	20W-24S	C5
-	NLNX	60451	3500	19W-24S	C5
-	NlxT	60432	3500	20W-23S	C4
-	NlxT	60433	3500	20W-23S	C4
-	NlxT	60451	3500	19W-24S	C5
-	OswT	60503	3201	33W-10S	A7
-	OswT	60543	3201	33W-10S	A7
-	SchT	60175	3019	38W-2N	A1
10	CmpT	60119	3018	39W-2N	E1
10	CmpT	60175	3018	39W-2N	D1
10	SCRL	60119	3018	39W-2N	E1
10	SCRL	60175	3018	39W-2N	D1
300	MTGY	60503	3200	34W-10S	E6
300	MTGY	60504	3200	34W-10S	E6
300	MTGY	60538	3200	34W-10S	E6
300	OswT	60503	3200	34W-10S	E6
300	OswT	60504	3200	34W-10S	E6
300	OswT	60538	3200	34W-10S	E6
300	OswT	60543	3200	34W-10S	E6
1400	SCRL	60174	3019	37W-2N	D1
2400	OMFD	60461	3507	3W-25S	B7
2500	PKFT	60466	3507	3W-25S	B7
3200	MTSN	60443	3506	4W-25S	E7
3200	MTSN	60466	3506	4W-25S	E7
3200	OMFD	60461	3506	4W-25S	E7
3200	PKFT	60466	3506	4W-25S	E7
3800	SCRL	60175	3019	38W-2N	A1
5300	MTSN	60443	3505	8W-25S	B7
6200	RchT	60443	3505	8W-25S	B7
6700	FftT	60423	3505	8W-25S	A7
6700	FKFT	60423	3505	8W-25S	A7
11200	MKNA	60448	3502	14W-25S	E7
11200	MKNA	60448	3590	14W-25S	E1
Lincoln Hwy SR-38					
-	SchT	60175	3019	38W-2N	A1
10	CmpT	60119	3018	39W-2N	E1
10	CmpT	60175	3018	39W-2N	D1
10	SCRL	60119	3018	39W-2N	E1
10	SCRL	60175	3018	39W-2N	D1
1400	SCRL	60174	3019	37W-2N	D1
3800	SCRL	60175	3019	38W-2N	A1
Lincoln Hwy US-30					
-	CHHT	60411	3507	3W-25S	C7
-	JLET	60431	3417	28W-19S	B4
-	JLET	60432	3500	20W-23S	C4
-	JLET	60435	3417	28W-19S	B4
-	NLNX	60433	3500	20W-24S	C5
-	NLNX	60451	3500	19W-24S	C5
-	NlxT	60432	3500	20W-23S	C4
-	NlxT	60433	3500	20W-23S	C4
-	NlxT	60451	3500	19W-24S	C5
-	OswT	60503	3201	33W-10S	A7
-	OswT	60543	3201	33W-10S	A7
300	MTGY	60503	3200	34W-10S	E6
300	MTGY	60504	3200	34W-10S	E6
300	MTGY	60538	3200	34W-10S	E6
300	OswT	60503	3200	34W-10S	E6
300	OswT	60504	3200	34W-10S	E6
300	OswT	60538	3200	34W-10S	E6
300	OswT	60543	3200	34W-10S	E6
2400	OMFD	60461	3507	3W-25S	B7
2500	PKFT	60466	3507	3W-25S	B7
3200	MTSN	60443	3506	4W-25S	E7
3200	MTSN	60466	3506	4W-25S	E7
3200	OMFD	60461	3506	4W-25S	E7
3200	PKFT	60466	3506	4W-25S	E7
5300	MTSN	60443	3505	8W-25S	B7
6200	RchT	60443	3505	8W-25S	B7
6700	FftT	60423	3505	8W-25S	A7
6700	FKFT	60423	3505	8W-25S	A7
11200	MKNA	60448	3502	14W-25S	E7
11200	MKNA	60448	3590	14W-25S	E1
E Lincoln Hwy					
10	FKFT	60423	3503	11W-25S	E7
100	FftT	60423	3503	11W-25S	E7
400	BlmT	60411	3508	0E-25S	D7
400	CHHT	60411	3508	0E-25S	D7
400	NLNX	60451	3501	16W-24S	E6
400	NlxT	60451	3501	17W-24S	D6
800	CHHT	60411	3509	1E-25S	A7
800	FDHT	60411	3509	1E-25S	A7
1200	NLNX	60451	3502	15W-25S	C7
1200	NlxT	60451	3502	15W-25S	C7
1400	BlmT	60411	3509	2E-25S	D7
1700	SLVL	60411	3509	2E-25S	D7
2400	BlmT	60411	3510	3E-25S	A7
2700	FftT	60448	3502	14W-25S	D7
2700	FftT	60451	3502	14W-25S	D7
2700	MKNA	60448	3502	14W-25S	D7
2700	MKNA	60451	3502	14W-25S	D7
2800	LYWD	60411	3510	3E-25S	A7
21400	BlmT	60411	3598	4E-25S	C1
21400	LYWD	60411	3598	4E-25S	C1
E Lincoln Hwy US-30					
10	FKFT	60423	3503	11W-25S	E7
100	FftT	60423	3503	11W-25S	E7
400	BlmT	60411	3508	0E-25S	D7
400	CHHT	60411	3508	0E-25S	D7
400	NLNX	60451	3501	16W-24S	E6
400	NlxT	60451	3501	17W-24S	D6
800	CHHT	60411	3509	1E-25S	A7
800	FDHT	60411	3509	1E-25S	A7
1200	NLNX	60451	3502	15W-25S	C7
1200	NlxT	60451	3502	15W-25S	C7
1400	BlmT	60411	3509	2E-25S	D7
1700	SLVL	60411	3509	2E-25S	D7
2400	BlmT	60411	3510	3E-25S	A7
2700	FftT	60448	3502	14W-25S	D7
2700	FftT	60451	3502	14W-25S	D7
2700	MKNA	60448	3502	14W-25S	D7
2700	MKNA	60451	3502	14W-25S	D7
2800	LYWD	60411	3510	3E-25S	A7
21400	BlmT	60411	3598	4E-25S	C1
21400	LYWD	60411	3598	4E-25S	C1
N Lincoln Hwy					
-	NARA	60542	3137	36W-4S	E1
N Lincoln Hwy SR-31					
-	NARA	60542	3137	36W-4S	E1
N Lincoln Hwy SR-56					
-	NARA	60542	3137	36W-4S	E1
W Lincoln Hwy					
-	FftT	60423	3503	11W-25S	E7
-	JLET	60431	3417	28W-19S	A3
-	JLET	60586	3417	28W-19S	A3
10	FKFT	60423	3503	12W-25S	C7
100	NLNX	60451	3501	18W-24S	A6
300	NlxT	60451	3501	18W-24S	A6
900	FKFT	60423	3591	13W-25S	A1
1100	NlxT	60451	3500	19W-24S	E5
1300	NLNX	60451	3500	19W-24S	E5
7200	FftT	60423	3505	9W-25S	A7
7200	FKFT	60423	3505	9W-25S	A7
7200	RchT	60443	3505	9W-25S	A7
7400	FftT	60423	3504	9W-25S	D7
7400	FKFT	60423	3504	9W-25S	E7
11100	MKNA	60448	3591	13W-25S	A1
22800	JLET	60544	3417	28W-19S	A3
22800	JLET	60586	3417	28W-19S	A3
22800	PnfT	60544	3417	28W-19S	A3
22800	PnfT	60586	3417	28W-19S	A3
22900	PNFD	60586	3417	28W-19S	A3
23000	PNFD	60544	3416	29W-19S	E2
23000	PNFD	60586	3416	29W-19S	E2
23000	PnfT	60544	3416	29W-19S	E2
23000	PnfT	60586	3416	29W-19S	E2
W Lincoln Hwy US-30					
-	FftT	60423	3503	11W-25S	E7
-	JLET	60431	3417	28W-19S	A3
10	FKFT	60423	3503	12W-25S	C7
100	NLNX	60451	3501	18W-24S	A6
300	NlxT	60451	3501	18W-24S	A6
900	FKFT	60423	3591	13W-25S	A1
1100	NlxT	60451	3500	19W-24S	E5
1300	NLNX	60451	3500	19W-24S	E5
7200	FftT	60423	3505	9W-25S	A7
7200	FKFT	60423	3505	9W-25S	A7
7200	RchT	60443	3505	9W-25S	A7
7400	FftT	60423	3504	9W-25S	D7
7400	FKFT	60423	3504	9W-25S	E7
11100	MKNA	60448	3591	13W-25S	A1
22800	JLET	60544	3417	28W-19S	A3
22800	JLET	60586	3417	28W-19S	A3
22800	PnfT	60544	3417	28W-19S	A3
22800	PnfT	60586	3417	28W-19S	A3
22900	PNFD	60586	3417	28W-19S	A3
23000	PNFD	60544	3416	29W-19S	E2
23000	PNFD	60586	3416	29W-19S	E2
23000	PnfT	60544	3416	29W-19S	E2
23000	PnfT	60586	3416	29W-19S	E2
Lincoln Ln					
200	WLNG	60090	2755	13W-17N	D5
400	FKFT	60423	3503	13W-25S	B7
800	CTSD	60525	3147	13W-6S	A4
800	LynT	60525	3147	13W-6S	A4
2700	WLMT	60091	2812	5W-13N	A6
N Lincoln Ln					
100	ANHT	60004	2807	17W-14N	B4
S Lincoln Ln					
300	ANHT	60005	2807	17W-13N	B6
W Lincoln Ln					
500	DSPN	60018	2862	15W-10N	A6
700	DSPN	60018	2861	16W-10N	E6
700	MPPT	60018	2861	16W-10N	E6
700	MPPT	60056	2861	16W-10N	E6
Lincoln Ln E					
3500	RBBN	60472	3348	4W-15S	D1
Lincoln Ln W					
4000	CTWD	60472	3348	5W-15S	C1
4300	CTWD	60445	3348	5W-15S	B1
4300	RBBN	60472	3348	5W-15S	B1
Lincoln Pk					
-	MDLN	60060	2590	19W-29N	C4
N Lincoln Pk W					
2000	CHCG	60614	2978	0W-2N	B6
Lincoln Pkwy					
10	CLLK	60014	2639	35W-26N	E3
Lincoln Pl					
100	DRGV	60515	3144	18W-4S	E1
600	CTCY	60409	3352	4E-17S	B6
1400	CTCY	60409	3430	4E-19S	B3
1400	HDPK	60035	2704	8W-21N	E5
4500	LSLE	60532	3143	23W-4S	A1
Lincoln Rd					
-	LslT	60563	3142	25W-4S	B1
-	NPVL	60563	3142	25W-4S	A1
3000	OKBK	60523	3086	15W-2S	A4
18100	HtdT	60033	2464	48W-37N	E1
E Lincoln Rd					
200	ANHT	60005	2861	17W-12N	B1
400	ANHT	60056	2861	17W-12N	B1
400	MPPT	60005	2861	17W-12N	B1
400	MPPT	60056	2861	17W-12N	B1
W Lincoln Rd					
100	GrtT	60041	2529	29W-33N	D3
100	GrtT	60051	2529	29W-33N	D3
100	LKMR	60051	2529	30W-33N	A3
100	MchT	60051	2529	29W-33N	C2
1800	LKMR	60051	2528	30W-33N	E3
1800	MchT	60051	2528	30W-33N	E3
1900	MHRY	60051	2528	31W-33N	D3
2100	MPPT	60005	2861	17W-12N	B1
2100	MPPT	60056	2861	17W-12N	B1
2300	ANHT	60005	2861	17W-12N	B1
2300	ANHT	60056	2861	17W-12N	B1
Lincoln Sq					
900	EGVV	60007	2914	18W-8N	E1
Lincoln St					
-	CbaT	60010	2697	26W-21N	D7
10	GNVW	60025	2864	9W-12N	D1
10	GNVW	60053	2864	9W-12N	D2
10	HRVD	60033	2406	50W-38N	B7
10	LIHL	60156	2693	35W-22N	E3
10	MNGV	60053	2864	9W-12N	D2
100	SMBG	60172	2912	23W-7N	E4
200	EGvT	60018	2862	15W-9N	A7
200	HFET	60169	2859	23W-10N	A5
200	HFET	60194	2859	23W-10N	A5
200	LMNT	60439	3270	19W-13S	D5
200	MHTN	60442	3677	19W-31S	D5
200	SMBG	60169	2859	23W-10N	A5
200	SMBG	60194	2859	23W-10N	A5
300	ALGN	60102	2694	33W-20N	E7
300	ALGN	60102	2747	33W-20N	D1
300	LKMR	60051	2529	29W-31N	C6
300	NndT	60051	2529	29W-31N	C6
300	ROSL	60172	2912	23W-7N	E4
400	SchT	60174	2908	34W-6N	D6
500	EVTN	60201	2867	2W-12N	B1
500	ROSL	60172	2913	23W-8N	A3
500	SmbT	60172	2913	23W-8N	A3
600	DRGV	60515	3144	20W-4S	B1
700	GNVW	60025	2810	8W-13N	D7
1000	EGVV	60007	2914	20W-8N	B2
1000	NCHI	60064	2537	10W-32N	A5
1000	WKGN	60085	2537	10W-32N	A5
1400	SMBG	60193	2913	23W-8N	A2
1400	SmbT	60193	2913	23W-8N	A2
1800	EVTN	60201	2866	3W-12N	E1
2400	FNPK	60164	2973	12W-2N	A6
2400	LydT	60131	2973	12W-3N	A6
2400	LydT	60164	2973	12W-3N	A6
3500	FNPK	60131	2973	12W-4N	A3
12800	BLID	60406	3277	2W-15S	C7
16700	HLCT	60428	3427	2W-20S	D4
16700	HLCT	60429	3427	2W-20S	D4
16700	MKHM	60428	3427	2W-20S	D4
17000	EHZC	60429	3427	2W-20S	D4
E Lincoln St					
10	GDLY	60407	4030	32W-43S	D2
100	MPPT	60056	2862	15W-12N	A1
100	PLTN	60067	2752	20W-16N	E7
100	PTON	60468	3861	9W-37S	A3
200	JLET	60433	3499	23W-24S	A5
400	PLTN	60067	2753	20W-16N	A7
400	PLTN	60074	2753	20W-16N	A7
1000	DSPN	60016	2862	15W-12N	B1
1000	MPPT	60016	2862	15W-12N	B1
N Lincoln St					
10	BTVA	60510	3078	35W-1S	B1
10	HNDL	60521	3146	15W-4S	A1
10	WTMT	60559	3145	18W-5S	B2
100	ELWD	60421	3675	25W-32S	B7
100	LMBD	60148	3026	20W-1N	B3
400	BDWD	60408	3942	31W-41S	A4
400	HNDL	60521	3086	15W-4S	A7
3900	DGvT	60559	3085	18W-4S	B7
3900	WTMT	60559	3085	18W-4S	A7
S Lincoln St					
10	BTVA	60510	3078	35W-1S	B2
10	HNDL	60521	3146	15W-5S	A2
10	WTMT	60559	3145	18W-5S	B3
100	BDWD	60408	3942	31W-41S	A6
100	ELWD	60421	3675	25W-32S	B7
300	LMBD	60148	3026	20W-0N	B4
800	LKPT	60441	3419	22W-19S	D3
1800	LMBD	60148	3084	20W-1S	B2
12300	BLID	60406	3277	2W-14S	C6
12300	BLID	60827	3277	2W-14S	C6
12300	CTPK	60406	3277	2W-14S	C6
12300	CTPK	60827	3277	2W-14S	C6
W Lincoln St					
-	MPPT	60056	2862	15W-12N	A1
100	PTON	60468	3860	10W-37S	D3
100	PTON	60468	3861	9W-37S	A3
500	MPPT	60056	2861	17W-12N	C1
2000	MPPT	60005	2861	17W-12N	B1
W Lincoln St SR-83					
-	MPPT	60056	2861	16W-12N	E1
-	MPPT	60056	2862	15W-12N	A1
Lincoln Ter					
200	BFGV	60089	2754	17W-18N	B3
Lincoln Wy					
-	ELWD	60421	3675	25W-32S	C7
Lincoln Mall Dr					
100	MTSN	60443	3594	5W-25S	B1
4700	MTSN	60443	3506	5W-25S	B7
Lincoln Meadows Cir					
1600	SMBG	60173	2859	21W-10N	E5
Lincoln Meadows Dr					
1600	SMBG	60173	2859	22W-10N	C6
N Lincoln Meadows Dr					
10	SMBG	60173	2859	22W-10N	C6
S Lincoln Meadows Dr					
10	SMBG	60173	2859	21W-10N	E5
Lincoln Oaks Dr					
10	WLBK	60527	3145	16W-6S	D5
Lincoln Park Ct					
2500	CTHL	60403	3497	27W-22S	D2
Lincolnshire Av					
1500	AURA	60506	3137	36W-5S	E3
Lincolnshire Ct					
200	BGBK	60440	3269	23W-11S	A1
200	SMBG	60193	2859	23W-10N	B6
1000	ELGN	60120	2855	32W-10N	C5
1300	CLSM	60188	2967	28W-3N	A6
Lincolnshire Dr					
10	LNSH	60069	2702	14W-22N	C3
100	CLLK	60014	2640	35W-24N	A6
3700	MchT	60050	2471	32W-36N	B3
7600	BRRG	60527	3208	14W-8S	C1
13500	ODPK	60462	3346	11W-16S	A2
13500	PlsT	60462	3346	11W-16S	A2
Lincolnshire Ln					
200	BGBK	60440	3269	23W-11S	A1
600	HFET	60169	2858	25W-10N	B5
Lincolnshire Ter					
-	CRTE	60417	3596	0E-28S	E7
N Lincolnway					
10	NARA	60542	3077	36W-3S	E7
10	NARA	60542	3137	36W-4S	E1
200	BtvT	60510	3077	36W-3S	E7
200	BtvT	60539	3077	36W-3S	E7
200	BtvT	60542	3077	36W-3S	E7
N Lincolnway SR-31					
10	NARA	60542	3077	36W-3S	E7
10	NARA	60542	3137	36W-4S	E1
200	BtvT	60510	3077	36W-3S	E7
200	BtvT	60539	3077	36W-3S	E7
200	BtvT	60542	3077	36W-3S	E7
S Lincolnway					
10	NARA	60542	3137	36W-4S	E1
100	NARA	60542	3138	36W-5S	A2
200	AURA	60542	3138	36W-5S	A2
400	AURA	60506	3138	36W-5S	A2
S Lincolnway SR-31					
10	NARA	60542	3137	36W-4S	E1
100	NARA	60542	3138	36W-5S	A2
200	AURA	60542	3138	36W-5S	A2
400	AURA	60506	3138	36W-5S	A2
S Lincolnway SR-56					
10	NARA	60542	3137	36W-4S	E1
100	NARA	60542	3138	36W-4S	A1
200	AURA	60506	3138	36W-4S	A2
Lincolnway Cir					
15200	PNFD	60544	3416	30W-18S	A1
Lincolnway Dr					
10	NLNX	60451	3502	16W-24S	A6
100	NlxT	60451	3502	16W-24S	A6
Lincoln-Way Ln					
20600	FftT	60423	3503	12W-24S	D6
20600	FKFT	60423	3503	12W-25S	D6
Lincolnway St					
24600	PNFD	60544	3416	30W-18S	A1
Lincolnwood Ct					
10	AntT	60081	2415	27W-38N	A6
10	FXLK	60081	2415	27W-38N	A6
2400	AURA	60504	3201	32W-9S	C4
Lincolnwood Dr					
600	SMWD	60107	2857	28W-10N	A6
2100	EVTN	60201	2866	4W-12N	D1
2100	EVTN	60203	2866	4W-12N	C1
2100	SKOK	60203	2866	4W-12N	C1
2600	EVTN	60201	2812	4W-13N	D7
2700	WLMT	60091	2812	4W-13N	D7
2700	WLMT	60201	2812	4W-13N	D7
8800	SKOK	60076	2866	4W-11N	D3
N Lincolnwood Dr					
6800	LNWD	60712	2919	6W-8N	E2
Lincolnwood Rd					
10	HDPK	60035	2758	7W-20N	C2
N Lind Av					
10	PvsT	60162	3028	14W-0S	D6
200	HLSD	60162	3028	14W-0S	D5
1200	BKLY	60163	3028	14W-0N	D3
5200	CHCG	60630	2919	6W-6N	D5
S Lind Av					
100	NHLK	60164	3028	14W-1N	D1
Lind Ln					
1600	GRNE	60031	2478	15W-35N	B5
Lind St					
900	JltT	60432	3499	22W-22S	D2
Linda Av					
10	BmdT	60188	3024	23W-2N	E1
Linda Ct					
500	AURA	60506	3137	38W-6S	A6
600	MRGO	60152	2634	49W-25N	B4
600	WDSK	60098	2524	40W-31N	E7
600	WDSK	60098	2525	40W-31N	A7
900	SchT	60177	2908	34W-7N	E4
900	SEGN	60177	2908	34W-7N	E4
2500	MaiT	60025	2864	9W-12N	C1
Linda Dr					
800	ALGN	60102	2748	33W-20N	A1
Linda Ln					
-	WMTN	60481	3853	29W-37S	A5
-	WmTp	60481	3853	29W-37S	A5

Block	City	ZIP	Map#	CGS	Grid
Linda Ln					
10	SMWD	60107	2856	29W-10N	E6
200	ElgT	60124	2853	37W-12N	C2
200	LYWD	60411	3510	4E-25S	C7
400	AddT	60101	2970	20W-3N	B5
400	ADSN	60101	2970	20W-3N	B5
1100	GLNC	60022	2758	6W-18N	C3
2900	AURA	60502	3139	33W-4S	A1
10000	MaiT	60016	2809	12W-12N	C7
10000	MaiT	60016	2863	12W-12N	C1
N Linda Ln					
700	ADSN	60101	2970	19W-4N	D3
18200	GRNE	60031	2476	18W-36N	E5
18200	WrnT	60031	2476	18W-36N	E5
18200	WrnT	60031	2477	18W-36N	A5
W Linda Ln					
400	AddT	60101	2970	19W-4N	D3
400	ADSN	60101	2970	19W-4N	D3
24400	LkvT	60046	2416	24W-39N	C6
24900	WldT	60564	3265	31W-11S	E2
24900	WldT	60564	3266	31W-11S	A2
N Linda Rd					
300	MHRY	60050	2528	32W-32N	B5
Linda Ter					
600	WLNG	60090	2755	15W-17N	A4
Lindale St					
600	EGvT	60007	2861	18W-10N	A6
600	EGVV	60007	2861	18W-10N	A6
Lindberg Ct					
500	ELGN	60123	2854	34W-10N	D6
Lindberg Ln					
400	NHBK	60062	2756	11W-18N	D4
Lindberg Rd					
400	BRWN	60402	3088	9W-2S	D4
400	RVSD	60402	3088	9W-2S	D4
400	RVSD	60546	3088	9W-2S	D4
W Lindbergh Dr					
28400	CbaT	60010	2696	28W-23N	E2
Lindemann Ct					
10	SEGN	60177	2908	34W-8N	C3
Linden Av					
-	KLWH	60043	2812	4W-14N	B4
-	WLMT	60043	2812	4W-14N	B4
10	BFGV	60090	2755	14W-20N	C2
10	BLWD	60104	3029	12W-0N	B5
10	BmdT	60157	2913	22W-6N	C7
10	BtlT	60560	3262	40W-13S	B5
10	FXLK	60020	2473	27W-36N	C4
10	GLNC	60022	2758	5W-17N	E6
10	GLNC	60093	2758	5W-16N	E7
10	LKFT	60045	2649	10W-24N	E7
10	MDLN	60060	2646	18W-27N	E1
100	DndT	60118	2801	33W-16N	B2
100	EDND	60118	2801	33W-16N	B2
100	JLET	60433	3499	23W-24S	A6
100	JLET	60436	3499	23W-24S	A6
100	OKPK	60302	3031	8W-0N	A3
100	WLMT	60091	2813	2W-13N	A6
200	RMVL	60446	3340	24W-16S	D4
300	LKFT	60045	2650	10W-24N	A7
400	AURA	60505	3200	35W-8S	B2
400	JltT	60433	3499	23W-24S	B6
600	ELGN	60120	2855	33W-11N	B4
700	WLMT	60091	2812	3W-13N	E6
1000	DRFD	60015	2703	11W-21N	D6
1000	HDPK	60035	2705	7W-21N	A6
1200	GNVW	60025	2811	7W-14N	A4
1200	PKRG	60068	2918	9W-7N	B3
1600	HRPK	60133	2911	27W-8N	D2
1800	HDPK	60035	2704	8W-22N	E4
1800	WKGN	60085	2479	10W-36N	E5
1900	CHCG	60631	2918	9W-7N	B4
1900	JNBG	60051	2471	31W-35N	D6
1900	JNBG	60051	2472	30W-35N	A6
1900	LynT	60525	3146	13W-6S	E4
1900	LynT	60558	3146	13W-6S	E4
1900	PKRG	60631	2918	9W-7N	B4
2000	WKGN	60087	2479	10W-36N	E4
3900	WNSP	60558	3086	13W-4S	E7
4300	AlqT	60102	2694	33W-21N	E5
4300	AlqT	60102	2695	33W-21N	A5
4500	ALGN	60102	2694	33W-21N	E5
4600	GNVW	60025	2809	12W-14N	B5
7600	DRN	60561	3207	17W-8S	B2
N Linden Av					
-	WKGN	60087	2479	10W-35N	E5
10	PLTN	60074	2806	20W-16N	A1
10	WTMT	60559	3145	17W-5S	B2
700	WKGN	60085	2479	10W-35N	E7
1200	PLTN	60074	2753	20W-17N	A5
5400	NpkT	60656	2918	9W-6N	B5
38500	BHPK	60099	2421	11W-38N	E7
38500	WKGN	60099	2421	11W-38N	E7
S Linden Av					
10	PLTN	60074	2806	20W-15N	A1
100	EMHT	60126	3028	15W-1N	B2
100	PLTN	60067	2806	20W-15N	A1
100	WTMT	60559	3145	17W-5S	B3
25500	MONE	60449	3683	6W-31S	A5
W Linden Av					
18600	WrnT	60030	2533	18W-32N	D6
21800	LkvT	60046	2417	21W-39N	C6
21900	LKVL	60046	2417	22W-39N	C6
Linden Av N					
700	OKPK	60302	3031	8W-1N	A2
1200	CHCG	60707	3031	8W-1N	A1
Linden Cir					
-	DGvT	60439	3270	20W-12S	B3
400	BCHR	60401	3774	0W-36S	C7
700	ITSC	60143	2914	19W-7N	C5
1000	WNSP	60558	3146	14W-6S	D4
1100	BCHR	60401	3864	0E-36S	E2
E Linden Cir					
-	HFET	60169	2859	23W-11N	A3
W Linden Cir					
-	HFET	60169	2859	23W-11N	A3
Linden Ct					
10	CRY	60013	2641	31W-24N	C6
10	NPVL	60540	3141	28W-6S	A5
10	SEGN	60177	2908	35W-7N	B4
100	SRGV	60554	3197	42W-7S	D1
400	FKFT	60423	3503	12W-25S	C7
500	GNVA	60134	3020	36W-0N	A4
700	BGBK	60440	3268	24W-12S	D2
900	WNSP	60558	3146	14W-6S	D4
W Linden Ct					
700	ITSC	60143	2914	19W-7N	D5
Linden Dr					
-	BCHR	60401	3864	0W-36S	C1
-	DndT	60118	2801	33W-14N	A5
100	FKFT	60423	3591	11W-26S	E2
100	OSWG	60543	3263	36W-13S	E6
100	OSWG	60543	3264	36W-13S	A6
100	SMWD	60107	2911	28W-8N	B2
200	RLKP	60073	2532	23W-33N	A2
400	RDLK	60073	2532	23W-33N	A2
600	CLSM	60188	2967	26W-3N	D5
2300	WDSK	60098	2581	40W-29N	E4
2300	WDSK	60098	2582	40W-29N	A4
3600	ISLK	60042	2586	30W-28N	B6
6500	OKFT	60452	3347	8W-18S	B7
7400	JSTC	60458	3148	10W-8S	D3
8900	TYPK	60487	3424	11W-21S	A6
17100	HLCT	60429	3427	4W-20S	A4
24300	PNFD	60585	3266	30W-13S	B5
24400	WldT	60585	3266	30W-13S	B5
N Linden Dr					
10	LtRT	60545	3259	48W-12S	B4
22600	LKBN	60010	2696	28W-22N	E3
S Linden Dr					
10	LtRT	60545	3259	48W-12S	B4
800	EMHT	60126	3028	15W-0S	B6
W Linden Dr					
6800	PSHT	60463	3275	8W-15S	A7
Linden Ln					
100	CHHT	60411	3507	1W-24S	E6
200	WLNG	60090	2755	14W-18N	C4
400	ANTH	60002	2357	23W-43N	E4
400	ANTH	60002	2358	23W-43N	A4
500	LYVL	60048	2591	16W-29N	C5
500	PTON	60468	3861	8W-37S	B2
500	WCDA	60084	2643	26W-26N	C2
700	YkTp	60126	3028	15W-0S	B7
900	GNVW	60025	2811	7W-14N	A4
1000	WNSP	60558	3146	14W-6S	D4
2000	PltT	60067	2805	20W-13N	E6
4200	RGMW	60008	2806	19W-12N	C7
6100	LynT	60525	3147	13W-6S	A5
34700	AvnT	60030	2476	19W-34N	B7
34700	AvnT	60030	2533	19W-34N	C1
34700	GYLK	60030	2533	19W-34N	C1
35000	TDLK	60030	2476	19W-34N	B7
E Linden Ln					
1600	MPPT	60056	2808	14W-14N	C5
N Linden Ln					
21200	KLDR	60047	2699	21W-21N	D6
42300	AntT	60002	2357	25W-42N	A6
S Linden Ln					
26700	CteT	60417	3685	0W-32S	C7
W Linden Ln					
14000	GNOK	60048	2592	14W-28N	D7
14000	LbvT	60045	2592	14W-28N	D7
14000	LbvT	60048	2592	14W-28N	D7
25100	AntT	60002	2357	25W-43N	B4
Linden Pl					
600	EVTN	60202	2867	2W-10N	B5
4700	DRGV	60515	3144	19W-5S	D2
N Linden Pl					
2400	CHCG	60647	2976	3W-3N	E5
Linden Rd					
10	ElaT	60047	2698	24W-23N	B3
200	BRTN	60010	2698	25W-20N	A7
200	LKZH	60047	2698	24W-23N	B2
200	NfdT	60062	2757	9W-18N	C3
500	FKFT	60423	3503	12W-25S	C7
1100	BtnT	60081	2414	30W-39N	B5
1400	NHBK	60062	2757	9W-17N	C5
1600	HMWD	60430	3427	2W-21S	D6
3600	PKFT	60466	3594	4W-26S	E2
3600	PKFT	60471	3594	4W-26S	E2
3600	RNPK	60471	3594	4W-26S	E2
4600	NndT	60014	2642	30W-27N	B1
W Linden Rd					
26500	AntT	60002	2356	26W-43N	D4
Linden Rd N					
300	ANHT	60004	2807	16W-15N	D2
300	PTHT	60004	2807	16W-15N	D2
300	PTHT	60070	2807	16W-15N	D2
Linden Rd S					
200	PTHT	60070	2807	16W-15N	D2
Linden Sq					
500	WNVL	60555	3080	30W-3S	B5
4200	ZION	60099	2421	12W-41N	C2
Linden St					
-	FTPK	60130	3030	9W-0N	C4
-	RVFT	60130	3030	9W-0N	C4
-	RVFT	60305	3030	9W-0N	C4
10	LIHL	60156	2694	35W-22N	A4
100	WNKA	60093	2812	5W-15N	B3
200	GNEN	60137	3025	23W-0N	A4
200	WHTN	60187	3025	23W-0N	A4
500	CRTE	60417	3685	1W-29S	B1
1600	DSPN	60018	2863	12W-9N	A6
N Linden St					
700	ITSC	60143	2914	19W-7N	C5
Lindengate Cir					
26600	PNFD	60585	3337	33W-15S	A3
Lindengate Ct					
13400	PNFD	60585	3337	33W-15S	B3
Lindenhurst Dr					
100	LNHT	60046	2476	20W-37N	A1
Linden Leaf Dr					
1000	GNVW	60025	2810	9W-13N	C6
Linden Oaks Ln					
-	NLNX	60451	3501	18W-24S	B5
Linden Park Ln					
1500	AURA	60504	3200	33W-8S	E3
1600	AURA	60504	3201	33W-8S	A3
Linden Park Pl					
100	HDPK	60035	2704	8W-22N	E4
100	HDPK	60035	2705	8W-22N	A4
Lindenwood Av					
800	AraT	60506	3199	38W-8S	B2
Lindenwood Cir					
5200	JLET	60586	3496	30W-22S	B2
Lindenwood Ct					
100	INCK	60061	2647	17W-25N	B6
100	VNHL	60061	2647	17W-25N	B6
1900	AraT	60506	3199	38W-8S	B2
4600	MTSN	60443	3506	5W-25S	B7
Lindenwood Dr					
100	WNVL	60555	3080	30W-3S	B5
1100	NtrT	60093	2811	5W-15N	E3
1100	WNKA	60093	2811	5W-15N	E3
4000	MTSN	60443	3506	5W-25S	C7
4000	OMFD	60461	3506	5W-25S	D7
W Lindenwood Dr					
18000	WrnT	60030	2534	18W-32N	A4
Lindenwood Ln					
2500	NPVL	60565	3204	24W-10S	C6
3000	GNVW	60025	2810	10W-13N	A5
3700	GNVW	60025	2809	11W-13N	E5
4500	NHBK	60062	2756	13W-18N	A2
8100	BGBK	60440	3205	22W-9S	C3
8100	BGBK	60517	3205	22W-9S	C3
8100	WDRG	60517	3205	22W-9S	C4
Linder Av					
-	MNGV	60077	2865	6W-10N	D5
300	NHFD	60093	2811	6W-15N	D2
300	NtrT	60093	2811	6W-15N	D2
7200	SKOK	60077	2865	6W-9N	C7
7600	BRBK	60459	3211	6W-8S	D1
8200	MNGV	60053	2865	6W-10N	D5
8600	OKLN	60453	3211	6W-9S	D4
8600	OKLN	60459	3211	6W-9S	D4
8800	SKOK	60053	2865	6W-11N	D3
9300	GfnT	60014	2638	38W-25N	E4
10300	OKLN	60453	3275	6W-12S	D1
13900	BmnT	60445	3347	6W-16S	D3
13900	CTWD	60445	3347	6W-16S	D3
14100	MDLN	60445	3347	6W-17S	E4
14500	BmnT	60452	3347	6W-17S	E4
14500	MDLN	60452	3347	6W-17S	E5
14500	OKFT	60445	3347	6W-17S	E4
14500	OKFT	60452	3347	6W-17S	E4
N Linder Av					
1400	CHCG	60651	3031	6W-1N	D1
1600	CHCG	60639	3031	6W-2N	D1
2400	CHCG	60639	2975	6W-3N	D5
2700	CHCG	60641	2975	6W-3N	D5
4300	CHCG	60630	2975	6W-5N	C1
5300	CHCG	60630	2919	6W-6N	C5
5500	CHCG	60646	2919	6W-6N	C5
S Linder Av					
4700	FTVW	60638	3149	6W-5S	D1
4700	StkT	60638	3149	6W-5S	D1
6300	CHCG	60638	3149	6W-7S	D5
7300	BDPK	60638	3149	6W-8S	D7
7300	BDPK	60638	3211	6W-8S	D1
Linder Ct					
5500	CTWD	60445	3347	6W-15S	D1
8400	MNGV	60053	2865	6W-10N	D4
8400	MNGV	60077	2865	6W-10N	D4
8400	SKOK	60077	2865	6W-10N	D4
14500	OKFT	60445	3347	6W-17S	E5
14500	OKFT	60452	3347	6W-17S	E5
Linder Ln					
-	PltT	60010	2751	24W-18N	C2
25400	GrtT	60041	2474	25W-35N	A6
Lindgren Ct					
2800	AURA	60503	3265	31W-11S	D1
Lindgren Tr					
2600	AURA	60503	3265	31W-11S	D1
Lindholm Ct					
700	NPVL	60565	3203	27W-10S	B6
Lindley Rd					
400	WTMT	60559	3145	18W-6S	A4
Lindley St					
4100	DRGV	60515	3084	19W-4S	C7
Lindon Ln					
10	VNHL	60061	2647	16W-24N	C6
Lindow Ln					
-	MRGO	60152	2634	48W-25N	E4
Lindrick Ct					
900	NPVL	60563	3141	28W-5S	B3
Lindrick Ln					
2600	AURA	60504	3201	32W-9S	C4
2600	NpvT	60504	3201	32W-9S	C4
Lindsay Av					
500	WKGN	60085	2480	10W-35N	A6
Lindsay Cir					
600	NARA	60542	3078	35W-3S	B7
Lindsay Ct					
10	LMNT	60439	3270	18W-13S	E5
500	WDND	60118	2800	35W-16N	C2
1200	MltT	60187	3024	23W-0N	E4
1200	WHTN	60187	3024	23W-0N	E3
2400	WCHI	60185	2965	32W-4N	C4
Lindsay Dr					
2100	NPVL	60564	3202	29W-9S	D5
13700	ODPK	60462	3346	10W-16S	B3
W Lindsay Dr					
10	RLKB	60073	2475	23W-35N	A5
Lindsay Ln					
400	WDND	60118	2800	35W-16N	C2
3500	AlqT	60014	2641	32W-25N	B5
10000	MKNA	60448	3503	12W-23S	C4
Lindsay St					
1000	JLET	60431	3497	28W-22S	A2
9400	ODHL	60487	3423	11W-20S	E3
Lindsey Av					
10	WNFD	60190	3023	27W-0N	D4
200	GYLK	60030	2532	21W-33N	D4
400	MltT	60187	3023	26W-0N	D4
Lindsey Ct E					
10	BGBK	60440	3268	25W-11S	C1
Lindsey Ct W					
10	BGBK	60440	3268	25W-11S	C1
Lindsey Ln					
100	BGBK	60440	3268	25W-12S	C3
300	BGBK	60490	3268	25W-12S	C3
600	BGBK	60440	3204	24W-11S	C7
6500	CPVL	60110	2747	36W-17N	A6
6500	DndT	60118	2747	36W-17N	A6
Lindwall Rd					
3500	HtdT	60033	2464	48W-35N	E5
Lindy Ln					
300	WMTN	60481	3943	27W-39S	D1
Lindy St					
200	FXLK	60041	2473	27W-36N	C5
Line Dr					
900	CmpT	60119	2962	40W-2N	B7
Line Rd					
13000	JLET	60447	3495	33W-23S	C4
13000	SwdT	60447	3495	33W-23S	C4
13000	TroT	60404	3495	33W-23S	C4
17000	JLET	60586	3415	33W-20S	B6
17000	NasT	60586	3415	33W-20S	B6
17000	PNFD	60586	3415	32W-19S	B4
18000	JLET	60431	3495	33W-21S	C1
18000	JLET	60586	3495	33W-21S	C1
Line St					
-	ITSC	60143	2914	19W-6N	C6
W Line St					
100	ITSC	60143	2914	19W-6N	C6
Lineas Ln					
200	GNVA	60134	3019	37W-1N	D3
Linebarger Ct					
500	ELWD	60421	3675	25W-32S	C7
W Linecrest Dr					
4300	ALSP	60803	3276	5W-13S	B4
Lingonberry Ct					
1300	LYVL	60048	2591	17W-30N	B2
Link Ct					
2700	FSMR	60422	3507	3W-23S	B3
W Link Ln					
23300	PnfT	60586	3416	29W-19S	E3
W Linklater Ct					
900	LGNG	60525	3147	13W-5S	A1
900	LynT	60525	3147	13W-5S	A1
Links Ct					
700	RVWD	60015	2703	12W-20N	A7
Linlar Dr					
10	BbyT	60119	3018	39W-1N	D4
Lin Lor Ct					
1600	ELGN	60123	2854	35W-11N	B4
Lin Lor Ln					
1500	ELGN	60123	2854	36W-11N	A4
Linn Av					
9700	SRPK	60176	2917	12W-6N	C7
Linn Ct					
10900	LynT	60525	3146	13W-6S	E5
10900	LynT	60525	3147	13W-6S	A5
N Linn Ct					
200	NARA	60542	3078	35W-3S	A7
Linn St					
300	CLLK	60014	2639	35W-25N	E5
Linne Av					
1200	JLET	60433	3587	23W-25S	C1
1200	JltT	60433	3587	23W-25S	C1
Linnea Ln					
9400	MaiT	60016	2863	11W-12N	C1
S Linneman Rd					
-	EGvT	60005	2861	16W-10N	D5
1000	MPPT	60056	2861	16W-11N	D4
1500	EGvT	60056	2861	16W-11N	D4
Linneman St					
1800	GNVW	60025	2810	9W-13N	C7
2900	NfdT	60025	2810	10W-13N	B7
3300	NfdT	60025	2809	10W-13N	E7
S Linn White Dr					
1300	CHCG	60605	3034	0E-1S	D7
Lin's Ln					
-	CmpT	60119	2961	42W-4N	C5
Linscott Av					
4300	DRGV	60515	3144	20W-4S	C1
Linsey Av					
400	SMBG	60194	2858	26W-11N	A4
W Linsey Ln					
16000	HmrT	60441	3420	20W-21S	C6
16000	NLNX	60441	3420	20W-21S	C6
Linton Ct					
1800	SMBG	60193	2912	25W-8N	A2
Lintz St					
300	LMNT	60439	3270	19W-14S	D6
Linus Ln					
10300	OKLN	60453	3275	6W-12S	E1
Linwood Ct					
400	SMBG	60193	2858	24W-10N	E6
Lioncrest Ct					
2000	RNPK	60471	3594	4W-26S	D2
Lioncrest Dr					
1000	RNPK	60471	3594	4W-26S	D3
Lionel Dr					
-	GYLK	60030	2532	21W-32N	D5
Lionel Rd					
200	RVSD	60546	3088	9W-3S	D6
300	LYNS	60534	3088	9W-3S	D6
300	LYNS	60546	3088	9W-3S	D6
Lions Ct					
100	LKZH	60047	2698	23W-23N	E2
Lions Dr					
-	DRFD	60015	2704	10W-21N	A7
10	LKZH	60047	2698	23W-23N	E2
100	BRTN	60010	2750	25W-20N	E1
100	EGVV	60007	2914	18W-9N	E1
Lions Rd					
600	SDWH	60548	3330	51W-15S	A2
700	LtRT	60548	3330	50W-15S	B2
700	SdwT	60548	3330	51W-15S	A2
17400	LtRT	60545	3330	50W-15S	B2
Lions Chase Ct					
12500	GfnT	60142	2691	41W-20N	D7
Lions Chase Ln					
-	HTLY	60142	2691	41W-20N	D7
12400	GfnT	60142	2691	41W-20N	D7
Lion's Club Dr					
-	MNSR	46321	3430		E7
Lions Club Dr					
-	MNSR	46321	3430		E7
Lion's Club Dr					
-	MNSR	46321	3510		E1
Lipizzan Ln					
700	WCDA	60084	2643	27W-26N	C2
Lippert Ln					
700	GLHT	60139	2969	22W-2N	C7
Lippincott Ln					
200	FXLK	60020	2473	27W-37N	C3
Lippincott Rd					
10	FXLK	60020	2473	27W-36N	C3
Lippitt Ct					
1100	SMBG	60193	2912	24W-9N	C1
Lippizan Ln					
2500	RLKP	60030	2532	22W-31N	B7
N Lipps Av					
4800	CHCG	60630	2919	6W-6N	D6
Lisa Blvd					
1000	AURA	60505	3138	34W-5S	D3
Lisa Cir					
1200	LYVL	60048	2590	18W-29N	E3
Lisa Ct					
10	LIHL	60156	2694	34W-22N	C4
1600	NPVL	60563	3140	29W-6S	D4
2300	RGMW	60008	2805	21W-14N	D4
2300	RGMW	60067	2805	21W-14N	D4
2600	NHBK	60062	2810	10W-15N	A2
15300	ODPK	60462	3346	10W-18S	B7
Lisa Ln					
10	HNWD	60047	2646	20W-24N	A6
300	LYWD	60411	3510	4E-25S	C7
400	SMWD	60107	2856	29W-10N	E6
500	ElgT	60124	2907	38W-8N	B3
500	SEGN	60124	2907	38W-8N	B3
800	ELGN	60120	2855	32W-10N	C5
4400	OKFT	60452	3426	5W-19S	B3
8500	HYHL	60457	3210	10W-10S	B4
21100	STGR	60475	3597	0E-27S	A4
Lisa Rd					
500	WDND	60118	2800	34W-15N	E3
Lisa St					
700	WDSK	60098	2524	42W-31N	B6
Lisadell Dr					
19400	TYPK	60477	3504	10W-23S	B3
Lisa Marie Ct					
1700	DRFD	60015	2703	12W-20N	C7
Liscanor Av					
9000	FftT	60448	3504	11W-23S	A3
9000	MKNA	60448	3504	11W-23S	A3
Lisdowney Dr					
700	LKPT	60441	3342	21W-18S	A7
Lisk Dr					
10	HNVL	60030	2532	21W-33N	C3
Liskeard Ct					
1000	WHTN	60187	3082	24W-1S	E2
Lisle Pl					
1100	LSLE	60532	3143	23W-5S	A2
E Lismore Cir					
20200	FftT	60423	3504	10W-24S	C5
W Lismore Cir					
20200	FftT	60423	3504	10W-24S	C5
Lismore Ct					
1100	LKZH	60047	2699	23W-21N	A6
16600	TYPK	60477	3424	9W-19S	E3
Lismore Dr					
1000	DSPN	60016	2808	13W-13N	D6
S Lismore Ln					
24900	MHTN	60442	3677	19W-30S	E3
Lismore St					
3600	FSMR	60422	3506	4W-23S	D3
Lissfannon Ct					
11900	ODPK	60467	3422	14W-20S	C5
Lisson Grv					
500	NLNX	60451	3502	15W-25S	B7
700	NLNX	60451	3590	15W-25S	B1
Lisson Rd					
1800	NPVL	60565	3204	24W-10S	C5
N Lister Av					
2200	CHCG	60614	2977	2W-2N	C6
2300	CHCG	60647	2977	2W-2N	B6
Liszka Ln					
200	OSWG	60543	3263	36W-13S	E6
Lita Av					
1500	VrnT	60015	2702	15W-20N	A7
Litchfield Ct					
10	LIHL	60156	2692	38W-22N	E3
200	GYLK	60030	2475	21W-35N	E6
200	GYLK	60030	2532	21W-34N	D1
2400	NPVL	60565	3203	27W-10S	B6
7200	LGGV	60047	2646	18W-25N	E5
S Litchfield Dr					
200	RDLK	60073	2531	25W-33N	A4
300	GrtT	60073	2531	25W-32N	A4
300	RDLK	60073	2530	25W-32N	E4
Litchfield Ln					
400	BRLT	60103	2910	30W-7N	B4
400	WynT	60103	2910	30W-7N	B4
2000	LIHL	60156	2692	38W-22N	E4
Litchfield Wy					
500	OSWG	60543	3263	36W-12S	E4
W Lithuanian Plaza Ct					
2400	CHCG	60629	3151	3W-7S	A6
2400	CHCG	60636	3151	3W-7S	A6
Litt Dr					
-	BLWD	60104	3028	13W-0N	E5
-	BLWD	60162	3028	13W-0N	E5
-	HLSD	60162	3028	13W-0N	E5
4100	HLSD	60162	3029	13W-0N	A5
S Little Dr					
4800	NndT	60051	2642	29W-27N	C1
N Little St					
5600	MchT	60050	2472	29W-37N	D2
Little Bend Rd					
10	BNHL	60010	2695	31W-20N	D7
10	BNHL	60010	2748	31W-20N	D1
Little Berry Ct					
1300	NPVL	60565	3204	24W-8S	E1
Little Big Horn Dr					
3000	JLET	60435	3497	27W-21S	C1
Little Cahill St					
10	TVLY	60013	2695	31W-22N	D3
Little City Dr					
1600	PltT	60067	2805	23W-14N	A4
1700	PltT	60195	2805	23W-14N	A5
Little Creek Ct					
10	SMWD	60107	2856	30W-10N	C5
Little Creek Dr					
100	HnrT	60120	2856	30W-10N	C5
100	SMWD	60107	2856	30W-10N	C5
100	SMWD	60120	2856	30W-10N	C5
400	HnrT	60107	2856	30W-10N	C5
W Little Creek Dr					
13400	HMGN	60491	3343	16W-16S	E4
Little Creek Ln					
2400	AURA	60506	3198	39W-8S	E1
Little Dorrit					
100	JLET	60432	3499	22W-23S	D4
100	JltT	60432	3499	22W-23S	D4
Little Elm Bnd					
8900	SKOK	60076	2866	4W-11N	B3
Little Falls Ct					
900	EGVV	60007	2914	20W-8N	B3
Little Falls Dr					
1000	ELGN	60120	2855	32W-12N	D1
Little Fawn Trc					
7400	NndT	60012	2583	36W-28N	D6
Littlefield Ct					
1400	LKFT	60045	2703	13W-24N	A1
Little Flower Ln					
2500	TNLK	53181	2354		A2
Little Fort Rd					
2000	WKGN	60087	2479	12W-36N	C4
Littlehip Ct					
10	SchT	60175	2907	38W-7N	A6
Little John Ct					
200	BRLT	60103	2910	29W-8N	D2
1300	HnrT	60120	2856	31W-10N	A6
1500	HDPK	60035	2704	10W-22N	B4
Little John Ln					
600	HRVD	60033	2406	49W-38N	C6
Little Marryat Rd					
10	TVLY	60013	2695	31W-23N	D2
W Little Melody Ln					
14000	LbvT	60045	2648	14W-26N	D3
14000	MTWA	60045	2648	14W-26N	D3
Little Moose Ln					
1400	NHBK	60062	2756	11W-17N	D6
Little Musky Cir					
-	BDWD	60481	3942	30W-40S	C2
Little Oak Pth					
-	SKOK	60076	2866	4W-11N	C3
Little Path Rd					
400	DSPN	60016	2862	14W-10N	C5
Little Peninsula Rd					
200	ELGN	60123	2800	35W-14N	B6
200	ELGN	60123	2801	33W-14N	B6
W Little Pond Rd					
22100	KLDR	60047	2699	22W-21N	B6
Little Rock Rd					
100	LtRT	60545	3259	47W-11S	C2
1500	PLNO	60545	3259	47W-11S	C2
4400	LtRT	60545	3331	48W-14S	A1
W Little St. Mary's Rd					
15000	MTWA	60048	2648	15W-27N	A1
Littlestone Cir					
3900	WldT	60564	3266	30W-12S	A3
Littlestone Ct					
3800	WldT	60564	3266	30W-12S	A3
Little Stonegate Rd					
200	CRY	60013	2695	31W-23N	C1
Littleton Ct					
10	HNVL	60030	2532	22W-33N	C3
Littleton Tr					
300	ELGN	60120	2855	31W-10N	E5
300	HnrT	60120	2855	31W-10N	E5
400	ELGN	60120	2856	31W-10N	A5
700	HnrT	60120	2856	31W-10N	A5

STREET Block	City	ZIP	Map#	CGS	Grid
E Littleton Tr					
100	HNVL	60030	2532	22W-33N	C3
N Littleton Tr					
100	HNVL	60030	2532	22W-33N	C3
Little Traverse Bay Dr					
-	FKFT	60423	3504	11W-24S	A6
Littlewoods Tr					
500	HshT	60140	2796	44W-14N	D5
Litturi Ct					
400	WCDA	60084	2643	26W-26N	D2
S Lituanica Av					
3100	CHCG	60608	3091	1W-3S	E4
3400	CHCG	60609	3091	1W-3S	E4
3500	CHCG	60608	3092	1W-3S	A5
3500	CHCG	60609	3092	1W-3S	A5
Lively Blvd					
10	EGVV	60007	2861	17W-9N	B7
800	WDDL	60191	2915	17W-7N	B5
900	EGVV	60007	2915	17W-7N	B4
N Lively Blvd					
10	EGVV	60007	2861	17W-10N	B5
Live Oak Ct					
18000	TYPK	60477	3425	8W-21S	B6
Live Oak Dr					
2500	CTHL	60403	3497	27W-22S	D1
2500	CTHL	60435	3497	27W-22S	D1
2500	JLET	60435	3497	27W-22S	D1
Live Oak Ln					
2500	BFGV	60089	2701	17W-22N	C3
Live Oak Rd					
3600	NndT	60012	2584	35W-28N	A6
N Livermore Av					
6200	CHCG	60646	2919	6W-7N	C3
Liverpool Ln					
1200	MDLN	60060	2590	19W-29N	B3
Livery Cir					
100	OKBK	60523	3084	18W-3S	E5
100	OKBK	60523	3085	18W-3S	A5
Livery Ct					
10	OKBK	60523	3084	18W-3S	E5
Livingston Av					
10	CPVL	60110	2747	34W-17N	E7
1000	HDPK	60035	2704	9W-23N	B3
Livingston Ct					
800	NPVL	60540	3202	29W-7S	D1
900	IVNS	60010	2751	25W-16N	A7
Livingston Dr					
400	NLNX	60451	3501	18W-24S	A6
Livingston Ln					
800	IVNS	60010	2751	25W-16N	A7
Livingston St					
500	FXLK	60050	2472	28W-37N	D2
1700	EVTN	60201	2813	3W-13N	E7
1700	EVTN	60201	2813	3W-13N	A7
E Livingston St					
10	GDLY	60407	4030	32W-43S	C3
Liz Dr					
10900	ODPK	60467	3423	13W-20S	A4
Lizabeth Ln					
1300	WKGN	60087	2479	11W-37N	E2
Lizette Ln					
3800	GNVW	60025	2809	11W-14N	D3
Llewellyn Av					
200	HIWD	60040	2704	9W-23N	C2
700	HDPK	60035	2704	9W-23N	C2
Lloyd Av					
10	GNEN	60137	3026	20W-0S	A7
10	GNEN	60148	3026	20W-0S	A7
10	MltT	60148	3026	20W-0S	A7
10	MltT	60148	3084	21W-2S	A3
100	MltT	60148	3083	21W-2S	E3
200	BmdT	60143	2914	21W-6N	A6
200	BmdT	60143	2970	21W-5N	A1
200	ITSC	60143	2914	21W-6N	A6
300	ITSC	60143	2970	21W-5N	A1
400	ADSN	60148	2970	21W-2N	A7
500	BmdT	60148	2970	21W-2N	A7
500	DRGV	60148	3084	21W-2S	A4
500	DRGV	60515	3084	21W-2S	A4
1400	WKGN	60085	2536	11W-33N	D2
2100	LMBD	60148	3084	21W-2S	A3
S Lloyd Av					
2100	LMBD	60148	3084	21W-1S	A2
2100	MltT	60148	3084	21W-1S	A2
2900	CHCG	60608	3091	1W-2S	D3
Lloyd Ct					
1400	MltT	60187	3082	25W-1S	B2
1400	WHTN	60187	3082	25W-1S	B2
S Lloyd Dr					
10700	WRTH	60482	3275	8W-12S	A2
W Lloyd Dr					
6600	WRTH	60482	3275	8W-12S	A3
Lloyd Ln					
700	BtvT	60510	3078	35W-3S	C6
700	NARA	60542	3078	35W-3S	C6
Lloyd Pl					
800	WNKA	60093	2759	5W-16N	B7
800	WNKA	60093	2812		B1
Lloyd St					
10	CRY	60013	2641	31W-24N	D7
Lloyd Eipers Dr					
-	BGBK	60440	3269	21W-12S	E2
-	WDRG	60440	3269	21W-12S	E2
-	WDRG	60517	3269	21W-12S	E2
N Lloyds Av					
800	JLET	60432	3499	23W-22S	B2
Loatonia Ct					
1500	LYVL	60048	2647	15W-27N	E1
Lobelia Cir					
2800	NPVL	60564	3266	29W-13S	C5
Lobelia Ct					
4800	JLET	60586	3416	30W-21S	C7
Lobelia Ln					
1800	JLET	60586	3416	30W-21S	C7
Loblolly Ct					
10	LMNT	60439	3271	17W-14S	D7
Loblolly Ln					
100	CmpT	60175	2962	39W-3N	E7
Loch Ln					
-	LKPT	60441	3419	21W-19S	E2
-	LktT	60441	3419	21W-19S	E2
10	SBTN	60010	2803	26W-15N	C2
1100	LKFT	60045	2650	9W-25N	C5
21400	LktT	60403	3417	26W-20S	D5
21500	PnfT	60403	3417	26W-20S	D5
21500	PnfT	60435	3417	26W-20S	D5
W Lochanora Dr					
22000	ElaT	60047	2645	22W-25N	A5
Lochbrook Ln					
10	IVNS	60010	2750	25W-16N	E7
Loch Glen Ct					
9400	LKWD	60014	2638	38W-24N	E7
9400	LKWD	60014	2639	38W-24N	A7
Loch Glen Dr					
7400	LKWD	60014	2639	38W-24N	A7
Loch Glen Ln					
200	MHRY	60050	2528	32W-31N	C6
Lochinvar Ln					
10	OKBK	60523	3085	18W-2S	A4
Lochleven Ln					
10	IVNS	60067	2752	22W-16N	B7
Loch Lomond Dr					
10	IVNS	60067	2752	22W-16N	A7
1300	CLLK	60014	2693	36W-23N	D2
Loch Lomond Ln					
500	PTHT	60070	2808	14W-14N	B3
Lochwood Dr					
500	CLLK	60012	2639	35W-27N	E1
500	CLLK	60012	2640	35W-27N	A1
Lochwood Pl					
9300	OrlT	60487	3423	11W-21S	E6
Lock Ln					
-	NndT	60050	2585	31W-30N	C2
Lock Pl					
500	WMTN	60481	3943	27W-39S	C1
S Lock St					
2800	CHCG	60608	3091	1W-2S	D3
Lockard Ln					
400	HIWD	60040	2704	9W-23N	C2
N Locke Ln					
1600	VNHL	60061	2647	17W-27N	B2
Lockerbie Ln					
100	WLMT	60091	2811	6W-13N	D7
Lockeslee Ct					
600	GRNE	60031	2477	16W-34N	D7
Lockman Cir					
10	ELGN	60123	2800	36W-13N	A7
Lockner Blvd					
2400	PnfT	60431	3417	28W-20S	A5
W Lockport Rd					
-	PNFD	60544	3338	29W-17S	D7
-	PnfT	60544	3338	29W-17S	D7
22300	PNFD	60544	3339	28W-17S	A7
22300	PnfT	60544	3339	28W-17S	A7
22300	RMVL	60446	3339	27W-17S	B7
22300	RMVL	60544	3339	27W-17S	B7
Lockport St					
100	LMNT	60439	3270	19W-13S	D5
W Lockport St					
10	PNFD	60544	3338	29W-17S	C7
10	PnfT	60544	3338	29W-17S	D7
1700	PNFD	60544	3337	31W-17S	E7
1700	PnfT	60544	3337	32W-18S	D7
24000	NasT	60543	3337	32W-17S	B7
24000	NasT	60544	3337	32W-17S	B7
24000	PnfT	60543	3337	32W-17S	B7
W Lockport St SR-126					
700	PNFD	60544	3338	30W-17S	B7
1000	PnfT	60544	3338	30W-17S	A7
1700	PNFD	60544	3337	31W-17S	E7
1700	PnfT	60544	3337	32W-18S	D7
24000	NasT	60543	3337	32W-17S	B7
24000	NasT	60544	3337	32W-17S	B7
24000	PnfT	60543	3337	32W-17S	B7
W Lockport St US-30					
400	PNFD	60544	3338	30W-17S	A7
1000	PnfT	60544	3338	30W-17S	A7
Lockridge Av					
16400	OKFT	60452	3426	5W-19S	B3
Locksley Dr					
100	SMWD	60107	2910	28W-9N	E1
100	SMWD	60107	2911	28W-9N	A1
Lockwood Av					
-	BmnT	60445	3347	6W-16S	E2
-	CTWD	60445	3347	6W-16S	E2
200	NHFD	60093	2811	6W-15N	D2
300	NtrT	60093	2811	6W-15N	D2
6800	SKOK	60077	2919	6W-8N	D1
7500	BDPK	60638	3211	6W-8S	E1
7500	BRBK	60459	3211	6W-9S	E3
7500	BRBK	60638	3211	6W-8S	E1
8600	OKLN	60453	3211	6W-9S	E4
8600	OKLN	60459	3211	6W-9S	E4
9300	SKOK	60077	2865	6W-11N	D2
10000	GNVW	60025	2811	6W-12N	D7
10000	GNVW	60077	2811	6W-12N	D7
10000	SKOK	60077	2811	6W-12N	D7
10300	OKLN	60453	3275	6W-12S	E1
15500	OKFT	60452	3347	6W-18S	E7
15900	OKFT	60452	3425	6W-19S	E2
16700	BmnT	60452	3425	6W-20S	E4
16700	BmnT	60477	3425	6W-20S	E4
16700	OKFT	60477	3425	6W-20S	E4
N Lockwood Av					
-	CHCG	60646	2919	6W-7N	D4
10	CHCG	60644	3031	6W-0N	D4
700	CHCG	60651	3031	6W-0N	D3
1600	CHCG	60639	3031	6W-2N	D1
2000	CHCG	60639	2975	6W-2N	D6
2700	CHCG	60641	2975	6W-3N	D5
4300	CHCG	60630	2975	6W-5N	D1
5300	CHCG	60630	2919	6W-6N	D5
6700	LNWD	60077	2919	6W-8N	D2
6700	LNWD	60712	2919	6W-8N	D2
6700	SKOK	60077	2919	6W-8N	D2
S Lockwood Av					
10	CHCG	60644	3031	6W-0S	D6
4700	FTVW	60638	3149	6W-5S	D1
4700	StkT	60638	3149	6W-5S	D2
6300	CHCG	60638	3149	6W-7S	D5
7100	BDPK	60638	3149	6W-8S	E7
7300	BDPK	60638	3211	6W-8S	E1
11900	ALSP	60803	3275	6W-14S	E5
E Lockwood Cir					
800	NPVL	60563	3141	26W-5S	E2
Lockwood Ct					
900	BTVA	60510	3078	36W-2S	A4
10600	OKLN	60453	3275	6W-12S	E2
Lockwood Ct E					
1100	BFGV	60089	2701	17W-21N	C6
Lockwood Ct W					
1100	BFGV	60089	2701	17W-21N	C6
Lockwood Dr					
1100	BFGV	60089	2701	17W-21N	C6
1800	GNOK	60048	2592	14W-30N	C2
N Lockwood Dr					
500	LKPT	60441	3420	21W-18S	A1
Lockwood Ln					
100	BMDL	60108	2969	22W-5N	B2
900	BTVA	60510	3077	36W-2S	E3
900	BTVA	60510	3078	36W-2S	A3
6300	GRNE	60031	2477	16W-34N	C7
Locust Av					
10	LGNG	60525	3087	12W-4S	C6
10	WynT	60185	2966	30W-3N	C5
100	WDSK	60098	2524	41W-32N	D5
200	WYNE	60184	2966	30W-3N	C5
200	WYNE	60185	2966	30W-3N	C5
500	GNVA	60134	3020	34W-1N	D2
3400	ISLK	60042	2586	28W-28N	D5
4600	GNVW	60025	2809	12W-14N	B5
Locust Av					
5100	BKLY	60163	3028	14W-0N	C5
5100	HLSD	60162	3028	14W-0N	C5
5100	HLSD	60163	3028	14W-0N	C5
17200	TYPK	60487	3424	11W-20S	A4
Locust Cir					
-	BmnT	60426	3426	5W-19S	B1
Locust Ct					
-	BmnT	60426	3426	5W-19S	B2
10	CTCY	60409	3429	2E-18S	C1
10	NPVL	60540	3141	27W-6S	B5
10	SEGN	60177	2908	35W-7N	B5
1100	BRLT	60103	2910	30W-7N	C4
1300	GYLK	60030	2475	21W-34N	D7
Locust Dr					
-	LbvT	60048	2592	15W-28N	B6
-	MTWA	60048	2592	15W-28N	B6
-	RLKP	60073	2532	22W-33N	A2
100	PTBR	60010	2642	28W-26N	E4
100	WcnT	60010	2642	28W-26N	E4
300	LIHL	60156	2694	35W-21N	A5
500	WLNG	60090	2754	16W-18N	E2
700	SYHW	60118	2800	35W-15N	D3
700	WDND	60118	2800	35W-15N	D3
17000	HLCT	60429	3426	4W-20S	E4
26100	WmTp	60481	3761	32W-34S	D5
Locust Ln					
-	LKPT	60441	3420	19W-20S	E4
200	NLNX	60451	3501	17W-24S	C4
200	NlxT	60451	3501	17W-24S	C5
400	ROSL	60172	2913	22W-7N	B5
600	DrrT	60098	2525	39W-31N	D7
700	BLVY	60098	2525	39W-31N	D7
1300	GNVW	60025	2865	8W-12N	A1
1400	GNVW	60025	2864	8W-12N	E1
6100	LynT	60525	3146	13W-6S	E5
6400	GRNE	60048	2534	16W-32N	D6
7500	JLET	60586	3415	33W-20S	A6
S Locust Ln					
400	PTON	60468	3860	10W-37S	D4
800	PtnT	60468	3860	10W-37S	D4
W Locust Ln					
1800	MPPT	60056	2861	17W-11N	C3
Locust Pl					
400	DRFD	60015	2756	11W-20N	E1
1700	RGMW	60008	2860	21W-12N	A1
1700	RGMW	60173	2860	21W-12N	A1
1700	SMBG	60173	2860	21W-12N	A1
S Locust Pl					
25900	MONE	60449	3683	6W-31S	A6
Locust Rd					
10	NtrT	60091	2812	5W-14N	A4
10	NtrT	60093	2812	5W-14N	A4
10	WLMT	60091	2812	5W-13N	A7
10	WLMT	60093	2812	5W-14N	A4
300	WNKA	60093	2812	5W-15N	A2
2500	HLCT	60430	3427	3W-21S	B5
2500	HMWD	60430	3427	3W-21S	B5
26800	CNHN	60410	3672	33W-31S	B6
Locust St					
10	CTCY	60409	3430		C2
10	HMND	46324	3430		C2
10	OSWG	60543	3263	37W-13S	C4
100	MRGO	60152	2634	49W-26N	C3
100	SEGN	60177	2908	34W-8N	D3
200	ELGN	60123	2854	34W-11N	D5
300	BTVA	60510	3078	35W-1S	C2
300	NARA	60542	3078	35W-3S	B7
700	WNKA	60093	2812	5W-16N	A1
800	WNKA	60093	2759	5W-16N	A7
1600	DSPN	60018	2863	12W-9N	B6
17800	ThtT	60438	3429	2E-21S	D6
18200	LNSG	60438	3429	2E-21S	D7
21100	MTSN	60443	3506	4W-25S	E7
21100	MTSN	60443	3594	4W-25S	E1
N Locust St					
10	AURA	60506	3138	36W-7S	A7
200	FKFT	60423	3503	12W-25S	D7
200	FKFT	60423	3591	12W-25S	D1
600	FftT	60423	3503	12W-25S	D7
S Locust St					
10	AURA	60506	3138	36W-7S	A7
100	FKFT	60423	3591	12W-26S	D2
W Locust St					
400	CHCG	60610	3034	0W-1N	A2
S Lode Dr					
6800	WRTH	60482	3275	8W-12S	A2
S Lodge Ln					
10	LMBD	60148	3026	19W-0N	D4
W Lodge Tr					
400	WLNG	60090	2754	16W-17N	C5
Lodgepole Ct					
1100	DRN	60561	3145	17W-7S	B6
Lodi Dr					
-	DrrT	60098	2581	41W-28N	E6
-	WDSK	60098	2581	41W-28N	E6
S Loeffel Steel Dr					
14100	RVDL	60827	3350	1W-16S	A3
Logan Av					
10	GNVA	60134	3020	35W-1N	A3
400	JLET	60433	3499	22W-24S	C6
400	JltT	60433	3499	22W-24S	C6
600	ELGN	60120	2855	33W-12N	A1
700	MHRY	60050	2528	33W-32N	A4
700	SCRL	60134	3020	35W-1N	A3
700	SCRL	60174	3020	35W-1N	A3
S Logan Av					
100	JLET	60433	3499	22W-24S	C5
100	JltT	60433	3499	22W-24S	C5
W Logan Blvd					
2200	CHCG	60618	2977	2W-3N	A5
2400	CHCG	60647	2977	3W-3N	A5
2700	CHCG	60647	2976	3W-3N	E5
Logan Ct					
900	BtnT	60099	2422	9W-41N	C1
900	ZION	60099	2422	9W-41N	C1
11600	OrlT	60467	3344	14W-16S	D3
W Logan Ct					
9900	BtnT	60099	2422	10W-41N	B1
Logan Dr					
13600	OrlT	60467	3344	14W-16S	D3
13800	ODPK	60467	3344	14W-16S	D3
Logan Lp					
10	HDPK	60035	2650	8W-24N	D7
Logan St					
10	BTVA	60510	3020	35W-0S	B7
400	HMND	46320	3352		D5
400	ROSL	60172	2912	23W-8N	E3
500	SmbT	60172	2912	23W-8N	E3
700	AURA	60505	3200	36W-8S	A2
1400	SmbT	60193	2912	23W-8N	E2
2600	HDPK	60035	2704	8W-23N	D2
E Logan St					
10	LMNT	60439	3270	19W-14S	D6
800	HMND	46320	3352		E6
W Logan St					
10	LMNT	60439	3270	19W-14S	C6
Logan Ter					
10	GLF	60029	2864	8W-11N	E2
10	GLF	60029	2865	8W-12N	A1
22700	AntT	60002	2417	22W-40N	B3
Loganberry Ln					
2200	JltT	60433	3588	21W-26S	A4
Loganbury Ct					
1100	ELGN	60120	2801	32W-12N	D7
Logan Ridge Ct					
1600	JLET	60586	3495	31W-21S	E1
Logsdon Ln					
1300	BFGV	60089	2701	17W-21N	A6
Lois Av					
100	LKPT	60441	3419	22W-20S	C5
100	LktT	60441	3419	22W-20S	C5
1000	PKRG	60068	2918	10W-7N	A4
1200	PKRG	60068	2917	10W-7N	E4
N Lois Av					
900	ADSN	60101	2970	19W-4N	D3
Lois Ct					
500	ANHT	60005	2861	17W-12N	B1
500	ANHT	60056	2861	17W-12N	B1
500	MPPT	60056	2861	17W-12N	B1
1400	PKRG	60068	2917	10W-7N	E4
1600	GNVA	60134	3020	36W-0N	A5
Lois Dr					
2200	RGMW	60008	2860	19W-12N	C2
9600	MaiT	60016	2863	10W-12N	E1
Lois Ln					
100	DRPK	60010	2751	23W-20N	D1
300	LKZH	60047	2698	23W-23N	D2
900	GNVW	60025	2811	7W-14N	B3
900	NHFD	60025	2811	7W-14N	B3
900	NHFD	60093	2811	7W-14N	B3
2100	WHTN	60187	3081	26W-1S	E1
N Lois Pl					
700	JLET	60435	3498	26W-23S	A3
Lois St					
200	LKPT	60441	3419	22W-20S	C6
200	LktT	60441	3419	22W-20S	C6
W Lois St					
25400	CNHN	60410	3672	31W-30S	E4
Lois Ann Ln					
1500	NPVL	60563	3140	29W-6S	D4
N Loleta Av					
6600	CHCG	60646	2919	7W-8N	C2
Lolo Pass					
2100	JLET	60586	3415	32W-21S	C7
Lombard Av					
800	GNEN	60137	3025	21W-0S	D7
10400	CHRG	60415	3275	7W-12S	C1
11000	ALSP	60482	3275	7W-12S	B3
11000	CHRG	60482	3275	7W-12S	B3
11000	WRTH	60482	3275	7W-12S	B3
N Lombard Av					
600	LMBD	60148	3026	19W-1N	C2
S Lombard Av					
10	LMBD	60148	3026	19W-0N	C5
100	OKPK	60302	3031	7W-0S	B5
400	OKPK	60304	3031	7W-1S	B7
1200	BRWN	60304	3031	7W-1S	B7
1200	BRWN	60402	3031	7W-1S	B7
1200	CCRO	60304	3031	7W-1S	B7
1200	CCRO	60402	3031	7W-1S	B7
1200	CCRO	60804	3031	7W-1S	B7
1300	YkTp	60148	3084	19W-1S	C1
1500	BRWN	60402	3089	7W-2S	B3
1500	CCRO	60804	3089	7W-2S	B3
3100	CCRO	60402	3089	7W-3S	B5
3800	SKNY	60402	3089	7W-3S	B6
Lombard Av N					
1100	OKPK	60302	3031	7W-1N	B1
1200	CHCG	60639	3031	7W-1N	B1
Lombard Cir					
10	LMBD	60148	3026	18W-0S	E6
Lombard Ct					
1700	GLHT	60139	2968	23W-3N	E6
Lombard Dr					
800	CLLK	60014	2639	37W-24N	B7
S Lombard Ln					
12300	ALSP	60803	3276	5W-14S	C6
Lombard Rd					
700	ADSN	60101	2970	20W-2N	B7
700	ADSN	60148	2970	20W-2N	B7
700	LMBD	60101	2970	20W-2N	B7
700	LMBD	60148	2970	20W-2N	B7
N Lombard Rd					
10	AddT	60101	2970	20W-4N	B3
10	ADSN	60101	2970	20W-3N	B5
900	ADSN	60148	2970	20W-2N	B7
900	LMBD	60148	2970	20W-2N	B7
900	LMBD	60148	3026	20W-2N	B1
S Lombard Rd					
10	AddT	60101	2970	20W-3N	B6
10	ADSN	60101	2970	20W-2N	B7
300	ITSC	60143	2914	20W-6N	B7
Lombard St					
3400	FNPK	60131	2973	11W-4N	D3
N Lombard St					
700	AddT	60126	2972	15W-2N	B6
700	EMHT	60126	2972	15W-3N	B6
Lombardi Ln					
-	AURA	60503	3265	32W-11S	C1
Lombardy Ct					
700	DRFD	60015	2703	11W-20N	D7
4300	HFET	60192	2804	24W-15N	B2
Lombardy Ln					
10	OSWG	60543	3263	37W-11S	D2
600	DRFD	60015	2703	11W-20N	D7
600	DRFD	60015	2756	11W-20N	D1
1400	NPVL	60540	3140	28W-6S	E5
4200	HFET	60192	2804	24W-15N	B2
Lomond Av					
10	LslT	60515	3143	21W-6S	D4
10	LslT	60516	3143	21W-6S	D4
5500	DRGV	60515	3143	21W-5S	D3
Lomond Dr					
-	IVNS	60067	2751	23W-16N	E7
10	IVNS	60067	2804	23W-16N	E1
300	MDLN	60060	2590	19W-28N	C6
London Av					
-	DGvT	60516	3206	20W-10S	B6
-	WDRG	60516	3206	20W-10S	B6
-	WDRG	60517	3206	20W-10S	B6
N London Av					
4700	CHCG	60630	2919	6W-5N	D7
London Ct					
600	BFGV	60089	2701	17W-22N	B5
1300	GYLK	60030	2475	21W-34N	D7
1500	NPVL	60563	3140	29W-5S	D3
E London Ct					
500	RLKB	60073	2475	22W-36N	B4
N London Ct					
10	SEGN	60177	2908	35W-8N	B4
S London Ct					
10	SEGN	60177	2908	35W-8N	B4
London Dr					
-	BMDL	60108	2969	23W-4N	A4
-	BMDL	60139	2969	23W-4N	A4
2100	GLHT	60139	2969	23W-4N	A4
3000	OMFD	60461	3507	3W-25S	A7
London Ln					
-	SRWD	60404	3583	32W-25S	D1
-	TroT	60404	3583	32W-25S	D1
1300	GNVW	60025	2810	8W-14N	D4
1300	GNVW	60025	2811	8W-14N	A5
18700	FftT	60448	3503	13W-22S	B1
18700	MKNA	60448	3503	13W-22S	B1
S London Ln					
12600	PSHT	60463	3274	9W-14S	D7
London Pl					
200	WLNG	60090	2755	15W-18N	A4
London Rd					
1300	NlxT	60451	3501	16W-23S	E3
1400	NLNX	60451	3501	16W-23S	E3
London Sq					
-	HFET	60169	2858	24W-11N	D4
London Tr					
400	MHRY	60050	2527	34W-32N	B5
London Bay					
10400	MKNA	60448	3503	13W-22S	B1
Londonberry Av					
1100	GNEN	60137	3025	21W-0S	E7
1100	GNEN	60137	3026	21W-0S	A7
Londonberry Ct					
1000	BGBK	60440	3205	21W-9S	E4
Londonberry Ln					
600	BGBK	60440	3205	21W-9S	E4
London Bridge Ct					
-	FftT	60423	3590	15W-26S	C2
London Bridge Dr					
11600	FftT	60423	3590	14W-26S	D1
11600	FftT	60448	3590	14W-26S	E1
11600	MKNA	60423	3590	14W-26S	D1
11600	MKNA	60448	3590	14W-26S	E1
Londonderry Ct					
200	MDLN	60060	2590	19W-28N	D6
3500	HFET	60067	2804	23W-14N	E4
Londonderry Dr					
6100	AlqT	60013	2641	31W-25N	C4
Londonderry Ln					
10	LNSH	60069	2702	14W-22N	C4
10	RVWD	60015	2702	14W-22N	D4
Loneflower Dr					
10	SjnT	46311	3598		C6
Lone Oak Rd					
7100	SPGV	60081	2413	31W-39N	D6
N Lone Oak Rd					
40000	BHPK	60099	2421	12W-40N	B4
40200	ZION	60099	2421	12W-40N	B4
Lone Oak Tr					
1200	AURA	60506	3137	37W-5S	C3
Lone Pine Ct					
20800	DRPK	60010	2698	23W-20N	D7
N Lone Rock Rd					
33200	WrnT	60030	2534	18W-33N	A3
Lonesome Rd					
-	HRVD	60033	2405	51W-39N	E5
Lone Star Dr					
2100	LKPT	60441	3419	22W-20S	D5
Lone Star Wy					
10600	HTLY	60142	2692	39W-21N	B6
Lone Tree Ct					
4300	AURA	60564	3202	30W-9S	B5
6300	GRNE	60031	2534	16W-34N	C2
W Lone Tree Ct					
27400	CNHN	60410	3672	33W-30S	B5
Lonetree Dr					
7800	MchT	60097	2469	36W-37N	D2
W Lone Tree Ln					
23100	ElaT	60047	2698	23W-23N	E1
23100	ElaT	60047	2699	23W-23N	A1
Long Av					
10	SmbT	60193	2912	25W-8N	B3
100	NARA	60542	3078	35W-3S	A6
2100	BlmT	60411	3597	2E-27S	D5
3600	JNBG	60050	2471	31W-35N	E6
7500	BDPK	60638	3211	6W-8S	D1
7500	BRBK	60638	3211	6W-8S	D1
7700	MNGV	60053	2865	6W-9N	D6
7700	MNGV	60077	2865	6W-9N	D6
7700	SKOK	60053	2865	6W-9N	D6
7900	BRBK	60459	3211	6W-9S	D3
8600	OKLN	60453	3211	6W-9S	D4
8600	OKLN	60459	3211	6W-9S	D4
9200	SKOK	60077	2865	6W-11N	D2
10300	OKLN	60453	3275	6W-12S	D1
13500	BmnT	60445	3347	6W-16S	E2
13500	CTWD	60445	3347	6W-16S	E4
13500	WthT	60445	3347	6W-16S	E4
14300	MDLN	60445	3347	6W-17S	E5
14300	MDLN	60452	3347	6W-17S	E5
14300	OKFT	60452	3347	6W-17S	E5
15900	OKFT	60452	3425	6W-19S	E2
16200	BmnT	60477	3425	6W-19S	E2
16200	OKFT	60477	3425	6W-19S	E2
N Long Av					
10	CHCG	60644	3031	6W-0N	D5
1400	CHCG	60651	3031	6W-1N	D1
1600	CHCG	60639	3031	6W-2N	D1
1600	CHCG	60639	2975	6W-2N	D7
2700	CHCG	60641	2975	6W-3N	D5
4300	CHCG	60630	2975	6W-5N	D1
5400	CHCG	60630	2919	6W-6N	D5
34600	GrtT	60041	2474	25W-34N	B7
S Long Av					
4700	FTVW	60638	3149	6W-5S	D1
4700	StkT	60638	3149	6W-5S	D2
6300	CHCG	60638	3149	6W-7S	D5
6400	BDPK	60638	3149	6W-7S	D5
N Long Dr					
39700	AntT	60002	2416	25W-39N	B4
Long Ln					
400	BGBK	60440	3268	24W-12S	E3
N Long Ln					
2200	MchT	60051	2529	30W-34N	A1
W Long Ln					
28300	WcnT	60084	2642	28W-26N	E3
28300	WcnT	60084	2643	28W-26N	A3
Long Rd					
-	GNVW	60091	2811	6W-13N	D7
800	GNVW	60025	2811	6W-13N	D7
900	WLMT	60091	2811	6W-13N	D7
Longacre Ct					
800	ISLK	60042	2586	28W-29N	E4
800	ISLK	60042	2587	27W-28N	A7
Long Acre Dr					
2700	NPVL	60564	3203	28W-10S	A7
Longacre Dr					
200	CmpT	60175	2906	41W-6N	A6

STREET Block	City	ZIP	Map#	CGS	Grid
Longacre Ln					
500	ISLK	60042	2586	28W-28N	E7
1200	WLNG	60090	2755	15W-16N	B7
Longacres Ln					
300	PltT	60067	2806	20W-13N	A6
300	SMBG	60067	2806	20W-13N	A7
Longaker Rd					
900	NHBK	60062	2757	8W-17N	E4
900	NHBK	60062	2758	8W-17N	A5
Long Bay Ct					
-	ANTH	60002	2357	25W-41N	B7
Long Beach Dr					
22900	FftT	60423	3591	13W-27S	B5
W Long Beach Dr					
25400	GrtT	60041	2474	25W-34N	A7
Long Beach Rd					
10	OswT	60538	3199	36W-10S	E7
10	OswT	60538	3200	36W-10S	A7
100	OSWG	60538	3200	36W-10S	A7
100	OSWG	60543	3200	36W-10S	A7
Longbeach Rd					
500	LKMR	60051	2529	29W-31N	D7
Longboat Ct					
1000	SMBG	60194	2858	24W-11N	D3
Longboat Dr					
1700	EGVV	60007	2913	22W-8N	C2
Longboat Ln					
800	SMBG	60194	2858	24W-11N	D3
Long Boat Keys Ln					
-	SMWD	60120	2856	30W-9N	C7
Longbow Ct					
10	SEGN	60177	2908	35W-7N	B5
1600	WLNG	60090	2754	16W-18N	D4
Long Bow Dr					
17200	LKPT	60441	3420	20W-20S	B5
Longbranch Ct					
1500	NPVL	60565	3204	25W-8S	B3
Longchamps Ct					
1300	GYLK	60030	2532	21W-34N	D1
S Longcommon Ln					
-	PNFD	60586	3415	31W-19S	D2
Long Common Pkwy					
-	ELGN	60123	2853	37W-11N	C4
-	ELGN	60124	2853	37W-11N	C4
-	ElgT	60123	2853	37W-11N	C4
-	ElgT	60124	2853	38W-10N	B5
-	ElgT	60124	2907	37W-9N	B1
Longcommon Rd					
-	RVSD	60546	3088	10W-3S	B5
500	BRWN	60402	3088	9W-2S	D3
500	BRWN	60546	3088	9W-2S	D4
Long Cove Ct					
10	LIHL	60156	2693	36W-22N	C4
600	RVWD	60015	2703	13W-20N	A7
Long Cove Dr					
10	LMNT	60439	3271	17W-15S	B7
10	LMNT	60439	3343	17W-15S	B1
600	LIHL	60156	2693	37W-22N	C4
Longest Dr					
-	GNVA	60134	3021	32W-1N	B4
2300	WCHI	60185	3021	32W-1N	B4
Longfellow Av					
400	DRFD	60015	2703	10W-21N	E6
400	DRFD	60015	2704	10W-20N	A7
400	GNEN	60137	3025	21W-0N	D5
3000	HLCT	60429	3427	3W-20S	A5
Longfellow Ct					
1600	WHTN	60187	3082	24W-2S	D3
Longfellow Dr					
100	WHTN	60187	3082	24W-1S	C3
Longfellow Ln					
600	MDLN	60060	2646	18W-26N	E2
Longfield Av					
10	NHLK	60164	2972	14W-2N	D6
Longfield Dr					
9600	HTLY	60142	2692	39W-22N	C4
Longfield Ln					
-	AvnT	60030	2476	20W-35N	A6
300	GYLK	60030	2476	20W-35N	A6
Longford Cir					
1200	ELGN	60120	2855	32W-11N	D4
Longford Ct					
10	OSWG	60543	3263	37W-11S	D2
100	ROSL	60172	2912	24W-7N	D5
200	ELGN	60120	2855	32W-11N	D3
1000	WTMT	60559	3145	17W-6S	C5
Longford Dr					
10	ELGN	60120	2855	31W-11N	D3
600	DSPN	60016	2808	13W-13N	D6
600	MPPT	60016	2808	13W-13N	D6
600	MPPT	60056	2808	13W-13N	D6
700	ROSL	60172	2912	24W-7N	D5
1000	WTMT	60559	3145	17W-6S	C5
3200	JLET	60431	3497	28W-25S	B7
3200	JLET	60431	3585	28W-25S	B1
3200	JLET	60436	3585	27W-25S	C1
6200	MHRY	60050	2527	35W-32N	A5
Longford Rd					
-	HRPK	60103	2911	27W-7N	C6
-	HRPK	60133	2911	27W-7N	C6
900	BRLT	60103	2911	27W-7N	C5
Longford St					
1200	WDRG	60517	3206	20W-9S	B3
Long Grove Ct					
3000	AURA	60504	3201	31W-8S	D3
Long Grove Dr					
700	AURA	60504	3201	31W-8S	D3
Long Grove Ln					
3000	AURA	60504	3201	31W-8S	D3
Long Grove Rd					
10	DRPK	60010	2752	22W-20N	A1
100	BRTN	60010	2751	23W-20N	D1
100	DRPK	60010	2751	23W-20N	D1
100	ElaT	60010	2751	23W-20N	E1
500	DRPK	60074	2752	22W-20N	C1
Long Grove Rd CO-A49					
10	DRPK	60010	2752	22W-20N	A1
100	BRTN	60010	2751	23W-20N	D1
100	DRPK	60010	2751	23W-20N	D1
100	ElaT	60010	2751	23W-20N	E1
500	DRPK	60074	2752	22W-20N	C1
W Long Grove Rd					
3400	ElaT	60047	2700	20W-20N	A7
3400	LGGV	60047	2700	20W-20N	A7
3500	KLDR	60047	2700	20W-20N	A7
20700	KLDR	60047	2699	21W-20N	D7
21400	ElaT	60074	2699	21W-20N	D7
21500	DRPK	60074	2752	21W-20N	C1
21500	ElaT	60074	2752	21W-20N	C1
21700	DRPK	60010	2752	21W-20N	C1
W Long Grove Rd CO-A49					
3400	ElaT	60047	2700	20W-20N	A7
3400	LGGV	60047	2700	20W-20N	A7
3500	KLDR	60047	2700	20W-20N	A7
20700	KLDR	60047	2699	21W-20N	D7
21400	ElaT	60074	2699	21W-20N	D7
W Long Grove Rd CO-A49					
21500	DRPK	60074	2752	21W-20N	C1
21500	ElaT	60074	2752	21W-20N	C1
21700	DRPK	60010	2752	21W-20N	C1
Long Hill Rd					
200	GRNE	60031	2535	14W-33N	B3
Long Lake Dr					
600	RDLK	60073	2531	24W-34N	D1
600	RLKB	60073	2531	24W-34N	D1
1300	AvnT	60073	2531	24W-34N	B1
1300	GrtT	60041	2531	24W-34N	B1
Longlane Rd					
700	NLNX	60451	3589	16W-25S	E1
Longleaf Dr					
100	NPVL	60540	3141	28W-6S	A5
Longley Ct					
14600	LKPT	60441	3421	18W-19S	B3
N Longmeadow Av					
6400	CHCG	60646	2919	6W-8N	E3
6400	LNWD	60646	2919	6W-8N	E3
6500	LNWD	60712	2919	6W-8N	E2
6700	LNWD	60077	2919	6W-8N	E2
6700	SKOK	60077	2919	6W-8N	E2
Long Meadow Cir					
500	SCRL	60174	2964	34W-3N	D6
26600	FmtT	60060	2646	20W-26N	A3
Long Meadow Ct					
200	OSWG	60543	3263	37W-13S	C5
26800	FmtT	60060	2646	20W-26N	A2
Longmeadow Ct					
10	BNHL	60010	2748	30W-16N	E6
10	BNHL	60010	2749	30W-16N	A6
700	CLSM	60188	2967	27W-3N	D6
800	LKBN	60010	2697	27W-24N	C1
N Long Meadow Ct					
20600	KLDR	60047	2699	20W-20N	E7
20600	KLDR	60047	2752	21W-20N	C1
W Long Meadow Ct					
15100	LKPT	60441	3420	18W-19S	E3
Long Meadow Dr					
-	HmrT	60441	3421	18W-19S	A3
-	LKPT	60441	3421	18W-19S	A3
800	SMBG	60193	2859	23W-9N	A7
900	SMBG	60193	2913	23W-9N	A1
Longmeadow Dr					
-	AURA	60504	3202	30W-8S	B1
-	LktT	60441	3418	25W-19S	B3
10	BNHL	60010	2748	30W-16N	E6
10	BNHL	60010	2749	30W-16N	A6
10	LNHT	60046	2476	20W-38N	A1
10	LNHT	60046	2418	20W-38N	A7
100	LNHT	60046	2418	20W-38N	A7
700	CLSM	60188	2967	27W-3N	D6
800	GNVA	60134	3020	34W-1N	E3
900	NfdT	60025	2809	10W-13N	E6
1600	GNVW	60025	2809	10W-14N	E4
2500	NHBK	60062	2809	10W-16N	E1
2500	NHBK	60062	2810	10W-16N	A1
4300	GRNE	60031	2535	14W-33N	C3
13300	HTLY	60142	2744	43W-19N	B3
20400	CTHL	60403	3418	25W-19S	B3
21000	LktT	60403	3418	26W-19S	A3
26300	FmtT	60060	2646	20W-26N	A3
W Long Meadow Dr					
14900	LKPT	60441	3421	18W-19S	A3
15100	LKPT	60441	3420	19W-19S	E3
Longmeadow Ln					
1000	LKFT	60045	2649	12W-26N	B3
1000	WNSP	60558	3146	14W-6S	D3
1100	GLNC	60022	2758	7W-18N	B4
1500	BRLT	60103	2966	30W-5N	B2
1700	HRPK	60133	2911	26W-8N	E2
12000	HMGN	60491	3422	15W-20S	C4
Longmeadow Pkwy					
-	ALGN	60102	2746	36W-19N	E4
-	ALGN	60102	2747	36W-19N	A4
-	DndT	60102	2746	36W-19N	E4
-	DndT	60118	2746	36W-19N	E4
Longmeadow Rd					
-	JNBG	60050	2471	31W-35N	E6
10	NHFD	60091	2811	6W-14N	D4
10	NHFD	60093	2811	6W-14N	D4
10	NtrT	60093	2811	6W-14N	E4
10	WLMT	60091	2811	6W-14N	D4
1100	NHBK	60062	2757	8W-18N	D3
3900	DRGV	60515	3084	18W-4S	E7
Longmoor Dr					
6800	GfnT	60014	2639	38W-25N	A5
6800	LKWD	60014	2639	38W-25N	A5
Long Oak Dr					
200	WCHI	60185	3022	30W-2N	B2
Longreen Rd					
-	LslT	60540	3142	25W-6S	C5
Long Ridge Ct					
1900	JLET	60586	3416	31W-20S	A6
Longridge Ct					
10	BFGV	60089	2701	16W-21N	D6
200	NPVL	60565	3203	26W-9S	E4
Longridge Dr					
100	BMDL	60108	2968	23W-5N	E2
Longridge Rd					
100	SchT	60175	2907	38W-7N	B5
W Long Run Ct					
13200	HMGN	60491	3343	16W-16S	E3
Long Run Dr					
-	OrlT	60467	3344	14W-16S	D4
11600	ODPK	60467	3344	14W-16S	D4
13700	HMGN	60491	3343	18W-16S	A3
Long Shadow Ln					
400	CmpT	60175	2962	40W-5N	B2
Longspur Ct					
1600	NPVL	60565	3203	26W-9S	E3
Longstreet Dr					
900	BRLT	60103	2911	28W-6N	B6
Longtree Ct					
-	SMBG	60173	2859	21W-12N	E1
1700	RGMW	60008	2860	21W-12N	A1
1700	RGMW	60173	2860	21W-12N	A1
1700	SMBG	60008	2860	21W-12N	A1
1700	SMBG	60173	2860	21W-12N	A1
Longtree Dr					
-	WLNG	60070	2754	15W-17N	E6
400	WLNG	60090	2754	15W-17N	E6
Longtree Ln					
1100	WLNG	60004	2754	16W-17N	E6
1100	WLNG	60090	2754	16W-17N	E6
Longvalley Ct					
1600	NHBK	60062	2756	11W-17N	C6
Longvalley Dr					
1700	NHBK	60062	2756	11W-16N	C7
E Long Valley Dr					
1200	PLTN	60074	2753	19W-17N	D5
1200	PltT	60074	2753	19W-17N	D5
Longvalley Rd					
1200	GNVW	60025	2811	8W-12N	A7
1400	GNVW	60025	2810	8W-12N	E7
Longview Ct					
10	SEGN	60177	2908	35W-7N	B4
800	SRGV	60554	3136	41W-5S	A2
Longview Dr					
-	BMDL	60139	2968	24W-4N	D4
-	GLHT	60139	2968	24W-4N	D4
200	GNVA	60134	3020	34W-1N	E3
300	BMDL	60108	2968	24W-4N	C4
400	ALGN	60102	2695	33W-22N	A4
400	AlqT	60102	2695	33W-22N	A4
500	ANTH	60002	2358	23W-42N	A6
500	SchT	60175	2963	36W-5N	E2
700	CTSD	60525	3147	12W-6S	B4
700	LynT	60525	3147	12W-6S	B4
2600	LSLE	60532	3142	24W-6S	C5
3200	PKCY	60085	2536	12W-33N	B3
13500	HMGN	60491	3342	19W-16S	E3
21200	FKFT	60423	3592	9W-25S	E1
Long View Ln					
500	PltT	60124	2852	40W-10N	B6
S Longview Ln					
14000	PnfT	60544	3339	27W-16S	C5
W Longview Ln					
600	PLTN	60067	2805	21W-15N	C2
N Longview Pt					
23300	LKBN	60010	2697	26W-23N	C2
Longview Rd					
300	WKGN	60087	2480	10W-36N	A4
1700	WKGN	60087	2479	11W-36N	D4
2000	NfdT	60062	2756	11W-16N	C7
Longwood Av					
500	GLNC	60022	2758	5W-17N	E4
Longwood Cir					
11300	ODPK	60467	3422	14W-20S	E5
Longwood Ct					
-	WDSK	60098	2582	38W-30N	E2
10	ALGN	60102	2695	33W-20N	A7
10	BFGV	60089	2754	17W-18N	A3
10	JLET	60432	3500	21W-23S	A3
10	JltT	60432	3500	21W-23S	A4
400	CHHT	60411	3507	2W-24S	D5
700	MNKA	60447	3672	34W-29S	A2
2000	RMVL	60446	3339	27W-17S	B6
N Longwood Ct					
600	GNWD	60425	3428	0W-21S	B7
S Longwood Ct					
13100	PlsT	60464	3346	10W-15S	C1
Longwood Dr					
-	BLVY	60098	2582	38W-30N	E2
-	HHLL	60051	2586	29W-29N	B3
-	NndT	60051	2586	30W-29N	B3
-	WDSK	60098	2582	38W-30N	E2
10	ALGN	60102	2694	33W-20N	E7
10	ALGN	60102	2747	33W-20N	E1
10	BRRG	60527	3146	14W-6S	C5
10	JLET	60432	3500	21W-23S	A3
10	JltT	60432	3500	21W-23S	A3
400	BFGV	60089	2754	17W-18N	A3
400	CHHT	60411	3507	2W-24S	D5
500	ALGN	60102	2695	33W-21N	A7
500	LKFT	60045	2650	10W-24N	B7
800	LKVL	60046	2417	22W-39N	C5
1100	LSLE	60532	3143	23W-6S	A5
11900	BLID	60406	3277	2W-14S	C5
11900	BLID	60643	3277	2W-14S	C5
11900	CHCG	60643	3277	2W-14S	C5
14100	SjnT	46311	3598		E5
17400	ODPK	60467	3422	14W-20S	D4
26500	LbvT	60045	2648	14W-26N	C2
27200	MTWA	60048	2648	14W-26N	C3
E Longwood Dr					
-	WDSK	60098	2582	38W-29N	D3
3200	CteT	60417	3598	3E-29S	B7
N Longwood Dr					
300	GNWD	60425	3508	0W-22S	B1
500	GNWD	60425	3428	0W-21S	C7
800	JLET	60432	3500	21W-22S	A2
S Longwood Dr					
-	BlmT	60411	3598	4E-28S	C6
-	CteT	60417	3598	4E-28S	C6
-	SjnT	46311	3598	4E-28S	C6
9500	CHCG	60620	3213	2W-11S	C7
9500	CHCG	60643	3213	2W-11S	C7
10200	CHCG	60643	3277	2W-12S	C2
11800	BLID	60406	3277	2W-13S	C5
11800	BLID	60643	3277	2W-13S	C5
W Longwood Dr					
-	WDSK	60098	2582	38W-29N	D3
26900	GrtT	60041	2473	27W-35N	C6
27000	FXLK	60041	2473	27W-35N	C6
Longwood Ln					
3000	AURA	60502	3078	33W-3S	E6
10400	OKLN	60453	3276	5W-12S	C1
Longwood Pl					
10	ELGN	60123	2854	35W-12N	C2
Longwood Rd					
6300	GRNE	60048	2534	16W-32N	D5
Longwood Ter					
100	MDLN	60060	2646	19W-26N	D2
Longwood Wy					
10	DPgT	60441	3342	20W-15S	A2
10	LMNT	60439	3342	20W-15S	A2
E Lonnquist Blvd					
10	MPPT	60056	2862	15W-11N	A2
W Lonnquist Blvd					
10	MPPT	60056	2862	15W-12N	A2
200	MPPT	60056	2861	17W-12N	B2
Lonnquist Dr					
3400	FNPK	60131	2973	12W-4N	C3
Lonsdale Av					
1600	NPVL	60540	3202	29W-7S	E1
Lonsdale Rd					
10	EGVV	60007	2914	19W-8N	D2
200	PTHT	60070	2808	15W-14N	A4
Looking Glass Ct					
2500	AURA	60502	3139	32W-7S	C6
Looking Post Av					
3700	NPVL	60564	3266	30W-11S	B1
Looking Post Ct					
3800	NPVL	60564	3266	30W-11S	A1
Look Out Ct					
600	NPVL	60540	3141	26W-7S	E7
600	NPVL	60540	3203	26W-8S	D2
Lookout Dr					
-	PGGV	60140	2797	43W-15N	C4
7300	MchT	60097	2469	36W-37N	E2
Lookout Ln					
700	CmpT	60175	2963	39W-5N	A2
700	SchT	60175	2963	39W-5N	A2
W Lookout Point Ct					
26200	CNHN	60410	3672	32W-30S	C5
N Lookout Pointe Rd					
23500	LKBN	60010	2697	27W-23N	B1
Loomes Av					
1900	DRGV	60516	3144	20W-7S	A6
Loomis Av					
-	EHZC	60429	3427	1W-20S	E5
-	HRVY	60429	3427	1W-20S	E5
-	ThtT	60426	3349	1W-16S	E4
14400	HRVY	60426	3349	1W-17S	E5
15600	HRVY	60426	3427	1W-19S	E2
16000	MKHM	60426	3427	1W-19S	E2
16000	MKHM	60428	3427	1W-19S	E2
17400	HMWD	60429	3427	1W-20S	E5
17900	HMWD	60430	3427	1W-21S	E7
18900	HMWD	60430	3507	1W-22S	E2
19100	HMWD	60430	3508	1W-23S	A3
S Loomis Av					
23600	CteT	60417	3596	1W-29S	A7
23600	CteT	60475	3596	1W-29S	A7
23600	STGR	60417	3596	1W-29S	A7
23600	STGR	60475	3596	1W-29S	A7
23900	CteT	60417	3685	1W-29S	A1
S Loomis Blvd					
4700	CHCG	60609	3151	1W-5S	D2
5500	CHCG	60636	3151	1W-8S	D7
7500	CHCG	60620	3213	1W-9S	D3
Loomis Ct					
13400	CTWD	60445	3347	6W-15S	E2
Loomis Ln					
13500	CTWD	60445	3347	6W-16S	E2
S Loomis Pl					
3600	CHCG	60609	3091	1W-3S	D5
N Loomis St					
10	NPVL	60540	3141	26W-6S	E5
100	CHCG	60607	3033	1W-0N	D4
400	NPVL	60563	3141	26W-5S	E4
S Loomis St					
10	CHCG	60607	3033	1W-1S	D7
10	NPVL	60540	3141	26W-6S	D5
1100	CHCG	60608	3033	1W-1S	D7
1500	CHCG	60608	3091	1W-2S	E3
3900	CHCG	60609	3091	1W-4S	D6
8700	CHCG	60620	3213	1W-11S	D6
9400	CHCG	60643	3213	1W-11S	D6
10300	CHCG	60643	3277	1W-12S	E1
12200	CTPK	60643	3277	1W-14S	E6
12500	CTPK	60827	3277	1W-14S	E6
W Loon Dr					
22000	AntT	60002	2417	22W-40N	C3
W Loon Lake Blvd					
-	LKVL	60046	2417	22W-40N	A4
22600	AntT	60002	2417	22W-40N	A4
Loon Lake Ct					
-	PGGV	60140	2798	40W-15N	B4
Loop Dr					
-	CHCG	60637	3152	0E-6S	D3
Loop Rd					
2300	ALGN	60102	2746	36W-18N	E4
E Loop Rd					
10	WHTN	60187	3082	24W-2S	D4
200	MltT	60187	3082	24W-3S	D5
W Loop Rd					
10	WHTN	60187	3082	24W-2S	C4
200	MltT	60187	3082	24W-3S	C5
Lootens Ct					
100	BTVA	60510	3078	36W-1S	A2
W Loral Av					
1300	JLET	60435	3498	25W-22S	B3
Loran Dr					
1700	GNVA	60134	3019	36W-0N	E4
1700	GNVA	60134	3020	36W-0N	A4
Lor Ann St					
600	SEGN	60177	2908	34W-8N	E4
Loras Ct					
-	CCHL	60478	3506	5W-22S	B1
Loras Ln					
7100	MchT	60097	2469	36W-36N	E3
18600	CCHL	60478	3506	5W-22S	B2
N Loras Ln					
9200	NLES	60714	2864	10W-11N	B2
N Lord Av					
10	CPVL	60110	2800	34W-17N	E1
100	CPVL	60110	2747	34W-17N	E7
S Lord Av					
10	CPVL	60110	2800	34W-16N	E1
Lord St					
10	ELGN	60123	2855	33W-10N	A6
100	ELGN	60123	2854	33W-10N	E6
Lorden Ct					
1100	AlqT	60013	2642	30W-25N	B4
Lore Ln					
1300	LMBD	60148	3084	20W-1S	B1
Loreen Ct					
600	OSWG	60543	3264	34W-11S	E1
Loreen Dr					
-	AraT	60502	3139	33W-5S	A3
-	AraT	60505	3139	33W-5S	A3
-	AURA	60502	3139	33W-5S	A3
-	AURA	60505	3139	33W-5S	A3
Lorel Av					
7000	SKOK	60077	2919	6W-8N	D1
7500	BDPK	60638	3211	6W-8S	E1
7500	BRBK	60459	3211	6W-9S	D3
7500	BRBK	60638	3211	6W-8S	E1
8600	OKLN	60453	3211	6W-9S	E4
8600	OKLN	60459	3211	6W-9S	E4
9200	SKOK	60077	2865	6W-11N	D2
10500	OKLN	60453	3275	6W-12S	E2
14700	MDLN	60445	3347	6W-17S	E5
14700	MDLN	60452	3347	6W-17S	E5
14700	OKFT	60452	3347	6W-17S	E5
15800	OKFT	60452	3425	6W-18S	E1
N Lorel Av					
10	CHCG	60644	3031	6W-0N	D5
1400	CHCG	60651	3031	6W-1N	D1
1600	CHCG	60639	3031	6W-2N	D1
2000	CHCG	60639	2975	6W-2N	D6
S Lorel Av					
4700	FTVW	60638	3149	6W-5S	D1
4700	StkT	60638	3149	6W-5S	D1
5000	CHCG	60638	3149	6W-5S	D1
6400	BDPK	60638	3149	6W-7S	D5
Lorelei Dr					
500	SMBG	60193	2912	24W-9N	E1
900	ZION	60099	2362	12W-42N	C7
1400	BtnT	60099	2421	12W-41N	C1
1400	ZION	60099	2421	12W-41N	C1
Loren Ct					
2600	ALGN	60102	2746	37W-19N	D2
S Loren Dr					
1000	JLET	60431	3585	28W-25S	B1
Loren Ln					
-	ALGN	60118	2746	37W-19N	C2
2600	ALGN	60102	2746	37W-19N	D2
Lorene Ct					
3400	WKGN	60087	2479	11W-38N	D1
Lorenz Av					
17000	LNSG	60438	3430	3E-20S	A4
18800	LNSG	60438	3510	3E-22S	B1
Lorete Ln					
1400	NHBK	60062	2756	11W-17N	D6
Loretta Av					
1100	JLET	60435	3498	25W-22S	B2
1300	JltT	60436	3586	24W-25S	D2
Loretta Dr					
200	CmpT	60175	2962	39W-3N	D7
N Loretto Av					
37000	LkvT	60046	2475	20W-37N	E2
Loretto Ln					
-	WHTN	60187	3082	25W-2S	A3
18700	CCHL	60478	3506	5W-22S	B2
18900	CCHL	60477	3506	5W-22S	B2
18900	RchT	60477	3506	5W-22S	B2
Lori Ct					
-	BMDL	60108	2913	22W-6N	B7
22700	RNPK	60471	3594	5W-27S	C5
Lori Dr					
-	GNVW	60025	2810	10W-15N	A3
Lori Ln					
500	PltT	60124	2906	39W-9N	D1
8800	ODPK	60462	3346	11W-16S	A4
11600	HTLY	60142	2745	40W-20N	A1
S Lori Ln					
10500	PSHL	60465	3274	9W-12S	D2
Lorie Ln					
900	LKZH	60047	2644	23W-24N	D7
900	LKZH	60047	2698	23W-24N	D1
Lorien Ct					
200	EDND	60118	2801	33W-16N	B2
W Lorient Dr					
3100	MHRY	60050	2528	32W-32N	C5
Lori Lyn Ln					
1400	NHBK	60062	2756	12W-17N	A6
1500	NfdT	60062	2756	12W-17N	A6
Lorin Ln					
4900	OKFT	60452	3348	6W-17S	A6
N Loring Av					
5200	CHCG	60630	2919	6W-6N	C5
Loriss Pl					
2600	CHCG	60007	2916	15W-8N	A2
Lorlyn Cir					
1000	BTVA	60510	3078	36W-0S	A1
Lorlyn Dr					
-	WnfT	60185	3022	29W-0S	E7
900	WCHI	60185	3022	29W-0S	D7
N Loron Av					
6800	CHCG	60646	2919	7W-8N	C1
Lorr Dr					
-	WDSK	60098	2581	42W-30N	B2
Lorraine Av					
10	DRGV	60517	3143	21W-7S	E6
10	WDRG	60517	3143	21W-7S	E6
400	WKGN	60085	2536	11W-34N	E1
500	WnfT	60555	3081	27W-3S	C6
500	WNVL	60555	3081	27W-3S	C6
900	WKGN	60085	2479	11W-35N	E6
2100	JltT	60433	3500	21W-24S	A5
2900	WKGN	60087	2479	11W-37N	E2
E Lorraine Av					
10	ADSN	60101	2970	18W-2N	E7
10	ADSN	60101	2971	18W-2N	A7
200	AddT	60101	2971	18W-2N	A7
200	AddT	60181	2971	18W-2N	A7
400	ADSN	60181	2971	18W-2N	A7
400	VLPK	60101	2971	18W-2N	A7
W Lorraine Av					
500	EMHT	60101	2971	17W-2N	C6
500	EMHT	60126	2971	17W-2N	C6
Lorraine Cir					
200	BMDL	60108	2968	24W-5N	D1
700	HDPK	60035	2704	8W-20N	D7
2500	GNVA	60134	3019	37W-1N	C3
Lorraine Ct					
10	ODHL	60013	2642	30W-26N	A3
700	LKPT	60441	3419	22W-20S	D4
22600	RNPK	60471	3594	6W-27S	A4
Lorraine Ct E					
1600	LKPT	60441	3419	22W-20S	D4
Lorraine Dr					
10	DGvT	60527	3207	17W-9S	D4
200	CLLK	60012	2640	34W-26N	C2
200	CLLK	60014	2640	34W-26N	C2
400	WnfT	60185	3081	28W-1S	A2
400	WnfT	60190	3081	28W-1S	A2
9700	CTSD	60525	3147	12W-6S	C4
W Lorraine Ln					
22800	JLET	60586	3417	28W-19S	A4
22800	PnfT	60586	3417	28W-19S	A4
Lorraine Pl					
1200	SMBG	60173	2859	22W-10N	D5
1300	WKGN	60085	2479	11W-35N	E6
S Lorraine Rd					
100	GNEN	60137	3025	23W-0S	A7
100	GNEN	60187	3025	23W-0S	A7
100	WHTN	60187	3025	23W-0S	A7
500	GNEN	60137	3083	23W-1S	A1
500	GNEN	60187	3083	23W-1S	A1
500	WHTN	60137	3083	23W-1S	A2
500	WHTN	60187	3083	23W-1S	A1
Lorraine St					
200	GNEN	60137	3025	23W-0S	A6
200	GNEN	60187	3025	23W-0S	A6
200	WHTN	60187	3025	23W-0S	A6
8000	BtnT	60081	2414	30W-39N	A4
8000	SPGV	60081	2414	30W-39N	A4
Lorraine Ter					
7000	SKNY	60402	3088	8W-4S	E6
Lorree Ln					
600	LIHL	60156	2694	34W-22N	C4
Lorry Ct					
700	MltT	60137	3083	21W-1S	D2
Los Angeles Av					
17900	HMWD	60430	3427	3W-21S	B7
Los Angeles Ct N					
17900	HMWD	60430	3427	3W-21S	B6
Los Angeles Ct S					
18100	HMWD	60430	3427	3W-21S	B7
Losey Ct					
10	LMNT	60439	3270	19W-14S	D6
Los Lagos Dr					
100	BMDL	60108	2968	24W-5N	D2
Los Palos Ln					
9000	PSHL	60465	3209	11W-11S	E7
9100	PSHL	60465	3209	11W-11S	E7
9100	PlsT	60480	3209	11W-11S	E7
Lost Boy Ln					
13500	HMGN	60491	3344	16W-16S	A3
13500	LMNT	60439	3344	16W-16S	A3
Lost Meadows Ln					
100	WnfT	60555	3080	29W-2S	D3
Lost View Ln					
500	CmpT	60175	2961	42W-5N	C2
S Lothair Av					
11100	CHCG	60643	3277	2W-13S	C3

STREET Block	City	ZIP	Map#	CGS	Grid
Lothair Dr					
500	LYVL	60048	2591	17W-28N	B6
W Lotta St					
100	GNWD	60425	3508	0W-22S	D2
Lotus Av					
7700	BRBK	60459	3211	6W-8S	D2
7800	MNGV	60053	2865	6W-9N	D6
7800	SKOK	60053	2865	6W-9N	D6
8600	OKLN	60453	3211	6W-9S	D4
8600	OKLN	60459	3211	6W-9S	D4
8900	SKOK	60077	2865	6W-11N	D2
N Lotus Av					
300	CHCG	60644	3031	6W-0N	D4
700	CHCG	60651	3031	6W-0N	D3
1600	CHCG	60639	3031	6W-2N	D1
2400	CHCG	60639	2975	6W-3N	D5
2800	CHCG	60641	2975	6W-3N	D4
5300	CHCG	60630	2919	6W-6N	C5
5500	CHCG	60646	2919	6W-6N	C5
38500	AntT	60081	2415	27W-38N	B6
41500	AntT	60002	2415	26W-41N	E1
41800	AntT	60002	2356	26W-41N	E7
S Lotus Av					
10	CHCG	60644	3031	6W-0S	D5
4700	FTVW	60638	3149	6W-5S	D1
4700	StkT	60638	3149	6W-5S	D2
5000	CHCG	60638	3149	6W-5S	D2
W Lotus Av					
26300	AntT	60002	2415	26W-38N	D6
Lotus Ct					
500	WLNG	60090	2754	16W-18N	D3
2200	NPVL	60565	3204	24W-10S	D5
Lotus Dr					
100	LKMR	60051	2529	29W-31N	D6
900	RDLK	60073	2531	24W-34N	D1
900	RLKB	60073	2531	24W-34N	D1
1300	RLKB	60073	2474	24W-35N	D6
1500	RLKH	60073	2474	24W-35N	D6
8800	HYHL	60457	3210	11W-10S	A4
Lotus Ln					
400	GNVW	60025	2810	10W-12N	A7
400	GNVW	60025	2864	10W-11N	A2
400	MaiT	60025	2864	10W-11N	A2
500	NfdT	60025	2810	10W-12N	A7
2500	CTHL	60403	3417	27W-21S	D6
Lotus Pl					
600	HDPK	60035	2704	9W-24N	B1
W Lotus Rd					
26000	AntT	60002	2415	26W-39N	E4
Lotus St					
100	WCDA	60084	2643	25W-27N	E1
Lotus Ridge Rd					
10	KdlT	60560	3333	42W-15S	E2
10	OswT	60560	3333	42W-15S	E2
Lotz Dr					
-	RVDL	60827	3350	1W-16S	A2
Lou Av					
6100	CLLK	60014	2640	35W-24N	B6
Lou Boudreau Blvd					
14200	DLTN	60419	3350	0E-16S	E3
N Loucks St					
10	AURA	60504	3200	34W-7S	E1
10	AURA	60505	3200	34W-7S	E1
100	AURA	60505	3138	34W-7S	E7
S Loucks St					
10	AraT	60504	3200	34W-8S	E1
10	AURA	60504	3200	34W-8S	E1
10	AURA	60505	3200	34W-8S	E1
Loudon Rd					
400	RVSD	60546	3088	9W-2S	C3
Louella Av					
5400	MchT	60050	2472	29W-37N	D2
Louetta Dr					
-	OrlT	60467	3423	13W-21S	B6
10400	ODPK	60467	3423	13W-21S	B6
Louetta Ln					
10800	ODPK	60467	3423	13W-21S	A6
10800	OrlT	60467	3423	13W-21S	A6
Loughborough Ct					
1000	WHTN	60187	3082	23W-1S	E2
Louis Av					
1000	ALGN	60102	2748	34W-19N	A2
1200	EGVV	60007	2861	17W-9N	C7
15900	SHLD	60473	3428	0E-18S	E1
E Louis Av					
10	LKFT	60045	2649	10W-24N	E6
10	LKFT	60045	2650	10W-24N	A6
W Louis Av					
10	LKFT	60045	2649	10W-24N	E6
Louis Ct					
5200	GRNE	60031	2478	15W-35N	A5
16800	SHLD	60473	3428	0E-19S	E3
Louis Dr					
200	WLSP	60480	3209	11W-9S	D2
Louis Rd					
-	JltT	60436	3587	23W-26S	A2
10	JltT	60433	3587	23W-26S	A2
Louis St					
2000	LydT	60160	2973	12W-2N	B7
2000	LydT	60164	2973	12W-2N	B7
2000	MLPK	60160	2973	12W-2N	B7
2000	MLPK	60164	2973	12W-2N	B7
3400	FNPK	60131	2973	12W-4N	B3
N Louis St					
10	MPPT	60056	2808	15W-13N	B7
S Louis St					
10	MPPT	60056	2808	15W-12N	B7
200	MPPT	60056	2862	15W-12N	B1
200	PLNO	60545	3259	48W-14S	C7
900	DSPN	60016	2862	15W-11N	B2
900	DSPN	60056	2862	15W-11N	B2
900	MPPT	60016	2862	15W-11N	B2
Louisa St					
300	SRWD	60404	3496	30W-24S	C7
E Louisa St					
-	SRWD	60404	3496	30W-24S	C7
N Louisa St					
300	SRWD	60404	3496	30W-24S	C7
Louisa May Alcott Ln					
100	CmpT	60175	2962	39W-4N	D5
Louis Bork Dr					
1400	BTVA	60510	3021	33W-0S	B6
1400	GnvT	60510	3021	33W-0S	B6
N Louise Av					
6100	CHCG	60646	2919	6W-7N	C3
Louise Ct					
-	RNPK	60471	3594	4W-27S	D5
100	WDDL	60191	2915	17W-5N	B7
500	LKZH	60047	2699	21W-22N	C4
3200	LNSG	60438	3510	4E-22S	B1
6700	HMND	46324	3430		E3
Louise Dr					
1600	SEGN	60177	2908	36W-7N	A4
3200	LNSG	60438	3510	4E-22S	B1
E Louise Dr					
18900	LNSG	60438	3510	4E-22S	B1
W Louise Dr					
18800	LNSG	60438	3510	4E-22S	B1
N Louise Ln					
1400	PLTN	60074	2752	21W-17N	C4
1400	PltT	60074	2752	21W-17N	C4
S Louise Ln					
1000	JLET	60431	3585	28W-25S	B1
W Louise Ln					
700	PTON	60468	3860	10W-37S	D4
N Louise Pl					
35500	GrtT	60041	2474	25W-35N	A5
Louise St					
1300	NndT	60014	2586	30W-27N	A7
1900	NndT	60014	2585	30W-27N	E7
3800	SKOK	60076	2866	4W-9N	B6
4800	SKOK	60077	2865	6W-9N	E6
Louisiana Ct					
3200	NCHI	60088	2593	12W-30N	C2
10700	ODPK	60467	3423	13W-21S	A7
Louisiana Dr					
1800	EGVV	60007	2913	22W-8N	D3
Louis Sherman Dr					
3000	SCHT	60411	3596	0W-27S	C5
3000	SCHT	60475	3596	0W-27S	C5
3000	STGR	60411	3596	0W-27S	C5
3000	STGR	60475	3596	0W-27S	C5
3300	CRTE	60417	3596	0W-27S	C5
Louisville Ln					
1700	CLLK	60014	2693	36W-22N	C3
Loulla St					
600	CteT	60417	3686	0E-31S	A5
Lourdes Dr					
-	HMGN	60491	3343	17W-18S	D7
-	HMGN	60491	3421	17W-18S	D1
Love Dr					
500	PTHT	60070	2808	13W-15N	E1
20400	LYWD	60411	3509	2E-24S	D5
20500	BlmT	60411	3509	2E-24S	D5
Love St					
600	EGvT	60007	2915	18W-8N	A1
600	EGVV	60007	2915	18W-8N	A1
Lovedale Ln					
10	NARA	60542	3138	36W-5S	A3
N Lovejoy Av					
5300	CHCG	60630	2919	7W-6N	C5
Loveland Ct					
100	GLBT	60136	2799	38W-14N	A5
19100	MKNA	60448	3502	15W-23S	C2
Loveland Dr					
200	GLHT	60139	2969	23W-3N	A4
Loveland Ln					
8400	PSHL	60465	3274	10W-12S	B2
Loveland St					
2700	NPVL	60564	3202	29W-10S	D6
S Loveland St					
12200	ALSP	60803	3276	5W-14S	B6
12800	ALSP	60803	3348	5W-15S	B1
Lovell Ct					
1100	EGVV	60007	2913	21W-8N	E2
Lovell St					
10	ELGN	60120	2854	34W-12N	E2
300	ELGN	60120	2855	33W-12N	A2
Loverock Av					
3300	STGR	60475	3596	0W-27S	C5
3400	CRTE	60417	3596	0W-28S	C6
W Lovers Ln					
18600	WrnT	60030	2533	18W-33N	E2
W Loves Ln					
2000	CteT	60417	3684	2W-29S	D2
2000	CteT	60466	3684	2W-29S	D2
2000	UYPK	60417	3684	2W-29S	D2
2000	UYPK	60466	3684	2W-29S	D2
Low Av					
800	WKGN	60085	2536	10W-34N	E1
800	WKGN	60085	2537	10W-34N	A1
1700	NndT	60050	2586	30W-29N	A4
Lowden Av					
10	WHTN	60187	3081	27W-1S	D2
10	WnfT	60187	3081	27W-1S	D2
500	GNEN	60137	3083	22W-1S	B1
E Lowden Av					
1000	WHTN	60187	3082	23W-1S	E1
E Lowden Ln					
1400	MPPT	60056	2808	14W-13N	C6
1500	DSPN	60016	2808	14W-13N	D6
1500	DSPN	60056	2808	14W-13N	D6
1500	MPPT	60016	2808	14W-13N	D6
Lowden St					
12300	HTLY	60142	2744	43W-19N	A2
Lowe Av					
-	BlmT	60411	3508	0W-24S	B4
500	CHHT	60411	3508	0W-24S	B5
1400	CHHT	60411	3508	0W-25S	B1
15600	HRVY	60426	3428	0W-18S	B1
15900	HRVY	60473	3428	0W-19S	B2
15900	SHLD	60426	3428	0W-19S	B2
16600	SHLD	60473	3428	0W-19S	B3
S Lowe Av					
-	RVDL	60827	3350	1W-15S	B2
2600	CHCG	60616	3092	0W-3S	A4
3900	CHCG	60609	3092	0W-4S	A6
5100	CHCG	60609	3152	0W-5S	A2
6300	CHCG	60621	3152	0W-7S	A5
7500	CHCG	60620	3214	0W-9S	A2
9400	CHCG	60628	3214	0W-11S	A6
11800	CHCG	60628	3278	0W-14S	B5
14500	HRVY	60426	3350	1W-16S	B4
14500	HRVY	60827	3350	1W-16S	B4
Lowe Rd					
1500	ALGN	60102	2695	32W-21N	A6
Lowe St					
3900	PKCY	60085	2535	13W-33N	E3
Lowell Av					
400	GNEN	60137	3025	21W-0N	D5
7400	LNWD	60076	2866	5W-9N	A7
7400	LNWD	60712	2866	5W-9N	A7
7800	SKOK	60076	2866	5W-10N	A5
16200	SHLD	60473	3428	0E-19S	E1
17300	HLCT	60429	3427	3W-20S	A5
N Lowell Av					
1600	CHCG	60639	3032	5W-1N	A1
1600	CHCG	60651	3032	5W-1N	A1
2800	CHCG	60639	2976	5W-3N	A4
4200	CHCG	60641	2976	5W-5N	A1
4300	CHCG	60630	2976	5W-5N	A1
4400	CHCG	60630	2920	5W-5N	A7
6100	CHCG	60646	2920	5W-7N	A3
6300	CHCG	60712	2920	5W-7N	A3
6300	LNWD	60712	2920	5W-7N	A3
7200	LNWD	60712	2866	5W-9N	A7
7300	LNWD	60076	2866	5W-9N	A7
7300	SKOK	60076	2866	5W-9N	A7
Lowell Cir					
1100	SMBG	60193	2858	24W-9N	C7
Lowell Dr					
300	SEGN	60177	2908	35W-8N	A2
7000	CPVL	60110	2748	32W-17N	D7
Lowell Ln					
200	YkTp	60148	3085	18W-1S	A1
700	YkTp	60181	3085	18W-1S	A1
800	NPVL	60540	3202	29W-8S	E1
1000	SMBG	60193	2858	24W-9N	C7
1600	LKFT	60045	2703	12W-23N	B1
Lowell Pl					
200	VNHL	60061	2647	17W-26N	B3
Lowell St					
2200	AURA	60506	3137	38W-6S	A6
Lowell Ter					
8800	SKOK	60076	2866	5W-11N	A3
Lower Horseshoe Dr					
400	TNLK	53181	2354		D1
Lowery Ct					
2700	ZION	60099	2421	11W-40N	D4
Lowestoft Ln					
500	EGVV	60007	2914	19W-8N	C2
Lowlands Dr					
-	GYLK	60030	2532	21W-34N	D2
Lowrie Ct					
400	ELGN	60120	2855	33W-11N	A4
Lowry St					
2200	AraT	60506	3198	38W-8S	E2
2200	AraT	60506	3199	38W-8S	A2
W Loy St					
300	LMBD	60148	3026	20W-1N	A2
N Loyola Av					
37800	BHPK	60087	2480	10W-38N	A1
38200	BHPK	60087	2422	10W-38N	A7
38200	BHPK	60099	2422	10W-38N	A7
W Loyola Av					
1000	CHCG	60626	2921	1W-8N	D2
1900	CHCG	60645	2921	2W-8N	B2
3800	LNWD	60712	2920	4W-8N	B2
Loyola Dr					
300	ELGN	60123	2853	36W-10N	E6
1100	LYVL	60048	2591	17W-29N	A3
1500	LslT	60565	3204	24W-8S	D2
1500	NPVL	60565	3204	24W-8S	D2
4400	MHRY	60050	2527	33W-32N	E5
Lra Dr					
200	AURA	60506	3137	38W-7S	B7
300	AURA	60506	3199	38W-7S	B1
W Luana Dr					
27500	GrtT	60041	2473	27W-35N	B6
Luana Rd					
10	JltT	60433	3587	23W-26S	A2
Luau Dr					
700	DSPN	60016	2862	14W-12N	D1
Lubliner Ter					
100	BtnT	60081	2414	29W-39N	D5
100	FXLK	60081	2414	29W-39N	D5
N Luby Ct					
35200	GrtT	60041	2473	26W-35N	D6
E Lucas Dr					
10	PSHL	60465	3274	10W-13S	A3
S Lucas Dr					
10	PSHL	60465	3274	11W-13S	A3
W Lucas Dr					
10	PSHL	60465	3274	11W-13S	A3
Lucas Ln					
400	PLNO	60545	3259	47W-14S	D7
Lucas Rd					
8900	CLLK	60012	2639	38W-27N	A1
8900	DrrT	60012	2639	38W-27N	A1
8900	DrrT	60098	2639	38W-27N	A1
9300	CLLK	60012	2638	38W-27N	E1
9300	CLLK	60098	2638	38W-27N	E1
9300	DrrT	60098	2638	38W-27N	E1
10500	DrrT	60098	2581	40W-28N	E6
10500	DrrT	60098	2582	40W-27N	B7
10500	WDSK	60098	2581	40W-28N	E6
Lucas St					
1000	CTCY	60409	3351	3E-17S	E5
1000	CTCY	60409	3352	3E-17S	A5
W Lucas St					
200	JLET	60436	3498	24W-24S	E6
Luce Blvd					
-	NCHI	60088	2537	10W-31N	A7
2400	NCHI	60088	2594	10W-31N	A1
E Lucent Ln					
-	LSLE	60532	3082	24W-4S	C7
-	NPVL	60532	3082	25W-4S	B7
-	NPVL	60563	3082	25W-4S	B7
W Lucent Ln					
1900	LSLE	60532	3082	25W-4S	B7
1900	MltT	60563	3082	25W-4S	B7
1900	NPVL	60532	3082	25W-4S	B7
1900	NPVL	60563	3082	25W-4S	B7
N Lucerne Av					
6000	CHCG	60646	2919	6W-7N	D3
Lucerne Ct					
100	WLNG	60090	2808	14W-15N	B1
700	MDLN	60060	2590	19W-28N	C6
Lucerne Dr					
1300	CLLK	60014	2693	36W-23N	D2
Lucerne Ln					
-	LYVL	60048	2591	18W-29N	A4
-	MDLN	60048	2591	18W-29N	A4
-	MDLN	60060	2591	18W-29N	A4
5700	LIHL	60156	2692	39W-23N	B2
Lucia Av					
1700	WKGN	60085	2536	11W-33N	D2
W Lucia Av					
2500	WKGN	60085	2536	12W-33N	C2
Lucile Av					
500	ELGN	60120	2855	32W-10N	C5
Lucille Av					
300	ELGN	60120	2855	32W-10N	C5
400	FRGV	60021	2696	29W-23N	B3
1100	TNLK	53181	2354		A1
Lucille Ct					
100	BRLT	60103	2911	28W-8N	A3
Lucille Dr					
-	MONE	60449	3683	6W-31S	A5
Lucille Ln					
200	SMBG	60193	2912	23W-8N	E2
1800	HRPK	60133	2911	27W-6N	D6
12500	PlsT	60464	3273	12W-14S	B7
Lucille St					
500	SEGN	60177	2908	34W-8N	E3
Lucina Av					
5400	MchT	60050	2472	29W-37N	D2
Lucinda					
900	BFGV	60089	2701	17W-21N	B7
Luckie Ct					
4100	ZION	60099	2362	12W-42N	B6
Lucky Ct					
700	OSWG	60543	3263	36W-11S	E1
Lucky Debonair Ct					
1700	WHTN	60187	3082	24W-2S	C3
Lucky Lake Ct					
27600	GNOK	60045	2648	13W-27N	D1
Lucky Lake Dr					
2300	GNOK	60045	2592	13W-27N	D7
13500	GNOK	60045	2648	13W-27N	E1
Lucre Ct					
100	SMBG	60173	2859	22W-10N	C5
Lucy Ct					
100	LKZH	60047	2698	23W-24N	D1
Lucy Dr					
7600	MchT	60097	2526	36W-34N	D1
Lucy Ln					
2900	FNPK	60131	2972	13W-3N	E5
2900	FNPK	60164	2972	13W-3N	E5
2900	LydT	60164	2972	13W-3N	E5
Lucylle Av					
1600	SCRL	60174	3020	34W-2N	D1
Lucylle Ct					
1800	SCRL	60174	3020	34W-2N	D2
Luda St					
600	ELGN	60120	2855	33W-13N	B1
Ludbury Ct					
11700	HTLY	60142	2744	42W-20N	A1
Ludbury Rdg					
11700	HTLY	60142	2744	42W-20N	A1
Ludeka Pl					
100	ELGN	60123	2854	34W-11N	D4
Ludeman Dr					
10	PKFT	60466	3595	3W-26S	A2
Ludington Cir					
1400	RMVL	60446	3417	26W-18S	E1
Ludington Ct					
3900	HRPK	60133	2967	27W-4N	D3
4100	HFET	60192	2804	24W-15N	C2
N Ludlam Av					
5200	CHCG	60630	2919	6W-6N	D5
Ludlow Av					
600	ELGN	60120	2855	33W-12N	B1
Ludwig Av					
100	CTHL	60403	3418	24W-21S	D7
100	CTHL	60435	3418	24W-21S	D7
Luella Av					
10	CTCY	60409	3351	2E-16S	D4
16500	SHLD	60473	3429	2E-19S	D3
S Luella Av					
-	CHCG	60617	3279	2E-11S	D1
-	CHCG	60633	3351	2E-15S	D2
-	CTCY	60409	3351	2E-15S	D2
7100	CHCG	60649	3153	2E-8S	D7
7500	CHCG	60649	3215	2E-9S	D2
7800	CHCG	60617	3215	2E-9S	D3
Luella Ct					
22100	SLVL	60411	3597	2E-26S	D3
Luis Munoz Marin Dr					
1000	CHCG	60622	3032	3W-1N	E2
W Lukas Av					
800	PLTN	60067	2805	22W-14N	C4
N Lullo Dr					
600	ADSN	60101	2970	18W-4N	E4
Lumber St					
1200	CRTE	60417	3685	1W-29S	B2
S Lumber St					
1400	CHCG	60607	3034	0W-1S	B7
1400	CHCG	60616	3034	0W-1S	B7
1600	CHCG	60616	3092	0W-2S	A2
2300	CHCG	60608	3091	1W-2S	E2
2300	CHCG	60608	3092		E2
Lumley Dr					
-	MchT	60097	2470	35W-37N	A3
-	RGWD	60097	2470	35W-37N	A3
Luna Av					
7700	BRBK	60459	3211	6W-8S	D2
7800	SKOK	60053	2865	6W-9N	C6
7800	SKOK	60077	2865	6W-9N	C6
8800	MNGV	60053	2865	6W-11N	C3
14100	BmnT	60445	3347	6W-16S	D4
14100	MDLN	60445	3347	6W-16S	D4
N Luna Av					
1400	CHCG	60651	3031	6W-1N	C1
1500	CHCG	60639	3031	6W-1N	C1
2400	CHCG	60639	2975	6W-3N	C5
2800	CHCG	60641	2975	6W-3N	C4
5200	CHCG	60630	2919	6W-6N	C5
5500	CHCG	60646	2919	6W-6N	C5
S Luna Av					
4700	FTVW	60638	3149	6W-5S	D1
4700	StkT	60638	3149	6W-5S	D2
5000	CHCG	60638	3149	6W-5S	D2
Lunar Av					
8900	ODPK	60462	3346	11W-17S	A5
Lunar Dr					
200	RDLK	60073	2531	23W-34N	D1
Lund Av					
10100	AlqT	60102	2695	33W-21N	A5
10400	AlqT	60102	2694	33W-21N	E5
Lund Ln					
600	BTVA	60510	3078	34W-2S	D3
Lundberg Av					
1300	BTVA	60510	3019	36W-0S	E7
Lundergan Av					
1500	PKRG	60068	2863	12W-10N	C4
Lundquist Dr					
-	AURA	60585	3265	32W-11S	B2
2100	AURA	60503	3201	33W-10S	A6
2400	OswT	60503	3201	33W-10S	B7
2600	AURA	60503	3265	33W-11S	B1
Lundstrom Ln					
400	DndT	60118	2747	35W-19N	D2
700	DndT	60102	2747	35W-19N	D2
N Lundy Av					
6200	CHCG	60646	2919	6W-7N	C3
Lundy Ln					
200	SMBG	60193	2859	23W-10N	B6
2000	LSLE	60532	3142	24W-6S	E5
Lunga Ct					
1000	RDLK	60073	2531	24W-34N	C1
Lunga Dr					
900	AvnT	60073	2531	24W-34N	C1
900	RDLK	60073	2531	24W-34N	C1
Lunt Av					
10	SMBG	60193	2913	23W-8N	A2
10	SmbT	60193	2913	23W-8N	A2
200	SMBG	60193	2912	23W-8N	E2
600	EGVV	60007	2915	17W-8N	B2
900	SmbT	60193	2912	24W-8N	D2
1600	DSPN	60018	2917	12W-8N	A1
4900	LNWD	60077	2919	6W-8N	E1
4900	LNWD	60712	2919	6W-8N	E1
5300	SKOK	60077	2919	6W-8N	D1
10400	RSMT	60018	2917	13W-8N	A1
10500	DSPN	60018	2916	13W-8N	E1
10500	RSMT	60018	2916	13W-8N	E1
W Lunt Av					
1100	CHCG	60626	2921	2W-8N	B1
2000	CHCG	60645	2921	2W-8N	B1
2600	CHCG	60645	2920	3W-8N	E1
4400	LNWD	60712	2920	5W-8N	A1
4600	LNWD	60712	2919	5W-8N	E1
4800	LNWD	60077	2919	6W-8N	E1
4800	SKOK	60077	2919	6W-8N	E1
5400	CHCG	60646	2919	6W-8N	C1
7200	CHCG	60631	2918	9W-8N	D1
7200	CHCG	60714	2918	9W-8N	D1
7200	NLES	60714	2918	9W-8N	D1
7700	CHCG	60068	2918	9W-8N	C1
7700	PKRG	60068	2918	9W-8N	C1
7700	PKRG	60631	2918	9W-8N	C1
Lupine Cir					
1500	GYLK	60030	2533	19W-31N	D6
2600	NPVL	60564	3266	29W-13S	D5
Lura Ln					
700	MRGO	60152	2634	49W-25N	B4
Lurilane Dr					
-	GNVW	60062	2809	12W-14N	B4
Lusted Ln					
-	BTVA	60510	3077	37W-2S	C3
-	BtvT	60510	3077	37W-2S	C3
Luther Av					
10	YkTp	60148	3026	18W-1S	E7
400	OKTR	60148	3084	18W-1S	E2
400	OKTR	60181	3084	18W-1S	E1
400	YkTp	60148	3084	18W-1S	E1
400	YkTp	60181	3084	18W-1S	E1
2100	JLET	60432	3499	22W-21S	C1
2100	LkdT	60432	3499	22W-21S	C1
2100	LkdT	60441	3419	22W-21S	C7
2100	LkdT	60441	3499	22W-21S	C1
N Luther Av					
1200	JLET	60432	3499	22W-22S	C1
S Luther Av					
1100	YkTp	60148	3026	18W-0S	E7
1300	YkTp	60148	3084	18W-1S	E1
1600	OKTR	60148	3084	18W-1S	E2
1600	OKTR	60181	3084	18W-1S	E2
1600	YkTp	60181	3084	18W-1S	E2
W Luther Av					
24500	AvnT	60073	2474	24W-35N	C6
Luther Dr					
700	RMVL	60446	3268	23W-14S	E7
700	RMVL	60446	3340	23W-15S	E1
800	WMTN	60481	3943	27W-39S	E1
Luther Ln					
100	FKFT	60423	3591	11W-26S	E2
800	CHHT	60411	3507	2W-24S	E6
1200	ANHT	60004	2806	18W-15N	E2
1600	PKRG	60068	2863	11W-10N	E4
W Luther St					
2600	CHCG	60608	3091	3W-2S	A2
Luthin Rd					
300	OKBK	60523	3086	15W-3S	A5
Lutter Dr					
-	CLLK	60013	2694	33W-23N	E1
900	CLLK	60014	2640	33W-24N	E7
900	CLLK	60014	2694	33W-23N	E1
Luxbridge Ct					
-	JLET	60431	3495	33W-22S	B1
Luxembourg Ct					
1000	CLSM	60188	2968	25W-4N	A4
Luzern Ct					
2600	WDRG	60517	3205	21W-9S	D3
LW Besinger Dr					
10	CPVL	60110	2748	33W-17N	B7
10	EDND	60110	2748	33W-17N	C7
Lydia Av					
-	ZION	60099	2421	11W-41N	D1
500	ADSN	60101	2969	21W-3N	D5
500	BmdT	60101	2969	21W-3N	D5
S Lydia Av					
13900	RBBN	60472	3348	4W-16S	E3
W Lydia Av					
3100	RBBN	60472	3348	4W-16S	D3
Lydia Ct					
-	ElgT	60124	2907	38W-8N	B3
-	SEGN	60124	2907	38W-8N	B3
10	HNWD	60047	2644	23W-24N	E7
Lydia St					
2600	WKGN	60085	2479	12W-33N	C7
Lyford Ln					
700	WHTN	60187	3082	25W-1S	B1
N Lyle Av					
300	ElgT	60123	2854	36W-11N	A3
500	ELGN	60123	2853	36W-12N	E2
800	ELGN	60123	2854	36W-12N	A1
1200	ELGN	60123	2800	36W-13N	A7
S Lyle Av					
10	ELGN	60123	2854	35W-11N	A5
W Lyle Ct					
14200	GNOK	60048	2592	14W-30N	D1
Lyle Ln					
3400	CRTE	60417	3597	1E-28S	B6
Lyman Av					
-	GNVW	60016	2809	11W-12N	C7
-	GNVW	60025	2809	11W-12N	C7
-	MaiT	60016	2809	11W-12N	C7
-	MaiT	60016	2863	11W-12N	C1
5200	DRGV	60515	3144	19W-6S	D4
5400	DRGV	60516	3144	19W-6S	D4
6500	HMND	46324	3430		D4
7200	DRGV	60516	3206	19W-8S	D1
7500	DRN	60516	3206	19W-8S	D2
7500	DRN	60561	3206	19W-8S	D2
7900	DGvT	60516	3206	19W-9S	D2
7900	DGvT	60561	3206	19W-9S	D2
10300	CHRG	60415	3275	7W-12S	C1
11000	ALSP	60482	3275	7W-12S	C3
11000	CHRG	60482	3275	7W-12S	C3
S Lyman Av					
300	DSPN	60016	2863	12W-11N	C3
300	MaiT	60016	2863	12W-11N	C3
500	OKPK	60302	3031	7W-0S	B5
500	OKPK	60304	3031	7W-0S	B5
700	PKRG	60016	2863	12W-11N	C4
700	PKRG	60068	2863	12W-11N	C4
1100	CCRO	60304	3031	7W-0S	B7
1100	CCRO	60804	3031	7W-0S	B7
5300	HMND	46320	3352		D6
5900	HMND	46320	3430		D1
6100	HMND	46324	3430		D1
Lyman Ct					
500	HDPK	60035	2758	7W-20N	C1
5900	DRGV	60516	3144	19W-6S	D4
Lyman Lp					
2500	BtlT	60560	3262	40W-13S	B5
Lyman St					
400	WnfT	60185	3022	30W-0N	B5
700	WCHI	60185	3022	30W-0N	B6
S Lyman St					
2900	CHCG	60608	3091	1W-2S	E3
Lyn Ct					
18500	HMWD	60430	3507	1W-22S	E1
Lyn Ln					
10	AlqT	60021	2695	30W-22N	E4
10	BNHL	60010	2695	30W-22N	E4

STREET Block	City	ZIP	Map#	CGS	Grid
Lyn Ln					
10	BNHL	60021	2695	30W-22N	E4
Lynbrook Dr					
100	BMDL	60108	2968	23W-5N	E2
Lynch Av					
-	BHPK	60087	2421	12W-39N	C6
-	BHPK	60099	2421	12W-39N	C6
N Lynch Av					
5300	CHCG	60630	2919	6W-6N	D5
39000	BHPK	60087	2421	12W-39N	C6
39000	WKGN	60087	2421	12W-39N	C6
Lynch Dr					
11800	HMGN	60491	3422	14W-18S	C1
11800	OrlT	60467	3422	14W-18S	C1
Lynch St					
10	ELGN	60123	2854	34W-11N	D4
Lynchburg Ct					
600	NPVL	60540	3142	25W-7S	B7
Lyncliff Dr					
10	BtlT	60543	3262	40W-13S	C4
Lynda Ct					
-	FXLK	60020	2414	28W-39N	D5
E Lynda Dr					
400	PLTN	60074	2753	20W-18N	B3
N Lynda Dr					
1600	PLTN	60074	2753	20W-18N	B4
E Lyndale Av					
10	NHLK	60164	2972	13W-2N	E6
300	LydT	60164	2973	13W-2N	A6
300	NHLK	60164	2973	13W-2N	A6
W Lyndale Av					
10	MDLN	60060	2590	19W-28N	D6
10400	LydT	60164	2973	13W-2N	A6
10400	NHLK	60164	2973	13W-2N	A6
Lyndale Ln					
2600	RVWD	60015	2755	13W-20N	E1
Lyndale Rd					
1600	MTGY	60506	3198	39W-9S	E5
W Lyndale St					
2100	CHCG	60647	2977	2W-2N	B6
2800	CHCG	60647	2976	3W-2N	E6
4500	CHCG	60639	2976	5W-2N	A6
8600	RVGV	60171	2973	10W-2N	E6
8600	RVGV	60171	2974	10W-2N	A6
E Lynden Ln					
600	ANHT	60005	2807	17W-13N	B5
Lyndhurst Ct					
800	NPVL	60563	3141	26W-5S	D3
800	NPVL	60563	3142	26W-6S	A4
Lyndhurst Ln					
1900	AURA	60503	3201	33W-10S	A6
Lyndon St					
7000	RSMT	60018	2917	13W-8N	A1
7100	DSPN	60018	2917	13W-8N	A1
Lyndsay Dr					
26300	CNHN	60410	3672	33W-32S	B7
26400	CNHN	60410	3761	33W-32S	B1
Lynette Dr					
-	LKFT	60045	2649	11W-24N	C7
Lynette Ln					
1100	LKFT	60045	2649	12W-24N	C7
3100	ISLK	60042	2586	29W-28N	C5
Lyngby Ct					
10	RVWD	60015	2703	13W-22N	A4
Lynn Av					
600	RMVL	60446	3340	24W-15S	D1
Lynn Blvd					
1600	AURA	60505	3138	34W-5S	D3
Lynn Cir					
1900	LbvT	60048	2591	16W-30N	C2
Lynn Ct					
100	WNVL	60555	3080	30W-2S	C3
200	DSPN	60016	2862	15W-11N	B3
400	CNHL	60514	3085	17W-4S	C7
400	CNHL	60559	3085	17W-4S	C7
400	WTMT	60559	3085	17W-4S	C7
500	GLHT	60139	3025	22W-2N	C1
2200	MTGY	60538	3198	39W-10S	D6
3000	EGVV	60005	2861	17W-10N	C5
3000	EGVV	60007	2861	17W-10N	C5
3000	MPPT	60005	2861	17W-10N	C5
E Lynn Ct					
1300	HMWD	60430	3507	1W-22S	E1
Lynn Dr					
-	SchT	60175	2963	38W-3N	B6
10	HNWD	60047	2645	21W-24N	E7
100	SCRL	60175	2963	38W-3N	B7
400	LslT	60540	3143	23W-7S	A7
1600	MngT	60152	2578	49W-30N	C2
2200	MTGY	60538	3198	39W-10S	D6
10400	ODPK	60467	3423	13W-21S	B7
W Lynn Dr					
200	PLTN	60067	2752	21W-16N	D6
Lynn Ln					
100	WLNG	60090	2755	14W-16N	C7
200	CHHT	60411	3507	1W-23S	E3
S Lynn Ln					
-	MONE	60449	3682	6W-31S	E6
25900	MONE	60449	3683	6W-31S	A5
S Lynn Pkwy					
100	NlxT	60448	3501	16W-22S	E2
Lynn Rd					
500	MltT	60148	3025	21W-1N	D2
7400	MchT	60097	2469	36W-36N	D3
E Lynn St					
10	SEGN	60177	2908	35W-8N	B3
W Lynn St					
10	SEGN	60177	2908	35W-8N	B3
23500	PNFD	60586	3416	29W-19S	D2
23500	PnfT	60586	3416	29W-19S	D2
Lynn Ter					
300	WKGN	60085	2536	11W-34N	C1
400	WKGN	60085	2479	11W-34N	C7
1200	HDPK	60035	2704	10W-23N	B2
Lynnann Ct					
500	MRGO	60152	2634	49W-25N	C4
Lynnbrook Dr					
10	PTHT	60070	2754	15W-16N	E7
10	PTHT	60070	2755	15W-16N	A7
Lynn Dale Dr					
42000	BtnT	60099	2362	12W-43N	B4
42000	PTPR	53158	2362	12W-43N	B4
42000	PTPR	60099	2362	12W-43N	B4
Lynne Ct					
14900	OKFT	60452	3347	6W-17S	E6
Lynne Dr					
-	EGVV	60007	2914	19W-8N	C2
-	TNLK	53181	2354		C2
Lynne Ln					
-	LMBD	60148	3084	20W-1S	B1
Lynnfield Ct					
3200	AURA	60504	3201	31W-9S	E3
Lynnfield Ln					
100	SMBG	60193	2858	26W-10N	A6
1100	BRLT	60103	2910	30W-7N	B5
1200	BRLT	60120	2910	30W-7N	B5
E Lynnwood Av					
200	ANHT	60004	2807	17W-15N	A2
W Lynnwood Av					
1400	ANHT	60004	2806	18W-15N	D2
Lynnwood Ct					
900	SRWD	60404	3496	30W-24S	B6
3000	SMWD	60107	2911	28W-8N	A2
10700	PlsT	60464	3345	13W-15S	A1
Lynnwood Ln					
8900	LKWD	60014	2639	38W-24N	A6
N Lynsee Ct					
4600	BHPK	60099	2421	13W-39N	A5
N Lynsee Ct SR-158					
4600	BHPK	60099	2421	13W-39N	A5
Lynwood Cir					
300	BMDL	60108	2968	24W-5N	C2
Lynwood Ct					
1600	FSMR	60422	3507	2W-23S	D3
Lynwood Dr					
10	LtRT	60545	3330	49W-14S	E1
3200	SCHT	60411	3596	1W-27S	A4
5800	OKLN	60453	3211	7W-10S	C5
8600	HYHL	60457	3210	10W-10S	A4
Lynwood Ln					
200	BMDL	60108	2968	24W-5N	C2
700	WHTN	60187	3082	25W-1S	B1
Lynwood St					
1700	CTHL	60403	3418	26W-21S	A6
2100	CTHL	60403	3417	26W-21S	E6
2300	LktT	60403	3417	26W-21S	E6
Lynx Ln					
200	OSWG	60543	3263	38W-11S	B2
Lynze Ln					
8800	FKFT	60423	3504	11W-24S	A5
Lyon Av					
400	WHTN	60187	3024	25W-0S	B6
S Lyon Av					
9300	CHCG	60619	3214	0E-10S	E5
Lyon Ct					
600	BFGV	60089	2701	17W-21N	B5
1000	AURA	60506	3138	35W-6S	B4
Lyon Dr					
500	BFGV	60089	2701	17W-21N	B5
Lyon Pl					
-	AURA	60506	3138	35W-6S	B4
Lyon Rd					
1100	BTVA	60510	3020	34W-0S	E7
Lyons Cir					
600	HDPK	60035	2704	8W-20N	D7
Lyons Ct					
1500	WKGN	60085	2536	11W-32N	D5
Lyons Rd					
200	BGBK	60440	3269	23W-11S	A1
300	BGBK	60440	3205	23W-11S	A7
Lyons St					
-	SKOK	60076	2865	5W-11N	E2
-	SKOK	60076	2866	5W-11N	A2
1300	EVTN	60201	2867	3W-11N	A2
1700	EVTN	60201	2866	3W-11N	E2
3300	SKOK	60203	2866	4W-11N	D2
5400	SKOK	60053	2865	6W-11N	C2
5400	SKOK	60077	2865	6W-11N	C2
6400	MNGV	60053	2865	8W-11N	A2
7200	MNGV	60053	2864	9W-11N	C2
7900	NLES	60053	2864	9W-11N	B2
8600	MaiT	60016	2863	10W-11N	E2
8600	MaiT	60016	2864	10W-11N	A2
8600	MaiT	60714	2864	10W-11N	A2
8600	NLES	60714	2864	10W-11N	A2
8700	HGKN	60525	3147	11W-7S	D6
E Lyons St					
800	HMND	46320	3430		E1
W Lyons St					
8000	MNGV	60053	2864	10W-11N	B2
8000	NLES	60053	2864	10W-11N	B2
8000	NLES	60714	2864	10W-11N	B2
Lyons Ridge Dr					
-	AlqT	60013	2642	29W-24N	C7
-	CRY	60013	2642	29W-24N	C7
Lyons Wood Ct					
37500	BHPK	60087	2480	10W-37N	A2
Lysle Rd					
300	WYNE	60184	2966	30W-5N	B3
Lyster Rd					
600	HIWD	60037	2704	9W-23N	D1
800	HDPK	60035	2650	9W-24N	C7
800	HDPK	60040	2650	9W-24N	C7
800	HDPK	60040	2704	9W-24N	C1
800	HIWD	60035	2650	9W-24N	C7
800	HIWD	60040	2650	9W-24N	C7
800	HIWD	60040	2704	9W-24N	C1
Lytham Ct					
400	WNFD	60190	3023	26W-1N	E2
N Lytle Dr					
100	PLTN	60074	2753	19W-16N	C7
S Lytle St					
800	CHCG	60607	3033	1W-0S	D6
1000	CHCG	60608	3033	1W-0S	D6
M					
M Ct					
10200	MKNA	60448	3503	12W-23S	C4
N Mabel Ct					
900	BDWD	60408	3941	32W-40S	E3
900	RedT	60408	3941	32W-40S	E3
Mabel St					
-	ELGN	60123	2854	34W-12N	D1
Mable Av					
-	LKZH	60047	2699	23W-22N	A4
1600	JltT	60433	3499	21W-24S	E6
Mable Ln					
600	BRLT	60103	2909	31W-8N	E2
N Macalpin Av					
6900	CHCG	60714	2919	7W-8N	A1
6900	NLES	60714	2919	7W-8N	A1
7000	CHCG	60646	2919	7W-8N	B1
Macalpin Cir					
1400	IVNS	60010	2751	25W-16N	A6
Macalpin Ct					
300	IVNS	60010	2751	25W-16N	A6
Macalpin Dr					
1100	IVNS	60010	2751	25W-16N	A6
MacArthur					
9100	MaiT	60016	2863	11W-11N	D3
MacArthur Av					
10	MltT	60188	3023	26W-1N	D3
10	MltT	60188	3024	26W-1N	A3
100	WNFD	60188	3023	26W-1N	D3
500	WNFD	60190	3023	26W-1N	D3
7000	MchT	60097	2469	36W-37N	E3
MacArthur Blvd					
800	MNSR	46321	3510		E1
2900	NHBK	60062	2756	11W-18N	D3
MacArthur Ct					
-	VNHL	60061	2647	17W-27N	C2
10	BFGV	60089	2754	17W-18N	C3
700	DLTN	60419	3350	0E-16S	E3
700	DLTN	60419	3351	1E-16S	A3
MacArthur Dr					
-	MchT	60097	2469	35W-37N	E2
-	RGWD	60097	2469	35W-37N	E2
10	NHLK	60164	2972	13W-3N	D5
10	WLBK	60527	3145	16W-6S	D5
200	LydT	60164	2972	13W-3N	D5
400	OKTR	60181	3085	17W-1S	C2
400	YkTp	60181	3085	17W-1S	C2
500	BFGV	60089	2754	17W-18N	C4
700	OKBK	60181	3085	17W-1S	C2
700	OKBK	60523	3085	17W-1S	C2
800	BlmT	60411	3507	2W-24S	D6
800	CHHT	60411	3507	2W-24S	D6
1300	WKGN	60087	2479	11W-37N	E2
2100	GNVW	60025	2864	9W-12N	D1
2300	MchT	60050	2527	34W-34N	D1
2400	MCLK	60050	2527	34W-34N	D1
6300	WDRG	60517	3143	22W-7S	C6
E MacArthur Dr					
600	PLTN	60074	2753	20W-16N	A7
N MacArthur Dr					
100	MPPT	60056	2807	16W-13N	D6
200	PLTN	60074	2753	20W-16N	A7
W MacArthur Dr					
10700	BHPK	60087	2479	11W-37N	E2
10700	BHPK	60087	2480	10W-37N	A2
Macbain Wy					
400	HFET	60010	2751	24W-16N	C7
400	IVNS	60010	2751	24W-16N	C7
N Macchesney Ct					
-	CHCG	60601	3034		E4
Maccomb Rd					
-	MmT	60037	2650	8W-24N	D7
MacDonald Ln					
2200	FSMR	60422	3507	2W-22S	C2
Macdonough St					
2100	NCHI	60088	2537	10W-31N	B7
2400	NCHI	60088	2594	10W-31N	B1
Macfarlane Cres					
2800	FSMR	60422	3507	3W-23S	A3
Macfarlane Dr					
2200	JLET	60435	3497	26W-22S	E2
Macgillis Dr					
10	RDLK	60073	2531	23W-33N	E3
S Macgillis Dr					
10	RDLK	60073	2531	23W-33N	E3
10	RDLK	60073	2532	23W-33N	A3
10	RLKP	60073	2532	23W-33N	A3
MacGregor Ct					
700	WDND	60118	2800	35W-16N	C1
MacGregor Rd					
100	LKPT	60441	3419	21W-18S	E1
100	LktT	60441	3419	21W-18S	E2
700	LKPT	60441	3341	21W-18S	E7
700	LktT	60441	3341	21W-18S	E7
Mach Dr					
22900	CRTE	60417	3597	0E-27S	A5
22900	STGR	60475	3597	0E-27S	A5
Macheath Cres					
2800	FSMR	60422	3507	3W-23S	A3
Machelle Dr					
200	AlqT	60013	2642	29W-24N	C6
Macher St					
1900	CTHL	60403	3417	26W-21S	E7
N Macie Ct					
500	ADSN	60101	2970	18W-4N	E4
Macintosh Ct					
100	GNEN	60137	3083	21W-1S	D2
15900	WDWH	60083	2419	16W-39N	E4
Macintosh Dr					
1200	WCDA	60084	2588	24W-28N	B6
Mack Dr					
27000	WcnT	60084	2643	27W-27N	C1
Mack Rd					
10	WnfT	60185	3080	29W-1S	D3
10	WnfT	60185	3081	28W-1S	B3
10	WnfT	60187	3081	27W-2S	D3
10	WnfT	60555	3080	29W-1S	D3
10	WnfT	60555	3081	28W-1S	B3
10	WNVL	60555	3080	29W-1S	D3
200	WnfT	60190	3081	28W-2S	A3
N Mack St					
400	JLET	60435	3498	25W-23S	C3
MacKenzie Dr					
900	ANTH	60002	2359	20W-42N	A7
S Mackenzie Dr					
15100	HMGN	60491	3344	15W-18S	C6
Mackenzie Ln					
1400	ELGN	60120	2855	31W-12N	E3
1400	HnrT	60120	2855	31W-12N	E3
Mackenzie Pl					
1000	MltT	60187	3024	23W-0N	E4
1000	WHTN	60187	3024	23W-0N	E4
Mackey Ln					
800	ELGN	60120	2855	32W-11N	C4
Mackie Pl					
5100	DRGV	60515	3144	19W-5S	D2
Mackinac Ct					
16400	HMGN	60491	3422	15W-19S	C3
Mackinac Ln					
-	LKMR	60041	2530	27W-32N	A5
-	LKMR	60051	2530	27W-32N	A5
Mackinac Rd					
12000	HMGN	60467	3422	15W-19S	C2
12000	HMGN	60491	3422	15W-19S	C3
12000	OrlT	60467	3422	15W-19S	C2
Mackinac St					
4500	LIHL	60156	2692	38W-22N	E4
Mackinaw Av					
300	CTCY	60409	3352	3E-17S	A6
1200	CTCY	60409	3430	3E-19S	A2
S Mackinaw Av					
-	CHCG	60617	3280	3E-12S	A3
8200	CHCG	60617	3216	4E-9S	A3
13000	CHCG	60633	3280	3E-14S	A7
13000	CHCG	60633	3352	3E-15S	A1
13900	BNHM	60633	3352	3E-16S	A3
S Mackinaw Av US-41					
8700	CHCG	60617	3216	4E-10S	A4
Mackinaw Ct					
100	NPVL	60565	3204	26W-10S	A5
Mackler Dr					
800	CHHT	60411	3507	2W-24S	E6
Macks Dr					
100	WLSP	60480	3209	12W-9S	B4
Maclaine Ln					
5400	HRPK	60133	2911	27W-6N	C6
Maclaren Ln					
200	LKBF	60044	2593	11W-28N	D6
Maclean Av					
-	NtrT	60043	2812	4W-14N	C4
-	NtrT	60093	2812	4W-14N	C4
700	KLWH	60043	2812	4W-14N	C4
700	KLWH	60093	2812	4W-14N	C4
700	WNKA	60043	2812	4W-14N	C4
700	WNKA	60093	2812	4W-14N	C4
Macom Dr					
-	NPVL	60564	3202	29W-9S	C4
1300	AURA	60564	3202	30W-9S	C4
Macomber St					
500	JLET	60433	3499	23W-24S	A6
Macon Av					
300	RMVL	60446	3340	24W-15S	D2
Macqueen Dr					
400	WnfT	60185	3022	31W-1N	A3
600	WCHI	60185	3022	31W-1N	A2
Macura St					
27300	AxST	60410	3672	34W-31S	A6
Macwood Dr					
4800	RcmT	60071	2412	33W-40N	D3
4800	RHMD	60071	2412	33W-40N	D3
Macy Ct					
-	ALGN	60118	2746	37W-19N	D2
Madach Ct					
10	DRPK	60010	2699	22W-20N	A7
Maddeline Ln					
22600	FKFT	60423	3592	10W-27S	C5
S Madden Dr					
4900	HMND	46320	3352		D5
Madeline Cir					
10	SMBG	60173	2859	21W-10N	E5
Madeline Dr					
7700	OswT	60560	3334	40W-15S	B3
W Madeline St					
400	JLET	60436	3498	24W-24S	D5
Madelyn Dr					
600	DSPN	60016	2808	13W-13N	D7
Madera Cir					
100	CPVL	60110	2748	33W-18N	C4
Madera Dr					
1700	WHTN	60187	3082	23W-2S	E3
Madera Ln					
2400	NPVL	60565	3204	24W-10S	C5
Madera St					
-	HRPK	60133	2911	26W-7N	E5
Madiera Ct					
2300	BFGV	60089	2701	16W-22N	E3
Madiera Dr					
800	SRWD	60404	3496	30W-24S	B6
Madiera Ln					
2200	BFGV	60089	2701	16W-22N	E4
Madisen Ln					
600	UYPK	60466	3684	3W-29S	B1
Madison					
100	WnfT	60187	3081	27W-2S	C3
Madison Av					
-	AntT	60002	2417	22W-41N	B2
-	BtnT	60081	2414	29W-38N	C6
-	BtnT	60096	2363	10W-42N	A6
-	WPHR	60096	2363	10W-42N	A6
200	CTCY	60409	3351	2E-17S	C5
300	GLNC	60022	2758	6W-17N	D6
400	DLTN	60409	3351	2E-17S	C5
400	FXLK	60041	2473	26W-35N	D5
400	WnfT	60187	3081	27W-2S	C4
400	WnfT	60555	3081	27W-2S	C4
600	SCRL	60174	3020	35W-2N	C1
900	BDWD	60408	3941	32W-41S	D4
900	WCDA	60084	2588	25W-28N	A6
1000	DYR	46311	3510		E6
1000	SCRL	60174	2964	34W-2N	C7
1100	WcnT	60084	2588	25W-28N	A6
1500	DYR	46311	3598		D1
1900	GRNE	60031	2477	16W-36N	E5
3100	LGPK	60513	3087	11W-3S	D6
3100	LGPK	60525	3087	11W-3S	D6
3900	BKFD	60513	3087	11W-4S	D7
4500	BKFD	60513	3147	11W-4S	D1
5800	HMND	46320	3352		E7
6200	HMND	46324	3430		E3
7800	MNSR	46321	3430		E6
8700	MNSR	46321	3510		E1
14700	HRVY	60426	3350	1W-17S	B5
15100	DLTN	60419	3351	2E-17S	C6
15500	ThtT	60473	3351	2E-18S	C7
15600	DLTN	60473	3351	2E-18S	C7
E Madison Av					
100	WHTN	60187	3024	24W-0S	D6
N Madison Av					
10	LGNG	60525	3087	12W-4S	B6
100	LGPK	60525	3087	12W-4S	B6
28500	WcnT	60084	2588	25W-28N	A5
41400	AntT	60002	2417	22W-41N	B1
S Madison Av					
10	LGNG	60525	3087	12W-4S	C7
300	LGNG	60525	3147	12W-5S	C2
5500	CTSD	60525	3147	12W-6S	C3
W Madison Av					
100	WHTN	60187	3024	25W-0S	C6
Madison Blvd					
-	DPgT	60490	3267	26W-13S	D6
700	BGBK	60490	3267	26W-13S	D6
Madison Ct					
-	SRWD	60404	3496	30W-22S	B2
400	OSWG	60543	3263	38W-13S	B5
400	EGVV	60007	2913	22W-8N	D2
800	ISLK	60042	2586	28W-27N	E7
1100	CPVL	60110	2748	32W-17N	D7
1300	SCRL	60174	2964	34W-2N	D7
6100	MNGV	60053	2865	7W-10N	B5
8800	MNSR	46321	3510		E1
13200	PNFD	60544	3338	31W-16S	A4
E Madison Ct					
400	EMHT	60126	3028	15W-0S	B5
W Madison Ct					
8300	NLES	60714	2864	10W-10N	A5
Madison Ct N					
1500	BFGV	60089	2701	16W-21N	D5
Madison Ct S					
1300	BFGV	60089	2701	16W-21N	D6
Madison Dr					
200	HnrT	60107	2856	29W-10N	D6
200	SMWD	60107	2856	29W-10N	D6
1300	BFGV	60089	2701	16W-21N	D6
W Madison Dr					
8400	NLES	60714	2864	10W-10N	A5
8600	NLES	60714	2863	10W-10N	E5
Madison Ln					
500	LNHT	60046	2418	19W-38N	D6
E Madison Pk					
1200	CHCG	60615	3153	1E-5S	A1
Madison Pl					
2100	EVTN	60202	2866	3W-10N	E5
Madison St					
-	HNDL	60523	3086	15W-3S	A6
-	MHTN	60442	3677	19W-31S	E5
10	ALGN	60102	2694	33W-20N	D7
10	BTVA	60510	3078	35W-0S	B1
10	CHCG	60644	3031	7W-0N	B5
10	FTPK	60130	3030	10W-0N	B5
10	FTPK	60153	3030	10W-0N	B5
10	FTPK	60305	3030	10W-0N	B5
10	LKPT	60441	3419	22W-19S	D3
10	LktT	60441	3419	22W-19S	D2
10	MYWD	60153	3030	10W-0N	B5
10	OKPK	60302	3031	7W-0N	B5
10	OKPK	60304	3031	7W-0N	B5
10	RVFT	60305	3030	10W-0N	B5
100	WnfT	60187	3081	27W-2S	C4
200	JLET	60435	3497	26W-23S	E4
200	MTGY	60538	3199	37W-9S	D4
300	WNFD	60190	3023	27W-0S	C7
400	EGvT	60018	2861	16W-9N	E7
400	EGvT	60018	2862	15W-9N	A7
500	WnfT	60555	3081	27W-2S	C4
600	EDND	60118	2801	33W-16N	B2
600	EVTN	60202	2867	3W-10N	A5
600	WNFD	60190	3081	27W-0S	C1
700	OKPK	60302	3030	8W-0N	E5
700	OKPK	60304	3030	8W-0N	E5
700	WNFD	60187	3081	27W-0S	C1
800	MYWD	60153	3029	11W-0N	D5
1100	FTPK	60302	3030	8W-0N	D5
1100	FTPK	60304	3030	8W-0N	D5
1600	EVTN	60202	2866	3W-10N	E5
2100	BLWD	60104	3029	11W-0N	D5
3300	LNSG	60438	3430	4E-21S	C6
3300	SKOK	60076	2866	4W-10N	D5
3500	OKBK	60523	3086	15W-3S	A6
3900	BLWD	60162	3029	13W-0S	A5
3900	HLSD	60162	3029	13W-0S	A5
4700	SKOK	60076	2865	5W-10N	E5
5000	HLSD	60162	3028	14W-0S	C5
5100	SKOK	60077	2865	6W-10N	D5
5300	MNGV	60077	2865	6W-10N	D5
5700	MNGV	60053	2865	7W-10N	B5
5800	BKLY	60163	3028	14W-0S	C5
5800	HLSD	60163	3028	14W-0S	C5
7400	HRPK	60133	2912	26W-9N	A1
7600	RVFT	60130	3030	9W-0N	C5
8500	DrrT	60012	2583	37W-27N	B7
24800	PNFD	60544	3338	31W-16S	A4
25000	PNFD	60544	3337	31W-16S	E4
E Madison St					
10	CHCG	60602	3034	0E-0N	C4
10	CHCG	60603	3034	0E-0N	C4
10	LMBD	60148	3026	18W-0N	D5
10	VLPK	60181	3027	17W-0N	B5
10	WKGN	60085	2537	9W-34N	B1
100	EMHT	60126	3027	16W-0N	C5
100	EMHT	60126	3028	15W-0N	A5
1000	LMBD	60181	3026	18W-0N	E5
1000	VLPK	60181	3026	18W-0N	E5
N Madison St					
10	AURA	60505	3200	35W-7S	C1
10	HNDL	60521	3146	16W-4S	A1
10	OSWG	60543	3263	37W-12S	C3
100	WDSK	60098	2524	41W-31N	D7
400	HNDL	60521	3086	15W-4S	A7
900	HNDL	60523	3086	16W-4S	A7
900	OKBK	60521	3086	16W-4S	A7
900	OKBK	60523	3086	16W-4S	A7
N Madison St SR-25					
10	OSWG	60543	3263	37W-12S	C3
N Madison St SR-120					
300	WDSK	60098	2524	41W-31N	D7
S Madison St					
-	WDSK	60098	2524	41W-31N	E7
10	AURA	60505	3200	35W-8S	C1
10	BRRG	60527	3208	16W-10S	A6
10	DGvT	60527	3208	16W-8S	A1
10	HNDL	60521	3146	16W-5S	A1
10	OSWG	60543	3263	37W-13S	B4
300	HPSR	60140	2796	46W-16N	A2
300	WDSK	60098	2581	41W-30N	D1
5400	DGvT	60521	3146	16W-6S	A3
5800	DGvT	60527	3146	16W-6S	A4
5900	BRRG	60527	3146	16W-6S	A5
6300	WLBK	60527	3146	15W-7S	A5
7200	WLBK	60527	3208	16W-9S	A3
S Madison St CO-8					
5400	DGvT	60521	3146	16W-6S	A3
5400	HNDL	60521	3146	16W-6S	A4
5800	DGvT	60527	3146	16W-6S	A4
5900	BRRG	60527	3146	16W-6S	A5
6300	WLBK	60527	3146	15W-7S	A5
7200	DGvT	60527	3208	16W-8S	A1
7200	WLBK	60527	3208	16W-8S	A1
7600	BRRG	60527	3208	15W-8S	A2
S Madison St US-34					
10	OSWG	60543	3263	37W-12S	C3
W Madison St					
10	CHCG	60602	3034	0W-0N	A4
10	CHCG	60603	3034	0W-0N	A4
10	LMBD	60148	3026	20W-0N	A5
10	VLPK	60181	3027	18W-0S	A5
100	CHCG	60606	3034	0W-0N	B4
100	EMHT	60126	3027	16W-0N	E5
100	YKVL	60560	3333	43W-15S	B2
300	VLPK	60181	3026	18W-0N	E5
400	CHCG	60661	3034	0W-0N	A4
500	MltT	60148	3026	20W-0N	A5
500	WKGN	60085	2537	10W-34N	A1
500	YkTp	60148	3026	20W-0N	A5
700	CHCG	60607	3034	0W-0N	A4
800	CHCG	60607	3033	0W-0N	A5
1500	CHCG	60612	3033	1W-0N	D5
2800	CHCG	60612	3032	4W-0N	C5
3100	CHCG	60624	3032	3W-0N	E5
4500	CHCG	60644	3032	5W-0N	A5
4700	CHCG	60644	3031	6W-0N	E5
5900	OKPK	60302	3031	7W-0N	B5
5900	OKPK	60304	3031	7W-0N	B5
6800	NLES	60714	2864	8W-10N	E5
25400	GrtT	60041	2474	25W-34N	A7
Madison Wy					
10800	HTLY	60142	2692	39W-21N	C6
Madison Ridge Ct					
1600	JLET	60586	3495	31W-21S	E1
Madlock Ct S					
1300	ELGN	60123	2800	36W-13N	A7
Madlock Ln					
1400	ELGN	60123	2800	36W-14N	A7
Madonna Av					
100	JLET	60436	3497	26W-24S	E6
Madrid Ct					
5700	HRPK	60133	2911	26W-7N	E5
Madsen Ct					
1600	WHTN	60187	3024	23W-0N	E4
1900	WHTN	60187	3025	23W-0N	A4
Madsen Dr					
200	BMDL	60108	2967	26W-4N	E3

STREET Block	City	ZIP	Map#	CGS	Grid
Madsen Dr					
200	BMDL	60108	2968	26W-4N	A3
200	BmdT	60108	2967	26W-4N	E3
200	BmdT	60188	2967	26W-4N	E3
Mae Ct					
1200	WLNG	60090	2754	16W-18N	D3
2200	WPHR	60096	2363	10W-41N	B7
Mae St					
800	WMTN	60481	3943	27W-39S	E1
Maeburn Ter					
-	CRTE	60417	3685	0E-29S	E1
-	CRTE	60417	3686	0E-29S	A1
Magellan Dr					
2800	MchT	60051	2472	29W-34N	C7
Magenta Ct					
1100	NPVL	60564	3267	28W-11S	A2
Mager Dr					
18000	TYPK	60487	3424	10W-21S	B7
N Maggie Ln					
400	RMVL	60446	3340	25W-15S	B2
W Maggie Ln					
-	PNFD	60586	3415	31W-20S	E4
1100	RMVL	60446	3340	25W-15S	B2
Maggies Wy					
19500	MKNA	60448	3502	15W-23S	C3
Magical Ln					
7500	GRNE	60031	2534	18W-34N	A1
Magna Dr					
700	RDLK	60073	2531	23W-34N	D1
700	RLKB	60073	2531	23W-34N	D1
N Magnet Av					
5300	CHCG	60630	2919	7W-6N	C5
Magnet Wy					
500	HtdT	60098	2524	43W-32N	A5
N Magnetics Blvd					
39100	NptT	60083	2420	15W-39N	B6
39100	WDWH	60083	2420	15W-39N	B6
Magnolia Av					
-	AddT	60101	2970	19W-2N	C7
-	ADSN	60101	2970	19W-2N	C7
-	ADSN	60101	3026	19W-2N	D1
10	BmdT	60148	2970	21W-2N	A7
100	BmdT	60148	2969	21W-3N	D6
300	MchT	60051	2529	29W-32N	C5
9200	FftT	60448	3503	11W-23S	E3
9200	FftT	60448	3504	11W-23S	A3
9200	MKNA	60448	3504	11W-23S	A3
N Magnolia Av					
900	JLET	60432	3499	22W-22S	C2
1400	CHCG	60622	3033	1W-1N	D1
1900	CHCG	60614	2977	1W-2N	D6
2700	CHCG	60657	2977	1W-3N	D5
3600	CHCG	60613	2977	1W-4N	D2
4400	CHCG	60613	2921	1W-5N	D7
5200	CHCG	60640	2921	1W-6N	D5
5500	CHCG	60660	2921	1W-6N	D5
6300	CHCG	60626	2921	1W-7N	D3
36700	WKGN	60087	2479	13W-36N	A3
36700	WrnT	60031	2479	13W-36N	A3
36700	WrnT	60087	2479	13W-36N	A3
38500	WDWH	60083	2421	13W-38N	A7
38500	WKGN	60083	2421	13W-38N	A7
Magnolia Cir					
600	LMBD	60148	3026	19W-0S	D6
Magnolia Ct					
-	SRWD	60404	3583	31W-25S	E1
10	SMWD	60107	2856	30W-10N	C5
300	BGBK	60440	3269	22W-13S	D4
300	SMBG	60193	2858	23W-10N	E6
600	HnrT	60120	2856	29W-12N	E2
700	OSWG	60543	3262	39W-11S	D1
1800	MHRY	60050	2528	32W-33N	C2
2900	AURA	60502	3079	32W-3S	C6
8100	FXLK	60020	2415	28W-39N	A5
8100	FXLK	60081	2415	28W-39N	A5
8800	ODPK	60462	3346	11W-17S	A5
12100	PNFD	60585	3266	30W-14S	B7
20400	FKFT	60423	3504	10W-24S	B6
Magnolia Ct E					
2300	BFGV	60089	2701	17W-22N	C4
Magnolia Ct W					
2200	BFGV	60089	2701	17W-22N	B4
Magnolia Dr					
-	BlmT	60425	3508	0E-22S	E1
-	GNWD	60425	3508	0E-22S	E1
-	RcmT	60071	2354	32W-42N	B6
-	SPGV	60071	2354	32W-42N	B6
200	NARA	60542	3077	37W-3S	C7
800	JLET	60435	3497	27W-22S	D3
800	TroT	60435	3497	27W-22S	D3
900	ALGN	60102	2695	32W-20N	C7
1000	CTHL	60403	3497	27W-22S	D3
1400	CLLK	60014	2693	37W-23N	C2
3200	MKHM	60428	3348	4W-18S	E7
3600	SPGV	60081	2354	32W-42N	B6
4400	RGMW	60008	2806	20W-12N	B7
5900	MchT	60097	2469	36W-37N	D1
16900	HLCT	60429	3426	4W-20S	E4
S Magnolia Dr					
13400	DPgT	60544	3340	26W-16S	A4
13400	RMVL	60544	3340	26W-16S	A4
15500	LktT	60544	3340	26W-16S	A3
W Magnolia Dr					
10	SMWD	60107	2856	30W-10N	C5
7900	FftT	60423	3504	10W-24S	C5
24300	AntT	60002	2416	24W-40N	C2
Magnolia Ln					
10	LNHT	60046	2476	19W-37N	B1
300	WYNE	60184	2966	30W-4N	B3
300	WYNE	60185	2966	30W-4N	B4
300	WynT	60185	2966	30W-4N	B4
500	EGVV	60007	2915	18W-8N	A2
500	WynT	60103	2966	30W-4N	B3
500	WynT	60184	2966	30W-4N	B3
800	NPVL	60540	3141	27W-7S	D7
800	NPVL	60540	3203	27W-7S	D1
1100	LYVL	60048	2647	16W-27N	D1
2000	HDPK	60035	2757	9W-20N	C2
2200	HnrT	60120	2856	29W-12N	D2
2400	GrtT	60041	2530	26W-34N	E1
2400	RDLK	60041	2530	26W-34N	E1
2400	RDLK	60073	2530	26W-34N	E1
4600	LIHL	60156	2692	38W-23N	E2
8900	TYPK	60487	3424	11W-21S	A5
12000	HMGN	60491	3344	15W-18S	C7
21100	ELWD	60421	3675	25W-30S	D4
21100	JknT	60421	3675	25W-30S	D4
N Magnolia Ln					
2900	WKGN	60083	2478	14W-37N	B1
S Magnolia Ln					
11400	ALSP	60803	3275	6W-13S	E4
26300	CNHN	60410	3672	32W-32S	C7
W Magnolia Ln					
1700	MPPT	60056	2861	17W-11N	C3
Magnolia Pkwy					
10	HNWD	60047	2646	19W-24N	B7
10	HNWD	60047	2700	19W-24N	B1
Magnolia Pl					
200	SCHT	60411	3595	2W-27S	D3
200	SCHT	60411	3596	1W-27S	A3
Magnolia Plz					
3000	SCHT	60411	3595	1W-27S	E3
Magnolia Rd					
700	BRTN	60010	2698	25W-20N	A7
1100	MDLN	60060	2590	19W-29N	B5
2000	HMWD	60430	3427	2W-21S	C6
Magnolia St					
-	GNVW	60062	2809	12W-14N	B4
300	GRNE	60031	2535	13W-34N	E1
300	GRNE	60031	2536	13W-34N	A1
700	GRNE	60031	2479	13W-35N	A7
1200	HRVD	60033	2405	51W-39N	E4
1400	GNVW	60025	2809	12W-14N	B5
2100	DSPN	60018	2863	12W-9N	B7
2300	DSPN	60018	2917	12W-9N	B1
6800	HRPK	60133	2911	27W-8N	D3
E Magnolia St					
10	ANHT	60005	2807	17W-12N	A7
W Magnolia St					
-	ANHT	60005	2806	18W-12N	E7
-	ANHT	60005	2807	18W-12N	A7
Magnolia Wy					
1400	CLSM	60188	2967	28W-3N	A5
Magnuson Ct					
800	BNHL	60010	2802	30W-15N	A2
800	BNHL	60118	2802	30W-15N	A2
Maha Ct					
5400	JLET	60586	3496	30W-22S	B2
Mahan Rd					
-	LkeC	60088	2594	10W-30N	A1
-	NCHI	60088	2594	10W-30N	A1
Mahogany Ct					
5300	GRNE	60031	2478	15W-35N	A5
Mahoney Dr					
-	BRRG	60527	3208	15W-10S	C6
-	DGvT	60527	3208	15W-10S	C6
Mahoney Pkwy					
17200	HLCT	60429	3427	3W-20S	B5
Maiden Ln					
10	EDND	60118	2801	33W-16N	A3
10	WDND	60118	2801	33W-15N	A3
500	GNEN	60137	3025	22W-0S	C7
6100	BtnT	60081	2472	29W-37N	D1
10000	RHMD	60071	2353	34W-41N	D7
S Maiden Ln					
1800	HMND	46394	3280		D4
Maidstone Ct					
300	SMBG	60194	2857	27W-11N	D3
N Maidstone Dr					
1200	VNHL	60061	2647	17W-26N	B2
Main Av					
-	CHCG	60613	2977	1W-5N	D1
Main Dr					
-	HGKN	60525	3147	12W-6S	C4
-	NPVL	60540	3141	27W-6S	B5
-	WynT	60184	2909	32W-6N	D6
10	CTSD	60525	3147	12W-6S	C4
10	WnfT	60185	3081	28W-2S	A3
10	WnfT	60555	3081	28W-2S	A3
10	WNVL	60185	3081	28W-2S	A3
10	WNVL	60555	3081	28W-2S	A3
1000	DRGV	60515	3144	20W-6S	B3
1000	DRGV	60516	3144	20W-5S	B3
Main Ln					
300	ELGN	60123	2854	35W-10N	B5
S Main Pl					
200	CLSM	60188	3024	24W-1N	C3
Main Rd					
-	ELGN	60123	2854	34W-10N	D7
Main St					
-	BHPK	60087	2479	12W-38N	B1
-	BtlT	60512	3261	41W-12S	E3
-	CHHT	60411	3595	2W-26S	C2
-	CHHT	60466	3595	2W-26S	C2
-	CnhT	60410	3674	29W-28S	A1
-	HbnT	60034	2350	41W-42N	E6
-	HNVL	60030	2532	22W-33N	B3
-	HNVL	60073	2532	22W-33N	B3
-	HTLY	60142	2692	39W-21N	C7
-	WKGN	60087	2479	12W-38N	B1
-	WPHR	60096	2363	9W-42N	D6
10	BbyT	60119	3075	43W-1S	A3
10	BbyT	60119	3076	41W-1S	A2
10	BbyT	60134	3076	39W-1S	D2
10	BbyT	60510	3076	41W-1S	A2
10	BTVA	60510	3077	38W-1S	A2
10	BtvT	60510	3077	37W-1S	C2
10	DRGV	60516	3144	19W-7S	C5
10	GNVW	60093	2810	8W-15N	E3
10	LMNT	60439	3270	19W-13S	E5
10	NCHI	60064	2537	10W-31N	A7
10	NCHI	60088	2537	10W-31N	A7
10	NHFD	60093	2810	8W-15N	E3
10	PKFT	60466	3595	3W-27S	B4
10	PKRG	60068	2918	10W-8N	A1
10	ROSL	60172	2913	23W-7N	A4
10	WNVL	60555	3080	28W-3S	E6
100	AlqT	60010	2696	28W-23N	D2
100	CbaT	60010	2696	29W-23N	D2
100	EVTN	60202	2867	2W-10N	C4
100	LKBF	60044	2593	11W-28N	E5
100	MYWD	60153	3030	10W-0N	A4
100	WCHI	60185	3022	29W-0N	D4
100	WNVL	60555	3081	28W-3S	B6
200	ANTH	53179	2357	23W-43N	E4
200	ANTH	60002	2357	23W-42N	E6
200	BTVA	60510	3078	36W-1S	A2
200	BtvT	60134	3077	38W-1S	E2
200	SlmT	53179	2357	23W-43N	E4
200	WDSK	60098	2524	41W-31N	D7
300	MltT	60137	3025	22W-1N	C2
400	DGvT	60516	3206	19W-9S	C4
400	GNCY	53128	2353		A3
500	BtvT	60134	3076	38W-1S	E2
500	BtvT	60510	3076	38W-1S	E2
500	DYR	46311	3510		E5
500	GLHT	60137	3025	22W-1N	C2
500	GLHT	60139	3025	22W-1N	C2
500	MltT	60139	3025	22W-1N	C2
500	MNSR	46321	3510		E5
500	PKCY	60085	2535	13W-33N	E3
700	WnfT	60185	3022	29W-0N	E4
800	BfdT	53128	2352		E3
800	CRTE	60417	3596	1W-28S	B7
800	CRTE	60417	3685	0W-30S	B2
800	GNCY	53128	2352		E3
900	MYWD	60153	3029	10W-0N	E3
900	MYWD	60160	3029	10W-0N	E3
1100	LmnT	60439	3271	18W-13S	A4
1100	MLPK	60160	3029	11W-0N	D3
1200	ANTH	60002	2416	23W-41N	E1
1200	AntT	60002	2357	23W-41N	E7
1200	AntT	60002	2416	23W-41N	E1
1300	BtvT	60539	3077	36W-1S	E2
1500	CteT	60417	3685	0W-30S	B3
1700	EVTN	60202	2866	3W-10N	E4
1900	BTVA	60539	3077	36W-1S	D2
2400	BLWD	60104	3029	11W-0N	D3
2400	MLPK	60104	3029	11W-0N	D3
2400	SKOK	60202	2866	3W-10N	D4
3300	SKOK	60076	2866	5W-10N	B4
3600	MHRY	60050	2528	32W-32N	B4
3900	DRGV	60515	3084	19W-4S	C7
4300	DRGV	60515	3144	19W-6S	C5
4300	LSLE	60532	3083	22W-4S	B7
4300	LSLE	60532	3143	23W-5S	A2
4700	SKOK	60076	2865	6W-10N	E4
4700	SKOK	60077	2865	6W-10N	E4
5300	MNGV	60077	2865	6W-10N	D4
5300	SKOK	60053	2865	6W-10N	E4
5400	LslT	60532	3143	23W-5S	A3
5700	MNGV	60053	2865	7W-10N	B4
6000	UNON	60180	2635	46W-25N	D4
6600	CrlT	60180	2635	46W-25N	D5
7100	DRGV	60516	3206	19W-8S	C1
7300	DRN	60516	3206	19W-8S	C1
8300	DGvT	60561	3206	19W-9S	C4
8300	DRN	60561	3206	19W-9S	C4
9600	HBRN	60034	2350	41W-42N	E6
12700	LmnT	60439	3272	16W-12S	A3
14700	HRVY	60426	3350	1W-18S	A6
18600	NlxT	60448	3502	15W-22S	B1
21100	MTSN	60443	3506	4W-25S	E7
21100	OMFD	60461	3506	4W-25S	E7
21400	KLDR	60047	2699	21W-23N	D3
21500	ElaT	60047	2699	21W-23N	D3
21600	MTSN	60443	3594	4W-26S	E2
21800	PKFT	60443	3594	4W-26S	E2
21800	PKFT	60466	3594	4W-27S	E3
21800	PKFT	60471	3594	4W-26S	E3
21800	RNPK	60471	3594	4W-27S	E4
22500	CstT	60481	3942	29W-41S	E6
22500	CstT	60481	3943	29W-41S	A6
23600	RedT	60408	3942	29W-41S	D6
23600	RedT	60481	3942	29W-41S	D6
Main St CO-5					
300	MltT	60137	3025	22W-1N	C2
500	GLHT	60137	3025	22W-1N	C2
500	GLHT	60139	3025	22W-1N	C2
500	MltT	60139	3025	22W-1N	C2
Main St CO-9					
10	DRGV	60516	3144	19W-7S	C5
3900	DRGV	60515	3084	19W-4S	C7
5500	DRGV	60515	3144	19W-6S	C3
7100	DRGV	60516	3206	19W-8S	C1
Main St CO-10					
10	BbyT	60119	3075	43W-1S	A3
10	BbyT	60119	3076	41W-1S	A2
10	BbyT	60134	3076	39W-1S	D2
10	BbyT	60510	3076	41W-1S	A2
10	BTVA	60510	3077	37W-1S	C2
10	BtvT	60510	3077	37W-1S	C2
200	BtvT	60134	3077	38W-1S	A2
500	BtvT	60134	3076	38W-1S	E2
500	BtvT	60510	3076	38W-1S	E2
2000	BTVA	60539	3077	36W-1S	D2
2000	BtvT	60539	3077	36W-1S	D2
Main St CO-B					
700	GNCY	53128	2353		A3
800	BfdT	53128	2352		E3
800	GNCY	53128	2352		E3
Main St CO-T65					
6000	UNON	60180	2635	46W-25N	D4
Main St SR-1					
800	CRTE	60417	3596	1W-28S	B7
800	CRTE	60417	3685	0W-30S	B2
1500	CteT	60417	3685	0W-30S	B3
Main St SR-22					
21400	KLDR	60047	2699	21W-23N	D3
21500	ElaT	60047	2699	21W-23N	D3
Main St SR-47					
-	HbnT	60034	2350	41W-42N	E6
9600	HBRN	60034	2350	41W-42N	E6
Main St SR-53					
5200	LSLE	60532	3143	23W-6S	B4
5400	LslT	60532	3143	23W-5S	A3
Main St SR-83					
200	ANTH	53179	2357	23W-43N	E4
200	ANTH	60002	2357	23W-42N	E6
200	SlmT	53179	2357	23W-43N	E4
1200	ANTH	60002	2416	23W-41N	E1
1200	AntT	60002	2357	23W-41N	E7
1200	AntT	60002	2416	23W-41N	E1
Main St SR-113					
22500	CstT	60481	3942	29W-41S	E6
22500	CstT	60481	3943	29W-41S	A6
23600	RedT	60408	3942	29W-41S	D6
23600	RedT	60481	3942	29W-41S	D6
E Main St					
-	HFET	60118	2801	32W-15N	E4
10	BCVL	60407	4030	33W-44S	B4
10	BlmT	60425	3508	0E-22S	E2
10	CHHT	60411	3596	1W-26S	B2
10	CPVL	60110	2800	34W-16N	E1
10	CRY	60013	2695	30W-23N	E1
10	EDND	60118	2801	32W-15N	C3
10	GDLY	60407	4030	32W-43S	D2
10	GNWD	60425	3508	0E-22S	E2
10	LKZH	60047	2698	23W-23N	E3
10	PLNO	60545	3259	46W-13S	E6
10	RLKP	60073	2532	22W-33N	B3
10	SCRL	60174	2964	35W-3N	B7
100	AlqT	60013	2696	30W-23N	B1
100	BDWD	60408	3942	31W-41S	B6
100	CbaT	60013	2696	29W-23N	D1
100	HNVL	60073	2532	22W-33N	A3
100	PTON	60468	3861	9W-37S	A3
100	YKVL	60560	3333	42W-15S	C2
200	CRY	60013	2696	30W-23N	B1
200	DLTN	60419	3350	0E-16S	D3
200	DLTN	60827	3350	0E-16S	D3
200	LKZH	60047	2699	23W-23N	A3
200	RVDL	60827	3350	0E-16S	D3
300	HNVL	60030	2532	22W-33N	B3
400	DndT	60118	2801	32W-15N	C3
400	RedT	60408	3942	31W-41S	B6
400	SCRL	60185	2965	32W-3N	C6
400	WynT	60185	2965	32W-3N	C6
500	SEGN	60177	2908	34W-8N	E2
700	DLTN	60419	3351	1E-16S	A3
700	ElgT	60177	2908	34W-8N	E2
900	LtRT	60545	3260	46W-13S	A6
900	PLNO	60545	3260	46W-13S	A6
2800	SCRL	60174	2965	33W-3N	A6
11100	HTLY	60142	2692	40W-20N	A7
11800	HTLY	60142	2691	40W-21N	E7
E Main St CO-A52					
11300	HTLY	60142	2692	40W-20N	A7
11800	HTLY	60142	2691	40W-21N	E7
E Main St SR-22					
200	LKZH	60047	2698	23W-23N	E3
200	LKZH	60047	2699	23W-23N	A3
E Main St SR-64					
10	SCRL	60174	2964	35W-3N	B7
400	SCRL	60185	2965	32W-3N	C6
400	WynT	60185	2965	32W-3N	C6
2800	SCRL	60174	2965	33W-3N	A6
E Main St SR-72					
-	HFET	60118	2801	32W-15N	E4
10	EDND	60118	2801	32W-15N	C3
400	DndT	60118	2801	32W-15N	C3
E Main St SR-113					
100	BDWD	60408	3942	31W-41S	B6
400	RedT	60408	3942	31W-41S	B6
E Main St SR-134					
10	RLKP	60073	2532	22W-33N	B3
100	HNVL	60073	2532	22W-33N	A3
300	HNVL	60030	2532	22W-33N	B3
E Main St US-14					
10	CRY	60013	2695	30W-23N	E1
N Main St					
-	BlmT	60425	3508	0W-22S	C1
10	ALGN	60102	2694	33W-21N	E6
10	CLLK	60014	2640	34W-26N	B3
10	GNEN	60137	3025	22W-0S	B7
10	LMBD	60148	3026	20W-1N	B2
10	MPPT	60056	2808	15W-13N	A6
10	NPVL	60540	3141	27W-6S	D5
100	ELBN	60119	3017	43W-2N	A2
100	GNWD	60425	3508	0W-22S	C1
100	MTGY	60538	3199	37W-9S	D4
100	SEGN	60177	2908	34W-8N	E3
100	WCDA	60084	2643	26W-27N	E1
100	WHTN	60187	3024	24W-0N	C4
100	WMTN	60481	3853	27W-38S	D6
400	WCDA	60084	2587	26W-27N	E7
500	NPVL	60563	3141	27W-5S	D3
600	CmpT	60119	3017	43W-2N	A2
600	CmpT	60151	3017	43W-2N	A2
600	ELBN	60151	3017	43W-2N	A2
600	WnfT	60185	3022	28W-0N	E4
600	WnfT	60185	3023	28W-0N	A4
800	MltT	60137	3025	22W-0N	B4
900	LMBD	60148	2970	20W-2N	B7
1000	AlqT	60102	2694	33W-21N	E6
1000	AURA	60506	3199	36W-9S	D4
1000	AURA	60538	3199	37W-9S	D4
1000	MTGY	60506	3199	37W-9S	D4
2000	WHTN	60188	3024	24W-0S	C6
2200	CLSM	60188	3024	24W-0S	C6
2200	MltT	60188	3024	24W-0S	C6
2900	BFGV	60061	2701	16W-23N	D2
2900	BFGV	60089	2701	16W-23N	D2
2900	VNHL	60061	2701	16W-23N	D2
2900	VrnT	60089	2701	16W-23N	D2
8600	RcmT	60071	2412	34W-40N	C3
8600	RHMD	60071	2412	34W-40N	C2
9700	RHMD	60071	2353	34W-43N	C4
11200	RcmT	60071	2353	34W-43N	C4
11500	GNCY	53128	2353	34W-43N	C4
11500	GNCY	60071	2353	34W-43N	C4
11500	RcmT	53128	2353	34W-43N	C4
22900	BFGV	60069	2701	16W-23N	D2
22900	VrnT	60069	2701	16W-23N	D2
24600	CbaT	60013	2642	28W-24N	E6
26800	WCDA	60084	2644	25W-26N	A2
26800	WcnT	60084	2644	25W-26N	A2
N Main St CO-5					
800	GNEN	60137	3025	22W-1N	C3
800	MltT	60137	3025	22W-0N	B4
N Main St CO-36					
2200	CLSM	60188	3024	24W-0S	C6
2200	MltT	60188	3024	24W-0S	C6
2200	WHTN	60187	3024	24W-1N	C3
2200	WHTN	60188	3024	24W-0S	C6
N Main St SR-31					
10	ALGN	60102	2694	33W-21N	E6
1000	AlqT	60102	2694	33W-21N	E6
N Main St SR-47					
100	ELBN	60119	3017	43W-2N	A2
600	CmpT	60119	3017	43W-2N	A2
600	CmpT	60151	3017	43W-2N	A2
600	ELBN	60151	3017	43W-2N	A2
N Main St SR-83					
10	MPPT	60056	2808	15W-13N	A6
N Main St US-12					
8600	RcmT	60071	2412	34W-40N	C3
8600	RHMD	60071	2412	34W-40N	C2
9700	RHMD	60071	2353	34W-43N	C4
11200	RcmT	60071	2353	34W-43N	C4
11500	GNCY	53128	2353	34W-43N	C4
11500	GNCY	60071	2353	34W-43N	C4
11500	RcmT	53128	2353	34W-43N	C4
S Main St					
-	CHCG	60456	3212	5W-10S	B4
-	CHCG	60805	3212	5W-10S	B4
10	ALGN	60102	2694	33W-20N	D7
10	CLLK	60014	2640	34W-25N	B5
10	ELBN	60119	3017	43W-1N	A3
10	GNEN	60137	3083	22W-1S	B1
10	GNVW	60093	2810	8W-15N	E3
10	LMBD	60148	3026	20W-0N	B5
10	MPPT	60056	2808	15W-12N	A7
10	NPVL	60540	3141	27W-7S	D6
10	OSWG	60543	3263	38W-13S	B5
10	SEGN	60177	2908	34W-8N	E3
10	SRGV	60554	3135	42W-7S	C7
100	BbyT	60119	3017	43W-1N	A3
100	BRLT	60103	2910	29W-8N	E3
100	MTGY	60538	3199	37W-9S	C5
100	WCDA	60084	2643	25W-27N	E2
100	WHTN	60187	3024	24W-0S	C7
100	WMTN	60481	3853	27W-38S	D7
200	BRkT	60554	3197	42W-7S	C1
200	LMNT	60439	3270	19W-14S	D6
200	MPPT	60056	2862	15W-12N	A1
200	SRGV	60554	3197	42W-7S	C1
200	YKVL	60560	3333	42W-15S	C3
500	WcnT	60084	2644	25W-26N	A2
500	OswT	60543	3263	38W-13S	B5
600	WnfT	60185	3022	28W-0N	E4
600	WnfT	60185	3023	28W-0N	A4
700	WHTN	60187	3082	24W-1S	C1
1200	LMBD	60148	3084	19W-2S	C3
1200	YkTp	60148	3084	20W-1S	B1
1400	ALGN	60102	2747	34W-20N	D1
1400	DndT	60102	2747	34W-20N	D1
1500	DndT	60118	2747	34W-19N	D2
8800	HMTN	60456	3212	5W-10S	B4
9000	HMTN	60453	3212	5W-10S	B5
9000	OKLN	60453	3212	5W-10S	B5
S Main St CO-V32					
600	CLLK	60014	2640	35W-24N	B6
S Main St SR-31					
10	ALGN	60102	2694	33W-20N	D7
1400	ALGN	60102	2747	34W-20N	D1
1400	DndT	60102	2747	34W-20N	D1
1500	DndT	60118	2747	34W-19N	D2
S Main St SR-47					
10	ELBN	60119	3017	43W-1N	A3
100	BbyT	60119	3017	43W-1N	A3
S Main St SR-83					
10	MPPT	60056	2808	15W-12N	A7
200	MPPT	60056	2862	15W-12N	A1
W Main St					
-	AlqT	60013	2696	28W-23N	D1
10	CHHT	60411	3596	1W-26S	A2
10	CPVL	60110	2800	34W-16N	D1
10	CRY	60013	2695	31W-23N	E1
10	EDND	60118	2801	34W-16N	A2
10	GNWD	60425	3508	0W-22S	D2
10	LKZH	60047	2698	23W-22N	E3
10	PLNO	60545	3259	47W-13S	C6
10	PNFD	60544	3338	30W-17S	C7
10	PnfT	60544	3338	29W-17S	E5
10	RLKP	60073	2532	23W-33N	A3
10	SCRL	60174	2964	36W-3N	A7
10	WDND	60118	2801	34W-16N	A2
100	BCVL	60407	4030	34W-44S	A4
100	BDWD	60408	3942	31W-41S	A5
100	PTON	60468	3861	9W-37S	A3
100	RDLK	60073	2531	23W-33N	E2
100	RDLK	60073	2532	23W-33N	A3
100	YKVL	60560	3333	43W-15S	C2
200	CPVL	60118	2800	35W-16N	D1
200	PTON	60468	3860	9W-37S	E3
300	BDWD	60408	3941	32W-41S	D5
300	WDND	60110	2800	35W-16N	D1
400	PNFD	60544	3339	28W-16S	A4
400	PnfT	60544	3339	28W-16S	A4
400	WDND	60118	2800	35W-16N	D2
700	BNVL	60106	2971	16W-5N	D1
900	SYHW	60118	2800	35W-16N	D2
1000	AlqT	60013	2695	32W-23N	B1
1100	SCRL	60174	2963	36W-3N	E7
1900	SCRL	60175	2963	36W-3N	D7
3700	SchT	60175	2963	37W-3N	B6
4800	MONE	60449	3683	6W-31S	A5
4800	MonT	60449	3683	6W-31S	B5
5500	MONE	60449	3682	6W-31S	E5
6800	NLES	60714	2864	8W-10N	E4
7000	MNGV	60053	2864	8W-10N	D4
7000	MNGV	60714	2864	8W-10N	D4
7700	MaiT	60714	2864	9W-10N	C5
18600	WrnT	60030	2533	18W-33N	E2
25000	GrtT	60041	2474	25W-34N	B7
27700	WcnT	60084	2643	27W-26N	A2
28300	CbaT	60010	2696	28W-23N	E2
28300	LKBN	60010	2696	28W-23N	E2
28300	WcnT	60084	2642	28W-26N	E2
28800	CbaT	60013	2696	28W-23N	D1
28900	AlqT	60010	2696	28W-23N	D2
W Main St CO-30					
200	CPVL	60110	2800	34W-16N	D1
200	CPVL	60118	2800	35W-16N	D1
200	WDND	60118	2800	35W-16N	D1
W Main St SR-22					
-	LKZH	60047	2698	24W-22N	C4
W Main St SR-64					
10	SCRL	60174	2964	36W-3N	A7
1100	SCRL	60174	2963	36W-3N	E7
1900	SCRL	60175	2963	36W-3N	D7
3700	SchT	60175	2963	37W-3N	B6
W Main St SR-72					
10	EDND	60118	2801	34W-16N	A2
10	WDND	60118	2801	34W-16N	A2
400	WDND	60118	2800	35W-16N	D2
900	SYHW	60118	2800	35W-16N	D2
W Main St SR-113					
100	BDWD	60408	3942	31W-41S	A5
300	BDWD	60408	3941	31W-41S	E5
W Main St SR-126					
10	PNFD	60544	3338	30W-17S	C7
10	PnfT	60544	3338	29W-17S	E5
400	PNFD	60544	3339	28W-16S	A4
400	PnfT	60544	3339	28W-16S	A4
W Main St SR-134					
10	RLKP	60073	2532	23W-33N	A3
100	RDLK	60073	2531	23W-33N	E2
100	RDLK	60073	2532	23W-33N	A3
W Main St US-14					
10	CRY	60013	2695	31W-23N	E1
Maine Av					
3300	NCHI	60088	2593	11W-30N	C2
Maine Ct					
17800	ODPK	60467	3423	13W-21S	A6
Maine Dr					
1800	EGVV	60007	2913	22W-9N	C1
Maine Tr					
4100	NndT	60012	2583	35W-27N	E7
4500	NndT	60012	2639	36W-27N	D1
Main Entrance Rd					
-	BTVA	60510	3078	33W-2S	E3
-	BtvT	60510	3078	33W-2S	E3
-	BtvT	60510	3079	33W-2S	A3
-	WnfT	60510	3079	33W-2S	A3
Mainsail Ct					
10	TDLK	60030	2533	19W-34N	C1
Mainsail Dr					
-	GYLK	60030	2533	18W-34N	D1
100	TDLK	60030	2533	19W-34N	D1
200	TDLK	60030	2476	19W-34N	C7
Main St Rd					
100	BtnT	60081	2414	29W-39N	C5
100	FXLK	60081	2414	29W-39N	D5
500	SPGV	60081	2414	29W-39N	C5
1900	SPGV	60081	2413	31W-39N	D4
Main St Rd CO-A7					
100	BtnT	60081	2414	29W-39N	D5
100	FXLK	60081	2414	29W-39N	D5
Main St Rd CO-A17					
200	BtnT	60081	2414	29W-39N	C5
200	FXLK	60081	2414	29W-39N	D5
500	SPGV	60081	2414	29W-39N	C5
1900	SPGV	60081	2413	31W-39N	D4
W Main Street Rd					
11900	HTLY	60142	2691	41W-21N	C7
12100	GfnT	60142	2691	41W-21N	E7
W Main Street Rd CO-A47					
11900	HTLY	60142	2691	41W-21N	C7
12100	GfnT	60142	2691	41W-21N	E7
Mair Ct					
600	BTVA	60510	3019	36W-0S	E7
Mair Dr					
-	AURA	60504	3201	33W-9S	A4
N Maison Ct					
200	EMHT	60126	3028	15W-1N	B2

STREET / Block City ZIP Map# CGS Grid

Maitland Dr
900 LKPT 60441 3419 21W-19S E3
Majestic Ct
- ALGN 60110 2747 36W-18N A4
- ALGN 60118 2747 36W-18N A4
- CPVL 60110 2747 36W-18N A4
400 GRNE 60031 2535 14W-33N C3
Majestic Dr
10 LMBD 60148 3084 19W-2S C3
500 ALGN 60102 2694 35W-20N A7
700 ALGN 60102 2747 35W-20N A1
1100 LKMR 60051 2529 29W-33N C3
1100 McHT 60051 2529 29W-33N C3
23900 CNHN 60410 3672 31W-29S E2
Majestic Ln
400 OSWG 60543 3264 34W-11S D2
600 LKVL 60046 2474 24W-37N D3
Majestic Wy
6600 CPVL 60110 2747 36W-18N A4
Majestic Oaks Dr
2900 SCRL 60174 2965 33W-4N A4
Majestic Oaks Ln
2400 SCRL 60174 2965 33W-4N A4
Majestic Pine St
21200 SRWD 60404 3584 31W-25S A1
Majic Wy
- RlyT 60152 2634 49W-25N C4
600 MRGO 60152 2634 49W-25N C4
Major Av
7700 BRBK 60459 3211 7W-9S D2
8600 MNGV 60053 2865 7W-11N C3
8700 OKLN 60453 3211 7W-10S D5
8700 OKLN 60459 3211 7W-10S D5
10500 OKLN 60453 3275 7W-12S D2
10800 CHRG 60415 3275 7W-12S D3
11000 ALSP 60482 3275 7W-12S D3
11000 CHRG 60482 3275 7W-12S D3
14200 BmnT 60445 3347 7W-16S D4
14700 BmnT 60452 3347 7W-17S D5
14700 OKFT 60452 3347 7W-17S D5
N Major Av
1600 CHCG 60639 3031 6W-0S E7
1600 CHCG 60651 3031 6W-0S E7
2000 CHCG 60639 2975 7W-2N C6
2700 CHCG 60634 2975 7W-3N C5
4300 CHCG 60630 2975 7W-5N C1
5500 CHCG 60630 2919 7W-7N C4
5500 CHCG 60646 2919 7W-7N C4
S Major Av
4900 CHCG 60638 3149 7W-5S C2
4900 StkT 60638 3149 7W-5S C2
6500 BDPK 60638 3149 7W-7S D5
12500 WthT 60463 3275 7W-14S D7
12500 WthT 60803 3275 7W-14S D7
12600 WthT 60445 3275 7W-14S D7
W Major Av
12600 BHPK 60099 2421 12W-39N B5
Major Dr
200 NHLK 60164 2972 13W-2N E7
300 NHLK 60164 2973 13W-2N A7
400 LydT 60164 2973 13W-2N A7
1300 JLET 60586 3496 31W-22S A1
W Makepiece Ln
- PNFD 60586 3415 31W-20S E4
Malcolm Ln
600 WDND 60118 2800 35W-16N B2
Malden Av
10 LGNG 60525 3087 13W-4S A6
200 LGPK 60525 3087 13W-3S A6
Malden Ct
800 SMBG 60193 2858 24W-10N C6
N Malden St
4400 CHCG 60613 2921 1W-5N D7
4400 CHCG 60640 2921 1W-5N D7
Maley Rd
- LMNT 60439 3271 16W-12S D3
E Malibou Ln
600 PLTN 60074 2753 20W-16N A6
Malibu Ct
10 BRRG 60527 3208 15W-10S B6
10 LsIT 60540 3142 25W-5S C4
200 BGBK 60440 3269 22W-11S C1
800 CLSM 60188 2968 26W-3N A5
W Malibu Ct
5100 MHRY 60050 2527 34W-31N D6
Malibu Dr
- LktT 60441 3340 25W-16S B4
100 RMVL 60446 3340 25W-16S B4
200 BGBK 60440 3269 22W-11S C1
300 BGBK 60440 3205 22W-11S C7
S Malibu Dr
23100 MhtT 60442 3588 19W-28S D6
23100 NLNX 60442 3588 19W-28S D6
23100 NLNX 60451 3588 19W-28S D6
Malibu Ln
700 LsIT 60540 3142 24W-5S C4
Malik Ct
2300 GNVW 60025 2864 9W-12N C1
Malinda Dr
8900 CmgT 60033 2406 49W-40N B2
Mall Dr
500 SMBG 60173 2859 21W-11N E3
W Mall Rd
28600 GrtT 60041 2472 28W-35N E6
W Mallard Av
25700 AntT 60002 2416 25W-40N A3
25900 AntT 60002 2415 26W-40N E3
Mallard Cir
900 SMBG 60193 2913 22W-9N B1
15200 ODPK 60462 3346 10W-18S B7
Mallard Ct
100 GYLK 60030 2533 19W-32N C4
300 MDLN 60061 2647 17W-25N B5
300 VNHL 60061 2647 17W-25N B5
500 LsIT 60540 3142 24W-5S C3
500 MltT 60187 3081 26W-2S D4
500 SMBG 60193 2913 22W-9N B1
500 WHTN 60187 3081 26W-2S D4
600 BmdT 60108 2968 25W-5N A2
600 BRLT 60103 2911 28W-8N A3
700 VrnT 60015 2755 15W-20N A1
1100 FXLK 60020 2414 28W-38N E6
3500 RGMW 60008 2806 20W-13N B6
23200 DRPK 60010 2698 23W-21N E7
S Mallard Ct
900 PLTN 60067 2805 22W-14N B3
Mallard Dr
400 VrnT 60015 2755 15W-20N A1
700 MRGO 60152 2634 49W-27N D1
700 NLNX 60451 3502 15W-25S B7
700 NLNX 60451 3590 15W-25S B1
1200 ELGN 60123 2800 35W-13N B7
2000 NHBK 60062 2757 10W-16N A7
2400 LNHT 60046 2418 19W-38N B7
3100 FSMR 60422 3507 4W-22S A1
3100 HMWD 60430 3506 4W-22S E1
Mallard Dr
3100 HMWD 60430 3507 4W-22S A1
3800 NPVL 60564 3266 29W-11S D2
5500 MTSN 60443 3505 6W-24S E5
14000 HMGN 60491 3344 15W-17S B5
N Mallard Dr
4100 ANHT 60004 2753 18W-20N D2
S Mallard Dr
600 PLTN 60067 2805 22W-14N B3
2400 PNFD 60544 3338 30W-16S C4
25400 CNHN 60410 3672 33W-30S B5
W Mallard Dr
1000 PLTN 60067 2805 22W-15N B2
Mallard Ln
- BmdT 60133 2968 25W-5N A2
- RHMD 60071 2353 34W-42N D5
10 BMDL 60108 2968 25W-4N A3
10 BmdT 60108 2968 25W-4N A3
100 LKFT 60045 2649 11W-25N E5
300 BRKT 60554 3197 42W-7S D1
300 SRGV 60554 3197 42W-7S D1
400 DRFD 60015 2756 11W-20N D1
600 OKBK 60523 3085 16W-3S D5
600 VrnT 60015 2755 15W-20N A1
700 ANHT 60004 2754 16W-17N D6
700 WLNG 60004 2754 16W-17N D6
700 WLNG 60090 2754 16W-17N D6
1000 GNCY 53128 2353 B1
1000 PTON 60468 3860 10W-38S C4
1100 HFET 60192 2856 30W-12N B2
1100 HnrT 60192 2856 30W-12N B2
2000 HRPK 60133 2967 27W-4N C3
2000 WDSK 60098 2582 39W-30N B2
4200 JLET 60586 3496 29W-22S D1
4300 JLET 60431 3496 29W-22S D1
16800 LKPT 60441 3420 19W-20S E4
E Mallard Ln
10 LKFT 60045 2649 10W-25N E5
8500 GLKT 60481 3761 33W-34S C5
8500 WmTp 60481 3761 33W-34S C4
N Mallard Ln
2500 RLKB 60073 2475 23W-36N A3
2700 LKVL 60046 2475 23W-36N A3
2700 LKVL 60073 2475 23W-36N A3
S Mallard Ln
- HMGN 60441 3342 19W-18S D6
- HmrT 60441 3342 19W-18S D6
1300 MPPT 60056 2861 16W-11N E3
15200 HMGN 60491 3342 19W-18S D7
W Mallard Ln
10 LKFT 60045 2649 11W-25N C5
14400 HMGN 60491 3344 15W-17S C5
Mallard Lndg
200 BGBK 60440 3269 22W-12S C2
Mallard Pt
200 LKBN 60010 2643 26W-24N D7
2800 ISLK 60042 2586 28W-29N D4
Mallard Rd
8800 TYPK 60487 3424 11W-21S A7
S Mallard St
2200 PNFD 60544 3338 30W-16S C4
Mallard Wy
7000 AlqT 60013 2642 30W-24N A7
7300 CRY 60013 2642 30W-24N A7
E Mallard Creek Dr
600 RLKB 60073 2475 22W-35N C6
Mallard Lake Rd
10 SchT 60175 2907 38W-6N A7
Mallard Point Dr
400 BtvT 60542 3077 37W-3S D7
Mallard Ridge Dr
- LkvT 60046 2475 21W-38N E1
- LNHT 60046 2475 21W-38N E1
Mallards Cove
200 BCHR 60401 3774 0W-35S D7
Mallect Ct
17600 UNON 60180 2635 46W-25N D4
Mallery Av
10 ELGN 60123 2854 34W-11N D5
Mallette Av
100 ThtT 60476 3428 0E-21S E6
100 TNTN 60476 3428 0E-21S E6
Mallette Rd
1600 AURA 60505 3139 33W-5S A2
Mall Loop Dr
- JLET 60435 3417 28W-20S A4
3200 JLET 60431 3417 28W-20S A4
N Mallory Av
10 BTVA 60510 3078 35W-1S A2
S Mallory Av
10 BTVA 60510 3078 35W-1S A2
Mallory Ct
- BRRG 60527 3146 15W-7S B6
1100 NPVL 60540 3202 29W-8S D2
2300 RGMW 60008 2805 21W-14N D4
2300 RGMW 60067 2805 21W-14N D4
Mallory Dr
2100 FmtT 60048 2590 19W-31N C1
2100 LYVL 60048 2590 19W-31N C1
E Mallory Dr
10 BbyT 60134 3076 39W-1S E1
S Mallory Dr
19900 FftT 60423 3504 9W-24S D4
W Mallory Dr
10 BbyT 60134 3076 39W-1S E1
Mallow Ct
2000 HRPK 60133 2967 27W-5N C1
2400 SMBG 60194 2857 26W-10N E5
Mallow Dr
8000 TYPK 60477 3424 10W-21S C6
Mallow Ridge Dr
16700 ODPK 60467 3423 13W-20S A4
Mallview Ln
400 BGBK 60440 3269 22W-12S B2
Malmesbury Ct
2500 AURA 60502 3139 32W-5S C3
Malmo Rd
2800 EGvT 60005 2861 16W-10N E5
2800 EGvT 60056 2861 16W-10N E5
2800 MPPT 60005 2861 16W-10N E5
2800 MPPT 60056 2861 16W-10N E5
Malmquist Rd
34200 GrtT 60041 2530 28W-34N A1
Malone St
12000 HTLY 60142 2691 41W-22N E3
Malory Ln
2000 HDPK 60035 2703 11W-22N E3
S Malta St
9900 CHCG 60643 3213 1W-11S D7
10000 CHCG 60643 3277 2W-12S D1
Malthusian Wy
- RVFT 60305 3030 9W-1N B2
Malvern Ln
10 VNHL 60061 2647 16W-25N C6
Malvina Ct
3500 NPVL 60564 3267 28W-11S A1
Manassas Ct
800 NPVL 60540 3203 27W-7S B1
1300 LGGV 60047 2700 18W-21N E6
Manassas Ln
1200 LGGV 60047 2700 18W-21N D6
S Manassas Ln
14100 PnfT 60544 3339 28W-17S B5
W Manawa Tr
500 MPPT 60056 2861 16W-12N E2
Mance St
- HGKN 60525 3147 12W-7S C5
Manchester Av
300 BTVA 60510 3078 34W-2S C3
600 WSTR 60154 3029 12W-0S C7
1400 WSTR 60154 3087 12W-1S C1
Manchester Blvd
1500 HFET 60169 2858 25W-12N A1
Manchester Cir
900 GYLK 60030 2533 19W-34N B2
900 SMBG 60193 2913 23W-9N B1
Manchester Ct
10 BFGV 60089 2754 17W-20N C2
10 FRGV 60021 2696 29W-22N B4
10 LIHL 60156 2692 38W-22N E4
10 LIHL 60156 2693 38W-22N A3
10 SMWD 60107 2856 29W-11N D4
100 SMBG 60193 2913 22W-7N D4
800 GNVA 60134 3020 34W-1N D3
800 WMTN 60481 3943 27W-39S E1
900 LKZH 60047 2644 24W-24N D7
900 SEGN 60177 2908 35W-8N B2
1000 NPVL 60563 3140 29W-5S D3
1200 CLLK 60014 2693 37W-23N C2
2400 WDRG 60517 3143 21W-7S E7
19500 MKNA 60448 3503 12W-23S D3
Manchester Dr
- HFET 60169 2858 25W-12N A1
10 BFGV 60089 2754 17W-20N C2
100 BRTN 60010 2750 25W-17N E5
1200 CLLK 60014 2693 36W-23N C2
1200 MDLN 60060 2590 19W-29N B3
5600 GRNE 60031 2534 16W-33N E3
7000 JLET 60586 3415 33W-21S B6
8200 BtlT 60512 3198 41W-10S A7
8200 BtlT 60538 3198 41W-10S A7
8200 MTGY 60512 3198 40W-10S B7
19200 MKNA 60448 3503 12W-23S D3
E Manchester Dr
10 CHHT 60411 3508 1W-24S A5
200 WLNG 60090 2755 14W-17N D5
N Manchester Dr
400 CHHT 60411 3508 1W-24S A5
W Manchester Dr
10 WLNG 60090 2755 14W-17N C5
Manchester Ln
- YKVL 60560 3333 42W-17S D6
10 EMHT 60126 3027 16W-0N E4
10 VNHL 60061 2647 17W-24N C6
200 PTBR 60010 2642 29W-26N D2
500 ElgT 60124 2853 37W-10N B6
600 WNVL 60555 3080 30W-1S B3
N Manchester Ln
100 BMDL 60108 2968 25W-5N C1
Manchester Mnr
7600 HRPK 60133 2912 26W-9N A1
Manchester Rd
10 WHTN 60187 3023 26W-0S E7
10 WNFD 60190 3023 27W-0S D7
400 OSWG 60543 3200 35W-10S B6
800 WHTN 60187 3024 25W-0S B6
900 LKZH 60047 2644 24W-24N D7
900 LKZH 60047 2698 24W-24N D1
1000 SMBG 60193 2913 23W-9N B1
Manchester St
800 NPVL 60563 3140 29W-5S E3
900 CRY 60013 2695 32W-23N B1
16400 TYPK 60477 3425 8W-19S A2
Manchester Wy
10 AURA 60506 3136 39W-7S E7
Manchester Course
800 GNVA 60134 3020 34W-1N E3
Manchester Mall
1100 MHRY 60050 2528 33W-33N A3
Manda Dr
11600 CrlT 60142 2743 45W-20N B1
Manda Ln
400 WLNG 60090 2754 16W-18N E3
Mandalay Ct
1000 NPVL 60563 3140 30W-5S B3
Mandam Village Dr
1700 JLET 60586 3415 32W-21S C7
1700 JLET 60586 3495 32W-21S C1
S Mandarin Ct
13800 LktT 60544 3340 26W-16S A4
Mandarin Ln
200 BmdT 60108 2967 26W-5N E2
Mandel Av
1200 HLSD 60162 3028 13W-1S E7
1200 WSTR 60154 3028 13W-1S E7
1200 WSTR 60162 3028 13W-1S E7
1400 WSTR 60154 3086 13W-1S E1
2100 HLSD 60154 3086 13W-1S E2
2100 HLSD 60162 3086 13W-1S E2
Mandel Ct
11000 WSTR 60154 3086 13W-1S E1
Mandel Ln
10 MPPT 60056 2808 13W-15N D3
10 MPPT 60070 2808 13W-15N D3
10 PTHT 60070 2808 13W-15N D3
N Mandel Ln
1400 MPPT 60056 2808 13W-14N D3
1400 MPPT 60070 2808 13W-14N D3
1400 PTHT 60070 2808 13W-14N D3
S Mandel St
10000 WldT 60503 3265 31W-11S D2
10000 WldT 60585 3265 31W-11S D2
N Mandell Av
6200 CHCG 60646 2919 7W-7N C3
Mandeville Ln
3700 NPVL 60564 3267 28W-12S A2
3800 NPVL 60564 3266 28W-12S E2
3800 WldT 60564 3266 28W-12S E2
Mandrake Dr
700 BTVA 60510 3078 34W-1S E3
Mandy Ln
- OSWG 60543 3200 34W-10S E7
Maneval Dr
- GYLK 60030 2533 20W-32N A4
Mango Av
8800 MNGV 60053 2865 7W-11N C3
N Mango Av
1600 CHCG 60639 3031 6W-0S E6
1600 CHCG 60651 3031 6W-0S E6
2000 CHCG 60639 2975 7W-2N C6
4400 CHCG 60630 2975 7W-5N C1
4400 CHCG 60634 2975 7W-5N C1
N Mango Av
5500 CHCG 60630 2919 7W-6N C5
5500 CHCG 60646 2919 7W-6N C5
Manhatas Tr
1000 ALGN 60102 2747 34W-19N E2
1000 DndT 60102 2747 34W-19N E2
Manhattan Dr
10800 HTLY 60142 2692 39W-21N B7
Manhattan Rd
10 JLET 60433 3587 23W-25S A1
10 JltT 60433 3587 21W-26S E2
2100 JltT 60421 3588 21W-26S A3
2100 JltT 60433 3588 21W-26S A3
Manhattan Rd US-52
10 JLET 60433 3587 23W-25S A1
10 JltT 60433 3587 22W-26S E2
2100 JltT 60421 3588 21W-26S A3
2100 JltT 60433 3588 21W-26S A3
W Manhattan Rd
- CnhT 60421 3674 27W-30S D5
- JknT 60421 3674 27W-30S D5
16000 MhtT 60442 3677 20W-30S D3
16100 JknT 60421 3677 21W-30S A4
16100 MhtT 60421 3677 20W-30S B4
19200 JknT 60421 3675 24W-30S E4
19800 ELWD 60421 3675 24W-30S D4
Manhattan St
1500 BGBK 60490 3267 26W-13S D5
W Manhattan Monee Rd
- MHTN 60442 3678 18W-31S A4
12800 MhtT 60442 3678 17W-30S C4
Manhatten Cir
600 MTGY 60543 3263 38W-11S A2
700 OSWG 60543 3263 38W-11S A2
Manico Ct
2000 CTHL 60403 3417 26W-21S E7
Manico Dr
2000 CTHL 60403 3417 26W-21S E7
N Manila Av
5300 CHCG 60630 2919 7W-6N C5
Manistee Av
200 BNHM 60409 3351 3E-17S E5
200 BNHM 60633 3351 3E-17S E5
200 CTCY 60409 3351 3E-17S E6
S Manistee Av
7900 CHCG 60617 3215 3E-9S E3
7900 CHCG 60649 3215 3E-9S E2
10300 CHCG 60617 3279 3E-11S E1
12600 CHCG 60633 3279 3E-14S E7
13100 CHCG 60633 3351 2E-15S D1
13900 BNHM 60633 3351 3E-16S E3
14500 BNHM 60409 3351 3E-16S E4
14500 CTCY 60409 3351 3E-16S E4
S Manistee Ct
14100 PnfT 60544 3339 27W-16S C5
Manito Tr
900 ALGN 60102 2747 34W-19N E2
900 DndT 60102 2747 34W-19N E2
W Manitoba Dr
7400 PSHT 60463 3274 9W-15S D7
Manitoba St
17100 LKPT 60441 3420 21W-20S A5
Manitoba Tr
28700 GrtT 60051 2472 28W-34N D7
Manitou Ct
16400 HMGN 60491 3422 15W-19S B2
Manitou Rd
12200 HMGN 60491 3422 15W-19S B3
Manitou St
700 CRY 60013 2695 32W-23N C1
Manitou Tr
2600 McHT 60051 2529 29W-34N D1
2700 GrtT 60051 2472 29W-34N D7
2700 McHT 60051 2472 29W-34N D7
Manitowac St
300 PKFT 60466 3595 3W-27S A5
W Manitowoc Ct
18000 WrnT 60030 2534 18W-33N A3
N Mankato Av
7000 CHCG 60646 2919 7W-8N B1
Manke Ln
- GwdT 60098 2524 41W-32N E4
Manley Rd
700 SCRL 60174 2963 36W-3N E6
700 SCRL 60174 2964 36W-3N A6
Mann Dr
- CHCG 60629 3150 3W-7S E6
- CHCG 60629 3151 3W-7S A6
5100 McHT 60072 2470 34W-37N D2
5100 RGWD 60072 2470 34W-37N D2
Mann Pl
100 ELGN 60120 2855 33W-12N A2
Mann St
4300 OKFT 60452 3426 5W-19S B2
Mannheim Rd
- CHCG 60176 2917 12W-6N B6
- CHCG 60666 2973 12W-5N B1
- SRPK 60176 2917 12W-6N B6
10 BLWD 60104 3029 13W-0N A3
10 BLWD 60160 3029 13W-0N A4
10 MLPK 60160 3029 13W-0N A4
300 DSPN 60016 2863 13W-10N A4
500 BLWD 60162 3029 12W-0N A4
500 HLSD 60162 3029 12W-0N A4
900 DSPN 60016 2862 13W-10N E5
1000 DSPN 60018 2862 13W-10N E6
1700 DSPN 60018 2863 13W-9N A6
2000 DSPN 60018 2917 13W-8N A1
2000 RSMT 60018 2917 13W-8N A1
2400 FNPK 60131 2973 12W-3N A4
2400 LydT 60131 2973 13W-3N A6
2400 LydT 60164 2973 13W-3N A6
2600 FNPK 60164 2973 13W-3N A5
2900 CHCG 60018 2917 12W-8N A2
3700 FNPK 60176 2973 13W-4N A2
3700 SRPK 60131 2973 13W-4N A2
3700 SRPK 60176 2973 13W-4N A2
6400 CHCG 60666 2917 12W-7N A3
6400 RSMT 60666 2917 12W-8N A3
Mannheim Rd US-12
- CHCG 60176 2917 12W-6N B6
- CHCG 60666 2973 12W-5N B1
- SRPK 60176 2917 12W-6N B6
10 BLWD 60104 3029 13W-0N A4
10 BLWD 60160 3029 13W-0N A4
10 MLPK 60160 3029 13W-0N A4
300 DSPN 60016 2863 13W-10N A4
500 BLWD 60162 3029 12W-0N A4
500 HLSD 60162 3029 12W-0N A4
1000 DSPN 60016 2862 13W-10N E6
1000 DSPN 60018 2862 13W-10N E6
1700 DSPN 60018 2863 13W-9N A6
2000 DSPN 60018 2917 13W-8N A1
2000 RSMT 60018 2917 13W-8N A1
2400 FNPK 60131 2973 12W-3N A4
2400 LydT 60131 2973 13W-3N A6
Mannheim Rd US-12
2400 LydT 60164 2973 13W-3N A6
2600 FNPK 60164 2973 13W-3N A5
2900 CHCG 60018 2917 12W-8N A2
3700 FNPK 60176 2973 13W-4N A2
3700 SRPK 60131 2973 13W-4N A2
3700 SRPK 60176 2973 13W-4N A2
6400 CHCG 60666 2917 12W-7N A3
6400 RSMT 60666 2917 12W-8N A3
Mannheim Rd US-20
10 BLWD 60104 3029 13W-0N A4
10 BLWD 60160 3029 13W-0N A4
10 MLPK 60160 3029 13W-0N A4
500 BLWD 60162 3029 12W-0N A4
500 HLSD 60162 3029 12W-0N A4
Mannheim Rd US-45
- CHCG 60176 2917 12W-6N B6
- CHCG 60666 2973 12W-5N B1
- SRPK 60176 2917 12W-6N B6
10 BLWD 60104 3029 13W-0N A4
10 BLWD 60160 3029 13W-0N A4
10 MLPK 60160 3029 13W-0N A4
300 DSPN 60016 2863 13W-10N A4
500 BLWD 60162 3029 12W-0N A4
500 HLSD 60162 3029 12W-0N A4
1000 DSPN 60016 2862 13W-10N E6
1000 DSPN 60018 2862 13W-10N E6
1700 DSPN 60018 2863 13W-9N A6
2000 DSPN 60018 2917 13W-8N A1
2000 RSMT 60018 2917 13W-8N A1
2400 FNPK 60131 2973 12W-3N A4
2400 LydT 60131 2973 13W-3N A6
2400 LydT 60164 2973 13W-3N A6
2600 FNPK 60164 2973 13W-3N A5
2900 CHCG 60018 2917 12W-8N A2
3700 FNPK 60176 2973 13W-4N A2
3700 SRPK 60131 2973 13W-4N A2
3700 SRPK 60176 2973 13W-4N A2
6400 CHCG 60666 2917 12W-7N A3
6400 RSMT 60666 2917 12W-8N A3
N Mannheim Rd
- BLWD 60160 3029 12W-1N A3
- HLSD 60154 3029 12W-0S A6
- WSTR 60154 3029 12W-0S A6
10 BLWD 60104 3029 12W-0S A5
10 HLSD 60104 3029 12W-0S A5
10 HLSD 60162 3029 12W-0S A5
100 BLWD 60162 3029 12W-0S A5
1500 MLPK 60160 3029 12W-1N A2
1500 SNPK 60160 3029 12W-1N A2
1500 SNPK 60165 3029 12W-1N A2
1800 MLPK 60164 3029 12W-1N A1
1800 MLPK 60165 3029 12W-1N A1
1800 SNPK 60164 3029 12W-1N A1
2000 LydT 60160 2973 12W-2N A7
2000 LydT 60164 2973 13W-2N A7
2000 MLPK 60160 2973 12W-2N A7
2000 NHLK 60160 2973 12W-2N A7
2000 NHLK 60164 2973 12W-2N A7
2300 LydT 60131 2973 13W-2N A7
N Mannheim Rd US-12
- BLWD 60160 3029 12W-1N A3
- HLSD 60154 3029 12W-0S A6
- WSTR 60154 3029 12W-0S A6
10 BLWD 60104 3029 12W-0S A5
10 HLSD 60104 3029 12W-0S A5
10 HLSD 60162 3029 12W-0S A5
100 BLWD 60162 3029 12W-0S A5
1500 MLPK 60160 3029 12W-1N A2
1500 SNPK 60160 3029 12W-1N A2
1500 SNPK 60165 3029 13W-1N A2
1800 MLPK 60164 3029 12W-1N A1
1800 MLPK 60165 3029 12W-1N A1
1800 SNPK 60164 3029 12W-1N A1
2000 LydT 60160 2973 12W-2N A7
2000 LydT 60164 2973 13W-2N A7
2000 MLPK 60160 2973 12W-2N A7
2000 NHLK 60160 2973 12W-2N A7
2000 NHLK 60164 2973 12W-2N A7
2300 LydT 60131 2973 13W-2N A7
N Mannheim Rd US-20
- BLWD 60160 3029 12W-1N A3
- HLSD 60154 3029 12W-0S A6
- MLPK 60160 3029 12W-1N A2
- SNPK 60160 3029 12W-1N A2
- SNPK 60165 3029 12W-1N A2
- WSTR 60154 3029 12W-0S A6
10 BLWD 60104 3029 12W-0S A5
10 HLSD 60104 3029 12W-0S A5
10 HLSD 60162 3029 12W-0S A5
100 BLWD 60162 3029 12W-0S A5
N Mannheim Rd US-45
- BLWD 60160 3029 12W-1N A3
- HLSD 60154 3029 12W-0S A6
- WSTR 60154 3029 12W-0S A6
10 BLWD 60104 3029 12W-0S A5
10 HLSD 60104 3029 12W-0S A5
10 HLSD 60162 3029 12W-0S A5
100 BLWD 60162 3029 12W-0S A5
1500 MLPK 60160 3029 12W-1N A2
1500 SNPK 60160 3029 12W-1N A2
1500 SNPK 60165 3029 12W-1N A2
1800 MLPK 60164 3029 12W-1N A1
1800 MLPK 60165 3029 12W-1N A1
1800 SNPK 60164 3029 12W-1N A1
2000 LydT 60160 2973 12W-2N A7
2000 LydT 60164 2973 13W-2N A7
2000 MLPK 60160 2973 12W-2N A7
2000 NHLK 60160 2973 12W-2N A7
2000 NHLK 60164 2973 12W-2N A7
2300 LydT 60131 2973 13W-2N A7
S Mannheim Rd
- BLWD 60104 3029 12W-0S A6
- HLSD 60104 3029 12W-0S A6
10 HLSD 60154 3029 12W-0S A6
10 HLSD 60162 3029 12W-0S A6
10 WSTR 60154 3029 13W-1S A7
100 WSTR 60162 3029 13W-1S A7
300 PvsT 60162 3029 13W-1S A7
1400 PvsT 60162 3087 12W-1S A1
1400 WSTR 60154 3087 12W-1S A1
1400 WSTR 60162 3087 12W-1S A1
2100 PvsT 60154 3087 12W-1S A2
2100 PvsT 60525 3087 12W-1S A2
S Mannheim Rd US-12
- BLWD 60104 3029 12W-0S A6
- HLSD 60104 3029 12W-0S A6
10 HLSD 60154 3029 12W-0S A6
10 HLSD 60162 3029 12W-0S A6
10 WSTR 60154 3029 13W-1S A7
100 WSTR 60162 3029 13W-1S A7
300 PvsT 60162 3029 13W-1S A7
1400 PvsT 60162 3087 12W-1S A1
1400 WSTR 60154 3087 12W-1S A1
1400 WSTR 60162 3087 12W-1S A1
2100 PvsT 60154 3087 12W-1S A2

Block	City	ZIP	Map#	CGS	Grid
S Mannheim Rd US-12					
2100	PvsT	60525	3087	12W-1S	A2
S Mannheim Rd US-20					
-	BLWD	60104	3029	12W-0S	A6
-	HLSD	60104	3029	12W-0S	A6
10	HLSD	60154	3029	12W-0S	A6
10	HLSD	60162	3029	12W-0S	A6
10	WSTR	60154	3029	13W-1S	A7
100	WSTR	60162	3029	13W-1S	A7
300	PvsT	60162	3029	13W-1S	A7
1400	PvsT	60162	3087	12W-1S	A1
1400	WSTR	60154	3087	12W-1S	A1
1400	WSTR	60162	3087	12W-1S	A1
2100	PvsT	60154	3087	12W-1S	A2
2100	PvsT	60525	3087	12W-1S	A2
S Mannheim Rd US-45					
-	BLWD	60104	3029	12W-0S	A6
-	HLSD	60104	3029	12W-0S	A6
10	HLSD	60154	3029	12W-0S	A6
10	HLSD	60162	3029	12W-0S	A6
10	WSTR	60154	3029	13W-1S	A7
100	WSTR	60162	3029	13W-1S	A7
300	PvsT	60162	3029	13W-1S	A7
1400	PvsT	60162	3087	12W-1S	A1
1400	WSTR	60154	3087	12W-1S	A1
1400	WSTR	60162	3087	12W-1S	A1
2100	PvsT	60154	3087	12W-1S	A2
2100	PvsT	60525	3087	12W-1S	A2
Manning Av					
100	MTGY	60538	3199	36W-9S	E5
200	WNVL	60555	3080	28W-3S	E6
200	WNVL	60555	3081	28W-3S	A5
1300	MTGY	60538	3200	36W-9S	A5
Manning Dr					
300	WDDL	60191	2970	18W-5N	E1
Manning Rd					
100	DRGV	60516	3206	18W-9S	E2
100	DRGV	60561	3206	18W-9S	E2
100	DRN	60516	3206	18W-9S	E2
100	HTLY	60140	2744	42W-17N	E7
100	RtdT	60140	2744	42W-17N	E7
100	RtdT	60140	2797	42W-16N	E1
300	DRN	60561	3206	19W-8S	D2
Manomet Ct					
600	SMBG	60173	2859	22W-11N	C3
Manomet Ln					
800	SMBG	60173	2859	22W-11N	C3
Manomet on Auburn					
10	RGMW	60008	2806	19W-14N	C3
Manor Av					
-	PTHT	60070	2807	15W-15N	E2
100	FXLK	60020	2472	28W-36N	E5
500	GYLK	60030	2533	20W-33N	A2
7600	MNSR	46321	3430		D7
8700	MNSR	46321	3510		D1
14100	DLTN	60419	3350	0E-16S	D3
N Manor Av					
4400	CHCG	60618	2920	3W-5N	E7
4400	CHCG	60625	2920	3W-5N	E7
37700	BHPK	60087	2479	10W-37N	E1
37700	BHPK	60087	2480	10W-37N	A1
38000	BHPK	60087	2422	10W-38N	A7
38500	WKGN	60099	2422	10W-38N	A7
W Manor Av					
10000	FNPK	60131	2973	12W-3N	B5
Manor Cir					
500	SMBG	60194	2857	26W-11N	E4
900	LYVL	60048	2591	16W-29N	E4
Manor Ct					
200	DLTN	60419	3350	0E-16S	D3
300	BGBK	60440	3269	22W-12S	C3
400	NLNX	60451	3501	18W-24S	B6
600	DSPN	60016	2862	14W-11N	C4
1300	ELGN	60123	2854	35W-12N	B2
3300	SKOK	60203	2866	4W-11N	D2
S Manor Ct					
10	JLET	60435	3498	25W-24S	C5
10	JLET	60436	3498	25W-24S	C5
W Manor Ct					
800	GNWD	60425	3428	0W-22S	B7
800	JLET	60436	3498	25W-24S	C5
Manor Dr					
10	DRFD	60015	2704	10W-21N	B6
10	MTSN	60443	3505	6W-24S	E5
10	NLNX	60451	3501	18W-24S	A6
200	BFGV	60089	2754	17W-20N	C1
1000	SMWD	60107	2857	28W-9N	A7
1200	WLMT	60091	2811	6W-14N	D4
2800	NHBK	60062	2809	11W-16N	D1
6300	BRRG	60527	3146	14W-7S	C5
16700	SHLD	60473	3429	2E-19S	C3
N Manor Dr					
3200	LNSG	60438	3510	4E-22S	B1
S Manor Dr					
400	PTON	60468	3860	9W-37S	D4
3200	LNSG	60438	3510	4E-22S	B1
W Manor Dr					
12500	HMGN	60491	3344	15W-17S	B6
24600	SRWD	60404	3496	30W-25S	B7
Manor Ln					
100	BMDL	60108	2969	22W-5N	B2
700	BmdT	60143	2913	21W-6N	D6
1500	NLES	60068	2863	11W-10N	D5
1500	NLES	60714	2863	11W-10N	D5
1500	PKRG	60068	2863	11W-10N	D5
1500	PKRG	60714	2863	11W-10N	D5
1700	MDLN	60060	2590	20W-28N	A6
2200	MchT	60051	2528	31W-33N	D3
15200	HMGN	60491	3343	18W-18S	B7
E Manor Ln					
400	VLPK	60181	3027	17W-1N	B2
400	YkTp	60181	3027	17W-1N	B2
N Manor Ln					
5600	CHCG	60631	2918	10W-7N	B5
5600	LydT	60631	2918	10W-7N	B5
5600	MaiT	60631	2918	10W-7N	B5
S Manor Ln					
23100	CNHN	60410	3584	29W-28S	E7
Manor Pl					
200	AURA	60506	3138	35W-6S	A4
400	AURA	60506	3137	36W-6S	E5
Manor Rd					
10	LKZH	60047	2698	24W-23N	C1
700	AlqT	60014	2640	33W-24N	E6
700	CLLK	60014	2640	33W-24N	E6
Manor St					
-	AlqT	60102	2695	31W-22N	C4
Manor Hill Ct					
300	LMBD	60148	3084	20W-1S	B1
Manor Hill Ln					
400	LMBD	60148	3084	20W-1S	B1
Manor Hill Pl					
700	SgrT	60506	3135	41W-5S	E3
700	SgrT	60506	3136	41W-5S	A3
700	SgrT	60554	3135	41W-5S	E3
700	SgrT	60554	3136	41W-5S	A3
N Manor Hill Rd					
30800	FmtT	60030	2588	24W-30N	D1
Manor Ln Dr					
100	FXLK	60020	2472	28W-36N	E4
Manor Oaks Dr					
1600	JLET	60586	3496	30W-21S	B1
W Mansard Ln					
1700	EGvT	60056	2861	17W-10N	C5
1700	MPPT	60056	2861	17W-10N	C5
Mansfield Av					
-	CHRG	60415	3275	7W-12S	C2
7500	BRBK	60459	3211	7W-8S	C1
8500	OKLN	60459	3211	7W-9S	C4
9300	MNGV	60053	2865	7W-11N	C2
9500	OKLN	60453	3211	7W-11S	C6
10300	OKLN	60453	3275	7W-12S	C1
11000	ALSP	60482	3275	7W-12S	C3
11000	CHRG	60482	3275	7W-12S	C3
Mansfield Ct					
300	BRLT	60103	2911	28W-7N	B5
700	OSWG	60543	3263	36W-12S	E4
800	SMBG	60194	2858	25W-11N	A3
1600	ROSL	60172	2912	25W-7N	B4
2800	WCHI	60185	2965	32W-4N	C4
Mansfield Dr					
1200	AURA	60502	3139	33W-5S	B4
1500	AURA	60505	3139	33W-5S	B3
9000	TYPK	60487	3424	11W-21S	A7
18000	TYPK	60487	3423	11W-21S	E7
Mansfield Ln					
19200	MKNA	60448	3503	12W-23S	C3
Mansfield St					
100	PGGV	60140	2798	41W-14N	B6
1200	WDRG	60517	3206	20W-9S	B3
S Mansfield St					
12300	ALSP	60803	3275	7W-14S	C7
Mansfield Wy					
200	ROSL	60172	2912	25W-7N	B4
600	OSWG	60543	3263	36W-12S	E4
W Manshire Pl					
100	MPPT	60056	2807	16W-14N	D4
Mansie Ct					
1700	WKGN	60048	2535	15W-32N	A6
1700	WrnT	60048	2535	15W-32N	A6
Mansion Heights Dr					
9200	AdnT	60033	2350	43W-41N	A7
14300	AdnT	60033	2349	43W-41N	E7
Manteca Ct					
700	UYPK	60466	3684	3W-29S	A2
Mantle Ln					
100	CLSM	60188	3024	24W-1N	D2
N Manton Av					
5700	CHCG	60646	2919	7W-7N	C4
Mantua Ct					
10	PKFT	60466	3595	4W-27S	A4
Mantua St					
200	PKFT	60466	3594	4W-27S	E4
200	PKFT	60466	3595	4W-27S	A4
Manu Ct					
2700	GNVW	60025	2809	11W-15N	E2
Manuel Ct					
-	AxST	60447	3672	32W-29S	C1
-	MNKA	60447	3672	32W-29S	C1
Manydown Ct					
4900	NPVL	60564	3266	28W-12S	E4
Manzella Ln					
1200	GNVW	60025	2810	10W-13N	A6
Maple					
-	ELGN	60120	2855	32W-10N	C7
Maple Av					
-	CHCG	60613	2977	1W-5N	D1
-	DndT	60118	2801	33W-15N	C4
-	EDND	60118	2801	33W-15N	C4
-	JNBG	60051	2472	30W-35N	A6
10	CPVL	60110	2800	34W-17N	E1
10	HIWD	60040	2704	9W-23N	D3
10	LKZH	60047	2698	23W-22N	D4
10	SchT	60174	2908	35W-6N	B6
100	AddT	60106	2971	17W-4N	B3
100	ADSN	60101	2971	17W-4N	B4
100	ADSN	60106	2971	17W-4N	B3
100	CPVL	60110	2747	34W-17N	E7
100	EVTN	60201	2813	2W-13N	B6
100	HDPK	60035	2704	8W-22N	E3
100	NARA	60542	3077	36W-3S	E7
100	WDSK	60098	2524	41W-32N	D5
100	WLMT	60091	2813	3W-13N	A6
200	DRGV	60515	3144	20W-6S	A4
200	SCHT	60411	3595	1W-27S	E4
200	SCHT	60411	3596	1W-27S	A4
200	WTMT	60515	3144	19W-5S	D2
200	WTMT	60559	3144	19W-5S	D2
300	SchT	60174	2964	35W-6N	B1
400	AddT	60191	2915	17W-6N	B6
400	AURA	60505	3200	35W-8S	B2
400	CPVL	60110	2748	33W-17N	B7
500	AvnT	60073	2532	22W-34N	B1
500	LKBF	60044	2594	10W-28N	A6
500	LSLE	60532	3142	24W-6S	D4
500	LSLE	60532	3143	23W-5S	A4
500	LSLE	60540	3142	24W-6S	C4
500	LslT	60532	3142	22W-5S	C4
500	LslT	60540	3142	24W-6S	C4
500	NPVL	60532	3142	24W-6S	C4
500	NPVL	60540	3142	24W-6S	C4
500	RLKB	60073	2532	22W-34N	B1
500	RLKP	60073	2532	22W-34N	B1
500	WLSP	60480	3209	12W-9S	C4
600	BmdT	60157	2913	21W-7N	D5
600	DLTN	60419	3350	0W-17S	B4
600	DLTN	60827	3350	0W-17S	B4
600	PlsT	60480	3209	12W-9S	C4
600	RVDL	60827	3350	0W-17S	B4
800	HMWD	60430	3428	1W-21S	A6
900	EVTN	60202	2867	2W-10N	B4
1200	BRWN	60304	3030	8W-1S	E7
1200	BRWN	60402	3030	8W-1S	E7
1200	EVTN	60201	2867	2W-10N	B4
1200	OKPK	60304	3030	8W-1S	E7
1200	WLMT	60091	2812	4W-13N	D6
1400	BRWN	60402	3088	8W-1S	E1
1400	DRGV	60516	3144	20W-6S	A4
1400	NHBK	60062	2757	9W-17N	C6
1500	LslT	60532	3142	24W-6S	D4
1600	HRPK	60133	2911	27W-8N	C3
1700	DGvT	60515	3144	20W-6S	A4
1700	DGvT	60516	3144	20W-6S	A4
1900	LslT	60515	3144	20W-6S	A4
1900	LslT	60516	3144	20W-6S	A4
2100	LslT	60515	3143	21W-6S	E4
2600	DRGV	60516	3143	21W-6S	D4
2600	NHBK	60062	2756	10W-17N	E6
2800	DRGV	60515	3143	22W-6S	D4
2800	LslT	60515	3143	22W-6S	D4
3100	BKFD	60513	3087	11W-3S	D5
3100	BKFD	60525	3087	11W-3S	D5
Maple Av					
3100	LGPK	60525	3087	11W-3S	D5
3600	MHRY	60050	2528	32W-33N	A3
3600	NfdT	60062	2756	12W-17N	B6
4000	RNPK	60471	3594	5W-26S	C3
4100	LYNS	60534	3088	9W-4S	D7
4100	SKNY	60402	3088	8W-4S	E7
4400	FTVW	60402	3088	8W-4S	E7
4500	BKFD	60513	3147	11W-4S	D1
4500	FTVW	60402	3148	8W-4S	E1
6300	BtnT	60081	2414	29W-38N	D7
8900	LynT	60480	3208	14W-10S	D5
8900	WLSP	60480	3208	14W-10S	D5
9900	OKLN	60453	3211	6W-11S	D7
10100	OKLN	60453	3275	6W-11S	D1
11300	HbnT	60034	2351	40W-42N	A7
11400	HBRN	60034	2351	40W-42N	A7
11900	BLID	60406	3277	3W-15S	B7
11900	BLID	60655	3277	3W-14S	B6
11900	CHCG	60655	3277	3W-14S	B6
12000	HBRN	60034	2350	41W-41N	E7
13000	BLID	60406	3343	3W-15S	B1
13100	LMNT	60439	3343	18W-15S	B2
13300	HMGN	60439	3343	18W-15S	B2
13300	HMGN	60491	3343	18W-15S	B2
13800	ODPK	60462	3346	10W-16S	B3
17500	CCHL	60478	3426	5W-21S	C5
18500	CCHL	60478	3506	5W-22S	C1
20800	FmtT	60060	2589	20W-28N	E5
20800	MDLN	60060	2589	20W-28N	E5
27000	FmtT	60060	2645	20W-27N	E2
Maple Av CO-17					
500	LSLE	60532	3142	24W-6S	D4
500	LSLE	60532	3143	23W-5S	A4
500	LSLE	60540	3142	24W-6S	C4
500	LslT	60532	3142	22W-5S	C4
500	LslT	60540	3142	24W-6S	C4
500	NPVL	60532	3142	24W-6S	C4
500	NPVL	60540	3142	24W-6S	C4
1400	DRGV	60515	3144	20W-6S	A4
1400	DRGV	60516	3144	20W-6S	A4
1500	LslT	60532	3142	24W-6S	D4
1700	DGvT	60515	3144	20W-6S	A4
1700	DGvT	60516	3144	20W-6S	A4
1900	LslT	60515	3144	20W-6S	A4
1900	LslT	60516	3144	20W-6S	A4
2100	LslT	60516	3143	21W-6S	E4
2600	DRGV	60516	3143	21W-6S	D4
2800	DRGV	60515	3143	22W-6S	D4
2800	LslT	60515	3143	22W-6S	D4
Maple Av SR-173					
11300	HbnT	60034	2351	40W-42N	A7
11400	HBRN	60034	2351	40W-42N	A7
12000	HBRN	60034	2350	41W-41N	E7
E Maple Av					
10	MDLN	60060	2590	18W-28N	E6
10	ROSL	60172	2913	23W-7N	B5
100	LYVL	60048	2591	16W-29N	D5
600	BKFD	60513	3087	12W-4S	D7
600	BKFD	60525	3087	12W-4S	C7
600	LGNG	60525	3087	12W-4S	C7
900	MDLN	60060	2591	18W-28N	A6
E Maple Av SR-176					
10	MDLN	60060	2590	18W-28N	E6
900	MDLN	60060	2591	18W-28N	A6
1000	LYVL	60048	2591	18W-28N	A6
N Maple Av					
-	NRIV	60546	3087	11W-2S	D2
10	FXLK	60020	2473	27W-36N	B4
100	BMDL	60108	2913	23W-6N	A7
100	BMDL	60108	2969	23W-5N	A1
100	EMHT	60126	3027	16W-1N	E1
100	FmtT	60060	2646	19W-26N	D3
100	PTHT	60070	2808	15W-15N	A3
100	WDDL	60191	2971	17W-5N	B1
200	WDDL	60191	2915	17W-5N	B7
300	OKPK	60302	3030	8W-0N	D3
400	AddT	60191	2915	17W-6N	B7
400	EMHT	60126	2971	16W-2N	E7
600	PLTN	60067	2752	22W-17N	C6
700	ITSC	60143	2914	19W-7N	C5
1100	BKFD	60513	3087	11W-2S	D3
1100	BKFD	60525	3087	11W-2S	D4
1100	LGPK	60525	3087	11W-2S	D3
1200	LGPK	60513	3087	11W-2S	D3
1500	PvsT	60513	3087	11W-2S	D3
1500	PvsT	60525	3087	11W-2S	D3
36300	GrtT	60041	2473	26W-36N	E4
38800	LkvT	60046	2417	21W-38N	D6
S Maple Av					
10	FXLK	60020	2473	27W-36N	B4
10	WKGN	60085	2536	11W-34N	E2
100	BMDL	60108	2968	23W-5N	E1
100	HLSD	60162	3028	13W-0S	E7
100	OKPK	60302	3030	8W-0S	D5
100	WCDA	60084	2643	26W-27N	E1
900	OKPK	60304	3030	8W-0S	D6
1100	BRWN	60304	3030	8W-0S	D7
1100	BRWN	60402	3030	8W-0S	D7
W Maple Av					
10	LGNG	60525	3087	12W-4S	B7
10	ROSL	60172	2913	23W-7N	A5
100	BmdT	60172	2912	23W-7N	E5
100	LYVL	60048	2591	16W-29N	D5
100	ROSL	60172	2912	23W-7N	E5
100	WCDA	60084	2643	26W-27N	E1
800	LGNG	60525	3147	13W-4S	A1
1100	FmtT	60060	2590	20W-28N	A6
1100	MDLN	60060	2590	20W-28N	A6
1400	WNSP	60525	3147	13W-4S	A1
1400	WNSP	60558	3147	13W-4S	A1
1900	FmtT	60060	2589	20W-28N	E6
1900	MDLN	60060	2589	20W-28N	E6
5700	BKLY	60162	3028	14W-0N	C4
5700	BKLY	60163	3028	14W-0N	C4
5700	HLSD	60162	3028	14W-0N	C4
8100	NRDG	60706	2918	10W-5N	B7
8200	NRDG	60706	2974	10W-5N	A1
8300	CHCG	60656	2974	10W-5N	A1
8300	CHCG	60706	2974	10W-5N	A1
18600	WrnT	60030	2533	18W-32N	E5
26000	AntT	60002	2356	26W-42N	E6
26000	GrtT	60041	2473	26W-35N	E5
26800	WcnT	60084	2642	28W-26N	E2
27900	WcnT	60084	2643	28W-26N	A2
28200	WcnT	60010	2643	28W-26N	A4
28300	WcnT	60010	2642	28W-26N	E4
W Maple Av SR-176					
1100	FmtT	60060	2590	20W-28N	A6
1100	MDLN	60060	2590	20W-28N	A6
1900	FmtT	60060	2589	20W-28N	E6
1900	MDLN	60060	2589	20W-28N	E6
Maple Av E					
-	ELGN	60120	2855	32W-10N	D7
Maple Cir					
1300	WDND	60118	2747	36W-17N	B7
Maple Cir					
2600	WDND	60118	2800	36W-16N	A1
Maple Ct					
10	CTCY	60409	3351	2E-16S	C4
10	GNVA	60134	3020	36W-1N	A3
10	SchT	60175	2963	37W-5N	C3
100	BMDL	60108	2968	23W-5N	E1
100	VrnT	60015	2702	15W-20N	B7
200	LKFT	60045	2650	9W-26N	B4
200	WNVL	60555	3080	29W-2S	B4
400	WCHI	60185	2966	30W-3N	B6
400	WynT	60185	2966	30W-3N	B6
500	BmdT	60157	2913	22W-5N	D7
600	EGVV	60007	2915	18W-8N	A1
600	ELBN	60119	3017	43W-2N	A2
600	FKFT	60423	3592	10W-26S	C2
600	MPPT	60056	2808	15W-13N	A5
800	UYPK	60466	3684	3W-30S	A2
900	BRLT	60103	2910	29W-6N	D6
900	DRFD	60015	2703	11W-21N	C6
1000	LKPT	60441	3419	21W-19S	E3
1500	MHRY	60050	2528	32W-33N	B3
4400	RGMW	60008	2806	19W-12N	C7
5500	LSLE	60532	3143	22W-6S	B4
5500	LslT	60532	3143	22W-6S	B4
6700	BGVW	60455	3148	9W-7S	C6
9100	SJHN	46373	3687		E1
9200	MNGV	60053	2864	9W-11N	C2
15400	OKFT	60452	3347	8W-18S	B7
15500	HMGN	60491	3344	16W-18S	A7
15500	HMGN	60491	3422	16W-18S	A1
16500	SHLD	60473	3428	0E-19S	E2
E Maple Ct					
200	ADSN	60101	2971	18W-3N	A5
400	GNWD	60425	3508	0E-22S	E1
N Maple Ct					
10	ADSN	60101	2971	18W-3N	A5
S Maple Ct					
100	PLTN	60067	2805	21W-15N	D1
W Maple Ct					
10	PNFD	60544	3338	29W-17S	D6
22000	KLDR	60047	2699	22W-21N	B6
Maple Dr					
-	ELWD	60421	3675	25W-31S	C5
400	WLNG	60090	2755	13W-17N	D5
500	BFGV	60089	2754	17W-18N	B2
500	SMWD	60107	2911	28W-9N	B2
7200	JSTC	60458	3148	10W-7S	B7
7400	MchT	60097	2469	36W-36N	D4
8800	ODPK	60462	3346	11W-17S	A5
9100	SJHN	46373	3687		E1
9500	RSMT	60018	2917	11W-7N	C3
15300	OKFT	60452	3347	8W-18S	A7
17500	LNSG	60438	3430	4E-20S	C5
E Maple Dr					
10	GNWD	60425	3508	0E-22S	E1
500	BlmT	60476	3509	0E-22S	A1
500	GNWD	60425	3509	0E-22S	A1
N Maple Dr					
800	CHHT	60411	3507	1W-24S	E6
800	CHHT	60411	3508	1W-24S	A6
43300	AntT	60002	2357	25W-43N	A4
W Maple Dr					
100	CHHT	60411	3507	1W-24S	E6
Maple Ln					
-	BmnT	60426	3426	5W-19S	B2
10	KdlT	60560	3333	43W-17S	A7
10	NPVL	60540	3141	26W-7S	D7
10	NLNX	60451	3501	18W-23S	B4
100	SchT	60174	2964	35W-5N	B2
200	GNVA	60134	3020	36W-1N	A3
200	HLSD	60162	3028	13W-0S	E5
200	MNSR	46321	3430		D7
200	ThtT	60476	3428	0E-21S	E6
200	TNTN	60476	3428	0E-21S	E6
300	BTVA	60510	3078	35W-0S	A1
300	EGVV	60007	2915	18W-8N	A2
300	RDLK	60073	2531	23W-33N	E2
300	SRWD	60404	3496	30W-23S	C4
400	DRN	60561	3145	17W-7S	C7
500	MltT	60137	3083	22W-1S	C2
600	SCRL	60134	3020	36W-1N	A3
600	SCRL	60174	3020	36W-1N	A3
700	BNVL	60106	2915	16W-6N	D7
700	HFET	60169	2858	24W-11N	D4
700	LynT	60458	3209	11W-8S	E1
800	PTHT	60070	2755	15W-16N	A6
800	WLNG	60090	2755	15W-16N	A6
900	BRLT	60103	2910	29W-6N	D6
1100	BTVA	60510	3077	36W-0S	E1
1100	PTHT	60090	2755	15W-16N	A6
1100	WNSP	60558	3146	14W-6S	D4
1200	GNVW	60025	2811	7W-14N	A4
1400	ELGN	60123	2854	36W-11N	A4
1600	WHTN	60187	3025	23W-0N	A4
1800	SYHW	60118	2800	34W-15N	D3
1900	RVWD	60015	2702	13W-22N	D4
2300	HDPK	60035	2704	8W-22N	E3
2300	RGMW	60008	2806	19W-12N	C7
3200	HLCT	60429	3426	4W-20S	E4
3200	HLCT	60429	3427	4W-20S	A4
4200	ZION	60099	2421	12W-41N	B1
5500	BmnT	60445	3347	6W-17S	D4
5500	MDLN	60445	3347	6W-17S	D4
6700	DRN	60559	3145	18W-7S	A7
6700	WTMT	60559	3145	18W-7S	A7
9200	MaiT	60016	2863	11W-11N	D3
15300	MKHM	60426	3348	4W-18S	E7
15300	MKHM	60428	3348	4W-18S	E7
22300	AntT	60002	2417	22W-40N	B2
N Maple Ln					
1900	ANHT	60004	2807	16W-16N	C1
S Maple Ln					
10	PTHT	60070	2808	15W-14N	A3
200	MPPT	60056	2808	15W-14N	A4
200	PTHT	60056	2808	15W-14N	A4
8900	HYHL	60457	3210	10W-10S	A5
W Maple Ln					
10	PSHT	60463	3275	8W-14S	B7
800	PTON	60468	3860	10W-37S	D4
1600	CteT	60417	3595	2W-28S	E6
1600	STGR	60417	3595	2W-28S	E6
1700	CteT	60475	3595	2W-28S	E6
8900	HYHL	60457	3209	11W-10S	E5
8900	HYHL	60457	3210	11W-10S	A5
17200	WrnT	60031	2534	17W-34N	C1
Maple Pl					
1700	SMBG	60173	2859	21W-12N	E1
S Maple Pl					
100	HPSR	60140	2795	46W-16N	E2
Maple Rd					
100	BRTN	60010	2698	25W-20N	A7
100	BRTN	60010	2751	25W-20N	A1
200	NLNX	60451	3500	19W-22S	E1
200	NLNX	60451	3501	18W-22S	A1
200	NlxT	60448	3501	18W-22S	A1
Maple Rd					
200	NlxT	60451	3501	18W-22S	A1
400	JLET	60432	3499	22W-23S	C3
400	JltT	60432	3499	22W-23S	C3
800	FSMR	60422	3506	4W-22S	D2
1300	JLET	60441	3500	19W-22S	D1
1300	JLET	60451	3500	19W-22S	D1
1300	NLNX	60441	3500	19W-22S	D1
1300	NlxT	60441	3500	19W-22S	D1
1300	NlxT	60451	3500	19W-22S	D1
2000	HMWD	60430	3427	2W-21S	C6
2000	JLET	60432	3500	20W-22S	B1
2000	JltT	60432	3500	20W-22S	B1
11200	FftT	60448	3502	14W-22S	E1
11200	MKNA	60448	3502	14W-22S	E1
11900	NlxT	60448	3502	15W-22S	B1
15800	NlxT	60432	3500	20W-22S	B1
Maple Rd US-6					
200	NLNX	60451	3500	19W-22S	E1
200	NLNX	60451	3501	18W-22S	A1
200	NlxT	60448	3501	18W-22S	A1
200	NlxT	60451	3501	18W-22S	A1
400	JLET	60432	3499	22W-23S	C3
400	JltT	60432	3499	22W-23S	C3
1300	JLET	60441	3500	19W-22S	D1
1300	JLET	60451	3500	19W-22S	D1
1300	NLNX	60441	3500	19W-22S	D1
1300	NlxT	60441	3500	19W-22S	D1
1300	NlxT	60451	3500	19W-22S	D1
2000	JLET	60432	3500	20W-22S	B1
2000	JltT	60432	3500	20W-22S	B1
15800	NlxT	60432	3500	20W-22S	B1
Maple Row					
200	NHFD	60093	2758	7W-16N	A7
Maple St					
-	BDWD	60408	3941	32W-41S	D6
-	RedT	60408	3941	32W-41S	D6
10	CLLK	60014	2640	35W-25N	A4
10	CNHL	60514	3145	16W-4S	E1
10	CTSD	60525	3147	12W-6S	C4
10	KdlT	60560	3333	44W-16S	A4
10	OSWG	60543	3263	37W-13S	B4
10	SRGV	60554	3135	42W-7S	C7
10	YKVL	60560	3333	44W-16S	A4
100	FRGV	60021	2695	30W-22N	E3
100	MYWD	60153	3030	10W-0N	A4
100	NndT	60051	2642	29W-27N	D1
100	RVFT	60305	3030	10W-0N	A4
200	BCHR	60401	3864	0W-36S	D1
200	GNEN	60137	3025	23W-0N	A4
300	MRGO	60152	2634	49W-26N	C3
400	WNKA	60093	2812	4W-15N	B1
700	MYWD	60153	3029	11W-0N	E4
800	WNSP	60558	3086	14W-4S	D7
900	WslT	60481	3943	27W-40S	E2
1000	AURA	60506	3137	37W-5S	D2
1000	LIHL	60156	2694	35W-22N	B4
1300	RLKB	60073	2474	23W-35N	D7
1400	DSPN	60018	2863	12W-9N	B7
1400	GNVW	60025	2809	12W-14N	B5
1600	GNVW	60062	2809	12W-14N	B5
1700	NHFD	60093	2811	7W-15N	C2
2200	DSPN	60018	2917	12W-8N	B1
2400	FNPK	60171	2973	11W-3N	D6
2400	RVGV	60171	2973	11W-3N	D6
3000	FNPK	60171	2973	11W-3N	D4
6300	RlyT	60152	2634	49W-24N	C7
6500	MNGV	60053	2865	8W-11N	A2
6600	MNGV	60053	2864	8W-11N	E2
7800	NLES	60053	2864	9W-11N	B2
7800	NLES	60714	2864	9W-11N	B2
15400	DLTN	60419	3350	0E-18S	E7
15400	SHLD	60473	3350	0E-18S	E7
16600	SHLD	60473	3428	0E-19S	E2
17500	LNSG	60438	3430	4E-21S	C5
19200	LNSG	60438	3510	4E-22S	C2
21100	MTSN	60443	3506	4W-25S	D7
21100	OMFD	60461	3506	4W-25S	D7
21200	MTSN	60443	3594	4W-25S	D1
Maple St CO-T58					
300	MRGO	60152	2634	49W-26N	C3
6300	RlyT	60152	2634	49W-25N	C4
E Maple St					
10	HNDL	60521	3146	15W-4S	B1
10	LMBD	60148	3026	18W-0N	E4
100	VLPK	60181	3027	17W-1N	B2
200	EMHT	60126	3027	17W-1N	B2
200	VLPK	60126	3027	17W-1N	B2
1100	LMBD	60181	3026	18W-0N	E4
1100	VLPK	60181	3026	18W-0N	E4
1200	ANHT	60005	2807	17W-13N	C6
2000	CteT	60417	3686	2E-30S	D2
N Maple St					
10	MPPT	60056	2808	15W-13N	A7
10	PLTN	60067	2805	21W-16N	D1
100	BDWD	60408	3941	32W-41S	D5
100	PLTN	60067	2752	21W-16N	D7
200	ADSN	60101	2971	17W-3N	B4
200	FKFT	60423	3503	12W-25S	D7
200	FKFT	60423	3591	12W-25S	D1
200	ITSC	60143	2914	19W-6N	C6
200	JLET	60432	3499	22W-23S	C4
800	PTHT	60070	2808	15W-16N	A1
2400	RVGV	60171	2974	10W-3N	A5
S Maple St					
10	FKFT	60423	3591	12W-26S	D2
10	MPPT	60056	2808	15W-12N	A7
100	BDWD	60408	3941	32W-41S	D6
100	ITSC	60143	2914	19W-6N	C7
100	PLTN	60067	2805	21W-15N	D1
200	MPPT	60056	2862	15W-12N	A1
900	DSPN	60016	2862	15W-11N	A3
900	ELGN	60123	2854	36W-10N	A5
900	ElgT	60123	2854	36W-10N	A5
900	MPPT	60016	2862	15W-11N	A3
27400	CteT	60401	3774	1W-33S	A2
W Maple St					
10	ANHT	60005	2807	18W-13N	A6
10	CHCG	60610	3034	0W-1N	B2
10	CHCG	60611	3034	0W-1N	B2
10	HNDL	60521	3146	15W-4S	A1
10	LMBD	60148	3026	20W-0N	B4
10	MDLN	60060	2590	19W-28N	C6
500	HNDL	60521	3145	16W-4S	E1
600	ANHT	60005	2806	18W-13N	E6
1000	FmtT	60060	2590	19W-28N	C6
1400	NLNX	60433	3500	19W-24S	D5
1400	NLNX	60451	3500	19W-24S	D5
1400	NlxT	60432	3500	19W-24S	D5
1400	NlxT	60451	3500	19W-24S	D5
3200	ENGN	60805	3212	4W-11S	E6
26500	AntT	60002	2356	26W-42N	D6
W Maple St SR-176					
10	MDLN	60060	2590	19W-28N	C6
1000	FmtT	60060	2590	19W-28N	C6

STREET Block City ZIP Map# CGS Grid

W Maple St US-30
1400 NLNX 60433 3500 19W-24S D5
1400 NLNX 60451 3500 19W-24S D5
1400 NlxT 60432 3500 19W-24S D5
1400 NlxT 60451 3500 19W-24S D5
Maple Ter
- WslT 60481 3943 27W-41S D6
1600 LSLE 60532 3142 23W-6S E4
1600 LslT 60532 3142 23W-6S E4
1600 LslT 60532 3143 23W-6S A4
4300 CCHL 60478 3506 5W-22S C1
Maple Tr
600 BGBK 60490 3267 26W-13S E4
Maple Wy
- ELGN 60120 2855 32W-9N C7
Maplebrook Ct
200 SMBG 60194 2859 22W-10N C5
Maplebrook Dr
- RchT 60443 3593 7W-26S C2
6200 MTSN 60443 3593 7W-26S C2
Maple Creek Dr
- TYPK 60477 3424 9W-22S E7
- TYPK 60477 3504 9W-22S E1
Maplecreek Dr
14600 ODPK 60467 3344 14W-17S D5
14600 OrlT 60467 3344 14W-17S D5
Maplecrest Av
900 JltT 60432 3499 22W-22S D2
Maple Crest Ct
9700 PSHL 60465 3209 11W-11S E7
Maplefield Rd
900 NPVL 60564 3203 27W-8S B2
900 NPVL 60565 3203 27W-8S B2
900 NpvT 60564 3203 27W-8S B2
Maple Glen Ct
5400 JLET 60586 3416 30W-20S C6
Maple Glen Dr
1800 JLET 60586 3416 30W-21S B7
Maple Hill Dr
4900 MCLK 60050 2470 34W-34N D7
Maple Hill Rd
10 GLNC 60022 2758 6W-18N D3
Maple Hills Ct
1500 NPVL 60563 3141 27W-5S B2
Maplehurst Ln
300 RtdT 60140 2798 40W-15N B4
400 PGGV 60140 2798 40W-15N B4
Maple Knoll Dr
1500 NPVL 60563 3141 26W-5S E3
Maple Leaf Ct
1700 WHTN 60187 3024 26W-0S A7
Maple Leaf Dr
3000 GNVW 60025 2810 10W-15N A3
3600 GNVW 60025 2809 10W-15N E3
Mapleleaf Dr
4300 MchT 60050 2472 30W-36N B4
Maple Ln Dr
6500 TYPK 60477 3425 8W-20S B3
Maple Park Ln
1600 AURA 60504 3200 34W-9S E3
1600 AURA 60504 3201 33W-9S A3
Maple Ridge Ct
900 FKFT 60423 3503 13W-25S B7
1400 CLSM 60188 2967 28W-4N A4
1400 WynT 60185 2967 28W-4N A4
1400 WynT 60188 2967 28W-4N A4
Maple Ridge Dr
2200 JLET 60586 3415 31W-21S E6
Maple Ridge Ln
100 MTGY 60538 3199 36W-9S E4
Maples Ct
600 NfdT 60025 2809 11W-13N D7
Mapleside Ct
2700 AURA 60502 3139 32W-7S D7
Mapleside Ln
2600 AURA 60502 3139 32W-7S C7
Mapleton Av
800 OKPK 60302 3031 7W-1N B2
Maple Trail Ct
10 BGBK 60490 3267 26W-13S E5
Maple Tree Ct
10 EMHT 60126 3027 16W-0S E7
Maple Tree Dr
10600 GwdT 60098 2525 39W-34N C1
Maple Tree Ln
100 WYNE 60184 2966 30W-4N B3
Mapletree Ln
100 DndT 60110 2748 33W-18N A6
N Maple Tree Ln
3000 WKGN 60083 2478 14W-37N D1
3300 WDWH 60083 2478 14W-37N D1
Mapleview Dr
26100 PNFD 60585 3337 32W-15S B3
Maplewood Av
- MKHM 60428 3427 3W-19S B2
100 MDLN 60060 2646 18W-26N D3
1400 HRPK 60133 2911 26W-8N E3
7000 HMND 46324 3430 E4
11100 HTLY 60142 2691 41W-20N C7
14700 HRVY 60426 3349 3W-17S B6
N Maplewood Av
800 CHCG 60612 3033 3W-1N A2
800 CHCG 60622 3033 3W-1N A2
1500 CHCG 60647 3033 3W-1N A1
2400 CHCG 60647 2977 3W-3N A5
4000 CHCG 60618 2977 3W-5N A1
4400 CHCG 60618 2921 3W-5N A7
4700 CHCG 60625 2921 3W-5N A7
5500 CHCG 60659 2921 3W-7N A4
6300 CHCG 60645 2921 3W-7N A3
7500 CHCG 60202 2867 3W-9N A6
7500 CHCG 60645 2867 3W-9N A6
7500 EVTN 60202 2867 3W-9N A6
S Maplewood Av
100 CHCG 60612 3033 3W-0S A5
200 NHLK 60164 3028 13W-1N E2
3500 CHCG 60608 3091 3W-3S A5
3500 CHCG 60632 3091 3W-3S A5
4900 CHCG 60632 3151 3W-5S A2
5500 CHCG 60629 3151 3W-7S B5
7600 CHCG 60652 3213 3W-8S A1
9600 ENGN 60805 3213 3W-11S B7
9800 CHCG 60805 3213 3W-11S B7
10000 CHCG 60655 3213 3W-11S B7
10200 CHCG 60655 3277 3W-12S B2
11800 BLID 60406 3277 3W-13S B5
11800 BLID 60655 3277 3W-13S B5
Maplewood Cir
2000 NPVL 60563 3140 30W-5S B3
Maplewood Ct
100 WNVL 60555 3080 30W-2S C4
700 WLBK 60527 3207 16W-8S E1
1700 GYLK 60030 2475 21W-34N C7
1700 RLKB 60030 2475 21W-34N C7
1800 LNHT 60046 2418 20W-38N A7
9200 ODHL 60487 3423 11W-19S E2
14000 GNOK 60048 2592 14W-30N D1
16400 TYPK 60477 3425 8W-19S A3
Maplewood Dr
- MRGO 60152 2634 49W-25N C4
10 VNHL 60061 2647 17W-25N B6
10 WNVL 60555 3080 30W-2S C4
100 ANTH 60002 2358 23W-43N A5
100 BGBK 60440 3268 23W-12S E2
100 INCK 60061 2647 17W-25N B6
200 NARA 60542 3077 36W-4S D7
300 LKMR 60051 2529 29W-32N D5
500 ANTH 60002 2357 23W-43N E5
600 MNKA 60447 3672 34W-29S A3
600 WHTN 60187 3082 25W-2S A3
800 ITSC 60143 2914 20W-6N A6
1800 LNHT 60046 2418 20W-38N A7
2000 GRNE 60031 2478 15W-36N A4
7200 JSTC 60458 3148 10W-7S B7
7200 JSTC 60458 3210 10W-8S A1
11300 PNFD 60585 3266 30W-13S B5
E Maplewood Dr
7600 MchT 60097 2526 36W-34N D1
8000 GwdT 60097 2526 37W-34N C1
S Maplewood Dr
2100 BLVY 60097 2526 37W-34N C1
2100 GwdT 60097 2526 37W-34N C1
2200 BLVY 60098 2526 37W-34N C1
2200 GwdT 60098 2526 37W-34N C1
Maplewood Ln
- AURA 60506 3136 39W-7S E7
- RchT 60443 3506 5W-25S B7
200 SMBG 60193 2859 22W-9N D7
300 CLLK 60014 2639 35W-26N E3
1100 ALGN 60102 2695 33W-20N A7
1700 GNVW 60025 2810 8W-13N E5
2100 JltT 60433 3587 21W-26S E3
S Maplewood Ln
200 BRLT 60103 2910 30W-8N C3
W Maplewood Ln
1000 BRLT 60103 2910 30W-8N C3
Maplewood Pl
5300 DRGV 60515 3144 19W-5S C3
Maplewood Rd
10 LKFT 60045 2650 9W-26N B3
100 RVSD 60546 3088 10W-3S B4
1900 NfdT 60062 2757 10W-18N B2
10800 CTSD 60525 3146 13W-7S E6
10800 CTSD 60525 3147 13W-7S A7
W Maplewood Rd
12700 BHPK 60099 2421 12W-39N B4
Maplewood St
9000 SJHN 46373 3598 E7
9000 SJHN 46373 3687 E1
Mappold Wy
1800 JLET 60435 3498 26W-22S A1
Mar Dr
1600 MchT 60051 2529 30W-33N B2
Mara Lynn Ct
500 RDLK 60073 2531 23W-31N E7
Maramel Dr
16200 HMGN 60491 3421 16W-19S E2
Marathon Ct
20500 OMFD 60461 3506 4W-24S E6
Marathon Dr
- NPVL 60585 3266 30W-13S C5
11300 PNFD 60585 3266 30W-13S C5
S Marathon Ln
11400 PNFD 60585 3266 30W-13S C5
Maray Av
100 NLNX 60451 3501 17W-25S D7
100 NlxT 60451 3501 17W-25S D7
Marberry Dr
- MPPT 60056 2808 15W-14N A3
- MPPT 60070 2808 15W-14N A3
10 PTHT 60070 2808 15W-14N A3
Marberry Ln
10 PTHT 60070 2808 15W-14N A3
Marbil Farms Rd
- MTGY 60538 3198 41W-9S A4
- SgrT 60538 3198 41W-9S A4
Marbilynn Dr
900 ELGN 60120 2855 32W-12N C1
E Marble Av
10 CTCY 46327 3352 D4
10 HMND 46327 3352 D4
Marble Ct
1000 LIHL 60156 2693 37W-22N C4
4000 AURA 60504 3202 30W-8S B2
Marble Ln
- CPVL 60110 2748 33W-19N B3
W Marble Pl
10 CHCG 60603 3034 0W-0S B5
100 CHCG 60606 3034 0W-0S B5
600 CHCG 60661 3034 0W-0S A5
Marble Rd
24200 CNHN 60410 3672 31W-29S E2
24200 CnhT 60410 3672 31W-29S E2
W Marble St
100 JLET 60435 3498 24W-23S E3
Marblehead Ct
100 LslT 60540 3142 25W-6S C4
Marblehead Rd
7400 MchT 60097 2469 36W-36N D3
7400 WRLK 60097 2469 36W-36N D3
Marble Hill Ct
10 SMBG 60193 2859 23W-10N B5
Marble Hill Dr
1200 LKZH 60047 2699 22W-22N C4
Marbridge Ct
10 NBRN 60010 2644 25W-26N B6
Marbury Ct
200 SEGN 60177 2908 35W-8N B3
Marbury Ln
10 BNHL 60010 2750 25W-17N E4
Marc Ct
10500 BHPK 60087 2480 10W-38N A1
Marcee Ln
1700 NHBK 60062 2757 9W-17N C5
Marcell St
- BCVL 60407 4030 34W-44S A4
Marcella Av
1600 JltT 60436 3586 24W-26S E2
Marcella Ln
200 WCHI 60185 3022 30W-2N B1
Marcella Rd
600 DSPN 60016 2808 14W-12N C7
600 MPPT 60056 2808 14W-12N C7
N Marcella Rd
10 DSPN 60016 2808 14W-13N C7
10 MPPT 60056 2808 14W-13N C6
Marcey Av
1100 WHTN 60187 3082 25W-1S A1
N Marcey St
1600 CHCG 60614 2977 1W-2N E7
March St
800 LKZH 60047 2699 22W-24N B1
900 LKZH 60047 2645 22W-24N B7
Marci Ct
1800 GLHT 60139 2968 24W-3N D5
Marci Ln
9600 HBRN 60034 2350 41W-41N E7
Marcia Ct
10 SEGN 60177 2908 36W-9N A2
300 BRLT 60103 2911 28W-8N A3
Marcie Ct
700 DRFD 60015 2703 12W-20N C7
Marco Ct
1300 DRN 60561 3207 18W-9S A3
Marcus Ct
1000 LKZH 60047 2645 22W-24N B7
E Marcus Ct
1400 PKRG 60068 2863 11W-10N E4
W Marcus Ct
1400 PKRG 60068 2863 11W-10N D4
Marcus Dr
- ADSN 60101 2970 20W-4N B2
400 LMBD 60148 3026 19W-1N C2
N Marcus St
40500 AntT 60002 2415 26W-40N E3
Marcy Av
2300 EVTN 60201 2866 4W-12N C1
2700 EVTN 60201 2812 4W-13N C7
2700 WLMT 60091 2812 4W-13N C7
2700 WLMT 60201 2812 4W-13N C7
Marcy Ln
1300 WLNG 60090 2754 16W-17N D4
Mardan Dr
3400 LGGV 60047 2700 19W-21N B7
E Mardan Dr
3400 LGGV 60047 2700 19W-21N B6
W Mardan Dr
3400 LGGV 60047 2700 19W-21N B6
Marden Ct
2700 NHBK 60062 2756 10W-17N E5
Mardjetko Dr
5200 HFET 60192 2802 30W-12N C7
Mardon Rd
200 WynT 60185 2967 27W-2N C7
Mare Ln
10 CmpT 60119 3018 41W-2N A1
Mare Barn Ln
300 WYNE 60184 2965 33W-5N A1
500 WYNE 60184 2964 33W-5N E1
N Mare Barn Ln
1100 ADSN 60101 2970 19W-4N C2
Marengo Av
800 FTPK 60130 3030 9W-1S D7
1400 FTPK 60130 3088 9W-1S D1
1500 NRIV 60130 3088 9W-1S D1
Marengo Ct
1300 NPVL 60564 3203 28W-10S A5
Marengo Ln
3800 WRLK 60097 2469 37W-35N B5
Marengo Rd
300 DhmT 60033 2406 49W-38N D6
300 DhmT 60033 2464 50W-36N A3
300 HRVD 60033 2406 49W-38N D6
300 HRVD 60033 2464 50W-36N A3
13300 CrlT 60142 2691 42W-21N A5
13300 GfnT 60142 2691 42W-21N B6
14100 CrlT 60180 2691 42W-21N A5
Marengo Rd CO-A47
13300 CrlT 60142 2691 42W-21N A5
13300 GfnT 60142 2691 42W-21N B6
14100 CrlT 60180 2691 42W-21N A5
Marengo Rd CO-T55
4600 DhmT 60033 2464 50W-36N A3
5000 HRVD 60033 2464 50W-36N A3
S Marengo Rd
100 HRVD 60033 2406 50W-38N A7
Margail Av
9300 MaiT 60016 2863 11W-11N D2
Margaret Av
10600 HTLY 60142 2692 40W-21N B6
N Margaret Av
20500 BFGV 60069 2754 16W-20N E1
20500 BFGV 60089 2754 16W-20N E1
20500 VrnT 60069 2754 16W-20N E1
20500 VrnT 60089 2754 16W-20N E1
20600 BFGV 60089 2701 15W-21N E6
20600 VrnT 60069 2701 15W-21N E6
Margaret Ct
- LYWD 60411 3510 3E-23S A3
800 SCRL 60174 3020 36W-2N A1
1600 LKMR 60051 2528 30W-33N E2
1600 LKMR 60051 2529 30W-33N A2
1600 MchT 60051 2529 30W-33N A2
1900 AraT 60505 3138 34W-5S D2
1900 AURA 60505 3138 34W-5S D2
2200 MTGY 60538 3198 40W-10S C6
W Margaret Ct
23200 PnfT 60586 3416 29W-19S E3
Margaret Dr
2200 MTGY 60538 3198 40W-10S C6
Margaret Ln
1600 AraT 60504 3138 34W-5S D3
1600 AraT 60505 3138 34W-5S D3
1600 AURA 60505 3138 34W-5S D3
8700 TYPK 60487 3424 10W-20S A4
Margaret Pl
600 ELGN 60120 2855 33W-11N B5
Margaret St
- BtnT 60081 2414 30W-40N B3
600 DLTN 60419 3350 0E-16S E4
600 WDSK 60098 2524 42W-31N B7
800 DSPN 60016 2862 13W-10N E4
1200 DSPN 60018 2862 13W-10N E5
E Margaret St
100 TNTN 60476 3428 0E-21S E6
500 ThtT 60476 3428 0E-21S E6
N Margaret St
40300 AntT 60002 2415 26W-40N E3
S Margaret St
10 JLET 60435 3498 26W-24S A6
10 JLET 60436 3498 26W-24S A6
600 RKDL 60436 3498 26W-24S B7
W Margaret St
100 TNTN 60476 3428 0W-21S B6
300 TNTN 60430 3428 0W-21S B6
4800 MONE 60449 3683 6W-31S A6
4800 MonT 60449 3683 6W-31S A6
5500 MONE 60449 3682 7W-31S E6
E Margaret Ter
10 CRY 60013 2641 30W-24N E7
W Margaret Ter
10 CRY 60013 2641 31W-24N D7
Margaret Curtis Ln
5100 CTWD 60445 3347 6W-16S E3
5100 MDLN 60445 3347 6W-16S E3
5100 MDLN 60445 3348 6W-16S A3
Margaret Mitchell St
10 CmpT 60175 2962 40W-4N C4
Margarets Ln
10 AraT 60505 3138 34W-6S E6
10 AURA 60505 3138 34W-6S E6
Margarets Courtyard
6900 TYPK 60477 3425 8W-19S A2
Margaret's Parkview Ests
- AraT 60504 3200 34W-8S D3
- AraT 60505 3200 34W-8S D3
- AURA 60504 3200 34W-8S E3
- AURA 60505 3200 34W-8S D3
Margarette St
100 WMTN 60481 3853 28W-37S C5
100 WmTp 60481 3853 28W-37S C5
Margate Ct
10 LIHL 60156 2692 38W-23N E2
10 LKZH 60047 2699 22W-22N B4
10 SMBG 60193 2859 23W-10N B5
100 LKBF 60044 2593 11W-29N E4
1300 NPVL 60540 3142 25W-7S C7
Margate Dr
600 LNSH 60069 2701 16W-22N E5
600 VrnT 60069 2701 16W-22N E5
1400 BFGV 60089 2701 16W-21N D5
Margate Ln
700 PTHT 60070 2808 14W-14N C3
1100 GNOK 60048 2592 14W-28N B5
1100 LYVL 60048 2592 15W-28N B5
Margate Ter
300 DRFD 60015 2704 10W-21N A7
W Margate Ter
800 CHCG 60640 2921 1W-6N E6
23500 ANTH 60002 2416 23W-41N E1
23500 AntT 60002 2416 23W-41N E1
Margate on Oxford
10 RGMW 60008 2805 20W-14N E4
Marge Ln
1000 GwdT 60098 2525 40W-32N A4
1000 WDSK 60098 2525 40W-32N A4
Margerita Av
8300 ODPK 60462 3346 10W-16S B4
Margie Ln
100 CmpT 60175 2961 41W-6N E1
5400 OKFT 60452 3425 6W-19S D1
5500 BmnT 60477 3425 6W-19S D1
5500 OKFT 60477 3425 6W-19S D1
Margo Ln
3000 NHBK 60062 2809 11W-16N D1
9700 MNSR 46321 3510 C4
Margot Ln
10 PlsT 60464 3346 10W-15S C1
Margraf Ct
200 DYR 46311 3598 D3
N Marguerite Dr
38900 BHPK 60099 2422 9W-39N C6
W Marguerite Ln
9600 BHPK 60099 2422 9W-38N C6
Marguerite St
- NndT 60014 2585 30W-27N E7
300 ELGN 60123 2854 34W-10N C6
600 SCRL 60174 2963 36W-3N E6
1500 NndT 60014 2586 30W-27N A7
1500 PKRG 60068 2863 11W-10N E6
Margust Ln
14700 HMGN 60491 3343 18W-17S B6
Marhil Ct
300 CLLK 60014 2639 35W-25N E4
Maria Av
2800 NHBK 60062 2756 11W-18N E3
Maria Ct
10 LKZH 60047 2698 23W-21N E6
300 MNKA 60447 3672 32W-29S C1
1500 WHTN 60187 3025 23W-0N A5
1900 SYHW 60118 2800 35W-15N D3
N Maria Ct
4600 CHCG 60656 2918 10W-5N A7
4700 CHCG 60706 2918 10W-5N A7
4700 NRDG 60706 2918 10W-5N A7
Maria Ln
- NLNX 60451 3501 18W-23S A4
Maria St
400 TNTN 60476 3428 0E-21S E6
Marian Av
24900 JknT 60421 3677 21W-30S A3
Marian Cir
500 BbyT 60554 3075 43W-3S A6
Marian Cir E
500 BbyT 60554 3075 43W-3S A6
Marian Cir N
600 BbyT 60554 3075 43W-3S A6
Marian Cir S
600 BbyT 60554 3075 43W-3S A6
Marian Cir W
500 BbyT 60554 3075 43W-3S A6
Marian Ct
300 BGBK 60440 3205 22W-11S D7
400 TRLK 60010 2643 26W-25N D4
Marian Dr
12700 LMNT 60439 3271 18W-14S A7
12700 LMNT 60439 3343 18W-15S A1
15600 HMGN 60491 3421 17W-18S C1
Marian Ln
2500 WLMT 60091 2812 5W-13N A5
Marian Pkwy
100 CLLK 60014 2640 35W-26N A3
Maricopa Ln
10 HFET 60169 2859 23W-11N A4
10 HFET 60194 2859 23W-11N A4
10 SMBG 60194 2859 23W-11N A4
100 HFET 60169 2858 23W-11N E4
Maridon Rd
7300 CTSD 60525 3209 12W-8S B1
Marie Av
- ALGN 60102 2694 34W-21N C6
600 BtlT 60560 3333 42W-14S D1
1200 JltT 60432 3499 22W-22S D2
W Marie Av
15700 VrnT 60069 2701 15W-20N E7
15900 BFGV 60069 2701 16W-20N E7
15900 BFGV 60089 2701 16W-20N E7
26200 AntT 60002 2356 26W-41N E7
26300 AntT 60002 2415 26W-41N E1
Marie Ct
10 SEGN 60177 2908 35W-9N B2
Marie Dr
10 DRGV 60516 3207 18W-8S A2
100 DRGV 60516 3206 18W-8S E2
100 IVNS 60010 2751 23W-17N D5
100 IVNS 60067 2751 23W-17N D5
500 SHLD 60473 3428 0E-19S E2
8600 SPGV 60081 2413 31W-40N E2
Marie Ln
300 SMBG 60193 2858 24W-10N D6
1600 GNVW 60025 2809 11W-14N E4
9200 SRPK 60176 2973 11W-5N C2
W Marie Pl
26100 AntT 60002 2356 26W-41N E7
Marie St
500 BRKT 60511 3196 45W-8S B3
1400 GNVA 60134 3019 36W-2N E2
1400 GNVA 60174 3019 36W-2N E2
1400 SCRL 60174 3019 36W-2N E2
Marie Curie Ln
500 WNVL 60555 3080 29W-2S E3
Mariel Cir
22400 DRPK 60010 2752 22W-20N B1
Mariemont Rd
- SRGV 60554 3136 41W-7S A7
Marietta Dr
5600 NndT 60014 2640 33W-26N E3
Marietta St
- MHRY 60050 2527 33W-32N E4
Marigold Cir
300 MTSN 60443 3593 7W-26S C2
Marigold Ct
700 NPVL 60540 3140 29W-7S D7
2300 AURA 60506 3137 38W-6S A5
Marigold Dr
2600 SLVL 60411 3597 3E-26S E3
Marigold Ln
10 ALGN 60102 2692 38W-20N E7
10 LIHL 60156 2692 38W-20N E7
1300 MNKA 60447 3672 33W-30S A3
1800 HRPK 60133 2911 27W-9N C2
1900 RDLK 60073 2531 25W-33N A3
W Marigold Ln
4700 MONE 60449 3683 5W-31S B4
Marigold Pl
300 JltT 60433 3500 21W-24S A6
16100 ODHL 60487 3424 11W-19S A2
Marigold Rd
13500 PNFD 60544 3337 31W-16S E3
Marigold St
1400 JLET 60433 3588 21W-25S A1
1400 JltT 60433 3588 21W-25S A1
Marik Rd
900 BLWD 60104 3029 12W-0S B5
Marikay Av
1500 AURA 60505 3138 34W-5S D3
Marilyn Av
600 GLHT 60139 2969 22W-2N C7
N Marilyn Av
100 NHLK 60164 2972 13W-2N E7
100 NHLK 60164 3028 13W-2N E1
S Marilyn Av
100 NHLK 60164 3028 13W-1N E1
Marilyn Ct
1400 RGMW 60008 2806 20W-14N A3
11100 ODPK 60467 3344 13W-16S E4
16500 ODHL 60487 3424 11W-19S A3
25300 WcnT 60084 2588 25W-29N A3
Marilyn Dr
1700 MTGY 60538 3198 41W-9S A4
2800 JLET 60432 3500 20W-22S C2
3800 RNPK 60471 3594 4W-27S D5
4500 LGGV 60047 2700 19W-23N C2
16900 TYPK 60477 3424 10W-20S C4
17000 OrlT 60477 3424 10W-20S C4
Marilyn Ln
500 NLNX 60451 3501 16W-25S E7
1700 AraT 60505 3138 34W-5S C3
1800 AraT 60504 3138 34W-5S C3
1800 AURA 60504 3138 34W-5S C3
N Marilyn Ln
25200 ElaT 60047 2645 21W-25N C5
25400 HNWD 60047 2645 21W-25N C5
36500 RLKB 60046 2475 21W-36N D4
36500 RLKB 60073 2475 21W-36N D4
36800 LkvT 60046 2475 21W-36N D3
Marilyn Ter
14000 ODPK 60467 3344 13W-16S E3
W Marilyn Ter
10 ADSN 60101 2970 18W-4N E4
Marilyn Wy
11200 MKNA 60423 3591 13W-26S A2
11200 MKNA 60448 3590 14W-26S E2
11200 MKNA 60448 3591 13W-26S A2
Marilynn Ln
14700 HMGN 60491 3343 18W-17S A6
Marimac Ln
100 VNHL 60061 2647 17W-24N C6
Marina Ct
500 WCDA 60084 2588 24W-28N C6
700 UYPK 60466 3684 3W-29S A2
Marina Dr
- ALSP 60803 3275 6W-14S D6
- PNFD 60585 3338 28W-15S E2
- WldT 60585 3338 28W-15S E2
10 DSPN 60016 2862 15W-12N B2
10 MTGY 60543 3263 37W-11S C1
100 MPPT 60056 2862 15W-12N B2
22600 PNFD 60585 3339 28W-15S A2
S Marina Dr
- DSPN 60016 2862 15W-12N B1
500 MPPT 60056 2862 15W-12N B1
Marina St
500 WCDA 60084 2588 25W-27N A7
Marina Ter E
800 BRLT 60103 2911 28W-7N B4
Marina Ter W
800 BRLT 60103 2911 28W-7N A4
Marine Dr
- CLSM 60133 2967 27W-4N D3
- CLSM 60188 2967 27W-4N D3
600 WCDA 60084 2587 26W-28N C6
600 WcnT 60084 2587 26W-28N C6
3800 HRPK 60133 2967 27W-4N D3
N Marine Dr
- CHCG 60613 2922 0W-5N A7
4000 CHCG 60613 2978 0W-5N A1
4400 CHCG 60640 2921 0W-5N E7
4400 CHCG 60640 2922 0W-5N A7
35500 GrtT 60020 2473 27W-35N B5
35800 FXLK 60020 2473 27W-35N A5
Mariner Ct
700 ELGN 60120 2855 31W-10N D6
2700 LYWD 60411 3510 3E-23S A3
Mariner Dr
600 ELGN 60120 2855 32W-10N D5
Mariner Ln
10 FXLK 60020 2473 27W-36N A3
Mariner Pt
700 SMBG 60194 2859 22W-10N C5
Marino Ct
10 AddT 60143 2914 19W-7N D4
10 ITSC 60143 2914 19W-7N D4
Marion Av
- WHTN 60187 3024 25W-0N A4
10 LKFT 60045 2649 10W-24N E7
10 MltT 60187 3024 25W-0N C4
100 FmtT 60060 2645 21W-26N E3

STREET Block	City	ZIP	Map#	CGS	Grid
Marion Av					
100	LKFT	60045	2650	10W-24N	A7
100	MltT	60187	3023	26W-0N	E4
200	GNEN	60137	3025	23W-0N	A4
300	AURA	60505	3200	35W-8S	A2
300	SCRL	60174	2964	35W-3N	B5
600	HDPK	60035	2758	7W-20N	A2
800	GNVA	60134	3020	35W-0N	A6
2800	LydT	60164	2972	14W-3N	D5
2800	NHLK	60164	2972	14W-3N	D5
3100	FNPK	60131	2972	14W-3N	D5
9100	MNGV	60053	2864	8W-11N	D2
9500	OKLN	60453	3211	7W-11S	B6
10000	CHRG	60415	3211	7W-11S	B7
10000	OKLN	60415	3211	7W-11S	B7
E Marion Av					
10	PTHT	60070	2808	15W-15N	A2
N Marion Av					
100	BRLT	60103	2911	28W-8N	A2
W Marion Av					
25600	GrtT	60041	2474	25W-35N	A6
Marion Ct					
10	BlmT	60411	3510	3E-25S	A7
10	LIHL	60156	2694	34W-21N	C5
200	BNVL	60106	2972	15W-5N	A2
300	WLNG	60090	2755	15W-17N	A5
1100	SRWD	60404	3496	30W-22S	A3
1400	GNVA	60134	3020	36W-1N	A4
3500	ISLK	60042	2586	29W-28N	D6
16000	SHLD	60473	3429	1E-18S	A1
N Marion Ct					
200	OKPK	60301	3030	8W-0N	E3
200	OKPK	60302	3030	8W-0N	E3
1200	CHCG	60622	3033	2W-1N	C1
W Marion Ct					
26800	FXLK	60041	2473	27W-35N	C6
26800	GrtT	60041	2473	27W-35N	C6
Marion Dr					
1000	SRWD	60404	3496	30W-22S	B3
1500	WMTN	60481	3853	28W-37S	A5
1500	WmTp	60481	3853	28W-37S	A5
8000	BGVW	60455	3210	10W-9S	B3
8000	BGVW	60458	3210	10W-9S	B3
8000	JSTC	60455	3210	10W-9S	B3
8000	JSTC	60458	3210	10W-9S	B3
15900	SHLD	60473	3429	1E-18S	A1
W Marion Dr					
18700	GRNE	60031	2476	18W-35N	D5
18700	WrnT	60046	2476	18W-35N	D5
Marion Ln					
10	SMWD	60107	2857	28W-11N	A4
Marion Rd					
10	WNFD	60190	3023	28W-0S	B7
10	WnfT	60190	3023	28W-0S	B7
W Marion Rd					
1000	ANHT	60004	2806	18W-15N	E2
Marion Sq					
600	OKBK	60523	3085	17W-3S	B5
Marion St					
-	MhtT	60442	3677	19W-30S	D4
100	MHTN	60442	3677	19W-30S	D4
200	BNVL	60106	2972	15W-5N	A2
400	ROSL	60172	2913	23W-7N	A4
1200	DSPN	60016	2862	13W-11N	E4
1400	SMBG	60193	2913	23W-8N	A2
1400	SmbT	60193	2913	23W-8N	A2
1500	SmbT	60172	2913	23W-8N	A2
1700	WHTN	60187	3025	23W-0N	A4
3000	ElgT	60124	2853	38W-11N	B4
E Marion St					
-	ThtT	60476	3428	0E-21S	E5
10	JLET	60436	3499	23W-24S	A5
100	EMHT	60126	3028	15W-1N	A2
100	JLET	60433	3499	23W-24S	A5
100	TNTN	60476	3428	0E-21S	D5
600	ANHT	60004	2807	17W-15N	B2
1000	PTHT	60004	2807	17W-15N	B2
N Marion St					
100	OKPK	60301	3030	8W-0N	E4
100	OKPK	60302	3030	8W-0N	E3
200	PLTN	60074	2753	20W-16N	A7
26500	WcnT	60084	2643	28W-26N	A2
S Marion St					
-	OKPK	60301	3030	8W-0N	E4
100	OKPK	60302	3030	8W-0N	E4
W Marion St					
10	JLET	60436	3498	24W-24S	E5
100	PTHT	60070	2808	15W-15N	A2
200	ANHT	60004	2807	18W-15N	A2
200	JLET	60435	3498	24W-24S	E5
200	TNTN	60476	3428	0E-21S	D5
500	PTHT	60070	2807	16W-15N	D2
Marion St N					
700	OKPK	60302	3030	8W-1N	D2
1200	CHCG	60302	3030	8W-1N	D1
1200	CHCG	60707	3030	8W-1N	D1
Marion Wy					
300	LslT	60540	3143	23W-7S	A6
800	CHHT	60411	3507	2W-24S	D6
Marion Graves Ct					
1700	NCHI	60064	2536	11W-32N	D6
Mariposa Av					
10	WKGN	60087	2480	10W-36N	B4
Marissa Ct					
10	BRRG	60527	3208	15W-11S	A6
13500	HMGN	60491	3343	16W-17S	D5
Marissa Tr					
9000	WRLK	60097	2469	38W-35N	A6
Mariwood Ct					
10	LslT	60540	3142	24W-6S	D4
Marjorie Pkwy					
18700	FftT	60448	3502	14W-22S	D1
Mark Av					
-	BHPK	60099	2421	12W-40N	C3
-	ZION	60099	2421	12W-40N	C3
200	GLHT	60139	2969	23W-2N	A7
600	DSPN	60016	2808	13W-13N	D7
600	DSPN	60056	2808	13W-13N	D7
600	MPPT	60056	2808	14W-13N	D7
1500	ELGN	60123	2854	36W-12N	A1
Mark Cir					
2000	BGBK	60490	3339	28W-14S	B1
2100	BGBK	60490	3267	28W-14S	B7
2100	PNFD	60490	3267	28W-14S	B7
Mark Ct					
100	OSWG	60543	3263	36W-11S	E1
200	WDSK	60098	2581	41W-30N	C2
1100	ANTH	60002	2359	20W-41N	A7
Mark Dr					
10	HNWD	60047	2646	20W-24N	A7
10	HNWD	60047	2700	20W-24N	A1
100	GNVW	60025	2811	6W-13N	C5
200	WldT	60564	3266	29W-11S	D2
E Mark Dr					
1500	MPPT	60056	2808	14W-13N	D7
Mark Ln					
-	ElaT	60047	2699	23W-24N	A1
-	HPSR	60140	2796	46W-15N	A3
-	NLNX	60451	3588	19W-27S	E5
10	FXLK	60020	2473	27W-36N	C3
300	HFET	60010	2857	27W-11N	D4
300	SMWD	60010	2857	27W-11N	D4
300	SMWD	60107	2857	27W-11N	D4
500	DGvT	60516	3206	19W-9S	D2
500	DRN	60516	3206	19W-9S	D2
500	DRN	60561	3206	19W-9S	D2
800	WLNG	60090	2754	16W-16N	D6
900	PTHT	60070	2754	16W-16N	D6
900	PTHT	60090	2754	16W-16N	D6
11600	OrlT	60467	3344	14W-16S	D3
16300	BmnT	60477	3425	7W-19S	C2
16300	TYPK	60477	3425	7W-19S	C2
S Mark Ln					
1700	RDLK	60073	2531	23W-31N	E7
1700	RDLK	60073	2588	23W-31N	E1
Mark St					
100	WDDL	60191	2915	18W-7N	A4
400	SCRL	60174	2964	36W-3N	A6
700	EGVV	60007	2915	17W-7N	B4
700	WDDL	60007	2915	17W-7N	B4
900	SEGN	60177	2908	34W-7N	D4
1000	SchT	60177	2908	34W-7N	D5
1200	BNVL	60106	2915	17W-7N	B4
W Mark Ter					
2000	MPPT	60056	2861	17W-12N	B1
Mark Carre Ct					
2600	LSLE	60532	3142	24W-5S	C2
Mark Collins Dr					
-	FDHT	60411	3597	1E-26S	B3
-	SLVL	60411	3597	1E-26S	B3
-	STGR	60411	3597	1E-26S	B3
Market Av					
1000	NPVL	60540	3204	25W-8S	B1
Market Ct					
900	VNHL	60061	2647	17W-26N	C3
Market Dr					
700	OSWG	60543	3264	34W-11S	C2
Market Mdws					
1200	NPVL	60540	3204	25W-8S	B1
Market Pl					
100	MHTN	60442	3677	19W-30S	D3
100	MhtT	60442	3677	19W-30S	D3
Market Sq					
200	LKFT	60045	2650		C2
Market St					
-	GYLK	60030	2533	19W-32N	D6
10	ELGN	60123	2854	35W-11N	A4
100	LKPT	60441	3419	22W-18S	D1
100	LktT	60441	3419	22W-18S	D1
400	WKGN	60085	2537	10W-33N	B3
1200	NPVL	60540	3204	25W-8S	B1
1400	DSPN	60016	2863	13W-11N	A3
2000	BLID	60406	3349	2W-15S	C1
2100	WLSP	60480	3209	12W-10S	B4
4200	DrrT	60012	2583	37W-27N	B7
5700	RHMD	60071	2353	34W-42N	C6
S Market St					
400	JLET	60436	3498	24W-24S	D6
Market Loop Dr					
500	WDND	60118	2800	34W-15N	D3
Market Place Dr					
-	BtlT	60560	3261	42W-14S	D7
-	YKVL	60560	3261	42W-14S	D7
Market Square Ct					
10	LKFT	60045	2650		C2
Marketview Dr					
1700	YKVL	60560	3261	42W-13S	D6
1900	BtlT	60560	3261	42W-13S	D6
Markev Ln					
100	NLNX	60451	3501	18W-24S	B4
Markey Ln					
1600	FSMR	60422	3507	2W-23S	D4
N Markham Av					
5900	CHCG	60646	2919	7W-7N	C4
Markham Dr					
14700	DLTN	60419	3350	0W-17S	C6
14700	HRVY	60426	3350	0W-17S	C6
Markle Rd					
32000	WmTp	60481	3943	28W-39S	B1
Marks Pl					
500	BbyT	60134	3018	39W-0N	D5
Mark Thomas Ln					
-	BRLT	60103	2911	28W-8N	B3
2500	HRPK	60133	2911	28W-8N	B3
Mark Twain St					
200	CmpT	60175	2962	40W-4N	C4
Mark Twain Tr					
800	BTVA	60510	3078	34W-2S	D5
Marlboro Cir					
1600	CPVL	60110	2748	32W-17N	D7
Marlboro Ct					
1300	BRLT	60103	2967	28W-5N	A1
Marlboro Dr					
1600	CTHL	60403	3498	25W-21S	C1
1700	CTHL	60403	3418	25W-21S	B7
Marlboro Rd					
7300	NndT	60012	2583	36W-27N	D7
Marlborough Ln					
10	MltT	60148	3084	21W-2S	A3
100	YkTp	60148	3084	20W-2S	A3
2400	DRN	60561	3206	19W-8S	D2
Marlborough Rd					
400	LMBD	60148	3084	20W-2S	A3
400	YkTp	60148	3084	20W-2S	A3
900	BRTN	60010	2698	25W-20N	A7
900	CbaT	60010	2698	25W-20N	A7
Marlbourgh Ct					
1300	MDLN	60060	2590	19W-27N	B7
Marleigh Ln					
1300	SEGN	60177	2908	36W-9N	A2
Marlene Av					
900	ELGN	60123	2854	36W-12N	A1
Marlene Ct					
100	WCDA	60084	2643	25W-27N	E2
W Marlene Ct					
24200	TroT	60404	3584	30W-25S	C1
Marley Cir					
7300	JLET	60586	3415	33W-21S	B7
Marley Ln					
-	FftT	60448	3503	13W-22S	B2
-	MKNA	60448	3503	13W-22S	B2
N Marley Rd					
100	NLNX	60451	3501	16W-24S	E6
100	NlxT	60451	3501	16W-24S	E6
1100	NlxT	60451	3502	16W-23S	A4
2700	NlxT	60448	3502	16W-23S	A4
S Marley Rd					
-	NlxT	60451	3501	16W-25S	E7
400	NLNX	60451	3501	16W-25S	E7
Marley Brook Ct					
11200	ODPK	60467	3422	14W-21S	E6
Marley Creek Blvd					
17700	ODPK	60467	3422	14W-21S	E6
Marley Creek Ct					
19200	FftT	60448	3502	14W-23S	D3
19200	MKNA	60448	3502	14W-23S	D3
Marley Creek Ln					
11300	ODPK	60467	3422	14W-21S	E6
S Marley Hills Rd					
18600	NlxT	60448	3502	15W-22S	C1
Marlin Av					
20100	LYWD	60411	3510	3E-23S	A4
Marlin Ct					
2700	HMWD	60430	3427	3W-21S	B7
20000	LYWD	60411	3510	3E-23S	A4
Marlin Dr					
10	MTGY	60543	3199	38W-11S	B7
26000	WmTp	60481	3761	32W-34S	D6
Marlin Ln					
18000	HMWD	60430	3427	3W-21S	B7
Mar Ln Dr					
1000	LKFT	60045	2649	12W-24N	C7
Marl Oak Dr					
2600	HDPK	60035	2704	9W-23N	B2
Marlowe Av					
1700	PKRG	60068	2917	11W-8N	E1
Marlowe Pl					
1100	VNHL	60061	2647	17W-27N	C2
Marls Ct					
1200	LslT	60563	3142	25W-5S	B3
1200	NPVL	60563	3142	25W-5S	A3
Marmion Av					
2000	JLET	60436	3497	26W-24S	E5
E Marmion Pl					
1800	CteT	60417	3686	2E-29S	D1
Marmion Academy Dr					
-	BtvT	60510	3078	34W-3S	C6
1300	AURA	60510	3078	34W-3S	C7
3000	AURA	60502	3078	34W-3S	D6
Marmon Dr					
-	WDRG	60517	3269	21W-12S	E3
300	BGBK	60440	3269	21W-12S	E3
300	WDRG	60440	3269	21W-12S	E3
Marne Rd					
1800	BGBK	60490	3267	27W-11S	C2
Marnel Rd					
10	OswT	60538	3199	36W-10S	D6
Maroon Dr					
1200	ELGN	60120	2855	32W-10N	D5
Maroon Bells Ct					
10	BGBK	60490	3267	27W-12S	D2
Maroon Bells Ln					
1600	BGBK	60490	3267	27W-12S	D2
Maros Ln					
10	OMFD	60461	3507	3W-25S	A7
E Marquardt Dr					
10	WLNG	60090	2755	14W-16N	C7
N Marquardt Ln					
2400	MchT	60051	2529	30W-34N	A1
Marquette Av					
200	BNHM	60409	3351	3E-17S	E5
200	BNHM	60633	3351	3E-17S	E5
200	CTCY	60409	3351	3E-17S	E6
400	CRY	60013	2696	30W-23N	A3
1500	NPVL	60565	3204	24W-8S	D3
S Marquette Av					
7800	CHCG	60617	3215	3E-8S	E1
7900	CHCG	60649	3215	3E-9S	E2
12600	CHCG	60633	3279	3E-14S	E7
13800	BNHM	60633	3351	3E-16S	E3
14500	BNHM	60409	3351	3E-16S	E4
14500	CTCY	60409	3351	3E-16S	E4
Marquette Ct					
10	BGBK	60440	3205	22W-10S	C5
800	VNHL	60061	2647	18W-25N	A6
1500	JLET	60435	3498	25W-23S	B4
1600	LKFT	60045	2649	13W-26N	A2
Marquette Dr					
200	BGBK	60440	3269	23W-13S	B5
200	RMVL	60446	3269	23W-13S	A5
E Marquette Dr					
2000	CHCG	60637	3153	2E-7S	C5
2000	CHCG	60649	3153	2E-7S	C5
E Marquette Dr US-41					
2000	CHCG	60637	3153	2E-7S	C5
2000	CHCG	60649	3153	2E-7S	C5
W Marquette Dr					
25700	GrtT	60041	2473	25W-36N	E5
25700	GrtT	60041	2474	25W-36N	A5
Marquette Dr N					
7800	TYPK	60477	3424	9W-21S	D5
Marquette Dr S					
7700	TYPK	60477	3424	9W-21S	D6
Marquette Ln					
1700	HFET	60169	2858	25W-12N	A1
Marquette Pl					
10	BFGV	60090	2755	14W-20N	C2
10	PKFT	60466	3595	3W-27S	A4
Marquette Rd					
10	HDPK	60035	2758	8W-20N	A2
10	NfdT	60062	2758	8W-20N	A2
1500	JLET	60435	3498	26W-23S	A4
E Marquette Rd					
10	CHCG	60621	3152	0E-7S	C5
10	CHCG	60637	3152	0E-7S	C6
1100	CHCG	60637	3153	1E-7S	A5
W Marquette Rd					
10	CHCG	60621	3152	0W-7S	B5
10	CHCG	60637	3152	0W-7S	C6
900	CHCG	60621	3151	2W-7S	C6
1100	CHCG	60636	3151	1W-7S	E6
2300	CHCG	60629	3151	2W-7S	B6
2900	CHCG	60629	3150	4W-7S	C6
4700	BDPK	60638	3150	5W-7S	A6
4700	CHCG	60638	3150	5W-7S	A6
Marquette St					
300	PKFT	60466	3594	4W-27S	E4
300	PKFT	60466	3595	4W-27S	A4
1900	NCHI	60064	2537	10W-31N	A6
1900	NCHI	60088	2537	10W-31N	A7
Marquis Ct					
-	WDRG	60517	3143	22W-7S	B6
Marquise St					
-	DMND	60416	3941	34W-40S	A3
Marriot Dr					
2100	WDND	60118	2800	34W-14N	E6
Marriott Dr					
-	LNSH	60069	2702	15W-22N	B3
Marryat Pl					
100	SMWD	60107	2856	29W-10N	D5
Marryat Rd					
10	TVLY	60013	2695	31W-23N	C3
Mars Pl					
10	MPPT	60056	2808	15W-14N	A3
10	PTHT	60070	2808	15W-14N	A3
Marsch Av					
100	MTGY	60538	3199	36W-9S	E4
Marseillaise Pl					
900	AURA	60506	3199	36W-7S	D1
Marseilles Cir					
500	BFGV	60089	2754	16W-20N	C1
600	BFGV	60089	2701	16W-20N	C7
Marseilles Ln					
3500	HLCT	60429	3426	4W-21S	E7
E Marseilles St					
200	VNHL	60061	2647	16W-24N	D7
Marsh Dr					
7100	LKWD	60014	2638	39W-24N	D6
Marsh Ln					
10	BTVA	60510	3077	37W-1S	C1
6000	MTSN	60443	3505	7W-24S	C6
N Marsha Dr					
800	PLTN	60067	2753	20W-17N	A6
Marshall Av					
10	BLWD	60104	3029	12W-0N	B3
500	AURA	60506	3199	36W-7S	E1
5400	MchT	60097	2469	36W-37N	E2
5400	WRLK	60097	2469	36W-37N	E2
6000	CHRG	60415	3275	7W-12S	C1
6000	OKLN	60453	3275	7W-12S	C1
26000	GrtT	60041	2473	26W-36N	E5
Marshall Blvd					
1200	AURA	60505	3138	34W-5S	E3
S Marshall Blvd					
1900	CHCG	60623	3090	3W-2S	E2
Marshall Ct					
100	NlxT	60448	3502	15W-22S	C1
700	BTVA	60510	3078	34W-1S	D2
1100	NPVL	60565	3204	25W-10S	C6
3800	BLWD	60104	3029	12W-0N	A4
E Marshall Ct					
800	PLTN	60074	2753	19W-18N	B3
W Marshall Ct					
-	WKGN	60083	2478	14W-37N	D2
Marshall Dr					
200	DSPN	60016	2862	15W-10N	A5
200	MPPT	60016	2862	15W-11N	A3
200	MPPT	60056	2862	15W-11N	A3
300	ANTH	60002	2357	24W-43N	D4
1400	DSPN	60018	2862	15W-10N	A6
1600	EGvT	60018	2862	15W-9N	A6
6300	WDRG	60517	3143	22W-7S	B6
W Marshall Dr					
22000	PnfT	60544	3339	27W-16S	C5
Marshall Ln					
10	MltT	60188	3024	25W-1N	A3
Marshall Pkwy					
1900	WKGN	60085	2536	11W-33N	D4
Marshall Rd					
200	BNVL	60106	2915	16W-5N	D7
300	PltT	60140	2797	41W-13N	E7
300	PltT	60140	2851	41W-12N	E2
400	NHBK	60062	2758	8W-17N	A5
400	OKTR	60181	3085	17W-1S	B2
400	YkTp	60181	3085	17W-1S	B1
500	NHBK	60062	2757	8W-17N	E5
E Marshall St					
1300	ANHT	60004	2807	17W-14N	C3
Marshall Ash Ct					
10	BGBK	60490	3267	26W-12S	E4
Marshall Ash St					
300	BGBK	60490	3267	26W-12S	E4
Marshfield Av					
3400	PKCY	60085	2536	13W-33N	A3
14100	DXMR	60426	3349	2W-16S	E4
14500	HRVY	60426	3349	2W-17S	E5
15600	HRVY	60426	3427	2W-19S	E2
16000	MKHM	60426	3427	2W-19S	E2
16100	MKHM	60428	3427	2W-19S	E3
16500	HLCT	60428	3427	2W-19S	E3
16500	HLCT	60429	3427	2W-19S	E3
18300	HMWD	60430	3427	2W-22S	E7
18300	HMWD	60430	3507	2W-22S	E1
N Marshfield Av					
400	CHCG	60612	3033	2W-0N	C3
400	CHCG	60622	3033	2W-0N	C3
1600	CHCG	60622	2977	2W-2N	C7
2400	CHCG	60614	2977	2W-3N	C5
3300	CHCG	60657	2977	2W-4N	C3
3500	CHCG	60613	2977	2W-4N	C3
7400	CHCG	60626	2867	2W-9N	C6
S Marshfield Av					
-	BLID	60406	3277	2W-15S	D7
-	CHCG	60608	3091	2W-1S	D1
-	CTPK	60406	3277	2W-15S	D7
700	CHCG	60612	3033	2W-0S	D6
3400	CHCG	60609	3091	2W-3S	D5
4700	CHCG	60609	3151	2W-5S	D2
5500	CHCG	60636	3151	2W-6S	D3
7500	CHCG	60620	3213	2W-9S	D3
11100	CHCG	60643	3277	2W-13S	D4
11700	CTPK	60643	3277	2W-13S	D4
12100	BLID	60643	3277	2W-14S	D5
12100	BLID	60827	3277	2W-14S	D6
12400	CTPK	60827	3277	2W-15S	D7
Marshfield Ct					
2900	ELGN	60124	2853	37W-11N	C3
Marshfield Dr					
2900	ELGN	60124	2853	37W-11N	C3
Marshfield Ln					
2200	AURA	60503	3201	33W-10S	B7
8800	ODHL	60487	3424	11W-19S	A2
W Marshfield Rd					
25600	LkvT	60046	2474	25W-37N	A1
N Marshfield St					
500	CHCG	60622	3033	2W-0N	C3
Marsh Hawk Wy					
29800	BCHR	60401	3864	0E-36S	E1
Marshland Wy					
1500	BLVY	60098	2526	38W-33N	A3
Marshman St					
200	HDPK	60035	2705	7W-21N	B7
Marsh Meadow Ln					
1900	RDLK	60073	2531	25W-33N	A2
Marshview Ct					
1400	WCHI	60185	2966	29W-2N	E7
Marske Av					
-	RNPK	60471	3594	4W-27S	E5
Marston Av					
10	MltT	60137	3083	22W-1S	D2
300	GNEN	60137	3083	23W-1S	A2
Marston Ct					
500	MltT	60137	3083	21W-1S	D2
Marston Ln					
2000	FSMR	60422	3507	2W-22S	C2
N Mart Ct					
600	PLTN	60067	2752	21W-16N	C6
W Mart Center Dr					
300	CHCG	60606	3034	0W-0N	A4
Martens St					
3400	FNPK	60131	2973	11W-4N	D3
Martha Av					
2400	ZION	60099	2421	12W-40N	C3
S Martha Av					
14500	BNHM	60633	3351	3E-16S	E4
14500	CTCY	60409	3351	3E-16S	E4
14500	CTCY	60633	3351	3E-16S	E4
Martha Ct					
300	LMBD	60148	3026	19W-0N	C4
Martha Dr					
1500	ELGN	60123	2854	35W-11N	B4
Martha Ln					
10	EVTN	60201	2866	4W-11N	D2
900	WDSK	60098	2581	40W-30N	E2
5300	BmnT	60452	3425	6W-20S	E4
5300	OKFT	60452	3425	6W-20S	E4
W Martha Ln					
1700	MPPT	60056	2861	17W-12N	C2
E Martha Pl					
2600	BNHM	60633	3351	3E-16S	E4
Martha St					
100	BNVL	60106	2971	16W-5N	D1
900	EGVV	60007	2914	20W-8N	B2
N Martha St					
600	LMBD	60148	3026	19W-1N	C2
S Martha St					
100	LMBD	60148	3026	19W-0N	C4
Marthas Dr					
-	BfdT	53128	2352		E2
-	GNCY	53128	2352		E2
Marti Rd					
17500	HMGN	60491	3422	15W-21S	B6
Martie Ln					
19400	MKNA	60448	3503	13W-23S	A3
Martin Av					
10	NPVL	60540	3141	27W-7S	C7
100	MTGY	60538	3199	36W-9S	D3
500	BtlT	60560	3333	42W-14S	D1
500	YKVL	60560	3333	42W-14S	D1
2800	LydT	60164	2972	14W-3N	C5
2800	NHLK	60164	2972	14W-3N	C5
3000	FNPK	60131	2972	14W-3N	C5
3000	FNPK	60164	2972	14W-3N	C5
3000	LydT	60131	2972	14W-3N	C5
18000	HMWD	60430	3427	2W-22S	D7
18400	HMWD	60430	3507	2W-22S	D1
N Martin Av					
200	WKGN	60085	2536	11W-34N	D1
1400	WKGN	60085	2479	11W-35N	D6
S Martin Av					
10	WKGN	60085	2536	11W-34N	D2
W Martin Av					
300	NPVL	60540	3141	27W-7S	C7
13200	BHPK	60083	2421	13W-39N	A6
13200	WDWH	60083	2421	13W-39N	A6
Martin Ct					
-	PLNO	60545	3260	45W-13S	C5
10	BlmT	60411	3510	3E-25S	A7
10	LMNT	60439	3272	15W-13S	B3
10	WDRG	60517	3143	22W-7S	C7
200	BMDL	60108	2968	24W-4N	C3
300	BRTN	60010	2751	25W-20N	B1
1300	JLET	60586	3496	31W-22S	A1
2500	NLNX	60451	3588	19W-27S	E5
2900	MhtT	60442	3588	19W-27S	E5
3300	RGMW	60008	2806	19W-13N	D6
18900	CCHL	60478	3506	5W-22S	B2
Martin Dr					
-	BTVA	60510	3077	37W-1S	D1
-	GnvT	60510	3077	37W-1S	D1
100	SEGN	60177	2908	35W-8N	C2
200	WDSK	60098	2525	40W-32N	A5
600	ELGN	60123	2908	35W-9N	C1
600	ELGN	60177	2908	35W-9N	C1
700	ELGN	60120	2855	32W-12N	C2
2600	SPGV	60081	2413	31W-41N	C1
2900	WDRG	60517	3143	22W-7S	D7
4900	HMND	46320	3352		D5
6300	DGvT	60527	3145	16W-7S	E5
6300	WLBK	60527	3145	16W-7S	E5
8700	HGKN	60525	3147	11W-7S	D6
11600	HTLY	60142	2692	40W-20N	A7
N Martin Dr					
800	PLTN	60067	2752	21W-17N	C6
800	PltT	60067	2752	21W-17N	C6
W Martin Dr					
19400	FmtT	60060	2646	19W-26N	C2
Martin Ln					
10	EGvT	60007	2861	17W-10N	B5
10	EGVV	60007	2861	17W-10N	B5
10	NHFD	60093	2811	7W-15N	A1
100	CHHT	60411	3508	0W-24S	B6
300	BMDL	60108	2968	24W-4N	D3
600	VrnT	60015	2755	15W-20N	B1
2600	RGMW	60008	2806	19W-13N	B6
5400	HRPK	60133	2911	27W-6N	C6
9000	BGVW	60455	3210	8W-10S	E5
18900	CCHL	60478	3506	5W-22S	B2
19000	CCHL	60477	3506	5W-22S	B2
19000	RchT	60477	3506	5W-22S	B2
S Martin Ln					
2200	ANHT	60005	2861	18W-11N	A3
W Martin Ln					
1700	MPPT	60056	2861	17W-12N	C2
Martin Rd N					
2100	MHRY	60050	2527	35W-34N	B1
5600	MchT	60050	2527	34W-34N	C1
Martin St					
6400	GfnT	60014	2639	38W-25N	A4
Martindale Dr					
10800	WSTR	60154	3086	13W-2S	E3
Martindale Dr E					
2400	WSTR	60154	3086	13W-2S	E3
Martindale Dr W					
2400	WSTR	60154	3086	13W-2S	D3
Martin France Cir					
6600	TYPK	60477	3425	8W-21S	B7
Martingale Dr					
300	WynT	60103	2966	29W-5N	D2
900	BRLT	60103	2910	29W-6N	D6
Martingale Ln					
900	RLKB	60046	2475	21W-36N	D4
900	RLKB	60073	2475	21W-36N	C4
W Martingale Ln					
12500	HMGN	60491	3344	15W-17S	A5

STREET Block	City	ZIP	Map#	CGS	Grid
Martingale Rd					
-	EGvT	60007	2914	21W-9N	A1
-	EGvT	60193	2860	20W-9N	A7
-	EGvT	60193	2914	21W-9N	A1
-	EGVV	60007	2914	21W-9N	A1
-	SMBG	60173	2860	21W-9N	A7
-	SMBG	60193	2860	21W-9N	A7
-	SmbT	60173	2860	21W-9N	A7
-	SmbT	60193	2860	21W-9N	A7
-	SmbT	60193	2914	21W-9N	A1
1900	WHTN	60187	3024	24W-0N	D4
N Martingale Rd					
-	SMBG	60193	2860	21W-9N	A6
-	SmbT	60173	2860	21W-10N	A6
-	SmbT	60193	2860	21W-9N	A6
10	SMBG	60173	2860	21W-10N	A5
Martingdale Av					
300	RMVL	60446	3340	24W-16S	E4
N Martin Luther King Jr Av					
10	WKGN	60085	2537	10W-34N	B1
S Martin Luther King Jr Av					
10	WKGN	60085	2537	10W-33N	A2
900	NCHI	60064	2537	10W-33N	A4
Martins Ln					
10	HDPK	60035	2650	9W-24N	D7
Martinson Ct					
900	NARA	60542	3077	38W-3S	B6
Marvel Av					
800	WDSK	60098	2524	41W-31N	E6
Marvell Ln					
900	HDPK	60035	2704	8W-21N	D6
Marvin Av					
10	FXLK	60020	2473	28W-36N	A3
Marvin Dr					
9900	HTLY	60142	2692	38W-22N	D4
Marvin Pkwy					
800	PKRG	60068	2863	11W-9N	E6
Marvin Pl					
300	WLNG	60090	2755	13W-17N	D5
Marvins Wy					
400	BFGV	60089	2701	16W-21N	E7
Marvo St					
10	NARA	60542	3137	36W-4S	E1
10	NARA	60542	3138	36W-4S	A1
W Marwood Av					
7400	EDPK	60707	2974	9W-3N	C6
N Marwood St					
2500	RVGV	60171	2974	10W-3N	A5
Marx Pl					
-	WCHI	60185	3022	29W-0N	D4
Mary Av					
1000	WPHR	60096	2363	10W-42N	B7
3400	PKCY	60085	2536	13W-33N	A2
N Mary Av					
43200	AntT	60002	2357	25W-43N	B4
Mary Cir					
600	RtdT	60136	2745	39W-17N	D6
Mary Ct					
10	CmpT	60175	2961	42W-5N	C3
10	SLVL	60411	3597	1E-27S	B4
100	BRLT	60103	2911	28W-8N	A3
200	RLKB	60073	2474	23W-35N	E5
800	MRGO	60152	2634	49W-25N	C4
4900	CCHL	60478	3506	6W-22S	A1
10900	NlxT	60448	3501	16W-23S	E2
10900	NlxT	60451	3501	16W-23S	E2
N Mary Ct					
36100	GrtT	60041	2473	26W-36N	D4
36400	LkvT	60046	2475	21W-36N	C4
36400	RLKB	60046	2475	21W-36N	C4
36400	RLKB	60073	2475	21W-36N	C4
W Mary Ct					
600	EMHT	60126	2971	17W-3N	C6
25100	PnfT	60586	3415	31W-20S	E5
Mary Dr					
-	CmpT	60175	2961	42W-4N	C4
100	BRkT	60511	3134	46W-7S	A7
13700	ODPK	60462	3345	11W-16S	E3
13700	OrlT	60462	3345	11W-16S	E3
20600	LktT	60403	3418	25W-19S	B3
20600	LktT	60441	3418	25W-19S	A3
22000	FKFT	60423	3590	14W-26S	D3
E Mary Dr					
10	CmpT	60175	2961	42W-4N	C3
N Mary Dr					
36700	LkvT	60046	2475	21W-36N	C3
W Mary Dr					
10	CmpT	60175	2961	42W-4N	C3
Mary Ln					
-	JLET	60435	3498	26W-22S	A2
10	CLLK	60014	2640	35W-25N	A5
10	HNWD	60047	2646	19W-24N	B7
100	CRY	60013	2695	31W-23N	C1
500	RtdT	60136	2745	39W-17N	D6
800	RtdT	60142	2745	39W-17N	D6
1100	NPVL	60540	3142	25W-7S	A6
2900	MchT	60051	2528	31W-33N	C3
10700	MKNA	60448	3503	13W-23S	B4
E Mary Ln					
100	SchT	60175	2963	38W-3N	A6
100	SCRL	60175	2963	38W-3N	A7
400	GDLY	60407	4030	32W-43S	D2
700	RedT	60408	4030	32W-43S	D2
N Mary Ln					
900	BDWD	60408	3941	32W-40S	E3
900	RedT	60408	3941	32W-40S	E3
S Mary Ln					
25600	CteT	60417	3687	3E-31S	A4
W Mary Ln					
200	SchT	60175	2963	38W-3N	A6
24900	PnfT	60586	3416	31W-20S	A5
25000	PnfT	60586	3415	31W-20S	E5
Mary Pl					
400	ELGN	60120	2855	33W-11N	A4
Mary St					
10	DSPN	60016	2863	13W-12N	A2
10	GLNC	60022	2759	5W-17N	A6
10	GLNC	60093	2759	5W-17N	A6
100	MTGY	60543	3263	38W-11S	A1
200	DYR	46311	3598		D3
200	GLNC	60022	2758	5W-17N	E6
200	GLNC	60093	2758	5W-17N	E6
S Mary St					
2500	CHCG	60608	3091	1W-2S	E2
Marya Ln					
800	SRWD	60404	3496	30W-24S	B5
Mary Ann Ct					
5500	BmnT	60477	3425	6W-19S	D2
5500	OKFT	60452	3425	6W-19S	D2
5500	OKFT	60477	3425	6W-19S	D2
Mary Ann Ln					
1600	LKPT	60441	3419	22W-20S	D4
18100	CCHL	60478	3426	5W-21S	B7
Maryann Ln					
3100	DYR	46311	3598		C5
W Mary Ann Rd					
26000	AntT	60002	2415	26W-41N	E2
Mary Anne St					
600	WDSK	60098	2524	42W-31N	B7
Mary Belle Cir					
-	BFGV	60089	2754	16W-20N	D1
Marybeth Ct					
600	DGvT	60527	3207	16W-9S	D4
N Marybrook Dr					
2200	PNFD	60544	3338	30W-16S	B4
Mary Byrne Dr					
800	SLVL	60411	3597	1E-27S	A4
800	STGR	60411	3597	1E-27S	A4
800	STGR	60475	3597	1E-27S	A4
Marycrest Dr					
-	RchT	60477	3506	6W-22S	A2
-	RchT	60478	3506	6W-22S	A2
18300	CCHL	60478	3426	6W-22S	A7
18300	CCHL	60478	3506	6W-22S	A1
W Mary Dale Av					
24000	ElaT	60047	2644	24W-25N	C6
Maryhill Ln					
200	ElgT	60124	2853	37W-11N	C4
Mary Jane Ln					
500	ADSN	60143	2970	19W-5N	D2
500	ADSN	60191	2970	19W-5N	D2
500	WDDL	60191	2970	19W-5N	D2
1100	WKGN	60099	2421	10W-38N	E6
1100	WKGN	60099	2422	10W-38N	A6
2000	PKRG	60068	2863	11W-9N	D6
Mary Kay Ln					
3000	GNVW	60025	2810	10W-15N	A2
Maryknoll Cir					
800	GNEN	60137	3083	21W-1S	D1
800	MltT	60137	3083	21W-1S	D1
Maryknoll Dr					
600	LKPT	60441	3341	21W-18S	D7
600	LktT	60441	3341	21W-18S	D7
Marylake Ln					
19000	CCHL	60478	3506	6W-22S	A2
19000	RchT	60477	3506	6W-22S	A2
19000	RchT	60478	3506	6W-22S	A2
Maryland Av					
2700	FSMR	60422	3507	3W-23S	B3
14200	DLTN	60419	3351	1E-16S	A4
15000	SHLD	60473	3351	1E-17S	A5
16200	SHLD	60473	3429	1E-19S	A1
S Maryland Av					
-	CHCG	60615	3152	1E-5S	E1
300	GNWD	60425	3509	1E-23S	A3
5600	CHCG	60637	3152	1E-6S	E3
7200	CHCG	60619	3152	1E-8S	E7
7500	CHCG	60619	3214	1E-9S	E3
9700	CHCG	60628	3214	1E-11S	E6
10400	CHCG	60628	3278	1E-12S	E1
13400	CHCG	60827	3350	0E-15S	E1
Maryland Ct					
17800	ODPK	60467	3423	12W-21S	C5
Maryland Dr					
1800	EGVV	60007	2913	22W-9N	D1
Maryland St					
3000	NCHI	60088	2593	12W-30N	B2
N Maryland St					
9000	NLES	60714	2864	10W-11N	B2
Mary Lee Ct					
13300	PNFD	60585	3337	31W-15S	E3
Mary Ln Ct					
10	CLLK	60014	2640	35W-25N	A5
W Marylou Av					
23000	CNHN	60410	3585	28W-27S	A4
Mary Lu Ln					
100	BFGV	60089	2754	17W-18N	B2
Marys Ln					
300	YkTp	60148	3084	19W-1S	D1
S Mary Therese Ln					
20100	FftT	60423	3504	10W-24S	D5
Maryview Ct					
300	MTSN	60443	3505	6W-24S	E5
Maryview Pkwy					
10	MTSN	60443	3505	6W-24S	E5
Maryville Dr					
-	DSPN	60016	2808	13W-13N	E7
900	LktT	60441	3419	21W-19S	E2
2800	MchT	60051	2528	31W-33N	C3
N Marywood Av					
1600	AURA	60505	3138	34W-5S	E3
1800	AraT	60505	3138	34W-5S	E2
W Marywood Av					
700	AraT	60504	3138	34W-5S	D3
700	AURA	60504	3138	34W-5S	D3
700	AURA	60505	3138	34W-5S	D3
900	AraT	60505	3138	34W-5S	D3
Marywood Cir					
10	WHTN	60187	3082	25W-2S	B3
Marywood Ct					
1200	AURA	60505	3138	34W-5S	E3
Marywood Ln					
10	BGBK	60440	3205	23W-10S	A6
N Masaryk Rd					
40800	AntT	60002	2416	24W-40N	B2
Maserati Dr					
1700	JLET	60435	3417	27W-21S	C7
1700	JLET	60435	3497	27W-21S	C1
Mashie Ct					
10	WDRG	60517	3143	23W-7S	B7
22100	FmtT	60060	2589	22W-29N	C5
Mashpee Ln					
300	SMBG	60194	2858	24W-10N	D5
Masland Ct					
600	NBRN	60010	2698	24W-22N	B5
Mason Av					
800	AURA	60506	3199	36W-8S	E3
7900	BRBK	60459	3211	7W-9S	C3
8800	MNGV	60053	2865	7W-11N	B3
9500	OKLN	60453	3211	7W-11S	C6
10300	CHRG	60415	3275	7W-12S	C1
10300	OKLN	60415	3275	7W-12S	C1
10300	OKLN	60453	3275	7W-12S	C1
11000	ALSP	60482	3275	7W-12S	C3
11000	CHRG	60482	3275	7W-12S	C3
N Mason Av					
10	CHCG	60644	3031	7W-0N	C5
1000	CHCG	60651	3031	7W-1N	B2
1600	CHCG	60639	3031	7W-2N	C1
2100	CHCG	60639	2975	7W-2N	B6
4000	CHCG	60634	2975	7W-5N	B1
4300	CHCG	60630	2975	7W-5N	B1
5400	CHCG	60630	2919	7W-6N	B5
5500	CHCG	60646	2919	7W-6N	B5
S Mason Av					
10	CHCG	60644	3031	7W-0S	C5
1100	CCRO	60644	3031	7W-0S	C7
1100	CCRO	60804	3031	7W-0S	C7
4900	StkT	60638	3149	7W-5S	C2
5100	CHCG	60638	3149	7W-5S	C2
7300	BDPK	60638	3149	7W-8S	C7
S Mason Av					
7300	BDPK	60638	3211	7W-8S	C1
12400	ALSP	60803	3275	7W-14S	C7
12700	ALSP	60463	3275	7W-15S	C7
12700	WthT	60463	3275	7W-15S	C7
12900	WthT	60463	3347	7W-15S	C1
W Mason Av					
400	JLET	60435	3498	26W-23S	A3
2000	JLET	60435	3497	26W-23S	E3
3300	JLET	60431	3497	28W-23S	B3
Mason Ct					
700	JLET	60435	3497	26W-23S	E3
1200	CHHT	60411	3508	0W-25S	C7
Mason Dr					
600	LGNG	60525	3147	13W-5S	A1
1300	WNSP	60525	3147	13W-5S	A1
1300	WNSP	60558	3147	13W-5S	A1
4000	HFET	60192	2804	23W-15N	D3
S Mason Dr					
-	CHCG	60644	3031	7W-0S	C5
-	OKPK	60304	3031	7W-0S	C5
-	OKPK	60644	3031	7W-0S	C5
700	LGNG	60525	3147	13W-5S	A2
Mason Ln					
-	CLLK	60014	2693	37W-22N	B4
-	CLLK	60156	2693	37W-22N	B4
400	LIHL	60156	2693	37W-22N	B4
800	DSPN	60016	2863	12W-10N	B4
8000	WDRG	60517	3206	21W-9S	A3
8500	TYPK	60487	3424	10W-21S	B6
14300	ODPK	60462	3345	11W-17S	E4
Mason Rd					
-	ELGN	60123	2799	37W-14N	E5
300	DndT	60124	2799	37W-15N	D5
300	ELGN	60124	2799	37W-15N	D5
300	GLBT	60124	2799	37W-15N	D5
300	GLBT	60136	2799	37W-15N	D5
Mason St					
-	BDWD	60408	3942	31W-41S	B5
10	CTCY	60409	3352	4E-18S	B7
10	HMND	46320	3352	4E-18S	C7
E Mason St					
10	CTCY	60409	3352		C7
10	HMND	46320	3352		C7
200	BDWD	60408	3942	31W-41S	B5
N Mason St					
100	BNVL	60106	2971	16W-5N	E1
S Mason St					
10	BNVL	60106	2971	16W-4N	E2
Mason Corte Dr					
1600	LKMR	60051	2528	31W-33N	E2
1600	LKMR	60051	2529	30W-33N	A2
1600	MchT	60051	2529	30W-33N	A2
Mason Hill Rd					
6100	BLVY	60050	2584	35W-30N	A2
6100	NndT	60012	2584	35W-30N	A2
6100	NndT	60050	2584	35W-30N	A2
6500	BLVY	60050	2583	37W-30N	B2
6500	NndT	60012	2583	37W-30N	E2
6500	NndT	60050	2583	37W-30N	B2
7000	BLVY	60098	2583	37W-30N	B2
7900	DrrT	60098	2583	37W-30N	B2
7900	NndT	60098	2583	37W-30N	B2
Massachusetts Av					
400	NPVL	60565	3203	27W-10S	C5
1100	JLET	60435	3498	25W-22S	B2
2200	NpvT	60565	3203	27W-10S	C5
Massachusetts Ct					
17800	ODPK	60467	3423	12W-21S	C5
Massasoit Av					
7700	BRBK	60459	3211	7W-9S	C2
8600	OKLN	60459	3211	7W-9S	D4
9100	OKLN	60453	3211	7W-11S	D6
10400	CHRG	60415	3275	7W-12S	D1
10400	OKLN	60453	3275	7W-12S	D1
11000	ALSP	60482	3275	7W-12S	D3
11000	CHRG	60482	3275	7W-12S	D3
14700	OKFT	60452	3347	7W-17S	D5
N Massasoit Av					
800	CHCG	60644	3031	7W-1N	C3
800	CHCG	60651	3031	7W-1N	C2
1500	CHCG	60639	3031	7W-1N	C1
S Massasoit Av					
5100	CHCG	60638	3149	7W-5S	C2
5100	StkT	60638	3149	7W-5S	C2
7300	BDPK	60638	3149	7W-8S	C7
7300	BDPK	60638	3211	7W-8S	D1
12500	WthT	60463	3275	7W-14S	D7
12500	WthT	60803	3275	7W-14S	D7
Massasoit Ct					
14800	OKFT	60452	3347	7W-17S	D5
Massasoit St					
100	MNKA	60447	3583	33W-28S	B7
Massel Ct					
10	BNVL	60106	2971	17W-4N	C4
Massena Av					
500	WKGN	60085	2480	10W-35N	A7
1000	WKGN	60085	2479	10W-35N	E7
Massey Av					
-	PNFD	60544	3416	29W-18S	D1
Massey Rd					
2400	DndT	60118	2801	32W-15N	C5
Mast Ct					
1200	FSMR	60422	3507	2W-23S	C2
Mastadon Dr					
200	FXLK	60041	2473	26W-36N	D5
Masters Ct					
1600	NPVL	60563	3140	30W-5S	B2
1600	NpvT	60563	3140	30W-5S	B2
Masters Ln					
600	RVWD	60015	2703	13W-20N	A7
2300	RLKB	60046	2475	21W-36N	C4
2300	RLKB	60073	2475	21W-36N	C4
N Masters Ln					
2000	RLKB	60046	2475	21W-36N	C5
2100	RLKB	60073	2475	21W-36N	C5
Masters Pkwy					
1000	AURA	60506	3136	39W-6S	E4
E Masters Tr					
200	VNHL	60061	2647	16W-27N	D2
W Matalina Ct					
26100	GrtT	60041	2473	26W-36N	E3
Matanuska Tr					
1100	MHRY	60050	2527	35W-33N	A3
W Matanuska Tr					
6500	MHRY	60050	2527	35W-33N	A4
Matena Dr					
400	OSWG	60543	3200	36W-11S	A7
400	OSWG	60543	3264	35W-11S	B2
Matfield Ct					
1000	SMBG	60193	2912	24W-9N	C1
Mather Av					
7000	CHRG	60415	3210	8W-11S	E7
S Mather Av					
11200	ALSP	60803	3275	6W-13S	E3
Mather Ct					
-	RMVL	60446	3268	24W-14S	D7
4600	NPVL	60564	3266	29W-12S	C4
Mather Dr					
4600	NPVL	60564	3266	29W-12S	C4
Mather Ln					
700	BTVA	60510	3078	34W-1S	D2
Mathew St					
10600	HTLY	60142	2692	40W-21N	A6
Mathews Ct					
24900	PNFD	60585	3338	31W-15S	A3
W Mathews Dr					
7200	FftT	60423	3504	9W-25S	E7
7200	FftT	60423	3505	9W-25S	A7
N Mathewson Ln					
10	BbyT	60134	3018	39W-0S	D6
S Mathewson Ln					
200	BbyT	60134	3018	39W-0S	D7
Mathias Ct					
100	NARA	60542	3078	35W-3S	C6
Mathon Dr					
-	WKGN	60085	2537		C2
Matisse Dr					
3500	SCRL	60175	2963	38W-3N	B6
Matlock Dr					
-	BtlT	60543	3262	40W-12S	C2
W Matson Av					
5900	CHCG	60646	2919	7W-7N	B3
Matson Ln					
1900	LSLE	60532	3082	23W-4S	E7
Matsushita Ln					
-	FNPK	60131	2973	11W-3N	D5
Mattande Ln					
1000	NPVL	60540	3141	26W-6S	E5
1000	NPVL	60540	3142	26W-6S	A4
Matter Ln					
200	BRkT	60511	3196	46W-8S	A1
S Matterhorn Cir					
11600	PSPK	60464	3274	10W-13S	C5
Matteson Av					
-	MTSN	60443	3506	6W-25S	A7
Matteson St					
-	ELWD	60421	3675	25W-32S	C7
10	GLBT	60136	2799	38W-16N	A1
100	DYR	46311	3598		D1
N Matteson St					
100	ELWD	60421	3675	25W-31S	C7
S Matteson St					
100	ELWD	60421	3675	25W-31S	C6
Matthew Av					
2000	TNLK	53181	2354		C1
Matthew Ct					
900	NPVL	60540	3202	29W-8S	D1
1900	ELGN	60123	2800	36W-13N	A7
S Matthew Ct					
1800	WKGN	60048	2535	15W-31N	A6
Matthew Dr					
1500	ALGN	60102	2746	37W-19N	D2
2000	MTGY	60538	3198	40W-10S	D5
Matthew Ln					
600	CLSM	60188	2967	26W-3N	D6
1700	AURA	60504	3201	33W-8S	A2
3000	HMWD	60430	3427	3W-22S	A7
3000	HMWD	60430	3507	3W-22S	A1
Matthew Pl					
2200	ZION	60099	2421	11W-40N	D3
W Matthew St					
23500	PNFD	60586	3416	29W-19S	D3
23500	PnfT	60586	3416	29W-19S	D3
Matthews Ct					
1800	BTVA	60510	3078	34W-3S	C5
Matthias Rd					
7200	DRGV	60516	3206	19W-8S	C1
S Mattox Ln					
21500	SRWD	60404	3584	30W-26S	C2
21500	TroT	60404	3584	30W-26S	C2
Matts Rd					
10	FXLK	60020	2472	28W-36N	E4
10	FXLK	60020	2473	28W-36N	A4
Maubert Ct					
1000	CLSM	60188	2968	25W-4N	B4
N Maud Av					
1900	CHCG	60614	2977	1W-2N	E7
Maude Av					
10	FXLK	60020	2473	27W-37N	A2
1800	JltT	60433	3499	21W-25S	E7
E Maude Av					
100	ANHT	60004	2807	17W-15N	B1
400	JLET	60433	3587	23W-25S	B1
400	JltT	60433	3587	23W-25S	B1
W Maude Av					
10	ANHT	60004	2807	18W-15N	A2
400	ANHT	60004	2806	18W-15N	E1
Maude St					
-	PLNO	60545	3259	47W-12S	D4
Maue Dr					
10500	ODPK	60467	3423	13W-21S	A6
Maumell St					
100	HNDL	60521	3086	15W-4S	B7
Maura Ct					
9200	FKFT	60423	3503	11W-24S	E5
9200	FKFT	60423	3504	11W-24S	A5
Maureen Ct					
500	LYWD	60411	3510	4E-25S	C7
2000	NlxT	60451	3502	15W-24S	B6
Maureen Dr					
100	ELGN	60123	2854	35W-11N	A5
200	WLNG	60090	2755	15W-17N	A5
300	WLNG	60090	2754	15W-17N	E5
1500	HFET	60192	2855	31W-12N	D1
2100	NlxT	60451	3502	15W-24S	B5
8600	SPGV	60081	2413	31W-40N	D2
Maureen Ln					
-	MTWA	60045	2648	14W-27N	D1
-	MTWA	60048	2648	14W-27N	D1
W Maurine Dr					
21300	LkvT	60046	2475	21W-36N	D3
Maurita Ct					
19500	MKNA	60448	3503	13W-23S	B3
Maurus Ct					
5400	LSLE	60532	3142	23W-5S	E3
N Mauser Dr					
39800	WDWH	60083	2420	13W-39N	E4
39900	NptT	60083	2420	13W-39N	E4
W Maverick Tr					
13200	HMGN	60491	3343	16W-18S	E7
Maves Dr					
200	BTVA	60510	3020	35W-0S	C7
Mavis Av					
100	SEGN	60177	2908	34W-9N	D1
N Mavis Ln					
700	ADSN	60101	2970	18W-4N	E3
Mavor Ln					
2600	HDPK	60035	2704	10W-23N	A2
Mawman Av					
600	LKBF	60044	2593	11W-28N	E5
E Mawman Av					
9800	BHPK	60087	2480	9W-37N	C2
W Mawman Av					
9900	BHPK	60087	2480	10W-37N	B2
12800	BHPK	60087	2479	12W-37N	A2
12800	WrnT	60087	2479	12W-37N	A2
Max Ct					
900	WCDA	60084	2588	25W-28N	A6
3000	ISLK	60042	2586	29W-28N	C5
Maxant Dr					
600	LMBD	60148	3084	19W-2S	D3
600	YkTp	60148	3084	19W-2S	D3
600	YkTp	60523	3084	19W-2S	D3
Maxey Ct					
3600	RBBN	60472	3348	4W-16S	D4
Maxim Dr					
2100	JltT	60436	3497	26W-25S	E7
2100	RKDL	60436	3497	26W-25S	E7
2100	RKDL	60436	3585	26W-25S	E1
Maxine Cohen Cir					
-	NHBK	60062	2756	11W-18N	D4
Maxine Cohen Dr					
-	NHBK	60062	2757	9W-18N	D3
E Maxon Ln					
200	SMWD	60107	2857	28W-10N	A5
S Maxon Ln					
100	SMWD	60107	2857	28W-10N	A5
Maxon Rd					
6200	CmgT	60033	2405	53W-39N	A4
Maxwell Cir					
100	HPSR	60140	2795	47W-15N	D4
Maxwell Ct					
-	ITSC	60143	2914	19W-7N	B5
10	WNFD	60190	3023	27W-0N	D4
Maxwell Dr					
6300	WDRG	60517	3143	22W-7S	C6
Maxwell St					
300	BCHR	60401	3864	0W-37S	C2
25300	MhtT	60442	3677	19W-30S	D4
W Maxwell St					
700	CHCG	60607	3034		E7
700	CHCG	60608	3034		E7
900	CHCG	60608	3033	1W-1S	E7
Maxwelton Rd					
400	EDND	60118	2801	33W-16N	B1
May Av					
100	GNEN	60137	3025	21W-0S	D6
1100	MchT	60050	2472	30W-36N	A4
1800	JNBG	60050	2471	30W-36N	E4
1800	JNBG	60050	2472	30W-36N	A4
5200	RHMD	60071	2353	34W-41N	C7
May Ct					
200	CHHT	60411	3507	1W-23S	E4
S May Ct					
25500	CNHN	60410	3672	31W-31S	E5
May Ln					
10	SchT	60174	2964	35W-6N	C1
3700	SPGV	60081	2413	32W-39N	B5
3800	RcmT	60081	2413	32W-39N	B5
May St					
-	LktT	60441	3419	22W-21S	C6
-	PLNO	60545	3260	45W-14S	C7
10	WCHI	60185	3022	30W-0S	C7
10	WnfT	60185	3022	30W-0S	C7
100	BNVL	60106	2972	15W-5N	A2
100	GYLK	60030	2532	21W-33N	D3
100	MHTN	60442	3677	19W-31S	E5
200	WKGN	60085	2537	10W-33N	A3
300	LKPT	60441	3419	23W-20S	B4
500	ELGN	60120	2855	33W-10N	B5
500	ROSL	60172	2913	23W-8N	A3
500	SmbT	60172	2913	23W-8N	A3
700	CTCY	60409	3352	3E-18S	B7
700	GNVA	60134	3020	35W-1N	B2
800	GNVA	60174	3020	35W-1N	B2
800	SCRL	60134	3020	35W-1N	B2
800	SCRL	60174	3020	35W-1N	B2
900	WKGN	60085	2536	10W-33N	E3
1300	NndT	60014	2586	30W-27N	B7
4000	HLSD	60162	3029	13W-0S	A7
4000	WSTR	60154	3029	13W-0S	A7
4000	WSTR	60162	3029	13W-0S	A7
9700	AlqT	60102	2695	32W-22N	C4
18300	HMWD	60430	3428	1W-22S	A7
18400	HMWD	60430	3508	1W-22S	A1
28900	AntT	60081	2414	28W-38N	D7
E May St					
100	EMHT	60126	3027	15W-0N	E4
100	EMHT	60126	3028	15W-0N	A4
800	HMND	46320	3352		E7
N May St					
10	ADSN	60101	2970	18W-3N	E5
10	CHCG	60607	3033	1W-0N	E4
10	JLET	60436	3498	25W-23S	C5
700	AURA	60506	3137	36W-6S	E5
800	CHCG	60622	3033	1W-1N	E2
1200	JLET	60435	3498	25W-22S	C1
1500	CTHL	60403	3498	25W-22S	C1
S May St					
10	AURA	60506	3137	36W-7S	E7
10	JLET	60435	3498	25W-24S	C6
10	JLET	60436	3498	25W-24S	C6
700	CHCG	60607	3033	1W-0S	E6
1100	CHCG	60608	3033	1W-0S	E6
1800	CHCG	60608	3091	1W-1S	E1
3600	CHCG	60609	3091	1W-3S	E5
4800	CHCG	60609	3151	1W-5S	E1
5500	CHCG	60621	3151	1W-8S	E7
7500	CHCG	60620	3213	1W-10S	E4
7500	CHCG	60621	3213	1W-8S	E1
9900	CHCG	60643	3213	1W-11S	E7
10200	CHCG	60643	3277	1W-12S	E1
12200	CTPK	60643	3277	1W-14S	E6
12700	CTPK	60827	3277	1W-15S	E7
25500	CNHN	60410	3672	32W-31S	E5
W May St					
27000	WcnT	60084	2643	27W-27N	C2
E Maya Ln					
-	PTHT	60070	2808	13W-15N	D3
1700	MPPT	60056	2808	13W-15N	D3
Mayan Ct					
1900	JLET	60435	3498	26W-22S	A2
Mayapple Ct					
1600	NPVL	60565	3204	24W-10S	D5
2500	NHBK	60062	2756	10W-16N	E7
2500	NHBK	60062	2757	9W-16N	B7
Mayapple Ln					
2100	NHBK	60062	2756	10W-16N	E7
2100	NHBK	60062	2757	10W-16N	A7
Mayberry Ct					
100	RGMW	60008	2805	21W-14N	D4
700	LIHL	60156	2693	37W-22N	B4
Mayberry Ln					
-	FKFT	60423	3592	9W-27S	D4
Mayborne Ln					
300	GNVA	60134	3019	37W-1N	C2

STREET Block	City	ZIP	Map#	CGS	Grid
Maybrook Dr					
1300	MYWD	60153	3030	10W-0S	A5
Maybrook Sq					
1300	MYWD	60153	3030	10W-0S	B5
Maycliff Dr					
14300	ODPK	60462	3346	10W-17S	A5
Maydell Ct					
19800	FftT	60477	3504	11W-23S	A4
19800	TYPK	60477	3504	11W-23S	A4
Mayer Av					
10	WLNG	60090	2755	14W-18N	B3
Mayer Ct					
200	DRFD	60015	2756	11W-20N	E2
Mayfair Av					
1600	WSTR	60154	3086	13W-2S	E3
3000	LGPK	60154	3086	13W-2S	E4
3000	LGPK	60525	3086	13W-2S	E4
3000	PvsT	60154	3086	13W-2S	E4
3000	PvsT	60525	3086	13W-2S	E4
3000	PvsT	60558	3086	13W-2S	E4
Mayfair Ct					
10	LMNT	60439	3270	18W-13S	E5
10	WNVL	60555	3080	30W-1S	C2
100	OSWG	60543	3200	35W-10S	A6
300	MNSR	46321	3510		D4
2400	NlxT	60433	3500	20W-23S	B4
4300	CCHL	60478	3426	5W-21S	C7
20900	MKNA	60448	3502	14W-25S	E7
Mayfair Ct N					
500	BFGV	60089	2754	17W-18N	B3
Mayfair Ct S					
600	BFGV	60089	2754	17W-18N	B4
Mayfair Dr					
-	LMNT	60439	3342	20W-15S	B1
10	AURA	60504	3202	30W-8S	A1
100	AddT	60106	2971	17W-4N	C4
600	CLSM	60188	2967	26W-4N	D5
900	LYVL	60048	2591	17W-27N	C7
1200	CPVL	60110	2748	32W-18N	D5
2400	JltT	60433	3500	20W-23S	B4
2400	NlxT	60433	3500	20W-23S	B4
4300	JNBG	60050	2472	30W-36N	A4
4300	MchT	60050	2472	30W-36N	A4
20900	MKNA	60448	3502	14W-25S	E7
Mayfair Ln					
-	MTSN	60443	3594	6W-25S	A1
10	AURA	60504	3202	30W-8S	A1
10	LNSH	60069	2702	13W-23N	D3
200	SEGN	60177	2908	35W-8N	B3
200	SMBG	60193	2859	21W-10N	E6
300	BFGV	60089	2754	17W-18N	B4
500	NPVL	60565	3203	27W-10S	C6
700	ALGN	60102	2694	35W-20N	B7
1100	GLNC	60022	2758	7W-18N	B4
1200	GYLK	60030	2532	21W-34N	C1
1300	GYLK	60030	2475	21W-34N	C7
7800	DRN	60561	3207	17W-8S	C2
9200	ODPK	60462	3345	11W-18S	E7
Mayfair Pl					
2200	MDLN	60060	2647	17W-25N	B5
N Mayfair Pl					
100	CHHT	60411	3508	1W-23S	A3
S Mayfair Pl					
10	CHHT	60411	3508	1W-23S	A4
Mayfair Rd					
10	MltT	60148	3084	21W-2S	A3
600	YkTp	60148	3084	20W-2S	A3
E Mayfair Rd					
600	ANHT	60005	2807	17W-13N	B6
1000	ANHT	60004	2807	17W-13N	B5
2500	ANHT	60056	2807	16W-13N	D5
2500	MPPT	60004	2807	16W-13N	D5
2500	MPPT	60056	2807	16W-13N	D5
Mayfair Wy					
100	MNSR	46321	3510		D4
Mayfield Av					
-	BmnT	60445	3347	7W-17S	C4
10	CLLK	60014	2639	37W-25N	B4
2000	JLET	60435	3497	26W-23S	E4
8300	BRBK	60459	3211	7W-9S	C4
8700	OKLN	60453	3211	7W-10S	C5
8700	OKLN	60459	3211	7W-10S	C5
9900	CHRG	60415	3211	7W-11S	C7
9900	CHRG	60453	3211	7W-11S	C7
10100	CHRG	60415	3275	7W-11S	C1
10100	OKLN	60415	3275	7W-11S	C1
10100	OKLN	60453	3275	7W-11S	C1
10300	CHRG	60453	3275	7W-12S	C1
11000	ALSP	60482	3275	7W-12S	C3
11000	CHRG	60482	3275	7W-12S	C3
N Mayfield Av					
10	CHCG	60644	3031	7W-0N	C4
1000	CHCG	60651	3031	7W-1N	C2
1600	CHCG	60639	3031	7W-2N	C1
1700	CHCG	60639	2975	7W-2N	C7
S Mayfield Av					
10	CHCG	60644	3031	7W-0S	C5
1100	CCRO	60644	3031	7W-0S	C7
1100	CCRO	60804	3031	7W-0S	C7
5100	CHCG	60638	3149	7W-5S	C2
5100	StkT	60638	3149	7W-5S	C2
6400	BDPK	60638	3149	7W-7S	C5
11500	ALSP	60482	3275	7W-13S	C4
11500	ALSP	60803	3275	7W-13S	C4
W Mayfield Av					
1200	JLET	60435	3498	25W-23S	B3
2200	JLET	60435	3497	26W-23S	E4
Mayfield Ct					
400	NPVL	60565	3203	27W-10S	B7
400	WldT	60565	3203	27W-10S	B7
500	MltT	60137	3083	21W-2S	D3
1900	RMVL	60446	3339	27W-17S	C5
2400	MTGY	60538	3198	39W-10S	D7
12500	ALSP	60803	3275	7W-14S	C6
Mayfield Dr					
-	GLHT	60139	3025	23W-1N	A2
-	MltT	60139	3025	23W-1N	A2
-	MltT	60188	3025	23W-1N	A2
100	BGBK	60440	3268	23W-11S	E1
100	SMWD	60107	2857	27W-10N	B5
800	RLKB	60073	2474	24W-34N	C7
2300	MTGY	60538	3198	39W-10S	D6
2600	PKRG	60068	2863	11W-10N	C4
Mayfield Ln					
100	MltT	60137	3083	21W-2S	D3
400	AURA	60504	3201	31W-8S	D2
1000	HFET	60169	2804	24W-12N	C7
10600	HTLY	60142	2692	39W-21N	C6
21600	DRPK	60010	2698	23W-21N	D5
Mayfield Pl					
19400	FftT	60423	3504	9W-23S	D3
19400	FftT	60477	3504	9W-23S	D3
19400	TYPK	60423	3504	9W-23S	D3
19400	TYPK	60477	3504	9W-23S	D3
Mayfield St					
900	CRY	60013	2695	32W-23N	B1
Mayflower					
3200	LGGV	60047	2700	19W-21N	B6
Mayflower Av					
10	LslT	60540	3142	25W-6S	B4
Mayflower Ct					
200	GRNE	60031	2535	14W-33N	C2
5400	RGMW	60008	2860	19W-12N	D1
Mayflower Dr					
10	BTVA	60510	3078	33W-1S	E1
Mayflower Ln					
200	BGBK	60490	3267	26W-11S	E1
200	BRLT	60103	2967	27W-5N	B1
400	HRPK	60103	2967	27W-5N	B1
400	HRPK	60133	2967	27W-5N	B1
10200	HTLY	60142	2692	39W-21N	C5
11000	ODPK	60467	3344	13W-16S	E3
11000	ODPK	60467	3345	13W-16S	A3
Mayflower Pl					
100	MltT	60187	3023	26W-0N	E5
Mayflower Rd					
10	VNHL	60061	2647	16W-25N	C5
N Mayflower Rd					
10	LKFT	60045	2650	9W-26N	C3
S Mayflower Rd					
10	LKFT	60045	2650	9W-25N	C4
Mayflower St					
2200	AURA	60506	3137	38W-6S	A6
Mayhaw					
-	CLLK	60012	2640	33W-27N	E1
Mayher Dr					
17700	ODPK	60467	3422	14W-21S	D6
May Kay St					
3300	ZION	60099	2422	10W-39N	A5
Mayland Villa					
14400	VrnT	60069	2702	14W-23N	B2
Mayland Villa Ct					
14400	VrnT	60069	2702	14W-23N	C2
S Mayleon Dr					
16300	PnfT	60586	3416	28W-19S	E3
Maynard Dr					
-	NLES	60714	2864	10W-12N	B1
2700	MaiT	60025	2864	10W-12N	B1
W Maynard Dr					
8200	MaiT	60025	2864	10W-12N	B1
8200	NLES	60714	2864	10W-12N	B1
W Maynard Ovl					
8300	NLES	60714	2864	10W-12N	A1
W Maynard Rd					
8300	NLES	60714	2864	10W-12N	A1
8500	GNVW	60025	2864	10W-12N	A1
N Maynard Ter					
9800	NLES	60714	2864	10W-11N	A2
Mayo Av					
1400	WHTN	60187	3082	25W-1S	A2
Mayo Ct					
-	YkTp	60126	3028	15W-0S	A6
7500	SPGV	60081	2414	30W-39N	A5
Mayo Dr					
15000	ODPK	60462	3346	11W-17S	A6
Mayo Ln					
300	BMDL	60101	2969	22W-4N	D2
300	BMDL	60108	2969	22W-4N	D2
300	BmdT	60101	2969	22W-4N	D2
Mayor Roger Byrne Blvd					
-	VNHL	60061	2647	16W-25N	D5
Mayors Row					
9100	ODHL	60487	3424	11W-19S	A2
W Maypole Av					
1600	CHCG	60607	3033	2W-0N	C4
1600	CHCG	60612	3033	2W-0N	C4
3100	CHCG	60612	3032	3W-0N	E4
3100	CHCG	60624	3032	4W-0N	D4
4500	CHCG	60644	3032	5W-0N	A4
4800	CHCG	60644	3031	6W-0N	E4
S Mayre Av					
10300	NPVL	60564	3266	30W-12S	B2
10300	WldT	60564	3266	30W-12S	B2
Mayre Rd					
-	WldT	60564	3266	30W-12S	B3
Mays					
-	NLNX	60451	3588	19W-26S	D3
Mays Lake Ct					
-	LktT	60403	3417	26W-19S	D2
Mays Lake Dr					
21400	LktT	60403	3417	26W-19S	E2
Maytree Ln					
400	PTON	60468	3860	10W-37S	C4
S Maywood Av					
5200	HMND	46320	3352		E6
Maywood Ct					
800	LYVL	60048	2647	16W-27N	D1
2600	RLKP	60030	2532	22W-31N	B7
Maywood Dr					
2200	BLWD	60104	3029	11W-0S	C5
2200	MYWD	60153	3029	11W-0S	C5
N Maywood Dr					
1400	MYWD	60153	3029	11W-0S	E5
S Maywood Dr					
1700	MYWD	60153	3029	11W-0S	D5
1900	BLWD	60104	3029	11W-0S	D5
Maywood Ln					
500	HFET	60169	2858	24W-11N	E4
500	LslT	60532	3143	22W-6S	C5
800	SMBG	60194	2858	26W-11N	A3
N Maywood Rd					
10	LKFT	60045	2650	10W-26N	B4
S Maywood Rd					
10	LKFT	60045	2650	10W-25N	B4
Mazalin Dr					
900	SRWD	60404	3496	30W-22S	C2
Mc 8th Dr					
-	CHCG	60616	3092		E2
McAdam Rd					
1800	DRN	60561	3144	18W-7S	E7
McAlister Av					
400	WKGN	60085	2537	10W-33N	A3
1000	NCHI	60064	2537	10W-32N	A4
S McAlister Av					
500	WKGN	60085	2537	10W-33N	A4
900	NCHI	60064	2537	10W-33N	A4
S McAllister Rd					
16500	JLET	60586	3417	28W-19S	A4
16500	PnfT	60586	3417	28W-19S	A4
McAndrews Gln					
-	BLVY	60050	2526	36W-31N	E7
-	MHRY	60050	2526	36W-31N	E7
McArdle Dr					
600	CLLK	60014	2640	33W-24N	D7
McAree Av					
39000	BHPK	60087	2421	11W-39N	C6
39000	BHPK	60099	2421	11W-39N	C6
39000	WKGN	60087	2421	12W-39N	C6
N McAree Rd					
10	WKGN	60085	2536	11W-34N	C1
400	WKGN	60085	2479	12W-33N	C7
1700	WKGN	60087	2479	12W-36N	C5
N McAree Rd					
1700	WkgT	60085	2479	12W-36N	C5
2600	BHPK	60087	2479	11W-37N	C3
3000	WkgT	60087	2479	12W-37N	C2
S McAree Rd					
700	WKGN	60085	2536	12W-33N	C4
900	NCHI	60064	2536	12W-33N	C4
900	WKGN	60064	2536	12W-33N	C4
McArthur Lp					
10	HDPK	60035	2650	9W-24N	D7
McBreen Av					
3200	RBBN	60472	3348	4W-16S	E3
McBride St					
400	ELGN	60120	2854	34W-12N	E2
McCabe Av					
1100	EGvT	60007	2915	16W-8N	D1
1100	EGVV	60007	2915	16W-8N	D1
3700	NndT	60014	2586	30W-28N	A6
McCabe Dr					
10	SMWD	60107	2857	28W-10N	A5
13500	OrlT	60467	3344	14W-16S	D3
13500	PlsT	60467	3344	14W-16S	D3
13800	ODPK	60467	3344	14W-16S	D3
McCabe Ln					
-	LKPT	60432	3420	20W-21S	B7
McCain Ct					
200	DSPN	60016	2862	15W-10N	B5
McCameron Av					
100	LktT	60441	3419	21W-18S	E1
1200	LktT	60441	3420	21W-18S	A1
1300	HmrT	60441	3420	20W-18S	A1
W McCampbell Dr					
6800	MonT	60449	3682	8W-30S	B4
McCannon Rd					
-	GwdT	60098	2524	41W-32N	E4
-	WDSK	60098	2524	41W-32N	D4
600	SgrT	60554	3196	44W-8S	E3
McCannon St					
10	SRGV	60554	3135	42W-7S	C7
McCarron Rd					
10	MltT	60137	3083	22W-2S	C4
S McCarron Rd					
17100	LKPT	60441	3420	18W-20S	E5
17100	LKPT	60491	3420	18W-20S	E5
17500	HMGN	60491	3421	18W-21S	A6
17700	HMGN	60491	3420	18W-21S	E6
McCarthy Dr					
-	CHCG	60616	3092		E2
McCarthy Rd					
10	BlmT	60466	3595	3W-27S	C4
10	PKFT	60466	3595	3W-27S	B4
400	LMNT	60439	3270	19W-13S	E5
1000	LMNT	60439	3271	17W-14S	D6
12200	LMNT	60439	3272	15W-14S	A6
12200	PlsT	60439	3272	15W-14S	A6
12200	PlsT	60464	3272	15W-14S	A6
12200	PSPK	60439	3272	15W-14S	A6
N McCarthy Rd					
38100	NptT	60031	2478	15W-38N	B1
38100	NptT	60083	2478	15W-38N	B1
38100	WDWH	60031	2478	15W-38N	B1
38100	WDWH	60083	2478	15W-38N	B1
38100	WKGN	60083	2478	15W-38N	B1
38100	WKGN	60087	2478	15W-38N	B1
S McCarthy Rd					
12400	PSHT	60463	3274	9W-14S	D7
12400	PSHT	60464	3274	9W-14S	D7
12400	PSPK	60464	3274	9W-14S	D7
W McCarthy Rd					
7700	PSHT	60463	3274	9W-14S	C6
7700	PSHT	60464	3274	9W-14S	C6
7700	PSPK	60463	3274	9W-14S	C6
7700	PSPK	60464	3274	9W-14S	C6
7800	PSPK	60463	3274	9W-14S	C6
9600	PlsT	60464	3273	13W-14S	B6
9600	PSPK	60464	3273	13W-14S	B6
11000	PlsT	60464	3272	14W-14S	D6
11000	PSPK	60464	3272	14W-14S	D6
11600	LmnT	60439	3272	14W-14S	C6
11600	PlsT	60439	3272	14W-14S	C6
11600	PSPK	60439	3272	14W-14S	C6
McCarthy St					
400	LMNT	60439	3270	19W-14S	E6
McCartney Dr					
2200	NPVL	60565	3203	26W-10S	E5
McChesney Rd					
-	WnfT	60510	3021	32W-0S	D6
-	WnfT	60510	3079	32W-0S	D1
300	WCHI	60185	3021	32W-0S	D7
McClaran Av					
700	AraT	60506	3199	38W-8S	A2
800	AraT	60538	3199	38W-8S	A2
McClean Av					
-	NHLK	60164	2972	13W-2N	E7
McClellan Av					
-	PNFD	60586	3416	29W-19S	E3
-	PnfT	60586	3416	29W-19S	E3
15900	PNFD	60544	3416	28W-19S	E2
15900	PnfT	60544	3416	28W-19S	E3
N McClellan Av					
6100	CHCG	60646	2919	7W-7N	C3
McClellan Ct					
100	BRLT	60103	2911	28W-7N	A5
McClellan Dr					
-	LkvT	60046	2417	21W-39N	E5
-	LNHT	60046	2417	21W-39N	E5
McClellan St					
100	BRLT	60103	2910	29W-7N	E5
100	BRLT	60103	2911	28W-7N	A5
McClennan Ct					
2700	NPVL	60563	3140	29W-5S	C3
McClintock Dr					
600	BRRG	60527	3208	14W-8S	C1
W McClintock Rd					
22700	CNHN	60410	3585	28W-27S	A5
22700	JLET	60410	3585	28W-27S	A5
23200	CNHN	60410	3584	29W-27S	D5
23900	CNHN	60436	3584	29W-27S	D6
McClure Av					
300	MHTN	60442	3677	19W-31S	D6
500	ELGN	60123	2854	34W-12N	D3
McClure Rd					
600	AraT	60502	3139	33W-6S	A5
600	AraT	60504	3139	33W-7S	A6
600	AraT	60505	3139	33W-6S	A6
600	AURA	60502	3139	33W-6S	A6
1300	AURA	60505	3139	33W-5S	A4
4300	GRNE	60031	2478	14W-34N	C7
N McClurg Ct					
300	CHCG	60611	3034	0E-0N	D3
McClurg Dr					
1000	BTVA	60510	3077	36W-2S	E4
McComb St					
100	HRVD	60033	2406	50W-38N	B7
E McConnell Av					
100	WCHI	60185	3022	29W-1N	C4
W McConnell Av					
100	WCHI	60185	3022	30W-1N	C4
McConnell Rd					
900	WDSK	60098	2581	41W-30N	E2
8900	DrrT	60098	2583	38W-29N	A4
9400	DrrT	60098	2582	38W-29N	E4
9800	WDSK	60098	2582	38W-29N	D4
McConnell St					
10200	RHMD	60071	2353	34W-42N	C7
10300	RcmT	60071	2353	34W-42N	C6
McConnoiche Ct					
900	WDND	60118	2800	35W-16N	B1
McConnor Pkwy					
1400	SMBG	60173	2859	21W-12N	E1
1400	SMBG	60173	2860	21W-12N	A1
1800	RGMW	60173	2860	20W-12N	A2
N McCook Av					
5900	CHCG	60646	2919	7W-7N	B4
McCook Ct					
200	BRLT	60103	2911	28W-7N	A5
McCord Trc					
10	PlsT	60464	3345	12W-15S	D1
10	PSPK	60464	3273	12W-15S	D7
10	PSPK	60464	3345	12W-15S	D1
S McCorkle Av					
25500	MONE	60449	3683	6W-31S	A5
McCormack Dr					
1500	HFET	60169	2858	25W-12N	B1
McCormick Av					
10	MltT	60137	3083	22W-1S	C2
1500	MDLN	60060	2647	17W-25N	A4
2900	BKFD	60513	3088	10W-2S	A4
3800	LYNS	60513	3088	10W-3S	A6
3800	LYNS	60534	3088	10W-3S	A6
McCormick Blvd					
1800	EVTN	60201	2866	3W-11N	E2
1800	EVTN	60201	2867	3W-12N	A1
2000	SKOK	60201	2866	4W-11N	D2
2000	SKOK	60203	2866	4W-11N	D2
7500	SKOK	60076	2866	4W-9N	D6
N McCormick Blvd					
6400	CHCG	60659	2920	4W-8N	D3
6400	LNWD	60659	2920	4W-8N	D3
6400	LNWD	60712	2920	4W-8N	D2
7100	LNWD	60076	2920	4W-8N	D1
7100	SKOK	60076	2920	4W-8N	D1
7200	SKOK	60076	2866	4W-9N	D7
McCormick Dr					
400	LKFT	60045	2650	9W-25N	B6
3400	MmT	60037	2704	8W-24N	D1
McCormick Ln					
-	HmrT	60441	3420	19W-20S	E5
-	LKPT	60441	3420	19W-20S	E5
800	WCHI	60185	3022	29W-1N	E2
1700	HRPK	60133	2967	27W-5N	D1
30600	WNVL	60555	3081	28W-3S	A7
McCormick Pl					
1400	WHTN	60187	3081	26W-1S	D2
N McCormick Rd					
6200	CHCG	60659	2920	4W-7N	D3
6200	LNWD	60659	2920	4W-7N	D3
6200	LNWD	60712	2920	4W-7N	D3
E McCormick Sq					
-	CHCG	60616	3092	0E-2S	D2
McCormick St					
1100	CLSM	60188	2968	26W-4N	A3
McCornack Rd					
10	GLBT	60136	2798	39W-15N	E4
10	RtdT	60124	2798	39W-15N	E4
10	RtdT	60136	2798	39W-15N	E4
W McCowan St					
25400	CNHN	60410	3672	31W-30S	E3
McCoy Dr					
-	AURA	60504	3202	30W-7S	A1
-	AURA	60505	3201	32W-8S	C1
-	NPVL	60504	3202	30W-7S	A1
-	NPVL	60540	3202	29W-7S	C1
-	NpvT	60504	3201	31W-7S	E1
-	PvsT	60141	3088	10W-1S	A1
2400	AURA	60502	3201	32W-8S	C1
2400	AURA	60504	3201	32W-8S	C1
2500	NpvT	60502	3201	32W-7S	C1
McCraren Rd					
1600	HDPK	60035	2704	9W-22N	B4
McCrea Dr					
100	CHCG	60624	3032	4W-0N	C4
McCreey Av					
200	GNEN	60137	3083	23W-1S	A2
300	WHTN	60137	3083	23W-1S	A2
300	WHTN	60187	3083	23W-1S	A2
McCullom St					
100	CLLK	60014	2640	35W-26N	B2
McCullom Lake Rd					
3600	MHRY	60050	2528	31W-33N	C2
3700	MchT	60050	2528	33W-34N	A1
4300	JNBG	60050	2528	33W-34N	A1
4300	MCLK	60050	2528	33W-34N	A1
4400	JNBG	60050	2471	33W-34N	A7
4400	MchT	60050	2470	33W-34N	D7
4400	MchT	60050	2471	33W-34N	A7
4400	MCLK	60050	2470	33W-34N	E7
4400	MCLK	60050	2471	33W-34N	A7
4600	JNBG	60050	2470	33W-34N	D7
5300	MchT	60097	2470	33W-34N	D7
6900	MchT	60097	2469	36W-35N	E5
McDaniel Av					
900	EVTN	60202	2866	3W-10N	D4
900	SKOK	60076	2866	3W-10N	D4
900	SKOK	60202	2866	3W-10N	D4
1900	EVTN	60201	2866	4W-12N	D1
1900	SKOK	60201	2866	4W-11N	D2
1900	SKOK	60203	2866	4W-11N	D2
2600	EVTN	60201	2812	3W-13N	D7
2700	WLMT	60091	2812	3W-13N	D7
2700	WLMT	60201	2812	3W-13N	D7
S McDaniel Ct					
13000	ALSP	60803	3348	5W-15S	A1
S McDaniel St					
12200	ALSP	60803	3276	5W-14S	A6
McDaniels Av					
1100	HDPK	60035	2704	8W-21N	D6
McDaniels Cir					
400	CNHL	60514	3145	17W-5S	C2
McDaniels St					
12700	ALSP	60803	3276	5W-15S	A7
McDermott Dr					
5200	BKLY	60163	3028	14W-0N	C3
S McDermott St					
2800	CHCG	60608	3091	1W-2S	D3
McDevitt Cir					
1500	EGVV	60007	2913	21W-9N	E1
1500	EGVV	60007	2914	21W-9N	A1
McDivitt Dr					
600	NLNX	60451	3589	18W-25S	A1
McDole Dr					
900	SgrT	60554	3136	40W-5S	B3
McDole Dr					
900	SRGV	60554	3136	40W-5S	B3
McDonald Av					
10	JLET	60431	3496	29W-24S	E5
100	WnfT	60185	3022	29W-0N	D5
1100	AraT	60506	3199	37W-8S	C1
1100	AURA	60506	3199	37W-8S	C1
McDonald Dr					
-	CNHN	60410	3584	29W-27S	E5
-	CnhT	60410	3584	29W-27S	E5
1400	HmrT	60441	3420	20W-18S	A1
1400	LKPT	60441	3420	20W-18S	B1
McDonald Ln					
10	FKFT	60423	3591	12W-25S	D1
McDonald Rd					
10	ElgT	60124	2907	38W-8N	A4
10	ElgT	60175	2907	38W-8N	A4
10	PltT	60124	2905	42W-8N	C4
10	PltT	60124	2906	39W-8N	D4
10	PltT	60175	2905	41W-8N	E4
10	PltT	60175	2906	39W-8N	D4
300	PltT	60140	2905	43W-8N	A3
300	PltT	60151	2905	43W-8N	A3
700	ElgT	60177	2907	36W-8N	D4
700	PltT	60124	2907	39W-8N	A4
700	PltT	60175	2907	39W-8N	A4
700	SEGN	60177	2907	36W-8N	D4
1700	SEGN	60175	2907	36W-8N	D4
McDonalds Ct					
24200	TroT	60404	3584	30W-25S	C1
McDonalds Dr					
2100	OKBK	60523	3085	16W-1S	E2
McDonough Dr					
-	HFET	60192	2802	30W-12N	B7
McDonough Rd					
1600	HFET	60192	2856	30W-12N	B1
1600	HnrT	60192	2856	30W-12N	B1
1800	HFET	60192	2802	30W-12N	B7
1800	HnrT	60120	2856	30W-12N	B1
5400	HnrT	60192	2802	30W-12N	B7
McDonough St					
1600	JLET	60436	3498	26W-24S	A6
2000	JLET	60436	3497	27W-24S	D6
2700	JLET	60431	3497	28W-24S	A6
2700	TroT	60436	3497	27W-24S	B6
3800	JLET	60431	3496	29W-24S	E6
3800	TroT	60431	3496	29W-24S	E6
3800	TroT	60431	3497	28W-24S	A6
W McDonough St					
10	JLET	60436	3498	24W-24S	E6
W McDonough St US-6					
10	JLET	60436	3498	24W-24S	E6
W McDonough St US-52					
10	JLET	60436	3498	24W-24S	E6
McDowell Av					
1600	AURA	60504	3201	33W-9S	B5
S McDowell Av					
4500	CHCG	60609	3091	1W-4S	D7
McDowell Rd					
100	NPVL	60563	3140	29W-5S	D2
1700	NpvT	60563	3140	29W-5S	C2
McDuffee Cir					
2500	NARA	60542	3076	39W-3S	D7
2800	NARA	60506	3076	39W-3S	D7
E McEldowney St					
10	CHHT	60411	3596	1W-25S	A1
W McEldowney St					
10	CHHT	60411	3596	1W-25S	A1
McEvilly Rd					
100	AxST	60447	3672	33W-28S	A1
100	MNKA	60447	3672	33W-28S	A1
25300	CnhT	60447	3672	32W-28S	C1
McGarity Rd					
10	PKFT	60466	3595	3W-27S	B4
McGaw Rd					
-	WrnT	60031	2535	14W-32N	C4
-	WrnT	60085	2535	13W-32N	E4
4500	WKGN	60085	2535	14W-32N	C4
McGilvary Dr					
20500	LktT	60403	3418	26W-19S	A3
20500	LktT	60441	3418	26W-19S	A3
W McGilvary Dr					
20500	CTHL	60403	3418	25W-19S	B3
20500	LktT	60403	3418	25W-19S	B3
McGinty St					
-	DMND	60416	3941	33W-39S	B2
N McGinty St					
-	DMND	60416	3941	33W-39S	B2
S McGinty St					
100	DMND	60416	3941	33W-40S	B2
McGlashen Dr					
10	SBTN	60010	2803	26W-13N	D5
McGlinnin Ct					
1000	LKFT	60045	2649	12W-27N	B2
McGonagle Ct					
100	CmpT	60119	3018	41W-2N	A2
McGovern St					
1600	HDPK	60035	2704	8W-22N	E5
McGovney St					
11000	MKNA	60448	3503	13W-23S	A4
McGowan Woods Rd					
-	CNHN	60410	3672	32W-29S	E2
-	CNHN	60447	3672	32W-29S	E2
25600	CnhT	60447	3672	32W-29S	D2
McGrath Dr					
300	OSWG	60543	3264	34W-11S	D2
S McGrath Dr					
16100	PnfT	60586	3416	29W-19S	E3
McGrath Ln					
400	WldT	60564	3266	29W-11S	D2
700	NPVL	60564	3266	29W-11S	D2
N McGraw Ct					
23600	LKBN	60010	2697	27W-23N	B1
McGraw Ln					
10	DndT	60118	2801	33W-15N	C4
10	EDND	60118	2801	33W-15N	C4
McGregor Ct					
10	HNWD	60047	2645	21W-24N	C7
McGregor Ln					
200	NpvT	60563	3140	30W-5S	B3
McGuire Pkwy					
11200	LmnT	60439	3271	17W-13S	B4
McGuire Rd					
18700	HtdT	60033	2464	49W-37N	B1
20100	DhmT	60033	2464	48W-37N	E2
20100	HRVD	60033	2464	48W-37N	E2
23500	CstT	60481	4031	29W-43S	E3
23500	RedT	60481	4031	29W-43S	E3
McGuire Rd CO-A22					
18700	HtdT	60033	2464	49W-37N	B1
20100	DhmT	60033	2464	48W-37N	E2
20100	HRVD	60033	2464	48W-37N	E2
McHenry Av					
-	MHRY	60050	2528	32W-31N	C6
-	NndT	60050	2528	32W-31N	C6
10	CLLK	60014	2640	35W-25N	A4

STREET Block	City	ZIP	Map#	CGS	Grid
McHenry Av					
100	CLLK	60014	2639	36W-24N	E6
200	WDSK	60098	2524	41W-31N	E7
800	CLLK	60014	2693	36W-24N	E1
2700	NPVL	60563	3140	29W-5S	C4
McHenry Av CO-V29					
300	CLLK	60014	2639	36W-24N	E6
800	CLLK	60014	2693	36W-24N	E1
McHenry Av SR-120					
200	WDSK	60098	2524	41W-31N	D7
McHenry Rd					
10	BFGV	60089	2754	16W-20N	C1
10	WLNG	60090	2755	15W-18N	A4
600	BFGV	60089	2701	17W-21N	B7
700	WLNG	60090	2754	16W-18N	D2
900	WLNG	60089	2754	16W-18N	D2
McHenry Rd SR-83					
10	BFGV	60089	2754	16W-20N	C1
400	WLNG	60090	2755	15W-18N	A3
500	WLNG	60090	2754	16W-18N	D2
600	BFGV	60089	2701	17W-21N	B7
900	WLNG	60089	2754	16W-18N	D2
McHenry Dam Rd					
-	NndT	60051	2585	31W-30N	D1
McHugh Rd					
300	BtlT	60560	3333	42W-14S	D1
300	YKVL	60560	3333	42W-15S	D1
1000	BtlT	60560	3261	42W-14S	D7
1000	YKVL	60560	3261	42W-14S	D7
McIntosh Av					
10	CNHL	60514	3145	17W-5S	D2
McIntosh Ct					
800	PTHT	60070	2808	13W-15N	E2
9000	LKWD	60014	2693	37W-23N	A1
McIntosh Dr					
7600	PlsT	60463	3346	9W-15S	D2
7600	PSHT	60462	3346	9W-15S	D2
7600	PSHT	60463	3346	9W-15S	D2
13400	ODPK	60462	3346	9W-15S	D2
McIntosh Ln					
900	JltT	60433	3499	22W-24S	D6
McIntyre Dr					
200	LktT	60441	3419	21W-18S	E1
N McIntyre St					
100	WMTN	60481	3853	27W-38S	D6
S McIntyre St					
100	WMTN	60481	3853	27W-38S	D6
McKay Cir					
900	GYLK	60030	2533	19W-34N	C1
McKay Dr					
200	SchT	60175	2907	36W-6N	E6
200	SchT	60175	2908	36W-6N	A6
McKay St					
1100	JltT	60432	3499	22W-22S	D2
1200	JLET	60432	3499	22W-22S	D2
1600	WKGN	60087	2479	11W-37N	D2
11000	LydT	60164	2972	13W-3N	D5
McKee St					
10	GnvT	60510	3077	38W-0S	B1
200	BTVA	60510	3077	37W-0S	D1
300	BTVA	60510	3078	36W-1S	A1
McKenna Ct					
10400	ODPK	60467	3423	13W-20S	B4
E McKenna Ct					
300	YkTp	60126	3028	15W-0S	B7
McKenna Dr					
2700	NLNX	60451	3589	18W-27S	B5
S McKenna Dr					
17000	PnfT	60586	3416	30W-20S	B5
17200	JLET	60586	3416	30W-20S	B6
McKenna Wy					
11200	FKFT	60423	3590	14W-28S	E6
McKenzie Av					
1400	HmrT	60441	3420	20W-18S	B1
1400	LktT	60441	3420	20W-18S	A1
16500	LKPT	60441	3420	20W-18S	B1
McKenzie Ct					
10	LIHL	60156	2692	39W-23N	D2
500	LKVL	60046	2417	22W-39N	B5
2400	AURA	60503	3201	32W-10S	C6
McKenzie Dr					
5400	LIHL	60156	2692	39W-23N	C2
McKenzie Station Dr					
800	LSLE	60532	3143	22W-5S	B2
McKibbin Rd					
-	HDPK	60037	2704	8W-23N	D1
-	MrnT	60037	2704	8W-23N	D1
McKinley Av					
10	FXLK	60020	2473	28W-36N	A3
10	GNVA	60134	3020	35W-1N	B3
10	LKVL	60046	2475	22W-37N	A1
10	STGR	60475	3596	1W-28S	A6
100	LYVL	60048	2591	17W-28N	C5
100	WKGN	60085	2537	10W-33N	A3
500	MDLN	60060	2590	18W-27N	E7
700	SCRL	60134	3020	35W-1N	B3
700	SCRL	60174	3020	35W-1N	B3
900	MDLN	60060	2591	18W-28N	A7
1100	CHHT	60411	3508	0W-25S	B7
4700	LSLE	60532	3143	23W-5S	A2
10900	HBRN	60034	2351	40W-41N	A7
12000	HBRN	60034	2350	41W-41N	E7
S McKinley Av					
500	ANHT	60005	2807	17W-13N	C6
11900	PlsT	60464	3273	11W-14S	E5
11900	PSPK	60464	3273	11W-14S	E5
14300	POSN	60469	3349	3W-17S	B4
W McKinley Av					
200	EMHT	60126	3027	16W-0N	D5
McKinley Ct					
900	LKPT	60441	3419	22W-19S	D3
McKinley Dr					
8800	AlqT	60010	2696	29W-23N	D2
McKinley Ln					
10	SMWD	60107	2856	29W-10N	E6
700	HNDL	60521	3146	14W-5S	C3
N McKinley Rd					
600	LKFT	60045	2650	10W-26N	A3
1400	LKFT	60045	2593	10W-28N	E7
1500	LKBF	60044	2593	10W-28N	E7
1500	LKBF	60045	2593	10W-28N	E7
McKinley St					
10	LIHL	60156	2693	35W-22N	E3
10	SCRL	60174	3020	35W-2N	B1
400	EGvT	60018	2861	16W-9N	E7
400	EGvT	60018	2862	15W-9N	A7
500	BTVA	60510	3078	36W-1S	A3
900	JLET	60436	3498	24W-25S	E7
1000	LKPT	60441	3419	22W-19S	D3
1200	JLET	60436	3586	24W-26S	E2
1200	JltT	60436	3586	24W-26S	E2
E McKinley St					
100	HRVD	60033	2406	50W-38N	B6
S McKinley St					
25700	MONE	60449	3682	7W-31S	E5
W McKinley St					
100	HRVD	60033	2406	50W-38N	A6
McKinley Woods Rd					
25300	CNHN	60410	3672	32W-30S	D5
25300	CnhT	60410	3672	32W-30S	D5
S McKinley Woods Rd					
24600	CNHN	60410	3672	32W-31S	D7
24600	CnhT	60410	3672	32W-31S	D7
24600	WilC	60410	3672	32W-32S	D7
26400	CNHN	60410	3761	32W-32S	D2
26400	CnhT	60410	3761	32W-32S	D2
26400	WilC	60410	3761	32W-32S	D2
McKinstry Dr					
100	ELGN	60123	2853	36W-11N	E4
100	ElgT	60123	2853	36W-11N	E4
McKone Ct					
4600	RGMW	60008	2805	20W-13N	E5
E McKone Ct					
400	ANHT	60005	2861	17W-12N	B1
McKool Av					
-	HRPK	60107	2911	27W-9N	C1
100	RMVL	60446	3341	27W-16S	A3
200	RMVL	60446	3340	24W-16S	E3
1500	HRPK	60133	2911	27W-9N	C1
1500	SMWD	60107	2911	27W-9N	C2
1500	SMWD	60133	2911	27W-9N	C1
McLaren Dr					
-	OSWG	60560	3334	39W-14S	E1
McLean Av					
300	BNVL	60106	2971	16W-5N	E1
9600	FNPK	60131	2973	12W-2N	C7
9600	FNPK	60164	2973	12W-2N	C7
9600	LydT	60164	2973	12W-2N	C7
9600	MLPK	60131	2973	12W-2N	C7
9600	MLPK	60164	2973	12W-2N	C7
W McLean Av					
1400	CHCG	60614	2977	1W-2N	D6
2000	CHCG	60647	2977	2W-2N	B6
3900	CHCG	60647	2976	4W-2N	B6
4300	CHCG	60639	2976	5W-2N	B6
4700	CHCG	60639	2975	6W-2N	E7
6400	CHCG	60707	2975	8W-2N	A7
10100	LydT	60164	2973	12W-2N	A7
10300	NHLK	60164	2973	12W-2N	A7
N McLean Blvd					
800	ELGN	60123	2854	35W-12N	B1
1100	ELGN	60123	2800	35W-13N	B7
S McLean Blvd					
10	ELGN	60123	2854	35W-10N	B7
100	ElgT	60177	2908	35W-8N	B2
100	SEGN	60177	2908	35W-7N	B4
300	SchT	60175	2908	35W-7N	B5
300	SchT	60177	2908	35W-7N	B5
300	SEGN	60175	2908	35W-7N	B5
900	ElgT	60123	2854	35W-9N	B7
1000	ELGN	60123	2908	35W-9N	B1
1000	ElgT	60123	2908	35W-9N	B1
1000	SEGN	60123	2908	35W-9N	B1
McLean Ct					
1700	GNVW	60025	2810	8W-13N	E6
McLellan Blvd					
-	BtlT	60543	3262	40W-12S	C3
2800	BtlT	60560	3262	40W-12S	B4
N McLeod Av					
6000	CHCG	60646	2919	7W-7N	A3
McMillan Ln					
4800	NndT	60012	2584	33W-28N	D5
McMillen Av					
1100	AraT	60506	3199	37W-8S	D2
McMillen Rd					
10	ANTH	60002	2357	23W-41N	E7
10	ANTH	60002	2358	23W-41N	A7
McMillen St					
200	GYLK	60030	2533	20W-32N	A4
W McMillin Dr					
25100	CNHN	60410	3672	31W-29S	E1
McMullin Cir					
23800	PNFD	60586	3416	29W-19S	C3
McNair Av					
100	AddT	60101	2971	17W-3N	B6
300	ADSN	60101	2971	17W-3N	B5
McNair Dr					
800	GnvT	60134	3019	38W-0S	A7
N McNally Ln					
31700	LKMR	60073	2530	27W-31N	B6
31700	VOLO	60073	2530	27W-31N	B6
31700	WcnT	60073	2530	27W-31N	B6
N McNeil St					
100	BCVL	60407	4030	33W-44S	B3
500	BvlT	60407	4030	33W-44S	B3
McNerney Dr					
10200	FNPK	60131	2973	12W-4N	A3
McPhee Dr					
800	LIHL	60156	2694	34W-22N	B4
E McQuown St					
600	SDWH	60548	3258	51W-14S	A7
McRae Ln					
1800	MDLN	60060	2590	20W-28N	A6
1900	FmtT	60060	2590	20W-28N	A6
N McRoberts St					
200	JLET	60432	3499	23W-23S	A4
McVicker Av					
8500	OKLN	60453	3211	7W-9S	C4
8700	BRBK	60459	3211	7W-10S	C5
8700	OKLN	60459	3211	7W-10S	C5
10300	CHRG	60415	3275	7W-12S	C1
N McVicker Av					
1600	CHCG	60302	3031	6W-0S	E7
1600	CHCG	60639	3031	6W-0S	E7
1600	OKPK	60302	3031	6W-0S	E7
1600	OKPK	60639	3031	6W-0S	E7
2100	CHCG	60639	2975	7W-2N	B6
4000	CHCG	60634	2975	7W-5N	B1
4300	CHCG	60630	2975	7W-5N	B1
4800	CHCG	60630	2919	7W-6N	B6
5500	CHCG	60646	2919	7W-7N	B4
7200	CHCG	60646	2865	7W-9N	B7
S McVicker Av					
5100	CHCG	60638	3149	7W-6S	C3
5100	StkT	60638	3149	7W-5S	C2
McVickers Av					
8800	MNGV	60053	2865	7W-11N	B3
S McVickers Av					
12400	WthT	60463	3275	7W-15S	C7
12900	WthT	60463	3347	7W-15S	C1
McWalter Dr					
-	ROSL	60172	2913	23W-8N	B3
Meacham Av					
10	PKRG	60068	2918	8W-8N	D1
900	NLES	60068	2864	10W-9N	B6
900	NLES	60714	2864	10W-9N	B6
900	PKRG	60068	2864	10W-9N	B6
N Meacham Ct					
8100	NLES	60714	2864	10W-10N	B5
Meacham Rd					
-	EGVV	60143	2913	21W-7N	D3
-	ITSC	60143	2913	21W-7N	D4
-	ITSC	60157	2913	21W-7N	D4
200	EGVV	60007	2859	21W-9N	E7
200	EGVV	60193	2859	21W-9N	E7
200	SmbT	60007	2859	21W-9N	E7
200	SmbT	60193	2859	21W-9N	E7
300	EGVV	60007	2913	21W-8N	E2
Meacham Rd CO-24					
-	EGVV	60143	2913	21W-7N	D3
-	ITSC	60143	2913	21W-7N	D4
-	ITSC	60157	2913	21W-7N	D4
N Meacham Rd					
-	SMBG	60193	2859	21W-10N	E5
1200	SMBG	60173	2859	21W-12N	E1
1300	ITSC	60143	2913	21W-7N	E4
1700	SMBG	60173	2805	21W-12N	E7
2500	PltT	60067	2805	20W-13N	E7
2500	PltT	60173	2805	20W-13N	E7
S Meacham Rd					
10	SMBG	60173	2859	21W-9N	E7
10	SMBG	60193	2859	21W-9N	E7
500	EGVV	60007	2859	21W-9N	E7
500	EGVV	60193	2859	21W-9N	E7
900	SmbT	60193	2859	21W-9N	E7
1000	SmbT	60007	2859	21W-9N	E7
1500	PltT	60008	2805	21W-14N	E5
1500	PltT	60067	2805	21W-13N	E6
1500	RGMW	60008	2805	21W-14N	E5
1500	RGMW	60067	2805	21W-14N	E5
2000	PltT	60173	2805	21W-13N	E6
2000	SMBG	60067	2805	21W-13N	E6
2000	SMBG	60173	2805	21W-13N	E6
Mead Av					
500	WcnT	60084	2644	25W-26N	A3
12000	HBRN	60034	2350	40W-42N	E6
12000	HBRN	60034	2351	40W-42N	A6
Mead Ct					
500	GNVA	60134	3020	35W-0N	A4
Mead St					
17100	LKPT	60441	3420	21W-20S	A5
Meade Av					
8500	BRBK	60459	3211	7W-9S	C4
8500	OKLN	60459	3211	7W-9S	C4
8700	OKLN	60453	3211	7W-11S	C6
8800	MNGV	60053	2865	7W-11N	B3
10000	CHRG	60415	3211	7W-11S	B7
N Meade Av					
1600	CHCG	60302	3031	6W-0S	E7
1600	CHCG	60639	3031	6W-0S	E7
1600	OKPK	60302	3031	6W-0S	E7
2100	CHCG	60639	2975	7W-2N	B6
2700	CHCG	60634	2975	7W-3N	B5
4300	CHCG	60630	2975	7W-5N	B1
4400	CHCG	60630	2919	7W-5N	B7
6100	CHCG	60646	2919	7W-7N	B3
7200	CHCG	60646	2865	7W-9N	B7
S Meade Av					
5100	CHCG	60638	3149	7W-6S	B3
5100	StkT	60638	3149	7W-5S	B2
7300	BDPK	60638	3149	7W-8S	C7
7300	BDPK	60638	3211	7W-8S	C1
12300	WthT	60463	3275	7W-14S	C6
12900	WthT	60463	3347	7W-15S	C1
Meade Blvd					
400	NARA	60506	3076	39W-3S	D7
400	NARA	60542	3076	39W-3S	E7
400	SgrT	60506	3076	39W-3S	D7
Meade Ct					
-	LNHT	60046	2417	21W-39N	D5
10	FXLK	60020	2472	28W-36N	E3
10	FXLK	60020	2473	28W-36N	A3
200	BRLT	60103	2911	28W-7N	A6
Meade Dr					
-	LNHT	60046	2417	21W-39N	D5
Meade Ln					
700	ROSL	60172	2912	24W-6N	C6
W Meade Ln					
1200	ANHT	60004	2753	18W-18N	E2
Meade Pl					
6700	DRGV	60516	3144	20W-7S	A7
Meade Rd					
100	WynT	60185	2966	30W-3N	B5
6700	DRGV	60516	3144	20W-7S	A7
Meade St					
10900	ODPK	60467	3423	13W-19S	A2
S Meader Rd					
17500	HMGN	60491	3421	17W-21S	C6
17500	HmrT	60448	3421	17W-21S	C6
17500	HmrT	60491	3421	17W-21S	C6
Meadow Av					
-	WnfT	60555	3080	29W-3S	C5
-	WNVL	60555	3080	29W-3S	C5
10	RKDL	60436	3498	25W-25S	B7
100	WDSK	60098	2524	41W-32N	C5
400	FKFT	60423	3503	12W-25S	C7
600	MltT	60148	3025	21W-1N	E3
W Meadow Av					
400	LMBD	60148	3026	20W-1N	A3
600	LMBD	60148	3025	21W-1N	E3
600	MltT	60148	3025	21W-1N	E3
600	MltT	60148	3026	21W-1N	A3
Meadow Cir					
12500	LKBF	60044	2593	12W-29N	B4
Meadow Ct					
10	SBTN	60010	2803	27W-13N	B5
10	SMBG	60193	2857	27W-10N	D5
100	ANTH	60002	2358	22W-43N	A5
100	DGvT	60527	3207	16W-9S	E3
300	MDLN	60061	2647	17W-25N	B5
300	VNHL	60061	2647	17W-25N	B5
500	WPHR	60096	2362	11W-42N	D5
600	DSPN	60016	2862	14W-12N	D1
600	EGvT	60007	2860	19W-9N	D7
600	EGVV	60007	2860	19W-9N	D7
600	EGVV	60007	2914	19W-9N	D1
600	RtdT	60140	2798	40W-15N	B3
1000	SMWD	60107	2857	28W-9N	B7
2900	DRN	60561	3206	20W-9S	B4
3600	OMFD	60461	3506	4W-24S	E5
8100	TYPK	60477	3424	10W-19S	C3
15300	OKFT	60452	3347	6W-18S	E7
20700	DRPK	60010	2698	23W-20N	E7
S Meadow Ct					
10	SBTN	60010	2803	27W-13N	B5
Meadow Dr					
10	SchT	60175	2964	35W-5N	B3
10	SCRL	60175	2964	35W-5N	A3
100	CTSD	60525	3147	12W-7S	B5
100	GNCY	53128	2353		B2
100	SRWD	60404	3496	30W-23S	C4
200	BfdT	53128	2353		B2
300	BtvT	60510	3078	34W-2S	C4
500	WldT	60565	3203	27W-10S	B5
500	MaiT	60025	2809	10W-13N	E7
600	NfdT	60025	2809	10W-13N	E7
600	WldT	60564	3203	28W-10S	B5
700	DSPN	60016	2862	14W-12N	D1
800	PltT	60124	2851	41W-9N	E7
800	PltT	60124	2852	41W-9N	A7
1100	BTVA	60510	3078	34W-2S	C4
1200	ALGN	60102	2747	34W-20N	D1
1200	AlqT	60102	2747	34W-20N	D1
2100	LNHT	60046	2418	20W-38N	A7
2100	LNHT	60046	2476	20W-38N	A1
2300	RGMW	60008	2806	19W-13N	C6
2700	SchT	60174	2964	35W-4N	A4
3200	PKCY	60085	2536	12W-33N	A4
5900	LSLE	60532	3142	23W-6S	E5
5900	LslT	60532	3142	23W-6S	E5
6700	NndT	60012	2640	35W-27N	A1
6800	NndT	60012	2639	35W-27N	E1
E Meadow Dr					
500	WLMT	60091	2812	5W-13N	B6
N Meadow Dr					
2300	WLMT	60091	2812	5W-13N	B6
S Meadow Dr					
2300	WLMT	60091	2812	5W-13N	A6
W Meadow Dr					
500	WLMT	60091	2812	5W-13N	A6
Meadow Ln					
-	AntT	60002	2417	22W-41N	B1
-	WldT	60585	3337	31W-15S	E1
10	DGvT	60439	3270	20W-11S	B1
10	LKZH	60047	2698	23W-22N	E3
10	NpvT	60564	3203	28W-10S	A5
10	ODHL	60013	2641	31W-26N	D3
10	WldT	60564	3203	28W-10S	A5
10	WLNG	60090	2755	14W-18N	B3
100	CLSM	60188	3024	24W-1N	D2
100	CTSD	60525	3147	13W-7S	B6
100	LynT	60525	3147	13W-7S	B6
100	WNKA	60093	2812	5W-15N	A3
200	CHHT	60411	3507	1W-25S	E6
200	NlxT	60451	3501	17W-25S	C7
300	LIHL	60156	2694	35W-21N	A5
300	PltT	60067	2806	20W-13N	A6
400	LYVL	60048	2591	16W-28N	E5
400	SmbT	60193	2912	25W-8N	B2
500	BCHR	60401	3864	0W-36S	C1
500	HRVD	60033	2464	50W-37N	A2
500	WPHR	60096	2362	11W-42N	D5
600	LSLE	60532	3143	22W-5S	B3
700	BRTN	60010	2750	25W-18N	E3
700	LMBD	60148	3084	19W-1S	D2
700	MRGO	60152	2634	49W-25N	C4
700	YkTp	60148	3084	19W-1S	D2
800	NARA	60542	3078	34W-3S	C5
900	ELGN	60123	2800	35W-13N	C7
900	LKFT	60045	2650	10W-27N	B2
900	SMWD	60107	2857	28W-9N	B7
1100	HFET	60169	2858	24W-11N	E3
1200	DRFD	60015	2703	11W-21N	D6
1300	MHRY	60050	2527	33W-33N	E3
1400	GNVW	60025	2811	7W-14N	A5
1600	BKBN	60015	2703	11W-22N	C4
1600	HDPK	60035	2704	10W-22N	A3
2100	NCHI	60064	2536	12W-31N	C7
2800	SMBG	60193	2857	27W-10N	D5
2800	SMBG	60194	2857	27W-10N	C5
3200	NfdT	60025	2810	10W-13N	A7
3400	NfdT	60025	2809	10W-13N	E7
5200	DRGV	60515	3144	20W-5S	B3
6300	WLBK	60527	3146	15W-7S	A6
6500	HMND	46324	3430		D2
7000	AlqT	60013	2642	29W-24N	D7
8000	TYPK	60477	3424	10W-19S	C3
8500	DRN	60561	3206	20W-9S	C4
8700	MNSR	46321	3510		D1
9400	DSPN	60016	2863	11W-11N	C2
10000	MaiT	60016	2809	11W-12N	D7
10000	MaiT	60016	2863	11W-12N	D1
10100	HBRN	60034	2350	41W-42N	E7
12700	PNFD	60585	3337	31W-15S	E1
13400	PNFD	60544	3337	31W-16S	E5
14600	FoxT	60560	3331	48W-17S	C7
14900	OrlT	60462	3346	9W-17S	C6
15000	DLTN	60419	3351	1E-17S	B6
15000	ODPK	60462	3346	9W-17S	C6
17700	UNON	60180	2635	46W-25N	C4
18500	HLCT	60429	3506	4W-22S	E1
18500	HLCT	60430	3506	4W-22S	E1
18500	HMWD	60429	3506	4W-22S	E1
18500	HMWD	60430	3506	4W-22S	E1
20200	DRPK	60010	2751	23W-20N	E1
20600	DRPK	60010	2698	23W-20N	D7
23400	CbaT	60010	2696	28W-23N	E2
23500	LKBN	60010	2696	28W-23N	E2
E Meadow Ln					
600	PLTN	60074	2753	20W-16N	B6
8000	BLVY	60097	2526	37W-34N	C1
8000	GwdT	60097	2526	37W-34N	C1
8000	McHT	60097	2526	37W-34N	C1
N Meadow Ln					
10	HNWD	60047	2645	22W-24N	A7
10	PNFD	60544	3415	31W-18S	E1
100	PNFD	60544	3337	31W-18S	E7
1000	MPPT	60056	2808	15W-14N	A4
1100	MPPT	60056	2807	15W-14N	E4
23500	CbaT	60013	2696	28W-23N	D2
26100	WcnT	60084	2644	25W-26N	A3
35400	GrtT	60041	2473	25W-35N	E6
39200	WDWH	60083	2420	14W-39N	D5
S Meadow Ln					
10	HNWD	60047	2645	22W-24N	A7
500	PTON	60468	3860	10W-37S	D4
1300	RDLK	60073	2531	23W-31N	E6
6500	HMND	46324	3430		D2
7600	AlqT	60013	2642	29W-24N	D7
10700	PSHL	60465	3274	10W-12S	B2
W Meadow Ln					
500	RDLK	60073	2531	24W-31N	D7
700	FmtT	60030	2531	24W-31N	D7
3100	GwdT	60097	2469	37W-35N	A6
3700	WRLK	60097	2469	37W-35N	A5
18300	WrnT	60031	2476	18W-36N	E4
18500	LGGV	60047	2646	18W-25N	D5
Meadow Ln W					
-	DndT	60118	2801	33W-14N	B5
Meadow Pl					
10	LKBN	60010	2643	26W-24N	E7
8100	MNSR	46321	3430		D6
Meadow Pth					
2600	NLNX	60451	3589	18W-27S	A5
Meadow Rd					
-	ADSN	60101	2970	18W-4N	E3
-	NtrT	60093	2812	4W-14N	B3
-	PSPK	60464	3272	14W-14S	D7
100	NpvT	60563	3080	30W-4S	B7
100	NpvT	60563	3140	30W-4S	B1
400	ADSN	60101	2969	21W-3N	D5
400	BmdT	60101	2969	21W-3N	D5
500	WNKA	60093	2812	4W-14N	C3
800	NHBK	60062	2757	9W-17N	B5
1000	GLNC	60022	2758	6W-18N	D3
N Meadow Rd					
32800	WrnT	60030	2533	18W-32N	E4
S Meadow Rd					
600	MHRY	60050	2528	32W-31N	C7
600	NndT	60050	2528	32W-31N	C7
Meadow St					
3400	NfdT	60062	2756	11W-16N	C6
3400	NHBK	60062	2756	11W-16N	C6
5100	MHRY	60050	2528	32W-32N	B4
5200	NndT	60010	2642	29W-26N	D2
5200	NndT	60051	2642	29W-26N	D2
Meadow Ter					
800	AURA	60505	3138	34W-6S	D5
4600	MLPK	60160	3029	13W-1N	A2
4600	NHLK	60160	3029	13W-1N	A2
4600	NHLK	60164	3029	13W-1N	A2
Meadow Tr					
300	BRLT	60103	2911	28W-7N	B5
Meadow Vw					
100	ANTH	60002	2357	23W-42N	E5
100	ANTH	60002	2358	22W-42N	B5
Meadow Wy					
1200	BRTN	60010	2698	24W-20N	C7
Meadow Bridge Dr					
-	PLTN	60008	2805	21W-14N	D5
-	RGMW	60008	2805	21W-14N	D5
-	RGMW	60067	2805	21W-13N	D5
Meadowbrook Ct					
100	LKZH	60047	2699	22W-22N	A3
600	LslT	60540	3142	25W-6S	B5
5500	RGMW	60008	2860	19W-12N	C1
Meadowbrook Dr					
200	BGBK	60440	3269	22W-11S	C1
200	NHFD	60093	2758	7W-16N	A7
1100	AURA	60504	3202	30W-9S	A3
1200	AURA	60564	3202	30W-9S	A4
1300	RLKB	60073	2474	23W-35N	E6
8300	BRRG	60527	3207	16W-9S	E3
8300	DGvT	60527	3207	16W-9S	E3
N Meadowbrook Dr					
2200	PNFD	60544	3338	30W-16S	C5
W Meadowbrook Dr					
17400	WrnT	60030	2534	17W-33N	B3
Meadowbrook Ln					
10	LKZH	60047	2699	22W-22N	B3
10	WLNG	60090	2755	14W-17N	C5
100	NCHI	60044	2593	12W-30N	B3
200	HNDL	60521	3146	15W-6S	B4
900	DRFD	60015	2704	10W-21N	A7
2400	WSTR	60154	3086	14W-2S	C3
5600	NndT	60014	2641	32W-26N	B3
6800	HRPK	60133	2912	26W-8N	A2
8000	ODPK	60462	3346	10W-18S	C7
Meadowbrook Rd					
800	ELWD	60421	3675	25W-31S	B5
Meadowbrook St					
5200	JLET	60586	3496	30W-22S	B1
Meadowbrook Industrial Ct					
5400	RGMW	60008	2860	19W-12N	C2
W Meadow Creek Ct					
1100	VNHL	60061	2646	18W-24N	E6
Meadow Creek Dr					
18800	MKNA	60448	3502	14W-22S	D2
Meadow Crest Cir					
3400	GRNE	60031	2479	13W-35N	A6
Meadowcrest Dr					
6700	DRGV	60516	3144	19W-7S	D7
16700	HMGN	60491	3422	15W-20S	C4
Meadowcrest Rd					
900	LGPK	60525	3087	12W-3S	B4
Meadowcroft Ln					
2200	GYLK	60030	2475	20W-35N	E6
Meadowdale Cir					
10000	BtnT	60081	2355	30W-41N	A7
10000	SPGV	60081	2354	30W-41N	E7
10000	SPGV	60081	2355	30W-41N	A7
E Meadowdale Cir					
-	HPSR	60140	2795	47W-16N	D1
W Meadowdale Cir					
-	HPSR	60140	2795	47W-16N	D1
Meadowdale Ct					
100	CPVL	60110	2748	33W-17N	B6
Meadowdale Dr					
600	RMVL	60446	3340	25W-15S	B1
16700	OKFT	60452	3426	6W-20S	A3
Meadowdale Ln					
2400	WDRG	60517	3205	21W-9S	D3
Meadow Grass Dr					
18700	WrnT	60046	2476	18W-37N	D3
Meadow Green Ct					
2500	AURA	60506	3136	39W-6S	E6
Meadow Green Dr					
300	NPVL	60565	3203	26W-10S	D5
Meadow Green Ln					
300	RLKB	60073	2474	23W-35N	E5
Meadow Hill Ct					
700	McHT	60050	2472	29W-37N	C2
Meadow Hill Ln					
400	RLKB	60073	2474	23W-35N	E5
5300	McHT	60050	2472	29W-37N	C2
16600	LKPT	60441	3342	20W-17S	A6
S Meadow Hill Ln					
13100	LMNT	60439	3344	16W-15S	A2
13200	LMNT	60439	3343	16W-15S	E2
W Meadow Hill Ln					
13100	LMNT	60439	3343	16W-15S	E1
Meadow Hill Rd					
10	BNHL	60010	2696	29W-20N	B7
10	BNHL	60010	2749	29W-20N	B2
Meadow Lake Ct					
-	ANTH	60002	2357	25W-41N	B7
700	LslT	60540	3142	25W-5S	B3
4800	RNPK	60471	3594	6W-26S	A3
Meadow Lake Dr					
500	LslT	60540	3142	25W-5S	C4
2300	NPVL	60564	3266	29W-12S	D3
4800	RNPK	60471	3594	6W-26S	A3
23600	WldT	60564	3266	29W-12S	D3
E Meadow Lake Dr					
1000	PLTN	60074	2753	19W-17N	C5
Meadow Lake Ln					
300	LKFT	60045	2649	13W-25N	A5
Meadow Lakes Blvd					
100	AURA	60504	3202	31W-8S	A2
Meadow Lakes Dr					
100	SRWD	60404	3495	31W-24S	E6
Meadowland Cir					
25600	PNFD	60585	3337	32W-15S	C1
Meadowland Dr					
1500	NPVL	60540	3140	28W-7S	E7
1500	NPVL	60540	3141	28W-7S	A7

STREET Block City ZIP Map# CGS Grid

Meadowland Dr
1500 NPVL 60540 3202 28W-7S E1
12000 HMGN 60491 3344 15W-17S C5
12000 OrlT 60467 3344 15W-17S C5
Meadow Lark
- LYWD 60411 3510 C6
10 DYR 46311 3510 C6
21300 KLDR 60047 2699 21W-21N D6
Meadowlark Cir
100 LNHT 60046 2476 19W-37N C1
Meadow Lark Ct
21500 FKFT 60423 3591 13W-26S A2
Meadowlark Ct
10 ROSL 60172 2912 24W-7N C4
300 CmpT 60175 2961 42W-5N D2
900 ANTH 60002 2358 21W-41N E7
1900 YKVL 60560 3333 42W-16S D5
2900 AURA 60502 3079 32W-3S C6
4300 GRNE 60031 2535 14W-34N C1
5000 NndT 60012 2640 35W-27N A1
13000 HMGN 60491 3344 16W-18S A7
Meadowlark Dr
100 HNWD 60047 2645 22W-26N C3
300 BGBK 60440 3268 23W-12S E3
600 WynT 60103 2966 29W-5N D1
800 PltT 60140 2851 42W-12N C1
2300 WCHI 60185 2966 29W-3N E5
2300 WynT 60185 2966 29W-3N E5
8800 TYPK 60487 3424 11W-21S A6
13100 PlsT 60462 3346 10W-15S B1
13100 PlsT 60464 3346 10W-15S B1
W Meadowlark Dr
900 MchT 60050 2472 29W-36N B3
Meadowlark Ln
- NPVL 60565 3203 27W-9S C3
10 CPVL 60110 2748 32W-17N C6
100 CTSD 60525 3147 12W-6S B5
100 NpvT 60565 3203 27W-9S C3
400 NHFD 60093 2811 7W-15N B2
1000 DGvT 60561 3207 17W-9S B3
1000 DRN 60561 3207 17W-9S B3
1000 GNVW 60025 2810 9W-13N B6
1200 GYLK 60030 2533 19W-33N C4
1900 YKVL 60560 3333 42W-16S D5
2700 EVTN 60201 2812 4W-13N B7
2900 WKGN 60087 2479 11W-37N D2
3400 PRGV 60012 2585 32W-27N B7
5700 JNBG 60050 2471 30W-37N E1
6000 BtnT 60050 2471 30W-37N E1
Meadowlark Rd
200 BMDL 60108 2968 24W-4N D3
300 BmdT 60108 2968 24W-4N E4
300 GLHT 60108 2968 24W-4N E4
300 GLHT 60139 2968 24W-4N E4
Meadowlawn Av
900 DRGV 60516 3144 19W-7S C6
W Meadow Lily Ct
24200 PNFD 60585 3338 30W-15S B2
Meadow Lily Dr
500 JLET 60431 3497 28W-24S B6
Meadow Ln Av
28000 MHRY 60050 2528 32W-32N A4
S Meadow Ln Dr
11500 MTPK 60803 3276 3W-13S E4
W Meadow Ln Dr
3100 MTPK 60803 3276 3W-13S E4
Meadow Ln Rd
28000 WcnT 60051 2587 28W-28N A6
28000 WcnT 60084 2587 28W-28N A6
W Meadow Mist Ln
300 RDLK 60073 2531 23W-31N E6
Meadowood Dr
10 OKBK 60523 3086 15W-1S B1
500 LKFT 60045 2649 12W-26N B3
Meadowood Ln
10 NHFD 60093 2811 7W-14N B3
S Meadowood Rd
24200 CteT 60417 3684 2W-29S D1
24200 UYPK 60417 3684 2W-29S D1
W Meadowood Estates Dr
- KLDR 60047 2699 21W-22N E4
- LGGV 60047 2699 21W-22N E4
Meadowoods Ln
27000 MTWA 60048 2648 14W-27N C2
Meadowridge Cir
700 CmpT 60175 2962 39W-3N E5
Meadow Ridge Dr
- JLET 60586 3496 31W-22S A1
800 WCHI 60185 3022 29W-1N E3
900 WnfT 60185 3022 29W-1N E3
6200 JLET 60586 3415 31W-21S D6
Meadowridge Dr
600 AURA 60504 3202 30W-8S A3
W Meadow Ridge Dr
17600 WrnT 60031 2477 17W-36N B5
Meadow Ridge Ln
400 PTHT 60070 2754 16W-16N D6
Meadowridge Ln
800 NLNX 60451 3589 19W-26S A3
Meadow Rose Ln
- YKVL 60560 3333 42W-16S D5
Meadowrue Ln
300 BTVA 60510 3078 34W-1S E2
N Meadows Blvd
600 ADSN 60101 2969 21W-4N E3
Meadows Ct
10 SchT 60175 2963 36W-5N E3
100 SRGV 60554 3135 42W-7S C6
N Meadows Ct
20700 KLDR 60047 2699 20W-20N E7
Meadows Dr
10 GLBT 60124 2799 38W-14N B6
10 GLBT 60136 2799 38W-14N B5
10 RtdT 60124 2799 38W-14N B6
10 SRGV 60554 3135 42W-7S C6
Meadows Ln
- DMND 60416 3941 33W-39S A2
2300 RLKB 60073 2475 21W-36N D4
Meadows Rd
700 GNVA 60134 3020 35W-0N B5
Meadowsedge Dr
- WDSK 60098 2581 41W-29N D4
Meadowsedge Ln
- SgrT 60506 3198 39W-8S D2
500 AURA 60506 3198 39W-8S D2
900 JLET 60436 3497 27W-25S C7
1000 JLET 60436 3585 27W-25S C1
2400 CPVL 60110 2746 37W-17N D6
Meadows Edge Tr
8400 TYPK 60477 3504 10W-23S B3
Meadowshire Ln
7200 NndT 60012 2583 36W-27N D7
7200 NndT 60012 2639 36W-27N D1
Meadowsweet Dr
10 BbyT 60119 3017 42W-1N C3

Meadow View Cir
1700 WKGN 60048 2534 15W-31N E6
1700 WKGN 60048 2535 15W-32N A6
Meadowview Cross
600 WCHI 60185 2966 29W-2N E7
700 WynT 60185 2966 29W-2N E7
Meadow View Ct
- HTLY 60140 2744 43W-19N A3
- HTLY 60142 2744 43W-19N A3
14200 ODPK 60462 3346 10W-16S B4
Meadowview Ct
100 MltT 60187 3023 26W-0N E4
200 CmpT 60175 2906 39W-6N E6
300 BMDL 60108 2969 22W-4N C3
700 LKVL 60046 2475 23W-37N A3
2000 NHBK 60062 2757 8W-16N D7
2300 AURA 60502 3201 33W-8S B1
2800 NHBK 60025 2809 11W-15N D1
N Meadow View Ct
25900 LKBN 60010 2643 27W-25N C4
Meadow View Dr
3900 SCRL 60175 2964 36W-5N A2
Meadowview Dr
- GNVW 60025 2809 11W-15N C2
- GNVW 60062 2809 11W-15N C2
- NHBK 60062 2809 11W-15N C2
500 WCDA 60084 2643 26W-26N C2
500 WCHI 60185 2966 29W-2N D7
500 WcnT 60084 2643 26W-26N C2
4200 NHBK 60025 2809 11W-15N C2
8800 ODHL 60487 3424 11W-19S A2
8800 ODPK 60462 3424 11W-19S A2
8800 ODPK 60487 3424 11W-19S A2
9000 HYHL 60457 3209 11W-9S E4
9000 HYHL 60480 3209 11W-9S E4
9000 LynT 60480 3209 11W-9S E4
9200 ODHL 60487 3423 11W-19S E2
9200 ODPK 60467 3423 11W-19S E2
9200 ODPK 60487 3423 11W-19S E2
18800 MKNA 60448 3502 14W-22S D2
N Meadow View Dr
500 SCRL 60175 2964 36W-5N A1
W Meadowview Dr
1900 RDLK 60073 2531 25W-33N A3
Meadowview Ln
100 AURA 60502 3201 32W-8S B2
200 LYLK 60175 2961 43W-5N A3
500 CmpT 60175 2961 43W-5N A2
1600 WslT 60481 3943 26W-40S E2
2100 YKVL 60560 3261 43W-13S B5
2900 MTGY 60538 3198 40W-10S B6
12800 HMGN 60491 3422 16W-18S A1
13100 HMGN 60491 3421 16W-18S E1
21000 SRWD 60404 3583 31W-25S E1
Meadowview Rd
10 NHFD 60093 2811 6W-14N E4
10 NtrT 60093 2811 6W-14N E3
800 BtvT 60510 3077 37W-2S C5
Meadowwood Av
1200 WDRG 60517 3206 20W-9S B3
8200 DRN 60517 3206 20W-9S B3
8200 DRN 60561 3206 20W-9S B3
Meadow Wood Dr
200 JLET 60431 3497 28W-23S B4
N Meadow Wood Dr
700 JLET 60431 3497 28W-23S B3
Meadowwood Ln
500 OSWG 60543 3262 39W-12S D2
600 WMTN 60481 3853 28W-39S B7
Meagan Ct
1000 NPVL 60540 3202 29W-8S D1
W Meagan Ct
5200 WKGN 60048 2535 15W-31N B6
Meagan Ln
10 LMNT 60439 3270 19W-14S C7
Meagan's Wy
- TNLK 53181 2354 D2
Meander Dr
1400 NPVL 60565 3203 26W-8S E2
18100 WrnT 60030 2534 18W-34N A1
18100 WrnT 60031 2534 18W-34N A1
18300 WrnT 60030 2533 18W-34N E1
Meandering Wy
3800 AlqT 60014 2641 33W-25N A4
Mears Pl
10 HIWD 60040 2704 9W-23N D2
Meath Cir
13600 HMGN 60491 3343 17W-16S D3
Meath Dr
2000 JLET 60431 3417 28W-21S B7
W Meath Dr
13600 HMGN 60491 3343 17W-16S D3
Mecan Dr
2200 NPVL 60564 3203 28W-10S A5
2200 NpvT 60564 3203 28W-10S A5
S Mecosta Ln
600 RMVL 60446 3417 26W-18S E2
600 RMVL 60446 3418 26W-18S A1
Meda Av
100 JLET 60433 3499 23W-24S B5
N Medford Av
6900 CHCG 60646 2919 7W-8N A1
Medford Cir
- LGGV 60047 2647 18W-24N A7
800 SMBG 60193 2859 23W-9N B7
800 SMBG 60193 2913 22W-7N D3
3800 NHBK 60062 2756 12W-17N B5
Medford Ct
3100 AURA 60504 3201 31W-8S D2
3100 BRLT 60103 2910 28W-9N E1
3100 BRLT 60107 2910 28W-9N E1
3100 SMWD 60103 2910 28W-9N E1
3100 SMWD 60107 2910 28W-9N E1
3200 ISLK 60042 2586 29W-28N B5
Medford Dr
400 SEGN 60177 2908 35W-8N B3
700 CLSM 60188 2967 27W-2N D7
W Medford Dr
600 PLTN 60067 2805 21W-14N C3
W Medical Center Dr
- NndT 60050 2528 32W-31N A7
4200 MHRY 60050 2528 33W-31N A7
Medill Av
9100 FNPK 60131 2973 11W-2N D6
9100 FNPK 60171 2973 11W-2N D6
E Medill Av
10 NHLK 60164 2972 13W-2N E6
300 LydT 60164 2973 13W-2N A6
300 NHLK 60164 2973 13W-2N A6
W Medill Av
1600 CHCG 60614 2977 2W-2N C6
2200 CHCG 60647 2977 3W-2N A6
2800 CHCG 60647 2976 3W-2N E6
4800 CHCG 60639 2975 6W-2N E6
6700 CHCG 60707 2974 8W-2N E6
6700 CHCG 60707 2975 8W-2N A6

W Medill Av
7100 EDPK 60707 2974 8W-2N D6
10000 LydT 60164 2973 12W-2N B6
10400 NHLK 60164 2973 13W-2N A6
W Medill St
- CHCG 60614 2977 1W-2N D6
N Medina Av
5800 CHCG 60646 2919 7W-7N B4
Medina Dr
13300 ODPK 60462 3346 11W-15S A2
Medinah
- MONE 60449 3683 6W-31S A5
Medinah Cir
2000 ELGN 60123 2907 36W-9N E1
W Medinah Cir
10 GLHT 60139 3024 24W-2N D1
Medinah Ct
10 LIHL 60156 2693 36W-21N D5
2100 PSHT 60463 3347 8W-15S B2
5500 GRNE 60031 2478 15W-36N A4
5600 GRNE 60031 2477 16W-36N D4
Medinah Dr
300 NPVL 60563 3140 30W-5S B2
300 NpvT 60563 3140 30W-5S B2
1200 BmdT 60143 2913 21W-6N E7
1200 BmdT 60143 2914 21W-6N A7
1200 ITSC 60143 2913 21W-6N E7
1200 ITSC 60143 2914 21W-6N A7
25500 MONE 60449 3683 6W-31S B5
Medinah Ln
- SRWD 60404 3583 31W-25S D2
100 TRLK 60010 2643 25W-25N E5
Medinah Rd
10 BMDL 60101 2969 21W-5N D1
10 BMDL 60108 2969 21W-5N D2
10 BMDL 60157 2913 22W-5N D7
10 BmdT 60101 2969 21W-5N D1
10 BmdT 60143 2913 22W-6N D7
10 BmdT 60157 2913 22W-6N D7
300 ITSC 60143 2913 22W-7N D4
300 ITSC 60157 2913 22W-7N D4
300 ROSL 60143 2913 22W-7N D4
300 ROSL 60157 2913 22W-7N D4
400 BMDL 60157 2969 21W-4N D2
400 BmdT 60108 2969 21W-4N D3
400 BmdT 60157 2969 21W-5N D1
700 BMDL 60101 2913 21W-5N D7
Medinah Rd CO-24
10 BMDL 60101 2969 21W-5N D1
10 BMDL 60108 2969 21W-5N D2
10 BMDL 60157 2913 22W-5N D7
10 BmdT 60101 2969 21W-5N D1
10 BmdT 60143 2913 22W-6N D7
10 BmdT 60157 2913 22W-6N D7
300 ITSC 60143 2913 22W-7N D4
300 ITSC 60157 2913 22W-7N D4
300 ROSL 60143 2913 22W-7N D4
300 ROSL 60157 2913 22W-7N D4
400 BMDL 60157 2969 21W-4N D3
400 BmdT 60108 2969 21W-4N D3
400 BmdT 60157 2969 21W-5N D1
700 BMDL 60101 2913 21W-5N D7
Medinah St
10 FXLK 60020 2473 27W-36N B3
900 BNVL 60106 2915 16W-5N D7
Medline Pl
- MDLN 60060 2646 18W-26N E4
- MDLN 60060 2647 18W-26N A4
Meed Ct
12900 PlsT 60464 3345 13W-15S B1
Meegan Wy
1400 EGVV 60007 2913 21W-8N E3
E Meeker Av
400 JLET 60432 3499 23W-22S B2
W Meeker Ct
28700 WcnT 60084 2642 28W-27N E2
Meer Park Ct
2500 CTHL 60403 3497 27W-22S D2
Megan Ct
700 WTMT 60559 3145 17W-6S B4
1300 MNKA 60447 3672 34W-30S A3
21300 MTSN 60443 3593 7W-25S C1
25000 LkvT 60046 2416 25W-38N B6
Megan Dr
26700 AxST 60410 3672 33W-31S B7
26700 CNHN 60410 3672 33W-31S B7
Megan Ann Ct
300 GNVA 60134 3020 34W-0N C4
Meghan Av
1000 ALGN 60102 2748 34W-19N A2
1400 ALGN 60102 2747 34W-19N E2
Meghan Ct N
26700 MonT 60449 3683 6W-32S A7
Mehring Av
2300 JNBG 60050 2471 31W-35N D5
S Meier Rd
200 MPPT 60005 2861 17W-12N B1
200 MPPT 60056 2861 17W-12N B1
800 ANHT 60005 2861 17W-11N B2
Meier St
300 EDND 60118 2801 33W-16N A2
Meigs Ct
10 BNVL 60106 2972 15W-5N A1
Meijer Dr
1300 ANHT 60005 2860 18W-11N E2
1300 ANHT 60008 2860 18W-11N E2
1300 RGMW 60008 2860 18W-11N E2
Meisch Ct
1500 NPVL 60563 3141 27W-5S D2
Meisinger Ln
10 NPVL 60540 3141 26W-7S D7
W Meister Av
100 EMHT 60126 3027 16W-0N E4
N Melanie Ct
10 CRTE 60417 3597 1E-28S B7
200 PltT 60067 2752 22W-16N B7
S Melanie Ct
10 CRTE 60417 3597 1E-28S B7
Melanie Ln
2500 NHBK 60062 2809 11W-15N D1
3600 CRTE 60417 3597 1E-28S B7
Melba Ln
200 HDPK 60035 2704 8W-23N E3
Melbourne Ct
10 LIHL 60156 2692 38W-22N E3
N Melbourne Ct
39300 BHPK 60083 2421 12W-39N B5
S Melbourne Ct
100 BMDL 60108 2969 23W-5N A1
Melbourne Ln
1700 AURA 60503 3201 32W-10S B5
2500 LIHL 60156 2692 38W-22N E3
Melbourne Pl
1100 BtnT 60081 2414 30W-39N B4
1100 SPGV 60081 2414 30W-39N B4

W Melbourne Pl
14200 LKPT 60441 3421 18W-19S B3
Melbourne St
1300 ELBN 60119 3017 43W-0N B5
Melbrook Dr
1000 MNSR 46321 3510 E1
Melbrooke Rd
10 ELGN 60123 2801 33W-13N A7
100 ELGN 60123 2800 35W-14N B6
Melcher Av
500 WnfT 60555 3081 27W-3S C6
500 WNVL 60555 3081 27W-3S C7
S Melchoir Pl
10 JLET 60432 3499 23W-24S B5
10 JLET 60433 3499 23W-24S B5
Melinda Dr
100 SEGN 60177 2908 35W-8N C2
Melinda Ln
200 BFGV 60089 2754 17W-18N C3
Melise Dr
1700 GNVW 60025 2810 8W-14N E4
Melissa Cir
400 RMVL 60446 3339 27W-18S D7
Melissa Ct
3000 JNBG 60051 2472 30W-34N A7
3000 LKMR 60051 2472 30W-34N A7
3600 JLET 60431 3417 28W-20S A5
S Melissa Ct
26500 MonT 60449 3683 6W-32S B7
Melissa Dr
10 LMNT 60439 3342 19W-15S D2
600 BGBK 60440 3269 21W-11S E1
10600 ODPK 60467 3423 13W-21S B7
W Melissa Dr
26400 CNHN 60410 3761 33W-32S C1
Melissa Ln
- AURA 60506 3136 39W-5S E2
Mellbrook Rd
100 BGBK 60440 3269 22W-12S D2
Mellody Rd
200 LKFT 60045 2649 11W-26N C4
Mellor Rd
300 MltT 60188 3024 25W-1N B3
Melo Ln
400 WnfT 60185 3022 30W-0S C7
Melody Ct
300 BGBK 60440 3269 23W-12S A2
500 SMBG 60194 2858 26W-11N A4
Melody Dr
100 WynT 60103 2967 28W-5N A2
Melody Ln
- LKFT 60045 2649 13W-26N A4
- WthT 60482 3275 7W-13S B5
200 DndT 60110 2748 33W-18N A5
200 VNHL 60061 2647 16W-25N C5
500 HDPK 60035 2758 7W-20N B1
600 NPVL 60540 3141 26W-7S D7
1300 AURA 60564 3201 31W-9S E4
E Melody Ln
100 WDSK 60098 2524 41W-32N D4
N Melody Ln
23300 ElaT 60047 2699 21W-23N E1
23500 KLDR 60047 2699 21W-23N D2
23600 ElaT 60047 2645 21W-24N E6
23600 HNWD 60047 2645 21W-24N E6
23600 KLDR 60047 2645 21W-24N E6
W Melody Ln
10 PNFD 60544 3338 29W-17S D5
10 PnfT 60544 3338 29W-17S D5
100 WDSK 60098 2524 41W-32N D4
N Melody Rd
33100 WKGN 60031 2535 14W-33N D4
33100 WrnT 60031 2535 14W-33N D4
Melon Ct
7500 GRNE 60031 2477 18W-35N A6
Melrose Av
10 WTMT 60559 3145 17W-4S B1
100 KLWH 60043 2812 4W-14N D4
100 SEGN 60177 2908 34W-9N D2
200 AURA 60505 3200 35W-9S A4
200 AURA 60538 3200 36W-9S A4
200 EMHT 60126 3028 15W-2N A1
200 MTGY 60505 3200 36W-9S A4
200 MTGY 60538 3200 36W-9S A4
400 GNEN 60137 3025 22W-0N B5
400 HLSD 60162 3028 13W-0N E5
500 AraT 60505 3200 35W-9S C4
1200 WKGN 60085 2536 11W-34N C2
1500 RLKB 60073 2475 22W-35N A6
2400 LydT 60164 2972 13W-3N E5
2400 NHLK 60164 2972 13W-3N E6
11200 FNPK 60131 2972 14W-4N C4
E Melrose Av
800 JltT 60433 3499 22W-25S C7
N Melrose Av
500 ELGN 60123 2854 35W-12N C3
S Melrose Av
10 ELGN 60123 2854 35W-11N C5
Melrose Ct
10 FRGV 60021 2696 30W-22N A4
400 ELGN 60123 2854 35W-10N C6
800 MHRY 60050 2527 33W-32N D4
3100 WLMT 60091 2811 6W-14N E5
11200 ODPK 60467 3344 14W-16S E4
Melrose Dr
200 TRLK 60010 2643 26W-25N D5
Melrose Ln
10 LNSH 60069 2702 14W-22N C3
200 LKWD 60014 2639 36W-25N C5
300 CLLK 60014 2639 36W-25N C5
300 WNFD 60190 3023 27W-1N C4
500 BCHR 60401 3864 0W-37S C2
S Melrose Ln
26700 CteT 60417 3685 0W-32S C7
Melrose St
800 NLNX 60451 3501 16W-25S E7
800 NlxT 60451 3501 16W-25S E7
900 NlxT 60451 3502 16W-25S A7
2100 JltT 60433 3500 21W-24S A5
2300 NlxT 60433 3500 21W-24S A5
W Melrose St
400 CHCG 60657 2978 0W-4N A3
1600 CHCG 60657 2977 2W-4N B3
2500 CHCG 60618 2977 3W-4N A3
2700 CHCG 60618 2976 3W-4N E3
4000 CHCG 60641 2976 5W-4N B3
5100 CHCG 60641 2975 7W-4N C3
5500 CHCG 60634 2975 7W-4N C3
6900 CHCG 60634 2974 8W-4N E4
Melshane Ct
10 LMNT 60439 3271 18W-13S A5
N Melva Av
43300 AntT 60002 2357 25W-43N B4
Melville Ct
17000 LKPT 60441 3420 21W-20S A4

Melvin Dr
200 NHBK 60062 2756 11W-18N E3
1000 HDPK 60035 2758 8W-20N A2
29600 LKBF 60044 2593 11W-29N E4
29600 ShdT 60044 2593 11W-29N E4
Melvin Pl
300 WLNG 60090 2755 14W-17N C5
Melvina Av
7700 BRBK 60459 3211 7W-9S B3
8700 OKLN 60453 3211 7W-11S B7
8700 OKLN 60459 3211 7W-10S B5
10000 CHRG 60415 3211 7W-11S B7
10000 OKLN 60415 3211 7W-11S B7
N Melvina Av
1600 CHCG 60639 3031 6W-0S E6
1600 OKPK 60302 3031 6W-0S E6
2600 CHCG 60639 2975 7W-3N B5
2700 CHCG 60634 2975 7W-3N B5
4200 CHCG 60630 2975 7W-5N B1
5200 CHCG 60630 2919 7W-6N B5
7100 CHCG 60646 2919 7W-8N B1
7200 CHCG 60646 2865 7W-9N B7
7200 CHCG 60714 2865 7W-9N B7
7200 NLES 60714 2865 7W-9N B7
S Melvina Av
5100 CHCG 60638 3149 7W-5S B2
5100 StkT 60638 3149 7W-5S B2
6400 BDPK 60638 3149 7W-7S B5
12400 PSHT 60463 3275 7W-14S C5
12700 WthT 60463 3275 7W-15S C7
Melvina Ct
10 ALGN 60102 2695 32W-21N A6
Memenas Pl
- JLET 60436 3498 24W-24S D5
Memorial Ct
200 CLLK 60014 2640 34W-25N B5
Memorial Dr
- DrrT 60098 2582 39W-28N C6
- PSPK 60464 3274 11W-14S A6
- VNHL 60061 2647 16W-24N D6
- WDSK 60098 2582 39W-28N C6
10 CTCY 60409 3352 4E-17S B6
10 HMND 46320 3352 4E-17S C6
100 BtnT 60081 2414 29W-38N C7
100 SPGV 60081 2414 29W-38N C7
200 CLLK 60014 2640 34W-25N C5
1100 CTCY 60409 3351 3E-17S E6
1900 DLTN 60409 3351 2E-17S C6
1900 DLTN 60419 3351 2E-17S C6
14600 DLTN 60419 3350 0E-17S E4
N Memorial Dr
800 CHHT 60411 3507 1W-24S E6
W Memorial Dr
100 CHHT 60411 3507 1W-24S E6
E Memorial Rd
10 BNVL 60106 2972 15W-4N A2
W Memorial Rd
100 BNVL 60106 2971 16W-5N E2
700 AddT 60106 2971 16W-5N D2
Memory Ct
1000 GNEN 60137 3025 21W-0S E6
Memory Ln
100 DndT 60110 2748 33W-17N A6
200 WTMT 60559 3145 18W-7S A6
1000 LKZH 60047 2698 24W-22N B4
E Memory Ln
- MPPT 60056 2808 15W-13N A6
W Memory Ln
- ANHT 60004 2807 15W-13N E6
10 MPPT 60056 2808 15W-13N A6
100 AddT 60101 2970 19W-3N D5
100 ADSN 60101 2970 19W-3N D5
200 MPPT 60056 2807 16W-13N E6
8000 CHCG 60656 2918 10W-6N B6
8000 CHCG 60706 2918 10W-6N B6
8000 NRDG 60706 2918 10W-6N B6
Memory Tr
5400 MchT 60050 2472 29W-37N C2
8400 GwdT 60097 2469 37W-35N B6
9000 WRLK 60097 2469 38W-35N A6
Memphis Cir
1000 EGVV 60007 2913 22W-8N D3
Memphis Pl
100 VNHL 60061 2647 17W-24N C6
Menard Av
7600 BRBK 60459 3211 7W-9S C2
8000 MNGV 60053 2865 7W-10N C5
8000 SKOK 60053 2865 7W-10N C5
8000 SKOK 60077 2865 7W-10N C5
8700 OKLN 60453 3211 7W-11S C6
8700 OKLN 60459 3211 7W-10S C5
10100 OKLN 60453 3275 7W-11S C1
10300 CHRG 60415 3275 7W-12S C1
11000 ALSP 60482 3275 7W-12S C3
11000 CHRG 60482 3275 7W-12S C3
14200 BmnT 60445 3347 7W-16S D4
14700 BmnT 60452 3347 7W-17S D6
14700 OKFT 60452 3347 7W-17S D6
N Menard Av
10 CHCG 60644 3031 7W-0N C5
700 CHCG 60651 3031 7W-0N C3
1500 CHCG 60639 3031 7W-1N C1
2100 CHCG 60639 2975 7W-2N C6
2700 CHCG 60634 2975 7W-3N C5
4300 CHCG 60630 2975 7W-5N C1
4900 CHCG 60630 2919 7W-6N C6
5500 CHCG 60646 2919 7W-7N C4
7500 NLES 60077 2865 7W-9N C7
7500 NLES 60714 2865 7W-9N C7
7500 SKOK 60077 2865 7W-9N C7
7500 SKOK 60714 2865 7W-9N C7
S Menard Av
10 CHCG 60644 3031 7W-0S C5
1100 CCRO 60644 3031 7W-0S C7
1100 CCRO 60804 3031 7W-0S C7
4900 StkT 60638 3149 7W-5S C2
5900 CHCG 60638 3149 7W-7S C5
6500 BDPK 60638 3149 7W-7S C6
12400 ALSP 60463 3275 7W-14S D7
12400 ALSP 60803 3275 7W-14S D7
12400 WthT 60463 3275 7W-14S D7
12400 WthT 60803 3275 7W-14S D7
Menard Dr
- YKVL 60560 3261 42W-13S C6
S Menard Pl
11700 ALSP 60803 3275 7W-13S D5
N Mendell St
1900 CHCG 60614 2977 1W-2N C6
1900 CHCG 60622 2977 1W-2N C6
Mendelsson Ct
300 WHTN 60187 3082 25W-2S C4
Mendingwall Dr
8300 WDRG 60517 3205 22W-9S D4
8400 BGBK 60440 3205 22W-9S D4
8400 WDRG 60440 3205 22W-9S D4

STREET Block	City	ZIP	Map#	CGS	Grid
Mendocino Ct					
700	UYPK	60466	3684	3W-29S	A2
Mendocino Dr					
7600	GRNE	60031	2476	18W-35N	E5
Mendon Ln					
10	SMBG	60193	2858	26W-10N	A6
N Mendota Av					
6800	CHCG	60646	2919	7W-8N	B1
6800	CHCG	60714	2919	7W-8N	B1
6800	NLES	60714	2919	7W-8N	B1
Mendota Dr					
16900	LKPT	60441	3420	21W-20S	A5
Mendota Ln					
600	RMVL	60446	3340	24W-15S	C1
Menlo Ct					
800	JLET	60431	3497	28W-25S	B7
W Menna Ln					
16300	VrnT	60069	2701	16W-23N	D3
Menno Dr					
300	NlxT	60451	3501	18W-23S	A4
Menoma Tr					
600	DndT	60102	2747	34W-19N	E2
1000	ALGN	60102	2747	34W-19N	E2
Menominee Dr					
600	ALGN	60102	2694	34W-21N	B6
600	LIHL	60102	2694	34W-21N	B6
600	LIHL	60156	2694	34W-21N	C5
N Menominee Dr					
100	MNKA	60447	3672	33W-28S	B1
S Menominee Dr					
200	MNKA	60447	3672	33W-28S	B1
Menominee Ln					
400	NPVL	60563	3141	26W-5S	D2
W Menominee Pkwy					
6600	PSHT	60463	3275	8W-14S	A6
Menominee Rd					
2600	WKGN	60087	2479	12W-36N	C4
Menomini Ct					
400	MltT	60187	3081	26W-2S	E4
Menomini Dr					
10	MltT	60187	3082	26W-2S	A4
200	MltT	60187	3081	26W-2S	E4
Menomini Ln					
2100	MltT	60187	3081	26W-2S	D4
2100	WHTN	60187	3081	26W-2S	D4
W Menomonee St					
100	CHCG	60614	2978	0W-2N	A7
Mensching Rd					
300	ROSL	60172	2912	24W-6N	E6
400	BmdT	60172	2912	24W-6N	E6
Meota St					
300	PKFT	60466	3595	3W-27S	A4
Merbach Ct					
900	BmdT	60188	2968	26W-3N	A5
900	CLSM	60188	2968	26W-3N	A5
Merbach Dr					
-	BMDL	60108	2968	26W-4N	A4
-	BmdT	60188	2968	26W-4N	A5
-	CLSM	60108	2968	26W-4N	A4
1100	CLSM	60188	2968	26W-4N	A4
Merc Ln					
16500	LKPT	60441	3342	20W-18S	B7
Mercantile Ct					
400	WLNG	60090	2755	15W-17N	B5
Mercedes Dr					
100	CLSM	60188	2968	25W-3N	B6
Mercer Ct					
2200	NPVL	60565	3204	24W-10S	C5
Merchant Ct					
8400	LKWD	60014	2693	37W-23N	A1
Merchant Dr					
1400	ALGN	60102	2746	35W-20N	E2
Merchants Dr					
-	GnvT	60134	3019	37W-0S	D6
1600	GNVA	60134	3019	37W-0S	D6
E Merchants Dr					
10	OSWG	60543	3200	36W-10S	A6
10	OswT	60538	3200	36W-10S	A6
10	OswT	60543	3200	36W-10S	A6
N Merchants Dr					
200	OSWG	60543	3200	36W-10S	A6
W Merchants Dr					
10	OSWG	60543	3200	36W-10S	A6
10	OswT	60538	3200	36W-10S	A6
10	OswT	60543	3200	36W-10S	A6
Mercury Ct					
300	WynT	60103	2966	29W-5N	D1
900	SMBG	60193	2912	25W-9N	B1
Mercury Dr					
1000	SMBG	60193	2912	25W-8N	A2
Mercy Dr					
800	MHRY	60050	2528	32W-31N	A7
800	NndT	60050	2528	32W-31N	A7
Mercy Ln					
400	AURA	60506	3137	36W-5S	E4
N Meredith Av					
6200	CHCG	60646	2919	7W-7N	C3
Meredith Dr					
10	RVWD	60015	2755	13W-20N	E1
Meredith Ln					
100	SMWD	60107	2857	28W-9N	A7
100	SMWD	60107	2911	28W-9N	A1
Meredith Pl					
300	VNHL	60061	2647	17W-26N	B3
700	GNEN	60137	3025	22W-1N	C3
Merganser Ct					
400	LNHT	60046	2476	19W-37N	C2
Merganser Ln					
-	PtnT	60468	3860	10W-38S	D5
10	BmdT	60108	2967	26W-5N	E2
600	PTON	60468	3860	10W-38S	D5
Merganser Cove					
13100	PNFD	60585	3339	28W-15S	A2
Merganzer Ct					
3300	GNVA	60134	3019	37W-0N	B4
Meribel Ct					
200	SMBG	60194	2857	27W-10N	D5
Meridian Ct					
600	WHTN	60187	3082	24W-1S	D2
1500	BRLT	60103	2967	27W-5N	B1
Meridian Dr					
2400	JLET	60431	3417	28W-20S	B6
2400	PnfT	60431	3417	28W-20S	B6
2500	NCHI	60088	2593	11W-30N	C2
3500	NCHI	60064	2593	12W-30N	C2
S Meridian Dr					
2100	NCHI	60088	2593	11W-29N	D3
Meridian Ln					
200	LKWD	60014	2639	37W-25N	C5
300	CLLK	60014	2639	37W-25N	C5
Meridian Pkwy					
4100	AURA	60504	3140	30W-6S	A5
4300	AURA	60540	3140	30W-6S	C5
Meridian Rd					
-	DGvT	60439	3207	18W-11S	A7
-	DGvT	60439	3271	18W-11S	A1

STREET Block	City	ZIP	Map#	CGS	Grid
Meridian Rd					
300	AURA	60563	3080	30W-4S	A7
300	AURA	60563	3140	30W-4S	A1
300	NPVL	60563	3140	30W-4S	A1
300	NpvT	60563	3080	30W-4S	A7
300	NpvT	60563	3140	30W-4S	A1
Meridian Wy					
-	BFGV	60089	2701	16W-22N	C4
-	VrnT	60089	2701	16W-22N	C4
500	ANTH	60002	2357	24W-42N	C5
Meridian Lakes Dr					
-	AURA	60540	3140	30W-6S	B5
800	AURA	60504	3140	30W-6S	B5
Merimac Ct					
400	ROSL	60172	2912	24W-7N	E5
Merion Dr					
300	CRY	60013	2642	30W-25N	A5
8800	ODPK	60462	3346	11W-18S	A7
9000	ODPK	60462	3345	11W-18S	E7
25700	MONE	60449	3683	6W-31S	B5
Merioneth Dr					
-	CRTE	60417	3596	0E-29S	E7
-	CRTE	60417	3685	0E-29S	E1
-	CteT	60417	3685	0E-29S	E1
Merit Club Ln					
1500	GRNE	60048	2534	16W-32N	D5
6200	WrnT	60048	2534	16W-32N	D5
Merle Dr					
1500	AURA	60502	3139	32W-5S	D3
1500	NpvT	60502	3139	32W-5S	D3
Merle Ln					
500	WLNG	60090	2755	15W-17N	A5
3400	GNVW	60062	2809	12W-14N	B4
3500	GNVW	60025	2809	12W-14N	B4
E Merle Ln					
400	WLNG	60090	2755	15W-17N	A5
S Merle Ln					
600	WLNG	60090	2755	15W-17N	A5
W Merle St					
600	VLPK	60181	3026	18W-1N	E2
Merlin Ct					
10	DRFD	60015	2756	11W-20N	D2
300	BGBK	60440	3205	22W-11S	C7
5700	OKFT	60452	3347	7W-18S	D6
S Merlin Ct					
22500	TroT	60404	3584	30W-27S	B5
Merlin Dr					
500	SMBG	60193	2859	22W-9N	C7
700	EGVV	60007	2859	22W-9N	C7
700	EGVV	60193	2859	22W-9N	C7
Merlo St					
200	BTVA	60510	3078	35W-2S	B3
Merlot Ct					
400	MTGY	60543	3198	39W-11S	D7
1900	WLNG	60090	2808	14W-15N	B2
7600	GRNE	60031	2476	18W-35N	E6
Merlot Ln					
24100	PNFD	60586	3416	30W-19S	B3
Mermaid Ct					
800	SMBG	60193	2912	24W-9N	D1
Merriam Dr					
-	AURA	60504	3202	30W-8S	B1
Merriford Ln					
100	ROSL	60172	2912	25W-7N	B4
N Merril St					
100	BCVL	60407	4030	34W-44S	A4
400	BvlT	60407	4030	34W-44S	A4
S Merril St					
100	BCVL	60407	4030	34W-44S	A4
Merrill Av					
-	MNGV	60714	2864	9W-11N	C3
-	NLES	60714	2864	9W-11N	C3
200	CTCY	60409	3351	2E-17S	D6
1200	ALGN	60102	2747	34W-20N	D1
9400	MNGV	60053	2864	9W-11N	C1
16600	SHLD	60473	3429	2E-19S	D3
21500	BlmT	60411	3597	2E-26S	D1
21500	SLVL	60411	3597	2E-26S	D2
S Merrill Av					
-	CHCG	60633	3351	2E-15S	C2
-	CTCY	60409	3351	2E-15S	C2
7200	CHCG	60649	3153	2E-8S	C7
7500	CHCG	60649	3215	2E-9S	C2
7800	CHCG	60617	3215	2E-9S	C2
Merrill Ct					
300	LYVL	60048	2591	16W-29N	D4
21600	SLVL	60411	3597	2E-26S	D2
Merrill Dr					
10	MltT	60187	3082	25W-1S	B2
10	WHTN	60187	3082	25W-1S	B2
Merrill Ln					
400	GYLK	60030	2533	20W-33N	B3
Merrill Rd					
10	SgrT	60554	3075	43W-4S	B7
10	SgrT	60554	3135	42W-4S	C1
10	SRGV	60554	3135	42W-4S	C1
Merrill St					
1000	WNKA	60093	2758	5W-16N	E7
1000	WNKA	60093	2759		B7
15400	CTCY	60409	3351	2E-18S	C7
15400	ThtT	60409	3351	2E-18S	C7
15400	ThtT	60473	3351	2E-18S	C7
E Merrill St					
800	HMND	46320	3430		E1
N Merrill St					
10	PKRG	60068	2864	9W-9N	C7
10	PKRG	60068	2918	9W-8N	C1
8000	NLES	60068	2864	9W-10N	C6
8000	NLES	60714	2864	9W-10N	C6
8200	MaiT	60714	2864	9W-10N	C5
S Merrill St					
300	CHCG	60631	2918	9W-8N	C1
300	PKRG	60068	2918	9W-8N	C1
300	PKRG	60631	2918	9W-8N	C1
W Merrill St					
200	BlmT	60425	3508	0W-22S	D1
200	GNWD	60425	3508	0W-22S	D1
Merrill New Rd					
600	SgrT	60506	3135	41W-5S	E3
600	SgrT	60554	3135	41W-5S	E3
700	SRGV	60554	3135	41W-5S	E3
Merrillwood Rd					
800	HNDL	60521	3086	15W-4S	A7
Merrimac Av					
7700	BRBK	60459	3211	7W-9S	B2
7800	MNGV	60053	2865	7W-9N	B6
7800	NLES	60714	2865	7W-9N	B6
8700	OKLN	60453	3211	7W-10S	B4
8700	OKLN	60459	3211	7W-10S	B4
10000	CHRG	60415	3211	7W-11S	B7
10000	OKLN	60415	3211	7W-11S	B7
N Merrimac Av					
1600	CHCG	60639	3031	6W-0S	E6
1600	OKPK	60302	3031	6W-0S	E6
2600	CHCG	60639	2975	7W-3N	B5
4400	CHCG	60630	2975	7W-5N	B1

STREET Block	City	ZIP	Map#	CGS	Grid
N Merrimac Av					
4400	CHCG	60634	2975	7W-5N	B1
4800	CHCG	60630	2919	7W-6N	A6
7000	CHCG	60646	2919	7W-8N	B1
7600	NLES	60714	2865	7W-9N	B6
7800	MNGV	60053	2865	7W-9N	B6
S Merrimac Av					
4700	StkT	60638	3149	7W-5S	B2
4900	CHCG	60638	3149	7W-6S	B3
Merrimac Cir					
900	NPVL	60540	3203	27W-8S	B1
Merrimac Ln					
3200	LGGV	60047	2700	19W-21N	B6
E Merrimac Ln					
-	BmdT	60188	2967	26W-4N	E4
3700	CLSM	60188	2967	26W-4N	E4
3700	HRPK	60133	2967	26W-4N	E4
N Merrimac Ln					
1200	HRPK	60133	2967	26W-4N	E3
S Merrimac Ln					
1400	HRPK	60133	2967	26W-4N	D3
W Merrimac Ln					
3700	HRPK	60133	2967	26W-4N	D3
Merrimac Pl					
1300	AURA	60506	3137	37W-6S	C6
Merrimac St					
300	PKFT	60466	3595	3W-27S	A5
700	CRY	60013	2695	32W-23N	B1
Merrimack Ct					
10	BGBK	60440	3205	23W-11S	A7
1200	CLLK	60014	2693	36W-23N	E1
Merrimack Ln					
-	BCHR	60401	3774	0W-35S	D6
Merri Oaks Rd					
-	CbaT	60010	2696	28W-21N	D6
500	BNHL	60010	2696	28W-21N	D6
S Merrion Av					
9500	CHCG	60617	3215	2E-11S	D6
S Merrion Ln					
8700	CHCG	60652	3212	5W-10S	B4
8700	HMTN	60456	3212	5W-10S	B4
8700	HMTN	60652	3212	5W-10S	B4
11600	MTPK	60803	3276	4W-13S	E4
W Merrion Ln					
3300	CHCG	60655	3276	4W-13S	E4
3300	MTPK	60655	3276	4W-13S	E4
3300	MTPK	60803	3276	4W-13S	E4
Merritt Ct					
700	NPVL	60540	3204	25W-7S	A1
Merritt Ln					
1800	LKFT	60045	2703	12W-23N	B2
Merritton Ct					
11400	FKFT	60423	3590	14W-27S	E4
Merritton Rd					
22400	FKFT	60423	3590	14W-27S	E4
Merriweather Ln					
600	DndT	60118	2800	36W-16N	A1
E Merriwood Ln					
400	RLKB	60073	2532	22W-34N	B1
W Merriwood Ln					
22200	RLKB	60073	2475	22W-34N	B7
Merry Ct					
10	CTSD	60525	3147	12W-6S	B4
Merry Ln					
800	OKBK	60523	3085	16W-1S	E1
Merry Oaks Rd					
10	SMWD	60107	2856	29W-9N	E7
300	SMWD	60107	2910	29W-9N	E1
400	HnrT	60107	2910	29W-9N	E1
400	HnrT	60120	2910	29W-9N	E1
Merrywell Ct					
3100	CPVL	60110	2747	36W-18N	A5
Merton Av					
100	GNEN	60137	3025	22W-0S	C6
900	WKGN	60087	2480	10W-36N	A5
1000	WKGN	60087	2479	10W-36N	E5
1100	WKGN	60085	2479	10W-36N	E5
9500	OKLN	60453	3211	7W-11S	B6
10000	CHRG	60415	3211	7W-11S	B7
10000	OKLN	60415	3211	7W-11S	B7
W Merton Rd					
26000	BRTN	60010	2697	26W-20N	E7
26000	CbaT	60010	2697	26W-20N	D7
Mertz Ct					
2000	LSLE	60532	3142	24W-6S	E5
Mery Ln					
-	WthT	60482	3275	7W-13S	B5
Mery Drew Pkwy					
-	FftT	60423	3504	10W-23S	C4
N Meryls Tr					
1900	PLTN	60074	2752	21W-18N	C3
S Meryton Ct					
9700	PSHL	60465	3210	10W-11S	A7
E Mesa Ct					
700	GDLY	60407	4030	32W-43S	D2
700	RedT	60408	4030	32W-43S	D2
Mesa Dr					
500	HFET	60169	2858	24W-11N	E3
700	ELGN	60123	2853	36W-9N	E7
700	NPVL	60565	3203	27W-10S	B7
800	ELGN	60123	2907	36W-9N	E1
900	LIHL	60156	2694	34W-21N	C5
1400	BGBK	60490	3267	26W-12S	E2
E Mesa Dr					
400	GDLY	60407	4030	32W-43S	D2
N Mesa Dr					
1200	JLET	60435	3497	27W-22S	C2
3100	TroT	60435	3497	27W-22S	C2
Mesa Ln					
-	AURA	60502	3078	33W-3S	E6
-	AURA	60502	3079	33W-3S	A6
N Mesa St					
200	GDLY	60407	4030	32W-43S	D2
Mesa Verde Ct					
500	CLSM	60188	2967	26W-3N	D6
Mescallero Ct					
100	NPVL	60563	3141	26W-4S	D2
Mesquite Dr					
14500	OrlT	60467	3344	14W-17S	E5
Messenger Blvd					
-	HMGN	60491	3421	17W-18S	C1
Messenger Cir					
300	NARA	60542	3077	37W-3S	B7
S Messenger Cir					
-	HmrT	60491	3421	17W-19S	B2
Messina Ct					
10	TYPK	60477	3505	8W-23S	B4
Messina Dr					
-	OMFD	60461	3507	3W-24S	A5
Messiner Dr					
11600	HTLY	60142	2744	42W-20N	B1
Messines Ridge Ct					
2300	JLET	60435	3417	27W-21S	C6
Messner Dr					
10	WLNG	60090	2755	14W-16N	C7

STREET Block	City	ZIP	Map#	CGS	Grid
Mestic Ct					
300	SEGN	60177	2908	34W-9N	E1
Metalmaster Wy					
-	MHRY	60050	2527	33W-31N	D7
-	MHRY	60050	2584	33W-31N	E1
Metawa Ln					
10	RVWD	60015	2702	14W-21N	C6
Metcalf Ct					
4600	JLET	60586	3416	29W-21S	D7
Metcalf Ln					
-	SRWD	60404	3495	31W-23S	E4
Metoyer Ct					
1700	WCHI	60185	2965	31W-4N	E4
1700	WynT	60185	2965	31W-4N	E4
S Metron Dr					
12900	CHCG	60633	3279	1E-14S	B7
W Metropole St					
7900	EDPK	60171	2974	9W-3N	B4
7900	EDPK	60707	2974	9W-3N	B4
Metropolitan Av					
-	BHPK	60087	2421	12W-39N	C6
-	BHPK	60099	2421	12W-39N	C6
700	BGBK	60490	3267	26W-13S	D6
2400	WKGN	60087	2479	12W-36N	C3
2600	BHPK	60087	2479	12W-36N	C3
N Metropolitan Av					
10	WKGN	60085	2536	12W-33N	C1
1300	WKGN	60085	2479	12W-35N	C6
1300	WkgT	60085	2479	12W-35N	C6
37400	WKGN	60087	2479	12W-37N	C2
37600	BHPK	60087	2479	12W-37N	C1
39000	BHPK	60087	2421	12W-38N	C6
39000	WKGN	60087	2421	12W-38N	C6
Metropolitan St					
400	AURA	60502	3139	31W-7S	E7
Metropolitan Wy					
600	DSPN	60016	2863	12W-11N	B3
Mettawa Ln					
13800	LbvT	60045	2648	13W-27N	D2
13800	MTWA	60045	2648	13W-27N	D2
Mettawa Woods Ln					
14000	MTWA	60045	2648	14W-26N	D4
Mettel Rd					
-	AraT	60542	3138	35W-5S	B2
-	AURA	60542	3138	35W-5S	B2
-	NARA	60542	3138	35W-5S	A2
1200	AraT	60505	3138	34W-4S	E2
1300	AraT	60504	3138	35W-5S	B2
1300	AURA	60504	3138	35W-5S	B2
E Metzen St					
100	HRVD	60033	2406	50W-38N	A7
W Metzen St					
200	HRVD	60033	2406	50W-38N	A7
800	CmgT	60033	2405	51W-38N	E7
800	HRVD	60033	2405	51W-38N	E7
N Meyer Av					
1600	CHCG	60614	2978	0W-2N	A7
Meyer Ct					
300	SMWD	60107	2857	27W-11N	D4
500	AraT	60506	3199	38W-8S	A1
500	AURA	60506	3199	38W-8S	A1
1200	NPVL	60564	3203	28W-10S	A6
1200	WldT	60564	3203	28W-10S	A6
1400	JLET	60586	3496	31W-22S	A1
1600	ELGN	60123	2854	35W-10N	A5
N Meyer Ct					
10	DSPN	60016	2862	14W-12N	C2
S Meyer Ct					
10	DSPN	60016	2862	14W-11N	C2
Meyer Dr					
100	ALGN	60102	2694	34W-21N	D6
1000	CLLK	60014	2640	33W-24N	E7
1000	CLLK	60014	2694	33W-24N	E1
5200	LSLE	60532	3143	22W-5S	C3
W Meyer Dr					
1200	ADSN	60101	2970	20W-4N	B3
Meyer Rd					
-	PLNO	60545	3259	48W-12S	B4
10	LtRT	60545	3259	48W-12S	B4
300	BNVL	60106	2915	16W-6N	E1
1300	HFET	60169	2858	25W-12N	B2
6200	WDRG	60517	3143	22W-6S	B5
7000	BtnT	60050	2413	30W-38N	E7
7000	BtnT	60081	2413	31W-39N	E5
7000	RcmT	60050	2413	30W-38N	E7
7000	SPGV	60050	2413	30W-38N	E7
7000	SPGV	60081	2413	31W-39N	E5
W Meyer Rd					
14000	WrnT	60031	2478	14W-37N	D2
Meyer St					
1400	ELGN	60123	2854	35W-10N	B5
Meyers Rd					
-	YkTp	60148	3084	18W-2S	E2
-	YkTp	60181	3084	18W-2S	E2
-	YkTp	60515	3084	18W-3S	E6
2700	OKBK	60523	3084	18W-2S	E4
2700	YkTp	60523	3084	18W-2S	E4
Meyers Rd CO-25					
-	YkTp	60148	3084	18W-2S	E2
-	YkTp	60181	3084	18W-2S	E2
-	YkTp	60515	3084	18W-3S	E6
2700	OKBK	60523	3084	18W-2S	E4
2700	YkTp	60523	3084	18W-2S	E4
S Meyers Rd					
1200	YkTp	60148	3026	18W-1S	E7
1300	YkTp	60148	3084	18W-1S	E1
1600	OKTR	60181	3084	18W-1S	E1
1600	YkTp	60181	3084	18W-1S	E1
2000	YkTp	60523	3084	18W-1S	E2
S Meyers Rd CO-25					
1200	YkTp	60148	3026	18W-1S	E7
1300	YkTp	60148	3084	18W-1S	E1
1600	OKTR	60181	3084	18W-1S	E1
1600	YkTp	60181	3084	18W-1S	E1
2000	YkTp	60523	3084	18W-2S	E2
Meyers St					
100	SRWD	60404	3496	30W-24S	C6
Meyerson Wy					
10	WLNG	60090	2755	14W-18N	C3
MGM Dr					
11700	ODPK	60467	3422	14W-21S	D7
Mgsr Cardiff Dr					
5100	OKLN	60453	3275	6W-12S	E1
Mgsr McNichols Dr					
5300	OKLN	60453	3211	6W-10S	D6
Mgsr Mulcahey St					
6900	CHCG	60626	2921	2W-8N	C1
M Hershman Dr					
1500	JLET	60431	3417	28W-21S	B7
Mia Dr					
1800	CTHL	60403	3418	26W-21S	A7
W Miami Av					
5900	CHCG	60646	2919	7W-7N	B3
Miami Ct					
10	NPVL	60563	3141	26W-4S	D2

STREET Block	City	ZIP	Map#	CGS	Grid
Miami Ln					
1300	DSPN	60018	2862	15W-10N	B6
Miami Rd					
1000	WLMT	60091	2812	5W-14N	A5
2000	WKGN	60087	2479	12W-36N	C4
3800	BLWD	60104	3029	12W-0N	A4
Miami St					
100	PKFT	60466	3595	4W-27S	A5
200	PKFT	60466	3594	4W-27S	E4
400	JLET	60432	3499	21W-23S	E4
400	JltT	60432	3499	21W-23S	E3
400	RNPK	60471	3594	4W-27S	E3
Michael Av					
100	MDLN	60060	2646	19W-27N	C1
2400	ZION	60099	2421	12W-40N	C3
3400	PKCY	60085	2536	13W-33N	A2
17700	CCHL	60478	3426	5W-21S	B6
Michael Ct					
10	LIHL	60156	2694	34W-22N	C5
10	LKZH	60047	2698	23W-21N	E5
400	DSPN	60016	2862	15W-11N	A3
400	SchT	60175	2907	36W-7N	E6
1000	GLHT	60139	3025	23W-1N	A2
1300	HFET	60192	2804	24W-15N	C3
5700	RGMW	60008	2805	21W-14N	C5
9300	MNGV	60053	2864	9W-11N	B2
18500	HLCT	60429	3506	4W-22S	D1
19300	MKNA	60448	3503	13W-23S	A3
34600	GrtT	60041	2472	28W-34N	E7
S Michael Ct					
2500	NndT	60051	2586	30W-29N	B4
Michael Dr					
1000	GLHT	60139	3025	23W-1N	A2
14000	ODPK	60462	3346	11W-16S	A4
18600	HLCT	60429	3506	4W-22S	D1
N Michael Dr					
1200	WDDL	60191	2915	18W-7N	A3
1500	EGvT	60007	2915	18W-7N	A3
S Michael Dr					
10300	BGVW	60455	3274	9W-12S	D1
10300	PSHL	60455	3274	9W-12S	D1
10300	PSHL	60465	3274	9W-12S	D1
15100	PnfT	60446	3339	27W-18S	D7
15100	PnfT	60544	3339	27W-18S	D7
15100	RMVL	60446	3339	27W-18S	D7
15300	PnfT	60544	3417	27W-18S	D1
22700	CNHN	60410	3584	29W-27S	E5
Michael Ln					
100	NlxT	60451	3501	18W-23S	B3
3800	GNVW	60025	2809	11W-15N	D2
3800	GNVW	60062	2809	11W-15N	D2
6200	MTSN	60443	3505	7W-24S	C5
W Michael Ln					
10	AddT	60101	2970	18W-4N	E4
10	ADSN	60101	2970	18W-4N	E4
Michael Mnr					
10	MaiT	60025	2864	10W-12N	B1
10	MaiT	60714	2864	10W-12N	B2
10	NLES	60714	2864	10W-12N	B2
300	GNVW	60025	2864	10W-12N	B1
400	GNVW	60025	2810	10W-12N	B7
Michael Rd					
10	DSPN	60016	2862	15W-11N	B3
10	PKFT	60466	3595	2W-27S	C4
Michael St					
500	CRTE	60417	3685	1W-30S	B3
1100	LKPT	60441	3419	21W-19S	E2
1100	LKPT	60441	3420	21W-19S	A2
2300	MchT	60097	2526	36W-34N	D1
2600	MchT	60097	2469	36W-34N	D7
10600	HTLY	60142	2692	40W-21N	A6
S Michael St					
200	MPPT	60056	2861	17W-12N	C1
Michael Browning Wy					
-	WCHI	60185	3022	29W-0S	D7
Michaele Dr					
15300	OKFT	60452	3347	6W-18S	E7
Michael John Ct					
4400	RNPK	60471	3594	5W-27S	C4
Michael John Dr					
10	NLES	60068	2864	10W-9N	B6
10	NLES	60714	2864	10W-9N	B6
10	PKRG	60068	2864	10W-9N	B6
Michael John Ln					
4400	RNPK	60471	3594	5W-27S	B4
Michael Jordan Dr					
-	AURA	60504	3140	30W-6S	C5
E Michael Manor Ln					
2200	ANHT	60004	2807	16W-15N	D1
Michael McFarlane Dr					
1400	CHCG	60640	2921	1W-6N	C5
Michael McGuire Dr					
-	LMBD	60148	3026	20W-0N	B4
Michaels Ln					
1000	LYVL	60048	2591	15W-27N	E7
S Michaels St					
24700	CteT	60417	3686	2E-30S	C2
Michael Todd Ter					
10300	GNVW	60025	2809	11W-13N	D6
10300	NfdT	60025	2809	11W-13N	D6
Michas Dr					
2300	JLET	60586	3416	31W-21S	A6
2300	PnfT	60586	3416	31W-21S	A6
Michaux Rd					
10	RVSD	60546	3088	9W-3S	C4
Michel Ln					
1500	AraT	60505	3138	33W-5S	E4
1500	AURA	60505	3138	33W-5S	E4
Michelangelo Dr					
400	BGBK	60440	3205	22W-11S	C7
Michele Ct					
10	BGBK	60490	3339	28W-15S	B1
Michele Dr					
1300	PLTN	60074	2753	19W-16N	C7
1600	MngT	60152	2578	49W-30N	C2
24800	PNFD	60544	3338	31W-16S	A3
25000	PNFD	60544	3337	31W-16S	E4
W Michele Ln					
21800	AntT	60002	2417	21W-40N	C3
Michelle Cir					
1300	SMBG	60173	2859	21W-10N	D4
Michelle Ct					
7900	ODPK	60462	3346	9W-17S	C4
12300	SlmT	53179	2357		B3
S Michelle Ct					
26600	MonT	60449	3683	6W-32S	B7
Michelle Dr					
600	BlmT	60411	3510	4E-25S	C7
700	LYWD	60411	3510	4E-25S	B7
Michelle Ln					
1100	LMBD	60148	3026	19W-0S	D7
8200	TYPK	60477	3424	10W-19S	B3
Michelle Pl					
100	SMBG	60173	2859	21W-11N	D4
Michelline Ct					
1400	HFET	60192	2804	24W-14N	C3

STREET Block City ZIP Map# CGS Grid

Michelline Ln
600 NHBK 60062 2756 12W-18N B4
Michels Av
3900 AURA 60505 3138 34W-6S D5
Michels St
700 AURA 60505 3138 34W-6S D5
Michigamme Rd
400 LKFT 60045 2649 11W-25N D4
Michigan Av
10 EDND 60118 2800 35W-16N C1
10 EDND 60118 2801 34W-16N A2
10 HDPK 60035 2704 9W-23N D3
10 HIWD 60040 2704 9W-23N D3
100 VLPK 60181 3085 18W-1S A1
100 YkTp 60148 3085 18W-1S A1
100 YkTp 60181 3085 18W-1S A1
200 OKTR 60181 3085 18W-1S A1
300 AURA 60506 3138 36W-6S A5
400 AURA 60506 3137 36W-6S E5
500 SEGN 60177 2908 35W-9N B2
700 ELGN 60123 2908 35W-9N B1
700 ELGN 60177 2908 35W-9N B1
900 WLMT 60091 2813 3W-14N A5
1100 WLMT 60091 2812 E4
1200 EVTN 60202 2867 2W-10N C4
1800 NPVL 60563 3140 29W-6S D4
4800 SRPK 60176 2917 12W-6N C7
5100 SRPK 60656 2917 12W-6N C7
13000 HTLY 60142 2744 42W-18N C4
14600 DLTN 60419 3350 0W-17S C5
14600 DLTN 60827 3350 0W-17S C5
14600 RVDL 60827 3350 0W-17S C5
15700 SHLD 60473 3350 0E-18S D7
15900 SHLD 60473 3428 0E-18S D1
26400 AntT 60002 2415 26W-38N D7
E Michigan Av
10 PLTN 60067 2805 20W-15N E3
N Michigan Av
10 ADSN 60101 2971 18W-3N A5
10 CHCG 60602 3034 0E-0N C4
10 CHCG 60603 3034 0E-0N C4
100 CHCG 60601 3034 0E-0N C4
100 EMHT 60126 3028 15W-1N A1
400 VLPK 60181 3027 18W-1N A2
900 CHCG 60611 3034 0E-0N C3
900 PNFD 60544 3338 30W-17S B6
5200 CHCG 60018 2917 12W-6N C6
5200 CHCG 60656 2917 12W-6N C6
5200 RSMT 60018 2917 12W-6N C6
5200 SRPK 60176 2917 12W-6N C6
5200 SRPK 60656 2917 12W-6N C6
S Michigan Av
10 ADSN 60101 2971 18W-3N A6
10 CHCG 60602 3034 0E-0S C4
10 CHCG 60603 3034 0E-0S C4
100 AddT 60101 3027 18W-2N A1
100 AddT 60181 3027 18W-2N A1
100 ADSN 60101 3027 18W-2N A1
100 CHCG 60604 3034 0E-0S C5
300 CHCG 60605 3034 0E-1S C7
1000 VLPK 60181 3027 18W-2N A1
1200 VLPK 60148 3027 18W-0S A7
1200 YkTp 60148 3027 18W-0S A7
1200 YkTp 60181 3027 18W-0S A7
1500 CHCG 60616 3034 0E-1S C7
1600 CHCG 60616 3092 0E-2S C2
1600 VLPK 60181 3085 18W-1S A2
1600 YkTp 60148 3085 18W-1S A2
1600 YkTp 60181 3085 18W-1S A2
3400 CHCG 60653 3092 0E-3S C4
4600 CHCG 60615 3092 0E-4S C7
4700 CHCG 60615 3152 0E-6S C3
6600 CHCG 60637 3152 0E-7S C5
7000 CHCG 60619 3152 0E-8S C7
7500 CHCG 60619 3214 0E-10S C4
9400 CHCG 60628 3214 0E-11S C6
10300 CHCG 60628 3278 0W-14S C6
13300 CHCG 60827 3350 0W-15S D1
13500 RVDL 60827 3350 0W-15S C2
14500 DLTN 60419 3350 0W-17S C4
14500 DLTN 60827 3350 0W-17S C4
W Michigan Av
10 PLTN 60067 2805 21W-15N D3
Michigan Blvd
- NHFD 60093 2811 6W-15N D3
- NtrT 60093 2811 6W-15N D2
- WNKA 60093 2811 6W-15N D2
W Michigan Blvd
9700 BHPK 60099 2422 9W-38N C6
Michigan Ct
10 VNHL 60061 2647 16W-26N D2
2600 NCHI 60088 2593 12W-30N C3
16200 LktT 60403 3418 25W-19S B3
18200 ODPK 60467 3423 13W-21S B7
S Michigan Ct
500 ADSN 60101 2971 18W-2N A6
Michigan Dr
100 BMDL 60108 2969 22W-5N D2
600 RMVL 60446 3340 24W-15S C1
10600 SPGV 60081 2355 30W-42N B5
Michigan Ln
600 EGVV 60007 2913 21W-8N D2
600 EGVV 60193 2913 21W-8N D2
Michigan Rd
300 FKFT 60423 3503 12W-25S D7
E Michigan Rd
100 NlxT 60451 3589 17W-25S C1
W Michigan Rd
100 NlxT 60451 3589 18W-25S B1
400 NLNX 60451 3589 18W-25S A1
Michigan St
200 ELGN 60120 2855 33W-11N A4
600 BDWD 60408 3942 31W-41S A4
700 WHTN 60187 3024 24W-0S D7
16100 LktT 60403 3418 25W-19S B2
E Michigan St
400 HMND 46320 3352 D5
N Michigan St
10 JLET 60433 3499 23W-23S A5
200 JLET 60432 3499 23W-23S A4
500 EMHT 60126 2972 15W-2N A7
Michigan Bay
- BHPK 60099 2422 9W-38N D6
Michigan City Rd
- HMND 46324 3430 4E-19S C1
10 CTCY 60409 3430 3E-18S A1
600 CTCY 60409 3352 3E-18S A7
1000 CTCY 60409 3351 2E-17S C6
1900 DLTN 60409 3351 2E-17S C6
1900 DLTN 60419 3351 2E-17S C6
Michigan Island Ct
- FKFT 60423 3504 11W-24S A6
Michigan Island Dr
- FKFT 60423 3504 11W-25S A6
Mickey Ln
2000 GNVW 60025 2810 8W-14N E3
2000 NHFD 60093 2810 8W-14N E3
Micou Dr
- FKFT 60423 3504 10W-25S B6
Mid America Plz
10 OKTR 60181 3085 17W-1S C2
Mid America Plz SR-83
10 OKTR 60181 3085 17W-1S C2
Midan Dr
800 BbyT 60119 3018 39W-1N D4
Middaugh Av
4300 DRGV 60515 3144 20W-4S B1
5500 DRGV 60516 3144 20W-6S B4
Middaugh Ct
6000 DRGV 60516 3144 20W-6S B5
Middaugh Dr
200 DGvT 60439 3206 20W-11S C7
400 DGvT 60439 3270 20W-11S C1
Middaugh Rd
200 CNHL 60514 3085 16W-4S D7
200 CNHL 60514 3145 16W-4S D1
200 CNHL 60559 3085 16W-4S D7
200 WTMT 60559 3085 16W-4S D7
Middaugh St
5800 DRGV 60516 3144 20W-6S B4
Midday Dr
1700 ZION 60099 2421 12W-41N B1
Middle Av
10 AURA 60506 3138 36W-7S A7
200 AURA 60506 3200 36W-7S A1
500 AURA 60506 3199 36W-8S E1
3600 JNBG 60050 2471 30W-35N E5
Middle Dr
- SMBG 60173 2805 22W-12N D7
- SMBG 60173 2859 21W-11N E2
- WLMT 60091 2813 2W-13N B5
Middle Fk
- VOLO 60041 2530 27W-33N B3
Middle Rd
200 LslT 60563 3142 25W-5S B3
200 NPVL 60563 3142 25W-5S B3
500 ELGN 60123 2854 34W-10N D7
4600 GRNE 60031 2535 14W-33N B2
Middle St
- WMTN 60481 3853 28W-38S C7
E Middle St
300 SEGN 60177 2908 34W-8N E3
500 BRLT 60103 2909 33W-8N B3
500 BRLT 60120 2909 33W-8N B3
500 ElgT 60177 2909 33W-8N A3
500 SEGN 60103 2909 33W-8N A3
500 SEGN 60120 2909 33W-8N B3
500 SEGN 60177 2909 33W-8N A3
800 ElgT 60177 2908 34W-8N E3
W Middle St
10 SEGN 60177 2908 34W-8N C3
Middleburg Ct
1300 NPVL 60540 3142 25W-7S B6
Middleburg Rd
1300 NPVL 60540 3142 25W-7S B6
Middlebury Av
8100 WDRG 60517 3206 20W-9S B3
8200 DRN 60561 3206 20W-9S B3
8200 WDRG 60561 3206 20W-9S B3
Middlebury Ct
10 SMWD 60107 2857 28W-12N B1
200 SMBG 60193 2859 21W-10N E6
Middlebury Ct E
3000 AURA 60504 3201 31W-9S D4
Middlebury Ct W
2900 AURA 60504 3201 31W-9S D4
Middlebury Dr
400 LKVL 60046 2475 21W-37N D2
1100 AURA 60504 3201 31W-10S D7
1600 AURA 60503 3201 31W-10S D7
2100 WldT 60503 3201 31W-10S D6
2400 WldT 60585 3201 31W-10S D7
Middlebury Ln
10 LNSH 60069 2702 13W-21N D5
500 EGVV 60007 2860 18W-9N E7
500 EGVV 60007 2914 18W-9N D1
1100 WLNG 60090 2754 16W-18N D3
1200 WLMT 60091 2812 5W-14N A4
1300 NtrT 60093 2812 5W-14N A4
5600 GRNE 60031 2534 16W-33N E6
Middlebury Rd
10 BNHL 60010 2748 30W-18N E2
600 EGVV 60007 2914 18W-9N E1
Middlecoff Ct
6500 WDRG 60517 3143 23W-7S A7
Middlecreek Ln
10 SchT 60175 2963 36W-4N D3
Middlefield Av
2000 AraT 60506 3199 38W-8S A2
Middlefield Ct
10 LIHL 60156 2693 38W-22N A3
Middleford Ct
10 SEGN 60177 2908 35W-9N B1
Middlefork Dr
1300 LKFT 60045 2649 12W-27N B2
Middlefork Rd
2000 NHFD 60093 2811 7W-16N B1
W Middle Fork Rd
24300 DRPK 60010 2698 24W-21N B5
24500 ElaT 60010 2698 24W-21N B5
25000 CbaT 60010 2698 24W-21N B5
Middlelane Ln
2600 AlqT 60013 2641 31W-25N D4
Middle Pinecreek Dr
14600 OrlT 60467 3344 14W-17S C5
S Middlepoint Av
25600 MONE 60449 3683 6W-31S A5
Middle Queensbury Ct
2500 AURA 60506 3136 39W-7S E7
Middlesax Dr
3200 LGGV 60047 2700 19W-21N C6
Middlesex Ct
10 LNSH 60069 2701 16W-23N E2
400 BFGV 60089 2754 16W-17N D4
Middlesex Dr
10 CPVL 60110 2748 33W-18N A4
3500 DrrT 60098 2583 37W-28N B6
Middleton Av
1100 LSLE 60532 3143 23W-4S A1
1700 LSLE 60532 3142 24W-4S D1
1700 LslT 60532 3142 23W-4S E1
N Middleton Av
10 PLTN 60067 2805 22W-16N B1
10 PltT 60067 2805 22W-16N B1
100 PLTN 60067 2752 22W-16N B7
100 PltT 60067 2752 22W-16N B7
S Middleton Av
10 PltT 60067 2805 22W-15N B1
400 PLTN 60067 2805 22W-15N B2
Middleton Ct
700 PLTN 60067 2805 22W-15N B3
1300 DSPN 60016 2808 13W-13N D6
1900 WHTN 60187 3082 25W-2S B4
2700 AURA 60503 3201 32W-10S D7
Middleton Dr
500 ROSL 60172 2912 24W-6N C6
1900 WHTN 60187 3082 25W-2S B4
N Middleton Dr
20800 KLDR 60047 2699 20W-20N E7
Middleton Ln
600 DSPN 60016 2808 13W-13N D6
800 BRLT 60103 2910 30W-7N B5
900 IVNS 60010 2804 25W-15N A1
6300 MHRY 60050 2527 35W-32N A5
N Middleton Pkwy
26000 FmtT 60060 2645 21W-26N D3
26000 HNWD 60047 2645 21W-26N D3
26000 HNWD 60060 2645 21W-26N D3
Middleton Pl
1000 LSLE 60532 3143 23W-4S B1
Middleton Rd
8900 DRN 60561 3206 19W-10S D5
Middletown Ln
10400 HTLY 60142 2692 39W-20N C7
Middletree Ln
10 HNWD 60047 2644 23W-24N D6
Middletree Rd
200 JltT 60433 3587 23W-25S A2
Midfield Dr
500 AURA 60506 3136 39W-7S D7
500 SgrT 60506 3136 39W-7S D7
Midfield Ln
600 NHBK 60062 2757 8W-16N E6
600 NHBK 60062 2758 8W-17N A6
Midhurst Ct
10 NPVL 60565 3203 26W-9S E5
2000 JLET 60435 3497 26W-22S E1
N Midhurst Ln
2000 JLET 60435 3497 26W-22S E1
Midhurst Rd
2100 DRGV 60516 3143 21W-7S E6
2100 DRGV 60516 3144 21W-7S A6
6500 DRGV 60516 3143 21W-7S E6
6500 WDRG 60517 3143 21W-7S E6
Midland Av
100 RKDL 60436 3498 25W-25S B7
100 RKDL 60436 3586 25W-25S B1
1600 HDPK 60035 2704 10W-21N B6
19100 FftT 60448 3503 13W-23S A2
19100 MKNA 60448 3503 13W-23S A3
N Midland Av
10 JLET 60435 3498 25W-23S B5
10 JLET 60436 3498 25W-23S B5
S Midland Av
10 JLET 60435 3498 25W-24S B6
10 JLET 60436 3498 25W-24S B6
10 MDLN 60060 2646 18W-27N D1
500 RKDL 60436 3498 25W-24S B6
W Midland Ct
1400 JLET 60436 3498 25W-24S B6
Midland Dr
2500 NPVL 60564 3203 28W-10S A7
E Midland Dr
- RDLK 60073 2532 23W-34N A2
100 RLKP 60073 2532 22W-33N A2
W Midland Dr
200 RDLK 60073 2532 23W-34N A2
200 RLKP 60073 2532 23W-34N A2
Midlane Dr
- NndT 60012 2640 35W-27N A2
100 CLLK 60012 2640 35W-27N A2
200 CLLK 60012 2639 35W-26N E2
1000 AURA 60505 3138 34W-5S D4
3000 WKGN 60083 2478 14W-37N D2
Midlothian Av
2000 HDPK 60035 2704 8W-22N D4
N Midlothian Rd
100 MDLN 60060 2590 19W-27N C7
600 FmtT 60060 2590 19W-30N C2
2300 FmtT 60048 2590 19W-30N C2
2300 LYVL 60048 2590 19W-30N C2
2300 LYVL 60060 2590 19W-30N C2
23000 ElaT 60047 2699 23W-23N A1
23000 LKZH 60047 2699 23W-23N A1
24000 ElaT 60047 2645 21W-25N C6
24000 LKZH 60047 2645 22W-24N B7
24300 HNWD 60047 2645 21W-25N C6
25500 ElaT 60060 2645 21W-25N D5
25500 HNWD 60060 2645 21W-25N D5
25800 FmtT 60060 2645 21W-25N E4
26000 LGGV 60060 2645 21W-26N E4
26200 FmtT 60047 2646 20W-26N A3
26200 FmtT 60060 2646 20W-26N A3
26200 LGGV 60047 2646 20W-26N A3
26200 LGGV 60060 2646 20W-26N A3
26500 MDLN 60047 2646 20W-26N A3
26500 MDLN 60060 2646 20W-26N A3
N Midlothian Rd CO-V73
700 FmtT 60060 2590 19W-30N C2
700 MDLN 60060 2590 19W-30N C2
2300 FmtT 60048 2590 19W-30N C2
2300 LYVL 60048 2590 19W-30N C2
2300 LYVL 60060 2590 19W-30N C2
S Midlothian Rd
10 MDLN 60060 2646 19W-27N C2
100 FmtT 60060 2646 19W-26N B2
500 LGGV 60047 2646 19W-26N B2
500 MDLN 60047 2646 19W-26N B2
Midlothian Tpk
4200 CTWD 60445 3348 5W-16S A3
4200 RBBN 60445 3348 5W-16S A3
4200 RBBN 60472 3348 5W-16S A3
4800 BmnT 60445 3348 5W-16S A3
5000 BmnT 60445 3347 7W-16S D4
5000 MDLN 60445 3347 7W-16S D4
5000 MDLN 60445 3348 5W-16S A3
5100 CTWD 60445 3347 6W-16S E3
W Midlothian Tpk
3600 RBBN 60472 3348 4W-16S C3
3800 CTWD 60472 3348 4W-16S C2
4100 CTWD 60445 3348 5W-16S C3
4100 RBBN 60445 3348 5W-16S C3
Midmar Ln
100 IVNS 60067 2752 22W-16N B7
Midnight Pth
- LKVL 60046 2475 23W-37N A2
Midnight Pass
500 ANTH 60002 2358 23W-42N A5
1000 NLNX 60451 3588 19W-27S E4
1000 NLNX 60451 3589 19W-27S A4
Mid Oak Ln
2600 MchT 60051 2528 31W-32N D5
Mid Oaks Ln
10 BNHL 60010 2750 27W-20N C1
Midway Av
1200 SCRL 60174 3020 34W-2N E1
Midway Ct
10 BNVL 60106 2972 15W-5N A1
10 CTCY 60409 3430 C3
10 HMND 46324 3430 C3
100 CLLK 60012 2640 35W-27N A1
1500 EGVV 60007 2861 17W-10N C6
Midway Dr
10 WLBK 60527 3207 16W-8S D2
200 MDLN 60060 2646 18W-27N D2
500 BTVA 60510 3078 36W-2S A4
500 DSPN 60018 2861 16W-10N E6
500 MPPT 60056 2861 16W-10N E6
3100 ISLK 60042 2586 28W-28N D5
Midway Ln
100 VNHL 60061 2647 16W-24N C6
1400 GNVW 60025 2810 10W-14N A5
Midway Pk
500 GNEN 60137 3025 21W-0N D4
W Midway Pk
5700 CHCG 60644 3031 7W-0N C3
5900 CHCG 60302 3031 7W-0N B3
5900 OKPK 60302 3031 7W-0N B3
Midway Rd
800 NHBK 60062 2757 8W-17N E4
1000 NHBK 60062 2758 8W-17N A5
Midway St
400 FRGV 60021 2696 29W-22N C3
W Midway St
28800 AlqT 60013 2696 28W-23N D1
28800 CbaT 60013 2696 28W-23N D1
Midway Plaisance Dr
- CHCG 60637 3152 1E-6S E3
- CHCG 60637 3153 1E-6S A4
Midwest Av
10600 HTLY 60142 2692 39W-21N C6
Midwest Ln
1100 WHTN 60187 3082 25W-1S A2
Midwest Rd
2200 OKBK 60181 3085 17W-2S B4
2200 OKBK 60523 3085 17W-2S B4
2300 YkTp 60523 3085 17W-2S B3
3400 OKBK 60559 3085 17W-3S B5
3500 WTMT 60523 3085 17W-3S B6
3500 WTMT 60559 3085 17W-3S B5
Midwest Rd CO-15
2200 OKBK 60181 3085 17W-2S B4
2200 OKBK 60523 3085 17W-2S B4
2300 YkTp 60523 3085 17W-2S B3
3400 OKBK 60559 3085 17W-3S B5
3500 WTMT 60523 3085 17W-3S B6
3500 WTMT 60559 3085 17W-3S B5
Midwest Club Pkwy
- YkTp 60523 3085 18W-3S A4
600 OKBK 60523 3085 18W-3S A4
700 OKBK 60523 3084 18W-3S E5
N Mies Van Der Rohe Wy
800 CHCG 60611 3034 D2
Mighell Rd
10 SgrT 60554 3196 43W-9S E5
10 SgrT 60554 3197 43W-8S A3
800 BtlT 60512 3196 43W-9S E4
800 BtlT 60545 3196 43W-9S E5
Mignin Dr
300 WNVL 60555 3080 29W-3S E6
Miguel Ct
- AxST 60447 3672 32W-29S C2
- MNKA 60447 3672 32W-29S C2
Mikan Ln
10 DPgT 60441 3341 23W-15S A3
10 DPgT 60446 3341 23W-15S A3
10 RMVL 60446 3341 23W-15S A3
Mikasa Ct
1000 JLET 60431 3496 29W-22S C2
Mike Ct
700 NPVL 60563 3140 29W-6S D4
Milan Av
800 JltT 60433 3499 22W-25S C7
Milan Ct
300 SMBG 60193 2858 23W-9N E7
Milan Ln
500 HFET 60169 2858 24W-11N E4
Milan Wy
7700 GRNE 60031 2533 18W-34N E1
Milano Dr
300 AlqT 60013 2695 32W-23N B2
300 CRY 60013 2695 32W-23N B2
Milbeck Av
700 EGVV 60007 2914 19W-8N D1
Milbeck Ct
700 EGVV 60007 2914 19W-8N D1
W Milbrook Dr
12800 HTLY 60142 2744 41W-20N C1
S Milbrook Ln
1700 ANHT 60005 2861 18W-12N A2
Milburn Av
100 CRTE 60417 3685 0W-29S C1
E Milburn Av
- DSPN 60016 2862 15W-12N B1
- MPPT 60016 2862 15W-12N B1
- MPPT 60056 2862 15W-12N B1
W Milburn Av
10 MPPT 60056 2862 15W-12N A1
700 MPPT 60056 2861 16W-12N E1
Milburn Ct
1100 LslT 60540 3142 25W-6S A5
1100 NPVL 60540 3142 25W-6S A5
Milburn Pk
10 EVTN 60201 2813 2W-12N C7
Milburn St
500 EVTN 60201 2813 2W-12N C7
Mildred Av
10 BmdT 60137 3025 23W-2N A1
100 CRY 60013 2696 30W-23N A3
200 GLHT 60139 3025 23W-2N A1
400 BmdT 60137 2969 23W-2N A7
400 GLHT 60139 2969 23W-2N A7
500 BmdT 60139 2969 23W-2N A7
500 GLHT 60137 2969 23W-2N A7
900 MltT 60137 3025 23W-1N A3
1300 SCRL 60174 3020 34W-2N D1
1500 ELGN 60123 2854 35W-12N B1
N Mildred Av
2600 CHCG 60614 2977 1W-3N E5
2700 CHCG 60657 2977 1W-3N E5
43300 AntT 60002 2357 25W-43N A4
Mildred Ct
11400 WLSP 60480 3208 14W-9S D4
Mildred Dr
500 MRGO 60152 2634 49W-25N C4
Mildred Ln
10 CHHT 60411 3508 1W-23S A4
1000 UYPK 60466 3684 3W-30S C3
Miles Av
400 JLET 60433 3499 23W-24S B6
500 JltT 60433 3499 23W-24S B6
N Miles Av
500 PNFD 60544 3338 29W-18S D7
W Milestone Dr
26300 PNFD 60585 3337 32W-14S B1
Milford Av
4600 OKFT 60452 3426 5W-19S B3
17000 TYPK 60477 3424 9W-20S D4
Milford Ct
200 BMDL 60108 2969 23W-5N A2
300 SMBG 60193 2858 24W-9N E7
1200 NPVL 60564 3267 28W-12S A2
Milford Ln
- AURA 60504 3140 30W-7S B6
200 BMDL 60108 2969 23W-5N A2
Milford Rd
300 DRFD 60015 2757 10W-20N A1
400 DRFD 60015 2756 10W-20N E1
Milford St
800 CRY 60013 2695 32W-23N B1
10200 PvsT 60162 3087 12W-1S A1
10200 WSTR 60154 3087 12W-1S A1
10200 WSTR 60162 3087 12W-1S A1
Milford Haven Wy
200 MNSR 46321 3510 D3
E Milida Ct
1200 ANHT 60004 2807 17W-16N C1
Milkweed Dr
5300 NPVL 60564 3266 29W-13S C5
W Mill Av
100 HPSR 60140 2795 47W-16N D2
Mill Cir
600 WLNG 60090 2755 13W-17N D6
Mill Ct
10 INCK 60061 2647 17W-25N B6
600 WKGN 60085 2537 10W-34N A1
1100 CLSM 60188 2967 27W-4N D4
N Mill Ct
36200 WrnT 60031 2476 18W-36N E4
W Mill Ct
1300 PLTN 60074 2753 20W-17N B4
Mill Ct E
9700 PlsT 60464 3345 12W-15S D1
Mill Dr
- RNPK 60471 3594 4W-26S D3
1600 MchT 60097 2469 36W-37N D1
N Mill Dr
5900 MchT 60097 2469 36W-37N D1
5900 RcmT 60097 2469 36W-37N D1
Mill Dr E
9700 PlsT 60464 3345 12W-15S D1
12900 PSPK 60464 3345 12W-15S D1
Mill Dr W
9800 PlsT 60464 3345 12W-15S C1
Mill Ln
2100 MchT 60051 2528 31W-33N E3
Mill Rd
200 ADSN 60143 2970 19W-5N D2
200 ADSN 60191 2970 19W-5N D2
200 WDDL 60191 2970 19W-5N D2
300 AddT 60101 2970 19W-4N D3
400 ITSC 60143 2970 19W-5N D1
400 ITSC 60191 2970 19W-5N D1
500 LinT 53147 2349 E1
700 ADSN 60101 2970 19W-5N D2
4600 MTGY 60543 3263 37W-12S C2
4600 OSWG 60543 3263 39W-11S A2
6000 OSWG 60543 3262 39W-12S E2
7200 BtlT 60543 3262 39W-11S D2
7400 BtlT 60512 3262 40W-11S B2
E Mill Rd
- LNSH 60015 2702 14W-22N D5
- LNSH 60069 2702 14W-22N D5
- VrnT 60015 2702 14W-22N D5
3900 RcmT 60071 2413 32W-40N A2
N Mill Rd
100 AddT 60101 2970 19W-3N D4
100 ADSN 60143 2970 19W-5N D1
100 ADSN 60191 2970 19W-5N D1
100 ITSC 60143 2970 19W-5N D1
100 ITSC 60191 2970 19W-5N D1
100 WDDL 60191 2970 19W-5N D1
200 ADSN 60143 2914 19W-5N D7
200 ITSC 60143 2914 19W-5N D7
200 WDDL 60143 2914 19W-5N D7
200 WDDL 60143 2970 19W-5N D1
200 WDDL 60191 2914 19W-5N D7
700 ADSN 60101 2970 19W-4N D3
32900 WrnT 60030 2534 17W-33N A3
33700 WrnT 60031 2534 17W-33N A3
S Mill Rd
10 ADSN 60101 2970 19W-3N D6
12800 PlsT 60464 3273 12W-15S D7
12800 PlsT 60464 3345 12W-15S D1
13000 PlsT 60462 3345 12W-15S D1
13000 PSPK 60464 3345 12W-15S D1
W Mill Rd
3600 RcmT 60071 2413 32W-40N B2
Mill St
- GnvT 60510 3019 37W-0S D7
- GnvT 60510 3077 37W-0S D1
- NPVL 60555 3081 27W-4S C7
- NPVL 60563 3081 27W-4S C7
- RcmT 60071 2413 32W-39N A4
- RcmT 60081 2413 32W-39N A4
- WNVL 60555 3081 27W-4S C7
- WNVL 60563 3081 27W-4S C7
10 NPVL 60563 3141 27W-4S C1
10 WNVL 60555 3141 27W-4S C1
10 WNVL 60563 3141 27W-4S C1
100 GLBT 60136 2799 39W-16N A1
100 WMTN 60481 3853 27W-38S D6
200 BTVA 60510 3019 37W-0S D7
200 BTVA 60510 3077 36W-1S D1
200 ELGN 60123 2854 34W-11N D3
200 YKVL 60560 3333 42W-15S C3
300 SEGN 60177 2908 34W-8N E3
600 ElgT 60177 2908 34W-8N E3
1300 CRTE 60417 3685 1W-29S B2
1600 DSPN 60016 2863 12W-11N A3
5500 RHMD 60071 2353 34W-42N C6
11600 HTLY 60142 2692 40W-20N A7
12000 HTLY 60142 2691 41W-20N E7
Mill St CO-32
- NPVL 60555 3081 27W-4S C7
- NPVL 60563 3081 27W-4S C7
- WNVL 60555 3081 27W-4S C7
- WNVL 60563 3081 27W-4S C7
10 NPVL 60563 3141 27W-4S C1
10 WNVL 60555 3141 27W-4S C1
10 WNVL 60563 3141 27W-4S C1
E Mill St
10 MTGY 60538 3199 36W-9S D4
100 WCDA 60084 2643 25W-27N E1
E Mill St CO-29
10 MTGY 60538 3199 36W-9S D4

STREET Block	City	ZIP	Map#	CGS	Grid
N Mill St					
10	NPVL	60540	3141	27W-6S	C5
300	NPVL	60563	3141	27W-6S	C4
400	PTON	60468	3860	9W-37S	E3
500	PtnT	60468	3860	9W-37S	E3
700	MHRY	60050	2528	33W-32N	A4
1100	PNFD	60544	3338	29W-17S	C6
1400	NpvT	60563	3141	27W-5S	C2
1900	WNVL	60555	3141	27W-4S	C1
1900	WNVL	60563	3141	27W-4S	C1
N Mill St CO-32					
900	NPVL	60563	3141	27W-4S	C1
1400	NpvT	60563	3141	27W-5S	C2
1900	WNVL	60555	3141	27W-4S	C1
1900	WNVL	60563	3141	27W-4S	C1
S Mill St					
10	NPVL	60540	3141	27W-6S	C5
200	PTON	60468	3860	9W-37S	E4
W Mill St					
100	MTGY	60538	3199	36W-9S	D4
100	WCDA	60084	2643	26W-27N	E1
5300	MONE	60449	3683	6W-31S	A6
5400	MONE	60449	3682	6W-31S	E6
Mill Tr					
1500	HDPK	60035	2703	10W-23N	E1
1600	LKFT	60045	2703	10W-23N	E1
Millard Av					
100	FRGV	60021	2696	30W-22N	A3
200	CLLK	60014	2639	37W-25N	A5
200	GfnT	60014	2639	37W-25N	A5
14300	MDLN	60445	3348	4W-17S	D4
15400	MKHM	60428	3348	4W-18S	D7
15500	MKHM	60428	3426	4W-18S	D1
21900	RNPK	60471	3594	4W-26S	E3
S Millard Av					
500	CHCG	60624	3032	4W-0S	C5
1200	CHCG	60623	3032	4W-1S	C7
1500	CHCG	60623	3090	4W-2S	D3
5100	CHCG	60632	3150	4W-5S	D2
6600	CHCG	60629	3150	4W-7S	D6
9100	ENGN	60805	3212	4W-10S	D5
9800	CHCG	60655	3212	4W-11S	D7
11700	CHCG	60655	3276	4W-13S	D5
11700	WthT	60655	3276	4W-13S	D5
11700	WthT	60803	3276	4W-13S	D5
12100	ALSP	60803	3276	4W-14S	D6
Millard Cir					
31900	WNVL	60555	3081	28W-3S	B6
S Millard St					
11900	ALSP	60803	3276	4W-14S	D5
11900	WthT	60803	3276	4W-14S	D5
Millay St					
300	CmpT	60175	2962	40W-3N	C6
Millbank Dr					
13100	PNFD	60585	3338	30W-15S	A2
13900	ODPK	60462	3346	10W-16S	C3
S Millboro Pl					
400	JLET	60436	3498	25W-24S	C6
Millbridge Ln					
6000	LSLE	60532	3142	23W-6S	E5
Millbridge Pkwy					
-	BCHR	60401	3774	0W-35S	D5
-	WshT	60401	3774	0W-34S	D5
Millbridge Rd					
-	LYNS	60534	3088	9W-3S	C6
-	RVSD	60534	3088	10W-3S	C6
-	RvsT	60534	3088	10W-3S	C6
-	RvsT	60546	3088	10W-3S	C6
100	RVSD	60546	3088	10W-3S	B6
Millbrook Ct					
10	ALGN	60102	2746	37W-19N	D2
100	DGvT	60516	3206	19W-9S	D3
1400	SMBG	60193	2858	25W-10N	B6
1700	GNVA	60134	3019	36W-1N	E3
1700	GNVA	60134	3020	36W-1N	A3
Millbrook Dr					
400	DGvT	60516	3206	19W-9S	E3
900	LKZH	60047	2699	22W-22N	B3
1400	ALGN	60102	2746	36W-20N	D1
1600	ALGN	60118	2746	37W-19N	D2
2000	BFGV	60069	2701	15W-22N	E3
2000	BFGV	60089	2701	15W-22N	E3
2000	LNSH	60069	2701	15W-22N	E3
2000	LNSH	60089	2701	15W-22N	E3
2200	AURA	60502	3201	32W-7S	B1
Millbrook Ln					
-	NPVL	60540	3203	27W-8S	B2
-	NPVL	60565	3203	27W-8S	B2
100	SMBG	60193	2858	25W-10N	B6
100	WLMT	60091	2811	6W-13N	E7
Millburn Ct					
1100	SCRL	60174	3020	36W-2N	A1
W Millburn Rd					
17200	OMCK	60083	2419	18W-38N	A7
18400	OMCK	60083	2418	18W-38N	E6
18600	LNHT	60046	2418	18W-38N	E6
18600	OMCK	60046	2418	18W-38N	E6
W Millburn Rd CO-A14					
17500	OMCK	60083	2419	18W-38N	A7
18400	OMCK	60083	2418	18W-38N	E6
18600	LNHT	60046	2418	18W-38N	E6
18600	OMCK	60046	2418	18W-38N	E6
Millburne Ct					
7200	BLVY	60050	2526	36W-31N	E6
Millburne Rd					
1600	LKFT	60045	2703	11W-23N	D1
Millcreek Cir					
800	ELGN	60123	2853	36W-12N	E1
Mill Creek Cir E					
10	BbyT	60134	3076	39W-1S	E1
Mill Creek Cir W					
10	BbyT	60134	3076	39W-1S	E1
Millcreek Ct					
-	ELGN	60123	2853	36W-12N	E1
400	LslT	60540	3142	25W-6S	B5
Mill Creek Dr					
1000	BFGV	60089	2754	17W-17N	A5
1400	ANHT	60004	2754	17W-17N	A5
1400	BFGV	60004	2754	17W-17N	A5
N Mill Creek Dr					
-	GnvT	60134	3018	38W-0S	E6
-	GnvT	60134	3019	38W-0S	A7
10	BbyT	60134	3018	39W-0N	E6
36400	WrnT	60031	2477	17W-36N	B4
36500	WrnT	60083	2477	17W-36N	B4
S Mill Creek Dr					
-	BbyT	60134	3018	39W-0S	E7
-	BbyT	60134	3076	39W-0S	E1
-	BbyT	60510	3076	39W-1S	E2
-	GnvT	60134	3018	39W-0S	E7
-	GnvT	60134	3019	38W-0S	A7
Mill Creek Ln					
24100	PNFD	60586	3416	30W-19S	B4
Millcreek Ln					
200	BMDL	60108	2969	22W-4N	B3
200	NPVL	60540	3142	25W-6S	B6
400	LslT	60540	3142	25W-7S	B6
1100	ALGN	60102	2694	35W-20N	A7
1100	ALGN	60102	2747	35W-20N	A1
2500	RGMW	60008	2805	21W-13N	D5
N Mill Creek Rd					
39400	NptT	60083	2419	16W-41N	D2
40000	WDWH	60083	2419	16W-41N	D2
41500	WDWH	60099	2419	16W-41N	D1
41600	WDWH	60099	2360	16W-41N	D7
W Mill Creek Crossing Dr					
17500	WrnT	60031	2477	17W-36N	B4
Millennium Dr					
-	CLLK	60012	2640	34W-26N	D2
-	ELGN	60123	2799	37W-13N	D7
-	ElgT	60123	2799	37W-13N	D7
18300	TYPK	60477	3425	8W-22S	A7
18300	TYPK	60477	3505	8W-22S	A1
Millennium Pkwy					
11500	PNFD	60585	3266	30W-13S	A5
11700	PNFD	60585	3265	31W-13S	E5
Miller Av					
200	JLET	60433	3499	23W-24S	B6
800	SMWD	60107	2911	27W-9N	C1
1100	OKPK	60302	3030	8W-1N	D2
1100	RVFT	60302	3030	8W-1N	D2
1100	RVFT	60305	3030	8W-1N	D2
2700	SCHT	60411	3596	1W-26S	A3
3300	SCHT	60475	3596	1W-27S	A4
3300	STGR	60475	3596	1W-27S	A4
S Miller Av					
10	JLET	60432	3499	23W-24S	B5
10	JLET	60433	3499	23W-24S	B5
Miller Ct					
300	GNEN	60137	3025	22W-0S	B6
1100	BTVA	60510	3078	34W-1S	E2
1900	HMWD	60430	3427	2W-21S	D7
W Miller Ct					
22000	PnfT	60544	3339	27W-16S	C5
Miller Dr					
-	AraT	60542	3077	37W-4S	C7
-	NARA	60542	3077	37W-4S	C7
300	ELGN	60123	2854	35W-10N	C5
3000	MHRY	60050	2528	32W-31N	C7
3700	GNVW	60025	2809	10W-15N	E2
18400	LNSG	60438	3430	4E-21S	C7
W Miller Dr					
22000	PnfT	60544	3339	27W-16S	C4
Miller Ln					
-	ANHT	60004	2754	17W-17N	A4
200	SchT	60175	2907	38W-6N	A7
300	WDDL	60191	2914	18W-5N	E7
800	BFGV	60089	2754	17W-17N	A4
6000	LSLE	60532	3142	23W-6S	E5
Miller Pkwy					
1300	MHRY	60050	2584	33W-30N	D2
Miller Pl					
900	PHNX	60426	3350	0W-18S	C7
900	SHLD	60426	3350	0W-18S	C7
900	SHLD	60473	3350	0W-18S	C7
Miller Rd					
-	GwdT	60098	2524	41W-32N	E4
-	HTLY	60142	2692	39W-23N	B2
-	LYNS	60534	3088	9W-3S	D6
-	LYNS	60546	3088	9W-3S	D6
-	RVSD	60546	3088	9W-3S	D6
-	WDSK	60098	2524	41W-32N	E4
10	CLLK	60014	2693	38W-22N	A4
10	CLLK	60156	2693	38W-22N	A4
10	ElaT	60047	2698	24W-23N	C1
10	HNWD	60047	2644	23W-24N	E7
10	HNWD	60047	2698	24W-23N	C1
10	LIHL	60156	2693	38W-22N	A4
10	LKZH	60047	2698	24W-23N	C1
200	CPVL	60110	2747	36W-17N	A6
200	DndT	60118	2747	35W-18N	C5
300	DndT	60110	2747	36W-18N	B5
300	NBRN	60010	2698	25W-24N	E1
500	CPVL	60118	2747	35W-18N	C5
500	LKBN	60010	2697	25W-24N	E1
500	LKBN	60010	2698	25W-24N	A1
500	NBRN	60010	2697	25W-24N	E1
1200	BtnT	60050	2472	30W-38N	A1
1200	JNBG	60050	2472	30W-38N	A1
1200	MchT	60050	2472	30W-38N	A1
1200	SPGV	60050	2472	30W-38N	A1
1200	SPGV	60081	2472	30W-38N	A1
1300	GNVA	60134	3019	37W-0S	D6
1600	NHBK	60062	2756	11W-16N	D6
1800	BtnT	60050	2471	31W-38N	E1
1800	JNBG	60050	2471	31W-38N	E1
2300	MchT	60050	2471	31W-38N	C1
2300	MchT	60081	2471	31W-38N	C1
2300	RcmT	60050	2471	31W-38N	C1
2300	RcmT	60081	2471	31W-38N	C1
2600	MchT	60072	2471	31W-38N	C1
2600	RcmT	60072	2471	31W-38N	C1
5200	GNWD	60097	2468	39W-37N	D3
5200	GNWD	60098	2468	39W-37N	D3
5200	GwdT	60034	2468	39W-37N	D1
5200	GwdT	60097	2468	39W-37N	D1
5200	GwdT	60098	2468	39W-37N	D1
5200	HbnT	60034	2468	39W-37N	D4
7400	LIHL	60014	2693	36W-22N	D4
7800	CPVL	60110	2746	37W-17N	E6
9000	GfnT	60156	2693	37W-22N	A4
9100	LIHL	60156	2692	39W-23N	C2
14200	LtRT	60545	3259	48W-11S	A2
14200	PLNO	60545	3259	48W-11S	A2
15100	LtRT	60545	3258	49W-11S	D2
22400	SCHT	60411	3596	0E-27S	D4
22400	SCHT	60475	3596	0E-27S	D4
22400	STGR	60411	3596	0E-27S	D4
22900	CRTE	60417	3596	0E-27S	D5
22900	STGR	60475	3596	0E-27S	D5
24600	ElaT	60010	2698	24W-24N	C1
Miller Rd CO-A42					
300	NBRN	60010	2698	25W-24N	A1
500	LKBN	60010	2697	25W-24N	E1
500	LKBN	60010	2698	25W-24N	A1
500	NBRN	60010	2697	25W-24N	E1
24600	ElaT	60010	2698	24W-24N	C1
24600	ElaT	60047	2698	24W-24N	C1
24600	LKZH	60047	2698	24W-24N	C1
N Miller Rd					
38600	LkvT	60046	2417	21W-38N	E6
38600	LNHT	60046	2417	21W-38N	E6
W Miller Rd					
-	ElaT	60010	2698	24W-24N	C1
-	ElaT	60047	2698	24W-24N	C1
-	LKZH	60047	2698	24W-24N	C1
500	LKBN	60010	2697	27W-23N	C1
500	NBRN	60010	2697	26W-24N	E1
19200	AntT	60046	2418	19W-40N	C3
19500	AntT	60002	2418	19W-40N	C3
20500	ANTH	60002	2418	20W-40N	A3
23100	ElaT	60047	2644	23W-24N	E7
23100	ElaT	60047	2645	23W-24N	A7
23100	HNWD	60047	2645	23W-24N	A7
23300	HNWD	60047	2644	23W-24N	E7
W Miller Rd CO-A42					
500	LKBN	60010	2697	27W-23N	C1
500	NBRN	60010	2697	26W-24N	E1
Miller St					
-	WshT	60401	3864	1W-36S	B1
10	AURA	60505	3200	34W-8S	D1
200	BCHR	60401	3864	0W-36S	D1
400	STGR	60475	3596	0E-27S	D4
S Miller St					
700	CHCG	60607	3033	1W-0S	E6
1600	CHCG	60608	3091	1W-1S	E1
Miller Cir Dr					
5300	MTSN	60443	3593	6W-25S	E1
5300	MTSN	60443	3594	6W-25S	A1
5400	MTSN	60443	3505	6W-25S	E7
Miller Oak Rd					
4100	MchT	60050	2471	33W-36N	A4
Millers Cross					
100	ITSC	60143	2914	19W-7N	C5
Millers Ln					
10	MPPT	60056	2807	16W-13N	D7
Millers Rd					
36400	SCRL	60175	2963	37W-2N	D7
E Millers Rd					
10	DSPN	60016	2862	14W-11N	C3
W Millers Rd					
10	DSPN	60016	2862	15W-11N	B3
700	DSPN	60016	2861	16W-11N	E3
700	MPPT	60016	2861	16W-11N	E3
700	MPPT	60056	2861	16W-11N	E3
Millet St					
1200	NPVL	60563	3141	26W-5S	D3
Millhurst Rd					
-	NvlT	60548	3330	50W-16S	B4
14500	FoxT	60545	3331	48W-16S	A4
14500	FoxT	60560	3331	48W-16S	A4
14500	LtRT	60545	3331	48W-16S	A4
14500	LtRT	60560	3331	48W-16S	A4
15200	FoxT	60541	3331	48W-16S	A4
16300	FoxT	60541	3330	49W-16S	E4
16300	FoxT	60545	3330	49W-16S	E4
16300	FoxT	60548	3330	49W-16S	E4
Millicent Ct					
10	SEGN	60177	2908	36W-9N	A1
Millington Ct					
2400	AURA	60504	3201	32W-8S	C1
Millington Ln					
100	AURA	60504	3201	32W-8S	C2
Millington Rd					
100	FoxT	60548	3330	51W-16S	B5
100	LtRT	60548	3330	51W-16S	B5
100	NvlT	60548	3330	51W-16S	B5
100	SdwT	60548	3330	51W-16S	B5
6500	FoxT	60541	3330	51W-17S	B6
6500	KdlC	60541	3330	51W-17S	B6
6500	KdlC	60548	3330	51W-17S	B6
Millington Wy					
100	SCRL	60174	2964	36W-3N	A6
Millis Ln					
100	SMBG	60193	2857	26W-10N	E6
Mill Meadows Ln					
10	ADSN	60101	2970	19W-3N	D6
W Millns Ct					
500	ADSN	60101	2970	19W-4N	D2
N Millns Ln					
1100	ADSN	60101	2970	19W-4N	D2
Millpond Ct					
2400	JLET	60586	3415	32W-20S	C6
Mill Pond Dr					
10	GLHT	60139	2968	24W-3N	D5
100	CLSM	60139	2968	24W-3N	D5
100	CLSM	60188	2968	24W-3N	D5
Millpond Ln					
2000	HRPK	60133	2967	27W-4N	C3
Mill Race Ln					
-	ODPK	60467	3423	13W-20S	A5
-	OrlT	60467	3423	13W-20S	A5
Millrace Ln					
800	NPVL	60565	3204	25W-9S	B3
Millrose Dr					
2600	AURA	60503	3265	32W-11S	C1
Mill Run Ct					
17100	ODHL	60487	3424	11W-20S	A4
17100	TYPK	60487	3424	11W-20S	A4
Mills Ct					
200	LKFT	60045	2650	10W-27N	A1
500	SchT	60175	2963	37W-4N	C4
Mills Rd					
-	JLET	60433	3500	21W-25S	A7
-	JltT	60433	3500	21W-25S	A7
10	JLET	60433	3587	23W-25S	A1
10	JLET	60436	3587	23W-25S	A1
10	JltT	60436	3587	23W-25S	A1
900	JltT	60433	3587	22W-25S	D1
1900	JLET	60433	3588	21W-25S	A1
1900	JltT	60433	3588	21W-25S	A1
E Mills Rd					
200	JLET	60433	3587	23W-25S	B1
200	JltT	60433	3587	23W-25S	B1
N Mills Rd					
40300	AntT	60002	2415	26W-40N	E3
Mills St					
200	HNDL	60521	3146	14W-4S	C1
600	HNDL	60521	3086	14W-4S	C7
W Millsdale Rd					
19200	JknT	60421	3675	25W-28S	C1
19200	JLET	60421	3675	26W-28S	A1
21200	CnhT	60421	3674	28W-30S	B3
21200	JknT	60421	3674	26W-29S	E1
21200	JLET	60421	3674	26W-29S	E1
Millsfell					
1100	WDND	60118	2800	34W-15N	D4
Mills Pond Rd					
2100	NndT	60014	2585	31W-27N	E7
Millstone Cir					
32500	LKMR	60051	2529	28W-32N	D5
E Millstone Cir					
1000	RLKB	60046	2475	21W-36N	D5
W Millstone Ct					
10	PSHL	60465	3274	10W-12S	B3
Mill Stone Dr					
800	CmpT	60175	2962	41W-5N	A1
E Millstone Dr					
800	RLKB	60046	2475	21W-36N	C5
N Millstone Dr					
2000	RLKB	60046	2475	21W-36N	D5
Millstone Ln					
1400	GRNE	60031	2477	17W-35N	B5
2700	RGMW	60008	2805	21W-13N	C5
Millstone Rd					
10	DRFD	60015	2704	9W-21N	B7
17900	HLCT	60429	3427	3W-21S	A6
Mill Stream Dr					
200	BGBK	60440	3268	24W-12S	E2
N Millstream Dr					
1300	MHRY	60050	2528	32W-33N	B3
W Millstream Dr					
3700	MHRY	60050	2528	32W-33N	B3
Millstream Ln					
300	OSWG	60543	3263	38W-12S	A3
Millstream Rd					
4700	SenT	60152	2635	47W-27N	B1
4700	SenT	60180	2635	47W-27N	B1
Millstream Rd CO-T64					
4700	SenT	60152	2635	47W-27N	B1
4700	SenT	60180	2635	47W-27N	B1
E Mill Valley Rd					
400	PLTN	60074	2753	20W-17N	A5
Millview Ct					
1000	BTVA	60510	3078	36W-2S	A3
Millview Dr					
500	BTVA	60510	3077	36W-1S	E2
900	BTVA	60510	3078	36W-2S	A4
1500	BtvT	60510	3078	36W-2S	A4
E Millwood Dr					
300	BRLT	60103	2911	28W-7N	B5
S Millwood Dr					
900	BRLT	60103	2911	27W-7N	C5
Millwood St					
700	CRY	60013	2695	32W-23N	C1
Milne Dr					
900	LKPT	60441	3419	21W-19S	E3
1200	LKPT	60441	3420	21W-19S	A3
1300	LktT	60441	3420	21W-19S	A4
Milo Ct					
200	WCHI	60185	3022	30W-0N	B4
N Miltimore Av					
5600	CHCG	60646	2919	7W-7N	C4
Milton Av					
-	GNEN	60137	3083	22W-1S	C2
400	GLNC	60022	2758	6W-17N	C4
700	MltT	60137	3083	22W-1S	C2
1800	NHBK	60062	2757	10W-17N	B5
2000	PKRG	60068	2863	11W-9N	D6
N Milton Av					
100	GNEN	60137	3025	22W-0S	C7
S Milton Av					
100	GNEN	60137	3083	22W-1S	C2
200	MltT	60137	3083	22W-1S	C2
Milton Ct					
10	CRY	60013	2642	29W-24N	B7
300	BMDL	60108	2969	22W-4N	B3
5500	RSMT	60018	2917	12W-6N	C5
Milton Dr					
600	NPVL	60563	3142	26W-6S	A4
700	LslT	60563	3142	26W-6S	A4
Milton Ln					
400	HFET	60169	2858	24W-11N	E4
700	SMBG	60194	2858	24W-11N	D4
1200	SMBG	60193	2912	25W-9N	C1
1700	WHTN	60187	3082	24W-2S	D3
Milton Pkwy					
5400	RSMT	60018	2917	12W-6N	C5
Milton Rd					
600	IVNS	60067	2751	23W-16N	E6
N Milton Rd					
25900	ElaT	60047	2644	24W-25N	C4
25900	HNWD	60047	2644	24W-25N	C5
W Milton Rd					
22800	FmtT	60060	2645	23W-26N	A3
22800	HNWD	60060	2645	23W-26N	A3
22900	FmtT	60047	2645	23W-26N	A3
23200	FmtT	60084	2644	23W-26N	D3
23200	FmtT	60084	2645	23W-26N	A3
23800	HNWD	60047	2644	23W-26N	D3
25900	ElaT	60047	2644	24W-25N	C4
Milton St					
400	WMTN	60481	3853	27W-38S	D6
Milton Bridge Ter					
900	FKFT	60423	3592	9W-26S	E3
900	FKFT	60423	3593	8W-26S	A2
Milwaukee Av					
-	AntT	60002	2416	23W-39N	E5
-	GRNE	60031	2478	14W-34N	B7
-	LKVL	60002	2416	23W-39N	E5
-	LKVL	60046	2416	23W-39N	E5
-	LKVL	60046	2475	22W-37N	C2
-	LkvT	60046	2416	23W-39N	E5
-	LkvT	60046	2475	22W-37N	C2
-	LkvT	60073	2475	22W-36N	C3
-	LYVL	60048	2647	16W-26N	E3
-	RLKB	60046	2475	21W-35N	C6
-	RLKB	60073	2475	22W-36N	C3
-	VNHL	60061	2647	16W-26N	E3
100	LNSH	60061	2702	15W-23N	A2
100	LNSH	60069	2702	15W-23N	A2
100	VNHL	60061	2702	15W-23N	A2
100	VNHL	60069	2702	15W-23N	A2
200	VrnT	60061	2702	15W-23N	A2
500	MaiT	60016	2809	10W-13N	E7
500	MaiT	60025	2809	10W-13N	E7
500	NfdT	60016	2809	10W-13N	E7
500	NfdT	60025	2809	11W-14N	C5
700	GNVW	60025	2809	11W-13N	C5
900	BFGV	60089	2755	14W-20N	C1
900	VrnT	60015	2755	14W-20N	C1
900	VrnT	60062	2755	14W-20N	C1
900	VrnT	60089	2755	14W-20N	C1
1000	BFGV	60089	2702	14W-20N	B7
1000	RVWD	60015	2702	14W-20N	B7
1000	RVWD	60015	2755	14W-20N	C1
1000	VrnT	60015	2702	14W-21N	B6
1400	LNSH	60015	2702	14W-21N	B6
1400	VrnT	60069	2702	14W-21N	B6
1600	GNVW	60062	2809	12W-14N	C4
1800	NfdT	60062	2809	12W-15N	B3
2800	PTHT	60062	2809	12W-15N	B3
2800	PTHT	60070	2809	12W-15N	B3
9700	GNVW	60025	2863	10W-12N	E1
9700	GNVW	60025	2864	10W-12N	A1
9700	MaiT	60016	2864	10W-12N	A1
9700	MaiT	60025	2863	11W-12N	E1
9700	MaiT	60025	2864	10W-12N	A1
9700	MaiT	60714	2864	10W-12N	A1
9700	NLES	60025	2864	10W-12N	A1
9700	NLES	60714	2864	10W-12N	A1
9800	MaiT	60016	2863	11W-12N	E1
20400	BFGV	60090	2755	14W-20N	C1
Milwaukee Av SR-21					
-	LYVL	60048	2647	16W-26N	E3
-	VNHL	60061	2647	16W-26N	E3
100	LNSH	60061	2702	15W-23N	A2
100	LNSH	60069	2702	15W-23N	A2
100	VNHL	60061	2702	15W-23N	A2
100	VNHL	60069	2702	15W-23N	A2
200	VrnT	60061	2702	15W-23N	A2
500	MaiT	60016	2809	10W-13N	E7
500	MaiT	60025	2809	10W-13N	E7
500	NfdT	60016	2809	10W-13N	E7
500	NfdT	60025	2809	11W-14N	C5
700	GNVW	60025	2809	11W-14N	C5
900	BFGV	60089	2755	14W-20N	C1
900	VrnT	60015	2755	14W-20N	C1
900	VrnT	60062	2755	14W-20N	C1
900	VrnT	60089	2755	14W-20N	C1
1000	BFGV	60089	2702	14W-20N	B7
1000	RVWD	60015	2702	14W-20N	B7
1000	RVWD	60015	2755	14W-20N	C1
1000	VrnT	60015	2702	14W-21N	B6
1400	LNSH	60015	2702	14W-21N	B6
1400	VrnT	60069	2702	14W-21N	B6
1600	GNVW	60062	2809	12W-14N	C4
1800	NfdT	60062	2809	12W-15N	B3
2800	PTHT	60062	2809	12W-15N	B3
2800	PTHT	60070	2809	12W-15N	B3
9700	GNVW	60025	2863	10W-12N	E1
9700	GNVW	60025	2864	10W-12N	A1
9700	MaiT	60016	2864	10W-12N	A1
9700	MaiT	60025	2863	11W-12N	E1
9700	MaiT	60025	2864	10W-12N	A1
9700	MaiT	60714	2864	10W-12N	A1
9700	NLES	60025	2864	10W-12N	A1
9700	NLES	60714	2864	10W-12N	A1
9800	MaiT	60016	2863	11W-12N	E1
20400	BFGV	60090	2755	14W-20N	C1
Milwaukee Av SR-83					
-	AntT	60002	2416	23W-39N	E5
-	LKVL	60002	2416	23W-39N	E5
-	LKVL	60046	2416	23W-39N	E5
-	LKVL	60046	2475	22W-37N	C2
-	LkvT	60046	2416	23W-39N	E5
-	LkvT	60046	2475	22W-37N	C2
-	LkvT	60073	2475	22W-36N	C3
-	RLKB	60046	2475	21W-35N	C6
-	RLKB	60073	2475	22W-36N	C3
Milwaukee Av US-45					
200	LNSH	60061	2702	15W-23N	A2
200	LNSH	60069	2702	15W-23N	A2
200	VNHL	60061	2702	15W-23N	A2
200	VNHL	60069	2702	15W-23N	A2
200	VrnT	60061	2702	15W-23N	A2
900	BFGV	60089	2755	14W-20N	C1
900	VrnT	60015	2755	14W-20N	C1
900	VrnT	60062	2755	14W-20N	C1
900	VrnT	60089	2755	14W-20N	C1
1000	BFGV	60089	2702	14W-20N	B7
1000	RVWD	60015	2702	14W-20N	B7
1000	RVWD	60015	2755	14W-20N	C1
1000	VrnT	60015	2702	14W-21N	B6
1400	LNSH	60015	2702	14W-21N	B6
1400	VrnT	60069	2702	14W-21N	B6
20400	BFGV	60090	2755	14W-20N	C1
N Milwaukee Av					
-	LKVL	60046	2475	22W-38N	B1
-	NfdT	60062	2809	12W-15N	A2
10	MTWA	60048	2647	15W-25N	E6
10	VNHL	60061	2647	15W-25N	E5
10	VNHL	60061	2648	15W-24N	A6
10	VrnT	60061	2647	15W-24N	E6
10	VrnT	60061	2648	15W-24N	A6
100	LKVL	60046	2417	22W-38N	A6
100	LYVL	60048	2591	16W-29N	D4
200	CHCG	60606	3034	0W-0N	A4
200	CHCG	60661	3034	0W-0N	A4
400	CHCG	60610	3034	0W-0N	A3
400	CHCG	60622	3034	0W-0N	A3
500	CHCG	60622	3033	1W-1N	D2
500	PTHT	60062	2809	13W-15N	A1
500	PTHT	60070	2809	12W-15N	A2
500	PTHT	60090	2809	13W-15N	A1
500	WhlT	60062	2809	13W-15N	A1
500	WhlT	60090	2809	13W-15N	A1
500	WLNG	60090	2755	14W-18N	C2
800	BFGV	60090	2755	14W-20N	C2
800	LkvT	60046	2417	23W-38N	A6
900	BFGV	60089	2755	14W-20N	C1
900	VrnT	60062	2755	14W-20N	C1
900	VrnT	60089	2755	14W-20N	C1
1500	CHCG	60647	3033	2W-1N	B1
1600	CHCG	60647	2977	2W-2N	A7
1700	LbvT	60048	2591	16W-30N	D2
2200	CHCG	60647	2976	3W-2N	E6
2700	CHCG	60618	2976	4W-3N	D5
3200	CHCG	60641	2976	5W-4N	B3
3900	CHCG	60641	2975	6W-5N	E1
4300	CHCG	60630	2975	6W-5N	E1
4400	CHCG	60630	2919	6W-5N	D7
5500	CHCG	60646	2919	7W-6N	B5
6300	CHCG	60631	2919	8W-7N	A3
6500	CHCG	60714	2919	8W-8N	A2
6500	NLES	60631	2919	8W-8N	A2
6500	NLES	60714	2919	7W-6N	C5
6600	NLES	60714	2918	8W-8N	E1
7200	NLES	60714	2864	9W-9N	D6
7500	CHCG	60631	2864	8W-9N	D7
7500	CHCG	60714	2864	8W-9N	D7
7500	NLES	60631	2864	9W-9N	D7
8300	MaiT	60714	2864	9W-9N	D6
9500	MaiT	60016	2864	9W-9N	D6
9600	GNVW	60025	2864	9W-9N	D6
9600	MaiT	60025	2864	9W-9N	D6
9600	NLES	60025	2864	9W-9N	D6
21800	LNSH	60069	2702	15W-22N	B4
21800	VrnT	60069	2702	14W-21N	B5
31000	LbvT	60048	2534	16W-31N	C7
31400	WKGN	60048	2534	16W-31N	D6
32700	GRNE	60048	2534	16W-32N	E5
32700	WrnT	60048	2534	16W-32N	E5
35000	GrtT	60041	2474	25W-35N	A7
N Milwaukee Av SR-21					
-	NfdT	60062	2809	12W-15N	A2
10	MTWA	60048	2647	15W-25N	E6
10	VNHL	60061	2647	15W-25N	E5
10	VNHL	60061	2648	15W-24N	A6
10	VrnT	60061	2647	15W-24N	E6
10	VrnT	60061	2648	15W-24N	A6
100	LYVL	60048	2591	16W-29N	D4
500	PTHT	60062	2809	13W-15N	A1
500	PTHT	60070	2809	13W-15N	A1
500	PTHT	60090	2809	13W-15N	A1
500	WhlT	60062	2809	13W-15N	A1
500	WhlT	60090	2809	13W-15N	A1
500	WLNG	60090	2755	14W-18N	C2
800	BFGV	60090	2755	14W-20N	C2
900	BFGV	60089	2755	14W-20N	C1
900	VrnT	60062	2755	14W-20N	C1
900	VrnT	60089	2755	14W-20N	C1
1700	LbvT	60048	2591	16W-30N	D2
7500	CHCG	60631	2864	9W-9N	D7
7500	CHCG	60714	2864	9W-9N	D7
7500	NLES	60631	2864	9W-9N	D7

STREET Block	City	ZIP	Map#	CGS	Grid
N Milwaukee Av SR-21					
7500	NLES	60714	2864	9W-9N	D6
8300	MaiT	60714	2864	9W-9N	D6
9500	MaiT	60016	2864	9W-9N	D6
9600	GNVW	60025	2864	9W-9N	D6
9600	MaiT	60025	2864	9W-9N	D6
9600	NLES	60025	2864	9W-9N	D6
21800	LNSH	60069	2702	15W-22N	B4
21800	VrnT	60069	2702	14W-21N	B5
31000	LbvT	60048	2534	16W-31N	C7
31400	WKGN	60048	2534	16W-31N	D6
32700	GRNE	60048	2534	16W-32N	E5
32700	WrnT	60048	2534	16W-32N	E5
N Milwaukee Av SR-83					
-	LKVL	60046	2475	22W-38N	B1
100	LKVL	60046	2417	23W-38N	A6
800	LkvT	60046	2417	23W-38N	A6
N Milwaukee Av US-45					
500	PTHT	60062	2809	13W-15N	A1
500	PTHT	60070	2809	13W-15N	A1
500	PTHT	60090	2809	13W-15N	A1
500	WhlT	60062	2809	13W-15N	A1
500	WhlT	60090	2809	13W-15N	A1
500	WLNG	60090	2755	14W-18N	C2
800	BFGV	60090	2755	14W-20N	C2
900	BFGV	60089	2755	14W-20N	C1
900	VrnT	60062	2755	14W-20N	C1
900	VrnT	60089	2755	14W-20N	C1
21800	LNSH	60069	2702	15W-22N	B4
21800	VrnT	60069	2702	14W-21N	B5
S Milwaukee Av					
10	LKVL	60046	2475	22W-37N	B1
10	WLNG	60090	2755	13W-17N	E5
100	LYVL	60048	2591	16W-28N	D6
100	VNHL	60061	2648	15W-24N	A7
100	VNHL	60061	2702	15W-24N	A1
100	VrnT	60061	2648	15W-24N	A7
100	VrnT	60061	2702	15W-24N	A1
600	WhlT	60090	2755	13W-16N	E7
1000	LYVL	60048	2647	16W-27N	E2
1000	PTHT	60070	2755	13W-16N	E7
1000	PTHT	60070	2808	13W-16N	E1
1000	PTHT	60070	2809	13W-16N	A1
1000	PTHT	60090	2809	13W-16N	A1
1000	WhlT	60090	2808	13W-16N	E1
1000	WhlT	60090	2809	13W-16N	A1
1200	VNHL	60061	2647	16W-27N	E2
1600	VNHL	60048	2647	16W-26N	E2
S Milwaukee Av SR-21					
10	WLNG	60090	2755	13W-17N	E5
100	LYVL	60048	2591	16W-28N	D6
100	VNHL	60061	2648	15W-24N	A7
100	VNHL	60061	2702	15W-24N	A1
100	VrnT	60061	2648	15W-24N	A7
100	VrnT	60061	2702	15W-24N	A1
600	WhlT	60090	2755	13W-16N	E7
1000	LYVL	60048	2647	16W-27N	E2
1000	PTHT	60070	2755	13W-16N	E7
1000	PTHT	60070	2808	13W-16N	E1
1000	PTHT	60070	2809	13W-16N	A1
1000	PTHT	60090	2809	13W-16N	A1
1000	WhlT	60090	2808	13W-16N	E1
1000	WhlT	60090	2809	13W-16N	A1
1200	VNHL	60061	2647	16W-27N	E2
1600	VNHL	60048	2647	16W-26N	E2
S Milwaukee Av SR-83					
10	LKVL	60046	2475	22W-37N	B1
S Milwaukee Av US-45					
10	WLNG	60090	2755	13W-17N	E5
600	WhlT	60090	2755	13W-16N	E7
1000	PTHT	60070	2755	13W-16N	E7
1000	PTHT	60070	2808	13W-16N	E1
1000	PTHT	60070	2809	13W-16N	A1
1000	PTHT	60090	2809	13W-16N	A1
1000	WhlT	60090	2808	13W-16N	E1
1000	WhlT	60090	2809	13W-16N	A1
Milwaukee Ct					
3800	CHCG	60641	2976	5W-4N	A2
Milwaukee Pl					
10	WLNG	60090	2755	14W-18N	D4
Milwaukee St					
5700	RHMD	60071	2353	34W-42N	C7
Mimosa Ct					
1700	GLHT	60139	2968	23W-3N	E6
Mimosa Dr					
7300	ODPK	60462	3346	9W-18S	E7
Mimosa Ln					
200	EGVV	60007	2914	18W-8N	E2
Minard Ln					
1300	GNOK	60048	2592	14W-29N	B5
Minear Dr					
300	LYVL	60048	2591	16W-29N	D3
N Minena St					
40500	AntT	60002	2415	26W-40N	E3
Mineola Rd					
10	FXLK	60020	2473	27W-37N	A3
Miner Dr					
500	BGBK	60440	3205	22W-10S	D6
Miner St					
200	BNVL	60106	2971	16W-4N	D2
300	AddT	60106	2971	16W-4N	D2
1200	DSPN	60016	2862	13W-11N	E3
1300	DSPN	60016	2863	13W-11N	A3
Miner St US-14					
1200	DSPN	60016	2862	13W-11N	E3
1300	DSPN	60016	2863	13W-11N	A3
E Miner St					
10	ANHT	60004	2807	16W-14N	D4
W Miner St					
10	ANHT	60004	2807	17W-14N	A4
200	ANHT	60005	2807	18W-14N	A4
1400	ANHT	60005	2806	18W-14N	D4
1700	RGMW	60008	2806	18W-14N	D4
Mineral Springs Dr					
300	MchT	60051	2528	31W-32N	D5
Minerva Av					
600	WCDA	60084	2587	26W-27N	C7
14200	DLTN	60419	3351	1E-17S	A5
15100	SHLD	60419	3351	1E-17S	A6
15400	DLTN	60473	3351	1E-18S	A7
15400	SHLD	60473	3351	1E-18S	A7
15900	SHLD	60473	3429	1E-18S	A1
S Minerva Av					
200	BlmT	60425	3509	1E-23S	A3
200	GNWD	60425	3509	1E-23S	A3
6300	CHCG	60637	3153	1E-7S	A5
Mines Dr					
-	CHCG	60616	3092	0E-1S	D1
Minette Ln					
500	CHHT	60411	3595	2W-25S	D1
Minetz Ct					
11600	OrlT	60467	3344	14W-16S	D2
Mini Dr					
3000	WKGN	60083	2478	14W-37N	D1
Mining Rd					
-	PltT	60124	2852	39W-10N	E6
Mink Tr					
1100	AlqT	60013	2642	30W-24N	A6
Minkler Rd					
3700	OSWG	60543	3262	39W-14S	E7
3700	OSWG	60560	3262	39W-14S	E7
3700	OSWG	60560	3334	39W-15S	E1
3700	OswT	60543	3262	39W-14S	E7
3700	OswT	60560	3262	39W-14S	E7
3700	OswT	60560	3334	39W-15S	E1
5300	OswT	60560	3334	39W-15S	E1
6200	KdlT	60560	3334	40W-16S	C4
Minnaqua Dr					
400	PTHT	60070	2807	16W-15N	D2
Minneapolis Av					
9600	FNPK	60131	2973	12W-3N	B4
N Minnehaha Av					
6300	CHCG	60646	2919	6W-8N	D2
6500	CHCG	60712	2919	6W-8N	D2
6600	LNWD	60077	2919	6W-8N	D2
6600	LNWD	60712	2919	6W-8N	D2
6600	SKOK	60077	2919	6W-8N	D2
Minneola St					
10	HNDL	60521	3086	15W-4S	A7
Minnesota Av					
-	ALSP	60406	3276	4W-14S	E7
-	ALSP	60406	3277	3W-14S	A7
-	ALSP	60803	3276	4W-14S	E7
-	ALSP	60803	3277	3W-14S	A7
-	BLID	60406	3276	4W-14S	E7
-	BLID	60803	3277	3W-14S	A7
2800	BLID	60406	3277	3W-14S	A7
W Minnesota Av					
200	PLTN	60067	2752	21W-16N	D7
Minnesota Cir					
400	CLSM	60188	2967	27W-2N	D7
Minnesota Ct					
3600	NCHI	60088	2593	12W-30N	C2
10800	ODPK	60467	3423	12W-21S	C5
Minnesota Dr					
1600	EGVV	60007	2913	21W-8N	D2
S Minnesota Dr					
6700	BDPK	60638	3148	8W-7S	E7
N Minnetonka Av					
6800	CHCG	60646	2919	6W-8N	D1
Minnick Av					
9500	OKLN	60453	3211	6W-10S	E6
10100	OKLN	60453	3275	6W-11S	E1
Minnie St					
10	CLLK	60014	2640	35W-26N	B3
Minniehaha Tr					
1200	DndT	60102	2747	34W-19N	E2
Minocqua Ct					
10	PKFT	60466	3595	3W-27S	A4
Minocqua St					
200	PKFT	60466	3595	4W-27S	A4
300	PKFT	60466	3594	4W-27S	E4
E Minooka Rd					
-	MNKA	60447	3583	34W-28S	A7
Minot Ct					
700	EGVV	60007	2913	21W-8N	D2
Mint Ln					
2100	GNVW	60025	2810	9W-14N	B3
Minthaven Ct					
100	GRNE	60031	2535	14W-34N	C1
Minthaven Rd					
1400	LKFT	60045	2703	13W-24N	A1
W Mint Julip Dr					
5200	ALSP	60803	3275	6W-13S	E4
Minto Ct					
3400	NPVL	60564	3266	30W-11S	B1
Minton Rd					
100	JltT	60436	3586	24W-26S	E2
Mintum Av					
-	BHPK	60087	2421	12W-38N	B6
Minuteman Cir					
6800	NndT	60012	2584	35W-27N	A7
Mionske Dr					
10	LKZH	60047	2698	23W-22N	E3
Mira St					
400	CLLK	60012	2640	35W-26N	A2
Mirador Dr					
-	BtvT	60510	3077	38W-3S	A6
-	BtvT	60542	3077	38W-3S	A6
-	NARA	60542	3077	38W-3S	A6
Miraflores Av					
100	WKGN	60087	2480	10W-36N	B4
Mirage Av					
2500	JLET	60586	3415	32W-20S	C6
Miramar Av					
100	LktT	60441	3419	21W-19S	D2
Miramar Ct					
2200	BFGV	60089	2701	16W-22N	D4
Miramar Ln					
2200	BFGV	60089	2701	16W-22N	D4
Miranda Ln					
4300	LGGV	60047	2700	19W-23N	C3
Miriam Av					
2400	ZION	60099	2421	12W-40N	C3
Miroballi Dr					
8600	HYHL	60457	3210	11W-9S	A4
Mirror Lake Dr					
1500	NPVL	60563	3141	28W-5S	A2
Mirta Cir					
10	LMNT	60439	3271	18W-14S	B7
Mishenauma Tr					
-	GrtT	60051	2472	28W-34N	D7
Misko Ct					
10	LMNT	60439	3271	18W-13S	A5
Mission Av					
14700	OKFT	60452	3347	6W-17S	E5
N Mission Av					
300	VLPK	60181	3026	18W-1N	E3
S Mission Blvd					
800	JLET	60431	3497	27W-24S	C6
800	JLET	60436	3497	27W-24S	C6
800	JLET	60436	3585	27W-25S	C1
800	TroT	60436	3497	27W-24S	B6
1000	JLET	60431	3585	27W-25S	C1
Mission Ct					
10	MltT	60187	3024	25W-1N	A3
10	MltT	60188	3024	25W-1N	A3
300	BMDL	60108	2912	25W-6N	A7
1500	BRLT	60103	2967	27W-5N	C1
Mission Dr					
-	BGBK	60490	3267	26W-13S	D4
-	PSPK	60464	3273	12W-14S	C7
700	UYPK	60466	3684	3W-30S	B3
4900	RNPK	60471	3594	6W-27S	B4
9900	PlsT	60464	3273	12W-15S	C7
N Mission Dr					
5100	CHCG	60656	2918	9W-6N	B6
5100	NRDG	60656	2918	9W-6N	B6
5100	NRDG	60706	2918	9W-6N	B6
Mission St					
-	GLHT	60139	2968	24W-3N	D5
-	GLHT	60188	2968	24W-3N	D5
300	CLSM	60188	2968	24W-3N	C5
Mission Creek Ct					
24100	PNFD	60586	3416	30W-19S	C3
Mission Hills Ct					
13500	ODPK	60462	3346	10W-16S	A2
Mission Hills Dr					
1700	ELGN	60123	2854	36W-9N	A7
1700	ELGN	60123	2908	36W-9N	A1
1800	ELGN	60123	2853	36W-9N	E7
2000	ELGN	60123	2907	36W-9N	E1
Mission Hills Ln					
1800	NfdT	60062	2756	12W-16N	B7
Mission Hills Rd					
1600	NfdT	60062	2756	12W-16N	B6
Mississippi Av					
-	JknT	60421	3675	26W-31S	A7
100	ELWD	60421	3675	26W-31S	A7
21500	CnhT	60421	3674	27W-31S	C7
21500	ELWD	60421	3674	27W-31S	C7
21500	JknT	60421	3674	27W-31S	D7
E Mississippi Av					
100	ELWD	60421	3675	25W-32S	C7
300	JknT	60421	3675	25W-32S	C7
S Mississippi Av					
10	JLET	60432	3499	23W-24S	B5
10	JLET	60433	3499	23W-24S	B5
Mississippi Ct					
10800	ODPK	60467	3423	12W-21S	C5
Mississippi Ln					
900	EGVV	60007	2913	22W-8N	D3
W Mississippi Rd					
19200	JknT	60421	3675	24W-32S	D7
19800	ELWD	60421	3675	24W-32S	D7
Mississippi St					
3000	NCHI	60064	2593	12W-30N	B2
3000	NCHI	60088	2593	12W-30N	B2
Missouri Ct					
17700	ODPK	60467	3423	13W-21S	A6
Missouri Dr					
1600	EGVV	60007	2913	21W-8N	D2
Missouri St					
-	NCHI	60064	2593	11W-30N	E1
2600	NCHI	60088	2593	11W-30N	E1
Mistflower Ct					
3900	NPVL	60564	3266	31W-11S	A1
Mistflower Ln					
2700	NPVL	60564	3266	30W-11S	A1
2700	WldT	60564	3266	30W-11S	B2
Misthaven Ln					
1400	ELGN	60123	2907	36W-8N	E3
Mistic Harbour Ln					
500	SMBG	60193	2858	24W-9N	E7
Mistwood Ct					
1100	DRGV	60515	3084	19W-3S	C5
1200	YKVL	60560	3261	42W-14S	E7
Mistwood Dr					
1600	LslT	60540	3204	24W-8S	C1
1600	NPVL	60540	3204	24W-8S	C1
23800	PNFD	60586	3416	29W-19S	C2
Mistwood Ln					
100	NARA	60542	3077	36W-3S	E7
200	CLLK	60012	2640	33W-26N	E3
200	CLLK	60014	2640	33W-26N	E3
1000	DRGV	60515	3084	19W-3S	C5
Mistwood Pl					
1100	DRGV	60515	3084	19W-3S	C5
Misty Ct					
10	SEGN	60177	2908	36W-9N	A2
2500	NPVL	60564	3203	28W-10S	A6
W Misty Dr					
700	PltT	60074	2752	21W-17N	C4
Misty Ln					
1400	BGBK	60490	3267	26W-12S	E3
16800	TYPK	60477	3424	8W-20S	E3
Misty Rdg					
200	LKMR	60051	2529	28W-32N	E4
Misty Brook Ln					
1000	JLET	60432	3500	20W-22S	B2
Misty Creek Dr					
-	AxST	60447	3672	33W-30S	B4
-	CnhT	60410	3672	33W-30S	C4
-	MNKA	60410	3672	33W-30S	C4
-	MNKA	60447	3672	34W-30S	A3
500	NLNX	60451	3501	18W-25S	A7
Misty Falls Cir					
-	FKFT	60423	3590	14W-27S	E4
Misty Falls Ln					
11400	FKFT	60423	3590	14W-27S	E4
S Misty Harbour Ln					
12700	PSPK	60464	3272	13W-14S	E7
12700	PSPK	60464	3273	13W-15S	A7
12700	PSPK	60464	3344	13W-15S	E1
Misty Hill Ln					
10	HNVL	60030	2532	22W-33N	C3
Misty Hill Rd					
10400	ODPK	60462	3345	13W-17S	B6
Misty Meadow Dr					
-	CNHN	60410	3672	33W-31S	C6
-	OrlT	60462	3346	10W-15S	C2
-	OrlT	60464	3346	10W-15S	C2
13200	PlsT	60462	3346	10W-15S	C2
13200	PSHT	60462	3346	10W-15S	C2
13200	PSHT	60464	3346	10W-15S	C1
Misty Pine Ct					
6100	NndT	60012	2584	35W-30N	B3
6200	RchT	60477	3425	7W-22S	C7
6200	TYPK	60477	3425	7W-22S	C7
Misty Pines Dr					
-	TYPK	60477	3425	7W-22S	C7
6200	RchT	60477	3425	7W-22S	C7
Misty Ridge Ct					
1900	AURA	60503	3201	33W-10S	B6
Misty Ridge Dr					
-	RMVL	60446	3268	24W-14S	D7
-	RMVL	60446	3340	24W-14S	E1
Misty Ridge Ln					
1800	AURA	60503	3201	33W-10S	A5
Misty Woods Rd					
2600	BFGV	60089	2701	16W-23N	C3
Mitchel Ct					
4400	LtRT	60545	3332	45W-14S	C1
Mitchel Dr					
-	LtRT	60545	3260	45W-14S	B7
-	PLNO	60545	3260	45W-14S	B7
-	PLNO	60545	3332	45W-14S	B1
E Mitchel Dr					
12000	LtRT	60545	3332	45W-14S	C1
W Mitchel Dr					
-	LtRT	60545	3332	45W-14S	B1
-	PLNO	60545	3332	45W-14S	B1
N Mitchell Av					
1600	ANHT	60004	2807	18W-15N	A1
1700	ANHT	60004	2806	18W-15N	E1
2800	ANHT	60004	2754	18W-17N	A5
S Mitchell Av					
10	ANHT	60005	2807	18W-13N	A7
500	EMHT	60126	3027	16W-0S	E6
S Mitchell Av					
1200	ANHT	60005	2861	18W-12N	A1
Mitchell Blvd					
1200	SMBG	60193	2912	24W-8N	E3
1500	SMBG	60172	2912	24W-8N	E3
Mitchell Cir					
10	WHTN	60187	3081	26W-2S	D4
Mitchell Ct					
200	BDWD	60408	3942	31W-40S	B4
600	GRNE	60031	2534	16W-33N	E3
1000	CLLK	60014	2694	33W-23N	E1
N Mitchell Ct					
10	AddT	60101	2970	21W-3N	A5
10	ADSN	60101	2970	21W-3N	A5
10	BmdT	60101	2970	21W-3N	A5
S Mitchell Ct					
10	ADSN	60101	2970	21W-3N	A6
W Mitchell Ct					
400	ANHT	60004	2807	18W-15N	A1
25000	AvnT	60041	2474	25W-35N	B6
25000	AvnT	60073	2474	25W-35N	B6
25000	GrtT	60041	2474	25W-35N	B5
25000	GrtT	60073	2474	25W-35N	B6
Mitchell Dr					
-	OswT	60503	3201	33W-11S	A7
-	OswT	60543	3201	33W-11S	A7
300	GYLK	60030	2532	21W-33N	D3
2000	OSWG	60543	3201	33W-11S	A7
2000	OSWG	60543	3265	33W-11S	A1
2500	WDRG	60517	3143	21W-7S	D6
16900	LKPT	60441	3421	18W-20S	A4
N Mitchell Dr					
3900	ANHT	60004	2754	18W-18N	A3
Mitchell Ln					
-	LKPT	60432	3420	20W-21S	B7
10	LslT	60540	3205	23W-8S	A1
17700	LKPT	60441	3420	20W-21S	B7
22100	AntT	60002	2417	22W-40N	C2
E Mitchell Ln					
1500	MPPT	60056	2808	14W-13N	D6
Mitchell Rd					
400	BmdT	60101	2969	22W-3N	B5
400	GLHT	60101	2969	22W-3N	B5
400	GLHT	60139	2969	22W-3N	B5
1100	AraT	60505	3138	35W-5S	C3
1100	AURA	60504	3138	35W-5S	C3
1100	AURA	60505	3138	35W-5S	C3
1100	AURA	60506	3138	35W-6S	B4
1200	AraT	60504	3138	35W-4S	C2
1900	AraT	60502	3138	35W-4S	C1
1900	NARA	60502	3138	35W-4S	C2
1900	NARA	60504	3138	35W-4S	C2
1900	NARA	60542	3138	35W-4S	C2
2000	AURA	60502	3138	34W-4S	C1
2500	AURA	60502	3078	35W-4S	C7
2500	NARA	60502	3078	35W-4S	C7
2500	NARA	60542	3078	35W-4S	C7
2600	AraT	60502	3078	34W-4S	C7
2600	AraT	60510	3078	34W-4S	C7
2600	AraT	60542	3078	34W-4S	C7
2600	AURA	60510	3078	34W-4S	C7
S Mitchell Rd					
3800	BCVL	60407	4030	33W-43S	A3
3800	BvlT	60407	4030	33W-43S	A3
Mitchell St					
700	WDSK	60098	2581	42W-30N	C1
N Mitchell St					
100	BCVL	60407	4030	34W-44S	A4
100	WMTN	60481	3853	27W-38S	D6
400	BvlT	60407	4030	34W-44S	A4
600	BDWD	60408	3942	31W-40S	B4
S Mitchell St					
100	BCVL	60407	4030	34W-45S	A6
100	WMTN	60481	3853	27W-38S	D6
200	BvlT	60407	4030	34W-45S	A6
500	GflT	60407	4030	34W-45S	A6
Mitchell Tr					
1300	EGVV	60007	2914	21W-8N	A3
N Mittel Blvd					
1200	WDDL	60191	2915	18W-7N	A4
1300	WDDL	60191	2914	18W-7N	E3
1500	EGvT	60007	2914	18W-7N	E3
Mittel Dr					
100	WDDL	60191	2915	18W-6N	A5
ML King Jr Dr					
-	LbvT	60044	2535	13W-31N	E7
-	LbvT	60044	2536	12W-31N	A7
-	WKGN	60085	2535	13W-31N	E7
-	WKGN	60085	2536	12W-31N	A7
1200	NCHI	60064	2536	11W-31N	E7
3100	ShdT	60044	2536	12W-31N	A7
ML King Jr Dr CO-A31					
-	LbvT	60044	2535	13W-31N	E7
-	LbvT	60044	2536	12W-31N	A7
-	WKGN	60085	2535	13W-31N	E7
-	WKGN	60085	2536	12W-31N	A7
3100	NCHI	60064	2536	12W-31N	B7
3100	ShdT	60044	2536	12W-31N	A7
Moate Ln					
10	BNHL	60010	2696	29W-21N	B7
Mobile Av					
8500	BRBK	60459	3211	7W-9S	B4
8700	OKLN	60453	3211	7W-10S	B4
8700	OKLN	60459	3211	7W-10S	B4
N Mobile Av					
1600	CHCG	60639	3031	6W-0S	E6
1600	OKPK	60302	3031	7W-2N	B1
1600	OKPK	60639	3031	7W-2N	B1
2600	CHCG	60639	2975	7W-3N	B5
4200	CHCG	60630	2975	7W-5N	B1
4200	CHCG	60634	2975	7W-5N	B1
5400	CHCG	60630	2919	7W-6N	A5
6300	CHCG	60646	2919	7W-7N	A3
S Mobile Av					
5100	CHCG	60638	3149	7W-5S	B2
5100	StkT	60638	3149	7W-5S	B2
6400	BDPK	60638	3149	7W-7S	B5
12700	PSHT	60463	3275	7W-15S	B7
12700	WthT	60463	3275	7W-15S	B7
Mobile Blvd					
3300	PKCY	60085	2536	12W-33N	A3
3300	WKGN	60085	2536	12W-33N	A3
Mobile Cir					
1000	EGVV	60007	2913	21W-8N	D3
Mobile Ct					
800	NPVL	60540	3203	28W-8S	A2
Mocassin Ct					
900	CLSM	60188	2968	26W-3N	A5
Mocassin Ln					
2500	CPVL	60110	2748	32W-18N	C4
Mockingbird Ct					
400	LNHT	60046	2476	19W-37N	B2
600	LslT	60540	3142	24W-5S	C3
600	SCRL	60175	2964	36W-5N	A2
1100	GYLK	60030	2533	19W-33N	B4
W Mockingbird Ct					
21500	KLDR	60047	2699	21W-21N	D5
Mocking Bird Dr					
700	ANTH	60002	2416	24W-41N	C1
Mockingbird Dr					
-	BCHR	60401	3864	0E-36S	E1
Mockingbird Ln					
10	DGvT	60527	3207	17W-10S	D6
10	OKBK	60523	3085	17W-2S	B4
10	YkTp	60523	3085	17W-2S	B4
100	WLNG	60090	2754	16W-18N	E4
200	NBRN	60010	2698	25W-23N	B1
18100	TYPK	60487	3424	11W-21S	A7
Moczygemba St					
600	LMNT	60439	3270	19W-14S	E6
Modaff Rd					
-	DPgT	60565	3203	26W-10S	D7
-	WldT	60565	3203	26W-10S	D7
10	NPVL	60565	3203	26W-10S	D6
10	NpvT	60565	3203	27W-9S	D3
1100	NPVL	60540	3203	26W-8S	D1
Model Ct					
100	RLKP	60073	2532	23W-33N	A4
12800	CTWD	60445	3275	6W-15S	E7
Model Airfield Rd					
23500	WynT	60184	2909	31W-6N	E7
Moders Av					
200	CRY	60013	2695	32W-23N	B2
Moe Dr					
-	CHCG	60616	3092	0E-2S	D2
E Moehling Dr					
200	MPPT	60056	2862	15W-12N	A1
Moeller St					
2100	DYR	46311	3598		D2
Moen Av					
10	RKDL	60436	3498	26W-25S	A7
1800	JltT	60436	3498	26W-25S	A7
2000	JltT	60436	3497	26W-25S	E7
2000	RKDL	60436	3497	26W-25S	E7
2200	TroT	60436	3497	26W-25S	E7
W Moffat St					
2000	CHCG	60622	2977	2W-2N	B7
2000	CHCG	60647	2977	2W-2N	B7
3100	CHCG	60647	2976	3W-2N	E7
Moffett Rd					
-	LKFT	60045	2594	10W-28N	A7
10	LKBF	60044	2594	10W-28N	A7
Mogra Dr					
2400	MchT	60050	2528	31W-34N	D1
S Mohave Ct					
17200	LKPT	60441	3420	21W-20S	A5
Mohave St					
200	HFET	60169	2858	23W-11N	E4
200	HFET	60169	2859	23W-10N	A4
200	SMBG	60169	2859	23W-10N	A4
200	SMBG	60194	2859	23W-10N	A4
Mohawk Av					
2400	WDRG	60517	3205	21W-8S	E1
Mohawk Ct					
10	BFGV	60089	2754	17W-18N	C3
10	SBTN	60010	2804	25W-13N	A5
800	ELGN	60120	2855	32W-12N	C2
1300	BRLT	60103	2967	28W-5N	A1
1300	SMBG	60193	2913	22W-8N	B2
1300	SmbT	60193	2913	22W-8N	B2
6400	IHPK	60525	3146	14W-7S	D6
W Mohawk Ct					
16200	LKPT	60441	3420	20W-20S	C4
Mohawk Dr					
10	CNHL	60514	3145	17W-5S	C2
10	SBTN	60010	2804	25W-13N	A5
10	TNTN	60476	3428	0E-20S	E5
100	CLSM	60188	2968	25W-2N	A7
100	NBRN	60010	2697	26W-22N	E3
200	BNVL	60106	2915	16W-5N	D7
600	RLKH	60073	2474	23W-35N	D5
800	ELGN	60120	2855	32W-12N	C1
1300	SmbT	60193	2913	23W-8N	B2
1500	SmbT	60172	2913	23W-8N	B2
7100	MchT	60097	2469	36W-36N	D4
Mohawk Ln					
2300	GNVW	60025	2809	11W-15N	C2
13500	ODPK	60462	3346	9W-16S	C2
25600	CNHN	60410	3672	32W-29S	E2
E Mohawk Ln					
1700	MPPT	60056	2808	13W-15N	D2
1700	PTHT	60070	2808	13W-15N	D2
Mohawk Rd					
1000	WLMT	60091	2812	5W-14N	A5
2600	WKGN	60087	2479	12W-36N	C4
3300	LinT	53147	2350		A2
3700	LinT	53147	2349		D2
3800	LinT	53184	2349		D2
S Mohawk Rd					
12300	PSPK	60464	3274	10W-14S	B6
Mohawk St					
10	CRY	60013	2695	32W-23N	B1
200	PKFT	60466	3595	4W-27S	A4
300	JltT	60432	3499	21W-23S	E4
300	PKFT	60466	3594	4W-27S	E4
400	JLET	60432	3499	21W-23S	E3
N Mohawk St					
1300	CHCG	60610	3034	0W-1N	A1
1600	CHCG	60610	2978	0W-2N	A7
1600	CHCG	60614	2978	0W-2N	A7
Mohawk Tr					
-	PltT	60124	2852	40W-10N	B6
10	BFGV	60089	2754	16W-18N	C3
10	LKZH	60047	2699	23W-22N	A3
100	ALGN	60102	2694	34W-21N	B6
100	ALGN	60102	2695	32W-21N	A6
100	AlqT	60102	2695	32W-21N	A5
100	LIHL	60102	2694	34W-21N	B6
100	LIHL	60156	2694	34W-21N	B5
100	LKZH	60047	2698	23W-22N	E3
1500	WLNG	60090	2754	16W-17N	D5
20000	OMFD	60461	3507	4W-24S	A5
20100	OMFD	60461	3506	4W-24S	E5
Mohegan Ln					
900	SMBG	60193	2912	24W-9N	D1
Moher Ct					
19400	MKNA	60448	3504	11W-23S	A3
Mohican Ct					
3900	JLET	60435	3417	27W-19S	C2
3900	JLET	60544	3417	27W-19S	C2
Mohican Dr					
10	MltT	60187	3081	26W-2S	E3
10	MltT	60187	3082	26W-2S	A3
2100	RLKH	60073	2474	23W-36N	D4
11800	ALGN	60102	2747	33W-20N	D1
11800	AlqT	60102	2747	33W-20N	D1
16700	LKPT	60441	3420	20W-20S	B4
Mohican Ln					
500	CmpT	60119	2961	43W-4N	A4
Mohican Rd					
500	CLSM	60188	2967	26W-3N	E6

Chicago 7-County Street Index

STREET Block	City	ZIP	Map#	CGS	Grid
Mohican Rd					
2200	WKGN	60087	2479	12W-36N	C4
Mohican Tr					
500	LIHL	60156	2694	34W-21N	B5
Mohler Ct					
1600	NPVL	60563	3141	27W-5S	C2
Mojave Ct					
7000	JLET	60586	3415	32W-20S	C5
Mojave Dr					
-	JLET	60586	3415	32W-20S	C5
Mokena St					
19600	MKNA	60448	3503	13W-23S	A4
N Moki Ln					
900	MPPT	60056	2808	13W-14N	E5
W Molidor Rd					
26300	GrtT	60041	2530	27W-33N	C3
26700	VOLO	60041	2530	26W-33N	C3
Moline Expwy					
-	BmnT	-	3425	7W-21S	D7
-	BmnT	-	3426	6W-21S	A6
-	CCHL	-	3426	6W-21S	B5
-	FftT	-	3503	12W-22S	B1
-	FftT	-	3504	9W-22S	D1
-	HLCT	-	3426	4W-20S	D4
-	HLCT	-	3427	3W-20S	A4
-	MKHM	-	3427	3W-20S	A4
-	MKNA	-	3503	12W-22S	D1
-	MKNA	-	3504	10W-22S	C1
-	ODPK	-	3503	12W-22S	B1
-	RchT	-	3425	7W-21S	D7
-	RchT	-	3505	8W-22S	A1
-	TYPK	-	3503	11W-22S	E1
-	TYPK	-	3504	10W-22S	C1
-	TYPK	-	3505	8W-22S	A1
Moline Expwy I-80					
-	BmnT	-	3425	7W-21S	D7
-	BmnT	-	3426	6W-21S	A6
-	CCHL	-	3426	6W-21S	A6
-	FftT	-	3503	12W-22S	B1
-	FftT	-	3504	9W-22S	D1
-	HLCT	-	3426	4W-20S	D4
-	HLCT	-	3427	3W-20S	A4
-	MKHM	-	3427	3W-20S	A4
-	MKNA	-	3503	12W-22S	D1
-	MKNA	-	3504	10W-22S	C1
-	ODPK	-	3503	12W-22S	B1
-	RchT	-	3425	7W-21S	D7
-	RchT	-	3505	8W-22S	A1
-	TYPK	-	3503	11W-22S	E1
-	TYPK	-	3504	10W-22S	C1
-	TYPK	-	3505	8W-22S	A1
Molitor Rd					
-	NpvT	60563	3139	31W-5S	D3
1000	AraT	60504	3138	34W-5S	D2
1000	AraT	60505	3138	34W-5S	D2
1000	AURA	60504	3138	34W-5S	D2
1000	AURA	60505	3138	34W-5S	D2
1500	AURA	60505	3139	33W-5S	A2
1700	AraT	60502	3139	33W-5S	A2
1700	AraT	60505	3139	33W-5S	A2
1700	AURA	60502	3139	33W-5S	A2
2100	NpvT	60502	3139	32W-5S	D3
Molly Ct					
2500	NLNX	60451	3588	19W-27S	E5
Molobay Ter					
900	BRLT	60103	2911	28W-7N	B5
Monaco Dr					
300	ROSL	60172	2912	24W-7N	E4
Monaghan Dr					
8400	FftT	60477	3504	10W-23S	B4
8400	TYPK	60477	3504	10W-23S	B4
S Monaghan Rd					
13500	HMGN	60491	3343	17W-16S	D2
13500	LMNT	60439	3343	17W-16S	D2
Monaldi Dr					
7900	MNSR	46321	3430		E6
Monaldi Pkwy					
2600	DYR	46311	3598		C3
Monarch Av					
-	NlxT	60451	3588	19W-27S	E5
1500	NLNX	60451	3588	19W-27S	D5
Monarch Cir					
1300	AURA	60564	3201	31W-9S	E5
3500	AURA	60564	3202	31W-9S	A4
Monarch Ct					
-	BHPK	60087	2421	11W-38N	E7
10	LIHL	60156	2692	38W-21N	D5
Monarch Dr					
10	SMWD	60107	2856	30W-9N	B7
10	SMWD	60107	2910	30W-9N	C1
500	CLLK	60014	2693	36W-23N	D1
Monarch Ln					
-	BHPK	60087	2421	11W-38N	E7
-	BHPK	60087	2479	11W-38N	E1
-	SEGN	60177	2907	37W-7N	D6
300	BGBK	60440	3268	23W-12S	E3
1100	HFET	60192	2804	24W-15N	C1
N Monarch Ln					
500	ADSN	60101	2970	20W-4N	A4
Monarch Birch Ct					
300	BRLT	60103	2910	30W-8N	A2
Monarch Birch Ln					
400	BRLT	60103	2910	30W-9N	A2
Monaville Rd					
10	LKVL	60046	2475	23W-36N	A3
10	LKVL	60073	2475	23W-36N	A3
10	RLKB	60073	2475	23W-36N	A3
200	LKVL	60046	2474	23W-36N	D3
400	LkvT	60046	2474	23W-36N	D3
Monaville Rd CO-A18					
10	LKVL	60046	2475	23W-36N	A3
10	LKVL	60073	2475	23W-36N	A3
10	RLKB	60073	2475	23W-36N	A3
200	LKVL	60046	2474	23W-36N	D3
400	LkvT	60046	2474	23W-36N	D3
E Monaville Rd					
10	LKVL	60046	2475	23W-36N	A3
10	LKVL	60073	2475	22W-36N	A3
10	LkvT	60046	2475	22W-36N	A3
10	LkvT	60073	2475	22W-36N	A3
10	RLKB	60046	2475	22W-36N	A3
10	RLKB	60073	2475	22W-36N	A3
E Monaville Rd CO-A18					
10	LKVL	60046	2475	23W-36N	A3
10	LKVL	60073	2475	22W-36N	A3
10	LkvT	60046	2475	22W-36N	A3
10	LkvT	60073	2475	22W-36N	A3
10	RLKB	60046	2475	22W-36N	A3
10	RLKB	60073	2475	22W-36N	A3
W Monaville Rd					
22400	LkvT	60046	2475	22W-36N	B3
22400	RLKB	60046	2475	22W-36N	B3
22400	RLKB	60073	2475	22W-36N	B3
22500	LkvT	60073	2475	22W-36N	B3
22600	LKVL	60046	2475	22W-36N	B3
22600	LKVL	60073	2475	22W-36N	B3
23700	LKVL	60046	2474	24W-37N	C3
23700	LkvT	60046	2474	24W-37N	C3
24800	GrtT	60046	2474	25W-37N	B3
25400	GrtT	60041	2474	25W-37N	A3
25400	LkvT	60041	2474	25W-37N	A3
W Monaville Rd CO-A18					
22400	LkvT	60046	2475	22W-36N	B3
22400	RLKB	60046	2475	22W-36N	B3
22400	RLKB	60073	2475	22W-36N	B3
22500	LkvT	60073	2475	22W-36N	B3
22600	LKVL	60046	2475	22W-36N	B3
22600	LKVL	60073	2475	22W-36N	B3
23700	LKVL	60046	2474	24W-37N	C3
23700	LkvT	60046	2474	24W-37N	C3
24800	GrtT	60046	2474	25W-37N	B3
25400	GrtT	60041	2474	25W-37N	A3
25400	LkvT	60041	2474	25W-37N	A3
E Mondamin St					
100	MNKA	60447	3583	33W-28S	B7
W Mondamin St					
100	MNKA	60447	3583	33W-28S	A7
Monday Dr					
1800	ELGN	60123	2800	36W-13N	A7
Mondelli Ln					
-	HMGN	60491	3342	19W-17S	E5
Mondovi Dr					
200	OSWG	60543	3200	36W-11S	A7
200	OSWG	60543	3264	36W-11S	A1
Monee Ct					
10	PKFT	60466	3595	3W-28S	B5
Monee Rd					
-	CteT	60417	3686	0E-31S	A5
10	BlmT	60466	3595	3W-28S	B5
10	MonT	60466	3595	3W-27S	B5
10	PKFT	60466	3595	3W-28S	B5
700	CteT	60417	3685	1W-31S	A5
1100	CRTE	60417	3684	1W-31S	E5
1100	CRTE	60417	3685	1W-31S	A5
1100	CteT	60417	3684	2W-31S	D5
1900	MonT	60417	3684	2W-31S	D5
1900	MonT	60449	3684	2W-31S	D5
W Monee Rd					
10	CRTE	60417	3685	0W-31S	C5
10	CteT	60417	3685	0W-31S	C5
W Monee Manhattan Rd					
5500	MONE	60449	3682	6W-31S	E4
5500	MONE	60449	3683	6W-30S	A4
5500	MonT	60449	3682	8W-30S	B4
5500	MonT	60449	3683	6W-30S	A4
5500	UYPK	60449	3683	6W-30S	A4
5600	MONE	60466	3682	7W-30S	D4
5600	UYPK	60449	3682	7W-30S	E4
5600	UYPK	60466	3682	7W-30S	D4
6800	GGnT	60449	3682	8W-31S	A4
Monestary Dr					
-	LSLE	60532	3142	23W-6S	E4
Monet Cir					
400	BGBK	60440	3205	22W-11S	C7
Monet Ct					
700	SMBG	60193	2858	24W-9N	E7
Monet Pl					
100	SCRL	60175	2963	38W-3N	B6
Monhegan Av					
1800	BCHR	60401	3774	0W-35S	D6
Moni Dr					
21600	NLNX	60451	3590	15W-26S	B2
S Monica Dr					
10	LKVL	60046	2475	22W-37N	C1
Monica Ln					
1400	NLNX	60451	3588	19W-27S	E5
W Monica St					
24000	CNHN	60410	3584	30W-28S	C7
24000	CnhT	60410	3584	30W-28S	C7
Monica Tr					
3500	NndT	60014	2641	32W-26N	A3
Monitor Av					
200	AURA	60505	3200	36W-9S	A3
7500	BRBK	60459	3211	7W-8S	C2
9100	OKLN	60453	3211	7W-10S	C5
10700	CHRG	60415	3275	7W-12S	C2
N Monitor Av					
1000	CHCG	60651	3031	7W-1N	C2
1600	CHCG	60639	3031	7W-2N	C1
2100	CHCG	60639	2975	7W-2N	C6
4000	CHCG	60634	2975	7W-5N	C1
4300	CHCG	60630	2975	7W-5N	C1
5400	CHCG	60630	2919	7W-6N	B5
6000	CHCG	60646	2919	7W-7N	B3
S Monitor Av					
900	CHCG	60644	3031	7W-0S	C6
1100	CCRO	60644	3031	7W-0S	C7
1100	CCRO	60804	3031	7W-0S	C7
4900	CHCG	60638	3149	7W-5S	C2
5100	StkT	60638	3149	7W-5S	C2
12700	ALSP	60463	3275	7W-15S	C7
12700	ALSP	60803	3275	7W-15S	C7
12700	WthT	60463	3275	7W-15S	C7
12900	WthT	60463	3347	7W-15S	C1
Monitor Dr					
3700	CLSM	60188	2967	26W-4N	D4
3700	HRPK	60133	2967	26W-4N	D4
Monitor Ln					
3200	LGGV	60047	2700	19W-21N	C6
Monitor St					
400	PKFT	60466	3507	3W-25S	B7
400	PKFT	60466	3595	3W-25S	B1
Monmouth Av					
1300	NPVL	60565	3204	24W-9S	C3
Monmouth Ct					
400	AURA	60504	3140	29W-6S	D6
Monmouth Dr					
1200	LMNT	60439	3271	18W-14S	A6
6900	JLET	60431	3495	32W-22S	C1
Monmouth Pl					
-	CRTE	60417	3685	0E-29S	D1
1700	DRGV	60516	3144	20W-7S	A7
E Monna St					
10	SRGV	60554	3135	42W-7S	D6
Monomoy St					
1200	AURA	60506	3137	37W-6S	C5
N Monon Av					
7000	CHCG	60646	2919	7W-8N	B1
Monona Av					
1300	AURA	60506	3137	37W-6S	C6
Monroe Av					
300	FXLK	60041	2473	26W-35N	D5
400	GLNC	60022	2758	6W-17N	D6
500	RVFT	60305	3030	9W-0N	D3
500	SCRL	60174	2964	35W-2N	C7
800	CPVL	60110	2748	32W-17N	D7
800	OKPK	60304	3030	8W-0S	E5
800	SCRL	60174	3020	35W-2N	C1
900	WCDA	60084	2588	25W-28N	A6
900	WPHR	60096	2363	10W-42N	A7
1100	WcnT	60084	2588	25W-28N	A6
1400	WPHR	60096	2422	10W-41N	A1
1500	EDPK	60707	3030	9W-1N	D1
1500	RVFT	60707	3030	9W-1N	D1
1800	GNVW	60025	2810	8W-14N	E4
6200	HMND	46324	3430		E2
7800	MNSR	46321	3430		E6
8700	MNSR	46321	3510		D1
8800	BKFD	60513	3087	11W-3S	D5
9500	BKFD	60525	3087	11W-3S	C5
9500	LGPK	60525	3087	11W-3S	C5
E Monroe Av					
900	LGPK	60525	3087	12W-3S	C5
1100	BKFD	60513	3087	12W-3S	C5
1100	BKFD	60525	3087	12W-3S	C5
W Monroe Av					
200	LGPK	60525	3087	12W-3S	B5
Monroe Ct					
10	SMWD	60107	2857	28W-10N	A6
900	VNHL	60061	2647	17W-26N	B4
1300	AURA	60506	3137	37W-6S	C5
1800	GNVW	60025	2810	8W-14N	E4
6000	MNGV	60053	2865	7W-10N	B5
25200	PNFD	60585	3337	31W-15S	E3
W Monroe Ct					
6900	NLES	60714	2864	8W-10N	E5
Monroe Dr					
600	LNHT	60046	2418	19W-39N	B5
1100	BRLT	60103	2910	29W-6N	C7
E Monroe Dr					
100	CHCG	60603	3034	0E-0S	C5
Monroe Ln					
1600	HRPK	60133	2911	26W-6N	E6
Monroe Pl					
500	WDDL	60191	2914	18W-5N	D7
Monroe Rd					
200	BGBK	60440	3205	22W-10S	C6
Monroe St					
10	ELGN	60123	2854	34W-11N	C4
10	NARA	60542	3078	36W-4S	A7
10	NARA	60542	3138	35W-4S	A1
10	OSWG	60543	3263	37W-12S	C4
200	EGvT	60018	2862	15W-9N	A7
400	DLTN	60419	3350	0E-16S	D4
600	AURA	60505	3138	34W-6S	C6
700	EVTN	60202	2867	3W-10N	A5
1100	FTPK	60304	3030	8W-0S	D5
1100	OKPK	60304	3030	8W-0S	D5
1300	LIHL	60156	2693	35W-22N	E4
1500	AlqT	60156	2693	35W-22N	E4
1600	EVTN	60202	2866	3W-10N	E5
2600	NARA	60542	3077	36W-4S	E7
3400	LNSG	60438	3430	4E-21S	C6
3900	BLWD	60104	3029	12W-0S	A5
3900	BLWD	60162	3029	12W-0S	A5
3900	HLSD	60162	3029	12W-0S	A5
4100	DrrT	60012	2583	36W-28N	C6
5000	RGWD	60072	2470	34W-36N	D4
5100	MTSN	60443	3506	6W-24S	A5
5200	SKOK	60077	2865	6W-10N	C5
5300	MNGV	60077	2865	6W-10N	C5
5800	MNGV	60053	2865	7W-10N	B5
7000	WLBK	60527	3146	16W-8S	A7
7600	FTPK	60130	3030	9W-0S	C5
E Monroe St					
10	CHCG	60603	3034	0E-0S	C5
10	VLPK	60181	3027	17W-0S	B5
100	EMHT	60126	3028	15W-0S	A5
N Monroe St					
10	HNDL	60521	3145	16W-4S	E1
400	HNDL	60521	3085	16W-4S	E7
S Monroe St					
5500	DGvT	60521	3145	16W-6S	E4
5500	HNDL	60521	3145	16W-6S	E4
W Monroe St					
-	WkgT	60031	2536	12W-33N	A1
10	CHCG	60603	3034	0W-0S	A5
10	VLPK	60181	3027	18W-0S	A5
100	CHCG	60606	3034	0W-0S	B5
400	CHCG	60661	3034	0W-0S	A5
400	EMHT	60126	3027	17W-0S	C5
700	CHCG	60607	3034	0W-0S	A5
800	CHCG	60607	3033	1W-0S	D5
1400	WKGN	60085	2536	11W-34N	E1
2000	CHCG	60612	3033	2W-0S	B5
2800	CHCG	60612	3032	3W-0S	E5
3100	CHCG	60624	3032	4W-0S	D5
4600	CHCG	60644	3032	5W-0S	A5
4800	CHCG	60644	3031	6W-0S	D5
7200	NLES	60714	2864	9W-10N	D5
7900	MaiT	60714	2864	9W-10N	B5
Monson Ct					
200	SMBG	60173	2859	21W-10N	E5
Montabello					
-	BMDL	60172	2912	24W-6N	C7
-	BmdT	60172	2912	24W-6N	C7
Montana Av					
3100	NCHI	60088	2593	11W-30N	C2
9900	FNPK	60131	2973	12W-3N	B6
E Montana Av					
10	GLHT	60139	2968	23W-3N	E6
300	GLHT	60139	2969	22W-3N	B6
W Montana Av					
10	GLHT	60139	2968	24W-3N	D6
Montana Ct					
10	CRY	60013	2642	30W-24N	A7
18200	ODPK	60467	3423	13W-21S	A7
Montana Dr					
10	CRY	60013	2696	30W-23N	A1
800	CRY	60013	2642	30W-24N	A7
Montana St					
10400	LydT	60131	2973	13W-3N	A6
10400	LydT	60164	2973	13W-3N	A6
10600	LydT	60164	2972	13W-3N	E6
10600	NHLK	60164	2972	13W-3N	E6
W Montana St					
900	CHCG	60614	2977	1W-3N	D5
2300	CHCG	60647	2977	2W-3N	A5
4400	CHCG	60639	2976	5W-3N	A5
4700	CHCG	60639	2975	6W-3N	D5
Montana Wy					
1500	EGVV	60007	2859	21W-9N	E7
Montauk Ct					
1400	BRLT	60103	2967	28W-5N	B1
Montauk Dr					
5000	JLET	60586	3496	30W-22S	B2
W Montauk Dr					
16500	LKPT	60441	3420	20W-20S	B5
Montauk Ln					
10	VNHL	60061	2647	17W-24N	C6
400	PGGV	60140	2798	41W-14N	A5
N Montclair Av					
100	GNEN	60137	3025	22W-0S	C6
S Montclair Av					
100	GNEN	60137	3083	22W-1S	C1
Montclair Ct					
10	CRY	60013	2695	33W-23N	A1
10	LIHL	60156	2692	38W-23N	E2
400	RMVL	60446	3340	24W-15S	D2
3300	JLET	60441	3417	27W-19S	C3
Montclair Dr					
-	ELGN	60123	2907	36W-8N	E3
-	SEGN	60123	2907	36W-8N	E3
10	CRY	60013	2695	33W-23N	A1
700	RDLK	60073	2531	23W-32N	E5
1900	LslT	60565	3204	24W-9S	D4
1900	NPVL	60565	3204	24W-9S	D4
Montclair Rd					
10	VNHL	60061	2701	17W-24N	B1
Montclaire Cir					
1300	SMBG	60173	2859	21W-10N	D5
Montclaire Ln					
3500	MTGY	60538	3198	40W-10S	C7
Montclaire Pl					
1200	SMBG	60173	2859	22W-10N	D5
N Mont Clare Av					
2500	CHCG	60707	2974	8W-3N	D5
2700	CHCG	60634	2974	8W-3N	D5
4800	CHCG	60656	2918	8W-6N	D6
4800	CHCG	60706	2918	8W-6N	D6
4800	HDHT	60706	2918	8W-6N	D7
Montclare Ct					
2700	AURA	60504	3201	32W-8S	C1
Montclare Ln					
100	AddT	60191	2971	17W-5N	B2
100	WDDL	60191	2971	17W-5N	B2
Montclare Lake Ct					
16300	LktT	60403	3417	26W-19S	E3
Montclare Lake Dr					
16300	LktT	60403	3417	26W-19S	E3
Montebello Dr					
10	VNHL	60061	2647	17W-24N	C6
Monte Carlo Wy					
-	JLET	60421	3586	24W-28S	D7
Montego Ct					
200	BMDL	60108	2912	25W-6N	B7
200	BmdT	60172	2912	25W-6N	B7
1200	EGVV	60007	2914	19W-8N	C3
Montego Dr					
500	EGVV	60007	2914	19W-8N	C3
Montego Bay Ct					
1000	RMVL	60446	3340	25W-16S	B4
Montego Colony St					
10	FXLK	60020	2414	28W-38N	D6
Monteith Av					
100	NlxT	60433	3500	20W-24S	C5
Monteith Ct					
10	VNHL	60061	2646	18W-25N	E5
Monterey Av					
100	OKTR	60181	3085	17W-1S	C2
400	OKBK	60181	3085	17W-1S	C2
19800	LYWD	60411	3510	3E-23S	A4
E Monterey Av					
10	SMBG	60193	2913	23W-8N	A2
400	SmbT	60193	2913	22W-8N	B2
N Monterey Av					
5000	CHCG	60656	2918	9W-6N	B6
5000	NRDG	60656	2918	9W-6N	B6
5000	NRDG	60706	2918	9W-6N	B6
S Monterey Av					
10	EMHT	60126	3027	17W-0N	C4
10	EMHT	60181	3027	17W-0N	C4
10	VLPK	60181	3027	17W-0N	C4
1400	ROSL	60172	2913	22W-8N	C2
1400	SmbT	60193	2913	22W-8N	C2
1500	OKTR	60181	3027	17W-0S	C7
W Monterey Av					
10	SMBG	60193	2913	23W-8N	A2
1600	CHCG	60643	3277	2W-13S	D3
Monterey Ct					
200	BGBK	60440	3269	22W-11S	C1
1100	NPVL	60540	3141	28W-6S	A5
1500	GRNE	60031	2478	14W-35N	B5
1700	HFET	60169	2858	25W-12N	A2
Monterey Dr					
-	NLNX	60451	3500	20W-24S	B5
10	VNHL	60061	2647	17W-24N	C6
200	BGBK	60440	3269	22W-11S	C1
200	GnvT	60510	3077	38W-1S	A1
300	BGBK	60440	3205	22W-11S	C7
500	CLLK	60014	2639	36W-24N	D7
1000	RMVL	60446	3340	25W-16S	B3
1400	GNVW	60025	2810	10W-14N	A4
2400	JLET	60586	3415	31W-20S	E6
2900	FSMR	60422	3507	3W-22S	A1
3100	HMWD	60430	3507	3W-22S	A1
4800	RNPK	60471	3594	6W-27S	A4
W Monterey Dr					
12000	HMGN	60491	3344	15W-18S	C6
12000	ODPK	60467	3344	15W-18S	C6
N Monterey Ln					
-	WDWH	60083	2478	14W-37N	C1
-	WKGN	60083	2478	14W-37N	D1
E Monterey Rd					
400	PLTN	60074	2753	20W-17N	A6
Monterra Dr					
2800	SPGV	60081	2413	31W-40N	D2
W Monterrey Dr					
21200	LktT	60544	3339	26W-16S	E3
Monterrey Ter					
500	FXLK	60050	2472	28W-37N	D2
500	GrtT	60050	2472	28W-37N	D2
500	MchT	60050	2472	28W-37N	D2
Montery Ct					
1000	UYPK	60466	3684	3W-30S	B3
Montesano Av					
700	WKGN	60087	2480	10W-36N	A4
1100	WKGN	60087	2479	11W-36N	E4
Montgomery Av					
900	AURA	60506	3199	37W-8S	D2
4700	DRGV	60515	3144	20W-5S	B2
S Montgomery Av					
4000	CHCG	60632	3091	3W-4S	A6
W Montgomery Av					
2600	CHCG	60632	3091	3W-4S	A6
Montgomery Ct					
900	NPVL	60540	3203	27W-8S	B1
1800	DRFD	60015	2703	12W-21N	B6
Montgomery Dr					
-	CRTE	60417	3596	0E-29S	E7
-	CRTE	60417	3685	0E-29S	E1
3300	LIHL	60156	2692	39W-23N	C2
9100	ODPK	60462	3346	10W-17S	A6
9200	ODPK	60462	3345	11W-17S	E5
Montgomery Ln					
10	VNHL	60061	2647	17W-24N	C6
100	GNVW	60025	2864	9W-12N	D1
200	WDDL	60191	2914	19W-5N	C7
Montgomery Rd					
-	AURA	60504	3202	30W-9S	A4
10	AraT	60504	3200	34W-9S	D4
10	AURA	60504	3200	34W-9S	D4
100	AraT	60538	3200	34W-9S	D4
100	AURA	60505	3200	34W-9S	D4
100	MTGY	60504	3200	34W-9S	D4
100	MTGY	60505	3200	36W-9S	A5
100	MTGY	60538	3199	36W-9S	E5
100	MTGY	60538	3200	36W-9S	A5
100	NpvT	60504	3201	32W-9S	C4
200	AURA	60564	3202	30W-9S	A4
500	AraT	60505	3200	36W-9S	A5
1300	WdfT	60015	2703	12W-21N	B6
1500	BKBN	60015	2703	12W-21N	B6
1600	AraT	60504	3201	33W-9S	A4
1600	AURA	60504	3201	33W-9S	A3
1600	DRFD	60015	2703	12W-21N	C7
2400	HDPK	60035	2704	8W-23N	E3
3400	AURA	60564	3201	31W-9S	E4
Montgomery Rd CO-29					
100	MTGY	60538	3199	36W-9S	E5
200	MTGY	60538	3200	36W-9S	A5
300	AURA	60505	3200	34W-9S	D4
300	MTGY	60505	3200	36W-9S	A5
500	AraT	60505	3200	36W-9S	A5
500	AraT	60538	3200	34W-9S	D4
1400	AraT	60504	3200	34W-9S	D4
1400	AURA	60504	3200	34W-9S	D4
1400	MTGY	60504	3200	34W-9S	D4
Montgomery St					
100	AURA	60505	3138	34W-7S	D7
100	GLNC	60022	2758	5W-17N	E5
W Montgomery St					
-	DSPN	60016	2861	16W-10N	E4
-	MPPT	60016	2861	16W-10N	E4
-	MPPT	60056	2861	16W-10N	E4
Montibello Dr					
5500	HRPK	60133	2911	26W-6N	D6
Monticello Av					
400	WTMT	60559	3085	17W-4S	C7
8000	SKOK	60076	2866	4W-10N	C5
8800	SKOK	60203	2866	4W-11N	C4
9500	EVTN	60201	2866	4W-11N	C2
N Monticello Av					
400	CHCG	60624	3032	4W-0N	C3
1400	CHCG	60651	3032	4W-1N	C1
1500	CHCG	60647	3032	4W-1N	C1
2200	CHCG	60647	2976	4W-2N	C6
3500	CHCG	60618	2976	4W-4N	C2
4300	CHCG	60625	2976	4W-5N	C1
5100	CHCG	60625	2920	4W-6N	C6
6000	CHCG	60659	2920	4W-7N	C3
6300	LNWD	60659	2920	4W-7N	C3
6400	LNWD	60712	2920	4W-8N	C2
S Monticello Av					
13300	RBBN	60472	3348	4W-16S	D2
Monticello Cir					
100	BGBK	60440	3269	23W-11S	B1
600	LKFT	60045	2649	12W-26N	B2
S Monticello Cir					
14100	PnfT	60544	3339	27W-16S	C5
Monticello Ct					
100	MltT	60137	3083	21W-2S	D3
1600	WHTN	60187	3082	25W-2S	B3
E Monticello Ct					
6700	GRNE	60031	2477	17W-35N	C6
W Monticello Ct					
6800	GRNE	60031	2477	17W-35N	B6
Monticello Dr					
10	DYR	46311	3510		C7
10	LYWD	60411	3510		C7
700	NPVL	60563	3141	26W-6S	E4
900	LslT	60563	3141	26W-6S	E4
1000	AraT	60506	3199	38W-8S	B3
Monticello Ln					
3200	LGGV	60047	2700	19W-21N	B6
W Monticello Ln					
23200	ElaT	60047	2644	23W-25N	E5
S Monticello Pl					
-	PvsT	60558	3086	14W-2S	D4
-	WSTR	60558	3086	14W-2S	D4
2500	WSTR	60154	3086	14W-2S	D3
W Monticello Pl					
11300	WSTR	60154	3086	14W-2S	D3
Monticello Rd					
10	MltT	60148	3083	21W-2S	E3
10	MltT	60148	3084	21W-2S	A3
400	MltT	60137	3083	21W-2S	D3
1600	HFET	60169	2858	23W-12N	E1
W Monticello Rd					
500	BTVA	60510	3078	35W-2S	A4
Monticello St					
700	EVTN	60201	2813	2W-13N	B7
E Monticello Wy					
7600	AlqT	60014	2641	33W-24N	A7
7600	CLLK	60014	2641	33W-24N	A7
Montmarte Av					
3300	HLCT	60429	3426	4W-21S	E7
Montrose Av					
-	SRPK	60176	2917	12W-5N	B7
-	SRPK	60176	2973	11W-5N	C1
500	CHCG	60666	2917	12W-5N	A7
E Montrose Av					
-	BNVL	60106	2971	16W-5N	C1
-	BNVL	60191	2971	16W-5N	C1
-	WDDL	60106	2971	16W-5N	C1
400	WDDL	60191	2971	17W-5N	C1
W Montrose Av					
-	CHCG	60613	2922	0W-5N	A7
-	CHCG	60640	2922	0W-5N	A7
300	EMHT	60126	3027	16W-0N	D4
500	ADSN	60143	2970	19W-5N	D1
500	ADSN	60191	2970	19W-5N	D1
500	ITSC	60143	2970	19W-5N	D1
500	ITSC	60191	2970	19W-5N	D1
500	WDDL	60191	2970	19W-5N	D1
600	CHCG	60613	2921	2W-5N	C7
600	CHCG	60640	2921	2W-5N	C7
1900	CHCG	60618	2921	2W-5N	B7
1900	CHCG	60625	2921	2W-5N	B7
2700	CHCG	60618	2920	3W-5N	E7
2700	CHCG	60625	2920	3W-5N	E7
3200	CHCG	60618	2976	4W-5N	D1
3200	CHCG	60625	2976	4W-5N	D1
3900	CHCG	60630	2976	4W-5N	B1
3900	CHCG	60641	2976	4W-5N	B1
4600	CHCG	60630	2975	7W-5N	B1
4600	CHCG	60641	2975	7W-5N	B1
5500	CHCG	60634	2975	6W-5N	C1
6300	HDHT	60706	2975	7W-5N	A1
6500	CHCG	60706	2975	8W-5N	A1
6600	CHCG	60634	2974	8W-5N	E1
6600	CHCG	60706	2974	8W-5N	E1
6600	HDHT	60706	2974	8W-5N	E1
7200	NRDG	60706	2974	10W-5N	A1
7700	NRDG	60634	2974	9W-5N	C1
8300	CHCG	60656	2974	10W-5N	A1

STREET Block	City	ZIP	Map#	CGS	Grid
W Montrose Av					
8500	CHCG	60634	2973	10W-5N	E1
8500	CHCG	60656	2973	10W-5N	E1
Montrose Blvd					
9900	SRPK	60176	2973	12W-5N	B1
Montrose Ct					
100	NPVL	60565	3204	25W-10S	A5
9000	LKWD	60014	2639	37W-24N	A6
Montrose Dr					
10	RMVL	60446	3340	24W-15S	D2
10	RMVL	60446	3341	23W-15S	A2
1700	AURA	60503	3201	32W-10S	B5
1700	AURA	60504	3201	32W-10S	B5
3100	LIHL	60156	2692	39W-23N	C2
W Montrose Rd					
25900	AntT	60002	2415	26W-38N	E6
25900	LkvT	60002	2415	26W-38N	E6
W Montrose Harbor Dr					
-	CHCG	60613	2922	0W-5N	B7
-	CHCG	60613	2978	0W-5N	B1
-	CHCG	60640	2922	0W-5N	B7
Montrose Park Pl					
10	ELGN	60123	2854	35W-12N	C2
W Montvale Av					
1600	CHCG	60643	3277	2W-13S	C3
Monument Av					
100	BRTN	60010	2750	25W-18N	E3
Monument Ct					
2200	GRNE	60031	2478	15W-36N	A4
Moody Av					
7700	BRBK	60459	3211	7W-8S	C2
8500	OKLN	60453	3211	7W-9S	C4
8500	OKLN	60459	3211	7W-9S	C4
8800	MNGV	60053	2865	7W-11N	B3
10400	CHRG	60415	3275	7W-12S	C1
N Moody Av					
1600	CHCG	60302	3031	6W-0S	E7
1600	CHCG	60639	3031	6W-0S	E7
1600	OKPK	60302	3031	6W-0S	E7
2600	CHCG	60639	2975	7W-3N	B5
4000	CHCG	60634	2975	7W-5N	B1
4200	CHCG	60630	2975	7W-5N	B1
5200	CHCG	60630	2919	7W-6N	B5
5600	CHCG	60646	2919	7W-7N	B4
7100	CHCG	60646	2865	7W-8N	B7
7100	CHCG	60714	2865	7W-8N	B7
7100	NLES	60714	2865	7W-8N	B7
S Moody Av					
5100	StkT	60638	3149	7W-5S	B2
5500	CHCG	60638	3149	7W-6S	B3
12400	WthT	60463	3275	7W-14S	C7
12900	WthT	60463	3347	7W-15S	C1
Moody Ct					
300	SEGN	60177	2909	33W-9N	B1
Moody St					
300	SCRL	60174	3020	35W-2N	B1
N Moody St					
35200	FXLK	60041	2473	27W-35N	C6
35200	GrtT	60041	2473	27W-35N	C6
Mooney Dr					
400	JLET	60435	3497	27W-23S	C4
Moon Hill Dr					
2900	NHBK	60062	2756	11W-17N	D5
Moon Lake Blvd					
-	SMBG	60169	2858	25W-12N	A2
-	SMBG	60194	2858	25W-12N	A2
1300	HFET	60169	2858	26W-12N	A2
1600	HFET	60169	2857	26W-12N	E2
Moonlight Ct					
10	MTSN	60443	3506	5W-24S	C5
2300	AURA	60503	3201	32W-10S	C7
2300	NPVL	60565	3203	27W-10S	C6
Moonlight Dr					
-	ElgT	60124	2853	38W-11N	B5
Moonlight Rd					
10	MTSN	60443	3506	5W-24S	C5
Moonlight Ridge Ct					
13500	HTLY	60142	2744	43W-19N	B2
Moon Rover Dr					
200	RDLK	60073	2531	24W-34N	D1
Moonstone Run					
1100	LIHL	60156	2693	36W-22N	D4
Moon Vista Ct					
700	NLNX	60451	3589	18W-27S	A4
Moore Av					
1300	SCRL	60174	3020	34W-2N	D2
1600	JltT	60433	3587	23W-26S	A2
1600	SMWD	60107	2911	28W-9N	B1
1800	JLET	60433	3587	23W-26S	A3
Moore Ct					
200	GYLK	60030	2532	21W-32N	E5
1100	ANTH	60002	2359	20W-41N	A7
1800	SCRL	60174	3020	34W-2N	D2
2400	NPVL	60564	3202	29W-10S	C6
Moore Dr					
-	BGBK	60440	3205	22W-11S	B7
700	EGVV	60007	2914	19W-9N	C1
8900	BGVW	60455	3210	9W-10S	D5
Moore Ln					
-	SRPK	60176	2973	11W-5N	C1
Moorefield Av					
-	NARA	60542	3077	37W-3S	C7
Moorefield Ct					
13100	LMNT	60439	3343	16W-15S	E1
W Moorefield Dr					
7600	FRfT	60423	3504	9W-24S	E5
Mooregate Tr					
10	HNWD	60047	2644	24W-25N	D4
Moorehead Cir					
-	FmtT	60048	2533	19W-31N	C7
-	LYVL	60048	2533	19W-31N	C7
Moorehead Dr					
100	BRLT	60103	2909	32W-8N	C3
800	AURA	60510	3078	34W-3S	D6
800	BTVA	60510	3078	34W-3S	D6
Mooresfield St					
400	ElgT	60124	2853	38W-10N	A6
Moorfield Rd					
400	RchT	60443	3593	8W-26S	B2
Moorings Dr					
10	PSHT	60463	3274	9W-13S	D5
S Moorings Dr					
1000	ANHT	60005	2807	17W-12N	B7
Moorings Ln					
14800	OKFT	60452	3347	7W-17S	C5
Moorland Av					
1100	SRWD	60404	3496	30W-23S	A4
W Moorland Dr					
12500	HMGN	60491	3344	15W-17S	B5
Moorland Ln					
1600	CLLK	60014	2693	37W-22N	B3
N Moorman St					
1300	CHCG	60622	3033	1W-1N	E1
Moose Ln					
10800	ODPK	60467	3423	13W-20S	A4
Moose Rd					
100	BtvT	60539	3077	36W-3S	E5
Moose St					
300	MTGY	60543	3263	38W-11S	B2
300	OSWG	60543	3263	38W-11S	B2
Mooseheart Rd					
10	BtvT	60539	3077	36W-3S	D6
10	BtvT	60542	3077	36W-3S	D6
10	NARA	60542	3077	36W-3S	D6
200	BtvT	60510	3077	37W-3S	C6
200	NARA	60539	3077	37W-3S	D6
Mooseheart Rd CO-71					
10	BtvT	60539	3077	36W-3S	D6
10	BtvT	60542	3077	36W-3S	D6
10	NARA	60542	3077	36W-3S	D6
200	BtvT	60510	3077	37W-3S	C6
200	NARA	60539	3077	37W-3S	D6
W Mooseheart Rd					
100	NARA	60542	3077	38W-3S	A6
200	BtvT	60506	3077	38W-3S	A6
200	BtvT	60542	3077	38W-3S	A6
200	NARA	60506	3077	38W-3S	A6
Moose Lake Dr					
-	BtvT	60542	3077	36W-3S	D6
Mora Ct					
1900	HRPK	60133	2912	26W-8N	A2
1900	SMBG	60193	2912	26W-8N	A2
Mora Rd					
100	CPVL	60110	2748	33W-18N	B4
Moraine Av					
6200	HMND	46324	3430		C2
8400	MNSR	46321	3430		C2
Moraine Ct					
-	AURA	60506	3198	40W-8S	C2
-	ISLK	60042	2587	28W-28N	A5
-	ISLK	60051	2587	28W-28N	A5
10	HnrT	60107	2856	29W-11N	E5
400	LslT	60540	3143	23W-7S	A7
14000	WDSK	60098	2581	43W-30N	A1
Moraine Dr					
-	AURA	60506	3198	40W-8S	C1
-	SgrT	60506	3198	40W-7S	C1
10	HnrT	60107	2856	29W-11N	E4
10	SMWD	60107	2856	29W-11N	E4
1000	SenT	60098	2581	43W-30N	A1
1000	WDSK	60098	2581	43W-30N	A1
8400	PSHL	60465	3274	10W-13S	B3
Moraine Rd					
100	HDPK	60035	2704	8W-23N	D3
Moraine St					
8900	SjnT	46311	3598		C7
9100	SjnT	46311	3687		D1
Moraine Tr					
-	RGWD	60072	2470	33W-37N	D1
Moraine Hill Dr					
200	CRY	60013	2696	30W-23N	B1
300	CRY	60013	2642	30W-24N	A7
Moraine Hills Dr					
14000	HTLY	60140	2744	43W-19N	A2
14000	HTLY	60142	2744	43W-19N	A2
Moraine Valley Rd					
2700	WCDA	60030	2588	24W-30N	B2
2700	WCDA	60084	2588	25W-30N	B2
Moran Dr					
-	SRWD	60404	3495	31W-23S	E5
-	TroT	60404	3495	31W-23S	E5
W Moran St					
200	JLET	60435	3498	25W-22S	C2
Moray Ct					
200	CRTE	60417	3596	0E-28S	E6
2800	AURA	60503	3201	31W-10S	D5
Moray Dr					
-	IVNS	60010	2803	25W-15N	E1
-	SBTN	60010	2803	25W-15N	E2
Moray Ter					
400	CRTE	60417	3596	0E-28S	E6
Morcambe Bay Dr					
2000	NlxT	60451	3590	15W-27S	B5
S Morel St					
16700	LKPT	60441	3420	19W-20S	D4
Moreland Av					
400	AddT	60101	2970	20W-3N	A5
500	BmdT	60101	2970	20W-3N	A5
600	ADSN	60101	2970	19W-3N	D5
E Moreland Av					
10	ADSN	60101	2970	19W-4N	D4
100	ADSN	60101	2971	18W-3N	A5
W Moreland Av					
400	ADSN	60101	2970	19W-3N	D5
N Moreland Dr					
5000	CHCG	60656	2918	9W-6N	B6
5000	NRDG	60656	2918	9W-6N	B6
5000	NRDG	60706	2918	9W-6N	B6
Morey Dr					
100	WDRG	60439	3270	20W-12S	B2
100	WDRG	60517	3270	20W-12S	B2
W Morey Ln					
24800	LkvT	60041	2474	24W-36N	B4
24800	LkvT	60046	2474	24W-36N	B4
N Morey St					
26700	WcnT	60084	2642	28W-26N	E2
Morgan Av					
1100	BKFD	60513	3087	11W-2S	D4
1100	LGPK	60513	3087	11W-2S	D4
1100	LGPK	60525	3087	11W-2S	D4
1500	PvsT	60525	3087	11W-2S	D4
9300	SKOK	60203	2866	4W-11N	D2
N Morgan Av					
100	WHTN	60187	3024	25W-0S	A7
S Morgan Av					
100	WHTN	60187	3024	25W-0S	A7
Morgan Cir					
-	FXLK	60081	2414	29W-39N	D4
1800	NPVL	60565	3204	24W-8S	E2
Morgan Ct					
10	BRRG	60527	3208	15W-10S	B5
10	OswT	60560	3334	40W-15S	C1
100	RMVL	60446	3339	27W-17S	C6
200	MHTN	60442	3677	19W-30S	D4
2200	RLKP	60030	2532	22W-31N	B7
3700	STGR	60475	3596	1W-28S	A6
6900	GRNE	60031	2477	17W-35N	B5
7900	DRN	60561	3206	19W-9S	C3
14100	GNOK	60048	2535	14W-31N	D7
W Morgan Ct					
12500	HMGN	60491	3344	15W-17S	B5
Morgan Dr					
-	CHCG	60637	3152	0E-6S	D3
1400	EGVV	60007	2913	21W-8N	E3
Morgan Ln					
10	BrnT	60010	2803	27W-14N	A5
10	SBTN	60010	2803	27W-14N	A5
300	FRGV	60021	2696	28W-22N	E3
400	CbaT	60010	2696	28W-22N	E3
400	HFET	60169	2858	24W-10N	E4
400	LKBN	60010	2696	28W-22N	E3
1200	BRLT	60103	2910	30W-6N	C7
16300	ODHL	60487	3423	11W-19S	E2
S Morgan Ln					
-	PNFD	60544	3338	30W-17S	A7
Morgan Pl					
10	HIWD	60040	2704	9W-23N	D3
Morgan St					
10	CLLK	60014	2640	34W-26N	C4
200	CHHT	60411	3596	0W-25S	C1
200	ELGN	60123	2854	34W-10N	D6
200	LKPT	60441	3419	22W-18S	D1
200	LktT	60441	3419	22W-18S	D1
200	YKVL	60560	3333	43W-15S	B3
3000	SCHT	60411	3596	1W-27S	A5
3000	SCHT	60475	3596	1W-27S	A5
3000	STGR	60475	3596	1W-28S	A6
3800	CteT	60417	3596	1W-28S	A7
3800	CteT	60475	3596	1W-28S	A7
14900	HRVY	60426	3350	1W-18S	A6
18200	HMWD	60430	3428	1W-21S	A7
18700	HMWD	60430	3508	1W-22S	A2
N Morgan St					
10	CHCG	60607	3033	1W-0N	E4
700	CHCG	60622	3033	1W-0N	E3
S Morgan St					
10	CHCG	60607	3033	1W-0S	E5
1000	CHCG	60608	3033	1W-1S	E7
1600	CHCG	60608	3091	1W-1S	E1
3400	CHCG	60609	3091	1W-4S	E6
4700	CHCG	60609	3151	1W-6S	E3
5500	CHCG	60621	3151	1W-8S	E7
7500	CHCG	60620	3213	1W-10S	E4
7500	CHCG	60621	3213	1W-8S	E1
9400	CHCG	60643	3213	1W-10S	E6
9600	CHCG	60643	3214	1W-11S	A6
10300	CHCG	60643	3278	1W-12S	A1
12200	CTPK	60643	3278	1W-14S	A6
12300	CTPK	60827	3278	1W-14S	A6
W Morgan St					
400	JLET	60436	3498	25W-24S	C6
Morgan Tr					
1400	MchT	60051	2529	30W-33N	A3
Morgan Wy					
13400	HTLY	60142	2744	42W-20N	B1
Morgana Ct					
1200	JLET	60447	3495	33W-22S	A2
Morgana Dr					
1200	JLET	60447	3495	33W-22S	A2
Morgan O'Brien					
-	DSPN	60016	2862	15W-12N	B2
Morgan Valley Dr					
10	OSWG	60543	3263	37W-14S	D7
10	OswT	60543	3263	37W-14S	D7
N Morley Rd					
43000	ANTH	60002	2357	24W-43N	C5
43000	AntT	60002	2357	24W-43N	C5
S Mormann Ln					
13900	HMGN	60491	3343	18W-16S	A4
Morning Dove Cir					
5300	RHMD	60071	2353	34W-42N	D5
Morning Dove Ct					
700	MltT	60187	3024	25W-1N	A3
W Morningdove Ct					
21500	KLDR	60047	2699	21W-21N	C5
Morning Dove Ln					
1300	ANTH	60002	2357	24W-41N	C7
1300	ANTH	60002	2416	24W-41N	C1
1300	AntT	60002	2416	24W-41N	C1
11000	SPGV	60081	2354	32W-43N	C5
21500	FKFT	60423	3591	13W-26S	A2
Morning Glory Ct					
1800	MTGY	60538	3199	36W-10S	E5
13000	HMGN	60491	3344	16W-18S	A7
Morning Glory Dr					
4500	MTSN	60443	3506	5W-24S	B6
Morning Glory Ln					
600	BRLT	60103	2910	29W-6N	D7
2400	CTHL	60403	3417	27W-21S	C7
11400	HTLY	60142	2691	41W-20N	D7
Morninglory Cir					
400	DRGV	60515	3144	18W-4S	E1
400	WTMT	60515	3144	18W-4S	E1
400	WTMT	60559	3144	18W-4S	E1
Morning Mist Pl					
13300	PNFD	60585	3337	33W-15S	B3
Morningside Av					
10	WynT	60185	2967	28W-3N	A6
600	AURA	60505	3200	34W-8S	C3
600	WnfT	60185	3023	28W-0N	A4
E Morningside Av					
10	LMBD	60148	3026	19W-0N	C5
Morningside Cir					
2200	CPVL	60110	2801	32W-16N	D1
Morningside Ct					
10	LIHL	60156	2693	37W-22N	A3
600	ROSL	60172	2913	22W-7N	C4
600	SMBG	60173	2859	22W-11N	C4
6000	GRNE	60031	2534	16W-34N	E1
Morning Side Dr					
900	UYPK	60466	3684	3W-30S	A3
Morningside Dr					
-	SHLD	60473	3350	0E-18S	D6
10	ROSL	60172	2913	22W-7N	C5
100	LKMR	60051	2529	29W-31N	D6
100	WcnT	60051	2529	29W-31N	D6
300	BMDL	60108	2969	22W-4N	C4
400	WynT	60103	2966	29W-5N	D1
400	YkTp	60181	3085	17W-1S	B1
500	OKTR	60181	3085	17W-1S	B1
500	RLKB	60073	2474	24W-35N	C6
600	LKFT	60045	2650	10W-24N	B7
600	NPVL	60563	3141	27W-6S	C4
800	SMBG	60173	2859	22W-11N	C4
1100	AvnT	60073	2474	24W-35N	C6
1100	ELGN	60123	2800	34W-13N	D7
1100	ELGN	60123	2854	34W-12N	D1
Morningside Ln					
700	GnvT	60510	3077	37W-0S	B1
2100	CPVL	60110	2801	32W-16N	D1
2100	EDND	60110	2801	32W-16N	D1
2100	EDND	60118	2801	32W-16N	D1
Morningside Ln E					
100	BFGV	60089	2701	16W-21N	C6
Morningside Ln W					
100	BFGV	60089	2701	16W-21N	C7
Morningside Pt					
600	ELGN	60123	2854	34W-13N	D1
Morningside Rd					
14400	ODPK	60462	3345	13W-17S	B5
Morning Song Ct					
1900	SMBG	60194	2858	26W-11N	A3
Morningstar Av					
-	WnfT	60185	3023	28W-0N	A5
400	WnfT	60190	3023	28W-0S	A7
Morningstar Ct					
1300	NPVL	60564	3203	28W-10S	A6
Morningstar Ln					
6500	JLET	60586	3415	32W-20S	D4
Morningview Ct					
5300	HFET	60192	2802	30W-12N	B7
Morningview Dr					
1900	HFET	60192	2802	30W-12N	C7
Morray Ct					
500	DSPN	60018	2862	15W-10N	A5
Morrhine Dr					
27600	GrtT	60041	2473	27W-35N	B6
Morrill Ln					
800	ELBN	60119	3017	43W-2N	A1
Morris Av					
-	LMBD	60148	3026	19W-0S	C7
10	BLWD	60104	3029	12W-0N	A3
500	MDLN	60060	2590	18W-28N	D6
600	HLSD	60162	3028	13W-0N	D4
600	YkTp	60148	3026	18W-0S	E7
700	BKLY	60162	3028	13W-0N	D4
700	BKLY	60163	3028	13W-0N	D4
700	HLSD	60163	3028	13W-0N	D4
18100	HMWD	60430	3427	2W-22S	C7
18400	HMWD	60430	3507	2W-22S	C1
W Morris Av					
-	GNEN	60137	3026	20W-0S	A7
-	GNEN	60148	3026	20W-0S	A7
10	LMBD	60148	3026	20W-0S	B7
800	ADSN	60101	2970	19W-3N	C4
Morris Ct					
10	WnfT	60555	3080	29W-2S	E4
100	WNVL	60555	3080	29W-2S	E4
700	LKMR	60051	2529	29W-32N	D4
700	LMBD	60148	3026	19W-0S	D7
800	BTVA	60510	3078	34W-3S	D6
1100	WKGN	60099	2421	11W-38N	E6
E Morris Dr					
600	PLTN	60074	2753	20W-16N	B7
N Morris Dr					
200	PLTN	60074	2753	19W-16N	C7
Morris Ln					
500	HNDL	60521	3086	16W-4S	A7
Morris St					
100	PKRG	60068	2864	10W-9N	A7
500	JLET	60436	3498	26W-24S	A6
600	RKDL	60436	3498	26W-25S	A7
E Morris St					
800	HMND	46320	3430		E1
S Morris St					
10	JLET	60435	3498	26W-24S	A5
10	JLET	60436	3498	26W-24S	A6
S Morris Hill Dr					
1800	MPPT	60056	2861	16W-10N	D5
E Morrison Av					
100	WhlT	60056	2808	13W-13N	E6
N Morrison Av					
600	PLTN	60067	2752	22W-16N	B6
Morrison Dr					
3900	GRNE	60031	2478	13W-35N	D6
Morrison Rd					
900	NHBK	60062	2757	8W-18N	D3
Morrow Av					
1200	NCHI	60064	2536	11W-31N	E7
1500	NCHI	60088	2536	11W-31N	E7
1800	NCHI	60064	2593	11W-31N	D1
1800	NCHI	60088	2593	11W-31N	D1
Mors Av					
200	WLNG	60090	2755	14W-17N	D5
Morse Av					
-	BHPK	60087	2421	12W-38N	B6
10	MltT	60187	3024	25W-1N	B3
10	MltT	60188	3024	25W-1N	B3
10	SmbT	60193	2913	23W-8N	A2
200	CLSM	60188	3024	25W-1N	B3
300	NHLK	60164	3028	13W-1N	E2
300	NHLK	60164	3029	13W-1N	A1
400	NHLK	60165	3029	13W-1N	A1
400	SNPK	60165	3029	13W-1N	A1
500	SMBG	60193	2912	24W-8N	D2
600	EGVV	60007	2915	17W-8N	B2
900	SmbT	60193	2912	24W-8N	D2
1600	DSPN	60018	2917	12W-8N	A2
4900	LNWD	60077	2919	6W-8N	E1
4900	LNWD	60712	2919	6W-8N	E1
4900	SKOK	60077	2919	6W-8N	D1
E Morse Av					
100	BRLT	60103	2910	28W-8N	E2
200	BRLT	60103	2911	28W-8N	A2
W Morse Av					
100	BRLT	60103	2910	29W-8N	E2
2000	CHCG	60626	2921	2W-8N	B1
2000	CHCG	60645	2921	2W-8N	A1
2600	CHCG	60645	2920	3W-8N	E1
4500	LNWD	60712	2920	5W-8N	A1
4800	LNWD	60077	2919	6W-8N	E1
4800	LNWD	60712	2919	6W-8N	E1
4800	SKOK	60077	2919	6W-8N	E1
5400	CHCG	60646	2919	6W-8N	D1
5400	SKOK	60646	2919	6W-8N	D1
Morse Dr					
300	NHLK	60164	3028	13W-1N	E1
Morse Ln					
2100	GLHT	60139	2969	23W-4N	A4
Morse St					
300	WHTN	60187	3024	25W-0N	B4
500	MltT	60187	3024	25W-0N	B4
700	MltT	60188	3024	25W-0N	B4
N Morse St					
-	MltT	60187	3024	25W-0N	B5
-	WHTN	60187	3024	25W-0N	B5
Mortimer Rd					
200	GLNC	60022	2758	6W-17N	E5
Morton Av					
1000	ELGN	60120	2855	33W-12N	B1
1200	AURA	60506	3137	36W-5S	D4
3100	LGPK	60513	3087	11W-3S	D4
3100	LGPK	60525	3087	11W-3S	D4
3500	BKFD	60513	3087	11W-3S	D6
3900	DRGV	60515	3084	20W-4S	A7
8500	MNGV	60053	2865	7W-10N	B4
Morton Ct					
5100	HMND	46320	3352		C6
W Morton Dr					
21800	LkvT	60046	2475	22W-36N	C3
Morton Rd					
-	CLSM	60188	2967	27W-3N	C6
500	WynT	60185	2967	27W-2N	C7
500	WynT	60185	3023	27W-2N	C1
700	CLSM	60185	2967	27W-3N	C6
1900	LSLE	60532	3082	23W-4S	E7
4400	HRPK	60133	2967	27W-5N	C1
Morton St					
300	BTVA	60510	3078	36W-1S	A3
800	HFET	60169	2858	24W-11N	E3
1100	BTVA	60510	3077	36W-1S	E3
W Morton St					
10500	BHPK	60087	2480	10W-37N	A1
Mortonsberry Dr					
900	NPVL	60540	3203	28W-8S	A1
Morven Ct					
800	NPVL	60563	3141	26W-6S	E4
Mosby Ct					
900	JLET	60431	3497	28W-25S	B7
Mosedale St					
10	SCRL	60174	3020	35W-2N	B1
Moseley Rd					
600	HDPK	60035	2705	8W-21N	A7
Moseley St					
100	ELGN	60123	2854	34W-10N	D5
N Moselle Av					
6800	CHCG	60714	2919	7W-8N	B1
6800	NLES	60714	2919	7W-8N	B1
6900	CHCG	60646	2919	7W-8N	B1
Moser Ln					
2200	ALGN	60102	2747	36W-19N	A4
Moss Ct					
1400	AURA	60504	3201	32W-9S	C4
8700	TYPK	60487	3424	10W-21S	B6
Moss Ln					
-	JltT	60433	3500	20W-24S	B6
2500	AURA	60504	3201	32W-9S	C4
2500	NLNX	60433	3500	20W-24S	B6
2500	NLNX	60451	3500	20W-24S	B6
2500	NlxT	60433	3500	20W-24S	B6
2700	NlxT	60451	3500	20W-24S	B6
E Moss St					
1000	HMND	46320	3430		E2
Mossfield Ct					
10	SgrT	60506	3136	40W-5S	A3
Mossheather Dr					
7700	JLET	60447	3495	33W-22S	A2
Motorola					
-	SMBG	60173	2805	21W-13N	D7
Motorola Pkwy					
-	LYVL	60048	2590	18W-29N	E4
-	LYVL	60060	2590	18W-29N	E4
-	MDLN	60060	2590	18W-29N	E4
600	FmtT	60048	2590	18W-29N	D4
600	FmtT	60060	2590	18W-29N	D4
Motz St					
1200	ELBN	60119	3017	43W-0N	B5
Moulin Ln					
3800	HFET	60192	2804	24W-14N	B3
Moulis Ter					
-	FXLK	60041	2473	26W-36N	C4
Moultrie Ct					
900	NPVL	60563	3140	29W-5S	C3
N Mound Av					
39000	AntT	60081	2415	27W-39N	B5
Mound Ct					
21800	JLET	60436	3585	28W-26S	A3
21800	TroT	60436	3585	28W-26S	A3
Mound Rd					
200	RKDL	60436	3498	25W-25S	C7
200	RKDL	60436	3586	26W-25S	A1
1600	RKDL	60436	3585	26W-25S	E1
W Mound Rd					
2200	RKDL	60436	3585	27W-25S	D1
2200	TroT	60436	3585	27W-25S	C2
2600	JLET	60436	3585	28W-26S	A3
4000	JLET	60436	3584	29W-26S	E3
4000	TroT	60436	3584	29W-26S	E3
24400	SRWD	60404	3584	31W-26S	A2
24400	SRWD	60431	3584	31W-26S	A2
24400	TroT	60404	3584	31W-26S	A2
24400	TroT	60431	3584	31W-26S	A2
24800	SRWD	60404	3583	31W-26S	E2
24800	TroT	60404	3583	31W-26S	E2
25700	SwdT	60447	3583	32W-25S	C2
Mound St					
100	WLSP	60480	3209	12W-9S	C3
200	ALGN	60102	2694	33W-21N	E6
400	FRGV	60021	2696	29W-22N	C3
E Mound St					
200	JLET	60433	3499	23W-24S	A5
Mount St					
700	WNVL	60555	3080	28W-3S	E5
Mountain Ct					
1700	DRFD	60015	2703	11W-22N	E5
1800	NPVL	60565	3204	25W-9S	B4
Mountain Dr					
800	DRFD	60015	2703	11W-22N	E5
Mountain Rd					
600	LKBF	60044	2594	10W-28N	B6
Mountain St					
200	ELGN	60123	2854	34W-11N	D4
1300	AraT	60505	3138	34W-6S	E5
1300	AURA	60505	3138	34W-6S	E5
1600	AURA	60502	3139	33W-6S	A5
1600	AURA	60505	3139	33W-6S	A5
Mountain Ash Ct					
7800	GRNE	60031	2476	18W-34N	E7
Mountain Ash Dr					
300	WYNE	60184	2966	30W-4N	B4
300	WynT	60184	2966	30W-4N	B4
300	WynT	60185	2966	30W-4N	B4
Mountain Glen Wy					
1000	CLSM	60188	2967	27W-3N	C5
Mountain Laurel Ct					
2400	ELGN	60124	2907	36W-9N	D1
Mountain Ridge Pass					
6500	JLET	60586	3495	32W-21S	C1
Mountainview Dr					
900	JLET	60432	3500	20W-22S	C2
Mt Carmel Dr					
15500	HMGN	60491	3421	17W-18S	C1
Mt Laurel Ct					
100	RMVL	60446	3339	26W-17S	E6
S Mt Pleasant Ct					
14000	PnfT	60544	3339	28W-17S	B5
Mt Pleasant Rd					
1000	WNKA	60093	2811	5W-15N	E2
1000	WNKA	60093	2812	5W-15N	A2
Mt Pleasant St					
-	NtrT	60093	2811	6W-15N	D2
-	WNKA	60093	2811	6W-15N	D2
700	WNKA	60093	2812	5W-15N	A2
1500	NHFD	60093	2811	6W-15N	D2
Mt Prospect Plz					
900	MPPT	60016	2808	14W-13N	B7
900	MPPT	60056	2808	14W-13N	B7
Mt Prospect Rd					
3300	AddT	60106	2972	14W-3N	B4
3300	AddT	60126	2972	14W-3N	B4
3300	BNVL	60106	2972	15W-3N	B4
3300	EMHT	60126	2972	14W-3N	B5
3300	FNPK	60131	2972	14W-3N	B4
3300	FNPK	60164	2972	14W-3N	B5
3300	LydT	60164	2972	14W-3N	B5
3500	BNVL	60131	2972	15W-3N	B4

Chicago 7-County Street Index

STREET Block	City	ZIP	Map#	CGS	Grid
N Mt Prospect Rd					
10	DSPN	60016	2862	15W-12N	B2
10	MPPT	60016	2862	15W-12N	B2
10	MPPT	60056	2862	15W-12N	B2
S Mt Prospect Rd					
10	DSPN	60016	2808	14W-12N	B7
10	DSPN	60056	2808	15W-12N	B7
10	MPPT	60016	2808	14W-12N	B7
10	MPPT	60056	2808	14W-12N	B7
200	DSPN	60016	2862	15W-12N	B1
200	MPPT	60016	2862	15W-12N	B1
200	MPPT	60056	2862	15W-12N	B1
900	DSPN	60018	2862	14W-10N	B5
1800	EGvT	60018	2862	14W-9N	B7
2200	DSPN	60018	2916	15W-8N	B1
2200	EGvT	60018	2916	15W-8N	B1
2200	MaiT	60018	2916	14W-9N	B1
2500	CHCG	60018	2916	14W-8N	C2
Mt Tabor Rd					
4500	CLLK	60098	2638	39W-26N	C2
4500	DrrT	60098	2638	39W-26N	C2
Mt Vernon Av					
800	LKFT	60045	2649	11W-24N	D7
Mt Vernon Ct					
800	GYLK	60030	2533	19W-34N	D1
800	NPVL	60563	3141	26W-5S	E4
1100	WHTN	60187	3082	23W-2S	E3
2500	AURA	60503	3201	32W-11S	C7
E Mt Vernon Ct					
6700	GRNE	60031	2477	17W-35N	A6
W Mt Vernon Ct					
6800	GRNE	60031	2477	17W-35N	B6
Mt Vernon Dr					
900	GYLK	60030	2533	19W-34N	C1
Mt Vernon Pl					
600	BTVA	60510	3078	35W-2S	A4
Mt Vernon Ter					
1200	NHBK	60062	2756	10W-17N	E5
Mourine Ln					
2900	MchT	60051	2528	31W-33N	C3
Mourning Dove Ct					
8200	WDRG	60517	3205	21W-9S	E3
Moutray Ln					
2400	NARA	60542	3076	39W-3S	D6
Mozart Av					
16700	MKHM	60428	3427	3W-20S	B3
16700	MKHM	60429	3427	3W-20S	B3
S Mozart Av					
14400	POSN	60469	3349	3W-17S	A5
14700	BmnT	60469	3349	3W-17S	A5
Mozart Ct					
300	WHTN	60187	3082	24W-2S	C4
N Mozart Dr					
1200	CHCG	60622	3032	3W-1N	E1
Mozart St					
-	WDSK	60098	2524	41W-33N	E3
12700	BLID	60406	3277	3W-15S	A7
13400	BLID	60406	3349	3W-16S	A2
N Mozart St					
100	PLTN	60067	2753	20W-16N	A7
200	CHCG	60612	3032	3W-0N	E4
800	CHCG	60622	3032	3W-1N	E2
2400	CHCG	60647	2976	3W-3N	E5
3600	CHCG	60618	2976	3W-4N	E2
4400	CHCG	60618	2920	3W-5N	E7
4400	CHCG	60625	2920	3W-5N	E7
5600	CHCG	60659	2920	3W-7N	E4
6300	CHCG	60645	2920	3W-7N	E3
S Mozart St					
1100	CHCG	60612	3032	3W-0S	E6
1100	CHCG	60623	3032	3W-0S	E7
3500	CHCG	60623	3091	3W-3S	A5
3500	CHCG	60632	3091	3W-3S	A5
5100	CHCG	60632	3151	3W-6S	A3
5400	CHCG	60629	3151	3W-7S	A5
7900	CHCG	60652	3213	3W-9S	A2
8700	ENGN	60805	3213	3W-10S	A4
Mudjekeewis Ter					
34700	GrtT	60051	2472	28W-34N	E7
Muehl Dr					
100	LKPT	60441	3419	21W-19S	D2
Mueller Cir					
16400	PNFD	60586	3415	31W-19S	E3
Mueller Ct					
-	PNFD	60586	3415	31W-19S	E4
Mueller Dr					
300	HLSD	60162	3029	13W-0S	A5
W Mueller St					
300	ANHT	60004	2807	18W-14N	A4
Muenich Ct					
10	HMND	46320	3352		C6
Muir Av					
700	ShdT	60044	2593	12W-29N	A5
1100	LbvT	60044	2593	13W-29N	A5
Muir Dr					
400	HmrT	60441	3420	20W-18S	A1
12500	HTLY	60142	2744	43W-19N	B3
Muirfield Av					
800	WKGN	60085	2479	11W-35N	D7
Muirfield Cir					
-	MltT	60187	3081	26W-1S	E3
10	WHTN	60187	3081	26W-1S	E3
1900	ELGN	60123	2853	36W-9N	E7
1900	ELGN	60123	2854	36W-9N	A7
Muirfield Ct					
10	LIHL	60156	2692	38W-22N	E3
1100	YKVL	60560	3333	42W-17S	C6
2500	SCRL	60174	2964	34W-4N	E4
9400	LKWD	60014	2638	38W-24N	E7
Muirfield Dr					
800	HRPK	60133	2912	25W-7N	A5
2000	YKVL	60560	3333	42W-16S	C5
10500	WldT	60564	3266	30W-12S	A3
16700	ODPK	60467	3423	13W-20S	B3
16700	OrlT	60467	3423	13W-20S	B3
N Muirfield Dr					
9300	GfnT	60014	2638	38W-24N	E7
9300	LKWD	60014	2638	38W-24N	E7
S Muirfield Dr					
9600	GfnT	60014	2638	38W-24N	E7
9600	LKWD	60014	2638	38W-24N	E7
Muirfield Ln					
400	RVWD	60015	2756	12W-20N	A1
Muirfield Rd					
800	IVNS	60067	2751	24W-17N	D5
Muirfield Tr					
2100	BGBK	60490	3339	28W-14S	B1
Muirhead Av					
700	NPVL	60565	3204	25W-8S	B2
1400	LslT	60565	3204	25W-8S	B2
Muirhead Ct					
800	PltT	60124	2852	41W-9N	A7
Muirhead Ln					
800	PltT	60124	2852	41W-9N	A7
Muirhead Rd					
10	PltT	60124	2852	41W-9N	A7
10	PltT	60124	2905	41W-9N	E2
10	PltT	60140	2852	41W-12N	A2
100	PltT	60124	2906	41W-9N	A1
Muirhead Rd CO-17					
10	PltT	60124	2852	41W-10N	A7
Muirwood Ct					
10	CRY	60013	2695	32W-23N	B3
400	VNHL	60061	2647	17W-25N	B6
3800	LGGV	60047	2700	20W-22N	B5
6600	LSLE	60532	3142	24W-7S	D6
Muirwood Dr					
10	GNEN	60137	3025	22W-1N	C3
Mulberry Av					
9900	OKLN	60453	3211	6W-11S	D7
10100	OKLN	60453	3275	6W-11S	D1
17400	TYPK	60487	3424	11W-20S	A5
17500	CCHL	60478	3426	5W-21S	B6
Mulberry Ct					
-	AntT	60002	2417	22W-39N	B4
-	AntT	60046	2417	22W-39N	B4
-	BGVW	60455	3274	9W-11S	D1
-	LkvT	60002	2417	22W-39N	B4
-	LkvT	60046	2417	22W-39N	B4
10	WNVL	60555	3080	30W-3S	B5
300	BRLT	60103	2911	28W-8N	B3
400	LKVL	60046	2417	22W-40N	B4
500	BFGV	60089	2754	17W-18N	B3
600	ALGN	60102	2694	34W-20N	C7
700	NPVL	60540	3141	28W-7S	B7
800	GYLK	60030	2532	21W-34N	C1
1600	ELGN	60123	2854	35W-10N	B5
2200	AURA	60506	3137	38W-6S	A5
8200	PSHL	60465	3274	10W-13S	B3
12600	HTLY	60142	2744	42W-19N	D3
15400	HMGN	60491	3344	16W-18S	A7
E Mulberry Ct					
400	GNWD	60425	3508	0E-22S	E1
400	GNWD	60425	3509	0E-22S	A2
2900	CteT	60417	3687	3E-29S	A2
Mulberry Dr					
-	MPPT	60056	2808	14W-14N	C4
10	HNWD	60047	2645	22W-24N	A6
300	WCHI	60185	2966	30W-3N	B6
300	WynT	60185	2966	30W-3N	B5
600	PTHT	60070	2808	14W-14N	B4
1500	LYVL	60048	2591	17W-30N	B3
1600	LKVL	60046	2417	22W-40N	B4
1800	MTGY	60538	3199	38W-9S	A5
E Mulberry Dr					
10	GNWD	60425	3508	0E-22S	E2
Mulberry Ln					
-	BGVW	60455	3274	9W-11S	D1
10	GNVW	60025	2811	6W-13N	D7
10	MltT	60137	3083	23W-3S	A5
200	EGVV	60007	2914	18W-8N	E3
400	WDDL	60191	2971	17W-5N	C2
900	SMWD	60107	2857	28W-9N	B7
1200	CLLK	60014	2639	37W-25N	A4
1300	CLLK	60013	2695	32W-23N	A1
1300	CRY	60013	2695	32W-23N	A1
1500	ELGN	60123	2854	35W-10N	A5
2500	NHBK	60062	2756	10W-16N	E7
3200	OKBK	60523	3084	18W-3S	E5
E Mulberry Ln					
1900	ANHT	60004	2807	16W-16N	D1
N Mulberry Ln					
1300	MPPT	60056	2808	14W-14N	C5
37000	GRNE	60031	2477	15W-37N	E3
37000	WDWH	60031	2477	15W-36N	E3
S Mulberry Ln					
10	MltT	60137	3083	22W-3S	B5
24500	CteT	60417	3687	3E-29S	B2
W Mulberry Ln					
1300	ANHT	60005	2806	18W-14N	D4
5200	MONE	60449	3683	6W-31S	A6
15900	WDWH	60031	2477	15W-37N	E3
15900	WrnT	60031	2477	16W-37N	E3
Mulberry Pl					
500	HDPK	60035	2704	8W-21N	E5
Mulberry Rd					
10	DRFD	60015	2757	10W-20N	B2
200	FKFT	60423	3503	12W-25S	C7
200	FKFT	60423	3591	12W-25S	C1
1700	MTGY	60538	3199	38W-9S	A4
E Mulberry Rd					
2200	JLET	60432	3500	21W-22S	A2
Mulberry St					
400	HMND	46324	3430		D3
6900	HRPK	60133	2911	27W-8N	D2
S Mulberry St					
13400	DPgT	60544	3340	26W-15S	A3
Mulberry Ter					
18300	CCHL	60478	3426	5W-22S	B7
Mulberry East Rd					
10	DRFD	60015	2757	10W-20N	B2
Mulcahey Dr					
100	DSPN	60016	2808	13W-13N	E7
Mulford Ct					
200	ELGN	60120	2855	32W-11N	C3
Mulford Dr					
10	ELGN	60120	2855	32W-11N	C3
Mulford Ln					
200	ROSL	60172	2912	24W-7N	C5
800	JLET	60431	3497	28W-25S	B7
Mulford St					
900	EVTN	60202	2867	2W-9N	A6
1700	EVTN	60202	2866	3W-9N	E6
3900	SKOK	60076	2866	5W-9N	A6
5200	SKOK	60077	2865	6W-9N	D6
5300	MNGV	60053	2865	6W-9N	D6
5300	MNGV	60077	2865	6W-9N	D6
5300	SKOK	60053	2865	6W-9N	D6
W Mulford St					
6100	NLES	60077	2865	7W-9N	B6
6100	NLES	60714	2865	7W-9N	B6
6100	SKOK	60077	2865	7W-9N	B6
7200	NLES	60714	2864	9W-9N	D6
Mulguy Ct					
2100	IVNS	60010	2751	25W-16N	A7
Mulguy Dr					
2100	IVNS	60010	2751	25W-16N	A7
Mulhern Ct					
300	YKVL	60560	3261	42W-13S	C6
Mulhern Dr					
10	BbyT	60119	3018	41W-1N	A2
10	CmpT	60119	3018	41W-1N	A2
Mullady Pkwy					
600	LYVL	60048	2591	16W-27N	E7
600	LYVL	60048	2647	15W-27N	E1
Mulligan Av					
7700	BRBK	60459	3211	7W-9S	B3
9100	OKLN	60453	3211	7W-10S	B5
N Mulligan Av					
2600	CHCG	60639	2975	7W-3N	A5
4200	CHCG	60630	2975	7W-5N	A1
4200	CHCG	60634	2975	7W-5N	A1
4800	CHCG	60630	2919	7W-6N	A6
4800	HDHT	60630	2919	7W-6N	A6
4800	HDHT	60706	2919	7W-6N	A6
5700	CHCG	60646	2919	7W-7N	A4
S Mulligan Av					
5100	CHCG	60638	3149	7W-5S	B2
5100	StkT	60638	3149	7W-5S	B2
Mulligan Ct					
-	FXLK	60081	2414	29W-39N	D5
N Mulligan Ct					
800	PLTN	60067	2752	21W-17N	C6
800	PltT	60067	2752	21W-17N	C6
Mulligan Dr					
10	WDRG	60517	3143	23W-7S	B6
1600	NPVL	60563	3140	30W-5S	B2
1600	NpvT	60563	3140	30W-5S	B2
Mullingar Ct					
100	SMBG	60193	2859	23W-9N	A7
W Mulloy Dr					
1500	ADSN	60101	2970	20W-4N	A3
Mulranny Dr					
13100	HMGN	60491	3343	16W-17S	E5
Mulrany Pl					
200	GYLK	60030	2532	21W-33N	D3
Mulrenen Ln					
-	KLDR	60047	2699	20W-22N	E3
-	KLDR	60047	2700	20W-22N	A3
Mumford Ct					
4400	HFET	60192	2804	24W-15N	C2
Mumford Dr					
4100	HFET	60192	2804	24W-15N	C1
Mundelein Rd					
1700	NPVL	60565	3204	24W-9S	D3
E Mundhank Rd					
10	HFET	60192	2804	25W-14N	A5
10	SBTN	60010	2803	26W-14N	D5
10	SBTN	60010	2804	25W-14N	A5
10	SBTN	60192	2804	25W-14N	A5
W Mundhank Rd					
10	SBTN	60010	2803	27W-13N	B6
Mundhawk Rd					
-	HFET	60010	2803	28W-12N	B7
-	HFET	60010	2857	28W-12N	B1
Munger Rd					
-	WynT	60185	2966	31W-4N	A4
10	BRLT	60103	2910	30W-6N	A7
10	BRLT	60103	2966	30W-4N	A3
10	BRLT	60120	2910	30W-7N	A5
10	BRLT	60184	2910	30W-6N	A7
10	BRLT	60184	2966	30W-4N	A3
10	WYNE	60184	2966	30W-4N	A3
10	WYNE	60185	2966	30W-4N	A3
10	WynT	60184	2910	30W-6N	A7
10	WynT	60184	2966	30W-4N	A3
Munhall Av					
700	SCRL	60174	2964	34W-2N	D7
Municipal Dr					
-	SRGV	60554	3135	43W-7S	B7
-	WSTR	60154	3029	12W-1S	B7
100	MRGO	60152	2634	49W-26N	B3
N Municipal Wy					
1900	RLKB	60073	2475	22W-35N	B5
W Municipal Complex					
100	CLLK	60014	2640	35W-26N	A3
N Munn Rd					
-	LkvT	60046	2475	21W-38N	E1
38200	LkvT	60046	2417	21W-38N	E7
38200	LNHT	60046	2417	21W-38N	E7
38200	LNHT	60046	2475	21W-38N	E1
Munroe Cir					
200	DSPN	60016	2862	15W-10N	B4
Munroe Cir S					
400	DSPN	60016	2862	15W-10N	A4
Munroe Dr					
300	BMDL	60108	2968	24W-4N	C4
300	BMDL	60139	2968	24W-4N	C4
300	GLHT	60139	2968	24W-4N	C4
Munroe St					
300	JLET	60436	3498	24W-24S	D6
Munshaw Ln					
700	CLLK	60014	2694	33W-23N	E1
Munson Dr					
-	CLSM	60185	2967	27W-3N	D7
-	WynT	60185	2967	27W-3N	D7
-	WynT	60188	2967	27W-3N	D7
700	CLSM	60188	2967	27W-3N	D6
Munson St					
-	PLNO	60545	3260	45W-14S	B7
Munster Rd					
10	LMNT	60439	3342	19W-15S	D1
Munz Rd					
-	CRTE	60417	3685	0W-30S	C4
E Munz Rd					
200	CRTE	60417	3685	0E-30S	E4
200	CteT	60417	3685	0E-30S	E4
200	CteT	60417	3686	0E-30S	A4
N Mura Ln					
1500	MPPT	60056	2808	13W-15N	E2
1800	PTHT	60056	2808	13W-15N	E2
1800	PTHT	60070	2808	13W-15N	E2
Murcer Ln					
1900	ELGN	60123	2800	36W-13N	A7
Murdock Ct					
1200	NPVL	60540	3204	24W-8S	C1
Murdstone Dr					
1300	NPVL	60563	3142	25W-4S	A2
Murer Ct					
100	WLNG	60090	2808	14W-15N	C1
Murfield Ct					
21800	FmT	60060	2589	21W-28N	C6
Muriel Ct					
400	WLNG	60090	2808	15W-16N	B1
2200	JltT	60433	3588	21W-26S	A3
2200	NlxT	60433	3588	21W-26S	A3
Muriel Rd					
-	AntT	60020	2414	28W-38N	E7
-	AntT	60081	2414	29W-38N	D7
-	FXLK	60020	2414	28W-38N	E7
-	FXLK	60081	2414	28W-38N	E7
100	BlnT	60081	2414	29W-38N	D7
Muriel St					
-	GfnT	60014	2638	38W-25N	E4
700	WDSK	60098	2581	42W-30N	C1
Murifield Dr					
5900	GRNE	60031	2534	16W-33N	D2
Murphy Av					
16900	HLCT	60429	3427	3W-20S	B4
22300	BlmT	60411	3598	3E-27S	A3
22300	SLVL	60411	3598	3E-27S	A3
Murphy Cir					
-	TYPK	60487	3423	11W-21S	E7
18200	OrlT	60487	3423	11W-21S	E7
21400	FKFT	60423	3591	12W-25S	D1
Murphy Dr					
100	RMVL	60446	3341	23W-16S	A3
200	RMVL	60446	3340	25W-16S	B4
800	JLET	60435	3497	27W-22S	C3
800	TroT	60435	3497	27W-22S	C3
Murphy Ln					
9000	SKOK	60076	2866	4W-11N	C3
S Murphy Ln					
24700	MonT	60449	3682	8W-30S	B3
Murphy Rd					
-	DPgT	60440	3206	20W-10S	A6
-	DPgT	60517	3206	21W-10S	A6
-	WDRG	60517	3206	21W-10S	A6
-	WDRG	60517	3270	20W-12S	C2
700	DGvT	60439	3270	20W-12S	C3
Murphy St					
100	WCDA	60084	2643	26W-27N	E1
3800	PKCY	60085	2535	13W-33N	E3
3800	WKGN	60085	2535	13W-33N	E3
Murphy Lake Ln					
100	PKRG	60068	2863	11W-9N	D7
Murphy Lake Rd					
100	PKRG	60068	2917	11W-9N	D1
Murray Av					
700	ELGN	60123	2854	34W-12N	C3
14300	DLTN	60419	3350	0E-16S	E4
Murray Ct					
800	SchT	60175	2907	38W-6N	A6
7500	JSTC	60458	3209	11W-8S	E1
9300	MNGV	60053	2864	9W-11N	B2
Murray Dr					
-	WDDL	60191	2971	17W-5N	B1
100	LslT	60540	3204	23W-8S	E1
5600	BKLY	60163	3028	14W-0N	C4
S Murray Dr					
26500	CteT	60417	3686	2E-32S	D7
Murray Ln					
-	DSPN	60016	2862	15W-10N	A4
600	DSPN	60016	2861	16W-10N	E4
600	MPPT	60016	2861	15W-10N	E4
600	MPPT	60056	2861	15W-10N	E4
Murray Rd					
500	SchT	60175	2907	38W-6N	A6
800	TRLK	60010	2643	27W-25N	C5
E Murray St					
900	HMND	46320	3352		E6
S Murvey Ct					
13600	HMGN	60491	3344	15W-16S	C2
W Murvey Dr					
12000	HMGN	60491	3344	15W-16S	C2
Muscovy Ln					
10	BmdT	60108	2968	26W-5N	A2
N Museum Blvd					
-	LYVL	60048	2647	16W-26N	E3
-	VNHL	60061	2647	16W-26N	E3
Museum Dr					
-	CrlT	60180	2635	45W-25N	E6
1500	HDPK	60035	2704	10W-23N	A2
E Museum Dr					
1700	CHCG	60637	3153	2E-6S	B3
S Museum Campus Dr					
-	CHCG	60616	3034	0E-1S	D7
-	CHCG	60616	3092	0E-1S	D1
1400	CHCG	60605	3034	0E-1S	D7
Musial Cir					
300	BGBK	60440	3205	23W-11S	A7
300	BGBK	60440	3269	23W-11S	A1
Musial Rd					
1200	TNLK	53181	2354		A2
1800	RdlT	53128	2353		E2
1800	RdlT	53181	2353		E2
1800	TNLK	53181	2353		E2
W Music Ct Dr					
3600	CHCG	60624	3032	4W-0S	C5
Muskegan Ct					
500	VNHL	60061	2647	18W-25N	A4
W Muskego Av					
25300	GrtT	60041	2474	25W-35N	A6
Muskegon Av					
200	BNHM	60409	3351	3E-17S	E5
200	BNHM	60633	3351	3E-17S	E5
200	CTCY	60409	3351	3E-17S	E6
S Muskegon Av					
7900	CHCG	60617	3215	3E-9S	E2
7900	CHCG	60649	3215	3E-9S	E2
10300	CHCG	60617	3279	3E-11S	E1
12600	CHCG	60633	3279	3E-14S	E7
13100	CHCG	60633	3351	2E-15S	D1
14500	BNHM	60409	3351	3E-16S	E4
14500	BNHM	60633	3351	3E-16S	E4
14500	CTCY	60409	3351	3E-16S	E4
Muskegon Wy					
1500	RMVL	60446	3417	26W-18S	E2
Muskie Ln					
26000	WmTp	60481	3761	32W-34S	D6
Mustang Ct					
10	RLKP	60030	2589	22W-30N	C2
10	SMWD	60107	2856	30W-10N	C6
1700	WHTN	60187	3082	23W-2S	E3
Mustang Dr					
300	OSWG	60543	3263	37W-14S	D7
2000	LslT	60565	3204	24W-8S	E2
2000	NPVL	60565	3204	24W-8S	E2
S Mustang Dr					
14300	HMGN	60491	3344	15W-17S	A5
14300	HmrT	60491	3344	15W-17S	A5
Mustang Ln					
800	NLNX	60451	3501	18W-25S	A7
Mustang Rd					
3400	JLET	60435	3417	27W-19S	D3
3400	JLET	60441	3417	27W-19S	D3
S Mustang Rd					
22700	FKFT	60423	3592	11W-27S	A4
Mustang Tr					
2100	GwdT	60098	2525	39W-34N	C1
Mutual Ter					
15600	SHLD	60473	3350	0E-18S	E7
Myang Av					
2500	MchT	60050	2528	31W-34N	D1
Myers Rd					
800	SgrT	60554	3136	40W-5S	B3
800	SGRV	60554	3136	40W-5S	B3
Myles Rd					
500	SchT	60175	2963	36W-5N	E2
Mylith Park Rd					
-	ISLK	60042	2586	28W-27N	E7
-	WcnT	60042	2586	28W-27N	E7
E Myrick Av					
10	ADSN	60101	2970	18W-3N	E5
10	ADSN	60101	2971	18W-3N	A5
W Myrick Av					
300	ADSN	60101	2970	19W-3N	D5
W Myrick St					
3700	CHCG	60652	3212	4W-8S	C2
Myrna Ct					
1700	SYHW	60118	2800	35W-16N	C3
Myrrh Ln					
11400	FKFT	60423	3590	14W-26S	E3
Myrtle Av					
-	ELGN	60120	2855	32W-10N	C6
10	OKTR	60181	3027	17W-1S	B7
10	YkTp	60181	3027	17W-1S	B7
10	YkTp	60181	3085	17W-1S	B1
300	OKTR	60181	3085	17W-1S	B1
14400	HRVY	60426	3349	1W-17S	E5
15600	HRVY	60426	3427	1W-18S	E1
16000	MKHM	60426	3427	1W-19S	E2
16000	MKHM	60428	3427	1W-19S	E2
N Myrtle Av					
100	EMHT	60126	3027	16W-1N	D1
100	VLPK	60181	3027	17W-1N	B3
500	EMHT	60126	2971	16W-2N	E7
S Myrtle Av					
100	EMHT	60126	3027	16W-1N	D2
100	VLPK	60181	3027	17W-0N	B4
1000	YkTp	60181	3027	17W-0S	B6
W Myrtle Av					
7100	CHCG	60631	2918	8W-7N	D3
Myrtle Ct					
18200	LNSG	60438	3430	4E-21S	C6
W Myrtle Dr					
1700	MPPT	60056	2861	17W-12N	C2
Myrtle Ln					
10	SMWD	60107	2856	29W-10N	E6
1100	DRFD	60015	2703	11W-21N	D6
3100	GNVW	60025	2809	11W-15N	D2
3100	GNVW	60062	2809	11W-15N	D2
3100	NHBK	60025	2809	11W-15N	D2
3100	NHBK	60062	2809	11W-15N	D2
W Myrtle Ln					
25900	GrtT	60041	2473	25W-35N	E6
Myrtle St					
10	WNFD	60190	3023	27W-0N	D5
100	WNKA	60093	2812	4W-15N	C3
600	WKGN	60085	2480	10W-35N	A7
700	WNFD	60190	3081	27W-0S	D1
700	WnfT	60187	3081	27W-0S	D1
700	WnfT	60190	3081	27W-0S	D1
E Myrtle St					
900	HMND	46394	3280		E4
N Myrtle St					
10900	HTLY	60142	2692	40W-21N	A6
27900	WcnT	60084	2587	25W-27N	E7
S Myrtle St					
11300	HTLY	60142	2692	40W-20N	A7
W Myrtle St					
1000	PLTN	60067	2752	22W-17N	B6
Myrtle Park St					
1400	SMBG	60193	2913	23W-8N	A2
1400	SmbT	60193	2913	23W-8N	A2
1500	SmbT	60172	2913	23W-8N	A2
Myrtlewood Ln					
500	WHTN	60187	3024	25W-0S	A7
Mystic Ct					
800	OSWG	60543	3263	36W-12S	E3
1100	CLSM	60188	2967	27W-4N	C3
Mystic Dr					
1700	JLET	60586	3415	32W-21S	C7
1700	JLET	60586	3495	32W-21S	C1
Mystic Ln					
-	RMVL	60446	3268	24W-14S	D7
Mystic Pl					
200	VNHL	60061	2647	17W-25N	C6
Mystic Trc					
8300	DGvT	60561	3207	17W-9S	B4
8300	DRN	60561	3207	17W-9S	B4
Mystic Cove					
1100	ANTH	60002	2357	24W-41N	D7
N					
Naber Av					
400	ANTH	60002	2357	24W-42N	D6
Nachtman Ct					
2000	GNEN	60137	3024	23W-0N	E4
2000	WHTN	60187	3024	23W-0N	E4
S Nacke Rd					
-	CRTE	60417	3684	2W-31S	D4
24700	CteT	60417	3684	2W-32S	D6
24700	UYPK	60417	3684	2W-30S	D2
Nacona Ln					
10	IHPK	60525	3146	13W-7S	E5
Nadelhoffer Ct					
-	WDRG	60517	3143	22W-7S	C7
-	WDRG	60517	3205	22W-8S	D1
Naden Ct					
100	YKVL	60560	3261	43W-13S	C6
S Nadia Dr					
21500	SRWD	60404	3584	30W-26S	B2
21500	TroT	60404	3584	30W-26S	B2
Nagel Blvd					
-	GnvT	60510	3020	34W-0S	D6
1300	BTVA	60510	3020	34W-0S	D6
Nagel Ct					
500	WCHI	60185	3022	29W-2N	D1
1300	WCHI	60185	2966	29W-2N	D7
2800	GNOK	60044	2593	13W-28N	A5
Nagle Av					
7700	BDPK	60638	3211	8W-8S	B1
7700	BRBK	60459	3211	8W-9S	B2
7700	BRBK	60638	3211	8W-8S	B1
8600	OKLN	60453	3211	8W-9S	B4
8600	OKLN	60459	3211	8W-9S	B4
9200	MNGV	60053	2865	8W-11N	A2
N Nagle Av					
1600	CHCG	60302	3031	8W-2N	A1
1600	CHCG	60707	3031	8W-2N	A1
1600	OKPK	60302	3031	8W-2N	A1
1700	CHCG	60707	2975	8W-2N	A7
4400	CHCG	60634	2975	8W-5N	A1
4400	HDHT	60706	2919	8W-5N	A7
4400	HDHT	60706	2975	8W-5N	A1
4500	CHCG	60630	2919	7W-6N	A6
4500	HDHT	60630	2919	7W-5N	A7
4800	CHCG	60656	2919	7W-6N	A6
4800	HDHT	60656	2919	7W-6N	A6
5600	CHCG	60631	2919	8W-7N	A3
7100	CHCG	60646	2919	8W-8N	A1
S Nagle Av					
5000	CHCG	60638	3149	8W-5S	B2
5100	FTVW	60638	3149	8W-5S	B2
5100	StkT	60638	3149	8W-5S	B2
10700	CHRG	60415	3275	8W-12S	B2
10700	CHRG	60482	3275	8W-12S	B2
10700	WRTH	60482	3275	8W-12S	B2
12100	PSHT	60463	3275	8W-14S	B6
Nan St					
2200	AraT	60502	3139	33W-4S	A1
2200	AURA	60502	3139	33W-4S	A1
Nanak Ct					
600	NPVL	60565	3204	25W-10S	B6

STREET Block	City	ZIP	Map#	CGS	Grid
Nancy Ct					
-	DrrT	60098	2581	42W-27N	C7
400	WldT	60564	3203	28W-10S	A6
500	WCDA	60084	2588	25W-28N	A6
500	WcnT	60084	2588	25W-28N	A6
5400	JLET	60586	3496	30W-22S	B1
N Nancy Ct					
25400	ElaT	60047	2645	21W-25N	C5
N Nancy Dr					
4400	AlqT	60014	2640	33W-25N	E5
S Nancy Dr					
4400	AlqT	60014	2640	33W-25N	E5
Nancy Ln					
10	CmpT	60124	2905	42W-7N	D6
10	CmpT	60175	2905	42W-7N	D6
300	WLNG	60090	2755	14W-17N	C5
600	LKMR	60051	2529	29W-31N	C6
600	NndT	60051	2529	29W-31N	C6
600	WYNE	60184	2965	31W-4N	D3
1700	AURA	60504	3201	33W-8S	A2
8600	ODPK	60462	3346	10W-18S	B7
S Nancy St					
25700	CteT	60417	3686	0E-31S	A5
Nancy Ann Ln					
800	ELGN	60120	2855	32W-11N	C5
Nancy Vallera Ln					
2800	JLET	60435	3497	27W-23S	C4
Nandina Ct					
10	BGBK	60490	3267	27W-12S	D3
Nanti St					
100	PKFT	60466	3595	4W-28S	A6
Nantucket Ct					
300	BRLT	60103	2911	28W-6N	B6
1300	CLSM	60188	2967	27W-4N	B3
1300	HFET	60192	2804	24W-15N	C2
2300	ELGN	60123	2907	36W-9N	E1
6700	GRNE	60031	2477	17W-35N	C6
Nantucket Dr					
-	JLET	60544	3417	27W-19S	B2
-	PnfT	60544	3417	27W-19S	B2
10	DGvT	60561	3207	17W-9S	C2
10	DRN	60561	3207	17W-9S	C2
3000	JLET	60435	3417	27W-19S	B2
Nantucket Hbr					
200	SMBG	60193	2913	23W-9N	B1
Nantucket Ln					
100	PltT	60010	2751	23W-18N	E3
2300	ELGN	60123	2907	36W-9N	E1
10600	HTLY	60142	2692	39W-21N	B6
Nantucket Rd					
400	NPVL	60565	3203	27W-10S	C5
1100	AURA	60506	3137	36W-5S	E4
7300	MchT	60097	2469	36W-37N	D2
Nantucket Wy					
500	ISLK	60042	2586	29W-28N	C5
Nantucket Cove					
7400	HRPK	60133	2912	26W-9N	A1
Naoma Dr					
600	CRTE	60417	3685	1W-30S	A2
S Napa Cir					
14100	PnfT	60544	3339	27W-16S	B5
Napa Dr					
1600	GRNE	60031	2477	18W-35N	A5
Napa Ln					
800	AURA	60502	3078	34W-3S	D6
Napa St					
700	CLSM	60188	2968	26W-3N	A5
800	CLSM	60188	2967	26W-3N	E5
Napa Tr					
900	SPGV	60081	2414	29W-40N	B2
Napa Suwe Ct					
1700	WCDA	60084	2588	25W-29N	B4
Napa Suwe Ln					
1600	WCDA	60084	2588	25W-29N	B4
N Naper Av					
5900	CHCG	60631	2919	8W-7N	A3
Naper Blvd					
-	LSLE	60540	3142	25W-7S	B6
-	LslT	60563	3142	25W-5S	B3
-	NPVL	60532	3142	25W-7S	C6
-	NPVL	60540	3204	25W-7S	B1
100	LslT	60565	3204	25W-9S	B3
400	LslT	60540	3142	25W-7S	C6
400	NPVL	60540	3142	25W-7S	C6
500	LSLE	60532	3142	25W-7S	C6
500	LslT	60532	3142	25W-7S	C6
700	NPVL	60565	3204	26W-10S	A6
N Naper Blvd					
-	LslT	60563	3142	25W-5S	B3
1500	NPVL	60563	3142	25W-5S	B3
N Naper Blvd CO-23					
-	LslT	60563	3142	25W-4S	B2
1500	NPVL	60563	3142	25W-5S	B2
S Naper Blvd					
10	LslT	60540	3142	24W-6S	C5
10	NPVL	60540	3142	24W-6S	C5
2600	NPVL	60565	3204	26W-10S	A6
Naperville Dr					
-	BGBK	60440	3268	24W-14S	E7
-	BGBK	60446	3268	24W-14S	E7
-	RMVL	60440	3268	24W-14S	E7
-	RMVL	60446	3268	24W-14S	E7
1100	RMVL	60446	3269	23W-14S	A6
Naperville Ln					
1500	BTVA	60510	3078	34W-2S	D5
Naperville Rd					
-	BRLT	60103	2856	30W-9N	B7
-	BRLT	60107	2856	30W-9N	B7
-	HnrT	60107	2856	30W-9N	B7
10	CNHL	60514	3085	16W-4S	D7
10	LSLE	60532	3082	25W-4S	B7
10	LSLE	60563	3082	25W-4S	B7
10	LslT	60563	3082	25W-4S	B7
10	MltT	60187	3082	25W-3S	C6
10	MltT	60563	3082	25W-3S	C6
10	NPVL	60532	3082	25W-4S	B7
10	NPVL	60563	3082	25W-4S	B7
10	RMVL	60446	3341	23W-14S	A1
10	WHTN	60187	3082	24W-3S	C5
100	BRLT	60103	2910	30W-8N	B3
100	CNHL	60514	3145	16W-4S	D1
100	HnrT	60103	2910	30W-8N	B2
100	LslT	60563	3082	25W-4S	B7
400	CNHL	60559	3145	17W-4S	C1
400	LSLE	60532	3142	25W-4S	B1
400	LSLE	60563	3142	25W-4S	B1
400	LslT	60563	3142	25W-4S	B1
400	NPVL	60532	3142	25W-4S	B1
400	NPVL	60563	3142	25W-4S	B1
400	WTMT	60559	3145	17W-4S	C1
Naperville Rd CO-23					
10	LSLE	60532	3082	25W-4S	B7
10	LSLE	60563	3082	25W-4S	B7
10	LslT	60563	3082	25W-4S	B7
10	MltT	60187	3082	25W-3S	C6
10	MltT	60563	3082	25W-3S	C6
Naperville Rd CO-23					
10	NPVL	60532	3082	25W-4S	B7
10	NPVL	60563	3082	25W-4S	B7
10	WHTN	60187	3082	24W-3S	C5
100	LslT	60532	3082	25W-4S	B7
400	LSLE	60532	3142	25W-4S	B1
400	LSLE	60563	3142	25W-4S	B1
400	LslT	60563	3142	25W-4S	B1
400	NPVL	60532	3142	25W-4S	B1
400	NPVL	60563	3142	25W-4S	B1
E Naperville Rd					
10	WTMT	60559	3145	17W-4S	B1
300	CNHL	60514	3145	17W-4S	B1
300	CNHL	60559	3145	17W-4S	B1
N Naperville Rd					
1600	LslT	60563	3142	25W-4S	B1
1600	NPVL	60563	3142	25W-4S	B1
N Naperville Rd CO-23					
1600	LslT	60563	3142	25W-4S	B1
1600	NPVL	60563	3142	25W-4S	B1
S Naperville Rd					
-	BGBK	60490	3267	28W-14S	A7
-	BGBK	60490	3339	28W-14S	A1
-	BGBK	60564	3267	28W-13S	B4
-	PNFD	60490	3267	28W-14S	A7
-	PNFD	60490	3339	28W-14S	A1
-	PNFD	60585	3339	28W-14S	A1
-	WldT	60490	3267	28W-13S	B4
200	PNFD	60544	3338	29W-17S	D6
200	WHTN	60187	3024	24W-0S	D7
700	WHTN	60187	3082	24W-2S	C4
1200	PnfT	60544	3338	29W-17S	C6
2000	MltT	60187	3082	24W-3S	C5
11200	BGBK	60585	3267	28W-13S	A5
11200	WldT	60564	3267	28W-13S	A5
11200	WldT	60585	3267	28W-13S	A5
11400	PNFD	60585	3267	28W-14S	A7
12700	BGBK	60490	3338	28W-15S	E1
12700	PNFD	60585	3338	28W-15S	E2
12700	WldT	60585	3338	28W-15S	E2
S Naperville Rd CO-23					
700	WHTN	60187	3082	24W-2S	C4
2000	MltT	60187	3082	24W-3S	C5
W Naperville Rd					
10	WTMT	60559	3145	18W-5S	A2
400	DRGV	60515	3144	18W-5S	E2
400	DRGV	60559	3144	18W-5S	E2
400	WTMT	60515	3144	18W-5S	E2
400	WTMT	60559	3144	18W-5S	E2
Naperville-Wheaton Rd					
200	LslT	60563	3142	25W-5S	B2
200	NPVL	60563	3142	25W-5S	B2
Napier Ct					
100	VNHL	60061	2646	18W-25N	E6
N Naples Av					
6000	CHCG	60631	2919	8W-7N	A3
6000	CHCG	60646	2919	8W-7N	A3
Naples Ct					
1400	BRLT	60103	2967	27W-6N	B1
Naples Dr					
10	WCDA	60084	2643	26W-26N	E2
10	WcnT	60084	2643	26W-26N	E2
Naples Ln					
900	DGvT	60439	3270	19W-12S	C2
900	DGvT	60517	3270	19W-12S	C2
900	WDRG	60517	3270	19W-12S	D2
N Napoleon Av					
5800	CHCG	60631	2919	8W-7N	A4
5800	CHCG	60646	2919	8W-7N	A4
Napoleon Dr					
1700	NPVL	60565	3204	25W-9S	B4
Narcissus Av					
2000	HRPK	60133	2911	27W-9N	C1
2100	HRPK	60107	2911	27W-9N	C1
2100	SMWD	60107	2911	27W-9N	C1
Narcissus Ct					
15100	ODPK	60462	3346	9W-18S	D6
Narcissus Ln					
7700	ODPK	60462	3346	9W-18S	D7
Nardis Dr					
700	VNHL	60061	2701	17W-24N	C1
Narraganset Dr					
1100	CLSM	60188	2967	27W-4N	B4
Narragansett Av					
7700	BDPK	60638	3211	7W-8S	B1
7700	BRBK	60459	3211	8W-9S	B2
7700	BRBK	60638	3211	7W-8S	B1
8700	MNGV	60053	2865	8W-10N	A4
N Narragansett Av					
10	CHCG	60706	2975	8W-5N	A1
10	HDHT	60706	2975	8W-5N	A1
1600	CHCG	60639	3031	8W-1N	A1
1600	CHCG	60707	3031	8W-1N	A1
1600	OKPK	60302	3031	8W-1N	A1
1600	OKPK	60639	3031	8W-1N	A1
1700	CHCG	60639	2975	7W-2N	A7
1700	CHCG	60707	2975	7W-2N	A7
2700	CHCG	60634	2975	8W-4N	A3
4200	CHCG	60630	2975	7W-5N	A1
4400	CHCG	60630	2919	7W-5N	A7
4400	HDHT	60630	2919	7W-5N	A7
4400	HDHT	60706	2919	7W-5N	A7
S Narragansett Av					
5100	CHCG	60638	3149	8W-6S	B4
5100	StkT	60638	3149	7W-5S	B2
7200	BDPK	60638	3149	7W-8S	B7
7300	BDPK	60638	3211	8W-8S	B1
Narragansett Ct					
300	CLLK	60012	2640	33W-26N	D2
Nary Ct					
1200	BTVA	60510	3077	36W-0S	E1
NASA Cir					
-	RLKB	60073	2531	24W-34N	D1
100	RDLK	60073	2531	24W-34N	D1
Nash Ct					
-	LYWD	60411	3509	2E-23S	D3
Nash Rd					
300	CLLK	60014	2639	36W-25N	D5
Nash St					
6400	DRGV	60516	3144	20W-7S	A6
N Nashotah Av					
5800	CHCG	60631	2919	8W-7N	A4
Nashua Ct					
700	CLLK	60012	2640	33W-26N	D2
Nashua Dr					
1100	NPVL	60540	3141	27W-7S	C7
1100	NPVL	60540	3203	26W-7S	E1
Nashua Ln					
1200	HRPK	60133	2911	26W-6N	D7
1200	HRPK	60133	2912	26W-6N	A6
Nashua St					
100	PKFT	60466	3595	3W-27S	A5
Nashville Av					
7700	BDPK	60638	3211	8W-8S	A1
7700	BRBK	60459	3211	8W-9S	A3
7700	BRBK	60638	3211	8W-8S	A1
Nashville Av					
8700	OKLN	60459	3211	8W-10S	A5
9200	MNGV	60053	2865	8W-11N	A2
9400	OKLN	60415	3211	8W-10S	A6
9500	CHRG	60415	3211	8W-11S	A7
9500	CHRG	60453	3211	8W-11S	A7
9500	GLF	60029	2865	8W-11N	A2
9500	GLF	60053	2865	8W-11N	A2
9500	OKLN	60453	3211	8W-11S	A7
10300	CHRG	60415	3275	8W-12S	A1
N Nashville Av					
1600	CHCG	60302	3031	8W-2N	A1
1600	CHCG	60707	3031	8W-2N	A1
1600	OKPK	60302	3031	8W-2N	A1
1700	CHCG	60707	2975	8W-2N	A7
4400	CHCG	60634	2975	8W-5N	A1
4400	CHCG	60706	2975	8W-5N	A1
4400	HDHT	60706	2975	8W-5N	A1
4800	CHCG	60656	2919	8W-6N	A6
4800	HDHT	60706	2919	8W-6N	A6
6400	CHCG	60631	2919	8W-8N	A2
S Nashville Av					
5100	CHCG	60638	3149	8W-6S	A4
5100	FTVW	60638	3149	8W-5S	A2
6400	BDPK	60638	3149	8W-7S	A5
10700	CHRG	60415	3275	8W-12S	A2
10700	WRTH	60415	3275	8W-12S	A2
10700	WRTH	60482	3275	8W-12S	A2
12300	PSHT	60463	3275	8W-14S	B6
Nashville Ct					
1100	NPVL	60540	3203	27W-8S	B1
Nashville Ln					
1700	CLLK	60014	2693	36W-22N	C4
Nassau Av					
500	BGBK	60440	3205	22W-10S	C6
N Nassau Av					
6000	CHCG	60631	2919	8W-7N	A3
6000	CHCG	60646	2919	8W-7N	A3
6100	CHCG	60631	2918	8W-7N	E3
Nassau Ct					
10	PKFT	60466	3595	3W-27S	B5
7100	FXLK	60020	2415	28W-39N	A6
Nassau Dr					
600	ROSL	60172	2912	24W-6N	D6
Nassau Ln					
800	GNVA	60134	3020	35W-0N	A4
Nassau St					
300	PKFT	60466	3595	3W-27S	B5
Nassau Colony St					
10	FXLK	60020	2414	29W-38N	B6
Natalie Ct					
400	MltT	60188	3023	26W-1N	E3
1000	ANTH	60002	2359	20W-41N	A7
1100	NPVL	60540	3202	29W-8S	D1
Natalie Dr					
300	WCHI	60185	3022	30W-2N	B1
5400	OKFT	60452	3347	6W-18S	E7
Natalie Ln					
1300	AURA	60504	3201	32W-9S	D4
W Natalie Ln					
10	ADSN	60101	2970	19W-3N	D5
100	AddT	60101	2970	19W-3N	D5
Natchez Av					
7700	BDPK	60638	3211	8W-8S	B1
7700	BRBK	60459	3211	8W-9S	B2
7700	BRBK	60638	3211	8W-8S	B1
8600	OKLN	60459	3211	8W-9S	B4
8900	MNGV	60053	2865	8W-11N	A2
9300	OKLN	60453	3211	8W-10S	B5
10200	CHRG	60415	3275	8W-11S	B1
N Natchez Av					
1600	CHCG	60302	3031	8W-2N	A1
1600	CHCG	60707	3031	8W-2N	A1
1600	OKPK	60302	3031	8W-2N	A1
2000	CHCG	60707	2975	8W-2N	A6
4400	CHCG	60634	2975	8W-5N	A1
4400	HDHT	60706	2919	8W-5N	A7
4400	HDHT	60706	2975	8W-5N	A1
4800	CHCG	60656	2919	8W-6N	A6
4800	HDHT	60656	2919	8W-6N	A6
7900	MNGV	60053	2865	8W-9N	A6
7900	MNGV	60714	2865	8W-9N	A6
7900	NLES	60714	2865	8W-9N	A6
S Natchez Av					
5100	CHCG	60638	3149	8W-6S	A3
5100	FTVW	60638	3149	8W-5S	A2
6500	BDPK	60638	3149	8W-7S	A5
10700	CHRG	60415	3275	8W-12S	B2
10700	CHRG	60482	3275	8W-12S	B2
10700	WRTH	60482	3275	8W-12S	B2
12100	PSHT	60463	3275	8W-14S	B6
W Natchez Ct					
22200	PnfT	60544	3339	27W-16S	B5
Natchez Tr					
13500	OrlT	60467	3344	14W-16S	D3
13500	PlsT	60467	3344	14W-16S	D3
Natchez Trc					
1800	ELGN	60123	2854	36W-12N	A2
1800	ElgT	60123	2854	36W-12N	A2
Natchez Trace Cir					
1200	NPVL	60540	3203	27W-8S	B2
Nathan Ct					
-	ALGN	60118	2746	37W-19N	D2
Nathan Ln					
1500	LYVL	60048	2591	18W-29N	A3
1700	LYVL	60048	2590	18W-29N	E3
7000	CPVL	60110	2746	36W-17N	E6
7000	CPVL	60110	2747	36W-17N	A6
7000	DndT	60118	2747	36W-17N	A6
Nathan Rd					
500	UYPK	60466	3684	3W-30S	C3
N Nathan Hale Dr					
36600	LkvT	60046	2475	21W-36N	E3
N Nathan Hale Dr CO-A18					
36800	LkvT	60046	2475	21W-36N	E3
S Nathan Hale Dr					
36200	LkvT	60046	2475	21W-36N	E4
Nathaniel Pl					
2300	EVTN	60202	2866	3W-10N	D4
National Av					
200	WCHI	60185	3022	29W-1N	E3
200	WnfT	60185	3022	29W-1N	D3
8800	MNGV	60053	2864	8W-11N	E3
8800	NLES	60053	2864	8W-11N	E3
8800	NLES	60714	2864	8W-11N	E3
W National Av					
900	ADSN	60101	2970	19W-3N	B5
National Ct					
-	SRWD	60404	3495	31W-24S	E5
-	SRWD	60404	3496	31W-24S	A5
National Dr					
200	SRWD	60404	3495	31W-24S	E5
300	SRWD	60404	3496	31W-24S	A6
National Pkwy					
-	SMBG	60193	2859	21W-10N	D5
1000	SMBG	60173	2859	22W-12N	D1
National St					
-	ELGN	60120	2855	33W-10N	A5
-	ELGN	60123	2855	33W-10N	A5
10	ELGN	60123	2854	34W-11N	E5
10	MltT	60188	3023	27W-1N	D3
10	WNFD	60190	3023	27W-1N	D3
10	WnfT	60185	3023	27W-1N	D3
10	WnfT	60190	3023	27W-1N	D3
100	WNFD	60185	3023	27W-1N	D3
600	WCHI	60185	3022	28W-1N	E3
600	WnfT	60185	3022	28W-1N	E3
6500	UNON	60180	2635	46W-25N	D5
E National St					
100	WCHI	60185	3022	29W-1N	C3
N National St					
8500	NLES	60714	2864	8W-10N	E4
W National St					
100	WCHI	60185	3022	30W-1N	C3
Nations Dr					
1500	GRNE	60031	2477	15W-35N	E5
1500	GRNE	60031	2478	15W-35N	A7
1500	WrnT	60031	2478	15W-35N	A7
Natoma Av					
-	BRBK	60459	3211	8W-10S	A5
-	OKLN	60459	3211	8W-10S	A5
1700	NCHI	60064	2536	12W-32N	C6
7700	BDPK	60638	3211	8W-8S	A1
7700	BRBK	60638	3211	8W-8S	A1
8700	OKLN	60453	3211	8W-10S	A5
8900	MNGV	60053	2865	8W-11N	A3
9700	CHRG	60415	3211	8W-11S	A7
9700	CHRG	60453	3211	8W-11S	A7
10300	CHRG	60415	3275	8W-12S	A1
12600	PSHT	60463	3275	8W-14S	B7
E Natoma Av					
10	ADSN	60101	2970	18W-3N	E5
10	ADSN	60101	2971	18W-3N	A5
N Natoma Av					
1600	CHCG	60707	3031	8W-2N	A1
1600	OKPK	60302	3031	8W-2N	A1
1700	CHCG	60707	2975	8W-2N	A7
2800	CHCG	60634	2975	8W-3N	A4
4800	CHCG	60656	2919	8W-6N	A6
4800	CHCG	60706	2919	8W-6N	A6
4800	HDHT	60706	2919	8W-6N	A6
5700	CHCG	60631	2918	8W-7N	E4
6200	CHCG	60631	2919	8W-7N	A3
6500	CHCG	60714	2919	8W-8N	A2
6500	NLES	60714	2919	8W-8N	A2
S Natoma Av					
5100	CHCG	60638	3149	8W-6S	A3
5100	FTVW	60638	3149	8W-5S	A2
11100	WRTH	60482	3275	8W-13S	A4
W Natoma Av					
200	ADSN	60101	2970	18W-3N	D5
Natoma Cir					
400	CLSM	60188	2968	25W-2N	B7
Natoma Ct					
10	OKBK	60523	3085	16W-3S	E5
600	ELGN	60120	2855	32W-10N	D6
900	JLET	60431	3497	28W-25S	B7
Natoma Dr					
10	OKBK	60523	3085	16W-3S	E4
600	ELGN	60120	2855	32W-10N	D6
W Natoma Dr					
16600	LKPT	60441	3420	20W-20S	B5
16700	LktT	60441	3420	20W-20S	B5
Natoma St					
400	PKFT	60466	3595	4W-28S	A5
Natoma Tr					
200	DndT	60102	2747	34W-19N	D2
Nature Ct					
1700	SMBG	60193	2912	25W-8N	A3
N Nature Ct					
1100	RLKB	60073	2474	24W-34N	C7
39600	WDWH	60083	2420	14W-39N	C5
Nature Dr					
6400	OKFT	60452	3347	8W-18S	B7
Nature Center Dr					
21500	OKBK	60523	3086	15W-3S	A5
Nature Creek Cir					
22500	FKFT	60423	3592	10W-27S	C4
Nature Creek Tr					
8000	FKFT	60423	3592	10W-27S	D4
Natures Ct					
1800	LNHT	60046	2418	20W-39N	A5
Natures Wy					
1600	LNHT	60046	2417	21W-39N	E4
1700	LNHT	60046	2418	20W-39N	A5
Natwick Ln					
200	SMBG	60193	2858	26W-10N	A6
Natwill Sq					
600	GNVA	60134	3020	35W-1N	B3
Naughton Dr					
15000	SHLD	60473	3351	1E-17S	A6
Nauset Ln					
100	SMBG	60194	2858	24W-10N	D5
Nautical Wy					
-	ElgT	60123	2853	36W-10N	E5
200	ELGN	60123	2853	36W-10N	E5
Nautilus Ct					
4100	NCHI	60088	2593	11W-31N	D1
Nautilus Ln					
1600	HRPK	60133	2967	27W-4N	C3
Nauvoo St					
100	PKFT	60466	3595	4W-28S	A5
200	PKFT	60466	3594	4W-28S	E5
Navaho Av					
22100	SLVL	60411	3597	2E-26S	E3
Navaho Rd					
2700	WKGN	60087	2479	12W-36N	C4
W Navaho Tr					
13400	HMGN	60491	3343	16W-16S	D3
N Navajo Av					
6200	CHCG	60646	2919	6W-7N	D3
6400	LNWD	60646	2919	6W-8N	D2
6600	LNWD	60712	2919	6W-8N	D2
6700	LNWD	60077	2919	6W-8N	D2
6700	SKOK	60077	2919	6W-8N	D2
Navajo Ct					
10	BRRG	60527	3208	14W-9S	D4
100	MchT	60051	2472	29W-34N	D7
100	MchT	60051	2529	29W-34N	D1
400	BGBK	60440	3268	23W-11S	E1
500	JLET	60451	3500	19W-23S	D3
E Navajo Ct					
12600	PSHT	60463	3275	8W-13S	A5
S Navajo Ct W					
12600	PSHT	60463	3275	8W-13S	A5
Navajo Dr					
200	BGBK	60440	3268	23W-11S	E1
400	JLET	60451	3500	19W-23S	D3
700	CPVL	60110	2748	32W-18N	C4
800	LIHL	60156	2694	34W-21N	C5
1100	BTVA	60510	3019	36W-0S	E7
4700	ALGN	60102	2747	33W-20N	D1
Navajo Dr					
4700	AlqT	60102	2747	33W-20N	D1
E Navajo Dr					
6600	PSHT	60463	3275	8W-14S	A7
S Navajo Dr					
12600	PSHT	60463	3275	8W-14S	A7
W Navajo Dr					
6700	PSHT	60463	3275	8W-14S	A7
Navajo Ln					
200	HFET	60169	2858	23W-10N	E5
200	RtdT	60142	2745	40W-18N	C4
Navajo St					
400	PKFT	60466	3595	4W-28S	A5
600	RLKH	60073	2474	23W-36N	D4
900	CLSM	60188	2967	26W-3N	E5
Navajo Tr					
100	BFGV	60089	2754	16W-18N	C3
100	GrtT	60051	2472	29W-34N	D7
100	MchT	60051	2472	29W-34N	D7
S Navajo Tr					
400	WLNG	60090	2754	16W-17N	D5
Navajo Trc					
17500	TYPK	60477	3424	10W-21S	C6
Navarone Dr					
1900	NPVL	60565	3203	27W-9S	D5
N Navarre Av					
5800	CHCG	60631	2919	8W-7N	A4
6000	CHCG	60631	2918	8W-7N	E3
Navy Blvd					
2600	GNVW	60025	2810	9W-14N	B4
Navy Ct					
1200	ELGN	60123	2907	36W-9N	E2
Nawakwa Ln					
10	KdlT	60560	3333	43W-17S	B7
S Na Wa Ta Av					
400	MPPT	60056	2861	16W-12N	E1
Nawata Pl					
400	PTHT	60070	2807	16W-15N	D2
Neal Av					
900	JLET	60433	3499	23W-25S	B7
1100	JLET	60433	3587	23W-25S	B1
Neal Cir					
18600	CCHL	60478	3506	6W-22S	A1
Neal Ct					
400	SMBG	60193	2859	22W-9N	B6
Nealy Rd					
13400	HTLY	60142	2744	42W-20N	B1
Nebel Ln					
700	DSPN	60018	2862	13W-9N	D7
Nebraska Cir					
500	CLSM	60188	2967	27W-2N	C7
Nebraska Ct					
3100	NCHI	60088	2593	11W-30N	C2
18100	ODPK	60467	3423	13W-21S	A7
Nebraska Dr					
1600	EGVV	60007	2913	21W-8N	D2
Nebraska St					
-	WDSK	60098	2524	41W-31N	D7
10	GNVA	60134	3020	34W-0N	D4
10400	FKFT	60423	3591	13W-26S	B2
10700	FftT	60423	3591	13W-26S	A2
E Nebraska St					
10	FKFT	60423	3591	11W-26S	E1
100	BbyT	60119	3017	43W-1N	A3
100	ELBN	60119	3017	43W-1N	A3
300	FKFT	60423	3592	11W-26S	A1
500	FftT	60423	3592	11W-26S	A1
W Nebraska St					
10	FKFT	60423	3591	12W-26S	D1
Nebraska A Ct					
300	FKFT	60423	3592	11W-26S	A1
Nebraska B Ct					
400	FKFT	60423	3592	11W-26S	A2
Ned Dr					
3900	NndT	60014	2641	32W-26N	A2
Needham Ct					
-	WNVL	60555	3141	27W-4S	B2
2500	AURA	60503	3201	32W-10S	C6
Needham Dr					
200	BMDL	60108	2968	24W-5N	C2
Needham Rd					
1100	NPVL	60563	3142	25W-6S	A4
3300	LtRT	60545	3260	46W-12S	A4
3300	PLNO	60545	3260	46W-13S	A6
3900	LtRT	60545	3259	46W-14S	E7
3900	LtRT	60545	3331	46W-14S	E1
3900	PLNO	60545	3259	46W-14S	E7
3900	PLNO	60545	3331	46W-14S	E1
Needle Creek Ct					
3600	NndT	60012	2584	35W-28N	A6
N Needlegrass Ct					
34000	GrtT	60073	2531	25W-33N	A2
N Needlegrass Dr					
34100	GrtT	60073	2531	25W-34N	A1
Needlegrass Pkwy					
500	ANTH	60002	2357	24W-42N	B5
Needles Ct					
-	HMGN	60491	3344	15W-16S	B3
1200	NPVL	60540	3142	25W-7S	A7
Needles Dr					
-	HMGN	60491	3344	15W-16S	B3
Neenah Av					
7700	BDPK	60638	3211	8W-8S	A1
7700	BRBK	60459	3211	8W-9S	A2
7700	BRBK	60638	3211	8W-8S	A1
9300	MNGV	60053	2865	8W-11N	A2
N Neenah Av					
2800	CHCG	60707	2975	8W-3N	A5
4400	CHCG	60634	2975	8W-5N	A1
4400	CHCG	60706	2975	8W-5N	A1
4400	HDHT	60706	2919	8W-5N	A7
4400	HDHT	60706	2975	8W-5N	A1
4900	CHCG	60656	2919	8W-6N	A6
6200	CHCG	60631	2919	8W-7N	A3
S Neenah Av					
5100	CHCG	60638	3149	8W-6S	A3
5100	FTVW	60638	3149	8W-5S	A2
10700	CHRG	60415	3275	8W-12S	B2
10700	WRTH	60415	3275	8W-12S	B2
10700	WRTH	60482	3275	8W-12S	B2
Neff Ct					
2100	LSLE	60532	3142	24W-6S	E5
Negaunee Ln					
10	LKFT	60045	2649	11W-25N	D4
Neil Av					
200	MPPT	60056	2808	14W-13N	B6
Neil Ct					
-	LktT	60441	3419	23W-21S	B7
800	WCDA	60084	2588	25W-28N	A6
Neil Ln					
900	GNVW	60025	2809	11W-13N	E6
900	NfdT	60025	2809	11W-13N	E6
1200	NCHI	60064	2536	11W-31N	E7
Neil Rd					
10	SRGV	60554	3135	42W-7S	D7

STREET Block	City	ZIP	Map#	CGS	Grid
Neilis Dr					
6600	JLET	60586	3415	32W-20S	D5
Nekoma Dr					
500	CLSM	60188	2967	27W-3N	D6
Nelli Ct					
800	NPVL	60563	3140	29W-5S	D4
Nellie Ct					
300	MaiT	60025	2864	9W-12N	B1
Nells Rd					
1400	LbvT	60048	2592	15W-29N	B3
Nelson Av					
600	RMVL	60446	3340	24W-15S	D1
3200	RBBN	60472	3348	4W-16S	D4
Nelson Cir					
600	WTMT	60559	3144	18W-7S	E6
1300	WHTN	60187	3082	24W-1S	D1
Nelson Ct					
300	BGBK	60440	3205	22W-9S	C4
600	GNVA	60134	3019	37W-1N	C2
4100	WDRG	60517	3142	23W-7S	E7
13700	PNFD	60544	3338	30W-16S	B4
W Nelson Ct					
-	WKGN	60083	2478	14W-37N	C2
Nelson Dr					
10	WYNE	60174	2964	34W-4N	D3
10	WYNE	60184	2964	34W-4N	D3
300	GNVA	60134	3019	37W-1N	C2
800	SCRL	60174	2964	34W-4N	D3
11200	HTLY	60142	2691	41W-20N	C7
Nelson Ln					
500	DSPN	60016	2808	14W-12N	D7
500	MPPT	60056	2808	14W-12N	D7
500	WTMT	60559	3144	18W-7S	E6
Nelson Rd					
-	SlmT	53104	2358	22W-43N	B4
-	SlmT	60002	2358	22W-43N	B4
10	NLNX	60451	3501	18W-24S	A6
10	NlxT	60451	3501	18W-24S	A6
400	ANTH	60002	2358	22W-43N	B4
400	AntT	60002	2358	22W-43N	B4
1300	NLNX	60451	3589	18W-27S	A5
1300	NlxT	60451	3589	18W-26S	A2
2700	MhtT	60442	3589	19W-27S	A5
2700	MhtT	60451	3589	19W-27S	A5
Nelson Sq					
2400	WSTR	60154	3086	13W-2S	E3
Nelson St					
-	RLKB	60073	2474	24W-35N	C7
10800	WSTR	60154	3086	13W-2S	E3
35100	AvnT	60073	2474	24W-35N	C7
W Nelson St					
1800	CHCG	60657	2977	2W-3N	B4
2600	CHCG	60618	2977	3W-3N	A4
2700	CHCG	60618	2976	3W-3N	E4
4000	CHCG	60641	2976	5W-3N	B4
4800	CHCG	60641	2975	6W-3N	E4
6000	CHCG	60634	2975	7W-3N	B4
6900	CHCG	60634	2974	8W-3N	E4
Nelson C White Pkwy					
10	MDLN	60060	2589	20W-28N	E6
Nelson Lake Rd					
10	BtvT	60510	3077	38W-2S	A4
500	BtvT	60134	3077	38W-1S	A2
N Neltnor Blvd					
100	WCHI	60185	3022	29W-1N	D4
300	WnfT	60185	3022	29W-1N	D3
N Neltnor Blvd SR-59					
100	WCHI	60185	3022	29W-1N	D4
300	WnfT	60185	3022	29W-1N	D3
S Neltnor Blvd					
100	WCHI	60185	3022	29W-0S	D7
200	WnfT	60185	3022	29W-0N	D5
S Neltnor Blvd SR-59					
100	WCHI	60185	3022	29W-0S	D7
200	WnfT	60185	3022	29W-0N	D5
Nemery Ct					
2400	WKGN	60085	2479	11W-35N	C6
N Nemesis Av					
13400	WrnT	60031	2478	13W-36N	E3
13400	WrnT	60031	2479	13W-36N	A3
13400	WrnT	60087	2479	13W-36N	A3
W Nemesis Av					
3400	WKGN	60087	2479	13W-36N	A3
3400	WrnT	60087	2479	13W-36N	A3
12700	WkgT	60087	2479	12W-36N	B3
N Neola Av					
6000	CHCG	60631	2918	8W-7N	E3
6000	CHCG	60631	2919	8W-7N	A3
Neola Ct					
10	KdlT	60560	3333	43W-18S	B7
Neola St					
300	PKFT	60466	3595	3W-27S	A5
Neosho St					
400	PKFT	60466	3595	4W-28S	A6
Nepil Av					
10	MltT	60187	3024	25W-0N	A5
Neptune Ct					
500	GNVW	60025	2810	10W-14N	A3
500	LslT	60540	3142	24W-6S	C4
Neptune Ln					
22000	RNPK	60471	3594	6W-26S	B3
Neptune Cove					
100	LKMR	60051	2529	28W-33N	D3
Nerbonne Av					
9400	FNPK	60131	2973	11W-4N	C3
Nerge Rd					
1000	EGVV	60007	2914	21W-8N	A2
1100	ITSC	60007	2914	20W-8N	A3
1100	ITSC	60143	2914	20W-8N	A3
1500	EGVV	60007	2913	22W-8N	D2
1900	EGVV	60172	2913	22W-8N	D2
1900	ROSL	60172	2913	22W-8N	D2
E Nerge Rd					
10	ROSL	60172	2913	23W-8N	B2
10	ROSL	60193	2913	23W-8N	B2
10	SmbT	60172	2913	23W-8N	B2
10	SmbT	60193	2913	23W-8N	A2
800	EGVV	60007	2913	23W-8N	B2
800	EGVV	60172	2913	23W-8N	B2
800	ROSL	60007	2913	23W-8N	B2
W NE Shore Dr					
1000	NndT	60051	2586	30W-29N	B4
1200	HHLL	60051	2586	30W-29N	B4
Neskola Ct					
1300	NPVL	60564	3203	28W-10S	A6
Nesler Rd					
10	PltT	60124	2852	39W-10N	E6
200	PltT	60124	2906	39W-9N	D1
500	ElgT	60124	2853	38W-11N	A5
500	PltT	60124	2853	38W-11N	A5
Ness Wy					
1800	MTGY	60538	3198	40W-9S	B5
Nestor St					
-	JLET	60432	3499	21W-23S	E4
-	JltT	60432	3499	21W-23S	E4
Netherby Wy					
-	FKFT	60423	3590	14W-27S	E4
Netherlands Dr					
10	ANTH	60002	2358	22W-42N	A5
Nettle Ln					
100	HnrT	60107	2856	30W-10N	B5
100	SMWD	60107	2856	30W-10N	B5
N Nettleton Av					
6000	CHCG	60631	2918	8W-7N	E3
Nettleton Wy					
3100	GNCY	53128	2353		A3
Neubauer Cir					
-	LNHT	60046	2476	19W-37N	D1
Neuberry Ridge Ct					
17000	LKPT	60441	3419	22W-20S	D5
Neuberry Ridge Dr					
17600	LKPT	60441	3419	22W-20S	D5
17600	LktT	60441	3419	22W-20S	D5
Neubert St					
-	LtRT	60545	3259	47W-12S	D4
-	PLNO	60545	3259	47W-12S	D4
Neudearborn Dr					
900	NpvT	60563	3140	30W-5S	C4
Neufairfield Dr					
800	JLET	60432	3500	20W-22S	B2
800	NlxT	60432	3500	20W-22S	B2
Neuhaven Dr					
900	ANTH	60002	2359	20W-42N	A7
Neustoneshire Blvd					
-	JLET	60431	3495	33W-22S	B1
Neutrenton Av					
100	ELGN	60120	2855	31W-11N	E4
100	HnrT	60120	2855	31W-11N	E4
Neuway Ln					
-	ANTH	60002	2418	20W-40N	A3
900	ANTH	60002	2417	21W-40N	E2
Neva Av					
200	GNVW	60025	2864	8W-12N	E1
7900	BRBK	60459	3210	8W-9S	E2
9300	BGVW	60455	3210	8W-10S	E6
9300	OKLN	60453	3210	8W-10S	E6
9300	OKLN	60455	3210	8W-10S	E6
N Neva Av					
500	ADSN	60101	2970	19W-4N	D3
1600	CHCG	60302	3030	8W-2N	D1
1600	CHCG	60707	3030	8W-2N	D1
1600	OKPK	60302	3030	8W-2N	D1
1700	CHCG	60707	2974	8W-2N	D7
2700	CHCG	60634	2974	8W-3N	D5
4200	NRDG	60706	2974	8W-5N	D1
4800	CHCG	60656	2918	8W-6N	D6
4800	CHCG	60706	2918	8W-6N	D6
4800	HDHT	60706	2918	8W-6N	D7
6500	CHCG	60631	2918	8W-8N	D2
6500	CHCG	60714	2918	8W-8N	D2
6500	NLES	60631	2918	8W-8N	D2
6500	NLES	60714	2918	8W-8N	D2
8200	NLES	60714	2864	8W-10N	D5
S Neva Av					
5100	CHCG	60638	3148	8W-5S	E2
Neva Ter					
200	BmdT	60143	2969	21W-5N	E1
300	BmdT	60143	2913	21W-6N	E6
300	BmdT	60157	2913	21W-6N	E6
400	ITSC	60143	2969	21W-5N	E1
Nevada Av					
10000	FNPK	60131	2973	12W-3N	B5
10400	LydT	60131	2973	13W-3N	A6
10400	LydT	60164	2973	13W-3N	A6
10600	LydT	60164	2972	13W-3N	E6
E Nevada Av					
10	GLHT	60139	2968	23W-3N	E6
W Nevada Av					
10	GLHT	60139	2968	24W-3N	D6
Nevada Ct					
1700	ODPK	60467	3423	13W-21S	A7
3700	NCHI	60088	2593	12W-30N	C2
Nevada Ln					
1500	EGVV	60007	2859	21W-9N	E7
Nevada St					
300	FKFT	60423	3592	11W-26S	A2
400	FftT	60423	3592	11W-26S	A2
W Nevada St					
1000	GNWD	60425	3428	1W-22S	A7
1100	HMWD	60425	3428	1W-22S	A7
1100	HMWD	60430	3428	1W-22S	A7
Nevada A Ct					
300	FKFT	60423	3592	11W-26S	A2
Nevada B Ct					
400	FKFT	60423	3592	11W-26S	A2
N Nevelier Rd					
40700	AntT	60002	2416	24W-40N	C2
S Neville Ct					
-	BMDL	60108	2969	23W-5N	A1
Neville Dr					
300	GYLK	60030	2532	21W-32N	E5
Neville Rd					
-	ISLK	60051	2586	29W-29N	D3
-	NndT	60051	2586	29W-29N	D3
28600	WcnT	60051	2586	28W-30N	E3
28600	WcnT	60051	2587	28W-30N	A3
Nevin Av					
10700	ALGN	60102	2694	34W-21N	C6
Nevis Dr					
1400	NPVL	60565	3204	24W-8S	C2
Nevqua St					
-	WnfT	60510	3080	30W-1S	A2
New Av					
-	LKPT	60441	3419	22W-18S	D1
-	LktT	60441	3419	22W-18S	D1
12300	DPgT	60441	3269	21W-14S	E7
12300	DPgT	60441	3270	21W-14S	A7
12300	DPgT	60441	3341	22W-17S	D6
12500	RMVL	60441	3341	22W-15S	D2
13900	LKPT	60441	3341	22W-17S	D5
13900	LktT	60441	3341	22W-16S	D4
E New Av					
10	LMNT	60439	3270	19W-13S	C5
S New Av					
300	LKPT	60441	3419	22W-18S	D1
300	LktT	60441	3419	22W-18S	D1
12200	DPgT	60441	3270	21W-14S	A6
12200	LmnT	60439	3270	21W-14S	A6
15200	LKPT	60441	3341	22W-18S	D7
15200	LktT	60441	3341	22W-18S	D7
W New Av					
10	LmnT	60439	3270	20W-14S	B6
200	DPgT	60441	3270	20W-14S	A6
New St					
200	LMBD	60148	3026	19W-0S	C6
2700	BLID	60406	3349	3W-15S	A1
E New St					
10	JLET	60432	3499	23W-24S	A5
10	JLET	60433	3499	23W-24S	A5
10	JLET	60436	3499	23W-24S	A5
N New St					
400	CHCG	60611	3034	0E-0N	D3
New Abby Dr					
10	IVNS	60010	2803	25W-16N	E1
10	IVNS	60010	2804	25W-16N	A1
New Albany Rd					
6300	LSLE	60532	3142	24W-7S	C6
N Newark Av					
5600	CHCG	60656	2918	8W-7N	E4
6100	CHCG	60631	2918	8W-7N	E3
6400	CHCG	60714	2918	8W-8N	E2
6500	NLES	60631	2918	8W-8N	E2
7100	NLES	60714	2918	8W-8N	E1
Newark Ln					
200	HFET	60169	2858	24W-10N	E5
S Newberg Ct					
14200	PnfT	60544	3339	27W-16S	C5
Newberry Av					
10	LGNG	60525	3087	12W-4S	C6
100	LYVL	60048	2591	16W-29N	D4
300	LGPK	60525	3087	12W-3S	C5
1500	PvsT	60525	3087	12W-2S	C4
4600	OKFT	60452	3426	5W-19S	B3
S Newberry Av					
1600	CHCG	60608	3092		E2
20700	FftT	60423	3504	10W-25S	D7
Newberry Ct					
10	AURA	60504	3201	31W-8S	E1
10	ELGN	60124	2853	37W-11N	D4
400	LKZH	60047	2699	22W-21N	A6
N Newberry Ct					
22400	KLDR	60047	2699	20W-22N	E4
Newberry Dr					
300	EGVV	60007	2859	22W-9N	C7
300	EGVV	60007	2913	22W-9N	C1
500	SMWD	60107	2857	27W-10N	C6
700	BTVA	60510	3078	34W-1S	D2
Newberry Ln					
1600	WHTN	60187	3082	24W-1S	D2
4200	JLET	60586	3496	29W-21S	D1
N Newberry Ln					
1000	MPPT	60056	2808	14W-14N	C5
W Newberry Ln					
25100	LkvT	60046	2474	25W-37N	B2
Newberry Wy					
24800	PNFD	60585	3338	31W-14S	A1
Newbold Rd					
7600	AlqT	60013	2642	29W-24N	C7
7600	AlqT	60013	2696	29W-23N	C1
New Bond Rd					
100	SgrT	60506	3135	41W-5S	E3
100	SgrT	60554	3135	41W-5S	E3
Newbridge Cir					
1700	ELGN	60123	2907	36W-8N	E3
New Bridge Ct					
200	RGMW	60067	2805	21W-13N	D5
600	BRTN	60010	2698	25W-20N	B7
N New Bridge Ct					
36000	WrnT	60031	2477	17W-36N	C4
Newbridge Dr					
1200	LKPT	60441	3342	21W-18S	A7
Newbridge Ln					
100	RDLK	60073	2532	23W-32N	A6
200	RDLK	60073	2531	23W-32N	E5
N New Britton Dr					
4000	HFET	60192	2804	24W-15N	C3
W New Britton Dr					
1200	HFET	60192	2804	24W-15N	C3
New Britton Rd					
800	CLSM	60188	2967	28W-3N	B6
N Newburg Av					
5900	CHCG	60631	2919	8W-7N	A4
5900	CHCG	60646	2919	8W-7N	A4
6100	CHCG	60631	2918	8W-7N	E3
Newburg Ct					
1100	CLSM	60188	2967	26W-4N	E4
Newburn Ct					
1600	WLNG	60090	2754	16W-18N	D3
Newbury Ct					
10	HNWD	60047	2700	20W-24N	A1
10	LIHL	60156	2692	39W-23N	D2
800	GYLK	60030	2533	19W-33N	B2
800	SMBG	60173	2859	22W-11N	C3
6000	GRNE	60031	2534	16W-33N	D3
16400	LktT	60403	3418	25W-19S	B4
Newbury Dr					
200	ISLK	60042	2586	29W-28N	C5
500	NndT	60042	2586	29W-28N	C5
900	CLLK	60014	2639	36W-24N	C7
7900	ODPK	60462	3346	9W-16S	D3
New Bury Ln					
200	YKVL	60560	3261	42W-13S	D5
Newbury Ln					
10	MDLN	60060	2646	20W-27N	B1
200	BGBK	60440	3269	23W-12S	A2
600	SMBG	60173	2859	22W-11N	C3
5900	MTSN	60443	3505	7W-25S	C7
S Newbury Pl					
300	ANHT	60005	2807	17W-13N	B5
Newbury St					
10600	WSTR	60154	3087	13W-2S	A3
New Castle Av					
7700	BDPK	60638	3211	8W-8S	A1
7700	BRBK	60459	3211	8W-9S	A2
7700	BRBK	60638	3211	8W-8S	A1
8100	BGVW	60455	3211	8W-9S	A3
8100	BGVW	60459	3211	8W-9S	A3
8100	BRBK	60459	3211	8W-9S	A3
8600	OKLN	60453	3211	8W-9S	A4
8600	OKLN	60459	3211	8W-9S	A4
Newcastle Av					
1200	WSTR	60154	3029	12W-1S	B7
1400	WSTR	60154	3087	12W-1S	B1
2100	PvsT	60154	3087	12W-1S	B2
9100	MNGV	60053	2864	8W-11N	E3
N Newcastle Av					
1600	CHCG	60302	3030	8W-1N	E1
1600	CHCG	60707	3030	8W-1N	E1
1600	OKPK	60302	3030	8W-1N	E1
2400	CHCG	60707	2974	8W-3N	E5
2700	CHCG	60634	2974	8W-3N	E4
4200	HDHT	60706	2974	8W-5N	E1
4700	HDHT	60706	2918	8W-5N	E7
4800	CHCG	60706	2918	8W-6N	E6
5400	CHCG	60656	2918	8W-6N	E5
6200	CHCG	60631	2918	8W-7N	E3
6400	CHCG	60714	2918	8W-8N	E2
6400	NLES	60714	2918	8W-8N	E2
6500	NLES	60631	2918	8W-8N	E2
8200	NLES	60714	2864	8W-10N	E5
S Newcastle Av					
5100	CHCG	60638	3149	8W-6S	A3
5100	FTVW	60638	3149	8W-5S	A2
5100	StkT	60638	3149	8W-5S	A2
New Castle Ct					
10	CLLK	60014	2694	35W-24N	A1
10	WDRG	60517	3206	20W-9S	B3
100	RGMW	60008	2805	22W-13N	B5
Newcastle Ct					
10	MDLN	60060	2647	17W-27N	B1
400	ROSL	60172	2912	24W-7N	E4
1300	BRLT	60103	2967	28W-5N	A2
1400	IVNS	60010	2751	25W-17N	A5
9000	TYPK	60487	3423	11W-21S	E7
9000	TYPK	60487	3424	11W-21S	A7
22600	DRPK	60010	2752	22W-20N	A1
E Newcastle Ct					
3100	WKGN	60087	2479	11W-37N	D2
S Newcastle Ct					
22300	TroT	60404	3584	30W-27S	C4
W Newcastle Ct					
3000	WKGN	60087	2479	11W-37N	D2
New Castle Dr					
-	AlqT	60013	2642	30W-25N	B6
-	CRY	60013	2642	30W-25N	A5
-	RMVL	60446	3339	27W-17S	C5
1100	LbvT	60048	2591	17W-30N	B3
1100	LYVL	60048	2591	17W-30N	B3
7500	FftT	60423	3504	9W-23S	E4
Newcastle Dr					
400	ROSL	60172	2912	24W-7N	D4
500	LKFT	60045	2649	12W-25N	B5
Newcastle Ln					
10	LNSH	60069	2703	13W-22N	A3
200	BGBK	60440	3269	22W-13S	D4
700	PTHT	60070	2808	14W-15N	C2
700	WLNG	60090	2808	14W-15N	C2
1000	AURA	60506	3137	37W-6S	C5
1200	HFET	60169	2858	25W-12N	B2
1300	BRLT	60103	2967	28W-5N	B1
W Newcastle Ln					
13100	BHPK	60083	2421	13W-39N	A6
New Castle Rd					
10	LslT	60540	3142	25W-6S	B4
Newcastle Rd					
500	NLNX	60451	3589	18W-25S	A1
3200	WKGN	60087	2479	11W-38N	D1
Newcastle St					
24100	PNFD	60585	3338	30W-15S	C1
Newcastle Wy					
16400	LKPT	60441	3421	18W-19S	A3
New Deerpath Rd					
-	AURA	60506	3136	39W-4S	E2
-	SgrT	60506	3136	39W-4S	E2
New Devon St					
9800	MNSR	46321	3510		C4
Newell Av					
700	CTCY	60409	3352	3E-18S	A7
Newell St					
100	WDSK	60098	2524	41W-31N	D7
New England Av					
-	BDPK	60638	3149	8W-7S	A6
-	NHBK	60062	2757	8W-18N	E2
7700	BDPK	60638	3211	8W-9S	A2
7700	BRBK	60638	3211	8W-9S	A2
8300	BGVW	60455	3211	8W-9S	A4
8300	BGVW	60459	3211	8W-9S	A4
8300	BRBK	60455	3211	8W-9S	A4
8700	BGVW	60453	3211	8W-10S	A4
8700	BRBK	60459	3211	8W-10S	A4
8700	OKLN	60453	3211	8W-10S	A4
8700	OKLN	60459	3211	8W-10S	A4
9100	MNGV	60053	2864	8W-11N	E3
9600	CHRG	60415	3211	8W-11S	A6
9600	CHRG	60453	3211	8W-11S	A6
15500	OKFT	60452	3347	8W-18S	A7
15600	BmnT	60452	3347	8W-18S	A7
15600	BmnT	60477	3347	8W-18S	A7
15700	BmnT	60477	3425	8W-18S	A1
16700	TYPK	60477	3425	8W-20S	A4
N New England Av					
1600	CHCG	60302	3030	8W-1N	E1
1600	CHCG	60707	3030	8W-1N	E1
1600	OKPK	60302	3030	8W-1N	E1
2400	CHCG	60707	2974	8W-3N	E5
2700	CHCG	60634	2974	8W-3N	E4
4200	HDHT	60634	2974	8W-5N	E1
4200	HDHT	60706	2974	8W-5N	E1
4400	HDHT	60706	2918	8W-5N	E7
4800	CHCG	60656	2918	8W-6N	E6
6400	CHCG	60631	2918	8W-8N	E2
6400	CHCG	60714	2918	8W-8N	E2
6400	NLES	60714	2918	8W-8N	E2
8300	MNGV	60053	2864	8W-10N	E5
8300	NLES	60714	2864	8W-10N	E5
S New England Av					
5100	StkT	60638	3148	8W-5S	E2
6300	CHCG	60638	3148	8W-7S	E5
6400	BDPK	60638	3148	8W-7S	E5
10700	WRTH	60482	3275	8W-12S	A2
Newfield Ct					
100	BFGV	60089	2701	16W-21N	C5
Newfield Dr					
10	BFGV	60089	2701	16W-21N	D6
Newfield Ln					
7600	TYPK	60477	3504	9W-23S	D3
N Newgard Av					
6400	CHCG	60626	2921	1W-8N	D2
6400	CHCG	60660	2921	1W-8N	D2
Newgate Av					
10	NPVL	60565	3203	26W-10S	E5
Newgate Ct					
-	BFGV	60069	2701	16W-21N	E5
-	VrnT	60069	2701	16W-21N	E5
10	LKZH	60047	2699	22W-22N	B4
300	SMBG	60193	2859	23W-10N	B5
1400	LYVL	60048	2591	17W-28N	A6
1600	BFGV	60089	2701	16W-21N	D5
1600	GRNE	60031	2477	17W-35N	A5
14000	ODPK	60462	3346	10W-16S	B3
Newgate Ln					
700	PTHT	60070	2808	14W-14N	C3
New Gross Point Rd					
-	NLES	60714	2865	7W-9N	C6
-	SKOK	60077	2865	7W-9N	C6
-	SKOK	60714	2865	7W-9N	C6
N New Hampshire Av					
5600	CHCG	60631	2918	8W-7N	E4
New Hampshire Ct					
17700	ODPK	60467	3423	12W-20S	C5
New Hampshire Tr					
4300	NndT	60012	2584	35W-27N	A7
4400	NndT	60012	2640	35W-27N	A1
6800	NndT	60012	2583	35W-27N	E7
New Haven Av					
400	AURA	60506	3138	36W-6S	A5
500	AURA	60506	3137	36W-6S	D5
3900	ANHT	60004	2753	19W-18N	D3
3900	PltT	60004	2753	19W-18N	D3
4200	GRNE	60031	2535	14W-33N	D3
New Haven Ct					
2300	NPVL	60564	3202	29W-10S	D5
5100	JLET	60586	3496	30W-22S	B1
New Haven Dr					
10	CLLK	60013	2695	33W-23N	A1
10	CRY	60013	2695	33W-23N	A1
300	CLLK	60013	2641	32W-24N	A7
300	CRY	60013	2641	32W-24N	A7
2400	NPVL	60564	3202	29W-10S	D6
Newhaven Dr					
10	ElaT	60047	2644	23W-25N	E5
10	HNWD	60047	2644	23W-25N	E5
W Newhaven Dr					
23400	ElaT	60047	2644	23W-25N	E5
23400	HNWD	60047	2644	23W-25N	E5
New Hope Rd					
100	LslT	60540	3142	25W-6S	B4
New House Ln					
200	RLKP	60073	2532	23W-33N	A3
W New Indian Trail Ct					
300	AURA	60506	3138	36W-5S	A4
New Jersey Ct					
17700	ODPK	60467	3423	13W-21S	A6
W Newkirk Dr					
400	PNFD	60544	3416	30W-18S	C1
N Newkirk Ln					
700	PLTN	60074	2753	19W-16N	D6
Newland Av					
700	RMVL	60446	3340	24W-15S	C3
7700	BDPK	60459	3210	8W-9S	E3
7700	BDPK	60638	3210	8W-8S	E2
7700	BRBK	60459	3210	8W-9S	E3
7700	BRBK	60638	3210	8W-8S	E2
8200	BGVW	60455	3210	8W-9S	E3
8200	BGVW	60459	3210	8W-9S	E3
8300	BRBK	60455	3210	8W-9S	E3
8500	BRBK	60459	3211	8W-9S	A4
8700	BGVW	60453	3211	8W-10S	A4
8700	BGVW	60455	3211	8W-10S	A4
8700	OKLN	60453	3211	8W-10S	A4
8700	OKLN	60459	3211	8W-10S	A4
N Newland Av					
1600	CHCG	60302	3030	8W-2N	E1
1600	CHCG	60707	3030	8W-1N	E1
1600	OKPK	60302	3030	8W-1N	E1
2300	CHCG	60707	2974	8W-3N	E5
3600	CHCG	60634	2974	8W-4N	E2
4200	HDHT	60634	2974	8W-5N	E1
4200	HDHT	60706	2974	8W-5N	E1
4200	NRDG	60634	2974	8W-5N	E1
4200	NRDG	60706	2974	8W-5N	E1
4700	HDHT	60706	2918	8W-5N	E7
5200	CHCG	60656	2918	8W-6N	E5
6400	CHCG	60631	2918	8W-8N	E2
8200	NLES	60714	2864	8W-10N	E5
S Newland Av					
5100	CHCG	60638	3148	8W-6S	E3
5100	StkT	60638	3148	8W-5S	E2
Newland Pl					
600	BmdT	60143	2913	21W-6N	E6
New Lenox Rd					
800	JLET	60433	3499	22W-24S	C7
800	JltT	60433	3499	22W-24S	D7
1600	JLET	60433	3500	21W-24S	A7
1600	JltT	60433	3500	21W-24S	A7
2100	NLNX	60433	3500	20W-24S	C6
2100	NLNX	60451	3500	20W-24S	D6
2100	NlxT	60433	3500	21W-24S	A7
2100	NlxT	60451	3500	20W-24S	D6
New London Ct					
1300	CLSM	60188	2967	28W-3N	B5
Newman Ct					
300	LKBF	60044	2594	10W-28N	A6
600	RMVL	60446	3340	24W-15S	C2
1500	NPVL	60564	3266	28W-11S	E1
Newman Pl					
4300	HFET	60067	2804	23W-15N	D2
4300	HFET	60192	2804	23W-15N	D2
4300	IVNS	60067	2804	23W-15N	D2
New Market Av					
3200	CPVL	60110	2747	36W-18N	A5
Newmarket Dr					
10500	WldT	60564	3266	30W-12S	B3
New Mexico Ct					
700	EGVV	60007	2913	21W-9N	E1
10900	ODPK	60467	3423	13W-21S	A6
New Mexico Tr					
600	EGVV	60007	2859	21W-9N	E7
600	EGVV	60007	2913	21W-9N	E1
New Mills Ct					
300	SMBG	60193	2859	23W-10N	B6
Newport Av					
10	EGVV	60007	2914	19W-8N	D3
600	WTMT	60559	3085	16W-4S	D7
W Newport Av					
800	CHCG	60657	2977	1W-4N	D3
1900	CHCG	60618	2977	2W-4N	B3
4000	CHCG	60618	2976	5W-4N	B3
4000	CHCG	60641	2976	5W-4N	B3
5500	CHCG	60634	2975	7W-4N	C3
5500	CHCG	60641	2975	7W-4N	C3
7000	CHCG	60634	2974	8W-4N	E3
Newport Blvd					
-	BRLT	60103	2911	28W-7N	B4
-	HRPK	60103	2911	27W-6N	D6
-	HRPK	60133	2911	27W-6N	D6
-	WynT	60103	2911	27W-7N	B5
Newport Cir					
-	PGGV	60140	2797	42W-15N	D4
400	OSWG	60543	3264	35W-11S	B1
600	LNHT	60046	2417	21W-39N	D6
2000	HRPK	60133	2911	27W-6N	C6
Newport Ct					
-	PGGV	60140	2797	42W-15N	D4
500	ISLK	60042	2586	29W-28N	C5
700	ElgT	60124	2853	37W-10N	C5
800	BFGV	60089	2701	18W-20N	A7
1700	GRNE	60031	2477	16W-36N	E5
N Newport Ct					
4000	ANHT	60004	2753	18W-18N	D3
S Newport Ct					
100	LKFT	60045	2649	13W-25N	A4
W Newport Ct					
1700	LKFT	60045	2649	13W-25N	A4
1700	VrnT	60045	2649	13W-25N	A4
Newport Dr					
-	HmrT	60441	3421	17W-19S	C2
-	HmrT	60491	3421	17W-19S	C2
-	LKPT	60441	3421	17W-19S	C2
100	BGBK	60440	3268	23W-12S	E2
400	NPVL	60565	3203	27W-10S	C5
500	ISLK	60042	2586	29W-28N	B6
2000	JLET	60431	3417	28W-21S	B7
5000	RGMW	60008	2860	19W-12N	B1
5100	OKFT	60452	3425	6W-20S	E3
5100	OKFT	60452	3426	6W-20S	A3

STREET Block	City	ZIP	Map#	CGS	Grid
Newport Dr					
7000	WDRG	60517	3143	21W-7S	E7
19300	MKNA	60448	3504	11W-23S	A3
24300	CRTE	60417	3685	1W-29S	A2
S Newport Dr					
12700	PlsT	60464	3273	12W-15S	C7
12700	PlsT	60464	3345	12W-15S	C1
Newport Hbr					
1000	SMBG	60193	2913	23W-9N	B1
Newport Ln					
-	MTGY	60506	3198	40W-9S	B4
-	MTGY	60538	3198	40W-9S	B5
100	YkTp	60523	3084	19W-2S	D4
300	AURA	60504	3201	31W-8S	E2
300	BRLT	60103	2911	28W-8N	B4
1400	IVNS	60010	2751	25W-17N	A6
2200	GNVA	60134	3019	36W-1N	D3
N Newport Ln					
-	WKGN	60083	2478	14W-37N	C1
4000	ANHT	60004	2753	19W-18N	D2
4000	PltT	60004	2753	18W-18N	D2
Newport Rd					
1800	DRGV	60516	3144	20W-7S	A7
1800	DRGV	60517	3144	20W-7S	A7
2400	NHBK	60062	2809	10W-16N	E1
2400	NHBK	60062	2810	10W-15N	A1
N Newport Rd					
1600	HFET	60169	2858	23W-12N	E1
W Newport Rd					
300	HFET	60169	2804	24W-12N	E7
Newport St					
1200	MDLN	60060	2647	17W-25N	A5
1700	GLHT	60139	2968	23W-3N	E5
5300	LSLE	60532	3142	23W-5S	E3
W Newport St					
700	ROSL	60172	2912	24W-6N	D6
Newport Tr					
100	MHRY	60050	2527	34W-32N	C6
Newport Wy					
3900	PltT	60004	2753	19W-18N	C3
Newport North St					
600	ROSL	60172	2912	24W-6N	D6
Newport S St					
600	ROSL	60172	2912	24W-6N	D6
New Salem St					
300	PKFT	60466	3595	3W-25S	B1
400	PKFT	60466	3507	3W-25S	B7
New Sutton Rd					
-	BNHL	60010	2803	28W-15N	A1
-	BrnT	60010	2803	28W-15N	A1
-	BrnT	60192	2802	28W-13N	E6
-	HnrT	60010	2802	29W-12N	D7
100	BNHL	60010	2750	27W-16N	B6
100	BrnT	60010	2750	27W-16N	B6
700	BNHL	60010	2802	28W-14N	E5
700	BNHL	60118	2802	28W-14N	E4
700	BrnT	60010	2802	28W-14N	E4
700	BrnT	60118	2802	28W-14N	E4
2500	HFET	60010	2802	29W-12N	D7
2500	HFET	60192	2802	28W-13N	E6
2700	SBTN	60010	2802	28W-13N	E6
New Sutton Rd SR-59					
-	BNHL	60010	2803	28W-15N	A1
-	BrnT	60010	2803	28W-15N	A1
-	BrnT	60192	2802	28W-13N	E6
-	HnrT	60010	2802	29W-12N	D7
100	BNHL	60010	2750	27W-16N	B6
100	BrnT	60010	2750	27W-16N	B6
700	BNHL	60010	2802	28W-14N	E5
700	BNHL	60118	2802	28W-14N	E4
700	BrnT	60010	2802	28W-14N	E4
700	BrnT	60118	2802	28W-14N	E4
2500	HFET	60010	2802	29W-12N	D7
2500	HFET	60192	2802	28W-13N	E6
2700	SBTN	60010	2802	28W-13N	E6
New Sutton Rd SR-68					
100	BNHL	60010	2750	27W-16N	B6
100	BrnT	60010	2750	27W-16N	B6
Newton Av					
10	GNEN	60137	3025	23W-0S	A7
300	GLHT	60137	3025	23W-1N	B2
300	GLHT	60139	3025	23W-1N	B2
300	MltT	60137	3025	23W-1N	B2
300	MltT	60139	3025	23W-1N	B2
700	BmdT	60137	3025	23W-1N	B2
1100	BTVA	60510	3077	36W-2S	E3
1200	BTVA	60510	3078	36W-2S	A4
1600	PKRG	60068	2918	9W-7N	B4
2000	CHCG	60631	2918	9W-7N	B4
2000	PKRG	60631	2918	9W-7N	B4
2600	NPVL	60564	3202	29W-10S	C5
S Newton Av					
1400	JLET	60433	3587	23W-25S	B1
1400	JltT	60433	3587	23W-25S	B1
Newton Ct					
400	BGBK	60440	3205	22W-11S	D7
600	SMBG	60194	2857	26W-11N	E4
1100	BTVA	60510	3077	36W-2S	E3
2600	AURA	60502	3079	32W-4S	C7
Newton Ln					
-	BbyT	60134	3076	39W-1S	D1
E Newton Pl					
300	JLET	60433	3499	23W-24S	A5
Newton Rd					
9600	HTLY	60142	2692	40W-22N	A4
Newton Sq					
10	BbyT	60134	3076	39W-1S	D1
Newton St					
200	HFET	60169	2858	23W-10N	E5
200	HFET	60194	2858	23W-10N	E5
200	SMBG	60194	2858	23W-10N	E5
Newton Wy					
19900	MKNA	60448	3503	12W-24S	D5
Newtown Ct E					
10	BFGV	60089	2701	16W-20N	D7
Newtown Ct W					
10	BFGV	60089	2701	16W-20N	D7
Newtown Dr					
10	BFGV	60089	2701	16W-20N	D7
400	BFGV	60069	2701	16W-20N	E7
400	VrnT	60069	2701	16W-20N	E7
New Trier Ct					
1000	WLMT	60091	2811	6W-14N	C5
N New Venice Wy					
43100	AntT	60002	2357	24W-43N	B4
S New Wilke Rd					
-	RGMW	60005	2806	19W-12N	D7
1100	ANHT	60005	2806	19W-12N	D7
1100	ANHT	60008	2806	19W-12N	D7
1100	RGMW	60008	2806	19W-12N	D7
1200	ANHT	60005	2860	19W-12N	D2
1400	RGMW	60005	2860	19W-12N	D1
1400	RGMW	60008	2860	19W-12N	D1
New York Av					
-	AURA	60502	3139	32W-7S	D7
-	AURA	60504	3139	32W-7S	D7
2400	NCHI	60088	2593	12W-29N	C3
N New York Av					
3200	BHPK	60087	2479	11W-37N	E1
3200	WKGN	60087	2479	11W-37N	E1
New York Ct					
11000	ODPK	60467	3423	13W-21S	A6
New York Ln					
400	EGVV	60007	2859	22W-9N	C7
400	EGVV	60007	2913	22W-9N	C1
New York St					
700	WKGN	60085	2479	11W-35N	E7
2200	WKGN	60087	2479	11W-36N	E4
E New York St					
-	AURA	60506	3138	35W-7S	B7
10	AURA	60505	3138	35W-7S	B7
400	AURA	60505	3200	34W-7S	C1
1500	AURA	60505	3139	32W-7S	C7
1700	AURA	60502	3139	32W-7S	C7
1900	AraT	60502	3139	33W-7S	B7
1900	AraT	60505	3139	33W-7S	B7
2800	AURA	60504	3139	31W-7S	E7
3100	NpvT	60502	3139	31W-7S	E7
3100	NpvT	60504	3139	31W-7S	E7
3500	AURA	60504	3140	30W-7S	B7
4200	NpvT	60504	3140	30W-7S	B7
4300	NPVL	60504	3140	30W-7S	B7
W New York St					
10	AURA	60505	3138	35W-7S	B7
10	AURA	60506	3138	35W-7S	A7
500	AURA	60506	3137	36W-7S	E7
W New York St SR-31					
100	AURA	60506	3138	35W-7S	A7
Neyer Cir					
10	NCHI	60088	2537	10W-31N	A6
Nez Perce Ct					
500	CLSM	60188	2967	27W-2N	C7
Nez Perce Ln					
400	LKVL	60046	2474	24W-37N	D2
400	LkvT	60046	2474	24W-37N	D2
Niada Ter					
400	HDPK	60035	2704	8W-23N	D3
E Niagara Av					
200	EMHT	60126	3028	15W-0N	A4
400	SMBG	60193	2913	22W-8N	B2
400	SmbT	60193	2913	22W-8N	B2
N Niagara Av					
6200	CHCG	60631	2918	8W-7N	E3
W Niagara Av					
10	SMBG	60193	2913	23W-8N	A2
Niagara Ct					
2100	ELGN	60123	2853	36W-12N	E2
W Niagara Ct					
22200	PnfT	60544	3339	27W-16S	B4
Niagara Dr					
600	BGBK	60440	3269	21W-11S	E1
Niagara St					
-	LKMR	60041	2530	28W-32N	A5
-	LKMR	60051	2530	28W-32N	A5
-	LMNT	60439	3271	17W-13S	B5
300	PKFT	60466	3595	3W-27S	A5
W Niagara Tr					
22200	PnfT	60544	3339	27W-16S	B5
Niagra Dr					
5700	WRLK	60097	2469	36W-37N	E1
Niagra Ln					
11600	HTLY	60142	2745	39W-20N	C1
Niagra St					
700	CLSM	60188	2967	26W-3N	E5
Niamh Ct					
22800	RNPK	60471	3594	4W-27S	D5
Niblick Ct					
3800	PRGV	60012	2585	31W-28N	D6
Niblick Knoll Ct					
28900	FmtT	60060	2589	22W-28N	C5
Nicanoa Ln					
3700	NPVL	60564	3266	30W-11S	B1
Niccon Tr					
600	DndT	60102	2747	34W-19N	E2
Nicholas Av					
1200	SCRL	60174	3020	34W-2N	D1
Nicholas Blvd					
700	EGvT	60007	2861	16W-9N	D7
700	EGVV	60007	2861	16W-9N	D7
700	EGVV	60007	2915	16W-9N	D1
2000	BNVL	60106	2915	16W-8N	D3
Nicholas Cir					
100	HPSR	60140	2795	47W-15N	E4
Nicholas Ct					
10	BGBK	60490	3267	26W-11S	E1
1500	NPVL	60563	3141	27W-5S	B2
2600	JLET	60586	3416	30W-20S	A5
3900	AURA	60504	3202	30W-8S	A3
5200	OKFT	60452	3425	6W-20S	E5
Nicholas Dr					
1400	BGBK	60490	3267	26W-11S	E1
Nicholas Ln					
9100	SPGV	60081	2414	29W-41N	C2
Nichole Ln					
600	GNVA	60134	3020	33W-1N	E2
600	GNVA	60134	3021	33W-1N	A2
600	SCRL	60134	3021	33W-1N	A2
600	SCRL	60174	3021	33W-1N	A2
Nicholl Av					
100	GNEN	60137	3025	22W-0S	C7
S Nicholl Av					
10	GNEN	60137	3083	22W-1S	C1
Nicholl Wy					
10	GNEN	60137	3083	22W-1S	C1
Nichols Av					
3500	FNPK	60131	2973	11W-4N	C3
Nichols Dr					
-	LYWD	60411	3509	2E-23S	D3
2800	SLVL	60411	3597	3E-26S	E3
2800	SLVL	60411	3598	3E-27S	A4
Nichols Ln					
1100	MYWD	60153	3030	10W-1N	A2
Nichols Rd					
13600	HbnT	60034	2350	42W-42N	B5
13800	AdnT	60034	2350	43W-43N	A4
14500	AdnT	60034	2349	43W-43N	E4
E Nichols Rd					
1000	PLTN	60074	2753	19W-18N	C2
W Nichols Rd					
-	ANHT	60004	2754	18W-18N	A3
-	ANHT	60089	2754	18W-18N	A3
-	BFGV	60004	2754	18W-18N	A3
-	BFGV	60089	2754	18W-18N	A3
-	ElaT	60004	2753	19W-18N	C2
-	ElaT	60047	2753	19W-18N	C2
500	BFGV	60004	2753	18W-18N	E3
500	BFGV	60089	2753	18W-18N	E3
2200	ANHT	60004	2753	19W-18N	C2
2200	PltT	60004	2753	19W-18N	C2
Nicholson Dr					
1600	HFET	60192	2856	30W-12N	B1
1600	HnrT	60192	2856	30W-12N	B1
Nicholson Rd					
-	HDPK	60035	2650	9W-24N	D6
-	LKFT	60035	2650	9W-24N	C7
Nicholson St					
1600	CTHL	60403	3498	24W-21S	D1
1600	JLET	60435	3498	24W-21S	D1
1700	CTHL	60403	3418	24W-21S	D7
N Nicholson St					
10	JLET	60436	3498	24W-23S	D5
800	JLET	60435	3498	24W-22S	D2
N Nickerson Av					
5800	CHCG	60631	2918	8W-7N	E4
N Nicklaus Ct					
1600	VNHL	60061	2647	16W-27N	D1
Nicklaus Ln					
9200	LKWD	60014	2692	38W-23N	E1
9300	LKWD	60014	2693	38W-23N	A1
N Nicklaus Ln					
-	WKGN	60083	2478	14W-37N	C2
W Nicklaus Wy					
24700	AntT	60002	2416	24W-39N	B4
24700	LkvT	60002	2416	24W-39N	B4
Nickolas Ct					
1800	GLHT	60139	2968	24W-3N	D5
Nickolsen Av					
100	WNFD	60190	3081	27W-0S	D1
Nicola Dr					
-	ELGN	60120	2855	32W-12N	D2
Nicole Av					
10	WCDA	60084	2643	26W-26N	E2
10	WcnT	60084	2643	26W-26N	E2
Nicole Ct					
15200	ODPK	60462	3346	10W-18S	B7
Nicole Dr					
-	WldT	60564	3202	29W-10S	D7
10	SEGN	60177	2907	37W-8N	C3
400	BRLT	60103	2911	27W-6N	C6
2900	NPVL	60564	3202	29W-10S	D7
N Nicole Ln					
1700	RLKB	60073	2475	23W-35N	A6
Nicole Finney Ct					
-	DLTN	60419	3351	1E-17S	A5
-	DLTN	60473	3351	1E-17S	A5
-	SHLD	60419	3351	1E-17S	A5
-	SHLD	60473	3351	1E-17S	A5
N Nicolet Av					
5800	CHCG	60631	2918	8W-7N	D4
Nicolette Av					
10	SMBG	60173	2859	21W-10N	D5
Nicolette Dr					
3400	CRTE	60417	3597	1E-28S	B5
3400	STGR	60475	3597	1E-28S	B5
Nicoll Wy					
10	GNEN	60137	3025	22W-0S	C7
Nicollet Ln					
11200	GfnT	60142	2691	41W-20N	D7
Nida Ct					
8800	HYHL	60457	3210	11W-10S	A5
Nielsen Dr					
8400	TYPK	60477	3424	10W-21S	B7
8400	TYPK	60487	3424	10W-21S	B7
N Nielsen Dr					
35100	AvnT	60073	2474	24W-35N	C6
Nielsen Plz					
-	GNVW	60062	2809	12W-15N	B1
10	NfdT	60062	2809	12W-15N	B2
10	PTHT	60062	2809	12W-15N	B2
W Nielson Dr					
-	LkvT	60073	2475	22W-36N	C3
-	RLKB	60073	2475	22W-36N	C3
21800	LkvT	60046	2475	21W-36N	C3
Nielson Ln					
500	DGvT	60527	3207	16W-10S	E6
8000	TYPK	60477	3424	10W-21S	C7
Niess Ct					
1400	GLHT	60139	2968	23W-2N	E7
Nightengale Cir					
1500	LNHT	60046	2417	21W-38N	E7
1500	LNHT	60046	2475	20W-38N	E1
S Nightengale Dr					
1000	PLTN	60067	2805	22W-14N	B4
Nightengale Ter					
18600	CCHL	60478	3506	6W-22S	A1
Nighthawk Ct					
3900	NPVL	60564	3266	29W-11S	D2
Nighthawk Wy					
6900	AlqT	60013	2642	30W-24N	A7
6900	CRY	60013	2642	30W-24N	A7
Nightingale Ct					
24000	PNFD	60585	3266	30W-14S	C7
Nightingale Ln					
1300	BRLT	60103	2967	28W-5N	B1
19000	CCHL	60478	3506	6W-22S	A2
Night Shade Ln					
800	SRWD	60404	3496	31W-22S	A3
Nightshade Ln					
-	JLET	60447	3495	33W-22S	A3
Night Song Ct					
1900	SMBG	60194	2857	26W-11N	E3
Nike Pkwy					
-	VNHL	60061	2647	16W-24N	D7
Nike Rd					
-	AddT	60101	2970	20W-2N	B7
-	ADSN	60101	2970	20W-2N	B7
Niles Av					
10	LKFT	60045	2649	10W-24N	E7
100	AddT	60101	2971	18W-4N	A4
100	ADSN	60101	2971	18W-4N	A4
100	LKFT	60045	2650	10W-24N	A7
7800	SKOK	60077	2865	6W-9N	E6
W Niles Av					
7100	NLES	60714	2864	8W-10N	D4
W Niles Ter					
6900	NLES	60714	2864	8W-9N	E7
Niles Center Rd					
7200	SKOK	60077	2865	6W-9N	D7
8800	SKOK	60076	2865	6W-11N	E3
9000	SKOK	60076	2866	5W-11N	A3
Nimco Dr					
1000	CLLK	60014	2640	33W-24N	D7
1000	CLLK	60014	2694	33W-24N	D1
Nimitz Av					
10	NCHI	60064	2537	10W-31N	A7
10	NCHI	60088	2537	10W-31N	A7
Nimitz Dr					
-	GNVW	60025	2810	9W-14N	C4
2000	DSPN	60018	2917	12W-8N	D2
5100	MchT	60097	2469	35W-37N	E3
Nimitz Rd					
400	OKTR	60181	3085	17W-1S	B2
Nina					
10	BRLT	60103	2910	31W-8N	A3
10	HnrT	60103	2910	31W-8N	A3
Nina Av					
3100	WLMT	60091	2811	6W-13N	E7
N Nina Av					
5700	CHCG	60631	2918	8W-7N	D4
Nippersink Av					
200	RDLK	60073	2531	24W-33N	D3
Nippersink Av SR-134					
200	RDLK	60073	2531	23W-33N	E3
W Nippersink Av					
1000	AvnT	60073	2531	24W-33N	C3
1000	RDLK	60073	2531	25W-33N	A3
25100	GrtT	60073	2531	25W-33N	A3
25700	GrtT	60041	2530	26W-33N	E3
25700	GrtT	60073	2530	26W-33N	E3
Nippersink Blvd					
10	FXLK	60020	2473	28W-36N	A3
Nippersink Dr					
100	GrtT	60050	2472	29W-37N	D1
100	MchT	60050	2472	29W-37N	D1
1200	MchT	60081	2472	29W-37N	D1
1500	BtnT	60081	2414	29W-38N	C7
1500	SPGV	60081	2414	29W-38N	C7
N Nippersink Dr					
2500	RHMD	60071	2353	34W-41N	D7
Nippersink Pl					
38000	AntT	60081	2414	29W-38N	B7
38000	AntT	60081	2472	29W-37N	B1
38000	BtnT	60081	2472	29W-37N	B1
38000	GrtT	60081	2472	29W-37N	B1
38000	MchT	60081	2472	29W-37N	B1
N Nippersink Pl					
37600	GrtT	60081	2472	28W-37N	E1
Nippersink Rd					
800	BtnT	60081	2414	29W-39N	B5
W Nippersink Rd					
26000	GrtT	60041	2530	26W-33N	D2
26000	GrtT	60073	2530	26W-33N	E3
26800	FXLK	60041	2530	26W-34N	C1
26800	VOLO	60041	2530	26W-34N	C1
27000	FXLK	60041	2473	27W-35N	B7
27000	VOLO	60041	2473	27W-34N	C7
27300	GrtT	60041	2473	27W-35N	B6
Nippersink St					
38200	AntT	60081	2414	29W-38N	D7
38200	BtnT	60081	2414	29W-38N	D7
Nippert Av					
200	RMVL	60446	3340	24W-16S	D3
Nippert Dr					
1200	SMWD	60107	2911	28W-9N	B1
Nish Rd					
1600	NndT	60012	2586	30W-28N	A6
1600	NndT	60014	2586	30W-28N	A6
1600	NndT	60050	2586	30W-28N	A6
1900	NndT	60012	2585	30W-28N	E6
1900	PRGV	60012	2585	31W-28N	D6
Niswender Ct					
4600	NPVL	60564	3266	29W-12S	C4
Niswender Dr					
4700	NPVL	60564	3266	29W-12S	C4
Nita Ln					
200	LYVL	60048	2591	16W-27N	D7
Niva Ct					
1900	WKGN	60087	2479	11W-36N	D5
Niven Ln					
5300	HRPK	60133	2911	27W-6N	C6
N Nixon Av					
6500	CHCG	60631	2918	8W-8N	D2
6500	CHCG	60714	2918	8W-8N	D2
6500	NLES	60714	2918	8W-8N	D2
S Noah Ter					
500	MPPT	60056	2861	17W-12N	B2
Noahs Lndg					
-	BFGV	60089	2701	16W-23N	D3
-	VrnT	60069	2701	16W-23N	D3
-	VrnT	60089	2701	16W-23N	D3
Nobes Av					
100	LktT	60441	3419	23W-21S	B6
Noble Av					
-	BHPK	60099	2421	12W-39N	C5
200	LKFT	60045	2650	10W-27N	A1
39300	BHPK	60087	2421	12W-39N	C6
Noble Cir					
200	VNHL	60061	2701	17W-24N	B1
Noble Ct					
-	NHBK	60062	2756	12W-17N	B5
Noble Dr					
-	WDRG	60517	3143	22W-7S	B6
1200	PTBR	60010	2642	28W-26N	D2
Noble Pkwy					
1000	PTBR	60010	2642	28W-26N	D2
N Noble St					
1500	CHCG	60622	3033	1W-1N	D1
Nodding Flower Ct					
24600	TRLK	60010	2643	26W-24N	C6
Noel Av					
800	JLET	60435	3498	25W-22S	C3
1000	WLNG	60090	2755	14W-16N	B6
9200	MaiT	60016	2863	11W-11N	D2
Noel Ct					
900	WTMT	60559	3145	18W-6S	B5
Noel Dr					
600	MDLN	60060	2646	18W-27N	E1
800	MDLN	60060	2591	18W-27N	A7
800	MDLN	60060	2647	18W-27N	A1
Noel Rd					
-	JknT	60421	3675	25W-29S	D3
-	JLET	60421	3675	25W-29S	D3
W Noel Rd					
-	CnhT	60421	3674	27W-29S	D3
-	ELWD	60421	3674	27W-29S	D3
-	JknT	60421	3674	27W-29S	D3
19300	JknT	60421	3675	24W-29S	E3
19800	JLET	60421	3675	24W-29S	D3
20800	ELWD	60421	3675	25W-29S	B3
Noelle Bnd					
800	LIHL	60156	2692	38W-22N	E4
Nogales St					
200	HFET	60169	2858	23W-10N	E5
200	HFET	60194	2858	23W-10N	E5
200	SMBG	60194	2858	23W-10N	E5
Noggle Ct					
2600	AURA	60503	3201	32W-10S	C6
2600	WldT	60503	3201	32W-10S	C6
N Nokomis Av					
6200	CHCG	60646	2919	6W-7N	D3
6400	CHCG	60712	2919	6W-8N	D2
6600	LNWD	60712	2919	6W-8N	D2
6700	LNWD	60077	2919	6W-8N	D2
6700	SKOK	60077	2919	6W-8N	D2
Nokomis Ln					
500	ElgT	60124	2907	38W-9N	A1
Nokomis St					
300	PKFT	60466	3595	3W-27S	B5
Nokomis Tr					
400	DndT	60102	2747	34W-19N	E3
34600	GrtT	60051	2472	28W-34N	E7
Nolan Av					
600	BmdT	60139	2969	22W-2N	C7
600	GLHT	60139	2969	22W-2N	C7
Nolan Ct					
15400	HMGN	60441	3342	19W-16S	D4
15400	HMGN	60491	3342	19W-16S	D4
Nolan Rd					
10	ELGN	60124	2907	38W-9N	A2
10	ElgT	60124	2907	38W-8N	A2
Nolen Dr					
400	SEGN	60177	2908	36W-7N	A4
Noll Dr					
3300	PKCY	60085	2536	12W-33N	A3
3300	WKGN	60085	2536	12W-33N	A3
Noll St					
10	PKCY	60085	2536	12W-33N	A1
10	WKGN	60085	2536	12W-33N	A1
N Nolton Av					
100	WLSP	60480	3209	12W-9S	C3
S Nolton Av					
100	WLSP	60480	3209	12W-9S	C4
600	PlsT	60480	3209	12W-9S	C4
Nona St					
2500	FNPK	60131	2973	12W-3N	C5
Nondorf St					
2100	DYR	46311	3598		D2
Noonan St					
2000	CTHL	60403	3417	26W-21S	D7
Nora Av					
200	GNVW	60025	2864	8W-12N	D1
9000	SPGV	60081	2413	31W-40N	D2
9400	OKLN	60453	3210	8W-10S	E6
N Nora Av					
3500	CHCG	60634	2974	8W-4N	E2
8000	NLES	60714	2864	8W-10N	D5
N Nora Pl					
37800	GrtT	60081	2472	28W-37N	E1
Norbert Dr					
10	HNWD	60047	2699	20W-24N	E1
10	HNWD	60047	2700	20W-24N	A1
S Norbury Av					
600	LMBD	60148	3026	19W-0S	C6
1600	LMBD	60148	3084	19W-1S	C2
1600	YkTp	60148	3084	19W-1S	C2
Norcia Dr					
-	LSLE	60532	3142	23W-5S	E4
Norcross Dr					
500	BTVA	60510	3078	34W-2S	D4
900	BtvT	60510	3078	34W-2S	D4
Nordic Ct					
600	LYVL	60048	2591	17W-28N	B6
700	BTVA	60510	3078	34W-1S	E2
2200	AURA	60504	3201	32W-8S	B3
Nordic Ln					
12900	LMNT	60439	3343	17W-15S	D1
Nordic Rd					
10	BmdT	60143	2970	21W-5N	A1
10	ITSC	60143	2970	21W-5N	A1
200	BMDL	60108	2969	22W-5N	B1
200	BmdT	60143	2969	21W-5N	E1
200	BtvT	60143	2969	21W-5N	E1
300	ADSN	60143	2970	20W-5N	B1
S Nordic Rd					
1800	EGvT	60005	2861	16W-10N	E5
1800	EGvT	60056	2861	16W-10N	E5
1800	MPPT	60056	2861	16W-10N	E5
Nordic St					
1100	BNVL	60106	2915	16W-6N	D6
Nordica Av					
200	GNVW	60025	2864	8W-12N	E1
7900	BGVW	60459	3210	8W-9S	E2
7900	BRBK	60459	3210	8W-9S	E2
9300	BGVW	60455	3210	8W-10S	E6
9300	OKLN	60453	3210	8W-10S	E6
9300	OKLN	60455	3210	8W-10S	E6
N Nordica Av					
1600	CHCG	60302	3030	8W-2N	E1
1600	CHCG	60707	3030	8W-2N	E1
1600	OKPK	60302	3030	8W-2N	E1
1700	CHCG	60707	2974	8W-2N	E7
3200	CHCG	60634	2974	8W-4N	E3
4300	NRDG	60706	2974	8W-5N	D1
4800	CHCG	60656	2918	8W-6N	E6
4800	HDHT	60656	2918	8W-6N	E6
4800	HDHT	60706	2918	8W-6N	E6
6200	CHCG	60631	2918	8W-7N	E3
6500	CHCG	60714	2918	8W-8N	E2
6500	NLES	60631	2918	8W-8N	E2
6500	NLES	60714	2918	8W-8N	E2
7500	NLES	60714	2864	8W-9N	E6
S Nordica Av					
5100	CHCG	60638	3148	8W-6S	E3
10700	WRTH	60482	3274	8W-12S	E2
Nordigan Dr					
10	WKGN	60087	2480	10W-36N	B3
Noreen Ct					
17600	WrnT	60031	2534	17W-34N	B2
Norelius Av					
1100	AvnT	60073	2474	24W-35N	C7
1100	RLKB	60073	2474	24W-35N	C7
Norfolk Av					
-	WTMT	60559	3145	17W-5S	B2
10	CNHL	60514	3145	17W-5S	B2
600	BRLT	60103	2910	30W-7N	C4
1200	CteT	60417	3596	1W-28S	A7
1300	WSTR	60154	3029	12W-1S	B7
1400	CteT	60417	3595	2W-28S	D7
1400	WSTR	60154	3087	12W-1S	B1
1800	MonT	60417	3595	2W-28S	C7
1800	MonT	60466	3595	2W-28S	C7
Norfolk Ct					
10	AURA	60502	3201	32W-8S	B1
100	ROSL	60172	2912	25W-7N	C4
2400	NPVL	60565	3204	25W-10S	B4
5300	GRNE	60031	2478	15W-35N	A5
12200	MKNA	60448	3502	15W-23S	C4
Norfolk Dr					
12800	HTLY	60142	2691	41W-20N	D7
Norfolk Ln					
1000	GYLK	60030	2532	20W-34N	E1
24000	PNFD	60585	3338	30W-15S	C2
Norfolk St					
1000	DRGV	60516	3144	20W-7S	B6
E Norfolk St					
-	CNHL	60514	3145	17W-5S	B2
10	WTMT	60559	3145	17W-5S	B2
W Norfolk St					
10	WTMT	60559	3145	18W-5S	A2
Norfork Rd					
2000	NHFD	60093	2811	7W-16N	B1
Norge Pkwy					
800	FRGV	60021	2696	29W-23N	C3
Noritake Ct					
4700	JLET	60431	3496	29W-22S	E2
W Norley Av					
800	JLET	60435	3498	25W-22S	B1

Block	City	ZIP	Map#	CGS	Grid
Norma Ct					
2700	MaiT	60025	2864	10W-12N	B1
W Norma Ct					
8200	MaiT	60025	2864	10W-12N	B1
8200	NLES	60714	2864	10W-12N	B1
Norma Ln					
2200	DYR	46311	3598		E2
3000	WKGN	60085	2536	12W-33N	B1
23100	CmgT	60033	2405	52W-39N	C5
Normal Av					
-	BlmT	60411	3508	0W-24S	C5
400	CHHT	60411	3508	0W-24S	C5
14300	HRVY	60426	3350	0W-17S	B4
14300	HRVY	60827	3350	0W-17S	B4
14300	RVDL	60827	3350	0W-17S	B4
S Normal Av					
2900	CHCG	60616	3092	0W-3S	A5
4400	CHCG	60609	3092	0W-4S	B7
5500	CHCG	60609	3152	0W-6S	B3
6300	CHCG	60621	3152	0W-7S	B5
7500	CHCG	60620	3214	0W-8S	B1
7500	CHCG	60621	3214	0W-8S	B1
9400	CHCG	60628	3214	0W-11S	B6
10300	CHCG	60628	3278	0W-13S	B4
13600	RVDL	60827	3350	0W-15S	B2
14500	HRVY	60426	3350	0W-16S	B4
14500	HRVY	60827	3350	0W-16S	B4
W Normal Av					
8400	NLES	60714	2864	10W-10N	A5
8600	NLES	60714	2863	10W-10N	E5
8700	NLES	60068	2863	10W-10N	E5
8700	PKRG	60068	2863	10W-10N	E5
S Normal Blvd					
7400	CHCG	60621	3152	0W-8S	B7
W Normal Ct					
8300	NLES	60714	2864	10W-10N	A5
W Normal Pkwy					
300	CHCG	60621	3152	0W-7S	B6
Norman Av					
900	GRNE	60031	2478	14W-35N	D7
3200	JLET	60431	3417	28W-19S	B4
3200	JLET	60435	3417	28W-19S	B4
3200	PnfT	60435	3417	28W-19S	B4
W Norman Av					
300	PNFD	60544	3416	29W-18S	C2
Norman Blvd					
1700	PKRG	60068	2917	11W-8N	E1
Norman Ct					
10	BRRG	60527	3208	15W-10S	B5
10	DSPN	60016	2862	15W-11N	A3
10	SMBG	60193	2913	23W-9N	A1
8400	LKWD	60014	2692	38W-23N	D1
Norman Dr					
100	MHRY	60050	2527	33W-32N	E6
800	HFET	60192	2804	23W-14N	D4
1400	DRN	60561	3207	18W-8S	A2
1500	DRGV	60516	3207	18W-8S	A2
1500	DRN	60516	3207	18W-8S	A2
E Norman Dr					
1200	PLTN	60074	2806	19W-16N	C1
N Norman Dr					
10	PLTN	60074	2753	19W-16N	D7
10	PLTN	60074	2806	19W-16N	D1
3800	WKGN	60085	2535	13W-31N	E6
W Norman Dr					
25800	AntT	60002	2415	25W-39N	E5
25800	AntT	60002	2416	25W-39N	A4
Norman Dr S					
2200	WKGN	60085	2535	13W-31N	E7
Norman Dr W					
2000	WKGN	60085	2535	13W-31N	E6
Norman Ln					
300	ROSL	60172	2912	24W-6N	C6
500	CRY	60013	2695	31W-24N	D1
1100	DRFD	60015	2703	10W-21N	E6
E Norman Ln					
100	WLNG	60090	2755	15W-17N	A5
N Norman Ln					
800	WLNG	60090	2755	15W-17N	A4
900	WLNG	60090	2754	15W-17N	E4
W Norman Ln					
100	WLNG	60090	2754	15W-17N	E4
Norman Rd					
100	BGBK	60440	3205	22W-10S	B6
Norman Wy					
100	BGBK	60440	3205	22W-10S	B6
Normandie Dr					
10	SgrT	60506	3135	41W-5S	E3
Normandie Ln					
400	RLKB	60073	2474	23W-35N	E5
Normandy Av					
7700	BDPK	60638	3211	8W-8S	A1
7700	BRBK	60459	3211	8W-9S	A3
7700	BRBK	60638	3211	8W-8S	A1
8500	OKLN	60459	3211	8W-9S	A4
8700	OKLN	60453	3211	8W-10S	A4
9300	MNGV	60053	2865	8W-11N	A2
9500	GLF	60029	2865	8W-11N	A2
9500	GLF	60053	2865	8W-11N	A2
9800	CHRG	60415	3211	8W-11S	A7
9800	CHRG	60453	3211	8W-11S	A7
10300	CHRG	60415	3275	8W-12S	A1
36500	LkvT	60046	2475	21W-36N	D4
36500	RLKB	60046	2475	21W-36N	D4
36500	RLKB	60073	2475	21W-36N	D4
N Normandy Av					
1600	CHCG	60707	3031	6W-0S	D6
1600	OKPK	60302	3031	6W-0S	D6
2400	CHCG	60707	2975	8W-3N	A5
3800	CHCG	60634	2974	8W-4N	E2
4200	CHCG	60634	2975	8W-5N	A1
4200	CHCG	60706	2974	8W-5N	E1
4200	HDHT	60706	2974	8W-5N	E1
4800	CHCG	60656	2918	8W-6N	E6
4800	HDHT	60706	2918	8W-6N	E6
6200	CHCG	60631	2919	8W-7N	A3
6300	CHCG	60631	2918	8W-8N	E2
6500	NLES	60631	2918	8W-8N	E2
6500	NLES	60714	2918	8W-8N	E2
S Normandy Av					
5100	CHCG	60638	3149	8W-6S	A4
5100	FTVW	60638	3149	8W-5S	A2
6400	BDPK	60638	3149	8W-7S	A5
10900	WRTH	60482	3275	8W-12S	A3
Normandy Cir					
10	SMBG	60173	2859	21W-10N	E5
Normandy Ct					
-	EGVV	60007	2913	21W-8N	E1
10	ODHL	60013	2642	30W-26N	A3
2900	WldT	60564	3202	30W-10S	A7
3700	AURA	60504	3202	30W-8S	A1
4400	LGGV	60047	2700	18W-23N	D2
N Normandy Ct					
1800	ANHT	60004	2807	16W-15N	C2
Normandy Dr					
4400	LSLE	60532	3142	24W-4S	C1
6700	BtnT	60081	2414	29W-38N	D6
16700	TYPK	60477	3425	8W-20S	B3
E Normandy Dr					
10	ADSN	60101	2971	18W-3N	A6
10	CHHT	60411	3508	1W-23S	A4
N Normandy Dr					
100	CHHT	60411	3508	1W-23S	A3
S Normandy Dr					
100	CHHT	60411	3508	1W-23S	A4
W Normandy Dr					
10	CHHT	60411	3508	0W-23S	B4
100	CHHT	60411	3507	1W-23S	E4
Normandy Ln					
200	GYLK	60030	2532	20W-33N	E2
300	GYLK	60030	2533	20W-33N	A2
500	PTBR	60010	2642	28W-26N	D3
700	GNVW	60025	2811	7W-13N	B6
700	LIHL	60142	2692	38W-21N	E5
700	LIHL	60156	2692	38W-21N	E5
1300	BRLT	60103	2967	27W-5N	B1
1900	GNVA	60134	3019	36W-1N	E3
3800	NHBK	60062	2756	12W-18N	B4
17900	HLCT	60429	3426	4W-21S	E6
19900	FftT	60448	3502	14W-24S	D5
19900	MKNA	60448	3502	14W-24S	D5
Normandy Pl					
2600	LSLE	60532	3142	24W-4S	C1
3000	EVTN	60201	2866	4W-12N	C1
S Normandy Rd					
1000	WKGN	60085	2535	14W-32N	C4
Normandy Woods Ct					
1600	AvnT	60030	2475	21W-35N	E7
1600	GYLK	60030	2475	21W-35N	E7
Normandy Woods Dr					
100	WNFD	60190	3081	27W-1S	B1
Norman Heck Ct					
100	HDPK	60037	2704	8W-23N	E2
Norman Nelson Ct					
200	ELGN	60123	2854	34W-11N	D3
Normantown Rd					
-	BGBK	60490	3339	26W-14S	E1
-	BGBK	60490	3340	26W-15S	A1
-	DPgT	60490	3339	26W-14S	E1
-	RMVL	60446	3340	26W-15S	A1
-	RMVL	60490	3339	26W-14S	E1
-	RMVL	60490	3340	26W-15S	A1
-	RMVL	60544	3339	26W-14S	E1
-	WldT	60585	3265	31W-11S	E2
100	AURA	60503	3201	31W-10S	E6
100	WldT	60503	3201	31W-10S	E6
100	WldT	60564	3201	31W-10S	E6
1300	AURA	60504	3201	31W-9S	E4
1300	AURA	60564	3201	31W-9S	E5
1400	RMVL	60544	3340	26W-15S	A1
1400	WldT	60544	3339	26W-15S	E2
11400	PNFD	60564	3265	31W-13S	E6
11400	PNFD	60585	3265	31W-13S	E6
11400	WldT	60564	3265	31W-13S	E6
12500	PNFD	60585	3337	31W-14S	E1
12500	WldT	60585	3337	31W-14S	E1
W Normantown Rd					
10	RMVL	60446	3340	25W-15S	A1
1000	RMVL	60544	3340	25W-15S	A1
Nor Oaks Ct					
600	WCHI	60185	3022	29W-1N	C3
Norridge Ln					
400	HFET	60169	2858	24W-10N	E4
W Norridge St					
7600	HDHT	60706	2918	9W-6N	C6
7600	NRDG	60706	2918	9W-6N	C6
Norris Av					
10	WynT	60185	2966	30W-4N	B5
100	WCHI	60185	3022	30W-0N	B5
200	WYNE	60184	2966	30W-4N	B5
200	WYNE	60185	2966	30W-4N	B5
400	WCHI	60185	2966	30W-3N	B6
Norris Dr					
10	BRRG	60527	3146	15W-6S	A5
10	DGvT	60527	3146	15W-6S	A5
Norris Rd					
10	BbyT	60506	3076	40W-4S	B7
10	BbyT	60554	3076	40W-3S	B6
10	SgrT	60506	3076	40W-4S	B7
100	SgrT	60506	3136	40W-4S	B1
100	SgrT	60554	3136	40W-5S	B3
100	SRGV	60554	3136	40W-5S	B3
500	SRGV	60506	3136	40W-5S	B3
Norris Rd CO-15					
10	BbyT	60506	3076	40W-3S	B7
10	SgrT	60506	3076	40W-3S	B7
Norris St					
2300	DXMR	60406	3349	2W-17S	C4
2300	POSN	60406	3349	2W-17S	C4
2300	POSN	60469	3349	2W-17S	C4
North Av					
-	AntT	60002	2416	25W-41N	B1
-	AntT	60002	2417	22W-41N	B1
-	AURA	60506	3200	36W-7S	A1
-	CLSM	60139	3024	24W-2N	D1
-	GfnT	60014	2638	38W-25N	E5
10	ANTH	60002	2358	23W-43N	A5
10	AntT	60002	2358	22W-43N	B5
10	AURA	60505	3200	35W-8S	A1
10	BmdT	60137	3025	23W-2N	A1
10	BmdT	60139	3025	23W-1N	A1
10	BmdT	60188	3024	25W-2N	A1
10	BmdT	60188	3025	23W-1N	A1
10	CLSM	60139	3023	26W-2N	D1
10	CLSM	60188	3024	24W-1N	D2
10	FXLK	60020	2473	27W-36N	A3
10	GLHT	60139	3024	24W-1N	C2
10	GLHT	60139	3025	23W-2N	A1
10	GLHT	60188	3024	24W-1N	C2
10	GLHT	60188	3025	23W-1N	A1
10	LKFT	60045	2649	10W-24N	E6
10	MltT	60148	3025	21W-1N	E1
10	SCRL	60174	2964	35W-3N	B6
10	WCHI	60185	2965	32W-3N	D6
10	WCHI	60185	2966	31W-3N	A6
10	WynT	60185	2965	32W-3N	D6
10	WynT	60185	2967	28W-2N	A7
10	WynT	60185	3023	26W-2N	E1
10	WynT	60188	3023	27W-2N	D1
100	BRTN	60010	2751	25W-20N	A1
100	HIWD	60040	2704	9W-23N	C2
100	PTPR	53158	2363	10W-43N	A4
100	SCRL	60185	2965	32W-3N	D6
100	WCDA	60084	2587	26W-27N	E7
100	WPHR	53158	2363	10W-43N	A4
100	WPHR	60096	2363	10W-43N	A4
200	ANTH	60002	2357	23W-43N	E5
200	BmdT	60188	3023	26W-2N	E1
200	BTVA	60510	3078	35W-0S	A1
200	MltT	60137	3025	22W-1N	C1
200	SCRL	60174	2965	32W-3N	C6
300	GLHT	60137	3025	23W-2N	A1
300	LYVL	60048	2591	16W-29N	E4
400	AntT	60002	2357	24W-42N	D5
400	BmdT	60148	3025	21W-2N	E1
400	GLHT	60148	3025	21W-2N	D1
400	LktT	60441	3419	22W-21S	C6
400	LMBD	60148	3025	21W-2N	E1
400	WKGN	60085	2480	10W-35N	A7
400	WKGN	60085	2537	10W-34N	A1
500	WCHI	60185	2967	28W-2N	A7
500	WynT	60185	2966	29W-2N	D7
600	CLLK	60014	2639	37W-25N	A5
600	GfnT	60014	2639	38W-25N	A5
800	DSPN	60016	2862	13W-11N	D3
1000	AURA	60504	3200	34W-8S	D2
1100	BKBN	60015	2703	11W-22N	D5
1100	BTVA	60510	3077	36W-0S	E1
1100	DRFD	60015	2703	11W-22N	C5
1100	HDPK	60035	2704	10W-23N	B2
1200	LKWD	60014	2639	37W-25N	B5
1300	AraT	60504	3200	34W-8S	E2
1300	RLKB	60073	2475	22W-35N	B6
1700	WKGN	60087	2480	10W-35N	A6
4500	GRNE	60031	2535	14W-34N	C1
North Av CO-A2					
10	ANTH	60002	2358	23W-43N	A5
10	AntT	60002	2358	22W-43N	B5
200	ANTH	60002	2357	23W-43N	E5
North Av SR-64					
-	CLSM	60139	3024	24W-2N	D1
10	BmdT	60137	3025	23W-2N	A1
10	BmdT	60188	3023	26W-2N	E1
10	BmdT	60188	3024	25W-2N	A1
10	CLSM	60188	3023	26W-2N	D1
10	CLSM	60188	3024	24W-1N	C2
10	GLHT	60139	3024	24W-1N	C2
10	GLHT	60139	3025	23W-2N	A1
10	GLHT	60188	3024	24W-1N	C2
10	GLHT	60188	3025	23W-1N	A1
10	MltT	60148	3025	21W-1N	E1
10	WCHI	60185	2965	32W-3N	D6
10	WCHI	60185	2966	31W-3N	A6
10	WynT	60185	2965	32W-3N	D6
10	WynT	60185	2966	29W-2N	D7
10	WynT	60185	2967	28W-2N	A7
10	WynT	60185	3023	26W-2N	E1
10	WynT	60188	3023	26W-2N	D1
100	SCRL	60185	2965	32W-3N	D6
200	BmdT	60139	3025	22W-2N	C1
200	MltT	60137	3025	22W-1N	C1
200	SCRL	60174	2965	32W-3N	C6
300	GLHT	60137	3025	23W-2N	A1
400	BmdT	60148	3025	21W-2N	E1
400	BmdT	60188	3025	23W-2N	A1
400	GLHT	60148	3025	21W-2N	D1
400	LMBD	60148	3025	21W-2N	E1
500	WCHI	60185	2967	28W-2N	A7
E North Av					
-	EMHT	60126	3027	17W-2N	B1
-	NHLK	60164	3029	13W-1N	A1
-	NHLK	60165	3029	13W-1N	A1
-	SNPK	60164	3029	13W-1N	A1
10	ADSN	60101	2971	18W-3N	A4
10	LKBF	60044	2593	10W-28N	E5
10	LMBD	60148	3026	19W-2N	C1
10	NHLK	60164	3028	13W-1N	E1
10	NPVL	60540	3141	26W-6S	E5
10	VLPK	60181	3027	17W-2N	B1
10	YkTp	60181	3027	17W-2N	B1
100	BRLT	60103	2910	29W-8N	E3
100	EMHT	60126	3028	15W-1N	A1
100	LKBF	60044	2594	10W-28N	A5
200	BRLT	60103	2911	28W-8N	A3
400	HRPK	60133	2911	28W-8N	B3
400	MLPK	60160	3029	13W-2N	A1
400	MLPK	60164	3029	13W-2N	A1
400	NHLK	60160	3029	13W-2N	A1
400	VLPK	60126	3027	17W-2N	B1
400	VLPK	60148	3026	19W-2N	C1
400	YkTp	60126	3027	17W-2N	B1
600	AddT	60148	3026	19W-2N	C1
1000	NPVL	60540	3142	26W-6S	A5
E North Av SR-64					
-	EMHT	60126	3027	17W-2N	B1
-	MLPK	60160	3029	13W-2N	A1
-	MLPK	60164	3029	13W-1N	A1
-	NHLK	60160	3029	13W-2N	A1
-	NHLK	60164	3029	13W-1N	A1
-	NHLK	60165	3029	13W-1N	A1
-	SNPK	60164	3029	13W-1N	A1
10	LMBD	60148	3026	19W-2N	C1
10	NHLK	60164	3028	13W-1N	E1
10	VLPK	60181	3027	17W-2N	B1
10	YkTp	60181	3027	17W-2N	B1
100	EMHT	60126	3028	15W-1N	A1
400	VLPK	60126	3027	17W-2N	B1
400	VLPK	60148	3026	19W-2N	C1
400	YkTp	60126	3027	17W-2N	B1
600	AddT	60148	3026	19W-2N	C1
N North Av					
-	MchT	60051	2528	31W-32N	C4
-	WKGN	60087	2480	10W-37N	A2
-	WkgT	60087	2480	10W-37N	A2
1800	MHRY	60050	2527	33W-33N	E2
37500	BHPK	60087	2480	10W-37N	A2
38200	BHPK	60087	2422	10W-38N	A7
39400	BHPK	60099	2422	10W-39N	A5
39400	ZION	60099	2422	10W-39N	A5
W North Av					
-	ADSN	60148	3026	18W-2N	D1
-	AntT	60002	2416	25W-41N	B1
-	EMHT	60126	3028	14W-1N	B1
-	FftT	60423	3505	9W-25S	A6
-	FKFT	60423	3504	9W-24S	E6
-	LMBD	60148	3025	21W-2N	E1
-	MLPK	60164	3029	12W-2N	B1
-	MTSN	60443	3505	9W-25S	A6
-	SNPK	60164	3029	12W-1N	A1
-	VLPK	60148	3026	18W-2N	D1
10	LKFT	60045	2649	11W-24N	E6
10	LMBD	60148	3026	20W-1N	A1
10	NHLK	60164	3028	14W-1N	C1
10	VLPK	60181	3027	18W-1N	A1
100	CHCG	60610	2978	0W-2N	A7
100	CHCG	60614	2978	0W-2N	A7
100	EMHT	60126	3027	16W-2N	D1
100	WCHI	60185	2966	30W-3N	C7
100	WynT	60185	2966	30W-3N	B7
200	ADSN	60101	3026	18W-2N	E1
200	ADSN	60181	3026	18W-2N	E1
200	BRLT	60103	2910	29W-8N	E3
200	VLPK	60101	3026	18W-2N	E1
200	VLPK	60181	3026	18W-2N	E1
400	AddT	60148	3026	19W-2N	D1
500	MLPK	60160	3030	10W-2N	A1
500	PvsT	60160	3030	10W-2N	A1
600	MLPK	60160	3029	12W-2N	B1
600	VLPK	60126	3027	17W-2N	C1
600	YkTp	60126	3027	17W-2N	C1
700	CHCG	60610	2977	1W-2N	D7
700	CHCG	60614	2977	1W-2N	D7
700	CHCG	60622	2977	1W-2N	D7
700	ShdT	60044	2593	12W-28N	A5
800	MchT	60051	2529	29W-32N	B5
1000	GNOK	60044	2593	12W-28N	A5
1900	CHCG	60622	3033	2W-1N	B1
1900	CHCG	60647	3033	2W-1N	B1
2500	MLPK	60165	3029	12W-2N	B1
2500	SNPK	60160	3029	12W-2N	B1
2500	SNPK	60165	3029	12W-2N	B1
2800	CHCG	60622	3032	3W-1N	E1
2800	CHCG	60647	3032	3W-1N	E1
3100	CHCG	60651	3032	3W-2N	D1
3900	CHCG	60639	3032	4W-2N	B1
4700	CHCG	60639	3031	7W-2N	C1
4700	CHCG	60651	3031	7W-2N	C1
5900	OKPK	60302	3031	7W-2N	B1
5900	OKPK	60639	3031	7W-2N	B1
5900	OKPK	60651	3031	7W-2N	B1
6000	CHCG	60302	3031	7W-2N	B1
6300	CHCG	60707	3031	7W-2N	A1
6700	CHCG	60302	3030	8W-2N	E1
6700	CHCG	60707	3030	8W-1N	E1
6700	OKPK	60302	3030	8W-1N	E1
7100	EDPK	60707	3030	8W-2N	D1
7100	OKPK	60305	3030	8W-2N	D1
7100	RVFT	60305	3030	8W-2N	D1
7100	RVFT	60707	3030	8W-2N	D1
7600	FftT	60423	3504	9W-24S	E6
8300	RVFT	60160	3030	10W-1N	B1
8300	RVFT	60171	3030	10W-1N	B1
8300	RVGV	60171	3030	10W-1N	B1
8400	MLPK	60171	3030	10W-1N	A1
8400	RVGV	60160	3030	10W-2N	A1
21400	ANTH	60002	2358	21W-43N	D4
21400	AntT	53104	2358	21W-43N	D4
21400	AntT	60002	2358	21W-43N	D4
21400	BtlT	53104	2358	21W-43N	D4
21400	BtlT	60002	2358	21W-43N	D4
23500	LkvT	60046	2416	23W-38N	E6
24100	ANTH	60002	2357	24W-42N	C5
24100	AntT	60002	2357	24W-42N	C5
W North Av CO-A2					
21400	ANTH	60002	2358	21W-43N	D4
21400	AntT	53104	2358	21W-43N	D4
21400	AntT	60002	2358	21W-43N	D4
21400	BtlT	53104	2358	21W-43N	D4
21400	BtlT	60002	2358	21W-43N	D4
W North Av SR-64					
-	ADSN	60148	3026	18W-2N	D1
-	EMHT	60126	3028	14W-1N	B1
-	LMBD	60148	3025	21W-2N	E1
-	MLPK	60164	3029	12W-2N	A1
-	SNPK	60164	3029	12W-1N	A1
-	VLPK	60148	3026	18W-2N	D1
10	LMBD	60148	3026	20W-1N	A1
10	NHLK	60164	3028	14W-1N	C1
10	VLPK	60181	3027	18W-1N	A1
100	CHCG	60610	2978	0W-2N	A7
100	CHCG	60614	2978	0W-2N	A7
100	EMHT	60126	3027	16W-2N	D1
100	WCHI	60185	2966	30W-3N	B7
100	WynT	60185	2966	30W-3N	B7
200	ADSN	60101	3026	18W-2N	E1
200	ADSN	60181	3026	18W-2N	E1
200	VLPK	60101	3026	18W-2N	E1
200	VLPK	60181	3026	18W-2N	E1
400	AddT	60148	3026	19W-2N	D1
500	MLPK	60160	3030	10W-2N	A1
500	PvsT	60160	3030	10W-2N	A1
600	MLPK	60160	3029	12W-2N	B1
600	VLPK	60126	3027	17W-2N	C1
600	YkTp	60126	3027	17W-2N	C1
700	CHCG	60610	2977	1W-2N	D7
700	CHCG	60614	2977	1W-2N	D7
700	CHCG	60622	2977	1W-2N	D7
1900	CHCG	60622	3033	2W-1N	B1
1900	CHCG	60647	3033	2W-1N	B1
2500	MLPK	60165	3029	12W-2N	B1
2500	SNPK	60160	3029	12W-2N	B1
2500	SNPK	60165	3029	12W-2N	B1
2800	CHCG	60622	3032	3W-1N	E1
2800	CHCG	60647	3032	3W-1N	E1
3100	CHCG	60651	3032	3W-2N	D1
3900	CHCG	60639	3032	4W-2N	B1
4700	CHCG	60639	3031	7W-2N	C1
4700	CHCG	60651	3031	7W-2N	C1
5900	OKPK	60302	3031	7W-2N	B1
5900	OKPK	60639	3031	7W-2N	B1
5900	OKPK	60651	3031	7W-2N	B1
6000	CHCG	60302	3031	7W-2N	B1
6300	CHCG	60707	3031	7W-2N	A1
6700	CHCG	60302	3030	8W-2N	E1
6700	CHCG	60707	3030	8W-1N	E1
6700	OKPK	60302	3030	8W-1N	E1
7100	EDPK	60707	3030	8W-2N	D1
7100	OKPK	60305	3030	8W-2N	D1
7100	RVFT	60305	3030	8W-2N	D1
7100	RVFT	60707	3030	8W-2N	D1
8300	RVFT	60160	3030	10W-1N	B1
8300	RVFT	60171	3030	10W-1N	B1
8300	RVGV	60160	3030	10W-2N	A1
8300	RVGV	60171	3030	10W-1N	B1
8400	MLPK	60171	3030	10W-1N	A1
North Blvd					
-	NndT	60051	2529	29W-31N	B6
10	CHCG	60302	3031	7W-0N	B4
10	CHCG	60644	3031	7W-0N	B4
10	OKPK	60302	3031	7W-0N	B4
100	MchT	60051	2529	29W-31N	B6
400	LKMR	60051	2529	29W-32N	B5
600	OKPK	60301	3031	8W-0N	A4
700	OKPK	60301	3030	8W-0N	E4
700	OKPK	60302	3030	8W-0N	E4
1100	OKPK	60305	3030	8W-0N	D4
1100	RVFT	60301	3030	8W-0N	D4
1100	RVFT	60305	3030	8W-0N	D4
E North Blvd					
10	CHCG	60610	2978	0E-2N	C7
10	CHCG	60614	2978	0E-2N	C7
W North Blvd					
10	CHCG	60610	2978	0W-1N	B7
10	CHCG	60614	2978	0W-1N	B7
North Brch					
10	GNVW	60093	2810	8W-15N	D2
N North Cir					
500	ITSC	60143	2914	20W-6N	B5
North Ct					
4600	NndT	60012	2640	35W-27N	A1
N North Ct					
500	PLTN	60067	2752	20W-16N	E6
600	PLTN	60067	2753	20W-16N	A6
S North Ct					
20700	FftT	60423	3504	9W-25S	D6
W North Ct					
27600	GrtT	60041	2473	27W-35N	B6
North Dr					
-	PLTN	60067	2805	22W-14N	B4
-	WslT	60481	3943	27W-41S	E5
100	SchT	60177	2908	34W-7N	D4
100	SEGN	60177	2908	34W-7N	D4
700	BbyT	60554	3075	43W-3S	A7
1500	MHRY	60050	2528	32W-33N	A3
1900	GNVW	60025	2811	7W-14N	A4
7300	MchT	60097	2469	36W-36N	D4
28500	CbaT	60010	2696	28W-23N	E2
W North Dr					
22000	AntT	60002	2417	22W-40N	C3
North Ln					
-	MPPT	60056	2861	17W-11N	C3
10	LKZH	60047	2698	23W-23N	D1
100	BmdT	60143	2969	21W-5N	E1
100	BmdT	60143	2970	21W-5N	A1
600	NpvT	60540	3141	27W-7S	B7
1600	NHBK	60062	2757	8W-16N	E6
2600	AlqT	60013	2641	31W-25N	D4
10000	RHMD	60071	2353	34W-42N	D7
North Pkwy					
10	PTHT	60070	2808	15W-15N	A2
200	PTHT	60070	2807	15W-15N	E2
North Pth					
700	WHTN	60187	3024	24W-0S	D6
North Rd					
1000	FRGV	60010	2696	29W-22N	C3
1000	FRGV	60021	2696	29W-22N	C3
1000	LKBN	60010	2696	29W-22N	C3
1000	LKBN	60021	2696	29W-22N	C3
9100	PlsT	60465	3273	11W-13S	E3
9100	PSHL	60465	3273	11W-13S	E3
W North Rd					
24700	LkvT	60046	2416	24W-39N	B5
North St					
-	MTSN	60443	3594	4W-26S	E1
-	PKFT	60443	3594	4W-26S	E1
-	PKFT	60466	3594	4W-26S	E1
-	RcmT	60081	2413	32W-39N	B4
-	SEGN	60177	2908	34W-8N	D2
10	AddT	60106	2915	17W-6N	C5
10	BtlT	60512	3261	42W-12S	E3
10	CHHT	60411	3595	3W-26S	C1
10	CHHT	60466	3595	3W-26S	C1
10	EDND	60118	2800	34W-16N	E2
10	MTSN	60443	3595	3W-25S	A1
10	OSWG	60543	3263	37W-12S	C3
10	PKFT	60443	3595	3W-25S	A1
10	PKFT	60466	3595	3W-25S	A1
100	BDWD	60408	3942	31W-41S	B5
100	EDND	60118	2801	34W-16N	A2
100	MchT	60081	2472	29W-37N	D1
100	WDSK	60098	2524	41W-31N	D7
200	ELGN	60120	2854	34W-10N	C6
200	ELGN	60120	2855	33W-11N	A3
200	WMTN	60481	3853	27W-38S	D5
400	CRTE	60417	3685	1W-29S	B2
600	GNVA	60134	3020	35W-1N	B3
1900	SPGV	60081	2413	30W-40N	E4
1900	SPGV	60081	2414	30W-40N	A4
3900	RcmT	60071	2413	32W-39N	A4
6700	TYPK	60477	3425	8W-20S	A5
11800	HTLY	60142	2692	40W-21N	A6
11900	HTLY	60142	2691	40W-21N	E6
E North St					
10	HNDL	60521	3086	15W-4S	B7
10	PLNO	60545	3259	47W-13S	D6
100	BCVL	60407	4030	33W-44S	A4
100	ELBN	60119	3017	43W-1N	A3
100	ITSC	60143	2914	19W-6N	C5
100	MHTN	60442	3677	19W-30S	E4
200	LKPT	60441	3419	21W-18S	E1
200	LktT	60441	3419	21W-18S	E1
200	MHTN	60442	3678	19W-31S	A4
300	PTON	60468	3861	9W-37S	A3
700	MhtT	60442	3678	18W-30S	A4
800	CLCY	60416	3941	34W-39S	A1
800	FlxT	60416	3941	34W-39S	A1
1100	LKPT	60441	3420	21W-18S	A1
1200	LKPT	60441	3342	21W-18S	A7
N North St					
38800	LkvT	60046	2417	21W-38N	C6
W North St					
-	PtnT	60468	3860	9W-37S	D3
10	HNDL	60521	3086	15W-4S	A7
10	HNVL	60030	2532	22W-33N	B3
10	PLNO	60545	3259	47W-13S	C6
100	BCVL	60407	4030	34W-44S	A4
100	ELWD	60421	3675	25W-32S	B7
100	ITSC	60143	2914	19W-6N	B6
100	MHTN	60442	3677	19W-30S	E4
100	PTON	60468	3860	9W-37S	E3
100	PTON	60468	3861	9W-37S	A3
500	HNDL	60521	3085	16W-4S	E7
500	MhtT	60442	3677	19W-30S	E4
1300	PltT	60067	2752	22W-17N	A5
1500	PLTN	60067	2752	22W-17N	A5
28200	WcnT	60084	2643	28W-27N	A1
W North St US-52					
100	MHTN	60442	3677	19W-30S	E4
500	MhtT	60442	3677	19W-30S	E4
W North Ter					
8400	NLES	60714	2864	10W-10N	A5
8500	PKRG	60068	2864	10W-10N	A5
8500	PKRG	60714	2864	10W-10N	A5
8600	NLES	60714	2863	10W-10N	E5
8600	PKRG	60068	2863	10W-10N	E5
8600	PKRG	60714	2863	10W-10N	E5
8700	NLES	60068	2863	10W-10N	E5
North Tr					
10	HNWD	60047	2644	23W-25N	E5
10	LMNT	60439	3272	15W-13S	B4
Northampton Cir					
500	EGvT	60007	2860	19W-9N	D7
500	EGVV	60007	2860	19W-9N	D7
Northampton Dr					
100	OSWG	60543	3263	37W-11S	D2
700	CLLK	60014	2640	35W-24N	A7
2600	RGMW	60008	2806	19W-12N	B7
N Northampton Dr					
10	GNVA	60134	3019	36W-1N	E3
S Northampton Dr					
10	GNVA	60134	3019	36W-1N	E4
Northampton Ln					
200	LNSH	60045	2648	14W-24N	D7
200	LNSH	60069	2648	14W-24N	D7
200	LNSH	60069	2702	14W-24N	D1
400	ROSL	60172	2912	25W-7N	B5

Block	City	ZIP	Map#	CGS	Grid
Northampton St					
600	WDSK	60098	2524	41W-31N	D6
W North Bank Dr					
200	CHCG	60606	3034	0W-0N	B4
200	CHCG	60610	3034	0W-0N	B4
North Branch Rd					
200	GNVW	60025	2810	8W-12N	E7
200	GNVW	60025	2864	8W-12N	E1
N North Branch St					
900	CHCG	60622	3033	1W-1N	E2
Northbridge Ct					
10600	PlsT	60462	3345	13W-15S	A2
10600	PlsT	60464	3345	13W-15S	A2
Northbridge Dr					
-	LIHL	60142	2692	39W-21N	C5
10200	HTLY	60142	2692	39W-21N	C5
10600	PlsT	60462	3345	13W-15S	A2
10600	PlsT	60467	3345	13W-15S	A2
Northbridge Pl					
1800	DRGV	60516	3144	20W-7S	A7
N Northbridge Rd					
25300	ElaT	60047	2644	23W-25N	E5
E North Broadway St					
400	LMBD	60148	3026	19W-0N	D4
Northbrook Av					
800	NHBK	60062	2757	8W-17N	E5
Northbrook Ct					
1000	HDPK	60035	2757	9W-18N	C2
1000	NHBK	60062	2757	9W-18N	C2
Northbrook Ct Dr					
-	DRFD	60015	2757	9W-18N	C2
-	HDPK	60015	2757	9W-18N	C2
-	HDPK	60035	2757	9W-18N	C2
-	NHBK	60062	2757	9W-18N	C2
Northbury Ct					
200	SMBG	60193	2859	22W-10N	C6
Northbury Ln					
1100	WLNG	60090	2754	15W-18N	E2
Northcliffe Wy					
900	LKFT	60045	2649	12W-26N	C3
Northcott Av					
4000	DRGV	60515	3084	20W-4S	B7
4700	DRGV	60515	3144	20W-5S	B2
N Northcott Av					
5600	CHCG	60631	2919	8W-7N	A4
6000	CHCG	60631	2918	8W-7N	D3
North Creek Dr					
-	GRNE	60031	2477	16W-36N	D4
-	GRNE	60083	2477	16W-36N	D4
-	WrnT	60031	2477	16W-36N	D4
-	WrnT	60083	2477	16W-36N	D4
2600	WDRG	60517	3205	22W-9S	D4
Northcrest Dr					
2700	LslT	60517	3143	22W-7S	C6
25500	CNHN	60410	3672	31W-29S	E1
25600	CNHN	60447	3672	31W-29S	E1
25600	CnhT	60447	3672	31W-29S	E1
Northcrest Rd					
10	LKZH	60047	2698	24W-23N	D1
North Croft Ct					
600	LKFT	60045	2649	11W-25N	C6
North Ct Dr					
-	WLBK	60527	3145	16W-7S	D6
Northeast Ct					
-	CTSD	60525	3147	13W-5S	A3
-	LynT	60525	3147	13W-5S	A3
Northeast Dr					
-	DRN	60561	3207	17W-8S	C1
Northeast Pkwy					
-	LNWD	60712	2920	4W-8N	C1
Northeast Pl					
800	DSPN	60016	2862	13W-10N	D4
W Northeast Shore Dr					
800	NndT	60051	2586	29W-29N	C4
North End Av					
100	EMHT	60126	2971	16W-3N	E6
100	EMHT	60126	2972	15W-3N	A6
300	AddT	60126	2972	15W-3N	A6
Norther Av					
-	BRTN	60010	2697	26W-20N	D7
Northern Av					
-	BHPK	60087	2421	12W-38N	B7
-	BHPK	60099	2421	12W-39N	B6
-	CHCG	60613	2977	1W-5N	D1
-	WKGN	60087	2421	12W-38N	B7
10	ShdT	60044	2593	12W-28N	B5
500	LKBF	60044	2593	12W-29N	B4
1400	WKGN	60085	2479	12W-35N	B5
1700	WkgT	60085	2479	12W-35N	B5
2000	NCHI	60064	2536	12W-31N	B7
N Northern Av					
2100	WKGN	60087	2479	12W-36N	B4
35200	WKGN	60085	2479	12W-35N	B6
35200	WkgT	60085	2479	12W-35N	B6
36100	WkgT	60087	2479	12W-36N	B5
37700	BHPK	60087	2479	12W-37N	B1
Northern Ct					
300	ISLK	60042	2586	28W-28N	E5
700	SchT	60175	2907	38W-7N	A5
Northern Dr					
800	LKPT	60441	3341	21W-18S	E7
800	LktT	60441	3341	21W-18S	E7
Northern Ter					
100	ISLK	60042	2586	28W-28N	D5
Northern Dancer Ln					
10	CmpT	60175	2906	39W-7N	E4
10	PltT	60175	2906	39W-7N	E4
Northern Light Ct					
200	NARA	60542	3137	38W-4S	A1
Northern Lights Wy					
500	NLNX	60451	3589	18W-27S	B5
2700	NlxT	60451	3589	18W-27S	B5
Northern View Ct					
900	BbyT	60119	3075	43W-0S	B1
Northfield Av					
100	HRVD	60033	2406	50W-39N	A5
1000	HRVD	60033	2405	51W-38N	E5
2600	WKGN	60085	2479	12W-35N	C7
2600	WkgT	60085	2479	12W-35N	C7
Northfield Ct					
10	LNSH	60069	2701	16W-23N	E2
1300	CmgT	60033	2406	50W-39N	A5
1300	HRVD	60033	2406	50W-39N	A5
1900	NPVL	60565	3203	26W-9S	D4
Northfield Dr					
-	LGGV	60047	2646	18W-24N	E6
-	VNHL	60047	2646	18W-25N	E6
-	VNHL	60061	2646	18W-25N	E6
100	MNKA	60447	3583	32W-28S	C7
400	JLET	60435	3497	27W-23S	C4
800	AURA	60505	3138	34W-6S	D4
1800	NPVL	60565	3203	26W-9S	E4
Northfield Ln					
7700	TYPK	60477	3504	9W-23S	D2
Northfield Plz					
10	NHFD	60093	2811	7W-15N	B1
Northfield Rd					
100	NHFD	60093	2811	7W-15N	C2
100	NtrT	60093	2811	7W-15N	C2
300	SchT	60175	2963	37W-5N	C2
9000	WDRG	60517	3206	20W-10S	B6
Northfield Sq					
1700	NHFD	60093	2811	6W-15N	C2
W North Fox Ln					
4600	MHRY	60050	2527	33W-32N	E4
E North Frontage Rd					
100	BGBK	60440	3269	22W-12S	C3
W North Frontage Rd					
10	BGBK	60440	3269	23W-13S	A4
400	BGBK	60440	3268	23W-13S	E5
Northgate Av					
2100	NHBK	60062	2758	7W-16N	A7
2100	NHBK	60093	2758	7W-16N	A7
2100	NHFD	60062	2758	7W-16N	A7
2100	NHFD	60093	2758	7W-16N	A7
Northgate Cir					
500	OSWG	60543	3263	38W-13S	B5
Northgate Ct					
400	RVSD	60546	3088	9W-2S	C3
1300	BRLT	60103	2910	30W-6N	B7
4400	CPVL	60110	2746	37W-18N	D5
4400	CPVL	60110	2747	36W-18N	A5
5900	WDRG	60517	3143	21W-6S	D5
Northgate Dr					
-	RcmT	60072	2413	33W-39N	A6
-	SPGV	60072	2413	33W-39N	A6
-	SPGV	60081	2413	33W-39N	A6
400	DYR	46311	3510		D5
600	OSWG	60543	3263	38W-13S	B5
1300	BRLT	60103	2910	30W-6N	B7
1300	BRLT	60103	2966	30W-5N	A1
4300	CPVL	60110	2747	36W-18N	A5
Northgate Ln					
600	SRWD	60404	3496	30W-23S	A4
Northgate Pkwy					
200	WLNG	60090	2755	14W-17N	B4
600	BFGV	60089	2755	15W-18N	B2
600	BFGV	60090	2755	15W-18N	B2
Northgate Pl					
100	BRRG	60527	3208	14W-8S	D2
Northgate Rd					
-	DGvT	60439	3207	18W-10S	A6
-	DGvT	60527	3207	18W-10S	A5
10	RVSD	60546	3088	9W-2S	C3
500	LNHT	60046	2418	20W-38N	A6
500	NLNX	60451	3501	17W-25S	C7
500	NLNX	60451	3589	17W-25S	C1
500	NlxT	60451	3501	17W-25S	C7
500	NlxT	60451	3589	17W-25S	C1
2200	FTPK	60130	3088	9W-2S	C2
2200	FTPK	60546	3088	9W-2S	C2
2200	NRIV	60546	3088	9W-2S	C2
Northgate St					
200	LKFT	60045	2650		C2
Northgate Wy					
7300	DRGV	60516	3206	19W-8S	D1
Northhampton Ct					
400	NPVL	60565	3203	27W-10S	C5
Northlake Pkwy					
1400	CPVL	60110	2801	33W-16N	B1
1400	EDND	60110	2801	33W-16N	B1
1500	CPVL	60118	2801	33W-16N	B1
1500	EDND	60118	2801	33W-16N	B1
Northland Av					
1500	HDPK	60035	2704	10W-21N	A5
Northland Dr					
12900	PNFD	60585	3337	31W-15S	D2
Northland Ln					
2000	YKVL	60560	3261	43W-13S	B5
S Northland Wy					
-	RMVL	60446	3417	26W-18S	E1
Northlane Rd					
2600	AlqT	60013	2641	31W-26N	C4
Northlight Passe					
100	LIHL	60156	2693	36W-22N	E4
Northmont Ct					
4400	JLET	60586	3416	29W-21S	D7
Northmont Dr					
4500	JLET	60586	3416	29W-21S	D7
Northmoor Av					
2400	WKGN	60085	2479	11W-35N	C6
Northmoor Ct					
1300	NHBK	60062	2757	10W-17N	A6
Northmoor Rd					
600	LKFT	60045	2650	10W-25N	B4
N North Park Av					
1300	CHCG	60610	3034	0W-1N	B1
1600	CHCG	60610	2978	0W-2N	B7
1600	CHCG	60614	2978	0W-2N	B7
S Northpoint Blvd					
800	PKCY	60085	2536	13W-33N	A4
800	WKGN	60085	2535	13W-33N	E4
800	WKGN	60085	2536	13W-33N	A4
Northpoint Ct					
10	BGBK	60440	3268	25W-12S	C4
Northpoint Dr					
1500	AURA	60504	3200	33W-9S	E5
1600	AURA	60504	3201	33W-9S	A5
1600	OswT	60504	3201	33W-9S	A5
Northpointe Rd					
-	WDWH	60083	2420	14W-39N	C5
Northport Dr					
500	EGVW	60007	2914	19W-8N	C3
Northridge Av					
100	BGBK	60440	3269	22W-11S	B1
Northridge Dr					
5500	GRNE	60031	2477	15W-35N	E6
5500	GRNE	60031	2478	15W-35N	A6
E North RR St					
200	BCVL	60407	4030	33W-44S	B3
Northrup Rd					
6700	CrlT	60180	2635	46W-24N	D6
6700	UNON	60180	2635	46W-24N	D6
Northshire Dr					
1700	JLET	60586	3415	33W-21S	A7
1700	JLET	60586	3495	33W-22S	B2
Northshore Av					
1800	DSPN	60018	2917	12W-8N	B2
N North Shore Av					
37800	BHPK	60087	2479	10W-38N	E1
38000	BHPK	60087	2421	10W-38N	E7
38000	WKGN	60099	2421	10W-38N	E7
W North Shore Av					
1000	CHCG	60626	2921	1W-8N	D2
2400	CHCG	60645	2921	3W-8N	A2
2600	CHCG	60645	2920	3W-8N	E2
3100	LNWD	60645	2920	3W-8N	D2
3300	LNWD	60712	2920	4W-8N	C2
5000	LNWD	60712	2919	6W-8N	D2
7200	CHCG	60631	2918	9W-8N	D2
7200	CHCG	60714	2918	9W-8N	D2
7200	NLES	60714	2918	9W-8N	D2
7700	CHCG	60068	2918	9W-8N	C2
7700	PKRG	60068	2918	9W-8N	C2
7700	PKRG	60631	2918	9W-8N	C2
Northshore Ct					
1100	BRTN	60010	2751	24W-20N	C1
Northshore Dr					
8800	GNVW	60025	2863	11W-12N	E1
8900	MaiT	60016	2863	11W-12N	E1
W Northshore Dr					
10	MDLN	60060	2646	19W-27N	D2
Northshore Rd					
10	ELGN	60123	2801	33W-13N	A7
200	ELGN	60123	2800	35W-14N	B6
Northside Av					
-	ROSL	60172	2913	23W-8N	A2
-	SmbT	60172	2913	23W-8N	A2
2800	MchT	60051	2528	32W-32N	C4
2800	MHRY	60051	2528	32W-32N	C4
Northside Dr					
1000	SRWD	60404	3496	30W-22S	B3
North-South Tollway					
-	ADSN	-	2969	21W-2N	E7
-	BGBK	-	3206	21W-10S	A6
-	BGBK	-	3270	20W-14S	A6
-	BmdT	-	2969	21W-3N	E6
-	BmdT	-	3025	21W-2N	E1
-	DPgT	-	3270	20W-13S	A5
-	DRGV	-	3083	21W-4S	D7
-	DRGV	-	3084	20W-2S	A3
-	DRGV	-	3143	22W-6S	C4
-	GNEN	-	3025	21W-0S	E7
-	HmrT	-	3342	20W-15S	B1
-	HmrT	-	3420	19W-20S	D5
-	LKPT	-	3342	20W-15S	B1
-	LKPT	-	3420	19W-20S	D5
-	LMBD	-	3025	21W-0S	E7
-	LMBD	-	3026	21W-0N	A5
-	LMBD	-	3083	21W-1S	E1
-	LMBD	-	3084	20W-2S	A3
-	LMNT	-	3270	20W-14S	A6
-	LMNT	-	3342	20W-15S	B1
-	LSLE	-	3083	21W-4S	D7
-	LSLE	-	3143	22W-4S	D1
-	LslT	-	3083	21W-4S	D7
-	LslT	-	3084	21W-4S	A7
-	LslT	-	3143	22W-6S	D5
-	MltT	-	3025	21W-0S	E7
-	MltT	-	3026	21W-0S	A5
-	MltT	-	3083	21W-1S	E1
-	NLNX	-	3420	19W-20S	D5
-	NLNX	-	3421	18W-21S	A7
-	NLNX	-	3501	18W-22S	B2
-	WDRG	-	3143	21W-7S	E6
-	WDRG	-	3205	21W-8S	E1
-	WDRG	-	3206	21W-8S	A2
-	WDRG	-	3270	21W-12S	A3
-	YkTp	-	3084	20W-2S	A3
North-South Tollway I-355					
-	ADSN	-	2969	21W-2N	E7
-	BGBK	-	3206	21W-10S	A6
-	BGBK	-	3270	21W-11S	A1
-	BmdT	-	2969	21W-3N	E6
-	BmdT	-	3025	21W-2N	E1
-	DPgT	-	3270	21W-13S	A5
-	DRGV	-	3083	21W-4S	D7
-	DRGV	-	3084	20W-2S	A3
-	DRGV	-	3143	21W-7S	E6
-	GNEN	-	3025	21W-0S	E7
-	HmrT	-	3342	20W-18S	C7
-	HmrT	-	3420	20W-19S	C2
-	LKPT	-	3342	20W-17S	C6
-	LKPT	-	3420	20W-18S	C1
-	LMBD	-	3025	21W-0S	E7
-	LMBD	-	3026	21W-0S	A5
-	LMBD	-	3083	21W-1S	E1
-	LMBD	-	3084	20W-2S	A3
-	LMNT	-	3270	20W-14S	A6
-	LMNT	-	3342	20W-15S	C1
-	LSLE	-	3083	21W-4S	D7
-	LSLE	-	3143	22W-5S	C3
-	LslT	-	3083	21W-4S	D7
-	LslT	-	3084	21W-4S	A7
-	LslT	-	3143	22W-5S	C2
-	MltT	-	3025	21W-0S	E7
-	MltT	-	3026	21W-0S	A5
-	MltT	-	3083	21W-1S	E1
-	NLNX	-	3420	18W-21S	E7
-	NLNX	-	3421	18W-21S	A7
-	NLNX	-	3501	18W-22S	A1
-	WDRG	-	3143	21W-7S	E6
-	WDRG	-	3205	21W-8S	E1
-	WDRG	-	3206	21W-8S	A2
-	WDRG	-	3270	21W-12S	A3
-	YkTp	-	3084	20W-2S	A3
Northstar Ct					
18500	TYPK	60487	3504	10W-22S	C1
N Northumberland Pass					
1900	PLTN	60074	2752	21W-18N	D3
Northview Ln					
400	HFET	60169	2804	24W-12N	D7
E North Water St					
100	CHCG	60611	3034	0E-0N	C3
Northway Ct					
300	GLNC	60022	2758	6W-17N	D5
900	HRPK	60133	2912	26W-9N	A1
Northway Dr					
10	BbyT	60119	3017	41W-1N	E3
7200	HRPK	60133	2912	26W-9N	A1
7800	HRPK	60133	2858	26W-9N	A7
8200	SMBG	60133	2858	26W-9N	A7
8200	SMBG	60193	2858	26W-9N	A7
Northwest Av					
100	LydT	60164	2972	14W-2N	C6
100	NHLK	60164	2972	14W-2N	C6
100	NHLK	60164	3028	14W-2N	C1
1300	WCHI	60185	3021	31W-2N	E1
1300	WCHI	60185	3022	31W-2N	A1
Northwest Ct					
-	LynT	60525	3147	13W-5S	A3
Northwest Dr					
-	WCHI	60185	3021	31W-2N	E1
Northwest Hwy					
-	CbaT	60010	2696	29W-22N	D4
-	CRY	60013	2696	29W-22N	B3
10	AlqT	60013	2696	29W-22N	B3
10	CRY	60013	2641	31W-24N	D7
10	FRGV	60010	2696	29W-22N	B3
10	FRGV	60021	2696	29W-22N	B3
800	AlqT	60013	2641	32W-24N	B7
800	AlqT	60014	2641	32W-24N	B6
800	CRY	60014	2641	32W-24N	B6
1000	FRGV	60010	2696	29W-22N	D4
1000	LKBN	60010	2696	29W-22N	D4
4100	CLLK	60014	2641	33W-24N	A6
4400	AlqT	60014	2640	33W-24N	E6
4400	CLLK	60014	2640	33W-25N	D6
Northwest Hwy US-14					
-	CbaT	60010	2696	29W-22N	D4
-	CRY	60013	2696	29W-22N	B3
10	AlqT	60013	2696	29W-22N	B3
10	CRY	60013	2641	31W-24N	D7
10	FRGV	60013	2696	29W-22N	B3
10	FRGV	60021	2696	29W-22N	B3
800	AlqT	60013	2641	32W-24N	B7
800	AlqT	60014	2641	32W-24N	B6
800	CRY	60014	2641	32W-24N	B6
1000	FRGV	60010	2696	29W-22N	D4
1000	LKBN	60010	2696	29W-22N	D4
1000	LKBN	60021	2696	29W-22N	D4
4100	CLLK	60014	2641	33W-24N	A6
4400	AlqT	60014	2640	33W-24N	E6
4400	CLLK	60014	2640	33W-25N	D6
E Northwest Hwy					
-	DSPN	60068	2863	12W-10N	C4
-	PKRG	60016	2863	12W-10N	C4
-	PKRG	60068	2863	12W-10N	C4
10	ANHT	60004	2807	16W-13N	C6
10	ANHT	60005	2807	16W-13N	C6
10	DSPN	60016	2862	14W-12N	C1
10	MPPT	60016	2862	14W-12N	B1
10	MPPT	60056	2808	15W-12N	A7
10	MPPT	60056	2862	13W-11N	D2
10	PLTN	60067	2752	20W-16N	E6
100	BRTN	60010	2751	25W-20N	A1
200	PLTN	60067	2753	20W-16N	A6
400	PLTN	60067	2806	19W-15N	C3
400	PLTN	60074	2806	19W-15N	C2
1700	DSPN	60016	2863	12W-11N	B4
2100	MPPT	60056	2807	16W-13N	D6
E Northwest Hwy US-14					
10	ANHT	60004	2807	16W-13N	C6
10	ANHT	60005	2807	16W-13N	C6
10	DSPN	60016	2862	14W-12N	C1
10	MPPT	60016	2862	14W-12N	B1
10	MPPT	60056	2808	15W-12N	A7
10	MPPT	60056	2862	13W-11N	D2
10	PLTN	60067	2752	20W-16N	E6
100	BRTN	60010	2751	25W-20N	A1
200	PLTN	60067	2753	20W-16N	A6
400	PLTN	60067	2806	19W-15N	C2
400	PLTN	60074	2806	19W-15N	C2
1700	DSPN	60016	2863	12W-11N	B4
2100	MPPT	60056	2807	16W-13N	D6
N Northwest Hwy					
10	PKRG	60068	2864	10W-9N	A7
10	PLTN	60067	2806	20W-15N	A1
10	PLTN	60074	2806	20W-15N	A1
100	BRTN	60010	2751	25W-20N	A1
100	PLTN	60067	2753	20W-16N	A7
100	PLTN	60074	2753	20W-16N	A7
600	PKRG	60068	2863	11W-10N	C5
1500	DSPN	60016	2863	11W-10N	C5
1500	DSPN	60068	2863	11W-10N	C5
1500	PKRG	60016	2863	11W-10N	C5
5000	CHCG	60630	2919	6W-6N	C6
5500	CHCG	60646	2919	7W-7N	B5
5700	CHCG	60631	2919	7W-6N	B5
5900	CHCG	60631	2918	9W-8N	C2
6800	PKRG	60068	2918	9W-8N	C2
N Northwest Hwy US-14					
10	PLTN	60067	2806	20W-15N	A1
10	PLTN	60074	2806	20W-15N	A1
100	BRTN	60010	2751	25W-20N	A1
100	PLTN	60067	2753	20W-16N	A7
100	PLTN	60074	2753	20W-16N	A7
S Northwest Hwy					
-	PLTN	60067	2751	23W-17N	E5
-	PltT	60067	2751	23W-17N	E5
10	CRY	60013	2695	30W-23N	E1
10	CRY	60013	2696	30W-23N	A2
10	PKRG	60068	2918	9W-8N	B1
10	PLTN	60067	2806	20W-15N	A1
10	PLTN	60074	2806	20W-15N	A1
100	AlqT	60013	2696	30W-23N	A2
100	BRTN	60010	2751	25W-18N	B2
100	FRGV	60013	2696	30W-23N	A2
400	CHCG	60631	2918	9W-8N	C1
1100	PltT	60010	2751	23W-17N	D4
S Northwest Hwy US-14					
-	PLTN	60067	2751	23W-17N	E5
-	PltT	60067	2751	23W-17N	E5
10	CRY	60013	2695	30W-23N	E1
10	CRY	60013	2696	30W-23N	A2
10	PLTN	60067	2806	20W-15N	A1
10	PLTN	60074	2806	20W-15N	A1
100	AlqT	60013	2696	30W-23N	A2
100	BRTN	60010	2751	25W-18N	A2
100	FRGV	60013	2696	30W-23N	A2
1100	PltT	60010	2751	23W-17N	D4
W Northwest Hwy					
-	FRGV	60010	2696	28W-22N	D4
-	PltT	60010	2751	23W-17N	E5
-	PltT	60067	2751	23W-17N	E5
10	ANHT	60005	2807	18W-14N	A4
10	MPPT	60056	2808	15W-12N	A7
10	PLTN	60067	2752	21W-16N	D6
100	BRTN	60010	2750	26W-20N	E1
200	MPPT	60056	2807	16W-13N	D6
300	ANHT	60004	2806	18W-14N	D3
300	ANHT	60005	2806	18W-14N	D3
500	BRTN	60010	2697	26W-20N	D7
500	PltT	60067	2752	21W-16N	C6
700	CbaT	60010	2697	27W-21N	B6
900	LKBN	60010	2697	27W-21N	B6
1300	ANHT	60004	2807	16W-13N	D6
1500	PLTN	60067	2751	23W-17N	E5
1800	ANHT	60074	2806	18W-14N	D3
1800	PLTN	60074	2806	18W-14N	D3
28100	LKBN	60010	2696	28W-22N	D4
28700	CbaT	60010	2696	28W-22N	D4
28900	FRGV	60021	2696	28W-22N	D4
28900	LKBN	60021	2696	28W-22N	D4
W Northwest Hwy US-14					
-	FRGV	60010	2696	28W-22N	D4
-	PltT	60010	2751	23W-17N	E5
-	PltT	60067	2751	23W-17N	E5
10	ANHT	60004	2807	18W-14N	A4
10	ANHT	60005	2807	18W-14N	A4
10	MPPT	60056	2808	15W-12N	A7
10	PLTN	60067	2752	21W-16N	D6
100	BRTN	60010	2750	26W-20N	E1
200	MPPT	60056	2807	16W-13N	D6
300	ANHT	60004	2806	18W-14N	D3
300	ANHT	60005	2806	18W-14N	D3
500	BRTN	60010	2697	26W-20N	D7
500	PltT	60067	2752	21W-16N	C6
700	CbaT	60010	2697	27W-21N	B6
900	LKBN	60010	2697	27W-21N	B6
1500	PLTN	60067	2751	23W-17N	E5
1800	ANHT	60074	2806	18W-14N	D3
1800	PLTN	60074	2806	18W-14N	D3
28100	LKBN	60010	2696	28W-22N	D4
28700	CbaT	60010	2696	28W-22N	D4
28900	FRGV	60021	2696	28W-22N	D4
28900	LKBN	60021	2696	28W-22N	D4
Northwest Pkwy					
-	FmtT	60060	2645	20W-27N	E2
-	FmtT	60060	2646	20W-27N	A2
-	SYHW	60118	2799	37W-15N	E3
-	SYHW	60124	2799	37W-15N	E3
2500	ELGN	60124	2799	37W-15N	D3
Northwest Pl					
800	DSPN	60016	2862	14W-10N	D4
Northwest Rd					
2800	MngT	60152	2578	50W-29N	B4
11100	PSHL	60465	3273	11W-13S	E3
Northwestern Av					
1000	GRNE	60031	2478	13W-35N	E6
1500	WrnT	60031	2478	13W-35N	E5
2800	WKGN	60087	2478	13W-37N	E2
2800	WrnT	60087	2478	13W-37N	E2
N Northwestern Av					
4000	WDWH	60083	2420	13W-38N	E6
36700	WrnT	60031	2478	13W-36N	E3
36800	WKGN	60031	2478	13W-36N	E3
36800	WKGN	60087	2478	13W-36N	E3
36800	WrnT	60087	2478	13W-36N	E3
Northwestern Ct					
300	BMDL	60108	2969	22W-4N	C4
Northwestern Dr					
5200	MTSN	60443	3505	6W-24S	E6
Northwest Tollway					
-	ANHT	-	2860	18W-11N	E3
-	ANHT	-	2861	17W-10N	B4
-	CHCG	-	2916	13W-8N	D1
-	CHCG	-	2917	11W-7N	D4
-	DndT	-	2799	37W-14N	E5
-	DndT	-	2800	35W-14N	B6
-	DSPN	-	2861	16W-9N	E6
-	DSPN	-	2862	15W-9N	A7
-	DSPN	-	2916	14W-8N	D1
-	DSPN	-	2917	12W-8N	A2
-	EGvT	-	2860	19W-12N	D2
-	EGvT	-	2861	16W-9N	E7
-	EGvT	-	2862	15W-9N	A7
-	EGVV	-	2861	17W-10N	B5
-	ELGN	-	2799	37W-14N	E5
-	ELGN	-	2800	35W-14N	B6
-	ELGN	-	2801	33W-13N	A7
-	ElgT	-	2801	33W-13N	B7
-	GLBT	-	2798	39W-16N	D2
-	GLBT	-	2799	37W-15N	C4
-	HFET	-	2802	29W-12N	D7
-	HFET	-	2803	27W-12N	C7
-	HFET	-	2804	24W-12N	D7
-	HnrT	-	2801	33W-13N	A7
-	HnrT	-	2802	30W-12N	C7
-	HPSR	-	2743	45W-19N	C3
-	HshT	-	2743	44W-18N	D4
-	HshT	-	2744	42W-18N	D5
-	HTLY	-	2744	42W-18N	D5
-	HTLY	-	2745	41W-17N	A7
-	MPPT	-	2861	17W-10N	B5
-	RGMW	-	2859	21W-12N	E1
-	RGMW	-	2860	19W-12N	C2
-	RSMT	-	2916	13W-8N	E1
-	RSMT	-	2917	12W-7N	B3
-	RtdT	-	2744	43W-18N	B5
-	RtdT	-	2745	41W-17N	A7
-	RtdT	-	2798	39W-16N	D2
-	RtdT	-	2799	38W-15N	A3
-	SMBG	-	2804	24W-12N	D7
-	SMBG	-	2805	23W-12N	B7
-	SMBG	-	2859	22W-12N	C1
-	SmbT	-	2805	23W-12N	B7
-	SmbT	-	2859	22W-12N	C1
Northwest Tollway I-90					
-	ANHT	-	2860	18W-11N	E3
-	ANHT	-	2861	17W-11N	A4
-	CHCG	-	2916	14W-8N	D1
-	CHCG	-	2917	11W-7N	E4
-	DndT	-	2799	37W-15N	C4
-	DndT	-	2800	36W-14N	A6
-	DSPN	-	2861	16W-9N	E6
-	DSPN	-	2862	15W-9N	A7
-	DSPN	-	2916	14W-8N	D1
-	DSPN	-	2917	12W-8N	A2
-	EGvT	-	2860	19W-12N	D2
-	EGvT	-	2861	16W-9N	E7
-	EGvT	-	2862	15W-9N	A7
-	EGVV	-	2861	16W-10N	D6
-	ELGN	-	2799	37W-15N	C4
-	ELGN	-	2800	35W-14N	B6
-	ELGN	-	2801	33W-13N	A7
-	ElgT	-	2801	33W-13N	A7
-	GLBT	-	2798	39W-16N	D2
-	GLBT	-	2799	37W-15N	C4
-	HFET	-	2802	29W-12N	D7
-	HFET	-	2803	28W-12N	A7
-	HFET	-	2804	24W-12N	D7
-	HnrT	-	2801	33W-13N	A7
-	HnrT	-	2802	31W-12N	A7
-	HPSR	-	2743	45W-19N	C3
-	HshT	-	2743	44W-18N	D4
-	HshT	-	2744	42W-18N	D5
-	HTLY	-	2744	43W-18N	B5
-	HTLY	-	2745	41W-17N	A7
-	MPPT	-	2861	17W-10N	B5
-	RGMW	-	2859	21W-12N	E1
-	RGMW	-	2860	21W-12N	A1
-	RSMT	-	2916	13W-8N	E1
-	RSMT	-	2917	12W-7N	B3
-	RtdT	-	2744	42W-18N	D5
-	RtdT	-	2745	41W-17N	A6
-	RtdT	-	2798	39W-16N	D2
-	RtdT	-	2799	38W-15N	A3
-	SMBG	-	2804	24W-12N	D7
-	SMBG	-	2805	23W-12N	B7
-	SMBG	-	2859	22W-12N	C1
-	SmbT	-	2805	23W-12N	B7
-	SmbT	-	2859	22W-12N	C1
Northwind Blvd					
1600	LYVL	60048	2590	18W-30N	D2
Northwind Cir					
2100	SMBG	60194	2858	26W-11N	A3
Northwind Dr					
-	LYWD	60411	3509	2E-23S	E3
200	LKVL	60046	2474	23W-37N	E3
2800	NLNX	60451	3502	15W-25S	C7
2800	NLNX	60451	3590	15W-25S	D1
5200	RNPK	60471	3593	6W-27S	E4
5200	RNPK	60471	3594	6W-27S	A5
Northwind Ln					
100	RtdT	60118	2746	38W-18N	B5

STREET Block City ZIP Map# CGS Grid

Northwind Ln
600 LKVL 60046 2474 23W-37N E3
600 LKVL 60046 2475 23W-37N A2
Northwood Av
- PKCY 60085 2535 13W-33N E2
Northwood Ct
- WCDA 60084 2588 24W-29N B4
E Northwood Ct
2400 ANHT 60004 2807 16W-15N D1
Northwood Dr
- WCDA 60084 2588 24W-29N B4
400 GLNC 60022 2758 7W-18N C3
E Northwood Dr
7200 MchT 60097 2469 36W-35N D6
7300 WRLK 60097 2469 36W-35N D6
Northwood Ln
- WCDA 60084 2588 24W-29N B4
2000 WDSK 60098 2524 41W-32N D4
Northwood Rd
100 RVSD 60546 3088 9W-2S C3
Northwood Tr
- LKVL 60046 2474 23W-36N E4
Northwoods Cir
1400 DRFD 60015 2703 11W-21N E5
Northwoods Ct
800 DRFD 60015 2703 11W-21N E5
6000 FoxT 60560 3332 46W-16S A4
7800 FKFT 60423 3592 9W-27S D4
Northwoods Dr
300 AddT 60106 2971 17W-4N C3
600 WnfT 60185 3023 27W-1N C2
700 WynT 60185 3023 27W-1N C2
800 DRFD 60015 2703 11W-21N E5
7800 FKFT 60423 3592 9W-27S D4
29400 LbvT 60048 2592 15W-29N B4
29400 LYVL 60048 2592 15W-29N B4
N Northwoods Dr
800 DRFD 60015 2703 11W-21N E5
38600 WDWH 60083 2420 14W-38N D6
S Northwoods Dr
800 DRFD 60015 2703 11W-21N E6
Northwoods Ln
100 BMDL 60108 2968 24W-5N C1
27000 MTWA 60048 2648 14W-27N C2
Norton Av
10 LMNT 60439 3270 19W-14S D6
400 BmdT 60137 2969 22W-2N B7
400 GLHT 60139 2969 22W-2N B7
E Norton Av
600 JLET 60432 3499 23W-23S B5
N Norton Av
600 MDLN 60060 2590 18W-28N E6
Norton Dr
10 LMNT 60439 3270 19W-14S D6
100 BMDL 60108 2969 23W-4N A3
Norton Ln
- BtlT 60560 3261 43W-13S B5
- YKVL 60560 3261 43W-13S B5
300 BMDL 60108 2969 23W-4N A3
Norton St
700 LMBD 60148 3026 18W-0S E7
700 YkTp 60148 3026 18W-0S E7
Norton Creek Dr
2700 WCHI 60185 2965 31W-4N D4
2700 WynT 60185 2965 31W-4N D4
Norwalk Ct
2900 AURA 60502 3139 32W-6S D4
5000 JLET 60586 3496 30W-22S C1
Norwalk Rd
1000 LMNT 60439 3270 18W-14S E7
1000 LMNT 60439 3271 18W-14S A7
Norway Cir
400 YKVL 60560 3333 43W-15S A3
Norway Ln
1500 PltT 60074 2753 19W-17N C4
Norway Pl
700 OSWG 60543 3262 39W-12S E3
E Norway Tr
3300 CteT 60417 3687 4E-29S C1
Norway Pine Ln
2800 NHBK 60062 2756 11W-16N E7
2800 NHBK 60062 2809 11W-16N E1
Norwell Ct
1300 SMBG 60193 2858 25W-9N C7
Norwell Ln
10 RDLK 60073 2589 23W-30N A2
100 RDLK 60073 2588 23W-30N E2
1600 SMBG 60193 2858 25W-9N B7
Norwich Ct
100 LKBF 60044 2593 11W-29N D4
200 MNSR 46321 3510 D4
700 CLLK 60012 2640 33W-26N D2
2000 GNVW 60025 2809 10W-14N E3
2200 NPVL 60565 3203 27W-10S C5
W Norwich Ct
22200 PnfT 60544 3339 28W-17S B5
Norwich Dr
- MNSR 46321 3510 D4
100 BRLT 60103 2909 32W-8N C3
Norwich Ln
11200 ODPK 60467 3344 14W-16S E3
W Norwich Ln
22200 PnfT 60544 3339 27W-16S B5
Norwich St
12900 PNFD 60585 3338 30W-15S C2
Norwick Ln
400 CLSM 60188 3024 24W-1N D3
Norwood Av
900 LslT 60540 3204 25W-8S A1
900 NPVL 60540 3204 25W-8S A1
1700 MLPK 60160 3029 11W-1N D2
W Norwood Av
1200 ITSC 60143 2914 21W-7N A4
1400 ITSC 60143 2913 21W-7N E4
Norwood Blvd
10 PKFT 60466 3595 3W-26S B2
Norwood Ct
100 RGMW 60008 2805 21W-14N D4
3100 SMWD 60107 2911 28W-8N A2
3300 JLET 60451 3500 19W-22S D2
8000 WDRG 60517 3205 22W-9S D3
W Norwood Ct
6600 HDHT 60706 2974 8W-5N E1
6600 HDHT 60706 2975 8W-5N A1
Norwood Dr
24200 PNFD 60585 3338 30W-15S B2
W Norwood Dr
8000 FftT 60423 3504 10W-24S C5
Norwood Ln
500 SMBG 60193 2858 24W-9N C7
900 BRLT 60103 2910 30W-7N C5
900 WynT 60103 2910 30W-7N C5
3300 JLET 60451 3500 19W-22S D2
Norwood Ln E
1000 AURA 60504 3201 31W-9S D3
Norwood Ln W
1100 AURA 60504 3201 31W-9S D3
Norwood St
9800 RSMT 60018 2917 12W-7N B4
W Norwood St
1800 CHCG 60660 2921 2W-7N B3
1900 CHCG 60659 2921 2W-7N B3
4300 CHCG 60646 2920 5W-7N A3
6200 CHCG 60646 2919 7W-7N A3
7700 CHCG 60631 2918 9W-7N C4
Norwood Ter
2700 GNVW 60025 2864 10W-12N B1
2700 MaiT 60025 2864 10W-12N B1
Norwood Square Dr
100 PKFT 60466 3595 3W-26S C2
Notis Ct
900 SMBG 60193 2912 24W-9N D1
Notre Dame Av
3200 JLET 60436 3497 26W-24S E5
6200 HRPK 60133 2911 26W-7N E4
E Notre Dame Av
1800 CteT 60417 3686 2E-29S D1
Notre Dame Dr
10 NPVL 60540 3141 26W-7S D7
700 MTSN 60443 3505 6W-25S E6
1100 LMNT 60439 3271 18W-14S A7
Notre Dame Ln
300 ELGN 60123 2853 36W-10N E6
Nottingham Av
200 GNVW 60025 2864 8W-12N E1
2900 MKHM 60428 3427 3W-19S A2
7900 BRBK 60459 3210 8W-9S E3
8200 BGVW 60455 3210 8W-9S E3
8200 BGVW 60459 3210 8W-9S E3
8200 BRBK 60455 3210 8W-9S E3
9500 OKLN 60415 3210 8W-11S E6
9500 OKLN 60453 3210 8W-11S E6
9700 CHRG 60415 3210 8W-11S E7
24100 PNFD 60585 3338 30W-15S C2
N Nottingham Av
3200 CHCG 60634 2974 8W-4N D3
4300 NRDG 60706 2974 8W-5N D1
4500 NRDG 60706 2918 8W-5N D7
4800 CHCG 60706 2918 8W-6N D6
4800 HDHT 60706 2918 8W-6N D6
5300 CHCG 60656 2918 8W-6N D5
5700 CHCG 60631 2918 8W-7N D4
7500 NLES 60714 2864 8W-9N E6
S Nottingham Av
6300 CHCG 60638 3148 8W-7S E5
7100 BDPK 60638 3148 8W-8S E7
7300 BDPK 60638 3210 8W-8S E1
7400 BGVW 60455 3210 8W-8S E1
7400 BGVW 60638 3210 8W-8S E1
Nottingham Ct
100 OSWG 60543 3263 36W-11S D2
200 CLLK 60014 2640 35W-24N A7
700 ISLK 60042 2586 29W-28N C6
1400 WLNG 60090 2754 15W-18N E3
2600 NPVL 60565 3203 27W-10S C6
4200 LSLE 60532 3082 24W-4S D7
7700 TYPK 60477 3424 9W-19S D2
16400 ODPK 60467 3423 13W-19S A3
S Nottingham Ct
16500 LKPT 60441 3421 18W-19S A3
Nottingham Dr
- ALGN 60102 2693 37W-21N C6
10 LNSH 60069 2702 13W-23N E3
100 BGBK 60440 3268 23W-11S E2
100 OSWG 60543 3263 37W-11S D2
700 BbyT 60119 3075 43W-2S A4
1900 AraT 60504 3138 35W-5S B2
1900 AURA 60504 3138 35W-5S B2
2100 NPVL 60565 3203 27W-10S B5
3800 LGGV 60047 2700 20W-22N B5
7400 TYPK 60477 3424 9W-19S D2
11700 HTLY 60142 2744 42W-20N C1
Nottingham Ln
- CLSM 60188 3024 25W-2N A1
- MDLN 60061 2647 17W-25N A5
- VNHL 60061 2647 17W-25N A5
600 CLLK 60014 2640 35W-24N A7
800 CLLK 60014 2639 35W-24N E7
800 CLLK 60014 2693 35W-23N E1
1000 HFET 60169 2804 24W-12N C7
1100 HnrT 60120 2856 31W-10N A5
1400 INCK 60060 2647 17W-25N B5
1400 MDLN 60060 2647 17W-25N A5
1800 WHTN 60187 3082 23W-2S E4
2000 NPVL 60565 3203 27W-10S B5
Nottingham Pl
- BHPK 60087 2422 9W-38N C7
Nottingham Rd
1800 WDRG 60517 3206 20W-9S A3
8000 TYPK 60477 3424 10W-19S C2
Notting Hill Rd
1300 ALGN 60102 2747 35W-19N B3
5200 GRNE 60031 2478 15W-36N A3
5400 GRNE 60031 2477 15W-36N E3
Nottingwood Av
16400 OKFT 60452 3426 5W-19S A2
Nottoway Ct
- RGMW 60008 2860 19W-11N B2
Nottoway Sq
- RGMW 60008 2860 19W-12N C1
Nova Ct
1200 WLNG 60090 2754 16W-18N D3
Novak Dr
17000 HLCT 60429 3427 3W-20S A4
Novean Pkwy
11800 DrrT 60098 2581 40W-29N E5
11800 DrrT 60098 2582 40W-29N A5
11800 WDSK 60098 2581 40W-29N E5
11800 WDSK 60098 2582 40W-29N A5
N Novy Rd
- BDWD 60408 3942 31W-40S B3
- BDWD 60481 3942 31W-40S B3
- RedT 60408 3942 31W-40S B3
- RedT 60481 3942 31W-40S B3
- WmTp 60408 3942 31W-40S B2
No Wake Av
21500 WMTN 60481 3853 26W-37S E4
Nowell Av
1000 JLET 60433 3499 23W-25S A7
1100 JLET 60433 3587 23W-25S A1
1100 JltT 60433 3587 23W-25S A1
Noyes Ct
2300 EVTN 60201 2867 2W-12N B1
Noyes St
600 EVTN 60201 2867 3W-12N A1
3300 EVTN 60201 2866 4W-12N B1
3300 SKOK 60076 2866 4W-12N B1
E Noyes St
400 ANHT 60005 2861 17W-12N B1
400 ANHT 60056 2861 17W-12N B1
400 MPPT 60056 2861 17W-12N B1
W Noyes St
200 ANHT 60005 2861 18W-12N A1
300 ANHT 60005 2860 18W-12N E1
Nuclear Dr
1200 WCHI 60185 3021 31W-2N E1
2400 JLET 60431 3417 28W-20S B6
2400 PnfT 60431 3417 28W-20S B6
Nueport Ct S
8200 WLSP 60480 3208 14W-9S D3
Nueport Dr S
8100 WLSP 60480 3208 14W-9S D3
Nueport Dr W
11400 WLSP 60480 3208 14W-9S D3
Nugent St
- GNWD 60425 3508 0E-23S D3
10 AddT 60101 2971 18W-4N A4
10 ADSN 60101 2971 18W-4N A4
Nugget Cir
6200 HRPK 60133 2911 26W-7N E4
Nunda Av
4300 NndT 60014 2585 30W-27N E7
Nunda Rd
8200 WRLK 60097 2469 37W-35N C5
Nunda Tr
500 CLLK 60012 2640 33W-27N D1
5000 NndT 60012 2640 34W-27N D1
Nursery Dr
7700 GRNE 60031 2476 18W-35N E5
7800 WrnT 60046 2476 18W-35N E5
Nusbaum Rd
11400 GwdT 60098 2468 40W-35N A7
Nutcracker Dr
- DRN 60561 3207 18W-8S A1
Nuthatch Ct
700 CmpT 60175 2961 42W-5N D2
Nuthatch Dr
100 WDSK 60098 2525 40W-32N A5
Nuthatch Wy
400 LNHT 60046 2476 19W-37N B2
Nutmeg Ct
1300 MPPT 60056 2807 16W-14N E3
1400 BRLT 60103 2967 27W-5N C1
Nutmeg Ln
1900 NPVL 60565 3204 24W-8S D2
4300 LSLE 60532 3142 24W-4S D1
Nuttall Rd
200 RVSD 60546 3088 9W-2S C3
Nutwood Ct
100 BGBK 60440 3269 22W-12S D2
W Nutwood Ct
7600 FftT 60423 3504 9W-24S D5
Ny-O-Da Pl
1300 HDPK 60035 2757 8W-20N E2

O

Oak
- MNGV 60053 2865 8W-10N A5
Oak Av
10 GYLK 60030 2532 20W-32N E4
10 HIWD 60040 2704 9W-23N D3
100 CPVL 60110 2747 34W-17N E7
100 HLSD 60162 3029 13W-0S A6
100 WDDL 60191 2971 17W-5N B1
200 DndT 60118 2747 35W-17N B7
200 WDDL 60191 2915 17W-6N B7
200 WDND 60118 2747 35W-17N B7
200 WTMT 60559 3145 17W-5S C3
400 AddT 60191 2915 17W-6N B7
600 LKBF 60044 2593 10W-28N E6
900 AURA 60506 3138 35W-6S A5
1000 WLNG 60070 2755 15W-16N A7
1000 WLNG 60090 2755 15W-16N A7
1100 PTHT 60070 2755 15W-16N A6
1200 EVTN 60202 2867 2W-10N B3
1300 LMNT 60439 3271 17W-14S B6
1800 EVTN 60201 2867 2W-11N B2
2000 HRPK 60133 2911 27W-8N C3
2100 NHBK 60062 2757 10W-17N A6
2500 NHBK 60062 2756 10W-17N E6
3100 BKFD 60513 3087 11W-3S E5
3600 NfdT 60062 2756 12W-17N B6
4300 LYNS 60534 3088 9W-4S D7
4500 BKFD 60513 3147 11W-4S E1
7200 OKPK 60302 3030 9W-0N D3
7200 RVFT 60302 3030 9W-0N C3
7200 RVFT 60305 3030 10W-0N B3
10400 CHRG 60415 3275 7W-12S B2
11000 CHRG 60482 3275 7W-12S B3
11000 WRTH 60482 3275 7W-12S B3
15900 OKFT 60452 3426 6W-19S A2
18600 BlmT 60411 3429 3E-22S E7
18600 LNSG 60411 3429 3E-22S E7
18600 LNSG 60438 3429 3E-22S E7
18700 BlmT 60411 3509 3E-22S E1
18700 LNSG 60411 3509 3E-22S E1
18700 LNSG 60438 3509 3E-22S E1
19100 CCHL 60478 3506 5W-23S D3
19400 LNSG 60411 3510 3E-23S B2
19400 LNSG 60438 3510 3E-23S B2
21500 LkvT 60046 2417 21W-38N D6
E Oak Av
100 WHTN 60187 3024 24W-0N D5
1000 LGPK 60525 3087 12W-3S C5
1100 BKFD 60513 3087 12W-3S C5
1100 BKFD 60525 3087 12W-3S C5
N Oak Av
- RLKB 60073 2475 22W-34N A7
100 BRLT 60103 2910 29W-8N E2
300 BRLT 60107 2910 28W-9N E1
300 SMWD 60107 2910 28W-9N E1
9400 MaiT 60016 2863 11W-11N D2
22200 AvnT 60030 2532 22W-34N C2
22200 RLKP 60073 2532 22W-34N C2
25200 GrtT 60041 2474 25W-34N B7
26000 FmtT 60060 2646 19W-26N C3
32300 WrnT 60030 2533 18W-32N E5
32400 GYLK 60030 2533 18W-32N E5
39400 AntT 60002 2416 25W-39N A5
S Oak Av
100 BRLT 60103 2910 29W-8N E3
4300 HMND 46327 3352 E4
W Oak Av
10 LGPK 60525 3087 12W-3S B5
10 LktT 60441 3419 22W-21S D7
100 WHTN 60187 3024 24W-0N C5
600 LktT 60432 3419 22W-21S D7
3800 MHRY 60050 2528 32W-32N A4
8100 NLES 60714 2864 10W-11N B3
14100 LbvT 60045 2648 14W-26N C2
14300 HMGN 60491 3343 17W-16S B4
16000 HmrT 60432 3420 20W-21S C7
16000 HmrT 60441 3420 20W-21S C7
16000 LKPT 60432 3420 21W-21S A7
16000 LKPT 60441 3420 21W-21S A7
16000 NLNX 60441 3420 20W-21S C7
W Oak Av
16600 LktT 60432 3420 21W-21S A7
16600 LktT 60441 3420 21W-21S A7
16800 LKPT 60432 3419 22W-21S D7
16800 LKPT 60441 3419 22W-21S D7
18800 LbvT 60060 2646 18W-26N D3
18800 MDLN 60060 2646 18W-26N D3
24800 LkvT 60046 2416 24W-39N B5
25800 AntT 60002 2415 26W-40N E4
25800 AntT 60002 2416 25W-40N A3
Oak Cir
300 WLMT 60091 2812 3W-13N D6
W Oak Cir
26000 GrtT 60041 2473 26W-36N E3
Oak Ct
- DGvT 60439 3270 20W-12S C3
- FKFT 60423 3504 10W-24S B6
10 CTCY 60409 3351 2E-16S C4
10 LMNT 60439 3270 19W-14S C6
10 OKBK 60523 3086 15W-3S B5
10 SchT 60175 2963 36W-5N D3
100 PltT 60010 2751 24W-18N C3
100 SRWD 60404 3496 29W-24S D5
200 MNKA 60447 3583 33W-28S C7
400 WNFD 60190 3023 27W-0S C2
700 CLLK 60014 2639 36W-25N C4
1000 FSMR 60422 3506 4W-22S E2
2100 NPVL 60565 3204 25W-9S A5
2900 SMBG 60193 2857 27W-10N C6
3200 HLCT 60429 3426 4W-20S E4
13500 LMNT 60439 3343 17W-15S B2
28400 LKBN 60010 2696 28W-22N E4
S Oak Ct
13000 PSHT 60463 3346 9W-15S D1
23500 CteT 60417 3595 2W-28S E6
W Oak Ct
12800 HMGN 60491 3422 16W-19S A2
13300 HMGN 60491 3343 16W-17S E5
19000 AvnT 60046 2476 19W-35N D5
19000 WrnT 60046 2476 19W-35N D5
Oak Dr
- BmnT 60426 3426 5W-19S A2
10 AlqT 60013 2641 31W-25N D4
10 CmpT 60175 2962 41W-5N A1
10 ElgT 60124 2907 38W-7N B4
10 ElgT 60175 2907 38W-7N B4
10 ODHL 60013 2641 31W-25N D4
10 SchT 60175 2907 38W-7N B4
100 NLNX 60451 3501 18W-24S B6
200 SRWD 60404 3496 30W-23S C4
400 WLNG 60090 2755 14W-17N C5
500 EDND 60118 2801 33W-16N B2
500 WcnT 60084 2644 25W-26N B3
700 GLNC 60022 2758 7W-17N C4
700 SchT 60174 2908 35W-7N B6
1000 BCHR 60401 3864 0W-36S C1
1500 MHRY 60050 2528 33W-33N A2
2500 DndT 60118 2800 36W-17N B1
2500 WDND 60118 2800 36W-17N B1
2700 DndT 60118 2747 36W-17N A7
2700 WDND 60118 2747 36W-17N A7
7700 MchT 60097 2469 36W-37N D2
39300 LkvT 60046 2416 24W-39N B5
40200 AntT 60002 2417 23W-40N A3
E Oak Dr
200 ELBN 60119 3017 43W-1N A3
N Oak Dr
33500 GrtT 60041 2530 26W-33N D3
W Oak Dr
11500 BHPK 60099 2421 11W-38N D7
11500 WKGN 60099 2421 11W-38N D7
Oak Ln
- CRTE 60417 3597 0E-29S A7
- CRTE 60417 3686 0E-29S A1
- CteT 60417 3686 0E-29S A1
- LGGV 60047 2700 19W-22N C4
- SEGN 60177 2907 37W-7N C4
10 AddT 60106 2971 17W-3N C4
10 BtlT 60560 3333 41W-14S E1
10 BtlT 60560 3334 41W-14S A1
10 HNWD 60047 2645 21W-24N D7
10 LKVL 60046 2475 23W-37N A1
10 LMNT 60439 3270 19W-14S C6
10 PKFT 60466 3595 3W-27S B5
10 WnfT 60555 3080 29W-2S E4
200 WynT 60185 2966 29W-3N D6
300 LynT 60458 3209 11W-8S E2
300 SchT 60174 2964 35W-5N B3
500 FXLK 60041 2473 27W-35N C5
600 WNFD 60190 3023 27W-0S B7
1000 ALGN 60102 2694 33W-21N E6
1000 ALGN 60102 2695 33W-21N A6
1100 WNSP 60558 3146 14W-6S D4
2200 ANHT 60005 2806 19W-12N D7
2200 RGMW 60005 2806 19W-12N D7
2200 RGMW 60008 2806 19W-12N C7
2700 HHLL 60051 2586 30W-29N A4
4900 GRNE 60031 2478 15W-35N B6
12500 PSPK 60464 3272 14W-14S E7
13200 LMNT 60439 3342 19W-15S E2
13400 OrlT 60462 3346 9W-15S D2
13400 PSHT 60462 3346 9W-15S D2
13400 PSHT 60463 3346 9W-15S D2
20100 LYWD 60411 3509 3E-23S E4
24000 CNHN 60404 3584 30W-26S C4
24000 TroT 60404 3584 30W-26S C4
34400 AvnT 60073 2532 21W-34N C1
N Oak Ln
10 GNWD 60425 3508 0E-22S E1
9600 MaiT 60016 2863 11W-12N D1
28300 LbvT 60048 2592 15W-28N B6
42200 AntT 60002 2357 25W-42N A6
S Oak Ln
10 GNWD 60425 3508 0E-22S E2
20700 FftT 60423 3504 9W-25S E6
23700 CteT 60417 3687 4E-30S B2
W Oak Ln
8100 NLES 60714 2864 10W-10N B5
11700 WPHR 60099 2362 11W-43N D4
14500 VrnT 60045 2702 14W-24N C1
25100 AntT 60002 2357 25W-43N B4
Oak Pl
14200 ODPK 60462 3345 12W-17S D4
W Oak Pl
9500 MaiT 60016 2863 11W-12N C1
Oak Rd
- GNVA 60134 3021 33W-1N A4
- GnvT 60134 3021 33W-1N A4
- GnvT 60185 3021 33W-1N A4
100 AlqT 60102 2695 32W-21N B5
200 SchT 60175 2963 36W-5N E2
400 SCRL 60185 2965 32W-3N C6
400 WynT 60185 2965 32W-3N C6
600 BRTN 60010 2698 25W-20N A7
600 BRTN 60010 2751 25W-20N A1
2100 HMWD 60430 3427 2W-21S C7
Oak Rd
15200 OKFT 60452 3347 8W-18S B6
S Oak Rd
- MonT 60449 3682 6W-32S E6
7600 MchT 60097 2469 36W-35N D5
7600 WRLK 60097 2469 36W-35N D5
25600 MONE 60449 3683 6W-31S A5
25900 MONE 60449 3682 6W-32S E6
Oak St
- AddT 60101 2971 17W-3N B4
- ADSN 60101 2971 17W-3N B4
- JltT 60436 3586 24W-26S E2
- MONE 60449 3683 6W-31S A4
- RcmT 60071 2413 33W-39N A4
10 AddT 60101 2970 19W-3N D4
10 ADSN 60101 2970 19W-3N D4
10 BtlT 60512 3261 41W-12S E3
10 CTSD 60525 3147 12W-6S C4
10 FKFT 60423 3591 12W-26S D2
10 HGKN 60525 3147 12W-7S C5
10 LKZH 60047 2698 23W-23N E3
10 NARA 60542 3077 36W-4S D7
10 NARA 60542 3078 36W-4S A7
10 PGGV 60140 2798 41W-13N B7
10 PltT 60140 2798 41W-13N B7
10 PTBR 60010 2642 29W-26N D4
10 WcnT 60010 2642 29W-26N D4
10 WTMT 60559 3145 17W-5S B3
10 YKVL 60512 3261 41W-12S E3
100 BDWD 60408 3942 31W-41S B5
100 BMDL 60108 2968 23W-5N E1
100 ELGN 60123 2854 34W-10N D5
100 ELGN 60123 2855 33W-10N A6
100 MYWD 60153 3030 10W-0N A4
100 NLNX 60451 3501 17W-24S C6
100 RVFT 60305 3030 10W-0N A4
100 WMTN 60481 3853 27W-39S D7
200 AraT 60506 3077 38W-4S A7
200 AraT 60542 3077 37W-4S C7
200 BTVA 60510 3078 35W-2S B3
200 FRGV 60021 2696 29W-23N B3
200 GNEN 60137 3025 23W-0N B4
200 TRLK 60010 2643 26W-25N C5
300 DSPN 60016 2863 13W-11N A3
300 JLET 60432 3499 22W-23S C4
300 JltT 60432 3499 22W-23S C4
300 PKRG 60068 2918 10W-8N B1
300 SCRL 60174 2964 35W-2N A7
300 SEGN 60177 2908 34W-8N D2
300 WKGN 60085 2537 10W-33N B3
400 DYR 46311 3598 D2
400 LKPT 60441 3419 21W-18S E1
400 LktT 60441 3419 21W-18S E1
400 WNKA 60093 2812 4W-15N B2
500 EGVV 60007 2860 18W-9N E7
500 EGVV 60007 2914 18W-9N E1
500 LYVL 60048 2591 16W-28N D6
600 LktT 60441 3341 21W-18S E7
600 ROSL 60172 2912 23W-6N E6
600 WDSK 60098 2524 42W-31N B6
700 GNVA 60134 3020 34W-1N D4
700 MYWD 60153 3029 11W-0N C4
800 BmdT 60172 2912 23W-6N E7
800 WNSP 60558 3086 14W-4S D6
900 SRGV 60554 3135 42W-4S D2
1000 SCRL 60174 3020 36W-2N A1
1100 WNKA 60093 2811 6W-15N E2
1200 SCRL 60174 3019 36W-2N E1
1600 CHHT 60411 3596 1W-25S A1
1600 HRPK 60133 2911 27W-7N D4
1700 SPGV 60081 2414 30W-39N A4
1800 BLID 60827 3277 2W-15S C7
1800 CTPK 60406 3277 2W-15S C7
1800 CTPK 60827 3277 2W-15S C7
1800 NHFD 60093 2811 7W-15N C2
2000 SchT 60174 3019 36W-2N D1
2000 SchT 60175 3019 36W-2N D1
2000 SCRL 60175 3019 36W-2N D1
2400 BLID 60406 3277 3W-15S B7
2400 FNPK 60131 2973 11W-3N D5
2400 FNPK 60171 2973 11W-3N D6
2500 HDPK 60035 2704 8W-23N E2
2500 SCRL 60175 2963 37W-2N C7
2700 HDPK 60037 2704 8W-23N E2
3100 BLWD 60104 3029 12W-0N B4
3200 HLCT 60429 3426 4W-20S E4
3500 FSMR 60422 3506 4W-22S E2
4600 BLWD 60104 3028 13W-0N E4
5100 BKLY 60104 3028 13W-0N E4
5100 BKLY 60162 3028 13W-0N E4
5100 BKLY 60163 3028 13W-0N E4
5100 HLSD 60162 3028 13W-0N E4
5200 OKLN 60453 3211 6W-10S E5
6000 CmgT 60033 2405 52W-38N B7
9200 ODPK 60462 3345 11W-17S E5
13900 HMGN 60491 3342 19W-16S E4
14100 HmrT 60491 3342 19W-16S E4
14200 DLTN 60419 3350 0E-16S E4
15300 SHLD 60473 3350 0E-18S E6
18200 LNSG 60438 3430 3E-21S A6
19300 FftT 60448 3503 11W-23S E3
19300 MKNA 60448 3503 11W-23S E3
21100 MTSN 60443 3506 4W-25S E7
21100 MTSN 60443 3594 4W-25S E1
21100 OMFD 60461 3506 4W-25S E7
27500 ISLK 60042 2586 28W-27N E7
27500 WcnT 60042 2586 28W-27N E7
27500 WcnT 60042 2642 28W-27N E1
38800 LkvT 60046 2417 21W-38N D6
Oak St CO-15
200 AraT 60506 3077 38W-4S A7
200 AraT 60542 3077 37W-4S C7
200 NARA 60542 3077 38W-4S A7
Oak St US-20
10 PGGV 60140 2798 41W-13N B7
10 PltT 60140 2798 41W-13N B7
E Oak St
10 ADSN 60101 2970 18W-3N E4
10 ADSN 60101 2971 18W-3N A4
10 CHCG 60610 3034 0E-1N C2
10 CHCG 60611 3034 0E-1N C2
10 FXLK 60020 2473 28W-37N A3
10 LIHL 60156 2694 35W-22N A4
200 VLPK 60181 3027 17W-1N B3
300 EMHT 60126 3027 17W-1N B3
300 VLPK 60126 3027 17W-1N B3
400 MDLN 60060 2646 18W-27N E1
700 AddT 60106 2971 17W-3N B4
700 ADSN 60106 2971 17W-3N B4
2000 CteT 60417 3686 2E-29S D2
N Oak St
10 CLLK 60014 2639 36W-27N E2
10 PLNO 60545 3259 47W-13S D6
10 PLTN 60067 2805 20W-16N E1
100 GNWD 60425 3508 0W-22S D1
200 CLLK 60012 2639 36W-27N E2

Block	City	ZIP	Map#	CGS Grid	
N Oak St					
200	EMHT	60126	3027	16W-2N	D1
200	ITSC	60143	2914	19W-6N	C6
200	NndT	60014	2639	36W-27N	E2
300	HNDL	60521	3086	15W-4S	B7
300	HNDL	60521	3146	15W-4S	C1
300	MPPT	60056	2807	16W-13N	E6
400	EMHT	60126	2971	16W-2N	D7
400	NndT	60012	2639	36W-26N	E2
500	WCHI	60185	3022	29W-1N	D3
500	WnfT	60185	3022	29W-1N	D3
800	RLKP	60073	2532	22W-34N	B1
1200	PLTN	60067	2752	20W-17N	E4
1400	PLTN	60074	2752	20W-17N	E4
1400	PltT	60074	2752	20W-17N	E4
2400	RVGV	60171	2974	10W-3N	A5
4500	NRDG	60706	2918	10W-5N	B7
7100	MchT	60097	2469	36W-36N	E4
33700	WrnT	60030	2533	18W-33N	E2
39000	FXLK	60020	2415	28W-39N	A6
39000	FXLK	60081	2415	28W-39N	A6
42300	AntT	60002	2356	26W-42N	D6
S Oak St					
10	CLLK	60014	2639	36W-25N	E4
10	HNDL	60521	3146	15W-5S	B1
100	HPSR	60140	2795	47W-16N	E2
200	ITSC	60143	2914	19W-6N	C6
200	PLTN	60067	2805	20W-15N	E2
300	PLNO	60545	3259	47W-14S	D7
700	WCHI	60185	3022	29W-0N	D6
W Oak St					
10	CHCG	60611	3034	0W-1N	B2
10	FXLK	60020	2473	28W-36N	A3
10	LIHL	60156	2693	35W-22N	E4
400	CHCG	60610	3034	0W-1N	A2
400	PNFD	60544	3338	30W-17S	C7
500	PTON	60468	3860	9W-37S	E2
600	PtnT	60468	3860	9W-37S	D2
21600	LkvT	60046	2417	21W-39N	D6
23100	PNFD	60544	3416	28W-19S	E3
23100	PnfT	60544	3416	28W-19S	E3
24400	AvnT	60073	2474	24W-35N	C6
24400	RLKB	60073	2474	24W-35N	C6
28200	WcnT	60084	2642	28W-27N	E2
28200	WcnT	60084	2643	28W-27N	A2
Oak Ter					
10	LKBF	60044	2594	10W-28N	A7
900	GLNC	60022	2758	6W-18N	D4
3100	ISLK	60042	2586	29W-28N	D5
N Oak Ter					
1100	RLKB	60073	2475	22W-34N	B7
W Oak Tr					
14300	HMGN	60491	3343	16W-17S	E5
21400	KLDR	60047	2699	21W-21N	D7
Oak Bluff Ct					
10	NPVL	60565	3203	26W-10S	E6
10	NPVL	60565	3204	26W-10S	A6
200	WCDA	60084	2644	24W-27N	B1
Oak Bluff Dr					
10	PltT	60124	2906	41W-9N	A2
Oak Bluff Ln					
-	DGvT	60439	3270	20W-12S	B3
N Oakbrook Cir					
2100	PLTN	60074	2753	19W-20N	C2
Oakbrook Ct					
300	BRLT	60103	2910	29W-8N	D4
Oak Brook Dr					
2700	OKBK	60523	3085	18W-2S	A4
Oakbrook Dr					
800	CLLK	60014	2641	33W-24N	A6
5200	JLET	60586	3496	30W-22S	B1
Oak Brook Rd					
100	OKBK	60523	3086	15W-2S	A4
100	PvsT	60523	3086	15W-2S	A4
800	OKBK	60523	3085	16W-2S	D4
2000	YkTp	60523	3085	17W-2S	B4
2800	OKBK	60523	3084	18W-2S	E4
3000	DRGV	60523	3084	18W-2S	E4
3000	YkTp	60523	3084	18W-2S	E4
11300	PvsT	60558	3086	14W-3S	D4
11300	WSTR	60154	3086	14W-3S	D4
11300	WSTR	60558	3086	14W-3S	D4
11400	WSTR	60523	3086	14W-3S	D4
Oakbrook Rd					
6500	FoxT	60541	3330	49W-17S	E6
6500	FoxT	60545	3330	49W-17S	E6
Oak Brook Rd CO-34					
100	OKBK	60523	3086	15W-2S	B4
100	PvsT	60523	3086	15W-2S	C4
800	OKBK	60523	3085	16W-2S	D4
2000	YkTp	60523	3085	17W-2S	B4
2800	OKBK	60523	3084	18W-2S	E4
3000	DRGV	60523	3084	18W-2S	E4
3000	YkTp	60523	3084	18W-2S	E4
Oak Brook Club Dr					
10	OKBK	60523	3085	16W-1S	D1
Oakbrook Estates Dr					
-	CLLK	60014	2641	32W-24N	A7
Oak Brook Hills Rd					
10	OKBK	60523	3085	18W-2S	A4
Oak Center Dr					
4800	OKLN	60453	3276	6W-11S	A1
4900	OKLN	60453	3211	6W-11S	E7
4900	OKLN	60453	3212	6W-11S	A7
N Oak Creek Cir					
25500	CbaT	60010	2644	25W-25N	A5
Oak Creek Ct					
10	AraT	60510	3078	35W-4S	C7
10	AraT	60542	3078	35W-4S	C7
10	BRRG	60527	3208	15W-10S	B6
10	NARA	60542	3078	35W-4S	C7
200	WynT	60185	3023	28W-2N	A1
14800	ODPK	60467	3344	14W-17S	D5
Oak Creek Dr					
-	PTHT	60070	2808	15W-15N	B1
-	PTHT	60090	2808	14W-15N	B1
10	BFGV	60089	2754	16W-18N	C4
10	BRRG	60527	3208	15W-10S	B6
10	OSWG	60560	3262	40W-14S	C7
10	OswT	60560	3262	40W-14S	C7
10	OswT	60560	3334	40W-14S	C1
200	WLNG	60090	2808	14W-15N	B1
400	LMBD	60148	3084	21W-1S	A2
400	YkTp	60148	3084	21W-1S	A2
500	WynT	60185	2967	28W-2N	B7
500	WynT	60185	3023	28W-2N	B1
Oakcreek Dr					
21300	RlyT	60152	2634	50W-24N	A6
Oak Creek Ln					
4300	LGGV	60047	2700	19W-22N	C3
Oakcreek Ln					
39300	LkvT	60046	2417	21W-39N	D5
Oak Creek Pkwy					
11800	HTLY	60142	2744	41W-18N	E4
Oak Creek Plz					
-	MDLN	60060	2646	18W-25N	E4
-	MDLN	60060	2647	18W-25N	A4
Oak Creek Rd					
10	RGMW	60008	2806	20W-13N	A6
200	RMVL	60446	3340	26W-17S	A6
200	RMVL	60544	3340	26W-17S	A6
Oak Crest Cir					
-	SchT	60174	2963	36W-3N	D5
-	SCRL	60174	2963	37W-3N	D5
1000	SCRL	60175	2963	37W-3N	D5
W Oak Crest Ct					
9000	PSHL	60465	3209	11W-11S	D6
Oak Crest Dr					
10	CPVL	60110	2748	33W-18N	A4
400	NARA	60510	3078	35W-3S	B5
400	NARA	60542	3078	35W-3S	B5
Oakcrest Dr					
11800	HTLY	60142	2691	41W-21N	E6
Oak Crest Ln					
900	SCRL	60175	2963	37W-3N	D6
Oakcrest Ln					
26100	PNFD	60585	3337	32W-15S	C2
43200	BtnT	53158	2362	12W-43N	B4
43200	BtnT	60099	2362	12W-43N	B5
43200	PTPR	53158	2362	12W-43N	B5
N Oakcrest Ln					
38500	WDWH	60083	2420	14W-38N	C6
Oak Crest Rd					
200	AlqT	60013	2696	29W-24N	C1
Oakcrest Rd					
4600	NndT	60012	2584	33W-27N	E7
4600	NndT	60012	2640	33W-27N	E1
Oakcrest St					
300	WKGN	60085	2536	11W-34N	E1
Oakdale Av					
100	MDLN	60060	2646	18W-26N	D2
100	PTPR	53158	2363	9W-43N	C5
100	WPHR	53158	2363	9W-43N	C5
100	WPHR	60096	2363	9W-43N	C5
200	NlxT	60432	3500	20W-24S	B5
200	NlxT	60433	3500	20W-24S	B5
300	LKFT	60045	2650	10W-24N	A6
400	GLNC	60022	2758	6W-16N	D6
900	WCDA	60084	2588	25W-28N	B6
3200	JNBG	60050	2471	31W-35N	D6
7100	HMND	46324	3430		E5
14900	HRVY	60426	3350	0W-17S	C6
W Oakdale Av					
300	CHCG	60657	2978	0W-3N	A4
1700	CHCG	60657	2977	2W-3N	B4
2200	CHCG	60618	2977	2W-3N	B4
3600	CHCG	60618	2976	4W-3N	C4
4000	CHCG	60641	2976	5W-3N	B4
4800	CHCG	60641	2975	6W-3N	D4
6900	CHCG	60634	2974	8W-3N	E4
Oakdale Cir					
2100	HRPK	60133	2911	27W-6N	C6
S Oakdale Cir					
13900	PnfT	60544	3339	27W-16S	C4
Oakdale Ct					
-	CRY	60013	2642	29W-24N	C7
2400	AURA	60504	3201	32W-9S	C4
8900	ODPK	60462	3346	11W-17S	A5
S Oakdale Ct					
13900	PnfT	60544	3339	27W-16S	B4
Oakdale Dr					
100	AddT	60106	2971	17W-3N	C4
200	ADSN	60101	2971	17W-3N	C4
200	ADSN	60106	2971	17W-3N	C4
500	EMHT	60106	2971	17W-3N	C5
500	EMHT	60126	2971	17W-3N	C5
900	ELGN	60123	2800	35W-13N	C7
5200	OKLN	60453	3275	6W-11S	D1
Oakdale Ln					
26600	FmtT	60060	2646	19W-26N	C2
Oakdale Rd					
1900	HFET	60169	2804	25W-12N	C7
1900	HFET	60169	2858	25W-12N	C1
Oakdale Ter					
2400	AlqT	60013	2641	31W-25N	D5
Oakdale Estates Dr					
2000	JLET	60586	3416	30W-21S	B7
Oakdene Dr					
10	BNHL	60010	2750	26W-18N	C3
10	BRTN	60010	2750	26W-18N	C2
Oakdene Dr E					
10	BNHL	60010	2750	26W-18N	C2
Oakdene Dr W					
200	BNHL	60010	2750	26W-18N	C3
Oaken Dr					
800	BRkT	60511	3196	45W-8S	C3
800	SgrT	60511	3196	45W-8S	C3
S Oakenwald Av					
4000	CHCG	60653	3092	1E-4S	E6
4200	CHCG	60653	3093	1E-4S	A7
Oakfern Ln					
1000	DRN	60561	3145	18W-7S	A7
Oakfield Ct					
2300	AURA	60503	3201	32W-10S	B6
Oakfield Dr					
2300	AURA	60503	3201	32W-10S	C6
22500	FKFT	60423	3592	9W-27S	D4
Oak Forest Av					
6000	BmnT	60477	3425	8W-20S	B4
6000	TYPK	60477	3425	8W-20S	B4
W Oak Forest Dr					
9700	BHPK	60099	2422	9W-38N	C6
E Oak Glen Dr					
100	BRLT	60103	2910	29W-7N	D4
200	BRLT	60103	2911	28W-8N	B3
S Oak Glen Dr					
400	BRLT	60103	2911	28W-7N	A4
W Oak Glen Dr					
100	BRLT	60103	2910	29W-7N	E4
Oak Grove Av					
-	WKGN	60031	2478	13W-37N	E2
-	WKGN	60083	2478	13W-37N	E2
-	WKGN	60087	2478	13W-37N	E2
7100	JSTC	60458	3148	11W-8S	A7
7300	JSTC	60458	3210	11W-8S	A2
9000	LynT	60480	3208	14W-10S	E5
N Oak Grove Av					
30100	LbvT	60048	2592	15W-30N	A2
Oak Grove Cir					
300	WCDA	60084	2643	26W-26N	D2
Oak Grove Dr					
-	LGGV	60047	2700	18W-22N	E3
10	HshT	60140	2743	46W-17N	A7
300	WCDA	60084	2643	26W-26N	D3
300	WcnT	60084	2643	26W-26N	D3
5300	LGGV	60047	2701	18W-22N	A3
12500	HTLY	60142	2744	42W-19N	D3
Oak Grove Ln					
1000	LKFT	60045	2649	12W-26N	B2
Oak Grove Rd					
10	WCHI	60185	3022	29W-1N	E3
10	WnfT	60185	3022	29W-1N	E3
800	JNBG	60051	2472	29W-35N	C6
3000	DRGV	60515	3084	20W-2S	B4
19300	AdnT	60033	2406	48W-41N	E1
19900	CmgT	60033	2406	50W-40N	A2
21200	HRVD	60033	2406	50W-40N	A2
21600	HRVD	60033	2405	51W-40N	E3
22000	CmgT	60033	2405	51W-40N	E3
Oak Grove Rd CO-A15					
19300	AdnT	60033	2406	48W-41N	E1
19900	CmgT	60033	2406	49W-41N	D1
Oak Grove Rd CO-T50					
22600	CmgT	60033	2405	51W-39N	D3
22600	HRVD	60033	2405	51W-39N	D3
S Oak Grove Rd					
6100	CmgT	60033	2405	52W-38N	B6
23000	HRVD	60033	2405	51W-39N	D4
S Oak Grove Rd CO-A20					
6100	CmgT	60033	2405	52W-38N	B6
Oakhaven Ct					
28500	GNOK	60044	2593	13W-28N	A6
Oak Hill Ct					
100	NARA	60542	3137	38W-4S	A1
1400	DRGV	60515	3084	20W-3S	B5
Oakhill Ct					
100	SCRL	60174	2964	36W-4N	A4
300	ANTH	60002	2358	22W-42N	B6
8600	HYHL	60457	3210	10W-10S	A4
Oak Hill Dr					
10	BtlT	60543	3262	39W-12S	E4
10	CmpT	60175	2961	41W-5N	E3
100	WDDL	60191	2915	17W-5N	A7
200	DndT	60118	2800	36W-15N	A5
500	DndT	60118	2799	36W-15N	E5
900	BtnT	60081	2414	29W-38N	C6
1200	DRGV	60515	3084	20W-3S	B5
2100	LSLE	60532	3142	24W-5S	D3
3400	MonT	60417	3594	4W-29S	E7
3400	MonT	60417	3595	4W-29S	A7
11800	HMGN	60491	3344	14W-18S	C7
11800	OrlT	60467	3344	14W-18S	C7
Oakhill Dr					
800	WTMT	60559	3085	16W-4S	D7
1000	AURA	60502	3139	32W-6S	D5
Oak Hill Ln					
1300	HPSR	60140	2795	47W-14N	E5
27600	MTWA	60048	2648	14W-27N	C1
Oakhill Ln					
3500	LGGV	60047	2700	20W-21N	A7
Oak Hill Rd					
-	NBRN	60010	2697	26W-24N	C1
200	LKBN	60010	2643	26W-24N	D7
1300	LKBN	60010	2697	26W-24N	C1
Oakhill Rd					
200	ODHL	60013	2641	31W-26N	D3
400	ELGN	60120	2855	33W-13N	B1
500	ELGN	60120	2801	33W-13N	B7
1000	DRGV	60515	3084	19W-3S	C5
N Oak Hill Rd					
25800	LKBN	60010	2643	27W-25N	B4
Oak Hill Colony St					
10	FXLK	60020	2414	28W-38N	D6
Oak Hills Ct					
10	CmpT	60119	2962	41W-3N	A6
W Oak Hills Ct					
7800	PSHT	60463	3346	9W-15S	D1
S Oak Hills Pkwy					
7900	PSHT	60463	3346	9W-15S	C2
Oak Hollow Ct					
-	CLLK	60014	2640	34W-25N	D4
Oak Hollow Rd					
-	CLLK	60014	2640	34W-25N	D4
Oakhurst Ct					
10	MTSN	60443	3505	7W-24S	D5
600	NPVL	60540	3140	29W-7S	D6
600	NPVL	60540	3141	27W-7S	B7
Oakhurst Dr					
500	NPVL	60540	3141	28W-7S	A7
N Oakhurst Dr					
100	AURA	60504	3201	32W-8S	C2
200	AURA	60504	3139	31W-7S	E7
500	AURA	60502	3139	31W-7S	D7
S Oakhurst Dr					
10	AURA	60504	3201	32W-8S	C1
Oakhurst Ln					
-	DRFD	60015	2703	12W-21N	B7
500	CPVL	60110	2748	33W-17N	A7
800	RVWD	60015	2703	12W-21N	B7
Oakhurst Rd					
10	MTSN	60443	3505	7W-24S	D5
N Oak Knoll Cir					
34600	WrnT	60031	2477	17W-34N	B7
34600	WrnT	60031	2534	17W-34N	C1
Oak Knoll Ct					
10	SMWD	60107	2857	26W-11N	E4
100	VOLO	60041	2530	27W-34N	C1
200	SMBG	60193	2859	22W-9N	D6
4300	NHBK	60062	2756	12W-18N	A3
W Oak Knoll Ct					
21000	KLDR	60047	2699	21W-20N	E7
Oak Knoll Dr					
10	LKVL	60046	2475	23W-37N	A1
500	LKFT	60045	2649	12W-24N	A7
1400	LKFT	60045	2703	12W-24N	A1
E Oak Knoll Dr					
10	HPSR	60140	2796	46W-15N	A4
10	HshT	60140	2796	46W-15N	A4
100	HPSR	60140	2795	46W-15N	E4
100	HshT	60140	2795	46W-15N	E4
E Oak Knoll Dr SR-72					
10	HPSR	60140	2796	46W-15N	A4
10	HshT	60140	2796	46W-15N	A4
100	HPSR	60140	2795	46W-15N	E4
100	HshT	60140	2795	46W-15N	E4
W Oak Knoll Dr					
100	HPSR	60140	2795	47W-15N	D3
100	HshT	60140	2795	47W-15N	C3
W Oak Knoll Dr SR-72					
100	HPSR	60140	2795	47W-15N	D3
100	HshT	60140	2795	47W-15N	C3
Oak Knoll Ln					
200	BMDL	60108	2969	22W-4N	C2
200	DndT	60118	2746	38W-17N	C7
200	RtdT	60118	2746	38W-17N	C7
200	WynT	60185	2966	29W-3N	D5
3000	CPVL	60110	2747	35W-17N	C6
4200	HFET	60192	2804	25W-15N	B2
7900	PSHT	60463	3346	9W-15S	C1
Oak Knoll Rd					
10	BNHL	60010	2750	27W-20N	B1
300	BNHL	60010	2697	27W-20N	A7
300	CbaT	60010	2697	27W-20N	A7
400	BNHL	60010	2696	28W-20N	D7
3200	CPVL	60110	2747	35W-17N	C6
3300	CPVL	60118	2747	35W-17N	C6
3300	DndT	60118	2747	35W-17N	C6
28300	WcnT	60051	2587	28W-28N	A6
W Oak Knoll Rd					
14000	WDWH	60083	2420	14W-39N	D6
Oak Knoll Rd N					
3600	PRGV	60012	2585	32W-27N	B7
Oak Knoll Rd S					
3600	PRGV	60012	2585	32W-27N	B7
Oak Knoll Ter					
100	HDPK	60035	2758	6W-20N	C2
200	NHBK	60062	2756	12W-18N	A3
300	NfdT	60062	2756	12W-18N	A3
Oak Lake Dr					
10	BNHL	60010	2696	28W-21N	D6
Oakland Av					
-	CTHL	60441	3418	24W-20S	C6
-	WDSK	60098	2524	42W-31N	B7
600	ELGN	60120	2855	33W-12N	B3
1600	CTHL	60403	3498	24W-21S	D1
1600	JLET	60435	3498	24W-21S	D1
1700	CTHL	60403	3418	25W-21S	C6
2600	WKGN	60085	2479	12W-35N	C7
6000	OKFT	60452	3347	7W-18S	C6
N Oakland Av					
700	JLET	60435	3498	24W-23S	D3
S Oakland Av					
10	EMHT	60126	3027	17W-0N	C3
10	EMHT	60181	3027	17W-0N	C3
10	VLPK	60181	3027	17W-0N	C3
1400	OKTR	60181	3027	17W-0S	C7
W Oakland Av					
27600	AntT	60081	2415	27W-38N	B7
Oakland Cir					
1300	NARA	60542	3077	37W-4S	B7
Oakland Ct					
1000	BRTN	60010	2751	24W-18N	B2
10500	HTLY	60142	2691	41W-21N	E5
Oakland Dr					
200	HDPK	60035	2758	7W-20N	B1
1000	BRTN	60010	2751	24W-18N	B3
1000	SMWD	60107	2857	28W-9N	B7
1500	LKVL	60046	2417	22W-39N	B4
10800	ODPK	60462	3345	13W-17S	A5
10800	ODPK	60467	3345	13W-17S	A5
22800	STGR	60475	3596	0E-27S	E5
23000	CRTE	60417	3597	0E-27S	A5
23000	STGR	60475	3597	0E-27S	A5
N Oakland Dr					
33500	WrnT	60030	2534	18W-33N	A3
W Oakland Dr					
25500	GrtT	60041	2474	25W-34N	A7
S Oakland Grv					
100	EMHT	60126	3027	17W-1N	C3
200	EMHT	60181	3027	17W-1N	C3
200	VLPK	60181	3027	17W-1N	C3
Oakland Ln					
800	BbyT	60506	3076	40W-3S	C7
2900	MCLK	60050	2470	34W-34N	D7
Oakland Ln W					
900	AURA	60504	3201	32W-9S	D3
Oakland St					
500	MTGY	60538	3200	35W-9S	B4
6000	BbyT	60506	3076	40W-3S	C7
6000	SgrT	60506	3076	40W-3S	C7
S Oakland Crescent St					
4000	CHCG	60653	3092	1E-4S	E6
Oakland Hills Ct					
-	HNWD	60047	2645	22W-26N	C4
Oaklane Rd					
25700	GrtT	60041	2473	25W-35N	E6
25700	GrtT	60041	2474	25W-35N	A6
Oak Lawn Av					
900	EMHT	60106	2971	16W-3N	D5
900	EMHT	60126	2971	16W-3N	D5
Oaklawn Av					
10	BtlT	60560	3262	40W-13S	B5
10	OSWG	60543	3263	37W-11S	D2
N Oaklawn Av					
200	EMHT	60126	3027	16W-1N	D1
700	EMHT	60126	2971	16W-3N	D6
Oak Lawn Ct					
100	SMBG	60195	2859	23W-12N	A2
Oaklawn Dr					
400	MltT	60137	3083	22W-2S	B4
Oak Lawn Farm Rd					
400	WYNE	60184	2965	32W-5N	B2
Oakleaf Av					
900	MchT	60050	2472	30W-36N	B4
W Oakleaf Av					
7800	EDPK	60707	2974	9W-3N	B5
7900	EDPK	60171	2974	9W-3N	B5
Oakleaf Cir					
2000	RLKB	60046	2475	21W-35N	D5
Oak Leaf Ct					
10	WDRG	60517	3205	21W-9S	D3
100	SchT	60174	2964	35W-5N	B3
500	JLET	60436	3497	26W-24S	E6
1200	CRTE	60417	3685	0W-29S	D1
2100	RLKB	60046	2475	21W-36N	D4
Oakleaf Ct					
10	ALGN	60102	2694	35W-21N	A6
900	NPVL	60540	3141	26W-6S	E5
1200	AURA	60506	3137	38W-5S	A4
N Oakleaf Ct					
27200	FmtT	60060	2645	21W-27N	E1
Oak Leaf Dr					
700	BbyT	60119	3075	43W-2S	A5
8300	WDRG	60517	3205	21W-9S	D4
Oakleaf Dr					
700	AddT	60106	2971	17W-3N	C4
700	ADSN	60101	2971	17W-3N	C4
700	ADSN	60106	2971	17W-3N	C4
1500	JNBG	60050	2472	30W-36N	A4
1500	MchT	60050	2472	30W-36N	A4
1900	MchT	60050	2471	30W-36N	E4
N Oakleaf Dr					
100	AddT	60106	2971	17W-3N	B5
100	ADSN	60101	2971	17W-3N	B5
100	ADSN	60106	2971	17W-3N	B5
Oak Leaf Ln					
-	NBRN	60010	2698	25W-22N	A3
10	LtRT	60545	3330	49W-14S	E1
Oakleaf Ln					
-	HTLY	60142	2691	41W-21N	E5
1400	WDSK	60098	2582	40W-30N	A2
2000	RLKB	60046	2475	21W-36N	D5
2100	RLKB	60073	2475	21W-35N	D5
3500	PRGV	60012	2584	33W-28N	E6
4300	LGGV	60047	2700	19W-22N	C3
Oakleaf Rd					
-	ALGN	60102	2694	35W-21N	A6
-	ALGN	60156	2694	35W-21N	A6
100	LIHL	60156	2694	35W-21N	A5
S Oakleaf Rd					
10	ALGN	60102	2694	35W-21N	A6
10	ALGN	60156	2694	35W-21N	A6
10	LIHL	60156	2694	35W-21N	A6
Oakleaf St					
2000	JLET	60436	3497	26W-24S	E6
Oak Leaf Ter					
800	NHBK	60062	2757	9W-17N	C4
Oakley Av					
-	LNSG	60438	3429	3E-20S	E4
600	JLET	60436	3498	25W-24S	B7
700	ELGN	60123	2854	34W-11N	C3
700	RKDL	60436	3498	25W-24S	C7
800	WKGN	60085	2480	10W-35N	B7
1000	DRFD	60015	2703	11W-21N	D6
1100	WNKA	60093	2758	5W-16N	E7
5100	HMND	46320	3352		D6
14300	DXMR	60406	3349	2W-17S	C5
14300	DXMR	60426	3349	2W-17S	C5
14300	ODPK	60462	3345	12W-17S	B5
14600	HRVY	60426	3349	2W-17S	C5
15600	HRVY	60428	3427	2W-18S	C1
15600	MKHM	60428	3427	2W-18S	C1
15900	ThtT	60428	3427	2W-19S	C2
18500	BlmT	60411	3429	3E-21S	E7
18500	LNSG	60411	3429	3E-21S	E7
N Oakley Av					
2800	CHCG	60647	2977	2W-3N	B5
2900	CHCG	60618	2977	2W-3N	B4
4700	CHCG	60625	2921	2W-6N	B6
6000	CHCG	60659	2921	2W-7N	A3
6800	CHCG	60645	2921	2W-8N	A1
7200	CHCG	60645	2867	2W-9N	A7
7500	CHCG	60202	2867	2W-9N	A7
7500	EVTN	60202	2867	2W-9N	A7
S Oakley Av					
1200	CHCG	60608	3033	2W-1S	B7
1200	CHCG	60612	3033	2W-1S	B7
1800	CHCG	60608	3091	2W-2S	B2
3400	CHCG	60609	3091	2W-3S	B5
4700	CHCG	60609	3151	2W-5S	B1
5200	HMND	46320	3352		D6
5500	CHCG	60636	3151	2W-6S	B3
7400	CHCG	60620	3213	2W-8S	B1
7400	CHCG	60636	3213	2W-8S	B1
9500	CHCG	60643	3213	2W-11S	B6
10200	CHCG	60643	3277	2W-12S	B1
11800	BLID	60406	3277	2W-13S	B5
11800	BLID	60643	3277	2W-13S	B5
N Oakley Blvd					
10	CHCG	60612	3033	2W-0N	B4
700	CHCG	60622	3033	2W-0N	B3
1500	CHCG	60647	3033	2W-1N	B1
S Oakley Blvd					
10	CHCG	60612	3033	2W-0S	B5
Oakley Ct					
10	WTMT	60559	3085	18W-3S	A6
15400	HRVY	60426	3349	2W-18S	C7
Oakley Dr					
8100	DRN	60561	3207	18W-9S	A3
Oakley Dr N					
10	WTMT	60559	3085	18W-3S	A6
Oakley Dr NW					
200	WTMT	60559	3085	18W-3S	A6
Oakley Dr S					
10	WTMT	60559	3085	18W-3S	A6
Oakley Dr SW					
200	OKBK	60523	3085	18W-3S	A6
200	WTMT	60559	3085	18W-3S	A6
Oakley Dr W					
1000	WTMT	60559	3085	18W-3S	A6
Oakley Ln					
10	WTMT	60559	3085	18W-3S	A6
Oak Ln Dr					
20700	OMFD	60461	3506	4W-25S	E7
Oak Ln Rd					
1700	FSMR	60422	3507	3W-23S	B4
1800	RchT	60461	3507	3W-23S	B4
Oak Manor Dr					
700	MRGO	60152	2634	50W-26N	B3
Oak Manor Rd					
1400	AraT	60504	3138	34W-5S	D3
Oak Meadow Ct					
-	LtRT	60545	3331	48W-15S	A2
10	SMWD	60107	2857	28W-12N	B2
300	SMBG	60193	2859	22W-10N	C6
1400	LMBD	60148	3084	20W-1S	A1
Oakmeadow Ct					
700	GYLK	60030	2475	21W-34N	C7
1100	GRNE	60031	2477	18W-35N	A6
1300	WLNG	60090	2754	16W-18N	D4
17200	HMGN	60491	3422	16W-20S	A4
Oak Meadow Ln					
2200	AURA	60502	3079	32W-3S	C7
Oak Meadows Dr					
300	AddT	60191	2971	17W-4N	B3
300	ADSN	60106	2971	17W-4N	C3
300	ADSN	60191	2971	17W-4N	C3
300	WDDL	60106	2971	17W-4N	B3
300	WDDL	60191	2971	17W-4N	B3
400	AddT	60106	2971	17W-4N	C3
E Oak Meadows Dr					
-	AddT	60101	2971	17W-4N	B3
-	AddT	60106	2971	17W-4N	B3
-	AddT	60191	2971	17W-4N	B3
-	ADSN	60101	2971	17W-4N	B3
-	ADSN	60106	2971	17W-4N	B3
E Oak Mill Ct					
700	ADSN	60101	2971	17W-3N	B5
N Oak Mill St					
100	ADSN	60101	2971	17W-3N	B5
Oakmont Av					
1100	FSMR	60422	3507	3W-23S	B3
Oakmont Ct					
-	WDSK	60098	2582	39W-30N	D2
10	LMNT	60439	3342	20W-15S	B2
10	SMWD	60107	2857	26W-11N	E4
Oakmont Dr					
-	BLVY	60098	2582	39W-30N	D2
-	WDSK	60098	2582	39W-30N	D2
10	DRFD	60015	2757	10W-20N	A2
100	ELGN	60123	2853	36W-11N	E4
100	ElgT	60123	2853	36W-11N	E4
300	BRLT	60103	2910	29W-8N	D4
300	CRY	60013	2642	30W-25N	A5
300	NPVL	60563	3140	30W-5S	B2
300	NpvT	60563	3140	30W-5S	B2
600	CmpT	60119	2962	41W-4N	A6
1200	LMNT	60439	3342	20W-15S	B2
2700	MTGY	60538	3198	40W-10S	C5
N Oakmont Dr					
1300	GLHT	60139	3024	24W-2N	E1
1500	VNHL	60061	2647	16W-26N	D2
Oakmont Ln					
400	SMBG	60173	2859	22W-11N	C4
600	WLNG	60090	2754	15W-18N	E2
600	WTMT	60559	3085	17W-3S	C6

Chicago 7-County Street Index

STREET Block City ZIP Map# CGS Grid

Oakmont Ln
900 OKBK 60523 3085 17W-3S C6
900 WTMT 60523 3085 17W-3S C6
5900 GRNE 60031 2534 16W-33N D2
5900 WrnT 60031 2534 16W-33N D2
Oakmont Rd
10 HDPK 60035 2705 7W-21N B6
N Oakmont Rd
1300 HFET 60169 2858 25W-12N B2
W Oakmont Rd
1200 HFET 60169 2858 25W-12N C2
Oakmont Wy
2300 DRN 60439 3206 19W-10S D6
Oakmont Plaza Dr
900 WTMT 60559 3085 16W-3S D6
Oak Park Av
- OKLN 60459 3211 8W-10S A6
500 BCHR 60401 3864 1W-36S B2
600 WshT 60401 3864 1W-36S B2
1200 BRWN 60304 3030 8W-1S E7
1200 BRWN 60402 3030 8W-1S E7
1200 OKPK 60304 3030 8W-1S E7
1500 BRWN 60402 3088 8W-1S E1
2000 BRWN 60402 3089 8W-4S A7
3800 SKNY 60402 3089 8W-4S A7
4400 FTVW 60402 3089 8W-4S A7
4500 FTVW 60402 3149 8W-4S A1
7700 BDPK 60638 3211 8W-8S A2
7700 BRBK 60459 3211 8W-9S A2
7700 BRBK 60638 3211 8W-8S A2
8700 BGVW 60453 3211 8W-10S A4
8700 BGVW 60455 3211 8W-10S A4
8700 OKLN 60453 3211 8W-11S A6
8700 OKLN 60455 3211 8W-10S A4
8800 MNGV 60053 2864 8W-11N E3
9600 CHRG 60415 3211 8W-11S A6
9600 CHRG 60453 3211 8W-11S A6
9600 OKLN 60415 3211 8W-11S A6
10300 CHRG 60415 3275 8W-12S A2
10300 CHRG 60482 3275 8W-12S A2
10300 WRTH 60415 3275 8W-12S A2
10300 WRTH 60482 3275 8W-12S A2
14500 BmnT 60445 3347 8W-17S A5
14500 BmnT 60452 3347 8W-18S A7
14500 OKFT 60445 3347 8W-17S A5
14500 OKFT 60452 3347 8W-18S A7
15600 BmnT 60477 3347 8W-18S A7
15700 BmnT 60452 3425 8W-18S A1
15700 BmnT 60477 3425 8W-18S A1
15700 OKFT 60452 3425 8W-18S A1
15800 TYPK 60452 3425 8W-18S A1
15800 TYPK 60477 3425 8W-19S A3
18200 RchT 60477 3425 8W-21S A7
18500 RchT 60477 3505 8W-22S A1
18500 TYPK 60477 3505 8W-23S A3
N Oak Park Av
100 OKPK 60301 3030 8W-0N E4
100 OKPK 60302 3030 8W-0N E3
1200 CHCG 60707 3030 8W-1N E1
1600 CHCG 60302 3030 8W-2N E1
1700 CHCG 60707 2974 8W-2N E7
2700 CHCG 60634 2974 8W-3N E6
4100 HDHT 60706 2974 8W-5N E1
4400 HDHT 60706 2918 8W-5N E7
4800 CHCG 60706 2918 8W-6N E6
5400 CHCG 60656 2918 8W-6N E6
6200 CHCG 60631 2918 8W-7N E3
6500 NLES 60631 2918 8W-8N E2
6500 NLES 60714 2918 8W-8N E2
7200 NLES 60714 2865 8W-9N E7
7400 NLES 60714 2864 8W-9N E7
S Oak Park Av
100 OKPK 60302 3030 8W-0S E5
400 OKPK 60304 3030 8W-0N E5
1100 BRWN 60304 3030 8W-0S E7
1100 BRWN 60402 3030 8W-0S E7
5900 CHCG 60638 3149 8W-7S A5
7300 BDPK 60638 3149 8W-8S A7
7300 BDPK 60638 3211 8W-8S A1
10700 CHRG 60415 3275 8W-12S A3
10700 WRTH 60415 3275 8W-12S A3
10700 WRTH 60482 3275 8W-13S A4
11900 PSHT 60463 3275 8W-14S A6
12900 PSHT 60463 3347 8W-15S A1
13000 WthT 60463 3347 8W-15S A1
Oak Park Av N
900 OKPK 60302 3030 8W-1N E1
Oak Park Ct
2500 CTHL 60403 3497 27W-22S D2
Oak Park Rd
5300 NndT 60013 2641 31W-26N D3
5300 ODHL 60013 2641 31W-26N D3
Oak Point Ct
- ANTH 60002 2357 25W-41N B7
Oak Pointe Dr
200 SchT 60175 2907 36W-7N E5
200 SchT 60175 2908 36W-7N A5
W Oak Pond Ln
15200 LbvT 60048 2592 15W-29N A5
15200 LYVL 60048 2592 15W-29N A5
Oak Rail Dr
2500 NlxT 60451 3590 16W-27S A5
2700 MhtT 60451 3590 16W-27S A5
Oak Ridge Av
10 HLSD 60162 3029 13W-0S A7
300 PvsT 60162 3029 13W-0S A7
Oakridge Av
200 HIWD 60040 2704 9W-23N C2
4600 OKFT 60452 3426 5W-19S B3
Oak Ridge Blvd
800 ELGN 60120 2856 31W-10N A7
Oak Ridge Cir
1000 BRTN 60010 2751 24W-18N B2
Oak Ridge Ct
400 LKBF 60044 2593 11W-29N D4
900 FKFT 60423 3503 13W-25S B7
1300 WLSP 60480 3209 12W-10S B4
26100 CNHN 60410 3672 32W-31S C6
Oakridge Ct
100 ANTH 60002 2357 23W-42N E5
200 BGBK 60440 3269 22W-11S C1
7600 NndT 60012 2583 36W-28N D6
N Oakridge Ct
1200 PLTN 60067 2752 22W-17N C5
S Oak Ridge Ct
14100 HMGN 60491 3343 16W-16S E4
W Oak Ridge Ct
7700 PSHT 60463 3346 9W-15S D1
Oak Ridge Dr
600 PltT 60124 2852 40W-10N B6
900 HnrT 60107 2856 29W-9N D7
900 SMWD 60107 2856 29W-9N D7
9000 JSTC 60458 3209 11W-9S E2
Oakridge Dr
700 RMVL 60446 3269 23W-14S A7
1000 GLNC 60022 2758 7W-18N C4
2200 AURA 60502 3079 32W-3S B6
S Oak Ridge Dr
13800 HMGN 60491 3343 16W-16S E3
W Oak Ridge Dr
7800 PSHT 60463 3274 9W-14S C6
7800 PSHT 60464 3274 9W-14S C6
7800 PSPK 60464 3274 9W-14S C6
Oak Ridge Dr E
100 BRRG 60527 3208 15W-10S A6
Oak Ridge Dr W
100 BRRG 60527 3208 15W-10S A6
Oak Ridge Ln
10 DRPK 60010 2751 23W-20N E2
10 PltT 60010 2751 23W-20N E2
700 GNCY 53128 2352 E3
900 WDSK 60098 2582 40W-30N A2
1300 MTGY 60538 3199 36W-9S E4
2600 JLET 60435 3417 27W-21S D7
Oakridge Ln
600 SchT 60174 2963 36W-3N E5
W Oak Ridge Ln
13200 HMGN 60491 3343 16W-16S E4
Oak Ridge Rd
- DndT 60110 2748 33W-17N B7
10 CmpT 60175 2906 40W-6N C7
300 SchT 60174 2964 35W-5N B2
300 WYNE 60174 2964 35W-5N B2
600 CPVL 60110 2801 33W-17N B1
600 CPVL 60118 2801 33W-17N B1
600 EDND 60110 2801 33W-17N B1
600 EDND 60118 2801 33W-17N B1
1000 CPVL 60110 2748 33W-17N B7
1000 CPVL 60118 2748 33W-17N B7
1000 EDND 60110 2748 33W-17N B7
1000 EDND 60118 2748 33W-17N B7
1200 BRTN 60010 2751 24W-18N C2
2600 NndT 60012 2583 36W-29N D5
W Oakridge Rd
200 NBRN 60010 2644 25W-25N A6
25300 CbaT 60010 2644 25W-25N A6
S Oak Ridge Tr
13100 PSHT 60463 3346 9W-15S D1
Oak Run Ct
10 SchT 60175 2963 36W-6N E1
Oaks Av
100 WCDA 60084 2643 26W-26N E2
W Oaks Av
9000 MaiT 60016 2863 11W-11N D2
N Oaks Ct
25600 CbaT 60010 2644 25W-25N A4
Oaks Ln
500 DndT 60118 2800 36W-16N A1
500 WDND 60118 2800 36W-16N A1
Oaksbury Ct
2900 RGMW 60008 2806 20W-13N A5
Oaksbury Ln
4100 RGMW 60008 2806 20W-13N A5
4300 PltT 60067 2806 20W-13N A5
E Oaksbury Ln
100 PltT 60067 2805 20W-13N E5
200 PltT 60067 2806 20W-13N A5
200 RGMW 60008 2806 20W-13N A5
Oakshire Ct
2600 AURA 60502 3139 32W-4S C1
7600 JLET 60586 3495 33W-21S A1
Oakshire Ln
500 HshT 60140 2796 44W-15N E4
Oakshore
1100 ANTH 60002 2418 20W-40N A2
Oak Shores Dr
10 FmtT 60060 2646 19W-26N C3
Oakside Ln
800 UYPK 60466 3684 3W-29S A2
N Oakside St
34600 FXLK 60041 2473 26W-34N D7
35700 GrtT 60041 2473 26W-34N D7
Oak Spring Ln
700 LbvT 60048 2592 15W-29N A4
W Oak Spring Rd
15100 GNOK 60048 2592 15W-29N B4
15100 LbvT 60048 2592 15W-29N B4
15100 LYVL 60048 2592 15W-29N A4
15600 LYVL 60048 2591 16W-29N E4
Oak Terrace Av
200 HIWD 60040 2704 9W-23N C2
Oak Terrace Ct
10 BTVA 60510 3020 35W-0S B7
Oakton Av
800 RMVL 60446 3340 24W-16S C4
21900 FKFT 60423 3591 13W-26S B3
Oakton Ct
200 MHRY 60050 2527 33W-32N E5
2500 LSLE 60532 3142 24W-6S D5
10700 FKFT 60423 3591 13W-26S B3
W Oakton Ct
6900 NLES 60714 2864 8W-10N E5
Oakton Dr
10 LMBD 60148 3084 19W-2S C3
Oakton Ln
100 LKVL 60046 2475 22W-37N B3
1100 NPVL 60540 3203 28W-8S A1
Oakton Pl
1600 DSPN 60018 2862 13W-9N E6
Oakton Rd
700 MTGY 60538 3199 38W-9S A5
1700 AraT 60538 3199 38W-9S A5
Oakton St
- CHCG 60068 2863 12W-10N B6
- DSPN 60018 2863 12W-10N B6
- MNGV 60714 2865 8W-10N A5
- NLES 60714 2865 8W-10N A5
100 EGVV 60007 2861 17W-9N B6
100 MHRY 60050 2527 33W-32N D5
600 EGvT 60007 2861 17W-9N B6
600 EVTN 60202 2867 3W-9N A6
900 NLES 60068 2864 10W-9N A6
900 NLES 60714 2864 10W-9N A6
900 PKRG 60068 2864 10W-9N A6
1300 PKRG 60068 2863 11W-10N D6
1700 EVTN 60202 2866 5W-10N A6
1900 EGvT 60005 2861 16W-9N D6
1900 EGVV 60005 2861 16W-9N D6
2300 SKOK 60076 2866 3W-10N D6
4700 SKOK 60076 2865 6W-10N D5
4700 SKOK 60077 2865 7W-9N A5
5300 MNGV 60053 2865 7W-9N A5
5300 MNGV 60077 2865 6W-10N D6
5500 SKOK 60053 2865 7W-9N A5
Oakton St SR-72
1500 EGVV 60007 2861 17W-9N C6
1800 EGvT 60007 2861 16W-9N D6
Oakton St SR-83
1800 EGvT 60007 2861 16W-9N D6
1800 EGVV 60007 2861 16W-9N C6
1900 EGvT 60005 2861 16W-9N D6
1900 EGVV 60005 2861 16W-9N D6
E Oakton St
10 ANHT 60004 2807 16W-14N C3
10 DSPN 60018 2862 14W-9N C6
1300 DSPN 60018 2863 12W-10N A6
1600 PTHT 60004 2807 16W-14N C3
1900 CHCG 60068 2863 12W-10N A6
2200 EGvT 60005 2861 16W-9N D6
2200 EGvT 60007 2861 16W-9N D6
2200 EGVV 60005 2861 16W-9N D6
2200 EGVV 60007 2861 16W-9N D6
2300 MPPT 60005 2861 16W-9N D6
2500 MPPT 60056 2861 16W-9N D6
2600 DSPN 60005 2861 16W-9N D6
2600 MPPT 60018 2861 16W-9N D6
E Oakton St SR-83
2200 EGvT 60005 2861 16W-9N D6
2200 EGvT 60007 2861 16W-9N D6
2200 EGVV 60005 2861 16W-9N D6
2200 EGVV 60007 2861 16W-9N D6
2300 MPPT 60005 2861 16W-9N D6
2500 MPPT 60056 2861 16W-9N D6
2600 DSPN 60005 2861 16W-9N D6
2600 DSPN 60018 2861 16W-9N D6
2600 MPPT 60018 2861 16W-9N D6
W Oakton St
- MNGV 60053 2864 8W-10N E5
10 ANHT 60004 2807 18W-14N A3
10 DSPN 60018 2862 15W-9N A6
500 ANHT 60004 2806 18W-15N D3
900 DSPN 60018 2861 16W-9N E6
900 EGvT 60005 2861 16W-9N E6
900 MPPT 60005 2861 16W-9N E6
900 MPPT 60018 2861 16W-9N E6
900 MPPT 60056 2861 16W-9N E6
1700 ANHT 60074 2806 18W-15N D3
1700 PLTN 60074 2806 18W-15N D3
6700 MNGV 60714 2864 8W-10N E5
6700 NLES 60714 2864 9W-10N B6
7500 NLES 60068 2864 9W-10N B6
7500 PKRG 60068 2864 9W-10N B6
W Oakton St SR-43
7000 NLES 60714 2864 8W-10N E5
W Oakton St SR-83
900 DSPN 60018 2861 16W-9N E6
900 EGvT 60005 2861 16W-9N E6
900 MPPT 60005 2861 16W-9N E6
900 MPPT 60018 2861 16W-9N E6
900 MPPT 60056 2861 16W-9N E6
Oak Trail Ct
10 PSHT 60463 3274 9W-14S C5
5000 LSLE 60532 3142 24W-5S E3
Oak Trail Dr
1100 LYVL 60048 2592 15W-27N A7
1200 MTWA 60048 2592 15W-27N B7
Oak Trails Dr
400 LslT 60517 3142 23W-7S E7
400 LslT 60540 3142 23W-7S E7
400 WDRG 60517 3142 23W-7S E7
2500 AURA 60506 3136 39W-6S E6
Oak Trails Rd
300 MaiT 60016 2863 12W-12N C1
Oaktree Cir
1900 RLKB 60046 2475 21W-35N D5
Oak Tree Ct
- PSPK 60464 3272 14W-14S E6
10 EMHT 60126 3027 16W-0S E7
6600 WDRG 60517 3143 22W-7S B6
Oaktree Ct
300 HFET 60169 2858 24W-11N E3
S Oak Tree Dr
10600 WRTH 60482 3274 9W-12S E2
Oak Tree Ln
- WDWH 60083 2420 14W-38N D6
100 PltT 60124 2906 40W-9N C1
300 WKGN 60085 2537 10W-34N A1
500 NHFD 60093 2811 7W-15N B1
2200 PKRG 60068 2863 11W-10N D4
2400 JLET 60586 3416 29W-20S E6
2400 PnfT 60586 3416 29W-20S E6
Oaktree Ln
11900 LMNT 60439 3271 17W-14S D6
Oak Tree Pl
6600 WDRG 60517 3143 22W-7S B6
E Oaktree Tr
1000 RLKB 60046 2475 21W-35N D5
NE Oaktree Tr
1900 RLKB 60046 2475 21W-35N D5
NW Oaktree Tr
1900 RLKB 60046 2475 21W-35N D5
1900 RLKB 60073 2475 21W-35N D5
Oakvale Rd
10 HDPK 60035 2705 7W-21N B6
Oak Valley Ct
800 CLLK 60014 2640 33W-25N E4
15900 HMGN 60491 3422 16W-19S A1
Oak Valley Dr
10 CRY 60013 2641 31W-24N C6
600 CLLK 60014 2640 33W-25N E4
2600 SPGV 60081 2413 31W-40N D2
Oak Valley Tr
12600 HMGN 60491 3422 16W-19S A2
Oakview Av
10 AURA 60505 3139 33W-7S A7
10 AURA 60505 3201 33W-7S A1
200 AraT 60505 3139 33W-7S A7
N Oakview Av
5500 CHCG 60631 2917 10W-6N E5
5500 CHCG 60656 2917 10W-6N E5
S Oakview Av
10 JLET 60433 3499 22W-24S D6
600 JltT 60433 3499 22W-24S D6
Oak View Ct
14200 WDSK 60098 2581 43W-30N A1
Oakview Ct
10 SEGN 60177 2907 37W-8N C3
10 WDRG 60517 3205 22W-9S D3
400 SMBG 60193 2858 24W-10N E6
2000 NlxT 60451 3502 15W-24S B5
S Oakview Ct
13300 PSHT 60463 3346 9W-15S D2
25600 CNHN 60410 3672 32W-31S C6
W Oak View Ct
12900 HMGN 60491 3422 16W-19S A2
Oak View Dr
100 WHTN 60187 3024 25W-0N A5
Oakview Dr
100 NLNX 60451 3501 17W-24S C5
100 NlxT 60451 3501 17W-24S C5
600 ALGN 60102 2694 34W-20N C7
600 ALGN 60102 2747 34W-20N C1
5200 LSLE 60532 3143 23W-5S B3
Oakview Ln
5200 GRNE 60031 2478 15W-36N A5
7800 WDRG 60517 3205 22W-9S D3
Oakview Rd
10 MTSN 60443 3505 7W-24S D4
N Oakview St
4700 CHCG 60706 2917 10W-5N E7
4700 NRDG 60706 2917 10W-5N E7
5200 CHCG 60656 2917 10W-6N E6
Oak View Ter
1300 WDSK 60098 2581 43W-30N A1
Oakville Dr
- DGvT 60516 3206 20W-10S B5
- WDRG 60516 3206 20W-10S B5
1300 WDRG 60517 3206 20W-10S B5
Oakwerth Ln
8000 BRRG 60527 3208 14W-9S C3
Oakwood Av
- AraT 60505 3138 34W-5S D3
100 LKVL 60046 2475 23W-37N A1
200 DGvT 60439 3206 20W-11S B7
200 DGvT 60516 3206 20W-11S B7
200 WDRG 60516 3206 20W-11S B7
200 WKGN 60085 2536 12W-33N A1
300 AURA 60505 3138 35W-6S C4
400 DGvT 60439 3270 20W-11S B1
400 LKFT 60045 2650 10W-26N A3
400 WDSK 60098 2581 41W-30N D1
400 WkgT 60085 2536 12W-33N A1
500 WkgT 60085 2479 12W-33N A7
600 WKGN 60085 2479 12W-33N A7
1100 WLMT 60091 2812 3W-13N D6
1200 DSPN 60016 2862 13W-10N E4
1200 DSPN 60016 2863 13W-10N A4
1300 HDPK 60035 2704 8W-21N E6
1400 HRPK 60133 2911 26W-8N E3
2800 MchT 60051 2471 31W-34N E7
4300 DRGV 60515 3144 20W-4S B1
7300 LYNS 60534 3088 9W-4S D6
17000 LNSG 60438 3430 3E-20S A4
17500 CCHL 60478 3426 5W-21S D6
18600 LNSG 60438 3510 3E-22S A1
18800 CCHL 60478 3506 5W-22S D2
19300 LNSG 60411 3510 3E-23S A3
19300 LYWD 60411 3510 3E-23S A3
N Oakwood Av
100 WCHI 60185 3022 29W-1N D4
100 WLSP 60480 3209 12W-9S B3
35600 GrtT 60041 2473 25W-35N E5
S Oakwood Av
100 WCHI 60185 3022 29W-0N D4
100 WLSP 60480 3209 12W-9S C4
600 PlsT 60480 3209 12W-9S C4
W Oakwood Av
26500 GrtT 60041 2473 26W-35N D7
Oakwood Blvd
10 ELGN 60120 2855 32W-11N C3
E Oakwood Blvd
400 CHCG 60653 3092 0E-4S D6
Oakwood Cir
5600 LGGV 60047 2701 17W-23N A1
Oakwood Ct
- LYWD 60411 3510 3E-23S A4
10 OSWG 60543 3263 37W-12S C3
10 WNVL 60555 3080 30W-2S C4
200 WHTN 60187 3082 25W-2S A3
300 PltT 60067 2806 20W-13N A6
700 WTMT 60559 3085 17W-4S C7
800 DSPN 60016 2862 13W-10N D4
900 GNEN 60137 3083 21W-1S E1
1000 SMBG 60193 2912 24W-9N C1
1300 MHRY 60050 2527 33W-33N D3
1800 JltT 60433 3587 21W-26S E3
2300 MchT 60051 2528 31W-33N E3
4400 AlqT 60102 2694 33W-21N E5
4500 ALGN 60102 2694 33W-21N E5
5100 OKFT 60452 3426 6W-19S A3
18900 CCHL 60478 3506 5W-22S D2
W Oakwood Ct
14200 GNOK 60048 2592 14W-30N D1
Oakwood Dr
- BNHL 60010 2697 26W-20N C7
- BRTN 60010 2697 26W-20N C7
- CbaT 60010 2697 26W-20N C7
- LKPT 60441 3420 19W-20S E4
10 EGvT 60007 2861 18W-10N A6
10 EGVV 60007 2861 18W-10N A6
10 NPVL 60540 3141 27W-7S D7
10 NPVL 60540 3203 27W-7S D1
10 OSWG 60543 3263 37W-12S D2
10 PlsT 60464 3273 13W-14S B7
10 PTHT 60070 2754 15W-16N E7
10 PTHT 60070 2755 14W-16N B7
10 SchT 60174 2964 35W-6N B1
100 BGBK 60440 3268 23W-12S E2
100 GNVA 60134 3020 34W-1N D3
100 SRWD 60404 3496 30W-24S C6
200 CRTE 60417 3685 0W-29S C1
200 GYLK 60030 2532 20W-33N E2
200 NARA 60542 3138 36W-4S A2
300 ANTH 60002 2358 23W-43N A5
300 SchT 60174 2908 35W-6N B7
300 SchT 60175 2963 38W-3N A6
400 RLKB 60073 2474 23W-35N D7
500 BbyT 60119 3017 43W-0N A5
500 ELBN 60119 3017 43W-0N A5
600 CNHL 60514 3085 17W-4S D7
600 CNHL 60559 3085 17W-4S D7
700 FKFT 60423 3503 12W-24S C6
1000 AvnT 60073 2474 24W-35N C7
1000 CLSM 60188 2967 27W-4N C4
1100 WTMT 60523 3085 17W-3S C5
1100 WTMT 60559 3085 17W-3S C5
2500 OMFD 60461 3507 3W-24S B6
3400 ISLK 60042 2586 28W-28N D6
5300 NndT 60013 2641 31W-26N D2
5300 ODHL 60013 2641 31W-26N D3
5800 LSLE 60532 3142 23W-6S E5
5800 LslT 60532 3142 23W-6S E5
5800 LslT 60532 3143 23W-6S A5
5900 LSLE 60532 3143 23W-6S A5
8600 CLLK 60014 2639 37W-25N B5
8600 LKWD 60014 2639 37W-25N B5
8700 HYHL 60457 3209 11W-10S E5
17500 HLCT 60429 3427 3W-21S A6
17500 TYPK 60487 3423 11W-21S E5
17500 TYPK 60487 3424 11W-21S A5
19900 MKNA 60448 3502 14W-24S D5
20100 MKNA 60448 3502 14W-24S D5
20100 NlxT 60448 3502 14W-24S D5
20100 NlxT 60451 3502 14W-24S D5
E Oakwood Dr
- LKBN 60010 2644 25W-24N A6
400 CbaT 60010 2644 25W-25N A5
400 NBRN 60010 2644 25W-25N A6
6000 FXLK 60020 2414 28W-39N E6
7300 MchT 60051 2469 36W-34N D7
7300 WRLK 60097 2469 36W-34N D7
N Oakwood Dr
800 MHRY 60050 2527 33W-32N D4
1100 FXLK 60020 2414 28W-39N E5
1900 ANHT 60004 2754 16W-16N D7
1900 ANHT 60004 2807 16W-16N D1
36000 GRNE 60031 2476 18W-36N E5
36000 WrnT 60031 2476 18W-36N E5
36500 LkvT 60046 2475 21W-36N E4
S Oakwood Dr
100 WDDL 60191 2971 18W-5N A1
200 WDDL 60191 2915 18W-5N A7
1100 MPPT 60056 2861 17W-11N C3
W Oakwood Dr
300 CmpT 60175 2906 41W-6N A7
400 CbaT 60010 2644 25W-25N A5
3200 JLET 60431 3497 28W-23S B3
3200 JLET 60435 3497 28W-23S B3
3200 TroT 60435 3497 28W-23S B3
4700 MHRY 60050 2527 33W-32N D4
13400 HMGN 60491 3343 16W-17S E5
Oakwood Ln
10 LNSH 60045 2702 14W-23N C3
10 LNSH 60069 2702 14W-23N C3
100 BMDL 60108 2969 22W-4N B3
100 BRLT 60103 2910 29W-7N E5
100 BRLT 60103 2911 28W-7N A5
100 WynT 60103 2910 29W-7N E5
200 WLNG 60090 2755 14W-18N D3
400 SEGN 60177 2908 35W-7N C4
1200 GNVW 60025 2811 7W-14N A3
1700 JltT 60433 3587 21W-26S E3
4100 MTSN 60443 3506 5W-25S C7
7100 CLLK 60012 2639 36W-26N E2
7300 NndT 60012 2639 36W-26N E2
Oakwood Pl
1500 BKBN 60015 2703 11W-21N C5
1500 DRFD 60015 2703 11W-21N C5
W Oakwood Pl
1000 WdfT 60015 2703 11W-23N D2
Oakwood Rd
- ElaT 60047 2699 22W-24N B1
- INCK 60060 2647 17W-24N A6
- MDLN 60060 2647 17W-24N A6
10 INCK 60061 2647 17W-24N A6
10 LKZH 60047 2699 22W-23N B1
10 VNHL 60061 2647 17W-24N B6
300 WCDA 60084 2587 26W-27N C7
300 WCDA 60084 2643 26W-27N C1
1600 NfdT 60062 2757 9W-18N B3
5600 LGGV 60047 2700 18W-23N E1
5600 LGGV 60047 2701 17W-24N A1
7600 WRLK 60097 2469 36W-34N C7
Oakwood St
100 WNFD 60190 3023 27W-0N C5
200 HMND 46324 3430 D3
200 YKVL 60560 3333 42W-15S D2
300 PKFT 60466 3595 3W-27S B5
400 WNFD 60185 3023 27W-0N C5
400 WnfT 60185 3023 27W-0N C5
400 WnfT 60190 3023 27W-0N C5
600 MNKA 60447 3672 34W-29S A3
900 GRNE 60031 2478 13W-35N D7
Oakwood Ter
600 BbyT 60119 3075 43W-2S A4
900 HNDL 60521 3086 15W-4S B6
2500 OMFD 60461 3507 3W-24S B6
Oakwood Manor Dr
6400 NndT 60012 2584 35W-29N A4
Oakworth Dr
8000 WRLK 60097 2469 36W-36N C3
Oasis Dr
2500 JLET 60586 3415 32W-20S C5
E Oasis Service Rd
- GNOK 60045 2648 13W-27N D1
- LbvT 60045 2648 13W-27N D1
- LKFT 60045 2648 13W-27N D1
- MTWA 60045 2648 13W-27N D1
Oatwind Rd
700 ElgT 60124 2853 37W-11N C3
W Oban Ct
14100 GNOK 60048 2535 14W-31N D7
Oberlin Ct
2200 NPVL 60565 3204 25W-10S C5
W Obermaier Ln
25600 LkvT 60046 2474 25W-37N A1
Oberweis Av
400 NARA 60542 3078 35W-3S B6
Oboe Ct
1200 WLNG 60090 2754 16W-18N D3
O'Brien Dr
- AURA 60502 3139 31W-7S D7
8800 ODHL 60487 3424 11W-19S A3
8800 ODPK 60462 3424 11W-19S A3
8800 ODPK 60487 3424 11W-19S A3
O'Brien St
700 HRVD 60033 2406 49W-38N C6
W O'Brien St
- CHCG 60607 3034 0W-1S A7
- CHCG 60608 3034 0W-1S A7
W Ocala Ct
22100 PnfT 60544 3339 28W-17S B5
Oceanside Ct
3000 JLET 60586 3415 32W-20S C4
Oceanside Ter
900 BRLT 60103 2911 28W-7N B4
Oceola Dr
600 ALGN 60102 2747 33W-20N D1
1900 AlqT 60102 2747 33W-20N D2
1900 DndT 60102 2747 33W-20N D2
Ocock Rd
17200 SenT 60180 2635 47W-26N B3
17200 UNON 60180 2635 47W-26N B3
18000 CrlT 60180 2635 47W-26N C3
O'Connel Ln
25400 MhtT 60442 3677 19W-31S D5
O'Connell Av
10200 MKNA 60448 3503 12W-23S C3
O'Connell Cir
1200 NLNX 60451 3501 16W-25S E7
1300 NLNX 60451 3589 16W-25S E1
O'Connell Dr
7000 CHRG 60415 3210 8W-11S E7
W O'Connell Dr
15000 HMGN 60491 3421 18W-21S A6
O'Connell Rd
21700 MRGO 60152 2634 50W-25N A3
O'Connell St
700 NLNX 60451 3589 16W-25S E1
10400 MKNA 60448 3503 13W-23S B3
O'Connor Dr
- JLET 60431 3495 32W-22S C2
100 DSPN 60016 2808 13W-13N E7
W O'Connor Dr
8000 EDPK 60171 2974 10W-3N B4
8000 EDPK 60707 2974 9W-3N B4
8000 RVGV 60171 2974 10W-3N A4

STREET Block	City	ZIP	Map#	CGS	Grid
Oconto Av					
9500	MNGV	60053	2864	9W-11N	D2
16700	TYPK	60477	3424	9W-20S	E3
N Oconto Av					
3000	CHCG	60707	2974	9W-3N	D4
3000	EDPK	60707	2974	9W-3N	D4
3100	CHCG	60634	2974	9W-3N	D4
3900	NRDG	60634	2974	9W-4N	D3
3900	NRDG	60706	2974	9W-4N	D3
4900	HDHT	60706	2918	9W-6N	D6
5100	CHCG	60706	2918	9W-6N	D6
5400	CHCG	60656	2918	9W-6N	D5
6500	CHCG	60631	2918	9W-8N	D2
7200	CHCG	60631	2864	9W-9N	D7
7500	NLES	60631	2864	9W-9N	D7
7600	NLES	60714	2864	9W-9N	D6
S Oconto Av					
7500	BGVW	60455	3210	9W-8S	E1
Oconto Ct					
1300	NPVL	60564	3203	28W-10S	A5
1300	WldT	60564	3203	28W-10S	A5
W Oconto Ct					
7200	WRTH	60482	3274	9W-12S	E2
Octavia Av					
-	MNGV	60053	2864	9W-11N	D2
N Octavia Av					
3000	CHCG	60707	2974	9W-3N	D4
3000	EDPK	60707	2974	9W-3N	D4
3100	CHCG	60634	2974	9W-3N	D4
3900	NRDG	60634	2974	9W-4N	D2
3900	NRDG	60706	2974	9W-4N	D2
4900	HDHT	60706	2918	9W-6N	D6
5100	CHCG	60656	2918	9W-6N	D6
5100	CHCG	60706	2918	9W-6N	D6
7100	CHCG	60631	2918	9W-8N	D1
7200	CHCG	60631	2864	9W-9N	D7
7500	NLES	60631	2864	9W-9N	D7
7700	NLES	60714	2864	9W-10N	D5
S Octavia Av					
7100	BGVW	60455	3148	9W-8S	E7
7300	BGVW	60455	3210	9W-8S	E1
10700	WRTH	60482	3274	9W-12S	E2
O'Dell Av					
7500	BGVW	60455	3210	9W-8S	D1
9200	MNGV	60053	2864	9W-11N	D2
16700	TYPK	60477	3424	9W-20S	E4
N O'Dell Av					
3000	CHCG	60707	2974	9W-3N	D4
3000	EDPK	60707	2974	9W-3N	D4
3100	CHCG	60634	2974	9W-3N	D4
4000	NRDG	60634	2974	9W-5N	D2
4000	NRDG	60706	2974	9W-5N	D1
4900	HDHT	60706	2918	9W-6N	D6
5100	CHCG	60706	2918	9W-6N	D6
5400	CHCG	60656	2918	9W-6N	D5
6900	CHCG	60631	2918	9W-8N	D1
7200	CHCG	60631	2864	9W-9N	D7
7500	NLES	60631	2864	9W-9N	D7
7500	NLES	60714	2864	9W-9N	D7
O'Dell Ct					
-	HDHT	60706	2918	9W-6N	D7
W O'Dell Ct					
7300	WRTH	60482	3274	9W-12S	E2
N Oden Av					
34600	GrtT	60041	2474	25W-34N	B7
W Odessa Ct					
22200	PnfT	60544	3339	27W-16S	B4
Odessa Dr					
-	MTSN	60443	3506	5W-24S	B6
Odlum Ct					
200	SMBG	60194	2857	27W-10N	D5
Odlum Dr					
2700	SMBG	60194	2857	27W-10N	D5
2800	SMBG	60193	2857	27W-10N	D5
O'Donahue Dr					
4300	JLET	60431	3496	29W-22S	D2
Odysseus Rd					
6700	AraT	60506	3199	37W-8S	C2
6700	AURA	60506	3199	37W-8S	D2
6700	MTGY	60506	3199	37W-8S	D3
6700	MTGY	60538	3199	37W-8S	D3
Odyssey Av					
-	NPVL	60563	3080	29W-4S	C7
-	NPVL	60563	3140	30W-4S	C1
Odyssey Blvd					
-	MTSN	60443	3505	8W-23S	B4
-	MTSN	60477	3505	8W-23S	B4
-	TYPK	60477	3505	8W-23S	B4
Odyssey Ct					
3300	NPVL	60563	3140	30W-4S	B1
Odyssey Dr					
10	TYPK	60477	3505	8W-23S	B4
Oeffling Ct					
900	MchT	60050	2472	29W-36N	B3
Oeffling Dr					
600	MchT	60050	2472	29W-36N	C3
1000	JNBG	60050	2472	30W-36N	B3
Off-Bradley Rd					
-	GNOK	60045	2592	13W-27N	D7
-	GNOK	60048	2592	13W-27N	D7
-	LbvT	60048	2592	13W-27N	D7
27600	GNOK	60045	2648	13W-27N	D1
27600	MTWA	60045	2648	13W-27N	D1
Office Dr					
-	WTMT	60559	3085	18W-3S	A6
Office Rd					
-	RcmT	60071	2412	35W-38N	B7
-	RcmT	60072	2412	35W-38N	B7
-	RcmT	60097	2412	35W-38N	B7
N Office St					
100	BDWD	60408	3941	32W-41S	E5
S Office St					
100	BDWD	60408	3941	32W-41S	E6
Official Rd					
6100	CLLK	60014	2640	35W-24N	B6
W Official Rd					
10	ADSN	60101	2970	18W-2N	E6
Offield Dr					
200	LKVL	60046	2416	23W-38N	E7
200	LKVL	60046	2474	23W-38N	E1
200	LkvT	60046	2416	23W-38N	E7
200	LkvT	60046	2474	23W-38N	E1
W Offner Rd					
13400	MhtT	60442	3767	16W-33S	E3
14400	WltT	60442	3767	19W-33S	A4
15000	MhtT	60442	3766	19W-33S	E4
15000	WltT	60442	3766	19W-33S	E4
16300	MhtT	60421	3766	19W-33S	E4
Offutt Ln					
300	AURA	60506	3138	36W-5S	A3
300	AURA	60542	3138	36W-5S	A3
300	NARA	60542	3138	36W-5S	A3
N Ogallah Av					
6600	CHCG	60631	2918	9W-8N	D2
Ogaw Tr					
-	DndT	60102	2747	34W-19N	E2
Ogden Av					
-	AURA	60540	3202	29W-8S	C1
-	CHCG	60610	3034	0W-1N	A1
-	HNDL	60521	3086	14W-3S	C6
-	LynT	60521	3086	14W-3S	C6
-	LynT	60558	3086	14W-3S	C6
-	NPVL	60563	3140	28W-6S	E5
-	OswT	60503	3201	33W-9S	A5
-	OswT	60504	3201	33W-9S	A5
10	DRGV	60515	3084	18W-4S	E7
10	DRGV	60515	3085	18W-4S	A7
10	LSLE	60563	3142	25W-5S	B2
10	LslT	60563	3142	25W-5S	B2
10	NPVL	60540	3140	29W-7S	E6
10	NPVL	60563	3142	25W-5S	B2
10	WTMT	60515	3084	18W-4S	E7
10	WTMT	60515	3085	18W-4S	A7
10	WTMT	60559	3084	18W-4S	E7
10	WTMT	60559	3085	18W-4S	A7
100	LSLE	60532	3142	25W-5S	C2
100	PvsT	60525	3086	13W-3S	E6
100	PvsT	60558	3086	14W-3S	D6
100	WNSP	60558	3086	14W-3S	D6
300	AURA	60504	3201	32W-8S	C3
300	NpvT	60504	3201	32W-9S	C3
400	LSLE	60532	3143	23W-4S	A1
400	LslT	60532	3143	23W-4S	A1
400	NPVL	60504	3202	29W-8S	C1
400	NPVL	60540	3202	30W-8S	C1
1200	DRGV	60515	3144	20W-4S	A1
1900	AraT	60504	3201	33W-9S	A5
2000	DRGV	60515	3143	21W-4S	D1
2500	LslT	60515	3143	21W-4S	D1
2700	DRGV	60532	3143	22W-4S	D1
3600	AURA	60504	3202	31W-8S	A2
6200	BRWN	60402	3089	8W-3S	A5
6200	CCRO	60402	3089	8W-3S	A5
6200	CCRO	60804	3089	8W-3S	A5
6800	BRWN	60402	3088	9W-4S	D6
7100	BRWN	60402	3088	9W-4S	C6
7100	LYNS	60534	3088	9W-4S	C6
7100	LYNS	60546	3088	9W-4S	C6
7100	RVSD	60402	3088	9W-4S	C6
7100	RVSD	60546	3088	9W-4S	C6
8700	BKFD	60513	3088	10W-4S	A6
8700	BKFD	60534	3088	10W-4S	A6
8800	BKFD	60513	3087	11W-4S	D6
9500	BKFD	60525	3087	11W-4S	D6
9500	LGNG	60525	3087	11W-4S	D6
Ogden Av US-34					
-	AURA	60540	3202	29W-8S	C1
-	HNDL	60521	3086	14W-3S	C6
-	LynT	60521	3086	14W-3S	C6
-	LynT	60558	3086	14W-3S	C6
-	NPVL	60563	3140	28W-6S	E5
-	OswT	60503	3201	33W-9S	A5
-	OswT	60504	3201	33W-9S	A5
10	DRGV	60515	3084	18W-4S	E7
10	DRGV	60515	3085	18W-4S	A7
10	LSLE	60563	3142	25W-5S	B2
10	LslT	60563	3142	25W-5S	B2
10	NPVL	60540	3140	28W-7S	E6
10	NPVL	60563	3142	25W-5S	B2
10	WTMT	60515	3084	18W-4S	E7
10	WTMT	60515	3085	18W-4S	A7
10	WTMT	60559	3084	18W-4S	E7
10	WTMT	60559	3085	18W-4S	A7
100	LSLE	60532	3142	25W-5S	C2
100	PvsT	60525	3086	13W-3S	E6
100	PvsT	60558	3086	14W-3S	D6
100	WNSP	60558	3086	14W-3S	D6
400	AURA	60504	3202	29W-8S	C1
400	LSLE	60532	3143	23W-4S	A1
400	LslT	60532	3143	23W-4S	A1
400	NPVL	60540	3202	30W-8S	C1
1200	DRGV	60515	3144	20W-4S	A1
1900	AraT	60504	3201	33W-9S	A5
2000	DRGV	60515	3143	21W-4S	D1
2100	AURA	60504	3201	33W-9S	A5
2400	NpvT	60504	3201	32W-9S	C3
2500	LslT	60515	3143	21W-4S	D1
2700	DRGV	60532	3143	22W-4S	D1
4300	NPVL	60504	3202	30W-8S	C1
7200	BRWN	60402	3088	9W-4S	C6
7200	LYNS	60402	3088	9W-4S	C6
7200	LYNS	60534	3088	9W-4S	C6
7200	LYNS	60546	3088	9W-4S	C6
7200	RVSD	60402	3088	9W-4S	C6
7200	RVSD	60546	3088	9W-4S	C6
8700	BKFD	60513	3088	10W-4S	A6
8700	BKFD	60534	3088	10W-4S	A6
8800	BKFD	60513	3087	11W-4S	D6
9500	BKFD	60525	3087	11W-4S	D6
9500	LGNG	60525	3087	11W-4S	D6
E Ogden Av					
10	HNDL	60521	3086	15W-4S	B6
10	LGNG	60525	3087	12W-4S	C6
10	NPVL	60563	3141	26W-5S	E4
10	WTMT	60559	3085	17W-4S	C7
100	CNHL	60514	3085	17W-4S	C7
100	CNHL	60559	3085	17W-4S	C7
100	WTMT	60514	3085	16W-4S	D7
400	LynT	60521	3086	15W-4S	C6
400	LynT	60558	3086	15W-4S	C6
800	CNHL	60521	3085	16W-4S	E7
800	HNDL	60521	3085	16W-4S	E7
800	WTMT	60521	3085	16W-4S	E7
900	NPVL	60563	3142	25W-5S	A2
1000	LslT	60563	3142	25W-5S	A2
1400	LSLE	60563	3142	25W-5S	A2
9600	BKFD	60513	3087	12W-4S	D6
9600	BKFD	60525	3087	12W-4S	D6
E Ogden Av US-34					
10	HNDL	60521	3086	15W-4S	B6
10	LGNG	60525	3087	12W-4S	C6
10	NPVL	60563	3141	26W-5S	E4
10	WTMT	60559	3085	17W-4S	C7
100	CNHL	60514	3085	17W-4S	C7
100	CNHL	60559	3085	17W-4S	C7
100	WTMT	60514	3085	16W-4S	D7
400	LynT	60521	3086	15W-4S	C6
400	LynT	60558	3086	15W-4S	C6
800	CNHL	60521	3085	16W-4S	E7
800	HNDL	60521	3085	16W-4S	E7
800	WTMT	60521	3085	16W-4S	E7
900	NPVL	60563	3142	25W-5S	A2
1000	LslT	60563	3142	25W-5S	A2
1400	LSLE	60563	3142	25W-5S	A2
9600	BKFD	60513	3087	12W-4S	D6
9600	BKFD	60525	3087	12W-4S	D6
N Ogden Av					
10	CHCG	60607	3033	1W-0N	D4
300	CHCG	60622	3033	1W-0N	D4
1400	CHCG	60610	3034		C1
W Ogden Av					
-	CNHL	60514	3085	16W-4S	E7
-	CNHL	60521	3085	16W-4S	E7
-	WTMT	60514	3085	16W-4S	E7
-	WTMT	60521	3085	16W-4S	E7
10	DGvT	60559	3085	18W-4S	A7
10	HNDL	60521	3086	15W-4S	A7
10	LGNG	60525	3087	12W-4S	C6
10	NPVL	60563	3141	28W-6S	B4
10	WTMT	60559	3085	18W-4S	A7
300	DRGV	60515	3085	18W-4S	A7
300	WTMT	60515	3085	18W-4S	A7
500	HNDL	60521	3085	16W-4S	E7
1200	LGPK	60525	3087	13W-4S	A6
1300	NPVL	60563	3140	28W-6S	E5
1500	CHCG	60607	3033	2W-0S	C5
1500	LGPK	60558	3087	13W-4S	A6
1500	NPVL	60540	3140	28W-6S	E5
1500	WNSP	60525	3087	13W-4S	A6
1500	WNSP	60558	3087	13W-4S	A6
1600	PvsT	60525	3087	13W-4S	A6
1600	PvsT	60558	3087	13W-4S	A6
2300	CHCG	60608	3033	3W-1S	A7
2300	CHCG	60612	3033	2W-1S	B7
2700	CHCG	60623	3033	3W-1S	A7
2800	CHCG	60623	3032	3W-1S	E7
2800	CHCG	60623	3090	4W-1S	D1
4400	CCRO	60804	3090	5W-2S	A2
4800	CCRO	60804	3089	7W-3S	C4
6100	BRWN	60402	3089	7W-3S	B4
6100	CCRO	60402	3089	7W-3S	B4
W Ogden Av US-34					
-	CNHL	60514	3085	16W-4S	E7
-	CNHL	60521	3085	16W-4S	E7
-	WTMT	60514	3085	16W-4S	E7
-	WTMT	60521	3085	16W-4S	E7
10	DGvT	60559	3085	18W-4S	A7
10	HNDL	60521	3086	15W-4S	A7
10	LGNG	60525	3087	12W-4S	C6
10	NPVL	60563	3141	28W-6S	A4
10	WTMT	60559	3085	18W-4S	A7
300	DRGV	60515	3085	18W-4S	A7
300	WTMT	60515	3085	18W-4S	A7
500	HNDL	60521	3085	16W-4S	E7
1200	LGPK	60525	3087	13W-4S	A6
1300	NPVL	60563	3140	28W-6S	E5
1500	LGPK	60558	3087	13W-4S	A6
1500	NPVL	60540	3140	28W-6S	E5
1500	WNSP	60525	3087	13W-4S	A6
1500	WNSP	60558	3087	13W-4S	A6
1600	PvsT	60525	3087	13W-4S	A6
1600	PvsT	60558	3087	13W-4S	A6
N Ogden Ln					
39000	BHPK	60083	2421	13W-39N	A6
Ogden Rd					
600	NLNX	60451	3501	18W-25S	B7
600	NlxT	60451	3501	18W-25S	B7
700	NlxT	60451	3589	18W-25S	B1
900	NLNX	60451	3589	18W-25S	B1
E Ogden St					
10	CTCY	60409	3352		C6
10	HMND	46320	3352		D6
Ogden Falls Blvd					
-	MTGY	60538	3200	34W-11S	E7
-	MTGY	60543	3200	34W-11S	E7
-	OSWG	60538	3200	34W-11S	E7
300	OSWG	60543	3200	34W-11S	E7
300	OSWG	60543	3264	34W-11S	E1
Ogilvie Ct					
-	ELGN	60123	2854	34W-10N	D6
Oglesby Av					
-	WrnT	60031	2535	13W-34N	E2
200	CTCY	60409	3351	2E-17S	D5
4000	GRNE	60031	2535	14W-34N	D2
S Oglesby Av					
-	CHCG	60633	3351	2E-15S	D2
-	CTCY	60409	3351	2E-15S	D2
6700	CHCG	60649	3153	2E-7S	D6
7500	CHCG	60649	3215	2E-9S	D2
7800	CHCG	60617	3215	2E-9S	D3
10300	CHCG	60617	3279	2E-11S	D1
Ogorman Dr					
11100	PSHL	60465	3274	10W-12S	A3
O'Hara Ter					
3300	AURA	60564	3201	31W-9S	E4
O'Hare Ct					
10	BNVL	60106	2972	15W-5N	A1
2600	WDRG	60517	3143	22W-7S	D7
S O'Hare Ct					
25200	MonT	60449	3682	8W-30S	B4
O'Hare Dr					
4100	HFET	60192	2804	24W-15N	D3
O'Hare Cargo Area Rd					
-	CHCG	60666	2916	14W-5N	C7
-	CHCG	60666	2972	14W-5N	C1
Ohio Av					
800	SCRL	60174	2964	35W-3N	C7
2400	NCHI	60088	2593	12W-29N	C3
3000	SCRL	60174	2965	33W-3N	A7
3800	WynT	60174	2965	33W-2N	B7
3800	WynT	60185	2965	33W-2N	B7
Ohio Ct					
1100	AURA	60505	3138	34W-6S	D4
1900	LSLE	60532	3142	23W-5S	E3
18100	ODPK	60467	3423	13W-21S	B7
Ohio Rd					
-	BtvT	60539	3077	36W-2S	E5
400	FftT	60423	3503	12W-25S	C7
400	FKFT	60423	3503	12W-25S	C7
Ohio St					
-	NCHI	60064	2593	11W-30N	E2
10	MYWD	60153	3030	10W-0N	A3
200	LslT	60540	3142	24W-5S	C3
600	SchT	60174	2908	34W-6N	D6
700	LSLE	60532	3143	22W-5S	B3
800	NCHI	60044	2593	11W-30N	E2
900	CLSM	60188	2967	26W-3N	E5
900	LKBF	60044	2593	11W-30N	E2
900	LKBF	60088	2593	11W-30N	E2
900	NCHI	60088	2593	11W-30N	E3
1900	LSLE	60532	3142	23W-5S	E3
E Ohio St					
10	CHCG	60610	3034	0E-0N	C3
10	CHCG	60611	3034	0E-0N	C3
10	JLET	60432	3499	23W-23S	A3
N Ohio St					
10	AURA	60504	3200	34W-8S	D1
10	AURA	60505	3200	34W-8S	D1
600	AraT	60505	3138	34W-6S	D5
1000	AURA	60505	3138	34W-6S	D4
S Ohio St					
10	AURA	60504	3200	34W-8S	D2
10	AURA	60505	3200	34W-8S	D2
W Ohio St					
10	CHCG	60610	3034	0W-0N	B3
10	CHCG	60611	3034	0W-0N	B3
700	CHCG	60622	3034	0W-0N	A3
W Ohio St					
1000	GNWD	60425	3508	1W-22S	A1
1000	HMWD	60425	3508	1W-22S	A1
1000	HMWD	60430	3508	1W-22S	A1
1200	CHCG	60622	3033	2W-0N	B3
1900	CHCG	60612	3033	3W-0N	A3
3000	CHCG	60612	3032	4W-0N	D3
3100	CHCG	60624	3032	4W-0N	C3
4600	CHCG	60644	3032	5W-0N	A3
4700	CHCG	60644	3031	6W-0N	E3
5900	OKPK	60302	3031	7W-0N	B3
Ohlendorf Rd					
3000	MonT	60449	3683	4W-31S	D6
3000	MonT	60449	3684	3W-31S	A6
Ojai Dr					
-	RchT	60443	3593	7W-27S	D3
-	RNPK	60443	3593	7W-27S	C3
Ojibwa Ln					
6100	MHRY	60050	2527	35W-33N	A3
Ojibwa Tr					
-	MPPT	60056	2861	16W-12N	D2
2300	RLKH	60073	2474	23W-36N	E4
S Ojibwa Tr					
400	MPPT	60056	2861	16W-12N	D1
W Okelly Dr					
28000	GrtT	60041	2530	28W-34N	A1
Oketo Av					
8800	MNGV	60714	2864	9W-11N	D4
8800	NLES	60714	2864	9W-11N	D4
9300	MNGV	60053	2864	9W-11N	D2
16700	TYPK	60477	3424	9W-20S	E3
N Oketo Av					
3000	CHCG	60707	2974	9W-3N	D4
3000	EDPK	60707	2974	9W-3N	D4
3100	CHCG	60634	2974	9W-3N	D4
3900	NRDG	60634	2974	9W-4N	D2
3900	NRDG	60706	2974	9W-5N	D1
4400	HDHT	60706	2918	9W-6N	D6
4400	NRDG	60706	2918	9W-5N	D7
5100	CHCG	60656	2918	9W-6N	D6
5100	CHCG	60706	2918	9W-6N	D6
6500	CHCG	60631	2918	9W-8N	D2
7200	CHCG	60631	2864	9W-9N	D7
7500	NLES	60631	2864	9W-9N	D7
8000	NLES	60714	2864	9W-10N	D5
8700	MNGV	60053	2864	9W-10N	D5
8700	NLES	60053	2864	9W-10N	D5
S Oketo Av					
7100	BGVW	60455	3148	9W-8S	D7
8900	BGVW	60455	3210	9W-10S	D5
10700	WRTH	60482	3274	9W-13S	E3
Oklahoma Av					
4200	NCHI	60088	2593	12W-30N	C3
Oklahoma Cir					
600	EGVV	60007	2859	21W-9N	E7
Oklahoma Ct					
-	OrlT	60467	3423	13W-21S	B7
-	OrlT	60487	3423	13W-21S	B7
4200	NCHI	60088	2593	12W-30N	C3
18200	ODPK	60467	3423	13W-21S	B7
Oklahoma Wy					
600	EGVV	60007	2859	21W-9N	E7
600	EGVV	60007	2913	21W-9N	E1
Okolona Ct					
800	NPVL	60540	3203	27W-8S	B1
Olandra Wy					
-	RtdT	60140	2798	40W-14N	B5
Olcott Av					
8800	NLES	60714	2864	9W-11N	D4
9200	MNGV	60053	2864	9W-11N	C2
15900	ODPK	60462	3424	9W-19S	E1
15900	ODPK	60477	3424	9W-19S	E1
15900	TYPK	60477	3424	9W-19S	E2
16700	OrlT	60477	3424	9W-20S	E4
N Olcott Av					
3000	CHCG	60707	2974	9W-3N	C4
3000	EDPK	60707	2974	9W-3N	C4
3900	CHCG	60634	2974	9W-4N	C2
3900	CHCG	60706	2974	9W-4N	C2
3900	NRDG	60706	2974	9W-4N	C2
4600	HDHT	60706	2918	9W-5N	C7
4600	NRDG	60706	2918	9W-5N	C7
5100	CHCG	60706	2918	9W-6N	C6
5400	CHCG	60656	2918	9W-6N	C5
6800	CHCG	60631	2918	9W-8N	C1
7200	CHCG	60631	2864	9W-9N	C7
7500	NLES	60631	2864	9W-9N	C7
8100	NLES	60714	2864	9W-10N	C4
8600	MNGV	60053	2864	9W-10N	C4
Olcott Ct					
17300	TYPK	60477	3424	9W-20S	E5
Old Arlington Ct					
900	ANHT	60004	2754	17W-17N	A4
900	BFGV	60004	2754	17W-17N	A4
900	BFGV	60089	2754	17W-17N	A4
N Old Arlington Heights Rd					
3200	ANHT	60004	2754	17W-17N	A5
3200	BFGV	60004	2754	17W-17N	A5
3200	BFGV	60089	2754	17W-17N	A5
Old Barn Cir					
1500	LYVL	60048	2591	17W-30N	A2
Old Barn Ct					
100	BFGV	60089	2701	16W-21N	C6
1500	BRLT	60103	2966	30W-5N	B2
16700	TYPK	60477	3424	10W-20S	C3
Old Barn Ln					
1000	LKFT	60045	2648	13W-24N	E7
1400	HDPK	60035	2704	8W-21N	D5
E Old Barn Ln					
700	ANHT	60005	2807	17W-12N	B7
W Old Barn Ln					
21300	ElaT	60047	2699	21W-23N	D1
Old Barn Rd					
-	BFGV	60089	2701	16W-21N	C6
10	HNWD	60047	2700	20W-23N	B1
10	LGGV	60047	2700	19W-23N	B1
10	LKBN	60010	2697	26W-24N	E1
100	LKBN	60010	2643	26W-24N	E7
600	DndT	60118	2747	35W-18N	B5
600	ElgT	60124	2853	37W-11N	C3
1500	BRLT	60103	2966	30W-5N	B2
Old Barrington Ct					
23500	LKBN	60010	2697	27W-23N	B2
Old Barrington Rd					
-	HFET	60192	2803	25W-13N	E6
-	SBTN	60010	2803	25W-13N	E6
N Old Barrington Rd					
10	LKBN	60010	2697	27W-23N	B1
100	CbaT	60010	2697	26W-21N	D5
100	NBRN	60010	2697	26W-21N	D5
Old Bartlett Rd					
-	BmT	60010	2803	27W-16N	A1
10	BNHL	60010	2750	27W-16N	A7
10	BNHL	60010	2803	27W-16N	A1
10	SBTN	60010	2803	27W-16N	A1
Old Bay Rd					
-	LKMR	60051	2472	30W-34N	B7
1200	JNBG	60051	2472	30W-34N	B7
Old Beach Rd					
800	DYR	46311	3598		E2
Old Bender Rd					
10	DSPN	60016	2863	12W-11N	B3
Old Bluff Rd					
-	DGvT	60439	3207	17W-11S	C7
-	DGvT	60439	3271	17W-11S	B1
Old Bond Ct					
1200	GNEN	60137	3026	20W-0S	A7
1200	GNEN	60148	3026	20W-0S	A7
1200	LMBD	60148	3026	20W-0S	A7
Old Brennan Hwy					
-	BmnT	60477	3426	6W-20S	A5
-	BmnT	60478	3426	6W-20S	A5
-	CCHL	60478	3426	6W-20S	A5
Old Briar Rd					
1600	HDPK	60035	2757	9W-20N	C2
Old Bridge Ct					
2400	NPVL	60564	3202	29W-10S	D6
Old Bridge Rd					
-	LKFT	60045	2649	13W-25N	A4
-	VrnT	60045	2649	13W-25N	A4
E Old Bridge Rd					
100	PLTN	60067	2752	20W-17N	E5
100	PLTN	60067	2753	20W-17N	A5
100	PLTN	60074	2753	20W-17N	A5
N Old Bridge Rd					
1000	PLTN	60067	2752	20W-17N	E4
Old Buffalo Grove Rd					
-	BFGV	60089	2754	16W-18N	C4
-	WhlT	60004	2754	16W-18N	C4
-	WhlT	60089	2754	16W-18N	C4
N Old Buffalo Grove Rd					
-	ANHT	60004	2754	16W-17N	C6
-	ANHT	60090	2754	16W-17N	C6
-	WLNG	60090	2754	16W-17N	C6
3500	BFGV	60004	2754	16W-17N	C4
3500	WhlT	60004	2754	16W-17N	C4
3500	WhlT	60089	2754	16W-17N	C4
Old Burlington Rd					
10	CmpT	60175	2962	39W-4N	D3
Old Cargo Rd					
500	CHCG	60666	2917	12W-6N	A6
Old Castle Dr					
11600	MKNA	60448	3502	14W-24S	D6
Old Castle Rd					
-	JLET	60435	3417	28W-21S	B6
3200	JLET	60431	3417	28W-21S	B6
Old Checker Ct					
700	BFGV	60089	2754	17W-20N	B1
Old Checker Rd					
800	BFGV	60089	2754	17W-20N	B1
Old Chicago Dr					
10	BGBK	60440	3269	23W-13S	B4
Old Church Rd					
1000	SMBG	60107	2857	27W-11N	D5
1000	SMBG	60194	2857	27W-11N	D5
1000	SMWD	60107	2857	27W-11N	D5
2000	AraT	60504	3138	34W-5S	D2
2000	AraT	60505	3138	34W-5S	D2
2000	AURA	60504	3138	34W-5S	D2
2000	AURA	60505	3138	34W-5S	D2
Old Coach Dr					
10	SBTN	60010	2803	26W-14N	D4
S Old Coach Tr					
19500	FftT	60423	3504	9W-23S	D3
Old College Rd					
300	LSLE	60540	3142	24W-7S	D7
300	LslT	60532	3142	24W-7S	D7
300	LslT	60540	3142	24W-7S	D7
400	LSLE	60532	3142	24W-7S	D7
Old Colony Rd					
1000	LKFT	60045	2649	11W-24N	D7
Old Country Wy					
300	WCDA	60084	2643	26W-27N	D1
400	WCDA	60084	2587	26W-27N	D7
Old Creek Ct					
600	BRTN	60010	2698	25W-21N	A7
700	EGVV	60007	2914	20W-8N	B3
1000	ELGN	60120	2801	32W-12N	D7
1100	DGvT	60517	3206	20W-8S	B2
1100	WDRG	60517	3206	20W-8S	B2
N Old Creek Ct					
36100	WrnT	60031	2477	17W-36N	B4
Old Creek Ln					
6000	MTSN	60443	3505	7W-24S	D6
N Old Creek Rd					
10	VNHL	60061	2647	16W-25N	D6
S Old Creek Rd					
10	VNHL	60061	2647	16W-24N	C6
Old Creek Rd N					
10	PSPK	60464	3272	14W-14S	D7
Old Creek Rd S					
10	PSPK	60464	3272	14W-15S	D7
10	PSPK	60464	3344	14W-15S	E1
Old Darby Ln					
100	PTPR	53158	2363	10W-43N	A4
100	WPHR	53158	2363	10W-43N	A4
100	WPHR	60096	2363	10W-43N	A4
Old Deerfield Rd					
1400	HDPK	60035	2704	9W-21N	C6
Old Dominion Ct					
1300	NPVL	60540	3142	25W-7S	B6
Old Dominion Rd					
1300	NPVL	60540	3142	25W-7S	B6
Old Draper Rd					
900	MchT	60050	2527	35W-32N	B4
900	MHRY	60050	2527	35W-32N	B4
Old Dundee Rd					
100	BNHL	60010	2750	27W-16N	B6
100	BrnT	60010	2750	27W-16N	B6
Olde English Ct					
100	RMVL	60446	3339	27W-17S	D5
Olde English Dr					
10	RMVL	60446	3339	27W-17S	D5
Olde Farm Rd					
1200	SMBG	60173	2805	21W-13N	D6
18200	ThtT	60438	3429	2E-21S	D6
18300	LNSG	60438	3429	2E-21S	D7
18500	BlmT	60411	3429	2E-21S	D7
18500	BlmT	60438	3429	2E-21S	D7
Olde Gatehouse Rd					
6800	TYPK	60477	3425	8W-19S	A3
Olde Ivey Rd					
800	SRWD	60404	3496	31W-24S	A7
Old Elm Dr					
200	BGBK	60440	3268	23W-11S	E1
16900	CCHL	60478	3426	4W-20S	D4
Old Elm Ln					
1000	GLNC	60022	2758	6W-18N	C3
Old Elm Pl					
900	GLNC	60022	2758	6W-18N	C4

STREET Block	City	ZIP	Map#	CGS	Grid
Old Elm Rd					
-	LKFT	60035	2649	10W-24N	E7
-	LKFT	60045	2649	11W-24N	E7
10	JltT	60433	3587	23W-25S	A1
10	JltT	60436	3587	23W-25S	A1
100	LNHT	60046	2476	20W-37N	A1
400	HDPK	60035	2650	10W-24N	A7
400	HIWD	60035	2650	9W-24N	C7
400	LKFT	60035	2650	10W-24N	A7
400	LKFT	60037	2650	9W-24N	C7
400	LKFT	60045	2650	10W-24N	A7
700	HDPK	60045	2650	10W-24N	B7
W Old Elm Rd					
10	LKFT	60045	2649	11W-24N	D7
Olde Mill Ln					
1900	MHRY	60050	2528	32W-34N	A2
2000	MchT	60050	2528	32W-34N	A2
Olde Mill Rd					
1800	JLET	60586	3416	30W-21S	C7
10600	ODPK	60467	3423	13W-20S	A5
Olde Oaks Rd					
1100	SMBG	60173	2805	21W-13N	D6
Old Eola Rd					
100	AURA	60502	3139	31W-6S	D5
100	NpvT	60502	3139	31W-6S	D5
Olde Post Rd					
7600	AlqT	60014	2641	33W-24N	A7
7600	CLLK	60014	2641	33W-24N	A7
Older Creek Ct					
-	RMVL	60446	3340	26W-17S	A6
-	RMVL	60544	3340	26W-17S	A6
Older Creek Dr					
200	RMVL	60446	3340	26W-17S	A6
200	RMVL	60544	3340	26W-17S	A6
Olde Salem Cir					
7200	HRPK	60133	2912	25W-9N	A1
7200	SMBG	60133	2912	25W-9N	A2
Olde Salem Rd					
7300	HRPK	60133	2912	26W-9N	A1
E Olde Virginia Ct					
1000	PLTN	60074	2753	19W-17N	B5
E Olde Virginia Rd					
1000	PLTN	60074	2753	19W-17N	C5
Olde Western Av					
13200	BLID	60406	3349	3W-15S	B1
Old Farm Ct					
10	LNHT	60046	2476	19W-38N	D1
26000	CNHN	60410	3672	33W-31S	C6
Old Farm Dr					
600	ROSL	60172	2912	24W-6N	D7
Old Farm Ln					
10	DndT	60110	2748	33W-18N	A5
100	CmpT	60175	2962	39W-6N	D1
100	WnfT	60555	3080	29W-2S	E3
200	CmpT	60175	2906	39W-6N	D7
6100	GRNE	60031	2534	16W-34N	D1
Old Farm Rd					
-	LYWD	60411	3510		C6
100	NHFD	60093	2811	7W-16N	A1
200	NfdT	60093	2811	7W-16N	A1
200	NHFD	60093	2758	7W-16N	A7
600	SchT	60175	2963	36W-4N	E4
700	MTSN	60443	3505	7W-24S	D6
800	SchT	60175	2964	36W-4N	A3
900	AvnT	60073	2531	24W-33N	C2
900	DYR	46311	3510		C6
900	RDLK	60073	2531	24W-33N	C2
21500	DRPK	60010	2698	24W-21N	C5
24000	MhtT	60442	3590	15W-29S	C7
Old Farm Tr					
26400	CNHN	60410	3672	33W-31S	C7
26500	AxST	60410	3672	33W-31S	C7
Old Fence Ct					
8300	WDRG	60517	3205	22W-9S	D4
N Old Fence Rd					
1100	ADSN	60101	2970	19W-4N	C2
Old Ferry Rd					
100	AURA	60502	3079	31W-4S	E7
Old Field Ln					
5500	LGGV	60047	2701	17W-22N	A3
Old Field Rd					
5500	LGGV	60047	2701	17W-22N	B3
Oldfield Rd					
100	DGvT	60516	3206	19W-10S	D5
100	DGvT	60561	3206	19W-10S	D5
100	DRN	60516	3206	19W-10S	D5
100	DRN	60561	3206	19W-10S	D5
Old Forge Ct					
600	UYPK	60466	3684	3W-30S	B4
S Old Forge Ct					
1200	PLTN	60067	2805	21W-14N	D4
Old Forge Ln					
600	UYPK	60466	3684	3W-30S	B4
Old Forge Rd					
100	ELGN	60123	2854	36W-11N	A3
1500	BRLT	60103	2966	30W-5N	B2
1500	BRLT	60184	2966	30W-5N	B2
1500	WYNE	60184	2966	30W-5N	B2
Old Frankfort Wy					
-	FKFT	60423	3591	12W-25S	D1
W Old Gages Lake Rd					
18400	WrnT	60030	2533	18W-33N	E2
Old Gary Av					
10	BMDL	60108	2968	25W-4N	B3
10	BMDL	60133	2968	25W-4N	B3
200	BmdT	60133	2968	25W-4N	B4
200	CLSM	60133	2968	25W-4N	B4
1200	BmdT	60188	2968	25W-4N	B4
1200	CLSM	60188	2968	25W-4N	B4
Old George Wy					
2300	LslT	60515	3143	21W-6S	E4
Old Georges Wy					
7900	PSHT	60463	3346	9W-15S	C2
20000	OMFD	60461	3506	4W-24S	D4
W Old Gilmer Rd					
25800	WcnT	60030	2587	26W-30N	E2
25800	WcnT	60084	2587	26W-30N	E2
25900	WcnT	60073	2587	26W-30N	E2
Old Glenview Rd					
2000	WLMT	60091	2812	5W-13N	A7
2100	EVTN	60201	2812	4W-13N	B7
2200	WLMT	60201	2812	4W-13N	B7
3200	SKOK	60077	2811	6W-13N	D7
3200	WLMT	60077	2811	6W-13N	D7
3200	WLMT	60091	2811	6W-13N	D7
3300	GNVW	60025	2811	6W-13N	D7
3300	GNVW	60091	2811	6W-13N	D7
Old Glory Ct					
2000	BtlT	60543	3262	41W-12S	B4
2000	BtlT	60560	3262	41W-12S	B4
Old Glory Dr					
2800	BtlT	60543	3262	40W-12S	B4
2800	BtlT	60560	3262	40W-12S	B4
Old Grand Av					
10	AddT	60106	2971	17W-3N	C5
10	EMHT	60106	2971	17W-3N	C5
10	EMHT	60126	2971	17W-3N	C5
100	ADSN	60106	2971	17W-3N	C5
100	EMHT	60101	2971	17W-3N	C5
700	ADSN	60101	2971	17W-3N	B5
4000	GRNE	60031	2478	14W-35N	D7
W Old Grand Av					
25600	GrtT	60041	2474	25W-36N	A4
W Old Grass Lake Rd					
25300	AntT	60002	2416	25W-40N	A3
Old Green Bay Rd					
10	GLNC	60093	2759	5W-16N	A7
10	WNKA	60093	2759	5W-17N	A6
100	GLNC	60022	2759	5W-17N	A6
700	GLNC	60022	2758	6W-18N	D4
10700	PTPR	53158	2362		A2
Old Grove Cir					
5500	BFGV	60047	2701	17W-22N	B3
5500	BFGV	60089	2701	17W-22N	B3
5500	LGGV	60047	2701	17W-22N	B3
Old Half Day Rd					
100	LNSH	60061	2702	15W-23N	A2
100	VrnT	60061	2702	15W-23N	A2
200	LNSH	60069	2702	15W-23N	A3
200	VrnT	60069	2702	15W-23N	A3
15300	VNHL	60061	2702	15W-23N	A2
15300	VNHL	60069	2702	15W-23N	A2
Oldham Av					
1000	LSLE	60532	3143	22W-4S	B1
3000	LSLE	60532	3142	25W-4S	C1
3000	LSLE	60563	3142	25W-4S	C1
3000	LslT	60532	3142	25W-4S	C1
3000	LslT	60563	3142	25W-4S	C1
Oldham Ct					
-	AraT	60502	3139	33W-6S	B4
-	AURA	60502	3139	33W-6S	B4
Oldham Rd					
3000	LSLE	60532	3142	25W-4S	B1
3000	LSLE	60563	3142	25W-4S	B1
3000	LslT	60532	3142	25W-4S	B1
3000	LslT	60563	3142	25W-4S	B1
14100	ODPK	60467	3344	14W-16S	D4
S Old Harlem Av					
6500	BDPK	60638	3148	9W-7S	E6
6500	CHCG	60638	3148	9W-7S	E6
Old Hart Rd					
10	BNHL	60010	2697	26W-20N	D7
10	BNHL	60010	2750	26W-20N	C1
Old Harter Rd					
800	SgrT	60554	3135	43W-5S	A2
800	SRGV	60554	3135	43W-5S	A2
W Old Hickory Ct					
18200	WrnT	60031	2534	18W-34N	A1
Old Hickory Ln					
500	LbvT	60048	2592	15W-29N	B5
500	LYVL	60048	2592	15W-29N	B5
Old Hickory Rd					
10	RGMW	60008	2806	19W-14N	C3
300	NLNX	60451	3501	18W-24S	A5
300	NlxT	60451	3501	18W-24S	A5
400	NlxT	60451	3500	19W-24S	E5
Old Hicks Rd					
2300	ElaT	60047	2753	19W-20N	B1
2300	LGGV	60047	2700	19W-20N	B7
2300	LGGV	60047	2753	19W-20N	B1
E Old Hicks Rd					
2000	PLTN	60074	2753	19W-18N	B2
2300	LGGV	60047	2753	19W-18N	B2
2300	LGGV	60074	2753	19W-18N	B2
N Old Hicks Rd					
1800	PLTN	60074	2753	19W-18N	B3
W Old Hideaway Rd					
28500	AlqT	60013	2642	28W-24N	D7
28500	CbaT	60013	2642	28W-24N	D7
Old Higgins Rd					
-	EDND	60118	2801	30W-14N	E4
-	HFET	60010	2803	27W-12N	C7
-	HFET	60010	2857	27W-12N	D1
-	HFET	60118	2801	30W-14N	E4
-	HFET	60118	2802	30W-14N	A4
-	HFET	60169	2857	26W-12N	E1
2700	EGvT	60007	2915	16W-8N	E1
2700	EGVV	60007	2915	16W-8N	E1
2800	EGVV	60007	2916	15W-8N	A1
2900	CHCG	60007	2916	15W-8N	A1
3000	CHCG	60018	2916	15W-8N	A1
3000	DSPN	60007	2916	15W-8N	A1
3000	DSPN	60018	2916	15W-8N	A1
Old Homestead Rd					
10	SchT	60175	2963	38W-6N	A1
400	CmpT	60175	2907	39W-6N	A7
400	SchT	60175	2907	39W-6N	A7
Old Hunt Rd					
-	NfdT	60062	2757	8W-16N	E7
-	NfdT	60062	2758	8W-16N	A7
-	NfdT	60093	2757	8W-16N	E7
-	NHBK	60062	2758	8W-16N	A7
-	NHBK	60093	2758	8W-16N	A7
-	NHFD	60093	2758	8W-16N	A7
10	NHBK	60062	2757	8W-16N	E7
10	NHBK	60093	2757	8W-16N	E7
10	NHFD	60093	2757	8W-16N	E7
300	FRGV	60021	2696	30W-22N	A4
700	AlqT	60010	2696	30W-22N	A4
700	AlqT	60021	2696	30W-22N	A4
Old IL-31-Frontage Rd					
6500	AlqT	60014	2640	33W-25N	E5
6600	CLLK	60014	2640	33W-25N	E5
W Old Indian Tr					
300	AURA	60506	3138	36W-6S	A4
400	AURA	60506	3137	36W-6S	E4
Old Indian Creek Ln					
4300	LGGV	60047	2700	18W-22N	D3
Old Iroquois Dr					
-	CbaT	60010	2697	25W-22N	E3
-	NBRN	60010	2697	25W-22N	E3
Old Irving Park Rd					
11500	CHCG	60666	2972	14W-5N	C1
Old Kent Dr					
2800	JLET	60435	3497	27W-23S	C5
Old Kerry Grv					
26600	CNHN	60410	3672	33W-32S	B7
26900	AxST	60410	3672	33W-32S	A7
W Old Kerry Grv					
-	CnhT	60410	3761	32W-32S	D1
-	WilC	60410	3761	32W-32S	D1
26200	CNHN	60410	3672	32W-32S	C7
26400	CNHN	60410	3761	32W-32S	C1
Old Kings Ct					
2300	SMBG	60194	2857	28W-12N	B2
2300	SMWD	60107	2857	28W-12N	B2
Old Kirk Rd					
-	GnvT	60185	3021	33W-0N	A5
300	GnvT	60134	3021	33W-0N	A5
Old Kress Rd					
200	WCHI	60185	3021	32W-0N	D4
Old Lafox Rd					
10	CmpT	60175	2962	40W-4N	C4
Old Lafox Rd CO-81					
10	CmpT	60175	2962	40W-5N	B2
Old Lagrange Rd					
18700	FftT	60448	3503	11W-22S	D1
18700	MKNA	60448	3503	12W-22S	D1
Old Lake Av					
42000	AntT	60002	2356	26W-42N	D7
Old Lake Rd					
10	HNWD	60047	2645	22W-24N	B6
Old Lake St					
200	BRLT	60120	2910	29W-9N	E1
200	HnrT	60107	2910	29W-9N	E1
200	HnrT	60120	2910	29W-9N	E1
200	SMWD	60107	2910	29W-9N	E1
200	SMWD	60120	2910	29W-9N	E1
300	BRLT	60103	2910	29W-9N	D1
300	HnrT	60103	2910	29W-9N	D1
Old Lemont Rd					
-	LmnT	60439	3270	19W-13S	D4
Old Lonesome Rd					
-	CmgT	60033	2405	51W-39N	D3
-	HRVD	60033	2405	51W-39N	E4
Old McHenry Rd					
-	LGGV	60047	2700	20W-23N	B2
100	ElaT	60047	2645	21W-24N	D7
100	HNWD	60047	2645	21W-24N	D7
100	HNWD	60047	2699	21W-24N	E1
100	KLDR	60047	2645	21W-24N	C7
100	KLDR	60047	2699	21W-24N	E1
500	ElaT	60047	2700	20W-23N	A1
500	HNWD	60047	2700	20W-23N	A1
500	KLDR	60047	2700	20W-23N	A1
Old McHenry Rd CO-V77					
-	LGGV	60047	2700	20W-23N	B2
100	ElaT	60047	2645	21W-24N	D7
100	HNWD	60047	2645	21W-24N	C7
100	HNWD	60047	2699	21W-24N	E1
100	KLDR	60047	2645	21W-24N	C7
100	KLDR	60047	2699	21W-24N	E1
500	ElaT	60047	2700	20W-23N	A1
500	HNWD	60047	2700	20W-23N	A1
500	KLDR	60047	2700	20W-23N	A1
N Old McHenry Rd					
100	LGGV	60047	2700	19W-22N	D4
1100	BFGV	60047	2700	18W-21N	E6
1100	BFGV	60089	2700	18W-21N	E6
1100	LGGV	60089	2700	18W-21N	E6
3300	ElaT	60047	2700	19W-22N	D4
24500	ElaT	60047	2645	21W-24N	C7
24500	HNWD	60047	2645	22W-24N	A7
24900	LKZH	60047	2645	22W-24N	A7
27000	ElaT	60047	2644	24W-25N	C4
27000	HNWD	60047	2644	24W-25N	C4
N Old McHenry Rd CO-V77					
100	LGGV	60047	2700	19W-22N	D4
1100	BFGV	60047	2700	18W-21N	E6
1100	BFGV	60089	2700	18W-21N	E6
1100	LGGV	60089	2700	18W-21N	E6
3300	ElaT	60047	2700	19W-22N	D4
24500	ElaT	60047	2645	21W-24N	C7
24500	HNWD	60047	2645	22W-24N	A7
24900	LKZH	60047	2645	22W-24N	A7
25800	ElaT	60047	2644	24W-25N	C4
25800	HNWD	60047	2644	23W-24N	E6
Old Meadow Ct					
900	CLSM	60188	2967	27W-3N	C5
4400	JLET	60586	3416	29W-21S	D7
Old Meadow Rd					
500	MTSN	60443	3505	7W-24S	D6
Old Midlothian Tpk					
10	BbyT	60119	3075	43W-2S	A4
Old Mill Cir					
-	LNSH	60045	2702	13W-23N	E2
Old Mill Ct					
10	BRRG	60527	3146	14W-7S	C7
10	BRTN	60010	2751	24W-18N	B2
1200	NPVL	60564	3203	28W-10S	A7
2800	GNVA	60134	3019	37W-0N	C4
Old Mill Dr					
100	SMBG	60193	2859	23W-9N	A6
N Old Mill Dr					
1000	PLTN	60067	2752	20W-17N	E5
Old Mill Ln					
-	BRRG	60527	3146	14W-7S	C7
200	HPSR	60140	2795	46W-15N	E3
300	BMDL	60108	2968	24W-4N	C3
300	HPSR	60140	2796	46W-15N	A3
300	HshT	60140	2796	46W-15N	A3
1000	HRPK	60133	2911	26W-9N	E1
1200	ALGN	60102	2695	32W-20N	A7
1200	EGVV	60007	2914	20W-8N	B3
2600	RGMW	60008	2805	21W-13N	C5
E Old Mill Ln					
10	BRRG	60527	3146	14W-7S	D7
N Old Mill Ln					
10	BRRG	60527	3146	14W-7S	C7
S Old Mill Ln					
10	BRRG	60527	3146	14W-7S	D7
W Old Mill Ln					
10	BRRG	60527	3146	14W-7S	C7
Old Mill Rd					
10	MTSN	60443	3505	7W-24S	C5
100	BRTN	60010	2751	24W-18N	C2
300	LtRT	60545	3259	47W-13S	D5
300	PLNO	60545	3259	47W-13S	D5
1100	HNDL	60521	3086	15W-3S	B6
1100	OKBK	60523	3086	15W-3S	B6
3200	NHBK	60062	2756	11W-16N	D7
3300	HDPK	60035	2650	10W-24N	A7
3300	HDPK	60035	2704	10W-24N	A1
3300	LKFT	60035	2650	10W-24N	A7
3300	LKFT	60045	2650	10W-24N	A7
3300	NHBK	60062	2809	11W-16N	C1
7900	FftT	60423	3504	10W-24S	C5
E Old Mill Rd					
10	HDPK	60035	2703	10W-24N	E1
10	LKFT	60045	2703	10W-24N	E1
W Old Mill Rd					
-	LNSH	60069	2702	13W-23N	D2
10	LKFT	60045	2703	11W-23N	D1
1700	LKFT	60045	2702	13W-24N	E1
2000	LNSH	60045	2702	13W-23N	E2
2000	VrnT	60045	2702	13W-23N	E2
2000	VrnT	60069	2702	13W-23N	E2
E Old Mill Tr					
10	ANTH	60002	2358	22W-42N	B6
W Old Mill Tr					
10	ANTH	60002	2358	23W-42N	A5
Old Mill Grove Rd					
10	LKZH	60047	2699	22W-21N	B5
1000	KLDR	60047	2699	22W-21N	B5
Old Minkler Rd					
3300	OswT	60543	3262	39W-13S	E5
3300	OswT	60560	3262	39W-13S	E5
W Old Monaville Rd					
24100	LkvT	60046	2474	24W-36N	C3
Old Monee Rd					
10	MonT	60466	3595	3W-28S	B5
10	PKFT	60466	3595	4W-28S	A6
200	MonT	60417	3594	4W-28S	E7
200	MonT	60466	3594	4W-28S	E7
200	PKFT	60466	3594	4W-28S	E7
W Old Monee Rd					
500	CRTE	60417	3685	1W-30S	B4
500	CteT	60417	3685	1W-30S	B4
1300	CRTE	60417	3684	2W-30S	E4
1300	CteT	60417	3684	2W-30S	D4
2000	MonT	60417	3684	2W-30S	D4
2000	MonT	60449	3684	2W-30S	D4
2000	UYPK	60417	3684	2W-30S	D4
2000	UYPK	60466	3684	2W-30S	D4
Old Mud Rd					
500	CteT	60417	3685	0E-31S	E6
500	CteT	60417	3686	0E-31S	A6
Old Naperville Rd					
500	LslT	60563	3142	25W-4S	B1
Old North Church Rd					
21200	FKFT	60423	3592	9W-25S	E1
W Old Northwest Hwy					
400	BRTN	60010	2750	26W-20N	D1
Old Oak Cir					
400	ALGN	60102	2695	33W-20N	A7
Old Oak Ct					
-	BmnT	60426	3426	5W-19S	A1
-	DGvT	60527	3208	15W-9S	B3
1200	HPSR	60140	2795	47W-15N	E4
1200	HshT	60140	2795	47W-15N	E4
Old Oak Ct E					
100	BFGV	60089	2754	16W-18N	C4
Old Oak Ct W					
100	BFGV	60089	2754	16W-18N	C4
Old Oak Dr					
-	BRLT	60103	2910	29W-9N	E1
-	BRLT	60107	2910	29W-9N	E1
-	SMWD	60103	2910	29W-9N	E1
-	SMWD	60107	2910	29W-9N	E1
-	SMWD	60107	2911	28W-8N	A2
10	BFGV	60089	2754	16W-18N	C3
10	NBRN	60010	2698	25W-22N	A3
10	WLNG	60089	2754	16W-18N	D3
2700	MchT	60050	2471	31W-34N	D7
W Old Oak Dr					
24000	FmtT	60060	2588	24W-28N	C6
Old Oak Ln					
24900	SRWD	60404	3584	31W-25S	A1
Old Oak Pl					
-	DRN	60561	3206	18W-10S	E5
1500	DRN	60561	3207	18W-10S	A5
Old Oak Rd					
6300	GRNE	60048	2534	16W-32N	D6
Old Oak Tr					
10	PSHT	60463	3274	9W-14S	C5
Old Oaks Ct					
1600	JLET	60586	3496	30W-21S	B1
Old Oaks Dr					
4600	LSLE	60532	3142	24W-5S	C2
Old Oaks Rd					
400	SgrT	60554	3135	43W-4S	A1
Old Orchard Av					
800	DRGV	60516	3206	19W-8S	D1
Old Orchard Ct					
10100	SKOK	60076	2812	5W-12N	A7
15700	ODPK	60462	3424	10W-18S	C1
W Old Orchard Dr					
16500	WDWH	60083	2419	16W-40N	D3
Old Orchard Ln E					
13300	DPgT	60441	3342	21W-15S	A2
13300	LktT	60441	3342	21W-15S	A2
Old Orchard Ln N					
16900	DPgT	60441	3342	21W-15S	A2
17000	DPgT	60441	3341	21W-15S	E2
Old Orchard Ln W					
13300	DPgT	60441	3341	21W-15S	E2
13300	LktT	60441	3341	21W-15S	E3
13300	RMVL	60441	3341	21W-15S	E3
Old Orchard Rd					
500	HRVD	60033	2406	49W-39N	B5
4000	EVTN	60076	2866	5W-12N	A1
4000	EVTN	60201	2866	5W-12N	A1
4000	SKOK	60076	2866	5W-12N	A1
4100	SKOK	60201	2866	5W-12N	B1
4700	SKOK	60076	2865	5W-12N	E1
4700	SKOK	60077	2865	6W-12N	D1
5200	SKOK	60077	2811	6W-12N	D7
5300	SKOK	60029	2811	7W-12N	C7
5700	GLF	60025	2811	7W-12N	C7
5700	GLF	60029	2811	7W-12N	C7
5700	GLF	60077	2811	7W-12N	C7
Old Orchard Tr					
-	PNFD	60585	3265	32W-14S	B7
-	WldT	60585	3265	32W-14S	B7
Old Orchard Shopping Ctr					
300	SKOK	60077	2865	6W-12N	E1
Old Peterson Rd					
1200	LbvT	60048	2591	18W-30N	A2
1200	LYVL	60048	2591	18W-30N	A2
W Old Peterson Rd					
18400	LbvT	60048	2590	18W-30N	E2
W Old Pine Ct					
18100	WrnT	60031	2534	18W-34N	A1
Old Plank Blvd					
6000	MTSN	60443	3593	8W-25S	B1
6300	RchT	60443	3593	8W-25S	B1
Old Plank Dr					
12500	NlxT	60451	3590	15W-26S	B2
Old Plank Rd					
3300	PKCY	60085	2536	13W-33N	A3
3300	WKGN	60085	2536	13W-33N	A3
N Old Plank Rd					
10	BNVL	60106	2971	16W-5N	E1
W Old Plank Rd					
18500	WrnT	60030	2533	18W-33N	D4
18900	GYLK	60030	2533	18W-33N	D4
Old Plank Road Tr					
-	MTSN	60443	3594	6W-25S	A1
Old Plum Grove Rd					
5200	RGMW	60067	2805	21W-13N	D5
5200	RGMW	60173	2805	21W-13N	D5
5200	SMBG	60067	2805	21W-13N	D5
5200	SMBG	60173	2805	21W-13N	D5
W Old Plum Grove Rd					
10	PltT	60008	2805	21W-13N	D5
10	PltT	60067	2805	21W-13N	D5
10	RGMW	60008	2805	21W-13N	D5
10	RGMW	60067	2805	21W-13N	D5
N Old Pond Ct					
2200	RLKB	60073	2475	23W-36N	A4
N Old Pond Ln					
2200	RLKB	60073	2475	23W-36N	A4
Old Post Rd					
10	OSWG	60543	3199	36W-11S	E7
10	OswT	60538	3199	36W-11S	D7
10	OswT	60538	3263	37W-11S	D1
10	OswT	60543	3263	37W-11S	C1
100	OSWG	60543	3263	36W-11S	E1
100	OSWG	60543	3264	36W-11S	A1
200	NHBK	60062	2757	8W-18N	D3
700	ANHT	60004	2754	17W-17N	B5
700	BFGV	60089	2754	17W-17N	B5
13600	OrlT	60467	3344	14W-16S	C3
E Old Post Rd					
2500	CteT	60417	3686	3E-29S	E1
2500	CteT	60417	3687	3E-29S	A1
S Old Post Rd					
23900	CteT	60417	3597	2E-29S	E7
24000	CteT	60417	3686	2E-29S	E1
S Old Prague Pth					
11500	PSPK	60464	3274	10W-13S	C4
Old Quarry Rd					
-	LMNT	60439	3270	20W-14S	C6
300	SchT	60174	2964	36W-4N	A4
300	SCRL	60174	2964	36W-4N	A4
300	SCRL	60175	2964	36W-4N	A4
N Old Rand Rd					
700	LKZH	60047	2698	24W-23N	C2
900	WCDA	60084	2587	26W-28N	D6
900	WcnT	60084	2587	26W-28N	D5
S Old Rand Rd					
10	LKZH	60047	2698	23W-22N	E3
400	LKZH	60047	2699	23W-22N	A4
25000	WcnT	60084	2644	25W-26N	B3
W Old Rand Rd					
-	WcnT	60010	2644	25W-26N	A3
-	WcnT	60084	2644	25W-26N	A3
Old Renwick Cir					
2900	JLET	60544	3417	27W-19S	C2
2900	PnfT	60544	3417	27W-19S	C2
Old Renwick Rd					
21600	JLET	60435	3417	27W-19S	D2
21600	PnfT	60435	3417	27W-19S	D2
21600	PnfT	60544	3417	27W-19S	B2
21700	JLET	60544	3417	27W-19S	B2
Old Renwick Tr					
-	JLET	60446	3417	27W-19S	C2
-	RMVL	60446	3417	27W-19S	C2
-	RMVL	60544	3417	27W-19S	C2
-	WilC	60544	3417	27W-19S	C2
2700	JLET	60435	3417	27W-19S	C2
3900	JLET	60544	3417	27W-19S	C2
Old Renwick Trail Ct					
3400	JLET	60435	3417	27W-19S	C3
Old River Rd					
4100	SRPK	60176	2973	11W-5N	D1
Old Rockland Rd					
29000	GNOK	60048	2592	14W-28N	C5
Old Route 30					
-	FKFT	60423	3503	12W-25S	C7
Old Route 34					
800	SDWH	60548	3330	51W-14S	A1
Old Route 45					
-	FftT	60448	3503	11W-22S	D1
-	MKNA	60448	3503	11W-22S	D1
W Old Russell Rd					
14000	NptT	60099	2361	14W-43N	D4
14000	WDWH	60099	2361	14W-43N	D4
Old St. Charles Rd					
-	WCHI	60185	2966	29W-2N	D7
-	WynT	60185	2966	29W-2N	D7
Old Saybrook on Auburn					
10	RGMW	60008	2806	19W-14N	B4
Old Schaumburg Rd					
-	SMBG	60173	2859	21W-10N	E6
-	SMBG	60193	2859	21W-10N	E6
W Old School Rd					
-	MTWA	60048	2592	15W-27N	A7
14000	MTWA	60045	2648	14W-27N	C1
14000	MTWA	60048	2648	15W-27N	A1
15300	LbvT	60048	2648	15W-27N	A1
Old Skokie Rd					
-	GRNE	60031	2535	13W-34N	E2
10	PKCY	60085	2535	13W-34N	E2
10	PKCY	60085	2536	13W-33N	A2
1200	HDPK	60035	2704	9W-22N	C5
Oldsmar Ln					
600	PKCY	60085	2536	12W-33N	B3
Old Spanish Tr					
11800	OrlT	60467	3344	14W-16S	C3
Old Stage Rd					
500	PGGV	60140	2798	41W-15N	A4
500	RtdT	60140	2798	41W-15N	A4
Old Stone Ct					
400	MNSR	46321	3510		D1
Old Stone Rd					
500	BGBK	60440	3268	24W-12S	E3
Old Surrey Rd					
400	DGvT	60521	3146	15W-6S	A4
400	DGvT	60527	3146	15W-6S	A4
400	HNDL	60521	3146	15W-6S	A4
Old Sutton Rd					
-	BrnT	60192	2802	28W-13N	D6
-	HFET	60010	2802	28W-13N	D6
-	HFET	60118	2802	28W-13N	D5
-	HFET	60192	2802	28W-13N	D6
10	BNHL	60118	2802	28W-15N	D3
10	BrnT	60010	2802	28W-13N	D6
10	BrnT	60118	2802	28W-15N	D3
100	BNHL	60010	2802	28W-14N	D4
200	BNHL	60010	2749	28W-16N	D6
300	AlqT	60010	2749	28W-16N	D6
Old Tamerack Ln					
10	ODPK	60462	3345	13W-16S	B4
10	OrlT	60462	3345	13W-16S	B4
Old Tavern Rd					
2300	LSLE	60532	3142	24W-4S	D1
2900	LslT	60532	3142	24W-4S	C1
2900	LslT	60563	3142	25W-4S	C1
4600	LSLE	60563	3142	24W-5S	D2
Old Tavern Rd E					
100	YkTp	60523	3084	19W-3S	D5
Old Tavern Rd W					
200	YkTp	60523	3084	19W-2S	D4
Old Timber Ct					
1100	HFET	60192	2804	24W-15N	C1
Old Timber Ln					
10	PSPK	60464	3272	13W-14S	E7
10	PSPK	60464	3273	13W-14S	A7
1200	HFET	60192	2804	24W-15N	C1
W Old Town Ct					
300	CHCG	60610	3034	0W-1N	A1
Old Trail Rd					
600	HDPK	60035	2704	9W-23N	B1
600	HIWD	60040	2704	9W-23N	C2
17800	HLCT	60429	3427	3W-21S	A6
Old US-41					
-	NptT	60083	2360	16W-42N	E7

STREET Block	City	ZIP	Map#	CGS	Grid
Old US-41					
42000	WDWH	60099	2360	16W-42N	E6
42500	NptT	60099	2360	16W-42N	D5
43000	BtlT	53142	2360	16W-43N	E4
43000	BtlT	60099	2360	16W-43N	E4
Old Valley Rd					
10	RGMW	60008	2806	20W-13N	A6
Old Walnut Cir					
-	WrnT	60031	2534	18W-34N	A1
300	GRNE	60031	2534	18W-34N	A1
400	GRNE	60031	2477	18W-34N	A7
N Old Walnut Cir					
34000	WrnT	60031	2534	18W-34N	A2
34400	GRNE	60031	2534	18W-34N	A1
Old Wayne Ct					
200	WynT	60185	2966	29W-3N	D6
Old Weiland Rd					
-	BFGV	60089	2701	15W-22N	E4
20000	BFGV	60069	2701	15W-22N	E4
20000	VrnT	60069	2701	15W-22N	E4
Old Westbury Ct					
700	CLLK	60012	2640	33W-27N	D1
Old Westbury Rd					
600	CLLK	60012	2640	33W-27N	D1
600	NndT	60012	2640	33W-27N	D1
Old Western Av					
2400	PKFT	60466	3595	3W-28S	C5
13300	BLID	60406	3349	3W-15S	B1
Old Wick Ln					
100	IVNS	60067	2752	22W-18N	B3
S Old Wilke Rd					
1200	ANHT	60005	2860	19W-12N	D1
1200	ANHT	60008	2860	19W-12N	D1
1200	RGMW	60005	2860	19W-12N	D1
1200	RGMW	60008	2860	19W-12N	D1
Old Williams Rd					
10	DndT	60102	2748	34W-18N	A4
800	CPVL	60110	2748	33W-18N	A4
800	DndT	60110	2748	33W-18N	A4
Old Willow Rd					
1800	GNVW	60062	2810	9W-15N	B3
1800	NHFD	60093	2811	7W-15N	B2
2600	GNVW	60025	2810	9W-15N	C3
2600	NHBK	60025	2810	9W-15N	C3
2600	NHBK	60062	2810	9W-15N	C3
E Old Willow Rd					
-	MPPT	60056	2808	13W-15N	D2
-	PTHT	60070	2808	13W-15N	D2
-	WLNG	60090	2808	13W-15N	D2
S Old Wilmington Rd					
26700	JknT	60421	3763	26W-32S	E2
Old Wolf Rd					
20500	FftT	60448	3503	13W-24S	A6
Old Wood Ct					
100	AURA	60506	3137	38W-7S	B7
S Old Wood Ct					
300	VNHL	60061	2647	16W-24N	C7
Old Wood Ln					
5500	LGGV	60047	2701	17W-22N	B4
N Old Woodford Rd					
41100	NptT	60083	2420	15W-41N	A1
41100	NptT	60099	2420	15W-41N	A1
Oldwoods Dr					
400	LslT	60517	3205	22W-9S	C4
400	LslT	60565	3205	22W-9S	C4
Old Woods Tr					
2600	JLET	60586	3416	29W-20S	C5
N Old Woods Tr					
36200	WrnT	60031	2477	17W-36N	B4
Old York Rd					
400	EMHT	60126	3028	15W-0S	A6
400	YkTp	60126	3028	15W-0S	A6
Oleander Av					
8800	MNGV	60053	2864	9W-11N	C3
8800	NLES	60714	2864	9W-11N	C4
9500	GNVW	60025	2864	9W-11N	C2
16700	OrlT	60477	3424	9W-20S	E3
16700	TYPK	60477	3424	9W-20S	E3
N Oleander Av					
3000	CHCG	60707	2974	9W-3N	C4
3000	EDPK	60707	2974	9W-3N	C4
3900	CHCG	60634	2974	9W-4N	C2
3900	CHCG	60706	2974	9W-4N	C2
3900	NRDG	60706	2974	9W-4N	C2
5200	CHCG	60656	2918	9W-6N	C6
5200	CHCG	60706	2918	9W-6N	C6
5200	HDHT	60706	2918	9W-6N	C6
6800	CHCG	60631	2918	9W-8N	C1
7200	CHCG	60631	2864	9W-9N	C7
7500	NLES	60631	2864	9W-9N	C7
8200	NLES	60714	2864	9W-10N	C4
8600	MNGV	60053	2864	9W-10N	C4
Oleander Ct					
-	NPVL	60540	3204	25W-8S	C1
1800	JLET	60586	3415	33W-21S	A7
2100	AURA	60502	3139	33W-5S	B4
Oleander Dr					
300	SMBG	60173	2859	21W-11N	E4
1800	JLET	60586	3415	33W-21S	A7
O'Leary Dr					
10	BNVL	60106	2972	15W-5N	B1
10	CHCG	60106	2972	15W-5N	B1
1200	JLET	60431	3496	29W-22S	D2
O'Leary Ln					
1700	LKBF	60044	2593	12W-28N	B7
1700	LKFT	60044	2593	12W-28N	B7
1700	LKFT	60045	2593	12W-28N	B7
N Ole Farm Rd					
2200	JLET	60586	3416	29W-21S	D6
W Ole Farm Rd					
4400	JLET	60586	3416	29W-21S	D6
Olesen Dr					
10	LslT	60540	3142	25W-7S	B7
10	LslT	60540	3204	25W-8S	A1
10	NPVL	60540	3142	25W-7S	B7
10	NPVL	60540	3204	25W-8S	A1
Olga Ln					
1100	LbvT	60060	2646	18W-26N	E3
1100	MDLN	60060	2646	18W-26N	E3
Olha Farm Wy					
16100	HMGN	60491	3421	17W-19S	C2
Olin Ct					
300	ALGN	60102	2694	33W-20N	E7
Olin Rd					
-	CnhT	60410	3674	28W-29S	A2
Olinger Ln					
300	BbyT	60134	3018	39W-0N	E6
Oliphant Av					
9300	MNGV	60053	2864	9W-11N	C2
N Oliphant Av					
6400	CHCG	60068	2918	9W-8N	C2
6400	CHCG	60631	2918	9W-8N	C2
6400	PKRG	60068	2918	9W-8N	C2
E Olive Av					
100	PTHT	60070	2808	15W-15N	A2
W Olive Av					
100	PTHT	60070	2808	15W-15N	A2
400	ANHT	60004	2807	16W-15N	D2
400	PTHT	60004	2807	16W-15N	D2
400	PTHT	60070	2807	16W-15N	D2
1400	CHCG	60660	2921	2W-7N	C4
3200	CHCG	60659	2920	4W-7N	D4
7200	CHCG	60631	2918	9W-7N	D4
7800	NpkT	60631	2918	9W-7N	B5
Olive Ct					
10	ELGN	60120	2855	32W-10N	C5
400	BmdT	60137	3025	23W-2N	A1
400	BmdT	60188	3025	23W-2N	A1
400	GLHT	60137	3025	23W-2N	A1
400	GLHT	60188	3025	23W-2N	A1
500	BmdT	60188	3024	23W-2N	E1
41900	AntT	60002	2356	25W-41N	E7
Olive Pkwy					
600	BRLT	60103	2910	29W-9N	D1
Olive Pl					
600	BGBK	60440	3205	22W-10S	B6
E Olive Pl					
500	JLET	60432	3499	23W-23S	B4
Olive Rd					
900	HMWD	60430	3428	1W-21S	A7
1800	HMWD	60430	3427	2W-21S	D7
3000	HLCT	60429	3427	3W-21S	A7
3000	HLCT	60430	3427	3W-21S	A7
Olive St					
100	WMTN	60481	3943	27W-39S	D1
400	EMHT	60126	3027	16W-0N	C3
600	WDSK	60098	2524	42W-31N	C6
800	ELGN	60120	2855	32W-10N	C5
800	HFET	60169	2858	24W-11N	E3
2200	BLID	60406	3277	2W-14S	B7
2500	JNBG	60050	2471	31W-35N	D5
E Olive St					
10	ANHT	60004	2807	17W-15N	B2
1000	PTHT	60004	2807	17W-15N	C2
1400	PLTN	60074	2806	19W-15N	D2
1500	ANHT	60004	2806	19W-15N	D2
1500	ANHT	60074	2806	19W-15N	D2
N Olive St					
35500	GrtT	60041	2474	25W-35N	A6
S Olive St					
20900	DPgT	60544	3340	26W-15S	A3
W Olive St					
10	ANHT	60004	2807	18W-15N	A2
100	EMHT	60126	3027	16W-0N	E3
1600	ANHT	60004	2806	18W-15N	D2
1700	PLTN	60074	2806	18W-15N	D2
Olive Hill Dr					
2000	BFGV	60089	2701	16W-22N	D4
2000	VrnT	60089	2701	16W-22N	D4
Olive Oyl Ct					
-	GYLK	60030	2533	19W-32N	C4
Oliver Av					
800	AURA	60506	3199	36W-8S	E3
900	AURA	60538	3199	36W-8S	E3
1000	MTGY	60506	3199	36W-8S	E3
1000	MTGY	60538	3199	36W-8S	E3
Oliver Ct					
100	SMBG	60193	2913	23W-9N	A1
200	LKVL	60046	2475	22W-37N	B2
300	WTMT	60559	3144	18W-6S	E5
300	WTMT	60559	3145	18W-6S	A5
Oliver Dr					
400	RtdT	60124	2798	39W-14N	E6
400	WTMT	60559	3144	18W-6S	E5
700	GLBT	60124	2798	39W-14N	E6
700	GLBT	60136	2798	39W-14N	E6
Oliver Pl					
10	JltT	60433	3500	21W-24S	A5
Oliver St					
100	BRLT	60103	2910	29W-8N	D3
Olivers Wy					
-	ElaT	60047	2645	22W-25N	A5
-	HNWD	60047	2645	22W-25N	A5
Oliver Wendell Homes St					
300	CmpT	60175	2962	40W-3N	C6
Olivia Av					
21500	SLVL	60411	3597	2E-26S	C2
Olivia Ct					
6000	MTSN	60443	3593	7W-25S	D1
S Olivia Ct					
26500	MonT	60449	3683	6W-32S	B7
Olivia Ln					
1500	HRPK	60133	2857	26W-9N	D7
17500	ODPK	60467	3423	13W-21S	A6
Olivia St					
1000	DSPN	60018	2862	13W-10N	E5
Oliviabrook Dr					
-	OKTR	60181	3085	17W-1S	C1
-	YkTp	60181	3085	17W-1S	C1
Ollerton Av					
3100	AURA	60502	3139	31W-6S	D5
Ollie Ct					
800	CPVL	60110	2748	33W-17N	B7
Olmstead Dr					
-	HFET	60010	2804	24W-15N	C1
4400	HFET	60192	2804	24W-15N	B2
Olmstead Rd					
-	CteT	60417	3684	3W-31S	B4
-	MonT	60417	3684	3W-31S	B4
-	UYPK	60417	3684	3W-31S	B4
600	MonT	60449	3684	3W-31S	B4
600	MonT	60466	3684	3W-31S	B4
600	UYPK	60449	3684	3W-30S	B4
600	UYPK	60466	3684	3W-31S	B4
N Olmsted Av					
6600	CHCG	60631	2918	9W-8N	C2
6800	PKRG	60068	2918	9W-8N	C2
Olmsted Dr					
1000	LKFT	60045	2649	12W-27N	B1
Olmsted Ln					
100	RDLK	60073	2588	23W-30N	E2
100	RDLK	60073	2589	23W-30N	A2
Olmsted Rd					
100	RVSD	60546	3088	9W-3S	D5
300	BRWN	60402	3088	9W-3S	E5
300	BRWN	60546	3088	9W-3S	E5
N Olsen Ct					
23100	LNSH	60069	2702	15W-23N	A2
23100	VrnT	60069	2702	15W-23N	A2
Olsen St					
300	YKVL	60560	3333	42W-15S	C3
Olson Ct					
300	BTVA	60510	3077	36W-0S	E1
300	GNVA	60134	3019	36W-1N	E3
Olson Dr					
300	BTVA	60510	3077	36W-0S	E1
400	BTVA	60510	3019	36W-0S	E7
Olson Rd					
6100	CrlT	60180	2635	46W-25N	E5
6100	SenT	60180	2635	45W-25N	E3
Olson St					
500	WDSK	60098	2524	41W-31N	D6
E Oltendorf Ct					
10	SMWD	60107	2857	28W-10N	A7
E Oltendorf Rd					
10	SMWD	60107	2857	28W-9N	A7
N Oltendorf Rd					
10	SMWD	60107	2857	28W-11N	A4
300	HFET	60010	2857	28W-11N	A4
300	HFET	60107	2857	28W-11N	A4
S Oltendorf Rd					
10	SMWD	60107	2857	28W-10N	A6
Olwin Av					
100	ElgT	60124	2853	37W-12N	D3
N Olympia Av					
5000	CHCG	60656	2918	9W-6N	C6
6600	CHCG	60631	2918	9W-8N	C2
E Olympia Cir					
10700	PSHL	60465	3274	10W-12S	B2
W Olympia Cir					
10700	PSHL	60465	3274	10W-12S	B2
Olympia Ct					
10	OKBK	60523	3084	18W-2S	E3
300	ELGN	60120	2855	31W-12N	E3
400	LslT	60540	3143	23W-7S	A7
Olympia Dr					
18000	CCHL	60478	3426	5W-21S	D7
S Olympia Dr					
22600	FftT	60423	3591	13W-27S	A5
Olympia Ln					
1000	ROSL	60172	2912	24W-7N	C5
3800	ISLK	60042	2586	30W-28N	B6
Olympia St					
100	PnfT	60435	3417	27W-20S	C5
Olympia Fields Ct					
-	HNWD	60047	2645	22W-26N	B2
-	HNWD	60060	2645	22W-26N	B2
Olympian Wy					
20500	OMFD	60461	3507	4W-25S	A6
20800	MTSN	60443	3506	4W-24S	D6
20800	OMFD	60461	3506	4W-24S	D6
21100	MTSN	60443	3594	5W-25S	C1
Olympic Blvd					
1400	JLET	60431	3585	28W-25S	A2
3300	JLET	60431	3584	29W-25S	E2
Olympic Ct					
10	LIHL	60156	2693	36W-21N	C5
2700	AURA	60503	3265	32W-11S	D1
Olympic Dr					
100	BGBK	60440	3269	22W-11S	C2
900	BTVA	60510	3020	34W-0S	D6
6800	BGVW	60455	3211	8W-10S	A5
6800	OKLN	60453	3211	8W-10S	A5
6800	OKLN	60455	3211	8W-10S	A5
6900	BGVW	60455	3210	8W-10S	E4
8700	BGVW	60459	3210	8W-10S	E4
11500	PNFD	60585	3266	30W-13S	C5
25700	MONE	60449	3683	6W-31S	B5
N Olympic Dr					
1800	VNHL	60061	2647	17W-27N	B1
Olympic Ln					
15100	LKPT	60441	3342	20W-18S	B7
Olympic Vil					
10	CHHT	60411	3507	2W-25S	D7
Olympus Dr					
10	NPVL	60540	3203	26W-8S	E2
10	TYPK	60477	3505	8W-23S	B4
1200	NPVL	60565	3203	26W-8S	E2
Omaha Cir					
1600	EGVV	60007	2913	21W-8N	D2
Omaha Ct					
800	CLSM	60188	2967	26W-3N	E5
1100	NPVL	60540	3204	25W-7S	A1
Omaha Dr					
-	YKVL	60560	3333	42W-14S	E1
8400	BRRG	60527	3208	14W-9S	D3
8400	LynT	60527	3208	14W-9S	D4
O'Malley Ct					
200	AURA	60506	3199	36W-8S	E1
1000	LKZH	60047	2645	22W-24N	B7
O'Malley Dr					
1000	LKZH	60047	2645	22W-24N	B7
Omni Dr					
10	SMBG	60193	2859	23W-9N	A7
N Onarga Av					
6500	CHCG	60631	2918	9W-8N	D2
Onarga St					
300	PKFT	60466	3595	3W-27S	B5
Onaway Tr					
1000	ALGN	60102	2747	34W-19N	E2
1000	DndT	60102	2747	34W-19N	E2
E Oneida Av					
-	BRLT	60103	2910	28W-8N	E3
100	EMHT	60126	3027	16W-0N	E5
100	EMHT	60126	3028	15W-0N	A5
200	BRLT	60103	2911	28W-8N	A3
N Oneida Av					
5000	NRDG	60706	2918	9W-6N	C6
6400	CHCG	60631	2918	9W-8N	C2
W Oneida Av					
100	BRLT	60103	2910	29W-8N	E3
Oneida Ct					
100	BMDL	60108	2968	25W-5N	B1
500	CLSM	60188	2967	27W-3N	D6
1600	MPPT	60056	2808	13W-15N	E3
Oneida Dr					
500	SmbT	60193	2913	22W-8N	B2
W Oneida Dr					
16400	LKPT	60441	3420	20W-20S	A5
Oneida Ln					
10	HNWD	60047	2646	20W-25N	B4
2400	NPVL	60563	3140	30W-5S	A4
N Oneida Ln					
1800	MPPT	60056	2808	13W-15N	E2
25400	LKBN	60010	2643	27W-25N	B5
Oneida Rd					
2200	WKGN	60087	2479	12W-36N	C4
7400	MchT	60097	2469	36W-36N	D3
W Oneida St					
200	JLET	60435	3498	25W-23S	C4
1800	JLET	60435	3497	26W-23S	E5
O'Neill Dr					
8800	DGvT	60527	3207	16W-10S	E5
O'Neill Rd					
7200	DRGV	60516	3206	20W-8S	C1
S O'Neill St					
10	JLET	60435	3498	25W-24S	C5
10	JLET	60436	3498	25W-24S	C5
W Onekema Dr					
6700	PSHT	60463	3275	8W-14S	A6
One Renaissance Pl					
10	PLTN	60067	2752	20W-16N	E6
Onie Ct					
10	CPVL	60118	2801	33W-16N	B2
10	EDND	60118	2801	33W-16N	B2
Onondaga Dr					
10	HNWD	60047	2646	20W-25N	B5
500	NBRN	60010	2697	26W-22N	E3
W Onondaga Tr					
13200	HMGN	60491	3343	16W-16S	E3
Ontario Av					
1300	SPGV	60081	2355	30W-42N	B5
1700	NPVL	60563	3140	29W-6S	D4
Ontario Ct					
-	NCHI	60088	2593	12W-30N	B3
10	OKPK	60302	3030	8W-0N	D3
Ontario Dr					
700	RMVL	60446	3340	25W-15S	C1
Ontario St					
10	CHCG	60644	3031	7W-0N	B3
10	OKPK	60302	3031	8W-0N	A3
100	FKFT	60423	3591	11W-26S	E3
400	JLET	60436	3586	24W-25S	D1
400	JltT	60436	3586	24W-25S	D1
600	OKPK	60301	3031	8W-0N	A3
800	OKPK	60302	3030	8W-0N	E3
1000	OKPK	60301	3030	8W-0N	D3
1100	RVFT	60301	3030	8W-0N	D3
1100	RVFT	60302	3030	8W-0N	D3
1100	RVFT	60305	3030	8W-0N	D3
16100	LktT	60403	3418	25W-19S	B2
E Ontario St					
10	CHCG	60610	3034	0E-0N	C3
10	CHCG	60611	3034	0E-0N	C3
S Ontario St					
500	VNHL	60061	2647	16W-24N	D7
W Ontario St					
10	CHCG	60610	3034	0W-0N	A3
10	CHCG	60611	3034	0W-0N	B3
1600	CHCG	60622	3033	2W-0N	C3
3900	CHCG	60624	3032	4W-0N	C3
Ontario Bay					
-	BHPK	60099	2422	9W-38N	D7
Ontarioville Rd					
1900	HRPK	60133	2911	27W-7N	D4
Onwentsia Av					
500	HDPK	60035	2704	8W-22N	D3
Onwentsia Ct					
1000	NPVL	60563	3141	28W-5S	A2
Onwentsia Rd					
200	VNHL	60061	2647	16W-25N	D5
E Onwentsia Rd					
10	LKFT	60045	2649	10W-25N	E4
10	LKFT	60045	2650	10W-25N	A4
W Onwentsia Rd					
10	LKFT	60045	2649	11W-25N	D4
Onyx Ct					
400	SMBG	60194	2857	26W-11N	E4
Onyx Rd					
-	AURA	60504	3202	30W-8S	B2
-	AURA	60564	3202	30W-8S	B2
-	NpvT	60564	3202	30W-8S	B2
Opal Av					
10	GLHT	60139	2968	23W-3N	E5
N Opal Av					
3200	EDPK	60707	2974	9W-4N	C4
4400	CHCG	60634	2974	9W-5N	B1
4400	NRDG	60706	2974	9W-5N	B1
4800	NRDG	60706	2918	9W-6N	B7
Opal Dr					
1900	AURA	60506	3137	38W-6S	B5
4400	HFET	60192	2804	24W-15N	C1
Opatrny Dr					
200	FRGV	60021	2696	29W-23N	B2
Open Pkwy					
-	HNWD	60060	2645	22W-25N	A4
Open Pkwy N					
10	HNWD	60060	2645	22W-26N	A4
Open Pkwy S					
10	HNWD	60047	2645	22W-25N	B4
10	HNWD	60060	2645	22W-25N	B4
Open Gate Rd					
2900	NndT	60012	2583	35W-28N	E5
Oplaine Rd					
1800	GNOK	60048	2592	14W-30N	C2
N Oplaine Rd					
10	GRNE	60031	2535	14W-34N	C1
400	GRNE	60031	2478	14W-34N	C7
30900	GNOK	60048	2592	14W-30N	C1
31000	GNOK	60048	2535	14W-31N	C7
31500	WKGN	60048	2535	14W-31N	C7
32300	WKGN	60085	2535	14W-31N	C7
32300	WrnT	60048	2535	14W-31N	C7
32300	WrnT	60085	2535	14W-31N	C7
32400	WrnT	60031	2535	14W-32N	C4
32800	WKGN	60031	2535	14W-33N	C4
N Oplaine Rd CO-W20					
10	GRNE	60031	2535	14W-34N	C1
400	GRNE	60031	2478	14W-34N	C7
30900	GNOK	60048	2592	14W-30N	C1
31000	GNOK	60048	2535	14W-31N	C7
31500	WKGN	60048	2535	14W-31N	C7
32300	WKGN	60085	2535	14W-31N	C7
32300	WrnT	60048	2535	14W-31N	C7
32300	WrnT	60085	2535	14W-31N	C7
32400	WrnT	60031	2535	14W-32N	C4
32800	WKGN	60031	2535	14W-33N	C4
S Oplaine Rd					
10	GRNE	60031	2535	14W-33N	C2
10	WrnT	60031	2535	14W-34N	C1
1000	WKGN	60031	2535	14W-33N	C4
1000	WKGN	60085	2535	14W-33N	C4
1700	GNOK	60048	2592	14W-30N	C2
S Oplaine Rd CO-W20					
10	GRNE	60031	2535	14W-33N	C2
10	WrnT	60031	2535	14W-34N	C1
1000	WKGN	60031	2535	14W-33N	C4
1000	WKGN	60085	2535	14W-33N	C4
Opus Pl					
1400	DRGV	60515	3084	20W-3S	B5
Orange Av					
16200	ODPK	60467	3422	13W-19S	E3
16600	OrlT	60467	3422	13W-19S	E3
N Orange Av					
3200	EDPK	60707	2974	9W-4N	B4
4400	CHCG	60634	2974	9W-5N	B1
4400	NRDG	60706	2974	9W-5N	B1
4800	NRDG	60706	2918	9W-6N	B7
5700	CHCG	60631	2918	9W-7N	B5
5700	NpkT	60631	2918	9W-7N	B5
Orange Ct					
1400	MPPT	60056	2807	16W-14N	E3
Orange Ln					
600	HFET	60169	2858	24W-10N	D5
5800	OKFT	60452	3347	7W-18S	D7
Orange St					
200	ELGN	60123	2854	34W-10N	D5
E Orange St					
100	YKVL	60560	3333	42W-15S	C3
W Orange St					
100	YKVL	60560	3333	43W-15S	B3
Orange & Black Dr					
-	SCRL	60174	2964	33W-4N	E4
-	SCRL	60174	2965	33W-4N	A4
Orange Blossom Dr					
15600	ODPK	60462	3346	9W-18S	D7
W Orange Blossom Ln					
20900	LktT	60544	3340	26W-16S	A3
Orange Brace Rd					
2800	RVWD	60015	2755	13W-20N	D1
3200	RVWD	60015	2702	13W-20N	D7
Orangery Ct					
-	CLSM	60133	2968	25W-4N	A4
1100	BmdT	60188	2968	25W-4N	A4
1100	CLSM	60188	2968	25W-4N	A4
Orberg Av					
-	BHPK	60087	2421	12W-38N	A6
Orbiter Dr					
200	RDLK	60073	2531	24W-34N	D1
Orchard					
100	GnvT	60134	3021	33W-1N	A4
100	GnvT	60185	3021	33W-1N	A4
Orchard Av					
10	BNVL	60106	2972	15W-5N	A1
10	OSWG	60543	3263	37W-12S	C2
100	HLSD	60162	3028	13W-0S	E7
200	BNVL	60106	2916	15W-5N	A7
200	CHCG	60106	2916	15W-5N	A7
200	PvsT	60162	3028	13W-0S	E7
700	AURA	60506	3138	35W-6S	B5
1000	MYWD	60153	3030	10W-0S	A5
1200	CHHT	60411	3507	2W-25S	D7
1600	SMBG	60193	2912	25W-8N	A3
12400	ALSP	60803	3276	5W-14S	B6
19800	LYWD	60411	3509	3E-23S	E4
25500	GrtT	60041	2474	25W-36N	A3
34300	WslT	60481	3943	27W-42S	E6
E Orchard Av					
800	MDLN	60060	2646	18W-27N	E1
900	MDLN	60060	2647	18W-27N	A1
N Orchard Av					
10	WKGN	60085	2536	11W-34N	D1
S Orchard Av					
10	WKGN	60085	2536	11W-33N	D2
W Orchard Av					
10	MDLN	60060	2646	19W-27N	C1
26300	AntT	60002	2356	26W-42N	D5
Orchard Cir					
800	LYVL	60048	2591	16W-29N	E4
1500	NPVL	60565	3204	25W-8S	A2
Orchard Coms					
8000	LGGV	60060	2645	20W-25N	E4
Orchard Coms E					
8000	LGGV	60060	2645	20W-25N	E5
Orchard Coms W					
8000	LGGV	60060	2645	20W-25N	E5
Orchard Ct					
100	PTON	60468	3860	9W-37S	E4
100	PTON	60468	3861	9W-37S	A4
300	WDSK	60098	2524	41W-32N	C5
500	DSPN	60016	2862	14W-11N	D3
600	ALGN	60102	2694	34W-20N	C7
600	ROSL	60172	2913	22W-6N	C6
900	BTVA	60510	3078	33W-2S	E3
1600	WCHI	60185	3022	29W-0S	E7
1600	WCHI	60185	3080	29W-1S	E1
1600	WnfT	60185	3080	29W-0S	E1
8000	LGGV	60060	2645	20W-25N	E4
8400	TYPK	60487	3424	10W-19S	B3
19700	LYWD	60411	3509	3E-23S	E3
W Orchard Ct					
500	RLKB	60073	2474	23W-35N	E7
Orchard Dr					
-	RGWD	60097	2469	35W-37N	E3
-	TYPK	60477	3424	9W-21S	E7
200	WDDL	60191	2915	18W-6N	A6
500	CRTE	60417	3685	1W-30S	B3
8600	HYHL	60457	3210	10W-10S	A4
21000	OMFD	60461	3507	3W-25S	A7
21000	PKFT	60466	3507	3W-25S	A7
27700	ISLK	60042	2587	28W-27N	A7
27700	WcnT	60042	2587	28W-27N	A7
27700	WcnT	60084	2587	28W-27N	A7
N Orchard Dr					
-	JNBG	60050	2470	33W-34N	E7
10	PKFT	60466	3595	3W-25S	B1
100	BGBK	60440	3268	24W-11S	D1
400	OMFD	60461	3507	3W-25S	A7
400	PKFT	60466	3507	3W-25S	A7
2700	MCLK	60050	2470	33W-34N	E7
S Orchard Dr					
10	PKFT	60466	3595	3W-27S	B5
100	BGBK	60440	3268	24W-12S	D3
700	BRTN	60010	2750	26W-18N	E3
W Orchard Dr					
4700	MCLK	60050	2470	34W-34N	D7
6300	PSHT	60463	3275	7W-14S	B6
8100	FftT	60423	3504	10W-24S	C5
27600	FXLK	60041	2473	27W-35N	B6
27600	GrtT	60041	2473	27W-35N	B6
Orchard Ln					
-	GNEN	60137	3083	23W-1S	A2
-	GNEN	60187	3083	23W-1S	A2
-	WHTN	60187	3083	23W-1S	A2
10	BKBN	60015	2703	11W-22N	D5
10	ElgT	60124	2853	37W-11N	B3
10	GLF	60029	2865	8W-12N	A1
10	HNWD	60047	2645	21W-24N	D6
10	LNHT	60046	2476	19W-37N	B1
200	BCHR	60401	3864	0W-36S	C1
300	BDWD	60408	3941	31W-42S	E6
300	BMDL	60108	2968	24W-5N	C1
300	HDPK	60035	2704	8W-23N	D3
400	WNKA	60093	2812	4W-15N	B2
500	GLNC	60022	2758	7W-18N	B4
500	WynT	60103	2966	29W-5N	D2
600	WYNE	60184	2965	31W-5N	D2
1200	HRVD	60033	2405	51W-39N	E5
1400	NHBK	60062	2757	9W-17N	C6
1500	GLHT	60139	2969	23W-2N	A7
1600	NndT	60050	2585	31W-30N	C2
1700	NHFD	60093	2811	6W-15N	C2
2000	CPVL	60110	2746	37W-17N	D6
2000	DndT	60110	2746	37W-17N	D7
2200	JLET	60435	3497	26W-22S	D2
2700	WLMT	60091	2812	5W-13N	A5
2800	BFGV	60089	2701	16W-23N	D2
2800	VrnT	60089	2701	16W-23N	D2
2900	WLMT	60091	2811	5W-13N	E5
3900	ElaT	60047	2700	19W-22N	C3
3900	LGGV	60047	2700	19W-22N	C3
4100	MTSN	60443	3506	5W-24S	C5
4600	NndT	60014	2640	33W-26N	E3
7000	HRPK	60133	2912	26W-8N	A2
7500	WDRG	60517	3206	21W-8S	A2
9100	BGVW	60455	3211	8W-10S	A5
10500	CHRG	60415	3275	8W-12S	B2

STREET Block City ZIP Map# CGS Grid

Orchard Ln
12800 ALSP 60803 3276 5W-15S B7
12800 ALSP 60803 3348 5W-15S B1
15000 HMGN 60491 3342 18W-16S E3
15000 HMGN 60491 3343 18W-16S A3
15300 OKFT 60452 3347 8W-18S B7
17100 CCHL 60478 3426 4W-20S D4
21800 DRPK 60010 2698 24W-21N B5
21800 ElaT 60010 2698 24W-21N B5
21800 NBRN 60010 2698 24W-21N B5
E Orchard Ln
10 PLTN 60067 2805 20W-15N E3
N Orchard Ln
800 WKGN 60085 2479 12W-35N C7
1000 WkgT 60085 2479 12W-35N C7
1700 RLKB 60073 2475 22W-35N B5
2600 LKVL 60046 2475 22W-35N B5
2600 LkvT 60046 2475 22W-35N B5
2600 RLKB 60046 2475 22W-35N B5
W Orchard Ln
18800 WrnT 60030 2533 18W-33N D3
22100 AntT 60002 2417 22W-40N C2
23600 PNFD 60586 3416 29W-19S D2
Orchard Pl
10 HNDL 60521 3146 15W-5S B1
100 OKTR 60181 3085 17W-1S C2
200 FXLK 60020 2473 27W-36N C3
2800 DSPN 60018 2917 12W-8N A2
3000 RSMT 60018 2917 12W-8N A2
7200 DRGV 60516 3206 19W-8S D1
W Orchard Pl
10 MPPT 60056 2861 16W-11N E2
10 MPPT 60056 2862 15W-11N A2
1200 RLKH 60073 2474 24W-35N C5
1400 ANHT 60005 2806 18W-13N D7
1400 RGMW 60005 2806 18W-13N D7
1400 RGMW 60008 2806 18W-13N D7
24700 AvnT 60073 2474 24W-35N B5
Orchard Rd
- AraT 60506 3077 38W-4S A7
- AraT 60506 3137 38W-4S A1
- AraT 60506 3198 38W-7S E1
- AraT 60542 3077 38W-4S A7
- AraT 60542 3137 38W-4S A1
- AURA 60506 3198 38W-7S E1
- BtlT 60560 3262 39W-13S E5
- BtvT 60506 3077 38W-3S A7
- BtvT 60510 3077 37W-3S C6
- BtvT 60539 3077 37W-3S C6
- BtvT 60542 3077 37W-3S B6
- MTGY 60538 3198 39W-10S E7
- MTGY 60543 3198 39W-10S E7
- MTGY 60543 3262 39W-11S E1
- NARA 60506 3136 38W-4S E2
- NARA 60506 3137 38W-4S A1
- NARA 60539 3077 37W-3S C6
- NARA 60542 3077 37W-3S B6
- OswT 60543 3262 39W-13S E4
- OswT 60560 3262 39W-13S E4
- SgrT 60506 3136 38W-5S E2
10 MltT 60187 3082 25W-2S A3
10 WHTN 60187 3082 25W-2S A4
200 NBRN 60010 2698 25W-23N A2
700 MltT 60555 3082 25W-2S A5
1100 AraT 60538 3198 39W-8S E2
1100 AURA 60538 3198 39W-8S E2
1100 MTGY 60506 3198 38W-8S E2
1200 AURA 60506 3136 39W-7S E7
3400 BtlT 60543 3262 39W-12S E4
3400 OSWG 60543 3262 39W-12S E3
7600 MchT 60097 2469 36W-35N D6
Orchard Rd CO-83
1100 AraT 60506 3198 39W-8S E2
1100 AraT 60538 3198 39W-8S E2
1100 AURA 60506 3198 39W-8S E2
1100 AURA 60538 3198 39W-8S E2
1100 MTGY 60506 3198 38W-8S E2
1100 MTGY 60538 3198 38W-8S E2
N Orchard Rd
3200 BHPK 60087 2479 11W-37N E1
3200 WKGN 60087 2479 11W-37N E1
26100 WcnT 60010 2642 28W-26N E3
26100 WcnT 60084 2642 28W-26N E3
42800 NptT 60099 2360 16W-42N E5
42800 WDWH 60099 2360 16W-42N E5
Orchard Row
500 CLLK 60014 2639 36W-26N D3
Orchard St
10 RDLK 60073 2531 23W-33N E3
100 ELGN 60123 2854 34W-10N D5
100 FRGV 60021 2696 29W-22N B3
300 ANTH 60002 2357 24W-42N D6
600 DRFD 60015 2703 10W-21N E7
1400 DSPN 60018 2863 12W-9N A6
2400 BLID 60406 3277 3W-14S A6
8800 WLSP 60480 3208 14W-10S D5
E Orchard St
10 ANHT 60005 2807 17W-13N A7
100 EMHT 60126 3027 16W-0N E4
100 EMHT 60126 3028 15W-0N A4
100 ITSC 60143 2914 19W-6N C6
N Orchard St
1600 CHCG 60610 2978 0W-2N A7
2100 CHCG 60614 2978 0W-2N A6
3100 CHCG 60657 2978 0W-3N A4
42300 AntT 60002 2357 25W-42N A6
S Orchard St
12200 ALSP 60803 3276 5W-14S B6
W Orchard St
10 ANHT 60005 2807 17W-13N A7
100 ITSC 60143 2914 19W-6N C6
Orchard Ter
10 LMBD 60148 3026 20W-0N B3
300 ROSL 60172 2913 23W-6N B6
3400 CRTE 60417 3596 0E-28S E6
3400 STGR 60475 3596 0E-28S E6
Orchard Tr
5200 MONE 60449 3683 6W-31S A6
5400 MONE 60449 3682 6W-31S E6
15100 LMNT 60439 3342 18W-15S E1
Orchard Beach Rd
1800 MchT 60050 2528 31W-33N D2
1800 MHRY 60050 2528 32W-33N C2
2600 MchT 60050 2471 31W-34N D7
Orchard Bluff Ln
39500 WDWH 60083 2419 15W-39N E4
39500 WDWH 60083 2420 15W-39N A4
39700 NptT 60083 2419 16W-39N E5
Orchard Gate Ln
- DRGV 60516 3144 18W-7S E6
- WTMT 60516 3144 18W-7S E6
- WTMT 60559 3144 18W-7S E6
1500 WTMT 60559 3145 18W-7S B6
Orchard Gateway
- NARA 60506 3137 38W-4S A1
Orchard-Gateway Rd
- AURA 60506 3136 39W-4S D2
- NARA 60506 3136 39W-4S D2
Orchard Gateway Rd
- NARA 60542 3137 38W-4S B2
1800 AURA 60506 3137 38W-4S B2
1800 NARA 60506 3137 38W-4S B2
Orchard Hill Ct
1200 VLPK 60181 3027 17W-0S B6
Orchard Lake Dr
1000 AURA 60506 3136 39W-6S E4
Orchard Pointe Dr
- JLET 60586 3496 31W-22S A2
Orchard Pond Ct
900 LKZH 60047 2698 24W-22N C4
Orchard Pond Dr
500 LKZH 60047 2698 24W-22N C4
Orchard Ridge Av
16700 HLCT 60428 3427 2W-20S C4
16700 HLCT 60429 3427 2W-20S C4
16700 MKHM 60428 3427 2W-20S C4
Orchards Pass
100 BRLT 60103 2910 29W-6N E6
Orchard Valley Dr
7200 BLVY 60050 2526 36W-31N D7
W Orchard Valley Dr
16500 GRNE 60031 2477 16W-35N D7
16500 WrnT 60031 2477 16W-35N C7
W Orchard Wy Dr
5300 MchT 60050 2527 34W-34N C1
Orchid Ct
10 SMWD 60107 2856 30W-10N B5
1700 HDPK 60035 2704 10W-22N A4
2400 NPVL 60540 3140 29W-7S C7
15300 ODPK 60462 3346 9W-18S D7
Orchid Dr
600 SHLD 60473 3350 0E-18S E7
3400 SjnT 46311 3598 C6
Orchid Ln
- LKPT 60441 3420 19W-20S D5
700 BRLT 60103 2910 29W-6N D7
2200 CTHL 60403 3417 27W-21S C6
15100 ODPK 60462 3346 9W-18S D6
N Orchid Ln
2100 ANHT 60004 2754 16W-16N C7
2100 ANHT 60004 2807 16W-16N C1
S Orchid Pth
600 MHRY 60050 2528 32W-31N C7
600 NndT 60050 2528 32W-31N C7
Orchid St
1600 AURA 60505 3139 33W-5S A3
S Orchid St
13200 DPgT 60544 3339 26W-15S E2
Ord Ct
200 BRLT 60103 2911 28W-7N A5
Oregon Av
10 WDND 60118 2801 34W-16N A3
400 WDND 60118 2800 34W-16N E2
1100 JLET 60435 3498 25W-22S B2
N Oregon Av
1200 JLET 60435 3498 25W-22S B2
Oregon Ct
3700 NCHI 60088 2593 12W-30N C2
S Oregon Dr
13900 PnfT 60544 3339 27W-16S C4
Oregon Ln
18100 ODPK 60467 3423 13W-21S B7
Oregon St
10 FKFT 60423 3591 12W-26S D2
Oregon Tr
700 ROSL 60172 2913 22W-8N C3
1500 EGVV 60007 2913 21W-9N E1
3200 OMFD 60461 3506 4W-24S E5
3200 OMFD 60461 3507 4W-24S A4
4700 MHRY 60050 2527 33W-31N E6
10600 HTLY 60142 2692 39W-21N B6
11800 OrlT 60467 3344 14W-16S C2
Oregon Trails
- DMND 60416 3941 33W-39S A2
Orenia Ct
8400 ODPK 60462 3346 10W-16S B3
Origin Al
- BbyT 60134 3018 39W-0N E5
Oriole Av
8800 MNGV 60053 2864 9W-11N C3
8800 MNGV 60714 2864 9W-11N C4
8800 NLES 60714 2864 9W-11N C4
17100 TYPK 60477 3424 9W-20S D5
E Oriole Av
400 EMHT 60126 3028 15W-0N B4
N Oriole Av
3200 CHCG 60634 2974 9W-4N C3
3200 CHCG 60707 2974 9W-4N C4
3200 EDPK 60707 2974 9W-4N C4
3900 CHCG 60706 2974 9W-4N A6
4400 NRDG 60706 2974 9W-5N C1
4500 NRDG 60706 2918 9W-5N C7
4600 HDHT 60706 2918 9W-5N C7
4900 CHCG 60656 2918 9W-6N C6
4900 CHCG 60706 2918 9W-6N C6
6800 CHCG 60631 2918 9W-8N C1
7200 CHCG 60631 2864 9W-9N C7
7500 NLES 60068 2864 9W-9N C7
7500 NLES 60631 2864 9W-9N C7
7500 PKRG 60068 2864 9W-9N C6
7500 PKRG 60631 2864 9W-9N C7
7600 PKRG 60714 2864 9W-9N C6
8200 NLES 60714 2864 9W-10N C4
8600 MNGV 60053 2864 9W-10N C4
N Oriole Av SR-72
- CHCG 60631 2918 9W-7N C4
Oriole Ct
10 HNWD 60047 2645 22W-26N B3
10 NPVL 60540 3203 26W-8S E2
10 WDRG 60517 3143 21W-7S E7
200 DYR 46311 3510 D6
600 GYLK 60030 2533 20W-33N A3
1100 ANTH 60002 2358 21W-41N E7
1500 LNHT 60046 2417 21W-38N E7
4400 GRNE 60031 2478 14W-34N C7
8500 ODPK 60462 3346 10W-18S B7
W Oriole Ct
1200 RDLK 60073 2531 24W-34N C1
Oriole Dr
- BlmT 60411 3509 3E-25S E7
- SmbT 60007 2913 22W-8N C2
- SmbT 60193 2913 22W-8N C2
600 SMWD 60107 2857 28W-9N B7
700 PtnT 60468 3860 10W-38S C5
700 PTON 60468 3860 10W-38S C5
1800 EGVV 60007 2913 22W-8N C2
8100 DGvT 60561 3207 17W-9S B3
8100 DRN 60561 3207 17W-9S B3
9300 MNSR 46321 3510 E2
Oriole Ln
- BMDL 60108 2968 23W-4N E4
- GLHT 60108 2968 23W-4N E4
10 GLHT 60139 2968 23W-4N E4
10 LslT 60540 3142 25W-5S C3
1500 JLET 60586 3496 29W-22S D1
2600 RGMW 60008 2806 19W-13N C6
W Oriole Ln
400 MPPT 60056 2807 15W-14N E5
600 ANHT 60004 2807 15W-14N E5
600 MPPT 60004 2807 15W-14N E5
Oriole Rd
10 MTSN 60443 3505 7W-24S D5
Oriole St
300 BMDL 60108 2968 23W-4N E4
400 GLHT 60108 2968 23W-4N E4
400 GLHT 60139 2968 23W-4N E4
Oriole Ter
200 CRY 60013 2641 30W-24N E7
Oriole Tr
600 MchT 60050 2472 29W-37N C1
1200 CLSM 60188 2967 28W-4N B5
8800 GwdT 60097 2469 38W-35N A7
N Oriole Tr
10 CLLK 60014 2639 36W-26N E4
S Oriole Tr
10 CLLK 60014 2639 35W-25N E4
W Oriole Tr
100 CRY 60013 2641 31W-24N D7
Orion Av
2400 BlmT 60411 3597 2E-26S D3
21500 SLVL 60411 3597 2E-26S D2
Orion Rd
300 BTVA 60510 3020 35W-0S C6
Orlan Brook Dr
15100 ODPK 60462 3346 10W-18S B7
15700 ODPK 60462 3424 10W-19S B1
Orland Ct
9000 ODPK 60462 3346 11W-17S A6
Orland Pkwy
- FftT 60448 3423 12W-21S D7
- OrlT 60487 3423 12W-21S D7
- TYPK 60448 3423 12W-21S D7
10300 FftT 60467 3423 13W-22S B7
10300 ODPK 60448 3503 13W-22S B1
10300 ODPK 60467 3423 12W-22S C7
10300 ODPK 60467 3503 13W-22S B1
18200 ODPK 60448 3423 12W-21S D7
18200 ODPK 60487 3423 12W-21S D7
18200 TYPK 60487 3423 12W-21S D7
Orland Park Pl
10 ODPK 60462 3345 11W-18S D6
Orland Square Dr
10 ODPK 60462 3345 11W-17S D6
Orland Woods Ln
17500 ODPK 60467 3422 14W-20S E5
Orleans Av
400 NPVL 60565 3204 25W-9S A3
500 LslT 60565 3204 25W-9S B3
Orleans Cir
1300 HDPK 60035 2704 8W-21N D7
1800 EGVV 60007 2913 22W-8N D3
Orleans Dr
700 HDPK 60035 2704 9W-20N D7
1100 MDLN 60060 2647 17W-25N A5
18100 HLCT 60429 3426 4W-21S E7
Orleans Ln
400 SMBG 60193 2858 25W-10N B6
Orleans Pl
800 WTMT 60559 3085 17W-4S C6
Orleans St
200 CPVL 60110 2747 34W-17N E6
N Orleans St
400 CHCG 60606 3034 0W-0N B3
1400 CHCG 60610 3034 0W-1N B1
1700 MHRY 60050 2528 32W-33N B2
2000 CHCG 60614 2978 0W-2N B6
W Orleans St
3700 MHRY 60050 2528 32W-33N A2
Orman Av
4600 ISLK 60042 2642 29W-27N C1
4600 ISLK 60051 2642 29W-27N C1
4600 NndT 60051 2642 29W-27N C1
Orogrande Ct
15300 OKFT 60452 3347 7W-18S B7
Orogrande St
15300 OKFT 60452 3347 7W-18S B7
Orr Ct
- NARA 60542 3076 39W-3S E7
Orr St
600 RKDL 60436 3498 26W-24S B7
Orrefors Ct
4700 JLET 60431 3496 29W-22S C2
Orrington Av
1800 EVTN 60201 2867 2W-11N B2
2500 EVTN 60201 2813 2W-12N B7
Orrington Ct
10 SMBG 60173 2859 22W-10N C5
500 LKZH 60047 2699 22W-21N A6
1300 WLNG 60090 2754 16W-18N D4
Orth Ct
1500 WHTN 60187 3081 26W-1S E2
Orth Dr
1500 WHTN 60187 3081 26W-1S E2
Orton Av
600 WCDA 60084 2643 26W-27N C1
Orwell Rd
1200 NPVL 60564 3267 28W-12S A2
1500 NPVL 60564 3266 28W-12S E2
1600 WldT 60564 3266 28W-12S E2
Ory Bridge Ct
6400 LSLE 60532 3142 23W-7S E6
Osage Av
5900 DRGV 60516 3144 19W-6S E5
7100 DRGV 60516 3206 19W-8S E1
N Osage Av
3200 EDPK 60707 2974 9W-4N B4
4400 CHCG 60634 2974 9W-5N B1
4400 NRDG 60706 2918 9W-5N B7
4400 NRDG 60706 2974 9W-5N B1
5700 CHCG 60631 2918 9W-7N B5
Osage Cir
500 CLSM 60188 2967 27W-3N D6
2800 WKGN 60087 2479 12W-36N C4
Osage Ct
600 DYR 46311 3598 E3
900 CPVL 60110 2748 32W-18N C4
8700 FKFT 60423 3504 10W-24S B6
S Osage Ct
100 RDLK 60073 2531 23W-33N E3
17100 LKPT 60441 3420 20W-20S C5
Osage Dr
100 NBRN 60010 2697 26W-22N E3
200 CmpT 60175 2962 39W-4N E4
300 BGBK 60490 3267 26W-12S D3
300 MltT 60137 3083 22W-3S B6
400 DYR 46311 3598 D3
900 NndT 60051 2528 31W-31N D7
1000 NndT 60051 2585 31W-30N D1
2500 GNVW 60025 2809 11W-15N C2
Osage Ln
- MDLN 60060 2646 18W-25N E5
300 NPVL 60540 3203 26W-8S D2
700 HFET 60169 2858 24W-10N D5
700 SMBG 60169 2858 24W-10N D5
700 SMBG 60194 2858 24W-10N D5
900 WLMT 60091 2812 5W-14N A5
2000 HRPK 60133 2911 27W-9N C1
18500 LGGV 60047 2646 18W-25N D4
18500 LGGV 60060 2646 18W-25N D4
E Osage Ln
400 PLTN 60074 2753 20W-18N A3
Osage Rd
10 BtlT 60543 3263 38W-12S A3
4400 MchT 60097 2469 36W-36N E4
Osage St
100 MNKA 60447 3583 33W-28S B7
100 WCDA 60084 2643 26W-27N D2
200 MNKA 60447 3672 33W-28S B1
300 PKFT 60466 3595 3W-27S B5
400 JltT 60432 3499 21W-23S E3
400 WCDA 60084 2587 26W-27N E7
Osage Ter
- WLNG 60089 2754 16W-20N D2
200 BFGV 60089 2754 16W-20N D2
800 WCDA 60084 2587 26W-28N C6
Osage Orange Rd
1300 GYLK 60030 2533 19W-32N C5
Osbron St
- PLNO 60545 3260 45W-13S C5
Oscar Av
10 JLET 60433 3499 23W-24S A7
10 JLET 60436 3499 23W-24S A7
10 JltT 60433 3499 23W-24S A7
Oscar Ct
5200 GRNE 60031 2478 15W-35N A6
Osceola Av
8800 NLES 60053 2864 9W-11N D4
8800 NLES 60714 2864 9W-11N D4
9100 MNGV 60053 2864 9W-11N D2
17300 TYPK 60477 3424 9W-20S E5
N Osceola Av
3000 CHCG 60707 2974 9W-3N D4
3000 EDPK 60707 2974 9W-3N D4
3100 CHCG 60634 2974 9W-3N D4
3900 CHCG 60706 2974 9W-4N C2
3900 NRDG 60706 2974 9W-5N C1
5200 CHCG 60706 2918 9W-6N C6
5200 HDHT 60706 2918 9W-6N C6
5500 CHCG 60656 2918 9W-6N D5
6800 CHCG 60631 2918 9W-8N D1
7200 CHCG 60631 2864 9W-9N D7
7500 NLES 60631 2864 9W-9N D7
8000 NLES 60714 2864 9W-10N D4
8600 MNGV 60053 2864 9W-10N D4
N Osceola St
100 MNKA 60447 3583 33W-28S B7
S Osceola St
100 MNKA 60447 3583 33W-28S B7
Osceola Tr
6600 IHPK 60525 3146 14W-7S D6
E Osgood St
10 JLET 60433 3499 23W-24S A5
10 JLET 60436 3499 23W-24S A5
W O'Shea Ct
1600 LKMR 60051 2529 30W-34N A2
1600 MchT 60051 2529 30W-34N A2
N Oshkosh Av
6500 CHCG 60068 2918 9W-8N C2
6500 PKRG 60068 2918 9W-8N C2
6700 CHCG 60631 2918 9W-8N C2
Osler Dr
100 NPVL 60540 3141 27W-7S C7
Oslo Ct
1800 MDLN 60060 2647 17W-25N A5
Osmond Av
900 ANTH 60002 2357 23W-42N D7
Ospray Ln
- NLNX 60451 3589 18W-27S B4
Osprey Cross
- BCHR 60401 3864 0E-36S E1
Osprey Ct
- SMWD 60107 2856 29W-9N D7
1900 BRLT 60103 2909 32W-8N D3
3300 GNVA 60134 3019 37W-0N B4
Osprey Ln
200 LNHT 60046 2476 19W-37N C2
4600 JLET 60586 3496 29W-22S D2
S Osprey Ln
1800 WKGN 60048 2535 14W-31N D6
Oster Dr
- ZION 60099 2362 12W-41N B7
Osterman Av
600 DRFD 60015 2703 11W-20N D7
Ostrander Av
1100 BKFD 60513 3087 11W-2S D4
1100 LGPK 60513 3087 11W-2S D4
1100 LGPK 60525 3087 11W-2S D4
1500 PvsT 60525 3087 11W-2S D4
Osullivan Dr
4300 JLET 60431 3496 29W-22S D2
Oswalt Av
100 BTVA 60510 3078 35W-2S C4
Oswego Av
8800 MNGV 60053 2864 9W-11N C3
8800 NLES 60714 2864 9W-11N C4
Oswego Dr
600 CLSM 60188 2967 27W-3N C6
Oswego Rd
400 NPVL 60540 3141 28W-7S A7
400 NpvT 60540 3141 28W-7S A7
400 NPVL 60540 3140 28W-7S E7
Oswego St
300 PKFT 60466 3595 3W-27S B5
N Oswego St
400 CHCG 60612 3033 2W-0N C3
400 CHCG 60622 3033 2W-0N C3
Othello Dr
3500 NPVL 60564 3266 28W-11S E2
Otis Av
400 DRGV 60515 3144 19W-4S D1
600 RKDL 60436 3498 26W-25S A7
Otis Pl
1100 NHBK 60062 2757 8W-17N E5
1100 NHBK 60062 2758 8W-17N A5
Otis Rd
- MTGY 60506 3199 37W-8S C3
10 BNHL 60010 2750 27W-18N C4
10 BRTN 60010 2750 27W-18N C4
200 BNHL 60010 2749 28W-18N E4
N Otsego Av
6500 CHCG 60631 2918 9W-8N C2
6600 CHCG 60068 2918 9W-8N C2
6600 PKRG 60068 2918 9W-8N C2
Otsego Ct
100 BMDL 60108 2968 25W-5N B1
Ott Av
500 GNEN 60137 3083 23W-1S A2
N Ott Av
10 GNEN 60137 3025 23W-0S A7
10 GNEN 60187 3025 23W-0S A7
10 WHTN 60187 3025 23W-0S A7
Ottawa Av
600 CHCG 60631 2864 9W-9N C7
600 PKRG 60631 2864 9W-9N C7
800 PKRG 60068 2864 9W-9N C6
1100 AURA 60506 3137 37W-6S C6
8800 MNGV 60053 2864 9W-11N C3
8800 MNGV 60714 2864 9W-11N C4
8800 NLES 60714 2864 9W-11N C4
17300 TYPK 60477 3424 9W-20S D5
N Ottawa Av
3200 CHCG 60634 2974 9W-4N C3
3200 EDPK 60707 2974 9W-4N C4
3900 CHCG 60706 2974 9W-4N C2
4400 NRDG 60706 2974 9W-5N C1
4500 HDHT 60706 2918 9W-5N C7
4500 NRDG 60706 2918 9W-5N C7
5600 CHCG 60656 2918 9W-6N C5
6600 CHCG 60068 2918 9W-8N C2
6600 PKRG 60068 2918 9W-8N C2
6800 CHCG 60631 2918 9W-8N C1
7200 CHCG 60631 2864 9W-9N C7
7500 PKRG 60631 2864 9W-9N C7
8000 NLES 60068 2864 9W-10N C5
8000 PKRG 60068 2864 9W-10N C5
8300 NLES 60714 2864 9W-10N C4
Ottawa Cir
- SRGV 60554 3136 41W-7S A6
Ottawa Ct
10 JSTC 60458 3209 11W-8S E1
10 NPVL 60563 3141 26W-5S D2
700 CLSM 60188 2967 26W-3N E5
1600 WLNG 60090 2754 16W-17N D5
Ottawa Dr
- AxST 60447 3583 34W-28S A6
- MNKA 60447 3583 34W-28S A6
300 BGBK 60440 3268 23W-11S E1
600 RLKH 60073 2474 23W-36N D4
1200 MhtT 60451 3589 16W-28S E6
1200 MhtT 60451 3590 16W-28S A6
S Ottawa Dr
16700 LKPT 60441 3420 20W-20S C4
Ottawa Ln
300 OKBK 60523 3085 16W-3S E4
900 WLMT 60091 2812 5W-14N A5
Ottawa Rd
2200 WKGN 60087 2479 12W-36N C4
4700 MchT 60097 2469 36W-36N E3
Ottawa St
300 PKFT 60466 3595 3W-27S B5
2200 DSPN 60016 2863 12W-11N C3
24500 PNFD 60544 3338 31W-18S A7
N Ottawa St
10 JLET 60432 3498 24W-23S E4
10 JLET 60436 3498 24W-23S E5
N Ottawa St SR-53
10 JLET 60432 3498 24W-23S E4
10 JLET 60436 3498 24W-23S E5
N Ottawa St US-6
10 JLET 60432 3498 24W-23S E5
10 JLET 60436 3498 24W-23S E5
S Ottawa St
10 JLET 60432 3498 24W-24S E5
10 JLET 60436 3498 24W-24S E6
1500 JLET 60436 3586 24W-25S E1
1500 JltT 60436 3586 24W-25S E2
S Ottawa St SR-53
10 JLET 60432 3498 24W-24S E5
10 JLET 60436 3498 24W-24S E5
S Ottawa St US-6
10 JLET 60432 3498 24W-24S E5
10 JLET 60436 3498 24W-24S E5
W Ottawa St
10 PNFD 60544 3338 30W-18S C7
Otter Ln
300 CmpT 60175 2961 43W-6N B1
Otter Tr
1300 AlqT 60013 2642 30W-24N A7
Otter Wy
600 OSWG 60543 3262 39W-11S E1
600 OSWG 60543 3263 39W-11S A1
Otter Creek Ln
2400 ELGN 60124 2853 36W-10N D6
Otter Tail Dr
- MRGO 60152 2634 49W-27N D1
Otter Tail Pl
- MRGO 60152 2634 49W-27N D1
Otto Av
5200 CHCG 60018 2917 12W-6N C6
5200 CHCG 60656 2917 12W-6N C6
5200 RSMT 60018 2917 11W-6N C5
5200 SRPK 60176 2917 12W-6N C6
5200 SRPK 60656 2917 12W-6N C6
Otto Blvd
1200 CHHT 60411 3508 1W-25S A7
1400 CHHT 60411 3596 1W-25S B1
E Otto Dr
10 NLNX 60451 3589 17W-26S C2
10 NlxT 60451 3589 17W-26S C2
W Otto Dr
100 NLNX 60451 3589 18W-26S B2
100 NlxT 60451 3589 18W-26S C2
Otto Ln
3200 EVTN 60201 2812 4W-13N C7
Otto Pl
5100 OKLN 60453 3211 6W-10S E5
6400 DRGV 60516 3144 20W-7S A6
Otto St
3200 LNSG 60438 3430 4E-22S B7
Otto Graham Ln
1100 WKGN 60099 2421 10W-38N E6
1100 WKGN 60099 2422 10W-39N A6
Ouilmette Ln
600 WLMT 60091 2812 4W-13N B6
Ouimet Ct
3700 WDRG 60517 3143 23W-7S A7
Our Lady Dr
- HMGN 60491 3421 17W-18S C1
Outer Dr
- CstT 60481 3942 30W-40S D3
- RedT 60408 3942 30W-40S D4
- RedT 60481 3942 30W-40S D4
N Outer Dr
300 WMTN 60481 3853 27W-38S D5
S Outer Dr
300 WMTN 60481 3853 27W-38S D5

Block	City	ZIP	Map#	CGS	Grid
Outer Cir Dr					
-	CstT	60481	3942	30W-40S	D4
-	DGvT	60439	3206	18W-10S	E6
-	DGvT	60439	3207	18W-10S	A6
-	RedT	60481	3942	30W-40S	D4
Outer Ring Rd					
-	BtvT	60502	3079	33W-2S	B4
-	BtvT	60510	3079	32W-3S	B5
-	WnfT	60510	3079	33W-2S	B4
Outrigger Ln					
-	PGGV	60140	2798	41W-14N	B5
Ovaltine Ct					
100	VLPK	60181	3027	17W-0N	B4
Overbeck Ln					
2800	WCHI	60185	2965	32W-4N	C4
N Overbrook Ct					
36100	WrnT	60031	2477	17W-36N	B5
Overbrook Rd					
10	SBTN	60010	2803	26W-14N	D3
Overcup Ct					
300	CmpT	60175	2962	39W-4N	E3
Overhill Av					
600	CHCG	60631	2864	9W-9N	C7
600	PKRG	60068	2864	9W-9N	C6
600	PKRG	60631	2864	9W-9N	C7
9300	MNGV	60053	2864	9W-11N	C2
16800	TYPK	60477	3424	9W-20S	D3
N Overhill Av					
3200	EDPK	60707	2974	9W-4N	C4
3600	CHCG	60634	2974	9W-4N	C2
4000	CHCG	60706	2974	9W-5N	C2
4000	NRDG	60706	2974	9W-5N	C1
4600	HDHT	60706	2918	9W-5N	C7
4600	NRDG	60706	2918	9W-5N	C7
5000	CHCG	60656	2918	9W-6N	C6
5000	CHCG	60706	2918	9W-6N	C6
6800	CHCG	60631	2918	9W-8N	C1
7200	CHCG	60631	2864	9W-9N	C7
7500	PKRG	60631	2864	9W-9N	C7
8000	NLES	60068	2864	9W-10N	C5
8000	NLES	60714	2864	9W-10N	C5
8000	PKRG	60068	2864	9W-10N	C5
Overhill Ct					
9300	MNGV	60053	2864	9W-11N	C2
N Overhill Dr					
23400	ElaT	60047	2699	21W-23N	D1
Overkamp Av					
-	AddT	60101	2970	19W-4N	D4
-	ADSN	60101	2970	19W-4N	D4
700	AddT	60101	2971	18W-4N	A3
700	ADSN	60101	2971	18W-4N	A3
Overland Ct					
-	CNHN	60410	3761	32W-32S	C1
700	ROSL	60172	2913	22W-8N	C3
Overland Dr					
100	AURA	60542	3137	36W-4S	E2
100	NARA	60542	3137	36W-4S	D2
22200	PnfT	60544	3339	27W-16S	B4
S Overland Dr					
26300	CNHN	60410	3761	32W-32S	C1
Overland Rd					
3600	NndT	60012	2585	30W-28N	E6
Overland Tr					
600	ROSL	60172	2913	22W-8N	C2
1600	DRFD	60015	2703	11W-22N	D5
4700	MHRY	60050	2527	33W-31N	E6
11900	HMGN	60491	3344	14W-16S	C3
11900	OrlT	60467	3344	14W-16S	C3
20000	OMFD	60461	3506	4W-24S	E5
Overland Pass					
3200	GNVW	60025	2809	11W-14N	C3
3200	NfdT	60062	2809	11W-14N	C3
N Overlook Cir					
700	RDLK	60073	2531	25W-34N	A1
Overlook Ct					
300	BNHL	60010	2748	30W-18N	E3
800	LKVL	60046	2475	23W-36N	A3
2300	NPVL	60563	3140	30W-5S	B4
2300	NpvT	60563	3140	30W-5S	B4
2500	YKVL	60512	3261	42W-13S	D4
2500	YKVL	60560	3261	42W-13S	D4
W Overlook Ct					
-	GrtT	60073	2531	25W-34N	A1
1900	RDLK	60073	2531	25W-34N	A1
Overlook Ct E					
800	FKFT	60423	3503	12W-24S	C6
Overlook Ct W					
800	FKFT	60423	3503	12W-24S	C6
Overlook Dr					
-	WLMT	60091	2813	2W-14N	B5
10	GLF	60029	2865	8W-12N	A1
10	GLF	60053	2865	8W-12N	A2
10	GNVW	60025	2865	8W-12N	A1
10	GNVW	60029	2865	8W-12N	A1
10	HNWD	60047	2645	22W-25N	B5
10	MNGV	60053	2865	7W-11N	A2
200	LKFT	60045	2650	9W-25N	A5
800	FKFT	60423	3503	12W-24S	C6
1300	GLF	60029	2864	8W-12N	E1
1300	GNVW	60025	2864	8W-12N	E1
1300	GNVW	60029	2864	8W-12N	E1
1500	GLF	60025	2864	8W-12N	E1
3400	RcmT	60071	2354	32W-43N	B4
3900	SPGV	60081	2413	32W-38N	A6
N Overlook Dr					
1600	JLET	60431	3497	28W-21S	A1
1600	PnfT	60431	3497	28W-21S	A1
Overlook Ln					
900	CLSM	60188	2967	27W-3N	B5
Overlook Pt					
10	LNSH	60069	2702	15W-22N	A4
N Overlook Tr					
300	RDLK	60073	2531	25W-34N	A1
W Overman Ct					
23700	PNFD	60585	3338	29W-15S	E3
23700	WldT	60585	3338	29W-15S	E3
Overstreet Ct					
2100	NPVL	60565	3204	25W-9S	B4
Overton Ct					
10	LMNT	60439	3270	18W-14S	E7
1100	NPVL	60540	3204	25W-7S	B1
Overton Dr					
1300	LMNT	60439	3270	18W-14S	E7
1300	LMNT	60439	3271	18W-14S	A7
SE Overton Dr					
3600	RcmT	60071	2413	32W-40N	B3
Overton Rd					
10	DMND	60416	3941	32W-40S	D2
Overview Cir					
-	ANTH	60002	2418	20W-40N	A2
Overview Dr					
2400	BFGV	60089	2701	16W-22N	D3
Owasco Av					
10	ELGN	60123	2854	34W-12N	D1
N Owen Av					
6900	CHCG	60631	2918	9W-8N	C1
6900	PKRG	60068	2918	9W-8N	C1
6900	PKRG	60631	2918	9W-8N	C1
Owen Ct					
300	OSWG	60543	3263	38W-11S	A2
300	PTHT	60070	2808	15W-15N	B2
Owen Dr					
10400	ODPK	60467	3423	13W-21S	B6
Owen Pl					
100	PTHT	60070	2808	15W-14N	B4
Owen St					
500	PTHT	60070	2808	15W-15N	B2
N Owen St					
10	MPPT	60056	2808	15W-13N	B6
S Owen St					
10	MPPT	60056	2808	15W-12N	B7
200	MPPT	60056	2862	15W-12N	B1
900	DSPN	60016	2862	15W-11N	B2
900	MPPT	60016	2862	15W-11N	B2
Owens Ct					
22800	FmtT	60060	2645	22W-26N	A2
Owens Rd					
-	AURA	60506	3136	40W-7S	B7
N Owens Rd					
20800	MKNA	60448	3502	14W-25S	E7
26600	FmtT	60060	2645	22W-27N	B2
26600	HNWD	60060	2645	22W-27N	B2
27000	HNWD	60047	2645	22W-27N	B2
27600	FmtT	60047	2645	22W-27N	B2
27800	MDLN	60060	2645	22W-27N	B1
S Owens Rd					
-	MKNA	60423	3590	14W-26S	E1
21800	FftT	60423	3590	14W-26S	E2
21800	FftT	60448	3590	14W-26S	E2
21800	MKNA	60448	3590	14W-26S	E2
Owl Ct					
10	WDRG	60517	3143	21W-7S	E7
8400	LKWD	60014	2693	38W-23N	A1
Owl Dr					
2200	JLET	60586	3415	31W-21S	E6
2200	JLET	60586	3416	31W-21S	A6
2900	RGMW	60008	2806	19W-13N	B6
Owl Ln					
2700	RGMW	60008	2806	19W-14N	B5
Owl Wy					
7000	AlqT	60013	2642	30W-24N	A6
Owl Creek Ln					
-	GRNE	60048	2534	16W-33N	C3
-	WrnT	60048	2534	16W-33N	C3
Oxbow Ct					
21300	ELWD	60421	3675	25W-30S	C5
Oxbow Ln					
600	BRTN	60010	2698	24W-20N	C7
600	BRTN	60010	2751	24W-20N	C1
3300	SCRL	60174	2965	33W-4N	B5
Oxbow Wy					
700	BRTN	60010	2698	24W-20N	C7
Oxer Ct					
200	LslT	60540	3143	23W-7S	A7
Oxford Av					
-	SRGV	60554	3135	42W-6S	B5
10	CNHL	60514	3145	17W-5S	C2
200	CNHL	60514	3085	17W-4S	C7
200	CNHL	60559	3085	17W-4S	C7
200	WTMT	60559	3085	17W-4S	C7
600	MTSN	60443	3506	6W-25S	A7
10300	CHRG	60415	3275	7W-12S	B2
11000	CHRG	60482	3275	7W-12S	B3
11000	WRTH	60482	3275	7W-12S	B3
N Oxford Av					
6700	CHCG	60631	2918	9W-8N	D2
Oxford Cir					
-	FXLK	60020	2415	28W-39N	A5
10	GYLK	60030	2475	20W-34N	E7
400	ROSL	60172	2912	25W-6N	B6
500	EGVV	60007	2913	21W-9N	D1
5700	GRNE	60031	2477	16W-36N	D4
Oxford Ct					
-	OSWG	60543	3200	35W-10S	A6
10	ALGN	60102	2695	33W-20N	A7
10	SEGN	60177	2908	35W-8N	B3
200	BMDL	60108	2969	23W-4N	A2
200	NPVL	60540	3142	25W-7S	B6
500	NLNX	60451	3501	18W-25S	B7
500	NlxT	60451	3501	18W-25S	B7
600	LNHT	60046	2418	19W-39N	C6
1000	OKTR	60148	3084	18W-1S	E2
1000	OKTR	60181	3084	18W-1S	E2
1000	YkTp	60148	3084	18W-1S	E2
1000	YkTp	60181	3084	18W-1S	E2
1100	HDPK	60035	2704	10W-23N	B2
1100	LKZH	60047	2699	21W-21N	C5
1300	LYVL	60048	2591	17W-29N	B3
1900	SMBG	60194	2858	26W-11N	A3
2000	FSMR	60422	3507	2W-23S	D3
2900	AURA	60502	3139	32W-5S	D4
3200	ISLK	60042	2586	29W-28N	B5
4000	SMWD	60107	2911	28W-9N	A1
9900	MKNA	60448	3503	12W-23S	D4
12100	LMNT	60439	3271	17W-14S	D6
W Oxford Ct					
900	PLTN	60067	2805	22W-14N	C3
Oxford Dr					
10	LNSH	60069	2702	14W-22N	C3
100	WNVL	60555	3080	30W-1S	C3
1400	BFGV	60089	2701	17W-21N	A5
1700	FmtT	60060	2590	19W-29N	C4
1700	MDLN	60060	2590	19W-29N	C4
2600	DRN	60561	3206	19W-9S	C2
10300	HTLY	60142	2692	39W-22N	C4
15000	OKFT	60452	3347	7W-18S	D6
15200	ODPK	60462	3345	11W-18S	E7
16100	MKHM	60428	3427	3W-19S	B3
16300	TYPK	60477	3425	8W-19S	A3
N Oxford Dr					
2700	MKHM	60428	3427	3W-19S	B2
S Oxford Dr					
2600	MKHM	60428	3427	3W-19S	B3
Oxford Ln					
-	LNHT	60046	2418	19W-38N	C6
10	GLHT	60139	3024	23W-2N	E1
10	GLHT	60139	3025	22W-2N	B1
100	OKTR	60181	3085	17W-1S	B1
100	YkTp	60181	3085	17W-1S	B1
200	BMDL	60108	2969	23W-4N	A3
200	LslT	60540	3204	25W-8S	A2
200	LslT	60565	3204	25W-8S	A2
300	CLLK	60014	2639	36W-25N	C6
300	LKWD	60014	2639	36W-25N	C6
400	LKVL	60046	2475	21W-37N	D2
400	NPVL	60565	3204	25W-8S	A2
600	ElgT	60124	2853	37W-10N	C5
900	WLMT	60091	2812	4W-14N	B5
1000	SEGN	60177	2908	35W-8N	B3
1000	WHTN	60187	3082	23W-2S	E4
1100	LKZH	60047	2699	21W-21N	C5
1100	SRWD	60404	3496	30W-24S	A7
1200	GNVW	60025	2811	7W-13N	A5
1200	HRPK	60133	2911	26W-9N	E1
1300	RDLK	60073	2531	24W-34N	C1
1900	HFET	60169	2804	26W-12N	A7
1900	HFET	60169	2858	25W-12N	B1
3000	NHBK	60062	2756	11W-16N	D7
Oxford Ln SR-50					
-	LNHT	60046	2418	19W-38N	C6
E Oxford Ln					
1100	ANHT	60004	2807	17W-16N	C1
S Oxford Ln					
12200	WldT	60585	3266	29W-14S	D7
Oxford Pl					
100	BMDL	60108	2969	23W-4N	A3
400	ROSL	60172	2912	24W-6N	C6
500	LktT	60441	3499	23W-21S	B1
800	WLNG	60090	2755	15W-18N	A3
10200	MNSR	46321	3510		E4
W Oxford Pl					
10	MPPT	60056	2808	15W-14N	A4
Oxford Rd					
10	CPVL	60102	2748	33W-18N	A4
10	CPVL	60110	2748	33W-18N	A4
10	DndT	60102	2748	33W-18N	A4
10	DndT	60110	2748	33W-18N	A4
10	LKFT	60045	2593	11W-28N	C6
10	LKFT	60045	2594	10W-27N	A7
100	BGBK	60440	3269	22W-12S	D2
100	KLWH	60043	2812	3W-14N	D4
100	TRLK	60010	2643	26W-25N	D5
200	DSPN	60016	2862	14W-11N	C3
200	NBRN	60010	2697	25W-23N	E1
200	NBRN	60010	2698	25W-23N	A1
800	DRFD	60015	2704	10W-21N	A7
900	GNEN	60137	3025	21W-0S	D6
2100	DSPN	60018	2862	14W-9N	C7
6400	WLBK	60527	3146	15W-7S	B6
E Oxford Rd					
400	NBRN	60010	2698	25W-23N	A2
Oxford St					
10	RGMW	60008	2805	20W-14N	E4
500	ELGN	60123	2854	34W-10N	E6
900	DRGV	60516	3144	19W-7S	C6
1400	BRLT	60103	2967	28W-4N	A3
1400	CLSM	60103	2967	28W-4N	A3
1400	CLSM	60188	2967	28W-4N	A3
7000	BGVW	60455	3210	8W-10S	E5
8700	WDRG	60517	3206	20W-10S	A5
10200	WSTR	60154	3087	13W-1S	A2
10700	WSTR	60154	3086	13W-1S	E1
Oxford Farm Ln					
-	WcnT	60042	2586	28W-28N	E5
28300	ISLK	60042	2586	28W-28N	E5
28300	ISLK	60051	2586	28W-28N	E5
28300	WcnT	60051	2586	28W-28N	E5
Oxfordshire Ln					
3200	SPGV	60081	2413	32W-39N	C5
Oxhill Ct					
2300	SMBG	60194	2857	26W-11N	E4
Oxley Ct					
1500	WLNG	60090	2754	16W-18N	D4
Oxmoor Ct					
500	SCRL	60175	2964	36W-5N	A2
Oxnard Ct					
-	RNPK	60443	3593	7W-27S	C4
Oxnard Dr					
1600	DRGV	60516	3144	20W-7S	B6
2100	DRGV	60516	3143	21W-7S	E6
Oxo Dr					
-	NlxT	60448	3502	14W-24S	D5
-	NlxT	60451	3502	14W-24S	D5
11900	MKNA	60448	3502	14W-24S	D5
Oyster Bay					
10	LKMR	60051	2529	28W-33N	E3
Ozanam Av					
9500	MaiT	60025	2864	9W-11N	C2
9500	MaiT	60053	2864	9W-12N	C2
9500	MNGV	60053	2864	9W-12N	C2
N Ozanam Av					
800	CHCG	60068	2918	9W-8N	C2
800	CHCG	60631	2918	9W-8N	C2
800	PKRG	60068	2918	9W-8N	C2
3200	EDPK	60707	2974	9W-4N	C4
4000	CHCG	60634	2974	9W-5N	C1
4000	CHCG	60706	2974	9W-5N	C2
4000	NRDG	60634	2974	9W-5N	C1
4000	NRDG	60706	2974	9W-5N	C1
4800	NRDG	60706	2918	9W-6N	C7
5100	CHCG	60656	2918	9W-6N	C6
5100	CHCG	60706	2918	9W-6N	C6
6900	PKRG	60631	2918	9W-8N	C1
8000	NLES	60068	2864	9W-10N	C6
8000	NLES	60714	2864	9W-10N	C5
8000	PKRG	60068	2864	9W-10N	C6
8200	MaiT	60714	2864	9W-10N	C5
Ozark Av					
15900	TYPK	60477	3424	9W-19S	D2
N Ozark Av					
-	PKRG	60068	2918	9W-8N	C2
3200	CHCG	60634	2974	9W-4N	C3
3200	EDPK	60707	2974	9W-4N	C4
4000	CHCG	60706	2974	9W-5N	C2
4000	NRDG	60706	2974	9W-5N	C1
4600	NRDG	60706	2918	9W-5N	C7
5600	CHCG	60656	2918	9W-7N	C5
6900	CHCG	60631	2918	9W-8N	C1
7000	PKRG	60631	2918	9W-8N	C1
7400	CHCG	60631	2864	9W-9N	C7
7400	PKRG	60068	2864	9W-9N	C7
7500	PKRG	60631	2864	9W-9N	C7
8000	NLES	60068	2864	9W-10N	C6
8000	NLES	60714	2864	9W-10N	C5
8000	PKRG	60068	2864	9W-10N	C6
8700	MNGV	60053	2864	9W-10N	C4
8700	MNGV	60714	2864	9W-10N	C4
Ozark Dr					
300	BGBK	60440	3268	23W-11S	E1
Ozark Pkwy					
1900	ALGN	60102	2748	32W-20N	B1
Ozark St					
8800	MNGV	60714	2864	9W-11N	C4
8800	NLES	60053	2864	9W-11N	C4
8800	NLES	60714	2864	9W-11N	C4
8900	MNGV	60053	2864	9W-11N	C3
Ozier Dr					
200	BTVA	60510	3020	34W-0S	C7
P					
Pace Av					
3300	PKCY	60085	2536	12W-33N	A3
3300	WKGN	60085	2536	12W-33N	A3
Pacer Tr					
10	SBTN	60010	2803	27W-14N	A5
W Pacesetter Pkwy					
400	RVDL	60827	3350	0W-15S	B2
Pacific Av					
-	GRNE	60031	2478	13W-35N	E6
800	HFET	60169	2857	26W-11N	E3
800	HFET	60194	2857	26W-11N	E3
800	SMWD	60107	2857	26W-11N	E4
3400	WkgT	60031	2479	13W-35N	A6
3400	WkgT	60085	2479	13W-35N	A6
3600	GRNE	60031	2479	13W-35N	A6
9600	FNPK	60131	2973	12W-4N	B3
N Pacific Av					
3200	EDPK	60171	2974	9W-4N	B4
3200	EDPK	60707	2974	9W-4N	B4
3600	CHCG	60634	2974	10W-4N	B2
5200	CHCG	60656	2918	10W-6N	B6
5200	LydT	60656	2918	10W-6N	B6
5200	NpkT	60656	2918	10W-6N	B6
W Pacific Av					
500	WKGN	60085	2480	10W-35N	A6
2800	WKGN	60085	2479	12W-35N	B6
3300	GRNE	60031	2479	12W-35N	A6
3300	WkgT	60031	2479	12W-35N	A6
12500	WkgT	60085	2479	12W-35N	B6
Pacific Ct					
400	WLNG	60090	2754	16W-17N	D5
9500	BRRG	60527	3208	16W-11S	A6
Pacific Dr					
200	BGBK	60440	3269	22W-11S	C1
300	BGBK	60440	3205	22W-11S	C7
500	NPVL	60563	3141	27W-6S	B4
S Pacific Dr					
11200	WRTH	60482	3274	9W-13S	E3
Pacific Rd					
2700	NCHI	60088	2593	11W-30N	C3
Pacific St					
10	FKFT	60423	3591	12W-26S	D2
Packard Dr					
-	BLID	60406	3349	2W-15S	B2
600	ELGN	60120	2855	32W-10N	D6
Packard Ln					
1900	GRNE	60031	2478	15W-36N	A4
S Packers Av					
4000	CHCG	60609	3091	1W-4S	D7
Packford Ln					
2700	AURA	60502	3079	32W-3S	B7
Paddington Av					
1700	NPVL	60563	3140	29W-5S	C4
Paddington Cres					
10200	MNSR	46321	3510		C5
Paddington Ct					
-	AURA	60505	3139	33W-5S	B3
Paddington Ln					
200	BGBK	60440	3268	25W-12S	B2
Paddington Rd					
8100	WDRG	60517	3206	20W-9S	A3
Paddock					
10	LMNT	60439	3272	15W-13S	B5
E Paddock Av					
9800	BHPK	60087	2480	9W-37N	C2
W Paddock Av					
10000	BHPK	60087	2480	10W-37N	B2
Paddock Cir					
200	GLHT	60139	2969	23W-3N	A6
Paddock Ct					
10	HNWD	60047	2644	23W-25N	D4
1200	AURA	60502	3078	34W-3S	E6
1800	NPVL	60565	3204	25W-9S	C4
1800	RLKP	60030	2532	22W-31N	B7
1900	WHTN	60187	3024	24W-0N	D4
2200	GNVA	60134	3019	36W-1N	D3
11000	ODPK	60467	3423	13W-18S	A1
Paddock Dr					
800	CLSM	60188	2967	27W-3N	C5
1400	GNVW	60025	2810	9W-15N	C2
E Paddock Dr					
1000	PLTN	60074	2753	19W-16N	C7
S Paddock Dr					
1200	WLNG	60090	2755	15W-16N	A7
W Paddock Dr					
500	WLNG	60090	2755	15W-16N	A7
Paddock Ln					
200	CmpT	60175	2961	42W-5N	C2
600	BTVA	60510	3019	36W-0S	E7
600	LYVL	60048	2591	16W-27N	E7
1600	LKFT	60045	2703	12W-23N	B1
1900	WHTN	60187	3024	24W-0N	D4
15300	HMGN	60491	3343	16W-18S	E7
25000	LKBN	60010	2643	27W-25N	C5
25000	TRLK	60010	2643	27W-25N	C5
Paddock Pl					
1300	BRLT	60103	2910	30W-6N	B7
1300	BRLT	60103	2966	30W-6N	B1
Paddock Rd					
800	BtnT	60081	2414	30W-40N	B3
800	FXLK	60081	2414	29W-40N	C3
Paddock St					
10	OswT	60538	3200	36W-10S	A7
E Paddock St					
10	CLLK	60014	2640	35W-25N	B4
W Paddock St					
10	CLLK	60014	2640	35W-25N	A4
12200	BHPK	60087	2479	12W-37N	B2
12200	WKGN	60087	2479	12W-37N	C2
Padre Ln					
-	ODPK	60467	3423	13W-21S	B6
Padre Island Dr					
-	PGGV	60140	2797	42W-15N	D5
Paganica Dr					
10	BNHL	60010	2697	27W-20N	C7
10	BNHL	60010	2750	27W-20N	C1
Page Av					
100	JLET	60432	3499	22W-23S	C4
100	JltT	60432	3499	22W-23S	C4
600	ELGN	60120	2855	33W-12N	B1
14100	DXMR	60426	3349	2W-16S	D4
14700	HRVY	60426	3349	2W-18S	D7
15600	HRVY	60426	3427	2W-18S	D1
16000	MKHM	60426	3427	2W-19S	D2
16000	MKHM	60428	3427	2W-19S	D2
16700	HLCT	60429	3427	2W-20S	D4
18500	HMWD	60430	3507	2W-22S	D1
N Page Av					
3200	RVGV	60171	2974	10W-4N	B4
3600	CHCG	60634	2974	10W-4N	B2
Page Ct					
1000	NPVL	60540	3141	27W-6S	B5
12900	BLID	60406	3277	2W-15S	D7
18300	HMWD	60430	3427	2W-22S	D7
Page Pl					
1900	NndT	60050	2585	30W-29N	E4
Page St					
-	BLID	60827	3277	2W-14S	D5
10	MltT	60190	3023	26W-0N	E5
100	WHTN	60187	3023	26W-0S	E7
100	WNFD	60190	3023	26W-0N	E5
12900	BLID	60406	3277	2W-15S	D7
12900	CTPK	60406	3277	2W-15S	D7
12900	CTPK	60827	3277	2W-15S	D7
N Page St					
200	HRVD	60033	2406	50W-38N	A6
200	MRGO	60152	2634	49W-26N	B2
1300	MRGO	60152	2578	49W-27N	B7
3300	ANHT	60004	2754	17W-17N	B4
S Page St					
100	HRVD	60033	2406	50W-38N	A7
100	MRGO	60152	2634	49W-26N	B3
11900	CHCG	60643	3277	2W-14S	D5
11900	CTPK	60643	3277	2W-14S	D5
11900	CTPK	60827	3277	2W-14S	D5
12600	CTPK	60406	3277	2W-15S	D7
12800	BLID	60406	3277	2W-15S	D7
12800	BLID	60827	3277	2W-15S	D7
Pagles Rd					
4000	DhmT	60033	2463	53W-37N	A1
Pagni Dr					
1100	EGVV	60007	2861	17W-10N	C5
Pagosa Springs Dr					
2200	AURA	60503	3265	32W-11S	C1
Pahl Rd					
700	EGVV	60007	2914	19W-9N	B1
Paige Ln					
800	HPSR	60140	2795	46W-15N	E3
Paige St					
-	PLNO	60545	3260	45W-14S	B7
Paine Av					
800	LNHT	60046	2418	19W-39N	B5
Paine St					
200	SEGN	60177	2908	35W-8N	B4
Painted Desert Ct					
10600	HTLY	60142	2745	39W-20N	C1
Painted Lake Ct					
1000	LKVL	60046	2417	22W-39N	C5
Painted Lakes Blvd					
-	LKVL	60046	2417	22W-39N	B4
-	LkvT	60046	2417	22W-39N	C5
Painters Lake Rd					
2000	HDPK	60035	2703	10W-22N	E4
2000	HDPK	60035	2704	10W-22N	A5
Paisley Ct					
1400	HFET	60010	2751	24W-16N	B7
Pakan Dr					
100	SchT	60174	2908	34W-7N	D5
Palace Ct					
500	SMBG	60194	2857	26W-11N	E4
Palace St					
400	AURA	60506	3138	35W-6S	A6
Palace Green Ln					
200	YkTp	60523	3084	19W-2S	D4
Paladino Dr					
10	RMVL	60446	3339	26W-17S	E5
Palamino Ct					
1200	BRLT	60103	2910	29W-6N	E7
Palamino Dr					
1200	MchT	60051	2529	30W-33N	A3
Palamino Pl					
100	WHTN	60187	3082	24W-2S	C3
Palamino St					
900	CLSM	60188	2967	26W-3N	E5
W Palatine Av					
6400	CHCG	60631	2919	8W-7N	A3
6400	CHCG	60646	2919	8W-7N	A3
6600	CHCG	60631	2918	8W-7N	E3
7700	PKRG	60068	2918	9W-7N	C3
7700	PKRG	60631	2918	9W-7N	C3
Palatine Rd					
-	IVNS	60010	2804	24W-15N	B1
-	SBTN	60010	2804	24W-15N	B1
1300	HFET	60010	2804	24W-15N	B1
1300	HFET	60192	2804	24W-15N	B1
E Palatine Rd					
-	ANHT	60004	2806	19W-16N	D1
-	NfdT	60090	2809	13W-15N	A1
-	PLTN	60004	2806	19W-16N	D1
-	PTHT	60070	2809	13W-15N	A1
-	WhlT	60090	2809	13W-15N	A1
10	ANHT	60004	2807	16W-15N	C1
10	BNHL	60010	2803	27W-15N	B1
10	BrnT	60010	2803	27W-15N	B1
10	IVNS	60010	2803	26W-16N	E1
10	PLTN	60067	2805	20W-15N	E1
100	PTHT	60070	2808	15W-16N	A1
300	PLTN	60067	2806	20W-16N	A1
300	SBTN	60010	2803	27W-16N	B1
300	WLNG	60070	2808	15W-16N	B1
300	WLNG	60090	2808	15W-16N	B1
1000	PLTN	60074	2806	19W-15N	C2
2600	PTHT	60004	2807	16W-16N	E1
2600	PTHT	60070	2807	16W-16N	E1
W Palatine Rd					
-	ANHT	60004	2806	18W-16N	E1
-	HFET	60192	2804	25W-15N	A1
-	PLTN	60074	2806	19W-16N	D1
-	WLNG	60090	2808	14W-16N	C1
10	ANHT	60004	2807	17W-16N	A1
10	IVNS	60010	2804	25W-15N	A1
10	PLTN	60067	2805	21W-16N	E1
10	PTHT	60070	2807	15W-15N	E1
10	PTHT	60070	2808	15W-15N	A1
10	SBTN	60010	2804	25W-15N	A1
200	PTHT	60004	2807	16W-16N	E1
300	BNHL	60010	2803	25W-15N	E1
300	BrnT	60010	2803	25W-15N	E1
300	IVNS	60010	2803	25W-15N	E1
400	WLNG	60070	2808	15W-16N	B1
700	PltT	60067	2805	21W-16N	E1
1200	IVNS	60067	2805	21W-16N	D1
1800	IVNS	60067	2804	23W-15N	E1
2400	HFET	60010	2804	23W-15N	D1
2400	IVNS	60192	2804	24W-15N	D1
Palatine Frontage Rd					
300	WLNG	60090	2808	14W-16N	B1
E Palatine Frontage Rd					
10	WLNG	60090	2808	14W-15N	C1
Palazzo Ct					
2400	BFGV	60089	2701	16W-22N	E3
Palazzo Dr					
10	ADSN	60101	2970	19W-3N	D5
2400	BFGV	60089	2701	16W-22N	E3
2500	BFGV	60069	2701	16W-22N	E3
2500	LNSH	60069	2701	16W-22N	E3
Palisades Av					
13900	HTLY	60142	2744	43W-19N	A2
14000	HTLY	60140	2744	43W-19N	A2
Palisades Dr					
10	OKBK	60523	3086	15W-1S	B1
1300	BGBK	60490	3339	28W-15S	A1
W Palisades Rd					
3100	MTPK	60803	3276	3W-13S	E4
Palisades Ln					
10	ODHL	60013	2641	31W-26N	C3

STREET Block	City	ZIP	Map#	CGS	Grid
Palisades Ln					
100	CTSD	60525	3147	12W-7S	B5
100	LynT	60525	3147	13W-7S	B5
1500	HFET	60192	2856	31W-12N	A2
Palisades Pt					
300	SMBG	60194	2859	22W-10N	C4
Palisades Rd					
8800	DGvT	60527	3207	16W-10S	E5
9500	BRRG	60527	3207	16W-11S	E6
E Palladium Dr					
400	JLET	60435	3498	26W-23S	A3
W Palladium Dr					
400	JLET	60435	3498	26W-23S	A3
Palm Ct					
500	CLLK	60014	2693	36W-22N	E3
1100	NPVL	60540	3141	28W-7S	B7
7900	ODPK	60462	3346	9W-18S	C7
15900	CTHL	60403	3418	25W-19S	B2
E Palm Ct					
200	RLKB	60073	2475	22W-36N	B4
Palm Dr					
100	DRPK	60010	2752	23W-18N	A2
100	PltT	60010	2752	23W-18N	A2
1100	WLNG	60090	2754	16W-17N	E4
7600	ODPK	60462	3346	9W-18S	D7
16000	CTHL	60403	3418	25W-19S	B2
W Palm Dr					
600	GNWD	60425	3428	0W-21S	B7
1700	MPPT	60056	2861	17W-11N	C3
Palm Ln					
3000	NHBK	60062	2756	11W-16N	D7
Palm St					
4900	NndT	60051	2642	29W-27N	D1
5200	NndT	60010	2642	29W-26N	D2
Palma Ln					
6400	MNGV	60053	2865	8W-11N	A2
7200	MNGV	60053	2864	9W-11N	D2
Palma Pl					
4400	SKOK	60076	2866	5W-11N	A2
5200	SKOK	60077	2865	6W-11N	D2
Palm Canyon Dr					
3600	NHBK	60062	2756	12W-17N	B4
Palmer Av					
300	HIWD	60040	2704	9W-23N	D2
500	AURA	60506	3199	38W-8S	A1
600	RMVL	60446	3340	24W-15S	D3
800	AraT	60506	3199	38W-8S	A2
2400	MonT	60449	3682	7W-30S	E3
2400	MonT	60466	3682	7W-30S	E3
2400	UYPK	60449	3682	7W-30S	E3
2400	UYPK	60466	3682	7W-30S	E3
9600	FNPK	60131	2973	12W-2N	C6
9600	FNPK	60164	2973	12W-2N	C6
9600	LydT	60164	2973	12W-2N	C6
18400	HMWD	60430	3507	2W-22S	C1
E Palmer Av					
10	ADSN	60101	2970	18W-3N	E6
10	NHLK	60164	2972	13W-2N	E6
300	ADSN	60101	2971	17W-3N	A6
300	LydT	60164	2973	13W-2N	A6
300	NHLK	60164	2973	13W-2N	A6
S Palmer Av					
-	POSN	60469	3349	3W-16S	B3
14800	POSN	60426	3349	3W-17S	B5
W Palmer Av					
10	NHLK	60164	2972	14W-2N	D6
10000	LydT	60164	2973	12W-2N	B6
10400	NHLK	60164	2973	13W-2N	A6
Palmer Blvd					
17200	HLCT	60429	3427	3W-20S	B5
17200	HLCT	60430	3427	3W-20S	B5
17300	HMWD	60430	3427	3W-20S	B5
Palmer Cir					
100	VNHL	60061	2647	17W-27N	C1
2100	AURA	60564	3202	30W-10S	C5
2200	NPVL	60564	3202	30W-10S	B5
18600	HMWD	60430	3507	2W-22S	C1
Palmer Ct					
10	BGBK	60490	3267	26W-11S	E2
100	YKVL	60560	3261	42W-13S	C6
300	RVWD	60015	2755	13W-20N	E1
300	RVWD	60015	2756	13W-20N	A1
1100	CLLK	60014	2639	37W-24N	B7
1100	FSMR	60422	3507	3W-22S	A1
4000	AURA	60564	3202	30W-9S	B4
W Palmer Ct					
24800	AntT	60002	2416	25W-40N	B4
Palmer Dr					
-	BGBK	60490	3267	26W-11S	E1
2000	AURA	60564	3202	30W-9S	B5
2000	NPVL	60564	3202	30W-9S	B5
2000	SMBG	60173	2805	21W-13N	C6
9700	LKWD	60014	2692	38W-23N	D1
N Palmer Dr					
100	EMHT	60126	3028	15W-1N	A2
S Palmer Dr					
100	BGBK	60490	3267	26W-12S	E2
100	EMHT	60126	3028	15W-1N	A2
Palmer Ln					
2000	GNOK	60048	2592	14W-29N	D3
E Palmer Ln					
1500	PLTN	60074	2753	19W-18N	C4
Palmer Pl					
1000	WKGN	60085	2480	10W-35N	A7
W Palmer Sq					
3000	CHCG	60647	2976	4W-2N	D6
Palmer St					
1000	DRGV	60516	3144	19W-7S	C6
W Palmer St					
2300	CHCG	60647	2977	2W-2N	A6
2800	CHCG	60647	2976	3W-2N	E6
3900	CHCG	60639	2976	5W-2N	A6
6200	CHCG	60639	2975	8W-2N	A6
6300	CHCG	60707	2975	8W-2N	A6
6800	CHCG	60707	2974	9W-2N	D6
7100	EDPK	60707	2974	9W-2N	D6
8600	RVGV	60171	2973	11W-2N	E6
8600	RVGV	60171	2974	10W-2N	A6
9000	FNPK	60131	2973	11W-2N	D6
9000	FNPK	60160	2973	11W-2N	D6
9000	FNPK	60171	2973	11W-2N	D6
9000	MLPK	60160	2973	11W-2N	D6
9000	RVGV	60131	2973	11W-2N	D6
9000	RVGV	60160	2973	11W-2N	D6
Palmer C Singleton Jr Dr					
-	MNSR	46321	3510		E4
Palmer Ranch Dr					
11000	NLNX	60451	3588	19W-27S	E4
Palmetto Ct					
1100	NPVL	60540	3141	28W-7S	B7
Palmgren Ct					
200	BFGV	60089	2754	16W-17N	D5
Palmgren Dr					
1900	GNVW	60025	2810	8W-13N	D7
E Palmieri Cir					
800	PKCY	60085	2536	12W-33N	B4
N Palmieri Cir					
3200	PKCY	60085	2536	12W-33N	B4
3200	WKGN	60085	2536	12W-33N	B4
S Palmieri Cir					
3200	PKCY	60085	2536	12W-33N	B4
W Palmieri Cir					
800	PKCY	60085	2536	12W-33N	B4
Palm Springs Ln					
2600	AURA	60502	3139	32W-6S	D4
2700	NpvT	60502	3139	32W-6S	D4
Palo Alto Dr					
-	RNPK	60443	3593	7W-27S	C3
Palomino Ct					
300	RLKP	60030	2589	22W-30N	C1
700	SYHW	60118	2799	37W-15N	D4
14500	HMGN	60491	3344	15W-17S	B5
Palomino Dr					
-	PLNO	60545	3260	46W-13S	A5
10	CmpT	60175	2906	41W-6N	A6
100	CmpT	60175	2962	40W-6N	B1
200	LslT	60540	3204	23W-8S	E2
200	LslT	60565	3204	23W-8S	E2
200	NPVL	60540	3204	23W-8S	E2
200	NPVL	60565	3204	23W-8S	E2
1500	AURA	60502	3139	32W-5S	D3
1600	NpvT	60502	3139	32W-5S	D3
S Palomino Dr					
18700	TroT	60404	3495	32W-22S	D2
Palomino Ln					
10	OswT	60543	3264	34W-13S	E5
N Palos Av					
900	PLTN	60067	2752	22W-17N	A5
1200	PltT	60067	2752	22W-17N	A5
1300	PltT	60010	2752	22W-17N	A5
1300	PltT	60074	2752	22W-17N	A5
S Palos Av					
12700	PSHT	60463	3274	9W-15S	E7
W Palos Av					
7200	PSHT	60463	3274	9W-15S	E7
7900	PSPK	60464	3274	9W-14S	C5
Palos Ct					
10	BGBK	60440	3268	24W-11S	D2
S Palos Dr					
10700	PSHL	60465	3274	10W-12S	B2
Palos Pl					
10500	PSHL	60465	3274	9W-12S	C2
Palos Rd					
300	GLNC	60022	2758	5W-17N	E5
Palos Springs Dr					
8800	ODPK	60462	3346	11W-15S	A1
Palos West Dr					
10400	PlsT	60464	3273	13W-14S	A7
Palwaukee Dr					
400	WLNG	60090	2755	14W-17N	C5
Pam Ct					
500	WLNG	60090	2754	16W-18N	E3
Pam Rd					
-	ELGN	60123	2801	33W-13N	A7
Pam Anne Dr					
1300	GNVW	60025	2809	10W-13N	E5
Pamarco Dr					
200	BTVA	60510	3078	35W-1S	B3
Pamela Cir					
400	HNDL	60521	3146	15W-5S	B4
Pamela Ct					
200	ANTH	60002	2357	23W-42N	E5
500	WnfT	60185	3081	28W-1S	A3
600	WCDA	60084	2588	25W-28N	A6
1300	NPVL	60540	3142	25W-7S	B6
3200	JLET	60431	3497	28W-23S	B4
4500	LGGV	60047	2700	19W-23N	B2
16100	OKFT	60452	3425	6W-19S	E2
Pamela Dr					
10	BNVL	60106	2972	15W-4N	A4
100	BGBK	60440	3205	22W-10S	B6
200	AddT	60126	2972	15W-4N	A4
1500	ELGN	60123	2854	35W-11N	B5
7600	MchT	60097	2469	36W-34N	D7
Pamela Dr N					
100	CHHT	60411	3508	1W-23S	A4
200	BlmT	60411	3508	1W-23S	A4
Pamela Dr S					
10	CHHT	60411	3508	1W-24S	A4
Pamela Ln					
6400	CHRG	60415	3275	8W-12S	B1
10800	ODPK	60467	3423	13W-21S	A5
Pamela Pl					
-	DLTN	60419	3350	0E-16S	D2
W Pamela Pl					
18500	WrnT	60031	2476	18W-36N	E4
Pamela Rd					
10	LKZH	60047	2698	24W-23N	C2
9400	GwdT	60097	2468	38W-35N	E6
9400	WRLK	60097	2468	38W-35N	E6
Pamela St					
500	GLBT	60136	2799	37W-15N	C3
Pamella Ln					
400	NfdT	60062	2756	12W-18N	B2
4000	NHBK	60062	2756	12W-18N	B2
Pampas Cir					
1800	BGBK	60490	3267	27W-12S	C3
1800	WldT	60490	3267	27W-12S	C3
Pampas Ct					
10	BGBK	60490	3267	26W-12S	D3
Pampas St					
1700	BGBK	60490	3267	27W-12S	C3
1800	WldT	60490	3267	27W-12S	C3
Pampered Chef Ln					
10	ADSN	60101	2969	21W-3N	E5
Pan Am Blvd					
2400	EGVV	60007	2915	16W-7N	E4
Panama Av					
300	HPSR	60140	2795	46W-15N	E3
300	HPSR	60140	2796	46W-15N	A3
E Panama Av					
100	HPSR	60140	2795	46W-15N	E3
N Panama Av					
3200	CHCG	60634	2974	10W-4N	B3
3200	RVGV	60171	2974	10W-4N	B4
3200	RVGV	60634	2974	10W-4N	B4
5400	CHCG	60656	2918	10W-6N	B5
5400	LydT	60656	2918	10W-6N	B5
Panasonic Ct					
-	FNPK	60131	2973	11W-3N	D5
Pandola Av					
-	JLET	60435	3497	28W-22S	A2
3200	JLET	60431	3497	28W-22S	A2
3800	JLET	60431	3496	29W-22S	E2
Panorama Ct					
700	AURA	60502	3139	32W-7S	C6
W Panorama Dr					
-	PltT	60067	2752	22W-17N	B5
800	PLTN	60067	2752	22W-17N	B5
Panorama Ln					
1300	GRNE	60031	2476	18W-35N	E6
1300	WrnT	60031	2476	18W-35N	E6
Panoramic Dr					
10200	FNPK	60131	2973	12W-4N	A3
Pansey Ln					
100	MTSN	60443	3593	7W-26S	C2
Panther Blvd					
-	RDLK	60073	2531	23W-34N	E1
Panther Dr					
10	RDLK	60073	2531	23W-34N	D1
W Pantigo Ln					
15200	HmrT	60491	3420	19W-19S	E2
Papago Ct					
10	NPVL	60563	3141	26W-5S	D2
Papaw Dr					
5200	NPVL	60564	3266	29W-13S	D5
Papermill Hill Dr					
600	BTVA	60510	3078	34W-2S	C4
600	BtvT	60510	3078	34W-2S	C4
Papoose Ct					
800	CLSM	60188	2967	26W-3N	E5
Papoose Rd					
1700	CPVL	60110	2748	32W-18N	C4
Papoose Lake Ct					
21500	LktT	60403	3417	26W-19S	D3
Papoose Lake Dr					
21400	LktT	60403	3417	26W-19S	D3
Pappas Ct					
1200	ELGN	60123	2800	35W-13N	B7
Pappas Dr					
1300	ELGN	60123	2800	35W-13N	A7
Papworth St					
10	BmdT	60108	2912	25W-6N	C7
10	BmdT	60172	2912	25W-6N	C7
10	MltT	60187	3024	25W-0N	B4
10	MltT	60188	3024	25W-0N	B4
200	ROSL	60172	2912	25W-6N	C7
300	WHTN	60187	3024	25W-0N	B4
Par Ct					
6000	GRNE	60031	2534	16W-33N	D3
Par Dr					
700	ALGN	60102	2693	37W-20N	C7
900	ALGN	60102	2746	37W-20N	C1
Par Ln					
10	ADSN	60143	2970	21W-5N	A1
10	BmdT	60143	2970	21W-5N	A1
100	BmdT	60143	2969	21W-5N	E1
Parade Ct					
20300	MngT	60152	2578	49W-28N	C5
Paradise Av					
1500	MLPK	60160	3029	13W-1N	A2
Paradise Cir					
2400	JLET	60586	3415	32W-20S	C6
Paradise Ct					
7000	JLET	60586	3415	33W-20S	B6
Paradise Ln					
-	BtlT	53104	2358		E3
600	LYVL	60048	2591	17W-29N	B4
7300	ODPK	60462	3346	9W-18S	E6
7300	OrlT	60462	3346	9W-18S	E6
W Paradise Ln					
20800	LkvT	60046	2475	21W-36N	E4
Paradise Pkwy					
200	OSWG	60543	3263	38W-13S	B6
Paradise Canyon Ct					
3900	AURA	60564	3202	30W-9S	B4
Parador Dr					
3700	NPVL	60564	3267	28W-11S	A2
E Parallel St					
300	PLTN	60067	2806	20W-15N	A1
300	PLTN	60074	2806	20W-15N	A1
Paramount Dr					
100	WDDL	60191	2970	18W-5N	E1
Paramount Pkwy					
900	BTVA	60510	3021	33W-0S	A7
1400	GnvT	60134	3021	33W-0S	A7
1400	GnvT	60510	3021	33W-0S	A7
Parc Ct					
700	LIHL	60156	2692	38W-22N	E4
Par Four Ct					
2400	JLET	60436	3497	27W-24S	D6
Par Four Ln					
2600	JLET	60436	3497	27W-24S	D6
Paris Av					
600	OSWG	60543	3264	35W-11S	B2
N Paris Av					
3000	RVGV	60171	2974	10W-3N	B4
3100	RVGV	60634	2974	10W-3N	B4
4400	CHCG	60634	2974	10W-5N	B1
4400	NRDG	60706	2974	10W-5N	B1
5400	CHCG	60656	2918	10W-6N	B5
N Paris Dr					
-	BHPK	60099	2421	13W-39N	A4
-	WDWH	60083	2421	13W-39N	A4
Paris Ln					
500	HFET	60169	2858	24W-10N	E5
500	SMBG	60194	2858	24W-10N	E5
Paris Rd					
2800	OMFD	60461	3507	3W-25S	A7
Park					
-	HGKN	60525	3147	12W-7S	C5
N Park					
-	DSPN	60018	2917	12W-8N	C2
S Park					
-	DSPN	60018	2917	12W-8N	C2
Park Av					
-	AntT	60081	2415	28W-38N	A6
-	BDWD	60408	3942	31W-41S	B5
-	DndT	60118	2801	33W-14N	A5
-	FXLK	60081	2415	28W-38N	A6
-	MKNA	60448	3503	11W-23S	E3
-	PvsT	60513	3087	11W-2S	E4
10	CNHL	60514	3145	17W-5S	C2
10	CRY	60013	2695	31W-24N	D1
10	CTCY	60409	3429	2E-19S	C1
10	FTPK	60130	3030	9W-0N	C5
10	GLNC	60022	2758	6W-17N	D5
10	GYLK	60030	2532	20W-33N	E4
10	HDPK	60035	2705	8W-22N	A4
10	LKVL	60046	2475	22W-37N	B1
10	LKZH	60047	2698	23W-22N	E3
10	LynT	60558	3209	11W-8S	E1
10	RVFT	60130	3030	9W-0N	C5
100	BMDL	60108	2969	23W-5N	A1
100	BRTN	60010	2750	25W-18N	E2
100	BRTN	60010	2751	25W-18N	A2
100	CPVL	60110	2748	33W-17N	A6
100	DndT	60110	2748	33W-18N	A6
100	EVTN	60201	2812	3W-13N	D7
100	LKFT	60045	2593	11W-28N	C6
100	LKFT	60045	2594	10W-27N	A7
100	SRGV	60554	3135	42W-6S	D5
100	WCDA	60084	2643	26W-27N	E1
100	WLMT	60091	2812	3W-13N	D6
100	WLMT	60201	2812	3W-13N	D7
200	ANTH	60002	2357	23W-42N	E6
200	HDPK	60035	2704	8W-22N	E4
200	SCRL	60174	2964	35W-3N	B6
Park Av					
200	SEGN	60177	2908	34W-8N	D4
200	WLNG	60090	2755	13W-17N	D4
300	GNVA	60134	3020	34W-1N	D3
300	GYLK	60030	2533	20W-32N	A4
400	ADSN	60101	2969	21W-3N	D6
400	AlqT	60021	2696	29W-22N	C4
400	BmdT	60101	2969	21W-3N	D6
400	CNHL	60559	3145	17W-5S	C3
400	RVFT	60305	3030	9W-0N	C4
400	SchT	60174	2908	35W-6N	B6
400	WTMT	60559	3145	17W-5S	C3
500	FXLK	60020	2473	28W-35N	A5
500	WPHR	60096	2363	9W-43N	C5
700	TNTN	60476	3428	0E-20S	E5
700	WNKA	60093	2812	4W-16N	B1
900	DRFD	60015	2703	11W-21N	E6
1000	FDHT	60411	3509	1E-25S	A7
1000	NCHI	60064	2537	10W-32N	A5
1000	WCDA	60084	2588	25W-28N	B6
1000	WKGN	60085	2537	10W-32N	A5
1200	CHHT	60411	3508	1W-25S	B7
1400	CHHT	60411	3596	1W-25S	B1
1500	EDPK	60707	3030	9W-1N	C1
1500	RVFT	60707	3030	9W-1N	C1
1600	HRPK	60133	2911	27W-8N	D2
2200	FTPK	60130	3088	9W-2S	C2
2200	FTPK	60546	3088	9W-2S	C2
2200	NRIV	60546	3088	9W-2S	C2
2500	RVSD	60546	3088	9W-2S	C3
2600	BKFD	60513	3087	11W-3S	E5
3700	CteT	60417	3596	1W-28S	A7
3700	CteT	60475	3596	1W-28S	A7
3700	STGR	60475	3596	1W-28S	A7
4500	BKFD	60513	3147	11W-4S	E1
5200	DRGV	60515	3144	19W-5S	D3
5800	BKLY	60163	3028	14W-1N	C2
6200	BRWN	60402	3089	7W-3S	B4
6200	CCRO	60402	3089	7W-3S	B4
6200	CCRO	60804	3089	7W-3S	B4
6200	DRGV	60516	3144	19W-6S	D5
6200	MNGV	60053	2865	7W-10N	A5
7200	SMMT	60501	3148	9W-5S	D2
7300	DGvT	60561	3207	18W-8S	A1
7300	DRN	60561	3207	18W-8S	A1
7600	SKOK	60077	2865	6W-9N	D6
13800	CHCG	60419	3350	0E-16S	D2
13800	CHCG	60827	3350	0E-16S	D2
13800	DLTN	60419	3350	0E-16S	D3
14300	HRVY	60426	3350	0W-17S	B5
14300	HRVY	60827	3350	0W-17S	B5
14300	RVDL	60827	3350	0W-17S	B5
14700	OKFT	60452	3347	6W-17S	D5
15600	HRVY	60426	3428	1W-18S	A1
15900	HRVY	60426	3427	1W-19S	E2
16000	HRVY	60428	3427	1W-19S	E2
16000	MKHM	60426	3427	1W-19S	E2
16000	MKHM	60428	3427	1W-19S	E2
16500	HLCT	60426	3427	1W-19S	E3
16500	HLCT	60429	3427	1W-19S	E3
16500	HRVY	60429	3427	1W-19S	E3
17000	EHZC	60429	3427	2W-21S	D5
17000	LNSG	60438	3430	3E-20S	A4
17500	EHZC	60430	3427	2W-20S	D5
17900	HMWD	60430	3427	2W-21S	C7
18800	LNSG	60438	3510	3E-22S	A1
19400	LNSG	60411	3510	3E-23S	A2
19500	LYWD	60411	3510	3E-23S	A2
19800	LYWD	60411	3509	3E-23S	E4
E Park Av					
-	GNOK	60044	2592	14W-28N	D5
-	GNOK	60045	2592	14W-28N	D5
-	SRGV	60554	3135	42W-6S	D5
100	EMHT	60126	3027	17W-1N	C2
100	EMHT	60126	3028	15W-1N	B2
100	LYVL	60048	2591	16W-28N	E5
100	WHTN	60187	3082	24W-1S	C1
200	BMDL	60108	2969	22W-5N	B1
400	AURA	60505	3200	35W-8S	B2
800	LYVL	60048	2592	15W-28N	A5
1000	LbvT	60048	2592	14W-28N	C6
1100	GNOK	60048	2592	14W-28N	C6
28300	WcnT	60084	2642	28W-26N	E2
E Park Av SR-176					
-	GNOK	60044	2592	14W-28N	D5
-	GNOK	60045	2592	14W-28N	D5
100	LYVL	60048	2591	16W-28N	E5
800	LYVL	60048	2592	15W-28N	A5
1000	LbvT	60048	2592	14W-28N	C6
1100	GNOK	60048	2592	14W-28N	C6
N Park Av					
10	HNDL	60521	3146	15W-4S	B1
10	WKGN	60085	2537	10W-33N	A1
200	AURA	60506	3138	36W-6S	A4
400	AURA	60506	3137	36W-6S	E4
400	LMBD	60148	3026	20W-1N	B2
600	WPHR	60096	2363	9W-42N	C5
1000	PLTN	60067	2752	22W-17N	A5
1200	PltT	60067	2752	22W-17N	A5
34500	GrtT	60041	2473	26W-34N	E7
34500	GrtT	60041	2530	26W-34N	E1
38800	BHPK	60099	2422	9W-38N	C6
39200	LkvT	60046	2416	24W-39N	C5
40700	AntT	60002	2416	25W-40N	A2
41500	BtnT	60099	2422	9W-41N	C1
41500	WPHR	60096	2422	9W-41N	C1
41500	ZION	60099	2422	9W-41N	C1
42600	AntT	60002	2356	27W-42N	A5
S Park Av					
-	BRLT	60103	2911	28W-8N	A2
-	BtnT	60099	2422	9W-41N	C1
-	WPHR	60096	2422	9W-41N	C1
10	ADSN	60101	2970	18W-3N	E5
10	WKGN	60085	2537	10W-34N	A2
100	HRVD	60033	2464	50W-37N	B1
100	LMBD	60148	3026	20W-0N	B4
700	WPHR	60096	2363	9W-42N	C6
1100	SMWD	60107	2857	28W-9N	A7
1200	SMWD	60107	2911	28W-9N	A2
2100	BRLT	60107	2911	28W-9N	A2
5500	HNDL	60521	3146	15W-6S	B4
5800	MNGV	60053	2865	7W-10N	B4
6000	BRRG	60527	3146	15W-6S	B5
7200	BRRG	60527	3208	15W-8S	B1
8100	DGvT	60527	3208	15W-9S	B3
27500	CteT	60401	3774	0E-33S	E3
27500	WshT	60401	3774	0E-34S	E4
28700	BCHR	60401	3774	0E-34S	E4
W Park Av					
10	BFGV	60069	2701	16W-23N	D2
10	BFGV	60089	2701	16W-23N	D2
10	SRGV	60554	3135	42W-6S	C5
10	VrnT	60069	2701	16W-23N	D2
10	VrnT	60089	2701	16W-23N	D2
100	AURA	60506	3138	35W-7S	B6
100	BMDL	60108	2968	23W-5N	E1
W Park Av					
100	BMDL	60108	2969	23W-5N	A1
100	EMHT	60126	3027	16W-1N	E2
100	LYVL	60048	2591	17W-28N	B6
100	WHTN	60187	3082	24W-1S	C1
300	ADSN	60101	2970	19W-3N	D6
400	RDLK	60073	2531	23W-33N	E3
500	AURA	60506	3137	36W-7S	E6
500	PNFD	60544	3338	29W-18S	D7
800	JLET	60436	3498	25W-24S	C6
1500	MDLN	60060	2591	17W-28N	A6
5600	CCRO	60804	3089	7W-3S	C4
7800	NLES	60714	2864	9W-11N	B3
20500	FmtT	60060	2590	20W-28N	A6
20500	MDLN	60060	2590	20W-28N	A6
20600	FmtT	60060	2589	20W-28N	E6
24800	LkvT	60046	2416	24W-39N	B4
25000	AntT	60002	2357	25W-42N	B5
27100	AntT	60002	2415	27W-38N	C6
W Park Av SR-176					
100	LYVL	60048	2591	17W-28N	B6
1500	MDLN	60060	2591	17W-28N	A6
Park Av W					
600	HDPK	60035	2704	9W-22N	B4
Park Blvd					
10	MltT	60137	3083	22W-2S	B4
100	EGVV	60007	2914	20W-7N	B4
100	ITSC	60143	2914	20W-7N	B4
200	CLLK	60012	2640	34W-26N	C3
200	CLLK	60014	2640	34W-26N	C3
200	GNEN	60137	3083	22W-2S	C3
300	MltT	60137	3025	22W-1N	C2
400	MltT	60532	3083	22W-3S	B6
600	GLHT	60137	3025	22W-1N	C2
700	GLHT	60139	3025	22W-1N	C2
17700	LNSG	60438	3430	3E-20S	A5
Park Blvd CO-5					
10	MltT	60137	3083	22W-2S	B4
200	GNEN	60137	3083	22W-2S	C3
400	MltT	60532	3083	22W-3S	B6
E Park Blvd					
10	VLPK	60181	3027	17W-0N	B4
N Park Blvd					
10	GNEN	60137	3025	22W-0S	C7
10	SMWD	60107	2857	28W-11N	B4
300	HFET	60010	2857	28W-11N	B4
S Park Blvd					
10	GNEN	60137	3083	22W-1S	C2
300	MltT	60137	3083	22W-1S	C2
900	SMWD	60107	2857	28W-9N	A7
S Park Blvd CO-5					
400	GNEN	60137	3083	22W-1S	C2
400	MltT	60137	3083	22W-1S	C2
W Park Blvd					
10	VLPK	60181	3027	18W-0N	A4
300	LMBD	60148	3026	18W-0N	E4
300	LMBD	60181	3026	18W-0N	E4
300	VLPK	60181	3026	18W-0N	E4
W Park Cres					
18800	WrnT	60046	2476	18W-34N	D7
Park Ct					
10	GLHT	60139	3024	23W-2N	E1
10	ROSL	60172	2913	23W-7N	A4
100	BGBK	60440	3269	21W-11S	D1
100	GLBT	60136	2798	39W-16N	E2
200	BLWD	60104	3029	12W-0N	A4
400	FRGV	60021	2696	29W-22N	B3
3000	RGMW	60008	2806	19W-13N	C5
13000	CTWD	60445	3347	6W-15S	E1
W Park Ct					
25300	LkvT	60046	2474	25W-37N	A1
Park Dr					
-	CHCG	60611	3034	0E-0N	D3
-	DndT	60118	2801	33W-14N	A5
-	HNWD	60047	2644	24W-24N	C7
-	NBRN	60010	2644	24W-24N	C7
-	RVFT	60305	3030	9W-0N	C4
10	GNVW	60025	2810	9W-13N	B6
100	PTBR	60010	2642	29W-25N	C4
200	PltT	60067	2805	20W-13N	E7
300	MRGO	60152	2634	50W-26N	A3
300	NHBK	60062	2758	7W-17N	A6
400	PltT	60067	2806	20W-13N	A6
500	KLWH	60043	2812	4W-14N	C4
600	FSMR	60422	3507	3W-22S	B2
600	HMWD	60430	3507	3W-22S	B2
700	WLMT	60091	2812	4W-14N	C4
900	MLPK	60160	3029	11W-1N	E1
1100	WMTN	60481	3943	27W-39S	D1
1300	AURA	60505	3200	34W-9S	D4
1300	MTGY	60505	3200	34W-9S	D4
1300	MTGY	60538	3200	34W-9S	D4
1600	SMBG	60194	2858	25W-10N	B5
3100	WRLK	60097	2469	36W-35N	D7
3200	ISLK	60042	2586	28W-28N	D5
3600	OMFD	60461	3506	4W-24S	E4
3700	FSMR	60422	3506	4W-24S	E4
N Park Dr					
-	CHCG	60601	3034	0E-0N	C4
-	CHCG	60611	3034	0E-0N	C3
10	BtlT	60560	3261	41W-14S	E7
10	BtlT	60560	3262	41W-14S	A7
200	GNWD	60425	3508	0W-22S	C1
300	GNWD	60425	3428	0W-22S	C7
1300	RLKB	60073	2474	23W-35N	E6
1500	MPPT	60056	2808	13W-15N	E3
1600	MPPT	60056	2809	13W-15N	A2
1800	PTHT	60070	2809	13W-15N	A2
3000	NndT	60013	2641	31W-26N	D2
3000	NndT	60014	2641	31W-26N	D2
3000	ODHL	60013	2641	31W-26N	D2
3000	ODHL	60014	2641	31W-26N	D2
34800	GrtT	60041	2472	28W-34N	E7
34800	GrtT	60051	2472	28W-34N	E7
36100	WrnT	60031	2476	18W-36N	E4
S Park Dr					
10	BtlT	60560	3333	41W-14S	E1
10	BtlT	60560	3334	41W-14S	A1
10	JLET	60435	3498	25W-24S	C6
10	JLET	60436	3498	25W-24S	C6
W Park Dr					
100	LMBD	60148	3026	20W-0S	B5
21400	RLKB	60046	2475	21W-36N	D4
21400	RLKB	60073	2475	21W-36N	D4
21600	LkvT	60046	2475	21W-36N	C4
22000	LkvT	60073	2475	21W-36N	C4
25100	AntT	60002	2357	25W-43N	B4
28600	CbaT	60010	2696	28W-23N	D2
Park Ln					
-	NLNX	60451	3501	18W-25S	A6
-	SCRL	60175	2964	35W-6N	A1
10	BtlT	60512	3198	40W-11S	B7
10	BtlT	60512	3262	40W-11S	B1
10	GLF	60029	2864	8W-12N	E1
10	GLF	60029	2865	8W-12N	A1
10	LKBF	60044	2593	11W-28N	E6

STREET Block	City	ZIP	Map#	CGS	Grid
Park Ln					
10	PKRG	60068	2863	11W-9N	D7
10	WldT	60564	3203	28W-10S	B6
100	DRFD	60015	2756	11W-20N	C2
200	CLLK	60014	2639	36W-25N	D5
200	FXLK	60041	2473	27W-35N	C5
200	ROSL	60172	2913	23W-7N	B4
200	SchT	60175	2964	35W-5N	B3
200	SLVL	60411	3597	2E-25S	D1
400	BRTN	60010	2751	25W-20N	A1
400	WDDL	60191	2914	18W-5N	E7
700	HFET	60192	2804	23W-15N	D2
700	WNKA	60093	2812	4W-16N	B1
1100	BtnT	60081	2414	30W-39N	B5
1100	GNVW	60025	2810	9W-13N	B6
1100	WNSP	60558	3146	14W-6S	D3
1400	FDHT	60411	3509	1E-25S	B7
2000	HDPK	60035	2705	8W-22N	A4
2600	TNLK	53181	2354		A3
4100	CCHL	60478	3426	5W-20S	C5
5100	MONE	60449	3683	6W-31S	A6
5200	CTWD	60445	3347	6W-15S	E1
5400	MONE	60449	3682	6W-31S	E6
6700	DRN	60559	3145	18W-7S	A6
6700	WTMT	60559	3145	18W-7S	A6
9400	MaiT	60016	2863	11W-11N	D2
9400	MaiT	60714	2863	11W-11N	D2
9400	NLES	60714	2863	11W-11N	D2
14700	ODPK	60462	3345	12W-17S	C5
14900	OrlT	60462	3346	9W-17S	D6
15400	DLTN	60419	3350	0E-18S	E7
15400	SHLD	60473	3350	0E-18S	E7
43100	NptT	60099	2361	14W-43N	C5
N Park Ln					
30100	LbvT	60048	2592	15W-30N	B3
42300	AntT	60002	2357	25W-42N	B6
N Park Ln W					
42300	AntT	60002	2357	25W-42N	A6
S Park Ln					
200	PLTN	60074	2806	19W-15N	B2
W Park Ln					
600	PNFD	60544	3338	30W-16S	C4
2700	ODHL	60013	2641	31W-26N	D3
8600	NLES	60714	2863	10W-10N	E4
8600	NLES	60714	2864	10W-10N	A4
8600	PKRG	60714	2863	10W-10N	E4
Park Ln E					
37400	LkvT	60046	2474	25W-37N	A2
Park Ln W					
37400	LkvT	60046	2474	25W-37N	A2
Park Mnr					
1200	AURA	60506	3137	37W-7S	C7
Park Pl					
-	AntT	60002	2357	25W-42N	B6
-	MHRY	60050	2528	32W-31N	A6
10	RVSD	60546	3088	10W-3S	B4
100	GYLK	60030	2532	20W-32N	E4
100	LYVL	60048	2591	16W-29N	D5
300	GLNC	60022	2758	6W-18N	C3
500	LMNT	60439	3270	19W-14S	C6
500	SchT	60174	2908	35W-6N	C7
700	LKBF	60044	2594	10W-28N	B6
700	WCDA	60084	2588	25W-28N	B7
900	LynT	60525	3146	14W-6S	E3
900	WNSP	60525	3146	14W-6S	E4
900	WNSP	60558	3146	14W-6S	E4
1400	BTVA	60510	3078	35W-2S	B4
1400	DSPN	60016	2863	13W-11N	A3
1500	BtvT	60510	3078	35W-2S	B4
1600	BGBK	60490	3267	26W-13S	D5
2300	EVTN	60201	2812	3W-13N	D7
3500	FSMR	60422	3506	4W-23S	E4
5700	CTWD	60445	3275	7W-15S	D7
5700	WthT	60445	3275	7W-15S	D7
7400	HMND	46324	3430		D4
9200	ODHL	60487	3423	11W-19S	E3
10100	AlqT	60102	2694	33W-21N	E5
10100	AlqT	60102	2695	33W-21N	A5
12700	WthT	60463	3275	7W-15S	D7
E Park Pl					
10	AURA	60505	3200	35W-7S	B1
1300	CHCG	60637	3153	1E-6S	A2
1800	WhlT	60004	2754	16W-17N	D4
N Park Pl					
42200	AntT	60002	2357	25W-42N	B6
S Park Pl					
5900	HMND	46320	3430		D1
W Park Pl					
-	GRNE	60031	2476	18W-34N	E7
-	GRNE	60046	2476	18W-34N	E7
10	AURA	60505	3138	35W-7S	C6
10	AURA	60505	3200	34W-9S	D3
300	ANHT	60004	2807	18W-14N	A4
500	ADSN	60101	2970	19W-4N	D3
18700	WrnT	60046	2476	18W-34N	E7
26200	AntT	60002	2356	26W-42N	E6
Park Plz					
500	GNEN	60137	3025	22W-0S	C7
16000	SHLD	60473	3428	0E-18S	E1
Park Rd					
100	LKMR	60051	2529	29W-31N	D6
1200	CRTE	60417	3685	1W-29S	B1
N Park Rd					
10	JltT	60433	3499	21W-23S	E4
10	LGNG	60525	3087	13W-4S	A7
200	BDWD	60408	3942	30W-41S	B6
200	RedT	60408	3942	30W-41S	B6
300	LGPK	60525	3087	13W-3S	A6
600	RDLK	60073	2532	23W-34N	A1
23500	ElaT	60047	2699	21W-23N	D2
S Park Rd					
10	JltT	60433	3499	21W-24S	E5
100	LGNG	60525	3087	13W-4S	B7
200	LGNG	60525	3147	13W-4S	A1
400	LMBD	60148	3026	20W-0S	B5
5500	CTSD	60525	3147	13W-6S	B3
5500	LynT	60525	3147	13W-6S	B3
W Park Rd					
100	RDLK	60073	2531	23W-34N	E1
100	RDLK	60073	2532	23W-34N	A1
Park Row					
10	ELGN	60120	2855	33W-11N	A4
500	GNEN	60137	3025	22W-0N	C5
Park St					
-	SenT	60180	2635	46W-25N	D4
-	WMTN	60481	3853	27W-38S	C7
10	OSWG	60543	3263	37W-12S	C3
10	PKFT	60466	3595	3W-26S	B2
100	ALGN	60102	2694	33W-21N	E6
100	GLBT	60136	2798	39W-16N	E2
100	WLSP	60480	3209	12W-9S	C3
100	WNFD	60190	3023	27W-0S	C7
200	BNVL	60106	2972	15W-5N	A2
200	HNDL	60521	3146	15W-6S	B4
300	ELGN	60120	2855	33W-11N	A3
300	WDSK	60098	2524	41W-31N	D6
400	BTVA	60510	3078	35W-0S	C1
500	BCHR	60401	3864	0W-36S	C2
500	DndT	60118	2801	33W-16N	B2
500	EDND	60118	2801	33W-16N	B2
600	GNCY	53128	2353		A3
800	BTVA	60510	3020	35W-0S	C7
1300	CRTE	60417	3685	0W-30S	C2
1700	NPVL	60563	3141	27W-4S	D2
2100	RGMW	60008	2806	19W-13N	C5
2600	FNPK	60131	2973	12W-3N	B5
5600	DGvT	60521	3145	16W-6S	E4
6100	UNON	60180	2635	46W-25N	D4
E Park St					
10	ANHT	60005	2807	17W-13N	B6
10	MDLN	60060	2590	18W-28N	D7
10	PLNO	60545	3259	47W-13S	D5
100	ELWD	60421	3675	25W-32S	B7
100	HRVD	60033	2406	50W-38N	B7
100	YKVL	60560	3333	42W-14S	C1
400	BtlT	60560	3333	42W-14S	D1
600	LtRT	60545	3259	47W-13S	D5
1800	ANHT	60004	2807	16W-13N	D6
N Park St					
-	HPSR	60140	2795	47W-16N	E2
10	ROSL	60172	2913	23W-7N	A4
10	WTMT	60559	3145	18W-5S	A2
100	MHTN	60442	3678	19W-30S	A4
100	WMTN	60481	3853	27W-39S	C7
200	MhtT	60442	3678	19W-30S	A4
500	DGvT	60559	3085	18W-4S	A7
500	DRGV	60559	3085	18W-4S	A7
500	WTMT	60559	3085	18W-4S	A7
1200	MHRY	60050	2528	32W-33N	B3
1600	McHT	60050	2528	32W-33N	C3
3800	OKBK	60523	3085	18W-4S	A7
3800	OKBK	60559	3085	18W-4S	A7
3800	YkTp	60559	3085	18W-4S	A7
33000	WrnT	60030	2533	18W-33N	D3
S Park St					
10	ROSL	60172	2913	23W-7N	A5
10	WTMT	60559	3145	18W-5S	A3
100	HPSR	60140	2795	47W-16N	E2
100	MHTN	60442	3678	19W-31S	A5
200	WMTN	60481	3853	27W-39S	C7
200	WMTN	60481	3943	27W-39S	C1
W Park St					
10	ANHT	60005	2807	18W-13N	A6
100	HRVD	60033	2406	50W-38N	A6
400	MDLN	60060	2590	19W-28N	C7
700	CmgT	60033	2405	50W-38N	E7
700	HRVD	60033	2405	51W-38N	E7
1300	ANHT	60005	2806	18W-13N	D6
25500	AntT	60002	2357	25W-43N	A4
28900	AlqT	60013	2696	28W-23N	D2
28900	CbaT	60013	2696	28W-23N	D2
Park Ter					
200	SCHT	60411	3595	1W-27S	E4
200	SCHT	60411	3596	1W-27S	A4
2400	HHLL	60051	2586	30W-29N	A3
N Park Ter					
43300	AntT	60002	2357	25W-43N	A4
S Park Ter					
800	CHCG	60605	3034	0W-0S	B6
W Park Ter					
23500	ANTH	60002	2416	23W-41N	E1
23500	AntT	60002	2416	23W-41N	E1
Park Wy					
-	AlqT	60102	2695	31W-22N	D4
100	FRGV	60021	2696	30W-22N	B3
Park Barrington Dr					
-	BrnT	60010	2751	25W-17N	A4
400	BRTN	60010	2751	25W-17N	A5
Park Barrington Wy					
500	BRTN	60010	2751	25W-17N	A5
Park Center Dr					
-	ODPK	60462	3424	9W-19S	E1
-	TYPK	60477	3424	9W-19S	D4
Park Central Dr N					
7800	TYPK	60477	3424	9W-21S	D5
Park Central Dr S					
7800	TYPK	60477	3424	9W-21S	D6
Parkchester Rd					
100	EGVV	60007	2914	19W-8N	C3
400	BFGV	60089	2701	16W-20N	E7
W Park Cir Dr					
100	WHTN	60187	3024	24W-0N	C4
Park Crest Ct					
1700	LYVL	60048	2590	18W-30N	E2
1700	LYVL	60048	2591	18W-30N	A2
Park Crest Dr					
1000	DGvT	60561	3207	17W-9S	B3
1000	DRN	60561	3207	17W-9S	B3
Parke Av					
9900	OKLN	60453	3212	5W-11S	A7
Parke Ln					
700	LslT	60540	3142	24W-5S	C4
Parker Av					
-	FNPK	60131	2973	12W-3N	B5
200	AURA	60505	3200	36W-9S	A3
200	AURA	60538	3200	36W-9S	A3
200	MTGY	60505	3200	36W-9S	A3
200	MTGY	60538	3200	36W-9S	A3
200	WCHI	60185	3022	29W-0N	C4
500	AraT	60505	3200	35W-9S	B3
1100	DRGV	60516	3144	19W-7S	C7
1300	JltT	60432	3499	22W-23S	D4
1800	NndT	60050	2585	30W-29N	E4
1800	NndT	60050	2586	30W-29N	A4
W Parker Av					
4000	CHCG	60639	2976	5W-3N	B5
4000	CHCG	60647	2976	5W-3N	B5
4800	CHCG	60639	2975	6W-3N	D5
Parker Ct					
100	WMTN	60481	3853	27W-38S	D5
200	AURA	60505	3200	36W-9S	A4
200	AURA	60538	3200	36W-9S	A4
200	MTGY	60505	3200	36W-9S	A4
200	MTGY	60538	3200	36W-9S	A4
600	GNVA	60134	3020	34W-1N	D2
2000	GwdT	60098	2524	41W-33N	D2
Parker Dr					
100	GYLK	60030	2532	21W-33N	D3
600	LMBD	60148	3026	19W-1N	D2
800	SMBG	60194	2858	24W-11N	D4
Parker Ln					
-	JNBG	60050	2471	32W-34N	C7
-	JNBG	60050	2528	32W-34N	C1
900	BFGV	60089	2701	17W-21N	A6
Parker Pl					
-	OSWG	60543	3265	33W-11S	A2
1200	EGVV	60007	2914	21W-8N	A2
1400	EGVV	60007	2913	21W-8N	E3
Parker Rd					
-	LmnT	60439	3271	17W-13S	D4
12900	LMNT	60439	3343	17W-15S	D2
13400	HMGN	60491	3343	16W-15S	D2
18400	NlxT	60448	3501	16W-23S	E3
19000	NlxT	60451	3501	16W-23S	E3
S Parker Rd					
13400	HMGN	60491	3343	17W-16S	D4
13400	LMNT	60439	3343	16W-16S	D2
15600	HMGN	60491	3421	17W-19S	D3
17900	HMGN	60448	3421	16W-21S	E6
17900	HmrT	60448	3421	16W-21S	E7
17900	HmrT	60491	3421	16W-21S	E7
18200	NlxT	60448	3421	16W-22S	E7
18200	NlxT	60448	3501	16W-22S	E1
18200	NlxT	60491	3421	16W-22S	E7
Parker St					
11000	MKNA	60448	3503	13W-23S	A3
11100	MKNA	60448	3502	14W-23S	E4
N Parker St					
700	AddT	60126	2972	15W-3N	B6
700	EMHT	60126	2972	15W-3N	B6
S Parker Ridge Dr					
16700	LKPT	60441	3420	19W-20S	C4
Parkes Dr					
1700	BDVW	60155	3087	11W-1S	D1
S Parkfalls Ct					
13700	PnfT	60544	3339	27W-16S	C4
Parkfield Ct					
1500	NPVL	60540	3202	28W-7S	E1
1500	NPVL	60540	3203	28W-7S	A1
Parkhill Cir					
900	AURA	60502	3139	32W-6S	C6
Park Hill Ct					
8700	HYHL	60457	3210	10W-10S	A5
20000	DRPK	60010	2751	23W-20N	E2
Park Hill Dr					
-	PltT	60010	2751	23W-20N	E2
20000	DRPK	60010	2751	23W-20N	E2
Parkhill Dr					
300	GNOK	60048	2592	14W-28N	C5
15700	ODPK	60462	3424	11W-18S	A1
15800	ODHL	60487	3424	11W-18S	A1
Park Hill Tr					
100	CLSM	60188	3024	25W-2N	A1
Parkland Ct					
500	OSWG	60543	3263	38W-12S	B3
13500	HMGN	60491	3343	16W-17S	D5
Parklane Av					
-	FNPK	60171	2973	11W-3N	D4
-	RVGV	60171	2973	11W-3N	D4
9100	FNPK	60131	2973	11W-3N	D4
Parklane Dr					
10	PSPK	60464	3273	12W-14S	C7
Parklawn Ct					
100	BGBK	60440	3269	22W-11S	D1
Park Ln Av					
1600	MHRY	60050	2527	34W-33N	D3
Park Ln Ct					
7000	WDRG	60517	3143	21W-7S	E6
Park Ln Dr					
2100	WDRG	60517	3144	21W-7S	A7
W Park Ln Dr					
3100	MTPK	60803	3276	3W-13S	E4
4300	ALSP	60803	3276	5W-14S	B6
6700	PSHT	60463	3347	8W-15S	A1
Park Ln Rd					
200	ELGN	60123	2800	34W-13N	E7
E Park Manor Ct					
400	BKLY	60163	3028	15W-0S	B5
400	EMHT	60126	3028	15W-0S	B5
Park Manor Dr					
10	DYR	46311	3598		C3
Parkmead Ln					
900	LKFT	60045	2649	12W-26N	C3
Park Meadow Dr					
10	LslT	60540	3142	24W-5S	D3
Park Meadow Ln					
100	BGBK	60440	3268	25W-11S	B1
Park Meadow Rd					
3200	PRGV	60050	2585	31W-28N	D5
Park Place Cir					
10	HNWD	60047	2645	21W-24N	D7
Park Place Ct					
-	TroT	60403	3497	27W-22S	D2
-	TroT	60435	3497	27W-22S	D2
400	NARA	60542	3137	38W-4S	A2
1200	CTHL	60403	3497	27W-22S	D2
S Park Place Dr					
200	BRLT	60103	2910	30W-8N	C3
22700	CNHN	60410	3584	29W-27S	E5
S Parkplace Dr					
800	PLTN	60067	2805	21W-14N	D3
W Park Place Dr					
1000	BRLT	60103	2910	30W-8N	C3
Park Plaine Av					
500	PKRG	60068	2863	11W-9N	D7
Park Rd Ct					
10	LMBD	60148	3026	20W-0N	B5
Park Ridge Blvd					
1100	PKRG	60068	2918	10W-7N	A3
1300	PKRG	60068	2917	10W-7N	E3
Park Ridge Ct					
100	AURA	60504	3201	31W-8S	E1
2500	CTHL	60403	3497	27W-22S	D2
Parkridge Ct					
1300	CLLK	60014	2693	36W-23N	D2
Park Ridge Dr					
2200	JLET	60586	3415	31W-21S	E6
Parkridge Dr					
1300	CLLK	60014	2693	36W-23N	D2
Park Ridge Ln					
100	AURA	60504	3201	31W-8S	E2
Park Ridge Pt					
-	DSPN	60068	2863	12W-10N	C4
1600	PKRG	60068	2863	12W-10N	C4
W Park River Ln					
24400	SRWD	60404	3584	30W-25S	B2
24400	TroT	60404	3584	30W-25S	B2
Parkrose Av					
2200	CTHL	60403	3417	26W-21S	D6
N Parks Av					
100	JLET	60432	3499	23W-23S	B4
Parks St					
-	ELWD	60421	3675	25W-32S	B7
Parkshore Dr					
500	SRWD	60404	3496	30W-23S	C4
E Park Shore East Ct					
1500	CHCG	60637	3153	1E-6S	B4
S Park Shore East Ct					
6100	CHCG	60637	3153	1E-6S	B4
Parkside Av					
10	CHHT	60411	3508	1W-24S	A6
100	AddT	60143	2914	19W-7N	D4
100	AURA	60505	3139	33W-7S	A7
100	AURA	60505	3201	33W-7S	A1
200	AraT	60505	3139	33W-7S	A7
200	ITSC	60143	2914	19W-6N	D7
400	WDDL	60143	2914	19W-6N	D7
400	WDDL	60191	2914	19W-6N	D7
500	WCHI	60185	3022	30W-0N	B6
1000	PKRG	60068	2863	11W-10N	E5
2900	McHT	60051	2528	31W-32N	C4
2900	MHRY	60051	2528	31W-32N	C4
6800	CTSD	60525	3147	13W-7S	A7
7600	NLES	60077	2865	7W-9N	C6
7600	NLES	60714	2865	7W-9N	C6
7600	SKOK	60077	2865	7W-9N	C6
7700	BRBK	60459	3211	7W-9S	D2
8600	OKLN	60459	3211	7W-9S	D4
8800	MNGV	60053	2865	7W-11N	C3
8900	OKLN	60453	3211	7W-11S	D6
10500	CHRG	60415	3275	7W-12S	D2
10500	OKLN	60453	3275	7W-12S	D2
11000	ALSP	60482	3275	7W-12S	D3
11000	CHRG	60482	3275	7W-12S	D3
14800	OKFT	60452	3347	7W-17S	D6
14900	HRVY	60426	3350	0W-17S	C6
16800	SHLD	60473	3428	0E-19S	E3
17100	BmnT	60477	3425	7W-20S	D5
E Parkside Av					
10	LMBD	60148	3026	19W-0N	C4
N Parkside Av					
10	GNEN	60137	3025	22W-0S	B7
400	CHCG	60644	3031	7W-0N	C3
700	CHCG	60651	3031	7W-0N	C3
1500	CHCG	60639	3031	7W-1N	C1
2000	CHCG	60639	2975	7W-2N	C6
4000	CHCG	60634	2975	7W-5N	C1
5400	CHCG	60630	2919	7W-6N	C5
5500	CHCG	60646	2919	7W-6N	C5
8900	MaiT	60068	2863	11W-11N	E3
8900	NLES	60714	2863	11W-11N	E3
9200	MaiT	60016	2863	11W-11N	E2
9200	PKRG	60068	2863	11W-11N	E3
9400	NLES	60016	2863	11W-11N	E2
S Parkside Av					
10	CHCG	60644	3031	7W-0S	C5
100	GNEN	60137	3083	22W-1S	B1
500	EMHT	60126	3027	16W-0S	E5
5100	CHCG	60638	3149	7W-5S	D2
5100	StkT	60638	3149	7W-5S	D2
12500	WthT	60463	3275	7W-14S	D7
12500	WthT	60803	3275	7W-14S	D7
12600	CTWD	60445	3275	7W-14S	D7
12600	WthT	60445	3275	7W-14S	D7
W Parkside Av					
10	LMBD	60148	3026	20W-0N	B4
Parkside Cir					
500	SMWD	60107	2857	28W-10N	A6
Parkside Ct					
10	ALGN	60102	2693	36W-21N	D7
10	BGBK	60490	3268	26W-13S	A4
10	NARA	60542	3137	38W-4S	A1
10	VNHL	60061	2647	17W-26N	C3
500	CLLK	60012	2639	35W-27N	E1
800	SMWD	60107	2857	28W-9N	A7
1100	CLSM	60188	2967	26W-4N	E4
5400	GRNE	60031	2478	15W-36N	A5
Parkside Dr					
-	AURA	60506	3136	41W-7S	A7
-	BFGV	60089	2701	16W-21N	C6
-	PNFD	60544	3415	31W-18S	E2
-	PnfT	60544	3415	31W-18S	E2
-	SRGV	60554	3136	41W-7S	A7
100	SRWD	60404	3495	31W-24S	E5
400	CLSM	60188	2967	26W-4N	E4
500	ELGN	60123	2854	34W-12N	C2
700	WHTN	60187	3024	25W-0S	B7
1300	BGBK	60490	3268	26W-13S	A4
1300	DPgT	60490	3268	26W-13S	A4
1400	BGBK	60490	3267	26W-13S	E4
1600	JLET	60586	3496	29W-21S	E1
1700	JLET	60586	3416	29W-21S	E7
1700	PnfT	60586	3416	29W-21S	E7
2100	MaiT	60068	2863	11W-11N	E3
2100	PKRG	60068	2863	11W-11N	E3
2200	MaiT	60016	2863	11W-11N	E3
2700	HDPK	60035	2704	10W-23N	A1
3300	WDRG	60517	3143	22W-6S	B5
6400	TYPK	60477	3425	8W-20S	B3
8000	FftT	60423	3504	10W-24S	C6
14600	DLTN	60419	3350	0W-17S	C5
15200	MKHM	60428	3349	3W-18S	A7
15600	HMGN	60491	3422	16W-18S	A1
N Parkside Dr					
3900	HFET	60192	2804	25W-15N	A3
S Parkside Dr					
200	HPSR	60140	2796	46W-16N	A2
500	RDLK	60073	2531	23W-32N	E5
1300	PLTN	60067	2805	21W-14N	C4
12800	PlsT	60464	3273	12W-15S	C7
12800	PlsT	60464	3345	12W-15S	C1
12900	PSPK	60464	3345	12W-15S	C1
13000	PlsT	60462	3345	12W-15S	C1
24500	CNHN	60410	3672	32W-31S	E6
W Parkside Dr					
400	PLTN	60067	2805	21W-14N	C4
1700	HFET	60192	2804	25W-15N	B2
Parkside Ln					
100	BNVL	60106	2971	16W-5N	D1
200	OSWG	60543	3263	37W-13S	B5
400	YKVL	60560	3333	42W-17S	D5
800	KdlT	60560	3333	41W-17S	E5
1100	DRFD	60015	2703	11W-21N	D6
1500	LynT	60525	3146	13W-6S	E4
1500	LynT	60525	3147	13W-6S	A4
11600	MKNA	60448	3502	14W-23S	D2
S Parkside Pl					
400	EMHT	60126	3027	16W-0N	E4
Parkside Rd					
10	LslT	60540	3142	26W-7S	A6
10	NPVL	60540	3142	26W-7S	A6
100	LslT	60540	3141	26W-7S	E7
700	NPVL	60540	3141	26W-7S	E7
Parkside Ter					
500	CLLK	60012	2639	35W-27N	E2
Parksleg Ct					
6400	LSLE	60532	3142	24W-7S	D6
Park Station Blvd					
-	ODPK	60462	3345	13W-18S	B7
-	ODPK	60462	3423	13W-18S	B1
Parkstone Dr					
100	CRY	60013	2641	30W-25N	E5
200	CRY	60013	2642	30W-25N	A5
Parktrail Ct					
200	SMBG	60173	2859	21W-10N	E5
Parkview W					
-	RMVL	60446	3339	28W-17S	B6
Park View Av					
10	CLLK	60012	2640	35W-26N	A2
10	CLLK	60014	2640	35W-26N	A2
Parkview Av					
10	BtlT	60560	3262	41W-13S	B5
10	WNVL	60555	3081	28W-3S	B6
600	WnfT	60555	3081	27W-3S	B6
800	RKDL	60436	3498	25W-24S	C7
900	JLET	60436	3498	25W-24S	C7
1000	CHHT	60411	3507	1W-25S	E6
1000	CHHT	60411	3508	1W-25S	A7
8400	BKFD	60513	3088	10W-3S	A5
8400	BKFD	60546	3088	10W-3S	B5
8400	RVSD	60546	3088	10W-3S	B5
16400	TYPK	60477	3424	9W-19S	D3
E Parkview Av					
300	EMHT	60126	3028	15W-0N	B4
S Parkview Av					
400	EMHT	60126	3028	15W-0N	B4
1200	HMND	46394	3280		E4
Parkview Blvd					
-	GNEN	60137	3025	21W-0S	E7
-	GNEN	60148	3025	21W-0S	E7
800	LMBD	60148	3025	21W-0S	E6
800	LMBD	60148	3026	21W-0S	A6
800	YkTp	60148	3026	21W-0S	A6
Park View Cir					
-	FXLK	60081	2414	28W-39N	D4
Parkview Cir					
-	RMVL	60446	3339	26W-18S	E7
700	EGVV	60007	2914	19W-9N	C1
1000	CLSM	60188	2967	27W-4N	C4
Parkview Cir E					
2000	HFET	60169	2804	25W-12N	B7
Parkview Cir W					
2000	HFET	60169	2804	25W-12N	B7
Park View Ct					
-	WLSP	60527	3208	13W-8S	E1
Parkview Ct					
400	CNHL	60514	3145	17W-6S	C3
400	HNVL	60030	2532	22W-33N	B2
400	RLKP	60073	2532	22W-33N	B2
400	WTMT	60514	3145	17W-6S	C3
500	LslT	60540	3142	24W-6S	C4
500	OSWG	60543	3263	37W-13S	C5
1100	CLSM	60188	2967	27W-4N	C4
2100	WLMT	60091	2812	4W-13N	B6
5500	CTWD	60445	3275	6W-15S	D7
E Parkview Ct					
400	ANHT	60005	2861	17W-12N	B1
700	BmdT	60157	2913	22W-7N	C4
700	ROSL	60172	2913	22W-7N	C4
Park View Dr					
1100	ANTH	60002	2359	20W-41N	A7
4500	MCLK	60050	2470	33W-34N	D7
10000	PlsT	60464	3273	12W-15S	C7
17800	CCHL	60478	3426	6W-21S	A6
Parkview Dr					
-	RMVL	60446	3339	27W-17S	D5
-	WcnT	60084	2587	26W-28N	E6
-	WPHR	60096	2362	11W-42N	E5
10	NHLK	60164	3028	13W-2N	D1
100	WCDA	60084	2587	26W-28N	E6
300	NHLK	60164	3029	12W-2N	A1
400	SMBG	60193	2912	25W-8N	C2
400	SmbT	60193	2912	25W-8N	C2
500	MltT	60137	3083	22W-2S	B4
1000	BTVA	60510	3020	36W-0S	A7
1000	HRPK	60133	2911	26W-9N	E1
1100	ELGN	60123	2800	35W-13N	C7
1100	ELGN	60123	2854	35W-13N	C1
1500	LYVL	60048	2591	16W-30N	D3
1800	LSLE	60532	3142	23W-4S	E1
2000	SHLD	60473	3429	2E-20S	D4
2300	AraT	60502	3139	33W-4S	A1
2300	AURA	60502	3139	33W-4S	A1
2800	MngT	60152	2578	50W-29N	B4
6900	DRGV	60516	3144	19W-7S	D7
8300	DGvT	60517	3206	20W-9S	B4
8300	DRN	60517	3206	20W-9S	B4
8300	DRN	60561	3206	20W-9S	B4
13400	ODPK	60462	3346	10W-15S	A2
22600	RNPK	60471	3594	5W-27S	B4
28500	WcnT	60042	2642	28W-27N	E1
34700	AntT	60002	2356	26W-42N	E7
E Parkview Dr					
900	SEGN	60177	2907	37W-7N	C6
W Park View Dr					
5100	MCLK	60050	2470	34W-34N	D7
W Parkview Dr					
200	ADSN	60101	2970	18W-3N	E6
900	SEGN	60177	2907	37W-7N	C6
26000	AntT	60002	2356	26W-41N	E7
Park View Ln					
10	ElaT	60047	2645	21W-24N	C7
10	HNWD	60047	2645	21W-24N	C7
Parkview Ln					
200	BDWD	60408	3942	31W-41S	A5
400	LKPT	60441	3419	22W-20S	D5
800	DSPN	60016	2863	12W-10N	B4
8000	FKFT	60423	3592	10W-27S	C4
W Parkview Ln					
8800	HYHL	60457	3210	11W-10S	A5
Parkview Pl					
400	BRRG	60527	3208	15W-9S	B4
W Parkview Pl					
28500	GrtT	60081	2472	28W-37N	E1
Parkview Rd					
-	BHPK	60099	2422	9W-38N	C7
10	GNVW	60053	2864	9W-12N	D2
10	MNGV	60053	2864	9W-12N	D2
10	RVSD	60546	3088	10W-3S	B5
100	BKFD	60513	3088	10W-3S	B5
100	BKFD	60546	3088	10W-3S	B5
200	GNVW	60025	2864	9W-12N	D1
Park View Ter					
300	BFGV	60089	2754	17W-17N	B4
300	WhlT	60004	2754	16W-17N	C4
300	WhlT	60089	2754	16W-17N	C4
E Parkview Ter					
400	ALGN	60102	2694	34W-20N	B7
N Parkview Ter					
-	CHCG	60618	2976	4W-4N	C2
1300	ALGN	60102	2694	34W-21N	B7
S Parkview Ter					
1300	ALGN	60102	2694	34W-20N	B7
W Parkview Ter					
400	ALGN	60102	2694	34W-20N	B7
Parkville Rd					
2000	SMBG	60194	2858	26W-11N	A4
Park Vista Ln					
-	AntT	60081	2414	29W-39N	D4
-	FXLK	60081	2414	29W-39N	D4
1500	AURA	60504	3200	33W-9S	E3
Parkway					
-	PTHT	60070	2808	15W-15N	A2
N Parkway					
-	EMHT	60126	2972	15W-3N	B5

Chicago 7-County Street Index

Block	City	ZIP	Map#	CGS	Grid
S Parkway					
-	EMHT	60126	2972	15W-3N	B5
Parkway Av					
100	LKZH	60047	2698	23W-23N	E2
200	DGvT	60559	3085	18W-4S	A7
200	WTMT	60559	3085	18W-4S	A7
300	BMDL	60108	2968	24W-5N	C2
500	ANTH	60002	2357	23W-42N	E5
600	ELGN	60120	2801	32W-12N	B7
4200	MHRY	60050	2527	33W-33N	E2
4200	MHRY	60050	2528	33W-33N	A2
N Parkway Av					
39400	AntT	60002	2416	25W-39N	A5
W Parkway Av					
23500	LKVL	60046	2416	23W-38N	E6
23500	LkvT	60046	2416	23W-38N	E6
Parkway Dr					
-	MltT	60187	3024	26W-0N	A5
10	MltT	60190	3023	26W-0N	D5
10	WNFD	60190	3023	26W-0N	D5
10	WnfT	60190	3023	27W-0N	D5
100	WHTN	60187	3024	24W-0N	D5
200	LNSH	60015	2702	15W-21N	B5
200	MltT	60187	3023	26W-0N	D5
200	VrnT	60015	2702	15W-21N	B5
200	VrnT	60069	2702	15W-21N	B5
200	WNFD	60187	3023	26W-0N	D5
300	AlqT	60013	2696	29W-23N	C2
300	LNSH	60069	2702	15W-21N	B5
N Parkway Dr					
10	NPVL	60540	3141	27W-6S	B5
3800	GNVW	60062	2809	12W-15N	B3
3800	NfdT	60062	2809	12W-15N	B3
S Parkway Dr					
10	NPVL	60540	3141	27W-6S	B5
3800	GNVW	60062	2809	12W-14N	B3
3800	NfdT	60062	2809	12W-14N	B3
W Parkway Dr					
3200	GNVW	60062	2809	12W-15N	B3
3200	NfdT	60062	2809	12W-15N	B3
Parkway Ln					
3700	ZION	60099	2362	12W-42N	C7
18800	MKNA	60448	3502	14W-22S	E2
21900	FKFT	60423	3591	13W-26S	B2
E Parkway Rd					
500	RVSD	60546	3088	9W-2S	D3
W Parkway Rd					
500	RVSD	60546	3088	9W-2S	D3
Parkway St					
100	BDWD	60408	3942	31W-41S	B6
100	DGvT	60527	3207	16W-9S	E3
100	RedT	60408	3942	31W-41S	B6
1200	DRGV	60515	3144	20W-5S	C2
N Parkway St					
600	EGvT	60007	2915	17W-8N	B3
600	EGVV	60007	2915	17W-8N	B3
Parkway Ter					
-	RVSD	60546	3088	9W-2S	D3
Parkway N Blvd					
-	RVWD	60015	2703	12W-21N	B7
10	DRFD	60015	2703	12W-20N	B7
10	DRFD	60015	2756	12W-20N	A1
10	RVWD	60015	2756	12W-20N	A1
Park West Blvd					
-	VrnT	60015	2755	15W-20N	B1
Parkwood Av					
500	PKRG	60068	2863	11W-9N	D7
600	RMVL	60446	3341	23W-15S	A1
700	RMVL	60446	3269	23W-14S	A7
Parkwood Cir					
400	SEGN	60177	2907	37W-7N	D4
1200	ALGN	60102	2694	34W-21N	B7
Parkwood Ct					
10	SMWD	60107	2857	27W-9N	C7
6300	OKFT	60452	3347	8W-17S	B6
E Parkwood Ct					
700	JLET	60432	3500	21W-23S	A3
W Parkwood Ct					
300	PLTN	60067	2805	21W-14N	D3
Parkwood Dr					
100	SMWD	60107	2857	27W-9N	C7
500	JLET	60432	3500	21W-22S	A2
500	JltT	60432	3500	21W-22S	A2
E Parkwood Dr					
7300	MchT	60097	2469	36W-35N	D6
7300	WRLK	60097	2469	36W-35N	D6
Parkwood Ln					
2400	DSPN	60018	2917	12W-8N	C1
2800	AURA	60502	3139	32W-5S	C3
2900	WDRG	60517	3205	22W-9S	C3
Parkwood Rd					
100	ELGN	60123	2800	33W-13N	E7
100	ELGN	60123	2801	33W-13N	A7
Parliament Av					
16300	TYPK	60477	3424	9W-19S	D2
Parliament Ct					
1200	LYVL	60048	2591	16W-29N	D3
1700	LKFT	60045	2703	13W-23N	A1
Parliament Dr E					
10	PSHT	60463	3274	9W-13S	D5
Parliament Dr W					
10	PSHT	60463	3274	9W-13S	D5
Parliament Ln					
3400	NPVL	60564	3202	30W-10S	B7
W Parliament Pl					
200	MPPT	60056	2807	16W-14N	D3
W Parliament St					
1200	CRTE	60417	3685	1W-29S	A1
N Parliament Wy					
10	MDLN	60060	2591	17W-27N	B7
10	MDLN	60060	2647	17W-27N	B1
N Parma Av					
37000	LkvT	60046	2475	20W-37N	E2
Parma Dr					
900	CRY	60013	2695	32W-23N	B2
Parmalee Pl					
300	WKGN	60087	2480	10W-36N	A5
Parnell Av					
-	BlmT	60411	3508	0W-24S	B4
400	CHHT	60411	3508	0W-24S	B5
14300	HRVY	60426	3350	0W-17S	B4
14300	HRVY	60827	3350	0W-17S	B4
14300	RVDL	60827	3350	0W-17S	B4
18000	TNTN	60430	3428	0W-21S	B7
S Parnell Av					
-	CHCG	60609	3092	0W-4S	A7
3500	CHCG	60616	3092	0W-3S	A5
5900	CHCG	60621	3152	0W-6S	A4
7400	CHCG	60620	3214	0W-8S	A1
7400	CHCG	60621	3214	0W-8S	A1
9400	CHCG	60628	3214	0W-11S	B7
10400	CHCG	60628	3278	0W-13S	B4
13600	RVDL	60827	3350	0W-15S	B2
14500	HRVY	60426	3350	0W-16S	B4
14500	HRVY	60827	3350	0W-16S	B4
Parnell Cir					
15000	HMGN	60491	3421	18W-21S	A6
Parrish Ct					
1400	DRGV	60515	3084	20W-3S	B6
Pars Pth					
100	ElgT	60124	2853	38W-9N	B7
100	ElgT	60124	2907	38W-9N	B1
Parsimony Ln					
3600	CHCG	60632	3150	4W-5S	D3
Parsons Av					
600	DSPN	60016	2862	13W-11N	E3
Parsons Rd					
500	CPVL	60110	2747	35W-17N	B6
500	DndT	60118	2747	35W-17N	B6
800	DndT	60110	2747	35W-17N	B6
Parthenon Wy					
3400	OMFD	60461	3506	4W-24S	D6
Partlow Dr					
400	NPVL	60564	3266	29W-11S	C2
400	WldT	60564	3266	29W-11S	C2
Parton Ct					
10	LNSH	60045	2702	13W-23N	D2
Partree Pl					
-	PNFD	60585	3337	31W-15S	E2
Partridge Av					
1100	BGBK	60440	3268	25W-12S	B4
1100	BGBK	60490	3268	25W-12S	B4
Partridge Cir					
1500	LNHT	60046	2417	21W-38N	E7
Partridge Ct					
100	GYLK	60030	2533	19W-32N	C4
200	ALGN	60102	2694	34W-21N	B6
600	LslT	60540	3142	24W-6S	C4
1600	RLKB	60073	2474	23W-35N	D6
1600	RLKH	60073	2474	23W-35N	D6
2900	AURA	60502	3079	32W-3S	D6
3300	SPGV	60081	2354	32W-42N	C5
S Partridge Ct					
900	PLTN	60067	2805	22W-14N	C3
W Partridge Ct					
1600	ANHT	60004	2753	18W-18N	D2
Partridge Dr					
-	JLET	60431	3496	29W-22S	D2
10	MltT	60187	3024	26W-1N	A3
10	MltT	60188	3024	26W-1N	A3
500	WCHI	60185	2966	29W-3N	D5
700	PNFD	60544	3338	30W-16S	B4
700	SMBG	60193	2913	22W-8N	C2
1200	JLET	60586	3496	29W-22S	D2
13500	ODPK	60462	3346	10W-16S	B2
13500	PlsT	60462	3346	10W-16S	B2
W Partridge Dr					
800	PLTN	60067	2805	22W-14N	B3
Partridge Ln					
-	BRLT	60103	2910	29W-6N	E6
-	WrnT	60031	2534	17W-33N	C2
10	PSPK	60464	3344	14W-15S	E1
300	WLNG	60090	2755	14W-18N	D3
400	VrnT	60015	2755	14W-20N	B1
900	LKZH	60047	2699	22W-22N	B5
1900	HDPK	60035	2704	10W-22N	A5
2400	NHBK	60062	2757	10W-17N	A5
2500	NHBK	60062	2756	10W-17N	E5
5800	LGGV	60047	2701	17W-23N	B1
9600	LKWD	60014	2638	38W-24N	D6
W Partridge Ln					
800	MPPT	60056	2861	16W-11N	D3
1400	ANHT	60004	2753	18W-18N	D2
1600	PltT	60004	2753	18W-18N	D2
12200	HMGN	60491	3344	15W-16S	B4
Partridge Pkwy					
600	GNCY	53128	2353		B2
Partridge Rd					
100	BtvT	60510	3077	38W-2S	A4
Partridge Sq					
10	OSWG	60543	3263	37W-12S	D2
Partridge St					
1600	WKGN	60087	2479	11W-37N	E3
Partridge Tr					
-	RHMD	60071	2353	34W-42N	D5
Partridge Hill Dr					
600	HFET	60169	2858	24W-11N	C4
Partridge Run Dr					
200	BDWD	60408	3942	31W-41S	B4
200	RedT	60481	3942	31W-41S	B4
Pas Ct					
800	NPVL	60563	3140	29W-5S	D4
Pasadena Av					
300	CTHL	60403	3418	24W-21S	D7
500	BCHR	60401	3864	0W-37S	C2
Pasadena Dr					
10	AraT	60538	3199	38W-10S	B5
W Pasadena Dr					
22000	PnfT	60544	3339	27W-16S	C4
Pasatiempo Dr					
4800	MONE	60449	3683	6W-31S	B4
Pasec Pl					
500	ElgT	60124	2907	38W-8N	A3
Paso Fino					
10	LMNT	60439	3272	15W-13S	A5
Pasquinelli Dr					
-	OKBK	60523	3085	16W-4S	D6
-	OKBK	60559	3085	16W-4S	D6
-	PNFD	60585	3266	30W-14S	C7
-	WldT	60585	3266	30W-14S	C7
600	CNHL	60514	3085	16W-4S	D7
600	CNHL	60559	3085	16W-4S	D7
600	WTMT	60559	3085	16W-4S	D6
Passage Ln					
2800	NLNX	60451	3590	15W-25S	C1
Passavant Av					
1100	AvnT	60073	2474	24W-34N	B7
1100	RLKB	60073	2474	24W-34N	B7
W Passavant Av					
24500	AvnT	60073	2474	24W-35N	C7
24600	RLKB	60073	2474	24W-35N	C7
Pastoral Dr					
25200	PNFD	60585	3337	32W-15S	D2
25200	WldT	60585	3337	32W-15S	D2
Pastoral Ln					
1800	HRPK	60133	2967	27W-5N	C2
Pasture Dr					
16400	LMNT	60439	3342	20W-15S	B1
Pasture Side Tr					
6400	RchT	60443	3593	8W-25S	B1
Pat Ct					
800	AURA	60504	3202	30W-8S	B3
Patch Av					
1500	BTVA	60510	3077	36W-0S	E1
Pater Ct					
8900	SPGV	60081	2413	31W-40N	D2
Pathfinder Ct					
3800	JLET	60435	3417	27W-19S	C2
Pathfinder Dr					
400	CmpT	60119	2961	43W-4N	A4
500	CmpT	60151	2961	43W-4N	A4
Pathfinder Ln					
3900	JLET	60435	3417	27W-19S	C2
3900	JLET	60544	3417	27W-19S	C2
Pathway Dr					
300	LKVL	60046	2474	23W-36N	E4
1500	NPVL	60565	3204	24W-9S	D4
E Patmore St					
1500	DMND	60416	3941	33W-40S	B2
Patricia Av					
16400	BmnT	60477	3425	7W-19S	C2
16500	TYPK	60477	3425	7W-19S	C3
Patricia Ct					
100	PLTN	60074	2806	19W-15N	C1
400	GYLK	60030	2532	21W-33N	D3
1100	SMBG	60193	2858	24W-10N	C6
1500	EGVV	60007	2913	21W-8N	E3
Patricia Dr					
-	ElaT	60047	2700	20W-23N	B2
-	LGGV	60047	2700	20W-23N	B2
100	SMBG	60193	2858	24W-10N	C6
300	CHHT	60411	3508	1W-23S	A3
300	CHHT	60430	3508	1W-23S	A3
300	HMWD	60430	3508	1W-23S	A3
700	ELGN	60120	2855	32W-12N	C2
6100	MTSN	60443	3593	7W-25S	C1
6300	RchT	60443	3593	8W-25S	C1
8600	LYNS	60534	3088	10W-4S	A6
8700	BKFD	60513	3088	10W-4S	A6
8700	BKFD	60534	3088	10W-4S	A6
Patricia Ln					
-	FftT	60448	3503	13W-24S	B4
-	GnvT	60134	3077	38W-1S	A2
-	HPSR	60140	2796	46W-15N	B3
-	RNPK	60471	3594	4W-27S	D5
-	SRGV	60554	3135	42W-7S	B7
10	BbyT	60134	3076	39W-1S	E2
10	BtlT	60560	3261	42W-13S	C5
10	GnvT	60134	3076	39W-1S	E1
10	PTHT	60070	2808	14W-15N	C3
10	YKVL	60560	3261	42W-13S	C5
200	BRLT	60103	2910	29W-8N	E2
400	AddT	60126	2972	15W-3N	A5
400	EMHT	60126	2972	15W-3N	A5
500	DSPN	60016	2808	14W-12N	C7
500	DSPN	60056	2808	14W-12N	C7
500	MPPT	60056	2808	14W-12N	C7
900	CRTE	60417	3597	1E-28S	A6
1500	GNVA	60134	3020	34W-1N	E2
1500	GNVA	60174	3020	34W-1N	E2
1500	SCRL	60174	3020	34W-2N	E2
1700	FSMR	60422	3507	3W-23S	A4
1700	SCRL	60134	3020	33W-2N	E2
2400	HMWD	60430	3427	3W-21S	B7
3100	PKCY	60085	2536	12W-33N	B3
3100	WKGN	60085	2536	12W-33N	B3
6000	MTSN	60443	3593	7W-25S	D1
8900	ODPK	60462	3424	11W-18S	A1
19600	MKNA	60448	3503	13W-23S	B4
37600	GrtT	60081	2472	28W-37N	E1
N Patricia Ln					
2400	MchT	60050	2471	31W-34N	C7
2400	MchT	60050	2528	31W-34N	C1
S Patricia Ln					
10	PLTN	60074	2806	19W-15N	C1
19700	FftT	60423	3504	9W-23S	D4
19700	FftT	60477	3504	9W-23S	D4
22800	CNHN	60410	3584	29W-27S	E6
23000	JLET	60410	3584	29W-27S	E6
Patricia Pkwy					
100	SMWD	60107	2856	29W-10N	E6
Patricia Pl					
1600	CTCY	60409	3351	2E-16S	D4
Patrick Av					
100	WLSP	60480	3209	12W-9S	B4
18100	CCHL	60478	3426	5W-21S	B7
Patrick Ct					
10	BlmT	60411	3510	3E-25S	A7
8800	WDRG	60517	3206	20W-10S	A5
11200	FKFT	60423	3590	14W-27S	E4
11200	FKFT	60423	3591	13W-27S	A4
15400	ODPK	60462	3346	10W-18S	B7
Patrick Dr					
1200	MDLN	60060	2590	19W-29N	B3
S Patrick Ln					
1200	PLTN	60067	2805	22W-14N	C4
Patrick St					
100	SEGN	60177	2908	34W-8N	E3
Patrick Henry Ct					
400	AURA	60504	3140	29W-6S	D5
Patrick Henry Pkwy					
-	PNFD	60490	3267	27W-14S	B7
1100	BGBK	60490	3267	27W-14S	B7
Patrick Henry Sq E					
500	YkTp	60523	3084	19W-3S	D5
Patrick Henry Sq N					
200	YkTp	60523	3084	19W-3S	D5
Patrick Henry Sq S					
-	YkTp	60523	3084	19W-3S	D5
Patrick Henry Sq W					
500	YkTp	60523	3084	19W-3S	D5
Patrick John Ct					
300	GNVA	60134	3020	34W-0N	C5
Patriot Blvd					
1300	GNVW	60025	2810	9W-15N	B3
2200	GNVW	60062	2810	9W-15N	B3
Patriot Ct					
-	BtlT	60560	3262	40W-13S	B4
10	CRY	60013	2641	31W-24N	D6
500	GRNE	60031	2534	17W-34N	A1
24400	CRTE	60417	3685	1W-29S	A2
25100	PNFD	60544	3337	31W-17S	E7
Patriot Dr					
1000	NLNX	60451	3589	18W-26S	B2
N Patriot Dr					
300	HNVL	60030	2532	22W-33N	C3
300	HNVL	60073	2532	22W-33N	C3
Patriot Ln					
-	SRWD	60404	3495	31W-24S	E6
900	HFET	60192	2804	24W-14N	D3
1100	CRY	60013	2641	31W-24N	D6
24300	CRTE	60417	3685	1W-29S	A1
Patriot Pkwy					
-	ELBN	60119	3017	43W-0N	B5
Patriot Wy					
-	VNHL	60061	2647	16W-24N	D7
12900	HTLY	60142	2744	43W-19N	B3
Patriot's Ln					
2800	NPVL	60563	3140	29W-6S	C4
2800	NpvT	60540	3140	29W-6S	C4
2800	NpvT	60563	3140	29W-6S	C4
Patriot Square Blvd					
-	PNFD	60544	3338	30W-17S	A5
Patriot Square Dr					
14500	PNFD	60544	3338	30W-17S	A6
Pattee Av					
-	ELBN	60119	3017	42W-0N	C5
Patten Av					
2700	GNVA	60134	3019	37W-0N	C5
E Patten Dr					
800	PLTN	60074	2753	19W-16N	B6
Patten Rd					
-	HDPK	60035	2704	8W-23N	E2
800	HDPK	60035	2650	9W-24N	D7
800	HIWD	60040	2650	9W-24N	D7
800	MrnT	60037	2650	9W-24N	D7
800	MrnT	60040	2650	9W-24N	D7
3100	HDPK	60037	2704	8W-24N	D1
3300	MrnT	60037	2704	8W-24N	D1
3400	MrnT	60040	2704	8W-24N	D1
Patterman Rd					
100	WnfT	60555	3080	29W-3S	D6
100	WNVL	60555	3080	29W-3S	D6
Patterson Av					
-	BtvT	60510	3077	38W-3S	A6
1400	NARA	60542	3077	38W-3S	B6
W Patterson Av					
600	CHCG	60613	2978	0W-4N	A2
1100	CHCG	60613	2977	1W-4N	D2
1900	CHCG	60618	2977	2W-4N	B2
4000	CHCG	60618	2976	5W-4N	B2
4000	CHCG	60641	2976	5W-4N	B2
4700	CHCG	60641	2975	6W-4N	D2
5600	CHCG	60634	2975	7W-4N	B2
7700	CHCG	60634	2974	9W-4N	C3
Patterson Ct					
6500	WDRG	60517	3143	21W-7S	D6
Patterson Rd					
-	BtlT	60512	3198	41W-10S	A7
-	MTGY	60512	3198	41W-10S	A7
10	JLET	60436	3499	24W-25S	A7
10	JltT	60436	3498	24W-25S	E7
10	JltT	60436	3499	24W-25S	A7
300	JltT	60436	3586	25W-26S	B3
600	JltT	60421	3586	25W-26S	B3
S Patterson Rd					
3600	JknT	60421	3586	26W-28S	B7
3600	JknT	60421	3675	26W-29S	B2
3600	JLET	60421	3586	26W-28S	B7
3600	JltT	60421	3586	26W-28S	B7
22400	JltT	60436	3586	26W-28S	B7
24200	ELWD	60421	3675	25W-29S	B2
W Patterson St					
23100	PNFD	60544	3416	29W-18S	D2
23100	PnfT	60544	3416	29W-18S	D2
Pattie Ln					
100	LYWD	60411	3510	4E-25S	C7
Patton Av					
200	OKTR	60181	3085	17W-1S	C1
200	YkTp	60181	3085	17W-1S	C1
1100	LIHL	60156	2693	35W-22N	E4
N Patton Av					
200	ANHT	60005	2806	18W-14N	E4
1500	ANHT	60004	2806	18W-15N	E1
2700	ANHT	60004	2753	18W-17N	E6
S Patton Av					
10	ANHT	60005	2806	18W-13N	E5
1200	ANHT	60005	2860	18W-12N	E1
S Patton Cir					
700	ANHT	60005	2806	18W-13N	E6
Patton Dr					
-	CHCG	60018	2917	13W-8N	A3
-	CHCG	60666	2917	13W-8N	A3
-	LslT	60532	3143	23W-5S	A4
-	RSMT	60018	2917	13W-8N	A3
400	BFGV	60089	2754	17W-18N	C4
3000	DSPN	60018	2917	12W-8N	C2
3200	WDRG	60517	3143	22W-7S	C7
5400	LSLE	60532	3143	23W-5S	A4
N Patton Dr					
4500	CHCG	60656	2918	10W-5N	A7
Patton St					
5100	MchT	60097	2469	36W-37N	E2
Patty Ln					
4700	RGWD	60072	2470	34W-36N	C3
8900	ODPK	60462	3346	11W-15S	A1
Patty Berg Ct					
3800	WDRG	60517	3143	23W-7S	A6
Patuxet Ct					
200	SMBG	60194	2858	24W-10N	C5
Paul Av					
1700	GLHT	60139	2969	23W-3N	B6
Paul Cir					
400	BRTN	60010	2751	25W-20N	B1
13000	WldT	60585	3338	29W-15S	C2
Paul Ct					
1100	FRGV	60021	2696	30W-22N	A3
16700	ODPK	60467	3423	13W-20S	A3
Paul St					
10	GYLK	60030	2532	20W-32N	E5
200	ELBN	60119	3017	43W-1N	B3
700	ISLK	60042	2642	29W-27N	B1
700	ISLK	60051	2642	29W-27N	B1
700	NndT	60051	2642	29W-27N	B1
1200	WKGN	60085	2536	11W-34N	E1
Paula Av					
1400	WHTN	60187	3082	25W-1S	A1
Paula Ct					
300	DRFD	60015	2756	12W-20N	C1
1800	SYHW	60118	2800	35W-16N	B2
13100	WldT	60585	3338	29W-15S	C2
Paula Ln					
1800	DSPN	60018	2917	12W-8N	B1
Paul Briese Ct					
6600	JLET	60586	3415	32W-20S	D5
Pauley Sq					
10	BbyT	60134	3018	39W-0N	E6
Paulina St					
1100	OKPK	60302	3030	8W-1N	D3
1100	RVFT	60302	3030	8W-1N	D3
1100	RVFT	60305	3030	8W-1N	D3
14300	DXMR	60426	3349	2W-17S	D5
14800	HRVY	60426	3349	2W-18S	D7
15600	HRVY	60426	3427	2W-19S	D1
16000	MKHM	60426	3427	2W-19S	D2
16100	MKHM	60428	3427	2W-19S	D3
16500	MKHM	60426	3427	2W-19S	D3
16800	HLCT	60429	3427	2W-20S	D4
N Paulina St					
10	CHCG	60612	3033	2W-0N	C4
1300	CHCG	60622	3033	2W-1N	C1
1600	CHCG	60622	2977	2W-2N	C7
2600	CHCG	60614	2977	2W-3N	C5
2600	CHCG	60657	2977	2W-3N	C5
4000	CHCG	60613	2977	2W-5N	C1
4400	CHCG	60640	2921	2W-5N	C7
5100	CHCG	60640	2921	2W-6N	C6
5500	CHCG	60660	2921	2W-6N	C5
7000	CHCG	60626	2921	2W-8N	C1
7600	CHCG	60626	2867	2W-9N	C6
S Paulina St					
500	CHCG	60612	3033	2W-0S	C6
1300	CHCG	60608	3033	2W-1S	C7
1600	CHCG	60608	3091	2W-2S	C2
4300	CHCG	60609	3091	2W-4S	C7
4700	CHCG	60609	3151	2W-5S	D2
5500	CHCG	60636	3151	2W-8S	D7
7500	CHCG	60620	3213	2W-10S	D4
11900	CHCG	60643	3277	2W-14S	D5
11900	CTPK	60643	3277	2W-14S	D5
11900	CTPK	60827	3277	2W-14S	D5
12100	BLID	60827	3277	2W-14S	D5
12700	BLID	60406	3277	2W-15S	D7
12700	CTPK	60406	3277	2W-15S	D7
Pauline Av					
-	BFGV	60069	2754	16W-20N	D1
-	NLES	60714	2864	10W-12N	B1
-	VrnT	60069	2754	16W-20N	D1
-	VrnT	60089	2754	16W-20N	D1
10	BFGV	60089	2754	16W-20N	D1
10	CLLK	60014	2639	38W-25N	A5
10	GfnT	60014	2639	38W-25N	A5
2600	MaiT	60025	2864	10W-12N	B1
W Pauline Av					
15700	BFGV	60069	2754	16W-20N	E1
15700	BFGV	60089	2754	16W-20N	E1
15700	VrnT	60069	2754	16W-20N	E1
15700	VrnT	60089	2754	16W-20N	E1
Pauline Cir					
10	SMBG	60173	2859	22W-10N	D5
1400	LbvT	60060	2646	18W-26N	E3
1400	MDLN	60060	2646	18W-26N	E3
Pauline Ct					
600	GLBT	60136	2799	37W-15N	C3
13200	PlsT	60462	3346	10W-15S	B1
Pauline Dr					
10	ELGN	60123	2854	35W-10N	A5
S Pauline Dr					
17400	PnfT	60586	3415	31W-20S	E6
W Pauline Dr					
25000	PnfT	60586	3416	31W-20S	A6
Pauline Pl					
-	PLNO	60545	3259	48W-13S	B5
N Pauline St					
41900	AntT	60002	2356	25W-41N	E7
W Pauling Rd					
13300	MhtT	60442	3767	18W-32S	B2
Paul Jones St					
500	NCHI	60088	2537	10W-31N	A7
2300	NCHI	60088	2594	10W-30N	A1
Paul Revere Ct					
400	AURA	60504	3140	29W-6S	D5
14700	PNFD	60544	3338	30W-17S	B6
Paul Revere Dr					
800	LYVL	60048	2591	15W-28N	E7
Paul Revere Ln					
200	DRGV	60515	3084	19W-2S	D4
200	DRGV	60523	3084	19W-2S	D4
200	YkTp	60523	3084	19W-2S	D4
14600	PNFD	60544	3338	30W-17S	B6
14600	PnfT	60544	3338	30W-17S	B6
Paulsen Av					
10	SCHT	60411	3596	1W-26S	B2
Paulson Dr					
6600	RlyT	60152	2634	50W-25N	A5
Paulson St					
4800	MchT	60050	2472	29W-36N	B3
Pauly Dr					
900	EGVV	60007	2861	17W-10N	B5
1300	GRNE	60031	2478	15W-35N	A6
Pau Puk Keewis					
34800	GrtT	60051	2472	28W-34N	E7
Pavilion Pl					
-	WldT	60585	3337	31W-15S	D2
25400	PNFD	60585	3337	31W-15S	D2
Pavilion Wy					
1600	PKRG	60068	2863	12W-10N	C4
Pavillion Rd					
6600	KdlT	60560	3332	44W-16S	D5
Pawnee Cir					
2800	GNVW	60025	2809	11W-15N	C2
Pawnee Dr					
10	TNTN	60476	3428	0E-20S	E4
10	TNTN	60476	3429	0E-20S	A4
500	LIHL	60156	2694	35W-21N	B5
700	CLSM	60188	2967	27W-3N	C7
800	CLSM	60185	2967	27W-3N	C7
800	WynT	60185	2967	27W-3N	C7
Pawnee Ln					
500	NPVL	60563	3141	26W-5S	E2
E Pawnee Ln					
1900	MPPT	60056	2808	13W-15N	E3
W Pawnee Ln					
13400	HMGN	60491	3343	16W-16S	E4
25200	CNHN	60410	3672	31W-28S	E1
Pawnee Rd					
1000	WLMT	60091	2812	5W-14N	B5
1500	CPVL	60110	2748	32W-18N	C4
2700	WKGN	60087	2479	12W-36N	C4
13500	ODPK	60462	3346	9W-16S	C2
13500	PSHT	60463	3346	9W-16S	C2
N Pawnee Rd					
24800	CbaT	60010	2644	25W-25N	A6
24800	LKBN	60010	2643	25W-24N	E6
24800	LKBN	60010	2644	25W-25N	A6
S Pawnee Rd					
12500	PSPK	60464	3274	10W-14S	A7
W Pawnee Rd					
8400	PSPK	60464	3274	10W-14S	B7
Pawnee St					
100	PNFD	60544	3416	31W-18S	A1
1200	JLET	60433	3587	22W-25S	C1
1200	JltT	60433	3587	22W-25S	C1
Paw Paw Av					
16400	ODPK	60467	3423	13W-19S	A3
Pawtucket Av					
200	ElgT	60124	2853	38W-10N	A5
Pawtucket Rd					
3000	NHBK	60062	2756	11W-17N	D5
Paxos Dr					
10	PSHL	60465	3274	9W-12S	C1
Paxson Ct					
10	BGBK	60440	3204	24W-10S	D5
Paxson Dr					
-	BGBK	60440	3204	24W-10S	D5
-	BGBK	60565	3204	24W-10S	E6
-	LslT	60565	3204	24W-10S	D5
Paxton Av					
-	CTCY	60409	3429	2E-19S	D1
-	CTCY	60473	3429	2E-18S	D1
-	ThtT	60409	3429	2E-18S	D1
-	ThtT	60473	3429	2E-18S	D1
10	CTCY	60409	3351	2E-16S	D4
7900	TYPK	60477	3424	9W-20S	D3
15400	ThtT	60409	3351	2E-18S	D7
15400	ThtT	60473	3351	2E-18S	D7
16600	SHLD	60473	3429	2E-18S	D3
17500	LNSG	60438	3429	2E-21S	D6

STREET Block	City	ZIP	Map#	CGS Grid	Grid
Paxton Av					
17600	ThtT	60438	3429	2E-21S	D6
22100	SLVL	60411	3597	2E-26S	D3
S Paxton Av					
-	CHCG	60633	3351	2E-15S	D2
-	CTCY	60409	3351	2E-15S	D2
4900	HMND	46320	3352		D5
6700	CHCG	60649	3153	2E-8S	C7
7500	CHCG	60649	3215	2E-9S	C2
7800	CHCG	60617	3215	2E-9S	C2
Paxton Ct					
2900	LSLE	60563	3142	24W-5S	C2
2900	LslT	60563	3142	24W-5S	C3
Paxton Dr					
500	NpvT	60563	3140	30W-5S	C3
1700	NPVL	60563	3140	29W-5S	C3
W Paxton Dr					
9700	BHPK	60099	2422	9W-39N	C6
Paxton Ln					
10	SMBG	60194	2858	25W-10N	B5
Paxton Pl					
600	CLSM	60188	2967	26W-2N	D7
Paxton Rd					
4800	OKLN	60453	3212	6W-11S	A7
4900	OKLN	60453	3211	6W-11S	E7
W Paydon Rd					
10	PNFD	60543	3337	33W-15S	A3
10	PNFD	60585	3337	33W-15S	A3
Payne Av					
1200	BTVA	60510	3077	36W-2S	E3
Payne Dr					
-	CHCG	60615	3152	0E-5S	E2
-	CHCG	60637	3152	0E-5S	E2
E Payne Dr					
-	CHCG	60615	3152	1E-5S	E2
Payne Rd					
1300	SMBG	60173	2859	22W-12N	D2
Payne St					
1500	EVTN	60201	2867	3W-12N	A1
1700	EVTN	60201	2866	3W-12N	E1
3300	SKOK	60076	2866	4W-12N	B1
5000	SKOK	60077	2865	6W-12N	E1
Payson Cir					
300	GLHT	60139	2969	23W-4N	B3
Payson St					
10	HFET	60169	2858	24W-10N	E5
Payton Cross					
-	JNBG	60050	2471	32W-34N	B7
Payton Ln					
500	BGBK	60440	3268	24W-12S	E3
Payton Run					
-	ANHT	60005	2807	16W-13N	C7
Peace Av					
100	BGBK	60490	3267	27W-11S	C2
Peace Blvd					
10	WCDA	60084	2643	26W-26N	E2
10	WcnT	60084	2643	26W-26N	E2
Peace Dr					
1000	WLNG	60090	2755	15W-16N	A6
Peace Ln					
-	BHPK	60099	2421	12W-40N	C3
-	ZION	60099	2421	12W-40N	C3
E Peacedale Ct					
24400	PnfT	60586	3416	30W-19S	B3
W Peacedale Ct					
24500	PnfT	60586	3416	30W-19S	B3
Peace Memorial Dr					
-	PlsT	60462	3345	12W-15S	B1
-	PlsT	60464	3345	12W-15S	B1
Peach Ln					
1700	SMBG	60194	2858	25W-11N	B3
Peach Pkwy					
10100	SKOK	60076	2811	7W-13N	B7
10100	SKOK	60076	2812	5W-12N	A7
Peach St					
-	CTHL	60435	3417	27W-20S	D6
-	PnfT	60435	3417	27W-20S	D6
100	PKFT	60466	3595	3W-27S	B4
Peachgate Ct					
2900	GNVW	60025	2810	10W-13N	B5
2900	NfdT	60025	2810	10W-13N	B5
Peachgate Ln					
3000	NfdT	60025	2810	10W-13N	A5
Peachgate Rd					
-	GNVW	60025	2810	10W-13N	A5
-	NfdT	60025	2810	10W-13N	A5
Peach Grove Ln					
3600	HLCT	60429	3426	4W-20S	D5
Peach Tree Av					
2900	SLVL	60411	3598	3E-26S	A3
Peachtree Cir					
2800	AURA	60502	3139	32W-6S	D4
Peach Tree Ct					
10	ALGN	60102	2747	36W-19N	A2
600	DYR	46311	3598		E3
Peachtree Ct					
10	ELGN	60120	2855	32W-11N	C4
300	BGBK	60440	3269	22W-13S	D4
500	CLLK	60014	2693	36W-23N	D3
700	LIHL	60156	2693	37W-22N	B4
900	VNHL	60061	2647	17W-26N	C3
1100	LslT	60540	3142	25W-6S	A5
1100	NPVL	60540	3142	25W-6S	A5
3500	JLET	60435	3417	27W-19S	D3
6400	OKFT	60452	3347	8W-18S	B7
Peachtree Dr					
8900	TYPK	60487	3424	11W-22S	A7
15500	ODPK	60462	3345	11W-18S	E7
15600	ODPK	60462	3423	11W-18S	E1
Peach Tree Ln					
10	WTMT	60559	3145	18W-7S	A6
200	EGVV	60007	2914	18W-8N	E3
800	GLNC	60022	2758	7W-17N	C5
1800	ALGN	60102	2747	36W-19N	A2
2000	ALGN	60102	2746	36W-19N	E2
2300	DYR	46311	3598		E3
Peachtree Ln					
-	JLET	60435	3417	27W-19S	D3
100	WCHI	60185	3022	30W-1N	C2
100	WDSK	60098	2524	41W-32N	D4
400	WNFD	60190	3023	26W-1N	E3
500	LKZH	60047	2698	24W-22N	C5
1000	DRFD	60015	2756	11W-20N	D2
1100	ELGN	60120	2855	32W-11N	D4
1400	LKPT	60441	3419	21W-20S	E4
2300	NHBK	60062	2757	10W-17N	A5
E Peachtree Ln					
600	LkvT	60046	2475	22W-36N	C4
600	LkvT	60073	2475	22W-36N	C4
600	RLKB	60073	2475	22W-36N	C4
1500	ANHT	60004	2754	16W-16N	C7
1900	WLNG	60090	2754	16W-16N	C7
N Peachtree Ln					
1300	MPPT	60056	2808	13W-14N	D4
S Peach Tree Ln					
11300	ALSP	60803	3275	6W-13S	E4
S Peach Tree Ln					
26200	MONE	60449	3682	6W-31S	E6
Peach Tree St					
6600	HRPK	60133	2911	27W-8N	D3
Peacock Av					
-	BHPK	60099	2421	12W-39N	B4
Peacock Ct					
500	NPVL	60565	3203	26W-9S	D3
4200	RGMW	60008	2806	19W-13N	B7
Peacock Ln					
1300	JLET	60586	3496	29W-22S	C2
3200	RGMW	60008	2806	20W-12N	B7
9400	TYPK	60487	3423	11W-21S	E6
W Peacock Rd					
12600	BHPK	60099	2421	12W-39N	B4
Peak Dr					
7800	PSHL	60465	3274	9W-13S	C4
Peale Av					
900	PKRG	60068	2918	9W-8N	B2
Peale St					
10	JltT	60433	3499	21W-24S	E6
Pear Av					
16400	ODPK	60467	3423	13W-19S	A3
Pearce's Ford Rd					
-	OSWG	60543	3264	36W-11S	A1
600	OSWG	60543	3199	38W-11S	A7
600	OSWG	60543	3263	36W-11S	E1
Pearl Av					
-	ELGN	60120	2855	32W-10N	C6
200	BmdT	60137	2969	22W-2N	B7
200	BmdT	60137	3025	23W-2N	B1
200	GLHT	60137	3025	23W-2N	B1
200	GLHT	60139	3025	23W-2N	B1
500	GLHT	60139	2969	23W-2N	B7
800	MHRY	60050	2528	32W-31N	C7
800	NndT	60050	2528	32W-31N	C7
1200	BmdT	60139	3025	22W-2N	B1
2800	LydT	60164	2972	14W-3N	C5
2800	NHLK	60164	2972	14W-3N	C5
3000	FNPK	60131	2972	14W-3N	C5
3000	LydT	60131	2972	14W-3N	C5
Pearl Ct					
-	TNLK	53181	2354		B1
1600	CLLK	60014	2693	36W-22N	D3
1600	NPVL	60563	3140	29W-5S	D2
Pearl Dr					
600	HFET	60169	2858	24W-10N	D5
Pearl Ln					
400	CRTE	60417	3685	0W-29S	B1
Pearl Rd					
10	WCHI	60185	3022	30W-0S	B6
10	WnfT	60185	3022	30W-0S	B6
Pearl St					
-	AntT	60081	2414	28W-38N	E7
-	McHT	60051	2528	32W-33N	C3
-	MHRY	60051	2528	32W-33N	C3
10	CRY	60013	2695	30W-23N	E1
200	CRY	60013	2696	30W-23N	A1
200	MTGY	60538	3199	37W-9S	D4
400	WCHI	60185	3022	30W-0N	B5
800	AURA	60505	3200	35W-9S	B4
800	WMTN	60481	3943	27W-39S	D1
900	HMND	46394	3280		E4
1200	MTGY	60505	3200	35W-9S	B4
1300	MTGY	60538	3200	35W-9S	B4
3200	FNPK	60131	2973	11W-4N	C4
3300	MHRY	60050	2528	32W-33N	C3
5100	CHCG	60018	2917	12W-6N	C6
5100	SRPK	60018	2917	12W-6N	C6
5100	SRPK	60176	2917	12W-6N	C6
5400	RSMT	60018	2917	12W-6N	B5
N Pearl St					
100	WLSP	60480	3209	12W-9S	B3
200	JLET	60435	3498	24W-23S	D4
39700	AntT	60002	2415	26W-39N	E4
Pearle Dr					
2600	DSPN	60018	2917	12W-8N	B2
Pearl Harbor Dr					
1600	JLET	60435	3497	27W-21S	C1
Pearlman Dr					
1000	LKZH	60047	2645	22W-24N	B7
Pearsall Pkwy					
1900	WKGN	60085	2536	11W-33N	D4
Pearson Cir					
300	NPVL	60563	3141	27W-5S	C4
Pearson Dr					
200	SchT	60174	2964	35W-5N	C2
200	WYNE	60174	2964	35W-5N	B2
600	BmdT	60172	2912	24W-6N	D6
600	ROSL	60172	2912	24W-6N	D6
800	JLET	60435	3497	26W-22S	E3
8500	DRN	60561	3206	20W-9S	C4
Pearson Rd					
800	CRY	60013	2695	32W-23N	B2
1200	GNOK	60048	2592	14W-29N	B3
1200	LbvT	60048	2592	14W-29N	B3
Pearson St					
600	DSPN	60016	2863	13W-10N	A4
E Pearson St					
10	CHCG	60610	3034	0E-1N	C2
10	CHCG	60611	3034	0E-1N	C2
W Pearson St					
10	CHCG	60611	3034		D2
500	CHCG	60610	3034	0W-1N	A2
1500	CHCG	60622	3033	1W-1N	D2
Pear Tree Cir					
24000	PNFD	60585	3266	30W-14S	C7
Pear Tree Ct					
3700	CCHL	60478	3426	4W-20S	D4
24100	PNFD	60585	3266	30W-14S	C7
Peartree Dr					
3700	LIHL	60156	2693	37W-22N	B4
Pear Tree Ln					
100	BRLT	60103	2910	29W-7N	E5
100	WynT	60103	2910	29W-7N	E5
900	WLNG	60090	2755	15W-16N	A7
N Peartree Ln					
10	ANHT	60004	2807	16W-14N	D4
1300	MPPT	60056	2808	13W-14N	D4
S Pear Tree Ln					
800	BRLT	60103	2910	28W-7N	E5
Pear Tree Rd					
1600	DRFD	60015	2703	12W-21N	C6
Pear Tree Wy					
12100	PNFD	60585	3266	30W-14S	B7
Pebble Cr					
3600	MHRY	60050	2528	32W-31N	B7
Pebble Ct					
10	BGBK	60440	3268	25W-11S	B1
400	SMBG	60193	2859	22W-9N	B7
700	MonT	60466	3684	3W-29S	A2
W Pebble Ct					
10	PSHL	60465	3274	10W-12S	B3
Pebble Dr					
900	WLNG	60090	2754	15W-18N	E4
900	WLNG	60090	2755	15W-18N	A4
N Pebble Dr					
2000	McHT	60051	2528	30W-34N	E1
2000	McHT	60051	2529	30W-33N	A2
S Pebble Dr					
12700	PlsT	60464	3273	12W-15S	D7
12700	PlsT	60464	3345	12W-15S	D1
12700	PSPK	60464	3273	12W-15S	D7
12700	PSPK	60464	3345	12W-15S	D1
W Pebble Dr					
9700	PlsT	60464	3273	12W-15S	D7
9700	PSPK	60464	3273	12W-15S	D7
Pebble Ln					
1400	CLLK	60014	2693	37W-23N	C2
5200	PRGV	60012	2584	34W-29N	D4
W Pebble Ln					
7400	FftT	60423	3504	9W-24S	E6
Pebble Beach Cir					
400	UYPK	60466	3684	2W-30S	C2
1600	ELGN	60123	2854	36W-9N	A7
1800	EGVV	60007	2859	22W-9N	C7
N Pebble Beach Cir					
1300	GLHT	60139	3024	24W-2N	D1
W Pebble Beach Cir					
10	GLHT	60139	3024	24W-2N	D1
Pebble Beach Ct					
10	LIHL	60156	2693	37W-21N	C5
10	NPVL	60563	3140	30W-4S	C1
10	NpvT	60563	3140	30W-4S	C1
400	UYPK	60466	3684	2W-30S	C3
900	GNVA	60134	3019	36W-0N	E5
1700	HFET	60169	2858	25W-12N	B2
Pebblebeach Ct					
1300	HRPK	60133	2911	26W-7N	E6
S Pebble Beach Ct					
27000	CteT	60417	3774	0W-33S	D2
Pebble Beach Dr					
1600	HFET	60169	2858	25W-12N	A2
1600	JLET	60586	3496	30W-21S	B1
1700	JLET	60586	3416	30W-21S	B7
Pebblebeach Dr					
5500	HRPK	60133	2911	26W-7N	E5
W Pebble Beach Dr					
4700	WKGN	60083	2478	14W-37N	C2
Pebble Beach Ln					
300	BRLT	60103	2910	29W-8N	C2
300	BRLT	60120	2910	30W-8N	C2
400	RVWD	60015	2756	13W-20N	A1
8800	ODPK	60462	3346	10W-16S	A3
Pebble Beach Rd					
3600	NHBK	60062	2756	12W-17N	B4
N Pebble Beach Wy					
1600	VNHL	60061	2647	17W-27N	B1
Pebblebrook Ct					
400	SRGV	60554	3197	42W-8S	D1
Pebblebrook Ln					
2500	RGMW	60008	2805	21W-13N	C5
7800	HRPK	60133	2857	26W-9N	D7
Pebblebrook Rd					
400	NHBK	60062	2758	8W-16N	A7
400	NHBK	60093	2758	8W-16N	A7
Pebble Creek Ct					
-	WRLK	60097	2469	37W-36N	B3
6000	GRNE	60031	2534	16W-33N	D3
14600	HMGN	60491	3343	17W-17S	C5
Pebble Creek Dr					
10	LKZH	60047	2699	22W-22N	B4
100	CbaT	60010	2643	26W-25N	E5
100	TRLK	60010	2643	26W-25N	E5
200	BMDL	60108	2969	22W-4N	C3
2100	LSLE	60532	3082	24W-4S	D7
2100	LslT	60532	3082	24W-4S	D7
2500	LSLE	60187	3082	24W-4S	D7
Pebblecreek Dr					
-	GNVW	60025	2810	8W-14N	E5
S Pebble Creek Dr					
14300	HMGN	60491	3343	17W-17S	C5
Pebble Creek Ln					
4400	LGGV	60047	2700	18W-22N	E3
16600	PNFD	60586	3416	30W-19S	C4
E Pebble Creek Rd					
400	PLTN	60074	2753	20W-16N	A6
Pebblecreek Tr					
100	CLSM	60188	2968	25W-3N	A6
Pebbleford Ln					
2500	GNVW	60025	2810	10W-15N	A2
Pebblefork Ln					
2300	NHFD	60093	2811	8W-15N	A2
N Pebble Lake Ct					
22500	FKFT	60423	3590	14W-27S	D4
S Pebble Lake Ct					
22600	FKFT	60423	3590	14W-27S	D4
Pebblestone Dr					
1700	RMVL	60446	3339	27W-17S	C5
Pebblestone Rd					
200	NPVL	60565	3203	26W-10S	D5
Pebblestone Wy					
-	BGBK	60490	3339	27W-15S	B1
Pebblestone Cove					
1400	WHTN	60187	3081	26W-1S	E2
Pebblewood Ct					
2400	AURA	60506	3136	39W-6S	E5
Pebblewood Ln					
10	NpvT	60563	3140	30W-5S	C2
1100	GLNC	60022	2758	7W-18N	B4
1600	NPVL	60563	3140	29W-5S	C2
1700	HFET	60192	2804	25W-15N	B2
17700	HLCT	60429	3427	3W-21S	A6
Pebblewood Tr					
-	NPVL	60563	3140	30W-5S	C2
10	NpvT	60563	3140	30W-5S	C2
Pecan Ct					
1000	NPVL	60540	3203	27W-8S	C1
Pecan Ln					
17500	TYPK	60487	3424	11W-21S	A5
Pecan Pl					
8200	FftT	60423	3504	10W-24S	C5
Pecan St					
2400	JLET	60435	3417	27W-20S	D5
2400	PnfT	60435	3417	27W-20S	D5
N Peck Av					
10	LGNG	60525	3087	13W-4S	A6
100	LGPK	60525	3087	13W-4S	A6
S Peck Av					
200	LGNG	60525	3087	13W-4S	A7
200	LGNG	60525	3147	13W-4S	A1
5500	CTSD	60525	3147	13W-6S	A4
5500	LynT	60525	3147	13W-6S	A4
Peck Pl					
700	ELGN	60120	2855	32W-10N	D6
Peck Rd					
10	GNVA	60134	3019	38W-1N	B3
10	GnvT	60134	3019	38W-1N	B3
10	SCRL	60175	2963	37W-3N	B6
400	GNVA	60134	3020	35W-0N	B5
700	SchT	60175	2963	37W-3N	B6
900	GnvT	60175	3019	37W-1N	B2
Peck Rd					
900	SchT	60175	3019	37W-1N	B2
900	SCRL	60175	3019	37W-1N	B2
Peck Rd CO-84					
10	GNVA	60134	3019	38W-1N	B3
10	GnvT	60134	3019	38W-1N	B3
400	SCRL	60175	2963	38W-2N	B7
900	GnvT	60175	3019	37W-1N	B2
900	SchT	60175	3019	37W-1N	B2
900	SCRL	60175	3019	37W-1N	B2
Pecos Cir					
100	CPVL	60110	2748	33W-18N	C4
E Pecos Ln					
900	MPPT	60056	2808	13W-14N	E4
W Peder Ln					
700	PLTN	60067	2752	21W-16N	C6
S Pedersen Dr					
41500	AntT	60002	2418	19W-41N	B1
41600	AntT	60002	2359	19W-41N	B7
W Pedersen Dr S					
19400	ANTH	60002	2359	19W-41N	C7
19400	AntT	60002	2359	19W-41N	C7
N Pedersen Ln					
42200	AntT	60002	2356	27W-42N	C6
Peebles Ct					
500	BTVA	60510	3019	36W-0S	D7
S Peebles Rd					
600	PLTN	60067	2805	22W-15N	A2
S Peerless Dr					
15900	PNFD	60544	3416	29W-19S	D2
15900	PNFD	60586	3416	29W-19S	D2
15900	PnfT	60586	3416	29W-19S	D3
Pegasus Ct					
1100	RLKP	60030	2589	22W-30N	C1
Peggy Ct					
-	WLNG	60090	2755	14W-17N	C5
21100	RlyT	60152	2634	50W-25N	B5
Peggy Ln					
1100	CHHT	60411	3507	2W-25S	D7
15700	BmnT	60477	3425	7W-18S	D1
15700	OKFT	60452	3347	7W-18S	D7
15700	OKFT	60452	3425	7W-18S	D1
Pegwood Dr					
1100	ELGN	60120	2855	32W-11N	D3
Peiffer Av					
10	LMNT	60439	3270	20W-14S	C7
E Peiffer Av					
10	LMNT	60439	3270	19W-14S	D6
W Peiffer Av					
10	LMNT	60439	3270	19W-14S	C6
Pekara Dr					
100	VrnT	60015	2702	15W-20N	B7
Pelham Ct					
300	LslT	60540	3205	23W-7S	A1
900	NPVL	60563	3140	29W-5S	D3
Pelham Rd					
1000	WNKA	60093	2811	5W-16N	E1
1000	WNKA	60093	2812	5W-16N	A1
Pelham St					
10100	WSTR	60154	3029	12W-1S	B7
10200	PvsT	60162	3029	12W-1S	A7
10200	WSTR	60162	3029	12W-1S	A7
Pelican Ct					
1300	ZION	60099	2362	11W-41N	D7
Pelican Dr					
8700	HGKN	60525	3147	11W-7S	E5
18000	TYPK	60487	3424	11W-21S	A6
Pelican Ln					
700	PTON	60468	3860	10W-38S	C5
Pelican Bay					
10	ROSL	60172	2912	24W-7N	C4
Pelicans Nest					
200	BCHR	60401	3864	0E-36S	E1
Pell Av					
200	RMVL	60446	3340	24W-16S	E3
200	RMVL	60446	3341	23W-16S	A3
Pell St					
10100	WSTR	60154	3087	12W-1S	B2
W Pellinore Dr					
24400	TroT	60404	3584	30W-27S	B5
Pember Cir					
900	WDHD	60118	2800	35W-16N	B1
S Pemberly Ct					
9700	PSHL	60465	3210	10W-11S	A7
Pembridge Av					
8200	WDRG	60517	3206	20W-9S	B3
Pembridge Dr					
800	LKFT	60045	2649	12W-27N	C1
2100	LIHL	60142	2692	39W-22N	C3
Pembridge Ln					
200	SMBG	60193	2859	23W-10N	B6
600	PTHT	60070	2808	14W-14N	B3
Pembridge Pl					
700	SRGV	60554	3135	41W-4S	E2
900	SRGV	60554	3136	41W-4S	A2
Pembridge Rd					
900	LKZH	60047	2699	22W-22N	B4
15300	ODPK	60462	3346	10W-18S	A7
Pembroke Av					
100	NlxT	60433	3500	20W-23S	B4
300	JLET	60432	3500	20W-23S	B4
2300	HFET	60169	2803	26W-12N	E7
17000	TYPK	60477	3424	9W-20S	D4
Pembroke Cir					
10	SMWD	60107	2856	29W-11N	D4
100	NCHI	60044	2593	13W-29N	A3
Pembroke Ct					
300	SMBG	60193	2857	26W-10N	E6
400	DRFD	60015	2756	11W-20N	D1
Pembroke Dr					
10	LKFT	60045	2649	10W-26N	E3
10	LKFT	60045	2650	10W-26N	A3
10	LNSH	60045	2702	14W-23N	C2
N Pembroke Dr					
1400	SEGN	60177	2908	36W-8N	A2
S Pembroke Dr					
-	SMBG	60194	2857	26W-10N	E6
10	SMBG	60193	2857	26W-10N	E6
1300	SEGN	60177	2908	36W-8N	A3
Pembroke Ln					
10	OKBK	60523	3085	17W-2S	B3
1400	WHTN	60187	3082	23W-1S	E2
9100	BGVW	60455	3211	8W-10S	A5
Pembroke Rd					
10	LslT	60540	3142	25W-6S	A6
10	NPVL	60540	3142	25W-6S	A6
4700	MTSN	60443	3506	5W-24S	B6
Pembroke on Duxbury					
10	RGMW	60008	2805	22W-13N	B6
Pembrook Cir					
1200	ROSL	60172	2912	25W-7N	B5
Pem Brook Ct					
1700	JLET	60586	3416	30W-21S	C7
Pembrook Ct					
10	BGBK	60440	3268	25W-11S	C1
10	FSMR	60422	3507	3W-22S	A1
Pembrook Ct					
10	FSMR	60430	3507	3W-22S	A1
800	CLSM	60188	3024	24W-1N	E2
5100	GRNE	60031	2478	15W-35N	B5
10800	FKFT	60423	3591	13W-26S	A2
Pembrook Ct N					
500	CLLK	60014	2693	36W-23N	D3
Pembrook Ct S					
500	CLLK	60014	2693	36W-22N	D3
Pembrook Dr					
10	IHPK	60525	3146	14W-6S	D4
21900	FKFT	60423	3591	13W-26S	A3
Pembrook Ln					
200	MDLN	60060	2591	18W-27N	A7
800	BGBK	60440	3268	24W-11S	C1
Pembroke Ct					
200	RLKB	60073	2475	22W-36N	B4
1900	RMVL	60446	3339	28W-17S	B6
Pembrooke Dr					
-	RMVL	60446	3339	27W-17S	C5
Pembrooke Ln					
300	GNEN	60137	3083	23W-1S	B2
9200	ODPK	60462	3345	11W-18S	E6
Pembrooke Rd					
10	OswT	60538	3199	36W-10S	E6
800	LYVL	60048	2591	17W-28N	C7
Pembury Wy					
10	SBTN	60010	2803	25W-15N	E3
10	SBTN	60010	2804	25W-15N	A2
Pemlico Ct					
10	GYLK	60030	2532	21W-34N	E1
Pence St					
100	LtRT	60545	3259	48W-14S	B7
100	PLNO	60545	3259	48W-14S	B7
Pendelton Ct					
1500	PLTN	60067	2752	21W-17N	D4
1500	PltT	60074	2752	21W-17N	D4
Pendelton St					
100	LktT	60441	3419	21W-19S	E2
Pendleton Ct					
3000	SCRL	60175	2964	36W-4N	A3
Pendleton Dr					
1200	LMNT	60439	3271	18W-14S	A7
Pendleton Ln					
1300	GNVW	60025	2810	8W-14N	D4
1300	GNVW	60025	2811	8W-14N	A5
Pendleton Pl					
10	OSWG	60543	3200	36W-10S	A6
10	OswT	60538	3200	36W-10S	A6
10	OswT	60543	3200	36W-10S	A6
W Pendleton Pl					
1000	MPPT	60056	2861	16W-12N	D1
Penefield Ln					
12900	HTLY	60142	2744	43W-19N	B3
Penfield Av					
800	JltT	60433	3499	22W-25S	C7
Penfield Dr					
700	CLSM	60188	2967	27W-3N	D6
10600	ODPK	60462	3345	13W-18S	A7
Penfield St					
500	BCHR	60401	3864	0W-36S	C2
900	WshT	60401	3864	1W-36S	B2
Penfold Pl					
1600	NHBK	60062	2757	10W-16N	A6
Peninsula Ct					
-	PGGV	60140	2797	42W-15N	C4
Peninsula Dr					
700	WCDA	60084	2588	25W-28N	A7
Peninsula Ln					
10	PTBR	60010	2642	29W-26N	C3
N Peninsula Rd					
37900	LkvT	60046	2474	25W-37N	A1
Penn Av					
1000	AURA	60506	3138	36W-6S	A5
Penn Blvd					
500	LNHT	60046	2418	19W-39N	B5
Penn Ct					
10	OSWG	60543	3263	37W-12S	C3
100	GNVW	60025	2810	10W-15N	B2
700	LNHT	60046	2418	19W-39N	B5
1600	CLLK	60014	2693	36W-22N	D3
1700	NPVL	60565	3204	24W-8S	D2
Penn Ln					
22300	CNHN	60410	3584	29W-27S	E5
N Penn Rd					
900	PNFD	60544	3338	30W-17S	C6
Penncross Dr					
5400	NPVL	60564	3266	29W-13S	D5
Penner Av					
6800	DRGV	60516	3144	20W-7S	A7
Penner Pl					
6800	DRGV	60516	3144	20W-7S	A7
Pennington Ct					
1700	NlxT	60451	3502	16W-24S	A5
W Pennington Ln					
7500	GGnT	60449	3682	8W-31S	A5
E Pennington Rd					
10	PnfT	60544	3338	29W-17S	D5
Pennsboro Ct					
1300	CLSM	60188	2967	28W-4N	B4
Pennsbury Ct					
10	BGBK	60440	3268	25W-11S	C1
200	RLKB	60073	2475	22W-36N	A4
1600	WLNG	60090	2754	16W-18N	D3
2300	SMBG	60194	2857	27W-11N	D3
3200	AURA	60502	3139	31W-6S	E4
4000	HRPK	60133	2967	27W-5N	C2
Pennsbury Ln					
1100	AURA	60502	3139	31W-6S	E4
2000	HRPK	60133	2967	27W-5N	C2
7100	GRNE	60031	2477	17W-35N	A6
Pennsylvania Av					
200	GNEN	60137	3025	23W-0N	A5
200	WHTN	60137	3025	23W-0N	A5
200	WHTN	60187	3025	23W-0N	A5
400	AURA	60506	3138	36W-6S	A6
700	ELGN	60123	2854	34W-11N	C4
1200	DSPN	60016	2862	15W-10N	B5
1200	DSPN	60018	2862	15W-10N	B5
1200	JLET	60435	3498	25W-22S	B1
1200	WPHR	60096	2363	10W-41N	B7
2500	NCHI	60088	2593	12W-30N	C3
12900	HTLY	60142	2744	43W-18N	C4
14200	DLTN	60419	3350	0E-16S	D3
Pennsylvania Ct					
1600	NPVL	60563	3141	28W-5S	B2
17600	ODPK	60467	3423	12W-20S	C5
E Pennsylvania Ct					
600	ANHT	60005	2861	17W-11N	B2
E Pennsylvania Dr					
600	PLTN	60074	2753	20W-18N	B2
Pennsylvania St					
1200	DSPN	60018	2862	15W-10N	B6
Pennview Ln					
2200	SMBG	60194	2858	26W-11N	A3
2300	SMBG	60194	2857	26W-11N	E3

STREET Block	City	ZIP	Map#	CGS	Grid
Pennway Cir					
-	WcnT	60084	2643	26W-26N	E3
Pennwood Ct					
1300	SMBG	60193	2859	21W-10N	D5
N Pennwood Ct					
2400	RLKB	60073	2475	22W-36N	B3
Pennwood Ln					
900	BGBK	60440	3268	25W-11S	C1
Penny Av					
100	EDND	60118	2801	33W-16N	B2
200	DndT	60118	2801	33W-16N	B2
Penny Av SR-68					
100	EDND	60118	2801	33W-16N	B2
200	DndT	60118	2801	33W-16N	B2
Penny Ct					
10	BGBK	60440	3268	25W-11S	C1
600	CLSM	60188	2967	26W-3N	D6
1700	BRLT	60103	2967	28W-4N	B3
Penny Ct N					
10400	FKFT	60423	3591	13W-26S	B2
Penny Ct S					
10400	FKFT	60423	3591	13W-26S	C2
Penny Ln					
10	BlmT	60411	3510	3E-25S	A7
10	SgrT	60506	3135	41W-5S	E3
10	SgrT	60554	3135	41W-5S	E3
10	WNVL	60555	3080	30W-1S	C2
100	BGBK	60440	3268	25W-11S	C1
200	GYLK	60030	2475	21W-34N	D7
200	GYLK	60030	2532	21W-34N	D1
300	PTON	60468	3860	9W-37S	E3
500	CLLK	60014	2693	36W-22N	D3
600	GRNE	60031	2477	18W-34N	A7
700	BFGV	60089	2701	17W-20N	A7
1000	MltT	60187	3082	25W-1S	B2
1000	WHTN	60187	3082	25W-1S	B2
1600	BRLT	60103	2967	28W-5N	B3
8100	RcmT	60071	2412	33W-40N	E3
10400	FKFT	60423	3591	13W-26S	B2
13800	HMGN	60491	3421	17W-19S	D2
N Penny Ln					
1100	PLTN	60067	2752	22W-17N	B5
1300	PnfT	60544	3338	29W-17S	D5
1600	SMBG	60173	2859	22W-12N	C1
Penny Rd					
10	BNHL	60010	2801	30W-15N	E2
10	BNHL	60118	2801	30W-15N	E2
10	CPVL	60110	2801	32W-16N	D1
10	CPVL	60118	2801	32W-16N	D1
10	EDND	60110	2801	30W-15N	E2
10	EDND	60118	2801	30W-15N	E2
300	BNHL	60010	2802	29W-15N	B2
300	BNHL	60118	2802	29W-15N	B2
300	BrnT	60010	2802	28W-15N	D3
300	BrnT	60118	2802	28W-15N	D3
Penny Rd CO-40					
10	BNHL	60010	2801	32W-16N	E2
10	BNHL	60118	2801	32W-16N	E2
10	CPVL	60110	2801	32W-16N	D1
10	CPVL	60118	2801	32W-16N	D1
10	EDND	60110	2801	32W-16N	E1
10	EDND	60118	2801	32W-16N	E1
E Penny Rd					
10	BrnT	60010	2803	26W-15N	D3
10	SBTN	60010	2803	26W-15N	D3
W Penny Rd					
10	BrnT	60010	2802	28W-15N	E3
10	BrnT	60010	2803	28W-15N	A3
10	BrnT	60118	2802	28W-15N	E3
10	SBTN	60010	2803	27W-15N	A3
100	BNHL	60010	2802	28W-15N	E3
100	BNHL	60118	2802	28W-15N	E3
Pennycress Ct					
500	BbyT	60119	3017	42W-1N	C4
Pennyroyal Cir					
2700	NPVL	60564	3266	29W-13S	C5
Penny Royal Pl					
10	WDRG	60517	3143	21W-7S	D7
Pennywood Dr					
5100	LSLE	60532	3142	24W-5S	D3
Penquin Ln					
400	VrnT	60015	2755	15W-20N	A1
Penrith Av					
700	EGVV	60007	2914	19W-8N	D1
Penrith Pl					
1500	SMBG	60194	2858	25W-10N	B5
W Pensacola Av					
1400	CHCG	60613	2977	1W-5N	C1
2000	CHCG	60618	2977	2W-5N	B1
3300	CHCG	60618	2976	4W-5N	D1
4700	CHCG	60641	2975	7W-5N	C1
5500	CHCG	60634	2975	7W-5N	C1
7100	NRDG	60706	2974	9W-5N	D1
Pensacola Ct					
1100	AURA	60502	3139	32W-6S	D4
Pensive Ln					
2000	NfdT	60062	2756	12W-16N	C7
Penstemon Cir					
1500	GYLK	60030	2533	19W-31N	D6
Penstemon Ln					
400	HshT	60140	2796	45W-16N	C1
Pentagon Dr					
10400	ODPK	60467	3423	13W-21S	B6
Pentwater Ct					
-	RMVL	60446	3417	26W-18S	E2
Pentwater Dr					
10	SBTN	60010	2803	27W-13N	A6
Pentwater Rd					
700	RMVL	60446	3417	26W-18S	E1
S Penwick Ct					
100	BMDL	60108	2969	23W-5N	A1
Peony Pl					
200	DRN	60561	3145	16W-7S	D7
Peoria Ct					
800	CLSM	60188	2967	27W-3N	D6
S Peoria Dr					
6200	CHCG	60621	3152	1W-6S	A4
Peoria St					
-	CHHT	60411	3508	1W-24S	B5
1200	CRTE	60417	3685	1W-29S	A2
3000	SCHT	60411	3596	1W-28S	A6
3000	SCHT	60475	3596	1W-28S	A6
3000	STGR	60475	3596	1W-28S	A6
14400	HRVY	60426	3350	1W-17S	A5
19300	BlmT	60411	3508	1W-23S	A3
19300	HMWD	60430	3508	1W-23S	A3
N Peoria St					
400	CHCG	60607	3033	1W-0N	E3
400	CHCG	60622	3033	1W-0N	E4
S Peoria St					
-	CHCG	60608	3091	1W-2S	E3
10	CHCG	60607	3033	1W-0S	E5
1300	CHCG	60608	3033	1W-1S	E7
4000	CHCG	60609	3091	1W-4S	E6
4900	CHCG	60609	3152	1W-6S	A3
5500	CHCG	60621	3152	1W-6S	A3
S Peoria St					
7500	CHCG	60621	3214	1W-8S	A1
9200	CHCG	60620	3214	1W-10S	A5
9900	CHCG	60643	3214	1W-11S	A7
10300	CHCG	60643	3278	1W-12S	A1
12200	CTPK	60643	3278	1W-14S	A6
12300	CTPK	60827	3278	1W-14S	A6
W Peotone Rd					
20800	FrnT	60481	3853	26W-37S	E5
20800	WMTN	60481	3853	26W-37S	E5
Pepper Ct					
100	WynT	60185	2966	29W-4N	E4
Pepper Rd					
10	LKBN	60010	2696	28W-21N	E5
300	CbaT	60010	2696	28W-21N	E5
W Pepper Rd					
21200	ElaT	60047	2699	21W-24N	D1
21200	KLDR	60047	2699	21W-24N	D1
Pepperell on Asbury					
10	RGMW	60008	2806	19W-14N	B3
Pepperidge Cir					
200	SMWD	60107	2857	27W-10N	C6
Pepperidge Ct					
400	AURA	60506	3199	38W-7S	A1
Pepperidge Dr					
10	NPVL	60540	3141	28W-6S	A5
Pepper Mill Ct					
10	BRRG	60527	3146	15W-7S	B5
S Peppermill Tr					
16000	HmrT	60491	3420	19W-19S	E2
Pepper Tree Ct					
2300	LSLE	60532	3142	24W-7S	D6
Peppertree Ct					
200	ElgT	60124	2907	37W-8N	B3
W Peppertree Ct					
20800	LktT	60544	3340	26W-16S	A3
Peppertree Dr					
12800	PNFD	60585	3337	33W-15S	A2
E Pepper Tree Dr					
10	PLTN	60067	2752	20W-17N	E5
N Pepper Tree Dr					
1100	PLTN	60067	2752	20W-17N	E4
1500	PltT	60074	2752	20W-17N	E4
Peppertree Ln					
10	ElgT	60124	2907	37W-8N	B4
10	ElgT	60177	2907	37W-8N	B4
10	SEGN	60177	2907	37W-8N	B4
200	AURA	60504	3140	29W-6S	D6
2600	WKGN	60085	2479	12W-35N	C6
2700	WkgT	60085	2479	12W-35N	C6
Pepper Valley Dr					
1900	GNVA	60134	3019	36W-1N	D4
Pepperwood Ct					
20200	FftT	60423	3504	10W-24S	C5
Pepperwood Dr					
100	BGBK	60440	3268	24W-12S	E2
9200	ODHL	60487	3423	11W-19S	E3
9300	ODPK	60467	3423	11W-19S	E3
Pepperwood Ln					
300	BMDL	60108	2969	23W-4N	B4
300	GLHT	60139	2969	23W-4N	B4
2100	GLHT	60108	2969	23W-4N	B4
Pepperwood Tr					
9000	ODHL	60487	3424	11W-19S	A3
9100	ODHL	60487	3423	11W-19S	E2
Pepplestone Dr					
-	AURA	60503	3201	33W-10S	B6
Pequot St					
1200	JLET	60433	3587	22W-25S	C1
1200	JltT	60433	3587	22W-25S	C1
Peraino Dr					
-	AlqT	60010	2749	28W-20N	D1
-	BNHL	60010	2749	28W-20N	D1
Percheron Ln					
100	WYNE	60184	2965	31W-5N	D3
Percy Ln					
-	ITSC	60143	2913	21W-6N	E5
Percy St					
200	ELGN	60120	2855	33W-11N	A5
Percy Julian Sq					
100	OKPK	60302	3031	7W-0S	C6
Perda Ln					
1000	DSPN	60016	2862	15W-10N	A5
Peregine Wy					
-	HPSR	60140	2795	47W-15N	D4
W Peregrine Ct					
1100	PLTN	60067	2805	22W-14N	B4
Peregrine Dr					
2300	NLNX	60451	3589	18W-27S	A4
W Peregrine Dr					
500	PLTN	60067	2805	21W-14N	C4
Peregrine Ln					
100	HNWD	60047	2645	21W-26N	C3
Peregrine Pkwy					
400	BRLT	60103	2910	30W-9N	B1
Peregrine Tr					
16000	CrlT	60142	2743	45W-20N	B1
Perennial Ln					
1600	HDPK	60035	2704	9W-22N	C5
Periano Cir					
-	BNHL	60010	2749	28W-20N	D1
Perimeter Dr					
-	SMBG	60173	2860	21W-11N	A3
1100	SMBG	60173	2859	21W-11N	E3
Periwinkle Ct					
2300	NPVL	60540	3140	29W-7S	D7
W Periwinkle Ct					
20800	LktT	60544	3340	26W-16S	A3
Periwinkle Ln					
100	BGBK	60490	3267	27W-12S	C2
600	AURA	60504	3201	33W-8S	A2
2100	NPVL	60540	3140	29W-7S	D7
2200	ALGN	60102	2695	32W-20N	C7
Periwinkle Wy					
400	PTHT	60070	2754	16W-16N	D7
N Periwinkle Wy					
2200	RLKB	60073	2475	23W-36N	A4
Perkins Ct					
600	WldT	60564	3202	28W-10S	E6
Perkins Rd					
12700	DrrT	60098	2581	41W-28N	C6
12700	WDSK	60098	2581	41W-28N	C6
14100	SenT	60098	2581	43W-28N	A6
Perna Ln					
1500	BTVA	60510	3078	34W-2S	D5
S Perona Ct					
100	DMND	60416	3941	33W-40S	C2
Perrie Dr					
300	EGVV	60007	2861	17W-9N	B7
Perry Av					
14700	DLTN	60419	3350	0W-17S	C5
14700	HRVY	60426	3350	0W-17S	C5
14700	SHLD	60426	3350	0W-17S	C5
14900	PHNX	60426	3350	0W-17S	B6
S Perry Av					
5500	CHCG	60609	3152	0W-6S	C3
S Perry Av					
6500	CHCG	60621	3152	0W-7S	C6
7400	CHCG	60620	3214	0W-8S	C1
7400	CHCG	60621	3214	0W-8S	C1
9400	CHCG	60628	3214	0W-11S	C6
10300	CHCG	60628	3278	0W-12S	C1
13400	RVDL	60827	3350	0W-15S	C1
Perry Ct					
1500	AURA	60505	3139	33W-5S	A3
Perry Dr					
800	ALGN	60102	2695	32W-20N	A7
5900	WDRG	60517	3143	21W-6S	D5
N Perry Dr					
1100	PltT	60067	2752	21W-17N	C5
Perry Ln					
600	HFET	60169	2858	24W-10N	D5
Perry Rd					
2700	FSMR	60422	3507	3W-23S	B4
Perry St					
100	ELGN	60123	2854	34W-10N	E5
1200	DSPN	60016	2862	13W-11N	E3
1300	CRTE	60417	3685	0W-29S	C2
1300	DSPN	60016	2863	13W-11N	A3
2500	NCHI	60088	2594	10W-30N	B1
Pershing Av					
-	GNEN	60137	3025	21W-0S	E6
10	LIHL	60156	2693	35W-22N	E4
10	MltT	60148	3083	21W-1S	E1
10	MltT	60148	3084	21W-1S	A1
100	BNVL	60106	2972	15W-5N	A1
300	WHTN	60187	3082	24W-1S	D1
700	GNEN	60137	3083	22W-1S	D1
1600	WHTN	60187	3083	23W-1S	A1
4400	DRGV	60515	3143	21W-4S	E1
4800	DRGV	60515	3144	21W-5S	A2
5500	LslT	60515	3144	21W-6S	A5
5500	LslT	60516	3144	21W-6S	A5
6100	DRGV	60516	3144	21W-6S	A5
N Pershing Av					
10	MDLN	60060	2646	19W-27N	C1
100	MDLN	60060	2590	19W-27N	C7
S Pershing Av					
10	MDLN	60060	2646	19W-27N	C1
Pershing Ct					
500	MDLN	60060	2646	19W-27N	C2
2700	WDRG	60517	3143	22W-7S	D7
Pershing Dr					
900	WCDA	60084	2588	25W-28N	B6
W Pershing Pl					
1900	CHCG	60609	3091	2W-4S	C6
Pershing Rd					
-	WKGN	60085	2537	10W-33N	B2
-	WKGN	60087	2480	9W-35N	B6
300	WKGN	60085	2480	9W-35N	C6
6200	BRWN	60402	3089	8W-3S	A6
6200	CCRO	60402	3089	8W-3S	A6
6200	CCRO	60804	3089	8W-3S	A6
6200	SKNY	60402	3089	8W-3S	A6
6800	BRWN	60402	3088	8W-3S	E6
6800	SKNY	60402	3088	8W-3S	E6
7100	LYNS	60534	3088	8W-3S	E6
7600	LYNS	60534	3088	9W-4S	C6
7600	RvsT	60534	3088	9W-4S	C6
7600	RvsT	60546	3088	9W-4S	C6
E Pershing Rd					
10	CHCG	60609	3092	0E-3S	C5
10	CHCG	60653	3092	0E-3S	D5
N Pershing Rd					
1800	WKGN	60085	2480	9W-36N	C5
1800	WKGN	60087	2480	9W-36N	C5
S Pershing Rd					
10	WKGN	60085	2537	10W-34N	B1
W Pershing Rd					
10	CHCG	60609	3092	0W-3S	B5
10	CHCG	60653	3092	0W-3S	B5
800	CHCG	60609	3091	1W-3S	E6
2400	CHCG	60632	3091	3W-3S	B6
2800	CHCG	60632	3090	4W-4S	D6
4800	CCRO	60632	3090	5W-3S	A6
4800	CCRO	60804	3090	5W-3S	A6
4800	CHCG	60804	3090	5W-3S	A6
4800	SKNY	60804	3090	5W-3S	A6
4900	CHCG	60804	3089	6W-3S	E6
5600	CCRO	60804	3089	7W-3S	C6
5600	SKNY	60402	3089	7W-3S	C6
5600	SKNY	60804	3089	7W-3S	C6
6100	BRWN	60402	3089	7W-4S	B6
6100	CCRO	60402	3089	7W-4S	B6
Pershing St					
1000	AURA	60506	3137	37W-5S	C3
Persico Ct					
21200	SRWD	60404	3584	31W-25S	A1
Persimmin Ln					
10	SEGN	60177	2907	37W-7N	C5
Persimmon Ct					
200	RLKB	60073	2475	23W-36N	A4
300	AURA	60504	3139	31W-6S	E5
300	BRLT	60103	2910	30W-9N	B2
800	SCRL	60174	2964	35W-3N	C5
1900	SMBG	60193	2912	26W-8N	A3
2000	NPVL	60565	3204	25W-9S	B4
10900	ODPK	60467	3345	13W-16S	A3
20600	FKFT	60423	3504	10W-24S	B6
25400	PNFD	60585	3337	31W-15S	D2
Persimmon Dr					
200	SCRL	60174	2964	35W-3N	C5
500	WCHI	60185	3022	29W-1N	E3
3500	ALGN	60102	2693	37W-20N	B7
13900	ODPK	60467	3345	13W-16S	A3
13900	OrlT	60467	3345	13W-16S	A3
Persimmon Ln					
10	SEGN	60177	2907	37W-7N	C5
300	OSWG	60543	3263	38W-13S	B5
400	BRLT	60103	2910	30W-9N	B2
900	MPPT	60056	2807	16W-14N	D3
23000	PnfT	60586	3416	28W-20S	E4
Persimmon St					
-	HRPK	60133	2911	27W-8N	D3
Persimmon Wy					
6500	GRNE	60048	2534	16W-32N	C5
Perth Av					
600	FSMR	60422	3507	3W-22S	B1
600	HMWD	60430	3507	3W-22S	B1
17900	HMWD	60430	3427	3W-22S	B7
Perth Cir					
9400	TYPK	60487	3423	11W-20S	E4
Perth Dr					
1000	SMBG	60194	2858	24W-10N	C5
4700	WldT	60564	3266	30W-12S	A4
Perth Rd					
10	CRY	60013	2695	31W-23N	D2
Perthshire Ln					
900	DYR	46311	3510		E7
Peschel Ct					
3100	DYR	46311	3598		D5
Peshtigo Av					
1300	NPVL	60564	3203	28W-10S	A5
1300	WldT	60564	3203	28W-10S	A5
N Peshtigo Ct					
500	CHCG	60611	3034	0E-0N	D3
Pesz Rd					
-	NndT	60042	2642	29W-27N	D1
N Pet Ln					
22000	BFGV	60089	2701	16W-22N	D5
22000	VrnT	60069	2701	16W-22N	D5
Pete Dye Dr					
-	LMNT	60439	3343	17W-15S	C1
10	LMNT	60439	3271	17W-14S	C7
Peter Ct					
100	BRLT	60103	2911	28W-8N	A3
800	INCK	60061	2647	17W-25N	A6
Peter Ln					
1600	RMVL	60446	3339	26W-18S	D7
Peter Rd					
200	MltT	60190	3023	26W-0N	E4
200	WNFD	60190	3023	26W-0N	E4
600	MltT	60187	3023	26W-0N	E4
2400	DSPN	60018	2917	12W-8N	B1
Peter St					
700	ISLK	60042	2642	29W-27N	B1
700	NndT	60042	2642	29W-27N	B1
700	NndT	60051	2642	29W-27N	B1
W Peter Ter					
8400	MaiT	60714	2864	10W-10N	A4
8400	NLES	60714	2864	10W-10N	A4
Peters Ct					
400	DGvT	60516	3206	20W-10S	B5
1000	LKZH	60047	2645	22W-24N	B7
Peters Dr					
400	DGvT	60516	3206	20W-10S	A5
400	WDRG	60516	3206	20W-10S	A5
400	WDRG	60517	3206	20W-10S	A5
Petersburg Ct					
1300	CLSM	60188	2967	28W-4N	B4
S Petersburg Dr					
13700	PnfT	60544	3339	27W-16S	C4
Petersdorf Rd					
100	BRLT	60103	2966	29W-5N	D3
100	WynT	60103	2966	29W-5N	D3
500	BRLT	60185	2966	29W-5N	D3
500	WynT	60185	2966	29W-5N	D3
Petersen Av					
10	BmdT	60148	3025	21W-2N	E1
10	LMBD	60148	3025	21W-2N	E1
1000	AURA	60505	3200	36W-9S	A3
Petersen Park Rd					
-	McHT	60050	2528	33W-34N	A1
-	MHRY	60050	2528	33W-34N	A1
Petersham Ln					
1500	SMBG	60173	2859	21W-10N	E4
Peterson Av					
200	BmdT	60188	3023	26W-2N	E1
200	GLHT	60139	3025	22W-2N	C1
200	PKRG	60068	2918	10W-7N	A4
700	BmdT	60139	3025	22W-2N	D1
1100	PKRG	60068	2917	10W-7N	E4
21300	SLVL	60411	3597	2E-26S	C2
N Peterson Av					
34600	GrtT	60041	2474	25W-34N	B7
W Peterson Av					
1600	CHCG	60660	2921	1W-7N	C3
1900	CHCG	60659	2921	2W-7N	B3
2700	CHCG	60659	2920	3W-7N	D3
3800	CHCG	60646	2920	4W-7N	B4
5700	CHCG	60646	2919	7W-7N	B3
6300	CHCG	60631	2919	8W-7N	A4
7100	CHCG	60631	2918	9W-7N	D4
W Peterson Av US-14					
1700	CHCG	60660	2921	2W-7N	B3
1900	CHCG	60659	2921	2W-7N	B3
2700	CHCG	60659	2920	3W-7N	D3
3800	CHCG	60646	2920	4W-7N	B4
5700	CHCG	60646	2919	5W-7N	E4
Peterson Ct					
-	PLNO	60545	3260	45W-13S	C5
10	WDRG	60517	3205	22W-9S	C3
2700	GNVA	60134	3019	37W-0N	C4
Peterson Dr					
700	WYNE	60184	2965	31W-5N	D2
1200	WLNG	60090	2755	14W-16N	C7
W Peterson Dr					
23200	PnfT	60586	3416	29W-19S	E3
Peterson Ln					
-	GRNE	60031	2478	14W-35N	D5
-	WrnT	60031	2478	14W-35N	D5
S Peterson Ln					
34900	WslT	60481	3943	26W-42S	E7
Peterson Pkwy					
100	CLLK	60014	2640	35W-26N	A3
Peterson Pl					
2000	BTVA	60510	3078	33W-3S	E6
Peterson Rd					
300	LbvT	60048	2591	17W-30N	A2
300	LYVL	60048	2591	17W-30N	A2
Peterson Rd SR-137					
300	LbvT	60048	2591	17W-30N	A2
300	LYVL	60048	2591	17W-30N	A2
W Peterson Rd					
-	LbvT	60048	2591	18W-30N	A2
-	LYVL	60048	2591	18W-30N	A2
1800	LbvT	60048	2590	18W-30N	E2
1800	LYVL	60048	2590	18W-30N	D2
19200	FrmT	60048	2590	18W-30N	D2
19500	FmtT	60060	2590	19W-30N	C2
19800	FmtT	60030	2590	20W-30N	A2
19800	GYLK	60030	2590	20W-30N	A2
19800	GYLK	60048	2590	20W-30N	B2
19800	RLKP	60030	2590	20W-30N	A2
20700	FmtT	60030	2589	21W-30N	D2
20700	GYLK	60030	2589	21W-30N	D2
20700	RLKP	60030	2589	21W-30N	D2
21500	FmtT	60060	2589	21W-30N	D2
22000	RLKP	60060	2589	22W-30N	B2
W Peterson Rd CO-A33					
-	LbvT	60048	2590	18W-30N	E2
-	LbvT	60048	2591	18W-30N	A2
-	LYVL	60048	2591	18W-30N	A2
1800	LYVL	60048	2590	18W-30N	D2
19200	FrmT	60048	2590	18W-30N	D2
19500	FmtT	60060	2590	19W-30N	C2
19800	FmtT	60030	2590	20W-30N	A2
19800	GYLK	60030	2590	20W-30N	A2
19800	GYLK	60048	2590	20W-30N	B2
19800	RLKP	60030	2590	20W-30N	A2
20700	FmtT	60030	2589	21W-30N	D2
20700	GYLK	60030	2589	21W-30N	D2
20700	RLKP	60030	2589	21W-30N	D2
21500	FmtT	60060	2589	21W-30N	D2
22000	RLKP	60060	2589	22W-30N	B2
W Peterson Rd SR-137					
-	LbvT	60048	2591	18W-30N	A2
W Peterson Rd SR-137					
-	LYVL	60048	2591	18W-30N	A2
Petit Ct					
24800	PNFD	60586	3416	31W-19S	A2
W Petite Av					
25000	ANTH	60002	2357	25W-42N	B5
25000	AntT	60002	2357	25W-42N	B5
N Petite Ct					
39200	LkvT	60046	2416	24W-39N	B5
N Petite Rd					
700	RDLK	60073	2531	23W-34N	E1
N Petite Ter					
39100	LkvT	60046	2416	24W-39N	B6
W Petite Lake Rd					
-	LKVL	60046	2417	23W-39N	A6
-	LkvT	60046	2417	23W-39N	A6
23400	LKVL	60046	2416	23W-39N	D6
23400	LkvT	60046	2416	23W-39N	D6
W Petite Lake Rd CO-A12					
-	LKVL	60046	2417	23W-39N	A6
-	LkvT	60046	2417	23W-39N	A6
23400	LKVL	60046	2416	23W-39N	D6
23400	LkvT	60046	2416	23W-39N	D6
N Petite Pass					
39400	AntT	60002	2416	25W-39N	A5
W Petoskey Ct					
22000	PnfT	60544	3339	27W-15S	C3
S Petoskey Dr					
13800	PnfT	60544	3339	27W-16S	C4
Petra Ct					
3800	NPVL	60564	3267	28W-11S	B2
Petrick Ln					
10	CLLK	60014	2640	35W-26N	B3
Petrie Cir					
10	SMWD	60107	2857	27W-11N	C4
W Petronella Dr					
14000	GNOK	60048	2592	14W-28N	D7
14000	LbvT	60045	2592	14W-28N	D7
14000	LbvT	60048	2592	14W-28N	D7
Petterson Ct					
1000	NPVL	60540	3141	27W-6S	B5
Petunia Cir					
10	MTSN	60443	3593	7W-26S	C1
Petunia Ct					
15600	ODPK	60462	3346	9W-18S	E7
Petworth Ct					
2200	NPVL	60565	3203	26W-10S	E5
Peyla Ln					
6400	JLET	60586	3415	32W-20S	D5
Peyton Dr					
10	CHHT	60411	3508	1W-23S	A3
Peyton St					
10	GNVA	60134	3020	35W-1N	C3
Pfaff Dr					
10	FKFT	60423	3591	11W-26S	E2
Pfeiffer Rd					
21100	FftT	60423	3504	11W-25S	B7
21100	FKFT	60423	3504	11W-25S	B7
21200	FftT	60423	3592	11W-26S	B2
21200	FKFT	60423	3592	11W-26S	B2
22700	GGnT	60423	3592	11W-27S	B4
Pfingsten Rd					
-	DRFD	60062	2756	11W-18N	E4
300	NHBK	60062	2756	11W-16N	E7
600	NfdT	60025	2809	11W-13N	E7
1500	GNVW	60025	2809	11W-14N	E4
2200	NHBK	60062	2809	11W-16N	E1
2300	GNVW	60062	2809	11W-15N	E3
N Pfingsten Rd					
-	DRFD	60062	2756	10W-20N	E2
-	NHBK	60062	2756	10W-20N	E2
10	DRFD	60015	2756	10W-20N	E2
S Pfingsten Rd					
10	DRFD	60015	2756	11W-18N	E2
10	DRFD	60062	2756	11W-18N	E2
10	NHBK	60062	2756	11W-18N	E2
Pfund Av					
400	AddT	60101	2971	17W-3N	B5
400	ADSN	60101	2971	17W-3N	B5
Pfund Ct					
100	OSWG	60543	3263	37W-12S	D3
Phaeton Ct					
1900	NPVL	60565	3204	25W-9S	A4
Phaeton Dr					
10	WLNG	60090	2754	16W-18N	D3
100	WLNG	60090	2755	15W-18N	A2
Phar Lap Dr					
10	CmpT	60175	2906	39W-7N	E4
10	PltT	60175	2906	39W-7N	E5
100	PltT	60124	2906	39W-7N	E5
Pheasant Av					
1500	TNLK	53181	2354		A3
1600	TNLK	53181	2353		E3
1900	RdlT	53181	2353		E3
Pheasant Cir					
13600	HMGN	60491	3342	19W-16S	E3
Pheasant Ct					
-	BTVA	60510	3020	35W-0S	A7
-	CteT	60417	3687	4E-29S	B1
10	MltT	60188	3023	26W-1N	E3
10	WDRG	60517	3143	21W-7S	D7
200	BMDL	60108	2968	24W-4N	D3
500	GYLK	60030	2533	20W-33N	A3
1200	HPSR	60140	2795	47W-15N	D4
1800	FSMR	60422	3507	3W-23S	A4
3400	GNVA	60134	3019	37W-1N	B3
4000	SCRL	60174	2965	32W-3N	C5
12700	PSHT	60463	3275	8W-15S	B7
19500	MKNA	60448	3502	14W-23S	D4
26500	WcnT	60084	2643	26W-26N	C2
W Pheasant Ct					
500	RLKB	60073	2474	23W-35N	E6
12800	HMGN	60491	3422	16W-19S	A1
Pheasant Dr					
100	CTSD	60525	3147	12W-7S	B5
200	BfdT	53128	2353		B1
200	GNCY	53128	2353		B1
600	OswT	60543	3265	33W-13S	A5
3200	RGMW	60008	2806	19W-13N	B6
7400	LKWD	60014	2639	37W-24N	A7
9400	TYPK	60487	3423	11W-21S	E6
N Pheasant Dr					
10	BNHL	60010	2696	28W-21N	D6
Pheasant Ln					
-	BTVA	60510	3020	35W-0S	A7
-	RHMD	60071	2353	34W-42N	D5
100	PltT	60010	2751	24W-18N	D3
200	BMDL	60108	2968	24W-4N	D3
600	VrnT	60015	2755	15W-20N	B5
1500	NlxT	60451	3590	16W-27S	A5
10700	GwdT	60098	2525	39W-34N	B1
14300	HMGN	60491	3344	15W-17S	B6
17600	CCHL	60478	3426	4W-21S	D6
19500	MKNA	60448	3502	14W-23S	D3
S Pheasant Ln					
14100	HMGN	60491	3344	15W-16S	B4

Chicago 7-County Street Index

STREET Block	City	ZIP	Map#	CGS	Grid
S Pheasant Ln					
25500	CNHN	60410	3672	33W-30S	A5
Pheasant Rd					
10	MTSN	60443	3505	7W-24S	D5
7600	MchT	60097	2469	36W-35N	D6
Pheasant Row					
10	LNSH	60015	2702	13W-22N	D4
10	LNSH	60069	2702	13W-22N	D4
10	RVWD	60015	2702	13W-22N	D4
Pheasant Run					
-	SCRL	60174	2965	32W-3N	C6
900	BtnT	60099	2362	12W-42N	B6
900	ZION	60099	2362	12W-42N	B6
1800	LGGV	60047	2753	18W-20N	E1
6900	NndT	60012	2583	36W-29N	E4
N Pheasant Run					
26400	FmtT	60060	2645	22W-26N	A3
Pheasant St					
2400	WDRG	60517	3143	21W-7S	E7
Pheasant Tr					
-	CteT	60417	3687	4E-29S	B2
10	SMWD	60107	2910	29W-9N	E1
100	DndT	60110	2748	33W-17N	A6
300	LIHL	60156	2694	35W-21N	A5
500	SCRL	60174	2965	32W-3N	C5
500	SCRL	60185	2965	32W-3N	C5
500	WCHI	60185	2965	32W-4N	C5
500	WynT	60185	2965	32W-3N	C5
600	FKFT	60423	3592	10W-26S	C1
1000	CLSM	60188	2967	28W-4N	B5
1300	HPSR	60140	2795	47W-14N	D5
1400	HshT	60140	2795	47W-14N	E5
1400	IVNS	60067	2805	23W-15N	A2
1400	PLTN	60067	2805	22W-15N	A2
1700	IVNS	60067	2804	23W-15N	E2
6500	AlqT	60013	2641	31W-25N	D5
20800	ElaT	60010	2698	23W-20N	E7
20900	DRPK	60010	2698	23W-21N	E6
21400	LKZH	60010	2698	23W-21N	E7
21400	LKZH	60047	2698	23W-21N	E7
26500	LKBN	60084	2643	26W-26N	C3
26500	WcnT	60084	2643	26W-26N	C3
26600	WCDA	60084	2643	26W-26N	C3
E Pheasant Tr					
8500	AxST	60481	3761	33W-33S	B4
8500	GLkT	60481	3761	33W-33S	B4
8500	WmTp	60481	3761	33W-33S	B4
W Pheasant Tr					
10	LIHL	60156	2693	35W-21N	E5
600	MchT	60050	2472	29W-37N	C1
1700	MPPT	60056	2861	17W-11N	C3
1800	ANHT	60005	2861	17W-11N	C3
Pheasant Chase Cir					
1300	BCHR	60401	3774	0W-35S	D7
Pheasant Chase Dr					
300	BGBK	60490	3268	26W-12S	A3
400	BGBK	60490	3267	26W-12S	E3
400	PNFD	60544	3338	30W-16S	B4
Pheasant Creek Dr					
3000	NHBK	60062	2756	11W-17N	D4
Pheasant Field Ln					
700	RtdT	60140	2798	40W-15N	C3
Pheasant Hill Dr					
-	BtvT	60542	3077	36W-3S	E7
Pheasant Hill Rd					
100	DRPK	60010	2751	23W-20N	E1
Pheasant Hollow Dr					
100	BRRG	60527	3146	14W-6S	C5
Pheasant Lake Dr					
8900	TYPK	60487	3424	11W-21S	A7
Pheasant Landing Dr					
-	PnfT	60586	3496	29W-21S	D1
1400	JLET	60586	3496	29W-21S	D1
Pheasant Ln Ct					
17600	CCHL	60478	3426	4W-21S	D6
Pheasant Meadow Ct					
200	GRNE	60031	2534	16W-34N	D2
Pheasant Ridge Ct					
300	LNHT	60046	2418	19W-38N	C7
400	DRN	60527	3145	17W-7S	D6
700	LKZH	60047	2699	22W-22N	C5
N Pheasant Ridge Ct					
2100	RLKB	60073	2474	23W-36N	E4
Pheasant Ridge Dr					
-	KLDR	60047	2699	21W-21N	C5
400	LKZH	60047	2698	23W-22N	E5
400	LKZH	60047	2699	23W-22N	A5
6100	JLET	60586	3415	31W-21S	E7
W Pheasant Ridge Dr					
12300	HTLY	60142	2744	42W-19N	D3
Pheasant Run Ct					
23900	WldT	60564	3266	29W-12S	C3
Pheasant Run Dr					
200	SchT	60175	2963	38W-4N	A5
Pheasant Run Ln					
1000	AURA	60504	3201	31W-9S	E3
Pheasant Run Pl					
1600	GNVA	60134	3020	36W-0S	A6
Pheasant Run Rd					
10	HNWD	60047	2644	24W-25N	C4
10	JLET	60433	3587	23W-26S	A3
10	JLET	60436	3587	23W-26S	A3
10	JltT	60433	3587	23W-26S	A3
10	JltT	60436	3587	23W-26S	A3
1500	HRVD	60033	2406	49W-39N	C5
Pheasant Run Tr					
100	NBRN	60010	2698	25W-23N	B3
Pheasant Trail Ct					
1400	HFET	60192	2856	30W-12N	B2
1400	HnrT	60192	2856	30W-12N	B2
N Pheasant Trail Ct					
4100	ANHT	60004	2753	18W-18N	D2
W Pheasant Trail Dr					
1500	ANHT	60004	2753	18W-18N	D2
Pheasant Walk Dr					
800	SMBG	60193	2913	22W-8N	C2
900	SMBG	60193	2859	23W-9N	A7
Phelps Av					
10	RMVL	60446	3340	23W-15S	E1
10	RMVL	60446	3341	23W-15S	A1
N Phelps Av					
1100	ANHT	60004	2807	16W-15N	D3
1100	PTHT	60004	2807	16W-15N	D3
2600	ANHT	60004	2754	16W-16N	D6
S Phelps Av					
10	ANHT	60004	2807	16W-13N	D6
Phelps Ct					
-	YKVL	60560	3333	42W-17S	D7
Phelps Dr					
-	BTVA	60510	3021	33W-0S	A7
Phelps Ln					
800	SRWD	60404	3496	30W-22S	B2
Philadelphia Av					
400	WTMT	60559	3085	17W-4S	C7
Philip Dr					
600	BRLT	60103	2856	30W-9N	B7
Philip Dr					
600	BRLT	60103	2910	30W-9N	B1
10600	HTLY	60142	2692	40W-21N	A6
Philippa Av					
10	WKGN	60085	2537	10W-34N	A1
Philips Wy					
-	ELGN	60120	2855	31W-11N	E5
Phillip Ct					
100	LKBF	60044	2593	11W-29N	D4
Phillip Dr					
-	BHPK	60099	2421	12W-40N	C3
-	GYLK	60046	2475	21W-36N	E5
-	ZION	60099	2421	12W-40N	C3
S Phillip Dr					
1800	MPPT	60056	2861	17W-10N	C5
E Phillip Rd					
10	VNHL	60061	2647	16W-25N	C4
W Phillip Rd					
10	VNHL	60061	2647	17W-25N	C4
Phillippa St					
200	HNDL	60521	3146	14W-4S	C1
300	HNDL	60521	3086	14W-4S	C7
Phillippi Creek Dr					
10	SMWD	60120	2856	30W-9N	C7
Phillips Av					
400	GNEN	60137	3025	22W-0S	B6
1800	NfdT	60062	2756	11W-16N	C7
1800	NHBK	60062	2756	11W-16N	C7
3000	SCHT	60411	3596	0W-27S	B5
3000	STGR	60411	3596	0W-27S	B5
3000	STGR	60475	3596	0W-28S	B6
S Phillips Av					
7200	CHCG	60649	3153	3E-8S	D7
7500	CHCG	60649	3215	3E-9S	D2
8300	CHCG	60617	3215	3E-9S	D3
Phillips Cir					
500	ANTH	60002	2357	24W-42N	D5
Phillips Ct					
100	CLSM	60139	3024	24W-2N	C1
100	CLSM	60188	3024	24W-2N	C1
100	GLHT	60139	3024	24W-2N	C1
500	LMBD	60148	3026	21W-0N	A4
Phillips Dr					
2100	GNVW	60025	2810	10W-14N	A3
Phillips Rd					
25800	WmTp	60481	3761	32W-34S	E6
Phillips Farm Rd					
-	WnfT	60510	3079	32W-1S	B2
Phlox Cir					
600	MTSN	60443	3506	5W-24S	B6
Phoenix Ct					
500	AURA	60505	3138	34W-6S	C5
Phoenix Dr					
1200	DSPN	60018	2862	15W-10N	B6
Phoenix Ln					
1300	JLET	60431	3497	28W-22S	B1
Phoenix Rd					
-	GLBT	60136	2799	38W-16N	B2
Phoenix Lake Av					
800	SMWD	60107	2857	27W-9N	D7
Phyllis Dr					
800	WMTN	60481	3943	27W-39S	E2
4300	NfdT	60062	2756	12W-18N	A2
4300	NHBK	60062	2756	12W-18N	A2
Phyllis Rd					
4000	NHBK	60062	2756	12W-18N	A3
4100	NfdT	60062	2756	12W-18N	A3
Piacenti Ln					
1100	CHHT	60411	3507	2W-25S	D7
N Picadilly Cir					
-	MPPT	60056	2808	15W-15N	A3
-	PTHT	60056	2808	15W-15N	A3
-	PTHT	60070	2808	15W-15N	A3
1400	MPPT	60056	2807	15W-14N	E3
Picadilly Ct					
1400	MPPT	60056	2807	16W-14N	D3
Picadilly Ln					
500	ANTH	60002	2357	24W-42N	C5
Picardy Cir					
600	NfdT	60062	2756	12W-18N	A4
600	NHBK	60062	2756	12W-18N	A4
Picardy Ct					
200	WnfT	60190	3081	28W-1S	A1
1600	LGGV	60047	2701	18W-20N	A7
Picardy Dr					
4000	NHBK	60062	2756	12W-18N	A4
Picardy Ln					
10	WLNG	60090	2755	14W-18N	C3
200	BGBK	60440	3268	25W-12S	B2
1300	HFET	60192	2804	24W-14N	C3
1600	LGGV	60047	2701	18W-20N	A7
Picasso Dr					
100	SCRL	60175	2963	38W-3N	A6
Piccadilly Cir					
1100	NPVL	60563	3140	29W-5S	D3
Piccadilly Ct					
1000	BGBK	60440	3205	21W-9S	D4
22200	RNPK	60471	3594	4W-27S	D3
Piccadilly Ln					
500	BGBK	60440	3205	21W-9S	D4
Piccadilly Rd					
500	MltT	60187	3082	25W-1S	A2
800	DRFD	60015	2704	9W-21N	B7
800	HDPK	60035	2704	9W-21N	B7
S Pick Av					
100	EMHT	60126	3027	17W-1N	C3
200	EMHT	60181	3027	17W-1N	C3
200	VLPK	60181	3027	17W-1N	C3
Pick Dr					
2400	GNVW	60025	2810	9W-12N	C7
Pick St					
800	WHTN	60187	3024	23W-0S	E6
Pickard Av					
700	ANTH	60002	2357	23W-42N	E6
S Pickens St					
10	GNWD	60425	3508	0E-22S	D2
Pickerel Ct					
400	NPVL	60565	3203	27W-10S	D6
Pickett Ct					
200	BRLT	60103	2911	28W-7N	B5
W Pickford Av					
10600	BHPK	60099	2422	10W-38N	A6
10700	WKGN	60099	2422	10W-38N	A6
Pickford Ct					
2300	MDLN	60060	2590	20W-29N	A4
Pickford Rd					
10	OswT	60538	3263	37W-11S	D1
Pickford St					
13000	BHPK	60087	2421	13W-38N	A6
13000	WDWH	60083	2421	13W-38N	A6
Pickus Ct					
600	WKGN	60085	2479	10W-34N	E7
Pickwick Ct					
-	JltT	60432	3499	22W-23S	D4
700	ALGN	60102	2695	33W-20N	A7
1300	NPVL	60563	3140	29W-5S	D3
W Pickwick Ct					
600	EGvT	60056	2861	16W-11N	D4
600	MPPT	60056	2861	16W-11N	D4
Pickwick Dr					
100	SMBG	60193	2913	22W-8N	C2
Pickwick Ln					
1800	NfdT	60025	2810	10W-14N	A4
E Pickwick Rd					
10	ANHT	60005	2861	18W-12N	A1
W Pickwick Rd					
10	ANHT	60005	2861	18W-12N	A1
Pickwick St					
100	JLET	60432	3499	22W-23S	D4
100	JltT	60432	3499	22W-23S	D4
Picnic Ct					
10	BGBK	60490	3267	27W-12S	C3
Picnic Rd					
2800	LslT	60565	3204	23W-9S	E4
Picnic St					
100	SRWD	60404	3496	30W-24S	C5
Pico Ct					
1300	JltT	60436	3586	24W-25S	D1
Pico St					
400	JLET	60436	3586	24W-25S	D1
400	JltT	60436	3586	24W-25S	D1
Picton Rd					
10	BMDL	60108	2913	23W-6N	A6
10	BMDL	60172	2913	23W-6N	A6
10	ROSL	60108	2913	23W-6N	A6
10	ROSL	60172	2912	23W-6N	E6
10	ROSL	60172	2913	23W-6N	A6
200	BmdT	60172	2912	23W-6N	E6
Piedmont Cir					
800	NPVL	60565	3204	25W-10S	B5
Pielet Dr					
-	SMMT	60501	3148	9W-6S	C4
Pier Av					
200	NPVL	60565	3204	25W-8S	A3
Pier Ct					
100	NPVL	60565	3204	25W-9S	A3
N Pier Ct					
3200	CHCG	60618	2977	3W-4N	A3
Pier Dr					
10	WTMT	60559	3145	18W-7S	B6
W Pier Dr					
10	WTMT	60559	3145	18W-7S	A6
Pierce Av					
10	MltT	60187	3024	25W-0N	A5
400	ROSL	60172	2913	22W-6N	C5
500	DYR	46311	3510		D5
18300	HMWD	60430	3428	1W-22S	A7
19100	HMWD	60430	3508	1W-23S	A2
N Pierce Av					
100	WHTN	60187	3024	25W-0S	A7
S Pierce Av					
100	WHTN	60187	3024	25W-0S	A7
W Pierce Av					
1600	CHCG	60622	3033	2W-1N	C1
3200	CHCG	60622	3032	4W-1N	D1
3200	CHCG	60651	3032	4W-1N	D1
Pierce Ct					
300	BGBK	60440	3269	23W-11S	A1
300	VNHL	60061	2647	17W-26N	B3
500	GYLK	60030	2533	20W-33N	A3
19100	HMWD	60430	3508	1W-23S	A3
Pierce Dr					
2000	SPGV	60081	2413	31W-39N	D5
Pierce Rd					
-	ITSC	60143	2914	19W-7N	C4
10	HDPK	60035	2758	7W-20N	C2
200	AddT	60143	2914	19W-7N	D4
1600	HFET	60169	2859	23W-12N	A1
1800	HFET	60169	2805	23W-12N	A7
W Pierce Rd					
200	ITSC	60143	2914	19W-7N	C4
Pierce St					
10	AURA	60505	3138	34W-7S	C6
100	NARA	60542	3138	36W-4S	A1
200	GLBT	60136	2799	38W-15N	C3
200	RtdT	60136	2799	38W-15N	C3
E Pierce St					
100	ELBN	60119	3017	43W-1N	A2
Pierce Ter					
18500	HMWD	60430	3508	1W-22S	A1
Pierceshire Rd					
7100	SPGV	60081	2413	32W-39N	B5
S Piermont Dr					
10	NBRN	60010	2644	24W-24N	B7
Pierport Ln					
500	RMVL	60446	3417	26W-18S	E1
N Pierre Dr					
26900	FmtT	60060	2646	19W-26N	C2
26900	MDLN	60060	2646	19W-26N	C2
Pierre Curie Ln					
600	WNVL	60555	3080	29W-2S	E4
Piers Dr					
8100	WDRG	60517	3205	21W-9S	E3
Pierson Dr					
900	BTVA	60510	3021	33W-0S	B7
Pierson St					
300	CLLK	60014	2639	36W-25N	E5
Pigeon Av					
100	WKGN	60085	2536	12W-33N	B1
Piikoi Ln					
5600	LbvT	60048	2591	15W-31N	E1
5600	WKGN	60048	2591	15W-31N	E1
Pike St					
-	LkvT	60046	2417	21W-38N	C6
Pikes Peak Ct					
-	JLET	60421	3675	24W-29S	D1
Pikes Peak Dr					
-	JknT	60421	3675	24W-29S	D1
-	JLET	60421	3675	24W-29S	D1
Pilcher Rd					
22800	PNFD	60544	3339	28W-15S	A3
22800	PNFD	60585	3339	28W-15S	A3
22900	PNFD	60544	3338	29W-15S	E3
22900	PNFD	60585	3338	29W-15S	E3
23100	PnfT	60544	3338	29W-15S	E3
23100	PnfT	60585	3338	29W-15S	E3
Pilgrim Ct					
100	BGBK	60440	3269	22W-12S	B2
N Pilgrim St					
10	BtvT	60539	3077	36W-2S	E5
S Pilgrim St					
10	BtvT	60539	3077	36W-3S	E5
Pilgrims Ct					
32500	LKMR	60051	2529	28W-32N	D4
Pilgrim's Pth					
200	GRNE	60031	2535	14W-33N	C2
Pilgrims Pass					
28700	LKMR	60051	2529	28W-32N	D4
N Pillow Hill Rd					
-	BtnT	60081	2414	29W-40N	D3
7800	AntT	60081	2414	29W-40N	D3
7800	FXLK	60081	2414	29W-40N	D3
Pillsbury Dr					
2000	GNVA	60134	3021	33W-1N	B3
2000	WnfT	60185	3021	33W-1N	B3
Pilsen Ct					
1300	NPVL	60563	3140	29W-5S	D2
Pilsen Rd					
600	WCHI	60185	3022	30W-1N	A2
600	WnfT	60185	3022	30W-1N	A2
Pima Ct					
10	NPVL	60563	3141	26W-5S	D2
S Pima Ct					
17000	LKPT	60441	3420	20W-20S	C4
N Pima Ln					
1300	MPPT	60056	2808	13W-14N	E4
Pimlico Ln					
900	BRLT	60103	2966	29W-5N	C1
Pimlico Pkwy					
700	SYHW	60118	2799	36W-15N	E4
700	SYHW	60118	2800	36W-15N	A4
1300	LYVL	60048	2647	15W-27N	E1
Pimpernel Ct					
900	NPVL	60540	3202	29W-8S	D1
Pindar St					
500	ELGN	60123	2854	34W-11N	D3
Pine Av					
-	AddT	60106	2971	17W-4N	C3
-	ADSN	60106	2971	17W-4N	C3
-	ANHT	60004	2754	17W-16N	B6
-	NCHI	60064	2536	12W-32N	B5
10	FXLK	60020	2473	27W-36N	B4
10	LGPK	60525	3087	12W-3S	B6
10	LKPT	60441	3419	23W-20S	B6
10	LktT	60441	3419	23W-20S	B6
10	LKZH	60047	2698	23W-22N	D4
10	RVSD	60546	3088	10W-3S	B5
200	WCHI	60185	3022	29W-1N	D2
200	WnfT	60185	3022	29W-1N	D2
300	AURA	60505	3138	35W-6S	C5
400	AddT	60191	2971	17W-5N	C1
400	WDDL	60106	2915	17W-6N	C6
400	WDDL	60191	2915	17W-6N	C7
400	WDDL	60191	2971	17W-5N	C1
700	ROSL	60172	2912	24W-7N	D5
1000	OMFD	60461	3506	4W-25S	D7
8800	GwdT	60097	2469	38W-35N	A6
9400	FftT	60448	3503	11W-23S	E3
E Pine Av					
10	BNVL	60106	2972	15W-5N	A2
N Pine Av					
10	CHCG	60644	3031	6W-0N	D4
700	ANHT	60004	2807	17W-14N	B3
700	CHCG	60651	3031	6W-0N	D3
2300	ANHT	60004	2754	17W-16N	B7
3800	BHPK	60099	2421	11W-38N	E7
3800	WKGN	60099	2421	11W-38N	E7
32000	WrnT	60030	2533	18W-32N	D5
S Pine Av					
10	ANHT	60004	2807	17W-14N	A5
100	ANHT	60005	2807	17W-13N	A6
1200	ANHT	60005	2861	17W-12N	A1
4300	HMND	46327	3352		E4
Pine Cir					
10	CRY	60013	2641	31W-24N	C6
3400	CPVL	60110	2747	36W-18N	A5
Pine Ct					
10	BRLT	60103	2966	28W-5N	E2
10	BRLT	60185	2966	28W-5N	E2
10	CLLK	60014	2640	35W-26N	A3
10	KdlT	60560	3333	43W-16S	A4
10	WynT	60185	2966	28W-5N	E2
300	NPVL	60540	3141	26W-7S	D7
600	LKBF	60044	2593	11W-28N	E5
600	WDSK	60098	2524	41W-31N	E6
1100	BTVA	60510	3078	34W-1S	E3
1200	GLNC	60022	2758	7W-18N	B3
1800	DSPN	60018	2863	12W-9N	A7
7900	DRN	60561	3207	18W-9S	A2
15700	OKFT	60452	3347	8W-18S	B7
17000	HLCT	60429	3427	4W-20S	A4
E Pine Ct					
2800	CteT	60417	3687	3E-29S	A2
N Pine Ct					
1100	ANHT	60004	2807	17W-15N	A3
W Pine Ct					
12300	BHPK	60099	2421	12W-40N	B4
Pine Dr					
400	GLHT	60139	3025	23W-1N	A2
400	MltT	60139	3025	23W-1N	A2
400	MltT	60188	3024	23W-1N	E2
400	MltT	60188	3025	23W-1N	A2
1800	MHRY	60050	2528	32W-33N	C2
15200	OKFT	60452	3347	8W-18S	B6
16000	TYPK	60477	3424	10W-19S	B2
19100	CCHL	60478	3506	5W-23S	C2
21400	SRWD	60404	3584	30W-25S	B2
21400	TroT	60404	3584	30W-25S	B2
Pine Ln					
-	LSLE	60532	3082	23W-4S	E7
10	HGKN	60525	3147	12W-7S	C5
100	LMBD	60148	3084	19W-1S	D1
200	BNVL	60106	2915	17W-5N	C7
200	LynT	60458	3209	11W-8S	E2
300	WDDL	60106	2915	17W-5N	C7
400	LKFT	60045	2650	10W-27N	A1
500	YkTp	60148	3084	19W-1S	D1
600	WNKA	60093	2811	5W-16N	E1
6700	CPVL	60110	2747	36W-18N	A5
N Pine Ln					
10	GNWD	60425	3508	0E-22S	E2
S Pine Ln					
10	GNWD	60425	3508	0E-22S	E2
W Pine Ln					
25100	AntT	60002	2357	25W-43N	B4
Pine Pkwy					
7800	DRN	60561	3207	18W-8S	A2
Pine Pl					
1100	NLNX	60451	3501	18W-24S	B5
1100	NlxT	60451	3501	18W-24S	B5
S Pine Pl					
12300	PSHT	60463	3275	7W-14S	C6
Pine Pt					
1200	GNVW	60025	2810	8W-13N	D5
Pine Rd					
10	SchT	60175	2907	38W-7N	B5
100	BRTN	60010	2697	25W-20N	E7
1600	HMWD	60430	3427	2W-21S	D6
1900	LSLE	60532	3082	23W-4S	E7
15700	OKFT	60452	3347	8W-18S	B7
Pine St					
-	ELGN	60123	2854	34W-12N	C2
-	MYWD	60153	3029	11W-0N	E4
-	RVFT	60305	3030	10W-0N	A4
-	WCDA	60084	2587	26W-27N	D7
-	WDDL	60191	2915	17W-6N	C6
-	WNKA	60093	2811	6W-16N	D1
10	AddT	60106	2915	17W-6N	C6
Pine St					
10	CPVL	60110	2748	32W-17N	C6
10	CTSD	60525	3147	12W-6S	C4
10	DRFD	60015	2756	11W-20N	D1
10	GYLK	60030	2532	20W-33N	E3
200	BCHR	60401	3774	0W-36S	D7
200	JLET	60435	3498	24W-23S	E4
300	BTVA	60510	3078	34W-1S	D3
300	MYWD	60153	3030	10W-0N	A4
300	WLSP	60480	3209	12W-9S	D3
400	CLLK	60014	2639	36W-25N	E4
600	DRFD	60015	2703	11W-20N	D7
600	SRGV	60554	3135	42W-4S	D1
600	WLMT	60091	2811	5W-13N	E6
700	WKGN	60085	2479	11W-35N	E7
700	WNKA	60093	2812	5W-16N	A1
1000	FRGV	60021	2696	30W-22N	A4
1000	SCRL	60174	3020	35W-2N	B1
1100	LIHL	60156	2694	35W-22N	A4
1300	BtvT	60510	3078	33W-2S	E3
1300	GNVW	60025	2810	8W-13N	D5
1500	SPGV	60081	2414	30W-38N	A6
1700	MHRY	60050	2528	32W-33N	C2
1800	DSPN	60018	2863	13W-9N	A7
1900	NHFD	60093	2811	7W-15N	B1
3100	BtvT	60510	3079	33W-2S	B3
6000	CmgT	60033	2405	52W-37N	A7
6000	DhmT	60033	2405	52W-37N	A7
8500	ODPK	60462	3346	11W-16S	A3
9100	ODPK	60462	3345	11W-16S	E3
11900	LmnT	60439	3271	17W-14S	B6
E Pine St					
10	ROSL	60172	2913	23W-7N	A5
10	SMWD	60107	2857	28W-10N	A6
200	EMHT	60126	3027	17W-1N	B3
200	VLPK	60126	3027	17W-1N	B3
200	VLPK	60181	3027	17W-1N	B3
700	WCHI	60185	3022	29W-1N	D3
N Pine St					
10	MPPT	60056	2808	15W-13N	A5
10	PTHT	60070	2808	15W-15N	A2
100	EMHT	60126	3028	15W-1N	A2
100	GNVA	60134	3020	36W-1N	A3
300	JLET	60435	3498	24W-23S	E4
500	WKGN	60085	2479	11W-34N	E7
500	WKGN	60085	2536	11W-34N	E1
1100	NLNX	60451	3501	18W-23S	B4
2600	WKGN	60087	2479	11W-37N	E3
3800	BHPK	60099	2421	11W-38N	E7
3800	WKGN	60087	2421	11W-38N	E7
3800	WKGN	60099	2421	11W-38N	E7
S Pine St					
10	GNVA	60134	3020	36W-1N	A3
10	MPPT	60056	2808	15W-12N	A7
10	PLTN	60067	2805	21W-15N	D1
100	NLNX	60451	3501	18W-25S	B7
100	PltT	60067	2805	21W-15N	D1
200	MPPT	60056	2862	15W-12N	A1
700	NLNX	60451	3501	18W-25S	B7
700	NlxT	60451	3589	18W-25S	B1
800	SMWD	60107	2857	28W-10N	A7
900	NLNX	60451	3589	18W-25S	B1
4800	ISLK	60042	2642	29W-27N	D1
4800	ISLK	60051	2642	29W-27N	D1
4800	NndT	60042	2642	29W-27N	D1
4900	NndT	60051	2642	29W-27N	D1
W Pine St					
10	BmdT	60172	2913	23W-7N	A5
10	ROSL	60172	2913	23W-7N	A5
100	BmdT	60172	2912	23W-7N	E5
100	ROSL	60172	2912	23W-7N	E5
1300	HHLL	60051	2586	30W-29N	A4
1300	NndT	60051	2586	30W-29N	A4
21500	LkvT	60046	2417	21W-38N	D6
26600	AntT	60002	2356	26W-42N	D6
Pine Ter					
3100	ISLK	60042	2586	29W-28N	D5
Pine Tr					
6400	TYPK	60477	3505	8W-22S	B1
Pine Wy					
11600	HTLY	60142	2745	40W-20N	A1
Pinebluff Ct					
8200	DRN	60561	3207	18W-9S	A3
Pinebrook Dr					
500	BGBK	60490	3267	26W-13S	E4
500	LMBD	60148	3084	20W-1S	A1
Pine Cone Ct					
2500	NPVL	60565	3204	25W-10S	B6
Pinecone Ct					
2800	AURA	60502	3079	32W-3S	C7
6200	LGGV	60047	2646	18W-24N	D7
6200	LGGV	60047	2700	18W-24N	D1
Pine Cone Dr					
6400	TYPK	60477	3425	8W-22S	B7
Pine Cone Ln					
10	SYHW	60118	2800	35W-16N	B2
W Pine Cone Ln					
24800	PNFD	60586	3416	31W-19S	A3
24800	PnfT	60586	3416	31W-19S	A3
Pinecove Ct					
1400	DRN	60561	3207	18W-9S	A3
Pine Creek Dr					
-	NARA	60542	3078	35W-4S	B7
-	NARA	60542	3138	35W-4S	B1
Pinecreek Dr					
100	NARA	60542	3078	35W-3S	B6
1900	AURA	60503	3201	33W-10S	B6
16500	LKPT	60441	3420	20W-19S	B3
N Pinecreek Dr					
11900	HMGN	60491	3344	14W-17S	C5
11900	OrlT	60467	3344	14W-17S	C5
S Pinecreek Dr					
11900	HMGN	60491	3344	14W-17S	C6
11900	ODPK	60467	3344	14W-17S	D5
11900	OrlT	60467	3344	14W-17S	C6
Pine Creek Ln					
-	PNFD	60586	3416	30W-19S	B4
Pine Creek Ter					
17400	WrnT	60030	2534	17W-33N	B2
Pine Crest Cir					
100	LKBN	60010	2643	26W-24N	E7
Pinecrest Cir					
11300	ODPK	60467	3422	14W-20S	E3
Pine Crest Ct					
2300	SPGV	60081	2413	31W-40N	E2
Pinecrest Ct					
-	BRRG	60527	3146	14W-7S	C5
10	BGBK	60440	3205	22W-10S	D6
200	AURA	60502	3139	32W-7S	C7
700	DGvT	60527	3146	15W-6S	A4
Pinecrest Dr					
600	PTHT	60070	2808	13W-15N	D1
900	SgrT	60554	3136	41W-4S	A2
900	SRGV	60554	3136	41W-4S	A2
3200	JLET	60435	3417	27W-19S	B4
3200	PnfT	60435	3417	27W-19S	B4

STREET Block	City	ZIP	Map#	CGS	Grid
Pinecrest Dr					
3700	CPVL	60110	2747	36W-18N	A5
Pinecrest Ln					
400	WLMT	60091	2812	4W-13N	B6
1800	LNHT	60046	2476	20W-38N	A1
2400	WSTR	60154	3086	14W-2S	D3
N Pinecrest Rd					
100	BGBK	60440	3269	21W-11S	D1
800	BGBK	60440	3205	21W-10S	D5
800	WDRG	60440	3205	21W-10S	D5
800	WDRG	60517	3205	21W-10S	D5
S Pinecrest Rd					
100	BGBK	60440	3269	22W-12S	D2
Pinecroft Dr					
200	ROSL	60172	2913	22W-7N	B5
Pine Croft Ln					
900	LKFT	60045	2649	12W-25N	C4
Pine Forest Ln					
800	PTHT	60070	2808	14W-14N	C3
Pine Grove Av					
100	AddT	60106	2971	16W-4N	D4
1300	RLKB	60073	2475	22W-35N	B7
Pinegrove Av					
34300	WslT	60481	3943	27W-42S	E6
N Pine Grove Av					
2700	CHCG	60614	2978	0W-3N	A5
2900	CHCG	60657	2978	0W-3N	A4
3500	CHCG	60613	2978	0W-4N	A2
38500	WKGN	60083	2421	13W-38N	A7
39000	WDWH	60083	2421	13W-39N	A6
Pine Grove Ct					
10	ALGN	60102	2693	36W-21N	D6
600	JLET	60451	3500	19W-23S	D3
600	NLNX	60451	3500	19W-23S	D3
1000	VNHL	60061	2646	18W-24N	D7
11900	ODPK	60467	3344	14W-18S	C6
Pinegrove Ct					
10	MltT	60137	3083	22W-2S	C4
800	MltT	60187	3024	24W-0N	D4
800	WHTN	60187	3024	24W-0N	D4
1100	AURA	60504	3201	32W-9S	D3
20000	FftT	60448	3503	12W-24S	D5
20000	MKNA	60448	3503	12W-24S	D5
N Pine Grove Ct					
21600	KLDR	60047	2699	22W-21N	B5
W Pine Grove Ct					
13200	HMGN	60491	3343	16W-17S	E5
Pinegrove Dr					
19900	FftT	60448	3503	12W-24S	D4
19900	MKNA	60448	3503	12W-24S	D5
S Pine Grove Dr					
14400	HMGN	60491	3343	16W-17S	E5
Pine Grove Ln					
1400	JLET	60451	3500	19W-23S	D3
1400	NLNX	60451	3500	19W-23S	D3
Pine Grove Rd					
10	LKMR	60051	2529	29W-32N	C5
Pine Grove St					
300	GRNE	60031	2536	13W-34N	A1
1000	GRNE	60031	2479	13W-35N	A6
Pineham Ct					
5200	LGGV	60047	2701	17W-22N	B4
Pine Hill Ct					
200	ANTH	60002	2358	22W-42N	B6
Pinehill Ct					
100	AraT	60542	3137	37W-4S	B1
100	NARA	60542	3137	37W-4S	B1
N Pinehill Ct					
300	PLTN	60067	2752	22W-16N	B7
300	PltT	60067	2752	22W-16N	B7
Pine Hill Dr					
800	ANTH	60002	2358	22W-42N	B6
16300	HMGN	60491	3421	17W-19S	C2
Pinehill Dr					
10	NARA	60542	3137	37W-4S	B1
Pine Hill Ln					
10	HNDL	60521	3085	16W-4S	E7
10	HNDL	60523	3085	16W-4S	E7
10	OKBK	60523	3085	16W-4S	E7
S Pine Hill Rd					
19900	FftT	60423	3504	10W-24S	C5
W Pine Hill Rd					
7800	FftT	60423	3504	9W-24S	D4
Pine Hills Rd					
200	CmpT	60175	2962	39W-3N	E6
Pine Hollow Rd					
5900	CPVL	60110	2747	36W-18N	A5
Pinehurst Av					
200	DSPN	60016	2862	14W-12N	C1
500	DSPN	60016	2808	14W-12N	C7
W Pinehurst Blvd					
2200	ADSN	60101	2969	21W-5N	E2
2200	BmdT	60101	2969	21W-5N	D2
W Pinehurst Cir					
10	GLHT	60139	3024	24W-2N	E1
Pinehurst Ct					
10	BRBK	60459	3211	7W-8S	C1
300	GRNE	60031	2534	18W-34N	A1
300	LslT	60540	3143	23W-7S	A6
300	PSHT	60463	3347	8W-15S	B1
700	OSWG	60543	3263	37W-13S	C5
800	NARA	60542	3078	35W-3S	C6
1900	LbvT	60048	2590	18W-30N	E1
5000	JNBG	60050	2472	30W-36N	B3
6600	LSLE	60532	3142	24W-7S	D6
Pinehurst Dr					
200	MDLN	60060	2590	20W-27N	A7
200	NpvT	60563	3140	30W-4S	B2
200	WNFD	60190	3023	26W-1N	D2
300	PSHT	60463	3347	8W-15S	B1
600	NARA	60542	3078	35W-3S	B6
1300	GNVW	60025	2810	9W-13N	C5
1400	DRN	60561	3207	18W-9S	A3
2400	AURA	60506	3136	39W-6S	E6
22900	FftT	60423	3591	13W-27S	A5
25700	MONE	60449	3683	6W-31S	B5
N Pinehurst Dr					
1300	VNHL	60061	2647	16W-26N	D2
Pinehurst Ln					
300	LslT	60540	3143	23W-7S	A6
600	BFGV	60089	2701	16W-20N	D7
700	OSWG	60543	3263	37W-13S	C5
800	SMBG	60193	2858	24W-9N	C7
800	SMBG	60193	2912	24W-9N	C1
1600	FSMR	60422	3507	2W-23S	D3
Pinehurst St					
-	ANTH	60002	2357	25W-41N	B7
Pine Lake Cir					
21700	KLDR	60047	2699	21W-21N	C6
E Pine Lake Cir					
300	VNHL	60061	2647	16W-26N	D2
Pine Lake Ct					
18300	TYPK	60477	3425	8W-22S	B7
N Pine Lake Ct					
21500	KLDR	60047	2699	21W-21N	C6
Pine Lake Dr					
1500	AURA	60564	3202	30W-9S	B5
6500	TYPK	60477	3505	8W-22S	B1
18300	TYPK	60477	3425	8W-22S	B7
Pine Lake Rd					
24700	MonT	60417	3683	4W-29S	E2
24700	MonT	60449	3683	4W-29S	E2
24700	MonT	60466	3683	4W-29S	D2
24700	UYPK	60466	3683	4W-29S	E2
25500	UYPK	60449	3683	5W-31S	D5
Pineland Ct					
2900	AURA	60504	3201	31W-8S	D3
Pinelands Rd					
200	SchT	60174	2964	35W-5N	C2
200	WYNE	60174	2964	35W-5N	C2
Pine Manor Dr					
400	WLMT	60091	2812	4W-13N	C6
Pine Meadow Ct					
1000	VNHL	60061	2646	18W-24N	E7
1400	LYVL	60048	2591	18W-29N	A3
1800	GRNE	60031	2478	15W-36N	B5
Pine Meadow Ln					
10	LYVL	60048	2591	18W-29N	A4
10	MDLN	60060	2591	18W-29N	A4
Pine Meadows Cir					
3000	CPVL	60110	2747	36W-18N	A5
Pine Needle Ln					
800	JLET	60432	3500	20W-22S	C2
Pine Needle Pass					
9100	BLVY	60097	2526	38W-34N	A1
Pine Needles Ct					
700	GnvT	60510	3019	37W-0S	B7
Pine Needles Dr					
-	LMNT	60439	3343	17W-15S	C1
Pine Oaks Cir					
1100	LKFT	60045	2649	12W-25N	B6
Pine Point Dr					
10	HDPK	60035	2758	6W-20N	C2
6500	TYPK	60477	3425	8W-20S	B4
S Pineprairie Dr					
18400	NlxT	60448	3422	16W-22S	A7
18400	NlxT	60448	3502	16W-22S	A1
Pine Ridge Ct					
1100	LslT	60540	3204	25W-8S	A1
1100	NPVL	60540	3204	25W-8S	A1
6300	TYPK	60477	3425	7W-22S	C7
N Pine Ridge Ct					
22300	FKFT	60423	3592	10W-27S	D4
Pine Ridge Dr					
-	FftT	60423	3592	10W-27S	B4
-	FKFT	60423	3592	10W-27S	B4
-	RchT	60477	3425	7W-22S	C7
10	JltT	60433	3587	23W-25S	A1
6300	TYPK	60477	3425	7W-22S	C7
Pineridge Dr N					
-	OSWG	60543	3262	39W-11S	D2
Pineridge Dr S					
100	OSWG	60543	3262	39W-11S	D2
Pine Ridge Ln					
100	MTGY	60538	3199	36W-9S	E4
Pine Row Ct					
200	BbyT	60119	3075	43W-2S	A4
Pines Blvd					
-	LKVL	60046	2474	23W-37N	E2
-	LKVL	60046	2475	23W-37N	A2
Pines Dr					
-	GYLK	60030	2533	18W-32N	D4
Pine Trace Ct					
1500	MonT	60417	3594	4W-29S	D7
1500	UYPK	60466	3594	4W-29S	D7
Pine Trail Dr					
700	RMVL	60446	3269	23W-14S	A7
Pine Trails Cir					
5200	JLET	60586	3496	30W-22S	B2
Pinetree Cir N					
900	BFGV	60089	2701	16W-21N	C5
Pinetree Cir S					
900	BFGV	60089	2701	16W-21N	C7
Pine Tree Ct					
-	LKVL	60046	2474	23W-36N	E3
-	OSWG	60543	3262	39W-11S	D2
10	EMHT	60126	3027	16W-0S	D6
1500	LSLE	60532	3082	23W-4S	E7
1500	LSLE	60532	3083	23W-4S	A7
2900	AURA	60502	3079	32W-3S	C7
Pinetree Ct					
700	RMVL	60446	3269	23W-14S	A6
6200	LGGV	60047	2646	18W-24N	E7
Pine Tree Dr					
-	OSWG	60543	3262	39W-11S	D2
1100	LKVL	60046	2474	23W-36N	E4
6200	LGGV	60047	2646	18W-24N	D7
6200	LGGV	60047	2700	18W-24N	D1
Pinetree Dr					
1400	NPVL	60565	3203	27W-8S	C2
1500	GRNE	60031	2478	15W-35N	A5
N Pinetree Dr					
1900	ANHT	60004	2807	17W-16N	B1
2000	ANHT	60004	2754	17W-16N	B7
Pine Tree Ln					
10	BRRG	60527	3208	15W-9S	B3
100	RVWD	60015	2703	13W-21N	A6
200	LGPK	60525	3087	12W-2S	B3
500	WDDL	60191	2971	17W-5N	C2
600	DRN	60561	3207	17W-8S	C2
600	WLBK	60527	3207	17W-8S	C2
900	WNKA	60093	2758	6W-16N	D7
Pinetree Ln					
300	SMBG	60193	2859	21W-9N	E6
1100	BRLT	60103	2910	29W-6N	E7
1100	LYVL	60048	2591	17W-28N	B5
Pine Tree Rd					
10	DRFD	60015	2757	9W-18N	B2
10	NfdT	60062	2757	9W-18N	B2
14700	ODPK	60462	3345	13W-17S	A6
Pine Tree Row					
10	LKZH	60047	2698	24W-23N	C1
Pinetree St					
6600	HRPK	60133	2911	27W-8N	D3
Pine Tuck Ter					
-	RVWD	60015	2702	13W-21N	E6
Pine Valley Dr					
1100	SMBG	60173	2805	21W-13N	D6
S Pine Valley Dr					
22900	FftT	60423	3591	13W-27S	B5
Pine Valley Rd					
10	RGMW	60008	2806	19W-14N	C4
N Pineview Blvd					
31300	LKMR	60051	2529	28W-31N	E7
Pineview Cir					
3200	CPVL	60110	2747	36W-18N	A5
Pine View Ct					
400	YkTp	60148	3084	19W-1S	D1
1500	DRN	60561	3207	18W-9S	A3
Pineview Ct					
7600	FKFT	60423	3592	9W-27S	E4
14400	OrlT	60467	3344	14W-17S	D5
Pine View Dr					
1000	JLET	60432	3500	20W-22S	B2
Pineview Dr					
11600	OrlT	60467	3344	14W-17S	D5
16700	HMGN	60491	3422	15W-20S	C4
E Pineview Dr					
10	RLKP	60073	2532	22W-33N	A3
200	HNVL	60073	2532	22W-33N	A3
W Pineview Dr					
200	RDLK	60073	2531	23W-33N	E2
300	HNVL	60073	2532	22W-33N	B3
300	RLKP	60073	2532	22W-33N	B3
22000	AntT	60002	2417	22W-40N	C2
Pineview Ln					
7600	FKFT	60423	3592	9W-27S	D4
Pine View St					
300	YkTp	60148	3084	19W-1S	D1
Pine View Pass					
500	LKVL	60046	2475	22W-37N	A2
Pine Wood Ct					
18300	TYPK	60477	3425	7W-21S	C7
Pinewood Ct					
6100	WLBK	60527	3145	16W-6S	D5
14500	OrlT	60467	3344	14W-17S	C5
Pinewood Dr					
400	NARA	60542	3077	37W-3S	D7
500	EGVV	60007	2915	18W-8N	A2
500	GLNC	60022	2758	7W-18N	B3
1000	DRGV	60516	3206	19W-8S	C1
14300	ODPK	60467	3344	14W-17S	C5
14300	OrlT	60467	3344	14W-17S	C5
14500	HMGN	60491	3344	14W-17S	C5
W Pinewood Dr					
3600	MonT	60449	3683	4W-31S	E5
Pinewood Ln					
-	MONE	60449	3683	6W-31S	A5
200	BMDL	60108	2969	22W-4N	B3
1200	CLLK	60014	2639	37W-25N	B4
1700	JltT	60433	3587	21W-26S	E3
4100	MTSN	60443	3506	5W-25S	C6
6500	TYPK	60477	3425	8W-22S	B7
S Pinewood Ln					
25500	MonT	60449	3683	4W-31S	E5
W Pinewood Ln					
15200	LbvT	60048	2592	15W-30N	B2
Pinewood Pl					
1000	DRGV	60516	3206	20W-8S	B1
Pinewood Rd					
5200	GRNE	60031	2478	15W-35N	A6
15100	HmrT	60441	3421	18W-20S	A4
15100	LKPT	60441	3420	19W-20S	E4
15100	LKPT	60441	3421	18W-20S	A4
Pine Woods Ct					
1400	MonT	60417	3683	4W-29S	D1
1400	MonT	60466	3683	4W-29S	D1
1400	UYPK	60417	3683	4W-29S	D1
1400	UYPK	60466	3683	4W-29S	D1
Pinewoods Dr					
400	NBRN	60010	2698	25W-22N	A3
Pine Woods Ln					
3200	CPVL	60110	2747	35W-18N	C6
Pingree Rd					
-	NndT	60014	2640	34W-25N	D5
900	CLLK	60014	2640	33W-24N	D7
6000	AlqT	60014	2640	34W-25N	D5
8100	CLLK	60014	2694	34W-23N	D1
8100	LIHL	60014	2694	34W-23N	D2
8100	LIHL	60156	2694	34W-23N	D2
Pinnacle Ct					
1600	AURA	60502	3079	33W-3S	A6
Pinnacle Dr					
10	RMVL	60441	3340	25W-17S	B5
10	RMVL	60446	3340	25W-17S	B5
1700	AURA	60502	3079	33W-3S	A6
N Pinnacle Dr					
-	LktT	60441	3340	25W-16S	B5
-	RMVL	60441	3340	25W-16S	B5
-	RMVL	60446	3340	25W-16S	B5
Pinney St					
10	AURA	60505	3138	35W-7S	B7
10	AURA	60506	3138	35W-7S	B7
Pin Oak Cir					
200	CRY	60013	2642	30W-24N	A7
11200	MKNA	60448	3502	14W-24S	E4
Pin Oak Ct					
10	CRY	60013	2642	30W-24N	A7
100	WNFD	60190	3023	27W-0S	C6
400	SCRL	60174	2964	34W-3N	D6
1200	MHRY	60050	2527	35W-33N	B3
1200	WHTN	60187	3081	26W-1S	E2
3700	LSLE	60187	3082	24W-3S	D6
3700	LSLE	60532	3082	24W-3S	D6
7600	JLET	60586	3495	33W-21S	A1
18000	TYPK	60477	3425	8W-21S	B6
S Pin Oak Ct					
16100	HMGN	60491	3422	16W-19S	A2
W Pin Oak Ct					
13200	HMGN	60491	3343	16W-16S	E4
Pin Oak Dr					
-	ELWD	60421	3675	25W-31S	B5
-	JknT	60421	3675	25W-31S	B5
-	PTHT	60070	2754	16W-16N	E6
-	WLNG	60004	2754	16W-16N	E6
-	WLNG	60070	2754	16W-16N	E6
200	WLMT	60091	2812	4W-13N	C6
7700	JLET	60586	3495	33W-21S	A1
Pinoak Dr					
300	NARA	60542	3077	36W-4S	D7
400	BRLT	60103	2910	29W-8N	E3
7800	MchT	60097	2526	36W-34N	C1
8100	BLVY	60097	2526	37W-34N	C1
8100	GwdT	60097	2526	37W-34N	C1
E Pinoak Dr					
2000	MPPT	60056	2808	13W-14N	E4
2000	WhlT	60025	2808	13W-14N	E4
2000	WhlT	60056	2808	13W-14N	E4
S Pinoak Dr					
300	BRLT	60103	2910	29W-8N	E4
W Pin Oak Dr					
12800	HMGN	60491	3344	16W-16S	A4
13000	HMGN	60491	3343	16W-16S	E4
Pin Oak Ln					
-	GRNE	60031	2477	17W-34N	B7
-	WrnT	60031	2477	17W-34N	B7
800	UYPK	60466	3684	3W-30S	B2
1000	PTHT	60070	2754	16W-16N	E7
1700	ELGN	60120	2856	31W-10N	A6
Pinoak Ln					
200	LslT	60540	3204	24W-8S	D2
Pin Oak Tr					
1100	AURA	60506	3137	37W-5S	D3
Pintail Ct					
600	BmdT	60108	2968	25W-5N	A2
700	VrnT	60015	2755	15W-20N	B1
E Pintail Ct					
1100	PLTN	60067	2805	22W-14N	B3
Pintail Dr					
700	NLNX	60451	3502	15W-25S	B7
700	NLNX	60451	3590	15W-25S	B1
Pintail Ln					
10	BmdT	60108	2968	25W-5N	A2
400	VrnT	60015	2755	15W-20N	B1
5800	LGGV	60047	2701	17W-23N	C2
Pintail Pl					
700	GNCY	53128	2353		B2
Pintail Rd					
12700	BGBK	60490	3339	28W-15S	A1
12700	BGBK	60585	3339	28W-15S	A1
12700	PNFD	60585	3339	28W-15S	A1
Pintail St					
500	VrnT	60015	2755	15W-20N	B1
Pinto Ct					
10	SMWD	60107	2856	30W-10N	C5
1400	GNVA	60134	3020	36W-0N	A5
1900	WHTN	60187	3082	24W-2S	E4
Pinto Dr					
300	BGBK	60440	3268	24W-11S	E1
Pinto Ln					
300	CmpT	60175	2906	41W-6N	A7
800	NHBK	60062	2756	12W-17N	A4
1200	RLKP	60030	2589	22W-30N	C1
Pinto St					
15300	HMGN	60491	3343	16W-18S	E7
Pinyon Pine Ct N					
100	BFGV	60089	2701	16W-23N	C2
Pinyon Pine Ct S					
10	BFGV	60089	2701	16W-23N	C2
N Pioneer Av					
3200	CHCG	60634	2974	10W-4N	B3
3200	RVGV	60171	2974	10W-4N	B4
3200	RVGV	60634	2974	10W-4N	B4
5400	CHCG	60656	2918	10W-6N	B5
Pioneer Ct					
-	WKGN	60085	2536	12W-33N	C3
10	OswT	60543	3265	33W-13S	A4
100	CmpT	60175	2962	39W-4N	E5
700	WCHI	60185	3022	29W-1N	E2
900	ROSL	60172	2912	24W-7N	C5
1400	WKGN	60085	2479	12W-35N	C6
2500	GNVA	60134	3019	37W-0N	D5
3200	JLET	60431	3497	28W-25S	B7
21400	FKFT	60423	3591	13W-25S	A1
Pioneer Dr					
100	MNKA	60447	3583	33W-28S	B7
100	MNKA	60447	3672	33W-28S	B1
N Pioneer Dr					
500	AddT	60101	2970	19W-4N	C4
500	ADSN	60101	2970	19W-4N	C4
Pioneer Ln					
2000	WLMT	60091	2812	4W-13N	B7
Pioneer Pkwy					
16300	LKPT	60441	3420	20W-19S	B3
Pioneer Pl					
200	NlxT	60451	3502	15W-25S	C7
Pioneer Rd					
1000	ALGN	60102	2694	33W-21N	E6
1000	ALGN	60102	2695	33W-21N	A6
1300	CTHL	60403	3497	26W-22S	E2
1300	CTHL	60435	3497	26W-22S	E2
1400	AlqT	60102	2695	33W-21N	A5
2100	EVTN	60201	2866	3W-12N	E1
2500	EVTN	60201	2812	3W-12N	E7
4000	JNBG	60050	2471	32W-35N	A5
4000	JNBG	60072	2471	32W-35N	A5
4000	MchT	60050	2471	32W-36N	A4
4000	MchT	60072	2471	32W-36N	A4
4600	RGWD	60072	2471	33W-37N	A2
5300	MchT	60072	2470	33W-37N	E1
5300	RcmT	60072	2412	33W-38N	E6
5300	RcmT	60072	2470	33W-37N	E1
5300	RGWD	60072	2470	33W-37N	E1
6500	RcmT	60071	2412	33W-38N	E6
N Pioneer Rd					
10	WKGN	60085	2536	12W-33N	C1
700	WKGN	60085	2479	12W-35N	C7
1000	WkgT	60085	2479	12W-35N	C7
S Pioneer Rd					
6800	RcmT	60071	2412	33W-39N	D5
6800	RcmT	60072	2412	33W-39N	E6
W Pioneer Rd					
23600	AlqT	60013	2696	28W-23N	D1
23600	CbaT	60013	2696	28W-23N	D1
Pioneer Tr					
10800	FKFT	60423	3591	13W-26S	A1
Pioneer Oaks Dr					
-	RGWD	60072	2470	33W-36N	E3
-	RGWD	60072	2471	33W-37N	A3
Pioneer Park Pl					
10	ELGN	60123	2854	35W-12N	B2
Piper Av					
200	NPVL	60565	3203	26W-10S	D5
Piper Ct					
3500	RGMW	60008	2806	20W-13N	B6
Piper Dr					
800	NLNX	60451	3501	18W-25S	A7
Piper Ln					
10	HNWD	60047	2645	21W-24N	C7
10	PTHT	60070	2808	13W-15N	D1
10	WLNG	60090	2808	13W-15N	D1
N Piper Ln					
37000	GrtT	60046	2474	25W-37N	B3
37000	LkvT	60046	2474	25W-37N	B2
Pipers Dr					
100	BRLT	60103	2910	29W-7N	E5
100	BRLT	60103	2911	28W-7N	A5
Pipers Wy					
7400	DRGV	60516	3206	19W-8S	D1
Pipestone Ct					
4500	NPVL	60564	3266	29W-12S	E3
W Pippin St					
3700	CHCG	60652	3212	4W-8S	C1
Pirates Cove					
-	RGMW	60067	2805	21W-13N	D6
-	SMBG	60067	2805	21W-13N	D6
-	SMBG	60173	2805	21W-13N	D6
Piscasow N					
10	CmgT	60033	2405	53W-38N	A6
Pistakee Dr					
4900	MchT	60050	2472	29W-37N	C2
Pistakee Pkwy					
500	FXLK	60020	2473	28W-35N	A5
N Pistakee Lake Rd					
10	FXLK	60020	2472	28W-36N	E3
10	FXLK	60020	2473	28W-36N	A3
S Pistakee Lake Rd					
10	FXLK	60020	2472	28W-36N	E4
Pistakee View Ct					
1000	JNBG	60051	2472	29W-35N	C5
Pitcher Dr					
3100	DRN	60561	3206	20W-9S	B4
Pitner Av					
900	EVTN	60202	2866	3W-10N	E4
1200	EVTN	60201	2866	3W-11N	E3
S Pitney Ct					
3000	CHCG	60608	3091	1W-2S	D3
Pit Run Dr					
-	CNHN	60481	3761	32W-33S	C3
W Pittner Av					
28700	AlqT	60013	2642	28W-24N	D7
28700	CbaT	60013	2642	28W-24N	D7
N Pittsburgh Av					
3200	CHCG	60634	2974	10W-4N	A4
3200	RVGV	60171	2974	10W-4N	A4
3200	RVGV	60634	2974	10W-4N	A4
5100	CHCG	60706	2918	10W-6N	A7
5200	CHCG	60656	2918	10W-6N	B6
5200	NRDG	60706	2918	10W-6N	B6
Pitz Ln					
100	BTVA	60510	3077	36W-1S	E2
Pitzen Rd					
3500	JNBG	60051	2472	29W-35N	C6
Piute Tr					
8000	TYPK	60477	3424	10W-21S	C6
Placer Ct					
1500	NPVL	60565	3203	26W-9S	D3
Placid Av					
100	GLHT	60139	2968	23W-3N	E6
100	GLHT	60139	2969	23W-3N	A6
Placid Ct					
200	EGVV	60007	2914	18W-8N	E2
5400	LSLE	60532	3142	24W-6S	E4
16700	LKPT	60441	3420	21W-20S	A4
Placid Ln					
1900	GNOK	60048	2592	14W-30N	C2
Placid Wy					
200	EGVV	60007	2914	18W-8N	E2
S Plahm Ct					
10700	WRTH	60482	3275	8W-12S	A2
Plain Av					
1300	AURA	60505	3138	34W-6S	E6
1600	AraT	60504	3139	33W-6S	A6
1600	AraT	60505	3139	33W-6S	A6
1800	AraT	60502	3139	33W-6S	B6
2000	AURA	60502	3139	33W-6S	B6
N Plainfield Av					
3200	CHCG	60634	2974	10W-4N	A4
3200	RVGV	60171	2974	10W-4N	A4
3200	RVGV	60634	2974	10W-4N	A4
5000	NRDG	60706	2918	10W-6N	A6
5300	CHCG	60656	2918	10W-6N	A6
Plainfield Ct					
200	VNHL	60061	2647	16W-27N	D1
Plainfield Dr					
1700	DSPN	60018	2862	13W-9N	D7
Plainfield Rd					
-	DGvT	60517	3206	19W-9S	C3
-	DRN	60517	3206	19W-9S	C3
10	DRGV	60516	3206	19W-9S	C3
10	DRGV	60561	3206	19W-9S	C3
10	DRN	60516	3206	19W-9S	C3
10	DRN	60561	3206	19W-9S	C3
100	BRRG	60527	3146	15W-7S	A7
100	DRN	60527	3145	16W-8S	D7
100	DRN	60561	3145	16W-8S	D7
100	WLBK	60527	3145	16W-8S	D7
100	WLBK	60527	3146	15W-7S	B6
100	WLBK	60561	3145	16W-8S	D7
200	DGvT	60516	3206	18W-8S	E3
300	DRN	60561	3207	17W-8S	B2
400	DRN	60527	3207	17W-8S	D1
400	JLET	60435	3498	26W-21S	A1
400	WLBK	60527	3207	17W-8S	D1
400	WLBK	60561	3207	17W-8S	D1
500	DGvT	60561	3206	19W-9S	C3
800	NasT	60543	3337	33W-16S	A4
800	PNFD	60543	3337	33W-16S	A4
800	PNFD	60585	3337	33W-16S	A4
900	OswT	60585	3337	33W-16S	A3
1500	CTHL	60403	3498	25W-22S	A1
1500	DRGV	60516	3207	18W-8S	A2
1500	DRN	60516	3207	18W-8S	A2
1500	JLET	60403	3498	25W-22S	A1
1600	CTHL	60403	3418	26W-21S	A7
1700	DRGV	60561	3207	18W-9S	A2
2000	CTHL	60403	3417	26W-21S	E7
2300	CTHL	60435	3417	26W-21S	D6
2300	CTHL	60435	3417	26W-20S	D6
2300	PnfT	60435	3417	26W-20S	D6
2400	LktT	60435	3417	27W-20S	C5
2600	JLET	60431	3417	27W-20S	C5
3100	OswT	60543	3263	37W-13S	D5
3100	OswT	60543	3264	36W-14S	A7
3500	OSWG	60543	3263	36W-14S	E7
8400	LYNS	60534	3088	10W-4S	A7
8700	BKFD	60513	3088	10W-4S	A7
8700	BKFD	60534	3088	10W-4S	A7
8800	BKFD	60513	3087	11W-4S	E7
8800	BKFD	60513	3147	11W-4S	E1
9100	MCCK	60513	3147	11W-4S	E1
9100	MCCK	60525	3147	11W-4S	E1
12000	IHPK	60558	3146	15W-7S	A7
12000	LynT	60558	3146	15W-7S	A7
Plainfield Rd CO-31					
-	DGvT	60517	3206	19W-9S	C3
-	DRN	60517	3206	19W-9S	C3
10	DRGV	60516	3206	19W-9S	C3
10	DRGV	60561	3206	19W-9S	C3
10	DRN	60516	3206	19W-9S	C3
10	DRN	60561	3206	19W-9S	C3
100	BRRG	60527	3146	15W-7S	C6
100	DRN	60527	3145	16W-8S	D7
100	DRN	60561	3145	16W-8S	D7
100	WLBK	60527	3145	16W-8S	D7
100	WLBK	60527	3146	15W-7S	B6
100	WLBK	60561	3145	16W-8S	D7
200	DGvT	60516	3206	18W-9S	E3
300	DRN	60561	3207	17W-8S	B2
400	DRN	60527	3207	17W-8S	D1
400	WLBK	60527	3207	17W-8S	D1
400	WLBK	60561	3207	17W-8S	D1
500	DGvT	60561	3206	19W-9S	C3
1500	DRGV	60516	3207	18W-8S	A2
1500	DRN	60516	3207	18W-8S	A2
1700	DRGV	60561	3207	18W-9S	A2
Plainfield Rd US-30					
400	JLET	60435	3498	26W-21S	A1
1500	CTHL	60403	3498	25W-22S	A1
1500	JLET	60403	3498	25W-22S	A1
1600	CTHL	60403	3418	26W-21S	A7
2000	CTHL	60403	3417	26W-21S	E7
2300	CTHL	60435	3417	26W-21S	D6
2300	LktT	60435	3417	26W-20S	D6
2300	PnfT	60435	3417	26W-20S	D6
2400	JLET	60435	3417	27W-20S	C5
2600	JLET	60431	3417	27W-20S	C5

STREET Block	City	ZIP	Map#	CGS	Grid
E Plainfield Rd					
10	CTSD	60525	3147	12W-5S	C2
10	LGNG	60525	3147	12W-5S	C2
500	MCCK	60525	3147	12W-5S	C2
W Plainfield Rd					
-	BRRG	60527	3146	14W-7S	D5
10	CTSD	60525	3147	13W-6S	A4
10	LGNG	60525	3147	13W-6S	A4
800	LynT	60525	3147	13W-6S	B3
1500	LynT	60525	3146	14W-6S	D5
2000	IHPK	60525	3146	13W-6S	E5
11400	IHPK	60558	3146	14W-7S	D5
11400	LynT	60558	3146	14W-7S	D5
Plainfield-Naperville Rd					
-	BGBK	60490	3267	28W-12S	B3
-	BGBK	60564	3267	28W-12S	B3
-	BGBK	60585	3267	28W-12S	B3
-	WldT	60490	3267	28W-12S	B3
-	WldT	60585	3267	28W-12S	B3
10	NpvT	60564	3203	28W-9S	B4
10	WldT	60564	3203	28W-11S	B7
10	NPVL	60564	3203	28W-9S	B4
100	NPVL	60564	3267	28W-11S	B1
100	NPVL	60565	3203	28W-9S	B4
100	NPVL	60565	3267	28W-11S	B1
100	NpvT	60565	3203	28W-9S	B4
100	WldT	60564	3267	28W-12S	B3
100	WldT	60565	3267	28W-11S	B1
Plainfield Naperville Rd					
200	NPVL	60540	3141	27W-7S	B7
200	NpvT	60540	3141	27W-7S	B7
Plainfield-Naperville Rd					
2100	WldT	60565	3203	28W-9S	B5
Plainfield-Naperville Rd CO-1					
400	NPVL	60564	3203	28W-9S	B4
400	NPVL	60565	3203	28W-9S	B4
400	NpvT	60564	3203	28W-9S	B4
400	NpvT	60565	3203	27W-8S	B3
S Plainfield Naperville Rd					
10	NPVL	60540	3203	27W-8S	B1
600	NPVL	60540	3141	27W-7S	B7
600	NpvT	60540	3141	27W-7S	B7
Plainfield-Oswego Rd					
6100	NasT	60543	3337	33W-17S	A6
6100	PNFD	60543	3337	33W-17S	A6
6100	PNFD	60585	3337	33W-17S	A6
6200	NasT	60544	3337	33W-17S	A7
Plains Ct					
800	CLSM	60188	2967	27W-3N	D7
S Plainsman Cir					
-	PNFD	60586	3416	29W-20S	C5
W Plainsman Cir					
23800	PNFD	60586	3416	29W-20S	C5
S Plainsman Ct					
23900	PNFD	60586	3416	30W-20S	C4
Plainview Ct					
10	BGBK	60440	3268	24W-12S	C3
Plainview Dr					
-	CNHN	60410	3672	33W-30S	A5
10	WldT	60564	3203	28W-10S	A5
10	WldT	60565	3203	28W-10S	A5
100	BGBK	60440	3268	24W-12S	D3
16500	MKHM	60428	3426	4W-19S	E3
16600	HLCT	60429	3426	4W-19S	E3
Plainview Rd					
1400	CPVL	60110	2801	33W-16N	C1
1400	EDND	60110	2801	33W-16N	B1
1400	EDND	60118	2801	33W-16N	B1
6400	GRNE	60031	2534	16W-34N	C1
Plaister Av					
1000	ShdT	60044	2593	13W-29N	A5
1100	LbvT	60044	2593	13W-29N	A5
Plamondon Ct					
600	MltT	60187	3082	25W-1S	B1
600	WHTN	60187	3082	25W-1S	B1
N Plamondon Dr					
500	AddT	60101	2970	20W-4N	A4
500	ADSN	60101	2970	20W-4N	A4
Plamondon Rd					
200	MltT	60187	3082	25W-1S	B2
200	WHTN	60187	3082	25W-1S	B2
W Plane Rest Dr					
2600	WKGN	60087	2479	12W-38N	C1
Plank Dr					
100	OSWG	60543	3263	37W-13S	D5
Plank Rd					
10	LslT	60563	3142	25W-5S	B3
10	NPVL	60563	3142	26W-6S	A4
10	PltT	60124	2852	40W-12N	B3
10	PltT	60140	2851	43W-13N	A1
10	PltT	60140	2852	40W-12N	B3
100	LSLE	60563	3142	25W-5S	B3
500	LslT	60563	3141	26W-6S	E4
500	NPVL	60563	3141	26W-6S	E4
700	ElgT	60124	2853	38W-11N	A3
700	NLNX	60451	3589	17W-25S	D1
700	PltT	60124	2853	38W-11N	A3
Plank Rd CO-22					
10	PltT	60124	2852	40W-12N	B3
10	PltT	60140	2851	43W-13N	A1
10	PltT	60140	2852	40W-12N	B3
700	ElgT	60124	2853	38W-11N	A3
700	PltT	60124	2853	38W-11N	A3
Plank Trail Ct					
21100	FKFT	60423	3504	9W-25S	E7
Plank Trail Dr					
-	FftT	60423	3504	9W-25S	E7
-	FKFT	60423	3504	9W-25S	E7
21200	FKFT	60423	3592	9W-25S	E1
Plant Rd					
1000	WLNG	60090	2755	13W-16N	D6
Plantain Ct					
900	CLLK	60014	2639	37W-24N	B6
Plantain Dr					
900	JLET	60447	3495	33W-22S	A3
1400	MNKA	60447	3672	33W-30S	A4
1500	CNHN	60410	3672	33W-30S	A4
Plantation Ct					
3200	NPVL	60564	3202	30W-10S	B5
Plantation Dr					
2900	CPVL	60110	2747	36W-17N	A6
W Plantation Rd					
25600	PnfT	60586	3415	32W-21S	D7
Plante Rd					
2700	NARA	60542	3076	39W-3S	D6
Planters Row					
100	GNVA	60134	3019	37W-1N	C3
Plate Dr					
500	DndT	60118	2801	32W-15N	D4
500	EDND	60118	2801	32W-15N	D4
E Plate Dr					
800	PLTN	60074	2753	19W-16N	B6
Plato Rd					
10	PltT	60124	2851	43W-10N	B6
10	PltT	60140	2851	43W-10N	A6
400	PltT	60124	2852	41W-10N	A6
Plato Rd CO-17					
400	PltT	60124	2851	41W-10N	E6
400	PltT	60124	2852	41W-10N	A6
Plato Rd CO-32					
10	PltT	60124	2851	43W-10N	B6
10	PltT	60140	2851	43W-10N	A6
400	PltT	60124	2852	41W-10N	A6
Platt Pl					
10	BbyT	60134	3018	39W-0N	E5
Platt St					
-	GNCY	53128	2353		A3
Platte Tr					
3200	OMFD	60461	3506	4W-24S	E5
Plattner Ct					
20300	FftT	60448	3502	14W-24S	E5
20300	MKNA	60448	3502	14W-24S	E5
Plattner Dr					
11200	MKNA	60448	3502	14W-24S	E5
W Plattner Dr					
5200	ALSP	60803	3275	6W-14S	E6
Player Ct					
10	BGBK	60490	3267	27W-12S	D3
9500	LKWD	60014	2692	38W-23N	E1
N Players Ct					
1700	VNHL	60061	2647	17W-27N	B2
E Playfield Dr					
12700	CTWD	60445	3275	6W-15S	E7
12900	CTWD	60445	3347	6W-15S	E1
W Playfield Dr					
12700	CTWD	60445	3275	6W-15S	E7
12900	CTWD	60445	3347	6W-15S	E1
Plaza Ct					
-	CHHT	60411	3507	1W-24S	E5
-	CHHT	60411	3508	1W-24S	A5
7500	WLBK	60527	3208	16W-8S	A1
Plaza Dr					
-	PTHT	60070	2808	13W-15N	E1
-	RGMW	60008	2806	19W-13N	B5
10	WDRG	60517	3205	21W-8S	E1
10	WTMT	60559	3085	17W-4S	B7
1100	JLET	60435	3498	25W-22S	B2
1100	NlxT	60451	3501	16W-24S	E4
5500	GRNE	60031	2477	15W-35N	E6
5500	GRNE	60031	2478	15W-35N	A6
N Plaza Dr					
800	JLET	60435	3498	25W-22S	B3
800	SMBG	60173	2859	21W-11N	E2
W Plaza Ln					
16200	NptT	60083	2419	16W-39N	E5
16200	WDWH	60083	2419	16W-39N	E5
Plaza 33 Service Rd					
-	SRPK	60176	2917	12W-5N	B7
Plaza Service Rd					
-	HLCT	60428	3427	3W-19S	C3
-	HLCT	60429	3427	3W-19S	C3
-	MKHM	60428	3427	3W-19S	B3
Pleasant Av					
10	HIWD	60040	2704	9W-23N	C3
100	GNEN	60137	3025	22W-1N	B3
100	MltT	60137	3025	22W-1N	B3
200	BmdT	60137	2969	22W-2N	B7
200	BmdT	60137	3025	22W-2N	B1
200	BmdT	60139	3025	22W-2N	B1
200	GLHT	60139	3025	22W-2N	B1
400	GLHT	60139	2969	22W-2N	B7
400	HDPK	60035	2758	7W-20N	A1
600	LMBD	60148	3026	21W-1N	A2
600	MltT	60137	3025	21W-1N	E2
600	MltT	60148	3026	21W-1N	A2
700	HDPK	60035	2705	7W-20N	A7
1600	MHRY	60050	2527	33W-33N	E3
1700	SCRL	60174	3020	34W-2N	D2
8700	HYHL	60457	3210	10W-10S	A4
9200	TYPK	60487	3423	11W-22S	E7
9300	FftT	60448	3423	11W-22S	E7
9300	FftT	60487	3423	11W-22S	E7
E Pleasant Av					
500	SDWH	60548	3258	51W-14S	A7
N Pleasant Av					
100	BMDL	60108	2913	22W-5N	B7
100	BMDL	60108	2969	22W-5N	B1
S Pleasant Av					
-	CHCG	60643	3213	2W-10S	C6
100	BMDL	60108	2969	22W-5N	B1
8800	CHCG	60620	3213	2W-10S	C4
Pleasant Blvd					
5600	CHRG	60415	3275	7W-12S	D2
5600	OKLN	60453	3275	7W-12S	D2
Pleasant Ct					
-	SRWD	60404	3496	31W-24S	A7
1100	BTVA	60510	3078	34W-1S	E3
1600	LYVL	60048	2591	18W-30N	A3
12800	CTWD	60445	3275	6W-15S	E7
15200	HMGN	60491	3342	19W-16S	E3
E Pleasant Ct					
24600	PnfT	60586	3416	30W-19S	A3
W Pleasant Ct					
24700	PnfT	60586	3416	30W-19S	A3
Pleasant Dr					
-	BRLT	60103	2967	28W-5N	A1
-	SRWD	60404	3495	31W-24S	E6
-	SRWD	60404	3496	31W-24S	A7
10	RtdT	60124	2799	39W-14N	A6
10	SMBG	60193	2859	23W-10N	A5
10	SMBG	60194	2859	23W-10N	A5
100	CHHT	60411	3507	1W-23S	E4
100	CHHT	60411	3508	0W-23S	B4
100	SEGN	60177	2908	34W-8N	E3
100	WynT	60103	2967	28W-5N	A1
200	EGVV	60007	2914	18W-8N	E2
200	HFET	60169	2859	23W-10N	A5
200	HFET	60194	2859	23W-10N	A5
200	RtdT	60124	2798	39W-14N	E6
400	SMBG	60193	2912	25W-8N	B2
400	SmbT	60193	2912	25W-8N	B2
1200	ELGN	60123	2800	35W-13N	C7
1400	CTHL	60403	3418	25W-21S	B7
2800	MchT	60050	2471	31W-34N	C7
2900	JNBG	60050	2471	31W-34N	C7
3100	WRLK	60097	2469	36W-35N	D7
22400	RNPK	60471	3594	6W-27S	B4
N Pleasant Dr					
200	GNWD	60425	3508	0W-22S	B1
400	GNWD	60425	3428	0W-22S	C7
800	ADSN	60101	2970	19W-4N	D3
1300	RLKB	60073	2474	23W-35N	E6
Pleasant Ln					
400	DSPN	60018	2862	15W-10N	A6
700	GNVW	60025	2811	7W-14N	B4
700	GNVW	60093	2811	7W-14N	B4
700	NHFD	60093	2811	7W-14N	B4
1400	GNVW	60025	2810	8W-14N	E4
5200	CTWD	60445	3275	6W-15S	E7
E Pleasant Ln					
10	LMBD	60148	3026	19W-1N	C2
700	VLPK	60181	3026	19W-1N	D2
W Pleasant Ln					
500	LMBD	60148	3026	20W-1N	A2
500	MltT	60148	3026	20W-1N	A2
Pleasant Pl					
-	WrnT	60046	2476	18W-34N	D7
500	ISLK	60042	2586	29W-28N	C5
600	SMWD	60107	2857	28W-9N	B7
1000	AraT	60505	3200	35W-9S	C4
1000	OKPK	60302	3030	8W-0N	E4
1100	LMNT	60439	3271	18W-14S	A7
1200	MTGY	60505	3200	35W-9S	C4
1200	MTGY	60538	3200	35W-9S	C4
10500	AURA	60505	3200	35W-9S	C3
N Pleasant Rd					
10	LKZH	60047	2698	24W-23N	C2
S Pleasant Rd					
10	LKZH	60047	2698	24W-22N	C3
W Pleasant Rd					
26500	GrtT	60041	2473	26W-36N	D4
Pleasant Run					
3200	GNVW	60025	2809	11W-14N	D3
3200	GNVW	60062	2809	11W-14N	D3
3200	NfdT	60062	2809	11W-14N	D3
Pleasant St					
10	BNVL	60106	2915	16W-5N	E7
10	HFET	60169	2858	24W-10N	D5
10	OKPK	60302	3031	8W-0N	A4
100	NLNX	60451	3501	16W-24S	E6
100	NlxT	60451	3501	16W-24S	E6
100	WDSK	60098	2524	42W-31N	B6
500	LinT	53147	2349		E1
800	FRGV	60021	2696	29W-23N	C2
900	DrrT	60098	2524	42W-31N	B6
1000	OKPK	60302	3030	8W-0N	E4
1100	FTPK	60130	3030	8W-0N	D4
1100	FTPK	60302	3030	8W-0N	D4
3400	NfdT	60062	2756	11W-16N	C6
3400	NHBK	60062	2756	11W-16N	C6
S Pleasant St					
100	JLET	60436	3498	24W-24S	D5
W Pleasant St					
600	VLPK	60181	3026	18W-1N	D2
700	LMBD	60148	3026	18W-1N	E2
Pleasant Ter					
200	RchT	60443	3593	8W-26S	B2
1100	AURA	60505	3138	34W-6S	C4
Pleasantdale Ct					
7100	CTSD	60525	3147	13W-8S	A7
Pleasantdale Dr					
10	DGvT	60439	3270	20W-11S	B1
7100	CTSD	60525	3147	13W-8S	A7
Pleasant Grove Rd					
21500	RlyT	60152	2634	50W-24N	A6
W Pleasant Hill Blvd					
10	PLTN	60067	2805	21W-15N	D2
Pleasant Hill Ct					
10	FKFT	60423	3591	12W-26S	C1
3600	NndT	60012	2584	34W-28N	C6
S Pleasant Hill Ct					
23700	CteT	60417	3598	3E-28S	A7
S Pleasant Hill Dr					
23600	CteT	60417	3598	3E-28S	A7
Pleasant Hill Ln					
1900	LSLE	60532	3142	23W-6S	E5
Pleasant Hill Rd					
10	BmdT	60188	3023	26W-2N	E1
10	CLSM	60188	3023	26W-2N	E1
10	MltT	60187	3023	26W-0S	E6
10	MltT	60188	3023	26W-1N	E2
10	MltT	60190	3023	26W-0S	E6
10	WHTN	60187	3023	26W-0S	E6
10	WNFD	60187	3023	26W-1N	E2
10	WNFD	60188	3023	26W-1N	E2
100	WNFD	60190	3023	26W-0S	E6
400	FKFT	60423	3591	12W-25S	C1
5100	NndT	60012	2584	34W-28N	B6
5100	PRGV	60012	2584	34W-28N	D6
6000	CLLK	60012	2584	34W-28N	B6
S Pleasant Hill Gate					
1000	WKGN	60085	2535	14W-32N	D4
Pleasant Knoll Dr					
1200	JLET	60435	3497	27W-22S	C2
Pleasant Oak Ct					
10	FXLK	60020	2473	28W-36N	A3
Pleasant Park Wy					
-	CHCG	60620	3213	2W-10S	C5
Pleasant Plains Dr					
200	SCRL	60175	2963	37W-2N	B7
Pleasant Run Ct					
2000	NPVL	60565	3204	24W-8S	E2
Pleasant Run Dr					
-	PTHT	60070	2755	15W-16N	A7
-	WLNG	60070	2755	15W-16N	A7
1100	WLNG	60090	2755	15W-16N	A7
1200	PTHT	60090	2755	15W-16N	A7
Pleasant Valley Rd					
11600	DrrT	60098	2638	40W-26N	A3
11600	DrrT	60142	2638	40W-26N	A3
Pleasant View Av					
8300	WLSP	60480	3208	14W-9S	D3
W Pleasant View Av					
25800	WcnT	60084	2587	25W-28N	E7
Pleasant View Dr					
1200	ELGN	60123	2800	35W-13N	C7
5100	ALGN	60102	2747	34W-20N	D1
E Pleasant View Dr					
10	BtlT	60543	3263	38W-12S	A4
N Pleasant View Dr					
5200	MchT	60050	2472	29W-37N	D2
W Pleasant View Dr					
10	BtlT	60543	3262	39W-12S	E4
10	BtlT	60543	3263	39W-12S	A4
300	MchT	60050	2472	29W-37N	D2
3100	MHRY	60050	2585	32W-30N	C1
3300	NndT	60050	2585	32W-30N	C1
Pleasant View Ln					
400	CmpT	60119	2962	41W-3N	A7
6100	AlqT	60013	2641	31W-25N	D4
6100	NndT	60013	2641	31W-25N	D4
Pleasantview Ln					
10	NHFD	60093	2811	7W-15N	B2
Pleasure Av					
3100	GwdT	60097	2469	38W-35N	A7
3300	WRLK	60097	2469	38W-35N	A7
E Pleasure Ct					
500	AURA	60506	3137	37W-6S	D6
N Pleasure Ct					
1000	AURA	60506	3137	37W-6S	D6
S Pleasure Ct					
1000	AURA	60506	3137	37W-6S	D6
W Pleasure Ct					
500	AURA	60506	3137	37W-6S	D6
Pleasure Dr					
200	BtlT	60560	3261	43W-14S	B7
200	MDLN	60060	2646	18W-26N	D3
200	YKVL	60560	3261	42W-14S	C7
Pleasureview Rd					
2100	AraT	60506	3199	38W-8S	A1
Plentywood Ln					
700	BNVL	60106	2971	16W-5N	D1
Plover Ct					
10	WDRG	60517	3143	21W-7S	E6
Plum Ct					
10	SYHW	60118	2800	35W-15N	C3
10	WNVL	60555	3080	30W-1S	C2
300	ELGN	60120	2855	33W-12N	A2
500	CLLK	60014	2693	36W-22N	D3
1400	MPPT	60056	2807	16W-14N	D3
1500	GYLK	60030	2475	21W-34N	D7
1600	DRGV	60515	3084	20W-3S	A6
8400	TYPK	60477	3424	10W-20S	B4
8400	TYPK	60487	3424	10W-20S	B4
Plum Ln					
1500	WTMT	60559	3145	18W-7S	A6
N Plum Pl					
20700	ElaT	60010	2698	23W-20N	E7
Plum St					
10	BtlT	60512	3261	41W-12S	E3
10	ELGN	60120	2854	34W-12N	E2
200	AURA	60506	3138	36W-6S	A6
200	ELGN	60120	2855	33W-12N	A2
200	LIHL	60156	2694	35W-22N	A4
500	AURA	60506	3137	36W-6S	E6
2400	CTHL	60435	3417	27W-20S	D6
2500	PnfT	60435	3417	27W-20S	D6
E Plum St					
400	SEGN	60177	2908	34W-8N	E3
W Plum St					
10	SEGN	60177	2908	34W-8N	D3
700	NndT	60051	2586	29W-28N	C5
Plumage St					
-	LkrT	60403	3417	26W-19S	D3
Plum Blossom Tr					
3300	RGMW	60067	2805	21W-13N	D6
Plum Creek Dr					
100	DYR	46311	3598		D2
300	WLNG	60090	2755	13W-17N	D6
Plum Grove Cir					
-	ANHT	60004	2754	17W-18N	A3
-	ANHT	60089	2754	17W-18N	A3
800	BFGV	60089	2754	17W-18N	A2
W Plum Grove Cir					
200	ANHT	60004	2754	18W-18N	A2
200	ANHT	60089	2754	18W-18N	A2
200	BFGV	60089	2754	18W-18N	A3
Plum Grove Ct					
1400	CLSM	60188	2967	28W-4N	A4
1400	WynT	60185	2967	28W-4N	A4
1400	WynT	60188	2967	28W-4N	A4
Plum Grove Dr					
3200	RGMW	60008	2860	20W-12N	B1
3300	RGMW	60008	2806	20W-12N	B7
Plum Grove Rd					
-	RGMW	60067	2805	21W-13N	D6
-	RGMW	60173	2805	21W-13N	D6
-	SMBG	60067	2805	21W-13N	D6
-	SMBG	60173	2805	21W-13N	D6
1800	PLTN	60008	2805	21W-14N	E4
1800	PLTN	60067	2805	21W-14N	E4
1800	RGMW	60008	2805	21W-14N	E4
2400	PltT	60008	2805	21W-14N	E4
2400	PltT	60067	2805	21W-14N	E4
12100	HTLY	60142	2744	42W-19N	D2
N Plum Grove Rd					
-	HFET	60169	2859	22W-11N	C4
-	HFET	60173	2859	22W-11N	C4
-	ROSL	60157	2913	22W-7N	C4
-	SMBG	60169	2859	22W-11N	C4
-	SMBG	60193	2859	22W-10N	C5
-	SMBG	60194	2859	22W-11N	C4
10	PLTN	60067	2805	21W-16N	E1
100	BmdT	60157	2913	22W-7N	C4
200	BmdT	60172	2913	22W-7N	C3
500	ROSL	60172	2913	22W-7N	C4
700	ROSL	60193	2913	22W-7N	C4
700	SmbT	60193	2913	22W-7N	C4
900	PLTN	60067	2752	20W-17N	E5
1000	SMBG	60173	2859	22W-11N	C2
20100	DRPK	60074	2752	21W-20N	E2
20100	ElaT	60074	2752	21W-20N	E2
20100	PltT	60074	2752	21W-20N	E2
20400	KLDR	60047	2752	21W-20N	E1
S Plum Grove Rd					
-	EGVV	60193	2913	22W-8N	C1
10	PLTN	60067	2805	20W-15N	E2
10	SMBG	60173	2859	22W-10N	C5
10	SMBG	60194	2859	22W-10N	C6
300	EGVV	60007	2859	22W-10N	C6
300	SMBG	60007	2859	22W-10N	C6
600	EGVV	60193	2859	22W-9N	C7
800	RGMW	60008	2805	21W-14N	E3
800	RGMW	60067	2805	21W-14N	E3
900	EGVV	60007	2913	22W-8N	C2
900	SMBG	60007	2913	22W-8N	C2
900	SMBG	60193	2913	22W-8N	C2
1400	EGVV	60172	2913	22W-8N	C2
1400	SmbT	60007	2913	22W-8N	C2
1400	SmbT	60172	2913	22W-8N	C2
1400	SmbT	60193	2913	22W-8N	C2
1500	ROSL	60172	2913	22W-8N	C2
1500	ROSL	60193	2913	22W-8N	C2
Plum Hollow Ct					
1000	NPVL	60563	3141	28W-5S	B4
Plum Island Dr					
3000	NHBK	60062	2756	11W-17N	D5
Plummer Av					
10	CTCY	60409	3352	4E-17S	C5
10	HMND	46320	3352	4E-17S	C5
Plumrose Ct					
10	SMBG	60194	2859	23W-10N	B5
Plumrose Ln					
-	SMBG	60193	2859	23W-10N	A5
10	SMBG	60194	2859	23W-10N	A5
2900	MchT	60050	2528	31W-33N	C2
Plum Tree Ct					
10	SMWD	60107	2857	26W-11N	D5
700	WLNG	60090	2754	16W-18N	D3
1200	SMBG	60193	2859	21W-10N	D6
Plumtree Ct					
300	BGBK	60440	3269	23W-12S	A3
S Plum Tree Ct					
1000	PLTN	60067	2805	21W-14N	C3
Plum Tree Dr					
900	CLLK	60014	2639	37W-24N	C7
900	CLLK	60014	2693	37W-24N	B1
15500	ODPK	60462	3346	10W-18S	B7
15600	ODPK	60462	3424	10W-18S	B1
Plumtree Dr					
2100	NPVL	60565	3204	25W-10S	B5
Plum Tree Ln					
100	WLMT	60091	2811	5W-13N	E7
500	ANTH	60002	2357	24W-42N	D6
1300	WNKA	60093	2758	6W-16N	E7
1500	AURA	60504	3200	33W-9S	E3
2400	PLTN	60008	2805	22W-13N	B5
2400	PLTN	60067	2805	22W-13N	B5
2400	RGMW	60008	2805	22W-13N	B5
2400	RGMW	60067	2805	22W-13N	B5
6800	HRPK	60133	2911	27W-8N	C3
7000	SMWD	60107	2911	27W-8N	C3
7000	SMWD	60133	2911	27W-8N	C3
Plumtree Ln					
100	WCHI	60185	3022	30W-1N	B2
S Plum Tree Ln					
1000	PLTN	60067	2805	21W-14N	C4
26100	MONE	60449	3683	6W-31S	A6
Plum Tree Rd					
100	DRFD	60015	2756	11W-20N	D2
2300	LNHT	60046	2476	20W-37N	B2
Plumtree Rd					
500	BNHL	60010	2696	29W-22N	C5
500	LKBN	60010	2696	28W-21N	E5
600	AlqT	60010	2696	29W-22N	C5
600	GNEN	60137	3025	22W-0N	D4
900	AlqT	60021	2696	29W-22N	C5
900	BNHL	60021	2696	29W-22N	C5
900	FRGV	60010	2696	29W-22N	C5
900	FRGV	60021	2696	29W-22N	C5
S Plum Valley Dr					
23600	CteT	60417	3598	3E-29S	A7
23900	CteT	60417	3687	3E-29S	A1
Plumwood Ct					
300	VNHL	60061	2647	16W-24N	E7
400	SMBG	60173	2859	22W-11N	C4
Plumwood Dr					
-	HFET	60169	2859	22W-11N	C4
-	SMBG	60169	2859	22W-11N	C4
800	SMBG	60173	2859	22W-11N	C4
1400	LYVL	60048	2591	17W-29N	B3
N Plumwood Dr					
20500	KLDR	60047	2700	20W-20N	A7
20500	KLDR	60047	2753	20W-20N	A1
20500	LGGV	60047	2700	20W-20N	A7
Pluskota Dr					
8000	ODPK	60462	3346	10W-16S	C3
Plymouth Av					
2600	WSTR	60154	3086	13W-2S	D3
Plymouth Cir					
1500	CPVL	60110	2748	32W-17N	D7
W Plymouth Cir					
22000	PnfT	60544	3339	27W-16S	C4
Plymouth Ct					
10	AURA	60504	3202	31W-8S	A1
10	LNSH	60069	2702	14W-22N	D3
10	NPVL	60565	3203	26W-9S	E4
10	SchT	60175	2907	36W-6N	E6
100	BRLT	60103	2911	28W-7N	A4
100	IVNS	60067	2805	23W-15N	A1
200	RLKB	60073	2475	23W-36N	A4
500	FKFT	60423	3592	9W-26S	E2
500	GRNE	60031	2535	14W-33N	C3
600	OSWG	60543	3264	35W-11S	B1
800	WCHI	60185	3022	29W-1N	D4
900	ALGN	60102	2695	33W-20N	A7
1100	CLSM	60188	2967	27W-4N	C4
1700	WHTN	60187	3082	23W-2S	E3
6200	DRGV	60516	3144	20W-6S	B5
7000	TYPK	60477	3425	8W-19S	A2
S Plymouth Ct					
300	CHCG	60604	3034	0W-0S	B5
1200	CHCG	60605	3034	0W-1S	C7
W Plymouth Ct					
1300	ANHT	60004	2753	18W-16N	D7
22100	PnfT	60544	3339	27W-16S	C4
Plymouth Dr					
-	PnfT	60544	3339	27W-16S	B5
100	IVNS	60067	2805	23W-15N	A1
200	CHHT	60411	3595	1W-26S	E1
200	SMWD	60107	2857	28W-11N	B4
16100	MKHM	60428	3427	3W-19S	B2
W Plymouth Dr					
1400	ANHT	60004	2753	18W-16N	D7
Plymouth Ln					
-	GfnT	60142	2744	41W-20N	D1
-	HTLY	60142	2744	41W-20N	D1
200	BGBK	60440	3269	23W-11S	A1
200	CLLK	60014	2639	35W-24N	E6
200	CLLK	60014	2640	35W-24N	A6
300	BMDL	60108	2969	23W-4N	A3
400	SMBG	60193	2858	25W-9N	B7
800	ISLK	60042	2586	29W-28N	B6
800	MchT	60051	2528	31W-32N	C4
1300	GNVW	60025	2810	8W-14N	E5
1300	GNVW	60025	2811	8W-14N	A5
1400	ELGN	60123	2854	35W-12N	B3
2000	NHBK	60062	2757	10W-16N	B7
Plymouth Pl					
10	LGPK	60525	3087	12W-3S	C6
1400	GNVW	60025	2810	8W-14N	E5
Plymouth Rd					
700	HFET	60192	2804	23W-14N	D3
6700	DRGV	60516	3144	20W-7S	B7
Plymouth St					
5500	DRGV	60515	3144	20W-6S	B4
6100	DGvT	60516	3144	20W-6S	B5
6100	DRGV	60516	3144	20W-6S	B5
E Plymouth St					
10	VLPK	60181	3027	17W-1N	B2
W Plymouth St					
10	VLPK	60181	3027	18W-1N	A2
300	VLPK	60181	3026	18W-1N	E2
Plymouth Farms Rd					
-	MDLN	60060	2647	17W-25N	B5
-	MDLN	60061	2647	17W-25N	B5
-	VNHL	60060	2647	17W-25N	B5
-	VNHL	60061	2647	17W-25N	B5
Pocahontas Tr					
300	LIHL	60156	2694	34W-21N	B5
Pocasset Ct					
100	SMBG	60193	2858	25W-10N	C6
W Pocasset Ct					
16500	LKPT	60441	3420	20W-20S	B5
Pocasset on Asbury					
10	RGMW	60008	2806	19W-14N	B3
Pochet Ct					
300	SMBG	60193	2858	24W-10N	D6
Pochet Ln					
200	SMBG	60193	2858	24W-10N	D6
Pockey Wy					
20100	ELWD	60421	3675	25W-31S	C5
Pocohontas Tr					
700	CLSM	60188	2967	26W-3N	E6
Pocono Rd					
-	JLET	60421	3675	24W-29S	D2
Podlin Dr					
400	BNVL	60131	2972	14W-4N	C2

STREET Block	City	ZIP	Map#	CGS	Grid
Poe Av					
17300	HLCT	60429	3427	3W-20S	A5
N Poe St					
1800	CHCG	60614	2977	1W-2N	E7
Poet Ct					
3400	NPVL	60564	3267	28W-11S	A1
Poets Ln					
2300	ALGN	60102	2746	36W-18N	E4
Pohlers Ct					
14400	DLTN	60419	3350	0E-16S	E4
Pohlman Ct					
200	LKZH	60047	2698	23W-23N	D1
Poinsetta Ln					
1100	BRLT	60103	2910	29W-6N	E7
Point Blvd					
2100	DndT	60123	2799	36W-15N	E4
2100	ELGN	60123	2799	36W-15N	E5
2100	ELGN	60123	2800	36W-14N	A5
2100	ELGN	60124	2799	37W-15N	E4
NW Point Blvd					
10	EGvT	60007	2861	18W-10N	A4
10	EGVV	60007	2861	18W-10N	A4
Point Ct					
300	ALGN	60102	2694	33W-21N	E6
S Point Ct					
1200	SMBG	60193	2913	22W-8N	C1
E Point Dr					
900	SMBG	60193	2913	22W-9N	C1
8800	MaiT	60016	2863	10W-11N	E3
8800	MaiT	60068	2863	10W-11N	E3
N Point Dr					
-	BtnT	60096	2363	8W-42N	E6
100	WPHR	60096	2363	9W-43N	D5
600	SMBG	60193	2913	22W-9N	C1
41200	AntT	60002	2416	23W-41N	D1
S Point Dr					
600	SMBG	60193	2913	22W-8N	C2
W Point Dr					
900	SMBG	60193	2913	22W-9N	C1
18500	TYPK	60477	3505	8W-22S	B1
Point Ln					
2600	HDPK	60035	2704	10W-23N	A3
Point Pl					
10	FXLK	60041	2473	26W-36N	D3
10	GrtT	60041	2473	26W-36N	D3
W Point Pl					
-	TYPK	60477	3505	8W-22S	B1
N Point St					
2000	CHCG	60647	2977	3W-2N	A6
2100	CHCG	60647	2976	4W-2N	D7
Pointe Blvd					
1900	AURA	60504	3201	33W-9S	B4
N Pointe Ct					
23800	LKBN	60010	2697	27W-23N	B1
S Pointe Ct					
5300	LGGV	60047	2701	18W-23N	A3
Pointe Dr					
-	AlqT	60014	2640	33W-24N	D6
-	CLLK	60014	2640	33W-24N	D6
100	NfdT	60062	2756	12W-18N	B2
100	NHBK	60015	2756	12W-18N	B2
100	NHBK	60062	2756	12W-18N	B2
100	WdfT	60015	2756	12W-18N	B2
5500	HMND	46320	3352		D6
17100	ODPK	60467	3423	13W-20S	A5
S Pointe Dr					
6700	RchT	60477	3425	8W-22S	A7
6700	TYPK	60477	3425	8W-22S	A7
N Point Marina Dr					
-	BtnT	60096	2363	8W-43N	E5
-	WPHR	60096	2363	8W-43N	E5
Point Oak Dr					
400	WNVL	60555	3080	29W-3S	D7
500	NPVL	60555	3080	29W-3S	D7
500	NPVL	60563	3080	29W-3S	D7
Point O Woods Ct					
10	LIHL	60156	2693	37W-22N	C4
Pokagon Tr					
300	DndT	60102	2747	34W-19N	E2
Polaris Dr					
10	LIHL	60156	2693	36W-22N	E4
Polaris Rd					
1500	BtnT	60081	2355	30W-42N	A5
1500	SPGV	60081	2355	30W-42N	A5
Police Plz					
10	GNVA	60134	3020	35W-1N	C4
Polk Av					
300	CPVL	60110	2748	32W-17N	D7
700	DYR	46311	3510		D6
3600	RNPK	60471	3594	4W-27S	D5
3800	RchT	60471	3594	4W-27S	D5
Polk Ct					
10	SMWD	60107	2856	29W-10N	D6
200	BRLT	60103	2911	28W-7N	A5
1000	VNHL	60061	2647	17W-26N	B3
1800	RGMW	60008	2805	20W-14N	E4
Polk St					
10	OSWG	60543	3263	37W-12S	C4
200	EGvT	60018	2862	15W-9N	A7
4000	RchT	60471	3594	5W-27S	C5
7400	HRPK	60133	2912	26W-9N	A1
7600	FTPK	60130	3030	9W-0S	C6
N Polk St					
34500	GrtT	60041	2473	26W-34N	E7
34500	GrtT	60041	2530	26W-34N	E1
S Polk St					
25700	MONE	60449	3682	7W-31S	E5
W Polk St					
10	CHCG	60605	3034	0W-0S	B6
200	CHCG	60607	3034	0W-0S	B6
1000	CHCG	60607	3033	1W-0S	E6
1600	CHCG	60612	3033	2W-0S	E6
2800	CHCG	60612	3032	4W-0S	D6
3100	CHCG	60624	3032	4W-0S	C6
4500	CHCG	60644	3032	5W-0S	A6
5200	CHCG	60644	3031	6W-0S	D6
Polk Tr					
2500	MHRY	60051	2528	31W-33N	D2
Pollitt Dr					
10	ElgT	60124	2853	38W-12N	B1
Polly Ct					
1000	ELGN	60120	2855	32W-12N	B1
Polly Ln					
2900	FSMR	60422	3507	3W-23S	A3
W Polo Av					
12700	WkgT	60087	2479	12W-36N	A5
12800	WkgT	60031	2479	12W-36N	A5
Polo Ct					
1400	BRLT	60103	2966	30W-6N	B1
2800	RLKP	60030	2532	22W-31N	B7
8200	LKWD	60014	2693	37W-23N	A1
Polo Dr					
-	OKBK	60523	3086	15W-2S	A4
10	SBTN	60010	2803	26W-14N	D5
600	MltT	60187	3024	25W-0S	A7
1000	LKFT	60045	2649	11W-24N	D7

STREET Block	City	ZIP	Map#	CGS	Grid
Polo Dr					
1400	BRLT	60103	2910	30W-6N	B7
1400	BRLT	60103	2966	30W-6N	B1
Polo Ln					
300	OKBK	60523	3084	18W-3S	E5
800	GNVW	60025	2811	7W-13N	B7
Polo Club Ct					
1700	GLHT	60139	2969	23W-3N	A6
Polo Club Dr					
200	GLHT	60139	2969	23W-3N	B6
6000	FoxT	60560	3332	46W-16S	A4
Poloma Dr					
8200	PlsT	60462	3346	10W-15S	B2
8200	PSHT	60462	3346	10W-15S	C2
8200	PSHT	60464	3346	10W-15S	C2
8500	ODPK	60462	3346	10W-15S	B2
Polo Ridge Ct					
-	BRRG	60527	3208	15W-10S	A5
-	DGvT	60527	3208	15W-10S	A5
W Polo Trail Dr					
13600	GNOK	60045	2592	13W-27N	D7
13900	GNOK	60048	2592	13W-27N	D7
Polson Pl					
200	JLET	60432	3499	23W-23S	B4
Polynesian Dr					
500	DSPN	60016	2808	13W-12N	E7
Pomeroon St					
800	NPVL	60540	3140	29W-7S	C7
800	NPVL	60540	3202	29W-7S	E1
Pomeroy Av					
10	CLLK	60014	2639	35W-25N	E4
10	CLLK	60014	2640	35W-25N	A4
Pomeroy Ct					
1200	SCRL	60174	3020	34W-2N	D1
3500	DRGV	60515	3084	20W-3S	B6
Pomeroy Rd					
10	OswT	60538	3199	36W-10S	E7
3300	DRGV	60515	3084	20W-3S	B5
Pomeroy St					
200	WCHI	60185	3022	30W-0N	B5
200	WnfT	60185	3022	30W-0N	B5
E Pomeroy St					
100	WCHI	60185	3022	29W-0N	D5
500	WnfT	60185	3022	29W-0N	D5
W Pomeroy St					
100	WCHI	60185	3022	30W-0N	C5
Pomfret Ct					
700	OSWG	60543	3263	36W-12S	E3
700	OSWG	60543	3264	36W-12S	A3
Pomo Ct					
2500	SLVL	60411	3597	2E-26S	E3
Pomona Ct					
1000	NPVL	60540	3141	28W-6S	B5
Pomona Ln					
2300	WLMT	60091	2812	5W-13N	A6
E Pompano Ln					
600	PLTN	60074	2753	20W-16N	B6
Ponca Dr					
1000	BTVA	60510	3020	36W-0S	A7
Ponca St					
4200	MHRY	60050	2528	33W-32N	A4
4400	MHRY	60050	2527	33W-32N	E5
N Ponce Av					
37100	LkvT	60046	2476	20W-37N	A2
N Ponchartrain Blvd					
6500	CHCG	60646	2919	7W-8N	C2
Pond Cir					
4500	JLET	60586	3416	29W-21S	D6
Pond Ct					
-	BGBK	60490	3267	28W-14S	A7
Pond Dr					
500	WDDL	60191	2915	18W-6N	A6
2000	BTVA	60510	3078	34W-2S	D5
N Pond Ln					
1700	LKFT	60045	2648	13W-25N	E5
1700	LKFT	60045	2649	13W-25N	A5
Pond St					
-	BDWD	60408	3942	31W-41S	B5
-	RedT	60408	3942	31W-41S	B5
Pond End Ln					
3000	WRLK	60097	2468	38W-35N	E6
3200	GwdT	60097	2468	38W-35N	E6
Ponder Pl					
10000	SPGV	60081	2355	30W-41N	A7
Ponderosa Ct					
100	BRTN	60010	2751	24W-20N	D1
1100	DRN	60561	3145	18W-7S	A7
1800	JltT	60433	3587	21W-26S	E3
1800	JltT	60433	3588	21W-26S	A3
7400	ODPK	60462	3346	9W-18S	E6
W Ponderosa Ct					
7900	ODPK	60462	3346	9W-18S	C6
Ponderosa Dr					
10	OswT	60560	3334	41W-15S	B2
10	RMVL	60446	3269	23W-14S	A7
200	CmpT	60175	2962	39W-3N	D6
600	BGBK	60440	3268	24W-12S	D2
S Ponderosa Dr					
12700	PSHT	60463	3274	9W-15S	D7
W Ponderosa Dr					
7600	PSHT	60463	3274	9W-15S	D7
Ponderosa Ln					
900	HFET	60010	2751	24W-16N	C7
N Ponderosa Pl					
400	JLET	60431	3497	28W-23S	B4
Pond Gate Dr					
500	BNHL	60010	2801	30W-14N	E3
500	BNHL	60010	2802	30W-14N	A3
500	BNHL	60118	2801	30W-14N	E3
500	BNHL	60118	2802	30W-14N	A3
Pond Point Rd					
-	WDSK	60098	2582	40W-29N	A4
1100	WDSK	60098	2581	40W-29N	E4
W Pond Ridge Cir					
17700	WrnT	60031	2477	18W-36N	A4
Pond Ridge Rd					
100	LYVL	60048	2591	17W-28N	B5
Ponds Ct					
700	OSWG	60543	3263	38W-12S	B3
N Pond Shore Dr					
26500	FmtT	60084	2644	23W-26N	E3
26600	FmtT	60060	2644	23W-26N	E3
Pondside Dr					
1700	NHBK	60062	2756	10W-16N	E7
Pond View Ct					
4800	LGGV	60047	2700	18W-23N	E1
18300	TYPK	60477	3425	8W-22S	B7
Pondview Ct					
800	SMBG	60194	2858	24W-10N	D5
Pond View Dr					
2600	ALGN	60102	2746	36W-20N	D1
6200	MTSN	60443	3505	7W-25S	C7
6600	RchT	60477	3425	8W-22S	B7
6600	TYPK	60477	3425	8W-22S	B7
23700	PNFD	60585	3338	30W-15S	C2

STREET Block	City	ZIP	Map#	CGS	Grid
Pondview Dr					
300	ANTH	60002	2357	24W-43N	D4
3800	HRPK	60133	2967	27W-4N	C3
N Pondview Dr					
300	PLTN	60067	2752	22W-16N	C7
W Pondview Dr					
28700	LKMR	60051	2529	28W-31N	D6
28800	WcnT	60051	2529	28W-31N	D6
Pond View Ln					
400	BRLT	60103	2910	29W-8N	D3
Pontarelli Ct					
1700	AURA	60504	3200	33W-10S	E5
Pontiac Av					
1100	NndT	60051	2585	31W-30N	D1
N Pontiac Av					
3200	CHCG	60634	2974	10W-4N	A3
3200	RVGV	60171	2974	10W-4N	A4
3200	RVGV	60634	2974	10W-4N	A4
4800	NRDG	60706	2918	10W-6N	A6
Pontiac Cir					
2200	NPVL	60565	3203	26W-10S	D5
Pontiac Ct					
600	RLKH	60073	2474	23W-35N	D6
Pontiac Dr					
1000	BTVA	60510	3020	36W-0S	A7
6300	IHPK	60525	3146	14W-7S	D6
Pontiac Ln					
200	VNHL	60061	2647	18W-25N	A5
500	BGBK	60440	3268	24W-11S	D1
500	CLSM	60188	2967	27W-3N	C7
Pontiac Rd					
1000	WLMT	60091	2812	5W-14N	A5
Pontiac St					
400	JltT	60432	3499	21W-23S	E3
Pontigo Glen Dr					
5100	JLET	60586	3496	30W-22S	C2
Ponto Dr					
7200	MNGV	60053	2864	9W-11N	D2
Pony Ln					
800	NHBK	60062	2756	12W-17N	A4
2800	NndT	60012	2584	35W-29N	B4
Pooks Hill Rd					
400	NBRN	60010	2698	25W-22N	A4
S Pool St					
3000	NndT	60051	2586	30W-29N	A5
Poole Ct					
10	BTVA	60510	3077	37W-1S	C2
Pope Blvd					
15500	VrnT	60015	2702	15W-20N	A7
W Pope Blvd					
15700	VrnT	60069	2754	16W-20N	E1
15700	VrnT	60089	2754	15W-20N	E1
16200	BFGV	60089	2754	16W-20N	D1
Pope Ct					
-	PLNO	60545	3260	45W-14S	B7
W Pope John Paul II Dr					
2400	CHCG	60609	3091	3W-4S	A7
2400	CHCG	60632	3091	3W-4S	A7
2400	CHCG	60632	3090	3W-4S	E7
Pope's Creek Cir					
1000	GYLK	60030	2532	20W-34N	E1
1000	GYLK	60030	2533	20W-34N	A1
Popeye Ln					
-	GYLK	60030	2533	19W-32N	C4
Poplar Av					
-	EVTN	60201	2812	3W-13N	E7
-	WLMT	60091	2812	3W-13N	E7
-	WLMT	60201	2812	3W-13N	E7
200	BmdT	60157	2913	22W-7N	C3
200	ROSL	60157	2913	22W-7N	C3
300	ANTH	60002	2357	23W-42N	D5
400	YkTp	60126	3028	15W-0S	B7
600	RMVL	60446	3340	24W-16S	D3
1600	HRPK	60133	2911	27W-8N	D2
2100	HRPK	60107	2911	27W-8N	C2
2100	SMWD	60107	2911	27W-8N	C2
2100	SMWD	60133	2911	27W-8N	C2
2300	EVTN	60201	2867	3W-12N	A1
2400	EVTN	60201	2866	3W-12N	E1
4100	RNPK	60471	3594	5W-26S	C3
16100	BmnT	60428	3427	3W-19S	B2
18300	HMWD	60430	3427	1W-22S	E7
18400	HMWD	60430	3507	1W-22S	E1
N Poplar Av					
10	FXLK	60020	2473	27W-36N	C4
300	BNVL	60106	2915	17W-6N	C7
300	WDDL	60106	2915	17W-6N	C7
400	WDDL	60191	2915	17W-6N	C7
1500	RLKB	60073	2475	22W-35N	B6
35500	GrtT	60041	2474	25W-35N	B5
42300	AntT	60002	2356	26W-42N	D6
S Poplar Av					
600	EMHT	60126	3028	15W-0S	A5
600	YkTp	60126	3028	15W-0S	B7
2700	CHCG	60608	3091	1W-2S	E3
3000	CHCG	60608	3092	1W-2S	A3
Poplar Blvd					
-	RMVL	60446	3340	24W-16S	C3
Poplar Cross					
-	PNFD	60543	3337	33W-14S	B1
-	PNFD	60585	3337	33W-14S	B1
Poplar Ct					
10	BFGV	60089	2754	17W-18N	B3
10	GLHT	60139	2968	23W-3N	E6
100	NHBK	60062	2755	13W-18N	E2
100	NHBK	60062	2756	13W-18N	A2
300	LNHT	60046	2476	19W-37N	C2
400	ELGN	60120	2855	33W-12N	B3
500	LYVL	60048	2591	16W-27N	C7
700	OSWG	60543	3263	37W-13S	C5
800	SBTN	60010	2803	25W-15N	E2
800	SBTN	60010	2804	25W-15N	A2
1000	LKZH	60047	2698	24W-22N	B3
1300	HMWD	60430	3507	1W-22S	E2
1400	LMBD	60148	3084	20W-1S	A1
14600	ODPK	60462	3346	11W-17S	A5
E Poplar Ct					
2700	CteT	60417	3687	3E-29S	A2
Poplar Dr					
10	KdlT	60560	3333	44W-16S	A4
100	EVTN	60201	2812	3W-13N	E7
100	WLMT	60091	2812	3W-13N	E6
100	WLMT	60201	2812	3W-13N	E7
300	WLNG	60090	2755	13W-17N	E5
300	YKVL	60560	3333	44W-15S	A3
400	YKVL	60560	3332	44W-15S	E3
3100	ISLK	60042	2586	28W-28N	D5
Poplar Ln					
10	CmpT	60175	2962	39W-5N	E3
10	CmpT	60175	2963	39W-5N	A3
100	LynT	60458	3209	11W-8S	E2
200	BCHR	60401	3864	0W-36S	D1
300	NLNX	60451	3501	17W-24S	C5
300	NlxT	60451	3501	17W-24S	C5
400	MaiT	60025	2809	10W-12N	E7
800	BGBK	60440	3268	24W-12S	C2

STREET Block	City	ZIP	Map#	CGS	Grid
Poplar Ln					
800	DRFD	60015	2756	11W-20N	E1
900	BRLT	60103	2910	29W-6N	D6
1600	GwdT	60098	2524	41W-32N	E5
1600	WDSK	60098	2524	41W-32N	E5
2000	SLVL	60411	3509	2E-25S	D7
2000	SLVL	60411	3597	2E-25S	D1
7200	DRN	60561	3207	16W-8S	D1
8200	PSHL	60465	3274	10W-13S	B3
17900	CCHL	60478	3426	6W-21S	A7
E Poplar Ln					
2800	CteT	60417	3687	3E-29S	A2
Poplar Pl					
-	FSMR	60422	3506	4W-23S	D2
-	RchT	60430	3506	4W-23S	D2
10	NARA	60542	3137	37W-4S	D1
100	AURA	60542	3137	37W-4S	D2
1700	SMBG	60173	2859	21W-12N	E1
N Poplar Pl					
10	LGNG	60525	3087	13W-4S	A7
Poplar Rd					
200	HDPK	60035	2757	9W-20N	D1
600	MltT	60137	3083	22W-2S	B4
3600	FSMR	60422	3506	4W-22S	D2
4600	RNPK	60471	3594	5W-26S	B3
9000	ODPK	60462	3346	11W-17S	A5
9100	ODPK	60462	3345	11W-17S	E5
S Poplar Rd					
100	LKFT	60045	2649	11W-25N	E4
Poplar St					
-	LkvT	60046	2417	21W-38N	D6
-	NPVL	60540	3203	28W-8S	B1
-	WcnT	60042	2586	28W-27N	E7
-	WslT	60481	3943	27W-41S	D6
10	GLHT	60139	2968	23W-3N	E6
10	GLHT	60139	2969	23W-3N	A6
200	WNKA	60093	2812	4W-15N	C2
300	CLLK	60014	2640	34W-26N	C3
800	AntT	60002	2356	26W-42N	D5
1100	LIHL	60156	2694	35W-22N	B4
1500	HHLL	60051	2586	30W-29N	A3
1500	NLES	60068	2863	11W-10N	E5
1500	NLES	60714	2863	11W-10N	E5
1500	PKRG	60068	2863	11W-10N	E5
2400	JLET	60435	3417	27W-20S	D5
2400	LktT	60403	3417	27W-20S	D5
2400	PnfT	60403	3417	27W-20S	D5
2400	PnfT	60435	3417	27W-20S	D5
8900	TYPK	60487	3424	11W-21S	A6
19500	FftT	60448	3503	11W-23S	E3
24400	AvnT	60073	2474	24W-35N	C6
24400	RLKB	60073	2474	24W-35N	C6
N Poplar St					
100	PLTN	60067	2752	22W-17N	A5
400	WKGN	60085	2537	9W-34N	C1
1000	WKGN	60085	2480	10W-35N	A6
1000	WKGN	60087	2480	10W-36N	A3
26700	WcnT	60084	2642	28W-26N	E2
39000	LkvT	60046	2417	21W-39N	D6
42600	AntT	60002	2356	26W-42N	D5
W Poplar St					
800	PLTN	60067	2752	22W-17N	C5
800	PltT	60067	2752	22W-17N	C5
Poplar Creek Ct					
700	SMWD	60107	2857	28W-10N	A6
15200	ODPK	60467	3344	14W-18S	E7
Poplar Creek Dr					
10	ELGN	60120	2855	32W-11N	D4
1400	HFET	60169	2857	26W-12N	E2
Poplar Creek Ln					
11200	ODPK	60467	3344	14W-18S	E6
Poplar Glen Ct					
5300	JLET	60586	3416	30W-21S	B7
Poplar Glen Dr					
-	JLET	60586	3416	30W-20S	C6
Poplarleaf Dr					
4400	MchT	60050	2472	30W-36N	B4
Poplar View Bnd					
2600	HnrT	60120	2856	31W-11N	A4
Popp Ln					
1700	LGGV	60047	2753	19W-20N	D1
Popple Ct					
2200	NPVL	60564	3266	29W-12S	D4
Poppy Dr					
-	RMVL	60446	3339	26W-17S	E6
Poppy Ln					
200	BNVL	60106	2915	16W-5N	E7
200	MTSN	60443	3593	7W-26S	C2
700	BRLT	60103	2910	29W-6N	D7
2100	CTHL	60403	3417	27W-21S	D6
2300	GNVW	60025	2810	9W-15N	C3
N Poppy Ln					
100	PNFD	60544	3337	31W-18S	E7
100	PNFD	60544	3415	31W-18S	E1
Porett Dr					
3900	GRNE	60031	2478	13W-35N	D5
3900	WrnT	60031	2478	13W-35N	D5
Port Dr					
-	FftT	60423	3503	11W-24S	E5
-	FKFT	60423	3503	11W-24S	E5
3900	HRPK	60133	2967	27W-4N	C3
Portage Av					
2500	WCDA	60084	2588	25W-30N	B2
N Portage Av					
1200	PLTN	60067	2752	22W-17N	A4
1200	PltT	60067	2752	22W-17N	A4
1300	PltT	60010	2752	22W-17N	A4
Portage Ct					
-	PNFD	60544	3415	31W-18S	E1
600	VNHL	60061	2647	18W-25N	A4
S Portage Ct					
13700	PnfT	60544	3339	27W-15S	C2
W Portage Ct					
1500	PLTN	60067	2752	22W-17N	A5
1500	PltT	60067	2752	22W-17N	A5
Portage Ln					
1200	WDSK	60098	2581	41W-30N	D2
4100	HFET	60192	2804	24W-15N	B2
5100	GRNE	60031	2478	15W-35N	B5
15600	PNFD	60544	3415	31W-18S	E2
Portage Run					
1500	GNVW	60025	2809	11W-14N	D5
Portage Tr					
7200	FTVW	60402	3148	9W-5S	D1
7200	FTVW	60534	3148	9W-5S	D1
7200	LYNS	60534	3148	9W-5S	D1
Portage Wy					
1800	ELGN	60123	2854	36W-12N	A3
1800	ElgT	60123	2854	36W-12N	A3
Portage Pass					
1600	DRFD	60015	2703	11W-22N	E5
Port Arthur Ct					
1400	HFET	60192	2804	24W-15N	B2
Port Center Dr					
1500	IVNS	60067	2805	23W-14N	A5
1500	PltT	60067	2805	23W-14N	A5

STREET Block	City	ZIP	Map#	CGS	Grid
Port Center Dr					
1700	PltT	60195	2805	23W-14N	A5
Portchester Cir					
1200	CLSM	60188	2967	27W-4N	B4
Port Clinton Ct E					
800	BFGV	60089	2701	17W-23N	B2
Port Clinton Ct W					
800	BFGV	60089	2701	17W-23N	A2
Port Clinton Rd					
-	BFGV	60089	2701	17W-23N	B2
2700	HDPK	60035	2704	8W-23N	E2
2700	HDPK	60037	2704	8W-23N	E2
5400	LGGV	60047	2700	18W-24N	E1
5400	LGGV	60047	2701	18W-23N	A2
W Port Clinton Rd					
-	BFGV	60061	2701	16W-23N	C2
-	VNHL	60061	2701	16W-23N	C2
5800	BFGV	60047	2701	17W-23N	B2
5800	BFGV	60089	2701	17W-23N	B2
5800	LGGV	60047	2701	17W-23N	B2
5800	LGGV	60089	2701	17W-23N	B2
15800	LNSH	60069	2701	15W-23N	E2
15800	LNSH	60069	2702	15W-23N	A2
15800	VNHL	60061	2702	15W-23N	A2
15800	VrnT	60069	2701	16W-23N	D2
16300	BFGV	60069	2701	16W-23N	D2
Port Cove					
100	CPVL	60110	2800	35W-16N	C1
Porten Rd					
200	NndT	60042	2642	29W-27N	C1
200	NndT	60051	2642	29W-27N	C1
300	ISLK	60042	2642	29W-27N	D1
300	ISLK	60051	2642	29W-27N	D1
Porter Av					
-	NCHI	60088	2594	10W-31N	A1
400	CLLK	60014	2639	36W-25N	E5
800	JLET	60432	3499	22W-23S	D3
800	JltT	60432	3499	22W-23S	D3
E Porter Av					
400	NPVL	60540	3141	26W-7S	E6
900	NPVL	60540	3142	26W-7S	A6
W Porter Av					
10	NPVL	60540	3141	27W-7S	D6
Porter Cir					
-	LNHT	60046	2417	21W-39N	E5
Porter Ct					
-	SCRL	60174	2963	36W-3N	E6
200	BRLT	60103	2911	28W-7N	B5
400	ELGN	60120	2855	33W-12N	B3
2700	GNVW	60025	2809	11W-15N	D2
2700	NHBK	60062	2809	11W-15N	D2
Porter Dr					
10	HNVL	60030	2532	22W-33N	A4
10	RLKP	60030	2532	22W-33N	A4
10	RLKP	60073	2532	22W-33N	A3
Porter Ln					
200	BGBK	60440	3205	22W-10S	B7
Porter Pl					
1200	LKPT	60441	3420	21W-19S	A3
Porter St					
-	TNLK	53181	2354		A2
400	LMNT	60439	3270	19W-13S	E5
500	NCHI	60088	2594	10W-31N	A1
600	WKGN	60085	2537	10W-34N	A1
700	WKGN	60085	2480	10W-34N	A7
800	JLET	60432	3499	22W-22S	D3
800	JltT	60432	3499	22W-22S	D3
900	WKGN	60085	2479	10W-34N	E7
N Porter St					
500	ELGN	60120	2855	33W-12N	B2
S Porter St					
10	ELGN	60120	2855	33W-11N	B4
Porter School Rd					
10	BNHL	60010	2696	28W-21N	E7
Portia Rd					
1500	GYLK	60030	2533	19W-32N	D6
Portland Av					
1200	CHHT	60411	3508	0W-25S	C7
1400	CHHT	60411	3596	0W-25S	C1
2500	BlmT	60411	3596	0W-26S	C2
S Portland Av					
4500	CHCG	60609	3092	0W-4S	B7
Portland Ct					
3100	AURA	60504	3201	31W-8S	E1
Portland Dr					
800	SMBG	60194	2858	25W-11N	B3
Portland Ln					
3100	AURA	60504	3201	31W-8S	D1
Port O Call Dr					
1300	PLTN	60074	2753	19W-17N	C4
Portree Ln					
600	LKZH	60047	2699	22W-22N	B4
Port Royal Cir					
100	AURA	60504	3201	32W-8S	C2
Port Royal Rd					
-	PGGV	60140	2797	42W-15N	D4
Portshire Ct					
3300	HFET	60067	2804	23W-14N	E4
Portshire Dr					
10	LNSH	60069	2702	13W-22N	D3
Portside Ct					
10	TDLK	60030	2533	19W-34N	C1
Portside Dr					
10	GrtT	60041	2529	28W-33N	E3
10	GrtT	60051	2529	28W-33N	E3
10	LKMR	60051	2529	28W-33N	D3
Portside Lakes Ct					
2200	JLET	60586	3416	30W-21S	A6
Portsmith Ct					
10	ALGN	60102	2694	35W-21N	A6
500	CLLK	60014	2693	36W-22N	D3
1700	BRLT	60103	2967	28W-4N	B3
2900	NPVL	60564	3202	30W-10S	B7
Portsmith Ln					
900	BGBK	60440	3268	25W-11S	C2
W Portsmith Ln					
1600	ANHT	60004	2753	18W-18N	D3
Portsmouth Av					
600	WSTR	60154	3029	12W-0S	B7
1400	WSTR	60154	3087	12W-1S	B1
2100	PvsT	60154	3087	12W-1S	B2
Portsmouth Cir					
1000	GRNE	60031	2477	17W-35N	C6
Portsmouth Ct					
10	ELGN	60124	2853	37W-11N	C4
10	SMBG	60194	2858	25W-10N	B5
100	DGvT	60561	3207	17W-9S	C3
100	GLHT	60139	3024	23W-1N	E2
100	GLHT	60139	3025	22W-1N	B2
1300	CLSM	60188	2967	28W-4N	B3
1400	NHBK	60062	2757	9W-17N	C5
1500	GYLK	60030	2475	21W-34N	D7
2200	AURA	60504	3201	32W-9S	B5
Portsmouth Dr					
400	DGvT	60561	3207	17W-9S	B3
600	ISLK	60042	2586	30W-28N	B6

STREET Block City ZIP Map# CGS Grid

Portsmouth Dr
600 PGGV 60140 2797 41W-14N E5
1800 LSLE 60532 3142 23W-5S E3
3400 ZION 60099 2362 11W-41N D7
8000 DRN 60561 3207 17W-9S C3
Portsmouth Ln
1600 SMBG 60194 2858 25W-10N A5
Portsmouth Pl
600 WLNG 60090 2755 15W-18N A3
Port Washington Ct
20300 FKFT 60423 3504 11W-24S A5
Port Washington Dr
8800 FKFT 60423 3504 11W-24S A6
Portwine Ct
1500 LYVL 60048 2591 17W-30N B2
Portwine Rd
- WhIT 60090 2755 13W-18N E4
- WLNG 60090 2755 13W-18N E4
10 ROSL 60172 2913 22W-7N B4
10 WLBK 60527 3145 16W-7S D6
200 RVWD 60015 2755 13W-20N E2
200 RVWD 60062 2755 13W-20N E2
200 VrnT 60015 2755 13W-20N E2
200 VrnT 60062 2755 13W-20N E2
200 WhIT 60062 2755 13W-18N E4
600 RVWD 60015 2702 13W-20N E7
Poss Rd
700 NpvT 60502 3139 31W-6S D5
Poss St
10 MltT 60137 3025 22W-1N B2
400 GLHT 60137 3025 22W-1N B2
400 GLHT 60139 3025 22W-1N B2
S Possum Dr
11100 PSHL 60465 3274 11W-13S A3
Possum Hllw
1600 LGPK 60525 3087 13W-2S A3
1600 PvsT 60525 3087 13W-2S A3
1600 WSTR 60525 3087 13W-2S A3
Post Cir
100 HNDL 60521 3146 15W-4S B1
Post Ct
800 SMWD 60107 2857 27W-10N C5
Post Ln
800 SMWD 60107 2857 27W-10N C5
N Post Pl
200 CHCG 60606 3034 E4
Post Rd
100 BRRG 60527 3146 14W-7S C6
400 SCRL 60174 2964 34W-3N D6
1200 AURA 60506 3137 36W-5S D4
2000 NfdT 60062 2756 12W-16N B7
2000 NfdT 60062 2809 12W-16N C1
2000 NHBK 60062 2809 12W-16N C1
S Post Rd
12300 PlsT 60464 3273 13W-14S A6
12300 PSPK 60464 3273 13W-14S A6
Post Oak Cir
100 WCHI 60185 2966 30W-2N B7
Post Oak Ct
1300 CTHL 60403 3497 27W-22S D1
W Post Oak Ct
14400 GNOK 60048 2592 14W-28N C5
Post Oak Pl
2000 SMBG 60173 2805 22W-13N B7
Postoffice Dr
- WNSP 60558 3146 14W-4S D1
Post Office Rd
- CHCG 60666 2916 14W-5N D7
- CHCG 60666 2972 13W-5N D1
Poston Rd
10 WLSP 60480 3209 12W-9S C2
Potawatami Tr
10 IHPK 60525 3146 13W-7S E6
Potawatomi Blvd
- WnfT 60510 3080 30W-1S A2
Potawatomi Dr
7200 PSHT 60463 3274 9W-15S D7
Potawatomi Rd
1400 GYLK 60030 2533 19W-32N C6
S Potawatomi Tr
13500 HMGN 60491 3343 16W-16S D3
N Potawatomie St
4400 CHCG 60656 2973 11W-5N E1
4700 CHCG 60706 2917 10W-5N E7
4700 NRDG 60706 2917 10W-5N E7
5200 CHCG 60656 2917 10W-6N E6
S Potawatomie Tr
24700 CNHN 60410 3672 32W-30S E3
Poteet Av
10 IVNS 60067 2804 23W-15N D2
100 IVNS 60010 2751 23W-16N D7
300 HFET 60192 2804 23W-15N D1
300 IVNS 60192 2804 23W-15N D2
Poteet Rd
10 IVNS 60010 2751 23W-16N D7
Potomac Av
700 NPVL 60565 3204 25W-10S B5
W Potomac Av
10 LMBD 60148 3026 20W-1N B2
1300 CHCG 60622 3033 1W-1N D1
2700 CHCG 60622 3032 3W-1N E1
3200 CHCG 60651 3032 4W-1N D1
4800 CHCG 60651 3031 7W-1N C1
5900 OKPK 60302 3031 7W-1N B1
Potomac Ct
10 BGBK 60440 3205 23W-11S A7
1000 GYLK 60030 2532 21W-34N E1
1300 CLSM 60188 2967 28W-4N B3
1400 GNVA 60134 3020 34W-0N E4
2300 LNHT 60046 2418 20W-39N B5
24400 CRTE 60417 3685 1W-29S A1
Potomac Dr
10 DYR 46311 3510 C7
10500 HTLY 60142 2692 39W-21N B6
Potomac Ln
200 WPHR 60096 2363 10W-43N A4
400 EGVV 60007 2859 22W-9N D7
400 EGVV 60007 2913 22W-9N D1
E Potomac Ln
1100 PLTN 60074 2753 19W-17N C5
Potomac Pl
2100 ELGN 60123 2853 36W-12N E2
Potowatomie Pnd
5400 WhIT 60062 2755 13W-18N D3
5400 WLNG 60062 2755 13W-18N D3
5400 WLNG 60090 2755 13W-18N D3
Potowatomi Trail Rd
100 LKZH 60047 2698 23W-22N E3
100 LKZH 60047 2699 23W-22N A3
Pottawatamie Ln
100 NlxT 60451 3502 15W-25S C7
E Pottawatomi Ct
1200 LGGV 60047 2700 19W-21N D7
S Pottawatomi Ct
12800 PSHT 60463 3274 9W-14S D6
W Pottawatomi Dr
- PSHT 60463 3274 9W-15S E7
Pottawatomie Tr
500 BTVA 60542 3078 34W-3S C5
500 NARA 60542 3078 34W-3S C5
700 BTVA 60510 3078 34W-3S D5
Pottawattami Dr
8900 SKOK 60076 2866 4W-11N B3
Pottawattomi Tr
8000 TYPK 60477 3424 10W-21S C6
Potter Ln
100 BNHL 60010 2802 30W-15N B1
Potter Rd
1100 PKRG 60068 2863 11W-10N D5
1800 DSPN 60016 2863 11W-10N D4
1800 PKRG 60016 2863 11W-10N D4
3200 GNVW 60025 2809 11W-14N C4
3500 GNVW 60062 2809 11W-14N C4
3500 NfdT 60062 2809 11W-14N C4
10000 MaiT 60016 2809 11W-12N D7
10000 MaiT 60016 2863 11W-12N D1
10000 NfdT 60016 2809 11W-12N D7
10000 NfdT 60025 2809 11W-12N D7
E Potter St
100 WDDL 60191 2971 17W-5N B1
400 AddT 60191 2971 17W-5N C1
W Potter St
- WDDL 60191 2971 18W-5N A1
300 WDDL 60191 2970 18W-5N E1
600 ADSN 60143 2970 19W-5N D1
600 WDDL 60143 2970 19W-5N D1
Pottowatamie Ct
400 OSWG 60543 3264 35W-11S B2
Pottowattomie Ct
10 NPVL 60563 3141 26W-4S D2
Pouley Rd
10 BbyT 60119 3017 42W-0N D5
10 CmpT 60119 3017 42W-2N D1
10 ELBN 60119 3017 42W-0N D5
Povalish Ct
10 LMNT 60439 3270 19W-13S C5
Powder Horn Ct
200 GLBT 60136 2799 38W-14N A5
200 RtdT 60136 2799 38W-14N A5
Powder Horn Dr
200 NHBK 60062 2757 9W-18N D3
1200 ALGN 60102 2695 32W-20N A7
Powderhorn Lake Wy
16100 LktT 60403 3417 26W-19S E2
Powder Park Rd
11400 HTLY 60142 2692 40W-20N A7
11400 HTLY 60142 2745 40W-20N A1
Powder River Pth
1900 ELGN 60123 2854 36W-12N A3
Powell Av
300 WKGN 60085 2537 10W-33N A3
3800 LYNS 60534 3088 9W-3S D6
3800 LYNS 60546 3088 9W-3S D6
3800 RVSD 60546 3088 9W-3S D6
9300 AURA 60506 3199 36W-8S D3
9300 AURA 60538 3199 36W-8S D3
Powell Ct
2800 NPVL 60563 3140 29W-5S C3
7000 DRGV 60516 3144 19W-7S C7
Powell Pl
7200 DRGV 60516 3206 20W-8S B1
W Powell Rd
9600 PlsT 60464 3273 12W-14S C7
9600 PSPK 60464 3273 12W-14S C7
Powell St
200 CNHL 60514 3145 16W-5S D3
3400 FNPK 60131 2972 14W-4N C4
6600 DRGV 60516 3144 20W-7S C7
7100 DRGV 60516 3206 20W-8S B1
S Power Ct
400 ADSN 60101 2970 18W-2N E6
S Powerhouse Dr
- LktT 60441 3419 23W-19S B2
- RMVL 60441 3419 23W-19S B2
Powers Ct
500 YKVL 60560 3261 43W-14S C7
8700 ODPK 60462 3424 10W-19S B1
Powers Rd
- GwdT 60098 2524 41W-32N E5
- HTLY 60142 2744 41W-19N E3
10 RtdT 60136 2745 40W-17N C7
10 RtdT 60142 2744 41W-19N E3
10 RtdT 60142 2745 40W-17N C7
400 RtdT 60136 2798 40W-16N B1
400 RtdT 60140 2798 40W-16N B1
900 WDSK 60098 2524 41W-32N E4
Powis Ct
1400 WCHI 60185 2965 31W-3N E7
1400 WynT 60185 2965 31W-3N E7
Powis Rd
- BRLT 60120 2909 31W-7N E5
- WynT 60120 2909 31W-7N E5
10 BRLT 60184 2909 31W-6N D7
10 WCHI 60185 2965 31W-3N E7
10 WYNE 60184 2965 31W-5N D1
10 WynT 60184 2909 31W-6N D7
10 WynT 60184 2965 31W-5N D1
10 WynT 60185 2965 31W-3N E7
400 WYNE 60185 2965 31W-4N E4
700 WCHI 60185 3021 31W-2N E1
1100 WynT 60185 3021 31W-2N E1
Powis Rd CO-18
100 WCHI 60185 2965 31W-3N E7
100 WynT 60185 2965 31W-3N E7
700 WCHI 60185 3021 31W-2N E1
1100 WynT 60185 3021 31W-2N E1
Pradel Dr
4200 NPVL 60564 3266 29W-12S D3
Prague Av
800 BFGV 60090 2755 14W-20N C2
Prague Ct
1600 NPVL 60563 3140 29W-5S D2
Prairie Av
10 HDPK 60035 2704 9W-23N C3
10 HIWD 60035 2704 9W-23N D3
10 HIWD 60040 2704 9W-23N C3
10 MltT 60187 3023 26W-0N E5
10 PKRG 60068 2918 10W-8N A1
10 WKGN 60085 2536 12W-33N C2
100 MltT 60137 3025 22W-1N B3
100 MltT 60190 3023 26W-0N E5
100 WLMT 60091 2812 3W-13N D6
100 WLMT 60201 2812 3W-13N E7
200 BmdT 60137 2969 22W-2N B7
200 BmdT 60137 3025 22W-2N B1
200 CTCY 60409 3351 2E-17S C5
200 GLHT 60137 3025 22W-2N B1
200 GLHT 60139 3025 22W-2N B1
200 LYVL 60048 2591 16W-28N D5
300 NPVL 60540 3141 26W-7S E6
400 BCHR 60401 3864 0W-37S C2
400 DRGV 60515 3144 20W-5S A2
400 WPHR 60096 2362 11W-43N D5
500 GNEN 60137 3025 22W-0N B4
500 WnfT 60555 3080 29W-3S C5
500 WNVL 60555 3080 29W-3S C5
600 MltT 60187 3024 25W-0N A5
800 BRLT 60103 2911 28W-7N A5
800 NPVL 60540 3142 26W-7S A6
1000 BrnT 60010 2751 25W-17N A4
1000 DRFD 60015 2703 11W-21N D6
1000 LKFT 60045 2649 11W-24N D7
1200 BRTN 60010 2751 25W-17N A4
1300 CHHT 60411 3507 1W-25S E7
1400 GLHT 60139 2969 22W-2N B7
1600 LKPT 60441 3419 23W-20S B4
1600 LktT 60441 3419 23W-20S B4
1600 NfdT 60062 2756 11W-16N C7
1600 NHBK 60062 2756 11W-17N C6
1800 PKRG 60068 2917 11W-8N D1
2000 DRGV 60515 3143 21W-5S E2
2300 EVTN 60201 2866 3W-12N E1
2400 DSPN 60016 2863 11W-11N C3
2400 MaiT 60016 2863 11W-11N C3
2500 EVTN 60201 2812 3W-12N E7
2900 BKFD 60513 3087 11W-4S E6
4000 SRPK 60176 2973 12W-5N C2
4200 MHRY 60050 2527 33W-33N E2
4200 MHRY 60050 2528 33W-33N A2
4400 BKFD 60513 3147 11W-4S E1
4500 MCCK 60513 3147 11W-4S E1
4500 MCCK 60525 3147 11W-4S E1
11600 HBRN 60034 2351 40W-41N A7
12000 HBRN 60034 2350 41W-41N E7
16000 SHLD 60473 3428 0E-18S D1
22100 SLVL 60411 3597 2E-26S C3
E Prairie Av
10 LMBD 60148 3026 19W-1N B3
400 DSPN 60016 2862 13W-11N D4
600 VLPK 60181 3026 19W-1N C3
1000 WHTN 60187 3024 23W-0N E5
1300 DSPN 60016 2863 13W-11N A4
1400 WHTN 60187 3025 23W-0N A5
N Prairie Av
10 JLET 60436 3498 25W-23S C5
10 MDLN 60060 2646 19W-27N D1
100 BMDL 60108 2913 22W-6N B7
100 BMDL 60108 2969 22W-5N B1
100 MDLN 60060 2590 19W-28N D7
800 JLET 60435 3498 25W-22S C1
1500 CTHL 60403 3498 25W-22S C1
1600 CTHL 60403 3418 25W-21S C7
41000 AntT 60002 2416 24W-41N D1
43100 WPHR 60096 2362 11W-43N D5
43100 WPHR 60099 2362 11W-43N D5
43300 BtnT 60099 2362 11W-43N D5
S Prairie Av
10 JLET 60435 3498 25W-24S C5
10 JLET 60436 3498 25W-24S C5
10 MDLN 60060 2646 19W-27N D1
100 BMDL 60108 2969 22W-5N B1
200 ANHT 60005 2807 16W-13N C7
200 ANHT 60005 2861 17W-12N B1
200 MPPT 60005 2861 17W-12N B1
200 MPPT 60056 2807 16W-13N C7
200 MPPT 60056 2861 17W-12N B1
300 EMHT 60126 3028 15W-0N A4
500 BRTN 60010 2751 25W-18N A3
500 FmtT 60060 2646 19W-27N D2
1400 CHCG 60605 3034 0E-1S C7
1900 CHCG 60616 3092 0E-2S C2
3800 CHCG 60653 3092 0E-3S C5
4600 CHCG 60615 3092 0E-4S C7
4700 CHCG 60615 3152 0E-5S C2
5400 CHCG 60637 3152 0E-6S C4
7000 CHCG 60619 3152 0E-8S D7
7500 CHCG 60619 3214 0E-10S D4
10000 CHCG 60628 3214 0E-11S D7
10300 CHCG 60628 3278 0E-12S D2
13200 CHCG 60827 3350 0E-15S D1
W Prairie Av
10 LMBD 60148 3026 20W-1N B3
100 WHTN 60187 3024 24W-0N C5
400 MltT 60187 3024 25W-0N B5
Prairie Cir
200 BGBK 60440 3268 24W-12S D2
1100 PTHT 60070 2754 16W-16N E6
W Prairie Cir
300 ITSC 60143 2914 19W-7N B5
Prairie Cross
300 PltT 60124 2852 40W-10N B6
5300 LGGV 60047 2701 17W-22N A4
22400 PNFD 60544 3339 28W-16S A4
22600 PnfT 60544 3339 28W-16S A4
Prairie Ct
- HDPK 60035 2757 9W-20N D2
- NHBK 60062 2757 9W-20N D2
400 RtdT 60140 2798 40W-16N C3
500 MltT 60190 3023 26W-0N D6
800 CLSM 60188 2967 27W-3N C6
1300 WCHI 60185 2966 29W-2N D7
1300 WCHI 60185 3022 29W-2N D1
1400 NARA 60542 3137 38W-4S B1
2500 GNVA 60134 3019 37W-0N D5
8000 TYPK 60477 3424 10W-19S C3
11900 LmnT 60439 3271 17W-14S B6
E Prairie Ct
10 HNWD 60047 2645 22W-27N B1
W Prairie Ct
10 HNWD 60047 2645 22W-27N B1
12300 HMGN 60491 3344 15W-17S B5
26200 CNHN 60410 3761 32W-32S C1
Prairie Dr
10 WTMT 60559 3085 18W-3S A6
100 MNKA 60447 3672 33W-28S B1
300 HRVD 60033 2464 50W-37N A1
400 SchT 60175 2963 38W-3N A6
900 ALGN 60102 2695 32W-20N B7
1000 ALGN 60102 2748 32W-20N B1
1600 PNFD 60544 3416 31W-18S A1
3400 SjnT 46311 3598 D6
3600 SPGV 60081 2413 32W-38N B6
8200 DrrT 60098 2583 37W-28N B6
16300 TYPK 60477 3424 10W-19S C3
N Prairie Dr
10 ADSN 60101 2970 20W-3N B5
S Prairie Dr
12000 ALSP 60803 3276 5W-14S C5
W Prairie Dr
4100 ALSP 60803 3276 5W-14S B5
12300 HMGN 60491 3344 15W-17S B5
12400 HTLY 60142 2744 42W-18N D4
Prairie Ln
- SRWD 60404 3495 31W-24S E7
- SRWD 60404 3496 29W-24S D7
10 ElaT 60047 2700 20W-23N A1
10 HNWD 60047 2700 20W-23N A1
10 WYNE 60185 2965 31W-4N E4
10 WYNE 60185 2966 31W-4N A4
200 LKZH 60047 2698 23W-22N E3
400 WMTN 60481 3943 27W-39S C2
800 BFGV 60089 2701 16W-20N D7
1000 BtlT 60560 3261 43W-14S C7
1200 YKVL 60560 3261 43W-14S C7
2000 WDRG 60517 3206 20W-10S A6
5800 RGMW 60067 2805 22W-14N C4
N Prairie Ln
22000 KLDR 60047 2699 21W-22N D4
22900 BFGV 60089 2701 16W-22N D3
22900 LNSH 60069 2701 16W-22N D3
22900 VrnT 60069 2701 16W-23N D3
W Prairie Ln
200 RDLK 60073 2531 23W-33N E3
10200 BHPK 60087 2480 10W-38N B1
Prairie Ln W
10 ODPK 60467 3344 14W-17S D5
Prairie Pth
- GYLK 60030 2533 19W-33N D2
Prairie Rd
400 RchT 60443 3593 8W-26S C2
700 GLNC 60022 2758 6W-17N C5
40400 AntT 60002 2416 24W-40N D3
E Prairie Rd
7400 LNWD 60076 2866 4W-9N B7
7400 LNWD 60712 2866 4W-9N B7
8400 SKOK 60076 2866 4W-10N C4
8800 SKOK 60203 2866 4W-11N C3
9400 EVTN 60201 2866 4W-11N D2
9400 SKOK 60201 2866 4W-11N D2
N Prairie Rd
22000 BFGV 60089 2701 16W-22N D5
22000 VrnT 60089 2701 16W-22N D5
22900 BFGV 60069 2701 16W-23N D2
22900 VrnT 60069 2701 16W-23N D2
N Prairie Rd CO-W17
22000 BFGV 60069 2701 16W-22N D5
22000 BFGV 60089 2701 16W-22N D5
22000 VrnT 60069 2701 16W-22N D5
22000 VrnT 60089 2701 16W-22N D5
NE Prairie Rd
6600 LNWD 60712 2920 4W-8N B2
7200 LNWD 60712 2866 4W-9N B7
7300 LNWD 60076 2866 4W-9N B7
7300 SKOK 60076 2866 4W-9N B7
S Prairie Rd
100 NLNX 60451 3501 17W-25S C7
Prairie Rdg
9700 RcmT 60071 2353 34W-41N C7
9700 RcmT 60071 2412 34W-41N C1
9700 RHMD 60071 2353 34W-41N C7
9700 RHMD 60071 2412 34W-41N C1
Prairie Sq
1900 SMBG 60173 2805 21W-12N E7
Prairie St
- BRkT 60511 3196 44W-8S D2
- BRkT 60554 3196 44W-8S D2
- PltT 60140 2798 41W-13N A7
- SgrT 60511 3196 44W-8S D2
10 AURA 60506 3136 40W-7S B7
10 AURA 60506 3198 40W-7S B1
10 BRkT 60554 3135 41W-7S E7
10 BRkT 60554 3197 42W-7S D1
10 MHTN 60442 3677 19W-30S E4
10 PGGV 60140 2798 41W-13N A7
10 SCRL 60174 2964 35W-2N B7
10 SgrT 60506 3198 40W-7S B1
10 SgrT 60554 3197 42W-8S B1
10 SgrT 60554 3198 40W-7S B1
10 SRGV 60506 3198 40W-7S B1
10 SRGV 60554 3135 41W-7S E7
10 SRGV 60554 3136 40W-7S B7
10 SRGV 60554 3197 42W-7S D1
10 SRGV 60554 3198 40W-7S B1
100 AURA 60506 3199 37W-7S B1
100 BDWD 60408 3942 31W-41S B6
100 SEGN 60177 2908 34W-8N D2
200 ELGN 60120 2854 33W-11N E4
300 ELGN 60120 2855 33W-11N A4
300 SCRL 60174 3020 36W-2N A1
700 SgrT 60554 3196 44W-8S D2
800 AraT 60506 3199 36W-7S D1
1100 SCRL 60174 3019 36W-2N E1
1700 SCRL 60175 3019 36W-2N D1
1800 GNVW 60025 2810 8W-13N D6
2000 BLID 60406 3277 2W-15S C7
2300 AraT 60506 3198 38W-7S E1
3000 FNPK 60131 2973 13W-3N A4
3300 MTSN 60443 3594 4W-26S E2
3300 MTSN 60443 3595 4W-26S A2
17600 UNON 60180 2635 46W-25N D5
E Prairie St
10 PLNO 60545 3259 47W-13S D5
100 CLLK 60014 2640 34W-26N C3
100 MRGO 60152 2634 49W-26N C2
200 NndT 60014 2640 34W-26N C3
N Prairie St
10 BTVA 60510 3078 35W-1S C1
10 CRY 60013 2695 31W-23N D1
700 BTVA 60510 3020 34W-0S C7
S Prairie St
10 BTVA 60510 3078 34W-1S C2
10 CRY 60013 2695 31W-23N D1
100 HPSR 60140 2795 47W-16N D2
700 NLNX 60451 3501 17W-25S C7
700 NlxT 60451 3501 17W-25S C7
700 NlxT 60451 3589 17W-25S C1
900 NLNX 60451 3589 17W-25S C1
W Prairie St
10 MHTN 60442 3678 19W-30S A4
100 MHTN 60442 3677 19W-30S E4
100 MRGO 60152 2634 50W-26N B2
2900 MHRY 60050 2528 31W-31N C6
Prairie Tr
- GwdT 60097 2469 38W-35N A6
- WRLK 60097 2469 38W-35N A6
900 GYLK 60030 2533 19W-32N D6
2100 RLKH 60073 2474 24W-36N D5
E Prairie Brook Dr
1200 PLTN 60074 2753 19W-17N C5
Prairie Center Dr
- SMBG 60193 2859 22W-10N C5
- SMBG 60194 2859 22W-10N C5
Prairie Clover Dr
900 RMVL 60446 3340 25W-15S C1
Prairie Creek Dr
- GRNE 60031 2477 16W-36N D5
Prairie Crossing Dr
- KdlT 60560 3333 42W-17S E5
- KdlT 60560 3334 41W-16S A5
- WynT 60185 2966 29W-2N D7
- YKVL 60560 3333 42W-17S E6
1400 WCHI 60185 2966 29W-2N D7
4000 SCRL 60175 2964 36W-5N A1
Prairie Crossing Ln
500 NLNX 60451 3501 18W-25S A6
Prairie Edge Dr
9500 WRLK 60097 2468 38W-35N E6
Prairie Estate Dr
1200 MhtT 60451 3589 16W-28S E6
1500 MhtT 60451 3590 16W-28S A6
Prairie Farm Dr
700 HshT 60140 2796 45W-16N C1
Prairie Grove Dr
- WldT 60585 3265 31W-14S E7
- WldT 60585 3266 31W-14S A7
24000 PNFD 60585 3266 30W-14S B7
24300 PNFD 60585 3338 30W-14S B1
24300 WldT 60585 3338 30W-14S B1
25000 PNFD 60585 3265 31W-14S E7
Prairie Hill Cir
400 RtdT 60140 2798 40W-15N B3
Prairie Hill Ct
900 AlqT 60013 2642 29W-24N B7
900 CRY 60013 2642 29W-24N B7
Prairie Hill Dr
13700 HMGN 60491 3342 19W-16S D3
13700 HmrT 60491 3342 19W-16S D3
Prairie Hill Ln
25800 WldT 60543 3265 32W-13S C6
25800 WldT 60585 3265 32W-13S C6
Prairie Knoll Dr
300 NPVL 60565 3203 26W-9S D4
Prairie Lake Ct
3600 AURA 60504 3202 31W-8S A2
N Prairie Lake Pl
22700 KLDR 60047 2699 21W-22N E3
Prairie Lake Rd
100 EDND 60110 2748 32W-17N E7
100 EDND 60110 2801 32W-16N E1
Prairie Landing Ct
- HNWD 60047 2645 22W-26N B2
- HNWD 60060 2645 22W-26N B2
Prairie Landing Ln
- SRWD 60404 3583 31W-25S E2
Prairie Lawn Rd
800 GNVW 60025 2810 10W-13N B7
800 NfdT 60025 2810 10W-13N B7
Prairie Meadow Ln
300 VNHL 60061 2646 18W-24N E7
Prairie Mist Dr
300 RDLK 60073 2531 25W-33N A2
Prairiemoor Ln
5500 LGGV 60047 2701 17W-22N B3
Prairie Oak Rd
4900 GRNE 60031 2478 15W-35N B6
Prairie Orchid Ln
1200 GYLK 60030 2533 19W-32N C5
Prairie Park Blvd
- BCHR 60401 3774 0W-35S C7
Prairie Park Dr
- WLNG 60090 2755 14W-18N C2
Prairie Path Ln
10 WNFD 60190 3023 27W-1N D4
10 WnfT 60190 3023 27W-1N D4
400 EMHT 60126 3027 16W-0N D4
800 JLET 60436 3497 27W-25S C7
1900 CPVL 60110 2746 37W-17N D6
Prairie Point Dr
- SEGN 60177 2909 33W-9N A1
Prairie Pointe Ln
10 SMWD 60107 2856 29W-10N D6
Prairie Pond Dr
13200 PNFD 60585 3337 32W-15S D2
Prairie Ridge Cir
1700 LNHT 60046 2417 20W-39N E4
1700 LNHT 60046 2418 20W-39N A5
Prairie Ridge Ct
- DGvT 60527 3207 16W-9S E4
- DGvT 60527 3208 16W-9S A4
1900 JLET 60586 3416 31W-21S A7
Prairie Ridge Ct N
31100 GNOK 60048 2592 14W-31N C1
Prairie Ridge Ct S
31000 GNOK 60048 2592 14W-31N C1
Prairie Ridge Dr
100 WDSK 60098 2581 41W-30N D2
200 MNKA 60447 3672 33W-29S A3
500 BtvT 60542 3077 37W-3S D6
1800 JLET 60586 3416 31W-21S A7
S Prairie Ridge Ln
- PNFD 60585 3265 32W-14S B7
Prairie Ridge Rd
- AlqT 60014 2641 33W-26N A4
5900 NndT 60014 2641 33W-26N A3
31000 GNOK 60048 2592 14W-31N C1
Prairie Rose Cir
600 MltT 60188 3024 25W-1N A3
Prairie Rose Ct
- PNFD 60585 3338 30W-15S C2
Prairie Rose Ln
5500 JNBG 60050 2471 31W-37N E2
Prairie Sage Ln
5000 NPVL 60564 3266 29W-13S C5
Prairie Scene
100 ANTH 60002 2357 23W-42N E5
100 ANTH 60002 2358 22W-42N B5
Prairie Side Dr
1700 JLET 60586 3495 33W-21S A1
Prairie Smoke Rd
- GYLK 60030 2533 19W-31N D6
- LbvT 60030 2533 19W-31N D6
Prairie Spring Dr
10 CmpT 60175 2962 40W-5N C2
Prairie Springs Dr
200 RDLK 60073 2530 25W-33N E2
Prairie Stone Pkwy
- HFET 60118 2802 29W-13N C5
5000 HFET 60192 2802 30W-13N B6
Prairie Trail Ct
1900 JLET 60586 3416 30W-21S C7
Prairie Trail Ln
3200 JNBG 60050 2471 32W-35N C5
22300 FKFT 60423 3592 10W-27S C3
Prairie Trail Rd
- GrtT 60041 2530 25W-33N E2
- RDLK 60041 2530 25W-33N E2
- RDLK 60073 2530 25W-33N E2
- RDLK 60073 2531 25W-33N A2
Prairie Valley Ct
200 ELBN 60119 3017 43W-2N A2
Prairie Valley Dr
10 CmpT 60175 2961 43W-5N B1
300 CmpT 60175 2905 43W-6N B7
Prairie Valley St
- CmpT 60151 3017 43W-2N A2
200 ELBN 60119 3017 43W-2N A2

STREET Block	City	ZIP	Map#	CGS	Grid
Prairie Valley St					
800	CmpT	60119	3017	43W-2N	B1
Prairie View Av					
100	GYLK	60030	2532	21W-33N	D2
Prairieview Av					
6800	WDRG	60517	3143	21W-7S	E7
6800	WDRG	60517	3144	21W-7S	A7
S Prairie View Av					
25700	CteT	60417	3686	3E-31S	E5
Prairieview Blvd					
1600	BGBK	60490	3267	26W-13S	D5
Prairie View Ct					
1000	NPVL	60563	3140	30W-5S	B3
Prairieview Ct					
10	BGBK	60490	3267	26W-13S	D5
100	OSWG	60543	3263	37W-13S	C5
Prairie View Dr					
-	GnvT	60134	3019	38W-0N	A5
-	MNKA	60447	3672	33W-30S	A4
100	PlsT	60464	3273	12W-14S	C7
200	GNVA	60134	3019	37W-1N	B2
Prairieview Dr					
100	OSWG	60543	3263	37W-13S	B5
N Prairie View Dr					
36700	LkvT	60046	2476	20W-36N	A3
39800	WDWH	60083	2420	14W-39N	D4
Prairie View Ln					
-	MTWA	60045	2648	14W-24N	C6
200	WLNG	60090	2755	14W-18N	D3
300	CmpT	60119	2962	41W-3N	A7
700	WDSK	60098	2581	40W-30N	E2
Prairieview Ln					
2500	AURA	60502	3079	31W-4S	D7
S Prairie View Ln					
1100	RDLK	60073	2531	23W-31N	E6
W Prairieview Ln					
17000	WrnT	60031	2534	17W-33N	C2
Prairieview Ln S					
2500	AURA	60502	3139	32W-4S	C1
2600	AURA	60502	3079	31W-4S	D7
Prairie View Pkwy					
1200	CRY	60013	2641	32W-24N	C6
Prairieview Pkwy					
400	HPSR	60140	2795	47W-15N	D3
Prairie View Rd					
-	GrtT	60073	2530	25W-34N	E1
-	RDLK	60073	2530	25W-34N	E1
3200	PRGV	60050	2585	31W-28N	D5
25700	GrtT	60073	2531	25W-34N	A1
Prairie View Tr					
32200	LKMR	60051	2529	28W-32N	D5
W Prairie Walk Ln					
200	RDLK	60073	2531	23W-31N	E6
Prairie Wind Dr					
1700	JLET	60435	3417	27W-21S	C7
1700	JLET	60435	3497	27W-21S	D1
Prairie Wind Rd					
3300	LGGV	60047	2700	19W-22N	C4
Prairiewood Ln					
-	TroT	60404	3583	31W-25S	E2
25300	SRWD	60404	3583	31W-25S	E2
Pralls Lp					
10	HDPK	60040	2704	9W-24N	C1
10	HIWD	60040	2704	9W-24N	C1
Prarie Av					
-	BNHM	60633	3352	3E-16S	A3
Prarie Crossing Dr					
2400	MTGY	60538	3198	40W-10S	B7
2500	BtlT	60512	3198	40W-10S	B7
2500	BtlT	60538	3198	40W-10S	B7
Prarieview Pkwy					
-	HPSR	60140	2795	47W-15N	D4
-	HshT	60140	2795	47W-15N	D4
N Prater Av					
10	NHLK	60164	3028	13W-2N	E1
100	NHLK	60164	2972	13W-2N	E7
800	LydT	60164	2972	13W-3N	D5
3100	FNPK	60131	2972	13W-3N	D5
3100	FNPK	60164	2972	13W-3N	D5
3100	LydT	60131	2972	13W-3N	D5
S Prater Av					
100	NHLK	60164	3028	13W-1N	E1
Pratt Av					
1600	DSPN	60018	2917	12W-8N	B2
1600	RSMT	60018	2917	12W-8N	A2
W Pratt Av					
3300	LNWD	60712	2920	4W-8N	C2
4700	LNWD	60712	2919	5W-8N	E2
4800	LNWD	60077	2919	6W-8N	D1
4800	SKOK	60077	2919	6W-8N	D1
5300	CHCG	60646	2919	6W-8N	D1
5300	LNWD	60646	2919	6W-8N	D1
5300	SKOK	60646	2919	6W-8N	D1
7200	CHCG	60631	2918	9W-8N	D2
7200	CHCG	60714	2918	9W-8N	D2
7200	NLES	60714	2918	9W-8N	D2
Pratt Av N					
400	SMBG	60193	2912	24W-8N	D2
Pratt Blvd					
10	ROSL	60172	2913	23W-8N	A2
10	ROSL	60193	2913	23W-8N	A2
10	SmbT	60172	2913	23W-8N	A2
10	SmbT	60193	2913	23W-8N	A2
100	SmbT	60172	2912	23W-8N	E2
100	SmbT	60193	2912	23W-8N	E2
600	EGVV	60007	2915	17W-8N	B2
2100	CHCG	60007	2915	16W-8N	D2
W Pratt Blvd					
1000	CHCG	60626	2921	2W-8N	C1
1900	CHCG	60645	2921	2W-8N	B1
2600	CHCG	60645	2920	3W-8N	E1
3100	LNWD	60712	2920	3W-8N	D2
Pratt Ct					
2000	EVTN	60201	2867	2W-11N	B2
4700	JLET	60586	3416	29W-21S	C7
E Pratt Dr					
1000	PLTN	60074	2753	19W-16N	C6
N Pratt Ln					
10	PNFD	60544	3416	30W-18S	C1
Pratt Rd					
200	WYNE	60184	2965	32W-5N	D1
16600	SdwT	60548	3258	51W-13S	A6
17500	LtRT	60548	3258	51W-13S	A6
Pratt St					
-	PLNO	60545	3260	45W-14S	C7
Pratt Woods Ct					
600	WYNE	60184	2965	31W-5N	D2
Pratum Av					
-	HnrT	60192	2802	29W-13N	C7
2300	HFET	60192	2802	29W-13N	C6
W Pratum Terra Dr					
14000	WDWH	60083	2420	14W-39N	D4
Preakness Ct					
3000	AURA	60502	3078	33W-3S	E6
Preakness Dr					
3100	AURA	60502	3078	33W-3S	E6
S Preakness Dr					
11300	PNFD	60585	3266	30W-13S	C5
Preakness Ln					
3600	RLKP	60030	2532	22W-31N	C7
Preakness Pl					
6700	GRNE	60031	2477	17W-35N	C6
Preble Av					
100	NCHI	60088	2593	10W-30N	E1
100	NCHI	60088	2594	10W-30N	A1
Preble Pl					
100	NCHI	60088	2593	10W-30N	E1
Precision Plz					
10	CLLK	60014	2640	33W-24N	E7
Precision Plz SR-31					
10	CLLK	60014	2640	33W-24N	E7
Precision Rd					
100	FXLK	60020	2473	27W-36N	B4
S Preller Av					
11100	WRTH	60482	3274	8W-13S	E3
Prelude Ct					
1100	NPVL	60564	3267	28W-11S	A1
W Premier Dr					
17700	WrnT	60031	2534	17W-33N	A2
Premium Outlets Blvd					
-	AURA	60502	3139	33W-4S	A1
1600	AraT	60502	3139	33W-4S	A2
1600	AraT	60504	3139	33W-4S	A2
1600	AURA	60502	3138	33W-4S	E1
1600	AURA	60504	3138	33W-4S	E1
1600	AURA	60504	3139	33W-4S	A2
Premrose Ct					
900	RMVL	60446	3340	25W-15S	C1
Premrose Dr					
900	RMVL	60446	3340	25W-15S	C1
W Prendergast Ln					
2100	MPPT	60056	2861	17W-12N	B2
Prentice Dr					
6300	LslT	60517	3143	21W-7S	D6
Prentiss Ct					
6400	DRGV	60516	3144	20W-7S	A6
Prentiss Dr					
1700	DRGV	60516	3144	21W-7S	A6
2000	DRGV	60516	3143	21W-7S	E6
2000	WDRG	60516	3143	21W-7S	E6
2000	WDRG	60517	3143	21W-7S	E6
Prescott					
1300	VOLO	60041	2530	27W-33N	C3
Prescott Av					
200	ElgT	60124	2853	38W-11N	A5
3900	LYNS	60534	3088	9W-4S	C7
4500	LYNS	60534	3148	9W-4S	C1
4600	MCCK	60534	3148	9W-4S	C1
N Prescott Av					
6100	CHCG	60646	2919	6W-7N	C3
Prescott Ct					
700	NPVL	60563	3141	28W-6S	A4
2000	AURA	60503	3201	32W-10S	C6
W Prescott Ct					
21300	KLDR	60047	2699	21W-23N	D2
Prescott Dr					
-	BtlT	60538	3198	40W-10S	B6
-	MTGY	60538	3198	40W-10S	B6
100	BRLT	60103	2909	32W-8N	B3
400	WNFD	60190	3023	26W-0N	E4
700	ROSL	60172	2912	24W-6N	C6
900	JLET	60432	3500	20W-22S	C2
Prescott Ln					
300	GRNE	60031	2477	17W-34N	A7
300	GRNE	60031	2534	18W-34N	A1
1100	CLLK	60014	2693	36W-23N	C1
2400	WSTR	60154	3086	14W-2S	D3
7300	CTSD	60525	3209	13W-8S	A1
Prescott Pl					
-	ADSN	60143	2970	20W-5N	A2
Prescott St					
700	WKGN	60085	2537	10W-33N	A4
900	NCHI	60064	2537	10W-33N	A4
Preservation Wy					
-	BtnT	60071	2354	31W-42N	E5
-	BtnT	60071	2355	30W-42N	A5
-	BtnT	60081	2355	30W-42N	A5
-	RcmT	60071	2354	31W-42N	E5
-	RdlT	53181	2355	30W-43N	A4
Preserve Av					
1000	NPVL	60564	3267	28W-12S	B3
Preserve Cir					
10	LNHT	60046	2476	19W-37N	C1
Preserve Ct					
10	HNWD	60047	2645	22W-27N	B1
4800	LGGV	60047	2700	18W-23N	E2
Preserve Pkwy					
4800	LGGV	60047	2700	18W-23N	E2
Preserve Tr					
1100	BRLT	60103	2910	30W-8N	C4
President Ct					
-	CLSM	60188	3024	24W-1N	E2
-	GLHT	60188	3024	24W-1N	E2
E President Ct					
-	MltT	60188	3024	23W-1N	E2
W President Ct					
-	MltT	60188	3024	24W-1N	D2
President St					
-	CLSM	60188	3024	24W-1N	E1
-	GLHT	60188	3024	24W-2N	E1
900	ELBN	60119	3017	43W-0N	A5
1200	GLHT	60139	3024	24W-2N	E1
1400	GLHT	60139	2968	24W-2N	E7
N President St					
100	WHTN	60187	3024	24W-0S	E6
1600	MltT	60187	3024	24W-0S	E6
2100	CLSM	60188	3024	24W-0S	E6
2100	MltT	60188	3024	24W-0S	E6
2100	WHTN	60188	3024	24W-0S	E6
S President St					
-	GLHT	60139	3024	24W-1N	E2
100	CLSM	60188	3024	24W-1N	E3
100	GLHT	60188	3024	24W-1N	E2
100	WHTN	60187	3024	23W-0S	E7
300	MltT	60188	3024	24W-1N	E3
500	MltT	60187	3024	24W-1N	E3
500	WHTN	60188	3024	24W-1N	E3
800	WHTN	60187	3082	24W-1S	E1
Presidential Av					
-	PNFD	60544	3338	30W-17S	A6
-	PnfT	60544	3337	31W-17S	E6
-	PnfT	60544	3338	31W-17S	A6
25100	PNFD	60544	3337	31W-17S	E6
Presidential Blvd					
200	OSWG	60543	3263	38W-12S	A3
Presidential Dr					
10	ROSL	60172	2912	24W-7N	E4
7100	GRNE	60031	2477	17W-34N	B7
7100	GRNE	60031	2534	17W-34N	A1
Presidential Ln					
200	ELGN	60123	2854	36W-11N	A3
Presidents Dr					
17700	HMWD	60430	3428	1W-21S	A6
Presidents Wy					
-	SRWD	60404	3496	31W-24S	A5
Presidio Ct					
100	SMBG	60195	2859	23W-12N	A2
Presley Cir					
11700	PNFD	60585	3265	31W-13S	E6
Prestancia Dr					
21000	FftT	60451	3502	14W-25S	D7
21000	MKNA	60448	3502	14W-25S	D7
21000	MKNA	60448	3590	14W-25S	D1
21000	MKNA	60451	3502	14W-25S	D7
Prestbury Ct					
700	NHBK	60062	2756	11W-18N	D4
Prestbury Dr					
1000	ELGN	60120	2855	32W-12N	D1
Prestige Ln					
300	RtdT	60124	2798	40W-14N	C6
Prestige Ct					
3600	NPVL	60564	3267	28W-11S	A1
N Prestige St					
500	JLET	60435	3497	27W-23S	D3
Preston Av					
10	ELGN	60120	2855	33W-11N	B4
N Preston Av					
400	ELGN	60120	2855	33W-12N	B3
Preston Cir					
400	LNHT	60046	2418	19W-38N	D7
Preston Ct					
-	BbyT	60134	3018	39W-0S	E7
10	ALGN	60102	2694	35W-21N	A6
800	LKVL	60046	2475	21W-37N	C2
6500	CPVL	60110	2747	36W-17N	A6
7100	GRNE	60031	2477	17W-35N	B5
W Preston Ct					
21200	FmtT	60060	2645	21W-26N	D3
Preston Dr					
500	BGBK	60440	3205	21W-10S	D6
7600	McHT	60097	2469	36W-34N	D7
Preston Ln					
-	BlmT	60411	3509	2E-23S	E4
-	LYWD	60411	3509	2E-23S	E4
-	OSWG	60543	3263	36W-12S	E4
-	OSWG	60543	3264	36W-12S	A4
600	SMBG	60193	2859	22W-9N	C7
2300	WDND	60118	2800	35W-16N	B1
Preston Pkwy					
10700	HTLY	60142	2692	39W-21N	C6
Preston Rd					
1500	NPVL	60563	3140	29W-5S	D4
Preston St					
1600	ALGN	60102	2694	35W-21N	A6
10400	WSTR	60154	3087	13W-2S	A3
Preston Lakes Ct					
2200	JLET	60586	3416	30W-21S	A6
Prestson Cir					
-	BbyT	60134	3018	39W-0S	E7
Prestwick Ct					
600	WDND	60118	2800	35W-16N	B2
4200	SCRL	60174	2965	33W-5N	A3
5100	JLET	60586	3416	30W-21S	B6
21300	LktT	60403	3417	26W-20S	E5
Prestwick Dr					
-	FKFT	60423	3593	9W-26S	A1
-	RchT	60443	3593	9W-26S	A1
600	FKFT	60423	3592	9W-26S	E1
1600	NPVL	60563	3140	30W-5S	B2
1600	NpvT	60563	3140	30W-5S	B2
1700	IVNS	60067	2804	23W-15N	E2
7500	TYPK	60477	3424	9W-20S	D4
21300	LktT	60403	3417	26W-20S	E5
N Prestwick Dr					
21000	CbaT	60010	2697	26W-21N	D7
Prestwick Ln					
10	RGMW	60008	2805	23W-12N	B7
100	WNFD	60190	3023	26W-1N	E2
400	WLNG	60090	2755	13W-17N	D5
1200	ITSC	60143	2913	21W-6N	E7
1200	ITSC	60143	2914	21W-6N	A7
3200	NHBK	60062	2756	11W-17N	C6
3300	NfdT	60062	2756	11W-17N	C6
8800	ODPK	60462	3346	11W-15S	A2
9000	LKWD	60014	2639	38W-24N	A7
Prestwick Pl					
4800	HFET	60010	2751	25W-16N	A7
4800	HFET	60010	2804	24W-16N	B1
W Prestwick St					
3700	MHRY	60050	2528	32W-33N	A2
Prestwicke Blvd					
-	GfnT	60156	2693	37W-21N	B6
200	ALGN	60102	2693	37W-21N	B6
Preswick Ct					
400	OSWG	60543	3263	36W-11S	E2
Preswick Ln					
2100	WDSK	60098	2582	39W-29N	D3
Price Av					
600	CTCY	60409	3352	4E-18S	B7
1200	CTCY	60409	3430	4E-19S	B2
Price Ct					
3200	JLET	60431	3497	28W-25S	B7
Price Dr					
1000	ELGN	60120	2855	32W-11N	D3
Price Ln					
700	DRFD	60015	2703	11W-20N	D7
Price Rd					
500	AraT	60506	3199	38W-8S	A1
500	AURA	60506	3199	38W-8S	A1
900	SgrT	60506	3136	40W-5S	B3
900	SgrT	60554	3136	40W-5S	B3
900	SRGV	60506	3136	40W-5S	B3
900	SRGV	60554	3136	40W-5S	B3
Price St					
600	CTCY	60409	3352	4E-17S	B6
Pride Ct					
4500	RGMW	60008	2805	20W-14N	E3
Prideham St					
6300	DRGV	60516	3144	20W-7S	A6
Prideland Dr					
200	SRWD	60404	3496	31W-24S	A6
Prides Run					
400	LIHL	60156	2693	36W-22N	D4
Prieboy Av					
3300	JLET	60431	3417	28W-20S	A5
3300	PnfT	60431	3417	28W-20S	A5
3400	JLET	60586	3417	28W-20S	A5
Prime Pkwy					
4400	MHRY	60050	2584	33W-30N	E1
4400	MHRY	60050	2585	33W-30N	A1
Prime Pointe Ct					
13800	HTLY	60140	2744	43W-19N	A4
13800	HTLY	60142	2744	43W-19N	A4
Primrose Av					
5500	LSLE	60532	3143	22W-6S	C4
5500	LslT	60532	3143	22W-6S	C4
Primrose Cir					
500	ROSL	60172	2912	24W-6N	D6
600	MTSN	60443	3506	5W-24S	B6
24000	PNFD	60585	3338	30W-15S	C2
Primrose Ct					
300	AURA	60504	3139	31W-7S	E7
1900	BRLT	60103	2909	32W-8N	D2
4200	ZION	60099	2362	12W-41N	B7
9200	FRGV	60021	2696	29W-22N	D3
11400	HTLY	60142	2691	41W-20N	D7
15300	ODPK	60462	3346	9W-18S	D7
20500	DRPK	60010	2698	23W-21N	E7
20500	DRPK	60010	2751	23W-20N	E1
N Primrose Ct					
34000	GrtT	60073	2531	25W-34N	A2
Primrose Dr					
10	SjnT	46311	3598		C6
2000	JLET	60586	3416	30W-21S	C7
Primrose Ln					
-	FRGV	60010	2696	29W-22N	D3
-	JLET	60586	3496	31W-22S	A2
-	SRWD	60404	3496	31W-22S	A2
10	OSWG	60543	3200	34W-10S	D7
100	BRLT	60103	2909	32W-8N	C2
400	BGBK	60490	3268	26W-12S	A3
500	NndT	60014	2640	34W-26N	C3
600	CLLK	60014	2640	34W-26N	D3
600	MTSN	60443	3506	5W-24S	B6
600	SMBG	60194	2858	26W-11N	A4
1500	GNVW	60025	2810	9W-14N	C5
2000	NPVL	60565	3204	25W-9S	C5
8200	FXLK	60081	2415	28W-39N	A5
9000	HYHL	60457	3209	11W-9S	E3
9100	FRGV	60021	2696	29W-22N	D3
11400	MKNA	60448	3502	14W-25S	E7
15000	WDWH	60083	2420	15W-38N	B7
15100	ODPK	60462	3346	9W-18S	D6
15100	OrlT	60462	3346	9W-18S	D6
27200	FmtT	60060	2645	22W-27N	C1
27200	HNWD	60047	2645	22W-27N	C1
27200	HNWD	60060	2645	22W-27N	C1
27200	MDLN	60047	2645	22W-27N	C1
27200	MDLN	60060	2645	22W-27N	C1
S Primrose Ln					
100	RDLK	60073	2531	23W-33N	E4
W Primrose Ln					
16400	LKPT	60441	3342	20W-18S	B7
Primrose Pth					
300	HshT	60140	2743	46W-17N	A7
N Primrose Pth					
38200	AntT	60081	2415	27W-38N	B7
Prince Ct					
1700	NPVL	60563	3140	29W-5S	D3
5800	LslT	60532	3143	22W-6S	B5
Prince Dr					
1200	SHLD	60419	3351	1E-18S	B6
1200	SHLD	60473	3351	1E-18S	B6
16200	SHLD	60473	3429	1E-19S	B3
Prince St					
2500	NHBK	60062	2809	10W-15N	E1
4300	DRGV	60515	3144	19W-5S	C2
Prince Charles Ct					
800	SMBG	60195	2858	24W-12N	D1
Prince Charles Ln					
800	HFET	60169	2858	24W-12N	D1
800	HFET	60195	2858	24W-12N	D1
800	SMBG	60169	2858	24W-12N	D1
800	SMBG	60195	2858	24W-12N	D1
Prince Crossing Rd					
-	WynT	60185	2966	29W-2N	E7
10	WCHI	60185	3022	29W-1N	E2
10	WynT	60185	3022	29W-2N	E2
100	WCHI	60185	2966	29W-2N	E7
400	WnfT	60185	3022	29W-0S	E7
500	WnfT	60190	3022	29W-0S	E7
Prince Crossing Rd CO-27					
300	WCHI	60185	3022	28W-0N	E5
300	WnfT	60185	3022	28W-0N	E5
Prince Edward Cir					
600	SMBG	60193	2913	22W-9N	C1
Prince Edward Dr					
600	EGVV	60007	2913	22W-9N	C1
600	SMBG	60007	2913	22W-9N	C1
600	SMBG	60193	2913	22W-9N	C1
Prince Edward Rd					
300	GNEN	60137	3083	22W-1S	B2
Prince George Ln					
200	YkTp	60523	3084	19W-2S	D4
Prince Lake Ct					
21200	LktT	60403	3417	26W-19S	E3
Prince Lake Dr					
21200	LktT	60403	3417	26W-19S	E3
Princess Av					
-	NLNX	60451	3588	19W-27S	D5
-	NlxT	60442	3588	19W-27S	D5
-	NlxT	60451	3588	19W-27S	D5
10400	CHRG	60415	3275	7W-12S	B2
11000	CHRG	60482	3275	7W-12S	B3
11000	WRTH	60482	3275	7W-12S	B3
Princess Cir					
1700	NPVL	60564	3266	28W-12S	E2
1700	NPVL	60564	3267	28W-12S	A2
Princess Ct					
10	WSTR	60154	3086	13W-2S	E3
2000	LKPT	60441	3419	22W-20S	D5
S Princess Ln					
25900	CteT	60417	3685	1W-31S	B5
Princess Elizabeth Ct					
17600	TYPK	60487	3424	11W-21S	A6
Princeton Av					
-	BHPK	60087	2421	12W-39N	B6
-	BHPK	60099	2421	12W-39N	C6
-	WKGN	60087	2421	12W-39N	B6
100	BNHL	60010	2750	25W-17N	E4
100	BrnT	60010	2750	25W-17N	E4
100	LktT	60441	3419	23W-21S	B7
200	BrnT	60010	2751	25W-17N	A4
300	ELGN	60123	2854	36W-10N	A6
600	BRTN	60010	2751	25W-17N	A4
800	LktT	60432	3419	22W-21S	C7
800	MTSN	60443	3505	7W-25S	E7
900	HDPK	60035	2704	9W-22N	D5
900	RMVL	60446	3340	25W-16S	C3
2600	EVTN	60201	2812	4W-13N	B7
3500	AURA	60504	3201	31W-8S	D1
3500	AURA	60504	3202	31W-8S	A1
14600	DLTN	60419	3350	0W-17S	B5
14600	DLTN	60827	3350	0W-17S	B5
14600	RVDL	60827	3350	0W-17S	B5
16100	TYPK	60477	3424	9W-19S	C2
N Princeton Av					
800	ANHT	60004	2806	18W-14N	D3
800	ANHT	60005	2806	18W-14N	D3
1000	VLPK	60181	2971	18W-2N	A7
1000	VLPK	60181	3027	18W-2N	A1
1100	ADSN	60101	2971	18W-2N	A7
N Princeton Av					
1100	ADSN	60181	2971	18W-2N	A7
1100	VLPK	60101	2971	18W-2N	A7
S Princeton Av					
100	ITSC	60143	2914	19W-6N	D7
200	ANHT	60005	2806	18W-13N	D6
300	VLPK	60181	3027	18W-0N	A5
500	ADSN	60143	2914	19W-5N	D7
1300	ANHT	60005	2860	18W-12N	D1
3500	CHCG	60616	3092	0W-3S	B5
4100	CHCG	60609	3092	0W-4S	B7
4700	CHCG	60609	3152	0W-6S	B3
5500	CHCG	60621	3152	0W-6S	B4
9500	CHCG	60620	3214	0W-11S	B6
9500	CHCG	60628	3214	0W-11S	B6
10300	CHCG	60628	3278	0W-12S	B1
Princeton Cir					
900	HRPK	60133	2911	26W-9N	E1
900	HRPK	60133	2912	26W-9N	A1
1800	NPVL	60565	3204	24W-8S	D2
21900	FKFT	60423	3591	13W-26S	B2
E Princeton Cir					
800	ISLK	60042	2586	28W-29N	E4
800	ISLK	60042	2587	28W-28N	A7
W Princeton Cir					
800	ISLK	60042	2586	28W-29N	E4
Princeton Ct					
10	HNWD	60047	2645	20W-25N	E5
10	LIHL	60156	2692	39W-23N	D2
10	NARA	60542	3137	36W-4S	D1
10	WNVL	60555	3080	30W-1S	C2
200	SRWD	60404	3496	30W-24S	B6
400	ELGN	60123	2854	36W-10N	A6
800	EMHT	60126	3028	15W-0S	B5
900	VNHL	60061	2647	17W-26N	C4
1000	WKGN	60085	2535	14W-33N	C4
1400	WHTN	60187	3082	24W-1S	E2
1500	SMBG	60193	2912	25W-9N	B1
1700	LKFT	60045	2649	13W-26N	A3
1800	GRNE	60031	2477	16W-35N	E5
4000	SMWD	60107	2911	28W-9N	A1
22100	FKFT	60423	3591	13W-26S	B3
E Princeton Ct					
600	RLKB	60073	2475	22W-36N	C4
S Princeton Ct					
10	ANHT	60005	2806	18W-13N	D5
13800	PnfT	60544	3339	27W-16S	C4
Princeton Dr					
400	NARA	60542	3137	37W-4S	D1
500	BGBK	60440	3268	24W-12S	E2
1000	RMVL	60446	3340	25W-16S	B3
1100	BRLT	60103	2910	30W-6N	C7
12300	HTLY	60142	2744	42W-19N	E2
12300	RtdT	60142	2744	42W-19N	E2
Princeton Ln					
100	GNVW	60025	2810	10W-15N	B2
400	DRFD	60015	2756	11W-20N	D1
600	NLNX	60451	3502	16W-25S	A7
700	NLNX	60451	3590	16W-25S	A1
1300	SMBG	60193	2912	25W-9N	B1
4300	GfnT	60156	2692	38W-23N	E2
4300	GfnT	60156	2693	38W-23N	A2
4400	LIHL	60156	2692	38W-23N	D2
6000	PSHT	60463	3275	7W-14S	C6
6000	WthT	60463	3275	7W-14S	C6
17700	CCHL	60429	3426	4W-21S	E6
17700	CCHL	60478	3426	4W-21S	E6
17700	HLCT	60429	3426	4W-21S	E6
Princeton Pl					
1200	WLMT	60091	2812	5W-14N	A4
Princeton Rd					
10	HNDL	60521	3146	14W-5S	C1
1600	FSMR	60422	3507	2W-23S	D4
1700	BlmT	60422	3507	2W-23S	D4
1700	CHHT	60422	3507	2W-23S	D4
Princeton St					
10	DSPN	60016	2862	14W-12N	C1
100	HFET	60169	2858	24W-10N	D5
E Princeton St					
500	PLTN	60074	2753	20W-17N	A5
S Princeton St					
200	ADSN	60101	2971	18W-3N	A6
Princeton Cir Dr					
-	HRPK	60133	2912	26W-8N	A3
Princetown Ct					
700	CLSM	60188	2967	27W-3N	D5
Principal Av					
400	MDLN	60060	2590	18W-28N	D5
W Prindiville St					
2700	CHCG	60647	2977	2W-3N	C5
N Prindle Av					
10	ANHT	60004	2807	16W-14N	D5
2200	ANHT	60004	2754	16W-16N	C7
2600	WLNG	60004	2754	16W-16N	D6
2600	WLNG	60090	2754	16W-16N	D6
S Prindle Av					
10	ANHT	60004	2807	16W-13N	D6
Pringle Dr					
1700	MngT	60152	2578	50W-29N	A3
W Prior St					
400	JLET	60436	3498	24W-24S	D5
Priscilla Av					
2900	HDPK	60035	2704	9W-23N	C2
E Priscilla Ln					
2400	CteT	60417	3597	3E-28S	E7
2500	CteT	60417	3598	3E-28S	A7
Pristine Pl					
16100	ODHL	60487	3424	11W-19S	A2
Private Dr					
-	GRNE	60031	2478	14W-36N	D5
-	MaiT	60016	2863	12W-12N	C1
8700	ODPK	60462	3346	10W-16S	A4
Private Ln					
200	ODHL	60013	2641	31W-26N	D3
Private Rd					
-	CbaT	60010	2643	27W-24N	C6
800	WNKA	60093	2759	5W-16N	A7
Privet Ct					
600	CmpT	60175	2905	41W-6N	E7
Privett Ct					
10	BGBK	60490	3267	26W-11S	E1
Proctor Av					
400	GYLK	60030	2533	20W-32N	A4
W Proctor Cir					
3900	ANHT	60004	2754	18W-18N	A3
Prodehl Dr					
1200	LKPT	60441	3420	21W-19S	A2
Production Dr					
300	SEGN	60177	2908	34W-9N	C1
1600	SCRL	60174	2964	34W-3N	E6
2600	SCRL	60174	2965	33W-3N	A6
W Proesel Av					
6400	CHCG	60659	2920	4W-8N	B3
6400	CHCG	60712	2920	4W-8N	B3
6400	LNWD	60712	2920	4W-8N	C2

Block	City	ZIP	Map#	CGS	Grid
Professional Plaza Dr					
1600	MHRY	60050	2585	32W-31N	A1
Progress Av					
600	MNSR	46321	3510		D3
Progress Dr					
900	GYLK	60030	2533	19W-32N	B4
E Progress Rd					
10	LMBD	60148	3026	19W-2N	C1
N Prologis Pkwy					
700	BGBK	60446	3268	24W-14S	D7
700	RMVL	60446	3268	24W-14S	D7
Promenade Ln					
1500	WHTN	60187	3082	25W-1S	A2
Promethian Wy					
20600	OMFD	60461	3507	3W-24S	B6
Promontory Ct					
500	SchT	60175	2907	38W-6N	B7
Promontory Dr					
-	PGGV	60140	2797	43W-15N	C4
5400	LGGV	60047	2701	17W-23N	A3
S Promontory Dr					
6400	CHCG	60637	3153	2E-7S	C5
Promontory Ln					
300	WCDA	60084	2644	25W-27N	A1
4700	JNBG	60050	2472	30W-36N	A3
5000	MchT	60050	2472	30W-36N	A3
5300	LGGV	60047	2701	18W-23N	A3
Prospect Av					
-	BtnT	60099	2422	8W-40N	E2
-	WKGN	60085	2536	11W-32N	C5
10	ADSN	60191	2970	19W-5N	D1
10	HDPK	60035	2705	8W-22N	A5
10	WDDL	60191	2970	19W-5N	D1
200	GNEN	60137	3025	22W-0S	B6
200	WDDL	60191	2914	19W-5N	D7
300	HDPK	60035	2704	8W-22N	E5
300	WDDL	60143	2914	19W-5N	D7
600	BRTN	60010	2750	25W-20N	E1
600	EMHT	60126	3027	16W-0S	E7
600	WNKA	60093	2812	5W-16N	B1
600	YkTp	60126	3027	16W-0S	E7
700	BRTN	60010	2697	25W-20N	E7
800	WLSP	60480	3209	12W-9S	C4
800	WNKA	60093	2759	5W-16N	A7
1200	DSPN	60018	2862	13W-9N	E7
1400	NCHI	60064	2536	11W-32N	C5
1600	DSPN	60018	2863	12W-9N	A7
2100	EVTN	60201	2866	4W-12N	C1
2500	EVTN	60201	2812	4W-12N	C7
4300	DRGV	60515	3084	18W-4S	E7
4300	DRGV	60515	3144	19W-4S	D1
4300	WNSP	60558	3086	14W-4S	D7
4300	WNSP	60558	3146	14W-4S	D1
5800	BKLY	60163	3028	14W-0N	C5
5800	HLSD	60162	3028	14W-0N	C5
5800	HLSD	60163	3028	14W-0N	C5
11300	ITSC	60143	2914	18W-6N	E6
E Prospect Av					
-	DSPN	60016	2862	15W-12N	B1
-	MPPT	60016	2862	15W-12N	B1
10	MPPT	60056	2808	14W-13N	B5
100	LKBF	60044	2594	10W-28N	A6
100	MPPT	60056	2862	15W-12N	A1
N Prospect Av					
-	AddT	60191	2914	19W-7N	D4
-	ITSC	60191	2914	19W-7N	D4
10	CNHL	60514	3145	16W-5S	D2
10	ITSC	60143	2914	18W-7N	D5
100	BRLT	60103	2911	28W-8N	A2
100	MDLN	60060	2590	18W-27N	E7
100	MDLN	60060	2646	18W-27N	E2
100	PKRG	60068	2864	10W-9N	B7
300	AddT	60143	2914	18W-7N	D5
900	NLES	60068	2864	10W-9N	B7
4800	NRDG	60706	2918	10W-6N	B7
5500	CHCG	60631	2918	10W-7N	A5
5500	CHCG	60656	2918	10W-6N	A5
5500	LydT	60631	2918	10W-6N	A5
5500	LydT	60656	2918	10W-6N	A5
5500	MaiT	60631	2918	10W-7N	A5
8800	NLES	60714	2864	10W-11N	B3
N Prospect Av CO-10					
-	AddT	60191	2914	19W-7N	D4
-	ITSC	60191	2914	19W-7N	D4
10	ITSC	60143	2914	18W-7N	D5
300	AddT	60143	2914	18W-7N	D5
S Prospect Av					
10	CNHL	60514	3145	16W-5S	D2
100	BRLT	60103	2911	28W-7N	A5
100	EMHT	60126	3027	16W-1N	E3
100	ITSC	60143	2914	18W-6N	D7
200	WDDL	60143	2914	18W-6N	D7
200	WDDL	60191	2914	18W-6N	D7
700	WynT	60103	2911	28W-7N	A4
1000	YkTp	60126	3027	16W-0S	E7
1100	PKRG	60068	2918	10W-7N	A3
1800	CHCG	60631	2918	10W-7N	A4
1800	PKRG	60631	2918	10W-7N	A4
9500	CHCG	60620	3213	2W-11S	D6
9500	CHCG	60643	3213	2W-11S	D6
10200	CHCG	60643	3277	2W-12S	D2
S Prospect Av CO-10					
100	ITSC	60143	2914	19W-6N	D7
200	WDDL	60143	2914	19W-6N	D7
200	WDDL	60191	2914	19W-6N	D7
W Prospect Av					
10	MPPT	60056	2808	15W-12N	A7
300	LKBF	60044	2593	11W-28N	D6
1000	MPPT	60056	2807	16W-13N	D6
26100	AntT	60002	2356	26W-42N	D5
Prospect Blvd					
800	ELGN	60120	2855	33W-12N	A2
Prospect Cir					
-	PGGV	60140	2797	42W-15N	C4
Prospect Ct					
10	PTHT	60070	2807	15W-15N	E3
900	NPVL	60540	3203	28W-8S	B1
1600	WHTN	60187	3083	23W-1S	A2
2500	AURA	60502	3079	31W-4S	E7
W Prospect Ct					
8000	NLES	60714	2864	10W-10N	B6
Prospect Dr					
-	BRTN	60010	2751	24W-18N	C2
10	LkvT	60046	2475	20W-37N	E1
10	LNHT	60046	2475	20W-37N	E1
10	PTHT	60070	2755	15W-16N	A6
10	WLNG	60090	2755	15W-16N	A6
100	FmtT	60060	2646	19W-26N	C2
100	PltT	60010	2751	24W-18N	C2
2300	AURA	60502	3139	31W-4S	E1
N Prospect Dr					
200	RLKP	60073	2532	22W-33N	B2
34000	WrnT	60030	2533	18W-33N	D2
Prospect Ln					
-	MTGY	60543	3263	37W-11S	B1
1000	DSPN	60018	2862	13W-9N	E6

Block	City	ZIP	Map#	CGS	Grid
Prospect Pl					
-	FXLK	60081	2414	29W-39N	D6
6800	BtnT	60081	2414	29W-38N	D6
11100	ODPK	60467	3423	13W-21S	A6
W Prospect Pl					
500	JLET	60436	3498	25W-24S	C6
Prospect Rd					
10	LKZH	60047	2698	24W-23N	C1
S Prospect Sq					
9100	CHCG	60620	3213	2W-10S	C5
Prospect St					
-	RcmT	60071	2353	34W-41N	C7
-	RHMD	60071	2353	34W-41N	C7
400	ELGN	60120	2855	33W-12N	A2
8300	DrrT	60012	2583	37W-27N	C7
8300	DrrT	60098	2583	37W-27N	C7
N Prospect St					
100	MRGO	60152	2634	49W-26N	C2
100	ROSL	60172	2913	23W-7N	A4
400	WHTN	60187	3024	23W-0S	E6
S Prospect St					
10	ROSL	60172	2913	23W-7N	A5
100	MRGO	60152	2634	49W-26N	C3
100	WHTN	60187	3024	23W-0S	E7
800	WHTN	60187	3082	23W-1S	E1
1500	WHTN	60187	3083	23W-1S	A2
N Prospect Manor Av					
10	MPPT	60056	2807	15W-13N	E6
Prosper Ct					
10	LIHL	60156	2694	34W-22N	C4
Prosperi Dr					
-	TYPK	60477	3505	8W-22S	A2
Proud Clarion Ct					
800	NPVL	60540	3141	26W-7S	E7
Provencal Dr					
700	BRRG	60527	3208	15W-10S	A6
700	DGvT	60527	3208	15W-10S	A6
S Provencal Dr					
14300	HMGN	60491	3343	16W-17S	D5
Provence Ct					
3500	SCRL	60175	2963	38W-3N	B6
Provence Dr					
3600	SchT	60175	2963	38W-3N	B5
3600	SCRL	60175	2963	38W-3N	B5
Provence Ln					
8400	WLSP	60480	3209	13W-9S	A3
Provence Pl					
800	LIHL	60156	2692	38W-22N	E4
Providence Av					
2500	AURA	60503	3201	32W-10S	C7
Providence Cir					
1300	ELGN	60120	2801	32W-12N	D7
Providence Ct					
10	CRY	60013	2695	33W-23N	A1
400	BGBK	60440	3269	22W-12S	C3
600	CLLK	60012	2640	33W-26N	D2
900	BFGV	60089	2700	18W-21N	E6
900	BFGV	60089	2701	18W-21N	A7
2300	NPVL	60565	3203	27W-10S	C5
6200	CPVL	60110	2747	36W-17N	A6
7200	LGGV	60047	2646	18W-25N	E5
Providence Dr					
-	CteT	60417	3774	0W-33S	D2
-	DRGV	60517	3144	21W-7S	A7
10	MTSN	60443	3505	6W-24S	E5
10	MTSN	60443	3506	6W-24S	A6
700	ALGN	60102	2694	35W-20N	A7
1400	LKMR	60051	2529	29W-33N	C3
1400	MchT	60051	2529	29W-33N	C3
2000	BRLT	60103	2909	32W-8N	C3
2000	WDRG	60517	3144	21W-7S	A7
2000	WDRG	60517	3206	21W-8S	A1
5700	HFET	60192	2856	31W-12N	A2
6100	CPVL	60110	2747	36W-17N	A6
30000	LbvT	60048	2591	17W-30N	B2
30000	LYVL	60048	2591	17W-30N	B2
N Providence Dr					
23100	KLDR	60047	2699	21W-23N	D3
Providence Ln					
-	LYWD	60411	3509	2E-24S	C5
10	SMWD	60107	2856	29W-9N	E7
200	WNFD	60190	3023	27W-0N	C4
400	WnfT	60185	3023	27W-0N	C4
400	WnfT	60190	3023	27W-0N	C4
600	CLLK	60012	2640	33W-26N	D2
600	LNHT	60046	2418	19W-39N	C6
600	NndT	60012	2640	33W-26N	D2
900	BFGV	60089	2700	18W-20N	E7
900	BFGV	60089	2701	18W-21N	A7
2700	MTGY	60538	3198	40W-10S	C6
2900	MTGY	60512	3198	40W-10S	B6
S Providence Ln					
700	RDLK	60073	2532	23W-32N	A5
700	RLKP	60030	2532	23W-32N	A5
W Providence Ln					
-	RDLK	60073	2531	23W-32N	E5
10	RDLK	60073	2532	23W-32N	A5
Providence Rd					
4500	GRNE	60031	2535	14W-33N	C3
E Providence Rd					
-	BRTN	60010	2697	25W-20N	E7
-	BRTN	60010	2698	25W-21N	A7
-	CbaT	60010	2697	25W-20N	E7
-	CbaT	60010	2698	25W-21N	A7
-	DRPK	60010	2698	25W-21N	A7
400	PLTN	60067	2753	20W-16N	A6
400	PLTN	60074	2753	20W-16N	A6
Providence Sq					
9400	ODPK	60467	3423	11W-19S	D2
Provident Av					
300	WNKA	60093	2812	5W-15N	A2
Province Dr					
-	LMNT	60439	3270	20W-14S	A7
Provincetown Ct					
10	LNSH	60069	2702	14W-23N	B2
Provincetown Dr					
700	CLSM	60188	2967	27W-3N	D5
1100	CCHL	60478	3506	5W-22S	C1
1100	HLCT	60429	3506	4W-22S	D1
Proviso Dr					
4700	BKLY	60163	3028	13W-1N	E3
4700	BLWD	60104	3028	13W-1N	E3
4700	BLWD	60104	3029	13W-0N	A3
4700	BLWD	60160	3028	13W-1N	E3
4700	MLPK	60160	3028	13W-1N	E3
4700	MLPK	60163	3028	13W-1N	E3
4800	BKLY	60160	3028	13W-1N	E3
Prunetree Ln					
800	CmpT	60175	2906	39W-6N	D7
Pruthmore Ct					
6400	LSLE	60532	3142	24W-6S	D5
Pruxne St					
-	LMNT	60439	3270	19W-13S	E5
W Pryor Av					
1700	CHCG	60643	3277	2W-12S	C2

Block	City	ZIP	Map#	CGS	Grid
Ptarmigan Ct					
2400	AURA	60502	3079	32W-3S	C6
Ptarmigan Pl					
400	LNHT	60046	2476	19W-37N	C2
Public Rd					
-	GrtT	60041	2474	25W-36N	A3
-	HMGN	60491	3342	19W-16S	D3
-	HmrT	60491	3342	19W-16S	D3
Public St					
-	VNHL	60061	2647	17W-24N	B7
10	PGGV	60140	2798	41W-14N	A7
Public Service Rd					
200	WKGN	60085	2536	12W-33N	B1
600	WKGN	60085	2479	12W-33N	B7
Public Works Dr					
6600	BRWN	60402	3089	8W-2S	A4
Pueblo Ct					
100	FKFT	60423	3503	12W-25S	D7
800	NPVL	60565	3203	27W-10S	B7
S Pueblo Ct					
13000	PSHT	60463	3346	9W-15S	E1
17200	LKPT	60441	3420	20W-20S	A5
Pueblo Dr					
200	BGBK	60440	3268	24W-11S	E1
500	JLET	60451	3500	19W-23S	D3
1000	BTVA	60510	3020	36W-0S	A7
2600	NndT	60051	2528	31W-31N	D7
W Pueblo Ln					
7200	PSHT	60463	3346	9W-15S	E1
Pueblo Rd					
10	OswT	60538	3199	36W-10S	E7
100	CPVL	60110	2748	33W-18N	B4
Pueblo Tr					
400	WLNG	60090	2754	16W-17N	C5
Pueblo Peak					
600	PltT	60124	2906	39W-9N	E1
Puffer Rd					
4600	DRGV	60515	3143	21W-5S	E2
5900	DRGV	60516	3143	21W-6S	E5
5900	LslT	60516	3143	21W-6S	E5
6500	WDRG	60516	3143	21W-7S	E6
6500	WDRG	60517	3143	21W-7S	E6
Puffin Cir					
10	BGBK	60440	3205	21W-10S	D5
Pulaski Av					
4500	LYNS	60534	3088	10W-4S	A7
4500	LYNS	60534	3148	10W-5S	A1
4500	MCCK	60525	3148	10W-5S	A2
4500	MCCK	60534	3148	10W-5S	A2
Pulaski Rd					
10	CTCY	60409	3352	3E-17S	A6
10	HMND	46320	3352	3E-17S	A6
1100	CTCY	60409	3351	2E-17S	D6
1700	ThtT	60409	3351	2E-17S	D6
1700	ThtT	60473	3351	2E-17S	D6
14000	CTWD	60445	3348	5W-17S	C5
14000	CTWD	60472	3348	5W-17S	C5
14200	MDLN	60445	3348	4W-16S	C4
15000	BmnT	60426	3348	4W-17S	C6
15000	MDLN	60426	3348	4W-17S	C6
15400	MDLN	60428	3348	4W-18S	C7
15400	MKHM	60426	3348	4W-18S	C7
15400	MKHM	60428	3348	4W-18S	C7
15600	BmnT	60426	3426	5W-21S	D6
15600	MKHM	60426	3426	5W-21S	D6
15600	MKHM	60428	3426	5W-21S	D6
15900	BmnT	60428	3426	4W-19S	C1
16300	OKFT	60428	3426	4W-19S	D3
16300	OKFT	60452	3426	4W-19S	D3
16500	MKHM	60452	3426	4W-19S	D3
16600	CCHL	60452	3426	4W-19S	D3
16600	CCHL	60478	3426	5W-20S	D4
17800	BmnT	60430	3426	4W-21S	D6
17800	CCHL	60430	3426	4W-21S	D6
18200	HLCT	60429	3426	4W-21S	D7
18300	CCHL	60478	3506	5W-22S	D2
18300	HLCT	60429	3506	5W-22S	D2
18500	CCHL	60422	3506	5W-22S	D2
18500	CCHL	60429	3506	5W-22S	D2
18500	FSMR	60422	3506	5W-22S	D2
18500	FSMR	60429	3506	5W-22S	D2
19000	FSMR	60430	3506	4W-22S	D2
19100	RchT	60430	3506	4W-23S	D2
19100	RchT	60478	3506	4W-23S	D3
19400	RchT	60443	3506	4W-23S	D3
N Pulaski Rd					
10	CHCG	60624	3032	4W-0N	B5
700	CHCG	60651	3032	4W-0N	C4
1500	CHCG	60639	3032	4W-1N	B1
1500	CHCG	60647	3032	4W-1N	B1
1600	CHCG	60639	2976	5W-2N	B7
1600	CHCG	60647	2976	5W-2N	B7
2700	CHCG	60618	2976	5W-5N	B1
2800	CHCG	60641	2976	5W-5N	B1
4300	CHCG	60625	2976	4W-5N	B1
4300	CHCG	60630	2976	4W-5N	B1
4400	CHCG	60625	2920	4W-5N	B7
4400	CHCG	60630	2920	4W-5N	B7
5400	CHCG	60646	2920	5W-5N	B7
5400	CHCG	60659	2920	5W-5N	B7
6300	CHCG	60712	2920	4W-7N	B3
6300	LNWD	60712	2920	4W-7N	B3
S Pulaski Rd					
10	CHCG	60624	3032	5W-1S	C7
1100	CHCG	60623	3032	4W-0S	C7
1500	CHCG	60623	3090	4W-4S	C7
3300	CHCG	60632	3090	4W-4S	C7
4600	CHCG	60632	3150	5W-6S	C4
5400	CHCG	60629	3150	4W-5S	C3
7400	CHCG	60629	3212	4W-8S	C1
7400	CHCG	60652	3212	5W-9S	C3
8700	CHCG	60456	3212	4W-10S	C4
8700	HMTN	60456	3212	4W-10S	C4
8700	HMTN	60652	3212	4W-10S	C4
8800	CHCG	60805	3212	5W-10S	C4
9000	ENGN	60805	3212	5W-11S	C7
9000	OKLN	60453	3212	5W-11S	C7
9300	ENGN	60453	3212	5W-11S	C7
9800	CHCG	60453	3212	4W-11S	C7
9800	CHCG	60655	3212	4W-11S	C7
10100	OKLN	60655	3212	4W-11S	C7
10200	CHCG	60655	3276	4W-12S	C2
10200	OKLN	60453	3276	4W-12S	C2
10200	OKLN	60655	3276	4W-11S	C1
10300	CHCG	60453	3276	4W-12S	C2
11300	ALSP	60655	3276	5W-13S	C4
11300	ALSP	60803	3276	5W-14S	C6
12900	ALSP	60803	3348	4W-15S	C1
13100	ALSP	60472	3348	4W-15S	C1
13100	CTWD	60472	3348	4W-16S	C2
13400	RBBN	60472	3348	4W-16S	C2
13800	CTWD	60445	3348	4W-16S	C3
W Pulaski Rd					
5200	MchT	60050	2527	34W-34N	D1
Pulawski St					
-	LMNT	60439	3270	19W-14S	E6

Block	City	ZIP	Map#	CGS	Grid
W Pullman Ct					
9200	MKNA	60448	3503	12W-22S	D1
Pullman Rd					
-	CrlT	60180	2635	46W-24N	C6
-	UNON	60180	2635	46W-24N	C6
500	RMVL	60446	3340	25W-15S	A2
Pulse Ln					
-	MRGO	60152	2634	48W-26N	D2
-	SenT	60152	2634	48W-26N	D2
Pump St					
-	BRTN	60010	2750	25W-20N	E1
Purchase Ct					
10	BGBK	60440	3205	22W-10S	C6
Purchase Dr					
6300	WDRG	60517	3143	23W-7S	B6
Purdue Av					
1300	NPVL	60565	3204	24W-9S	C4
S Purdue Av					
300	JLET	60436	3497	26W-24S	E6
Purdue Ln					
300	ELGN	60123	2853	36W-10N	E6
800	MTSN	60443	3505	6W-25S	E7
Purdue Pl					
-	CLLK	60012	2640	33W-27N	E1
-	CLLK	60012	2641	33W-27N	A1
4900	NndT	60012	2640	33W-27N	E1
Purdy Ln					
400	CNHL	60514	3145	17W-6S	C3
Purify Dr					
10	ELGN	60120	2855	33W-9N	A7
10	ElgT	60120	2855	33W-9N	A7
Puritan Dr					
19100	MKNA	60448	3503	13W-23S	B2
Purity Dr					
-	WNFD	60190	3023	28W-0S	A6
-	WnfT	60190	3023	28W-0S	A6
W Purley Ct					
15400	HMGN	60491	3342	19W-16S	D3
Purnell Rd					
200	WnfT	60185	3081	28W-1S	A2
200	WnfT	60187	3081	28W-1S	A2
200	WnfT	60190	3081	28W-1S	A2
600	WnfT	60185	3080	29W-1S	E1
Purnell St					
10	MltT	60188	3024	25W-1N	B3
10	WHTN	60187	3024	25W-1N	B3
200	CLSM	60188	3024	25W-1N	B3
400	MltT	60187	3024	25W-0N	B4
Putnam Ct					
800	OSWG	60543	3263	36W-12S	E4
Putnam Dr					
900	LKPT	60441	3419	21W-19S	E3
2300	NPVL	60565	3203	26W-10S	E5
Putnam Ln					
400	SMBG	60193	2912	24W-9N	E1
Putnam St					
300	WDSK	60098	2581	42W-30N	C1
Putney Pl					
14000	ODPK	60462	3346	10W-16S	C4
Putter Ct					
200	JLET	60435	3497	27W-23S	D4
Pyndale Dr					
4800	MHRY	60050	2527	33W-32N	D5
Pynsky Rd					
3400	GNVW	60025	2809	11W-15N	C3
Pyott Rd					
100	ALGN	60102	2694	34W-21N	C6
100	LIHL	60156	2694	34W-23N	B2
800	CLLK	60014	2640	35W-24N	B7
800	CLLK	60156	2640	35W-24N	B7
800	LIHL	60156	2640	35W-24N	B7
8000	CLLK	60156	2694	34W-23N	B2
Pyott Rd CO-V32					
100	ALGN	60102	2694	34W-21N	C6
100	LIHL	60156	2694	34W-23N	B2
800	CLLK	60014	2640	35W-24N	B7
800	CLLK	60156	2640	35W-24N	B7
800	LIHL	60156	2640	35W-24N	B7
8000	CLLK	60156	2694	34W-23N	B2
Pyramid Dr					
7000	JLET	60586	3415	32W-20S	C5
7000	NasT	60586	3415	32W-20S	B5

Q

Block	City	ZIP	Map#	CGS	Grid
Quadrangle Dr					
300	BGBK	60440	3269	23W-12S	A3
Quail Cir					
200	LNHT	60046	2417	21W-38N	E7
W Quail Cir					
7300	FftT	60423	3504	9W-24S	E5
Quail Cross					
9400	TYPK	60487	3423	11W-21S	E5
10900	RHMD	60071	2353	34W-42N	D5
Quail Ct					
10	WDRG	60517	3143	21W-7S	E7
200	BDWD	60408	3942	31W-41S	B4
500	CmpT	60175	2961	42W-5N	C2
1300	ANTH	60002	2416	24W-41N	C1
1700	WDSK	60098	2524	41W-32N	C5
1800	FSMR	60422	3507	3W-23S	A4
2100	RGMW	60008	2806	19W-13N	D6
2400	AURA	60502	3079	32W-3S	D6
2500	JNBG	60050	2471	31W-37N	D1
12700	PSHT	60463	3275	8W-15S	B7
16100	ODHL	60487	3423	11W-19S	E2
19300	JknT	60421	3675	24W-30S	E3
23300	DRPK	60010	2698	23W-21N	E6
W Quail Ct					
400	PNFD	60544	3338	30W-16S	C4
1600	ANHT	60004	2753	18W-18N	D2
21500	KLDR	60047	2699	21W-21N	D5
Quail Dr					
10	LKFT	60045	2649	11W-25N	E6
200	BfdT	53128	2353		B1
200	GNCY	53128	2353		B1
400	NPVL	60565	3203	26W-9S	D3
1200	JLET	60586	3496	29W-22S	C1
11000	MKNA	60448	3503	13W-22S	A1
Quail Hl					
-	HMGN	60441	3421	18W-20S	A5
-	HMGN	60491	3421	18W-20S	A5
-	LKPT	60441	3421	18W-20S	A4
-	LKPT	60491	3421	18W-20S	A4
Quail Ln					
-	ELGN	60123	2800	35W-13N	C7
-	HMGN	60491	3344	15W-16S	B4
100	CTSD	60525	3147	12W-6S	B5
2100	RGMW	60008	2806	19W-13N	C6
2600	NHBK	60062	2809	10W-15N	E2
Quail Pth					
100	FXLK	60041	2473	27W-35N	C7
Quail Run					
10	LIHL	60156	2694	35W-21N	A5
700	IVNS	60067	2804	23W-14N	E4

Block	City	ZIP	Map#	CGS	Grid
Quail St					
-	BtvT	60539	3077	36W-3S	D6
-	BtvT	60542	3077	36W-3S	D6
4200	ZION	60099	2362	12W-42N	B7
Quail Tr					
9400	TYPK	60487	3423	11W-21S	E5
E Quail Tr					
17500	TYPK	60487	3423	11W-21S	E5
W Quail Tr					
17500	TYPK	60487	3423	11W-21S	E5
S Quail Wk					
1300	MPPT	60056	2861	16W-11N	E3
Quail Wy					
1600	CLLK	60014	2693	37W-22N	A3
Quail Cove					
2500	CPVL	60110	2746	37W-17N	D6
Quail Creek Dr					
500	GYLK	60030	2533	20W-33N	A3
Quailhaven Ct					
100	GRNE	60031	2534	16W-34N	D2
Quail Hollow Ct					
10	HNWD	60047	2700	20W-23N	B1
10	NPVL	60540	3142	26W-6S	A5
S Quail Hollow Ct					
200	RDLK	60073	2531	24W-32N	C4
Quail Hollow Dr					
200	BCHR	60401	3774	0W-35S	D6
400	WLNG	60090	2755	15W-18N	B3
15100	ODPK	60462	3346	10W-18S	B6
Quail Hollow Ln					
-	FmtT	60060	2645	22W-26N	A4
-	HNWD	60060	2645	22W-26N	A4
W Quail Hollow Ln					
1200	PLTN	60067	2805	22W-14N	B4
Quail Hollow Rd					
10	HNWD	60047	2700	20W-23N	B1
Quail Ridge Ct					
10600	WldT	60564	3266	29W-12S	D3
Quail Ridge Dr					
100	WTMT	60559	3085	16W-3S	D5
12100	HTLY	60142	2744	42W-18N	E4
17700	LKPT	60441	3419	22W-20S	D5
Quail Run Av					
1100	BGBK	60440	3268	25W-12S	A4
1100	BGBK	60490	3268	25W-12S	A4
Quail Run Ct					
10	WNFD	60190	3023	27W-0S	D6
100	CLSM	60188	3024	25W-2N	B1
400	DRN	60527	3145	17W-7S	D6
13600	HMGN	60491	3342	19W-16S	D3
Quail Run Dr					
10	MltT	60187	3023	26W-0N	E4
10	MltT	60187	3024	26W-0N	A4
600	PNFD	60544	3338	30W-16S	B4
Quail Run Rd					
500	MTSN	60443	3505	7W-24S	C6
Quails Roost Dr					
2000	NLNX	60451	3590	15W-25S	B1
2000	NlxT	60451	3590	15W-25S	B1
Quaker Ln					
1300	MPPT	60056	2808	13W-15N	E2
1300	PTHT	60070	2808	13W-15N	E2
Quaker Hill Ct					
400	AURA	60504	3140	30W-7S	A7
1000	ELGN	60120	2855	32W-12N	D2
Quaker Hill Ln					
900	LYVL	60048	2591	17W-29N	A4
Quaker Hollow Ct N					
1500	BFGV	60089	2701	16W-21N	E5
Quaker Hollow Ct S					
1500	BFGV	60089	2701	16W-21N	E6
Quaker Hollow Ln					
1800	SMWD	60107	2857	26W-11N	D4
E Quaker Hollow Ln					
300	RLKB	60073	2475	22W-36N	B4
N Quaker Hollow Ln					
2200	RLKB	60073	2475	22W-36N	B4
W Quaker Ridge Ct					
500	VNHL	60061	2647	17W-26N	B3
Quality Dr					
13800	HTLY	60142	2744	42W-18N	E5
Quanset Ct					
1000	SMBG	60194	2858	24W-10N	C5
Quantock Ln					
-	OswT	60560	3334	40W-15S	C2
Quark Ct					
200	BTVA	60510	3078	35W-2S	B5
Quarry Cir					
200	SgrT	60506	3135	41W-6S	E4
Quarry Ct					
10	SEGN	60177	2908	34W-9N	D2
Quarry Dr					
300	BGBK	60490	3268	25W-12S	B3
Quarry Ln					
300	ALGN	60102	2748	33W-19N	A2
300	AlqT	60102	2748	33W-19N	A2
Quarry Rd					
-	DGvT	60439	3270	19W-12S	E3
-	DGvT	60439	3271	18W-12S	A2
Quarry St					
10	JltT	60436	3586	24W-25S	E2
200	SEGN	60177	2908	34W-8N	C2
Quarter Horse Ct					
1700	WHTN	60187	3082	24W-2S	C3
Quarterhorse Ct					
10	SMWD	60107	2856	30W-10N	C5
Quarterhouse Ct					
1200	SCRL	60174	2964	34W-4N	D5
Quartz Ct					
11600	FKFT	60423	3590	14W-27S	D4
Quassey Av					
400	ShdT	60044	2593	12W-29N	B5
1100	LbvT	60044	2593	13W-29N	A5
Quassey St					
400	ShdT	60044	2593	12W-29N	C5
Quayside Ct					
10	ALGN	60102	2693	37W-20N	A7
Quebec Pl					
700	WTMT	60559	3085	17W-4S	C7
Queen Dr					
600	OSWG	60543	3264	34W-11S	C1
Queen Ann Ln					
1000	LKZH	60047	2698	23W-21N	E5
1200	GRNE	60031	2478	14W-35N	B6
17300	TYPK	60477	3424	10W-20S	C5
Queen Ann Rd					
3600	GNWD	60098	2468	40W-36N	B4
3600	GwdT	60098	2468	40W-36N	B4
5100	GwdT	60034	2468	40W-37N	B2
5100	HbnT	60034	2468	40W-37N	B2
Queen Anne Ct					
3700	SCRL	60174	2965	33W-4N	B4
N Queen Anne Rd					
10	BLVY	60098	2525	39W-31N	B6
10	DrrT	60098	2525	39W-31N	B6
10	GwdT	60098	2525	39W-31N	B6

STREET Block	City	ZIP	Map#	CGS	Grid
N Queen Anne Rd					
10	WDSK	60098	2525	39W-31N	B6
2600	GwdT	60098	2468	40W-34N	B7
S Queen Anne Rd					
10	BLVY	60098	2525	39W-31N	B7
10	DrrT	60098	2525	39W-31N	B7
Queen Anne St					
600	WDSK	60098	2524	41W-31N	C6
Queen Elizabeth Ct					
3700	SCRL	60174	2965	33W-4N	B4
Queen Elizabeth Ln					
17300	TYPK	60477	3424	10W-21S	C5
Queen Mary Ln					
17300	TYPK	60477	3424	10W-20S	C5
Queens Ct					
10	WSTR	60154	3086	13W-2S	E3
100	SMBG	60193	2859	23W-9N	A7
800	PLTN	60074	2753	19W-18N	B2
1100	NPVL	60563	3140	29W-5S	D3
1600	WLNG	60090	2754	16W-18N	D3
1700	CPVL	60110	2748	33W-18N	B5
7500	DRGV	60516	3206	18W-8S	E2
7500	DRN	60516	3206	18W-8S	E2
11900	MKNA	60448	3502	14W-23S	D3
S Queens Ct					
22500	TroT	60404	3584	30W-27S	B4
Queens Ln					
100	TNTN	60476	3428	0E-20S	D5
300	ThtT	60476	3428	0E-20S	E5
800	GNVW	60025	2811	7W-14N	B4
800	GNVW	60093	2811	7W-14N	B4
800	NHFD	60093	2811	7W-14N	B4
Queens Pkwy					
300	BRLT	60103	2910	29W-8N	E2
Queens Rd					
18700	HMWD	60430	3508	1W-22S	A2
Queens Wy					
10	LNSH	60069	2702	13W-22N	E3
2500	NHBK	60062	2809	10W-15N	E1
Queensbridge Dr					
-	LYWD	60411	3509	2E-23S	D4
Queensburg Ct					
10	ALGN	60102	2693	37W-21N	B6
N Queensburg Ct					
2100	PLTN	60074	2753	20W-20N	B1
N Queensburg Ln					
2100	PLTN	60074	2753	19W-18N	C3
Queensbury Cir					
1600	HFET	60169	2858	25W-12N	A1
Queensbury Ct					
900	NPVL	60563	3140	29W-5S	E3
2000	LMBD	60148	3083	21W-1S	E2
N Queensbury Ct					
2500	AURA	60506	3136	39W-7S	E7
N Queensbury Ln					
1000	BHPK	60083	2421	13W-39N	A5
1000	BHPK	60099	2421	13W-39N	A5
N Queensbury Ln SR-158					
4400	BHPK	60099	2421	13W-39N	A5
Queens Cove					
100	BRTN	60010	2751	25W-18N	B3
5800	LslT	60532	3143	22W-6S	B5
Queens Gate Cir					
700	SRGV	60554	3135	41W-5S	E2
Queensgreen Cir					
1300	NPVL	60563	3140	29W-5S	E3
Queensgreen Ct					
1500	NPVL	60563	3140	29W-5S	E2
Queensport Dr					
1700	CLLK	60014	2693	37W-22N	B4
Queenswood Ct					
800	WHTN	60187	3082	25W-1S	B2
Queenswood Ln					
500	WHTN	60187	3082	24W-1S	D2
Queenswood Rd					
100	BGBK	60440	3269	21W-11S	D2
Queen Victoria Ln					
8200	TYPK	60477	3424	10W-20S	B5
8300	TYPK	60487	3424	10W-20S	B5
Quentin Rd					
2600	RGMW	60008	2805	22W-13N	C6
2600	RGMW	60173	2805	21W-13N	C5
2600	SMBG	60008	2805	21W-13N	C5
2600	SMBG	60173	2805	21W-13N	C6
2800	RGMW	60067	2805	22W-13N	C6
21300	KLDR	60047	2699	21W-21N	C6
21600	LKZH	60047	2699	21W-21N	C5
Quentin Rd CO-V62					
21300	KLDR	60047	2699	21W-21N	C6
21600	LKZH	60047	2699	21W-21N	C5
N Quentin Rd					
10	PLTN	60067	2805	22W-16N	C1
10	PltT	60067	2805	22W-16N	C1
100	PLTN	60067	2752	22W-16N	C7
100	PltT	60067	2752	22W-16N	C7
800	PltT	60067	2752	21W-17N	C5
1500	PltT	60074	2752	21W-17N	C5
1900	PLTN	60074	2752	21W-20N	C2
2300	DRPK	60010	2752	22W-20N	C1
2300	PltT	60010	2752	22W-18N	C2
20000	DRPK	60074	2752	22W-20N	C1
20600	DRPK	60047	2752	22W-20N	C1
20600	DRPK	60074	2699	22W-20N	C7
20600	KLDR	60047	2752	22W-20N	C1
20800	ElaT	60074	2699	21W-21N	C7
20800	KLDR	60074	2699	21W-21N	C7
22000	KLDR	60047	2699	21W-22N	C3
22000	LKZH	60047	2699	21W-22N	C3
22600	ElaT	60047	2699	21W-22N	C3
23500	HNWD	60047	2699	21W-23N	C2
24200	ElaT	60047	2645	21W-24N	C7
24200	HNWD	60047	2645	21W-24N	C7
N Quentin Rd CO-V62					
20000	DRPK	60010	2752	22W-20N	C1
20000	DRPK	60074	2752	22W-20N	C1
20000	PltT	60010	2752	22W-20N	C2
20000	PltT	60074	2752	22W-20N	C2
20600	DRPK	60047	2752	22W-20N	C1
20600	DRPK	60074	2699	22W-20N	C7
20600	KLDR	60047	2699	22W-20N	C7
20600	KLDR	60047	2752	22W-20N	C1
20800	ElaT	60074	2699	21W-21N	C7
20800	KLDR	60074	2699	21W-21N	C7
22000	LKZH	60047	2699	21W-22N	C3
22600	ElaT	60047	2699	21W-22N	C3
23500	HNWD	60047	2699	21W-23N	C2
24200	ElaT	60047	2645	21W-24N	C7
24200	HNWD	60047	2645	21W-24N	C7
S Quentin Rd					
10	PLTN	60067	2805	22W-14N	C3
10	PltT	60067	2805	22W-14N	C3
1300	RGMW	60067	2805	21W-14N	C4
1400	RGMW	60008	2805	21W-14N	C4
Quick Av					
7200	OKPK	60302	3030	9W-0N	C3
7200	RVFT	60302	3030	9W-0N	C3
7200	RVFT	60305	3030	9W-0N	C3
Quiet Tr					
600	PltT	60124	2852	40W-10N	B6
S Quiet Oak Ln					
27100	CteT	60417	3774	0W-33S	C1
Quigley Dr					
100	DSPN	60016	2808	13W-13N	E6
100	WhlT	60056	2808	13W-13N	E6
S Quigley Rd					
29300	WltT	60442	3767	17W-35S	C7
Quigley St					
300	MDLN	60060	2646	19W-27N	C1
Quill Ln					
900	GwdT	60098	2524	40W-32N	E4
900	GwdT	60098	2525	40W-32N	A4
W Quill Ln					
4400	WKGN	60085	2535	14W-32N	C5
Quin Ct					
800	NPVL	60563	3140	29W-5S	D4
Quince Ct					
900	MPPT	60056	2808	13W-14N	D4
3600	DRGV	60515	3084	19W-3S	C6
N Quince Ln					
900	MPPT	60056	2808	13W-14N	D5
Quincy Av					
1100	JNBG	60051	2472	30W-35N	B6
1600	NPVL	60540	3140	29W-6S	D5
1600	NPVL	60563	3140	29W-6S	E5
Quincy Cir					
10	SBTN	60010	2803	27W-15N	A2
Quincy Ct					
10	DGvT	60527	3145	16W-7S	E5
100	BMDL	60108	2969	23W-5N	B2
200	SMBG	60193	2912	23W-9N	E1
300	RMVL	60446	3340	25W-16S	C3
500	LNHT	60046	2418	19W-38N	C6
600	CLSM	60188	2967	27W-3N	D6
800	ISLK	60042	2586	29W-28N	B6
1200	WLNG	60090	2754	16W-18N	E2
1300	ELGN	60120	2855	31W-11N	E4
1900	GLHT	60139	2968	23W-3N	E5
1900	GRNE	60031	2477	16W-36N	E5
3000	AURA	60504	3201	31W-9S	D4
3200	JLET	60431	3497	28W-25S	B7
4000	SMWD	60107	2911	28W-8N	A2
Quincy Dr					
700	ROSL	60172	2912	24W-7N	D5
6400	WLBK	60527	3145	16W-7S	E6
S Quincy Dr					
7500	WLBK	60527	3207	16W-8S	E1
Quincy Ln					
200	ROSL	60172	2912	24W-7N	D5
3000	AURA	60504	3201	31W-9S	D4
Quincy St					
-	MYWD	60153	3029	10W-0S	E5
500	MYWD	60153	3030	10W-0S	A5
E Quincy St					
10	RVSD	60546	3088	9W-3S	D5
10	WTMT	60559	3145	17W-5S	B2
100	EMHT	60126	3028	15W-0S	A6
300	BRWN	60402	3088	9W-3S	D5
300	CNHL	60514	3145	17W-5S	B2
300	CNHL	60559	3145	17W-5S	B2
300	RVSD	60402	3088	9W-3S	D5
N Quincy St					
100	HNDL	60521	3145	16W-4S	E1
400	HNDL	60521	3085	16W-4S	E7
S Quincy St					
10	HNDL	60521	3145	16W-5S	E1
900	DGvT	60521	3145	16W-5S	E3
6700	WLBK	60527	3145	16W-7S	E7
7300	WLBK	60527	3207	16W-8S	E1
W Quincy St					
10	WTMT	60559	3145	18W-5S	A2
100	BKFD	60513	3088	10W-3S	B5
100	BKFD	60546	3088	10W-3S	B5
100	CHCG	60604	3034	0W-0S	B5
100	CHCG	60606	3034	0W-0S	B5
100	RVSD	60546	3088	10W-3S	B5
300	DRGV	60515	3145	18W-5S	A2
300	DRGV	60559	3145	18W-5S	A2
500	CHCG	60661	3034	0W-0S	A5
700	CHCG	60607	3034	0W-0S	A5
4800	CHCG	60644	3031	6W-0S	B5
Quincy Bridge Ln					
-	MaiT	60016	2809	11W-13N	D7
-	NfdT	60016	2809	11W-13N	D7
600	NfdT	60025	2809	11W-13N	D7
Quindel Av					
10	SMBG	60193	2859	23W-10N	A5
Quinlan Ln					
500	WDSK	60098	2524	42W-31N	C7
Quinlan Rd					
4200	MaiT	60016	2809	11W-13N	D7
4200	NfdT	60016	2809	11W-13N	D7
4200	NfdT	60025	2809	11W-12N	D7
S Quinn Av					
21400	MTSN	60443	3594	4W-25S	D1
Quinn Ct					
1700	JLET	60586	3496	29W-21S	D1
Quinn Dr					
1600	JLET	60586	3496	29W-21S	D1
S Quinn Dr					
12500	ALSP	60803	3276	4W-14S	D6
Quinn Pl					
900	DYR	46311	3598		E4
Quinn Rd					
600	McHT	60051	2528	31W-32N	D4
S Quinn St					
2700	CHCG	60608	3091	1W-2S	E3
Quinsey Ln					
10	BtlT	60560	3333	42W-15S	D1
9200	YKVL	60560	3333	42W-15S	D1
Quist Ct					
300	AvnT	60030	2532	21W-32N	D4
300	GYLK	60030	2532	21W-32N	D4
R					
Raabe Ln					
10	LNSH	60069	2702	15W-22N	A5
Rabbit Ct					
2700	SPGV	60081	2413	31W-40N	D2
Rabbit Run					
100	FXLK	60041	2473	27W-35N	C6
N Rabbit Hill Ln					
36600	GrtT	60041	2473	26W-36N	E3
Raccoon Curv					
10700	ODPK	60467	3423	13W-20S	A4
Raccoon Cove					
3000	ISLK	60042	2586	29W-29N	D5
N Race Av					
900	ANHT	60005	2806	18W-14N	D3
1200	ANHT	60004	2806	18W-15N	D3
W Race Av					
1800	CHCG	60622	3033	2W-0N	B3
1900	CHCG	60612	3033	2W-0N	B3
4700	CHCG	60644	3031	6W-0N	E3
4700	CHCG	60644	3032	5W-0N	A3
5900	OKPK	60302	3031	7W-0N	B3
Race Ct					
1900	JLET	60431	3417	28W-21S	A7
Race St					
1500	WNSP	60558	3086	14W-4S	C7
Rachel Av					
100	JLET	60436	3587	23W-26S	B3
100	JltT	60436	3586	24W-26S	E3
100	JltT	60436	3587	23W-26S	B3
Rachel Cir					
400	RMVL	60446	3339	27W-18S	D7
Rachel Ct					
-	PLNO	60545	3260	45W-13S	B6
400	RMVL	60446	3339	27W-18S	D7
9300	ODHL	60487	3423	11W-19S	E3
Rachel Dr					
9200	WRLK	60097	2468	38W-35N	E6
9200	WRLK	60097	2469	38W-35N	A6
18300	NlxT	60448	3421	17W-22S	D7
18300	NlxT	60448	3501	17W-22S	D1
26100	AxST	60410	3672	33W-31S	B7
26100	CNHN	60410	3672	33W-31S	B7
Rachel Ln					
-	McHT	60050	2472	30W-37N	B2
1400	BFGV	60089	2753	18W-18N	E3
2000	AURA	60502	3079	33W-3S	B7
2000	BtvT	60502	3079	33W-3S	B7
5400	JNBG	60050	2472	30W-37N	B2
10400	ODPK	60467	3423	13W-21S	B6
Rachel Rd					
100	WLSP	60480	3209	12W-10S	B4
Rachell Rd					
-	AURA	60506	3199	37W-8S	C3
-	MTGY	60506	3199	37W-8S	C3
-	MTGY	60538	3199	37W-8S	C3
N Racine Av					
10	CHCG	60607	3033	1W-0N	E4
800	CHCG	60622	3033	1W-1N	E2
1900	CHCG	60614	2977	1W-2N	D7
2700	CHCG	60657	2977	1W-3N	D4
3500	CHCG	60613	2977	1W-3N	D4
4400	CHCG	60613	2921	1W-5N	D7
4400	CHCG	60640	2921	1W-5N	D7
S Racine Av					
10	CHCG	60607	3033	1W-1S	E7
1000	CHCG	60608	3033	1W-0S	E6
1600	CHCG	60608	3091	1W-1S	E1
3400	CHCG	60609	3091	1W-4S	E6
4700	CHCG	60609	3151	1W-6S	E4
5500	CHCG	60621	3151	1W-6S	E3
5500	CHCG	60636	3151	1W-6S	E3
7500	CHCG	60620	3213	1W-11S	E6
7500	CHCG	60621	3213	1W-8S	E1
9400	CHCG	60643	3213	1W-11S	E6
10300	CHCG	60643	3277	1W-12S	E1
12700	CTPK	60643	3277	1W-15S	E7
12700	CTPK	60827	3277	1W-15S	E7
29900	WshT	60401	3774	1W-36S	A7
29900	WshT	60401	3864	1W-36S	A2
W Racine Av					
25400	GrtT	60041	2474	25W-34N	A7
Racine Cir					
800	EGVV	60007	2913	22W-8N	D2
Racine Ct					
10	LKZH	60047	2698	23W-23N	E2
Racine Ln					
500	BGBK	60440	3205	22W-10S	C6
Racine Pl					
100	MDLN	60060	2590	18W-28N	D6
Racquet Club Ct					
200	HNDL	60521	3146	15W-6S	A4
W Racquet Club Dr					
700	AddT	60101	2970	19W-2N	D6
700	ADSN	60101	2970	19W-2N	D6
Raday Dr					
15100	MDLN	60445	3348	4W-18S	D6
Radcliff Cir					
500	DRFD	60015	2756	11W-20N	D1
W Radcliff Ct					
5800	MHRY	60050	2527	34W-34N	B1
Radcliff Dr					
200	BGBK	60440	3268	24W-12S	E2
Radcliff Ln					
1400	AURA	60502	3139	31W-5S	D3
Radcliff Rd					
100	LSLE	60563	3142	25W-5S	B3
400	LslT	60563	3142	25W-4S	B1
Radcliffe Av					
300	DSPN	60016	2862	14W-12N	C1
500	DSPN	60016	2808	14W-12N	C7
S Radcliffe Av					
200	DSPN	60016	2862	14W-11N	C3
Radcliffe Ct					
100	GNVW	60025	2810	10W-15N	A2
300	BMDL	60108	2968	24W-5N	C2
Radcliffe Dr					
2000	AraT	60506	3199	38W-8S	B3
3900	NHBK	60062	2756	12W-17N	B5
Radcliffe Ln					
900	SMBG	60193	2858	25W-9N	C7
900	SMBG	60193	2912	25W-9N	C1
Radcliffe Rd					
1200	BFGV	60089	2754	17W-17N	A5
8700	TYPK	60487	3424	10W-21S	B6
Radcliffe Wy					
300	HNDL	60521	3086	15W-4S	B7
300	HNDL	60521	3146	15W-4S	B1
Radclyffe Ct					
1000	ELGN	60120	2855	32W-10N	C5
Raddant Rd					
2300	AURA	60502	3138	34W-4S	D1
N Raddant Rd					
10	BTVA	60510	3078	34W-0S	D1
500	BTVA	60510	3020	34W-0S	D6
1000	GnvT	60510	3020	34W-0S	D6
S Raddant Rd					
100	AURA	60502	3078	34W-3S	D6
100	AURA	60510	3078	34W-3S	D6
100	BTVA	60510	3078	34W-3S	D6
300	BtvT	60510	3078	34W-2S	D4
E Radford Ct					
2600	ANHT	60004	2807	16W-15N	C2
Radford Dr					
1100	AURA	60502	3139	32W-6S	D4
Radford Ln					
100	VLPK	60181	3085	18W-1S	A1
100	YkTp	60181	3085	18W-1S	A1
Radley Cir					
10	SMBG	60173	2859	22W-10N	D5
Radner Ln					
10	CRTE	60417	3596	0W-28S	D7
Radnor Ct					
1700	GNVA	60134	3020	36W-1N	A3
Radnor Dr					
500	ROSL	60172	2912	24W-6N	C6
S Rado Dr E					
14100	HMGN	60491	3343	16W-16S	E4
Rado Dr N					
13100	HMGN	60491	3343	16W-16S	E4
Rado Dr S					
13100	HMGN	60491	3343	16W-16S	E4
Rado Dr W					
14100	HMGN	60491	3343	16W-16S	E4
Rado Ln					
-	HMGN	60491	3343	16W-16S	E4
Rae Av					
500	LKVL	60046	2416	23W-38N	E6
500	LkvT	60046	2416	23W-38N	E6
Rae Ln					
400	LKVL	60046	2416	23W-38N	E6
400	LkvT	60046	2416	23W-38N	E6
W Rae Ln					
18300	WrnT	60031	2476	18W-36N	E4
18300	WrnT	60031	2477	18W-36N	A4
Raes Creek Ct					
10	BGBK	60490	3267	27W-12S	C3
10	WldT	60490	3267	27W-12S	C3
Raes Creek Dr					
1700	BGBK	60490	3267	27W-12S	C4
1800	WldT	60490	3267	27W-12S	C4
Raffel Rd					
10	GwdT	60098	2525	40W-33N	A3
10	WDSK	60098	2525	40W-33N	A4
2000	GwdT	60098	2468	40W-34N	A7
Rago Av					
1100	DRFD	60015	2703	11W-21N	D5
Rahill Ct					
1100	CTHL	60403	3418	25W-21S	C7
Raider Ln					
-	MltT	60137	3083	22W-2S	B4
N Rail					
-	CLCY	60416	3941	34W-39S	A1
Rail Ln					
12500	PSPK	60464	3273	13W-14S	A7
Railroad Av					
-	ANTH	60002	2357	23W-42N	E6
-	BLWD	60104	3028	13W-0N	E3
-	BLWD	60104	3029	13W-0N	A3
-	LKVL	60046	2417	22W-38N	A7
-	LKVL	60046	2475	22W-37N	A1
10	BNVL	60106	2971	16W-5N	E1
10	GYLK	60030	2532	20W-33N	E3
10	GYLK	60030	2533	20W-33N	A3
100	BNVL	60106	2972	15W-5N	A1
200	CNHL	60514	3145	16W-5S	D2
300	DRGV	60515	3143	22W-5S	C2
300	RDLK	60073	2531	23W-33N	D2
500	AvnT	60073	2531	23W-34N	D2
800	CNHL	60521	3145	16W-5S	E2
800	GNVW	60025	2810	8W-13N	E6
800	HNDL	60521	3145	16W-5S	E2
1700	EVTN	60201	2867	2W-11N	B2
1900	MYWD	60153	3029	11W-0N	D3
17400	LNSG	60438	3430	3E-20S	A4
Railroad Av SR-134					
300	RDLK	60073	2531	23W-33N	D2
500	AvnT	60073	2531	23W-34N	D2
E Railroad Av					
100	BRLT	60103	2910	28W-8N	E3
100	BRLT	60103	2911	28W-8N	A3
N Railroad Av					
-	HLSD	60162	3028	14W-0S	D6
-	HLSD	60162	3029	13W-0S	A6
100	NHLK	60164	2972	14W-2N	C7
100	NHLK	60164	3028	14W-2N	C1
W Railroad Av					
10	BRLT	60103	2910	29W-8N	E3
10	PLTN	60067	2805	22W-14N	B4
5800	CHCG	60644	3031	7W-0S	C6
5900	CHCG	60304	3031	7W-0S	C6
5900	OKPK	60304	3031	7W-0S	C6
Railroad Dr					
-	DGvT	60439	3207	17W-11S	B7
-	DGvT	60439	3270	19W-12S	E3
-	DGvT	60439	3271	17W-11S	B1
-	LMNT	60439	3270	19W-12S	E3
Railroad St					
-	MHTN	60442	3677	19W-30S	E4
-	MltT	60137	3025	22W-1N	B3
10	CLLK	60014	2640	35W-26N	B3
10	EDND	60118	2801	33W-16N	A2
10	GLBT	60136	2799	39W-16N	A1
10	PGGV	60140	2798	41W-14N	B6
100	SRGV	60554	3135	42W-7S	C7
200	ALGN	60102	2694	34W-20N	D7
300	JLET	60436	3498	24W-24S	D7
300	WDSK	60098	2524	41W-31N	C6
400	WMTN	60481	3853	28W-38S	C6
400	WYNE	60184	2965	32W-5N	C2
600	JltT	60436	3498	24W-24S	D7
700	RKDL	60436	3498	25W-25S	C7
8300	DrrT	60012	2583	37W-27N	B7
Railroad St US-6					
400	JLET	60436	3498	24W-24S	D7
600	JltT	60436	3498	24W-24S	D7
700	RKDL	60436	3498	25W-25S	C7
E Railroad St					
-	SdwT	60548	3330	51W-14S	A1
100	HRVD	60033	2406	50W-38N	B7
100	MRGO	60152	2634	49W-26N	B2
700	SDWH	60548	3330	51W-14S	A1
800	HMND	46320	3280		E3
800	HMND	46394	3280		E3
N Railroad St					
100	MTGY	60538	3199	37W-9S	D4
100	PTON	60468	3861	8W-37S	B3
500	BDWD	60408	3942	31W-41S	A4
S Railroad St					
10	BDWD	60408	3942	30W-41S	C6
100	MTGY	60538	3199	37W-9S	C5
100	PTON	60468	3861	9W-37S	A3
W Railroad St					
100	MRGO	60152	2634	50W-26N	A2
21600	MngT	60152	2634	50W-26N	A2
Railway Dr					
500	NPVL	60563	3140	30W-6S	C4
Rainbow Cir					
-	ODPK	60467	3422	14W-20S	E3
Rainbow Ct					
400	SYHW	60118	2800	35W-15N	C3
Rainbow Dr					
-	BtlT	53104	2358		D3
-	MRGO	60152	2634	49W-26N	D2
100	SYHW	60118	2800	35W-16N	C2
N Rainbow Dr					
700	GNWD	60425	3508	0W-22S	B1
W Rainbow Dr					
200	GNWD	60425	3508	0W-22S	B1
Rainbow Ln					
100	TVLY	60013	2695	31W-23N	C2
E Rainbow Ln					
1800	CteT	60417	3686	2E-31S	D5
Rainbow Rd					
100	NBRN	60010	2698	24W-21N	B5
1100	ELGN	60123	2801	33W-13N	A7
21500	DRPK	60010	2698	24W-21N	C6
21500	ElaT	60010	2698	24W-21N	C5
Rainbow Ter					
800	SEGN	60177	2908	35W-9N	B1
E Rainbow Bay					
1600	PLTN	60074	2753	18W-18N	D3
Rainey Dr					
-	CHCG	60637	3152	0E-6S	D3
Rainford Ct					
8600	LynT	60480	3208	14W-9S	E4
8600	WLSP	60480	3208	14W-9S	E4
Rainford Dr					
-	FftT	60423	3504	10W-24S	C5
Rainier Wy					
200	FXLK	60020	2473	27W-35N	C5
Rainmaker Run					
200	LIHL	60156	2693	36W-21N	D5
Rainsford Dr					
9400	HTLY	60142	2692	40W-22N	A4
Raintree Ct					
10	CRY	60013	2695	32W-23N	B2
100	AURA	60504	3140	30W-7S	A7
400	GNEN	60137	3083	22W-1S	B2
600	BFGV	60089	2701	17W-23N	B2
600	CLSM	60188	2967	28W-3N	B6
4900	JNBG	60050	2472	30W-36N	A3
5800	WTMT	60559	3144	18W-6S	E4
6500	LSLE	60532	3142	24W-7S	E6
21100	FKFT	60423	3504	11W-25S	A7
26100	CNHN	60410	3672	33W-31S	C7
Rain Tree Dr					
1000	BGBK	60440	3205	22W-9S	C4
Raintree Dr					
400	GNEN	60137	3083	22W-1S	B2
400	OSWG	60543	3264	34W-11S	D1
500	MltT	60137	3083	22W-1S	C2
700	NPVL	60540	3141	28W-7S	A7
800	NPVL	60540	3203	28W-7S	A1
6100	NndT	60012	2584	35W-30N	B2
6100	NndT	60050	2584	35W-30N	B2
15200	ODPK	60462	3346	10W-18S	A7
Raintree Ln					
3900	NHBK	60062	2756	12W-17N	B5
5700	WTMT	60559	3144	18W-6S	E4
8600	ODPK	60462	3346	10W-18S	A7
8900	FKFT	60423	3504	11W-25S	A7
Rain Tree Pl					
10	BNHL	60010	2695	30W-21N	E5
Raintree Rd					
-	AURA	60504	3140	30W-7S	B7
600	BFGV	60089	2701	17W-23N	B2
1900	YKVL	60560	3333	42W-16S	D5
8500	TYPK	60487	3424	10W-20S	B5
N Rain Tree Rd					
43400	AntT	60002	2357	25W-43N	A4
Rainwood Dr					
1000	AURA	60506	3137	37W-6S	B5
Rainy Lake Ct					
1000	LKVL	60046	2417	22W-39N	C5
Raleigh Ct					
10	PSHT	60463	3274	9W-13S	D5
100	WDDL	60191	2970	18W-5N	E2
400	ElgT	60124	2853	37W-11N	C4
700	NHBK	60062	2757	8W-17N	E4
1200	GLHT	60139	3024	24W-2N	E1
1600	WHTN	60187	3082	24W-1S	C2
2400	SMBG	60193	2857	26W-10N	E6
E Raleigh Ct					
100	BMDL	60108	2969	23W-5N	A1
W Raleigh Ct					
1500	ANHT	60004	2753	18W-16N	D6
N Raleigh Dr					
23500	VrnT	60069	2701	16W-23N	D2
Raleigh Ln					
1700	HFET	60169	2858	26W-12N	A1
Raleigh Pl					
400	TRLK	60010	2643	26W-25N	D5
1900	HFET	60169	2858	25W-12N	C1
W Raleigh Pl					
200	MPPT	60056	2807	15W-14N	E3
Raleigh Rd					
200	KLWH	60043	2812	3W-14N	D4
600	GNVW	60025	2810	8W-13N	E6
600	GNVW	60025	2811	8W-13N	A7
800	MDLN	60060	2590	19W-28N	C6
6300	WLBK	60527	3146	15W-7S	B6
Raleigh St					
10900	WSTR	60154	3086	13W-2S	E3
N Raleigh St					
2500	ANHT	60004	2753	18W-16N	D6
Raleigh Tr					
200	RMVL	60446	3339	27W-17S	D6
Ralmark Ln					
3300	GNVW	60025	2809	10W-14N	E5
3300	GNVW	60025	2810	10W-14N	A5
Ralph Av					
900	GRNE	60031	2478	14W-35N	D7
Ralph Ct					
300	ISLK	60042	2586	29W-28N	D5
700	WHTN	60187	3024	25W-0N	B5
Ralph Judd Ct					
10	SgrT	60506	3136	41W-5S	A4
Ralph Waldo Emerson Ln					
200	CmpT	60175	2962	40W-4N	C5
Ram Rd					
100	ANTH	60002	2358	23W-41N	A7
Ramada Lake Cross					
-	ELGN	60123	2853	36W-10N	E5
Ramble Rd					
300	LIHL	60156	2694	35W-21N	B6
8300	GwdT	60097	2469	37W-35N	B6
N Ramble Rd					
1500	MHRY	60050	2527	33W-33N	E3
W Ramble Rd					
4400	MHRY	60050	2527	33W-33N	E2
Rambler Ct					
700	SMWD	60107	2857	28W-10N	B7
Rambler Ln					
400	SMWD	60107	2857	28W-10N	B6
500	HDPK	60035	2758	7W-20N	B2
Rambler Pl					
400	SMWD	60107	2857	28W-10N	B6
Ramblewood Ct					
400	LKZH	60047	2699	22W-22N	A3
Ramblewood Dr					
300	GNEN	60137	3083	23W-1S	B2
1400	HRPK	60133	2857	27W-9N	D7
1500	SMWD	60107	2857	27W-9N	D7
1500	SMWD	60133	2857	27W-9N	D7

STREET Block	City	ZIP	Map#	CGS	Grid
Ramblewood Ln					
10	LKZH	60047	2699	22W-22N	A3
Rambling Rd					
12000	HMGN	60491	3344	15W-17S	B5
12000	OrlT	60467	3344	15W-17S	C6
Ramblin Rose Ln					
-	PltT	60124	2852	41W-10N	A5
Ramer Rd					
22800	CmgT	60033	2405	52W-38N	C6
22800	HRVD	60033	2405	51W-38N	D6
Ramer Rd CO-A20					
22800	CmgT	60033	2405	52W-38N	C6
22800	HRVD	60033	2405	51W-38N	D6
Ramm Dr					
100	AURA	60503	3201	31W-10S	E6
100	AURA	60564	3201	31W-10S	E6
100	WldT	60503	3201	31W-10S	E6
100	WldT	60564	3201	31W-10S	E6
N Rammer Av					
10	ANHT	60004	2807	16W-14N	D5
S Rammer Av					
10	ANHT	60004	2807	16W-13N	D5
Ramona Av					
300	ELGN	60120	2855	32W-10N	C5
N Ramona Av					
6600	CHCG	60646	2919	6W-8N	D2
6600	CHCG	60712	2919	6W-8N	D2
6600	LNWD	60712	2919	6W-8N	D2
6700	LNWD	60077	2919	6W-8N	D2
6700	SKOK	60077	2919	6W-8N	D2
Ramona Ln					
10	SchT	60174	2964	34W-6N	C1
Rampart Ct					
1800	NPVL	60565	3204	25W-9S	B4
W Rampart Rd					
1600	ADSN	60101	2970	20W-4N	A4
1700	BmdT	60101	2970	20W-4N	A4
Ramsay Rd					
100	DRFD	60015	2704	10W-21N	A6
Ramschell St					
9100	HTLY	60142	2691	41W-22N	E3
Ramsden Rd					
-	PLNO	60545	3259	48W-13S	B5
Ramsey Cir					
2200	SMBG	60194	2857	28W-12N	B2
Ramsey Dr					
300	RMVL	60446	3339	27W-17S	D7
Ramsgate Cir					
7700	HRPK	60133	2857	26W-9N	E7
Ramsgate Ct					
800	NPVL	60540	3142	25W-7S	C7
Ramsgate Dr					
10	PSPK	60464	3272	14W-14S	D7
Ramsgate Ln					
-	LKMR	60051	2472	30W-35N	A7
3100	JNBG	60051	2472	30W-35N	A6
E Rana Dr					
3000	CteT	60417	3687	3E-31S	B5
Rance Rd					
10	OswT	60543	3265	33W-12S	A4
10	WldT	60543	3265	33W-12S	A4
W Rance Ter					
3300	LNWD	60712	2920	4W-8N	D2
Ranch Rd					
200	CPVL	60118	2747	35W-17N	B7
200	DndT	60118	2747	35W-17N	B7
200	WDND	60118	2747	35W-17N	B7
400	ELGN	60123	2800	34W-13N	E7
600	WHTN	60187	3024	24W-0N	D4
1100	LKFT	60045	2649	13W-24N	A7
1600	MchT	60051	2529	30W-33N	A2
N Ranch Rd					
31200	LbvT	60030	2533	18W-31N	D7
Ranchland Dr					
13300	PNFD	60544	3338	31W-16S	A4
Rancho Ln					
1900	MaiT	60016	2863	11W-11N	D3
Ranch View Ct					
1100	BFGV	60089	2701	17W-21N	A6
Ranch View Dr					
1300	LslT	60540	3204	24W-9S	D3
1300	LslT	60565	3204	24W-9S	D3
1300	NPVL	60565	3204	24W-9S	D3
Ranchwood Dr					
800	SRWD	60404	3496	30W-24S	B6
Rand Av					
10	FXLK	60020	2473	27W-36N	A3
W Rand Ct					
20700	ElaT	60074	2752	20W-20N	E1
Rand Dr					
400	MchT	60050	2472	29W-37N	C1
400	SPGV	60050	2472	29W-37N	C1
Rand Rd					
-	WcnT	60073	2587	27W-29N	C3
-	WcnT	60084	2587	27W-29N	C3
10	DRPK	60010	2699	22W-21N	B7
10	DRPK	60047	2699	22W-21N	B7
10	DSPN	60016	2808	14W-12N	C7
10	KLDR	60010	2699	22W-21N	B7
10	KLDR	60047	2699	22W-21N	B6
10	LKZH	60010	2699	22W-21N	B6
10	MPPT	60016	2808	14W-12N	C7
10	MPPT	60056	2808	14W-12N	C7
300	DSPN	60016	2862	13W-12N	E2
300	LKZH	60047	2699	22W-21N	B6
600	DRPK	60074	2699	21W-20N	C7
600	ElaT	60047	2699	21W-20N	C7
600	ElaT	60074	2699	21W-20N	D7
600	KLDR	60074	2699	21W-20N	C7
1200	DSPN	60016	2863	13W-11N	A3
2000	PLTN	60074	2753	20W-18N	A3
Rand Rd SR-53					
2000	PLTN	60074	2753	20W-18N	A3
Rand Rd US-12					
10	DRPK	60010	2699	22W-21N	B7
10	DRPK	60047	2699	22W-21N	B7
10	DSPN	60016	2808	14W-12N	C7
10	KLDR	60010	2699	22W-21N	B7
10	KLDR	60047	2699	22W-21N	B6
10	LKZH	60010	2699	22W-21N	B6
10	MPPT	60016	2808	14W-12N	C7
10	MPPT	60056	2808	14W-12N	C7
300	DSPN	60016	2862	13W-12N	E2
300	LKZH	60047	2699	22W-21N	B6
600	DRPK	60074	2699	21W-20N	C7
600	ElaT	60047	2699	21W-20N	C7
600	ElaT	60074	2699	21W-20N	D7
600	KLDR	60074	2699	21W-20N	C7
1200	DSPN	60016	2863	13W-11N	A2
2000	PLTN	60074	2753	20W-18N	A3
E Rand Rd					
10	ANHT	60004	2754	17W-16N	A7
10	ANHT	60004	2807	16W-15N	C2
10	MPPT	60056	2808	15W-13N	A5
900	DSPN	60016	2808	14W-13N	B7
900	MPPT	60016	2808	14W-13N	B7

STREET Block	City	ZIP	Map#	CGS	Grid
E Rand Rd					
1200	PTHT	60004	2807	17W-15N	C2
2400	MPPT	60004	2807	16W-14N	D3
2400	MPPT	60056	2807	16W-14N	D3
2400	WhlT	60004	2807	16W-14N	D3
2500	ANHT	60056	2807	16W-14N	E4
E Rand Rd US-12					
10	ANHT	60004	2754	17W-16N	A7
10	ANHT	60004	2807	16W-15N	C2
10	MPPT	60056	2808	15W-13N	A5
900	DSPN	60016	2808	14W-13N	B7
900	MPPT	60016	2808	14W-13N	B7
1200	PTHT	60004	2807	17W-15N	C2
2400	MPPT	60004	2807	16W-14N	D3
2400	MPPT	60056	2807	16W-14N	D3
2400	WhlT	60004	2807	16W-14N	D3
2500	ANHT	60056	2807	16W-14N	E4
N Rand Rd					
-	WcnT	60073	2587	27W-29N	C4
10	LKZH	60047	2698	24W-23N	C1
200	WCDA	60084	2643	26W-27N	D2
200	WcnT	60084	2643	26W-26N	D2
600	WCDA	60084	2587	26W-29N	C4
700	ElaT	60010	2698	24W-23N	C1
800	ElaT	60047	2698	24W-23N	C1
800	WcnT	60084	2587	26W-29N	C4
900	ElaT	60047	2644	24W-24N	C7
2100	PLTN	60074	2753	20W-18N	A2
2100	PltT	60074	2753	20W-18N	A2
2300	DRPK	60074	2752	21W-20N	E1
2300	ElaT	60074	2752	21W-20N	E1
2300	PltT	60074	2752	21W-20N	E1
20200	KLDR	60074	2752	21W-20N	E1
20400	KLDR	60047	2752	21W-20N	D1
24000	ElaT	60010	2644	24W-24N	C7
24000	NBRN	60010	2644	24W-24N	C7
24000	NBRN	60047	2644	24W-24N	C7
24200	HNWD	60047	2644	24W-24N	C7
24200	LKZH	60047	2644	24W-24N	C7
25800	ElaT	60084	2644	24W-25N	C4
25900	FmtT	60084	2644	24W-26N	B4
25900	WcnT	60084	2644	24W-26N	B3
26200	WcnT	60010	2644	25W-26N	B3
29000	WCDA	60073	2587	26W-29N	C5
N Rand Rd SR-53					
1600	PLTN	60074	2753	20W-18N	B4
N Rand Rd SR-59					
-	WcnT	60073	2587	27W-29N	C4
200	WCDA	60084	2643	26W-27N	D1
200	WcnT	60084	2643	26W-26N	D2
600	WCDA	60084	2587	26W-29N	C4
800	WcnT	60084	2587	26W-29N	C4
29000	WCDA	60073	2587	26W-29N	C5
N Rand Rd US-12					
-	WcnT	60073	2587	27W-29N	C4
10	LKZH	60047	2698	24W-23N	C1
200	WCDA	60084	2643	26W-27N	D1
200	WcnT	60084	2643	26W-26N	D2
600	WCDA	60084	2587	26W-28N	D6
700	ElaT	60010	2698	24W-23N	C1
700	ElaT	60047	2698	24W-23N	C1
800	WcnT	60084	2587	26W-29N	C4
900	ElaT	60047	2644	24W-24N	C7
900	NBRN	60047	2644	24W-24N	C7
2100	PLTN	60074	2753	20W-18N	A2
2100	PltT	60074	2753	20W-18N	A2
2300	DRPK	60074	2752	21W-20N	E1
2300	ElaT	60074	2752	21W-20N	E1
2300	PltT	60074	2752	21W-20N	E1
20200	KLDR	60074	2752	21W-20N	E1
20400	KLDR	60047	2752	21W-20N	D1
24000	ElaT	60010	2644	24W-24N	C7
24000	NBRN	60010	2644	24W-24N	C7
24200	HNWD	60047	2644	24W-24N	C7
24200	LKZH	60047	2644	24W-24N	C7
25800	ElaT	60084	2644	24W-25N	C4
25900	FmtT	60084	2644	24W-26N	B4
25900	WcnT	60010	2644	25W-26N	B3
25900	WcnT	60084	2644	24W-26N	B3
29000	WCDA	60073	2587	26W-29N	C5
S Rand Rd					
-	LKZH	60047	2698	23W-21N	E5
400	WCDA	60084	2643	26W-26N	E2
400	WcnT	60084	2643	26W-26N	E2
900	LKZH	60047	2699	22W-21N	A5
1000	VLPK	60181	3027	18W-0S	A6
1100	KLDR	60047	2699	22W-21N	A5
1100	LKZH	60010	2699	22W-21N	B6
26400	WCDA	60084	2644	25W-26N	A3
26400	WcnT	60010	2644	25W-26N	A3
26400	WcnT	60084	2644	25W-26N	A3
S Rand Rd SR-59					
400	WCDA	60084	2643	26W-26N	E2
400	WcnT	60084	2643	26W-26N	E2
S Rand Rd US-12					
10	LKZH	60047	2698	23W-22N	D4
400	WCDA	60084	2643	26W-26N	E2
400	WcnT	60084	2643	26W-26N	E2
900	LKZH	60047	2699	22W-21N	A5
1100	KLDR	60047	2699	22W-21N	A5
1100	LKZH	60010	2699	22W-21N	B6
26400	WCDA	60084	2644	25W-26N	A3
26400	WcnT	60010	2644	25W-26N	A3
26400	WcnT	60084	2644	25W-26N	A3
W Rand Rd					
-	ANHT	60074	2753	18W-16N	E6
-	PltT	60074	2753	19W-17N	D5
10	ANHT	60004	2754	18W-16N	A7
10	MPPT	60056	2807	15W-14N	E4
10	MPPT	60056	2808	15W-14N	A5
10	VLPK	60181	3027	18W-0S	A6
100	LKMR	60051	2529	29W-32N	C5
100	WcnT	60051	2529	29W-31N	D6
400	ANHT	60004	2753	18W-16N	E6
500	MchT	60051	2529	30W-32N	B5
600	ANHT	60056	2807	15W-14N	E4
700	ANHT	60004	2807	16W-14N	E4
700	MPPT	60004	2807	16W-14N	E4
1200	PltT	60004	2753	18W-16N	E6
W Rand Rd SR-120					
100	LKMR	60051	2529	29W-32N	C5
100	WcnT	60051	2529	29W-31N	D6
500	MchT	60051	2529	30W-32N	B5
W Rand Rd US-12					
-	ANHT	60074	2753	18W-16N	E6
-	PltT	60074	2753	19W-17N	D5
10	ANHT	60004	2754	18W-16N	A7
10	MPPT	60056	2807	15W-14N	E4
10	MPPT	60056	2808	15W-14N	A5
400	ANHT	60004	2753	18W-16N	E6
600	ANHT	60056	2807	15W-14N	E4
700	ANHT	60004	2807	16W-14N	E4
700	MPPT	60004	2807	16W-14N	E4
1200	PltT	60004	2753	18W-16N	E6
Randall Ct					
600	JltT	60433	3499	23W-24S	B6

STREET Block	City	ZIP	Map#	CGS	Grid
Randall Ct					
600	MRGO	60152	2634	49W-25N	C4
1100	GNVA	60134	3019	37W-0N	D5
1400	AURA	60506	3137	37W-7S	C6
Randall Ln					
2400	PltT	60004	2753	19W-18N	C2
Randall Rd					
-	SCRL	60174	2963	36W-3N	D5
-	SCRL	60175	2963	36W-3N	D5
10	ALGN	60102	2746	37W-18N	E4
10	ALGN	60118	2746	37W-18N	E4
10	DndT	60102	2746	36W-19N	E3
10	DndT	60118	2746	37W-17N	E7
10	DndT	60118	2799	37W-16N	E1
10	ELGN	60123	2853	36W-10N	E7
10	ELGN	60123	2907	36W-9N	E2
10	ELGN	60124	2799	37W-16N	E1
10	ELGN	60124	2853	36W-10N	E6
10	ELGN	60124	2907	36W-8N	E2
10	ElgT	60123	2907	36W-8N	E2
10	ElgT	60123	2853	36W-10N	E6
10	ElgT	60124	2907	36W-8N	E2
10	SchT	60174	2963	37W-3N	D6
10	SchT	60175	2963	37W-3N	D6
10	WDND	60118	2746	37W-17N	E7
10	WDND	60118	2799	37W-16N	E1
100	SCRL	60134	3019	37W-0N	D5
100	SCRL	60174	3019	37W-0N	D5
100	SCRL	60175	3019	37W-2N	D1
200	GNVA	60134	3019	37W-0N	D5
200	SchT	60175	2907	37W-6N	D7
200	SEGN	60124	2907	36W-8N	D3
200	SEGN	60177	2907	37W-7N	D6
300	CPVL	60118	2746	36W-17N	E7
300	SEGN	60175	2907	37W-7N	D6
300	WDND	60110	2746	36W-17N	E7
900	GNVA	60174	3019	37W-0N	D5
2300	CPVL	60110	2746	36W-18N	E6
2300	DndT	60110	2746	36W-18N	E6
8700	AlqT	60014	2693	36W-23N	E2
8700	CLLK	60014	2693	36W-23N	E3
9000	AlqT	60156	2693	36W-23N	E3
9100	CLLK	60156	2693	36W-23N	E3
9100	LIHL	60014	2693	36W-22N	E3
9100	LIHL	60156	2693	36W-22N	E3
Randall Rd CO-34					
-	SCRL	60174	2963	36W-3N	D5
-	SCRL	60175	2963	36W-3N	D5
10	ALGN	60102	2746	37W-18N	E4
10	ALGN	60118	2746	37W-18N	E4
10	DndT	60102	2746	36W-19N	E3
10	DndT	60118	2746	37W-17N	E7
10	DndT	60118	2799	37W-16N	E1
10	ELGN	60123	2853	36W-10N	E6
10	ELGN	60123	2907	36W-8N	E2
10	ELGN	60124	2799	37W-16N	E1
10	ELGN	60124	2853	36W-10N	E6
10	ELGN	60124	2907	36W-8N	E2
10	ElgT	60123	2907	36W-8N	E2
10	ElgT	60124	2853	36W-10N	E6
10	ElgT	60124	2907	36W-8N	E2
10	SchT	60174	2963	37W-3N	D6
10	SchT	60175	2963	37W-3N	D6
10	WDND	60118	2746	37W-17N	E7
10	WDND	60118	2799	37W-16N	E1
100	SCRL	60134	3019	37W-0N	D5
100	SCRL	60174	3019	37W-0N	D5
100	SCRL	60175	3019	37W-2N	D1
200	GNVA	60134	3019	37W-0N	D5
200	SchT	60175	2907	37W-6N	D7
200	SEGN	60124	2907	36W-8N	D3
200	SEGN	60177	2907	37W-7N	D6
300	CPVL	60110	2746	36W-17N	E7
300	CPVL	60118	2746	36W-17N	E7
300	SEGN	60175	2907	37W-7N	D6
300	WDND	60110	2746	36W-17N	E7
900	GNVA	60174	3019	37W-0N	D5
2300	DndT	60110	2746	36W-18N	E5
Randall Rd CO-V29					
8700	AlqT	60014	2693	36W-23N	E3
8700	CLLK	60014	2693	36W-23N	E3
9000	AlqT	60156	2693	36W-23N	E3
9100	CLLK	60156	2693	36W-23N	E3
9100	LIHL	60014	2693	36W-22N	E3
9100	LIHL	60156	2693	36W-22N	E3
N Randall Rd					
-	BtvT	60510	3077	37W-3S	C6
-	BtvT	60539	3077	37W-3S	C6
-	BtvT	60542	3077	37W-3S	C6
-	CLLK	60014	2693	36W-22N	E4
-	CLLK	60156	2693	36W-22N	E4
-	DndT	60123	2799	36W-15N	E4
-	NARA	60506	3137	37W-4S	C2
-	NARA	60539	3077	37W-3S	C6
-	NARA	60542	3137	37W-4S	C1
10	ALGN	60102	2693	36W-21N	E6
10	AraT	60542	3077	37W-3S	C6
10	AURA	60506	3137	37W-6S	C4
10	BTVA	60510	3077	36W-1S	D1
10	DndT	60124	2799	37W-14N	E6
10	ELGN	60118	2799	36W-15N	E4
10	ELGN	60123	2799	36W-15N	E4
10	ELGN	60123	2853	37W-12N	D3
10	ELGN	60124	2799	36W-15N	E4
10	ElgT	60123	2799	36W-13N	E7
10	ElgT	60123	2853	37W-12N	D3
10	ElgT	60124	2853	37W-12N	D3
10	LIHL	60102	2693	36W-21N	E6
10	NARA	60542	3077	37W-3S	C7
10	SYHW	60118	2799	36W-15N	E4
10	WDND	60118	2799	37W-16N	E3
100	SCRL	60174	2963	36W-3N	D7
100	SCRL	60175	2963	36W-3N	D7
200	BTVA	60510	3019	37W-0S	D7
200	DndT	60118	2799	37W-16N	E2
200	LIHL	60156	2693	36W-22N	E4
200	SYHW	60124	2799	37W-15N	E4
300	SchT	60174	2963	36W-3N	D7
300	SchT	60175	2963	36W-3N	D7
400	GnvT	60134	3019	37W-0S	D7
400	GnvT	60510	3019	37W-0S	D7
500	BTVA	60134	3019	37W-0S	D7
500	ELGN	60124	2853	37W-12N	D3
500	GNVA	60134	3019	37W-0S	D7
1700	AURA	60542	3137	37W-5S	C2
N Randall Rd CO-34					
-	BtvT	60510	3077	37W-3S	C6
-	BtvT	60539	3077	37W-3S	C6
-	BtvT	60542	3077	37W-3S	C6
-	DndT	60123	2799	36W-15N	E4
-	NARA	60506	3137	37W-4S	C2
-	NARA	60539	3077	37W-3S	C6
-	NARA	60542	3137	37W-4S	C1
10	AraT	60542	3077	37W-3S	C7
10	AURA	60506	3137	37W-6S	C4

STREET Block	City	ZIP	Map#	CGS	Grid
N Randall Rd CO-34					
10	BTVA	60510	3077	36W-1S	D1
10	DndT	60124	2799	37W-14N	E6
10	ELGN	60118	2799	36W-15N	E4
10	ELGN	60123	2799	36W-15N	E4
10	ELGN	60123	2853	37W-12N	D3
10	ELGN	60124	2799	36W-15N	E4
10	ElgT	60123	2799	36W-13N	E7
10	ElgT	60123	2853	37W-12N	D3
10	ElgT	60124	2799	36W-13N	E7
10	ElgT	60124	2853	37W-12N	D3
10	NARA	60542	3077	37W-3S	C7
10	SYHW	60118	2799	36W-15N	E4
10	WDND	60118	2799	37W-16N	E3
100	SCRL	60174	2963	36W-3N	D7
100	SCRL	60175	2963	36W-3N	D7
200	BTVA	60510	3019	37W-0S	D7
200	DndT	60118	2799	37W-16N	E2
200	SYHW	60124	2799	37W-15N	E4
300	SchT	60174	2963	36W-3N	D7
300	SchT	60175	2963	36W-3N	D7
400	GnvT	60134	3019	37W-0S	D7
400	GnvT	60510	3019	37W-0S	D7
500	BTVA	60134	3019	37W-0S	D7
500	ELGN	60124	2853	37W-12N	D3
500	GNVA	60134	3019	37W-0S	D7
1700	AURA	60542	3137	37W-5S	C2
N Randall Rd CO-V29					
-	CLLK	60014	2693	36W-22N	E4
-	CLLK	60156	2693	36W-22N	E4
10	ALGN	60102	2693	36W-21N	E6
10	LIHL	60102	2693	36W-21N	E6
10	LIHL	60156	2693	36W-22N	E4
S Randall Rd					
-	BtvT	60542	3077	37W-3S	C6
-	NARA	60539	3077	37W-3S	C6
-	NARA	60542	3077	37W-3S	C6
10	ALGN	60102	2693	36W-21N	E6
10	AURA	60506	3137	37W-7S	C7
10	BTVA	60510	3077	36W-1S	D3
10	BTVA	60539	3077	36W-1S	D3
10	BtvT	60539	3077	36W-1S	D3
10	LIHL	60102	2693	36W-21N	E6
10	LIHL	60156	2693	36W-21N	E6
10	SchT	60174	2963	37W-2N	D7
10	SchT	60175	2963	37W-2N	D7
10	SCRL	60174	2963	37W-2N	D7
10	SCRL	60175	2963	37W-2N	D7
100	ELGN	60123	2853	36W-10N	E5
100	ELGN	60124	2853	36W-10N	E5
200	BtvT	60510	3077	36W-1S	D3
300	SchT	60174	3019	37W-2N	D1
300	SchT	60175	3019	37W-2N	D1
300	SCRL	60174	3019	37W-2N	D1
300	SCRL	60175	3019	37W-2N	D1
400	AraT	60506	3199	37W-7S	C1
400	AURA	60506	3199	37W-7S	C1
1400	GNVA	60134	3019	37W-0N	D6
1500	ALGN	60102	2746	36W-20N	E1
1800	BTVA	60134	3019	37W-0S	D6
1800	BTVA	60510	3019	37W-0S	D6
1800	GnvT	60134	3019	37W-0S	D6
1800	GnvT	60510	3019	37W-0S	D6
11100	AlqT	60102	2746	36W-20N	E1
S Randall Rd CO-34					
-	BtvT	60542	3077	37W-3S	C6
-	NARA	60539	3077	37W-3S	C6
-	NARA	60542	3077	37W-3S	C6
10	BTVA	60510	3077	36W-1S	D3
10	BTVA	60539	3077	36W-1S	D3
10	BtvT	60539	3077	36W-1S	D3
10	SchT	60174	2963	37W-2N	D7
10	SchT	60175	2963	37W-2N	D7
10	SCRL	60174	2963	37W-2N	D7
10	SCRL	60175	2963	37W-2N	D7
100	ELGN	60123	2853	36W-10N	E5
100	ELGN	60124	2853	36W-10N	E5
200	BtvT	60510	3077	36W-1S	D3
300	SchT	60174	3019	37W-2N	D1
300	SchT	60175	3019	37W-2N	D1
300	SCRL	60174	3019	37W-2N	D1
300	SCRL	60175	3019	37W-2N	D1
1400	GNVA	60134	3019	37W-0N	D6
1500	ALGN	60102	2746	36W-19N	E2
1800	BTVA	60134	3019	37W-0S	D6
1800	BTVA	60510	3019	37W-0S	D6
1800	GnvT	60134	3019	37W-0S	D6
1800	GnvT	60510	3019	37W-0S	D6
S Randall Rd CO-V29					
10	ALGN	60102	2693	36W-21N	E7
10	LIHL	60102	2693	36W-21N	E6
10	LIHL	60156	2693	36W-21N	E6
11100	AlqT	60102	2746	36W-20N	E1
11900	ALGN	60102	2746	36W-20N	E1
Randall St					
10	EGVV	60007	2861	18W-10N	A5
100	HRVD	60033	2406	50W-38N	B7
600	DRGV	60515	3144	19W-5S	D3
Randall Ridge Ct					
2800	ELGN	60124	2853	37W-11N	C3
Randall Ridge Dr					
2700	ELGN	60124	2853	37W-11N	C4
E Rand Grove Village Ln					
700	PLTN	60074	2753	20W-18N	B3
N Randhill Dr					
35000	FXLK	60041	2473	27W-35N	B6
35000	GrtT	60041	2473	27W-35N	B6
Randi Dr					
1900	AURA	60504	3201	33W-9S	A3
Randi Ln					
600	HFET	60169	2858	24W-11N	C4
W Randich Rd					
26000	GrtT	60041	2473	26W-37N	E2
Randolph					
-	BLWD	60104	3029	12W-0N	B4
Randolph Ct					
400	NBRN	60010	2698	25W-22N	B3
8700	WDRG	60517	3206	20W-10S	B5
W Randolph Ct					
5000	HLSD	60162	3028	14W-0N	D4
Randolph St					
-	LMBD	60148	3026	19W-0N	C4
-	RVFT	60305	3030	10W-0N	A4
10	OKPK	60302	3031	8W-0N	A4
100	WNKA	60093	2758	6W-16N	E7
300	MYWD	60153	3030	10W-0N	A4
400	GLNC	60022	2758	6W-17N	E6
700	MYWD	60153	3029	11W-0N	C4
800	OKPK	60302	3030	8W-0N	E4
1100	FTPK	60130	3030	9W-0N	D4
1100	FTPK	60302	3030	9W-0N	C4
3400	LNSG	60438	3430	4E-21S	B6
4100	BLWD	60104	3029	13W-0N	A4
4600	BLWD	60104	3028	13W-0N	E4
7500	RVFT	60130	3030	9W-0N	C4

STREET Block	City	ZIP	Map#	CGS	Grid
E Randolph St					
10	CHCG	60602	3034	0E-0N	C4
10	CHCG	60603	3034	0E-0N	C4
400	CHCG	60601	3034	0E-0N	C4
W Randolph St					
10	CHCG	60601	3034	0W-0N	C4
10	CHCG	60602	3034	0W-0N	C4
100	CHCG	60606	3034	0W-0N	B4
300	EMHT	60126	3027	16W-0N	D4
700	CHCG	60607	3034	0W-0N	A4
700	CHCG	60661	3034	0W-0N	A4
800	CHCG	60607	3033	1W-0N	E4
2000	CHCG	60612	3033	2W-0N	B4
3100	CHCG	60612	3032	3W-0N	E3
4800	HLSD	60162	3028	14W-0N	D4
E Randville Dr					
1100	PLTN	60074	2753	19W-17N	B5
Randy Rd					
300	CLSM	60188	3024	24W-2N	C1
3000	JLET	60431	3497	28W-23S	B4
3000	JLET	60435	3497	28W-23S	B4
Raneys Ln					
14300	ODPK	60462	3345	12W-17S	C4
Ranger Ct					
1900	NCHI	60088	2593	11W-30N	D1
Ranger Dr					
500	CHHT	60411	3507	2W-24S	C6
Ranier Dr					
5400	LSLE	60532	3142	24W-6S	D4
Rankin Dr					
15900	LktT	60441	3418	26W-19S	A2
15900	LktT	60446	3418	26W-19S	A3
15900	RMVL	60441	3418	26W-19S	A3
15900	RMVL	60446	3418	26W-19S	A3
E Ranney Av					
100	VNHL	60061	2647	16W-24N	D7
300	VNHL	60061	2701	16W-24N	D1
Raoul Wallenberg Dr					
-	SKOK	60029	2811	6W-12N	C7
-	SKOK	60077	2811	7W-12N	C7
Raphael Av					
400	BFGV	60089	2754	15W-20N	E1
400	VrnT	60069	2754	15W-20N	E1
400	VrnT	60089	2754	15W-20N	E1
N Raphael Av					
20500	BFGV	60089	2754	15W-20N	E1
20500	VrnT	60069	2754	15W-20N	E1
20500	VrnT	60089	2754	15W-20N	E1
20700	VrnT	60069	2701	15W-20N	E7
Raphael Cir					
400	BGBK	60440	3205	22W-11S	C7
Raphael Ct					
3100	SCRL	60175	2963	37W-3N	B7
Raphael St					
13100	LMNT	60439	3343	18W-15S	A2
Rapidan Ct					
500	NPVL	60540	3142	25W-7S	B6
Rapids Ct					
1500	NPVL	60565	3203	26W-8S	D3
Raptor Ln					
-	AURA	60503	3201	31W-10S	E6
Raptor Tr					
8300	LKWD	60014	2693	37W-23N	A1
W Rascher Av					
2000	CHCG	60640	2921	2W-6N	B5
2500	CHCG	60625	2921	3W-6N	A5
2600	CHCG	60625	2920	3W-6N	E5
6200	CHCG	60630	2919	7W-6N	A5
6600	CHCG	60656	2919	8W-6N	A5
7900	NpkT	60656	2918	9W-6N	B5
8000	LydT	60656	2918	10W-6N	B5
8100	CHCG	60656	2918	10W-6N	B5
W Raska Ln					
25500	LkvT	60046	2474	25W-37N	A2
Ratfield Rd					
20700	RlyT	60152	2634	49W-25N	B5
Rathbone Av					
800	AraT	60506	3199	37W-8S	D2
800	AURA	60506	3199	37W-8S	D2
W Rathfarn Dr					
14400	HMGN	60491	3343	18W-17S	B6
S Rathje Rd					
200	PtnT	60468	3860	10W-37S	D3
200	PTON	60468	3860	10W-37S	D3
Ratray Dr					
1100	ALGN	60102	2747	33W-20N	D1
N Ratzlaff St					
100	CmgT	60033	2405	50W-38N	E7
100	HRVD	60033	2405	50W-38N	E7
N Raub St					
600	JLET	60435	3498	24W-23S	D3
Raupp Blvd					
10	BFGV	60089	2754	17W-18N	C3
Raven Ct					
-	LYWD	60411	3509	2E-23S	D3
10	BGBK	60490	3267	26W-12S	E3
4400	GRNE	60031	2535	14W-34N	C1
Raven Dr					
10	AURA	60506	3136	39W-7S	D7
1400	BGBK	60490	3267	26W-12S	E3
5500	MTSN	60443	3505	6W-24S	E5
Raven Hl					
1500	WHTN	60187	3081	26W-1S	E2
Raven Ln					
-	LYWD	60411	3509	2E-23S	D3
100	BMDL	60108	2968	23W-4N	E3
100	BMDL	60108	2969	23W-4N	A3
3800	RGMW	60008	2806	19W-13N	C7
W Raven Ln					
1000	PLTN	60067	2805	22W-15N	B2
N Raven Rd					
200	SRWD	60404	3496	30W-23S	B4
S Raven Rd					
100	SRWD	60404	3496	30W-24S	C6
W Raven St					
6200	CHCG	60646	2919	7W-7N	A3
6300	CHCG	60631	2919	7W-7N	A3
6600	CHCG	60631	2918	8W-7N	E3
Ravengate Ct					
11100	ODPK	60467	3422	14W-19S	E2
Ravenglass Ridge Rd					
3700	NndT	60012	2583	36W-28N	E6
Ravenna					
-	LGGV	60047	2646	18W-25N	E5
-	VNHL	60047	2646	18W-25N	E5
-	VNHL	60061	2646	18W-25N	E5
Ravenscraig Ln					
10	IVNS	60067	2752	22W-17N	B4
10	IVNS	60067	2805	22W-15N	A1
N Ravenswood Av					
3400	CHCG	60657	2977	2W-4N	C3
3600	CHCG	60613	2977	2W-5N	C1
4400	CHCG	60613	2921	2W-5N	C7
4400	CHCG	60640	2921	2W-5N	C7
6000	CHCG	60660	2921	2W-7N	C3
6300	CHCG	60626	2921	2W-7N	C3

STREET Block City ZIP Map# CGS Grid

Ravenswood Ct
700 LKZH 60047 2699 22W-22N B4
Ravina Ct
800 BTVA 60510 3078 34W-1S E3
Ravina Dr
7700 BtnT 60081 2414 30W-39N B4
7700 SPGV 60081 2414 30W-39N B4
Ravine Av
200 WKGN 60085 2537 10W-33N A3
300 LKBF 60044 2594 10W-28N A6
900 MchT 60051 2529 29W-32N B5
E Ravine Av
200 WLSP 60480 3209 12W-9S C3
N Ravine Av
39500 AntT 60002 2415 26W-39N E5
W Ravine Av
200 WLSP 60480 3209 12W-9S C3
300 RDLK 60073 2531 23W-33N E3
Ravine Ct
- ElgT 60124 2907 37W-9N D1
200 NBRN 60010 2644 24W-25N B4
Ravine Dr
- AntT 60081 2415 27W-39N B5
10 HDPK 60035 2705 7W-22N A5
100 CmpT 60175 2961 42W-5N D2
400 HDPK 60035 2704 8W-22N E5
400 WPHR 60096 2363 9W-43N C5
1800 GRNE 60031 2478 15W-36N B5
2100 BtnT 60099 2422 10W-41N A1
2100 ZION 60099 2422 10W-41N A1
2200 ZION 60099 2421 11W-41N E1
4100 NndT 60012 2583 36W-27N E7
13000 LMNT 60439 3342 19W-15S E1
E Ravine Dr
41500 BtnT 60099 2422 10W-41N B1
N Ravine Dr
500 HNVL 60030 2532 22W-34N B2
500 HNVL 60073 2532 22W-34N B2
500 RLKP 60073 2532 22W-34N B2
35000 GrtT 60041 2473 27W-35N B6
W Ravine Dr
10100 BtnT 60099 2422 10W-41N B1
10100 ZION 60099 2422 10W-41N B1
24800 LkvT 60046 2416 24W-39N B5
28600 CbaT 60010 2696 28W-23N E2
Ravine Ln
100 ElaT 60010 2644 24W-25N B4
100 NBRN 60010 2644 24W-25N B4
1600 CPVL 60110 2748 33W-17N C7
1600 CPVL 60110 2801 33W-16N C1
1600 HDPK 60035 2704 8W-22N E5
Ravine Rd
100 HNDL 60521 3086 15W-4S B7
600 CPVL 60110 2748 33W-17N B7
600 EDND 60118 2748 33W-17N B7
600 EDND 60118 2801 33W-16N B1
900 WNKA 60093 2759 5W-16N A7
1000 NARA 60542 3077 36W-3S E6
W Ravine Rd
21300 ElaT 60047 2699 21W-23N D1
21600 HNWD 60047 2699 21W-23N C1
Ravine Ter
1600 HDPK 60035 2705 8W-22N A5
Ravine Wy
2500 GNVW 60025 2810 9W-15N D2
2500 NHBK 60062 2810 9W-15N D2
W Ravine Crest Dr
24800 LkvT 60046 2416 24W-39N B5
Ravine Forest Dr
10 LKBF 60044 2593 10W-28N E6
10 LKBF 60044 2594 10W-28N A6
Ravine Glade St
100 GLNC 60022 2758 5W-17N E5
W Ravine Hills Ct
1200 PLTN 60067 2805 22W-14N B4
Ravine Park Dr
300 LKFT 60045 2594 10W-27N A7
Ravine Park Ln
1600 AURA 60504 3201 33W-8S A2
Ravine Woods Dr
26000 CNHN 60410 3672 32W-30S C4
26300 AxST 60447 3672 32W-30S C4
26300 CNHN 60447 3672 32W-30S C4
S Ravinia Av
- ODPK 60467 3423 12W-18S D1
14200 ODPK 60462 3345 12W-18S D7
15400 ODPK 60462 3423 12W-18S D1
Ravinia Cir
3300 AURA 60504 3201 31W-8S E2
Ravinia Ct
1100 SRWD 60404 3496 30W-24S B6
9700 ODPK 60462 3345 12W-17S D4
Ravinia Dr
100 SRWD 60404 3496 30W-24S B5
600 GRNE 60031 2476 18W-35N E7
6500 TYPK 60477 3425 8W-20S B4
Ravinia Ln
2500 WDRG 60517 3205 21W-8S D1
9700 ODPK 60462 3345 12W-17S D4
Ravinia Pl
100 ODPK 60462 3345 12W-18S D6
Ravinia Rd
500 HDPK 60035 2705 8W-21N A7
Ravinia Ter
900 LKZH 60047 2698 24W-23N C2
Ravinia Glen Pl
700 HDPK 60035 2758 7W-20N B2
Ravinia Park Rd
200 HDPK 60035 2758 7W-20N B2
Ravinoaks Ln
10 HDPK 60035 2705 7W-21N B6
Ravisloe Ln
- HMWD 60430 3427 3W-21S B7
S Ravisloe Ln
22600 FftT 60423 3591 13W-27S B5
Ravisloe Ter
17800 CCHL 60478 3426 5W-21S C7
Rawhide Dr
- PltT 60124 2852 39W-10N E6
Rawls Rd
10 DSPN 60018 2862 14W-10N C6
Rawson Bridge Rd
- WcnT 60010 2642 28W-26N D3
- WcnT 60084 2642 28W-26N D3
600 NndT 60013 2642 29W-26N C3
600 PTBR 60010 2642 29W-26N C3
Rawson Bridge Rd CO-V47
- PTBR 60010 2642 28W-26N D3
- WcnT 60010 2642 28W-26N D3
- WcnT 60084 2642 28W-26N D3
S Rawson Bridge Rd
800 AlqT 60013 2642 29W-24N B7
800 CRY 60013 2642 29W-24N B7
6000 NndT 60013 2642 30W-24N B6
W Rawson Bridge Rd
10 AlqT 60013 2641 31W-25N E4

W Rawson Bridge Rd
10 ODHL 60013 2641 31W-25N E4
800 AlqT 60013 2642 30W-26N A4
800 NndT 60013 2642 30W-26N A4
800 ODHL 60013 2642 30W-26N A4
900 NndT 60013 2641 30W-26N E4
Raxburg Ct
10 LIHL 60156 2692 38W-22N D3
Ray Av
200 WnfT 60185 3022 29W-1N D3
400 WCHI 60185 3022 29W-1N D3
Ray St
- NCHI 60064 2536 11W-31N E7
- NCHI 60088 2536 11W-31N E7
500 GNVA 60134 3020 35W-0N B5
600 WNVL 60555 3080 28W-3S E6
600 WNVL 60555 3081 28W-3S A6
2400 NCHI 60088 2593 11W-30N E1
4400 CLLK 60012 2640 33W-26N E2
4400 NndT 60012 2640 33W-26N E2
5600 MchT 60050 2472 29W-37N D2
Ray C Moses Dr
- AraT 60505 3200 34W-9S C3
900 AURA 60505 3200 34W-9S D3
Raycraft Rd
2400 GwdT 60098 2524 42W-34N C1
N Raye Dr
200 CHHT 60411 3507 1W-23S E3
200 CHHT 60411 3508 1W-23S A4
W Raye Dr
100 CHHT 60411 3507 1W-23S E3
Raymay Dr
400 JltT 60433 3499 21W-24S E6
Raymond Av
100 BRTN 60010 2750 26W-20N E2
1100 BKFD 60513 3087 11W-3S D4
1100 LGPK 60513 3087 11W-3S D4
1100 LGPK 60525 3087 11W-3S D4
1500 PvsT 60525 3087 11W-2S D4
4500 BKFD 60513 3147 11W-4S D1
4600 BKFD 60525 3147 11W-4S D1
4600 MCCK 60513 3147 11W-4S D1
4600 MCCK 60525 3147 11W-4S D1
9200 OKLN 60453 3211 6W-10S E6
Raymond Ct
500 SMBG 60193 2859 22W-9N B7
11000 HTLY 60142 2745 40W-20N A1
11000 RtdT 60142 2745 40W-20N A2
Raymond Dr
- CLLK 60014 2640 33W-24N E7
- FmtT 60030 2589 23W-30N A1
- FmtT 60073 2589 23W-30N A1
- GLBT 60136 2799 38W-15N B4
10 NPVL 60563 3140 28W-6S E4
1200 JLET 60431 3497 28W-22S A2
1300 AraT 60505 3200 34W-9S C4
1300 MTGY 60505 3200 34W-9S C4
1300 MTGY 60538 3200 34W-9S C4
1500 PnfT 60431 3497 28W-22S A1
1800 NHBK 60062 2810 9W-16N B1
2200 RDLK 60073 2589 23W-30N A2
4200 HLSD 60162 3028 13W-0S E5
4200 HLSD 60162 3029 13W-0S A5
12400 NlxT 60448 3502 15W-22S B2
19200 JknT 60421 3675 24W-29S E1
23700 CteT 60417 3597 2E-28S E7
Raymond Dr CO-1
600 NPVL 60563 3140 28W-6S E4
Raymond Dr CO-13
900 NPVL 60563 3140 29W-5S E2
N Raymond Dr
1600 JLET 60431 3417 28W-21S A7
1600 PnfT 60431 3417 28W-21S A7
Raymond Rd
- BFGV 60069 2754 16W-20N D1
- BFGV 60089 2754 16W-20N D1
- VrnT 60069 2754 16W-20N D1
100 BRkT 60511 3196 45W-8S C3
100 SgrT 60511 3196 45W-8S C3
1200 GLBT 60136 2799 38W-15N B4
Raymond St
200 ELGN 60120 2855 33W-10N A5
900 ElgT 60120 2855 33W-9N A7
900 ElgT 60177 2855 33W-9N A7
1100 SEGN 60177 2855 33W-9N A7
1200 SEGN 60177 2909 33W-9N A1
1300 SEGN 60177 2908 34W-9N E1
N Raynor Av
10 JLET 60435 3498 25W-23S D4
10 JLET 60436 3498 24W-23S D5
1500 CTHL 60403 3498 25W-21S C1
1700 CTHL 60403 3418 24W-21S D7
S Raynor Av
- JLET 60435 3498 24W-23S D5
10 JLET 60436 3498 25W-24S D5
600 RKDL 60436 3498 25W-24S C7
S Raynor Av US-52
- JLET 60435 3498 24W-23S D5
10 JLET 60436 3498 25W-24S D5
Rays Ln
200 MDLN 60060 2646 18W-26N D3
Rayson Ln
8800 TYPK 60487 3424 11W-21S A6
Ray Sternal Ln
- RMVL 60441 3340 24W-18S E7
Read St
300 LKPT 60441 3419 21W-19S E2
E Reader St
200 ELBN 60119 3017 43W-1N A2
Reading Cir
1600 CPVL 60110 2748 32W-18N C5
Reading Ct
1200 WHTN 60187 3082 23W-1S E2
W Reading Ct
100 PLTN 60067 2805 21W-14N D3
Reading Dr
500 BRLT 60103 2910 29W-7N C4
Reagan Blvd
1600 MHRY 60051 2528 31W-33N D3
1700 MchT 60051 2528 31W-33N D3
2300 BGBK 60490 3339 28W-14S B1
21400 BGBK 60544 3339 27W-14S B1
21900 WldT 60490 3339 27W-14S B1
21900 WldT 60544 3339 27W-14S B1
22700 BGBK 60585 3339 28W-14S B1
22700 PNFD 60585 3339 28W-14S B1
Reagan Dr
400 OSWG 60543 3263 38W-12S A3
Reagan Pl
400 GYLK 60030 2533 20W-32N A5
Ream Dr
200 ELBN 60119 3017 43W-2N A1
Reardon Dr
300 JLET 60435 3497 27W-23S C4
Reba Ct
10 MNGV 60053 2865 7W-10N B5

Reba Pl
700 EVTN 60202 2867 2W-10N B5
Reba St
5400 MNGV 60077 2865 6W-10N D5
5400 SKOK 60077 2865 6W-10N D5
5700 MNGV 60053 2865 7W-10N C5
Reba Ln Rd
1100 ELGN 60123 2801 33W-13N A7
Rebecca Av
- ELGN 60120 2855 32W-10N D7
Rebecca Cir
2100 MTGY 60538 3198 40W-10S C6
Rebecca Ct
900 SMBG 60193 2912 24W-9N D1
2800 MTGY 60538 3198 40W-10S C5
23200 NPVL 60564 3202 29W-11S E7
23200 WldT 60564 3202 29W-11S D7
Rebecca Dr
10 BNHL 60010 2802 28W-15N D2
1300 HFET 60169 2858 25W-12N A2
1700 RMVL 60446 3339 27W-17S D7
2800 NLNX 60451 3500 20W-24S C5
Rebecca Ln
400 BGBK 60440 3268 24W-13S D4
500 WnfT 60190 3023 28W-0S B7
1700 AURA 60504 3201 33W-8S A3
2400 GNVW 60025 2810 10W-15N A2
N Rebecca Ln
22600 KLDR 60047 2699 21W-22N E4
N Rebecca Rd
100 JLET 60435 3497 27W-23S C4
S Rebecca Rd
1300 LMBD 60148 3084 20W-1S B1
1300 YkTp 60148 3084 20W-1S B1
N Rebecca St
10 GNWD 60425 3508 0E-22S D2
100 CLLK 60014 2640 34W-26N B3
S Rebecca St
10 GNWD 60425 3508 0E-22S D2
Reber St
200 WHTN 60187 3024 24W-0S C7
Reckinger Rd
900 AraT 60505 3138 34W-5S D4
1100 AURA 60505 3138 34W-5S D4
1500 AURA 60505 3139 33W-5S A4
1600 AraT 60502 3139 33W-5S A4
1600 AraT 60505 3139 33W-5S A4
1600 AURA 60502 3139 33W-5S A4
Recreation Dr
200 BGBK 60440 3269 22W-12S C2
N Recreation Dr
3400 CHCG 60613 2978 0W-4N A2
N Recreation Dr SR-19
- CHCG 60613 2978 0W-5N A1
Recreation Rd
- ELGN 60123 2801 33W-13N A7
Red Dr
13100 LMNT 60439 3343 17W-15S C2
S Red Ln
26700 CteT 60417 3687 4E-32S C7
W Red Apple Rd
- PNFD 60543 3265 33W-14S B7
- PNFD 60585 3265 33W-14S B7
Red Bark Ln
8100 AlqT 60013 2696 29W-23N D1
Red Barn Ct
2100 WDSK 60098 2582 39W-29N C3
2900 AURA 60503 3201 31W-10S D6
Red Barn Dr
2900 AURA 60503 3201 31W-10S D6
2900 WldT 60503 3201 31W-10S D6
3400 WRLK 60097 2469 38W-35N A6
Red Barn Ln
100 BRTN 60010 2751 24W-18N B2
100 NHFD 60093 2811 7W-15N A3
200 CmpT 60175 2905 41W-7N E5
700 ELGN 60124 2853 36W-9N D7
800 ELGN 60124 2907 36W-9N D1
Red Barn Rd
10 HshT 60140 2795 47W-15N D4
10 MTSN 60443 3505 7W-24S C4
10 RchT 60477 3505 7W-24S C4
2000 WDSK 60098 2582 39W-29N C3
2700 BLVY 60012 2583 36W-28N E5
2700 NndT 60012 2583 36W-28N E5
6800 NndT 60012 2584 35W-28N A5
Red Barn Tr
500 BGBK 60490 3268 26W-13S A4
Red Bay Ct
500 SchT 60175 2907 38W-7N A4
Redberry Cir
13400 DPgT 60544 3339 26W-15S E3
13400 DPgT 60544 3340 26W-16S A3
13500 RMVL 60544 3340 26W-16S A3
W Redberry Ct
21000 DPgT 60544 3339 26W-16S E3
Redbird Ct
200 BMDL 60108 2968 24W-4N D3
Redbird Ln
- CLLK 60012 2640 35W-27N A1
4900 NndT 60012 2640 35W-27N A1
Redbird Rd
300 BMDL 60108 2968 24W-4N D3
300 BMDL 60139 2968 24W-4N D3
300 GLHT 60139 2968 24W-4N D3
Red Bridge Ct
500 LKZH 60047 2699 22W-22N A3
Redbridge Ct
1300 GYLK 60030 2532 21W-34N E1
Red Bridge Rd
10 LKZH 60047 2699 22W-22N A4
Redbud Av
1000 BCHR 60401 3864 0W-36S D1
Red Bud Cir
- LKPT 60432 3420 20W-21S B7
200 SYHW 60118 2800 36W-15N A3
Red Bud Ct
10 BGBK 60490 3267 27W-12S D2
700 BRLT 60103 2910 29W-9N D1
2400 AURA 60502 3079 32W-3S C7
3600 DRGV 60515 3084 20W-3S B6
3900 PRGV 60012 2641 32W-27N A1
Redbud Ct
- WRLK 60097 2469 37W-36N B3
10 LIHL 60156 2693 37W-22N A4
300 CmpT 60175 2961 42W-5N D2
300 FKFT 60423 3503 13W-25S B7
13600 LktT 60544 3339 26W-16S E3
Redbud Dr
- LNHT 60046 2476 19W-37N D1
100 JltT 60433 3587 23W-25S A2
100 JltT 60436 3587 23W-25S A2
300 NPVL 60540 3203 27W-7S C1
S Redbud Dr
13600 LktT 60544 3339 26W-16S E3
13700 LktT 60544 3340 26W-16S A4

Red Bud Ln
2400 AURA 60502 3079 32W-4S C7
6900 WDRG 60517 3143 21W-7S D7
Redbud Ln
- SRGV 60554 3135 42W-4S D1
200 BTVA 60510 3078 36W-1S A1
800 WLMT 60091 2811 5W-13N E5
800 WLMT 60091 2812 5W-13N A5
1400 GNVW 60025 2810 8W-14N D5
S Red Bud Ln
15500 HmrT 60441 3420 20W-18S B1
15500 LKPT 60441 3420 20W-18S B1
W Redbud Ln
18200 WrnT 60030 2534 18W-34N A1
18200 WrnT 60031 2534 18W-34N A1
Red Bud Pl
200 BFGV 60089 2754 16W-20N D1
Red Bud Rd
1700 BGBK 60490 3267 27W-12S C2
Redbud Rd
10 RGMW 60008 2806 19W-14N C3
Redcastle Dr
9000 FftT 60477 3504 11W-23S A4
9000 TYPK 60477 3504 11W-23S A4
Red Cedar Dr
100 SMWD 60107 2857 27W-10N C6
Red Cedar Ln
13300 DPgT 60544 3339 26W-15S E2
Red Cedar Rd
400 LKVL 60046 2474 23W-36N E4
Red Cedar Tr
15500 HMGN 60491 3344 15W-18S C7
Redcliffe St
1200 WDRG 60517 3206 20W-9S B3
W Red Cloud Dr
16000 LKPT 60441 3420 20W-20S C5
Red Cloud Ln
10 PltT 60124 2852 39W-9N E7
Red Clover Ct
12100 PNFD 60585 3265 31W-14S E7
Red Clover Dr
800 AURA 60504 3202 30W-9S A3
900 AURA 60564 3202 30W-9S A3
Red Clover Ln
12100 PNFD 60585 3265 31W-14S E7
Red Coach Ln
200 NHBK 60062 2757 9W-18N C3
600 ALGN 60102 2695 32W-20N A7
E Redcoat Dr
13100 LMNT 60439 3343 16W-15S E2
N Redcoat Dr
13300 LMNT 60439 3343 16W-15S D2
S Redcoat Dr
13500 LMNT 60439 3343 16W-15S E2
W Redcoat Dr
13300 LMNT 60439 3343 16W-15S D2
Red Cypress Ct
- CRY 60013 2642 29W-24N C7
Red Cypress Dr
500 CRY 60013 2642 29W-24N B7
Red Deer Rd
500 RDLK 60073 2531 24W-33N C2
Redden Ct
700 SCRL 60174 2964 36W-3N A6
Redding Ct
- OSWG 60543 3263 36W-13S E5
Reddington Dr
1000 AURA 60502 3139 32W-6S C4
Redeker Rd
1200 DSPN 60016 2862 13W-12N E2
1300 DSPN 60016 2863 13W-11N A2
Red Field Ct
5100 JLET 60586 3496 30W-22S C2
N Redfield Ct
200 PKRG 60068 2863 11W-9N D7
S Redfield Ct
300 PKRG 60068 2917 11W-8N D1
Redfield Dr
- CHCG 60629 3150 4W-7S D6
- CHCG 60629 3151 3W-7S A7
Redfield Rd
1100 NPVL 60563 3140 29W-5S D2
Redford Ln
5400 HRPK 60133 2911 27W-6N C6
5500 BRLT 60103 2911 27W-6N C6
5500 HRPK 60103 2911 27W-6N C6
Red Fox Cir
1200 SDWH 60548 3258 51W-14S A7
Red Fox Ct
1400 SCRL 60174 2964 34W-3N D5
13200 LMNT 60439 3343 16W-15S E2
Red Fox Ln
- OKBK 60523 3085 16W-1S E1
100 EGVV 60007 2859 22W-9N C6
400 LKFT 60045 2650 10W-25N A5
1900 GNOK 60048 2592 14W-30N C1
Red Fox Run
10 MTGY 60538 3199 36W-10S D5
Redgate Ct
700 SchT 60175 2907 36W-6N D7
Red Gate Ln
5900 FoxT 60560 3332 46W-16S B4
Red Gate Rd
10 SchT 60175 2963 36W-5N D1
200 SchT 60175 2964 35W-5N B2
200 SCRL 60175 2963 36W-5N E2
200 SCRL 60175 2964 36W-5N A2
Red Haw Ln
10 LKZH 60047 2699 22W-22N A4
10 SchT 60174 2963 36W-3N D6
1900 SCRL 60174 2963 36W-3N D6
2000 SCRL 60175 2963 36W-3N D6
Red Haw Rd
10 NHBK 60062 2757 9W-17N D4
10 RGMW 60008 2806 19W-14N C4
Red Hawk Ct
10 CmpT 60175 2962 40W-5N C2
10 OswT 60543 3264 35W-14S C7
Red Hawk Dr
- PnfT 60586 3416 31W-21S A6
- SCRL 60174 2964 34W-4N E5
10 OswT 60543 3264 35W-14S C7
800 ANTH 60002 2357 24W-41N C7
900 ANTH 60002 2416 24W-41N B1
2200 JLET 60586 3416 31W-21S A6
Red Hawk Ln
10600 SPGV 60081 2354 32W-42N C6
Red Hawk Pth
100 GLBT 60136 2799 38W-16N C2
Red Hawk Rd
- HPSR 60140 2795 47W-15N D4
Red Hawk Ridge Ct
2400 AURA 60503 3201 32W-11S C7
Red Hawk Ridge Dr
2500 AURA 60503 3201 32W-11S C7
2500 AURA 60503 3265 32W-11S C1

W Redhead Ct
10 RLKB 60073 2475 23W-36N A3
Redhead Ln
100 BmdT 60108 2967 26W-5N E2
100 BmdT 60133 2967 26W-5N E2
Red Hill Ln
10 SBTN 60010 2804 25W-13N A5
Redhill Tr
100 CLSM 60188 2968 25W-3N B6
Red Hills Rd
14000 HTLY 60140 2744 44W-19N A2
14000 HTLY 60142 2744 44W-19N A2
Redhorse Ln
500 YKVL 60560 3333 44W-15S A3
Reding Cir
- DSPN 60016 2863 12W-12N C2
9600 MaiT 60016 2863 12W-12N C1
Redington Dr
400 SEGN 60177 2907 37W-7N D5
Red Leaf Cir
- LKWD 60098 2638 39W-25N C4
Red Leaf Dr
500 RtdT 60140 2798 40W-15N B3
Red Maple Dr
1700 JLET 60586 3495 33W-21S A1
Red Maple Ln
600 MltT 60187 3082 25W-2S A4
600 ROSL 60172 2912 24W-6N D6
600 WHTN 60187 3082 25W-2S A4
2000 AURA 60502 3079 33W-4S B7
Redmond Ct
600 BNVL 60106 2972 15W-4N B3
Redmond Dr
100 GLBT 60136 2799 38W-16N B1
100 RtdT 60136 2799 38W-16N B1
N Redmond St
- FlxT 60416 3941 33W-39S B2
10 DMND 60416 3941 33W-39S B2
S Redmond St
10 DMND 60416 3941 33W-40S B2
Red Oak Av
10 AddT 60106 2971 17W-4N C3
200 ADSN 60106 2971 17W-4N B3
500 BNVL 60106 2971 16W-4N D3
Red Oak Cir
3200 CPVL 60110 2747 35W-17N C6
N Red Oak Cir
1100 RLKB 60073 2474 24W-34N C7
Red Oak Ct
10 BFGV 60089 2754 17W-18N B3
200 WCHI 60185 3022 30W-2N C1
700 BRLT 60103 2910 29W-9N D1
700 LslT 60563 3141 26W-5S E3
700 NPVL 60563 3141 26W-5S E3
1200 ELGN 60120 2855 32W-11N D4
2400 JLET 60586 3415 33W-20S A6
W Red Oak Ct
12800 HMGN 60491 3422 16W-19S A2
Red Oak Dr
10 MltT 60137 3083 23W-3S A5
500 BbyT 60119 3075 43W-2S A5
700 BRLT 60103 2856 29W-9N D7
700 BRLT 60103 2910 29W-9N D1
700 BRLT 60120 2910 29W-9N D1
900 SMWD 60103 2856 29W-9N D7
900 SMWD 60107 2856 29W-9N D7
2100 RDLK 60073 2531 25W-33N A2
2400 DYR 46311 3598 D3
2900 HtdT 60033 2464 48W-35N E6
5500 HFET 60192 2856 31W-12N A2
7100 NndT 60012 2583 36W-27N E7
7500 JLET 60586 3415 33W-20S A6
19800 MKNA 60448 3502 14W-24S D4
N Red Oak Dr
34500 WrnT 60031 2534 17W-34N C1
34600 WrnT 60031 2477 17W-34N C7
Red Oak Ln
- SPGV 60081 2413 30W-39N E5
- SPGV 60081 2414 30W-39N A5
10 NHBK 60062 2757 9W-20N C2
500 HDPK 60035 2757 9W-20N C1
600 HDPK 60035 2704 9W-20N C7
700 UYPK 60466 3684 3W-29S B2
1000 LKVL 60046 2475 21W-37N D1
1000 LNHT 60046 2475 21W-37N D1
2000 SCRL 60174 2964 34W-3N D6
2200 JNBG 60050 2471 31W-36N E3
3700 LSLE 60187 3082 24W-3S D6
3700 LSLE 60532 3082 24W-3S D6
4500 LGGV 60047 2700 19W-23N D2
8200 ODPK 60462 3346 10W-16S B2
E Red Oak Ln
200 CteT 60417 3687 4E-32S B7
W Red Oak Ln
24600 TroT 60404 3584 30W-26S B3
Red Oak Rd
200 NfdT 60062 2757 9W-18N B3
200 NHBK 60062 2757 9W-18N B3
25700 AxST 60410 3672 33W-31S B6
25700 CNHN 60410 3672 33W-31S B6
Red Oak St
100 BNVL 60106 2972 15W-4N A3
Red Oak Ter
600 HDPK 60035 2704 9W-20N C7
N Red Oak Ter
38700 WDWH 60083 2420 14W-38N D6
Red Oak Tr
10 CRY 60013 2641 31W-24N C6
2400 CTHL 60403 3497 27W-22S D1
Red Oaks Tr
1100 AURA 60506 3137 37W-5S D3
Redondo Dr
- RNPK 60443 3593 7W-27S C4
400 DGvT 60516 3206 19W-9S E3
400 DRN 60516 3206 19W-9S E3
1000 RMVL 60446 3340 25W-16S B3
Redondo Ln
7800 ODPK 60462 3346 9W-16S C3
7800 OrlT 60462 3346 9W-16S D3
Red Pine Av
4900 GRNE 60031 2478 15W-36N A4
4900 WrnT 60031 2478 15W-36N A4
Red Pine Ct
20600 FmtT 60060 2646 20W-26N A3
Red Pine Tr
6800 DRN 60561 3145 18W-7S A7
Redpoll Ct
1600 NPVL 60565 3204 26W-9S A3
Red Ridge Cir
10 SBTN 60010 2803 27W-15N A2
Red River Ct
100 NPVL 60565 3204 26W-10S A5
Red Rock Dr
400 LNHT 60046 2418 20W-38N A6
Red Rock Ln
300 ElgT 60124 2853 38W-10N A6

STREET Block	City	ZIP	Map#	CGS	Grid
Red Rock Pt					
400	LKMR	60051	2529	29W-32N	D5
Red Rose Dr					
100	SCRL	60175	2963	37W-3N	B7
Red Silver Ct					
1200	DRGV	60515	3084	20W-3S	B6
Red Sky Dr					
300	SCRL	60175	2963	37W-2N	B7
400	SCRL	60175	3019	37W-2N	B1
Redspire Ct					
10	BGBK	60490	3268	25W-12S	A3
Red Spruce Tr					
10	LKVL	60046	2475	22W-37N	A2
S Red Stable Ln					
25600	CNHN	60410	3672	33W-31S	C5
Red Stable Wy					
800	OKBK	60515	3084	18W-3S	E6
800	OKBK	60523	3084	18W-3S	E6
800	YkTp	60515	3084	18W-3S	E6
10500	NPVL	60564	3266	29W-12S	D3
10500	WldT	60564	3266	29W-12S	D3
Red Star Dr					
13200	PNFD	60585	3337	31W-15S	D3
Redstart Rd					
10	NPVL	60565	3203	26W-9S	D3
10	NPVL	60565	3204	26W-9S	A3
Redstone Dr					
25700	MhtT	60442	3678	16W-31S	E5
Red Tail Cir					
1000	ANTH	60002	2358	21W-41N	E7
Red Tail Dr					
10	FmtT	60060	2645	22W-26N	B3
10	HNWD	60060	2645	22W-26N	B3
Redtail Dr					
7800	LKWD	60014	2639	37W-24N	A7
7900	LKWD	60014	2693	37W-23N	A1
8400	GfnT	60156	2693	37W-23N	A2
Red Tail Ln					
500	YKVL	60560	3261	43W-13S	B5
Redtail Rdg					
500	ELGN	60123	2853	36W-12N	E2
Red Top Dr					
100	LYVL	60048	2647	16W-27N	E1
900	LYVL	60048	2648	15W-27N	A1
Red Top Ln					
1400	CNHN	60410	3672	33W-30S	A4
1400	MNKA	60447	3672	33W-30S	A4
N Redtop Rd					
34000	GrtT	60073	2531	25W-34N	A1
Red Wing Ct					
10	WDRG	60517	3143	21W-7S	E7
Redwing Ct					
10	MltT	60188	3023	26W-1N	E3
200	BMDL	60108	2968	24W-4N	D3
500	AvnT	60030	2533	20W-32N	A5
500	GYLK	60030	2533	20W-32N	A5
3500	NPVL	60564	3266	30W-11S	B2
3900	RGMW	60008	2806	20W-13N	B6
Red Wing Dr					
900	RedT	60408	3941	32W-40S	D4
6700	WDRG	60517	3143	21W-7S	E7
Redwing Dr					
100	MltT	60188	3023	26W-1N	E3
100	WDSK	60098	2525	40W-32N	A5
200	GwdT	60098	2525	40W-32N	A5
300	BGBK	60440	3268	24W-11S	D1
300	VrnT	60015	2755	14W-20N	B1
600	GNVA	60134	3020	36W-0S	A6
1300	ANTH	60002	2416	24W-41N	C1
3400	NPVL	60564	3266	30W-11S	B1
Red Wing Ln					
-	CNHN	60410	3672	34W-31S	A6
27200	AxST	60410	3672	34W-31S	A6
27200	AxST	60447	3672	34W-31S	A6
Redwing Ln					
100	NBRN	60010	2644	25W-24N	A6
300	VrnT	60015	2755	14W-20N	B1
4600	LGGV	60047	2700	19W-24N	D1
Redwing Pkwy					
1300	ANTH	60002	2417	21W-41N	E1
1300	AntT	60002	2417	21W-41N	E1
W Redwing Pl					
23300	ElaT	60010	2751	23W-20N	E1
Redwing St					
-	LYWD	60411	3509	2E-23S	D3
E Redwing St					
400	RLKB	60073	2475	22W-35N	C6
Redwood Av					
200	EGVV	60007	2861	17W-9N	B7
200	NlxT	60451	3501	17W-23S	C4
1600	HRPK	60133	2911	27W-8N	D2
20100	LYWD	60411	3510	3E-23S	A4
S Redwood Av					
1500	EGvT	60005	2861	16W-11N	D4
1500	EGvT	60056	2861	16W-11N	D4
1500	MPPT	60056	2861	16W-11N	D4
Redwood Ct					
10	SMWD	60107	2857	27W-10N	C6
10	WNVL	60555	3080	30W-1S	C2
200	VNHL	60061	2647	17W-25N	B5
200	WHTN	60187	3082	25W-2S	A3
500	NARA	60542	3077	36W-3S	D7
3100	FSMR	60422	3507	3W-22S	A1
3800	SPGV	60081	2354	32W-42N	B7
8000	FXLK	60020	2415	28W-39N	A6
8000	FXLK	60081	2415	28W-39N	A6
9300	MaiT	60016	2863	11W-12N	D1
17000	ODHL	60487	3424	11W-20S	A4
W Redwood Ct					
15300	LKPT	60441	3342	20W-18S	B7
Redwood Dr					
-	AlqT	60013	2642	30W-24N	A7
-	BNHL	60102	2695	32W-20N	B7
-	YKVL	60560	3333	42W-14S	E1
100	ELWD	60421	3675	25W-31S	B5
400	CRY	60013	2642	30W-24N	A7
500	AURA	60506	3137	38W-7S	B6
900	ALGN	60102	2695	32W-20N	B7
1000	ALGN	60102	2748	32W-20N	C1
1100	ALGN	60010	2748	31W-20N	C1
1100	BNHL	60010	2748	31W-20N	C1
1900	RLKB	60073	2474	23W-35N	E5
13800	ODPK	60462	3346	10W-16S	B3
22700	RNPK	60471	3594	6W-27S	B5
N Redwood Dr					
4400	CHCG	60634	2974	10W-5N	B1
4400	NRDG	60706	2974	10W-5N	B1
4800	NRDG	60706	2918	10W-6N	B7
5400	CHCG	60656	2918	10W-6N	B5
5400	LydT	60656	2918	10W-6N	B5
5600	CHCG	60631	2918	10W-7N	B5
5600	LydT	60631	2918	10W-7N	B5
5600	MaiT	60631	2918	10W-7N	B5
S Redwood Dr					
1400	MPPT	60056	2861	16W-11N	D3
W Redwood Dr					
21200	DPgT	60544	3339	26W-15S	E3
21200	LktT	60544	3339	26W-15S	E3
Redwood Ln					
-	HMWD	60430	3507	3W-22S	A1
10	HNWD	60047	2644	23W-25N	D5
100	BRTN	60010	2751	24W-20N	D2
200	CmpT	60175	2962	39W-4N	E3
400	SMBG	60193	2858	24W-9N	E7
500	LSLE	60532	3143	22W-4S	C1
600	FSMR	60422	3507	3W-22S	A1
600	GLNC	60022	2758	6W-16N	C6
600	HMWD	60422	3507	3W-22S	A1
700	GNVW	60025	2811	7W-13N	B7
800	BRLT	60103	2911	28W-7N	A5
1000	MNKA	60447	3672	34W-29S	A3
1700	CPVL	60110	2748	32W-18N	C5
1700	MHRY	60050	2528	32W-33N	C2
1900	NHBK	60062	2757	10W-17N	B4
17500	TYPK	60487	3424	11W-21S	A5
19500	FftT	60448	3503	11W-23S	E4
E Redwood Ln					
600	ANHT	60004	2807	17W-16N	B1
S Redwood Ln					
21200	SRWD	60404	3584	31W-25S	A2
W Redwood Ln					
15000	GNOK	60048	2592	15W-30N	B2
15000	LbvT	60048	2592	15W-30N	B2
Redwood Rd					
500	BGBK	60440	3269	21W-11S	D1
Redwood St					
10	CPVL	60110	2748	32W-18N	C5
7400	AlqT	60014	2640	33W-24N	D7
Redwood Tr					
10	WLNG	60090	2754	15W-17N	E4
Reed Av					
2100	JNBG	60050	2471	31W-35N	E6
Reed Ct					
10	HNWD	60047	2589	22W-27N	B7
10	HNWD	60047	2645	22W-27N	B1
800	ADSN	60101	2969	21W-4N	E3
40300	WDWH	60083	2419	16W-40N	E3
Reed Rd					
-	BDWD	60408	3941	32W-42S	C6
-	BvlT	60407	3941	32W-42S	C6
-	BvlT	60408	3941	32W-42S	C6
-	BvlT	60416	3941	32W-42S	C6
-	RedT	60408	3941	32W-42S	C6
700	GnvT	60134	3021	33W-0N	A4
800	GnvT	60134	3020	33W-0N	E4
1300	ZION	60099	2362	12W-41N	B7
10000	GfnT	60156	2692	38W-22N	E5
10000	HTLY	60156	2692	38W-22N	D5
10000	LlHL	60142	2692	38W-22N	E5
10000	LlHL	60156	2692	38W-22N	E5
10300	GfnT	60142	2692	39W-22N	C5
11100	HTLY	60142	2692	40W-21N	B5
E Reed Rd					
-	BDWD	60408	3941	33W-42S	C6
-	BvlT	60408	3941	33W-42S	C6
-	RedT	60408	3941	33W-42S	C6
7200	BvlT	60407	3941	33W-41S	B6
7200	BvlT	60416	3941	33W-41S	B6
Reed St					
600	BCHR	60401	3864	0W-36S	B2
25200	CNHN	60410	3672	31W-30S	E3
26100	GrtT	60041	2530	26W-34N	E1
E Reed St					
100	BDWD	60408	3942	31W-42S	B6
300	RedT	60408	3942	31W-42S	B6
N Reed St					
10	JLET	60435	3498	25W-23S	C4
10	JLET	60436	3498	25W-23S	C5
S Reed St					
10	JLET	60435	3498	25W-24S	C6
10	JLET	60436	3498	25W-24S	C6
W Reed St					
100	BDWD	60408	3942	31W-41S	A6
Reedham Pass					
100	SMBG	60194	2858	25W-10N	B5
Reedsworth Ct					
10	ALGN	60102	2693	38W-20N	A7
S Reedwood Dr					
10	JLET	60435	3498	25W-24S	B5
10	JLET	60436	3498	25W-24S	B6
Reef Ct					
800	WLNG	60090	2755	15W-16N	A6
Reef Rd					
700	LKPT	60441	3342	21W-18S	A7
N Reef Rd					
500	LKPT	60441	3420	21W-18S	A1
600	LKPT	60441	3342	21W-18S	A7
Rees Rd					
100	BRLT	60120	2910	31W-7N	A4
Reese Av					
500	EDND	60118	2801	33W-16N	B2
2600	EVTN	60201	2812	4W-13N	D7
2700	WLMT	60091	2812	4W-13N	D7
2700	WLMT	60201	2812	4W-13N	D7
E Reese St					
900	HMND	46394	3280		E4
E Reeves Ct					
9600	FNPK	60131	2973	12W-4N	C3
W Reeves Ct					
9700	FNPK	60131	2973	12W-4N	C3
Reeves Dr					
1700	GLHT	60139	2968	24W-3N	D6
Reeves Rd					
2400	JLET	60436	3585	27W-26S	D2
S Reeves Rd					
13900	RBBN	60472	3348	4W-16S	E3
Reeves St					
-	ELBN	60119	3017	42W-0N	C4
Reflection Ct					
2900	JLET	60586	3415	32W-20S	C5
Reflection Dr					
2500	NPVL	60564	3202	30W-11S	C7
2900	JLET	60586	3415	32W-20S	C4
3000	NasT	60586	3415	32W-20S	B4
Reflections					
-	RMVL	60446	3340	26W-17S	A5
Reflections Dr					
2200	AraT	60502	3139	32W-7S	B6
2200	AURA	60502	3139	32W-7S	B6
Regal Ct					
10	ALGN	60102	2694	35W-20N	A7
200	ROSL	60172	2912	25W-7N	C4
300	CNHL	60514	3145	16W-6S	D3
300	DGvT	60514	3145	16W-6S	D3
1900	SMBG	60194	2858	25W-11N	A4
4900	CTWD	60445	3348	6W-16S	A2
N Regal Ct					
400	ADSN	60101	2970	20W-4N	A4
Regal Dr					
-	CLLK	60014	2640	34W-25N	D4
Regal Ln					
-	AURA	60506	3198	40W-8S	C2
-	SgrT	60506	3198	40W-8S	C2
600	ALGN	60102	2694	35W-20N	A7
800	ALGN	60102	2747	35W-20N	A1
Regalia Ct					
500	IVNS	60010	2751	24W-16N	C6
Regalia Dr					
400	HFET	60010	2751	24W-16N	C7
400	IVNS	60010	2751	24W-16N	C7
Regal Oaks Ct					
7100	OSWG	60560	3262	40W-14S	C7
7100	OswT	60560	3262	40W-14S	C7
Regan Blvd					
300	BNHL	60010	2748	32W-18N	D4
Regan Ct					
1000	NlxT	60451	3501	17W-23S	D4
1500	HFET	60192	2804	24W-15N	B2
1600	NLNX	60451	3501	17W-23S	D4
Regan Dr					
500	EDND	60118	2801	33W-15N	B3
Regan Ln					
-	HNWD	60047	2589	22W-27N	B7
-	HNWD	60060	2589	22W-27N	B7
10	HNWD	60047	2645	22W-27N	B1
Regan Rd					
2400	PnfT	60431	3417	28W-20S	A6
3400	JLET	60431	3417	28W-20S	A6
W Regan Rd					
10	NlxT	60448	3502	15W-22S	B2
12300	MKNA	60448	3502	15W-23S	B3
12600	NlxT	60448	3501	16W-23S	E3
13200	NlxT	60451	3501	16W-23S	E3
13400	NLNX	60451	3501	16W-23S	E3
Regatta Pt					
300	SMBG	60194	2859	22W-11N	C4
Regency Blvd					
-	BNHL	60010	2802	28W-14N	E5
-	BrnT	60010	2802	28W-14N	E5
-	SgrT	60554	3135	41W-6S	E5
200	SRGV	60554	3135	41W-6S	E5
Regency Ct					
10	SMWD	60107	2856	29W-9N	E7
200	BRLT	60103	2910	29W-8N	D3
300	AURA	60504	3202	30W-8S	A2
1000	SRWD	60404	3496	30W-24S	B6
1100	SMBG	60193	2912	24W-8N	C2
1200	VNHL	60061	2647	16W-26N	D3
1300	ROSL	60172	2912	25W-6N	B5
1400	CTCY	60409	3429	2E-19S	D3
1700	MPPT	60056	2808	13W-14N	D4
2000	GNVA	60134	3019	36W-1N	E4
2600	NPVL	60565	3203	27W-10S	B6
5700	GRNE	60031	2534	16W-33N	E3
8300	WLSP	60480	3208	13W-9S	E3
S Regency Ct E					
10	ANHT	60004	2807	16W-14N	E5
S Regency Ct W					
10	ANHT	60004	2807	16W-14N	D5
Regency Dr					
-	BMDL	60139	2969	22W-4N	B4
-	FKFT	60423	3591	13W-26S	B3
-	GLHT	60101	2969	22W-3N	C5
100	BRLT	60103	2910	29W-8N	D3
100	GLHT	60139	2969	22W-3N	C5
100	LMBD	60148	3084	19W-2S	C3
200	BMDL	60108	2969	22W-4N	B4
500	LKZH	60047	2698	24W-22N	C4
600	DRPK	60047	2698	24W-22N	C5
600	DSPN	60016	2808	14W-12N	D7
1100	SMBG	60193	2912	24W-8N	C2
4300	GNVW	60025	2809	11W-13N	C7
4300	NfdT	60025	2809	11W-13N	C7
11000	WSTR	60154	3086	13W-2S	E4
22400	RNPK	60471	3594	4W-27S	D4
N Regency Dr					
1200	VNHL	60061	2647	16W-26N	D3
N Regency Dr E					
10	ANHT	60004	2807	16W-14N	E5
N Regency Dr W					
10	ANHT	60004	2807	16W-14N	D5
S Regency Dr E					
10	ANHT	60004	2807	16W-13N	D5
10	ANHT	60056	2807	16W-14N	E5
10	MPPT	60056	2807	16W-14N	E5
S Regency Dr W					
10	ANHT	60004	2807	16W-13N	D5
10	MPPT	60056	2807	16W-14N	D5
W Regency Dr					
4400	WKGN	60048	2535	14W-31N	C6
Regency Ln					
1000	CLSM	60188	2967	27W-4N	D4
1000	LYVL	60048	2591	17W-28N	B6
1100	LKFT	60045	2593	12W-27N	B7
1300	GYLK	60030	2475	21W-35N	D7
1300	GYLK	60046	2475	21W-35N	D7
1300	RLKB	60046	2475	21W-35N	D7
Regency Pkwy					
12100	HTLY	60142	2744	42W-19N	E2
12100	RtdT	60142	2744	42W-19N	E2
Regency Grove Dr					
1300	DRN	60561	3207	18W-8S	A2
Regency Park Dr					
700	CLLK	60014	2693	36W-23N	D1
W Regency Ridge Dr					
1400	JLET	60436	3498	25W-24S	B6
Regency Woods Dr					
2200	LSLE	60187	3082	24W-3S	D6
2200	LSLE	60532	3082	24W-3S	D6
2200	MltT	60187	3082	24W-3S	D6
2200	MltT	60532	3082	24W-3S	D6
Regent Blvd					
-	SRWD	60404	3583	31W-25S	E1
Regent Cir					
10	SMBG	60193	2859	23W-10N	B5
Regent Ct					
-	DMND	60416	3941	34W-40S	A3
10	BRRG	60527	3208	15W-10S	B5
10	LKZH	60047	2699	21W-22N	C4
10	OKBK	60523	3085	17W-2S	C4
300	LNHT	60046	2418	19W-38N	C7
Regent Ct E					
10	BFGV	60089	2754	17W-18N	A3
Regent Ct W					
10	BFGV	60089	2754	17W-18N	A3
Regent Dr					
-	FmtT	60060	2590	20W-27N	A7
10	GLBT	60136	2799	38W-14N	B6
10	OKBK	60523	3085	17W-2S	C5
200	BFGV	60089	2754	17W-18N	A3
300	WLNG	60090	2755	14W-18N	A4
600	CLLK	60014	2693	36W-23N	D2
1100	MDLN	60060	2646	19W-27N	B1
1200	MDLN	60060	2590	20W-27N	B7
1300	NfdT	60062	2756	12W-17N	C5
1300	NHBK	60062	2756	12W-17N	C6
Regent Dr					
3400	HFET	60067	2804	23W-14N	E4
15100	ODPK	60462	3345	11W-17S	E6
19500	MKNA	60448	3503	12W-23S	C3
Regent Ln					
10	LNSH	60069	2702	13W-22N	E3
600	PTHT	60070	2808	14W-14N	B3
1400	FDHT	60411	3509	1E-25S	B6
Regent Rd					
500	UYPK	60466	3684	3W-30S	C3
Regent St					
200	GNEN	60137	3025	22W-0S	B6
400	ELGN	60120	2855	33W-10N	A5
500	SEGN	60177	2908	34W-8N	D2
800	NLNX	60451	3501	16W-25S	E7
800	NlxT	60451	3501	16W-25S	E7
900	NLNX	60451	3502	16W-25S	A7
900	NlxT	60451	3502	16W-25S	A7
S Regents Rd					
16100	HmrT	60441	3420	19W-19S	D2
16100	HmrT	60491	3420	19W-19S	D2
Regent Wood Rd					
10	GNVW	60025	2810	8W-15N	E3
10	NHFD	60093	2810	8W-15N	E3
10	NHFD	60093	2811	7W-15N	A3
Regina Ct					
700	WDSK	60098	2524	42W-32N	C5
S Regina Ln					
12600	PSPK	60464	3274	9W-14S	D7
N Regina Rd					
40200	AntT	60002	2417	21W-40N	C3
N Regis Ct					
700	PLTN	60067	2752	21W-16N	C6
700	PltT	60067	2752	21W-16N	C6
N Regis Hall Rd					
38500	OMCK	60083	2419	16W-38N	D7
Regner Ln					
800	MchT	60051	2472	29W-34N	B7
Regner Rd					
600	MchT	60051	2472	29W-34N	C7
2600	MchT	60051	2529	29W-34N	C1
Rehm Ct					
1800	LSLE	60532	3142	23W-6S	E6
W Reiche Ln					
-	LKMR	60051	2529	30W-34N	A1
1500	MchT	60051	2529	30W-34N	A2
1900	MchT	60051	2528	30W-34N	E1
Reichert Av					
1700	SLVL	60411	3597	2E-27S	C4
E Reichert Dr					
3200	CteT	60417	3687	4E-31S	B6
3200	HnrT	46311	3687	4E-31S	B5
Reichman St					
100	JLET	60433	3499	23W-24S	A7
100	JltT	60433	3499	23W-24S	A7
Reid Pl					
-	NpvT	60502	3139	31W-6S	D5
Reid St					
1300	WNSP	60558	3086	14W-4S	D7
Reidel Dr					
1500	MDLN	60060	2647	17W-25N	B4
N Reigate Ln					
30900	GNOK	60048	2592	14W-31N	C1
31100	GNOK	60048	2535	14W-31N	C7
Reiger Ct					
11200	BtnT	60081	2355	30W-43N	A4
11200	SPGV	60081	2355	30W-43N	A4
Reiland Dr					
4600	CLLK	60012	2640	33W-26N	E2
4600	NndT	60012	2640	33W-26N	E2
4600	NndT	60014	2640	33W-26N	E2
Reilly Ln					
800	LKFT	60045	2649	12W-25N	C4
Reilly Pl					
4900	LSLE	60532	3143	23W-5S	A2
S Reilly Ter					
7700	CHCG	60652	3212	4W-8S	D2
Reimann Av					
400	SDWH	60548	3330	51W-14S	A1
600	SDWH	60548	3258	51W-14S	A7
Reimers Dr					
10	AURA	60506	3137	38W-7S	B7
N Rein Ct					
31500	GNOK	60048	2535	14W-31N	C7
Reindeer Tr					
700	CmpT	60175	2962	39W-5N	D2
W Reindeer Tr					
-	LkvT	60046	2416	23W-38N	D6
Reinking Rd					
-	PGGV	60140	2797	41W-15N	E4
10	PGGV	60140	2798	40W-14N	B6
10	PltT	60140	2798	40W-13N	B7
10	RtdT	60140	2744	43W-17N	B7
10	RtdT	60140	2797	41W-15N	E3
10	RtdT	60140	2798	41W-14N	B6
Reinking Rd CO-7					
10	PGGV	60140	2798	40W-14N	B6
10	PltT	60140	2798	40W-13N	B7
Reinzi Ln					
10	HIWD	60040	2704	9W-24N	D1
Reising Av					
400	AURA	60505	3138	35W-7S	C6
W Reiter Dr					
14800	HMGN	60441	3421	18W-20S	A4
14800	HMGN	60491	3421	18W-20S	A4
14800	LKPT	60441	3421	18W-20S	A4
14800	LKPT	60491	3421	18W-20S	A4
14900	HMGN	60491	3420	19W-20S	E4
14900	LKPT	60441	3420	19W-20S	E4
14900	LKPT	60491	3420	19W-20S	E4
Reiter Rd					
2500	NLNX	60451	3589	19W-27S	A5
Reliance Ct					
500	MTGY	60543	3262	39W-11S	D1
500	OSWG	60543	3262	39W-11S	D1
Reliance Ln					
10	LNSH	60069	2702	13W-22N	D3
Relstar Ct					
3800	NPVL	60564	3267	28W-11S	B2
Rembrandt Ct					
5800	HRPK	60133	2911	26W-7N	E4
Rembrandt Dr					
500	ANTH	60002	2358	23W-42N	A5
Remin Ln					
10	JltT	60433	3587	23W-25S	B1
Remington Av					
-	ELBN	60119	3017	42W-0N	C5
Remington Blvd					
-	DPgT	60490	3268	25W-14S	A6
100	BGBK	60440	3269	23W-13S	A4
400	BGBK	60440	3268	24W-13S	D4
1000	BGBK	60446	3268	25W-13S	B6
1000	BGBK	60490	3268	25W-13S	B6
1000	RMVL	60446	3268	25W-13S	B6
1000	RMVL	60490	3268	25W-13S	B6
1400	BGBK	60490	3340	26W-14S	A1
Remington Blvd					
1500	BGBK	60490	3339	26W-14S	D1
1500	BGBK	60544	3339	26W-14S	D1
1500	DPgT	60490	3339	26W-14S	D1
W Remington Cir					
-	SMBG	60173	2859	23W-12N	A2
10	SMBG	60195	2859	23W-12N	A2
Remington Ct					
1400	GYLK	60030	2532	21W-34N	D1
7000	WDRG	60517	3144	20W-7S	B6
Remington Dr					
-	VOLO	60041	2530	27W-33N	C3
100	BNHL	60010	2749	30W-17N	A6
100	BrnT	60010	2749	30W-17N	A6
100	SCRL	60175	2963	37W-3N	C6
200	BRLT	60103	2909	32W-8N	C4
2200	NPVL	60565	3204	25W-10S	B5
3100	NndT	60013	2641	32W-26N	C3
3100	NndT	60014	2641	32W-26N	C3
S Remington Dr					
22400	CNHN	60410	3584	29W-27S	D5
Remington Ln					
-	BbyT	60506	3076	40W-3S	C6
-	NARA	60506	3076	40W-3S	C6
1400	RDLK	60073	2531	25W-34N	B1
W Remington Ln					
-	SMBG	60195	2859	23W-12N	A2
Remington Rd					
10	SMBG	60173	2859	23W-12N	B2
10	SMBG	60195	2859	23W-12N	A2
Remmington Tr					
-	NndT	60050	2527	34W-31N	C6
5400	MHRY	60050	2527	34W-31N	C6
Remora Ct					
4000	NCHI	60088	2593	11W-30N	D1
N Rena Av					
39300	AntT	60002	2416	25W-39N	A4
Renaissance Blvd					
10	OKTR	60181	3085	18W-1S	A2
Renaissance Cir					
12500	HMGN	60491	3344	15W-17S	B4
Renaissance Dr					
800	CLSM	60188	2967	26W-3N	E5
1400	PKRG	60068	2863	12W-10N	C5
Renard Cir					
3400	SCRL	60175	2963	38W-3N	B6
Renard Ln					
2900	SCRL	60175	2963	37W-3N	B6
Renaux Blvd					
10	SCRL	60175	2963	38W-3N	B6
Rene Ct					
1000	PKRG	60068	2864	10W-10N	A6
Renee Av					
5300	NndT	60014	2641	33W-26N	A2
Renee Ct					
500	GNVA	60134	3019	36W-1N	D2
Renee Dr					
10	SEGN	60177	2908	35W-8N	C2
Renee Ter					
200	WLNG	60090	2755	15W-17N	A5
W Renier St					
12500	BHPK	60087	2421	12W-38N	B7
12500	WKGN	60087	2421	12W-38N	B7
Renken Dr					
1500	NCHI	60064	2536	11W-32N	D5
1500	WKGN	60085	2536	11W-32N	D5
Renmore Rd					
14400	HMGN	60491	3343	18W-17S	B6
Renn Ct					
500	WHTN	60187	3024	25W-0S	B7
Renner Dr					
300	ELGN	60123	2854	36W-10N	A6
300	ElgT	60123	2854	36W-10N	A6
Rennes Ct					
3000	NHBK	60062	2756	11W-17N	D6
Rennet Dr					
1300	NPVL	60565	3203	27W-8S	C2
Rennie Smith Dr					
3200	SCHT	60411	3596	0W-27S	C4
3200	SCHT	60475	3596	0W-27S	C4
Reno Ct					
-	GNEN	60137	3083	23W-1S	A1
Renouf Dr					
200	WnfT	60555	3080	29W-2S	D4
Renwick Rd					
-	LktT	60441	3419	23W-19S	A2
-	RMVL	60441	3419	23W-19S	A2
19200	CTHL	60441	3418	24W-19S	E2
19200	LktT	60441	3418	24W-19S	E2
19200	RMVL	60441	3418	24W-19S	E2
19500	CTHL	60403	3418	25W-18S	B2
19500	LktT	60403	3418	25W-18S	B2
E Renwick Rd					
10	PNFD	60544	3416	29W-18S	E2
10	PNFD	60586	3416	29W-18S	D2
300	PnfT	60544	3416	29W-18S	E2
400	PnfT	60544	3417	28W-19S	A2
700	PNFD	60544	3417	28W-18S	B2
W Renwick Rd					
10	PNFD	60544	3416	30W-19S	B2
10	PNFD	60586	3416	30W-19S	B2
1400	PnfT	60544	3416	31W-19S	A2
1400	PnfT	60586	3416	31W-19S	A2
1500	PnfT	60544	3415	31W-18S	E2
1500	PnfT	60586	3415	31W-18S	E2
1600	PNFD	60544	3415	31W-18S	E2
1800	PNFD	60586	3415	32W-19S	C2
20500	CTHL	60403	3418	25W-18S	B2
20500	LktT	60403	3418	25W-18S	B2
20500	LktT	60441	3418	26W-18S	B2
20700	LktT	60446	3418	26W-18S	A2
20700	RMVL	60441	3418	26W-18S	A2
20700	RMVL	60446	3418	26W-18S	A2
21000	LktT	60403	3417	26W-18S	E2
21000	LktT	60441	3417	26W-18S	E2
21000	LktT	60446	3417	26W-18S	E2
21000	RMVL	60446	3417	27W-18S	C2
21500	JLET	60403	3417	26W-18S	D2
21500	JLET	60446	3417	26W-18S	D2
21700	JLET	60446	3417	27W-18S	C2
21700	JLET	60544	3417	27W-18S	C2
21700	PnfT	60435	3417	27W-18S	D2
21700	PnfT	60544	3417	27W-18S	C2
21700	RMVL	60544	3417	27W-18S	C2
21700	WilC	60544	3417	27W-18S	C2
24800	NasT	60544	3415	32W-18S	B2
Renwick Park Dr					
15900	PNFD	60544	3416	30W-19S	B2
15900	PNFD	60586	3416	30W-19S	B2
15900	PnfT	60586	3416	30W-19S	B2
Repton Rd					
10	RVSD	60546	3088	9W-2S	C3
Republic Av					
10	JLET	60435	3497	26W-23S	E5
10	JLET	60436	3497	26W-23S	E5
500	ELBN	60119	3017	43W-0N	A5

STREET Block City ZIP Map# CGS Grid

Republic Ct
600 SMBG 60193 2859 23W-9N A7
W Republic Dr
1000 ADSN 60101 2970 19W-3N C6
Republic Rd
200 BTVA 60510 3078 35W-1S A1
500 BTVA 60510 3020 35W-0S A7
Reque Rd
- WynT 60185 2966 31W-3N A7
500 WCHI 60185 2966 31W-2N A7
E Reseda Pkwy
100 PLTN 60067 2752 20W-17N E5
200 PLTN 60067 2753 20W-17N A5
300 PLTN 60074 2753 20W-17N A5
Reservation Rd
6100 OswT 60560 3334 39W-15S D3
N Reserve Av
4400 CHCG 60656 2973 11W-5N E1
5200 CHCG 60656 2917 10W-6N E6
Reserve Cir
300 CNHL 60514 3145 17W-6S C4
22500 PNFD 60544 3339 28W-16S A5
Reserve Ct
400 JLET 60431 3496 28W-23S E4
600 SchT 60175 2907 37W-7N B5
600 SchT 60177 2907 37W-7N B6
600 SEGN 60175 2907 37W-7N B6
600 SEGN 60177 2907 37W-7N B6
900 FXLK 60041 2473 27W-35N C6
1700 HDPK 60035 2703 10W-23N E3
1700 HDPK 60035 2704 10W-22N A3
2700 AURA 60502 3139 32W-5S C3
Reserve Dr
- ALGN 60102 2746 37W-20N B2
- ElgT 60124 2907 37W-9N D1
- GfnT 60102 2746 37W-20N A2
- SCRL 60175 2963 36W-6N E1
200 SchT 60175 2964 35W-6N A1
200 SCRL 60175 2964 36W-6N A1
300 CLLK 60012 2639 36W-26N E2
300 NndT 60014 2639 36W-26N D2
400 CLLK 60014 2639 36W-26N D2
1100 ELGN 60124 2907 37W-9N D2
8900 LynT 60480 3208 14W-10S C5
8900 WLSP 60480 3208 14W-10S C5
Reserve Ln
700 JLET 60431 3496 28W-23S E3
3900 JLET 60431 3497 28W-23S A3
Reskin Rd
700 LMBD 60148 3026 19W-1N D2
W Resthaven Ter
25400 AntT 60002 2416 25W-39N A5
Reston Cir
300 RMVL 60446 3339 27W-17S D7
Reston Ct
100 ROSL 60172 2912 24W-7N E5
Reston Ln
- RtdT 60118 2746 38W-17N C7
- RtdT 60118 2799 38W-16N C1
N Reta Av
3500 CHCG 60613 2977 1W-4N E3
3500 CHCG 60657 2977 1W-4N E3
Retreat Ct
10 CmpT 60175 2961 42W-5N D2
Retta Ct
1000 JLET 60433 3499 23W-25S A7
Reuben Dr
23600 PNFD 60586 3416 29W-19S D3
23600 PnfT 60586 3416 29W-19S D3
N Reuter Dr
10 ANHT 60005 2806 18W-14N D4
S Reuter Dr
10 ANHT 60005 2806 18W-13N D6
Reuter St
2600 FNPK 60131 2973 12W-3N C5
Reva Bay Ln
- FXLK 60081 2415 27W-39N A6
Revell Ct
8000 ODPK 60462 3346 10W-17S C4
Revere Av
500 WTMT 60559 3085 17W-3S C6
Revere Cir
1500 SMBG 60193 2858 25W-10N B6
Revere Ct
10 BGBK 60440 3205 22W-10S D5
10 DRFD 60015 2704 10W-20N B7
800 WTMT 60559 3085 17W-4S D6
1000 LMBD 60148 3026 18W-0S E5
1000 NPVL 60540 3142 24W-7S C7
1200 CRTE 60417 3685 1W-29S A1
1200 NLNX 60451 3589 18W-26S B2
1600 MTGY 60538 3199 36W-10S E5
1600 MTGY 60538 3200 36W-10S A5
6500 GRNE 60031 2477 17W-35N B6
15700 OKFT 60452 3347 7W-18S D7
15700 OKFT 60452 3425 7W-18S D1
Revere Dr
10 HDPK 60035 2757 8W-18N D2
10 NHBK 60062 2757 8W-18N D2
10 SBTN 60010 2803 27W-14N B4
400 CLLK 60012 2640 35W-26N A2
N Revere Dr
30300 LbvT 60048 2591 16W-30N E2
Revere Ln
900 ISLK 60042 2586 30W-28N B5
1800 EGVV 60007 2859 22W-9N C7
W Revere Ln
500 PLTN 60067 2805 21W-14N C3
Revere Pl
- PLNO 60545 3259 47W-13S C5
1100 VNHL 60061 2647 17W-26N B3
Revere Rd
600 MaiT 60025 2809 10W-13N E7
800 GNEN 60137 3025 21W-0S D6
800 NfdT 60025 2809 10W-13N E6
800 SEGN 60177 2908 35W-8N C3
900 GNVW 60025 2809 10W-13N E6
6700 DRGV 60516 3144 20W-7S A7
10600 MKNA 60448 3503 13W-23S A3
11100 FftT 60448 3502 14W-23S E3
11100 MKNA 60448 3502 14W-23S E3
Revere St
10 SEGN 60177 2908 35W-8N C3
1900 CHHT 60411 3595 2W-26S D2
Revere House Ln
10 BbyT 60134 3076 39W-1S E1
10 GnvT 60134 3076 38W-1S E1
Reverend C Clarke Dr
2500 NCHI 60064 2593 11W-31N C1
Reverend Edw H Baseheart Dr
1600 CHCG 60640 2921 2W-6N C5
Reverend Morrison Blvd
100 EGVV 60007 2914 18W-8N E1
Reverend Rogers Dr
5500 BRBK 60459 3211 6W-9S D2
Reverend Walton Dr
100 LktT 60441 3419 23W-21S B7
Revier Park Ct
2500 CTHL 60403 3497 27W-22S D2
S Rex Blvd
100 EMHT 60126 3027 16W-1N D3
Rexford Rd
3800 CTWD 60445 3348 4W-17S C4
3800 CTWD 60472 3348 4W-17S C4
3800 MDLN 60445 3348 4W-17S C4
3800 RBBN 60472 3348 4W-17S C4
Rexford St
13100 BLID 60406 3349 2W-15S B1
S Rexford St
12200 ALSP 60803 3276 5W-14S A6
E Reynolds Dr
1300 PLTN 60074 2753 19W-16N C7
N Reynolds Dr
300 PLTN 60074 2753 19W-16N D7
Reynolds Ln
15500 OKFT 60452 3347 7W-18S D7
15700 OKFT 60452 3425 7W-18S D1
Rhea Dr
12100 PNFD 60585 3266 29W-14S C7
12100 WldT 60585 3266 29W-14S C7
12400 PNFD 60585 3338 29W-14S C1
12400 WldT 60585 3338 29W-14S C1
Rhema Dr
10 BlmT 60411 3507 1W-23S E3
10 BlmT 60430 3507 1W-23S E3
10 CHHT 60411 3507 1W-23S E3
Rhett Pl
1400 WDSK 60098 2524 40W-32N E5
Rhiannon Ct
4800 PLTN 60067 2805 21W-14N E4
4800 RGMW 60067 2805 21W-14N E4
Rhine Av
100 BGBK 60490 3267 27W-11S C2
Rhode Av
5700 HMND 46320 3352 E7
6000 HMND 46320 3430 E1
6800 HMND 46324 3430 E3
Rhode Ct
7900 SjnT 46311 3598 E5
Rhode Island Av
4200 NCHI 60088 2593 12W-29N C3
Rhode Island Ct
4200 NCHI 60088 2593 12W-29N C3
17600 ODPK 60467 3423 13W-21S A6
Rhode Island Tr
6600 NndT 60012 2583 35W-27N E7
6600 NndT 60012 2584 35W-27N A7
Rhodes Av
2700 LydT 60164 2972 14W-3N C5
2700 NHLK 60164 2972 14W-3N C5
3000 FNPK 60131 2972 14W-3N C4
3000 LydT 60131 2972 14W-3N C5
N Rhodes Av
2400 RVGV 60171 2973 11W-3N E6
S Rhodes Av
3100 CHCG 60616 3092 0E-3S D4
3500 CHCG 60653 3092 0E-3S D5
6000 CHCG 60637 3152 0E-7S D6
7000 CHCG 60619 3152 0E-8S D7
7500 CHCG 60619 3214 0E-9S D2
10000 CHCG 60628 3214 0E-11S D7
10300 CHCG 60628 3278 0E-12S D2
13100 CHCG 60827 3278 0E-15S E7
13100 CHCG 60827 3350 0E-15S D1
19100 BlmT 60425 3508 0E-23S E2
19100 GNWD 60425 3508 0E-23S E3
Rhodes Ct
1100 WHTN 60187 3082 24W-1S E2
7000 WDRG 60517 3144 20W-7S B6
Rhodes Ln
1200 NPVL 60540 3203 28W-8S A1
Rhodes St
800 WDSK 60098 2524 42W-31N C6
Rhonda Dr
500 LKPT 60441 3420 21W-19S A2
6600 CmgT 60033 2405 52W-38N B6
Ribbon Ct
5100 MONE 60449 3683 6W-31S A6
Ribbon Dr
4900 MONE 60449 3683 6W-31S B6
Rice Av
- MLPK 60160 3029 10W-1N E3
- MYWD 60153 3029 10W-1N E3
- MYWD 60153 3030 10W-1N A3
- MYWD 60160 3029 10W-1N E3
100 BLWD 60104 3029 12W-0N B5
Rice Ct
900 NPVL 60565 3204 25W-10S C5
Rice St
600 HDPK 60035 2705 7W-20N B7
600 HDPK 60035 2758 7W-20N B1
900 MLPK 60160 3029 11W-1N D3
1600 WKGN 60087 2479 11W-37N E2
W Rice St
- CHCG 60622 3032 3W-1N E2
1800 CHCG 60622 3033 2W-1N C2
3300 CHCG 60651 3032 4W-1N D2
4700 CHCG 60651 3031 6W-1N E2
5900 OKPK 60302 3031 7W-1N B3
Rice Lake Sq
10 MltT 60187 3082 24W-3S D5
10 WHTN 60187 3082 24W-3S D5
Rich Ct
10 PKFT 60466 3595 4W-27S A3
17200 JknT 60421 3677 21W-30S A3
Rich Ln
600 BRLT 60103 2909 31W-8N E2
Rich Rd
200 PKFT 60466 3595 3W-27S A3
Richard Av
10 MltT 60187 3023 26W-1N D4
10 MltT 60190 3023 26W-1N D4
200 MltT 60188 3023 26W-1N D3
200 WNFD 60190 3023 26W-1N D3
1000 BKLY 60163 3028 14W-1N C3
1700 AraT 60505 3138 34W-5S E3
1700 AURA 60505 3138 34W-5S E3
4300 OKFT 60452 3426 5W-19S B2
9200 FNPK 60131 2973 11W-3N D5
N Richard Av
100 EMHT 60126 3028 15W-1N B2
S Richard Av
11900 PSHT 60463 3274 9W-14S D6
13200 NlxT 60448 3501 16W-22S E2
Richard Ct
10 ADSN 60101 2970 19W-3N D6
200 FXLK 60020 2473 27W-37N B1
300 ISLK 60042 2586 29W-28N D5
2800 MHRY 60051 2528 31W-33N D3
E Richard Ct
700 GDLY 60407 4030 32W-43S D2
700 RedT 60408 4030 32W-43S D2
S Richard Ct
300 VNHL 60061 2647 17W-24N A7
Richard Dr
- CLLK 60014 2640 33W-25N E4
10 ElgT 60124 2907 38W-8N B3
700 WldT 60564 3266 28W-11S E1
800 PKCY 60085 2536 12W-33N B4
6100 AlqT 60014 2640 33W-25N E4
Richard Ln
700 EGvT 60007 2861 16W-9N D7
700 EGvT 60007 2915 16W-9N D1
700 EGVV 60007 2915 16W-9N D1
36800 LkvT 60046 2475 22W-36N B3
W Richard Pl
11400 BHPK 60099 2421 11W-39N D5
Richard Rd
100 NPVL 60540 3142 25W-7S A6
800 DYR 46311 3598 E2
1000 ELGN 60123 2800 34W-13N E7
1000 ELGN 60123 2854 34W-13N E1
1900 DRN 60561 3206 18W-8S E1
Richard St
- SRGV 60554 3135 42W-7S D6
200 PLNO 60545 3259 47W-14S C7
1800 AURA 60506 3137 38W-6S A5
W Richard St
- FNPK 60131 2973 11W-3N D5
- RVGV 60131 2973 11W-3N D5
8700 RVGV 60171 2973 11W-3N E5
Richard E Bush Ct
1600 WKGN 60085 2536 11W-32N D5
Richard J Brown
- PGGV 60140 2797 42W-15N D4
Richards Av
1400 DRGV 60516 3206 20W-8S B1
Richards Ct
200 WPHR 60096 2362 11W-43N E4
200 WPHR 60096 2363 10W-43N A4
1700 FSMR 60422 3507 2W-23S D4
8300 TYPK 60477 3424 10W-20S C3
N Richards Ct
23000 VrnT 60069 2701 16W-23N D2
Richards Dr
16500 TYPK 60477 3424 10W-20S C4
N Richards Dr
100 PLTN 60074 2753 19W-16N D7
100 PLTN 60074 2806 19W-16N D1
S Richards Dr
6400 CHCG 60637 3153 2E-7S C5
6400 CHCG 60649 3153 2E-7S C5
Richards Rd
- SRWD 60404 3496 30W-22S B3
7200 BGVW 60455 3210 9W-11S E6
Richards St
10 GNVA 60134 3020 35W-1N B3
800 SCRL 60134 3020 35W-1N B3
800 SCRL 60174 3020 35W-1N B3
1700 JltT 60433 3587 23W-26S B2
S Richards St
- JltT 60433 3499 23W-24S A6
10 JLET 60432 3499 23W-24S A5
10 JLET 60433 3499 23W-24S A5
1100 JLET 60433 3587 23W-25S B1
1100 JltT 60433 3587 23W-25S B1
Richard S McClaughry Dr
- MNSR 46321 3510 D4
S Richardson Av
13900 RBBN 60472 3348 4W-16S E3
Richardson Dr
300 DndT 60118 2801 33W-15N A4
Richardson Ln
7600 TYPK 60477 3504 9W-23S D3
Richardson Rd
- EDND 60118 2801 33W-15N B4
10 DndT 60118 2801 32W-15N C4
8400 BtnT 60081 2414 30W-40N A2
8400 SPGV 60081 2414 30W-40N A2
9700 BtnT 60081 2355 30W-41N A7
9700 SPGV 60081 2355 30W-41N A7
Richardson Rd CO-V43
9300 BtnT 60081 2414 30W-40N A2
9300 SPGV 60081 2414 30W-40N A2
9700 BtnT 60081 2355 30W-41N A7
9700 SPGV 60081 2355 30W-41N A7
Richert Ct
300 ELGN 60120 2855 33W-10N A5
Richert Rd
200 WDDL 60191 2915 17W-6N B5
Richfield Av
1600 HDPK 60035 2704 9W-21N C6
Richfield Ct
1200 DGvT 60517 3206 20W-8S B2
1200 WDRG 60517 3206 20W-8S B2
Richfield Ln
- HDPK 60035 2704 9W-21N C6
Richfield Tr
300 RMVL 60446 3339 27W-18S D7
Richland Ct
3200 AURA 60504 3201 31W-8S E1
Richland Ln
3100 AURA 60504 3201 31W-8S E2
Richmond Av
- MKHM 60429 3427 3W-19S A3
- YKVL 60560 3333 42W-17S E6
10 LGPK 60525 3087 12W-3S A6
400 WTMT 60559 3145 17W-6S C4
15900 MKHM 60428 3427 3W-19S A2
E Richmond Av
1000 LGPK 60525 3087 12W-3S C6
1100 BKFD 60513 3087 12W-3S C6
1100 BKFD 60525 3087 12W-3S C6
N Richmond Av
200 CNHL 60514 3085 17W-4S C7
200 CNHL 60514 3145 17W-4S C1
200 CNHL 60559 3085 17W-4S C7
200 CNHL 60559 3145 17W-4S C1
200 WTMT 60514 3085 17W-4S C7
200 WTMT 60514 3145 17W-4S C1
200 WTMT 60559 3085 17W-4S C7
200 WTMT 60559 3145 17W-4S C1
S Richmond Av
- CHCG 60652 3213 3W-10S A4
- CHCG 60805 3213 3W-10S A4
- ENGN 60805 3213 3W-10S A4
10 CNHL 60514 3145 17W-5S C3
10 CNHL 60559 3145 17W-5S C3
6000 DGvT 60527 3145 17W-6S C5
6000 DGvT 60559 3145 17W-6S C5
6000 WTMT 60527 3145 17W-6S C5
6000 WTMT 60559 3145 17W-7S C6
6500 DGvT 60561 3145 17W-7S C6
6500 DRN 60527 3145 17W-7S C6
6700 DRN 60561 3145 17W-7S C7
7100 DRN 60561 3207 17W-8S C1
14400 POSN 60469 3349 3W-17S A4
14900 BmnT 60469 3349 3W-17S A5
W Richmond Av
25300 AntT 60002 2416 25W-39N A5
Richmond Cir
- SEGN 60177 2909 33W-9N A1
500 LKZH 60047 2698 24W-22N C4
Richmond Ct
10 LKZH 60047 2698 24W-22N C4
100 ROSL 60172 2912 24W-7N E5
300 RMVL 60446 3339 27W-17S D7
400 OSWG 60543 3200 35W-11S B7
800 NPVL 60540 3141 27W-7S C7
900 EGVV 60007 2913 21W-8N D2
1000 DYR 46311 3510 C6
1900 SMBG 60194 2858 25W-11N B3
4000 MTSN 60443 3594 5W-26S D2
10600 PlsT 60462 3345 13W-15S A2
N Richmond Ct
22300 KLDR 60047 2699 20W-22N E4
Richmond Dr
100 BGBK 60440 3268 24W-12S E2
200 RMVL 60446 3339 27W-17S D7
300 PnfT 60446 3339 27W-17S D7
300 PnfT 60544 3339 27W-17S D7
400 ROSL 60172 2912 24W-7N E5
700 OSWG 60543 3200 35W-11S B7
2200 WHTN 60187 3083 23W-3S A5
Richmond Ln
- GfnT 60142 2691 41W-20N D7
- GfnT 60142 2744 41W-20N D1
- HTLY 60142 2744 41W-20N D1
10 AURA 60504 3201 32W-8S C1
200 LKWD 60014 2639 37W-25N B5
400 CLLK 60014 2639 37W-25N B6
1200 WLMT 60091 2812 4W-14N D4
1300 BRLT 60103 2967 28W-5N A1
1300 KLWH 60043 2812 4W-14N D4
1400 ALGN 60102 2747 35W-19N B4
1800 LGGV 60047 2753 18W-20N D1
1800 VrnT 60047 2753 18W-20N D1
Richmond Pl
300 VNHL 60061 2647 17W-24N B7
Richmond Rd
300 KLWH 60043 2812 4W-14N D4
500 DndT 60118 2800 36W-16N A2
600 DndT 60118 2799 36W-16N E1
1400 TNLK 53181 2353 D3
1800 RdlT 53128 2353 E1
1800 RdlT 53181 2353 E1
1800 TNLK 53128 2353 E1
4100 JNBG 60050 2471 33W-36N A4
4100 JNBG 60072 2471 33W-36N A4
4100 MchT 60072 2471 33W-36N A4
4100 RGWD 60072 2470 33W-36N D4
4100 RGWD 60072 2471 33W-36N A4
4400 MchT 60072 2470 33W-36N E4
5700 RcmT 60072 2470 33W-36N E4
6200 RcmT 60072 2412 34W-38N D7
6600 RcmT 60071 2412 34W-38N D7
8400 WRLK 60097 2469 37W-35N B5
12500 RcmT 60071 2353 D4
12500 RHMD 60071 2353 D4
12500 TNLK 60071 2353 D4
21600 MTSN 60443 3594 5W-26S D2
Richmond Rd CO-O
1400 TNLK 53181 2353 D3
Richmond Rd CO-P
1400 TNLK 53181 2353 D3
1800 RdlT 53128 2353 E1
1800 RdlT 53181 2353 E1
1800 TNLK 53128 2353 E1
12500 RcmT 60071 2353 D4
12500 RHMD 60071 2353 D4
12500 TNLK 60071 2353 D4
Richmond Rd SR-31
4100 JNBG 60050 2471 33W-36N A4
4100 JNBG 60072 2471 33W-36N A4
4100 MchT 60072 2471 33W-36N A4
4100 RGWD 60072 2470 33W-36N D4
4100 RGWD 60072 2471 33W-36N A4
4400 MchT 60072 2470 33W-36N E4
5700 RcmT 60072 2470 33W-36N E4
6200 RcmT 60072 2412 34W-38N D7
6600 RcmT 60071 2412 34W-38N D7
N Richmond Rd
1300 MHRY 60050 2528 32W-33N B3
1900 MchT 60050 2528 32W-33N B2
2500 JNBG 60050 2528 32W-34N B1
2700 JNBG 60050 2471 32W-34N B7
2700 MchT 60050 2471 32W-34N B7
3900 JNBG 60072 2471 32W-35N A5
3900 MchT 60072 2471 32W-35N A5
N Richmond Rd SR-31
1300 MHRY 60050 2528 32W-33N B3
1900 MchT 60050 2528 32W-33N B2
2500 JNBG 60050 2528 32W-34N B1
2700 JNBG 60050 2471 32W-34N B7
2700 MchT 60050 2471 32W-34N B7
3900 JNBG 60072 2471 32W-35N A5
3900 MchT 60072 2471 32W-35N A5
S Richmond Rd
17500 JLET 60586 3415 32W-21S D7
17500 PnfT 60586 3415 32W-21S D7
Richmond St
10 PLTN 60067 2752 21W-16N E7
200 EVTN 60202 2866 3W-9N E6
700 CNHL 60514 3145 17W-5S C3
700 CNHL 60559 3145 17W-5S C3
700 WTMT 60514 3145 17W-5S C3
700 WTMT 60559 3145 17W-5S C3
1600 JLET 60435 3498 26W-23S A5
13300 RBBN 60406 3349 3W-16S A2
13300 WthT 60406 3349 3W-15S A1
13400 BLID 60406 3349 3W-16S A2
16700 HLCT 60428 3427 3W-20S A3
16700 HLCT 60429 3427 3W-20S A3
16700 MKHM 60428 3427 3W-20S A3
16700 MKHM 60429 3427 3W-20S A3
E Richmond St
10 WTMT 60559 3145 17W-5S B3
300 CNHL 60514 3145 17W-5S B3
300 CNHL 60559 3145 17W-5S B3
N Richmond St
800 CHCG 60622 3032 3W-1N E2
2400 CHCG 60647 2976 3W-3N E5
3600 CHCG 60618 2976 3W-4N E2
4400 CHCG 60618 2920 3W-5N E7
4400 CHCG 60625 2920 3W-5N E7
5600 CHCG 60659 2920 3W-7N E4
6300 CHCG 60645 2920 3W-7N E3
S Richmond St
300 CHCG 60612 3032 3W-0S E5
1100 CHCG 60623 3032 3W-0S E7
3500 CHCG 60632 3090 3W-3S E5
4600 CHCG 60632 3150 3W-5S E1
5400 CHCG 60629 3150 3W-7S E5
7700 CHCG 60652 3212 3W-8S E1
7900 CHCG 60652 3213 3W-9S A2
W Richmond St
- DRGV 60515 3145 18W-5S A3
- DRGV 60559 3145 18W-5S A3
10 WTMT 60559 3145 18W-5S A3
600 JLET 60435 3498 25W-23S C5
1300 ANHT 60004 2806 18W-16N D1
1500 ANHT 60004 2753 18W-16N D7
2700 JLET 60435 3497 27W-23S C5
Richmond Park Dr
3000 TNLK 53181 2354 B3
Richnee Ln
3400 RGMW 60008 2805 20W-13N E6
Richter Rd
100 BTVA 60510 3077 36W-1S E1
Richton Dr
1900 WHTN 60187 3082 25W-2S B4
14800 LKPT 60441 3421 18W-20S A4
Richton Pl
1000 RNPK 60471 3594 4W-26S D3
Richton Rd
10 CRTE 60417 3596 0W-28S C7
300 STGR 60417 3596 0W-28S C7
300 STGR 60475 3596 0W-28S C7
1700 CteT 60417 3595 2W-28S E6
1700 CteT 60475 3595 2W-28S D5
1700 STGR 60417 3595 2W-28S E6
1700 STGR 60475 3595 2W-28S E6
2000 BlmT 60466 3595 2W-28S D6
21600 MTSN 60443 3594 4W-26S D2
21800 RNPK 60471 3594 4W-26S D3
E Richton Rd
10 CRTE 60417 3596 0E-28S D7
400 CRTE 60417 3597 1E-28S A7
800 CteT 60417 3597 3E-28S E7
2500 CteT 60417 3598 3E-29S A7
W Richton Rd
10 CRTE 60417 3596 1W-28S B7
10 CRTE 60475 3596 1W-28S B7
10 CteT 60417 3596 1W-28S A6
10 CteT 60475 3596 1W-28S A6
10 STGR 60417 3596 1W-28S B7
10 STGR 60475 3596 1W-28S A6
300 CteT 60417 3595 1W-28S E6
300 CteT 60475 3595 1W-28S E6
300 STGR 60475 3595 1W-28S E6
400 STGR 60417 3595 1W-28S E6
Richton Square Rd
22300 RNPK 60471 3594 4W-27S D5
22700 RchT 60471 3594 4W-27S D4
22900 MonT 60466 3594 4W-27S D5
Richwood Ct
4200 NPVL 60564 3267 28W-12S A3
Richwood Ter
10 BlmT 60430 3507 2W-23S E3
10 FSMR 60422 3507 2W-23S D3
10 FSMR 60430 3507 2W-23S D3
Rick Ct
100 MTGY 60543 3263 38W-11S A1
1200 JLET 60431 3497 28W-22S A2
E Rickard Dr
10 BtlT 60543 3262 40W-12S D3
W Rickard Dr
10 BtlT 60543 3262 40W-12S C3
Rickerman Rd
14400 HmrT 60441 3342 20W-17S B5
Rickert Ct
6000 LSLE 60532 3142 24W-6S E5
Rickert Dr
- NPVL 60540 3140 29W-7S E7
- NPVL 60540 3202 28W-8S E1
1200 NPVL 60540 3203 28W-8S A1
1200 NPVL 60564 3203 27W-8S B2
1200 NPVL 60565 3203 27W-8S B2
Rickert Ln
15000 LKPT 60441 3421 18W-20S A4
Rickert Rd
5000 CLLK 60014 2640 33W-25N D5
Rickey Dr
1400 JLET 60433 3588 21W-25S A1
1400 JltT 60433 3588 21W-25S A1
Rider Ct
- FKFT 60423 3590 14W-28S E6
Rider Wy
- FKFT 60423 3590 14W-28S E6
Rider Ridge Dr
- MKNA 60448 3590 14W-25S D1
Riderwood Rd
10 NBRN 60010 2644 24W-25N B6
Ridge Av
- WDDL 60191 2914 18W-8N E3
100 BMDL 60108 2969 23W-5N A1
100 CHCG 60202 2867 2W-9N B6
100 CHCG 60645 2867 2W-9N B6
100 CLLK 60014 2639 36W-26N D3
100 EVTN 60202 2867 2W-9N B6
100 WNKA 60093 2812 5W-15N B3
200 CLLK 60012 2639 36W-26N D3
300 CNHL 60514 3145 17W-5S C3
300 EGVV 60007 2860 18W-9N E7
400 CNHL 60559 3145 17W-5S C3
400 WTMT 60559 3145 17W-5S C3
500 EGvT 60007 2860 18W-9N E7
500 EGvT 60007 2914 18W-9N E1
500 EGVV 60007 2914 18W-8N E1
700 WCDA 60084 2588 25W-28N B7
800 MDLN 60060 2646 18W-26N E3
1200 EVTN 60201 2867 2W-10N B5
2200 AURA 60504 3201 32W-9S B4
2400 EVTN 60201 2813 2W-13N B7
2600 AlqT 60102 2695 31W-22N D4
2800 WKGN 60085 2536 12W-33N B2
5100 BKLY 60163 3028 14W-0N C5
5800 HLSD 60162 3028 14W-0N C5
5800 HLSD 60163 3028 14W-0N C5
12300 PSPK 60464 3274 11W-14S A6
14300 ODPK 60462 3345 12W-17S B5
E Ridge Av
300 EMHT 60126 3028 15W-0N B4
N Ridge Av
10 ANHT 60005 2806 18W-14N E5
10 MPPT 60056 2807 15W-13N E7
800 LMBD 60148 2970 20W-2N B7
800 LMBD 60148 3026 20W-2N B1
1900 ANHT 60004 2806 18W-16N E1
2500 ANHT 60004 2754 18W-16N A6
3900 ANHT 60004 2753 18W-18N E2
4200 VrnT 60004 2753 18W-18N E2
4200 VrnT 60089 2753 18W-18N E2
5600 CHCG 60640 2921 1W-7N D4
5600 CHCG 60660 2921 1W-7N D4
6300 CHCG 60626 2921 2W-7N C2

STREET Block City ZIP Map# CGS Grid

N Ridge Av
36600 GrtT 60041 2473 26W-36N E3
N Ridge Av US-14
5600 CHCG 60640 2921 1W-7N D4
5600 CHCG 60660 2921 1W-7N D4
S Ridge Av
10 ANHT 60005 2806 18W-13N E6
1100 ANHT 60005 2860 18W-12N E1
W Ridge Av
10 PTHT 60070 2807 15W-15N E1
10 PTHT 60070 2808 15W-15N A1
N Ridge Blvd
6400 CHCG 60626 2921 2W-8N B2
6400 CHCG 60660 2921 2W-8N C2
6500 CHCG 60645 2921 2W-8N B2
7200 CHCG 60645 2867 2W-9N B7
7500 CHCG 60202 2867 2W-9N B6
7500 EVTN 60202 2867 2W-9N B6
Ridge Cir
10 SMWD 60107 2857 27W-10N C6
3500 CPVL 60110 2747 35W-17N B6
N Ridge Cir
40800 AntT 60002 2417 22W-40N B2
Ridge Cross
5400 HRPK 60133 2911 27W-6N D6
5500 BRLT 60103 2911 27W-6N D6
5500 BRLT 60133 2911 27W-6N D6
Ridge Ct
- BRRG 60527 3208 15W-9S A2
10 BGBK 60440 3204 25W-11S C7
10 LNHT 60046 2476 20W-38N A1
10 SEGN 60177 2908 36W-9N A1
400 LIHL 60156 2693 37W-21N B5
400 ROSL 60172 2913 22W-6N B5
400 WCDA 60084 2644 25W-27N A1
600 SMBG 60193 2859 22W-9N B7
900 EGVV 60007 2914 18W-8N E1
900 EVTN 60202 2867 2W-10N A4
4000 ZION 60099 2362 12W-41N C7
6000 LslT 60532 3143 22W-6S B5
7200 SPGV 60081 2413 32W-39N B5
9000 WLSP 60527 3208 14W-10S C5
N Ridge Ct
10 SMWD 60107 2857 27W-11N C4
26200 FmtT 60060 2646 19W-26N C3
26200 LGGV 60047 2646 19W-26N C3
W Ridge Ct
500 ANHT 60004 2806 18W-15N E2
Ridge Dr
400 SchT 60175 2963 38W-3N A6
500 ELBN 60119 3017 43W-2N B2
500 WNVL 60555 3080 29W-2S C4
700 MRGO 60152 2634 49W-25N B4
900 SRWD 60404 3496 30W-23S B4
1100 TroT 60404 3496 30W-23S A4
2100 GNVW 60025 2810 9W-15N C3
2300 NfdT 60062 2809 11W-16N D1
2300 NHBK 60062 2809 11W-15N C1
4900 GRNE 60031 2478 15W-35N B6
6500 CHRG 60415 3275 8W-12S A2
10000 CHCG 60614 2978 0W-2N B6
10600 WRTH 60415 3275 8W-12S A2
10600 WRTH 60482 3275 8W-12S A2
19200 MKNA 60448 3503 11W-23S E3
N Ridge Dr
1900 CHCG 60614 2978 0W-2N B6
S Ridge Dr
1600 ANHT 60005 2860 18W-12N E2
W Ridge Dr
100 SgrT 60506 3136 39W-6S D5
22500 AntT 60002 2358 22W-42N B6
Ridge Ln
10 BRLT 60103 2966 30W-5N B3
10 BRLT 60184 2966 30W-5N B3
10 GNVA 60134 3020 34W-1N E4
10 WYNE 60184 2966 30W-5N B3
100 LKFT 60045 2649 10W-26N E2
200 LIHL 60156 2693 37W-21N B5
1100 WNSP 60558 3146 14W-6S D4
1500 DSPN 60018 2862 15W-10N A6
2000 WDRG 60517 3206 21W-8S A2
3600 GwdT 60097 2469 37W-35N B6
3600 WRLK 60097 2469 37W-35N B6
8800 ODHL 60487 3424 11W-19S A2
S Ridge Ln
22600 FftT 60423 3591 13W-27S B5
Ridge Pl
500 SMWD 60107 2857 27W-10N B6
N Ridge Pl
6400 LGGV 60047 2646 18W-24N E6
6400 VNHL 60061 2646 18W-24N E6
Ridge Rd
- AxST 60447 3583 33W-27S A6
- LSLE 60563 3142 25W-5S C3
- LslT 60563 3142 25W-5S C3
- NasT 60543 3337 33W-16S A6
- OswT 60543 3265 33W-14S A7
- OswT 60543 3337 33W-14S A1
- OswT 60585 3337 33W-15S A2
- PNFD 60543 3265 33W-14S A7
- TNTN 60476 3428 0W-21S C6
10 AlqT 60010 2749 28W-20N D2
10 BNHL 60010 2749 28W-20N D2
10 HDPK 60035 2757 9W-20N D1
10 LMNT 60439 3270 19W-14S C6
10 LNSG 60438 3430 C6
10 MNSR 46321 3430 C6
10 NHBK 60062 2757 9W-20N D1
10 NpvT 60565 3203 27W-10S B5
10 WldT 60565 3203 27W-10S B5
100 EVTN 60201 2812 4W-13N C7
100 WLMT 60091 2812 4W-13N C7
100 WLMT 60201 2812 4W-13N C7
200 DndT 60118 2747 35W-18N C4
200 NARA 60510 3078 35W-3S A6
300 AlqT 60010 2696 29W-21N D5
300 BNHL 60010 2696 29W-21N D7
300 EGVV 60007 2860 18W-9N E7
300 KLWH 60043 2812 4W-13N C6
300 KLWH 60091 2812 4W-14N C6
300 NARA 60542 3078 35W-3S B6
300 WLMT 60043 2812 4W-14N C5
400 BfdT 53147 2351 D1
400 EGvT 60007 2860 18W-9N E7
400 ROSL 60172 2913 22W-6N B5
400 TNTN 60430 3428 0W-21S C6
500 HMWD 60430 3428 1W-21S C7
500 NtrT 60043 2812 4W-13N C6
500 NtrT 60091 2812 4W-14N C4
500 NtrT 60093 2812 4W-13N C6
600 SEGN 60177 2908 36W-9N A1
700 MltT 60137 3083 21W-1S D2
1000 HDPK 60035 2704 10W-22N A4
1100 WTMT 60527 3145 17W-7S B6
1100 WTMT 60559 3145 17W-7S B6
1800 LNSG 60438 3429 3E-21S E6

Ridge Rd
1800 ThtT 60438 3429 2E-21S C6
2100 HMWD 60430 3427 2W-21S C6
2300 AlqT 60013 2641 31W-25N D4
2300 ODHL 60013 2641 31W-25N D4
2500 AURA 60504 3201 32W-9S C4
2600 HDPK 60035 2703 11W-23N E2
2600 LKFT 60035 2703 11W-23N E2
2600 LKFT 60045 2703 11W-23N E2
2700 NpvT 60504 3201 32W-9S C4
3300 ISLK 60042 2586 28W-28N E6
3300 SPGV 60081 2413 32W-39N B5
4000 SPGV 60072 2413 32W-39N A6
4000 ZION 60099 2362 12W-41N C7
6300 PNFD 60543 3337 33W-14S A1
6300 PNFD 60585 3337 33W-14S A1
6500 DRN 60527 3145 17W-7S B6
6500 DRN 60561 3145 17W-7S B6
7900 OrlT 60462 3346 9W-16S D3
12700 JLET 60447 3495 33W-23S A3
12700 SwdT 60447 3495 33W-23S A4
15000 SwdT 60447 3583 34W-26S A3
15600 MNKA 60447 3583 33W-26S A3
27000 WCDA 60084 2644 25W-27N A2
27000 WcnT 60084 2644 25W-27N A2
E Ridge Rd
300 ANHT 60004 2754 17W-16N B7
N Ridge Rd
- SwdT 60447 3583 34W-28S A7
10 LKFT 60045 2649 11W-26N C4
100 MchT 60050 2526 36W-33N D4
100 MchT 60098 2526 36W-32N D6
100 MNKA 60447 3583 34W-28S A7
100 NndT 60050 2526 36W-32N D6
100 NndT 60098 2526 36W-32N D6
200 AxST 60447 3583 34W-28S A7
500 MHRY 60050 2526 36W-33N D4
2100 MchT 60097 2526 36W-33N D2
8000 AxST 60410 3672 34W-31S A6
8000 CNHN 60410 3672 34W-31S A6
8000 CNHN 60447 3672 33W-31S A7
8000 CNHN 60450 3672 33W-32S A7
8400 AxST 60410 3672 33W-31S A6
8900 MNKA 60447 3672 34W-31S A6
33000 WrnT 60030 2533 18W-33N E4
S Ridge Rd
- AxST 60447 3672 33W-30S A3
10 LKFT 60045 2649 11W-25N D6
100 MchT 60050 2526 36W-31N D6
100 MchT 60098 2526 36W-31N D6
100 NndT 60050 2526 36W-31N D6
100 NndT 60098 2526 36W-31N D6
200 BLVY 60050 2526 36W-31N D6
200 BLVY 60098 2526 36W-31N D6
1000 MNKA 60447 3672 34W-29S A3
1400 LKFT 60045 2703 11W-24N E1
1600 HDPK 60035 2703 11W-23N E1
2000 AxST 60410 3672 33W-30S A5
2000 CNHN 60410 3672 34W-30S A5
2000 MNKA 60410 3672 34W-30S A5
10800 JLET 60586 3415 33W-21S A7
10800 NasT 60586 3415 33W-21S A7
11600 JLET 60447 3495 33W-22S A1
11600 JLET 60586 3495 33W-21S A1
23100 JknT 60421 3587 22W-28S E7
23100 JLET 60421 3587 22W-28S E7
23100 JLET 60433 3587 22W-28S E7
W Ridge Rd
200 VLPK 60181 3027 18W-1N A2
600 VLPK 60181 3026 18W-1N E2
21200 KLDR 60047 2699 21W-23N D1
21300 ElaT 60047 2699 21W-23N D1
28200 WcnT 60051 2587 28W-28N A6
Ridge Sq
- EGVV 60007 2914 18W-8N E1
Ridge St
10 ALGN 60102 2694 33W-20N E7
100 WCDA 60084 2644 25W-27N A1
300 ALGN 60102 2747 33W-20N E1
300 WMTN 60481 3943 27W-39S D1
300 YKVL 60560 3333 42W-15S C2
800 HMND 46324 3430 E2
27700 FXLK 60041 2473 27W-35N B6
27700 GrtT 60041 2473 27W-35N B6
E Ridge St
100 BDWD 60408 3942 31W-41S B6
100 RedT 60408 3942 31W-41S B6
W Ridge St
100 YKVL 60560 3333 43W-15S B2
8700 RVGV 60171 2973 10W-3N E1
15900 LKPT 60441 3420 19W-20S D4
Ridge Ter
200 PKRG 60068 2918 10W-8N B1
800 EVTN 60201 2813 2W-12N B7
Ridge Tr
- CLSM 60188 2967 27W-3N C5
W Ridge Tr
200 PLTN 60067 2752 21W-17N D5
Ridge Wy
1000 WMTN 60481 3943 26W-39S E1
Ridge Connector Dr
10000 CHCG 60614 2978 0W-2N B6
Ridge Cove Dr
- CHRG 60415 3274 8W-12S E2
Ridgecroft Ln
10 BNHL 60010 2696 29W-20N B7
Ridge Farm Rd
10 BRRG 60527 3146 15W-6S B5
Ridgefield Av
1700 ALGN 60102 2747 36W-19N B3
Ridgefield Cir
1000 CLSM 60188 2967 27W-4N C3
Ridgefield Ct
10 ALGN 60102 2747 36W-19N A3
3200 JLET 60441 3417 27W-19S D4
Ridgefield Dr
400 ROSL 60172 2912 24W-6N D5
15400 MHTN 60442 3677 19W-30S E3
E Ridgefield Dr
2400 CteT 60417 3687 3E-31S A5
Ridgefield Ln
- TYPK 60477 3504 9W-23S E3
10 WLBK 60527 3146 15W-7S B6
200 NPVL 60565 3203 26W-9S D4
800 BFGV 60089 2701 17W-21N B6
900 WLNG 60090 2755 15W-16N B6
Ridgefield Rd
10 OSWG 60543 3263 36W-11S D1
10 OswT 60538 3263 36W-11S D1
500 NLNX 60451 3501 18W-25S A7
7800 CLLK 60012 2639 36W-27N C1
7800 NndT 60012 2639 36W-27N C1
8000 DrrT 60012 2639 36W-27N C1
8100 CLLK 60012 2583 37W-27N A7
8100 DrrT 60012 2583 37W-27N A7
8900 DrrT 60098 2583 38W-27N A7

Ridgefield Rd CO-A38
8500 DrrT 60012 2583 37W-27N A7
8600 CLLK 60012 2583 37W-27N A7
8900 DrrT 60098 2583 38W-27N A7
Ridgefield Rd CO-V25
7800 CLLK 60012 2639 36W-27N C1
7800 NndT 60012 2639 36W-27N C1
8000 DrrT 60012 2639 36W-27N C1
8100 CLLK 60012 2583 37W-27N C7
8100 DrrT 60012 2583 37W-27N C7
Ridge Grove Ln
3000 HDPK 60035 2703 10W-23N E1
Ridgeland Av
- CHCG 60613 2977 1W-5N D1
- CteT 60417 3774 1W-32S B1
- PSHT 60445 3347 8W-16S B3
- PSHT 60463 3347 8W-16S B3
- WCHI 60185 3022 29W-0N D5
10 FXLK 60020 2473 27W-36N B4
10 LSLE 60532 3142 25W-5S B2
10 LSLE 60563 3142 25W-5S B2
10 LslT 60563 3142 25W-5S B2
10 NPVL 60563 3142 25W-4S B2
10 WnfT 60185 3022 29W-1N D3
200 WDSK 60098 2581 42W-30N C1
900 MDLN 60060 2590 19W-28N D6
1200 BRWN 60304 3031 7W-1S B7
1200 BRWN 60402 3031 7W-1S B7
1200 OKPK 60304 3031 7W-1S B7
1500 BRWN 60402 3089 8W-4S B7
3800 SKNY 60402 3089 8W-4S B7
4200 StkT 60402 3089 8W-4S B7
8700 BRBK 60459 3211 8W-10S B5
8700 OKLN 60453 3211 8W-10S B5
8700 OKLN 60459 3211 8W-10S B5
9400 CHRG 60415 3211 8W-10S B6
9400 CHRG 60453 3211 8W-10S B6
9400 OKLN 60415 3211 8W-10S B6
10200 CHRG 60415 3275 8W-12S B2
10600 CHRG 60482 3275 8W-12S B2
10600 WRTH 60415 3275 8W-12S B2
10600 WRTH 60482 3275 8W-12S B2
14500 BmnT 60445 3347 8W-16S B3
15000 BmnT 60452 3347 8W-18S B7
15000 OKFT 60452 3347 8W-18S B7
15700 OKFT 60452 3425 7W-18S B1
16300 TYPK 60477 3425 8W-20S B4
17700 BmnT 60477 3425 8W-21S B6
18000 LNSG 60438 3429 2E-21S C6
18000 ThtT 60438 3429 2E-21S C6
18200 RchT 60477 3425 7W-21S C7
18400 RchT 60477 3505 7W-22S C1
18400 TYPK 60477 3505 7W-22S C1
19300 MTSN 60443 3505 8W-23S C4
19300 TYPK 60443 3505 7W-23S C4
21000 MTSN 60443 3593 7W-25S C1
21000 RchT 60443 3505 8W-25S C7
21000 RchT 60443 3593 8W-26S C3
22000 RNPK 60443 3593 8W-26S C3
22600 MonT 60449 3593 8W-26S C3
N Ridgeland Av
200 EMHT 60126 3027 16W-1N D1
400 EMHT 60126 2971 16W-2N D7
900 OKPK 60302 3031 7W-1N A1
1200 CHCG 60639 3031 7W-1N B1
1200 OKPK 60639 3031 7W-1N B1
S Ridgeland Av
100 OKPK 60302 3031 8W-0N A4
400 OKPK 60304 3031 7W-0N A5
1100 BRWN 60304 3031 7W-0S A7
1100 BRWN 60402 3031 7W-0S A7
6700 CHCG 60649 3153 2E-7S B6
7500 CHCG 60649 3215 2E-8S B1
8200 CHCG 60617 3215 2E-9S B2
10700 CHRG 60415 3275 7W-13S B3
10700 CHRG 60482 3275 7W-13S B3
10700 WRTH 60415 3275 7W-13S B3
10700 WRTH 60482 3275 8W-14S B7
11400 ALSP 60803 3275 8W-14S B7
11500 WRTH 60803 3275 8W-13S B5
11600 WthT 60482 3275 8W-13S B5
11800 PSHT 60463 3275 8W-14S B5
11800 PSHT 60482 3275 8W-14S B5
11800 PSHT 60803 3275 8W-14S B5
11800 WthT 60463 3275 8W-14S B5
11800 WthT 60803 3275 8W-14S B5
13000 PSHT 60463 3347 8W-15S B1
13000 WthT 60463 3347 7W-15S B1
13300 BmnT 60445 3347 8W-15S B1
13300 PSHT 60445 3347 8W-15S B1
20000 MTSN 60443 3505 8W-24S C6
20800 RchT 60443 3505 7W-25S C7
23100 MonT 60449 3593 8W-28S C7
23100 MonT 60471 3593 8W-28S C7
23100 RchT 60443 3593 8W-28S C7
23100 RchT 60471 3593 8W-28S C7
23900 MonT 60449 3682 8W-32S C7
25700 MONE 60449 3682 8W-32S C7
W Ridgeland Av
200 WKGN 60085 2480 10W-35N A7
1600 WKGN 60085 2479 11W-35N C7
Ridgeland Dr
2200 LNHT 60046 2476 20W-37N B1
Ridgeland Ln
10 CTSD 60525 3147 12W-7S B6
4000 NfdT 60062 2756 12W-17N A6
4000 NHBK 60062 2756 12W-17N A6
S Ridgeland Rd
29500 WllT 60468 3861 8W-39S C7
Ridgeland St
700 FRGV 60021 2696 29W-22N C3
Ridgeland Manor Dr
21100 MTSN 60443 3505 7W-25S D7
21100 MTSN 60443 3593 7W-25S C1
Ridgelawn Tr
400 BTVA 60510 3078 34W-2S C5
Ridgelee Rd
1600 HDPK 60035 2757 9W-20N D2
Ridge Line Rd
10 CmpT 60175 2906 39W-7N E6
10 CmpT 60175 2907 39W-7N A5
800 SchT 60175 2907 38W-7N A5
Ridge Ln Av
300 HRVD 60033 2464 50W-37N A1
Ridgely Ct
1400 NPVL 60540 3142 25W-7S C7
Ridgemont Ct
1800 MTGY 60538 3199 36W-10S D6
Ridgemont Dr
19500 TYPK 60477 3504 10W-23S B4
Ridgemont Ln
5700 CHRG 60415 3275 7W-12S D2
N Ridgemoor Av
10 MDLN 60060 2646 19W-27N C1
400 MDLN 60060 2590 19W-28N C7

Ridgemoor Ct
300 WLBK 60527 3146 15W-7S A6
Ridge Moor Dr
1800 JLET 60586 3496 31W-21S A1
1900 JLET 60586 3416 31W-21S A7
Ridgemoor Dr
500 WLBK 60527 3145 16W-7S E6
500 WLBK 60527 3146 16W-7S A6
Ridgemoor Dr W
800 WLBK 60527 3145 16W-7S E6
Ridgemoor Tr
- WDSK 60098 2582 38W-30N D2
Ridgemore Dr
1900 BRLT 60103 2909 32W-8N C3
Ridgemore Rd
21000 MKNA 60448 3502 14W-25S E7
Ridge Point Dr
6800 BmnT 60452 3347 8W-18S A6
6800 OKFT 60452 3347 8W-18S A6
Ridgepoint Dr
8100 BRRG 60527 3208 15W-9S B3
Ridgestone Dr
- LslT 60540 3205 23W-8S A2
- LslT 60565 3205 23W-8S A2
Ridgeview Ct
600 CmpT 60175 2962 39W-3N E6
Ridgeview Dr
- BrnT 60010 2803 25W-15N E2
300 BfdT 53128 2352 E3
300 GNCY 53128 2352 E3
500 MHRY 60050 2527 33W-31N E7
1000 IVNS 60010 2803 25W-15N E2
1000 IVNS 60010 2804 25W-15N A1
1000 SBTN 60010 2803 25W-15N E1
1100 MHRY 60050 2584 33W-30N D1
Ridgeview Ln
- SRGV 60554 3135 43W-7S A6
600 LslT 60540 3142 24W-5S D3
20200 MngT 60152 2578 49W-30N C2
Ridgeview St
10 WynT 60185 2967 27W-3N C6
400 DRGV 60516 3206 19W-8S D1
600 DRGV 60516 3144 19W-8S D7
Ridgeway Av
100 AURA 60506 3199 37W-8S C1
800 AraT 60506 3199 36W-8S D1
800 MNSR 46321 3430 E6
8700 SKOK 60076 2866 4W-10N C4
9200 SKOK 60203 2866 4W-11N C2
9500 EVTN 60201 2866 4W-11N C2
14300 MDLN 60445 3348 4W-17S D4
15400 MKHM 60428 3348 4W-18S D7
15500 MKHM 60428 3426 4W-18S D1
22300 RNPK 60471 3594 4W-27S D4
23000 MonT 60466 3594 4W-27S D5
N Ridgeway Av
400 CHCG 60624 3032 4W-0N C3
1300 CHCG 60651 3032 4W-1N C1
1500 CHCG 60647 3032 4W-1N C1
2300 CHCG 60647 2976 4W-3N C5
3700 CHCG 60618 2976 4W-4N C2
4300 CHCG 60625 2976 4W-5N C1
4800 CHCG 60625 2920 4W-6N C6
6200 CHCG 60659 2920 4W-7N C3
6300 LNWD 60659 2920 4W-7N C3
7000 LNWD 60076 2920 4W-8N C1
7000 LNWD 60712 2920 4W-8N C1
7000 SKOK 60076 2920 4W-8N C1
S Ridgeway Av
1400 CHCG 60623 3032 4W-1S C7
1500 CHCG 60623 3090 4W-2S C3
5000 CHCG 60632 3150 4W-5S C2
7100 CHCG 60629 3150 4W-8S C7
7500 CHCG 60652 3212 4W-8S D1
9100 CHCG 60805 3212 4W-10S D5
9100 ENGN 60805 3212 4W-11S D6
9800 CHCG 60655 3212 4W-11S D7
10300 CHCG 60655 3276 4W-12S D1
11700 WthT 60803 3276 4W-13S D4
11900 ALSP 60803 3276 4W-14S D5
13300 RBBN 60472 3348 4W-16S D3
Ridgeway Ct
900 SMBG 60194 2858 24W-11N D4
1100 ELGN 60123 2800 35W-13N C7
Ridgeway Dr
5900 WDRG 60517 3143 22W-6S D5
Ridgeway Ln
100 LYVL 60048 2592 15W-28N B5
Ridgeway Rd
200 MchT 60051 2529 29W-32N C6
N Ridgeway Rd
5000 MchT 60072 2470 35W-37N B2
5000 RGWD 60072 2470 35W-37N B2
S Ridgeway Rd
4100 RGWD 60072 2470 35W-36N B4
Ridgeway St
1300 RLKB 60073 2475 22W-35N B7
2300 EVTN 60201 2866 4W-12N C1
2500 EVTN 60201 2812 4W-12N C7
N Ridgeway St
1500 RLKB 60073 2475 22W-35N B6
Ridgeway Tr
600 MHRY 60050 2526 36W-32N E4
Ridgewood Av
10 RMVL 60446 3269 23W-14S A7
200 AddT 60106 2971 16W-4N D3
200 BNVL 60106 2971 16W-4N D3
300 GNEN 60137 3025 23W-0S A4
900 MchT 60051 2529 30W-32N B5
1300 JLET 60432 3499 22W-23S D3
1300 JltT 60432 3499 22W-23S D3
17000 LNSG 60438 3430 3E-20S A4
18800 LNSG 60438 3510 3E-22S A1
E Ridgewood Av
1000 JLET 60432 3499 22W-23S C4
1000 JltT 60432 3499 22W-23S C4
N Ridgewood Av
4800 CHCG 60656 2917 10W-6N E7
4800 CHCG 60706 2917 10W-6N E7
4800 NRDG 60706 2917 10W-6N E7
Ridgewood Cir
1100 LIHL 60156 2693 36W-22N C4
1400 DRGV 60516 3144 20W-6S B5
Ridgewood Ct
100 BGBK 60440 3268 25W-12S B2
200 LKZH 60047 2699 22W-22N B3
200 WNVL 60555 3080 30W-2S B4
600 OKBK 60523 3084 18W-3S E6
900 WCHI 60185 3022 29W-2N D2
2400 AURA 60502 3139 32W-5S C3
2700 DYR 46311 3598 D4
S Ridgewood Ct
5400 CHCG 60615 3153 1E-5S A2
W Ridgewood Ct
1200 VNHL 60061 2647 17W-26N B3

Ridgewood Dr
10 SchT 60175 2963 36W-6N D1
100 WDSK 60098 2581 41W-30N C2
300 BMDL 60108 2968 24W-5N C1
500 ANTH 60002 2357 24W-42N C5
500 CRY 60013 2695 32W-23N B2
500 SMWD 60107 2856 29W-10N D5
700 RDLK 60073 2531 23W-34N E1
900 HDPK 60035 2705 8W-21N A6
900 WCHI 60185 3022 29W-2N D1
1000 BGBK 60440 3268 25W-12S B2
1100 HDPK 60035 2704 8W-21N E6
1200 NHBK 60062 2757 9W-17N D5
5500 WNSP 60558 3146 14W-6S D4
5800 LynT 60525 3146 14W-6S D4
10400 PlsT 60464 3345 13W-15S A1
13000 PlsT 60462 3345 13W-15S B1
14800 OKFT 60452 3347 7W-17S B5
16000 HMGN 60491 3421 16W-19S E2
16000 HMGN 60491 3422 16W-19S A2
17700 HLCT 60429 3427 3W-21S A6
E Ridgewood Dr
10 SchT 60175 2963 36W-5N E1
100 SchT 60175 2907 36W-6N E7
600 SCRL 60175 2963 36W-5N E2
Ridgewood Ln
- ElaT 60047 2700 19W-22N C3
- LGGV 60047 2700 19W-22N C3
10 DYR 46311 3598 C4
400 BFGV 60069 2754 16W-20N E1
400 BFGV 60089 2754 16W-20N E1
400 LYVL 60048 2591 17W-29N B4
400 VrnT 60069 2754 16W-20N E1
600 ElgT 60124 2799 38W-13N A7
900 CLLK 60014 2639 37W-24N B7
1000 CLLK 60014 2693 37W-23N B1
1200 LKVL 60046 2474 23W-36N E4
1700 HFET 60192 2804 25W-15N A3
7500 BRRG 60527 3208 14W-8S D1
E Ridgewood Ln
1700 GNVW 60025 2811 7W-14N A4
N Ridgewood Ln
1000 PLTN 60067 2753 20W-17N A5
22700 KLDR 60047 2699 21W-22N D3
W Ridgewood Ln
100 SchT 60175 2907 36W-6N D7
100 SchT 60175 2963 36W-6N D1
1800 GNVW 60025 2811 7W-14N A4
Ridgewood Pl
900 HDPK 60035 2705 8W-21N A7
Ridgewood Rd
10 EGVV 60007 2861 18W-10N A6
100 RVSD 60546 3088 10W-3S B5
200 BKFD 60513 3088 10W-3S B5
200 BKFD 60546 3088 10W-3S B5
2100 LSLE 60532 3142 24W-7S D6
Riding Hood Ln
900 SchT 60175 2963 37W-4N D3
Ridings Ln
700 SCRL 60174 2965 33W-4N A5
Riedle Ct
17900 HMWD 60430 3427 2W-21S C6
Riedy Pl
4900 LSLE 60532 3143 23W-5S A2
Riedy Rd
500 LSLE 60532 3143 23W-5S B2
Riegel Rd
18100 HMWD 60430 3427 1W-21S E7
18400 HMWD 60430 3507 1W-22S E2
18900 BlmT 60430 3507 1W-22S E2
19100 CHHT 60411 3507 1W-23S E3
19100 CHHT 60430 3507 1W-23S E3
S Riegel Farm Rd
1300 MonT 60449 3684 3W-30S C4
1300 MonT 60466 3684 3W-30S C4
1300 UYPK 60449 3684 3W-30S C4
1300 UYPK 60466 3684 3W-30S C4
Riegel Oaks Ln
10 BlmT 60430 3507 1W-22S E2
10 HMWD 60430 3507 2W-22S E2
Rieger St
- OMFD 60461 3507 3W-25S C7
Rieser Cir
100 NPVL 60565 3203 26W-9S E4
E Rietveld Dr
1300 CteT 60417 3686 2E-29S C2
Riffles St
100 SRWD 60404 3496 30W-24S C5
Riford Rd
500 GNEN 60137 3025 22W-0N D4
800 MltT 60137 3025 22W-0N C4
Rigby Rd
3900 NndT 60012 2583 36W-27N D7
Rigi Rd
10 NPVL 60563 3080 30W-4S C7
10 WNVL 60563 3080 30W-4S C7
Riivendell Dr
2100 NlxT 60451 3502 15W-24S B5
Riley Av
- PTHT 60070 2808 14W-15N B3
100 LktT 60441 3419 23W-21S B7
Riley Ct
2200 NPVL 60564 3266 29W-12S D4
Riley Dr
- JLET 60431 3495 32W-22S C1
300 MRGO 60152 2634 49W-25N C4
Riley Ln
500 LKZH 60047 2699 22W-22N C4
Riley Rd
8400 WRLK 60097 2469 37W-35N B5
Riley St
10 ELGN 60123 2855 33W-10N A6
Rill Ct
1400 NPVL 60565 3203 26W-8S E2
E Rimbach St
10 CTCY 60409 3352 C6
10 HMND 46320 3352 C6
E Rimini Ct
300 PLTN 60067 2753 20W-16N A6
300 PLTN 60074 2753 20W-16N A6
S Rincker Rd
26000 CteT 60417 3686 1E-31S C6
Rinear Rd
800 ANTH 60002 2358 23W-42N A6
Ring Ct
900 HDPK 60035 2704 9W-21N B7
5700 HRPK 60133 2911 26W-7N D5
Ring Rd
- EGvT 60008 2860 20W-12N B2
- NPVL 60565 3203 26W-10S D5
- RGMW 60008 2860 20W-12N B2
- VNHL 60061 2647 16W-26N E4
1300 CTCY 60409 3429 2E-19S D2
2600 JLET 60431 3417 28W-20S B5
Ringland Rd
700 RVWD 60015 2702 13W-20N D7

Chicago 7-County Street Index

STREET Block	City	ZIP	Map#	CGS	Grid
Ringling Rd					
500	CLLK	60014	2639	36W-25N	D5
Ring Neck Ct					
10	BmdT	60108	2967	26W-4N	E3
Ringneck Dr					
100	GLHT	60139	2968	24W-3N	D6
Ring Neck Ln					
10	BmdT	60108	2967	26W-5N	E2
300	BmdT	60133	2967	26W-5N	E2
Ringwood Rd					
800	LKFT	60045	2650	9W-25N	B4
3700	JNBG	60050	2470	34W-35N	C6
3700	MchT	60050	2470	34W-35N	C6
3700	MchT	60097	2470	34W-35N	D5
3700	RGWD	60072	2470	33W-36N	E3
3700	RGWD	60097	2470	34W-36N	D5
4300	MchT	60050	2471	33W-37N	A2
4300	MchT	60072	2470	33W-36N	E3
4300	MchT	60072	2471	33W-37N	A2
4300	MchT	60081	2471	33W-37N	A2
4300	RGWD	60072	2471	33W-37N	A2
N Ringwood Rd					
1700	MchT	60050	2527	34W-34N	C2
1700	MHRY	60050	2527	34W-33N	C2
2600	MchT	60050	2470	34W-34N	C7
2600	MHRY	60050	2470	34W-34N	C7
3000	JNBG	60050	2470	34W-34N	C7
3000	MchT	60097	2470	34W-34N	C7
W Ringwood Rd					
300	MchT	60050	2472	29W-37N	D2
1000	JNBG	60050	2472	30W-36N	B3
1700	JNBG	60050	2471	30W-36N	E3
2000	MchT	60050	2471	31W-37N	D2
2100	MchT	60081	2471	31W-37N	D2
3700	MchT	60072	2471	31W-37N	D2
W Rinn Av					
-	HPSR	60140	2795	47W-16N	E2
Rio Grande Cir					
2400	NPVL	60565	3204	25W-10S	B6
Rio Grande Ct					
2400	NPVL	60565	3204	25W-10S	B6
Rio Poco Av					
-	MNKA	60447	3672	32W-29S	C2
Riordan Rd					
400	VLPK	60181	3027	17W-0S	B7
400	YkTp	60181	3027	17W-0S	B7
E Riordan Rd					
400	VLPK	60181	3027	17W-0S	C7
400	YkTp	60181	3027	17W-0S	C7
500	OKTR	60181	3027	17W-0S	C7
Rio Verde Av					
6200	OKFT	60452	3347	7W-18S	B6
Rio Vista Rd					
400	GNVW	60025	2811	8W-12N	A7
Riparian Dr					
1500	NPVL	60565	3203	26W-9S	D3
Riparian Rd					
10	HDPK	60035	2704	8W-23N	E3
Ripley Ct					
300	NPVL	60565	3203	26W-9S	D4
Ripon Rd					
4500	NndT	60012	2584	33W-27N	E7
4500	NndT	60012	2640	33W-27N	E1
Rippburger Rd					
10	PltT	60124	2851	41W-10N	E6
10	PltT	60140	2851	41W-11N	E4
Rippburger Rd CO-33					
700	PltT	60124	2851	41W-10N	E6
Ripple Rdg					
8100	DRN	60561	3207	17W-9S	B3
Ripple Brook Ct					
500	LKZH	60010	2699	22W-21N	A6
500	LKZH	60047	2699	22W-21N	A6
700	ELGN	60120	2855	32W-12N	C2
Ripplebrook Ct					
200	SMBG	60173	2859	21W-11N	E3
Ripple Brook Ln					
700	ELGN	60120	2855	32W-12N	C2
Ripple Ridge Cove					
900	DRN	60561	3207	17W-9S	B3
Rippling Ridge Ct					
7700	GRNE	60031	2476	18W-34N	E7
Risch Ct					
-	WCHI	60185	3022	29W-1N	C2
-	WnfT	60185	3022	29W-1N	C2
Risen Star Ln					
300	OSWG	60543	3264	34W-11S	D2
Rising Ct					
10300	WDRG	60517	3270	20W-12S	B2
Rita Av					
1200	SCRL	60174	3020	34W-2N	D1
5200	NndT	60014	2641	33W-26N	A2
Rita Ct					
100	BRLT	60103	2911	28W-8N	A3
Rita Dr					
3800	RNPK	60471	3594	4W-27S	D5
23500	CmgT	60033	2405	52W-38N	B6
Rita Ln					
8100	BtnT	60081	2414	30W-40N	B3
Rita Rd					
2400	DSPN	60016	2863	11W-11N	C3
18100	TYPK	60477	3425	8W-21S	B7
N Ritchie Ct					
1300	CHCG	60610	3034		C1
W Riteway Rd					
14100	MTWA	60048	2648	14W-27N	D1
Ritter Dr					
500	BTVA	60510	3078	34W-2S	D5
500	NARA	60510	3078	34W-2S	C5
500	NARA	60542	3078	34W-2S	C5
Ritter St					
1400	NARA	60542	3077	37W-3S	B7
Riva Ct					
500	WHTN	60187	3082	24W-1S	D2
Riva Rdg					
10	LMNT	60439	3272	15W-13S	B5
Rivanna Ct					
100	NPVL	60565	3204	25W-10S	A5
Riva Ridge Ct					
800	NPVL	60540	3142	25W-7S	A7
Riva Ridge Dr					
-	LYVL	60048	2648	15W-27N	A1
1500	LYVL	60048	2647	15W-27N	E1
River Av					
-	ITSC	60191	2914	18W-6N	E6
-	WDDL	60191	2914	18W-6N	E6
River Ct					
200	MNKA	60447	3672	32W-28S	D1
S River Ct					
300	PNFD	60544	3416	30W-18S	A2
300	PnfT	60544	3416	30W-18S	A2
River Dr					
10	LNSG	60438	3430		C4
10	MNSR	60438	3430		C4
10	NPVL	60565	3203	27W-10S	D7
10	TVLY	60013	2695	31W-23N	C3
10	WldT	60565	3203	27W-10S	D7
100	CRY	60013	2695	31W-23N	C3
400	LslT	60565	3204	25W-8S	A2
400	MNSR	46321	3430		D5
400	NPVL	60565	3204	25W-8S	A2
500	MltT	60137	3025	21W-1N	D2
700	GLHT	60137	3025	21W-1N	D2
700	HMND	46324	3430		E5
800	CLSM	60188	2967	27W-3N	D5
900	GNVW	60025	2810	8W-13N	E6
1200	CTCY	60409	3430	3E-19S	A2
1500	GLHT	60139	3025	21W-1N	D2
4500	LSLE	60532	3143	23W-5S	A2
7600	BtnT	60081	2414	30W-39N	A4
7600	SPGV	60081	2414	30W-39N	A4
8000	MNGV	60053	2865	7W-10N	A5
E River Dr					
300	CHCG	60611	3034	0E-0N	C3
1200	DSPN	60018	2863	12W-10N	B5
N River Dr					
29700	LbvT	60048	2592	15W-29N	A3
W River Dr					
200	SCRL	60174	2964	36W-3N	A6
River Ln					
10	WNFD	60190	3023	27W-0S	B6
10	WnfT	60190	3023	27W-0S	B6
N River Ln					
10	GNVA	60134	3020	35W-1N	C3
S River Ln					
10	GNVA	60134	3020	35W-1N	C4
River Rd					
-	BtnT	60081	2414	30W-39N	A4
-	FrnT	60481	3853	27W-37S	C3
-	TroT	60404	3496	31W-23S	A4
-	WMTN	60481	3853	27W-37S	C3
-	WmTp	60481	3853	27W-37S	C3
10	LMNT	60439	3270	19W-13S	D5
10	NPVL	60563	3141	28W-6S	A4
10	SchT	60175	2964	35W-6N	B1
10	WNVL	60555	3081	28W-4S	A7
100	DRFD	60015	2757	9W-20N	B2
100	LKBN	60010	2643	27W-24N	B7
100	SchT	60175	2908	35W-6N	B7
100	SRWD	60404	3496	31W-23S	A4
300	NPVL	60555	3140	29W-4S	E1
300	NPVL	60563	3140	29W-4S	E1
300	WNVL	60555	3140	29W-4S	E1
300	WNVL	60563	3140	29W-4S	E1
500	WNVL	60555	3141	28W-4S	A1
1300	SEGN	60177	2908	34W-9N	E1
2600	CHCG	60018	2917	11W-8N	C2
2600	DSPN	60018	2917	11W-8N	C2
2600	RSMT	60018	2917	11W-8N	C3
3000	NRIV	60546	3088	10W-2S	B4
3600	HLCT	60429	3506	4W-22S	D1
4000	SRPK	60176	2973	11W-5N	D1
4500	SRPK	60176	2917	11W-6N	D6
5100	SRPK	60656	2917	11W-6N	C6
5500	LSLE	60532	3143	23W-6S	A4
5500	LslT	60532	3143	23W-6S	A4
6100	HGKN	60525	3148	11W-6S	A5
6500	HGKN	60525	3147	11W-8S	D7
6500	HGKN	60525	3209	12W-8S	C1
6500	WLSP	60525	3209	12W-8S	C1
10700	BtlT	60545	3333	43W-15S	A1
10700	BtlT	60560	3333	43W-15S	A1
10700	YKVL	60560	3333	43W-15S	A1
10900	BtlT	60545	3332	44W-15S	E2
12000	LtRT	60545	3332	44W-15S	E2
14200	LtRT	60545	3331	47W-15S	D3
19000	MngT	60152	2578	48W-28N	E6
19000	SenT	60152	2578	48W-28N	E6
20800	SRWD	60404	3584	31W-26S	A2
21300	TroT	60404	3584	31W-25S	A2
22200	TroT	60447	3584	31W-27S	B5
River Rd CO-1					
10	NPVL	60563	3140	28W-6S	E4
10	NPVL	60563	3141	28W-6S	A4
10	WNVL	60555	3081	28W-4S	A7
River Rd CO-3					
300	NPVL	60555	3140	29W-4S	E1
300	NPVL	60563	3140	29W-4S	E1
300	WNVL	60555	3140	29W-4S	E1
300	WNVL	60563	3140	29W-4S	E1
500	WNVL	60555	3141	28W-4S	A1
River Rd CO-13					
100	WNVL	60555	3081	28W-4S	A7
River Rd CO-V50					
100	LKBN	60010	2643	27W-24N	B7
E River Rd					
10	MTGY	60538	3199	37W-10S	C6
10	OswT	60538	3199	37W-10S	C6
N River Rd					
-	WMTN	60481	3853	29W-36S	A2
-	WmTp	60481	3853	29W-36S	A2
-	WrnT	60031	2535	15W-33N	A4
10	ALGN	60102	2694	33W-20N	E7
10	DSPN	60016	2863	13W-12N	A1
10	NARA	60542	3078	36W-3S	A7
10	NPVL	60540	3141	28W-6S	A5
100	FRGV	60021	2696	30W-23N	B2
100	MaiT	60016	2863	13W-12N	A1
100	NndT	60051	2528	31W-32N	D6
300	ALGN	60102	2695	33W-21N	A6
400	NPVL	60563	3141	28W-6S	A4
400	WhlT	60056	2808	13W-13N	E5
500	NARA	60510	3078	36W-3S	A7
600	MPPT	60056	2808	13W-13N	E5
600	WhlT	60025	2808	13W-13N	E5
700	DSPN	60016	2808	13W-12N	A7
700	DSPN	60016	2809	13W-12N	A7
700	MaiT	60016	2808	13W-12N	E7
700	MaiT	60016	2809	13W-12N	A7
900	MPPT	60025	2808	13W-14N	E5
1000	MHRY	60051	2528	32W-33N	C4
1300	MPPT	60056	2809	13W-15N	A3
1300	WhlT	60025	2809	13W-14N	A3
1300	WhlT	60056	2809	13W-15N	A3
1300	WhlT	60062	2809	13W-15N	A3
1400	MchT	60051	2528	32W-33N	C3
1500	PTHT	60070	2809	13W-15N	A3
2900	AlqT	60102	2695	32W-21N	C5
3000	BNHL	60102	2695	32W-22N	C5
5200	CHCG	60018	2917	11W-6N	C6
5200	CHCG	60656	2917	11W-6N	C6
5200	SRPK	60176	2917	11W-6N	C6
5200	SRPK	60656	2917	11W-6N	C6
5300	RSMT	60018	2917	11W-6N	C5
6200	DSPN	60018	2917	11W-7N	C4
23500	CbaT	60013	2696	28W-23N	D1
30500	LbvT	60048	2591	16W-30N	E1
31100	WKGN	60048	2591	16W-30N	E1
31200	WKGN	60048	2534	16W-31N	E7
31500	LbvT	60048	2534	16W-31N	E7
32000	WKGN	60048	2535	15W-31N	A6
32000	WrnT	60048	2535	15W-31N	A6
N River Rd CO-V45					
100	MchT	60051	2528	31W-32N	C4
100	NndT	60051	2528	31W-32N	D6
1000	MHRY	60051	2528	32W-33N	C4
N River Rd SR-25					
10	NARA	60542	3078	36W-3S	A7
500	NARA	60510	3078	36W-3S	A7
N River Rd US-45					
10	DSPN	60016	2863	13W-12N	A1
100	MaiT	60016	2863	13W-12N	A1
400	WhlT	60056	2808	13W-13N	E5
600	MPPT	60056	2808	13W-13N	E5
600	WhlT	60025	2808	13W-13N	E5
700	DSPN	60016	2808	13W-12N	E6
700	DSPN	60016	2809	13W-12N	A7
700	MaiT	60016	2808	13W-12N	E7
700	MaiT	60016	2809	13W-12N	A7
900	MPPT	60025	2808	13W-14N	E5
1300	MPPT	60056	2809	13W-15N	A3
1300	WhlT	60025	2809	13W-14N	A3
1300	WhlT	60056	2809	13W-15N	A3
1300	WhlT	60062	2809	13W-15N	A3
1500	PTHT	60070	2809	13W-15N	A3
S River Rd					
-	ISLK	60042	2586	29W-28N	C5
-	ISLK	60051	2586	29W-28N	C5
-	TroT	60404	3496	30W-22S	A3
10	ALGN	60102	2694	33W-20N	E7
10	DSPN	60016	2863	12W-10N	A4
10	NARA	60542	3138	35W-5S	B2
10	NPVL	60540	3141	28W-6S	A6
10	PNFD	60544	3416	30W-18S	B1
10	PnfT	60544	3416	30W-18S	B2
100	AURA	60542	3138	35W-5S	B2
100	FRGV	60021	2696	30W-22N	A3
100	NndT	60051	2528	31W-31N	D6
100	NpvT	60540	3141	28W-7S	A6
200	AURA	60504	3138	35W-5S	B3
200	NARA	60504	3138	35W-5S	B2
400	ALGN	60102	2747	33W-20N	D1
400	PnfT	60586	3416	31W-19S	A3
800	NPVL	60540	3203	28W-8S	A1
900	NndT	60051	2585	31W-30N	E1
1100	DSPN	60018	2863	12W-9N	B7
1200	MPPT	60056	2809	12W-15N	A2
1200	PTHT	60070	2809	12W-15N	A2
1200	WhlT	60056	2809	12W-15N	A2
1200	WhlT	60062	2809	12W-15N	A2
1500	HHLL	60051	2586	30W-30N	A2
1500	NndT	60051	2586	30W-30N	A1
2300	CHCG	60018	2917	12W-8N	C1
2300	DSPN	60018	2917	12W-8N	C1
3100	NndT	60042	2586	29W-29N	C5
15900	PNFD	60586	3416	31W-19S	A3
18300	JLET	60586	3496	30W-22S	A2
18300	PnfT	60586	3496	30W-22S	A1
18300	SRWD	60404	3496	31W-22S	A2
21100	FftT	60423	3504	10W-25S	C7
21100	FftT	60423	3592	10W-25S	C1
S River Rd CO-V45					
-	ISLK	60042	2586	29W-28N	C5
-	ISLK	60051	2586	29W-28N	C5
100	NndT	60051	2528	31W-31N	D6
900	NndT	60051	2585	31W-30N	E1
1500	HHLL	60051	2586	30W-30N	A2
1500	NndT	60051	2586	30W-30N	A1
3100	NndT	60042	2586	29W-29N	C5
S River Rd SR-25					
10	NARA	60542	3138	35W-5S	B2
100	AURA	60542	3138	35W-5S	B2
200	AURA	60504	3138	35W-5S	B2
200	NARA	60504	3138	35W-5S	B2
S River Rd US-12					
-	DSPN	60016	2863	13W-11N	A3
S River Rd US-45					
10	DSPN	60016	2863	13W-11N	A2
1200	MPPT	60056	2809	12W-15N	A2
1200	PTHT	60070	2809	12W-15N	A2
1200	WhlT	60056	2809	12W-15N	A2
1200	WhlT	60062	2809	12W-15N	A2
SE River Rd					
1300	MTGY	60538	3199	37W-9S	D5
1800	OswT	60538	3199	37W-10S	D5
SE River Rd SR-25					
1300	MTGY	60538	3199	37W-9S	D5
1800	OswT	60538	3199	37W-10S	D5
W River Rd					
-	AxST	60450	3761	32W-33S	C4
-	CnhT	60410	3761	31W-33S	E2
10	ELGN	60123	2801	33W-13N	A7
300	ELGN	60123	2800	34W-13N	E7
25800	CNHN	60481	3761	32W-33S	C4
25800	CnhT	60481	3761	32W-33S	C4
33200	CstT	60481	3943	28W-40S	C2
33200	WMTN	60481	3943	28W-40S	C2
River St					
-	CmgT	60033	2405	51W-39N	C4
100	WMTN	60481	3853	27W-38S	D7
100	YKVL	60560	3333	43W-15S	C2
300	BtlT	60560	3333	43W-15S	C2
600	JLET	60436	3498	24W-24S	E7
1200	AURA	60506	3138	35W-5S	A3
1200	AURA	60542	3138	35W-5S	A3
1200	NARA	60542	3138	35W-5S	A3
1600	DSPN	60016	2863	12W-11N	A3
9400	SRPK	60176	2917	11W-6N	D6
N River St					
10	BTVA	60510	3078	35W-1S	C1
10	EDND	60118	2801	33W-16N	A2
10	SEGN	60177	2908	34W-8N	D3
100	MTGY	60538	3199	36W-9S	E4
400	AURA	60506	3199	36W-9S	E3
400	MTGY	60506	3199	36W-9S	E3
700	AURA	60505	3138	35W-6S	B5
700	AURA	60506	3138	35W-6S	B5
800	BTVA	60510	3020	35W-0S	B7
23400	CbaT	60013	2696	28W-23N	D2
N River St SR-31					
10	AURA	60506	3138	35W-7S	A7
S River St					
10	AURA	60506	3138	35W-7S	A7
10	BTVA	60510	3078	35W-3S	A6
10	EDND	60118	2801	33W-15N	A3
10	SEGN	60177	2908	34W-8N	D3
100	AURA	60506	3200	36W-7S	A1
100	MTGY	60538	3199	37W-9S	C5
300	AURA	60506	3138	35W-7S	A7
300	BtvT	60510	3078	35W-2S	C4
1000	MTGY	60506	3199	36W-8S	E3
2000	NARA	60510	3078	35W-3S	A5
2500	NARA	60542	3078	36W-3S	A6
S River St SR-25					
10	BTVA	60510	3078	35W-3S	A6
300	BtvT	60510	3078	35W-2S	C4
2000	NARA	60510	3078	35W-3S	A5
2500	NARA	60542	3078	36W-3S	A6
S River St SR-31					
10	AURA	60506	3138	35W-7S	A7
100	AURA	60506	3200	36W-7S	A1
S River Tr					
24500	CNHN	60410	3672	32W-29S	D3
W River Tr					
25300	PTBR	60010	2643	27W-25N	A5
River Ash Ct					
1200	BRLT	60103	2910	30W-9N	B1
Rivera Vista					
8900	CLLK	60014	2639	37W-26N	A3
8900	DrrT	60014	2639	37W-26N	A3
River Bend Dr					
-	MNSR	46321	3430		D5
Riverbend Dr					
6000	LSLE	60532	3143	23W-6S	A5
W River Bend Dr					
5200	WKGN	60048	2535	15W-31N	A6
River Bend Ln					
-	PnfT	60586	3416	31W-20S	A6
2400	JLET	60586	3416	30W-20S	A6
Riverbend Ln					
1100	LSLE	60532	3143	23W-6S	A5
Riverbend Pl					
6100	LSLE	60532	3143	23W-6S	B5
River Bend Rd					
10	MTGY	60538	3199	37W-10S	D5
400	NPVL	60540	3141	27W-7S	B6
11300	ODPK	60467	3422	14W-21S	E6
Riverbend Rd					
26100	CNHN	60410	3672	32W-31S	C6
River Birch Blvd					
-	CLLK	60012	2640	33W-27N	E1
-	CLLK	60012	2641	33W-27N	A1
River Birch Ct					
3100	MHRY	60050	2528	32W-33N	C2
River Birch Dr					
600	YKVL	60560	3333	43W-15S	A2
5700	HFET	60192	2856	31W-12N	A2
Riverbirch Dr					
-	BtvT	60502	3078	33W-3S	E6
3100	AURA	60502	3078	33W-3S	E6
River Birch Ln					
-	YKVL	60560	3333	43W-15S	B2
River Birch Wy					
1700	GRNE	60048	2534	17W-32N	C6
River Bluff Cir					
300	NPVL	60540	3141	27W-6S	B6
River Bluff Ct					
100	CPVL	60110	2747	35W-17N	D7
700	SRWD	60404	3496	30W-24S	C7
River Bluff Dr					
300	CPVL	60110	2747	35W-17N	D7
700	SRWD	60404	3496	30W-24S	C7
700	TroT	60404	3496	30W-24S	C7
River Bluff Rd					
10	ELGN	60120	2854	34W-12N	E1
300	ELGN	60120	2855	33W-12N	A1
Riverboat Center Blvd					
3500	JLET	60431	3585	28W-25S	B2
Riverboat Center Dr					
1300	JLET	60431	3585	28W-25S	B2
Rivercrest Ct					
1500	MDLN	60060	2590	19W-29N	B4
5100	CTWD	60445	3347	6W-15S	E2
Rivercrest Dr					
13100	CTWD	60445	3347	6W-15S	E1
13100	CTWD	60445	3348	6W-15S	A1
S Rivercrest Dr					
13300	PNFD	60585	3338	29W-15S	E3
13300	WldT	60585	3338	29W-15S	E3
River Crossing Dr					
-	SRWD	60404	3584	30W-25S	B1
-	TroT	60404	3584	30W-25S	C1
-	TroT	60431	3584	30W-25S	C1
S Riverdale Av					
13200	CHCG	60827	3350	0E-15S	D1
Riverdale Ct					
10	ALGN	60102	2693	36W-21N	D6
Riverdale Dr					
300	NHBK	60062	2758	7W-16N	A7
300	NHFD	60093	2758	7W-16N	A7
N Riverdale Dr					
4500	MchT	60050	2472	29W-36N	C4
S Riverdale Rd					
3100	NndT	60051	2586	30W-28N	A5
River Edge Dr					
300	DPgT	60441	3341	23W-15S	A3
300	RMVL	60446	3341	23W-15S	A3
River Falls Dr					
3100	NHBK	60062	2756	11W-17N	D6
River Forest Blvd					
-	JLET	60586	3495	33W-21S	A1
River Forest Ct					
800	BNVL	60106	2972	15W-4N	B4
River Forest Dr					
800	BNVL	60106	2972	15W-4N	B4
Riverfront					
1700	AlqT	60013	2642	29W-25N	C4
River Front Cir					
400	NPVL	60540	3141	27W-6S	C6
N River Glen Av					
200	EMHT	60126	2971	17W-2N	C7
200	EMHT	60126	3027	17W-2N	C1
River Glen Dr					
4300	JLET	60431	3496	29W-22S	D2
River Glen Rd					
10	WnfT	60185	3022	29W-0S	E7
400	WCHI	60185	3022	29W-0S	D7
River Grange Rd					
10	SchT	60175	2908	36W-6N	A7
10	SCRL	60175	2908	36W-6N	A7
100	SchT	60175	2907	36W-6N	E7
W River Grove Av					
8400	RVGV	60171	2974	10W-3N	A5
River Grove Ct					
400	VNHL	60061	2701	16W-23N	E1
River Grove Ln					
400	VNHL	60061	2701	16W-23N	D1
400	VNHL	60069	2701	16W-23N	D1
400	VrnT	60069	2701	16W-23N	D1
Riverhead Dr					
-	JLET	60421	3675	24W-29S	E2
River Highlands Dr					
10	HNWD	60047	2645	22W-26N	A2
10	HNWD	60060	2645	22W-26N	A2
River Hills Ct					
-	BGBK	60490	3339	27W-15S	B1
River Hills Ln					
2300	BGBK	60490	3339	28W-14S	A1
2400	BGBK	60490	3267	28W-14S	A7
Riveria Blvd					
5200	JLET	60586	3496	31W-22S	A2
N Riveria Dr					
37300	LkvT	60046	2476	20W-37N	A2
37400	LNHT	60046	2476	20W-37N	A2
Riverlea Cir					
2100	NPVL	60565	3204	25W-9S	A5
W River Loft Ct					
2300	CHCG	60618	2977	2W-3N	A4
River Mill Pkwy					
600	WhlT	60090	2755	13W-17N	E6
600	WLNG	60090	2755	13W-17N	D6
Rivermist Ct					
2400	NPVL	60565	3203	26W-10S	E6
River Mist Dr					
100	OSWG	60543	3263	37W-11S	C2
River Oak Dr					
600	LslT	60565	3204	25W-9S	B4
600	NPVL	60565	3204	24W-9S	C4
River Oaks W					
400	CTCY	60409	3429	2E-19S	E1
River Oaks Cir E					
10	BFGV	60069	2701	16W-23N	D1
10	VrnT	60069	2701	16W-23N	D1
River Oaks Cir W					
10	BFGV	60069	2701	16W-23N	D1
10	VrnT	60069	2701	16W-23N	D1
River Oaks Ct					
800	ISLK	60042	2586	28W-29N	E4
River Oaks Ctr					
10	CTCY	60409	3429	3E-19S	E1
River Oaks Dr					
10	CTCY	60409	3430	4E-19S	B1
10	HMND	46324	3430	4E-19S	C2
300	WNVL	60555	3080	29W-2S	C4
500	RVFT	60305	3030	10W-0N	B3
1000	CTCY	60409	3429	3E-18S	E1
7600	OswT	60560	3334	40W-14S	B1
14500	LNSH	60045	2702	14W-23N	B1
14500	VrnT	60069	2702	14W-23N	B1
River Oaks Ln					
500	ISLK	60042	2586	28W-28N	E6
24700	SRWD	60404	3496	30W-25S	B7
River Oaks Rd					
1800	RDLK	60073	2531	25W-33N	A3
River Oaks Center Dr					
10	CTCY	60409	3429	3E-19S	E2
River Park Dr					
3100	JNBG	60051	2471	31W-35N	E7
5400	WKGN	60048	2535	15W-31N	A7
5500	WKGN	60048	2534	15W-31N	E7
W River Park Dr					
12800	HTLY	60142	2744	41W-20N	C2
River Ridge Cir					
1600	NPVL	60565	3204	25W-9S	A4
River Ridge Ct					
300	NPVL	60565	3204	25W-9S	A4
River Ridge Dr					
10	DndT	60118	2800	35W-14N	D5
10	SYHW	60118	2800	35W-15N	D4
10	WDND	60118	2800	35W-14N	D5
300	ELGN	60123	2800	34W-14N	E6
400	SCRL	60175	2964	36W-5N	A1
River Ridge St					
1900	NHBK	60062	2758	7W-16N	A7
1900	NHFD	60093	2758	7W-16N	A7
River Run Blvd					
-	MTGY	60543	3263	37W-12S	B3
-	OSWG	60543	3263	38W-12S	B3
River Run Ct					
100	OSWG	60543	3263	37W-12S	B3
24800	SRWD	60404	3584	31W-25S	A1
Rivers Dr					
200	LKBF	60044	2593	11W-29N	D4
200	ShdT	60044	2593	11W-29N	D4
Rivers Bend Ct					
10	LKBN	60010	2643	27W-25N	B5
Rivers Bend Dr					
10	LKBN	60010	2643	27W-25N	B5
Rivers Edge Ct					
100	MNKA	60447	3583	32W-28S	C7
Rivers Edge Dr					
300	MNKA	60447	3583	32W-28S	C7
500	CnhT	60447	3583	32W-28S	D7
800	CnhT	60447	3672	32W-28S	D1
800	MNKA	60447	3672	32W-28S	D1
28600	AlqT	60013	2696	28W-24N	D1
28600	CbaT	60013	2642	28W-24N	D7
28600	CbaT	60013	2696	28W-24N	D1
N Riversedge Ter					
5200	CHCG	60630	2920	5W-6N	B5
Rivershire Ct					
300	LNSH	60069	2702	14W-22N	B4
Rivershire Ln					
10	LNSH	60069	2702	15W-22N	B4
Rivershire Pl					
500	LNSH	60069	2702	14W-22N	B4
N River Shore Dr					
24600	CbaT	60013	2643	27W-24N	A6
Riverside Av					
10	WDND	60118	2801	34W-15N	A3
100	WNVL	60555	3080	29W-2S	C4
200	SCRL	60174	2964	35W-2N	B7
700	SCRL	60174	3020	35W-2N	C1
1800	GNVA	60134	3020	34W-2N	C2
1800	SCRL	60134	3020	34W-2N	C2
4300	LYNS	60534	3088	10W-4S	B7
4500	LYNS	60534	3148	10W-4S	B1
4600	MCCK	60525	3148	10W-4S	B1
4600	MCCK	60534	3148	10W-4S	B1
8400	BKFD	60513	3088	10W-3S	A6
8400	BKFD	60546	3088	10W-3S	B5
8400	RVSD	60546	3088	10W-3S	B5
14900	HRVY	60426	3350	0W-17S	C6
14900	SHLD	60426	3350	0W-17S	C6
14900	SHLD	60473	3350	0W-17S	C6
Riverside Av SR-25					
900	SCRL	60174	3020	35W-2N	C1
1800	GNVA	60134	3020	34W-2N	C2
1800	SCRL	60134	3020	34W-2N	C2
N Riverside Av					
6500	NLES	60714	2918	8W-8N	E1
6500	NLES	60714	2919	8W-8N	A1
S Riverside Av					
500	SEGN	60177	2908	34W-8N	D4
700	SchT	60177	2908	34W-8N	D4
Riverside Ct					
200	VLPK	60181	3027	17W-0N	C4
700	WMTN	60481	3943	28W-39S	B1
1600	GNVW	60025	2810	8W-14N	E4
Riverside Dr					
-	EMHT	60126	3027	17W-0S	C5
-	FftT	60423	3591	13W-27S	A5
-	VLPK	60126	3027	17W-0S	C5
-	VLPK	60181	3027	17W-0S	C5
10	BtlT	60560	3334	41W-14S	A1
10	DRFD	60015	2756	11W-20N	E2
10	SchT	60174	2908	35W-7N	B6

STREET Block City ZIP Map# CGS Grid

Riverside Dr
10 SchT 60174 2964 35W-6N B1
100 MTGY 60538 3199 36W-9S D3
100 NfdT 60093 2811 7W-15N C3
100 NHFD 60093 2811 7W-15N C3
200 BGBK 60440 3269 22W-11S C1
200 DLTN 60419 3350 0W-17S B5
400 CLLK 60014 2639 36W-25N D6
400 LKWD 60014 2639 36W-25N D6
400 PTBR 60010 2642 29W-25N D4
500 LYVL 60048 2592 15W-28N A6
600 LYVL 60048 2591 15W-28N E6
600 PKRG 60068 2863 11W-9N C7
2000 JLET 60586 3416 29W-21S D6
3400 NHFD 60091 2811 6W-14N D4
3400 WLMT 60091 2811 6W-14N D4
3500 NndT 60014 2586 30W-28N A6
3600 JNBG 60050 2471 32W-35N C5
4500 NndT 60014 2642 30W-27N B1
4800 LYNS 60534 3148 10W-5S B1
4800 MCCK 60525 3148 10W-5S B1
4800 MCCK 60534 3148 10W-5S B1
5100 RNPK 60471 3594 6W-27S A4
6500 TYPK 60477 3425 8W-20S B3
6700 BRWN 60402 3089 8W-2S A2
6800 BRWN 60402 3088 8W-2S E3
7100 BRWN 60546 3088 8W-2S D3
7100 RVSD 60546 3088 8W-2S D3
9800 HTLY 60142 2692 39W-22N C4
14700 SHLD 60426 3350 0W-17S C6
14900 PHNX 60426 3350 0W-17S C6
E Riverside Dr
14700 DLTN 60419 3350 0W-17S C5
14700 HRVY 60426 3350 0W-17S C5
14700 SHLD 60426 3350 0W-17S C5
14700 SHLD 60473 3350 0W-17S C5
N Riverside Dr
- WrnT 60031 2478 14W-35N B6
10 SHLD 60473 3350 0E-17S D6
300 GRNE 60031 2535 15W-34N A1
500 GRNE 60031 2478 14W-35N B6
1200 MHRY 60050 2528 32W-34N C2
1600 MchT 60050 2528 32W-33N C3
2300 JNBG 60050 2528 32W-34N C1
2500 JNBG 60050 2471 32W-35N C6
2500 MchT 60050 2471 32W-35N C6
7100 NLES 60714 2864 8W-9N E7
7100 NLES 60714 2918 8W-8N E1
24100 CbaT 60013 2642 28W-24N E7
N Riverside Dr SR-21
- WrnT 60031 2478 14W-35N B6
300 GRNE 60031 2535 15W-34N A1
500 GRNE 60031 2478 14W-35N B6
S Riverside Dr
- GRNE 60048 2534 16W-33N E4
10 ELGN 60120 2854 34W-11N E4
10 ELGN 60123 2854 34W-11N E4
200 VLPK 60181 3027 17W-0N C5
700 GRNE 60031 2534 16W-33N E4
700 GRNE 60031 2535 15W-33N A3
700 MHRY 60050 2528 31W-31N C7
700 NndT 60050 2528 31W-31N C7
800 EMHT 60126 3027 17W-0S C6
2600 NndT 60050 2585 30W-29N E4
2700 NndT 60050 2586 30W-29N A4
S Riverside Dr SR-21
- GRNE 60048 2534 16W-33N E4
700 GRNE 60031 2534 16W-33N E4
700 GRNE 60031 2535 15W-33N A3
W Riverside Dr
100 LKMR 60051 2529 29W-32N D5
2200 NndT 60050 2585 31W-30N D2
4400 JLET 60586 3416 29W-21S D6
15000 LNSH 60069 2702 15W-23N A3
24000 CNHN 60436 3584 30W-27S C5
24000 CNHN 60447 3584 30W-27S C5
27800 AntT 60002 2356 28W-42N A6
Riverside Pkwy
200 WNVL 60555 3080 29W-2S D3
Riverside Pl
- RtdT 60118 2799 38W-16N C1
N Riverside Plz
10 CHCG 60606 3034 D5
S Riverside Plz
10 CHCG 60606 3034 D5
Riverside Rd
10 RVSD 60546 3088 9W-3S C5
W Riverside Rd
14600 LNSH 60069 2702 14W-22N B4
14600 VrnT 60069 2702 14W-22N B4
Riverside St
10 BtlT 60560 3334 41W-15S A2
2600 FNPK 60131 2973 12W-3N B5
Riverside Island Dr
100 FXLK 60020 2472 28W-37N E2
Riverside Preserve Dr
- MTWA 60048 2648 15W-25N A4
Riverstone Ct
2800 AURA 60502 3139 31W-6S D5
Riverstone Dr
900 AURA 60502 3139 31W-6S D6
Riverstream Dr
3100 MHRY 60050 2528 32W-32N C4
River Terrace Dr
800 JNBG 60051 2472 29W-35N B5
1800 JNBG 60051 2471 31W-35N E6
River Terrace Ln
11600 HTLY 60142 2744 41W-20N D1
W Riverton Ct
7600 FftT 60423 3504 9W-23S D4
Rivertowne Ct
4200 JLET 60586 3416 29W-21S E6
Rivertowne Dr
- PnfT 60586 3416 29W-21S E6
4100 JLET 60586 3416 29W-21S E6
River Valley Dr
700 SchT 60177 2908 34W-7N D5
700 SEGN 60177 2908 34W-7N D5
Riverview Av
10 FXLK 60020 2473 28W-37N A2
100 LktT 60441 3419 23W-21S B7
1400 DSPN 60018 2863 13W-9N A6
2100 AlqT 60021 2695 31W-22N E4
River View Ct
100 SchT 60175 2908 36W-7N A6
400 MNKA 60447 3583 32W-28S C7
Riverview Ct
10 BtlT 60543 3263 39W-13S A4
W Riverview Ct
12600 HTLY 60142 2744 41W-20N D1
River View Dr
3900 SCRL 60175 2964 35W-5N A2
Riverview Dr
- DndT 60118 2801 33W-14N A5
10 AlqT 60102 2695 32W-21N B7
10 WNVL 60555 3081 28W-3S A5

Riverview Dr
200 ALGN 60102 2695 32W-21N B7
200 CPVL 60110 2747 35W-17N D6
300 SEGN 60177 2855 33W-9N A7
300 SEGN 60177 2909 33W-9N A1
500 SHLD 60473 3350 0E-18S E7
700 ALGN 60102 2694 33W-21N E6
800 SHLD 60473 3351 1E-18S A7
1200 JLET 60431 3496 29W-22S E2
1300 SEGN 60177 2908 33W-9N E1
4000 JNBG 60050 2472 30W-35N B5
4300 MchT 60050 2472 30W-36N B4
5100 LSLE 60532 3143 23W-6S A4
5500 LslT 60532 3143 23W-6S A4
N Riverview Dr
41600 AntT 60002 2356 26W-41N E7
S Riverview Dr
2400 HHLL 60051 2585 30W-29N E3
2400 HHLL 60051 2586 30W-29N A4
W Riverview Dr
26000 AntT 60002 2356 26W-41N E7
W Riverview Pkwy
2700 CHCG 60618 2977 3W-4N A3
W Riverview Pl
26000 AntT 60002 2356 26W-41N E7
Riverview Rd
- ALGN 60102 2694 33W-21N D6
500 NPVL 60540 3141 27W-6S D6
Riverview St
10 NARA 60542 3138 36W-4S A2
Riverwald Dr
3900 LYNS 60534 3088 10W-4S B6
3900 RvsT 60534 3088 10W-4S B6
3900 RvsT 60546 3088 10W-4S B6
Riverwalk Ct
10 PTBR 60010 2642 29W-26N D3
W Riverwalk Ct
24000 PNFD 60544 3338 30W-17S C5
River Walk Dr
700 WLNG 60090 2755 13W-17N D6
Riverwalk Dr
- BFGV 60090 2755 14W-20N C2
2400 JLET 60586 3416 29W-20S C5
2400 PnfT 60586 3416 29W-20S D6
N River Walk Dr
2900 CHCG 60618 2977 2W-3N A4
N Riverwalk Dr
- BFGV 60090 2755 14W-20N C1
- VrnT 60062 2755 14W-20N C1
Riverwalk Ln
100 NndT 60010 2642 29W-26N D2
100 NndT 60051 2642 29W-26N D2
100 PTBR 60010 2642 29W-26N D3
Riverway Rd
8300 AlqT 60013 2696 29W-23N C1
N River West Ct
1500 MPPT 60056 2808 13W-15N E3
1500 MPPT 60056 2809 13W-15N A3
1500 WhlT 60056 2809 13W-15N A3
1500 WhlT 60062 2809 13W-15N A3
River Wood Ct
2900 AURA 60502 3079 32W-3S C6
Riverwood Ct
- PNFD 60586 3416 30W-19S B3
10 BtlT 60543 3262 40W-13S D4
Riverwood Dr
10 BtlT 60543 3262 39W-12S D4
10 OSWG 60543 3262 39W-12S D4
1100 ALGN 60102 2747 34W-19N E2
1700 ALGN 60102 2748 34W-19N A3
16300 PNFD 60586 3416 30W-19S B4
Riverwood Ln
10 BtlT 60543 3262 39W-12S D4
N Riverwoods Blvd
- LbvT 60045 2648 13W-26N D3
26100 MTWA 60045 2648 13W-26N D4
Riverwoods Ct
2800 RVWD 60015 2702 13W-21N E6
River Woods Dr
2200 NPVL 60565 3204 26W-10S A5
Riverwoods Dr
600 SchT 60174 2908 35W-6N B7
1700 MLPK 60160 3030 10W-1N B1
1700 MLPK 60171 3030 10W-1N B1
1700 RVGV 60171 3030 10W-1N B1
Riverwoods Rd
10 LNSH 60045 2702 14W-23N D2
10 LNSH 60069 2702 14W-22N D5
10 MTWA 60045 2648 14W-24N D6
10 RVWD 60015 2702 13W-22N D4
800 VrnT 60045 2648 14W-24N D6
1000 LNSH 60045 2648 14W-24N D7
1000 LNSH 60069 2648 14W-24N D7
2100 LNSH 60015 2702 14W-22N D4
2200 RVWD 60015 2703 13W-21N A6
3000 VrnT 60015 2702 13W-21N D6
Riverwoods Rd CO-W24
10 LNSH 60045 2702 14W-23N D2
10 LNSH 60069 2702 14W-22N D5
10 MTWA 60045 2648 14W-24N D6
10 RVWD 60015 2702 13W-22N D4
800 VrnT 60045 2648 14W-24N D6
1000 LNSH 60045 2648 14W-24N D7
1000 LNSH 60069 2648 14W-24N D7
2100 LNSH 60015 2702 14W-22N D4
2200 RVWD 60015 2703 13W-21N A6
3000 VrnT 60015 2702 13W-21N D6
Riviera Ct
10 LIHL 60156 2693 36W-21N C5
200 WynT 60185 2967 28W-4N A4
3700 NHBK 60062 2756 12W-17N B4
21800 FmtT 60060 2589 21W-28N C6
Riviera Dr
4800 MONE 60449 3683 6W-31S B5
13100 PNFD 60585 3338 30W-15S C2
E Riviera Dr
10700 SPGV 60081 2355 30W-42N B5
W Riviera Dr
10700 SPGV 60081 2355 30W-43N B5
Riviera Pkwy
8900 ODPK 60462 3346 11W-17S A4
Rizzi Ln
- CLSM 60103 2967 28W-4N A3
- CLSM 60188 2967 28W-4N A3
1700 BRLT 60103 2967 28W-4N A3
Roach Av
9000 BKFD 60513 3087 11W-2S E4
9100 BKFD 60525 3087 11W-2S D4
9100 LGPK 60525 3087 11W-2S D4
S Road To Barns
21600 MltT 60187 3082 24W-3S C6
N Roadway Ln
10 LNSH 60069 2701 16W-21N E5
10 VrnT 60069 2701 16W-21N E5
W Roan Ln
25600 TroT 60404 3495 32W-22S D3

Roanoake Av
1500 AURA 60506 3137 37W-6S B5
Roanoake Ct
700 NPVL 60565 3204 25W-10S B6
6700 GRNE 60031 2477 17W-35N B5
Roanoake Dr
- RMVL 60446 3339 27W-17S D7
Roanoke Av
3600 CPVL 60110 2747 36W-18N A5
Roanoke Ct
10 BGBK 60440 3205 23W-11S A7
10 BRRG 60527 3208 15W-9S A4
1000 DYR 46311 3510 C6
1500 LGGV 60047 2700 18W-20N D7
W Roanoke Ct
700 PLTN 60067 2805 21W-15N C1
700 PltT 60067 2805 21W-15N C1
W Roanoke Dr
1300 ANHT 60004 2753 18W-16N D6
Roaring Brook Ln
700 ALGN 60102 2694 35W-20N B7
Roaring Creek Dr
2000 AURA 60503 3201 33W-10S A6
W Rob Av
17200 JknT 60421 3677 21W-30S A3
Rob Rd
10 MPPT 60056 2861 16W-12N D1
Robbie Ct
1100 DRFD 60015 2703 11W-21N D6
Robbie Ln
10 BmdT 60101 2969 21W-4N E4
W Robbie Ln
1700 MPPT 60056 2861 17W-12N C1
Robbin Dr
100 RMVL 60446 3269 23W-14S A7
Robbins Ct
1000 WHTN 60187 3024 23W-0N E4
Robbins St
300 WNFD 60190 3023 27W-0N C5
Robert Av
10 PTHT 60070 2808 15W-16N A1
10 WLNG 60090 2808 15W-16N A1
300 WLNG 60090 2754 15W-17N E5
Robert Ct
10 HNWD 60047 2646 20W-24N A7
100 BRLT 60103 2911 28W-8N A3
100 JLET 60435 3497 27W-23S C4
200 BMDL 60157 2913 22W-6N C7
200 BmdT 60157 2913 22W-6N C7
200 GLHT 60139 3025 23W-1N A2
1800 AURA 60506 3137 38W-6S B5
2300 RDLK 60073 2588 23W-30N E2
17500 WrnT 60031 2534 17W-34N A2
Robert Dr
200 ELGN 60123 2854 35W-10N B5
700 WDSK 60098 2524 42W-32N C5
S Robert Dr
1300 MPPT 60056 2861 16W-11N D3
Robert Ln
- BtlT 60512 3198 41W-11S A7
1100 CRTE 60417 3597 1E-28S B6
1600 NPVL 60564 3267 28W-12S A3
1700 NPVL 60564 3266 28W-12S E2
1800 WldT 60564 3266 28W-12S E2
Robert Rd
10 OSWG 60543 3263 36W-12S E3
600 SchT 60174 2908 34W-6N D7
6100 AlqT 60013 2641 31W-25N D4
8800 DRN 60561 3206 19W-10S D5
13100 HTLY 60142 2744 43W-18N B4
Robert St
- JltT 60436 3586 24W-25S D2
700 AURA 60506 3137 36W-6S D5
Roberta Av
10 BmdT 60188 3024 23W-2N E1
10 GLHT 60139 3024 23W-2N E1
10 GLHT 60188 3024 23W-2N E1
N Roberta Av
100 NHLK 60164 2972 13W-2N E7
100 NHLK 60164 3028 13W-2N E1
600 LydT 60164 2972 13W-3N E5
900 FNPK 60131 2972 13W-3N E5
900 FNPK 60164 2972 13W-3N E5
900 LydT 60131 2972 13W-3N E5
S Roberta Av
10 NHLK 60164 3028 13W-1N E1
100 MLPK 60160 3028 13W-1N E1
100 MLPK 60164 3028 13W-1N E1
200 NHLK 60160 3028 13W-1N E2
Roberta Ct
10 BFGV 60089 2754 16W-18N C3
100 BmdT 60188 3024 23W-2N E1
100 GLHT 60188 3024 23W-2N E1
500 RDLK 60073 2531 23W-34N E2
1200 GLHT 60139 3024 24W-2N E1
W Roberta Dr
10 LMNT 60439 3270 19W-14S C7
Roberta Ln
200 CHHT 60411 3508 1W-24S A5
5000 RNPK 60471 3594 6W-27S A4
E Roberta St
10 LMNT 60439 3270 19W-14S D7
S Robert Emmett Dr
17500 HMGN 60441 3421 18W-21S A6
17500 HMGN 60491 3421 18W-21S A6
17800 NLNX 60441 3421 18W-21S A6
N Robert Frost Cir
500 CmpT 60175 2962 39W-4N D4
S Robert Frost Cir
300 CmpT 60175 2962 39W-4N D4
Robert I Stuart Sports Complex
- MTGY 60506 3198 39W-9S D3
- SgrT 60506 3198 39W-9S D3
Robert Louis Dr
15700 PNFD 60544 3416 30W-18S B1
Robert Lowell Pl
10 CmpT 60175 2962 40W-4N D5
Robert Parker Coffin Rd
100 LGGV 60047 2700 19W-21N D6
Robert Penn Warren Cove
400 CmpT 60175 2962 39W-4N D4
Robert P Weidling Dr
800 WMTN 60481 3943 27W-39S E1
Roberts Av
2500 WKGN 60087 2479 12W-37N C3
Roberts Ct
10 WDRG 60517 3143 22W-7S C7
900 BTVA 60510 3078 36W-2S A3
3600 HLCT 60429 3506 4W-22S E1
N Roberts Ct
25800 CbaT 60010 2643 28W-25N A4
25800 WcnT 60010 2643 28W-25N A4
Roberts Dr
10 NPVL 60564 3266 28W-12S E2
10 WldT 60564 3266 28W-12S E2

Roberts Dr
2100 BDVW 60155 3087 11W-1S D1
2900 WDRG 60517 3143 22W-7S C7
7000 LslT 60517 3205 22W-8S C1
7000 WDRG 60517 3205 22W-8S C1
7000 WDRG 60540 3205 22W-8S C1
N Roberts Dr
100 GDLY 60407 4030 32W-43S D2
400 GNWD 60425 3428 0W-22S B7
400 GNWD 60425 3508 0W-22S B1
Roberts Ln
- MPPT 60056 2808 13W-15N D2
- PTHT 60070 2808 13W-15N D2
- WLNG 60090 2808 13W-15N D2
200 BTVA 60510 3078 36W-2S A3
300 WDDL 60191 2971 17W-4N B2
700 BTVA 60510 3077 36W-1S E3
26400 CbaT 60010 2643 26W-25N D4
26400 TRLK 60010 2643 26W-25N D4
W Roberts Ln
26200 CbaT 60010 2643 26W-25N D5
Roberts Rd
- NLNX 60451 3501 17W-25S D7
- PTBR 60010 2642 29W-27N D1
- WcnT 60084 2642 28W-26N D3
10 IVNS 60010 2751 24W-16N D7
10 IVNS 60067 2804 24W-15N D1
100 BGBK 60440 3205 22W-10S B7
100 NlxT 60451 3501 17W-25S D7
100 WldT 60565 3203 27W-11S C7
200 TRLK 60010 2643 26W-25N D4
300 WPHR 60096 2363 10W-42N A5
600 CmpT 60119 2962 41W-3N A6
800 SDWH 60548 3258 51W-14S A7
4000 ISLK 60042 2586 28W-27N D7
4000 NndT 60042 2586 28W-27N D7
4100 WcnT 60042 2586 29W-27N D7
4600 NndT 60042 2642 29W-27N D1
4600 NndT 60051 2642 29W-27N D1
5000 WcnT 60010 2642 29W-27N D1
27100 LKBN 60010 2643 27W-25N B4
27700 CbaT 60010 2643 27W-25N C4
Roberts Rd CO-V45
- PTBR 60010 2642 29W-27N D1
- WcnT 60084 2642 28W-26N D3
200 TRLK 60010 2643 26W-25N D4
4000 ISLK 60042 2586 28W-27N D7
4000 NndT 60042 2586 28W-27N D7
4100 WcnT 60042 2586 29W-27N D7
4600 NndT 60042 2642 29W-27N D1
4600 NndT 60051 2642 29W-27N D1
5000 WcnT 60010 2642 29W-27N D1
27100 LKBN 60010 2643 27W-25N B4
27700 CbaT 60010 2643 27W-25N B4
S Roberts Rd
6800 BDPK 60458 3148 9W-7S C7
6800 BGVW 60455 3148 9W-7S C7
6800 BGVW 60458 3148 9W-7S C7
7000 JSTC 60455 3148 9W-7S C7
7000 JSTC 60458 3148 9W-7S C7
7400 BGVW 60455 3210 10W-8S C2
7400 JSTC 60455 3210 10W-8S C2
7400 JSTC 60458 3210 10W-10S C6
7500 BGVW 60458 3210 10W-8S C2
8600 HYHL 60457 3210 10W-10S C6
8600 HYHL 60458 3210 10W-10S C6
9600 HYHL 60465 3210 9W-11S C6
9600 PSHL 60465 3210 9W-11S C6
9700 PSHL 60457 3210 9W-11S C7
10100 PSHL 60465 3274 10W-12S C2
W Roberts Rd
28000 CbaT 60010 2643 28W-25N A4
28000 LKBN 60010 2643 27W-25N A4
28100 WcnT 60010 2643 28W-25N A4
28300 PTBR 60010 2643 28W-25N A4
28400 PTBR 60010 2642 28W-26N E3
28400 WcnT 60010 2642 28W-26N E3
28700 WcnT 60084 2642 28W-26N E3
28800 PTBR 60084 2642 28W-26N D3
29000 NndT 60042 2586 28W-27N D7
29000 NndT 60042 2642 29W-27N D1
29000 NndT 60051 2586 29W-27N D7
29000 NndT 60051 2642 29W-27N D1
29000 WcnT 60042 2586 28W-27N D7
29400 ISLK 60042 2586 28W-27N D7
29400 ISLK 60051 2586 28W-27N D7
W Roberts Rd CO-V45
28000 CbaT 60010 2643 28W-25N A4
28000 LKBN 60010 2643 27W-25N A4
28100 WcnT 60010 2643 28W-25N A4
28300 PTBR 60010 2643 28W-25N A4
28400 PTBR 60010 2642 28W-26N E3
28400 WcnT 60010 2642 28W-26N E3
28700 WcnT 60084 2642 28W-26N E3
28800 PTBR 60084 2642 28W-26N D3
29000 NndT 60042 2586 28W-27N D7
29000 NndT 60042 2642 29W-27N D1
29000 NndT 60051 2586 29W-27N D7
29000 NndT 60051 2642 29W-27N D1
29000 WcnT 60042 2586 28W-27N D7
29400 ISLK 60042 2586 28W-27N D7
29400 ISLK 60051 2586 28W-27N D7
Roberts St
10 NARA 60542 3137 36W-4S E1
200 PNFD 60544 3416 29W-18S C1
1800 WMTN 60481 3943 27W-40S D4
1800 WslT 60481 3943 27W-40S D4
11600 FftT 60448 3502 14W-23S D4
11600 MKNA 60448 3502 14W-23S D4
Roberts Cove
200 BlmT 60422 3507 2W-24S D5
200 CHHT 60422 3507 2W-24S D4
200 FSMR 60422 3507 2W-24S D4
Robertson Av
10 LKZH 60047 2698 23W-22N D4
9600 OKLN 60453 3211 6W-11S D6
Robertson Blvd
10 LGGV 60047 2700 20W-22N B4
Robertson Ln
2300 FSMR 60422 3507 2W-23S C2
E Robertson St
- PLTN 60067 2752 20W-16N E7
- PLTN 60067 2753 20W-16N A7
400 PLTN 60074 2753 20W-16N A7
W Robertson St
10 PLTN 60067 2752 21W-16N D7
W Roberts Ridge Rd
4800 MonT 60449 3683 6W-32S A7
5300 MonT 60449 3682 6W-32S E7
Robert V Sabonjian Pl
400 WKGN 60085 2537
Robert York Av
600 DRFD 60015 2703 11W-20N E7
600 DRFD 60015 2756 10W-20N E1
Robey Av
1000 DRGV 60516 3144 19W-7S C7

Robey Av
14600 DXMR 60426 3349 2W-17S D6
14600 HRVY 60426 3349 2W-18S D7
Robey St
10 ELGN 60123 2855 33W-10N A6
14100 DXMR 60426 3349 2W-17S D5
14400 HRVY 60426 3349 2W-17S D5
16700 HLCT 60428 3427 2W-20S D4
16700 HLCT 60429 3427 2W-20S D4
16700 MKHM 60428 3427 2W-20S D4
Robin Av
1500 MLPK 60160 3028 13W-1N E2
Robin Cir
1500 HFET 60169 2858 25W-12N B2
Robin Ct
100 BMDL 60108 2968 23W-4N E3
100 PNFD 60544 3416 31W-18S A1
600 GYLK 60030 2533 20W-33N B2
600 ROSL 60172 2912 23W-6N E6
800 DYR 46311 3510 D6
900 ANTH 60002 2416 24W-41N C1
1200 EGVV 60007 2914 21W-8N A1
3600 SPGV 60081 2413 32W-39N B5
4400 GRNE 60031 2478 14W-34N C7
8100 TYPK 60477 3504 10W-23S C4
8800 HYHL 60457 3209 11W-9S E4
9000 ODHL 60487 3424 11W-19S A2
S Robin Ct
1800 WKGN 60048 2535 14W-31N D6
W Robin Ct
25400 WcnT 60084 2588 25W-29N A4
Robin Dr
100 BlmT 60411 3509 3E-25S E7
1100 CLSM 60188 2967 28W-4N B4
1200 EGVV 60007 2914 21W-8N A1
8800 MaiT 60016 2863 11W-11N D4
8800 PKRG 60016 2863 11W-11N D4
8800 PKRG 60068 2863 11W-11N D4
Robin Ln
10 SHLD 60473 3350 0E-18S D7
10 WnfT 60185 3023 28W-1N B2
200 DndT 60110 2748 33W-18N A5
200 WDDL 60143 2914 19W-5N D7
200 WDDL 60191 2914 19W-5N D7
200 WDDL 60191 2970 19W-5N D1
300 WYNE 60184 2964 34W-5N D2
600 GLNC 60022 2758 6W-16N D6
800 JLET 60432 3499 22W-22S C1
800 PltT 60140 2851 42W-12N C1
900 BTVA 60510 3020 36W-0S A7
1600 GNVW 60025 2809 11W-14N D4
1600 LSLE 60532 3142 23W-5S E3
1700 HFET 60169 2858 25W-12N B2
2100 RGMW 60008 2806 19W-14N B4
2300 ELGN 60123 2853 36W-12N E2
6100 AlqT 60014 2640 33W-25N E4
10500 ODPK 60467 3423 13W-20S B3
18300 HMWD 60430 3427 3W-22S A7
18300 HMWD 60430 3507 3W-22S A1
S Robin Ln
3200 ISLK 60042 2586 30W-28N B5
3200 NndT 60042 2586 30W-28N B5
3200 NndT 60051 2586 30W-28N B5
W Robin Ln
1200 MPPT 60056 2861 16W-11N D2
24900 WldT 60564 3265 31W-11S E2
24900 WldT 60564 3266 31W-11S A2
Robin Rd
10 CPVL 60110 2748 32W-18N C6
1500 BKBN 60015 2703 11W-22N C4
21100 DhmT 60033 2464 50W-36N B3
25200 TRLK 60010 2643 27W-25N C5
N Robin Rd
9800 NLES 60714 2864 10W-12N B1
34700 GrtT 60041 2473 26W-34N D7
Robin Rdg
500 ELGN 60123 2853 36W-12N D2
Robin St
- HGKN 60525 3147 11W-7S D5
Robincrest Dr
3200 NHBK 60062 2756 11W-16N D7
Robincrest Ln
100 LNHT 60046 2417 21W-38N E7
1900 GNVW 60025 2810 8W-13N D7
N Robincrest Ln
1700 GNVW 60025 2810 8W-13N D7
S Robincrest Ln
1700 GNVW 60025 2810 8W-13N D7
Robin Crest Rd
10 HNWD 60047 2644 23W-24N E7
Robin Glen Ln
200 ElgT 60124 2907 37W-8N D4
200 SEGN 60124 2907 37W-8N D4
200 SEGN 60177 2907 37W-8N D4
Robin Hill Ct
400 NPVL 60540 3203 27W-7S C1
Robin Hill Dr
10 NPVL 60540 3141 27W-7S C7
200 SRWD 60404 3496 30W-23S B5
300 NPVL 60540 3203 27W-7S C1
8900 DrrT 60098 2583 37W-28N A5
S Robin Hill Dr
8900 DrrT 60098 2583 37W-28N A5
Robinhood Cir
10 OSWG 60543 3263 37W-12S D2
Robin Hood Ct
10 LNSH 60069 2702 13W-23N E3
Robinhood Ct
300 BGBK 60440 3269 23W-11S A1
400 SMWD 60107 2857 28W-10N B5
Robinhood Dr
10 OSWG 60543 3263 36W-11S D2
400 AraT 60504 3138 35W-5S C2
400 AURA 60504 3138 35W-5S C2
400 SMWD 60107 2857 28W-10N B5
1100 HnrT 60120 2856 31W-10N A6
8700 ODHL 60462 3424 10W-19S A3
8700 ODHL 60487 3424 10W-19S A3
8700 ODPK 60462 3424 10W-20S B4
17000 ODPK 60487 3424 10W-20S B4
17000 TYPK 60487 3424 10W-20S B4
Robin Hood Ln
10 NHFD 60093 2811 7W-15N B2
Robinhood Ln
700 LGPK 60525 3087 12W-3S C5
E Robinhood Ln
1800 ANHT 60004 2807 16W-15N C1
Robin Hood Pl
1500 HDPK 60035 2704 10W-22N B5
Robinhood St
10800 WSTR 60154 3086 13W-2S E2
E Robinhood Wy
10 BGBK 60440 3205 22W-11S B7
W Robinhood Wy
100 BGBK 60440 3205 23W-11S B1
300 BGBK 60440 3269 23W-11S B1

STREET Block	City	ZIP	Map#	CGS	Grid
Robin Hood Ranch					
10	OKBK	60523	3086	15W-3S	A5
Robin's Nest Ct					
100	NARA	60542	3137	37W-4S	B1
Robinson Av					
800	SMWD	60107	2911	27W-9N	B1
9100	FNPK	60131	2973	11W-4N	D3
Robinson Ct					
300	BRWN	60402	3088	9W-3S	D5
300	RVSD	60402	3088	9W-3S	D5
300	RVSD	60546	3088	9W-3S	D5
N Robinson Dr					
500	PLTN	60074	2753	19W-16N	B6
Robinson Ln					
200	WTMT	60559	3145	18W-6S	A4
Robinson St					
1000	ELBN	60119	3017	43W-0N	A5
8900	SjnT	46311	3598		D7
9700	SjnT	46311	3687		D2
S Robinson St					
3100	CHCG	60608	3091	1W-3S	D4
Robinson Wy					
200	BTVA	60510	3078	34W-1S	E2
Robinwood Ct					
600	WHTN	60187	3082	24W-3S	D6
S Robinwood Ct					
10	RVWD	60015	2702	13W-22N	E4
Robinwood Dr					
1200	ELGN	60123	2800	35W-13N	B7
1300	AURA	60506	3137	36W-5S	E3
2000	ALGN	60102	2746	36W-20N	D1
2000	ALGN	60102	2747	35W-20N	A1
Robinwood Ln					
300	WHTN	60187	3082	24W-3S	D6
1600	RVWD	60015	2702	13W-22N	E5
2000	LNSH	60069	2702	13W-22N	E4
Rob Roy Cir					
15700	OKFT	60452	3425	7W-18S	C1
Rob Roy Ct					
100	SMBG	60194	2857	26W-10N	E5
500	IVNS	60067	2752	22W-16N	B7
2100	HRPK	60133	2967	27W-5N	C1
Rob Roy Dr					
8400	ODPK	60462	3424	10W-18S	B1
15500	OKFT	60452	3347	7W-18S	C7
15700	OKFT	60452	3425	7W-18S	C1
15800	BmnT	60477	3425	7W-18S	C1
Rob Roy Ln					
10	PTHT	60070	2808	14W-14N	B3
Rob Roy Pl					
900	DRGV	60516	3206	19W-8S	C1
Robsart Pl					
100	KLWH	60043	2812	3W-14N	D4
Robsart Rd					
10	KLWH	60043	2812	3W-14N	E4
Robson Dr					
200	LKPT	60441	3420	21W-18S	A1
200	LktT	60441	3420	21W-18S	A1
Robyn Ct					
500	PTHT	60070	2808	14W-15N	B2
Rocbaar Dr					
200	RMVL	60446	3269	23W-14S	A7
Rochdale Cir					
10	YkTp	60148	3084	19W-1S	D1
E Rochdale Pl					
1400	CHCG	60615	3153	1E-5S	A2
Rochefort Ln					
10	WYNE	60184	2909	33W-6N	B7
10	WYNE	60184	2965	32W-6N	C1
Rochelle Ct					
10	LIHL	60156	2692	39W-23N	D2
1900	WLNG	60090	2808	14W-15N	C2
Rochelle Ln					
17100	ODPK	60462	3424	10W-20S	B4
17100	ODPK	60487	3424	10W-20S	B4
17100	TYPK	60487	3424	10W-20S	B4
Rochelle Ter					
600	LMBD	60148	3026	20W-1N	B2
Rochester Av					
8800	BKFD	60513	3087	11W-4S	D7
8800	BKFD	60513	3088	10W-4S	D7
8800	BKFD	60534	3088	10W-4S	B7
8800	LYNS	60534	3088	10W-4S	B7
9500	LGNG	60513	3087	11W-4S	D7
9500	LGNG	60525	3087	11W-4S	D7
Rochester Ct					
10	ALGN	60102	2694	35W-20N	A7
600	SMBG	60194	2858	26W-11N	A4
Rochester Dr					
2000	MTGY	60506	3198	39W-8S	E3
2000	MTGY	60506	3199	38W-8S	A3
2000	MTGY	60538	3198	39W-8S	E3
2000	MTGY	60538	3199	38W-8S	A3
4900	HFET	60010	2751	24W-16N	C7
Rock Ct					
-	PNFD	60586	3415	31W-19S	E4
2300	NPVL	60565	3203	27W-10S	B6
2300	WldT	60565	3203	27W-10S	B6
Rock Dr					
-	PnfT	60586	3415	31W-19S	E3
25300	PNFD	60586	3415	31W-19S	D4
Rock Pkwy					
3400	WKGN	60087	2479	11W-38N	D1
Rock Rd					
-	BTVA	60134	3020	35W-0S	A7
-	BTVA	60510	3020	35W-0S	A7
-	DGvT	60439	3207	18W-11S	B7
-	DGvT	60439	3271	18W-11S	A1
-	GnvT	60134	3020	35W-0S	A7
10	RMVL	60446	3341	23W-16S	A3
E Rock St					
10	PLNO	60545	3259	47W-14S	D7
W Rock St					
10	PLNO	60545	3259	47W-14S	C7
Rockbluff Wy					
13800	HMGN	60491	3343	17W-17S	C4
Rockbridge Dr					
800	NPVL	60540	3142	25W-7S	B7
Rockbridge Rd					
900	NPVL	60540	3142	25W-7S	C7
Rock Canyon					
2300	NLNX	60451	3588	19W-27S	E4
Rock Cove Ct					
1300	HFET	60192	2804	24W-15N	C2
Rock Cove Dr					
4300	HFET	60192	2804	24W-15N	C2
Rock Creek Blvd					
1500	JLET	60431	3585	28W-26S	A2
3700	JLET	60431	3584	29W-26S	E2
Rock Creek Cir					
12700	HTLY	60142	2744	42W-19N	D3
Rock Creek Rd					
800	LtRT	60545	3196	46W-10S	A7
1100	LtRT	60545	3260	46W-11S	A1
1600	LtRT	60545	3259	47W-12S	E4
1600	PLNO	60545	3259	47W-12S	E4
Rock Dove Ct					
5800	LGGV	60047	2701	17W-23N	C1
Rockefeller Av					
8400	BKFD	60513	3088	10W-3S	A5
8400	BKFD	60546	3088	10W-3S	A5
8400	RVSD	60546	3088	10W-3S	A5
Rockefeller Cir					
13500	PNFD	60544	3338	30W-16S	B3
Rockefeller Ct					
24500	PNFD	60544	3338	30W-16S	A3
Rockefeller Dr					
2200	GNVA	60134	3019	36W-1N	D2
Rockefeller Rd					
400	LKFT	60045	2650	9W-25N	B5
E Rocket Cir					
10	PKFT	60466	3595	3W-27S	B4
W Rocket Cir					
10	PKFT	60466	3595	3W-27S	A3
Rock Fish Ln					
12900	PNFD	60585	3337	31W-15S	D2
Rockford Av					
10	FTPK	60130	3030	9W-0N	C4
200	RVFT	60130	3030	9W-0N	C4
200	RVFT	60305	3030	9W-0N	C4
W Rockford St					
25300	GrtT	60041	2474	25W-35N	A7
Rock Gate Ln					
10	GLNC	60022	2758	6W-18N	D3
Rock Glen Ln					
800	SchT	60175	2908	35W-6N	A7
Rock Hall Cir					
300	GYLK	60030	2533	20W-34N	A2
Rock Hall Ct					
200	GYLK	60030	2533	20W-34N	A2
Rockhurst Rd					
100	BGBK	60440	3269	21W-11S	D1
Rockingham Dr					
-	JLET	60421	3675	25W-29S	C1
Rockingham Rd					
22100	RNPK	60471	3594	5W-26S	B3
Rocking Horse Ln					
10	FmtT	60030	2589	22W-30N	A1
10	RLKP	60030	2589	22W-30N	A1
Rock Island Av					
600	JLET	60436	3498	25W-25S	C7
600	RKDL	60436	3498	25W-25S	C7
N Rock Island Av					
34800	GrtT	60041	2474	25W-34N	A7
Rock Island Tr					
12300	HTLY	60140	2744	43W-19N	A3
12300	HTLY	60142	2744	43W-19N	A3
Rock Lake Rd					
12200	SlmT	53179	2357		B3
12700	AntT	53179	2357		C4
12700	AntT	60002	2357		C4
Rockland Av					
-	ElgT	60124	2853	38W-10N	B6
600	LKBF	60044	2593	11W-28N	E5
Rockland Dr					
1800	AURA	60503	3201	32W-10S	C6
W Rockland Ln					
15300	LbvT	60048	2592	15W-28N	A6
Rockland Rd					
400	CLLK	60014	2639	36W-26N	E3
500	LKBF	60044	2593	12W-28N	B6
500	ShdT	60044	2593	12W-28N	B6
600	LKFT	60044	2593	12W-28N	B6
600	LKFT	60045	2593	12W-28N	B6
1000	GNOK	60044	2593	11W-28N	C6
1300	GNOK	60044	2592	13W-28N	D6
1300	LbvT	60044	2592	13W-28N	E5
1500	GNOK	60045	2592	13W-28N	D6
1500	LbvT	60045	2592	13W-28N	D6
Rockland Rd SR-176					
10	LKBF	60044	2593	11W-28N	D6
300	ShdT	60044	2593	12W-28N	C6
600	LKFT	60044	2593	12W-28N	B6
600	LKFT	60045	2593	12W-28N	B6
1000	GNOK	60044	2593	11W-28N	C6
1300	GNOK	60044	2592	13W-28N	D6
1300	LbvT	60044	2592	13W-28N	E5
1500	GNOK	60045	2592	13W-28N	D6
1500	LbvT	60045	2592	13W-28N	D6
E Rockland Rd					
200	LYVL	60048	2591	16W-28N	E6
800	LbvT	60048	2592	15W-28N	A6
800	LYVL	60048	2592	15W-28N	A6
W Rockland Rd					
100	LYVL	60048	2591	16W-28N	C6
14600	GNOK	60048	2592	15W-28N	A6
14600	LbvT	60048	2592	15W-28N	A6
15600	LYVL	60048	2592	15W-28N	A6
Rockledge Dr					
10	RMVL	60446	3268	23W-14S	E7
S Rockledge Dr					
1300	PLTN	60067	2805	21W-14N	C4
Rocklyn Ct					
100	BGBK	60440	3269	23W-12S	B2
Rockne Ct					
2100	SMBG	60194	2858	26W-10N	A5
Rockpointe Ct					
5200	GRNE	60031	2478	15W-35N	A6
Rockport Dr					
1000	CLSM	60188	2967	27W-4N	C3
Rockport Ln					
2600	NPVL	60564	3202	29W-10S	C7
Rock Rd Dr					
500	DndT	60118	2801	32W-15N	D4
500	EDND	60118	2801	32W-15N	D3
Rock Rd Ln					
1000	EDND	60118	2801	32W-15N	D3
E Rockridge Dr					
-	DMND	60416	3941	33W-40S	B4
Rock Ridge Rd					
10	BNHL	60010	2696	29W-21N	B5
Rock River Ct					
10	ALGN	60102	2693	36W-21N	D6
10	NPVL	60565	3204	26W-10S	A6
Rock Rose Dr					
300	ElaT	60047	2698	23W-21N	E5
300	ElaT	60047	2699	23W-21N	A5
300	LKZH	60047	2698	23W-21N	E5
300	LKZH	60047	2699	23W-21N	A5
Rock Run Dr					
20400	JLET	60431	3496	29W-24S	E6
20400	TroT	60431	3496	29W-25S	E7
20700	TroT	60431	3584	29W-25S	D1
N Rock Run Dr					
1200	CTHL	60403	3497	26W-22S	D2
1200	CTHL	60435	3497	26W-22S	D2
1200	TroT	60435	3497	26W-22S	D2
Rocksbury Ct					
800	BTVA	60510	3078	33W-1S	E3
Rock Springs Ct					
500	NPVL	60565	3203	27W-10S	C5
Rock Springs Dr					
1100	JLET	60435	3497	27W-22S	C2
W Rock Springs Ln					
12800	HTLY	60142	2744	41W-20N	C1
Rock Springs Rd					
600	NPVL	60565	3203	27W-10S	B5
700	WldT	60565	3203	27W-10S	B5
900	NPVL	60564	3203	28W-10S	B5
900	WldT	60564	3203	28W-10S	B5
Rockspur Tr					
3800	NndT	60012	2584	34W-28N	C7
Rockton Tr					
13300	HTLY	60142	2744	43W-19N	B3
Rockville Ln					
-	RtdT	60118	2746	38W-17N	B7
Rockwell Av					
300	SchT	60174	2964	35W-5N	B2
14700	HRVY	60426	3349	3W-17S	B6
14700	HRVY	60469	3349	3W-17S	B6
14700	POSN	60426	3349	3W-17S	B6
14700	POSN	60469	3349	3W-17S	B6
15500	HRVY	60426	3427	3W-18S	B1
15500	MKHM	60426	3349	3W-18S	B7
15500	MKHM	60426	3427	3W-18S	B1
16100	BmnT	60428	3427	3W-19S	B2
16100	MKHM	60428	3427	3W-19S	B2
17100	HLCT	60429	3427	3W-20S	B4
17100	HLCT	60430	3427	3W-20S	B4
17600	HMWD	60430	3427	3W-21S	B6
Rockwell Ct					
-	LKMR	60051	2530	28W-31N	A6
400	BRRG	60527	3208	15W-8S	B2
Rockwell Dr					
-	LKMR	60051	2530	28W-32N	A5
Rockwell Ln					
-	WldT	60585	3265	31W-13S	E6
25000	PNFD	60585	3265	31W-13S	E6
Rockwell Rd					
500	AraT	60506	3199	38W-8S	A1
500	AURA	60506	3199	38W-8S	A1
Rockwell St					
-	OMFD	60461	3507	3W-25S	B7
-	OMFD	60461	3595	3W-25S	B1
-	OMFD	60466	3595	3W-25S	B1
-	PKFT	60461	3507	3W-25S	B7
-	PKFT	60461	3595	3W-25S	B1
-	PKFT	60466	3507	3W-25S	B7
-	PKFT	60466	3595	3W-25S	B1
100	WNVL	60555	3080	28W-3S	E5
E Rockwell St					
100	ANHT	60005	2807	17W-13N	A6
N Rockwell St					
600	CHCG	60612	3033	3W-0N	A3
700	CHCG	60622	3033	3W-0N	A3
1500	CHCG	60647	3033	3W-1N	A1
2400	CHCG	60647	2977	3W-3N	A5
3300	CHCG	60618	2977	3W-4N	A3
4400	CHCG	60618	2921	3W-5N	A7
5200	CHCG	60625	2921	3W-6N	A5
5500	CHCG	60659	2921	3W-7N	A4
6300	CHCG	60645	2921	3W-7N	A3
7400	CHCG	60645	2867	3W-9N	A7
7500	CHCG	60202	2867	3W-9N	A7
7500	EVTN	60202	2867	3W-9N	A7
S Rockwell St					
100	CHCG	60612	3033	3W-0S	A5
1200	CHCG	60608	3033	3W-1S	A7
1500	CHCG	60608	3091	3W-1S	A1
3500	CHCG	60632	3091	3W-4S	A7
4800	CHCG	60632	3151	3W-6S	A4
5400	CHCG	60629	3151	3W-7S	A6
7400	CHCG	60629	3213	3W-8S	A1
7500	CHCG	60652	3213	3W-9S	A3
8700	CHCG	60805	3213	3W-10S	A4
8700	ENGN	60805	3213	3W-10S	A4
11400	CHCG	60655	3277	3W-13S	B3
W Rockwell St					
-	ANHT	60005	2807	18W-13N	A6
600	ANHT	60005	2806	18W-13N	E6
Rockwood Dr					
-	EGVV	60007	2861	17W-9N	B7
2400	JLET	60432	3500	20W-22S	B2
Rockwood Ln					
-	BtvT	60542	3077	38W-3S	A6
-	NARA	60542	3076	38W-3S	E6
-	NARA	60542	3077	38W-3S	A6
Rockwood Rd					
-	RGWD	60072	2470	34W-36N	C4
Rocky Wy					
10	OswT	60538	3199	37W-10S	C7
Rocky Beach Rd					
1100	JNBG	60051	2472	30W-35N	B6
Rocky Creek Rd					
-	PNFD	60544	3415	31W-19S	D3
-	PNFD	60586	3415	32W-19S	D3
-	PnfT	60544	3415	32W-19S	D3
W Rocky Creek Rd					
-	PNFD	60544	3415	32W-19S	D3
-	PNFD	60586	3415	32W-19S	D3
-	PnfT	60544	3415	32W-19S	D3
Rocky Hill Cir					
1000	JLET	60432	3500	20W-22S	B2
N Rocky Top Rd					
28500	GNOK	60048	2592	14W-28N	C6
28500	LbvT	60048	2592	14W-28N	C6
Rocky Valley Wy					
800	CLSM	60188	2967	27W-3N	C5
Rodao Dr					
15100	ODPK	60467	3344	14W-18S	D7
Rodeck Ln					
100	AddT	60106	2971	17W-3N	C4
Rodenburg Rd					
10	ROSL	60172	2912	24W-6N	C7
600	BmdT	60172	2912	24W-7N	C4
600	SMBG	60172	2912	24W-7N	C4
600	SMBG	60193	2912	24W-7N	C4
1000	BMDL	60172	2912	24W-6N	C7
1200	SmbT	60193	2912	25W-8N	C2
S Rodenburg Rd					
1800	SMBG	60193	2912	25W-8N	C3
Rodeo Cir					
10	CRY	60013	2695	32W-24N	B1
Rodeo Dr					
-	BGBK	60490	3268	26W-14S	A6
-	DPgT	60490	3268	26W-14S	A6
-	RMVL	60446	3268	26W-14S	A6
-	RMVL	60490	3268	26W-14S	A6
10	BRRG	60527	3208	15W-10S	B6
200	FmtT	60030	2589	22W-30N	A1
200	RLKP	60030	2589	22W-30N	A1
1500	BGBK	60490	3267	27W-14S	C6
1500	DPgT	60490	3267	26W-13S	E6
21600	BGBK	60585	3267	27W-14S	D6
21600	PNFD	60490	3267	27W-13S	B6
21600	PNFD	60585	3267	27W-13S	B6
22200	WldT	60564	3267	28W-13S	A6
Rodeo Dr					
22200	WldT	60585	3267	28W-13S	A6
Roder Av					
3200	GNVW	60025	2864	10W-12N	A1
3200	MaiT	60025	2864	10W-12N	A1
Roder Ct					
1600	SMWD	60107	2911	28W-9N	B1
Rodger Ct					
10	NlxT	60448	3502	15W-22S	B2
Rodgers Ct					
10	DGvT	60561	3207	18W-8S	B1
100	WLBK	60527	3146	15W-7S	A6
1200	LKZH	60047	2645	22W-24N	A7
Rodgers Dr					
6400	WLBK	60527	3146	15W-7S	A6
6600	BRRG	60527	3146	15W-7S	A6
Rodgers Ln					
1100	LKZH	60047	2645	22W-24N	B7
1200	HNWD	60047	2645	22W-24N	B7
Rodgers St					
2500	NCHI	60088	2594	10W-31N	A1
W Rodmell Ct					
14100	GNOK	60048	2535	14W-31N	D7
Rodney Ct					
600	LKPT	60441	3420	21W-19S	A2
Rodney Ln					
800	ELGN	60120	2855	32W-10N	C5
Rodney St					
500	LKPT	60441	3420	21W-19S	A2
Roe Ct					
400	DRGV	60516	3206	19W-8S	E1
W Roeland Ct					
7600	FftT	60423	3504	9W-24S	D4
Roesner Dr					
3200	MKHM	60426	3348	4W-18S	E6
3200	MKHM	60428	3348	4W-18S	E6
Roger Av					
600	KLWH	60043	2812	4W-14N	C4
700	NtrT	60093	2812	4W-14N	C4
3200	PKCY	60085	2536	12W-33N	A2
Roger Ln					
6200	HGKN	60525	3147	12W-7S	D5
Roger Rd					
300	DRN	60561	3145	16W-8S	D7
600	GNEN	60137	3025	21W-0N	D4
700	WDSK	60098	2524	41W-32N	E5
12200	GwdT	60098	2524	41W-32N	E5
Roger St					
700	ALGN	60102	2694	34W-21N	C6
4900	MchT	60050	2472	30W-36N	B3
W Roger Edwards Av					
1800	WKGN	60085	2479	11W-35N	D5
Rogers Av					
300	WNVL	60555	3081	28W-3S	A7
600	RMVL	60446	3340	24W-15S	E1
600	WNVL	60555	3080	28W-3S	E7
1600	MHRY	60050	2527	33W-33N	D2
1700	GNVW	60025	2810	8W-14N	E4
N Rogers Av					
5200	CHCG	60630	2919	6W-6N	D5
5600	CHCG	60646	2919	5W-7N	E4
5700	CHCG	60646	2920	5W-7N	A4
6100	CHCG	60659	2920	4W-7N	C3
7200	CHCG	60626	2867	2W-9N	B7
7200	CHCG	60645	2867	2W-9N	B7
Rogers Ct					
200	WnfT	60185	3023	28W-0N	A5
900	WKGN	60085	2536	10W-34N	E1
900	WKGN	60085	2537	10W-34N	A1
Rogers Rd					
700	RMVL	60446	3268	24W-14S	E7
700	RMVL	60446	3340	24W-14S	E1
1000	GRNE	60031	2478	15W-35N	B6
3100	NndT	60012	2584	33W-28N	E5
3100	PRGV	60012	2584	33W-28N	E5
16100	FoxT	60541	3330	50W-17S	B6
16100	FoxT	60541	3331	49W-17S	A6
16900	FoxT	60548	3330	49W-17S	D6
17400	KdlC	60541	3330	50W-17S	B6
17400	KdlC	60548	3330	50W-17S	B6
17400	NvlT	60548	3330	50W-17S	B6
Rogers St					
400	DRGV	60515	3144	19W-5S	D2
Rogers Farm Rd					
100	BRRG	60527	3146	15W-7S	B5
100	WLBK	60527	3146	15W-7S	B5
Roger Williams Av					
10	HDPK	60035	2705	8W-20N	A7
Rogina Dr					
3400	JLET	60431	3497	28W-22S	A1
N Rohde Av					
700	BKLY	60162	3028	13W-0N	E4
700	BKLY	60163	3028	13W-0N	E4
700	BLWD	60104	3028	13W-0N	E4
700	HLSD	60104	3028	13W-0N	E4
700	HLSD	60162	3028	13W-0N	E4
Rohe Ln					
1100	CRTE	60417	3685	0W-29S	C1
Rohlwing Rd					
-	EGvT	60193	2914	20W-9N	A1
-	SmbT	60193	2914	20W-9N	A1
10	ADSN	60101	2970	21W-3N	A5
10	BmdT	60143	2914	20W-6N	A7
10	ITSC	60143	2914	20W-6N	A7
100	AddT	60101	2970	21W-5N	A1
100	ADSN	60143	2970	21W-5N	A1
100	BmdT	60101	2970	21W-5N	A1
100	BmdT	60143	2970	21W-5N	A1
400	ITSC	60143	2970	20W-5N	A1
700	EGvT	60007	2914	21W-8N	A1
700	EGVV	60007	2914	20W-7N	A4
800	PLTN	60074	2806	19W-15N	B2
1000	ITSC	60007	2914	21W-8N	A3
1100	AddT	60143	2914	21W-7N	A4
1400	ANHT	60005	2806	20W-14N	A5
1400	ANHT	60008	2806	20W-14N	A5
1400	RGMW	60008	2806	20W-14N	A5
Rohlwing Rd SR-53					
10	ADSN	60101	2970	21W-3N	A5
10	BmdT	60143	2914	20W-6N	A7
10	ITSC	60143	2914	20W-6N	A7
100	AddT	60101	2970	21W-5N	A1
100	ADSN	60143	2970	21W-5N	A1
100	BmdT	60101	2970	21W-5N	A1
100	BmdT	60143	2970	21W-5N	A1
400	ITSC	60143	2970	20W-5N	A1
800	EGVV	60007	2914	20W-7N	A4
1000	ITSC	60007	2914	21W-8N	A3
1100	AddT	60143	2914	21W-7N	A4
N Rohlwing Rd					
10	PLTN	60074	2806	20W-16N	B1
100	PLTN	60074	2753	19W-17N	B5
200	AddT	60101	2970	21W-4N	A3
200	ADSN	60101	2970	21W-4N	A3
200	BmdT	60143	2970	21W-4N	A3
200	ITSC	60143	2914	21W-7N	A5
N Rohlwing Rd					
500	BmdT	60148	2970	20W-2N	A7
600	BmdT	60101	2970	21W-4N	A3
700	ADSN	60148	2970	20W-2N	A7
800	ADSN	60101	3026	20W-2N	A1
800	ADSN	60148	3026	20W-2N	A1
800	LMBD	60148	3026	20W-2N	A1
1000	AddT	60148	3026	20W-2N	A1
1000	ADSN	60143	2970	21W-4N	A3
1000	BmdT	60143	2970	21W-4N	A3
N Rohlwing Rd SR-53					
200	AddT	60101	2970	21W-4N	A3
200	ADSN	60101	2970	21W-4N	A3
200	BmdT	60143	2914	20W-6N	A6
200	ITSC	60143	2914	21W-7N	A5
500	BmdT	60148	2970	20W-2N	A7
600	BmdT	60101	2970	21W-4N	A3
700	ADSN	60148	2970	20W-2N	A7
800	ADSN	60101	3026	20W-2N	A1
800	ADSN	60148	3026	20W-2N	A1
800	LMBD	60148	3026	20W-2N	A1
1000	AddT	60148	3026	20W-2N	A1
1000	ADSN	60143	2970	21W-4N	A3
1000	BmdT	60143	2970	21W-4N	A3
S Rohlwing Rd					
10	PLTN	60074	2806	20W-15N	B2
300	ADSN	60101	2970	21W-3N	A6
300	BmdT	60101	2970	21W-3N	A6
400	BmdT	60148	2970	20W-2N	A6
S Rohlwing Rd SR-53					
300	ADSN	60101	2970	21W-3N	A6
300	BmdT	60101	2970	21W-3N	A6
400	BmdT	60148	2970	20W-2N	A6
Rohrer Dr					
7500	DRGV	60516	3206	18W-8S	E2
Rohrsen Rd					
10	PltT	60124	2851	43W-11N	A4
10	PltT	60140	2851	43W-11N	A4
300	PltT	60124	2852	41W-11N	A4
Rohrssen Rd					
10	HFET	60120	2856	31W-12N	A1
10	HFET	60192	2856	30W-12N	A1
10	HnrT	60120	2856	31W-11N	A4
10	HnrT	60192	2856	31W-12N	A1
700	ELGN	60120	2856	31W-10N	A5
Rokosz Ln					
1400	DYR	46311	3510		D7
1500	DYR	46311	3598		D1
Roland Av					
300	WMTN	60481	3853	27W-37S	D5
Roland Dr					
8800	AlqT	60010	2696	29W-23N	D2
W Rolf Rd					
23600	PNFD	60586	3416	29W-20S	D5
23600	PnfT	60586	3416	29W-20S	D5
Rolland Ct					
15900	MhtT	60442	3677	19W-31S	D5
Rolland Dr					
300	GLHT	60139	2969	23W-4N	A4
15700	MhtT	60442	3677	19W-31S	D5
Rolland Pl					
10	FXLK	60020	2473	28W-36N	A3
Roller Dr					
-	WDSK	60098	2582	39W-29N	C3
Rolling Dr					
700	LSLE	60532	3143	22W-5S	B3
N Rolling Ln					
1800	ANHT	60004	2807	16W-15N	D1
Rolling Glen Dr					
3600	LGGV	60047	2700	19W-22N	C4
Rolling Green Dr					
10	CbaT	60010	2643	25W-25N	E6
10	TRLK	60010	2643	25W-25N	E6
Rolling Green St					
600	GRNE	60031	2534	16W-33N	D3
Rolling Grove Ct					
1400	NPVL	60540	3141	28W-7S	A7
Rolling Hill Dr					
2300	DYR	46311	3598		E2
Rolling Hills Ct					
10	LIHL	60156	2693	38W-22N	A3
1400	BFGV	60089	2701	16W-21N	C5
Rolling Hills Dr					
10	BNHL	60010	2748	30W-16N	E6
10	BNHL	60010	2749	30W-16N	A7
1400	CLLK	60014	2693	37W-22N	A3
4400	LIHL	60156	2692	38W-22N	E3
4500	LIHL	60156	2693	38W-22N	A3
Rolling Hills Rd					
3700	CPVL	60110	2747	35W-17N	B6
N Rolling Hills Rd					
32800	WrnT	60030	2533	18W-33N	E4
Rolling Knolls Av					
10	HnrT	60120	2856	31W-11N	A4
Rolling Ln Rd					
800	JNBG	60051	2472	30W-35N	B6
Rolling Meadow Dr					
12900	LMNT	60439	3342	20W-15S	B1
Rolling Meadows Ct					
10	BGBK	60440	3268	24W-12S	C3
Rolling Meadows Dr					
2600	NPVL	60564	3203	28W-10S	B7
Rolling Meadows Ln					
12300	HTLY	60142	2744	43W-19N	B2
Rolling Oaks Dr					
1300	CLSM	60188	2967	28W-3N	A5
1300	WynT	60185	2967	28W-3N	A5
1300	WynT	60188	2967	28W-3N	A5
Rolling Oaks Rd					
10	SRGV	60554	3197	42W-8S	C1
2600	SPGV	60081	2413	31W-39N	C5
Rolling Pass					
800	GNVW	60025	2810	9W-13N	B6
1400	BCHR	60401	3774	0E-35S	D7
Rolling Prairie Ct					
1300	HFET	60192	2804	24W-15N	C2
Rolling Ridge Ln					
10	LNHT	60046	2418	20W-38N	A7
10	LNHT	60046	2476	20W-38N	A1
Rolling Ridge Rd					
10	NfdT	60093	2811	8W-16N	A1
10	NHFD	60093	2810	8W-16N	E1
10	NHFD	60093	2811	8W-15N	A1
Rollingridge Rd					
2900	NPVL	60564	3266	30W-11S	B2
2900	WldT	60564	3266	29W-11S	C2
Rollingwood Ct					
-	AURA	60506	3137	37W-7S	B6
3800	TroT	60431	3497	28W-23S	A4
Rollingwood Dr					
500	SRWD	60404	3496	30W-23S	B3
Rolling Wood Ln					
200	LKBN	60010	2643	26W-24N	D7
Rollingwood Ln					
300	TroT	60431	3497	28W-23S	B4
400	JLET	60431	3497	28W-23S	B4

STREET Block	City	ZIP	Map#	CGS	Grid
Rollingwood Rd					
900	HDPK	60035	2704	8W-21N	D6
Rolling Woods					
-	WKGN	60048	2534	16W-32N	D6
6300	GRNE	60048	2534	16W-32N	D6
Rollingwoods Ln					
1900	RVWD	60015	2702	13W-22N	E4
Rollins Ct					
1900	NPVL	60565	3204	24W-9S	C4
Rollins Rd					
10	FXLK	60020	2473	27W-36N	C5
400	FXLK	60041	2473	26W-35N	C5
600	GrtT	60041	2473	26W-35N	D5
Rollins Rd CO-A20					
10	FXLK	60020	2473	27W-36N	B5
400	FXLK	60041	2473	26W-35N	C5
600	GrtT	60041	2473	26W-35N	D5
E Rollins Rd					
10	RLKB	60073	2475	22W-35N	A6
700	RLKB	60046	2475	22W-35N	A6
900	GYLK	60046	2475	22W-35N	A6
E Rollins Rd CO-A20					
10	RLKB	60073	2475	22W-35N	A6
700	RLKB	60046	2475	22W-35N	A6
900	GYLK	60046	2475	22W-35N	A6
N Rollins Rd					
-	GRNE	60031	2476	18W-35N	E5
-	WrnT	60031	2476	18W-35N	E5
-	WrnT	60046	2476	18W-35N	E5
N Rollins Rd CO-A20					
-	GRNE	60031	2476	18W-35N	E5
-	WrnT	60031	2476	18W-35N	E5
-	WrnT	60046	2476	18W-35N	E5
W Rollins Rd					
-	GRNE	60031	2476	18W-35N	D5
10	RLKB	60073	2475	23W-35N	A6
200	RLKB	60073	2474	23W-35N	E6
500	RLKH	60073	2474	23W-35N	E6
1000	AvnT	60073	2474	23W-35N	E6
19000	AvnT	60046	2476	18W-35N	D5
19000	WrnT	60046	2476	18W-35N	D5
20500	AvnT	60046	2475	21W-35N	E5
20500	GYLK	60030	2475	21W-35N	E5
20500	GYLK	60030	2476	20W-35N	A5
20800	GYLK	60046	2475	21W-35N	E5
21300	RLKB	60046	2475	21W-35N	D5
24800	GrtT	60041	2474	23W-35N	E6
24800	GrtT	60073	2474	23W-35N	E6
25900	GrtT	60041	2473	26W-35N	E5
W Rollins Rd CO-A20					
-	GRNE	60031	2476	18W-35N	D5
10	RLKB	60073	2475	23W-35N	A6
200	RLKB	60073	2474	23W-35N	E6
500	RLKH	60073	2474	23W-35N	E6
1000	AvnT	60073	2474	23W-35N	E6
19000	AvnT	60046	2476	18W-35N	D5
19000	WrnT	60046	2476	18W-35N	D5
20500	AvnT	60046	2475	21W-35N	E5
20500	GYLK	60030	2475	21W-35N	E5
20500	GYLK	60030	2476	20W-35N	A5
20800	GYLK	60046	2475	21W-35N	E5
21300	RLKB	60046	2475	21W-35N	D5
24800	GrtT	60041	2474	23W-35N	E6
24800	GrtT	60073	2474	23W-35N	E6
25900	GrtT	60041	2473	26W-35N	E5
Rollo Blvd					
3400	PKCY	60085	2536	13W-33N	A3
Rolls Av					
13300	ClmT	60406	3349	2W-15S	D2
13300	ClmT	60827	3349	2W-15S	D2
Rolls Rd					
400	ALGN	60102	2693	35W-21N	E7
Rollwind Rd					
200	GNVW	60025	2811	8W-12N	A7
200	GNVW	60025	2865	8W-12N	A1
Rollyn L Anderson Ln					
-	GLBT	60136	2799	38W-16N	A1
S Roma Rd					
8600	PSPK	60464	3274	10W-14S	A7
Roma Jean Pkwy					
100	BRLT	60103	2911	28W-9N	A1
100	SMWD	60103	2911	28W-9N	A2
100	SMWD	60107	2911	28W-9N	A2
Roman Cir					
100	BGBK	60440	3269	21W-11S	E1
E Romans Rd					
300	EMHT	60126	2972	15W-2N	B7
300	EMHT	60164	2972	15W-2N	B7
300	NHLK	60164	2972	15W-2N	B7
Romayne Av					
200	JLET	60436	3497	26W-24S	E6
Romeo Cir					
300	PlfT	60124	2852	39W-11N	E4
Romeo Ct					
1300	LYVL	60048	2591	18W-30N	A3
Romeo Dr					
100	PlfT	60124	2852	39W-11N	E5
Romeo Rd					
300	DPgT	60544	3340	26W-15S	A3
300	RMVL	60441	3340	26W-15S	A3
300	RMVL	60446	3340	26W-15S	A3
300	RMVL	60544	3340	26W-15S	A3
E Romeo Rd					
10	DPgT	60441	3341	23W-15S	A3
10	DPgT	60446	3341	23W-15S	A3
10	LkrT	60441	3341	22W-16S	C3
10	LkrT	60446	3341	23W-15S	A3
10	RMVL	60441	3341	22W-16S	C3
10	RMVL	60446	3341	23W-15S	A3
W Romeo Rd					
500	RMVL	60446	3340	24W-15S	D3
W Romeoville Rd					
100	DPgT	60441	3341	23W-15S	A3
100	DPgT	60446	3341	23W-15S	A3
100	RMVL	60441	3341	23W-15S	A3
100	RMVL	60446	3340	24W-15S	E3
100	RMVL	60446	3341	23W-15S	A3
W Romero Av					
20400	LkvT	60046	2476	20W-37N	A2
Romford Ct					
500	ROSL	60172	2912	24W-6N	D6
Romiga Ln					
10	PSPK	60464	3272	13W-14S	E7
10	PSPK	60464	3273	13W-14S	A7
Romke Rd					
10	BrlT	60140	2796	46W-13N	B7
10	HPSR	60140	2796	45W-14N	C5
10	HshT	60140	2796	45W-14N	C5
Romm Ct					
2100	SMBG	60194	2857	27W-11N	D3
2100	SMBG	60194	2858	26W-10N	A5
Romona Ct					
2800	WLMT	60091	2811	5W-14N	E5
Romona Rd					
500	WLMT	60091	2811	5W-13N	E6
1100	NtrT	60091	2812	5W-14N	A4
Romona Rd					
1100	NtrT	60093	2812	5W-14N	A4
1100	WLMT	60091	2812	5W-14N	A4
Ron Ct					
14800	HMGN	60441	3421	18W-20S	A5
14900	HMGN	60491	3420	18W-20S	E5
14900	HMGN	60491	3421	18W-20S	A5
17200	JknT	60421	3677	21W-30S	A3
Rona Dr					
2400	AlqT	60013	2641	31W-25N	D4
Ronald Dr					
1000	JLET	60435	3497	27W-22S	D2
W Ronald Dr					
400	ADSN	60101	2970	19W-4N	D3
Ronald Ln					
300	OKBK	60523	3085	16W-2S	E3
4400	AlqT	60014	2640	33W-25N	E4
Ronald Rd					
3200	GNVW	60025	2864	10W-12N	A1
3200	MaiT	60025	2864	10W-12N	A1
3400	CRTE	60417	3597	1E-28S	B6
3400	STGR	60475	3597	1E-28S	B6
3700	CteT	60417	3597	1E-28S	B7
Ronald St					
11600	HTLY	60142	2692	40W-21N	A5
N Ronald St					
4600	CHCG	60656	2918	8W-5N	E7
4600	CHCG	60706	2918	8W-5N	E7
4600	HDHT	60706	2918	8W-5N	E7
4600	NRDG	60706	2918	8W-5N	E7
Ronald Ter					
800	RLKB	60073	2474	24W-34N	D7
Ronald J Bragassi Mem Blvd					
-	SMMT	60501	3148	9W-5S	D3
RJ Bragassi Mem Blvd SR-171					
-	SMMT	60501	3148	9W-5S	D3
Ronald Reagan Memorial Tollway					
-	AraT	-	3138	34W-4S	E2
-	AraT	-	3139	32W-4S	B2
-	AURA	-	3136	38W-5S	E2
-	AURA	-	3137	36W-5S	E2
-	AURA	-	3138	36W-5S	A2
-	AURA	-	3139	33W-4S	B2
-	BbyT	-	3075	43W-3S	A6
-	DRGV	-	3083	21W-4S	E7
-	DRGV	-	3084	21W-4S	A7
-	EMHT	-	3028	14W-0S	C6
-	HLSD	-	3028	15W-1S	B7
-	LMBD	-	3084	19W-2S	C4
-	LSLE	-	3083	23W-4S	A7
-	LSLE	-	3142	25W-4S	B1
-	LSLE	-	3143	23W-4S	A1
-	LslT	-	3083	21W-4S	D7
-	LslT	-	3084	21W-4S	A7
-	LslT	-	3142	23W-4S	E1
-	LslT	-	3143	23W-4S	A1
-	NARA	-	3137	36W-5S	E2
-	NARA	-	3138	36W-4S	A2
-	NPVL	-	3140	31W-4S	A1
-	NPVL	-	3141	27W-4S	C1
-	NPVL	-	3142	25W-4S	B1
-	NpvT	-	3139	32W-4S	B2
-	NpvT	-	3140	31W-4S	A1
-	OKBK	-	3028	15W-1S	B7
-	OKBK	-	3084	20W-3S	B5
-	OKBK	-	3085	17W-2S	C3
-	OKBK	-	3086	15W-1S	A2
-	PvsT	-	3028	14W-0S	B6
-	SgrT	-	3075	42W-4S	D7
-	SgrT	-	3135	41W-4S	E1
-	SgrT	-	3136	40W-4S	B1
-	SRGV	-	3135	41W-4S	E1
-	SRGV	-	3136	41W-4S	A1
-	WNVL	-	3141	27W-4S	C1
-	YkTp	-	3028	14W-0S	B6
-	YkTp	-	3084	19W-2S	C4
-	YkTp	-	3086	15W-1S	A2
Ronald Reagan Mem Tollway I-88					
-	AraT	-	3138	36W-4S	A2
-	AraT	-	3139	32W-4S	B2
-	AURA	-	3136	38W-5S	E2
-	AURA	-	3137	36W-5S	E2
-	AURA	-	3138	36W-5S	A2
-	AURA	-	3139	33W-4S	B2
-	BbyT	-	3075	43W-3S	A6
-	DRGV	-	3083	21W-4S	E7
-	DRGV	-	3084	19W-2S	C4
-	EMHT	-	3028	14W-0S	C6
-	HLSD	-	3028	15W-1S	B7
-	LMBD	-	3084	19W-2S	C4
-	LSLE	-	3083	23W-4S	A7
-	LSLE	-	3142	25W-4S	B1
-	LSLE	-	3143	23W-4S	A1
-	LslT	-	3083	22W-4S	B7
-	LslT	-	3084	21W-4S	A7
-	LslT	-	3142	23W-4S	E1
-	LslT	-	3143	23W-4S	A1
-	NARA	-	3137	36W-5S	E2
-	NARA	-	3138	34W-4S	C2
-	NPVL	-	3140	31W-4S	A1
-	NPVL	-	3141	27W-4S	C1
-	NPVL	-	3142	25W-4S	A1
-	NpvT	-	3139	32W-4S	B2
-	NpvT	-	3140	31W-4S	A1
-	OKBK	-	3028	15W-1S	B7
-	OKBK	-	3084	20W-3S	B5
-	OKBK	-	3085	17W-2S	B3
-	OKBK	-	3086	15W-1S	A2
-	PvsT	-	3028	14W-0S	C6
-	SgrT	-	3075	42W-4S	D7
-	SgrT	-	3135	41W-4S	E1
-	SgrT	-	3136	40W-4S	B1
-	SRGV	-	3135	41W-4S	E1
-	SRGV	-	3136	40W-4S	C2
-	WNVL	-	3141	27W-4S	C1
-	YkTp	-	3028	14W-0S	B6
-	YkTp	-	3084	19W-2S	C4
-	YkTp	-	3086	15W-1S	A2
R Reagan Mem Tollway SR-56					
-	AURA	-	3136	38W-5S	E2
-	AURA	-	3137	36W-5S	E2
-	NARA	-	3137	36W-5S	E2
-	SgrT	-	3136	39W-5S	E2
Ronan Ct					
10	LIHL	60156	2692	38W-23N	E3
1400	LYVL	60048	2591	17W-30N	B3
Ronan Dr					
3000	LIHL	60156	2692	38W-23N	E2
3100	GfnT	60156	2692	38W-23N	E2
3300	GfnT	60014	2692	38W-23N	E2
3300	LKWD	60014	2692	38W-23N	E2
Ronan Rd					
-	HDPK	60035	2650	9W-24N	D7
-	HDPK	60040	2650	9W-24N	D7
Ronan Rd					
-	HIWD	60040	2650	9W-24N	D7
10	HIWD	60040	2704	9W-24N	D1
N Ronda Rd					
100	MHRY	60050	2528	32W-32N	C5
S Ronda Rd					
100	MHRY	60050	2528	32W-31N	C6
Rondi Ct					
2700	SPGV	60081	2413	31W-39N	D6
Rondorey Rd					
25100	JknT	60421	3675	24W-30S	D4
Ronhill Dr					
10	KdlT	60560	3333	43W-18S	B7
S Ron Lee Ct					
20800	TroT	60404	3496	30W-25S	C7
Ron Lee Dr					
20900	TroT	60404	3584	30W-25S	C1
Ronnie Ct					
900	JLET	60435	3498	25W-22S	C2
W Ronnie Ct					
24200	TroT	60404	3496	30W-25S	C7
Ronnie Dr					
300	BFGV	60089	2701	17W-21N	C6
Ronsu Ln					
200	SchT	60175	2963	37W-5N	D2
Ronzheimer Av					
1500	SCRL	60174	3020	34W-2N	D1
Rood St					
-	BtlT	60560	3262	40W-12S	B4
Roof Av					
700	RMVL	60446	3340	24W-16S	C3
Rooke Ct					
400	DGvT	60516	3206	20W-10S	B5
W Rookery Cir					
1800	RDLK	60073	2531	25W-33N	B2
Rookery Dr					
16200	LktT	60403	3417	26W-19S	E3
Rookery Ln					
400	JLET	60431	3497	28W-23S	A4
Rooney Ct					
2000	HRPK	60133	2911	27W-6N	C6
Rooney Dr					
800	JLET	60435	3497	27W-22S	D3
800	TroT	60435	3497	27W-22S	D3
1000	CTHL	60403	3497	27W-22S	D3
1000	TroT	60403	3497	27W-22S	D3
Roosa Ln					
1600	EGVV	60007	2913	21W-8N	E3
Roosevelt					
-	SMBG	60173	2859	21W-12N	E1
Roosevelt Av					
10	SchT	60174	2908	34W-6N	D6
100	WCDA	60084	2587	26W-27N	E7
1100	GNVW	60025	2810	9W-13N	C6
17000	LKPT	60441	3420	21W-20S	A4
17500	HMWD	60430	3427	2W-21S	C5
S Roosevelt Av					
400	ANHT	60005	2807	17W-13N	B6
W Roosevelt Av					
100	BNVL	60106	2971	16W-5N	E1
200	BNVL	60106	2972	15W-5N	A1
1200	JLET	60435	3498	25W-22S	B2
N Roosevelt Blvd					
1400	SMBG	60173	2859	21W-12N	E2
1400	SMBG	60173	2860	21W-12N	A1
Roosevelt Ct					
-	AddT	60191	2971	17W-5N	C1
-	WDDL	60191	2971	17W-5N	C1
10	BNVL	60106	2972	15W-5N	A1
100	AURA	60505	3138	35W-7S	B7
500	AvnT	60030	2533	20W-32N	A5
500	GYLK	60030	2533	20W-32N	A5
Roosevelt Dr					
-	HTLY	60140	2744	43W-19N	B3
-	OSWG	60543	3263	38W-12S	A3
500	LYVL	60048	2591	17W-28N	C7
600	OSWG	60543	3264	35W-12S	B2
1000	VNHL	60061	2647	17W-27N	C2
13600	HTLY	60142	2744	43W-19N	B3
E Roosevelt Dr					
-	CHCG	60605	3034	0E-1S	D6
600	HMND	46394	3280		E5
Roosevelt Ln					
8400	RVGV	60171	2974	10W-3N	A5
Roosevelt Rd					
-	EMHT	60126	3027	17W-1S	C7
-	EMHT	60126	3028	15W-1S	A7
-	EMHT	60181	3027	17W-0S	C7
-	EMHT	60523	3027	17W-1S	C7
-	EMHT	60523	3028	15W-1S	A7
-	HLSD	60154	3028	14W-1S	C7
-	OKBK	60126	3028	15W-1S	A7
-	OKBK	60181	3027	16W-1S	E7
-	OKBK	60523	3027	17W-1S	C7
-	OKBK	60523	3028	15W-1S	A7
-	OKTR	60126	3027	17W-0S	C7
-	WHTN	60137	3025	23W-0S	A7
-	WSTR	60154	3028	14W-1S	C7
-	WSTR	60162	3028	14W-1S	C7
-	YkTp	60126	3028	14W-1S	B7
-	YkTp	60523	3028	15W-1S	B7
10	GnvT	60134	3021	33W-0N	A4
10	GnvT	60185	3021	33W-0N	A4
10	WCHI	60185	3021	33W-0N	B4
10	WCHI	60185	3022	29W-0S	E7
10	WHTN	60187	3081	28W-1S	B1
10	WHTN	60190	3081	28W-1S	A1
10	WNFD	60187	3081	27W-1S	D1
10	WNFD	60190	3081	28W-1S	A1
10	WnfT	60185	3022	29W-0S	E7
10	WnfT	60187	3081	28W-1S	A1
10	WnfT	60190	3022	29W-0S	D7
10	WnfT	60190	3081	28W-1S	A1
100	OKTR	60181	3027	17W-1S	C7
100	YkTp	60181	3027	17W-1S	C7
200	GNEN	60137	3025	21W-0S	D7
200	GNEN	60187	3025	23W-0S	A7
200	VLPK	60181	3027	17W-0S	C7
200	WHTN	60187	3025	23W-0S	A7
600	WnfT	60190	3080	28W-0S	E1
700	HRPK	60133	2912	26W-9N	A1
700	WDSK	60098	2581	41W-30N	D2
900	MltT	60137	3025	21W-0S	D7
1000	GNEN	60148	3025	21W-0S	E7
1000	MltT	60148	3025	21W-0S	E7
4000	HLSD	60162	3029	13W-1S	A7
4000	PvsT	60162	3029	13W-1S	A7
4000	WSTR	60154	3029	13W-1S	A7
4000	WSTR	60162	3029	13W-1S	A7
6200	BRWN	60304	3031	8W-1S	A7
6200	BRWN	60402	3031	8W-1S	A7
6200	CCRO	60304	3031	8W-1S	A7
6200	CCRO	60402	3031	8W-1S	A7
6200	CCRO	60804	3031	8W-1S	A7
6200	OKPK	60304	3031	8W-1S	A7
6700	BRWN	60304	3030	8W-0S	E7
Roosevelt Rd					
6700	BRWN	60402	3030	8W-0S	E7
6700	OKPK	60304	3030	8W-0S	E7
7100	BRWN	60130	3030	8W-0S	D7
7100	FTPK	60130	3030	9W-0S	C7
7100	OKPK	60130	3030	8W-0S	D7
8300	PvsT	60130	3030	9W-0S	C7
8400	FTPK	60153	3030	10W-0S	A7
8400	MYWD	60153	3030	10W-0S	A7
8400	PvsT	60153	3030	10W-0S	A7
11900	HLSD	60162	3028	14W-1S	C7
11900	PvsT	60126	3028	14W-0S	C7
11900	PvsT	60162	3028	14W-1S	C7
Roosevelt Rd SR-38					
-	EMHT	60126	3027	17W-1S	C7
-	EMHT	60126	3028	15W-1S	A7
-	EMHT	60181	3027	16W-1S	D7
-	EMHT	60523	3027	17W-1S	C7
-	EMHT	60523	3028	15W-1S	A7
-	HLSD	60154	3028	14W-1S	C7
-	OKBK	60126	3028	15W-1S	A7
-	OKBK	60181	3027	16W-1S	E7
-	OKBK	60523	3027	17W-1S	C7
-	OKBK	60523	3028	15W-1S	A7
-	OKTR	60126	3027	17W-1S	C7
-	WHTN	60137	3025	23W-0S	A7
-	WSTR	60154	3028	14W-1S	C7
-	WSTR	60162	3028	14W-1S	C7
-	YkTp	60126	3028	14W-0S	B7
-	YkTp	60523	3028	15W-1S	B7
10	GnvT	60134	3021	33W-0N	A4
10	GnvT	60185	3021	33W-0N	A4
10	WCHI	60185	3021	33W-0N	B4
10	WCHI	60185	3022	29W-0S	E7
10	WHTN	60187	3081	28W-1S	A1
10	WHTN	60190	3081	28W-1S	A1
10	WNFD	60187	3081	27W-1S	D1
10	WNFD	60190	3081	28W-1S	A1
10	WnfT	60185	3022	29W-0S	E7
10	WnfT	60187	3081	28W-1S	A1
10	WnfT	60190	3022	29W-0S	D7
10	WnfT	60190	3081	28W-1S	A1
100	OKTR	60181	3027	17W-1S	C7
100	YkTp	60181	3027	17W-1S	C7
200	GNEN	60137	3025	21W-0S	D7
200	GNEN	60187	3025	23W-0S	A7
200	VLPK	60181	3027	17W-0S	C7
200	WHTN	60187	3025	23W-0S	A7
600	WnfT	60190	3080	28W-0S	E1
900	MltT	60137	3025	21W-0S	D7
1000	GNEN	60148	3025	21W-0S	E7
1000	MltT	60148	3025	21W-0S	E7
4000	HLSD	60162	3029	13W-1S	A7
4000	PvsT	60162	3029	13W-1S	A7
4000	WSTR	60154	3029	13W-1S	A7
4000	WSTR	60162	3029	13W-1S	A7
11900	HLSD	60162	3028	14W-1S	C7
11900	PvsT	60126	3028	14W-0S	C7
11900	PvsT	60162	3028	14W-1S	C7
E Roosevelt Rd					
10	CHCG	60605	3034	0E-0S	C6
10	LMBD	60148	3026	19W-0S	D7
10	OKTR	60181	3027	17W-0S	B7
10	VLPK	60181	3027	17W-0S	B7
10	YkTp	60148	3026	19W-0S	D7
100	WCHI	60185	3022	29W-0S	C7
100	WHTN	60187	3024	24W-0S	D7
200	WnfT	60185	3022	29W-0S	C7
1600	WHTN	60187	3025	23W-0S	A7
1800	GNEN	60137	3025	23W-0S	A7
1800	GNEN	60187	3025	23W-0S	A7
1800	WHTN	60137	3025	23W-0S	A7
E Roosevelt Rd SR-38					
10	LMBD	60148	3026	19W-0S	D7
10	OKTR	60181	3027	17W-0S	B7
10	VLPK	60181	3027	17W-0S	B7
10	YkTp	60148	3026	19W-0S	D7
100	WCHI	60185	3022	29W-0S	C7
100	WHTN	60187	3024	24W-0S	D7
200	WnfT	60185	3022	29W-0S	C7
1600	WHTN	60187	3025	23W-0S	A7
1800	GNEN	60137	3025	23W-0S	A7
1800	GNEN	60187	3025	23W-0S	A7
1800	WHTN	60137	3025	23W-0S	A7
W Roosevelt Rd					
-	GNEN	60137	3025	21W-0S	E7
-	GNEN	60148	3025	21W-0S	E7
-	GnvT	60134	3021	32W-0N	C4
-	GnvT	60185	3021	32W-0N	C4
-	MltT	60137	3025	21W-0S	E7
-	MltT	60148	3025	21W-0S	E7
10	CHCG	60605	3034	0W-1S	B7
10	LMBD	60148	3026	20W-0S	B7
10	VLPK	60181	3027	18W-0S	A7
100	CHCG	60607	3034	0W-1S	B6
100	FTPK	60130	3030	10W-0S	A7
100	FTPK	60153	3030	10W-0S	A7
100	MYWD	60153	3030	10W-1S	A7
100	PvsT	60130	3030	10W-0S	A7
100	PvsT	60153	3030	10W-1S	A7
100	WCHI	60185	3022	31W-0N	A5
100	WHTN	60187	3082	25W-1S	A1
100	WnfT	60185	3022	30W-0S	C6
300	MYWD	60141	3030	10W-0S	A7
300	PvsT	60141	3030	10W-1S	A7
300	YkTp	60148	3027	18W-0S	A7
300	YkTp	60181	3027	18W-0S	A7
400	GNEN	60137	3026	20W-0S	A7
400	GNEN	60148	3026	20W-0S	A7
400	WnfT	60510	3022	30W-0S	B6
600	WCHI	60510	3022	30W-0S	B6
700	CHCG	60608	3034	0W-0S	A6
700	MltT	60148	3026	20W-0S	A7
700	MYWD	60153	3029	11W-0S	E7
700	PvsT	60141	3029	11W-0S	D7
700	PvsT	60153	3029	11W-0S	D7
800	BDVW	60153	3029	10W-0S	E7
800	BDVW	60155	3029	12W-0S	C7
800	CHCG	60607	3033	2W-0S	C7
800	CHCG	60608	3033	2W-0S	B7
1200	WCHI	60185	3021	32W-0N	C4
1500	CHCG	60612	3033	1W-0S	D7
1600	MltT	60187	3082	25W-1S	A1
1900	MltT	60187	3081	26W-1S	D1
1900	WHTN	60187	3081	26W-1S	D1
2100	WHTN	60190	3081	26W-1S	D1
2100	WNFD	60190	3081	26W-1S	D1
2100	WnfT	60187	3081	26W-1S	D1
2100	WnfT	60190	3081	26W-1S	D1
2500	WSTR	60154	3029	12W-1S	C7
2500	WSTR	60155	3029	12W-1S	C7
2700	CHCG	60623	3033	3W-1S	A7
2800	CHCG	60612	3032	4W-0S	D7
2800	CHCG	60623	3032	4W-0S	D7
3100	CHCG	60624	3032	3W-1S	E7
4500	CCRO	60644	3032	5W-0S	A7
W Roosevelt Rd					
4500	CCRO	60804	3032	5W-0S	A7
4500	CHCG	60644	3032	5W-0S	A7
4600	CHCG	60804	3032	5W-0S	A7
4800	CCRO	60644	3031	6W-0S	D7
4800	CCRO	60804	3031	6W-0S	D7
4800	CHCG	60644	3031	6W-0S	D7
5900	CCRO	60304	3031	7W-0S	B7
5900	OKPK	60304	3031	7W-0S	B7
5900	OKPK	60644	3031	7W-0S	B7
6100	BRWN	60304	3031	7W-0S	B7
6100	BRWN	60402	3031	7W-0S	B7
6100	CCRO	60402	3031	7W-0S	B7
9800	BDVW	60154	3029	12W-0S	C7
10300	HLSD	60162	3029	12W-1S	A7
10300	PvsT	60162	3029	12W-1S	A7
10300	WSTR	60162	3029	12W-1S	A7
10900	HLSD	60154	3028	13W-0S	E7
10900	HLSD	60162	3028	13W-0S	E7
10900	WSTR	60154	3028	13W-0S	E7
10900	WSTR	60162	3028	13W-0S	E7
18800	WrnT	60046	2476	18W-35N	D7
18900	TDLK	60046	2476	18W-35N	D7
W Roosevelt Rd SR-38					
-	GNEN	60137	3025	21W-0S	E7
-	GNEN	60148	3025	21W-0S	E7
-	GnvT	60134	3021	32W-0N	C4
-	GnvT	60185	3021	32W-0N	C4
-	MltT	60137	3025	21W-0S	E7
-	MltT	60148	3025	21W-0S	E7
10	LMBD	60148	3026	20W-0S	B7
10	VLPK	60181	3027	18W-0S	A7
100	WCHI	60185	3022	31W-0N	A5
100	WHTN	60187	3082	25W-1S	A1
100	WnfT	60185	3022	30W-0S	C6
300	YkTp	60148	3027	18W-0S	A7
300	YkTp	60181	3027	18W-0S	A7
400	GNEN	60137	3026	20W-0S	A7
400	GNEN	60148	3026	20W-0S	A7
400	WnfT	60510	3022	30W-0S	B6
600	WCHI	60510	3022	30W-0S	B6
700	MltT	60148	3026	20W-0S	A7
1200	WCHI	60185	3021	32W-0N	C4
1600	MltT	60187	3082	25W-1S	A1
1900	MltT	60187	3081	26W-1S	D1
1900	WHTN	60187	3081	26W-1S	D1
2100	WHTN	60190	3081	26W-1S	D1
2100	WNFD	60190	3081	26W-1S	D1
2100	WnfT	60187	3081	26W-1S	D1
2100	WnfT	60190	3081	26W-1S	D1
10900	HLSD	60154	3028	13W-0S	E7
10900	HLSD	60162	3028	13W-0S	E7
10900	WSTR	60154	3028	13W-0S	E7
10900	WSTR	60162	3028	13W-0S	E7
Roosevelt St					
10	AlqT	60156	2693	35W-23N	E3
10	LIHL	60156	2693	35W-23N	E3
10	SCRL	60174	3020	35W-2N	B2
200	EGvT	60018	2862	15W-9N	A7
300	DSPN	60018	2862	15W-9N	A7
E Roosevelt St					
100	HRVD	60033	2406	50W-38N	B6
W Roosevelt St					
100	HRVD	60033	2406	50W-38N	A6
5600	MONE	60449	3682	7W-31S	E5
N Root Ct					
8100	NLES	60714	2864	10W-10N	A5
S Root Dr					
26300	CteT	60417	3686	0E-32S	A6
Root Ln					
2100	AlqT	60013	2695	31W-22N	E3
Root St					
300	PKRG	60068	2864	10W-9N	A7
400	NLNX	60451	3501	17W-24S	C6
1300	CTHL	60403	3418	26W-21S	A6
2000	CTHL	60403	3417	26W-21S	E6
2300	LktT	60403	3417	26W-21S	E6
N Root St					
10	AURA	60505	3200	35W-7S	B1
700	AURA	60505	3138	35W-6S	C5
8800	NLES	60714	2864	10W-11N	A3
S Root St					
10	AURA	60505	3200	35W-7S	B1
W Root St					
10	CHCG	60609	3092	0W-4S	B6
10	CHCG	60653	3092	0W-4S	C6
Roppolo Av					
700	EGvT	60007	2861	16W-9N	D7
700	EGvT	60007	2915	16W-9N	D1
700	EGVV	60007	2915	16W-9N	D1
Roppolo Ln					
600	EGvT	60007	2861	16W-9N	D7
Rosada Dr					
3800	NPVL	60564	3267	28W-12S	A2
Rosalie Ct					
100	HNDL	60521	3145	16W-5S	E2
W Rosalie Rd					
200	PltT	60074	2752	21W-18N	D2
Rosalie St					
1300	EVTN	60201	2813	3W-12N	A7
Rosalind St					
-	JLET	60441	3499	23W-21S	B1
-	JltT	60432	3499	23W-21S	B1
-	LktT	60441	3499	23W-21S	B1
800	JLET	60432	3499	22W-22S	C1
900	LktT	60432	3499	22W-22S	C1
17000	HmrT	60432	3500	20W-22S	B1
17000	JltT	60432	3500	20W-22S	B1
17000	LktT	60432	3500	20W-22S	B1
17000	NlxT	60432	3500	20W-22S	B1
Rosanne Ln					
500	LKPT	60441	3419	22W-20S	D4
Rosanne St					
600	LKPT	60441	3419	22W-20S	D4
800	LktT	60441	3419	22W-20S	D4
Rosarie Dr					
15100	HMGN	60491	3343	16W-18S	D7
Rosary Ln					
800	JLET	60435	3497	27W-22S	C3
800	TroT	60435	3497	27W-22S	C3
W Roscoe St					
600	CHCG	60657	2977	2W-4N	B3
600	CHCG	60657	2978	0W-4N	A3
1900	CHCG	60618	2977	3W-4N	A3
4000	CHCG	60618	2976	5W-4N	B3
4000	CHCG	60641	2976	5W-4N	B3
4700	CHCG	60641	2975	7W-4N	C3
5500	CHCG	60634	2975	8W-4N	A3
7200	CHCG	60634	2974	9W-4N	B3
Roscommon Ct					
20900	MKNA	60448	3502	14W-25S	E7
Roscommon Wy					
1400	LMNT	60439	3271	18W-14S	B7
Rose Av					
-	SRGV	60554	3136	41W-7S	A7
10	FXLK	60020	2473	27W-36N	B4

STREET Block	City	ZIP	Map#	CGS	Grid
Rose Av					
200	CTHL	60403	3418	24W-21S	D7
200	CTHL	60435	3418	24W-21S	E7
200	LktT	60435	3418	24W-21S	E7
400	ISLK	60042	2586	28W-28N	E6
600	SchT	60174	2908	35W-7N	B6
800	DSPN	60016	2862	13W-11N	D4
800	PTHT	60070	2808	14W-15N	C3
1200	CLSM	60188	2967	28W-3N	B5
1700	PLTN	60074	2753	19W-18N	B3
2700	MHRY	60050	2470	34W-34N	C7
2700	MHRY	60050	2527	34W-34N	C1
3800	WNSP	60558	3086	14W-4S	D6
4000	LYNS	60534	3088	10W-4S	A7
4900	DRGV	60515	3143	21W-5S	E2
4900	LslT	60515	3143	21W-5S	E2
5800	CTSD	60525	3147	12W-6S	D4
6600	GfnT	60014	2639	38W-25N	A5
6700	LKWD	60014	2639	38W-25N	A5
18400	LNSG	60438	3429	2E-21S	D7
N Rose Av					
10	ADSN	60101	2970	19W-3N	D5
200	PKRG	60068	2863	11W-9N	D7
38500	LkvT	60046	2416	24W-38N	D7
S Rose Av					
10	PKRG	60068	2917	11W-8N	D1
W Rose Av					
400	ADSN	60101	2970	19W-3N	D5
18800	LbvT	60060	2646	18W-26N	D3
24000	ElaT	60047	2644	24W-25N	C5
Rose Blvd					
10	SBTN	60010	2803	26W-13N	D5
1300	ANHT	60004	2754	18W-18N	A3
1300	BFGV	60004	2754	18W-18N	A3
1300	BFGV	60089	2754	18W-18N	A3
1400	BFGV	60089	2753	18W-18N	E3
1600	ANHT	60004	2753	18W-18N	E3
1600	BFGV	60004	2753	18W-18N	E3
Rose Cir					
1600	RMVL	60446	3339	26W-17S	D6
Rose Ct					
10	LMNT	60439	3270	20W-14S	C7
600	LslT	60532	3143	22W-6S	B4
700	PTHT	60070	2808	14W-15N	C3
1000	WDSK	60098	2524	40W-31N	E6
1000	WDSK	60098	2525	40W-31N	A6
1100	BRLT	60103	2910	29W-6N	D7
1400	CLSM	60188	2967	28W-3N	A5
1600	RMVL	60446	3339	26W-17S	E6
1700	WHTN	60187	3082	24W-2S	D3
2100	SMBG	60194	2858	26W-11N	A4
4600	WPHR	60096	2362	11W-42N	D5
5700	BKLY	60163	3028	14W-0N	C4
5700	HLSD	60162	3028	14W-0N	C4
5800	CTSD	60525	3147	12W-6S	C4
E Rose Ct					
400	GNWD	60425	3508	0E-22S	E1
400	GNWD	60425	3509	0E-22S	A2
W Rose Ct					
22000	LkvT	60046	2475	22W-36N	C3
Rose Ct E					
1300	BFGV	60089	2754	18W-18N	A3
Rose Ct W					
1300	BFGV	60089	2754	18W-18N	A3
Rose Dr					
200	NARA	60542	3078	35W-3S	A7
300	FftT	60423	3504	10W-24S	C5
500	MLPK	60160	3030	10W-1N	A1
7300	MchT	60097	2469	36W-37N	E2
7300	WRLK	60097	2469	36W-37N	E2
15400	SHLD	60473	3351	0E-18S	A7
15500	SHLD	60473	3350	0E-18S	E7
Rose Dr E					
-	ROSL	60172	2913	22W-7N	B4
Rose Dr W					
-	ROSL	60172	2913	22W-7N	B4
Rose Ln					
-	BRLT	60103	2856	31W-9N	A7
-	ELGN	60103	2856	31W-9N	A7
10	ElaT	60047	2645	22W-25N	A5
10	HNWD	60047	2645	22W-25N	A5
400	BRLT	60103	2910	31W-9N	A1
700	HRVD	60033	2464	50W-37N	A1
700	MTSN	60443	3506	5W-25S	C6
800	PTHT	60070	2755	15W-16N	A6
800	PTHT	60090	2755	15W-16N	A6
800	WLNG	60090	2754	15W-16N	E6
800	WLNG	60090	2755	15W-16N	A6
900	NPVL	60540	3203	27W-7S	C1
1600	RMVL	60446	3339	26W-17S	D6
18700	FftT	60448	3502	14W-22S	D1
E Rose Ln					
400	GDLY	60407	4030	32W-43S	D2
400	RedT	60408	4030	32W-43S	D2
S Rose Ln					
25600	MONE	60449	3683	5W-31S	C5
Rose Pl					
10	CNHL	60514	3145	16W-5S	D2
Rose Rd					
600	LKZH	60047	2699	22W-23N	A2
Rose St					
-	EMHT	60126	3027	17W-1N	B3
-	VLPK	60126	3027	17W-1N	B3
-	VLPK	60181	3027	17W-1N	B3
10	AURA	60505	3200	34W-8S	A1
100	BNVL	60106	2972	15W-5N	A2
2000	FNPK	60131	2973	12W-4N	C3
2000	FNPK	60164	2973	12W-2N	C7
2000	LydT	60164	2973	12W-2N	C7
2000	MLPK	60131	2973	12W-2N	C7
2000	MLPK	60164	2973	12W-2N	C7
2400	LydT	60131	2973	11W-3N	C6
3600	SRPK	60131	2973	12W-4N	C3
4500	SRPK	60176	2973	11W-5N	C1
4700	AlqT	60014	2640	33W-24N	D6
5000	SRPK	60176	2917	11W-6N	C6
17800	LNSG	60438	3429	2E-21S	D6
19700	LYWD	60411	3509	2E-23S	D4
E Rose St					
10	GNWD	60425	3508	0E-22S	E2
N Rose St					
10	PLTN	60067	2805	21W-16N	D1
100	PLTN	60067	2752	21W-16N	D7
5200	CHCG	60018	2917	11W-6N	C6
5200	CHCG	60656	2917	11W-6N	C6
5200	RSMT	60018	2917	11W-6N	C6
5200	SRPK	60176	2917	11W-6N	C6
5200	SRPK	60656	2917	11W-6N	C6
S Rose St					
10	PLTN	60067	2805	21W-15N	D1
W Rose St					
10	GNWD	60425	3508	0E-22S	D2
Rose Ter					
100	TRLK	60010	2643	26W-24N	D6
200	LKFT	60045	2650	10W-27N	A1
1900	LNSH	60069	2702	13W-22N	D4
Rose Ter					
1900	RVWD	60015	2702	13W-22N	D4
N Rose Ter					
1900	RVWD	60015	2702	13W-22N	D4
Rose Ann Ct					
3600	MchT	60097	2470	34W-35N	B5
Rosebrook Cir					
-	PvsT	60558	3086	13W-2S	E4
-	WSTR	60558	3086	13W-2S	E4
3000	WSTR	60154	3086	13W-2S	E4
Rosebud Av					
6600	GfnT	60014	2639	38W-25N	A5
Rosebud Ct					
300	BGBK	60440	3269	23W-12S	A2
1600	WHTN	60187	3082	24W-2S	D3
Rosebud Dr					
-	SCRL	60175	2964	36W-6N	A1
N Rosebud Dr					
500	LMBD	60148	3084	19W-1S	D2
S Rosebud Dr					
500	LMBD	60148	3084	19W-1S	D2
Rosebud Ln					
1700	AURA	60504	3201	33W-9S	A3
N Rosebud Ln					
1300	ADSN	60101	2970	20W-5N	B1
Rosebud Pl					
16100	ODHL	60487	3424	11W-19S	A2
Rosebury Av					
8100	WDRG	60517	3206	20W-9S	B3
Rosebury Dr					
8000	FftT	60423	3504	10W-25S	C6
Rose Bush Ln					
500	DYR	46311	3510		C6
500	DYR	46321	3510		C6
500	LYWD	60411	3510		C6
500	MNSR	46321	3510		C6
Rosebush Ln					
500	OSWG	60543	3263	38W-13S	B6
Rosecrans Ct					
-	GNEN	60137	3083	23W-1S	A2
300	BRLT	60103	2911	28W-7N	B5
Rosecrans Rd					
-	ANTH	60002	2418	18W-41N	E1
-	AntT	60002	2418	18W-41N	E1
-	BtnT	60083	2420	13W-41N	E1
-	BtnT	60099	2420	13W-41N	E1
-	BtnT	60099	2421	12W-41N	B1
-	NptT	60002	2418	18W-41N	E1
-	NptT	60002	2419	16W-41N	D1
-	NptT	60083	2418	18W-41N	E1
-	NptT	60083	2419	16W-41N	D1
-	NptT	60083	2420	15W-41N	A1
-	NptT	60099	2420	15W-41N	A1
-	OMCK	60083	2418	18W-41N	E1
-	OMCK	60083	2419	17W-41N	A1
-	WDWH	60083	2419	16W-41N	D1
-	WDWH	60083	2420	13W-41N	E1
-	WDWH	60083	2421	13W-41N	A1
-	WDWH	60099	2419	16W-41N	D1
-	WDWH	60099	2420	13W-41N	E1
-	WDWH	60099	2421	13W-41N	A1
-	ZION	60099	2420	13W-41N	E1
Rosecrans Rd SR-173					
-	ANTH	60002	2418	18W-41N	E1
-	AntT	60002	2418	18W-41N	E1
-	BtnT	60083	2420	13W-41N	E1
-	BtnT	60099	2420	13W-41N	E1
-	BtnT	60099	2421	12W-41N	B1
-	NptT	60002	2418	18W-41N	E1
-	NptT	60002	2419	16W-41N	D1
-	NptT	60083	2418	18W-41N	E1
-	NptT	60083	2419	16W-41N	D1
-	NptT	60083	2420	15W-41N	A1
-	NptT	60099	2420	15W-41N	A1
-	OMCK	60083	2418	18W-41N	E1
-	OMCK	60083	2419	17W-41N	A1
-	WDWH	60083	2419	16W-41N	D1
-	WDWH	60083	2420	13W-41N	E1
-	WDWH	60083	2421	13W-41N	A1
-	WDWH	60099	2419	16W-41N	D1
-	WDWH	60099	2420	13W-41N	E1
-	WDWH	60099	2421	13W-41N	A1
-	ZION	60099	2420	13W-41N	E1
Rosecroft Ln					
3300	NPVL	60564	3202	30W-10S	B7
Rosedale Av					
10	BMDL	60108	2912	23W-6N	E7
10	BmdT	60108	2912	23W-6N	E7
100	BmdT	60172	2912	23W-6N	E6
100	CLLK	60014	2640	35W-25N	A4
100	ROSL	60172	2912	23W-6N	E6
400	PKCY	60085	2535	13W-33N	E3
500	BMDL	60108	2968	24W-5N	D1
500	BmdT	60108	2968	24W-5N	D1
600	WKGN	60085	2535	13W-33N	E3
N Rosedale Av					
10	AURA	60506	3137	37W-7S	B6
36200	WKGN	60087	2478	13W-36N	E3
36200	WrnT	60031	2478	13W-36N	E3
36300	WKGN	60031	2478	13W-36N	E3
38600	WDWH	60083	2420	13W-38N	E7
S Rosedale Av					
10	AURA	60506	3137	37W-7S	B7
200	AURA	60506	3199	37W-7S	B1
W Rosedale Av					
1200	CHCG	60660	2921	1W-7N	D4
2800	MchT	60051	2528	31W-33N	D3
2800	MHRY	60051	2528	31W-33N	C3
6100	CHCG	60646	2919	7W-7N	A4
6300	CHCG	60631	2919	8W-7N	A4
7600	CHCG	60631	2918	9W-7N	C4
7800	CHCG	60068	2918	9W-7N	C4
7800	PKRG	60068	2918	9W-7N	C4
7800	PKRG	60631	2918	9W-7N	C4
Rosedale Ct					
100	BMDL	60108	2968	23W-5N	E1
1700	AURA	60506	3137	37W-6S	B6
N Rosedale Ct					
200	RDLK	60073	2531	23W-34N	E1
S Rosedale Ct					
200	RDLK	60073	2531	23W-34N	E1
Rosedale Dr					
200	LKMR	60051	2529	29W-32N	D5
Rosedale Ln					
800	HFET	60169	2804	25W-12N	C7
Rosedale Rd					
600	NfdT	60025	2809	10W-13N	E7
Rosedale Ter					
600	CRTE	60417	3596	0E-28S	E7
600	CRTE	60417	3597	0E-28S	A7
Rosefield Ln					
900	AURA	60504	3202	30W-9S	A3
Rosefield Tr					
-	TYPK	60477	3504	9W-23S	D2
Rosegate Ct					
1200	AURA	60504	3202	30W-9S	A4
Roseglen Wy					
2400	AURA	60506	3198	39W-8S	E1
Rosehall Ct					
1500	INCK	60061	2647	17W-25N	A5
Rosehall Dr					
10	LKZH	60047	2698	23W-22N	E4
Rosehall Ln					
1600	ELGN	60123	2907	36W-8N	E3
2400	AURA	60503	3201	32W-10S	C5
S Rosehall Ln					
500	RDLK	60073	2531	23W-32N	E5
Rosehedge Dr					
6600	LGGV	60047	2646	19W-24N	C7
Rose Hill Ct					
-	KdlT	60560	3334	40W-16S	C4
10	ALGN	60102	2746	36W-18N	E4
Rosehill Ct					
300	DGvT	60516	3206	18W-9S	E3
1900	RMVL	60446	3339	27W-17S	C6
2200	NPVL	60565	3204	25W-10S	B5
Rosehill Dr					
-	BGBK	60440	3268	24W-11S	E2
300	LMNT	60439	3270	19W-14S	D6
E Rosehill Dr					
1400	ANHT	60004	2807	16W-16N	C1
1900	ANHT	60004	2754	16W-16N	D7
W Rosehill Dr					
1600	CHCG	60660	2921	2W-7N	C4
Rose Hill Ln					
-	KdlT	60560	3334	40W-16S	C4
Rosehill Ln					
100	DGvT	60516	3206	18W-9S	E3
Rosel Ct					
800	CTHL	60403	3418	25W-21S	C7
W Roseland Ct					
26100	GrtT	60041	2473	26W-36N	E3
Roselawn St					
10	CTCY	60409	3430		C3
10	HMND	46324	3430		C3
Roselle Ct					
600	LKVL	60046	2475	22W-37N	C1
Roselle Rd					
10	IVNS	60067	2805	22W-16N	A1
10	PLTN	60067	2805	22W-16N	A1
300	BMDL	60108	2913	23W-6N	A6
300	BMDL	60172	2913	23W-6N	A6
300	IVNS	60067	2752	22W-16N	A7
300	ROSL	60108	2913	23W-6N	A6
300	ROSL	60172	2913	23W-6N	A6
Roselle Rd CO-4					
300	BMDL	60108	2913	23W-6N	A6
300	BMDL	60172	2913	23W-6N	A6
300	ROSL	60108	2913	23W-6N	A6
300	ROSL	60172	2913	23W-6N	A6
N Roselle Rd					
10	SMBG	60193	2859	23W-10N	A5
10	SMBG	60194	2859	23W-10N	A5
200	HFET	60169	2859	23W-12N	A2
200	HFET	60194	2859	23W-10N	A4
300	ROSL	60172	2913	23W-7N	A4
400	SMBG	60169	2859	23W-11N	A4
1000	HFET	60173	2859	23W-12N	A2
1000	HFET	60195	2859	23W-12N	A2
1000	SMBG	60173	2859	23W-12N	A2
1000	SMBG	60195	2859	23W-12N	A2
2000	PltT	60195	2805	22W-13N	A6
2000	SMBG	60195	2805	23W-12N	A7
2100	PLTN	60067	2805	22W-13N	A6
2100	PltT	60067	2805	22W-13N	A6
N Roselle Rd CO-4					
10	ROSL	60172	2913	23W-7N	A4
S Roselle Rd					
10	IVNS	60067	2805	22W-14N	A4
10	PLTN	60067	2805	22W-14N	A4
10	ROSL	60172	2913	23W-7N	A5
10	SMBG	60193	2859	23W-10N	A6
10	SMBG	60194	2859	23W-9N	A6
700	BMDL	60108	2913	23W-6N	A6
700	ROSL	60108	2913	23W-6N	A6
800	SMBG	60193	2859	23W-9N	A1
1300	SmbT	60193	2913	23W-8N	A2
1400	ROSL	60193	2913	23W-8N	A2
1400	SmbT	60172	2913	23W-8N	A2
1700	PltT	60067	2805	22W-14N	A5
1700	PltT	60195	2805	22W-13N	A5
S Roselle Rd CO-4					
10	ROSL	60172	2913	23W-7N	A5
700	BMDL	60108	2913	23W-6N	A6
700	ROSL	60108	2913	23W-6N	A6
Rose Manor Ter					
3600	MKHM	60428	3426	4W-19S	D2
Rose Marie Dr					
2700	GwdT	60097	2469	37W-34N	C7
2700	WRLK	60097	2469	37W-34N	C7
Rosemarie Dr					
1400	JNBG	60050	2472	30W-36N	A5
Rosemarie Ln					
16000	LktT	60441	3417	26W-19S	E3
16200	LktT	60403	3417	26W-19S	E3
Rosemarie St					
800	ALGN	60102	2694	34W-21N	C6
Rosemary Av					
100	IVNS	60010	2751	24W-16N	C6
Rosemary Ct					
1400	DYR	46311	3510		C7
1500	DYR	46311	3598		C1
2200	MTGY	60538	3198	39W-10S	D6
5800	CTSD	60525	3147	12W-6S	C4
S Rosemary Ct					
13900	LktT	60544	3339	26W-16S	D4
Rosemary Dr					
1300	BGBK	60490	3339	28W-15S	A1
Rosemary Ln					
1200	NHBK	60062	2757	9W-18N	D3
1800	GRNE	60031	2478	15W-36N	A5
N Rosemary Ln					
6800	NLES	60714	2918	8W-8N	E1
S Rosemary Ln					
11700	ALSP	60803	3276	5W-13S	B5
Rosemary Rd					
800	LKFT	60045	2650	9W-26N	B3
1600	HDPK	60035	2757	9W-20N	C1
21000	FKFT	60423	3591	14W-26S	A3
Rosemary Ter					
800	DRFD	60015	2703	10W-21N	E7
Rosemear Av					
3500	BKFD	60513	3088	10W-3S	A5
3800	BKFD	60534	3088	10W-4S	A6
3800	LYNS	60513	3088	10W-4S	A6
3800	LYNS	60534	3088	10W-4S	A6
Rosemere Ct					
8100	WLSP	60480	3208	14W-9S	D3
Rosemery Ln					
12600	PSPK	60464	3274	9W-14S	C7
Rosemont Av					
10	ROSL	60172	2913	23W-7N	A3
Rosemont Av					
100	ROSL	60172	2912	23W-7N	E3
600	PKRG	60068	2918	10W-7N	A3
1900	AraT	60506	3199	38W-8S	A2
2000	MTGY	60506	3199	38W-8S	A2
10000	RSMT	60018	2917	12W-7N	B3
W Rosemont Av					
900	CHCG	60660	2921	1W-7N	D3
2100	CHCG	60659	2921	3W-7N	A3
3500	CHCG	60659	2920	4W-7N	B3
4400	CHCG	60646	2920	5W-7N	A3
4700	CHCG	60646	2919	6W-7N	E3
W Rosemont Dr					
3000	JLET	60435	3497	27W-23S	C4
3200	JLET	60431	3497	28W-23S	B4
W Rosemont Ln					
23700	LkvT	60046	2416	23W-38N	D6
Rosemont St					
9900	RSMT	60018	2917	12W-7N	B3
Rosenfelder Ct					
200	GNVA	60134	3020	36W-1N	A4
Rosenthal Dr					
-	CLLK	60014	2640	34W-25N	B6
Rose Tree Ln					
10	LNHT	60046	2476	19W-37N	B1
N Rosetree Ln					
1600	MPPT	60056	2808	13W-15N	D3
W Roseview Dr					
8400	MaiT	60714	2864	10W-10N	A4
8400	NLES	60714	2864	10W-10N	A4
8500	PKRG	60068	2864	10W-10N	A4
8500	PKRG	60714	2864	10W-10N	A4
Rosewind Dr					
7400	JLET	60586	3415	33W-21S	A6
Rosewood Av					
-	CteT	60417	3774	1W-33S	B1
200	AURA	60505	3200	36W-8S	A2
200	BFGV	60089	2754	17W-18N	C3
200	PLNO	60545	3259	47W-13S	C5
600	WNKA	60093	2812	5W-15N	A1
700	WNKA	60093	2759		B7
900	NPVL	60563	3142	26W-5S	A2
1200	DRFD	60015	2756	11W-20N	C1
6700	HMND	46324	3430		C3
12900	PSPK	60464	3274	11W-14S	A6
N Rosewood Av					
35000	GrtT	60041	2473	26W-35N	D7
Rosewood Cross					
400	LNHT	60046	2476	19W-37N	C2
Rosewood Ct					
10	CRY	60013	2695	32W-22N	B3
10	SMWD	60107	2856	30W-10N	B5
200	WTMT	60559	3085	17W-4S	B7
300	NHBK	60062	2758	7W-17N	A5
900	BRLT	60103	2910	29W-6N	E6
1200	ELGN	60120	2855	32W-11N	D4
1200	SMBG	60193	2859	21W-10N	D5
1900	DRN	60516	3206	18W-8S	E2
2700	WDRG	60517	3205	21W-9S	D3
4200	LIHL	60156	2693	37W-22N	A4
9300	MaiT	60016	2863	11W-12N	C1
N Rosewood Ct					
1200	PLTN	60067	2752	22W-17N	B5
2400	RLKB	60073	2475	22W-36N	B4
S Rosewood Ct					
20100	FftT	60423	3504	10W-24S	C5
Rosewood Dr					
-	HnrT	60107	2856	30W-10N	B5
-	HnrT	60120	2856	30W-10N	B5
10	HNWD	60047	2645	21W-24N	D6
10	ROSL	60172	2912	24W-7N	D5
100	SMWD	60107	2856	30W-10N	B5
400	CPVL	60110	2748	33W-17N	B6
600	WCHI	60185	3022	29W-2N	D1
900	WnfT	60185	3022	29W-2N	E2
12400	HMGN	60491	3344	15W-17S	B6
17600	LNSG	60438	3429	2E-20S	D5
17700	ThtT	60438	3429	2E-21S	D5
S Rosewood Dr					
19900	FftT	60423	3504	10W-24S	C5
W Rosewood Dr					
3000	JLET	60435	3497	27W-23S	C4
Rosewood Ln					
-	MKNA	60448	3503	13W-22S	A1
10	CHHT	60411	3508	1W-23S	A3
100	BlmT	60411	3508	1W-23S	A3
100	BtvT	60510	3077	38W-3S	B6
1200	CLLK	60014	2693	36W-23N	D2
1700	JNBG	60050	2472	30W-36N	A3
9500	FftT	60448	3503	11W-23S	E3
17500	TYPK	60487	3424	11W-21S	A5
24700	MHTN	60442	3677	19W-30S	E3
E Rosewood Ln					
10	RLKB	60073	2475	22W-36N	A4
N Rosewood Ln					
2300	RLKB	60073	2475	22W-36N	A4
W Rosewood Ln					
10	RLKB	60073	2475	23W-36N	A4
Rosewood Pl					
3100	DRGV	60515	3084	19W-3S	D5
3100	DRGV	60523	3084	19W-3S	D5
3100	YkTp	60523	3084	19W-3S	D5
Rosewood Rd					
10	RGMW	60008	2806	19W-14N	B4
Rosewood St					
1100	SRWD	60404	3496	30W-24S	B5
7200	HRPK	60133	2911	27W-9N	D2
34100	WslT	60481	3943	27W-41S	E5
Rosewood Ter					
1000	LYVL	60048	2591	16W-27N	C7
17700	CCHL	60478	3426	5W-21S	B6
Rosiclaire Ct					
3000	SCHT	60411	3595	1W-27S	E4
W Rosiland Rd					
400	PLTN	60074	2752	21W-18N	C3
Rosinweed Ln					
5500	NPVL	60564	3266	29W-13S	D5
E Rosita Dr					
1300	PLTN	60074	2753	19W-16N	C7
Roslara Ct					
200	BRLT	60103	2910	29W-8N	E2
Roslyn Cir					
2600	HDPK	60035	2704	8W-23N	E3
Roslyn Ct					
1000	SMBG	60194	2858	24W-11N	C4
Roslyn Ct E					
2800	BFGV	60089	2701	16W-23N	D2
Roslyn Ln					
1100	SMBG	60194	2858	24W-11N	C4
2500	HDPK	60035	2704	8W-23N	E2
2700	HDPK	60037	2704	8W-23N	E2
Roslyn Ln E					
2800	BFGV	60069	2701	16W-23N	D2
2800	BFGV	60089	2701	16W-23N	D2
2800	VrnT	60069	2701	16W-23N	D2
2800	VrnT	60089	2701	16W-23N	D2
Roslyn Pl					
400	TRLK	60010	2643	26W-25N	D5
W Roslyn Pl					
400	CHCG	60614	2978	0W-3N	A5
Roslyn Rd					
10	DRGV	60515	3145	18W-4S	A1
10	WTMT	60515	3145	18W-5S	A2
10	WTMT	60559	3145	18W-5S	A2
100	BRTN	60010	2697	26W-20N	E7
100	CbaT	60010	2697	26W-20N	E7
400	EDND	60118	2801	33W-16N	A1
500	KLWH	60043	2812	4W-14N	D3
900	GNEN	60137	3025	21W-0S	D6
900	MTSN	60443	3506	4W-25S	D7
900	OMFD	60461	3506	4W-25S	D7
1400	SmbT	60172	2913	23W-8N	B2
1600	SmbT	60193	2913	23W-8N	A3
1700	ROSL	60172	2913	23W-8N	A3
3300	OKBK	60523	3084	18W-3S	E5
3900	DRGV	60515	3085	18W-4S	A7
4300	DRGV	60515	3084	18W-4S	E7
4300	DRGV	60515	3144	18W-4S	E1
4300	DRGV	60559	3084	18W-4S	E7
4300	DRGV	60559	3144	18W-4S	E1
4300	WTMT	60515	3084	18W-4S	E7
4300	WTMT	60515	3144	18W-4S	E1
4300	WTMT	60559	3084	18W-4S	E7
4300	WTMT	60559	3144	18W-4S	E1
4500	DRGV	60559	3145	18W-4S	A1
W Roslyn Rd					
26000	BRTN	60010	2697	26W-20N	D7
26000	CbaT	60010	2697	26W-20N	D7
Roslyn Ter					
700	EVTN	60201	2813	2W-13N	B6
800	WLMT	60091	2813	2W-13N	B6
Rosner Dr					
600	ROSL	60172	2913	22W-7N	C5
Rosos Pkwy					
5600	LGGV	60047	2701	17W-23N	B1
Ross Av					
-	AvnT	60073	2531	24W-34N	C2
-	RDLK	60073	2531	24W-34N	C2
10	CRY	60013	2695	30W-23N	E1
100	SEGN	60177	2908	34W-9N	D1
S Ross Av					
6500	CHCG	60621	3152	0W-7S	B5
Ross Cres					
1700	SLVL	60411	3597	2E-27S	C4
Ross Ct					
1200	DRGV	60515	3144	20W-5S	C3
Ross Dr					
-	NlxT	60448	3501	17W-22S	D1
5900	WDRG	60517	3143	21W-6S	D5
Ross Ln					
25800	PNFD	60585	3337	32W-15S	C3
Ross St					
800	JLET	60435	3498	25W-22S	C3
N Ross St					
700	JLET	60435	3498	24W-22S	D3
W Ross St					
200	JLET	60435	3498	24W-22S	E2
Rossell Av					
1100	OKPK	60302	3031	8W-1N	A1
1200	CHCG	60707	3031	8W-1N	A1
Rossford Ln					
100	NLNX	60451	3500	20W-24S	B5
100	NlxT	60433	3500	20W-24S	B5
400	NLNX	60433	3500	20W-24S	B5
Rossi Ln					
100	BDWD	60408	3942	31W-42S	B7
Rossini Ct					
10	WHTN	60187	3082	24W-2S	C4
Rossiter Ct					
2200	JLET	60586	3416	29W-21S	D6
Rossiter Pkwy					
2100	JLET	60586	3416	29W-21S	D7
Rosslare Ct					
10	CRY	60013	2641	31W-24N	D6
Rosslyn Ln					
100	IVNS	60067	2752	22W-16N	B7
Rossmere Ct					
800	NPVL	60540	3142	25W-7S	B7
Rotary Dr					
-	BrnT	60010	2751	25W-17N	B4
10	BRTN	60010	2751	25W-17N	B4
Roth Av					
100	PltT	60010	2751	24W-18N	C2
Roth Ct					
1200	WLNG	60090	2754	16W-18N	E2
Roth Dr					
-	JLET	60431	3495	32W-22S	D1
-	JLET	60586	3495	32W-22S	D1
Roth Rd					
2200	OSWG	60543	3264	34W-13S	E5
2200	OswT	60543	3264	34W-13S	E5
Roth Ter					
3700	SKOK	60076	2866	4W-10N	C4
Rothbury Ct					
300	LKBF	60044	2593	11W-29N	D4
1100	SMBG	60193	2913	22W-9N	B1
Rothbury Dr					
400	BGBK	60440	3205	22W-10S	D7
Rothbury Ln					
1700	AURA	60503	3201	32W-10S	C5
Rothenburg Rd					
10500	DGvT	60439	3270	19W-12S	D2
10500	WDRG	60517	3270	19W-12S	D2
Rotolo Ct					
800	BTVA	60510	3078	34W-2S	D3
Rotterdam Dr					
10	ANTH	60002	2358	23W-42N	A6
Rotunda Wy					
-	AvnT	60030	2533	19W-33N	C3
-	GYLK	60030	2533	19W-33N	C3
Roulock Rd					
10	OswT	60538	3199	36W-10S	E6
Roundabout					
800	WDND	60118	2800	34W-15N	D3
Round Barn Rd					
10	BNHL	60010	2750	27W-17N	C4
13300	PNFD	60585	3337	31W-15S	E3
13300	PNFD	60585	3338	31W-15S	A3
13400	PNFD	60544	3338	31W-15S	A3
Round Hill Ct					
300	BGBK	60440	3205	22W-11S	D7
4900	JNBG	60050	2472	30W-36N	A3
Round House Rd					
-	CRTE	60417	3685	0E-31S	E5
-	CteT	60417	3685	0E-31S	E5
Round House St					
100	BDWD	60408	3942	31W-41S	B5
Round Lake Dr					
1400	RLKB	60073	2475	23W-35N	A6
Round Lake Rd					
-	AvnT	60073	2531	24W-34N	C1
-	RDLK	60073	2531	24W-34N	C1

STREET Block	City	ZIP	Map#	CGS	Grid
Round Lake Rd SR-134					
-	AvnT	60073	2531	24W-34N	C1
-	RDLK	60073	2531	24W-34N	C1
Roundstone Av					
25700	PNFD	60585	3337	32W-14S	C1
25700	WldT	60585	3337	32W-14S	C1
Roundstone Ln					
10	BNHL	60010	2748	30W-17N	E5
W Roundstone Wy					
4400	WKGN	60085	2535	14W-32N	C4
Round Up Rd					
6100	MHRY	60050	2527	35W-32N	A4
Rourke Dr					
2500	AURA	60503	3201	33W-11S	B7
2500	AURA	60503	3265	33W-11S	B1
Rouse St					
100	MDLN	60060	2590	18W-27N	E7
100	MDLN	60060	2646	18W-27N	E2
Route 1 Cto					
-	CHHT	60411	3508	1W-25S	A6
Route 1 Cto SR-1					
-	CHHT	60411	3508	1W-25S	A6
Routh Ct					
200	SMBG	60195	2859	23W-12N	A2
Rowan Ct					
300	NPVL	60540	3203	26W-8S	D1
Rowe Av					
800	PKRG	60068	2863	11W-9N	D6
W Rowe Av					
27500	AntT	60081	2415	27W-38N	B7
Rowe Rd					
10	BbyT	60119	3017	43W-0S	A7
S Rowell Av					
200	JLET	60433	3499	22W-24S	C6
400	JltT	60433	3499	22W-24S	C6
900	JLET	60433	3587	23W-26S	C3
900	JltT	60433	3587	23W-26S	C3
Rowell Rd					
100	HPSR	60140	2796	46W-16N	A2
S Rowell Rd					
23100	JknT	60421	3587	23W-28S	C7
23100	JLET	60421	3587	22W-28S	C6
23100	JLET	60433	3587	22W-28S	C6
Rowland Av					
300	MRGO	60152	2634	50W-26N	A2
Rowland Rd					
6300	GfnT	60142	2638	40W-25N	A4
Rowlett Av					
800	LydT	60164	2972	13W-3N	E5
Rowley Ct					
4100	SMWD	60107	2911	28W-9N	A1
S Rowley Ln					
16300	LKPT	60441	3420	20W-19S	A3
W Rowley Rd					
1800	PNFD	60544	3415	31W-18S	E1
1800	PnfT	60544	3415	31W-18S	E1
Roxanne Av					
300	BNVL	60106	2972	15W-4N	A2
Roxborough Pl					
100	IVNS	60010	2751	24W-17N	C6
Roxbury Ct					
10	DSPN	60018	2862	15W-10N	B5
10	SEGN	60177	2908	35W-9N	B1
100	WNVL	60555	3080	29W-2S	C3
900	HRPK	60133	2857	26W-9N	E7
900	HRPK	60133	2858	26W-9N	A7
900	RDLK	60073	2531	23W-32N	E6
3000	JLET	60435	3417	27W-19S	C3
7200	LGGV	60047	2646	18W-25N	E5
Roxbury Dr					
500	NPVL	60565	3203	27W-10S	C5
1300	AURA	60502	3139	31W-5S	D3
Roxbury Ln					
10	DSPN	60018	2862	15W-10N	B5
800	SMBG	60194	2858	24W-11N	D4
1400	WCDA	60084	2588	24W-28N	C5
2400	MTGY	60538	3198	39W-10S	D6
Roy Av					
1600	JltT	60433	3499	21W-24S	E5
N Roy Av					
100	NHLK	60164	2972	13W-2N	E6
100	NHLK	60164	3028	13W-2N	E1
800	LydT	60164	2972	13W-3N	E5
1500	MLPK	60160	3028	13W-1N	E2
1500	NHLK	60160	3028	13W-1N	E2
S Roy Av					
100	NHLK	60164	3028	13W-1N	E1
200	MLPK	60160	3028	13W-1N	E2
200	NHLK	60160	3028	13W-1N	E2
Roy Dr					
500	WDDL	60191	2970	19W-5N	D1
W Roy Dr					
600	VLPK	60181	3026	19W-1N	D1
Roy St					
100	NLNX	60451	3501	17W-25S	C7
100	NlxT	60451	3501	17W-25S	C7
700	DYR	46311	3598		E4
16400	OKFT	60452	3426	5W-19S	B2
17100	LNSG	60438	3430	4E-20S	B4
19100	LNSG	60438	3510	4E-22S	B2
Royal Blvd					
1100	ELGN	60123	2854	36W-12N	A2
2000	ELGN	60123	2853	36W-12N	E2
2400	ELGN	60124	2853	36W-12N	D2
Royal Ct					
-	CTWD	60445	3348	6W-16S	A2
10	LNSH	60069	2702	13W-22N	E3
100	BMDL	60108	2968	23W-5N	E1
200	ANHT	60004	2807	16W-15N	D2
200	PTHT	60004	2807	16W-15N	D2
200	PTHT	60070	2807	16W-15N	D2
900	SMBG	60193	2858	24W-9N	D7
1100	WHTN	60187	3024	25W-0N	B4
1400	ELGN	60123	2854	35W-12N	B2
1700	AURA	60503	3201	33W-10S	B5
2800	NLNX	60451	3588	19W-25S	D5
10200	MKNA	60448	3503	12W-23S	C4
17300	SHLD	60473	3429	2E-20S	D4
S Royal Ct					
300	PLTN	60067	2805	21W-15N	E2
Royal Dr					
1300	MTGY	60538	3200	34W-9S	D4
2400	LMBD	60148	3084	19W-2S	C3
2700	NHBK	60062	2756	10W-17N	E6
8800	BRRG	60527	3208	15W-10S	B5
9000	DGvT	60527	3208	15W-10S	B5
W Royal Dr					
1400	ADSN	60101	2970	20W-5N	B2
Royal Ln					
10	BMDL	60108	2968	24W-5N	E1
800	WDND	60118	2800	34W-16N	D3
1800	AURA	60503	3201	33W-10S	B5
2900	NLNX	60442	3588	19W-27S	D5
2900	NLNX	60451	3588	19W-27S	D5
W Royal Ln					
600	PTON	60468	3860	9W-37S	D4
Royal Rd					
18700	GNWD	60425	3508	1W-22S	A2
18700	HMWD	60430	3508	1W-22S	A2
Royal Wy					
10	BNHL	60010	2748	32W-18N	E4
Royal & Ancient Dr					
3900	SCRL	60174	2965	33W-5N	A3
Royal Ashdown Ct					
2800	SCRL	60174	2965	33W-4N	A4
Royal Birkdale Dr					
1800	VNHL	60061	2647	17W-27N	C1
24500	WldT	60564	3266	30W-12S	A3
Royal Blackheath Ct					
900	NPVL	60563	3141	27W-5S	B3
Royal Bombay Ct					
1000	NPVL	60563	3141	28W-5S	A3
Royal County Down Dr					
24200	WldT	60564	3266	30W-12S	B3
Royal Creek Ln					
15200	ODPK	60467	3344	14W-18S	E7
Royal Crest Ct					
700	BGBK	60440	3205	22W-10S	D5
S Royal Crest Dr					
26100	CteT	60417	3687	3E-31S	A6
Royal Dornach Ct					
3800	WldT	60564	3266	30W-12S	A3
Royal Dublin Ln					
700	DYR	46311	3510		E7
Royale Ln					
17900	HLCT	60429	3426	4W-21S	E6
Royal Fox Ct					
2600	SCRL	60174	2965	33W-4N	A3
Royal Fox Dr					
2600	SCRL	60174	2965	33W-4N	A3
4400	WYNE	60174	2965	33W-5N	A2
4400	WYNE	60184	2965	33W-5N	A2
Royal Foxhunt Rd					
15100	ODPK	60462	3346	11W-18S	A7
Royal Georgian Rd					
15100	ODPK	60462	3346	11W-18S	A7
Royal Glen Ct					
400	OKBK	60523	3028	15W-1S	B7
6500	LSLE	60532	3142	23W-7S	E6
15500	ODPK	60467	3345	13W-18S	A7
Royal Glen Dr					
700	CRY	60013	2695	32W-23N	B2
1100	GNEN	60137	3026	20W-0S	A7
1100	GNEN	60148	3026	20W-0S	A7
1100	LMBD	60148	3026	20W-0S	A7
10800	ODPK	60467	3345	13W-18S	A7
Royal Glen Ln					
800	CLSM	60188	2967	27W-4N	C5
Royal Gorge Ct					
12500	MKNA	60448	3502	15W-23S	B4
12600	NlxT	60448	3502	15W-23S	B4
Royal Kings Ct					
2700	SCRL	60174	2965	33W-4N	A4
Royal Lytham Ct					
2700	SCRL	60174	2965	33W-4N	A3
Royal Lytham Dr					
2500	SCRL	60174	2965	33W-4N	A3
24600	WldT	60564	3266	30W-12S	A3
Royal Melbourne Dr					
4400	LGGV	60047	2700	18W-23N	E2
Royal Oak Ct					
10	LIHL	60156	2693	37W-22N	A3
17900	TYPK	60477	3425	8W-21S	B6
Royal Oak Dr					
700	MRGO	60152	2634	50W-26N	B3
N Royal Oak Dr					
10	VNHL	60061	2646	18W-25N	E6
S Royal Oak Dr					
10	VNHL	60061	2646	18W-24N	E6
W Royal Oak Dr					
900	VNHL	60061	2647	18W-24N	A6
1000	VNHL	60061	2646	18W-24N	E6
Royal Oak Ln					
-	WrnT	60030	2534	18W-33N	A2
1200	LIHL	60156	2693	38W-22N	A3
1300	GNVW	60025	2810	8W-13N	E5
1300	GNVW	60025	2811	8W-13N	A5
N Royal Oak Ln					
33500	WrnT	60030	2534	18W-33N	A3
Royal Oak Rd					
500	LslT	60540	3204	24W-8S	E1
500	LslT	60540	3205	23W-8S	A1
1500	DRN	60561	3207	18W-9S	A4
1600	DRN	60561	3206	18W-10S	E4
Royal Oaks Ct					
10	BtlT	60512	3262	41W-12S	A3
Royal Oaks Dr					
400	WDDL	60191	2971	17W-5N	C2
N Royal Oaks Dr					
10	BtlT	60512	3262	41W-12S	A3
S Royal Oaks Dr					
10	BtlT	60512	3262	41W-12S	A3
W Royal Oaks Dr					
10	BtlT	60512	3262	41W-12S	A3
Royal Oaks Ln					
10900	ODPK	60467	3344	13W-17S	E5
10900	ODPK	60467	3345	13W-17S	A5
Royal Porthcawl Dr					
10500	WldT	60564	3266	30W-12S	A3
Royal Portrush Dr					
3800	WldT	60564	3266	30W-12S	A4
Royal Queens Ct					
3000	SCRL	60174	2965	33W-4N	A4
Royal Ridge Dr					
2000	NHBK	60062	2757	8W-16N	E7
2200	NHBK	60062	2810	8W-16N	E1
E Royal Ridge Dr					
2400	CteT	60417	3686	3E-31S	E6
2500	CteT	60417	3687	3E-31S	A6
Royal St. Anne Ct					
4200	SCRL	60174	2965	33W-5N	A3
Royal St. George					
300	VNHL	60061	2647	16W-27N	D2
Royal St. George Dr					
600	NPVL	60563	3141	27W-6S	B4
1400	NpvT	60563	3141	27W-5S	B3
Royal St. Georges Ct					
2400	SchT	60174	2964	34W-4N	D3
2400	SCRL	60174	2964	34W-4N	D3
2400	SCRL	60174	2965	33W-4N	A4
Royal St. James Ct					
2700	SCRL	60174	2965	33W-4N	A4
Royal Swan Ln					
8700	DRN	60561	3206	19W-10S	E5
Royal Troon Ct					
2400	RVWD	60015	2756	13W-20N	A1
4100	SCRL	60174	2965	33W-5N	B2
Royal Troon Dr					
2400	AURA	60503	3201	32W-11S	C7
Royal Vale Dr					
10	OKBK	60523	3084	18W-2S	E4
10	OKBK	60523	3085	18W-2S	A3
Royal Windyne Ct					
4300	SCRL	60174	2965	33W-5N	A3
Royal Woods Dr					
-	NndT	60013	2641	32W-26N	C3
3100	NndT	60014	2641	32W-26N	C3
Royal Worlington Dr					
23600	WldT	60564	3266	29W-12S	C3
N Royce Av					
800	JLET	60432	3499	23W-22S	B3
Royce Blvd					
800	OKTR	60181	3085	18W-1S	A2
Royce Ct					
200	BMDL	60108	2969	23W-4N	B3
W Royce Ct					
7600	FftT	60423	3504	9W-24S	E6
Royce Dr					
100	BMDL	60108	2969	23W-4N	B3
Royce Ln					
200	ROSL	60172	2912	24W-7N	D5
Royce Rd					
10	NPVL	60565	3204	24W-10S	C6
10	OswT	60543	3264	35W-14S	C7
100	BGBK	60440	3205	23W-10S	A6
100	BGBK	60565	3205	23W-10S	A6
300	BGBK	60440	3204	24W-10S	E6
300	BGBK	60565	3204	25W-10S	B6
500	NPVL	60440	3204	24W-10S	D6
Royce Woods Ct					
200	NPVL	60565	3204	25W-10S	A6
N Rozanne Dr					
700	ADSN	60101	2970	18W-4N	E3
W Rozanne Dr					
10	ADSN	60101	2970	18W-4N	E3
S Ruble St					
-	CHCG	60607	3034		E7
1600	CHCG	60616	3092	0W-1S	A1
Rub of the Green Ln					
900	BNHL	60010	2697	27W-20N	C7
Ruby Ct					
11600	FKFT	60423	3590	14W-27S	E4
Ruby Dr					
-	PGGV	60140	2797	42W-15N	C4
Ruby St					
300	CNHL	60514	3145	17W-5S	C3
400	CNHL	60559	3145	17W-5S	C3
400	WTMT	60559	3145	17W-5S	C3
2000	MLPK	60160	2973	12W-2N	C7
2000	MLPK	60164	2973	12W-2N	C7
2200	LydT	60164	2973	12W-2N	C6
2800	FNPK	60131	2973	12W-3N	C5
3600	SRPK	60131	2973	12W-4N	C3
3600	SRPK	60176	2973	12W-4N	C3
4800	SRPK	60176	2917	12W-6N	C7
5200	OKLN	60453	3211	6W-10S	E5
5900	RSMT	60018	2917	12W-7N	B3
N Ruby St					
1900	LydT	60164	2973	12W-2N	C7
1900	MLPK	60160	2973	12W-2N	C7
1900	MLPK	60160	3029	12W-2N	C1
1900	MLPK	60164	2973	12W-2N	C7
S Ruby St					
25900	MONE	60449	3683	6W-31S	A6
W Ruby St					
100	JLET	60432	3498	24W-23S	E3
100	JLET	60435	3498	24W-22S	D3
W Ruby St SR-53					
100	JLET	60432	3498	24W-23S	E3
100	JLET	60435	3498	24W-23S	E3
Rucci Ct					
10	BRRG	60527	3146	14W-7S	C6
Rudat Ct					
600	CLLK	60014	2639	36W-24N	E6
Rudd Ct					
1500	WKGN	60048	2535	14W-32N	C5
4000	GRNE	60031	2535	13W-34N	D1
Rudolph Ct					
1700	RMVL	60446	3417	27W-18S	D1
10800	BtnT	60081	2355	30W-42N	A5
Rudolph Dr					
1200	NHBK	60062	2757	9W-18N	D2
Rudolph St					
1200	CTCY	60409	3430	3E-19S	A1
W Rueben St					
23400	PnfT	60586	3416	29W-19S	D3
23500	PNFD	60586	3416	29W-19S	D3
Rue Chamonix					
500	DRPK	60010	2752	22W-20N	C1
Rue Foret					
10	LKFT	60045	2649	12W-26N	B4
Rue Jardin					
100	DRPK	60010	2752	22W-20N	B2
100	PltT	60010	2752	22W-20N	B2
100	PltT	60074	2752	22W-20N	B2
Rue Orleanais					
500	DRPK	60010	2752	22W-20N	C1
Rue Paris Av					
-	IVNS	60067	2805	22W-14N	A5
-	PLTN	60067	2805	22W-14N	A5
-	PltT	60067	2805	22W-14N	A5
Rue Royale					
500	DRPK	60010	2752	22W-20N	C1
500	DRPK	60074	2752	22W-20N	C1
Rue St. James Pl					
-	PltT	60067	2805	22W-14N	A5
Rue Touraine					
100	DRPK	60010	2752	22W-20N	C2
100	PltT	60010	2752	22W-20N	C2
100	PltT	60074	2752	22W-20N	C2
Ruff St					
25400	WldT	60585	3265	31W-11S	D2
Ruffled Feathers Ct					
10	HNWD	60047	2645	21W-26N	C2
Ruffled Feathers Dr					
10	LMNT	60439	3271	17W-14S	D7
10	LMNT	60439	3343	17W-15S	C1
S Ruga Ct					
10	ADSN	60101	2970	18W-3N	E5
Rugby Ct					
10	GLHT	60139	2968	23W-4N	E4
3200	WKGN	60087	2479	11W-37N	D1
Rugby Pl					
10	ELGN	60120	2855	33W-11N	A4
300	SMBG	60194	2858	24W-11N	C4
Rugby Rd					
10	LKZH	60047	2698	24W-23N	C1
200	NBRN	60010	2698	25W-23N	A1
W Rugeley Ct					
1100	ADSN	60101	2970	19W-3N	B4
Rugeley Rd					
100	WNSP	60558	3146	13W-5S	E2
100	WNSP	60558	3147	13W-5S	A2
Rugen Rd					
2100	GNVW	60025	2810	9W-14N	D5
3700	GNVW	60025	2809	11W-13N	D5
Ruggles Ct					
10	HMGN	60491	3344	14W-16S	C4
10	ODPK	60467	3344	14W-16S	C4
10	OrlT	60467	3344	14W-16S	C4
Ruhff St					
7800	CmgT	60033	2405	51W-39N	D4
7800	HRVD	60033	2405	51W-39N	D4
W Ruhl Rd					
-	PltT	60074	2752	21W-18N	C3
500	PLTN	60074	2752	21W-18N	C3
Ruidoso Ct					
1400	LYVL	60048	2647	16W-27N	D1
N Rule Ct					
33300	WrnT	60030	2533	18W-33N	E3
Rule St					
900	BTVA	60510	3077	36W-2S	E3
Rumford Blvd					
3300	ElgT	60124	2853	38W-11N	A5
Rumford Ct					
3200	AURA	60504	3201	31W-8S	E3
Rumford on Asbury					
10	RGMW	60008	2806	19W-14N	B3
N Rumple Ln					
500	ADSN	60101	2970	21W-4N	A4
Rumsey Av					
4500	OKLN	60453	3212	5W-10S	A5
Rumsey Pl					
100	WTMT	60559	3145	17W-6S	B5
W Rundell Pl					
1000	CHCG	60607	3033	1W-0S	E5
Rundle Ct					
500	BTVA	60510	3078	34W-2S	C3
Runge St					
3600	FNPK	60131	2972	14W-4N	C3
3600	LydT	60131	2972	14W-4N	C3
Running Brook Farm Blvd					
-	JNBG	60050	2471	32W-34N	B7
-	MchT	60050	2471	32W-34N	B7
W Running Creek Ct					
17600	WrnT	60031	2477	17W-36N	B5
Running Deer Ln					
400	GLBT	60136	2799	38W-16N	C3
Running Deer Tr					
500	ElgT	60124	2907	37W-8N	C3
Running Iron Dr					
6000	NndT	60012	2584	35W-29N	B4
Runway					
-	NLNX	60451	3590	15W-27S	B4
Runyan Dr					
900	LKPT	60441	3419	21W-19S	E3
1100	LKPT	60441	3420	21W-19S	A3
Runyard Av					
300	WPHR	60096	2363	9W-43N	C5
Runyard Pl					
1700	WKGN	60085	2536	11W-34N	D2
E Runyard Wy					
24800	SlmT	53179	2357		C3
W Runyard Wy					
25100	SlmT	53179	2357		C3
Rural St					
1000	AraT	60505	3138	34W-6S	D6
1000	AURA	60505	3138	34W-6S	D6
Rush Ct					
400	LKZH	60047	2699	23W-21N	A5
Rush St					
400	ROSL	60172	2913	23W-6N	B6
2000	SLVL	60411	3509	2E-25S	D7
N Rush St					
300	ITSC	60143	2914	19W-6N	C6
400	CHCG	60611	3034	0E-0N	C3
1000	CHCG	60610	3034	0E-1N	C2
S Rush St					
200	ITSC	60143	2914	19W-6N	C6
200	ROSL	60172	2913	23W-7N	B5
Rushford Pl					
24700	PNFD	60585	3338	30W-15S	A2
Rushing Ct					
1000	LKVL	60046	2417	22W-39N	C5
Rushmore Av					
-	LKMR	60051	2530	28W-32N	A4
Rushmore Dr					
100	BRLT	60103	2909	32W-8N	D3
100	BRLT	60120	2909	32W-8N	D3
100	ELGN	60120	2909	32W-8N	D3
11600	PNFD	60585	3266	30W-13S	A5
Rushmore Ln					
10600	HTLY	60142	2745	39W-20N	C1
Rushmore Rd					
10	FXLK	60020	2473	26W-36N	C4
10	FXLK	60041	2473	26W-36N	C4
N Rushmore Rd					
100	FXLK	60020	2473	27W-36N	C3
Rushwood Av					
1100	SRWD	60404	3496	30W-23S	A4
Ruskin Cir					
400	EGVV	60007	2860	19W-9N	C7
Ruskin Ct					
800	SMBG	60193	2858	25W-9N	C7
800	SMBG	60193	2912	24W-9N	D1
Ruskin Dr					
500	EGVV	60007	2860	19W-9N	C7
500	EGVV	60007	2914	19W-9N	B1
Russel Ct					
400	GwdT	60098	2524	41W-32N	D4
400	WDSK	60098	2524	41W-32N	D4
N Russel St					
100	MPPT	60056	2807	15W-13N	E6
Russell Av					
-	GRNE	60031	2535	14W-34N	B2
100	PTPR	53158	2363	10W-43N	B5
100	WPHR	53158	2363	10W-43N	B5
100	WPHR	60096	2363	10W-43N	B5
4100	PKCY	60085	2535	14W-34N	D2
4400	WrnT	60031	2535	14W-33N	C2
N Russell Av					
800	AURA	60506	3137	36W-6S	E5
38000	BHPK	60087	2480	10W-38N	B1
38300	BHPK	60087	2422	10W-38N	B7
38400	BHPK	60099	2422	10W-38N	B7
S Russell Av					
10	AURA	60506	3137	36W-7S	E7
W Russell Ct					
1400	ANHT	60005	2860	19W-12N	D1
Russell Dr					
-	CHCG	60637	3152	0E-6S	D3
-	MTGY	60538	3200	36W-9S	A4
1400	HFET	60192	2855	31W-12N	E2
1800	LSLE	60532	3142	23W-4S	E1
6100	ELGN	60120	2855	32W-12N	D2
11400	HTLY	60142	2692	40W-21N	A6
N Russell Dr					
30500	VOLO	60073	2587	27W-30N	B2
W Russell Ln					
24400	FmtT	60060	2588	24W-29N	C4
24500	FmtT	60084	2588	24W-29N	C4
24500	WCDA	60084	2588	24W-29N	C4
Russell Pl					
900	MDLN	60060	2646	18W-26N	D3
Russell Rd					
10	PltT	60124	2852	41W-11N	A5
300	PltT	60124	2851	41W-10N	E5
700	WYNE	60184	2965	31W-5N	D2
1300	PTPR	53158	2363	10W-43N	B4
1300	WPHR	53158	2363	10W-43N	B4
1300	WPHR	60096	2363	10W-43N	B4
3300	BtnT	53158	2362		E4
3300	BtnT	60096	2362		E4
3300	BtnT	60099	2362	11W-43N	E4
3300	PTPR	53158	2362		E4
3300	WPHR	53158	2362		E4
3300	WPHR	60096	2362		E4
Russell Rd CO-33					
10	PltT	60124	2852	41W-11N	A5
300	PltT	60124	2851	41W-10N	E5
W Russell Rd					
11400	BtnT	53158	2362	11W-43N	D4
11400	BtnT	60096	2362	11W-43N	E4
11400	BtnT	60099	2362		C4
11400	PTPR	53158	2362		C4
12600	PTPR	60099	2362		C4
13000	NptT	53158	2362		C4
13000	NptT	60099	2362		C4
13400	NptT	60099	2361	14W-43N	C4
13400	PTPR	53158	2361	14W-43N	C4
13400	WDWH	53158	2361	14W-43N	C4
13400	WDWH	60099	2361	14W-43N	C4
13400	ZION	60099	2361	14W-43N	C4
13800	PTPR	60099	2361	14W-43N	C4
16100	NptT	60099	2360	16W-43N	D5
16100	WDWH	60099	2360	16W-43N	D5
W Russell Rd CO-A1					
11900	BtnT	53158	2362	12W-43N	C4
11900	BtnT	60099	2362		C4
11900	PTPR	53158	2362		C4
12600	PTPR	60099	2362		C4
13000	NptT	53158	2362		C4
13000	NptT	60099	2362		C4
13400	NptT	60099	2361	14W-43N	C4
13400	PTPR	53158	2361	14W-43N	C4
13400	WDWH	53158	2361	14W-43N	C4
13400	WDWH	60099	2361	14W-43N	C4
13400	ZION	60099	2361	14W-43N	C4
13800	PTPR	60099	2361	14W-43N	C4
16100	NptT	60099	2360	16W-42N	E5
16100	WDWH	60099	2360	16W-42N	E5
W Russell Rd SR-142					
-	NptT	60099	2360	16W-43N	D5
-	WDWH	60099	2360	16W-43N	D5
Russell St					
10	CTCY	60409	3352		C6
10	HMND	46320	3352		D6
500	WLNG	60090	2754	15W-17N	E5
600	ELGN	60120	2855	33W-10N	B6
8300	AlqT	60013	2696	29W-23N	D2
E Russell St					
100	BRTN	60010	2750	26W-18N	D2
100	BRTN	60010	2751	25W-18N	A2
300	HMND	46320	3352		D6
W Russell St					
200	JLET	60435	3498	24W-22S	D1
300	BRTN	60010	2750	26W-18N	E2
Russellwood Ct					
300	SMBG	60193	2857	26W-9N	E7
1100	BFGV	60089	2701	16W-21N	D6
Russelwood Ct					
4600	HRPK	60133	2967	27W-5N	C1
Russet Av					
400	NPVL	60565	3203	27W-8S	D3
Russet Cir					
10	LKZH	60047	2698	24W-22N	C5
Russet Ln					
700	SMWD	60107	2857	28W-10N	B7
Russet Wy					
4000	CCHL	60478	3426	5W-20S	C5
4000	GNVW	60062	2809	11W-15N	D3
E Russet Wy					
10	PLTN	60067	2752	20W-17N	E5
200	PLTN	60067	2753	20W-17N	A5
200	PLTN	60074	2753	20W-17N	A5
Russett Ct					
600	SMBG	60193	2858	23W-9N	E7
3800	NHBK	60062	2756	12W-17N	B5
Russett Dr					
1700	NndT	60050	2585	31W-30N	D2
Russett Ln					
300	HDPK	60035	2757	9W-20N	C1
3700	NHBK	60062	2756	12W-17N	B5
4700	SKOK	60076	2811	7W-13N	B7
4700	SKOK	60076	2812	5W-13N	A7
Russett Wy E					
-	MDLN	60060	2647	17W-25N	B5
200	MDLN	60061	2647	17W-25N	B5
200	VNHL	60061	2647	17W-25N	B5
Russett Wy S					
300	MDLN	60061	2647	17W-25N	B5
300	VNHL	60061	2647	17W-25N	B5
Russetwood Ct					
1100	WLNG	60004	2754	15W-17N	E6
1100	WLNG	60090	2754	15W-17N	E6
Russetwood Dr					
-	ANHT	60004	2807	16W-15N	D2
-	PTHT	60070	2807	16W-15N	D2
Russinwood Ct					
200	PltT	60124	2852	39W-11N	D5
Russo Blvd					
-	AURA	60503	3201	32W-11S	C7
-	AURA	60503	3265	32W-11S	C1
Rust St					
200	WLSP	60480	3209	12W-9S	B4
E Rust Tr					
200	WLSP	60480	3209	11W-9S	D2
Rust Tr N					
400	WLSP	60480	3209	12W-9S	D2
Rust Tr W					
200	WLSP	60480	3209	12W-9S	D2
Rustic Dr					
200	NBRN	60010	2698	25W-23N	A1
300	WLNG	60090	2755	13W-17N	D5
N Rustic Dr					
39000	LkvT	60046	2417	21W-39N	D6
Rustic Ln					
300	ALGN	60102	2747	35W-19N	C2
28800	AlqT	60013	2696	28W-23N	D1
28800	CbaT	60013	2696	28W-23N	D1
E Rustic Ln					
10	RLKB	60073	2475	22W-36N	A4
W Rustic Ln					
10	RLKB	60073	2475	23W-36N	A5
Rustic Wood Ln					
27000	PNFD	60585	3337	33W-15S	A2
Rustling Birch Wy					
26400	PNFD	60585	3337	33W-15S	B3

STREET Block	City	ZIP	Map#	CGS	Grid
Rusty Dr					
2400	DSPN	60018	2917	12W-8N	B1
W Rusty Dr					
1700	MPPT	60056	2861	17W-12N	C1
Rusty Rd					
10	LMNT	60439	3272	15W-13S	A4
Rusty Scupper					
100	LKMR	60051	2529	28W-33N	D4
Rutgers Ct					
10	ElaT	60060	2645	20W-25N	E5
10	HNWD	60047	2645	20W-25N	E5
100	GNVW	60025	2810	10W-15N	A2
400	DGvT	60516	3206	20W-10S	B6
1700	NPVL	60565	3204	24W-9S	C3
Rutgers Dr					
300	DGvT	60516	3206	20W-10S	B5
300	DGvT	60517	3206	20W-10S	B5
300	WDRG	60516	3206	20W-10S	B6
300	WDRG	60517	3206	20W-10S	B5
Rutgers Ln					
500	EGVV	60007	2913	22W-9N	D1
3800	NHBK	60062	2756	12W-17N	A5
Ruth Av					
-	BHPK	60087	2421	12W-38N	B6
200	SCRL	60174	3020	34W-2N	C1
2200	PKRG	60068	2863	11W-10N	D5
Ruth Cir					
300	BGBK	60440	3205	23W-11S	A7
Ruth Ct					
1000	MRGO	60152	2634	49W-25N	B3
11000	CrlT	60142	2691	43W-21N	A6
11000	GfnT	60142	2691	43W-21N	A6
N Ruth Ct					
22200	KLDR	60047	2699	21W-22N	E4
Ruth Dr					
10	NlxT	60448	3502	16W-22S	A2
400	DGvT	60439	3206	19W-10S	E6
700	ELGN	60123	2854	35W-12N	A2
8600	DGvT	60516	3206	19W-9S	E4
18700	NlxT	60448	3501	16W-22S	E2
Ruth Rd					
-	GfnT	60142	2692	39W-20N	B7
10900	HTLY	60142	2692	39W-20N	B7
Ruth St					
10	HMND	46320	3352	4E-18S	C7
100	CTCY	60409	3352	4E-18S	C7
3000	FNPK	60131	2973	13W-3N	A4
7700	DYR	46311	3598		E4
7700	SjnT	46311	3598		E4
E Ruth St					
10	CTCY	60409	3352		C7
10	HMND	46320	3352		C7
Ruthenbeck Ln					
800	NLNX	60451	3501	16W-25S	E7
900	NlxT	60451	3501	16W-25S	E7
Rutherford Av					
7700	BDPK	60638	3211	8W-8S	A1
7700	BRBK	60459	3211	8W-9S	A3
7700	BRBK	60638	3211	8W-8S	A1
9500	OKLN	60453	3211	8W-11S	A7
9800	CHRG	60415	3211	8W-11S	A7
9800	OKLN	60415	3211	8W-11S	A7
N Rutherford Av					
1600	CHCG	60707	3030	8W-2N	E1
1600	OKPK	60302	3030	8W-2N	E1
2400	CHCG	60707	2974	8W-3N	E5
3700	CHCG	60634	2974	8W-4N	E2
4300	HDHT	60706	2974	8W-5N	E1
4800	CHCG	60656	2918	8W-6N	E6
4800	CHCG	60706	2918	8W-6N	E6
4800	HDHT	60706	2918	8W-6N	E6
S Rutherford Av					
5100	CHCG	60638	3149	8W-6S	A4
5100	FTVW	60638	3149	8W-5S	A2
10700	WRTH	60482	3275	8W-12S	A3
Rutherford Dr					
8000	WDRG	60517	3206	21W-9S	A3
Rutherford Ln					
9000	ODPK	60462	3346	11W-18S	A6
Ruth Fitzgerald Dr					
-	PNFD	60586	3415	32W-19S	D4
2400	JLET	60586	3415	32W-20S	D5
Ruth Lake Ct					
700	DGvT	60527	3146	16W-6S	A5
Rutland Cir					
2800	NPVL	60564	3202	29W-10S	C5
Rutland Ct					
1500	SMBG	60173	2859	21W-10N	E5
Rutland Dr					
-	MKNA	60448	3502	15W-23S	B4
Rutland Ln					
1500	SMBG	60173	2859	21W-10N	E5
Rutland Rd					
2600	NPVL	60564	3202	29W-10S	C5
Rutledge St					
400	OMFD	60461	3595	3W-25S	C1
400	OMFD	60466	3595	3W-25S	C1
400	PKFT	60466	3595	3W-25S	C1
Ruzich Dr					
100	BRLT	60103	2909	31W-8N	D3
100	ELGN	60120	2909	31W-8N	E3
Ryan Cir					
400	MTSN	60443	3505	7W-24S	D5
Ryan Ct					
500	WDND	60118	2800	34W-15N	E3
500	WTMT	60514	3145	17W-6S	C4
500	WTMT	60559	3145	17W-6S	C4
800	BTVA	60510	3078	34W-1S	D2
2500	NPVL	60564	3203	28W-10S	B6
9300	WRLK	60097	2468	38W-35N	E5
9300	WRLK	60097	2469	38W-35N	A5
19800	MKNA	60448	3503	13W-23S	B4
E Ryan Ct					
200	ANHT	60005	2861	17W-12N	B1
Ryan Dr					
2800	NLNX	60451	3589	18W-27S	B5
2800	NlxT	60451	3589	18W-27S	B5
Ryan Ln					
100	SRWD	60404	3495	31W-24S	E5
500	WDND	60118	2800	34W-15N	E3
17500	ODPK	60467	3423	13W-21S	A6
W Ryan Ln					
-	PNFD	60586	3415	31W-20S	E5
Ryan Pkwy					
1300	ALGN	60102	2748	32W-20N	A1
Ryan Pl					
400	LKFT	60045	2650	10W-26N	A4
Ryan Rd					
-	RchT	60443	3593	7W-26S	C3
-	RNPK	60443	3593	7W-26S	C3
-	ROSL	60172	2912	25W-7N	B4
4000	GRNE	60031	2478	13W-36N	D4
7100	DRGV	60516	3144	20W-8S	A7
7100	DRGV	60516	3206	20W-8S	A1
7100	WDRG	60516	3144	20W-8S	A7
7100	WDRG	60516	3206	20W-8S	A1
S Ryan Rd					
9000	HMTN	60456	3212	5W-10S	B5
9000	OKLN	60453	3212	5W-10S	B5
Ryan St					
100	WMTN	60481	3853	27W-39S	D7
N Ryan St					
1700	MHRY	60050	2528	32W-33N	A2
Ryan Wy					
-	NndT	60012	2640	35W-27N	A1
-	ROSL	60172	2912	25W-7N	B4
500	CLLK	60012	2640	35W-27N	A1
Rycon Dr					
13000	HMGN	60491	3422	16W-21S	A5
Rydal St					
2800	MhtT	60442	3590	15W-27S	B5
2800	MhtT	60451	3590	15W-27S	B5
2800	NlxT	60442	3590	15W-27S	B5
2800	NlxT	60451	3590	15W-27S	B5
Ryders Ln					
1500	HDPK	60035	2704	10W-22N	A5
Rye Ct					
10	BGBK	60440	3205	22W-10S	C6
1100	BTVA	60510	3078	34W-2S	E3
Rye Rd					
100	MDLN	60060	2590	19W-29N	D5
Ryegrass Cir					
500	AURA	60504	3201	33W-8S	A2
Ryegrass Ct					
500	AURA	60504	3201	33W-8S	B2
Ryegrass Tr					
500	AURA	60504	3201	33W-8S	B2
Ryehill Cir					
16200	ODPK	60467	3423	13W-19S	A2
Ryehill Ct					
1200	JLET	60431	3496	29W-22S	D2
1200	JLET	60586	3496	29W-22S	D2
Ryehill Dr					
1000	JLET	60431	3496	29W-22S	D2
1100	JLET	60586	3496	29W-22S	D2
Ryeland Dr					
8000	FftT	60423	3504	10W-24S	C5
Ryerson Av					
300	ELGN	60123	2854	33W-10N	E5
Rylane Ct					
24500	SRWD	60404	3584	30W-25S	B1
Rynberk Ct					
14200	HmrT	60441	3342	20W-16S	B4
Ryson Ct					
1100	WHTN	60187	3082	23W-3S	E5
Rywick Ct					
3700	RGMW	60008	2806	20W-13N	A5

S

STREET Block	City	ZIP	Map#	CGS	Grid
Saber Ct					
2100	NPVL	60565	3203	26W-9S	D5
W Sable Av					
600	ADSN	60101	2970	19W-5N	D2
Sable Dr					
2700	GNVW	60025	2810	9W-14N	B4
W Sable Dr					
900	ADSN	60101	2970	19W-4N	C2
1200	AddT	60101	2970	20W-4N	B2
Sable Ln					
1700	EGvT	60056	2861	17W-10N	C5
1700	MPPT	60056	2861	17W-10N	C5
Sable Oaks Ct					
2200	NPVL	60564	3202	30W-10S	B5
Sable Oaks Dr					
2200	NPVL	60564	3202	30W-10S	B5
Sable Ridge Dr					
1400	JLET	60447	3495	33W-22S	A3
Sac Rd					
4500	MchT	60097	2470	35W-36N	A4
N Sacomano Ln					
24000	ElaT	60047	2699	22W-24N	A1
Sacramento Av					
-	BmnT	60406	3349	3W-17S	A4
-	POSN	60469	3349	3W-17S	A4
12600	ALSP	60406	3277	3W-14S	A6
12600	ALSP	60803	3277	3W-14S	A6
12600	BLID	60406	3277	3W-15S	A7
12600	BLID	60803	3277	3W-14S	A6
13100	BLID	60406	3349	3W-15S	A1
13300	RBBN	60406	3349	3W-16S	A2
13300	WthT	60406	3349	3W-16S	A2
13700	BLID	60472	3349	3W-16S	A2
13700	RBBN	60472	3349	3W-16S	A2
15100	BmnT	60428	3349	3W-18S	A6
15100	BmnT	60469	3349	3W-18S	A6
15100	MKHM	60428	3349	3W-18S	A6
17900	HLCT	60429	3427	3W-21S	A7
17900	HMWD	60430	3427	3W-21S	A7
18500	HMWD	60422	3507	3W-22S	A1
18500	HMWD	60430	3507	3W-22S	A1
N Sacramento Av					
1000	CHCG	60622	3032	3W-1N	E2
2200	CHCG	60647	2976	3W-2N	E6
3500	CHCG	60618	2976	3W-5N	E1
4400	CHCG	60618	2920	3W-5N	E7
4400	CHCG	60625	2920	3W-5N	E7
5600	CHCG	60659	2920	3W-7N	E4
6300	CHCG	60645	2920	3W-7N	E3
7200	CHCG	60645	2866	3W-9N	E7
7500	EVTN	60202	2866	3W-9N	E7
S Sacramento Av					
-	CHCG	60805	3212	3W-10S	E4
-	ENGN	60805	3212	3W-10S	E4
2200	CHCG	60623	3090	3W-2S	E3
3500	CHCG	60632	3090	3W-3S	E5
5100	CHCG	60632	3150	3W-6S	E3
5400	CHCG	60629	3150	3W-7S	E5
7900	CHCG	60652	3212	3W-9S	E2
10300	CHCG	60655	3276	3W-12S	E1
11100	CHCG	60655	3277	3W-13S	A3
11200	MTPK	60655	3277	3W-13S	A3
11200	MTPK	60803	3277	3W-13S	A3
13800	BLID	60406	3349	3W-16S	A2
13800	BLID	60472	3349	3W-16S	A2
13800	RBBN	60472	3349	3W-16S	A2
14600	POSN	60469	3349	3W-17S	A5
14800	MKHM	60428	3349	3W-17S	A5
14800	MKHM	60469	3349	3W-17S	A5
14900	BmnT	60428	3349	3W-17S	A5
14900	BmnT	60469	3349	3W-17S	A5
N Sacramento Blvd					
700	CHCG	60612	3032	3W-0N	E3
700	CHCG	60622	3032	3W-0N	E3
S Sacramento Blvd					
10	CHCG	60612	3032	3W-0S	E6
1100	CHCG	60623	3032	3W-0S	E7
Sacramento Ct					
600	ELGN	60123	2854	36W-12N	A2
1400	GRNE	60031	2476	19W-35N	C5
1600	CPVL	60110	2748	33W-18N	B6
Sacramento Dr					
-	MTPK	60803	3276	4W-13S	E5
1200	CPVL	60110	2748	33W-18N	C5
1300	HRPK	60133	2911	26W-7N	E4
S Sacramento Dr					
-	CHCG	60612	3032	3W-1S	E7
1200	CHCG	60623	3032	3W-1S	E7
1500	CHCG	60623	3090	3W-1S	E1
11500	MTPK	60803	3276	3W-13S	E4
Sacramento Dr N					
-	CHCG	60629	3150	3W-7S	E6
Sacramento Dr S					
-	CHCG	60629	3150	3W-7S	E7
W Sacramento Sq					
3000	CHCG	60612	3032	3W-0N	E3
Saddle Ct					
10	BRRG	60527	3208	15W-10S	B4
12700	HTLY	60142	2744	42W-19N	E3
W Saddle Ct					
17600	WrnT	60031	2534	17W-34N	B1
Saddle Dr					
3200	PnfT	60435	3417	27W-19S	C4
Saddle Ln					
200	FRGV	60021	2696	28W-22N	D3
500	AraT	60504	3138	35W-5S	C3
500	AURA	60504	3138	35W-5S	C3
900	RLKB	60073	2475	21W-36N	C4
1000	LMNT	60439	3271	18W-13S	A5
1500	AURA	60505	3138	34W-5S	C3
21300	MKNA	60448	3590	14W-25S	D1
N Saddle Ln					
34200	WrnT	60031	2534	17W-34N	B1
Saddle Rd					
600	MltT	60187	3024	26W-0S	A7
Saddle Rdg					
-	BtnT	60050	2472	30W-37N	A1
600	CLLK	60012	2640	35W-27N	B1
5700	JNBG	60050	2472	30W-37N	A1
5700	MchT	60050	2472	30W-37N	A1
N Saddle Row					
1300	ADSN	60101	2970	20W-5N	B2
Saddle Run					
400	LKFT	60045	2649	11W-25N	D5
E Saddle Back Rd					
200	VNHL	60061	2647	16W-25N	D6
N Saddlebook Ct					
-	MNKA	60447	3672	33W-30S	B4
Saddlebred Ct					
8600	FKFT	60423	3504	10W-25S	B7
Saddlebred Tr					
10100	GwdT	60098	2525	39W-34N	D2
Saddle Brook Cir					
1400	ALGN	60102	2694	34W-20N	B7
Saddlebrook Ct					
600	OSWG	60543	3263	38W-13S	B5
S Saddlebrook Ct					
-	MNKA	60447	3672	33W-30S	B4
Saddle Brook Dr					
100	OKBK	60523	3084	18W-3S	E6
100	OKBK	60523	3085	17W-3S	B6
Saddlebrook Dr					
-	FmtT	60060	2589	22W-30N	B2
-	RLKP	60030	2532	22W-31N	C7
-	RLKP	60030	2589	22W-30N	B2
-	RLKP	60060	2589	22W-30N	B2
10	CmpT	60175	2962	41W-3N	A5
2500	NPVL	60564	3202	30W-10S	B6
E Saddlebrook Dr					
-	RLKP	60030	2532	21W-31N	D7
S Saddlebrook Dr					
19000	TroT	60404	3495	32W-22S	D3
Saddlebrook Ln					
-	MNKA	60447	3672	33W-30S	B3
-	SRGV	60554	3197	42W-8S	D1
12200	LMNT	60439	3272	16W-14S	A6
E Saddlebrook Ln					
400	VNHL	60061	2647	16W-26N	D3
S Saddle Brook Ln					
14300	HMGN	60491	3343	17W-17S	C5
S Saddlebrook Ln					
-	MNKA	60447	3672	33W-30S	B4
Saddlebrook Rd					
1300	BRLT	60103	2966	30W-5N	B1
Saddle Club Dr					
-	ELGN	60118	2799	36W-15N	E4
-	ELGN	60124	2799	37W-15N	E4
-	SYHW	60118	2799	37W-15N	E4
S Saddle Creek Dr					
23500	MhtT	60442	3590	15W-28S	B7
Saddle Creek Ln					
900	CLLK	60014	2693	37W-22N	C3
Saddle Creek Tr					
1100	BLVY	60050	2583	36W-31N	D1
7400	BLVY	60050	2526	36W-31N	D7
Saddle Hill Rd					
1600	GNOK	60048	2592	14W-30N	C3
Saddle Oaks Dr					
7100	AlqT	60013	2642	29W-24N	C7
7100	CRY	60013	2642	29W-24N	C7
Saddle Ridge Ct					
400	WNVL	60555	3081	27W-3S	C6
2500	JLET	60432	3500	20W-22S	B2
6500	LGGV	60047	2646	18W-24N	D6
S Saddle Ridge Ct					
1000	PLTN	60067	2805	22W-14N	B3
Saddle Ridge Dr					
1000	JLET	60432	3500	20W-22S	B2
Saddle Ridge Ln					
6500	LGGV	60047	2646	18W-24N	D7
Saddleridge Pl					
1400	BRLT	60103	2966	30W-5N	B1
Saddle Ridge Tr					
1100	CRY	60013	2695	32W-24N	B1
Saddle Run Ln					
300	BCHR	60401	3774	0W-35S	D6
Saddleshire Ct					
-	RLKP	60030	2589	22W-30N	B1
N Saddletree Ln					
10	CbaT	60010	2698	25W-22N	A4
10	NBRN	60010	2698	25W-22N	A4
Saddlewood Ct					
10	SgrT	60506	3135	41W-5S	E3
Saddlewood Dr					
700	WCDA	60084	2643	27W-26N	C2
700	WcnT	60084	2643	27W-26N	C2
800	GNEN	60137	3025	23W-1N	A3
800	MltT	60137	3025	23W-1N	A3
W Saddlewood Dr					
16500	LKPT	60441	3342	20W-18S	A7
Sadie Ln					
-	WcnT	60084	2643	26W-26N	E2
Sadler Av					
300	ELGN	60120	2855	32W-10N	C5
Safford Av					
700	LKBF	60044	2593	12W-29N	B4
700	ShdT	60044	2593	12W-29N	A4
Saffron Ct					
10900	ODPK	60467	3423	13W-20S	A3
Saffron Ln					
100	BGBK	60490	3267	27W-12S	C2
Sagamore Cir					
2500	AURA	60503	3201	32W-11S	C7
2500	AURA	60503	3265	32W-11S	C1
Sagamore Ct					
200	SMBG	60194	2858	24W-10N	D5
2400	AURA	60503	3265	32W-11S	C1
Sagamore Dr					
900	SMBG	60194	2858	24W-10N	C5
Saganashkee Ln					
2900	NPVL	60564	3266	30W-11S	B1
2900	WldT	60564	3266	30W-11S	B1
Sage Cir					
1200	JLET	60447	3495	33W-22S	A2
Sage Ct					
10	BGBK	60490	3267	26W-13S	E5
1500	GRNE	60031	2477	18W-35N	A5
13100	HMGN	60491	3343	16W-18S	E7
30900	GNOK	60048	2592	14W-30N	D1
Sage Dr					
1400	BGBK	60490	3267	26W-13S	E5
1400	BGBK	60490	3268	25W-13S	A5
13000	HTLY	60142	2744	43W-19N	B3
Sage Ln					
4900	LGGV	60047	2700	19W-23N	C1
8200	BtnT	60081	2414	30W-40N	B3
Sage Pkwy					
-	AlqT	60013	2641	32W-24N	A7
-	CRY	60013	2641	32W-24N	A7
S Sage St					
24900	CNHN	60410	3672	31W-30S	E4
Sage Brush Cir					
300	RDLK	60073	2531	23W-32N	E4
Sagebrush Ct					
-	LKVL	60046	2474	23W-37N	E3
10	SMWD	60107	2856	30W-10N	C5
3600	JNBG	60050	2471	32W-35N	C5
36500	WrnT	60046	2476	18W-36N	D4
Sage Brush Ln					
21100	MKNA	60448	3590	14W-25S	D1
Sagebrush Ln					
15000	LKPT	60441	3421	18W-20S	A4
Sagebrush Rd					
400	NPVL	60565	3203	26W-9S	D4
Sagebrush Tr					
1100	CRY	60013	2695	32W-24N	B1
Saggers Ln					
4800	AlqT	60014	2640	33W-24N	D6
4800	CLLK	60014	2640	33W-24N	D6
Saginaw Av					
200	BNHM	60409	3351	3E-17S	E5
200	BNHM	60633	3351	3E-17S	E5
200	CTCY	60409	3351	3E-17S	E6
S Saginaw Av					
7500	CHCG	60649	3153		E7
7800	CHCG	60617	3215	3E-8S	E1
7900	CHCG	60649	3215	3E-9S	E2
12600	CHCG	60633	3279	3E-14S	E7
13800	BNHM	60633	3351	3E-16S	E3
14500	BNHM	60409	3351	3E-16S	E4
14500	CTCY	60409	3351	3E-16S	E4
Saginaw Ct					
900	CLSM	60188	2967	26W-3N	E5
1900	NPVL	60565	3203	26W-9S	D4
Saginaw Pl					
10	PKFT	60466	3594	4W-27S	E4
Saginaw St					
10	LIHL	60156	2692	38W-22N	E4
Sahara Ct					
6900	JLET	60586	3415	32W-20S	C4
Sahara Dr					
6700	JLET	60586	3415	32W-20S	C4
Sahler Av					
8800	BKFD	60513	3147	11W-4S	E1
9500	BKFD	60525	3147	11W-4S	D1
9500	LGNG	60525	3147	11W-4S	D1
Sailboat Bay					
4600	LSLE	60532	3142	25W-5S	B2
Sailboat Cove					
-	LSLE	60532	3142	24W-4S	C2
Sailfish Dr					
2800	HMWD	60430	3427	3W-21S	B6
Sailor Ln					
18300	LNSG	60438	3429	3E-21S	E7
Saindon Dr					
100	PltT	60124	2852	39W-11N	E5
St. Albans Cir					
2600	NPVL	60564	3202	29W-10S	D7
St. Albans St					
9600	HBRN	60034	2351	40W-41N	A7
St. Albans on Oxford					
10	RGMW	60008	2805	22W-13N	B6
St. Albert Ct					
21700	MKNA	60448	3590	14W-26S	E2
St. Andrew Cir					
1200	ITSC	60143	2914	21W-6N	A7
St. Andrew's Cir					
900	GNVA	60134	3019	36W-0N	D5
1500	ELGN	60123	2854	35W-9N	A7
St. Andrew's Ct					
10	NpvT	60563	3140	30W-5S	B2
400	WCHI	60185	2966	30W-3N	B6
500	CLLK	60014	2639	36W-24N	D6
1000	ALGN	60102	2747	35W-20N	A1
St. Andrews Ct					
4100	SCRL	60174	2965	33W-5N	A3
St. Andrew's Ct					
12700	LMNT	60439	3270	19W-14S	D7
12700	LMNT	60439	3342	19W-15S	E1
15100	ODPK	60462	3346	10W-18S	C6
20100	OMFD	60461	3507	3W-24S	C5
St. Andrew's Dr					
-	GLHT	60139	3024	24W-2N	D1
200	BGBK	60440	3205	22W-10S	C5
500	CRTE	60417	3596	0E-28S	E6
600	CRTE	60417	3597	0E-28S	A7
1900	LbvT	60048	2590	18W-30N	E1
2000	JLET	60586	3416	30W-21S	C7
2400	OMFD	60461	3507	3W-24S	B5
8200	ODPK	60462	3346	10W-18S	C7
N St. Andrew's Dr					
1300	GLHT	60139	3024	24W-2N	D1
1500	VNHL	60061	2647	17W-27N	B2
S St. Andrew's Dr					
300	WDDL	60191	2970	18W-4N	E2
W St. Andrew's Dr					
10	GLHT	60139	3024	24W-2N	D1
St. Andrew's Ln					
10	WynT	60185	2966	30W-4N	C4
300	GRNE	60031	2477	17W-34N	B7
500	CLLK	60014	2639	36W-24N	D6
500	IVNS	60067	2752	22W-16N	A7
E St. Andrew's Ln					
10	DRFD	60015	2757	9W-20N	B1
W St. Andrew's Ln					
10	DRFD	60015	2757	10W-20N	B1
St. Andrew's St					
-	LNSG	60438	3429	1E-21S	B7
-	ThtT	60438	3429	1E-21S	B7
St. Andrew's Wy					
800	FKFT	60423	3592	9W-26S	D3
St. Andrew's Trace Ln					
200	WynT	60185	2966	29W-4N	D4
St. Ann Dr					
1600	HRPK	60133	2911	27W-6N	D6
St. Anne Ct					
1200	LMNT	60439	3271	18W-13S	B4
St. Anne's Ct					
3500	AURA	60504	3139	31W-6S	E6
24400	WldT	60564	3266	30W-12S	B4
St. Anne's Dr					
2800	MTGY	60538	3198	40W-10S	C6
St. Anthony Ct					
1200	LMNT	60439	3271	18W-13S	B4
St. Anton Ct					
2800	LSLE	60532	3142	24W-7S	C7
St. Armand Ct					
10	WLNG	60090	2754	15W-18N	E4
St. Armand Ln					
10	WLNG	60090	2754	15W-18N	E4
W St. Aubin Dr					
600	ADSN	60101	2970	19W-4N	D2
St. Barthelemy Ln					
3400	AURA	60504	3201	31W-8S	E1
St. Bonaventure Ct					
1200	LMNT	60439	3271	17W-13S	C4
St. Brendans Ct					
1200	LMNT	60439	3271	18W-14S	A7
S St. Cecilia Dr					
500	MPPT	60056	2861	17W-12N	B2
St. Charles Ct					
300	LKPT	60441	3419	21W-19S	E2
St. Charles Dr					
1200	LKPT	60441	3420	21W-19S	A2
St. Charles Pl					
10	GLNC	60022	2758	7W-20N	B2
10	HDPK	60035	2758	7W-20N	B2
3700	BLWD	60104	3029	12W-0N	B3
E St. Charles Pl					
500	LMBD	60148	3026	19W-0N	D3
St. Charles Rd					
10	BmdT	60188	3023	26W-2N	E2
10	BmdT	60188	3024	26W-1N	A2
10	CLSM	60188	3023	26W-2N	E2
10	CLSM	60188	3024	26W-1N	A2
10	GNEN	60137	3025	23W-1N	B3
10	MltT	60137	3025	23W-1N	A3
10	MltT	60188	3024	24W-1N	D2
10	WynT	60185	2967	28W-2N	A7
10	WynT	60188	3023	27W-2N	D1
100	WCHI	60185	2966	29W-2N	E7
100	WynT	60185	2966	29W-2N	E7
100	WynT	60185	3023	27W-2N	C1
300	MltT	60188	3025	23W-1N	A3
400	LMBD	60148	3025	21W-0N	E3
400	MltT	60148	3025	21W-1N	D3
400	MYWD	60153	3030	10W-0N	A4
800	MYWD	60153	3029	10W-0N	E4
2100	BLWD	60104	3029	12W-0N	B4
4700	BLWD	60104	3028	13W-0N	E3
5000	BKLY	60104	3028	13W-0N	E3
5000	BKLY	60163	3028	14W-0N	D3
5000	BLWD	60163	3028	13W-0N	E3
St. Charles Rd CO-7					
10	BmdT	60188	3023	26W-2N	E2
10	BmdT	60188	3024	26W-1N	A2
10	CLSM	60188	3023	26W-2N	E2
10	CLSM	60188	3024	26W-1N	A2
10	GNEN	60137	3025	23W-1N	B3
10	MltT	60137	3025	23W-1N	A3
10	MltT	60188	3024	24W-1N	D2
10	WynT	60188	3023	27W-2N	D1
100	WynT	60185	3023	27W-2N	C1
300	MltT	60188	3025	23W-1N	A3
400	LMBD	60148	3025	21W-0N	E3
400	MltT	60148	3025	21W-1N	D3
E St. Charles Rd					
-	BKLY	60163	3028	15W-0N	B3
-	EMHT	60163	3028	15W-0N	B3
10	VLPK	60181	3027	17W-0N	B3
100	EMHT	60126	3028	15W-0N	A3
200	EMHT	60126	3027	17W-0N	B3
200	EMHT	60181	3027	17W-0N	B3
200	VLPK	60126	3027	17W-0N	B3
400	LMBD	60148	3026	19W-1N	D3
800	LMBD	60181	3026	18W-1N	E3
800	VLPK	60181	3026	18W-1N	E3
W St. Charles Rd					
100	EMHT	60126	3027	17W-1N	C3
300	VLPK	60181	3026	18W-1N	E3
400	LMBD	60148	3026	18W-1N	E3
400	LMBD	60181	3026	18W-1N	E3
500	EMHT	60181	3027	17W-1N	C3
500	VLPK	60181	3027	17W-1N	C3
600	MltT	60148	3026	20W-0N	A4
700	LMBD	60148	3025	21W-0N	E3
700	MltT	60148	3025	21W-0N	E3
700	VLPK	60181	3027	17W-1N	B3
W St. Charles Rd CO-7					
600	LMBD	60148	3026	20W-0N	A4
600	MltT	60148	3026	20W-0N	A4
700	LMBD	60148	3025	21W-0N	E3
700	MltT	60148	3025	21W-0N	E3
St. Charles St					
300	ELGN	60120	2855	33W-9N	B7
900	ElgT	60120	2855	33W-9N	B7
900	ElgT	60177	2855	33W-9N	B7
1100	ElgT	60120	2909	33W-9N	B1
1100	ElgT	60177	2909	33W-9N	B1
St. Charles St SR-25					
800	ELGN	60120	2855	33W-9N	B7
900	ElgT	60120	2855	33W-9N	B7
900	ElgT	60177	2855	33W-9N	B7
1100	ElgT	60120	2909	33W-9N	B1
1100	ElgT	60177	2909	33W-9N	B1
St. Christopher Ct					
600	AraT	60506	3199	38W-8S	A2
St. Clair Ct					
1600	GRNE	60031	2476	18W-35N	E5
1800	HRPK	60133	2967	27W-5N	D2
St. Clair Ln					
-	NlxT	60451	3589	16W-26S	E2
1800	HRPK	60133	2967	27W-5N	C2
S St. Clair Ln					
10	VNHL	60061	2646	18W-24N	E6
W St. Clair Ln					
1000	VNHL	60061	2646	18W-24N	E6

STREET Block City ZIP Map# CGS Grid

N St. Clair St
500 CHCG 60611 3034 0E-0N C3
St. Claire Cir
10 SMBG 60173 2859 21W-10N D5
St. Claire Ct
1200 LMNT 60439 3271 17W-13S C4
St. Claire Dr
- RMVL 60446 3340 24W-15S D1
St. Claire Pl
1200 SMBG 60173 2859 22W-10N D5
St. Colette Ct
1200 LMNT 60439 3271 18W-13S B4
St. Croix Av
1300 NPVL 60564 3203 28W-10S A5
1300 WldT 60564 3203 28W-10S A5
St. Croix Ct
10 AURA 60504 3201 31W-8S E1
St. Cronan Ct
10 CRY 60013 2641 31W-24N E6
St. Francis Av
2200 JLET 60436 3497 26W-24S E6
2300 JNBG 60050 2471 31W-35N E5
St. Francis Cir
100 OKBK 60523 3085 17W-3S C5
St. Francis Ct
100 BMDL 60108 2913 22W-5N C7
100 BMDL 60157 2913 22W-5N C7
100 BmdT 60157 2913 22W-5N C7
1200 WHTN 60187 3081 26W-1S E2
W St. Francis Rd
- FKFT 60448 3503 11W-24S E5
7200 FftT 60423 3504 11W-24S A5
7200 FftT 60423 3505 9W-24S A5
8400 FKFT 60423 3504 11W-24S A5
9200 FftT 60423 3503 11W-24S E5
9200 FKFT 60423 3503 11W-24S E5
S St. George Ct
600 LKFT 60045 2648 14W-25N C6
W St. George Ct
2700 CHCG 60647 2976 4W-2N D7
2700 CHCG 60647 2977 2W-3N C5
St. George Dr
10 RGMW 60008 2805 23W-12N B7
10 RGMW 60008 2806 20W-15N A3
St. George Ln
100 MTGY 60543 3263 38W-11S A1
St. Germain Pl
10 SCRL 60175 2963 38W-3N B6
3700 SchT 60175 2963 38W-3N B6
W St. Helen St
2700 CHCG 60647 2977 2W-3N C5
St. Ives Ct
300 MNSR 46321 3510 D3
3000 RNPK 60471 3594 4W-26S D2
St. Ives Ln
10 VNHL 60061 2647 16W-25N C6
3000 RNPK 60471 3594 4W-26S D3
St. James Ct
200 MltT 60137 3083 23W-2S A4
1400 GRNE 60031 2476 19W-35N C5
5600 OKLN 60453 3275 7W-12S D1
6300 BRRG 60527 3146 14W-7S D5
6600 DRGV 60516 3144 19W-7S D6
8100 ODPK 60462 3346 10W-18S C6
10400 CHRG 60415 3275 7W-12S D1
21000 MKNA 60448 3502 14W-25S E7
W St. James Ct
1300 IVNS 60067 2805 22W-15N A2
1300 PLTN 60067 2805 22W-15N A2
St. James Dr
8000 ODPK 60462 3346 10W-18S C7
St. James Pkwy
200 SRGV 60554 3135 42W-6S D5
St. James Pl
900 PKRG 60068 2918 10W-8N A2
1200 GNEN 60137 3026 20W-0S A7
1200 GNEN 60148 3026 20W-0S A7
1200 LMBD 60148 3026 20W-0S A7
1200 LYVL 60048 2591 17W-29N B4
W St. James Pl
400 CHCG 60614 2978 0W-3N A5
1500 ANHT 60005 2806 18W-14N D4
St. James St
- AntT 60081 2414 28W-38N D7
- BtnT 60081 2414 28W-38N D7
2000 ANHT 60005 2806 19W-14N C4
2000 ANHT 60008 2806 19W-14N C4
3100 RGMW 60008 2806 19W-14N B4
E St. James St
200 ANHT 60004 2807 17W-14N A4
N St. James St
10 WKGN 60085 2537 10W-34N A1
S St. James St
10 WKGN 60085 2537 10W-34N A2
W St. James St
10 ANHT 60004 2807 17W-14N A4
800 ANHT 60005 2806 18W-14N E4
St. James Wy
400 WynT 60185 2966 29W-4N D6
12200 LMNT 60439 3271 16W-14S D6
St. James Gate
500 BGBK 60440 3269 22W-13S C4
500 RMVL 60440 3269 22W-13S C4
500 WDRG 60440 3269 22W-13S C4
St. John Av
10 WNFD 60190 3023 27W-0N D4
St. John Dr
10 HNWD 60047 2646 19W-24N B7
10 HNWD 60047 2700 19W-24N B1
10600 MKNA 60448 3503 13W-24S B4
St. John Ln
8600 MaiT 60016 2863 10W-11N E3
8600 MaiT 60016 2864 10W-11N A3
St. John St
900 ELGN 60120 2855 33W-12N A1
St. John's Av
- GLNC 60022 2758 7W-20N C2
10 HDPK 60035 2758 7W-20N C2
600 HDPK 60035 2705 8W-21N A6
St. Johns Av
1800 HDPK 60035 2704 8W-22N E5
St. John's Av
1800 HDPK 60035 2704 8W-22N E3
2700 HDPK 60037 2704 8W-23N D2
3700 JNBG 60050 2471 31W-35N E5
St. John's Ct
500 OKBK 60523 3085 17W-3S B4
N St. John's Ct
5800 CHCG 60646 2920 5W-7N A4
St. John's Pl
600 AddT 60101 2970 19W-3N D5
600 ADSN 60101 2970 19W-3N D5
W St. Johns Pl
- AddT 60101 2970 19W-3N C5
- ADSN 60101 2970 19W-3N C5
W St. John's Pl
800 PLTN 60067 2752 22W-16N C7
St. John's Rd
400 GwdT 60098 2524 41W-32N D5
400 WDSK 60098 2524 41W-32N D5
1000 GwdT 60098 2525 40W-32N A5
1000 WDSK 60098 2525 40W-32N A5
St. Joseph Av
10 JLET 60436 3497 26W-24S E6
400 AURA 60505 3138 35W-6S C5
W St. Joseph Av
8500 CHCG 60656 2918 10W-6N A6
St. Joseph Ct
1200 LMNT 60439 3271 17W-13S C4
10700 FftT 60448 3503 13W-23S A4
10700 MKNA 60448 3503 13W-23S A4
St. Joseph Creek Rd
4700 LSLE 60532 3143 22W-4S B1
St. Joseph's Ct
4900 MchT 60097 2469 36W-36N E3
St. Joseph's Dr
700 OKBK 60523 3085 17W-3S B5
St. Josephs Wy
200 YKVL 60560 3333 42W-17S C6
St. Jude Av
100 JLET 60436 3497 26W-24S E6
St. Jude Ct
1600 GNVA 60134 3020 36W-0N A6
St. Kitts Ct
3400 AURA 60504 3201 31W-8S E1
St. Lawrence Av
4000 MTSN 60443 3594 5W-25S C1
S St. Lawrence Av
- CHCG 60827 3278 0E-15S E7
4100 CHCG 60653 3092 0E-4S D7
4600 CHCG 60615 3092 0E-4S D7
4700 CHCG 60615 3152 0E-5S D1
6000 CHCG 60637 3152 0E-8S D7
7000 CHCG 60619 3152 0E-8S D7
7500 CHCG 60619 3214 0E-10S D4
10000 CHCG 60628 3214 0E-11S E7
11100 CHCG 60628 3278 0E-13S E3
13100 CHCG 60827 3350 0E-15S E1
19100 BlmT 60425 3508 0E-23S E3
19100 GNWD 60425 3508 0E-23S E3
St. Lo Ct
10 ODHL 60013 2641 30W-26N E2
10 ODHL 60013 2642 30W-26N A2
St. Louis Av
8300 SKOK 60076 2866 4W-10N C5
8700 SKOK 60203 2866 4W-10N D4
14400 MDLN 60445 3348 4W-17S E6
14800 MDLN 60426 3348 4W-17S E5
14800 MKHM 60426 3348 4W-17S E5
15700 MKHM 60428 3426 4W-19S E2
N St. Louis Av
200 CHCG 60624 3032 4W-0N D4
1300 CHCG 60651 3032 4W-1N D1
1600 CHCG 60647 3032 4W-1N D1
2400 CHCG 60647 2976 4W-3N D5
3600 CHCG 60618 2976 4W-4N D2
4300 CHCG 60625 2976 4W-5N D1
4400 CHCG 60625 2920 4W-5N D7
5500 CHCG 60659 2920 4W-6N C5
6400 LNWD 60659 2920 4W-8N C3
6400 LNWD 60712 2920 4W-8N C2
S St. Louis Av
10 CHCG 60624 3032 4W-0S D5
1100 CHCG 60623 3032 4W-1S D7
1500 CHCG 60623 3090 4W-1S D1
3700 CHCG 60632 3090 4W-3S D5
5000 CHCG 60632 3150 4W-5S D3
5900 CHCG 60629 3150 4W-7S D5
7500 CHCG 60652 3212 4W-9S D2
9100 ENGN 60805 3212 4W-11S D6
10200 CHCG 60805 3276 4W-11S D1
10300 CHCG 60655 3276 4W-13S D4
10300 ENGN 60805 3276 4W-11S D1
11600 MTPK 60655 3276 4W-13S D4
11600 MTPK 60803 3276 4W-13S D4
13300 RBBN 60472 3348 4W-15S D1
13300 WthT 60472 3348 4W-15S D1
St. Louis St
100 JLET 60433 3499 23W-24S A5
N St. Louis St
100 ELWD 60421 3675 25W-32S C7
S St. Louis St
100 ELWD 60421 3675 25W-31S C6
St. Mark's Ct
400 OKBK 60523 3085 17W-3S C4
1500 EVTN 60201 2867 2W-11N A3
N St. Mark's Pl
1500 PLTN 60067 2752 21W-17N D4
1500 PltT 60074 2752 21W-18N D4
St. Mark's Wy
600 WynT 60185 2966 29W-4N D3
St. Mary Cir
13500 ODPK 60462 3346 10W-16S A2
St. Mary's Ln
10 LNHT 60046 2476 19W-38N C1
St. Mary's Pkwy
10 BFGV 60089 2754 16W-18N C2
10 WLNG 60089 2754 16W-18N C2
St. Mary's Rd
- MKNA 60448 3502 14W-23S E4
St. Marys Rd
7700 MTWA 60045 2648 15W-24N B7
7700 MTWA 60048 2648 15W-24N B7
7700 VrnT 60045 2648 15W-24N B7
7700 VrnT 60048 2648 15W-24N B7
7700 VrnT 60069 2648 15W-24N B7
St. Mary's Rd
11000 MKNA 60448 3503 13W-23S A3
N St. Mary's Rd
100 GNOK 60048 2592 14W-30N B3
100 LYVL 60048 2592 15W-29N B5
600 LbvT 60048 2592 15W-29N B5
25000 MTWA 60045 2648 14W-24N B6
25000 MTWA 60048 2648 15W-27N B1
25000 VrnT 60045 2648 14W-24N B6
25000 VrnT 60048 2648 14W-24N B6
26100 LbvT 60048 2648 15W-26N B2
27500 MTWA 60048 2592 15W-27N B7
N St. Mary's Rd CO-W19
100 GNOK 60048 2592 14W-30N B3
100 LYVL 60048 2592 15W-29N B5
600 LbvT 60048 2592 15W-29N B5
25000 MTWA 60045 2648 14W-24N B6
25000 MTWA 60048 2648 15W-27N B1
25000 VrnT 60045 2648 14W-24N B6
25000 VrnT 60048 2648 14W-24N B6
26100 LbvT 60048 2648 15W-26N B2
27500 MTWA 60048 2592 15W-27N B7
S St. Mary's Rd
200 GNOK 60048 2592 14W-28N B7
200 LbvT 60048 2592 14W-28N B7
200 LYVL 60048 2592 15W-28N B6
400 MTWA 60048 2592 14W-28N B7
S St. Mary's Rd CO-W19
200 GNOK 60048 2592 14W-28N B7
200 LbvT 60048 2592 14W-28N B7
200 LYVL 60048 2592 15W-28N B6
400 MTWA 60048 2592 14W-28N B7
E St. Mary's St
100 MNKA 60447 3583 33W-28S B7
W St. Mary's St
100 MNKA 60447 3583 33W-28S A7
2700 CHCG 60647 2976 4W-2N D7
2700 CHCG 60647 2977 2W-3N C5
St. Michael Ct
200 OKBK 60523 3085 17W-3S C5
N St. Michael's Ct
1600 CHCG 60614 2978 C7
St. Michel Ct
3300 SCRL 60175 2963 37W-3N B7
St. Michel Ln
3000 SCRL 60175 2963 37W-3N C7
St. Mihiel Dr
100 WnfT 60187 3081 28W-1S B1
100 WnfT 60190 3081 28W-1S B1
St. Moritz Ct
10 EMHT 60126 3027 16W-0S D6
St. Moritz Dr
10 PSPK 60464 3274 10W-13S C5
400 GNEN 60137 3025 23W-0N A5
8300 SPGV 60081 2413 32W-40N C3
8800 RcmT 60071 2413 32W-40N C3
8800 RcmT 60081 2413 32W-40N C3
W St. Olaf Av
25200 GrtT 60041 2474 25W-34N B7
St. Paschals Dr
3300 OKBK 60523 3085 16W-3S D4
3300 OKBK 60559 3085 17W-3S D4
3300 WTMT 60559 3085 17W-3S D4
St. Patrick Rd
- DGvT 60439 3270 19W-11S E1
- DGvT 60439 3271 18W-11S A1
St. Paul Av
1300 GRNE 60031 2478 14W-35N D6
3300 BLWD 60104 3029 12W-0N B5
4000 BLWD 60162 3029 12W-0N A5
4000 HLSD 60162 3029 12W-0N A5
St. Paul Blvd
300 CLSM 60188 2968 24W-2N C7
400 GLHT 60139 2968 24W-2N D7
400 GLHT 60188 2968 24W-2N D7
St. Paul Ct
4800 HLSD 60162 3028 14W-0N D4
W St. Paul's Av
200 CHCG 60614 2978 0W-2N B7
2000 CHCG 60622 2977 2W-2N B7
2200 CHCG 60647 2977 2W-2N B7
3600 MHRY 60050 2528 32W-32N B5
4800 CHCG 60639 2975 6W-2N E7
St. Peter St
900 ANTH 60002 2357 24W-42N D6
St. Peter's Av
- AURA 60506 3199 36W-8S E3
St. Regis Ct
10 EMHT 60126 3027 16W-0S D6
St. Regis Dr
2000 LMBD 60148 3084 19W-1S D2
St. Regis Pl
- LMBD 60148 3084 19W-1S C2
St. Stephen's Grn
800 OKBK 60523 3085 17W-3S C5
800 OKBK 60559 3085 17W-3S C5
800 WTMT 60559 3085 17W-3S C5
2400 NHBK 60062 2757 10W-17N A5
St. Therese Blvd
- WKGN 60085 2536 12W-33N C2
St. Thomas Wy
500 WynT 60185 2966 29W-4N D3
St. Thomas Colony St
10 FXLK 60020 2414 28W-38N D6
St. Tropaz Cir
- FXLK 60020 2415 27W-39N B5
St. Tropez Ct
- HDPK 60035 2704 8W-21N D7
7100 FXLK 60020 2415 27W-39N B5
St. Tropez Dr
4400 LSLE 60532 3142 24W-4S C1
St. Tropez Pl
2600 LSLE 60532 3142 24W-4S C1
St. Vincent Ct
11400 MKNA 60448 3590 14W-26S E2
St. Vincents Dr
1300 LMNT 60439 3271 18W-14S B7
St. William Dr
1100 LYVL 60048 2591 17W-29N A3
Sak Dr
800 CTHL 60403 3418 25W-21S C6
Sakas Dr
200 DSPN 60016 2863 13W-11N A2
Salado Ct
100 SMBG 60195 2859 23W-12N A2
Salceda Ct
800 MDLN 60060 2590 19W-29N C4
Salceda Dr
500 MDLN 60060 2590 19W-29N C4
1000 FmtT 60060 2590 19W-29N C4
2200 NHBK 60062 2810 10W-16N A1
Salceda Ln
500 MDLN 60060 2590 19W-29N C4
Salem Av
10 LslT 60540 3142 25W-6S B4
1700 WKGN 60085 2536 11W-33N D2
2000 JNBG 60051 2471 31W-35N E7
N Salem Av
10 ANHT 60005 2806 18W-14N E4
800 ANHT 60004 2806 18W-14N E3
S Salem Av
10 ANHT 60005 2806 18W-14N E5
Salem Blvd
2000 ZION 60099 2422 10W-40N A3
2300 ZION 60099 2421 11W-40N E3
N Salem Blvd
1300 ANHT 60004 2806 18W-15N E2
Salem Cir
10 EVTN 60201 2866 4W-11N D2
10 SKOK 60201 2866 4W-11N D2
10 SKOK 60203 2866 4W-11N D2
600 OSWG 60543 3200 35W-11S B7
600 OSWG 60543 3264 35W-11S B1
Salem Ct
10 WNVL 60555 3080 30W-2S C3
100 BMDL 60108 2969 23W-5N B2
200 SYHW 60118 2799 36W-15N E3
1500 GNVA 60134 3020 34W-0N E4
1600 EGVV 60007 2859 21W-9N D7
1800 GRNE 60031 2477 15W-36N E5
2400 WDRG 60517 3143 21W-7S E7
3200 AURA 60504 3201 31W-8S E1
3500 ISLK 60042 2586 30W-28N B6
4700 RNPK 60471 3594 5W-26S B3
6500 LGGV 60047 2646 18W-24N D6
17000 TYPK 60477 3424 9W-20S D4
E Salem Ct
18700 LNSG 60438 3510 4E-22S B1
N Salem Ct
600 PLTN 60074 2753 20W-16N A6
S Salem Ct
700 SMBG 60193 2858 24W-9N D6
W Salem Ct
18700 LNSG 60438 3510 4E-22S B1
N Salem Dr
- SMBG 60195 2858 24W-11N D3
10 HFET 60169 2858 24W-10N D5
10 SMBG 60169 2858 24W-10N D5
10 SMBG 60193 2858 24W-10N D5
10 SMBG 60194 2858 24W-11N D4
4100 ANHT 60004 2753 18W-18N E2
S Salem Dr
10 HFET 60169 2858 24W-10N D6
10 JLET 60435 3498 25W-24S C5
10 JLET 60436 3498 25W-24S C5
10 SMBG 60169 2858 24W-10N D6
10 SMBG 60193 2858 24W-10N D6
10 SMBG 60194 2858 24W-10N D6
800 SMBG 60193 2912 24W-9N D1
Salem Ln
10 SKOK 60203 2866 4W-11N D2
800 CPVL 60110 2748 33W-18N B5
N Salem Ln
2200 RLKB 60073 2475 22W-36N B4
S Salem Ln
1100 ANHT 60005 2806 18W-12N E7
1100 ANHT 60005 2860 18W-12N E1
Salem Rd
1900 ELGN 60123 2854 36W-11N A3
7100 MchT 60097 2469 36W-36N D3
7300 WRLK 60097 2469 36W-36N D3
Salem Sq
400 BGBK 60440 3269 22W-12S B2
Salem Wk
- GNVW 60062 2809 12W-14N B4
3400 NfdT 60062 2809 12W-14N B4
Salem Lake Dr
10 ElaT 60047 2700 20W-22N A4
10 KLDR 60047 2700 20W-22N A4
10 LGGV 60047 2700 19W-22N B5
Salenz Ln
100 JLET 60436 3497 27W-24S D5
Salford Ct
10 ALGN 60102 2694 35W-21N A6
1200 WHTN 60187 3082 23W-3S E5
Salford Dr
100 ALGN 60102 2694 35W-21N A6
1200 SMBG 60193 2913 22W-8N C2
Salim Pl
1000 LMNT 60439 3270 19W-14S C7
Salina Av
400 SchT 60174 2908 35W-6N C7
Salinas Dr
- MKNA 60448 3504 11W-22S A1
Salisbury Av
8000 LYNS 60534 3088 10W-4S B6
Salisbury Ct
1600 WHTN 60187 3083 23W-2S A3
Salisbury Dr
100 MNSR 46321 3510 C4
100 NPVL 60565 3203 27W-10S C5
W Salisbury Dr
17700 GRNE 60031 2477 17W-36N B5
17700 WrnT 60031 2477 17W-36N A5
W Salisbury Ln
1800 LKFT 60045 2648 13W-24N E6
Salix Cir
2600 NPVL 60564 3202 28W-10S E6
2700 NPVL 60564 3203 28W-10S A7
N Salk Rd
3200 BFGV 60089 2754 16W-17N D5
3200 WhlT 60004 2754 16W-17N D5
3200 WhlT 60089 2754 16W-17N D5
3300 BFGV 60004 2754 16W-17N D4
W Sallmon Av
12200 WKGN 60087 2479 12W-37N C3
12600 BHPK 60087 2479 12W-37N B3
12900 WrnT 60087 2479 12W-37N A3
Sally Cir
14000 SenT 60098 2581 43W-28N A5
Sally Ct
600 ROSL 60172 2912 23W-6N E6
3800 GNVW 60025 2809 11W-13N D6
Sally Dr
3400 BlmT 60475 3596 1W-28S A6
3400 STGR 60475 3596 1W-28S A6
Sally Ln
9200 SRPK 60176 2973 11W-5N D2
Salma St
5400 JLET 60586 3496 30W-22S B2
Salt Creek Cir
3600 OKBK 60523 3086 15W-3S A6
Salt Creek Ct
2700 WCDA 60084 2588 25W-30N B2
Salt Creek Ln
10 HNDL 60521 3086 15W-3S B6
W Salt Creek Ln
3000 ANHT 60005 2806 20W-14N B3
3000 ANHT 60008 2806 20W-14N B3
3000 RGMW 60005 2806 20W-14N B3
Salt Creek Rd
10 ROSL 60172 2913 22W-7N C4
Salt Lake Dr
100 BMDL 60108 2969 22W-5N D2
Saltmeadow Dr
2500 NPVL 60564 3266 29W-13S C5
Salt River Ct
10 NPVL 60565 3204 26W-10S A6
Salvatori Ct
8000 ODPK 60462 3346 10W-16S C3
Salvia Ln
900 JLET 60447 3495 33W-22S A2
Salvington Pl
1400 BFGV 60089 2754 16W-17N E4
1400 WLNG 60090 2754 16W-17N D4
Samantha Cir
600 GNVA 60134 3019 37W-0N C5
Samantha Ct
500 AURA 60502 3139 32W-7S D7
S Samantha Ct
26600 CNHN 60410 3761 33W-32S B1
Samantha Dr
- LKZH 60047 2698 24W-23N C1
- NBRN 60010 2698 24W-23N C1
- PltT 60067 2805 22W-16N B1
Sammons Ct
10 BGBK 60440 3268 24W-13S C5
Samoset Ct
500 SMBG 60193 2858 24W-10N E6
Samoset Ln
10 SMBG 60193 2858 24W-10N D6
Samoset Tr
8900 SKOK 60076 2866 4W-11N C3
9100 SKOK 60203 2866 4W-11N C3
Sampson St
10 NCHI 60088 2537 10W-31N A7
2300 NCHI 60088 2594 10W-30N A2
Samson Ct
1000 UYPK 60466 3684 3W-30S C3
Samson Dr
900 UYPK 60466 3684 3W-30S C3
Samson Wy
700 NfdT 60062 2756 12W-18N A4
N Samson Wy
2300 WKGN 60087 2479 11W-36N E4
Samstag Ct
1100 NPVL 60563 3142 25W-5S A3
Samuel Ct
100 SMWD 60107 2911 28W-9N A1
1200 NPVL 60540 3202 29W-8S D2
1600 GRNE 60031 2476 19W-36N C5
Samuel Dr
10 SMWD 60107 2856 30W-10N B6
10 SMWD 60107 2857 28W-9N A7
10 SMWD 60107 2911 28W-9N A1
Samuel Adams Dr
14500 PNFD 60544 3338 30W-17S B6
Samuel Clemens Dr
- CmpT 60175 2962 40W-4N B4
Samuel Langhorn Clemens Course
300 CmpT 60175 2962 40W-4N C4
San Bernardino Dr
17500 ODPK 60467 3423 13W-21S B6
Sanborn Cir
2000 JLET 60586 3416 29W-21S D7
E Sanborn Dr
1200 PLTN 60074 2753 19W-16N C6
N Sanborn Dr
800 PLTN 60074 2753 19W-17N C6
San Carlos Rd
10 MNKA 60447 3672 32W-29S C2
Sancastle Dr
9600 PlsT 60465 3209 11W-11S D7
9600 PlsT 60480 3209 12W-11S D7
9600 PSHL 60465 3209 12W-11S D7
Sanchez Dr
100 WNVL 60555 3080 30W-2S C4
Sanctuary Ct
- VNHL 60061 2701 16W-23N E2
- WCDA 60084 2588 24W-29N B3
200 HNVL 60030 2532 21W-33N C2
2200 GRNE 60031 2478 15W-36N A4
3000 JLET 60435 3497 27W-23S C3
S Sanctuary Ct
900 VNHL 60061 2701 16W-23N E1
W Sanctuary Ct
12900 LKBF 60044 2593 12W-29N A4
Sanctuary Dr
- NLNX 60451 3501 17W-24S D5
- NlxT 60451 3501 16W-24S E5
800 LKVL 60046 2475 21W-37N C1
800 LNHT 60046 2475 21W-37N C1
E Sanctuary Dr
100 ISLK 60042 2586 28W-27N D7
100 NndT 60042 2586 28W-28N D7
Sanctuary Ln
- MTWA 60048 2648 14W-26N B3
200 LYLK 60175 2961 43W-5N B3
600 JLET 60435 3497 27W-23S B3
700 NPVL 60540 3140 28W-7S E7
700 NPVL 60540 3202 29W-8S D1
W Sanctuary Ln
12700 LKBF 60044 2593 12W-29N A4
12900 ShdT 60044 2593 13W-29N A4
Sand Ct
16000 WDWH 60083 2477 16W-37N E2
Sandalwood Ct
10 BGBK 60440 3268 25W-11S B2
10 SMWD 60107 2857 26W-11N E4
900 BRLT 60103 2911 27W-7N C5
2700 BFGV 60089 2701 17W-23N B2
3000 AURA 60504 3201 31W-8S D2
8400 DRN 60561 3206 20W-9S C4
Sandalwood Dr
- FftT 60423 3591 13W-26S A3
- FKFT 60423 3591 13W-26S A3
100 NPVL 60540 3203 27W-8S C1
7300 TYPK 60477 3424 9W-21S E5
8500 DRN 60561 3206 20W-9S C4
11200 FKFT 60423 3590 14W-26S D3
13500 ODPK 60462 3346 10W-16S B2
Sandalwood Ln
10 BNHL 60010 2750 26W-18N C3
100 BGBK 60440 3268 25W-11S A1
300 SMBG 60193 2859 21W-10N E6
900 CLLK 60014 2639 37W-24N B7
1000 CLLK 60014 2693 37W-23N B1
1600 JNBG 60050 2472 30W-36N A4
Sandalwood Rd
2700 BFGV 60089 2701 17W-23N B3
3000 LGGV 60047 2701 17W-23N B2
3000 LGGV 60089 2701 17W-23N B3
Sanday Ln
700 IVNS 60010 2751 25W-16N A7
Sandbank Dr E
1700 PNFD 60544 3337 31W-18S E7
Sandbank Dr W
1800 PNFD 60544 3337 31W-18S E7
Sandbar
10 LKMR 60051 2529 28W-33N E3
W Sand Bar Ct
1400 RLKB 60073 2474 24W-34N B7
Sandberg Ln
- LtRT 60545 3259 46W-12S E4
- PLNO 60545 3259 47W-12S D3
Sandbloom Rd
10 ALGN 60102 2748 33W-19N A3
10 DndT 60102 2748 33W-19N A3
700 AlqT 60102 2748 34W-19N A2
Sandburg Ct
2000 GLHT 60139 2969 23W-3N A4
9900 PlsT 60464 3345 12W-15S C1
13000 PlsT 60462 3345 12W-15S C1
Sandburg Dr
1400 SMBG 60173 2859 21W-10N E5
2100 AURA 60506 3137 38W-6S A5
5000 MHRY 60050 2527 34W-32N D5
Sandburg St
400 OMFD 60461 3595 3W-25S B1
400 OMFD 60466 3595 3W-25S B1

Chicago 7-County Street Index

STREET Block	City	ZIP	Map#	CGS	Grid
Sandburg St					
400	PKFT	60466	3595	3W-25S	B1
N Sandburg Ter					
1200	CHCG	60610	3034	0W-1N	B1
1500	CHCG	60610	2978		D7
1500	CHCG	60614	2978		D7
Sandcastle Dr					
2200	DYR	46311	3598		E2
Sandcastle Ln					
-	PGGV	60140	2797	42W-15N	C4
Sandcherry Ln					
1300	WCHI	60185	3022	30W-2N	B1
Sand Creek Ct					
24500	PNFD	60586	3416	30W-19S	B3
Sand Creek Dr					
600	CLSM	60188	2967	27W-3N	C6
Sand Creek Ln					
-	PnfT	60586	3416	30W-19S	B3
16300	PNFD	60586	3416	30W-19S	B3
Sandell Pl					
600	JltT	60433	3499	23W-24S	B6
Sander Ct					
1500	PTHT	60070	2808	15W-16N	A1
1500	WLNG	60070	2808	15W-16N	A1
1500	WLNG	60090	2808	15W-16N	A1
Sanderling Ct					
900	ANTH	60002	2358	21W-42N	E7
Sanders Ct					
300	YKVL	60560	3333	42W-15S	D2
600	GRNE	60031	2534	15W-33N	E3
6000	CPVL	60110	2747	36W-17N	A6
Sanders Dr					
8800	MaiT	60016	2863	11W-11N	E2
Sanders Ln					
5700	CTSD	60525	3147	13W-6S	A4
5700	LynT	60525	3147	13W-6S	A4
Sanders Rd					
-	NHBK	60015	2756	12W-18N	A2
-	RVWD	60015	2756	12W-18N	A2
-	WdfT	60015	2756	12W-18N	A2
10	NfdT	60062	2756	12W-18N	A2
10	NHBK	60062	2756	12W-16N	B6
400	WldT	60564	3266	29W-11S	D1
2300	GNVW	60062	2809	12W-15N	B1
2300	NfdT	60062	2809	12W-15N	B2
2400	PTHT	60062	2809	12W-15N	B2
Sanderson Av					
14300	DLTN	60419	3350	0E-16S	E4
Sandgate Ct					
1900	NPVL	60565	3203	26W-9S	E4
Sandhill Ct					
1300	ANTH	60002	2416	24W-41N	C1
Sandholm St					
10	GNVA	60134	3020	34W-1N	D4
Sandhurst Cir					
300	GNEN	60137	3083	23W-1S	B2
Sandhurst Ct					
10	SMWD	60107	2857	26W-11N	E4
600	CLSM	60188	2967	26W-4N	E4
1100	BFGV	60089	2701	16W-21N	D6
1200	SMBG	60193	2859	22W-10N	D6
1500	MltT	60187	3081	26W-1S	D2
1500	WHTN	60187	3081	26W-1S	D2
Sandhurst Dr					
800	SDWH	60548	3258	51W-14S	A7
800	SdwT	60548	3258	51W-14S	A7
1100	BFGV	60089	2701	16W-21N	C6
Sandhurst Ln					
200	SEGN	60177	2908	35W-8N	A2
1100	CLSM	60188	2967	26W-4N	E4
Sandhurst Rd					
10	MDLN	60060	2647	17W-27N	A1
San Diego Av					
18000	HMWD	60430	3427	3W-21S	A7
San Diego Pl					
600	BRLT	60103	2911	28W-7N	B4
Sand Island Ct					
2100	NPVL	60564	3266	29W-12S	E4
Sand Lake Rd					
-	OMCK	60083	2477	17W-37N	A2
-	WrnT	60083	2477	17W-37N	A2
E Sand Lake Rd					
2100	LNHT	60046	2476	19W-37N	B2
W Sand Lake Rd					
19000	LNHT	60046	2476	19W-37N	D2
19000	OMCK	60046	2476	19W-37N	C2
19000	OMCK	60083	2476	19W-37N	C2
W Sandlake Rd					
16000	WDWH	60083	2477	16W-37N	E2
16300	OMCK	60083	2477	17W-37N	C2
16300	WrnT	60083	2477	17W-37N	C2
Sandler Ct					
1000	MDLN	60060	2590	20W-28N	A6
Sandlewood Ct					
900	LKZH	60047	2699	22W-22N	B4
Sandlewood Ln					
-	LKVL	60046	2474	23W-37N	E2
4200	HFET	60192	2804	24W-15N	B2
Sand Lily Dr					
5300	NPVL	60564	3266	29W-13S	D5
Sando Ln					
1300	WDSK	60098	2581	42W-30N	C2
Sandpebble Cir					
1100	ALGN	60102	2694	34W-20N	C7
Sandpebble Dr					
500	SMBG	60193	2912	24W-9N	D1
1500	PTHT	60070	2808	15W-16N	B1
1500	WLNG	60070	2808	15W-16N	B1
1500	WLNG	60090	2808	15W-16N	B1
Sandpebble Ln					
300	AURA	60504	3139	31W-6S	E5
300	AURA	60504	3140	29W-6S	D6
Sandpiper					
100	LKMR	60051	2529	28W-33N	D4
Sandpiper Ct					
-	AURA	60504	3140	31W-7S	A7
-	SPGV	60081	2354	32W-43N	C5
10	MltT	60188	3023	26W-1N	E3
600	ALGN	60102	2694	35W-20N	B7
700	MonT	60466	3684	3W-29S	A2
900	BRLT	60103	2911	27W-7N	C4
1200	GYLK	60030	2533	19W-33N	C4
1200	JLET	60586	3496	29W-22S	D2
9100	ODPK	60462	3346	11W-17S	A6
W Sandpiper Ct					
800	PLTN	60067	2805	22W-14N	C4
Sandpiper Dr					
500	LNHT	60046	2476	19W-37N	B3
600	NLNX	60451	3589	18W-27S	A4
2500	LkvT	60046	2476	19W-37N	C3
3400	AURA	60504	3139	31W-7S	E7
3800	CLSM	60133	2967	27W-4N	C3
3800	CLSM	60188	2967	27W-4N	C3
3800	HRPK	60133	2967	27W-4N	C3
Sandpiper Ln					
10	HNWD	60047	2645	22W-26N	C3
100	LKFT	60045	2649	11W-25N	E5
500	VrnT	60015	2755	15W-20N	B2
1100	NPVL	60540	3203	26W-8S	E1
1200	NPVL	60540	3204	26W-8S	A2
1200	WDSK	60098	2581	41W-30N	D2
4700	JLET	60586	3496	29W-22S	C2
E Sandpiper Ln					
10	LKFT	60045	2649	10W-25N	E5
W Sandpiper Ln					
10	LKFT	60045	2649	11W-25N	C5
Sandpiper Rd					
-	ALGN	60102	2694	35W-21N	B7
Sandpiper Tr					
2500	WCHI	60185	2966	29W-3N	D5
Sandpiper Cove					
23100	PNFD	60585	3339	28W-15S	A3
Sandra Av					
1100	LydT	60164	2972	14W-3N	D5
1100	NHLK	60164	2972	14W-3N	D5
3000	FNPK	60131	2972	14W-3N	D4
Sandra Ct					
10	LtRT	60548	3258	50W-13S	B6
300	GLHT	60139	2969	23W-3N	B6
11400	MKNA	60448	3590	14W-26S	E2
Sandra Dr					
600	UYPK	60466	3684	3W-29S	B2
Sandra Ln					
300	CHHT	60411	3507	2W-24S	D5
400	ELGN	60120	2855	32W-10N	C5
500	CRY	60013	2641	31W-24N	D7
600	WLNG	60090	2755	15W-17N	A4
8900	HYHL	60457	3209	11W-10S	E5
8900	HYHL	60457	3210	11W-10S	A5
13700	CTWD	60445	3347	6W-16S	D3
13800	BmnT	60445	3347	6W-16S	D3
24900	PNFD	60544	3337	31W-16S	E4
24900	PNFD	60544	3338	31W-16S	A4
Sandra St					
3700	FNPK	60131	2972	14W-4N	D3
3700	LydT	60131	2972	14W-4N	D3
Sandridge Ct					
2300	LYWD	60411	3509	2E-24S	E5
Sandridge Dr					
20600	LYWD	60411	3509	2E-24S	E5
Sandridge Ln					
2200	DYR	46311	3598		E2
Sands Rd					
6100	AlqT	60014	2641	33W-25N	A5
6100	NndT	60014	2641	33W-25N	A5
6800	AlqT	60014	2640	33W-25N	E6
6800	CLLK	60014	2640	33W-24N	E6
6800	CLLK	60014	2641	33W-25N	A5
7000	CRY	60014	2640	33W-25N	E6
Sandstone Ct					
-	MTGY	60538	3198	40W-9S	B4
1000	AURA	60502	3139	32W-6S	C4
3300	LIHL	60156	2693	37W-21N	C5
11700	FKFT	60423	3590	14W-27S	D3
E Sandstone Ct					
10	SEGN	60177	2907	37W-7N	C6
W Sandstone Ct					
10	SEGN	60177	2907	37W-7N	C6
Sandstone Dr					
800	LYVL	60048	2591	16W-29N	E3
1400	PTHT	60070	2808	15W-16N	A1
1400	WLNG	60090	2808	15W-16N	A1
S Sandstone Dr					
-	BvlT	60416	3941	33W-40S	B4
-	DMND	60416	3941	33W-40S	B4
W Sandstone Dr					
13700	HMGN	60491	3343	17W-17S	C5
Sandstone Pkwy					
-	MTGY	60538	3198	40W-9S	B4
Sandwald Rd					
10	HTLY	60142	2744	43W-17N	B7
10	RtdT	60142	2744	43W-17N	B7
Sandwedge Pl					
500	GRNE	60031	2534	16W-33N	D3
E Sandwich Rd					
2800	SdwT	60548	3258	51W-13S	A5
Sandwick Ct					
1000	HDPK	60035	2704	9W-22N	C5
Sandy Ct					
-	MonT	60449	3683	5W-31S	D5
-	UYPK	60449	3683	5W-31S	D5
500	HRVD	60033	2464	50W-37N	A1
500	LYVL	60048	2591	16W-27N	C7
E Sandy Ct					
500	GDLY	60407	4030	32W-43S	D2
W Sandy Ct					
15100	NptT	60083	2420	15W-38N	B7
15100	WDWH	60083	2420	15W-38N	B7
15100	WDWH	60083	2478	15W-38N	B1
17600	WrnT	60031	2534	17W-34N	B1
Sandy Dr					
-	AntT	60002	2359	20W-41N	A7
1200	ANTH	60002	2359	20W-41N	A7
1600	JLET	60432	3499	21W-23S	E4
Sandy Ln					
200	LtRT	60545	3259	47W-14S	D7
200	PLNO	60545	3259	47W-14S	D7
400	DSPN	60016	2862	15W-11N	A3
400	LYVL	60048	2591	16W-27N	C7
400	WLMT	60091	2812	4W-13N	B6
1500	AURA	60506	3137	36W-5S	E3
3100	GNVW	60025	2810	10W-15N	A2
7200	TYPK	60477	3424	9W-20S	E3
Sandy Beach Rd					
1100	ELGN	60123	2801	33W-13N	A7
Sandy Bluff Rd					
3700	LtRT	60545	3258	50W-14S	C7
3700	LtRT	60545	3330	50W-16S	D4
4800	LtRT	60548	3330	50W-16S	D4
5800	FoxT	60541	3330	49W-16S	D5
5800	FoxT	60545	3330	49W-16S	D5
5800	FoxT	60548	3330	49W-16S	D5
Sandy Creek Dr					
1900	ELGN	60123	2854	36W-11N	A3
2300	ALGN	60102	2746	36W-18N	E4
Sandy Hook St					
1400	WHTN	60187	3081	26W-1S	D2
Sandy Knoll Dr					
25900	CNHN	60410	3672	32W-30S	D5
Sandy Pass Rd					
1300	LKZH	60047	2699	22W-21N	A6
Sandy Point Ln					
200	LKZH	60047	2698	24W-23N	C2
Sandy Pointe Ln					
700	RLKP	60073	2532	21W-34N	C2
Sandy Ridge Dr					
3000	SCHT	60475	3596	0W-27S	C5
3000	STGR	60475	3596	0W-27S	C5
Sanford Av					
2000	NLNX	60451	3588	19W-27S	D4
Sanford Ct					
1300	GNVW	60025	2810	8W-13N	E5
Sanford Ln					
1300	GNVW	60025	2810	8W-13N	E5
San Francisco Ter					
800	BRLT	60103	2911	28W-7N	B4
Sangamon Ct					
10	PKFT	60466	3594	4W-27S	E5
200	BRLT	60103	2967	28W-5N	A1
Sangamon St					
200	PKFT	60466	3594	4W-27S	E5
200	PKFT	60466	3595	4W-27S	A5
300	RNPK	60471	3594	4W-27S	E4
600	CHHT	60411	3508	1W-24S	A6
3000	SCHT	60411	3596	1W-27S	A5
3000	SCHT	60475	3596	1W-27S	A5
3000	STGR	60475	3596	1W-28S	A6
3800	CteT	60475	3596	1W-28S	A7
14400	HRVY	60426	3350	1W-17S	A5
N Sangamon St					
10	CHCG	60607	3033	1W-0N	E4
600	CHCG	60622	3033	1W-0N	E3
S Sangamon St					
-	CRTE	60417	3596	1W-29S	A7
-	CRTE	60417	3685	1W-29S	A1
-	CteT	60417	3685	1W-29S	A1
10	CHCG	60607	3033	1W-0S	E5
1300	CHCG	60608	3033	1W-1S	E7
1800	CHCG	60608	3091	1W-1S	E1
3500	CHCG	60609	3091	1W-3S	E5
5200	CHCG	60609	3151	1W-5S	E2
5500	CHCG	60621	3151	1W-6S	E4
7200	CHCG	60621	3152	1W-8S	A7
7500	CHCG	60620	3214	1W-9S	A3
7500	CHCG	60621	3214	1W-8S	A1
9900	CHCG	60643	3214	1W-11S	A7
10300	CHCG	60643	3278	1W-12S	A2
12200	CTPK	60643	3278	1W-14S	A6
12200	CTPK	60827	3278	1W-14S	A6
23900	CteT	60417	3596	1W-29S	A7
Sangmeister Rd					
-	FftT	60423	3591	13W-26S	C2
10	FKFT	60423	3591	12W-26S	D2
San Juan Rd					
100	CPVL	60110	2748	33W-18N	B4
San Luis Ct					
2700	NPVL	60565	3203	27W-10S	C7
San Luis Ln					
10400	ODPK	60467	3423	13W-20S	B5
10400	OrlT	60467	3423	13W-20S	B5
San Mateo Dr					
1000	RMVL	60446	3340	25W-16S	B3
2600	JLET	60586	3415	31W-20S	E6
2600	PNFD	60586	3415	31W-20S	E6
San Rem Av					
20500	LkvT	60046	2476	20W-37N	A2
20800	LkvT	60046	2475	20W-37N	E2
San Simeon Dr					
1100	HRPK	60133	2912	26W-7N	A6
1200	HRPK	60133	2911	26W-6N	D6
Sans Souci Dr					
300	AURA	60506	3199	38W-7S	A1
2300	AURA	60506	3198	39W-7S	D1
Santa Anita Dr					
1100	HRPK	60133	2912	26W-6N	A6
1300	HRPK	60133	2911	26W-6N	E6
Santa Barbara Ct					
6200	JLET	60586	3415	31W-20S	E6
Santa Barbara Dr					
5600	HRPK	60133	2911	26W-6N	D6
Santa Barbara Rd					
300	LKMR	60051	2529	29W-32N	D5
Santa Cruz Dr					
5500	HRPK	60133	2911	26W-6N	E6
Santa Cruz Ln					
10400	ODPK	60467	3423	13W-21S	B5
10400	OrlT	60467	3423	13W-21S	B5
Santa Fe Av					
600	CPVL	60110	2748	32W-18N	D4
Santa Fe Ct					
10	WLSP	60480	3208	14W-10S	D5
700	CLSM	60188	2967	26W-3N	E6
10600	HTLY	60142	2692	39W-21N	C6
Santa Fe Dr					
1800	NPVL	60563	3140	30W-6S	C4
6700	HGKN	60525	3147	12W-7S	D7
7000	HGKN	60525	3209	12W-8S	C1
7600	HGKN	60480	3209	12W-8S	C1
Santa Fe Ln					
100	LynT	60480	3208	14W-10S	D5
100	WLSP	60480	3208	14W-10S	D6
Santa Fe Pkwy					
-	UNON	60180	2635	46W-24N	C6
Santa Fe Rd					
1200	RMVL	60446	3340	25W-15S	B2
Santa Fe St					
1000	BRLT	60103	2910	30W-7N	C4
Santa Fe Tr					
400	BmdT	60108	2968	25W-5N	B1
400	CRY	60013	2641	32W-24N	C7
500	PltT	60124	2906	39W-9N	E1
700	BmdT	60108	2912	25W-5N	B7
700	BmdT	60172	2912	25W-5N	B7
700	PltT	60124	2852	39W-9N	E7
3300	OMFD	60461	3506	4W-24S	E5
10600	HTLY	60142	2692	39W-21N	B6
13600	OrlT	60467	3344	14W-16S	C2
Santa Fe Trails					
-	DMND	60416	3941	34W-39S	A2
Santa Maria Dr					
800	NPVL	60540	3141	26W-7S	D7
Santa Rosa Av					
900	WHTN	60187	3024	24W-0N	D5
Santa Rosa Dr					
500	DSPN	60018	2916	14W-8N	C1
S Santee Ct					
17100	LKPT	60441	3420	20W-20S	B5
N Santee Ln					
1300	MPPT	60056	2808	13W-14N	E4
Santos Av					
100	MNKA	60447	3672	32W-29S	D1
Santuit Ct					
800	SMBG	60194	2858	24W-10N	D5
Sapling Ln					
600	DRFD	60015	2703	12W-20N	C7
600	DRFD	60015	2756	12W-20N	C1
Sapphire Ct					
1500	GRNE	60031	2476	19W-36N	C5
11600	FKFT	60423	3590	14W-27S	D3
Sapphire Dr					
700	BGBK	60490	3267	26W-13S	E5
Sapphire Dr N					
4500	HFET	60192	2804	24W-15N	B1
Sapphire Dr W					
1400	HFET	60192	2804	24W-15N	B1
Sapphire Ln					
-	PGGV	60140	2797	42W-15N	C4
1800	AURA	60506	3137	38W-6S	A4
Sara Av					
400	LMNT	60439	3270	19W-14S	E7
Sara Ct					
10	SEGN	60177	2908	36W-9N	A2
1100	BTVA	60510	3077	36W-2S	E3
23700	CteT	60417	3597	2E-28S	E7
Sara Ln					
10	BNHL	60010	2750	25W-17N	E4
600	MRGO	60152	2634	49W-25N	C4
600	NPVL	60565	3204	25W-8S	B2
Sara Rd					
18700	FftT	60448	3502	14W-22S	D2
Sara Ann Ln					
6300	OKFT	60452	3425	8W-18S	B1
Sarah Av					
100	SRWD	60404	3496	29W-24S	C6
3700	FNPK	60131	2973	12W-4N	B2
3700	FNPK	60176	2973	12W-4N	B2
3700	SRPK	60131	2973	12W-4N	B2
3700	SRPK	60176	2973	12W-4N	B2
S Sarah Blvd					
1200	VNHL	60061	2702	15W-23N	A2
Sarah Ct					
-	LtRT	60545	3260	46W-14S	A7
-	PLNO	60545	3260	46W-14S	A7
200	WLNG	60090	2755	15W-17N	A4
400	WDDL	60191	2970	18W-5N	D1
2800	ELGN	60124	2853	37W-11N	C4
17800	CCHL	60478	3426	4W-21S	D6
23700	AntT	60002	2416	23W-40N	D2
Sarah Dr					
10	AlqT	60014	2640	34W-26N	D4
10	CLLK	60014	2640	34W-26N	D3
500	ADSN	60143	2970	19W-5N	D1
500	ADSN	60191	2970	19W-5N	D1
500	ITSC	60143	2970	19W-5N	D1
500	ITSC	60191	2970	19W-5N	D1
500	WDDL	60191	2970	19W-5N	D1
1000	JNBG	60050	2472	30W-37N	B2
3800	ZION	60099	2421	12W-40N	C3
N Sarah Dr					
37500	WDWH	60083	2477	16W-37N	E2
W Sarah Dr					
21300	LkvT	60046	2475	21W-36N	D3
Sarah Ln					
700	NfdT	60062	2756	12W-18N	A4
900	AraT	60502	3139	33W-6S	A5
900	AURA	60502	3139	33W-6S	A5
3600	CCHL	60478	3426	4W-21S	D6
Sarah St					
2400	LydT	60164	2973	12W-3N	B6
2500	FNPK	60131	2973	12W-3N	B5
3600	FNPK	60176	2973	12W-4N	B3
3600	SRPK	60176	2973	12W-4N	B3
23300	PNFD	60544	3338	29W-16S	D4
Sarah Constant Ln					
900	SMBG	60194	2857	27W-11N	D3
Sarahs Grove Ln					
10	SMBG	60193	2858	24W-10N	E5
10	SMBG	60193	2859	23W-10N	A6
Sarana Av					
100	WnfT	60185	3022	29W-0N	D5
1300	WCHI	60185	3022	29W-0S	D7
Saranac Ct					
100	BMDL	60108	2968	25W-5N	B1
2400	GNVW	60025	2809	11W-15N	C2
Saranac Ln					
1100	NHBK	60062	2756	10W-17N	E5
2400	GNVW	60025	2809	11W-15N	D3
Saranell Av					
1400	NPVL	60540	3203	28W-8S	A1
1500	NPVL	60540	3202	28W-8S	E1
Sarasota Dr					
-	PGGV	60140	2797	42W-15N	D4
300	SMWD	60107	2857	28W-11N	A4
1100	WLNG	60090	2754	16W-18N	E3
W Sarasota Dr					
5300	MHRY	60050	2527	34W-32N	C5
Sarasota Ln					
800	CLLK	60014	2639	37W-24N	C7
Sara Spring Dr					
-	FftT	60423	3591	13W-27S	A5
Saratoga Av					
3900	DRGV	60515	3084	19W-4S	C7
4300	DRGV	60515	3144	20W-5S	C2
6300	DRGV	60516	3144	20W-7S	C6
Saratoga Cir					
400	ALGN	60102	2693	36W-20N	C7
E Saratoga Cir					
800	ISLK	60042	2587	28W-27N	A7
800	WcnT	60042	2587	28W-27N	A7
W Saratoga Cir					
800	ISLK	60042	2586	28W-29N	E4
800	ISLK	60042	2587	27W-27N	A7
Saratoga Ct					
10	RLKP	60030	2589	22W-30N	B1
10	SEGN	60177	2908	35W-8N	C3
100	VNHL	60061	2647	16W-26N	D3
200	GRNE	60031	2534	16W-34N	C1
500	OSWG	60543	3263	37W-13S	B5
1100	NPVL	60564	3267	28W-11S	A2
1500	GNOK	60048	2592	14W-30N	C3
Saratoga Dr					
-	CPVL	60110	2801	33W-17N	A1
10	BTVA	60510	3077	36W-1S	E2
10	GLHT	60139	2968	24W-3N	D5
400	AURA	60502	3139	32W-7S	C7
500	CHHT	60411	3507	2W-24S	C5
1100	CLSM	60188	2967	27W-3N	B5
3700	JLET	60435	3417	27W-19S	C2
6800	BGVW	60455	3211	8W-10S	A4
6900	BGVW	60455	3210	8W-10S	E4
11000	ODPK	60467	3422	14W-19S	E2
11000	ODPK	60467	3423	13W-19S	A2
N Saratoga Dr					
900	PLTN	60074	2753	20W-17N	B5
Saratoga Ln					
200	RMVL	60446	3339	27W-17S	C6
700	BFGV	60089	2754	17W-17N	B5
1500	GNVW	60025	2810	10W-14N	A5
Saratoga Pkwy					
900	SYHW	60118	2799	36W-15N	E4
900	SYHW	60118	2800	36W-15N	A4
Saratoga Rd					
1000	NPVL	60564	3267	28W-11S	A2
4500	RNPK	60471	3594	5W-26S	B3
Saratoga St					
10	DGvT	60439	3206	19W-11S	C7
400	DGvT	60439	3270	19W-11S	C1
1800	NCHI	60064	2593	11W-30N	D1
1800	NCHI	60088	2593	11W-30N	C1
Sarazen Ct					
3900	WDRG	60517	3143	23W-7S	A6
N Sarazen Dr					
2200	VNHL	60061	2591	17W-27N	B7
Sard Av					
700	AURA	60506	3199	36W-8S	E3
900	AURA	60538	3199	36W-8S	E3
1000	MTGY	60538	3199	36W-8S	D3
Sard Pl					
200	HIWD	60040	2704	9W-23N	C3
Sargo Ct					
4100	NCHI	60088	2593	11W-31N	D1
Sarini Ln					
-	NndT	60012	2583	36W-28N	D5
Sarkis Dr					
12000	MKNA	60448	3502	15W-23S	C3
Sarson Wy					
700	HRPK	60133	2912	25W-9N	A1
Sartor Av					
400	AraT	60502	3139	33W-7S	B6
400	AraT	60504	3139	33W-7S	B6
400	AraT	60505	3139	33W-7S	B6
S Sarver Dr					
20700	SRWD	60404	3496	30W-25S	C7
20700	TroT	60404	3496	30W-25S	C7
20900	TroT	60404	3584	30W-25S	C1
21000	SRWD	60404	3584	30W-25S	C1
Sashay Ct					
1400	GRNE	60031	2476	19W-36N	C5
Sassabee St					
10	PKFT	60466	3594	4W-27S	E4
Sassafras Dr					
1300	WCHI	60185	3022	30W-2N	B1
1300	WynT	60185	3022	30W-2N	B1
Sassafras Ln					
4500	WldT	60564	3265	31W-12S	E3
4700	WldT	60564	3266	31W-12S	A4
Satellite Dr					
2400	JLET	60431	3417	28W-20S	B6
2400	PnfT	60431	3417	28W-20S	B6
Satinwood Ct N					
300	BFGV	60089	2701	16W-22N	C4
Satinwood Ct S					
300	BFGV	60089	2701	16W-22N	C4
Satinwood Ter					
300	BFGV	60089	2701	17W-22N	B4
300	VrnT	60089	2701	16W-22N	C4
Sauble Wy					
-	RMVL	60446	3417	26W-18S	E1
Saucer Ct					
10	SBTN	60010	2803	27W-13N	B6
N Sauganash Av					
6100	CHCG	60646	2920	5W-7N	A3
6400	LNWD	60712	2919	6W-8N	D2
6700	CHCG	60646	2919	6W-8N	D2
6700	LNWD	60646	2919	6W-8N	D2
6800	SKOK	60646	2919	6W-8N	C1
Sauganash Ct					
1500	GRNE	60031	2476	19W-36N	C5
N Sauganash Ln					
5900	CHCG	60646	2920	5W-7N	B4
Sauganash St					
300	PKFT	60466	3594	4W-27S	E5
300	RNPK	60471	3594	4W-27S	E5
Saugatuck Rd					
10	OswT	60538	3199	36W-11S	D7
10	OswT	60538	3200	36W-10S	A7
100	OSWG	60538	3200	36W-10S	A7
100	OSWG	60543	3200	36W-10S	A7
Saugatuck St					
400	PKFT	60466	3594	4W-27S	E5
Saugatuck Tr					
800	VNHL	60061	2647	18W-24N	A6
Saugatuk Cir					
600	RMVL	60446	3417	26W-18S	E1
Saugatuk Ct					
1500	RMVL	60446	3417	26W-18S	E1
Saugus Ln					
200	SMBG	60173	2859	21W-10N	E5
Sauk Blvd					
-	WnfT	60510	3080	30W-2S	A3
Sauk Ct					
-	LKVL	60046	2474	23W-35N	E5
-	RLKB	60073	2474	23W-35N	E5
10	PKFT	60466	3595	3W-27S	B4
500	CLSM	60188	2967	26W-3N	D6
Sauk Dr					
100	BTVA	60510	3078	35W-2S	C5
100	BtvT	60510	3078	35W-2S	B5
3000	MhtT	60451	3590	16W-28S	A6
3000	NlxT	60442	3590	16W-28S	A6
3000	NlxT	60451	3590	16W-28S	A6
17400	HmrT	60441	3420	20W-20S	B5
17400	LKPT	60441	3420	20W-20S	B6
Sauk Ln					
400	BGBK	60440	3268	23W-11S	E1
N Sauk Ln					
1400	MPPT	60056	2808	13W-14N	E3
Sauk Pth					
500	OKBK	60523	3085	16W-3S	D5
Sauk Tr					
-	BlmT	60411	3595	2W-27S	E4
-	SCHT	60411	3595	2W-27S	E4
10	BlmT	60466	3595	2W-27S	C4
10	IHPK	60525	3146	13W-7S	E6
10	PKFT	60466	3595	2W-27S	C4
300	PKFT	60466	3594	4W-27S	E3
400	RNPK	60471	3594	6W-26S	A3
900	NndT	60051	2528	31W-31N	D7
1000	NndT	60051	2585	31W-30N	D1
5300	RchT	60471	3593	6W-26S	E3
5300	RNPK	60471	3593	7W-26S	C3
5400	RchT	60443	3593	8W-26S	A3
5400	RNPK	60443	3593	8W-26S	A3
6500	FKFT	60443	3593	8W-27S	A3
7100	FKFT	60423	3593	8W-27S	A3
E Sauk Tr					
10	CHHT	60411	3596	0W-27S	B4
10	SCHT	60411	3596	0W-27S	B4
200	SCHT	60475	3596	0E-27S	D3
300	BlmT	60411	3596	0W-27S	C4
300	BlmT	60475	3596	0W-27S	C4
300	STGR	60411	3596	0W-27S	C4
300	STGR	60475	3596	0W-27S	C4
500	BlmT	60411	3597	0E-26S	A3
500	SLVL	60411	3597	2E-26S	D3
500	STGR	60411	3597	0E-26S	A3
500	STGR	60475	3597	0E-26S	A3
2700	BlmT	60411	3598	3E-26S	A2
3600	DYR	46311	3598	4E-26S	C2
E Sauk Tr US-30					
3600	BlmT	60411	3598	4E-26S	C2
3600	DYR	46311	3598	4E-26S	C2
W Sauk Tr					
-	FKFT	60423	3593	9W-26S	A3
-	RchT	60443	3593	9W-26S	A3
10	FKFT	60423	3591	11W-26S	E2
10	SCHT	60411	3596	1W-27S	A4

STREET Block	City	ZIP	Map#	CGS	Grid
W Sauk Tr					
200	SCHT	60411	3595	1W-27S	E4
300	BlmT	60411	3595	2W-27S	E4
300	BlmT	60466	3595	2W-27S	E4
300	FKFT	60423	3592	9W-26S	E3
8800	FftT	60423	3592	11W-26S	A2
Sauk Pointe Dr					
22400	SLVL	60411	3597	1E-27S	B3
Saunders Rd					
-	VrnT	60045	2648	13W-25N	E5
10	LKFT	60045	2648	13W-25N	E4
10	NHBK	60015	2756	12W-20N	A2
10	NHBK	60062	2756	12W-20N	A2
10	RVWD	60015	2756	12W-20N	A1
10	WdfT	60015	2756	12W-20N	A1
400	DRFD	60015	2756	12W-20N	A1
600	DRFD	60015	2703	12W-20N	A7
600	RVWD	60015	2703	12W-20N	A7
21600	FmtT	60060	2589	21W-29N	C4
Saunders Rd CO-W24					
10	NHBK	60015	2756	12W-20N	A2
10	NHBK	60062	2756	12W-20N	A2
10	RVWD	60015	2756	12W-20N	A1
10	WdfT	60015	2756	12W-20N	A1
400	DRFD	60015	2756	12W-20N	A1
600	DRFD	60015	2703	12W-20N	A7
600	RVWD	60015	2703	12W-20N	A7
N Saunders Rd					
25500	LKFT	60045	2648	13W-25N	E5
25500	VrnT	60045	2648	13W-25N	E5
Sausalito Ct					
1100	BRLT	60103	2911	27W-7N	C5
N Savage Rd					
39700	LkvT	60002	2417	20W-39N	E4
39700	LkvT	60046	2417	20W-39N	E4
39700	LNHT	60046	2417	20W-39N	E4
39800	ANTH	60002	2418	20W-40N	A2
39800	AntT	60002	2418	20W-40N	A3
39800	LkvT	60002	2418	20W-39N	A4
39800	LkvT	60046	2418	20W-39N	A4
39800	LNHT	60046	2418	20W-39N	A4
Savanna Ct					
-	KdlT	60560	3334	40W-16S	C4
N Savanna Ct					
100	LKFT	60045	2649	12W-26N	B3
Savanna Dr					
-	HPSR	60140	2795	47W-16N	D1
2300	WCDA	60084	2588	25W-29N	A3
13300	PNFD	60544	3338	31W-16S	A4
13600	PNFD	60544	3337	31W-16S	E3
13700	PNFD	60585	3337	31W-16S	E3
Savanna Ln					
-	LKWD	60142	2638	39W-25N	C5
1200	WDSK	60098	2581	41W-30N	D2
3300	MTSN	60443	3594	4W-26S	E1
W Savanna Ln					
21600	KLDR	60047	2699	21W-22N	D5
Savanna Grove Ln					
2400	WDSK	60098	2582	40W-28N	A5
Savannah Cir					
900	NPVL	60540	3141	27W-7S	B7
900	NPVL	60540	3203	28W-8S	A2
Savannah Ct					
-	ALGN	60102	2746	36W-20N	D1
1400	GRNE	60031	2476	19W-35N	C5
1700	AURA	60502	3079	33W-3S	A6
10500	HTLY	60142	2692	39W-21N	C5
22500	LKBN	60010	2697	27W-22N	B4
N Savannah Ct					
10	RDLK	60073	2531	25W-32N	A4
Savannah Dr					
2800	AURA	60502	3079	33W-3S	A6
E Savannah Dr					
200	RMVL	60446	3340	25W-16S	C4
W Savannah Dr					
200	RMVL	60446	3340	25W-16S	C4
Savannah Ln					
-	ALGN	60102	2746	36W-20N	D1
-	HRPK	60133	2912	25W-8N	A3
600	CLLK	60014	2640	33W-26N	D3
1400	SMBG	60193	2912	25W-8N	A2
10600	HTLY	60142	2692	39W-21N	C5
N Savannah Pkwy					
10	RDLK	60073	2531	25W-33N	A3
S Savannah Pkwy					
10	RDLK	60073	2531	25W-33N	A3
W Savannah Pkwy					
2000	RDLK	60073	2531	25W-32N	A4
Savannah Rd					
2000	ELGN	60123	2853	36W-12N	E2
2000	ELGN	60123	2854	36W-12N	A2
Savannah Tr					
-	CbaT	60010	2697	27W-22N	A4
-	LKBN	60010	2697	27W-22N	A4
E Savannah Tr					
27500	LKBN	60010	2697	27W-22N	A4
W Savannah Tr					
28000	LKBN	60010	2696	28W-22N	E3
28000	LKBN	60010	2697	28W-22N	A3
Savanna Lakes Ct					
500	ElgT	60124	2907	38W-9N	A2
Savanna Lakes Dr					
500	ElgT	60124	2907	39W-9N	A2
700	PltT	60124	2907	38W-9N	A2
Savanna Springs Dr					
600	LKVL	60046	2475	22W-36N	A3
800	LKVL	60073	2475	23W-36N	A3
800	RLKB	60073	2475	23W-36N	A3
Saville Row					
10	BNHL	60010	2696	30W-21N	A5
Savoy Ct					
10	LIHL	60156	2692	39W-23N	C2
400	SMBG	60193	2858	24W-9N	D6
500	INCK	60061	2647	17W-24N	A6
800	LKZH	60047	2698	23W-22N	E4
1000	EGVV	60007	2914	20W-8N	B3
2300	AURA	60503	3201	32W-10S	C5
Savoy Dr					
200	SRWD	60404	3496	31W-23S	A4
5400	LIHL	60156	2692	39W-23N	C2
W Savoy Dr					
200	RDLK	60073	2531	23W-32N	E4
Savoy Ln					
-	BGBK	60440	3268	25W-12S	C3
-	BGVW	60455	3274	9W-11S	D1
-	BlmT	60411	3509	2E-23S	D3
-	LYWD	60411	3509	2E-23S	D3
100	CRY	60013	2695	33W-23N	A1
2700	MTGY	60538	3198	40W-10S	C6
4200	MHRY	60050	2585	33W-30N	A2
Savoy Club Ct					
-	BRRG	60480	3208	14W-9S	D2
-	BRRG	60527	3208	14W-9S	D2
-	WLSP	60480	3208	14W-9S	D2
W Sawgrass Blvd					
-	WKGN	60083	2478	14W-37N	C2
Sawgrass Ct					
1500	ELGN	60123	2854	35W-9N	B7
2300	RVWD	60015	2756	12W-20N	A1
8000	ODPK	60462	3346	10W-18S	C7
Sawgrass Dr					
-	MONE	60449	3683	6W-31S	A4
10	BRBK	60459	3211	7W-8S	C1
10	LMNT	60439	3343	17W-15S	B1
200	PSHT	60463	3275	7W-14S	B5
200	PSHT	60463	3347	8W-15S	E5
2900	AURA	60502	3079	33W-3S	A6
5200	RNPK	60471	3593	6W-27S	E5
5200	RNPK	60471	3594	6W-27S	A5
Sawgrass Ln					
200	PSHT	60463	3347	8W-15S	B1
500	HPSR	60140	2795	47W-15N	C3
500	HshT	60140	2795	47W-15N	C3
10300	HTLY	60142	2692	39W-21N	B5
14900	HMGN	60491	3343	17W-17S	C6
Sawgrass St					
1700	VNHL	60061	2647	16W-27N	D1
Saw Horse Dr					
5200	HFET	60192	2802	30W-12N	C7
Sawmill Cr					
-	DGvT	60439	3207	17W-11S	B7
Sawmill Ln					
1100	ALGN	60102	2693	35W-20N	E7
1100	ALGN	60102	2694	35W-20N	A7
1100	ALGN	60102	2746	35W-20N	E1
1100	ALGN	60102	2747	35W-20N	A1
28700	LKMR	60051	2529	28W-32N	D5
Saw Mill Rd					
200	NPVL	60565	3203	26W-9S	D5
Sawmill Tr					
700	SCRL	60174	2964	34W-4N	D3
700	WYNE	60174	2964	34W-4N	D3
700	WYNE	60184	2964	34W-4N	D3
Sawmill Creek Dr					
8000	DRN	60561	3206	18W-9S	E3
Sawyer Av					
-	MKHM	60426	3348	4W-17S	E6
-	MKHM	60445	3348	4W-17S	E6
-	WHTN	60187	3025	23W-0S	A6
10	LGNG	60525	3087	12W-4S	C7
200	GNEN	60137	3025	23W-0S	A6
200	WHTN	60137	3025	23W-0S	A6
13300	RBBN	60472	3348	4W-16S	E2
14500	MDLN	60445	3348	4W-17S	E5
15600	MKHM	60428	3349	4W-18S	A7
15600	MKHM	60428	3427	4W-19S	A3
16600	HLCT	60428	3427	4W-19S	A3
16600	HLCT	60429	3427	4W-19S	A3
N Sawyer Av					
-	CHCG	60651	3032	4W-1N	D2
500	CHCG	60624	3032	4W-0N	D3
2700	CHCG	60647	2976	4W-3N	D5
3600	CHCG	60618	2976	4W-4N	D2
4300	CHCG	60625	2976	4W-5N	D1
4700	CHCG	60625	2920	4W-6N	D6
5500	CHCG	60659	2920	4W-6N	D5
S Sawyer Av					
1200	CHCG	60623	3032	4W-1S	D7
1200	CHCG	60624	3032	4W-1S	D7
1500	CHCG	60623	3090	4W-1S	D1
4300	CHCG	60632	3090	4W-4S	E7
5100	CHCG	60632	3150	4W-6S	E3
5400	CHCG	60629	3150	4W-6S	E4
7700	CHCG	60652	3212	4W-8S	E1
9100	ENGN	60805	3212	4W-10S	E5
10200	CHCG	60655	3276	4W-12S	E1
10200	CHCG	60805	3276	4W-11S	E1
10200	ENGN	60805	3276	4W-11S	E1
Sawyer Ct					
7700	GRNE	60031	2476	18W-35N	E6
8200	DRN	60561	3207	17W-9S	C3
32300	LKMR	60051	2529	28W-32N	E5
Sawyer Rd					
200	DndT	60118	2747	36W-18N	B5
400	CPVL	60110	2747	35W-18N	B5
7600	DRN	60561	3207	17W-8S	C2
Sawyer St					
9100	HTLY	60142	2691	41W-23N	E2
Saxon Ct					
1000	ELGN	60120	2855	32W-10N	C5
Saxon Ln					
600	LYVL	60048	2591	16W-28N	C6
1300	NPVL	60564	3266	28W-11S	E1
1300	NPVL	60564	3267	28W-11S	A1
Saxon Pl					
800	BFGV	60089	2754	16W-17N	D4
800	BFGV	60090	2754	16W-17N	D4
800	WLNG	60090	2754	16W-17N	D4
Saxony Dr					
900	HDPK	60035	2705	8W-21N	A7
1000	HDPK	60035	2704	8W-21N	E6
W Saxony Dr					
24000	LkvT	60046	2474	24W-37N	D1
W Saxony Ln					
27600	CNHN	60410	3672	33W-30S	A5
27600	MNKA	60410	3672	33W-30S	A5
27600	MNKA	60447	3672	33W-30S	A5
Saxony Rd					
-	HDPK	60035	2704	8W-21N	E7
-	HDPK	60035	2705	8W-21N	A6
Saybrook Ct					
700	RMVL	60446	3269	23W-14S	A6
Saybrook Ln					
800	BFGV	60089	2701	18W-20N	A7
Sayer Rd					
200	BRLT	60103	2910	30W-7N	C5
200	WynT	60103	2910	30W-7N	C5
300	HnrT	60103	2910	30W-8N	C4
E Sayles Dr					
800	PLTN	60074	2753	19W-16N	B6
Saylesville Ln					
1100	SMBG	60193	2912	25W-9N	C1
S Saylor Av					
500	EMHT	60126	3027	16W-0N	E5
Saylor St					
1000	DRGV	60516	3144	19W-7S	C6
Sayre Av					
7600	BDPK	60455	3210	8W-9S	E4
7600	BDPK	60459	3210	8W-9S	E4
7600	BDPK	60638	3210	8W-8S	E1
7600	BGVW	60455	3210	8W-9S	E4
7600	BGVW	60638	3210	8W-8S	E1
7800	BRBK	60455	3210	8W-9S	E4
8200	BGVW	60459	3210	8W-9S	E3
8700	BGVW	60453	3210	8W-10S	E6
8700	BRBK	60459	3210	8W-10S	E4
8700	OKLN	60459	3210	8W-10S	E4
9100	MNGV	60053	2864	8W-11N	E2
9300	OKLN	60455	3210	8W-10S	E6
9500	OKLN	60453	3210	8W-11S	E6
9600	CHRG	60453	3210	8W-11S	E6
9600	OKLN	60415	3210	8W-11S	E6
Sayre Av					
9700	CHRG	60415	3210	8W-11S	E7
15500	OKFT	60452	3347	8W-18S	A7
15600	BmnT	60477	3347	8W-18S	A7
15600	BmnT	60477	3425	8W-18S	A1
15600	ODPK	60462	3347	8W-18S	A7
15600	ODPK	60462	3425	8W-18S	A1
15600	ODPK	60477	3425	8W-18S	A1
16700	TYPK	60477	3425	8W-20S	A4
N Sayre Av					
1600	CHCG	60302	3030	8W-2N	E1
1600	CHCG	60707	3030	8W-2N	E1
1600	OKPK	60302	3030	8W-2N	E1
1700	CHCG	60707	2974	8W-2N	E7
2700	CHCG	60634	2974	8W-3N	E4
4200	HDHT	60706	2974	8W-5N	E1
4200	NRDG	60706	2974	8W-5N	E1
4400	HDHT	60706	2918	8W-5N	E7
4400	NRDG	60706	2918	8W-5N	E7
4700	CHCG	60706	2918	8W-5N	E7
4700	HDHT	60656	2918	8W-5N	E7
5400	CHCG	60656	2918	8W-6N	E5
6200	CHCG	60631	2918	8W-7N	E3
6500	NLES	60631	2918	8W-8N	E2
6500	NLES	60714	2918	8W-8N	E2
S Sayre Av					
-	BDPK	60638	3148	8W-8S	E7
5100	CHCG	60638	3148	8W-5S	E3
5100	StkT	60638	3148	8W-5S	E2
7300	BDPK	60638	3210	8W-8S	E1
7500	BDPK	60455	3210	8W-8S	E1
7500	BGVW	60455	3210	8W-8S	E1
7500	BGVW	60638	3210	8W-8S	E1
Sayton Rd					
10	FXLK	60020	2473	28W-36N	A4
Scanlon Dr					
600	WLNG	60090	2754	15W-18N	E2
Scarboro Dr					
1800	GLHT	60139	2969	23W-3N	B5
Scarboro Ln					
-	SMBG	60193	2859	21W-9N	D6
Scarborough Ct					
14600	OKFT	60452	3347	7W-17S	D5
W Scarborough Ct					
300	BMDL	60108	2968	25W-5N	C1
Scarborough Dr					
-	GRNE	60031	2476	18W-35N	E5
-	WrnT	60046	2476	18W-35N	E5
28500	GNOK	60044	2592	13W-28N	D6
28500	GNOK	60044	2593	12W-28N	A6
Scarborough Ln					
-	BmnT	60445	3347	6W-17S	D5
-	BmnT	60452	3347	6W-17S	D5
5500	OKFT	60452	3347	6W-17S	D5
Scarborough on Oxford					
10	RGMW	60008	2805	22W-13N	B6
Scarbrough Cir					
600	HFET	60169	2858	25W-10N	B5
Scarlet Ct					
10	BGBK	60490	3267	26W-13S	E5
1600	BRLT	60103	2910	31W-9N	A2
N Scarlet Ct					
1200	ADSN	60101	2970	20W-5N	A2
Scarlet Dr					
1500	BGBK	60490	3267	26W-13S	E5
10800	ODPK	60467	3423	13W-20S	A4
N Scarlet Dr					
1200	ADSN	60101	2970	20W-5N	A2
Scarlet Hawthorne Ct					
10	WDRG	60517	3143	21W-7S	E7
Scarlet Oak Ln					
2100	LSLE	60532	3142	24W-6S	E6
Scarlet Oaks Cir					
1000	AURA	60506	3137	37W-5S	D3
Scarlett Ter					
3400	NndT	60014	2641	32W-26N	B3
Scarlett Wy					
1500	WDSK	60098	2524	40W-32N	E5
Scarlett Oak Ct					
1700	JLET	60586	3495	33W-21S	A1
Scarlett Oak Dr					
7600	JLET	60586	3495	33W-21S	A1
Scarsdale Ct					
10	WDRG	60517	3206	20W-9S	A3
200	SMBG	60193	2859	22W-10N	C6
S Scarsdale Ct					
900	ANHT	60005	2807	17W-13N	B7
Scarsdale Rd					
10	OswT	60538	3199	37W-10S	C7
Scarth Ln					
19400	MKNA	60448	3503	13W-23S	B4
Scenic Ct					
16100	WDWH	60083	2419	16W-39N	E4
Scenic Dr					
-	BMDL	60108	2968	24W-5N	E1
200	ALGN	60102	2747	34W-20N	D1
200	TRLK	60010	2643	26W-25N	C5
8100	BRRG	60527	3208	14W-9S	E3
8100	WLSP	60480	3208	14W-9S	E3
Scenic Ln					
10	FXLK	60020	2473	28W-36N	A5
Scenic Rd					
100	FXLK	60020	2473	28W-36N	A4
Scenic Rdg					
12100	HTLY	60142	2744	42W-19N	E3
Scenicwood Ln					
3000	WDRG	60517	3205	22W-9S	C3
Schaaf Ct					
22100	RNPK	60471	3594	6W-26S	A3
Schaefer Rd					
12600	BtlT	60545	3332	45W-14S	B1
12600	LtRT	60545	3332	45W-14S	B1
N Schaefer Rd					
4000	ANHT	60004	2753	18W-18N	D2
4200	ANHT	60004	2753	18W-18N	D2
4200	VrnT	60004	2753	18W-18N	D2
4200	VrnT	60047	2753	18W-18N	D2
4200	VrnT	60089	2753	18W-18N	D2
Schaeffer Ct					
14200	HmrT	60441	3342	20W-16S	B4
Schaeffer Rd					
-	ANHT	60004	2753	18W-20N	D2
-	LGGV	60047	2700	18W-20N	D7
-	VrnT	60004	2753	18W-20N	D2
1400	LGGV	60047	2753	18W-20N	D1
1800	VrnT	60047	2753	18W-20N	D2
1800	VrnT	60089	2753	18W-20N	D2
Schaffer Ln					
700	NBRN	60010	2698	24W-22N	B5
Schaid Ct					
2600	JNBG	60050	2471	32W-34N	B7
Schaller Dr					
-	MYWD	60153	3088	10W-1S	A1
-	PvsT	60141	3088	10W-1S	A1
-	PvsT	60153	3088	10W-1S	A1
Schank Av					
28500	FmtT	60060	2589	21W-28N	E6
Schank Av					
28500	MDLN	60060	2589	21W-28N	E6
Schaumburg Ct					
100	SMBG	60193	2859	22W-10N	B6
Schaumburg Rd					
1000	HnrT	60107	2856	30W-10N	B5
1000	HnrT	60120	2856	30W-10N	B5
1000	SMWD	60107	2856	30W-10N	B5
1000	SMWD	60120	2856	30W-10N	B5
E Schaumburg Rd					
-	SMBG	60173	2860	21W-10N	A6
10	SMBG	60193	2859	22W-10N	C5
10	SMBG	60194	2859	23W-10N	A5
10	SMWD	60107	2857	27W-10N	C5
700	SMBG	60173	2859	22W-10N	D5
1000	SMBG	60193	2857	27W-10N	C5
1000	SMBG	60194	2857	27W-10N	C5
W Schaumburg Rd					
10	SMBG	60193	2859	23W-10N	A5
10	SMBG	60194	2859	23W-10N	A5
10	SMWD	60107	2856	29W-11N	D5
10	SMWD	60107	2857	28W-11N	A5
100	HnrT	60107	2856	28W-11N	E5
100	SMBG	60193	2858	26W-10N	A5
100	SMBG	60194	2858	26W-10N	A5
400	HFET	60169	2858	24W-10N	E5
400	HFET	60193	2858	24W-10N	E5
500	SMBG	60169	2858	24W-10N	E5
700	HnrT	60120	2856	29W-11N	D5
700	SMWD	60120	2856	29W-11N	D5
2000	SMBG	60193	2857	26W-10N	D6
2000	SMBG	60194	2857	26W-10N	D6
Scheel Dr					
10	DGvT	60527	3207	17W-10S	C4
Scheer Dr					
8500	TYPK	60487	3424	10W-21S	B7
S Scheer Rd					
22400	FftT	60423	3590	15W-27S	D5
22400	FKFT	60423	3590	15W-27S	D5
22400	FKFT	60451	3590	15W-27S	D5
22400	NlxT	60451	3590	15W-27S	D5
22600	NlxT	60423	3590	15W-27S	D5
23000	MhtT	60442	3590	15W-27S	D5
23000	NlxT	60442	3590	15W-27S	D5
23100	GGnT	60442	3590	15W-28S	D6
23900	GGnT	60423	3590	14W-29S	D7
23900	MhtT	60423	3590	14W-29S	D7
S Scheid Ln					
2500	NndT	60051	2586	29W-29N	B4
Scheldrup St					
2900	DRGV	60515	3084	20W-2S	B4
Schelter Rd					
100	LNSH	60069	2702	15W-22N	A3
200	LNSH	60069	2701	15W-22N	E4
500	VrnT	60069	2701	15W-22N	E4
Scheuring Pl					
1900	MTGY	60538	3199	38W-9S	A4
Schey Ct					
1700	NPVL	60565	3204	26W-9S	A3
N Schick Pl					
-	CHCG	60610	3034	0W-1N	A1
Schick Rd					
10	BRLT	60103	2966	29W-5N	D2
10	BRLT	60103	2967	27W-5N	B2
10	HRPK	60103	2967	27W-5N	B2
10	HRPK	60133	2967	27W-5N	B2
10	WynT	60103	2966	29W-5N	D2
10	WynT	60103	2967	28W-5N	B2
100	BMDL	60108	2968	25W-5N	B2
100	BmdT	60108	2968	25W-5N	B2
400	BMDL	60172	2968	26W-5N	A2
400	BmdT	60108	2967	28W-5N	B2
400	BmdT	60133	2967	28W-5N	A2
400	BmdT	60172	2968	26W-5N	A2
500	ADSN	60143	2970	20W-5N	A1
500	BmdT	60133	2968	25W-5N	A2
500	BmdT	60143	2970	20W-5N	A1
500	WynT	60133	2967	26W-5N	D2
Schick Rd CO-50					
100	HRPK	60133	2967	27W-5N	D2
400	BMDL	60108	2968	26W-5N	A2
400	BMDL	60172	2968	26W-5N	A2
400	BmdT	60108	2967	28W-5N	A2
400	BmdT	60133	2967	28W-5N	A2
400	BmdT	60172	2968	26W-5N	A2
500	BmdT	60108	2968	25W-5N	A2
500	BmdT	60133	2968	25W-5N	A2
500	WynT	60133	2967	26W-5N	D2
E Schick Rd					
100	BMDL	60108	2969	22W-5N	B1
W Schick Rd					
-	BmdT	60108	2968	25W-5N	B1
100	BMDL	60108	2968	24W-5N	D1
100	BMDL	60108	2969	23W-5N	A1
400	BMDL	60172	2968	25W-5N	B1
Schiedler Dr					
1200	BTVA	60510	3078	34W-2S	E4
1200	BtvT	60510	3078	34W-2S	E4
W Schiedler Dr					
1000	BTVA	60510	3078	34W-2S	D4
1000	BtvT	60510	3078	34W-2S	D4
Schierhorn Ln					
3300	FNPK	60131	2973	11W-4N	D4
Schiller Av					
200	AURA	60505	3138	34W-7S	D7
1900	WLMT	60091	2812	5W-13N	B5
Schiller Blvd					
9300	FNPK	60131	2973	13W-3N	A4
Schiller St					
10	LKZH	60047	2698	23W-23N	E1
600	ELGN	60123	2854	34W-12N	D2
600	ITSC	60143	2914	19W-6N	D6
E Schiller St					
10	CHCG	60610	3034	0E-1N	C1
100	EMHT	60126	3027	16W-1N	E2
100	EMHT	60126	3028	15W-1N	A2
200	VLPK	60181	3027	17W-1N	B1
200	YkTp	60181	3027	17W-1N	B1
N Schiller St					
200	PLTN	60067	2752	20W-16N	E7
W Schiller St					
-	VLPK	60181	3027	18W-1N	A1
10	CHCG	60610	3034	0W-1N	B1
1900	CHCG	60622	3033	2W-1N	B1
Schillerstrom Ct					
1700	WHTN	60187	3082	23W-2S	E3
Schilling Av					
1000	CHHT	60411	3507	1W-25S	E6
1200	CHHT	60411	3508	1W-25S	A6
1400	CHHT	60411	3596	1W-25S	A1
1500	CHHT	60411	3595	1W-25S	E1
Schilling Dr					
700	DYR	46311	3598		E3
N Schilling Rd					
6400	CHCG	60666	2917	13W-8N	A3
Schillinger Ct					
3600	WldT	60564	3266	28W-11S	E1
Schillinger Dr					
10	WldT	60564	3266	29W-11S	D2
700	NPVL	60564	3266	29W-12S	D3
Schimdt Ct					
-	PLNO	60545	3260	45W-13S	C6
Schimdt St					
-	PLNO	60545	3260	45W-13S	C6
Schindel Dr					
600	AURA	60505	3200	34W-8S	D3
Schirra Ct					
1500	EGVV	60007	2913	21W-9N	E1
E Schirra Dr					
800	PLTN	60074	2753	19W-16N	B7
N Schirra Dr					
500	PLTN	60074	2753	19W-16N	B7
W Schlesser Dr					
28600	LKMR	60051	2529	28W-31N	E6
Schlick Av					
-	BmdT	60157	2913	22W-7N	D5
W Schlosser Ct					
15000	NptT	60083	2420	15W-38N	B7
15000	WDWH	60083	2420	15W-38N	B7
Schmale Ct					
1800	CLSM	60188	2968	24W-3N	D5
1800	GLHT	60139	2968	24W-3N	D5
1800	GLHT	60188	2968	24W-3N	D5
Schmale Rd					
-	BMDL	60188	2968	24W-4N	D4
-	CLSM	60108	2968	24W-4N	D4
10	BMDL	60108	2968	24W-3N	D5
10	BMDL	60139	2968	24W-3N	D5
10	GLHT	60108	2968	24W-3N	D5
10	GLHT	60139	2968	24W-2N	D7
100	CLSM	60188	2968	24W-2N	D7
100	CLSM	60188	3024	24W-2N	D1
100	GLHT	60188	2968	24W-2N	D7
400	CLSM	60139	3024	24W-2N	D1
400	GLHT	60139	3024	24W-2N	D1
400	GLHT	60188	3024	24W-2N	D1
1800	CLSM	60139	2968	24W-3N	D5
Schmale Rd CO-36					
-	BMDL	60188	2968	24W-4N	D4
-	CLSM	60108	2968	24W-4N	D4
10	BMDL	60108	2968	24W-3N	D5
10	BMDL	60139	2968	24W-3N	D5
10	GLHT	60108	2968	24W-3N	D5
10	GLHT	60139	2968	24W-2N	D7
100	CLSM	60188	2968	24W-2N	D7
100	CLSM	60188	3024	24W-2N	D1
100	GLHT	60188	2968	24W-2N	D7
400	CLSM	60139	3024	24W-2N	D1
400	GLHT	60139	3024	24W-2N	D1
400	GLHT	60188	3024	24W-2N	D1
1800	CLSM	60139	2968	24W-3N	D5
N Schmale Rd					
100	CLSM	60139	3024	24W-2N	D1
100	CLSM	60188	3024	24W-2N	D1
100	GLHT	60139	3024	24W-2N	D1
100	GLHT	60188	3024	24W-2N	D1
N Schmale Rd CO-36					
100	CLSM	60139	3024	24W-2N	D1
100	CLSM	60188	3024	24W-2N	D1
100	GLHT	60139	3024	24W-2N	D1
100	GLHT	60188	3024	24W-2N	D1
S Schmale Rd					
100	CLSM	60188	3024	24W-1N	D2
100	GLHT	60188	3024	24W-1N	D2
200	MltT	60188	3024	24W-1N	D3
400	WHTN	60188	3024	24W-1N	C3
S Schmale Rd CO-36					
100	CLSM	60188	3024	24W-1N	D3
100	GLHT	60188	3024	24W-1N	D2
200	MltT	60188	3024	24W-1N	D3
400	WHTN	60188	3024	24W-1N	C3
Schmidt Dr					
10	DYR	46311	3598		C4
100	HPSR	60140	2795	47W-15N	D4
Schmidt Ln					
5600	OswT	60560	3334	40W-15S	D3
N Schmidt Ln					
900	BDWD	60408	3942	31W-40S	A3
W Schmidt Ln					
100	BDWD	60408	3942	31W-40S	A4
N Schmidt Rd					
400	BGBK	60440	3204	24W-11S	E7
600	BDWD	60408	3942	31W-40S	A4
800	BGBK	60440	3268	24W-14S	E6
800	RMVL	60440	3268	24W-14S	E6
800	RMVL	60446	3268	24W-14S	E6
S Schmidt Rd					
100	BGBK	60440	3268	24W-12S	E3
Schmidt St					
8100	BtnT	60081	2414	30W-40N	A3
Schneider Av					
1100	OKPK	60302	3030	8W-1N	D2
1100	RVFT	60302	3030	8W-1N	D2
1100	RVFT	60305	3030	8W-1N	D2
Schneider Ct					
100	NARA	60542	3138	35W-4S	C1
Schneider Dr					
600	SEGN	60177	2908	34W-9N	C2
900	SEGN	60177	2854	34W-9N	C7
W Schneider Ln					
2900	MchT	60050	2471	31W-34N	C7
3000	JNBG	60050	2471	32W-34N	C7
Schober Ct					
10	CRY	60013	2695	31W-23N	D1
Schock Dr					
800	SRWD	60404	3496	29W-22S	D3
Schoenbeck Rd					
10	WLNG	60090	2754	16W-17N	E6
300	WLNG	60004	2754	16W-17N	E6
700	PTHT	60070	2754	16W-17N	E6
N Schoenbeck Rd					
-	ANHT	60056	2807	16W-14N	E4
-	MPPT	60004	2807	16W-14N	E4
10	MPPT	60056	2807	16W-15N	E3
10	PTHT	60070	2807	15W-15N	E3
700	ANHT	60004	2807	15W-15N	E1
800	PTHT	60004	2807	15W-15N	E1
1000	PTHT	60070	2754	15W-16N	E7
1200	WLNG	60004	2754	15W-16N	E7
1200	WLNG	60090	2754	15W-16N	E7
2100	ANHT	60004	2754	16W-16N	E7
2200	PTHT	60004	2754	16W-16N	E7
Schoenherr Av					
1400	BGBK	60490	3267	26W-13S	E5
1400	BGBK	60490	3268	25W-13S	A5
Schoger Dr					
10	NPVL	60564	3202	31W-10S	A6
10	WldT	60564	3202	31W-10S	A5
100	WldT	60564	3201	31W-10S	E5
200	AURA	60503	3201	31W-10S	E5
200	AURA	60564	3201	31W-10S	E5

STREET Block City ZIP Map# CGS Grid

Schomer Av
700 AURA 60505 3200 35W-8S C2
Schomer Ct
1900 AraT 60505 3138 34W-5S D2
1900 AURA 60505 3138 34W-5S D2
Schomer Ln
10 LtRT 60545 3259 46W-12S E3
10 LtRT 60545 3260 46W-12S A3
10 PLNO 60545 3259 46W-12S E3
Schomer Rd
600 AraT 60504 3138 34W-5S C2
600 AraT 60505 3138 34W-5S C2
600 AURA 60504 3138 34W-5S C2
700 AURA 60505 3138 34W-5S C2
Schonback Ct
- BTVA 60510 3077 37W-2S B3
- BtvT 60510 3077 37W-2S B3
School Av
400 YkTp 60148 3084 18W-1S E2
700 MTSN 60443 3506 5W-25S B7
School Ct
- FXLK 60020 2473 27W-37N B3
200 MRGO 60152 2634 49W-26N C3
800 LMBD 60148 3026 18W-0S E6
900 RDLK 60073 2531 24W-33N D2
School Dr
- MHRY 60051 2528 31W-33N D3
- NHBK 60062 2810 10W-16N A1
100 RDLK 60073 2531 24W-33N D3
500 FRGV 60021 2696 29W-22N B3
2100 RGMW 60008 2806 19W-14N C5
3500 CCHL 60429 3426 4W-21S D6
3500 CCHL 60478 3426 4W-21S D6
3500 HLCT 60429 3426 4W-21S D6
3500 HLCT 60478 3426 4W-21S E6
3600 BmnT 60430 3426 4W-21S D6
3600 CCHL 60430 3426 4W-21S D6
E School Ln
200 PTHT 60070 2808 15W-14N B3
S School Ln
100 PTHT 60070 2808 15W-14N A4
200 MPPT 60056 2808 15W-14N A4
200 PTHT 60056 2808 15W-14N A4
School Rd
100 SRWD 60404 3496 29W-24S C5
300 CmpT 60175 2962 40W-4N C4
4300 RGWD 60072 2470 34W-36N D3
School St
- DRFD 60015 2703 11W-21N C6
- MYWD 60153 3029 11W-0N E5
10 GNVA 60134 3020 34W-1N D3
10 GYLK 60030 2532 21W-33N D3
10 YkTp 60148 3026 18W-0S E7
10 YkTp 60148 3084 18W-1S E1
100 LYVL 60048 2591 16W-29N D4
100 MYWD 60153 3030 10W-0N A5
100 WDDL 60191 2915 18W-6N A6
100 WMTN 60481 3853 28W-38S C7
200 WDDL 60191 2914 18W-6N E6
400 LMBD 60148 3026 18W-0S E7
400 WYNE 60184 2965 32W-5N D2
500 MNSR 46321 3430 D6
900 LSLE 60532 3143 23W-5S E4
1600 CHHT 60411 3596 1W-25S A1
2800 FSMR 60422 3507 3W-22S A2
3800 OKBK 60515 3084 18W-3S E6
3800 OKBK 60523 3084 18W-3S E6
3800 YkTp 60515 3084 18W-3S E6
3900 DGvT 60515 3084 18W-4S E6
5900 BKLY 60163 3028 14W-0N C5
5900 OKFT 60452 3347 7W-18S C6
8100 WLSP 60525 3208 13W-9S E3
8200 WLSP 60480 3208 13W-9S E3
8500 MNGV 60053 2865 7W-10N B4
15900 SHLD 60473 3428 0E-18S E1
17700 LNSG 60438 3430 3E-21S A6
E School St
10 NPVL 60540 3141 26W-6S E5
N School St
- PTHT 60070 2808 15W-15N A3
10 CRY 60013 2695 31W-23N D1
10 DMND 60416 3941 33W-39S C2
10 MPPT 60056 2808 15W-13N A7
100 BDWD 60408 3942 31W-40S A4
800 ADSN 60101 2970 18W-4N E3
7300 NLES 60714 2864 8W-9N E7
S School St
10 CRY 60013 2695 31W-23N D1
10 DMND 60416 3941 33W-40S C2
10 MPPT 60056 2808 15W-12N A7
100 BDWD 60408 3942 31W-41S A6
100 GDLY 60407 4030 32W-43S D3
300 MPPT 60056 2862 15W-12N A1
600 LMBD 60148 3026 18W-0S E6
900 DSPN 60016 2862 15W-11N A3
900 MPPT 60016 2862 15W-11N A2
13600 RVDL 60827 3350 0W-16S B3
14500 DLTN 60419 3350 0W-16S B3
14500 DLTN 60827 3350 0W-16S B4
W School St
10 GNWD 60425 3508 0E-22S D1
10 VLPK 60181 3027 18W-0N A4
100 LtRT 60545 3259 47W-14S D7
100 PLNO 60545 3259 47W-14S C7
300 LMBD 60148 3026 18W-0N E4
300 LMBD 60181 3026 18W-0N E4
300 VLPK 60181 3026 18W-0N E4
900 CHCG 60657 2977 2W-4N B3
1900 CHCG 60618 2977 2W-4N B3
2900 CHCG 60618 2976 3W-4N E3
4000 CHCG 60641 2976 5W-4N B3
4700 CHCG 60641 2975 7W-4N C3
5500 CHCG 60634 2975 7W-4N B3
6700 CHCG 60634 2974 10W-4N B3
Schoolgate Ct
500 NLNX 60451 3589 17W-25S D1
Schoolgate Rd
900 NLNX 60451 3589 17W-26S D2
School House Ct
10 PKFT 60466 3595 3W-26S B3
School House Ln
1800 AURA 60506 3137 38W-7S B7
Schoolhouse Ln
500 BbyT 60134 3018 39W-0N D4
S Schoolhouse Ln
14300 LktT 60441 3341 21W-17S E5
School House Rd
100 YKVL 60560 3333 43W-15S C3
School House Rd SR-126
100 YKVL 60560 3333 43W-15S C3
N Schoolhouse Rd
100 NLNX 60451 3502 15W-25S B7
100 NlxT 60451 3502 15W-25S B7
500 MKNA 60448 3502 15W-24S A5
500 MKNA 60451 3502 15W-24S B5
19600 NlxT 60448 3502 15W-23S A4
S Schoolhouse Rd
100 NLNX 60451 3502 15W-25S B7
100 NlxT 60451 3502 15W-25S B7
700 NLNX 60451 3590 16W-27S B5
700 NlxT 60451 3590 16W-27S B5
2900 MhtT 60442 3590 15W-27S B5
2900 MhtT 60451 3590 15W-27S B5
2900 NlxT 60442 3590 15W-27S B5
19100 MKNA 60448 3503 13W-24S B5
19700 FftT 60448 3503 13W-24S B5
Schooner Ct
900 RLKP 60073 2532 22W-34N B1
1500 ZION 60099 2362 11W-41N D7
Schooner Dr
600 NLNX 60451 3502 15W-25S C7
Schooner Ln
100 LKBN 60010 2696 28W-23N E1
100 LKBN 60010 2697 28W-23N A1
600 EGVV 60007 2913 22W-8N D2
600 EGVV 60193 2913 22W-8N D2
1400 HRPK 60133 2967 27W-4N D3
Schooner Pt
600 SMBG 60194 2859 23W-10N A5
Schoors Ln
100 RdlT 53181 2354 C2
100 TNLK 53181 2354 C2
Schorie Av
100 JltT 60433 3499 21W-24S E6
W Schorsch St
6500 CHCG 60634 2975 8W-4N A3
W Schrader Dr
3400 CHCG 60624 3032 4W-0N D4
Schrader Ln
2300 NARA 60542 3076 39W-3S E7
Schramm Ct
1400 WTMT 60559 3144 18W-7S E6
Schramm Dr
1400 WTMT 60559 3144 18W-7S E6
Schreiber Av
10 ROSL 60172 2913 23W-8N A3
100 ROSL 60172 2912 23W-8N E3
W Schreiber Av
1600 CHCG 60626 2921 2W-8N C2
3900 LNWD 60712 2920 4W-8N B2
6600 CHCG 60631 2919 8W-8N A2
7100 CHCG 60631 2918 8W-8N D2
W Schriber Av
800 JLET 60435 3498 25W-22S C2
S Schroeder Av
500 PtnT 60468 3860 9W-37S E4
500 PTON 60468 3860 9W-37S E4
W Schroeder Dr
15100 HmrT 60491 3420 19W-19S E2
S Schroeder Ln
1600 NndT 60050 2584 33W-30N E2
Schrum Rd
10 CTCY 60409 3430 4E-19S C2
10 HMND 46324 3430 4E-19S C2
Schryver Av
100 WDSK 60098 2581 41W-30N C2
Schubert Av
10400 FNPK 60131 2973 13W-3N A5
10400 FNPK 60164 2973 13W-3N A5
10400 LydT 60131 2973 13W-3N A5
10400 LydT 60164 2973 13W-3N A5
10600 LydT 60164 2972 13W-3N E5
E Schubert Av
10 GLHT 60139 2968 23W-3N E6
100 GLHT 60139 2969 23W-3N A6
W Schubert Av
10 GLHT 60139 2968 24W-3N D6
100 CLSM 60188 2968 24W-3N D6
100 GLHT 60188 2968 24W-3N D6
600 CHCG 60614 2978 0W-3N A5
700 CHCG 60614 2977 1W-3N E5
2300 CHCG 60647 2977 3W-3N A5
3300 CHCG 60647 2976 5W-3N B5
3900 CHCG 60639 2976 5W-3N B5
4800 CHCG 60639 2975 7W-3N B5
6700 CHCG 60707 2974 8W-3N E5
6700 CHCG 60707 2975 8W-3N A5
7200 EDPK 60707 2974 9W-3N D5
Schubert Ct
300 WHTN 60187 3082 24W-2S C4
1700 GLHT 60139 2968 24W-3N D6
Schubert Dr
- TroT 60436 3584 30W-26S C3
24100 TroT 60404 3584 30W-26S C3
Schubert Ln
600 WDSK 60098 2524 41W-33N E3
N Schubert St
100 PLTN 60067 2753 20W-16N A7
Schuett St
300 ALGN 60102 2747 33W-20N D1
Schuette Cir
11600 DrrT 60098 2525 40W-31N A7
Schuette Dr
900 WDSK 60098 2524 40W-31N E6
900 WDSK 60098 2525 40W-31N A6
3700 WRLK 60097 2469 38W-35N A5
Schuldt Dr
100 LKZH 60047 2698 23W-23N D2
Schuler Dr
1700 BTVA 60510 3021 33W-0S A6
Schulte St
200 DYR 46311 3598 D2
Schultz Dr
- LNSG 60438 3430 4E-21S C7
N Schultz Dr
3200 LNSG 60438 3430 4E-21S B7
S Schultz Dr
3200 LNSG 60438 3430 4E-21S B7
Schultz Ln
23100 BlmT 60466 3595 2W-28S D6
23100 CteT 60475 3595 2W-28S D6
Schultz Rd
5500 HtdT 60033 2464 48W-37N E1
6100 AdnT 60033 2406 48W-38N E7
6100 HtdT 60033 2406 48W-38N E7
Schultz St
400 LMNT 60439 3270 19W-14S E6
900 LMNT 60439 3271 18W-14S A6
W Schultz St
25400 WldT 60585 3265 31W-11S D2
Schumacher Dr
1500 BGBK 60490 3267 26W-13S E5
2000 NPVL 60540 3202 29W-8S E1
Schumann St
- GwdT 60098 2524 41W-33N E3
- WDSK 60098 2524 41W-33N E3
Schuster Ln
10 BtvT 60510 3077 37W-3S C5
Schuster St
1800 JltT 60433 3499 21W-25S E7
1900 JltT 60433 3500 21W-25S A7
Schwab St
100 TNTN 60476 3428 0E-21S E6
Schwartz Av
4400 LSLE 60532 3142 23W-5S E2
4400 LslT 60532 3142 23W-4S E1
Schweitzer Rd
16800 JknT 60421 3587 21W-27S E6
16800 JknT 60421 3588 21W-27S A6
16800 JknT 60442 3588 21W-27S A6
16800 JLET 60421 3587 21W-27S E6
16800 JLET 60421 3588 21W-27S A6
16800 JLET 60433 3587 21W-27S E6
16800 JltT 60421 3587 21W-27S E6
16800 JltT 60421 3588 21W-27S A6
16800 MhtT 60421 3588 21W-27S A6
16800 MhtT 60442 3588 21W-27S A6
16800 NlxT 60421 3588 21W-27S A6
16800 NlxT 60442 3588 21W-27S A6
17600 JknT 60433 3587 23W-27S E6
18700 JLET 60436 3587 23W-28S A6
18700 JltT 60433 3587 23W-28S A6
Schweizer Rd
- JltT 60436 3586 25W-27S B6
20800 JknT 60421 3585 26W-27S E6
20800 JknT 60421 3586 26W-27S A6
20800 JLET 60421 3585 26W-27S E6
20800 JltT 60421 3585 26W-27S E6
20800 JltT 60421 3586 26W-27S A6
20800 TroT 60421 3585 26W-27S E6
W Schweizer Rd
- JknT 60421 3588 20W-27S B5
- JknT 60442 3588 20W-27S B5
- JltT 60421 3588 20W-27S B5
- MhtT 60421 3588 20W-27S B5
- MhtT 60442 3588 20W-27S B5
- NlxT 60421 3588 20W-27S B5
- NlxT 60442 3588 20W-27S B5
19200 JknT 60421 3586 24W-27S D6
19200 JknT 60436 3586 24W-27S D6
19200 JLET 60421 3586 24W-27S D6
19200 JLET 60421 3587 24W-28S A6
19200 JLET 60436 3586 24W-27S D6
19200 JLET 60436 3587 24W-28S A6
19200 JltT 60421 3586 24W-27S D6
19200 JltT 60436 3586 24W-27S D6
22200 CnhT 60421 3585 27W-28S C6
22200 JLET 60421 3585 27W-28S C6
N Schwerman Rd
26700 FmtT 60060 2644 23W-26N E2
26700 FmtT 60084 2644 23W-26N E2
W Schwerman Rd
- FmtT 60047 2645 21W-26N C3
22600 FmtT 60060 2645 22W-26N B3
22600 HNWD 60047 2645 22W-26N B3
22600 HNWD 60060 2645 22W-26N B3
23000 FmtT 60060 2644 23W-26N E2
23000 FmtT 60084 2644 23W-26N E2
Science Dr
- CHCG 60637 3153 2E-6S B3
Science Rd
10 GNWD 60425 3508 0W-22S C2
Scioto Dr
25700 MONE 60449 3683 6W-31S B5
Scot Ct
900 GRNE 60031 2534 16W-33N E4
Scot Dr
200 NpvT 60563 3140 30W-5S C3
Scotch Ln
3000 RVWD 60015 2755 13W-20N D1
Scotch Rd
300 OswT 60543 3265 33W-13S A6
300 WldT 60543 3265 33W-13S A6
300 WldT 60585 3265 33W-13S A6
Scotch Pine Ct
2000 LKPT 60441 3419 22W-20S D4
Scotch Pine Dr
6400 TYPK 60477 3425 8W-22S B7
Scotch Pine Ln
2100 NHBK 60062 2756 11W-16N D7
Scotch Pine Tr
6800 DRN 60561 3145 18W-7S A7
Scotdale Rd
10 LGPK 60525 3087 12W-2S B3
10 PvsT 60525 3087 12W-2S B3
Scoter Ct
12800 PNFD 60585 3339 28W-15S A1
Scotland Ct
14200 GNOK 60048 2535 14W-31N D7
Scotland Rd
400 LKMR 60051 2529 29W-31N C6
400 NndT 60051 2529 29W-31N C6
Scots Cir
9900 LKWD 60014 2638 38W-24N D7
Scots Ct
500 IVNS 60067 2752 22W-16N B6
Scots Ln
7100 LKWD 60014 2639 38W-24N A6
Scotsglen
- NLNX 60451 3590 15W-26S B3
Scotsglen Rd
15500 ODPK 60462 3345 13W-18S A7
15600 ODPK 60462 3423 13W-18S A1
Scott Av
- BNHM 60633 3352 3E-16S A3
100 GLNC 60093 2759 5W-16N A6
100 SchT 60177 2908 35W-7N B6
200 SEGN 60177 2908 35W-7N B6
200 WNKA 60093 2759 5W-16N A7
400 GNEN 60137 3025 21W-0N E4
400 MltT 60137 3025 21W-0N E4
500 GYLK 60030 2532 21W-33N D4
1000 CHHT 60411 3507 2W-25S E7
1100 WNKA 60093 2758 6W-16N D7
1400 CHHT 60411 3595 2W-25S E1
2900 JNBG 60050 2528 31W-34N C1
2900 McHT 60050 2528 31W-34N C1
N Scott Av
20700 CbaT 60010 2697 26W-20N D7
20800 BRTN 60010 2697 26W-20N D7
Scott Blvd
1500 GNVA 60134 3020 36W-1N A3
Scott Cir
1900 CPVL 60110 2748 32W-18N D5
5100 LSLE 60563 3142 24W-5S C3
Scott Cres
1500 FSMR 60422 3507 3W-23S A3
Scott Ct
- HmrT 60441 3420 20W-18S B1
100 WTMT 60559 3145 17W-6S B4
200 BRLT 60103 2911 28W-7N A6
400 ROSL 60172 2913 23W-8N B5
600 FXLK 60041 2473 26W-34N D7
700 NlxT 60451 3502 15W-24S C5
1100 CLSM 60188 2967 26W-4N E4
1100 NPVL 60540 3204 26W-7S A1
2300 RLKB 60073 2475 21W-36N C4
2900 LSLE 60563 3142 24W-5S C3
4400 AlqT 60014 2640 33W-25N E4
6300 TYPK 60477 3425 7W-20S B4
14500 PNFD 60544 3337 31W-17S E6
17200 LktT 60403 3417 26W-20S E5
W Scott Ct
13100 BHPK 60083 2421 13W-39N A6
Scott Dr
- BDVW 60141 3087 10W-1S E1
- BDVW 60155 3087 10W-1S E1
- OMFD 60461 3506 4W-25S E6
- OMFD 60461 3507 3W-24S A6
- PvsT 60141 3087 10W-1S E1
- PvsT 60141 3088 10W-1S A1
100 EDND 60118 2801 32W-16N C2
200 PvsT 60141 3029 10W-1S E7
200 PvsT 60141 3030 10W-1S A7
400 BMDL 60108 2968 25W-4N D2
400 HmrT 60441 3420 20W-18S B1
600 ELGN 60123 2854 35W-12N B2
600 SMBG 60193 2913 22W-8N C1
10300 HTLY 60142 2692 39W-22N C4
10400 LIHL 60142 2692 39W-22N C4
22000 RNPK 60471 3594 6W-26S A3
25100 PNFD 60544 3337 31W-17S E6
W Scott Dr
3600 ALSP 60803 3276 4W-14S D6
Scott Ln
- ANTH 60002 2359 20W-42N A7
500 RMVL 60446 3339 27W-18S D7
500 RMVL 60446 3417 27W-18S D1
2200 AURA 60502 3079 32W-3S B7
5200 OKLN 60453 3211 6W-11S E7
6100 AlqT 60014 2640 33W-25N E4
6100 NndT 60014 2640 33W-25N E4
6600 AlqT 60014 2641 33W-25N A5
6600 BRLT 60103 2911 27W-8N C3
6600 HRPK 60133 2911 27W-8N C3
14000 ODPK 60462 3346 9W-16S D4
Scott Lp
10 HDPK 60035 2650 9W-24N D7
Scott Pl
800 LYVL 60048 2592 15W-28N A7
Scott Rd
10 BbyT 60554 3075 43W-4S A7
10 BRkT 60554 3134 45W-4S C2
10 SgrT 60554 3075 43W-4S A7
10 SgrT 60554 3134 45W-4S C2
100 CbaT 60010 2698 25W-22N A5
100 NBRN 60010 2698 25W-22N A5
2100 NHBK 60062 2757 10W-16N A7
Scott Rd CO-48
10 BRkT 60554 3134 45W-4S C2
10 SgrT 60554 3134 45W-4S D2
W Scott Rd
10 CbaT 60010 2697 26W-21N D5
25800 NBRN 60010 2697 25W-22N E5
Scott St
- MDLN 60060 2646 20W-27N B1
- PLNO 60545 3259 47W-13S C5
10 EGvT 60007 2861 17W-10N B5
10 EGVV 60007 2861 17W-10N B5
200 LKFT 60045 2650 10W-27N A2
200 MTGY 60538 3199 37W-9S C4
200 WLNG 60090 2754 16W-17N D5
400 ALGN 60102 2747 33W-20N E1
800 DndT 60102 2747 33W-20N E2
1600 GLHT 60139 2969 23W-3N A6
2000 LydT 60164 2973 12W-2N B7
2000 MLPK 60160 2973 12W-2N B7
2000 MLPK 60164 2973 12W-2N B7
2300 FNPK 60131 2973 12W-3N B6
3600 FNPK 60176 2973 12W-4N B3
3600 SRPK 60176 2973 12W-4N B3
4300 OKFT 60452 3426 5W-19S B2
4800 SRPK 60176 2917 12W-6N B7
20000 MKNA 60448 3503 13W-24S A5
E Scott St
10 CHCG 60610 3034 0E-1N C1
10 CHCG 60611 3034 0E-1N C1
N Scott St
- DSPN 60018 2917 12W-7N B3
10 JLET 60432 3499 23W-23S A4
10 JLET 60433 3499 23W-23S A5
100 WHTN 60187 3024 24W-0N D5
6000 RSMT 60018 2917 12W-7N B3
43300 AntT 60002 2356 26W-43N D4
N Scott St SR-53
10 JLET 60432 3499 23W-23S A4
10 JLET 60433 3499 23W-23S A5
N Scott St US-6
10 JLET 60432 3499 23W-23S A5
10 JLET 60433 3499 23W-23S A5
S Scott St
300 EMHT 60126 3027 17W-0N C3
2200 DSPN 60018 2863 12W-9N B7
2300 DSPN 60018 2917 12W-8N B1
W Scott St
600 CHCG 60610 3034 0W-1N A1
W Scott Ter
2000 MPPT 60056 2861 17W-12N B1
Scottdale Cir
1500 WHTN 60187 3082 23W-3S E5
1700 WHTN 60187 3083 23W-3S A5
2100 MltT 60137 3083 23W-3S A5
2100 MltT 60187 3083 23W-3S A5
Scottdale Ct
2200 WHTN 60187 3083 23W-3S A5
Scott Foresman Rd
- GNVW 60025 2810 8W-14N D5
Scottish Pine Ct
2900 BFGV 60089 2701 17W-23N B2
Scottlynne Dr
2800 PKRG 60068 2863 11W-9N C7
Scotts Ct
300 BGBK 60440 3205 22W-10S C5
Scottsbridge Rd
2800 DPgT 60565 3203 26W-10S E6
2800 NPVL 60565 3203 26W-10S E6
S Scottsdale Av
8100 CHCG 60652 3212 5W-9S A2
Scottsdale Cir
3400 NPVL 60564 3202 30W-10S B6
Scottsdale Ct
3300 NPVL 60564 3202 30W-10S B6
Scottsdale Ln
1000 JLET 60432 3500 20W-22S C2
Scottsvale Av
600 ANHT 60004 2807 16W-14N D4
Scottswood Rd
10 RVSD 60546 3088 10W-3S B6
Scotty Av
700 ALGN 60102 2694 34W-21N C6
700 LIHL 60102 2694 34W-21N C6
700 LIHL 60156 2694 34W-21N C6
Scotty Ln
400 DYR 46311 3598 D4
Scoville Av
1200 BRWN 60304 3031 8W-1S A7
1200 BRWN 60402 3031 8W-1S A7
1200 OKPK 60304 3031 8W-1S A7
3100 BRWN 60402 3089 8W-3S A4
3900 SKNY 60402 3089 8W-4S A7
N Scoville Av
100 OKPK 60302 3031 8W-0N A3
S Scoville Av
300 OKPK 60302 3031 8W-0N A5
500 OKPK 60304 3031 8W-0S A5
1100 BRWN 60304 3031 8W-0S A7
1100 BRWN 60402 3031 8W-0S A7
E Scranton Av
10 LKBF 60044 2593 10W-28N E6
100 LKBF 60044 2594 10W-28N A6
W Scranton Av
10 LKBF 60044 2593 11W-28N E6
W Scranton Av SR-176
- LKBF 60044 2593 11W-28N E6
Scribner St
200 JLET 60432 3499 22W-23S D4
200 JltT 60432 3499 22W-23S D4
Scully Ct
200 SMBG 60193 2859 23W-10N A6
Scully Dr
- MHRY 60050 2527 34W-33N D3
10 SMBG 60193 2859 23W-10N A6
N Scully Dr
1200 MHRY 60050 2527 34W-33N D3
S Sea Biscuit Ct
13900 HMGN 60491 3344 15W-16S C3
Sea Biscuit Ln
1300 HRPK 60133 2911 26W-6N E6
Seabrook Ct
400 LslT 60540 3142 24W-5S C4
Seabury Cir
1200 CLSM 60188 2967 27W-4N C4
Seabury Rd
10 BGBK 60440 3269 22W-11S D1
Seacrest Ln
800 BRLT 60103 2911 27W-7N B5
Seadragon Ct
4100 NCHI 60088 2593 11W-31N D1
Sea Eagle Ct
40300 AntT 60002 2416 23W-40N E3
Seafarer Dr
200 TDLK 60030 2533 18W-34N D1
600 SMBG 60193 2912 24W-9N D1
Seagull Ln
11700 PSHT 60463 3274 9W-13S C5
E Sea Horse Dr
10 LkeC 60085 2537 9W-34N B1
10 WKGN 60085 2480 9W-34N C7
10 WKGN 60085 2537 9W-34N B1
Seahorse Pl
4100 NCHI 60088 2593 12W-31N C1
Sealmaster Dr
- AraT 60502 3139 33W-4S A1
- AraT 60504 3139 33W-4S A1
- AURA 60502 3139 33W-4S A1
- AURA 60504 3139 33W-4S A1
Seaman Rd
10100 HbnT 60034 2351 39W-42N C6
Sean Dr
500 SRWD 60404 3496 30W-23S C4
17500 ODPK 60467 3423 13W-21S A6
Seanor Av
200 WnfT 60185 3022 29W-1N D4
Seapines Dr
7800 ODPK 60462 3346 9W-18S C7
Searl St
- PLNO 60545 3260 45W-13S C5
Searle Pkwy
4800 SKOK 60076 2865 6W-10N E5
4800 SKOK 60077 2865 6W-10N E5
N Sears Blvd
32800 GYLK 60030 2533 18W-32N E4
32800 WrnT 60030 2533 18W-33N E3
Sears Cir
- ELBN 60119 3017 43W-0N B4
Sears Ln
500 WHTN 60187 3024 24W-0S D6
Sears Pkwy
- HFET 60118 2802 30W-13N B5
- HFET 60192 2802 30W-13N B5
Sears Rd
13600 LtRT 60545 3196 46W-10S A7
13600 LtRT 60545 3259 47W-11S C1
Sears St
100 PLNO 60545 3259 47W-13S D6
Seaside Ct
800 SMBG 60193 2912 24W-9N D1
Seasons Ridge Blvd
- MTGY 60538 3199 36W-10S E5
- MTGY 60538 3200 36W-10S A5
Seaton Ct
- RDLK 60073 2531 23W-32N D6
200 LKZH 60047 2698 23W-22N E4
400 INCK 60061 2647 17W-25N A5
1700 AURA 60503 3201 32W-10S C5
Seaton Dr
400 RDLK 60073 2531 23W-32N E6
Seaton Ln
1600 ELGN 60123 2907 36W-8N E3
1600 SMBG 60194 2858 25W-10N B5
Seaton St
1300 ELBN 60119 3017 43W-0N B5
Seaver Ln
2100 HFET 60169 2857 26W-12N E2
2100 HFET 60169 2858 26W-12N A2
Seavey Rd
10 BbyT 60119 3075 43W-3S A5
10 BbyT 60506 3076 39W-2S E5
10 BbyT 60510 3076 39W-2S E5
10 BbyT 60554 3075 42W-3S D5
10 BbyT 60554 3076 39W-2S E5
10 NARA 60510 3076 39W-2S E5
200 BtvT 60510 3076 38W-2S E5
200 BtvT 60510 3077 38W-3S A5
Seaview Ct
1000 SMBG 60193 2912 24W-9N E1
Seaview Dr
1800 AURA 60503 3201 31W-10S D6
3800 HRPK 60133 2967 27W-4N D3
Seawolf Pl
- NCHI 60088 2593 11W-31N D1
Sebastian Ct
4800 NPVL 60564 3266 28W-12S E4
Sebastian Dr
- GwdT 60098 2524 40W-32N E4
4700 NPVL 60564 3266 28W-12S E4
Sebby Ln
100 LKZH 60047 2698 23W-23N E1

STREET Block	City	ZIP	Map#	CGS	Grid
Seberger Dr					
500	MNSR	46321	3430		D7
Sebring Cir					
1200	ELGN	60120	2855	32W-11N	D3
Sebring Dr					
1000	ELGN	60120	2855	32W-11N	D3
Second Av					
-	HbnT	60034	2351	40W-41N	B7
Second St					
200	WDSK	60098	2524	41W-31N	C6
1300	TNLK	53181	2354		A2
Secretariat Ct					
10	CmpT	60175	2906	39W-7N	E4
10	PltT	60175	2906	39W-7N	E4
10	RLKP	60030	2589	22W-30N	B1
100	WHTN	60187	3082	24W-2S	C3
900	SCRL	60174	2964	34W-3N	D5
3000	AURA	60502	3078	34W-3S	E6
Secretariat Dr					
900	NPVL	60540	3142	25W-7S	A7
3000	AURA	60502	3078	34W-3S	E6
Secretariat Ln					
-	OswT	60543	3264	34W-11S	C2
500	OSWG	60543	3264	34W-11S	C2
S Secretariat Ln					
13700	HMGN	60491	3344	15W-16S	B3
Secret Forest Dr					
-	DGvT	60527	3207	16W-11S	E7
Sect					
-	FmtT	60060	2588	23W-27N	D7
300	FXLK	60041	2473	27W-34N	C7
300	FXLK	60041	2530	27W-34N	C1
300	VOLO	60041	2473	27W-34N	B7
300	VOLO	60041	2530	27W-34N	C1
Sedge Blvd					
5000	HFET	60192	2802	29W-13N	C5
Sedge Ct					
7600	GRNE	60031	2476	18W-35N	E6
16100	WDWH	60083	2419	16W-40N	E3
Sedge St					
3900	ZION	60099	2362	12W-41N	B7
N Sedgefield Ct					
2100	RLKB	60073	2475	22W-36N	B4
Sedgegrass Tr					
1800	AURA	60504	3201	33W-8S	A2
Sedge Meadow Av					
600	RMVL	60446	3340	25W-15S	C1
Sedge Meadow Ct					
-	WRLK	60097	2469	37W-36N	B4
600	RMVL	60446	3340	25W-15S	B1
Sedge Pass					
1400	MNKA	60447	3672	33W-30S	A4
Sedgewick Cir					
200	SCRL	60174	2964	36W-3N	A6
Sedgewick Ct					
300	CLLK	60012	2640	33W-26N	D2
Sedgewick Dr					
500	LYVL	60048	2591	17W-29N	B4
11600	HTLY	60142	2744	42W-20N	C1
Sedgewick Rd					
-	LtRT	60545	3259	48W-13S	A5
17300	LtRT	60545	3258	49W-13S	D5
17300	LtRT	60548	3258	50W-12S	B4
17300	SdwT	60548	3258	50W-12S	B4
Sedgewick St					
300	CPVL	60110	2747	34W-17N	E7
Sedgewicke Ct					
2000	RMVL	60446	3339	28W-17S	B6
Sedgewicke Dr					
100	RMVL	60446	3339	27W-17S	B6
Sedgewood Av					
1800	AURA	60503	3201	33W-10S	B5
Sedgewood Ct					
10	ALGN	60102	2747	36W-18N	B4
1400	RDLK	60073	2531	24W-34N	B1
Sedgewood Tr					
1100	ALGN	60102	2747	35W-18N	B4
Sedgfield Ct					
2300	SMBG	60194	2857	26W-10N	E5
Sedgley Ct					
6000	BRRG	60527	3146	15W-6S	B4
Sedgwick Ct					
10	OSWG	60543	3263	36W-11S	D1
2300	NPVL	60564	3202	29W-10S	D6
Sedgwick Dr					
10600	PlsT	60464	3273	13W-14S	A7
Sedgwick Rd					
10	OSWG	60543	3263	37W-11S	D2
N Sedgwick St					
1200	CHCG	60610	3034	0W-1N	A1
1600	CHCG	60610	2978	0W-2N	A7
1600	CHCG	60614	2978	0W-2N	B7
Sedona Av					
-	AraT	60504	3200	33W-9S	E5
-	AraT	60504	3201	33W-9S	A5
-	AURA	60504	3200	33W-9S	E5
-	AURA	60504	3201	33W-9S	A5
Sedona Ct					
5000	GRNE	60031	2478	15W-35N	B5
Sedona Ln					
900	JLET	60432	3500	20W-22S	C2
Sedona Rd					
-	LKMR	60041	2530	27W-32N	A5
-	LKMR	60051	2530	27W-32N	A6
N Seebert St					
10	CRY	60013	2695	31W-23N	D1
S Seebert St					
10	CRY	60013	2695	31W-23N	D1
Seegers Av					
10	EGVV	60007	2861	17W-10N	C6
Seegers Rd					
600	DSPN	60016	2862	14W-11N	D2
E Seegers Rd					
10	ANHT	60005	2861	17W-11N	A2
W Seegers Rd					
10	ANHT	60005	2861	18W-11N	A2
S See Gwun Av					
200	MPPT	60056	2807	16W-12N	E7
200	MPPT	60056	2861	16W-12N	E1
Seekonk Av					
3000	ElgT	60124	2853	37W-11N	B4
Seeley Av					
900	PKRG	60068	2863	11W-9N	E6
1000	FDHT	60411	3509	1E-25S	A7
1600	FDHT	60411	3597	1E-25S	A1
3900	DRGV	60515	3084	20W-4S	B7
4300	DRGV	60515	3144	20W-4S	B1
13000	BLID	60406	3277	2W-15S	C7
13100	BLID	60406	3349	2W-15S	C1
14000	DXMR	60406	3349	2W-16S	C3
14100	DXMR	60426	3349	2W-16S	D4
14600	HRVY	60426	3349	2W-17S	D6
N Seeley Av					
100	CHCG	60612	3033	2W-0N	C4
2300	CHCG	60647	2977	2W-2N	B6
2900	CHCG	60618	2977	2W-3N	B4
N Seeley Av					
4400	CHCG	60618	2921	2W-5N	B7
4800	CHCG	60625	2921	2W-6N	B6
6000	CHCG	60659	2921	2W-7N	B3
6900	CHCG	60645	2921	2W-8N	B1
7300	CHCG	60645	2867	2W-9N	B7
7500	CHCG	60202	2867	2W-9N	B7
7500	EVTN	60202	2867	2W-9N	B7
S Seeley Av					
10	CHCG	60612	3033	2W-0S	B5
2300	CHCG	60608	3091	2W-2S	B2
3500	CHCG	60609	3091	2W-3S	C5
4700	CHCG	60609	3151	2W-5S	C1
5500	CHCG	60636	3151	2W-6S	C3
8300	CHCG	60620	3213	2W-9S	C3
9500	CHCG	60643	3213	2W-11S	C6
10200	CHCG	60643	3277	2W-11S	C1
Seeley St					
-	BtlT	60543	3262	40W-12S	C2
-	OSWG	60560	3334	39W-15S	E1
Seely Av					
300	DGvT	60439	3206	20W-11S	B7
Seers Ct					
200	SMBG	60173	2859	22W-10N	D4
Seers Dr					
800	SMBG	60173	2859	22W-10N	C4
S Seeser St					
10	JLET	60435	3498	24W-24S	D5
10	JLET	60436	3498	24W-24S	D5
Seger St					
-	WLMT	60091	2811	5W-13N	E6
Sehrig					
-	NLNX	60433	3588	19W-26S	D3
-	NLNX	60451	3588	19W-26S	D3
Sehring St					
400	JLET	60436	3586	24W-25S	D1
400	JltT	60436	3586	24W-25S	D2
Seibury St					
-	JLET	60431	3495	33W-22S	B1
Seil Rd					
-	TroT	60404	3496	30W-24S	B7
1000	SRWD	60404	3496	30W-25S	B7
W Seil Rd					
24000	SRWD	60431	3496	30W-25S	C7
24000	TroT	60404	3496	30W-25S	C7
24000	TroT	60431	3496	30W-25S	C7
24800	SRWD	60404	3496	31W-24S	A7
25200	SRWD	60404	3495	31W-24S	E7
25500	TroT	60404	3495	32W-25S	C7
25600	SwdT	60447	3495	32W-25S	C7
Seiler Ct					
3100	WldT	60565	3203	27W-11S	C7
Seiler Dr					
2600	NPVL	60565	3203	27W-10S	C7
2800	WldT	60565	3203	27W-10S	C7
Seine Ct					
3400	HLCT	60429	3426	4W-21S	E7
W Seipp St					
2600	CHCG	60652	3213	3W-9S	A3
Selborne Rd					
600	RVSD	60546	3088	9W-2S	D3
Selby Rd					
1500	NPVL	60563	3140	29W-5S	D3
Selfridge Ct					
-	PNFD	60586	3415	31W-19S	E2
Selfridge Rd					
15900	PNFD	60586	3415	31W-19S	E2
Selig Pl					
7300	DRGV	60516	3206	20W-8S	B1
Selkirk Ct					
1900	IVNS	60010	2751	25W-16N	B6
9100	GfnT	60014	2639	38W-25N	A5
9100	LKWD	60014	2639	38W-25N	A5
Selkirk Dr					
400	SMBG	60194	2858	25W-11N	C4
Selkirk St					
1400	FSMR	60422	3506	4W-23S	D3
Sell Rd					
100	CHCG	60007	2916	15W-8N	A1
Sell St					
10	CHCG	60007	2916	15W-8N	A2
10	DSPN	60007	2916	15W-8N	A2
10	DSPN	60018	2916	15W-8N	A2
Selleck St					
1300	CRTE	60417	3685	0W-30S	C2
Sellstrom Dr					
10	PLTN	60067	2806	20W-15N	A1
10	PLTN	60074	2806	20W-15N	A1
W Selma Av					
7300	SMMT	60501	3148	9W-5S	D2
Selma Ln					
1000	NPVL	60540	3202	29W-8S	D1
Selmarten Rd					
1800	AURA	60505	3139	33W-5S	A2
Selva Ln					
13800	ODPK	60462	3346	9W-16S	D4
13800	OrlT	60462	3346	9W-16S	D4
Selwyn Ln					
100	BFGV	60089	2754	16W-17N	D5
Seminary Av					
100	AURA	60505	3200	35W-8S	A2
2400	DSPN	60016	2863	11W-11N	C3
2400	MaiT	60016	2863	11W-11N	C3
E Seminary Av					
100	WHTN	60187	3024	24W-0S	D6
N Seminary Av					
10	PKRG	60068	2917	11W-8N	D2
200	PKRG	60068	2863	11W-9N	E7
600	WDSK	60098	2524	41W-32N	D5
1900	CHCG	60614	2977	1W-2N	E7
2100	GwdT	60098	2524	41W-33N	D4
2800	CHCG	60657	2977	1W-3N	E4
3800	CHCG	60613	2977	1W-4N	E2
N Seminary Av SR-47					
600	WDSK	60098	2524	41W-32N	D5
2100	GwdT	60098	2524	41W-33N	D4
S Seminary Av					
10	PKRG	60068	2917	11W-8N	E1
100	WDSK	60098	2524	41W-31N	E7
200	WDSK	60098	2581	41W-30N	E1
W Seminary Av					
100	WHTN	60187	3024	24W-0S	C6
Seminary Cir					
800	GNEN	60137	3083	21W-1S	D1
Seminary Dr					
100	DYR	46311	3510		C6
100	SchT	60174	2964	34W-5N	D1
500	DYR	46321	3510		C5
500	MNSR	46321	3510		C5
Seminary Rd					
-	SchT	60174	2908	34W-6N	D7
-	SchT	60174	2964	34W-5N	C1
W Seminole Av					
100	EMHT	60126	3027	16W-0N	E4
Seminole Ct					
600	RLKH	60073	2474	23W-36N	D4
Seminole Ct					
2400	RVWD	60015	2756	13W-20N	A1
7300	DRN	60561	3207	17W-8S	B1
7400	WDRG	60517	3205	21W-8S	E1
8100	ODPK	60462	3346	10W-18S	C7
11600	FftT	60448	3502	14W-23S	D4
11600	MKNA	60448	3502	14W-23S	D4
28400	FmtT	60060	2589	21W-28N	C6
Seminole Dr					
100	NBRN	60010	2697	26W-22N	E3
800	ELGN	60120	2855	32W-12N	C1
6600	MchT	60097	2469	36W-36N	D4
6600	MchT	60097	2470	35W-36N	A4
7000	DRN	60561	3145	17W-8S	B7
7100	DRN	60561	3207	17W-8S	B1
N Seminole Dr					
4400	GNVW	60025	2809	11W-15N	C2
S Seminole Dr					
4400	GNVW	60025	2809	11W-15N	C2
Seminole Ln					
300	CLSM	60188	2968	25W-2N	A7
300	CLSM	60188	3024	25W-2N	A1
400	BGBK	60440	3268	23W-11S	E1
400	WNFD	60190	3023	26W-1N	E2
1600	CPVL	60110	2748	32W-18N	D4
E Seminole Ln					
1700	MPPT	60056	2808	13W-15N	E2
1700	PTHT	60070	2808	13W-15N	E2
1800	PTHT	60056	2808	13W-15N	E2
2000	MPPT	60056	2809	13W-15N	A2
2000	PTHT	60070	2809	13W-15N	A2
2100	WhlT	60056	2809	13W-15N	A2
2100	WhlT	60062	2809	13W-15N	A2
Seminole Rd					
900	WLMT	60091	2812	5W-14N	A5
1000	WLMT	60091	2811	5W-14N	E5
1400	ALGN	60102	2695	32W-21N	A6
2200	WKGN	60087	2479	12W-36N	C4
S Seminole Rd					
12200	PSPK	60464	3274	10W-14S	B6
Seminole St					
300	PKFT	60466	3594	4W-27S	E5
300	RNPK	60471	3594	4W-27S	E5
W Seminole St					
5600	CHCG	60646	2919	7W-7N	C4
7400	CHCG	60631	2918	9W-7N	C4
7800	NpkT	60631	2918	9W-7N	B4
8000	MaiT	60631	2918	10W-7N	B4
Seminole Tr					
500	LIHL	60156	2694	34W-21N	C5
W Seminole Tr					
13500	HMGN	60491	3343	16W-16S	D3
Semmler Ct					
17900	TYPK	60487	3424	10W-21S	B6
Semmler Dr					
17900	TYPK	60487	3424	10W-21S	B7
Senate Dr					
9000	MaiT	60016	2863	11W-11N	D3
9300	DSPN	60016	2863	11W-11N	D3
Senator Ln					
1400	FDHT	60411	3509	1E-25S	B7
Seneca Av E					
10	ElaT	60047	2646	19W-25N	B5
10	HNWD	60047	2646	19W-25N	B5
Seneca Av W					
10	HNWD	60047	2646	20W-25N	B5
Seneca Ct					
10	BRRG	60527	3208	14W-9S	D3
10	SMWD	60107	2856	29W-10N	E6
200	BGBK	60440	3268	24W-11S	E1
Seneca Dr					
10	OswT	60538	3199	37W-10S	D6
200	MltT	60187	3081	26W-2S	E4
200	WHTN	60187	3081	26W-2S	E4
500	AURA	60506	3137	37W-6S	C6
1800	HRPK	60133	2967	27W-5N	C2
W Seneca Dr					
16600	LKPT	60441	3420	20W-20S	B5
Seneca Ln					
400	BGBK	60440	3268	24W-11S	E1
800	CLSM	60188	2967	27W-3N	C7
E Seneca Ln					
1900	MPPT	60056	2808	13W-15N	E2
2000	MPPT	60056	2809	12W-15N	A2
Seneca Rd					
900	WLMT	60091	2812	5W-14N	A5
2900	WKGN	60087	2479	12W-36N	B4
4000	WRLK	60097	2469	37W-36N	B5
S Seneca Rd					
12800	PSHT	60463	3274	9W-15S	E7
12900	PSHT	60463	3346	9W-15S	E1
Seneca St					
10	ELGN	60120	2854	34W-12N	E3
200	ELGN	60120	2855	33W-12N	A3
300	PKFT	60466	3594	4W-27S	E5
300	RNPK	60471	3594	4W-27S	E5
400	JLET	60436	3586	24W-25S	D2
400	JltT	60436	3586	24W-25S	D2
Seneca Tr					
100	BMDL	60108	2912	25W-5N	B7
100	BMDL	60108	2968	25W-5N	B1
100	BmdT	60108	2912	25W-5N	B7
100	BmdT	60172	2912	25W-5N	B7
800	RLKH	60073	2474	24W-36N	D4
Seneca Wy					
200	BGBK	60440	3268	24W-11S	D1
Seneca Lake Cir					
16100	LktT	60403	3417	26W-19S	E2
Senerity Ct					
1700	ANTH	60002	2417	21W-40N	D2
W Senior Pl					
6700	CHCG	60634	2974	8W-5N	E1
6700	HDHT	60706	2974	8W-5N	E1
Senior League					
2200	MDLN	60060	2590	19W-29N	C4
Senna Ct					
300	NPVL	60565	3203	26W-10S	D6
Sennett St					
600	BTVA	60510	3019	37W-0S	C7
Seno Dr					
-	HLSD	60162	3028	13W-0S	E6
-	HLSD	60162	3029	13W-0S	A6
Senon Dr					
400	LMNT	60439	3271	18W-13S	A5
S Senour Av					
2500	CHCG	60608	3091	1W-2S	E2
September Blvd					
6800	HNWD	60047	2646	19W-25N	B4
6800	LGGV	60047	2646	19W-25N	B4
September Ct					
2000	JLET	60431	3417	28W-21S	A7
September Dr					
3000	JLET	60431	3417	28W-21S	A7
3000	PnfT	60431	3417	28W-21S	A7
3100	PnfT	60431	3416	29W-21S	E7
Sequoia Av					
19400	LYWD	60411	3510	3E-23S	A3
Sequoia Cir					
1400	YKVL	60560	3260	44W-14S	E7
Sequoia Ct					
-	OSWG	60543	3263	36W-13S	E6
10	HnrT	60107	2856	30W-10N	B6
200	ANTH	60002	2358	22W-42N	B5
400	SMBG	60193	2858	23W-9N	E7
600	CLSM	60188	2967	27W-3N	D6
700	NPVL	60540	3140	28W-7S	E7
700	NPVL	60540	3141	28W-7S	A7
2100	LKPT	60441	3419	22W-20S	D5
5300	GRNE	60031	2478	15W-35N	A5
6300	JLET	60586	3415	31W-20S	D6
7700	ODPK	60462	3346	9W-18S	D6
10400	SPGV	60081	2354	32W-42N	A6
E Sequoia Ct					
7800	ODPK	60462	3346	9W-18S	D6
W Sequoia Ct					
7900	ODPK	60462	3346	9W-18S	C6
Sequoia Dr					
10	MltT	60137	3083	22W-3S	C5
1400	AURA	60506	3137	38W-5S	A3
1800	HRPK	60133	2911	27W-8N	D3
2600	GrtT	60051	2472	29W-34N	C7
2600	GrtT	60051	2529	29W-34N	D1
2600	MchT	60051	2472	29W-34N	C7
2600	MchT	60051	2529	29W-34N	D1
Sequoia Ln					
10	DRFD	60015	2757	10W-20N	B1
600	FSMR	60422	3507	3W-22S	A1
1400	DRGV	60516	3207	18W-8S	A2
1400	DRN	60516	3207	18W-8S	A2
1400	DRN	60561	3207	18W-8S	A2
Sequoia Rd					
10	HNWD	60047	2646	20W-25N	A5
1100	NPVL	60540	3141	28W-7S	A7
1100	NpvT	60540	3141	28W-7S	A7
1500	NPVL	60540	3140	28W-7S	E7
W Sequoia Rd					
7600	PSHT	60463	3346	9W-15S	D1
Sequoia St					
10	LKFT	60045	2649	11W-25N	E4
15200	OKFT	60452	3347	7W-18S	C6
Sequoia Tr					
400	CRY	60013	2641	32W-24N	B7
400	ROSL	60172	2913	22W-8N	B3
1400	GNVW	60025	2810	8W-14N	E4
2700	GrtT	60051	2472	29W-34N	D7
2700	MchT	60051	2472	29W-34N	D7
5400	NndT	60012	2584	34W-27N	C7
Sequoia Wy					
1800	LKPT	60441	3419	22W-20S	D4
Sequoit Av					
-	ANTH	60002	2357	23W-42N	E6
-	ANTH	60002	2358	23W-42N	A6
Sequoit Rd					
2200	WKGN	60087	2479	11W-36N	C4
Sequoya Ln					
11200	IHPK	60525	3146	14W-6S	D5
Seraph Holmes Ct					
500	WNVL	60555	3080	29W-2S	E4
W Serbian Dr					
7800	CHCG	60631	2918	10W-7N	B4
8000	MaiT	60631	2918	10W-7N	B4
Serena Dr					
100	CHHT	60411	3507	1W-23S	E4
300	BlmT	60430	3507	1W-23S	E4
Serenade Ct					
200	SMBG	60193	2858	23W-9N	E7
Serendipity Dr					
800	AURA	60504	3201	33W-9S	A4
1100	AURA	60504	3200	33W-9S	E3
Serene Lake Wy					
16500	LktT	60403	3418	26W-19S	A3
21100	LktT	60403	3417	26W-19S	E3
Serenity N					
200	RMVL	60446	3340	26W-17S	A6
200	RMVL	60544	3340	26W-17S	A6
Serenity S					
200	RMVL	60446	3340	26W-17S	A6
200	RMVL	60544	3340	26W-17S	A6
Serenity Dr					
1600	ANTH	60002	2417	21W-40N	D2
S Serenity Dr					
16100	PnfT	60586	3416	30W-19S	B3
Serenity Ln					
2000	WDSK	60098	2582	39W-29N	C3
3000	NPVL	60564	3202	30W-11S	B7
Serenity Pth					
11000	BtnT	60071	2354	30W-42N	E5
Sergeant Cir					
1800	JLET	60586	3416	29W-21S	D7
1800	PnfT	60586	3416	29W-21S	D7
Sergo Dr					
-	MCCK	60525	3147	11W-5S	D3
W Sergo Dr					
9400	MCCK	60525	3147	11W-5S	D3
W Serranda Dr					
16800	WrnT	60030	2534	16W-33N	C3
16800	WrnT	60048	2534	16W-33N	C3
Serrienne Ln					
700	WYNE	60184	2965	32W-5N	B1
Service Rd					
-	LbvT	60045	2648	13W-27N	D2
-	MTWA	60045	2648	13W-27N	D2
Sesame Dr					
1000	BNVL	60106	2972	14W-4N	B3
1000	BNVL	60131	2972	14W-4N	C3
Sessions Wk					
1700	HFET	60169	2858	25W-12N	B1
4700	NndT	60012	2639	36W-27N	D1
Setauket Av					
10	LslT	60540	3142	25W-6S	B4
Seth St					
500	BGBK	60440	3204	24W-10S	D5
Seton Ct					
100	SMWD	60107	2857	27W-10N	C5
800	WLNG	60090	2755	15W-17N	A6
Seton Dr					
16100	SHLD	60473	3429	1E-18S	B1
Seton Pl					
100	SMWD	60107	2857	27W-10N	C5
9400	ODHL	60487	3423	11W-19S	E3
9400	ODPK	60467	3423	11W-19S	E3
9400	ODPK	60487	3423	11W-19S	E3
Seton Rd					
1600	NfdT	60062	2757	9W-18N	C3
1600	NHBK	60062	2757	9W-18N	B3
Seton Creek Dr					
10	OSWG	60543	3264	35W-11S	A1
Seton Hall Dr					
1900	NPVL	60565	3204	24W-9S	C4
Setter St					
-	ELBN	60119	3017	42W-0N	C6
Settlement Dr					
500	CmpT	60175	2962	40W-4N	B4
Settlers Blvd					
-	AURA	60506	3136	41W-7S	A6
-	SRGV	60554	3136	41W-7S	A6
Settlers Ct					
200	NPVL	60565	3203	26W-10S	E6
1900	MHRY	60050	2528	32W-33N	A2
Settlers Dr					
100	NPVL	60565	3203	26W-10S	E6
Settlers Ln					
-	FKFT	60423	3503	12W-24S	D6
Settlers Pkwy					
3000	ElgT	60124	2853	37W-11N	B4
Settlers Sq					
-	LKFT	60045	2649	11W-24N	C7
Settlers Grove Rd					
300	PGGV	60140	2798	41W-15N	A4
300	RtdT	60140	2798	41W-15N	A4
Settlers Pond Ct					
10800	FKFT	60423	3591	13W-25S	A1
Settlers Pond Dr					
21300	FKFT	60423	3591	13W-25S	A1
Settlers Pond Wy					
11500	ODPK	60467	3422	14W-21S	D6
Sevan Ct					
19600	MKNA	60448	3502	15W-23S	C4
Seven Bridges Dr					
3500	WDRG	60517	3143	22W-7S	B6
Seven Gables Rd					
24800	MltT	60187	3082	24W-2S	C3
24800	WHTN	60187	3082	24W-2S	C3
Seven Pines Cir					
300	HDPK	60035	2757	8W-20N	E1
Seven Pines Rd					
1300	SMBG	60193	2859	21W-10N	E6
Severn Ct					
1400	NPVL	60565	3203	27W-8S	C2
Seville Av					
500	NPVL	60565	3203	27W-10S	C5
Seville Cir					
2400	NHBK	60062	2810	10W-15N	A1
Seville Ct					
1500	JNBG	60050	2472	30W-36N	A3
1500	WLNG	60090	2754	16W-18N	D3
1900	SMBG	60193	2912	25W-8N	A3
Seward St					
400	PKFT	60466	3507	3W-25S	A7
500	ROSL	60172	2912	23W-8N	E3
500	SmbT	60172	2912	23W-8N	E3
1400	SMBG	60193	2912	23W-8N	E2
1400	SmbT	60193	2912	23W-8N	E2
1600	EVTN	60202	2867	3W-10N	A5
1900	EVTN	60202	2866	3W-10N	E5
W Seward St					
6900	NLES	60714	2864	8W-10N	E5
Sexauer Av					
200	ELGN	60123	2854	35W-11N	B3
300	ElgT	60123	2854	35W-11N	B3
Sextant Dr					
10	GYLK	60030	2533	19W-34N	D1
10	TDLK	60030	2533	19W-34N	D1
Sexton Dr					
10	GLHT	60139	2968	24W-4N	D4
Sexton St					
600	AURA	60505	3200	35W-8S	A2
Seybrooke Ct					
700	CLLK	60012	2640	33W-26N	D2
Seybrooke Ln					
600	CLLK	60012	2640	34W-26N	D2
600	NndT	60012	2640	34W-26N	D2
Seymour Av					
-	CHCG	60666	2972	13W-4N	E2
-	FNPK	60666	2972	13W-4N	E2
1000	DSPN	60016	2862	15W-10N	A5
1100	DSPN	60018	2862	15W-10N	A5
1400	NCHI	60064	2536	11W-32N	E6
1400	WKGN	60085	2536	11W-32N	E6
9300	SRPK	60176	2973	11W-4N	C2
10400	FNPK	60131	2973	13W-5N	A2
10400	SRPK	60131	2973	13W-5N	A2
10600	FNPK	60131	2972	13W-4N	E2
N Seymour Av					
10	MDLN	60060	2646	18W-27N	D1
100	MDLN	60060	2590	18W-27N	D7
S Seymour Av					
10	GYLK	60030	2532	20W-32N	E4
10	MDLN	60060	2646	18W-27N	D1
Shabbona Av					
800	SCRL	60174	2964	35W-3N	B6
Shabbona Dr					
200	MNKA	60447	3583	33W-28S	B7
200	MNKA	60447	3672	33W-28S	B1
300	PKFT	60466	3594	4W-27S	E4
300	PKFT	60466	3595	4W-27S	A4
19300	TYPK	60477	3504	9W-23S	E3
Shabbona Ln					
4400	LSLE	60532	3142	24W-4S	D1
Shabbona Rd					
6500	IHPK	60525	3146	14W-7S	D6
Shabbona St					
-	WnfT	60510	3080	30W-1S	A3
Shabbona Tr					
200	BTVA	60510	3020	35W-0S	B7
1000	BTVA	60510	3019	36W-0S	E7
Shabona Ln					
900	WLMT	60091	2811	5W-14N	E5
Shabonee Ter					
2900	NHBK	60062	2756	11W-17N	E5
E Shabonee Tr					
300	MPPT	60056	2862	15W-12N	B1
W Shabonee Tr					
10	MPPT	60056	2862	15W-12N	A1
300	MPPT	60056	2861	16W-12N	E1
Shadblow Dr					
-	GNEN	60137	3083	23W-1S	A2
N Shaddle Av					
10	MDLN	60060	2646	18W-27N	E1
200	MDLN	60060	2590	18W-27N	E7
S Shaddle Av					
10	MDLN	60060	2646	18W-27N	E1
Shade Cove Ct					
11800	ODPK	60467	3344	14W-18S	D7
Shade Tree Cir					
8600	LKWD	60014	2639	37W-25N	B5
8700	CLLK	60014	2639	37W-25N	B5
Shade Tree Ct					
10	ALGN	60102	2746	36W-18N	E4
Shadow Ct					
-	OSWG	60543	3263	36W-13S	E4
Shadow Dr					
500	DhmT	60033	2463	50W-37N	E1
500	HRVD	60033	2463	50W-37N	E1
Shadow Ln					
8800	BLVY	60097	2526	38W-34N	A1
8800	WRLK	60097	2526	38W-34N	A1

Block	City	ZIP	Map#	CGS	Grid
Shadowbend Dr					
100	WLNG	60090	2755	13W-18N	D3
Shadowbrook Ct					
-	OSWG	60543	3263	36W-12S	E4
5600	WKGN	60048	2534	16W-32N	E5
Shadow Creek Cir					
10	PSHT	60463	3347	7W-15S	B1
W Shadow Creek Cir					
200	VNHL	60061	2591	17W-27N	A7
Shadow Creek Ct					
-	KdlT	60560	3334	41W-16S	B3
-	OswT	60560	3334	41W-16S	B3
10	LIHL	60156	2693	37W-22N	C4
400	LslT	60540	3204	25W-8S	A1
400	PSHT	60463	3347	8W-15S	B1
N Shadow Creek Ct					
2100	VNHL	60061	2591	17W-27N	A7
Shadow Creek Dr					
400	PSHT	60463	3347	7W-15S	B1
5100	OKFT	60452	3425	6W-19S	E1
5100	OKFT	60452	3426	6W-19S	A1
W Shadow Creek Dr					
300	VNHL	60061	2591	17W-27N	B7
300	VNHL	60061	2647	17W-27N	B1
Shadow Creek Ln					
-	LslT	60540	3204	26W-8S	A1
-	OswT	60560	3334	41W-15S	A3
300	RVWD	60015	2756	13W-20N	A1
Shadow Hill Dr					
-	ElgT	60124	2853	38W-10N	A7
-	PltT	60124	2852	39W-10N	E7
-	PltT	60124	2853	38W-10N	A7
Shadow Hills Ln					
2300	AURA	60503	3201	32W-11S	B7
2300	AURA	60503	3265	32W-11S	C1
E Shadow Lake Ter					
1300	PLTN	60074	2753	19W-18N	C3
Shadow Lake Bay					
400	ROSL	60172	2913	22W-8N	C3
Shadowood Dr					
3100	NndT	60012	2584	34W-28N	C5
Shadowood Ln					
200	NHFD	60093	2811	7W-16N	A1
900	CLLK	60014	2639	37W-24N	B7
Shadow Ridge Ct					
200	PSPK	60464	3272	14W-14S	E6
Shadow Ridge Dr					
-	PlsT	60464	3272	14W-14S	E6
-	PSPK	60464	3272	14W-14S	E6
Shadowrock Ct					
4200	GRNE	60031	2535	14W-33N	D2
Shadow Wood Wy					
-	PNFD	60544	3416	30W-18S	B1
-	PnfT	60544	3416	30W-18S	B1
Shady Av					
700	GNVA	60134	3020	35W-0N	B4
Shady Ct					
800	AURA	60506	3136	38W-6S	E5
4400	RGMW	60008	2805	20W-13N	E5
Shady Dr					
100	NndT	60051	2529	30W-31N	B6
3100	WRLK	60097	2469	36W-35N	D7
E Shady Dr					
200	PltT	60067	2806	20W-14N	A5
Shady Ln					
10	DRPK	60010	2752	23W-20N	A2
10	MDLN	60060	2646	18W-26N	E3
10	PltT	60010	2752	23W-20N	A2
100	BGBK	60440	3268	24W-12S	D2
100	BRLT	60103	2910	29W-7N	E4
200	DRGV	60515	3084	18W-4S	E7
200	FXLK	60041	2473	27W-36N	C4
200	MRGO	60152	2634	49W-26N	D3
200	NBRN	60010	2698	25W-23N	A2
300	ElgT	60124	2907	37W-8N	B3
300	SchT	60174	2908	35W-6N	B7
300	SEGN	60124	2907	37W-8N	B3
300	SRWD	60404	3496	30W-23S	C4
500	DndT	60118	2747	36W-17N	A7
500	LbvT	60060	2646	18W-26N	E3
500	WynT	60185	2966	30W-3N	B5
700	AURA	60506	3136	38W-6S	E5
900	AURA	60506	3137	38W-6S	A5
1000	GNEN	60137	3025	21W-0S	E5
1000	MltT	60148	3026	21W-0S	A7
1000	YkTp	60148	3026	21W-0S	A7
1100	RLKB	60073	2474	24W-34N	C7
1100	WHTN	60187	3024	23W-0N	E5
1400	SMBG	60173	2859	21W-10N	E5
2200	HDPK	60035	2704	10W-22N	A3
2800	TNLK	53181	2353		E3
6500	BRRG	60527	3146	14W-7S	C6
8300	GwdT	60097	2469	37W-35N	B6
8900	HYHL	60457	3209	11W-9S	E3
9900	ODPK	60462	3345	12W-18S	C7
13800	HTLY	60142	2744	42W-20N	A1
E Shady Ln					
18300	LbvT	60060	2646	18W-26N	E3
18300	MDLN	60060	2646	18W-26N	E3
N Shady Ln					
200	EMHT	60126	2971	17W-2N	C7
200	EMHT	60126	3027	17W-2N	C1
40200	AntT	60002	2417	22W-40N	A3
W Shady Ln					
-	FmtT	60060	2645	21W-26N	D3
400	BRTN	60010	2750	26W-18N	D3
500	BNHL	60010	2750	26W-18N	D3
13800	HMGN	60491	3343	17W-17S	D5
15800	HmrT	60491	3420	19W-18S	C1
21200	ElaT	60047	2645	21W-24N	D7
21200	KLDR	60047	2645	21W-24N	D7
E Shady Wy					
700	ANHT	60005	2861	17W-11N	B3
Shadybrook Ln					
200	AURA	60504	3201	31W-7S	E1
300	AURA	60504	3139	31W-6S	E5
Shadydell Av					
100	MDLN	60060	2646	18W-26N	D2
Shady Glen Dr					
25200	CNHN	60410	3672	32W-30S	D5
Shady Grove Ct					
2000	NPVL	60565	3204	24W-8S	E2
E Shady Grove Ct					
2500	CteT	60417	3687	3E-29S	A1
Shady Grove Ln					
600	BFGV	60089	2701	17W-21N	B7
W Shady Hollow Ln					
700	MchT	60050	2472	29W-36N	C3
Shady Ln Ct					
1000	RLKB	60073	2474	23W-34N	E7
W Shady Ln Rd					
400	PLTN	60074	2752	21W-18N	D2
Shady Oaks Ct					
10	CmpT	60175	2962	39W-5N	E3
600	ELGN	60120	2855	32W-12N	C2
N Shady Oaks Dr					
400	ELGN	60120	2855	32W-11N	D3
Shady Oaks Ln					
4600	NndT	60012	2640	33W-27N	D1
S Shady Oaks Tr					
24200	CteT	60417	3687	3E-29S	B1
E Shady Pines Ct					
300	PLTN	60067	2753	20W-17N	A5
300	PLTN	60074	2753	20W-17N	A5
Shady Trail Ct					
4200	NPVL	60564	3267	28W-12S	B2
Shady Tree Ln					
900	WLNG	60090	2755	15W-16N	A7
Shadywood Ln					
100	EGvT	60007	2861	18W-9N	A7
100	EGVV	60007	2861	18W-9N	A7
100	SMWD	60107	2856	29W-10N	E5
Shady Wy Dr					
600	WNFD	60190	3023	27W-0S	B6
600	WnfT	60190	3023	27W-0N	B6
Shafer Av					
1400	BGBK	60490	3267	26W-13S	E6
Shafer Ct					
6400	DSPN	60018	2917	11W-7N	C3
6400	RSMT	60018	2917	11W-7N	C3
Shaffner Rd					
10	WHTN	60187	3081	27W-1S	D2
10	WHTN	60190	3081	27W-1S	D1
10	WNFD	60190	3081	27W-1S	D1
10	WnfT	60187	3081	27W-1S	D2
10	WnfT	60190	3081	27W-1S	D1
Shaftesbury St					
100	CLSM	60188	2968	25W-4N	A4
Shag Bark Ct					
400	ALGN	60102	2694	34W-20N	C7
11700	BRRG	60527	3208	14W-9S	C3
Shagbark Ct					
300	SMBG	60193	2858	23W-10N	E6
400	PltT	60010	2751	23W-18N	D2
400	ROSL	60172	2912	24W-6N	D6
800	FKFT	60423	3503	13W-24S	B6
1000	NLNX	60451	3588	19W-26S	E3
1100	HFET	60192	2804	24W-15N	C1
1200	FXLK	60020	2414	28W-39N	E5
1300	CLSM	60188	2967	28W-3N	A6
1700	NPVL	60565	3204	25W-9S	B3
4900	GRNE	60031	2478	15W-35N	B5
6500	LSLE	60532	3142	23W-7S	E6
8400	WDRG	60517	3205	22W-9S	C4
8600	ODPK	60462	3346	10W-18S	B6
22900	PnfT	60586	3416	28W-20S	E5
S Shagbark Ct					
200	RDLK	60073	2531	24W-32N	C4
Shagbark Dr					
-	WldT	60585	3266	30W-14S	B7
500	ELGN	60123	2853	36W-12N	D2
500	ElgT	60123	2853	36W-12N	D2
800	BtvT	60510	3078	35W-2S	B5
1200	DSPN	60018	2863	12W-10N	B5
1400	BGBK	60490	3267	26W-11S	E2
12100	PNFD	60585	3266	30W-14S	B7
Shag Bark Ln					
700	DRFD	60015	2704	9W-20N	B7
1500	NHBK	60062	2757	9W-17N	C5
7900	BRRG	60527	3208	14W-9S	D3
Shagbark Ln					
-	WHTN	60187	3024	25W-0N	B5
10	AURA	60506	3136	39W-6S	D5
10	FoxT	60541	3331	48W-17S	A7
10	PvsT	60523	3086	14W-2S	C4
10	SgrT	60506	3136	39W-6S	D5
10	WSTR	60523	3086	14W-2S	C4
100	MltT	60137	3083	22W-3S	B6
100	WYNE	60184	2909	33W-6N	B7
400	LNHT	60046	2418	20W-38N	A6
400	ROSL	60172	2912	24W-6N	E6
800	NARA	60542	3137	37W-4S	C1
3100	HLCT	60429	3427	3W-21S	A7
22900	STGR	60475	3596	0E-27S	E5
22900	STGR	60475	3597	0E-27S	A5
E Shag Bark Ln					
10	SMWD	60107	2857	28W-11N	A4
N Shagbark Ln					
3100	LGGV	60047	2700	19W-21N	D5
23200	ElaT	60047	2644	23W-24N	E7
23200	ElaT	60047	2698	23W-24N	E1
28300	GNOK	60048	2592	15W-28N	B6
28300	LbvT	60048	2592	15W-28N	B6
28300	MTWA	60048	2592	15W-28N	B6
38200	NptT	60083	2420	14W-38N	C7
38200	WDWH	60083	2420	14W-38N	C7
W Shagbark Ln					
22400	AntT	60002	2417	22W-40N	B3
Shagbark Rd					
10	LKBF	60044	2593	12W-28N	C5
10	RGMW	60008	2806	20W-13N	A6
10	ShdT	60044	2593	12W-28N	C5
200	WynT	60185	2966	29W-3N	D6
800	NLNX	60451	3589	19W-26S	A3
1000	NLNX	60451	3588	19W-26S	E3
25000	MTWA	60045	2648	14W-25N	D6
E Shagbark Tr					
2900	CteT	60417	3687	3E-30S	A3
S Shagbark Tr					
2300	ANHT	60005	2861	17W-11N	B3
Shaker Ct					
2400	NPVL	60564	3202	29W-10S	D5
11700	ODPK	60467	3344	14W-18S	D6
E Shaker Ct					
400	RLKB	60073	2475	22W-36N	B4
Shaker Ln					
500	LKZH	60047	2699	22W-21N	A5
Shakespeare Av					
3900	LYNS	60534	3088	9W-4S	C6
3900	RvsT	60534	3088	9W-4S	C6
3900	RvsT	60546	3088	9W-4S	C6
W Shakespeare Av					
1400	CHCG	60614	2977	1W-2N	D6
2000	CHCG	60647	2977	2W-2N	D6
2800	CHCG	60647	2976	3W-2N	E6
4300	CHCG	60639	2976	5W-2N	A6
4700	CHCG	60639	2975	6W-2N	E6
6800	CHCG	60707	2974	8W-2N	E6
Shakespeare Ct					
800	GYLK	60030	2533	20W-33N	B2
1800	SMBG	60194	2858	25W-10N	A5
Shakespeare Dr					
500	GYLK	60030	2533	20W-33N	B2
Shakespeare Ln					
3600	NPVL	60564	3266	28W-11S	E2
3600	WldT	60564	3266	28W-11S	E2
Shakespeare St					
100	WMTN	60481	3853	27W-38S	D6
11100	WSTR	60154	3086	13W-1S	E2
Shales Pkwy					
500	ELGN	60120	2855	31W-11N	E3
500	HnrT	60120	2855	31W-10N	E5
Shales St					
7200	AlqT	60014	2640	33W-24N	D6
Shalestone Ct					
11700	FKFT	60423	3590	14W-27S	D4
Shallow Cove Rd					
500	LKZH	60047	2699	22W-21N	A7
Swallow Ridge Dr					
-	RcmT	60071	2353	34W-43N	C4
-	RHMD	60071	2353	34W-43N	C4
Shallow Ridge Rd					
-	BCHR	60401	3864	0E-36S	E1
Shaman Dr					
1400	BGBK	60490	3267	26W-12S	E2
Shambliss Ct					
1000	BFGV	60089	2700	18W-21N	E7
Shambliss Ln					
800	BFGV	60089	2700	18W-21N	E6
Shamrock Ct					
1100	LslT	60540	3204	24W-8S	D1
1600	AURA	60505	3138	34W-5S	E3
Shamrock Dr					
2900	ElgT	60124	2853	37W-10N	C7
Shamrock Ln					
1200	PGGV	60140	2797	42W-15N	E4
W Shamrock Ln					
4100	MHRY	60050	2528	33W-31N	A7
4100	NndT	60050	2528	33W-31N	A7
4300	MHRY	60050	2527	33W-31N	E7
4300	MHRY	60050	2584	33W-31N	E1
4300	MHRY	60050	2585	33W-30N	A1
Shanahan Ct					
800	NPVL	60540	3142	25W-7S	B7
Shanahan Dr					
1600	ElgT	60123	2907	36W-8N	E4
1600	ElgT	60177	2907	36W-8N	E4
1600	ElgT	60177	2908	36W-8N	A4
1600	SEGN	60177	2907	36W-8N	E4
1600	SEGN	60177	2908	36W-8N	A4
W Shandon Dr					
25800	GrtT	60041	2473	25W-36N	E4
25800	GrtT	60041	2474	25W-36N	A4
Shandrew Dr					
800	NPVL	60540	3202	29W-8S	C1
W Shanklin Ct					
14300	GNOK	60048	2592	14W-31N	C1
Shannock Ln					
900	SMBG	60193	2912	24W-9N	D1
Shannon Av					
21200	MTSN	60443	3593	7W-25S	C1
W Shannon Av					
26200	AntT	60002	2356	26W-42N	D5
Shannon Blvd					
-	BbyT	60134	3076	39W-0S	E1
Shannon Ct					
10	LMNT	60439	3342	19W-15S	D1
200	DSPN	60016	2862	15W-11N	A3
200	MPPT	60016	2862	15W-11N	A3
200	MPPT	60056	2862	15W-11N	A3
500	NLNX	60451	3500	20W-24S	C6
1300	MNKA	60447	3672	34W-30S	A3
2200	DRN	60561	3206	19W-10S	D5
2800	NHBK	60062	2756	11W-17N	E5
3600	JLET	60431	3417	28W-20S	A4
11900	ODPK	60467	3422	14W-20S	C5
16800	TYPK	60477	3424	10W-20S	C3
25300	MhtT	60442	3677	19W-30S	D4
Shannon Dr					
200	PTHT	60070	2808	14W-15N	B2
1000	AURA	60505	3138	34W-5S	D3
6200	MHRY	60050	2527	35W-32N	B4
6300	AlqT	60013	2641	31W-25N	C4
16900	TYPK	60477	3424	10W-20S	C4
25100	MhtT	60442	3677	19W-30S	D4
N Shannon Dr					
33000	WrnT	60030	2534	17W-33N	B4
S Shannon Dr					
600	RMVL	60446	3418	26W-18S	A1
13500	HMGN	60491	3343	17W-16S	C3
W Shannon Dr					
13100	BHPK	60083	2421	13W-39N	A5
13200	BHPK	60099	2421	13W-39N	A5
Shannon Ln					
10	RGMW	60008	2806	20W-14N	A4
2800	NLNX	60451	3500	20W-24S	C6
N Shannon Ln					
1700	PLTN	60074	2753	19W-18N	C3
Shannon Rd					
400	DRFD	60015	2757	9W-20N	B1
2400	NHBK	60062	2757	10W-17N	A5
2500	NHBK	60062	2756	11W-17N	E5
Shannon Sq					
10	BbyT	60134	3076	39W-0S	E1
E Shannon St					
100	ELBN	60119	3017	43W-1N	A3
Shannondale Rd					
2200	GNOK	60048	2535	14W-31N	B7
2200	GNOK	60048	2592	14W-31N	C1
2200	WKGN	60048	2535	14W-31N	B7
Shannon Lake Ct					
800	WTMT	60559	3145	17W-6S	B4
Sharen Ct					
3200	JLET	60431	3497	28W-22S	B2
Shari Ln					
800	MDLN	60060	2646	18W-26N	E2
1000	LYVL	60048	2591	17W-28N	B6
1700	AURA	60504	3201	33W-8S	A2
Shark Ct					
4100	NCHI	60088	2593	11W-31N	D1
Sharon Av					
700	PKCY	60085	2536	12W-33N	A4
Sharon Ct					
-	ELGN	60120	2855	32W-10N	B5
100	NARA	60542	3078	35W-3S	B6
16400	ODPK	60467	3423	11W-19S	D3
16500	ODHL	60487	3424	11W-19S	A3
18900	LNSG	60438	3510	4E-22S	B1
Sharon Dr					
100	SYHW	60118	2800	35W-16N	B3
200	BRTN	60010	2751	24W-20N	B1
500	CLLK	60014	2639	36W-24N	E6
600	DrrT	60098	2525	40W-31N	A7
2800	NLNX	60451	3500	20W-24S	C6
15300	HMGN	60491	3344	15W-18S	C7
N Sharon Dr					
500	WDSK	60098	2524	40W-31N	E6
800	ADSN	60101	2970	19W-4N	D3
S Sharon Dr					
-	DrrT	60098	2582	40W-30N	A1
800	DrrT	60098	2525	40W-31N	A7
Sharon Ln					
-	YKVL	60560	3333	44W-15S	A2
100	NARA	60542	3078	35W-3S	B6
900	SMBG	60193	2858	24W-10N	C6
6200	HGKN	60525	3147	11W-7S	D5
10100	HBRN	60034	2350	41W-42N	E7
10500	MKNA	60448	3503	13W-23S	B4
S Sharon Ln					
25500	CteT	60417	3687	3E-31S	B4
Sharon Pl					
3300	BHPK	60099	2422	10W-39N	A5
3300	ZION	60099	2422	10W-39N	A5
Sharon Wy					
500	BGBK	60440	3205	22W-10S	B6
S Sharons Wy					
-	PNFD	60586	3415	31W-20S	D5
Sharp Ct					
800	ELBN	60119	3017	43W-2N	A1
Sharp Dr					
-	PLNO	60545	3259	47W-13S	C5
100	MHTN	60442	3677	19W-30S	E4
800	SRWD	60404	3496	29W-23S	D3
13500	PNFD	60544	3338	29W-16S	D4
13500	PnfT	60544	3338	29W-16S	D4
W Sharp Rd					
19200	JknT	60421	3586	24W-28S	D7
19200	JknT	60421	3587	24W-28S	A7
19200	JLET	60421	3586	24W-28S	D7
19200	JLET	60421	3587	24W-28S	A7
Sharron Ct					
10	HNDL	60521	3146	14W-5S	C1
Shasta Dr					
2400	LSLE	60532	3142	24W-6S	D4
Shasta Daisy Ct					
2400	ELGN	60124	2907	36W-9N	E1
Shattuck Ct					
100	SMBG	60194	2858	24W-10N	C5
Shattuck Ln					
900	SMBG	60194	2858	24W-10N	D5
Shaun Dr					
2200	INCK	60060	2647	17W-25N	B5
2200	MDLN	60060	2647	17W-25N	B5
Shauna Dr					
2500	MTGY	60538	3198	40W-10S	D5
Shaw Av					
1400	NPVL	60564	3203	28W-11S	A7
Shaw Ct					
600	SMBG	60194	2857	28W-12N	B1
Shaw Dr					
10	WNVL	60555	3080	30W-2S	C4
Shaw St					
11000	WSTR	60154	3086	13W-1S	E2
Shawford Wy					
10	HDPK	60035	2703	11W-23N	E2
10	LKFT	60035	2703	11W-23N	E2
10	LKFT	60045	2703	11W-23N	E2
1100	ELGN	60120	2855	32W-12N	D1
1300	ELGN	60120	2801	32W-12N	D7
Shawmut Av					
-	BKFD	60513	3087	12W-4S	C6
400	LGNG	60525	3087	12W-4S	C6
600	LGNG	60513	3087	12W-4S	C6
Shawn Ct					
400	WLNG	60090	2808	15W-16N	B1
Shawn Ln					
400	PTHT	60070	2808	14W-15N	B2
700	DSPN	60016	2862	15W-11N	B4
N Shawnee Av					
33700	WrnT	60030	2534	17W-33N	B2
Shawnee Cir					
200	BRLT	60103	2967	28W-5N	A1
Shawnee Ct					
200	BRLT	60103	2967	28W-5N	A1
1000	HRVD	60033	2406	49W-38N	C7
Shawnee Dr					
100	CLSM	60188	2968	25W-2N	B7
200	BGBK	60440	3268	24W-11S	E1
200	CLSM	60188	3024	25W-2N	A1
200	MNKA	60447	3583	33W-28S	C6
16300	LKPT	60441	3420	20W-20S	B4
Shawnee Ln					
10	LKFT	60045	2649	11W-25N	E4
100	HRVD	60033	2406	49W-38N	C7
Shawnee Rd					
2200	WKGN	60087	2479	12W-36N	B4
S Shawnee Rd					
12800	PSHT	60463	3274	9W-15S	D7
12900	PSHT	60463	3346	9W-15S	D1
Shawnee St					
300	PKFT	60466	3594	4W-27S	E5
300	RNPK	60471	3594	4W-27S	E5
Shawnee Tr					
10	IHPK	60525	3146	13W-7S	E6
800	LIHL	60156	2694	34W-21N	C5
800	ROSL	60172	2913	22W-8N	C2
1400	RVWD	60015	2702	13W-21N	E5
1600	NHBK	60062	2756	11W-16N	D6
Shawno Dr					
-	AURA	60505	3138	33W-6S	E5
Shay Ct					
300	WLNG	60090	2755	15W-18N	A3
Shay Rd					
200	WLNG	60090	2755	15W-18N	A3
Shea Av					
16700	HLCT	60428	3427	2W-20S	D4
16700	HLCT	60429	3427	2W-20S	D4
17000	MKHM	60428	3427	2W-20S	D4
Shea Dr					
200	CHHT	60422	3507	2W-24S	D5
Sheahen Ct					
1800	HDPK	60035	2704	8W-22N	D5
Shearwater Ct					
10	HNWD	60047	2645	22W-26N	B3
W Shedron Wy					
1000	LMBD	60148	3083	21W-1S	E1
1000	LMBD	60148	3084	21W-1S	A1
Sheehan Av					
600	GNEN	60137	3083	22W-1S	C1
Sheehan Ct					
2600	NPVL	60564	3202	29W-10S	C6
Sheehan Dr					
10	LKVL	60046	2475	22W-37N	C1
2200	NPVL	60564	3202	29W-10S	C6
Sheeler Av					
3000	WKGN	60085	2479	12W-33N	B7
3000	WkgT	60085	2479	12W-33N	B7
Sheffer Rd					
-	NpvT	60502	3139	31W-6S	D4
400	AraT	60502	3139	33W-6S	A5
400	AURA	60502	3139	33W-6S	A5
700	AURA	60505	3138	34W-6S	C5
1000	AraT	60505	3138	34W-6S	D5
1600	AraT	60505	3139	33W-6S	A5
1700	AURA	60505	3139	33W-6S	A5
Sheffield Av					
100	JLET	60432	3499	23W-21S	B1
100	JLET	60441	3499	23W-21S	B1
100	LktT	60441	3499	23W-21S	B1
500	DYR	46311	3510		D5
1500	DYR	46311	3598		D1
8100	SjnT	46311	3598		D6
9100	SjnT	46311	3687		D2
9800	HnrT	46311	3687		D3
10100	MNSR	46321	3510		E4
N Sheffield Av					
1500	CHCG	60622	3033	1W-1N	E1
1600	CHCG	60614	2977	1W-2N	E6
1600	CHCG	60622	2977	1W-2N	E7
2700	CHCG	60657	2977	1W-3N	E5
3500	CHCG	60613	2977	1W-4N	E3
S Sheffield Av					
2400	HMND	46320	3280		E6
2400	HMND	46327	3280		E7
2400	HMND	46394	3280		E6
3000	HMND	46327	3352		D2
Sheffield Cir					
-	SgrT	60554	3135	41W-5S	E3
-	SRGV	60554	3135	41W-5S	E3
3000	OMFD	60461	3507	3W-25S	A7
Sheffield Ct					
10	ALGN	60102	2747	36W-19N	A3
10	CRY	60013	2641	31W-25N	D6
10	LKZH	60010	2698	24W-21N	D6
10	LNSH	60069	2702	14W-22N	D4
10	SEGN	60177	2908	36W-9N	A1
10	SMWD	60107	2856	29W-11N	D4
100	MltT	60137	3083	22W-2S	C3
300	ROSL	60172	2912	25W-7N	C4
600	LKFT	60045	2649	12W-25N	B6
800	GYLK	60030	2533	20W-33N	B3
1300	CLSM	60188	2967	28W-3N	B5
1500	ELGN	60123	2800	35W-13N	B7
1600	AURA	60504	3201	32W-9S	B5
4400	GRNE	60031	2535	14W-34N	B1
7300	GGnT	60449	3682	9W-31S	A5
12500	PlsT	60464	3273	13W-14S	A7
N Sheffield Ct					
2400	RLKB	60073	2475	22W-36N	B4
Sheffield Dr					
200	SMBG	60194	2857	27W-10N	C5
900	CLLK	60014	2640	35W-24N	A7
900	CLLK	60014	2694	35W-24N	A1
1300	ELGN	60123	2800	36W-13N	A7
2800	NLNX	60451	3500	20W-24S	C5
7800	PSHL	60465	3274	9W-12S	C1
14100	HMGN	60491	3344	15W-16S	B4
14100	HmrT	60491	3344	15W-16S	B4
24200	PNFD	60585	3338	30W-15S	B2
24200	WldT	60585	3338	30W-15S	B2
W Sheffield Dr					
300	BMDL	60108	2968	24W-5N	C1
Sheffield Ln					
10	OKBK	60523	3086	15W-2S	B3
100	VNHL	60061	2647	17W-24N	B7
100	VNHL	60061	2701	16W-24N	C1
200	GNEN	60137	3025	23W-0N	A5
600	BGBK	60440	3205	21W-9S	E4
600	WDRG	60440	3205	21W-9S	E4
600	WDRG	60517	3205	21W-9S	E4
700	WNVL	60555	3080	30W-2S	B3
1200	GNVW	60025	2811	7W-13N	A5
1800	GNVA	60134	3019	36W-1N	E3
1900	WHTN	60187	3083	23W-2S	A4
2000	WHTN	60187	3082	23W-2S	E4
6600	WLBK	60527	3146	15W-7S	A6
15300	ODPK	60462	3346	11W-18S	A7
W Sheffield Ln					
13100	BHPK	60083	2421	13W-39N	A5
Sheffield Pl					
100	MltT	60137	3083	22W-2S	C3
Sheffield Rd					
10	MltT	60137	3083	22W-2S	C3
10	OswT	60538	3200	36W-10S	A7
400	NPVL	60565	3204	25W-9S	A4
Shefield Av					
1200	MDLN	60060	2590	19W-29N	B4
Sheila Av					
500	GNVA	60134	3019	36W-0N	E4
Sheila Dr					
800	JLET	60435	3497	27W-22S	D3
800	TroT	60435	3497	27W-22S	D3
1000	CTHL	60403	3497	27W-22S	D3
Sheila Ln					
1400	INCK	60060	2647	17W-25N	B5
1400	MDLN	60060	2647	17W-25N	A5
Sheila Pl					
600	LMBD	60148	3026	20W-1N	B2
Sheila St					
1900	WDSK	60098	2524	41W-32N	D4
2400	LydT	60131	2973	12W-3N	C6
2400	LydT	60164	2973	12W-3N	C6
2500	FNPK	60131	2973	12W-3N	C5
Shelbourne Ct					
900	HRPK	60133	2858	26W-9N	A7
Shelburne Dr					
-	HmrT	60441	3420	19W-20S	E5
10	OKBK	60523	3085	17W-2S	C3
300	CLSM	60188	2967	26W-2N	E7
Shelburne Ln					
400	SRGV	60554	3135	42W-5S	D3
Shelburne Farms Dr					
-	WnfT	60190	3023	28W-0N	B5
Shelby Ct					
10	VNHL	60061	2647	18W-24N	A6
1500	GRNE	60031	2476	18W-35N	E5
S Shelby Ct					
1900	CHCG	60608	3091	1W-1S	E1
W Shelby St					
10	JLET	60436	3498	24W-24S	E6
Sheldon Av					
200	DRGV	60515	3144	18W-5S	E2
700	AURA	60506	3137	37W-6S	D5
Sheldon Ct					
200	BbyT	60134	3018	39W-0S	E6
800	WHTN	60187	3082	24W-1S	D2
1100	NPVL	60540	3202	28W-8S	E1
Sheldon Dr					
1300	GYLK	60046	2475	21W-35N	D5
1400	ELGN	60120	2855	31W-10N	E6
21100	GYLK	60073	2475	21W-35N	D5
21100	RLKB	60046	2475	21W-35N	D5
21100	RLKB	60073	2475	21W-35N	D5
Sheldon Ln					
10	HDPK	60035	2758	7W-20N	B2
10	NtrT	60062	2758	7W-20N	B2
400	BbyT	60134	3018	39W-0S	D6
Sheldon Rd					
9600	HTLY	60142	2692	40W-22N	B4
Sheldrake Dr					
1600	ANHT	60004	2754	16W-17N	D6
1600	ANHT	60090	2754	16W-17N	D6
1600	WLNG	60090	2754	16W-17N	D6
Shelia St					
100	MHTN	60442	3677	19W-31S	E5

STREET Block	City	ZIP	Map#	CGS	Grid
Shell Ct					
10	MTGY	60543	3263	38W-11S	B1
800	SMBG	60193	2912	24W-9N	D1
Shell Dr					
2000	LYVL	60048	2590	18W-30N	D2
Shellbark Dr					
12200	HMGN	60491	3422	15W-20S	B4
Shelley Ct					
10	EGVV	60007	2914	19W-9N	D1
1500	DRN	60561	3207	18W-8S	A1
1800	HDPK	60035	2703	10W-23N	E3
3100	WDRG	60517	3205	22W-9S	C3
10500	BLVY	60098	2525	39W-31N	C7
10500	DrrT	60098	2525	39W-31N	C7
11000	WSTR	60154	3086	13W-1S	E2
Shelley Dr					
10	BmdT	60143	2913	21W-6N	E7
10	BmdT	60143	2914	21W-6N	A7
10	ITSC	60143	2914	21W-6N	A7
Shelley Ln					
100	WHTN	60187	3082	24W-2S	C3
500	CHHT	60411	3595	2W-25S	C1
W Shelley Ln					
14200	WDWH	60083	2420	14W-38N	D7
E Shelley Rd					
10	EGVV	60007	2914	19W-9N	D1
W Shelley Rd					
10	EGVV	60007	2914	19W-9N	D1
Shelley St					
11000	WSTR	60154	3086	13W-1S	E2
Shellingham Dr					
2700	LSLE	60532	3142	24W-6S	C5
Shell Lake Dr					
10	WldT	60564	3202	29W-10S	E6
Shelly Ct					
500	WLNG	60090	2755	14W-17N	D5
Shelly Ln					
900	MKNA	60448	3502	15W-23S	C4
900	NlxT	60451	3502	15W-23S	C4
2700	AURA	60504	3201	32W-8S	D2
12700	PNFD	60585	3337	32W-15S	C2
12700	WldT	60585	3337	32W-15S	C2
Shelter Rd					
10200	DGvT	60527	3207	17W-11S	C7
10200	DGvT	60527	3271	17W-11S	C1
Shelton Ln					
1500	CLLK	60014	2693	36W-23N	D3
Shenandoah Cir					
3100	CPVL	60110	2747	35W-18N	B5
Shenandoah Ct					
10	BGBK	60440	3205	23W-11S	A7
10	BRRG	60527	3208	15W-10S	C5
300	DRFD	60015	2757	9W-20N	B1
2500	AURA	60503	3265	31W-11S	D1
6200	NndT	60012	2584	35W-28N	B6
10800	HTLY	60142	2745	39W-20N	B1
N Shenandoah Ct					
1900	ANHT	60004	2806	18W-16N	E1
Shenandoah Dr					
200	RMVL	60446	3340	25W-16S	C3
700	CLSM	60188	2967	27W-3N	C5
2100	AURA	60503	3265	32W-11S	D1
3000	CPVL	60110	2747	36W-17N	A6
3700	NndT	60012	2584	35W-28N	B7
10700	HTLY	60142	2745	39W-20N	C1
11000	ODPK	60467	3345	13W-18S	A7
11000	OrlT	60467	3345	13W-18S	A7
11100	OrlT	60467	3344	14W-18S	E7
15600	ODPK	60467	3422	13W-18S	E1
15600	OrlT	60467	3422	13W-18S	E1
N Shenandoah Dr					
1900	ANHT	60004	2753	18W-16N	E7
1900	ANHT	60004	2806	20W-15N	A2
Shenandoah Ln					
10	HNWD	60047	2646	20W-25N	A5
1500	NPVL	60563	3141	26W-5S	E2
1900	SCRL	60174	2965	33W-4N	B4
2500	ElaT	60047	2753	19W-20N	C1
2500	LGGV	60047	2753	19W-20N	C1
8800	BRRG	60527	3208	15W-10S	C5
Shenandoah Rd					
10	DRFD	60015	2757	10W-20N	B1
Shenandoah Tr					
400	ELGN	60123	2853	36W-12N	E3
400	ELGN	60123	2854	36W-12N	A3
12700	PNFD	60585	3337	32W-15S	D1
W Shenandoah Tr					
13100	WDWH	60083	2421	13W-41N	A1
Shenk Rd					
34000	CstT	60481	3942	29W-41S	E6
Shenstone Rd					
300	RVSD	60546	3088	9W-3S	D4
400	BRWN	60402	3088	9W-3S	D4
400	RVSD	60402	3088	9W-3S	D4
Shepard Av					
100	WLNG	60090	2755	14W-17N	B5
Shepard Cir					
1500	EGVV	60007	2914	21W-9N	A1
Shepard Ct					
700	GRNE	60031	2534	16W-33N	E3
Shepard Dr					
300	ELGN	60123	2854	35W-10N	B6
14200	DLTN	60419	3350	0E-16S	E3
14200	DLTN	60419	3351	0E-16S	A4
Shepard Ln					
700	BRRG	60527	3208	15W-10S	A5
Shepard Rd					
700	GRNE	60031	2534	16W-33N	D3
2000	HFET	60169	2804	24W-12N	D7
Shepherd Ct					
2900	WDRG	60517	3143	22W-7S	C7
Shepherd Dr					
1300	NPVL	60565	3203	27W-8S	C2
1900	DSPN	60018	2862	13W-9N	E7
Shepherd Ln					
500	GNVA	60134	3019	37W-1N	C2
800	ELBN	60119	3017	43W-2N	B1
N Shepherd Hills Ln					
300	MHRY	60050	2528	32W-32N	B5
W Shepherd Hills Ln					
3500	MHRY	60050	2528	32W-32N	B5
Shepherds Crossing Dr					
-	BHPK	60099	2421	12W-40N	C3
-	ZION	60099	2421	12W-40N	C3
W Shepley Rd					
24100	CNHN	60436	3584	30W-27S	C5
24100	CNHN	60447	3584	30W-27S	C5
24100	TroT	60404	3584	30W-27S	C5
24100	TroT	60447	3584	30W-27S	C5
24700	TroT	60404	3583	32W-27S	E5
24700	TroT	60447	3583	32W-27S	E5
25900	SwdT	60447	3583	32W-27S	C5
Sheppard Ct					
3700	JLET	60435	3417	27W-19S	C2
Sheppey Ct					
1000	NPVL	60565	3203	27W-8S	B3
Sherbon Ln					
10	CLLK	60014	2640	35W-24N	A7
Sherborn Ln					
2000	SMBG	60193	2858	26W-10N	A6
2200	SMBG	60193	2857	26W-10N	E6
Sherborne Ct					
800	LYVL	60048	2591	17W-29N	B4
Sherbrook Ln					
100	MltT	60137	3083	23W-2S	A4
Sherbrooke Ct					
300	CLLK	60012	2640	33W-26N	E2
Sheri Ct					
9000	ODPK	60462	3346	11W-16S	A3
Sheri Ln					
9000	ODPK	60462	3345	11W-16S	E3
9000	ODPK	60462	3346	11W-16S	A3
Sheri St					
10	WldT	60565	3203	27W-11S	D7
10	WldT	60565	3267	27W-11S	D1
Sheridan Av					
10	CNHL	60514	3145	16W-5S	D3
200	HIWD	60040	2704	9W-23N	C2
9000	BKFD	60513	3087	11W-3S	E6
13100	BLID	60406	3349	3W-15S	A1
13100	WthT	60406	3349	3W-15S	A1
W Sheridan Av					
18800	GRNE	60031	2476	18W-35N	D7
18800	GRNE	60046	2476	18W-35N	D7
18800	TDLK	60046	2476	18W-35N	D7
18800	WrnT	60046	2476	18W-35N	D7
Sheridan Cir					
900	NPVL	60563	3140	29W-5S	C3
Sheridan Ct					
10	WDRG	60517	3143	22W-6S	C5
100	WKGN	60085	2480	10W-35N	B6
200	NLNX	60451	3501	18W-24S	A5
600	LKZH	60047	2699	21W-22N	C4
1500	WLNG	60090	2754	16W-18N	D3
1900	BFGV	60089	2701	17W-22N	B4
2200	LGGV	60047	2700	19W-21N	C7
2700	NPVL	60563	3140	29W-5S	C3
Sheridan Dr					
300	WLBK	60527	3207	17W-8S	C1
600	WCDA	60084	2588	25W-28N	A6
2800	WDRG	60517	3143	22W-6S	C5
7500	DRN	60561	3207	17W-8S	C1
7500	WLBK	60561	3207	17W-8S	C1
E Sheridan Dr					
300	BRLT	60103	2911	28W-7N	B5
N Sheridan Dr					
35000	GrtT	60041	2473	27W-35N	B6
35500	GrtT	60020	2473	27W-35N	A5
S Sheridan Dr					
800	BRLT	60103	2911	28W-7N	B5
Sheridan Ln					
400	SMBG	60193	2859	23W-9N	B7
Sheridan Pl					
800	DRGV	60515	3144	19W-4S	C1
2800	EVTN	60201	2813	2W-13N	B6
2800	WLMT	60091	2813	2W-13N	B6
6100	BtnT	60081	2414	29W-38N	D7
6100	BtnT	60081	2472	29W-37N	D1
E Sheridan Pl					
10	LKBF	60044	2593	10W-28N	E6
10	LKBF	60044	2594	10W-28N	A6
N Sheridan Pl					
38000	BHPK	60087	2480	10W-38N	B1
W Sheridan Pl					
10	LKBF	60044	2593	11W-28N	D6
Sheridan Rd					
-	LKBF	60044	2593	11W-28N	D5
-	LKMR	60051	2529	29W-31N	C6
-	NCHI	60088	2537	10W-31N	A7
-	WKGN	60085	2537	10W-32N	A4
10	GLNC	60022	2758	6W-18N	D2
10	HDPK	60035	2758	6W-20N	C2
10	KLWH	60043	2812	3W-14N	E4
10	KLWH	60091	2812	3W-14N	E4
10	WLMT	60091	2812	3W-14N	E4
100	GLNC	60022	2759	5W-17N	A6
100	GLNC	60093	2759	5W-16N	A6
100	PTPR	53158	2363	9W-43N	C4
100	WLMT	60091	2813	2W-14N	A5
100	WPHR	53158	2363	9W-43N	C4
100	WPHR	60096	2363	9W-42N	C5
300	EVTN	60091	2813	2W-13N	B6
300	HIWD	60040	2704	9W-24N	C1
300	WLBK	60527	3207	17W-8S	D2
300	WLMT	60201	2813	2W-13N	B6
300	WNKA	60093	2812	4W-15N	C2
400	CHCG	60626	2867	1W-9N	D6
400	HIWD	60037	2704	9W-24N	C1
500	HDPK	60035	2705	7W-21N	C7
700	HIWD	60035	2704	9W-24N	C1
700	HIWD	60040	2650	9W-24N	C7
900	HDPK	60035	2650	9W-24N	C7
900	HDPK	60040	2650	9W-24N	C7
900	HIWD	60035	2650	9W-24N	C7
900	LKFT	60035	2650	9W-24N	C7
900	LKFT	60037	2650	9W-24N	C7
900	LKFT	60045	2650	10W-25N	B5
900	WNKA	60093	2759	5W-16N	A6
1000	DRFD	60015	2703	11W-21N	D6
1000	NCHI	60064	2537	10W-31N	A7
1300	LKBF	60088	2593	10W-30N	E2
1300	NCHI	60044	2593	10W-30N	E2
1300	NCHI	60088	2593	10W-30N	E2
1400	BtnT	60096	2422	9W-41N	B1
1400	BtnT	60099	2422	9W-41N	B1
1400	WPHR	60096	2422	9W-41N	B1
1700	ZION	60099	2422	10W-40N	B4
1800	HDPK	60035	2704	8W-22N	E4
1900	BFGV	60089	2701	17W-22N	B4
2500	EVTN	60201	2813	2W-13N	B7
2800	NCHI	60064	2593	10W-30N	E1
3400	BHPK	60099	2422	10W-39N	B6
16900	EVTN	60201	2867	2W-11N	C3
16900	EVTN	60202	2867	2W-11N	C3
Sheridan Rd SR-32					
10400	PTPR	53158	2363		C1
12700	WPHR	53158	2363		C4
12700	WPHR	60096	2363		C4
Sheridan Rd SR-137					
-	WKGN	60085	2537	10W-32N	A4
100	PTPR	53158	2363	9W-43N	C4
100	WPHR	53158	2363	9W-43N	C4
100	WPHR	60096	2363	9W-42N	C6
1000	NCHI	60064	2537	10W-31N	A7
1400	BtnT	60096	2422	9W-41N	B1
1400	BtnT	60099	2422	9W-41N	B1
1400	WPHR	60096	2422	9W-41N	B1
1700	ZION	60099	2422	10W-40N	B4
3400	BHPK	60099	2422	10W-39N	B6
E Sheridan Rd					
10	LKBF	60044	2593	10W-28N	E6
10	LKBF	60044	2594	10W-28N	A7
400	LKFT	60045	2594	10W-28N	A7
N Sheridan Rd					
-	CHCG	60613	2978		A2
10	LKFT	60045	2650	10W-26N	B3
10	WKGN	60085	2537	10W-34N	B1
100	LKMR	60051	2529	28W-32N	E6
500	WKGN	60085	2480	10W-35N	B6
1400	LKFT	60045	2594	10W-28N	A7
1500	LKBF	60044	2594	10W-27N	A7
1700	WKGN	60087	2480	10W-35N	B6
2500	BHPK	60087	2480	10W-36N	B3
2500	WkgT	60087	2480	10W-36N	B3
2800	CHCG	60614	2978	0W-3N	A4
2800	CHCG	60657	2978	0W-3N	A4
3900	CHCG	60613	2977	1W-4N	E2
4400	CHCG	60613	2921	1W-5N	E7
4400	CHCG	60640	2921	1W-6N	E6
5500	CHCG	60660	2921	1W-6N	E4
6400	CHCG	60626	2921	1W-8N	D1
7100	CHCG	60626	2867	1W-9N	D7
7700	EVTN	60202	2867	1W-9N	D6
37800	BHPK	60099	2480	9W-37N	B1
38200	BHPK	60087	2422	9W-38N	B7
38400	BHPK	60099	2422	9W-38N	B7
38700	LkvT	60002	2415	26W-38N	E6
38900	AntT	60002	2415	26W-39N	E6
N Sheridan Rd SR-137					
1800	WKGN	60085	2480	10W-36N	B5
1800	WKGN	60087	2480	9W-37N	B2
2500	BHPK	60087	2480	10W-36N	B3
2500	WkgT	60087	2480	10W-36N	B3
37800	BHPK	60099	2480	9W-37N	B1
38200	BHPK	60087	2422	9W-38N	B7
38400	BHPK	60099	2422	9W-38N	B7
S Sheridan Rd					
10	LKFT	60045	2650	9W-25N	B5
10	WKGN	60085	2537	10W-33N	B2
100	LKMR	60051	2529	29W-31N	D6
W Sheridan Rd					
400	LKMR	60051	2529	29W-31N	C6
600	CHCG	60613	2978	0W-4N	A2
700	CHCG	60613	2977	1W-4N	E2
700	NndT	60051	2529	29W-31N	C6
1000	CHCG	60626	2921	1W-7N	D2
1000	CHCG	60660	2921	1W-7N	D2
Sheridan Sq					
500	EVTN	60202	2867	1W-10N	C5
Sheridan St					
10	ELGN	60123	2854	34W-11N	D4
300	PKFT	60466	3595	3W-25S	A1
600	AURA	60505	3138	34W-6S	C6
600	DLTN	60419	3350	0E-16S	E3
W Sheridan St					
200	LKFT	60436	3498	24W-24S	E6
Sheridan AC C					
2200	WKGN	60085	2536	11W-33N	D3
N Sheridan Oaks Dr					
42500	NptT	60002	2360	18W-42N	A5
Sheridans Tr					
16700	ODPK	60467	3423	13W-20S	A3
16900	OrlT	60467	3423	13W-20S	A4
Sheringham Dr					
1000	NPVL	60565	3203	27W-8S	B2
Sherington Ct					
10	BGBK	60440	3269	22W-12S	C2
Sherlock St					
200	FKFT	60423	3591	12W-26S	D1
Sherman Av					
100	MTGY	60538	3199	36W-9S	E4
200	MTGY	60538	3200	36W-9S	A4
300	AURA	60505	3200	36W-9S	A4
300	LslT	60563	3141	26W-5S	E3
300	MTGY	60505	3200	36W-9S	A4
300	NPVL	60563	3141	26W-5S	E3
400	AraT	60505	3200	36W-9S	A4
400	ELGN	60120	2855	33W-10N	B5
400	EVTN	60202	2867	2W-9N	B6
600	MLPK	60160	3030	10W-1N	A2
900	MLPK	60160	3029	11W-1N	E2
900	MYWD	60153	3029	11W-1N	E2
900	MYWD	60160	3029	11W-1N	E2
1200	EVTN	60201	2867	2W-10N	B4
1400	NCHI	60064	2536	11W-32N	D5
1500	GNVA	60134	3020	36W-1N	A3
1800	GNVA	60134	3019	36W-1N	E3
2300	NCHI	60064	2593	11W-31N	D1
2500	EVTN	60201	2813	2W-12N	B7
3400	WkgT	60031	2479	13W-35N	A6
3400	WkgT	60085	2479	13W-35N	A6
3600	GRNE	60031	2479	13W-35N	A6
5600	DGvT	60515	3144	20W-6S	A4
5600	DGvT	60516	3144	20W-6S	A4
5600	DRGV	60515	3144	20W-6S	A4
9100	BKFD	60513	3087	11W-3S	E5
E Sherman Av					
300	EMHT	60126	3028	15W-0N	B4
N Sherman Av					
1100	LslT	60563	3141	26W-5S	E3
1100	NPVL	60563	3141	26W-5S	E3
S Sherman Av					
14300	POSN	60469	3349	3W-17S	B4
W Sherman Av					
3000	WKGN	60085	2479	12W-35N	B6
3000	WkgT	60085	2479	12W-35N	B6
3300	GRNE	60031	2479	12W-35N	A6
3300	WkgT	60031	2479	12W-35N	A6
Sherman Blvd					
1300	NndT	60014	2586	30W-27N	A7
1900	NndT	60014	2585	30W-27N	E7
Sherman Ct					
100	BRLT	60103	2911	28W-7N	A5
200	JLET	60433	3499	23W-24S	A6
Sherman Dr					
-	CHCG	60609	3151	1W-5S	D2
5900	WDRG	60517	3143	22W-6S	C5
16700	HRVY	60426	3428	1W-20S	B4
N Sherman Dr					
1900	MHRY	60050	2527	34W-33N	D2
W Sherman Dr					
5300	MHRY	60050	2527	34W-33N	C2
5900	MchT	60050	2527	34W-34N	B2
Sherman Pl					
200	WKGN	60085	2537	10W-34N	A1
1300	EVTN	60201	2867	2W-11N	B3
1300	EVTN	60202	2867	2W-11N	B3
1500	DSPN	60016	2863	13W-11N	A1
Sherman Rd					
-	ALGN	60102	2693	36W-20N	E7
-	ALGN	60102	2746	36W-20N	E1
1400	RMVL	60440	3269	22W-13S	C5
1400	RMVL	60441	3269	22W-13S	C5
1400	RMVL	60446	3269	22W-13S	C5
22200	BlmT	60411	3596	0E-27S	E5
22200	BlmT	60475	3596	0E-27S	E5
22200	STGR	60411	3596	0E-27S	E5
22200	STGR	60475	3596	0E-27S	E5
22900	CRTE	60417	3596	0E-27S	E5
Sherman St					
-	WCHI	60185	3022	30W-0S	B6
-	WnfT	60185	3022	30W-0S	B6
10	CLLK	60014	2640	35W-26N	B3
100	BRLT	60103	2911	28W-7N	A5
400	PKFT	60466	3595	3W-25S	A1
700	AraT	60505	3138	34W-6S	D5
700	AURA	60505	3138	34W-6S	D5
800	JltT	60433	3499	23W-25S	A7
1000	DRGV	60515	3144	19W-4S	C1
1000	JLET	60433	3499	23W-25S	A7
10900	ODPK	60467	3423	13W-19S	A3
18200	LNSG	60438	3430	4E-21S	C7
18700	LNSG	60438	3510	4E-22S	B1
E Sherman St					
100	PLTN	60067	2752	20W-16N	E7
S Sherman St					
200	JLET	60433	3499	23W-24S	A5
W Sherman St					
10	PLTN	60067	2752	21W-16N	E7
Shermead Rd					
10	OswT	60538	3199	36W-10S	E6
Shermer Ct					
1300	GNVW	60025	2810	9W-13N	C5
Shermer Rd					
10	GNVW	60025	2864	9W-11N	D2
10	GNVW	60053	2864	9W-11N	D2
10	MNGV	60053	2864	9W-11N	D2
400	GNVW	60025	2810	9W-13N	C6
800	NHBK	60062	2757	9W-17N	C5
2100	NHBK	60062	2810	10W-15N	B3
2200	GNVW	60062	2810	10W-15N	B3
2500	NHBK	60025	2810	10W-15N	B3
8800	NLES	60714	2864	8W-11N	D3
N Shermer Rd					
8200	NLES	60714	2864	8W-10N	E4
8700	MNGV	60053	2864	8W-10N	E4
Sherry Ln					
100	CHHT	60411	3507	1W-23S	E4
100	JLET	60433	3587	23W-25S	B1
100	JltT	60433	3587	23W-25S	B1
400	RVWD	60015	2755	13W-20N	E1
500	RVWD	60015	2702	13W-20N	E7
9000	MaiT	60016	2863	11W-11N	E2
9000	NLES	60016	2863	11W-11N	E2
9000	NLES	60714	2863	11W-11N	E2
W Sherry Ln					
1800	ADSN	60101	2970	21W-4N	A4
Sherwick Rd					
10	OSWG	60543	3263	37W-11S	D1
Sherwin Av					
2000	DSPN	60018	2863	12W-9N	B7
4900	LNWD	60077	2865	6W-9N	E7
4900	LNWD	60712	2865	6W-9N	E7
4900	SKOK	60712	2865	6W-9N	E7
5000	SKOK	60077	2865	6W-9N	D7
W Sherwin Av					
1100	CHCG	60626	2867	1W-9N	C7
2400	CHCG	60645	2867	3W-9N	A7
2700	CHCG	60645	2866	3W-9N	E7
3800	LNWD	60076	2866	4W-9N	B7
3800	LNWD	60712	2866	4W-9N	B7
4800	LNWD	60077	2865	6W-9N	E7
4800	LNWD	60712	2865	6W-9N	E7
4800	SKOK	60077	2865	6W-9N	E7
4800	SKOK	60712	2865	6W-9N	E7
5900	CHCG	60646	2865	7W-9N	B7
6000	CHCG	60714	2865	7W-9N	B7
6000	NLES	60714	2865	7W-9N	B7
7700	CHCG	60068	2864	9W-9N	C7
7700	CHCG	60631	2864	9W-9N	C7
7700	PKRG	60068	2864	9W-9N	C7
Sherwood Av					
10	LKVL	60046	2475	22W-37N	A1
700	AURA	60506	3137	37W-6S	B5
1100	ELGN	60120	2855	33W-12N	B1
1300	ELGN	60120	2801	33W-13N	B7
2200	WSTR	60154	3086	13W-2S	E2
2900	MKHM	60428	3427	3W-19S	A2
4500	DRGV	60515	3144	19W-4S	D1
Sherwood Cir					
7700	HRPK	60133	2857	26W-9N	E7
N Sherwood Cir					
100	BMDL	60108	2968	24W-5N	C1
Sherwood Ct					
10	LIHL	60156	2693	37W-22N	C4
10	MDLN	60060	2647	17W-27N	A1
100	DRGV	60516	3206	18W-8S	E2
100	ROSL	60172	2912	25W-7N	B4
300	BGBK	60440	3205	22W-11S	C7
600	RMVL	60446	3269	23W-14S	A6
700	NPVL	60565	3203	27W-10S	B6
900	LKPT	60441	3342	21W-18S	A7
1300	GRNE	60031	2478	14W-35N	B5
W Sherwood Ct					
1600	PLTN	60067	2752	23W-17N	A5
Sherwood Dr					
-	CLSM	60188	3024	25W-2N	A2
-	PTHT	60070	2807	15W-16N	E1
10	LNSH	60069	2702	13W-23N	D3
10	OSWG	60543	3263	37W-12S	D3
100	CRY	60013	2695	30W-24N	E1
100	CRY	60013	2696	30W-23N	A1
100	WDDL	60191	2971	17W-5N	C2
300	AURA	60504	3138	35W-5S	B2
400	AraT	60504	3138	35W-5S	B2
400	SMWD	60107	2857	27W-10N	B6
900	LKBF	60044	2593	12W-28N	C7
900	LKFT	60044	2593	12W-28N	C7
900	LKFT	60045	2593	12W-28N	C7
900	PTHT	60070	2754	15W-16N	E7
1000	WLNG	60070	2754	15W-16N	E7
1000	WLNG	60090	2754	15W-16N	E7
4100	NndT	60012	2583	35W-27N	E7
4300	NndT	60012	2639	36W-27N	D1
8700	ODPK	60462	3424	10W-19S	B2
16100	TYPK	60487	3424	10W-19S	B2
E Sherwood Dr					
400	ADSN	60101	2971	17W-3N	B5
Sherwood Ln					
600	SMBG	60193	2859	22W-10N	C6
1400	GNVA	60134	3020	36W-0N	A5
N Sherwood Ln					
1100	PLTN	60067	2752	23W-17N	A5
Sherwood Pl					
1900	WHTN	60187	3082	25W-2S	B4
W Sherwood Pl					
800	JLET	60435	3498	25W-23S	C3
Sherwood Rd					
-	GNVW	60025	2811	6W-13N	C6
10	HnrT	60120	2856	31W-10N	A6
10	SMWD	60107	2856	31W-10N	A6
10	SMWD	60120	2856	31W-10N	A6
700	LGPK	60525	3087	12W-3S	C4
1300	WLMT	60091	2811	6W-13N	C6
1600	HDPK	60035	2704	10W-22N	B5
1700	DSPN	60016	2863	12W-11N	B3
E Sherwood Rd					
1800	ANHT	60004	2807	16W-15N	D1
Sherwood St					
1800	WLSP	60480	3209	12W-10S	B4
Sherwood Ter					
10	LKBF	60044	2593	12W-28N	C7
Sherwood Tr					
-	ODHL	60013	2641	31W-26N	D3
Sherwood Forest Dr					
3200	RcmT	60081	2413	32W-39N	B5
3200	SPGV	60081	2413	32W-39N	B5
Sheryl Ln					
400	GNVW	60025	2810	10W-12N	B7
400	GNVW	60025	2864	10W-12N	B1
400	GNVW	60714	2864	10W-12N	B1
400	NLES	60714	2864	10W-12N	B1
W Sheryl Lynn Dr					
14200	WDWH	60083	2420	14W-39N	D5
Shetland Ct					
900	RLKP	60030	2589	22W-30N	C1
1700	AURA	60502	3139	32W-5S	C3
W Shetland Ct					
16700	HmrT	60441	3420	20W-18S	A1
16700	LKPT	60441	3420	20W-18S	A1
Shetland Dr					
-	MTGY	60506	3198	40W-9S	C4
900	FKFT	60423	3592	9W-26S	E2
900	FKFT	60423	3593	9W-26S	A3
1200	MDLN	60060	2590	19W-29N	B3
1800	WHTN	60187	3083	23W-3S	A5
2600	AURA	60502	3139	32W-5S	C3
14500	HMGN	60491	3344	15W-17S	B5
17100	TYPK	60487	3424	11W-20S	A4
Shetland Ln					
-	MTGY	60506	3198	40W-9S	B4
-	MTGY	60538	3198	40W-9S	B5
2500	AURA	60502	3139	32W-5S	C3
2500	NpvT	60502	3139	32W-5S	C3
Shetland Pl					
4000	ZION	60099	2362	12W-41N	C7
Shetland Rd					
900	CmpT	60175	2906	41W-7N	A6
1800	NPVL	60565	3204	24W-8S	D2
2100	IVNS	60010	2751	25W-16N	A7
Shey Dr					
6200	ALSP	60803	3275	7W-13S	B5
6200	WRTH	60482	3275	7W-13S	B5
6200	WRTH	60803	3275	7W-13S	B5
W Shiawassie Dr					
6600	PSHT	60463	3275	8W-14S	A7
Shibley Av					
800	PKRG	60068	2863	11W-9N	E6
S Shield Av					
-	CHCG	60607	3034	0W-0S	B6
Shield Ct					
300	BGBK	60440	3205	22W-11S	C7
Shields Av					
900	WPHR	60096	2363	10W-42N	B6
1300	CHHT	60411	3508	0W-25S	C7
1400	CHHT	60411	3596	0W-25S	C1
8800	BKFD	60513	3087	11W-4S	D7
8800	BKFD	60513	3088	11W-4S	A7
8800	BKFD	60534	3088	11W-4S	A7
8800	LYNS	60534	3088	11W-4S	A7
9500	LGNG	60513	3087	11W-4S	D7
9500	LGNG	60525	3087	11W-4S	D7
S Shields Av					
2600	CHCG	60616	3092	0W-3S	B4
4300	CHCG	60609	3092	0W-4S	B7
4700	CHCG	60609	3152	0W-5S	B1
5500	CHCG	60621	3152	0W-6S	B3
S Shields Dr					
-	WKGN	60085	2536	13W-32N	A5
Shient Rd					
-	WslT	60481	3943	27W-41S	D4
Shiller St					
-	ELGN	60123	2854	34W-12N	D2
Shilling Ct					
10	BGBK	60440	3205	22W-10S	D6
21700	FKFT	60423	3591	13W-26S	B2
Shilling Rd					
10500	FKFT	60423	3591	13W-26S	B2
Shiloh Blvd					
900	ZION	60099	2422	9W-40N	B3
Shiloh Cir					
800	NPVL	60540	3203	27W-8S	B1
Shiloh Ct					
10	BRRG	60527	3208	15W-9S	A4
300	ELGN	60120	2855	32W-11N	C3
S Shiloh Ct					
900	JLET	60431	3497	28W-25S	B7
Shiloh Dr					
1900	JNBG	60050	2471	30W-35N	E5
1900	JNBG	60050	2472	30W-35N	A5
2200	AURA	60503	3265	32W-11S	B1
2200	LGGV	60047	2700	19W-21N	C7
2300	AURA	60503	3201	32W-11S	B7
W Shiloh Dr					
900	ANHT	60004	2753	18W-16N	E7
Shiloh Ln					
300	ELGN	60120	2855	32W-11N	C3
Shimer Ct					
1000	NPVL	60565	3204	25W-10S	C6
Shimmering View Ct					
9200	FKFT	60423	3503	11W-24S	E5
Shimmering View Dr					
-	FftT	60423	3504	11W-24S	A5
-	FKFT	60423	3504	11W-24S	A5
Shingle Oak Dr					
-	WCHI	60185	2966	30W-2N	B7
-	WynT	60185	2966	30W-2N	B7
Shining Moon Pth					
100	GLBT	60136	2799	37W-16N	C2
Shining Water Dr					
600	CLSM	60188	2967	27W-3N	C6
Shinnecook Dr					
-	MONE	60449	3683	6W-31S	A5
Shipland Dr					
200	CLLK	60012	2639	35W-27N	E1
200	CLLK	60012	2640	35W-27N	A1
300	NndT	60012	2639	36W-27N	E1
Shipston St					
8200	ODPK	60462	3346	10W-16S	B3
Shire Cir					
1300	IVNS	60067	2805	22W-14N	A4
1300	PLTN	60067	2805	22W-14N	A4
Shire Ct					
1500	GRNE	60031	2476	18W-35N	E5
1700	WHTN	60187	3082	24W-2S	C3
3400	NPVL	60564	3267	28W-11S	A1
8500	FKFT	60423	3592	10W-25S	B1

STREET Block City ZIP Map# CGS Grid

Shire Dr
15500 ODPK 60467 3423 13W-18S A1
Shire Tr
10 SBTN 60010 2803 27W-13N A6
Shires Ct
200 LslT 60540 3205 23W-8S A1
200 WNFD 60190 3023 27W-0N D4
Shires Ln
200 SCRL 60174 2964 34W-4N D4
Shirewood Farm Rd
10 HshT 60140 2795 47W-14N C5
Shirley Av
1100 SMWD 60107 2911 28W-9N B1
22100 SLVL 60411 3597 2E-26S D3
Shirley Ct
200 WHTN 60187 3024 26W-0S A7
16400 SHLD 60473 3428 0E-19S E2
Shirley Dr
1300 CTCY 60409 3430 4E-19S C3
17500 LNSG 60438 3430 4E-20S C5
Shirley Ln
200 GrtT 60050 2472 29W-35N D6
200 GrtT 60051 2472 29W-35N D6
200 MchT 60050 2472 29W-35N D6
13000 HTLY 60142 2744 43W-19N C3
S Shirley Ln
12200 ALSP 60803 3276 5W-14S C6
W Shirley Ln
4100 ALSP 60803 3276 5W-14S C6
Shirley Pkwy
900 NlxT 60451 3502 16W-24S A6
Shirley Rd
37000 WrnT 60031 2478 14W-37N D3
W Shirley Rd
21000 ElaT 60074 2752 21W-20N E1
21000 KLDR 60047 2752 21W-20N E1
21000 KLDR 60074 2752 21W-20N E1
W Shirra Ct
1600 ANHT 60004 2753 18W-16N D6
Shoal Dr
3800 HRPK 60133 2967 26W-4N E3
Shoal Creek Ct
10 LIHL 60156 2693 37W-22N C5
2400 RVWD 60015 2756 13W-20N A1
Shoal Creek Dr
25500 MONE 60449 3683 6W-31S B5
N Shoal Creek Ter
1700 VNHL 60061 2647 17W-27N B2
Shoals Dr
1100 LKPT 60441 3341 21W-18S E7
1100 LktT 60441 3341 21W-18S E7
1200 LKPT 60441 3342 21W-18S A7
Shoe Factory Rd
- ELGN 60120 2855 32W-12N D1
- HFET 60010 2803 27W-12N D7
- HFET 60010 2856 29W-12N D1
- HFET 60010 2857 28W-12N A1
- HFET 60120 2855 31W-12N E1
- HFET 60169 2803 27W-12N D7
- HFET 60169 2857 27W-12N C1
- HFET 60192 2855 32W-12N D1
- HnrT 60010 2856 29W-12N C1
- HnrT 60120 2855 31W-12N E1
- HnrT 60192 2855 31W-12N E1
10 HFET 60120 2856 31W-12N A1
10 HFET 60192 2856 31W-12N A1
10 HnrT 60120 2856 31W-12N A1
10 HnrT 60192 2856 31W-12N A1
600 HFET 60120 2802 30W-12N B7
600 HFET 60192 2802 30W-12N B7
600 HnrT 60120 2802 30W-12N A7
600 HnrT 60192 2802 30W-12N A7
S Sholer Av
7100 BGVW 60455 3148 9W-8S C7
7300 BGVW 60455 3210 9W-8S C1
Shome Ct
300 NPVL 60565 3203 26W-9S D4
Shoop Cir
1200 GNVA 60134 3019 37W-0N C5
1200 GnvT 60134 3019 37W-0N C5
Shoop Dr
1100 GNVA 60134 3019 37W-0N C5
1100 GnvT 60134 3019 37W-0N C5
Shooting Star Ct
2400 ELGN 60124 2853 36W-9N E7
Shooting Star Dr
4300 ISLK 60042 2586 28W-27N E7
4400 ISLK 60042 2642 28W-27N E1
Shootingstar Rd
800 GYLK 60030 2533 19W-31N C7
N Shore Av
6400 BtnT 60081 2414 29W-38N D7
39100 AntT 60002 2415 26W-39N D5
Shore Ct
10 MTGY 60543 3263 38W-11S B1
100 BRRG 60527 3207 16W-9S E3
100 BRRG 60527 3208 16W-9S A3
900 SMBG 60193 2913 23W-9N A1
1400 WLNG 60090 2754 16W-18N D4
S Shore Ct
1400 BRTN 60010 2751 24W-20N C1
Shore Dr
10 BRRG 60527 3207 16W-9S E3
10 BRRG 60527 3208 16W-9S A3
10 MTGY 60543 3263 37W-11S B1
10 SMBG 60193 2913 23W-9N A1
200 HRVY 60426 3350 1W-16S A4
200 HRVY 60827 3350 1W-16S A4
200 RVDL 60827 3350 1W-16S A4
37400 LkvT 60046 2474 25W-37N A2
E Shore Dr
- BHPK 60099 2422 9W-38N C7
100 SRWD 60404 3496 29W-24S D5
100 SRWD 60431 3496 29W-24S D5
9600 OKLN 60453 3211 6W-11S D6
N Shore Dr
- BHPK 60099 2422 9W-38N B7
100 LKVL 60046 2417 23W-38N A6
100 ODHL 60013 2641 31W-26N D3
400 CLLK 60014 2639 37W-25N B4
700 WCDA 60084 2588 25W-28N A6
900 LKBF 60044 2593 12W-28N C7
900 LKBF 60045 2593 12W-28N C7
900 LKFT 60045 2593 12W-28N C7
1100 WcnT 60084 2588 25W-28N A6
39400 AntT 60081 2415 27W-39N A5
39400 FXLK 60081 2415 27W-39N A5
NE Shore Dr
1300 HHLL 60051 2586 30W-29N A4
1300 NndT 60051 2586 30W-29N A4
S Shore Dr
- BHPK 60099 2422 9W-38N B7
900 LKWD 60014 2639 37W-25N C5
W Shore Dr
10 GYLK 60030 2532 21W-33N D4
4200 MHRY 60050 2528 33W-33N A2
W Shore Dr
4400 MHRY 60050 2527 33W-33N E2
4500 WRLK 60097 2469 36W-36N C4
5300 MchT 60050 2527 34W-33N C2
9500 OKLN 60453 3211 6W-11S D6
S Shore Ln
10 LKZH 60047 2698 24W-22N D4
200 LKFT 60045 2648 13W-25N E5
Shore Pl
- AntT 60081 2414 28W-39N E5
- FXLK 60081 2414 28W-39N E5
Shore Rd
1000 NPVL 60563 3140 31W-5S A3
26400 FXLK 60041 2473 26W-36N D3
26400 GrtT 60041 2473 26W-36N D3
Shore Acres Cir
200 LKBF 60044 2594 10W-30N A2
Shore Acres Dr
- LKBF 60044 2593 10W-29N E3
400 LKBF 60044 2594 10W-30N A2
Shoreacres Dr
- HNWD 60047 2645 22W-26N B2
S Shore Cove
- ANTH 60002 2418 20W-40N A3
Shoreham Cir
22500 DRPK 60010 2752 22W-20N B1
Shorehill Dr
5100 MHRY 60050 2527 34W-33N D2
Shoreland Ct
1000 RLKB 60073 2475 23W-34N A7
Shoreline Cir
100 SMBG 60173 2859 22W-10N C5
100 SMBG 60194 2859 22W-10N C5
Shore Line Ct
1800 RMVL 60446 3339 27W-17S C6
Shoreline Ct
- PGGV 60140 2798 41W-15N B4
100 SCRL 60174 2964 36W-4N A4
300 GLNC 60022 2759 5W-17N A5
Shoreline Dr
- PGGV 60140 2798 41W-15N B4
200 PKRG 60068 2863 11W-9N D7
500 GYLK 60030 2533 18W-33N D2
600 WrnT 60030 2533 18W-33N D2
700 AURA 60504 3202 31W-9S A3
1100 AURA 60504 3201 31W-9S E3
1500 SCRL 60174 2964 36W-4N A4
3800 HRPK 60133 2967 27W-4N D3
N Shoreline Dr
35000 GrtT 60041 2473 26W-35N D6
Shoreline Rd
- NBRN 60010 2697 26W-24N E1
10 LKBN 60010 2697 26W-24N D1
5000 LKBN 60010 2643 26W-25N D6
5000 TRLK 60010 2643 26W-25N D6
Shorely Dr
500 BRTN 60010 2751 25W-20N B1
N Shoreside Ct
1200 PLTN 60067 2752 22W-17N C5
Shoreside Dr
10 SBTN 60010 2803 27W-15N B2
Shorewood Ct
- GLHT 60139 3025 23W-1N A2
800 BRLT 60103 2911 27W-7N B4
4400 HFET 60192 2804 25W-15N A1
6100 LSLE 60532 3142 24W-6S D5
Shorewood Dr
- CLSM 60139 3024 23W-1N E2
- CLSM 60188 3024 23W-1N E2
10 GLHT 60139 3024 23W-1N E2
100 GLHT 60139 3025 23W-1N A2
300 GLHT 60137 3025 23W-1N A2
300 MltT 60137 3025 23W-1N A2
300 MltT 60139 3025 23W-1N A2
500 SRWD 60404 3496 30W-23S C4
800 BRLT 60103 2911 27W-7N B4
E Shorewood Dr
400 RLKB 60073 2475 22W-35N B7
600 RLKB 60030 2475 22W-35N B7
N Shorewood Dr
2600 MchT 60050 2528 31W-34N D1
2700 MchT 60050 2471 31W-34N D7
W Shorewood Dr
22300 RLKB 60073 2475 22W-34N B7
Shorewood Dr N
4400 HFET 60192 2804 25W-15N A2
Shorewood Dr W
1700 HFET 60192 2804 25W-15N A1
Shorewood Ln
100 SRWD 60404 3496 30W-24S C6
W Shorewood Rd
21100 AvnT 60030 2475 21W-35N E7
21100 GYLK 60030 2475 21W-35N D7
21300 GYLK 60046 2475 21W-35N D7
21300 RLKB 60046 2475 21W-35N D7
21800 RLKB 60030 2475 21W-35N D7
21900 RLKB 60073 2475 22W-35N C7
Short Av
1700 HRPK 60107 2911 27W-9N C2
1700 HRPK 60133 2911 27W-9N C2
1700 SMWD 60107 2911 27W-9N C2
Short Dr
13500 CTWD 60445 3347 6W-16S D2
Short Ln
500 GNVW 60025 2810 9W-12N C7
Short Pl
- ALGN 60102 2694 33W-20N E7
Short St
- GNVA 60134 3020 34W-1N C2
- LkvT 60046 2474 25W-38N A1
- LSLE 60532 3142 23W-5S E2
- MchT 60050 2472 29W-37N D2
- SPGV 60081 2413 31W-39N E5
10 CNHL 60514 3145 16W-5S D3
100 LKMR 60051 2529 29W-31N D6
100 WDND 60118 2801 34W-15N A4
200 CPVL 60118 2800 34W-16N E1
200 CRY 60013 2695 31W-23N E1
200 EDND 60118 2800 34W-16N E1
200 LMNT 60439 3270 19W-14S D6
300 CLLK 60014 2640 34W-26N C3
300 LSLE 60532 3143 23W-5S A3
300 WDSK 60098 2524 41W-31N C7
1600 ALGN 60102 2695 32W-21N A5
1600 AlqT 60102 2695 32W-21N A5
34100 WslT 60481 3943 27W-41S D5
N Short St
37600 LkvT 60046 2474 25W-37N A2
S Short St
2700 CHCG 60608 3091 1W-2S D3
14500 POSN 60469 3349 2W-17S B4
W Short St
28000 CbaT 60013 2643 28W-24N A6
Short Ter
1500 DSPN 60018 2862 15W-10N A6
Shortwood Dr
800 JLET 60432 3500 20W-22S B2
Shoshone Rd
2800 WKGN 60087 2479 12W-36N C4
S Shoshone Rd
12700 PSHT 60463 3274 9W-15S D7
Shoshone Tr
8000 TYPK 60477 3424 10W-21S C6
Shoshonee Tr
1700 WLNG 60090 2754 16W-17N D5
S Shoshoni Dr
14000 HMGN 60491 3343 16W-16S D4
Shoshoni Tr
10 LKVL 60046 2475 22W-38N C1
400 LKVL 60046 2417 22W-38N B7
Shotkoski Dr
5100 HFET 60192 2802 30W-12N C7
Shower St
300 BtnT 60081 2414 29W-38N D6
Showers St
- BtnT 60081 2414 29W-38N C6
Showplace Dr
2600 NPVL 60564 3202 30W-10S C6
2600 WldT 60564 3202 30W-10S C7
Shreffler Dr
13100 PNFD 60585 3337 31W-15S E2
Shriners Dr
500 ADSN 60101 2969 21W-4N E4
Shriver Ct
13700 PNFD 60544 3338 30W-16S B4
Shuler St
700 ELGN 60123 2854 35W-11N C4
Shuman Blvd
10 NPVL 60563 3141 27W-4S D1
Shumard Ln
- WldT 60564 3265 31W-12S E4
S Shumway Av
10 BTVA 60510 3078 35W-1S B2
W Shure Dr
1100 ANHT 60004 2753 18W-17N D4
Sibelius Ct
200 WHTN 60187 3082 24W-2S C4
W Sibelius Ln
16700 WrnT 60031 2477 16W-35N C7
W Sibley Av
10 CHCG 60631 2864 9W-9N B7
10 PKRG 60068 2864 9W-9N B7
10 PKRG 60631 2864 9W-9N B7
Sibley Blvd
- DLTN 60409 3351 1E-17S C5
- DLTN 60419 3351 1E-17S C5
10 CTCY 60409 3352 3E-17S B5
10 HMND 46320 3352 4E-17S C5
1100 CTCY 60409 3351 2E-17S C5
Sibley Blvd SR-83
- DLTN 60409 3351 1E-17S C5
- DLTN 60419 3351 1E-17S C5
1400 CTCY 60409 3351 2E-17S C5
E Sibley Blvd
10 DLTN 60419 3350 0E-17S D5
10 HRVY 60426 3349 1W-17S E5
10 SHLD 60419 3350 0E-17S D5
100 DLTN 60473 3350 0E-17S D5
100 HRVY 60426 3350 1W-17S A5
400 HRVY 60419 3350 0W-17S B5
500 SHLD 60426 3350 1W-17S A5
500 SHLD 60473 3350 1W-17S A5
700 DLTN 60419 3351 1E-17S A5
700 DLTN 60473 3351 1E-17S A5
800 SHLD 60419 3351 1E-17S A5
800 SHLD 60473 3351 1E-17S A5
1400 DLTN 60409 3351 1E-17S A5
E Sibley Blvd SR-83
10 HRVY 60426 3349 1W-17S E5
10 SHLD 60419 3350 0E-17S D5
100 DLTN 60473 3350 0E-17S D5
100 HRVY 60426 3350 1W-17S A5
400 DLTN 60419 3350 1W-17S A5
400 HRVY 60419 3350 0W-17S B5
500 HRVY 60426 3350 1W-17S A5
500 SHLD 60473 3350 1W-17S A5
700 DLTN 60419 3351 1E-17S A5
700 DLTN 60473 3351 1E-17S A5
800 SHLD 60419 3351 1E-17S A5
800 SHLD 60473 3351 1E-17S A5
1400 DLTN 60409 3351 1E-17S A5
W Sibley Blvd
10 DLTN 60419 3350 0W-17S C5
10 HRVY 60426 3349 2W-17S D5
10 SHLD 60419 3350 0W-17S C5
10 SHLD 60473 3350 0W-17S C5
100 DXMR 60426 3349 2W-17S D5
200 HRVY 60426 3350 0W-17S C5
200 SHLD 60426 3350 0W-17S C5
2200 POSN 60426 3349 2W-17S C5
2200 POSN 60469 3349 2W-17S C5
W Sibley Blvd SR-83
10 DLTN 60419 3350 0W-17S C5
10 HRVY 60426 3349 2W-17S D5
10 SHLD 60419 3350 0W-17S C5
10 SHLD 60473 3350 0W-17S C5
100 DXMR 60426 3349 2W-17S D5
200 HRVY 60426 3350 0W-17S C5
200 SHLD 60426 3350 0W-17S C5
2200 POSN 60426 3349 2W-17S C5
2200 POSN 60469 3349 2W-17S C5
Sibley Dr
100 MNKA 60447 3583 32W-28S C7
200 CnhT 60447 3583 32W-28S C7
200 MNKA 60447 3672 32W-28S C1
N Sibley Dr
40000 AntT 60002 2416 25W-40N B3
E Sibley St
10 CHCG 60631 2864 9W-9N C7
10 CTCY 60409 3352 D6
10 HMND 46320 3352 D6
10 PKRG 60068 2864 9W-9N C7
10 PKRG 60631 2864 9W-9N C7
200 NLES 60068 2864 9W-9N C7
200 NLES 60631 2864 9W-9N C7
200 NLES 60714 2864 9W-9N C7
W Sibley St
1600 PKRG 60068 2863 11W-9N D7
Sibling Ct
2900 NPVL 60564 3202 29W-10S D7
Sicilia
- BMDL 60172 2912 24W-6N C7
Sidney Av
- AddT 60101 3026 19W-2N D1
- AddT 60148 3026 19W-2N D1
10 ADSN 60148 3025 21W-2N E1
10 ADSN 60148 3026 21W-2N A1
10 BmdT 60137 3025 23W-2N B1
10 BmdT 60148 3025 21W-2N E1
10 GLHT 60137 3025 22W-2N B1
10 GLHT 60139 3025 23W-2N A1
Sidney Av
10 LMBD 60148 3025 21W-2N E1
10 LMBD 60148 3026 21W-2N A1
200 AddT 60101 3027 18W-2N A1
200 AddT 60181 3027 18W-2N A1
200 ADSN 60101 3027 18W-2N A1
300 AddT 60181 3026 18W-2N E1
300 ADSN 60101 3026 18W-2N E1
300 ADSN 60181 3027 18W-2N A1
400 BmdT 60139 3025 22W-2N B1
W Sidney Av
100 VLPK 60181 3027 18W-2N A1
Sidney Ct
10 SchT 60175 2907 38W-7N B6
E Sidney Ct
200 ADSN 60181 3027 17W-2N B1
200 VLPK 60181 3027 17W-2N B1
Sidwell Ct
- SCRL 60174 2964 34W-2N E7
Siebert Ct
1400 NPVL 60565 3204 24W-8S D2
Sieberts Ridge Rd
300 BNHL 60010 2696 28W-21N E5
300 LKBN 60010 2696 28W-21N E5
Siedschlag Rd
900 BtnT 60081 2355 30W-42N B5
900 SPGV 60081 2355 30W-42N B6
10100 FXLK 60081 2355 30W-42N B6
11000 RdlT 53181 2355 30W-42N B5
Siefert Ct
100 MltT 60187 3023 26W-1N D3
100 MltT 60190 3023 26W-1N D3
100 WNFD 60190 3023 26W-1N D3
Siegle Dr
16300 LktT 60403 3418 26W-19S A4
Siegmund St
200 JLET 60433 3499 22W-24S D6
300 JltT 60433 3499 22W-24S D5
Siems Cir
10 ROSL 60172 2913 23W-6N A6
Siems Dr
10 GLHT 60139 2968 23W-4N E4
Siena Dr
11000 FKFT 60423 3591 13W-27S A5
11100 FftT 60423 3591 13W-27S A5
Sienna Ct
10 BGBK 60440 3205 21W-10S E5
200 SMBG 60193 2858 24W-10N C6
200 SMBG 60193 2859 23W-9N A7
1000 RDLK 60073 2531 23W-32N E6
1600 INCK 60061 2647 17W-25N A6
1600 WLNG 60090 2808 14W-15N B1
Sienna Dr
600 SMBG 60193 2859 23W-9N A7
700 RDLK 60073 2531 23W-32N E5
700 SMBG 60193 2858 23W-9N E7
800 SMBG 60193 2912 24W-9N E1
3200 LIHL 60156 2692 39W-23N C2
W Sienna Dr
20400 LkvT 60046 2476 20W-37N A2
20800 LkvT 60046 2475 20W-37N E2
Sierra Av
300 NPVL 60565 3203 27W-10S D6
2400 JLET 60586 3415 32W-20S C5
Sierra Ct
10 LIHL 60156 2694 34W-21N C6
400 NPVL 60565 3203 27W-10S D6
800 GRNE 60031 2476 18W-35N E7
1000 UYPK 60466 3684 3W-30S B3
1800 RMVL 60446 3339 27W-17S D6
6900 JLET 60586 3415 32W-20S C6
7000 DRN 60561 3145 17W-7S C7
Sierra Dr
6900 DRN 60561 3145 17W-7S B7
15500 OKFT 60452 3347 7W-18S C7
Sierra Ln
400 BGBK 60440 3268 23W-11S E2
700 LslT 60540 3142 24W-5S C4
W Sierra Ln
9000 PSHL 60465 3209 11W-11S E7
Sierra Pl
300 GRNE 60031 2533 18W-34N E1
500 GRNE 60031 2476 18W-34N E7
Sierra Rd
10 OswT 60538 3199 36W-10S E7
Sierra Rdg
1000 NLNX 60451 3588 19W-27S E5
1000 NLNX 60451 3589 19W-27S A5
W Sierra St
7000 CHCG 60620 3214 0W-9S B3
Sierra Tr
- PnfT 60446 3339 27W-17S D6
200 CRY 60013 2695 32W-23N B1
200 RMVL 60446 3339 27W-17S D6
300 CRY 60013 2641 32W-24N B7
Sierra Canyon
2600 NLNX 60451 3588 19W-27S E5
Sierra Highlands Ct
1600 JLET 60586 3496 31W-21S A1
Sierra Highlands Dr
1600 JLET 60586 3496 31W-21S A1
Sierra Pass
- SMBG 60194 2857 27W-11N D3
Sierra Pass Dr
100 SMBG 60194 2857 27W-10N D5
Sierra Rose Cir
500 JLET 60431 3497 28W-23S A3
3900 JLET 60431 3496 28W-23S E3
Sierra Woods Ct
8200 CPVL 60110 2746 36W-17N E6
Sierra Woods Ln
8000 CPVL 60110 2746 36W-17N E6
Siesta Ct
100 CPVL 60110 2748 33W-18N B5
Siesta Dr
300 NLNX 60451 3501 18W-25S B7
Siesta Rd
100 CPVL 60110 2748 33W-18N B5
Siesta Keys Ln
1100 SMWD 60120 2856 30W-10N C7
Sievert Ct
100 BNVL 60106 2915 16W-6N E5
100 CHCG 60106 2915 16W-6N E5
Sieverwood Ct
10 SMWD 60107 2857 26W-11N E4
Sigmund Rd
700 NPVL 60563 3141 27W-5S B2
Signal Dr
1600 NPVL 60565 3204 25W-9S C3
Signal Ln
400 GYLK 60030 2533 20W-32N A5
Signal Hill Rd
100 NBRN 60010 2697 26W-23N D3
400 NBRN 60010 2698 25W-23N A3
Signature Dr
200 BMDL 60108 2969 22W-4N B2
Signe Ct
300 LKBF 60044 2593 11W-29N D4
Sigwalt Ct
2700 RGMW 60008 2806 19W-14N C5
Sigwalt St
3400 RGMW 60008 2806 20W-14N B5
E Sigwalt St
10 ANHT 60005 2807 17W-13N A5
W Sigwalt St
100 ANHT 60005 2807 18W-13N A5
400 ANHT 60005 2806 18W-14N E5
Silbury Ct
500 MHRY 60050 2527 33W-32N D5
Silbury Dr
100 BRLT 60103 2909 31W-8N E3
Silentbrook Ln
5400 RGMW 60008 2805 21W-14N C5
5600 RGMW 60067 2805 21W-14N C5
Silk Oak Dr
5400 WldT 60564 3266 31W-13S A5
Silk Oak Ln
600 CLLK 60014 2640 33W-26N D3
600 NndT 60014 2640 33W-26N D3
1200 BRLT 60103 2910 30W-9N B2
Silktree Cir
21200 DPgT 60544 3339 26W-15S E3
Sill Av
1000 AURA 60506 3199 37W-8S D2
Silo Ct
10 GRNE 60031 2534 16W-34N C1
S Silo Ct
15100 HMGN 60491 3343 16W-18S E6
S Silo Dr
15100 HMGN 60491 3343 16W-18S E7
W Silo Dr
7400 FftT 60423 3504 9W-24S E6
Siloam Av
10 FXLK 60020 2473 27W-36N A3
Silo Hill Dr
1100 GYLK 60030 2533 19W-32N C5
Silo Ridge Dr
10 ODPK 60467 3344 14W-17S D6
Silo Ridge Rd E
10 ODPK 60467 3344 14W-17S E6
Silo Ridge Rd N
10 ODPK 60467 3344 14W-17S D6
Silo Ridge Rd S
10 ODPK 60467 3344 14W-17S D6
Silo Ridge Rd W
10 ODPK 60467 3344 14W-17S D6
Silvana Ct
1000 SMBG 60173 2859 22W-11N D4
Silvana Dr
400 PltT 60124 2905 41W-9N E2
400 PltT 60124 2906 41W-9N A2
Silver Cir
1300 BRLT 60103 2967 28W-5N A1
Silver Ct
200 ELGN 60123 2854 34W-11N D4
1300 BRLT 60103 2967 28W-6N A1
7800 OrlT 60462 3346 9W-17S D6
Silver Ln
100 MLPK 60160 3030 10W-1N A2
N Silver Ln
1400 PnfT 60544 3338 29W-17S D5
1500 PLTN 60074 2753 19W-17N C4
1500 PltT 60074 2753 19W-17N C4
Silver St
300 ELGN 60123 2854 34W-11N D3
Silver Tr
10 NARA 60542 3077 37W-3S C6
10 NARA 60542 3137 37W-4S C1
Silverado Ct
10 BGBK 60490 3267 27W-12S D2
Silverado Dr
- JLET 60421 3675 25W-29S C2
Silverado St
100 BGBK 60490 3267 27W-12S D3
Silver Aspen Cir
500 CLLK 60014 2639 36W-24N E7
500 CLLK 60014 2693 36W-23N D1
Silverberry Ct
- JLET 60431 3497 28W-24S B7
Silver Berry Dr
500 CLLK 60014 2640 34W-26N D3
Silver Charm Dr
- OSWG 60543 3264 34W-11S D2
Silver Creek Ct
3800 AURA 60564 3202 30W-9S A4
16600 PNFD 60586 3416 30W-19S C4
Silver Creek Dr
600 JLET 60431 3497 28W-24S B7
2400 LydT 60164 2973 12W-3N B6
2600 FNPK 60131 2973 12W-3N B5
Silver Creek Ln
- MLPK 60160 3029 11W-1N D1
Silver Creek Rd
500 GwdT 60098 2524 41W-32N D5
500 WDSK 60098 2524 41W-32N D5
Silverdale Dr
8900 ODPK 60462 3346 11W-17S A6
Silver Falls Ct
- JLET 60431 3497 28W-24S B6
Silver Fox Dr
700 JLET 60431 3497 28W-24S B7
S Silver Fox Dr
12900 LMNT 60439 3343 16W-15S D1
Silvergate Ct
1600 GRNE 60031 2476 18W-35N E5
Silver Glen Ct
100 SchT 60175 2908 36W-6N A6
Silver Glen Rd
10 CmpT 60124 2905 42W-7N E6
10 CmpT 60151 2905 43W-7N B6
10 CmpT 60175 2905 42W-7N D6
10 CmpT 60175 2906 41W-7N A6
10 SchT 60175 2907 37W-6N D6
10 SchT 60177 2907 37W-6N D6
10 SEGN 60177 2907 37W-6N D6
100 SchT 60175 2908 36W-6N A6
600 MHRY 60050 2526 36W-32N D5
700 CmpT 60175 2907 38W-6N A6
1900 SEGN 60175 2907 37W-6N D6
Silver Glen Rd CO-5
10 CmpT 60124 2905 42W-7N E6
10 CmpT 60151 2905 43W-7N B6
10 CmpT 60175 2905 42W-7N D6
10 CmpT 60175 2906 41W-7N A6
10 SchT 60175 2907 37W-6N D6
10 SchT 60177 2907 37W-6N D6
10 SEGN 60177 2907 37W-6N D6
100 SchT 60175 2908 36W-6N A6
700 CmpT 60175 2907 38W-6N A6
700 SEGN 60175 2907 37W-6N D6
Silver Hill Cir
1000 JLET 60432 3500 21W-22S A2

STREET Block	City	ZIP	Map#	CGS	Grid
W Silver Lake Av					
22500	ANTH	60002	2358	22W-42N	B6
22500	AntT	60002	2358	22W-42N	B7
Silver Lake Ct					
-	PGGV	60140	2798	41W-15N	A4
Silver Lake Dr					
8000	ODPK	60462	3346	10W-17S	C5
8000	OrlT	60462	3346	10W-17S	C5
W Silver Lake Dr					
10600	FftT	60423	3591	13W-27S	B5
Silver Lake Rd					
-	CRY	60013	2695	31W-24N	D1
400	CRY	60013	2641	31W-24N	D7
6500	AlqT	60013	2641	31W-24N	D6
N Silver Lake Rd					
1900	ANHT	60004	2807	16W-16N	E1
Silver Lake Tr					
6000	AlqT	60013	2641	31W-25N	D4
6000	NndT	60013	2641	31W-25N	D4
6000	ODHL	60013	2641	31W-25N	D4
Silver Lakes Rd					
-	AlqT	60013	2641	31W-25N	D5
Silverleaf Blvd					
300	MltT	60187	3024	25W-0N	A5
N Silverleaf Blvd					
300	CLSM	60188	2968	26W-2N	A7
Silver Leaf Ct					
-	JLET	60431	3497	28W-24S	B7
Silverleaf Ct					
13000	PNFD	60585	3337	33W-15S	B2
W Silverleaf Ct					
21000	DPgT	60544	3340	25W-16S	B3
Silver Leaf Dr					
500	JLET	60431	3497	28W-24S	B7
Silverleaf Dr					
-	ADSN	60101	2969	21W-4N	E4
26400	PNFD	60585	3337	33W-15S	B2
Silver Leaf Ln					
-	GrtT	60041	2530	26W-34N	E1
-	GrtT	60073	2530	26W-34N	E1
-	RDLK	60041	2530	26W-34N	E1
500	RDLK	60073	2530	26W-34N	E1
S Silverleaf Rd					
13400	DPgT	60544	3340	26W-15S	A3
Silver Linden Ln					
2100	BFGV	60089	2701	17W-22N	B4
Silver Maple Ct					
1500	NPVL	60563	3141	26W-5S	E2
Silver Maple Dr					
12200	HMGN	60491	3422	15W-19S	C1
Silver Maple Ln					
2400	JLET	60433	3587	23W-27S	B4
2400	JltT	60433	3587	23W-27S	B4
Silver Moon Lake Wy					
16300	LktT	60403	3418	26W-19S	A3
21100	LktT	60403	3417	26W-19S	E3
Silver Oaks Cir					
1800	AURA	60504	3201	33W-8S	A3
E Silver Oaks Dr					
100	RLKB	60073	2475	22W-36N	B5
N Silver Oaks Dr					
-	LkvT	60046	2475	22W-36N	B4
-	LkvT	60073	2475	22W-36N	B4
300	RLKB	60073	2475	22W-36N	B4
Silver Pine Dr					
-	HFET	60010	2751	24W-16N	C7
1100	HFET	60010	2804	24W-16N	C1
1600	NHBK	60062	2756	11W-16N	D6
Silverpine Dr					
2200	GNVW	60025	2810	9W-13N	C5
Silver Ridge Dr					
-	JLET	60586	3415	32W-21S	D7
-	JLET	60586	3495	31W-22S	D1
400	SchT	60175	2907	36W-6N	E7
Silver Rock Dr					
1800	CTHL	60403	3417	27W-21S	D7
2500	JLET	60435	3417	27W-21S	D7
Silver Rock Ln					
500	BFGV	60089	2701	17W-21N	B7
Silverside Dr					
-	FKFT	60423	3504	10W-23S	B4
19500	TYPK	60477	3504	10W-23S	B4
19700	FftT	60477	3504	10W-23S	B4
Silverspring Ct					
1600	AURA	60504	3201	33W-9S	B4
Silverspring Dr					
-	ElgT	60124	2853	38W-10N	A5
Silver Spur Ct					
2700	NPVL	60565	3203	27W-10S	B7
Silver Spur Dr					
10	LMNT	60439	3272	15W-13S	B4
Silverstone Dr					
-	BNHL	60110	2748	32W-19N	C3
-	CPVL	60110	2748	33W-19N	B3
-	DndT	60110	2748	33W-19N	B3
E Silver Strand Cir					
1500	PLTN	60074	2753	19W-18N	C3
Silver Stream Dr					
26200	CNHN	60410	3672	32W-30S	C4
N Silverton Ct					
10	PltT	60067	2805	22W-15N	B2
Silverton Dr					
-	GYLK	60030	2532	21W-32N	E5
Silver Tree Cir					
10	CRY	60013	2641	31W-24N	C6
Silverwillow Dr					
1800	GNVW	60025	2810	8W-14N	D4
Silverwood Ct					
300	SMBG	60193	2859	22W-9N	D7
800	LKZH	60047	2699	22W-21N	A5
1100	WLNG	60090	2754	16W-18N	E2
Simms Ct					
-	PLNO	60545	3259	48W-13S	B5
Simms St					
200	AURA	60505	3200	35W-8S	B3
1200	AraT	60504	3200	34W-8S	E3
1300	AURA	60504	3200	34W-8S	E3
1700	AURA	60504	3201	33W-8S	A3
Simo Dr					
24000	PNFD	60586	3416	30W-19S	B2
Simon Ct					
800	GNVA	60134	3019	37W-0N	C5
W Simon Ct					
25800	AntT	60002	2416	25W-39N	A4
Simon Ln					
-	BtlT	60512	3198	40W-10S	B7
-	MTGY	60512	3198	40W-10S	B7
N Simonds Dr					
-	CHCG	60613	2922	0W-5N	A7
-	CHCG	60640	2921	0W-6N	E5
-	CHCG	60640	2922	0W-6N	A5
Simonds Wy					
-	HDPK	60035	2650	9W-24N	C7
-	HDPK	60037	2650	9W-24N	C7
-	HDPK	60040	2650	9W-24N	C7
-	HIWD	60035	2650	9W-24N	C7
Simonds Wy					
-	LKFT	60035	2650	9W-24N	C7
-	LKFT	60037	2650	9W-24N	C7
-	LKFT	60045	2650	9W-24N	C7
Simone Dr					
300	DSPN	60016	2808	14W-12N	C7
300	DSPN	60016	2862	14W-12N	C1
Simons Rd					
500	OswT	60543	3337	33W-14S	A1
500	OswT	60585	3337	33W-14S	A1
500	PNFD	60543	3337	33W-14S	A1
500	PNFD	60585	3337	33W-14S	A1
Simonsen Ln					
2800	GNVW	60025	2810	10W-13N	B6
Simotes Ln					
26100	CNHN	60481	3761	32W-33S	D3
26100	CnhT	60481	3761	32W-33S	D3
Simplon Cir					
300	LYWD	60411	3598	4E-25S	C1
Simpson Av					
300	LKBF	60044	2594	10W-28N	B6
Simpson Ct					
1800	MTGY	60538	3198	40W-9S	A5
Simpson Pkwy					
-	MTGY	60506	3198	40W-9S	C4
-	MTGY	60538	3198	41W-9S	A5
-	SgrT	60538	3198	41W-9S	A5
Simpson St					
-	SKOK	60076	2866	5W-12N	B2
10	GNVA	60134	3020	34W-0N	D4
800	EVTN	60201	2867	2W-12N	B1
1100	MDLN	60060	2646	18W-26N	D3
1700	EVTN	60201	2866	3W-11N	E2
2900	EVTN	60203	2866	4W-12N	C2
2900	SKOK	60203	2866	4W-12N	C1
7000	MNGV	60053	2864	8W-11N	D2
Sims Ln					
100	SchT	60175	2908	36W-7N	A6
Simsbury Ct					
-	OSWG	60543	3263	36W-13S	D5
2300	NPVL	60564	3202	29W-10S	D5
Sinatra Ln					
5400	HRPK	60133	2911	27W-6N	C6
Sinclair Av					
6400	BRWN	60402	3089	8W-3S	A4
S Sinclair Dr					
-	PNFD	60585	3265	32W-14S	C7
-	WldT	60585	3265	32W-14S	C7
Sinde Cir					
10	RMVL	60446	3341	23W-16S	A3
Sinderson St					
5900	CmgT	60033	2405	53W-37N	A7
5900	DhmT	60033	2405	53W-37N	A7
5900	DhmT	60033	2463	53W-37N	A1
Singapore Ln					
400	CPVL	60110	2747	35W-17N	D6
Singer Av					
400	LMNT	60439	3270	19W-14S	D6
Single Oak Ct					
34100	GrtT	60041	2530	26W-34N	D1
Singleton Dr					
1100	ROSL	60172	2912	24W-7N	C5
Singleton Pl					
400	JLET	60436	3586	24W-25S	D1
400	JltT	60436	3586	24W-25S	D1
Singletree Ln					
700	LslT	60565	3204	23W-8S	E3
Singletree Rd					
100	ODPK	60467	3344	14W-17S	D6
Sinker Bay					
10	LKMR	60051	2529	28W-33N	E3
Sinnett St					
12100	HTLY	60142	2691	41W-22N	E3
Sioux Av					
100	BNHL	60010	2748	32W-18N	D5
100	BNHL	60110	2748	32W-18N	D5
100	CPVL	60110	2748	32W-18N	D4
2400	WDRG	60517	3205	21W-8S	E1
N Sioux Av					
7000	CHCG	60646	2919	7W-8N	B1
Sioux Ct					
10	MltT	60187	3082	26W-2S	A4
10	NPVL	60563	3141	26W-5S	D2
1200	MhtT	60451	3589	16W-28S	E6
1200	MhtT	60451	3590	16W-28S	A6
Sioux Dr					
200	BGBK	60440	3268	23W-11S	E1
500	BTVA	60510	3019	36W-0S	E7
800	ELGN	60120	2855	32W-12N	C1
800	RLKH	60073	2474	24W-36N	D5
W Sioux Dr					
16600	LKPT	60441	3420	20W-20S	B5
Sioux Ln					
300	CLSM	60188	2968	26W-2N	A7
4200	MHRY	60050	2528	33W-32N	A4
N Sioux Ln					
1900	MPPT	60056	2808	13W-14N	E5
S Sioux Ln					
13000	PSHT	60463	3346	9W-15S	E1
Sioux Rd					
2100	WKGN	60087	2479	11W-36N	C4
7800	ODPK	60462	3346	9W-16S	C2
Sioux St					
300	PKFT	60466	3594	4W-27S	E5
300	RNPK	60466	3594	4W-27S	E5
300	RNPK	60471	3594	4W-27S	E5
Sioux Tr					
300	LIHL	60156	2694	34W-21N	B5
2700	GNVW	60025	2809	11W-15N	D2
2700	GNVW	60062	2809	11W-15N	D2
6400	IHPK	60525	3146	14W-7S	D6
Sippel Dr					
17900	TYPK	60487	3424	10W-21S	B6
Sir Barton Ct					
1000	NPVL	60540	3142	26W-7S	A7
S Sir Galahad Ln					
1300	MPPT	60056	2861	16W-11N	E3
N Sir John Dr					
39000	LkvT	60046	2416	24W-39N	C6
S Sir Lancelot Ln					
1300	MPPT	60056	2861	16W-11N	E3
Sirus Av					
400	AURA	60506	3137	37W-6S	C5
Sir William Ln					
1000	LKFT	60045	2649	12W-24N	B7
Sisson St					
1400	LKPT	60441	3419	22W-20S	D4
Sister Ct					
11400	HTLY	60142	2692	40W-21N	A6
Sisters Av					
2100	NPVL	60564	3202	29W-10S	D7
Sisters Ct					
2400	NPVL	60564	3202	29W-10S	D7
N Sistina Av					
37100	LkvT	60046	2476	20W-37N	A2
E Sitka Ln					
1800	MPPT	60056	2808	13W-14N	D3
Sivert Dr					
800	WDDL	60191	2915	17W-7N	B5
900	EGVV	60007	2915	17W-7N	B5
S Sivic St					
-	ANHT	60005	2807	17W-12N	C7
-	MPPT	60056	2807	17W-12N	C7
Siwiha Dr					
200	GYLK	60030	2532	21W-33N	D3
Six Flags Dr					
-	GRNE	60031	2478	15W-34N	A7
-	GRNE	60031	2535	15W-34N	A1
-	WrnT	60031	2535	15W-34N	A1
Six Flags Pkwy					
-	GRNE	60031	2478	15W-35N	A6
Six Pines Dr					
10	RMVL	60446	3269	23W-14S	A6
Sizer Rd					
700	GRNE	60031	2534	16W-33N	D3
Sjogren Ct					
1700	WHTN	60187	3082	24W-2S	D3
Skate Ct					
4100	NCHI	60088	2593	11W-31N	D1
Skender Ct					
13800	HMGN	60491	3343	18W-16S	A3
S Skidmore Ct					
19600	FftT	60423	3504	9W-23S	D4
Skidmore Dr					
900	ANTH	60002	2357	23W-42N	E6
Ski Hill Rd					
10	FRGV	60021	2696	29W-23N	C2
Skillen Ln					
10	FXLK	60020	2473	28W-36N	A3
Skinner Dr					
1500	TNLK	53181	2354		A3
Skinner St					
-	DMND	60416	3941	33W-39S	C2
E Skinner St					
2300	DMND	60416	3941	33W-40S	C2
Skipjack Pl					
4100	NCHI	60088	2593	12W-31N	C1
Skipping Stone Ln					
400	DGvT	60521	3146	15W-6S	A4
400	HNDL	60521	3146	15W-6S	A4
Skokiana Ter					
4100	SKOK	60076	2866	5W-11N	B2
Skokie					
-	WNKA	60093	2811	6W-16N	D1
Skokie Av					
500	HDPK	60035	2704	8W-22N	D3
Skokie Blvd					
10	HDPK	60035	2757	8W-18N	E2
10	NfdT	60062	2757	8W-18N	E3
10	NHBK	60062	2757	8W-18N	E2
400	NHBK	60062	2758	8W-18N	A4
1200	GLNC	60062	2758	8W-18N	A4
7400	LNWD	60712	2865	6W-9N	E7
7400	SKOK	60077	2865	6W-9N	E7
7400	SKOK	60712	2865	6W-9N	E7
9700	SKOK	60076	2865	6W-12N	E1
10000	SKOK	60076	2811	5W-13N	E7
10000	SKOK	60077	2811	5W-13N	E7
10000	WLMT	60076	2811	6W-12N	E7
10000	WLMT	60077	2811	6W-12N	E7
10000	WLMT	60091	2811	5W-13N	E7
Skokie Blvd SR-50					
7400	LNWD	60712	2865	6W-9N	E7
7400	SKOK	60077	2865	6W-9N	E7
7400	SKOK	60712	2865	6W-9N	E7
7500	SKOK	60076	2865	6W-9N	E7
Skokie Blvd US-41					
7500	SKOK	60077	2865	6W-9N	E7
9700	SKOK	60076	2865	6W-12N	E1
10000	SKOK	60076	2811	5W-13N	E7
10000	SKOK	60077	2811	5W-13N	E7
10000	WLMT	60076	2811	6W-12N	E7
10000	WLMT	60077	2811	6W-12N	E7
10000	WLMT	60091	2811	5W-13N	E7
Skokie Ct					
300	WLMT	60091	2811	5W-13N	E6
Skokie Hwy					
-	GRNE	60031	2535	13W-34N	E1
-	HDPK	-	2757	8W-20N	E1
-	NCHI	60064	2536	12W-32N	A6
-	NCHI	60085	2536	12W-32N	A5
-	NfdT	-	2757	8W-20N	E1
-	NHBK	-	2757	8W-20N	E1
-	NptT	60031	2420	15W-39N	A5
-	NptT	60031	2478	15W-38N	A1
-	NptT	60083	2360	16W-41N	E7
-	NptT	60083	2419	16W-41N	E2
-	NptT	60083	2420	15W-40N	A4
-	NptT	60099	2360	16W-41N	E7
-	PKCY	-	2535	13W-33N	E2
-	PKCY	-	2536	13W-33N	A3
-	ShdT	60044	2536	12W-31N	B7
-	WDWH	60031	2420	15W-39N	A5
-	WDWH	60031	2478	15W-37N	A1
-	WDWH	60083	2360	16W-41N	E7
-	WDWH	60083	2419	16W-41N	E2
-	WDWH	60083	2420	15W-39N	A5
-	WDWH	60099	2360	16W-42N	E7
-	WKGN	-	2535	13W-33N	E3
-	WKGN	60064	2536	12W-32N	A6
-	WKGN	60085	2536	12W-32N	A6
-	WrnT	60031	2478	15W-37N	A1
Skokie Hwy US-41					
-	GRNE	60031	2535	13W-34N	E1
-	HDPK	-	2757	8W-20N	E1
-	NCHI	60064	2536	12W-32N	A6
-	NCHI	60085	2536	12W-32N	A6
-	NfdT	-	2757	8W-20N	E1
-	NHBK	-	2757	8W-20N	E1
-	NptT	60031	2420	15W-39N	A5
-	NptT	60031	2478	15W-37N	A1
-	NptT	60083	2360	16W-41N	E7
-	NptT	60083	2419	16W-41N	E2
-	NptT	60083	2420	15W-40N	A4
-	NptT	60099	2360	16W-41N	E7
-	PKCY	-	2535	13W-33N	E2
-	PKCY	-	2536	13W-33N	A3
-	ShdT	60044	2536	12W-31N	B7
-	WDWH	60031	2420	15W-39N	A5
-	WDWH	60031	2478	15W-37N	A1
-	WDWH	60083	2360	16W-41N	E7
-	WDWH	60083	2419	16W-41N	E2
-	WDWH	60083	2420	15W-39N	A5
-	WDWH	60099	2360	16W-42N	E7
-	WKGN	-	2535	13W-33N	E3
-	WKGN	60064	2536	12W-32N	A6
-	WKGN	60085	2536	12W-32N	A6
-	WrnT	60031	2478	15W-37N	A1
N Skokie Hwy					
-	NCHI	60064	2536	12W-31N	B7
-	ShdT	60044	2536	12W-31N	B7
N Skokie Hwy					
-	WKGN	60085	2536	12W-31N	B7
100	LKFT	60044	2593	11W-28N	C7
300	GRNE	60031	2535	13W-34N	E1
300	LKFT	60045	2593	11W-28N	C7
900	LKFT	60045	2649	11W-26N	C3
900	ShdT	60044	2593	12W-31N	B1
1000	GRNE	60031	2478	13W-35N	E6
1100	NCHI	60088	2593	12W-31N	B1
1300	WrnT	60031	2478	15W-37N	A2
1400	ShdT	60088	2593	12W-31N	B1
2300	WDWH	60031	2478	15W-37N	A2
2800	NCHI	60044	2593	12W-29N	B3
2800	NCHI	60064	2593	12W-29N	B3
2800	ShdT	60064	2593	12W-29N	B3
3600	LKBF	60044	2593	12W-29N	B4
N Skokie Hwy US-41					
-	NCHI	60064	2536	12W-31N	B7
-	ShdT	60044	2536	12W-31N	B7
-	WDWH	60031	2478	15W-37N	A2
-	WKGN	60085	2536	12W-31N	B7
100	LKFT	60045	2593	11W-28N	C7
300	GRNE	60031	2535	13W-34N	E1
300	LKFT	60044	2593	11W-28N	C7
900	LKFT	60045	2649	11W-26N	C3
900	NCHI	60044	2593	12W-31N	B1
900	ShdT	60044	2593	12W-31N	B1
1000	GRNE	60031	2478	13W-35N	E7
1100	NCHI	60088	2593	12W-31N	B1
1300	WrnT	60031	2478	15W-37N	A2
1400	ShdT	60088	2593	12W-31N	B1
2800	NCHI	60064	2593	12W-29N	B3
2800	ShdT	60064	2593	12W-29N	B3
30000	LKBF	60044	2593	12W-29N	B4
S Skokie Hwy					
1200	LKFT	60035	2650	10W-24N	A7
1200	LKFT	60045	2649	11W-25N	D5
1200	LKFT	60045	2650	10W-24N	A7
1300	LKFT	60035	2649	10W-24N	E7
S Skokie Hwy US-41					
1200	LKFT	60035	2650	10W-24N	A7
1200	LKFT	60045	2649	11W-25N	D5
1200	LKFT	60045	2650	10W-24N	A7
1300	LKFT	60035	2649	10W-24N	E7
Skokie Ln					
400	BGBK	60440	3268	23W-11S	E1
N Skokie Ln					
300	GLNC	60022	2758	6W-16N	D6
S Skokie Ln					
600	GLNC	60022	2758	6W-16N	D6
Skokie Rd					
-	NHFD	60093	2811	6W-14N	D5
-	SKOK	60076	2811	5W-13N	E7
-	SKOK	60077	2811	5W-13N	E7
-	WLMT	60076	2811	5W-13N	E7
-	WLMT	60077	2811	5W-13N	E7
-	WLMT	60091	2811	6W-14N	D5
-	WLMT	60093	2811	6W-14N	D5
Skokie Rd US-41					
-	NHFD	60093	2811	6W-14N	D5
-	SKOK	60076	2811	5W-13N	E7
-	SKOK	60077	2811	5W-13N	E7
-	WLMT	60076	2811	5W-13N	E7
-	WLMT	60077	2811	5W-13N	E7
-	WLMT	60091	2811	6W-14N	D5
-	WLMT	60093	2811	6W-14N	D5
E Skokie Rd					
200	ShdT	60044	2593	12W-29N	C5
Skokie Ditch					
-	KLWH	60043	2812	3W-15N	D3
Skokie Ridge Dr					
1000	GLNC	60022	2758	7W-18N	C4
Skokie Valley Rd					
-	HDPK	60035	2757	9W-20N	D1
10	LKBF	60044	2593	12W-28N	C5
10	NHBK	60062	2757	8W-20N	E2
10	ShdT	60044	2593	12W-28N	C5
500	HDPK	60035	2704	9W-21N	C7
3100	LKFT	60045	2704	10W-24N	A1
3300	LKFT	60035	2704	10W-24N	A1
Skokie Valley Rd US-41					
-	HDPK	60035	2757	9W-20N	D1
-	LKBF	60044	2593	12W-29N	B4
-	ShdT	60044	2593	12W-29N	B4
500	HDPK	60035	2704	9W-21N	C7
3100	LKFT	60045	2704	10W-24N	A1
3300	LKFT	60035	2704	10W-24N	A1
Sky Crest Dr					
28500	FmtT	60060	2589	22W-28N	C6
Skye Ct					
1500	FSMR	60422	3506	4W-23S	D3
S Skye Dr					
19500	FftT	60423	3504	9W-23S	E4
Skye Ln					
600	IVNS	60010	2751	24W-16N	B6
Skye Wy					
-	MTGY	60506	3198	40W-9S	B4
Skyelar Ct					
-	HDPK	60035	2757	9W-20N	C2
W Skyhawk Av					
1900	WKGN	60087	2479	11W-38N	D1
Skyhawk Ln					
-	JNBG	60050	2471	30W-37N	E2
Sky Hill Rd					
200	WCDA	60084	2644	25W-27N	A1
Skylane Dr					
10	NpvT	60564	3202	29W-9S	D4
2200	NPVL	60564	3202	29W-10S	D7
N Skylar Ct					
1500	VNHL	60061	2647	16W-26N	D2
Skylark Ct					
200	BRLT	60103	2967	28W-5N	A1
W Skylark Ct					
1000	PLTN	60067	2805	22W-14N	B4
Skylark Dr					
300	BMDL	60108	2968	24W-4N	D3
300	BMDL	60139	2968	24W-4N	D3
300	GLHT	60108	2968	24W-4N	D3
300	GLHT	60139	2968	24W-4N	D3
W Skylark Dr					
1000	PLTN	60067	2805	22W-14N	B4
Skylark Ln					
400	VrnT	60015	2755	14W-20N	B1
1400	JLET	60586	3496	29W-22S	D1
Skyler Ln					
24000	PNFD	60586	3416	30W-19S	B3
E Skyline Cir					
-	LKVL	60046	2418	20W-39N	A5
Skyline Ct N					
25700	PNFD	60585	3337	32W-15S	D2
Skyline Ct S					
25700	PNFD	60585	3337	32W-15S	D2
Skyline Dr					
-	BDWD	60408	3942	30W-41S	D6
-	RedT	60408	3942	30W-41S	D6
-	RedT	60481	3942	30W-41S	D6
Skyline Dr					
100	DndT	60110	2748	33W-17N	B6
100	SchT	60174	2964	34W-6N	C1
200	BRTN	60010	2750	25W-18N	E3
200	CPVL	60110	2748	33W-18N	B6
500	ALGN	60102	2694	34W-20N	C7
500	FRGV	60021	2696	29W-23N	B2
500	GnvT	60510	3019	37W-0S	C7
600	GnvT	60510	3077	37W-0S	B1
800	BTVA	60510	3019	37W-0S	B7
2800	NndT	60012	2584	35W-29N	B4
7200	JSTC	60458	3148	10W-8S	A7
8700	DGvT	60527	3207	16W-10S	E5
12700	PNFD	60585	3337	32W-15S	C2
16400	TYPK	60477	3425	8W-19S	B3
Skyridge Dr					
1300	CLLK	60014	2693	36W-23N	E2
Skytrain Ln					
400	GNVW	60025	2810	10W-14N	A3
400	GNVW	60062	2810	10W-14N	A3
Sky View					
-	NLNX	60451	3590	15W-27S	B4
Skyvue Ln					
300	SMBG	60194	2857	26W-10N	E5
Skywater Dr					
1700	SMBG	60008	2806	21W-12N	A7
1700	SMBG	60173	2805	21W-12N	E7
1700	SMBG	60173	2806	21W-12N	A7
Skyway Dr					
-	FftT	60423	3590	14W-26S	D1
W Skyway Dr					
3100	MHRY	60050	2528	32W-32N	C5
Slade Av					
10	ELGN	60120	2854	34W-12N	E2
600	ELGN	60120	2855	33W-12N	B2
E Slade St					
10	PLTN	60067	2805	20W-16N	E1
W Slade St					
10	PLTN	60067	2805	21W-16N	D1
Slaker Ct					
500	NARA	60542	3078	35W-3S	B6
Slalom Ln					
30800	WMTN	60481	3853	26W-37S	E4
Slate Dr					
6700	CPVL	60110	2748	33W-19N	C2
Slate Rd					
3800	AURA	60504	3202	30W-8S	A2
Slater Av					
-	AURA	60506	3136	40W-7S	B7
-	SRGV	60554	3136	40W-7S	B7
Slawin Ct					
500	MPPT	60056	2808	14W-13N	C5
Slayton Ct					
7000	WDRG	60517	3143	22W-7S	C7
E Slayton Dr					
800	PLTN	60074	2753	19W-16N	B6
Slayton Ln					
1900	GLHT	60139	2968	24W-3N	D5
Sleeping Bear Rd					
8900	SKOK	60076	2866	4W-11N	B3
Sleeping Bear Tr					
400	GLBT	60136	2799	38W-16N	C2
Sleepy Hllw					
2000	NHBK	60062	2756	11W-16N	C7
Sleepy Hollow Ct					
1200	DRN	60561	3207	18W-9S	B3
1700	HFET	60195	2859	23W-12N	A1
1700	SMBG	60195	2859	23W-12N	A1
Sleepy Hollow Ln					
-	BGBK	60446	3268	24W-14S	D7
-	PNFD	60586	3416	30W-19S	A4
-	RMVL	60446	3268	24W-14S	D7
300	ADSN	60101	2971	18W-2N	A7
300	ADSN	60181	2971	18W-2N	A7
500	CPVL	60110	2747	36W-18N	A5
500	DndT	60110	2747	36W-18N	A5
500	DndT	60118	2747	36W-18N	A5
1200	DRN	60561	3207	18W-9S	A3
6200	GRNE	60031	2534	16W-34N	D1
6200	LSLE	60532	3142	23W-7S	E6
Sleepy Hollow Rd					
10	ALGN	60102	2747	36W-19N	A3
10	DndT	60102	2747	36W-19N	A3
10	DndT	60118	2747	36W-17N	B7
10	SYHW	60118	2800	36W-15N	A4
10	WDND	60118	2747	36W-17N	B7
400	CPVL	60110	2747	36W-17N	B7
400	CPVL	60118	2747	36W-17N	B6
400	DndT	60123	2800	36W-14N	B6
400	ELGN	60123	2800	36W-14N	B6
500	ALGN	60110	2747	36W-18N	A4
500	ALGN	60118	2747	36W-18N	A4
500	DndT	60110	2747	36W-17N	B7
600	DndT	60118	2800	36W-16N	B2
600	WDND	60118	2800	36W-16N	B2
1300	GNVW	60025	2810	8W-13N	E5
N Sleight St					
10	NPVL	60540	3141	26W-6S	E5
900	NPVL	60563	3141	26W-5S	E3
S Sleight St					
10	NPVL	60540	3141	26W-7S	E7
S Sligo Wy					
18100	BmnT	60478	3426	6W-21S	B7
18100	CCHL	60478	3426	6W-21S	B7
W Sligo Wy					
4800	CCHL	60478	3426	6W-21S	A7
Slingerland Dr					
300	SMBG	60193	2858	25W-9N	A7
Slippery Rock Ct					
1800	NPVL	60565	3204	24W-9S	D4
W Slippery Rock Dr					
500	PLTN	60067	2805	21W-14N	C4
Slippery Rock Rd					
1800	NPVL	60565	3204	24W-9S	D4
Sloane Ln					
5800	NndT	60014	2641	32W-26N	B3
Slocum Lake Rd					
100	WCDA	60084	2643	26W-27N	D1
W Slocum Lake Rd					
25500	WCDA	60084	2643	26W-27N	D1
26000	WcnT	60084	2643	26W-27N	C1
N Slusser St					
10	GYLK	60030	2532	20W-33N	E3
S Slusser St					
10	GYLK	60030	2532	20W-32N	E4
Small Ct					
700	NPVL	60563	3140	29W-6S	E4
Small Dr					
-	SMBG	60193	2857	27W-10N	D6
E Small Ln					
1400	MPPT	60056	2808	14W-13N	C6
W Small St					
600	MchT	60050	2472	29W-37N	C2
Smalley Ct					
2400	WDND	60118	2800	35W-16N	B1

STREET Block	City	ZIP	Map#	CGS	Grid
Smallmouth Ln					
-	BDWD	60481	3942	30W-40S	C2
-	RedT	60481	3942	30W-40S	D2
Small Tree Ct					
200	WNVL	60555	3080	30W-2S	B4
Smethwick Ln					
10	EGVV	60007	2914	19W-9N	D1
W Smethwick Ln					
2100	HFET	60169	2858	25W-12N	B1
Smiley Rd					
23400	CstT	60481	4031	29W-42S	E1
23400	RedT	60408	4031	29W-42S	E1
23400	RedT	60481	4031	29W-42S	E1
W Smiley Rd					
100	RedT	60408	4031	30W-42S	C1
24400	RedT	60481	4031	30W-42S	C1
Smitana Rd					
4000	AlqT	60014	2641	33W-25N	A6
4000	CLLK	60014	2640	33W-25N	D5
4000	CLLK	60014	2641	33W-25N	A6
4000	CRY	60014	2640	33W-25N	D5
4000	CRY	60014	2641	33W-25N	A6
Smith Av					
400	ShdT	60044	2593	12W-29N	B5
W Smith Av					
200	JLET	60435	3498	24W-22S	E2
S Smith Blvd					
500	AURA	60505	3200	34W-8S	D2
Smith Ct					
300	SEGN	60177	2908	34W-9N	E1
900	BTVA	60510	3078	36W-2S	A3
1600	SMWD	60107	2857	27W-11N	D4
4600	GNWD	60097	2469	38W-36N	A4
11800	HTLY	60142	2745	40W-20N	A1
Smith Dr					
500	HPSR	60140	2796	46W-15N	A3
11300	HTLY	60142	2745	41W-19N	B2
11700	RtdT	60142	2745	40W-20N	A2
W Smith Ln					
8100	RVGV	60171	2974	10W-3N	B4
Smith Rd					
-	DMND	60416	3941	32W-40S	D2
-	NHBK	60062	2756	11W-16N	D6
10	BbyT	60119	3075	43W-0S	B1
10	BRLT	60185	2966	29W-4N	E3
10	WCHI	60185	2965	32W-4N	D5
10	WYNE	60184	2966	31W-4N	A4
10	WYNE	60185	2966	31W-4N	A4
10	WynT	60185	2966	31W-4N	A4
100	SCRL	60174	2965	32W-3N	B6
100	SCRL	60185	2965	32W-3N	B6
100	WYNE	60185	2965	31W-4N	E4
100	WynT	60184	2966	30W-4N	C4
400	WYNE	60184	2965	31W-4N	E4
400	WynT	60185	2965	31W-4N	E4
700	BRLT	60103	2966	28W-4N	E3
700	LslT	60532	3143	22W-6S	B4
700	WynT	60103	2966	28W-4N	E3
800	BbyT	60119	3017	42W-0S	C7
1200	DPgT	60441	3270	21W-14S	A7
1200	DPgT	60441	3342	20W-15S	A1
1200	LMNT	60439	3270	21W-14S	A7
1200	LMNT	60439	3342	20W-15S	A1
1200	LSLE	60532	3143	23W-6S	A4
1300	HmrT	60441	3342	20W-17S	A5
1300	LktT	60441	3342	20W-17S	A5
5200	NndT	60014	2641	33W-26N	A3
6000	AlqT	60014	2641	33W-26N	A4
14700	LKPT	60441	3342	20W-17S	A6
17700	LtRT	60545	3258	50W-11S	B1
W Smith Rd					
100	BvlT	60407	4030	33W-43S	C3
100	GDLY	60407	4030	33W-43S	C3
100	RedT	60407	4030	33W-43S	C3
12800	MhtT	60442	3678	18W-29S	B2
13600	MHTN	60442	3678	18W-29S	B2
15400	MHTN	60442	3677	19W-29S	D2
15400	MhtT	60442	3677	19W-29S	D2
Smith St					
-	NtrT	60093	2811	6W-15N	E3
-	WNKA	60093	2811	6W-15N	E3
10	FKFT	60423	3591	12W-25S	D1
10	SchT	60177	2908	35W-7N	B6
400	ShdT	60044	2593	12W-29N	C5
600	WDSK	60098	2581	41W-30N	E1
800	GNEN	60137	3025	21W-0S	D6
2400	RGMW	60008	2805	21W-14N	D5
2400	RGMW	60067	2805	21W-14N	D5
N Smith St					
10	AURA	60505	3200	34W-7S	D1
10	PLTN	60067	2805	21W-16N	D1
100	AURA	60505	3138	34W-7S	D7
100	PLTN	60067	2752	21W-17N	D5
1500	PltT	60074	2752	21W-17N	D5
41900	AntT	60002	2356	25W-41N	E7
S Smith St					
10	AURA	60505	3200	34W-8S	D2
900	PLTN	60067	2805	21W-14N	D4
1200	RGMW	60067	2805	21W-14N	D4
Smithfield Ct					
1000	GRNE	60031	2477	18W-35N	A6
2400	AURA	60503	3265	32W-11S	C1
Smithfield Ln					
2400	AURA	60503	3265	32W-11S	C1
Smithwood Dr					
10	MNGV	60053	2865	7W-10N	B4
Smoketree Cir					
1300	BRLT	60103	2910	30W-9N	B1
Smoke Tree Ct					
3100	HLCT	60429	3427	3W-21S	A6
Smoke Tree Ln					
-	AURA	60506	3137	36W-5S	E2
-	AURA	60542	3137	36W-5S	E2
-	NARA	60542	3138	36W-5S	A2
10	NARA	60542	3137	36W-5S	E2
3600	NndT	60012	2584	35W-28N	B6
Smoketree Ln					
400	BRLT	60103	2910	30W-9N	B2
Smoke Tree Rd					
600	DRFD	60015	2704	9W-20N	B7
Smokey Ct					
1600	NPVL	60563	3141	26W-4S	D1
Smokey Ridge Dr					
6100	JLET	60586	3495	31W-21S	E1
Smythe Ct					
1400	GRNE	60031	2476	19W-36N	C5
Snapdragon Ct					
10	RMVL	60446	3339	26W-17S	E5
1600	HDPK	60035	2704	10W-22N	A4
Snapdragon Rd					
2200	NPVL	60564	3266	29W-13S	D5
Snapjack Cir					
4700	NPVL	60564	3266	29W-12S	D4
Snead Ct					
10	BGBK	60490	3267	26W-12S	D3
6300	WDRG	60517	3143	23W-7S	A6
Snead St					
1800	BGBK	60490	3267	27W-12S	C4
1800	WldT	60490	3267	27W-12S	C4
Snow Ct					
1200	BTVA	60510	3077	36W-2S	E4
Snow Dr					
1100	ELBN	60119	3017	43W-2N	A1
Snow St					
10	SRGV	60554	3135	43W-7S	B7
Snowberry Ct					
1500	DRGV	60515	3084	20W-3S	B6
W Snowberry Ct					
21000	DPgT	60544	3340	26W-15S	A2
Snowberry Ln					
1300	CLLK	60014	2639	37W-25N	A5
1300	GfnT	60014	2639	37W-25N	A5
1300	WCHI	60185	3022	30W-2N	C1
1300	WynT	60185	3022	30W-2N	C1
1400	WCHI	60185	2966	30W-2N	C7
W Snowberry Ln					
20900	DPgT	60544	3340	26W-15S	A2
Snowbird Ct					
500	CmpT	60175	2961	41W-4N	E4
Snowbird Ln					
2600	NPVL	60564	3266	29W-11S	C2
3900	NHBK	60062	2756	12W-17N	B5
Snow Cap Ct					
600	GRNE	60031	2476	18W-34N	E7
Snow Creek Rd					
2000	NPVL	60564	3266	29W-12S	D3
Snowdown Ct					
1000	NPVL	60540	3204	25W-8S	B1
Snow Drift Cir					
400	BRLT	60103	2910	30W-9N	A1
Snow Drift Ct					
300	BRLT	60103	2910	30W-9N	A2
Snowdrop Ln					
5600	LslT	60532	3143	22W-6S	C4
Snowhill Ct					
800	GNEN	60137	3083	21W-1S	D1
Snowmass Ct					
2700	JLET	60586	3416	31W-20S	A5
Snowmass Ln					
-	MKNA	60448	3502	15W-23S	B4
-	NlxT	60448	3502	15W-23S	B3
Snowshoe Tr					
28700	GrtT	60051	2472	28W-34N	E7
N Snuff Valley Rd					
23300	AlqT	60013	2696	28W-23N	D1
23300	CbaT	60013	2696	28W-23N	D1
Snug Harbor Dr					
6500	WLBK	60527	3145	16W-7S	D6
6600	DRN	60527	3145	16W-7S	D6
6600	DRN	60561	3145	16W-7S	D6
6600	WLBK	60561	3145	16W-7S	D6
Sobieski St					
600	LMNT	60439	3270	19W-14S	E6
Soccer Dr					
10200	WldT	60503	3265	32W-11S	D2
10200	WldT	60585	3265	32W-11S	D2
Sodaro Av					
500	BMDL	60157	2913	23W-6N	B7
Sodaro Rd					
500	BMDL	60157	2913	22W-6N	B7
Soderquist Ct					
2400	GNVA	60134	3019	37W-0N	D5
Sodman Ct					
24500	AntT	60002	2416	24W-40N	C2
E Soffel Av					
100	MLPK	60160	3028	13W-1N	E2
100	NHLK	60160	3028	13W-1N	E2
100	NHLK	60164	3028	13W-1N	E2
300	MLPK	60160	3029	13W-1N	A2
300	NHLK	60160	3029	13W-1N	A2
300	NHLK	60164	3029	13W-1N	A2
400	NHLK	60165	3029	13W-1N	A2
400	SNPK	60165	3029	13W-1N	A2
W Soffel Av					
-	SNPK	60160	3029	12W-1N	B1
10	NHLK	60164	3028	14W-1N	D1
2900	MLPK	60160	3029	12W-1N	B1
3200	MLPK	60165	3029	12W-1N	B1
3200	SNPK	60165	3029	12W-1N	B1
4600	NHLK	60160	3029	13W-1N	A2
4600	NHLK	60164	3029	13W-1N	A2
Soffel Ter					
-	MLPK	60160	3028	13W-1N	E2
4600	MLPK	60160	3029	13W-1N	A2
S Sohl Av					
4900	HMND	46320	3352		D7
4900	HMND	46327	3352		D5
5900	HMND	46320	3430		E1
Sojourn Rd					
600	NLNX	60451	3501	16W-25S	E7
700	NLNX	60451	3589	16W-25S	E1
Sokol Ct					
2300	DRN	60439	3206	19W-10S	D6
Sola Dr					
100	GLBT	60136	2799	38W-16N	A2
Sola Rd					
-	GLBT	60136	2799	38W-16N	B2
Solar Dr					
100	LYVL	60048	2591	15W-28N	E5
Solar Ln					
800	GNVW	60025	2811	7W-13N	B7
Soldier Ct					
1300	ELBN	60119	3017	43W-0N	B5
25200	PNFD	60544	3337	31W-17S	E7
W Soldier Dr					
-	PNFD	60544	3338	30W-17S	A7
-	PnfT	60544	3338	30W-17S	A7
Soldiers Rd					
700	ELGN	60123	2854	34W-9N	D7
Soleri Dr					
4000	BmnT	60430	3426	5W-21S	C7
4000	CCHL	60430	3426	5W-21S	C7
4000	CCHL	60478	3426	5W-21S	C7
Solfisburg Av					
900	AURA	60505	3138	34W-7S	D6
1300	AraT	60505	3138	34W-7S	D6
1500	AraT	60505	3139	33W-7S	A6
1500	AURA	60505	3139	33W-7S	A6
E Solidarity Dr					
600	CHCG	60605	3034	0E-1S	D7
Solitude Ln					
3000	AURA	60502	3079	33W-3S	A6
Solomon Ct					
5200	GRNE	60031	2478	15W-35N	A6
E Solon Rd					
2600	RcmT	60081	2413	31W-40N	C4
2600	SPGV	60081	2413	31W-40N	C4
2900	RcmT	60071	2413	31W-40N	C4
2900	SPGV	60071	2413	31W-40N	C4
N Solon Rd					
8000	RcmT	60071	2413	33W-41N	A2
8700	RHMD	60071	2413	32W-40N	A2
N Solon Rd					
9600	RcmT	60071	2354	32W-41N	A7
9600	SPGV	60071	2354	32W-41N	A7
9600	SPGV	60081	2354	32W-41N	A7
S Solon Rd					
5300	MchT	60050	2471	32W-37N	A2
5300	MchT	60072	2471	33W-37N	A1
5300	MchT	60081	2471	33W-37N	A1
5300	RcmT	60072	2471	33W-37N	A1
5300	RcmT	60081	2471	33W-37N	A1
6100	RcmT	60072	2413	33W-39N	A5
6100	RcmT	60081	2413	33W-39N	A5
6100	SPGV	60072	2413	33W-39N	A5
6100	SPGV	60081	2413	33W-39N	A5
7200	RcmT	60071	2413	32W-39N	A5
W Solon Rd					
4100	RcmT	60071	2412	33W-39N	D4
4100	RcmT	60071	2413	33W-39N	A4
4100	RcmT	60081	2413	33W-39N	A4
Somer Ln					
10800	ODPK	60462	3423	13W-18S	A1
10800	ODPK	60467	3423	13W-18S	A1
Somerfield Dr					
1300	BGBK	60490	3268	26W-13S	A5
1400	BGBK	60490	3267	26W-13S	E6
Somerfield Ln					
1700	CLLK	60014	2693	36W-22N	D4
Somerglen Ct					
15600	ODPK	60467	3423	13W-18S	A1
Somerglen Dr					
-	ODPK	60462	3423	13W-18S	B1
-	ODPK	60467	3423	13W-18S	A1
Somerglen Ln					
10800	ODPK	60462	3423	13W-18S	A1
10800	ODPK	60467	3345	13W-18S	A7
10800	ODPK	60467	3423	13W-18S	B1
Somerset Av					
1000	DRFD	60015	2703	11W-21N	D6
W Somerset Av					
6400	CHCG	60631	2919	8W-7N	A4
6400	CHCG	60646	2919	8W-7N	A4
Somerset Cir					
800	HRPK	60133	2912	26W-8N	A3
N Somerset Cir					
14500	GNOK	60048	2535	14W-31N	C7
S Somerset Cir					
14500	GNOK	60048	2535	14W-31N	C7
W Somerset Cir					
31200	GNOK	60048	2535	14W-31N	C7
Somerset Ct					
-	ANHT	60004	2807	17W-15N	C2
-	NLNX	60451	3590	16W-25S	A1
-	PTHT	60004	2807	17W-15N	C2
10	SBTN	60010	2804	24W-14N	C4
100	WLBK	60527	3146	15W-7S	A6
200	LslT	60540	3142	24W-6S	C4
200	NlxT	60451	3502	16W-25S	A7
400	ALGN	60102	2694	34W-20N	B7
400	AURA	60504	3140	30W-7S	D2
400	WYNE	60184	2966	30W-4N	A4
900	CLSM	60188	2967	27W-3N	D5
1400	MDLN	60060	2590	20W-29N	A5
1500	SMBG	60193	2858	25W-10N	B6
1800	GRNE	60031	2477	15W-35N	E5
1900	RMVL	60446	3339	27W-17S	C5
9000	ODPK	60462	3346	11W-17S	A6
14100	HMGN	60491	3344	15W-16S	C4
21900	FKFT	60423	3591	13W-26S	A3
E Somerset Ct					
400	RLKB	60073	2475	22W-36N	B4
N Somerset Ct					
25500	ElaT	60047	2645	23W-25N	A5
Somerset Dr					
-	BCHR	60401	3774	0W-35S	D7
-	WDND	60118	2800	36W-16N	A3
10	OswT	60538	3263	37W-11S	D1
100	SMWD	60107	2857	28W-11N	A4
200	SRGV	60554	3135	41W-6S	E5
300	HFET	60010	2857	28W-11N	B4
300	HFET	60107	2857	28W-11N	B4
600	CmpT	60175	2905	41W-6N	E7
800	CLSM	60188	2967	27W-3N	D5
1100	GNVW	60025	2811	7W-13N	A6
1800	GLHT	60139	2969	22W-3N	B5
1900	RMVL	60446	3339	27W-17S	C5
7500	CrlT	60152	2634	48W-24N	E6
7500	CrlT	60152	2635	48W-24N	A7
Somerset Ln					
10	BFGV	60089	2701	16W-20N	D7
100	BGBK	60440	3269	22W-12S	B3
300	MDLN	60061	2647	17W-25N	B5
300	VNHL	60061	2647	17W-25N	B5
400	NLNX	60451	3501	16W-25S	E7
400	NlxT	60451	3501	16W-25S	E7
500	CLLK	60014	2640	35W-24N	A7
500	NHFD	60093	2811	7W-15N	A2
700	DRN	60561	3207	17W-8S	C2
1100	EGVV	60007	2914	19W-8N	C2
1200	SMBG	60193	2858	25W-10N	B6
1300	ITSC	60143	2914	19W-8N	D3
1500	WHTN	60187	3082	25W-2S	B4
1700	MDLN	60060	2590	20W-29N	A5
1800	NHBK	60062	2757	10W-16N	B7
3400	CRTE	60417	3596	0W-28S	D6
10200	HTLY	60142	2692	39W-22N	C4
N Somerset Ln					
200	ANHT	60005	2807	16W-13N	C6
1200	WDRG	60517	3206	20W-10S	B6
S Somerset Ln					
1200	WDRG	60517	3206	20W-11S	B7
W Somerset Ln					
9800	PSPK	60464	3273	12W-14S	C7
Somerset Pl					
900	NlxT	60451	3502	16W-25S	A7
Somerset Rd					
100	WLBK	60527	3146	15W-7S	A6
11800	ODPK	60467	3344	14W-16S	C4
11900	HMGN	60491	3344	14W-16S	C4
Somerset St					
800	NLNX	60451	3501	16W-25S	E7
800	NlxT	60451	3501	16W-25S	E7
800	NlxT	60451	3502	16W-25S	A7
21000	SRWD	60404	3583	31W-25S	E1
Somerset Acres					
800	JLET	60451	3500	19W-22S	E2
Somerset Hills Ct					
10	HNWD	60047	2645	22W-26N	B3
10	HNWD	60060	2645	22W-26N	B3
400	RVWD	60015	2756	13W-20N	A1
Somerset Mall					
1000	MHRY	60050	2528	33W-32N	A4
Somersworth Pl					
2100	HFET	60169	2858	26W-12N	A1
Somerton Dr					
4900	HFET	60010	2751	24W-16N	C7
Somme Ct					
3000	JLET	60435	3417	27W-21S	C6
Somme St					
2800	JLET	60435	3417	27W-21S	C6
Sommerset Av					
2600	WSTR	60154	3087	13W-2S	A3
Sommerset Ct					
1000	ELGN	60120	2855	32W-10N	D5
Sommerset Dr					
300	GYLK	60030	2533	20W-32N	A5
Sommerset Ln					
10	LNSH	60069	2703	13W-22N	A3
Sommerset Hills Ct					
-	HNWD	60060	2645	22W-26N	B4
Sommersville Ct					
600	MTSN	60443	3506	5W-24S	B6
Somonauk Ct					
10	PKFT	60466	3594	4W-27S	E5
Somonauk St					
200	PKFT	60466	3594	4W-27S	E5
200	PKFT	60466	3595	4W-27S	A5
300	RNPK	60466	3594	4W-27S	E5
300	RNPK	60471	3594	4W-27S	E5
E Somonauk St					
100	YKVL	60560	3333	42W-14S	C1
400	BtlT	60560	3333	42W-14S	D1
W Somonauk St					
100	YKVL	60560	3333	43W-14S	B1
Songbird Cir					
10400	ODPK	60467	3423	13W-20S	B4
Songbird Ln					
12200	HTLY	60142	2744	42W-18N	E4
Song Sparrow Ct					
1900	SMBG	60173	2805	21W-12N	E7
Sonia Ln					
2500	FNPK	60131	2973	12W-3N	C5
Sonlight Ct					
10400	BHPK	60087	2422	10W-38N	A7
W Sonny Ln					
100	BNVL	60106	2971	16W-3N	E4
Sonoma Cir					
3300	LIHL	60156	2692	39W-23N	B2
Sonoma Ct					
-	JLET	60586	3415	31W-20S	E6
10	LIHL	60156	2692	39W-23N	B2
1300	GRNE	60031	2477	18W-35N	A6
1600	RMVL	60446	3339	26W-17S	D5
Sonoma Dr					
-	BGBK	60490	3267	27W-13S	C4
-	WldT	60490	3267	27W-13S	C4
10	RMVL	60446	3339	26W-17S	D5
Sonoma Ln					
1000	AURA	60502	3078	34W-3S	D6
Sonoma Rd					
100	NLNX	60433	3500	20W-24S	B5
100	NLNX	60451	3500	20W-24S	B5
100	NlxT	60433	3500	20W-24S	B5
100	NlxT	60451	3500	20W-24S	B5
Sonoma Tr					
8600	SPGV	60081	2414	29W-40N	B2
Sonoma Pass					
-	LKMR	60051	2530	28W-32N	A5
Sonora Ct					
6300	JLET	60586	3415	31W-20S	D6
Sonora Dr					
10	OSWG	60538	3200	35W-10S	A7
10	OSWG	60543	3200	36W-10S	A6
10	OswT	60538	3200	36W-10S	A6
10	OswT	60543	3200	36W-10S	A6
Soo Line Dr					
10	GYLK	60030	2532	21W-32N	D5
Soo Line Ln					
4400	SRPK	60176	2973	11W-5N	C1
Soper Av					
300	BRRG	60527	3208	15W-8S	A1
300	DGvT	60527	3208	15W-8S	A1
300	WLBK	60527	3208	15W-8S	A1
Soper Ct					
1300	NPVL	60563	3140	29W-5S	D2
Sophia Dr					
6100	MTSN	60443	3505	7W-25S	D7
6100	MTSN	60443	3593	7W-25S	C1
Sophia Ln					
18700	WrnT	60046	2476	18W-36N	D4
Sophia St					
100	WCHI	60185	3022	29W-1N	C4
S Sophies Ln					
1800	HMND	46394	3280		E4
Soreng Av					
9500	SRPK	60176	2973	12W-4N	C2
Sorenger Rd					
-	ANTH	60002	2358	21W-41N	E7
-	ANTH	60002	2359	20W-41N	B7
Sorensen Ct					
9700	MKNA	60448	3503	12W-24S	D4
Sorrel					
10	LMNT	60439	3272	15W-13S	A5
Sorrel Ct					
800	CLSM	60188	2967	27W-3N	C5
Sorrel Dr					
3400	NHBK	60062	2756	11W-18N	C3
17800	LKPT	60441	3420	20W-21S	A6
Sorrel Row					
2700	LIHL	60156	2692	38W-22N	E3
Sorrel Ter					
4400	AlqT	60014	2640	33W-25N	E4
Sorrell Ct					
10	SchT	60175	2907	38W-7N	A6
Sorrento Dr					
10	PSHT	60463	3275	8W-14S	B5
Souders Av					
-	ELBN	60119	3017	42W-0N	C5
Souster Av					
10	ELGN	60123	2855	33W-10N	A6
100	ELGN	60123	2854	33W-10N	E6
South Av					
10	GLNC	60022	2759	5W-17N	A5
100	GLNC	60022	2758	6W-17N	D5
100	LktT	60441	3419	23W-21S	B6
100	WKGN	60085	2537	10W-33N	B3
200	SCRL	60174	2964	35W-2N	B7
300	AURA	60505	3200	35W-8S	B2
900	MDLN	60060	2646	18W-26N	D3
9800	SRPK	60176	2917	12W-6N	B7
E South Av					
100	HPSR	60140	2795	46W-15N	E3
300	HPSR	60140	2796	46W-15N	A3
W South Av					
24600	LkvT	60041	2474	24W-36N	C5
26300	GrtT	60041	2473	26W-36N	D5
28200	WcnT	60084	2643	28W-26N	A2
South Blvd					
10	CHCG	60302	3031	8W-0N	A4
10	CHCG	60644	3031	8W-0N	A4
10	OKPK	60302	3031	8W-0N	A4
600	EVTN	60202	2867	3W-10N	A5
South Blvd					
800	OKPK	60302	3030	8W-0N	E4
1100	FTPK	60130	3030	8W-0N	D4
1100	OKPK	60130	3030	8W-0N	D4
1600	EVTN	60202	2866	3W-10N	E5
South Brch					
10	GNVW	60093	2810	8W-15N	D3
South Ct					
1700	BTVA	60510	3078	34W-2S	C5
2900	RGMW	60008	2806	19W-13N	C5
28600	GrtT	60041	2472	28W-34N	E7
28600	GrtT	60051	2472	28W-34N	E7
W South Ct					
27700	GrtT	60041	2473	27W-35N	B6
South Dr					
-	BTVA	60510	3019	37W-0S	C7
-	DndT	60102	2747	33W-20N	D2
-	GnvT	60134	3019	37W-0S	C7
-	GnvT	60510	3019	37W-0S	C7
-	WLNG	60090	2808	14W-16N	D1
100	TRLK	60010	2643	26W-24N	D6
200	SchT	60177	2908	34W-7N	D5
200	SEGN	60177	2908	34W-7N	D5
400	ALGN	60102	2747	35W-19N	C2
400	AlqT	60102	2747	35W-19N	C2
700	BRRG	60521	3146	14W-6S	C4
7400	MchT	60097	2469	36W-36N	D5
South Ln					
-	MPPT	60056	2861	17W-11N	C3
-	SCRL	60175	2964	35W-6N	B1
200	GLNC	60022	2758	6W-17N	E5
600	NPVL	60540	3141	27W-7S	B7
600	NpvT	60540	3141	27W-7S	B7
700	SchT	60175	2964	35W-6N	B1
1700	NHBK	60062	2757	8W-16N	E7
1700	NHBK	60062	2758	8W-16N	A7
2600	AlqT	60013	2641	31W-25N	D4
3000	DSPN	60018	2917	12W-8N	B3
South Pk					
800	WPHR	60096	2363	9W-42N	C6
1400	WPHR	60096	2422	9W-41N	C1
South Pkwy					
10	PTHT	60070	2807	15W-15N	E2
10	PTHT	60070	2808	15W-15N	A2
South Rd					
100	GNCY	53128	2353		C3
100	RdlT	53128	2353		C3
100	RdlT	53181	2353		C3
100	TNLK	53128	2353		C3
400	ELGN	60123	2854	34W-10N	E6
500	LslT	60532	3143	22W-6S	B4
600	PLTN	60074	2752	21W-18N	C2
600	PltT	60074	2752	21W-18N	C2
1000	FRGV	60021	2696	29W-22N	C4
1300	LSLE	60532	3143	23W-6S	A4
1500	RchT	60477	3505	8W-23S	B2
1500	TYPK	60477	3505	8W-23S	B2
4900	GRNE	60031	2478	15W-35N	B7
9100	PlsT	60465	3273	11W-13S	E3
9100	PSHL	60465	3273	11W-13S	E3
W South Rd					
-	KLDR	60047	2699	21W-23N	D2
24100	ElaT	60047	2699	21W-23N	D2
South St					
-	ElgT	60124	2853	38W-10N	A6
-	PltT	60124	2852	39W-10N	E6
-	PltT	60124	2853	39W-10N	A6
-	WMTN	60481	3853	28W-38S	C7
10	BtlT	60512	3261	41W-12S	E3
10	CHHT	60411	3595	3W-26S	B2
10	CHHT	60466	3595	3W-26S	B2
10	CRY	60013	2695	31W-23N	D2
10	FXLK	60020	2473	28W-36N	A3
10	GNVA	60134	3020	35W-1N	A4
10	PKFT	60466	3595	3W-26S	B2
10	WDND	60118	2801	34W-15N	A3
100	CLLK	60014	2640	35W-25N	A4
100	DYR	46311	3598		C3
100	JLET	60436	3498	24W-25S	E7
100	MchT	60081	2472	29W-37N	D1
100	SEGN	60177	2908	34W-8N	D3
300	ELGN	60123	2854	34W-11N	D5
400	BRTN	60010	2751	25W-18N	A3
400	MNSR	46321	3430		D7
400	MRGO	60152	2634	50W-26N	B3
400	WDND	60118	2800	34W-15N	E3
600	LKPT	60441	3419	22W-20S	D4
700	LktT	60441	3419	22W-20S	D4
1400	NndT	60014	2586	30W-28N	A7
1700	ElgT	60123	2854	36W-10N	A5
1700	GNVA	60134	3019	36W-1N	E4
2000	ELGN	60123	2853	36W-10N	E5
2000	ElgT	60123	2853	36W-10N	E5
2100	RGMW	60008	2806	19W-13N	C5
2300	ELGN	60124	2853	36W-10N	D5
4200	MHRY	60050	2528	33W-32N	A4
5500	RHMD	60071	2353	34W-42N	C7
6600	TYPK	60477	3425	8W-20S	B5
17600	UNON	60180	2635	46W-25N	D5
23900	DhmT	60033	2405	53W-37N	A7
28900	GrtT	60081	2472	29W-37N	D1
E South St					
-	ANHT	60005	2807	17W-13N	A5
-	BbyT	60119	3017	43W-1N	A3
10	PLNO	60545	3259	47W-13S	D6
100	EMHT	60126	3027	16W-0N	E4
100	EMHT	60126	3028	15W-0N	A4
200	ELBN	60119	3017	43W-1N	A3
200	PTON	60468	3861	9W-37S	A4
400	WllT	60468	3861	9W-37S	A4
700	WDSK	60098	2581	41W-31N	E1
E South St US-34					
10	PLNO	60545	3259	47W-13S	D6
W South St					
10	ANHT	60005	2807	18W-13N	A5
10	PLNO	60545	3259	47W-14S	C7
100	WDSK	60098	2581	42W-31N	C1
200	PTON	60468	3860	9W-37S	E4
500	ANHT	60005	2806	18W-13N	E5
1100	DrrT	60098	2581	43W-30N	A2
1200	LtRT	60545	3259	48W-14S	B7
14000	SenT	60098	2581	43W-30N	A2
28800	CbaT	60013	2696	28W-23N	D1
W South St CO-A35					
100	WDSK	60098	2581	42W-31N	C1
1100	DrrT	60098	2581	43W-30N	A2
14000	SenT	60098	2581	43W-30N	A2
W South St US-34					
10	PLNO	60545	3259	47W-14S	C7
South Access Rd					
-	CHCG	60666	2972	14W-5N	C1
Southampton Ct					
1600	WHTN	60187	3082	25W-2S	B3
1700	GNVA	60134	3019	36W-1N	E4
Southampton Dr					
300	GNVA	60134	3019	36W-1N	E4

Block	City	ZIP	Map#	CGS	Grid
Southampton Dr					
2700	RGMW	60008	2860	19W-11N	B2
Southbridge Ct					
1700	SMBG	60194	2858	25W-11N	B3
South Bridge Dr					
800	AURA	60506	3137	36W-5S	D4
Southbridge Ln					
1000	SMBG	60194	2858	25W-11N	B3
1100	HFET	60169	2858	25W-11N	B3
1100	SMBG	60169	2858	25W-11N	B3
2200	NHBK	60062	2757	10W-16N	A7
E South Broadway Av					
400	LMBD	60148	3026	19W-0N	D4
Southbrook Dr					
22600	SLVL	60411	3597	2E-27S	C5
Southbury Blvd					
-	OSWG	60543	3263	36W-12S	E4
Southbury Ct					
10	SMWD	60107	2857	28W-12N	B2
300	SMBG	60193	2859	21W-10N	D6
6500	LSLE	60532	3142	25W-7S	C6
Southbury Ln					
1000	WLNG	60090	2754	15W-18N	E3
Southcote Rd					
10	RVSD	60546	3088	9W-2S	C3
Southcreek Pkwy					
-	RMVL	60441	3340	25W-17S	C6
-	RMVL	60446	3340	25W-17S	C6
Southcrest Dr					
2600	LslT	60517	3143	21W-7S	D6
Southeast Ct					
-	CTSD	60525	3147	13W-6S	A3
Southeast Pl					
1100	DSPN	60016	2862	14W-10N	D5
1100	DSPN	60018	2862	13W-10N	D5
Southeastern Ct					
10	GNCY	53128	2353		A4
N South Elgin Blvd					
10	SEGN	60177	2908	34W-8N	E2
S South Elgin Blvd					
10	SEGN	60177	2908	34W-8N	E3
South End Ln					
13300	CTWD	60445	3347	6W-15S	D2
Southend Rd					
16200	JLET	60435	3417	27W-19S	B3
16200	PnfT	60435	3417	27W-19S	B3
Southern Ter					
100	ISLK	60042	2586	28W-28N	D6
N Southern Hills Dr					
2800	WKGN	60083	2478	14W-37N	C1
3000	WDWH	60083	2478	14W-37N	C1
Southfield Av					
-	CRTE	60417	3684	1W-29S	E1
-	CRTE	60417	3685	1W-29S	A1
-	CteT	60417	3684	1W-29S	E1
-	CteT	60417	3685	1W-29S	A1
Southfield Ct					
19400	TYPK	60477	3504	9W-23S	D3
Southfield Dr					
10	VNHL	60061	2646	18W-25N	E6
200	BCHR	60401	3864	0W-37S	C3
200	MNKA	60447	3583	32W-28S	D7
200	MNKA	60447	3672	32W-28S	D1
1400	AURA	60504	3200	33W-10S	E5
1900	BRLT	60103	2909	32W-8N	D3
7100	BGVW	60455	3210	8W-10S	E5
8800	BGVW	60453	3210	8W-10S	E5
8800	OKLN	60453	3210	8W-10S	E5
Southfield Ln					
19400	TYPK	60477	3504	9W-23S	D3
E South Frontage Rd					
10	BGBK	60440	3269	22W-12S	C3
W South Frontage Rd					
-	BGBK	60446	3268	24W-14S	D6
10	BGBK	60440	3269	23W-13S	A4
400	BGBK	60440	3268	24W-13S	E5
Southgate					
10	LKFT	60045	2650		C2
Southgate Av					
100	CHHT	60411	3508	0W-24S	B6
2100	NHFD	60093	2758	7W-16N	A7
Southgate Ct					
10	BRRG	60527	3208	14W-8S	D2
10	SCRL	60174	2964	34W-4N	E5
1100	AURA	60504	3201	32W-9S	C3
1500	BRLT	60103	2966	30W-5N	B2
Southgate Dr					
200	NHBK	60062	2758	7W-17N	A6
200	VNHL	60061	2647	17W-24N	B7
Southgate Rd					
600	NLNX	60451	3589	17W-26S	C2
1500	BRLT	60103	2966	30W-5N	C2
Southgate Tr					
26400	PTBR	60010	2643	27W-25N	A5
Southgate Course					
10	SCRL	60174	2964	34W-4N	E5
Southhampton Dr					
4600	ISLK	60042	2642	29W-27N	C1
4700	ISLK	60051	2642	29W-27N	C1
South Hills Dr					
100	LKBN	60010	2643	26W-25N	D6
100	TRLK	60010	2643	26W-25N	C6
Southland Av					
1600	HDPK	60035	2704	10W-21N	B6
Southland Dr					
10	BlmT	60411	3509	2E-23S	C3
10	LYWD	60411	3509	2E-23S	C3
Southlane Dr					
400	OKTR	60181	3085	17W-1S	B1
400	YkTp	60181	3085	17W-1S	B1
Southlawn Pl					
1400	AURA	60506	3199	37W-7S	B1
S Southmeadow Ln					
700	LKFT	60045	2648	13W-25N	E6
W Southmeadow Ln					
-	LKFT	60045	2648	13W-25N	E6
Southmoor Dr					
-	PlsT	60462	3345	11W-15S	D1
-	PlsT	60464	3345	11W-15S	E1
Southmoor Ln					
800	RLKB	60073	2531	24W-34N	D1
900	RDLK	60073	2531	24W-34N	D1
Southmoor Rd					
200	HMND	46324	3430		D4
South Park Av					
15400	DLTN	60419	3350	0E-18S	E6
15400	SHLD	60419	3350	0E-18S	E6
15400	SHLD	60473	3350	0E-18S	E7
15900	SHLD	60473	3428	0E-19S	E3
17300	SHLD	60476	3428	0E-20S	E4
Southport Av					
900	LSLE	60532	3143	23W-4S	A1
N Southport Av					
2000	CHCG	60614	2977	1W-2N	D6
2700	CHCG	60657	2977	1W-3N	D5
3500	CHCG	60613	2977	1W-4N	D3

Block	City	ZIP	Map#	CGS	Grid
Southport Ct					
1500	ZION	60099	2362	11W-41N	D7
1900	RMVL	60446	3339	27W-17S	C6
Southport Dr					
3300	ISLK	60042	2586	30W-28N	A5
N Southport Rd					
10	MDLN	60060	2646	20W-27N	B1
100	MDLN	60060	2590	20W-27N	B7
S Southport Rd					
100	MDLN	60060	2646	20W-27N	B1
Southridge Dr					
100	GRNE	60031	2534	16W-34N	D2
100	WrnT	60031	2534	16W-34N	D2
6100	JLET	60586	3415	31W-21S	D6
Southridge Ter					
900	NHBK	60062	2758	7W-16N	A7
900	NHBK	60093	2758	7W-16N	A7
900	NHFD	60093	2758	7W-16N	A7
Southridge Tr					
1100	ALGN	60102	2747	36W-18N	B4
E South RR St					
100	BCVL	60407	4030	33W-44S	A3
W South RR St					
100	BCVL	60407	4030	34W-44S	A3
South Shore Dr					
100	ISLK	60042	2586	28W-28N	D6
E South Shore Dr					
2400	CHCG	60649	3153	3E-7S	D6
E South Shore Dr US-41					
2400	CHCG	60649	3153	3E-7S	D6
S South Shore Dr					
5300	CHCG	60615	3153	2E-5S	B2
5500	CHCG	60637	3153	2E-6S	B3
6700	CHCG	60649	3153	3E-7S	D6
7700	CHCG	60649	3215	3E-8S	E1
7800	CHCG	60617	3216	3E-8S	A1
7800	CHCG	60649	3216	3E-9S	A1
S South Shore Dr US-41					
6700	CHCG	60637	3153	3E-7S	D6
6700	CHCG	60649	3153	3E-7S	D6
7700	CHCG	60649	3215	3E-8S	E1
7800	CHCG	60617	3216	3E-8S	A1
7800	CHCG	60649	3216	3E-9S	A1
Southside Av					
700	MchT	60051	2529	29W-32N	B5
Southview Av					
8400	BKFD	60513	3088	10W-3S	A6
8400	BKFD	60534	3088	10W-3S	A6
8400	LYNS	60534	3088	10W-3S	A6
8500	LYNS	60513	3088	10W-3S	A6
8800	BKFD	60513	3087	11W-4S	E6
9500	BKFD	60525	3087	11W-3S	D6
9500	LGNG	60513	3087	11W-3S	D6
9500	LGNG	60525	3087	11W-3S	D6
9500	LGPK	60525	3087	11W-3S	D6
12400	WKGN	60085	2479	12W-35N	B6
12400	WkgT	60085	2479	12W-35N	A6
Southview Dr					
800	WDSK	60098	2581	41W-30N	E2
15700	ODPK	60467	3423	13W-18S	A1
W Southview St					
12300	WKGN	60085	2479	12W-35N	C6
12300	WkgT	60085	2479	12W-35N	C6
E South Water St					
-	CHCG	60601	3034		E4
W South Water Market					
100	CHCG	60608	3033	1W-1S	E7
Southway Ct					
300	GLNC	60022	2758	6W-17N	D5
Southwell Ct					
5200	LGGV	60047	2701	18W-22N	A4
Southwest Ct					
-	CTSD	60525	3147	13W-5S	A3
-	LynT	60525	3147	13W-5S	A3
Southwest Hwy					
-	HMGN	60448	3422	15W-21S	C7
-	NlxT	60448	3422	15W-21S	C7
4100	CHCG	60652	3212	5W-10S	B5
4100	HMTN	60456	3212	5W-10S	B5
4100	HMTN	60652	3212	5W-10S	B5
4300	OKLN	60453	3212	5W-10S	B5
4900	OKLN	60453	3211	7W-10S	D5
10000	CHRG	60415	3211	8W-11S	B7
10100	CHRG	60415	3275	8W-12S	A1
10300	CHRG	60482	3275	8W-12S	A1
10300	WRTH	60415	3275	8W-12S	A1
10300	WRTH	60482	3275	8W-12S	A1
10500	CHRG	60415	3274	9W-12S	D2
10500	CHRG	60482	3274	9W-12S	D2
10500	WRTH	60482	3274	10W-14S	C6
10600	WRTH	60415	3274	8W-12S	E2
10800	PSHL	60465	3274	10W-14S	C6
10800	PSHL	60482	3274	10W-14S	C6
11200	PSHT	60465	3274	10W-14S	C6
11300	ODPK	60467	3422	14W-21S	D6
11400	PSHT	60463	3274	9W-13S	D4
11800	PSHT	60464	3274	9W-13S	C5
11800	PSPK	60464	3274	11W-15S	A7
12600	PlsT	60464	3346	11W-15S	A1
12600	PSPK	60464	3346	11W-15S	A1
13000	NlxT	60448	3502	15W-22S	B1
13000	ODPK	60462	3346	11W-15S	A1
13000	PlsT	60462	3346	11W-15S	A1
13000	PSPK	60462	3346	11W-15S	A1
13100	NlxT	60448	3501	17W-22S	D1
13100	ODPK	60462	3345	12W-16S	D4
13100	OrlT	60462	3345	12W-16S	D4
13100	PlsT	60462	3345	12W-16S	D4
14000	NLNX	60451	3501	17W-22S	B1
14000	NlxT	60451	3501	17W-22S	C1
17700	OrlT	60467	3422	14W-21S	D6
17900	HMGN	60491	3422	14W-21S	C7
Southwest Hwy SR-7					
10600	CHRG	60415	3274	9W-12S	E2
10600	CHRG	60482	3274	9W-12S	E2
10600	WRTH	60415	3274	9W-12S	E2
10600	WRTH	60482	3274	10W-14S	C6
10800	PSHL	60465	3274	10W-14S	C6
10800	PSHL	60482	3274	10W-14S	C6
11200	PSHT	60465	3274	10W-14S	C6
11400	PSHT	60463	3274	9W-13S	D4
11800	PSHT	60464	3274	9W-13S	C5
11800	PSPK	60464	3274	11W-15S	A7
12600	PlsT	60462	3346	11W-15S	A1
12600	PSPK	60464	3346	11W-15S	A1
13000	ODPK	60462	3346	11W-15S	A1
13000	PlsT	60462	3346	11W-15S	A1
13000	PSPK	60462	3346	11W-15S	A1
13100	ODPK	60462	3345	12W-16S	D4
13100	OrlT	60462	3345	12W-16S	D4
13100	PlsT	60462	3345	12W-16S	D4
Southwest Hwy US-6					
-	HMGN	60448	3422	15W-21S	C7
-	NlxT	60448	3422	15W-21S	C7
11300	ODPK	60467	3422	14W-21S	D6
13000	NlxT	60448	3502	15W-22S	B1

Block	City	ZIP	Map#	CGS	Grid
Southwest Hwy US-6					
13100	NlxT	60448	3501	17W-22S	D1
14000	NLNX	60451	3501	17W-22S	B1
14000	NlxT	60451	3501	17W-22S	C1
17700	OrlT	60467	3422	14W-21S	D6
17900	HMGN	60491	3422	14W-21S	C7
Southwest Ln					
10	GnvT	60134	3020	33W-0N	E5
Southwest Pl					
1100	DSPN	60016	2862	14W-10N	D5
1100	DSPN	60018	2862	14W-10N	D5
Southwick Ct					
-	MTSN	60443	3594	6W-25S	A1
200	VNHL	60061	2647	16W-26N	C2
7200	FKFT	60423	3592	9W-27S	E4
7200	FKFT	60423	3593	9W-27S	A3
Southwick Dr					
700	ALGN	60102	2694	35W-20N	A7
4800	MTSN	60443	3594	6W-25S	A1
7200	FKFT	60423	3592	9W-27S	E3
7300	FKFT	60423	3593	9W-27S	A4
7300	FKFT	60443	3593	9W-27S	A4
Southwick Ln					
200	SMBG	60173	2859	21W-10N	E5
Southwicke Dr					
-	BRLT	60103	2856	30W-9N	C7
-	SMWD	60103	2856	30W-9N	C7
10	SMWD	60107	2856	30W-9N	C7
Southwind Blvd					
2200	BRLT	60103	2909	33W-8N	B3
Southwind Cir					
2100	SMBG	60194	2858	26W-11N	A3
Southwind Ct					
300	LKVL	60046	2474	23W-36N	E3
Southwind Dr					
200	LKVL	60046	2474	23W-36N	E3
200	LKVL	60046	2475	23W-36N	A3
700	CPVL	60110	2747	35W-17N	D6
1200	NHBK	60062	2756	12W-17N	B5
1300	NfdT	60062	2756	12W-17N	B6
2600	NLNX	60451	3590	15W-26S	C1
5200	RchT	60471	3593	6W-27S	E5
5200	RNPK	60471	3593	6W-27S	E5
5200	RNPK	60471	3594	6W-27S	A5
South Winds Cross					
11200	ODPK	60467	3422	14W-21S	E7
Southwood Cir					
100	SMWD	60107	2857	27W-9N	C7
Southwoods Ln					
27000	MTWA	60048	2648	14W-27N	C2
Southworth Cir					
7300	JLET	60586	3415	33W-21S	B7
Souwanas Tr					
-	AlqT	60102	2748	33W-20N	A2
200	ALGN	60102	2747	34W-19N	E2
200	ALGN	60102	2748	33W-20N	A2
200	DndT	60102	2747	33W-20N	D2
Sova Ln					
500	WNVL	60555	3080	29W-2S	C4
Spaatz Av					
7200	MchT	60097	2469	36W-37N	E2
7300	WRLK	60097	2469	36W-37N	E2
Spafford St					
900	ANTH	60002	2357	23W-42N	D7
Spalding Av					
-	ELBN	60119	3017	42W-0N	C5
Spalding Dr					
100	NPVL	60540	3141	27W-7S	C7
1200	MDLN	60060	2646	20W-27N	B1
Spalding St					
600	GNEN	60137	3025	22W-0N	C5
W Spangler Av					
100	EMHT	60126	2971	16W-3N	E6
Spangler Rd					
10	RMVL	60446	3341	23W-16S	A3
16300	JLET	60544	3417	28W-19S	A4
16300	JLET	60586	3417	28W-19S	A4
16300	PNFD	60586	3417	28W-19S	A4
16300	PnfT	60544	3417	28W-19S	A4
16300	PnfT	60586	3417	28W-19S	A4
W Spangler Rd					
17200	JknT	60421	3677	21W-29S	A3
17200	JLET	60421	3677	21W-29S	A3
17200	JLET	60442	3677	21W-29S	A3
17200	MhtT	60421	3677	21W-29S	A3
17200	MhtT	60442	3677	21W-29S	A3
Spangler's Farm Dr					
15700	PNFD	60544	3416	30W-18S	C2
15800	PNFD	60586	3416	30W-18S	C2
Spaniel Dr					
16500	HMGN	60491	3422	15W-19S	C3
Spanky Ct					
500	RDLK	60073	2531	23W-34N	E2
N Sparkle Ct					
700	OSWG	60543	3264	34W-11S	E1
S Sparkle Ct					
800	OSWG	60543	3264	34W-11S	E1
Sparrow Av					
1500	MLPK	60160	3028	13W-1N	E2
Sparrow Cir					
1900	RDLK	60073	2531	25W-33N	A3
Sparrow Ct					
10	AURA	60504	3202	31W-8S	A1
10	CPVL	60110	2748	32W-17N	D7
500	LNHT	60046	2476	19W-37N	C3
13100	HMGN	60491	3343	16W-18S	E7
S Sparrow Ct					
1900	WKGN	60048	2535	14W-31N	D6
W Sparrow Ct					
900	PLTN	60067	2805	22W-15N	C2
Sparrow Dr					
100	BlmT	60411	3509	3E-25S	E7
200	WDSK	60098	2525	40W-32N	A5
Sparrow Ln					
100	BGBK	60490	3267	27W-12S	D3
300	BRLT	60103	2967	28W-5N	B2
Sparrow Rd					
10	CPVL	60110	2748	32W-17N	D6
Sparta Ct					
800	VNHL	60061	2647	18W-25N	A5
20600	OMFD	60461	3507	3W-25S	B7
Sparta Ln					
2700	OMFD	60461	3507	3W-25S	B7
Spartan Dr					
1700	ELGN	60123	2854	36W-10N	A6
Spartan Wy					
-	OMFD	60461	3506	4W-25S	E6
Spartina Ln					
2200	NPVL	60564	3266	29W-13S	D5
Spathis Dr					
11100	PSHL	60465	3274	10W-13S	A3
Spaulding Av					
-	MKHM	60426	3348	4W-17S	E6
-	MKHM	60445	3348	4W-17S	E6
-	POSN	60406	3349	2W-17S	C4
-	POSN	60469	3349	2W-17S	C4

Block	City	ZIP	Map#	CGS	Grid
Spaulding Av					
2000	WDND	60118	2800	35W-16N	B1
2200	DXMR	60406	3349	2W-17S	C4
2900	WKGN	60085	2536	12W-33N	B1
14500	DXMR	60426	3349	2W-17S	D5
14500	HRVY	60426	3349	2W-17S	D5
14500	MDLN	60445	3348	4W-17S	E5
15600	MKHM	60428	3348	4W-18S	E7
15600	MKHM	60428	3426	4W-18S	E1
16600	HLCT	60428	3426	4W-19S	E3
16600	HLCT	60429	3426	4W-19S	E3
N Spaulding Av					
700	CHCG	60651	3032	4W-0N	D3
800	CHCG	60624	3032	4W-1N	D2
1500	CHCG	60647	3032	4W-1N	D1
2400	CHCG	60647	2976	4W-3N	D5
3600	CHCG	60618	2976	4W-4N	D2
4300	CHCG	60625	2976	4W-5N	D1
4400	CHCG	60625	2920	4W-5N	D7
5500	CHCG	60659	2920	4W-6N	D5
6400	LNWD	60712	2920	4W-8N	D2
S Spaulding Av					
10	CHCG	60624	3032	4W-0S	D5
1200	CHCG	60623	3032	4W-1S	D7
1500	CHCG	60623	3090	4W-2S	D2
3700	CHCG	60632	3090	4W-3S	D6
5000	CHCG	60632	3150	4W-6S	E3
7100	CHCG	60629	3150	4W-8S	E7
7700	CHCG	60652	3212	4W-8S	E1
9300	ENGN	60805	3212	4W-10S	E6
10200	CHCG	60655	3276	4W-12S	E1
10200	CHCG	60805	3276	4W-11S	E1
10200	ENGN	60805	3276	4W-11S	E1
11400	CHCG	60803	3276	4W-13S	E4
11400	MTPK	60803	3276	4W-13S	E4
13300	RBBN	60472	3348	4W-16S	E2
14200	RBBN	60406	3348	4W-16S	E4
W Spaulding Av					
2300	DXMR	60406	3349	3W-17S	B4
2300	POSN	60406	3349	3W-17S	B4
2300	POSN	60469	3349	3W-17S	B4
Spaulding Ct					
2000	WDND	60118	2800	35W-16N	C1
Spaulding Rd					
10	BRLT	60103	2909	32W-9N	D2
10	BRLT	60120	2909	31W-9N	E2
10	ELGN	60120	2909	31W-9N	E2
10	HnrT	60103	2909	31W-9N	E2
10	HnrT	60120	2909	31W-9N	E2
400	BRLT	60103	2910	30W-9N	B1
Spaulding St					
-	NCHI	60064	2536	11W-31N	E7
-	NCHI	60088	2536	11W-31N	E7
2400	NCHI	60088	2593	11W-30N	E1
2400	ShdT	60088	2593	11W-30N	E2
2800	NCHI	60064	2593	11W-30N	E1
S Spaulding School Dr					
11100	WldT	60564	3266	29W-14S	C7
11100	WldT	60585	3266	29W-14S	C7
Speckman Ct					
10	BGBK	60440	3204	24W-10S	E5
Speckman Leedle Rd					
-	BfdT	53147	2351		B2
-	HbnT	53147	2351		B4
-	HbnT	60034	2351		B4
Spector Rd					
1300	NlxT	60451	3501	18W-23S	A4
Spectrum Dr					
2700	ELGN	60124	2799	37W-16N	D2
Speechley Blvd					
700	BKLY	60162	3028	13W-0N	E4
700	BKLY	60163	3028	13W-0N	E4
700	BLWD	60104	3028	13W-0N	E4
700	HLSD	60104	3028	13W-0N	E4
700	HLSD	60162	3028	13W-0N	E4
1400	BKLY	60104	3028	13W-0N	E4
1400	BLWD	60163	3028	13W-0N	E4
Speedway Blvd					
-	JLET	60421	3587	23W-27S	B5
-	JLET	60433	3587	23W-27S	B5
Spella Dr					
-	ALGN	60102	2746	36W-20N	D1
Spencer Av					
1500	WLMT	60091	2812	4W-13N	C6
4700	LSLE	60532	3143	23W-5S	B2
22500	SLVL	60411	3598	3E-27S	A4
S Spencer Av					
1400	BKLY	60163	3028	13W-0N	E4
1400	BLWD	60104	3028	13W-0N	E4
1400	BLWD	60163	3028	13W-0N	E4
Spencer Ct					
-	SRWD	60404	3495	31W-23S	E4
10	DRFD	60015	2756	11W-20N	C2
1500	GRNE	60031	2476	19W-36N	C5
S Spencer Ct					
13000	ALSP	60803	3276	5W-15S	A7
13000	ALSP	60803	3348	5W-15S	A1
Spencer Ln					
-	ElaT	60010	2698	24W-23N	C1
-	LKZH	60047	2698	24W-23N	C1
-	NBRN	60010	2698	24W-23N	C1
1300	BTVA	60510	3077	36W-1S	E1
W Spencer Ln					
4600	ALSP	60803	3276	5W-15S	A7
Spencer Pl					
5200	LIHL	60156	2692	38W-21N	E6
Spencer Rd					
800	JLET	60433	3587	22W-25S	D2
800	JltT	60433	3587	22W-25S	D2
1500	JLET	60433	3588	21W-25S	A2
1500	JltT	60433	3588	21W-25S	A2
16900	NlxT	60433	3588	21W-25S	A2
S Spencer Rd					
100	NLNX	60451	3501	16W-25S	E7
100	NlxT	60451	3501	16W-25S	E7
600	NLNX	60451	3589	16W-26S	E3
600	NlxT	60451	3589	16W-27S	E4
1800	NlxT	60442	3589	16W-27S	E4
22700	MhtT	60442	3589	16W-27S	E5
22700	MhtT	60451	3589	16W-27S	E5
W Spencer Rd					
-	NLNX	60433	3588	19W-25S	D1
-	NLNX	60451	3588	19W-25S	D1
-	NlxT	60433	3588	19W-25S	D1
-	NlxT	60451	3588	19W-25S	D1
14900	NLNX	60451	3589	18W-26S	A1
14900	NlxT	60451	3589	18W-26S	A1
Spencer St					
10	JltT	60433	3499	22W-24S	C7
100	WCHI	60185	3022	29W-0N	C4
E Spencer St					
100	ELWD	60421	3675	25W-32S	B7
N Spencer St					
10	AURA	60505	3200	35W-7S	C1
100	AURA	60505	3138	35W-7S	C7

Block	City	ZIP	Map#	CGS	Grid
S Spencer St					
10	AURA	60505	3200	35W-8S	C2
1000	AraT	60505	3200	35W-9S	C4
1200	AraT	60538	3200	35W-9S	C4
1200	MTGY	60505	3200	35W-9S	C4
1300	MTGY	60538	3200	35W-9S	C4
12200	ALSP	60803	3276	5W-14S	A6
W Spencer St					
10	ELWD	60421	3675	25W-32S	B7
Spencer Wy					
-	SRWD	60404	3495	31W-23S	E5
Spenser Ct					
2700	NHBK	60062	2756	10W-18N	E3
3300	NPVL	60564	3267	28W-11S	A1
Spero Ct					
1400	WHTN	60187	3024	23W-0N	E5
Sperry Ct					
400	AURA	60505	3200	35W-8S	B2
2700	BTVA	60510	3077	37W-1S	C1
Spice Cir					
1900	NPVL	60565	3204	24W-8S	D2
Spicebush Ct					
400	YKVL	60560	3333	43W-16S	B4
Spicebush Ln					
600	AURA	60504	3201	33W-8S	A2
600	AURA	60505	3201	33W-8S	A2
16800	ODPK	60467	3423	13W-20S	B4
Spiegelhoff Rd					
1600	TNLK	53181	2353		E1
Spike Horn Ln					
2300	NPVL	60564	3266	29W-12S	D4
Spikes Dr					
-	OSWG	60543	3264	35W-11S	C1
Spindletree Av					
700	NPVL	60565	3204	25W-9S	B4
Spine Rd					
-	CHCG	60176	2917	12W-5N	B7
-	CHCG	60666	2917	12W-5N	B7
-	SRPK	60176	2917	12W-5N	B7
-	SRPK	60666	2917	12W-5N	B7
Spinnaker Ct					
-	PGGV	60140	2797	42W-15N	C4
10	TDLK	60030	2533	19W-34N	C1
1900	AURA	60503	3201	31W-10S	D5
Spinnaker Dr					
800	NLNX	60451	3590	15W-25S	C1
2500	AURA	60503	3201	32W-10S	C5
Spinnaker Ln					
1200	HRPK	60133	2967	27W-4N	D3
Spinnaker Pt					
600	SMBG	60194	2859	23W-10N	A5
Spinnaker St					
-	PGGV	60140	2797	42W-15N	C4
1000	ELGN	60123	2907	36W-9N	E2
1000	ELGN	60123	2908	36W-9N	A2
Spinnaker Cove					
300	CPVL	60110	2800	35W-16N	C1
Spinner Ct					
2800	NPVL	60565	3203	27W-10S	C7
Spinney Run Rd					
-	GRNE	60031	2534	15W-33N	E3
Spinning Wheel Rd					
10	HNDL	60521	3086	15W-4S	B6
Spinny Run Rd					
-	GRNE	60031	2534	15W-33N	E3
Spire Dr					
12200	LMNT	60439	3271	17W-14S	D6
Spirea Ln					
20400	CTHL	60403	3418	25W-19S	B2
20400	LktT	60403	3418	25W-19S	B2
Spirit Dr					
800	MTSN	60443	3505	7W-25S	D7
N Spitz Dr					
3600	WKGN	60087	2421	11W-38N	D7
3600	WKGN	60087	2479	11W-37N	D2
38300	BHPK	60099	2421	11W-38N	D7
38300	WKGN	60099	2421	11W-38N	D7
S Spitzer Rd					
300	BRLT	60103	2910	31W-8N	A4
300	BRLT	60120	2910	31W-8N	A4
300	ELGN	60103	2910	31W-8N	A4
300	HnrT	60103	2910	31W-8N	A4
W Split Oak Cir					
1200	RLKB	60073	2474	24W-34N	C7
Split Oak Rd					
10	NPVL	60565	3203	26W-9S	E4
Split Rail					
10	LMNT	60439	3272	15W-13S	B5
Splitrail Ct					
400	CmpT	60175	2906	39W-6N	D7
W Split Rail Ct					
13000	HMGN	60491	3344	16W-16S	A3
Split Rail Dr					
900	CLSM	60188	2967	27W-3N	D5
16300	LKPT	60441	3420	20W-19S	B3
S Split Rail Dr					
13800	HMGN	60491	3343	16W-16S	E3
13900	HMGN	60491	3344	16W-16S	A4
Splitrail Ln					
300	CmpT	60175	2906	39W-6N	D7
N Spojnia Rd					
2200	MchT	60050	2527	34W-34N	D1
N Spokane Av					
6300	CHCG	60646	2919	6W-7N	D3
6500	CHCG	60712	2919	6W-8N	D2
6500	LNWD	60712	2919	6W-8N	D2
N Sponable St					
10	MRGO	60152	2634	50W-26N	A2
Spoon Ct					
29000	FmtT	60060	2589	21W-28N	C5
Sports Club Dr					
-	AvnT	60030	2532	21W-31N	C6
-	GYLK	60030	2532	21W-31N	D6
100	FmtT	60030	2532	21W-31N	D6
100	HNVL	60030	2532	21W-31N	C6
Sportsman Dr					
10	DMND	60416	3941	33W-39S	B1
N Sprague Av					
-	CHCG	60018	2917	12W-6N	B6
-	SRPK	60018	2917	12W-6N	B6
-	SRPK	60176	2917	12W-6N	B6
Spring Av					
-	GNEN	60137	3025	21W-0N	D5
300	MltT	60137	3025	21W-0S	D7
900	SCRL	60174	3020	34W-2N	C1
E Spring Av					
10	SEGN	60177	2908	34W-8N	D4
N Spring Av					
10	LGNG	60525	3087	12W-4S	B7
200	LGPK	60525	3087	12W-3S	B5
S Spring Av					
10	LGNG	60525	3087	12W-4S	B7
300	LGNG	60525	3147	12W-5S	B2
1200	CTSD	60525	3147	12W-5S	B3
W Spring Av					
10	NPVL	60540	3141	27W-6S	C5

STREET Block	City	ZIP	Map#	CGS	Grid
Spring Bluff					
300	WPHR	60096	2363	8W-43N	E5
Spring Ct					
-	BtnT	60081	2414	30W-39N	A4
200	BMDL	60108	2969	22W-4N	B2
200	NARA	60542	3077	37W-4S	B7
200	ROSL	60172	2913	23W-7N	B5
500	GNVA	60134	3020	34W-0N	D4
600	BmdT	60157	2913	22W-6N	D6
600	ROSL	60157	2913	22W-6N	D6
700	MonT	60466	3684	3W-29S	A2
800	LKZH	60047	2699	22W-21N	A5
900	DRN	60561	3207	17W-9S	B3
1500	SPGV	60081	2355	30W-41N	A7
4800	RNPK	60471	3594	6W-26S	A3
13000	HMGN	60491	3344	16W-18S	A7
N Spring Ct					
28000	FmtT	60060	2588	24W-28N	D7
Spring Ct N					
100	CPVL	60110	2747	35W-17N	C7
Spring Ct W					
400	CPVL	60110	2747	35W-17N	C7
400	CPVL	60110	2800	35W-17N	C1
Spring Dr					
-	BGVW	60458	3210	10W-9S	C2
-	JSTC	60458	3210	10W-9S	C2
-	WDSK	60098	2581	41W-30N	D2
400	MRGO	60152	2634	49W-25N	B4
N Spring Dr					
23400	CbaT	60010	2696	28W-23N	E2
S Spring Dr					
12100	PSPK	60464	3274	11W-14S	A6
Spring Ln					
10	BNHL	60010	2695	31W-20N	D7
10	BNHL	60010	2748	31W-20N	D1
100	WNKA	60093	2811	5W-15N	E3
300	VNHL	60061	2647	16W-25N	C5
900	LKFT	60045	2650	9W-26N	C2
1000	ShdT	60044	2593	11W-29N	D3
6000	MTSN	60443	3505	7W-24S	C6
8000	GwdT	60098	2525	38W-33N	E3
13700	ODPK	60467	3344	13W-16S	E3
22000	RNPK	60471	3594	6W-26S	A3
Spring Rd					
-	FXLK	60002	2356	28W-42N	A6
-	MchT	60050	2527	34W-34N	D1
10	OKTR	60181	3027	16W-1S	D7
10	OKTR	60181	3085	16W-1S	E2
100	OKBK	60523	3085	16W-1S	E2
100	OKTR	60523	3085	16W-1S	E2
200	FXLK	60041	2473	27W-35N	C5
600	GNVW	60025	2810	8W-13N	E7
2800	MCLK	60050	2470	33W-34N	D7
3000	JNBG	60050	2470	33W-34N	D7
3400	OKBK	60523	3086	15W-3S	A5
3700	HNDL	60521	3086	15W-3S	B6
3700	OKBK	60521	3086	15W-3S	A6
4900	OKLN	60453	3212	6W-11S	A7
5000	MCLK	60050	2527	34W-34N	D1
27800	AntT	60002	2356	28W-42N	A6
E Spring Rd					
1200	BDWD	60408	3941	32W-40S	C4
1200	BvlT	60416	3941	33W-40S	B4
1200	DMND	60408	3941	32W-40S	C4
1200	DMND	60416	3941	33W-40S	B4
1200	RedT	60408	3941	32W-40S	C4
S Spring Rd					
300	EMHT	60126	3027	16W-0N	D4
Spring St					
-	BRTN	60010	2751	25W-18N	A2
-	BtlT	60560	3333	41W-14S	E1
-	YKVL	60560	3333	41W-14S	E1
10	CRY	60013	2695	31W-23N	D2
10	ROSL	60172	2913	23W-7N	B5
100	AlqT	60013	2695	31W-23N	E2
100	AURA	60505	3138	35W-7S	B7
100	BTVA	60510	3078	35W-1S	C1
100	CPVL	60110	2800	34W-16N	E1
100	FRGV	60021	2696	29W-23N	B2
100	WLSP	60480	3209	12W-9S	C3
300	PKRG	60068	2918	10W-8N	B1
400	GNVA	60134	3020	34W-1N	D4
500	AURA	60505	3200	34W-7S	C1
2400	WDRG	60517	3205	21W-9S	E3
4000	WNSP	60558	3086	14W-4S	C7
25000	MHTN	60442	3677	19W-30S	E4
E Spring St					
100	YKVL	60560	3333	42W-15S	D1
400	BtlT	60560	3333	42W-15S	D1
N Spring St					
10	ELGN	60120	2854	33W-12N	E3
S Spring St					
10	ELGN	60120	2854	33W-11N	E4
W Spring St					
-	ELGN	60123	2908	36W-8N	A2
100	SEGN	60177	2908	34W-8N	D3
100	YKVL	60560	3333	43W-14S	C1
300	JLET	60435	3498	24W-23S	E4
1100	ElgT	60177	2908	35W-8N	A2
Spring Bay Dr					
200	LSLE	60532	3142	24W-6S	D4
200	LSLE	60540	3142	24W-6S	D4
200	LslT	60540	3142	24W-6S	D4
Spring Beach Wy					
100	AlqT	60013	2696	30W-23N	A2
100	CRY	60013	2696	30W-23N	A2
Spring Bluff Dr					
500	CPVL	60110	2747	36W-18N	B5
500	DndT	60110	2747	36W-18N	B5
500	DndT	60118	2747	36W-18N	B4
Springbrook					
-	PNFD	60586	3415	32W-19S	D2
Spring Brook Ct					
1400	RLKB	60073	2531	25W-34N	B1
1500	RLKB	60073	2474	24W-34N	B7
Springbrook Ct					
-	ALGN	60102	2693	36W-21N	C6
10	BGBK	60490	3268	26W-13S	A6
10	HnrT	60107	2856	30W-10N	B7
100	MDLN	60060	2590	20W-27N	B7
100	MHRY	60050	2527	34W-31N	D6
200	CLSM	60188	2968	25W-3N	A6
11700	ODPK	60467	3422	14W-20S	D6
Springbrook Dr					
10	NpvT	60565	3203	27W-10S	B5
10	WldT	60565	3203	27W-10S	B5
300	MDLN	60060	2590	19W-27N	B7
600	AURA	60506	3137	36W-5S	E3
600	AURA	60542	3137	36W-5S	E3
600	NARA	60542	3137	36W-5S	E3
7600	JLET	60586	3415	33W-21S	A7
E Springbrook Dr					
100	BMDL	60108	2969	23W-5N	B1
Springbrook Ln					
700	BGBK	60490	3268	26W-13S	A5
N Springbrook Ln					
36000	WrnT	60031	2477	17W-36N	B5
Springbrook Rd					
2700	BLVY	60012	2583	35W-28N	E5
2700	NndT	60012	2583	35W-28N	E5
4800	PTPR	53158	2362		B3
6800	PTPR	53158	2361		E2
Springbrook Rd CO-ML					
4800	PTPR	53158	2362		B3
6800	PTPR	53158	2361		E2
Springbrook Shopping Ctr					
-	BMDL	60108	2969	23W-5N	A1
Spring Cove Dr					
-	ELGN	60123	2854	35W-11N	A3
-	ElgT	60123	2854	35W-11N	B3
200	BCHR	60401	3774	0W-35S	D7
800	SMBG	60193	2912	24W-9N	E1
1000	SMBG	60193	2858	24W-9N	D7
Springcreek					
-	RtdT	60118	2746	38W-18N	B5
Spring Creek Cir					
200	SMBG	60173	2859	21W-10N	E4
300	SMBG	60173	2860	20W-10N	A6
800	WldT	60565	3203	27W-11S	B7
800	WldT	60565	3267	27W-11S	B1
Spring Creek Ct					
10	HNWD	60047	2645	21W-25N	D5
800	EGVV	60007	2914	20W-8N	B3
14100	GNOK	60048	2592	14W-30N	D2
Spring Creek Dr					
10	SBTN	60010	2803	27W-15N	A2
11900	HTLY	60142	2744	42W-19N	C2
18400	TYPK	60477	3424	9W-22S	E7
18400	TYPK	60477	3504	9W-22S	E1
Spring Creek Ln					
1100	ELGN	60120	2855	32W-12N	C1
2000	MHRY	60050	2528	32W-34N	A2
2100	MchT	60050	2528	32W-34N	A2
11200	ODPK	60467	3344	14W-18S	E6
11200	OrlT	60467	3344	14W-18S	E7
16300	PNFD	60586	3416	30W-19S	B3
Springcreek Ln					
-	WDSK	60098	2524	41W-32N	D5
Spring Creek Rd					
-	ALGN	60102	2695	32W-21N	B7
10	AlqT	60010	2696	29W-21N	C7
10	BNHL	60010	2696	30W-21N	A7
700	BfdT	53128	2351		E1
1100	ELGN	60120	2855	32W-12N	C1
1200	ELGN	60120	2801	32W-12N	C7
1700	AlqT	60010	2695	31W-21N	D7
1700	BNHL	60010	2695	31W-21N	D7
3100	AlqT	60102	2695	32W-21N	C7
3100	BNHL	60102	2695	32W-21N	C7
14200	HMGN	60491	3343	18W-16S	B3
Spring Creek St					
18700	NLNX	60451	3500	19W-22S	E2
Spring Cress Ct					
400	WCHI	60185	3022	29W-2N	D1
Spring Cress Ln					
400	WCHI	60185	3022	29W-2N	D1
Springcrest Rd					
10	EDND	60118	2801	33W-16N	A2
Springdale Av					
3000	GNVW	60025	2810	10W-13N	A6
3700	GNVW	60025	2809	11W-13N	E5
Springdale Cir					
1200	NPVL	60564	3203	28W-10S	A7
Spring Dale Dr					
1800	SPGV	60081	2354	30W-41N	E7
1800	SPGV	60081	2355	30W-41N	A7
9900	BtnT	60081	2355	30W-41N	A7
Springdale Dr					
500	LslT	60540	3142	24W-6S	C4
Springdale Ln					
100	BMDL	60108	2968	24W-5N	C2
1200	EGVV	60007	2914	18W-8N	E2
1200	EGVV	60007	2915	18W-8N	A2
W Springdale Ln					
5100	MHRY	60050	2527	34W-33N	D3
Springdale Rd					
10	OSWG	60538	3200	36W-10S	A7
10	OSWG	60543	3200	36W-10S	A7
10	OswT	60538	3200	36W-10S	A7
Springer Dr					
600	LMBD	60148	3084	20W-1S	A2
Spring Farm Rd					
700	LKVL	60046	2417	22W-39N	C5
Springfield Av					
10	JLET	60435	3497	26W-23S	E5
10	JLET	60436	3497	26W-23S	E5
1000	DRFD	60015	2703	11W-21N	E6
8800	SKOK	60076	2866	4W-11N	C3
9200	SKOK	60203	2866	4W-11N	C2
9200	EVTN	60201	2866	4W-11N	C2
14100	CTWD	60445	3348	4W-16S	D4
14900	MDLN	60445	3348	4W-17S	D6
15700	MKHM	60428	3426	4W-19S	D1
17600	CCHL	60478	3426	4W-21S	D6
17900	BmnT	60430	3426	4W-21S	D7
17900	CCHL	60430	3426	4W-21S	D7
17900	HLCT	60429	3426	4W-21S	D7
18700	FSMR	60422	3506	4W-22S	D2
18700	HLCT	60422	3506	4W-22S	D2
18700	HLCT	60429	3506	4W-22S	D2
19000	RchT	60430	3506	4W-22S	D2
N Springfield Av					
400	CHCG	60624	3032	4W-0N	C3
900	CHCG	60651	3032	4W-1N	C2
1500	CHCG	60647	3032	4W-1N	C1
2100	CHCG	60647	2976	4W-2N	C6
4200	CHCG	60618	2976	4W-5N	C1
4300	CHCG	60625	2976	4W-5N	C1
5000	CHCG	60625	2920	4W-6N	B6
6100	CHCG	60659	2920	4W-7N	B3
6300	CHCG	60712	2920	4W-7N	B3
6300	LNWD	60712	2920	4W-7N	B3
S Springfield Av					
10	CHCG	60624	3032	4W-0S	C5
1100	CHCG	60623	3032	4W-1S	C7
1600	CHCG	60623	3090	4W-2S	C2
4400	CHCG	60632	3090	4W-4S	C7
4600	CHCG	60632	3150	4W-5S	C1
5400	CHCG	60629	3150	4W-8S	C7
7500	CHCG	60652	3212	4W-8S	C1
9100	CHCG	60805	3212	4W-10S	C5
9100	ENGN	60805	3212	4W-11S	C5
10100	CHCG	60655	3212	4W-11S	C7
11500	ALSP	60655	3276	4W-13S	C4
11500	ALSP	60803	3276	4W-14S	C5
11500	CHCG	60655	3276	4W-13S	C4
11500	WthT	60655	3276	4W-13S	C4
11500	WthT	60803	3276	4W-14S	C5
13300	CTWD	60472	3348	4W-15S	C2
13300	RBBN	60472	3348	4W-15S	C2
13800	CTWD	60445	3348	4W-16S	C3
S Springfield Av					
13900	RBBN	60445	3348	4W-16S	C3
Springfield Ct					
600	ROSL	60172	2912	24W-6N	D7
14300	PNFD	60544	3337	31W-17S	E5
Springfield Dr					
-	BMDL	60172	2968	24W-5N	D1
-	BmdT	60108	2912	24W-5N	D7
-	BmdT	60172	2912	24W-5N	D7
-	BmdT	60172	2968	24W-5N	D1
200	BMDL	60108	2968	25W-4N	C3
600	ROSL	60172	2912	24W-6N	D6
900	BMDL	60108	2912	24W-6N	D7
900	BMDL	60172	2912	24W-5N	D7
Springfield Ln					
-	SRWD	60404	3496	31W-24S	A7
Springfield St					
200	SchT	60174	2908	34W-6N	D6
300	PKFT	60466	3595	3W-25S	A1
400	PKFT	60466	3507	3W-25S	A7
Springfield Ter					
200	DSPN	60018	2862	15W-10N	B5
Springfield Wy					
-	SCRL	60175	2963	38W-2N	B7
Spring Garden Cir					
1000	NPVL	60563	3142	26W-5S	A2
Spring Garden Ct					
10	LIHL	60156	2693	37W-22N	A3
Spring Garden Dr					
10	OswT	60538	3199	36W-10S	D6
Spring Green Dr					
1000	JLET	60433	3588	21W-25S	A1
1000	JltT	60433	3500	21W-25S	A7
1000	JltT	60433	3588	21W-25S	A1
1800	WHTN	60187	3081	26W-1S	E2
1800	WHTN	60187	3082	26W-1S	A2
2900	DRN	60561	3206	20W-9S	B4
Spring Green Wy					
700	BTVA	60510	3077	37W-0S	C1
700	GnvT	60510	3077	37W-0S	B1
900	GnvT	60510	3019	37W-0S	C7
Spring Grove Rd					
3600	JNBG	60050	2471	31W-36N	D3
4100	MchT	60050	2471	31W-36N	D5
5000	MchT	60081	2471	31W-37N	D2
5300	JNBG	60081	2471	31W-37N	D2
5600	RcmT	60050	2471	31W-37N	D1
5600	RcmT	60081	2471	31W-37N	D1
6100	RcmT	60050	2413	31W-38N	D7
6100	RcmT	60081	2413	31W-38N	D7
6300	SPGV	60081	2413	31W-38N	D7
Spring Grove Rd CO-V40					
3600	JNBG	60050	2471	31W-36N	D3
4100	MchT	60050	2471	31W-36N	D5
5000	MchT	60081	2471	31W-37N	D2
5300	JNBG	60081	2471	31W-37N	D2
5600	RcmT	60050	2471	31W-37N	D1
5600	RcmT	60081	2471	31W-37N	D1
6100	RcmT	60050	2413	31W-38N	D7
6100	RcmT	60081	2413	31W-38N	D7
6300	SPGV	60081	2413	31W-38N	D7
W Spring Grove Rd					
26000	AntT	60002	2356	26W-41N	E7
Spring Haven Ct					
1900	MTGY	60538	3199	36W-10S	E6
Springhaven Dr					
100	GRNE	60031	2535	14W-34N	C1
900	LYVL	60048	2591	17W-29N	A4
Springhill Cir					
800	NPVL	60563	3142	25W-5S	A2
E Springhill Cir					
500	NPVL	60563	3142	25W-5S	A4
W Springhill Cir					
500	NPVL	60563	3142	25W-6S	A4
Springhill Ct					
100	RMVL	60446	3339	27W-17S	C6
700	ELGN	60120	2855	32W-12N	C2
Spring Hill Dr					
200	CPVL	60110	2800	35W-16N	D1
200	CPVL	60118	2800	35W-16N	D1
200	WDND	60110	2800	35W-16N	D1
200	WDND	60118	2800	35W-16N	D1
900	NHBK	60062	2756	11W-17N	D4
Springhill Dr					
100	BGBK	60440	3268	24W-12S	E2
200	BmdT	60157	2913	22W-6N	C6
200	ROSL	60157	2913	22W-6N	C6
200	ROSL	60172	2913	22W-6N	C6
1000	NPVL	60563	3142	25W-5S	A3
1100	ALGN	60102	2747	35W-19N	B2
1400	AlqT	60102	2747	35W-19N	B2
Spring Hill Ln					
10	PNFD	60544	3338	29W-17S	D6
2300	LNHT	60046	2418	20W-38N	B7
Springhill Ring Rd					
-	CPVL	60118	2800	35W-16N	D2
600	WDND	60118	2800	35W-16N	D2
N Springinsguth Rd					
10	SMBG	60193	2858	25W-10N	B5
10	SMBG	60194	2858	25W-10N	B5
500	HFET	60169	2858	25W-10N	B4
500	HFET	60194	2858	25W-10N	B4
S Springinsguth Rd					
-	SmbT	60193	2912	25W-8N	B3
10	SMBG	60193	2858	25W-9N	B7
10	SMBG	60193	2858	25W-9N	B7
1900	SMBG	60193	2912	25W-8N	B3
Springlake Av					
10	HNDL	60521	3146	14W-5S	C2
Spring Lake Ct					
3800	JLET	60435	3417	27W-19S	D2
3900	LIHL	60156	2693	37W-22N	B4
Spring Lake Dr					
-	MKNA	60448	3504	10W-22S	B1
10	WldT	60564	3202	29W-10S	D6
100	ITSC	60143	2914	20W-6N	A7
200	RDLK	60073	2531	25W-33N	A2
1000	BmdT	60143	2914	20W-6N	A7
Springlake Dr					
3800	HRPK	60133	2967	27W-4N	C3
3900	CLLK	60014	2693	37W-22N	B4
3900	LIHL	60156	2693	37W-22N	A4
W Spring Lake Dr					
12200	HMGN	60491	3344	15W-17S	B6
Springlake Ln					
300	AURA	60504	3140	31W-7S	A7
Spring Lake Rd					
-	JLET	60403	3417	27W-19S	D2
-	LktT	60403	3417	27W-19S	D2
2400	JLET	60435	3417	27W-19S	D2
Spring Leaf					
600	JLET	60431	3497	28W-24S	B6
1400	WDND	60118	2800	34W-15N	D5
Spring Leaf Dr					
2600	SPGV	60081	2413	31W-39N	D5
Springleaf Dr					
100	BGBK	60440	3268	24W-12S	D2
Spring Leaf St					
-	JLET	60431	3497	28W-24S	B6
-	TroT	60436	3497	28W-24S	B6
W Spring Meadow Ct					
14300	GNOK	60048	2592	14W-28N	C5
Spring Meadow Ln					
-	LYWD	60411	3509	2E-23S	E3
S Spring Meadows Dr					
17900	HMGN	60491	3422	15W-21S	B6
Spring Mill Dr					
800	HFET	60169	2858	24W-11N	E3
1000	HFET	60195	2858	24W-11N	E3
1000	SMBG	60195	2858	24W-11N	E3
Springmist Ct					
300	BGBK	60440	3269	22W-13S	D4
Spring Oaks Dr					
100	WDDL	60191	2971	17W-5N	B2
Spring Point Dr					
200	CPVL	60110	2747	35W-17N	C7
200	CPVL	60110	2800	35W-17N	C1
Spring Pointe Ln					
-	ANTH	60002	2417	20W-40N	E3
Spring Ridge Dr					
400	CLLK	60012	2639	35W-26N	E2
1800	JLET	60586	3416	31W-21S	A7
2200	SPGV	60081	2413	31W-39N	D5
W Spring Ridge Dr					
1800	ANHT	60004	2753	19W-18N	D3
1800	PltT	60004	2753	19W-18N	D3
Springs Blvd					
5700	NndT	60012	2584	34W-28N	B5
Springside Av					
5500	DRGV	60515	3144	20W-6S	B4
6100	DGvT	60516	3144	20W-7S	B6
6100	DRGV	60516	3144	20W-7S	B6
7100	DRGV	60516	3206	20W-8S	B1
Springside Ct					
-	OSWG	60543	3263	36W-12S	D4
10	BFGV	60089	2754	17W-20N	B1
1800	JLET	60586	3415	33W-20S	A5
Springside Dr					
200	ElgT	60124	2853	38W-10N	A5
1800	CTHL	60403	3417	27W-21S	D7
1800	JLET	60586	3415	33W-21S	A7
1900	NPVL	60565	3203	26W-9S	D5
S Springside Dr					
10	RDLK	60073	2531	25W-33N	A3
Springside Ln					
300	BFGV	60089	2754	17W-20N	B1
Springside Pl					
1500	DRGV	60516	3144	20W-7S	B7
Springside St					
-	PNFD	60586	3415	32W-19S	C3
Spring Song Ct					
700	NARA	60542	3137	38W-4S	A2
Spring South Rd					
400	SMBG	60193	2912	25W-8N	B2
400	SmbT	60193	2912	25W-8N	B2
Springtide Ln					
17100	HLCT	60429	3426	4W-20S	E5
Springvale Rd					
10	WynT	60185	2967	27W-3N	C6
100	CLSM	60188	2967	27W-3N	C6
100	WynT	60188	2967	27W-3N	C6
Spring Valley Ct					
200	RDLK	60073	2530	26W-33N	E2
800	SMBG	60193	2859	22W-10N	C5
1200	CLSM	60188	2967	28W-4N	B4
2400	AURA	60503	3265	32W-11S	C1
Spring Valley Dr					
-	BRLT	60103	2967	28W-4N	B4
-	CLSM	60103	2967	28W-4N	B4
-	CLSM	60133	2967	28W-4N	B4
-	HRPK	60103	2967	28W-4N	B4
-	HRPK	60133	2967	28W-4N	B4
10	BMDL	60101	2913	22W-5N	D7
10	BmdT	60157	2913	22W-5N	C7
200	BMDL	60108	2913	22W-5N	B7
1000	CLSM	60188	2967	28W-4N	B4
1600	ELBN	60119	3017	43W-0N	B6
Spring Valley Ln					
10	SMWD	60107	2857	28W-10N	B5
Spring Valley Rd					
3700	LGGV	60047	2700	20W-21N	A5
Spring Valley Wy					
200	RDLK	60073	2530	25W-33N	E2
Spring View Ct					
-	PNFD	60586	3415	31W-19S	D2
Springview Ct					
1500	WLNG	60090	2754	16W-17N	D5
Spring View Dr					
16300	LKPT	60441	3420	20W-19S	B3
Springview Dr					
16600	LKPT	60441	3420	20W-19S	C3
Springview Ln					
13900	ODPK	60467	3344	14W-16S	D4
W Springwell Av					
26000	AntT	60002	2415	26W-39N	D5
S Spring Willow Bay					
700	PLTN	60067	2805	22W-15N	B3
Springwood Av					
500	EDND	60118	2801	33W-15N	B3
Springwood Cir					
500	EDND	60118	2801	33W-16N	B3
Springwood Ct					
10	ROSL	60172	2913	23W-8N	A3
500	EDND	60118	2801	33W-15N	B3
E Springwood Ct					
300	RLKB	60073	2475	22W-36N	B4
Springwood Dr					
-	INCK	60060	2647	17W-25N	A5
-	INCK	60061	2647	17W-25N	A5
-	WDSK	60098	2581	41W-29N	D5
100	NPVL	60540	3141	27W-7S	C7
400	JLET	60431	3497	28W-24S	A6
400	ROSL	60172	2913	23W-8N	A3
400	TroT	60431	3497	28W-24S	A6
1300	SMBG	60173	2859	21W-10N	D5
1300	SMBG	60193	2859	21W-10N	D5
18300	WrnT	60030	2533	18W-34N	E1
N Springwood Dr					
1200	PLTN	60074	2753	20W-17N	B5
Springwood Ln					
10	CmpT	60119	2961	42W-3N	D7
100	BNHL	60010	2749	29W-16N	C6
18200	WrnT	60030	2534	18W-34N	A1
Springwood Wy					
400	BGBK	60440	3204	25W-11S	C7
Sproat Av					
8700	BRBK	60459	3211	6W-10S	E5
8700	OKLN	60453	3211	6W-10S	E5
8700	OKLN	60459	3211	6W-10S	E5
Spruance Pl					
800	DSPN	60016	2862	15W-10N	B4
Spruce Av					
10	FXLK	60020	2473	27W-36N	B4
10	WKGN	60087	2480	10W-36N	B4
100	BNVL	60106	2971	17W-5N	C1
300	LKFT	60045	2650	10W-27N	A1
500	AddT	60106	2915	17W-6N	C6
500	BNVL	60191	2915	17W-6N	C6
500	WDDL	60191	2915	17W-6N	C6
600	LKFT	60045	2594	10W-27N	B7
1200	BNVL	60106	2915	17W-7N	C3
1200	EGVV	60007	2915	17W-7N	C3
1400	HRPK	60133	2911	26W-8N	E3
1600	DSPN	60018	2862	13W-9N	E7
1600	HDPK	60035	2704	10W-22N	A5
S Spruce Av					
100	AddT	60191	2971	17W-5N	C1
100	WDDL	60191	2971	17W-5N	C1
Spruce Ct					
10	LMNT	60439	3270	20W-14S	C6
10	WNVL	60555	3080	30W-1S	C2
200	YKVL	60560	3333	43W-15S	B2
400	SMBG	60193	2858	24W-10N	E6
600	BtlT	60543	3263	39W-12S	A3
600	OSWG	60543	3263	39W-12S	A3
1200	LYVL	60048	2647	16W-27N	D1
1500	LMBD	60148	3084	20W-1S	A1
2600	RGMW	60008	2806	20W-14N	B5
2800	GNVA	60134	3019	37W-0N	C5
13500	LMNT	60439	3343	17W-15S	C2
19100	MKNA	60448	3502	15W-23S	C2
S Spruce Ct					
12300	PSHT	60463	3275	7W-14S	B6
24800	CteT	60417	3687	3E-30S	B2
W Spruce Ct					
6400	MONE	60449	3682	8W-32S	C6
Spruce Dr					
-	CPVL	60110	2800	34W-16N	D1
-	CPVL	60118	2800	34W-16N	D1
-	WLNG	60090	2754	16W-18N	E2
300	NPVL	60540	3203	27W-8S	C1
400	SMBG	60193	2858	24W-10N	E6
600	PTHT	60070	2808	15W-15N	A1
800	SMWD	60107	2857	28W-10N	A7
1100	GNVW	60025	2810	9W-13N	D6
2600	DndT	60118	2747	36W-17N	A7
2600	WDND	60118	2747	36W-17N	A7
8400	ODPK	60462	3346	10W-16S	B3
E Spruce Dr					
400	PLTN	60074	2753	20W-18N	A3
S Spruce Dr					
19900	FftT	60423	3504	10W-24S	C4
W Spruce Dr					
2400	RDLK	60073	2530	26W-34N	E1
22000	AntT	60002	2417	22W-40N	C2
Spruce Ln					
-	PNFD	60544	3337	31W-16S	E4
200	CHHT	60411	3507	1W-24S	E5
300	CLLK	60014	2639	36W-25N	D5
300	EGVV	60007	2914	18W-8N	E2
300	EGVV	60007	2915	18W-8N	A2
300	GNEN	60137	3083	23W-2S	A3
500	LSLE	60532	3143	22W-4S	C1
700	BRLT	60103	2910	29W-6N	D6
1200	ELGN	60120	2855	32W-11N	D4
1400	WTMT	60559	3144	18W-7S	E6
2400	LYWD	60411	3509	3E-23S	E4
4500	MHRY	60050	2527	33W-33N	E2
9200	TYPK	60487	3423	11W-20S	E4
15100	BmnT	60452	3347	8W-18S	B6
15100	OKFT	60452	3347	8W-18S	B6
20400	CTHL	60403	3418	25W-19S	B2
20400	LktT	60403	3418	25W-19S	B2
S Spruce Ln					
10	GNWD	60425	3508	0E-22S	E2
W Spruce Ln					
20900	DPgT	60544	3340	26W-15S	A2
Spruce Rd					
200	NfdT	60062	2757	9W-18N	B3
300	AddT	60106	2971	17W-4N	C2
300	AddT	60191	2971	17W-4N	C2
300	WDDL	60106	2971	17W-4N	C2
300	WDDL	60191	2971	17W-4N	C2
500	BGBK	60440	3269	21W-11S	D1
700	BRTN	60010	2698	25W-20N	A7
700	FKFT	60423	3503	12W-25S	C6
2500	HMWD	60430	3427	3W-21S	B5
W Spruce Rd					
21200	ElaT	60047	2699	21W-23N	D1
21200	KLDR	60047	2699	21W-23N	D1
Spruce St					
-	NtrT	60093	2811	6W-15N	D1
10	LKZH	60047	2698	23W-22N	E3
100	AURA	60506	3138	36W-7S	A7
200	GNVW	60025	2864	9W-12N	D1
300	SEGN	60177	2908	34W-8N	E2
400	HMND	46324	3430		E3
400	NARA	60542	3078	35W-3S	B7
500	AURA	60506	3137	36W-7S	E7
600	GNVW	60025	2810	9W-13N	D7
800	BTVA	60510	3078	34W-2S	C3
800	DRFD	60015	2703	11W-21N	D7
800	WNKA	60093	2812	5W-15N	A1
900	SRGV	60554	3135	41W-4S	D2
1000	GLHT	60139	3025	23W-1N	A2
1000	GRNE	60031	2478	15W-35N	A6
1000	WrnT	60031	2478	15W-35N	A6
1100	LIHL	60156	2694	35W-22N	A4
1100	WNKA	60093	2811	5W-15N	E1
1400	NHBK	60062	2757	9W-17N	B6
1500	HHLL	60051	2586	30W-29N	A4
1500	SPGV	60081	2414	30W-38N	A6
N Spruce St					
2700	RVGV	60171	2973	11W-3N	E5
39000	LkvT	60046	2417	21W-39N	C5
W Spruce St					
26500	AntT	60002	2356	26W-42N	D6
Spruce Ter					
2800	ISLK	60042	2586	29W-28N	D5
N Spruce Ter					
1900	ANHT	60004	2807	17W-16N	B1
Spruce Creek Ct					
24400	PNFD	60586	3416	30W-19S	B3
Sprucecreek Ln					
14600	OrlT	60467	3344	14W-17S	C5
14700	ODPK	60467	3344	14W-17S	D5
Spruce Hill Ct					
13000	LMNT	60439	3342	19W-15S	E1
Spruce Pointe Ct					
2100	GRNE	60031	2478	15W-36N	A4
Spruce Pointe Dr					
5100	GRNE	60031	2478	15W-36N	A4
5100	WrnT	60031	2478	15W-36N	B4
Spruce Slip St					
10	JLET	60433	3499	22W-24S	C5
10	JLET	60436	3499	22W-24S	C5

STREET Block	City	ZIP	Map#	CGS	Grid
Spruce Tree Dr					
500	CRY	60013	2642	30W-24N	B7
500	CRY	60013	2696	30W-24N	B1
Spruce Tree Ln					
700	ALGN	60102	2747	35W-19N	C2
Sprucewood Av					
2100	DSPN	60018	2862	14W-9N	D7
2200	DSPN	60018	2916	14W-9N	D1
7100	WDRG	60517	3205	22W-8S	D1
Sprucewood Ct					
200	RLKB	60073	2474	23W-36N	E5
200	RLKB	60073	2475	22W-35N	A5
1900	NPVL	60565	3204	25W-9S	C4
17000	LKPT	60441	3420	19W-20S	E4
Sprucewood Dr					
-	LKPT	60441	3420	19W-20S	E5
S Sprucewood Dr					
1100	MPPT	60056	2861	17W-11N	C3
Sprucewood Ln					
1300	DRFD	60015	2756	11W-20N	C1
1800	GRNE	60031	2478	15W-36N	A5
1800	LNHT	60046	2418	20W-38N	A7
3200	NHFD	60091	2811	6W-14N	D4
3200	NHFD	60093	2811	6W-14N	D4
3200	WLMT	60091	2811	6W-14N	D4
4700	MTSN	60443	3506	5W-25S	B7
4700	RchT	60443	3506	5W-25S	B7
W Sprucewood Ln					
10	RLKB	60073	2475	23W-35N	A5
15600	LbvT	60048	2592	15W-30N	A3
Sprucewood Rd					
3100	WLMT	60091	2811	6W-14N	D5
Spuce Dr					
-	BmnT	60426	3426	5W-19S	A2
Spuhler Dr					
10	BTVA	60510	3077	36W-1S	D2
10	BtvT	60510	3077	36W-1S	D2
10	BtvT	60539	3077	36W-1S	D2
Spur Ct					
10	SMWD	60107	2856	30W-10N	C5
1200	WLNG	60090	2754	16W-18N	E2
W Spur Ct					
26400	CNHN	60410	3672	33W-31S	C5
Spur Ln					
10	CmpT	60175	2962	41W-4N	A5
1600	AURA	60502	3139	32W-5S	C3
Spyglass Cir					
10	PSHT	60463	3347	8W-15S	B2
8200	ODPK	60462	3346	10W-18S	C7
28600	FmtT	60060	2589	21W-28N	C5
Spyglass Ct					
-	LMNT	60439	3271	17W-14S	D7
10	LIHL	60156	2693	37W-21N	C5
10	NPVL	60563	3140	30W-4S	C1
10	NpvT	60563	3140	30W-4S	C1
400	LslT	60540	3143	23W-7S	A7
600	NARA	60542	3078	35W-3S	B5
800	HDPK	60035	2704	9W-23N	C3
1400	ITSC	60143	2913	21W-6N	E6
2300	RVWD	60015	2756	13W-20N	A1
28700	FmtT	60060	2589	21W-28N	C5
Spyglass Dr					
-	BmnT	60445	3347	8W-16S	B2
-	PSHT	60445	3347	8W-16S	B2
-	PSHT	60463	3347	8W-16S	B2
Spyglass Ln					
900	NHBK	60062	2756	12W-17N	B5
Spyglass Cove					
100	CPVL	60110	2800	35W-16N	C1
Spyglass Hl					
-	MONE	60449	3683	6W-31S	B4
Spy Glass Hill Ct					
700	ELGN	60123	2854	35W-10N	B7
Spy Glass Ridge Rd					
3700	NndT	60012	2584	35W-28N	A6
Squanto Ct					
10	SMBG	60193	2858	24W-10N	D6
Square Barn Rd					
-	GfnT	60102	2693	37W-20N	A7
-	GfnT	60156	2693	37W-20N	A7
500	ALGN	60102	2746	38W-19N	A2
500	GfnT	60102	2746	38W-19N	A2
500	RtdT	60118	2746	38W-19N	A2
500	RtdT	60142	2746	38W-19N	A2
11600	ALGN	60102	2693	37W-20N	A7
Squaw Rd					
26500	GrtT	60041	2473	26W-36N	D4
Squaw Valley Tr					
2700	AURA	60503	3265	32W-11S	C1
Squibb Dr					
3200	RGMW	60008	2860	20W-12N	B1
Squire Cir					
-	BtlT	60560	3262	40W-13S	B4
Squire Ct					
10	SBTN	60010	2803	26W-14N	D3
1000	AURA	60505	3138	34W-5S	D3
Squire Dr					
1000	AraT	60505	3138	34W-5S	D3
1000	AURA	60505	3138	34W-5S	D3
3400	MngT	60152	2578	49W-28N	C5
Squire Ln					
10	BmdT	60157	2913	22W-7N	D5
10	SCRL	60174	2964	34W-4N	E4
1400	BRLT	60103	2966	30W-5N	B1
6200	WLBK	60527	3145	17W-6S	D5
26200	CNHN	60410	3672	32W-31S	C6
W Squire Ln					
1500	ADSN	60101	2970	20W-5N	B1
Squire Pl					
10	PSHT	60463	3274	9W-14S	D5
Squire Rd					
10	ElaT	60047	2645	21W-24N	C6
10	HNWD	60047	2645	21W-24N	C6
Squires Ln					
9600	RcmT	60071	2412	33W-41N	E1
9600	RHMD	60071	2412	33W-41N	E1
Squires Mill Ct					
1800	JLET	60431	3417	28W-21S	A7
Squires Mill Rd					
-	JLET	60431	3416	29W-21S	E7
3600	JLET	60431	3417	28W-21S	A7
Squirrel Dr					
8200	SPGV	60081	2413	31W-40N	D3
Squirrel St					
500	JLET	60432	3499	22W-23S	D3
Squirrel Tr					
1600	AlqT	60013	2642	30W-24N	A6
SR-1 Chicago Rd					
1100	CHHT	60411	3508	1W-25S	A7
1500	CHHT	60411	3596	1W-28S	B6
2500	SCHT	60411	3596	1W-26S	A2
3000	SCHT	60475	3596	1W-27S	B4
3000	STGR	60475	3596	1W-27S	B4
3700	CRTE	60417	3596	1W-28S	B7
3700	CRTE	60475	3596	1W-28S	B7
SR-1 Dixie Hwy					
-	CteT	60417	3774	0W-32S	C1
27500	CteT	60401	3774	0W-33S	C3
27600	WshT	60401	3774	0W-35S	C6
28600	BCHR	60401	3774	0W-35S	C6
SR-1 S Dixie Hwy					
300	BCHR	60401	3864	0W-36S	C2
300	WshT	60401	3864	0W-37S	C2
1100	BCHR	60401	3774	0W-36S	C7
25300	CRTE	60417	3685	0W-30S	B4
25300	CteT	60417	3685	0W-32S	B6
26700	CteT	60417	3774	0W-32S	C1
26900	CteT	60401	3774	0W-33S	C2
SR-1 Halsted St					
-	EHZC	60426	3428	0W-20S	B4
-	EHZC	60473	3428	0W-20S	B4
14300	HRVY	60426	3350	1W-17S	A4
14300	HRVY	60827	3350	1W-16S	A4
14300	RVDL	60827	3350	1W-16S	A4
15200	PHNX	60426	3350	0W-18S	B7
15600	HRVY	60426	3428	1W-21S	B7
16900	SHLD	60426	3428	0W-20S	B4
16900	SHLD	60473	3428	0W-20S	B4
17100	EHZC	60429	3428	0W-20S	B5
17300	EHZC	60430	3428	0W-20S	B5
17300	HMWD	60429	3428	0W-20S	B5
17300	HMWD	60430	3428	0W-20S	B5
18000	GNWD	60425	3428	0W-21S	B7
18000	HMWD	60425	3428	0W-21S	B7
SR-1 S Halsted St					
-	RVDL	60827	3278	0W-15S	A7
100	CHHT	60411	3508	1W-23S	B4
9900	CHCG	60628	3214	1W-11S	A7
9900	CHCG	60643	3214	1W-11S	A7
10300	CHCG	60628	3278	1W-13S	A3
10300	CHCG	60643	3278	1W-13S	A3
12200	CTPK	60628	3278	1W-14S	A6
12200	CTPK	60643	3278	1W-14S	A6
12200	CTPK	60827	3278	1W-14S	A6
13100	RVDL	60827	3350	1W-17S	A4
14500	HRVY	60426	3350	1W-16S	A4
14500	HRVY	60827	3350	1W-16S	A4
18300	GNWD	60425	3428	0W-22S	B7
18300	GNWD	60425	3508	1W-24S	B5
18300	HMWD	60430	3428	0W-22S	B7
18500	HMWD	60425	3508	1W-24S	B5
18500	HMWD	60430	3508	1W-24S	B5
19100	BlmT	60411	3508	1W-23S	B3
19100	GNWD	60411	3508	1W-23S	B3
SR-1 Main St					
800	CRTE	60417	3596	1W-28S	B7
800	CRTE	60417	3685	0W-29S	B1
1500	CteT	60417	3685	0W-30S	B3
SR-1 Route 1 Cto					
-	CHHT	60411	3508	1W-24S	B6
SR-1 Vincennes Rd					
-	PHNX	60426	3350	1W-18S	B7
14900	HRVY	60426	3350	1W-18S	B7
SR-7 E 9th St					
-	LKPT	60441	3420	21W-19S	A2
100	LKPT	60441	3419	22W-19S	C3
1100	LktT	60441	3419	21W-19S	E2
SR-7 W 9th St					
-	RMVL	60441	3419	23W-19S	B2
10	LKPT	60441	3419	22W-19S	C3
500	LktT	60441	3419	23W-19S	B2
SR-7 W 143rd St					
9800	ODPK	60462	3345	12W-16S	C4
10600	OrlT	60462	3345	13W-16S	B4
10700	ODPK	60467	3345	13W-16S	A4
10700	OrlT	60467	3345	13W-16S	A4
10900	ODPK	60467	3344	14W-17S	E6
10900	OrlT	60467	3344	14W-17S	E6
SR-7 E 159th St					
1200	LKPT	60441	3420	21W-18S	A2
1200	LktT	60441	3420	21W-18S	A2
1300	HmrT	60441	3420	21W-18S	A2
SR-7 W 159th St					
11200	ODPK	60467	3422	14W-18S	E1
11200	OrlT	60467	3422	14W-18S	E1
11800	HMGN	60491	3422	14W-18S	C1
13000	HMGN	60491	3421	18W-19S	A1
13900	HmrT	60491	3421	17W-18S	C1
14800	HmrT	60491	3420	20W-19S	B2
15400	HmrT	60441	3420	19W-19S	C1
16000	LKPT	60441	3420	20W-19S	C2
16000	LKPT	60491	3420	20W-19S	C2
16600	LktT	60441	3420	20W-18S	A2
SR-7 Broadway St					
2100	CTHL	60403	3418	24W-21S	E6
2100	CTHL	60435	3418	24W-21S	E6
2100	CTHL	60441	3418	24W-21S	E6
2100	LktT	60435	3418	24W-21S	E6
15800	LktT	60441	3419	23W-19S	A2
15800	RMVL	60441	3419	23W-19S	A2
16200	CTHL	60441	3419	23W-19S	A2
17000	LktT	60441	3418	24W-20S	E5
SR-7 N Broadway St					
1600	CTHL	60403	3498	24W-21S	E1
1600	CTHL	60435	3498	24W-21S	E1
1600	JLET	60435	3498	24W-21S	E1
1600	LktT	60435	3498	24W-21S	E1
1700	CTHL	60403	3418	24W-21S	E7
1700	CTHL	60435	3418	24W-21S	E7
1800	LktT	60435	3418	24W-21S	E7
2000	CTHL	60441	3418	24W-21S	E6
SR-7 N Larkin Av					
10	JLET	60435	3498	26W-23S	A4
10	JLET	60436	3498	26W-23S	A5
1200	JLET	60403	3498	26W-22S	A1
SR-7 S Larkin Av					
-	JltT	60436	3586	26W-25S	A1
10	JLET	60435	3498	26W-24S	A5
10	JLET	60436	3498	26W-24S	A5
600	JltT	60436	3498	26W-24S	A7
600	JLET	60436	3498	26W-25S	A7
1200	RKDL	60436	3498	26W-25S	A7
1200	RKDL	60436	3586	26W-25S	A1
SR-7 Southwest Hwy					
10600	CHRG	60415	3274	9W-12S	E2
10600	CHRG	60482	3274	9W-12S	E2
10600	WRTH	60415	3274	9W-12S	E2
10600	WRTH	60482	3274	9W-12S	E2
10800	PSHL	60465	3274	9W-12S	C5
10800	PSHL	60482	3274	9W-12S	D2
11200	PSHT	60465	3274	9W-13S	C5
11400	PSHT	60463	3274	9W-13S	C5
11800	PSHT	60464	3274	9W-13S	C5
11800	PSPK	60464	3274	11W-14S	A7
12600	PlsT	60464	3346	11W-15S	A1
12600	PSPK	60464	3346	11W-15S	A1
13000	ODPK	60462	3346	11W-15S	A1
13000	PlsT	60462	3346	11W-15S	A1
13000	PSPK	60462	3346	11W-15S	A1
13100	ODPK	60462	3345	11W-16S	E3
13100	OrlT	60462	3345	11W-16S	E3
13100	PlsT	60462	3345	11W-16S	E3
SR-7 Theodore St					
200	CTHL	60403	3498	25W-22S	C1
200	CTHL	60435	3498	24W-21S	E1
200	JLET	60435	3498	25W-22S	C1
1400	JLET	60403	3498	25W-21S	B1
SR-7 Wolf Rd					
14300	ODPK	60467	3344	13W-17S	E4
14300	OrlT	60467	3344	13W-17S	E4
15600	ODPK	60467	3422	15W-19S	B1
15600	OrlT	60467	3422	15W-19S	B1
SR-19 E Chicago St					
-	ELGN	60123	2854	34W-11N	E4
10	ELGN	60120	2854	34W-11N	E4
300	ELGN	60120	2855	33W-11N	B4
1400	HnrT	60120	2855	31W-10N	E5
SR-19 W Chicago St					
100	ELGN	60123	2854	34W-11N	E4
SR-19 Irving Park Rd					
-	CHCG	60176	2973	12W-5N	C1
-	CHCG	60634	2973	12W-5N	C1
-	CHCG	60666	2973	12W-5N	A1
-	ELGN	60120	2855	31W-10N	E5
-	FNPK	60131	2973	13W-5N	A1
-	HnrT	60120	2855	31W-10N	E5
-	ROSL	60157	2913	22W-7N	C5
-	ROSL	60172	2913	22W-7N	C5
-	SRPK	60666	2973	12W-5N	A1
10	BmdT	60143	2913	22W-6N	D5
10	BmdT	60143	2914	18W-6N	E7
10	BmdT	60157	2913	22W-6N	D5
10	HnrT	60107	2856	30W-10N	B5
10	HnrT	60120	2856	30W-10N	B5
10	ITSC	60143	2914	18W-6N	E7
100	SMWD	60107	2856	30W-10N	B5
100	SMWD	60120	2856	30W-10N	B5
400	ITSC	60143	2913	21W-6N	E6
800	HRPK	60133	2912	24W-8N	C3
800	SMBG	60133	2912	26W-9N	A2
1200	HRPK	60133	2911	27W-9N	C1
1600	ELGN	60120	2856	31W-10N	A5
1700	HRPK	60107	2911	27W-9N	D1
1700	SMWD	60107	2911	27W-9N	D1
1700	SMWD	60133	2911	27W-9N	D1
9200	SRPK	60176	2973	12W-5N	A1
SR-19 E Irving Park Rd					
10	BNVL	60106	2972	15W-5N	A1
10	ROSL	60172	2913	23W-7N	A4
10	SMWD	60107	2857	28W-9N	A7
100	ITSC	60143	2914	19W-6N	C6
100	WDDL	60191	2915	17W-5N	B7
400	BmdT	60157	2913	22W-7N	C5
400	BNVL	60106	2915	17W-5N	C7
400	CHCG	60106	2972	15W-5N	A1
400	ROSL	60157	2913	22W-7N	C5
800	SMWD	60107	2911	27W-9N	C1
900	BNVL	60131	2972	14W-5N	B1
900	CHCG	60131	2972	14W-5N	B1
900	HRPK	60107	2911	27W-9N	C1
900	HRPK	60133	2911	27W-9N	C1
900	SMWD	60133	2911	27W-9N	C1
1100	WDDL	60143	2914	19W-6N	D7
1200	WDDL	60191	2914	19W-6N	D7
1300	ITSC	60191	2914	18W-6N	E7
11500	CHCG	60666	2972	14W-5N	C1
SR-19 W Irving Park Rd					
-	BNVL	60131	2972	14W-5N	C1
-	CHCG	60131	2972	14W-5N	D2
-	CHCG	60176	2973	11W-5N	E2
-	CHCG	60634	2973	10W-5N	E2
-	CHCG	60666	2972	14W-5N	D2
-	FNPK	60131	2972	14W-5N	D2
-	FNPK	60666	2972	13W-5N	E2
10	BNVL	60106	2915	16W-5N	E7
10	ROSL	60172	2913	21W-6N	D5
10	SMWD	60107	2856	29W-10N	D6
100	ROSL	60172	2912	23W-7N	E4
100	SMBG	60172	2912	23W-7N	E4
100	WDDL	60191	2915	17W-5N	C7
200	ITSC	60143	2914	19W-6N	C6
200	WDDL	60191	2914	18W-6N	E7
400	ITSC	60191	2914	18W-6N	E7
400	SMBG	60193	2912	24W-7N	D3
400	WDDL	60143	2914	18W-6N	E7
600	CHCG	60613	2978	0W-5N	A1
700	CHCG	60613	2977	3W-4N	A2
700	HnrT	60107	2856	29W-10N	D6
700	SmbT	60193	2912	25W-8N	B2
900	HnrT	60120	2856	29W-10N	C6
900	SMWD	60120	2856	29W-10N	C6
1200	BmdT	60143	2914	21W-6N	A6
1400	BmdT	60143	2913	21W-6N	E6
1400	ITSC	60143	2913	21W-6N	E6
1800	SMBG	60133	2912	25W-8N	A2
1900	CHCG	60618	2977	2W-5N	B1
1900	HRPK	60133	2912	25W-9N	A2
2700	CHCG	60618	2976	3W-4N	E2
3900	CHCG	60641	2976	5W-4N	A2
4600	CHCG	60641	2975	7W-4N	B2
5500	CHCG	60634	2975	6W-5N	C2
6600	CHCG	60634	2974	8W-4N	D2
7100	NRDG	60634	2974	8W-5N	D2
7100	NRDG	60706	2974	8W-5N	D2
7300	CHCG	60706	2974	9W-4N	D2
SR-19 N Recreation Dr					
-	CHCG	60613	2978	0W-4N	A1
SR-21					
32500	GRNE	60048	2534	16W-32N	D5
32500	WrnT	60048	2534	16W-32N	D5
SR-21 Milwaukee Av					
-	LYVL	60048	2647	16W-26N	E3
-	VNHL	60061	2647	16W-26N	E3
100	LNSH	60061	2702	15W-23N	A2
100	LNSH	60069	2702	15W-23N	A1
100	VNHL	60061	2702	15W-23N	A2
100	VNHL	60069	2702	15W-23N	A2
200	VrnT	60061	2702	15W-23N	A2
300	VrnT	60069	2702	15W-23N	A2
500	MaiT	60016	2809	10W-13N	E7
500	MaiT	60025	2809	10W-13N	E7
500	NfdT	60016	2809	10W-13N	E7
500	NfdT	60025	2809	11W-13N	E7
700	GNVW	60025	2809	11W-13N	D6
900	BFGV	60089	2755	14W-20N	C1
900	VrnT	60062	2755	14W-20N	C1
900	VrnT	60069	2755	14W-20N	C1
900	VrnT	60089	2755	14W-20N	C1
1000	BFGV	60089	2702	14W-20N	B7
1000	RVWD	60015	2702	14W-20N	B7
1000	RVWD	60015	2755	14W-20N	C1
1000	VrnT	60015	2702	14W-20N	B7
1400	LNSH	60015	2702	14W-21N	B5
1600	GNVW	60062	2809	12W-14N	C4
1800	NfdT	60062	2809	12W-14N	C4
2800	PTHT	60062	2809	12W-15N	A2
2800	PTHT	60070	2809	12W-15N	A2
9700	GNVW	60025	2863	10W-12N	E1
SR-21 Milwaukee Av					
9700	GNVW	60025	2864	10W-12N	A1
9700	MaiT	60016	2864	10W-12N	A1
9700	MaiT	60025	2863	10W-12N	E1
9700	MaiT	60025	2864	10W-12N	A1
9700	MaiT	60714	2864	10W-12N	A1
9700	NLES	60025	2864	10W-12N	A1
9700	NLES	60714	2864	10W-12N	A1
9800	MaiT	60016	2863	10W-12N	E1
20400	BFGV	60090	2755	14W-20N	C1
SR-21 N Milwaukee Av					
-	NfdT	60062	2809	12W-15N	A2
-	VrnT	60061	2647	15W-25N	E6
10	VNHL	60061	2648	15W-24N	A7
10	VrnT	60061	2648	15W-24N	A7
100	LYVL	60048	2591	16W-29N	D4
100	MTWA	60048	2647	15W-25N	E6
100	VNHL	60061	2647	15W-25N	E6
500	PTHT	60062	2809	13W-15N	A1
500	PTHT	60070	2809	13W-15N	A1
500	PTHT	60090	2809	13W-15N	A1
500	WhlT	60062	2809	13W-15N	A1
500	WhlT	60090	2809	13W-15N	A1
500	WLNG	60090	2755	13W-16N	E6
800	BFGV	60090	2755	14W-20N	C2
900	BFGV	60089	2755	14W-20N	C1
900	VrnT	60062	2755	14W-20N	C1
900	VrnT	60089	2755	14W-20N	C1
1700	LbvT	60048	2591	16W-30N	D2
7500	CHCG	60631	2864	9W-9N	D7
7500	CHCG	60714	2864	9W-9N	D7
7500	NLES	60631	2864	9W-9N	D7
7500	NLES	60714	2864	9W-9N	D6
8300	MaiT	60714	2864	9W-10N	C5
9500	MaiT	60016	2864	10W-11N	A2
9600	GNVW	60025	2864	10W-12N	A1
9600	MaiT	60025	2864	10W-12N	A1
9600	NLES	60025	2864	10W-12N	A1
21800	LNSH	60069	2702	15W-21N	B5
21800	VrnT	60069	2702	14W-21N	B5
31000	LbvT	60048	2534	16W-31N	C7
31400	WKGN	60048	2534	16W-31N	D6
32200	WrnT	60048	2534	16W-32N	D5
32700	GRNE	60048	2534	16W-32N	E5
SR-21 S Milwaukee Av					
10	WLNG	60090	2755	14W-18N	D4
100	LYVL	60048	2591	16W-28N	D5
100	VNHL	60061	2648	15W-24N	A7
100	VNHL	60061	2702	15W-24N	A1
100	VrnT	60061	2648	15W-24N	A7
100	VrnT	60061	2702	15W-24N	A1
600	WhlT	60090	2755	13W-17N	E5
1000	LYVL	60048	2647	15W-25N	E5
1000	PTHT	60070	2755	13W-16N	E7
1000	PTHT	60070	2808	13W-16N	E1
1000	PTHT	60070	2809	13W-16N	A1
1000	PTHT	60090	2809	13W-16N	A1
1000	WhlT	60090	2808	13W-16N	E1
1000	WhlT	60090	2809	13W-16N	A1
1200	VNHL	60061	2647	15W-25N	E5
1600	VNHL	60048	2647	16W-26N	E2
SR-21 N Riverside Dr					
-	WrnT	60031	2478	15W-35N	B5
300	GRNE	60031	2535	15W-34N	B1
500	GRNE	60031	2478	15W-35N	B5
SR-21 S Riverside Dr					
-	GRNE	60031	2535	15W-34N	A1
-	GRNE	60048	2534	16W-33N	E4
700	GRNE	60031	2534	16W-31N	C7
SR-22					
-	CbaT	60010	2696	29W-22N	C3
-	CbaT	60010	2697	26W-22N	D4
-	CbaT	60010	2698	25W-22N	A4
-	ElaT	60047	2699	22W-22N	B3
-	ElaT	60047	2700	18W-22N	D3
-	KLDR	60047	2699	22W-22N	B3
-	KLDR	60047	2700	18W-22N	D3
-	LGGV	60047	2700	18W-23N	E3
-	LGGV	60047	2701	18W-23N	A3
-	LKBN	60010	2696	29W-22N	C3
-	LKBN	60010	2697	28W-22N	A3
-	NBRN	60010	2697	26W-22N	D4
200	LKZH	60047	2699	23W-23N	A3
600	LKZH	60047	2698	24W-22N	C4
1000	FRGV	60010	2696	29W-22N	D3
1000	FRGV	60021	2696	29W-22N	C3
1000	LKZH	60047	2698	24W-22N	C4
23100	ElaT	60010	2698	24W-22N	B4
23100	ElaT	60047	2698	24W-22N	B4
23100	NBRN	60010	2698	25W-22N	B4
SR-22 BYP					
300	LKZH	60047	2698	23W-22N	E4
SR-22 Half Day Rd					
10	LNSH	60045	2702	14W-23N	C2
10	LNSH	60069	2702	14W-23N	C2
10	VrnT	60069	2702	13W-23N	D2
800	HDPK	60035	2703	11W-23N	E3
800	WdfT	60015	2703	11W-23N	D3
1100	BKBN	60015	2703	11W-23N	D3
1300	HDPK	60035	2704	10W-23N	A3
2200	VrnT	60015	2703	13W-23N	A2
2300	LNSH	60069	2703	12W-23N	B3
2300	VrnT	60069	2703	12W-23N	B3
SR-22 W Half Day Rd					
-	LGGV	60089	2701	17W-23N	B3
-	VrnT	60089	2701	16W-22N	D3
10	LNSH	60069	2702	13W-23N	E2
100	BFGV	60069	2701	16W-22N	C3
100	BFGV	60089	2701	16W-22N	C3
100	VrnT	60069	2701	16W-22N	C3
400	LNSH	60069	2701	15W-22N	E3
5500	BFGV	60047	2701	17W-23N	A3
5500	LGGV	60047	2701	17W-22N	A3
14400	LNSH	60045	2702	14W-23N	C2
14500	VrnT	60069	2702	13W-23N	E2
SR-22 Main St					
21400	KLDR	60047	2699	21W-23N	D3
21500	ElaT	60047	2699	21W-23N	D3
SR-22 W Main St					
-	LKZH	60047	2698	24W-22N	C4
SR-23					
-	HRVD	60033	2464	50W-35N	A5
-	MngT	60152	2578	50W-28N	B5
-	MRGO	60152	2578	50W-28N	B6
-	MRGO	60152	2634	50W-25N	B4
-	RlyT	60152	2634	50W-25N	B4
2000	DhmT	60033	2464	50W-35N	A5
SR-23 N State St					
-	MngT	60152	2578	50W-27N	B7
100	MRGO	60152	2634	50W-25N	B3
1400	MRGO	60152	2578	50W-27N	B7
SR-23 S State St					
100	MRGO	60152	2634	50W-26N	B2
1100	RlyT	60152	2634	50W-25N	B3
SR-25					
-	ELGN	60120	2855	33W-12N	B1
SR-25					
10	SchT	60120	2908	34W-6N	D7
10	SchT	60120	2909	33W-7N	A5
10	SchT	60174	2964	34W-6N	D1
10	SCRL	60174	2964	35W-5N	C1
200	SchT	60174	2908	34W-6N	D7
300	WYNE	60174	2964	35W-5N	C2
400	BRLT	60120	2909	33W-9N	B1
400	BRLT	60177	2909	33W-9N	B1
400	ElgT	60120	2909	33W-9N	B1
400	ElgT	60177	2909	33W-9N	B2
400	SchT	60103	2909	33W-7N	A5
400	SchT	60177	2909	33W-7N	A5
400	SEGN	60120	2909	33W-9N	B1
400	SEGN	60177	2909	33W-9N	B1
500	BRLT	60103	2909	33W-7N	B4
500	MTGY	60538	3199	37W-10S	C6
500	OSWG	60543	3263	37W-12S	C2
500	OswT	60538	3199	37W-10S	C7
500	OswT	60538	3263	37W-11S	C1
500	OswT	60543	3199	37W-10S	C7
500	OswT	60543	3263	37W-12S	C2
600	SEGN	60103	2909	33W-8N	B3
SR-25 N 5th Av					
10	SCRL	60174	2964	35W-3N	B7
SR-25 S 5th Av					
10	SCRL	60174	2964	35W-3N	B7
SR-25 Aurora Av					
700	AURA	60505	3138	35W-6S	C5
900	AURA	60504	3138	35W-6S	B4
900	AURA	60506	3138	35W-6S	B4
1100	AURA	60542	3138	35W-5S	B4
SR-25 N Bennett St					
10	GNVA	60134	3020	34W-1N	C3
800	SCRL	60134	3020	34W-1N	C2
800	SCRL	60174	3020	34W-1N	C2
SR-25 S Bennett St					
10	GNVA	60134	3020	34W-1N	C4
SR-25 Bluff City Blvd					
500	ELGN	60120	2855	33W-10N	B6
SR-25 N Broadway					
10	AURA	60505	3138	35W-7S	B7
SR-25 S Broadway					
10	AURA	60505	3138	35W-7S	B7
10	AURA	60505	3200	35W-8S	A1
700	AURA	60505	3199	36W-9S	E3
800	MTGY	60505	3199	36W-8S	E3
800	MTGY	60538	3199	36W-8S	E3
SR-25 S Broadway Rd					
1000	AURA	60505	3199	36W-8S	E3
1000	MTGY	60505	3199	36W-8S	E3
1000	MTGY	60538	3199	36W-9S	E3
SR-25 Crissey Av					
-	BTVA	60510	3020	35W-0S	C6
-	GNVA	60510	3020	35W-0S	C6
200	GNVA	60134	3020	34W-1N	C4
SR-25 Dundee Av					
10	CPVL	60110	2801	33W-16N	C2
10	EDND	60110	2801	33W-16N	C2
10	EDND	60118	2801	33W-16N	C2
600	DndT	60118	2801	33W-14N	C6
1100	ELGN	60120	2855	33W-12N	B1
1300	ELGN	60120	2801	33W-14N	C6
1500	DndT	60120	2801	33W-14N	C6
1500	ELGN	60118	2801	33W-14N	C6
SR-25 Elgin Rd					
1600	BNHL	60110	2748	33W-19N	C2
1600	CPVL	60110	2748	33W-19N	C2
1900	DndT	60110	2748	32W-19N	C2
2100	ALGN	60102	2748	32W-19N	C2
2100	ALGN	60110	2748	32W-19N	C2
2100	BNHL	60010	2748	32W-19N	C2
2100	BNHL	60102	2748	32W-19N	C2
SR-25 JFK Memorial Dr					
-	EDND	60118	2801	33W-16N	C1
10	CPVL	60110	2748	33W-17N	C6
200	EDND	60110	2748	33W-17N	C7
800	CPVL	60110	2801	33W-16N	C1
800	EDND	60110	2801	33W-16N	C1
SR-25 N Kennedy Dr					
10	CPVL	60110	2748	33W-17N	C6
100	BNHL	60110	2748	33W-18N	C4
SR-25 N Liberty St					
10	ELGN	60120	2855	33W-11N	B4
SR-25 S Liberty St					
10	ELGN	60120	2855	33W-11N	B4
SR-25 N Madison St					
10	OSWG	60543	3263	37W-12S	C3
SR-25 N River Rd					
10	NARA	60542	3078	36W-4S	A7
500	NARA	60510	3078	36W-3S	A6
SR-25 S River Rd					
10	NARA	60542	3138	35W-4S	A1
100	AURA	60542	3138	35W-4S	A1
200	AURA	60504	3138	35W-4S	A1
200	NARA	60504	3138	35W-4S	A1
SR-25 SE River Rd					
1300	MTGY	60538	3199	36W-9S	D4
1800	OswT	60538	3199	37W-10S	D5
SR-25 S River St					
10	BTVA	60510	3078	35W-1S	C2
300	BtvT	60510	3078	35W-2S	C4
2000	NARA	60510	3078	35W-3S	A5
2500	NARA	60542	3078	36W-3S	A6
SR-25 Riverside Av					
900	SCRL	60174	3020	35W-0N	C5
1800	GNVA	60134	3020	34W-2N	C2
1800	SCRL	60134	3020	34W-2N	C2
SR-25 St. Charles St					
800	ELGN	60120	2855	33W-10N	B6
900	ElgT	60120	2855	33W-9N	B7
900	ElgT	60177	2855	33W-9N	B7
1100	ElgT	60120	2909	33W-9N	B1
1100	ElgT	60177	2909	33W-9N	B1
SR-25 N Washington Av					
10	BTVA	60510	3078	35W-1S	C1
800	BTVA	60510	3020	35W-0S	C7
1200	GNVA	60134	3020	35W-0S	C6
1200	GNVA	60510	3020	35W-0S	C6
SR-25 E Wilson St					
100	BTVA	60510	3078	35W-1S	C2
SR-31					
-	ALGN	60013	2694	33W-22N	E3
-	ALGN	60102	2694	33W-23N	E1
-	AlqT	60013	2694	33W-22N	E3
-	AlqT	60014	2640	33W-26N	E3
-	AlqT	60014	2694	33W-23N	E1
-	AlqT	60102	2694	33W-23N	E1
-	CLLK	60012	2584	33W-30N	E2
-	CLLK	60012	2640	33W-27N	E1
-	CLLK	60013	2694	33W-23N	E1
-	CLLK	60014	2640	33W-24N	E7
-	CLLK	60014	2694	33W-24N	E1
-	CRY	60013	2694	33W-23N	E2
-	CRY	60014	2694	33W-23N	E2
-	DndT	60102	2747	34W-19N	D2

STREET Block	City	ZIP	Map#	CGS	Grid
SR-31					
-	LIHL	60013	2694	33W-22N	E4
-	LIHL	60014	2694	33W-23N	E2
-	LIHL	60102	2694	33W-23N	E1
-	LIHL	60156	2694	33W-22N	E3
-	MHRY	60050	2584	33W-30N	E2
-	MHRY	60050	2585	33W-30N	A2
-	MTGY	60538	3199	37W-10S	B6
-	NndT	60012	2584	33W-30N	E2
-	NndT	60012	2640	33W-27N	E1
-	NndT	60014	2640	33W-26N	E3
-	NndT	60050	2584	33W-28N	E5
-	NndT	60050	2585	33W-30N	A2
-	PRGV	60012	2584	33W-28N	E5
-	PRGV	60050	2584	33W-29N	E3
10	DndT	60118	2747	34W-19N	D4
10	SchT	60174	2964	36W-4N	A5
10	SchT	60175	2964	35W-5N	B1
10	SchT	60177	2908	34W-7N	C5
10	SCRL	60174	2964	36W-4N	A5
10	SCRL	60175	2964	35W-5N	B1
100	CPVL	60110	2747	35W-17N	C6
200	SchT	60175	2908	35W-6N	A7
200	SCRL	60175	2908	35W-6N	A7
200	SEGN	60177	2908	34W-7N	D5
400	SEGN	60175	2908	35W-7N	B5
600	MTGY	60543	3199	37W-10S	B7
1300	MTGY	60543	3263	37W-11S	B2
1900	OSWG	60543	3263	37W-11S	B2
7000	RcmT	60071	2412	34W-39N	D5
7000	RcmT	60072	2412	34W-39N	D6
7800	RHMD	60071	2412	34W-40N	C3
SR-31 N 1st St					
10	GNVA	60134	3020	35W-1N	C3
500	SCRL	60174	3020	35W-2N	C2
SR-31 S 1st St					
10	GNVA	60134	3020	35W-1N	C3
SR-31 N 2nd St					
10	SCRL	60174	2964	35W-3N	B7
2700	SchT	60174	2964	35W-5N	B1
2700	SCRL	60175	2964	35W-5N	B1
SR-31 S 2nd St					
10	SCRL	60174	2964	35W-3N	B7
SR-31 N 8th St					
100	WDND	60118	2800	34W-15N	E4
400	CPVL	60110	2800	34W-15N	E4
400	CPVL	60118	2800	34W-15N	E4
400	WDND	60110	2800	34W-15N	E4
SR-31 S 8th St					
-	DndT	60118	2800	34W-15N	E4
100	WDND	60118	2800	34W-16N	E2
SR-31 N Batavia Av					
10	BTVA	60510	3078	35W-0S	B1
500	BTVA	60510	3020	35W-0S	B7
600	BTVA	60134	3020	35W-0S	B7
600	GNVA	60134	3020	35W-0S	B7
SR-31 S Batavia Av					
10	BTVA	60510	3078	35W-1S	B2
200	BtvT	60510	3077	36W-3S	E6
200	BtvT	60510	3078	36W-3S	A6
200	BtvT	60539	3077	36W-3S	E6
200	BtvT	60539	3078	36W-3S	A6
200	BtvT	60542	3077	36W-3S	E6
600	GNVA	60134	3020	35W-0N	B4
SR-31 W Elm St					
3600	MHRY	60050	2528	32W-33N	B3
SR-31 N Front St					
100	MHRY	60050	2528	32W-32N	A5
SR-31 S Front St					
100	MHRY	60050	2528	32W-31N	A6
400	NndT	60050	2528	32W-31N	A7
1000	MHRY	60050	2585	33W-30N	A1
1000	NndT	60050	2585	33W-30N	A1
SR-31 Gale St					
100	AURA	60506	3200	36W-7S	A1
SR-31 Geneva Rd					
600	SCRL	60174	2964	35W-2N	B7
600	SCRL	60174	3020	35W-1N	C2
1300	GNVA	60134	3020	35W-2N	C2
SR-31 Green Bay Rd					
10400	PTPR	53158	2362		A4
12600	NptT	53158	2362		A4
12600	NptT	60099	2362		A4
SR-31 N La Fox St					
10	SEGN	60177	2908	34W-7N	D4
1500	ELGN	60123	2854	34W-9N	E7
1500	ELGN	60177	2854	34W-9N	E7
1500	ELGN	60177	2908	34W-9N	D1
1500	SEGN	60123	2854	34W-9N	E7
1500	SEGN	60177	2854	34W-9N	E7
SR-31 S La Fox St					
10	SEGN	60177	2908	34W-8N	D3
400	SchT	60177	2908	34W-7N	D4
SR-31 N Lake St					
10	AURA	60506	3138	35W-7S	A7
1300	AURA	60542	3138	36W-5S	A3
1300	NARA	60542	3138	36W-5S	A3
SR-31 S Lake St					
10	AURA	60506	3138	35W-7S	A7
100	MTGY	60538	3199	37W-8S	D3
100	MTGY	60543	3199	37W-10S	B6
200	AURA	60506	3200	36W-7S	A1
300	AURA	60506	3199	37W-8S	D3
1000	MTGY	60506	3199	37W-8S	D3
1100	AraT	60506	3199	37W-8S	D3
SR-31 N Lincoln Hwy					
-	NARA	60542	3137	36W-4S	E1
SR-31 N Lincolnway					
10	NARA	60542	3077	36W-4S	E7
10	NARA	60542	3137	36W-4S	E1
200	BtvT	60510	3077	36W-3S	E6
200	BtvT	60539	3077	36W-3S	E6
200	BtvT	60542	3077	36W-3S	E6
SR-31 S Lincolnway					
10	NARA	60542	3137	36W-4S	E1
100	NARA	60542	3138	35W-5S	A4
200	AURA	60542	3138	35W-5S	A4
400	AURA	60506	3138	35W-5S	A4
SR-31 N Main St					
10	ALGN	60102	2694	33W-20N	D7
1000	AlqT	60102	2694	33W-21N	E6
SR-31 S Main St					
10	ALGN	60102	2694	33W-20N	D7
1400	ALGN	60102	2747	34W-20N	D1
1400	DndT	60102	2747	34W-20N	D1
1500	DndT	60118	2747	34W-19N	D2
SR-31 W New York St					
100	AURA	60506	3138	36W-7S	A7
SR-31 Precision Plz					
10	CLLK	60014	2640	33W-24N	E7
SR-31 Richmond Rd					
4100	JNBG	60050	2471	33W-35N	A5
4100	JNBG	60072	2471	33W-35N	A5
4100	MchT	60072	2471	33W-35N	A5
4100	RGWD	60072	2470	33W-36N	E4
4100	RGWD	60072	2471	33W-36N	A4
4400	MchT	60072	2470	33W-36N	E4
5700	RcmT	60072	2470	33W-36N	E4
6200	RcmT	60072	2412	34W-38N	D7
6600	RcmT	60071	2412	34W-38N	D6
SR-31 N Richmond Rd					
1300	MHRY	60050	2528	32W-34N	B1
1900	MchT	60050	2528	32W-33N	B2
2500	JNBG	60050	2528	32W-34N	B1
2700	JNBG	60050	2471	32W-35N	B6
2700	MchT	60050	2471	32W-34N	B7
3900	JNBG	60072	2471	32W-35N	A5
3900	MchT	60072	2471	32W-35N	A5
SR-31 N River St					
10	AURA	60506	3138	35W-7S	A7
SR-31 S River St					
10	AURA	60506	3138	35W-7S	A7
100	AURA	60506	3200	36W-7S	A1
SR-31 N State St					
10	ELGN	60123	2854	34W-9N	E7
1100	ELGN	60123	2800	34W-13N	D7
1700	DndT	60123	2800	34W-14N	E6
1700	WDND	60118	2800	34W-14N	E6
1700	WDND	60123	2800	34W-14N	E6
SR-31 S State St					
10	ELGN	60123	2854	34W-11N	E4
700	SEGN	60123	2854	34W-9N	E7
2100	WDND	60118	2800	34W-14N	E6
SR-31 N Western Av					
-	DndT	60118	2747	35W-17N	C6
10	CPVL	60110	2800	34W-16N	D1
100	CPVL	60110	2747	35W-17N	D7
SR-31 S Western Av					
10	CPVL	60110	2800	34W-16N	D1
10	CPVL	60118	2800	34W-16N	D1
100	WDND	60110	2800	34W-16N	E2
100	WDND	60118	2800	34W-16N	E2
SR-32 Sheridan Rd					
10400	PTPR	53158	2363		C3
12700	WPHR	53158	2363		C4
12700	WPHR	60096	2363		C4
SR-38					
-	CmpT	60151	3017	43W-2N	A1
-	ELBN	60151	3017	43W-2N	A1
10	CmpT	60119	3017	43W-2N	A1
10	CmpT	60119	3018	39W-2N	E1
10	ELBN	60119	3017	43W-2N	B1
200	SchT	60175	3019	37W-2N	C1
200	SCRL	60175	3019	37W-2N	D1
SR-38 Lincoln Hwy					
-	SchT	60175	3019	38W-2N	B1
10	CmpT	60119	3018	39W-2N	E1
10	CmpT	60175	3018	39W-2N	E1
10	SCRL	60119	3018	39W-2N	E1
10	SCRL	60175	3018	39W-2N	E1
1400	SCRL	60174	3019	36W-2N	E2
3800	SCRL	60175	3019	38W-2N	A1
SR-38 Roosevelt Rd					
-	EMHT	60126	3027	17W-1S	B7
-	EMHT	60126	3028	15W-1S	B7
-	EMHT	60181	3027	17W-1S	B7
-	EMHT	60523	3027	16W-1S	E7
-	EMHT	60523	3028	15W-1S	A7
-	HLSD	60154	3028	13W-0S	D7
-	OKBK	60126	3028	15W-1S	A7
-	OKBK	60181	3027	16W-1S	E7
-	OKBK	60523	3027	16W-1S	E7
-	OKBK	60523	3028	15W-1S	A7
-	OKTR	60126	3027	17W-1S	B7
-	WHTN	60137	3025	23W-0S	A7
-	WSTR	60162	3028	13W-0S	D7
-	YkTp	60126	3028	15W-1S	B7
-	YkTp	60523	3028	14W-1S	B7
10	GnvT	60134	3021	33W-0N	B4
10	GnvT	60185	3021	33W-0N	B4
10	WCHI	60185	3021	33W-0N	B4
10	WCHI	60185	3022	29W-0S	E7
10	WHTN	60187	3081	27W-1S	D1
10	WHTN	60190	3081	27W-1S	D1
10	WNFD	60187	3081	27W-1S	D1
10	WNFD	60190	3081	27W-1S	D1
10	WnfT	60185	3022	29W-0S	E7
10	WnfT	60187	3081	27W-1S	D1
10	WnfT	60190	3022	28W-0S	E7
10	WnfT	60190	3081	27W-1S	D1
100	YkTp	60181	3027	17W-1S	C7
200	GNEN	60137	3025	21W-1S	E7
200	GNEN	60187	3025	23W-0S	A7
200	OKTR	60181	3027	17W-1S	B7
200	VLPK	60181	3027	17W-0S	C7
200	WHTN	60137	3025	23W-0S	A7
600	WnfT	60190	3080	28W-0S	E1
900	MltT	60137	3025	21W-1S	E7
1000	GNEN	60148	3025	21W-0S	E7
1000	MltT	60148	3025	21W-0S	E7
4000	HLSD	60162	3029	13W-1S	A7
4000	PvsT	60162	3029	13W-1S	A7
4000	WSTR	60154	3029	13W-1S	A7
4000	WSTR	60162	3029	13W-0S	A7
4300	HLSD	60162	3028	14W-1S	D7
4300	PvsT	60162	3028	14W-1S	D7
4400	WSTR	60154	3028	13W-0S	E7
11900	PvsT	60126	3028	15W-1S	B7
SR-38 E Roosevelt Rd					
10	LMBD	60148	3026	18W-0S	E7
10	OKTR	60181	3027	17W-0S	B7
10	VLPK	60181	3027	17W-0S	B7
10	YkTp	60148	3026	18W-0S	E7
100	WCHI	60185	3022	29W-0S	C7
100	WHTN	60187	3024	23W-0S	E7
200	WnfT	60185	3022	29W-0S	C7
1600	WHTN	60187	3025	23W-0S	A7
1800	GNEN	60137	3025	23W-0S	A7
1800	GNEN	60187	3025	23W-0S	A7
1800	WHTN	60137	3025	23W-0S	A7
SR-38 W Roosevelt Rd					
-	GnvT	60134	3021	32W-0N	B4
-	GnvT	60185	3021	32W-0N	B4
-	MltT	60137	3025	21W-0S	E7
10	LMBD	60148	3026	20W-0S	B7
10	VLPK	60181	3027	18W-0S	A7
100	WCHI	60185	3022	30W-0S	A6
100	WHTN	60187	3082	25W-1S	A1
100	WnfT	60185	3022	30W-0S	C6
300	YkTp	60148	3027	18W-0S	A7
300	YkTp	60181	3027	18W-0S	A7
400	GNEN	60137	3026	20W-0S	A7
400	GNEN	60148	3026	20W-0S	A7
400	WnfT	60185	3022	30W-0S	B6
600	WCHI	60510	3022	30W-0S	B6
700	GNEN	60137	3025	23W-1S	A7
700	GNEN	60148	3025	23W-1S	A7
700	MltT	60137	3025	23W-1S	A7
700	MltT	60148	3026	20W-0S	A7
1200	WCHI	60185	3021	31W-0N	E5
1600	MltT	60187	3082	25W-1S	A1
1900	MltT	60187	3081	27W-1S	C1
1900	WHTN	60187	3081	27W-1S	C1
2100	WHTN	60190	3081	26W-1S	D1
2100	WNFD	60190	3081	26W-1S	D1
2100	WnfT	60187	3081	26W-1S	D1
2100	WnfT	60190	3081	26W-1S	D1
10900	HLSD	60154	3028	13W-0S	E7
10900	HLSD	60162	3028	13W-0S	E7
10900	WSTR	60154	3028	13W-0S	E7
10900	WSTR	60162	3028	13W-0S	E7
SR-38 E State St					
10	GNVA	60134	3020	35W-1N	C3
600	GNVA	60134	3021	32W-0N	C4
600	GNVA	60185	3021	32W-0N	C4
600	GnvT	60134	3021	32W-0N	C4
600	GnvT	60185	3021	32W-0N	C4
1200	GnvT	60134	3020	33W-1N	E4
SR-38 W State St					
10	GNVA	60134	3020	36W-1N	A3
1700	GNVA	60134	3019	36W-2N	E2
1900	SCRL	60134	3019	36W-1N	E2
1900	SCRL	60174	3019	36W-1N	E2
SR-43 Harlem Av					
-	CHCG	60402	3148	8W-5S	E2
-	CHCG	60501	3148	8W-5S	E2
-	CHCG	60638	3148	8W-5S	E2
-	FftT	60477	3505	9W-23S	A2
-	FTVW	60402	3148	9W-5S	E1
-	FTVW	60501	3148	8W-5S	E2
-	LYNS	60534	3148	9W-5S	E1
-	SMMT	60501	3148	8W-5S	E2
-	SMMT	60534	3148	9W-5S	E2
-	TYPK	60477	3505	8W-22S	A1
1100	BRWN	60130	3030	8W-0S	D7
1100	BRWN	60304	3030	8W-0S	D7
1100	BRWN	60402	3030	8W-0S	D7
1100	FTPK	60130	3030	8W-0S	D7
1100	OKPK	60130	3030	8W-0S	D7
1100	OKPK	60304	3030	8W-0S	D7
1500	BRWN	60130	3088	9W-1S	D1
1500	BRWN	60402	3088	9W-1S	D1
1500	FTPK	60130	3088	8W-1S	D1
1500	NRIV	60130	3088	9W-1S	D1
2100	BRWN	60546	3088	9W-1S	D2
2100	NRIV	60546	3088	9W-1S	D2
2500	RVSD	60546	3088	9W-2S	D3
2800	RVSD	60402	3088	9W-2S	D3
3600	LYNS	60402	3088	8W-3S	E5
3600	LYNS	60534	3088	8W-3S	E5
3600	LYNS	60546	3088	8W-3S	E5
3800	SKNY	60402	3088	8W-3S	E6
4200	SKNY	60534	3088	8W-4S	E7
4400	FTVW	60402	3088	8W-4S	E7
4400	FTVW	60534	3088	8W-4S	E7
4600	FTVW	60534	3148	8W-4S	E1
15900	ODPK	60462	3424	9W-19S	E1
15900	TYPK	60477	3424	9W-19S	E2
16300	OrlT	60477	3424	8W-19S	E2
18200	TYPK	60477	3425	8W-21S	A7
SR-43 N Harlem Av					
10	FTPK	60130	3030	8W-0N	D4
10	FTPK	60302	3030	9W-0N	D5
10	FTPK	60304	3030	9W-0N	D5
10	OKPK	60130	3030	8W-0N	D4
10	OKPK	60302	3030	9W-0S	D6
10	OKPK	60304	3030	9W-0N	D5
400	OKPK	60301	3030	8W-0N	D4
400	OKPK	60305	3030	9W-0S	D6
400	RVFT	60301	3030	8W-0N	D4
400	RVFT	60302	3030	9W-0S	D6
400	RVFT	60305	3030	9W-0S	D6
1500	CHCG	60302	3030	8W-1N	D1
1500	CHCG	60707	3030	8W-1N	D1
1500	EDPK	60707	3030	8W-1N	D1
1500	RVFT	60707	3030	8W-1N	D1
1700	CHCG	60707	2974	8W-2N	D7
1700	EDPK	60707	2974	8W-2N	D7
2700	CHCG	60634	2974	9W-3N	D5
3900	CHCG	60634	2974	9W-3N	D5
3900	NRDG	60706	2974	9W-3N	D5
4400	HDHT	60706	2918	8W-5N	D7
4400	NRDG	60706	2918	8W-5N	D7
4700	CHCG	60656	2918	8W-6N	D7
4700	CHCG	60706	2918	8W-6N	D7
4700	HDHT	60656	2918	8W-6N	D7
5600	CHCG	60631	2918	9W-6N	D6
6500	CHCG	60714	2918	9W-6N	D6
6500	NLES	60714	2918	9W-6N	D6
7200	CHCG	60631	2864	8W-9N	D7
7200	CHCG	60714	2864	8W-9N	D7
7200	NLES	60714	2864	8W-9N	D7
7500	NLES	60631	2864	8W-9N	D7
SR-43 S Harlem Av					
-	BGVW	60453	3210	8W-10S	E6
-	FftT	60477	3505	9W-23S	A3
-	OKLN	60415	3210	8W-11S	E6
-	OKLN	60453	3210	8W-11S	E6
-	OKLN	60455	3210	8W-11S	E6
-	PlsT	60463	3346	9W-16S	E2
-	SMMT	60534	3148	9W-5S	E2
-	TYPK	60423	3505	8W-23S	A3
-	TYPK	60477	3505	8W-23S	A3
10	FTPK	60130	3030	9W-0S	D5
10	FTPK	60302	3030	9W-0S	D5
10	FTPK	60304	3030	9W-0S	D5
10	OKPK	60302	3030	9W-0S	D5
10	OKPK	60304	3030	9W-0S	D5
700	OKPK	60130	3030	9W-0S	D6
5100	CHCG	60402	3148	9W-5S	E1
5100	CHCG	60501	3148	9W-5S	E1
5100	CHCG	60638	3148	9W-5S	E1
5100	FTVW	60402	3148	9W-5S	E1
5100	FTVW	60501	3148	9W-5S	E1
5100	SMMT	60501	3148	9W-5S	E1
6300	BDPK	60501	3148	8W-7S	E5
6300	BDPK	60638	3148	8W-7S	E5
6700	BGVW	60455	3148	9W-7S	E6
6700	BGVW	60501	3148	9W-7S	E6
6700	BGVW	60638	3148	9W-7S	E6
6800	BDPK	60455	3148	9W-7S	E7
7300	BDPK	60638	3210	8W-8S	E1
7300	BGVW	60455	3210	9W-8S	E1
7300	BGVW	60638	3210	8W-8S	E1
7700	BGVW	60459	3210	8W-8S	E2
7700	BRBK	60455	3210	8W-8S	E2
7700	BRBK	60459	3210	8W-8S	E2
9800	BGVW	60415	3210	8W-11S	E7
9800	CHRG	60415	3210	8W-11S	E7
9900	CHRG	60455	3210	8W-11S	E7
10100	BGVW	60415	3274	8W-11S	E1
10100	BGVW	60455	3274	8W-11S	E1
10100	CHRG	60415	3274	9W-15S	E7
10100	PSHL	60415	3274	8W-11S	E1
10100	PSHL	60455	3274	8W-11S	E1
10100	PSHL	60465	3274	8W-11S	E1
10400	WRTH	60415	3274	9W-15S	E7
10400	WRTH	60482	3274	9W-15S	E7
10500	CHRG	60482	3274	9W-15S	E7
11600	PSHT	60463	3274	8W-13S	E5
11600	WRTH	60463	3274	8W-13S	E5
12800	PSHT	60463	3346	9W-16S	E2
13500	BmnT	60445	3346	9W-17S	E6
13500	BmnT	60462	3346	9W-16S	E2
13500	WthT	60445	3346	9W-17S	E6
13500	WthT	60462	3346	9W-16S	E2
13500	WthT	60463	3346	9W-17S	E6
13700	OrlT	60462	3346	8W-16S	E3
14100	BmnT	60452	3346	8W-16S	E4
14100	OrlT	60445	3346	8W-16S	E4
14100	OrlT	60452	3346	9W-17S	E4
15100	ODPK	60462	3346	9W-18S	E6
15200	OKFT	60452	3346	9W-18S	E6
15700	ODPK	60462	3424	9W-18S	E1
15800	TYPK	60477	3424	9W-18S	E1
19700	FftT	60423	3505	9W-24S	A6
19700	MTSN	60443	3505	9W-24S	A6
19700	RchT	60423	3505	9W-24S	A6
20600	FKFT	60423	3505	8W-25S	A7
20600	RchT	60443	3505	8W-25S	A7
21500	FKFT	60423	3593	9W-27S	A5
21500	RchT	60443	3593	9W-27S	A5
22400	FKFT	60443	3593	9W-27S	A5
SR-43 W Oakton St					
7000	NLES	60714	2864	8W-10N	E5
SR-43 Waukegan Rd					
-	LbvT	60044	2535	13W-31N	E7
-	WKGN	60085	2535	13W-31N	E7
10	DRFD	60015	2757	10W-20N	A2
10	DRFD	60062	2757	10W-20N	A2
10	GNVW	60025	2864	8W-12N	E1
10	GNVW	60053	2864	8W-12N	E2
10	MNGV	60025	2864	8W-12N	E1
10	MNGV	60053	2864	8W-10N	E4
100	GNVW	60025	2810	8W-13N	E6
100	GNVW	60093	2810	8W-15N	E3
100	NHFD	60025	2810	8W-15N	E3
100	NHFD	60093	2810	8W-15N	E2
300	NHBK	60062	2810	8W-15N	E2
400	NfdT	60062	2757	10W-18N	B3
600	DRFD	60015	2703	11W-21N	E6
600	DRFD	60015	2756	10W-20N	E1
600	NHBK	60062	2757	9W-18N	B4
1300	LbvT	60044	2592	13W-30N	E1
1300	LbvT	60064	2592	13W-30N	E2
1300	NCHI	60044	2592	13W-30N	E2
1600	BKBN	60015	2703	11W-22N	D5
2100	NHFD	60062	2810	8W-16N	E1
2100	WdfT	60015	2703	11W-23N	C3
8400	MNGV	60714	2864	8W-10N	E4
8400	NLES	60714	2864	8W-10N	E4
SR-43 N Waukegan Rd					
10	LKBF	60044	2593	12W-28N	B6
10	LKFT	60044	2593	12W-28N	B6
10	LKFT	60045	2593	12W-28N	B6
10	LKFT	60045	2649	12W-25N	B6
10	ShdT	60044	2593	12W-28N	B5
700	LbvT	60044	2593	13W-29N	A3
700	NCHI	60044	2593	13W-30N	A2
1200	NCHI	60064	2593	13W-30N	A2
1700	LKBF	60045	2593	12W-28N	B7
8000	NLES	60714	2864	8W-10N	E5
8300	MNGV	60053	2864	8W-10N	E5
8300	MNGV	60714	2864	8W-10N	E5
29500	LbvT	60064	2593	13W-29N	A4
SR-43 S Waukegan Rd					
-	PKCY	60085	2535	13W-33N	E4
10	DRFD	60015	2757	10W-18N	A2
10	DRFD	60062	2757	10W-18N	A2
10	LKFT	60045	2649	12W-25N	C4
10	NfdT	60062	2757	10W-18N	A2
800	WKGN	60085	2535	13W-33N	E4
1000	WrnT	60085	2535	13W-32N	E4
1200	LKFT	60045	2703	11W-23N	C2
1600	BKBN	60015	2703	11W-23N	C2
1600	BKBN	60045	2703	11W-23N	C2
1600	WdfT	60015	2703	11W-23N	C2
1600	WdfT	60045	2703	11W-23N	C2
2100	LbvT	60044	2535	13W-31N	E7
SR-47					
-	BRkT	60554	3135	42W-7S	C7
-	BRkT	60554	3197	42W-7S	C1
-	CLLK	60098	2638	40W-26N	A3
-	DrrT	60098	2638	40W-26N	A4
-	DrrT	60142	2638	40W-26N	A3
-	GfnT	60098	2638	40W-25N	A4
-	GfnT	60142	2638	40W-25N	A4
-	GfnT	60142	2692	40W-23N	A1
-	GwdT	60098	2524	41W-34N	D1
-	HTLY	60140	2744	41W-17N	E6
-	HTLY	60142	2638	40W-24N	A7
-	HTLY	60142	2691	40W-20N	E7
-	HTLY	60142	2692	40W-21N	A5
-	HTLY	60142	2744	42W-18N	E5
-	LIHL	60142	2692	40W-23N	A1
-	LKWD	60142	2638	40W-25N	A5
-	RtdT	60140	2744	42W-17N	E6
-	RtdT	60142	2744	42W-18N	E5
-	WDSK	60098	2524	41W-33N	D4
-	YKVL	60512	3197	42W-10S	C7
10	PGGV	60140	2797	43W-14N	B5
10	PltT	60124	2851	43W-10N	B6
10	PltT	60124	2905	43W-8N	B3
10	PltT	60151	2905	43W-8N	A3
10	RtdT	60140	2797	43W-13N	B7
10	SgrT	60506	3197	42W-10S	C7
10	SgrT	60554	3197	42W-10S	C7
10	SRGV	60554	3197	42W-8S	C2
100	BbyT	60119	3075	43W-3S	A6
100	SgrT	60554	3075	43W-4S	B7
200	CmpT	60151	2961	43W-3N	A7
200	PltT	60140	2797	43W-13N	B7
200	PltT	60140	2851	43W-12N	B1
200	SgrT	60554	3135	42W-7S	C7
200	SRGV	60554	3135	42W-7S	C7
300	BbyT	60119	3017	43W-0S	A7
600	CmpT	60119	3017	43W-2N	A1
600	CmpT	60151	3017	43W-2N	A1
600	ELBN	60119	3017	43W-2N	A1
600	ELBN	60151	2961	43W-2N	A7
600	ELBN	60151	3017	43W-2N	A1
800	BtlT	60512	3197	42W-10S	C7
900	BbyT	60554	3075	43W-3S	A5
2000	BtlT	60512	3261	42W-14S	C7
2000	YKVL	60512	3261	42W-14S	C7
2000	YKVL	60545	3261	42W-14S	C7
2000	YKVL	60560	3261	42W-14S	C7
2200	BtlT	60560	3261	42W-12S	C3
8000	KdlT	60560	3333	42W-18S	D7
10300	HbnT	60034	2350	41W-42N	E6
10300	HBRN	60034	2350	41W-42N	E6
11500	HbnT	53147	2350	41W-42N	E6
11500	LinT	53147	2350	41W-42N	E6
SR-47 N Bridge St					
100	YKVL	60560	3333	42W-15S	C2
1100	YKVL	60560	3261	42W-14S	C7
1200	BtlT	60560	3261	42W-14S	C7
2400	YKVL	60512	3261	42W-13S	C5
2600	BtlT	60512	3261	42W-12S	C3
SR-47 S Bridge St					
100	YKVL	60560	3333	43W-16S	C4
1300	KdlT	60560	3333	43W-16S	C4
SR-47 N Eastwood Dr					
10	WDSK	60098	2524	41W-31N	E7
SR-47 S Eastwood Dr					
10	WDSK	60098	2524	41W-31N	E7
200	WDSK	60098	2581	40W-30N	E2
2800	DrrT	60098	2581	40W-29N	E5
SR-47 Main St					
-	HbnT	60034	2350	41W-42N	E6
9600	HBRN	60034	2350	41W-41N	E7
SR-47 N Main St					
100	ELBN	60119	3017	44W-1N	A3
600	CmpT	60119	3017	43W-2N	A1
600	CmpT	60151	3017	43W-2N	A1
600	ELBN	60151	3017	43W-2N	A1
SR-47 S Main St					
10	ELBN	60119	3017	44W-1N	A3
100	BbyT	60119	3017	44W-1N	A3
SR-47 N Seminary Av					
600	WDSK	60098	2524	41W-33N	D3
2100	GwdT	60098	2524	41W-33N	D4
SR-47 Vine St					
10400	HTLY	60142	2692	40W-21N	A5
10800	HTLY	60142	2691	40W-21N	E6
SR-50					
-	PtnT	60468	3860	9W-38S	E6
-	PtnT	60468	3861	9W-38S	A4
-	PTON	60468	3860	9W-38S	E6
-	PTON	60468	3861	9W-38S	A4
SR-50 Cicero Av					
-	ALSP	60803	3348	5W-15S	A1
-	CTWD	60803	3348	5W-15S	A1
13100	CTWD	60445	3348	5W-15S	A1
13900	BmnT	60445	3348	5W-16S	A3
14300	MDLN	60445	3348	6W-18S	A7
14700	MDLN	60452	3348	6W-18S	A7
14800	OKFT	60452	3348	5W-17S	A5
14900	OKFT	60445	3348	5W-17S	A6
15700	BmnT	60426	3426	6W-21S	B7
15700	BmnT	60452	3426	6W-21S	B7
15700	OKFT	60426	3426	5W-18S	A1
15700	OKFT	60452	3426	6W-21S	B7
16700	BmnT	60477	3426	5W-20S	A3
17000	BmnT	60478	3426	6W-20S	B4
17000	CCHL	60477	3426	6W-20S	B4
17000	CCHL	60478	3426	6W-20S	B4
18400	CCHL	60478	3506	6W-25S	B7
18800	CCHL	60477	3506	5W-22S	B2
18800	RchT	60477	3506	5W-22S	B2
19900	MTSN	60443	3506	6W-24S	B4
19900	RchT	60443	3506	6W-24S	B4
21100	MTSN	60443	3594	6W-26S	B2
21900	RNPK	60471	3594	6W-26S	B2
22700	UYPK	60471	3594	6W-27S	B5
22900	UYPK	60449	3594	6W-27S	B5
SR-50 N Cicero Av					
10	CHCG	60644	3031	5W-0N	E5
700	CHCG	60651	3031	6W-1N	E2
1500	CHCG	60639	3031	5W-1N	E1
1600	CHCG	60639	2975	5W-2N	E7
2700	CHCG	60641	2975	6W-5N	E1
4300	CHCG	60630	2975	5W-5N	E1
4400	CHCG	60630	2919	5W-5N	E7
5600	CHCG	60646	2919	6W-7N	E4
6300	CHCG	60712	2919	6W-7N	E3
6300	LNWD	60712	2919	6W-6N	E5
7200	LNWD	60712	2865	6W-9N	E7
7300	SKOK	60077	2865	6W-9N	E7
7300	SKOK	60712	2865	6W-9N	E7
SR-50 S Cicero Av					
-	CTWD	60445	3348	5W-15S	A1
-	CTWD	60803	3348	5W-15S	A1
-	MonT	60466	3683	6W-29S	B2
-	UYPK	60466	3683	6W-29S	B2
10	CHCG	60644	3031	5W-0S	E5
800	CHCG	60644	3032	5W-0S	A6
1000	CCRO	60804	3032	5W-0S	A7
1000	CHCG	60804	3032	5W-0S	A7
1500	CCRO	60804	3090	5W-1S	A1
3400	SKNY	60804	3090	5W-3S	A5
3700	CCRO	60632	3090	5W-3S	A6
3700	CHCG	60804	3090	5W-3S	A6
4200	CHCG	60632	3090	6W-4S	A7
4200	CHCG	60638	3090	5W-4S	A7
4600	CHCG	60632	3150	5W-6S	A3
4600	CHCG	60638	3150	5W-6S	A3
6100	CHCG	60629	3150	6W-7S	A6
6400	BDPK	60638	3150	5W-7S	A6
7100	BDPK	60629	3150	5W-8S	A7
7400	BDPK	60638	3212	5W-8S	A1
7400	BRBK	60459	3212	6W-8S	A1
7400	CHCG	60629	3212	5W-8S	A1
7400	CHCG	60638	3212	5W-8S	A1
7400	CHCG	60652	3212	6W-8S	A1
7700	CHCG	60459	3212	6W-8S	A1
8600	HMTN	60453	3212	6W-9S	A4
8600	HMTN	60456	3212	6W-9S	A4
8600	HMTN	60459	3212	6W-9S	A4
8600	HMTN	60652	3212	6W-9S	A4
8600	OKLN	60453	3212	6W-9S	A4
8600	OKLN	60459	3212	6W-9S	A4
8900	OKLN	60456	3212	6W-10S	A4
10200	OKLN	60453	3276	5W-13S	A3
11000	ALSP	60453	3276	5W-12S	A3
11000	ALSP	60655	3276	5W-12S	A3
11000	ALSP	60803	3276	5W-12S	A3
11000	CHCG	60453	3276	5W-12S	A3
11000	CHCG	60655	3276	5W-12S	A3
11100	CHCG	60803	3276	5W-13S	A4
13100	ALSP	60803	3348	5W-15S	A1
23100	MonT	60449	3594	6W-28S	B7
23100	RNPK	60471	3594	6W-28S	B5
23100	UYPK	60449	3594	6W-28S	B6
23100	UYPK	60471	3594	6W-28S	B5
24000	MonT	60449	3683	6W-31S	A5
SR-50 S Governors Hwy					
-	MonT	60466	3683	6W-29S	B2
-	UYPK	60466	3683	6W-29S	B2
400	PTON	60468	3861	9W-37S	A4
400	WltT	60468	3861	9W-37S	A4
600	PtnT	60468	3861	9W-37S	A4
25100	MonT	60449	3683	6W-30S	A3
25100	UYPK	60449	3683	6W-30S	A3
25300	MONE	60449	3683	6W-30S	A3
25600	MONE	60449	3682	7W-31S	E6

Block	City	ZIP	Map#	CGS	Grid
SR-50 S Governors Hwy					
26200	MonT	60449	3682	7W-32S	E7
SR-50 N Harlem Av					
100	PTON	60468	3861	9W-37S	A2
200	WIIT	60468	3861	9W-37S	A2
300	PtnT	60468	3861	9W-37S	A2
SR-50 S Harlem Av					
100	PTON	60468	3861	8W-37S	A3
100	WIIT	60468	3861	8W-37S	A3
SR-50 Hastings Ct					
3500	GRNE	60031	2477	16W-36N	E3
SR-50 Oxford Ln					
-	LNHT	60046	2418	19W-38N	C6
SR-50 Skokie Blvd					
7400	LNWD	60712	2865	6W-9N	E7
7400	SKOK	60077	2865	6W-9N	E7
7400	SKOK	60712	2865	6W-9N	E7
7500	SKOK	60076	2865	6W-9N	E7
SR-53					
-	ANHT	-	2753	18W-16N	D7
-	ANHT	-	2806	19W-15N	B2
-	BCVL	60407	4030	33W-44S	B3
-	BDWD	60408	3942	30W-41S	B5
-	BFGV	60047	2700	18W-21N	D6
-	BFGV	60089	2700	18W-21N	D6
-	BGBK	60440	3205	22W-9S	C5
-	BvlT	60407	4030	33W-43S	B3
-	CstT	60481	3942	30W-40S	D3
-	DRGV	60137	3083	22W-2S	D4
-	DRGV	60515	3083	22W-2S	D4
-	EGvT	-	2860	20W-10N	A6
-	EGvT	-	2914	20W-9N	A1
-	EGVV	-	2914	20W-9N	A1
-	ELWD	60421	3675	25W-32S	C7
-	FrnT	60421	3763	27W-35S	E6
-	FrnT	60481	3763	27W-35S	E6
-	FrnT	60481	3853	27W-36S	E2
-	GDLY	60407	4030	33W-44S	B4
-	GNEN	60137	3025	21W-0S	E7
-	GNEN	60137	3083	22W-1S	D1
-	GNEN	60148	3025	21W-0S	E7
-	LGGV	60089	2700	18W-21N	D6
-	LMBD	60148	3025	21W-0S	E7
-	LMBD	60148	3026	20W-1N	A1
-	LslT	60517	3205	22W-8S	B1
-	LslT	60532	3083	23W-4S	B7
-	LslT	60540	3143	22W-7S	B7
-	LslT	60540	3205	22W-8S	B1
-	LslT	60565	3205	22W-8S	B1
-	MltT	60137	3083	22W-3S	C6
-	MltT	60148	3026	20W-1N	A1
-	MltT	60515	3083	22W-2S	D4
-	MltT	60532	3083	22W-3S	B6
-	PLTN	-	2753	18W-16N	D7
-	PLTN	-	2806	19W-15N	C2
-	PltT	-	2753	18W-16N	D7
-	PltT	-	2806	20W-13N	A6
-	RedT	60408	3941	32W-42S	E7
-	RedT	60408	4030	32W-42S	E1
-	RedT	60481	3942	30W-40S	D3
-	RGMW	-	2806	20W-13N	A6
-	RGMW	-	2860	20W-12N	A1
-	SMBG	-	2806	20W-13N	A7
-	SMBG	-	2860	20W-12N	A1
-	WDRG	60517	3205	22W-8S	B1
-	WDRG	60565	3205	22W-8S	B1
-	WMTN	60481	3853	27W-36S	E2
-	WMTN	60481	3942	29W-39S	E2
-	WMTN	60481	3943	29W-39S	A1
-	WmTp	60481	3763	26W-35S	E7
-	WmTp	60481	3853	27W-36S	E2
-	WmTp	60481	3942	29W-39S	E2
-	WmTp	60481	3943	29W-39S	A1
1100	LGGV	60047	2700	18W-21N	D6
25600	JknT	60421	3675	24W-31S	D6
SR-53 EXT					
-	ANHT	-	2753	19W-18N	C3
-	ElaT	-	2753	19W-18N	C2
-	PLTN	-	2753	19W-18N	C3
-	PltT	-	2753	19W-18N	D4
SR-53 E Baltimore St					
100	WMTN	60481	3853	27W-38S	D6
SR-53 W Baltimore St					
200	WMTN	60481	3853	27W-38S	C7
SR-53 Biesterfield Rd					
1000	EGVV	60007	2914	21W-8N	A2
SR-53 Bolingbrook Dr					
-	BGBK	60440	3269	22W-13S	B6
-	RMVL	60446	3269	22W-13S	B6
SR-53 N Bolingbrook Dr					
-	LslT	60565	3205	22W-10S	C5
100	BGBK	60440	3269	23W-11S	B1
300	BGBK	60440	3205	23W-11S	B7
600	DPgT	60440	3205	22W-10S	B5
SR-53 S Bolingbrook Dr					
-	RMVL	60446	3269	23W-13S	B5
500	BGBK	60440	3269	23W-13S	B4
SR-53 Bridge St					
100	WMTN	60481	3853	28W-39S	C7
SR-53 Broadway St					
2100	CTHL	60403	3418	24W-21S	E6
2100	CTHL	60435	3418	24W-21S	E6
2100	CTHL	60441	3418	24W-21S	E6
2100	LktT	60435	3418	24W-21S	E6
15700	LktT	60441	3419	23W-18S	A1
15700	RMVL	60441	3419	23W-18S	A1
16200	CTHL	60441	3419	23W-19S	A2
17000	LktT	60441	3418	24W-20S	E5
SR-53 N Broadway St					
700	JLET	60435	3498	24W-23S	E3
1600	CTHL	60403	3498	24W-21S	E1
1600	CTHL	60435	3498	24W-21S	E1
1600	LktT	60435	3498	24W-21S	E1
1700	CTHL	60403	3418	24W-21S	E7
1700	CTHL	60435	3418	24W-21S	E7
1800	LktT	60435	3418	24W-21S	E7
2000	CTHL	60441	3418	24W-21S	E6
SR-53 Bryant Av					
10	GNEN	60137	3025	22W-0S	D7
SR-53 N Chicago St					
500	JLET	60432	3499	23W-23S	A3
SR-53 S Chicago St					
-	JknT	60421	3587	23W-28S	A7
-	JLET	60432	3499	23W-23S	A5
-	JLET	60436	3498	24W-24S	E5
200	JLET	60433	3499	24W-24S	A6
600	JLET	60436	3499	24W-25S	A7
600	JltT	60436	3499	23W-25S	A7
900	JLET	60433	3587	23W-25S	A1
900	JLET	60436	3587	23W-25S	A1
900	JltT	60433	3587	24W-26S	A2
900	JltT	60436	3587	24W-26S	A2
2400	JLET	60421	3587	23W-27S	A6
SR-53 E Columbia St					
10	JLET	60432	3499	23W-23S	A4

Block	City	ZIP	Map#	CGS	Grid
SR-53 N Columbine Av					
10	LMBD	60148	3026	21W-0N	A3
300	MltT	60148	3026	21W-1N	A2
SR-53 S Columbine Av					
10	LMBD	60148	3026	21W-0S	A6
500	MltT	60148	3026	21W-0N	A5
500	YkTp	60148	3026	21W-0N	A5
1000	MltT	60148	3025	21W-0S	E7
1100	GNEN	60137	3025	21W-0S	E7
1100	GNEN	60148	3025	21W-0S	E7
1100	LMBD	60148	3025	21W-0S	E7
SR-53 E Dundee Rd					
-	PltT	60004	2753	19W-18N	D4
900	PLTN	60074	2753	19W-18N	B4
1500	PltT	60074	2753	19W-18N	C4
SR-53 W Dundee Rd					
-	ANHT	60004	2753	19W-18N	D4
-	PltT	60004	2753	19W-18N	D4
-	PltT	60074	2753	19W-18N	D4
SR-53 Fairview Av					
-	GNEN	60137	3025	21W-0S	E7
-	GNEN	60148	3025	21W-0S	E7
-	LMBD	60148	3025	21W-0S	E7
-	MltT	60148	3025	21W-0S	E7
SR-53 N Front St					
100	BDWD	60408	3942	31W-41S	B5
200	RedT	60408	3942	31W-41S	B5
200	RedT	60481	3942	30W-41S	B5
SR-53 S Front St					
100	BDWD	60408	3942	31W-41S	B6
300	RedT	60408	3942	31W-41S	B6
700	RedT	60408	3941	32W-42S	E7
SR-53 Hicks Rd					
2700	ElaT	60047	2753	20W-20N	A2
2700	ElaT	60074	2753	20W-20N	A2
2700	LGGV	60047	2753	20W-20N	A2
2700	LGGV	60074	2753	20W-20N	A2
2700	PLTN	60074	2753	20W-20N	A2
20700	ElaT	60047	2700	20W-20N	B7
20700	LGGV	60047	2700	20W-21N	B7
SR-53 N Hicks Rd					
2100	PLTN	60074	2753	20W-20N	A2
2300	ElaT	60047	2753	20W-18N	A2
2300	ElaT	60074	2753	20W-18N	A2
2300	LGGV	60047	2753	20W-18N	A2
2300	LGGV	60074	2753	20W-18N	A2
SR-53 N Independence Blvd					
10	LktT	60446	3341	23W-16S	A4
10	RMVL	60441	3341	23W-16S	A5
10	RMVL	60446	3341	23W-16S	A4
300	DPgT	60441	3341	23W-15S	A3
300	DPgT	60446	3341	23W-15S	A3
700	RMVL	60446	3269	23W-14S	B7
SR-53 S Independence Blvd					
14200	LktT	60441	3341	23W-17S	A6
14200	RMVL	60441	3341	23W-17S	A6
14200	RMVL	60446	3341	23W-16S	A5
SR-53 W Jackson St					
10	JLET	60432	3498	24W-23S	E4
SR-53 Lincoln Av					
-	LSLE	60532	3083	23W-4S	A7
-	LslT	60532	3083	23W-4S	A7
4300	LSLE	60532	3143	23W-6S	B5
SR-53 Main St					
5200	LSLE	60532	3143	23W-5S	A3
5400	LslT	60532	3143	23W-5S	A3
SR-53 N Ottawa St					
10	JLET	60436	3498	24W-23S	E5
400	JLET	60432	3498	24W-23S	E5
SR-53 S Ottawa St					
10	JLET	60432	3498	24W-23S	E5
10	JLET	60436	3498	24W-24S	E5
SR-53 Rand Rd					
2000	PLTN	60074	2753	20W-18N	A3
SR-53 N Rand Rd					
1600	PLTN	60074	2753	19W-18N	B4
SR-53 Rohlwing Rd					
10	ADSN	60101	2970	20W-4N	A4
10	BmdT	60143	2914	20W-6N	A7
100	AddT	60101	2970	20W-5N	A2
100	ADSN	60143	2970	21W-5N	A1
100	BmdT	60101	2970	20W-5N	A2
100	BmdT	60143	2970	21W-5N	A1
400	ITSC	60143	2970	21W-5N	A1
800	EGVV	60007	2914	21W-8N	A2
1000	ITSC	60007	2914	21W-8N	A3
1000	ITSC	60143	2914	21W-8N	A3
1100	AddT	60143	2914	21W-7N	A4
SR-53 N Rohlwing Rd					
200	AddT	60101	2970	20W-4N	A3
200	ADSN	60101	2970	20W-4N	A3
200	BmdT	60143	2914	20W-6N	A6
200	ITSC	60143	2914	20W-6N	A6
500	BmdT	60148	2970	20W-2N	A7
600	BmdT	60101	2970	20W-4N	A4
700	ADSN	60148	2970	20W-2N	A7
800	ADSN	60101	3026	21W-2N	A1
800	ADSN	60148	3026	21W-2N	A1
800	LMBD	60148	3026	21W-2N	A1
1000	AddT	60148	3026	20W-2N	A1
1000	ADSN	60143	2970	20W-5N	A2
1000	BmdT	60143	2970	20W-5N	A2
SR-53 S Rohlwing Rd					
300	ADSN	60101	2970	20W-3N	A6
300	BmdT	60101	2970	20W-3N	A6
400	BmdT	60148	2970	20W-2N	A6
SR-53 W Ruby St					
100	JLET	60432	3498	24W-23S	E3
100	JLET	60435	3498	24W-23S	E3
SR-53 N Scott St					
10	JLET	60432	3499	23W-23S	A5
10	JLET	60433	3499	23W-23S	A5
SR-53 E Washington St					
10	JLET	60432	3499	23W-23S	A5
10	JLET	60433	3499	23W-23S	A5
10	JLET	60436	3499	23W-23S	A5
SR-56					
-	SgrT	-	3135	41W-7S	D6
-	SgrT	-	3136	40W-5S	C2
-	SRGV	-	3135	41W-7S	D6
SR-56 Butterfield Rd					
-	WnfT	60563	3080	30W-3S	B6
10	AURA	60502	3079	33W-3S	B6
10	AURA	60510	3079	33W-3S	B6
10	BtvT	60502	3079	33W-3S	B6
10	DRGV	60137	3083	22W-2S	D4
10	MltT	60137	3083	22W-2S	C4
10	MltT	60187	3082	24W-3S	E5
10	MltT	60515	3083	22W-2S	D4
10	MltT	60555	3082	25W-3S	A5
10	OKTR	60181	3085	17W-1S	B2
10	WHTN	60187	3081	27W-2S	B4
10	WHTN	60187	3082	23W-3S	E5
10	WHTN	60187	3083	23W-2S	A4
10	WHTN	60555	3082	25W-3S	B5
10	WnfT	60185	3081	28W-2S	B4

Block	City	ZIP	Map#	CGS	Grid
SR-56 Butterfield Rd					
10	WnfT	60510	3079	31W-3S	E6
10	WnfT	60555	3081	27W-2S	B4
10	WNVL	60555	3080	29W-3S	E5
10	WNVL	60555	3081	28W-2S	B4
100	AraT	60510	3078	35W-4S	C7
100	AraT	60542	3078	35W-4S	C7
100	MltT	60187	3081	27W-2S	B4
100	MltT	60187	3083	23W-2S	A4
100	MltT	60555	3081	27W-2S	B4
100	NARA	60510	3078	35W-4S	C7
100	NARA	60542	3078	35W-4S	C7
100	WNVL	60185	3081	28W-2S	A5
100	WNVL	60563	3080	30W-3S	C6
100	YkTp	60181	3085	17W-1S	B2
200	WHTN	60137	3083	23W-2S	A4
300	AURA	60563	3080	30W-3S	B6
400	WnfT	60555	3080	29W-3S	D6
500	OKBK	60181	3085	18W-2S	A2
500	OKBK	60523	3085	17W-1S	B2
500	OKTR	60523	3085	17W-1S	B2
500	WHTN	60555	3081	27W-2S	B4
500	WnfT	60187	3081	27W-2S	B4
500	YkTp	60148	3084	19W-2S	D3
500	YkTp	60523	3084	20W-2S	B4
600	AraT	60502	3078	34W-4S	C7
600	AURA	60502	3078	35W-4S	A7
600	AURA	60510	3078	34W-3S	C7
600	NARA	60502	3078	34W-4S	C7
700	AURA	60502	3080	30W-3S	B6
700	AURA	60510	3080	31W-3S	A6
700	OKBK	60148	3084	19W-2S	E3
700	OKBK	60523	3084	20W-2S	B4
700	WnfT	60502	3080	30W-3S	B6
700	WnfT	60510	3080	30W-3S	B6
800	DRGV	60148	3084	21W-2S	A4
800	DRGV	60515	3084	21W-2S	A4
800	MltT	60148	3084	21W-2S	A4
800	MltT	60515	3084	21W-2S	A4
1000	LMBD	60148	3084	19W-2S	C4
1000	LMBD	60515	3084	19W-2S	C4
2000	DRGV	60515	3083	23W-2S	A4
2100	DRGV	60148	3083	21W-2S	E4
2100	MltT	60148	3083	21W-2S	E4
2700	YkTp	60523	3085	18W-2S	A3
4000	BLWD	60104	3029	13W-0N	A5
4000	HLSD	60162	3029	13W-0N	A5
4100	HLSD	60104	3029	13W-0N	A5
4200	BLWD	60162	3029	13W-0N	A5
4300	BLWD	60104	3028	13W-0N	E5
4300	BLWD	60162	3028	13W-0N	E5
4300	HLSD	60162	3028	13W-0N	E5
5200	BKLY	60163	3028	14W-0S	C5
5200	HLSD	60163	3028	14W-0S	C5
5900	BKLY	60162	3028	14W-0S	C5
5900	EMHT	60162	3028	14W-0S	C6
6000	EMHT	60126	3028	14W-0S	B6
SR-56 E Butterfield Rd					
-	LMBD	60148	3084	19W-2S	D3
100	EMHT	60126	3027	16W-0S	D7
100	EMHT	60126	3028	15W-0S	A6
100	BKLY	60162	3028	15W-0S	B6
500	BKLY	60163	3028	15W-0S	B6
500	EMHT	60162	3028	15W-0S	B6
SR-56 W Butterfield Rd					
-	EMHT	60181	3027	16W-1S	D7
-	OKTR	60181	3027	16W-1S	D7
100	EMHT	60126	3027	16W-0S	E6
SR-56 N Lincoln Hwy					
-	NARA	60542	3137	36W-4S	E1
SR-56 S Lincolnway					
10	NARA	60542	3137	36W-4S	E1
10	NARA	60542	3138	36W-4S	A1
200	AURA	60542	3138	36W-4S	A2
SR-56 R Reagan Mem Tollway					
-	AURA	-	3136	38W-5S	E2
-	AURA	-	3137	38W-5S	A2
-	NARA	-	3137	36W-5S	E2
-	SgrT	-	3136	41W-6S	A6
SR-56 E State St					
10	NARA	60542	3078	36W-4S	A7
10	NARA	60542	3138	36W-4S	A1
SR-56 W State St					
-	NARA	60542	3138	36W-4S	A1
SR-56 Washington Blvd					
4000	BLWD	60104	3029	12W-0N	A4
4000	BLWD	60162	3029	12W-0N	A4
4000	HLSD	60162	3029	13W-0N	A4
4100	HLSD	60104	3029	13W-0N	A4
SR-58 Dempster St					
4800	SKOK	60076	2865	6W-11N	E4
4800	SKOK	60077	2865	6W-11N	E4
5600	MNGV	60053	2865	8W-10N	A4
6700	MNGV	60053	2864	8W-10N	E4
SR-58 Golf Rd					
-	ELGN	60120	2855	31W-12N	E3
-	HFET	60010	2856	29W-11N	E3
-	HFET	60010	2857	28W-12N	A3
-	HFET	60120	2856	29W-11N	E3
-	HnrT	60120	2855	31W-12N	E3
-	RGMW	60173	2860	20W-12N	A2
-	SMBG	60173	2860	20W-12N	A2
500	HFET	60192	2856	30W-11N	B3
500	HnrT	60120	2856	30W-11N	B3
500	HnrT	60192	2856	30W-11N	B3
1100	ANHT	60005	2860	18W-12N	E2
1100	RGMW	60008	2860	21W-11N	A2
1700	GNVW	60025	2864	10W-11N	B2
1700	GNVW	60053	2864	10W-11N	B2
1700	MNGV	60053	2864	10W-11N	B2
2100	EGvT	60007	2860	21W-11N	A2
2100	RGMW	60007	2860	19W-12N	C2
2200	EGvT	60008	2860	21W-11N	A2
2400	MaiT	60025	2864	9W-12N	C2
2400	MaiT	60053	2864	9W-12N	C2
2500	MaiT	60714	2864	9W-12N	B2
6900	MNGV	60025	2864	8W-12N	E2
9200	MaiT	60016	2863	11W-12N	D2
9200	NLES	60016	2863	11W-12N	D2
9200	NLES	60714	2863	11W-12N	D2
9500	DSPN	60016	2863	11W-12N	C2
SR-58 E Golf Rd					
10	ANHT	60005	2861	17W-11N	B2
10	HFET	60169	2859	23W-12N	A2
10	HFET	60173	2859	23W-12N	A2
10	HFET	60195	2859	23W-12N	A2
10	SMBG	60169	2859	23W-12N	A2
10	SMBG	60195	2859	23W-12N	A2
500	DSPN	60016	2862	13W-12N	E2
600	MPPT	60005	2861	17W-11N	B2
600	MPPT	60056	2861	17W-11N	B2
1300	DSPN	60016	2863	12W-12N	B2
1400	SMBG	60173	2859	23W-11N	A2
1700	MaiT	60016	2863	12W-12N	B2
2000	EGvT	60007	2860	20W-11N	A2
2000	EGvT	60008	2860	20W-11N	A2

Block	City	ZIP	Map#	CGS	Grid
SR-58 E Golf Rd					
2000	RGMW	60008	2860	20W-12N	A2
2000	RGMW	60173	2860	20W-12N	A2
2000	SMBG	60173	2860	20W-12N	A2
SR-58 W Golf Rd					
-	HFET	60010	2857	27W-12N	C3
10	DSPN	60016	2862	15W-11N	A3
10	HFET	60169	2859	23W-12N	A2
10	HFET	60173	2859	23W-12N	A2
10	HFET	60195	2859	23W-12N	A2
10	MPPT	60016	2862	15W-11N	A3
10	MPPT	60056	2862	15W-11N	A3
10	SMBG	60169	2859	23W-12N	A2
10	SMBG	60173	2859	23W-12N	A2
10	SMBG	60195	2859	23W-12N	A2
300	DSPN	60016	2861	16W-11N	E3
300	DSPN	60056	2862	15W-11N	B2
300	HFET	60169	2858	25W-11N	B2
300	HFET	60195	2858	23W-12N	E2
300	MPPT	60016	2861	16W-11N	E3
300	MPPT	60056	2861	16W-11N	D3
300	SMBG	60169	2858	24W-11N	E2
300	SMBG	60195	2858	24W-11N	E2
500	ANHT	60005	2860	18W-11N	E2
700	RGMW	60008	2860	18W-12N	E2
900	HFET	60194	2858	24W-12N	D2
1600	SMBG	60194	2858	25W-12N	B2
2000	ANHT	60005	2861	17W-11N	B2
2000	MPPT	60005	2861	17W-11N	B2
2100	HFET	60169	2857	27W-11N	C3
2100	HFET	60194	2857	27W-11N	C3
2100	SMBG	60194	2857	27W-11N	C3
8000	MaiT	60025	2864	10W-12N	B2
8000	MaiT	60053	2864	10W-12N	B2
8000	MaiT	60714	2864	10W-12N	B2
8000	MNGV	60053	2864	10W-12N	B2
8000	NLES	60714	2864	10W-12N	B2
8100	MaiT	60016	2864	10W-12N	A2
8500	NLES	60016	2864	10W-12N	A2
8700	MaiT	60016	2863	10W-12N	E2
8700	MaiT	60714	2863	11W-12N	E2
8700	NLES	60016	2863	11W-12N	E2
8700	NLES	60714	2863	11W-12N	E2
SR-58 Summit St					
600	ELGN	60120	2855	32W-12N	C3
1300	HnrT	60120	2855	32W-12N	C3
SR-58 Waukegan Rd					
8800	MNGV	60053	2864	8W-11N	E3
9500	GNVW	60025	2864	8W-11N	E2
9500	GNVW	60053	2864	8W-11N	E2
9500	MNGV	60025	2864	8W-11N	E2
SR-59					
-	ANTH	60002	2416	24W-41N	D1
-	AntT	60002	2416	24W-38N	B6
-	AntT	60046	2416	24W-38N	B6
-	AURA	60504	3140	30W-7S	C7
-	AURA	60504	3202	30W-8S	C1
-	AURA	60540	3140	29W-7S	C6
-	AURA	60540	3202	30W-8S	C1
-	AURA	60555	3080	30W-3S	C6
-	AURA	60563	3080	30W-3S	C6
-	AURA	60563	3140	29W-6S	C5
-	AURA	60564	3202	29W-8S	C2
-	CbaT	60010	2643	26W-24N	E6
-	CbaT	60010	2697	25W-22N	E3
-	CbaT	60084	2643	26W-25N	D4
-	FXLK	60020	2473	26W-36N	D4
-	FXLK	60041	2530	27W-34N	B1
-	GrtT	60041	2473	27W-35N	B7
-	GrtT	60041	2530	27W-34N	B1
-	GrtT	60073	2530	27W-32N	B5
-	JLET	60404	3496	30W-21S	C1
-	JLET	60586	3496	30W-21S	C1
-	LKBN	60010	2643	26W-24N	E6
-	LKBN	60010	2697	26W-24N	E1
-	LKMR	60041	2530	27W-32N	B5
-	LKMR	60073	2530	27W-31N	C7
-	LkvT	60002	2416	24W-40N	C4
-	LkvT	60046	2416	24W-40N	C4
-	LkvT	60046	2474	25W-38N	B1
-	NBRN	60010	2643	26W-24N	E7
-	NBRN	60010	2697	26W-23N	E2
-	NPVL	60504	3140	30W-7S	C7
-	NPVL	60504	3202	30W-8S	C1
-	NPVL	60540	3140	30W-6S	C5
-	NPVL	60540	3202	30W-8S	C1
-	NPVL	60563	3080	29W-3S	C7
-	NPVL	60563	3140	30W-6S	C5
-	NPVL	60564	3202	29W-8S	C2
-	NPVL	60585	3266	29W-13S	C4
-	NpvT	60504	3202	29W-8S	C2
-	NpvT	60540	3140	30W-6S	C5
-	NpvT	60563	3140	30W-6S	C5
-	PnfT	60586	3496	30W-21S	C1
-	TRLK	60010	2643	26W-24N	E6
-	TRLK	60084	2643	26W-25N	D4
-	VOLO	60041	2530	27W-32N	B5
-	VOLO	60073	2530	27W-32N	B5
-	VOLO	60073	2587	27W-31N	C1
-	WCDA	60073	2587	27W-29N	C3
-	WCDA	60084	2587	27W-29N	C3
-	WCHI	60185	2966	30W-3N	C6
-	WCHI	60185	3022	30W-2N	C1
-	WCHI	60185	3080	29W-1S	D1
-	WcnT	60073	2530	27W-31N	C7
-	WcnT	60073	2587	27W-30N	C2
-	WcnT	60084	2587	27W-29N	C3
-	WcnT	60084	2643	26W-25N	D4
-	WnfT	60185	3080	29W-1S	D1
-	WnfT	60555	3080	29W-3S	C5
-	WNVL	60185	3080	29W-1S	C2
-	WNVL	60555	3080	30W-3S	C7
-	WNVL	60563	3080	30W-3S	C6
-	WYNE	60103	2966	30W-4N	C3
-	WynT	60185	3022	30W-2N	C1
10	PNFD	60544	3416	30W-19S	C4
10	WldT	60564	3202	30W-10S	C6
100	PnfT	60544	3416	29W-18S	C2
300	PNFD	60544	3338	30W-18S	C7
400	NPVL	60564	3266	30W-11S	C2
400	NpvT	60564	3202	29W-8S	C2
400	WldT	60564	3266	30W-11S	C2
500	WYNE	60184	2966	30W-2N	C7
500	WYNE	60185	2966	30W-4N	C3
500	WynT	60184	2966	30W-2N	C7
500	WynT	60185	2966	30W-4N	C3
600	WynT	60103	2966	30W-2N	C7
700	FXLK	60041	2473	27W-34N	B7
900	ANTH	60002	2357	24W-42N	D6
1000	PnfT	60544	3338	29W-17S	C6
2800	PNFD	60585	3338	30W-18S	C7
12100	PNFD	60585	3266	29W-14S	C7
12100	WldT	60585	3266	29W-14S	C7
12200	WldT	60585	3338	29W-14S	C1
SR-59 N Barrington Rd					
25900	CbaT	60084	2643	26W-26N	D4

Block	City	ZIP	Map#	CGS	Grid
SR-59 N Barrington Rd					
25900	TRLK	60010	2643	26W-26N	D4
25900	TRLK	60084	2643	26W-26N	D4
25900	WcnT	60084	2643	26W-26N	D3
26300	WCDA	60084	2643	26W-26N	D3
SR-59 Brook Forest Av					
-	JLET	60404	3496	30W-21S	C1
-	PnfT	60586	3496	30W-21S	C1
100	SRWD	60404	3496	30W-21S	C1
100	SRWD	60431	3496	29W-23S	C5
900	JLET	60431	3496	30W-21S	C1
1100	JLET	60586	3496	30W-21S	C1
SR-59 Cottage St					
100	SRWD	60404	3496	29W-24S	C5
100	SRWD	60431	3496	29W-24S	C5
800	TroT	60404	3496	29W-24S	C6
800	TroT	60431	3496	29W-24S	C6
SR-59 S Division St					
-	PNFD	60586	3416	29W-19S	C3
SR-59 Grand Av					
-	GrtT	60041	2474	25W-37N	A3
-	LkvT	60041	2474	25W-37N	A3
-	LkvT	60046	2474	25W-37N	B1
SR-59 E Grand Av					
500	FXLK	60020	2473	26W-36N	D4
500	FXLK	60041	2473	26W-36N	D4
SR-59 W Grand Av					
-	GrtT	60041	2474	25W-36N	A3
26000	GrtT	60041	2473	26W-36N	E4
26200	FXLK	60041	2473	26W-36N	D4
26500	FXLK	60020	2473	26W-36N	D4
SR-59 Hawthorne Rd					
10	BNHL	60010	2750	25W-18N	E3
10	BRTN	60010	2750	25W-18N	E3
SR-59 N Hough St					
-	NBRN	60010	2697	25W-22N	E4
100	BRTN	60010	2750	25W-20N	E2
700	BRTN	60010	2697	25W-20N	E7
700	CbaT	60010	2697	25W-20N	E7
SR-59 S Hough St					
100	BRTN	60010	2750	25W-18N	E2
SR-59 Lake St					
300	ANTH	60002	2357	24W-41N	D7
SR-59 N Neltnor Blvd					
100	WCHI	60185	3022	29W-1N	D4
300	WnfT	60185	3022	29W-2N	C1
SR-59 S Neltnor Blvd					
100	WCHI	60185	3022	29W-0N	D4
200	WnfT	60185	3022	29W-0N	D5
SR-59 New Sutton Rd					
-	BNHL	60010	2803	28W-15N	A1
-	BrnT	60010	2803	28W-15N	A1
-	BrnT	60192	2802	28W-13N	E6
-	HnrT	60010	2802	29W-12N	D7
100	BNHL	60010	2750	27W-16N	A7
100	BrnT	60010	2750	27W-16N	B6
700	BNHL	60010	2802	28W-14N	E5
700	BNHL	60118	2802	28W-14N	E4
700	BrnT	60010	2802	28W-14N	E3
700	BrnT	60118	2802	28W-14N	E3
2500	HFET	60010	2802	29W-12N	D7
2500	HFET	60192	2802	28W-13N	E6
2700	SBTN	60010	2802	28W-13N	E6
SR-59 N Rand Rd					
200	WCDA	60084	2643	26W-27N	D1
200	WcnT	60084	2643	26W-26N	D2
600	WCDA	60084	2587	26W-27N	D7
800	WcnT	60084	2587	26W-28N	D6
29000	WCDA	60073	2587	26W-29N	C5
29500	WcnT	60073	2587	27W-29N	C4
SR-59 S Rand Rd					
400	WCDA	60084	2643	26W-26N	D2
400	WcnT	60084	2643	26W-26N	D2
SR-59 Sutton Rd					
-	BRLT	60103	2856	29W-9N	C7
-	BRLT	60107	2856	30W-9N	C7
-	BRLT	60120	2856	30W-9N	C7
-	BRLT	60120	2910	30W-6N	C6
-	HFET	60010	2856	29W-12N	D1
-	SMWD	60103	2856	29W-9N	C7
-	SMWD	60103	2910	30W-9N	C1
-	SMWD	60107	2910	30W-9N	C1
-	SMWD	60120	2910	30W-9N	C1
10	BRLT	60103	2910	30W-6N	C6
10	BRLT	60103	2966	30W-5N	C1
10	WYNE	60184	2966	30W-5N	C3
10	WynT	60103	2910	30W-8N	C4
10	WynT	60103	2966	30W-5N	C2
10	WynT	60184	2966	30W-5N	C3
200	HFET	60107	2856	29W-11N	D3
200	HFET	60120	2856	29W-11N	D3
200	HnrT	60107	2856	29W-12N	D2
200	HnrT	60120	2856	29W-12N	D2
200	SMWD	60107	2856	29W-12N	D2
200	SMWD	60120	2856	29W-12N	D2
SR-59 S Sutton Rd					
10	HnrT	60107	2856	29W-11N	D5
10	HnrT	60120	2856	29W-11N	D5
10	SMWD	60107	2856	29W-10N	D5
10	SMWD	60120	2856	29W-11N	D5
SR-60					
-	FmtT	60030	2531	24W-31N	C7
-	FmtT	60030	2588	23W-30N	E1
-	FmtT	60030	2589	21W-29N	D4
-	FmtT	60060	2589	21W-29N	D4
-	FmtT	60060	2590	20W-28N	A6
-	FmtT	60073	2588	23W-30N	E1
-	FmtT	60073	2589	23W-30N	A1
-	LbvT	60060	2646	18W-26N	D4
-	LGGV	60047	2646	19W-26N	C3
-	MDLN	60060	2589	20W-28N	E6
-	MDLN	60060	2590	20W-28N	A6
-	RDLK	60030	2588	23W-30N	E1
-	RDLK	60030	2589	23W-30N	A2
-	RDLK	60073	2588	23W-30N	E1
-	RDLK	60073	2589	23W-30N	A1
-	RLKP	60030	2589	22W-30N	B3
-	RLKP	60060	2589	22W-30N	B3
-	VOLO	60030	2530	26W-31N	E7
-	VOLO	60030	2531	25W-31N	B7
-	VOLO	60073	2530	26W-31N	E7
-	VrnT	60060	2646	18W-26N	D4
-	WcnT	60030	2530	26W-31N	E7
-	WcnT	60030	2531	25W-31N	B7
700	FmtT	60060	2646	19W-26N	B2
700	MDLN	60060	2646	19W-26N	B2
SR-60 W Kennedy Rd					
-	LbvT	60045	2648	13W-25N	E4
-	VrnT	60045	2649	13W-25N	A4
700	LKFT	60045	2649	12W-25N	C4
1800	LKFT	60045	2648	13W-25N	E4
1800	VrnT	60045	2648	13W-25N	E4
SR-60 Townline Rd					
-	LbvT	60045	2648	13W-26N	E4
-	LKFT	60045	2648	13W-26N	E4
-	MTWA	60045	2648	14W-26N	D4

STREET Block	City	ZIP	Map#	CGS	Grid
SR-60 Townline Rd					
-	MTWA	60048	2648	15W-26N	A4
-	VNHL	60061	2648	15W-26N	A4
-	VrnT	60045	2648	13W-26N	D4
-	VrnT	60048	2648	14W-26N	D4
200	MDLN	60060	2646	18W-25N	E4
800	MDLN	60060	2647	17W-25N	A4
1300	VNHL	60060	2647	17W-26N	B4
1500	VNHL	60061	2647	17W-26N	B4
SR-60 E Townline Rd					
-	VNHL	60061	2648	15W-26N	B4
-	VrnT	60048	2648	15W-26N	B4
10	VNHL	60061	2647	16W-26N	C4
700	VrnT	60048	2647	15W-26N	E4
SR-60 W Townline Rd					
10	VNHL	60061	2647	17W-26N	C4
400	MDLN	60060	2647	17W-26N	B4
400	VNHL	60060	2647	17W-26N	B4
SR-62 Algonquin Rd					
-	HFET	60010	2804	23W-14N	E4
-	HFET	60192	2804	23W-14N	E4
-	RGMW	60008	2806	20W-12N	A7
-	SBTN	60010	2804	23W-14N	E4
-	SBTN	60192	2804	23W-14N	E4
10	BNHL	60010	2750	27W-16N	A7
10	BNHL	60010	2803	27W-15N	C1
10	BrnT	60010	2750	27W-16N	A7
10	BrnT	60010	2803	27W-15N	C1
10	SBTN	60010	2803	27W-15N	C1
100	ALGN	60102	2748	32W-19N	C2
100	ALGN	60110	2748	32W-19N	C2
100	BNHL	60010	2748	32W-20N	A1
100	BNHL	60010	2749	29W-16N	B6
100	BNHL	60102	2748	32W-19N	C2
100	BNHL	60110	2748	32W-19N	C2
2200	ANHT	60005	2860	19W-12N	D1
2200	ANHT	60008	2860	19W-12N	D1
2200	RGMW	60005	2860	19W-12N	D1
2200	RGMW	60008	2860	19W-12N	C1
SR-62 E Algonquin Rd					
-	RGMW	60067	2806	20W-12N	A7
10	ALGN	60102	2694	33W-20N	E7
10	ANHT	60005	2861	18W-11N	A3
200	PLTN	60067	2805	22W-13N	B6
200	PltT	60173	2805	22W-13N	B6
200	SMBG	60173	2805	22W-13N	B6
800	ALGN	60102	2695	33W-20N	A7
1000	EGvT	60005	2861	16W-10N	D5
1000	EGvT	60056	2861	16W-10N	D5
1500	MPPT	60005	2861	16W-10N	E5
1500	PltT	60067	2805	20W-13N	E7
1500	SMBG	60067	2805	20W-13N	E7
1600	MPPT	60056	2861	16W-10N	E5
1700	SMBG	60067	2806	21W-12N	A7
1700	SMBG	60173	2806	21W-12N	A7
1900	ALGN	60102	2748	32W-20N	B2
1900	AlqT	60102	2748	32W-20N	B2
2000	RGMW	60008	2806	21W-12N	A7
2000	RGMW	60173	2806	21W-12N	A7
2000	SMBG	60008	2806	21W-12N	A7
2200	ALGN	60110	2748	33W-19N	C2
2200	BNHL	60010	2748	33W-19N	C2
2200	BNHL	60102	2748	33W-19N	C2
2200	BNHL	60110	2748	33W-19N	C2
SR-62 W Algonquin Rd					
10	ALGN	60102	2694	33W-20N	E7
10	ANHT	60005	2861	18W-11N	A3
300	DSPN	60016	2861	16W-10N	E5
300	DSPN	60018	2861	16W-10N	E5
300	MPPT	60016	2861	16W-10N	E5
300	MPPT	60018	2861	16W-10N	E5
300	MPPT	60056	2861	16W-10N	E5
400	ANHT	60005	2860	18W-11N	E2
400	ANHT	60008	2860	18W-11N	E2
500	EGvT	60056	2861	16W-10N	E5
700	HFET	60067	2804	23W-14N	E4
700	HFET	60192	2804	23W-14N	D4
700	PltT	60067	2804	23W-14N	E4
700	PltT	60192	2804	23W-14N	E4
700	PltT	60195	2804	23W-14N	E4
700	RGMW	60008	2860	18W-11N	E2
1000	RGMW	60005	2860	18W-11N	E2
1100	PLTN	60067	2805	22W-13N	B6
1100	PltT	60173	2805	22W-13N	B6
1100	SMBG	60173	2805	22W-13N	B6
1300	SBTN	60010	2804	24W-14N	C4
1300	SBTN	60192	2804	24W-14N	C4
1400	HFET	60010	2804	24W-14N	C4
1400	PltT	60067	2805	21W-13N	E7
1400	PltT	60195	2805	21W-13N	E7
1500	EGvT	60005	2861	16W-10N	D4
1600	IVNS	60067	2804	23W-14N	E5
1600	IVNS	60067	2805	21W-13N	E7
1600	IVNS	60195	2804	23W-14N	E5
1700	ANHT	60056	2861	17W-11N	C4
1700	MPPT	60005	2861	17W-10N	C4
1800	HFET	60195	2804	23W-14N	E4
SR-64					
10	CmpT	60119	2961	42W-4N	D4
10	CmpT	60175	2961	41W-4N	E4
10	CmpT	60175	2962	41W-4N	A4
10	LYLK	60151	2961	43W-4N	A3
300	SchT	60175	2963	37W-3N	D7
400	CmpT	60175	2963	37W-3N	D7
400	LYLK	60175	2961	43W-4N	A3
SR-64 W Eugenie St					
100	CHCG	60614	2978	0W-2N	B7
SR-64 N Lasalle Dr					
1600	CHCG	60610	2978	0W-2N	B7
1600	CHCG	60614	2978	0W-2N	B7
SR-64 W La Salle Dr					
-	CHCG	60614	2978	0W-1N	A7
SR-64 E Main St					
10	SCRL	60174	2964	35W-3N	B7
400	SCRL	60185	2965	32W-3N	C6
400	WynT	60185	2965	32W-3N	C6
2800	SCRL	60174	2965	33W-3N	A6
SR-64 W Main St					
10	SCRL	60174	2964	35W-3N	B7
1100	SCRL	60174	2963	36W-3N	E7
1900	SCRL	60175	2963	36W-3N	D7
3700	SchT	60175	2963	38W-3N	B6
SR-64 North Av					
-	CLSM	60139	3024	24W-2N	D1
-	SCRL	60174	2965	33W-3N	A6
10	BmdT	60137	3025	23W-1N	B1
10	BmdT	60139	3025	23W-1N	A1
10	BmdT	60188	3023	26W-2N	E1
10	BmdT	60188	3025	23W-1N	A1
10	CLSM	60188	3023	26W-2N	D1
10	GLHT	60139	3024	23W-1N	E1
10	GLHT	60139	3025	23W-1N	B1
10	GLHT	60188	3025	23W-1N	A1
10	MltT	60148	3025	21W-1N	E1
10	WCHI	60185	2965	32W-3N	D6
10	WCHI	60185	2966	29W-2N	D7

STREET Block	City	ZIP	Map#	CGS	Grid
SR-64 North Av					
10	WynT	60185	2965	32W-3N	D6
10	WynT	60185	2966	30W-3N	B6
10	WynT	60185	2967	28W-2N	B7
10	WynT	60185	3023	26W-2N	D1
10	WynT	60188	3023	27W-2N	D1
100	BmdT	60188	3024	25W-2N	A1
100	SCRL	60185	2965	32W-3N	D6
200	MltT	60137	3025	22W-1N	C1
300	GLHT	60137	3025	23W-1N	B1
400	BmdT	60148	3025	21W-2N	E1
400	CLSM	60188	3024	25W-2N	A1
400	GLHT	60148	3025	21W-2N	D1
400	LMBD	60148	3025	21W-2N	E1
500	WCHI	60185	2967	28W-2N	B7
700	GLHT	60188	3024	23W-2N	E1
SR-64 E North Av					
-	MLPK	60160	3029	13W-2N	A1
-	MLPK	60164	3029	13W-2N	A1
-	NHLK	60160	3029	13W-2N	A1
-	NHLK	60164	3028	15W-1N	B1
-	NHLK	60164	3029	13W-1N	A1
-	NHLK	60165	3029	13W-1N	A1
-	SNPK	60164	3029	13W-1N	A1
10	LMBD	60148	3026	19W-1N	C1
10	VLPK	60181	3027	17W-2N	B1
10	YkTp	60181	3027	17W-2N	A1
100	EMHT	60126	3027	17W-1N	B1
100	EMHT	60126	3028	15W-1N	A1
400	VLPK	60126	3027	17W-2N	B1
400	VLPK	60148	3026	19W-2N	D1
400	YkTp	60126	3027	17W-2N	B1
600	AddT	60148	3026	19W-2N	D1
SR-64 W North Av					
-	ADSN	60148	3026	18W-2N	D1
-	EMHT	60126	3028	14W-2N	B1
-	LMBD	60148	3025	21W-2N	E1
-	MLPK	60164	3029	12W-2N	A1
-	SNPK	60164	3029	12W-1N	A1
-	VLPK	60148	3026	18W-2N	D1
10	LMBD	60148	3026	21W-1N	A1
10	NHLK	60164	3028	13W-1N	E1
10	VLPK	60181	3027	18W-2N	A1
100	CHCG	60610	2978	0W-2N	B7
100	CHCG	60614	2978	0W-2N	B7
100	EMHT	60126	3027	16W-2N	E1
100	WCHI	60185	2966	30W-3N	C7
100	WynT	60185	2966	29W-3N	C7
200	ADSN	60181	3026	18W-2N	E1
200	VLPK	60101	3026	18W-2N	E1
300	AddT	60148	3026	21W-1N	A1
300	VLPK	60181	3026	18W-1N	E1
500	ADSN	60101	3026	18W-1N	E1
500	MLPK	60160	3030	10W-2N	A1
500	PvsT	60160	3030	10W-2N	A1
600	MLPK	60160	3029	12W-1N	A1
600	VLPK	60126	3027	17W-2N	C1
600	YkTp	60126	3027	17W-2N	C1
700	CHCG	60610	2977	1W-1N	E7
700	CHCG	60614	2977	1W-1N	E7
700	CHCG	60622	2977	1W-1N	E7
1900	CHCG	60622	3033	3W-1N	A1
1900	CHCG	60647	3033	3W-1N	A1
2500	MLPK	60165	3029	12W-1N	A1
2500	SNPK	60160	3029	12W-1N	A1
2500	SNPK	60165	3029	12W-1N	A1
2800	CHCG	60622	3032	3W-1N	E1
2800	CHCG	60647	3032	3W-1N	E1
3100	CHCG	60651	3032	3W-2N	D1
3900	CHCG	60639	3032	4W-2N	B1
4700	CHCG	60639	3031	8W-1N	A1
4700	CHCG	60651	3031	8W-1N	A1
5900	OKPK	60302	3031	7W-2N	B1
5900	OKPK	60639	3031	7W-2N	B1
5900	OKPK	60651	3031	7W-2N	B1
6000	CHCG	60302	3031	7W-2N	B1
6300	CHCG	60707	3031	7W-2N	A1
6700	CHCG	60302	3030	8W-2N	E1
6700	CHCG	60707	3030	10W-1N	A1
6700	OKPK	60302	3030	10W-1N	A1
7100	EDPK	60707	3030	8W-2N	D1
7100	OKPK	60305	3030	8W-2N	E1
7100	RVFT	60305	3030	8W-2N	D1
7100	RVFT	60707	3030	8W-2N	D1
8300	RVFT	60160	3030	10W-1N	B1
8300	RVFT	60171	3030	10W-1N	B1
8300	RVGV	60160	3030	10W-2N	A1
8400	MLPK	60171	3030	10W-1N	A1
8400	RVGV	60171	3030	10W-2N	A1
SR-68					
-	CPVL	60118	2801	32W-16N	D1
600	CPVL	60110	2801	32W-16N	D1
600	EDND	60110	2801	32W-16N	D1
600	EDND	60118	2801	32W-16N	D1
SR-68 Algonquin Rd					
100	BNHL	60010	2750	27W-16N	A7
100	BrnT	60010	2750	27W-16N	A7
SR-68 Barrington Av					
500	CPVL	60110	2801	33W-16N	C2
500	DndT	60118	2801	33W-16N	B2
500	EDND	60110	2801	33W-16N	C2
500	EDND	60118	2801	33W-16N	B2
SR-68 Dundee Rd					
-	BNHL	60010	2801	30W-15N	E1
-	BRTN	60010	2750	25W-17N	E5
-	CPVL	60110	2801	32W-16N	D1
-	CPVL	60118	2801	32W-16N	D1
-	EDND	60110	2801	30W-15N	E1
-	EDND	60118	2801	32W-16N	D1
-	GLNC	60062	2758	8W-17N	A4
-	IVNS	60010	2750	25W-17N	E5
-	NtrT	60062	2758	8W-17N	A4
-	PLTN	60067	2751	23W-17N	E5
-	PltT	60067	2751	23W-17N	E5
-	WhlT	60062	2755	13W-18N	E4
-	WhlT	60062	2756	13W-18N	A4
-	WhlT	60090	2755	13W-18N	E4
-	WhlT	60090	2756	13W-18N	A4
-	WLNG	60062	2755	13W-18N	E4
-	WLNG	60090	2755	13W-18N	E4
-	WLNG	60090	2756	13W-18N	A4
10	BNHL	60010	2750	26W-17N	D5
100	BNHL	60010	2802	30W-15N	A1
200	BNHL	60010	2749	28W-16N	E7
400	NHBK	60062	2758	8W-17N	A4
500	NHBK	60062	2757	8W-17N	E4
2000	IVNS	60010	2751	23W-17N	D5
2000	IVNS	60067	2751	23W-17N	D5
2000	PltT	60010	2751	23W-17N	E5
2500	NHBK	60062	2756	10W-18N	E4
4100	NfdT	60062	2756	13W-18N	A4
SR-68 E Dundee Rd					
-	BFGV	60004	2754	15W-18N	E4
-	PltT	60004	2753	19W-18N	D4
-	WhlT	60090	2755	13W-18N	E4
-	WLNG	60062	2755	13W-18N	E4

STREET Block	City	ZIP	Map#	CGS	Grid
SR-68 E Dundee Rd					
10	BRTN	60010	2750	26W-17N	D5
10	BRTN	60010	2751	25W-17N	A5
10	IVNS	60010	2750	26W-17N	D5
10	IVNS	60010	2751	25W-17N	A5
10	PLTN	60067	2752	20W-18N	E4
10	PLTN	60067	2753	20W-17N	A4
10	PLTN	60074	2752	20W-18N	E4
10	PLTN	60074	2753	20W-17N	A4
10	PltT	60074	2752	20W-18N	E4
10	PltT	60074	2753	20W-17N	A4
10	WLNG	60090	2755	13W-18N	E4
100	IVNS	60067	2751	23W-17N	D5
100	PltT	60067	2753	20W-18N	A4
300	BFGV	60090	2754	16W-18N	D4
600	ANHT	60004	2754	15W-18N	E4
600	BFGV	60089	2754	15W-18N	E4
1000	ANHT	60089	2754	17W-18N	A4
SR-68 W Dundee Rd					
-	PltT	60004	2753	19W-18N	D4
-	PltT	60074	2753	19W-18N	D4
10	BFGV	60089	2754	16W-18N	C4
10	BFGV	60090	2754	16W-18N	D4
10	WLNG	60089	2754	16W-18N	D4
10	WLNG	60090	2755	14W-18N	C4
100	PLTN	60067	2752	21W-18N	E4
100	PltT	60074	2752	21W-18N	E4
500	PLTN	60074	2752	21W-17N	C4
700	ANHT	60004	2753	18W-17N	E4
700	BFGV	60089	2753	18W-17N	E4
700	PltT	60067	2752	21W-17N	C4
800	WLNG	60090	2754	15W-18N	E4
1200	ANHT	60004	2754	17W-18N	A4
1200	ANHT	60089	2754	17W-18N	A4
1200	PltT	60010	2752	22W-17N	A4
1500	PLTN	60010	2752	23W-17N	A4
1700	PLTN	60010	2751	24W-17N	C5
1700	PLTN	60067	2751	24W-17N	C5
1700	PltT	60010	2751	24W-17N	C5
1800	PltT	60067	2751	23W-17N	E5
SR-68 New Sutton Rd					
100	BNHL	60010	2750	26W-17N	C6
100	BrnT	60010	2750	27W-16N	B6
SR-68 Penny Av					
100	EDND	60118	2801	32W-16N	D1
200	DndT	60118	2801	32W-16N	D1
SR-71					
4000	OSWG	60543	3263	38W-13S	A5
5000	OswT	60543	3263	38W-13S	A5
5600	OSWG	60543	3262	39W-13S	E5
5600	OswT	60543	3262	39W-13S	E5
5600	OswT	60560	3262	40W-14S	C7
6600	OSWG	60560	3262	40W-14S	C7
7300	OswT	60560	3334	40W-14S	C1
7900	KdlT	60560	3334	40W-15S	B2
8000	KdlT	60560	3333	41W-16S	E4
8000	YKVL	60560	3333	41W-16S	E4
11000	KdlT	60560	3332	45W-17S	D7
11600	FoxT	60560	3332	45W-17S	C7
SR-71 Stagecoach Tr					
-	KdlT	60560	3333	43W-16S	B5
-	YKVL	60560	3333	43W-16S	B5
SR-71 E Stagecoach Tr					
100	KdlT	60560	3333	42W-16S	C5
100	YKVL	60560	3333	43W-16S	C5
SR-72					
-	DndT	60118	2799	36W-16N	E2
-	DndT	60118	2800	36W-16N	B2
-	ELGN	60124	2799	37W-16N	E2
-	HPSR	60140	2795	47W-15N	C3
-	HPSR	60140	2796	44W-15N	D4
-	HshT	60140	2795	47W-15N	C3
-	HshT	60140	2796	44W-15N	E4
-	HshT	60140	2797	44W-15N	A4
-	PGGV	60140	2797	44W-15N	A4
-	PGGV	60140	2798	41W-15N	A3
-	RtdT	60136	2798	39W-16N	E2
-	RtdT	60140	2797	44W-15N	A4
-	RtdT	60140	2798	39W-16N	E2
-	WDND	60118	2800	36W-16N	B2
SR-72 W Higgins Av					
7200	CHCG	60631	2918	9W-7N	D5
7200	CHCG	60656	2918	9W-7N	D5
SR-72 Higgins Rd					
-	DndT	60118	2800	36W-16N	B2
-	DndT	60136	2799	37W-16N	C2
-	EGvT	60007	2860	18W-10N	E5
-	SYHW	60118	2800	35W-16N	B2
-	WDND	60118	2800	35W-16N	B2
10	GLBT	60136	2798	39W-16N	E2
10	RtdT	60136	2798	40W-16N	C2
10	RtdT	60140	2798	40W-16N	C2
500	GLBT	60136	2799	38W-16N	B2
500	RtdT	60118	2799	38W-16N	B2
500	RtdT	60136	2799	38W-16N	B2
700	CHCG	60631	2918	10W-7N	A4
700	PKRG	60068	2918	10W-7N	A4
700	PKRG	60631	2918	10W-7N	A4
1500	CHCG	60018	2917	11W-7N	E4
1500	CHCG	60068	2917	11W-7N	E4
1500	CHCG	60631	2917	11W-7N	E4
1500	PKRG	60068	2917	11W-7N	E4
1500	PKRG	60631	2917	11W-7N	E4
2000	PKRG	60018	2917	11W-7N	D4
2500	DndT	60118	2799	37W-16N	C2
2500	DndT	60124	2799	37W-16N	D2
2500	ELGN	60118	2799	37W-16N	C2
2500	ELGN	60124	2799	37W-16N	C2
SR-72 E Higgins Rd					
-	EGvT	60007	2860	20W-11N	A4
-	SMBG	60007	2860	20W-11N	A4
10	EGvT	60007	2861	17W-10N	B5
10	EGVV	60007	2861	17W-9N	C6
10	GLBT	60136	2799	38W-16N	A2
10	HFET	60169	2859	23W-11N	A3
600	HFET	60173	2859	22W-11N	C3
600	SMBG	60169	2859	22W-11N	C3
600	SMBG	60173	2859	22W-11N	C3
1700	SMBG	60173	2860	19W-10N	C5
2400	EGVV	60007	2915	16W-9N	E1
2600	EGvT	60007	2915	16W-9N	E1
SR-72 W Higgins Rd					
-	CHCG	60018	2916	13W-8N	E1
-	DSPN	60018	2916	13W-8N	E1
-	EDND	60118	2801	30W-14N	E4
-	HFET	60118	2801	30W-14N	E4
-	HFET	60192	2802	28W-13N	E6
-	PKRG	60018	2917	11W-7N	D4
-	PKRG	60068	2917	11W-7N	D4
10	BrnT	60010	2803	27W-13N	A6
10	HFET	60169	2859	21W-11N	E4
10	HFET	60195	2859	21W-11N	E4
10	SBTN	60010	2803	27W-13N	B7
100	SMBG	60169	2859	23W-11N	A3
100	SMBG	60195	2859	23W-11N	A3
200	BrnT	60010	2802	28W-13N	E6

STREET Block	City	ZIP	Map#	CGS	Grid
SR-72 W Higgins Rd					
200	HFET	60010	2802	28W-13N	D5
200	HFET	60118	2802	28W-13N	E6
200	HFET	60195	2858	23W-11N	E3
200	SBTN	60010	2802	28W-13N	E6
200	SMBG	60195	2858	23W-11N	E3
500	SMBG	60194	2858	24W-12N	D2
600	HFET	60169	2858	26W-12N	A1
600	SMBG	60169	2858	24W-12N	D2
1000	HFET	60194	2858	24W-12N	D2
2200	HFET	60169	2857	27W-12N	D1
2600	HFET	60010	2857	26W-12N	E1
2600	HFET	60169	2803	27W-12N	D7
2900	HFET	60010	2803	27W-12N	D7
7700	PKRG	60631	2918	9W-7N	B4
8300	CHCG	60068	2918	10W-7N	B4
8300	CHCG	60631	2918	10W-7N	B4
8300	PKRG	60068	2918	10W-7N	B4
8400	CHCG	60018	2917	10W-7N	E4
8400	CHCG	60068	2917	10W-7N	E4
8400	CHCG	60631	2917	10W-7N	E4
8400	PKRG	60631	2917	10W-7N	E4
9300	RSMT	60018	2917	12W-7N	C3
9300	RSMT	60068	2917	11W-7N	D4
9600	DSPN	60018	2917	12W-7N	C3
10200	CHCG	60666	2917	13W-8N	A2
10200	RSMT	60666	2917	12W-8N	A2
10700	CHCG	60666	2916	13W-8N	E2
10700	RSMT	60018	2916	13W-8N	E2
10700	RSMT	60666	2916	13W-8N	E2
SR-72 E Main St					
-	HFET	60118	2801	32W-15N	E4
10	EDND	60118	2801	32W-15N	E4
400	DndT	60118	2801	32W-15N	E4
SR-72 W Main St					
10	EDND	60118	2801	33W-16N	A2
10	WDND	60118	2801	33W-16N	A2
400	WDND	60118	2800	34W-16N	E2
900	SYHW	60118	2800	35W-16N	D2
SR-72 E Oak Knoll Dr					
10	HPSR	60140	2796	46W-15N	A3
10	HshT	60140	2796	46W-15N	A3
100	HPSR	60140	2795	48W-15N	B3
100	HshT	60140	2795	48W-15N	B3
SR-72 W Oak Knoll Dr					
100	HPSR	60140	2795	47W-15N	E3
100	HshT	60140	2795	47W-15N	C3
SR-72 Oakton St					
1500	EGVV	60007	2861	17W-9N	C6
1800	EGvT	60007	2861	16W-9N	D6
SR-72 N Oriole Av					
-	CHCG	60631	2918	9W-7N	C4
SR-72 Touhy Av					
2500	EGvT	60007	2915	16W-9N	E1
2500	EGvT	60018	2915	16W-9N	E1
2500	EGVV	60007	2915	16W-9N	E1
SR-72 E Touhy Av					
200	CHCG	60018	2916	14W-8N	C1
200	DSPN	60018	2916	15W-8N	B1
200	MaiT	60018	2916	14W-8N	C1
SR-72 W Touhy Av					
10	DSPN	60018	2916	14W-8N	B1
10	EGvT	60018	2916	15W-8N	B1
10	MaiT	60018	2916	14W-8N	C1
300	CHCG	60007	2916	15W-8N	A1
300	CHCG	60018	2916	15W-8N	A1
2800	EGvT	60007	2915	15W-8N	E1
2800	EGvT	60018	2915	15W-8N	E1
2800	EGVV	60007	2915	15W-8N	E1
2800	EGVV	60007	2916	15W-8N	A1
2800	EGVV	60018	2915	15W-8N	E1
2800	EGVV	60018	2916	15W-8N	A1
SR-83					
-	ANTH	60002	2416	23W-41N	E1
-	AntT	60002	2416	23W-41N	E1
-	BFGV	60047	2700	18W-21N	E6
-	BFGV	60089	2700	18W-21N	E6
-	BFGV	60089	2701	18W-21N	A6
-	FmtT	60060	2589	20W-28N	E6
-	FmtT	60060	2590	20W-28N	A6
-	LbvT	60060	2646	18W-26N	D4
-	LGGV	60060	2646	18W-25N	E4
-	LGGV	60061	2646	18W-25N	E5
-	LGGV	60089	2700	18W-21N	E6
-	LGGV	60089	2701	18W-21N	A6
-	LKVL	60002	2416	23W-40N	E4
-	LKVL	60046	2416	23W-40N	E4
-	MDLN	60047	2646	18W-25N	E4
-	MDLN	60060	2589	20W-28N	E6
-	MDLN	60060	2590	20W-28N	A6
-	RLKB	60073	2475	21W-35N	C6
-	VNHL	60047	2646	18W-24N	E6
-	VrnT	60060	2646	18W-26N	D4
700	FmtT	60060	2646	19W-26N	B2
700	MDLN	60060	2646	18W-25N	E4
4200	LGGV	60047	2700	18W-22N	E5
4200	VrnT	60047	2700	18W-22N	E5
6300	LGGV	60047	2646	18W-24N	E6
6300	VNHL	60061	2646	18W-24N	E6
34400	AvnT	60030	2533	20W-34N	A1
34400	GYLK	60030	2532	20W-34N	E1
34400	GYLK	60030	2533	20W-34N	A1
34600	AvnT	60030	2475	21W-34N	E7
34600	GYLK	60030	2475	21W-34N	E7
34800	GYLK	60046	2475	21W-35N	D7
34800	RLKB	60046	2475	21W-35N	D7
SR-83 111th St					
-	PlsT	60464	3272	14W-12S	D3
-	PlsT	60464	3273	13W-13S	A3
-	PlsT	60480	3273	13W-13S	A3
12200	LMNT	60439	3272	14W-13S	C3
12200	LmnT	60464	3272	15W-12S	B3
SR-83 119th St					
7400	PSHT	60463	3274	9W-14S	D5
7900	PSHT	60464	3274	9W-13S	C5
7900	PSPK	60464	3274	9W-13S	C5
SR-83 W 127th St					
4800	ALSP	60803	3276	5W-14S	A7
5100	ALSP	60803	3275	6W-14S	E7
5200	ALSP	60445	3275	6W-14S	E7
5200	CTWD	60445	3275	6W-14S	E7
SR-83 147th St					
3200	MDLN	60445	3348	4W-17S	E5
3200	POSN	60445	3348	4W-17S	E5
3200	POSN	60469	3348	4W-17S	E5
SR-83 W 147th St					
2300	DXMR	60426	3349	2W-17S	C5
2300	HRVY	60426	3349	2W-17S	C5
2300	POSN	60426	3349	3W-17S	C5
2300	POSN	60469	3349	3W-17S	A5
3100	MDLN	60445	3348	3W-17S	E5
3100	POSN	60445	3348	3W-17S	E5
3100	POSN	60469	3348	5W-17S	B5
SR-83 Antioch Rd					
10900	SlmT	53179	2357	23W-42N	E5
12700	ANTH	53179	2357	23W-42N	E5

STREET Block	City	ZIP	Map#	CGS	Grid
SR-83 Antioch Rd					
12700	ANTH	60002	2357	23W-42N	E5
SR-83 S Archer Av					
10800	LMNT	60439	3272	16W-12S	A3
SR-83 Barron Blvd					
-	AvnT	60030	2533	20W-32N	A5
-	AvnT	60048	2533	20W-32N	A5
-	GYLK	60048	2533	20W-32N	A5
10	GYLK	60030	2533	20W-34N	A1
SR-83 N Barron Blvd					
34200	AvnT	60030	2533	20W-34N	A1
34200	GYLK	60030	2533	20W-34N	A1
SR-83 Busse Rd					
200	EGVV	60007	2861	17W-9N	C7
600	EGvT	60007	2861	17W-9N	C7
900	EGVV	60007	2915	17W-8N	C1
1000	BNVL	60106	2915	16W-7N	C4
SR-83 W Cal Sag Rd					
-	PlsT	60480	3273	12W-13S	B3
-	PSHT	60463	3275	7W-14S	B5
5400	ALSP	60445	3275	6W-14S	E7
5400	ALSP	60803	3275	8W-14S	A5
5400	CTWD	60445	3275	6W-14S	E7
5500	ALSP	60463	3275	8W-14S	A5
5500	WthT	60463	3275	6W-14S	D6
5500	WthT	60803	3275	8W-14S	A5
8000	PSHT	60463	3274	10W-13S	C5
8000	PSHT	60464	3274	10W-13S	C5
8000	PSPK	60464	3274	10W-13S	C5
8500	PlsT	60464	3274	11W-13S	A4
8600	PlsT	60464	3273	11W-13S	E4
SR-83 Cicero Av					
-	ALSP	60803	3348	5W-15S	A1
-	CTWD	60803	3348	5W-15S	A1
13100	CTWD	60445	3348	5W-15S	A1
13900	BmnT	60445	3348	5W-16S	A3
14300	MDLN	60445	3348	5W-17S	A4
SR-83 S Cicero Av					
-	CTWD	60445	3348	5W-15S	A1
-	CTWD	60803	3348	5W-15S	A1
12700	ALSP	60803	3276	6W-15S	A7
13100	ALSP	60803	3348	5W-15S	A1
SR-83 W College Dr					
6300	PSHT	60463	3275	8W-14S	B5
6300	WthT	60463	3275	8W-14S	B5
7400	PSHT	60463	3274	9W-13S	E5
7900	PSHT	60464	3274	9W-13S	C5
7900	PSPK	60464	3274	9W-13S	C5
SR-83 Elmhurst Rd					
600	MPPT	60016	2861	15W-11N	E3
900	DSPN	60016	2861	15W-10N	E4
900	MPPT	60056	2861	15W-10N	E4
SR-83 N Elmhurst Rd					
10	MPPT	60056	2808	15W-15N	A3
10	MPPT	60070	2808	15W-15N	A3
10	PTHT	60070	2808	15W-13N	A7
10	WLNG	60090	2755	15W-18N	A4
900	PTHT	60070	2755	15W-16N	A7
1000	PTHT	60090	2755	15W-16N	A7
1100	PTHT	60056	2808	15W-14N	A4
SR-83 S Elmhurst Rd					
10	MPPT	60056	2808	15W-14N	A3
10	MPPT	60070	2808	15W-14N	A3
10	PTHT	60056	2808	15W-14N	A3
10	PTHT	60070	2808	15W-14N	A3
10	WLNG	60090	2755	15W-18N	A4
400	MPPT	60056	2861	16W-9N	E6
800	MPPT	60016	2861	15W-10N	E4
900	DSPN	60016	2861	15W-11N	E3
900	PTHT	60090	2755	15W-17N	A6
1400	DSPN	60018	2861	15W-10N	E6
1400	MPPT	60018	2861	15W-10N	E6
SR-83 Glenwood Dyer Rd					
2400	BlmT	60411	3510	4E-25S	B6
2400	LYWD	60411	3509	3E-24S	E5
2400	LYWD	60411	3510	4E-25S	B6
SR-83 Ivanhoe Rd					
-	AvnT	60030	2533	20W-32N	A5
-	AvnT	60048	2533	20W-32N	A5
-	FmtT	60030	2533	20W-31N	A6
-	FmtT	60030	2590	20W-31N	A1
-	FmtT	60048	2533	20W-31N	A7
-	FmtT	60048	2590	20W-31N	A1
-	FmtT	60060	2589	20W-28N	E5
-	FmtT	60060	2590	20W-29N	A3
-	GYLK	60030	2533	20W-32N	A5
-	GYLK	60030	2590	20W-30N	B1
-	GYLK	60048	2533	20W-32N	A5
-	GYLK	60048	2590	20W-30N	B1
-	MDLN	60060	2589	20W-28N	E5
-	MDLN	60060	2590	20W-29N	A3
-	RLKP	60030	2590	20W-30N	A2
SR-83 Kingery Expwy					
600	HNDL	60521	3085	16W-4S	D6
600	HNDL	60559	3085	16W-4S	D6
600	OKBK	60523	3085	16W-4S	D6
600	OKBK	60559	3085	16W-4S	D6
600	WTMT	60559	3085	16W-4S	D6
900	WTMT	60523	3085	16W-3S	D6
SR-83 Kingery Hwy					
-	AddT	60101	2971	17W-3N	C5
-	AddT	60106	2971	17W-4N	C4
-	AddT	60191	2971	17W-4N	C2
-	ADSN	60101	2971	17W-3N	C4
-	ADSN	60106	2971	17W-3N	C4
-	ADSN	60126	2971	17W-2N	C7
-	BNVL	60007	2915	16W-7N	C4
-	BNVL	60106	2971	17W-2N	C7
-	BNVL	60191	2971	16W-5N	C1
-	CNHL	60514	3085	16W-4S	E7
-	CNHL	60514	3145	16W-4S	E1
-	CNHL	60521	3085	16W-4S	E7
-	CNHL	60521	3145	16W-7S	E6
-	CNHL	60527	3145	16W-6S	E4
-	DGvT	60439	3271	16W-11S	E1
-	DGvT	60514	3145	16W-6S	E4
-	DGvT	60521	3145	16W-6S	E4
-	DGvT	60527	3271	16W-12S	E1
-	EGVV	60007	2915	17W-6N	C6
-	EMHT	60101	2971	17W-3N	C6
-	EMHT	60126	2971	17W-2N	C7
-	EMHT	60126	3027	17W-0N	C4
-	EMHT	60181	3027	17W-0S	C7
-	HNDL	60521	3085	16W-3S	D6
-	HNDL	60521	3145	16W-7S	E6
-	HNDL	60559	3085	16W-3S	D6
-	LmnT	60439	3271	16W-11S	E1
-	LmnT	60439	3272	16W-12S	A2
-	OKBK	60181	3085	16W-1S	D2
-	OKBK	60521	3085	16W-3S	D6
-	OKBK	60523	3085	16W-3S	D6
-	OKBK	60559	3085	16W-3S	D6
-	OKTR	60126	3027	17W-0S	C7
-	OKTR	60181	3027	17W-0S	C7
-	OKTR	60181	3085	16W-3S	D6
-	OKTR	60523	3085	16W-3S	D6

STREET Block	City	ZIP	Map#	CGS	Grid
SR-83 Kingery Hwy					
-	VLPK	60126	2971	17W-2N	C7
-	VLPK	60126	3027	17W-0N	C3
-	VLPK	60181	3027	17W-0N	C3
-	WDDL	60106	2971	17W-2N	C7
-	WDDL	60191	2971	17W-5N	C1
-	WTMT	60514	3085	16W-4S	E7
-	WTMT	60521	3085	16W-4S	E7
-	WTMT	60523	3085	16W-3S	D6
-	WTMT	60559	3085	16W-4S	D7
300	DGvT	60527	3207	16W-11S	E7
400	BNVL	60106	2915	17W-6N	C6
400	BRRG	60527	3207	16W-9S	E4
6300	DGvT	60527	3145	16W-6S	E5
6300	WLBK	60527	3145	16W-7S	E5
6600	DRN	60527	3145	16W-7S	E6
6600	WLBK	60561	3145	16W-7S	E6
6700	DRN	60561	3145	16W-7S	E6
7100	WLBK	60527	3207	16W-10S	E6
7200	DRN	60527	3207	16W-8S	E1
7200	DRN	60561	3207	16W-8S	E1
SR-83 S Kingery Hwy					
7600	WLBK	60527	3207	16W-8S	E2
SR-83 W Lincoln St					
-	MPPT	60056	2861	15W-12N	E1
-	MPPT	60056	2862	15W-12N	A1
SR-83 Main St					
200	ANTH	53179	2357	23W-43N	E4
200	ANTH	60002	2357	23W-43N	E4
200	SlmT	53179	2357	23W-43N	E4
1200	ANTH	60002	2416	23W-41N	E1
1200	AntT	60002	2357	23W-41N	E7
1200	AntT	60002	2416	23W-41N	E1
SR-83 N Main St					
10	MPPT	60056	2808	15W-13N	A7
SR-83 S Main St					
10	MPPT	60056	2808	15W-12N	A7
200	MPPT	60056	2862	15W-12N	A1
SR-83 McHenry Rd					
10	BFGV	60089	2754	16W-18N	D2
400	WLNG	60090	2755	15W-16N	A7
500	WLNG	60090	2754	15W-18N	E3
600	BFGV	60089	2701	17W-20N	B7
900	WLNG	60089	2754	16W-18N	D2
SR-83 Mid America Plz					
10	OKTR	60181	3085	16W-1S	D2
SR-83 Milwaukee Av					
-	AntT	60002	2416	23W-39N	E4
-	LKVL	60002	2416	23W-39N	E4
-	LKVL	60046	2416	23W-39N	E4
-	LKVL	60046	2417	22W-38N	A7
-	LKVL	60046	2475	21W-35N	D7
-	LkvT	60046	2416	23W-39N	E4
-	LkvT	60046	2417	22W-38N	A7
-	LkvT	60046	2475	21W-35N	D7
-	LkvT	60073	2475	22W-36N	C3
-	RLKB	60046	2475	21W-35N	C6
-	RLKB	60073	2475	22W-36N	C3
SR-83 N Milwaukee Av					
-	LKVL	60046	2475	22W-38N	B1
100	LKVL	60046	2417	22W-38N	B7
800	LkvT	60046	2417	23W-39N	A6
SR-83 S Milwaukee Av					
10	LKVL	60046	2475	22W-37N	B1
SR-83 Oakton St					
1800	EGvT	60007	2861	16W-9N	D6
1800	EGVV	60007	2861	16W-9N	C6
1900	EGvT	60005	2861	16W-9N	D6
1900	EGVV	60005	2861	16W-9N	D6
SR-83 E Oakton St					
2200	EGvT	60005	2861	16W-9N	D6
2200	EGvT	60007	2861	16W-9N	D6
2200	EGVV	60005	2861	16W-9N	D6
2200	EGVV	60007	2861	16W-9N	D6
2300	MPPT	60005	2861	16W-9N	D6
2500	MPPT	60056	2861	16W-9N	E6
2600	DSPN	60018	2861	16W-9N	E6
2600	MPPT	60018	2861	16W-9N	E6
SR-83 W Oakton St					
900	DSPN	60018	2861	16W-9N	E6
900	EGvT	60005	2861	16W-9N	E6
900	MPPT	60005	2861	16W-9N	E6
900	MPPT	60018	2861	16W-9N	E6
900	MPPT	60056	2861	16W-9N	E6
SR-83 Sibley Blvd					
-	DLTN	60409	3351	1E-17S	C5
-	DLTN	60419	3351	1E-17S	C5
1400	CTCY	60409	3351	2E-18S	E7
SR-83 E Sibley Blvd					
10	HRVY	60426	3349	1W-17S	E5
10	SHLD	60419	3350	0E-17S	D5
10	SHLD	60473	3350	0E-17S	D5
100	DLTN	60473	3350	0E-17S	D5
100	HRVY	60426	3350	1W-17S	A5
400	DLTN	60419	3350	0W-17S	B5
400	HRVY	60419	3350	0W-17S	B5
500	SHLD	60426	3350	0W-17S	C5
700	DLTN	60419	3351	0E-17S	A5
700	DLTN	60473	3351	1E-17S	A5
800	SHLD	60419	3351	1E-17S	A5
800	SHLD	60473	3351	1E-17S	A5
1400	DLTN	60409	3351	1E-17S	B5
SR-83 W Sibley Blvd					
10	DLTN	60419	3350	0E-17S	E5
10	HRVY	60426	3349	2W-17S	E5
10	SHLD	60419	3350	0E-17S	E5
10	SHLD	60473	3350	0E-17S	E5
100	DXMR	60426	3349	2W-17S	D5
200	HRVY	60426	3350	0W-17S	C5
200	SHLD	60426	3350	0W-17S	C5
2200	POSN	60426	3349	2W-17S	C5
2200	POSN	60469	3349	2W-17S	C5
SR-83 Torrence Av					
400	CTCY	60409	3351	3E-17S	E5
900	CTCY	60409	3429	2E-21S	E7
1400	CTCY	60438	3429	3E-19S	E3
1400	LNSG	60409	3429	3E-19S	E2
1400	LNSG	60438	3429	3E-19S	E3
18500	BlmT	60411	3429	3E-21S	E7
18500	LNSG	60411	3429	3E-21S	E7
19000	BlmT	60411	3509	2E-23S	E3
19000	LNSG	60411	3509	3E-22S	E1
19000	LNSG	60438	3509	3E-22S	E1
19300	LYWD	60411	3509	2E-23S	E3
SR-102 S Water St					
100	WMTN	60481	3853	27W-38S	D7
800	WMTN	60481	3943	27W-39S	E2
1200	WslT	60481	3943	27W-40S	E2
SR-113					
-	BDWD	60408	3942	30W-41S	C6
-	CstT	60481	3942	29W-41S	D6
-	RedT	60408	3942	30W-41S	D6
-	RedT	60481	3942	30W-41S	D6
22100	CstT	60481	3943	27W-42S	D7
SR-113 W Coal City Rd					
-	DMND	60408	3941	32W-39S	E2
SR-113 W Coal City Rd					
-	DMND	60416	3941	32W-39S	E2
-	DMND	60481	3941	32W-39S	E2
500	BDWD	60408	3941	31W-39S	E2
500	BDWD	60481	3941	31W-39S	E2
500	RedT	60408	3941	31W-39S	E2
500	WmTp	60481	3941	31W-39S	E2
SR-113 E Division St					
800	BvlT	60416	3941	34W-39S	A2
800	CLCY	60416	3941	34W-39S	A2
900	DMND	60416	3941	34W-39S	A2
2900	DMND	60408	3941	32W-39S	D2
2900	DMND	60481	3941	32W-39S	D2
SR-113 N Division St					
100	BDWD	60408	3942	32W-41S	E5
500	RedT	60408	3941	32W-41S	E5
1100	BDWD	60481	3941	31W-40S	E2
1100	WmTp	60481	3941	31W-40S	E2
SR-113 Main St					
22500	CstT	60481	3942	29W-41S	E6
22500	CstT	60481	3943	28W-41S	B6
23600	RedT	60408	3942	29W-41S	D6
23600	RedT	60481	3942	29W-41S	D6
SR-113 E Main St					
100	BDWD	60408	3942	30W-42S	C6
400	RedT	60408	3942	31W-41S	B6
SR-113 W Main St					
100	BDWD	60408	3942	31W-41S	A5
400	BDWD	60408	3941	31W-41S	E5
SR-120					
-	LKMR	60051	2529	30W-32N	A4
-	MchT	60050	2527	35W-33N	A2
-	MchT	60051	2528	32W-33N	C3
-	MchT	60051	2529	30W-32N	A4
-	MchT	60097	2527	35W-33N	A2
-	MHRY	60050	2526	35W-33N	E2
-	MHRY	60050	2527	35W-33N	B2
-	MHRY	60051	2528	32W-33N	C3
-	MHRY	60097	2526	35W-33N	E2
-	MHRY	60097	2527	35W-33N	A2
100	HbnT	53147	2350		D4
100	HbnT	60034	2350		D4
100	LinT	53147	2350		D2
1200	GwdT	60098	2525	40W-32N	A5
1200	WDSK	60098	2525	40W-32N	A5
7800	BLVY	60097	2526	35W-33N	E2
7800	BLVY	60098	2526	35W-33N	E2
7800	GwdT	60098	2526	35W-33N	E2
7800	MchT	60050	2526	36W-33N	D2
7800	MchT	60097	2526	36W-33N	D2
7800	MchT	60098	2526	36W-33N	D2
7800	WRLK	60098	2526	37W-33N	B2
8700	BLVY	60098	2525	38W-33N	E2
SR-120 Belvidere Rd					
-	AvnT	60030	2531	24W-32N	C5
-	AvnT	60073	2531	24W-32N	C5
-	GRNE	60031	2535	14W-33N	D3
-	GrtT	60030	2531	24W-32N	B5
-	GrtT	60073	2530	26W-31N	E6
-	GrtT	60073	2531	24W-32N	B5
-	LKMR	60041	2530	27W-31N	A6
-	LKMR	60051	2529	28W-31N	D6
-	LKMR	60051	2530	28W-31N	A6
-	LKMR	60073	2530	27W-31N	B6
-	PKCY	60085	2535	13W-33N	D3
-	RDLK	60073	2531	24W-32N	C5
-	VOLO	60051	2530	27W-31N	A6
-	VOLO	60051	2530	26W-31N	E6
-	VOLO	60073	2531	25W-32N	A6
-	WcnT	60051	2529	28W-31N	E6
-	WcnT	60051	2530	28W-31N	A6
-	WcnT	60073	2530	27W-31N	A6
-	WKGN	60031	2535	14W-33N	D3
2900	PKCY	60085	2536	13W-33N	A3
2900	WKGN	60085	2536	13W-33N	A3
3800	WKGN	60085	2535	13W-33N	D3
SR-120 E Belvidere Rd					
-	GYLK	60030	2532	21W-33N	C4
10	HNVL	60030	2532	22W-33N	C3
400	GYLK	60030	2533	20W-32N	A5
700	AvnT	60030	2533	20W-32N	A5
SR-120 W Belvidere Rd					
-	GRNE	60031	2534	15W-33N	E4
-	GRNE	60048	2534	16W-33N	D4
-	WrnT	60030	2534	17W-32N	B4
-	WrnT	60031	2534	15W-33N	E4
-	WrnT	60048	2534	18W-32N	A4
-	WrnT	60048	2535	15W-33N	B4
10	GYLK	60030	2532	21W-32N	E4
10	HNVL	60030	2532	22W-33N	A4
10	HNVL	60073	2532	22W-33N	A4
100	RDLK	60073	2532	23W-32N	A4
100	RLKP	60030	2532	23W-32N	A4
100	RLKP	60073	2532	23W-32N	A4
300	AvnT	60030	2532	21W-32N	D4
700	AvnT	60030	2531	23W-32N	D4
700	AvnT	60073	2531	24W-32N	D4
700	RDLK	60073	2531	23W-32N	D4
1800	AvnT	60030	2533	18W-32N	D4
1800	GYLK	60030	2533	19W-32N	C4
2000	WrnT	60030	2533	19W-32N	C4
4200	GRNE	60031	2535	14W-33N	D3
4200	WKGN	60031	2535	14W-33N	D3
4200	WKGN	60085	2535	14W-33N	D3
4400	WrnT	60031	2535	14W-33N	C3
18000	GYLK	60030	2534	18W-32N	A4
SR-120 Belvidere St					
100	WKGN	60085	2537	10W-33N	B2
2600	WKGN	60085	2536	12W-33N	C3
SR-120 E Church St					
100	WDSK	60098	2524	41W-31N	D7
SR-120 W Church St					
10	WDSK	60098	2524	41W-31N	D7
SR-120 Elm St					
-	MchT	60050	2527	34W-33N	B2
-	MHRY	60050	2527	34W-33N	B2
SR-120 W Elm St					
3300	MchT	60051	2528	32W-33N	C3
3300	MHRY	60050	2528	30W-32N	E4
3300	MHRY	60051	2528	32W-33N	C3
4300	MHRY	60050	2527	35W-33N	B2
5200	MchT	60050	2527	34W-33N	C2
SR-120 N Madison St					
300	WDSK	60098	2524	41W-31N	D7
SR-120 McHenry Av					
200	WDSK	60098	2524	41W-31N	D7
SR-120 W Rand Rd					
100	LKMR	60051	2529	30W-32N	A4
100	WcnT	60051	2529	29W-31N	D6
500	MchT	60051	2529	30W-32N	A4
SR-120 Washington St					
10	WDSK	60098	2524	42W-31N	C6
800	DrrT	60098	2524	42W-31N	C6
800	GwdT	60098	2524	42W-31N	C6
13900	HtdT	60098	2524	42W-32N	A5
SR-126					
-	PnfT	60543	3337	33W-18S	B7
-	PnfT	60544	3337	33W-18S	B7
700	NasT	60543	3337	32W-18S	C7
700	NasT	60544	3337	32W-18S	C7
5000	KdlT	60560	3334	41W-17S	A5
8000	YKVL	60560	3334	41W-17S	A5
8700	KdlT	60560	3333	41W-16S	E5
8700	YKVL	60560	3333	41W-16S	E5
SR-126 W Lockport St					
700	PNFD	60544	3338	30W-18S	A7
1000	PnfT	60544	3338	30W-18S	A7
1700	PNFD	60544	3337	31W-17S	E7
1700	PnfT	60544	3337	31W-17S	E7
24000	NasT	60543	3337	32W-17S	B7
24000	NasT	60544	3337	32W-17S	B7
24000	PnfT	60543	3337	32W-17S	B7
SR-126 W Main St					
10	PNFD	60544	3338	29W-17S	D6
10	PnfT	60544	3338	29W-17S	D6
400	PNFD	60544	3339	28W-16S	A4
400	PnfT	60544	3339	28W-16S	A4
SR-126 School House Rd					
100	YKVL	60560	3333	41W-16S	E5
SR-129					
-	BCVL	60407	4030	33W-43S	B3
-	BDWD	60407	3941	32W-42S	E7
-	BDWD	60407	4030	32W-43S	C2
-	BDWD	60408	3941	32W-42S	E7
-	GDLY	60407	4030	32W-43S	C2
-	RedT	60407	3941	32W-42S	E7
-	RedT	60407	4030	32W-43S	C2
-	RedT	60408	3941	32W-42S	E7
-	RedT	60408	3942	30W-39S	D1
-	RedT	60481	3942	30W-39S	D1
-	WMTN	60481	3942	30W-39S	D1
-	WmTp	60408	3942	30W-39S	D1
-	WmTp	60481	3942	30W-39S	D1
SR-129 N Washington St					
100	BDWD	60408	3942	30W-41S	C4
100	RedT	60481	3942	30W-41S	C4
200	RedT	60408	3942	30W-40S	D3
200	WMTN	60481	3942	29W-40S	D2
200	WmTp	60408	3942	29W-40S	D2
200	WmTp	60481	3942	29W-40S	D2
SR-129 S Washington St					
100	BDWD	60408	3942	31W-41S	A6
300	RedT	60408	3942	31W-42S	A7
400	BDWD	60407	3941	31W-42S	E7
400	BDWD	60408	3941	31W-42S	E7
400	RedT	60407	3941	31W-42S	E7
400	RedT	60408	3941	31W-42S	E7
SR-131 Green Bay Rd					
600	LKBF	60044	2593	11W-28N	D5
1000	NCHI	60044	2593	11W-29N	D4
1000	NCHI	60064	2536	12W-32N	B5
1000	NCHI	60088	2593	11W-30N	C1
1000	ShdT	60044	2593	11W-29N	D4
1000	ShdT	60088	2593	11W-29N	D4
1000	WKGN	60064	2536	12W-32N	B4
1000	WKGN	60085	2536	12W-32N	B4
2400	NCHI	60064	2593	11W-30N	C1
SR-131 N Green Bay Rd					
10	WKGN	60085	2536	12W-33N	B1
400	WKGN	60085	2479	12W-33N	B7
700	WkgT	60085	2479	12W-35N	B7
1400	WkgT	60031	2479	12W-35N	A6
2100	WKGN	60087	2479	12W-36N	A4
2100	WkgT	60087	2479	12W-36N	A4
36900	BHPK	60087	2479	12W-36N	A4
38300	BHPK	60087	2421	12W-38N	B7
38300	WKGN	60087	2421	12W-38N	B7
39000	BHPK	60083	2421	12W-39N	B6
39000	BHPK	60099	2421	12W-39N	B4
40800	BtnT	60099	2421	12W-40N	B2
40800	WDWH	60099	2421	12W-40N	B2
41000	ZION	60099	2421	12W-41N	B2
41700	ZION	60099	2362	12W-41N	A7
42000	BtnT	60099	2362	13W-42N	A7
42500	NptT	60099	2362	12W-41N	A7
43400	NptT	53158	2362	13W-43N	A4
43400	PTPR	53158	2362	13W-43N	A4
SR-131 S Green Bay Rd					
10	WKGN	60085	2536	12W-33N	B3
900	NCHI	60064	2536	12W-33N	B4
900	WKGN	60064	2536	12W-33N	B4
SR-132 Grand Av					
-	WKGN	60085	2537	10W-34N	B1
3300	GRNE	60031	2479	13W-34N	A7
3300	WKGN	60031	2479	12W-35N	A7
3300	WKGN	60085	2479	12W-35N	A7
3700	GRNE	60031	2478	14W-34N	D7
5300	WrnT	60031	2478	15W-35N	A6
5800	WrnT	60031	2477	18W-35N	A5
6000	GRNE	60031	2477	18W-35N	A5
7600	GRNE	60031	2476	18W-36N	E5
7600	WrnT	60031	2476	18W-36N	E5
SR-132 E Grand Av					
10	LKVL	60046	2475	22W-38N	A1
1000	LkvT	60046	2475	21W-38N	D1
1700	LNHT	60046	2475	20W-37N	E1
1700	LNHT	60046	2476	20W-37N	A2
2000	LkvT	60046	2476	20W-37N	A2
SR-132 W Grand Av					
10	LKVL	60046	2475	21W-37N	E1
200	LKVL	60046	2474	24W-37N	D1
400	LkvT	60046	2474	23W-38N	E1
18400	GRNE	60031	2476	18W-36N	E5
18400	WrnT	60031	2476	18W-36N	E5
18700	WrnT	60046	2476	18W-36N	E5
18900	LkvT	60046	2476	18W-36N	D5
19400	LNHT	60046	2476	19W-36N	C3
20800	LkvT	60046	2475	20W-37N	E1
20800	LNHT	60046	2475	20W-37N	E1
SR-134					
-	AvnT	60073	2531	24W-34N	B1
-	GrtT	60041	2474	25W-34N	B7
-	GrtT	60073	2531	25W-34N	B1
-	RDLK	60073	2474	25W-34N	B7
-	RDLK	60073	2531	24W-34N	B1
SR-134 W Big Hollow Rd					
-	GrtT	60041	2474	25W-34N	A7
-	RDLK	60073	2474	25W-34N	B7
27200	FXLK	60041	2473	27W-34N	C7
27200	GrtT	60041	2473	26W-34N	D7
SR-134 E Main St					
10	RLKP	60073	2532	22W-33N	A3
100	HNVL	60073	2532	22W-33N	A3
300	HNVL	60030	2532	22W-33N	B3
SR-134 W Main St					
10	RLKP	60073	2532	22W-33N	B3
100	RDLK	60073	2532	22W-33N	B3
SR-134 Nippersink Av					
200	RDLK	60073	2531	23W-33N	E3
SR-134 Railroad Av					
300	RDLK	60073	2531	23W-33N	E2
SR-134 Railroad Av					
500	AvnT	60073	2531	23W-34N	D2
SR-134 Round Lake Rd					
-	AvnT	60073	2531	24W-34N	D1
-	RDLK	60073	2531	24W-34N	C1
SR-137 Amstutz Expwy					
-	NCHI	60044	2593	11W-30N	E2
-	NCHI	60064	2536	10W-31N	E7
-	NCHI	60064	2537	10W-31N	A7
-	NCHI	60064	2593	10W-31N	E1
-	NCHI	60088	2593	11W-30N	E1
-	WKGN	60085	2480	10W-35N	B6
-	WKGN	60085	2537	10W-34N	B1
-	WKGN	60087	2480	10W-35N	B6
SR-137 S Amstutz Expwy					
-	WKGN	60085	2537	10W-33N	B3
SR-137 Buckley Rd					
-	AvnT	60030	2533	20W-32N	B6
-	AvnT	60048	2533	20W-32N	B6
-	FmtT	60048	2533	19W-31N	B6
-	FmtT	60048	2590	18W-30N	E2
-	GNOK	60044	2590	15W-30N	B2
-	GYLK	60030	2533	20W-32N	B6
-	GYLK	60048	2533	20W-32N	B6
-	LbvT	60044	2592	13W-30N	E1
-	LbvT	60044	2593	13W-30N	A1
-	LbvT	60048	2590	19W-31N	D1
-	LbvT	60064	2592	13W-30N	E1
-	LYVL	60048	2590	19W-31N	D1
-	NCHI	60044	2592	13W-30N	E1
-	ShdT	60088	2593	12W-30N	A2
10	LbvT	60048	2591	16W-30N	D2
10	LYVL	60048	2591	16W-30N	D2
1500	NCHI	60088	2593	12W-30N	A2
2000	NCHI	60064	2593	12W-30N	A2
2100	GNOK	60048	2592	15W-30N	B2
3400	ShdT	60044	2593	12W-30N	A2
3400	ShdT	60064	2593	12W-30N	A2
3500	NCHI	60044	2593	12W-30N	A2
SR-137 W Buckley Rd					
1100	LbvT	60048	2592	15W-30N	A2
14400	GNOK	60048	2592	14W-30N	C1
15700	LbvT	60048	2591	15W-30N	E2
SR-137 S Genesee St					
500	WKGN	60085	2537	10W-33N	B3
900	NCHI	60064	2537	10W-33N	B4
SR-137 E Greenwood Av					
10	WKGN	60085	2480	10W-36N	B5
10	WKGN	60087	2480	10W-36N	B5
SR-137 Peterson Rd					
300	LbvT	60048	2591	16W-30N	E2
300	LYVL	60048	2591	16W-30N	E2
SR-137 W Peterson Rd					
-	LbvT	60048	2591	18W-30N	A2
-	LYVL	60048	2591	18W-30N	A2
SR-137 Sheridan Rd					
-	WKGN	60085	2537	10W-32N	A4
100	PTPR	53158	2363	9W-43N	C4
100	WPHR	53158	2363	9W-43N	C4
100	WPHR	60096	2363	9W-42N	B6
1000	NCHI	60064	2537	10W-32N	A5
1400	BtnT	60096	2422	9W-41N	B1
1400	BtnT	60099	2422	9W-41N	B1
1400	WPHR	60096	2422	9W-41N	B1
1700	ZION	60099	2422	10W-39N	B4
3400	BHPK	60099	2422	10W-39N	B6
SR-137 N Sheridan Rd					
1800	WKGN	60085	2480	10W-36N	B5
1800	WKGN	60087	2480	10W-36N	B5
2500	BHPK	60087	2480	10W-36N	B3
2500	WkgT	60087	2480	10W-36N	B3
37800	BHPK	60099	2480	9W-37N	B1
38200	BHPK	60087	2422	9W-38N	B7
38400	BHPK	60099	2422	10W-38N	B7
SR-142 W Russell Rd					
-	NptT	60099	2360	16W-43N	D5
-	WDWH	60099	2360	16W-43N	D5
SR-158 N Lynsee Ct					
4600	BHPK	60099	2421	13W-39N	A5
SR-158 N Queensbury Ln					
4400	BHPK	60099	2421	13W-39N	A5
SR-171					
-	LYNS	60534	3088	10W-4S	A7
-	LYNS	60534	3148	10W-4S	A1
-	MCCK	60525	3148	10W-5S	A2
-	MCCK	60534	3148	10W-4S	A1
-	SMMT	60501	3148	9W-5S	C3
-	SMMT	60525	3148	10W-5S	B2
SR-171 1st Av					
-	FTPK	60130	3030	10W-1S	A7
-	FTPK	60153	3030	10W-1S	A7
-	MYWD	60130	3088	10W-3S	B5
-	MYWD	60153	3088	10W-3S	B5
-	NRIV	60141	3088	10W-1S	A2
-	NRIV	60546	3088	10W-1S	A2
-	PvsT	60130	3088	10W-3S	B5
-	PvsT	60141	3088	10W-3S	B5
-	PvsT	60153	3030	10W-1S	A7
-	PvsT	60153	3088	10W-3S	B5
1900	MLPK	60160	3030	10W-1N	A1
1900	MLPK	60171	3030	10W-1N	A1
1900	PvsT	60160	3030	10W-1N	A1
1900	RVGV	60160	3030	10W-2N	A1
1900	RVGV	60171	3030	10W-2N	A1
2100	MYWD	60130	3030	10W-1S	A7
2100	MYWD	60153	3030	10W-1S	A7
2100	PvsT	60130	3030	10W-1S	A7
3900	BKFD	60513	3088	10W-4S	B6
3900	LYNS	60534	3088	10W-4S	A6
3900	RVSD	60513	3088	10W-4S	B6
3900	RVSD	60546	3088	10W-4S	B6
SR-171 N 1st Av					
10	MYWD	60153	3030	10W-0N	A4
700	MLPK	60153	3030	10W-1N	A2
700	MLPK	60160	3030	10W-1N	A1
700	RVFT	60305	3030	10W-1N	A3
1600	MLPK	60160	2974	10W-2N	A7
1600	MLPK	60171	3030	10W-2N	A1
1600	PvsT	60160	3030	10W-1N	A1
1600	RVGV	60160	2974	10W-2N	A7
1600	RVGV	60160	3030	10W-2N	A1
1600	RVGV	60171	2974	10W-2N	A7
1600	RVGV	60171	3030	10W-2N	A1
SR-171 S 1st Av					
-	BKFD	60513	3088	10W-2S	A3
-	LYNS	60534	3088	10W-3S	B6
-	PvsT	60130	3030	10W-0S	A7
-	PvsT	60153	3030	10W-0S	A7
-	RVSD	60513	3088	10W-3S	B6
-	RVSD	60546	3088	10W-2S	B4
100	MYWD	60153	3030	10W-0N	A4
100	RVFT	60305	3030	10W-0N	A4
1700	FTPK	60130	3030	10W-0S	A6
1700	FTPK	60153	3030	10W-0S	A6
1700	MYWD	60130	3030	10W-0S	A6
2200	NRIV	60141	3088	10W-2S	A2
SR-171 S 1st Av					
2200	NRIV	60546	3088	10W-2S	A2
2200	PvsT	60141	3088	10W-1S	A2
2500	BKFD	60546	3088	10W-2S	A3
SR-171 Archer Av					
-	JSTC	60458	3209	11W-9S	E2
-	JSTC	60480	3209	11W-9S	E2
-	LmnT	60439	3272	15W-11S	B1
-	LmnT	60480	3208	15W-11S	C7
-	LmnT	60480	3272	15W-11S	B1
-	PlsT	60480	3208	14W-11S	D6
8000	WLSP	60480	3209	11W-9S	D3
9000	PlsT	60480	3209	13W-10S	A5
13900	HmrT	60441	3342	20W-17S	A5
13900	HmrT	60491	3342	20W-17S	A5
14400	LktT	60441	3342	20W-17S	A5
14500	LKPT	60441	3342	21W-17S	A5
14700	LKPT	60441	3341	21W-17S	E6
14700	LktT	60441	3341	21W-17S	E6
SR-171 S Archer Av					
-	JSTC	60458	3209	11W-9S	D3
-	JSTC	60458	3210	11W-8S	A2
-	JSTC	60480	3209	11W-9S	E2
-	WLSP	60480	3209	11W-9S	E2
10800	LMNT	60439	3272	16W-13S	A4
11300	LMNT	60439	3271	17W-14S	B7
12700	LMNT	60439	3343	18W-15S	A1
12900	LMNT	60439	3342	18W-15S	E1
13400	HMGN	60439	3342	19W-15S	D2
13400	HMGN	60491	3342	19W-15S	D2
13500	HMGN	60441	3342	19W-16S	D3
13500	HmrT	60441	3342	19W-16S	D3
13500	HmrT	60491	3342	19W-16S	D3
SR-171 S Archer Rd					
5500	SMMT	60501	3148	9W-6S	C5
6300	BDPK	60501	3148	9W-7S	C5
6600	BDPK	60455	3148	9W-7S	C6
6700	BGVW	60455	3148	9W-7S	C6
6700	BGVW	60501	3148	9W-7S	C6
6800	BDPK	60458	3148	9W-7S	C6
6800	BGVW	60458	3148	9W-7S	C6
7000	JSTC	60458	3148	10W-7S	B7
7000	JSTC	60501	3148	10W-7S	B7
7300	JSTC	60458	3210	10W-8S	A1
SR-171 Collins St					
1000	JLET	60432	3499	23W-22S	A2
1400	JLET	60441	3499	23W-21S	A1
1400	JltT	60432	3499	23W-22S	A1
1400	LktT	60432	3499	23W-21S	A1
1400	LktT	60441	3499	23W-21S	A1
SR-171 N Collins St					
400	JLET	60432	3499	23W-23S	A4
SR-171 N Cumberland Av					
-	CHCG	60068	2918	10W-6N	A5
-	PKRG	60068	2918	10W-6N	A5
3200	RVGV	60171	2974	10W-4N	A4
3200	RVGV	60634	2974	10W-4N	A4
3700	CHCG	60634	2974	10W-2N	A6
4200	CHCG	60656	2974	10W-2N	A6
4200	CHCG	60706	2974	10W-2N	A6
4200	NRDG	60706	2974	10W-2N	A6
4600	CHCG	60656	2918	10W-5N	A7
4600	CHCG	60706	2918	10W-5N	A7
4600	NRDG	60656	2918	10W-5N	A7
4600	NRDG	60706	2918	10W-5N	A7
5500	CHCG	60631	2918	10W-6N	A5
SR-171 Forbes Rd					
-	NRIV	60546	3088	10W-3S	B4
-	RVSD	60546	3088	10W-3S	B4
SR-171 RJ Bragassi Mem Blvd					
-	SMMT	60501	3148	9W-6S	D3
SR-171 N State St					
100	LKPT	60441	3419	22W-18S	D1
200	LktT	60441	3419	22W-18S	D1
600	LKPT	60441	3341	21W-17S	E6
SR-171 S State St					
100	LKPT	60441	3419	23W-21S	B6
2300	LktT	60441	3419	23W-20S	B5
3500	JLET	60432	3499	23W-21S	A1
3500	JLET	60441	3499	23W-21S	A1
3500	JltT	60432	3499	23W-21S	A1
3500	LktT	60432	3499	23W-21S	A1
3500	LktT	60441	3499	23W-21S	A1
SR-171 N Thatcher Av					
2500	RVGV	60171	2974	10W-3N	A5
3000	CHCG	60634	2974	10W-3N	A4
3000	RVGV	60634	2974	10W-3N	A4
SR-173					
-	AdnT	60033	2406	48W-38N	D6
-	ANTH	60002	2357	25W-42N	B6
-	ANTH	60002	2358	23W-41N	A7
-	ANTH	60002	2417	21W-41N	D1
-	ANTH	60002	2418	20W-41N	B1
-	AntT	60002	2356	26W-41N	E7
-	AntT	60002	2357	23W-41N	E7
-	AntT	60002	2358	23W-41N	A7
-	AntT	60002	2417	21W-41N	D1
-	AntT	60002	2418	20W-41N	B1
-	BtnT	60071	2354	31W-42N	E6
-	BtnT	60071	2355	30W-42N	A6
-	BtnT	60081	2355	30W-42N	A6
-	BtnT	60099	2421	12W-41N	B1
-	CmgT	60033	2406	48W-38N	D6
-	FXLK	60002	2355	29W-42N	C6
-	FXLK	60002	2356	28W-42N	A6
-	FXLK	60081	2355	29W-42N	C6
-	HRVD	60033	2406	49W-38N	C6
-	RcmT	60071	2352	36W-42N	E6
-	RcmT	60071	2353	35W-42N	A6
-	RcmT	60071	2354	31W-42N	E6
-	RcmT	60081	2354	32W-42N	C6
-	RHMD	60071	2353	35W-42N	B6
-	SPGV	60071	2354	32W-42N	A6
-	SPGV	60081	2354	31W-42N	E6
-	SPGV	60081	2355	29W-42N	C6
-	WDWH	60099	2421	12W-41N	B1
3100	ZION	60099	2421	11W-41N	D1
9300	HbnT	60034	2351	39W-42N	D7
9300	HbnT	60034	2352	38W-42N	A7
9300	HbnT	60071	2352	38W-42N	A7
12100	HBRN	60034	2350	41W-41N	E7
23000	CmgT	60033	2405	51W-37N	E7
23000	DhmT	60033	2405	51W-38N	D7
23000	HRVD	60033	2405	52W-38N	C7
SR-173 21st St					
1200	ZION	60099	2422	10W-41N	B2
SR-173 Bethlehem Av					
-	ZION	60099	2421	11W-41N	E1
SR-173 W Brink St					
100	DhmT	60033	2406	50W-37N	A7
100	HRVD	60033	2406	50W-37N	A7
800	DhmT	60033	2405	51W-38N	E7
800	HRVD	60033	2405	50W-38N	E7
SR-173 E Diggins St					
100	HRVD	60033	2406	50W-38N	B6

STREET Block	City	ZIP	Map#	CGS	Grid
SR-173 N Division St					
100	HRVD	60033	2406	50W-38N	B7
SR-173 S Division St					
100	HRVD	60033	2406	50W-38N	B7
SR-173 Kenosha St					
5300	RcmT	60071	2353	34W-42N	D6
5300	RHMD	60071	2353	34W-42N	D6
SR-173 Maple Av					
11300	HbnT	60034	2351	40W-41N	A7
11400	HBRN	60034	2351	40W-42N	A7
12000	HBRN	60034	2350	41W-41N	E7
SR-173 Rosecrans Rd					
-	ANTH	60002	2418	18W-41N	D1
-	AntT	60002	2418	18W-41N	D1
-	BtnT	60083	2420	13W-41N	E1
-	BtnT	60099	2420	13W-41N	E1
-	BtnT	60099	2421	12W-41N	B1
-	NptT	60002	2418	18W-41N	D1
-	NptT	60002	2419	17W-41N	C1
-	NptT	60083	2418	18W-41N	D1
-	NptT	60083	2419	18W-41N	A1
-	NptT	60083	2420	15W-41N	B1
-	NptT	60099	2420	15W-41N	B1
-	OMCK	60083	2418	18W-41N	D1
-	OMCK	60083	2419	18W-41N	A1
-	WDWH	60083	2419	16W-41N	D1
-	WDWH	60083	2420	13W-41N	E1
-	WDWH	60083	2421	11W-41N	E2
-	WDWH	60099	2419	17W-41N	C1
-	WDWH	60099	2420	13W-41N	E1
-	WDWH	60099	2421	11W-41N	E2
-	ZION	60099	2420	13W-41N	E1
SR-176					
-	DrrT	60142	2638	40W-26N	A3
-	FmtT	60047	2589	22W-28N	B6
-	FmtT	60060	2589	22W-27N	B7
-	FmtT	60060	2644	23W-27N	E1
-	FmtT	60084	2644	23W-27N	D1
-	HNWD	60047	2589	21W-28N	D6
-	HNWD	60060	2589	22W-28N	C6
-	ISLK	60042	2586	28W-27N	E7
-	ISLK	60042	2587	28W-27N	A7
-	ISLK	60051	2586	28W-27N	E7
-	MDLN	60060	2589	21W-28N	D6
-	NndT	60042	2586	30W-28N	A5
-	NndT	60051	2586	28W-27N	E7
-	WcnT	60042	2587	28W-27N	A7
-	WcnT	60084	2587	28W-27N	A7
1600	NndT	60012	2586	30W-28N	A6
1600	NndT	60014	2586	30W-28N	A6
1600	NndT	60050	2586	30W-28N	A5
2000	NndT	60012	2585	30W-27N	E7
2000	NndT	60014	2585	30W-27N	E7
2000	PRGV	60014	2585	30W-27N	E7
2400	NndT	60014	2641	31W-27N	D1
2400	PRGV	60014	2641	31W-27N	D1
3000	NndT	60013	2641	31W-27N	C1
3000	PRGV	60013	2641	31W-27N	C1
3200	PRGV	60012	2641	32W-27N	B1
3500	CLLK	60012	2641	32W-27N	B1
3800	CLLK	60014	2641	32W-26N	A2
4100	CLLK	60012	2640	33W-26N	E2
4100	CLLK	60014	2640	33W-26N	E2
4100	NndT	60014	2640	33W-26N	E2
8000	CLLK	60014	2639	36W-26N	D3
8000	NndT	60012	2639	36W-26N	D3
8200	DrrT	60014	2639	37W-26N	C3
9100	CLLK	60014	2638	38W-26N	E2
9100	CLLK	60098	2638	38W-26N	E2
9100	CLLK	60098	2639	38W-26N	A3
9100	DrrT	60014	2638	38W-26N	E2
9100	DrrT	60098	2638	38W-26N	E2
9100	DrrT	60098	2639	38W-26N	A3
18600	SenT	60152	2634	48W-27N	E1
18600	SenT	60152	2635	47W-27N	A1
18600	SenT	60180	2635	46W-27N	E1
SR-176 E Liberty St					
100	WCDA	60084	2643	25W-27N	E1
300	WCDA	60084	2644	23W-27N	E1
1000	FmtT	60084	2644	24W-27N	B1
1000	WcnT	60084	2644	25W-27N	B1
SR-176 W Liberty St					
-	FmtT	60060	2644	23W-27N	D1
-	FmtT	60084	2644	24W-27N	C1
-	ISLK	60042	2587	28W-27N	A7
-	ISLK	60042	2643	28W-27N	A1
-	ISLK	60084	2587	28W-27N	A7
-	ISLK	60084	2643	27W-27N	B1
-	WcnT	60042	2587	28W-27N	A7
-	WcnT	60042	2643	28W-27N	A1
-	WcnT	60084	2587	28W-27N	A7
100	WCDA	60084	2643	26W-27N	D2
600	WcnT	60084	2643	27W-27N	B1
SR-176 E Maple Av					
10	MDLN	60060	2590	18W-28N	D6
900	MDLN	60060	2591	18W-28N	A6
1000	LYVL	60048	2591	18W-28N	A6
SR-176 W Maple Av					
1100	FmtT	60060	2590	19W-28N	B6
1100	MDLN	60060	2590	19W-28N	B6
1900	FmtT	60060	2589	21W-28N	E6
1900	MDLN	60060	2589	21W-28N	E6
SR-176 W Maple St					
10	MDLN	60060	2590	19W-28N	D6
1000	FmtT	60060	2590	19W-28N	C6
SR-176 E Park Av					
-	GNOK	60044	2592	14W-28N	D5
-	GNOK	60045	2592	14W-28N	D5
100	LYVL	60048	2591	16W-28N	D5
800	LYVL	60048	2592	15W-28N	B5
1000	LbvT	60048	2592	13W-28N	D5
1100	GNOK	60048	2592	13W-28N	D5
SR-176 W Park Av					
100	LYVL	60048	2591	18W-28N	A6
1500	MDLN	60060	2591	17W-28N	A6
SR-176 Rockland Rd					
10	LKBF	60044	2593	11W-28N	D6
300	ShdT	60044	2593	12W-28N	C6
600	LKFT	60044	2593	12W-28N	B6
600	LKFT	60045	2593	12W-28N	B6
1000	GNOK	60044	2593	11W-28N	D6
1300	GNOK	60044	2592	13W-28N	E5
1300	LbvT	60044	2592	13W-28N	E5
1500	GNOK	60045	2592	13W-28N	E5
1500	LbvT	60045	2592	13W-28N	E5
SR-176 W Scranton Av					
-	LKBF	60044	2593	11W-28N	E6
SR-176 E State Rd					
100	ISLK	60042	2586	28W-28N	D6
400	WcnT	60042	2586	28W-28N	E7
SR-176 W State Rd					
100	ISLK	60042	2586	29W-28N	D6
600	ISLK	60051	2586	29W-28N	C5
600	NndT	60042	2586	29W-28N	C5
600	NndT	60051	2586	29W-28N	C5
SR-176 Telegraph St					
100	MRGO	60152	2634	49W-26N	D1
20000	SenT	60152	2634	48W-27N	D1
SR-176 E Terra Cotta Av					
10	CLLK	60012	2640	35W-26N	B3
10	CLLK	60014	2640	35W-26N	B3
300	NndT	60012	2640	34W-26N	C3
300	NndT	60014	2640	34W-26N	C3
SR-176 W Terra Cotta Av					
10	CLLK	60012	2640	35W-26N	A3
10	CLLK	60014	2640	35W-26N	A3
200	CLLK	60014	2639	38W-26N	A3
300	NndT	60014	2639	35W-26N	E3
600	CLLK	60012	2639	36W-26N	D3
600	NndT	60012	2639	36W-26N	D3
SR-312 E Chicago St					
800	HMND	46327	3352		E4
SR-312 Gostlin St					
10	BNHM	60633	3352		C4
10	HMND	46327	3352		C4
SR-394 Bishop Ford Mem Expwy					
-	BlmT	-	3429	1E-21S	B7
-	BlmT	-	3509	1E-24S	B5
-	BlmT	-	3597	1E-26S	C2
-	FDHT	-	3509	1E-24S	C6
-	GNWD	-	3509	1E-22S	B2
-	LYWD	-	3509	1E-23S	B3
-	SHLD	-	3429	1E-20S	B5
-	SLVL	60411	3597	1E-26S	C2
-	ThtT	-	3429	1E-21S	B7
SR-394 Calumet Expwy					
-	CRTE	60417	3597	1E-28S	C6
-	CRTE	60417	3686	1E-30S	C2
-	CteT	60401	3774	0W-33S	C2
-	CteT	60417	3597	1E-28S	C6
-	CteT	60417	3685	0W-32S	D7
-	CteT	60417	3686	1E-30S	C2
-	CteT	60417	3774	0W-32S	C1
-	SLVL	60411	3597	1E-27S	C4
-	STGR	60411	3597	1E-28S	C6
-	STGR	60475	3597	1E-27S	C4
SR-394 Kingery Expwy					
-	SHLD	-	3429	1E-20S	B3
SR-912 Cline Av					
-	HMND	-	3280		E7
Srr Ln					
5000	BbyT	60119	3018	40W-1N	B4
Staben Av					
600	PKCY	60085	2536	12W-33N	B3
600	WKGN	60085	2536	12W-33N	B3
Stable Ct					
-	RLKP	60030	2589	21W-31N	C1
Stable Ln					
-	HMGN	60491	3421	16W-21S	E7
-	HmrT	60448	3421	16W-21S	D7
-	HmrT	60491	3421	16W-21S	D7
400	LKFT	60045	2649	11W-25N	C5
Stable Rd					
6200	WDRG	60517	3143	22W-6S	B5
Stable Wy					
10	LNHT	60046	2418	19W-38N	D7
10	LNHT	60046	2476	19W-38N	D1
Stableford Dr					
100	GNEN	60137	3024	23W-1N	E3
Stableford Ln					
4200	AURA	60564	3202	30W-9S	B4
Stables Ct					
10	HIWD	60040	2704	9W-24N	D1
Stables Ct E					
700	HIWD	60040	2704	9W-24N	D1
Stables Ct W					
700	HIWD	60040	2704	9W-24N	D1
Stables Ct Wy					
100	HIWD	60040	2704	8W-24N	D1
Stablewood Ln					
300	LKFT	60045	2649	13W-25N	A6
Stacey Ct					
4400	RNPK	60471	3594	5W-27S	B4
Stacey Dr					
600	NLNX	60451	3589	18W-27S	A5
Stacia Ct					
2800	JLET	60431	3417	28W-20S	A5
Stacie Ct					
700	NPVL	60563	3140	29W-6S	D4
Stackinghay Dr					
3500	NPVL	60564	3266	30W-11S	A2
Stacy Cir					
2200	MTGY	60538	3198	40W-10S	C6
Stacy Ct					
10	MaiT	60025	2864	9W-12N	C1
10	MaiT	60053	2864	9W-12N	C2
10	MNGV	60053	2864	9W-12N	C2
100	GNEN	60137	3025	22W-1N	C3
100	MltT	60137	3025	22W-1N	C3
2300	MTGY	60538	3198	40W-10S	C6
5400	RGMW	60008	2805	21W-13N	C5
5400	RGMW	60067	2805	21W-13N	C5
Stacy Ct N					
-	GNEN	60137	3025	22W-0N	B4
N Stadium Dr					
100	JLET	60435	3497	27W-23S	D5
Stadium St					
-	SCRL	60174	2964	33W-3N	E5
-	SCRL	60174	2965	33W-4N	A5
Staffeld Dr					
200	WldT	60564	3266	29W-11S	D1
N Staffire Dr					
10	SMBG	60193	2857	26W-10N	E6
10	SMBG	60194	2857	26W-10N	E5
S Staffire Dr					
-	SMBG	60194	2857	26W-10N	E6
10	SMBG	60193	2857	26W-10N	E6
Staffmark Ln					
200	SMBG	60193	2859	23W-10N	A6
Stafford Av					
400	NPVL	60540	3142	25W-7S	A6
Stafford Cir					
1500	EGVV	60007	2914	21W-9N	A1
Stafford Ct					
300	BGBK	60440	3205	22W-11S	C7
300	LNHT	60046	2418	19W-38N	D7
300	LNSH	60046	2702	13W-23N	D1
900	NLNX	60451	3589	18W-25S	A1
2100	JLET	60586	3415	31W-21S	E7
9800	MKNA	60448	3503	12W-23S	D4
Stafford Dr					
100	WLNG	60090	2755	13W-18N	D3
200	MDLN	60060	2590	19W-27N	B7
500	NLNX	60451	3501	18W-25S	A7
500	NLNX	60451	3589	18W-25S	A1
500	ROSL	60172	2912	24W-6N	C6
2900	MKHM	60428	3427	3W-19S	A2
N Stafford Dr					
4600	MchT	60050	2472	29W-36N	C4
W Stafford Dr					
12600	BHPK	60083	2421	12W-39N	B5
12600	BHPK	60099	2421	12W-39N	B5
Stafford Ln					
10	OKBK	60523	3086	15W-2S	B3
500	GNEN	60137	3083	22W-1S	B2
Stafford Pl					
100	CRTE	60417	3596	0W-28S	C6
500	WNVL	60555	3081	28W-3S	A5
600	WNVL	60555	3080	28W-3S	E5
Stafford Sq					
-	RGMW	60008	2860	19W-11N	B2
Stafford St					
2000	JLET	60586	3415	31W-21S	D7
Stafford Wy					
300	BGBK	60440	3205	22W-11S	D7
Stafney Dr					
200	BTVA	60510	3078	34W-1S	E2
Stag Tr					
1400	AlqT	60013	2642	30W-24N	A6
Stagecoach Ct					
400	GNEN	60137	3025	22W-1N	B3
Stagecoach Rd					
11800	ODPK	60467	3344	14W-16S	C3
11800	OrlT	60467	3344	14W-16S	C3
Stagecoach Run					
400	GNEN	60137	3025	22W-1N	B3
400	MltT	60137	3025	22W-1N	B3
Stagecoach Tr					
-	KdlT	60560	3333	43W-16S	B5
-	YKVL	60560	3333	43W-16S	B5
Stagecoach Tr SR-71					
-	KdlT	60560	3333	43W-16S	B5
-	YKVL	60560	3333	43W-16S	B5
E Stagecoach Tr					
100	KdlT	60560	3333	42W-16S	C5
100	YKVL	60560	3333	42W-16S	C5
E Stagecoach Tr SR-71					
100	KdlT	60560	3333	42W-16S	C5
100	YKVL	60560	3333	42W-16S	C5
Staggs Leap Tr					
13000	PNFD	60585	3337	32W-15S	C2
13000	WldT	60585	3337	32W-15S	C2
Staghorn Dr					
1500	JLET	60431	3495	31W-22S	E1
1500	JLET	60586	3495	31W-22S	E1
1500	PnfT	60586	3495	31W-22S	E1
Staghorn Ln					
-	NARA	60542	3137	37W-4S	C1
Stainfield Dr					
10	LtRT	60545	3259	47W-11S	C1
Stair St					
6400	DRGV	60516	3144	20W-7S	A6
Stairway Dr					
2000	HRPK	60133	2911	27W-6N	C6
2000	WynT	60133	2911	27W-6N	C6
Stakes Ln					
-	RLKP	60030	2532	21W-31N	C7
Stalford Rd					
6500	CTSD	60525	3147	13W-7S	A6
6500	LynT	60525	3147	13W-7S	A6
Stallion Ct					
2000	WHTN	60187	3083	23W-3S	A5
2400	RLKP	60030	2532	22W-31N	B7
Stamford Ct					
200	RMVL	60446	3339	27W-17S	C6
800	SMBG	60193	2858	23W-9N	E7
1000	AURA	60502	3139	31W-6S	D5
Stamford Ln					
200	RMVL	60446	3339	27W-17S	C6
Stamford Pl					
900	SRGV	60554	3135	41W-4S	E2
Standish Ct					
100	ELGN	60123	2854	34W-10N	E5
400	BGBK	60440	3269	22W-12S	C3
700	BTVA	60510	3078	36W-2S	A4
1100	NPVL	60540	3204	26W-8S	A1
Standish Dr					
10	DRFD	60015	2757	10W-20N	B1
Standish Ln					
10	SMBG	60193	2858	25W-10N	C6
10	SMBG	60194	2858	25W-10N	C6
200	YkTp	60148	3085	18W-1S	A1
700	YkTp	60181	3085	17W-1S	B1
Standish St					
300	CHHT	60411	3595	2W-26S	D2
400	ELGN	60123	2854	34W-10N	D5
Stanford Av					
1100	DRGV	60516	3144	19W-7S	C7
1100	DRGV	60516	3206	20W-8S	B1
Stanford Cir					
-	LGGV	60047	2647	17W-24N	B7
600	EGVV	60007	2860	19W-9N	C7
1400	CPVL	60110	2748	32W-18N	D5
Stanford Ct					
1700	LKFT	60045	2649	13W-26N	A2
1900	ELGN	60123	2854	36W-10N	A6
W Stanford Ct					
9200	MKNA	60448	3503	12W-22S	D2
Stanford Dr					
400	MRGO	60152	2634	50W-26N	B3
400	SRWD	60404	3496	30W-24S	B7
1800	NPVL	60565	3204	25W-9S	C4
6800	BGVW	60455	3211	8W-10S	A5
6900	BGVW	60455	3210	8W-10S	E5
22600	FKFT	60423	3592	10W-27S	C4
N Stanford Dr					
2800	ANHT	60004	2754	16W-17N	C5
Stanford Ln					
600	BFGV	60089	2754	17W-17N	B5
700	CLSM	60188	2967	27W-4N	D4
5200	MTSN	60443	3505	6W-24S	E6
5200	MTSN	60443	3506	6W-24S	A6
Stanford St					
4300	NndT	60012	2640	33W-27N	E1
4300	NndT	60012	2641	33W-27N	A1
Stanhope Ct					
500	NPVL	60565	3204	25W-9S	B4
Stanhope Dr					
100	WLBK	60527	3145	16W-6S	D5
Stanley Av					
10	PKRG	60068	2918	9W-8N	B2
200	WKGN	60085	2480	10W-35N	A6
3700	RvsT	60546	3088	9W-3S	C6
3800	LYNS	60534	3088	9W-3S	C6
3800	RvsT	60534	3088	9W-3S	C6
4300	DRGV	60515	3084	18W-4S	E7
4300	DRGV	60515	3144	19W-4S	D1
6400	BRWN	60402	3089	8W-3S	A4
6800	BRWN	60402	3088	8W-3S	E4
7100	BRWN	60546	3088	8W-3S	E4
7100	RVSD	60546	3088	8W-3S	E4
Stanley Blvd					
1200	CTCY	60409	3430	4E-19S	B3
Stanley Ct					
2100	SMBG	60194	2858	26W-11N	A3
Stanley Rd					
10	SRGV	60554	3135	42W-7S	D7
N Stanley Rd					
34400	FXLK	60041	2473	27W-34N	B7
34400	FXLK	60041	2530	27W-34N	B1
34400	GrtT	60041	2473	27W-34N	B7
34400	GrtT	60041	2530	27W-34N	B1
Stanley St					
10	EGvT	60007	2861	17W-10N	B6
10	MltT	60190	3023	26W-0S	E6
100	EGVV	60007	2861	17W-10N	B6
100	WNFD	60190	3023	26W-0S	E6
1800	NHBK	60062	2757	9W-16N	B7
Stansbury Ln					
-	LKWD	60014	2638	38W-25N	E4
Stansted Rd					
9000	WDRG	60517	3206	20W-10S	B6
S Stanton Av					
1200	HMND	46320	3280		E3
1200	HMND	46394	3280		E3
Stanton Cir					
2300	LIHL	60156	2692	38W-22N	D3
Stanton Ct					
10	LIHL	60156	2692	38W-22N	D3
10	LKZH	60047	2699	22W-22N	C4
10	SMBG	60193	2859	23W-10N	B5
E Stanton Ct					
300	RLKB	60073	2475	22W-36N	B4
Stanton Ct E					
200	BFGV	60089	2701	16W-21N	D5
Stanton Ct N					
1900	ANHT	60004	2807	18W-16N	A1
Stanton Ct S					
2600	AURA	60502	3139	32W-4S	C1
Stanton Ct W					
200	BFGV	60089	2701	16W-21N	D5
Stanton Dr					
10	SchT	60174	2964	34W-6N	C1
100	BRLT	60103	2909	31W-8N	D3
200	BFGV	60089	2701	16W-21N	D5
900	NPVL	60540	3204	25W-8S	B1
22000	AntT	60002	2417	22W-40N	C2
Stanton Ln					
33200	GrtT	60041	2530	26W-33N	C3
33200	VOLO	60041	2530	26W-33N	C3
W Stanton Ln					
400	CteT	60417	3774	0W-32S	C1
Stanton Rd					
200	MltT	60137	3083	22W-2S	C4
1000	LKZH	60047	2699	22W-22N	B4
Stanton St					
400	PKFT	60466	3595	3W-25S	A1
900	BTVA	60510	3078	34W-1S	D3
W Stanton Bay Rd					
26100	GrtT	60041	2473	26W-36N	E3
N Stanton Point Rd					
36600	FXLK	60041	2473	26W-36N	D4
36600	GrtT	60041	2473	26W-36N	E3
N Stanwich Rd					
1600	VNHL	60061	2647	17W-27N	B2
Stanyon Ct					
200	BMDL	60108	2969	22W-4N	C3
Stanyon Ln					
200	BMDL	60108	2969	22W-4N	C2
Star Av					
1300	AURA	60505	3138	34W-5S	D4
Star Ct					
9200	FKFT	60423	3503	11W-24S	E5
Star Dr					
5600	HRPK	60133	2911	26W-7N	E6
Star Ln					
10	SBTN	60010	2803	27W-13N	B6
500	SgrT	60506	3197	42W-9S	C5
500	SgrT	60554	3197	42W-9S	C5
1000	NLNX	60451	3589	17W-26S	C2
1000	NlxT	60451	3589	17W-26S	C2
13500	HmrT	60441	3342	20W-16S	A3
13500	LMNT	60439	3342	20W-16S	A3
N Star Ln					
200	JLET	60435	3497	27W-23S	D4
Starboard Ct					
10	TDLK	60030	2533	19W-34N	D1
Starboard Dr					
3900	HRPK	60133	2967	27W-4N	D3
Starboard Pt					
700	SMBG	60194	2859	23W-10N	A5
Star Grass Ct					
-	LKVL	60046	2474	23W-37N	D2
Star Grass Ln					
-	AURA	60506	3136	39W-5S	D4
Stargrass Ln					
10	BbyT	60119	3017	42W-1N	C4
10	ELBN	60119	3017	42W-1N	C4
200	SjnT	46311	3598		D5
Stark Dr					
100	CLSM	60133	2968	25W-4N	B4
100	CLSM	60188	2968	25W-4N	B4
8700	LynT	60527	3208	14W-10S	D4
E Stark Dr					
600	PLTN	60074	2753	20W-16N	B7
N Stark Dr					
400	PLTN	60074	2753	20W-17N	A6
Stark Pl					
1100	DSPN	60016	2862	15W-10N	B5
1100	DSPN	60018	2862	15W-10N	B5
S Stark St					
2500	CHCG	60608	3091	1W-2S	E2
Starling Ct					
300	BMDL	60108	2969	22W-4N	C4
700	LslT	60540	3142	24W-5S	C3
Starling Ln					
-	LNHT	60046	2476	19W-37N	C1
10	NPVL	60565	3203	26W-9S	E3
2800	RGMW	60008	2806	19W-13N	B6
Starlite Ct					
1100	NPVL	60564	3203	28W-10S	A7
Star Lite Dr					
2600	NLNX	60433	3500	20W-24S	B5
2600	NLNX	60451	3500	20W-24S	B5
2600	NlxT	60433	3500	20W-24S	B5
Star Pass					
2900	NLNX	60451	3589	18W-27S	A5
Starr Dr					
10	ALGN	60102	2695	32W-21N	B6
10	AlqT	60102	2695	32W-21N	A6
1500	JltT	60433	3587	23W-25S	A1
Starr Rd					
1000	WNKA	60093	2812	5W-16N	A1
W Starry Ln					
21200	ElaT	60047	2699	21W-23N	D1
21200	KLDR	60047	2699	21W-23N	D1
Starved Rock Pl					
13900	HTLY	60142	2744	43W-19N	A2
Starwood Ct					
10	BGBK	60490	3267	27W-11S	B2
Starwood Dr					
100	BGBK	60490	3267	27W-11S	D2
Starwood Pass					
300	LIHL	60156	2693	36W-22N	D4
State Av					
10	SCRL	60174	2964	35W-3N	B7
E State Pkwy					
10	SMBG	60195	2859	23W-12N	A1
700	SMBG	60173	2859	22W-12N	C1
N State Pkwy					
1200	CHCG	60610	3034	0W-1N	B1
1200	CHCG	60611	3034	0W-1N	B1
State Rd					
-	OKLN	60453	3211	8W-9S	B4
-	OKLN	60459	3211	8W-9S	B4
5100	BDPK	60459	3211	6W-8S	E1
5100	BDPK	60638	3211	6W-8S	E1
5100	BRBK	60459	3211	7W-9S	B4
5100	BRBK	60638	3211	6W-8S	E1
E State Rd					
100	ISLK	60042	2586	28W-28N	D6
400	WcnT	60042	2586	28W-28N	E7
E State Rd SR-176					
100	ISLK	60042	2586	28W-28N	D6
400	WcnT	60042	2586	28W-28N	E7
S State Rd					
7300	BDPK	60638	3150	6W-8S	A7
7300	BDPK	60638	3211	6W-8S	E1
7300	BDPK	60638	3212	6W-8S	A1
7300	BRBK	60459	3211	6W-8S	E1
7300	CHCG	60629	3150	6W-8S	A7
W State Rd					
100	ISLK	60042	2586	29W-28N	C5
600	ISLK	60051	2586	29W-28N	C5
600	NndT	60042	2586	29W-28N	C5
600	NndT	60051	2586	29W-28N	C5
W State Rd SR-176					
100	ISLK	60042	2586	29W-28N	C5
600	ISLK	60051	2586	29W-28N	C5
600	NndT	60042	2586	29W-28N	C5
600	NndT	60051	2586	29W-28N	C5
State St					
-	ELGN	60123	2854	34W-11N	E5
-	HMGN	60439	3342	19W-15S	D2
-	HMGN	60441	3342	19W-17S	D6
-	HMGN	60491	3342	19W-17S	D6
-	HmrT	60441	3342	19W-17S	D6
-	HmrT	60491	3342	19W-17S	D6
10	CTCY	60409	3352	3E-17S	A4
10	HMND	46320	3352	4E-17S	C5
100	BTVA	60510	3078	35W-1S	C1
100	LMNT	60439	3270	19W-13S	D5
200	BlmT	60411	3508	0W-24S	D5
200	BlmT	60425	3508	0W-24S	D5
200	CHHT	60411	3508	0W-24S	D5
200	CHHT	60425	3508	0W-24S	D5
200	YKVL	60560	3333	43W-15S	C2
400	DSPN	60016	2862	14W-12N	C2
700	BNHM	60633	3352	3E-17S	A4
700	CTCY	60633	3352	3E-17S	A4
1200	LMNT	60439	3342	19W-15S	D2
1400	BlmT	60411	3596	0W-27S	D4
1400	CHHT	60411	3596	0W-27S	D4
1600	BNHM	60409	3351	2E-16S	D4
1600	BNHM	60633	3351	2E-16S	D4
1600	CTCY	60409	3351	2E-17S	C4
1600	CTCY	60633	3351	2E-16S	D4
2700	SCHT	60411	3596	0E-26S	D3
3100	SCHT	60475	3596	0E-27S	D4
3100	STGR	60411	3596	0E-27S	D4
3100	STGR	60475	3596	0E-27S	D4
4800	AlqT	60014	2640	33W-24N	D6
4800	CLLK	60014	2640	33W-24N	D6
14600	DLTN	60419	3350	0W-17S	C5
14600	DLTN	60827	3350	0W-17S	C4
14600	RVDL	60827	3350	0W-17S	C4
15000	SHLD	60419	3350	0W-18S	D7
15000	SHLD	60473	3350	0W-18S	D7
15900	SHLD	60473	3428	0W-19S	D2
16800	SHLD	60476	3428	0W-19S	D3
16800	TNTN	60476	3428	0W-19S	D3
23000	CRTE	60417	3596	0E-27S	D5
E State St					
-	SchT	60177	2908	34W-8N	D3
10	GNVA	60134	3020	34W-1N	D4
10	HMND	46320	3352		C5
10	NARA	60542	3138	36W-4S	A1
100	NARA	60542	3078	35W-4S	A7
100	SEGN	60177	2908	34W-8N	E3
500	JLET	60432	3499	23W-23S	A3
600	GNVA	60134	3021	33W-1N	A4
600	GNVA	60185	3021	33W-1N	A4
600	GnvT	60134	3021	33W-1N	A4
600	GnvT	60185	3021	33W-1N	A4
1200	GnvT	60134	3020	33W-1N	E4
2200	BNHM	60409	3351	3E-17S	E4
2200	BNHM	60633	3351	3E-17S	E4
2200	CTCY	60409	3351	3E-17S	E4
2200	CTCY	60633	3351	3E-17S	E4
2700	BNHM	60633	3352	3E-17S	A4
2700	CTCY	60409	3352	3E-17S	A4
2700	CTCY	60633	3352	3E-17S	A4
E State St SR-38					
10	GNVA	60134	3020	34W-1N	C4
600	GNVA	60134	3021	33W-1N	A4
600	GNVA	60185	3021	33W-1N	A4
600	GnvT	60134	3021	33W-1N	A4
600	GnvT	60185	3021	33W-1N	A4
1200	GnvT	60134	3020	33W-1N	E4
E State St SR-56					
10	NARA	60542	3078	36W-4S	A7
10	NARA	60542	3138	36W-4S	A1
N State St					
-	MngT	60152	2578	50W-27N	B7
10	AURA	60505	3200	34W-7S	C1
10	CHCG	60602	3034	0E-0N	C4
10	CHCG	60603	3034	0E-0N	C4
10	ELGN	60123	2854	34W-12N	D2
10	GNWD	60425	3508	0W-22S	D1
100	ADSN	60101	2971	18W-3N	A5
100	AURA	60505	3138	34W-7S	C7
100	BlmT	60425	3508	0W-22S	D1
100	CHCG	60601	3034	0E-0N	C4
100	HPSR	60140	2795	47W-16N	E1
100	LKPT	60441	3419	22W-18S	D1
100	MRGO	60152	2634	50W-27N	B1
200	LktT	60441	3419	22W-18S	D1
300	CHCG	60610	3034	0E-0N	C3
300	CHCG	60611	3034	0E-0N	C3
400	JLET	60432	3499	23W-23S	A4
600	LKPT	60441	3341	21W-18S	D7
1100	ELGN	60123	2800	34W-13N	D7
1400	MRGO	60152	2578	50W-27N	B7
1700	DndT	60123	2800	34W-14N	E6
1700	WDND	60118	2800	34W-14N	E6
1700	WDND	60123	2800	34W-14N	E6

Block	City	ZIP	Map#	CGS	Grid
N State St CO-36					
100	HPSR	60140	2795	47W-16N	E2
N State St SR-23					
-	MngT	60152	2578	50W-27N	B7
100	MRGO	60152	2634	50W-27N	B1
1400	MRGO	60152	2578	50W-27N	B7
N State St SR-31					
10	ELGN	60123	2854	34W-12N	D2
1100	ELGN	60123	2800	34W-13N	D7
1700	DndT	60123	2800	34W-14N	E6
1700	WDND	60118	2800	34W-14N	E6
1700	WDND	60123	2800	34W-14N	E6
N State St SR-171					
100	LKPT	60441	3419	22W-18S	D1
200	LktT	60441	3419	22W-18S	D1
600	LKPT	60441	3341	21W-18S	D7
S State St					
-	CHHT	60411	3508	0E-23S	D4
-	CHHT	60425	3508	0E-23S	D4
10	AURA	60505	3200	34W-8S	C1
10	CHCG	60602	3034	0E-0S	C4
10	CHCG	60603	3034	0E-0S	C5
10	ELGN	60123	2854	34W-10N	E6
10	GNWD	60425	3508	0E-22S	D2
100	BlmT	60425	3508	0E-23S	D3
100	CHCG	60604	3034	0E-0S	C5
100	HPSR	60140	2795	46W-15N	E3
100	LKPT	60441	3419	23W-20S	B5
100	MHTN	60442	3677	19W-31S	E5
100	MRGO	60152	2634	49W-26N	B3
300	MHTN	60442	3678	19W-31S	A5
500	MhtT	60442	3678	19W-31S	A5
600	CHCG	60605	3034	0E-1S	C7
700	SEGN	60123	2854	34W-9N	E7
1100	AraT	60505	3200	34W-9S	C4
1100	RlyT	60152	2634	50W-25N	B3
1200	MTGY	60505	3200	34W-9S	C4
1200	MTGY	60538	3200	34W-9S	C4
1500	CHCG	60616	3034	0W-1S	C7
1900	CHCG	60616	3092	0E-2S	C3
2100	WDND	60118	2800	34W-14N	E6
2300	LktT	60441	3419	23W-20S	B5
3400	CRTE	60417	3596	0W-28S	D6
3400	LktT	60441	3499	23W-21S	A1
3400	STGR	60475	3596	0W-28S	D6
3500	JLET	60432	3499	23W-21S	A1
3500	JLET	60441	3499	23W-21S	A1
3500	JltT	60432	3499	23W-21S	A1
3500	LktT	60432	3499	23W-21S	A1
3600	CHCG	60609	3092	0W-4S	C7
3600	CHCG	60653	3092	0W-4S	C7
4600	CHCG	60615	3092	0W-4S	C7
4700	CHCG	60609	3152	0W-5S	C1
4700	CHCG	60615	3152	0W-5S	C1
5400	CHCG	60637	3152	0E-8S	C7
5500	CHCG	60621	3152	0E-8S	C7
7000	CHCG	60619	3152	0E-8S	C7
7400	CHCG	60619	3214	0E-8S	C1
7400	CHCG	60620	3214	0E-8S	C1
7400	CHCG	60621	3214	0E-8S	C1
9400	CHCG	60628	3214	0W-11S	C7
10300	CHCG	60628	3278	0W-14S	C6
13600	RVDL	60827	3350	0W-15S	C2
14500	DLTN	60419	3350	0W-17S	C4
14500	DLTN	60827	3350	0W-17S	C4
25200	CRTE	60417	3685	0E-30S	E4
25200	CteT	60417	3685	0E-30S	E4
S State St CO-36					
100	HPSR	60140	2795	46W-15N	E3
S State St SR-23					
100	MRGO	60152	2634	49W-26N	B3
1100	RlyT	60152	2634	50W-25N	B3
S State St SR-31					
10	ELGN	60123	2854	34W-10N	E7
700	SEGN	60123	2854	34W-9N	E7
2100	WDND	60118	2800	34W-14N	E6
S State St SR-171					
100	LKPT	60441	3419	23W-20S	B5
2300	LktT	60441	3419	23W-20S	B5
3400	LktT	60441	3499	23W-21S	A1
3500	JLET	60432	3499	23W-21S	A1
3500	JLET	60441	3499	23W-21S	A1
3500	JltT	60432	3499	23W-21S	A1
3500	LktT	60432	3499	23W-21S	A1
S State St US-52					
100	MHTN	60442	3677	19W-31S	E5
300	MHTN	60442	3678	19W-31S	A5
500	MhtT	60442	3678	19W-31S	A5
W State St					
-	NARA	60542	3138	36W-4S	A1
10	GNVA	60134	3020	35W-1N	B3
10	SchT	60177	2908	34W-8N	D3
10	SEGN	60177	2908	34W-8N	D3
200	SCRL	60174	2964	35W-3N	A7
300	NARA	60542	3137	36W-4S	D1
1700	GNVA	60134	3019	36W-1N	E2
1900	SCRL	60134	3019	36W-1N	E2
1900	SCRL	60174	3019	36W-1N	E2
W State St SR-38					
10	GNVA	60134	3020	35W-1N	B3
1700	GNVA	60134	3019	36W-1N	E2
1900	SCRL	60134	3019	36W-1N	E2
1900	SCRL	60174	3019	36W-1N	E2
W State St SR-56					
-	NARA	60542	3138	36W-4S	A1
State Line Av					
1100	CTCY	60409	3430		C3
1100	HMND	46324	3430		C3
7200	CTCY	46324	3430	4E-20S	C4
7500	LNSG	60438	3430	4E-21S	C6
7500	MNSR	46321	3430	4E-21S	C6
S State Line Av					
10	HMND	46320	3352	4E-17S	C5
5400	CTCY	60409	3352	4E-18S	C7
5900	CTCY	60409	3430	4E-18S	C1
5900	HMND	46320	3430	4E-18S	C1
6100	HMND	46324	3430	4E-18S	C1
State Line Rd					
900	BtnT	60081	2355		A4
900	RdlT	53181	2355		A4
900	RdlT	60081	2355	29W-43N	B4
1000	SPGV	60081	2355	30W-43N	B4
1300	CTCY	60409	3430	4E-20S	C4
1300	HMND	46324	3430	4E-20S	C4
1400	BtnT	60071	2355	30W-43N	A4
1600	BtnT	53181	2354	30W-43N	E4
1600	BtnT	60071	2354	30W-43N	E4
1600	RcmT	53181	2354	30W-43N	E4
1600	RcmT	60071	2354	30W-43N	E4
1600	RcmT	60081	2354	32W-43N	C4
1600	RdlT	53181	2354	32W-43N	C4
1600	RdlT	60071	2354	31W-43N	D4
1600	RdlT	60081	2354	32W-43N	C4
3000	TNLK	53181	2354	32W-43N	B4
3000	TNLK	60071	2354	32W-43N	B4
4000	AdnT	53147	2349	44W-43N	C4
4000	AdnT	60033	2349		A3
4000	AdnT	60034	2349	44W-43N	C4
4000	LinT	53147	2349		A3
4000	LinT	60033	2349		A3
4300	LinT	53184	2349		A3
10300	BfdT	53147	2351	40W-43N	A4
10300	BfdT	60034	2351	40W-43N	A4
10300	HbnT	53147	2351	40W-43N	A4
10300	HbnT	60034	2351	40W-43N	A4
10700	LinT	53147	2351	40W-43N	A4
10700	LinT	60034	2351	40W-43N	A4
11600	CteT	60417	3687		C7
11600	HnrT	46311	3687		C7
12000	HbnT	53147	2350		D4
12000	HbnT	60034	2350		D4
12000	LinT	53147	2350		D4
12000	LinT	60034	2350	41W-43N	E4
State Line Rd CO-CK					
900	BtnT	60081	2355		A4
900	RdlT	53181	2355		A4
900	RdlT	60081	2355	29W-43N	B4
1000	SPGV	60081	2355	30W-43N	B4
1400	BtnT	60071	2355	30W-43N	A4
1600	BtnT	53181	2354	30W-43N	E4
1600	BtnT	60071	2354	30W-43N	E4
1600	RcmT	53181	2354	30W-43N	E4
1600	RcmT	60071	2354	30W-43N	E4
1600	RcmT	60081	2354	32W-43N	C4
1600	RdlT	53181	2354	32W-43N	C4
1600	RdlT	60071	2354	31W-43N	D4
1600	RdlT	60081	2354	32W-43N	C4
S State Line Rd					
600	CTCY	60409	3352	4E-17S	C6
600	HMND	46320	3352	4E-17S	C6
13900	BNHM	60633	3352		C2
13900	HMND	46327	3352	4E-15S	C2
23700	CteT	60417	3598	4E-29S	C7
23700	SjnT	46311	3598	4E-29S	C7
24000	CteT	60417	3687		C2
24000	SjnT	46311	3687		C2
25000	HnrT	46311	3687	4E-32S	C7
W State Line Rd					
16500	BtlT	53142	2360		D4
16500	BtlT	60099	2360	16W-43N	D4
16500	NptT	53142	2360		D4
16500	NptT	60099	2360	16W-43N	D4
16800	BtlT	60002	2360		D4
16800	NptT	60002	2360		D4
18500	AntT	60002	2359		C4
18500	BtlT	53142	2359		C4
18500	BtlT	60002	2359		C4
18500	NptT	53142	2359		C4
18500	NptT	60002	2359		C4
19800	BtlT	53104	2359		B4
W State Line Rd CO-WG					
16500	BtlT	53142	2360		D4
16500	BtlT	60099	2360	16W-43N	D4
16500	NptT	53142	2360		D4
16500	NptT	60099	2360	16W-43N	D4
16800	BtlT	60002	2360		D4
16800	NptT	60002	2360		D4
18500	AntT	60002	2359		C4
18500	BtlT	53142	2359		C4
18500	BtlT	60002	2359		C4
18500	NptT	53142	2359		C4
18500	NptT	60002	2359		C4
19800	BtlT	53104	2359		B4
Stately Oaks Cir					
14300	HMGN	60491	3342	19W-17S	D5
14300	HmrT	60491	3342	19W-17S	D5
Stately Oaks Dr					
15600	HMGN	60491	3342	19W-17S	D5
15700	HmrT	60441	3342	19W-17S	D5
E State Park Rd					
500	AntT	60081	2414	28W-39N	E4
500	FXLK	60081	2414	28W-39N	E4
N State Park Rd					
-	MchT	60081	2472	29W-37N	D1
6100	AntT	60081	2472	29W-38N	D1
6100	BtnT	60081	2472	29W-38N	D1
6100	GrtT	60081	2472	29W-38N	D1
6500	AntT	60081	2414	29W-38N	D7
6500	BtnT	60081	2414	29W-38N	D7
6500	FXLK	60020	2414	29W-38N	D7
6500	FXLK	60081	2414	29W-38N	D7
N State Park Rd CO-A7					
7000	BtnT	60081	2414	29W-38N	D7
7000	FXLK	60020	2414	28W-39N	D6
7000	FXLK	60081	2414	29W-38N	D7
N State Park Rd CO-A17					
-	MchT	60081	2472	29W-37N	D1
6100	AntT	60081	2472	29W-38N	D1
6100	BtnT	60081	2472	29W-38N	D1
6100	GrtT	60081	2472	29W-38N	D1
6500	AntT	60081	2414	29W-38N	D7
6500	FXLK	60020	2414	29W-38N	D7
6500	FXLK	60081	2414	29W-38N	D7
6800	BtnT	60081	2414	29W-38N	D6
W State Park Rd					
2300	MHRY	60050	2585	32W-30N	C2
2300	NndT	60050	2585	32W-30N	B2
States Ln					
24500	SRWD	60404	3496	30W-25S	B7
24500	SRWD	60404	3584	30W-25S	B1
24500	TroT	60404	3496	30W-25S	B7
S States Ln					
20900	SRWD	60404	3584	30W-25S	B1
State St Br					
-	SchT	60177	2908	34W-8N	D3
-	SEGN	60177	2908	34W-8N	D3
Station Blvd					
-	AURA	60504	3140	30W-7S	B6
Station Dr					
-	ITSC	60143	2914	18W-5N	E7
-	ITSC	60191	2914	18W-5N	E7
-	WDDL	60143	2914	18W-5N	E7
200	WDDL	60191	2914	18W-5N	E7
200	WDDL	60191	2970	18W-5N	E1
3400	MTSN	60443	3594	4W-25S	E1
Station St					
500	LinT	53147	2349		E1
24800	PNFD	60585	3266	31W-14S	A7
24800	WldT	60585	3266	31W-14S	A7
E Station St					
-	BRTN	60010	2751	25W-18N	A2
100	BRTN	60010	2750	26W-18N	D2
W Station St					
100	BRTN	60010	2750	25W-18N	E2
Station Park Cir					
10	GYLK	60030	2532	21W-32N	D5
Station Park Dr					
-	GYLK	60030	2532	21W-32N	D5
Staton Ln					
-	JLET	60586	3495	32W-21S	C1
Statton St					
4500	DRGV	60515	3144	19W-4S	D1
N Stauffer Dr					
10	NPVL	60540	3141	28W-6S	B5
S Stauffer Dr					
10	NPVL	60540	3141	28W-6S	B5
Staunton Ct					
100	BGBK	60440	3269	22W-11S	D1
Staunton Rd					
400	NPVL	60565	3204	25W-9S	B4
N Stave St					
2000	CHCG	60647	2977	3W-2N	A6
2100	CHCG	60647	2976	4W-2N	D7
Staycoff Ln					
-	CHCG	60652	3212	5W-10S	A4
-	HMTN	60652	3212	5W-10S	A4
8700	HMTN	60456	3212	5W-10S	A4
Stayton Ln					
-	LGGV	60047	2700	19W-21N	D7
Steadman Av					
200	WNVL	60555	3081	28W-3S	A6
Steamboat Cir					
2600	JLET	60586	3416	31W-20S	A5
2600	PnfT	60586	3416	31W-20S	A5
Steamboat Dr					
100	GLBT	60136	2799	39W-15N	A4
Steamboat Ln					
100	BGBK	60490	3267	26W-12S	D3
Steamboat Rd					
600	NPVL	60565	3203	27W-10S	B7
Steamboat Springs Dr					
12400	MKNA	60448	3502	15W-23S	B4
12400	NlxT	60448	3502	15W-23S	B4
Stearman Dr					
10	NPVL	60564	3202	29W-9S	C4
600	NpvT	60564	3202	29W-9S	C4
Stearns Rd					
10	BRLT	60103	2910	31W-7N	A5
10	BRLT	60120	2909	32W-7N	C5
10	BRLT	60120	2910	31W-7N	A5
10	BRLT	60184	2909	31W-7N	E5
10	SchT	60120	2909	32W-7N	C5
10	WynT	60120	2909	32W-7N	C5
10	WynT	60184	2909	31W-7N	E5
100	BRLT	60103	2911	28W-6N	A6
500	WynT	60103	2911	28W-6N	A6
Stearns Rd CO-29					
10	BRLT	60103	2910	31W-7N	A5
10	BRLT	60120	2909	32W-7N	C5
10	BRLT	60120	2910	31W-7N	A5
10	BRLT	60184	2909	31W-7N	E5
10	SchT	60120	2909	32W-7N	C5
10	WynT	60120	2909	32W-7N	C5
10	WynT	60184	2909	31W-7N	E5
100	BRLT	60103	2911	28W-6N	A6
500	WynT	60103	2911	28W-6N	A6
E Stearns Rd					
-	BRLT	60133	2911	27W-7N	D6
-	HRPK	60103	2911	27W-6N	C6
-	HRPK	60133	2911	27W-6N	C6
200	BRLT	60103	2911	27W-6N	C6
200	WynT	60103	2911	27W-6N	B6
E Stearns Rd CO-29					
-	BRLT	60133	2911	27W-7N	D6
-	HRPK	60103	2911	27W-6N	C6
-	HRPK	60133	2911	27W-6N	C6
200	BRLT	60103	2911	27W-6N	C6
200	WynT	60103	2911	27W-6N	B6
W Stearns Rd					
100	BRLT	60103	2910	29W-7N	E6
500	BRLT	60120	2910	30W-7N	A5
W Stearns Rd CO-29					
100	BRLT	60103	2910	29W-7N	D6
500	BRLT	60120	2910	30W-7N	A5
W Stearns School Rd					
15100	GRNE	60031	2478	15W-36N	A4
15100	WrnT	60031	2478	15W-36N	A4
15800	GRNE	60031	2477	16W-36N	D4
15800	WrnT	60031	2477	18W-36N	A3
16300	GRNE	60083	2477	16W-36N	D4
16300	WrnT	60083	2477	18W-36N	A3
17700	OMCK	60031	2477	17W-36N	A3
17700	OMCK	60083	2477	18W-36N	A3
Stech St					
100	DYR	46311	3598		C2
Steck Ct					
10	BGBK	60440	3204	24W-10S	D5
Stedhall Rd					
18400	HMWD	60430	3507	3W-22S	B1
18500	FSMR	60422	3507	3W-22S	B1
Steel St					
800	ELGN	60123	2854	34W-12N	D1
Steele Ct					
400	WKGN	60085	2537	10W-34N	B1
Steeple Cir					
300	PltT	60124	2905	43W-8N	B3
Steeple Ct					
8600	FXLK	60081	2414	29W-40N	C2
Steeple Dr					
100	BFGV	60089	2754	16W-20N	D2
8500	TYPK	60487	3424	10W-20S	B5
Steeple Run					
3800	AlqT	60014	2641	33W-25N	A4
Steeple Brook Ct					
2000	NPVL	60565	3204	24W-8S	E2
W Steeplebush Ln					
25800	GrtT	60073	2530	25W-34N	E1
Steeple Chase					
500	CmpT	60175	2961	42W-5N	C2
Steeplechase Blvd					
-	OSWG	60543	3264	34W-11S	C1
E Steeple Chase Cir					
2300	WKGN	60048	2535	15W-31N	A7
2300	WKGN	60048	2592	15W-31N	A1
W Steeple Chase Cir					
2300	WKGN	60048	2535	15W-31N	A7
2300	WKGN	60048	2592	15W-31N	A1
Steeplechase Ct					
200	SMBG	60173	2859	21W-11N	E3
200	SMBG	60173	2860	21W-10N	A5
500	MHRY	60050	2527	34W-32N	B5
800	SCRL	60174	2964	35W-3N	C5
1500	GNOK	60048	2592	14W-30N	C2
2400	SPGV	60081	2354	31W-42N	D6
Steeple Chase Dr					
25000	PNFD	60585	3265	31W-14S	E7
Steeplechase Dr					
10	HNWD	60047	2644	23W-25N	E4
7600	FKFT	60423	3592	9W-25S	D1
7700	FftT	60423	3592	9W-25S	D1
Steeplechase Ln					
10	NfdT	60093	2811	8W-16N	A1
10	NHFD	60093	2811	8W-16N	A1
2300	SPGV	60081	2354	31W-42N	E6
W Steeplechase Ln					
1200	PLTN	60067	2805	22W-14N	A3
Steeplechase Pkwy					
11300	ODPK	60467	3422	14W-20S	E4
Steeplechase Rd					
10	BNHL	60010	2750	28W-20N	A1
100	BNHL	60010	2749	28W-20N	E2
500	SCRL	60174	2964	35W-3N	C5
1300	BRLT	60103	2966	30W-5N	C1
Steeplechase Wy					
200	LIHL	60156	2692	38W-20N	D7
3400	RLKP	60030	2532	22W-31N	C7
3400	RLKP	60030	2589	22W-31N	C1
Steeple Pointe Blvd					
5600	GRNE	60031	2477	15W-36N	E4
Steeple Ridge Ct					
10	OKBK	60523	3084	18W-3S	E5
10	OKBK	60523	3085	18W-3S	A6
Steeple Run Dr					
10	LslT	60540	3142	24W-6S	C4
200	LSLE	60532	3142	24W-6S	C4
200	LSLE	60540	3142	24W-6S	C4
Steeples Rd					
13700	LMNT	60439	3271	17W-14S	D6
Steepleside Dr					
8100	BRRG	60480	3208	14W-9S	D3
8100	BRRG	60527	3208	14W-9S	D3
8100	WLSP	60480	3208	14W-9S	D3
Steepleview Ln					
13800	LMNT	60439	3271	17W-14S	C6
Stefan Ct					
3000	LSLE	60563	3142	25W-5S	C2
Steffanie Ct					
3200	JLET	60451	3500	19W-23S	D3
Steffen Dr					
1800	HFET	60192	2855	31W-12N	E1
Steger Rd					
-	UYPK	60471	3594	6W-27S	B5
3600	MonT	60466	3594	4W-27S	D5
3600	PKFT	60466	3594	4W-27S	D5
3600	RNPK	60466	3594	4W-27S	D5
3600	RNPK	60471	3594	4W-27S	D5
5100	RchT	60471	3594	6W-27S	A5
5100	UYPK	60449	3594	6W-27S	A5
E Steger Rd					
10	CRTE	60417	3596	0E-27S	D5
10	STGR	60475	3596	0E-27S	D5
600	CRTE	60417	3597	1E-27S	B5
600	STGR	60475	3597	1E-27S	B5
1400	STGR	60411	3597	1E-27S	B5
1600	CteT	60417	3597	2E-27S	D5
1600	SLVL	60411	3597	2E-27S	D5
1700	BlmT	60411	3597	2E-27S	E5
2500	BlmT	60411	3598	3E-27S	B5
2500	CteT	60417	3598	3E-27S	A5
3500	SjnT	46311	3598	4E-28S	C5
W Steger Rd					
10	STGR	60475	3596	1W-27S	A5
100	BlmT	60475	3596	1W-27S	A5
300	BlmT	60466	3595	2W-27S	D5
300	BlmT	60475	3595	1W-27S	E5
300	CteT	60475	3595	2W-27S	D5
300	STGR	60475	3595	1W-27S	E5
2200	MonT	60466	3595	2W-27S	C5
2200	MonT	60475	3595	2W-27S	C5
2200	PKFT	60466	3595	2W-27S	C5
4800	RchT	60471	3593	6W-27S	E5
4800	RchT	60471	3594	6W-28S	A5
4800	RNPK	60471	3593	6W-27S	E5
4800	RNPK	60471	3594	6W-28S	A5
4800	UYPK	60449	3593	6W-27S	E5
4800	UYPK	60449	3594	6W-28S	A5
5600	MonT	60449	3593	7W-27S	C5
5600	MonT	60471	3593	7W-27S	D5
5600	RchT	60443	3593	8W-27S	A5
5600	UYPK	60471	3593	7W-27S	E5
6600	FKFT	60423	3593	8W-27S	B5
6600	FKFT	60449	3593	8W-27S	A5
6900	FftT	60423	3592	9W-27S	E5
6900	FKFT	60423	3592	9W-27S	E5
6900	GGnT	60423	3592	9W-27S	E5
8800	FftT	60423	3591	13W-27S	B5
8800	GGnT	60423	3591	13W-27S	B5
10800	FKFT	60423	3591	13W-27S	B5
11200	FftT	60423	3590	14W-27S	E5
11200	FKFT	60423	3590	14W-27S	E5
11300	GGnT	60423	3590	14W-27S	E5
11900	MhtT	60423	3590	14W-27S	D5
11900	MhtT	60442	3590	14W-27S	D5
11900	NlxT	60423	3590	14W-27S	D5
11900	NlxT	60442	3590	14W-27S	D5
11900	NlxT	60451	3590	14W-27S	D5
18800	LbvT	60030	2533	18W-31N	D7
Steger-Monee Rd					
23900	MonT	60417	3594	4W-28S	E7
23900	MonT	60417	3683	4W-29S	E1
23900	MonT	60466	3594	4W-28S	E7
23900	UYPK	60466	3683	4W-29S	E1
Stein St					
1100	JLET	60432	3499	22W-22S	C3
1100	JltT	60432	3499	22W-22S	C3
Steinbeck Ct					
1000	NPVL	60540	3202	28W-8S	E1
Steiner Ct					
10	ALGN	60102	2692	38W-21N	E6
10	LIHL	60156	2692	38W-21N	E6
S Steiner Rd					
14500	PNFD	60544	3337	32W-17S	D6
14500	PnfT	60544	3337	32W-17S	D6
Steinert Rd					
2400	TNLK	53181	2354		A2
Steinley Av					
1400	JltT	60433	3587	22W-26S	D3
Stella Blvd					
3700	CteT	60417	3596	1W-28S	A7
3700	STGR	60417	3596	1W-28S	A7
3700	STGR	60475	3596	1W-28S	B6
Stella Ct					
500	ELGN	60120	2855	33W-11N	B4
3200	ZION	60099	2421	11W-40N	D2
Stella St					
400	ELGN	60120	2855	33W-11N	A4
Stellar Ln					
12700	PNFD	60585	3339	28W-15S	A2
Stellon St					
-	DMND	60416	3941	33W-39S	A2
E Stellon St					
1500	DMND	60416	3941	33W-39S	C2
Stenman Dr					
1600	BTVA	60510	3078	34W-2S	D4
1900	BtvT	60510	3078	34W-2S	D5
Stepeeple Hl					
8600	HYHL	60457	3209	11W-10S	E4
N Stephan Dr					
400	PLTN	60067	2752	21W-16N	C6
600	PltT	60067	2752	21W-16N	C6
Stephanie Ct					
100	BRLT	60103	2911	28W-8N	A3
S Stephanie Ct					
26500	MonT	60449	3683	6W-32S	A7
Stephanie Dr					
500	LKPT	60441	3420	21W-19S	A2
Stephanie Ln					
10	GNEN	60137	3025	22W-0S	C7
11600	FftT	60448	3502	14W-22S	D2
11600	MKNA	60448	3502	14W-22S	D2
Stephen Av					
900	ELGN	60123	2854	36W-12N	A1
Stephen Ct					
-	AraT	60502	3139	33W-6S	B5
-	AURA	60502	3139	33W-6S	B5
8400	WDRG	60517	3205	21W-9S	D4
10900	MKNA	60448	3503	13W-23S	A2
Stephen Dr					
1800	MTGY	60538	3199	38W-9S	A5
10300	CHRG	60415	3275	8W-12S	A1
S Stephen Dr					
13300	PlsT	60464	3345	13W-15S	B2
Stephen St					
10	LMNT	60439	3270	19W-13S	D5
1800	AraT	60502	3139	33W-6S	A5
1900	AURA	60502	3139	33W-6S	A5
Stephens St					
10	MTSN	60443	3506	6W-24S	A5
Stepp Dr					
5400	SMMT	60501	3148	9W-5S	C3
Stepstone Ln					
2200	HRPK	60133	2967	27W-5N	B2
Sterbenz Ct					
300	ANTH	60002	2358	22W-42N	B5
Sterkel Rd					
-	NARA	60506	3076	39W-3S	D6
Sterling Av					
-	AntT	60081	2415	28W-38N	A6
-	FXLK	60081	2415	28W-38N	A6
-	SEGN	60177	2907	37W-7N	C4
600	FSMR	60422	3507	3W-22S	B2
600	FSMR	60430	3507	2W-22S	C1
600	HMWD	60430	3507	2W-22S	C1
800	GNVA	60134	3019	37W-0N	C5
800	GnvT	60134	3019	37W-0N	C5
1000	JLET	60432	3499	22W-23S	D4
1000	JltT	60432	3499	22W-23S	D4
17400	CCHL	60478	3426	4W-20S	D5
17400	HLCT	60429	3426	4W-20S	D5
17400	HLCT	60478	3426	4W-20S	D5
E Sterling Av					
800	WCHI	60185	3022	29W-0N	E5
N Sterling Av					
800	PLTN	60067	2752	22W-16N	B6
900	PltT	60067	2752	22W-17N	B5
900	PltT	60074	2752	22W-17N	B5
Sterling Cir					
10	WHTN	60187	3082	24W-2S	D4
300	AlqT	60013	2641	31W-25N	D5
300	CRY	60013	2641	31W-25N	D5
Sterling Ct					
-	DMND	60416	3941	33W-40S	C3
200	BMDL	60108	2969	23W-4N	B2
200	GNCY	53128	2353		B3
600	NPVL	60540	3142	25W-7S	A7
700	BRLT	60103	2911	28W-8N	B3
1800	SCRL	60174	2964	34W-3N	D5
2600	ELGN	60124	2853	37W-11N	D4
17100	LKPT	60441	3419	22W-20S	D5
17300	SHLD	60473	3429	2E-20S	D4
18500	WrnT	60030	2533	18W-34N	E2
N Sterling Ct					
2400	RLKB	60073	2475	22W-36N	B4
Sterling Dr					
10	HmrT	60441	3342	20W-16S	B3
100	BMDL	60108	2969	23W-4N	B3
1000	LMNT	60439	3342	20W-16S	B3
1200	MDLN	60060	2590	19W-29N	B3
2400	MchT	60050	2528	31W-34N	D1
2600	MchT	60050	2471	31W-34N	D7
11800	ODPK	60467	3344	14W-16S	C4
16600	LMNT	60439	3270	20W-14S	A7
17000	LKPT	60441	3419	22W-20S	D5
W Sterling Dr					
7600	FftT	60423	3504	9W-24S	D6
Sterling Ln					
-	NptT	60099	2361	15W-42N	A5
100	BMDL	60108	2969	23W-4N	B3
100	EVTN	60201	2812	4W-13N	C7
100	NHFD	60093	2811	7W-15N	B2
100	WLMT	60091	2812	4W-13N	C7
100	WLMT	60201	2812	4W-13N	C7
9800	SRPK	60176	2973	12W-4N	B2
14000	HTLY	60142	2744	42W-20N	A1
42900	WDWH	60099	2361	15W-42N	A5
Sterling Pkwy					
10	GNCY	53128	2353		B4
10	RcmT	53128	2353		B4
Sterling Rd					
300	KLWH	60043	2812	4W-14N	C4
600	IVNS	60067	2751	23W-16N	E6
3600	DRGV	60515	3084	19W-4S	D7
3600	YkTp	60515	3084	19W-4S	D7
4200	DRGV	60515	3144	19W-4S	D1
Sterling St					
-	LynT	60458	3209	12W-8S	D1
-	WLSP	60458	3209	12W-8S	D1
-	WLSP	60480	3209	12W-8S	D1
Sterling St E					
400	LynT	60458	3209	11W-8S	E2
Sterling St W					
600	LynT	60458	3209	11W-8S	E2
Sterling Heights Ct					
-	ANTH	60002	2417	21W-40N	D3
Sterling Heights Dr					
700	ANTH	60002	2417	21W-40N	D3
700	AntT	60002	2417	21W-40N	D3
N Sterling Heights Rd					
10	VNHL	60061	2647	18W-25N	A6
S Sterling Heights Rd					
10	VNHL	60061	2647	18W-24N	A6
Sterling Lake Ct					
-	LktT	60403	3417	26W-19S	E4
-	LktT	60403	3418	26W-19S	A4
Sterling Lake Dr					
-	LktT	60403	3417	26W-19S	E4
-	LktT	60403	3418	26W-19S	A4
Sterling Oaks Ct					
-	SRWD	60404	3584	31W-25S	A2
Sterling Ridge Blvd					
-	CRY	60013	2641	31W-25N	D5
Sterling Woods Ln					
-	ElgT	60124	2907	38W-8N	B3
-	SEGN	60124	2907	38W-8N	B3
Stern Av					
200	CTHL	60403	3498	24W-21S	D1
200	CTHL	60435	3498	24W-21S	E1
3000	SCRL	60174	2965	33W-2N	A7

STREET Block	City	ZIP	Map#	CGS	Grid
Stern Av					
3700	WynT	60174	2965	33W-2N	B7
3700	WynT	60185	2965	33W-2N	B7
Stetson Av					
600	SCRL	60174	2965	33W-2N	A7
600	SCRL	60174	3021	33W-2N	A1
N Stetson Av					
100	CHCG	60601	3034	0E-0N	C4
Steuban Rd					
800	NndT	60051	2529	29W-31N	B6
W Steuben St					
1700	CHCG	60643	3277	2W-13S	D3
Steven Ct					
10	ALGN	60102	2694	34W-21N	B6
14800	LMNT	60439	3271	18W-15S	A7
14800	LMNT	60439	3343	18W-15S	A1
Steven Dr					
8800	MaiT	60016	2863	11W-12N	E2
8800	MaiT	60714	2863	11W-12N	E2
8800	NLES	60016	2863	11W-12N	E2
8800	NLES	60714	2863	11W-12N	E2
Steven Ln					
2500	NHBK	60062	2809	11W-15N	C1
Steven Pl					
8400	TYPK	60487	3424	10W-19S	B2
Stevens Av					
300	JLET	60432	3499	22W-23S	C4
300	JltT	60432	3499	22W-23S	C4
N Stevens Av					
6000	CHCG	60646	2920	4W-7N	B3
6000	CHCG	60659	2920	4W-7N	B3
Stevens Ct					
400	GYLK	60030	2533	19W-32N	C5
500	SYHW	60118	2800	36W-15N	A3
600	WNVL	60555	3080	29W-2S	C5
1500	NARA	60542	3077	38W-3S	B7
Stevens Dr					
10	SMBG	60173	2859	21W-10N	E5
1700	GNVW	60025	2810	8W-13N	E5
8700	BRBK	60459	3211	6W-10S	E4
8700	OKLN	60453	3211	6W-10S	E4
8700	OKLN	60459	3211	6W-10S	E4
W Stevens Dr					
400	AddT	60101	2970	19W-3N	D4
400	ADSN	60101	2970	19W-3N	D4
Stevens Ln					
200	ElgT	60124	2907	38W-8N	A3
200	SEGN	60124	2907	38W-8N	A3
22700	WMTN	60481	3853	28W-38S	A6
22700	WmTp	60481	3853	29W-38S	A6
Stevens Rd					
10	ElgT	60124	2907	38W-7N	B5
10	ElgT	60175	2907	38W-8N	B4
10	SchT	60175	2907	38W-7N	B4
200	SEGN	60124	2907	38W-7N	B5
Stevens St					
10	GNVA	60134	3020	35W-1N	C3
600	NPVL	60540	3141	27W-6S	C5
7700	DRN	60561	3207	18W-8S	A2
Stevens Glen Rd					
200	SchT	60175	2907	38W-7N	A5
Steven Smith St					
1200	JLET	60431	3496	28W-22S	E2
Stevenson Ct					
1000	BmdT	60143	2913	22W-7N	D4
1000	BmdT	60157	2913	22W-7N	D4
1000	ROSL	60143	2913	22W-7N	D4
1000	ROSL	60157	2913	22W-7N	D4
Stevenson Dr					
10	BFGV	60089	2701	16W-23N	E3
10	LNSH	60069	2701	16W-23N	E3
400	BGBK	60440	3269	22W-12S	C3
500	LYVL	60048	2591	17W-28N	A6
9100	MaiT	60016	2863	11W-11N	D3
E Stevenson Dr					
10	GLHT	60139	2968	23W-3N	E6
100	GLHT	60139	2969	23W-3N	A5
W Stevenson Dr					
10	GLHT	60139	2968	24W-3N	D6
100	CLSM	60188	2968	24W-3N	D6
100	GLHT	60188	2968	24W-3N	D6
Stevenson Expwy					
-	BDPK	-	3147	11W-7S	E6
-	BDPK	-	3148	10W-6S	B4
-	CHCG	-	3089	6W-4S	E6
-	CHCG	-	3090	5W-4S	A6
-	CHCG	-	3091	3W-3S	A4
-	CHCG	-	3092	0W-2S	A2
-	CTSD	-	3146	14W-7S	D7
-	CTSD	-	3147	13W-7S	A7
-	FTVW	-	3089	6W-4S	D7
-	FTVW	-	3148	9W-5S	E2
-	FTVW	-	3149	8W-5S	A1
-	HGKN	-	3147	11W-7S	E7
-	IHPK	-	3146	14W-7S	D7
-	SKNY	-	3089	6W-4S	E7
-	SMMT	-	3148	9W-5S	C2
-	StkT	-	3089	6W-4S	D7
Stevenson Expwy I-55					
-	BDPK	-	3147	11W-7S	E7
-	BDPK	-	3148	10W-6S	B4
-	CHCG	-	3089	6W-4S	E6
-	CHCG	-	3090	5W-4S	A6
-	CHCG	-	3091	3W-3S	A4
-	CHCG	-	3092	0W-2S	A2
-	CTSD	-	3146	14W-7S	D7
-	CTSD	-	3147	13W-7S	A7
-	FTVW	-	3089	6W-4S	D7
-	FTVW	-	3148	8W-5S	E2
-	FTVW	-	3149	8W-5S	A1
-	HGKN	-	3147	11W-7S	E7
-	IHPK	-	3146	14W-7S	D7
-	SKNY	-	3089	6W-4S	E7
-	SMMT	-	3148	9W-5S	C2
-	StkT	-	3089	6W-4S	D7
N Stevenson Ln					
10	DSPN	60016	2808	14W-13N	C7
10	MPPT	60056	2808	14W-13N	C7
Stevenson Pl					
400	VNHL	60061	2647	17W-26N	B3
Stevenson Rd					
400	SEGN	60177	2908	35W-9N	C2
Stevenson St					
400	MRGO	60152	2634	49W-26N	C1
Steves Farm Dr					
10	SEGN	60177	2908	34W-9N	C1
Steward Ln					
1800	JLET	60586	3415	33W-21S	B7
E Steward St					
10	PLNO	60545	3259	47W-13S	C6
W Steward St					
500	PLNO	60545	3259	47W-13S	C6
Stewart Av					
-	AURA	60502	3138	35W-4S	C1
-	WslT	60481	3943	27W-42S	E6
200	WKGN	60085	2480	10W-35N	A6
200	YkTp	60148	3084	19W-1S	C1
300	WDSK	60098	2581	42W-30N	C1
400	PKRG	60068	2918	10W-8N	A1
500	LMBD	60148	3084	19W-1S	C2
600	DLTN	60419	3350	0E-17S	E5
600	ELGN	60120	2801	32W-12N	B7
600	NARA	60542	3138	35W-4S	B1
1000	CTCY	60409	3352	3E-17S	A5
1400	CTCY	60409	3351	2E-17S	C5
1400	PKRG	60068	2917	11W-8N	E1
1500	CHHT	60411	3596	0W-25S	C1
1700	DSPN	60018	2863	12W-10N	B5
2500	BlmT	60411	3596	0W-26S	C2
2600	EVTN	60201	2812	3W-13N	E7
3300	CRTE	60417	3596	0W-27S	C5
3300	STGR	60475	3596	0W-27S	C5
18000	HMWD	60430	3427	3W-22S	B7
18200	LNSG	60438	3430	4E-21S	B6
18400	HMWD	60430	3507	3W-22S	B1
N Stewart Av					
100	LYVL	60048	2591	16W-28N	D5
200	LMBD	60148	3026	19W-1N	C3
38500	BHPK	60087	2422	10W-38N	B7
38500	BHPK	60099	2422	10W-38N	B7
S Stewart Av					
-	YkTp	60148	3026	19W-0S	C7
10	LMBD	60148	3026	19W-0N	C5
100	LYVL	60048	2591	16W-28N	D6
300	AddT	60101	2970	19W-3N	C6
300	ADSN	60101	2970	19W-3N	C6
1600	CHCG	60616	3092	0W-1S	B1
2200	LMBD	60148	3084	19W-2S	C3
3800	CHCG	60609	3092	0W-3S	B5
5500	CHCG	60609	3152	0W-6S	B3
5900	CHCG	60621	3152	0W-7S	B6
7500	CHCG	60620	3214	0W-8S	B1
7500	CHCG	60621	3214	0W-8S	B1
11100	CHCG	60628	3278	0W-14S	B5
13700	RVDL	60827	3350	0W-16S	B2
W Stewart Av					
28100	AntT	60081	2415	28W-38N	A7
Stewart Ct					
300	LkT	60441	3419	21W-18S	E1
600	GRNE	60031	2534	15W-33N	E3
1000	JLET	60431	3496	29W-22S	E2
E Stewart Ct					
600	HMND	46394	3280		D4
Stewart Dr					
-	BvlT	60416	3941	33W-40S	C3
-	DMND	60408	3941	33W-40S	C3
-	DMND	60416	3941	33W-40S	C3
-	WLBK	60514	3145	16W-6S	D4
200	NPVL	60563	3140	30W-5S	B2
200	NpvT	60563	3140	30W-5S	B3
1500	DRN	60561	3207	18W-9S	A2
5900	WLBK	60527	3145	16W-6S	D4
Stewart Ln					
2100	WDND	60118	2800	35W-16N	B2
Stewart Rd					
-	OswT	60543	3265	33W-13S	A6
Stewart St					
200	WMTN	60481	3853	27W-38S	C6
400	BTVA	60510	3078	34W-1S	D2
Stewart Ter					
-	CRTE	60417	3596	0E-29S	E7
-	CRTE	60417	3597	0E-29S	A7
Stewart Wy					
-	BlmT	60411	3508	0W-24S	C5
-	CHHT	60411	3508	0W-24S	C5
W Stewart Ridge Dr					
-	PNFD	60585	3265	32W-14S	C7
-	WldT	60585	3265	32W-14S	C7
Stewert Dr					
3200	DRN	60561	3206	20W-9S	B4
Stickley Ln					
200	LIHL	60156	2692	38W-21N	E5
Stickney Av					
7200	BGVW	60455	3148	9W-8S	C7
7500	BGVW	60455	3210	9W-8S	C2
Stickney Run					
8100	BLVY	60098	2583	37W-30N	C2
Stieg Rd					
2000	SenT	60098	2581	43W-29N	A4
2000	WDSK	60098	2581	43W-29N	A4
W Stiehr Rd					
13700	NptT	60083	2420	13W-40N	E3
13700	WDWH	60083	2420	13W-40N	E3
Stiers Ct					
2000	AURA	60510	3078	34W-3S	D5
2000	BTVA	60510	3078	34W-3S	D5
S Stiles Dr					
900	ADSN	60101	2970	19W-2N	D7
900	ADSN	60101	3026	19W-2N	D1
Still Hill Dr					
3000	MHRY	60050	2528	32W-31N	C7
N Stilling Blvd					
-	MchT	60050	2528	31W-34N	D1
2700	MchT	60050	2471	31W-34N	D7
Stilling Ln					
2100	NndT	60050	2585	31W-29N	D3
Still Meadows Ln					
200	BbyT	60119	3017	42W-1N	D4
Still Water Ct					
200	RGMW	60067	2805	22W-13N	B5
Stillwater Ct					
10	ALGN	60102	2693	36W-21N	C6
10	AURA	60506	3137	38W-7S	A7
200	OSWG	60543	3263	38W-12S	B3
300	WCDA	60084	2644	25W-27N	A1
400	NPVL	60565	3204	25W-10S	A5
700	LKZH	60047	2699	22W-22N	A4
1000	YKVL	60560	3333	42W-14S	D1
2000	RMVL	60544	3417	27W-18S	B1
2900	JLET	60586	3415	32W-20S	C4
W Stillwater Ct					
17400	WrnT	60031	2477	17W-36N	B4
Stillwater Dr					
10	HNVL	60030	2532	22W-33N	C3
Stillwater Ln					
600	BRTN	60010	2698	25W-20N	B7
Stillwater Rd					
-	WRLK	60097	2469	37W-36N	B3
1000	ELGN	60120	2855	32W-12N	C2
N Stillwater Rd					
1900	ANHT	60004	2807	16W-16N	D1
Stillwell Av					
100	RKDL	60436	3498	25W-25S	B7
Stillwell Ct					
800	WHTN	60187	3082	24W-2S	D3
3200	WDRG	60517	3143	22W-7S	B6
Stillwell Dr					
300	BFGV	60089	2754	17W-18N	C3
3000	DSPN	60018	2917	12W-8N	B2
3100	RSMT	60018	2917	12W-8N	B3
5200	MchT	60097	2469	36W-37N	E2
5300	RGWD	60097	2469	36W-37N	E2
Stillwell Pl					
4000	OKLN	60453	3276	5W-12S	C2
Stillwell Rd					
200	OKTR	60181	3085	17W-1S	C1
E Stimmel St					
100	WCHI	60185	3022	29W-0N	D5
500	WnfT	60185	3022	29W-0N	D5
W Stimmel St					
100	WCHI	60185	3022	30W-0N	C5
300	WnfT	60185	3022	30W-0N	B5
Stirling Av					
1000	BlmT	60411	3507	2W-25S	D7
1000	CHHT	60411	3507	2W-25S	D7
Stirling Ct					
-	LKWD	60014	2692	39W-23N	D1
2100	HRPK	60133	2967	27W-5N	C1
2900	MTGY	60538	3198	40W-9S	B5
Stirling Ln					
10	CNHL	60514	3145	16W-6S	D4
10	RGMW	60008	2806	20W-15N	A3
10	WLBK	60514	3145	16W-6S	D4
10	WLBK	60527	3145	16W-6S	D4
100	SMBG	60194	2857	26W-10N	E5
600	PTHT	60070	2808	14W-14N	C4
1800	MTGY	60538	3198	40W-9S	B5
Stirling Rd					
2100	BKBN	60015	2703	11W-22N	C4
Stirlingshire Ct					
300	BLVY	60050	2526	36W-31N	D6
Stirrup Ct					
-	RLKP	60030	2532	22W-31N	B7
10	LMNT	60439	3271	18W-13S	A5
S Stirrup Ct					
14500	HMGN	60491	3344	15W-17S	B5
Stirrup Ln					
10	CmpT	60175	2962	40W-4N	B5
100	BRRG	60527	3146	14W-7S	C6
700	NLNX	60451	3501	17W-23S	D3
1000	LMNT	60439	3271	18W-13S	A5
2100	WHTN	60187	3082	23W-3S	E5
2100	WHTN	60187	3083	23W-3S	A5
Stirrup Pl					
100	BRRG	60527	3146	14W-7S	C6
Stirrup Cup Ct					
10	SCRL	60174	2964	34W-4N	D4
Stockberry Ln					
2700	WCHI	60185	2965	32W-4N	B5
Stockbridge Ct					
500	LKFT	60045	2648	13W-25N	E5
700	SMBG	60194	2858	25W-11N	B4
1000	ELGN	60120	2855	32W-12N	D1
Stockbridge Dr					
700	CLSM	60188	2967	27W-3N	D6
Stockbridge Ln					
6500	LGGV	60047	2646	18W-24N	D6
6500	LGGV	60060	2646	18W-24N	D6
Stockbridge Pl					
800	ELGN	60120	2855	32W-12N	D2
800	HFET	60192	2855	32W-12N	D2
Stockholm Av					
26500	GrtT	60041	2530	26W-33N	D3
Stockley Rd					
700	DRGV	60516	3206	19W-8S	D1
700	DRN	60516	3206	19W-8S	D1
Stockport Ct					
200	ROSL	60172	2912	25W-7N	C5
Stock Port Ln					
200	SMBG	60193	2859	23W-10N	B6
Stockton Av					
1000	DSPN	60018	2862	13W-9N	E7
1800	DSPN	60018	2863	12W-9N	B7
12900	PNFD	60585	3338	30W-15S	B2
18500	HMWD	60422	3507	3W-22S	A1
18500	HMWD	60430	3507	3W-22S	A1
Stockton Ct					
1000	AURA	60502	3139	32W-6S	B4
1000	VNHL	60061	2647	17W-26N	C3
1500	BRLT	60103	2967	28W-5N	B2
2900	NPVL	60564	3202	29W-9S	C4
E Stockton Ct					
400	RLKB	60073	2475	22W-36N	B4
W Stockton Ct					
18000	WrnT	60031	2477	18W-36N	A4
Stockton Dr					
-	JLET	60421	3586	24W-28S	E7
-	JLET	60421	3675	24W-28S	D1
10	GYLK	60030	2475	21W-35N	E7
10	GYLK	60030	2532	21W-34N	D1
100	AvnT	60030	2475	21W-35N	E7
1800	HFET	60169	2858	25W-12N	C1
1800	NHFD	60093	2811	7W-15N	C3
N Stockton Dr					
1600	CHCG	60614	2978	0W-2N	B7
Stockton Ln					
1500	CLLK	60014	2693	36W-22N	D3
2200	AURA	60502	3139	33W-6S	B4
2700	NPVL	60564	3202	29W-9S	C4
9900	HTLY	60142	2692	40W-22N	A4
13900	ODPK	60467	3344	14W-16S	E3
N Stockton Ln					
39100	BHPK	60083	2421	13W-39N	A5
Stockton St					
-	WNKA	60093	2811	6W-15N	D2
Stoddard Av					
-	MltT	60188	3024	23W-0N	E4
-	WHTN	60188	3024	23W-0N	E4
1400	WHTN	60187	3024	23W-0N	E4
1600	MltT	60187	3024	23W-0N	E4
Stoffa Av					
500	ELBN	60119	3017	43W-0N	A4
N Stokes Av					
-	CHCG	60018	2917	12W-6N	B6
-	SRPK	60018	2917	12W-6N	B6
-	SRPK	60176	2917	12W-6N	B6
Stoll Rd					
11100	FKFT	60423	3591	13W-27S	A4
11200	FKFT	60423	3590	14W-27S	E4
N Stolp Av					
10	AURA	60505	3138	35W-7S	B7
10	AURA	60506	3138	35W-7S	A7
S Stolp Av					
10	AURA	60505	3138	35W-7S	B6
10	AURA	60506	3138	35W-7S	B6
W Stolting Rd					
8600	NLES	60714	2863	10W-10N	E4
8600	NLES	60714	2864	10W-10N	A4
8600	PKRG	60714	2863	10W-10N	E4
Stone Av					
10	NARA	60542	3078	35W-4S	A7
200	LKZH	60047	2699	22W-22N	C3
300	AddT	60101	2970	18W-4N	E4
300	AddT	60101	2971	18W-4N	A4
300	AddT	60106	2971	17W-4N	B4
300	ADSN	60101	2970	18W-4N	E4
300	ADSN	60101	2971	18W-4N	A4
300	AURA	60505	3200	36W-8S	A1
400	ADSN	60101	2969	21W-4N	E4
400	BmdT	60101	2969	21W-4N	E4
E Stone Av					
10	AddT	60101	2971	18W-4N	A4
10	LKFT	60045	2649	10W-24N	E6
10	LKFT	60045	2650	10W-24N	A6
300	ADSN	60101	2971	17W-4N	B4
N Stone Av					
100	LGNG	60525	3087	12W-4S	B6
200	LGPK	60525	3087	12W-3S	B5
S Stone Av					
10	LGNG	60525	3087	12W-4S	B7
300	LGNG	60525	3147	12W-5S	B2
1200	CTSD	60525	3147	12W-5S	B3
W Stone Av					
10	LKFT	60045	2649	11W-24N	E6
300	ADSN	60101	2970	19W-4N	D4
1400	AddT	60101	2970	20W-4N	A4
1700	BmdT	60101	2970	20W-4N	A4
Stone Cl					
-	GNVA	60134	3019	37W-1N	C3
Stone Ct					
200	NLNX	60451	3500	19W-24S	D5
E Stone Ct					
800	AddT	60101	2971	17W-4N	B4
800	AddT	60106	2971	17W-4N	B4
800	ADSN	60101	2971	17W-4N	B4
N Stone Ct					
1000	NPVL	60563	3142	25W-5S	A3
S Stone Ct					
3500	JLET	60436	3498	25W-24S	C6
W Stone Ct					
26900	GrtT	60041	2530	26W-33N	C2
Stone Dr					
400	SCRL	60174	2964	34W-3N	E7
2000	NndT	60051	2586	29W-30N	C2
Stone Ln					
-	BlmT	60411	3509	2E-25S	D7
-	FDHT	60411	3509	2E-25S	D7
-	SLVL	60411	3509	2E-25S	D7
1100	SLVL	60411	3509	2E-25S	D7
Stone Pl					
300	WLNG	60090	2755	14W-17N	D5
W Stone Rd					
200	VLPK	60181	3027	18W-1N	A1
400	VLPK	60181	3026	18W-1N	E1
Stone St					
200	SEGN	60177	2908	34W-8N	D2
500	DSPN	60016	2862	14W-12N	C1
N Stone St					
1200	CHCG	60610	3034	0E-1N	C1
1200	CHCG	60611	3034	0E-1N	C1
W Stone St					
100	JLET	60435	3498	24W-23S	E3
Stone Bluff Dr					
-	RMVL	60544	3339	27W-18S	C7
Stonebriar Ct					
-	LslT	60540	3204	24W-8S	C2
Stonebriar Dr					
-	LslT	60540	3204	24W-8S	C1
Stonebriar Ln					
500	PltT	60124	2852	40W-11N	B5
W Stonebriar Wy					
26400	CNHN	60410	3672	33W-31S	B6
Stonebridge Blvd					
2600	AURA	60502	3139	32W-5S	C3
Stonebridge Cir					
1400	WHTN	60187	3081	26W-1S	E2
Stonebridge Ct					
1100	ELGN	60120	2855	32W-12N	D2
1300	BRLT	60103	2967	28W-5N	A1
1600	NLNX	60451	3588	19W-26S	E3
1600	WHTN	60187	3081	26W-2S	E3
2600	JLET	60586	3415	32W-20S	C5
18600	WrnT	60030	2533	18W-34N	E1
39700	LkvT	60002	2416	24W-39N	C4
E Stonebridge Ct					
800	PLTN	60074	2806	19W-15N	B1
W Stonebridge Ct					
10	PSHL	60465	3274	10W-12S	B3
Stonebridge Dr					
-	ANHT	60004	2753	18W-16N	E6
-	ANHT	60004	2754	18W-16N	A7
-	HMGN	60491	3344	15W-16S	B3
-	HmrT	60491	3344	15W-16S	B3
600	BGBK	60490	3268	26W-13S	A5
1400	NLNX	60451	3588	19W-26S	E3
1900	NlxT	60451	3588	19W-26S	E3
2700	JLET	60586	3415	32W-20S	C5
3900	ZION	60099	2362	12W-41N	B7
16100	HMGN	60491	3421	17W-19S	C2
17500	HLCT	60429	3427	3W-21S	A6
N Stonebridge Dr					
-	ANHT	60004	2753	18W-16N	E6
W Stonebridge Dr					
-	LkvT	60046	2416	24W-39N	C4
24500	AntT	60002	2416	24W-40N	C4
24500	LkvT	60002	2416	24W-40N	C4
Stonebridge Ln					
10	SchT	60175	2963	36W-5N	E3
100	PltT	60124	2852	41W-11N	A4
700	BFGV	60089	2754	17W-17N	B5
700	CLLK	60014	2693	36W-23N	C1
2500	NHBK	60062	2757	10W-18N	A4
N Stonebridge Ln					
34100	WrnT	60030	2533	18W-34N	E1
W Stonebridge Ln					
13000	HTLY	60142	2744	42W-20N	C1
Stonebridge Rd					
700	FKFT	60423	3503	13W-24S	B6
Stonebridge Sq					
-	HLCT	60429	3427	3W-21S	A5
Stonebridge Tr					
1300	WHTN	60187	3081	26W-1S	E2
5700	MHRY	60050	2527	34W-32N	C5
Stonebridge Wy					
100	MDLN	60060	2646	20W-27N	B1
900	DGvT	60439	3270	19W-12S	D2
900	DGvT	60517	3270	19W-12S	D2
900	WDRG	60517	3270	19W-12S	D2
Stonebridge Woods Cross					
13600	HMGN	60491	3421	17W-19S	C2
Stone Brook Ct					
600	EGVW	60007	2914	20W-8N	B3
Stonebrook Ct					
10	SBTN	60010	2803	27W-13N	B6
Stonebrook Dr					
-	GRNE	60031	2477	17W-35N	B5
-	RMVL	60446	3417	27W-18S	B1
-	RMVL	60544	3339	27W-18S	B7
-	RMVL	60544	3417	27W-18S	B1
Stonebrook Rd					
100	MTSN	60443	3506	5W-24S	C5
3000	LSLE	60532	3142	25W-7S	C6
Stonebrooke Ct					
9400	TYPK	60487	3423	11W-20S	D5
Stone Canyon Cir					
500	IVNS	60010	2750	25W-17N	E6
500	IVNS	60010	2751	25W-17N	A6
800	BRTN	60010	2751	25W-17N	A6
Stone Canyon Wy					
-	IVNS	60010	2750	25W-17N	E6
Stonecastle Ln					
6100	GfnT	60014	2638	38W-25N	E4
6100	LKWD	60014	2638	38W-25N	E4
Stonechase Ct					
-	CNHN	60410	3672	32W-30S	D5
Stone Cir Ct					
600	SMBG	60194	2859	22W-10N	C5
Stone Cir Dr					
4900	OKLN	60453	3212	6W-11S	A7
Stone Creek Blvd					
8600	FKFT	60423	3592	10W-27S	B5
E Stone Creek Cir					
900	CLLK	60014	2693	37W-22N	C3
W Stone Creek Cir					
1000	CLLK	60014	2693	37W-22N	C3
Stone Creek Ct					
200	NPVL	60565	3203	26W-8S	E2
3500	JLET	60435	3417	27W-19S	C3
12900	HTLY	60142	2744	42W-18N	D4
Stonecreek Ct					
13200	HMGN	60491	3343	16W-17S	E6
Stone Creek Dr					
10	ElaT	60047	2645	23W-24N	A7
10	HNWD	60047	2645	22W-24N	A7
10	LMNT	60439	3272	15W-13S	B4
300	BGBK	60440	3205	22W-9S	C4
Stonecreek Dr					
18400	HLCT	60429	3426	4W-22S	D7
18400	HLCT	60429	3506	4W-22S	E1
Stonecrest Ct					
300	PltT	60124	2852	40W-11N	B4
Stonecrest Dr					
200	PltT	60124	2852	40W-11N	B4
Stonecrop Ct					
800	CmpT	60175	2962	39W-5N	D2
Stonecrop Ln					
-	JLET	60447	3495	33W-22S	A2
Stonefence Ct					
100	AURA	60506	3137	38W-7S	A7
Stone Fence Ln					
-	GNVA	60134	3020	34W-1N	D2
-	GnvT	60134	3020	34W-1N	D2
S Stone Fence Rd					
200	VNHL	60061	2647	16W-24N	C7
Stonefield Cir					
900	IVNS	60067	2751	23W-17N	D6
Stonefield Ct					
200	SMBG	60173	2860	20W-10N	A5
Stonefield Dr					
10	GLHT	60139	2968	23W-4N	E4
Stonefield Pl					
800	ROSL	60172	2912	24W-6N	D6
Stonefield Wy					
-	BTVA	60510	3077	36W-1S	E1
Stonegate					
-	HPSR	60140	2795	47W-16N	D1
2100	AURA	60506	3137	38W-7S	A7
Stone Gate Cir					
400	SMBG	60193	2859	23W-9N	A7
Stonegate Cir					
10	LNSH	60069	2702	14W-23N	C3
Stonegate Ct					
10	ALGN	60102	2747	36W-19N	A2
10	BFGV	60089	2754	17W-18N	A2
100	GNEN	60137	3083	22W-1S	C1
300	WLBK	60527	3146	15W-7S	A6
700	LYVL	60048	2591	17W-29N	C4
900	JLET	60435	3497	26W-22S	E3
1100	BRLT	60103	2966	30W-5N	C1
3100	FSMR	60422	3507	3W-22S	A1
Stone Gate Dr					
-	MRGO	60152	2634	49W-25N	C5
700	HDPK	60035	2758	7W-20N	A2
Stonegate Dr					
-	MTGY	60538	3198	41W-9S	A4
100	OSWG	60543	3263	37W-12S	C3
2700	NndT	60012	2583	36W-29N	E4
8000	TYPK	60477	3504	10W-23S	C4
26500	AntT	60002	2415	26W-38N	D6
S Stonegate Dr					
14600	HMGN	60491	3343	16W-17S	E5
W Stonegate Dr					
26500	AntT	60002	2415	26W-38N	D6
27400	AntT	60081	2415	27W-38N	B7
Stonegate Dr E					
10	PTHT	60070	2754	15W-16N	E7
10	PTHT	60070	2755	15W-16N	A7
10	WLNG	60090	2755	15W-16N	A7
Stonegate Dr W					
10	ANHT	60004	2754	16W-16N	E7
10	PTHT	60070	2754	15W-16N	E7
Stonegate Ln					
10	LKFT	60045	2650	9W-25N	C4
10	SMWD	60107	2857	28W-11N	A4
2200	WHTN	60187	3081	26W-2S	D3
2900	NHBK	60062	2756	11W-17N	D5
13900	ODPK	60467	3344	14W-16S	E4
Stonegate Rd					
-	DndT	60102	2746	36W-18N	E4
10	BFGV	60089	2754	17W-18N	A2
10	LGPK	60525	3087	12W-2S	B3
100	CRY	60013	2695	31W-23N	C2
100	TVLY	60013	2695	31W-23N	C2
200	ALGN	60102	2694	35W-20N	D4
200	CNHL	60514	3085	16W-4S	D7
200	CNHL	60514	3145	16W-4S	D1
200	CNHL	60559	3085	16W-4S	D7
200	WTMT	60559	3085	16W-4S	D7
300	NLNX	60451	3589	17W-25S	C1
300	NlxT	60451	3589	17W-25S	C1
700	LYVL	60048	2591	17W-29N	C4
1200	NPVL	60540	3141	28W-7S	A6
1400	ALGN	60102	2747	36W-19N	A2
1400	NPVL	60540	3140	28W-7S	E6
2300	ALGN	60102	2693	36W-21N	D6
2300	ALGN	60102	2746	36W-18N	E4
2400	ALGN	60118	2746	36W-18N	E5
2400	CPVL	60110	2746	36W-18N	E5
3300	WKGN	60087	2479	11W-37N	D1
N Stonegate Rd					
38600	AntT	60081	2415	27W-38N	B6
W Stonegate Rd					
13800	NptT	60083	2420	13W-40N	D3
13800	WDWH	60083	2420	13W-40N	D3
Stonegate Ter					
600	GLNC	60022	2758	7W-17N	B5
Stoneham Ct					
100	BGBK	60440	3269	22W-11S	D1

STREET Block	City	ZIP	Map#	CGS	Grid
Stoneham St					
100	WDDL	60106	2915	17W-6N	C7
100	WDDL	60191	2915	17W-6N	C7
1100	BNVL	60106	2915	16W-6N	D7
Stone Harbor Ct					
1400	HFET	60192	2804	25W-15N	A2
Stone Harbor Dr N					
4300	HFET	60192	2804	24W-15N	C2
Stone Harbor Dr W					
1400	HFET	60192	2804	25W-15N	A2
Stonehaven					
800	IVNS	60067	2804	23W-14N	E3
Stonehaven Av					
500	EGvT	60007	2860	19W-9N	D7
500	EGVV	60007	2860	19W-9N	D7
Stonehaven Cir					
1100	AURA	60564	3202	30W-9S	B4
Stonehaven Ct					
900	ELGN	60124	2853	37W-12N	C1
Stone Haven Dr					
10	HNWD	60047	2645	20W-24N	E7
10	HNWD	60047	2646	20W-24N	A7
Stonehaven Dr					
900	ELGN	60124	2853	37W-12N	C1
2200	JLET	60586	3416	30W-21S	B6
4400	LGGV	60047	2700	18W-22N	E3
Stone Haven Ln					
14600	HMGN	60491	3343	18W-17S	A6
Stonehaven Wy					
2100	LSLE	60532	3142	24W-7S	D6
Stonehearth Ln					
10	IHPK	60525	3146	13W-7S	E5
10	IHPK	60525	3147	12W-7S	B6
Stonehearth Sq					
10	IHPK	60525	3147	12W-7S	B6
Stoneheather Av					
1800	AURA	60503	3201	33W-10S	A5
Stonehedge Ct					
-	LslT	60540	3205	23W-8S	B1
900	CLLK	60014	2639	38W-24N	A7
900	CLLK	60014	2693	37W-23N	B1
1500	WLNG	60090	2754	16W-18N	D3
N Stonehedge Ct					
2100	RLKB	60073	2475	22W-36N	B5
Stonehedge Dr					
200	LslT	60540	3205	23W-8S	A1
1000	SMBG	60194	2858	24W-11N	D2
W Stonehedge Dr					
900	AddT	60101	2970	19W-3N	C5
900	ADSN	60101	2970	19W-3N	C5
S Stonehedge Ln					
900	PLTN	60067	2805	21W-14N	C3
Stonehedge Rd					
500	SCRL	60174	2964	35W-3N	C5
Stonehenge Ct					
10	BRRG	60527	3208	14W-8S	D2
800	CLSM	60188	2967	28W-3N	B5
900	NPVL	60563	3140	29W-5S	D3
1500	AURA	60502	3139	32W-5S	C3
Stonehenge Dr					
2400	AURA	60502	3139	32W-5S	C3
8200	ODPK	60462	3346	10W-16S	B3
19200	MKNA	60448	3503	12W-23S	C3
Stonehenge Ln					
200	TRLK	60010	2643	26W-25N	E5
Stonehill Ct					
700	SRGV	60554	3135	41W-5S	E2
1500	WHTN	60187	3081	26W-1S	D2
Stone Hill Dr					
10400	ODPK	60467	3423	13W-20S	B5
13400	HTLY	60142	2744	43W-19N	B3
Stonehill Ln					
200	SMBG	60193	2859	23W-10N	B5
Stonehill Rd					
10	OSWG	60543	3263	36W-12S	D3
Stonehurst Av					
-	DrrT	60098	2581	41W-28N	D6
-	WDSK	60098	2581	41W-28N	D6
Stonehurst Ct					
3200	JLET	60431	3497	28W-25S	B7
Stonehurst Dr					
10	ELGN	60120	2855	32W-11N	D4
700	ROSL	60172	2912	24W-7N	D5
Stonehurst Ln					
300	ROSL	60172	2912	24W-7N	D5
Stoneleat Rd					
500	SchT	60175	2963	36W-4N	E3
Stoneleigh Ct					
1600	LKFT	60045	2703	13W-23N	A1
2400	NPVL	60564	3202	29W-10S	D6
Stoneleigh Ln					
300	OSWG	60543	3264	36W-11S	A1
Stone Manor Cir					
200	BTVA	60510	3078	35W-1S	B3
W Stone Manor Ct					
17600	WrnT	60030	2534	17W-33N	B4
N Stone Manor Dr					
32700	WrnT	60030	2534	17W-32N	B4
Stone Marsh Ln					
100	NBRN	60010	2644	24W-25N	B5
Stonemill Av					
-	AddT	60101	2970	19W-4N	C4
500	ADSN	60101	2970	19W-4N	C4
W Stonemill Av					
-	AddT	60101	2970	19W-4N	C4
-	ADSN	60101	2970	19W-4N	C4
Stonemill Ln					
200	OSWG	60543	3264	36W-11S	A1
W Stoneoak Wy					
13900	HMGN	60491	3343	17W-17S	C5
Stone Ridge Cir					
1500	YKVL	60560	3260	44W-14S	E7
Stone Ridge Ct					
1500	YKVL	60560	3260	44W-14S	E7
Stoneridge Ct					
-	PltT	60124	2852	40W-11N	B4
5200	MTSN	60443	3594	6W-25S	A1
Stone Ridge Dr					
10	SBTN	60010	2803	26W-15N	C2
Stoneridge Dr					
100	DYR	46311	3598		D5
11100	ODPK	60467	3422	14W-21S	E6
11100	ODPK	60467	3423	12W-21S	C5
11100	OrlT	60467	3422	14W-21S	E6
Stone Ridge Ln					
1600	ALGN	60102	2747	36W-19N	B3
S Stone Ridge Ln					
24500	CteT	60417	3687	3E-29S	A2
Stoneridge Rd					
10	RGMW	60008	2806	19W-14N	B3
Stonewall Av					
2400	WDRG	60517	3143	21W-6S	D5
4300	DRGV	60515	3144	20W-5S	A2
5500	DGvT	60515	3144	20W-6S	A4
5900	DGvT	60516	3144	20W-6S	A5
6600	DRGV	60516	3144	20W-7S	A7
Stonewall Ct					
700	SMBG	60173	2859	22W-11N	C3
2500	WDRG	60517	3143	21W-6S	D5
Stonewall Dr					
8000	ODPK	60462	3346	10W-16S	C3
Stonewall Ln					
2700	JLET	60435	3417	27W-19S	C3
Stonewall St					
-	DRGV	60516	3144	20W-6S	A5
Stonewater Cross					
11300	HTLY	60142	2691	41W-20N	C7
11500	HTLY	60142	2744	41W-20N	D1
Stonewater Dr					
2800	NPVL	60564	3202	29W-10S	C7
Stonewater Ln					
400	OSWG	60543	3263	38W-12S	A3
Stonewier Pt					
7100	NndT	60050	2526	36W-31N	E7
7100	NndT	60050	2583	36W-30N	E1
Stonewood Cir					
-	CLSM	60188	2968	26W-4N	A4
300	CLSM	60188	2967	26W-4N	E4
Stonewood Dr					
10	SCRL	60174	2964	34W-4N	C4
W Stonewood Dr					
13100	HMGN	60491	3343	16W-17S	E5
Stonewood Pl					
100	AURA	60506	3137	38W-7S	B7
Stoneybrook Ct					
21500	KLDR	60047	2699	22W-21N	C6
Stoney Brook Dr					
600	NPVL	60565	3204	25W-9S	B4
Stoney Brook Ln					
-	BLID	60406	3349	3W-15S	B1
Stoneybrook Ln					
100	BMDL	60108	2969	22W-4N	C3
2600	AURA	60502	3079	32W-4S	C7
Stoneybrooke					
-	LMNT	60439	3342	20W-15S	B1
Stoney Creek Ln					
500	HRVD	60033	2464	50W-37N	A2
Stoney Island Av					
-	DLTN	60419	3351	1E-17S	C4
-	DLTN	60473	3351	2E-18S	C6
-	FDHT	60411	3509	2E-25S	C7
-	SLVL	60411	3509	2E-25S	C7
10	CTCY	60409	3351	2E-17S	C5
4100	GRNE	60031	2535	14W-34N	D1
18000	LNSG	60438	3429	1E-21S	C6
18000	ThtT	60438	3429	1E-21S	C6
18700	BlmT	60411	3429	2E-22S	C7
18700	BlmT	60411	3509	1E-24S	C5
18700	BlmT	60438	3429	2E-22S	C7
19000	LYWD	60411	3509	1E-24S	C5
S Stoney Island Av					
24500	CteT	60417	3686	2E-30S	D2
N Stoney Kirk Ct					
25600	ElaT	60047	2645	23W-25N	A4
Stonington Av					
300	BCHR	60401	3774	0W-35S	D6
2000	HFET	60169	2803	26W-12N	E7
Stonington Ct					
1000	SMBG	60193	2912	24W-9N	C1
2100	NPVL	60564	3202	29W-9S	D5
S Stonington Dr					
10	PLTN	60074	2806	19W-15N	B1
Stony Brook Ct					
25100	CNHN	60410	3672	32W-30S	C4
Stonybrook Ct					
300	ALGN	60102	2694	34W-21N	B6
Stonybrook Dr					
2500	JLET	60586	3416	31W-20S	A5
Stonybrook St					
2300	WCDA	60084	2588	25W-29N	A3
Stony Creek Dr					
10	PSHL	60465	3274	10W-12S	B3
5200	OKLN	60453	3275	6W-12S	E2
Stony Creek Ln					
900	YKVL	60560	3332	44W-15S	E2
900	YKVL	60560	3333	44W-15S	A2
Stony Hill Ln					
500	CLLK	60012	2639	36W-27N	E1
Stony Island Av					
18100	LNSG	60438	3429	1E-21S	C6
23300	CHCG	60617	3279	2E-12S	B1
S Stony Island Av					
5600	CHCG	60637	3153	1E-8S	B7
6600	CHCG	60649	3153	1E-8S	B7
7000	CHCG	60619	3153	1E-7S	B6
7500	CHCG	60649	3215	2E-8S	B1
8000	CHCG	60617	3215	1E-10S	B5
8000	CHCG	60619	3215	1E-10S	B5
9400	CHCG	60628	3215	1E-10S	B5
10300	CHCG	60617	3279	2E-13S	C5
12700	CHCG	60633	3279	2E-14S	C7
S Stony Island Ext					
-	CHCG	60617	3215	1E-11S	B7
-	CHCG	60628	3215	1E-11S	B7
-	CHCG	60628	3279	1E-12S	B1
Stony Man Ct					
-	PNFD	60585	3337	32W-15S	C1
Stoos Ln					
900	NPVL	60540	3141	26W-7S	D7
Stope Creek Dr					
2800	JLET	60435	3417	27W-19S	C3
Store St					
100	PGGV	60140	2798	40W-14N	B6
100	RtdT	60140	2798	40W-14N	B6
Stork Ct					
2900	RGMW	60008	2806	19W-14N	C4
Stormy Ct					
1900	SMBG	60193	2912	26W-8N	A2
W Story St					
25300	CNHN	60410	3672	31W-30S	E4
Storybook Dr					
-	BtlT	60512	3262	40W-11S	C1
Story Book Ln					
10	LNSH	60069	2702	13W-23N	E2
N Story Book Ln					
23000	LNSH	60069	2702	13W-23N	E3
N Stough St					
10	HNDL	60521	3145	16W-4S	E1
S Stough St					
10	HNDL	60521	3145	16W-5S	E3
5500	DGvT	60521	3145	16W-6S	E3
6500	WLBK	60527	3145	16W-7S	E6
W Stoughton Av					
25100	GrtT	60041	2474	25W-34N	B7
Stoughton Cir					
2300	AURA	60502	3139	32W-7S	C7
Stoughton Ct					
1100	SMBG	60194	2858	24W-10N	C5
Stoughton Dr					
2200	AURA	60502	3139	32W-7S	B7
Stout Ct					
600	GRNE	60031	2534	15W-33N	E3
Stover Rd					
-	BrnT	60010	2750	27W-16N	C7
-	BrnT	60010	2803	27W-15N	C1
10	BNHL	60010	2750	27W-16N	C7
10	BNHL	60010	2803	27W-16N	C1
Stowaway Bay					
100	LKMR	60051	2529	28W-33N	E4
Stowe Cir					
1800	EGVV	60007	2859	22W-9N	D7
2100	NPVL	60564	3202	29W-10S	D5
Stowe Ct					
2500	NHBK	60062	2756	10W-18N	E3
2500	NHBK	60062	2757	10W-18N	A3
2600	JLET	60586	3416	30W-20S	B5
6600	LSLE	60532	3142	24W-7S	D7
S Stowe Ct					
10400	PSHL	60465	3274	10W-12S	A2
Stowell Av					
700	SMWD	60107	2911	27W-9N	B2
Stowell Ct					
700	SMWD	60107	2911	28W-9N	B2
Stradford Cir					
700	BFGV	60089	2754	17W-18N	A4
Stradford Ln					
15100	ODPK	60462	3345	11W-18S	E7
Strandhill Dr					
13200	PlsT	60462	3345	11W-15S	D2
Strassburg Av					
22300	SLVL	60411	3597	2E-27S	D4
Stratford Av					
1600	WSTR	60154	3087	13W-1S	A2
2600	WSTR	60525	3087	13W-2S	A3
S Stratford Av					
700	EMHT	60126	3028	15W-0S	B6
800	YkTp	60126	3028	15W-0S	B6
Stratford Cir					
300	SMWD	60107	2857	28W-9N	A7
7200	FXLK	60020	2415	28W-39N	A5
Stratford Ct					
10	IHPK	60525	3146	13W-7S	E5
10	MltT	60137	3083	22W-2S	C3
10	SEGN	60177	2908	35W-7N	C5
100	NPVL	60540	3141	28W-6S	A5
300	AURA	60504	3202	30W-8S	A2
400	MHRY	60050	2527	33W-32N	D5
400	SMWD	60107	2857	28W-9N	B7
700	LKVL	60046	2475	22W-37N	C2
800	FKFT	60423	3503	13W-24S	B6
800	GYLK	60030	2533	20W-34N	B2
1100	ELGN	60120	2855	32W-10N	D5
1100	ISLK	60042	2586	30W-28N	B6
1200	LKZH	60047	2699	21W-21N	C6
1500	JLET	60435	3498	26W-23S	A4
1600	LKFT	60045	2703	13W-23N	A2
1600	WLNG	60090	2754	15W-18N	E3
3200	LbvT	60044	2593	13W-30N	A3
3300	NCHI	60044	2593	13W-30N	A3
21000	MKNA	60448	3502	14W-25S	E7
Stratford Dr					
-	BtvT	60506	3077	38W-3S	A6
-	NARA	60506	3077	38W-3S	A6
-	NARA	60542	3077	38W-3S	A6
10	BMDL	60108	2968	25W-4N	B2
200	GNVA	60134	3019	36W-1N	E3
1300	GRNE	60031	2478	14W-35N	C6
8400	TYPK	60487	3424	10W-21S	B7
11000	WLSP	60480	3208	13W-9S	E3
W Stratford Dr					
23600	WldT	60585	3266	29W-14S	D7
Stratford Ln					
-	CPVL	60118	2746	37W-18N	C4
100	VLPK	60181	3085	18W-1S	A1
200	IVNS	60010	2751	23W-16N	D6
200	OKTR	60181	3085	18W-1S	A1
200	YkTp	60181	3085	18W-1S	A1
300	SMWD	60107	2857	28W-9N	A7
300	WLBK	60527	3146	15W-7S	A6
600	SMBG	60193	2913	22W-9N	C1
700	ElgT	60124	2853	37W-11N	B5
800	DRGV	60516	3144	19W-6S	C5
900	DYR	46311	3510		E5
900	MDLN	60060	2646	18W-26N	E3
1000	ALGN	60102	2747	34W-19N	E2
1000	ALGN	60102	2748	34W-19N	A2
1000	HRPK	60133	2911	26W-9N	E1
1100	LKZH	60047	2699	21W-21N	C6
2100	GNVW	60025	2809	10W-14N	E3
9000	PSHL	60465	3209	11W-11S	E7
E Stratford Ln					
400	RLKB	60073	2475	22W-36N	B3
N Stratford Ln					
2500	RLKB	60073	2475	22W-36N	B4
W Stratford Ln					
13100	HTLY	60142	2744	42W-20N	C1
Stratford Pl					
10	DGvT	60561	3207	17W-9S	B3
10	MltT	60137	3083	22W-2S	C3
300	BMDL	60108	2968	24W-4N	C3
1200	NHBK	60062	2756	12W-17N	C5
7600	DRN	60561	3207	17W-8S	B2
W Stratford Pl					
100	MPPT	60056	2807	15W-14N	E4
100	MPPT	60056	2808	15W-14N	A4
500	CHCG	60657	2978	0W-4N	A3
Stratford Rd					
-	CLLK	60012	2641	33W-27N	A1
-	PRGV	60012	2641	33W-27N	A1
-	PRGV	60014	2641	33W-27N	A1
10	MltT	60137	3083	22W-2S	D3
10	OswT	60538	3199	36W-10S	E7
100	DSPN	60016	2862	14W-12N	C2
900	DRFD	60015	2703	11W-21N	D6
1500	BKBN	60015	2703	11W-21N	D6
1800	HDPK	60035	2704	9W-20N	C7
11000	MKNA	60448	3502	14W-25S	E7
N Stratford Rd					
1000	PTHT	60004	2807	16W-14N	C3
1700	ANHT	60004	2807	16W-15N	C1
3000	ANHT	60004	2754	16W-17N	C5
S Stratford Rd					
100	ANHT	60004	2807	16W-13N	C5
Stratham Cir					
10	NBRN	60010	2644	25W-24N	B7
Stratham Ct					
1000	SMBG	60193	2912	24W-9N	C1
Stratham Pl					
2200	HFET	60169	2857	26W-12N	E1
2200	HFET	60169	2858	26W-12N	A1
Strath Erin St					
1600	HDPK	60035	2704	9W-20N	C7
Strathmore Ct					
10	BFGV	60089	2754	17W-18N	A4
200	BMDL	60108	2969	23W-4N	B3
400	BRLT	60103	2910	30W-7N	B4
Strathmore Ln					
200	BMDL	60108	2969	23W-4N	B3
7800	HRPK	60133	2857	26W-9N	E7
Strathmore Ter					
10	SEGN	60177	2908	35W-8N	C3
Straton Cir					
600	WDND	60118	2800	36W-16N	A2
Straton Ct					
-	MKNA	60448	3502	15W-23S	C3
Stratton Av					
-	BHPK	60087	2480	9W-37N	B2
Stratton Dr					
-	LMNT	60439	3270	20W-14S	B7
Stratton Ln					
3100	AURA	60502	3139	31W-5S	E3
N Stratton Ln					
100	MPPT	60056	2808	14W-13N	C6
S Stratton Ln					
7000	GRNE	60031	2477	17W-35N	B5
Stratton St					
3300	ElgT	60124	2853	38W-11N	A4
Stratton Pond Ct					
1600	SMBG	60194	2858	25W-11N	B4
Stratton Pond Ln					
1600	SMBG	60194	2858	25W-11N	B4
Strauss Ct					
-	WDSK	60098	2524	41W-33N	E3
Strauss Ln					
10	OMFD	60461	3506	4W-25S	E7
Strawberry Ct					
700	AURA	60506	3137	38W-6S	B5
1200	BRLT	60103	2967	28W-5N	A2
Strawberry Flds					
600	GRNE	60031	2477	18W-34N	A7
Strawberry Ln					
100	YKVL	60560	3261	43W-13S	B6
2200	GNVW	60025	2810	10W-15N	A3
13300	ODPK	60462	3346	10W-15S	B2
Strawberry Hill Dr					
600	GLNC	60022	2758	7W-17N	C5
1400	LKPT	60441	3419	21W-20S	E4
Strawbridge Ct					
1300	NPVL	60565	3204	24W-8S	D2
Strawflower Ct					
10	RMVL	60446	3340	25W-17S	B5
Streamside Dr					
200	HRVY	60426	3350	1W-17S	B4
Streamtown Ct					
14200	ODPK	60462	3346	10W-16S	C4
E Streamwood Blvd					
10	SMWD	60107	2857	28W-10N	A6
W Streamwood Blvd					
10	SMWD	60107	2856	29W-10N	E6
10	SMWD	60107	2857	28W-10N	A6
Streamwood Ct					
2600	AURA	60502	3079	32W-4S	C7
W Streamwood Ct					
18400	WrnT	60031	2476	18W-36N	E4
Streamwood Dr					
3700	HLCT	60429	3506	4W-22S	D1
14300	OrlT	60467	3344	14W-17S	C5
N Streamwood Dr					
36300	WrnT	60031	2476	19W-36N	D3
36400	WrnT	60031	2477	18W-36N	A4
Streamwood Ln					
6100	MTSN	60443	3505	7W-24S	C6
N Streamwood Ln					
1100	VNHL	60061	2647	16W-26N	C3
N Streeter Dr					
-	CHCG	60611	3034	0E-0N	D3
Streit Rd					
18300	HtdT	60033	2464	48W-36N	E4
20200	DhmT	60033	2464	50W-36N	B4
21600	DhmT	60033	2463	52W-36N	C4
Streit Rd CO-A27					
23500	DhmT	60033	2463	52W-36N	B4
Streitz Dr					
2800	JLET	60435	3497	27W-23S	C4
Strenger Ln					
1800	RVWD	60015	2702	13W-22N	E4
22400	LNSH	60015	2702	13W-22N	E4
22400	LNSH	60069	2702	13W-22N	E4
Stretch Run Rd					
-	RLKP	60030	2532	22W-31N	C7
Strieff Av					
100	CHHT	60411	3507	1W-24S	E5
100	CHHT	60411	3508	1W-24S	A5
Strieff Ln					
1200	FSMR	60422	3507	3W-23S	B3
N Strieff Ln					
300	GNWD	60425	3508	1W-22S	A1
W Strieff Ln					
700	GNWD	60425	3508	1W-22S	B1
Stripe Ct					
100	WKGN	60085	2536	10W-34N	E2
Stripmine Rd					
22800	WMTN	60481	3853	28W-38S	A7
22800	WmTp	60481	3853	28W-38S	B7
32100	BDWD	60481	3941	32W-39S	E2
32100	WmTp	60481	3941	32W-39S	E2
32100	WmTp	60481	3942	31W-39S	A1
32600	BDWD	60408	3941	32W-39S	E2
32600	RedT	60408	3941	32W-39S	E2
Stritch Dr					
1300	MDLN	60060	2591	18W-28N	A6
Strom Dr					
700	WDND	60118	2800	34W-15N	E4
Strome Ln					
100	IVNS	60067	2752	22W-18N	B4
Stronach Dr					
-	PNFD	60586	3415	32W-19S	C3
-	PnfT	60544	3415	32W-19S	C3
Strong Av					
400	JLET	60433	3499	23W-24S	B6
400	JltT	60433	3499	23W-24S	B6
Strong Rd					
4600	NndT	60014	2640	33W-26N	D3
Strong St					
500	BGBK	60440	3204	24W-10S	E5
E Strong St					
10	WLNG	60090	2755	14W-18N	C3
W Strong St					
10	WLNG	60090	2755	14W-18N	C3
3800	CHCG	60625	2920	4W-6N	B6
3900	CHCG	60630	2920	4W-6N	B6
4800	CHCG	60630	2919	6W-6N	E6
6300	CHCG	60656	2919	8W-6N	A6
6600	CHCG	60656	2918	8W-6N	E6
7100	HDHT	60656	2918	8W-6N	D6
7600	HDHT	60706	2918	9W-6N	C6
8200	NRDG	60706	2918	10W-6N	A6
N Struckman Av					
2700	RVGV	60171	2974	10W-3N	A5
Struckman Blvd					
100	BRLT	60103	2910	30W-6N	C7
100	BRLT	60103	2967	28W-6N	A1
Struckmon Blvd					
1400	BRLT	60103	2967	28W-5N	A2
1400	WynT	60103	2967	28W-5N	A2
Stryker Av					
800	RKDL	60436	3498	25W-25S	B7
S Stryker Av					
10	JLET	60435	3498	25W-24S	B6
10	JLET	60436	3498	25W-24S	B6
Stuart Av					
200	AURA	60505	3138	34W-7S	D7
16400	ODPK	60467	3423	13W-19S	A3
S Stuart Av					
700	EMHT	60126	3028	15W-0S	B5
Stuart Cir					
800	FKFT	60423	3592	9W-26S	D2
Stuart Ct					
10	BlmT	60411	3510	3E-25S	A7
1100	NPVL	60540	3204	25W-7S	B1
S Stuart Ct					
700	EMHT	60126	3028	15W-0N	B5
Stuart Dr					
500	CLSM	60188	2967	26W-3N	D6
900	BRLT	60103	2911	28W-6N	B6
N Stuart Dr					
2600	ANHT	60004	2754	17W-16N	B6
Stuart Ln					
1800	IVNS	60067	2751	23W-16N	E7
5800	OKFT	60452	3347	7W-18S	C7
10000	LKWD	60014	2638	39W-24N	D6
S Stuart Ln					
400	PLTN	60067	2805	21W-15N	C2
400	PltT	60067	2805	21W-15N	C2
Stuart Rd					
200	LktT	60441	3419	21W-18S	E1
Stuart St					
500	GYLK	60030	2532	20W-33N	E3
Stuart Kaplan Ct					
2700	AURA	60503	3265	32W-11S	C1
Stuart Kaplan Dr					
2600	AURA	60503	3265	32W-11S	C1
Stuarton Dr					
100	WHTN	60187	3082	25W-2S	B3
Stuart on Oxford					
10	RGMW	60008	2805	22W-13N	B6
Stuarts Dr					
700	SCRL	60174	2965	33W-3N	A5
Stub Av					
1300	AvnT	60073	2474	24W-35N	C6
1300	RLKB	60073	2474	24W-35N	C6
W Stub Av					
24500	AvnT	60073	2474	24W-35N	C6
Stubblefield Ct					
2500	AURA	60502	3079	32W-4S	C7
Stubby Av					
3600	JNBG	60050	2471	30W-35N	E5
Studio Dr					
100	SBTN	60010	2803	26W-13N	D6
Studio Ln					
1100	RVWD	60015	2703	13W-21N	A6
W Stuenkel Rd					
3600	MonT	60417	3594	4W-28S	D7
3600	MonT	60466	3594	4W-28S	D7
3600	PKFT	60417	3594	4W-28S	E7
3600	PKFT	60466	3594	4W-28S	D7
3700	UYPK	60466	3594	4W-28S	D7
5600	MonT	60449	3593	9W-28S	A7
5600	MonT	60471	3593	7W-28S	D7
5600	UYPK	60449	3593	7W-28S	D7
6400	GGnT	60423	3593	9W-28S	A7
6400	GGnT	60449	3593	9W-28S	A7
7200	FKFT	60423	3592	9W-28S	E7
7200	FKFT	60423	3593	9W-28S	A7
7200	GGnT	60423	3592	11W-28S	B7
8800	GGnT	60423	3591	12W-28S	D7
11200	GGnT	60423	3590	14W-29S	E7
11200	MhtT	60423	3590	14W-29S	E7
12000	MhtT	60442	3590	15W-29S	D7
Sturbridge Ct					
1400	HFET	60192	2804	24W-15N	B2
N Sturbridge Dr					
4100	HFET	60192	2804	24W-15N	B2
W Sturbridge Dr					
1100	HFET	60192	2804	24W-15N	C2
Sturbridge Pl					
1800	DRGV	60516	3144	20W-7S	A7
Sturbridge Wy					
10	PltT	60124	2906	40W-8N	C2
Sturgeon Bay Ct					
1400	SMBG	60173	2859	21W-10N	E5
1400	SMBG	60193	2859	21W-10N	E5
S Sturges Pkwy					
300	EMHT	60126	3027	16W-1N	E3
Sturgis Ct					
100	DndT	60118	2747	36W-17N	A7
Sturm Rd					
22200	DRPK	60047	2699	22W-20N	B7
22200	ElaT	60047	2699	22W-20N	B7
22200	KLDR	60047	2699	22W-20N	B7
Sturnbridge Ct					
900	SMBG	60173	2859	22W-11N	C3
Sturnbridge Ln					
600	SMBG	60173	2859	22W-11N	C3
Sturtz St					
100	BRTN	60010	2750	25W-18N	E3
Subiaco Dr					
5400	LSLE	60532	3142	24W-6S	E4
Suburban Ln					
7000	BGVW	60455	3148	9W-7S	C6
Suda Dr					
10	GRNE	60031	2535	13W-34N	D1
Sudbury Ct					
8100	BLVY	60098	2526	37W-32N	C5
Sudbury Cir					
400	OSWG	60543	3263	37W-14S	B7
Sudbury Ct					
800	SMBG	60193	2912	24W-9N	D1
2700	WCHI	60185	2965	32W-4N	C5
Sudbury Dr					
800	JLET	60435	3497	26W-22S	E2
1900	HFET	60169	2858	26W-12N	A1
Sudbury Ln					
2200	GNVA	60134	3019	36W-1N	D4
Sudbury St					
2000	NPVL	60564	3202	29W-9S	D5
W Suddard Pl					
10000	BHPK	60087	2480	10W-38N	B1
W Suddard St					
12700	BHPK	60087	2479	12W-38N	B1
12700	WKGN	60087	2479	12W-38N	B1
Sudeneew Dr					
1400	JNBG	60050	2472	30W-36N	A3
Sue Ct					
100	CHHT	60411	3507	1W-23S	E4
100	CHHT	60411	3508	1W-23S	A4
W Sue Ln					
100	RGMW	60067	2805	21W-13N	D6

STREET Block City ZIP Map# CGS Grid

W Sue Ln
100 SMBG 60173 2805 21W-13N D6
Suffield Ct
- OSWG 60543 3263 36W-12S E4
300 GNVA 60134 3020 34W-1N E3
4000 SKOK 60076 2866 5W-11N B3
5100 SKOK 60077 2865 6W-11N D3
5400 MNGV 60053 2865 6W-11N D3
5400 SKOK 60053 2865 6W-11N D3
E Suffield Ct
10 WTMT 60559 3145 18W-7S B5
S Suffield Ct
100 WTMT 60559 3145 18W-7S A6
W Suffield Ct
10 WTMT 60559 3145 18W-7S A5
1500 ANHT 60004 2753 18W-16N D6
Suffield Dr
100 DGvT 60516 3206 20W-10S A5
100 WDRG 60517 3206 20W-10S A5
7900 ODPK 60462 3346 9W-16S C4
10800 PlsT 60464 3273 13W-15S A7
E Suffield Dr
1200 ANHT 60004 2754 17W-16N C6
2000 WLNG 60090 2754 16W-16N C6
W Suffield Dr
10 ANHT 60004 2754 17W-16N A6
Suffield Sq
800 LNSH 60069 2703 13W-22N A4
Suffield St
2500 DSPN 60016 2863 11W-11N C3
2500 MaiT 60016 2863 11W-11N C3
7200 MNGV 60053 2864 9W-11N D3
Suffield Ter
800 SMBG 60193 2859 23W-9N B7
800 SMBG 60193 2913 23W-9N A1
900 NHBK 60062 2756 12W-17N B4
5400 MNGV 60053 2865 6W-11N D3
5400 SKOK 60053 2865 6W-11N D3
5400 SKOK 60077 2865 6W-11N D3
Suffolk
- RGMW 60008 2860 19W-12N C1
Suffolk Av
600 WSTR 60154 3029 12W-0S B7
1400 WSTR 60154 3087 12W-1S B1
2100 PvsT 60154 3087 12W-1S B2
Suffolk Ct
- MKNA 60448 3502 15W-24S B5
- MKNA 60451 3502 15W-24S B5
700 HFET 60192 2804 23W-15N D3
700 SMWD 60107 2857 28W-10N B6
900 LYVL 60048 2648 15W-27N A1
1000 GRNE 60031 2477 17W-35N B6
S Suffolk Ct
14900 HMGN 60491 3344 15W-17S A6
Suffolk Dr
300 CLLK 60014 2639 36W-24N E7
Suffolk Ln
10 GYLK 60030 2475 20W-34N E7
400 OKBK 60523 3085 18W-3S A6
2400 JltT 60433 3500 20W-23S B4
2400 NlxT 60433 3500 20W-23S B4
3900 HFET 60192 2804 23W-15N D3
N Suffolk Ln
10 LKFT 60045 2649 12W-26N C4
S Suffolk Ln
10 LKFT 60045 2649 12W-25N C4
Suffolk Pl
700 SMWD 60107 2857 28W-10N B6
Suffolk St
1200 NPVL 60563 3141 26W-5S D3
Suffolk Wy
- FmtT 60030 2589 22W-30N B2
- RLKP 60030 2589 22W-30N B2
Suffork Rd
2000 NHFD 60093 2811 7W-16N B1
Sugar Ct
1300 NPVL 60563 3140 28W-5S E4
Sugar Ln
10 SRGV 60554 3135 42W-7S C7
Sugarbush Ln
7700 WLBK 60527 3207 17W-8S D2
Sugar Creek Ct
10 LIHL 60156 2693 38W-22N A3
1400 NPVL 60563 3141 28W-5S A3
1600 JltT 60433 3587 23W-26S B2
Sugar Creek Dr
1300 JltT 60433 3587 23W-25S B1
Sugar Ford Wy
500 JltT 60433 3587 23W-25S B1
Sugarloaf Ct
5400 JLET 60586 3416 30W-20S A5
Sugar Loaf Ln
3800 SKOK 60076 2866 4W-11N B3
Sugar Maple Ct
- JLET 60586 3495 33W-21S A1
Sugar Maple Dr
1600 JLET 60586 3495 33W-21S A1
Sugar Pine Cir
2800 NHBK 60062 2756 11W-16N E7
Sugar Pine Ct
9400 MaiT 60016 2863 11W-12N D1
Sugar Valley Ln
1500 JltT 60433 3587 23W-25S A2
Sugar Valley Rd
300 JltT 60433 3587 23W-25S A1
Sulgrave Ct
300 BGBK 60440 3205 22W-9S C4
Sulkey Dr
34000 WrnT 60030 2534 18W-34N A2
Sulky Dr
15100 HMGN 60491 3343 16W-18S D7
Sulky Rd
100 SchT 60174 2909 33W-6N A7
100 WYNE 60174 2909 33W-6N A7
100 WYNE 60184 2909 33W-6N A7
100 WYNE 60184 2965 33W-6N A1
Sulley Dr
200 BbyT 60134 3018 39W-0N D5
Sulley Pl
400 BbyT 60134 3018 39W-0N D5
Sulley Sq
200 BbyT 60134 3018 39W-0N D5
Sullivan Cir
400 BGBK 60440 3205 22W-11S C7
Sullivan Ct
800 CTHL 60403 3418 25W-21S C7
W Sullivan Ct
2000 MPPT 60056 2861 17W-12N B1
Sullivan Dr
- VNHL 60061 2647 17W-25N C6
400 INCK 60061 2647 17W-25N B6
Sullivan Ln
400 BDWD 60408 3942 31W-41S A4
600 UYPK 60466 3684 3W-30S B2
Sullivan Rd
100 AURA 60506 3138 36W-5S A3

Sullivan Rd
100 AURA 60542 3138 36W-5S A3
100 NARA 60542 3138 36W-5S A3
300 NARA 60506 3138 36W-5S A3
400 AURA 60506 3137 36W-5S D3
400 NARA 60506 3137 36W-5S E3
400 NARA 60542 3137 36W-5S E3
600 AURA 60542 3137 36W-5S E3
E Sullivan Rd
100 AURA 60504 3138 35W-5S B3
100 AURA 60542 3138 35W-5S B3
200 AURA 60505 3138 35W-5S B3
W Sullivan Rd
200 AURA 60506 3136 39W-5S D3
200 SgrT 60506 3136 39W-5S D3
Sullivan St
100 MRGO 60152 2634 49W-26N C2
W Sullivan St
400 CHCG 60610 3034 0W-1N A1
Sullivan Lake Blvd
- WcnT 60051 2530 28W-31N A6
400 LKMR 60051 2530 28W-31N A6
W Sullivan Lake Rd
900 GrtT 60041 2529 28W-33N D3
900 GrtT 60051 2529 28W-33N D3
900 LKMR 60051 2529 28W-33N D3
900 MchT 60051 2529 28W-33N D3
27600 GrtT 60041 2530 27W-33N A4
27600 LKMR 60041 2530 27W-33N A4
27600 VOLO 60041 2530 27W-33N B4
27800 LKMR 60051 2530 27W-33N A4
29000 LKMR 60041 2529 28W-33N E4
Sullivan Pass
- GfnT 60156 2692 38W-21N E5
5300 LIHL 60156 2692 38W-21N E5
Sumac Av
3800 ISLK 60042 2586 28W-28N D6
N Sumac Av
10 WKGN 60085 2536 11W-34N D1
100 NndT 60051 2529 29W-31N B6
S Sumac Av
700 WKGN 60085 2536 11W-33N D3
Sumac Cir
2300 GNVW 60025 2810 9W-13N C6
Sumac Ct
100 SCRL 60174 2964 36W-4N A4
100 SMBG 60193 2859 23W-10N A6
900 LNHT 60046 2476 19W-37N C2
1100 BRLT 60103 2910 30W-7N C4
21300 DRPK 60010 2698 23W-21N E6
Sumac Dr
500 AURA 60506 3198 39W-8S D2
700 SMWD 60107 2857 28W-9N B7
2500 JLET 60435 3417 27W-19S D2
3400 JLET 60441 3417 27W-19S D3
7300 MchT 60097 2469 36W-37N E2
7300 WRLK 60097 2469 36W-37N D2
Sumac Ln
- LktT 60544 3339 26W-16S D3
- WrnT 60030 2533 18W-34N E1
10 ELGN 60120 2855 32W-11N D4
10 SMBG 60193 2858 23W-10N E6
10 SMBG 60194 2858 23W-10N E6
100 SMBG 60193 2859 23W-10N A6
700 WNKA 60093 2758 6W-16N D7
700 WNKA 60093 2811 6W-16N D1
N Sumac Ln
900 MPPT 60056 2808 13W-14N E4
Sumac Rd
200 HDPK 60035 2757 9W-20N D1
200 WhlT 60090 2755 13W-16N E7
200 WLNG 60090 2755 13W-16N E7
500 HDPK 60035 2704 9W-21N C7
9600 MaiT 60016 2863 11W-12N D1
Sumac St
200 WslT 60481 3943 27W-40S D3
2500 WDRG 60517 3143 21W-7S D7
Sumac Tr
1100 HFET 60192 2804 24W-15N C1
Summer Blvd
500 LKMR 60051 2530 28W-32N A5
Summer Ct
800 BFGV 60089 2701 17W-22N B4
Summer Ln
800 NLNX 60451 3501 16W-25S E7
7900 DGvT 60516 3206 18W-9S E2
Summer St
100 SRWD 60404 3496 30W-24S C5
E Summer St
800 HMND 46320 3352 E7
Summerall Dr
6400 WDRG 60517 3143 22W-7S B6
Summer Breeze Ct
500 NARA 60542 3137 38W-4S A2
Summerbreeze Ct
300 BGBK 60440 3269 22W-13S D4
Summer Breeze Ln
1700 AURA 60504 3201 33W-9S A3
Summercrest Av
16700 ODPK 60467 3422 14W-20S E3
Summerdale Av
500 GNEN 60137 3025 22W-0S C7
2200 BDVW 60155 3087 11W-2S D2
W Summerdale Av
1800 CHCG 60640 2921 2W-6N B5
2500 CHCG 60625 2921 3W-6N A5
2600 CHCG 60625 2920 3W-6N E5
4300 CHCG 60630 2920 5W-6N A5
6900 CHCG 60656 2918 8W-6N D5
7900 LydT 60656 2918 10W-6N B5
7900 NpkT 60656 2918 10W-6N B5
8600 CHCG 60656 2917 10W-6N E5
Summerdale Ln
200 ALGN 60102 2693 37W-21N B6
600 ROSL 60172 2912 24W-6N D6
Summerdale St
11200 WSTR 60154 3086 14W-2S D3
Summerfield Ct
10 BRLT 60107 2856 29W-9N D7
200 RMVL 60446 3339 27W-17S D6
600 MltT 60187 3082 25W-2S A4
600 WHTN 60187 3082 25W-2S A4
1000 ROSL 60172 2912 24W-6N E7
5200 JLET 60586 3496 30W-21S C1
W Summerfield Ct
- KLDR 60047 2699 21W-22N E4
Summerfield Dr
200 NIBK 60062 2758 7W-16N A7
200 RMVL 60446 3339 27W-17S C6
300 ROSL 60172 2912 24W-6N E6
1000 BMDL 60108 2912 24W-6N D7
1000 BMDL 60172 2912 24W-6N D7
1400 AURA 60504 3200 34W-9S E5
14400 NLNX 60441 3501 17W-22S B1
14400 NlxT 60441 3501 17W-22S B1
14400 NlxT 60451 3501 17W-22S B1

Summerfield Dr
37000 LkvT 60046 2474 25W-37N A3
W Summerfield Dr
1000 LKFT 60045 2649 12W-26N B2
N Summerfields Dr
33700 WrnT 60030 2534 17W-33N C2
33700 WrnT 60031 2534 17W-33N C2
Summergate Ct
18700 MKNA 60448 3502 14W-22S E1
Summer Glen Ct
300 NARA 60542 3137 38W-4S A1
Summergrove Dr
13400 PNFD 60585 3337 33W-15S A3
Summer Hill Ct
800 ANTH 60002 2358 22W-42N B6
Summerhill Ct
2500 AURA 60506 3198 39W-8S E2
19600 TYPK 60477 3504 10W-23S C3
Summer Hill Dr
10 DYR 46311 3598 C4
Summerhill Dr
10 MDLN 60060 2646 20W-27N B1
700 AURA 60506 3198 39W-8S E2
1000 MTGY 60506 3198 39W-8S E2
1000 SgrT 60506 3198 39W-8S E2
1100 LSLE 60532 3143 23W-6S A5
3300 WDRG 60517 3143 23W-6S A5
3400 LslT 60532 3143 22W-6S B5
4800 BmnT 60478 3426 6W-21S A7
Summer Hill Ln
- LKWD 60098 2638 39W-25N C4
- LKWD 60142 2638 39W-25N C4
300 WLNG 60090 2755 14W-18N C3
Summerhill Ln
1500 CRY 60013 2695 33W-23N A2
Summerhill Pl
100 MltT 60137 3083 23W-2S A4
Summerhouse Dr
- PNFD 60585 3337 31W-15S E2
Summer Isle Ln
700 IVNS 60010 2751 25W-16N A7
Summerlin Dr
- AURA 60503 3201 33W-10S A5
- OswT 60503 3201 33W-10S A5
1900 AURA 60503 3200 33W-10S E6
Summerlyn Dr
- AntT 60002 2357 24W-42N C5
500 ANTH 60002 2357 24W-42N C5
Summer Ridge Ln
11900 HTLY 60142 2744 43W-19N C2
Summerset Ct
500 NPVL 60565 3203 27W-8S C2
N Summerside Dr
39300 AntT 60002 2416 25W-39N A5
Summer Song Ct
1900 SMBG 60194 2858 26W-12N A2
Summersweet Ln
400 BRLT 60103 2910 30W-9N B2
Summerton Pl
1700 NHBK 60062 2757 10W-16N B7
W Summerview Dr
12800 HTLY 60142 2691 41W-20N C7
Summerville Dr
5300 MchT 60097 2469 36W-37N E2
Summerwind Ct
100 NARA 60542 3077 38W-3S B7
Summerwind Dr
- JLET 60586 3415 33W-21S B7
Summerwind Ln
2400 MTGY 60538 3198 40W-10S C7
Summerwood
1200 SYHW 60118 2800 35W-15N D4
1200 WDND 60118 2800 35W-15N D4
Summit Av
10 EDND 60118 2801 33W-16N A2
10 OKTR 60181 3027 17W-1S B7
10 OKTR 60181 3085 17W-1S B1
10 PKRG 60068 2918 9W-8N B1
10 VLPK 60181 3027 17W-1S B7
10 YkTp 60181 3085 17W-1S B1
100 HIWD 60040 2704 9W-23N D3
200 WDSK 60098 2524 42W-32N C5
400 CHCG 60631 2918 9W-8N C1
400 OKBK 60523 3085 17W-1S B2
400 OKTR 60523 3085 17W-1S B2
400 WCHI 60185 3022 29W-0N D4
500 OKBK 60181 3085 17W-1S B2
700 LKFT 60045 2649 10W-26N E2
800 FmtT 60084 2588 24W-28N B7
800 WCDA 60084 2588 24W-28N B7
1100 AraT 60504 3200 34W-8S E1
1100 AURA 60504 3200 34W-8S E1
1300 FDHT 60411 3509 1E-25S B7
1400 AraT 60505 3200 33W-8S E1
1400 AURA 60505 3200 33W-8S E1
2600 HDPK 60035 2704 9W-23N B2
3400 HDPK 60035 2650 9W-24N B7
3500 LKFT 60045 2650 9W-24N B7
17100 HLCT 60429 3427 3W-20S B4
Summit Av CO-15
10 OKTR 60181 3027 17W-1S B7
10 OKTR 60181 3085 17W-1S B1
10 VLPK 60181 3027 17W-1S B7
10 YkTp 60181 3085 17W-1S B1
400 OKBK 60523 3085 17W-1S B2
400 OKTR 60523 3085 17W-1S B2
500 OKBK 60181 3085 17W-1S B2
N Summit Av
10 PKRG 60068 2864 10W-9N B7
10 PKRG 60068 2918 8W-8N D2
200 VLPK 60181 3027 17W-1N B3
S Summit Av
10 VLPK 60181 3027 17W-0N B3
1200 YkTp 60181 3027 17W-0S B6
1500 OKTR 60181 3027 17W-0S B7
8500 CHCG 60620 3214 1W-9S A3
Summit Ct
- CLSM 60188 2967 28W-4N B4
300 SMBG 60193 2859 23W-9N B7
700 LKVL 60046 2475 23W-36N A3
22300 MKNA 60448 3502 15W-23S C3
E Summit Ct
1700 DRFD 60015 2703 11W-22N E5
N Summit Ct
- RLKH 60073 2474 23W-35N D5
700 LNHT 60046 2418 20W-39N A5
S Summit Ct
- RLKH 60073 2474 23W-35N D5
W Summit Ct
1700 DRFD 60015 2703 11W-22N E5
Summit Dr
- GLBT 60124 2799 38W-14N A5
- RtdT 60124 2799 38W-14N A5
10 GLBT 60136 2799 38W-14N A5
10 SMBG 60193 2859 23W-9N B7
10 SMBG 60194 2859 23W-10N B6

Summit Dr
100 LslT 60563 3142 25W-4S B1
100 WNFD 60190 3023 27W-0S B7
200 TRLK 60010 2643 26W-25N C5
300 LKPT 60441 3419 21W-19S E3
700 DRFD 60015 2703 11W-22N D5
700 HDPK 60015 2703 10W-22N E5
800 SMBG 60193 2913 23W-8N B2
1200 SmbT 60193 2913 23W-8N B2
2600 GNVW 60025 2810 8W-15N E2
7200 MchT 60097 2469 36W-37N E1
7200 WRLK 60097 2469 36W-37N E1
N Summit Dr
10 SMBG 60193 2859 22W-10N B5
10 SMBG 60194 2859 22W-10N B5
23300 CbaT 60010 2696 28W-23N E2
W Summit Dr
17500 WrnT 60030 2534 17W-33N B3
Summit Ln
- PGGV 60140 2797 42W-14N D5
700 VNHL 60061 2647 17W-25N B4
800 BGBK 60440 3268 24W-12S C2
Summit Pl
- LKFT 60045 2649 10W-27N E2
Summit Rd
700 LKZH 60047 2698 23W-23N D1
7100 DRN 60561 3144 18W-8S E7
7100 DRN 60561 3206 18W-8S E1
Summit St
- SchT 60174 2908 34W-6N D7
10 ELGN 60120 2854 34W-12N E3
200 ALGN 60102 2747 33W-20N E1
400 GNVA 60134 3020 34W-1N D3
600 DRGV 60515 3144 19W-5S D3
600 ELGN 60120 2855 32W-12N D2
800 GNEN 60137 3024 23W-1N E3
800 WHTN 60137 3024 23W-1N E3
800 WHTN 60187 3024 23W-1N E3
800 WNKA 60093 2812 5W-16N A1
1300 HnrT 60120 2855 32W-12N D2
Summit St SR-58
600 ELGN 60120 2855 32W-12N D2
1300 HnrT 60120 2855 32W-12N D2
N Summit St
800 JLET 60435 3498 24W-22S E2
1300 WHTN 60187 3024 23W-0N E4
2000 GNEN 60137 3024 23W-0N E4
2000 WHTN 60137 3024 23W-0N E4
35300 AvnT 60073 2474 24W-35N C6
S Summit St
- PNFD 60586 3415 32W-19S D3
100 WHTN 60187 3024 23W-0S E7
400 BRTN 60010 2751 25W-18N A3
700 BrnT 60010 2751 25W-18N A3
Summit Ter
10 LKZH 60047 2698 24W-23N C2
Summit Tr
5900 JLET 60586 3415 31W-21S E6
Summit Wy
3100 DYR 46311 3598 D5
Summit Creek Dr
800 SRWD 60404 3496 29W-22S D3
900 JLET 60404 3496 29W-22S D2
900 JLET 60431 3496 29W-22S D2
Summit Hills Ln
1000 NPVL 60563 3141 28W-5S A4
Summit Pass
- CLSM 60188 2967 28W-3N B5
N Sumner Av
10 AURA 60504 3200 34W-8S E1
10 AURA 60505 3200 34W-8S E1
100 AURA 60505 3138 34W-7S E7
S Sumner Av
500 AraT 60504 3200 34W-8S E2
1100 WHTN 60187 3082 24W-1S D1
W Sumner Av
100 PTON 60468 3860 9W-37S E3
100 PTON 60468 3861 9W-37S A3
Sumner Cir
1000 GRNE 60031 2477 17W-35N B6
Sumner Ct
2000 JLET 60586 3415 33W-21S A7
Sumner St
300 GNCY 53128 2353 A3
900 WDSK 60098 2524 41W-31N D6
12200 LMNT 60439 3271 18W-14S B6
E Sumner St
100 HRVD 60033 2406 49W-39N D5
N Sumner St
800 ADSN 60101 2970 18W-4N E3
S Sumner St
100 WHTN 60187 3024 24W-0S D7
W Sumner St
100 HRVD 60033 2406 49W-39N D5
Sumpter Dr
4000 MTSN 60443 3594 5W-26S C2
Sumter Ct
800 NPVL 60540 3203 27W-8S B1
1500 LGGV 60047 2700 18W-20N E7
Sumter Dr
500 DndT 60118 2800 36W-16N A1
1500 LGGV 60047 2700 18W-20N E7
4100 MTSN 60443 3594 5W-26S C2
Sunbrook St
500 SEGN 60177 2908 35W-8N C3
Sunburst Ct
700 NLNX 60451 3501 18W-23S A4
Sunburst Ln
1300 NfdT 60062 2756 12W-17N B6
1300 NHBK 60062 2756 12W-17N B5
3700 NPVL 60564 3202 30W-11S A7
Sunburst Pt
23100 FKFT 60423 3590 14W-28S E6
Sunbury Dr
200 SCRL 60175 2963 37W-2N B7
Sunbury Ln
- CPVL 60118 2746 37W-18N D5
Sunbury Rd
500 SEGN 60177 2908 35W-8N B3
1100 ElgT 60177 2908 35W-8N B3
Sunbury St
10100 HTLY 60142 2692 39W-20N C7
Suncast Ln
1800 BTVA 60510 3021 33W-0S B6
Sun City Blvd
- HTLY 60140 2744 43W-18N A4
13100 HTLY 60142 2744 43W-18N B4
Suncrest Av
- WDSK 60098 2581 41W-28N D6
Suncrest Ct
500 AURA 60506 3198 39W-8S E2
Suncrest Dr
- AraT 60506 3198 39W-8S E2
500 AURA 60506 3198 39W-8S E2
Suncrest Ln
1500 BGBK 60490 3267 26W-13S D4

Sundance Cir
4400 HFET 60192 2804 24W-15N C1
Sun Dance Ct
200 CmpT 60175 2962 40W-5N C2
Sundance Ct
10 MTSN 60443 3506 5W-24S C5
500 CLSM 60188 2967 27W-3N D6
1700 PNFD 60544 3416 31W-18S A1
4400 HFET 60192 2804 24W-15N D2
Sundance Dr
400 BRLT 60103 2911 27W-7N C5
500 BGBK 60440 3268 24W-11S D1
Sundance Rd
10 MTSN 60443 3506 5W-24S C4
W Sundance Tr
11600 MKNA 60448 3502 14W-25S D7
Sunderland Ct
1000 WHTN 60187 3082 25W-1S B3
2100 NPVL 60565 3203 26W-9S E5
Sunderlin Dr
11600 HTLY 60142 2744 42W-20N A1
Sunderlin Rd
13100 PNFD 60585 3337 31W-15S E2
Sunderlin St
500 WKGN 60085 2537 10W-33N A3
Sun Dew Ct
900 AURA 60504 3202 30W-9S B3
Sundial Ln
8300 BtnT 60081 2414 29W-40N C3
8300 FXLK 60081 2414 29W-40N C3
Sundown Ct
300 WCDA 60084 2644 25W-27N A1
Sundown Dr
1200 AraT 60506 3199 37W-8S C2
1300 AURA 60506 3199 37W-8S C2
Sundown Ln
- BtlT 53104 2358 E3
1700 JNBG 60050 2472 30W-36N A3
6500 OswT 60543 3262 39W-13S D5
6500 OswT 60560 3262 40W-13S B6
Sundown Rd
200 SEGN 60177 2908 35W-9N B1
Sundowner Rd
6200 WDRG 60517 3143 22W-6S B5
Sun Drop Av
6900 WDRG 60517 3143 21W-7S D7
Sundrop Cir
1700 HDPK 60035 2704 10W-22N A3
Sun Drop Ct
10 WDRG 60517 3143 21W-7S D7
Sundrop Ct
1900 BRLT 60103 2909 32W-8N D2
Sundrop Dr
2300 GNVW 60025 2810 9W-15N C3
Sun Drop Ln
- AURA 60506 3136 39W-6S D5
- SgrT 60506 3136 39W-6S D5
Sunfish Cir
10 BDWD 60481 3942 30W-40S C2
Sunfish Ln
26000 WmTp 60481 3761 32W-34S D6
Sunfish Pt
700 SMBG 60194 2859 22W-10N C5
Sunflower Cir
1400 GYLK 60030 2533 19W-31N C6
Sun Flower Ct
10 BGBK 60440 3205 21W-10S D5
600 NARA 60542 3137 37W-4S C1
Sunflower Ct
400 YKVL 60560 3333 43W-16S B5
1400 AxST 60447 3672 33W-30S A3
1400 MNKA 60447 3672 33W-30S A3
1600 RMVL 60446 3339 26W-17S D5
2300 AURA 60506 3137 38W-6S A5
2700 NHBK 60025 2809 11W-15N D2
8000 FXLK 60081 2415 27W-39N A6
15300 ODPK 60462 3346 9W-18S D7
S Sunflower Ct
13400 PNFD 60585 3337 31W-15S D3
Sunflower Dr
- GnvT 60134 3019 37W-0N B5
10 PltT 60124 2906 40W-9N C2
900 GNVA 60134 3019 37W-0N B5
1500 RMVL 60446 3339 26W-17S E5
6000 MTSN 60443 3505 7W-24S C6
Sunflower Ln
100 BRLT 60103 2909 32W-8N C2
500 DYR 46311 3510 C6
1300 AxST 60447 3672 33W-29S A3
1300 MNKA 60447 3672 33W-29S A3
4600 HFET 60192 2804 24W-15N C1
11600 CrlT 60142 2743 44W-20N B1
Sunhill Ln
10 LMNT 60439 3272 16W-14S A7
Sun Lake Ct
1200 LKVL 60046 2417 22W-39N C5
Sun Lake Rd
700 LKVL 60046 2417 22W-39N C5
Sunlight Ct
2400 AURA 60502 3079 32W-3S C6
Sunmeadow Dr
5200 JLET 60586 3496 30W-22S B1
Sunningdale Ct
10600 WldT 60564 3266 30W-12S A3
Sunningdale Dr
4500 WldT 60564 3266 30W-12S A3
W Sunny Ct
19500 FmtT 60060 2646 19W-26N C3
Sunny Dr
100 ALGN 60102 2694 33W-21N E6
Sunny Ln
- BRTN 60010 2750 25W-20N E1
- WthT 60482 3275 7W-13S B5
700 BRTN 60010 2697 25W-20N E7
700 CbaT 60010 2697 25W-20N E7
14800 ODPK 60462 3346 10W-17S C6
14800 OrlT 60462 3346 10W-17S C6
Sunnybrook Dr
1100 NPVL 60540 3141 28W-6S A5
1400 NPVL 60540 3140 28W-6S E5
Sunnybrook Ln
400 MltT 60187 3024 26W-0S A7
400 WHTN 60187 3024 26W-0S A7
Sunnybrook Rd
100 GNEN 60137 3083 21W-1S D1
100 MltT 60137 3083 21W-1S D2
300 LMBD 60137 3083 21W-1S D2
300 LMBD 60148 3083 21W-1S D2
26000 GrtT 60041 2530 26W-34N E1
26000 GrtT 60073 2530 26W-34N E1
26000 RDLK 60041 2530 26W-34N E1
26000 RDLK 60073 2530 26W-34N E1
Sunny Creek Dr
- PSHL 60465 3274 10W-12S C2
Sunnydale Blvd
700 SMWD 60107 2857 27W-9N C7

STREET Block City ZIP Map# CGS Grid

Sunnydale Blvd
1000 SMWD 60107 2911 27W-9N C2
Sunny Dale Ct
500 WynT 60103 2966 29W-5N D1
Sunnydale Dr
2300 WDRG 60517 3143 21W-7S E7
Sunnydale Ln
1900 LSLE 60532 3142 24W-7S E6
Sunnydale St
2000 DRGV 60516 3144 21W-7S A7
2000 DRGV 60517 3144 21W-7S A7
2000 WDRG 60517 3144 21W-7S A7
3000 BDVW 60155 3087 11W-2S D2
Sunny Dell Ct
1900 YKVL 60560 3333 42W-16S D5
Sunny Dell Ln
- YKVL 60560 3333 42W-16S D5
Sunny Hill Cir
400 PltT 60124 2905 43W-8N B3
Sunnymere Ct
25600 PNFD 60585 3337 32W-15S D3
Sunnymere Dr
25700 PNFD 60585 3337 32W-15S D3
Sunnyridge Ct
700 MltT 60187 3082 25W-2S A4
Sunnyside Av
100 CLLK 60014 2639 37W-25N B4
100 WNFD 60190 3023 27W-0S C6
200 ITSC 60143 2914 19W-6N D7
200 MNSR 46321 3430 D5
200 WDDL 60191 2971 17W-5N B1
400 GRNE 60031 2535 14W-33N D3
400 SchT 60174 2908 35W-6N B7
400 WDDL 60143 2914 19W-6N D7
400 WDDL 60191 2914 19W-6N D7
400 WHTN 60187 3024 25W-0S B7
700 TNTN 60476 3428 0E-20S E5
800 WCDA 60084 2588 25W-27N B7
1200 CHHT 60411 3507 1W-25S E7
1300 HDPK 60035 2704 10W-21N A5
1400 CHHT 60411 3595 1W-25S E1
1600 WSTR 60154 3087 13W-2S A3
1900 DYR 46311 3598 C2
2600 WSTR 60525 3087 13W-2S A3
2700 BKFD 60513 3087 11W-3S E5
3000 LGPK 60525 3087 13W-2S A4
4500 BKFD 60513 3147 11W-4S E1
9800 SRPK 60176 2973 12W-5N B1
E Sunnyside Av
100 LYVL 60048 2591 16W-28N E5
N Sunnyside Av
33300 GRNE 60031 2535 14W-33N C3
35500 GrtT 60041 2474 25W-35N A6
S Sunnyside Av
100 EMHT 60126 3027 16W-1N D3
W Sunnyside Av
800 CHCG 60640 2921 1W-5N E7
1900 CHCG 60625 2921 3W-5N A7
2700 CHCG 60625 2920 4W-5N C7
4000 CHCG 60630 2920 5W-5N B7
4800 CHCG 60630 2919 7W-5N C7
6300 HDHT 60630 2919 7W-5N A7
6300 HDHT 60706 2919 7W-5N A7
6800 HDHT 60706 2918 8W-5N D7
8200 NRDG 60706 2918 10W-5N A7
8300 CHCG 60706 2918 10W-5N A7
8400 CHCG 60656 2918 10W-5N A7
8500 CHCG 60656 2917 11W-5N E7
Sunnyside Cir
1600 NHBK 60062 2756 10W-16N E7
Sunnyside Ct
3400 NPVL 60564 3266 30W-11S B1
9900 SRPK 60176 2973 12W-5N B1
Sunnyside Dr
300 BmdT 60143 2913 21W-6N E6
1200 BKLY 60163 3028 14W-0N D3
2000 BHPK 60099 2421 12W-41N B2
2000 ZION 60099 2421 12W-41N B2
2500 MTGY 60506 3198 39W-9S E5
4800 HLSD 60162 3028 14W-0N D4
W Sunnyside Dr
1300 JNBG 60050 2472 30W-35N A5
Sunnyside Ln
- JLET 60432 3500 20W-22S C2
1200 RLKB 60073 2474 23W-34N E7
1200 RLKB 60073 2475 23W-34N A7
Sunnyside Pk
10 BTVA 60510 3020 35W-0S B7
Sunnyside Pl
100 LYVL 60048 2591 16W-28N D5
Sunnyside Rd
100 LKMR 60051 2529 29W-32N D5
200 BmdT 60157 2913 22W-6N C6
200 ROSL 60172 2913 22W-6N C6
3600 DrrT 60098 2581 42W-27N A7
25900 LkvT 60002 2415 25W-38N E6
Sunnyside St
3100 RcmT 60071 2354 B4
3100 TNLK 53181 2354 B4
3100 TNLK 60071 2354 B4
Sunnyside Beach Dr
1300 JNBG 60050 2472 30W-35N A5
1900 JNBG 60050 2471 30W-35N E6
Sunnyslope
10 PSPK 60464 3272 13W-14S E7
Sunnyview Rd
1200 LYVL 60048 2591 17W-30N B3
1500 LbvT 60048 2591 17W-30N B3
Sunpivot Cir
- GYLK 60030 2533 19W-33N C2
S Sunridge Dr
10100 WldT 60564 3265 31W-11S E2
Sunridge Ln
10 BFGV 60089 2701 15W-21N E5
10 BFGV 60089 2754 16W-20N D1
Sunrise Av
10 DGvT 60527 3207 16W-9S E4
400 LKBF 60044 2594 10W-28N B6
900 AddT 60101 2971 17W-3N B6
900 ADSN 60101 2971 17W-3N B6
5800 CNHL 60514 3145 16W-6S D4
5800 DGvT 60514 3145 16W-6S D4
5800 DGvT 60527 3145 16W-6S D4
5800 WLBK 60527 3145 16W-6S D4
7200 DRN 60561 3207 16W-8S E1
Sunrise Cir
300 GLNC 60022 2758 5W-17N E5
300 GLNC 60022 2759 5W-17N A5
2000 AURA 60503 3201 32W-10S B7
Sunrise Ct
10 STGR 60475 3596 0W-27S C5
600 CLSM 60188 2968 25W-3N A6
800 ELGN 60123 2854 34W-10N C5
1700 MTGY 60538 3199 36W-10S E5
1800 NPVL 60565 3204 25W-9S C4
2300 AURA 60503 3201 32W-10S B7
Sunrise Ct
3200 JLET 60441 3417 26W-20S E4
Sunrise Dr
- RMVL 60446 3268 24W-14S E7
- RMVL 60446 3340 24W-14S D1
100 SRWD 60404 3496 30W-23S C4
100 WLNG 60090 2755 14W-17N C4
400 MchT 60050 2472 29W-37N C1
800 SEGN 60177 2907 37W-7N D6
12900 LMNT 60439 3342 20W-15S B1
E Sunrise Dr
25500 MONE 60449 3682 7W-31S D4
N Sunrise Dr
2100 RLKB 60073 2475 23W-36N A4
S Sunrise Dr
25700 MONE 60449 3682 7W-31S D5
26200 MonT 60449 3682 7W-31S D6
Sunrise Ln
10 ALGN 60102 2748 33W-20N A1
200 LKZH 60047 2698 24W-23N C3
700 ROSL 60172 2912 24W-6N D7
900 SchT 60174 2963 36W-3N D5
1300 GRNE 60031 2478 15W-35N A6
1700 JltT 60433 3587 23W-26S B2
2300 AURA 60503 3201 32W-10S B7
2700 NLNX 60451 3589 18W-27S B5
8900 ODPK 60462 3424 11W-18S A1
9100 ODPK 60462 3423 11W-18S E1
13500 HMGN 60491 3343 16W-17S D5
15500 ODPK 60462 3346 11W-18S A7
N Sunrise Ln
4800 NRDG 60706 2918 9W-6N B7
Sunrise Pl
800 ROSL 60172 2912 24W-6N D7
Sunrise Rd
400 NPVL 60563 3140 30W-4S A1
400 NpvT 60563 3140 30W-4S A1
700 GNOK 60048 2592 14W-29N C4
W Sunrise Rd
600 EMHT 60126 2971 17W-3N C6
Sunrise View St
3100 MHRY 60050 2585 32W-30N C1
Sun River Dr
22700 FKFT 60423 3590 14W-27S D5
Sun River Pt
22700 FKFT 60423 3590 14W-27S E4
Sunset
2900 AddT 60101 2971 17W-3N B5
Sunset Av
10 BtlT 60560 3262 41W-13S B4
10 GNEN 60137 3025 22W-0S B7
10 MltT 60148 3025 21W-1N E2
200 AURA 60506 3138 35W-6S A5
300 WnfT 60185 3022 28W-0N E5
600 WCHI 60185 3022 28W-0N E5
1400 CHHT 60411 3507 2W-25S C7
1400 CHHT 60411 3595 2W-25S C1
1400 WKGN 60087 2479 11W-36N D4
1800 MHRY 60050 2527 34W-33N D2
2800 FSMR 60422 3507 3W-23S A3
3500 GRNE 60031 2478 13W-36N E4
3500 WKGN 60087 2478 13W-36N E4
3600 MKHM 60428 3426 4W-19S D1
3800 WrnT 60087 2478 13W-36N D4
3800 WrnT 60087 2478 13W-36N D4
5700 CTSD 60525 3147 13W-6S A4
5700 LynT 60525 3147 13W-6S A4
7300 CTSD 60525 3209 13W-8S A1
14800 OKFT 60452 3347 6W-17S D6
Sunset Av CO-A19
1400 WKGN 60087 2479 11W-36N D4
3500 GRNE 60031 2478 13W-36N E4
3500 WKGN 60087 2478 13W-36N E4
3800 WrnT 60031 2478 13W-36N D4
3800 WrnT 60087 2478 13W-36N D4
E Sunset Av
10 LMBD 60148 3026 19W-1N D2
700 VLPK 60181 3026 19W-1N D2
N Sunset Av
24200 CbaT 60013 2642 28W-24N E7
33000 WrnT 60030 2533 18W-33N D3
S Sunset Av
10 LGNG 60525 3087 13W-4S A7
200 LGNG 60525 3147 13W-5S A1
500 LynT 60525 3147 13W-5S A1
1000 EMHT 60126 3027 16W-0S D7
W Sunset Av
10 LMBD 60148 3026 20W-1N B2
100 VLPK 60181 3027 18W-1N A2
600 MltT 60148 3025 21W-1N E2
600 MltT 60148 3026 21W-1N A2
26000 AntT 60002 2415 27W-38N C6
Sunset Blvd
- BCHR 60401 3864 0E-36S E2
Sunset Cir
700 SMWD 60107 2857 27W-10N C6
Sunset Ct
- BCHR 60401 3864 0E-36S E2
- MonT 60466 3684 3W-29S B2
10 BNVL 60106 2972 15W-5N A1
10 HNWD 60047 2700 20W-23N A1
10 STGR 60475 3596 0W-27S C5
10 WNVL 60555 3080 30W-3S C5
100 BmdT 60172 2912 24W-6N C7
200 LKZH 60047 2698 23W-22N E4
200 VNHL 60061 2647 16W-24N E6
300 NHBK 60062 2758 7W-16N A6
400 GNEN 60137 3025 22W-0S B7
700 DRFD 60015 2703 11W-20N E7
700 UYPK 60466 3684 3W-29S A2
800 NARA 60542 3137 37W-4S C1
1900 ZION 60099 2421 12W-41N B2
2000 SHLD 60473 3429 2E-20S D4
3200 JLET 60441 3417 26W-20S E4
5000 RGMW 60067 2805 21W-13N D5
14700 OKFT 60452 3347 6W-17S D5
24700 FmtT 60060 2588 24W-29N C4
25600 CnhT 60447 3672 32W-29S D1
S Sunset Ct
15000 HMGN 60491 3343 17W-17S D6
Sunset Ct N
40200 AntT 60002 2416 24W-40N C3
Sunset Ct S
40200 AntT 60002 2416 24W-40N C3
Sunset Dr
- ELGN 60118 2801 33W-14N B6
- ELGN 60120 2801 33W-14N B6
10 CmpT 60175 2962 41W-6N A1
10 CRY 60013 2695 30W-24N E1
10 WNVL 60555 3080 30W-3S C5
100 BmdT 60157 2913 22W-6N D7
100 DndT 60110 2748 33W-18N A5
100 LYVL 60048 2591 16W-29N C5
100 WDDL 60191 2971 18W-5N A1
100 WLMT 60091 2811 5W-13N E7
200 BTVA 60510 3078 34W-2S D3
Sunset Dr
200 BtvT 60510 3078 34W-2S D3
200 LKWD 60014 2639 37W-25N B6
200 NHFD 60093 2758 7W-16N A7
200 SchT 60174 2964 35W-5N B3
200 SCRL 60174 2964 35W-5N B3
300 SchT 60175 2963 38W-3N A6
400 CLLK 60014 2639 37W-25N B6
400 ELGN 60123 2854 35W-10N C5
400 WLMT 60091 2812 5W-13N A6
500 RDLK 60073 2531 23W-34N E1
600 DndT 60118 2801 33W-14N A5
600 NPVL 60540 3141 26W-7S D7
600 RLKB 60073 2531 23W-34N E1
800 HshT 60140 2796 44W-14N D5
800 SRWD 60404 3496 30W-23S C4
1000 RLKB 60073 2474 23W-35N D6
1000 WMTN 60481 3943 27W-40S D2
1100 HHLL 60051 2586 30W-29N B3
1100 NndT 60051 2586 30W-29N B3
1300 SMBG 60193 2913 22W-8N B2
1300 SmbT 60193 2913 22W-8N B2
1400 ROSL 60172 2913 22W-8N B2
1400 SmbT 60172 2913 22W-8N B2
1500 TNLK 53181 2354 A3
1500 WslT 60481 3943 27W-40S D2
1600 TNLK 53181 2353 E3
1700 HHLL 60051 2585 30W-29N E3
1800 HRPK 60133 2911 27W-6N D6
1900 RdlT 53181 2353 D3
2000 DSPN 60018 2917 12W-8N B3
2100 IVNS 60067 2804 23W-16N D1
5100 RGMW 60067 2805 21W-13N D5
6900 GfnT 60014 2639 37W-24N B6
15100 DLTN 60419 3351 1E-17S B6
22000 RNPK 60471 3594 6W-26S A3
28900 LKMR 60051 2529 28W-31N D6
28900 WcnT 60051 2529 28W-31N D6
E Sunset Dr
10 VLPK 60181 3027 17W-1N B2
300 ANHT 60004 2754 17W-16N B7
7600 MchT 60097 2469 36W-35N D5
N Sunset Dr
23700 ElaT 60047 2698 23W-23N E1
40200 AntT 60002 2416 24W-40N C3
S Sunset Dr
25800 MONE 60449 3682 7W-31S D5
25800 MonT 60449 3682 7W-31S D5
W Sunset Dr
- LMBD 60148 3026 19W-1N D2
100 LKMR 60051 2529 29W-31N D6
100 WcnT 60051 2529 29W-31N D6
200 VLPK 60181 3027 18W-1N A2
300 VLPK 60181 3026 18W-1N E2
500 GNWD 60425 3428 0W-21S B7
7600 EDPK 60707 2974 9W-3N B5
7900 EDPK 60171 2974 9W-3N B5
8300 GwdT 60097 2469 37W-35N A6
Sunset Dr S
40500 AntT 60002 2416 24W-40N B3
Sunset Ln
10 ALGN 60102 2747 33W-20N E1
10 ALGN 60102 2748 33W-20N A1
10 NLNX 60451 3500 20W-24S B5
10 NlxT 60433 3500 20W-24S B5
100 BGBK 60440 3269 22W-11S C1
100 LKZH 60047 2698 24W-23N C3
200 ANTH 60002 2358 23W-43N A4
200 MDLN 60060 2646 19W-27N D2
200 MNSR 46321 3430 D7
300 GLNC 60022 2758 7W-18N B4
300 WLNG 60090 2755 14W-17N B5
700 SRWD 60404 3496 30W-24S C6
1600 BKBN 60015 2703 12W-22N C5
2000 SHLD 60473 3429 2E-20S D4
2300 LNHT 60046 2476 20W-37N B1
3400 FNPK 60131 2973 12W-4N B3
3600 FNPK 60176 2973 12W-4N B3
3600 SRPK 60176 2973 12W-4N B3
3700 NHBK 60062 2756 12W-18N B3
4100 JNBG 60050 2472 30W-36N A5
4800 BmnT 60478 3426 6W-21S A6
4800 CCHL 60478 3426 6W-21S A6
11100 HTLY 60142 2691 41W-20N E7
21700 BlmT 60411 3598 4E-26S B2
W Sunset Ln
25100 LkvT 60046 2416 25W-38N B7
25800 CbaT 60010 2697 25W-21N E5
Sunset Pl
10 LKBF 60044 2593 10W-28N E7
10 LKBF 60044 2594 10W-28N A7
10 LKFT 60045 2649 10W-26N E2
Sunset Rd
- NHFD 60093 2811 6W-15N D3
700 BtnT 60081 2414 30W-38N A7
700 SPGV 60050 2414 30W-38N A7
700 SPGV 60081 2414 30W-38N A7
700 WHTN 60187 3082 25W-1S A1
700 WNKA 60093 2812 5W-15N A3
800 GNVA 60134 3020 35W-0N A5
1000 WNKA 60093 2811 5W-15N E3
1200 NtrT 60093 2811 5W-15N E3
1600 HDPK 60035 2704 9W-22N D4
1700 NndT 60050 2585 31W-30N D3
2000 BtnT 60050 2413 31W-38N D7
2000 BtnT 60050 2414 30W-38N A7
2000 BtnT 60081 2413 31W-38N D7
2000 RcmT 60050 2413 31W-38N D7
2000 SPGV 60050 2413 31W-38N D7
2000 SPGV 60081 2413 31W-38N D7
2100 RcmT 60081 2413 31W-38N D7
2400 HLCT 60429 3427 3W-20S C4
4100 MTSN 60443 3506 5W-24S C4
8100 DGvT 60527 3207 16W-9S D3
E Sunset Rd
10 MPPT 60056 2862 15W-11N A2
N Sunset Rd
2200 PLTN 60074 2752 21W-18N C2
W Sunset Rd
10 CbaT 60010 2697 25W-21N E6
10 MPPT 60056 2862 15W-11N A2
300 BRTN 60010 2750 26W-18N E3
300 MPPT 60056 2861 16W-11N E2
400 BNHL 60010 2750 26W-18N D3
8600 NLES 60714 2863 10W-10N E5
8600 NLES 60714 2864 10W-10N A5
8600 PKRG 60714 2863 10W-10N E5
26000 AntT 60002 2356 26W-43N E4
Sunset St
400 MRGO 60152 2634 50W-26N B2
1000 BtlT 60560 3261 42W-14S C7
1000 YKVL 60560 3261 42W-14S C7
1000 YKVL 60560 3333 42W-14S C1
Sunset Ter
- BMDL 60108 2913 22W-6N B7
- BmdT 60108 2913 22W-6N B7
Sunset Ter
100 BmdT 60157 2913 22W-6N C7
200 CLLK 60014 2640 35W-25N B4
400 LKBF 60044 2593 11W-28N D6
600 BMDL 60157 2913 22W-6N B7
800 WKGN 60087 2480 10W-36N A4
1000 WKGN 60087 2479 10W-36N E4
1400 WNSP 60558 3086 14W-4S C7
E Sunset Ter
1400 ANHT 60004 2807 16W-14N C5
W Sunset Ter
1200 ANHT 60005 2806 18W-14N D5
Sunset Tr
200 NLNX 60451 3501 17W-25S C7
300 NlxT 60451 3501 17W-25S C7
2600 RVWD 60015 2702 13W-21N E6
3200 NfdT 60062 2809 11W-16N C1
3200 NHBK 60062 2809 11W-16N C1
Sunset North
43100 AntT 60002 2356 26W-43N D4
Sunset Park Dr
10 DndT 60118 2801 33W-14N C5
Sunset Pointe
300 RMVL 60446 3340 25W-16S C3
Sunset Ridge Ct
8300 ODPK 60462 3346 10W-18S B6
E Sunset Ridge Ct
16700 LKPT 60441 3420 20W-20S C4
S Sunset Ridge Ct
15700 ODPK 60462 3424 10W-18S C1
Sunset Ridge Dr
100 DrrT 60098 2524 42W-31N A6
100 GwdT 60098 2524 42W-32N B6
100 WDSK 60098 2524 42W-31N A6
400 BRLT 60103 2966 29W-5N D1
400 WynT 60103 2966 29W-5N D1
4400 JLET 60586 3416 29W-21S D7
4400 PnfT 60586 3416 29W-21S D7
15100 ODPK 60462 3346 10W-18S B6
15600 ODPK 60462 3424 9W-18S C1
16700 CCHL 60478 3426 4W-20S D3
Sunset Ridge Rd
100 GNVW 60025 2811 8W-15N A3
100 NHFD 60093 2811 8W-15N A2
100 WLBK 60527 3146 15W-7S A5
600 NfdT 60093 2811 8W-15N A2
800 NHBK 60062 2758 8W-17N A4
1700 NHBK 60093 2758 8W-16N A7
1800 NHFD 60093 2758 8W-16N A7
2000 NfdT 60093 2758 8W-16N A7
14000 DrrT 60098 2524 43W-31N A6
14000 SenT 60098 2524 43W-31N A6
14000 WDSK 60098 2524 43W-31N A6
Sunset Strip
100 JLET 60435 3497 27W-23S D5
Sunset View Rd
10 DRPK 60010 2751 23W-20N E1
Sunshine Av
10 AvnT 60030 2476 19W-35N D6
10 AvnT 60046 2476 19W-35N D6
10 TDLK 60030 2476 19W-35N D6
10 TDLK 60046 2476 19W-35N D6
W Sunshine Av
19000 AvnT 60030 2476 19W-35N D6
19000 AvnT 60046 2476 19W-35N D6
19000 TDLK 60030 2476 19W-35N D6
19000 TDLK 60046 2476 19W-35N D6
19000 WrnT 60046 2476 19W-35N D6
N Sunshine Cir
100 PNFD 60544 3415 31W-18S E1
200 PNFD 60544 3337 31W-18S E7
W Sunshine Cir
1800 PNFD 60544 3415 31W-18S E1
Sunshine Ct
10 BGBK 60490 3267 26W-11S E2
400 OSWG 60543 3200 34W-11S E7
500 ALGN 60102 2747 33W-20N E1
900 LKPT 60441 3419 21W-20S E4
W Sunshine Ct
1800 PNFD 60544 3415 31W-18S E1
Sunshine Dr
100 BGBK 60490 3268 26W-11S A2
200 BGBK 60490 3267 26W-11S E1
400 OKTR 60181 3027 17W-1S B7
400 YkTp 60181 3027 17W-1S B7
Sunshine Ln
100 WDSK 60098 2524 41W-32N D4
1700 ZION 60099 2421 12W-41N E2
4200 LGGV 60047 2700 18W-22N E4
8600 ODPK 60462 3346 11W-15S A2
20000 DRPK 60010 2752 22W-20N B1
34300 GrtT 60041 2530 26W-34N E1
34300 GrtT 60073 2530 26W-34N E1
34300 RDLK 60041 2530 26W-34N E1
34300 RDLK 60073 2530 26W-34N E1
36800 LkvT 60046 2475 21W-36N D3
Suntone Dr
15800 SHLD 60473 3350 0W-18S C7
15800 SHLD 60473 3428 0W-18S C1
Sun Tree Ct
1300 AURA 60564 3202 31W-9S A4
Sunvale Ct
200 ElgT 60124 2907 38W-8N A3
Sunvale Dr
100 ElgT 60124 2907 38W-8N A4
100 ElgT 60175 2907 38W-8N A4
Sun Valley Ct
2900 JLET 60586 3416 30W-20S A5
Sunvalley Ct
10 LIHL 60156 2693 36W-21N C5
S Sun Valley Ct
10500 PSHL 60465 3274 10W-12S A2
Sun Valley Dr
2800 AlqT 60013 2641 31W-25N C5
2800 JLET 60586 3416 30W-20S A5
W Sun Valley Dr
8400 PSHL 60465 3274 10W-12S B2
Sunvalley Rd
2400 LSLE 60532 3142 24W-7S C7
2400 LslT 60532 3142 24W-7S C7
2400 LslT 60540 3142 24W-7S C7
2900 NPVL 60540 3142 24W-7S C7
Sunview Dr
17600 UNON 60180 2635 46W-25N D4
Sunview Ln
1200 WNKA 60093 2811 6W-16N E1
Superior Av
300 CTCY 60409 3352 3E-17S A6
400 MNSR 46321 3510 D3
1100 BtnT 60081 2355 30W-42N B5
1100 SPGV 60081 2355 30W-43N B4
1200 CTCY 60409 3430 3E-19S A2
Superior Cir
- NLNX 60451 3501 16W-24S E5
200 BRLT 60103 2967 28W-5N A1
Superior Ct
10 SMBG 60193 2859 23W-10N A6
700 NPVL 60563 3140 29W-6S D4
1400 SPGV 60081 2355 30W-43N A4
1600 GRNE 60031 2476 18W-35N E5
20500 CTHL 60403 3418 25W-19S B2
20500 LktT 60403 3418 25W-19S B2
Superior Dr
- BMDL 60101 2969 22W-5N D2
- BmdT 60101 2969 22W-5N D2
300 BMDL 60108 2969 22W-5N D2
600 RMVL 60446 3340 24W-15S D1
Superior St
10 CHCG 60644 3031 7W-0N B3
10 MYWD 60153 3030 10W-0N A3
10 OKPK 60302 3031 8W-0N A3
300 AURA 60505 3138 33W-7S E7
1000 MLPK 60160 3029 11W-0N E3
1000 MYWD 60153 3029 11W-0N E3
1000 MYWD 60160 3029 10W-0N E3
1000 OKPK 60302 3030 8W-0N D3
1100 RVFT 60302 3030 8W-0N D3
1100 RVFT 60305 3030 8W-0N D3
1500 AURA 60505 3139 33W-7S A7
3500 NCHI 60088 2593 12W-30N B2
5800 BKLY 60163 3028 14W-0N C3
E Superior St
10 CHCG 60610 3034 0E-0N C3
10 CHCG 60611 3034 0E-0N C3
S Superior St
400 VNHL 60061 2647 16W-24N C7
W Superior St
10 CHCG 60610 3034 0W-0N A3
10 CHCG 60611 3034 0W-0N C3
2000 CHCG 60622 3033 2W-0N B3
2100 CHCG 60612 3033 3W-0N A3
4600 CHCG 60644 3032 5W-0N A3
4700 CHCG 60644 3031 6W-0N E3
5900 OKPK 60302 3031 7W-0N B3
Superior Bay
- BHPK 60099 2422 9W-38N D6
Superstition Ct
7000 JLET 60586 3415 32W-20S C5
Supreme Dr
400 BNVL 60106 2915 16W-7N D5
400 CHCG 60106 2915 16W-7N E4
N Suraya Dr
41200 AntT 60002 2416 23W-41N E1
Surf Ct
400 LslT 60540 3142 24W-5S D3
500 WLNG 60090 2754 16W-17N D5
900 BRLT 60103 2911 27W-7N C4
2600 LYWD 60411 3509 3E-23S E2
Surf Dr
200 NLNX 60451 3501 18W-24S B5
Surf St
300 EMHT 60126 3027 16W-0N D4
1800 NndT 60050 2586 30W-29N A4
W Surf St
600 CHCG 60657 2978 0W-3N A4
1700 CHCG 60657 2977 2W-3N C4
Surf Ter
600 WCDA 60084 2587 26W-27N C7
Surfside Pl
300 GLNC 60022 2759 5W-17N A5
Surfside Pt
600 SMBG 60194 2859 23W-10N A4
Surrey
10 LMNT 60439 3272 15W-14S A6
Surrey Av
500 LslT 60565 3204 25W-8S A2
500 NPVL 60565 3204 25W-8S A2
Surrey Ct
- MKNA 60451 3502 15W-24S B5
10 BNHL 60010 2696 29W-22N B4
10 DRPK 60010 2699 22W-20N A7
10 RLKP 60030 2589 22W-30N B2
200 BRLT 60103 2910 29W-7N C6
400 LslT 60565 3204 25W-8S B2
400 NPVL 60565 3204 25W-8S B2
700 SMWD 60107 2857 28W-9N B7
800 SYHW 60118 2800 35W-15N C4
900 JLET 60431 3497 28W-25S B7
900 JLET 60431 3585 27W-25S C1
1000 GRNE 60031 2477 17W-35N C6
1200 ALGN 60102 2747 34W-20N B1
2500 AURA 60506 3136 39W-7S E7
14300 HMGN 60491 3344 15W-17S C4
N Surrey Ct
2400 CHCG 60614 2977 1W-3N D5
S Surrey Ct
12800 PlsT 60464 3273 12W-15S C7
12800 PlsT 60464 3345 12W-15S C1
Surrey Dr
10 BbyT 60119 3017 43W-0S A6
10 ELGN 60123 2854 35W-11N B4
10 GNEN 60137 3026 21W-0S A7
10 GNEN 60148 3026 21W-0S A7
10 MltT 60148 3026 21W-0S A7
100 BMDL 60108 2969 23W-4N A3
100 CLSM 60188 3024 25W-2N A1
100 GNEN 60137 3025 21W-0S E7
100 GNEN 60148 3025 21W-0S E7
100 LMBD 60148 3025 21W-0S E7
700 SMWD 60107 2857 28W-9N B7
1500 WHTN 60187 3082 25W-1S A2
7700 DRN 60561 3206 19W-8S D2
8400 TYPK 60487 3424 10W-19S B2
Surrey Ln
- PnfT 60586 3416 29W-19S E3
10 BNHL 60010 2696 29W-22N C4
10 CLLK 60014 2640 35W-24N A7
10 LNSH 60045 2702 14W-23N D2
100 BRRG 60527 3146 14W-7S C7
100 BRTN 60010 2751 24W-20N C2
300 BMDL 60108 2969 23W-4N A3
300 CRTE 60417 3596 0E-28S E6
400 LNHT 60046 2418 20W-38N A7
600 GNVW 60025 2811 7W-13N B7
700 SYHW 60118 2800 35W-15N B4
800 ALGN 60102 2747 34W-20N B1
900 EGVV 60007 2913 22W-8N C1
900 NHBK 60062 2757 9W-17N D5
900 SMBG 60007 2913 22W-8N C1
900 SMBG 60193 2913 22W-8N C1
1000 ITSC 60143 2914 19W-7N D5
1600 LKFT 60045 2703 11W-23N E1
3000 HLCT 60429 3427 3W-21S A6
3500 ElaT 60047 2700 20W-21N A6
3500 LGGV 60047 2700 20W-21N A6
12300 HMGN 60491 3344 15W-17S B4
S Surrey Ln
1500 ANHT 60005 2860 18W-12N E1
W Surrey Ln
10 BNHL 60010 2696 29W-22N C4
600 ALGN 60102 2694 34W-20N B7

STREET Block	City	ZIP	Map#	CGS	Grid
W Surrey Ln					
600	ALGN	60102	2747	34W-20N	B1
Surrey Ln E					
10	AlqT	60021	2696	29W-22N	C4
10	BNHL	60010	2696	29W-22N	C4
W Surrey Pk					
8700	PSHL	60465	3210	10W-11S	A7
Surrey Rd					
10	OswT	60538	3199	36W-10S	E6
10	WYNE	60184	2964	34W-5N	E1
10	WYNE	60184	2965	33W-6N	A1
100	WYNE	60184	2909	33W-6N	B7
200	WLNG	60090	2755	15W-18N	A2
400	WHTN	60187	3024	24W-0N	D4
1500	BTVA	60510	3020	34W-0S	C6
1500	GNVA	60134	3020	34W-0S	C6
1500	GNVA	60510	3020	34W-0S	C6
1500	GnvT	60510	3020	34W-0S	C6
W Surrey Rd					
900	ADSN	60101	2970	19W-4N	C3
1200	AddT	60101	2970	20W-4N	B3
Surrey St					
1200	BTVA	60510	3020	34W-0S	C6
S Surrey Hill Ct					
10	PSHT	60463	3274	9W-14S	D6
Surrey Hill Rd					
10	PSHT	60463	3274	9W-14S	D6
W Surrey Park Ln					
-	ANHT	60008	2860	19W-12N	D1
-	RGMW	60008	2860	19W-12N	D1
1800	ANHT	60005	2860	19W-12N	D1
Surrey Ridge Dr					
500	CRY	60013	2695	32W-23N	B2
S Surrey Ridge Dr					
1500	ANHT	60005	2861	18W-12N	A2
Surrey Ridge Rd					
6200	LSLE	60532	3142	24W-6S	C6
Surrey Woods Dr					
400	SCRL	60174	2964	34W-3N	D6
Surridge Ct					
1500	MDLN	60060	2646	20W-27N	B2
Surry Ln					
-	UYPK	60466	3684	3W-30S	B4
Surryse Rd					
-	LKZH	60047	2698	23W-22N	E4
300	LKZH	60047	2699	23W-22N	A4
Surveyor St					
-	GYLK	60030	2533	19W-31N	D6
Susan Cir E					
100	PKCY	60085	2536	12W-33N	B2
Susan Cir N					
3200	PKCY	60085	2536	12W-33N	A2
Susan Cir S					
3200	PKCY	60085	2536	12W-33N	A2
Susan Cir W					
100	PKCY	60085	2536	12W-33N	A2
Susan Ct					
400	BDWD	60408	3941	31W-41S	E4
500	SMBG	60193	2859	22W-9N	C7
900	ALGN	60102	2748	32W-20N	A2
1000	EGVV	60007	2913	21W-8N	E3
N Susan Ct					
8100	NLES	60714	2864	10W-10N	A5
Susan Dr					
10	MPPT	60056	2861	16W-12N	C1
1300	DSPN	60018	2862	15W-10N	A5
Susan Ln					
100	STGR	60475	3596	1W-28S	A5
400	DRFD	60015	2756	12W-20N	C1
16800	ODPK	60467	3423	13W-20S	A4
16800	OrlT	60467	3423	13W-20S	A4
S Susan Ln					
24200	MhtT	60442	3677	20W-29S	C1
25500	CteT	60417	3687	3E-31S	B4
Susan St					
400	RMVL	60446	3339	27W-18S	D7
400	RMVL	60446	3417	27W-18S	D1
1200	JLET	60431	3497	28W-22S	A2
Susanna Wy					
2000	CTHL	60403	3417	26W-21S	E7
Sussex Av					
2900	MKHM	60428	3427	3W-19S	A2
3700	AURA	60504	3139	31W-6S	E6
3700	AURA	60504	3140	31W-6S	A6
Sussex Cir					
10	VNHL	60061	2701	17W-24N	C1
100	SMBG	60193	2859	23W-10N	B6
Sussex Ct					
-	RGMW	60008	2806	19W-12N	B7
10	LIHL	60156	2692	38W-22N	D3
10	LKZH	60047	2699	22W-22N	B4
10	NPVL	60540	3142	25W-6S	B5
100	ROSL	60172	2912	25W-7N	B4
400	BFGV	60089	2754	16W-17N	D4
400	PKCY	60085	2535	13W-33N	E2
500	EGVV	60007	2860	18W-9N	E7
500	EGVV	60007	2914	18W-9N	E1
7000	WDRG	60517	3144	21W-7S	A7
9800	MKNA	60448	3503	12W-23S	D3
14500	OKFT	60452	3347	6W-17S	D5
16100	MKHM	60428	3427	3W-19S	A2
Sussex Dr					
900	NHBK	60062	2756	11W-17N	D4
4400	MHRY	60050	2527	33W-33N	E3
4400	MHRY	60050	2528	32W-32N	B4
16400	ODPK	60462	3424	10W-19S	B3
W Sussex Dr					
23700	CNHN	60410	3584	29W-27S	D6
Sussex Ln					
-	CPVL	60118	2746	37W-18N	C5
200	LKFT	60045	2649	12W-26N	C3
500	ALGN	60102	2694	35W-20N	A7
600	CLLK	60014	2639	35W-24N	E6
1000	WHTN	60187	3082	23W-2S	E4
1100	LYVL	60048	2591	17W-29N	B3
2300	GNVW	60062	2809	11W-15N	D3
Sussex Rd					
10	LslT	60540	3142	25W-6S	B5
100	NPVL	60540	3142	25W-6S	B5
800	CLSM	60188	2967	28W-3N	B5
6800	TYPK	60477	3425	8W-19S	A2
W Sussex Rd					
25800	JLET	60586	3415	32W-21S	D7
25800	PnfT	60586	3415	32W-21S	D7
Sussex Ter					
700	CRTE	60417	3597	0E-28S	A7
Sussex Wk					
1700	HFET	60169	2858	25W-12N	B1
Sussex Corner Ln					
700	PTHT	60070	2808	14W-14N	C4
Sussex Creek Dr					
7600	DRN	60561	3207	17W-8S	C2
Susy Ln					
9200	SRPK	60176	2973	11W-5N	D2
Sutcliff Ct					
10	ALGN	60102	2694	35W-20N	B7
Sutcliffe Cir					
300	VNHL	60061	2647	17W-24N	B7
Sutcliffe Ct					
2000	RMVL	60446	3339	28W-17S	B6
Sutcliffe Dr					
2000	RMVL	60446	3339	27W-17S	B6
Sutherland Ct					
600	SBTN	60010	2803	25W-15N	E2
1600	JLET	60586	3495	33W-21S	B1
7200	NasT	60586	3495	33W-21S	B1
N Sutherland Ct					
800	PLTN	60074	2753	19W-17N	B6
Sutherland Dr					
900	CLLK	60014	2639	36W-24N	D7
1000	CLLK	60014	2693	36W-23N	D1
3800	PKCY	60085	2535	13W-33N	E2
Sutherland Ln					
200	BMDL	60108	2969	23W-4N	A3
400	PTHT	60070	2808	14W-14N	C4
Sutherland Pl					
2000	HFET	60169	2858	25W-12N	B1
N Suthers Ln					
2300	PltT	60074	2752	21W-18N	C2
Sutter Dr					
1300	HRPK	60133	2911	26W-7N	E4
3200	OrlT	60487	3423	11W-21S	E7
Sutton Av					
-	SRGV	60554	3135	42W-6S	C4
Sutton Cir					
700	WLNG	60090	2755	15W-18N	A3
1400	FmtT	60084	2588	24W-28N	C5
1400	WCDA	60084	2588	24W-28N	C5
1500	WCDA	60060	2588	24W-28N	C5
Sutton Ct					
-	CPVL	60118	2746	37W-18N	C4
-	SRGV	60554	3135	42W-6S	C4
10	NCHI	60088	2593	12W-29N	C3
200	BMDL	60108	2969	22W-4N	C3
600	WLNG	60090	2755	15W-18N	A3
700	LKVL	60046	2475	22W-37N	C2
800	LNSH	60069	2703	13W-22N	A3
1400	VNHL	60061	2647	16W-26N	D2
2000	JLET	60435	3497	26W-22S	E3
2600	NndT	60051	2528	31W-31N	D6
2600	WldT	60564	3202	28W-10S	E6
9100	ODPK	60462	3345	11W-17S	E6
9100	ODPK	60462	3346	11W-17S	A6
W Sutton Ct					
1000	PLTN	60067	2752	22W-17N	B6
Sutton Dr					
800	NHBK	60062	2756	12W-17N	B4
1000	CLLK	60014	2639	36W-24N	D7
2100	SEGN	60177	2907	37W-7N	C6
Sutton Ln					
1700	SMBG	60194	2858	25W-10N	A5
2200	AURA	60502	3139	32W-6S	B5
Sutton Pl					
-	HNDL	60521	3146	15W-6S	B4
400	DGvT	60561	3207	17W-9S	B2
1000	SCRL	60174	2964	34W-3N	C5
1400	GRNE	60031	2476	18W-35N	E6
1600	BGBK	60490	3267	26W-13S	D5
9200	TYPK	60487	3423	11W-21S	E6
10200	MNSR	46321	3510		E4
N Sutton Pl					
1300	CHCG	60610	3034	0W-1N	B1
W Sutton Pl					
5600	MONE	60449	3682	7W-31S	E4
Sutton Rd					
-	BRLT	60103	2856	30W-9N	C7
-	BRLT	60107	2856	30W-9N	C7
-	BRLT	60120	2856	30W-9N	C7
-	BRLT	60120	2910	30W-6N	C6
-	HFET	60010	2856	29W-12N	D1
-	HFET	60120	2856	29W-11N	D3
-	SMWD	60103	2856	30W-9N	C7
-	SMWD	60103	2910	30W-9N	C1
-	SMWD	60107	2910	30W-9N	C1
-	SMWD	60120	2910	30W-9N	C1
10	BRLT	60103	2910	30W-6N	C6
10	BRLT	60103	2966	30W-5N	C2
10	WYNE	60184	2966	30W-5N	C3
10	WynT	60103	2910	30W-8N	C4
10	WynT	60103	2966	30W-5N	C2
10	WynT	60184	2966	30W-5N	C3
200	HFET	60107	2856	29W-11N	D3
200	HFET	60120	2856	29W-11N	D3
200	HnrT	60107	2856	29W-11N	D3
200	HnrT	60120	2856	29W-11N	D3
200	SMWD	60107	2856	29W-11N	D3
200	SMWD	60120	2856	29W-11N	D3
Sutton Rd SR-59					
-	BRLT	60103	2856	30W-9N	C7
-	BRLT	60107	2856	30W-9N	C7
-	BRLT	60120	2856	30W-9N	C7
-	BRLT	60120	2910	30W-6N	C6
-	HFET	60010	2856	29W-12N	D1
-	SMWD	60103	2856	30W-9N	C7
-	SMWD	60103	2910	30W-9N	C1
-	SMWD	60107	2910	30W-9N	C1
-	SMWD	60120	2910	30W-9N	C1
10	BRLT	60103	2910	30W-6N	C6
10	BRLT	60103	2966	30W-5N	C2
10	WYNE	60184	2966	30W-5N	C3
10	WynT	60103	2910	30W-8N	C4
10	WynT	60103	2966	30W-5N	C2
10	WynT	60184	2966	30W-5N	C3
200	HFET	60107	2856	29W-11N	D3
200	HFET	60120	2856	29W-11N	D3
200	HnrT	60107	2856	29W-11N	D3
200	HnrT	60120	2856	29W-11N	D3
200	SMWD	60107	2856	29W-11N	D3
200	SMWD	60120	2856	29W-11N	D3
S Sutton Rd					
10	HnrT	60107	2856	29W-10N	C6
10	HnrT	60120	2856	29W-10N	C6
10	SMWD	60107	2856	30W-9N	C7
10	SMWD	60120	2856	29W-10N	C6
S Sutton Rd SR-59					
10	HnrT	60107	2856	29W-10N	C6
10	HnrT	60120	2856	29W-10N	C6
10	SMWD	60107	2856	30W-9N	C7
10	SMWD	60120	2856	29W-10N	C6
Sutton St					
300	YKVL	60560	3333	42W-17S	D6
3000	ElgT	60124	2853	37W-11N	B4
Sutton Dale Ln					
10400	FKFT	60423	3591	13W-26S	B1
Suttondale Rd					
6300	GfnT	60098	2638	40W-25N	A4
6300	GfnT	60142	2638	40W-25N	A4
Sutton Woods Ct					
3000	PRGV	60012	2585	31W-28N	C6
Sutton Woods Dr					
3600	PRGV	60012	2585	31W-28N	C6
Suwanee St					
300	PKFT	60466	3594	4W-27S	E4
Suzann Ter					
1500	NHBK	60062	2757	9W-16N	C6
Suzanne Dr					
600	WNFD	60190	3023	27W-0N	D4
Suzanne Ln					
700	SPGV	60081	2414	29W-41N	B1
800	ELGN	60120	2855	32W-11N	C5
W Suzanne Rd					
13400	HTLY	60142	2744	43W-18N	B4
Suzanne St					
600	GLBT	60136	2799	37W-15N	C3
700	WDSK	60098	2524	42W-31N	B7
Suzy Ct					
200	LtRT	60545	3259	48W-14S	B7
200	PLNO	60545	3259	48W-14S	B7
S Swain Av					
800	EMHT	60126	3027	16W-0S	E6
E Swain St					
100	ELBN	60119	3017	43W-1N	A3
Swainwood Dr					
2000	GNVW	60025	2810	9W-13N	C6
Swallow Av					
100	BMDL	60108	2968	23W-4N	E3
Swallow Ct					
10	WDRG	60517	3143	21W-7S	E7
800	VrnT	60015	2755	15W-20N	A1
22900	DRPK	60010	2699	23W-20N	A7
Swallow Ln					
400	VrnT	60015	2755	15W-20N	A1
2900	RGMW	60008	2806	19W-13N	B6
10600	ODPK	60467	3423	13W-20S	B4
Swallow Rd					
1500	TNLK	53181	2354		A3
1600	TNLK	53181	2353		E3
Swallow St					
800	VrnT	60015	2755	15W-20N	A1
1300	NPVL	60565	3204	26W-9S	A3
Swallow Wy					
7000	AlqT	60013	2642	30W-24N	A6
W Swallowtail Dr					
4400	WKGN	60085	2535	14W-32N	C4
Swallow Tail Ln					
10800	FftT	60423	3591	13W-26S	A2
10800	FKFT	60423	3591	13W-26S	A2
Swamp Angel Rd					
200	AdnT	60033	2349		A3
200	LinT	53147	2349		A2
200	LinT	53184	2349		A2
200	LinT	60033	2349		A3
Swan Blvd					
400	VrnT	60015	2755	15W-20N	A1
Swan Cir					
10	BGBK	60440	3205	21W-10S	D6
5400	HFET	60192	2856	30W-12N	B1
Swan Ct					
400	VrnT	60015	2755	15W-20N	A1
4700	JLET	60586	3496	29W-22S	C1
W Swan Ct					
21500	KLDR	60047	2699	21W-21N	D6
Swan Dr					
10	DYR	46311	3510		D6
600	GYLK	60030	2533	20W-33N	A3
1100	ELBN	60119	3017	43W-0N	B5
18600	MKNA	60448	3502	14W-22S	E1
Swan Ln					
800	VrnT	60015	2755	15W-20N	A1
2000	BTVA	60510	3078	33W-3S	E5
2000	ELGN	60123	2854	36W-12N	A1
2100	RGMW	60008	2806	19W-14N	B4
4200	ZION	60099	2362	12W-42N	B6
Swan Wy					
7000	AlqT	60013	2642	30W-24N	A6
Swanberg Ln					
19600	MKNA	60448	3503	13W-23S	B4
Swanberg Rd					
10	CmpT	60151	2905	42W-6N	C7
10	CmpT	60175	2905	42W-6N	C7
10	CmpT	60175	2961	42W-5N	C1
Swandyke Ct					
2500	NPVL	60565	3203	27W-10S	B6
Swan Lake Ct					
500	WnfT	60187	3081	27W-1S	B2
Swan Lake Dr					
500	WnfT	60187	3081	28W-1S	B2
W Swann St					
200	CHCG	60609	3092	0W-4S	B7
Swansea Ct					
1100	SMBG	60193	2912	25W-9N	C1
1400	NPVL	60565	3203	27W-8S	B3
Swanson Av					
-	PLNO	60545	3259	47W-12S	C4
Swanson Ct					
1800	GRNE	60031	2478	13W-36N	E5
Swanson Dr					
900	BTVA	60510	3078	34W-0S	D1
Swanson Rd					
-	LIHL	60014	2693	37W-22N	B3
-	LIHL	60156	2693	37W-22N	B3
1700	CLLK	60014	2693	37W-22N	B3
1700	LIHL	60156	2693	37W-22N	B3
8400	GfnT	60014	2693	37W-22N	B3
8400	GfnT	60156	2693	37W-22N	B3
Swanstone Ct					
22500	FKFT	60423	3590	14W-27S	E4
Swansway					
20500	DRPK	60010	2699	22W-20N	B7
20500	DRPK	60010	2752	22W-20N	B1
Swaps Ct					
10	OKBK	60523	3084	18W-2S	E3
10	OKBK	60523	3085	18W-2S	A3
W Swaps Ct					
12300	HMGN	60491	3344	15W-16S	B3
Swarthmore Dr					
1900	AraT	60506	3199	38W-8S	B3
E Swarthmore Rd					
7600	NndT	60050	2526	36W-31N	C6
7600	NndT	60098	2526	36W-31N	C6
7900	BLVY	60098	2526	36W-31N	C6
7900	DrrT	60098	2526	36W-31N	C6
N Swarthmore Rd					
10	BLVY	60098	2526	37W-32N	C5
10	DrrT	60098	2526	37W-31N	C6
Swartmore Ct					
900	SMBG	60193	2912	25W-9N	B1
Sweet Bay Ct					
1100	NPVL	60540	3203	26W-7S	E1
Sweet Bay Dr					
-	NndT	60012	2584	35W-30N	A2
Sweetbay Ln					
1300	WCHI	60185	2966	30W-2N	C7
1300	WCHI	60185	3022	30W-2N	C1
Sweetbriar Av					
2100	CTHL	60403	3417	26W-21S	D7
Sweetbriar Ct					
10	SEGN	60177	2908	35W-8N	C3
Sweetbriar Ln					
1400	ELGN	60123	2907	36W-8N	E3
1900	DRGV	60516	3144	18W-7S	E7
1900	DRN	60516	3144	18W-7S	E6
1900	DRN	60561	3144	18W-7S	E6
2400	PvsT	60154	3086	14W-2S	D3
2400	WSTR	60154	3086	14W-2S	D3
Sweetbriar Pl					
10	PLNO	60545	3259	47W-13S	D5
Sweetbroom Ct					
2700	NPVL	60564	3266	29W-13S	C4
Sweetbroom Rd					
2600	NPVL	60564	3266	29W-13S	C4
Sweet Clover Ct					
2400	ELGN	60124	2853	36W-9N	E7
W Sweet Clover Rd					
300	RDLK	60073	2531	23W-32N	E4
Sweet Clover Wy					
2800	WCDA	60030	2588	24W-30N	B2
2800	WCDA	60084	2588	24W-30N	B2
Sweetflower Dr					
900	HFET	60169	2858	25W-11N	B3
Sweet Gum St					
300	BGBK	60490	3267	26W-12S	E3
Sweet Maggie Ln					
3500	NPVL	60564	3266	30W-11S	A2
Sweetwater Ct					
10	LIHL	60156	2693	36W-22N	D4
8200	DRN	60561	3207	17W-9S	B3
Sweetwater Dr					
-	GwdT	60098	2524	40W-32N	E4
-	WDSK	60098	2524	40W-32N	E4
W Sweetwater Dr					
13600	HMGN	60491	3343	16W-17S	D5
Sweetwater Ln					
2800	JNBG	60050	2471	31W-36N	C4
11900	HTLY	60142	2744	41W-20N	C2
Sweetwater Rdg					
1100	LIHL	60156	2693	36W-22N	D4
Sweetwater Tr					
1000	NLNX	60451	3588	19W-27S	E4
1000	NLNX	60451	3589	19W-27S	A4
Sweetwood Ct					
10	IHPK	60525	3146	13W-7S	E5
Sweitzer Rd					
300	AlqT	60102	2695	33W-21N	A5
Swenson Av					
3000	SCRL	60174	2965	33W-2N	A7
3000	SCRL	60174	3021	33W-2N	A1
3700	WynT	60185	3021	33W-2N	B1
N Swift Ct					
26300	WcnT	60084	2643	26W-26N	D3
Swift Dr					
1800	OKBK	60523	3086	15W-1S	B1
Swift Ln					
10	NPVL	60565	3203	26W-8S	E2
10	NPVL	60565	3204	26W-8S	A2
Swift Rd					
10	ADSN	60101	2969	21W-3N	E4
10	BmdT	60101	2969	21W-4N	E2
10	BmdT	60148	2969	21W-3N	E6
10	BmdT	60148	3025	21W-1N	D3
200	BmdT	60143	2969	21W-5N	E1
300	MltT	60137	3025	21W-1N	D3
300	MltT	60148	3025	21W-1N	D3
400	ITSC	60143	2969	21W-5N	E1
Swift Rd CO-54					
-	MltT	60148	3025	21W-2N	E1
10	ADSN	60101	2969	21W-3N	E6
10	BmdT	60101	2969	21W-3N	E6
10	BmdT	60148	2969	21W-3N	E6
10	BmdT	60148	3025	21W-2N	E1
Swift Arrow Dr					
16700	LKPT	60441	3420	20W-19S	B3
Swilly Ct					
11800	ODPK	60467	3422	14W-21S	D5
Swim Beach Rd					
500	WnfT	60185	3081	28W-2S	A4
500	WnfT	60555	3081	28W-2S	A4
500	WNVL	60185	3081	28W-2S	A4
500	WNVL	60555	3081	28W-2S	A4
Swinburne Pl					
1100	VNHL	60061	2647	17W-26N	B3
Swindon Pl					
1900	HFET	60169	2858	26W-12N	A1
Swinford Ct					
10	BGBK	60440	3205	23W-10S	B6
11500	MKNA	60448	3502	14W-24S	E5
Swinford Ln					
11400	MKNA	60448	3502	14W-24S	D6
Swinford Rd					
600	BRLT	60103	2911	27W-7N	D5
600	BRLT	60133	2911	27W-7N	D5
600	HRPK	60133	2911	27W-7N	D5
Swing Ct					
300	JLET	60435	3497	27W-23S	D4
Swinton Ct					
-	ELBN	60119	3017	42W-0N	C6
Swinton St					
-	WNKA	60093	2811	6W-15N	D2
Switchgrass Ct					
1200	MNKA	60447	3672	33W-29S	B3
Switchgrass Dr					
100	RDLK	60073	2531	25W-33N	A2
200	MNKA	60447	3672	33W-29S	B3
Switch Grass Ln					
5000	NPVL	60564	3266	29W-13S	D5
Switchgrass Ln					
500	GYLK	60030	2533	19W-32N	D5
Switzer Rd					
200	PltT	60124	2852	40W-12N	C2
200	PltT	60140	2852	40W-12N	C2
Sword Wy					
400	BGBK	60440	3205	21W-11S	D7
Sybil Dr					
1900	CTHL	60403	3417	26W-21S	E7
Sycamor Ln					
1700	GRNE	60031	2478	15W-35N	A5
Sycamore Av					
10	CPVL	60110	2748	32W-17N	C6
100	SMWD	60107	2911	28W-8N	B3
200	BmdT	60157	2913	22W-7N	C5
400	ROSL	60157	2913	22W-6N	C6
500	ROSL	60172	2913	22W-6N	C6
500	SchT	60174	2908	34W-6N	D7
1600	HRPK	60133	2911	27W-8N	C2
2400	HRPK	60107	2911	27W-8N	B2
18200	CCHL	60478	3426	5W-21S	C7
Sycamore Cir					
500	WCDA	60084	2643	26W-26N	C2
Sycamore Ct					
-	DGvT	60439	3270	20W-12S	B3
-	LNHT	60046	2476	19W-37N	C2
10	BGBK	60490	3267	26W-12S	B3
10	CTCY	60409	3429	2E-18S	C1
900	HFET	60192	2804	24W-14N	D4
1400	LMBD	60148	3084	20W-1S	A1
6500	MHRY	60050	2527	35W-33N	A4
7400	ODPK	60462	3346	9W-18S	E6
8600	FXLK	60020	2415	28W-39N	A5
8700	HYHL	60457	3209	11W-10S	E4
8800	TYPK	60487	3424	11W-20S	A4
12700	HTLY	60142	2744	42W-19N	D3
S Sycamore Ct					
15400	LKPT	60441	3342	20W-18S	B7
W Sycamore Ct					
100	PLTN	60067	2805	21W-15N	E2
21400	LktT	60544	3339	26W-16S	E3
Sycamore Dr					
-	ElaT	60047	2699	23W-24N	A1
-	HLCT	60429	3426	4W-20S	E5
10	MltT	60137	3083	23W-3S	B5
10	MonT	60466	3595	2W-28S	C6
10	NPVL	60540	3203	27W-8S	D1
10	PKFT	60466	3595	2W-28S	C6
100	BGBK	60490	3267	26W-12S	E2
100	HNWD	60047	2644	23W-25N	D5
400	DYR	46311	3598		D3
500	EGVV	60007	2915	18W-8N	A3
500	RDLK	60073	2532	23W-34N	A2
500	RLKP	60073	2532	23W-34N	A2
800	SRWD	60404	3495	31W-25S	E7
900	SRWD	60404	3583	31W-25S	E1
2600	WKGN	60085	2479	12W-35N	C6
7600	ODPK	60462	3346	9W-18S	D6
8900	HYHL	60457	3209	11W-10S	E4
8900	HYHL	60457	3210	11W-10S	A4
9100	HYHL	60480	3209	11W-10S	E4
9100	PlsT	60480	3209	11W-10S	E4
10500	CHRG	60415	3275	8W-12S	B2
17500	HMWD	60430	3427	2W-21S	D5
S Sycamore Dr					
19900	FftT	60423	3504	10W-24S	C4
W Sycamore Dr					
21300	LktT	60544	3339	26W-16S	E3
Sycamore Ln					
-	HDPK	60035	2705	7W-22N	B5
10	CLLK	60014	2639	36W-26N	D3
10	WNFD	60190	3023	27W-1N	D3
100	FKFT	60423	3591	11W-26S	E2
200	MNSR	46321	3430		D7
500	WLNG	60090	2754	15W-17N	E6
600	GLNC	60022	2758	7W-17N	B5
600	GYLK	60030	2475	21W-34N	C7
600	GYLK	60046	2475	21W-34N	C7
600	RLKB	60046	2475	21W-34N	C7
700	SYHW	60118	2800	35W-16N	D2
700	WDND	60118	2800	35W-16N	D3
800	BTVA	60510	3078	36W-2S	A4
900	BRLT	60103	2910	29W-6N	D6
1300	MTGY	60538	3199	36W-9S	E5
1400	NHBK	60062	2757	9W-17N	C6
1500	AURA	60504	3201	32W-9S	B4
4400	RGMW	60008	2806	20W-12N	B7
4900	OKFT	60452	3426	6W-20S	A4
11200	PSHL	60465	3274	10W-13S	C4
N Sycamore Ln					
10	GNWD	60425	3508	0E-22S	E2
10	NARA	60542	3077	36W-4S	D7
400	BtvT	60542	3077	36W-4S	D7
1000	MPPT	60056	2808	14W-14N	C5
S Sycamore Ln					
10	GNWD	60425	3508	0E-22S	E2
10	NARA	60542	3137	36W-4S	D1
12700	PSHT	60463	3274	9W-15S	D7
12900	PSHT	60463	3346	9W-15S	E1
Sycamore Pl					
10	HDPK	60035	2705	7W-22N	A5
1500	SMBG	60173	2805	21W-12N	E7
Sycamore Rd					
-	BtlT	60560	3260	44W-14S	E7
500	BFGV	60089	2754	17W-18N	B3
600	BRTN	60010	2750	25W-20N	E1
700	BRTN	60010	2697	26W-21N	E7
700	SchT	60175	2907	38W-7N	B5
1500	YKVL	60560	3260	44W-14S	E7
1800	HMWD	60430	3427	2W-21S	D7
W Sycamore Rd					
26500	AntT	60002	2356	26W-43N	D5
27000	AxST	60410	3672	33W-31S	A6
27000	CNHN	60410	3672	33W-31S	A6
Sycamore St					
-	NlxT	60451	3500	19W-23S	E4
10	WynT	60185	2967	27W-3N	B6
300	NlxT	60451	3501	18W-24S	A4
300	WCHI	60185	3022	29W-0N	D5
1000	BCHR	60401	3864	0W-36S	D1
1100	LIHL	60156	2694	35W-22N	A4
1200	ELGN	60123	2907	36W-8N	E2
1200	ELGN	60123	2908	36W-8N	A2
1600	DSPN	60018	2863	12W-9N	B6
1700	TNLK	53181	2354		D1
2200	CTHL	60403	3417	26W-21S	D6
2800	DSPN	60018	2917	12W-8N	A2
19500	FftT	60448	3503	11W-23S	E4
19500	MKNA	60448	3503	11W-23S	E4
S Sycamore St					
24700	JknT	60421	3675	24W-30S	E3
W Sycamore St					
200	VNHL	60061	2647	17W-26N	B3
Sydenham St					
100	MchT	60081	2472	29W-37N	D1
N Sylvan Av					
38800	WDWH	60083	2421	13W-38N	A6
Sylvan Cir					
900	NPVL	60540	3141	26W-7S	E6
900	NPVL	60540	3142	26W-7S	A6
Sylvan Ct					
10	EGVV	60007	2914	19W-9N	D1
600	BTVA	60510	3078	34W-1S	D2
1600	CHHT	60411	3507	2W-23S	D3
1600	FSMR	60411	3507	2W-23S	D3
1600	FSMR	60422	3507	2W-23S	D3
Sylvan Dr					
-	LKWD	60014	2693	37W-23N	B1
-	LYVL	60048	2591	17W-27N	C7
10	CmpT	60119	2962	41W-3N	A7
5700	WRLK	60097	2469	36W-37N	E1
25100	AntT	60002	2357	25W-43N	A4
N Sylvan Dr					
100	FmtT	60060	2645	21W-26N	D3
S Sylvan Dr					
21100	ElaT	60047	2645	21W-26N	D4
21100	ElaT	60060	2645	21W-26N	D4
21100	FmtT	60047	2645	21W-26N	D4
21100	FmtT	60060	2645	21W-26N	D4
W Sylvan Dr					
10	FmtT	60060	2645	21W-26N	D3
W Sylvan Dr N					
-	FmtT	60060	2645	21W-26N	E4
Sylvan Ln					
200	CmpT	60175	2961	42W-5N	D2

STREET Block	City	ZIP	Map#	CGS	Grid
Sylvan Pl					
600	BTVA	60510	3078	34W-1S	E2
Sylvan Rd					
-	BGBK	60440	3269	22W-11S	D1
10	LKBF	60044	2594	10W-28N	A6
200	GLNC	60022	2758	6W-18N	C3
Sylvander Dr					
21500	DRPK	60010	2698	24W-21N	B5
21500	ElaT	60010	2698	24W-21N	B5
Sylvan Glen Ct					
10	BRRG	60527	3207	16W-10S	E5
10	BRRG	60527	3208	16W-10S	A6
Sylvan Meadow Dr					
26100	CNHN	60410	3672	32W-30S	D4
Sylvester Pl					
1600	HDPK	60035	2705	7W-22N	A5
N Sylvester St					
24600	CbaT	60013	2643	28W-24N	A6
Sylvia Ln					
10	NPVL	60540	3203	26W-8S	E1
100	SchT	60174	2964	34W-6N	D1
Sylviawood Av					
500	PKRG	60068	2863	11W-9N	D7
Symonds Dr					
100	HNDL	60521	3146	15W-4S	B1
Symphony Dr					
700	AURA	60504	3200	33W-9S	E3
Symphony St					
800	LKFT	60045	2593	12W-27N	C7
Symphony Wy					
10	ELGN	60120	2854	34W-11N	E3
Syracuse Av					
1800	NPVL	60565	3204	24W-9S	D3
Syracuse Ct					
5000	JLET	60586	3496	30W-22S	C1
Syracuse Ln					
-	HRPK	60133	2858	25W-9N	A7
-	HRPK	60133	2912	25W-9N	A1
-	HRPK	60193	2858	25W-9N	A7
1600	SMBG	60193	2912	25W-9N	A1
1900	SMBG	60193	2858	25W-9N	A7
Syril Dr					
10	GNVA	60134	3020	36W-1N	A3

T

STREET Block	City	ZIP	Map#	CGS	Grid
T St					
200	AURA	60505	3200	35W-8S	B1
N T St					
25400	AntT	60002	2357	25W-42N	A6
Taana Rd					
-	BbyT	60134	3018	39W-0S	E7
Table St					
300	LktT	60441	3419	22W-18S	D1
Tacoma Ct					
200	RMVL	60446	3339	27W-17S	C6
Tacoma Dr					
600	CLSM	60188	2967	27W-3N	D6
Tacoma St					
1000	CPVL	60110	2748	33W-17N	C6
Tadmore Ct					
500	SMBG	60194	2858	25W-11N	A4
Taelevale Ct					
12800	HMGN	60491	3422	15W-20S	A4
Taffy Ct					
4700	RcmT	60071	2412	33W-40N	E3
Taft Av					
300	GNEN	60137	3083	23W-1S	B1
1000	WHTN	60187	3082	23W-1S	E1
1600	WHTN	60187	3083	23W-1S	A1
1700	PLTN	60067	2805	20W-14N	E4
1700	RGMW	60008	2805	20W-14N	E4
1700	RGMW	60067	2805	20W-14N	E4
N Taft Av					
10	HLSD	60162	3028	14W-0S	C6
10	PvsT	60162	3028	14W-0S	C6
300	BKLY	60163	3028	14W-0N	C4
300	HLSD	60163	3028	14W-0S	C5
Taft Cir					
700	HRPK	60133	2912	26W-9N	A1
Taft Ct					
10	SMWD	60107	2856	29W-10N	D6
300	GNVW	60025	2811	6W-13N	C6
Taft Dr					
300	OSWG	60543	3263	38W-12S	A3
E Taft Dr					
10	SHLD	60473	3428	0E-19S	D2
W Taft Dr					
10	SHLD	60473	3428	0W-19S	C2
400	HRVY	60426	3428	0W-19S	B2
400	SHLD	60426	3428	0W-19S	B2
Taft Rd					
-	BRRG	60521	3146	14W-5S	C3
900	HNDL	60521	3146	14W-5S	C3
Taft St					
-	DSPN	60018	2862	15W-9N	A7
100	EGvT	60018	2862	15W-9N	A7
11400	RcmT	60071	2354	32W-43N	B4
11500	TNLK	53181	2354	32W-43N	B4
11500	TNLK	60071	2354	32W-43N	B4
S Taft St					
25700	MONE	60449	3682	7W-31S	E5
Tag Wy					
400	CLLK	60014	2640	34W-25N	D5
Taggart Ct					
5600	LGGV	60047	2701	17W-23N	A1
Tahoe Ct					
600	CLSM	60188	2967	27W-3N	D6
2500	AURA	60503	3201	32W-11S	C7
25800	ElaT	60060	2646	19W-25N	C4
Tahoe Dr					
100	BGBK	60440	3268	25W-12S	B2
200	CHHT	60411	3507	1W-23S	E4
W Tahoe Dr					
19100	ElaT	60060	2646	19W-25N	C4
Tahoe Ln					
-	LktT	60544	3339	26W-17S	D5
-	MKNA	60448	3502	15W-23S	B4
-	RMVL	60446	3339	26W-17S	D5
-	RMVL	60544	3339	26W-17S	D5
2800	SPGV	60081	2413	31W-40N	C2
16000	CTHL	60403	3418	25W-19S	B2
16000	LktT	60403	3418	25W-19S	B2
Tahoe Pkwy					
1900	ALGN	60102	2748	32W-20N	B1
Tahoe St					
-	LKPT	60441	3342	21W-17S	A6
10	TNTN	60476	3428	0E-20S	E5
400	PKFT	60466	3594	4W-28S	E6
E Tahoe Tr					
500	PLTN	60074	2753	20W-16N	B6
Tahoe Cir Dr					
1600	WLNG	60090	2754	16W-17N	C5
1700	ANHT	60004	2754	16W-17N	C5
N Tahoma Av					
6900	CHCG	60646	2919	7W-8N	B1

STREET Block	City	ZIP	Map#	CGS	Grid
S Tail Feathers Dr					
20900	MKNA	60448	3502	14W-25S	D7
Takeda Pkwy					
10	NHBK	60015	2756	12W-20N	B2
10	NHBK	60062	2756	12W-20N	B2
10	WdfT	60015	2756	12W-20N	B2
Talaga Dr					
2800	ALGN	60102	2693	36W-21N	D6
2800	LIHL	60102	2693	36W-21N	D6
2800	LIHL	60156	2693	36W-21N	D6
3000	ALGN	60156	2693	36W-21N	D6
Talala St					
400	PKFT	60466	3594	4W-28S	E6
400	PKFT	60466	3595	4W-28S	A6
Talamore Blvd					
-	GfnT	60142	2691	41W-22N	E3
-	HTLY	60142	2691	40W-22N	E3
11600	HTLY	60142	2692	40W-22N	A3
Talandis Dr					
2400	SLVL	60411	3597	2E-26S	E3
Talbot Av					
10	WNVL	60555	3080	30W-3S	B5
100	WnfT	60510	3080	30W-3S	B5
100	WnfT	60555	3080	30W-3S	B5
800	ShdT	60044	2593	12W-29N	A4
1000	LbvT	60044	2593	13W-29N	A4
Talbot Dr					
1400	NPVL	60565	3203	27W-8S	B3
Talbot Ln					
1000	GYLK	60030	2532	20W-34N	E1
E Talbot St					
700	ANHT	60004	2807	17W-15N	B2
Talbots Ln					
1000	EGVV	60007	2914	20W-8N	B2
Talcot St					
400	LMNT	60439	3270	19W-13S	D5
Talcott Av					
10	CLLK	60014	2640	34W-26N	C3
W Talcott Av					
6700	CHCG	60656	2918	8W-7N	D4
6900	CHCG	60631	2918	9W-7N	C4
7700	CHCG	60068	2918	9W-7N	C4
7700	PKRG	60068	2918	9W-7N	C4
Talcott Ct					
10	CLLK	60014	2640	34W-26N	C4
100	BGBK	60440	3269	22W-11S	D1
S Talcott Dr					
1000	WKGN	60085	2535	14W-32N	C4
Talcott Pl					
200	PKRG	60068	2918	10W-7N	B3
Talcott Rd					
9100	WDRG	60517	3206	20W-11S	B7
N Talcott Rd					
10	PKRG	60068	2917	11W-9N	D1
100	PKRG	60068	2863	11W-9N	C7
W Talcott Rd					
10	CHCG	60068	2918	9W-7N	C3
10	CHCG	60631	2918	9W-7N	C3
10	PKRG	60068	2918	10W-8N	A2
1400	PKRG	60068	2917	11W-8N	E2
Talia Ln					
2500	NHBK	60062	2809	11W-15N	C1
Taliesin Dr					
2300	AURA	60506	3198	39W-7S	D1
2300	AURA	60506	3199	38W-7S	A1
Talismon Ct					
-	JNBG	60050	2471	32W-34N	C7
400	CLLK	60012	2640	35W-26N	A2
800	FXLK	60041	2473	27W-35N	C6
Talismon Dr					
10	CLLK	60012	2640	35W-26N	A2
10	CLLK	60014	2640	35W-26N	B2
Talismon Ln					
-	JNBG	60050	2471	32W-34N	C7
Talismon Wy					
900	FXLK	60041	2473	27W-35N	C6
Talladaga Dr					
-	JLET	60421	3675	24W-29S	D1
Tall Grass Cir					
400	LKZH	60047	2699	22W-22N	A4
Tall Grass Ct					
-	HnrT	60107	2856	29W-11N	D3
-	HnrT	60120	2856	29W-11N	D3
900	SCRL	60174	2964	34W-3N	C5
1500	NLNX	60451	3500	19W-24S	E6
4200	ZION	60099	2421	12W-41N	B1
6900	SPGV	60081	2413	32W-38N	B6
Tallgrass Ct					
1500	ALGN	60102	2694	35W-21N	B6
3600	JLET	60435	3417	27W-19S	C3
25500	CNHN	60410	3672	32W-31S	C5
W Tall Grass Ct					
10	RLKB	60073	2475	23W-36N	A3
31500	LKMR	60051	2529	28W-31N	E6
Tall Grass Dr					
-	WldT	60564	3266	30W-11S	A2
300	HRVD	60033	2464	50W-37N	A2
600	BGBK	60440	3205	21W-10S	E5
3000	NPVL	60564	3202	30W-11S	A7
3000	WldT	60564	3202	30W-11S	A7
3200	NPVL	60564	3266	30W-11S	B1
Tallgrass Dr					
300	BRLT	60103	2911	28W-7N	B5
23700	PNFD	60585	3338	29W-15S	C2
S Tall Grass Dr					
20900	MKNA	60448	3502	14W-25S	D7
Tall Grass Ln					
1600	LKFT	60045	2649	13W-24N	A6
Tallgrass Ln					
200	OswT	60560	3334	39W-15S	D2
600	LKVL	60046	2475	22W-37N	B2
Tall Grass Rd					
10	NLNX	60451	3500	19W-24S	E6
Tall Grass Tr					
800	MTSN	60443	3505	7W-25S	C6
Tallgrass Tr					
13500	ODPK	60462	3346	11W-16S	A2
W Tall Grass Tr					
12900	HTLY	60142	2744	41W-20N	C1
W Tallgrass Tr					
26100	CNHN	60410	3672	32W-31S	C5
Tallman Av					
200	RMVL	60446	3340	24W-16S	E4
200	RMVL	60446	3341	23W-16S	A4
Tall Oak Ct					
12600	HTLY	60142	2744	42W-19N	E3
W Tall Oak Dr					
10	HNVL	60030	2532	22W-33N	B3
10	HNVL	60073	2532	22W-33N	B3
Tall Oaks Ct					
10	BGBK	60440	3205	21W-10S	D5
400	ELGN	60123	2853	36W-11N	D3
1100	NPVL	60540	3204	24W-8S	C1
5300	JLET	60586	3496	30W-21S	C1
N Tall Oaks Ct					
21800	KLDR	60047	2699	20W-21N	E5

STREET Block	City	ZIP	Map#	CGS	Grid
Tall Oaks Dr					
-	ANTH	60002	2418	20W-40N	A3
-	ElgT	60123	2853	36W-11N	D3
-	ElgT	60124	2853	36W-11N	D3
1300	CLSM	60188	2967	28W-3N	A6
1400	WynT	60185	2967	28W-3N	A6
1400	WynT	60188	2967	28W-3N	A6
1600	JLET	60586	3496	30W-21S	B1
1700	JLET	60586	3416	30W-20S	C6
1800	AURA	60505	3138	33W-5S	E2
1800	AURA	60505	3139	33W-5S	A2
2400	ELGN	60123	2853	36W-11N	D3
4900	RGWD	60072	2470	34W-37N	C2
5400	LGGV	60047	2701	18W-23N	A2
E Tall Oaks Dr					
300	ITSC	60143	2914	19W-7N	C4
N Tall Oaks Dr					
21500	KLDR	60047	2699	20W-21N	E5
21700	LGGV	60047	2699	20W-21N	E5
Tall Oaks Ln					
1200	WHTN	60187	3024	25W-0N	A5
4500	RGMW	60008	2805	20W-13N	E6
4600	RGMW	60067	2805	20W-13N	E6
Tall Oaks Tr					
500	BbyT	60119	3075	43W-1S	A3
Tall Pines Dr					
-	DRN	60559	3145	17W-7S	B7
1100	DRN	60561	3145	17W-7S	B6
Tall Pines Ln					
13400	DPgT	60544	3340	26W-15S	A3
Tall Pines Rd					
10	PltT	60124	2905	43W-8N	B3
Tall Spruce Dr					
26400	PNFD	60585	3337	33W-15S	B2
Tall Timbers Rd					
1100	SMBG	60173	2805	21W-13N	D6
Tall Tree Ct					
5300	LSLE	60532	3142	24W-5S	D3
25200	CNHN	60410	3672	32W-30S	C4
Tall Tree Ln					
1200	SMWD	60107	2910	29W-9N	E1
1400	DRFD	60015	2703	12W-21N	C6
1700	JNBG	60050	2472	30W-36N	A3
Tall Tree Rd					
-	GNVW	60025	2810	8W-14N	D5
Talltree Ter					
1000	LYVL	60048	2591	16W-27N	D7
Tall Trees Cir					
100	BRTN	60010	2751	24W-20N	C2
Tall Trees Ct					
4500	PltT	60067	2805	20W-14N	E5
Tall Trees Dr					
100	BRTN	60010	2751	24W-20N	D1
E Tall Trees Ln					
200	PltT	60067	2805	20W-14N	E5
200	PltT	60067	2806	20W-14N	A5
Tallwood Pl					
1600	AURA	60506	3137	37W-7S	B6
W Tallyho Ct					
1400	ADSN	60101	2970	20W-5N	B1
Tally Ho Dr					
200	VNHL	60061	2647	17W-24N	B7
N Tallyho Dr					
1300	ADSN	60101	2970	20W-5N	B1
Tally Ho Ln					
8900	ODPK	60462	3346	11W-18S	A7
Talma St					
400	AURA	60505	3200	35W-8S	B3
1200	AraT	60505	3200	35W-9S	B4
1200	MTGY	60505	3200	35W-9S	B4
1300	MTGY	60538	3200	35W-9S	B4
W Talmadge Av					
10000	BHPK	60099	2422	10W-38N	A6
10700	WKGN	60099	2422	10W-38N	A6
Talman Av					
-	AntT	60002	2357	24W-42N	B6
14900	HRVY	60426	3349	3W-17S	B6
14900	POSN	60426	3349	3W-17S	B6
14900	POSN	60469	3349	3W-17S	B6
15000	MKHM	60426	3349	3W-17S	B6
N Talman Av					
600	CHCG	60612	3033	3W-0N	A3
1400	CHCG	60622	3033	3W-1N	A1
1500	CHCG	60647	3033	3W-1N	A1
2100	CHCG	60647	2977	3W-3N	A5
3200	CHCG	60618	2977	3W-4N	A3
4700	CHCG	60625	2921	3W-6N	A6
5600	CHCG	60659	2921	3W-7N	A4
6300	CHCG	60645	2921	3W-7N	A3
7400	CHCG	60645	2867	3W-9N	A7
S Talman Av					
1200	CHCG	60608	3033	3W-1S	A7
1200	CHCG	60612	3033	3W-1S	A7
3900	CHCG	60632	3091	3W-4S	A6
4900	CHCG	60632	3151	3W-6S	A3
5700	CHCG	60629	3151	3W-6S	A4
7900	CHCG	60652	3213	3W-9S	A2
8700	ENGN	60805	3213	3W-10S	A4
9900	CHCG	60655	3213	3W-11S	A7
9900	CHCG	60805	3213	3W-11S	A7
10300	CHCG	60655	3277	3W-12S	A1
Talon Cir					
3000	AURA	60503	3201	31W-10S	D6
Talon Ct					
23700	AntT	60002	2416	23W-40N	E3
Talon Dr					
1800	NLNX	60451	3590	16W-25S	A1
1900	NlxT	60451	3590	16W-25S	B1
Talon Tr					
-	BRLT	60103	2966	29W-5N	D2
-	WynT	60103	2966	29W-5N	D2
Tama Ct					
700	CLSM	60188	2967	26W-3N	E6
Tamahawk Ln					
1700	NPVL	60564	3202	28W-10S	E7
Tamaira St					
-	LtRT	60545	3260	46W-14S	B7
-	PLNO	60545	3260	46W-14S	B7
-	PLNO	60545	3332	45W-14S	B1
Tamar Ln					
17300	TYPK	60487	3424	10W-20S	B5
Tamara Ct					
1300	WKGN	60085	2536	11W-34N	E1
Tamara Dr					
200	PltT	60124	2905	41W-9N	E1
N Tamarac Blvd					
600	ADSN	60101	2969	21W-4N	E3
Tamarac Dr					
800	CLSM	60188	2967	26W-3N	D6
1000	CPVL	60110	2748	33W-17N	A7
1000	CPVL	60110	2801	33W-17N	A1
Tamarack Av					
10	LslT	60540	3203	26W-8S	E1
10	NPVL	60540	3203	26W-8S	D1
Tamarack Cir					
3600	PRGV	60012	2641	32W-27N	B1

STREET Block	City	ZIP	Map#	CGS	Grid
Tamarack Ct					
10	CRY	60013	2695	32W-23N	A2
10	WNFD	60190	3023	27W-1N	D3
100	LNHT	60046	2476	19W-36N	C3
4600	PRGV	60012	2641	32W-27N	A1
5100	HFET	60010	2751	24W-16N	C7
N Tamarack Ct					
1200	MHRY	60050	2527	35W-33N	A3
W Tamarack Ct					
21600	LktT	60544	3339	26W-16S	D4
Tamarack Dr					
10	MltT	60137	3083	23W-3S	A5
10	WNFD	60190	3023	27W-1N	D3
100	BGBK	60440	3268	24W-12S	E2
200	BMDL	60108	2969	22W-4N	C2
400	WcnT	60084	2644	25W-26N	A2
600	FmtT	60084	2644	25W-26N	B2
800	ALGN	60102	2747	33W-20N	E2
800	DRN	60561	3145	17W-8S	B7
1200	BRLT	60103	2910	30W-9N	B1
2000	JLET	60432	3500	21W-23S	A3
2200	LslT	60515	3143	21W-5S	E3
N Tamarack Dr					
36300	GrtT	60041	2474	25W-36N	A4
S Tamarack Dr					
600	MltT	60137	3083	22W-3S	B5
1000	MPPT	60056	2861	17W-11N	C3
1100	ANHT	60005	2861	17W-11N	B3
1100	ANHT	60056	2861	17W-11N	B3
13700	LktT	60544	3339	26W-16S	E4
Tamarack Dr N					
4900	HFET	60010	2751	24W-16N	C7
Tamarack Dr W					
1100	HFET	60010	2751	24W-16N	C7
Tamarack Ln					
-	HMGN	60467	3422	15W-20S	C4
-	ODPK	60467	3422	15W-20S	C4
100	BNHL	60010	2802	28W-15N	D1
1000	LYVL	60048	2591	16W-27N	D7
8000	GlkT	60450	3761	33W-34S	A4
12000	HMGN	60491	3422	15W-20S	C4
13700	ODPK	60462	3346	10W-16S	A3
Tamarack St					
400	MonT	60466	3594	4W-28S	E6
400	MonT	60466	3595	4W-28S	A6
400	PKFT	60466	3594	4W-28S	D6
400	PKFT	60466	3595	4W-28S	A6
N Tamarack Tr					
3800	PRGV	60012	2641	32W-27N	A1
S Tamarack Tr					
3800	PRGV	60012	2641	32W-27N	A1
Tamarind Dr					
3400	NHBK	60062	2756	11W-18N	C3
Tamarind Ln					
3600	HLCT	60429	3426	4W-20S	D5
Tamarisk Ct					
10	LIHL	60156	2693	36W-21N	D5
3600	NndT	60012	2584	34W-28N	C6
Tamarisk Ln					
10	DRFD	60015	2757	9W-20N	B2
Tamarisk Tr					
3800	NndT	60012	2584	34W-28N	C6
Tamaroa Ter					
8900	SKOK	60076	2866	4W-11N	C3
Tamarou Rd					
500	NPVL	60565	3203	27W-8S	C2
Tameling					
7900	PSHL	60465	3274	9W-12S	C2
Tameling Ct					
400	ELGN	60103	2910	31W-8N	A3
400	HnrT	60103	2910	31W-8N	A3
Tameling Dr					
16400	HmrT	60441	3342	20W-16S	A4
16700	LktT	60441	3342	20W-16S	A4
Tamer Ln					
900	GNVW	60025	2809	11W-13N	E6
Tamerisk Ln					
500	CLLK	60014	2639	36W-24N	D6
Tamerisk Ter					
600	CLLK	60014	2639	36W-24N	D6
Tamerton Pkwy					
300	BRRG	60527	3208	15W-9S	B3
N Tami Ln					
35500	GrtT	60041	2474	25W-35N	A6
Tamiami Dr					
6300	LslT	60517	3143	22W-7S	D6
Tammanny Ln					
200	RMVL	60446	3339	27W-17S	C6
N Tammi Ter					
41700	AntT	60002	2359	19W-41N	B7
Tamms Ln					
800	BGBK	60440	3268	24W-12S	C2
Tammy Dr					
18700	NlxT	60448	3501	16W-22S	E1
Tam O Shanter Cir					
800	BGBK	60440	3205	22W-10S	C5
Tam O Shanter Ct					
800	BGBK	60440	3205	22W-10S	C5
20000	OMFD	60461	3507	3W-24S	B5
S Tam O Shanter Ct					
26800	CteT	60417	3685	0W-32S	D7
26800	CteT	60417	3774	0W-33S	D2
W Tam O Shanter Dr					
10	CteT	60417	3774	0W-32S	C1
Tampa St					
200	MonT	60466	3595	4W-28S	A6
200	PKFT	60466	3594	4W-28S	E6
200	PKFT	60466	3595	4W-28S	A6
Tamworth Pl					
10	SMBG	60194	2858	25W-10N	A5
S Tan Ct					
1900	CHCG	60616	3092	0W-1S	B1
N Tana Ln					
400	JLET	60435	3497	27W-23S	D3
Tanaga Basin					
2500	NLNX	60451	3588	19W-27S	E5
2800	MhtT	60442	3588	19W-27S	E5
2800	MhtT	60451	3588	19W-27S	E5
Tanaga Canyon					
1200	NLNX	60451	3588	19W-27S	E5
Tanager Ct					
100	NPVL	60565	3203	26W-8S	E3
200	RMVL	60446	3339	27W-17S	C6
200	VrnT	60015	2755	14W-20N	B1
400	MltT	60148	3025	21W-1N	D2
700	CmpT	60175	2961	42W-5N	C2
900	ANTH	60002	2358	21W-41N	E7
900	ANTH	60002	2417	21W-41N	E1
1800	JLET	60435	3498	26W-22S	A2
24300	DRPK	60010	2698	24W-21N	C5
Tanager Dr					
100	BMDL	60108	2968	23W-4N	E3
100	BMDL	60108	2969	23W-4N	A3
200	WDSK	60098	2525	40W-32N	A5
400	GwdT	60098	2525	40W-32N	A5

STREET Block	City	ZIP	Map#	CGS	Grid
Tanager Ln					
300	LNHT	60046	2476	19W-37N	C2
500	WCHI	60185	2966	29W-3N	D5
600	NLNX	60451	3589	18W-27S	A4
700	GNVA	60134	3020	36W-0S	A6
700	WynT	60185	2966	29W-3N	E5
Tanager Tr					
3500	PRGV	60012	2585	32W-27N	B7
Tanager Wy					
1700	LGGV	60047	2700	19W-20N	D7
Tanbark Ct					
600	DGvT	60516	3206	19W-9S	C4
Tanbark Dr					
8200	TYPK	60477	3424	10W-19S	C3
8300	TYPK	60487	3424	10W-19S	B3
Tandragee Dr					
9200	PlsT	60462	3345	11W-15S	E1
Tang Blvd					
-	HPSR	60140	2743	46W-19N	B2
-	HshT	60140	2743	46W-19N	A2
Tanglewood Av					
1600	HRPK	60133	2911	27W-9N	D1
N Tanglewood Av					
1400	PLTN	60067	2752	21W-18N	D4
W Tanglewood Av					
300	PLTN	60067	2752	21W-17N	D4
E Tanglewood Cir					
10100	PlsT	60464	3345	12W-15S	C1
12700	PlsT	60464	3273	12W-15S	C7
W Tanglewood Cir					
12700	PlsT	60464	3273	12W-15S	C7
12700	PlsT	60464	3345	12W-15S	C1
13000	PlsT	60462	3345	12W-15S	C1
Tanglewood Ct					
10	BtvT	60510	3077	38W-2S	B4
10	HNWD	60047	2644	24W-24N	D7
10	IHPK	60525	3146	13W-6S	E5
200	EGVV	60007	2861	18W-9N	A7
400	VNHL	60061	2647	17W-25N	B6
500	ALGN	60102	2695	32W-21N	A7
600	LKFT	60045	2649	12W-25N	B6
700	DRFD	60015	2704	10W-20N	B7
2000	HDPK	60035	2757	9W-20N	C2
2300	AURA	60506	3136	39W-7S	D7
2300	AURA	60506	3137	38W-7S	A7
17800	HLCT	60429	3427	3W-21S	A6
N Tanglewood Ct					
28500	LbvT	60048	2592	15W-28N	A6
S Tanglewood Ct					
200	RDLK	60073	2531	24W-32N	C4
W Tanglewood Ct					
10000	PlsT	60464	3345	12W-15S	C1
Tanglewood Ct N					
700	FKFT	60423	3503	12W-24S	C6
Tanglewood Ct S					
700	FKFT	60423	3503	12W-25S	C6
Tanglewood Dr					
10	BtvT	60510	3077	38W-2S	B3
10	GNEN	60137	3025	21W-0S	D7
100	EGVV	60007	2861	18W-9N	A6
100	GRNE	60031	2535	14W-33N	D4
200	SMWD	60107	2856	29W-10N	D5
400	CRY	60013	2642	30W-24N	B7
600	ALGN	60102	2695	32W-20N	B7
800	WLNG	60090	2755	15W-16N	A6
1400	CLLK	60014	2693	36W-23N	C3
1800	GNVW	60025	2810	8W-14N	D4
2200	AURA	60506	3137	38W-7S	A7
2200	AURA	60506	3199	38W-7S	A1
2300	AURA	60506	3136	39W-7S	D7
2300	LSLE	60532	3142	24W-7S	D7
17400	LKPT	60441	3420	20W-20S	C5
W Tanglewood Dr					
200	ANHT	60004	2754	18W-17N	A5
500	ANHT	60004	2753	18W-17N	E5
Tanglewood Dr W					
19700	JknT	60421	3675	24W-30S	D4
Tanglewood Ln					
10	ELGN	60120	2854	33W-12N	E1
10	HNWD	60047	2644	24W-24N	D7
300	WNVL	60555	3080	29W-3S	D5
500	FKFT	60423	3503	12W-24S	C6
700	WLBK	60527	3145	16W-7S	E7
11600	HTLY	60142	2744	42W-20N	B1
E Tanglewood Ln					
100	NPVL	60563	3141	26W-5S	D3
Tanglewood Rd					
500	RchT	60443	3593	8W-26S	B2
Tanglewood St					
1400	FSMR	60422	3507	3W-22S	A2
1400	RchT	60422	3507	3W-22S	A2
Tanglewood Tr					
600	MHRY	60050	2527	34W-32N	C5
Tangley Oaks Tr					
3000	LSLE	60532	3142	25W-5S	C2
3000	LSLE	60563	3142	25W-5S	C2
3000	LslT	60532	3142	25W-5S	C2
3000	LslT	60563	3142	25W-5S	C2
Tangly Ct					
10	BGBK	60440	3205	22W-9S	C4
Tangueray Dr					
-	GRNE	60031	2533	18W-34N	E1
-	WrnT	60031	2533	18W-34N	E2
34300	WrnT	60030	2533	18W-34N	E2
Tannahill Dr					
3900	WKGN	60031	2478	13W-36N	D4
3900	WKGN	60087	2478	13W-36N	D4
Tanner Rd					
-	AraT	60506	3077	38W-3S	A7
-	BtvT	60506	3077	38W-3S	A7
10	BbyT	60506	3076	40W-3S	B7
10	NARA	60506	3076	40W-3S	C7
200	AraT	60506	3076	38W-3S	E7
200	BtvT	60506	3076	38W-3S	E7
200	NARA	60542	3076	39W-3S	E7
200	SgrT	60506	3076	39W-3S	E7
Tanner Rd CO-15					
-	AraT	60506	3077	38W-3S	A7
-	BtvT	60506	3077	38W-3S	A7
10	BbyT	60506	3076	40W-3S	B7
10	NARA	60506	3076	40W-3S	C7
200	AraT	60506	3076	38W-3S	E7
200	BtvT	60506	3076	38W-3S	E7
200	NARA	60542	3076	39W-3S	E7
200	SgrT	60506	3076	39W-3S	E7
Tannery Ridge Rd					
1100	ELGN	60120	2855	32W-12N	C1
E Tano Ln					
1800	MPPT	60056	2808	13W-14N	E3
2000	WhlT	60025	2808	13W-14N	E3
2000	WhlT	60056	2808	13W-14N	E3
Tanoak Ct					
300	BRLT	60103	2910	29W-8N	E4
Tanoak Ln					
100	NPVL	60540	3203	26W-8S	D1

STREET Block	City	ZIP	Map#	CGS	Grid
Tansy Rd					
4000	AURA	60504	3202	30W-9S	B3
Tantallon Ln					
100	IVNS	60067	2752	22W-18N	B4
Tantalum Dr					
10	NCHI	60064	2536	10W-31N	E7
Tantalum Pl					
-	NCHI	60064	2536	10W-31N	E7
Tanwood Ln					
10	VNHL	60061	2647	17W-25N	B5
Tanya Tr					
29800	LbvT	60048	2592	15W-29N	A3
Taos Ct					
6700	LSLE	60532	3142	24W-7S	D7
W Taos Dr					
8700	PSHL	60465	3274	10W-12S	A1
Taos Pl					
500	ElgT	60124	2907	38W-8N	A3
Tappan St					
900	WDSK	60098	2524	41W-32N	D5
Tapper Av					
5700	HMND	46320	3352		E7
5900	HMND	46320	3430		E1
7700	HMND	46324	3430		E5
7900	MNSR	46321	3430		E6
Tappingo Dr					
800	NPVL	60540	3202	29W-7S	D1
Tara Ct					
10	LKZH	60047	2698	23W-21N	E6
800	WHTN	60187	3082	24W-2S	D3
900	WDSK	60098	2581	42W-30N	B1
1100	JLET	60431	3496	29W-22S	D2
19300	MKNA	60448	3503	12W-23S	C3
N Tara Ct					
36000	GrtT	60041	2474	25W-36N	A4
Tara Dr					
100	WDSK	60098	2581	42W-30N	B2
2200	ELGN	60123	2853	36W-11N	E4
25600	CbaT	60010	2643	25W-25N	E5
25600	CbaT	60010	2644	25W-25N	A5
25800	TRLK	60010	2643	25W-25N	E5
S Tara Dr					
13500	HMGN	60491	3343	17W-16S	C3
Tara Ln					
100	WCHI	60185	3022	30W-2N	C1
1500	LKFT	60045	2593	11W-27N	E7
N Tara Ln					
400	ADSN	60101	2970	19W-4N	D4
Tara St					
600	NlxT	60451	3589	17W-26S	D3
Tara Belle Pkwy					
1300	AURA	60504	3201	31W-9S	E5
1300	AURA	60564	3201	31W-9S	E5
Tara Hill Rd					
8900	DRN	60561	3206	19W-10S	D5
Taralon Tr					
800	LIHL	60156	2692	38W-22N	E4
Tarbat Ct					
700	IVNS	60010	2751	24W-16N	C6
Tarenbrook Ct					
200	DGvT	60527	3207	16W-9S	D3
Tarmac					
-	NLNX	60451	3590	15W-27S	B4
-	NlxT	60451	3590	15W-27S	B4
Tarpey Ln					
2700	RVGV	60171	2974	10W-3N	A5
Tarpon Ct					
500	SMBG	60193	2912	24W-9N	E1
2700	HMWD	60430	3427	3W-21S	A6
17900	HLCT	60429	3427	3W-21S	A7
Tarrington Dr					
4800	HFET	60010	2804	24W-16N	B1
4900	HFET	60010	2751	24W-16N	B7
Tarrington Wy					
300	BGBK	60440	3205	22W-11S	D7
Tartan Dr					
-	CLLK	60012	2583	37W-27N	B7
-	CLLK	60012	2639	37W-27N	B1
-	DrrT	60012	2583	37W-27N	B7
Tartan Ln					
10	NpvT	60563	3140	30W-5S	C3
W Tartan Rd					
7400	FftT	60423	3504	9W-23S	E4
Tartan Tr					
4000	ZION	60099	2362	12W-41N	C7
Tartan Lakes Cir					
10	WTMT	60559	3085	17W-3S	C5
Tartan Lakes Ct					
10	WTMT	60559	3085	17W-3S	C6
Tartan Lakes Dr					
10	OKBK	60523	3085	17W-3S	C6
10	WTMT	60523	3085	17W-3S	C5
10	WTMT	60559	3085	17W-3S	C5
Tartan Lakes Wy					
10	WTMT	60559	3085	17W-3S	C6
Tartan Ridge Rd					
-	HNDL	60521	3146	14W-6S	C3
10	BRRG	60521	3146	14W-6S	C3
Tartans Ct					
1500	WDND	60118	2800	35W-16N	C2
Tartans Dr					
-	CPVL	60110	2800	35W-16N	C1
400	SYHW	60118	2800	35W-16N	C2
400	WDND	60118	2800	35W-16N	C1
Tarton Ct					
1000	MltT	60187	3024	23W-0N	E4
1000	WHTN	60187	3024	24W-0N	E4
Tarvin Ln					
26000	GrtT	60041	2473	26W-35N	E5
N Tash St					
-	DMND	60416	3941	33W-39S	B2
Tatara Bridge Ct					
-	FftT	60423	3590	14W-26S	D2
N Tatge Av					
-	BRLT	60103	2911	28W-8N	A3
100	BRLT	60103	2910	28W-8N	E2
Tatum Ln					
8200	FKFT	60423	3592	10W-27S	C4
Taub Dr					
200	DRFD	60015	2757	10W-20N	B2
Tauber Ct					
700	NLNX	60451	3501	16W-25S	E7
Tauber Rd					
700	NLNX	60451	3501	16W-25S	E7
700	NLNX	60451	3589	16W-25S	E1
Taubert Av					
200	BTVA	60510	3019	36W-0S	E7
200	BTVA	60510	3077	36W-0S	E1
Taun Ct					
12200	SlmT	53179	2357		B3
Taunton Ct					
1000	SMBG	60193	2912	24W-9N	C1
Taunton St					
-	ElgT	60124	2853	38W-11N	B5
Taupo Ln					
400	DRFD	60015	2756	10W-20N	E1
400	DRFD	60015	2757	10W-20N	A1
Taurus Ct					
10500	WDSK	60098	2582	39W-30N	C2
Taus Cir					
-	YKVL	60560	3333	42W-14S	E1
Tawny Ct					
1900	JLET	60435	3498	26W-22S	A2
Taylor Av					
200	GNEN	60137	3025	22W-0S	C6
800	AURA	60506	3137	36W-6S	D5
1100	HDPK	60035	2704	9W-22N	C5
3600	RNPK	60471	3594	4W-27S	D4
E Taylor Av					
100	BRLT	60103	2911	28W-8N	A2
S Taylor Av					
100	OKPK	60302	3031	7W-0N	B4
500	OKPK	60304	3031	7W-0S	B5
1100	CCRO	60304	3031	7W-0S	B7
1100	CCRO	60804	3031	7W-0S	B7
Taylor Av N					
1100	OKPK	60302	3031	7W-1N	B1
1200	CHCG	60302	3031	7W-1N	B1
1200	CHCG	60639	3031	7W-1N	B1
Taylor Ct					
-	JNBG	60050	2471	32W-34N	C7
-	SMWD	60107	2856	29W-10N	D6
10	BGBK	60440	3268	25W-12S	A4
10	BGBK	60490	3268	25W-12S	A4
10	DRFD	60015	2756	11W-20N	C2
200	BFGV	60089	2701	16W-22N	D3
300	VNHL	60061	2647	17W-26N	B3
13600	PNFD	60544	3338	30W-16S	B3
21200	MTSN	60443	3593	7W-25S	C1
S Taylor Ct					
-	PNFD	60586	3415	32W-19S	D3
Taylor Dr					
900	GRNE	60031	2534	16W-33N	E4
6300	WDRG	60517	3143	22W-7S	C6
Taylor Ln					
-	JNBG	60050	2471	32W-34N	C7
N Taylor Ln					
21000	CbaT	60010	2697	26W-21N	D7
W Taylor Ln					
3800	BtnT	60099	2421	12W-41N	A1
3800	WDWH	60099	2421	12W-41N	A1
Taylor Rd					
10	MltT	60137	3083	22W-2S	C3
1000	RMVL	60441	3340	25W-16S	B5
1000	RMVL	60446	3340	25W-16S	B5
1100	LktT	60441	3340	25W-16S	A5
1100	LktT	60446	3340	25W-16S	B5
1100	LktT	60544	3340	25W-16S	A5
19000	RMVL	60441	3341	23W-16S	A5
19000	RMVL	60446	3341	23W-16S	A5
E Taylor Rd					
10	LMBD	60148	3026	19W-0S	D6
W Taylor Rd					
10	LMBD	60148	3026	20W-0S	B6
1300	LktT	60441	3340	26W-17S	A5
1300	LktT	60544	3340	26W-17S	A5
1300	RMVL	60441	3340	26W-17S	A5
1300	RMVL	60446	3340	26W-17S	A5
20900	LktT	60446	3339	27W-16S	D5
20900	LktT	60446	3340	26W-16S	A5
20900	LktT	60544	3339	27W-16S	D5
20900	RMVL	60446	3339	27W-16S	D5
21200	RMVL	60544	3339	26W-16S	D5
21300	PnfT	60446	3339	27W-16S	D5
21300	PnfT	60544	3339	27W-16S	D5
26400	BRTN	60010	2697	26W-21N	D7
26400	CbaT	60010	2697	26W-21N	C7
Taylor St					
-	SMBG	60133	2912	25W-9N	A1
-	SMBG	60193	2912	25W-9N	A1
200	MTGY	60538	3199	36W-9S	D4
600	HRPK	60133	2912	25W-9N	A1
1700	DRGV	60516	3144	20W-7S	A6
7600	FTPK	60130	3030	9W-0S	C6
13100	PNFD	60585	3337	32W-15S	D2
E Taylor St					
700	SDWH	60548	3258	51W-14S	A7
N Taylor St					
100	MRGO	60152	2634	49W-26N	B2
1300	MRGO	60152	2578	49W-27N	B7
S Taylor St					
100	MRGO	60152	2634	49W-26N	B2
W Taylor St					
-	CHCG	60605	3034	0W-0S	B6
-	CHCG	60607	3034	0W-0S	B6
400	JLET	60435	3498	25W-23S	C4
800	CHCG	60607	3033	2W-0S	C6
2200	JLET	60435	3497	26W-23S	E4
2400	CHCG	60612	3033	3W-0S	A6
2800	CHCG	60612	3032	3W-0S	E6
3900	CHCG	60624	3032	5W-0S	B6
5600	CHCG	60644	3031	7W-0S	C6
Taylor Caldwell St					
300	CmpT	60175	2962	40W-3N	C6
Taylor Glen Dr					
2700	NLNX	60451	3589	18W-27S	B5
2900	NLNX	60442	3589	18W-27S	B5
Taylor Lake Ct					
19500	FmtT	60060	2646	19W-26N	C3
Taylorsport Ln					
1100	WNKA	60093	2759	5W-17N	A6
Taynton Ln					
10	SBTN	60010	2804	25W-15N	B1
Tay River Dr					
100	CPVL	60110	2800	35W-17N	D1
100	CPVL	60118	2800	35W-16N	D1
100	WDND	60118	2800	35W-16N	D1
Tayside Ln					
8900	TYPK	60487	3424	11W-20S	A5
Teaberry Ct					
5400	RGMW	60008	2860	19W-12N	C1
Teak Cir					
4000	WldT	60564	3266	31W-12S	A3
Teak Ln					
200	SMWD	60107	2857	27W-10N	C6
2400	AURA	60506	3198	39W-8S	E2
Teakwood Ct					
1200	NPVL	60540	3203	28W-7S	A1
8400	ODPK	60462	3346	10W-18S	B6
Teakwood Dr					
200	MltT	60137	3083	22W-3S	C5
17100	TYPK	60487	3423	11W-20S	E4
S Teakwood Dr					
13700	HMGN	60491	3343	16W-16S	E3
Teakwood Ln					
1300	CLLK	60014	2639	37W-26N	A4
Teal Av					
400	ELGN	60123	2854	34W-12N	D1
1000	PTON	60468	3860	10W-38S	C4
Teal Ct					
10	BmdT	60108	2968	25W-5N	A2
400	GYLK	60030	2533	20W-32N	A5
600	SMBG	60193	2859	23W-9N	B7
1100	PLTN	60067	2805	22W-15N	B3
1400	HFET	60192	2856	30W-12N	B2
3500	RGMW	60008	2806	19W-13N	B6
5800	LGGV	60047	2701	17W-23N	C2
23200	DRPK	60010	2698	23W-21N	E7
N Teal Ct					
2400	PNFD	60544	3338	30W-16S	C4
Teal Dr					
700	NLNX	60451	3502	15W-25S	B7
700	NLNX	60451	3590	15W-25S	C1
14600	HMGN	60491	3344	15W-17S	B5
Teal Ln					
200	BDWD	60408	3942	31W-41S	B4
1500	WLNG	60090	2754	16W-17N	D6
5800	LGGV	60047	2701	17W-23N	B2
E Teal Ln					
8600	GLkT	60481	3761	33W-34S	C4
8600	WmTp	60481	3761	33W-34S	C4
Teal Rd					
300	LNHT	60046	2418	19W-38N	B7
Teal Tr					
-	RHMD	60071	2353	34W-42N	D5
1000	GNCY	53128	2353		B1
Teal Bay Ct					
3100	AURA	60503	3201	31W-10S	E5
Tealwood Ct					
10	ALGN	60102	2747	35W-18N	B4
10	CRY	60013	2695	32W-22N	A3
Tealwood Dr					
6500	LSLE	60532	3142	24W-7S	C6
Tealwood Rd					
100	OswT	60538	3199	36W-10S	E6
100	OswT	60538	3200	36W-10S	A6
Tearle Ct					
1500	FSMR	60422	3506	4W-23S	D3
Teasel Ln					
700	AURA	60504	3202	30W-9S	B3
1000	AURA	60564	3202	30W-9S	B3
Tea Tree Ln					
11200	FKFT	60423	3590	14W-26S	E2
Tebay Pl					
400	SMBG	60194	2858	25W-11N	A4
Tec Air Av					
8000	WLSP	60480	3209	12W-9S	D3
Tech Ct					
2200	WDSK	60098	2581	41W-29N	E4
Tech Dr					
-	EVTN	60201	2867	2W-12N	C1
Tech Rd					
-	DGvT	60439	3207	17W-11S	C7
Techni Ln					
-	LktT	60441	3340	24W-18S	E7
-	RMVL	60441	3340	24W-17S	E7
Techni Rd					
-	LktT	60441	3340	24W-17S	E6
-	RMVL	60441	3340	24W-17S	E6
Technology Blvd					
-	WCHI	60185	3021	32W-0S	C6
Technology Dr					
-	LMBD	60148	3084	19W-2S	D3
-	YkTp	60148	3084	19W-2S	D3
-	YkTp	60523	3084	19W-2S	D3
500	NPVL	60563	3141	28W-5S	B3
2400	ELGN	60124	2799	37W-15N	D3
2400	SYHW	60118	2799	37W-15N	D3
2400	SYHW	60124	2799	37W-15N	D3
Technology Wy					
800	LYVL	60048	2590	18W-29N	E4
Techny Ct					
1800	NfdT	60062	2757	9W-16N	C7
1800	NHBK	60062	2757	9W-16N	C7
Techny Rd					
1200	NHBK	60062	2757	10W-16N	A7
1600	NfdT	60062	2757	9W-16N	C7
2600	NHBK	60062	2756	10W-16N	E7
3300	NfdT	60062	2756	11W-16N	C7
E Techny Rd					
-	ANHT	60004	2754	17W-16N	A7
W Techny Rd					
-	ANHT	60004	2754	17W-16N	A7
500	ANHT	60004	2753	18W-16N	E7
Teckler Blvd					
7100	CLLK	60014	2640	35W-24N	A6
Tecoma Dr					
3800	NndT	60012	2584	34W-28N	C6
Tecumseh Dr					
100	BGBK	60490	3267	26W-12S	E2
1400	MchT	60050	2527	35W-33N	B3
1400	MHRY	60050	2527	34W-33N	B3
Tecumseh Ln					
11200	IHPK	60525	3146	14W-7S	D6
Tecumseh Tr					
300	LIHL	60156	2694	34W-21N	C5
Ted Av					
3400	PKCY	60085	2536	13W-33N	A2
Ted Ln					
800	ELGN	60120	2855	32W-10N	C5
Tedd Rd					
-	HMGN	60491	3422	15W-21S	C7
E Tedy Ct					
1100	RLKB	60073	2475	21W-36N	D4
N Tedy Ln					
2200	RLKB	60073	2475	21W-36N	D4
2400	LkvT	60046	2475	21W-36N	D4
2400	RLKB	60046	2475	21W-36N	D4
Tee Ct N					
3600	CRTE	60417	3596	0W-28S	D6
Tee Ct S					
3600	CRTE	60417	3596	0W-28S	D6
Tee Ln					
10	BmdT	60143	2970	21W-5N	A2
200	BMDL	60108	2969	22W-5N	B2
200	BmdT	60143	2969	21W-5N	E1
200	CPVL	60110	2748	32W-17N	C7
Tee Rd					
100	CPVL	60110	2748	32W-17N	C7
Teebrook Dr					
8400	ODPK	60462	3346	10W-18S	B7
Tee Girl Ct					
2000	NPVL	60564	3202	29W-10S	E7
Teela Ln					
500	MaiT	60016	2809	12W-12N	B7
Teepee Ln					
-	RMVL	60446	3339	27W-17S	B6
N Tee Side Ct					
39700	AntT	60002	2416	25W-39N	B4
Teeway St					
100	JLET	60435	3417	27W-20S	C5
100	PnfT	60435	3417	27W-20S	C5
Teft Av					
10	ELGN	60120	2855	32W-11N	C4
S Tehle Rd					
19700	JknT	60421	3675	24W-30S	D4
Tek Dr					
600	CLLK	60014	2640	33W-24N	D7
Telegraph Rd					
900	LKFT	60045	2649	12W-24N	B7
1300	LKFT	60045	2703	12W-24N	B1
1700	BKBN	60015	2703	11W-22N	D4
1700	DRFD	60015	2703	11W-22N	D5
5500	MchT	60097	2469	36W-37N	E2
5500	WRLK	60097	2469	36W-37N	E2
Telegraph St					
100	MRGO	60152	2634	49W-26N	C1
20000	SenT	60152	2634	48W-27N	D1
Telegraph St SR-176					
100	MRGO	60152	2634	49W-26N	C1
20000	SenT	60152	2634	48W-27N	D1
Televista Ct					
100	VNHL	60061	2647	17W-24N	C6
Telling Ct					
10	PLNO	60545	3259	48W-14S	B6
Tellis Ln					
2100	LSLE	60532	3142	24W-6S	E5
Telluride Ct					
10	GLBT	60136	2799	38W-15N	A4
10	RtdT	60136	2799	38W-15N	A3
500	BRLT	60103	2910	30W-9N	B1
2700	JLET	60586	3416	31W-20S	A5
6800	LSLE	60532	3142	24W-7S	C7
N Telluride Ct					
700	VNHL	60061	2647	17W-25N	B4
Telluride Dr					
400	GLBT	60136	2799	38W-15N	A4
Telluride Ln					
-	MKNA	60448	3502	15W-23S	B4
Telser Rd					
200	ElaT	60047	2699	22W-23N	B3
200	LKZH	60047	2699	22W-23N	B2
N Telser Rd					
23000	ElaT	60047	2699	22W-23N	B3
23000	LKZH	60047	2699	22W-23N	B3
Tempel Ct					
10	WNKA	60093	2812	4W-14N	C3
Tempel Dr					
1800	LYVL	60048	2590	19W-30N	D1
Templar Dr					
1900	NPVL	60565	3203	26W-9S	D4
Temple Av					
300	HDPK	60035	2704	8W-23N	D2
300	HIWD	60035	2704	8W-23N	D2
300	HIWD	60040	2704	8W-23N	D2
Temple Ct					
300	GLNC	60022	2758	6W-17N	D5
Temple Dr					
10	BmdT	60157	2913	22W-7N	C5
10	ROSL	60157	2913	22W-6N	D5
200	BmdT	60143	2913	21W-6N	E6
Temple Ln					
3100	WLMT	60091	2811	6W-13N	D6
Temple St					
5200	OKFT	60452	3347	6W-17S	E5
Temple Garden Ct					
10	SCRL	60174	3020	34W-2N	E2
Templeton Ct					
1600	MDLN	60060	2590	20W-28N	A6
Templeton Dr					
10	OSWG	60543	3263	37W-13S	D5
Templeton St					
100	NCHI	60044	2593	13W-30N	A3
Tenby Wy					
200	ALGN	60102	2693	37W-21N	B6
Tenaqua Ln					
-	DRFD	60015	2703	12W-20N	B7
-	DRFD	60015	2756	12W-20N	B1
Tennessee Av					
10	DRN	60527	3207	17W-10S	C4
5500	CNHL	60514	3145	17W-6S	D4
5500	DGvT	60514	3145	17W-6S	D4
5600	WLBK	60514	3145	17W-6S	C4
6300	WLBK	60527	3145	17W-7S	D6
6600	DRN	60527	3145	17W-7S	D6
6700	DRN	60561	3145	17W-7S	C7
7400	DRN	60561	3207	17W-8S	D1
7400	WLBK	60527	3207	17W-8S	D1
7400	WLBK	60561	3207	17W-8S	D1
7900	DGvT	60527	3207	17W-9S	C3
Tennessee Ct					
3700	NCHI	60088	2593	12W-30N	C2
Tennessee Dr					
7300	DRN	60527	3207	17W-8S	D1
7300	DRN	60561	3207	17W-8S	D1
7300	WLBK	60527	3207	17W-8S	D1
7300	WLBK	60561	3207	17W-8S	D1
Tennessee Ln					
900	EGVV	60007	2913	22W-8N	D3
18100	ODPK	60467	3423	13W-21S	A7
Tenneyson Ct					
10	LIHL	60156	2692	38W-21N	D6
Tennis Ln					
10	VNHL	60061	2647	18W-24N	A6
Tennis Club Ln					
10	HFET	60192	2803	26W-13N	D6
10	SBTN	60010	2803	26W-13N	D6
Tennyson Ct					
100	ELGN	60120	2855	33W-11N	A4
Tennyson Dr					
100	WHTN	60187	3082	24W-1S	C2
Tennyson Ln					
1100	NPVL	60540	3203	28W-8S	A1
2000	HDPK	60035	2703	11W-22N	E3
Tennyson Pl					
1100	VNHL	60061	2647	17W-26N	B3
2700	HLCT	60429	3427	3W-20S	A5
Tennyson Rd					
400	BRLT	60103	2910	28W-7N	E4
400	BRLT	60103	2911	28W-7N	A4
Ten Pin Ln					
1100	WKGN	60099	2421	10W-38N	E7
1100	WKGN	60099	2422	10W-39N	A6
Tenuta Ct					
700	OMFD	60461	3507	3W-24S	B6
Teonia Woods Dr					
-	RGMW	60067	2805	20W-13N	E5
4600	RGMW	60008	2805	20W-13N	E5
Tepee Av					
2100	CPVL	60110	2748	32W-18N	C4
Teresa Ln					
-	WCHI	60185	2966	30W-3N	B6
Teresa St					
-	GfnT	60014	2638	38W-25N	E5
9100	CLLK	60014	2639	38W-25N	A4
9100	GfnT	60014	2639	38W-25N	A5
Teri Ln					
500	BtlT	60560	3333	42W-15S	D1
500	YKVL	60560	3333	42W-15S	D1
1500	ALGN	60102	2747	34W-19N	E3
1500	ALGN	60102	2748	34W-19N	A3
Terminal Av					
9400	SKOK	60077	2865	6W-11N	D2
Terminal Ct					
-	LktT	60441	3340	24W-17S	E6
-	RMVL	60441	3340	24W-17S	E6
Terminal Dr					
1000	MPPT	60005	2861	16W-10N	D6
W Terminal Dr					
2400	EGvT	60005	2861	16W-10N	D6
2400	MPPT	60005	2861	16W-10N	D6
W Termunde Dr					
4100	ALSP	60803	3276	5W-14S	B5
Tern Ct					
2800	RGMW	60008	2806	20W-14N	B5
W Tern Dr					
1100	PLTN	60067	2805	22W-14N	B3
Terney Ln					
600	BbyT	60134	3018	39W-0N	D5
Terney Sq					
600	BbyT	60134	3018	39W-0N	D5
Terrace					
10	LKZH	60047	2698	23W-22N	D4
Terrace Av					
800	ELGN	60120	2855	32W-11N	C4
1500	WKGN	60085	2480	10W-35N	B6
1700	JLET	60435	3498	26W-23S	A4
2400	LYWD	60411	3509	3E-23S	E4
W Terrace Av					
1400	JNBG	60050	2472	30W-36N	A4
1400	MchT	60050	2472	30W-36N	A4
Terrace Blvd					
12700	PNFD	60585	3337	31W-15S	E1
Terrace Ct					
10	BmdT	60157	2913	21W-7N	E5
500	OSWG	60543	3263	38W-13S	B6
700	ELGN	60120	2855	32W-11N	B4
700	SMBG	60193	2859	22W-9N	B7
1100	DRFD	60015	2756	11W-20N	D2
1100	GLNC	60022	2758	6W-18N	C3
16300	ODHL	60487	3423	11W-19S	E2
W Terrace Ct					
300	PLTN	60067	2805	21W-14N	D3
Terrace Ct E					
-	PSPK	60464	3345	12W-15S	C1
9800	PlsT	60464	3345	12W-15S	D1
Terrace Ct W					
-	PlsT	60462	3345	12W-15S	C1
9800	PlsT	60464	3345	12W-15S	C1
Terrace Dr					
-	CLLK	60014	2640	33W-24N	E6
10	CHHT	60411	3507	1W-23S	E4
10	CHHT	60411	3508	0W-23S	B4
10	LNSG	46321	3430		C7
10	LNSG	60438	3430		C7
10	MltT	60137	3083	22W-2S	D4
10	MNSR	46321	3430		C7
100	MDLN	60060	2647	18W-26N	A2
100	TRLK	60010	2643	26W-25N	D5
200	CNHL	60514	3145	16W-5S	D3
300	BRLT	60103	2910	29W-8N	D3
400	BmdT	60157	2913	21W-7N	E5
500	ALGN	60102	2694	34W-20N	B7
500	CLLK	60014	2641	33W-24N	A6
3200	MHRY	60050	2585	32W-31N	C1
6400	TYPK	60477	3425	8W-19S	B2
6500	DRGV	60516	3144	20W-7S	B6
7200	JSTC	60458	3148	10W-8S	B7
9800	PlsT	60464	3345	12W-15S	C1
15100	HRVY	60426	3349	2W-18S	C6
15600	OKFT	60452	3347	7W-18S	C7
15700	OKFT	60452	3425	7W-18S	C1
15800	BmnT	60477	3425	7W-18S	C1
W Terrace Dr					
800	GNWD	60425	3508	0W-22S	B1
9000	MaiT	60016	2863	11W-12N	D1
9000	NLES	60016	2863	11W-12N	D1
9000	NLES	60714	2863	11W-12N	D1
Terrace Ln					
10	RMVL	60446	3340	23W-15S	E1
10	RMVL	60446	3341	23W-15S	A1
400	OSWG	60543	3263	38W-13S	B5
400	SEGN	60177	2907	37W-7N	C5
1000	GNVW	60025	2810	9W-13N	B6
11000	HLSD	60154	3086	13W-2S	E3
11000	HLSD	60162	3086	13W-2S	E3
11000	WSTR	60154	3086	13W-2S	E3
12700	CTWD	60445	3275	6W-15S	E7
14900	MDLN	60445	3348	5W-17S	C6
E Terrace Ln					
10	DSPN	60016	2862	14W-11N	C4
N Terrace Ln					
37400	GrtT	60081	2472	28W-37N	D2
Terrace Pl					
200	BFGV	60089	2754	17W-18N	A3
E Terrace Pl					
9000	MaiT	60016	2863	11W-11N	D2
9000	NLES	60016	2863	11W-11N	D2
9000	NLES	60714	2863	11W-11N	D2
N Terrace Pl					
9400	MaiT	60016	2863	11W-11N	D2
9400	MaiT	60714	2863	11W-11N	D2
9400	NLES	60714	2863	11W-11N	D2
Terrace Rd					
600	BbyT	60506	3076	40W-3S	C7
1500	HMWD	60430	3507	1W-22S	E2
1800	FSMR	60422	3507	2W-22S	D2
W Terrace St					
10	VLPK	60181	3027	18W-1N	A2
400	VLPK	60181	3026	18W-1N	E3
700	LMBD	60148	3026	18W-1N	D3
Terrace Wy					
600	PLNO	60545	3259	47W-13S	D5
Terrace Lake Dr					
800	AURA	60504	3201	32W-9S	C3
Terrace View Dr					
1100	AURA	60504	3201	32W-9S	C3
E Terra Cotta Av					
10	CLLK	60012	2640	33W-26N	D3
10	CLLK	60014	2640	33W-26N	D3
300	NndT	60012	2640	33W-26N	D3
300	NndT	60014	2640	33W-26N	D3
3100	NndT	60013	2641	32W-26N	C3
3100	NndT	60014	2641	32W-26N	B3
E Terra Cotta Av SR-176					
10	CLLK	60012	2640	33W-26N	D3
10	CLLK	60014	2640	33W-26N	D3
300	NndT	60012	2640	33W-26N	D3
300	NndT	60014	2640	33W-26N	D3
W Terra Cotta Av					
10	CLLK	60012	2640	35W-26N	A3
10	CLLK	60014	2640	35W-26N	A3
200	CLLK	60014	2639	36W-26N	E3
300	NndT	60014	2639	35W-26N	E3
600	CLLK	60012	2639	35W-26N	D3
600	NndT	60012	2639	36W-26N	D3

STREET Block City ZIP Map# CGS Grid

W Terra Cotta Av SR-176
10 CLLK 60012 2640 35W-26N A3
10 CLLK 60014 2640 35W-26N A3
200 CLLK 60014 2639 36W-26N E3
300 NndT 60014 2639 35W-26N E3
600 CLLK 60012 2639 36W-26N D3
600 NndT 60012 2639 36W-26N D3
W Terra Cotta Pl
1700 CHCG 60614 2977 2W-3N C5
Terra Cotta Rd
4000 NndT 60012 2584 34W-27N D7
4000 PRGV 60012 2584 34W-27N D7
4300 NndT 60012 2640 34W-26N D2
4700 CLLK 60012 2640 34W-26N D2
5300 CLLK 60014 2640 34W-26N D3
5600 NndT 60014 2640 34W-26N D3
6000 AlqT 60014 2640 34W-26N D4
Terra Firma Ln
100 VOLO 60041 2530 27W-34N C1
Terra Joe Rd
- SBTN 60010 2803 25W-14N E4
Terra Meadow Cir
100 VOLO 60041 2530 27W-34N C1
N Terramere Av
4000 ANHT 60004 2753 18W-18N E2
Terramere Ln
200 LIHL 60156 2692 38W-21N E5
Terrance Dr
200 NPVL 60565 3203 26W-8S D2
Terrance Ferry Dr
- JLET 60431 3496 29W-22S E1
3600 JLET 60431 3497 28W-22S A1
Terrapin Ct
23100 CNHN 60447 3584 31W-28S A6
23100 TroT 60447 3584 31W-28S A6
Terra Springs Cir
200 VOLO 60041 2530 27W-34N C2
Terra Springs Dr
- FXLK 60041 2530 27W-34N C1
100 VOLO 60041 2530 27W-34N C1
Terra Vista Ct
100 VOLO 60041 2530 27W-34N C2
Terra Vita Ct
10 SBTN 60010 2803 26W-14N D4
Terra Vita Dr
10 SBTN 60010 2803 26W-14N E4
Terre Dr
800 GNOK 60048 2592 15W-29N B4
800 LbvT 60048 2592 15W-29N B4
Terrence Dr
- NLNX 60451 3589 16W-25S E1
- NLNX 60451 3590 16W-25S A1
- NlxT 60451 3589 16W-25S E1
Terri Cir
1600 NPVL 60563 3140 29W-6S D4
Terri Ct
100 MHTN 60442 3678 18W-31S B5
Terrier Ct
12100 HMGN 60491 3422 15W-19S C3
Terri Lyn Ln
4100 NfdT 60062 2756 12W-17N A6
4100 NHBK 60062 2756 12W-17N A6
Territorial Ct
10 BGBK 60440 3268 24W-13S D5
Territorial Dr
500 BGBK 60440 3268 24W-13S D5
500 BGBK 60490 3268 24W-13S C4
Terry Av
500 AraT 60506 3199 37W-8S D2
500 AURA 60506 3199 37W-7S D1
Terry Ct
10 CHHT 60411 3508 1W-23S A3
100 WDSK 60098 2524 41W-32N C5
400 GwdT 60098 2524 41W-32N C5
600 ROSL 60172 2913 22W-7N C4
1300 GLHT 60139 3025 22W-2N C1
14200 ODPK 60462 3346 11W-16S A4
16500 OKFT 60452 3426 5W-19S B3
Terry Dr
10 ROSL 60172 2913 22W-7N B4
1600 JLET 60436 3585 27W-26S D2
3900 NndT 60014 2641 32W-26N A2
8800 ODPK 60462 3346 11W-16S A4
E Terry Dr
10 SRGV 60554 3135 42W-7S D6
N Terry Dr
400 JLET 60435 3497 27W-23S D3
700 TroT 60435 3497 27W-23S D3
N Terry Dr E
36800 LkvT 60046 2475 22W-36N C3
N Terry Dr W
36800 LkvT 60046 2475 22W-36N B3
S Terry Dr
10300 BGVW 60455 3274 9W-12S D1
10300 PSHL 60455 3274 9W-12S D1
10300 PSHL 60465 3274 9W-12S D2
W Terry Dr N
22200 LkvT 60046 2475 22W-37N B3
W Terry Dr S
22200 LkvT 60046 2475 22W-36N B3
Terry Ln
200 BMDL 60108 2969 22W-4N C3
200 NlxT 60451 3501 17W-25S D7
200 VLPK 60181 3027 17W-0S B6
600 NARA 60542 3078 35W-3S B7
700 CTSD 60525 3147 12W-6S B4
700 LynT 60525 3147 12W-6S B4
3000 BDVW 60155 3087 11W-2S D2
16300 OKFT 60452 3426 5W-19S B2
N Terry Ln
40400 AntT 60002 2416 24W-40N D3
W Terry Ln
2200 BDVW 60155 3087 11W-2S D2
24200 AntT 60002 2416 24W-40N D2
Terry Rd
600 GLHT 60139 3025 22W-2N C1
1400 GLHT 60139 2969 22W-2N C7
Terry Tr
10 DGvT 60527 3207 17W-10S D5
Terry Ellen Ln
100 NLNX 60451 3501 18W-23S B3
100 NlxT 60451 3501 18W-23S B3
W Terwilliger Av
100 HPSR 60140 2795 47W-16N D2
500 HshT 60140 2795 47W-16N D2
Teske Blvd
10 PKCY 60085 2536 13W-33N A2
S Tess Ln
1300 RDLK 60073 2531 23W-31N D6
W Tess Ln
600 FmtT 60030 2531 23W-31N D6
600 RDLK 60073 2531 23W-31N D6
Tessington Ct
1900 NlxT 60451 3502 16W-24S A5
Testa Dr
1000 LynT 60458 3209 11W-8S D2
1000 WLSP 60458 3209 11W-8S D2
1000 WLSP 60480 3209 11W-8S D2
S Testa Dr
10 NPVL 60540 3140 28W-6S E5
Teton Cir
500 CLSM 60188 2967 27W-2N D7
17400 LKPT 60441 3420 20W-20S B5
Teton Ct
500 NPVL 60565 3203 27W-8S C2
13500 ODPK 60462 3346 9W-16S D2
17400 LKPT 60441 3420 20W-20S B5
Teton Dr
- AURA 60503 3265 32W-11S D1
16400 LKPT 60441 3420 20W-20S B5
Teton Pkwy
2000 ALGN 60102 2748 32W-20N B1
Teton Rd
7800 ODPK 60462 3346 9W-16S C2
Tetryl Rd
- ELWD 60421 3763 28W-33S B4
Teverton Ln
800 CLLK 60014 2640 35W-24N A7
N Tewes Ct
38300 BHPK 60087 2422 10W-38N A7
38300 BHPK 60099 2422 10W-38N A7
Tewes Ln
1100 WKGN 60099 2421 10W-38N E7
1100 WKGN 60099 2422 10W-38N A7
Tewkesbury Ln
10 SBTN 60010 2804 25W-15N B1
Tewksbury Cir
500 OSWG 60543 3263 36W-11S E2
Tewksbury Ct
500 OSWG 60543 3263 36W-12S E2
Texas Av
1200 JLET 60435 3498 25W-22S B2
Texas Ct
- NCHI 60088 2593 11W-30N C2
800 CLSM 60188 2967 27W-2N D7
10500 ODPK 60467 3423 13W-21S B7
Texas St
700 EGVV 60007 2913 21W-9N E1
Thacker Ct
400 SMBG 60173 2859 21W-11N D4
E Thacker St
10 DSPN 60016 2862 13W-11N E4
400 HFET 60169 2859 22W-11N B4
400 HFET 60194 2859 22W-11N B4
400 SMBG 60194 2859 22W-11N B4
1000 SMBG 60169 2859 22W-11N C4
1000 SMBG 60173 2859 22W-10N D4
1300 DSPN 60016 2863 13W-10N A4
W Thacker St
10 DSPN 60016 2862 15W-11N B4
10 HFET 60169 2859 23W-11N A4
10 HFET 60194 2859 23W-11N A4
10 SMBG 60194 2859 23W-11N A4
200 HFET 60169 2858 23W-11N E4
Thackeray Av
16800 BmnT 60452 3425 6W-20S E4
16800 OKFT 60452 3425 6W-20S E4
Thackeray Dr
100 BGBK 60440 3268 25W-11S B2
100 BGBK 60490 3268 25W-11S B2
700 HDPK 60035 2704 8W-21N E7
700 HDPK 60035 2705 8W-21N A7
N Thackeray Dr
1000 PLTN 60067 2752 20W-17N E5
Thackeray Ln
600 FRGV 60021 2696 30W-22N A4
Thackery Ct
1200 NPVL 60564 3203 28W-11S A7
Thackery Dr
- BGBK 60440 3268 25W-12S B3
Thackery Ln
100 NHFD 60093 2811 7W-15N B3
1000 NPVL 60564 3203 28W-11S B7
1000 NPVL 60564 3267 28W-11S B1
6300 GRNE 60048 2534 16W-32N D5
W Thackery Pl
100 MPPT 60056 2807 16W-14N D4
Thaddeus Cir
500 MltT 60137 3083 21W-2S D4
Thames Cir
900 SMBG 60193 2913 22W-9N C1
Thames Ct
1600 WHTN 60187 3082 23W-2S E3
1600 WHTN 60187 3083 23W-2S A3
Thames Dr
200 SRWD 60404 3496 31W-23S A4
400 DGvT 60516 3206 20W-10S B6
400 DGvT 60517 3206 20W-10S B6
400 WDRG 60517 3206 20W-10S B6
600 SMBG 60193 2913 22W-9N C1
Thames Pkwy
200 PKRG 60068 2917 11W-8N D1
Thames Ter
1300 ROSL 60172 2912 25W-6N B6
Thames River Ln
2000 NLNX 60451 3590 15W-25S B1
Thatcher Av
10 FTPK 60130 3030 10W-0N B5
10 RVFT 60130 3030 10W-0N B5
400 RVFT 60305 3030 10W-0N B4
1300 EDPK 60707 3030 9W-1N B1
1300 RVFT 60707 3030 9W-1N B1
N Thatcher Av
1600 EDPK 60171 2974 9W-2N B7
1600 EDPK 60707 2974 9W-2N B7
1600 EDPK 60707 3030 9W-2N B1
1600 RVFT 60305 3030 9W-2N B1
1600 RVFT 60707 3030 9W-2N B1
2000 RVGV 60171 2974 10W-2N B6
3000 CHCG 60634 2974 10W-3N A5
3000 RVGV 60634 2974 10W-3N A5
N Thatcher Av SR-171
2500 RVGV 60171 2974 10W-3N A5
3000 CHCG 60634 2974 10W-3N A5
3000 RVGV 60634 2974 10W-3N A5
Thatcher Dr
3900 AURA 60504 3202 30W-8S B3
4000 AURA 60564 3202 30W-8S B3
4000 NpvT 60564 3202 30W-8S B3
4700 NPVL 60564 3266 29W-13S D4
N Thatcher Ln
1100 ADSN 60101 2970 19W-4N C2
Thatcher Rd
2800 DRGV 60515 3143 22W-5S D3
4200 CHCG 60634 2974 10W-5N A1
4300 NRDG 60706 2974 10W-5N A1
4500 NRDG 60706 2918 10W-5N A7
Thatcher Tr
1100 WDND 60118 2800 35W-16N B1
Thaxted Cir
3200 OMFD 60461 3507 4W-25S A7
S Thaxter Av
500 WKGN 60085 2536 12W-33N B3
Thaxton Ct
2400 NPVL 60565 3204 25W-10S B6
Thayer Av
300 JltT 60432 3499 22W-23S C4
400 JLET 60432 3499 22W-23S C4
Thayer Ct
- EVTN 60201 2812 4W-13N B7
3500 AURA 60504 3201 31W-9S E3
3500 NpvT 60504 3201 31W-9S E3
Thayer Rd
9300 GwdT 60034 2468 40W-38N A1
9300 GwdT 60097 2468 40W-38N A1
9300 GwdT 60097 2469 38W-38N A1
9300 GwdT 60098 2468 40W-38N A1
9300 HbnT 60034 2468 40W-38N A1
9300 HbnT 60034 2469 38W-38N A1
9300 HbnT 60097 2469 38W-38N A1
Thayer St
3500 EVTN 60201 2812 5W-13N B7
E Thayer St
- MPPT 60056 2808 15W-13N A6
1500 DSPN 60016 2808 14W-13N D6
1500 DSPN 60056 2808 14W-13N D6
W Thayer St
- MPPT 60056 2807 15W-13N E6
- MPPT 60056 2808 15W-13N A6
The Court of Chapelwood
10 NHBK 60062 2756 11W-17N C5
The Court of Charlwood
10 NHBK 60062 2756 12W-17N C5
The Court of Cobblestone
10 NHBK 60062 2756 11W-17N C5
The Court of Greenway
10 NHBK 60062 2756 11W-17N C4
The Court of Harbinger Falls
10 NHBK 60062 2756 11W-17N C4
The Court of Hidden Bay
10 NHBK 60062 2756 11W-17N C4
The Court of Hidden Well
10 NHBK 60062 2756 11W-17N C4
The Court of Muirwood
10 NHBK 60062 2756 12W-17N C5
The Court of Stone Cr
10 NHBK 60062 2756 11W-17N D5
Theda Ln
2100 RGMW 60008 2806 20W-14N A4
The Hague
500 PTON 60468 3860 9W-37S D3
Theisen Av
22400 SLVL 60411 3598 3E-27S A4
Theisen Tr
100 GnvT 60510 3077 37W-1S B1
The Lane
100 HNDL 60521 3086 15W-4S A7
Thelen Dr
5200 MchT 60050 2472 29W-37N D2
Thelin Ct
100 WLMT 60091 2811 5W-13N E7
1100 BTVA 60510 3077 36W-2S E4
1100 BTVA 60510 3078 36W-2S A4
1600 EVTN 60201 2867 3W-11N A3
Thelma Cir
13100 WldT 60585 3338 29W-15S D2
Thelma Ct
300 WLNG 60090 2754 15W-17N E5
Thelma Ln
100 CHHT 60411 3507 1W-23S E4
Thelma St
10 MHTN 60442 3678 18W-31S A5
The Mews
2700 NHBK 60062 2756 10W-18N E4
Theobald Rd
5500 MNGV 60053 2865 7W-10N C4
Theodore Av
22500 SLVL 60411 3598 3E-27S A4
Theodore Ct
700 RMVL 60446 3268 25W-14S C7
Theodore Dr
100 OSWG 60543 3263 37W-13S D5
E Theodore Ln
100 ITSC 60143 2914 19W-7N C5
W Theodore Ln
100 ITSC 60143 2914 19W-7N C5
W Theodore Rd
- JLET 60447 3495 33W-21S B1
5800 JLET 60586 3496 31W-21S A1
25200 TroT 60586 3495 31W-21S E1
25300 JLET 60431 3495 31W-22S D1
25300 PnfT 60586 3495 31W-21S E1
25300 TroT 60431 3495 31W-21S E1
25800 JLET 60586 3495 33W-21S B1
Theodore St
10 CTHL 60435 3498 24W-22S D1
10 JLET 60435 3498 24W-22S D1
10 LktT 60435 3498 24W-21S E1
200 CTHL 60403 3498 24W-22S E1
1400 JLET 60403 3498 25W-21S B1
2000 CTHL 60403 3497 26W-21S D1
2000 JLET 60403 3497 28W-21S B1
2100 CTHL 60435 3497 26W-21S E1
3000 JLET 60431 3497 28W-21S B1
3300 PnfT 60431 3497 28W-21S B1
Theodore St SR-7
200 CTHL 60403 3498 24W-22S D1
200 CTHL 60435 3498 24W-22S D1
200 JLET 60435 3498 24W-22S D1
1400 JLET 60403 3498 25W-21S B1
W Theodore St
- TroT 60586 3496 29W-21S D1
3800 JLET 60431 3496 29W-21S E1
3800 PnfT 60431 3496 29W-21S E1
3800 PnfT 60431 3497 28W-21S A1
24100 JLET 60404 3496 30W-21S C1
24100 JLET 60586 3496 29W-21S D1
24100 PnfT 60586 3496 29W-21S D1
The Pines
700 HNDL 60521 3086 15W-4S A7
The Point St
1200 BRTN 60010 2751 24W-20N C1
Theresa Av
- BtlT 60543 3262 40W-12S B3
2600 WKGN 60085 2479 12W-35N C6
S Theresa Cir
11000 PSHL 60465 3274 10W-12S B3
Theresa Ct
700 YkTp 60523 3084 19W-2S D4
Theresa Dr
- LmnT 60439 3271 18W-13S B5
Theresa Ln
100 YkTp 60523 3084 19W-2S D4
800 CHHT 60411 3507 1W-24S E6
16600 TYPK 60477 3424 8W-19S E3
16600 TYPK 60477 3425 8W-19S A3
Therese Ct
600 DGvT 60527 3207 16W-9S D3
9200 ODPK 60462 3345 11W-16S E3
Therese Ln
19600 MKNA 60448 3503 13W-24S B4
Therese Ter
600 DSPN 60016 2808 13W-13N D7
The Strand
2400 NHBK 60062 2809 10W-15N E1
2400 NHBK 60062 2810 10W-15N A1
10100 WSTR 60154 3029 12W-0S B7
Thicket Ct
13600 HMGN 60491 3343 16W-16S E3
T Hickey Dr
2800 CTHL 60403 3417 27W-21S C7
2800 JLET 60435 3417 27W-21S C7
3100 JLET 60431 3417 27W-21S B7
Thierry Ln
200 PTHT 60070 2808 14W-15N B2
Thillen Dr
10 FXLK 60020 2473 27W-36N A3
Thimbleweed Ct
4900 LGGV 60047 2700 19W-23N C1
Thimbleweed Rd
1400 GYLK 60030 2533 19W-31N C7
Thimbleweed Tr
4900 LGGV 60047 2700 19W-23N C1
Third Av
- HbnT 60034 2351 40W-41N B7
Third St
200 WDSK 60098 2524 41W-31N C6
Thistle Ct
10 RchT 60443 3593 8W-26S C2
10 SMWD 60107 2856 30W-10N C5
100 SMBG 60194 2857 26W-10N E5
1500 BFGV 60089 2701 16W-21N D5
4700 HRPK 60133 2967 27W-5N C1
6600 AlqT 60013 2642 29W-25N C5
13000 HMGN 60491 3422 16W-18S A1
S Thistle Ct
100 RDLK 60073 2531 23W-33N E3
Thistle Dr
300 BGBK 60440 3268 25W-12S B3
300 BGBK 60490 3268 25W-12S B3
Thistle Ln
- GNVW 60025 2810 9W-14N C5
200 LKZH 60047 2699 22W-22N C3
600 PTHT 60070 2808 14W-14N B4
4000 ZION 60099 2362 12W-42N C7
4800 LIHL 60156 2692 38W-23N D2
S Thistle Ln
19500 FftT 60423 3504 9W-23S E3
Thistle Rd
2100 GNVW 60025 2810 9W-14N C5
Thistledawn Ct
600 MltT 60188 3024 25W-1N A3
Thistledown Ct
3900 RLKP 60030 2532 22W-31N C7
Thistle Hill Ct
2000 NPVL 60565 3204 24W-8S E2
Thistlewood Ct
8400 DRN 60561 3207 18W-9S A4
Thistlewood Dr
15300 ODPK 60462 3346 10W-18S A7
Thistlewood Ln
7600 FKFT 60423 3504 9W-25S D7
8600 ODPK 60462 3346 11W-18S A7
Thomas Av
400 FTPK 60130 3030 9W-0S D5
7100 BGVW 60455 3148 9W-8S D7
7300 BGVW 60455 3210 9W-8S D1
Thomas Blvd
900 MDLN 60060 2647 18W-27N A1
Thomas Ct
- GLHT 60139 3024 24W-2N D1
- PLNO 60545 3260 45W-14S B7
10 GYLK 60030 2532 21W-32N E5
10 RNPK 60471 3594 4W-26S D3
100 BRLT 60103 2911 28W-8N A3
100 NlxT 60448 3502 15W-22S C2
100 WCDA 60084 2643 26W-26N D2
700 LYVL 60048 2591 17W-29N B4
700 MDLN 60060 2646 18W-27N E1
1600 FSMR 60422 3507 2W-23S E4
2500 CTHL 60403 3497 27W-22S D1
14100 ODPK 60462 3345 11W-16S E4
S Thomas Ct
2600 NndT 60051 2586 29W-29N C4
15100 PnfT 60544 3339 27W-18S C7
W Thomas Ct
28400 GrtT 60041 2472 28W-34N E7
Thomas Dr
- RMVL 60446 3340 25W-15S B1
300 WCHI 60185 3022 30W-2N B1
400 NBRN 60010 2698 25W-22N B3
800 BNVL 60106 2915 16W-7N E5
1200 WDSK 60098 2524 42W-32N C6
5000 RNPK 60471 3594 6W-27S A4
13900 ODPK 60462 3345 11W-16S E5
20600 LktT 60403 3418 25W-19S A3
20600 LktT 60441 3418 25W-19S A3
Thomas Ln
- BtlT 60512 3198 41W-11S A7
100 NlxT 60451 3501 17W-23S C4
15700 OKFT 60452 3425 7W-18S D1
17900 CCHL 60478 3426 5W-21S B7
Thomas Pl
10 LKFT 60045 2649 10W-27N E1
Thomas Rd
10 MltT 60187 3023 26W-0N E4
100 BGBK 60440 3205 22W-10S B6
100 MltT 60187 3024 25W-0N B4
100 WHTN 60187 3024 25W-0N B4
600 BNVL 60106 2915 16W-6N E5
E Thomas Rd
1000 MltT 60187 3024 23W-0N E4
1000 WHTN 60187 3024 23W-0N E4
1600 WHTN 60187 3025 23W-0N A4
W Thomas Rd
13400 HTLY 60142 2744 43W-18N B4
Thomas St
10 CHCG 60651 3031 7W-1N B2
10 OKPK 60302 3031 7W-1N B2
200 AlqT 60013 2695 31W-23N E2
200 CRY 60013 2695 31W-23N E2
200 OMFD 60461 3595 3W-25S B1
200 OMFD 60466 3595 3W-25S B1
200 PKFT 60461 3595 3W-25S B1
200 PKFT 60466 3595 3W-25S B1
800 BlmT 60411 3507 2W-24S D6
800 CHHT 60411 3507 2W-24S D6
800 OKPK 60302 3030 9W-1N D2
1100 OKPK 60305 3030 9W-1N D2
1200 HMWD 60430 3507 1W-22S E2
1200 HMWD 60430 3508 1W-22S A2
1200 MLPK 60160 3029 11W-1N D2
7800 RVFT 60305 3030 9W-1N B2
8000 BGVW 60455 3210 10W-9S B3
8000 JSTC 60455 3210 10W-9S B3
8000 JSTC 60458 3210 10W-9S B3
E Thomas St
10 ANHT 60004 2807 16W-15N C2
1000 PTHT 60004 2807 16W-15N C2
1500 ANHT 60004 2806 19W-15N D2
1500 PLTN 60004 2806 19W-15N D2
1700 PTHT 60070 2807 16W-15N C2
W Thomas St
10 ANHT 60004 2807 18W-15N A2
400 ANHT 60004 2806 18W-15N D2
600 EMHT 60126 3027 17W-1N C3
700 VLPK 60126 3027 17W-1N B3
700 VLPK 60181 3027 17W-1N B3
1400 CHCG 60622 3033 1W-1N D2
1700 PLTN 60074 2806 18W-15N D2
2700 CHCG 60622 3032 3W-1N E2
3200 CHCG 60651 3032 4W-1N D2
4800 CHCG 60651 3031 7W-1N C2
5900 OKPK 60302 3031 7W-1N B2
Thomas Atkinson Rd
- IVNS 60067 2805 23W-16N A1
1700 IVNS 60067 2804 23W-16N E1
1800 IVNS 60067 2751 23W-16N E7
S Thomas Dillon Dr
22400 CNHN 60410 3584 29W-28S D6
22400 CNHN 60436 3584 29W-28S D6
22400 TroT 60410 3584 29W-27S D4
22400 TroT 60436 3584 29W-27S D4
Thomas Jefferson Ct
400 AURA 60504 3140 29W-6S D6
Thomas Jefferson Dr
14500 PNFD 60544 3338 30W-17S A6
Thomas More Dr
100 ELGN 60123 2854 35W-11N A4
Thomas More Ter
1100 MPPT 60056 2807 15W-14N E4
Thomas Payne
400 AURA 60504 3140 29W-6S D5
Thomas Rottman Memorial Dr
- WPHR 60096 2363 10W-42N A6
Thomasville Ln
1700 CLLK 60014 2693 36W-22N C4
1800 LIHL 60156 2693 36W-22N C4
W Thome Av
1600 CHCG 60660 2921 2W-7N B3
2200 CHCG 60659 2921 2W-7N B3
4400 CHCG 60646 2920 5W-7N A3
Thompson Av
100 PTPR 53158 2363 10W-43N B4
100 WPHR 53158 2363 10W-43N B4
100 WPHR 60096 2363 10W-42N B6
600 NARA 60542 3138 35W-4S B1
800 SchT 60174 2908 35W-6N B6
1800 BtnT 60099 2422 10W-41N B2
1800 ZION 60099 2422 10W-41N B2
Thompson Blvd
- BFGV 60069 2701 16W-21N E5
- VrnT 60069 2701 16W-21N E5
900 BFGV 60089 2701 18W-21N A6
1100 LGGV 60089 2701 17W-21N A6
Thompson Ct
- BFGV 60089 2701 17W-21N B6
18400 TYPK 60477 3424 9W-22S D7
18400 TYPK 60477 3504 9W-22S D1
E Thompson Dr
10 WHTN 60187 3082 24W-2S C3
S Thompson Dr
1200 CHCG 60623 3032 3W-1S E7
1600 WHTN 60187 3082 24W-2S C3
Thompson Ln
500 LKVL 60046 2474 23W-37N E2
2000 AURA 60505 3139 33W-5S A2
Thompson Rd
1300 BLVY 60097 2526 37W-33N A3
1300 BLVY 60098 2526 37W-33N A3
1300 GwdT 60098 2526 37W-33N A3
1900 WRLK 60097 2526 37W-34N B1
2500 BLVY 60097 2469 37W-34N B7
2500 WRLK 60097 2469 37W-35N B5
2800 GwdT 60097 2469 37W-35N B5
4000 GNWD 60097 2469 37W-35N B5
9100 GwdT 60098 2525 38W-32N D4
E Thompson St
200 HRVD 60033 2406 49W-38N D6
N Thompson St
35200 AvnT 60073 2474 24W-35N C7
W Thompson St
100 HRVD 60033 2406 50W-38N A7
800 CmgT 60033 2405 51W-38N E7
800 HRVD 60033 2405 51W-38N E7
Thompsons Cir
600 IVNS 60067 2804 23W-14N E3
Thompsons Wy
600 IVNS 60067 2804 23W-14N E3
Thor Dr
1400 IVNS 60067 2804 23W-14N E4
1400 IVNS 60067 2805 23W-14N A4
S Thoreau Ct
1800 SMBG 60193 2912 25W-9N B1
Thoreau Dr
600 ELGN 60120 2855 31W-10N E6
N Thoreau Dr
1500 SMBG 60173 2805 21W-12N E7
1900 PltT 60067 2805 21W-12N E7
1900 SMBG 60067 2805 21W-12N E7
Thoria Ct
400 BTVA 60510 3020 34W-0S C6
Thoria Rd
300 BTVA 60510 3020 35W-0S C6
1400 GNVA 60134 3020 35W-0S C6
1400 GNVA 60510 3020 35W-0S C6
W Thorn Ln
2000 CteT 60417 3684 2W-29S D1
Thorn Rd
300 BMDL 60108 2912 25W-6N B6
300 BMDL 60172 2912 25W-6N B6
300 BmdT 60108 2912 25W-6N B6
300 BmdT 60172 2912 25W-6N B6
400 BMDL 60108 2968 25W-5N B1
400 BMDL 60172 2968 25W-5N B1
400 BmdT 60172 2968 25W-5N B1
500 HRPK 60133 2912 25W-6N B6
500 HRPK 60172 2912 25W-6N B6
Thorn St
1500 CHHT 60411 3596 1W-25S A1
Thornapple Ct
200 BFGV 60089 2754 17W-20N A1
Thorn Apple Dr
12200 HMGN 60491 3422 15W-20S C4
Thornapple Dr
100 NPVL 60540 3141 28W-7S B6
100 NpvT 60540 3141 28W-7S B7

STREET Block City ZIP Map# CGS Grid

Thornapple Dr
800 NPVL 60540 3203 28W-7S B1
Thornapple Ln
- MRGO 60152 2634 49W-25N C4
400 LYVL 60048 2591 16W-27N C7
800 GLNC 60022 2758 7W-17N C5
1200 NHBK 60062 2757 9W-17N D4
N Thornapple Ln
32800 WmT 60030 2534 18W-32N A4
W Thornapple Ln
15800 WDWH 60031 2477 16W-37N E3
15800 WDWH 60031 2478 15W-37N A3
Thornapple Rd
10 SchT 60174 2963 36W-3N E5
100 BKBN 60015 2703 12W-22N B4
Thornapple Wy
1800 AURA 60504 3201 33W-8S A3
Thornapple Tree Dr
10 BbyT 60554 3075 43W-3S A7
10 SgrT 60554 3075 43W-3S A7
Thornbark Ct
4400 HFET 60192 2804 24W-15N C2
Thornbark Dr
4400 HFET 60067 2804 24W-15N C1
4400 HFET 60192 2804 24W-15N C1
4400 IVNS 60067 2804 24W-15N C1
4400 IVNS 60192 2804 24W-15N C1
4800 HFET 60010 2804 24W-16N C1
5100 HFET 60010 2751 24W-16N C7
5100 IVNS 60010 2751 24W-16N C7
Thornberry Cir
14100 PNFD 60544 3337 31W-16S E5
Thornberry Ct
1500 WKGN 60048 2535 14W-32N C5
14100 PNFD 60544 3337 31W-16S E5
Thornberry Dr
12300 LMNT 60439 3270 20W-14S B7
12600 DPgT 60441 3270 20W-14S A7
24800 PNFD 60544 3337 31W-16S E5
24900 PNFD 60544 3338 31W-16S A5
Thornberry Ln
3100 MaiT 60025 2864 10W-12N A1
3300 GNVW 60025 2863 10W-12N E1
3300 GNVW 60025 2864 10W-12N A1
3300 MaiT 60025 2863 11W-12N E1
Thornberry Wy
3800 LIHL 60156 2693 37W-22N B4
Thorn Bluff Ln
- RcmT 60071 2353 34W-43N D4
Thornbury Ct
200 OSWG 60543 3263 36W-11S E2
600 BRLT 60103 2855 31W-9N E7
600 BRLT 60103 2856 31W-9N A7
22400 DRPK 60010 2752 22W-20N B1
Thornbury Dr
200 OSWG 60543 3263 36W-11S E2
700 BRLT 60103 2855 31W-9N E7
700 BRLT 60120 2855 31W-9N E7
700 BRLT 60120 2909 31W-9N E1
1600 BRLT 60103 2909 31W-9N E1
E Thornbury Ln
900 LbvT 60048 2592 15W-29N B4
900 LYVL 60048 2592 15W-29N B4
1000 GNOK 60048 2592 15W-29N B4
Thorncliff Dr
300 GLHT 60139 2969 23W-4N B4
Thorn Creek Dr
10 PKFT 60466 3595 3W-28S B6
800 JLET 60436 3497 27W-25S C7
S Thorn Creek Ln
24200 CRTE 60417 3684 2W-29S D1
24200 CteT 60417 3684 2W-29S D1
Thorn Creek Rd
- BlmT 60425 3429 0E-21S A7
- BlmT 60476 3429 0E-21S A7
- ThtT 60476 3428 0E-21S E6
- ThtT 60476 3429 0E-21S A7
- TNTN 60476 3428 0E-21S E6
Thorncrest Ln
500 BTVA 60510 3078 35W-2S B5
500 BtvT 60510 3078 35W-2S B5
Thorncroft Dr
400 WYNE 60184 2965 33W-5N A1
Thorndale Av
- BNVL 60191 2915 17W-7N C4
10 AddT 60143 2914 19W-7N D4
10 AddT 60191 2914 19W-7N D4
10 BmdT 60157 2913 21W-7N D5
10 BNVL 60106 2915 16W-7N D4
10 CHCG 60068 2918 10W-7N B4
10 CHCG 60106 2915 16W-6N E5
10 CHCG 60631 2918 10W-7N B4
10 ITSC 60191 2914 18W-7N D4
10 PKRG 60068 2918 10W-7N B4
10 WDDL 60191 2915 18W-7N A4
200 EGvT 60007 2861 18W-9N A7
200 EGVV 60007 2861 18W-9N A7
300 ITSC 60143 2914 20W-7N A4
300 ROSL 60172 2913 22W-7N C5
300 WDDL 60143 2914 18W-7N D4
300 WDDL 60191 2914 18W-7N D4
400 BmdT 60143 2913 21W-7N D5
400 EGvT 60007 2915 17W-9N B1
400 EGVV 60007 2915 17W-9N B1
400 ITSC 60143 2913 21W-7N D5
500 PKCY 60085 2535 13W-33N D3
2400 BmnT 60428 3427 3W-19S B2
2500 MKHM 60428 3427 3W-19S B2
Thorndale Av CO-26
- BNVL 60191 2915 17W-7N C4
10 AddT 60191 2914 19W-7N D4
10 BNVL 60106 2915 16W-7N D4
10 CHCG 60106 2915 16W-6N E5
10 ITSC 60143 2914 18W-7N D4
10 ITSC 60191 2914 18W-7N D4
10 WDDL 60191 2915 18W-7N A4
100 AddT 60143 2914 20W-7N A4
300 WDDL 60143 2914 18W-7N D4
300 WDDL 60191 2914 18W-7N D4
E Thorndale Av
10 ROSL 60172 2913 23W-7N A4
10 WDDL 60191 2915 17W-7N B4
100 EGVV 60007 2915 17W-7N B4
300 EGVV 60191 2915 17W-7N C4
500 BNVL 60106 2915 17W-7N C4
500 BNVL 60191 2915 17W-7N C4
500 EGVV 60106 2915 17W-7N C4
E Thorndale Av CO-26
10 WDDL 60191 2915 17W-7N B4
100 EGVV 60007 2915 17W-7N B4
300 EGVV 60191 2915 17W-7N C4
500 BNVL 60106 2915 17W-7N C4
500 BNVL 60191 2915 17W-7N C4
500 EGVV 60106 2915 17W-7N C4
W Thorndale Av
10 ROSL 60172 2913 23W-7N A4
W Thorndale Av
800 ITSC 60143 2914 21W-7N A4
900 CHCG 60660 2921 1W-7N D4
1400 BmdT 60143 2913 21W-7N E4
1400 BmdT 60157 2913 21W-7N E4
1400 ITSC 60143 2913 21W-7N E4
2400 CHCG 60659 2921 3W-7N A4
4000 CHCG 60659 2920 5W-7N B4
4200 CHCG 60646 2920 5W-7N B4
6100 CHCG 60646 2919 7W-7N B4
6700 CHCG 60631 2918 8W-7N E4
7700 CHCG 60068 2918 9W-7N B4
7700 PKRG 60068 2918 9W-7N B4
Thorndale Ct
10 SEGN 60177 2908 34W-7N C5
100 SMWD 60107 2856 29W-10N E5
400 BFGV 60089 2754 16W-20N D1
800 LKZH 60047 2699 22W-21N C5
1000 WLNG 60090 2754 15W-18N E2
1200 ELGN 60120 2855 32W-10N D5
17500 LKPT 60441 3341 22W-18S D7
Thorndale Dr
400 BFGV 60089 2754 16W-20N D1
500 ELGN 60120 2855 31W-10N D5
S Thorndale Dr
19900 FftT 60423 3504 10W-24S C5
Thorndale Ln
1100 LKZH 60047 2699 22W-21N C5
E Thorndale Ln
500 SEGN 60177 2908 34W-7N C4
N Thorndale Ln
400 SEGN 60177 2908 35W-7N C4
W Thorndale Pl
38600 LkvT 60046 2416 23W-38N D7
Thorndon Ridge Rd
10 BbyT 60119 3075 43W-1S B1
Thorne Ct
- CHHT 60411 3508 0W-25S C6
Thorne Ln
400 LKFT 60045 2650 9W-26N B3
Thorne St
300 BTVA 60510 3077 37W-0S C1
600 JLET 60436 3498 25W-25S C7
600 RKDL 60436 3498 25W-25S C7
Thorneapple Ln
1600 ALGN 60102 2695 32W-20N B7
1700 ALGN 60102 2748 32W-20N B1
S Thorne Grove Dr
100 VNHL 60061 2646 18W-24N E6
Thornemeadow Cir
40700 WDWH 60083 2419 16W-40N D2
Thorne Tree Rd
10 SchT 60174 2963 36W-3N D5
900 SchT 60175 2963 36W-3N D5
Thornewood Ln
900 ALGN 60102 2695 32W-20N B7
900 ALGN 60102 2748 32W-20N A1
Thorney Lea Ter
800 SMBG 60193 2858 24W-9N D7
Thornfield Ct
1600 ROSL 60172 2912 25W-7N B4
Thornfield Ln
10 HNWD 60047 2644 24W-25N D4
1500 ROSL 60172 2912 25W-7N B4
Thorngate Dr
10 FmtT 60060 2589 21W-29N D5
10 HNWD 60047 2589 21W-28N C6
8400 ODPK 60462 3346 10W-18S B7
Thorngate Ln
- WdfT 60015 2756 12W-20N A1
200 WNFD 60190 3023 26W-1N E2
400 RVWD 60015 2756 13W-20N A1
500 RVWD 60015 2703 13W-20N A7
Thornham Dr
- MKNA 60448 3503 13W-23S B2
Thornhill Ct
10 BRRG 60527 3208 14W-8S D2
10 CRY 60013 2641 30W-25N E5
200 NPVL 60565 3203 26W-9S E4
300 SMBG 60193 2859 21W-10N E6
1200 GNVA 60134 3019 37W-0N D6
3500 OswT 60560 3334 40W-15S C3
22900 DRPK 60010 2699 23W-20N A7
22900 LKBN 60010 2643 26W-24N E7
Thornhill Dr
400 CLSM 60188 3024 24W-1N D3
Thornhill Ln
10 LKBN 60010 2643 26W-24N E7
400 WLNG 60090 2754 15W-18N E3
E Thornhill Ln
400 PLTN 60074 2753 20W-17N A4
Thornhill Rd
1800 IVNS 60067 2751 23W-16N E6
Thornhill Farm Rd
100 SCRL 60175 2964 35W-4N A3
Thornhouse Cres
500 NlxT 60451 3500 19W-24S E5
Thornhurst Rd
100 BGBK 60440 3269 22W-11S D1
Thornley Ct
2500 AURA 60504 3201 32W-8S C2
Thornly Rd
10 SchT 60174 2963 36W-3N E5
Thornmeadow Rd
300 RVWD 60015 2755 14W-20N D1
500 RVWD 60015 2702 14W-20N D7
Thornridge Dr
- KLDR 60047 2699 22W-21N B5
W Thornridge Dr
22100 KLDR 60047 2699 22W-21N B5
Thornton Av
16600 SHLD 60473 3428 0E-19S D2
Thornton Ct
800 SMBG 60193 2913 22W-8N C1
Thornton Ln
800 BFGV 60089 2754 17W-17N A5
900 ANHT 60004 2754 17W-17N A5
Thornton Rd
- DXMR 60426 3349 2W-16S D3
- HRVY 60426 3349 1W-16S E4
- SHLD 60426 3428 0W-18S B1
- SHLD 60473 3428 0W-18S B1
- ThtT 60426 3349 2W-16S E3
13500 BLID 60406 3349 1W-16S E4
13600 DXMR 60406 3349 1W-16S E4
Thornton St
100 LKPT 60441 3419 22W-19S D2
400 LktT 60441 3419 22W-19S D2
1100 LKPT 60441 3420 21W-18S A2
E Thornton St
600 HMND 46320 3352 E7
Thornton Wy
9800 HTLY 60142 2692 39W-22N C4
10000 GfnT 60142 2692 39W-22N C5
10000 GfnT 60156 2692 39W-22N C5
10000 HTLY 60156 2692 39W-22N C5
Thornton Lansing Rd
900 ThtT 60476 3428 0E-21S E6
900 TNTN 60476 3428 0E-21S E6
1000 ThtT 60476 3429 0E-21S A6
1100 ThtT 60438 3429 0E-21S A6
1600 LNSG 60438 3429 1E-21S C5
Thornton-Lansing Rd
2400 LNSG 60438 3429 3E-21S E6
Thorntree Ct
600 BRLT 60103 2911 28W-8N B3
Thorntree Dr
2200 PltT 60067 2805 20W-13N E7
2200 SMBG 60067 2805 20W-13N E7
2200 SMBG 60173 2805 20W-13N E7
Thorn Tree Ln
10 WNKA 60093 2812 5W-15N A3
1100 HDPK 60035 2704 8W-21N D6
Thorntree Ln
10 LKBF 60044 2593 12W-28N B5
10 ShdT 60044 2593 12W-28N B6
2000 PltT 60067 2805 20W-13N E6
4400 RGMW 60008 2806 20W-12N B7
Thorntree Rd
27300 FmtT 60060 2645 21W-27N E1
27400 MDLN 60060 2645 21W-27N E1
Thorntree Ter
700 RchT 60443 3593 8W-26S B2
E Thorntree Ter
600 ANHT 60004 2754 17W-16N B7
Thorn Valley Ln
400 LKBF 60044 2593 11W-29N D4
Thornwood Av
- SEGN 60175 2907 37W-7N D5
500 SEGN 60177 2907 37W-7N D5
1900 KLWH 60043 2812 4W-14N C5
1900 KLWH 60091 2812 4W-14N C5
2300 WLMT 60091 2812 5W-14N A5
3100 GNVW 60025 2810 10W-14N A5
3100 NfdT 60025 2810 10W-14N A5
3500 WLMT 60091 2811 6W-14N D5
4000 MTSN 60443 3506 5W-24S C5
4000 OMFD 60461 3506 5W-24S C5
Thornwood Blvd
- SchT 60175 2907 37W-7N D6
- SEGN 60175 2907 37W-7N D6
- SEGN 60177 2907 37W-7N D6
27000 PNFD 60585 3337 33W-15S A2
Thornwood Cir
2000 SCRL 60174 2963 36W-3N D6
20800 OMFD 60461 3506 4W-25S E7
Thornwood Ct
900 SchT 60174 2963 37W-3N D6
900 SCRL 60174 2963 37W-3N D6
1100 LKZH 60047 2698 24W-23N B3
17200 SHLD 60473 3429 0E-20S A4
Thornwood Dr
10 FSMR 60422 3507 2W-23S D3
500 BFGV 60089 2754 17W-18N B3
500 SHLD 60473 3428 0E-20S E3
600 NPVL 60540 3141 26W-7S D7
600 SHLD 60473 3429 0E-20S A4
800 SchT 60174 2963 36W-3N D6
800 SCRL 60174 2963 36W-3N D6
1200 SMBG 60193 2913 23W-8N A2
1400 DRGV 60516 3144 20W-6S B4
9200 TYPK 60487 3423 11W-20S E4
20700 OMFD 60461 3506 4W-25S E6
E Thornwood Dr
400 SEGN 60177 2907 37W-7N C4
2400 LNHT 60046 2476 19W-37N B2
N Thornwood Dr
300 MHRY 60050 2527 34W-32N D5
S Thornwood Dr
300 LNHT 60046 2476 20W-37N B2
SE Thornwood Dr
2300 LNHT 60046 2476 20W-37N B2
W Thornwood Dr
400 SEGN 60177 2907 37W-7N C5
5100 MHRY 60050 2527 34W-32N D5
Thornwood Ln
300 LKBF 60044 2593 11W-28N D6
300 WNVL 60555 3080 29W-3S D5
500 NHFD 60093 2811 7W-15N A2
800 GNVW 60025 2811 8W-13N A7
1100 CLLK 60014 2639 37W-25N A4
1600 HDPK 60035 2704 10W-23N A3
1800 NHBK 60062 2757 10W-17N B4
1900 RVWD 60015 2702 13W-22N E4
3400 GNVW 60025 2809 10W-14N E5
3400 GNVW 60025 2810 10W-14N A5
3400 NfdT 60025 2810 10W-14N A5
4200 JLET 60586 3496 29W-22S D1
W Thornwood Ln
1800 MPPT 60056 2861 17W-11N C3
15300 HMGN 60491 3342 19W-17S D6
15500 HmrT 60491 3342 19W-17S D5
Thornwood St
1500 WHTN 60187 3081 26W-1S E3
7200 HRPK 60133 2911 27W-9N D1
Thornwood Wy
- PNFD 60585 3337 33W-15S A2
200 SEGN 60177 2907 37W-8N C3
Thorobred Ln
10 SYHW 60118 2800 35W-15N B3
Thoroughbred Cir
1000 SCRL 60174 2964 34W-3N D5
Thoroughbred Dr
16200 WmT 60083 2477 16W-37N D2
N Thoroughbred Dr
36600 WmT 60031 2477 17W-36N B4
36600 WmT 60083 2477 17W-36N B4
Thoroughbred Ln
300 ROSL 60172 2912 24W-7N E4
300 SMBG 60172 2912 23W-7N E3
3500 JLET 60435 3417 27W-19S D3
3800 PnfT 60544 3417 27W-19S D2
Thoroughbred Tr
2200 GwdT 60098 2525 39W-34N C1
N Thorpe Av
42200 BhT 60099 2362 11W-42N D6
Thorsen Ln
500 BTVA 60510 3019 36W-0S E7
N Thorsen Ln
8100 GLkT 60450 3761 33W-33S A4
Thorton Wy
1400 MDLN 60060 2646 20W-27N B2
Thousand Oaks Dr
1100 BRLT 60103 2910 30W-6N C7
Thrasher St
200 BMDL 60108 2968 24W-5N E2
Three Farms Av
1900 NPVL 60540 3202 29W-8S D2
Three Forks Dr
2100 JLET 60586 3415 32W-21S C7
Three Lakes Ct
4100 LGGV 60047 2700 18W-21N E5
Three Lakes Dr
10 NHBK 60062 2810 8W-16N E1
10 NHFD 60093 2810 8W-15N E1
4100 LGGV 60047 2700 18W-21N E5
Three Lakes Rd
10 BNHL 60010 2750 27W-18N B2
Three Oaks Rd
10 AlqT 60013 2642 29W-24N C7
10 CbaT 60013 2642 29W-24N C7
600 CRY 60013 2642 29W-24N C7
1800 AlqT 60013 2641 30W-24N E7
1800 CRY 60013 2641 32W-24N A7
3900 CLLK 60014 2641 32W-24N A7
4000 AlqT 60014 2641 33W-24N A7
4300 AlqT 60014 2640 33W-24N D7
4300 CLLK 60014 2640 33W-24N D7
S Three Willow Ct
800 PLTN 60067 2805 22W-14N B3
Thresher St
4000 NCHI 60088 2593 11W-30N D1
Throop St
- HRVY 60426 3427 1W-20S E5
- HRVY 60429 3427 1W-20S E5
500 CHCG 60607 3033 1W-0S D6
17100 EHZC 60429 3427 1W-20S E5
17400 HMWD 60429 3427 1W-20S E5
17400 HMWD 60430 3427 1W-20S E5
N Throop St
10 CHCG 60607 3033 1W-0N D4
100 WDSK 60098 2524 41W-31N C7
1500 CHCG 60622 3033 1W-1N D1
1700 CHCG 60622 2977 1W-2N D7
S Throop St
100 WDSK 60098 2524 41W-31N D7
200 CHCG 60607 3033 1W-0S D5
200 WDSK 60098 2581 41W-30N D1
1300 CHCG 60608 3033 1W-1S D7
2500 CHCG 60608 3091 1W-2S E3
4700 CHCG 60609 3151 1W-5S E2
5500 CHCG 60636 3151 1W-6S E3
7600 CHCG 60620 3213 1W-8S E1
9400 CHCG 60643 3213 1W-11S E7
10300 CHCG 60643 3277 1W-13S E3
12200 CTPK 60643 3277 1W-14S E6
12200 CTPK 60827 3277 1W-15S E7
Thrun Dr
1200 BTVA 60510 3078 34W-2S E4
Thrush Cir
200 LNHT 60046 2476 19W-37N C1
Thrush Ct
10 BGBK 60440 3205 21W-10S D5
3100 RGMW 60008 2806 19W-13N B6
21400 DRPK 60010 2698 23W-21N E6
Thrush Ln
100 NPVL 60540 3203 26W-8S E2
2900 RGMW 60008 2806 19W-13N B6
Thrush St
10 CPVL 60110 2748 32W-17N D6
Thrush Creek Dr
- RcmT 60071 2353 34W-43N D4
- RHMD 60071 2353 34W-43N D4
Thunder Rdg
200 LIHL 60156 2693 36W-21N D5
E Thunderbird Ct
3100 AURA 60503 3201 31W-10S E7
W Thunderbird Ct
2900 AURA 60503 3201 31W-10S D7
Thunderbird Dr
6400 IHPK 60525 3146 14W-7S D6
Thunderbird Ln
1000 NPVL 60563 3141 28W-5S A3
3300 PRGV 60012 2584 33W-28N E6
Thunderbird Rd
200 BfdT 53128 2352 B2
Thunderbird Tr
100 CLSM 60188 2968 25W-2N A7
600 CLSM 60188 2967 26W-2N E7
800 WynT 60185 2967 27W-2N D7
800 WynT 60188 2967 27W-2N D7
Thunder Gap Ct
10 ElgT 60124 2907 38W-9N A1
Thurlow Dr
- DGvT 60527 3207 16W-9S E4
- DGvT 60527 3208 16W-9S A4
Thurlow St
10 DGvT 60527 3208 16W-10S A5
10 HNDL 60521 3146 16W-5S A1
5600 DGvT 60521 3146 16W-6S A4
6400 DGvT 60527 3146 16W-7S A6
6400 WLBK 60527 3146 16W-7S A6
Thurman Av
100 NPVL 60565 3204 25W-10S C5
Thurnau Rd
10 PGGV 60140 2797 43W-15N B4
10 RtdT 60140 2797 43W-15N B4
Thurston Ct
2400 AURA 60502 3139 32W-5S B3
E Thurston Dr
1200 PLTN 60074 2753 19W-16N C6
W Thurston Pl
1000 ANHT 60004 2753 18W-18N E2
Thyme Ln
21000 FKFT 60423 3590 14W-26S E3
Thyne Ct
1200 WLNG 60090 2754 16W-18N D3
Thyra Ln
1000 IVNS 60067 2804 23W-14N E4
1500 IVNS 60067 2805 23W-14N A3
Tia Juana Dr
300 LKMR 60051 2529 29W-32N C5
Tiara Ct
1100 NPVL 60564 3267 28W-12S A2
Tiburon Ct
1300 HRPK 60133 2911 26W-6N E6
Tiburon St
- RNPK 60443 3593 7W-27S C4
Tichfield Ter
2700 JNBG 60050 2471 31W-35N D6
W Ticknor Ct
1300 SMBG 60193 2912 25W-8N B2
Tickseed Dr
- ZION 60099 2362 12W-41N B7
Ticonderoga Ln
400 NPVL 60563 3141 26W-5S E2
Ticonderoga Pl
7200 DRGV 60516 3206 20W-8S B1
Ticonderoga Rd
6800 DRGV 60516 3144 20W-7S B7
7300 DRGV 60516 3206 20W-8S B1
Tide Ct
800 WLNG 60090 2755 15W-16N A6
Tidewater Ln
- ElgT 60124 2853 37W-9N D7
Tieri Ln
23200 CteT 60475 3595 2W-28S D6
23200 PKFT 60466 3595 2W-28S D6
Tierney Ct
23600 AntT 60002 2416 23W-40N D2
Tierney Ln
900 BTVA 60510 3078 34W-2S D3
Tiffany Cir
10 SBTN 60010 2803 27W-13N B5
Tiffany Ct
700 ANTH 60002 2357 24W-42N C6
1200 INCK 60061 2647 17W-25N A5
2700 NPVL 60565 3203 27W-10S D6
N Tiffany Ct
21500 KLDR 60047 2700 20W-21N A5
W Tiffany Ct
7900 PSHL 60465 3274 9W-12S C2
Tiffany Dr
300 WKGN 60085 2536 11W-34N D1
500 WKGN 60085 2479 11W-34N D7
2000 SMBG 60194 2858 26W-10N A5
2100 SMBG 60194 2857 26W-10N E5
2200 CteT 60417 3597 2E-28S E7
7300 ODPK 60462 3424 9W-18S E1
Tiffany Ln
200 ROSL 60172 2912 23W-6N E6
1100 LYVL 60048 2590 18W-29N E3
1100 LYVL 60060 2590 18W-29N E3
1100 MDLN 60060 2590 18W-29N E3
9100 FRGV 60021 2696 28W-22N D3
Tiffany Pl
4700 JLET 60431 3496 29W-22S E2
N Tiffany Rd
42200 ANTH 60002 2357 24W-42N C6
42500 AntT 60002 2357 24W-42N C6
Tiffany St
2600 AURA 60503 3201 32W-10S D6
Tiffany Farms Rd
- AntT 60002 2357 24W-42N C5
700 ANTH 60002 2357 24W-42N C5
Tiger Ct
10 BGBK 60490 3267 26W-12S D3
Tiger Dr
16000 LKPT 60441 3420 20W-20S C5
Tiger Ln
- TYPK 60477 3424 9W-21S D6
Tiger St
200 BGBK 60490 3267 26W-12S D3
Tiger Tr
- WHTN 60187 3081 27W-2S D4
- WnfT 60187 3081 27W-2S D4
Tiger Lily
13100 PNFD 60585 3337 31W-15S D2
Tiger Lily Ln
1300 JLET 60435 3498 25W-22S B1
2400 GRNE 60031 2478 14W-36N D4
W Tiger Tail Ct
17000 GRNE 60031 2534 17W-33N C2
17000 WmT 60031 2534 17W-33N C2
Tiger Trails
- WSTR 60154 3086 13W-1S E2
Tilbury Ln
200 WLNG 60090 2755 15W-18N A3
Tilche Ln
3700 NndT 60014 2641 32W-26N B3
N Tilden Av
10 LGNG 60525 3087 12W-3S C6
S Tilden Av
10 LGNG 60525 3087 12W-4S C7
Tilden Ln
100 BGBK 60440 3268 25W-12S B2
W Tilden St
- CHCG 60607 3033 1W-0S E6
- CHCG 60607 3034 D6
Tile Line Rd
4600 NndT 60012 2640 35W-27N A1
Tilia Ct
10 SMWD 60107 2856 30W-10N B5
Tilipi Ct
10 SMBG 60193 2858 24W-10N D5
Tilipi Ln
600 SMBG 60193 2858 24W-10N D5
Tiller St
600 ELBN 60119 3017 43W-2N B1
Tilson Ln
1900 RMVL 60446 3339 27W-17S C6
Timber Cir
400 SCRL 60174 2964 36W-3N A6
Timber Ct
10 BGBK 60440 3269 23W-12S A3
10 OKBK 60523 3085 16W-1S E1
10 OswT 60560 3334 40W-15S C1
100 GLBT 60136 2799 39W-14N A5
100 SMWD 60107 2857 28W-10N A5
100 WNFD 60190 3023 27W-1N D3
1200 NLNX 60451 3588 19W-26S E3
1900 GRNE 60031 2478 15W-36N A4
4900 OKFT 60452 3426 6W-20S A3
8800 TYPK 60487 3424 11W-20S A4
13000 PSHT 60463 3347 7W-15S C1
25400 TRLK 60010 2643 26W-25N D5
Timber Dr
- ELGN 60123 2854 35W-13N B1
10 WnfT 60555 3080 29W-3S D5
10 WNVL 60555 3080 29W-3S D5
100 PNFD 60544 3415 31W-18S E1
100 PNFD 60544 3416 31W-18S A1
300 HRVD 60033 2464 50W-37N A1
1200 EGVV 60007 2914 21W-8N A2
1200 SYHW 60118 2800 36W-15N A3
7000 TYPK 60477 3424 9W-21S D6
16900 LKPT 60441 3420 19W-20S E4
24900 JknT 60421 3675 24W-30S E3
W Timber Dr
1100 ELGN 60123 2854 35W-12N B1
Timber Dr N
19200 JknT 60421 3675 24W-30S E3
Timber Dr S
19300 JknT 60421 3675 24W-30S E4
Timber Ln
10 ANTH 60002 2358 23W-43N A4
10 LNHT 60046 2476 19W-37N C1
10 NHBK 60062 2757 9W-17N C5
10 SlmT 53104 2358 23W-43N A4
10 SlmT 60002 2358 23W-43N A4
10 VNHL 60061 2647 17W-26N C3
10 WynT 60185 2967 28W-3N B7
100 GLNC 60022 2758 6W-18N D3
100 ISLK 60042 2586 28W-27N D7
100 LGPK 60525 3087 12W-2S B3
100 NndT 60042 2586 28W-27N D7
200 BtnT 60081 2414 29W-38N D6
200 CLSM 60188 2967 28W-3N B7
200 WynT 60188 2967 28W-3N B6
400 CLSM 60185 2967 28W-3N B6
500 FKFT 60423 3592 10W-26S C2
500 LKFT 60045 2650 10W-24N A6
800 DRN 60561 3207 17W-8S B1
1000 WLMT 60091 2812 4W-14N B5

STREET Block	City	ZIP	Map#	CGS	Grid
Timber Ln					
1100	DGvT	60561	3207	17W-8S	B1
1100	HDPK	60035	2650	10W-24N	A7
1100	LKFT	60035	2650	10W-24N	A7
1300	SEGN	60177	2908	36W-8N	A3
1800	GLHT	60139	2969	23W-3N	A5
2000	WHTN	60187	3081	26W-1S	E2
11900	PSPK	60464	3274	10W-14S	C5
N Timber Ln					
18000	WrnT	60030	2534	18W-33N	A3
W Timber Ln					
100	HPSR	60140	2795	47W-15N	E3
12800	HMGN	60491	3422	16W-21S	A6
15400	LbvT	60048	2592	15W-29N	A3
25200	LkvT	60046	2474	25W-37N	B2
Timber Pl					
800	NLNX	60451	3589	18W-26S	A3
1200	NLNX	60451	3588	19W-26S	E3
Timber Rdg					
100	LKBN	60010	2643	26W-24N	D7
Timber Ter					
10	CRY	60013	2641	32W-24N	C6
Timber Tr					
10	SMWD	60107	2856	28W-10N	E5
10	SMWD	60107	2857	28W-10N	A5
100	CmpT	60175	2961	42W-5N	D1
100	ISLK	60042	2586	29W-27N	D7
100	ISLK	60051	2586	29W-27N	D7
100	NndT	60042	2586	29W-27N	D7
100	WcnT	60042	2586	29W-27N	D7
300	BTVA	60510	3020	35W-0S	B7
500	RVWD	60015	2702	13W-20N	E7
1500	WHTN	60187	3082	25W-1S	A1
2200	JLET	60586	3416	31W-21S	A6
2200	PnfT	60586	3416	31W-21S	A6
5900	JLET	60586	3415	31W-21S	E6
7100	MHRY	60050	2526	36W-32N	D4
13000	PSHT	60463	3347	7W-15S	B1
21200	SRWD	60404	3584	31W-25S	A1
Timbercreek Ct					
10	KdlT	60560	3332	44W-17S	E7
21300	SRWD	60404	3584	31W-25S	A2
Timber Creek Dr					
300	RLKP	60073	2532	23W-33N	A3
12700	HTLY	60142	2744	43W-19N	B3
Timbercreek Dr					
-	LNHT	60046	2476	19W-36N	C3
E Timbercreek Dr					
10	KdlT	60560	3332	44W-17S	E7
N Timber Creek Dr					
10	RLKP	60073	2532	23W-33N	A4
W Timbercreek Dr					
10	KdlT	60560	3332	44W-17S	E7
Timber Creek Ln					
3100	NPVL	60564	3203	27W-11S	B7
3100	NPVL	60565	3203	27W-11S	B7
3100	WldT	60565	3203	27W-11S	B7
3300	WldT	60565	3267	27W-11S	B1
Timbercreek Pl					
10	KdlT	60560	3332	44W-18S	E7
Timbercrest Ct					
300	SMBG	60193	2858	23W-10N	E6
Timbercrest Dr					
100	SMBG	60193	2858	23W-10N	E6
400	BbyT	60119	3017	43W-0S	A7
3600	JLET	60431	3497	28W-23S	A4
E Timberedge Ct					
3000	CteT	60417	3687	3E-29S	B1
Timber Edge Dr					
-	EMHT	60126	3028	15W-1S	A7
-	EMHT	60523	3028	16W-1S	A7
-	EMHT	60523	3086	15W-1S	A1
-	OKBK	60126	3028	16W-1S	A7
-	OKBK	60523	3027	16W-1S	E7
-	OKBK	60523	3028	16W-1S	A7
-	OKBK	60523	3086	15W-1S	A1
11900	ODPK	60467	3344	14W-18S	C7
Timber Edge Ln					
100	PlsT	60464	3273	12W-14S	C7
Timbergate Dr					
700	CmpT	60175	2962	40W-3N	B5
Timber Glen Dr					
-	GLBT	60124	2798	39W-14N	D5
-	GLBT	60136	2798	39W-14N	D5
-	RtdT	60124	2798	39W-14N	D5
Timber Hill Ct					
3000	AURA	60504	3201	31W-9S	D3
Timberhill Dr					
10	CLLK	60014	2639	37W-25N	B4
Timber Hill Ln N					
3000	AURA	60504	3201	31W-9S	D3
Timber Hill Rd					
10	BFGV	60089	2754	17W-18N	A3
600	DRFD	60015	2703	11W-20N	D7
600	DRFD	60015	2756	11W-20N	D1
700	HDPK	60035	2758	7W-20N	A2
Timber Lake Ct					
21400	LktT	60403	3417	26W-19S	E3
Timberlake Ct					
1000	AURA	60506	3137	37W-6S	C5
Timber Lake Dr					
800	ANTH	60002	2417	21W-40N	D2
2700	JLET	60435	3417	27W-19S	C3
2700	JLET	60441	3417	27W-19S	C3
Timberlake Dr					
100	DGvT	60527	3207	16W-10S	D5
1100	AURA	60506	3137	37W-6S	B4
Timberlake Pkwy					
10	CbaT	60010	2644	25W-25N	A6
Timber Lake Rd					
-	ElaT	60047	2644	24W-25N	C5
-	NBRN	60047	2644	24W-25N	C5
10	CbaT	60010	2644	25W-25N	B5
10	NBRN	60010	2644	25W-25N	B5
W Timber Lake Rd					
25500	CbaT	60010	2644	25W-25N	A5
25700	CbaT	60010	2643	26W-25N	E5
N Timberland Tr					
40700	WDWH	60083	2420	13W-40N	E3
40700	WDWH	60083	2421	13W-40N	A2
40700	ZION	60099	2421	13W-40N	A2
W Timberlane Ct					
13900	HMGN	60491	3343	17W-17S	C5
Timberlane Dr					
10	NpvT	60563	3140	30W-6S	A4
4000	NfdT	60062	2756	12W-16N	A7
N Timberlane Dr					
1100	PLTN	60067	2753	20W-17N	A5
S Timberlane Dr					
12500	PSPK	60464	3274	9W-14S	C7
Timberlane Rd					
10	MTSN	60443	3505	7W-24S	D5
4600	NndT	60014	2642	30W-27N	B1
Timberlea Ct					
3900	CCHL	60478	3426	4W-20S	D5
N Timberlea Dr					
900	PLTN	60067	2752	20W-17N	E5
W Timberlea Ln					
22300	KLDR	60047	2699	22W-21N	B6
Timber Leaf Ln					
10	RVWD	60015	2702	13W-21N	D7
Timber Lee Ct					
900	LslT	60540	3142	25W-7S	B7
900	NPVL	60540	3142	25W-7S	B7
Timberline Ct					
10	LMNT	60439	3270	20W-14S	C6
10400	ODPK	60462	3345	13W-17S	B6
E Timberline Ct					
2900	CteT	60417	3687	3E-29S	B1
Timberline Dr					
10	LmnT	60439	3270	20W-14S	C6
200	TroT	60431	3497	28W-23S	B4
600	BGBK	60490	3267	26W-13S	E5
700	GNVW	60025	2811	7W-13N	B6
1200	BRLT	60103	2910	30W-9N	B1
1200	JLET	60431	3497	28W-22S	B2
1300	PnfT	60431	3497	28W-22S	B2
Timberline Ln					
10	RVWD	60015	2702	14W-21N	C7
Timberline Pl					
10	LMNT	60439	3270	20W-14S	B6
Timberline Rd					
10	WCHI	60185	2966	29W-2N	D7
10	WynT	60185	2966	29W-3N	D6
Timberline Tr					
2100	GwdT	60098	2525	39W-34N	C1
S Timberline Tr					
24200	CteT	60417	3687	3E-29S	A1
Timber Ln Ct					
1100	LslT	60540	3142	25W-6S	A5
1100	NPVL	60540	3142	26W-6S	A5
Timber Ln Dr					
100	PLTN	60067	2752	20W-17N	E4
100	PLTN	60067	2753	20W-17N	A4
1600	MTGY	60538	3199	36W-10S	E5
Timbermill Ct					
10	BGBK	60490	3267	27W-12S	D3
Timber Mill Dr					
20500	FftT	60423	3504	10W-25S	C7
Timber Oaks Dr					
300	NARA	60542	3077	36W-3S	E7
3300	JLET	60431	3497	28W-23S	B4
3300	TroT	60431	3497	28W-23S	B4
Timber Pass					
1100	FmtT	60060	2590	19W-29N	B4
1100	MDLN	60060	2590	20W-29N	B4
Timber Ridge Ct					
-	TNLK	53181	2354		A1
500	SchT	60175	2963	36W-5N	E1
800	WTMT	60559	3145	17W-6S	C4
6100	IHPK	60525	3146	14W-6S	E5
6100	LynT	60525	3146	14W-6S	E5
15200	ODPK	60467	3344	14W-18S	D7
N Timber Ridge Ct					
21600	KLDR	60047	2699	22W-21N	C5
Timber Ridge Dr					
10	BtlT	60543	3262	40W-13S	B5
10	BtlT	60560	3262	40W-13S	B6
10	WNFD	60190	3023	27W-1N	D3
300	BRLT	60103	2910	29W-8N	D2
400	CLSM	60188	3024	23W-1N	E3
500	MltT	60187	3024	23W-1N	E3
500	MltT	60188	3024	23W-1N	E3
500	RtdT	60124	2798	39W-14N	E5
12300	PTPR	53158	2362		A4
25800	CNHN	60410	3672	32W-30S	D5
Timber Ridge Dr N					
-	DGvT	60527	3207	16W-9S	E4
-	DGvT	60527	3208	16W-9S	A4
Timber Ridge Dr S					
-	DGvT	60527	3207	16W-9S	E4
-	DGvT	60527	3208	16W-9S	A4
Timber Ridge Rd					
-	MTSN	60443	3593	8W-26S	C2
2000	HFET	60192	2804	23W-13N	D5
2000	HFET	60195	2804	23W-13N	D5
2000	PltT	60195	2804	23W-13N	D5
21700	RchT	60443	3593	8W-26S	B2
Timbers Ct					
600	SCRL	60174	2964	36W-3N	A6
Timbers Pl					
400	SCRL	60174	2964	36W-3N	A6
Timbers Tr					
100	SCRL	60174	2964	36W-3N	A6
800	SCRL	60174	2963	36W-3N	E6
Timbers Bluff Tr					
200	BCHR	60401	3774	0W-35S	D7
Timbers Edge Ln					
3700	GNVW	60025	2809	12W-14N	B4
3700	GNVW	60062	2809	12W-14N	B4
Timbers Pointe Dr E					
8600	TYPK	60487	3424	11W-22S	A7
Timber Springs Ct					
900	JLET	60432	3500	20W-22S	B2
Timber Springs Dr					
800	JLET	60432	3500	20W-22S	B2
Timber Trail Ct					
500	LslT	60565	3204	25W-9S	B3
500	NPVL	60565	3204	25W-9S	B3
Timber Trail Dr					
10	OKBK	60523	3085	16W-1S	E1
600	LslT	60565	3204	25W-9S	B3
600	NPVL	60565	3204	25W-9S	B3
2300	PRGV	60012	2585	31W-28N	D6
Timber Trails Blvd					
-	GLBT	60124	2799	38W-14N	B5
-	RtdT	60124	2799	38W-14N	B5
100	GLBT	60136	2799	38W-14N	B5
Timber Trails Ct					
100	GLBT	60136	2799	39W-15N	A4
Timber Trails Rd					
1100	DGvT	60516	3206	20W-10S	C5
1100	DGvT	60561	3206	20W-10S	C5
1100	DRN	60516	3206	20W-10S	C5
1100	DRN	60561	3206	20W-10S	C5
1100	WDRG	60517	3206	20W-10S	B5
9000	ODPK	60462	3345	11W-16S	E3
9000	ODPK	60462	3346	11W-16S	A3
Timbertrails Rd					
2100	LSLE	60532	3142	24W-7S	D6
Timberview					
10	LMNT	60439	3272	15W-13S	B4
Timber View Dr					
10	OKBK	60523	3027	16W-1S	E7
Timberview Dr					
6200	LSLE	60532	3142	24W-6S	D5
16400	PNFD	60586	3417	28W-19S	A4
16400	PnfT	60586	3417	28W-19S	A4
S Timberview Dr					
20000	FftT	60448	3503	13W-24S	B5
20000	MKNA	60448	3503	13W-24S	B5
Timberview Ln					
10	BtlT	60560	3262	41W-13S	B6
11200	LynT	60525	3146	14W-6S	E4
11200	LynT	60558	3146	14W-6S	D4
Timber Wood Cir					
-	PNFD	60585	3337	33W-15S	A1
Timber Wood Ct					
2400	JLET	60432	3500	20W-22S	B2
Timberwood Ct					
25700	CnhT	60447	3672	32W-29S	D1
Timberwood Dr					
500	LKZH	60047	2699	22W-22N	B4
23900	CnhT	60447	3672	32W-29S	D1
25700	CNHN	60410	3672	32W-29S	D2
Timberwood Ln					
10	RVWD	60015	2702	14W-21N	D7
600	ALGN	60102	2695	32W-20N	A7
8900	TYPK	60487	3424	11W-22S	A7
Timber Wood Wy					
-	OswT	60543	3337	33W-15S	A1
-	OswT	60585	3337	33W-15S	A2
-	PNFD	60543	3337	33W-15S	A2
-	PNFD	60585	3337	33W-15S	A2
Timber Woods Ln					
1600	WKGN	60048	2535	15W-32N	A5
Timer Dr					
11200	HTLY	60142	2692	40W-21N	A6
Timer Dr E					
10700	HTLY	60142	2692	40W-21N	B6
Timer Dr W					
10700	HTLY	60142	2692	40W-21N	A6
Times Dr					
1500	DSPN	60018	2862	13W-10N	E6
Times Square Rd					
10	ELGN	60120	2855	33W-10N	A5
Timke Rd					
6200	LslT	60517	3143	22W-6S	D5
6200	WDRG	60517	3143	22W-6S	D6
Timothy Ct					
400	SMBG	60193	2859	22W-9N	B6
700	EDND	60118	2801	33W-15N	B3
8900	ODPK	60462	3346	11W-16S	A3
Timothy Dr					
200	WldT	60565	3203	27W-11S	C7
2200	GNVW	60025	2810	9W-14N	C5
14000	ODPK	60462	3346	11W-16S	A4
Timothy Ln					
10	CTCY	60409	3351	2E-16S	C4
10	MltT	60188	3024	26W-1N	A3
10	NlxT	60448	3501	16W-22S	E2
700	DSPN	60016	2808	13W-13N	D7
1000	WDSK	60098	2524	40W-31N	E6
1000	WDSK	60098	2525	40W-31N	A7
N Timothy Ln					
200	MHRY	60050	2528	32W-32N	B5
W Timothy Ln					
3700	MHRY	60050	2528	32W-32N	B5
Timothy St					
4100	ZION	60099	2362	12W-42N	C6
Timothy Ter					
25300	WcnT	60084	2588	25W-29N	A4
Timrick Dr					
10	MNSR	46321	3430		C7
10	MNSR	46321	3510		D1
Timsbury Ct					
7400	GRNE	60031	2477	18W-35N	A5
Tim Tam Cir					
900	NPVL	60540	3142	26W-7S	A7
W Tim Tam Ct					
12300	HMGN	60491	3344	15W-16S	B3
Tina Ln					
1500	FSMR	60422	3507	2W-23S	E4
Tina Ter					
200	ElgT	60124	2853	37W-12N	D2
300	ELGN	60124	2853	37W-12N	D2
Tinbury Pl					
200	CRTE	60417	3596	0W-28S	C6
Tinder					
5500	RGMW	60008	2860	19W-12N	D2
Tinker Av					
-	ELGN	60123	2854	34W-12N	D1
500	WNVL	60555	3081	27W-3S	B6
Tinker Wy					
1200	GNVW	60025	2810	8W-13N	D5
Tinley Dr					
600	AURA	60506	3137	36W-5S	E3
Tinley Park Dr					
6700	TYPK	60477	3425	8W-20S	A3
N Tinman St					
10	DMND	60416	3941	33W-39S	B2
Tinnerella Av					
1300	SMWD	60107	2911	27W-9N	C1
Tioga Av					
200	BNVL	60106	2915	16W-5N	D7
Tioga Ct					
900	CLSM	60188	2967	26W-3N	E5
Tioga St					
300	PKFT	60466	3594	4W-28S	E6
Tioga Tr					
10	LKBN	60010	2643	26W-24N	D6
10	TRLK	60010	2643	26W-24N	D6
300	AddT	60191	2971	17W-5N	B1
300	WDDL	60191	2971	17W-5N	B1
Tipi Ln					
10	ElgT	60124	2907	38W-9N	B1
600	ElgT	60124	2853	38W-9N	B7
Tipperary Ct					
10	DrrT	60098	2526	37W-31N	C6
10	NndT	60098	2526	37W-31N	C6
700	SMBG	60193	2859	23W-9N	A7
13000	PNFD	60585	3338	31W-15S	A2
Tipperary Ln					
12700	PNFD	60585	3338	31W-15S	A1
Tipperary St					
600	GLBT	60136	2799	38W-15N	C4
Tipton Av					
17800	HMWD	60430	3427	2W-21S	C6
Tiree Ct					
1500	FSMR	60422	3506	4W-23S	D3
Tisbury Ln					
100	LKFT	60045	2649	12W-26N	C4
1000	SMBG	60193	2912	24W-9N	D1
Titonka St					
400	PKFT	60466	3594	4W-28S	E6
Titsworth Ct					
300	AURA	60505	3200	35W-8S	A1
Titus Pl					
600	BbyT	60134	3018	39W-0N	D5
Tiverton Ct					
10	ALGN	60102	2693	37W-21N	A6
900	SMBG	60193	2912	24W-9N	C1
Tiverton Ln					
200	CRTE	60417	3596	0W-28S	C6
Tiverton Rd					
600	LKFT	60045	2649	12W-26N	C3
Tivoli Pl					
10	ELGN	60123	2854	35W-12N	C2
Tivoli Ter					
2600	JNBG	60050	2471	31W-35N	D6
Toastmaster Dr					
1400	ELGN	60120	2801	32W-12N	D7
1400	ELGN	60120	2855	32W-12N	D1
Tobey Ct					
1000	SMBG	60194	2858	24W-10N	C5
Tobin Ct					
1100	WKGN	60085	2536	11W-32N	D5
S Tod Dr					
10400	PSHL	60465	3274	9W-12S	C2
E Todd Av					
100	WDSK	60098	2524	41W-31N	D6
W Todd Av					
10	WDSK	60098	2524	41W-31N	C6
Todd Ct					
10	CRTE	60417	3685	1W-30S	A2
800	DRFD	60015	2703	10W-21N	E7
Todd St					
200	PKFT	60466	3595	3W-25S	C1
400	OMFD	60461	3595	3W-25S	C1
400	OMFD	60466	3595	3W-25S	C1
W Todd St					
26500	AntT	60002	2356	26W-43N	D4
Todd Ter					
200	LYWD	60411	3598	4E-25S	C1
Todd Farm Ct					
1300	ELGN	60123	2800	35W-13N	B7
Todd Farm Dr					
1000	ELGN	60123	2854	35W-13N	B1
1300	ELGN	60123	2800	35W-13N	A7
Todor Ct					
10	BRRG	60527	3208	15W-10S	B4
Tod William Dr					
8700	ODPK	60462	3346	11W-16S	A3
Toft Av					
800	ANTH	60002	2357	23W-42N	E6
Toftrees Tr					
2200	ELGN	60123	2853	36W-12N	E1
Tollgate Rd					
-	WDND	60123	2800	34W-14N	E6
500	DndT	60123	2800	34W-14N	E6
500	ELGN	60123	2800	34W-14N	E6
Tollview Av					
900	AURA	60505	3138	33W-6S	E4
5100	AraT	60505	3138	33W-6S	E4
Toll View Ct					
200	GLBT	60136	2798	39W-16N	E2
Tollview Dr					
600	EHZC	60429	3428	0W-20S	B4
600	EHZC	60473	3428	0W-20S	B4
600	SHLD	60429	3428	0W-20S	B4
600	SHLD	60473	3428	0W-20S	B4
3000	RGMW	60008	2860	20W-12N	B1
Tollview Rd					
10	ELGN	60123	2801	33W-13N	A7
100	ELGN	60123	2800	35W-14N	B6
Toll View Ter					
100	GLBT	60136	2798	39W-16N	E2
S Tom Pkwy					
1800	CHCG	60616	3092	0W-1S	B1
Tomah Av					
400	PTHT	60070	2807	16W-15N	D2
Tomahawk Ct					
100	BGBK	60440	3268	24W-11S	D1
200	CLSM	60188	2968	25W-2N	A7
2400	CPVL	60110	2748	32W-18N	C4
33000	WrnT	60030	2534	18W-33N	A4
Tomahawk Dr					
10	MltT	60187	3081	26W-2S	E3
10	MltT	60187	3082	26W-2S	A3
10	WHTN	60187	3081	26W-2S	E3
Tomahawk Ln					
100	TRLK	60010	2643	26W-25N	D4
200	LKBN	60084	2643	26W-25N	D4
500	CLLK	60012	2640	34W-27N	B1
Tomahawk Rd					
900	DYR	46311	3598		E3
Tomahawk Rdg					
1600	NlxT	60451	3590	16W-27S	A4
Tomahawk St					
400	PKFT	60466	3594	4W-28S	E6
Tomahawk Tr					
-	RLKB	60073	2474	23W-35N	D6
700	RLKH	60073	2474	24W-35N	D5
Tomahawk Lake Ct					
16200	LktT	60403	3417	26W-19S	D4
Tomaszewski St					
600	LMNT	60439	3270	18W-14S	E6
Tomawadee Dr					
800	PKRG	60068	2863	11W-9N	E6
Tomcat Ln					
500	AURA	60505	3200	34W-8S	C2
Tomcin Tr					
5100	OKLN	60453	3275	6W-12S	E2
Tomich Ct					
1700	CTHL	60403	3418	26W-21S	A7
Tom Lambrecht Dr					
-	RMVL	60441	3418	24W-18S	E1
Tomlin Cir					
10	BRRG	60527	3146	14W-6S	C5
Tomlin Dr					
700	BRRG	60521	3146	14W-6S	C4
700	BRRG	60527	3146	14W-6S	C4
Tomlinson Ct					
5600	MHRY	60050	2527	34W-34N	C1
Tomlinson Dr					
5700	MHRY	60050	2527	34W-34N	B1
5900	MHRY	60050	2470	35W-34N	B7
Tommy Tr					
-	BCVL	60407	4030	33W-43S	B3
Toms Trail Dr					
100	SchT	60175	2963	38W-3N	A6
Ton Av					
17400	LNSG	60438	3430	3E-20S	A4
Tonell Av					
100	NLNX	60451	3501	17W-25S	D7
100	NlxT	60451	3501	17W-25S	D7
Tonelli Tr					
400	LKPT	60441	3420	21W-19S	A2
Toni St					
10	SchT	60174	3021	33W-2N	B1
10	WynT	60185	3021	33W-2N	B1
Toni Marie Ln					
6900	MONE	60449	3682	8W-32S	B7
S Tonne Dr					
-	ANHT	60005	2861	18W-12N	A2
Tonne Rd					
300	EGVV	60007	2861	18W-9N	A7
600	EGVV	60007	2915	18W-8N	A2
2000	EGvT	60007	2915	17W-8N	A3
2100	WDDL	60007	2915	18W-8N	A3
2100	WDDL	60191	2915	18W-8N	A3
Tonset Ct					
100	SMBG	60193	2858	25W-10N	B6
Tonset Ln					
1400	SMBG	60193	2858	25W-10N	B6
Tonti Dr					
3100	JLET	60431	3417	28W-20S	B4
3100	JLET	60435	3417	28W-20S	B4
Tonto Ct					
700	CLSM	60188	2967	26W-3N	E6
N Tonty Av					
6800	CHCG	60646	2919	7W-8N	B1
W Tooker Pl					
10	CHCG	60610	3034	0W-1N	B2
N Topanga Dr					
900	PLTN	60074	2753	20W-17N	A6
Topanga Tr					
26500	FmtT	60060	2644	23W-26N	E3
26500	FmtT	60084	2644	23W-26N	E3
Topanga Canyon					
11800	FKFT	60423	3590	14W-27S	D5
Topaz Dr					
4500	HFET	60192	2804	24W-15N	C1
Topaz Ln					
400	BRLT	60103	2910	31W-9N	A1
Topeka Ct					
500	CLSM	60188	2967	27W-3N	D6
Topeka Dr					
-	GYLK	60030	2532	21W-32N	E5
600	CPVL	60110	2748	33W-17N	B6
Topeka St					
400	PKFT	60466	3594	4W-28S	E6
Topp Ln					
1500	GNVW	60025	2810	8W-14N	E5
Topsoil Dr					
-	WCHI	60185	3022	30W-0S	B6
Torch Pkwy					
28100	WNVL	60555	3081	28W-3S	B7
Tordi Ln					
-	CnhT	60421	3674	27W-29S	E3
-	JknT	60421	3674	27W-29S	E3
Tori Ct					
10	BRRG	60527	3208	15W-10S	B5
Torino Dr					
200	CRY	60013	2695	32W-23N	B2
Toro Cir					
100	CPVL	60110	2748	33W-18N	B4
Toronto Ct					
4000	HRPK	60133	2967	27W-4N	D3
Toronto St					
700	BRkT	60511	3196	45W-8S	C3
Torphin Hill Ct					
4700	WldT	60564	3266	30W-12S	A4
Torrence Av					
200	BNHM	60409	3351	3E-17S	E4
200	BNHM	60633	3351	3E-17S	E4
200	CTCY	60409	3351	2E-18S	E7
900	CTCY	60409	3429	2E-19S	E3
1400	CTCY	60438	3429	3E-19S	E3
1400	LNSG	60409	3429	3E-19S	E2
1400	LNSG	60438	3429	3E-19S	E3
18500	BlmT	60411	3429	3E-21S	E7
18500	LNSG	60411	3429	3E-21S	E7
19000	BlmT	60411	3509	2E-22S	E2
19000	LNSG	60411	3509	3E-22S	E1
19000	LNSG	60438	3509	3E-22S	E1
19300	LYWD	60411	3509	3E-24S	E6
20900	FDHT	60411	3509	2E-24S	E6
21100	SLVL	60411	3509	3E-25S	E7
21300	BlmT	60411	3597	2E-25S	E1
21300	SLVL	60411	3597	2E-26S	E2
22900	CteT	60417	3597	2E-27S	E5
Torrence Av SR-83					
400	CTCY	60409	3351	2E-18S	E7
900	CTCY	60409	3429	2E-19S	E3
1400	CTCY	60438	3429	3E-19S	E3
1400	LNSG	60409	3429	3E-19S	E2
1400	LNSG	60438	3429	3E-19S	E3
18500	BlmT	60411	3429	3E-21S	E7
18500	LNSG	60411	3429	3E-21S	E7
19000	BlmT	60411	3509	2E-22S	E2
19000	LNSG	60411	3509	3E-22S	E1
19000	LNSG	60438	3509	3E-22S	E1
19300	LYWD	60411	3509	2E-23S	E3
Torrence Av US-6					
1100	CTCY	60409	3429	2E-19S	E3
1400	CTCY	60438	3429	3E-19S	E3
1400	LNSG	60409	3429	3E-19S	E2
1400	LNSG	60438	3429	3E-19S	E3
S Torrence Av					
3700	HMND	46327	3352		E3
9500	CHCG	60617	3215	3E-11S	E7
10300	CHCG	60617	3279	2E-12S	E3
11700	CHCG	60633	3279	3E-14S	E7
13000	CHCG	60633	3351	3E-15S	E1
13800	BNHM	60633	3351	2E-17S	E5
14500	BNHM	60409	3351	3E-16S	E4
14500	CTCY	60409	3351	3E-16S	E4
23100	BlmT	60411	3597	2E-28S	E6
23100	CteT	60417	3597	2E-28S	E6
Torrence Pl					
9400	SjnT	46311	3687		E1
Torrence St					
8400	SjnT	46311	3598		E6
Torrey Cir					
7300	JLET	60586	3415	33W-21S	B7
Torrey Ct					
20500	FKFT	60423	3504	10W-24S	B6
Torrey Dr					
-	CmpT	60175	2962	39W-3N	D6
Torrey Tr					
1400	JNBG	60050	2472	30W-36N	A3
1400	MchT	60050	2472	30W-36N	A3
Torrey Pine Cir					
5200	LGGV	60047	2701	17W-22N	A4
Torrey Pine Ln					
2800	LSLE	60532	3142	24W-6S	C5
Torrey Pines Ct					
-	LslT	60540	3204	26W-8S	A1
1000	DRN	60561	3145	18W-7S	A7
21000	LktT	60544	3340	26W-16S	A3
Torrey Pines Dr					
-	ELGN	60123	2854	35W-9N	B7
15600	ODPK	60462	3346	11W-18S	A7
15600	ODPK	60462	3424	11W-18S	A1
20700	LktT	60544	3340	26W-16S	A3
20800	RMVL	60544	3340	26W-16S	A3
Torrey Pines Pkwy					
3600	NHBK	60062	2756	12W-17N	B4
W Torrey Pines Wy					
300	VNHL	60061	2647	17W-26N	B2
Torri Ln					
800	ELGN	60120	2855	32W-10N	C5
Torrington Ct					
-	OSWG	60543	3263	36W-12S	E3
Torrington Dr					
300	BMDL	60108	2968	24W-5N	C2

Block	City	ZIP	Map#	CGS	Grid
Torrington Dr					
700	NPVL	60565	3203	27W-8S	C3
Torrin Rocks Cove					
10	IVNS	60010	2750	26W-16N	D7
Torry Pkwy					
1800	LbvT	60048	2591	17W-30N	B2
1800	LYVL	60048	2591	17W-30N	B2
Torry Pines Ct					
10	LIHL	60156	2693	36W-21N	D5
300	MltT	60188	3023	26W-1N	E3
300	WNFD	60190	3023	26W-1N	E3
Torwood Cir					
2000	JLET	60586	3416	30W-21S	B7
Tory Ct					
800	SMBG	60173	2859	22W-10N	C5
2800	LSLE	60532	3142	24W-6S	C5
Tory Ln					
10	RGMW	60008	2805	20W-14N	E4
10	RGMW	60008	2806	20W-14N	A4
Tosca Dr					
200	WDDL	60191	2915	17W-5N	B7
Toscana Dr					
22900	FftT	60423	3591	13W-27S	A5
22900	FKFT	60423	3591	13W-27S	A5
Tosoana					
-	BMDL	60172	2912	24W-6N	C7
-	BmdT	60172	2912	24W-6N	C7
Totem Tr					
900	NndT	60051	2528	31W-31N	D7
1000	NndT	60051	2585	31W-31N	D1
Tottenham					
-	JLET	60431	3495	33W-22S	B2
Tottenham Ln					
100	EGVV	60007	2914	19W-8N	C3
Touhy Av					
-	LNWD	60712	2919	6W-9N	E1
600	EGVV	60007	2915	17W-8N	B1
2500	EGvT	60007	2915	16W-9N	E1
2500	EGvT	60018	2915	16W-9N	E1
5000	SKOK	60077	2919	6W-8N	D1
5300	SKOK	60077	2865	6W-9N	C7
5400	NLES	60077	2865	6W-9N	C7
5400	NLES	60714	2865	6W-9N	C7
Touhy Av SR-72					
2500	EGvT	60007	2915	16W-9N	E1
2500	EGvT	60018	2915	16W-9N	E1
2500	EGVV	60007	2915	16W-9N	E1
E Touhy Av					
200	CHCG	60018	2916	14W-9N	C1
200	DSPN	60018	2916	14W-9N	C1
200	MaiT	60018	2916	14W-8N	C1
1200	RSMT	60018	2916	13W-9N	E1
1300	DSPN	60018	2917	13W-9N	A1
1300	RSMT	60018	2917	13W-9N	A1
2100	CHCG	60018	2917	12W-8N	B1
E Touhy Av SR-72					
200	CHCG	60018	2916	14W-9N	C1
200	DSPN	60018	2916	14W-9N	C1
200	MaiT	60018	2916	14W-8N	C1
W Touhy Av					
-	CHCG	60018	2917	11W-9N	D1
-	SKOK	60077	2919	5W-8N	E1
10	CHCG	60068	2918	9W-9N	C1
10	CHCG	60631	2918	8W-8N	D1
10	DSPN	60018	2916	15W-8N	A1
10	EGvT	60018	2916	15W-8N	A1
10	MaiT	60018	2916	15W-8N	A1
10	PKRG	60068	2918	10W-8N	A1
10	PKRG	60631	2918	9W-9N	C1
300	CHCG	60007	2916	15W-8N	A1
300	CHCG	60018	2916	15W-8N	A1
1200	CHCG	60626	2867	1W-9N	D7
1300	PKRG	60068	2917	11W-8N	D1
1900	CHCG	60645	2867	3W-9N	A7
2700	CHCG	60645	2866	3W-9N	E7
2800	EGvT	60007	2915	15W-8N	E1
2800	EGvT	60018	2915	15W-8N	E1
2800	EGVV	60007	2915	15W-8N	E1
2800	EGVV	60007	2916	15W-8N	A1
2800	EGVV	60018	2915	15W-8N	E1
2800	EGVV	60018	2916	15W-8N	A1
3000	CHCG	60645	2920	4W-8N	D1
3100	LNWD	60076	2920	3W-9N	D1
3100	LNWD	60645	2920	3W-9N	D1
3100	LNWD	60712	2920	3W-9N	D1
3100	SKOK	60076	2920	3W-9N	D1
3100	SKOK	60645	2920	3W-9N	D1
3300	SKOK	60712	2920	4W-9N	D1
4700	LNWD	60712	2919	5W-8N	E1
5600	NLES	60077	2865	7W-9N	C7
5600	NLES	60714	2865	8W-9N	A7
5600	SKOK	60077	2865	7W-9N	C7
5700	CHCG	60646	2865	8W-9N	A7
5700	CHCG	60714	2865	8W-9N	A7
5700	NLES	60646	2865	8W-9N	A7
6600	NLES	60714	2864	8W-9N	E7
7100	CHCG	60714	2918	8W-8N	D1
7100	NLES	60714	2918	8W-8N	D1
W Touhy Av SR-72					
10	DSPN	60018	2916	15W-8N	A1
10	EGvT	60018	2916	15W-8N	A1
10	MaiT	60018	2916	15W-8N	A1
300	CHCG	60007	2916	15W-8N	A1
300	CHCG	60018	2916	15W-8N	A1
2800	EGvT	60007	2915	15W-8N	E1
2800	EGvT	60018	2915	15W-8N	E1
2800	EGVV	60007	2915	15W-8N	E1
2800	EGVV	60007	2916	15W-8N	A1
2800	EGVV	60018	2915	15W-8N	E1
2800	EGVV	60018	2916	15W-8N	A1
Touhy Ct					
100	EGvT	60018	2916	14W-9N	C1
100	MaiT	60018	2916	14W-9N	C1
Toulon Ct					
1400	HDPK	60035	2704	8W-21N	D7
1400	HDPK	60035	2757	8W-20N	D1
Toulon Dr					
100	BFGV	60089	2754	16W-20N	C1
3100	NHBK	60062	2756	11W-17N	D6
Tour Ct					
700	RVWD	60015	2703	13W-20N	A7
Touraine Ter					
600	NHBK	60062	2756	12W-18N	B4
E Tournament Dr					
100	ElaT	60047	2645	22W-25N	B5
100	HNWD	60047	2645	22W-25N	B5
100	HNWD	60060	2645	22W-25N	B5
Tournament Dr E					
-	HNWD	60047	2645	22W-25N	B5
Tournament Dr N					
10	HNWD	60047	2645	22W-26N	B2
10	HNWD	60060	2645	22W-26N	B3
Tournament Dr S					
10	ElaT	60047	2645	22W-25N	B4
10	FmtT	60060	2645	22W-26N	B3
10	HNWD	60047	2645	22W-26N	B3
Tournament Dr S					
10	HNWD	60060	2645	22W-26N	B3
Towanda Ct					
10	PKFT	60466	3595	4W-28S	A6
Towanda St					
200	PKFT	60466	3594	4W-28S	E6
200	PKFT	60466	3595	4W-28S	A6
Tower					
-	NLNX	60451	3590	15W-26S	B3
Tower E					
-	HDPK	60035	2650	9W-24N	D7
Tower W					
-	HDPK	60035	2650	9W-24N	D7
-	HDPK	60040	2650	9W-24N	C7
Tower Av					
21100	MTSN	60443	3594	4W-25S	D1
Tower Blvd					
400	CLSM	60188	2968	24W-3N	C6
400	GLHT	60139	2968	24W-3N	C6
400	GLHT	60188	2968	24W-3N	C6
Tower Cir					
-	BmnT	60426	3426	5W-19S	B1
4000	SKOK	60076	2866	5W-11N	B2
20800	OMFD	60461	3507	4W-25S	A7
Tower Ct					
10	DGvT	60516	3206	19W-8S	D1
10	GRNE	60031	2535	13W-34N	E2
100	FRGV	60021	2696	30W-22N	B4
16600	TYPK	60477	3424	10W-19S	C3
E Tower Ct					
900	PLTN	60074	2753	19W-18N	B2
N Tower Ct					
6400	LNWD	60712	2919	6W-8N	E2
Tower Dr					
-	OKBK	60181	3085	18W-2S	A2
-	OKBK	60523	3085	18W-2S	A2
-	OKTR	60181	3085	18W-2S	A2
100	BRRG	60527	3146	14W-7S	C7
1800	AlqT	60021	2695	30W-22N	E4
1800	GNVW	60025	2810	9W-14N	B4
2600	HHLL	60051	2586	30W-29N	A4
3900	RNPK	60471	3594	4W-26S	D3
10600	ODPK	60467	3423	13W-20S	A3
E Tower Dr					
100	TRLK	60010	2643	26W-25N	D5
N Tower Dr					
300	HNVL	60030	2532	22W-33N	C3
S Tower Dr					
900	MPPT	60056	2862	15W-11N	A2
W Tower Dr					
200	TRLK	60010	2643	27W-25N	C5
Tower Ln					
10	OKTR	60181	3085	16W-1S	D1
10	WTMT	60559	3145	17W-5S	B3
100	EGVV	60007	2860	18W-9N	E7
200	EGvT	60007	2860	18W-9N	E7
600	YKVL	60560	3333	42W-14S	C1
1000	BNVL	60007	2915	17W-7N	C4
1000	BNVL	60106	2915	17W-7N	C4
1000	EGVV	60007	2915	17W-7N	C4
1200	AlqT	60013	2696	30W-23N	A2
1200	CRY	60013	2696	30W-23N	A2
S Tower Ln					
900	MPPT	60056	2862	15W-11N	A2
Tower Pkwy					
300	LNSH	60069	2702	15W-22N	A4
Tower Pl					
-	OKTR	60181	3085	18W-1S	A2
500	FRGV	60021	2696	30W-22N	B3
W Tower Pl					
100	PLTN	60067	2752	21W-16N	D7
Tower Rd					
-	GLNC	60062	2758	7W-16N	B7
-	GLNC	60093	2758	7W-16N	B7
-	NfdT	60093	2758	6W-16N	C7
-	NHFD	60093	2758	7W-16N	B7
-	SCRL	60174	2965	32W-3N	C6
-	WynT	60174	2965	32W-3N	C6
10	DRGV	60515	3084	18W-4S	E6
10	DRGV	60515	3085	18W-4S	A6
10	SCRL	60185	2965	32W-3N	D7
10	WCHI	60185	2965	32W-3N	C7
100	DGvT	60515	3084	18W-4S	E6
100	WynT	60185	2965	32W-3N	C6
600	MDLN	60060	2646	18W-26N	E2
700	WNKA	60093	2759	5W-16N	A7
900	MDLN	60060	2647	18W-26N	A2
1000	WNKA	60093	2758	6W-16N	C7
1100	SMBG	60173	2859	22W-12N	D1
1700	HRPK	60133	2911	27W-9N	D1
8300	WLSP	60480	3208	13W-9S	E3
N Tower Rd					
10	OKBK	60523	3084	18W-2S	E2
10	YkTp	60148	3084	18W-2S	E2
10	YkTp	60181	3084	18W-2S	E2
10	YkTp	60523	3084	18W-2S	E2
W Tower Rd					
300	BRTN	60010	2750	26W-18N	E3
Tower St					
400	GNCY	53128	2353		A3
Tower Bridge Dr					
-	FftT	60423	3590	14W-26S	D2
Tower Bridge Rd					
2000	NLNX	60451	3502	15W-25S	B7
Tower Cir Dr					
-	SMBG	60173	2805	22W-12N	D7
Tower Hill Dr					
200	SCRL	60175	2963	37W-2N	C7
1200	WDRG	60517	3206	20W-11S	B7
Tower Hill Rd					
100	GLBT	60136	2798	39W-16N	E1
100	GLBT	60136	2799	39W-16N	A1
100	RtdT	60136	2798	39W-16N	E1
Towering Oaks Ct					
1100	BRLT	60103	2910	30W-6N	C7
Tower Manor Dr					
900	WNKA	60093	2759	5W-16N	A7
N Towers Cir Dr					
6500	LNWD	60712	2919	6W-8N	E2
Towers Keep					
100	HDPK	60035	2650	9W-24N	D7
Towhee Ct					
1800	JLET	60435	3498	26W-22S	A2
Towhee Ln					
1500	NPVL	60565	3204	26W-8S	A3
S Towle Av					
3700	HMND	46327	3352		D3
Towle St					
8500	SjnT	46311	3598		D6
Town Ctr					
-	ELWD	60421	3675	25W-32S	C7
Town Dr					
1900	NPVL	60565	3203	26W-9S	E4
1900	NPVL	60565	3204	26W-9S	A4
Town Pl					
700	HNDL	60521	3145	16W-5S	E2
Town Rd					
-	WnfT	60510	3080	30W-0S	B1
200	WCHI	60185	3022	30W-0N	B5
200	WCHI	60510	3022	30W-0S	B7
200	WnfT	60185	3022	30W-0S	B7
200	WnfT	60510	3022	30W-0S	B7
Town Sq					
10	WHTN	60187	3082	24W-2S	D4
Town St					
400	WLNG	60090	2755	15W-17N	B4
Town Acres Ln					
100	ROSL	60172	2913	23W-7N	A4
Town Center Blvd					
-	DndT	60118	2799	37W-16N	C1
-	RtdT	60118	2746	38W-17N	A7
-	RtdT	60118	2799	38W-16N	C1
-	RtdT	60136	2746	38W-17N	A7
-	RtdT	60136	2799	38W-16N	A1
100	GLBT	60136	2799	38W-16N	A1
Town Center Dr					
-	AvnT	60073	2531	24W-34N	C1
-	RDLK	60073	2531	24W-34N	C1
Towncenter Dr					
10	MonT	60466	3684	3W-29S	A1
10	UYPK	60466	3684	3W-29S	A1
Town Center Ln					
200	GLHT	60139	2969	23W-4N	A4
Town Center Rd					
100	MTSN	60443	3594	6W-25S	A1
200	MTSN	60443	3506	6W-25S	B7
14300	HMGN	60491	3343	16W-17S	E4
Town Crest Dr					
100	NLNX	60451	3501	17W-23S	C4
100	NlxT	60451	3501	17W-23S	C4
Towne Av					
900	BTVA	60510	3078	36W-2S	A3
1000	BTVA	60510	3077	36W-2S	E3
E Towne Blvd					
2400	ANHT	60004	2754	16W-16N	D7
2400	ANHT	60004	2807	16W-16N	E1
2400	PTHT	60004	2807	16W-16N	E1
2400	PTHT	60070	2807	16W-16N	E1
Towne Ct					
500	GLBT	60136	2799	37W-15N	C4
Towne St					
300	GLBT	60136	2799	37W-15N	C3
Towne Center Blvd					
-	SRWD	60404	3495	31W-23S	E4
Towner Ct					
300	GLHT	60139	2969	23W-3N	A5
1000	BGBK	60440	3268	25W-11S	B2
Towner Dr					
1000	BGBK	60440	3268	25W-11S	B2
Towner Ln					
1900	GLHT	60139	2969	23W-3N	A5
Townes Cir					
1200	AURA	60502	3139	31W-5S	D4
Towne Trail Dr					
14300	GNOK	60048	2535	14W-31N	C7
Town Hall Dr					
600	RMVL	60446	3340	23W-15S	E1
Town Hall Rd					
10	CmpT	60119	2961	42W-3N	D7
10	CmpT	60175	2961	41W-3N	E6
Townline Coms					
-	VNHL	60061	2647	16W-25N	D4
Townline Rd					
-	LbvT	60045	2648	13W-26N	E4
-	LKFT	60045	2648	13W-26N	E4
-	MTWA	60045	2648	14W-26N	D4
-	MTWA	60048	2648	14W-26N	B4
-	VNHL	60061	2648	14W-26N	B4
-	VrnT	60045	2648	13W-26N	D4
-	VrnT	60048	2648	14W-26N	B4
200	MDLN	60060	2646	18W-25N	E4
300	NPVL	60555	3080	29W-3S	D7
300	NPVL	60563	3080	29W-3S	D7
300	WNVL	60555	3081	28W-3S	A7
600	WNVL	60555	3080	28W-4S	E7
800	MDLN	60060	2647	18W-25N	A4
1300	VNHL	60060	2647	17W-26N	B4
1500	VNHL	60061	2647	17W-26N	B4
18700	FftT	60448	3502	14W-23S	D3
18700	NlxT	60448	3502	15W-24S	B6
18900	MKNA	60448	3502	15W-24S	B5
19900	NlxT	60451	3502	15W-24S	B6
Townline Rd SR-60					
-	LbvT	60045	2648	13W-26N	E4
-	LKFT	60045	2648	13W-26N	E4
-	MTWA	60045	2648	14W-26N	D4
-	MTWA	60048	2648	14W-26N	B4
-	VNHL	60061	2648	14W-26N	B4
-	VrnT	60045	2648	13W-26N	D4
-	VrnT	60048	2648	14W-26N	B4
200	MDLN	60060	2646	18W-25N	E4
800	MDLN	60060	2647	18W-25N	A4
1300	VNHL	60060	2647	17W-26N	B4
1500	VNHL	60061	2647	17W-26N	B4
E Townline Rd					
-	VNHL	60061	2648	15W-26N	A4
-	VrnT	60048	2648	15W-26N	A4
10	VNHL	60061	2647	16W-25N	D4
700	VrnT	60048	2647	16W-25N	D4
E Townline Rd SR-60					
-	VNHL	60061	2648	15W-26N	A4
-	VrnT	60048	2648	15W-26N	A4
10	VNHL	60061	2647	16W-25N	D4
700	VrnT	60048	2647	16W-25N	D4
W Town Line Rd					
23400	AntT	60002	2416	24W-40N	D4
23400	AntT	60046	2416	24W-40N	D4
23400	LKVL	60002	2416	24W-40N	D4
23400	LKVL	60046	2416	24W-40N	D4
23400	LkvT	60002	2416	24W-40N	D4
23400	LkvT	60046	2416	24W-40N	D4
W Townline Rd					
-	HNVL	60030	2532	22W-32N	B6
10	VNHL	60061	2647	17W-25N	B4
400	MDLN	60060	2647	17W-26N	B4
400	VNHL	60060	2647	17W-26N	B4
700	AvnT	60030	2531	24W-32N	C6
700	FmtT	60030	2531	24W-32N	C6
700	RDLK	60073	2531	24W-32N	C6
12700	BHPK	60087	2479	12W-38N	B1
12700	WKGN	60087	2479	13W-38N	A1
12800	NptT	60087	2479	13W-38N	A1
12800	WrnT	60087	2479	13W-38N	A1
13400	WKGN	60087	2478	13W-37N	E1
22700	FmtT	60030	2532	22W-31N	A6
22700	RDLK	60073	2532	22W-31N	A6
22700	RLKP	60030	2532	22W-31N	A6
W Townline Rd SR-60					
10	VNHL	60061	2647	17W-25N	B4
400	MDLN	60060	2647	17W-26N	B4
400	VNHL	60060	2647	17W-26N	B4
Town Mall Dr					
-	LKZH	60047	2699	23W-22N	A3
Town Place Cir					
300	BFGV	60089	2754	16W-20N	C1
Town Place Pkwy					
-	BFGV	60089	2754	16W-20N	C1
Townsend Blvd					
7000	JLET	60586	3415	33W-21S	B7
Townsend Cir					
10	NPVL	60565	3203	26W-10S	E5
Townsend Ct					
1900	JLET	60586	3415	33W-21S	A7
Townsend Dr					
-	OSWG	60543	3265	33W-11S	A1
Town Square Dr					
-	RGMW	60008	2806	19W-13N	B5
Towpath Ct					
600	MltT	60187	3082	25W-2S	A3
1700	NPVL	60565	3204	25W-9S	B3
Towpath Ln					
1000	WMTN	60481	3943	28W-39S	C1
W Tow Path Ln					
25200	CNHN	60410	3672	31W-29S	E2
25200	CnhT	60410	3672	31W-29S	E2
Trace Dr					
-	BFGV	60089	2754	18W-18N	A4
800	BFGV	60089	2753	18W-18N	E4
Tracey Ct					
400	WTMT	60559	3145	18W-7S	A6
4000	GNVW	60025	2809	11W-13N	D6
Tracie Dr					
1100	LKZH	60047	2698	23W-21N	E6
S Tracy Av					
13800	RVDL	60827	3350	0W-16S	B2
Tracy Ct					
900	SMBG	60193	2913	23W-9N	A1
2000	HRPK	60133	2911	27W-6N	D6
Tracy Ln					
300	ElgT	60124	2853	38W-10N	B6
1100	LYVL	60048	2591	16W-27N	D7
2000	ALGN	60102	2746	36W-18N	E4
2000	ALGN	60102	2747	36W-18N	A4
2400	AURA	60506	3136	39W-7S	E7
W Tracy Ln					
24100	AntT	60002	2416	24W-40N	D2
Tracy Pl					
200	WNVL	60555	3081	28W-3S	A5
Tracy St					
18300	HmrT	60448	3421	17W-22S	D7
18300	NlxT	60448	3421	17W-22S	D7
E Tracy St					
2000	DMND	60416	3941	33W-39S	B1
2000	FlxT	60416	3941	33W-39S	B1
Tracy Ter					
400	DSPN	60016	2808	14W-12N	C7
Tracy Tr					
500	CLLK	60014	2640	34W-25N	D6
Tracy Wy					
100	BGBK	60440	3205	22W-10S	B6
Trade St					
10	AURA	60504	3202	30W-8S	C1
Trading Post Ln					
3800	JLET	60435	3417	27W-19S	C2
3800	JLET	60544	3417	27W-19S	C2
Tradition Blvd					
3800	SchT	60175	2963	36W-5N	E2
3800	SCRL	60175	2963	36W-5N	E2
Tradition Dr					
-	SCRL	60174	2964	33W-3N	E5
200	WKGN	60087	2480	10W-36N	B3
Traditions Dr					
3800	OMFD	60461	3506	4W-24S	D5
3900	MTSN	60443	3506	4W-24S	D5
19900	FSMR	60422	3506	4W-24S	D4
N Traer Ter					
36300	WrnT	60031	2476	18W-36N	E4
36500	WrnT	60031	2477	18W-36N	A4
Trafalager Sq					
10	LNSH	60069	2702	15W-23N	B2
10	VrnT	60069	2702	15W-23N	B2
Trafalgar Ct					
300	BGBK	60440	3205	22W-9S	C4
8000	ODPK	60462	3346	10W-16S	C3
13600	OrlT	60462	3346	10W-16S	C2
Trafalger Ct					
2000	RMVL	60446	3339	27W-17S	B6
Trafalger Dr					
1900	RMVL	60446	3339	27W-17S	C6
Trafalger Ln E					
1600	AURA	60504	3201	32W-9S	C4
Trafalger Ln W					
1600	AURA	60504	3201	32W-9S	B4
N Trail Ct					
26600	MTWA	60045	2648	13W-26N	D3
W Trail Ct					
400	GYLK	60030	2532	21W-33N	D2
W Trail Dr					
13800	MTWA	60045	2648	13W-26N	D3
13900	LbvT	60045	2648	13W-26N	D3
Trail Crest Ln					
-	LNHT	60046	2418	19W-38N	C7
Trail Ridge Ct					
10	HnrT	60107	2856	30W-10N	C5
10	HnrT	60120	2856	30W-10N	C5
10	SMWD	60107	2856	30W-10N	C5
10	SMWD	60120	2856	30W-10N	C5
Trail Ridge St					
1800	ANHT	60004	2753	19W-18N	D2
1800	PltT	60004	2753	19W-18N	D2
Trails Dr					
-	OMFD	60461	3506	4W-24S	E5
10	SMBG	60193	2859	22W-10N	C5
10	SMBG	60194	2859	22W-10N	C5
Trails Edge Dr					
1800	NHBK	60062	2757	9W-16N	C7
Trails End					
10	ElgT	60124	2853	38W-9N	B7
Trails End Ct					
1900	NPVL	60565	3204	25W-9S	B4
W Trails End Ct					
13100	HMGN	60491	3343	16W-16S	E4
S Trails End Dr					
13900	HMGN	60491	3343	16W-16S	E3
Trails End Ln					
1500	BGBK	60490	3267	26W-13S	D4
Trailsend Ln					
1000	JLET	60431	3585	27W-25S	C1
1000	JLET	60436	3585	27W-25S	C1
Trails End Rd					
400	MltT	60137	3025	23W-1N	A3
400	MltT	60188	3024	23W-1N	E3
400	MltT	60188	3025	23W-1N	A3
Trailside Ct					
300	CLSM	60188	2968	26W-4N	A4
4400	HFET	60192	2804	24W-15N	C2
N Trailside Ct					
1400	PLTN	60067	2752	21W-17N	C4
1400	PLTN	60074	2752	21W-17N	C4
1400	PltT	60074	2752	21W-17N	C4
Trailside Dr					
400	LKZH	60047	2699	22W-22N	A4
1300	BCHR	60401	3774	0W-35S	D7
15300	HMGN	60491	3344	16W-18S	A7
15500	HMGN	60491	3422	16W-18S	A1
15700	HMGN	60491	3421	16W-18S	E1
Trailside Ln					
400	DSPN	60016	2863	12W-11N	C3
900	BRLT	60103	2911	27W-7N	C5
2200	WCDA	60084	2588	25W-29N	B3
Trailway Dr					
14500	VrnT	60045	2648	14W-24N	C7
Trailway St					
2600	HDPK	60035	2704	10W-24N	A1
Trailwood Ct					
200	NHBK	60062	2756	12W-18N	A3
1400	CLLK	60014	2693	36W-23N	C2
Trailwood Dr					
1400	CLLK	60014	2693	36W-23N	C3
Trailwood Ln					
100	NHBK	60062	2756	12W-18N	A2
Tralee Ct					
600	SMBG	60193	2859	23W-9N	A7
800	GRNE	60031	2479	13W-35N	A7
3500	AURA	60564	3202	31W-9S	A5
Tralee Ln					
100	MHRY	60050	2527	35W-32N	A6
1200	LKPT	60441	3342	21W-18S	A7
Tralee Tr					
18200	TYPK	60477	3424	10W-21S	C7
18200	TYPK	60487	3424	10W-21S	C7
Tramore Ct					
3700	NPVL	60564	3267	28W-11S	B1
9500	PlsT	60462	3345	11W-15S	D1
Tramore Ln					
19300	FftT	60448	3504	11W-23S	A3
19500	MKNA	60448	3504	11W-23S	A4
S Trankle Ct					
5000	HMND	46327	3352		E5
Transam Plaza Dr					
-	OKBK	60181	3085	18W-2S	A2
-	OKBK	60523	3085	18W-2S	A2
10	OKTR	60181	3085	18W-2S	A2
Transportation Av					
-	BtnT	60099	2422	9W-41N	C2
-	ZION	60099	2422	9W-40N	C2
Transportation Dr					
-	BlmT	60411	3509	2E-25S	D7
-	FDHT	60411	3509	2E-25S	D7
-	SLVL	60411	3509	2E-25S	D7
-	SLVL	60411	3597	2E-25S	D1
Transworld Rd					
4200	SRPK	60176	2973	13W-5N	A1
Trapet Av					
16700	HLCT	60428	3427	2W-20S	C4
16700	HLCT	60429	3427	2W-20S	C4
16700	MKHM	60428	3427	2W-20S	C4
Trapp Ln					
1200	WNKA	60093	2811	6W-16N	E1
Trappers Ct					
100	DPgT	60565	3203	26W-10S	E6
100	NPVL	60565	3203	26W-10S	E6
1900	MHRY	60050	2528	32W-33N	A2
Trask Rd					
700	AURA	60505	3138	34W-6S	D5
1200	AraT	60505	3138	34W-5S	D4
Trask St					
100	AURA	60505	3138	34W-7S	D7
100	AURA	60505	3200	34W-7S	D1
100	MHTN	60442	3677	19W-31S	E5
Traube Av					
400	CNHL	60514	3145	17W-4S	C1
400	CNHL	60559	3145	17W-4S	C1
400	WTMT	60559	3145	17W-4S	C1
E Traube Av					
10	WTMT	60559	3145	17W-4S	B1
300	CNHL	60514	3145	17W-4S	B1
300	CNHL	60559	3145	17W-4S	B1
W Traube Av					
10	DRGV	60515	3144	18W-4S	E1
10	DRGV	60559	3144	18W-4S	E1
10	WTMT	60515	3144	18W-4S	E1
10	WTMT	60559	3144	18W-4S	E1
10	WTMT	60559	3145	18W-4S	A1
300	DRGV	60559	3145	18W-4S	A1
Traube St					
7600	NRIV	60546	3088	9W-2S	C2
Traudel Ct					
200	BDWD	60408	3941	32W-41S	D6
Travelaire Av					
400	NPVL	60565	3203	27W-9S	D5
Traver Av					
200	GNEN	60137	3025	23W-0S	A6
200	WHTN	60137	3025	23W-0S	A6
200	WHTN	60187	3025	23W-0S	A6
Travers Av					
100	GNEN	60137	3025	23W-0S	A7
100	WHTN	60137	3025	23W-0S	A7
100	WHTN	60187	3025	23W-0S	A7
600	CHHT	60411	3507	2W-24S	C6
600	OMFD	60461	3507	2W-24S	C6
700	BlmT	60411	3507	2W-24S	C6
Travers Ct					
600	CHHT	60411	3507	2W-24S	C5
Travers Ln					
700	FSMR	60422	3507	2W-22S	C2
Traverse Ct					
200	RMVL	60446	3339	27W-17S	C6
13800	HTLY	60142	2744	43W-19N	A3
Travis Ct					
200	SMBG	60195	2859	23W-12N	A2
Travis Pkwy					
-	ROSL	60172	2912	25W-7N	B4
Traymore Dr					
3300	JLET	60431	3497	28W-22S	B1
Treadway Rd					
900	MNSR	46321	3510		E4
Treasure Dr					
-	OSWG	60543	3200	34W-11S	E7
-	OswT	60503	3201	33W-11S	A7
-	OswT	60543	3201	33W-11S	A7
400	OSWG	60543	3201	33W-11S	A7
400	OSWG	60543	3264	33W-11S	E1
400	OSWG	60543	3265	33W-11S	A1
Treasure Ln					
10	RVWD	60015	2755	13W-20N	E1
Treaty Ln					
3400	HFET	60192	2804	23W-14N	D4
Trebes Dr					
-	DhmT	60033	2464	49W-36N	C4
Tree Ln					
800	PTHT	60070	2808	13W-15N	E2

STREET Block	City	ZIP	Map#	CGS	Grid
N Tree Rd					
21000	KLDR	60047	2699	22W-21N	C7
Treebark Ct					
10	SMBG	60193	2858	24W-10N	E5
Treebark Dr					
10	HFET	60169	2858	24W-10N	E5
10	HFET	60193	2858	24W-10N	E5
10	SMBG	60193	2858	24W-10N	E5
Tree Farm Ct					
2000	BFGV	60089	2701	17W-22N	B4
Treehouse Ct					
10	BGBK	60490	3267	27W-12S	B3
10	MTSN	60443	3506	5W-24S	C4
S Treehouse Ln					
10	RDLK	60073	2531	23W-33N	E3
W Treehouse Ln					
200	RDLK	60073	2531	23W-33N	E3
Treehouse Rd					
-	RchT	60443	3506	5W-24S	C5
10	MTSN	60443	3506	5W-24S	C5
Tree Line					
100	ANTH	60002	2357	23W-42N	E5
100	ANTH	60002	2358	23W-42N	A5
Treeline Ct					
900	LKPT	60441	3419	21W-18S	E1
1500	NPVL	60565	3204	25W-8S	B3
33800	WrnT	60030	2534	17W-33N	B2
E Treeline Dr					
1100	LKPT	60441	3419	21W-18S	E1
1100	LKPT	60441	3420	21W-18S	A1
Treesdale Ct					
3100	NPVL	60564	3202	30W-10S	B5
Treesdale Wy					
800	JLET	60447	3495	33W-22S	B3
1100	JLET	60431	3495	33W-22S	B3
Treetop Dr					
9800	ODPK	60462	3345	12W-18S	C7
Tree Top Ln					
-	AlqT	60014	2640	33W-24N	E7
700	CLLK	60014	2640	33W-24N	E7
Treetop Ln					
-	SRWD	60404	3495	31W-24S	E7
500	GRNE	60031	2476	18W-34N	E7
800	SchT	60174	2963	36W-3N	D5
W Treetop Rd					
28400	GrtT	60041	2472	28W-35N	E6
Tree Tops Ln					
10	MltT	60187	3082	25W-2S	B3
Treeview Ln					
700	RLKP	60073	2532	23W-33N	A3
Trefoil Ct					
1200	NPVL	60563	3141	26W-5S	D3
Tregonwell Ct					
10	ALGN	60102	2693	37W-20N	A7
Trelliage Av					
25200	PNFD	60585	3337	31W-15S	E1
Tremont Av					
-	KdlT	60560	3333	41W-17S	E6
2200	AURA	60502	3139	32W-6S	B6
Tremont Cir					
-	LGGV	60047	2701	17W-24N	B1
Tremont Ct					
-	LbvT	60048	2534	16W-31N	E7
2000	WKGN	60048	2534	15W-31N	E7
S Tremont Ln					
900	RDLK	60073	2531	23W-32N	E5
W Tremont Ln					
500	RDLK	60073	2531	23W-32N	D6
Tremont Rd					
10	FXLK	60020	2472	28W-36N	E4
Tremont St					
6300	WLBK	60527	3146	15W-7S	A5
W Tremont St					
400	CHCG	60621	3152	0W-6S	B3
Trenker Dr					
23500	LKVL	60046	2416	23W-39N	E4
23500	LkvT	60046	2416	23W-39N	E4
Trent Av					
1600	NPVL	60563	3140	29W-5S	D2
Trent Ct					
10	BGBK	60490	3267	27W-12S	D4
10	BRRG	60527	3208	14W-8S	D1
1700	GNEN	60137	3083	23W-1S	A2
1700	GNEN	60187	3083	23W-1S	A2
1700	WHTN	60187	3083	23W-1S	A2
2000	GNVW	60025	2809	10W-14N	E4
8700	TYPK	60487	3424	10W-20S	B5
Trent Dr					
-	BTVA	60510	3077	37W-0S	D1
-	GnvT	60510	3077	37W-0S	D1
Trent Ln					
600	SMBG	60193	2859	22W-9N	C7
Trent Rd					
10	HNWD	60047	2646	20W-24N	A7
7300	DRGV	60516	3206	19W-8S	D1
Trent Wy					
-	WCHI	60185	2966	30W-3N	C6
Trenton Av					
10	SEGN	60177	2908	35W-8N	C3
14100	ODPK	60462	3345	11W-16S	E4
Trenton Ct					
10	SBTN	60010	2803	27W-14N	B4
200	SMBG	60193	2859	22W-10N	C6
400	AURA	60504	3140	30W-7S	A7
4700	LGGV	60047	2700	18W-23N	D1
19500	MKNA	60448	3503	12W-23S	C3
Trenton Dr					
200	RMVL	60446	3339	27W-17S	B6
Trenton Ln					
1500	BRLT	60103	2967	27W-5N	C1
6700	DRN	60561	3145	17W-7S	C7
Trenton Rd					
2000	WKGN	60048	2535	15W-31N	A7
Trenton Wy					
19300	MKNA	60448	3503	12W-23S	C3
Trescott St					
1400	MDLN	60060	2646	20W-27N	B1
Trestle Ct					
500	GYLK	60030	2533	20W-32N	A5
Trevi Dr					
-	CLSM	60133	2968	25W-4N	A4
-	CLSM	60188	2968	25W-4N	A4
Trevino Cir					
1700	BGBK	60490	3267	27W-12S	C3
Trevino Ct					
10	BGBK	60490	3267	27W-12S	C3
Trevino Ln					
39000	AntT	60002	2416	24W-40N	C4
39000	LkvT	60002	2416	24W-40N	C4
N Trevino Ter					
1900	VNHL	60061	2647	17W-27N	B1
Trevino Wy					
8400	LKWD	60014	2692	38W-23N	D1
Trevor Cir					
-	RNPK	60443	3593	7W-26S	C3
1100	LYVL	60048	2590	18W-29N	E3
N Trevor Rd					
43100	AntT	60002	2357	24W-43N	C4
43200	ANTH	60002	2357	24W-43N	C4
43400	AntT	53179	2357	24W-43N	C4
43400	SlmT	53179	2357	24W-43N	C4
Trey Rd					
7100	MchT	60050	2526	36W-32N	E5
W Trey Rd					
-	MchT	60050	2526	36W-32N	E5
Treyburn Rd					
3200	NPVL	60564	3202	30W-10S	B5
Tribal Ct					
6700	LGGV	60047	2646	19W-25N	C5
Tributary Ln					
700	PltT	60124	2852	41W-9N	A7
Tricia Ln					
10	BNHL	60010	2802	28W-15N	D2
Trick Cir Ct					
21500	WMTN	60481	3853	26W-37S	E4
Trieste Ln					
200	WynT	60185	2967	28W-3N	A7
Triggs Av					
200	ELGN	60123	2854	35W-11N	B3
300	ElgT	60123	2854	35W-11N	B3
N Trillium					
38400	AntT	60081	2415	27W-38N	B7
Trillium Blvd					
-	HFET	60118	2802	29W-13N	C5
5200	HFET	60192	2802	30W-13N	B6
Trillium Ct					
-	SRWD	60404	3496	31W-22S	A2
10	YKVL	60560	3333	42W-16S	C4
600	CmpT	60175	2962	40W-5N	D2
1200	BTVA	60510	3078	34W-1S	E1
1600	LKFT	60045	2649	13W-24N	A7
22500	CbaT	60010	2697	26W-22N	C4
22500	LKBN	60010	2697	26W-22N	C4
40000	WDWH	60083	2419	16W-40N	E4
Trillium Ct E					
-	AURA	60506	3136	39W-6S	D6
Trillium Ct W					
-	AURA	60506	3136	39W-6S	D6
Trillium Dr					
10	SjnT	46311	3598		C6
Trillium Ln					
-	SRWD	60404	3496	31W-22S	A2
-	WDSK	60098	2581	41W-29N	D5
1000	BRLT	60103	2911	28W-6N	B6
1100	WynT	60103	2911	28W-6N	B6
1700	RVWD	60015	2702	13W-22N	E5
2200	NPVL	60565	3204	24W-10S	D6
2400	HDPK	60035	2704	8W-23N	D3
2400	HIWD	60040	2704	8W-23N	D3
13800	PNFD	60544	3337	31W-16S	E4
Trillium Tr					
700	LKZH	60047	2699	23W-22N	A4
1000	WCHI	60185	3022	29W-2N	D1
4900	LGGV	60047	2700	19W-23N	C2
N Trillium Wy					
34100	GrtT	60073	2531	25W-34N	A1
Trim Creek Ct					
200	BCHR	60401	3864	0E-36S	E1
Trim Creek Ln					
-	BCHR	60401	3864	0E-36S	E1
Trinity Cir					
7900	TYPK	60477	3504	9W-23S	D3
Trinity Ct					
100	EVTN	60201	2866	4W-12N	C1
400	BFGV	60089	2754	16W-17N	D4
700	CLSM	60188	2967	27W-4N	D4
5600	GRNE	60031	2477	15W-36N	E4
14000	WDSK	60098	2581	43W-30N	A1
Trinity Dr					
1200	CLSM	60188	2967	27W-4N	D4
6200	LSLE	60532	3142	24W-7S	D6
8700	ODPK	60462	3424	10W-19S	A1
9100	CRY	60013	2694	33W-22N	E3
9100	LIHL	60014	2694	33W-22N	E3
9100	LIHL	60156	2694	33W-22N	E3
W Trinity Dr					
1100	AddT	60101	2970	19W-5N	C2
1100	ADSN	60101	2970	19W-5N	C2
19600	FmtT	60060	2646	19W-26N	C2
19600	MDLN	60060	2646	19W-26N	C2
Trinity Ln					
300	OKBK	60523	3085	17W-3S	B5
300	OKBK	60559	3085	17W-3S	B5
300	WTMT	60559	3085	17W-3S	B5
400	WynT	60185	2966	29W-4N	D3
Trinity Pl					
1200	LYVL	60048	2591	17W-29N	B3
5200	MTSN	60443	3505	6W-24S	E5
5200	MTSN	60443	3506	6W-24S	A5
Trinity Rd					
-	OKBK	60523	3085	17W-3S	C4
Trinity Ter					
-	ElgT	60123	2853	36W-12N	E3
500	ELGN	60123	2853	36W-12N	E3
N Trinity Ter					
40500	AntT	60002	2416	24W-40N	D3
Triple Crown Ct					
100	WHTN	60187	3082	24W-2S	C4
1200	BRLT	60103	2910	29W-6N	E7
1500	SCRL	60174	2964	34W-3N	D5
Triple Oaks Farm Dr					
300	RtdT	60136	2798	40W-15N	C3
300	RtdT	60140	2798	40W-15N	C3
Tripp Av					
-	PvsT	60141	3030	10W-1S	A7
-	PvsT	60141	3088	10W-1S	A1
7400	LNWD	60076	2866	5W-9N	B7
7400	LNWD	60712	2866	5W-9N	B7
9000	SKOK	60076	2866	5W-11N	B2
14300	CTWD	60445	3348	5W-17S	C4
14300	MDLN	60445	3348	5W-17S	C4
N Tripp Av					
500	CHCG	60624	3032	5W-0N	B3
1400	CHCG	60651	3032	5W-1N	B1
1500	CHCG	60639	3032	5W-1N	B1
1600	CHCG	60639	2976	5W-2N	B7
2800	CHCG	60641	2976	5W-3N	B4
4300	CHCG	60630	2976	5W-5N	B1
4400	CHCG	60630	2920	5W-5N	B7
6000	CHCG	60646	2920	5W-7N	B3
6300	CHCG	60712	2920	5W-7N	B3
7000	LNWD	60712	2920	5W-8N	B1
7200	LNWD	60712	2866	5W-9N	B7
7300	LNWD	60076	2866	5W-9N	B7
7300	SKOK	60076	2866	5W-9N	B7
S Tripp Av					
1200	CHCG	60623	3032	5W-1S	B7
1200	CHCG	60624	3032	5W-1S	B7
1500	CHCG	60623	3090	5W-1S	B1
4300	CHCG	60632	3090	5W-4S	B7
4700	CHCG	60632	3150	5W-5S	B2
6700	CHCG	60629	3150	5W-7S	B6
S Tripp Av					
7700	CHCG	60652	3212	5W-8S	B1
8600	HMTN	60456	3212	5W-9S	B4
8600	HMTN	60652	3212	5W-9S	B4
9100	OKLN	60453	3212	5W-10S	B5
10200	OKLN	60453	3276	5W-12S	B1
11000	CHCG	60655	3276	5W-12S	B3
11000	OKLN	60655	3276	5W-12S	B3
11600	ALSP	60803	3276	5W-13S	B4
Tripp Ct					
10700	OKLN	60453	3276	5W-12S	B2
S Tripp St					
13300	RBBN	60472	3348	5W-15S	C2
13400	CTWD	60445	3348	5W-15S	C2
13400	CTWD	60472	3348	5W-15S	C2
Trisha Ct					
-	MONE	60449	3682	8W-32S	B7
Tristam Ct					
1000	WDND	60118	2800	35W-16N	C1
Tri State Pkwy					
-	GRNE	60031	2534	16W-34N	E1
-	WrnT	60031	2534	16W-34N	E1
600	GRNE	60031	2477	16W-35N	E6
1300	WrnT	60031	2477	16W-35N	D6
Tri State International					
10	LNSH	60069	2703	13W-23N	A3
Tri-State Tollway					
-	ALSP	-	3275	8W-13S	B4
-	ALSP	-	3276	6W-14S	A6
-	ALSP	-	3348	5W-15S	B1
-	BGVW	-	3210	9W-9S	C4
-	BKBN	-	2703	12W-20N	B7
-	BKLY	-	3028	14W-0S	C5
-	BmnT	-	3348	4W-17S	E4
-	BmnT	-	3349	3W-17S	A4
-	BRRG	-	3146	14W-7S	D6
-	CHCG	-	2863	12W-9N	C7
-	CHCG	-	2917	12W-8N	C1
-	CHRG	-	3210	8W-11S	E7
-	CHRG	-	3274	8W-11S	E1
-	CHRG	-	3275	7W-13S	C5
-	CTSD	-	3146	13W-8S	E7
-	CTSD	-	3147	13W-8S	A7
-	CTSD	-	3209	13W-8S	A1
-	CTWD	-	3348	4W-16S	D4
-	DRFD	-	2703	12W-20N	B7
-	DRFD	-	2756	12W-20N	B2
-	DSPN	-	2863	12W-11N	C3
-	DSPN	-	2917	12W-8N	C1
-	EHZC	-	3427	1W-20S	E4
-	EHZC	-	3428	0W-20S	C4
-	EMHT	-	3028	14W-0S	C5
-	FNPK	-	2972	13W-4N	E3
-	FNPK	-	2973	12W-4N	A3
-	GNOK	-	2535	14W-31N	D7
-	GNOK	-	2592	14W-28N	C7
-	GNOK	-	2648	14W-27N	D1
-	GNVW	-	2809	11W-13N	C7
-	GRNE	-	2477	16W-37N	E2
-	GRNE	-	2535	14W-33N	C4
-	HGKN	-	3209	12W-8S	C1
-	HLCT	-	3427	2W-20S	C4
-	HLSD	-	3028	14W-0S	C5
-	HNDL	-	3086	14W-4S	C7
-	HNDL	-	3146	14W-6S	D4
-	HYHL	-	3210	9W-9S	C4
-	IHPK	-	3146	14W-7S	D6
-	JSTC	-	3209	12W-8S	C2
-	JSTC	-	3210	10W-9S	B4
-	LbvT	-	2535	14W-31N	D7
-	LbvT	-	2592	14W-28N	C7
-	LbvT	-	2648	14W-27N	D1
-	LKFT	-	2648	13W-25N	E6
-	LKFT	-	2702	13W-24N	E1
-	LKFT	-	2703	13W-23N	A2
-	LNSG	-	3429	2E-20S	D4
-	LNSH	-	2703	12W-22N	A3
-	LydT	-	2972	13W-4N	E3
-	LydT	-	2973	13W-4N	A3
-	LynT	-	3086	14W-3S	C6
-	LynT	-	3146	14W-6S	D4
-	LynT	-	3147	13W-8S	A7
-	LynT	-	3209	12W-8S	D2
-	MaiT	-	2809	11W-13N	C7
-	MaiT	-	2863	12W-11N	C3
-	MDLN	-	3348	4W-16S	D4
-	MKHM	-	3349	3W-17S	A6
-	MKHM	-	3427	2W-20S	C4
-	MTWA	-	2592	14W-28N	D7
-	MTWA	-	2648	13W-27N	D1
-	NfdT	-	2756	12W-20N	B2
-	NfdT	-	2809	11W-13N	C6
-	NHBK	-	2756	12W-18N	A3
-	NHBK	-	2809	12W-16N	C1
-	NHLK	-	2972	14W-2N	C7
-	NHLK	-	3028	14W-2N	C1
-	NptT	-	2360	16W-41N	C7
-	NptT	-	2419	17W-41N	C1
-	NptT	-	2477	16W-38N	E1
-	OKBK	-	3086	14W-1S	C2
-	OMCK	-	2419	17W-41N	C1
-	OMCK	-	2477	16W-37N	E2
-	PKRG	-	2863	12W-10N	C4
-	POSN	-	3349	3W-17S	A5
-	PvsT	-	3028	14W-0S	C6
-	PvsT	-	3086	14W-3S	C5
-	RBBN	-	3348	4W-16S	D4
-	RSMT	-	2917	12W-8N	C3
-	RVWD	-	2703	12W-22N	A3
-	SHLD	-	3428	0W-20S	C4
-	SHLD	-	3429	1E-20S	A4
-	SRPK	-	2917	12W-6N	C6
-	SRPK	-	2973	12W-4N	A3
-	ThtT	-	3429	2E-20S	C4
-	TNTN	-	3428	0W-20S	C4
-	VrnT	-	2648	13W-25N	E6
-	VrnT	-	2702	13W-24N	E1
-	VrnT	-	2703	12W-20N	B7
-	WdfT	-	2703	12W-20N	B7
-	WdfT	-	2756	12W-20N	B1
-	WDWH	-	2360	17W-41N	C7
-	WDWH	-	2419	16W-40N	D3
-	WDWH	-	2477	16W-37N	E1
-	WhlT	-	2756	12W-18N	A4
-	WKGN	-	2535	14W-31N	D6
-	WLNG	-	2756	12W-16N	A6
-	WLSP	-	3209	12W-8S	C1
-	WNSP	-	3086	14W-4S	C7
-	WNSP	-	3146	14W-4S	C1
-	WrnT	-	2477	16W-37N	E2
-	WrnT	-	2478	15W-34N	A7
-	WrnT	-	2535	14W-32N	C5
-	WRTH	-	3275	8W-13S	B4
-	WthT	-	3275	7W-13S	B4
Tri-State Tollway I-80					
-	EHZC	-	3427	1W-20S	E4
Tri-State Tollway I-80					
-	EHZC	-	3428	0W-20S	C4
-	HLCT	-	3427	2W-20S	D4
-	LNSG	-	3429	2E-20S	C4
-	SHLD	-	3428	0W-20S	C4
-	SHLD	-	3429	1E-20S	A4
-	ThtT	-	3429	1E-20S	A4
-	TNTN	-	3428	0W-20S	C4
Tri-State Tollway I-94					
-	BKBN	-	2703	12W-20N	B7
-	DRFD	-	2703	12W-21N	B5
-	DRFD	-	2756	12W-20N	B1
-	GNOK	-	2535	14W-31N	D6
-	GNOK	-	2592	14W-29N	D5
-	GNOK	-	2648	13W-27N	D1
-	GRNE	-	2477	16W-37N	E2
-	GRNE	-	2535	15W-33N	A2
-	LbvT	-	2535	14W-31N	D7
-	LbvT	-	2592	14W-29N	D5
-	LbvT	-	2648	13W-26N	E2
-	LKFT	-	2648	13W-25N	E6
-	LKFT	-	2702	13W-24N	E1
-	LKFT	-	2703	13W-23N	A2
-	LNSH	-	2703	12W-22N	A3
-	MTWA	-	2592	14W-28N	D7
-	MTWA	-	2648	13W-27N	D1
-	NptT	-	2360	16W-42N	D6
-	NptT	-	2419	17W-41N	C1
-	NptT	-	2477	16W-38N	E1
-	OMCK	-	2419	17W-41N	C1
-	OMCK	-	2477	16W-37N	E2
-	RVWD	-	2703	12W-22N	A3
-	VrnT	-	2648	13W-25N	E6
-	VrnT	-	2702	13W-24N	E1
-	VrnT	-	2703	12W-22N	A3
-	WdfT	-	2703	12W-20N	B7
-	WdfT	-	2756	12W-20N	B1
-	WDWH	-	2360	17W-41N	C7
-	WDWH	-	2419	17W-41N	C1
-	WDWH	-	2477	16W-37N	E1
-	WKGN	-	2535	14W-32N	C5
-	WrnT	-	2477	16W-38N	E1
-	WrnT	-	2478	15W-34N	A7
-	WrnT	-	2535	14W-33N	B4
Tri-State Tollway I-294					
-	ALSP	-	3275	7W-13S	C5
-	ALSP	-	3276	6W-14S	A6
-	ALSP	-	3348	5W-15S	B1
-	BGVW	-	3210	9W-11S	E7
-	BKLY	-	3028	14W-0S	C5
-	BmnT	-	3348	4W-17S	E4
-	BmnT	-	3349	3W-17S	A4
-	BRRG	-	3146	14W-7S	D6
-	CHCG	-	2863	12W-9N	C7
-	CHCG	-	2917	12W-8N	C1
-	CHRG	-	3210	8W-11S	E7
-	CHRG	-	3274	8W-11S	E1
-	CHRG	-	3275	7W-13S	C5
-	CTSD	-	3146	13W-8S	E7
-	CTSD	-	3147	13W-8S	A7
-	CTSD	-	3209	13W-8S	A1
-	CTWD	-	3348	4W-16S	D4
-	DRFD	-	2756	12W-18N	B2
-	DSPN	-	2863	12W-11N	C3
-	DSPN	-	2917	12W-8N	C1
-	EHZC	-	3427	1W-20S	E4
-	EHZC	-	3428	0W-20S	C4
-	EMHT	-	3028	14W-0S	C5
-	FNPK	-	2972	13W-4N	E3
-	FNPK	-	2973	12W-4N	A3
-	GNVW	-	2809	11W-13N	C7
-	HGKN	-	3209	12W-8S	C1
-	HLCT	-	3427	3W-19S	B3
-	HLSD	-	3028	14W-0S	C5
-	HNDL	-	3086	14W-4S	C7
-	HNDL	-	3146	14W-4S	C1
-	HYHL	-	3210	9W-9S	C4
-	IHPK	-	3146	14W-7S	D6
-	JSTC	-	3209	12W-8S	C2
-	JSTC	-	3210	9W-9S	C4
-	LNSG	-	3429	2E-20S	D4
-	LydT	-	2972	13W-4N	E3
-	LydT	-	2973	13W-4N	A3
-	LynT	-	3086	14W-3S	C6
-	LynT	-	3146	14W-6S	D4
-	LynT	-	3147	13W-8S	A7
-	LynT	-	3209	12W-8S	D2
-	MaiT	-	2809	11W-13N	C7
-	MaiT	-	2863	12W-11N	C3
-	MDLN	-	3348	4W-16S	D4
-	MKHM	-	3349	3W-17S	B6
-	MKHM	-	3427	2W-20S	C4
-	NfdT	-	2756	12W-18N	A3
-	NfdT	-	2809	11W-13N	C7
-	NHBK	-	2756	12W-18N	A3
-	NHBK	-	2809	12W-16N	C1
-	NHLK	-	2972	14W-2N	C7
-	NHLK	-	3028	14W-2N	C1
-	OKBK	-	3086	14W-1S	C2
-	PKRG	-	2863	12W-10N	C4
-	POSN	-	3349	3W-17S	A5
-	PvsT	-	3028	14W-0S	C6
-	PvsT	-	3086	14W-1S	B1
-	RBBN	-	3348	5W-16S	C2
-	RSMT	-	2917	12W-8N	C3
-	SHLD	-	3428	0W-20S	C4
-	SHLD	-	3429	1E-20S	A4
-	SRPK	-	2917	12W-6N	C6
-	SRPK	-	2973	12W-4N	A2
-	ThtT	-	3429	1E-20S	A4
-	TNTN	-	3428	0W-20S	C4
-	WdfT	-	2756	12W-20N	B1
-	WhlT	-	2756	12W-18N	A4
-	WLNG	-	2756	12W-16N	A6
-	WLSP	-	3209	12W-8S	C2
-	WNSP	-	3086	14W-4S	C7
-	WNSP	-	3146	14W-4S	C1
-	WRTH	-	3275	8W-13S	B4
-	WthT	-	3275	7W-13S	B4
Triton Ln					
10	NPVL	60540	3203	26W-8S	D1
W Triton Wy					
5700	MONE	60449	3682	7W-31S	D5
N Triumph Ct					
500	HNVL	60030	2532	22W-33N	B2
Triumvera Dr					
-	MaiT	60016	2809	11W-13N	D7
-	NfdT	60016	2809	11W-13N	D7
3900	NfdT	60025	2809	11W-13N	D7
Trojak Ln					
2700	AraT	60502	3079	33W-4S	B7
2700	AURA	60502	3079	33W-4S	B7
Troon Cir					
900	FKFT	60423	3593	9W-26S	A2
Troon Ct					
400	WNFD	60190	3023	26W-1N	E2
Troon Dr					
3000	BtlT	60512	3198	40W-10S	B6
3000	BtlT	60538	3198	41W-10S	B6
3000	MTGY	60538	3198	41W-10S	B6
Troon Ln					
-	BHPK	60083	2421	12W-39N	B6
-	CRTE	60417	3596	0E-29S	E7
-	CRTE	60417	3685	0E-29S	E1
Troon St					
1300	CCHL	60478	3506	4W-23S	D3
1300	FSMR	60422	3506	4W-23S	D3
Troon Ter					
900	FKFT	60423	3593	9W-26S	A3
N Troons Cross					
1900	PLTN	60074	2752	21W-18N	D3
Troost Av					
900	FTPK	60130	3030	9W-0S	C7
Trotter Ct					
10	WHTN	60187	3082	24W-2S	D3
800	RLKP	60030	2589	22W-30N	C2
Trotter Ln					
600	CmpT	60119	2962	40W-3N	B6
700	CmpT	60175	2962	40W-3N	B6
Trotter Ln N					
10	CmpT	60175	2962	40W-4N	B5
Trotter Ln S					
10	CmpT	60175	2962	40W-3N	B5
Trottier Ct					
-	ALGN	60118	2746	37W-19N	C3
-	DndT	60118	2746	37W-19N	C3
Trotwood Ct					
10	BFGV	60089	2701	16W-21N	D6
Trout Av					
1200	ELGN	60120	2801	32W-12N	B7
Trout Rd					
300	BTVA	60510	3077	37W-0S	C1
Trout St					
100	SRWD	60404	3496	30W-24S	C5
400	WslT	60481	3943	27W-40S	D3
Trout Farm Rd					
400	BGBK	60440	3204	24W-11S	E7
Trout Lilly Ln					
1000	DRN	60561	3145	17W-7S	B7
Troutman Dr					
100	BRLT	60103	2909	32W-8N	C3
Trout Park Blvd					
400	ELGN	60120	2801	33W-13N	B7
Trout Valley Rd					
100	TVLY	60013	2695	31W-23N	C2
Trout View Ct					
16700	BmnT	60477	3425	7W-20S	D3
Trowbridge Cir					
10	LKBF	60044	2593	11W-29N	D4
Trowbridge Ct					
1600	WHTN	60187	3082	23W-2S	E3
2100	GNVW	60025	2809	10W-14N	E3
Trowbridge Rd					
200	EGVV	60007	2914	19W-8N	C3
Trowbridge Wy					
2300	LSLE	60532	3142	24W-6S	D5
Troxel Av					
10	RMVL	60441	3340	24W-16S	E5
10	RMVL	60446	3340	24W-16S	E4
Troy Av					
13600	RBBN	60472	3348	3W-16S	E3
15100	MKHM	60428	3349	3W-18S	A7
15700	MKHM	60428	3427	3W-18S	A1
S Troy Av					
14400	BmnT	60469	3348	3W-17S	E4
14400	POSN	60469	3348	3W-17S	E4
14700	MKHM	60428	3348	3W-17S	E5
14700	MKHM	60469	3348	3W-17S	E5
Troy Cir					
2400	OMFD	60461	3507	3W-25S	B7
Troy Ct					
200	RMVL	60446	3339	27W-17S	C6
Troy Dr					
-	LMBD	60148	3026	20W-1N	A3
3800	PKCY	60085	2535	13W-33N	E3
3800	WKGN	60085	2535	13W-33N	E3
S Troy Dr					
11500	MTPK	60803	3276	3W-13S	E4
Troy Ln					
200	LMBD	60148	3026	20W-1N	A3
Troy St					
10	FXLK	60020	2473	27W-36N	B3
N Troy St					
500	CHCG	60612	3032	3W-0N	E3
700	CHCG	60622	3032	3W-0N	E3
1600	CHCG	60647	2976	3W-2N	E7
3500	CHCG	60618	2976	3W-4N	D2
4400	CHCG	60618	2920	3W-5N	D7
5100	CHCG	60625	2920	3W-6N	D6
6000	CHCG	60659	2920	3W-7N	D3
6300	CHCG	60645	2920	3W-7N	D3
S Troy St					
-	ENGN	60652	3212	3W-10S	E4
100	CHCG	60612	3032	3W-0S	E5
1100	CHCG	60623	3032	3W-1S	E7
1600	CHCG	60623	3090	3W-1S	E1
4300	CHCG	60632	3090	3W-4S	E7
5500	CHCG	60629	3150	3W-7S	E5
5500	CHCG	60632	3150	3W-6S	E4
7500	CHCG	60652	3212	3W-8S	E1
8700	ENGN	60805	3212	3W-10S	E5
10300	CHCG	60655	3276	3W-12S	E2
11200	MTPK	60655	3276	3W-13S	E3
11400	MTPK	60803	3276	3W-13S	E4
Trudy Ln					
1000	FXLK	60020	2415	28W-39N	A6
Truman Ct					
10	SMWD	60107	2856	29W-10N	D6
S Truman Ct					
25800	MONE	60449	3682	7W-31S	D5
Truman Dr					
500	OSWG	60543	3263	38W-12S	A3
Truman Ln					
10	SMWD	60107	2856	29W-10N	E6
Truman St					
300	DSPN	60018	2862	15W-9N	A7
300	EGvT	60018	2862	15W-9N	A7
500	BGBK	60440	3204	24W-10S	E5
7400	HRPK	60133	2912	25W-9N	A1
E Truman St					
700	HMND	46320	3352		E6
S Truman St					
25700	MONE	60449	3682	7W-31S	D5
Trumbull Av					
8300	SKOK	60076	2866	4W-10N	D5
8700	SKOK	60203	2866	4W-10N	D4
14400	MDLN	60445	3348	4W-17S	E5
14800	MDLN	60426	3348	4W-17S	E5
14800	MKHM	60426	3348	4W-17S	E6
15700	MKHM	60428	3426	4W-19S	E2
N Trumbull Av					
500	CHCG	60624	3032	4W-0N	D3

STREET Block	City	ZIP	Map#	CGS	Grid
N Trumbull Av					
700	CHCG	60651	3032	4W-0N	D3
2300	RVGV	60171	2973	10W-2N	E6
6400	CHCG	60659	2920	4W-8N	D3
6400	LNWD	60659	2920	4W-8N	D3
6400	LNWD	60712	2920	4W-8N	D2
S Trumbull Av					
300	CHCG	60624	3032	4W-0S	D5
1400	CHCG	60623	3032	4W-1S	D7
1500	CHCG	60623	3090	4W-2S	D2
4300	CHCG	60632	3090	4W-4S	D7
4600	CHCG	60632	3150	4W-5S	D1
5500	CHCG	60629	3150	4W-6S	D3
7500	CHCG	60652	3212	4W-8S	D1
9100	ENGN	60805	3212	4W-10S	D5
10200	CHCG	60655	3276	4W-12S	D1
10200	CHCG	60805	3276	4W-11S	D1
10200	ENGN	60805	3276	4W-11S	D1
12300	ALSP	60803	3276	4W-14S	D6
12300	WthT	60803	3276	4W-14S	D6
12500	BLID	60406	3276	4W-14S	E6
12500	BLID	60803	3276	4W-14S	E6
13400	RBBN	60472	3348	4W-15S	E2
Truro Ct					
300	SMBG	60194	2858	24W-10N	C4
Tryall Dr					
1000	DYR	46311	3510		E6
Tryon St					
-	GfnT	60014	2638	38W-25N	E5
N Tryon St					
100	WDSK	60098	2524	41W-31N	C7
23900	CNHN	60410	3672	31W-29S	E2
23900	CnhT	60410	3672	31W-29S	E2
S Tryon St					
100	WDSK	60098	2524	41W-31N	E7
300	WDSK	60098	2581	41W-30N	C1
24400	CNHN	60410	3672	31W-29S	E3
24400	CnhT	60410	3672	31W-29S	E3
E Tryon Grove Rd					
5600	RcmT	60071	2412	34W-40N	C3
5600	RHMD	60071	2412	35W-40N	A3
E Tryon Grove Rd CO-A16					
5600	RcmT	60071	2412	34W-40N	C3
5600	RHMD	60071	2412	35W-40N	A3
Tubeway Dr					
100	CLSM	60188	3024	25W-1N	A2
200	MltT	60188	3024	25W-1N	A2
Tucci St					
-	AvnT	60030	2533	20W-32N	A5
-	AvnT	60048	2533	20W-32N	A5
-	GYLK	60030	2533	20W-32N	A5
Tuckaway Ct					
200	MltT	60188	3023	26W-1N	E3
200	WNFD	60188	3023	26W-1N	E3
200	WNFD	60190	3023	26W-1N	E3
Tucker Av					
400	SchT	60174	2908	35W-6N	C7
W Tucker Ln					
4400	WKGN	60085	2535	14W-32N	C4
Tucker Rd					
500	PtnT	60468	3861	9W-37S	A4
500	PTON	60468	3861	9W-37S	A4
500	WlIT	60468	3861	9W-37S	A4
Tucson Dr					
2800	JLET	60432	3500	20W-22S	C2
Tucumcari Tr					
100	BmdT	60108	2968	25W-5N	B1
Tudor Cir					
8300	WLSP	60480	3208	13W-9S	E3
Tudor Ct					
200	BGBK	60440	3205	22W-11S	C7
300	GLNC	60022	2758	6W-17N	D5
700	SRGV	60554	3135	41W-4S	E2
900	LKZH	60047	2698	24W-22N	C4
10200	MNSR	46321	3510		E4
Tudor Dr					
-	NpvT	60540	3140	29W-6S	D4
-	NpvT	60563	3140	29W-6S	D4
100	BRTN	60010	2751	24W-18N	D2
700	NPVL	60563	3140	29W-5S	D4
1300	MDLN	60060	2590	20W-29N	A5
Tudor Ln					
200	SMBG	60193	2859	23W-10N	B6
1700	NHBK	60062	2757	9W-16N	B6
1700	NLNX	60451	3589	16W-26S	E3
1700	NlxT	60442	3589	16W-26S	E3
1700	NlxT	60451	3589	16W-26S	E3
6700	WTMT	60559	3145	18W-7S	B7
8000	TYPK	60477	3424	10W-20S	C3
Tudor Pl					
10	KLWH	60043	2812	3W-14N	E4
10	WLMT	60043	2812	3W-14N	E4
10	WLMT	60091	2812	3W-14N	E4
Tudor Rd					
15400	OKFT	60452	3347	7W-18S	C7
Tufton Ct					
1900	NPVL	60564	3202	29W-9S	C4
Tufton St					
24400	PNFD	60585	3338	30W-15S	B2
Tufts Ct					
1700	NPVL	60565	3204	24W-9S	D3
Tuggles Ct					
600	BTVA	60510	3078	34W-2S	D4
Tuggles Ln					
1300	BTVA	60510	3078	34W-2S	D4
1300	BtvT	60510	3078	34W-2S	D4
Tugwell St					
4000	FNPK	60131	2972	13W-4N	E2
Tuileries Pl					
10	ELGN	60123	2854	35W-12N	B2
Tulane Dr					
1500	LslT	60565	3204	24W-8S	D3
1500	NPVL	60565	3204	24W-9S	D3
W Tulip Av					
4500	MONE	60449	3683	5W-31S	B5
Tulip Cir					
-	ISLK	60051	2586	29W-29N	C4
-	NndT	60051	2586	29W-29N	C4
100	ISLK	60042	2586	29W-29N	C4
200	MTSN	60443	3593	7W-26S	D2
Tulip Ct					
200	SMBG	60193	2857	26W-10N	E6
1400	WLNG	60090	2754	16W-18N	D3
15300	ODPK	60462	3346	9W-18S	C7
Tulip Dr					
3300	HLCT	60429	3426	4W-20S	E4
E Tulip Dr					
300	GNWD	60425	3508	0E-22S	E1
400	GNWD	60425	3509	0E-22S	A1
Tulip Ln					
-	BmnT	60426	3426	5W-19S	A1
-	PNFD	60586	3415	32W-19S	C4
-	PnfT	60544	3415	32W-19S	C4
800	NPVL	60540	3141	27W-7S	C7
800	NPVL	60540	3203	27W-7S	C1
1200	BRLT	60103	2910	29W-6N	C7
Tulip Ln					
2500	CTHL	60403	3417	27W-21S	D7
17700	TYPK	60477	3424	10W-21S	C6
Tulip St					
3700	NndT	60014	2586	30W-28N	A6
E Tulip Wy					
900	PLTN	60074	2753	19W-18N	B4
Tulip Tree Ct					
1200	LKVL	60046	2474	23W-36N	E4
Tuliptree Ct					
1500	GNVW	60025	2810	8W-14N	E5
Tulip Tree Ln					
-	LKVL	60046	2474	23W-36N	E4
2400	DYR	46311	3598		D3
Tuliptree Ln					
11900	HTLY	60142	2744	42W-19N	D2
Tullamore Ct					
700	SMBG	60193	2859	23W-9N	A7
Tullamore Dr					
8500	TYPK	60477	3504	10W-23S	B3
Tullamore Ter					
200	RchT	60443	3593	8W-26S	B1
Tulley Av					
8700	BRBK	60459	3211	6W-10S	E4
8700	OKLN	60459	3211	6W-10S	E4
9000	OKLN	60453	3211	6W-10S	E5
Tully Pl					
200	PTHT	60070	2808	15W-14N	A4
Tully Rd					
-	BDWD	60481	3942	30W-40S	C2
Tulsa Av					
300	CPVL	60110	2748	33W-17N	B6
Tulsa Ct					
300	CPVL	60110	2748	33W-17N	B6
Tuma Rd					
10	BtlT	60560	3261	42W-14S	E7
100	BtlT	60560	3333	41W-14S	E1
100	YKVL	60560	3333	41W-14S	E1
200	BtlT	60560	3334	41W-14S	A1
4300	YKVL	60560	3261	41W-14S	E7
Tumblebrook Ct					
10	BRRG	60527	3207	16W-10S	E6
Tummy Tooth Ln					
100	BDWD	60481	3942	30W-40S	C2
100	RedT	60481	3942	30W-40S	C2
Tunbridge Ct					
1900	ALGN	60102	2747	35W-20N	A1
2000	ALGN	60102	2746	35W-20N	E1
Tunbridge Tr					
1200	ALGN	60102	2746	35W-20N	E1
1900	ALGN	60102	2747	35W-20N	A1
Tupelo Dr					
10	NPVL	60540	3203	27W-8S	D2
10	NPVL	60540	3204	25W-8S	A2
Tuppence Ct					
10500	FKFT	60423	3591	13W-26S	B2
Tuppeny Ct					
1500	ROSL	60172	2912	25W-7N	A4
S Tures Ln					
700	DSPN	60018	2862	13W-9N	D7
Turf Ct					
1600	RLKP	60030	2532	22W-31N	B7
1600	RLKP	60030	2589	22W-31N	B1
Turf Ln					
400	WHTN	60187	3024	24W-0N	D4
14400	HMGN	60491	3344	15W-17S	B5
N Turf Hill Dr					
27600	FmtT	60060	2645	21W-27N	C1
27600	HNWD	60047	2645	21W-27N	C1
27600	HNWD	60060	2645	21W-27N	C1
27600	MDLN	60060	2645	21W-27N	C1
S Turf Hill Dr					
27500	FmtT	60060	2645	21W-27N	D1
27500	HNWD	60047	2645	21W-27N	D1
27500	HNWD	60060	2645	21W-27N	D1
27500	MDLN	60060	2645	21W-27N	D1
Turfway Ln					
1300	BRLT	60103	2966	30W-5N	C1
1300	WynT	60103	2966	30W-5N	C1
Turicum Rd					
400	LKFT	60045	2650	9W-25N	C5
Turkey Ct					
1400	IVNS	60067	2805	23W-14N	A3
Turkey Tr					
1400	IVNS	60067	2805	23W-14N	A3
Turkey Hill Rd					
100	TVLY	60013	2695	32W-22N	C3
Turkey Run Dr					
600	RLKH	60073	2474	24W-35N	D5
Turkey Run Rd					
100	TVLY	60013	2695	32W-23N	C2
Turks Cap Rd					
1400	GYLK	60030	2533	19W-31N	C7
Turlington Av					
14700	HRVY	60426	3350	1W-17S	A6
15600	HRVY	60426	3428	1W-18S	A1
Turnberry Ct					
10	BRRG	60527	3208	15W-10S	A5
10	GfnT	60156	2693	38W-23N	A2
700	SRWD	60404	3496	31W-24S	A6
800	HRPK	60133	2912	25W-7N	B5
1400	GNVA	60134	3020	36W-0N	A5
2900	SCRL	60174	2965	33W-4N	A4
5100	JLET	60586	3416	30W-21S	B6
24200	WldT	60564	3266	30W-12S	B3
Turnberry Dr					
10	PlsT	60464	3346	10W-15S	C1
10	PSHT	60464	3346	10W-15S	C1
500	NARA	60542	3078	35W-3S	B5
3100	MHRY	60050	2528	32W-31N	B6
4400	BmdT	60133	2912	25W-6N	A6
4400	BmdT	60172	2912	25W-6N	A6
4400	HRPK	60133	2912	25W-7N	B5
4400	HRPK	60172	2912	25W-6N	A6
4800	HFET	60010	2804	24W-16N	C1
4900	ROSL	60133	2912	25W-7N	A5
4900	ROSL	60172	2912	25W-7N	A5
9000	BRRG	60527	3208	15W-10S	A5
10800	FftT	60423	3591	13W-27S	A5
10800	GGnT	60423	3591	13W-27S	B5
Turnberry Ln					
-	GfnT	60156	2693	38W-23N	A1
-	GNEN	60137	3083	23W-1S	A2
-	LGGV	60047	2700	20W-22N	A5
-	MTGY	60506	3198	40W-9S	B4
400	WNFD	60190	3023	26W-1N	D2
500	ANTH	60002	2357	24W-42N	C5
800	NHBK	60062	2757	8W-16N	D7
800	WLBK	60527	3145	16W-7S	E5
1300	MDLN	60060	2590	19W-29N	B5
8900	TYPK	60487	3424	11W-20S	A4
13500	HmrT	60491	3344	15W-16S	B3
Turnberry Rd					
2600	SCRL	60174	2965	33W-4N	A4
Turnberry Tr					
9100	LKWD	60014	2639	38W-24N	A6
Turnberry Tr					
9200	LKWD	60014	2638	38W-24N	E6
15100	LMNT	60439	3342	19W-15S	E1
W Turnberry Tr					
7500	LKWD	60014	2638	38W-24N	E7
7800	GfnT	60014	2638	38W-24N	D7
Turnbridge Cir					
800	NPVL	60540	3142	25W-7S	C7
Turnbridge Ct					
1700	MTGY	60538	3199	36W-10S	D5
Turnbridge Dr					
100	SRWD	60404	3496	31W-23S	A4
Turnbull Dr					
1300	RLKB	60073	2474	24W-35N	D7
1500	RLKH	60073	2474	24W-35N	D7
Turnbull St					
-	ELBN	60119	3017	42W-0N	C5
Turnbull Woods Ct					
10	HDPK	60035	2758	7W-20N	A2
10	NtrT	60062	2758	7W-20N	A2
Turnbury Ct					
10	HNWD	60047	2645	22W-26N	B3
Turnbury Dr					
-	MNKA	60447	3672	34W-29S	A3
Turner Av					
-	WCHI	60185	3022	29W-1N	C3
10	EGVV	60007	2914	19W-8N	D3
10	ITSC	60143	2914	19W-8N	D3
300	BmdT	60157	2913	22W-6N	C6
300	ROSL	60157	2913	22W-6N	C6
400	ROSL	60172	2913	22W-6N	C6
600	BmdT	60172	2912	23W-6N	E5
600	ROSL	60172	2912	23W-6N	E5
800	GNEN	60137	3025	22W-0S	D6
13300	RBBN	60472	3348	4W-16S	E2
14000	RBBN	60406	3348	4W-16S	E4
14700	MDLN	60445	3348	4W-17S	E6
14700	MKHM	60426	3348	4W-17S	E5
14700	MKHM	60445	3348	4W-17S	E5
15600	MKHM	60428	3348	4W-18S	E7
15600	MKHM	60428	3426	4W-18S	E1
16600	HLCT	60428	3426	4W-19S	E3
16600	HLCT	60429	3426	4W-19S	E3
E Turner Av					
300	ROSL	60172	2913	22W-6N	B6
600	BmdT	60157	2913	22W-6N	C6
S Turner Av					
9100	ENGN	60805	3212	4W-10S	E5
10200	CHCG	60655	3276	4W-11S	E1
10200	CHCG	60805	3276	4W-11S	E1
10200	ENGN	60805	3276	4W-11S	E1
W Turner Av					
10	BmdT	60172	2913	23W-6N	A6
10	ROSL	60172	2913	23W-6N	A6
100	BmdT	60172	2912	23W-6N	E6
Turner Ct					
100	WCHI	60185	3022	30W-0N	C4
4800	CCHL	60478	3506	6W-22S	A2
Turner Ln					
100	WMTN	60481	3853	27W-38S	E7
1500	HRPK	60133	2911	26W-6N	E6
Turner Rd					
300	AraT	60504	3138	35W-5S	C4
300	AURA	60504	3138	35W-5S	B4
Turner St					
10	GLBT	60136	2799	38W-16N	A2
Turnham Green Rd					
-	GRNE	60031	2478	15W-36N	A3
Turning Shore Dr					
10	SBTN	60010	2803	27W-14N	C3
Turnmill Ln					
500	WynT	60185	2966	29W-4N	D3
Turret Ct					
900	MDLN	60060	2647	18W-26N	A3
Turtle Run					
11200	ODPK	60467	3422	14W-21S	E7
Turtle St					
100	SRWD	60404	3496	30W-24S	C5
N Turtle Bay Rd					
1800	VNHL	60061	2647	17W-27N	B1
Turtle Cove Ct					
1900	NPVL	60565	3204	25W-9S	B4
E Turtle Creek Cir					
1300	PLTN	60074	2753	19W-17N	C5
Turtle Creek Ct					
800	WldT	60565	3203	27W-11S	B7
Turtle Creek Dr					
1800	AURA	60503	3201	33W-10S	A6
Turtlecreek Dr					
2600	HLCT	60429	3427	3W-21S	B5
17700	HMWD	60430	3427	3W-21S	B6
Turtle Creek Ln					
1500	RDLK	60073	2531	24W-34N	B1
W Turtle Creek Ln					
1500	RDLK	60073	2531	25W-34N	B1
Turtledove Ln					
700	NLNX	60451	3589	18W-27S	A4
Turtle Pond Ct					
500	LKZH	60047	2699	22W-22N	A4
Turtle Pond Ln					
-	ODPK	60462	3346	9W-15S	D2
-	PSHT	60462	3346	9W-15S	D2
13400	PSHT	60463	3346	9W-15S	C2
Turtle Run Ct					
18100	ODPK	60467	3422	14W-21S	E7
Turvey Ct					
5300	DRGV	60515	3144	20W-5S	B3
Turvey Rd					
1300	DRGV	60515	3144	20W-5S	B3
Tuscan Ct					
-	OKBK	60523	3086	15W-1S	A1
Tuscan Vw					
-	ELGN	60124	2853	37W-10N	D7
-	ElgT	60124	2853	37W-9N	D7
Tuscany Ct					
1400	GNVW	60025	2811	8W-14N	A3
2000	RMVL	60446	3339	27W-17S	B6
2100	NHFD	60093	2811	8W-14N	A3
Tuscany Dr					
-	SMWD	60107	2856	30W-9N	C7
-	SMWD	60120	2856	30W-9N	C7
400	ALGN	60102	2692	38W-21N	E6
400	ALGN	60102	2693	38W-21N	A6
400	GfnT	60102	2693	38W-21N	A6
Tuscany Ln					
1100	NPVL	60564	3267	28W-11S	A2
1900	RMVL	60446	3339	27W-17S	C6
Tuscany Ter					
-	MTGY	60543	3262	39W-11S	D1
-	OSWG	60543	3262	40W-11S	D1
Tuscarora Ct					
16500	LKPT	60441	3420	20W-20S	B4
N Tuscarora Ct					
25500	LKBN	60010	2643	27W-25N	B5
Tuscola Av					
10	SchT	60174	2908	34W-6N	D7
Tussell St					
3200	NPVL	60564	3203	28W-11S	B7
3200	NPVL	60564	3267	28W-11S	B1
Tustamena Tr					
6300	MHRY	60050	2527	35W-33N	A3
Tuthill Rd					
200	LslT	60563	3142	25W-5S	B2
200	NPVL	60563	3142	25W-5S	B2
Tuttle Av					
10	CNHL	60514	3145	17W-5S	C2
Tuttle Ct					
-	ROSL	60172	2913	22W-8N	C2
-	ROSL	60193	2913	22W-8N	C2
Tuttle Dr					
8600	PSHL	60465	3274	10W-13S	A3
Tuttle Pl					
10	CmpT	60175	2906	39W-7N	E6
Tuttle Rd					
11000	SlmT	53179	2356		B1
Tuttle Rd CO-B					
11000	SlmT	53179	2356		B1
Tuxedo Ln					
500	AlqT	60013	2642	29W-25N	C4
500	NndT	60013	2642	29W-25N	C4
Twain Ct					
4600	JLET	60586	3416	29W-20S	D6
Tweed Rd					
10	FXLK	60020	2473	27W-36N	C3
1800	IVNS	60067	2751	23W-17N	E5
Twelve Oaks Pkwy					
800	WDSK	60098	2524	41W-32N	E5
Twickenham Ct					
10	ALGN	60102	2693	38W-21N	A6
Twilight Av					
3100	NPVL	60564	3266	30W-11S	B1
Twilight Dr					
2200	AURA	60503	3201	32W-10S	B6
Twilight Ln					
10	CTCY	60409	3351	2E-16S	C4
100	NLNX	60451	3501	17W-25S	C7
800	WLNG	60090	2755	15W-16N	A6
900	PTHT	60070	2754	15W-16N	E6
900	WLNG	60090	2754	15W-16N	E6
Twilight Tr					
300	SMWD	60107	2857	28W-10N	A6
Twilight Wy					
1200	BGBK	60490	3339	28W-14S	A1
Twilight Pass					
-	BFGV	60089	2701	17W-20N	B7
Twin Dr					
2300	LbvT	60045	2648	13W-27N	D2
2300	MTWA	60045	2648	13W-27N	D2
Twin Ln					
600	AraT	60504	3138	34W-5S	C3
600	AURA	60504	3138	34W-5S	C3
S Twin Creek Ln					
14300	HMGN	60491	3343	18W-17S	A5
Twin Creeks Ct					
200	BGBK	60440	3205	22W-9S	C4
Twin Creeks Dr					
300	BGBK	60440	3205	22W-9S	C4
Twin Eagles Ct					
10	HNWD	60047	2645	22W-27N	B2
Twin Elms Ln					
1000	BTVA	60510	3077	37W-2S	D3
Twin Falls Dr					
2700	JLET	60586	3415	32W-20S	C5
Twin Fountain Ct					
2400	JLET	60586	3415	33W-20S	B6
Twining Av					
4200	BLWD	60104	3029	13W-0N	A4
4600	BLWD	60104	3028	13W-0N	E4
5000	BKLY	60104	3028	13W-0N	E4
5000	BKLY	60163	3028	13W-0N	E4
5000	BLWD	60163	3028	13W-0N	E4
Twin Knolls Dr					
3100	LGGV	60047	2700	18W-21N	D5
W Twin Lakes Blvd					
17800	WrnT	60030	2534	18W-33N	A4
Twin Lakes Ct					
2200	JLET	60586	3416	31W-21S	A6
W Twin Lakes Ct					
14400	GNOK	60048	2592	14W-28N	C5
Twin Lakes Dr					
5500	JLET	60586	3416	30W-21S	A6
11200	ODPK	60467	3422	14W-21S	D7
15500	HMGN	60491	3344	15W-18S	C7
15500	HMGN	60491	3422	15W-18S	C1
E Twin Lakes Dr					
1200	PLTN	60074	2806	19W-15N	C2
Twin Lakes Ln					
4600	LGGV	60047	2700	19W-23N	D1
Twin Lakes Rd					
100	BfdT	53128	2353		B1
100	GNCY	53128	2353		B1
100	RdlT	53128	2353		B1
500	BfdT	53128	2352		E1
Twin Lakes Rd CO-B					
100	BfdT	53128	2353		B1
100	GNCY	53128	2353		B1
100	RdlT	53128	2353		B1
S Twin Oak Ct					
16100	HMGN	60491	3422	16W-19S	A2
Twin Oaks Blvd					
1800	BFGV	60089	2701	17W-22N	B5
Twin Oaks Ct					
1900	BFGV	60089	2701	17W-22N	B5
S Twin Oaks Ct					
13800	HMGN	60491	3342	18W-16S	E3
Twin Oaks Dr					
10	JLET	60431	3497	28W-23S	B5
10	JLET	60435	3497	28W-23S	B5
10	OKBK	60523	3027	16W-1S	E7
10	WnfT	60187	3081	27W-2S	C3
10	WnfT	60555	3081	27W-2S	C3
100	OKBK	60523	3085	16W-1S	E1
500	LKVL	60046	2416	23W-38N	E6
500	LkvT	60046	2416	23W-38N	E6
2800	HDPK	60035	2704	10W-23N	B2
3400	WRLK	60097	2468	38W-35N	E4
3800	WRLK	60097	2469	38W-35N	A5
N Twin Oaks Dr					
37100	WrnT	60046	2476	18W-37N	E3
Twin Oaks Ln					
6300	LSLE	60532	3142	24W-7S	D6
9200	MaiT	60016	2863	11W-11N	D3
Twin Oaks St					
1100	BNVL	60106	2915	16W-6N	D7
Twin Pines Ct					
-	SchT	60175	2963	36W-5N	E1
Twin Pines Dr					
100	WNVL	60555	3080	29W-3S	D5
Twin Pond Rd					
25700	LKBN	60010	2643	27W-25N	C4
Twin Rail Dr					
500	MNKA	60447	3583	34W-28S	A7
Twin Silo Dr					
100	SchT	60175	2907	37W-6N	C7
100	SchT	60175	2963	37W-6N	C1
Twisted Oak Ct					
800	ALGN	60102	2747	34W-20N	C1
3300	MHRY	60050	2528	32W-33N	B2
Twisted Oak Ln					
500	BFGV	60089	2701	17W-20N	B7
700	BFGV	60089	2754	17W-20N	A1
Two Paths Dr					
2900	WDRG	60517	3205	22W-9S	C4
Two River Ct					
200	RMVL	60446	3339	27W-17S	C6
Twyford Rd					
3200	WKGN	60087	2479	11W-37N	D1
Tyburn Dr					
1200	SMBG	60194	2858	25W-10N	C5
Tye Ct					
100	WCHI	60185	3022	29W-0N	C4
Tyler Av					
-	ELGN	60123	2854	35W-12N	B2
700	DYR	46311	3510		D6
2800	WKGN	60087	2479	12W-36N	B3
2900	WkgT	60087	2479	12W-36N	B3
W Tyler Av					
12400	WKGN	60087	2479	12W-36N	B3
12400	WkgT	60087	2479	12W-36N	B3
13400	WrnT	60031	2478	13W-36N	E3
13400	WrnT	60031	2479	13W-36N	A3
13400	WrnT	60087	2479	13W-36N	A3
24300	AvnT	60073	2531	24W-34N	C1
24400	RDLK	60073	2531	24W-34N	C1
Tyler Ct					
10	SMWD	60107	2856	29W-10N	D6
100	LKZH	60047	2698	24W-22N	C3
200	LYVL	60048	2591	16W-28N	D7
400	VNHL	60061	2647	17W-26N	B3
1200	LKVL	60046	2417	22W-39N	C5
2900	WDRG	60517	3143	22W-6S	C5
Tyler Dr					
500	CPVL	60110	2748	32W-17N	C7
1100	SMBG	60193	2913	23W-9N	A1
2000	LYWD	60411	3509	2E-24S	D5
3500	JLET	60431	3417	28W-21S	A7
3500	PnfT	60431	3417	28W-21S	A7
5900	WDRG	60517	3143	22W-6S	C5
20500	BlmT	60411	3509	2E-24S	D5
22400	RNPK	60471	3594	5W-27S	C4
Tyler Ln					
1200	ELGN	60123	2800	34W-13N	E7
Tyler Rd					
-	SCRL	60174	3020	34W-2N	D1
100	SCRL	60174	2964	34W-3N	D6
700	LtRT	60545	3258	50W-11S	C2
10700	PTPR	53158	2362		E1
E Tyler Rd					
1600	SCRL	60174	3020	34W-2N	E1
1900	SCRL	60174	3021	33W-2N	A1
N Tyler Rd					
200	SCRL	60174	2964	34W-3N	D6
S Tyler Rd					
1400	SCRL	60174	3020	34W-2N	E1
1800	GNVA	60134	3020	34W-2N	E2
1800	GNVA	60174	3020	34W-2N	E2
1800	SCRL	60134	3020	34W-2N	E2
Tyler St					
-	EGvT	60007	2861	15W-9N	E7
-	EGVV	60007	2861	15W-9N	E7
500	EGvT	60018	2861	16W-9N	E7
500	EGvT	60018	2862	15W-9N	A7
E Tyler St					
10	OSWG	60543	3263	37W-12S	C4
W Tyler St					
10	OSWG	60543	3263	37W-12S	C4
Tyler Tr					
1600	MchT	60051	2528	31W-33N	D2
1600	MHRY	60051	2528	31W-33N	D3
Tyler Creek Ct					
300	YKVL	60560	3333	44W-15S	A2
Tyler Creek Plz					
10	ELGN	60123	2854	35W-13N	B1
Tyler Creek St					
100	GLBT	60136	2798	39W-16N	E1
Tylerton Cir					
800	GYLK	60030	2532	20W-34N	E2
Tyme Ct					
1100	GRNE	60031	2477	17W-35N	B6
W Tymore Ct					
1100	PLTN	60067	2805	22W-14N	C4
Tyndall Ct					
15500	MhtT	60442	3677	19W-31S	D5
Tyne Ct					
600	IVNS	60010	2751	24W-16N	B6
Tyrell Av					
1400	PKRG	60068	2863	11W-10N	D5
Tyrnbury Dr					
-	LSLE	60532	3142	24W-6S	C5
N Tyrone Pl					
37500	GrtT	60081	2472	28W-37N	D2
Tyrrell Rd					
-	GLBT	60118	2746	38W-17N	A7
-	GLBT	60136	2746	38W-17N	A7
-	RtdT	60118	2746	38W-17N	A7
-	RtdT	60118	2799	38W-17N	B1
-	RtdT	60136	2746	38W-17N	A7
10	GLBT	60136	2799	37W-14N	C5
10	RtdT	60136	2799	38W-16N	B3
500	DndT	60124	2799	37W-14N	C5
500	DndT	60136	2799	37W-14N	C6
500	GLBT	60124	2799	37W-14N	C5
Tyrrell Rd CO-59					
10	GLBT	60136	2799	37W-14N	C5
10	RtdT	60136	2799	38W-16N	B3
200	RtdT	60118	2799	38W-16N	B3
500	DndT	60124	2799	37W-14N	C5
500	DndT	60136	2799	37W-14N	C6
500	GLBT	60124	2799	37W-14N	C5
Tyson Rd					
2200	BDVW	60155	3087	11W-1S	D1
Tzoumar Ln					
-	JLET	60436	3498	26W-24S	A6
U					
Ugland Dr					
3300	JLET	60432	3500	19W-23S	D4
Ullian Av					
1600	JLET	60436	3586	24W-26S	E2
1600	JltT	60436	3586	24W-26S	E2
Ulm Pl					
10	HNDL	60521	3146	15W-5S	B2
Umbdenstock Rd					
10	ELGN	60123	2907	36W-8N	E3
10	ElgT	60123	2907	36W-8N	E4
10	ElgT	60177	2907	36W-8N	E4
10	SEGN	60123	2907	36W-8N	E3

STREET Block	City	ZIP	Map#	CGS	Grid
Umbdenstock Rd					
10	SEGN	60177	2907	36W-8N	E4
Una Av					
300	LMNT	60439	3270	19W-14S	E7
500	LslT	60517	3205	22W-9S	C4
500	LslT	60565	3205	22W-9S	C4
500	WDRG	60517	3205	22W-9S	C4
500	WDRG	60565	3205	22W-9S	C4
Uncas Ln					
400	CmpT	60119	2961	43W-4N	B4
Underhill Ct					
9000	LKWD	60014	2639	37W-24N	A6
Underwood Dr					
10	BbyT	60134	3018	39W-0S	E6
Underwood Pl					
900	HIWD	60040	2704	9W-23N	C3
1000	HDPK	60035	2704	9W-23N	B3
Underwood Ter					
1100	WHTN	60187	3082	24W-1S	D1
Union Av					
10	BTVA	60510	3078	35W-1S	B2
400	SCRL	60174	3020	34W-2N	D2
600	BRLT	60103	2910	29W-7N	C4
700	RMVL	60446	3340	24W-15S	C2
1000	CHHT	60411	3508	0W-25S	B7
1500	CHHT	60411	3596	0W-25S	B1
1600	BGBK	60490	3267	26W-13S	D6
2500	BlmT	60411	3596	0W-26S	B2
3000	SCHT	60411	3596	0W-27S	B4
3000	STGR	60411	3596	0W-27S	B4
3000	STGR	60475	3596	1W-28S	B6
3600	CRTE	60417	3596	1W-28S	B6
3700	STGR	60417	3596	1W-28S	B7
13700	RVDL	60827	3350	1W-15S	A2
14400	HRVY	60426	3350	1W-17S	A5
15600	HRVY	60426	3428	0W-19S	B2
19300	MKNA	60448	3503	13W-23S	A3
E Union Av					
100	WHTN	60187	3024	24W-0S	D6
N Union Av					
200	CHCG	60661	3034	0W-0N	A4
400	CHCG	60610	3034	0W-0N	A3
S Union Av					
1200	CHCG	60607	3034	0W-1S	A7
1400	CHCG	60616	3034	0W-1S	A7
1700	CHCG	60616	3092	0W-1S	A1
3400	CHCG	60609	3092	0W-4S	A7
4700	CHCG	60609	3152	0W-6S	A3
5500	CHCG	60621	3152	0W-6S	A3
7500	CHCG	60620	3214	0W-8S	A1
7500	CHCG	60621	3214	0W-8S	A1
9400	CHCG	60628	3214	0W-11S	A6
10300	CHCG	60628	3278	0W-13S	A3
14200	ODPK	60462	3345	12W-16S	C4
14200	RVDL	60827	3350	1W-16S	A4
14500	HRVY	60426	3350	1W-16S	A4
14500	HRVY	60827	3350	1W-16S	A4
W Union Av					
500	WHTN	60187	3024	25W-0S	B6
Union Cir					
10	WHTN	60187	3024	25W-0S	B6
400	EGVV	60007	2913	21W-9N	D1
Union Ct					
700	ELGN	60123	2854	34W-10N	D5
1000	BRLT	60103	2910	30W-7N	C4
1200	WLNG	60090	2754	16W-18N	D2
2500	LGGV	60047	2700	19W-20N	C7
N Union Ct					
100	PNFD	60544	3416	29W-18S	C1
Union Dr					
700	UYPK	60466	3684	3W-30S	C3
N Union Rd					
-	GfnT	60142	2638	40W-25N	A6
4700	SenT	60180	2635	46W-26N	D3
5100	UNON	60180	2635	46W-26N	D3
N Union Rd CO-T65					
4700	SenT	60180	2635	46W-26N	D3
5100	UNON	60180	2635	46W-26N	D3
S Union Rd					
6600	CrlT	60180	2635	46W-24N	C6
6600	UNON	60180	2635	46W-24N	C6
7900	GfnT	60142	2691	41W-22N	E3
7900	HTLY	60142	2691	41W-22N	E3
10000	HTLY	60142	2692	40W-22N	A5
S Union Rd CO-T65					
6600	CrlT	60180	2635	46W-24N	C6
6600	UNON	60180	2635	46W-24N	C6
W Union Rd					
-	UNON	60180	2635	47W-25N	C4
18700	CrlT	60152	2635	47W-25N	A4
18700	CrlT	60180	2635	47W-25N	A4
W Union Rd CO-A42					
-	UNON	60180	2635	47W-25N	C4
18700	CrlT	60152	2635	47W-25N	A4
18700	CrlT	60180	2635	47W-25N	A4
W Union Rd CO-T65					
-	CrlT	60180	2635	46W-25N	C4
-	UNON	60180	2635	46W-25N	C4
Union St					
-	WDRG	60517	3206	20W-10S	A5
10	CLLK	60014	2640	35W-25N	A5
10	FXLK	60020	2472	28W-36N	E4
100	GLBT	60136	2799	39W-16N	A1
200	CLLK	60014	2639	35W-25N	E5
400	GNVA	60134	3020	35W-1N	B2
1800	BLID	60827	3277	2W-15S	C7
1800	CTPK	60406	3277	2W-15S	C7
1800	CTPK	60827	3277	2W-15S	C7
2200	BLID	60406	3277	3W-15S	A7
10000	HBRN	60034	2351	40W-41N	A7
19500	MKNA	60448	3503	13W-23S	A3
N Union St					
10	AURA	60505	3200	35W-7S	C1
10	ELGN	60123	2854	34W-11N	D4
100	AURA	60505	3138	34W-7S	C7
S Union St					
10	AURA	60505	3200	35W-9S	C3
10	ELGN	60123	2854	34W-11N	D4
10	JLET	60432	3499	23W-24S	A5
10	JLET	60433	3499	23W-24S	A5
1000	AraT	60505	3200	35W-9S	C4
1200	MTGY	60505	3200	35W-9S	C4
1200	MTGY	60538	3200	35W-9S	C4
W Union St					
300	PNFD	60544	3416	29W-18S	C1
Union Mill Dr					
2000	AURA	60503	3201	31W-10S	E6
Union Pacific Dr					
-	GYLK	60030	2532	21W-32N	E5
Union Special Plz					
10	HTLY	60142	2691	40W-21N	E6
Unit Ct					
5700	HRPK	60133	2911	26W-7N	E5
United Dr					
-	MTGY	60506	3198	38W-9S	E3
-	MTGY	60538	3198	38W-9S	E3
United Dr					
-	MTGY	60538	3199	38W-9S	A3
United Ln					
2300	EGVV	60007	2915	16W-7N	E4
United Pkwy					
4100	SRPK	60176	2973	13W-5N	A1
Unity Ct					
-	SRWD	60404	3495	31W-24S	E6
University Av					
800	MTSN	60443	3506	5W-25S	C7
2100	WKGN	60085	2479	11W-34N	C7
3000	HDPK	60035	2704	9W-23N	B1
3200	WkgT	60085	2479	12W-33N	A7
3400	GRNE	60031	2479	13W-34N	A7
3400	HDPK	60035	2650	9W-24N	B7
3500	LKFT	60045	2650	9W-24N	B7
3800	GRNE	60031	2478	13W-34N	E7
14200	DLTN	60419	3351	1E-16S	B4
15400	DLTN	60473	3351	1E-18S	B7
15400	SHLD	60419	3351	1E-18S	B7
15400	SHLD	60473	3351	1E-18S	B7
16000	SHLD	60473	3429	1E-18S	B1
S University Av					
200	GNWD	60425	3509	1E-23S	A3
4400	CHCG	60653	3093	1E-4S	A7
5100	CHCG	60615	3153	1E-6S	A3
5500	CHCG	60637	3153	1E-6S	A3
7100	CHCG	60619	3153	1E-8S	A7
8000	CHCG	60619	3215	1E-9S	A2
9500	CHCG	60628	3215	1E-11S	A6
University Cir					
-	NCHI	60088	2593	11W-30N	D2
10	HNWD	60047	2645	20W-24N	E6
10	HNWD	60047	2646	20W-25N	A6
University Cross					
-	MonT	60449	3594	6W-29S	A7
-	MonT	60449	3683	6W-29S	A1
University Ct					
-	FSMR	60422	3507	2W-23S	D4
10	BFGV	60089	2754	16W-17N	D5
2300	NPVL	60565	3204	25W-10S	C5
16400	SHLD	60473	3429	1E-19S	A2
University Dr					
-	LYVL	60048	2591	18W-28N	A6
-	MDLN	60060	2590	18W-28N	E6
-	MDLN	60060	2591	18W-28N	A6
10	ANHT	60004	2754	16W-17N	C5
10	BFGV	60089	2754	16W-17N	C5
100	FmtT	60060	2646	19W-26N	C2
200	MPPT	60056	2808	14W-13N	B5
200	MPPT	60056	2862	15W-12N	A1
2000	NPVL	60565	3204	24W-10S	C5
9000	MNSR	46321	3510		E1
E University Dr					
10	ANHT	60004	2754	17W-17N	A5
900	BFGV	60004	2754	17W-17N	B5
900	BFGV	60089	2754	17W-17N	B5
W University Dr					
10	ANHT	60004	2754	18W-17N	A5
300	ANHT	60004	2753	18W-17N	E5
University Dr E					
-	RMVL	60441	3419	23W-18S	A1
100	RMVL	60441	3341	23W-18S	A7
University Dr N					
-	RMVL	60441	3341	23W-18S	A7
University Dr S					
-	RMVL	60441	3419	23W-18S	A1
100	RMVL	60441	3418	24W-18S	E1
University Dr W					
-	RMVL	60441	3419	23W-18S	A1
300	RMVL	60441	3341	23W-18S	A7
University Ln					
200	EGVV	60007	2859	22W-9N	C7
200	SMBG	60007	2859	22W-9N	C7
200	SMBG	60193	2859	22W-9N	C7
1900	LSLE	60532	3142	23W-5S	E3
W University Ln					
800	CHCG	60607	3034		E7
800	CHCG	60608	3034		E7
University Pkwy					
-	PKFT	60466	3594	5W-29S	C7
10	RMVL	60441	3341	23W-18S	A7
400	CteT	60417	3684	3W-29S	C2
400	MonT	60466	3684	3W-29S	B1
400	UYPK	60417	3684	3W-29S	C2
400	UYPK	60466	3684	3W-29S	B1
1100	MonT	60417	3684	3W-29S	B1
4400	MonT	60417	3594	5W-28S	D7
4400	UYPK	60466	3594	5W-28S	B7
4500	MonT	60466	3594	5W-28S	B7
4600	MonT	60449	3594	5W-28S	B7
4600	UYPK	60449	3594	5W-28S	B7
4800	MonT	60449	3593	6W-28S	E7
4800	UYPK	60449	3593	6W-28S	E7
24000	MonT	60417	3683	5W-29S	D1
24000	MonT	60466	3683	5W-29S	D1
24000	UYPK	60417	3683	5W-29S	D1
24000	UYPK	60466	3683	5W-29S	D1
W University Pkwy					
3300	MonT	60417	3683	4W-29S	E1
3300	MonT	60417	3684	4W-29S	A1
3300	MonT	60466	3683	4W-29S	E1
3300	MonT	60466	3684	4W-29S	A1
3300	UYPK	60466	3683	4W-29S	E1
3600	UYPK	60417	3683	4W-29S	E1
University Pl					
600	EVTN	60201	2867	2W-11N	B2
700	WHTN	60187	3024	24W-0S	D6
University St					
100	CLLK	60014	2640	35W-25N	A4
700	HRVD	60033	2406	49W-38N	C6
2200	CTHL	60403	3417	26W-21S	D6
2200	DSPN	60016	2863	12W-11N	C3
2200	MaiT	60016	2863	12W-11N	C2
University Center Dr					
1200	GYLK	60030	2533	19W-34N	C2
Uno Cir					
10	JLET	60435	3497	26W-23S	E5
Upland Dr					
-	TYPK	60487	3423	11W-21S	E6
17900	OrlT	60487	3423	11W-21S	E6
E Upland Dr					
4600	NndT	60012	2640	35W-27N	A1
W Upland Dr					
4700	CLLK	60012	2639	35W-27N	E1
4700	NndT	60012	2639	35W-27N	E1
Upper Dr					
-	WLMT	60091	2813	2W-13N	B5
Upper Brandon Dr					
800	AURA	60506	3137	36W-5S	D4
N Upper Columbus Dr					
-	CHCG	60603	3034	0E-0N	C4
100	CHCG	60601	3034	0E-0N	C4
Upper Express Dr					
-	CHCG	60018	2916	13W-8N	D1
Upper Pond Rd					
10	SBTN	60010	2803	27W-14N	B3
Ups Wy					
-	HGKN	60525	3209	13W-8S	B1
10	WLSP	60525	3209	13W-8S	A1
Upton Rd					
-	BGBK	60440	3269	21W-11S	E2
Upton on Asbury					
10	RGMW	60008	2806	19W-15N	B3
S Urban Av					
9100	CHCG	60619	3214	0E-10S	C5
Ursula Dr					
10800	WLSP	60480	3208	13W-9S	E4
10800	WLSP	60480	3209	13W-9S	A4
Ursuline Av					
500	LslT	60565	3204	25W-9S	B3
500	NPVL	60565	3204	25W-9S	B3
US-6					
-	AxST	60410	3672	34W-30S	A5
-	CNHN	60410	3672	34W-30S	A5
-	JLET	60433	3499	23W-24S	A5
-	JLET	60436	3499	23W-24S	A5
-	MNKA	60447	3672	34W-30S	A5
US-6 159th St					
-	SHLD	60409	3429	1E-19S	C1
-	SHLD	60473	3429	1E-19S	C1
1400	CTCY	60409	3429	2E-18S	E1
4700	BmnT	60426	3426	5W-18S	B1
4700	BmnT	60452	3426	5W-18S	A1
4700	OKFT	60426	3426	5W-18S	B1
4700	OKFT	60452	3426	5W-18S	B1
5100	OKFT	60452	3425	7W-19S	C1
5400	BmnT	60452	3425	6W-18S	D1
5400	BmnT	60477	3425	6W-18S	D1
6400	TYPK	60477	3425	8W-19S	B1
6700	TYPK	60452	3425	8W-19S	A1
6900	ODPK	60462	3425	8W-19S	A1
6900	ODPK	60477	3425	8W-19S	A1
US-6 E 159th St					
10	HRVY	60426	3427	1W-18S	E1
100	HRVY	60426	3428	1W-18S	A1
300	HRVY	60473	3428	0W-18S	B1
300	SHLD	60426	3428	0W-18S	B1
300	SHLD	60473	3428	0W-18S	B1
US-6 W 159th St					
-	OKFT	60426	3426	5W-18S	B1
-	OKFT	60452	3426	5W-18S	B1
10	HRVY	60426	3427	2W-18S	E1
200	HRVY	60428	3427	2W-18S	C1
200	MKHM	60428	3427	2W-19S	C1
200	ThtT	60428	3427	2W-18S	C1
2300	BmnT	60428	3427	2W-19S	C1
2300	MKHM	60426	3427	2W-19S	C1
3300	MKHM	60428	3426	4W-19S	E1
3800	BmnT	60426	3426	4W-19S	E1
3800	MKHM	60426	3426	4W-19S	E1
7000	ODPK	60462	3425	8W-19S	A1
7000	ODPK	60477	3425	8W-19S	A1
7000	TYPK	60477	3425	8W-19S	A1
7100	ODPK	60462	3424	11W-19S	A1
7100	TYPK	60477	3424	11W-19S	A1
7200	ODPK	60477	3424	9W-19S	E1
7600	TYPK	60462	3424	9W-18S	D1
8000	TYPK	60487	3424	10W-19S	B1
8700	ODHL	60462	3424	10W-19S	A1
8700	ODHL	60487	3424	10W-19S	A1
8700	ODPK	60487	3424	10W-19S	A1
9100	ODHL	60487	3423	11W-19S	E1
9100	ODPK	60462	3423	11W-19S	E1
9200	ODHL	60462	3423	11W-19S	E1
9300	ODPK	60467	3423	11W-19S	E1
9900	OrlT	60462	3423	12W-18S	C1
9900	OrlT	60467	3423	12W-18S	C1
10800	ODPK	60467	3422	13W-18S	E1
10800	OrlT	60467	3422	13W-18S	E1
US-6 E 162nd St					
10	SHLD	60473	3428	0E-19S	D1
700	SHLD	60473	3429	0E-18S	A1
US-6 W 162nd St					
10	SHLD	60473	3428	0E-19S	E1
500	HRVY	60426	3428	0W-18S	B1
500	HRVY	60473	3428	0W-18S	B1
500	SHLD	60426	3428	0W-18S	B1
US-6 Borman Expwy					
-	HMND		3430		D5
-	LNSG		3430		D5
-	MNSR		3430		D5
US-6 E Cass St					
10	JLET	60432	3499	23W-23S	A4
US-6 Channahon Rd					
-	JltT	60436	3498	25W-25S	C7
-	RKDL	60436	3498	25W-25S	C7
1200	JltT	60436	3586	26W-25S	A2
1600	JLET	60436	3585	28W-27S	B4
1600	JltT	60436	3585	28W-27S	B4
1600	RKDL	60436	3586	25W-25S	B1
3200	TroT	60436	3585	28W-26S	B3
3400	JLET	60410	3585	28W-27S	B4
US-6 S Chicago St					
-	JLET	60432	3499	23W-23S	A5
-	JLET	60436	3498	24W-24S	E5
10	JLET	60433	3499	23W-24S	A5
10	JLET	60436	3499	23W-24S	A5
US-6 N Collins St					
10	JLET	60432	3499	23W-23S	A5
US-6 W Eames St					
22000	CNHN	60410	3585	28W-27S	A5
22000	JLET	60410	3585	28W-27S	A5
23000	CnhT	60410	3585	28W-27S	A5
23200	CNHN	60410	3584	29W-28S	D7
23200	CnhT	60410	3584	29W-28S	D7
23200	JLET	60410	3584	29W-28S	D7
25300	CNHN	60410	3672	31W-30S	E4
25800	CnhT	60410	3672	32W-30S	D5
26100	AxST	60447	3672	32W-30S	C5
26100	CNHN	60447	3672	32W-30S	C5
27100	AxST	60410	3672	33W-30S	A5
27100	MNKA	60447	3672	33W-30S	A5
US-6 E Jackson St					
400	JLET	60432	3499	23W-23S	B4
US-6 E Jefferson St					
10	JLET	60432	3499	23W-23S	A5
US-6 Kingery Expwy					
-	LNSG		3429	3E-20S	E4
-	LNSG		3430	3E-20S	A4
-	MNSR		3430	4E-20S	C4
US-6 Maple Rd					
200	NLNX	60451	3500	19W-22S	D1
200	NLNX	60451	3501	18W-22S	A1
200	NlxT	60448	3501	18W-22S	B1
200	NlxT	60451	3501	18W-22S	B1
400	JLET	60432	3499	22W-23S	C3
400	JltT	60432	3499	23W-23S	B4
1300	JLET	60441	3500	19W-22S	D1
1300	JLET	60451	3500	19W-22S	D1
1300	NLNX	60441	3500	19W-22S	D1
US-6 Maple Rd					
1300	NlxT	60441	3500	19W-22S	D1
1300	NlxT	60451	3500	19W-22S	D1
2000	JLET	60432	3500	21W-22S	A2
2000	JltT	60432	3500	21W-22S	A2
15800	NlxT	60432	3500	19W-22S	C1
US-6 W McDonough St					
10	JLET	60436	3498	24W-24S	E6
US-6 N Ottawa St					
10	JLET	60432	3498	24W-23S	E5
10	JLET	60436	3498	24W-23S	E5
US-6 S Ottawa St					
10	JLET	60432	3498	24W-23S	E5
10	JLET	60436	3498	24W-24S	E5
US-6 Railroad St					
400	JLET	60436	3498	24W-25S	D7
600	JltT	60436	3498	24W-24S	D7
700	RKDL	60436	3498	25W-25S	C7
US-6 N Scott St					
10	JLET	60432	3499	23W-23S	A5
10	JLET	60433	3499	23W-23S	A5
US-6 Southwest Hwy					
-	HMGN	60448	3422	15W-21S	C7
-	NlxT	60448	3422	15W-21S	C7
11300	ODPK	60467	3422	14W-21S	E5
13000	NlxT	60448	3502	15W-22S	B1
13100	NlxT	60448	3501	17W-22S	D1
14000	NLNX	60451	3501	17W-22S	B1
14000	NlxT	60451	3501	17W-22S	C1
17700	OrlT	60467	3422	14W-21S	D6
17900	HMGN	60491	3422	14W-21S	C7
US-6 Torrence Av					
1100	CTCY	60409	3429	3E-19S	E3
1400	CTCY	60438	3429	3E-19S	E3
1400	LNSG	60409	3429	3E-19S	E2
1400	LNSG	60438	3429	3E-19S	E3
US-6 E Washington St					
10	JLET	60432	3499	23W-23S	A5
10	JLET	60433	3499	23W-23S	A5
10	JLET	60436	3499	23W-23S	A5
US-6 Wolf Rd					
15900	ODPK	60467	3422	13W-19S	E1
15900	OrlT	60467	3422	13W-19S	E1
US-12					
-	BfdT		2353		B1
-	BtnT	60050	2472	29W-38N	C1
-	BtnT	60081	2414	29W-38N	C6
-	BtnT	60081	2472	29W-38N	C1
-	FXLK	60020	2472	28W-37N	E2
-	FXLK	60020	2473	28W-36N	A3
-	FXLK	60041	2473	27W-34N	B7
-	FXLK	60041	2530	27W-34N	B1
-	GNCY	-	2353		B1
-	GNCY	60071	2353		C4
-	GrtT	60020	2473	27W-34N	B7
-	GrtT	60041	2473	27W-35N	B7
-	GrtT	60041	2530	27W-34N	B1
-	GrtT	60073	2530	27W-32N	B5
-	GrtT	60081	2472	29W-37N	D1
-	LKMR	60041	2530	27W-32N	B5
-	LKMR	60073	2530	27W-31N	C7
-	MchT	60050	2472	29W-38N	D1
-	MchT	60081	2472	29W-37N	D1
-	RcmT	53128	2353		C4
-	RcmT	60071	2353		C4
-	RHMD	60071	2353		C4
-	SPGV	60050	2414	29W-38N	C7
-	SPGV	60050	2472	29W-38N	C1
-	SPGV	60081	2413	32W-39N	B5
-	SPGV	60081	2414	29W-38N	C7
-	SPGV	60081	2472	29W-38N	C1
-	VOLO	60041	2530	27W-32N	B5
-	VOLO	60073	2530	27W-32N	B5
-	VOLO	60073	2587	27W-31N	C1
-	WCDA	60073	2587	27W-29N	C3
-	WCDA	60084	2587	27W-29N	C3
-	WcnT	60073	2530	27W-31N	C7
-	WcnT	60073	2587	27W-31N	C1
-	WcnT	60084	2587	27W-29N	C3
4100	RcmT	60071	2413	33W-40N	A4
4100	RcmT	60081	2413	32W-39N	A4
4300	RcmT	60071	2412	34W-40N	D3
4300	RHMD	60071	2412	34W-40N	D3
US-12 95th St					
-	HYHL	60457	3209	11W-10S	E6
-	PlsT	60457	3209	11W-10S	E6
-	PlsT	60465	3209	11W-10S	E6
-	PlsT	60480	3209	11W-10S	E6
-	PSHL	60457	3209	11W-10S	E6
-	PSHL	60465	3209	11W-10S	E6
US-12 E 95th St					
10	CHCG	60619	3214	0E-10S	C6
10	CHCG	60620	3214	0E-10S	C6
10	CHCG	60628	3214	0E-10S	C6
900	CHCG	60619	3215	1E-10S	A5
900	CHCG	60628	3215	1E-10S	A5
1500	CHCG	60617	3215	1E-10S	B5
3000	CHCG	60617	3216	3E-11S	A5
US-12 W 95th St					
-	BGVW	60453	3210	8W-10S	E6
-	BGVW	60455	3210	8W-10S	E6
-	BGVW	60457	3210	9W-11S	D6
-	CHCG	60619	3214	0W-10S	C6
-	HYHL	60455	3210	9W-11S	D6
-	OKLN	60453	3210	8W-10S	E6
-	OKLN	60455	3210	8W-10S	E6
10	CHCG	60620	3214	0W-10S	C6
10	CHCG	60628	3214	0W-11S	C6
700	CHCG	60643	3214	0W-10S	A6
1000	CHCG	60620	3213	1W-10S	E6
2300	CHCG	60805	3213	2W-10S	B6
2300	ENGN	60805	3213	2W-10S	B6
2400	CHCG	60643	3213	3W-10S	B6
2900	ENGN	60805	3212	3W-10S	E6
3900	ENGN	60453	3212	4W-10S	C6
3900	OKLN	60453	3212	4W-10S	C6
4900	OKLN	60453	3211	6W-10S	E6
6300	CHRG	60415	3211	7W-10S	B6
6300	CHRG	60453	3211	7W-10S	B6
6300	OKLN	60415	3211	7W-10S	B6
7600	HYHL	60457	3210	9W-11S	D6
8700	HYHL	60465	3210	10W-10S	A6
8700	PSHL	60457	3210	10W-10S	A6
8700	PSHL	60465	3210	10W-10S	A6
8900	HYHL	60457	3209	11W-10S	E6
8900	HYHL	60465	3209	11W-10S	E6
8900	PSHL	60465	3209	11W-10S	E6
9000	PlsT	60457	3209	11W-10S	E6
9000	PlsT	60465	3209	11W-10S	E6
9000	PlsT	60480	3209	11W-10S	E6
9000	PSHL	60457	3209	11W-10S	E6
US-12 S Ewing Av					
9500	CHCG	60617	3216	4E-10S	B5
US-12 Graceland Av					
800	DSPN	60016	2862	13W-10N	E4
US-12 S Indianapolis Av					
-	CHCG	60617	3280	4E-11S	C1
-	HMND	60617	3280	4E-11S	C1
10000	CHCG	60617	3216	4E-11S	B7
10600	HMND	46320	3280	4E-11S	C1
US-12 S Indianapolis Blvd					
1000	HMND	46320	3280		D3
1000	HMND	46394	3280		E4
10500	CHCG	60617	3280		C1
10500	HMND	60617	3280	4E-11S	C1
US-12 La Grange Rd					
-	LynT	60458	3209	11W-8S	D2
-	LynT	60480	3209	11W-9S	D3
-	LynT	60525	3209	11W-8S	D2
-	PlsT	60480	3209	11W-9S	D4
-	WLSP	60458	3209	11W-9S	D2
-	WLSP	60480	3209	11W-8S	D2
-	WLSP	60525	3209	12W-8S	D1
US-12 N La Grange Rd					
-	PvsT	60154	3087	12W-2S	A2
-	WSTR	60154	3087	12W-2S	A2
10	LGNG	60525	3087	12W-4S	C6
100	LGPK	60525	3087	12W-4S	C6
1000	PvsT	60525	3087	12W-3S	B4
US-12 S La Grange Rd					
-	CTSD	60525	3147	12W-8S	C7
-	HGKN	60525	3209	12W-8S	C1
-	WLSP	60525	3209	12W-8S	C1
10	LGNG	60525	3087	12W-4S	C7
300	LGNG	60525	3147	12W-4S	C1
6000	HGKN	60525	3147	12W-6S	C5
US-12 N Main St					
8600	RcmT	60071	2412	34W-40N	C3
8600	RHMD	60071	2412	34W-41N	C1
9700	RHMD	60071	2353	34W-41N	C7
11200	RcmT	60071	2353	34W-43N	C5
11500	GNCY	53128	2353	34W-43N	C4
11500	GNCY	60071	2353	34W-43N	C4
11500	RcmT	53128	2353	34W-43N	C4
US-12 Mannheim Rd					
-	CHCG	60176	2917	12W-6N	B6
-	CHCG	60666	2973	12W-5N	B1
-	DSPN	60016	2863	13W-11N	A3
-	SRPK	60176	2917	12W-6N	B6
10	BLWD	60104	3029	12W-0N	A3
10	BLWD	60160	3029	12W-1N	A3
10	MLPK	60160	3029	12W-1N	A3
500	BLWD	60162	3029	12W-0N	A4
500	HLSD	60162	3029	12W-0N	A4
1000	DSPN	60016	2862	13W-10N	E5
1000	DSPN	60018	2862	13W-10N	E5
1700	DSPN	60018	2863	13W-9N	A6
2000	DSPN	60018	2917	13W-9N	A1
2000	RSMT	60018	2917	13W-9N	A1
2400	FNPK	60131	2973	13W-3N	A6
2400	LydT	60131	2973	13W-3N	A6
2400	LydT	60164	2973	13W-3N	A6
2600	FNPK	60164	2973	13W-3N	A5
2900	CHCG	60018	2917	12W-8N	A2
3700	FNPK	60176	2973	13W-4N	A3
3700	SRPK	60131	2973	13W-4N	A3
3700	SRPK	60176	2973	13W-4N	A3
6400	CHCG	60666	2917	12W-8N	A3
6400	RSMT	60666	2917	12W-8N	A3
US-12 N Mannheim Rd					
-	BLWD	60104	3029	12W-1N	A3
-	BLWD	60160	3029	12W-1N	A3
-	HLSD	60154	3029	12W-0S	A6
-	WSTR	60154	3029	12W-0S	A6
10	HLSD	60104	3029	12W-0S	A6
10	HLSD	60162	3029	12W-0S	A6
100	BLWD	60162	3029	12W-0S	A5
1500	MLPK	60160	3029	12W-1N	A2
1500	SNPK	60160	3029	12W-1N	A2
1500	SNPK	60165	3029	12W-1N	A2
1800	MLPK	60164	3029	12W-1N	A1
1800	MLPK	60165	3029	12W-1N	A1
1800	SNPK	60164	3029	12W-1N	A1
2000	LydT	60160	2973	12W-2N	A7
2000	LydT	60164	2973	12W-2N	A7
2000	MLPK	60160	2973	12W-2N	A7
2000	NHLK	60160	2973	12W-2N	A7
2000	NHLK	60164	2973	12W-2N	A7
2300	LydT	60131	2973	12W-2N	A6
US-12 S Mannheim Rd					
-	BLWD	60104	3029	12W-0S	A6
-	HLSD	60104	3029	12W-0S	A6
10	HLSD	60154	3029	12W-0S	A6
10	HLSD	60162	3029	12W-0S	A6
10	WSTR	60154	3029	12W-0S	A6
100	WSTR	60162	3029	12W-0S	A7
300	PvsT	60162	3029	12W-0S	A7
1400	PvsT	60162	3087	12W-1S	A1
1400	WSTR	60154	3087	12W-1S	A1
1400	WSTR	60162	3087	12W-1S	A1
2100	PvsT	60154	3087	12W-1S	A2
2100	PvsT	60525	3087	12W-1S	A2
US-12 Rand Rd					
10	DRPK	60010	2699	22W-21N	B7
10	DRPK	60047	2699	22W-21N	B7
10	DSPN	60016	2808	14W-12N	C7
10	KLDR	60010	2699	22W-21N	B7
10	KLDR	60047	2699	22W-21N	B7
10	LKZH	60010	2699	22W-21N	B6
10	MPPT	60016	2808	14W-12N	C7
10	MPPT	60056	2808	14W-12N	B7
300	DSPN	60016	2862	13W-11N	E2
300	LKZH	60047	2699	22W-21N	B6
600	DRPK	60074	2699	21W-20N	C7
600	DRPK	60074	2752	21W-20N	D1
600	ElaT	60047	2699	21W-20N	C7
600	ElaT	60074	2699	21W-20N	D7
600	ElaT	60074	2752	21W-20N	D1
600	KLDR	60074	2699	21W-20N	C7
1200	DSPN	60016	2863	13W-11N	A2
2000	PLTN	60074	2753	20W-18N	A3
US-12 E Rand Rd					
10	ANHT	60004	2754	17W-16N	A7
10	MPPT	60056	2808	15W-13N	A5
200	ANHT	60004	2807	15W-13N	E4
900	DSPN	60016	2808	14W-13N	B7
900	MPPT	60016	2808	14W-13N	B7
1200	PTHT	60004	2807	17W-15N	C2
2400	MPPT	60004	2807	16W-14N	D3
2400	MPPT	60056	2807	16W-14N	D3
2400	WhlT	60004	2807	16W-14N	D3
2500	ANHT	60004	2807	16W-14N	E6
US-12 N Rand Rd					
-	WcnT	60073	2587	27W-29N	C4
10	LKZH	60047	2698	24W-23N	C2
200	WCDA	60084	2643	26W-26N	D2
200	WcnT	60084	2643	26W-26N	D2
600	WCDA	60084	2587	27W-30N	C1
700	ElaT	60010	2698	24W-23N	C1
700	ElaT	60047	2698	24W-23N	C1
800	WcnT	60084	2587	26W-28N	D6

STREET Block	City	ZIP	Map#	CGS	Grid
US-12 N Rand Rd					
900	ElaT	60047	2644	24W-24N	C7
900	NBRN	60047	2644	24W-24N	C7
1200	PLTN	60074	2753	20W-18N	B3
2100	PltT	60074	2753	20W-18N	A2
2300	DRPK	60074	2752	20W-18N	E2
2300	ElaT	60074	2752	20W-18N	E2
2300	PltT	60074	2752	20W-18N	E2
20200	KLDR	60074	2752	21W-20N	E1
20400	KLDR	60047	2752	21W-20N	D1
24000	ElaT	60010	2644	24W-24N	C7
24000	NBRN	60010	2644	24W-24N	C7
24200	HNWD	60047	2644	24W-24N	C7
24200	LKZH	60047	2644	24W-24N	C7
25800	ElaT	60084	2644	24W-25N	C4
25900	FmtT	60084	2644	24W-26N	B4
25900	WcnT	60010	2644	25W-26N	B3
25900	WcnT	60084	2644	24W-26N	B3
29000	WCDA	60073	2587	26W-29N	C5
US-12 S Rand Rd					
10	LKZH	60047	2698	23W-22N	E5
400	WCDA	60084	2643	26W-27N	D1
900	LKZH	60047	2699	21W-20N	C7
1100	KLDR	60047	2699	22W-21N	A5
1100	LKZH	60010	2699	22W-21N	B6
26400	WCDA	60084	2644	25W-26N	A3
26400	WcnT	60010	2644	25W-26N	A3
26400	WcnT	60084	2644	25W-26N	A3
26500	WcnT	60084	2643	25W-26N	E3
US-12 W Rand Rd					
-	ANHT	60074	2753	19W-17N	D5
-	PltT	60074	2753	19W-17N	D5
10	ANHT	60004	2754	17W-16N	A7
10	MPPT	60056	2808	15W-13N	B6
300	MPPT	60056	2807	15W-14N	E4
400	ANHT	60004	2753	18W-17N	D6
600	ANHT	60056	2807	15W-14N	E4
700	ANHT	60004	2807	16W-14N	E4
700	MPPT	60004	2807	16W-14N	E4
1200	PltT	60004	2753	18W-17N	D6
US-12 S River Rd					
-	DSPN	60016	2863	13W-11N	A3
US-14					
-	CmgT	60033	2406	50W-39N	B5
-	DhmT	60033	2464	50W-36N	B3
-	HRVD	60033	2406	49W-40N	C3
-	HRVD	60033	2464	50W-36N	B3
-	HtdT	60033	2464	48W-35N	E5
-	SenT	60098	2581	43W-30N	A1
7600	CLLK	60014	2639	36W-26N	D3
7600	NndT	60012	2639	36W-26N	D3
7800	CLLK	60012	2639	36W-26N	C2
7900	DrrT	60012	2639	37W-26N	C2
7900	DrrT	60014	2639	37W-26N	C2
US-14 N Broadway St					
5200	CHCG	60640	2921	1W-6N	D5
5500	CHCG	60660	2921	1W-6N	D4
US-14 Caldwell Av					
7900	MNGV	60053	2864	8W-10N	E4
7900	NLES	60714	2864	8W-10N	E4
US-14 N Caldwell Av					
-	NLES	60053	2865	8W-9N	A6
6000	CHCG	60646	2919	6W-7N	D3
6800	CHCG	60714	2919	7W-8N	B1
6800	NLES	60714	2919	7W-8N	B1
7200	CHCG	60646	2865	8W-9N	A7
7200	CHCG	60714	2865	8W-9N	A7
7200	NLES	60646	2865	8W-9N	A7
7200	NLES	60714	2865	8W-9N	A6
7900	MNGV	60053	2865	8W-9N	A6
7900	MNGV	60714	2865	8W-9N	A6
8000	MNGV	60053	2864	8W-10N	E5
8000	MNGV	60714	2864	8W-10N	E5
8000	NLES	60714	2864	8W-10N	E5
US-14 Crystal St					
10	CRY	60013	2695	31W-23N	E1
US-14 Dempster St					
-	DSPN	60068	2863	12W-10N	C4
1200	NLES	60714	2863	10W-10N	E4
1200	PKRG	60068	2863	10W-10N	E4
1200	PKRG	60068	2864	10W-10N	A4
1200	PKRG	60714	2863	10W-10N	E4
1200	PKRG	60714	2864	10W-10N	A4
1500	NLES	60068	2863	11W-11N	E4
2000	MaiT	60016	2863	11W-11N	D4
2000	PKRG	60016	2863	11W-11N	D4
2300	DSPN	60016	2863	12W-10N	C4
6900	MNGV	60053	2864	8W-10N	E4
7000	NLES	60053	2864	8W-10N	E4
7000	NLES	60714	2864	8W-10N	E4
US-14 W Dempster St					
7000	MNGV	60053	2864	8W-11N	E4
7000	NLES	60053	2864	8W-11N	E4
7000	NLES	60714	2864	8W-11N	E4
7100	MNGV	60714	2864	8W-11N	D4
8500	PKRG	60068	2864	10W-10N	A4
8500	PKRG	60714	2864	10W-10N	A4
US-14 N Division St					
100	HRVD	60033	2406	50W-38N	B7
1800	CmgT	60033	2406	50W-39N	B4
US-14 S Division St					
100	HRVD	60033	2406	50W-38N	B7
300	HRVD	60033	2464	50W-37N	B1
800	DhmT	60033	2464	50W-37N	B2
US-14 E Main St					
10	CRY	60013	2695	30W-23N	E1
US-14 W Main St					
10	CRY	60013	2695	31W-23N	E1
US-14 Miner St					
1200	DSPN	60016	2862	13W-11N	E3
1300	DSPN	60016	2863	12W-11N	A4
US-14 Northwest Hwy					
-	CbaT	60010	2696	29W-22N	D4
-	CRY	60013	2696	30W-23N	A2
10	AlqT	60013	2696	30W-23N	A2
10	CRY	60013	2641	31W-24N	D7
10	CRY	60013	2695	31W-24N	D1
10	FRGV	60013	2696	30W-23N	A2
10	FRGV	60021	2696	29W-22N	C3
800	AlqT	60013	2641	32W-24N	B7
800	AlqT	60014	2641	31W-24N	D7
800	CRY	60014	2641	31W-24N	D7
1000	FRGV	60010	2696	29W-22N	D4
1000	LKBN	60010	2696	29W-22N	D4
1000	LKBN	60021	2696	29W-22N	D4
4100	CLLK	60014	2641	33W-24N	A6
4400	AlqT	60014	2640	33W-24N	E6
4400	CLLK	60014	2640	33W-24N	E6
US-14 E Northwest Hwy					
10	ANHT	60004	2807	17W-14N	A4
10	ANHT	60005	2807	17W-14N	A4
10	DSPN	60016	2862	14W-12N	C1
10	MPPT	60016	2862	14W-12N	B1
10	MPPT	60056	2808	15W-12N	A7
10	MPPT	60056	2862	13W-11N	E3
10	PLTN	60067	2752	20W-16N	E6
100	BRTN	60010	2751	25W-20N	A1
200	PLTN	60067	2753	20W-16N	A7
400	PLTN	60067	2806	20W-15N	A1
400	PLTN	60074	2806	20W-15N	A1
1700	DSPN	60016	2863	12W-11N	A4
2100	MPPT	60056	2807	16W-13N	D6
US-14 N Northwest Hwy					
10	PLTN	60067	2806	20W-16N	A1
10	PLTN	60074	2806	20W-16N	A1
100	BRTN	60010	2751	25W-20N	A2
100	PLTN	60074	2753	20W-16N	A7
300	PLTN	60067	2753	20W-16N	A7
US-14 S Northwest Hwy					
-	PLTN	60067	2751	23W-17N	E5
-	PltT	60067	2751	23W-17N	E5
10	CRY	60013	2695	30W-23N	E1
10	CRY	60013	2696	30W-23N	A2
10	PLTN	60067	2806	18W-14N	D3
10	PLTN	60074	2806	18W-14N	D3
100	AlqT	60013	2696	30W-23N	A2
100	BRTN	60010	2751	24W-17N	D4
100	FRGV	60013	2696	30W-23N	A2
1100	PltT	60010	2751	23W-17N	D4
US-14 W Northwest Hwy					
-	FRGV	60010	2696	28W-22N	D4
-	PltT	60010	2751	23W-17N	E5
-	PltT	60067	2751	23W-17N	E5
10	ANHT	60004	2807	17W-14N	A4
10	ANHT	60005	2807	17W-14N	A4
10	MPPT	60056	2808	15W-12N	A7
10	PLTN	60067	2752	22W-17N	A5
200	MPPT	60056	2807	15W-12N	E7
500	ANHT	60004	2806	18W-14N	E4
500	ANHT	60005	2806	18W-14N	E4
500	BRTN	60010	2697	26W-20N	D7
500	BRTN	60010	2750	26W-20N	D1
500	PltT	60067	2752	21W-16N	C6
800	CbaT	60010	2697	27W-21N	B7
900	LKBN	60010	2697	28W-21N	A5
1500	PLTN	60067	2751	23W-17N	E5
1800	ANHT	60074	2806	19W-14N	D3
1800	PLTN	60074	2806	19W-14N	D3
28300	LKBN	60010	2696	28W-21N	E5
28700	CbaT	60010	2696	28W-22N	D4
28900	FRGV	60021	2696	28W-22N	D4
28900	LKBN	60021	2696	28W-22N	D4
US-14 W Peterson Av					
1700	CHCG	60660	2921	2W-7N	B3
1900	CHCG	60659	2921	2W-7N	B3
2700	CHCG	60659	2920	3W-7N	E3
3800	CHCG	60646	2920	4W-7N	B4
4700	CHCG	60646	2919	5W-7N	E4
US-14 N Ridge Av					
5600	CHCG	60640	2921	1W-7N	D4
5600	CHCG	60660	2921	1W-7N	D4
US-14 N Virginia St					
10	CLLK	60014	2639	37W-27N	A1
10	NndT	60012	2639	36W-26N	D3
US-14 S Virginia St					
10	CLLK	60014	2639	36W-25N	D4
US-14 W Virginia St					
100	CLLK	60014	2640	35W-24N	A6
200	CLLK	60014	2639	35W-25N	E5
US-14 Waukegan Rd					
8500	MNGV	60053	2864	8W-10N	E4
US-20					
-	ELGN	-	2854	35W-10N	A5
-	ElgT	-	2853	36W-11N	E5
-	ElgT	-	2854	35W-10N	A5
10	HPSR	60140	2743	44W-17N	E6
10	HPSR	60140	2796	44W-16N	E2
10	HPSR	60140	2797	43W-15N	B4
10	HshT	60140	2796	44W-16N	E2
10	HshT	60140	2797	43W-15N	B4
10	PGGV	60140	2797	43W-14N	C5
10	PltT	60124	2852	39W-12N	D2
10	PltT	60140	2798	40W-13N	B7
10	PltT	60140	2852	39W-12N	E3
10	RtdT	60140	2797	43W-15N	B4
200	HshT	60140	2743	46W-19N	A2
300	PGGV	60140	2798	41W-13N	A7
500	PltT	60140	2797	41W-13N	E7
700	PltT	60124	2853	38W-12N	A3
800	CrlT	60140	2743	46W-19N	A2
800	CrlT	60142	2743	46W-19N	A2
US-20 95th St					
-	HYHL	60457	3209	11W-10S	E6
-	PlsT	60457	3209	11W-10S	E6
-	PlsT	60465	3209	11W-10S	E6
-	PlsT	60480	3209	11W-10S	E6
-	PSHL	60457	3209	11W-10S	E6
-	PSHL	60465	3209	11W-10S	E6
US-20 E 95th St					
10	CHCG	60619	3214	0E-10S	C6
10	CHCG	60620	3214	0E-10S	C6
10	CHCG	60628	3214	0E-10S	C6
900	CHCG	60619	3215	1E-10S	A5
900	CHCG	60628	3215	1E-10S	A5
1500	CHCG	60617	3215	1E-10S	B5
3000	CHCG	60617	3216	3E-11S	A5
US-20 W 95th St					
-	BGVW	60453	3210	8W-10S	E6
-	BGVW	60455	3210	8W-10S	E6
-	BGVW	60457	3210	9W-11S	E6
-	CHCG	60619	3214	0W-10S	C6
-	HYHL	60455	3210	9W-11S	D6
-	OKLN	60453	3210	8W-10S	E6
-	OKLN	60455	3210	8W-10S	E6
10	CHCG	60620	3214	0W-11S	C6
10	CHCG	60628	3214	0W-10S	C6
700	CHCG	60643	3214	0W-10S	A6
1000	CHCG	60620	3213	1W-10S	D6
2300	CHCG	60805	3213	2W-10S	B6
2400	CHCG	60643	3213	3W-10S	B6
2400	ENGN	60805	3213	3W-10S	B6
2900	ENGN	60805	3212	3W-10S	E6
3900	ENGN	60453	3212	4W-10S	E6
3900	OKLN	60453	3212	4W-10S	C6
4900	OKLN	60453	3211	6W-10S	E6
6300	CHRG	60415	3211	7W-10S	B6
6300	CHRG	60453	3211	7W-10S	B6
6300	OKLN	60415	3211	7W-10S	B6
7600	HYHL	60457	3210	9W-11S	E6
8700	HYHL	60465	3210	10W-10S	A6
8700	PSHL	60457	3210	10W-10S	A6
8700	PSHL	60465	3210	10W-10S	A6
8900	HYHL	60457	3209	11W-10S	E6
8900	HYHL	60465	3209	11W-10S	E6
8900	PSHL	60465	3209	11W-10S	E6
9000	PlsT	60457	3209	11W-10S	E6
9000	PlsT	60465	3209	11W-10S	E6
9000	PlsT	60480	3209	11W-10S	E6
9000	PSHL	60457	3209	11W-10S	E6
US-20 Brier Hill Rd					
10	HshT	60140	2743	44W-17N	E6
400	HshT	60140	2796	44W-16N	E2
US-20 Eisenhower Expwy					
-	EMHT	-	2971	16W-2N	E7
-	EMHT	-	2972	15W-2N	A7
-	EMHT	-	3028	15W-2N	B1
US-20 S Ewing Av					
9500	CHCG	60617	3216	4E-10S	B5
US-20 E Grant Hwy					
100	MRGO	60152	2634	49W-26N	B2
11400	CrlT	60140	2743	45W-20N	A1
11400	CrlT	60142	2743	45W-20N	A1
11600	HPSR	60140	2743	45W-20N	A1
11600	HshT	60140	2743	45W-20N	A1
19200	CrlT	60152	2634	48W-25N	E4
19200	CrlT	60180	2634	48W-25N	E4
US-20 S Grant Hwy					
6500	CrlT	60152	2635	47W-24N	B7
6500	CrlT	60180	2635	47W-24N	B7
US-20 W Grant Hwy					
100	MRGO	60152	2634	50W-26N	A2
US-20 S Indianapolis Av					
-	CHCG	60617	3280	4E-11S	C1
-	HMND	60617	3280	4E-11S	C1
10000	CHCG	60617	3216	4E-11S	B7
10600	HMND	46320	3280	4E-11S	C1
US-20 S Indianapolis Blvd					
1000	HMND	46320	3280		D3
1000	HMND	46394	3280		E4
10500	CHCG	60617	3280		C1
10500	HMND	60617	3280	4E-11S	C1
US-20 La Grange Rd					
-	LynT	60458	3209	11W-8S	D2
-	LynT	60480	3209	11W-9S	D3
-	LynT	60525	3209	11W-8S	D2
-	PlsT	60480	3209	11W-9S	D4
-	WLSP	60458	3209	11W-9S	D2
-	WLSP	60480	3209	11W-9S	D2
-	WLSP	60525	3209	12W-8S	D2
US-20 N La Grange Rd					
-	PvsT	60154	3087	12W-2S	A2
-	WSTR	60154	3087	12W-2S	A2
10	LGNG	60525	3087	12W-4S	C6
100	LGPK	60525	3087	12W-4S	C6
1000	PvsT	60525	3087	12W-3S	B4
US-20 S La Grange Rd					
-	HGKN	60525	3147	12W-8S	C7
-	HGKN	60525	3209	12W-8S	C1
-	WLSP	60525	3209	12W-8S	C1
10	LGNG	60525	3087	12W-4S	C7
300	LGNG	60525	3147	12W-4S	C1
5200	CTSD	60525	3147	12W-5S	C3
US-20 Lake St					
-	AddT	60101	2971	17W-3N	B5
-	BmdT	60133	2911	26W-7N	E5
-	BRLT	60103	2856	31W-9N	A7
-	BRLT	60120	2856	31W-9N	A7
-	ELGN	-	2855	32W-10N	D6
-	ELGN	60103	2856	31W-10N	A7
-	ELGN	60120	2856	31W-10N	A7
-	HnrT	60120	2856	31W-9N	A7
10	AddT	60101	2970	21W-5N	A2
10	ADSN	60101	2970	20W-4N	B2
10	ADSN	60143	2970	21W-5N	A2
10	BMDL	60101	2969	22W-5N	D1
10	BmdT	60101	2969	21W-5N	E1
10	BmdT	60101	2970	20W-4N	B2
10	BmdT	60143	2970	20W-4N	B2
10	BmdT	60172	2912	25W-6N	C6
10	ROSL	60172	2912	25W-6N	C6
100	ADSN	60101	2969	21W-5N	E1
100	BMDL	60108	2969	22W-5N	D1
100	BmdT	60143	2969	21W-5N	E2
200	AddT	60143	2970	20W-5N	A2
200	HRPK	60133	2911	26W-7N	E5
300	HRPK	60133	2912	25W-6N	B6
300	HRPK	60172	2912	25W-6N	B6
400	BmdT	60133	2912	25W-6N	A6
400	BmdT	60157	2969	21W-5N	E1
600	BMDL	60108	2912	24W-6N	D7
600	BMDL	60172	2912	24W-6N	D7
US-20 E Lake St					
10	ADSN	60101	2971	18W-3N	A5
10	MLPK	60160	3028	13W-1N	E2
10	NHLK	60164	3028	13W-1N	D2
100	BMDL	60108	2969	23W-5N	A1
100	BRLT	60103	2910	28W-9N	E2
100	BRLT	60103	2911	28W-8N	B2
100	BRLT	60107	2910	28W-9N	E1
100	SMWD	60103	2910	28W-9N	E2
100	SMWD	60103	2911	28W-8N	B2
100	SMWD	60107	2910	28W-9N	E2
100	SMWD	60107	2911	28W-8N	B2
200	AddT	60101	2971	17W-3N	A5
200	BRLT	60107	2911	28W-9N	A2
300	EMHT	60101	2971	17W-3N	C6
300	EMHT	60126	2971	17W-3N	C6
1000	BmdT	60133	2911	26W-7N	E5
1000	BmdT	60133	2912	26W-7N	A5
1000	HRPK	60133	2911	26W-7N	E5
1000	HRPK	60133	2912	26W-7N	A5
US-20 W Lake St					
-	EMHT	60101	2971	17W-3N	C6
-	SMWD	60120	2910	30W-9N	C1
10	ADSN	60101	2970	18W-3N	E4
10	NHLK	60164	3028	13W-1N	E2
100	AddT	60101	2970	20W-4N	B3
100	BMDL	60108	2968	23W-5N	E1
100	BMDL	60108	2969	23W-5N	B1
100	BmdT	60108	2968	23W-5N	E1
200	BMDL	60108	2912	24W-6N	E7
200	BMDL	60172	2912	24W-6N	E7
200	BmdT	60108	2912	24W-5N	E7
200	ROSL	60108	2912	24W-6N	E7
200	ROSL	60172	2912	24W-6N	E7
300	AddT	60101	2971	17W-3N	C6
300	EMHT	60126	2971	16W-2N	D6
500	BRLT	60103	2910	29W-9N	D1
500	BRLT	60107	2910	29W-9N	D1
500	BRLT	60120	2910	29W-9N	D1
500	HnrT	60120	2910	29W-9N	D1
500	SMWD	60107	2910	29W-9N	D1
600	BRLT	60103	2911	28W-8N	B2
600	HRPK	60133	2911	28W-8N	B2
600	SMWD	60107	2911	28W-8N	B2
1100	BRLT	60103	2856	30W-9N	B7
1100	BRLT	60107	2856	30W-9N	B7
1100	HnrT	60107	2856	30W-9N	B7
1100	SMWD	60107	2856	30W-9N	C7
1400	BRLT	60120	2856	30W-9N	B7
1400	HnrT	60120	2856	30W-9N	B7
2200	BRLT	60133	2911	27W-8N	C3
4100	MLPK	60160	3029	13W-1N	A2
4100	MLPK	60165	3029	13W-1N	A2
4100	SNPK	60160	3029	13W-1N	A2
4100	SNPK	60165	3029	13W-1N	A2
4700	MLPK	60160	3028	13W-1N	E2
US-20 Mannheim Rd					
10	BLWD	60104	3029	12W-0N	A3
10	BLWD	60160	3029	12W-1N	A3
10	MLPK	60160	3029	12W-1N	A3
500	BLWD	60162	3029	12W-0N	A4
500	HLSD	60162	3029	12W-0N	A4
US-20 N Mannheim Rd					
-	BLWD	60104	3029	12W-1N	A3
-	BLWD	60160	3029	12W-1N	A3
-	HLSD	60154	3029	12W-0S	A6
-	MLPK	60160	3029	12W-1N	A2
-	SNPK	60160	3029	12W-1N	A2
-	SNPK	60165	3029	12W-1N	A2
-	WSTR	60154	3029	12W-0S	A6
10	HLSD	60104	3029	12W-0S	A6
10	HLSD	60162	3029	12W-0S	A6
100	BLWD	60162	3029	12W-0S	A5
US-20 S Mannheim Rd					
-	BLWD	60104	3029	12W-0S	A6
-	HLSD	60104	3029	12W-0S	A6
10	HLSD	60154	3029	12W-0S	A6
10	HLSD	60162	3029	12W-0S	A6
10	WSTR	60154	3029	12W-0S	A6
100	WSTR	60162	3029	12W-0S	A7
300	PvsT	60162	3029	12W-0S	A7
1400	PvsT	60162	3087	12W-1S	A1
1400	WSTR	60154	3087	12W-1S	A1
1400	WSTR	60162	3087	12W-1S	A1
2100	PvsT	60154	3087	12W-1S	A2
2100	PvsT	60525	3087	12W-1S	A2
US-20 Oak St					
10	PGGV	60140	2798	40W-13N	B7
10	PltT	60140	2798	40W-13N	B7
US-20 Villa St					
-	ELGN	-	2855	31W-10N	E6
US-20 BUS Villa St					
-	ELGN	60120	2855	32W-10N	D6
US-20 E Villa St					
1500	ELGN	60120	2855	31W-10N	E7
1500	ELGN	60120	2856	30W-9N	B7
1600	ELGN	60103	2856	31W-10N	A7
US-30					
-	AURA	60543	3265	32W-12S	C3
-	AURA	60585	3265	32W-12S	C3
-	BRkT	60554	3135	42W-7S	C7
-	BRkT	60554	3197	42W-7S	C1
-	BtlT	60512	3198	40W-9S	B5
-	BtlT	60538	3198	40W-9S	B5
-	MTGY	60506	3198	39W-9S	D5
-	MTGY	60538	3198	41W-10S	A5
-	MTGY	60538	3199	36W-10S	E6
-	OswT	60538	3199	37W-10S	D5
-	OswT	60538	3200	36W-10S	A6
-	PNFD	60544	3338	31W-15S	A3
-	PNFD	60585	3338	31W-15S	A3
-	PnfT	60544	3338	31W-16S	A5
-	SgrT	60506	3198	41W-9S	A5
-	SgrT	60538	3198	41W-9S	A5
-	SgrT	60554	3134	45W-6S	C6
-	SRGV	-	3135	43W-7S	B6
-	WldT	60585	3265	33W-11S	B2
-	WldT	60585	3337	31W-14S	E1
-	WldT	60585	3338	31W-15S	A3
10	SgrT	60506	3197	42W-9S	C5
10	SgrT	60554	3197	42W-9S	C5
10	SRGV	60554	3197	42W-8S	C2
800	BtlT	60512	3197	42W-9S	C5
US-30 E 14th St					
10	CHHT	60411	3508	1W-25S	A7
300	BlmT	60411	3508	0W-25S	D7
US-30 W 14th St					
10	CHHT	60411	3508	1W-25S	A7
100	CHHT	60411	3507	1W-25S	E7
700	OMFD	60461	3507	2W-25S	C7
US-30 E Cass St					
10	JLET	60432	3499	21W-23S	E4
800	JltT	60432	3499	21W-23S	E4
1800	JLET	60433	3499	21W-23S	E4
1800	JltT	60433	3499	21W-23S	E4
1900	JltT	60432	3500	21W-23S	A4
1900	JltT	60433	3500	21W-23S	A4
2000	NlxT	60432	3500	21W-23S	A4
2000	NlxT	60433	3500	21W-23S	A4
2500	JLET	60432	3500	20W-23S	B4
US-30 W Cass St					
10	JLET	60432	3498	24W-23S	E4
100	JLET	60435	3498	24W-23S	E4
US-30 N Center St					
100	JLET	60435	3498	24W-23S	E4
US-30 N Collins St					
10	JLET	60432	3499	23W-23S	A5
US-30 E Jefferson St					
10	JLET	60432	3499	23W-23S	A5
US-30 W Jefferson St					
10	JLET	60432	3498	24W-23S	E5
200	JLET	60435	3498	24W-23S	E5
US-30 S Joliet Rd					
10	PNFD	60544	3416	29W-18S	D1
300	PNFD	60544	3338	29W-18S	C7
300	PNFD	60586	3416	29W-18S	E2
US-30 Joliet St					
10	BlmT	60411	3598		C2
10	DYR	46311	3598		C2
US-30 Lincoln Hwy					
-	CHHT	60411	3507	3W-25S	C7
-	JLET	60431	3417	28W-19S	B4
-	JLET	60432	3500	20W-23S	C4
-	JLET	60435	3417	28W-19S	B4
-	NLNX	60433	3500	20W-24S	C5
-	NLNX	60451	3500	19W-24S	C5
-	NlxT	60432	3500	20W-24S	C5
-	NlxT	60433	3500	20W-23S	C4
-	NlxT	60451	3500	19W-24S	C5
-	OswT	60503	3201	33W-11S	A7
-	OswT	60543	3201	33W-11S	A7
300	MTGY	60503	3200	33W-10S	E6
300	MTGY	60504	3200	33W-10S	E6
300	MTGY	60538	3200	33W-10S	E6
300	OswT	60503	3200	33W-10S	E6
300	OswT	60504	3200	33W-10S	E6
300	OswT	60538	3200	33W-10S	E6
300	OswT	60543	3200	33W-10S	E6
2400	OMFD	60461	3507	3W-25S	A7
2500	PKFT	60466	3507	3W-25S	A7
3200	MTSN	60443	3506	4W-25S	E7
3200	MTSN	60466	3506	4W-25S	E7
3200	OMFD	60461	3506	4W-25S	E7
3200	PKFT	60466	3506	4W-25S	E7
5300	MTSN	60443	3505	7W-25S	C7
6200	RchT	60443	3505	7W-25S	C7
6700	FftT	60423	3505	8W-25S	A7
6700	FKFT	60423	3505	8W-25S	A7
11200	FKFT	60423	3591	13W-25S	B1
11200	MKNA	60448	3502	14W-25S	E7
11200	MKNA	60448	3590	14W-25S	E1
11200	MKNA	60448	3591	13W-25S	B1
US-30 E Lincoln Hwy					
10	FKFT	60423	3503	11W-25S	E7
100	FftT	60423	3503	11W-25S	E7
400	BlmT	60411	3508	0E-25S	E7
400	CHHT	60411	3508	0E-25S	E7
400	NLNX	60451	3501	17W-24S	D6
400	NlxT	60451	3501	17W-24S	D6
800	CHHT	60411	3509	1E-25S	A7
800	FDHT	60411	3509	1E-25S	A7
1200	NLNX	60451	3502	16W-25S	A7
1200	NlxT	60451	3502	16W-25S	A7
1400	BlmT	60411	3509	3E-25S	E7
1700	SLVL	60411	3509	3E-25S	E7
2400	BlmT	60411	3510	3E-25S	A7
2700	FftT	60448	3502	14W-25S	D7
2700	FftT	60451	3502	14W-25S	D7
2700	MKNA	60448	3502	14W-25S	D7
2700	MKNA	60451	3502	14W-25S	D7
2800	LYWD	60411	3510	3E-25S	A7
21400	BlmT	60411	3598		D2
21400	LYWD	60411	3598		D2
US-30 W Lincoln Hwy					
-	JLET	60431	3417	26W-21S	E6
900	FKFT	60423	3591	13W-25S	B1
1000	NLNX	60451	3501	17W-25S	D6
1000	NlxT	60451	3501	17W-25S	D6
1100	NlxT	60451	3500	19W-24S	E5
1300	NLNX	60451	3500	19W-24S	E5
7200	FftT	60423	3505	9W-25S	A7
7200	FKFT	60423	3505	9W-25S	A7
7200	RchT	60443	3505	9W-25S	A7
7400	FftT	60423	3504	9W-25S	E7
7400	FKFT	60423	3504	9W-25S	E7
9200	FftT	60423	3503	13W-25S	B7
9200	FKFT	60423	3503	13W-25S	B7
11100	MKNA	60448	3591	14W-25S	A1
22800	JLET	60544	3417	26W-21S	E6
22800	JLET	60586	3417	26W-21S	E6
22800	PnfT	60544	3417	28W-19S	A3
22800	PnfT	60586	3417	28W-19S	A3
22900	PNFD	60586	3417	28W-19S	A3
23000	PNFD	60544	3416	29W-18S	D1
23000	PNFD	60586	3416	29W-18S	D1
23000	PnfT	60544	3416	29W-18S	D1
23000	PnfT	60586	3416	29W-18S	D1
US-30 W Lockport St					
400	PNFD	60544	3338	30W-17S	C7
1000	PnfT	60544	3338	30W-17S	A7
US-30 W Maple St					
1400	NLNX	60433	3500	19W-24S	D5
1400	NLNX	60451	3500	19W-24S	D5
1400	NlxT	60432	3500	19W-24S	D5
1400	NlxT	60451	3500	19W-24S	D5
US-30 Plainfield Rd					
400	JLET	60435	3498	25W-22S	B1
1500	CTHL	60403	3498	25W-22S	A1
1500	JLET	60403	3498	25W-22S	A1
1600	CTHL	60403	3418	26W-21S	A7
2000	CTHL	60403	3417	26W-21S	E7
2300	CTHL	60435	3417	26W-21S	D6
2300	LktT	60435	3417	26W-20S	D6
2300	PnfT	60435	3417	26W-20S	D6
2400	JLET	60435	3417	27W-20S	D5
2600	JLET	60431	3417	27W-20S	C5
US-30 E Sauk Tr					
3600	BlmT	60411	3598	4E-26S	C2
3600	DYR	46311	3598	4E-26S	C2
US-30 US Highway 34					
1200	MTGY	60538	3200	34W-10S	E6
1200	MTGY	60543	3200	34W-10S	E6
1200	OSWG	60538	3200	34W-10S	E6
1200	OSWG	60543	3200	34W-10S	E6
1200	OswT	60543	3200	34W-10S	E6
US-30 US Route 30					
-	MTGY	60538	3199	37W-9S	B5
US-30 W Western Av					
200	JLET	60432	3498	24W-23S	E4
200	JLET	60435	3498	24W-23S	E5
US-34					
-	LtRT	60545	3258	49W-14S	E7
-	LtRT	60545	3259	48W-14S	C7
-	LtRT	60545	3330	50W-14S	C1
-	LtRT	60548	3330	49W-14S	D1
-	MTGY	60543	3200	34W-10S	D6
-	MTGY	60543	3263	38W-12S	B3
-	OSWG	60543	3200	34W-10S	D6
-	OswT	60543	3263	37W-12S	B3
-	PLNO	60545	3258	49W-14S	E7
-	PLNO	60545	3259	47W-14S	C7
-	SDWH	60548	3330	50W-14S	B1
-	YKVL	60560	3262	41W-13S	A6
1000	LtRT	60545	3260	46W-13S	A6
1000	PLNO	60545	3260	46W-13S	A6
6000	BtlT	60543	3262	39W-12S	E4
6000	OSWG	60543	3262	39W-12S	E4
9100	BtlT	60560	3261	42W-14S	E7
9100	YKVL	60560	3261	42W-14S	E7
11400	BtlT	60560	3260	44W-14S	E6
11400	YKVL	60560	3260	44W-14S	E6
11900	BtlT	60545	3260	44W-13S	D6
11900	YKVL	60545	3260	44W-13S	D6
US-34 Chicago Rd					
10	OSWG	60543	3263	37W-12S	C3
US-34 E Church St					
600	SDWH	60548	3330	51W-15S	A2
1000	SdwT	60548	3330	51W-15S	A2
1400	LtRT	60548	3330	51W-14S	B1
US-34 S Madison St					
10	OSWG	60543	3263	37W-12S	C3
US-34 Ogden Av					
-	HNDL	60521	3086	14W-3S	C6
-	LynT	60521	3086	14W-3S	C6
-	LynT	60558	3086	14W-3S	C6
-	NPVL	60563	3140	28W-6S	E5
-	OswT	60503	3201	33W-9S	A5
-	OswT	60504	3201	33W-9S	A5
10	DRGV	60515	3084	18W-4S	E7
10	DRGV	60515	3085	18W-4S	A7
10	LGPK	60525	3087	13W-4S	B6
10	LGPK	60558	3087	13W-4S	B6
10	LSLE	60563	3142	25W-5S	B2
10	LslT	60563	3142	25W-5S	B2
10	NPVL	60540	3140	29W-7S	D7
10	NPVL	60540	3202	29W-7S	D1
10	NPVL	60563	3142	25W-5S	B2
10	PvsT	60525	3087	13W-4S	B6
10	PvsT	60558	3087	13W-4S	B6
10	WNSP	60558	3087	13W-4S	B6
10	WTMT	60515	3084	18W-4S	E7
10	WTMT	60515	3085	18W-4S	A7
10	WTMT	60559	3084	18W-4S	E7

STREET Block	City	ZIP	Map#	CGS	Grid
US-34 Ogden Av					
10	WTMT	60559	3085	18W-4S	A7
100	LSLE	60532	3142	23W-5S	E2
100	PvsT	60525	3086	13W-3S	E6
100	PvsT	60558	3086	15W-4S	A7
100	WNSP	60558	3086	15W-4S	A7
400	AURA	60540	3202	29W-8S	C1
400	LSLE	60532	3143	22W-4S	C1
400	LslT	60532	3143	22W-4S	C1
1200	DRGV	60515	3144	21W-4S	A1
1900	AraT	60504	3201	33W-9S	A5
2000	DRGV	60515	3143	23W-4S	A2
2100	AURA	60504	3201	33W-9S	B4
2400	NpvT	60504	3201	32W-9S	C3
2500	LslT	60515	3143	21W-4S	D1
2700	DRGV	60532	3143	22W-4S	D1
3600	AURA	60504	3202	30W-8S	B1
4300	NPVL	60504	3202	30W-8S	C1
7200	BRWN	60402	3088	9W-3S	D6
7200	LYNS	60402	3088	9W-3S	D6
7200	LYNS	60534	3088	9W-3S	D6
7200	LYNS	60546	3088	9W-3S	D6
7200	RVSD	60402	3088	9W-3S	D6
7200	RVSD	60546	3088	9W-3S	D6
8700	BKFD	60513	3088	10W-4S	A6
8700	BKFD	60534	3088	10W-4S	A6
8800	BKFD	60513	3087	11W-4S	E6
9500	BKFD	60525	3087	11W-4S	D6
9500	LGNG	60525	3087	11W-4S	D6
US-34 E Ogden Av					
10	LGNG	60525	3087	12W-4S	C6
10	NPVL	60563	3141	28W-6S	A4
10	WTMT	60559	3085	17W-4S	B7
100	CNHL	60514	3085	16W-4S	D7
100	CNHL	60559	3085	16W-4S	D7
100	WTMT	60514	3085	16W-4S	D7
400	HNDL	60521	3086	15W-4S	C6
400	LynT	60521	3086	15W-4S	C6
400	LynT	60558	3086	15W-4S	C6
800	CNHL	60521	3085	16W-4S	E7
800	HNDL	60521	3085	16W-4S	E7
800	WTMT	60521	3085	16W-4S	E7
1000	LslT	60563	3142	25W-5S	A3
1000	NPVL	60563	3142	26W-5S	A3
1400	LSLE	60563	3142	25W-5S	B2
9600	BKFD	60513	3087	12W-4S	D6
9600	BKFD	60525	3087	12W-4S	D6
US-34 W Ogden Av					
-	CNHL	60514	3085	16W-4S	E7
-	CNHL	60521	3085	16W-4S	E7
-	WTMT	60514	3085	16W-4S	E7
-	WTMT	60521	3085	16W-4S	E7
-	WTMT	60559	3085	16W-4S	E7
10	DGvT	60559	3085	18W-4S	B7
10	HNDL	60521	3086	15W-4S	A7
10	LGNG	60525	3087	12W-4S	C6
10	NPVL	60563	3141	27W-5S	D4
300	DRGV	60515	3085	18W-4S	A7
300	WTMT	60515	3085	18W-4S	A7
500	HNDL	60521	3085	16W-4S	E7
1200	LGPK	60525	3087	13W-3S	A6
1300	NPVL	60563	3140	29W-6S	E5
1500	LGPK	60558	3087	13W-3S	A6
1500	NPVL	60540	3140	28W-6S	E5
1500	WNSP	60525	3087	13W-3S	A6
1500	WNSP	60558	3087	13W-3S	A6
1600	PvsT	60525	3087	13W-3S	A6
1600	PvsT	60558	3087	13W-3S	A6
US-34 E South St					
10	PLNO	60545	3259	46W-13S	E6
700	LtRT	60545	3260	46W-13S	A6
700	PLNO	60545	3260	46W-13S	A6
US-34 W South St					
10	PLNO	60545	3259	47W-14S	D6
US-34 US Highway 34					
1200	MTGY	60538	3200	34W-10S	D7
1200	MTGY	60543	3200	34W-10S	D7
1200	OSWG	60538	3200	34W-10S	D7
1200	OSWG	60543	3200	34W-10S	D7
1200	OswT	60543	3200	34W-10S	E6
7200	BtlT	60543	3262	40W-13S	C4
7200	BtlT	60560	3262	40W-13S	C4
US-34 E Veterans Pkwy					
10	BtlT	60560	3261	42W-14S	D7
10	YKVL	60560	3261	42W-14S	C7
US-34 W Veterans Pkwy					
-	BtlT	60560	3260	44W-14S	E7
-	YKVL	60560	3260	44W-14S	E7
10	YKVL	60560	3261	43W-14S	A7
200	BtlT	60560	3261	43W-14S	A7
US-34 W Washington St					
-	OswT	60543	3263	37W-12S	B3
10	OSWG	60543	3263	37W-12S	C4
US-41					
-	BtlT	-	2360		E4
-	GRNE	60031	2535	13W-34N	E1
-	NptT	-	2360		E4
-	PTPR	-	2360		E1
US-41 E 85th St					
3200	CHCG	60617	3216	4E-9S	A3
US-41 E 87th St					
3200	CHCG	60617	3216	4E-9S	A3
US-41 S Baker Av					
8400	CHCG	60617	3216	3E-9S	A3
US-41 Borman Expwy					
-	HMND	-	3430		E5
US-41 S Burley Av					
8500	CHCG	60617	3216	4E-9S	A3
US-41 Calumet Av					
6200	HMND	46320	3430		E1
6200	HMND	46324	3430		E1
US-41 S Calumet Av					
1400	HMND	46394	3280		E7
2100	HMND	46320	3280		E5
2500	HMND	46327	3280		E7
3000	HMND	46320	3352		E5
3000	HMND	46327	3352		E5
5900	HMND	46320	3430		E2
6100	HMND	46324	3430		E2
US-41 S Coast Guard Dr					
6400	CHCG	60637	3153	2E-7S	C5
6400	CHCG	60649	3153	2E-7S	C5
US-41 Edens Expwy					
-	GLNC	-	2758	7W-16N	B7
-	HDPK	-	2757	8W-20N	E2
-	NfdT	-	2757	8W-18N	E2
-	NfdT	-	2811	7W-15N	C1
-	NHBK	-	2757	8W-18N	E3
-	NHBK	-	2758	7W-17N	A4
-	NHFD	-	2758	7W-16N	B7
-	NHFD	-	2811	6W-14N	D4
-	NtrT	-	2758	7W-18N	A4
-	NtrT	-	2811	6W-14N	D4
US-41 S Ewing Av					
9200	CHCG	60617	3216	4E-10S	A5
US-41 W Foster Av					
900	CHCG	60640	2921	1W-6N	E5
1900	CHCG	60625	2921	2W-6N	B5
US-41 S Indianapolis Av					
-	HMND	46320	3280	4E-11S	C1
-	HMND	60617	3280	4E-11S	C1
10000	CHCG	60617	3216	4E-11S	B7
10300	CHCG	60617	3280	4E-11S	C1
US-41 S Indianapolis Blvd					
1000	HMND	46320	3280		D2
1000	HMND	46394	3280		D3
10500	CHCG	60617	3280		C1
10500	HMND	60617	3280	4E-11S	C1
US-41 N Lake Shore Dr					
-	CHCG	-	2921	0W-6N	E6
-	CHCG	-	2922	0W-5N	A7
-	CHCG	-	2978	0W-4N	A2
-	CHCG	-	3034	0E-0N	D3
-	CokC	-	3034	0E-0N	D4
US-41 S Lake Shore Dr					
-	CHCG	-	3092	1E-3S	E4
-	CHCG	-	3093	1E-4S	A6
-	CHCG	-	3153	2E-5S	B1
-	CokC	60637	3153	2E-6S	C3
10	CHCG	60601	3034	0E-1S	D7
10	CHCG	60603	3034	0E-1S	D7
100	CHCG	60604	3034	0E-0S	D5
300	CHCG	60605	3034	0E-0S	D5
1500	CHCG	60616	3034	0E-1S	D7
5300	CHCG	60637	3153	2E-7S	D5
US-41 Lincoln Av					
7400	LNWD	60076	2866	5W-9N	A7
7400	LNWD	60712	2866	5W-9N	A7
7400	SKOK	60076	2866	5W-9N	A7
7400	SKOK	60712	2866	5W-9N	A7
7500	SKOK	60076	2865	5W-9N	E7
7500	SKOK	60077	2865	5W-9N	E7
US-41 N Lincoln Av					
5200	CHCG	60625	2921	3W-6N	A5
5500	CHCG	60659	2921	1W-6N	D5
5600	CHCG	60659	2920	3W-7N	E4
6300	LNWD	60659	2920	4W-7N	C3
6300	LNWD	60712	2920	3W-7N	E4
7200	LNWD	60076	2866	5W-9N	A7
7200	LNWD	60712	2866	5W-9N	A7
7200	SKOK	60076	2866	5W-9N	A7
7200	SKOK	60712	2866	5W-9N	A7
US-41 S Mackinaw Av					
8700	CHCG	60617	3216	4E-10S	B6
US-41 E Marquette Dr					
2000	CHCG	60637	3153	2E-7S	C5
2000	CHCG	60649	3153	2E-7S	C5
US-41 Skokie Blvd					
7500	SKOK	60076	2865	5W-9N	E7
7500	SKOK	60077	2865	5W-9N	E7
10000	SKOK	60076	2811	5W-12N	E7
10000	SKOK	60077	2811	5W-12N	E7
10000	WLMT	60076	2811	6W-12N	E7
10000	WLMT	60077	2811	6W-12N	E7
10000	WLMT	60091	2811	5W-13N	E7
US-41 Skokie Hwy					
-	GRNE	60031	2535	13W-34N	E1
-	HDPK	-	2757	8W-18N	E3
-	NCHI	60064	2536	13W-32N	A4
-	NCHI	60085	2536	12W-32N	A6
-	NfdT	-	2757	8W-20N	D1
-	NHBK	-	2757	8W-18N	E3
-	NptT	60031	2420	15W-39N	A5
-	NptT	60031	2478	15W-38N	A1
-	NptT	60083	2360	16W-41N	E7
-	NptT	60083	2419	16W-40N	E2
-	NptT	60083	2420	15W-40N	A4
-	NptT	60099	2360	16W-42N	E6
-	PKCY	-	2535	13W-33N	E2
-	PKCY	-	2536	13W-33N	A4
-	ShdT	60044	2536	12W-31N	B7
-	WDWH	60031	2420	15W-39N	A5
-	WDWH	60031	2478	15W-38N	A1
-	WDWH	60083	2360	16W-41N	E7
-	WDWH	60083	2419	16W-40N	E2
-	WDWH	60083	2420	15W-39N	A5
-	WDWH	60099	2360	16W-42N	E6
-	WKGN	-	2535	13W-33N	E3
-	WKGN	60064	2536	12W-32N	A5
-	WKGN	60085	2536	13W-33N	A4
-	WrnT	60031	2478	15W-37N	A1
US-41 N Skokie Hwy					
-	NCHI	60064	2536	12W-31N	B7
-	ShdT	60044	2536	12W-31N	B7
-	WDWH	60031	2478	15W-37N	A2
-	WKGN	60085	2536	12W-31N	B7
100	LKFT	60045	2593	11W-28N	C7
300	GRNE	60031	2535	13W-34N	E1
300	LKFT	60044	2593	11W-28N	C7
900	LKFT	60045	2649	11W-24N	E6
1000	GRNE	60031	2478	13W-35N	D6
1100	NCHI	60088	2593	12W-30N	B2
1300	WrnT	60031	2478	15W-37N	A3
1400	ShdT	60088	2593	12W-30N	B2
2800	NCHI	60044	2593	12W-28N	C6
2800	NCHI	60064	2593	12W-28N	C6
2800	ShdT	60044	2593	12W-28N	C6
2800	ShdT	60064	2593	12W-28N	C6
3600	LKBF	60044	2593	12W-29N	B4
US-41 S Skokie Hwy					
1200	LKFT	60035	2650	10W-24N	A7
1200	LKFT	60045	2649	10W-24N	E7
1200	LKFT	60045	2650	10W-24N	A7
1300	LKFT	60035	2649	10W-24N	E7
US-41 Skokie Rd					
-	NHFD	60093	2811	5W-13N	E6
-	SKOK	60076	2811	5W-13N	E7
-	SKOK	60077	2811	5W-13N	E7
-	WLMT	60076	2811	5W-13N	E7
-	WLMT	60077	2811	5W-13N	E7
-	WLMT	60091	2811	5W-13N	E6
-	WLMT	60093	2811	5W-13N	E6
US-41 Skokie Valley Rd					
-	HDPK	60035	2757	9W-20N	D1
-	LKBF	60044	2593	12W-29N	C5
-	ShdT	60044	2593	12W-29N	C5
500	HDPK	60035	2704	10W-23N	A2
3100	LKFT	60045	2704	10W-24N	A1
3300	LKFT	60035	2704	10W-24N	A1
US-41 E South Shore Dr					
2400	CHCG	60649	3153	3E-7S	D6
US-41 S South Shore Dr					
6700	CHCG	60637	3153	2E-7S	D5
6700	CHCG	60649	3153	2E-7S	D5
7700	CHCG	60649	3215	3E-8S	E1
7800	CHCG	60617	3216	3E-8S	A1
7800	CHCG	60649	3216	3E-8S	A1
US-45					
-	ANTH	60002	2359	19W-42N	C6
-	AntT	60002	2359	19W-42N	C7
-	AntT	60002	2418	19W-41N	C1
US-45					
-	AntT	60046	2418	19W-40N	C3
-	AvnT	60046	2476	19W-35N	D5
-	BtlT	53104	2359	20W-43N	B4
-	BtlT	60002	2359	20W-43N	B4
-	FmtT	60048	2533	19W-31N	D7
-	FmtT	60048	2590	19W-30N	D1
-	GRNE	60031	2476	18W-35N	D6
-	GRNE	60046	2476	18W-34N	E7
-	GRNE	60046	2533	18W-34N	E1
-	LbvT	60030	2533	19W-31N	D6
-	LbvT	60048	2533	19W-31N	D7
-	LbvT	60048	2590	19W-31N	D1
-	LkvT	60046	2418	19W-39N	D5
-	LkvT	60046	2476	19W-36N	D3
-	LkvT	60083	2418	19W-39N	D5
-	LNHT	60046	2418	19W-38N	D7
-	LNHT	60046	2476	19W-36N	D3
-	LNHT	60083	2418	19W-39N	D5
-	LNSH	60069	2702	15W-23N	A2
-	LYVL	60048	2590	19W-30N	D1
-	MDLN	60060	2646	18W-25N	E5
-	OMCK	60046	2418	19W-38N	D7
-	OMCK	60046	2476	19W-37N	D1
-	OMCK	60083	2418	19W-38N	D7
-	OMCK	60083	2476	19W-38N	D1
-	TDLK	60046	2533	18W-34N	E1
-	VNHL	60061	2701	16W-23N	D1
-	VNHL	60061	2702	15W-23N	A2
-	VNHL	60069	2702	15W-23N	A2
-	VrnT	60061	2647	16W-24N	C7
-	VrnT	60061	2701	16W-24N	D1
-	VrnT	60069	2701	16W-24N	D1
-	WrnT	60031	2476	18W-34N	E7
-	WrnT	60046	2476	19W-36N	D3
-	WrnT	60046	2533	18W-34N	E1
10	AvnT	60030	2533	18W-33N	D4
10	GYLK	60030	2533	18W-34N	E1
33100	WrnT	60030	2533	18W-33N	D3
33800	TDLK	60030	2533	18W-34N	E1
34200	TDLK	60031	2533	18W-34N	D1
34200	WrnT	60031	2533	18W-33N	D1
34300	GRNE	60031	2533	18W-34N	E1
US-45 96th Av					
-	PlsT	60464	3273	12W-13S	D4
-	PlsT	60465	3273	12W-13S	D4
-	PlsT	60480	3273	12W-13S	D4
US-45 Bristol Rd					
-	BtlT	60002	2359		B4
10700	BtlT	53104	2359	19W-42N	C6
11900	BtlT	53142	2359		B3
12400	AntT	60002	2359		B4
US-45 N Des Plaines River Rd					
-	DSPN	60016	2808	13W-13N	E6
-	WhlT	60056	2808	13W-13N	E6
US-45 Downing Cir					
-	GRNE	60031	2477	16W-36N	E3
US-45 Graceland Av					
800	DSPN	60016	2862	13W-10N	E4
US-45 La Grange Rd					
-	LynT	60458	3209	12W-8S	C1
-	LynT	60480	3209	12W-8S	C1
-	LynT	60525	3209	11W-8S	D2
-	MKNA	60448	3423	12W-22S	D7
-	PlsT	60480	3209	11W-11S	D7
-	PlsT	60480	3273	12W-12S	D1
-	WLSP	60458	3209	12W-8S	C1
-	WLSP	60480	3209	12W-8S	C1
-	WLSP	60525	3209	12W-8S	D2
16700	ODHL	60467	3423	11W-20S	D3
16700	ODHL	60487	3423	11W-20S	D3
16700	ODPK	60467	3423	11W-20S	D3
16700	OrlT	60467	3423	11W-20S	D3
16700	OrlT	60487	3423	11W-20S	D3
16900	TYPK	60487	3423	11W-20S	D4
18200	FftT	60448	3423	12W-21S	D7
18200	ODPK	60448	3423	12W-21S	D7
18200	ODPK	60487	3423	12W-21S	D7
18200	TYPK	60448	3423	12W-21S	D7
19100	MKNA	60448	3503	12W-24S	E6
19200	FftT	60448	3503	12W-24S	E6
19800	FKFT	60423	3503	11W-23S	E4
19800	FKFT	60448	3503	11W-23S	E4
19800	MKNA	60423	3503	11W-23S	E4
US-45 N La Grange Rd					
-	PvsT	60154	3087	12W-2S	A2
-	WSTR	60154	3087	12W-2S	A2
10	LGNG	60525	3087	12W-4S	C6
100	FKFT	60423	3503	11W-25S	E7
100	LGPK	60525	3087	12W-4S	C6
600	FftT	60423	3503	11W-25S	E6
1000	PvsT	60525	3087	12W-3S	B4
US-45 S La Grange Rd					
-	CTSD	60525	3147	12W-8S	C7
-	HGKN	60525	3209	12W-8S	C1
-	PlsT	60480	3273	12W-13S	D4
-	WLSP	60525	3209	12W-8S	C1
10	LGNG	60525	3087	12W-4S	C7
200	FKFT	60423	3591	14W-28S	A6
300	LGNG	60525	3147	12W-4S	C1
6000	HGKN	60525	3147	12W-6S	C5
11800	PlsT	60464	3273	12W-15S	D7
11800	PSPK	60464	3273	12W-15S	D7
12700	PSPK	60464	3345	12W-15S	D1
13000	PlsT	60462	3345	11W-15S	D1
13000	PSPK	60462	3345	11W-15S	D1
13400	OrlT	60462	3345	11W-15S	D2
13500	ODPK	60462	3345	11W-16S	D2
15700	ODPK	60462	3423	12W-18S	D1
15800	ODPK	60467	3423	12W-20S	D5
16600	ODHL	60467	3423	12W-19S	D3
16600	ODHL	60487	3423	12W-19S	D3
16600	ODPK	60487	3423	12W-19S	D3
16600	OrlT	60467	3423	12W-19S	D3
16600	OrlT	60487	3423	12W-19S	D3
20000	FKFT	60423	3503	11W-24S	E5
20000	FKFT	60448	3503	11W-24S	E5
20600	FftT	60423	3503	12W-24S	E6
21800	FftT	60423	3591	14W-28S	A6
22900	GGnT	60423	3591	14W-28S	A6
US-45 Lake St					
1000	MDLN	60060	2590	19W-28N	D5
1200	FmtT	60048	2590	19W-29N	D4
1200	FmtT	60060	2590	19W-29N	D4
1200	LYVL	60048	2590	19W-29N	D4
1200	MDLN	60048	2590	19W-29N	D4
US-45 N Lake St					
10	MDLN	60060	2646	19W-27N	D1
100	MDLN	60060	2590	19W-28N	D7
1200	FmtT	60048	2590	18W-29N	D4
1200	FmtT	60060	2590	18W-29N	D4
1200	LYVL	60048	2590	18W-29N	D4
1200	MDLN	60048	2590	18W-29N	D4
US-45 S Lake St					
10	MDLN	60060	2646	18W-25N	E4
1000	LbvT	60060	2646	18W-26N	E3
US-45 Mannheim Rd					
-	CHCG	60176	2917	12W-6N	B6
-	CHCG	60666	2917	12W-7N	A3
-	CHCG	60666	2973	12W-5N	B1
-	DSPN	60016	2863	13W-11N	A3
-	SRPK	60176	2917	12W-6N	B6
-	SRPK	60176	2973	12W-5N	B1
10	BLWD	60104	3029	12W-0N	A3
10	BLWD	60160	3029	12W-1N	A3
10	MLPK	60160	3029	12W-1N	A3
500	BLWD	60162	3029	12W-0N	A4
500	HLSD	60162	3029	12W-0N	A4
1000	DSPN	60016	2862	13W-10N	E5
1000	DSPN	60018	2862	13W-10N	E5
1700	DSPN	60018	2863	13W-9N	A6
2000	DSPN	60018	2917	13W-9N	A1
2000	RSMT	60018	2917	13W-9N	A1
2400	FNPK	60131	2973	13W-3N	A6
2400	LydT	60131	2973	13W-3N	A6
2400	LydT	60164	2973	13W-3N	A6
2600	FNPK	60164	2973	13W-3N	A5
2900	CHCG	60018	2917	12W-8N	A2
3700	FNPK	60176	2973	13W-4N	A3
3700	SRPK	60131	2973	13W-4N	A3
6400	RSMT	60666	2917	12W-8N	A3
US-45 N Mannheim Rd					
-	BLWD	60104	3029	13W-1N	A3
-	BLWD	60160	3029	13W-1N	A3
-	HLSD	60154	3029	12W-0S	A6
-	WSTR	60154	3029	12W-0S	A6
10	HLSD	60104	3029	12W-0S	A6
10	HLSD	60162	3029	12W-0S	A6
100	BLWD	60162	3029	12W-0S	A5
1500	MLPK	60160	3029	13W-1N	A2
1500	SNPK	60160	3029	12W-1N	A2
1500	SNPK	60165	3029	12W-1N	A2
1800	MLPK	60164	3029	12W-1N	A1
1800	MLPK	60165	3029	12W-1N	A1
1800	SNPK	60164	3029	12W-1N	A1
2000	LydT	60160	2973	12W-2N	A7
2000	LydT	60164	2973	12W-2N	A7
2000	MLPK	60160	2973	12W-2N	A7
2000	NHLK	60160	2973	12W-2N	A7
2000	NHLK	60164	2973	12W-2N	A7
2300	LydT	60131	2973	12W-2N	A6
US-45 S Mannheim Rd					
-	BLWD	60104	3029	12W-0S	A6
-	HLSD	60104	3029	12W-0S	A6
10	HLSD	60154	3029	12W-0S	A6
10	HLSD	60162	3029	12W-0S	A7
10	WSTR	60154	3029	13W-0S	A6
100	WSTR	60162	3029	12W-0S	A7
300	PvsT	60162	3029	12W-0S	A7
1400	PvsT	60162	3087	12W-1S	A1
1400	WSTR	60154	3087	13W-1S	A1
1400	WSTR	60162	3087	12W-1S	A1
2100	PvsT	60154	3087	12W-1S	A2
2100	PvsT	60525	3087	12W-1S	A2
US-45 Milwaukee Av					
200	LNSH	60061	2702	15W-23N	A2
200	LNSH	60069	2702	15W-23N	A2
200	VNHL	60061	2702	15W-23N	A2
200	VNHL	60069	2702	15W-23N	A2
200	VrnT	60061	2702	15W-23N	A2
300	VrnT	60069	2702	15W-23N	A2
900	BFGV	60089	2755	14W-20N	C1
900	VrnT	60015	2755	14W-20N	C1
900	VrnT	60062	2755	14W-20N	C1
900	VrnT	60089	2755	14W-20N	C1
1000	BFGV	60089	2702	14W-20N	B7
1000	RVWD	60015	2702	14W-20N	B7
1000	RVWD	60015	2755	14W-20N	C1
1000	VrnT	60015	2702	14W-20N	B7
1400	LNSH	60015	2702	14W-21N	B6
20400	BFGV	60090	2755	14W-20N	C1
US-45 N Milwaukee Av					
500	PTHT	60062	2809	13W-15N	A1
500	PTHT	60070	2809	13W-15N	A1
500	PTHT	60090	2809	13W-15N	A1
500	WhlT	60062	2809	13W-15N	A1
500	WhlT	60090	2809	13W-15N	A1
500	WLNG	60090	2755	13W-17N	D5
800	BFGV	60090	2755	14W-20N	C2
900	BFGV	60089	2755	14W-20N	C1
900	VrnT	60062	2755	14W-20N	C1
900	VrnT	60089	2755	14W-20N	C1
21800	LNSH	60069	2702	15W-21N	B5
21800	VrnT	60069	2702	14W-21N	B5
US-45 S Milwaukee Av					
10	WLNG	60090	2755	14W-18N	D4
600	WhlT	60090	2755	13W-17N	E5
1000	PTHT	60070	2755	13W-16N	E7
1000	PTHT	60070	2808	13W-16N	E1
1000	PTHT	60070	2809	13W-16N	A1
1000	PTHT	60090	2809	13W-16N	A1
1000	WhlT	60070	2808	13W-16N	E1
1000	WhlT	60090	2809	13W-16N	A1
US-45 N River Rd					
10	DSPN	60016	2863	13W-12N	A2
100	MaiT	60016	2863	13W-12N	A1
400	WhlT	60056	2808	13W-13N	E6
600	MPPT	60056	2808	13W-13N	E6
600	WhlT	60025	2808	13W-13N	E6
700	DSPN	60016	2808	13W-12N	E7
700	DSPN	60016	2809	13W-12N	A7
700	MaiT	60016	2808	13W-12N	E7
700	MaiT	60016	2809	13W-12N	A7
900	MPPT	60025	2808	13W-14N	E5
1300	MPPT	60056	2809	13W-14N	A3
1300	WhlT	60025	2809	13W-14N	A3
1300	WhlT	60056	2809	13W-14N	A3
1300	WhlT	60062	2809	13W-14N	A3
1500	PTHT	60070	2809	13W-15N	A2
US-45 S River Rd					
10	DSPN	60016	2863	13W-11N	A2
1200	MPPT	60056	2809	13W-15N	A2
1200	PTHT	60070	2809	12W-15N	A2
1200	WhlT	60056	2809	13W-15N	A2
1200	WhlT	60062	2809	13W-15N	A2
US-45 US Highway 45					
400	AvnT	60030	2533	18W-32N	D4
400	GYLK	60030	2533	18W-32N	D5
700	WrnT	60030	2533	18W-32N	D5
US-45 N US Highway 45					
31100	FmtT	60048	2533	19W-31N	D7
31100	LbvT	60048	2533	19W-31N	D7
31200	GYLK	60030	2533	19W-31N	D7
31200	LbvT	60030	2533	19W-31N	D7
32000	WrnT	60030	2533	18W-32N	D5
US-52					
-	JltT	60421	3588	21W-27S	B5
-	JltT	60433	3588	21W-27S	B4
-	MHTN	60442	3677	20W-29S	D2
-	MHTN	60442	3678	18W-32S	A6
-	MHTN	60442	3767	18W-34S	C4
-	MhtT	60442	3588	20W-27S	B5
US-52					
-	MhtT	60442	3677	20W-29S	D2
-	MhtT	60442	3678	19W-31S	A6
-	MhtT	60442	3767	18W-34S	C4
-	NlxT	60421	3588	20W-27S	B5
-	NlxT	60433	3588	21W-27S	B5
-	NlxT	60442	3588	20W-27S	B5
-	WltT	60442	3767	17W-35S	C7
US-52 S Cedar Rd					
27700	MhtT	60442	3767	17W-33S	C3
27800	WltT	60442	3767	17W-33S	C3
US-52 S Chicago St					
-	JLET	60436	3498	24W-24S	E6
400	JLET	60433	3499	24W-24S	A6
400	JLET	60436	3499	24W-24S	A6
600	JltT	60436	3499	23W-25S	A7
US-52 Doris Av					
10	JLET	60433	3499	23W-25S	A7
10	JLET	60436	3499	23W-25S	A7
10	JltT	60436	3499	23W-25S	A7
US-52 Gardner St					
1000	JLET	60433	3499	23W-25S	A7
1000	JLET	60436	3499	23W-25S	A7
1100	JLET	60433	3587	23W-25S	A1
1100	JltT	60433	3587	23W-25S	A1
US-52 W Jefferson St					
-	SwdT	60447	3495	32W-24S	C6
100	SRWD	60404	3496	30W-23S	C5
100	SRWD	60431	3496	30W-23S	C5
800	JLET	60435	3498	26W-24S	A5
800	JLET	60436	3498	26W-24S	A5
1200	TroT	60404	3496	31W-23S	A5
1800	JLET	60435	3497	27W-24S	C5
1800	JLET	60436	3497	27W-24S	C5
2800	JLET	60431	3497	27W-23S	C5
3200	TroT	60431	3497	28W-23S	B5
3700	JLET	60431	3496	31W-24S	A5
3700	TroT	60431	3496	31W-24S	A5
24200	SRWD	60404	3495	31W-23S	E5
24200	TroT	60404	3495	31W-23S	E5
US-52 W Joliet Rd					
13000	WltT	60442	3767	16W-35S	E7
US-52 Manhattan Rd					
10	JLET	60433	3587	23W-25S	A1
10	JltT	60433	3587	23W-25S	A1
2100	JltT	60421	3588	20W-28S	B6
2100	JltT	60433	3588	20W-28S	B6
US-52 W McDonough St					
10	JLET	60436	3498	24W-24S	E6
US-52 W North St					
100	MHTN	60442	3677	19W-30S	E4
500	MhtT	60442	3677	19W-30S	D3
US-52 S Raynor Av					
-	JLET	60435	3498	24W-23S	D5
10	JLET	60436	3498	24W-24S	D5
US-52 S State St					
100	MHTN	60442	3677	19W-31S	E4
300	MHTN	60442	3678	18W-32S	B7
500	MhtT	60442	3678	19W-31S	A5
USG Dr					
1900	FmtT	60048	2590	18W-29N	D3
1900	FmtT	60060	2590	18W-29N	D3
1900	LYVL	60048	2590	18W-29N	D3
US Highway 34					
1200	MTGY	60538	3200	34W-10S	E6
1200	MTGY	60543	3200	34W-10S	D6
1200	OSWG	60538	3200	34W-10S	E6
1200	OSWG	60543	3200	34W-10S	E6
1200	OswT	60543	3200	34W-10S	E6
7200	BtlT	60543	3262	40W-13S	C4
7200	BtlT	60560	3262	40W-13S	C4
US Highway 34 US-30					
1200	MTGY	60538	3200	34W-10S	E6
1200	MTGY	60543	3200	34W-10S	E6
1200	OSWG	60538	3200	34W-10S	E6
1200	OSWG	60543	3200	34W-10S	E6
1200	OswT	60543	3200	34W-10S	E6
US Highway 34 US-34					
1200	MTGY	60538	3200	34W-10S	E6
1200	MTGY	60543	3200	34W-10S	D6
1200	OSWG	60538	3200	34W-10S	E6
1200	OSWG	60543	3200	34W-10S	D6
1200	OswT	60543	3200	34W-10S	E6
7200	BtlT	60543	3262	40W-13S	C4
7200	BtlT	60560	3262	40W-13S	C4
US Highway 45					
400	AvnT	60030	2533	18W-32N	D4
400	GYLK	60030	2533	18W-32N	D5
700	WrnT	60030	2533	18W-32N	D5
US Highway 45 US-45					
400	AvnT	60030	2533	18W-32N	D4
400	GYLK	60030	2533	18W-32N	D5
700	WrnT	60030	2533	18W-32N	D5
N US Highway 45					
31100	FmtT	60048	2533	19W-31N	D7
31100	LbvT	60048	2533	19W-31N	D7
31200	GYLK	60030	2533	19W-31N	D7
31200	LbvT	60030	2533	19W-31N	D7
32000	WrnT	60030	2533	18W-32N	D5
N US Highway 45 US-45					
31100	FmtT	60048	2533	19W-31N	D7
31100	LbvT	60048	2533	19W-31N	D7
31200	GYLK	60030	2533	19W-31N	D7
31200	LbvT	60030	2533	19W-31N	D7
32000	WrnT	60030	2533	18W-32N	D5
US Route 30					
-	MTGY	60538	3199	37W-9S	B5
US Route 30 US-30					
-	MTGY	60538	3199	37W-9S	B5
Usufruct Av					
10	CHCG	60616	3092	0W-3S	B4
Utah Cir					
700	EGVV	60007	2913	21W-9N	E1
Utah Ct					
3700	NCHI	60088	2593	12W-30N	C1
10500	ODPK	60467	3423	13W-21S	B7
Utah St					
10	FKFT	60423	3591	12W-26S	D2
700	EGVV	60007	2859	21W-9N	E7
700	EGVV	60007	2913	21W-9N	E1
Ute Ln					
700	CLSM	60188	2967	26W-3N	E6
W Ute Ln					
7200	PSHT	60463	3346	9W-15S	E1
Ute Rd					
4600	MchT	60097	2469	35W-36N	E4
Uteg St					
100	CLLK	60014	2640	35W-25N	A5
200	CLLK	60014	2639	35W-25N	E5
Utica Av					
13600	RBBN	60472	3349	3W-16S	A3
S Utica Av					
-	CHCG	60652	3212	3W-10S	E4
-	ENGN	60652	3212	3W-10S	E4
8700	ENGN	60805	3212	3W-10S	E5

STREET Block City ZIP Map# CGS Grid

Utility Ct
7600 SPGV 60081 2413 31W-39N E4
W Utley Rd
300 EMHT 60126 3027 16W-1N D2
Utopia Ln
300 SchT 60175 2963 38W-3N B6
Uvedale Ct
400 RVSD 60546 3088 9W-2S C3
Uvedale Rd
200 RVSD 60546 3088 9W-2S C4
Uxbridge Dr
8100 ODPK 60462 3346 10W-16S C4

V

Vacation Vil
- FXLK 60020 2414 29W-38N B6
- FXLK 60081 2414 29W-38N B6
Vachel Lindsey St
400 CmpT 60175 2962 40W-3N C6
Vada Ct
1800 SMBG 60193 2912 25W-8N A2
Vail Av
14300 DXMR 60426 3349 2W-17S C5
14700 HRVY 60426 3349 2W-17S C6
N Vail Av
10 ANHT 60005 2807 17W-14N A5
1800 ANHT 60004 2807 17W-15N A1
S Vail Av
1000 ANHT 60005 2807 18W-12N A7
1200 ANHT 60005 2861 18W-12N A1
Vail Ct
100 GLBT 60136 2799 39W-15N A4
100 WHTN 60187 3082 24W-2S D3
500 WLNG 60090 2754 16W-18N E3
1100 NPVL 60540 3202 28W-8S E2
2800 LSLE 60532 3142 24W-7S C7
3700 JLET 60451 3500 19W-22S E2
8000 LGGV 60060 2645 20W-25N E4
15100 ODPK 60467 3344 14W-18S D6
Vail Dr
100 FKFT 60423 3503 12W-25S D7
500 FftT 60423 3503 12W-25S D7
3100 RcmT 60081 2413 32W-40N C3
3100 SPGV 60081 2413 32W-40N C3
6700 WTMT 60559 3145 18W-7S A6
W Vail Dr
8700 PSHL 60465 3274 10W-12S A2
Vail Ln
1900 GLHT 60139 2969 23W-3N A5
8800 DGvT 60516 3206 20W-10S B6
8800 DGvT 60517 3206 20W-10S B6
8800 WDRG 60517 3206 20W-10S B6
Vail Colony St
10 FXLK 60020 2414 28W-38N D6
Vail Ridge Dr
- JLET 60586 3495 32W-21S D1
W Val Ct
1500 MchT 60051 2529 30W-33N A3
Valayna Dr
1300 AURA 60504 3201 32W-9S D4
Vale Av
- SRGV 60554 3135 42W-6S C5
Vale Ct
- WLSP 60480 3208 14W-9S E3
- WLSP 60525 3208 14W-9S E3
100 LslT 60517 3143 21W-7S D6
Vale Rd
10 CLSM 60185 2967 27W-2N D7
10 CLSM 60188 2967 27W-2N D7
10 WynT 60185 2966 29W-2N C7
10 WynT 60185 2967 27W-2N D7
10 WynT 60185 3022 29W-2N D1
10 WynT 60188 2967 27W-2N D7
Vale St
1600 MchT 60051 2529 30W-32N A5
Valencia Av
- BRTN 60010 2751 25W-20N A1
E Valencia Av
400 BRTN 60010 2751 25W-20N A1
Valencia Ct
10 NpvT 60563 3140 30W-5S C4
1400 CTCY 60409 3429 2E-19S D3
Valencia Dr
800 SRWD 60404 3496 30W-24S C7
2000 NHBK 60062 2810 10W-15N A1
Valencia Ln
- ALGN 60102 2746 37W-20N B2
Valencia Pkwy
- RtdT 60118 2746 38W-17N C7
- RtdT 60118 2799 38W-16N B1
Valencia Wy
1500 MDLN 60060 2590 19W-29N C4
Valene Dr
600 PKCY 60085 2535 13W-33N E3
Valentina Dr
15100 ODPK 60462 3346 10W-18S A6
Valentine Ct
- NBRN 60010 2644 24W-25N C6
24400 ElaT 60047 2644 24W-25N C6
24400 NBRN 60047 2644 24W-25N C6
N Valentine Rd
27900 WcnT 60084 2588 25W-27N A7
Valentine St
10 CPVL 60110 2747 34W-17N E7
Valentine Wy
- OSWG 60543 3265 33W-11S B2
Valerian Ln
500 WDSK 60098 2581 41W-30N D2
Valerie Ct
200 MaiT 60025 2864 9W-12N B1
17700 ODPK 60467 3423 13W-21S A6
Valerie Dr
500 BlmT 60411 3510 4E-25S C7
500 LYWD 60411 3510 4E-25S C7
4600 AlqT 60014 2640 33W-25N D4
4800 CLLK 60014 2640 33W-25N D4
N Valerie Ln
500 ADSN 60101 2970 18W-4N E4
E Valerio Rd
- WmTp 60416 3941 33W-39S B1
8000 CLCY 60416 3941 33W-39S B1
8000 DMND 60416 3941 33W-39S B1
8000 FlxT 60416 3941 33W-39S A1
Valewood Ct
10 SMWD 60107 2856 29W-9N D7
Valewood Dr
1100 BRLT 60107 2856 29W-9N D7
1100 HnrT 60107 2856 29W-9N D7
1100 SMWD 60107 2856 29W-9N D7
Valewood Rd
100 WynT 60185 2966 29W-3N C6
900 BRLT 60103 2910 29W-6N C6
Valhalla Cir
300 CLLK 60014 2641 33W-24N A6
Valhalla Ct
10 LIHL 60156 2693 36W-22N C4
W Valhalla Ter
400 VNHL 60061 2647 17W-27N B1
E Vallette St
100 EMHT 60126 3027 16W-1N E3
400 BKLY 60163 3028 15W-0N B4
400 EMHT 60126 3028 15W-0N B4
W Vallette St
100 EMHT 60126 3027 16W-0N E4
Valle Vista Ct
200 MNKA 60447 3672 32W-29S C2
Valley
- ELGN 60120 2855 32W-10N C6
Valley Av
- MchT 60051 2529 29W-32N B6
200 AURA 60505 3138 35W-7S C7
800 GNEN 60137 3025 21W-0S D6
N Valley Av
1000 JLET 60432 3499 23W-22S B2
S Valley Cir
600 PLTN 60067 2805 21W-14N C3
Valley Ct
1300 LbvT 60048 2590 18W-30N E1
8100 PSHL 60465 3274 10W-12S C3
10600 ODPK 60462 3345 13W-17S A6
N Valley Ct
300 BRTN 60010 2751 24W-20N C1
Valley Dr
- SchT 60174 2908 34W-6N D7
10 AlqT 60013 2641 31W-26N E3
10 BNHL 60010 2749 28W-18N D4
10 ODHL 60013 2641 31W-26N E3
100 BGBK 60440 3268 24W-12S D2
100 CmpT 60151 3017 43W-2N A1
100 ELBN 60119 3017 43W-2N A1
200 LNHT 60046 2476 20W-37N B1
400 NPVL 60563 3141 28W-6S A4
600 LMNT 60439 3270 19W-14S C6
7400 FoxT 60541 3331 48W-17S A7
8000 PSHL 60465 3274 10W-12S C3
17100 ODPK 60462 3424 10W-20S B4
17100 ODPK 60487 3424 10W-20S B4
17100 TYPK 60487 3424 10W-20S B4
22700 RNPK 60471 3594 6W-27S A5
23900 ElaT 60047 2699 21W-23N D1
W Valley Dr
5200 RcmT 60071 2353 34W-41N C7
5200 RHMD 60071 2353 34W-41N C7
18000 WrnT 60030 2534 18W-33N A3
Valley Ln
- HFET 60195 2858 24W-11N E3
- SMBG 60169 2858 24W-12N E2
- SMBG 60195 2858 24W-11N E3
700 BmdT 60143 2913 21W-6N D5
800 GNVA 60134 3020 34W-1N E4
800 LKPT 60441 3419 21W-19S D3
1000 HFET 60169 2858 24W-11N E3
5000 SMWD 60107 2911 28W-9N A2
E Valley Ln
- SMWD 60107 2911 28W-9N A1
200 ANHT 60004 2754 17W-16N B7
S Valley Ln
800 PLTN 60067 2805 21W-14N C3
W Valley Ln
600 PLTN 60067 2805 21W-14N C3
Valley Pkwy E
1600 JltT 60433 3587 23W-26S B2
Valley Pkwy W
1700 JltT 60433 3587 23W-26S B2
Valley Rd
- MHRY 60050 2528 32W-32N C5
- WPHR 60096 2362 11W-42N E5
10 BmdT 60172 2912 23W-7N E5
10 HDPK 60035 2758 7W-20N B2
10 INCK 60061 2647 17W-24N B6
10 LMBD 60148 3083 21W-2S E3
10 MltT 60148 3083 21W-2S E3
10 NtrT 60062 2758 7W-20N B2
10 ROSL 60172 2912 23W-7N E5
10 VNHL 60061 2647 17W-24N B6
100 MltT 60137 3083 21W-1S E1
200 TVLY 60013 2695 31W-22N C3
300 BtvT 60542 3077 36W-3S E6
300 NARA 60542 3077 36W-3S E6
400 LKFT 60045 2649 10W-25N E6
600 GNEN 60137 3025 21W-0S E7
600 MltT 60137 3025 21W-0S E7
700 LKFT 60045 2650 10W-24N A7
800 GLNC 60022 2758 7W-17N C4
1100 BKBN 60015 2703 11W-22N D4
1100 HDPK 60035 2650 10W-24N A7
1100 LKFT 60035 2650 10W-24N A7
2100 NHBK 60062 2756 11W-16N C7
N Valley Rd
100 BRTN 60010 2751 24W-20N C1
20800 KLDR 60047 2699 21W-21N E7
23400 ElaT 60047 2699 21W-23N C1
S Valley Rd
- BRTN 60010 2751 24W-18N C2
100 MHRY 60050 2528 32W-31N C6
1000 LMBD 60148 3083 21W-1S E1
W Valley Rd
400 ITSC 60143 2914 20W-6N B7
28400 GrtT 60041 2472 28W-35N E6
Valley St
- MchT 60051 2529 30W-32N A5
100 BRLT 60103 2910 29W-8N E3
12600 NlxT 60448 3502 15W-22S B1
Valley Wy
400 NHBK 60062 2758 8W-16N A7
400 NHBK 60093 2758 8W-16N A7
400 NHFD 60093 2758 8W-16N A7
500 NHFD 60093 2757 8W-16N E7
Valley Brook Dr
11500 ODPK 60467 3422 14W-20S D5
Valley Castle Ln
8600 TYPK 60477 3504 10W-23S B3
Valley Creek Dr
1900 ELGN 60123 2854 36W-12N A2
2100 ELGN 60123 2853 36W-12N E2
Valley Falls St
- ElgT 60124 2853 38W-11N B4
Valley Forge Av
200 SEGN 60177 2908 35W-7N C4
Valley Forge Ct
400 AURA 60504 3140 30W-7S A7
1600 WHTN 60187 3082 24W-2S E3
Valley Forge Dr
2800 JLET 60435 3417 27W-21S C7
17300 TYPK 60477 3424 10W-20S C5
Valley Forge Ln
500 MDLN 60060 2646 19W-27N C2
Valley Forge Pl
1600 DRGV 60516 3144 20W-7S B7
Valley Forge Rd
2600 LSLE 60532 3142 24W-7S C6
N Valley Hill Rd
10 BLVY 60098 2526 36W-32N C4
200 GwdT 60098 2526 37W-32N C4
7500 MchT 60050 2526 36W-32N C4
7500 MchT 60098 2526 36W-32N C4
7500 MHRY 60050 2526 36W-32N C4
S Valley Hill Rd
10 BLVY 60098 2526 37W-31N B6
600 BLVY 60098 2583 37W-31N B1
600 DrrT 60098 2583 37W-31N B1
Valley Lake Dr
1000 IVNS 60067 2805 22W-14N A4
1200 SMBG 60173 2859 23W-12N A1
1200 SMBG 60195 2858 23W-12N E2
1200 SMBG 60195 2859 23W-12N A1
1400 PLTN 60067 2805 22W-14N A4
Valley Lakes Blvd
- RDLK 60073 2531 25W-33N A3
Valley Lo Ln
2000 GNVW 60025 2810 8W-15N E3
Valley Park Dr
500 LYVL 60048 2591 16W-28N E6
Valley Ridge Ct
1600 NPVL 60565 3204 24W-9S D4
Valley Ridge Dr
- JLET 60586 3495 32W-21S D1
Valley Stream Dr
800 PGGV 60140 2798 41W-15N A5
800 WLNG 60090 2755 15W-18N A3
900 WLNG 60090 2754 16W-18N E3
1000 PGGV 60140 2797 41W-14N E5
Valley View Cir
6300 LGGV 60047 2700 19W-24N D1
Valley View Ct
10 LMNT 60439 3342 20W-15S A2
100 ALGN 60102 2694 33W-21N E6
200 WLMT 60091 2811 5W-13N E7
700 AURA 60502 3139 32W-7S C6
1500 NPVL 60565 3204 24W-9S D4
8100 TYPK 60477 3424 10W-20S C5
14500 OrlT 60467 3344 14W-17S D5
Valleyview Ct
12900 PNFD 60585 3338 29W-15S D2
Valley View Dr
10 DPgT 60441 3342 20W-15S A2
10 LMNT 60439 3342 20W-15S A2
100 DGvT 60527 3207 16W-10S E5
200 MltT 60148 3025 21W-1N E1
200 SCRL 60175 2963 37W-2N C7
200 WLMT 60091 2811 5W-13N E7
400 GNCY 53128 2352 E3
400 SCRL 60175 3019 37W-2N C1
500 ADSN 60101 2969 22W-3N D5
500 ANTH 60002 2357 24W-42N D6
500 BMDL 60101 2969 22W-3N D5
500 BmdT 60101 2969 22W-3N D5
700 SmbT 60193 2912 25W-8N B2
800 DRGV 60516 3144 19W-7S D7
1600 SMBG 60193 2912 25W-8N B2
8000 TYPK 60477 3424 10W-20S C5
Valleyview Dr
10 MltT 60137 3025 22W-1N C2
14400 OrlT 60467 3344 14W-17S D5
E Valleyview Dr
400 BRLT 60103 2911 27W-7N C5
N Valley View Dr
33000 GrtT 60073 2531 25W-33N B3
33000 RDLK 60073 2531 25W-33N B3
33000 WrnT 60030 2533 18W-33N D3
W Valley View Dr
- WcnT 60051 2529 29W-31N D6
100 LKMR 60051 2529 29W-32N D6
13100 HMGN 60491 3421 16W-19S E2
Valley View Ln
2300 CteT 60417 3684 2W-29S C1
2300 MltT 60417 3684 2W-29S C1
2300 MonT 60417 3684 2W-29S C1
2300 MonT 60466 3684 2W-29S C1
6300 LGGV 60047 2646 19W-24N C7
6300 LGGV 60047 2700 19W-24N D1
7800 WDRG 60517 3205 21W-9S E3
Valleyview Ln
100 DYR 46311 3598 C5
100 SjnT 46311 3598 D5
Valley View Pl
1600 JltT 60432 3499 21W-22S E2
Valley View Rd
300 LKBN 60010 2643 26W-24N D7
700 DndT 60118 2747 35W-18N B5
1900 NHFD 60093 2758 7W-16N A7
2800 WDWH 60031 2478 15W-37N A2
2800 WDWH 60083 2478 15W-37N A2
3800 PRGV 60012 2585 32W-27N C7
4000 PRGV 60012 2641 32W-27N C1
4000 PRGV 60014 2641 32W-27N C1
4800 NndT 60013 2641 31W-26N C3
4800 NndT 60014 2641 31W-26N C3
4800 PRGV 60013 2641 32W-27N C1
4900 ODHL 60013 2641 31W-26N C2
4900 ODHL 60014 2641 31W-26N C2
5900 AlqT 60013 2641 31W-26N C3
5900 AlqT 60014 2641 31W-26N C3
6600 HRPK 60133 2911 26W-8N D3
Valley View Tr
800 CLSM 60188 2967 27W-3N C5
Valleywood Dr
100 CteT 60417 3596 1W-28S A7
100 CteT 60475 3596 1W-28S A7
100 STGR 60475 3596 1W-28S A7
Valor Ct
2000 GNVW 60025 2810 9W-14N B3
S Valor Ct
300 PLTN 60074 2806 19W-15N D2
Valor Dr
2600 GNVW 60025 2810 9W-14N B4
Valparaiso Dr
9600 MNSR 46321 3510 E3
Vals Ct
10 LYWD 60411 3598 4E-25S C1
Val Verde Ct
1300 JLET 60586 3496 30W-22S B2
W Van Ct
12400 BHPK 60099 2421 12W-40N B3
12400 ZION 60099 2421 12W-40N B3
Van St
500 ELGN 60123 2854 34W-11N D4
Vana Dr
100 WLSP 60480 3209 12W-9S D3
300 CPVL 60110 2747 34W-17N E7
Van Acker Rd
10 HTLY 60140 2744 42W-17N D6
10 HTLY 60142 2744 42W-17N D6
N Van Auken St
400 EMHT 60126 2972 15W-2N A6
800 AddT 60126 2972 15W-2N A6
S Van Beverin Dr
12000 ALSP 60803 3276 5W-14S C5
Van Buren Av
700 SCRL 60174 2964 34W-3N D6
900 DYR 46311 3510 D6
900 SCRL 60174 3020 35W-2N C1
1100 WCDA 60084 2588 25W-28N B6
1100 WcnT 60084 2588 25W-28N B6
1200 DSPN 60018 2862 13W-10N E5
1200 DSPN 60018 2863 13W-10N A5
6100 HMND 46324 3430 D2
7800 MNSR 46321 3430 D5
E Van Buren Av
100 NPVL 60540 3141 26W-6S E5
W Van Buren Av
500 NPVL 60540 3141 27W-6S C5
Van Buren Ct
900 VNHL 60061 2647 17W-26N B4
1300 AURA 60506 3137 37W-6S C5
8400 MNSR 46321 3430 D7
Van Buren St
- HLSD 60162 3028 14W-0S C6
- MYWD 60104 3029 11W-0S D6
- MYWD 60153 3030 10W-0S A6
- RGWD 60072 2470 34W-36N D4
10 CHCG 60644 3031 7W-0S B5
10 OKPK 60304 3031 8W-0S A5
10 OKPK 60644 3031 7W-0S B5
100 WMTN 60481 3853 27W-38S D6
300 CLLK 60014 2639 36W-25N E5
300 EGvT 60018 2862 15W-9N A7
800 OKPK 60304 3030 8W-0S E5
1000 DSPN 60018 2862 13W-10N E5
1000 MYWD 60153 3029 11W-0S C6
2500 BLWD 60104 3029 12W-0S C6
3800 HLSD 60104 3029 12W-0S A6
3800 HLSD 60162 3029 12W-0S A6
7600 FTPK 60130 3030 9W-0S C5
7700 RVFT 60130 3030 9W-0S C5
7700 RVFT 60305 3030 9W-0S C5
14400 DLTN 60419 3351 0E-16S A4
E Van Buren St
10 CHCG 60604 3034 0E-0S C5
10 CHCG 60605 3034 0E-0S C5
10 JLET 60432 3499 23W-23S A4
10 OSWG 60543 3263 37W-12S D4
100 EMHT 60126 3027 16W-0N C5
100 EMHT 60126 3028 15W-0S A6
100 MRGO 60152 2634 49W-26N B2
100 WDSK 60098 2524 41W-31N D7
400 VLPK 60181 3027 17W-0S C6
N Van Buren St
10 BTVA 60510 3078 35W-1S C1
10 EDND 60118 2801 33W-16N A2
500 CPVL 60118 2801 33W-16N A1
700 BTVA 60510 3020 35W-0S C7
S Van Buren St
10 BTVA 60510 3078 35W-1S C2
10 EDND 60118 2801 33W-16N A2
100 GDLY 60407 4030 32W-43S C2
W Van Buren St
10 CHCG 60604 3034 0W-0S B5
10 CHCG 60605 3034 0W-0S B5
10 JLET 60432 3498 24W-23S E4
10 OSWG 60543 3263 37W-12S C4
100 CHCG 60606 3034 0W-0S B5
100 CHCG 60607 3034 0W-0S A5
100 EMHT 60126 3027 16W-0S E6
100 MRGO 60152 2634 50W-26N B2
100 WDSK 60098 2524 41W-31N D7
500 CHCG 60661 3034 0W-0S A5
800 CHCG 60607 3033 1W-0S E5
1500 CHCG 60612 3033 2W-0S B5
2800 CHCG 60612 3032 3W-0S E5
3500 CHCG 60624 3032 4W-0S D5
4600 CHCG 60644 3032 5W-0S A5
4700 CHCG 60644 3031 6W-0S E5
26100 GrtT 60041 2473 26W-34N E7
Vance Ct
100 LKBN 60010 2696 28W-23N E1
100 LKBN 60010 2697 28W-23N A1
Vance St
- YkTp 60148 3026 20W-0N A5
100 LMBD 60148 3026 20W-0N A4
Vancina Ln
100 NLNX 60451 3502 15W-25S B7
100 NlxT 60451 3502 15W-25S B7
Vandalia St
300 ELGN 60123 2854 34W-10N D5
Van Dam Rd
- CTCY 60409 3429 1E-19S C1
- SHLD 60409 3429 1E-19S C1
15900 SHLD 60473 3429 1E-19S B1
Van Damin Av
300 GNEN 60137 3025 22W-0S D6
Vandenburgh Dr
- SBTN 60010 2803 26W-13N C6
Vanderbilt Ct
2000 NPVL 60565 3204 24W-9S C5
Vanderbilt Dr
500 NLNX 60451 3502 16W-25S A7
700 NLNX 60451 3590 16W-25S B1
2100 GNVA 60134 3019 36W-1N D2
2100 SCRL 60134 3019 36W-1N D2
2100 SCRL 60174 3019 36W-1N D2
S Vanderbilt Dr
18800 MKNA 60448 3503 11W-22S E1
E Vandermeer Dr
10 ANTH 60002 2358 22W-42N A5
W Vandermeer Dr
10 ANTH 60002 2358 23W-42N A5
S Vanderpoel Av
9200 CHCG 60620 3213 2W-10S D5
9500 CHCG 60643 3213 2W-11S D6
Vanderwalker Ln
400 BlmT 60430 3507 1W-23S E3
400 CHHT 60411 3507 1W-23S E3
E Vandrunen Dr
2500 CteT 60417 3686 3E-31S E5
2500 CteT 60417 3687 3E-31S A5
Van Drunen Rd
15600 PHNX 60426 3350 0W-18S C7
15600 PHNX 60473 3350 0W-18S C7
15600 SHLD 60426 3350 0W-18S C7
15600 SHLD 60473 3350 0W-18S C7
15600 SHLD 60473 3428 0W-18S C1
Vandustrial Dr
1000 WTMT 60559 3145 18W-6S A5
Vandustrial Ln
16000 HRVY 60426 3428 0W-18S B1
16000 SHLD 60426 3428 0W-18S B1
16000 SHLD 60473 3428 0W-18S B1
Van Dyke Dr
10 ANTH 60002 2358 23W-42N A5
Van Dyke Ln
1800 CPVL 60110 2746 37W-17N D6
Van Dyke Rd
- PNFD 60544 3338 30W-18S B7
- PNFD 60544 3416 30W-18S A1
- PNFD 60586 3415 31W-19S E3
1200 JLET 60431 3495 33W-22S B2
1200 JLET 60447 3495 33W-22S B2
S Van Dyke Rd
1400 PNFD 60544 3338 30W-17S B6
12200 PNFD 60585 3266 30W-14S B7
12200 WldT 60585 3266 30W-14S B7
12300 PNFD 60585 3338 30W-15S B2
12300 WldT 60585 3338 30W-14S B1
14800 PnfT 60544 3338 30W-17S B7
Van Emmon Rd
7800 OswT 60560 3334 41W-15S A2
8100 KdlT 60560 3333 42W-15S D2
8100 OswT 60560 3333 42W-15S D2
9300 YKVL 60560 3333 42W-15S D2
E Van Emmon St
100 YKVL 60560 3333 42W-15S C2
300 KdlT 60560 3333 42W-15S D2
W Van Emmon St
100 YKVL 60560 3333 43W-15S B2
Vanessa Ln
400 BGBK 60440 3268 24W-13S E4
Van Gogh Cir
400 BGBK 60440 3205 22W-11S C7
Van Gough Dr
300 PTON 60468 3860 9W-37S E3
Van Horn Ct
2200 JLET 60586 3416 29W-21S D6
W Van Horn Ln
23400 PNFD 60586 3416 29W-20S E5
23400 PnfT 60586 3416 29W-20S E5
N Van Horn St
100 BCVL 60407 4030 34W-44S A4
400 BvlT 60407 4030 34W-44S A4
S Van Horn St
100 BCVL 60407 4030 34W-44S A4
Vanilla Grass Dr
3400 NPVL 60564 3266 30W-11S A1
Vankalker Dr
2000 CteT 60417 3686 2E-31S D6
Van Meter Ct
1600 GLHT 60139 2968 23W-3N E6
Van Meter Dr
1400 GLHT 60139 2968 23W-2N E7
Van Meter St
1600 GLHT 60139 2968 23W-2N E7
Vanna Ct
300 HLSD 60162 3028 13W-0S E5
N Van Nortwick Av
10 BTVA 60510 3078 36W-1S A1
500 BTVA 60510 3020 36W-0S A7
700 BTVA 60134 3020 36W-0S A7
700 GnvT 60134 3020 36W-0S A7
S Van Nortwick Av
10 BTVA 60510 3078 36W-1S A2
Van Nortwick Cir
500 BTVA 60510 3020 36W-0S A7
Van Nortwick Ct
600 BTVA 60510 3020 35W-0S A7
Van Nostrand Pl
600 ELGN 60120 2855 33W-10N B5
Van Patten Wood
13900 NptT 60099 2361 15W-42N A6
Vans Dr
10100 FKFT 60423 3591 12W-26S C2
Van Selow Dr
- DSPN 60018 2917 11W-7N D3
Vantage Dr
- SRWD 60404 3495 31W-24S E7
- SRWD 60404 3496 31W-24S A7
2400 ELGN 60124 2799 37W-15N E4
Vantage Ln
- GNVW 60025 2810 10W-15N A3
3600 GNVW 60025 2809 10W-15N E3
Vantage St
2000 WDRG 60517 3144 21W-7S A7
Van Tassel Dr
1000 SYHW 60118 2800 36W-15N B3
Vantroba Dr
10 GLHT 60139 2968 23W-2N E7
100 BmdT 60137 2969 23W-2N A7
100 GLHT 60137 2969 23W-2N A7
100 GLHT 60139 2969 23W-2N A7
S Van Vlissingen Rd
9600 CHCG 60617 3215 2E-11S C7
N Vapor Ln
6400 MNGV 60053 2865 8W-9N A6
6400 MNGV 60714 2865 8W-9N A6
6400 NLES 60714 2865 8W-9N A6
Vardon
- CRTE 60417 3596 0E-29S E7
- CRTE 60417 3685 0E-29S E1
- CteT 60417 3685 0E-29S E1
Vardon Ct
3800 WDRG 60517 3143 23W-7S A7
Vardon Ln
2000 FSMR 60422 3507 2W-22S C2
2000 HMWD 60430 3507 2W-22S C2
Vardon Pl
2400 FSMR 60422 3507 3W-22S C2
E Vargo Ln
1000 ANHT 60004 2754 17W-16N C7
Varonen Av
2600 WKGN 60087 2479 12W-36N C4
Varsity Dr
600 ELGN 60120 2855 32W-10N C6
4900 LSLE 60532 3142 23W-5S E3
Vassar Ct
1700 SMBG 60193 2912 25W-9N B1
Vassar Dr
1800 LslT 60565 3204 24W-9S D4
1800 NPVL 60565 3204 24W-9S D4
Vassar Ln
400 DSPN 60016 2862 14W-12N C1
500 DSPN 60016 2808 14W-12N C7
800 SMBG 60193 2912 25W-9N B1
Vattman Rd
- LKFT 60037 2650 9W-24N C6
Vaughn Cir
- NpvT 60502 3139 32W-7S C7
400 AURA 60502 3139 32W-7S C7
Vaughn Ct
1300 AURA 60504 3201 32W-9S C4
Vaughn Rd
500 AURA 60502 3139 32W-7S C7
500 NpvT 60502 3139 32W-7S C7
600 AURA 60502 3201 32W-7S C1
600 AURA 60504 3201 32W-7S C1
600 NpvT 60502 3201 32W-7S C1
Vaupell Av
2400 HHLL 60051 2586 29W-29N B4
2400 NndT 60051 2586 29W-29N B4

STREET Block City ZIP Map# CGS Grid

Vaysee Ct
15200 HMGN 60491 3342 19W-16S E3
Velvent Bent Ct
5300 NPVL 60564 3266 29W-13S D5
Venard Rd
3100 DRGV 60515 3084 20W-3S B5
Venetian Ct
1100 NPVL 60540 3142 25W-7S A7
S Venetian Ct
13700 HMGN 60491 3344 15W-16S C3
Venetian Dr
- BGBK 60440 3269 22W-12S D2
W Venetian Dr
25500 GrtT 60041 2474 25W-34N A7
Venetian Ln
2500 ElgT 60124 2907 37W-9N D1
2600 ElgT 60124 2853 37W-9N D7
Venetian Wy
200 CmpT 60119 2961 42W-4N C4
W Venetian Wy
10 HMGN 60491 3344 15W-16S C3
10 OrlT 60467 3344 15W-16S C3
Venetian Wy Cir
10 WHTN 60187 3082 24W-1S D2
Veneto
- BMDL 60172 2912 24W-6N C7
- BmdT 60172 2912 24W-6N C7
Veneto Ct
- SMWD 60107 2856 30W-9N C7
Venezia Dr
11000 FKFT 60423 3591 13W-27S A5
Venice Av
10 FXLK 60020 2473 27W-36N B3
3300 MHRY 60050 2528 32W-33N B3
Venice Ct
- NfdT 60025 2809 11W-13N D6
600 SMBG 60193 2858 24W-9N E7
Venice Dr
- ElgT 60124 2907 37W-8N C2
Venice Ln
10400 ODPK 60467 3423 13W-21S B6
10400 OrlT 60467 3423 13W-21S B6
Venice Rd
100 LKMR 60051 2529 29W-31N D7
N Venn Rd
41700 AntT 60002 2357 25W-41N A7
42000 AntT 60002 2356 25W-42N E6
Venson Ct
1800 JLET 60435 3498 26W-22S A2
Ventura Ct
10 NPVL 60540 3141 28W-6S A5
6300 JLET 60586 3415 31W-20S D5
Ventura Dr
2400 JLET 60586 3415 31W-20S E6
N Ventura Dr
900 PLTN 60074 2753 20W-17N A5
3700 ANHT 60004 2753 18W-18N D3
Ventura St
15200 OKFT 60452 3347 7W-18S C6
Ventura Club Dr
300 ROSL 60172 2913 22W-7N B4
Ventura Dove
- RNPK 60443 3593 7W-27S C4
Venture St
4800 LSLE 60532 3143 22W-5S B2
Venuti Dr
- AURA 60504 3202 30W-7S C1
Vera Ct
500 JLET 60436 3497 26W-24S E6
15900 OKFT 60452 3425 6W-19S D1
Vera Ln
- EGvT 60007 2861 16W-9N D7
- EGVV 60007 2861 16W-9N D7
800 WLNG 60090 2754 15W-17N E5
800 WLNG 60090 2755 15W-17N A5
1100 WLNG 60004 2754 15W-17N E5
2600 CteT 60417 3687 3E-29S A2
Verbena Ct
400 NPVL 60565 3203 27W-10S D5
Verbena Dr
9100 MNSR 46321 3510 E2
Verbena Ln
200 WDSK 60098 2581 41W-30N C2
Verbend Pth
14000 HTLY 60142 2744 42W-20N A1
W Vercoe Av
2600 BHPK 60087 2479 12W-37N C3
2600 WKGN 60087 2479 12W-37N C3
Verda Ln
900 LKFT 60045 2649 12W-26N C3
N Verde Av
1700 ANHT 60004 2806 18W-15N E1
Verde Ct
1600 MDLN 60060 2590 19W-29N C4
S Verde Ct
1700 MPPT 60056 2861 17W-12N C1
Verde Dr
200 SMBG 60173 2859 22W-10N D4
N Verde Dr
1900 ANHT 60004 2806 18W-16N D1
2000 ANHT 60004 2753 18W-16N E7
S Verde Dr
1700 MPPT 60056 2861 17W-12N C1
W Verde Dr
1700 MPPT 60056 2861 17W-12N C1
Verde Ln
400 EGVV 60007 2915 18W-9N A1
1500 MDLN 60060 2590 19W-29N C4
Verde Vista Ct
700 ELGN 60123 2853 36W-9N E7
Verdi Ct
- WDSK 60098 2524 40W-33N E3
200 WHTN 60187 3082 24W-2S C4
Verdi St
600 WDSK 60098 2524 41W-33N E3
2700 GwdT 60098 2524 41W-33N E3
Verdin Ln
1600 NPVL 60565 3203 26W-9S E3
Verdun Ct
2300 JLET 60435 3417 27W-21S C6
Verdun Dr
500 WnfT 60190 3081 28W-1S A2
2200 JLET 60435 3417 27W-21S C6
Veretta Ct
200 MHRY 60050 2527 33W-31N D6
Verhaeghe Rd
900 CmpT 60175 2905 42W-6N E6
Veridian Wy
800 CRY 60013 2695 32W-23N B2
Verity St
800 AraT 60506 3199 38W-8S A2
Vermette Cir
1800 JLET 60586 3416 30W-21S C7
Vermette Rd
24800 PNFD 60585 3337 31W-15S E2
24800 PNFD 60585 3338 31W-15S A2

Vermillion Ct
2600 NPVL 60565 3204 25W-10S A6
E Vermillion Ln
1600 PLTN 60074 2753 19W-18N C3
Vermillion St
- PLNO 60545 3259 48W-13S B5
Vermont Av
- NHBK 60062 2757 8W-18N E2
10 AURA 60505 3200 33W-7S E1
200 AURA 60505 3138 33W-7S E7
4200 NCHI 60088 2593 12W-30N C2
W Vermont Av
600 CHCG 60628 3278 0W-15S A7
700 CHCG 60643 3278 0W-15S A7
1000 CTPK 60643 3278 1W-15S A7
1000 CTPK 60827 3277 1W-15S E7
1000 CTPK 60827 3278 1W-15S A7
1500 BLID 60406 3277 1W-15S D7
1500 BLID 60827 3277 1W-15S D7
1500 CTPK 60406 3277 1W-15S D7
2600 WKGN 60087 2479 12W-36N C3
12700 WkgT 60087 2479 12W-36N B4
13400 WKGN 60087 2478 13W-36N E3
13400 WmT 60031 2478 13W-36N E3
13400 WmT 60031 2479 13W-36N A3
13400 WmT 60087 2479 13W-36N A3
Vermont Cir
10 BGBK 60440 3205 22W-10S C6
Vermont Ct
- NCHI 60088 2593 12W-30N C2
1200 NPVL 60540 3203 27W-8S C2
1700 RGMW 60008 2806 20W-14N A3
18100 ODPK 60467 3423 13W-21S B7
N Vermont Ct
21300 KLDR 60047 2700 20W-21N A6
Vermont Dr
300 EGVV 60007 2859 22W-9N D7
1600 EGVV 60193 2859 22W-9N D7
1600 SmbT 60193 2859 22W-9N D7
Vermont Pl
1800 BLID 60406 3349 2W-15S C1
Vermont Rd N
200 FKFT 60423 3591 12W-25S C1
Vermont Rd W
600 FKFT 60423 3591 12W-25S C1
Vermont St
1400 PLTN 60067 2806 20W-14N A3
1400 RGMW 60008 2806 20W-14N A3
1700 BLID 60406 3277 2W-15S D7
1700 CTPK 60406 3277 2W-15S D7
1700 CTPK 60827 3277 2W-15S D7
1800 BLID 60406 3349 3W-15S A1
2000 RGMW 60008 2805 20W-14N E4
2600 WhtT 60406 3349 3W-15S A1
E Vermont St
10 VLPK 60181 3027 17W-1N B2
S Vermont St
400 PLTN 60067 2805 20W-15N E2
1100 RGMW 60067 2805 21W-14N D4
1300 PLTN 60008 2805 21W-14N D4
1300 RGMW 60008 2805 21W-14N D4
W Vermont St
10 VLPK 60181 3027 18W-1N A2
300 VLPK 60181 3026 18W-1N E2
13500 WKGN 60087 2478 13W-36N E4
13500 WmT 60031 2478 13W-36N E4
Vermont Tr
6400 NndT 60012 2584 35W-27N A7
Vern St
- FXLK 60050 2472 29W-37N D2
5600 GrtT 60050 2472 29W-37N D2
5600 GrtT 60081 2472 29W-37N D2
5600 MchT 60050 2472 29W-37N D2
5600 MchT 60081 2472 29W-37N D2
Vernal Ln
2800 NPVL 60564 3202 29W-10S C5
Verne Cir
10 BRTN 60010 2751 25W-20N B2
Verne Ln
800 FSMR 60422 3507 3W-22S B2
Vernon Av
100 WHTN 60187 3024 26W-0S A7
200 GLNC 60022 2758 6W-16N D6
200 WNKA 60022 2758 6W-16N D7
200 WNKA 60093 2758 6W-16N D7
1400 PKRG 60068 2863 11W-10N E4
2900 BKFD 60513 3087 11W-3S E5
4600 BKFD 60513 3147 11W-4S E1
4600 MCCK 60513 3147 11W-4S E1
4600 MCCK 60525 3147 11W-4S E1
S Vernon Av
2800 CHCG 60616 3092 0E-2S D3
4300 CHCG 60653 3092 0E-4S D7
6900 CHCG 60637 3152 0E-8S D7
7000 CHCG 60619 3152 0E-8S D7
7500 CHCG 60619 3214 0E-8S D1
10000 CHCG 60628 3214 0E-11S D7
10300 CHCG 60628 3278 0E-13S D3
13100 CHCG 60827 3278 0E-15S D7
13100 CHCG 60827 3350 0E-15S D1
W Vernon Av
1400 JLET 60435 3498 26W-22S A2
Vernon Cir
1900 EGVV 60007 2913 22W-9N C1
Vernon Ct
10 SEGN 60177 2908 35W-7N C4
500 OSWG 60543 3200 35W-10S C4
900 VNHL 60061 2647 17W-26N C4
2700 WDRG 60517 3143 22W-6S C5
N Vernon Ct
28600 LbvT 60048 2592 15W-28N A6
Vernon Ct N
600 BFGV 60089 2754 17W-18N B3
Vernon Ct S
700 BFGV 60089 2754 17W-18N B4
Vernon Dr
10 MchT 60051 2529 29W-31N C6
10 NndT 60051 2529 29W-31N C6
100 BGBK 60440 3269 22W-11S D1
1000 GNVW 60025 2810 8W-13N E6
2000 ELGN 60123 2853 36W-11N E4
N Vernon Dr
100 GDLY 60407 4030 32W-43S D2
Vernon Ln
- ANHT 60004 2754 17W-18N B4
- GYLK 60030 2532 21W-34N D1
500 BFGV 60089 2754 17W-18N B3
1300 BRLT 60103 2967 28W-5N A1
Vernon St
- BKFD 60513 3147 11W-5S E2
- MCCK 60513 3147 11W-5S E2
- MCCK 60525 3147 11W-5S E2
2200 BLID 60406 3277 2W-14S B6
S Vernon St
3300 CHCG 60616 3092 0E-3S D4

Vernon Tr
10 RVWD 60015 2702 13W-21N D5
10 VrnT 60015 2702 13W-21N D5
W Vernon Park Pl
- CHCG 60607 3034 D6
1000 CHCG 60607 3033 1W-0S E6
Vernon Ridge Dr
21700 FmtT 60060 2589 22W-29N C5
W Verona Av
20400 LkvT 60046 2476 20W-37N A2
20400 LNHT 60046 2476 20W-37N A2
20700 LkvT 60046 2475 20W-37N E2
Verona Ct
600 SMBG 60193 2858 24W-9N E7
Verona Dr
600 PltT 60124 2852 39W-11N D5
900 CRY 60013 2695 32W-23N B2
Verona Ridge Dr
- AURA 60506 3136 39W-5S D4
Veronica Cir
300 BRLT 60103 2909 32W-8N D2
Veronica Ct
600 NLNX 60451 3501 17W-25S D7
Veronica St
- LtRT 60545 3260 45W-14S B7
- PLNO 60545 3260 46W-14S B7
W Verret St
400 EMHT 60126 3027 16W-0S D7
Verrill Av
10 AddT 60101 2971 18W-4N A4
100 ADSN 60101 2971 18W-4N A4
Versailles Av
2500 NPVL 60540 3140 29W-7S D7
2500 NPVL 60540 3202 29W-7S D1
Versailles Cir
600 EGVV 60007 2914 19W-9N C1
Versailles Ct
10 BMDL 60108 2968 24W-5N D1
10 WLNG 60090 2808 14W-15N C2
600 IVNS 60010 2751 24W-17N B5
Versailles Dr
- OKTR 60181 3085 17W-1S B1
- YKTp 60181 3085 17W-1S B1
300 NHBK 60062 2756 12W-18N C3
Versailles Ln
500 BRLT 60103 2909 31W-9N E1
500 BRLT 60103 2910 31W-9N A1
500 BRLT 60120 2909 31W-9N E1
18000 HLCT 60429 3426 4W-21S E7
18000 HLCT 60429 3427 4W-21S A7
Versailles Pkwy
700 OSWG 60543 3264 35W-11S C2
Versailles Rd
3700 HFET 60192 2804 24W-14N B3
Vertin Blvd
500 JLET 60431 3496 30W-22S C2
500 SRWD 60404 3496 31W-22S A2
Vesper Ct
3900 NPVL 60564 3267 28W-12S A2
21800 DRPK 60010 2698 23W-21N D5
Vesper St
21500 LktT 60403 3417 26W-19S D3
Vest Av
10 NPVL 60563 3142 26W-5S A3
600 LslT 60563 3142 26W-5S A3
Vesta Dr
2400 JLET 60431 3417 28W-20S A6
2400 PnfT 60431 3417 28W-20S A6
Vetel St
15200 PNFD 60544 3416 30W-18S B1
Veteran Av
- ELBN 60119 3017 42W-0N C4
Veterans Blvd
6900 BRRG 60527 3146 15W-7S B7
Veterans Dr
- NRIV 60546 3088 9W-2S D3
- RVSD 60546 3088 9W-2S D3
W Veterans Dr
2400 POSN 60469 3349 3W-17S B5
Veterans Pkwy
- BGBK 60446 3268 25W-13S C5
- MHRY 60050 2584 33W-30N E2
- MHRY 60050 2585 33W-30N A2
- NndT 60050 2584 33W-30N E2
10 NLNX 60451 3501 18W-24S A6
10 NlxT 60451 3501 18W-24S A6
100 BGBK 60440 3268 25W-12S B3
100 BGBK 60490 3268 25W-12S B3
500 AddT 60101 2970 19W-4N C4
500 ADSN 60101 2970 19W-4N C4
600 DPgT 60440 3268 25W-13S C5
600 DPgT 60446 3268 24W-13S C5
12100 RMVL 60440 3268 24W-14S E7
12100 RMVL 60446 3268 24W-14S E7
E Veterans Pkwy
10 BtlT 60560 3261 42W-14S D7
10 YKVL 60560 3261 42W-14S D7
E Veterans Pkwy US-34
10 BtlT 60560 3261 42W-14S D7
10 YKVL 60560 3261 42W-14S D7
W Veterans Pkwy
- BtlT 60560 3260 44W-14S E7
- YKVL 60560 3260 44W-14S E6
10 YKVL 60560 3261 43W-14S A7
200 BtlT 60560 3261 43W-14S A7
W Veterans Pkwy US-34
- BtlT 60560 3260 44W-14S E6
- YKVL 60560 3260 44W-14S E6
10 YKVL 60560 3261 43W-14S A7
200 BtlT 60560 3261 43W-14S A7
Veterans Memorial Pkwy
- SgrT 60554 3135 43W-6S A6
- SRGV 60554 3135 43W-6S A6
S Vetter Rd
23400 CnhT 60421 3585 27W-28S D7
23400 CnhT 60421 3674 27W-29S D1
23400 JLET 60421 3585 27W-28S D7
VFW Dr
- NPVL 60540 3141 27W-6S B5
Vial Pkwy
5700 LynT 60525 3146 13W-6S E4
E Viator Ct
1000 ANHT 60004 2807 17W-15N B3
Via Veneto Dr
1800 GNVA 60134 3020 34W-1N E2
1800 GNVA 60174 3020 34W-1N E2
1800 SCRL 60134 3020 34W-1N E2
1800 SCRL 60174 3020 34W-2N E2
Vicarage Dr
15500 PNFD 60544 3338 30W-16S B3
15500 PNFD 60585 3338 30W-16S B3
Vicki Ln
2400 NHBK 60062 2809 11W-15N D1
Vickie Ln
3100 NCHI 60064 2536 12W-32N B5

Vicksburg Ct
600 NPVL 60540 3203 27W-8S C1
2200 AURA 60503 3265 32W-11S B1
Vicksburg Ln
2600 AURA 60503 3265 32W-11S B1
Vicky Ln
16700 ODHL 60487 3424 11W-20S A3
S Vicky Ln
10400 PSHL 60465 3274 9W-12S C2
Vicky St
13100 WldT 60585 3338 29W-15S D2
Victor Av
1200 ELGN 60120 2801 32W-12N C7
2300 MaiT 60025 2864 9W-12N B1
Victor Dr
5200 MHRY 60050 2527 34W-33N D2
Victor Ln
100 LKZH 60047 2699 21W-22N C4
1800 HRPK 60133 2967 27W-5N C1
8600 MaiT 60016 2863 10W-11N E3
8600 MaiT 60016 2864 10W-11N A3
W Victor Ln
5600 WKGN 60048 2534 15W-31N E7
Victor Pkwy
10 CLLK 60014 2639 36W-25N E4
Victor Pl
10000 AlqT 60102 2694 33W-21N E5
Victor Rd
700 AraT 60504 3138 34W-5S C3
Victor St
5100 DRGV 60515 3145 18W-5S A3
5400 DRGV 60559 3145 18W-5S A3
5400 WTMT 60559 3145 18W-5S A3
Victor Ter
1700 GRNE 60031 2478 15W-35N A5
Victoria Av
- BKLY 60163 3028 14W-0N C3
600 BtlT 60560 3333 42W-14S D1
2900 MchT 60050 2528 32W-32N C4
2900 MHRY 60050 2528 32W-32N C4
S Victoria Av
3700 HMND 46327 3352 C2
Victoria Cir
10 WCDA 60084 2643 26W-26N E2
900 BlmT 60411 3510 4E-25S C7
900 BlmT 60411 3598 4E-25S C1
900 LYWD 60411 3510 4E-25S C7
900 LYWD 60411 3598 4E-25S C1
E Victoria Cir
100 NARA 60542 3077 38W-3S B7
300 NARA 60542 3137 37W-4S C1
Victoria Ct
10 GRNE 60031 2535 14W-34N D1
10 OKBK 60523 3085 17W-2S C3
500 NPVL 60540 3141 26W-7S D6
700 BGBK 60440 3205 22W-9S D6
1200 ALGN 60102 2694 34W-20N C7
6100 MTSN 60443 3593 7W-25S C1
6100 OKFT 60452 3347 7W-18S C7
12000 HMGN 60491 3344 15W-17S C5
Victoria Dr
700 WDSK 60098 2524 42W-32N C5
800 MTGY 60538 3199 38W-9S A5
900 ISLK 60042 2586 30W-27N B7
1000 FRGV 60021 2696 29W-22N D3
3800 RNPK 60471 3594 4W-27S D4
4000 HFET 60192 2804 24W-15N C3
5600 OKFT 60452 3347 7W-18S C7
6600 BmnT 60452 3347 8W-18S A7
E Victoria Dr
300 NHLK 60164 3028 13W-1N E1
300 NHLK 60164 3029 13W-1N A1
N Victoria Dr
700 PLTN 60074 2753 19W-16N D6
4000 HFET 60192 2804 24W-15N C2
W Victoria Dr
- EGvT 60056 2861 17W-10N C5
1700 MPPT 60056 2861 17W-10N C5
Victoria Ln
10 HNWD 60047 2645 21W-24N D7
10 LNSH 60069 2702 14W-22N D4
10 RVWD 60015 2702 14W-22N D4
200 EGVV 60007 2914 18W-9N E1
200 WNFD 60190 3023 27W-0N C4
300 ElgT 60124 2853 38W-10N B6
400 GLHT 60139 3025 22W-1N B2
400 MltT 60137 3025 22W-1N B2
400 WDDL 60191 2970 19W-5N D1
500 ITSC 60143 2970 19W-5N D1
500 ITSC 60191 2970 19W-5N D1
500 OSWG 60543 3199 36W-11S E7
500 OSWG 60543 3200 36W-11S A7
600 SMBG 60193 2858 24W-10N D6
800 EGVV 60007 2915 18W-8N A2
3200 WKGN 60087 2478 15W-37N B1
4500 JLET 60586 3416 29W-21S D7
15100 LbvT 60048 2592 15W-29N B4
15100 LYVL 60048 2592 15W-29N B4
N Victoria Ln
10 SMWD 60107 2857 28W-11N B4
S Victoria Ln
10 SMWD 60107 2857 28W-10N B5
26100 CteT 60417 3687 3E-31S A6
W Victoria Ln
100 BHPK 60083 2421 13W-39N A5
200 ANHT 60005 2861 18W-12N A2
500 ANHT 60005 2860 18W-12N E2
Victoria Pl
10700 ODPK 60467 3423 13W-20S A3
Victoria Rd
600 DSPN 60016 2862 15W-11N B4
1700 MDLN 60060 2590 20W-28N A6
Victoria St
200 BRTN 60010 2751 25W-20N A1
900 ANTH 60002 2357 23W-42N E7
1000 NCHI 60064 2536 10W-32N E5
1000 WKGN 60085 2536 10W-32N E5
S Victoria St
23500 CnhT 60410 3584 30W-28S C7
W Victoria St
1400 CHCG 60660 2921 1W-7N C4
3200 CHCG 60659 2920 4W-7N D4
4000 CHCG 60646 2920 5W-7N B4
7700 CHCG 60068 2918 9W-7N B4
7700 CHCG 60631 2918 9W-7N B4
7700 PKRG 60068 2918 9W-7N B4
W Victoria Crossing Ct
15100 LKPT 60441 3420 18W-19S E3
W Victoria Crossing Wy
14600 LKPT 60441 3421 18W-19S B3
Victoria Lakes Ct
2100 JLET 60586 3416 31W-21S A6
Victoria Lakes Dr
2100 JLET 60586 3416 31W-21S A7
Victorian Dr
10 NLNX 60451 3500 19W-24S D6

Victorian Dr
10 NlxT 60451 3500 19W-24S D6
3200 LGGV 60047 2700 19W-21N C6
19300 FftT 60448 3502 14W-23S D3
19300 MKNA 60448 3502 14W-23S D4
Victoria Park Cir
1500 AURA 60504 3200 33W-8S E2
Victory Ct
1200 AURA 60506 3137 37W-6S C5
Victory Dr
300 PKFT 60466 3595 3W-27S B4
1200 LYVL 60048 2591 17W-28N B6
E Victory Dr
- LNHT 60046 2475 21W-37N D1
Victory Ln
800 LynT 60458 3209 11W-8S E1
1500 RLKP 60030 2532 22W-31N B7
Victory Pkwy
400 AddT 60126 2972 15W-3N A5
500 AddT 60101 2971 17W-3N B5
600 EMHT 60126 2972 15W-3N A5
E Victory Pkwy
100 AddT 60126 2972 15W-3N A5
100 EMHT 60126 2972 15W-3N A5
N Victory St
10 WKGN 60085 2536 10W-34N E1
S Victory St
10 WKGN 60085 2536 10W-33N E3
900 NCHI 60064 2536 10W-33N E4
Victory Lake Wy
21400 LktT 60403 3417 26W-19S D2
Vida Av
7700 GfnT 60014 2638 39W-24N D7
7700 LKWD 60014 2638 39W-24N D6
S Vienna Av
11500 PSPK 60464 3274 10W-13S C4
View Ct
500 NPVL 60540 3141 26W-7S E7
View St
200 CLLK 60012 2640 34W-26N C2
500 WDND 60118 2801 33W-15N A3
E View St
400 LMBD 60148 3026 19W-1N D3
N View St
10 AURA 60506 3137 36W-7S E7
200 AURA 60506 3138 36W-6S A5
S View St
10 AURA 60506 3137 36W-7S E7
W View St
300 LMBD 60148 3026 20W-1N A3
View High
- NLNX 60451 3590 15W-27S B4
Viewpoint Dr
900 LIHL 60156 2694 34W-21N C5
Viewpointe Dr
900 SCRL 60174 3020 35W-2N B1
Viewside
- NLNX 60442 3589 17W-27S D4
Vigilance Ct
10 BGBK 60440 3205 22W-10S C6
S Viking Blvd
10 NasT 60543 3337 33W-18S A7
10 NasT 60544 3337 33W-18S A7
Viking Ct
1000 BTVA 60510 3078 34W-1S D3
Viking Dr
- FSMR 60422 3507 3W-22S A2
- RchT 60422 3507 3W-22S A2
500 BTVA 60510 3078 34W-1S D2
1400 BTVA 60134 3019 37W-0S C6
1400 BTVA 60510 3019 37W-0S C6
1400 GNVA 60134 3019 37W-0S C6
1400 GnvT 60134 3019 37W-0S C6
Viking Ln
- RMVL 60446 3340 24W-15S D3
Villa Av
200 LKVL 60046 2475 22W-38N B1
400 NPVL 60540 3141 26W-7S E7
N Villa Av
10 AddT 60101 2971 17W-3N A5
10 ADSN 60101 2971 17W-3N A5
10 EMHT 60126 3027 17W-1N B3
10 EMHT 60181 3027 17W-1N B3
10 VLPK 60126 3027 17W-1N B2
10 VLPK 60181 3027 17W-1N B2
500 YkTp 60181 3027 17W-1N B2
700 YkTp 60126 3027 17W-1N B2
900 VLPK 60101 2971 17W-2N B7
900 VLPK 60181 2971 17W-2N B7
N Villa Av CO-28
10 AddT 60101 2971 17W-3N A5
10 ADSN 60101 2971 17W-3N A5
800 VLPK 60181 3027 17W-2N B1
900 VLPK 60101 2971 17W-2N B7
900 VLPK 60181 2971 17W-2N B7
S Villa Av
10 AddT 60101 2971 17W-3N B6
10 ADSN 60101 2971 17W-3N B6
10 EMHT 60126 3027 17W-0N B5
10 EMHT 60181 3027 17W-0N B5
10 VLPK 60126 3027 17W-0N B5
10 VLPK 60181 3027 17W-0N B5
400 AddT 60181 2971 17W-2N B6
400 ADSN 60181 2971 17W-2N B6
400 VLPK 60101 2971 17W-2N B6
1200 YkTp 60181 3027 17W-0S B6
1500 OKTR 60181 3027 17W-0S B7
S Villa Av CO-28
10 AddT 60101 2971 17W-3N B6
10 ADSN 60101 2971 17W-3N B6
400 AddT 60181 2971 17W-2N B6
400 ADSN 60181 2971 17W-2N B6
400 VLPK 60101 2971 17W-2N B6
Villa Ct
11500 ALSP 60803 3276 5W-13S B4
14000 ODPK 60462 3346 10W-16S B3
N Villa Ct
38700 LkvT 60046 2417 21W-38N C6
Villa Dr
38600 LkvT 60046 2416 23W-38N D6
E Villa Dr
900 DSPN 60016 2862 13W-10N D4
W Villa Dr
900 DSPN 60016 2862 14W-10N D4
N Villa Ln
2600 MchT 60051 2471 31W-34N E7
2600 MchT 60051 2528 31W-34N E1
Villa Pl
200 ELGN 60120 2855 33W-11N A4
Villa Rd
100 SMWD 60107 2857 28W-10N B5
Villa St
10 ELGN 60120 2854 33W-11N E4
700 ELGN 60120 2855 32W-10N B5
Villa St US-20
- ELGN - 2855 31W-10N E6

STREET Block	City	ZIP	Map#	CGS	Grid
Villa St US-20 BUS					
700	ELGN	60120	2855	32W-10N	B5
E Villa St					
1500	ELGN	60120	2855	31W-10N	E6
1500	ELGN	60120	2856	31W-10N	A7
1600	ELGN	60103	2856	31W-10N	A7
E Villa St US-20					
1500	ELGN	60120	2855	31W-10N	E6
1500	ELGN	60120	2856	31W-10N	A7
1600	ELGN	60103	2856	31W-10N	A7
Villa Wy					
100	BMDL	60108	2968	24W-5N	E1
Villa Cir Dr					
100	RGMW	60008	2805	21W-13N	C5
100	SMBG	60008	2805	21W-13N	C5
100	SMBG	60173	2805	21W-13N	C5
Village Cir					
-	WLSP	60480	3209	12W-10S	B5
700	MRGO	60152	2634	49W-27N	D1
Village Coms					
4900	MTSN	60443	3506	6W-24S	A6
5000	MTSN	60443	3505	6W-24S	E6
Village Ct					
10	ELGN	60120	2855	32W-11N	C3
10	SEGN	60177	2908	35W-7N	C4
100	CLSM	60188	2968	25W-2N	B7
100	DSPN	60016	2862	14W-12N	C1
600	GLNC	60022	2758	6W-17N	C5
800	MRGO	60152	2634	49W-27N	D1
1000	DRN	60561	3207	17W-8S	B1
1100	LKZH	60047	2699	22W-21N	A5
1400	BFGV	60089	2701	16W-21N	D5
1700	CLLK	60014	2693	36W-22N	E3
2400	AURA	60504	3201	32W-9S	C4
13200	CTWD	60445	3347	6W-15S	E1
N Village Ct					
200	PLTN	60067	2752	21W-16N	E7
W Village Ct					
800	CHCG	60608	3034		E7
900	CHCG	60608	3033	1W-1S	E7
Village Dr					
-	DRGV	60516	3144	18W-7S	E6
10	NHLK	60164	2972	13W-2N	E7
200	MPPT	60056	2862	15W-12N	A1
300	CLSM	60188	2968	25W-2N	B7
300	NHLK	60164	2973	13W-2N	A7
1200	LmnT	60439	3271	18W-13S	B4
1400	ANHT	60004	2806	18W-15N	E2
3700	HLCT	60429	3506	4W-22S	D1
E Village Dr					
-	NHLK	60164	2972	13W-2N	D7
N Village Dr					
900	AvnT	60073	2531	24W-34N	C1
900	RLKB	60073	2474	24W-34N	C7
900	RLKB	60073	2531	24W-34N	C1
Village Grn					
-	LNSH	60061	2702	15W-23N	A2
-	VNHL	60061	2702	15W-23N	A2
Village Ln					
200	BRLT	60103	2967	28W-5N	A2
1000	GRNE	60031	2477	18W-35N	A7
13100	CTWD	60445	3347	6W-15S	E1
17500	LKPT	60441	3419	22W-21S	D6
17500	LktT	60441	3419	22W-21S	D6
Village Pl					
10	HNDL	60521	3146	15W-5S	B2
Village Rd					
-	LIHL	60014	2693	36W-22N	E3
-	LIHL	60156	2693	36W-22N	E3
100	DGvT	60527	3207	16W-9S	E4
700	CLLK	60014	2693	37W-22N	C3
Village Tr					
200	MHRY	60050	2527	33W-31N	E6
W Village Center Dr					
24500	PNFD	60544	3338	30W-18S	B7
Village Center Pkwy					
1000	AURA	60506	3136	39W-6S	E4
1800	MTGY	60538	3200	36W-10S	A6
Village Cir Dr					
10300	PlsT	60464	3345	12W-15S	B1
Village Creek Dr					
100	LIHL	60156	2693	35W-21N	E5
Village Green Blvd					
30000	WNVL	60555	3081	27W-3S	B7
Village Green Ct					
1600	DRFD	60015	2703	12W-21N	C7
2900	AURA	60504	3201	31W-8S	D2
31000	WNVL	60555	3081	27W-3S	B7
Village Green Dr					
2600	AURA	60504	3201	32W-8S	D3
13200	HTLY	60142	2744	41W-18N	E4
Village Green Rd					
400	NPVL	60540	3141	27W-7S	B6
Village Grn					
-	LNSH	60069	2702	15W-23N	B2
Village Grove Dr					
1000	EGVV	60007	2914	19W-8N	D2
Village Hall Dr					
600	CRY	60013	2695	31W-23N	C2
Village In the Lk					
-	EGVV	60007	2914	19W-8N	C1
Village Quarter Rd					
800	WDND	60118	2800	34W-15N	E3
Village Square Ln					
4500	BKFD	60513	3147	11W-5S	E1
Village Station Blvd					
-	NLNX	60442	3589	17W-26S	C3
-	NLNX	60451	3589	17W-26S	C3
Village Station Ln					
10	GYLK	60030	2532	21W-32N	E5
Village View Dr					
2000	YKVL	60560	3333	42W-16S	C5
Village West Dr					
3500	HLCT	60429	3506	4W-22S	E1
18300	HLCT	60429	3426	4W-22S	E7
Village Woods Dr					
10	CteT	60417	3774	0W-32S	C1
Villa Maria Rd					
10	SchT	60174	2908	34W-6N	C7
Villanova Dr					
1700	NPVL	60565	3204	24W-9S	C3
2000	JNBG	60050	2471	31W-36N	E4
W Villa Rica Rd					
22800	AntT	60002	2417	22W-40N	A3
23100	AntT	60046	2417	23W-40N	A3
23100	LKVL	60046	2417	23W-40N	A3
Villas Ct					
800	DRFD	60015	2704	10W-21N	B7
800	DRFD	60035	2704	10W-21N	B7
800	HDPK	60015	2704	10W-21N	B7
800	HDPK	60035	2704	10W-21N	B7
Villa Verde Rd					
10	ANHT	60004	2753	18W-17N	E4
10	ANHT	60004	2754	18W-17N	A4
10	ANHT	60089	2753	18W-17N	E4
10	BFGV	60089	2753	18W-17N	E4
Villa Verde Rd					
10	BFGV	60089	2754	18W-17N	A4
Villa Vista Dr					
1000	RLKB	60073	2474	24W-34N	C7
1200	AvnT	60073	2474	24W-34N	C7
Villa Vista Rd					
-	FXLK	60081	2414	29W-39N	D5
7300	BtnT	60081	2414	29W-39N	D5
Vilmin Rd					
800	LtRT	60545	3259	48W-11S	C1
Vimy Ridge Dr					
2800	JLET	60435	3417	27W-21S	B6
2900	JLET	60431	3417	27W-21S	B6
Vinan Dr					
2900	LydT	60164	2972	13W-3N	E5
Vinca Ln					
-	OSWG	60543	3263	36W-13S	E6
Vincennes Av					
1200	CHHT	60411	3508	1W-25S	A7
1500	CHHT	60411	3596	1W-25S	B1
S Vincennes Av					
3500	CHCG	60653	3092	0E-4S	D7
4600	CHCG	60615	3092	0E-4S	D7
4700	CHCG	60615	3152	0E-5S	D1
7000	CHCG	60621	3152	0W-8S	B7
7500	CHCG	60620	3214	0W-9S	A3
7500	CHCG	60621	3214	0W-8S	B1
9100	CHCG	60620	3213	1W-11S	E6
9400	CHCG	60643	3213	1W-11S	E7
10300	CHCG	60643	3277	2W-13S	D3
11800	BLID	60406	3277	2W-13S	C5
11800	BLID	60643	3277	2W-13S	C5
Vincennes Rd					
-	PHNX	60426	3350	0W-17S	B6
-	PHNX	60426	3428	0W-18S	B1
300	SHLD	60476	3428	0E-20S	D4
300	TNTN	60473	3428	0E-20S	D4
300	TNTN	60476	3428	0E-20S	D4
11900	BLID	60406	3277	2W-14S	C6
11900	BLID	60643	3277	2W-14S	C6
11900	CHCG	60643	3277	2W-14S	C6
14400	HRVY	60426	3349	1W-17S	E4
14400	HRVY	60426	3350	1W-17S	A5
14400	ThtT	60426	3349	1W-17S	E4
15500	PHNX	60473	3350	0W-18S	B7
15500	SHLD	60426	3350	0W-18S	B7
15500	SHLD	60473	3350	0W-18S	B7
15700	HRVY	60426	3428	0W-18S	B1
15700	HRVY	60473	3428	0W-18S	B1
15700	SHLD	60426	3428	0W-18S	B1
15700	SHLD	60473	3350	0W-19S	D3
18300	BlmT	60425	3428	0W-22S	D7
18300	BlmT	60476	3428	0W-22S	D7
18400	BlmT	60425	3508	0W-22S	C1
Vincennes Rd SR-1					
-	PHNX	60426	3350	1W-18S	B7
14900	HRVY	60426	3350	1W-17S	A6
Vincennes St					
1300	CRTE	60417	3685	1W-30S	B3
Vincent Ct					
10	LslT	60565	3205	23W-8S	A2
300	LKBF	60044	2594	10W-28N	A6
1600	NPVL	60564	3267	28W-12S	A3
W Vincent Ct					
26300	GrtT	60041	2473	26W-36N	D4
N Vincent Dr					
100	BGBK	60490	3267	26W-11S	E2
S Vincent Dr					
100	BGBK	60490	3267	26W-12S	E2
W Vincent Dr					
-	PNFD	60543	3337	33W-14S	B1
Vincent Pl					
200	ELGN	60123	2854	34W-11N	D4
Vine Av					
10	HDPK	60035	2705	8W-22N	A3
10	PKRG	60068	2918	10W-7N	B3
100	HDPK	60035	2704	8W-22N	D4
100	LKFT	60045	2650	10W-26N	A3
300	GNEN	60137	3025	23W-0S	B6
1900	CHCG	60631	2918	10W-7N	B4
1900	PKRG	60631	2918	10W-7N	B4
8800	GwdT	60097	2469	38W-34N	A7
14800	HRVY	60426	3349	1W-18S	E7
15600	HRVY	60426	3427	1W-18S	E1
16000	MKHM	60426	3427	1W-19S	E2
16000	MKHM	60428	3427	1W-19S	E2
N Vine Av					
4800	NRDG	60706	2918	10W-6N	B7
5500	CHCG	60656	2918	10W-6N	B5
5500	LydT	60631	2918	10W-6N	B5
5500	MaiT	60631	2918	10W-6N	B5
5600	CHCG	60631	2918	10W-7N	B5
Vine Ct					
300	WLMT	60091	2812	5W-13N	B6
400	HMND	46324	3430		D2
Vine Ln					
-	EGVV	60193	2913	22W-8N	D1
600	EGVV	60007	2913	22W-9N	D1
2800	NndT	60012	2584	35W-29N	B4
Vine St					
10	CTCY	60409	3430		C2
10	ELGN	60123	2854	34W-11N	D4
100	AURA	60506	3138	35W-7S	A7
100	NLNX	60451	3501	18W-24S	B6
100	WMTN	60481	3853	27W-39S	D7
300	BRRG	60527	3208	15W-8S	A1
300	DGvT	60527	3208	15W-8S	A1
300	WCHI	60185	3022	30W-0N	C4
300	WDSK	60098	2581	41W-30N	D1
300	WLMT	60091	2812	5W-13N	A7
400	HMND	46324	3430		D2
400	NlxT	60451	3501	18W-24S	B5
500	LKPT	60441	3419	22W-19S	B2
900	SMWD	60107	2857	28W-9N	B1
900	WNKA	60093	2759	5W-16N	B7
1500	RLKB	60073	2475	22W-35N	C6
3500	MHRY	60050	2585	32W-31N	B1
5200	OKFT	60452	3347	6W-17S	D6
6400	UNON	60180	2635	46W-25N	D5
6900	IHPK	60525	3146	14W-7S	E7
7600	FTPK	60130	3030	9W-0N	C5
7600	RVFT	60130	3030	9W-0N	C5
7600	RVFT	60305	3030	9W-0N	C5
10100	HTLY	60142	2692	40W-21N	A6
10700	HTLY	60142	2691	40W-20N	E7
13300	BLID	60406	3349	3W-15S	A1
Vine St SR-47					
10400	HTLY	60142	2692	40W-21N	A6
10700	HTLY	60142	2691	40W-20N	E7
N Vine St					
10	HNDL	60521	3146	15W-4S	A1
400	HNDL	60521	3086	15W-4S	A7
600	JLET	60435	3498	24W-22S	D2
1600	CHCG	60610	2978	0W-2N	A7
1600	CHCG	60614	2978	0W-2N	A7
S Vine St					
100	HNDL	60521	3146	15W-5S	A2
200	BRRG	60527	3208	15W-10S	A5
200	DGvT	60527	3208	15W-10S	A5
7100	BRRG	60527	3146	15W-8S	A7
7100	DGvT	60527	3146	15W-8S	A7
W Vine St					
10	ANHT	60004	2807	18W-14N	A3
600	ANHT	60004	2806	18W-14N	E4
1200	ANHT	60005	2806	18W-14N	D4
N Vinelane Av					
38600	AntT	60081	2415	27W-38N	B6
Vinewood Av					
700	WLSP	60480	3209	12W-9S	D3
Vineyard Ct					
2300	ELGN	60123	2907	36W-9N	E1
2300	NPVL	60564	3202	29W-10S	D5
Vineyard Dr					
900	GRNE	60031	2476	18W-35N	E6
1700	WrnT	60031	2476	18W-35N	E6
Vineyard Ln					
900	AURA	60502	3078	34W-3S	D6
900	AURA	60510	3078	34W-3S	D6
1200	LYVL	60048	2591	17W-30N	B3
1500	BtnT	60081	2355	30W-43N	A4
1500	SPGV	60081	2355	30W-43N	A4
2500	RLKB	60073	2475	22W-36N	B3
Vinings Dr					
300	BMDL	60108	2968	24W-4N	C3
Vintage Ct					
14300	ODPK	60462	3346	11W-17S	A4
Vintage Dr					
400	LIHL	60156	2693	36W-21N	C5
1300	JLET	60431	3497	28W-22S	B1
16100	PNFD	60586	3416	30W-19S	B3
Vintage Ln					
200	BFGV	60089	2754	17W-20N	C1
S Vintage Ln					
700	RDLK	60073	2531	23W-32N	E5
Vintage Wy					
800	FXLK	60081	2414	29W-40N	C3
800	SPGV	60081	2414	29W-40N	B2
Vintage Knoll Dr					
900	PNFD	60544	3338	29W-17S	D6
Viola Ct					
100	RGMW	60008	2805	21W-14N	D4
700	SMBG	60194	2858	26W-11N	A4
Viola Ln					
200	PTHT	60070	2807	15W-15N	E1
Violet Av					
200	FRGV	60021	2696	29W-23N	C2
Violet Cir					
700	NPVL	60540	3140	29W-7S	D7
Violet Ct					
-	JLET	60447	3495	33W-22S	A2
-	LKVL	60046	2474	23W-37N	D3
1600	HDPK	60035	2704	10W-23N	A3
15600	ODPK	60462	3346	9W-18S	E7
Violet Dr					
200	RMVL	60446	3339	26W-17S	E6
900	BmdT	60172	2912	25W-6N	A6
900	HRPK	60133	2912	25W-6N	A6
900	HRPK	60172	2912	25W-6N	A6
N Violet Dr					
26100	LbvT	60060	2646	18W-26N	D3
W Violet Dr					
1100	HHLL	60051	2586	30W-29N	B3
1100	NndT	60051	2586	30W-29N	B3
Violet Ln					
-	JLET	60447	3495	33W-22S	A2
200	BTVA	60510	3078	34W-1S	E2
3100	NHBK	60062	2756	11W-16N	D7
3400	SjnT	46311	3598		D5
4000	MTSN	60443	3506	5W-25S	C6
S Violet Ln					
25600	MONE	60449	3683	5W-31S	B4
Violet Rd					
18300	LNSG	60438	3429	2E-21S	E7
Violet St					
1400	CLSM	60185	2967	28W-3N	A5
1400	CLSM	60188	2967	28W-3N	A5
1400	WynT	60185	2967	28W-3N	A5
1600	AURA	60505	3139	33W-5S	A3
2400	GNVW	60025	2810	9W-15N	C3
Violetta Av					
800	JLET	60432	3499	21W-22S	E3
800	JltT	60432	3499	21W-22S	E3
W Virell Dr					
22000	AntT	60002	2417	22W-40N	C3
Virgie Pl					
400	WCHI	60185	3022	29W-1N	D4
Virgil Av					
600	ELGN	60120	2855	32W-10N	C6
N Virgil Av					
42300	AntT	60002	2357	25W-42N	B6
Virgina Ln					
6200	MTSN	60443	3505	7W-24S	C5
Virginia Av					
10	BMDL	60108	2912	25W-5N	B7
10	BmdT	60108	2912	25W-6N	B7
10	BmdT	60137	3025	23W-2N	A1
10	BmdT	60172	2912	25W-6N	B7
300	WnfT	60555	3081	27W-3S	B6
400	BmdT	60137	2969	23W-2N	A7
400	WNVL	60555	3081	27W-3S	B6
500	BlmT	60411	3510	4E-25S	B7
500	BmdT	60139	2969	23W-2N	A7
500	GLHT	60137	2969	23W-2N	A7
500	GLHT	60139	2969	23W-2N	A7
500	LYWD	60411	3510	4E-25S	B7
1100	LYVL	60048	2590	18W-29N	E3
1400	DRGV	60515	3084	20W-4S	B7
1400	LYVL	60048	2591	18W-30N	A3
2600	NCHI	60088	2593	12W-30N	C3
2900	MchT	60050	2528	31W-32N	C3
2900	MHRY	60050	2528	31W-32N	C5
5500	CNHL	60514	3145	17W-6S	C4
5500	DGvT	60514	3145	17W-6S	C4
5700	WLBK	60514	3145	17W-6S	C4
5800	WLBK	60527	3145	17W-6S	C4
6800	CHRG	60415	3210	8W-11S	E7
6800	CHRG	60415	3211	8W-11S	A7
9900	CHRG	60415	3275	8W-11S	A1
N Virginia Av					
200	GNWD	60425	3508	1W-22S	B7
500	GNWD	60425	3428	1W-22S	B7
4500	CHCG	60625	2921	3W-5N	A7
5200	CHCG	60625	2920	3W-6N	E5
5500	CHCG	60659	2920	3W-6N	E5
25000	ElaT	60047	2644	24W-25N	C6
Virginia Ct					
100	SMWD	60107	2856	30W-10N	B6
100	SMWD	60107	2910	29W-9N	E1
600	NPVL	60540	3203	27W-8S	C1
700	SchT	60174	2908	34W-6N	D6
1100	BRLT	60103	2910	29W-6N	E7
Virginia Ct					
1800	ELGN	60123	2854	36W-12N	A1
4200	NCHI	60088	2593	12W-30N	C3
5300	GRNE	60031	2478	15W-35N	A5
7200	FKFT	60423	3592	9W-25S	E1
7200	FKFT	60423	3593	9W-25S	A1
7500	WLBK	60527	3207	16W-8S	E2
9200	ODPK	60462	3345	11W-16S	E3
Virginia Dr					
200	SEGN	60177	2908	34W-8N	C2
1200	WTMT	60559	3144	18W-7S	E6
1600	EGVV	60007	2913	22W-8N	D3
E Virginia Dr					
1300	PLTN	60074	2753	19W-16N	C7
S Virginia Dr					
17500	PnfT	60586	3415	32W-21S	D6
Virginia Ln					
500	AddT	60126	2972	15W-3N	A5
500	EMHT	60126	2972	15W-3N	A5
1100	NtrT	60091	2811	5W-14N	E5
1100	NtrT	60093	2811	5W-14N	E5
1100	WLMT	60091	2811	5W-14N	E5
2500	NHBK	60062	2810	10W-15N	A2
2700	GNVW	60025	2810	10W-12N	B7
18000	HMGN	60491	3422	16W-21S	A7
18300	NlxT	60448	3422	16W-22S	A7
18300	NlxT	60448	3502	16W-22S	A1
18300	NlxT	60491	3422	16W-22S	A7
N Virginia Ln					
900	AddT	60126	2972	15W-3N	A5
900	EMHT	60126	2972	15W-3N	A5
29200	WcnT	60084	2588	25W-29N	A4
29600	WCDA	60084	2588	25W-29N	A4
Virginia Pkwy					
-	SMBG	60193	2859	23W-10N	A6
11900	FftT	60448	3502	14W-22S	C2
11900	MKNA	60448	3502	14W-22S	C2
Virginia Pl					
300	WLNG	60090	2755	13W-17N	D5
2700	HMWD	60430	3427	3W-21S	B6
Virginia Rd					
10	CLLK	60014	2640	35W-24N	A6
400	BmdT	60172	2912	25W-6N	B6
400	ROSL	60172	2912	25W-6N	B6
800	HDPK	60035	2704	9W-21N	C7
8000	CLLK	60014	2694	34W-23N	C2
8000	LIHL	60014	2694	34W-23N	C2
8200	CLLK	60156	2694	34W-23N	C1
8200	LIHL	60156	2694	34W-23N	C2
9200	ALGN	60013	2694	33W-22N	E3
9200	AlqT	60013	2694	33W-22N	E3
Virginia Rd CO-V33					
10	CLLK	60014	2640	35W-24N	A6
8000	CLLK	60014	2694	34W-23N	C2
8000	LIHL	60014	2694	34W-23N	C2
8200	CLLK	60156	2694	34W-23N	C1
8200	LIHL	60156	2694	34W-23N	C2
9200	ALGN	60013	2694	33W-22N	E3
9200	AlqT	60013	2694	33W-22N	E3
Virginia St					
100	WNFD	60190	3023	27W-0N	C5
300	BNVL	60106	2972	15W-4N	A2
1000	CTCY	60409	3351	3E-18S	E7
1000	CTCY	60409	3352	3E-18S	A7
2300	PKRG	60068	2863	11W-9N	D6
E Virginia St					
700	JLET	60432	3499	22W-23S	C4
N Virginia St					
10	CLLK	60014	2639	36W-26N	D3
100	NndT	60012	2639	36W-26N	D3
N Virginia St US-14					
10	CLLK	60014	2639	36W-26N	D3
100	NndT	60012	2639	36W-26N	D3
S Virginia St					
10	CLLK	60014	2639	36W-25N	D4
S Virginia St US-14					
10	CLLK	60014	2639	36W-25N	D4
W Virginia St					
100	CLLK	60014	2640	35W-25N	A5
100	EMHT	60126	3027	16W-1N	E2
200	CLLK	60014	2639	35W-25N	E5
W Virginia St US-14					
100	CLLK	60014	2640	35W-25N	A5
200	CLLK	60014	2639	35W-25N	E5
N Virginia Lake Ct					
800	PLTN	60074	2753	19W-17N	C6
N Virn Allen Ct					
700	PLTN	60067	2752	21W-16N	C6
Viscaya Dr					
7200	AntT	60081	2415	27W-38N	B6
7200	FXLK	60081	2415	27W-38N	B6
Vision Av					
2500	JLET	60586	3415	32W-20S	C6
Vision Ct					
-	AURA	60506	3136	39W-4S	D2
-	SgrT	60506	3136	39W-4S	D2
Vista Av					
10	AddT	60148	3026	19W-2N	D1
10	YkTp	60148	3084	19W-1S	D2
700	LMBD	60148	3084	19W-1S	D2
N Vista Av					
600	LMBD	60148	3026	19W-1N	D2
S Vista Av					
10	ADSN	60101	2970	19W-3N	D5
400	AddT	60101	2970	19W-2N	D6
Vista Cir					
-	NPVL	60563	3140	30W-5S	C3
10	NpvT	60563	3140	30W-5S	C3
Vista Ct					
10	GLHT	60139	2968	23W-4N	E4
200	MNKA	60447	3672	32W-28S	C1
200	WLMT	60091	2812	5W-13N	A7
1800	SMBG	60193	2912	25W-8N	A2
2200	NHBK	60062	2810	10W-15N	A1
W Vista Ct					
26100	GrtT	60041	2473	26W-34N	E7
Vista Dr					
-	BRRG	60527	3208	13W-8S	E2
-	ISLK	60051	2642	29W-27N	C1
-	NndT	60042	2642	29W-27N	C1
-	NndT	60051	2642	29W-27N	C1
-	WLSP	60527	3208	13W-8S	E2
200	BGBK	60490	3267	26W-11S	D1
200	WLMT	60091	2812	5W-13N	A7
600	OSWG	60543	3263	37W-13S	C6
900	GRNE	60031	2476	18W-35N	E6
1100	WMTN	60481	3943	27W-39S	C2
1500	WslT	60481	3943	27W-40S	C2
2300	WDRG	60517	3143	21W-7S	E7
4500	ISLK	60042	2586	29W-27N	C7
4500	ISLK	60042	2642	29W-27N	C1
8200	ODPK	60462	3346	10W-16S	C3
15500	OKFT	60452	3347	7W-18S	C7
17800	CCHL	60478	3426	6W-21S	A6
N Vista Dr					
600	ALGN	60102	2747	33W-20N	E1
N Vista Dr					
900	ALGN	60102	2748	32W-20N	A1
S Vista Dr					
-	DndT	60102	2747	33W-20N	E2
600	ALGN	60102	2747	33W-20N	E2
900	ALGN	60102	2748	32W-20N	A2
Vista Dr W					
800	ALGN	60102	2747	33W-20N	E2
Vista Ln					
-	MNKA	60447	3672	32W-28S	C1
10	LKBN	60010	2697	27W-23N	B2
400	EDND	60118	2801	32W-16N	C2
500	EDND	60110	2801	32W-16N	C2
1400	CRTE	60417	3685	0W-30S	C2
1700	HFET	60169	2858	25W-12N	B2
N Vista Ln					
600	JLET	60435	3498	24W-23S	E3
S Vista Ln					
400	PNFD	60544	3338	30W-18S	B7
Vista Rd					
100	LKZH	60047	2698	24W-23N	D2
N Vista Rd					
2700	ANHT	60004	2754	17W-17N	B6
Vista Ter					
3200	MHRY	60050	2528	32W-31N	C7
E Vista Ter					
1800	LNHT	60046	2418	20W-39N	A5
Vista Tr					
2400	ElgT	60124	2853	37W-9N	D7
Vista Wk					
1400	HFET	60169	2858	25W-12N	B2
Vista Lake Dr					
1600	ANTH	60002	2417	20W-40N	E2
Vista View Dr					
100	WCDA	60084	2587	26W-28N	E6
Vita Dr					
400	WLNG	60090	2755	14W-17N	D5
Vita Ln					
100	BDWD	60408	3942	31W-42S	B6
Vivaldi Ct					
10	WHTN	60187	3082	24W-2S	C4
Vivaldi St					
2300	GwdT	60098	2524	41W-33N	E4
2300	WDSK	60098	2524	41W-33N	E4
Vivian Ct					
18000	ODPK	60467	3423	13W-21S	A6
Vivian Tr					
-	ELGN	60120	2855	32W-11N	C5
Vivian Wy Ct					
1600	LKMR	60051	2528	30W-33N	E2
Vivienne Dr					
21100	MTSN	60443	3505	7W-25S	C7
21100	MTSN	60443	3593	7W-25S	C1
Viviparous Wy					
7500	HDHT	60706	2918	9W-5N	C7
7500	NRDG	60706	2918	9W-5N	C7
Voce Ct					
8500	AlqT	60013	2696	29W-23N	D2
Vogay Ln					
2800	NfdT	60062	2809	12W-15N	B2
2800	PTHT	60062	2809	12W-15N	B2
Vogt St					
6500	TYPK	60477	3425	8W-20S	B4
Volbrecht Ct					
1600	SHLD	60473	3429	2E-20S	C4
Volbrecht Rd					
17500	LNSG	60438	3429	1E-20S	C5
17500	ThtT	60438	3429	1E-20S	C5
S Volbrecht Rd					
23100	CteT	60417	3597	1E-28S	C6
23100	SLVL	60411	3597	2E-28S	C5
24000	CteT	60417	3686	1E-29S	C1
Volid Dr					
1400	HFET	60169	2858	25W-12N	B2
Volintine Farm Rd					
10	BtvT	60510	3077	37W-2S	C5
Volkamer Tr					
1300	EGVV	60007	2913	21W-8N	E3
Volkening Cir					
500	HshT	60140	2796	44W-14N	E5
Volks Ct					
100	NARA	60542	3078	35W-4S	B7
Vollbrecht Dr					
1600	SHLD	60473	3429	2E-20S	C4
Vollbrecht Rd					
17000	SHLD	60473	3429	1E-20S	C4
17200	ThtT	60473	3429	1E-20S	C4
Vollmer Rd					
-	BlmT	60411	3508	0W-23S	B4
-	BlmT	60411	3509	1E-23S	B4
-	CHHT	60411	3508	1W-23S	A4
-	LYWD	60411	3509	1E-23S	B4
1400	CHHT	60411	3507	1W-24S	E4
1500	FSMR	60422	3507	2W-23S	C4
1800	BlmT	60411	3507	2W-23S	D4
1800	BlmT	60422	3507	2W-23S	D4
1800	CHHT	60422	3507	2W-23S	D4
2000	OMFD	60422	3507	2W-23S	D4
2000	OMFD	60461	3507	2W-23S	D4
2100	BlmT	60461	3507	2W-23S	C4
2400	FSMR	60461	3507	2W-23S	C4
2400	RchT	60461	3507	2W-23S	C4
3200	FSMR	60422	3506	4W-23S	E4
3200	OMFD	60422	3506	4W-23S	E4
3200	OMFD	60461	3506	4W-23S	E4
3800	MTSN	60443	3506	6W-23S	A4
3800	RchT	60443	3506	4W-23S	D4
4700	RchT	60477	3506	6W-23S	A4
5000	MTSN	60443	3505	6W-23S	E4
5000	RchT	60477	3505	6W-23S	E4
5600	MTSN	60477	3505	7W-23S	D4
6300	TYPK	60443	3505	6W-23S	E4
6300	TYPK	60477	3505	6W-23S	E4
W Vollmer Rd					
6400	MTSN	60443	3505	8W-23S	B4
6400	MTSN	60477	3505	8W-23S	B4
6400	RchT	60477	3505	8W-23S	B4
6400	TYPK	60443	3505	8W-23S	B4
6400	TYPK	60477	3505	8W-23S	B4
6700	RchT	60423	3505	8W-23S	B4
6700	TYPK	60423	3505	8W-23S	B4
6800	FftT	60423	3505	8W-23S	A4
Volo Village Rd					
26300	LKMR	60073	2530	27W-31N	B6
26300	VOLO	60073	2530	27W-31N	B6
27200	WcnT	60073	2530	27W-31N	B6
27400	LKMR	60041	2530	27W-31N	B6
27400	VOLO	60041	2530	27W-31N	B6
Voltaire Ln					
3400	SchT	60175	2963	38W-3N	B6
3400	SCRL	60175	2963	38W-3N	B5
Voltz Ct					
1600	NHBK	60062	2757	9W-16N	D6
Voltz Rd					
200	NHBK	60062	2758	7W-17N	A6
500	NHBK	60062	2757	8W-17N	D6

STREET Block	City	ZIP	Map#	CGS	Grid
Voltz Rd					
1100	NfdT	60062	2757	9W-17N	D6
Volz Av					
100	LktT	60441	3419	22W-21S	C6
N Volz Dr E					
3200	ANHT	60004	2754	17W-17N	C4
N Volz Dr W					
3100	ANHT	60004	2754	17W-17N	B5
Von Av					
5600	MONE	60449	3682	7W-31S	E4
Von Braun Tr					
1500	EGVV	60007	2914	21W-8N	A3
1600	EGVV	60007	2913	21W-8N	E3
Vonder Ln					
300	GNVA	60134	3020	34W-0N	C5
Von Drash Dr					
1300	DRN	60561	3207	18W-9S	A3
Von Esch Rd					
2300	JLET	60431	3416	28W-20S	E6
2300	PnfT	60431	3416	28W-20S	E6
2300	PnfT	60586	3416	28W-20S	E6
2500	JLET	60431	3417	28W-20S	A5
2500	JLET	60586	3417	28W-20S	A5
2500	PnfT	60431	3417	28W-20S	A5
2500	PnfT	60586	3417	28W-20S	A5
Von Hoff Dr					
1800	BTVA	60510	3078	34W-3S	D5
Vos Ct					
-	ANTH	60002	2416	24W-41N	D1
Vose Dr					
900	GRNE	60031	2534	16W-33N	D4
Voss Dr					
10700	ODPK	60467	3423	13W-21S	A6
Voyager Dr					
700	BRLT	60103	2911	28W-7N	B4
Voyager Ln					
-	JLET	60435	3417	27W-20S	B5
3000	JLET	60431	3417	27W-20S	B5
Vrin Ct					
10	LYWD	60411	3598	4E-25S	B1
Vulcan Blvd					
1900	BRLT	60120	2909	32W-9N	C1
1900	ELGN	60120	2909	32W-9N	D1
1900	HnrT	60120	2909	32W-9N	C1
W					
Waban Ct					
10	SMBG	60193	2858	25W-10N	A6
Waban Ln					
1800	SMBG	60193	2858	25W-10N	A6
Wabansia Av					
400	MTGY	60538	3200	35W-9S	B5
W Wabansia Av					
1300	CHCG	60622	2977	1W-2N	D7
2400	CHCG	60647	2977	3W-2N	A7
2800	CHCG	60647	2976	5W-2N	B7
3900	CHCG	60639	2976	5W-2N	B7
4800	CHCG	60639	2975	8W-2N	A7
6300	CHCG	60707	2975	8W-2N	A7
6700	CHCG	60707	2974	8W-2N	E7
7100	EDPK	60707	2974	9W-2N	C7
Wabash Av					
10	SchT	60174	2908	34W-6N	E6
5100	OKLN	60453	3211	6W-11S	E6
14600	DLTN	60827	3350	0W-17S	C5
14600	RVDL	60827	3350	0W-17S	C5
15000	DLTN	60419	3350	0E-17S	D6
15000	SHLD	60473	3350	0E-17S	D6
15900	SHLD	60473	3428	0E-18S	D1
N Wabash Av					
10	CHCG	60602	3034		D5
10	CHCG	60603	3034		D5
10	GNWD	60425	3508	0E-22S	D1
100	CHCG	60601	3034	0E-0N	C4
300	CHCG	60611	3034	0E-0N	C3
1000	JLET	60432	3499	23W-22S	B2
35700	AvnT	60073	2474	24W-35N	C5
S Wabash Av					
-	CHCG	60619	3214	0E-10S	C4
-	CHCG	60628	3214	0E-11S	C6
10	CHCG	60602	3034	0E-0S	C4
10	CHCG	60603	3034	0E-0S	C4
10	GNWD	60425	3508	0E-22S	D2
100	CHCG	60604	3034	0E-0S	C5
300	CHCG	60605	3034	0E-1S	C7
1400	CHCG	60616	3034	0E-1S	C7
2500	CHCG	60616	3092	0E-2S	C3
3600	CHCG	60653	3092	0E-4S	C6
4500	HMND	46327	3352		D4
4600	CHCG	60615	3092	0E-4S	C7
4700	CHCG	60615	3152	0E-5S	C2
5400	CHCG	60637	3152	0E-6S	C4
7000	CHCG	60619	3152	0E-7S	C6
10300	CHCG	60628	3278	0E-12S	C1
13700	RVDL	60827	3350	0W-15S	C2
14500	DLTN	60419	3350	0W-17S	C4
14500	DLTN	60827	3350	0W-17S	C4
Wabash Ct					
800	CLSM	60188	2967	26W-3N	E5
2600	NPVL	60565	3204	25W-10S	A6
15600	SHLD	60473	3350	0E-18S	D7
Wabash St					
100	WMTN	60481	3853	27W-39S	D7
300	ELGN	60123	2854	34W-10N	D5
9800	SjnT	46311	3687		D2
N Wabash St					
-	MHTN	60442	3677	19W-31S	D5
S Wabash St					
100	MHTN	60442	3677	19W-31S	E5
Wabasso Pl					
300	MNKA	60447	3583	33W-28S	B6
N Wabasso St					
300	MNKA	60447	3583	33W-28S	B7
S Wabasso St					
100	MNKA	60447	3583	33W-28S	B7
Wabena Av					
1100	MNKA	60447	3672	33W-29S	A3
N Wabena Av					
-	MNKA	60447	3583	33W-28S	B7
-	SwdT	60447	3583	33W-28S	B7
S Wabena Av					
100	MNKA	60447	3583	33W-28S	B7
300	AxST	60447	3672	33W-28S	B1
1200	MNKA	60447	3672	33W-30S	A3
Wabena Ct					
300	MNKA	60447	3672	33W-29S	A3
Wabena Dr					
1000	MNKA	60447	3672	33W-29S	A3
Wabican Tr					
1200	DndT	60102	2747	34W-19N	E2
Wachter Ln					
9000	HYHL	60457	3209	11W-10S	E5
Wacker Dr					
600	BtIT	60560	3333	42W-14S	D1
600	YKVL	60560	3333	42W-14S	D1
E Wacker Dr					
100	CHCG	60601	3034	0E-0N	C4
N Wacker Dr					
10	CHCG	60606	3034	0W-0N	B4
S Wacker Dr					
10	CHCG	60606	3034	0W-0S	B5
300	CHCG	60607	3034	0W-0S	B5
W Wacker Dr					
10	CHCG	60601	3034	0W-0N	B4
100	CHCG	60606	3034	0W-0N	B4
25500	LkvT	60046	2474	25W-37N	A2
E Wacker Pl					
10	CHCG	60601	3034	0E-0N	C4
Waco Dr					
800	CLSM	60188	2967	27W-3N	B5
Waco Ln					
500	CPVL	60110	2748	33W-17N	B6
Waddington Rd					
20600	DRPK	60010	2698	23W-20N	D7
N Wade Av					
-	WcnT	60084	2588	25W-29N	A5
Wade Ct					
3400	MrnT	60037	2704	8W-24N	D1
Wade Ln					
-	BTVA	60510	3077	37W-1S	B2
-	BtvT	60510	3077	37W-1S	B2
Wade St					
900	HDPK	60035	2705	7W-21N	B7
2400	EVTN	60201	2866	3W-11N	D2
28900	WcnT	60084	2588	25W-28N	A5
Wadham Ct					
1600	WHTN	60187	3082	23W-2S	E3
Wadham Pl					
1500	WHTN	60187	3082	23W-1S	E2
Wadsworth Av					
800	WKGN	60085	2537	10W-32N	A5
900	NCHI	60064	2537	10W-32N	A5
Wadsworth Pl					
1100	VNHL	60061	2647	17W-26N	B3
Wadsworth Rd					
1500	WHTN	60187	3082	24W-1S	C2
8400	WLSP	60480	3208	13W-9S	E4
W Wadsworth Rd					
-	BtnT	60099	2422	9W-39N	B6
2200	BHPK	60087	2421	11W-38N	D6
2200	BHPK	60099	2421	12W-39N	B6
2200	WKGN	60087	2421	11W-39N	D6
2200	WKGN	60099	2421	12W-39N	B6
4000	NptT	60083	2420	15W-39N	A6
4000	WDWH	60083	2420	13W-38N	D6
10000	BHPK	60099	2422	9W-39N	C6
12600	BHPK	60083	2421	12W-39N	A6
12600	WDWH	60083	2421	13W-39N	A6
15800	NptT	60083	2419	16W-39N	D6
15800	WDWH	60083	2419	15W-39N	E6
16100	OMCK	60083	2419	16W-39N	D6
W Wadsworth Rd CO-A9					
2200	BHPK	60087	2421	11W-38N	D6
2200	BHPK	60099	2421	12W-39N	B6
2200	WKGN	60087	2421	11W-39N	D6
2200	WKGN	60099	2421	12W-39N	B6
4000	NptT	60083	2420	15W-39N	A6
4000	WDWH	60083	2420	13W-38N	D6
10000	BHPK	60099	2422	10W-39N	B6
12600	BHPK	60083	2421	12W-39N	A6
12600	WDWH	60083	2421	13W-39N	A6
15800	NptT	60083	2419	16W-39N	D6
15800	WDWH	60083	2419	15W-39N	E6
16100	OMCK	60083	2419	16W-39N	D6
Wagman St					
4100	OKFT	60452	3426	5W-19S	B2
Wagner Av					
1100	JLET	60435	3498	25W-22S	B2
4000	SRPK	60176	2973	12W-5N	C2
Wagner Ct					
700	WNVL	60555	3080	28W-3S	E7
3100	AURA	60502	3078	34W-3S	E6
Wagner Dr					
10	CRY	60013	2695	31W-24N	E1
10	NHLK	60164	2972	13W-3N	D6
W Wagner Dr					
6800	MonT	60449	3682	8W-30S	B3
Wagner Ln					
10	McHT	60051	2528	31W-32N	D5
12700	WDSK	60098	2581	41W-30N	C3
Wagner Rd					
10	BTVA	60510	3078	34W-3S	E5
10	BtvT	60510	3078	34W-3S	E5
10	NHFD	60093	2811	7W-14N	B5
10	WldT	60564	3266	29W-11S	D1
10	WNVL	60555	3080	29W-3S	E6
600	GNVW	60025	2811	7W-13N	B7
2000	NHFD	60025	2811	7W-14N	B3
2100	BTVA	60502	3078	34W-3S	E6
3000	AURA	60502	3078	34W-3S	E7
17500	LtRT	60545	3258	51W-12S	A4
17500	LtRT	60548	3258	51W-12S	A4
17500	SdwT	60548	3258	51W-12S	A4
Wagon Ct					
10	DRPK	60010	2699	22W-20N	A7
Wagon Dr					
600	NLNX	60451	3501	17W-23S	D3
600	NlxT	60451	3501	17W-23S	D3
Wagon Rd					
-	PltT	60124	2852	39W-10N	E7
Wagontire Rd					
300	SchT	60175	2907	38W-7N	A5
Wagon Trail Ct					
28400	LKMR	60051	2529	28W-32N	E5
Wagon Trail Rd					
28400	LKMR	60051	2529	28W-32N	D5
Wagon Wheel Ct					
10	BGBK	60490	3268	26W-13S	A5
N Wagon Wheel Ct					
25300	CbaT	60010	2643	25W-25N	E5
Wagon Wheel Ln					
10	BNHL	60010	2696	29W-22N	C4
Wagonwood Rd					
100	AvnT	60073	2531	24W-33N	C3
100	RDLK	60073	2531	24W-33N	C3
Wahl St					
12600	ALSP	60406	3277	3W-14S	A6
12600	ALSP	60803	3277	3W-14S	A6
12600	BLID	60406	3277	3W-15S	A7
Waikiki Dr					
400	DSPN	60016	2862	14W-12N	D1
Wainlow Av					
400	WKGN	60085	2536	11W-33N	E3
Wainsford Dr					
600	HFET	60169	2858	25W-11N	C4
Wainwright Ct					
3000	HDPK	60037	2704	8W-23N	E2
N Wainwright Ct					
2000	PLTN	60074	2753	19W-18N	B3
Wainwright Dr					
300	NHBK	60062	2756	11W-18N	D3
5300	McHT	60097	2469	36W-37N	E2
6600	WDRG	60517	3143	22W-7S	C7
6800	LslT	60517	3143	22W-7S	C7
Wainwright Pl					
4000	OKLN	60453	3276	5W-12S	C3
Wainwright Rd					
400	OKTR	60181	3085	17W-1S	C1
N Waiola Av					
10	LGNG	60525	3087	12W-4S	B6
200	LGPK	60525	3087	12W-3S	B5
S Waiola Av					
10	LGNG	60525	3087	12W-4S	B7
300	LGNG	60525	3147	12W-5S	B2
Wait Rd					
2700	NPVL	60564	3266	29W-12S	C4
Waitkus Dr					
10	LMNT	60439	3272	15W-13S	B4
10	LmnT	60464	3272	15W-13S	B4
Wakeby Ln					
1300	SMBG	60193	2858	25W-10N	C6
Wakefield Ct					
10	BFGV	60089	2701	16W-20N	C7
100	AURA	60506	3137	38W-7S	A7
500	NPVL	60563	3142	25W-6S	A4
1500	MDLN	60060	2646	20W-27N	B1
W Wakefield Ct					
12600	BHPK	60083	2421	12W-39N	B5
Wakefield Dr					
1000	ELGN	60120	2855	32W-12N	D2
3000	CPVL	60110	2748	32W-17N	D7
3000	CPVL	60110	2801	32W-16N	D1
3000	EDND	60110	2801	32W-16N	D1
3000	EDND	60118	2801	32W-16N	D1
7500	DRN	60561	3206	19W-8S	D2
W Wakefield Dr					
4100	BHPK	60083	2421	12W-39N	B5
Wakefield Ln					
10	BFGV	60089	2701	15W-21N	E5
10	BFGV	60089	2754	17W-20N	B1
10	GNVA	60134	3019	36W-1N	D3
200	SMBG	60193	2858	24W-10N	C6
1100	BRLT	60103	2910	30W-7N	B5
5200	LGGV	60047	2701	17W-22N	A4
9800	HTLY	60142	2692	39W-22N	C4
Wakefield Rd					
600	GRNE	60031	2534	16W-33N	E3
Wakefield St					
10500	WSTR	60154	3087	13W-2S	A3
10500	WSTR	60525	3087	13W-2S	A3
10700	WSTR	60154	3086	13W-2S	E3
Wake Island Dr					
1700	JLET	60435	3417	27W-21S	D7
1700	JLET	60435	3497	27W-21S	C1
Wakeman Av					
1000	WHTN	60187	3024	23W-0N	E5
1600	WHTN	60187	3025	23W-0N	A5
Wakeman Ct					
1800	WHTN	60187	3025	23W-0N	A5
Wake Robin Ct					
10	WDRG	60517	3143	21W-7S	D7
Wake Robin Ln					
600	HDPK	60035	2705	7W-20N	C7
Wakeview Rd					
26500	LKBN	60010	2643	27W-25N	B5
26500	PTBR	60010	2643	27W-25N	A5
Wakia Ct					
10	HNWD	60047	2646	20W-25N	B5
Wakigan Tr					
1000	ALGN	60102	2747	34W-19N	E2
1000	DndT	60102	2747	34W-19N	E2
Walbridge Ct					
10	ALGN	60102	2693	37W-21N	B6
Walcott Ct					
-	EMHT	60126	3027	16W-0S	D6
Walcott Rd					
2100	AURA	60504	3201	33W-9S	B3
Wald St					
3200	GNVW	60025	2864	10W-12N	A1
3200	MaiT	60025	2864	10W-12N	A1
Walden Cir					
1400	AURA	60506	3137	38W-5S	B3
Walden Ct					
10	SMWD	60107	2857	28W-11N	A5
400	RMVL	60446	3269	23W-14S	A6
800	SMBG	60193	2912	25W-9N	A1
1000	BGBK	60440	3268	25W-11S	B1
14500	OKFT	60452	3347	6W-17S	D5
Walden Dr					
200	GLNC	60022	2758	6W-18N	D4
1300	ELGN	60120	2855	31W-10N	E6
12900	PNFD	60585	3338	29W-15S	C2
N Walden Dr					
700	PLTN	60067	2752	21W-16N	C6
700	PltT	60067	2752	21W-16N	C6
Walden Ln					
100	LKVL	60046	2475	23W-37N	A1
400	PTHT	60070	2754	16W-16N	D7
800	LKFT	60045	2650	9W-25N	B5
1100	DRFD	60015	2703	10W-21N	E6
1600	DRN	60561	3207	18W-8S	A1
3100	WLMT	60091	2811	6W-14N	E5
7100	DRN	60561	3145	18W-8S	A7
E Walden Ln					
2200	ANHT	60004	2754	16W-16N	D7
2200	ANHT	60004	2807	16W-16N	D1
S Walden Ln					
24000	CteT	60417	3598	3E-29S	A7
24000	CteT	60417	3687	3E-29S	A1
W Walden Ln					
14100	WDWH	60083	2420	14W-39N	D5
S Walden Pkwy					
9700	CHCG	60643	3213	2W-11S	C7
10100	CHCG	60643	3277	2W-12S	C1
Walden Rd					
100	JltT	60433	3587	23W-26S	A2
600	WNKA	60093	2812	5W-16N	A1
1000	LKFT	60045	2650	9W-25N	C4
12400	HMGN	60491	3344	15W-16S	B4
Walden Tr					
10	SMWD	60107	2857	28W-11N	A4
Walden Wy					
-	GRNE	60031	2477	17W-36N	B5
-	WrnT	60031	2477	17W-36N	A4
Walden Oaks Dr					
1100	WDSK	60098	2581	41W-30N	E2
Walden Office Sq					
-	RGMW	60008	2806	21W-12N	A7
-	SMBG	60008	2806	21W-12N	A7
1800	SMBG	60173	2806	21W-12N	A7
Waldman Dr					
300	PKFT	60466	3594	4W-26S	E2
300	PKFT	60466	3595	4W-26S	A2
W Waldo Av					
10100	BHPK	60099	2422	10W-39N	B6
10100	ZION	60099	2422	10W-39N	B6
12000	BHPK	60087	2421	12W-39N	C6
12000	BHPK	60099	2421	12W-39N	C6
12200	BHPK	60083	2421	12W-39N	C6
Waldo Erickson Dr					
-	WNSP	60558	3146	14W-4S	D1
Waldorf Ct					
10	EMHT	60126	3027	16W-0S	D6
Waldorth Ct					
600	MltT	60187	3082	25W-1S	A2
600	WHTN	60187	3082	25W-1S	A2
E Waldron Dr					
500	CHCG	60605	3034	0E-1S	D7
500	CHCG	60616	3034	0E-1S	D7
Wales Ct					
1200	SRWD	60404	3496	31W-24S	A5
Wales Dr					
1400	WHTN	60187	3082	24W-1S	D2
Walker Av					
10	CNHL	60514	3145	16W-5S	D2
10	HDPK	60035	2704	8W-23N	D2
10	HDPK	60037	2704	8W-23N	D2
10	HDPK	60040	2704	8W-23N	D2
10	HIWD	60040	2704	8W-23N	D2
1600	SMWD	60107	2911	28W-9N	B1
Walker Ct					
1000	ANTH	60002	2417	20W-41N	E1
1100	ELBN	60119	3017	43W-2N	A1
20600	FKFT	60423	3504	10W-24S	B6
Walker Dr					
-	ANTH	60002	2359	20W-41N	B7
-	CmpT	60119	3017	43W-2N	A1
-	CmpT	60151	3017	43W-2N	A1
-	ELBN	60151	3017	43W-2N	A1
200	BGBK	60440	3205	22W-10S	B6
200	ELBN	60119	3017	43W-2N	A1
1300	ANTH	60002	2417	20W-41N	E1
N Walker Ln E					
3100	ANHT	60004	2754	17W-17N	C5
N Walker Ln W					
3100	ANHT	60004	2754	17W-17N	C5
Walker Pl					
10	ELGN	60120	2855	33W-11N	A4
100	MDLN	60060	2590	18W-28N	D6
Walker Rd					
10	BrlT	60140	2795	48W-14N	A6
10	HshT	60140	2795	49W-16N	A1
11200	LMNT	60439	3271	17W-14S	B7
Walker Rd CO-46					
10	BrlT	60140	2795	48W-14N	A6
10	HshT	60140	2795	49W-16N	A1
W Walker Rd					
10	NasT	60586	3415	33W-19S	A4
10	PNFD	60586	3415	33W-19S	A4
Walker St					
500	HNDL	60521	3086	15W-4S	B7
1300	WNSP	60558	3086	14W-4S	D7
1400	WNSP	60558	3146	14W-4S	C1
7900	CmgT	60033	2405	51W-39N	D3
7900	HRVD	60033	2405	51W-39N	D3
N Walker St					
100	BDWD	60408	3941	31W-41S	E4
S Walker St					
100	BDWD	60408	3941	31W-41S	E6
100	BDWD	60408	3942	31W-41S	A6
Walker Wy					
600	NLNX	60451	3501	17W-23S	D4
600	NlxT	60451	3501	17W-23S	D4
Walking Ridge St					
4000	NndT	60012	2583	36W-28N	D7
N Walkup Av					
10	CLLK	60014	2640	35W-26N	B3
200	CLLK	60012	2640	35W-26N	B3
S Walkup Av					
10	CLLK	60014	2640	35W-25N	B4
Walkup Ln					
6300	CLLK	60012	2640	35W-27N	A1
6300	NndT	60012	2640	35W-27N	A1
Walkup Rd					
300	CLLK	60012	2640	35W-26N	B2
300	CLLK	60014	2640	35W-26N	B3
2600	BLVY	60012	2584	35W-29N	B4
2600	NndT	60012	2584	35W-28N	B7
4100	CLLK	60012	2584	35W-27N	B7
4400	NndT	60012	2640	35W-26N	B2
Walkup Rd CO-V34					
300	CLLK	60012	2640	35W-26N	B2
300	CLLK	60014	2640	35W-26N	B3
2600	BLVY	60012	2584	35W-29N	B4
2600	NndT	60012	2584	35W-27N	B7
4100	CLLK	60012	2584	35W-27N	B7
4400	NndT	60012	2640	35W-26N	B2
Wall Av					
2700	WKGN	60087	2479	12W-36N	B3
3000	WkgT	60087	2479	12W-36N	B3
W Wall Av					
12600	WKGN	60087	2479	12W-36N	B3
12600	WkgT	60087	2479	12W-36N	B3
12900	WrnT	60087	2479	13W-36N	A3
13500	WrnT	60031	2478	13W-36N	E3
Wall Pl					
5800	DRGV	60516	3144	19W-6S	E4
Wall St					
-	BMDL	60108	2968	24W-4N	D4
-	BMDL	60139	2968	24W-4N	D4
100	GLHT	60139	2968	24W-4N	D4
100	GNVA	60134	3020	34W-1N	C3
1500	NPVL	60563	3140	29W-5S	C2
1600	MPPT	60056	2861	16W-10N	E5
N Wall St					
200	DMND	60416	3941	33W-39S	B2
W Wall St					
23300	LKVL	60046	2417	23W-39N	A5
23300	LkvT	60046	2417	23W-39N	A5
23400	LKVL	60046	2416	23W-39N	E5
23400	LkvT	60046	2416	23W-39N	E5
Wallace Av					
100	CLLK	60014	2640	35W-25N	A5
400	WnfT	60187	3081	27W-2S	C3
1700	SCRL	60174	2964	34W-2N	D7
1700	SCRL	60174	3020	34W-2N	E1
1900	NCHI	60064	2536	11W-31N	D7
2300	NCHI	60064	2593	11W-31N	D1
3000	SCHT	60411	3596	0W-27S	B5
3000	STGR	60411	3596	0W-27S	B5
3000	STGR	60475	3596	0W-28S	B6
Wallace Ct					
1100	CHHT	60411	3507	1W-25S	E7
E Wallace Ct					
100	BRLT	60103	2911	28W-7N	A6
Wallace Dr					
100	AlqT	60013	2696	29W-23N	D2
100	CbaT	60013	2696	29W-23N	D2
100	DGvT	60516	3206	20W-10S	B5
100	WDRG	60516	3206	20W-10S	B5
100	WDRG	60517	3206	20W-10S	B5
2500	FSMR	60422	3507	3W-22S	B2
Wallace Rd					
100	LKFT	60045	2649	12W-25N	C5
100	WnfT	60187	3081	27W-2S	C3
Wallace St					
-	BlmT	60411	3508	0W-24S	B4
100	NLNX	60451	3501	18W-24S	B5
100	NlxT	60451	3501	18W-24S	B5
400	CHHT	60411	3508	0W-24S	B5
1400	CHHT	60411	3596	0W-25S	B1
2500	BlmT	60411	3596	0W-26S	B2
6100	CHCG	60621	3152	0W-6S	A4
14300	HRVY	60426	3350	1W-17S	B4
14300	HRVY	60827	3350	1W-17S	B4
14300	RVDL	60827	3350	1W-17S	B4
14700	DLTN	60419	3350	0W-17S	B6
14700	HRVY	60419	3350	0W-17S	B6
14700	SHLD	60426	3350	0W-17S	B6
14800	PHNX	60426	3350	0W-17S	B6
15700	HRVY	60426	3428	0W-18S	B1
16200	SHLD	60473	3428	0W-19S	B1
17000	SHLD	60426	3428	0W-20S	B4
E Wallace St					
100	BRLT	60103	2910	29W-7N	E5
100	BRLT	60103	2911	28W-7N	A6
100	JLET	60436	3498	24W-24S	E5
S Wallace St					
2500	CHCG	60616	3092	0W-3S	A4
3300	CHCG	60609	3092	0W-4S	A6
4700	CHCG	60609	3152	0W-5S	A1
7600	CHCG	60620	3214	0W-8S	A1
9400	CHCG	60628	3214	0W-11S	A6
10300	CHCG	60628	3278	0W-14S	B5
13600	RVDL	60827	3350	0W-15S	B2
14500	HRVY	60426	3350	1W-16S	B4
14500	HRVY	60827	3350	1W-16S	B4
W Wallace St					
10	JLET	60433	3499	22W-24S	C5
10	JLET	60436	3498	24W-24S	E5
10	JLET	60436	3499	22W-24S	C5
Wallace Wy					
-	WDRG	60517	3269	21W-12S	E2
300	RMVL	60446	3339	27W-17S	C7
600	BGBK	60440	3269	21W-12S	E2
600	BGBK	60517	3269	21W-12S	E2
600	WDRG	60440	3269	21W-12S	E2
Wallbank Av					
4700	DRGV	60515	3144	20W-5S	B2
W Wallen Av					
1600	CHCG	60626	2921	2W-8N	C2
3700	LNWD	60712	2920	4W-8N	C2
Wallen Dr					
4700	AlqT	60014	2640	33W-25N	E5
4700	CLLK	60014	2640	33W-25N	E5
Wallen Pl					
1200	DRGV	60516	3144	20W-6S	C5
N Waller Av					
400	CHCG	60644	3031	7W-0N	C3
700	CHCG	60651	3031	7W-0N	C3
1500	CHCG	60639	3031	7W-1N	C1
S Waller Av					
10	CHCG	60644	3031	7W-0S	C5
1100	CCRO	60644	3031	7W-0S	C7
1100	CCRO	60804	3031	7W-0S	C7
Waller St					
4200	DrrT	60012	2583	36W-28N	C6
Walleye Cir					
10	BDWD	60481	3942	30W-39S	D2
Walleye Ln					
10	BDWD	60481	3942	30W-40S	C2
10	RedT	60481	3942	30W-40S	C2
28500	WmTp	60481	3761	32W-34S	D6
Wallin Dr					
15100	PNFD	60544	3338	31W-18S	A7
15100	PnfT	60544	3338	30W-18S	A7
15200	PNFD	60544	3416	31W-18S	A1
Wallingford Ln					
20000	DRPK	60010	2752	22W-20N	B1
20000	PltT	60010	2752	22W-20N	B2
20000	PltT	60074	2752	22W-20N	B2
S Wallingford Rd					
28300	WltT	60442	3767	17W-34S	E4
Wallingford Tr					
14400	WltT	60442	3767	18W-35S	C7
Wallington Dr					
1800	NlxT	60451	3590	16W-27S	A5
W Wally Ct					
26500	GrtT	60041	2473	26W-35N	D6
Walnut					
-	HGKN	60525	3147	12W-7S	C5
Walnut Av					
200	ELGN	60123	2854	34W-10N	D5
200	WLNG	60090	2755	14W-17N	D4
300	NHFD	60093	2811	6W-15N	C1
600	LKBF	60044	2593	10W-28N	E6
600	SCRL	60174	2964	35W-3N	C7
700	BRTN	60010	2698	25W-20N	A7
900	HRPK	60133	2912	26W-8N	A3
900	SMBG	60193	2912	26W-8N	A3
1200	HRPK	60133	2911	27W-8N	C3
1500	WLMT	60091	2812	4W-14N	C5
2300	BRLT	60103	2911	27W-8N	C3
2300	BRLT	60133	2911	27W-8N	C3
2300	HRPK	60103	2911	27W-8N	C3
2500	GNVA	60134	3019	37W-0N	C4
2600	EVTN	60201	2812	3W-13N	E7
2700	WLMT	60201	2812	3W-13N	E7
3500	WLMT	60091	2811	6W-14N	D5
4500	LSLE	60515	3143	22W-5S	D2
5000	DRGV	60515	3143	22W-5S	D3
5400	DRGV	60516	3143	22W-6S	D4
5400	LslT	60515	3143	22W-6S	D4
5400	LslT	60516	3143	22W-6S	D4
6300	LslT	60517	3143	22W-7S	D6
7500	WDRG	60517	3205	21W-8S	D2
9000	FNPK	60131	2973	11W-3N	D4
9000	FNPK	60171	2973	11W-3N	D4
9000	RVGV	60171	2973	11W-3N	D4
18500	CCHL	60478	3506	5W-22S	C1
34300	WslT	60481	3943	27W-42S	E6
E Walnut Av					
900	DSPN	60016	2862	13W-10N	E5
1200	DSPN	60016	2863	13W-10N	A4
N Walnut Av					
100	ITSC	60143	2914	19W-6N	C6
100	WDDL	60191	2971	17W-5N	B1
300	WDDL	60191	2915	17W-6N	B7
400	AddT	60191	2915	17W-6N	B7
500	ANHT	60005	2806	18W-14N	E4
1900	ANHT	60004	2806	18W-16N	E1
2500	ANHT	60004	2754	18W-16N	A6
4000	ANHT	60004	2753	18W-18N	E2
26100	FmtT	60060	2646	19W-26N	C4
26100	LGGV	60047	2646	19W-26N	C4

STREET Block City ZIP Map# CGS Grid

S Walnut Av
100 ANHT 60005 2806 18W-13N E5
100 ITSC 60143 2914 19W-6N C7
1200 ANHT 60005 2860 18W-12N E1
W Walnut Av
10 DSPN 60016 2862 15W-10N B4
14400 HMGN 60491 3343 18W-16S B4
Walnut Cir
10 SgrT 60506 3136 41W-5S A4
300 BGBK 60440 3205 23W-11S A7
300 BGBK 60440 3269 23W-11S A1
1400 CLSM 60188 2967 28W-4N A4
1700 NfdT 60062 2757 10W-18N B3
2100 DRFD 60062 2757 10W-18N B3
24000 PNFD 60585 3266 30W-14S B6
Walnut Ct
10 MDLN 60060 2646 18W-27N E2
500 ANTH 60002 2357 24W-42N D5
800 DSPN 60016 2862 13W-10N D5
800 MRGO 60152 2634 49W-27N C1
1500 LMBD 60148 3084 20W-1S A1
1600 WHTN 60187 3082 25W-1S A2
1700 SPGV 60081 2414 30W-38N A6
2100 GNVW 60025 2864 9W-12N C1
2200 HRPK 60133 2911 27W-8N C3
3300 ISLK 60042 2586 29W-28N D5
3900 RGMW 60008 2806 20W-13N A6
9300 MaIT 60016 2863 11W-12N D1
11600 BRRG 60527 3208 14W-9S D3
15600 HMGN 60491 3422 16W-18S A1
E Walnut Ct
- LslT 60517 3143 21W-6S D5
N Walnut Ct
10 SMWD 60107 2856 29W-11N D4
2500 ANHT 60004 2754 18W-16N A6
S Walnut Ct
10 MDLN 60060 2646 18W-27N E1
W Walnut Ct
- LslT 60517 3143 22W-6S D5
10 ROSL 60172 2913 23W-6N A6
Walnut Dr
- GNVA 60134 3020 35W-0N B5
10 HNWD 60047 2645 21W-24N E7
10 KdlT 60560 3333 42W-16S C5
10 LIHL 60156 2694 35W-21N B5
10 NARA 60542 3077 37W-3S C6
10 NARA 60542 3137 37W-4S C1
10 WNFD 60190 3023 27W-1N D3
10 YKVL 60560 3333 42W-16S C5
100 SCRL 60174 2963 36W-2N D7
100 SCRL 60174 3019 36W-2N D1
100 SMWD 60107 2856 29W-10N E5
100 SRWD 60404 3495 31W-24S E5
700 DRN 60561 3207 17W-8S C2
800 SYHW 60118 2800 35W-15N C4
1000 VrnT 60015 2702 15W-20N A7
1300 RLKB 60073 2474 23W-35N D7
1400 DndT 60118 2747 36W-17N A7
1400 WDND 60118 2747 36W-17N A7
1400 WDSK 60098 2524 41W-32N D5
1600 RLKH 60073 2474 23W-35N D7
2400 AlqT 60013 2641 31W-25N D5
2600 McHT 60097 2469 36W-34N C7
2600 McHT 60097 2526 36W-34N C1
S Walnut Dr
10 NARA 60542 3137 37W-4S D1
Walnut Ln
- LslT 60517 3143 22W-6S D5
- WDRG 60517 3143 22W-6S D5
10 DndT 60118 2799 36W-15N E5
10 SBTN 60010 2803 27W-15N B3
10 SgrT 60506 3136 41W-5S A3
200 EGVV 60007 2914 18W-8N E3
200 LynT 60458 3209 11W-8S E2
200 OKBK 60523 3085 16W-1S E1
300 EGVV 60007 2915 18W-8N A3
700 MRGO 60152 2634 49W-27N C1
1100 NHBK 60062 2757 10W-17N B5
3300 MHRY 60050 2528 32W-33N C2
9000 TYPK 60487 3423 11W-20S E5
9000 TYPK 60487 3424 11W-20S A5
10800 MKNA 60448 3503 13W-23S A4
N Walnut Ln
10 GNWD 60425 3509 0E-22S A1
10 SMBG 60193 2858 25W-10N A5
100 SMBG 60194 2857 26W-10N E5
500 SMBG 60194 2858 26W-10N A5
1100 HFET 60169 2858 25W-11N A3
1100 SMBG 60169 2858 25W-11N A3
S Walnut Ln
10 GNWD 60425 3509 0E-22S A2
10 SMBG 60193 2858 25W-9N A7
10 SMBG 60194 2858 26W-10N A6
500 SMBG 60133 2858 25W-9N A7
W Walnut Ln
17300 WrnT 60031 2534 17W-34N C1
21000 LktT 60544 3339 26W-16S E4
21000 LktT 60544 3340 26W-16S A4
Walnut Pl
5400 DRGV 60515 3143 22W-5S D3
S Walnut Pl
- HPSR 60140 2795 47W-16N D2
Walnut Rd
100 TNLK 53181 2354 C1
200 MltT 60137 3025 21W-0N E4
400 LKFT 60045 2650 10W-26N A2
600 WCDA 60084 2587 26W-27N C7
2900 HMWD 60430 3427 3W-21S A6
15200 OKFT 60452 3347 8W-18S B7
S Walnut Rdg
11500 PSPK 60464 3274 10W-13S B5
Walnut St
- FNPK 60131 2973 11W-3N E4
- FNPK 60171 2973 11W-3N D4
- MYWD 60153 3029 11W-0N E4
- NndT 60014 2586 30W-28N A6
- RVGV 60171 2973 11W-3N D4
10 ALGN 60102 2747 33W-20N E1
10 ALGN 60102 2748 33W-20N A1
10 CNHL 60514 3145 16W-4S D1
10 CPVL 60110 2748 32W-18N C5
10 FKFT 60423 3591 12W-26S D2
10 JLET 60432 3499 22W-23S D4
100 JltT 60432 3499 22W-23S D4
100 LYVL 60048 2591 16W-29N D3
100 PKFT 60466 3594 4W-26S E3
200 LbvT 60048 2591 16W-29N D3
200 MYWD 60153 3030 10W-0N A4
200 WNKA 60093 2812 4W-15N B2
200 YKVL 60560 3333 42W-15S C1
300 BmdT 60157 2913 22W-6N C6
300 BTVA 60510 3078 36W-1S A1
300 ROSL 60157 2913 22W-6N C6
400 BtlT 60560 3333 42W-14S D1
500 BmdT 60172 2912 23W-6N E6
500 BmdT 60172 2913 23W-6N A6
Walnut St
500 LMNT 60439 3270 19W-14S D6
500 ROSL 60172 2912 23W-6N E6
600 HDPK 60035 2704 8W-21N E5
600 WKGN 60085 2479 10W-35N E7
700 GNEN 60137 3025 22W-0N D5
700 WLSP 60480 3209 12W-9S D3
900 DRFD 60015 2703 11W-21N E7
1300 WKGN 60085 2480 10W-35N A6
1400 WNSP 60558 3086 14W-4S C7
1500 HNDL 60521 3086 14W-4S C7
1500 PKRG 60068 2863 11W-10N E5
1700 WKGN 60087 2480 10W-36N A4
2000 BLID 60406 3277 2W-15S C7
5400 RHMD 60071 2353 34W-42N C5
8500 ODPK 60462 3346 10W-16S B2
19300 MKNA 60448 3503 11W-23S E3
19400 FftT 60448 3503 11W-23S E3
27500 WcnT 60042 2586 28W-27N E7
27500 WcnT 60042 2642 28W-27N E1
27600 ISLK 60042 2586 28W-27N E7
E Walnut St
10 ROSL 60172 2913 23W-6N B6
400 HNDL 60521 3146 15W-4S B1
500 PTON 60468 3861 8W-37S A3
N Walnut St
10 SEGN 60177 2908 34W-8N D2
100 BDWD 60408 3941 32W-41S D5
100 EMHT 60126 3027 16W-2N D1
200 BNVL 60106 2915 16W-5N E7
400 EMHT 60126 2971 16W-2N D7
700 ITSC 60143 2914 19W-7N C5
39000 LkvT 60046 2417 21W-39N C5
S Walnut St
10 PLTN 60067 2805 21W-15N C1
10 SEGN 60177 2908 34W-8N D3
100 BNVL 60106 2971 16W-5N E1
100 PltT 60067 2805 21W-15N C1
200 BDWD 60408 3941 32W-41S D6
200 BlmT 60425 3509 0E-23S A2
200 GNWD 60425 3509 0E-23S A2
200 RedT 60408 3941 32W-41S D6
400 MDLN 60060 2646 18W-27N E2
800 BmdT 60108 2913 22W-6N B6
800 BmdT 60157 2913 22W-6N B6
800 ROSL 60172 2913 22W-6N B6
24600 CteT 60417 3686 2E-29S D2
W Walnut St
10 HNDL 60521 3146 15W-4S A1
100 SCRL 60174 2964 35W-2N A7
400 MPPT 60056 2807 15W-13N E7
600 CHCG 60661 3034 0W-0N A4
600 HNDL 60521 3145 16W-4S E1
600 MDLN 60060 2646 18W-26N E2
700 CHCG 60607 3034 0W-0N A4
1000 SCRL 60174 2963 36W-2N E7
1600 CHCG 60607 3033 2W-0N C4
1600 CHCG 60612 3033 2W-0N C4
2800 CHCG 60612 3032 4W-0N D4
3100 CHCG 60624 3032 4W-0N D4
4600 CHCG 60644 3032 5W-0N A4
Walnut St S
24700 JknT 60421 3675 24W-30S D3
S Walnut Ter
- HYHL 60457 3210 10W-11S B7
- HYHL 60465 3210 10W-11S B7
9900 PSHL 60465 3210 10W-11S B7
Walnut Creek Dr
- FftT 60423 3504 10W-24S B6
- FKFT 60423 3504 10W-24S B6
1400 ELGN 60123 2907 36W-8N E3
1400 ElgT 60123 2907 36W-8N E3
Walnut Creek Ln
10 BtlT 60543 3262 39W-12S E3
400 DRGV 60515 3143 22W-5S C2
400 LSLE 60532 3143 22W-5S C2
Walnut Glen Dr
- CLLK 60014 2639 37W-24N B6
- GfnT 60014 2639 37W-24N B6
Walnut Grove Ct
10 LIHL 60156 2693 38W-22N A3
Walnut Hill Av
1400 GNVA 60134 3020 34W-2N D2
1400 GNVA 60174 3020 34W-1N D2
1400 SCRL 60174 3020 34W-1N D2
Walnut Manor Ct
2900 NndT 60012 2584 35W-29N A4
Walnut Oaks Dr
600 ROSL 60172 2913 23W-6N A6
Walnut Park Ln
1600 AURA 60504 3201 33W-9S A3
Walnut Ridge Ct
900 FKFT 60423 3503 13W-25S B7
S Walnut Ridge Ct
300 FKFT 60423 3503 13W-25S B7
300 FKFT 60423 3591 13W-26S B1
Walnut Ridge Dr
1300 MTGY 60538 3199 36W-9S E4
Walona Av
100 NLNX 60451 3501 17W-25S D7
100 NlxT 60451 3501 17W-25S D7
Walpole Ln
900 SMBG 60193 2912 24W-9N D1
Walpole Rd
10 EGVV 60007 2914 19W-8N D2
Walredon Av
8300 BRRG 60527 3208 15W-9S B4
Walsh Cir
200 YKVL 60560 3333 43W-16S B5
Walsh Ct
500 YKVL 60560 3333 43W-16S B4
Walsh Dr
- KdlT 60560 3333 43W-16S B5
1100 YKVL 60560 3333 43W-16S B5
W Walsh Ln
8100 RVGV 60171 2974 10W-3N B4
S Walsh Rd
- MhtT 60442 3767 19W-34S A5
27100 MHTN 60442 3767 19W-33S A3
27100 WltT 60442 3767 19W-33S A3
N Walsh St
500 JLET 60435 3498 24W-23S D3
Walsh Wy
2400 JLET 60435 3497 27W-23S D4
Walter Av
200 EGvT 60007 2860 19W-9N C7
200 EGVV 60007 2860 19W-9N C7
800 DSPN 60016 2862 13W-11N D3
900 AURA 60505 3200 34W-8S D2
S Walter Av
5500 HMND 46320 3352 D7
Walter Ct
10 LIHL 60156 2694 34W-22N C3
10 NlxT 60448 3502 15W-22S C2
100 BMDL 60108 2969 23W-5N A1
200 ELGN 60123 2854 35W-10N C5
Walter Dr
100 BMDL 60101 2969 22W-4N D4
100 BMDL 60108 2969 22W-4N D4
100 BmdT 60101 2969 22W-4N D4
200 ROSL 60172 2913 23W-7N A4
700 NlxT 60451 3502 15W-24S C4
13900 CTWD 60445 3348 6W-16S A3
Walter Dr CO-24
100 BMDL 60101 2969 22W-4N D4
100 BMDL 60108 2969 22W-4N D4
100 BmdT 60101 2969 22W-4N D4
W Walter Dr
10500 PlsT 60464 3345 13W-15S B2
Walter Ln
400 WldT 60564 3266 29W-11S D1
W Walter Ln
3800 ALSP 60803 3276 4W-15S C7
Walter St
300 YKVL 60560 3333 42W-15S C3
900 LMNT 60439 3270 19W-14S D7
17100 LNSG 60438 3430 4E-20S B4
18700 LNSG 60438 3510 4E-22S B1
W Walter St
200 EMHT 60126 3027 16W-1N E2
Walter Adamic Ln
6400 JLET 60586 3415 32W-20S D5
Walter Hagen Ln
14100 BmnT 60445 3347 6W-16S E4
14100 MDLN 60445 3347 6W-16S E4
14100 MDLN 60445 3348 6W-16S A4
Walter Payton Dr
- SMBG 60173 2859 21W-12N D2
- SMBG 60173 2860 21W-12N A2
Walters Av
2000 NHBK 60062 2757 10W-17N A6
2500 NHBK 60062 2756 11W-17N E6
3600 NfdT 60062 2756 11W-17N E6
E Walters Ln
100 ITSC 60143 2914 19W-7N C5
W Walters Ln
- ITSC 60143 2914 19W-7N C5
Walter Strawn Dr
- CnhT 60421 3763 27W-32S D1
- ELWD 60421 3763 27W-32S D1
- JknT 60421 3763 27W-32S D1
W Walter Zimny Dr
2300 DXMR 60406 3349 3W-17S B5
2300 POSN 60406 3349 3W-17S B5
2300 POSN 60469 3349 3W-17S B5
Waltham Ct
10 WNVL 60555 3080 30W-2S C3
Waltham Ln
1100 BRLT 60103 2910 30W-7N B5
Waltham Pl
400 DGvT 60561 3207 17W-9S C3
Waltham St
10 CTCY 60409 3352 4E-18S B7
10 HMND 46320 3352 4E-18S C7
E Waltham St
10 CTCY 60409 3352 D7
10 HMND 46320 3352 D7
300 HMND 46320 3430 D1
Walton Av
15200 PHNX 60426 3350 0W-18S B7
Walton Ct
2000 NPVL 60565 3203 26W-9S D4
S Walton Dr
- CHCG 60617 3216 4E-10S C6
Walton Ln
700 GYLK 60030 2533 20W-33N B3
17900 HMWD 60430 3428 1W-21S A6
E Walton Pl
10 CHCG 60610 3034 0E-1N C2
10 CHCG 60611 3034 0E-1N C2
Walton St
- DSPN 60016 2862 13W-12N E1
- DSPN 60016 2863 13W-12N A1
100 BRTN 60010 2751 25W-18N A2
500 MYWD 60153 3030 10W-1N A2
700 MYWD 60153 3029 11W-1N D3
800 MLPK 60160 3029 10W-1N E2
800 MYWD 60160 3029 10W-1N E2
W Walton St
10 CHCG 60610 3034 0W-1N B2
10 CHCG 60611 3034 0W-1N B2
1300 CHCG 60622 3033 1W-1N D2
3000 CHCG 60622 3032 3W-1N E2
4200 CHCG 60651 3032 5W-1N B2
4700 CHCG 60651 3031 6W-1N E2
5900 OKPK 60302 3031 7W-1N B2
Walton Heath Dr
10600 WldT 60564 3266 30W-12S C3
Waltonian Ter
100 FXLK 60020 2473 27W-37N B2
Waltshire Rd
4700 McHT 60050 2471 32W-36N B3
Walt Whitman Rd
10 CmpT 60175 2962 39W-3N D5
Waltz Ct
800 PTHT 60070 2808 15W-16N A1
W Waltz Dr
10 WLNG 60090 2755 14W-17N C6
Walworth St
100 GNCY 53128 2353 A3
Walworth St CO-H
100 GNCY 53128 2353 A3
Walz Dr
10 WHTN 60187 3081 27W-1S D2
10 WnfT 60187 3081 27W-1S D2
Wampum Ct
900 CLSM 60188 2967 26W-3N E5
Wanda Ln
1000 WDSK 60098 2581 40W-30N E2
N Wanda Ln
400 PLTN 60067 2752 21W-16N D7
Wanda Pl
5700 DRGV 60516 3144 19W-6S D4
Wanda Lea Ln
1200 PLNO 60545 3259 48W-12S B4
Wander Wy
10 ALGN 60102 2694 35W-21N A6
10 ALGN 60156 2694 35W-21N A6
10 LIHL 60156 2694 35W-21N A5
6500 AlqT 60013 2641 31W-25N D5
Wandsworth Cir
400 ROSL 60172 2912 25W-7N B5
Wanskuck St
3300 ElgT 60124 2853 38W-11N A4
S Wa Pella Av
10 MPPT 60056 2807 16W-12N E7
200 MPPT 60056 2861 16W-12N E1
E Wapella St
100 MNKA 60447 3583 33W-28S B7
500 CnhT 60447 3583 33W-28S B7
W Wapella St
100 MNKA 60447 3583 33W-28S B7
Wapoos Ct
200 SMBG 60194 2858 24W-10N D5
Warbler Cir
600 HDPK 60035 2704 9W-23N C1
Warbler Ct
200 LNHT 60046 2476 19W-37N C1
500 HDPK 60035 2704 9W-23N C1
S Warbler Ct
1800 WKGN 60048 2535 14W-31N D6
Warbler Dr
500 BGBK 60440 3205 21W-10S D5
1500 NPVL 60565 3203 26W-9S E3
Warbler Ln
600 NLNX 60451 3589 18W-27S A4
17000 ODPK 60467 3423 13W-20S A4
Warbler Pl
2900 HDPK 60035 2704 9W-23N C1
E Ward Av
300 JLET 60432 3499 23W-23S B3
Ward Ct
24500 SRWD 60404 3496 30W-25S B7
N Ward Ln
35500 GrtT 60041 2474 25W-35N B6
Ward Rd
1100 BTVA 60510 3077 36W-1S E1
1100 BTVA 60510 3078 36W-1S A1
Ward St
600 AURA 60505 3138 34W-6S D6
Ware Rd
11800 GwdT 60098 2524 41W-33N E4
11800 GwdT 60098 2525 40W-33N A4
11800 WDSK 60098 2524 41W-33N D4
11800 WDSK 60098 2525 40W-33N A4
Wareham Ln
10 SMBG 60193 2858 25W-10N A6
10 SMBG 60194 2858 25W-10N A6
Ware Woods Dr
600 SchT 60175 2963 36W-4N E4
Warington Ln
1000 HFET 60169 2858 24W-11N C3
Warkworth Ln
100 IVNS 60067 2752 22W-16N B7
Warm Springs Ct
2300 NPVL 60564 3202 29W-10S D6
Warm Springs Ln
2400 NPVL 60564 3202 29W-10S C6
Warne Ct
800 ELBN 60119 3017 43W-2N A1
Warner Av
400 LMNT 60439 3270 19W-14S D6
12600 BHPK 60087 2479 12W-37N B2
W Warner Av
1400 CHCG 60613 2977 1W-5N D1
1900 CHCG 60618 2977 2W-5N B1
3200 CHCG 60618 2976 4W-5N D1
4800 CHCG 60641 2975 6W-5N E1
6400 CHCG 60634 2975 8W-5N A1
Warner Cir
10 LMNT 60439 3270 19W-14S D7
Warner Ln
100 BbyT 60134 3018 39W-0S E6
S Warner St
100 HPSR 60140 2795 46W-15N E3
800 HshT 60140 2795 46W-15N E3
W Warner St
12000 BHPK 60087 2479 12W-37N C2
12000 WKGN 60087 2479 12W-37N C2
S Warner Bridge Rd
29000 WltT 60442 3766 20W-35S B7
Warren Av
- WMTN 60481 3853 27W-38S E6
10 NLNX 60451 3501 18W-25S B7
10 WNVL 60555 3081 28W-3S A7
100 AURA 60505 3200 36W-8S A2
100 BMDL 60108 2969 22W-5N C1
400 PKRG 60068 2917 11W-8N E2
600 RKDL 60436 3498 25W-25S B7
700 DRGV 60515 3144 19W-5S C2
2100 BLWD 60104 3029 11W-0N C5
2100 DRGV 60515 3143 21W-5S E2
2100 MYWD 60153 3029 11W-0N C5
2200 IVNS 60067 2804 23W-15N D1
3400 GRNE 60085 2536 13W-34N A2
3400 PKCY 60085 2536 13W-34N A2
3700 BLWD 60162 3029 12W-0N A5
4000 HLSD 60162 3029 13W-0N A5
4200 HLSD 60162 3028 13W-0N E5
5100 BKLY 60163 3028 14W-0N C5
5100 HLSD 60163 3028 14W-0N C5
9700 OKLN 60453 3211 6W-11S D7
S Warren Av
400 PLTN 60074 2806 19W-15N D3
W Warren Av
17400 WrnT 60030 2534 17W-33N B2
25000 LkvT 60046 2416 25W-38N B7
W Warren Blvd
600 CHCG 60661 3034 D5
1500 CHCG 60607 3033 3W-0N A4
1500 CHCG 60612 3033 3W-0N A4
2800 CHCG 60612 3032 3W-0N E5
3100 CHCG 60624 3032 3W-0N E4
Warren Cir
3100 OMFD 60461 3507 3W-25S A7
Warren Ct
200 WNVL 60555 3080 29W-3S D5
500 HNDL 60521 3086 16W-4S A7
500 WDDL 60191 2914 19W-5N D7
2600 AURA 60504 3201 32W-9S C4
5900 MNGV 60053 2865 7W-10N B5
Warren Dr
12200 NlxT 60448 3502 15W-22S C2
E Warren Dr
- NlxT 60448 3502 15W-22S C1
Warren Ln
300 GYLK 60030 2532 21W-32N D4
1000 VNHL 60061 2646 18W-25N E5
N Warren Ln
- BHPK 60099 2421 13W-39N A5
N Warren Ovl
300 GNVW 60025 2864 10W-12N A1
300 GNVW 60714 2864 10W-12N A1
300 NLES 60714 2864 10W-12N A1
Warren Rd
400 GNVW 60025 2810 10W-12N A7
400 GNVW 60025 2864 10W-11N A2
400 GNVW 60714 2864 10W-11N A2
400 NLES 60025 2864 10W-11N A2
400 NLES 60714 2864 10W-11N A2
N Warren Rd
9900 GNVW 60025 2864 10W-12N A1
9900 GNVW 60714 2864 10W-12N A1
9900 NLES 60025 2864 10W-12N A1
9900 NLES 60714 2864 10W-12N A1
Warren St
- BLWD 60104 3029 11W-0N D5
10 CTCY 60409 3352 4E-18S B7
Warren St
10 HMND 46320 3352 4E-18S C7
100 MYWD 60153 3030 10W-0N A5
700 MYWD 60153 3029 11W-0N E5
1900 EVTN 60202 2866 3W-10N E5
3800 SKOK 60076 2866 4W-10N C5
4900 SKOK 60077 2865 6W-10N E5
5400 MNGV 60077 2865 6W-10N D5
5700 MNGV 60053 2865 7W-10N C5
7400 FTPK 60130 3030 9W-0N D5
E Warren St
10 CTCY 60409 3352 C7
10 HMND 46320 3352 C7
Warren Ter
400 HNDL 60521 3086 15W-4S A7
Warren-Allen Dr
100 WDDL 60191 2915 17W-7N B5
Warren Dorris Dr
2800 JLET 60435 3497 27W-23S C4
Warrenville Av
10 WHTN 60187 3081 27W-2S C4
10 WnfT 60187 3081 27W-2S C4
100 WHTN 60555 3081 27W-2S D4
100 WnfT 60555 3081 27W-2S D4
Warrenville Rd
- NPVL 60555 3081 27W-4S C7
- NPVL 60563 3081 27W-4S C7
- WNVL 60555 3081 27W-4S C7
10 NPVL 60532 3082 25W-4S B7
10 NPVL 60563 3082 25W-4S C7
10 WNVL 60555 3080 29W-3S E6
200 WNVL 60563 3081 27W-4S D7
400 DRGV 60532 3143 22W-4S D1
400 LSLE 60532 3143 22W-4S C1
400 LslT 60532 3143 22W-4S C1
500 LSLE 60532 3083 23W-4S B7
500 LslT 60563 3082 25W-4S C7
700 LSLE 60532 3082 23W-4S E7
1100 MltT 60187 3082 25W-1S B2
1100 WHTN 60187 3082 25W-1S B2
1400 LslT 60532 3083 23W-4S A7
1500 LslT 60532 3082 23W-4S E7
2100 LSLE 60532 3142 24W-4S D1
2200 DRGV 60515 3143 21W-4S E1
2600 LSLE 60515 3143 21W-4S D1
Warrenville Rd CO-3
10 LSLE 60532 3082 25W-4S B7
10 NPVL 60532 3082 25W-4S B7
10 NPVL 60563 3082 25W-4S C7
200 WNVL 60563 3081 27W-4S D7
300 WNVL 60555 3081 27W-4S C7
400 DRGV 60532 3143 22W-4S D1
400 LSLE 60532 3143 22W-4S C1
400 LslT 60532 3143 22W-4S C1
400 NPVL 60555 3081 27W-4S C7
400 NPVL 60563 3081 27W-4S C7
500 LslT 60563 3082 25W-4S C7
1400 LSLE 60532 3083 23W-4S A7
1400 LslT 60532 3083 23W-4S A7
1500 LslT 60532 3082 23W-4S E7
2100 LSLE 60532 3142 24W-4S D1
2200 DRGV 60515 3143 21W-4S E1
2600 LSLE 60515 3143 21W-4S D1
Warrenville Rd CO-32
- NPVL 60555 3081 27W-4S C7
- NPVL 60563 3081 27W-4S C7
- WNVL 60563 3081 27W-4S C7
400 WNVL 60555 3081 27W-3S C7
E Warrenville Rd
1000 LslT 60563 3081 26W-4S E7
1000 NPVL 60563 3081 26W-4S E7
1000 NPVL 60563 3082 25W-4S A7
1100 LslT 60563 3082 25W-4S A7
E Warrenville Rd CO-3
1000 LslT 60563 3081 26W-4S E7
1000 NPVL 60563 3081 26W-4S E7
1000 NPVL 60563 3082 25W-4S A7
1100 LslT 60563 3082 25W-4S A7
W Warrenville Rd
100 LslT 60563 3081 27W-4S D7
100 NPVL 60555 3081 27W-4S D7
100 NPVL 60563 3081 27W-4S D7
100 WNVL 60555 3081 27W-4S D7
100 WNVL 60563 3081 27W-4S D7
W Warrenville Rd CO-3
100 LslT 60563 3081 27W-4S D7
100 NPVL 60555 3081 27W-4S D7
100 NPVL 60563 3081 27W-4S D7
100 WNVL 60555 3081 27W-4S D7
100 WNVL 60563 3081 27W-4S D7
Warrington Ct
10 LKBF 60044 2593 11W-29N D4
2100 GNVW 60025 2809 10W-14N E3
Warrington Dr
10 LKBF 60044 2593 11W-29N D4
Warrington Ln
1600 CLLK 60014 2693 36W-22N D3
Warrington Rd
10 VNHL 60061 2647 16W-25N C5
800 DRFD 60015 2704 10W-21N A7
N Warrington Rd
10 DSPN 60016 2862 14W-12N C2
100 MPPT 60016 2862 14W-12N C1
100 MPPT 60056 2862 14W-12N C1
S Warrington Rd
10 DSPN 60016 2862 14W-12N C2
Warrior Dr
600 RLKH 60073 2474 24W-35N D5
Warsaw Av
4500 LYNS 60534 3148 10W-4S A1
4500 MCCK 60525 3148 10W-4S A1
4500 MCCK 60534 3148 10W-4S A1
E Warson Ct
10 VNHL 60061 2647 16W-27N C1
N Warwick Av
300 WTMT 60559 3145 17W-4S B1
500 WTMT 60559 3085 17W-4S B7
S Warwick Av
100 WTMT 60559 3145 17W-5S B3
1400 HMND 46394 3280 E4
7600 DRN 60561 3207 17W-8S B2
W Warwick Av
4000 CHCG 60618 2976 5W-4N B2
4000 CHCG 60641 2976 5W-4N B2
5500 CHCG 60634 2975 7W-4N B2
5500 CHCG 60641 2975 7W-4N C2
Warwick Cir N
1000 HFET 60169 2858 24W-11N C3
Warwick Cir S
1100 HFET 60169 2858 24W-11N C3
Warwick Ct
10 LIHL 60156 2692 38W-21N D7
10 PKFT 60466 3595 3W-26S A3
10 SEGN 60177 2908 35W-7N C4
10 SMWD 60107 2857 26W-11N E4
100 SMBG 60193 2858 25W-10N A6

Block	City	ZIP	Map#	CGS	Grid
Warwick Ct					
200	BGBK	60440	3269	21W-11S	D1
700	CLSM	60188	2967	27W-4N	D4
700	LKZH	60047	2699	22W-22N	C5
1100	GYLK	60030	2532	21W-34N	D1
1200	DRFD	60015	2703	11W-21N	E6
1600	WLNG	60090	2754	16W-18N	D3
1700	GNEN	60137	3083	23W-1S	A2
1700	GNEN	60187	3083	23W-1S	A2
1700	WHTN	60187	3083	23W-1S	A2
2400	AURA	60503	3201	32W-10S	C6
5800	OKFT	60452	3347	7W-18S	D6
E Warwick Ct					
2600	ANHT	60004	2807	16W-15N	C2
Warwick Dr					
100	GLHT	60139	2968	24W-3N	D5
200	NPVL	60565	3204	25W-9S	B4
600	CLSM	60188	2967	26W-4N	E4
900	MTSN	60443	3505	7W-25S	D7
3600	CRTE	60417	3596	0W-28S	C7
15400	OKFT	60452	3347	7W-18S	D7
Warwick Ln					
10	LNSH	60069	2703	13W-22N	A3
100	KLWH	60043	2812	3W-14N	D4
200	LIHL	60156	2692	38W-21N	D6
200	LKWD	60014	2639	37W-25N	C5
300	BMDL	60108	2968	24W-5N	C2
400	CLLK	60014	2639	37W-25N	C6
700	LKZH	60047	2699	22W-21N	C5
800	LYVL	60048	2591	17W-28N	C7
900	KLDR	60047	2699	21W-21N	C6
1000	EGVV	60007	2915	18W-8N	A2
1600	SMBG	60193	2858	26W-10N	A6
2100	GNVW	60025	2809	10W-14N	E3
2200	SMBG	60193	2857	26W-10N	E6
10800	OrlT	60467	3423	13W-20S	A4
Warwick Pl					
10	ELGN	60120	2855	33W-11N	A4
Warwick Rd					
200	KLWH	60043	2812	4W-14N	C3
200	LKFT	60045	2649	12W-26N	C3
200	TRLK	60010	2643	26W-25N	D5
300	DRFD	60015	2704	10W-21N	A6
600	DRFD	60015	2703	10W-21N	E6
600	WNKA	60093	2812	4W-14N	C3
E Warwick Rd					
400	PLTN	60074	2753	20W-16N	A6
Warwick St					
100	PKFT	60466	3595	3W-26S	A3
E Warwick St					
600	BRTN	60010	2751	25W-18N	B2
Warwick Wy					
600	WYNE	60184	2966	30W-4N	A4
800	WYNE	60185	2966	31W-4N	A4
Wasco Rd					
10	CmpT	60175	2962	40W-4N	C3
Wasdale Av					
1300	EGVV	60007	2914	19W-8N	D3
1300	ITSC	60143	2914	19W-8N	D3
W Waseca Pl					
1600	CHCG	60643	3277	2W-13S	D3
Washburn Dr					
100	BbyT	60134	3018	39W-0N	E6
Washburn Pl					
300	BbyT	60134	3018	39W-0N	E6
Washburn St					
100	ELGN	60123	2854	34W-10N	D5
200	WDSK	60098	2581	41W-30N	E1
Washburn Wy					
1300	LKPT	60441	3420	21W-19S	A2
W Washburne Av					
1200	CHCG	60608	3033	1W-1S	D7
Washington Av					
-	AntT	60081	2415	27W-38N	A7
10	LGNG	60525	3087	12W-4S	D7
10	SMWD	60107	2856	29W-10N	E6
100	HIWD	60037	2704	9W-23N	D2
100	HIWD	60040	2704	9W-23N	C2
100	WNFD	60190	3023	27W-0S	C7
300	GLNC	60022	2758	6W-17N	D5
300	HDPK	60035	2704	9W-23N	C2
300	WLMT	60091	2813	3W-13N	A5
400	LKBF	60044	2593	11W-28N	C5
400	WnfT	60190	3023	28W-0S	A6
600	WnfT	60185	3022	28W-0S	E7
600	WnfT	60185	3023	28W-0S	A7
700	BtnT	60096	2363	10W-42N	A6
700	SCRL	60174	2964	35W-2N	C7
700	WLMT	60091	2812	3W-13N	E5
700	WPHR	60096	2363	10W-42N	A6
900	WCDA	60084	2588	25W-28N	A6
1100	WcnT	60084	2588	25W-28N	A6
2700	NCHI	60088	2593	11W-30N	C2
3400	WLMT	60091	2811	6W-13N	D6
3800	LYNS	60534	3088	9W-3S	C6
3800	RvsT	60534	3088	9W-3S	C6
3800	RvsT	60546	3088	9W-3S	C6
4200	MTSN	60443	3594	5W-25S	C1
8400	BKFD	60513	3088	10W-3S	A5
8400	BKFD	60546	3088	10W-3S	A5
8400	RVSD	60546	3088	10W-3S	A5
8700	BKFD	60513	3087	11W-3S	E5
9500	BKFD	60525	3087	11W-3S	D5
9500	LGPK	60525	3087	11W-3S	C5
9800	OKLN	60453	3211	6W-11S	D7
10200	OKLN	60453	3275	6W-12S	D1
11900	BLID	60406	3277	2W-14S	C5
11900	BLID	60643	3277	2W-14S	C5
11900	CHCG	60643	3277	2W-14S	C5
14700	HRVY	60426	3350	1W-17S	A6
17500	HMWD	60430	3427	2W-21S	C6
E Washington Av					
10	LKBF	60044	2593	10W-28N	E5
100	HPSR	60140	2795	46W-16N	E2
100	LKBF	60044	2594	10W-28N	A5
300	HPSR	60140	2796	46W-16N	A2
2800	NCHI	60088	2593	12W-30N	C3
N Washington Av					
10	BTVA	60510	3078	35W-0S	C1
10	PKRG	60068	2864	9W-9N	B7
10	PKRG	60068	2918	8W-8N	D2
700	BTVA	60510	3020	35W-0S	C7
900	NLES	60068	2864	10W-9N	B6
900	NLES	60714	2864	10W-9N	B6
1200	GNVA	60134	3020	35W-0S	C7
1200	GNVA	60510	3020	35W-0S	C7
28500	WCDA	60084	2588	25W-28N	A6
28500	WcnT	60084	2588	25W-28N	A5
N Washington Av SR-25					
10	BTVA	60510	3078	35W-0S	C1
700	BTVA	60510	3020	35W-0S	C7
1200	GNVA	60134	3020	35W-0S	C7
1200	GNVA	60510	3020	35W-0S	C7
S Washington Av					
10	BTVA	60510	3078	35W-1S	C2
300	PKRG	60068	2918	9W-8N	B1

Block	City	ZIP	Map#	CGS	Grid
S Washington Av					
1900	CHCG	60631	2918	9W-7N	B4
1900	PKRG	60631	2918	9W-7N	B4
10700	OKLN	60453	3275	6W-12S	D2
W Washington Av					
100	LKBF	60044	2593	11W-28N	D5
500	ShdT	60044	2593	12W-28N	C5
23700	LKVL	60046	2416	23W-38N	E6
23700	LkvT	60046	2416	23W-38N	D6
Washington Blvd					
10	CHCG	60302	3031	7W-0N	B4
10	CHCG	60644	3031	7W-0N	B4
10	MDLN	60060	2647	18W-27N	A2
10	MYWD	60153	3030	10W-0N	A4
10	OKPK	60302	3031	8W-0N	A4
10	RVFT	60305	3030	10W-0N	B4
10	SMBG	60169	2858	24W-10N	D5
10	SMBG	60193	2858	24W-10N	D5
200	MTGY	60543	3263	38W-12S	B3
200	OSWG	60543	3263	38W-12S	B3
300	GYLK	60030	2533	20W-32N	A5
600	HFET	60169	2858	24W-11N	E4
700	MYWD	60153	3029	11W-0N	D4
800	OKPK	60302	3030	8W-0N	E4
1100	FTPK	60302	3030	8W-0N	D4
2100	BLWD	60104	3029	12W-0N	B4
3900	BLWD	60162	3029	12W-0N	A4
3900	HLSD	60162	3029	12W-0N	B4
4100	HLSD	60104	3029	12W-0N	B4
7600	FTPK	60130	3030	9W-0N	C4
7600	RVFT	60130	3030	9W-0N	C4
Washington Blvd SR-56					
4000	BLWD	60104	3029	12W-0N	B4
4000	BLWD	60162	3029	12W-0N	A4
4000	HLSD	60162	3029	12W-0N	B4
4100	HLSD	60104	3029	12W-0N	B4
E Washington Blvd					
10	LMBD	60148	3026	19W-0N	C5
1100	LMBD	60181	3026	18W-0N	E5
1100	VLPK	60181	3026	18W-0N	E5
W Washington Blvd					
100	LMBD	60148	3026	20W-0N	B5
500	CHCG	60606	3034	0W-0N	A4
500	CHCG	60661	3034	0W-0N	A4
700	CHCG	60607	3034	0W-0N	A4
800	CHCG	60607	3033	1W-0N	D4
1500	CHCG	60612	3033	1W-0N	D4
2800	CHCG	60612	3032	4W-0N	D4
3400	CHCG	60624	3032	5W-0N	A4
4500	CHCG	60644	3032	5W-0N	A4
5100	CHCG	60644	3031	7W-0N	C4
5900	CHCG	60302	3031	7W-0N	B4
5900	OKPK	60302	3031	7W-0N	B4
Washington Cir					
10	LKFT	60045	2650	10W-26N	A4
S Washington Cir					
10	HNDL	60521	3146	15W-5S	A3
Washington Ct					
-	PKRG	60068	2918	10W-7N	B3
10	JLET	60435	3417	28W-19S	B3
10	MDLN	60060	2647	18W-27N	A1
10	PKFT	60466	3594	4W-26S	E3
10	PnfT	60435	3417	28W-19S	B3
10	SMWD	60107	2856	29W-10N	E6
100	WTMT	60559	3085	18W-4S	A7
200	PLTN	60067	2805	21W-15N	D1
300	VNHL	60061	2647	17W-26N	B3
700	HDPK	60035	2758	7W-20N	A1
1000	BRLT	60103	2910	30W-6N	C6
1200	WLMT	60091	2812	3W-13N	D5
1300	AURA	60506	3137	37W-6S	C5
1600	GNVA	60134	3021	33W-2N	A2
17700	ODPK	60467	3423	13W-21S	A6
Washington Dr					
-	OMFD	60461	3507	3W-25S	C7
-	SRWD	60404	3495	31W-24S	E6
10	DMND	60416	3941	33W-39S	B1
4300	RNPK	60471	3594	5W-27S	B4
N Washington Dr					
9000	MaiT	60016	2863	11W-11N	D3
Washington Ln					
-	PKRG	60068	2918	9W-7N	B3
Washington Pk					
100	WKGN	60085	2536	11W-33N	E2
1300	NCHI	60064	2536	11W-32N	E5
Washington Pkwy					
200	FKFT	60423	3591	12W-25S	C1
21100	FKFT	60423	3503	13W-25S	A7
Washington Pl					
400	HDPK	60035	2758	7W-20N	A1
600	GLNC	60022	2758	6W-17N	C5
1200	PKRG	60068	2918	9W-7N	C3
Washington Rd					
10	LKFT	60045	2650	10W-26N	A2
10	MaiT	60025	2864	10W-12N	B1
10	MaiT	60053	2864	10W-12N	B2
10	MaiT	60714	2864	10W-12N	B2
10	MNGV	60053	2864	10W-12N	B2
300	GNVW	60025	2864	10W-12N	B1
400	GNVW	60025	2810	10W-12N	B7
Washington Sq					
200	EGVV	60007	2914	18W-8N	E1
200	WDDL	60191	2914	19W-5N	D7
Washington St					
-	BGBK	60490	3267	27W-14S	D7
-	BGBK	60490	3339	27W-14S	D1
-	BGBK	60544	3339	27W-14S	D1
-	BNVL	60106	2971	16W-4N	E2
-	EGvT	60007	2861	15W-9N	E7
-	EGvT	60018	2861	16W-9N	E7
-	EGVV	60007	2861	15W-9N	E7
-	LktT	60441	3341	22W-16S	D3
-	PTON	60468	3861	9W-37S	A2
-	RMVL	60441	3341	22W-16S	D3
10	AddT	60106	2915	17W-6N	C5
10	ALGN	60102	2694	34W-20N	D7
10	FXLK	60020	2473	26W-36N	D4
10	FXLK	60041	2473	26W-36N	D4
10	GNVW	60025	2864	9W-12N	D1
10	GNVW	60053	2864	9W-12N	D2
10	MNGV	60053	2864	9W-12N	D2
10	WDSK	60098	2524	42W-31N	B6
100	AURA	60505	3200	35W-7S	A1
100	BMDL	60108	2969	23W-5N	A1
100	BRTN	60010	2750	27W-20N	C1
100	BRTN	60010	2751	27W-20N	A1
100	EGvT	60018	2862	15W-9N	A7
100	PKFT	60466	3594	4W-26S	E3
100	WDND	60118	2801	34W-16N	A2
100	WKGN	60085	2537		C2
200	CLLK	60014	2639	36W-25N	E5
200	ELGN	60123	2854	34W-11N	D4
400	AddT	60191	2915	17W-6N	B6
400	GNVW	60025	2810	9W-12N	D7
400	HMND	46320	3430		D1
400	HMND	46324	3430		D1

Block	City	ZIP	Map#	CGS	Grid
Washington St					
400	WDDL	60191	2915	17W-6N	B6
400	WDND	60118	2800	34W-16N	E2
500	DLTN	60419	3350	0E-16S	D3
700	DGvT	60561	3145	18W-8S	A7
700	DRN	60561	3145	18W-8S	A7
700	EVTN	60202	2867	2W-10N	B5
800	DrrT	60098	2524	42W-31N	B6
800	GwdT	60098	2524	42W-31N	B6
1000	BRLT	60103	2910	30W-6N	C7
1000	CHHT	60411	3508	0W-25S	C7
1000	WKGN	60085	2536	10W-34N	E2
1200	CRTE	60417	3685	1W-29S	A2
1300	LIHL	60156	2693	35W-22N	E4
1500	AlqT	60156	2693	35W-22N	E4
1600	EVTN	60202	2866	3W-10N	E5
3000	PKCY	60085	2536	12W-33N	B2
3200	FNPK	60131	2973	11W-4N	D4
3300	LNSG	60438	3430	4E-21S	B6
3300	MHRY	60050	2528	32W-33N	B3
3400	GRNE	60031	2536	13W-34N	A2
3400	GRNE	60085	2536	13W-34N	A2
3700	MNSR	46321	3430	4E-21S	C6
3700	OKBK	60521	3086	15W-3S	A6
3700	OKBK	60523	3086	15W-3S	A6
3800	HNDL	60521	3086	15W-3S	A6
3900	DRGV	60515	3084	19W-4S	D7
3900	GRNE	60031	2535	13W-34N	E1
4300	DRGV	60515	3144	19W-5S	C2
4300	WrnT	60031	2535	15W-34N	A1
4600	HLSD	60162	3028	14W-0N	D5
4600	SKOK	60076	2866	5W-10N	A5
4700	SKOK	60076	2865	6W-10N	E5
5100	BKLY	60163	3028	14W-0N	C5
5100	HLSD	60163	3028	14W-0N	C5
5200	SKOK	60077	2865	6W-10N	D5
5300	DRGV	60516	3144	19W-6S	D4
5300	MNGV	60077	2865	6W-10N	D5
5800	MNGV	60053	2865	7W-10N	B5
6000	CHRG	60415	3275	7W-12S	B1
6000	GRNE	60031	2534	16W-34N	E1
6000	WrnT	60031	2534	16W-34N	E1
7200	FTPK	60302	3030	9W-0N	D4
7200	OKPK	60302	3030	9W-0N	D4
7400	FTPK	60130	3030	9W-0N	D5
7400	HRPK	60133	2912	26W-8N	A3
8000	DGvT	60516	3206	19W-9S	D3
8700	DRN	60516	3206	19W-10S	D4
8700	DRN	60561	3206	19W-10S	D4
13700	PKCY	60085	2535	13W-34N	E1
13900	HtdT	60098	2524	42W-32N	A5
17400	UNON	60180	2635	46W-25N	D4
Washington St CO-A22					
3000	PKCY	60085	2536	12W-33N	B2
3000	WKGN	60085	2536	12W-33N	B2
3400	GRNE	60031	2536	13W-34N	A2
3400	GRNE	60085	2536	13W-34N	A2
3900	GRNE	60031	2535	13W-34N	E1
4300	WrnT	60031	2535	15W-34N	A1
6000	GRNE	60031	2534	16W-34N	E1
6000	WrnT	60031	2534	16W-34N	E1
13700	PKCY	60085	2535	13W-34N	E1
Washington St SR-120					
10	WDSK	60098	2524	42W-31N	B6
800	DrrT	60098	2524	42W-31N	B6
800	GwdT	60098	2524	42W-31N	B6
13900	HtdT	60098	2524	42W-32N	A5
E Washington St					
-	CHCG	60603	3034	0E-0N	C4
10	CHCG	60602	3034	0E-0N	C4
10	JLET	60436	3499	23W-23S	A5
10	OSWG	60543	3263	37W-12S	C4
10	PLTN	60067	2805	20W-15N	E1
10	RDLK	60073	2532	23W-34N	A2
10	RLKP	60073	2532	22W-33N	C3
10	VLPK	60181	3027	17W-0N	B5
100	BNVL	60106	2972	15W-4N	A2
100	HRVD	60033	2406	50W-38N	A7
100	ITSC	60143	2914	19W-6N	C7
100	JLET	60432	3499	23W-24S	A5
100	JLET	60433	3499	23W-24S	A5
100	MRGO	60152	2634	49W-26N	C2
100	WCHI	60185	3022	29W-0N	D4
100	YKVL	60560	3333	42W-15S	C3
400	HNVL	60030	2532	22W-34N	B2
400	HNVL	60073	2532	22W-34N	B2
600	JltT	60432	3499	22W-24S	D5
800	WnfT	60185	3022	29W-0N	D4
900	JltT	60433	3499	22W-24S	C5
1100	WDDL	60143	2914	19W-6N	D7
1200	DSPN	60016	2862	13W-11N	E3
1200	WDDL	60191	2914	19W-6N	D7
1300	DSPN	60016	2863	13W-11N	A3
2000	JltT	60433	3500	21W-24S	A5
2300	NLNX	60433	3500	20W-24S	B5
2300	NLNX	60451	3500	21W-24S	A5
2300	NlxT	60433	3500	20W-24S	B5
2400	NlxT	60451	3500	20W-24S	B5
2800	NlxT	60432	3500	20W-24S	B5
E Washington St CO-A22					
10	RDLK	60073	2532	23W-34N	A2
10	RLKP	60073	2532	22W-33N	C3
400	HNVL	60030	2532	22W-34N	B2
400	HNVL	60073	2532	22W-34N	B2
E Washington St SR-53					
10	JLET	60432	3499	23W-23S	A5
10	JLET	60433	3499	23W-23S	A5
10	JLET	60436	3499	23W-23S	A5
E Washington St US-6					
10	JLET	60432	3499	23W-23S	A5
10	JLET	60433	3499	23W-23S	A5
10	JLET	60436	3499	23W-23S	A5
N Washington St					
-	MaiT	60631	2918	10W-6N	B5
10	CPVL	60110	2800	34W-17N	E1
10	HNDL	60521	3146	15W-4S	A1
10	NPVL	60540	3141	27W-6S	D5
10	WTMT	60559	3145	18W-5S	A2
100	BDWD	60408	3942	30W-40S	D3
100	CPVL	60110	2747	34W-17N	E7
100	LKPT	60441	3419	22W-18S	D1
100	RedT	60481	3942	30W-40S	D3
200	RedT	60408	3942	30W-40S	D3
200	WMTN	60481	3942	29W-40S	D2
200	WmTp	60408	3942	29W-40S	D2
200	WmTp	60481	3942	29W-40S	D2
300	NPVL	60563	3141	26W-4S	D2
500	HNDL	60521	3086	15W-4S	A6
800	WMTN	60481	3853	27W-38S	D5
900	OKBK	60521	3086	15W-4S	A6
900	OKBK	60523	3086	15W-4S	A6
1600	WHTN	60187	3024	24W-0N	D4
1800	NPVL	60563	3081	26W-4S	E7
2100	LslT	60563	3081	26W-4S	E7
3800	DGvT	60559	3085	18W-4S	A7
3800	OKBK	60523	3085	18W-4S	A7

Block	City	ZIP	Map#	CGS	Grid
N Washington St					
3800	YkTp	60559	3085	18W-4S	A7
4100	WTMT	60559	3085	18W-4S	A7
5300	CHCG	60656	2918	10W-6N	B5
5300	LydT	60656	2918	10W-6N	B5
5300	NpkT	60656	2918	10W-6N	B5
5500	LydT	60631	2918	10W-6N	B5
5500	NpkT	60631	2918	10W-6N	B5
8000	NLES	60068	2864	9W-10N	B6
8000	PKRG	60068	2864	9W-10N	B6
8100	MaiT	60714	2864	10W-10N	B5
8800	NLES	60714	2864	10W-11N	B3
9000	MNGV	60053	2864	10W-11N	B3
9000	MNGV	60714	2864	9W-11N	B3
9000	NLES	60053	2864	10W-11N	B3
9500	MaiT	60025	2864	10W-11N	B3
9500	MaiT	60053	2864	10W-11N	B3
N Washington St SR-129					
100	BDWD	60408	3942	30W-40S	D3
100	RedT	60481	3942	30W-40S	D3
200	RedT	60408	3942	30W-40S	D3
200	WMTN	60481	3942	29W-40S	D2
200	WmTp	60408	3942	29W-40S	D2
200	WmTp	60481	3942	29W-40S	D2
S Washington St					
10	CPVL	60110	2800	34W-16N	E1
10	CPVL	60118	2800	34W-16N	E1
10	EDND	60110	2800	34W-16N	E2
10	EDND	60118	2800	34W-16N	E2
10	HNDL	60521	3146	15W-5S	A2
10	NPVL	60540	3141	27W-7S	D6
10	WTMT	60559	3145	18W-5S	A3
100	BDWD	60408	3942	31W-42S	A7
100	LKPT	60441	3419	22W-19S	D2
100	WMTN	60481	3853	27W-38S	D6
200	WHTN	60187	3024	24W-0S	D7
300	EMHT	60126	3027	16W-0N	E4
300	RedT	60408	3942	31W-42S	A7
400	BDWD	60407	3941	32W-42S	E7
400	BDWD	60408	3941	32W-42S	E7
400	RedT	60407	3941	32W-42S	E7
400	RedT	60408	3941	32W-42S	E7
1000	NPVL	60540	3203	26W-8S	E1
1100	LslT	60540	3203	26W-8S	E1
1100	WHTN	60187	3082	24W-1S	D1
1200	LslT	60540	3204	26W-9S	A4
1200	NPVL	60540	3204	26W-9S	A4
2300	NPVL	60565	3203	26W-10S	E5
2600	NPVL	60565	3204	26W-10S	A6
5700	BRRG	60521	3146	15W-6S	A4
5700	BRRG	60527	3146	15W-6S	A4
7100	DGvT	60561	3145	18W-8S	A7
7100	DGvT	60561	3207	18W-8S	A1
7100	DRN	60561	3145	18W-8S	A7
7100	DRN	60561	3207	18W-8S	A1
S Washington St SR-129					
100	BDWD	60408	3942	31W-42S	A7
300	RedT	60408	3942	31W-42S	A7
400	BDWD	60407	3941	32W-42S	E7
400	BDWD	60408	3941	32W-42S	E7
400	RedT	60407	3941	32W-42S	E7
400	RedT	60408	3941	32W-42S	E7
W Washington St					
-	OswT	60543	3263	38W-12S	B3
10	CHCG	60602	3034	0W-0N	B4
10	JLET	60432	3498	24W-24S	E5
10	JLET	60436	3498	24W-24S	E5
10	OSWG	60543	3263	38W-12S	B3
10	PLTN	60067	2805	21W-15N	E1
10	RDLK	60073	2532	23W-34N	A1
10	RLKP	60073	2532	23W-34N	A2
10	VLPK	60181	3027	18W-0N	A5
100	CHCG	60606	3034	0W-0N	B4
100	HRVD	60033	2406	50W-38N	A7
100	ITSC	60143	2914	19W-6N	C7
100	MRGO	60152	2634	50W-26N	A2
100	WCHI	60185	3022	30W-0N	B4
200	RDLK	60073	2531	23W-34N	E1
300	LMBD	60148	3026	19W-0S	D6
300	LMBD	60181	3026	19W-0S	D6
300	VLPK	60181	3026	19W-0S	D6
400	AddT	60106	2971	16W-4N	D2
400	BNVL	60106	2971	16W-4N	D2
400	CHCG	60661	3034	0W-0N	A4
400	JLET	60435	3498	24W-23S	D5
500	YKVL	60560	3333	43W-15S	B3
800	CmgT	60033	2405	51W-38N	E7
800	HRVD	60033	2405	51W-38N	E7
1200	WCHI	60185	3021	31W-0N	E5
17000	GRNE	60031	2534	17W-34N	B1
17000	WrnT	60031	2534	17W-34N	B1
18200	WrnT	60030	2534	17W-34N	B1
18300	GRNE	60031	2533	18W-34N	E1
18300	WrnT	60030	2533	18W-34N	E1
18300	WrnT	60031	2533	18W-34N	E1
18500	GRNE	60030	2533	18W-34N	E1
18700	TDLK	60030	2533	18W-34N	E1
18900	GYLK	60030	2533	19W-34N	C1
18900	TDLK	60031	2533	18W-34N	D1
19400	AvnT	60030	2533	19W-34N	C1
20700	GYLK	60030	2532	21W-34N	C2
21600	AvnT	60030	2532	21W-34N	C2
21700	AvnT	60073	2532	21W-34N	C2
21700	HNVL	60030	2532	21W-34N	C2
22500	AntT	60002	2417	22W-41N	B1
W Washington St CO-A22					
10	RDLK	60073	2532	23W-34N	A1
10	RLKP	60073	2532	23W-34N	A2
200	RDLK	60073	2531	23W-34N	E1
17000	GRNE	60031	2534	17W-34N	B1
17000	WrnT	60031	2534	17W-34N	B1
18200	WrnT	60030	2534	17W-34N	B1
18300	GRNE	60031	2533	18W-34N	E1
18300	WrnT	60030	2533	18W-34N	E1
18300	WrnT	60031	2533	18W-34N	E1
18500	GRNE	60030	2533	18W-34N	E1
18700	TDLK	60030	2533	18W-34N	E1
18900	GYLK	60030	2533	19W-34N	C1
18900	TDLK	60031	2533	18W-34N	D1
19400	AvnT	60030	2533	19W-34N	C1
20700	GYLK	60030	2532	21W-34N	C2
21600	AvnT	60030	2532	21W-34N	C2
21700	AvnT	60073	2532	21W-34N	C2
21700	HNVL	60030	2532	21W-34N	C2
W Washington St US-34					
-	OswT	60543	3263	38W-12S	B3
10	OSWG	60543	3263	38W-12S	B3
Washington Ter					
10	WKGN	60085	2536	12W-33N	C1
S Washington Park Ct					
4000	CHCG	60615	3152	0E-5S	D1
Washington Park Rd					
2600	MchT	60051	2471	31W-34N	E7
2600	MchT	60051	2528	31W-34N	E1
Washitay Av					
10	HNWD	60047	2646	20W-25N	B4

Block	City	ZIP	Map#	CGS	Grid
Washo Ct					
100	LKZH	60047	2698	23W-21N	E5
Washo Dr					
200	LKZH	60047	2698	23W-21N	E5
Washo Ln					
-	LKZH	60047	2698	23W-21N	E5
Washtenaw Av					
14800	HRVY	60426	3349	3W-17S	B6
14800	POSN	60426	3349	3W-17S	B6
14800	POSN	60469	3349	3W-17S	B6
15000	MKHM	60426	3349	3W-17S	B6
15600	MKHM	60428	3427	3W-18S	A1
N Washtenaw Av					
200	CHCG	60612	3033	3W-0N	A4
700	CHCG	60622	3033	3W-1N	A2
1500	CHCG	60647	3033	3W-1N	A1
2400	CHCG	60647	2977	3W-3N	A5
2800	CHCG	60618	2977	3W-3N	A4
4700	CHCG	60625	2921	3W-6N	A6
5300	CHCG	60625	2920	3W-6N	E5
5600	CHCG	60659	2920	3W-7N	E4
6300	CHCG	60645	2920	3W-7N	E3
7200	CHCG	60645	2866	3W-9N	E7
7500	CHCG	60202	2866	3W-9N	E7
7500	EVTN	60202	2866	3W-9N	E7
S Washtenaw Av					
-	CHCG	60805	3213	3W-10S	A4
10	CHCG	60612	3033	3W-0S	A5
1000	CHCG	60608	3033	3W-1S	A7
1600	CHCG	60608	3091	3W-2S	A2
3500	CHCG	60632	3091	3W-3S	A5
4600	CHCG	60632	3151	3W-5S	A1
5400	CHCG	60629	3151	3W-8S	A7
7500	CHCG	60652	3213	3W-9S	A2
9600	ENGN	60805	3213	3W-11S	A7
9800	CHCG	60655	3213	3W-11S	A7
10200	CHCG	60655	3277	3W-12S	A1
Washtenaw Ln					
10	ALGN	60102	2748	33W-20N	A1
10	AlqT	60102	2748	33W-20N	A1
Watch Ct					
300	ELGN	60120	2855	33W-11N	A5
Watch St					
200	ELGN	60120	2855	33W-10N	A5
S Water Rd					
10	ElgT	60124	2853	38W-10N	A6
500	ElgT	60124	2907	38W-9N	B1
Water St					
-	BtnT	60081	2414	29W-39N	C5
-	WMTN	60481	3853	27W-38S	C6
10	EDND	60118	2801	34W-16N	A2
10	PKFT	60466	3595	3W-26S	B2
100	NPVL	60540	3141	27W-6S	D6
200	TNTN	60476	3428	0E-21S	E5
600	EDND	60118	2800	34W-16N	E2
800	EDND	60110	2800	34W-16N	E2
5700	AURA	60505	3138	35W-7S	B6
5700	AURA	60506	3138	35W-7S	B6
E Water St					
10	WKGN	60085	2537	10W-34N	B2
N Water St					
10	GNVA	60134	3020	34W-1N	C3
100	BTVA	60510	3078	35W-1S	B1
100	WMTN	60481	3853	27W-38S	C6
600	SEGN	60177	2908	34W-8N	D2
S Water St					
10	AURA	60505	3138	35W-7S	B7
10	AURA	60505	3200	35W-7S	B1
10	BTVA	60510	3078	35W-1S	B2
10	SEGN	60177	2908	34W-8N	D3
100	WMTN	60481	3853	27W-39S	D7
200	JLET	60436	3498	24W-24S	E6
800	WMTN	60481	3943	27W-39S	D1
1200	WslT	60481	3943	27W-40S	E2
S Water St SR-102					
100	WMTN	60481	3853	27W-39S	D7
800	WMTN	60481	3943	27W-39S	D1
1200	WslT	60481	3943	27W-40S	E2
W Water St					
100	WKGN	60085	2537	10W-34N	B2
Water Bridge Rd					
-	LSLE	60532	3082	25W-4S	B7
Waterbury Av					
500	GRNE	60031	2535	14W-33N	D3
Waterbury Cir					
10	OSWG	60543	3200	34W-10S	E7
200	LKVL	60046	2475	23W-37N	A2
1800	GNVW	60025	2810	8W-15N	D2
2300	AURA	60504	3201	32W-8S	B2
N Waterbury Cir					
1400	PLTN	60074	2753	20W-17N	A4
Waterbury Ct					
10	LKZH	60047	2699	21W-22N	C4
100	MltT	60187	3023	26W-0N	E4
400	NPVL	60565	3203	27W-10S	C5
2000	WDND	60118	2800	35W-16N	C1
5300	CTWD	60445	3347	6W-16S	E3
8100	WDRG	60517	3205	21W-9S	E3
Waterbury Dr					
200	RDLK	60073	2531	23W-32N	E5
500	AURA	60504	3201	32W-8S	C2
700	MltT	60187	3023	26W-0N	E4
2400	WDRG	60517	3205	21W-9S	E3
5300	BmnT	60445	3347	6W-16S	E3
5300	CTWD	60445	3347	6W-16S	E3
W Waterbury Dr					
400	RDLK	60073	2531	23W-32N	E5
Waterbury Ln					
-	LNSH	60069	2701	16W-22N	D3
-	VrnT	60069	2701	16W-22N	D3
10	SMBG	60193	2859	23W-10N	A6
10	SMBG	60194	2859	23W-10N	A6
400	ROSL	60172	2912	25W-7N	C5
2400	BFGV	60089	2701	16W-22N	D3
5300	CTWD	60445	3347	6W-16S	E3
Waterbury Pl					
5500	LIHL	60156	2692	39W-21N	D6
Waterbury Wy					
5300	CTWD	60445	3347	6W-16S	E3
Water Chase					
-	NLNX	60442	3589	17W-27S	D4
Watercolor Pl					
1700	GYLK	60030	2533	18W-33N	D2
Watercress Dr					
900	NPVL	60540	3141	26W-7S	E7
Watercress Rd					
-	FoxT	60560	3332	46W-16S	A4
Watercress Wy					
1800	HDPK	60035	2704	10W-22N	A4
Watercrest Ct					
10	SBTN	60010	2803	27W-13N	A6
1600	RMVL	60446	3339	26W-17S	E7
Waterfall Ct					
7700	GRNE	60031	2533	18W-34N	E1
Waterfall Ln					
-	BRLT	60103	2967	27W-5N	B2

Block	City	ZIP	Map#	CGS	Grid
Waterfall Ln					
600	ELGN	60124	2853	36W-10N	D7
2100	HRPK	60133	2967	27W-5N	B2
Waterfall Pl					
6900	DRGV	60516	3144	19W-7S	C7
Waterfall St					
-	NPVL	60540	3140	29W-6S	D4
-	NPVL	60563	3140	29W-6S	D4
-	NpvT	60540	3140	29W-6S	D4
-	NpvT	60563	3140	29W-6S	D4
Waterfall Glen Blvd					
9200	DRN	60439	3206	19W-10S	D6
Water Falls Ct					
2500	JLET	60586	3415	32W-20S	C6
Waterfield Dr					
-	BtvT	60510	3078	34W-2S	C5
600	BTVA	60510	3078	34W-2S	C5
Waterford					
-	NLNX	60442	3589	17W-27S	D4
Waterford Dr					
-	LNSG	60438	3429	2E-20S	D3
Waterford Blvd					
-	WldT	60585	3338	31W-15S	A1
12700	PNFD	60585	3338	31W-15S	A1
Waterford Ct					
100	NPVL	60540	3140	28W-6S	E5
300	CLSM	60188	2967	26W-4N	E3
300	MHRY	60050	2527	35W-32N	A5
400	WLBK	60527	3146	15W-7S	A5
500	ROSL	60172	2912	24W-7N	D5
600	LKZH	60047	2699	23W-21N	A5
800	WMTN	60481	3943	27W-39S	E1
1000	DSPN	60016	2808	13W-13N	D6
1800	HDPK	60035	2704	10W-22N	A4
2600	AURA	60502	3139	32W-4S	C1
12900	PNFD	60585	3338	31W-15S	A2
22300	TroT	60404	3584	30W-27S	C4
W Waterford Ct					
2100	RDLK	60073	2531	25W-33N	A3
14400	GNOK	60048	2592	14W-29N	C5
Waterford Dr					
-	AURA	60505	3201	33W-8S	A3
100	WLBK	60527	3146	15W-7S	A6
100	WNFD	60190	3023	27W-0N	C4
200	LKZH	60047	2698	23W-21N	E5
200	PTHT	60070	2808	14W-15N	C2
300	LKZH	60047	2699	23W-21N	A6
400	DGvT	60527	3146	15W-7S	A6
400	LNHT	60046	2418	19W-38N	B6
400	WnfT	60185	3023	27W-0N	C4
400	WnfT	60190	3023	27W-0N	C4
500	GYLK	60030	2532	21W-33N	D2
500	OSWG	60543	3263	36W-11S	E1
600	DSPN	60016	2808	13W-13N	D6
600	HRPK	60133	2912	25W-9N	A1
900	AURA	60504	3201	33W-9S	A4
2400	CTHL	60403	3417	27W-21S	D7
3200	JLET	60431	3417	28W-21S	B7
6500	MHRY	60050	2526	35W-32N	E6
6500	MHRY	60050	2527	35W-32N	A5
6900	BLVY	60050	2526	35W-32N	E6
8300	TYPK	60477	3424	10W-20S	B4
8300	TYPK	60487	3424	10W-20S	B4
10400	PvsT	60162	3087	13W-1S	A1
10400	WSTR	60154	3087	13W-1S	A1
10400	WSTR	60162	3087	13W-1S	A1
N Waterford Dr					
10	RDLK	60073	2531	25W-33N	A3
10	SMBG	60194	2859	22W-10N	C5
S Waterford Dr					
10	RDLK	60073	2531	25W-33N	A3
Waterford Ln					
-	BCHR	60401	3774	0W-35S	C7
200	CmpT	60175	2906	40W-6N	C6
200	WynT	60185	2966	29W-4N	D4
400	IVNS	60010	2751	24W-17N	C5
500	SEGN	60177	2908	35W-7N	C4
900	EGVV	60007	2914	20W-8N	A2
900	NHBK	60062	2757	8W-16N	D7
2000	WDRG	60517	3206	20W-10S	A6
2500	LIHL	60156	2692	38W-22N	E3
9300	ODPK	60462	3423	11W-18S	E1
19200	FftT	60448	3504	11W-23S	A3
19200	MKNA	60448	3504	11W-23S	A3
E Waterford Ln					
1600	PLTN	60074	2753	18W-18N	D3
W Waterford Ln					
15600	MHTN	60442	3677	19W-30S	D3
Waterford Rd					
600	ElgT	60124	2853	37W-10N	B7
1000	BRLT	60103	2911	27W-7N	D5
1400	AraT	60542	3077	37W-4S	B7
1400	NARA	60542	3077	37W-4S	B7
S Waterford Rd					
600	SMBG	60193	2859	23W-9N	A7
Waterford Tr					
26300	CNHN	60410	3672	33W-32S	B7
26400	CNHN	60410	3761	33W-32S	B1
Waterford Wy					
3200	ISLK	60042	2586	29W-28N	B5
3200	ISLK	60051	2586	29W-28N	B5
3200	NndT	60051	2586	29W-28N	B5
4200	GRNE	60031	2535	14W-33N	D3
Waterford Cut					
900	CLLK	60014	2693	37W-23N	C1
Waterfront Av					
2800	ALGN	60102	2693	36W-21N	D6
Waterfront Cir					
15900	PNFD	60544	3416	29W-19S	E2
Waterfront Ct					
10	ALGN	60102	2693	36W-21N	D6
Waterfront Dr					
8700	PSHL	60465	3274	11W-13S	A3
Waterfront Ln					
-	PGGV	60140	2798	41W-15N	B4
Watergate Dr					
10	SBTN	60010	2803	27W-14N	C3
Water Leaf Dr					
2200	NPVL	60564	3202	29W-10S	C5
Waterleaf Ln					
2400	WDSK	60098	2582	40W-28N	A5
Water Lily Ct					
24000	PNFD	60585	3338	30W-15S	C2
Water Lily Ln					
-	WCDA	60030	2588	24W-30N	C2
N Waterloo Ct					
3000	CHCG	60657	2978	0W-3N	A4
Waterman Av					
200	ANHT	60004	2807	16W-15N	D2
200	PTHT	60004	2807	16W-15N	D2
200	PTHT	60070	2807	16W-15N	D2
N Waterman Av					
1100	PTHT	60004	2807	16W-15N	D3
1200	PTHT	60070	2807	16W-15N	D2
1500	ANHT	60004	2807	16W-15N	D2
2500	ANHT	60004	2754	16W-16N	D6
2500	WLNG	60090	2754	16W-16N	D6
2600	ANHT	60090	2754	16W-16N	D6
S Waterman Av					
10	ANHT	60004	2807	16W-13N	D6
600	MPPT	60056	2807	16W-13N	D6
Waterman Ct					
1700	JLET	60586	3495	33W-21S	B1
15200	SHLD	60473	3351	1E-17S	A6
Waterman Dr					
200	BGBK	60440	3268	24W-12S	C2
15000	DLTN	60419	3351	1E-17S	A5
15000	SHLD	60419	3351	1E-17S	A5
15000	SHLD	60473	3351	1E-17S	A5
Waters Rd					
-	AntT	60002	2356	26W-43N	D4
Waters Edge					
500	LMBD	60148	3084	20W-1S	A2
Waters Edge Cir					
2900	AURA	60504	3139	31W-7S	D7
2900	AURA	60504	3201	31W-7S	D1
Waters Edge Ct					
500	NHBK	60062	2757	9W-18N	D4
Waters Edge Dr					
-	GLHT	60139	2969	23W-4N	A3
400	MHRY	60050	2527	34W-32N	D5
500	SEGN	60177	2907	37W-7N	C5
700	LKVL	60046	2475	22W-38N	C1
1700	CNHN	60410	3672	34W-30S	A4
1700	MNKA	60447	3672	34W-30S	A4
11000	ODPK	60467	3422	14W-21S	D7
11000	ODPK	60467	3423	13W-21S	A7
Watersedge Dr					
4300	ISLK	60042	2586	28W-27N	E7
N Waters Edge Dr					
100	GLHT	60139	2969	23W-4N	A3
S Waters Edge Dr					
100	GLHT	60139	2969	23W-4N	A3
Waters Edge Ln					
1200	NHBK	60062	2757	9W-18N	C3
Waterside Cir					
11500	ODPK	60467	3422	14W-21S	D7
Waterside Ct					
300	NPVL	60540	3141	27W-6S	B6
900	AURA	60502	3139	32W-6S	C5
2400	WCDA	60084	2588	25W-29N	B3
Waterside Dr					
600	SEGN	60177	2907	37W-7N	C5
1300	BGBK	60490	3268	26W-13S	A5
1400	BGBK	60490	3267	26W-13S	E5
2300	AURA	60502	3139	32W-6S	B5
N Waterside Ln					
36900	GrtT	60041	2474	25W-36N	A3
36900	LkvT	60041	2474	25W-36N	A3
36900	LkvT	60046	2474	25W-36N	A3
Waterside Pl					
10	BRRG	60527	3208	14W-8S	D1
Water Stone Cir					
-	TroT	60431	3496	29W-24S	E6
200	JLET	60431	3496	29W-24S	E6
1200	WCDA	60084	2588	25W-28N	B6
Waterstone Dr					
-	AURA	60502	3139	31W-6S	D5
Water Stone Wy					
300	JLET	60431	3496	29W-24S	E6
Waterstone Wy					
7500	LslT	60565	3205	23W-8S	A2
Water Thrush Ct					
900	ANTH	60002	2358	21W-41N	E7
Waterton Dr					
10	HnrT	60107	2856	29W-11N	E5
10	SMWD	60107	2856	29W-11N	E5
Water Tower Ct					
1600	WHTN	60187	3082	26W-2S	A3
S Water Tower Dr					
2900	CteT	60417	3687	3E-31S	B5
Water Tower Ln					
2800	DRN	60561	3206	20W-9S	C4
Watertower Pl					
2000	CTHL	60403	3417	27W-21S	D7
Water Tower Rd					
1200	CPVL	60118	2800	35W-16N	D1
1200	WDND	60118	2800	35W-16N	D1
Watertower Rd					
-	DGvT	60439	3206	18W-11S	E7
S Waterview Av					
3100	NndT	60051	2586	30W-28N	A5
Waterview Cir					
800	VNHL	60061	2647	18W-24N	A7
1000	ANTH	60002	2417	20W-40N	E2
1100	ANTH	60002	2418	20W-40N	A2
Waterview Ct					
10	LKBN	60010	2643	26W-24N	C7
10	LKBN	60010	2697	26W-23N	C1
600	NPVL	60563	3140	29W-6S	D4
Waterview Dr					
700	RLKP	60073	2532	21W-34N	C1
Waterview Ter					
19900	FftT	60423	3503	11W-24S	E5
19900	FftT	60448	3503	11W-24S	E5
19900	FKFT	60423	3503	11W-24S	E5
Waterville Ln					
1600	SMBG	60194	2858	25W-11N	B4
Waterway Ct					
7000	JLET	60586	3415	32W-20S	C6
11600	ODPK	60467	3422	14W-21S	D7
24900	SRWD	60404	3584	31W-25S	A1
S Watkins Av					
11400	CHCG	60643	3277	2W-13S	D4
11800	BLID	60406	3277	2W-13S	C5
11800	BLID	60643	3277	2W-13S	C5
Watkins Ct					
3600	MKHM	60428	3426	4W-19S	E3
Watkins Ln					
1500	NPVL	60540	3140	28W-7S	E7
Watkins St					
200	MTGY	60538	3199	37W-9S	C5
W Watling Rd					
1000	ANHT	60004	2806	18W-15N	D3
Watres Pl					
300	ELGN	60120	2855	33W-11N	B5
Watseka Av					
10	SchT	60174	2908	34W-6N	D6
Watseka St					
400	PKFT	60466	3594	4W-26S	E3
N Watson Av					
35500	GrtT	60041	2473	26W-35N	E5
Watson Cir					
8300	LKWD	60014	2692	38W-23N	E1
Watson Ct					
10300	PlsT	60464	3345	13W-15S	A1
Watson Ln					
2400	ELGN	60124	2799	37W-14N	D6
W Watson Rd					
5800	MONE	60449	3682	7W-32S	E7
5800	MonT	60449	3682	7W-32S	E7
Watson St					
-	DMND	60416	3941	33W-40S	A3
300	AURA	60505	3200	35W-8S	B2
1000	AraT	60505	3200	35W-9S	B4
1300	MTGY	60505	3200	35W-9S	B4
1300	MTGY	60538	3200	35W-9S	B4
Watters Ct					
17600	LKPT	60441	3420	20W-21S	B6
Watters Dr					
16500	LKPT	60441	3420	20W-21S	B6
Wattles Ct					
2100	JLET	60586	3416	29W-21S	D7
N Watts Av					
37700	GrtT	60081	2472	28W-37N	E1
37900	AntT	60081	2472	28W-37N	E1
38000	AntT	60081	2414	28W-38N	E7
Waubansee Dr					
100	MNKA	60447	3672	33W-28S	B1
6400	IHPK	60525	3146	14W-7S	D6
Waubansee Ln					
-	IHPK	60525	3146	14W-7S	D6
Waubansee Rd					
100	BKFD	60513	3088	10W-3S	B6
100	BKFD	60546	3088	10W-3S	B6
100	RVSD	60546	3088	10W-3S	B5
Waubansie Ln					
4400	LSLE	60532	3142	24W-4S	D1
Waubonsee Dr					
-	PLNO	60545	3260	46W-13S	B6
-	SgrT	60554	3135	43W-5S	B3
-	SRGV	60554	3135	43W-5S	B3
Waubonsee Tr					
400	BTVA	60510	3020	35W-0S	A7
Waubonsee Cir Dr					
400	OSWG	60543	3263	36W-11S	E1
500	OSWG	60543	3264	36W-11S	A1
Waubonsie Av					
1000	AURA	60506	3138	35W-5S	A3
1000	AURA	60542	3138	35W-5S	A3
Wauchope Dr					
1300	ELGN	60123	2800	34W-13N	E7
Wauconda Rd					
500	WCDA	60084	2588	24W-28N	B7
600	FmtT	60084	2588	24W-28N	B7
1000	FmtT	60060	2588	24W-28N	B6
1000	WCDA	60060	2588	24W-28N	B7
W Wauconda Rd					
1300	NndT	60051	2586	30W-28N	A5
Waukegan Av					
200	HDPK	60035	2704	9W-23N	D2
200	HIWD	60035	2704	9W-23N	D2
200	HIWD	60040	2704	9W-23N	D2
Waukegan Rd					
-	LbvT	60044	2535	13W-31N	E7
-	WKGN	60085	2535	13W-31N	E7
10	DRFD	60015	2757	10W-20N	A1
10	DRFD	60062	2757	10W-20N	A1
10	GNVW	60025	2864	8W-11N	E3
10	GNVW	60053	2864	8W-12N	E2
10	MNGV	60025	2864	8W-11N	E3
10	MNGV	60053	2864	8W-11N	E3
100	GNVW	60025	2810	8W-13N	E6
100	GNVW	60093	2810	8W-15N	E3
100	NHFD	60025	2810	8W-15N	E3
100	NHFD	60093	2810	8W-15N	E1
300	NHBK	60062	2810	8W-15N	E2
400	NfdT	60062	2757	9W-18N	B4
600	DRFD	60015	2703	11W-21N	E6
600	NHBK	60062	2757	9W-16N	D6
1300	LbvT	60044	2592	13W-31N	E1
1300	LbvT	60064	2592	13W-31N	E1
1300	NCHI	60044	2592	13W-31N	E1
1600	BKBN	60015	2703	11W-23N	D3
2100	NHFD	60062	2810	8W-16N	E1
2100	WdfT	60015	2703	11W-23N	D3
8400	MNGV	60714	2864	8W-10N	E4
8400	NLES	60714	2864	8W-10N	E4
Waukegan Rd SR-43					
-	LbvT	60044	2535	13W-31N	E7
-	WKGN	60085	2535	13W-31N	E7
10	DRFD	60015	2757	10W-20N	A1
10	DRFD	60062	2757	10W-20N	A1
10	GNVW	60025	2864	8W-11N	E3
10	GNVW	60053	2864	8W-12N	E2
10	MNGV	60025	2864	8W-11N	E3
10	MNGV	60053	2864	8W-11N	E3
100	GNVW	60025	2810	8W-13N	E6
100	GNVW	60093	2810	8W-15N	E3
100	NHFD	60025	2810	8W-15N	E3
100	NHFD	60093	2810	8W-15N	E1
300	NHBK	60062	2810	8W-15N	E2
400	NfdT	60062	2757	9W-18N	B4
600	DRFD	60015	2703	11W-21N	E6
600	NHBK	60062	2757	9W-16N	D6
1300	LbvT	60044	2592	13W-31N	E1
1300	LbvT	60064	2592	13W-31N	E1
1300	NCHI	60044	2592	13W-31N	E1
1600	BKBN	60015	2703	11W-23N	D3
2100	NHFD	60062	2810	8W-16N	E1
2100	WdfT	60015	2703	11W-23N	D3
8400	MNGV	60714	2864	8W-10N	E4
8400	NLES	60714	2864	8W-10N	E4
Waukegan Rd SR-58					
8800	MNGV	60053	2864	8W-11N	E3
9500	GNVW	60025	2864	8W-11N	E2
9500	GNVW	60053	2864	8W-11N	E2
9500	MNGV	60025	2864	8W-11N	E2
Waukegan Rd US-14					
8500	MNGV	60053	2864	8W-10N	E4
N Waukegan Rd					
10	LKBF	60044	2593	12W-28N	B6
10	LKFT	60044	2593	12W-28N	B6
10	LKFT	60045	2593	12W-28N	B6
10	LKFT	60045	2649	12W-27N	C2
700	LbvT	60064	2593	13W-29N	A4
1200	LbvT	60044	2593	13W-30N	A2
1200	NCHI	60044	2593	13W-29N	A4
1200	NCHI	60064	2593	13W-30N	A2
1300	LbvT	60044	2592	13W-30N	E1
1300	NCHI	60044	2592	13W-30N	E1
1700	LKBF	60045	2593	12W-28N	B7
7200	NLES	60714	2864	8W-9N	E6
8300	MNGV	60053	2864	8W-10N	E5
8300	MNGV	60714	2864	8W-10N	E5
30000	ShdT	60044	2593	13W-30N	A3
N Waukegan Rd SR-43					
10	LKBF	60044	2593	12W-28N	B6
10	LKFT	60044	2593	12W-28N	B6
10	LKFT	60045	2593	12W-28N	B6
10	LKFT	60045	2649	12W-27N	C2
10	ShdT	60044	2593	12W-28N	B5
700	LbvT	60044	2593	13W-29N	A4
700	NCHI	60044	2593	13W-29N	A4
1200	NCHI	60064	2593	13W-30N	A2
1300	LbvT	60044	2592	13W-30N	E1
1300	NCHI	60044	2592	13W-30N	E1
1700	LKBF	60045	2593	12W-28N	B7
8000	NLES	60714	2864	8W-10N	E5
8300	MNGV	60053	2864	8W-10N	E5
8300	MNGV	60714	2864	8W-10N	E5
29500	LbvT	60064	2593	13W-29N	A4
S Waukegan Rd					
-	PKCY	60085	2535	13W-32N	E6
10	DRFD	60015	2757	10W-18N	A2
10	DRFD	60062	2757	10W-18N	A2
10	LKFT	60045	2649	12W-24N	B6
10	NfdT	60062	2757	10W-18N	A2
800	WKGN	60085	2535	13W-32N	E4
1000	WrnT	60085	2535	13W-32N	E4
1200	LKFT	60045	2703	12W-23N	C1
1600	BKBN	60015	2703	11W-23N	C2
1600	BKBN	60045	2703	11W-23N	C2
1600	WdfT	60015	2703	11W-23N	C2
1600	WdfT	60045	2703	11W-23N	C2
2100	LbvT	60044	2535	13W-31N	E7
S Waukegan Rd SR-43					
-	PKCY	60085	2535	13W-32N	E6
10	DRFD	60015	2757	10W-18N	A2
10	DRFD	60062	2757	10W-18N	A2
10	LKFT	60045	2649	12W-24N	B6
10	NfdT	60062	2757	10W-18N	A2
800	WKGN	60085	2535	13W-32N	E4
1000	WrnT	60085	2535	13W-32N	E4
1200	LKFT	60045	2703	12W-23N	C1
1600	BKBN	60015	2703	11W-23N	C2
1600	BKBN	60045	2703	11W-23N	C2
1600	WdfT	60015	2703	11W-23N	C2
1600	WdfT	60045	2703	11W-23N	C2
2100	LbvT	60044	2535	13W-31N	E7
Waukegan St					
3300	MHRY	60050	2528	32W-32N	B4
N Waukesha Av					
6700	SKOK	60646	2919	6W-8N	C2
6800	CHCG	60646	2919	6W-8N	C1
Waupaca Ct					
2400	NPVL	60564	3203	28W-10S	A6
Wausau Av					
15900	SHLD	60473	3428	0E-18S	D1
Wausau Ct					
16400	SHLD	60473	3428	0E-19S	D2
Wausau Ln					
1600	GRNE	60031	2478	15W-35N	B5
Waveland Av					
-	ADSN	60101	2970	19W-4N	D3
10	GRNE	60031	2535	13W-34N	E1
1000	BNVL	60106	2972	14W-4N	C3
1000	BNVL	60131	2972	14W-4N	C3
9600	SRPK	60176	2973	12W-4N	B3
10400	FNPK	60131	2973	13W-4N	A2
10400	FNPK	60176	2973	13W-4N	A2
10400	SRPK	60131	2973	13W-4N	A2
10500	FNPK	60131	2972	13W-4N	E3
N Waveland Av					
38500	WDWH	60083	2420	13W-38N	E7
38500	WKGN	60083	2420	13W-38N	E7
W Waveland Av					
600	CHCG	60613	2978	0W-4N	A2
700	CHCG	60613	2977	2W-4N	C2
1900	CHCG	60618	2977	2W-4N	B2
2800	CHCG	60618	2976	4W-4N	D2
3900	CHCG	60641	2976	5W-4N	A2
4700	CHCG	60641	2975	7W-4N	C2
5500	CHCG	60634	2975	7W-4N	B2
8000	CHCG	60634	2974	10W-4N	A2
Waveland Rd					
600	LKFT	60045	2650	10W-24N	A6
Waveland St					
500	GRNE	60031	2478	13W-34N	E7
Wavely Ct					
800	AURA	60502	3139	32W-6S	C5
Waverley Ln					
200	SMBG	60193	2858	25W-10N	A6
Waverly Av					
10	CNHL	60514	3145	16W-5S	D2
400	SMWD	60107	2857	28W-10N	B6
700	WNVL	60555	3080	29W-2S	C4
1400	WSTR	60154	3087	13W-1S	A1
14700	MDLN	60445	3348	4W-17S	C5
15100	BmnT	60445	3348	5W-18S	B6
15200	OKFT	60445	3348	5W-18S	B6
15300	OKFT	60452	3348	5W-18S	B7
S Waverly Av					
800	MPPT	60056	2861	16W-11N	D2
Waverly Cir					
-	YKVL	60560	3333	42W-17S	D6
1600	SCRL	60174	2964	34W-4N	D5
Waverly Ct					
10	ALGN	60102	2746	36W-19N	E3
10	PKFT	60466	3594	4W-27S	E3
200	CPVL	60110	2748	33W-17N	B7
200	WLBK	60527	3145	16W-7S	D6
500	NLNX	60451	3501	18W-24S	A6
800	NPVL	60563	3141	26W-5S	E4
1800	CTHL	60403	3418	25W-21S	C7
9200	DRN	60439	3206	19W-10S	D6
E Waverly Ct					
1500	ANHT	60004	2754	16W-16N	C7
N Waverly Ct					
300	ELGN	60120	2855	32W-11N	C3
S Waverly Ct					
300	ELGN	60120	2855	32W-11N	C3
W Waverly Ct					
300	ANHT	60004	2754	18W-16N	A6
1600	ANHT	60004	2753	18W-16N	D6
Waverly Dr					
200	BtnT	60081	2414	29W-38N	D7
200	BtnT	60081	2472	29W-38N	D1
200	ELGN	60120	2855	32W-11N	C3
300	MDLN	60060	2646	20W-27N	B1
1100	LKVL	60046	2474	23W-36N	E3
E Waverly Dr					
600	ANHT	60004	2754	17W-16N	B6
Waverly Ln					
700	WLNG	60090	2755	15W-18N	A3
1700	ALGN	60102	2747	36W-19N	A2
2000	ALGN	60102	2746	36W-19N	E2
E Waverly Ln					
1900	ANHT	60004	2754	16W-16N	D7
1900	WLNG	60090	2754	16W-16N	D7
Waverly Pl					
2000	WKGN	60085	2479	11W-35N	D7
E Waverly Pl					
1200	ANHT	60004	2754	17W-16N	C6
N Waverly Pl					
100	MPPT	60056	2807	16W-13N	D7
900	JLET	60435	3498	25W-22S	C1
1500	CTHL	60403	3498	25W-22S	C1
S Waverly Pl					
100	MPPT	60056	2807	16W-12N	D7
300	MPPT	60056	2861	16W-12N	D1
Waverly Rd					
900	GNEN	60137	3025	21W-0S	D5
1300	HDPK	60035	2705	7W-21N	B5
E Waverly Rd					
300	ANHT	60004	2754	17W-16N	B6
W Waverly Rd					
10	ANHT	60004	2754	17W-16N	A6
100	BRTN	60010	2697	26W-20N	E7
Waverly St					
300	PKFT	60466	3594	4W-26S	E3
300	PKFT	60466	3595	4W-27S	A3
1600	CTHL	60403	3498	25W-21S	C1
1600	JLET	60435	3498	25W-21S	C1
N Waverly St					
10	MPPT	60056	2807	16W-13N	D7
W Waverly St					
12700	BHPK	60099	2421	13W-40N	A2
12900	WDWH	60083	2421	13W-40N	A2
Waverly Wy					
1800	MTGY	60538	3198	40W-9S	B5
Waxwing Av					
10	NPVL	60565	3203	26W-8S	D2
10	NPVL	60565	3204	26W-8S	A2
Waxwing Ct					
1600	SMBG	60173	2805	21W-12N	E7
S Waxwing Ln					
1800	WKGN	60048	2535	14W-31N	C6
N Way Av					
-	LkvT	60046	2416	23W-38N	E6
Wayewood Ln					
600	LslT	60565	3204	23W-8S	E2
Wayfaring Ln					
2700	LSLE	60532	3142	24W-6S	C5
Wayland Av					
500	KLWH	60043	2812	4W-14N	C4
3000	ElgT	60124	2853	37W-11N	C4
Wayland Ct					
1900	SMBG	60193	2858	25W-10N	A6
Wayland Ln					
1900	SMBG	60193	2858	26W-10N	A6
2200	NPVL	60565	3203	26W-10S	D5
S Wayman Ln					
14000	RBBN	60472	3348	4W-16S	E3
W Wayman St					
600	CHCG	60661	3034	0W-0N	A4
700	CHCG	60607	3034	0W-0N	A4
800	CHCG	60607	3033	1W-0N	E4
4600	CHCG	60644	3032	5W-0N	A4
Wayne Av					
900	DRFD	60015	2703	11W-21N	D7
1400	GLHT	60139	2969	22W-2N	D7
2600	PnfT	60435	3417	27W-20S	C6
N Wayne Av					
2100	CHCG	60614	2977	1W-2N	D6
2700	CHCG	60657	2977	1W-3N	D5
3900	CHCG	60613	2977	1W-4N	D2
5200	CHCG	60640	2921	1W-6N	D5
6200	CHCG	60660	2921	1W-7N	D3
6800	CHCG	60626	2921	1W-8N	D1
Wayne Ct					
10	PKFT	60466	3595	4W-26S	A2
200	BRLT	60103	2911	28W-8N	A2
Wayne Dr					
500	CmpT	60175	2961	41W-4N	E5
700	CRTE	60417	3685	1W-30S	A3
1200	DSPN	60018	2862	13W-10N	D5
Wayne Ln					
10	HNWD	60047	2644	23W-24N	D7
E Wayne Pl					
200	WLNG	60090	2755	15W-17N	B5
N Wayne Pl					
600	WLNG	60090	2755	15W-17N	A4
S Wayne Pl					
500	WLNG	60090	2755	15W-17N	A5
W Wayne Pl					
10	WLNG	60090	2755	15W-17N	A4
Wayne St					
300	PKFT	60466	3595	4W-26S	A2
6300	UNON	60180	2635	46W-25N	D4
Wayne Oaks Ln					
10	WynT	60185	2967	28W-2N	A7
Waynesburg St					
2200	NPVL	60565	3203	26W-10S	D6
Waynewood Dr					
10	WCHI	60185	3022	30W-2N	C1
10	WynT	60185	3022	30W-2N	C1
Wayside Dr					
4800	ISLK	60042	2642	29W-27N	C2
4800	ISLK	60051	2642	29W-26N	C2
4800	NndT	60042	2642	29W-26N	C2
4800	NndT	60051	2642	29W-26N	C2
4900	NndT	60013	2642	29W-26N	C2
S Wayside Dr					
1200	OKTR	60181	3027	17W-0S	C7
1200	VLPK	60181	3027	17W-0S	C7
N Wayside Pl					
32900	WrnT	60030	2533	18W-33N	E4
W Wayside Pl					
25100	LkvT	60046	2474	25W-37N	B2
Weatherbee Av					
900	DRGV	60516	3144	19W-7S	C6
Weatherbee Pl					
900	DRGV	60516	3144	19W-7S	D6
Weatherford Ct					
300	LKBF	60044	2593	11W-29N	D5
Weatherford Ln					
200	NPVL	60565	3203	26W-10S	D5
Weather Hill Dr					
200	WLBK	60527	3145	16W-7S	D6
E Weathersfield Wy					
10	SMBG	60193	2859	23W-9N	B7
700	EGVV	60007	2859	22W-9N	C7
700	SMBG	60007	2859	22W-9N	C7
W Weathersfield Wy					
-	SMWD	60107	2857	26W-10N	E6
-	SMWD	60193	2857	26W-10N	E6
10	SMBG	60193	2859	23W-9N	A7
200	SMBG	60193	2858	26W-10N	A6
2200	SMBG	60193	2857	26W-10N	E6
W Weathersfield Wy Ct					
500	SMBG	60193	2858	24W-9N	D7
Weatherstone Ln					
1500	ELGN	60123	2854	35W-12N	B1
Weatherstone Rd					
100	PltT	60010	2751	23W-18N	D2
4200	NndT	60014	2641	33W-26N	A3
N Weatherstone Rd					
20400	KLDR	60047	2752	20W-20N	E1
20600	KLDR	60047	2699	21W-20N	E7
Weatherstone Wy					
5700	JNBG	60050	2472	30W-37N	A1
5700	MchT	60050	2472	30W-37N	A1
Weather Vane Ln					
15300	HMGN	60491	3343	16W-18S	E7
Weathervane Ln					
3700	NndT	60012	2583	36W-28N	E6

STREET Block	City	ZIP	Map#	CGS	Grid
Weathervane Ln					
32700	LKMR	60051	2529	28W-32N	D4
Weathervane Wy					
15700	PNFD	60544	3416	30W-18S	B2
15800	PNFD	60586	3416	30W-18S	B2
15800	PnfT	60586	3416	30W-18S	B2
E Weaver Cir					
500	BbyT	60134	3018	39W-0N	D5
W Weaver Cir					
500	BbyT	60134	3018	39W-0N	D5
Weaver Dr					
100	CRY	60013	2695	30W-23N	E1
200	CRY	60013	2696	30W-23N	A1
Weaver Ln					
10	BbyT	60134	3018	39W-0N	E5
2800	BTVA	60510	3077	37W-1S	C1
Weaver Pkwy					
4200	WNVL	60555	3141	27W-4S	B1
Weaver St					
-	OSWG	60560	3334	39W-15S	E2
Webb St					
10	CTCY	60409	3352	4E-18S	B7
10	GYLK	60030	2533	20W-33N	A4
10	HMND	46320	3352	4E-18S	C7
2100	CTHL	60403	3417	26W-21S	E7
E Webb St					
10	CTCY	60409	3352		C7
10	HMND	46320	3352		D7
Weber Ct					
300	CRY	60013	2641	31W-24N	D7
19300	MKNA	60448	3503	13W-23S	A3
Weber Dr					
-	GNVA	60134	3019	38W-1N	B4
-	GnvT	60134	3019	38W-1N	B4
10	SchT	60174	2908	35W-6N	C7
10	SchT	60174	2964	35W-5N	C1
500	WYNE	60174	2964	35W-5N	C2
2900	AURA	60502	3139	31W-7S	D7
4200	ANHT	60005	2806	19W-12N	D7
4200	RGMW	60005	2806	19W-12N	D7
4200	RGMW	60008	2806	19W-12N	D7
4900	ANHT	60005	2860	19W-12N	D1
4900	ANHT	60008	2860	19W-12N	D1
4900	RGMW	60008	2860	19W-12N	D1
5000	RGMW	60005	2860	19W-12N	D1
Weber Ln					
5100	SKOK	60077	2865	6W-12N	D1
Weber Rd					
1400	SCRL	60174	3020	33W-2N	E1
1900	CTHL	60403	3418	26W-21S	A7
2300	CTHL	60441	3418	25W-21S	A6
16200	LktT	60403	3418	25W-19S	A3
16200	LktT	60441	3418	26W-19S	A3
19100	MKNA	60448	3503	13W-23S	A2
N Weber Rd					
-	BGBK	60440	3204	26W-11S	A7
-	BGBK	60490	3204	26W-10S	A7
-	DPgT	60490	3204	26W-10S	A7
-	DPgT	60565	3204	26W-10S	A7
-	NPVL	60565	3204	26W-10S	A7
100	BGBK	60440	3268	25W-11S	A1
100	BGBK	60490	3268	25W-11S	A1
S Weber Rd					
-	BGBK	60446	3268	25W-14S	A6
-	DPgT	60446	3268	26W-14S	A7
-	DPgT	60544	3268	26W-13S	A4
-	RMVL	60544	3268	26W-13S	A4
10	LktT	60441	3340	25W-18S	A7
10	LktT	60446	3340	25W-18S	A7
10	LktT	60544	3340	26W-17S	A6
10	RMVL	60441	3340	26W-17S	A6
10	RMVL	60446	3340	25W-18S	A7
100	BGBK	60440	3268	25W-12S	A2
100	BGBK	60490	3268	25W-12S	A2
200	RMVL	60544	3340	26W-17S	A6
400	LktT	60441	3418	26W-18S	A1
400	LktT	60446	3418	26W-18S	A1
400	RMVL	60441	3418	26W-18S	A1
400	RMVL	60446	3418	26W-18S	A1
500	DPgT	60440	3268	25W-13S	A4
500	DPgT	60490	3268	25W-13S	A4
700	RMVL	60446	3268	26W-13S	A4
700	RMVL	60490	3268	25W-13S	A6
11000	DPgT	60446	3340	26W-15S	A2
11000	DPgT	60544	3340	26W-15S	A2
15700	LktT	60403	3418	26W-18S	A1
Weber Park Pl					
9300	SKOK	60077	2865	6W-11N	E2
Webford Av					
500	DSPN	60016	2862	13W-11N	E3
1300	DSPN	60016	2863	12W-11N	B3
Webley Ct					
700	SMBG	60193	2859	22W-9N	C7
Webley Ln					
600	SMBG	60193	2859	22W-9N	C7
Webster Av					
10	HDPK	60037	2704	9W-23N	D2
10	HIWD	60037	2704	9W-23N	D2
10	HIWD	60040	2704	9W-23N	D2
200	BmdT	60157	2913	22W-6N	C6
200	ROSL	60157	2913	22W-6N	C6
400	BmdT	60172	2912	25W-6N	A6
500	BmdT	60133	2912	25W-6N	A6
500	HRPK	60133	2912	25W-6N	A6
500	HRPK	60172	2912	25W-6N	A6
600	WHTN	60187	3024	24W-0S	E6
700	BRLT	60103	2910	29W-6N	D6
E Webster Av					
300	EMHT	60126	3028	15W-0N	B3
W Webster Av					
300	CHCG	60614	2978	0W-2N	A6
700	CHCG	60614	2977	1W-2N	E6
1900	CHCG	60647	2977	2W-2N	E6
2000	JLET	60436	3497	26W-24S	E5
Webster Ct					
100	ALGN	60102	2747	33W-20N	E1
300	SMBG	60193	2858	25W-10N	B6
1700	WHTN	60187	3024	24W-0N	E4
Webster Ln					
10	SMBG	60193	2858	25W-10N	B6
10	SMBG	60194	2858	25W-10N	B5
400	WldT	60564	3266	29W-11S	D1
900	SMBG	60193	2912	25W-9N	B1
1200	DSPN	60016	2862	13W-10N	E5
1200	DSPN	60018	2862	13W-10N	E5
2200	DSPN	60018	2916	13W-9N	D1
Webster Pl					
100	VNHL	60061	2647	17W-26N	B4
5900	DRGV	60516	3144	19W-6S	C4
Webster St					
10	BTVA	60510	3078	35W-1S	B2
10	ALGN	60102	2747	33W-20N	D1
100	MTGY	60538	3199	37W-9S	D4
100	NPVL	60563	3141	27W-4S	C2
100	NpvT	60563	3141	27W-5S	D2
5300	DRGV	60515	3144	19W-5S	C3
Webster St					
5400	DRGV	60516	3144	19W-6S	C4
7200	DGvT	60516	3206	19W-8S	C1
7200	DRGV	60516	3206	19W-8S	C1
7300	DRN	60516	3206	19W-8S	C1
E Webster St					
100	JLET	60432	3499	23W-23S	A4
N Webster St					
10	AURA	60505	3200	34W-8S	D1
10	NPVL	60540	3141	27W-6S	D5
500	NPVL	60563	3141	27W-6S	D4
1400	NpvT	60563	3141	27W-5S	D3
2400	EDPK	60171	2974	10W-3N	B6
2400	EDPK	60707	2974	10W-3N	B6
S Webster St					
400	NPVL	60540	3141	27W-7S	D6
500	AraT	60504	3200	34W-8S	D2
W Webster St					
10	JLET	60432	3498	24W-23S	E4
Wedel Ln					
800	GNVW	60025	2810	10W-13N	B6
800	NfdT	60025	2810	10W-13N	B6
Wedgefield Cir					
1500	NPVL	60563	3141	27W-5S	C2
Wedgefield Ct					
2300	AURA	60502	3139	32W-6S	B5
Wedgefield Ln					
300	BMDL	60108	2968	24W-4N	C2
Wedgemere Dr					
12300	HTLY	60142	2744	43W-19N	A3
Wedgemere Pl					
400	LYVL	60048	2591	16W-28N	E6
Wedgeport Cir					
100	RMVL	60446	3339	27W-17S	C6
Wedgeport Ct					
100	RMVL	60446	3339	27W-17S	C6
Wedgewood Av					
1400	DSPN	60018	2862	14W-10N	C6
16600	HLCT	60429	3426	4W-19S	E3
16600	MKHM	60428	3426	4W-19S	E3
Wedgewood Cir					
10	LIHL	60156	2692	38W-21N	E6
300	BMDL	60108	2968	24W-5N	D2
300	RMVL	60446	3339	27W-17S	B7
Wedgewood Ct					
200	LsIT	60540	3143	23W-7S	A7
300	WLBK	60527	3146	15W-7S	A7
500	HNDL	60521	3086	16W-4S	A7
800	BFGV	60089	2701	17W-23N	B3
800	LNHT	60046	2417	21W-39N	E5
800	WMTN	60481	3943	27W-39S	E1
1700	LKFT	60045	2703	13W-23N	A2
4600	LSLE	60532	3142	24W-4S	D2
6100	MTSN	60443	3505	7W-24S	C4
W Wedgewood Ct					
14300	WDWH	60083	2420	14W-39N	D4
24000	PNFD	60586	3416	30W-19S	C3
Wedgewood Dr					
10	HNWD	60047	2645	23W-24N	A6
10	JltT	60436	3586	24W-26S	E2
10	SEGN	60177	2908	35W-8N	B3
100	DRPK	60010	2752	23W-18N	A3
100	ElgT	60124	2799	38W-13N	A7
100	ElgT	60124	2853	38W-13N	A1
100	PltT	60010	2752	23W-18N	A3
600	CLLK	60014	2639	37W-24N	C6
600	HRPK	60133	2912	25W-9N	A1
900	GNVW	60025	2810	9W-13N	B6
1400	LKFT	60045	2703	13W-23N	A2
1600	GRNE	60031	2478	14W-35N	D5
2700	NPVL	60565	3203	27W-10S	C7
8500	BRRG	60527	3208	15W-9S	B4
8500	DGvT	60527	3208	15W-9S	B4
W Wedgewood Dr					
22300	AntT	60002	2417	22W-40N	C2
Wedgewood Ln					
900	AURA	60506	3137	37W-6S	C5
1800	SMBG	60193	2858	25W-10N	A6
6600	WLBK	60527	3146	15W-7S	A6
26800	CNHN	60410	3672	33W-32S	B7
N Wedgewood Ln					
-	MPPT	60056	2807	16W-13N	D5
1100	MPPT	60056	2808	15W-14N	A4
24000	LKBN	60010	2643	27W-24N	C7
24000	LKBN	60010	2697	27W-23N	C1
Wedgewood Rd					
10	MTSN	60443	3505	7W-24S	C4
Wedgewood Tr					
400	MHRY	60050	2527	34W-32N	B5
Wedgewood Wy					
100	BGBK	60440	3205	22W-11S	B7
Wedgewood Glens Dr					
14200	ODPK	60462	3346	10W-16S	C4
Wedgwood Dr					
-	BDVW	60154	3029	12W-0S	C6
-	BDVW	60155	3029	12W-0S	C6
-	WSTR	60154	3029	12W-0S	B6
-	WSTR	60155	3029	12W-0S	C6
12200	HMGN	60491	3422	15W-20S	B4
Wee Ct					
700	JLET	60432	3499	22W-23S	C4
W Weed St					
-	CHCG	60611	3034	0E-0N	D3
800	CHCG	60610	3033	1W-1N	E1
900	CHCG	60622	3033	1W-1N	E1
Weeg Wy					
1500	PKRG	60068	2863	11W-10N	E4
Weeping Beech Ln					
-	CmpT	60175	2906	39W-6N	D7
Weeping Willow Dr					
800	WLNG	60090	2755	15W-16N	A6
2700	LSLE	60532	3142	24W-6S	C5
Weeping Willow Ln					
1100	LYVL	60048	2647	16W-27N	D1
Weeping Willow Rd					
-	CTSD	60525	3147	12W-7S	C6
-	HGKN	60525	3147	12W-7S	C6
W Weeping Willow Rd					
300	RDLK	60073	2531	23W-33N	E4
Wegner Dr					
300	WCHI	60185	3022	31W-0N	A5
W Wegner Rd					
100	LKMR	60051	2529	28W-31N	D6
100	WcnT	60051	2529	28W-31N	D6
400	NndT	60051	2529	29W-31N	C7
We Go Ct					
300	DRFD	60015	2756	12W-20N	B1
We Go Tr					
1600	DRFD	60015	2756	12W-20N	C1
S We Go Tr					
10	MPPT	60056	2807	16W-12N	D7
100	MPPT	60056	2861	16W-12N	D1
Wehrheim Rd					
10	DRPK	60010	2752	23W-20N	A2
10	PltT	60010	2752	23W-20N	A2
Wehrli Dr					
600	NPVL	60540	3141	26W-7S	E6
700	LsIT	60540	3141	26W-7S	E7
Wehrli Rd					
100	LsIT	60540	3204	24W-9S	C3
100	NPVL	60540	3204	24W-8S	C1
200	LsIT	60565	3204	24W-9S	D4
400	NPVL	60565	3204	24W-9S	D4
2100	BGBK	60440	3204	24W-9S	D4
2100	BGBK	60565	3204	24W-9S	D4
Wehrli Rd CO-40					
100	LsIT	60540	3204	24W-8S	C1
100	NPVL	60540	3204	24W-8S	C1
200	LsIT	60565	3204	24W-8S	C2
Wehrman Av					
3700	FNPK	60131	2973	12W-4N	B2
3700	FNPK	60176	2973	12W-4N	B2
4300	SRPK	60176	2973	12W-5N	B1
Wehrman Pl					
10100	SRPK	60176	2973	12W-4N	B2
W Weich Rd					
19200	FmtT	60060	2646	19W-26N	C4
Weidner Ct					
10	BFGV	60089	2754	17W-18N	B3
Weidner Ct S					
800	BFGV	60089	2754	17W-18N	B4
Weidner Rd					
-	VrnT	60089	2754	17W-20N	A2
100	BFGV	60089	2754	17W-18N	A4
Weigel Dr					
900	BNVL	60106	2971	16W-3N	D5
900	EMHT	60106	2971	16W-3N	D5
900	EMHT	60126	2971	16W-3N	D5
Weiland Rd					
100	BFGV	60089	2754	16W-18N	D2
100	WLNG	60089	2754	16W-18N	D2
100	WLNG	60090	2754	16W-18N	D2
300	BFGV	60069	2754	16W-20N	D1
300	VrnT	60069	2754	16W-20N	D1
300	VrnT	60089	2754	16W-20N	D1
800	BFGV	60089	2701	16W-21N	E6
1200	BFGV	60069	2701	16W-21N	E6
1600	VrnT	60069	2701	16W-21N	E5
1600	VrnT	60089	2701	16W-21N	E5
Weiland Rd CO-W17					
100	BFGV	60089	2754	16W-20N	D2
100	WLNG	60089	2754	16W-20N	D2
300	BFGV	60069	2754	16W-20N	D1
300	VrnT	60069	2754	16W-20N	D1
300	VrnT	60089	2754	16W-20N	D1
800	BFGV	60089	2701	16W-21N	E6
1200	BFGV	60069	2701	16W-21N	E6
1600	VrnT	60069	2701	16W-21N	E5
1600	VrnT	60089	2701	16W-21N	E5
S Weiler Rd					
100	EGvT	60005	2861	16W-9N	E6
Weimer Av					
10	LMNT	60439	3270	19W-14S	D7
Weingart Rd					
-	LKMR	60051	2472	30W-35N	A7
3100	JNBG	60051	2472	30W-35N	B7
Weinhold Dr					
22800	PNFD	60585	3339	28W-15S	A1
22900	PNFD	60585	3338	28W-15S	E1
W Weis Ln					
16600	LKPT	60441	3420	20W-19S	A3
Weiss Tr					
21400	RlyT	60152	2634	50W-25N	A5
Welch Cir					
500	LKBN	60010	2696	28W-23N	E1
W Welch Ct					
7000	MonT	60449	3682	8W-30S	B4
Welch St					
500	GLBT	60136	2799	38W-15N	B4
Welch Wy					
18700	CCHL	60478	3506	6W-22S	A2
Weld Rd					
10	ELGN	60123	2854	35W-10N	A5
10	ELGN	60124	2853	37W-11N	C4
10	ElgT	60123	2853	35W-10N	A5
10	ElgT	60124	2853	37W-11N	C4
200	ELGN	60123	2853	37W-11N	C4
400	ElgT	60123	2853	36W-11N	E5
Weldwood Dr					
200	ELGN	60124	2853	37W-10N	D5
Well Ct					
10	PKFT	60466	3595	3W-26S	A2
Well St					
100	PKFT	60466	3595	3W-26S	B2
Welland Ct					
-	FKFT	60423	3590	14W-27S	E3
1400	ROSL	60172	2912	25W-7N	C4
Weller Dr					
100	PnfT	60544	3338	29W-16S	D4
Weller Ln					
2800	NHBK	60062	2756	11W-17N	E6
S Weller Ln					
100	MPPT	60056	2807	16W-12N	D7
100	MPPT	60056	2861	16W-12N	D1
Wellesley Cir					
10	NHBK	60062	2756	12W-18N	A2
13200	PNFD	60585	3338	30W-15S	B3
Wellesley Ct					
10	HNWD	60047	2699	22W-23N	C1
100	GNVW	60025	2810	10W-15N	A2
200	SMBG	60193	2858	25W-10N	A6
2300	NPVL	60564	3202	29W-10S	E5
13300	PNFD	60585	3338	30W-15S	B3
Wellesley Ln					
200	SMBG	60193	2858	25W-10N	A6
Wellingborough Ct					
10	SBTN	60010	2804	25W-15N	A2
Wellington Av					
-	FNPK	60131	2972	13W-3N	E4
-	FNPK	60131	2973	13W-3N	A4
10	MDLN	60060	2590	19W-28N	D6
100	ELGN	60120	2854	34W-10N	C7
100	ELGN	60120	2853	33W-11N	A4
200	EGVV	60007	2914	19W-8N	C2
400	LSLE	60563	3142	24W-5S	C2
400	LsIT	60563	3142	24W-5S	C2
500	LsIT	60532	3142	24W-5S	C2
1000	LYVL	60048	2591	17W-29N	B3
2200	LSLE	60532	3142	24W-5S	D2
2400	WSTR	60154	3086	13W-2S	D3
W Wellington Av					
300	CHCG	60657	2978	0W-3N	A4
700	CHCG	60657	2977	2W-3N	B4
1900	CHCG	60618	2977	2W-3N	B4
2700	CHCG	60618	2976	3W-3N	E4
3900	CHCG	60641	2976	5W-3N	B4
4700	CHCG	60641	2975	7W-3N	C4
5500	CHCG	60634	2975	8W-3N	A4
6700	CHCG	60634	2974	8W-3N	E4
7200	CHCG	60707	2974	9W-3N	C4
7200	EDPK	60707	2974	9W-3N	C4
W Wellington Av					
7900	EDPK	60171	2974	9W-3N	B4
Wellington Cir					
100	GRNE	60031	2535	14W-34N	D1
800	AURA	60506	3137	37W-6S	C5
Wellington Ct					
-	RGMW	60008	2806	19W-13N	B5
-	SMBG	60173	2859	23W-12N	B1
10	LNSH	60069	2703	13W-22N	A4
100	GYLK	60030	2532	21W-33N	D2
400	LKVL	60046	2475	22W-37N	C2
500	MDLN	60060	2590	19W-28N	D7
500	NLNX	60451	3502	15W-25S	B7
900	AURA	60506	3137	37W-6S	C5
1900	NPVL	60565	3204	25W-9S	B4
2000	GNVA	60134	3019	36W-1N	E3
2500	EVTN	60201	2812	5W-12N	A7
3600	HLCT	60429	3426	4W-20S	D5
N Wellington Ct					
1300	PLTN	60067	2752	21W-18N	D4
W Wellington Ct					
27000	LKBN	60010	2643	27W-24N	C7
Wellington Ct N					
1200	BFGV	60089	2701	16W-21N	D6
Wellington Ct S					
1200	BFGV	60089	2701	16W-21N	D6
Wellington Dr					
-	GfnT	60156	2692	39W-22N	D5
-	HTLY	60156	2692	39W-22N	D5
100	BMDL	60108	2968	24W-5N	C2
100	CLLK	60014	2640	35W-24N	A7
200	CLLK	60014	2639	36W-24N	E7
300	LKMR	60051	2529	29W-34N	C1
300	MchT	60051	2529	29W-34N	C1
300	SMWD	60107	2857	28W-11N	B4
500	DYR	46311	3510		E6
500	MNSR	46321	3510		E6
4400	LGGV	60047	2700	18W-23N	D2
5200	MHRY	60050	2527	34W-32N	D5
10000	HTLY	60142	2692	39W-22N	D5
17400	HLCT	60429	3426	4W-20S	D5
N Wellington Dr					
1200	PLTN	60067	2752	21W-17N	D5
W Wellington Dr					
200	PLTN	60067	2752	21W-17N	D5
Wellington Ln					
400	BGBK	60440	3269	22W-12S	B2
700	CRY	60013	2641	32W-24N	C6
Wellington Pkwy					
600	NLNX	60451	3502	15W-25S	B7
700	NLNX	60451	3590	15W-25S	B1
Wellington Pl					
1800	HFET	60169	2858	26W-12N	A1
1900	DRGV	60516	3144	20W-7S	A6
20400	CTHL	60403	3418	25W-19S	B3
Wellington Rd					
10	NHBK	60062	2757	9W-18N	C2
1900	WDRG	60517	3206	20W-9S	A3
S Wellington Rd					
1000	WKGN	60085	2535	14W-32N	C4
Wellington St					
-	BtnT	60081	2414	29W-39N	C5
-	LydT	60164	2972	14W-3N	D4
500	ELGN	60120	2855	33W-10N	A6
10800	FNPK	60131	2972	13W-3N	E4
10800	LydT	60131	2972	13W-3N	E4
Wellman Av					
1000	MTGY	60538	3200	36W-9S	A4
Wellner Rd					
600	NPVL	60540	3141	26W-7S	E7
Wells Av					
10	DXMR	60426	3349	1W-17S	E5
10	HRVY	60426	3349	1W-17S	E5
Wells Ct					
800	DYR	46311	3598		E3
N Wells Dr					
28000	WCDA	60084	2587	25W-28N	E7
28000	WcnT	60084	2587	25W-28N	E7
Wells Ln					
-	AntT	60002	2356	27W-42N	C6
Wells St					
10	FXLK	60020	2473	28W-37N	A2
6300	DRGV	60516	3144	20W-7S	B6
N Wells St					
10	CHCG	60602	3034	0W-0N	B4
10	CHCG	60603	3034	0W-0N	B4
10	CHCG	60606	3034	0W-0N	B4
100	CHCG	60601	3034	0W-0N	B4
300	CHCG	60610	3034	0W-0N	B3
1600	CHCG	60610	2978	0W-2N	B7
1600	CHCG	60614	2978	0W-2N	B7
S Wells St					
10	CHCG	60602	3034	0W-0S	B5
10	CHCG	60603	3034	0W-0S	B5
10	CHCG	60606	3034	0W-0S	B5
100	CHCG	60604	3034	0W-0S	B5
300	CHCG	60605	3034	0W-0S	B6
300	CHCG	60607	3034	0W-0S	B6
3500	CHCG	60609	3092	0W-3S	B5
3500	CHCG	60616	3092	0W-3S	B5
4700	CHCG	60609	3152	0W-5S	B1
5500	CHCG	60621	3152	0W-5S	B1
Wells Wy					
3400	JLET	60431	3497	28W-24S	A6
3400	TroT	60431	3497	28W-24S	A6
E Wellsley Ct					
6700	GRNE	60031	2477	17W-35N	C5
W Wellsley Ct					
6800	GRNE	60031	2477	17W-35N	A6
S Wellston Ln					
600	RMVL	60446	3417	26W-18S	E1
E Wellwood Dr					
1200	LKPT	60441	3420	21W-18S	A1
1300	HmrT	60441	3420	21W-18S	A1
Welsh Av					
-	AraT	60502	3139	33W-7S	B7
-	AraT	60505	3139	33W-7S	B7
-	AURA	60502	3139	33W-7S	B7
-	AURA	60505	3139	33W-7S	B7
Welsh Dr					
4600	AURA	60502	3139	33W-7S	B7
4600	AURA	60505	3139	33W-7S	B7
Welsh Ln					
9400	HTLY	60142	2692	40W-22N	B3
Welter Ct					
14300	HMGN	60491	3344	16W-17S	A4
Welter Dr					
200	WDDL	60191	2914	19W-5N	D7
200	WDDL	60191	2970	19W-5N	D1
Welton Ct					
1500	NPVL	60565	3203	26W-9S	E3
Welwyn Av					
1800	DSPN	60018	2863	12W-9N	B7
Welwyn Ct					
100	NCHI	60044	2593	13W-29N	A3
Welwyn St					
100	NCHI	60044	2593	12W-29N	A3
Wembley Ct					
800	ELGN	60120	2855	32W-12N	D2
2400	GRNE	60031	2478	15W-36N	A3
Wembley Dr					
900	ISLK	60042	2586	30W-28N	B6
3100	ZION	60099	2362	11W-41N	D7
11600	HTLY	60142	2744	42W-20N	B1
11800	MKNA	60448	3502	14W-23S	D3
Wembley Rd					
10	OSWG	60543	3199	36W-11S	E7
10	OswT	60538	3199	36W-11S	E7
Wembly Dr					
10	WNVL	60555	3080	30W-2S	C4
Wenberg St					
900	JLET	60432	3499	22W-23S	C4
E Wenberg St					
700	JLET	60432	3499	23W-23S	B4
S Wenbriar Sq					
400	ADSN	60101	2971	18W-2N	A6
Wend Dr					
11000	WCHI	60185	3022	29W-0S	D6
11000	WnfT	60185	3022	29W-0S	D6
E Wend St					
10	LMNT	60439	3270	19W-14S	D7
W Wend St					
10	LMNT	60439	3270	19W-14S	C7
Wendall Av					
700	WCHI	60185	3022	29W-1N	D3
W Wendell St					
300	CHCG	60610	3034	0W-1N	A2
Wendover Ct					
200	BMDL	60108	2968	24W-5N	C2
1400	WHTN	60187	3024	23W-0N	E4
Wendover Dr					
2400	NPVL	60565	3203	26W-10S	E6
Wendt Av					
500	EDND	60118	2801	33W-16N	B2
Wendt St					
-	ALGN	60118	2746	37W-19N	D3
Wendy Dr					
1100	NHBK	60062	2757	9W-17N	D5
2500	NPVL	60565	3203	27W-10S	B7
Wenholz Av					
10	EDND	60118	2800	34W-16N	E2
10	EDND	60118	2801	34W-16N	A2
Wenmoth Ln					
700	GnvT	60134	3019	38W-0N	A5
Wenmoth Rd					
10	GnvT	60510	3077	38W-0S	B1
300	BTVA	60510	3077	38W-1S	B2
300	BtvT	60510	3077	38W-1S	B2
600	GnvT	60134	3019	38W-0S	B7
600	GnvT	60510	3019	38W-0S	B7
Wennamacher Av					
900	AURA	60505	3138	35W-6S	C5
Wennes Ct					
500	HNDL	60521	3086	15W-3S	A6
500	OKBK	60523	3086	15W-3S	A6
Wenona Ln					
700	MltT	60187	3082	25W-2S	A3
Wenonah Av					
-	BRWN	60304	3030	8W-1S	E7
500	OKPK	60302	3030	8W-0S	E5
500	OKPK	60304	3030	8W-0S	E5
1200	BRWN	60402	3030	8W-1S	E7
1400	BRWN	60402	3088	8W-1S	E1
3800	SKNY	60402	3088	8W-4S	E6
4400	FTVW	60402	3088	8W-4S	E7
4500	FTVW	60402	3148	8W-4S	E1
Wenonah Tr					
28800	GrtT	60051	2472	28W-34N	D7
N Wente Ct					
800	PLTN	60074	2753	19W-17N	B6
Wentworth					
1200	VOLO	60041	2530	27W-33N	C3
Wentworth Av					
-	SHLD	60473	3428	0W-20S	C4
-	TNTN	60473	3428	0W-20S	C4
-	TNTN	60476	3428	0W-20S	C4
10	CTCY	60409	3352	4E-18S	C7
10	GLNC	60022	2759	5W-17N	A6
100	GLNC	60022	2758	5W-17N	E6
900	CTCY	60409	3430	4E-19S	C2
1100	CHHT	60411	3508	0W-25S	C7
1500	CHHT	60411	3596	0W-26S	C2
1600	LNSG	60438	3430	4E-20S	C5
2500	BlmT	60411	3596	0W-26S	C2
14800	DLTN	60419	3350	0W-17S	C5
14900	HRVY	60426	3350	0W-17S	C5
15500	SHLD	60473	3350	0W-18S	C7
18700	LNSG	60438	3510	4E-22S	C1
19400	LNSG	60411	3510	4E-22S	C2
22700	SCHT	60475	3596	0W-27S	D5
22700	STGR	60475	3596	0W-27S	D5
22800	CRTE	60417	3596	0W-27S	C5
S Wentworth Av					
1700	CHCG	60616	3092	0W-1S	B1
3400	CHCG	60609	3092	0W-3S	B4
4700	CHCG	60609	3152	0W-5S	B1
5500	CHCG	60621	3152	0W-8S	B7
7400	CHCG	60620	3214	0W-8S	B1
7400	CHCG	60621	3214	0W-8S	B1
9400	CHCG	60628	3214	0W-11S	B7
10300	CHCG	60628	3278	0W-14S	C6
13400	RVDL	60827	3350	0W-15S	C1
14500	DLTN	60419	3350	0W-17S	C4
14500	DLTN	60827	3350	0W-17S	C4
Wentworth Cir					
300	BMDL	60108	2968	24W-5N	D2
400	CRY	60013	2642	30W-25N	A5
N Wentworth Cir					
1700	RMVL	60446	3339	27W-17S	C7
S Wentworth Cir					
1700	RMVL	60446	3339	27W-17S	C7
Wentworth Ct					
-	CRY	60013	2642	30W-25N	B5
600	WNFD	60190	3023	26W-1N	E2
1400	VNHL	60061	2647	16W-26N	D2
2200	NPVL	60565	3203	26W-10S	E6
Wentworth Dr					
-	ALGN	60102	2692	38W-21N	E6
-	GfnT	60102	2692	38W-21N	E6
-	LIHL	60156	2692	38W-21N	E6
10600	WldT	60564	3266	30W-12S	B3
Wentworth Ln					
300	BMDL	60108	2968	24W-5N	D2
300	BRLT	60103	2967	28W-5N	B2
2400	AURA	60502	3139	32W-5S	B3
Wenz Av					
6500	HGKN	60525	3147	11W-7S	D6
Werch Dr					
10000	WDRG	60439	3270	20W-12S	B2
10000	WDRG	60517	3270	20W-12S	B2

Chicago 7-County Street Index

STREET Block	City	ZIP	Map#	CGS	Grid
N Werden Rd					
27000	WcnT	60084	2644	25W-27N	A1
Werline Av					
1000	FDHT	60411	3509	1E-25S	A7
Wermes Av					
1400	AURA	60505	3200	33W-8S	E1
Wern Av					
3000	HDPK	60035	2704	9W-23N	C2
3000	HIWD	60040	2704	9W-23N	C2
Wernecke Rd					
1500	GfnT	60142	2691	42W-20N	B7
1500	HTLY	60142	2691	42W-20N	B7
1500	HTLY	60142	2744	42W-20N	B1
Wescot Ln					
500	BRLT	60103	2966	29W-4N	D3
500	BRLT	60185	2966	29W-4N	D3
500	WynT	60185	2966	29W-4N	D3
Wescott Ct					
10	BGBK	60440	3204	24W-10S	D5
Wescott Ln					
10	SBTN	60010	2803	26W-13N	D6
Wescott Rd					
800	BGBK	60440	3204	24W-10S	D5
1400	NHBK	60062	2757	10W-17N	A6
Wesemann Dr					
-	DndT	60118	2799	37W-16N	D1
-	ELGN	60124	2799	37W-16N	D1
-	WDND	60118	2799	37W-16N	D1
Wesglen Pkwy					
-	LktT	60446	3339	26W-17S	E5
-	LktT	60544	3339	26W-17S	E5
100	RMVL	60446	3339	26W-17S	E5
Weslake Pkwy					
-	PnfT	60446	3339	27W-16S	D5
-	PnfT	60544	3339	27W-16S	D5
-	RMVL	60544	3339	27W-16S	D5
1700	RMVL	60446	3339	27W-17S	C5
Wesley Av					
-	BRWN	60304	3031	8W-1S	A7
10	LKVL	60046	2475	23W-37N	A1
100	OKPK	60302	3031	8W-0N	A5
300	NPVL	60565	3203	26W-10S	D5
400	OKPK	60304	3031	8W-0N	A5
900	EVTN	60202	2867	3W-10N	A4
1200	BRWN	60402	3031	8W-1S	A7
1900	EVTN	60201	2867	3W-11N	A2
3900	BRWN	60402	3089	8W-4S	A6
3900	SKNY	60402	3089	8W-4S	A6
S Wesley Av					
500	OKPK	60302	3031	8W-0S	A5
500	OKPK	60304	3031	8W-0S	A5
1100	BRWN	60304	3031	8W-0S	A7
1100	BRWN	60402	3031	8W-0S	A7
Wesley Ct					
1400	LbvT	60060	2646	18W-26N	E3
1400	WTMT	60559	3145	18W-7S	A6
1500	GNVA	60134	3020	33W-1N	E2
N Wesley Ct					
5200	CHCG	60018	2917	11W-6N	C6
5200	CHCG	60656	2917	11W-6N	C6
5200	RSMT	60018	2917	11W-6N	C6
Wesley Dr					
900	CLLK	60014	2639	36W-24N	C7
900	PKRG	60068	2863	11W-9N	C6
N Wesley Dr					
200	ADSN	60101	2970	19W-4N	C4
Wesley Ln					
400	WTMT	60559	3145	18W-7S	A6
900	ALGN	60102	2748	32W-20N	A1
1000	ALGN	60102	2695	32W-20N	A7
Wesley Rd					
6300	WLBK	60527	3146	15W-7S	A5
N Wesley Rd					
36200	GrtT	60041	2473	26W-36N	E4
Wesley St					
100	BRTN	60010	2751	24W-20N	B2
E Wesley St					
100	WHTN	60187	3024	24W-0S	C7
W Wesley St					
100	WHTN	60187	3024	25W-0S	B6
Wesley Ter					
-	SRPK	60176	2917	11W-6N	C7
4200	SRPK	60176	2973	11W-5N	C1
N Wesley Ter					
5200	CHCG	60018	2917	11W-6N	C6
5200	CHCG	60656	2917	11W-6N	C6
5200	SRPK	60176	2917	11W-6N	C6
5200	SRPK	60656	2917	11W-6N	C6
Weslyan St					
100	LktT	60441	3419	23W-21S	B7
Wesmere Pkwy					
-	JLET	60586	3496	31W-21S	A1
1500	JLET	60586	3416	30W-21S	A7
2300	PnfT	60586	3416	30W-21S	B6
Wesmere Lakes Ct					
5500	JLET	60586	3416	30W-21S	A7
Wesmere Lakes Dr					
2000	JLET	60586	3416	30W-21S	A6
S Wespark Av					
1900	HMND	46394	3280		E5
Wespark Blvd					
-	RMVL	60446	3340	26W-17S	A5
Wespark Cir					
-	RMVL	60446	3339	26W-17S	E5
-	RMVL	60446	3340	26W-17S	A6
N Wespark Pkwy					
-	LktT	60446	3339	26W-17S	E5
-	LktT	60544	3339	26W-17S	E5
-	RMVL	60446	3339	26W-17S	E5
S Wespark Pkwy					
-	RMVL	60446	3339	26W-17S	E6
Wessex Dr					
-	DndT	60118	2800	36W-16N	A2
2600	WDND	60118	2800	36W-16N	A2
Wessling Dr					
1300	NfdT	60062	2756	12W-17N	B5
1300	NHBK	60062	2756	12W-17N	B5
West Av					
-	ODPK	60462	3423	12W-18S	C1
-	SMBG	60173	2860	21W-12N	A2
10	RVSD	60546	3088	10W-3S	B5
500	AddT	60106	2971	16W-3N	C5
500	EMHT	60106	2971	17W-3N	C5
500	EMHT	60126	2971	17W-3N	C5
800	WDSK	60098	2524	42W-31N	B6
6800	HRPK	60133	2911	27W-8N	C2
7000	HRPK	60107	2911	27W-8N	C2
7000	SMWD	60107	2911	27W-8N	C2
7000	SMWD	60133	2911	27W-8N	C2
14300	ODPK	60462	3345	12W-17S	C4
15700	HRVY	60426	3428	1W-18S	A1
N West Av					
100	EMHT	60126	3027	17W-1N	C1
400	EMHT	60126	2971	17W-2N	C7
38700	LKVL	60046	2416	23W-38N	E6
38700	LkvT	60046	2416	23W-38N	E6
S West Av					
100	EMHT	60126	3027	17W-1N	C3
800	WKGN	60085	2535	14W-32N	D4
800	WrnT	60031	2535	14W-32N	C4
W West Av					
3900	MHRY	60050	2528	32W-33N	A3
West Blvd					
800	MchT	60051	2529	29W-32N	B5
West Brch					
1300	GNVW	60093	2810	8W-15N	D3
West Ct					
100	BTVA	60510	3078	35W-2S	B5
600	SHLD	60473	3428	0E-18S	E1
900	NPVL	60563	3141	27W-5S	C3
West Dr					
-	SMBG	60173	2805	22W-12N	D7
-	SMBG	60173	2859	21W-11N	E2
10	NHLK	60164	3028	14W-2N	D1
100	LKBN	60010	2643	27W-25N	C4
100	TRLK	60010	2643	27W-25N	C4
200	WKGN	60085	2536	12W-33N	B1
1000	SchT	60177	2908	34W-7N	D4
1400	WPHR	60096	2363	10W-41N	B7
1400	WPHR	60096	2422	10W-41N	B1
1700	CTCY	60409	3429	2E-19S	D1
25900	NPVL	60563	3140	29W-5S	E2
N West Dr					
10	BtlT	60543	3263	38W-12S	A3
S West Dr					
10	BtlT	60543	3263	38W-12S	A4
W West Dr					
25700	WcnT	60084	2588	25W-28N	A7
West Ln					
-	BNHL	60010	2750	27W-17N	C5
10	LKBN	60010	2697	27W-23N	B2
200	LKZH	60047	2698	23W-23N	D1
300	GNVA	60134	3020	36W-1N	A3
600	SCRL	60134	3020	36W-1N	A3
600	SCRL	60174	3020	36W-1N	A3
N West Ln					
32500	AvnT	60030	2531	24W-32N	C5
32500	AvnT	60073	2531	24W-32N	C5
W West Ln					
5200	MCLK	60050	2470	34W-34N	D7
West Rd					
-	JLET	60421	3587	23W-27S	B4
-	JLET	60433	3587	23W-27S	B4
-	SEGN	60123	2854	34W-9N	E7
100	BMDL	60108	2968	24W-5N	E1
600	ELGN	60123	2854	34W-9N	D7
N West Rd					
10	LMBD	60148	3026	20W-1N	A2
West St					
-	GrtT	60081	2472	29W-37N	B1
-	HPSR	60140	2795	47W-16N	D2
-	MchT	60081	2472	29W-37N	B1
-	NPVL	60555	3141	27W-4S	C2
-	WMTN	60481	3943	27W-39S	D1
10	BtlT	60512	3261	42W-12S	E3
10	CLSM	60188	3024	25W-1N	C3
10	MltT	60187	3024	25W-1N	C3
10	MltT	60188	3024	25W-1N	C3
10	NPVL	60563	3141	27W-5S	C2
10	NPVL	60565	3203	27W-11S	C7
10	NpvT	60563	3141	27W-5S	C2
10	WldT	60565	3203	27W-11S	C7
10	WldT	60565	3267	27W-11S	C1
10	WNVL	60555	3141	27W-4S	C1
10	WNVL	60563	3141	27W-4S	C1
100	MNKA	60447	3583	33W-28S	A7
100	SRGV	60554	3135	42W-7S	C7
200	GNVA	60134	3020	36W-1N	A3
300	GRNE	60031	2535	14W-34N	C1
400	LktT	60441	3419	21W-18S	D1
400	YKVL	60560	3333	43W-14S	B1
500	LYVL	60048	2591	16W-29N	C4
500	PKCY	60085	2535	13W-33N	E3
500	WnfT	60555	3081	27W-3S	C6
500	WNVL	60555	3081	27W-3S	C6
600	WHTN	60187	3024	25W-1N	C6
900	HRVD	60033	2406	50W-38N	A6
1300	LKPT	60441	3419	22W-20S	D4
4200	DrrT	60012	2583	37W-27N	B7
10100	RHMD	60071	2353	34W-42N	C7
18200	LNSG	60438	3430	4E-21S	C6
N West St					
10	AURA	60505	3200	35W-7S	C1
10	NPVL	60540	3141	27W-6S	C5
10	PLNO	60545	3259	47W-13S	C6
10	WKGN	60085	2537	10W-34N	A1
100	MRGO	60152	2634	50W-26N	A2
100	PTON	60468	3860	9W-37S	E3
100	WHTN	60187	3024	25W-0S	C6
500	PtnT	60468	3860	9W-37S	E3
1000	NPVL	60563	3141	27W-5S	C4
2000	MLPK	60160	2973	11W-2N	E6
2000	RVGV	60171	2973	11W-3N	E6
4800	MchT	60050	2472	29W-37N	C3
28900	GrtT	60081	2472	28W-37N	D1
28900	MchT	60081	2472	28W-37N	D1
S West St					
10	AURA	60505	3200	35W-7S	C1
10	NPVL	60540	3141	27W-6S	C5
10	PLNO	60545	3259	47W-14S	C7
10	WKGN	60085	2537	10W-33N	A2
100	MRGO	60152	2634	50W-26N	A2
100	PTON	60468	3860	9W-37S	E4
100	WHTN	60187	3024	25W-0S	C7
500	PtnT	60468	3860	9W-37S	E4
600	LtRT	60545	3259	47W-14S	D7
700	WHTN	60187	3082	25W-1S	C1
800	NPVL	60540	3203	27W-8S	B1
West Tr					
10	GYLK	60030	2532	21W-33N	D3
West Tr N					
400	GYLK	60030	2532	21W-33N	D2
400	HNVL	60030	2532	21W-33N	D2
W West Acres Rd					
1200	JLET	60435	3498	25W-23S	B4
Westberry Ct					
1000	LKZH	60047	2699	22W-24N	A1
Westberry Ln					
8400	TYPK	60487	3424	10W-19S	B1
Westbourne Av					
-	SRGV	60554	3135	42W-6S	C4
Westbourne Ln					
800	BFGV	60089	2701	17W-20N	B7
800	BFGV	60089	2754	17W-20N	B1
Westbourne Pkwy					
-	DndT	60102	2747	36W-19N	B3
1300	ALGN	60102	2747	36W-19N	B3
Westbridge Ct					
1700	SMBG	60194	2858	25W-11N	A3
4400	HFET	60192	2804	24W-15N	B2
17500	TYPK	60487	3424	10W-21S	B5
Westbridge Ln					
1600	HFET	60169	2858	25W-11N	B3
1600	SMBG	60194	2858	25W-11N	B3
Westbridge Rd					
8700	TYPK	60487	3424	11W-21S	A5
Westbrook Cir					
100	NPVL	60565	3203	26W-10S	D5
Westbrook Ct					
10	ALGN	60102	2747	35W-18N	B4
1700	JLET	60586	3495	33W-22S	B2
Westbrook Dr					
-	HMGN	60491	3422	14W-21S	C6
-	NPVL	60540	3202	29W-8S	C1
2400	FNPK	60131	2973	12W-3N	B6
2400	LydT	60164	2973	12W-3N	C6
4000	AURA	60504	3202	30W-8S	B1
4400	NPVL	60504	3202	29W-8S	C1
7400	JLET	60586	3495	33W-21S	A1
17400	ODPK	60467	3422	14W-21S	C6
Westbrook Ln					
-	GRNE	60031	2477	16W-36N	C5
West Brook Rd					
-	FKFT	60423	3591	13W-26S	A3
N West Brook Rd					
2400	EDPK	60707	2974	9W-3N	B6
Westbrook Corporate Ctr					
10	HLSD	60154	3086	14W-2S	D2
10	HLSD	60162	3086	14W-2S	D2
10	WSTR	60154	3086	14W-2S	D2
Westburg St					
1600	GLHT	60139	2969	23W-3N	A6
Westbury Cir					
1400	NARA	60542	3077	38W-4S	B7
Westbury Ct					
300	NPVL	60565	3203	26W-9S	D4
600	WNVL	60555	3080	29W-2S	E4
Westbury Dr					
-	AlqT	60013	2641	32W-24N	C7
-	AlqT	60014	2641	32W-24N	C7
-	CRY	60013	2641	32W-24N	C7
-	CRY	60014	2641	32W-24N	C7
700	ALGN	60102	2694	35W-20N	A7
1000	HFET	60067	2804	24W-15N	D2
1000	HFET	60192	2804	24W-15N	B2
1000	IVNS	60067	2804	24W-15N	D2
2000	WDRG	60517	3206	21W-9S	A3
4700	LGGV	60047	2700	18W-23N	D3
Westbury Ln					
-	AraT	60502	3139	33W-6S	B5
-	AURA	60502	3139	33W-6S	B5
Westcanton Ct					
1300	DRFD	60015	2703	11W-21N	E6
Westchester Blvd					
-	PvsT	60525	3087	12W-1S	B2
600	WSTR	60154	3029	12W-1S	B7
1400	WSTR	60154	3087	12W-1S	B1
2100	PvsT	60154	3087	12W-1S	B2
Westchester Cir					
-	LGGV	60047	2647	17W-24N	A7
900	SMBG	60193	2913	22W-9N	B1
Westchester Ct					
10	BGBK	60440	3205	22W-10S	C5
200	MltT	60137	3083	23W-2S	A4
1200	BFGV	60089	2701	16W-21N	E6
2400	AURA	60506	3136	39W-6S	E6
Westchester Dr					
900	HRPK	60133	2912	26W-8N	A2
900	SMBG	60193	2912	26W-8N	A2
1200	HRPK	60133	2911	26W-8N	E2
1300	GLHT	60139	3025	22W-2N	B1
1400	GLHT	60139	2969	23W-2N	A7
Westchester Ln					
700	BGBK	60440	3205	22W-10S	C5
W Westchester Ln					
4400	WKGN	60048	2535	14W-32N	C6
Westchester Rd					
400	SMBG	60193	2913	22W-9N	B1
1200	BFGV	60089	2701	16W-21N	C6
N West Cir Av					
5700	CHCG	60631	2918	8W-7N	D4
Westcliff Ln					
800	DRFD	60015	2704	10W-21N	A7
West End Av					
10	DRGV	60559	3144	18W-5S	E2
10	WTMT	60515	3144	18W-5S	E2
10	WTMT	60559	3144	18W-5S	E2
W West End Av					
4000	CHCG	60624	3032	5W-0N	B4
4500	CHCG	60644	3032	5W-0N	A4
5300	CHCG	60644	3031	6W-0N	D4
5900	CHCG	60302	3031	7W-0N	B4
5900	OKPK	60302	3031	7W-0N	B4
West End Dr					
10	ALGN	60102	2747	34W-20N	C1
N West End Dr					
-	MCLK	60050	2470	34W-34N	D7
1300	RLKB	60073	2475	22W-35N	A7
39000	AntT	60081	2415	27W-39N	B6
39000	FXLK	60081	2415	27W-39N	B6
W West End Dr					
3700	CHCG	60624	3032	4W-0N	C4
West End Ln					
-	VNHL	60061	2647	17W-26N	B3
West End Rd					
10	ROSL	60172	2912	24W-7N	E5
100	BmdT	60172	2912	24W-7N	E5
N West End Rd					
28000	WcnT	60084	2587	25W-28N	E7
Wester Blvd					
-	PGGV	60140	2797	41W-15N	E4
-	PGGV	60140	2798	41W-14N	A5
Westerfield Dr					
800	WLMT	60091	2812	3W-14N	E4
900	KLWH	60043	2812	3W-14N	E4
900	WLMT	60043	2812	3W-14N	E4
Westerfield Pl					
100	GYLK	60030	2533	20W-32N	A4
Westerhoff Dr					
4300	LSLE	60532	3142	23W-4S	E1
Westeria Ct					
1400	WynT	60103	2967	28W-5N	A2
Western					
-	BRTN	60010	2697	26W-20N	D7
-	BRTN	60010	2750	26W-20N	D1
Western Av					
-	BTVA	60510	3077	36W-1S	E2
-	CHCG	60613	2977	1W-5N	D1
-	FSMR	60430	3507	3W-23S	C3
-	HMWD	60422	3507	3W-23S	C3
-	MHTN	60442	3677	19W-30S	D3
-	MhtT	60442	3677	19W-30S	D3
10	HIWD	60040	2704	9W-23N	C3
200	WHTN	60187	3024	25W-0S	B6
300	CNHL	60514	3145	17W-5S	C3
400	GNEN	60137	3025	23W-0N	B4
500	DGvT	60527	3207	17W-9S	C4
Western Av					
500	DGvT	60561	3207	17W-9S	C4
500	GLHT	60137	3025	23W-1N	B2
500	GLHT	60139	3025	23W-1N	B2
500	GNVA	60134	3020	36W-0S	A6
700	BmdT	60137	3025	23W-1N	B2
700	FSMR	60422	3507	3W-24S	C5
700	HDPK	60035	2704	9W-23N	C1
700	NLNX	60451	3501	18W-25S	B7
700	NLNX	60451	3589	18W-25S	B1
700	NlxT	60451	3501	18W-25S	B7
700	NlxT	60451	3589	18W-25S	B1
800	MltT	60137	3025	23W-0N	B4
800	NHBK	60062	2757	10W-16N	A7
1300	CHHT	60411	3507	3W-25S	C7
1300	OMFD	60461	3507	3W-25S	C7
1300	WKGN	60085	2479	11W-35N	E6
1400	OMFD	60411	3507	3W-25S	C7
1500	CHHT	60411	3595	3W-28S	C5
1500	GnvT	60134	3020	36W-0N	A6
1500	OMFD	60411	3595	3W-25S	C1
1500	OMFD	60461	3595	3W-25S	C1
1500	OMFD	60466	3595	3W-25S	C1
1500	PKFT	60411	3595	3W-28S	C5
1500	PKFT	60466	3595	3W-28S	C5
1600	CHHT	60466	3595	3W-28S	C5
1600	NfdT	60062	2756	12W-16N	C6
1600	NHBK	60062	2756	12W-16N	C6
1800	FSMR	60461	3507	2W-23S	C4
1800	WKGN	60087	2479	11W-35N	E6
1900	NndT	60050	2585	30W-29N	E4
2100	BTVA	60134	3019	36W-0S	E7
2100	BTVA	60510	3019	36W-0S	E7
2100	GNVA	60134	3019	36W-0S	E7
2100	GnvT	60134	3019	36W-0S	E7
3500	HDPK	60035	2650	9W-24N	C7
3500	LKFT	60035	2650	9W-24N	C7
3500	LKFT	60045	2650	9W-24N	C7
3600	BlmT	60466	3595	2W-27S	C4
3800	MonT	60466	3595	2W-27S	C5
3800	WNSP	60558	3086	14W-4S	C7
4400	LSLE	60532	3142	24W-4S	D2
4900	DRGV	60515	3143	21W-5S	E2
4900	LslT	60515	3143	21W-5S	E2
5600	DGvT	60514	3145	17W-6S	C4
5600	WTMT	60514	3145	17W-6S	C4
5700	DGvT	60559	3145	17W-6S	C4
5700	WTMT	60559	3145	17W-6S	C4
5800	WLBK	60514	3145	17W-6S	C4
5800	WLBK	60527	3145	17W-7S	C6
5800	WLBK	60559	3145	17W-6S	C4
6000	DGvT	60527	3145	17W-7S	C6
6000	WTMT	60527	3145	17W-6S	C5
6500	DRN	60527	3145	17W-7S	C6
6700	DRN	60561	3145	17W-7S	C7
7200	DRN	60561	3207	17W-8S	C1
11900	BLID	60406	3277	3W-15S	B7
11900	BLID	60643	3277	3W-14S	B6
11900	BLID	60655	3277	3W-14S	B6
11900	CHCG	60643	3277	3W-14S	B6
11900	CHCG	60655	3277	3W-14S	B6
13500	BLID	60406	3349	3W-16S	B2
13800	DXMR	60406	3349	2W-16S	B3
13800	POSN	60406	3349	2W-16S	B3
13900	POSN	60469	3349	2W-16S	B3
14900	HRVY	60426	3349	2W-18S	C7
15500	HRVY	60428	3349	3W-18S	C7
15600	HRVY	60426	3427	3W-18S	C1
15600	HRVY	60428	3427	3W-18S	C1
15600	MKHM	60428	3427	3W-18S	C1
15700	MKHM	60426	3427	3W-18S	C1
15900	BmnT	60428	3427	3W-19S	C2
15900	ThtT	60428	3427	3W-19S	C2
16700	HLCT	60428	3427	2W-20S	C4
16700	HLCT	60429	3427	2W-20S	C4
17500	HLCT	60430	3427	3W-21S	C6
17500	HMWD	60430	3427	3W-21S	C6
18400	HMWD	60430	3507	3W-22S	C1
20300	BlmT	60411	3507	3W-24S	C6
23500	CteT	60417	3595	3W-28S	C7
23500	MonT	60417	3595	3W-28S	C7
23900	CteT	60466	3595	2W-29S	C7
24000	CteT	60417	3684	2W-29S	C2
24000	CteT	60466	3684	2W-29S	C2
24000	MonT	60417	3684	2W-29S	C2
24000	MonT	60466	3684	2W-29S	C2
24000	UYPK	60417	3684	2W-29S	C2
24000	UYPK	60466	3684	2W-29S	C2
E Western Av					
600	LMBD	60148	3026	19W-1N	D3
N Western Av					
-	DndT	60118	2747	35W-17N	D6
10	CHCG	60612	3033	2W-0N	B4
10	CPVL	60110	2800	34W-16N	D1
10	LKFT	60045	2650	10W-26N	A3
10	PKRG	60068	2917	11W-8N	D2
100	BRLT	60103	2910	29W-8N	E3
100	CPVL	60110	2747	35W-17N	D6
500	AURA	60506	3137	37W-6S	C6
700	CHCG	60622	3033	2W-0N	B3
700	PKRG	60068	2863	11W-9N	E6
1100	PKRG	60714	2863	10W-10N	E5
1200	LKFT	60045	2649	10W-27N	E1
1300	LKFT	60045	2593	10W-27N	E7
1500	CHCG	60647	3033	3W-1N	A1
1600	CHCG	60647	2977	2W-2N	A7
1800	MaiT	60016	2863	11W-11N	E3
1800	MaiT	60068	2863	11W-11N	E3
1800	NLES	60068	2863	11W-11N	E3
1800	NLES	60714	2863	11W-11N	E2
2700	CHCG	60618	2977	3W-2N	A6
4400	CHCG	60618	2921	2W-5N	A7
4400	CHCG	60625	2921	2W-5N	A7
5500	CHCG	60659	2921	2W-6N	A5
6300	CHCG	60645	2921	3W-8N	A1
7200	CHCG	60645	2867	2W-9N	A7
7500	CHCG	60202	2867	2W-9N	A7
7500	EVTN	60202	2867	2W-9N	A7
8800	GNVW	60025	2863	11W-12N	E1
8800	MaiT	60714	2863	11W-11N	E2
8800	NLES	60016	2863	11W-11N	E1
N Western Av SR-31					
-	DndT	60118	2747	35W-17N	D6
10	CPVL	60110	2800	34W-16N	D1
100	CPVL	60110	2747	35W-17N	D6
S Western Av					
10	AURA	60506	3137	37W-7S	C7
10	CHCG	60612	3033	3W-0S	B6
10	CPVL	60110	2800	34W-16N	D1
10	CPVL	60118	2800	34W-16N	D1
10	PKRG	60068	2917	10W-7N	E3
100	BRLT	60103	2910	29W-8N	E4
100	WDND	60110	2800	34W-16N	E2
100	WDND	60118	2800	34W-16N	E2
200	AURA	60506	3199	37W-7S	C1
200	LKFT	60045	2650	10W-25N	A4
S Western Av					
300	DSPN	60016	2862	13W-11N	E3
1100	CHCG	60608	3033	2W-0S	B7
1100	HDPK	60035	2650	9W-24N	C7
1100	LKFT	60035	2650	9W-24N	C7
1600	CHCG	60608	3091	3W-4S	B7
3400	CHCG	60632	3091	3W-3S	B5
4300	CHCG	60609	3091	2W-4S	B7
4700	CHCG	60609	3151	3W-7S	B6
4700	CHCG	60632	3151	3W-7S	B6
5400	CHCG	60629	3151	2W-5S	B3
5500	CHCG	60636	3151	2W-6S	B3
7400	CHCG	60652	3151	2W-8S	B7
7500	CHCG	60620	3213	3W-11S	B7
7500	CHCG	60636	3213	2W-8S	B1
7500	CHCG	60652	3213	3W-11S	B7
9000	ENGN	60620	3213	2W-10S	B5
9400	CHCG	60643	3213	2W-10S	B6
9400	CHCG	60805	3213	2W-10S	B5
9400	ENGN	60805	3213	2W-10S	B5
9800	CHCG	60655	3213	2W-11S	B7
10200	CHCG	60643	3277	3W-13S	B4
10200	CHCG	60655	3277	3W-13S	B4
11800	BLID	60406	3277	2W-13S	B5
11800	BLID	60643	3277	2W-13S	B5
11800	BLID	60655	3277	2W-13S	B5
14000	DXMR	60406	3349	2W-16S	B3
14000	POSN	60406	3349	2W-16S	B3
14000	POSN	60469	3349	2W-17S	C5
14500	DXMR	60426	3349	2W-17S	C5
14500	POSN	60426	3349	2W-17S	C5
14600	HRVY	60426	3349	2W-17S	C5
24500	CteT	60417	3684	3W-30S	C2
24500	UYPK	60417	3684	3W-31S	C5
24500	UYPK	60466	3684	3W-31S	C5
25300	MonT	60417	3684	3W-30S	C4
25300	MonT	60449	3684	3W-30S	C4
S Western Av SR-31					
10	CPVL	60110	2800	34W-16N	D1
10	CPVL	60118	2800	34W-16N	D1
100	WDND	60110	2800	34W-16N	E2
100	WDND	60118	2800	34W-16N	E2
W Western Av					
200	JLET	60432	3498	24W-23S	E4
200	JLET	60435	3498	24W-23S	D4
W Western Av US-30					
200	JLET	60432	3498	24W-23S	E4
200	JLET	60435	3498	24W-23S	E4
S Western Blvd					
3300	CHCG	60608	3091	2W-3S	B4
3400	CHCG	60609	3091	2W-3S	B5
Western Ct					
2100	LSLE	60532	3142	24W-4S	D1
Western Dr					
-	NARA	60506	3076	39W-3S	D7
-	NARA	60542	3076	39W-3S	D7
1600	WCHI	60185	3021	31W-1N	D3
N Western Ln					
600	ADSN	60101	2969	21W-4N	E3
Western Pl					
500	HDPK	60035	2650	9W-24N	C7
Western St					
300	HFET	60169	2858	24W-11N	D4
Westfield Av					
-	FftT	60477	3504	9W-23S	E3
-	TYPK	60477	3504	9W-23S	E3
Westfield Ct					
-	TYPK	60477	3504	9W-23S	D3
Westfield Dr					
-	WrnT	60031	2478	15W-36N	A4
700	SCRL	60174	3020	36W-2N	A2
1800	AURA	60504	3200	33W-10S	E5
1900	GRNE	60031	2478	15W-36N	A4
2200	DRGV	60516	3143	21W-7S	E6
2400	ELGN	60124	2799	37W-14N	D5
Westfield Ln					
10	DSPN	60018	2862	15W-10N	B5
800	SMBG	60193	2912	24W-9N	D1
3600	GNVW	60025	2809	10W-15N	E2
Westfield Rd					
2000	JLET	60435	3497	26W-22S	E2
Westfield Wy					
200	BrnT	60010	2749	30W-17N	A5
1000	MDLN	60060	2590	20W-28N	B5
Westfield Course					
500	GNVA	60134	3020	34W-1N	E2
Westgate Av					
100	EGVV	60007	2860	18W-9N	E6
100	EGVV	60007	2861	18W-9N	A6
200	CHHT	60411	3507	1W-24S	E5
Westgate Ct					
500	SMWD	60107	2857	27W-10N	C6
6100	WDRG	60517	3143	21W-6S	E5
13300	ODPK	60462	3346	11W-15S	A2
Westgate Dr					
-	LNSH	60069	2701	15W-23N	E3
10	AURA	60506	3137	37W-6S	B6
100	ELGN	60123	2853	36W-11N	E3
300	PKFT	60466	3594	4W-26S	E3
300	PKFT	60466	3595	4W-26S	A3
400	RNPK	60471	3594	4W-26S	E3
700	PKCY	60085	2536	12W-33N	B3
S Westgate Dr					
200	CLSM	60188	3024	25W-1N	A2
200	PtnT	60468	3860	10W-37S	D3
12700	PSHT	60463	3275	8W-15S	A7
12800	PSHT	60463	3347	8W-15S	A1
Westgate Ln					
-	BtlT	60512	3198	41W-11S	A7
3000	PnfT	60435	3417	27W-19S	B3
3100	JLET	60431	3417	27W-19S	B3
Westgate Rd					
-	DGvT	60439	3206	19W-11S	D7
-	DGvT	60439	3207	18W-10S	A6
-	DRN	60439	3206	19W-11S	D7
400	DRFD	60015	2704	10W-21N	A6
600	DRFD	60015	2703	10W-21N	E6
N Westgate Rd					
10	DSPN	60016	2808	14W-13N	C7
10	DSPN	60016	2862	14W-12N	C2
10	MPPT	60016	2808	14W-13N	C7
800	MPPT	60056	2808	14W-14N	C5
1200	PTHT	60070	2808	14W-14N	C5
S Westgate Rd					
200	DSPN	60016	2862	14W-11N	C3
Westgate St					
100	DrrT	60098	2526	37W-31N	C6
1100	OKPK	60301	3030	8W-0N	D4
1100	RVFT	60301	3030	8W-0N	D4
1100	RVFT	60305	3030	8W-0N	D4
S Westgate St					
400	ADSN	60101	2970	18W-2N	E7
900	ADSN	60101	3026	18W-2N	E1
Westgate Ter					
300	SMWD	60107	2857	27W-10N	C6
1900	DRFD	60015	2704	10W-21N	B6

Chicago 7-County Street Index

STREET Block	City	ZIP	Map#	CGS	Grid
Westgate Ter					
1900	HDPK	60035	2704	10W-21N	B7
W Westgate Ter					
1200	CHCG	60607	3033	1W-0S	D6
Westgate Valley Dr					
-	PSHT	60463	3347	8W-15S	B1
-	WthT	60463	3347	8W-15S	B1
Westglen Dr					
400	NPVL	60565	3203	27W-8S	C2
1500	NpvT	60565	3203	27W-8S	C3
Westhampton Ct					
10	AURA	60504	3202	30W-8S	A1
West Hampton Dr					
1300	JLET	60586	3496	30W-22S	C1
Westhaven Cir					
10	GNVA	60134	3019	37W-1N	B3
Westhaven Ct					
4800	HFET	60010	2804	24W-16N	B1
Westhaven Dr					
900	WHTN	60187	3082	25W-1S	A1
Westhill Cir					
4900	JLET	60586	3416	30W-21S	C6
W Westinghouse Ct					
9200	MKNA	60448	3503	12W-22S	D1
Westings Av					
2000	NPVL	60563	3140	29W-4S	C1
N Westlake Av					
41100	AntT	60002	2416	25W-41N	A1
Westlake Ct					
-	CRY	60013	2641	32W-24N	C6
Westlake Dr					
10	BNHL	60010	2803	27W-15N	A1
10	BrnT	60010	2803	27W-15N	A1
10	SBTN	60010	2803	27W-15N	A1
600	ELBN	60119	3017	43W-2N	B1
3100	CRY	60013	2641	32W-24N	C7
West Lake Rd					
17200	LNSG	60438	3430	3E-20S	A4
Westlake Ter					
4200	MLPK	60160	3029	13W-1N	A2
4200	MLPK	60165	3029	13W-1N	A2
4200	SNPK	60165	3029	13W-1N	A2
W Westlane Av					
28800	GrtT	60081	2472	29W-37N	D1
N Westlawn Av					
500	AURA	60506	3137	37W-6S	B6
S Westlawn Av					
10	AURA	60506	3137	37W-7S	B7
200	AURA	60506	3199	37W-7S	B1
Westleigh Ct					
10	OswT	60538	3199	37W-11S	D7
2400	AURA	60504	3201	32W-9S	C5
6100	LSLE	60532	3142	24W-6S	C5
Westleigh Dr					
-	GNVW	60025	2810	8W-15N	D2
-	NHBK	60062	2810	8W-15N	D2
-	NHFD	60093	2810	8W-15N	E2
E Westleigh Rd					
10	LKFT	60045	2649	10W-25N	E5
100	LKFT	60045	2650	9W-25N	C5
W Westleigh Rd					
10	LKFT	60045	2649	11W-25N	C5
Westley Ct					
200	BGBK	60440	3268	24W-12S	D2
Westley Ln					
1300	DndT	60118	2747	35W-17N	C7
1300	WDND	60118	2747	35W-17N	C7
1300	WDND	60118	2800	35W-16N	B1
Westley Rd					
400	GLNC	60022	2758	7W-18N	B3
Westline Dr					
2400	JLET	60431	3417	28W-20S	A6
2400	PnfT	60431	3417	28W-20S	A6
West Mary Ln					
100	SchT	60175	2963	38W-3N	A7
100	SCRL	60175	2963	38W-3N	A7
West Mead St					
200	PKCY	60085	2535	13W-33N	E2
Westmere Dr					
5300	JLET	60586	3416	30W-21S	B6
Westmere Rd					
100	DSPN	60016	2862	15W-11N	B3
Westmere St					
10	DSPN	60016	2862	15W-11N	B3
Westminister Ct					
300	OSWG	60543	3200	35W-10S	B6
Westminster Av					
3700	CCHL	60478	3426	4W-20S	D5
3700	HLCT	60429	3426	4W-20S	D5
Westminster Cir					
500	ROSL	60172	2912	25W-6N	B6
Westminster Ct					
10	LIHL	60156	2693	38W-22N	A3
200	SMBG	60193	2857	27W-10N	D6
1400	DRN	60561	3207	18W-9S	A3
S Westminster Ct					
200	RDLK	60073	2531	25W-33N	A3
Westminster Dr					
-	CLSM	60188	3024	25W-2N	A1
-	PvsT	60558	3086	13W-2S	E4
-	WSTR	60558	3086	13W-2S	E4
200	BMDL	60108	2912	24W-6N	D7
300	BRRG	60527	3208	15W-10S	B5
400	DGvT	60516	3206	20W-10S	B6
400	DGvT	60517	3206	20W-10S	B6
400	WDRG	60517	3206	20W-10S	B6
1500	NPVL	60563	3140	29W-5S	D3
4000	CCHL	60430	3426	4W-21S	D6
4000	CCHL	60478	3426	5W-21S	C6
4100	RNPK	60471	3594	5W-27S	C4
9000	WDRG	60516	3206	20W-11S	C7
11000	WSTR	60154	3086	13W-2S	E4
15500	ODPK	60462	3345	11W-18S	E7
15600	ODPK	60462	3423	11W-18S	E1
19500	MKNA	60448	3502	14W-23S	D4
N Westminster Dr					
300	PLTN	60067	2752	22W-16N	B7
Westminster Ln					
-	GRNE	60031	2478	15W-36N	A3
900	MNSR	46321	3510		E5
1100	EGVV	60007	2914	20W-8N	A2
2500	AURA	60506	3136	39W-6S	E5
3200	ISLK	60042	2586	30W-28N	B5
3800	GRNE	60031	2477	16W-36N	E3
21300	SRWD	60404	3583	31W-25S	E2
Westminster Ln CO-MB					
6800	GRNE	60031	2477	16W-36N	E3
Westminster Pl					
10	LKFT	60045	2650		C2
100	MNSR	46321	3510		C4
500	MDLN	60060	2590	20W-28N	A7
3600	MHRY	60050	2528	32W-31N	B7
Westminster Rd					
1100	JLET	60435	3498	26W-22S	A2
E Westminster Rd					
10	LKFT	60045	2649	10W-26N	E2
100	LKFT	60045	2650	10W-26N	A2
N Westminster Rd					
800	JLET	60435	3498	26W-22S	A3
W Westminster Rd					
10	LKFT	60045	2649	11W-26N	E2
Westminster St					
2200	WHTN	60187	3082	23W-3S	E5
Westminster Wy					
-	LNSH	60069	2702	13W-23N	E3
10	LNSH	60069	2703	13W-23N	A3
Westmont Dr					
600	CNHL	60514	3085	17W-4S	C7
600	CNHL	60559	3085	17W-4S	C7
600	WTMT	60559	3085	17W-4S	C7
N Westmoor Av					
36400	LkvT	60046	2474	24W-36N	B3
Westmoor Ct					
10	AURA	60502	3201	32W-8S	C1
Westmoor Dr					
3100	MchT	60097	2469	36W-34N	D7
3100	WRLK	60097	2469	36W-34N	D7
Westmoor Rd					
900	WNKA	60093	2812	5W-16N	A1
1100	WNKA	60093	2811	5W-16N	E1
Westmoor Tr					
1200	WNKA	60093	2811	6W-16N	E1
N Westmore Av					
10	LMBD	60148	3026	18W-1N	E3
10	LMBD	60181	3026	18W-1N	E3
300	VLPK	60181	3026	18W-1N	E2
700	ADSN	60101	3026	18W-1N	E1
700	ADSN	60181	3026	18W-1N	E1
700	VLPK	60101	3026	18W-1N	E1
Westmore Dr					
13900	HTLY	60142	2744	42W-20N	A1
Westmore Grove Dr					
1800	JLET	60586	3416	31W-21S	A7
Westmoreland Av					
200	WKGN	60085	2536	11W-34N	D1
700	WKGN	60085	2479	11W-35N	D6
Westmoreland Ct					
10	WDRG	60517	3143	21W-7S	D7
1300	NPVL	60540	3142	25W-6S	B5
Westmoreland Dr					
-	LGGV	60047	2646	18W-24N	E7
200	WLMT	60091	2812	5W-13N	A7
300	VNHL	60061	2647	18W-24N	A7
800	VNHL	60061	2646	18W-24N	E7
6600	WDRG	60517	3143	22W-7S	D6
N Westmoreland Dr					
2100	PLTN	60074	2753	19W-18N	B3
Westmoreland Ln					
-	LslT	60540	3142	25W-6S	B5
10	NPVL	60540	3142	25W-6S	B5
N Westmoreland Rd					
900	LKFT	60045	2649	11W-27N	C2
S Westmore-Meyers Rd					
-	LMBD	60148	3026	18W-0N	E4
-	LMBD	60181	3026	18W-0N	E5
-	VLPK	60181	3026	18W-0N	E5
-	YkTp	60148	3026	18W-0S	E7
Westmorland Av					
2800	MhtT	60442	3590	15W-27S	B5
2800	NlxT	60442	3590	15W-27S	B5
2800	NlxT	60451	3590	15W-27S	B5
Westnedge Ln					
2300	JLET	60435	3497	26W-23S	D3
N Westnedge Rd					
500	JLET	60435	3497	26W-23S	D3
Weston Av					
300	AURA	60505	3200	35W-8S	A2
1900	YKVL	60560	3333	42W-16S	D5
N Weston Av					
500	ELGN	60123	2854	35W-12N	B3
S Weston Av					
10	ELGN	60123	2854	35W-11N	B4
Weston Cir					
1000	BTVA	60510	3078	34W-2S	D3
Weston Ct					
10	SEGN	60177	2908	36W-8N	A3
10	SMWD	60107	2856	29W-11N	E4
200	BRLT	60103	2909	32W-8N	B3
300	MchT	60051	2472	29W-34N	D7
800	ELBN	60119	3017	43W-2N	A1
E Weston Ct					
600	RLKB	60073	2475	22W-36N	C4
Weston Dr					
700	CLLK	60014	2693	36W-23N	D1
W Weston Dr					
1200	ANHT	60004	2753	18W-18N	D3
Weston Ln					
100	FmtT	60060	2646	19W-27N	B1
100	MDLN	60060	2646	19W-27N	B1
1900	SMBG	60193	2858	25W-10N	A6
Weston Ridge Dr					
400	NPVL	60563	3140	30W-6S	B5
Westove Ct					
300	LslT	60540	3142	25W-6S	B4
Westover Av					
2200	FTPK	60130	3088	9W-2S	C2
2200	FTPK	60546	3088	9W-2S	C2
2200	NRIV	60546	3088	9W-2S	C2
2500	RVSD	60546	3088	9W-2S	C3
Westover Ct					
100	SMBG	60193	2858	25W-10N	B6
Westover Ln					
10	SMBG	60193	2858	25W-10N	B6
1000	SMBG	60193	2912	25W-9N	B1
Westover Rd					
10	HIWD	60035	2704	9W-24N	C1
10	HIWD	60040	2704	9W-24N	C1
2000	BtvT	60510	3077	38W-3S	A6
2000	BtvT	60542	3077	38W-3S	A6
2000	NARA	60510	3076	39W-3S	E6
2000	NARA	60542	3076	39W-3S	E6
2000	NARA	60542	3077	38W-3S	A6
3400	HDPK	60035	2650	9W-24N	C7
3400	HIWD	60035	2650	9W-24N	C7
N West Park Av					
38700	LKVL	60046	2416	23W-38N	E6
38700	LkvT	60046	2416	23W-38N	E6
West Park Dr					
100	TNLK	53181	2354		C1
Westpark Pl					
-	DRPK	60074	2752	21W-20N	C1
West Park Front St					
1000	JLET	60436	3498	25W-24S	B6
Westphalian Ct					
1700	RLKP	60030	2532	22W-31N	B7
1700	RLKP	60030	2589	22W-31N	B1
N West Pointe Dr					
-	VNHL	60061	2647	18W-25N	A5
Westport Dr					
400	PGGV	60140	2798	41W-14N	A5
8100	WLSP	60480	3208	14W-9S	D3
N Westport Dr					
600	JLET	60431	3497	28W-23S	B3
S Westport Dr					
10100	PlsT	60464	3345	12W-15S	C1
12700	PlsT	60464	3273	12W-15S	C7
W Westport Dr					
7900	FftT	60423	3504	10W-24S	C5
Westport Rdg					
1100	CLLK	60014	2693	36W-23N	D2
Westport Wy					
10600	MKNA	60448	3503	13W-23S	B3
Westport Ridge Ct					
1200	CLLK	60014	2693	36W-23N	D2
Westridge Blvd					
100	BRLT	60103	2909	32W-8N	C4
100	HnrT	60103	2909	32W-8N	C4
100	HnrT	60120	2909	32W-8N	C4
1800	BRLT	60120	2909	32W-8N	D3
1800	ELGN	60120	2909	32W-8N	D3
Westridge Ct					
600	AURA	60504	3201	32W-8S	B2
1900	RMVL	60446	3339	27W-17S	C5
13400	HTLY	60142	2744	43W-19N	B3
Westridge Dr					
600	AURA	60504	3201	33W-8S	B2
2900	WDRG	60517	3205	22W-8S	C2
3300	ISLK	60042	2586	28W-28N	E6
Westridge Pl					
1800	AURA	60504	3201	33W-8S	A2
N Westridge Pl					
1200	ADSN	60101	2970	20W-5N	B2
West Ridge Rd					
200	JLET	60431	3497	28W-23S	A4
700	TroT	60431	3497	28W-23S	A4
Westridge Rd					
3400	JLET	60431	3497	28W-23S	B4
3400	TroT	60431	3497	28W-23S	A4
Westshire Dr					
1100	JLET	60435	3498	25W-22S	B2
N Westshire Dr					
800	JLET	60435	3498	25W-22S	B3
Westshore Dr					
100	SRWD	60404	3496	30W-24S	C6
900	FXLK	60020	2414	28W-38N	E6
N West Shore Dr					
40100	AntT	60002	2416	23W-40N	E3
N Westshore Dr					
200	CHCG	60601	3034	0E-0N	D4
W West Shore Dr					
100	FmtT	60060	2646	19W-26N	C2
W Westshore Dr					
5100	MchT	60050	2527	34W-34N	C1
Westside Rd					
700	BfdT	53147	2351		A1
700	LinT	53147	2351		A1
Westside Tr					
1400	ZION	60099	2362	12W-41N	C7
West Spring Dr					
100	TNLK	53181	2354		C1
Westview Av					
600	YkTp	60148	3084	18W-1S	E2
16700	SHLD	60473	3428	0W-20S	C4
17000	TNTN	60473	3428	0W-20S	B4
17000	TNTN	60476	3428	0W-20S	B4
17100	SHLD	60476	3428	0W-20S	C4
17200	EHZC	60429	3428	0W-20S	C4
17200	EHZC	60473	3428	0W-20S	C4
Westview Ct					
200	CmpT	60175	2906	39W-7N	E5
E Westview Ct					
100	ADSN	60101	2971	18W-2N	A7
Westview Dr					
1000	EGVV	60007	2914	18W-8N	E2
2000	DSPN	60018	2862	13W-9N	D7
2200	DSPN	60018	2916	13W-9N	D1
3200	GNVW	60025	2809	11W-14N	C4
3200	NfdT	60025	2809	11W-14N	D4
3200	NfdT	60062	2809	11W-14N	C4
3300	GNVW	60062	2809	11W-14N	C4
6800	OKFT	60452	3347	8W-18S	A7
S Westview Dr					
13100	PSHT	60463	3346	9W-15S	C2
Westview Ln					
-	RLKH	60073	2474	23W-35N	E5
400	YkTp	60148	3084	18W-1S	E2
1900	RLKB	60073	2474	23W-35N	E5
5100	LSLE	60532	3143	22W-5S	C3
5100	LslT	60532	3143	22W-5S	C3
7500	LslT	60517	3205	22W-8S	C3
7500	LslT	60540	3205	22W-8S	C3
7500	WDRG	60517	3205	22W-9S	C4
8200	BGBK	60440	3205	22W-9S	C4
8200	BGBK	60517	3205	22W-9S	C4
Westview Rd					
100	NtrT	60093	2811	5W-15N	E3
100	WNKA	60093	2811	5W-15N	E3
1100	GNVW	60025	2811	7W-13N	A7
Westview St					
10	HFET	60169	2858	24W-10N	D5
100	ELGN	60124	2853	37W-12N	D2
100	ElgT	60124	2853	37W-12N	D2
Westward Dr					
2100	SPGV	60081	2413	31W-39N	E5
Westward Tr					
1100	CLSM	60188	2967	27W-3N	B5
Westward Ho Dr					
10	NHLK	60164	3028	14W-2N	C1
200	NHLK	60164	2972	14W-2N	C7
Westwaukee Rd					
10	WKGN	60085	2536	12W-33N	B1
Westway Wk					
15900	TYPK	60477	3424	9W-19S	E1
Westwind Ct					
10	HNWD	60047	2644	23W-25N	E5
2100	NPVL	60565	3204	25W-9S	A5
7100	TYPK	60477	3425	8W-20S	A3
West Wind Dr					
600	CPVL	60110	2747	35W-17N	D6
Westwind Dr					
-	AxST	60447	3672	33W-30S	B4
-	KdlT	60560	3333	43W-16S	B4
-	MNKA	60447	3672	33W-30S	B4
10	NpvT	60563	3140	30W-6S	A4
700	BGBK	60440	3268	24W-12S	D2
700	NLNX	60451	3502	15W-25S	C7
700	NLNX	60451	3590	15W-25S	C1
16700	TYPK	60477	3425	8W-20S	D3
22800	RNPK	60471	3593	6W-27S	E5
22900	RchT	60471	3593	6W-27S	E5
W Westwind Dr					
17200	WmT	60031	2477	17W-36N	B5
West Winds Ln					
18200	ODPK	60467	3422	14W-21S	E7
N Westwood Av					
-	LMBD	60181	3026	19W-1N	D3
200	VLPK	60181	3026	19W-1N	D3
500	LMBD	60148	3026	19W-1N	D2
S Westwood Av					
700	ADSN	60101	2970	19W-2N	D7
900	ADSN	60101	3026	19W-2N	D1
1000	AddT	60148	3026	18W-2N	D1
1100	ADSN	60148	3026	18W-2N	D1
W Westwood Av					
800	JLET	60436	3498	25W-24S	C6
Westwood Cir					
2700	CPVL	60110	2746	36W-17N	E6
2700	CPVL	60110	2747	36W-17N	A6
Westwood Ct					
10	IHPK	60525	3146	13W-7S	E6
10	PKFT	60466	3595	3W-26S	A2
200	SRWD	60404	3496	30W-24S	A5
300	VNHL	60061	2647	16W-24N	E7
400	CLLK	60014	2639	36W-24N	E7
600	WLNG	60090	2754	16W-17N	D6
1300	NHBK	60062	2757	10W-17N	A6
14200	WDSK	60098	2581	43W-30N	A2
17000	ODHL	60487	3424	11W-20S	A4
E Westwood Ct					
2500	CPVL	60110	2747	36W-17N	A6
S Westwood Ct					
26700	CNHN	60410	3761	32W-32S	C1
W Westwood Ct					
2600	CPVL	60110	2747	35W-17N	B7
Westwood Dr					
-	WKGN	60085	2536	12W-33N	C2
10	IHPK	60525	3146	13W-7S	E6
10	PKFT	60466	3595	3W-26S	A3
300	BRTN	60010	2750	26W-18N	D3
300	SRWD	60404	3496	30W-24S	B6
900	SMBG	60173	2805	21W-13N	C6
2200	HLSD	60154	3086	13W-2S	E3
2200	HLSD	60162	3086	13W-2S	E3
2200	WSTR	60154	3086	13W-2S	E3
3300	GwdT	60097	2469	37W-35N	B6
3500	WRLK	60097	2469	37W-35N	B6
7000	CPVL	60110	2747	36W-18N	A5
7100	CPVL	60110	2746	36W-18N	E5
7700	EDPK	60707	2974	9W-3N	B5
7900	EDPK	60171	2974	9W-3N	B5
8800	ODHL	60487	3424	11W-20S	A4
14500	ODPK	60462	3345	12W-17S	C5
N Westwood Dr					
300	WHTN	60187	3024	25W-0S	A6
5000	MchT	60050	2472	29W-36N	C3
S Westwood Dr					
10900	PSHL	60465	3274	9W-12S	C3
16300	LKPT	60441	3420	20W-19S	B3
26700	CNHN	60410	3761	32W-32S	C2
W Westwood Dr					
800	GNWD	60425	3508	0W-22S	B1
Westwood Ln					
-	BlmT	60411	3510	4E-24S	B6
-	LYWD	60411	3510	4E-24S	B6
10	LNSH	60069	2702	13W-22N	D5
10	SchT	60175	2963	36W-5N	D1
500	GLNC	60022	2758	7W-18N	B3
700	WLMT	60091	2811	5W-13N	E5
3100	LNSH	60015	2702	13W-22N	D5
3100	VrnT	60015	2702	13W-22N	D5
N Westwood Ln					
2300	PltT	60074	2752	21W-18N	D2
S Westwood Ln					
2200	PltT	60067	2805	20W-13N	E7
2300	SMBG	60067	2805	21W-12N	E7
2300	SMBG	60173	2805	21W-12N	E7
Westwood Pl					
18700	WmT	60031	2476	18W-36N	D4
18700	WmT	60046	2476	18W-36N	D4
W Westwood Pl					
18600	WmT	60031	2476	18W-36N	E4
18600	WmT	60046	2476	18W-36N	E4
Westwood Sq					
10	IHPK	60525	3146	14W-6S	D5
Westwood Tr					
14100	WDSK	60098	2581	43W-30N	A2
W Westwood Tr					
1100	ADSN	60101	2970	19W-4N	B4
Westwoods Ct					
700	CmpT	60175	2961	42W-4N	D3
Westwoods Dr					
10	CmpT	60175	2961	42W-4N	D4
Westwoods Ln					
14600	MTWA	60048	2648	14W-27N	C1
Wethersfield Ln					
100	BGBK	60440	3269	22W-12S	C2
Wethington Dr					
200	WCDA	60084	2644	25W-27N	B1
Wetumka Ct					
500	WLNG	60090	2754	16W-17N	D5
Wetzel Ct					
10	WKGN	60085	2536	11W-34N	D1
Wexford Cir					
1900	WHTN	60187	3081	26W-1S	E1
1900	WHTN	60187	3082	26W-1S	A1
Wexford Ct					
10	CRY	60013	2641	31W-24N	E6
10	LIHL	60156	2692	38W-22N	D3
10	LMNT	60439	3271	18W-13S	A5
300	CLSM	60188	2968	25W-4N	B4
500	SCRL	60175	2964	36W-4N	A3
700	GYLK	60030	2533	20W-33N	B3
800	NPVL	60540	3142	25W-7S	B7
900	LYVL	60048	2591	17W-28N	C7
1000	WHTN	60187	3082	26W-1S	A1
1100	DSPN	60016	2808	13W-13N	D6
7100	BLVY	60050	2526	36W-31N	E6
16600	TYPK	60477	3424	9W-19S	E3
Wexford Dr					
300	LMNT	60439	3270	18W-13S	E5
500	LMNT	60439	3271	18W-13S	A5
1000	WTMT	60559	3145	17W-6S	B5
11200	MKNA	60448	3502	14W-25S	E7
12700	PNFD	60585	3338	31W-15S	A1
Wexford Ln					
2300	LIHL	60156	2692	38W-22N	D3
3200	JLET	60431	3417	28W-21S	B6
15300	ODPK	60462	3346	11W-18S	A7
Wexford Pl					
1500	AURA	60564	3202	30W-9S	A5
Weybridge Dr					
10	CmpT	60175	2906	41W-7N	A6
Weybridge Ln					
10	NBRN	60010	2644	25W-24N	A6
Weyers Ct					
1400	SMBG	60193	2912	25W-8N	B2
Weymouth Av					
200	ElgT	60124	2853	38W-10N	A6
Weymouth Cir					
600	HRPK	60133	2912	25W-9N	A1
Weymouth Ct					
100	SMBG	60193	2858	26W-10N	A6
Weymouth Ln					
100	SMBG	60193	2858	25W-10N	A6
Weyrauch St					
400	WCHI	60185	3022	30W-0N	C5
Whalen Ct					
600	NARA	60542	3077	37W-3S	B6
Whalen Ln					
6500	JLET	60586	3415	32W-20S	D5
Whaler Ct					
10	TDLK	60030	2533	19W-34N	D1
Whaler Ln					
1800	HRPK	60133	2967	27W-4N	D3
Whalom Ln					
600	SMBG	60173	2859	22W-11N	C3
Wharf Dr					
2200	WDRG	60517	3205	21W-9S	E3
Wharton Dr					
500	LKFT	60045	2648	13W-25N	E5
Wheat Dr					
25200	PNFD	60585	3337	31W-15S	E2
Wheat Ln					
600	WDDL	60191	2915	18W-6N	A5
Wheatberry Ct					
600	MltT	60188	3024	25W-1N	A3
Wheatberry Dr					
10	MltT	60187	3024	25W-1N	A3
10	MltT	60188	3024	25W-1N	A3
Wheatfield Av					
-	SgrT	60554	3135	42W-4S	C1
-	SRGV	60554	3135	42W-4S	C1
Wheatfield Ct					
2600	AURA	60502	3079	32W-4S	C7
Wheatfield Dr					
1900	RMVL	60446	3339	27W-17S	B7
7800	FftT	60423	3504	9W-24S	D6
E Wheatfield Ln					
900	RLKB	60046	2475	21W-36N	C5
Wheatfield Rd					
300	MTSN	60443	3505	7W-24S	C5
Wheatfield St					
6600	WDRG	60517	3143	21W-7S	D6
Wheatland Cir					
3400	GNVA	60134	3019	37W-1N	B3
Wheatland Ct					
1000	CLLK	60014	2639	37W-24N	B7
1000	CLLK	60014	2693	37W-24N	B1
1100	YKVL	60560	3261	41W-14S	E7
2800	NPVL	60564	3202	29W-10S	C7
Wheatland Dr					
900	CLLK	60014	2639	37W-24N	B7
1000	CLLK	60014	2693	37W-24N	B1
1100	SRWD	60404	3496	30W-23S	A5
Wheatland Ln					
700	BGBK	60490	3268	26W-13S	A5
Wheatland Ln E					
800	AURA	60504	3201	31W-8S	D3
Wheatlands Wy					
10500	HTLY	60142	2692	39W-21N	C6
Wheaton Av					
400	MltT	60187	3082	24W-1S	C2
400	WHTN	60187	3082	24W-1S	C2
N Wheaton Av					
200	WHTN	60187	3024	24W-0S	C6
S Wheaton Av					
200	WHTN	60187	3024	24W-0S	C7
700	WHTN	60187	3082	24W-1S	C1
W Wheaton Av					
-	YKVL	60512	3261	43W-12S	B3
100	YKVL	60560	3261	43W-12S	B3
Wheaton Ct					
1800	WHTN	60187	3024	24W-0N	C4
Wheaton Ln					
7200	FXLK	60020	2415	28W-39N	A5
Wheaton Pl					
1000	WHTN	60187	3024	24W-0N	C5
Wheaton Rd					
10	BMDL	60108	2912	24W-6N	C7
10	BmdT	60108	2912	24W-6N	C7
10	BmdT	60172	2912	24W-6N	C7
200	ROSL	60172	2912	24W-6N	C7
Wheaton Oaks Ct					
1100	WHTN	60187	3024	25W-0N	B5
Wheaton Oaks Dr					
900	WHTN	60187	3024	25W-0N	A5
W Wheatstone Dr					
15300	HmrT	60491	3420	19W-19S	E2
Wheel Ct					
10	DRPK	60010	2699	22W-20N	A7
Wheeler Av					
600	JLET	60436	3498	25W-25S	C7
700	RKDL	60436	3498	25W-24S	C7
S Wheeler Av					
10	JLET	60435	3498	25W-24S	C6
10	JLET	60436	3498	25W-24S	C6
Wheeler Ct					
10	LMNT	60439	3270	18W-13S	E5
10	LMNT	60439	3271	17W-13S	B5
900	LYVL	60048	2591	16W-29N	D4
Wheeler Dr					
200	LMNT	60439	3270	18W-13S	E5
300	LMNT	60439	3271	18W-13S	A5
400	GNVA	60134	3020	35W-1N	C3
7000	ODPK	60462	3346	9W-18S	E7
7000	ODPK	60462	3347	8W-18S	A7
9000	ODPK	60462	3345	11W-18S	E7
Wheeler Rd					
10	SgrT	60554	3134	44W-5S	D4
10	SgrT	60554	3135	43W-5S	A4
10	SRGV	60554	3134	44W-5S	D4
10	SRGV	60554	3135	43W-5S	A4
500	BRKT	60554	3134	44W-5S	D4
W Wheeler Rd					
10	NasT	60544	3415	33W-18S	A2
10	NasT	60586	3415	33W-18S	A2
10	PNFD	60586	3415	33W-18S	A2
10	PnfT	60544	3415	33W-18S	A2
1000	BRKT	60554	3134	45W-5S	C4
1000	SRGV	60554	3134	45W-5S	C4
Wheeler St					
-	ELBN	60119	3017	42W-0N	C6
600	WDSK	60098	2524	41W-31N	C6
2000	DRGV	60516	3144	21W-7S	A7
2000	WDRG	60516	3144	21W-7S	A7
2000	WDRG	60517	3144	21W-7S	A6
2100	WDRG	60517	3143	21W-7S	E6
W Wheeler St					
-	ANHT	60004	2807	17W-16N	A1
Wheeling Av					
10	WLNG	60090	2755	14W-17N	C5
Wheeling Rd					
10	WLNG	60090	2755	14W-16N	B7
1400	WLNG	60090	2808	14W-16N	B1
N Wheeling Rd					
10	PTHT	60070	2808	15W-15N	B2
400	PTHT	60090	2808	15W-15N	B2
400	WLNG	60090	2808	15W-15N	B2

STREET Block	City	ZIP	Map#	CGS	Grid
N Wheeling Rd					
500	MPPT	60056	2808	14W-13N	B5
1200	PTHT	60056	2808	15W-14N	B5
S Wheeling Rd					
10	PTHT	60070	2808	15W-14N	B4
100	MPPT	60056	2808	15W-14N	B4
200	PTHT	60056	2808	15W-14N	B4
Wheelock St					
300	ELGN	60123	2854	34W-10N	E5
Wheelwood Ct					
3600	HLCT	60429	3426	4W-20S	D5
Whelan St					
500	LKPT	60441	3419	22W-20S	C4
Wherry Ln					
9200	ODPK	60462	3345	11W-18S	E7
Whidah Ct					
200	SMBG	60194	2858	24W-10N	C5
Whidden Av					
10	WKGN	60085	2536	11W-34N	C2
1700	DRGV	60516	3144	20W-7S	A5
Whiffin Pl					
4900	DRGV	60515	3144	19W-5S	D2
Whigam Rd					
3100	RVWD	60015	2702	13W-21N	D6
Whigham Rd					
900	RVWD	60015	2702	13W-21N	D6
Whildin Rd					
100	BGRK	60554	3134	46W-7S	A6
100	BRKT	60511	3134	46W-7S	A6
100	BRKT	60554	3134	46W-7S	A6
Whipperwill Ct					
1000	SRWD	60404	3496	30W-23S	B5
Whipple Av					
200	BTVA	60510	3078	36W-1S	A2
15700	MKHM	60428	3427	3W-18S	A1
W Whipple Dr					
3100	MTPK	60803	3276	3W-13S	E4
Whipple Ln					
400	WTMT	60559	3144	18W-7S	E6
400	WTMT	60559	3145	18W-7S	A6
Whipple St					
14000	BLID	60406	3349	3W-16S	A3
N Whipple St					
400	CHCG	60612	3032	3W-0N	E3
2000	CHCG	60647	2976	3W-2N	E6
3400	CHCG	60618	2976	3W-4N	E3
4400	CHCG	60618	2920	3W-5N	E7
4900	CHCG	60625	2920	3W-6N	E6
5800	CHCG	60659	2920	3W-7N	E4
6800	CHCG	60645	2920	3W-8N	E1
S Whipple St					
10	CHCG	60612	3032	3W-0S	E5
1100	CHCG	60623	3032	3W-0S	E6
2200	CHCG	60623	3090	3W-2S	E3
4200	CHCG	60632	3090	3W-4S	E7
5500	CHCG	60629	3150	3W-7S	E5
5500	CHCG	60632	3150	3W-6S	E3
7600	CHCG	60652	3212	3W-8S	E1
10200	CHCG	60805	3276	3W-11S	E1
10200	ENGN	60805	3212	3W-11S	E7
10200	ENGN	60805	3276	3W-11S	E1
11300	CHCG	60655	3276	3W-13S	E3
11300	MTPK	60655	3276	3W-13S	E4
11300	MTPK	60803	3276	3W-13S	E4
14500	POSN	60469	3349	3W-17S	A5
14700	MKHM	60428	3349	3W-17S	A5
14700	POSN	60428	3349	3W-17S	A5
Whipple Tree Rd					
10	WLNG	60090	2755	15W-18N	A3
Whippoorwill Ct					
10	ROSL	60172	2912	24W-7N	C4
Whippoorwill Dr					
1200	NndT	60014	2642	30W-27N	A1
S Whippoorwill Ln					
1000	PLTN	60067	2805	22W-14N	C4
Whirlaway Av					
1000	NPVL	60540	3142	26W-7S	A7
1200	LslT	60540	3142	25W-7S	A7
Whirlaway Ct					
-	RLKP	60030	2532	21W-31N	C7
-	RLKP	60030	2589	21W-31N	C1
10	CmpT	60119	2961	43W-4N	B4
300	WHTN	60187	3082	24W-2S	C4
1700	GLHT	60139	2969	23W-3N	A6
14000	HMGN	60491	3344	15W-16S	C4
Whirlaway Dr					
10	CmpT	60119	2961	42W-4N	C4
500	CmpT	60175	2906	39W-7N	E5
500	CmpT	60175	2961	42W-4N	C4
3300	NHBK	60062	2809	11W-16N	C1
3400	NfdT	60062	2809	11W-16N	C1
3500	NfdT	60062	2756	12W-16N	B7
Whirlaway Ln					
1300	HRPK	60133	2911	26W-6N	E6
Whisper Ln					
200	SRWD	60404	3496	30W-24S	C6
Whisper Creek Dr					
10	NLNX	60451	3500	19W-24S	E6
Whispering Ct					
10	SMWD	60107	2856	29W-10N	D6
300	BGBK	60440	3269	23W-12S	A3
W Whispering Ct					
1700	ADSN	60101	2970	20W-4N	A4
Whispering Dr					
10	SMWD	60107	2856	29W-10N	D7
Whispering Tr					
500	HshT	60140	2796	44W-15N	D5
Whispering Hill Dr					
11600	ODPK	60467	3422	14W-21S	D6
11600	OrlT	60467	3422	14W-21S	D6
W Whispering Hill Ln					
6900	GGnT	60449	3682	8W-31S	A4
6900	MonT	60449	3682	8W-31S	A4
Whispering Hills Ct					
1200	NPVL	60540	3141	28W-6S	A5
Whispering Hills Dr					
1100	NPVL	60540	3203	28W-8S	A2
1200	NPVL	60540	3202	28W-8S	E2
N Whispering Hills Dr					
10	NPVL	60540	3140	28W-6S	E5
S Whispering Hills Dr					
10	NPVL	60540	3140	28W-6S	E5
500	NPVL	60540	3141	28W-7S	A7
800	NPVL	60540	3203	28W-7S	A1
Whispering Hills Rd					
200	NPVL	60540	3140	29W-6S	D5
200	NPVL	60540	3141	28W-6S	A5
Whispering Lake Dr					
100	PlsT	60464	3273	12W-14S	C7
Whispering Meadow Ln					
6700	MchT	60072	2470	35W-37N	A3
6700	MchT	60097	2470	35W-37N	A2
6700	RGWD	60097	2470	35W-37N	A2
W Whispering Oak Ct					
12300	HTLY	60142	2744	42W-19N	D3
Whispering Oaks Ct					
100	WCHI	60185	3080	29W-0S	C1
700	PLTN	60074	2753	20W-18N	B3
1800	JLET	60586	3416	30W-21S	B7
2800	BFGV	60089	2701	16W-23N	C2
3100	WDRG	60517	3205	22W-9S	C3
E Whispering Oaks Ct					
600	PLTN	60074	2753	20W-18N	A2
Whispering Oaks Dr					
-	BbyT	60119	3017	43W-0S	A7
-	BFGV	60061	2701	16W-23N	C2
-	VNHL	60061	2701	16W-23N	C2
1600	JLET	60586	3496	30W-21S	B1
2900	BFGV	60089	2701	16W-23N	C2
5300	JLET	60586	3416	30W-21S	B7
N Whispering Oaks Dr					
700	PLTN	60074	2753	20W-18N	A3
Whispering Oaks Ln					
-	GYLK	60030	2532	21W-33N	E2
100	PltT	60010	2751	23W-18N	E3
1900	SRGV	60554	3134	44W-7S	E7
S Whispering Oaks Ln					
25000	CteT	60417	3687	3E-30S	B3
W Whispering Oaks Ln					
200	RDLK	60073	2531	23W-33N	E3
Whispering Pines Ct					
300	IVNS	60010	2751	25W-16N	A7
Whispering Pines Rd					
400	LNHT	60046	2418	20W-38N	B6
Whispering Pines Tr					
-	DrrT	60098	2583	37W-30N	B2
E Whispering Springs Cir					
1300	PLTN	60074	2753	18W-18N	D4
Whispering Springs Ln					
600	PltT	60124	2906	40W-9N	C1
Whispering Trail Ct					
800	SchT	60175	2907	36W-6N	D6
Whispering Trail Rd					
10	SchT	60175	2908	36W-7N	A6
100	SchT	60175	2907	36W-7N	D5
Whispering Trails Ct					
3900	HFET	60192	2804	25W-15N	B3
Whispering Trails Dr					
-	WldT	60585	3266	30W-14S	B6
3600	HFET	60192	2804	25W-14N	A3
24200	PNFD	60585	3266	30W-14S	B6
Whispering Wheat Ln					
24500	CbaT	60013	2642	28W-24N	D6
Whispering Willow Ct					
1700	WKGN	60048	2535	15W-32N	A6
Whispering Willows St					
300	SchT	60174	2908	34W-7N	D5
Whispering Winds Dr					
600	NpvT	60563	3140	30W-6S	A4
Whispering Woods Cir					
26000	PNFD	60585	3337	32W-15S	C2
Whispering Woods Ct					
26300	PNFD	60585	3337	32W-15S	B2
Whisper Meadow Ct					
5300	JLET	60586	3496	30W-22S	B2
Whisper Pointe					
-	CLSM	60188	2968	25W-3N	A6
Whispers Creek Ct					
10	HNWD	60047	2645	22W-26N	C2
Whisperwoods Ct					
3100	NfdT	60062	2756	11W-16N	D7
3100	NHBK	60062	2756	11W-16N	D7
Whistler Ct					
1500	AURA	60564	3202	30W-9S	C5
1500	NPVL	60564	3202	30W-9S	C5
Whistler Rd					
100	HDPK	60035	2650	9W-24N	D7
100	HDPK	60040	2650	9W-24N	D7
100	HIWD	60040	2650	9W-24N	D7
300	HIWD	60035	2650	9W-24N	C7
Whitaker Ct					
100	NndT	60098	2526	36W-31N	C6
Whitaker Tr					
300	MHRY	60050	2527	34W-31N	D6
Whitby Cir					
10	LNSH	60069	2702	13W-22N	E4
Whitby Ct					
10	LNSH	60069	2702	13W-22N	E3
500	BGBK	60440	3205	22W-10S	D7
Whitchurch Ct					
1000	WHTN	60187	3082	24W-1S	E2
2600	NPVL	60564	3202	29W-10S	C5
Whitchurch Ln					
2600	NPVL	60564	3202	29W-10S	D5
Whitcomb Av					
1200	DSPN	60018	2862	13W-9N	D6
1200	DSPN	60018	2863	13W-10N	A5
N Whitcomb Dr					
600	PLTN	60074	2753	19W-16N	C6
White Av					
1100	AraT	60506	3199	37W-8S	D1
1300	AURA	60506	3199	37W-8S	C1
1800	JltT	60433	3587	22W-26S	D2
7900	LYNS	60534	3088	10W-4S	B7
S White Av					
10	JLET	60433	3499	22W-24S	D5
300	JltT	60433	3499	22W-24S	D5
White Ct					
600	GRNE	60031	2534	16W-33N	E3
6800	WDRG	60517	3143	22W-7S	C7
White Dr					
2900	WDRG	60517	3143	22W-7S	C7
White Ln					
100	MNKA	60447	3583	33W-28S	B7
900	NLNX	60451	3589	18W-25S	A1
N White Ln					
500	HNVL	60030	2532	22W-33N	C2
White Pl					
1700	DRGV	60516	3206	20W-8S	A1
White Rd					
2200	ANTH	60002	2417	21W-40N	D3
2200	AntT	60002	2417	21W-40N	D3
W White Rd					
-	AntT	60002	2417	21W-40N	D3
4500	ANTH	60002	2417	20W-41N	E2
20800	ANTH	60002	2418	20W-41N	A2
20800	AntT	60002	2418	20W-41N	A2
White St					
300	GYLK	60030	2532	20W-32N	E4
300	GYLK	60030	2533	20W-32N	A4
1000	DSPN	60016	2863	12W-10N	A5
1200	DSPN	60018	2863	12W-10N	A6
3900	RcmT	60071	2413	33W-39N	A4
N White St					
10	FKFT	60423	3591	11W-25S	E1
100	FKFT	60423	3503	11W-25S	E7
S White St					
10	FKFT	60423	3591	11W-26S	E1
White Tr					
1500	EGvT	60007	2914	21W-8N	A1
1500	EGVV	60007	2913	21W-9N	E1
1500	EGVV	60007	2914	21W-9N	A1
White Ash Ct					
2400	JLET	60586	3415	33W-20S	A6
25100	PNFD	60585	3265	31W-14S	E7
White Ash Dr					
-	PNFD	60585	3265	31W-14S	E7
-	WldT	60585	3265	31W-14S	E7
7200	JSTC	60458	3148	10W-8S	A7
White Ash Ln					
4400	WldT	60564	3266	31W-12S	A3
White Ash Rd					
4200	NndT	60014	2641	33W-26N	A3
Whitebark Ct					
700	NPVL	60540	3141	28W-7S	A7
White Barn Ln					
10	GRNE	60031	2534	16W-34N	D1
White Barn Rd					
2300	AURA	60502	3079	32W-4S	C7
7000	NndT	60012	2583	36W-28N	E5
E White Barn Rd					
10	VNHL	60061	2647	16W-24N	C7
W White Barn Rd					
10	VNHL	60061	2647	17W-24N	C7
Whiteberry Av					
-	WldT	60564	3265	31W-12S	E2
-	WldT	60564	3266	31W-12S	A2
White Birch Ct					
600	MltT	60187	3082	25W-2S	A4
White Birch Dr					
4200	LSLE	60532	3082	23W-4S	E7
4200	LSLE	60532	3083	23W-4S	A7
White Birch Ln					
10	WTMT	60559	3085	18W-3S	A6
400	MltT	60187	3082	25W-2S	A4
600	LKZH	60047	2699	22W-22N	B4
2300	JLET	60435	3497	27W-23S	D4
6000	MTSN	60443	3505	7W-24S	C6
White Birch Rd					
500	LNHT	60046	2418	19W-38N	B6
White Branch Ct					
100	BFGV	60089	2701	16W-21N	D6
White Branch Ct N					
100	SMBG	60194	2857	27W-11N	D3
White Branch Ct S					
100	SMBG	60194	2857	27W-11N	D3
White Bridge Ct					
7500	HRPK	60133	2911	26W-9N	E1
White Bridge Ln					
900	HRPK	60133	2912	26W-9N	A1
1000	HRPK	60133	2911	26W-8N	E2
Whitebridge Ln					
100	WNKA	60093	2759		A6
White Bridge Rd					
100	SchT	60175	2964	36W-5N	A3
100	SCRL	60175	2964	36W-5N	A3
Whitebridge Hill Dr					
100	GLNC	60093	2759	5W-17N	A6
100	WNKA	60093	2759	5W-17N	A6
Whitebridge Hill Rd					
1100	GLNC	60093	2759	5W-17N	A6
1100	WNKA	60093	2759	5W-17N	A6
Whitecaps Ct					
-	PGGV	60140	2798	41W-14N	B5
White Chapel Ct					
10	ALGN	60102	2747	35W-19N	B3
White Chapel Ln					
1100	ALGN	60102	2747	35W-19N	B3
White Chappel Dr					
1800	MPPT	60056	2861	17W-11N	C4
Whitecliffe Dr					
2000	RMVL	60446	3339	27W-17S	B5
White Cloud Dr					
3800	SKOK	60076	2866	4W-11N	C3
6500	RchT	60443	3505	8W-25S	B7
21100	RchT	60443	3593	8W-25S	B1
White Clover Ct					
34300	GrtT	60073	2531	25W-34N	A1
White Deer Cir					
10800	ODPK	60467	3423	13W-20S	A4
White Deer Dr					
200	DGvT	60439	3207	18W-10S	A5
200	DRN	60439	3207	18W-10S	A5
3600	ALGN	60102	2746	37W-20N	B1
N White Deer Tr					
400	VNHL	60061	2647	16W-27N	D2
White Eagle Dr					
1400	AURA	60564	3202	30W-9S	A4
1500	NPVL	60564	3202	30W-9S	A5
2200	JLET	60586	3416	31W-21S	A6
White Eagle Dr W					
3900	AURA	60504	3202	30W-9S	A4
3900	AURA	60564	3202	30W-9S	A4
White Face Ct					
10600	WDSK	60098	2582	39W-30N	C1
White Fawn Tr					
100	DRGV	60516	3144	18W-6S	E4
Whitefeather Ln					
100	GLBT	60136	2799	38W-16N	C3
White Fence Ct					
200	VNHL	60061	2647	16W-24N	C6
S White Fence Ct					
20300	FftT	60423	3504	9W-24S	E6
White Fence Ln					
1600	GNOK	60048	2592	14W-30N	C2
N White Fence Ln					
1100	ADSN	60101	2970	19W-5N	C2
Whitefence Rd					
1400	BRLT	60103	2966	30W-5N	B1
White Fence Tr					
10	SMWD	60107	2856	30W-10N	C5
White Fence Wy					
500	CmpT	60175	2962	40W-5N	B2
White Gate Ct					
500	PltT	60010	2751	23W-18N	D2
Whitegate Ct					
700	MPPT	60056	2807	16W-12N	E7
Whitegate Dr					
900	MPPT	60056	2807	16W-12N	D7
Whitegate Rd					
3200	JLET	60431	3417	28W-21S	B7
Whitehall					
-	NLNX	60442	3589	17W-27S	D4
-	NLNX	60451	3589	17W-27S	D4
Whitehall Av					
10	NHLK	60164	2972	14W-2N	D7
300	MLPK	60160	2973	13W-2N	A7
300	MLPK	60164	2973	13W-2N	A7
300	NHLK	60160	2973	13W-2N	A7
300	NHLK	60164	2973	13W-2N	A7
Whitehall Ct					
10	BFGV	60089	2754	17W-18N	A2
10	SMWD	60107	2857	26W-11N	E4
100	GYLK	60030	2533	19W-33N	C3
200	WNVL	60555	3080	30W-2S	B4
700	SMBG	60194	2858	25W-11N	A4
1000	BGBK	60440	3205	21W-9S	D4
1200	LKZH	60047	2699	21W-21N	C5
1500	BTVA	60510	3077	36W-1S	D1
1600	WLNG	60090	2754	16W-18N	D3
1900	JltT	60433	3587	23W-26S	A3
2400	AURA	60504	3201	32W-8S	C2
4500	ALGN	60102	2693	38W-21N	A6
E Whitehall Ct					
600	RLKB	60073	2475	22W-36N	C4
S Whitehall Ct					
100	PLTN	60067	2805	22W-15N	B1
W Whitehall Ct					
21800	AntT	60002	2417	21W-40N	C3
Whitehall Dr					
-	LYWD	60411	3509	2E-23S	D4
-	MDLN	60060	2647	17W-25N	B5
900	BFGV	60089	2754	17W-18N	A2
1000	ANHT	60004	2754	17W-18N	A2
1000	ANHT	60089	2754	17W-18N	A2
1000	NHBK	60062	2757	9W-17N	C5
S Whitehall Dr					
-	MDLN	60060	2647	17W-25N	B6
200	PLTN	60067	2805	22W-15N	A2
W Whitehall Dr					
-	ANHT	60089	2754	18W-18N	A2
-	BFGV	60089	2754	18W-18N	A2
200	ANHT	60004	2754	18W-18N	A2
300	ANHT	60004	2753	18W-20N	D2
Whitehall Gdn					
9700	MNSR	46321	3510		D4
Whitehall Gdns					
10200	MNSR	46321	3510		D5
Whitehall Ln					
2500	NPVL	60564	3202	29W-9S	C5
4000	ALGN	60102	2693	37W-21N	A6
4200	RNPK	60471	3594	5W-26S	C3
9200	ODPK	60462	3345	11W-18S	E7
Whitehall Rd					
-	NLNX	60442	3589	17W-26S	D3
-	NLNX	60451	3589	17W-26S	D3
-	NlxT	60451	3589	17W-26S	D3
Whitehall St					
1100	LMBD	60148	3083	21W-1S	E2
White Hall Ter					
300	BMDL	60108	2968	24W-4N	C3
Whitehall Wy					
500	BGBK	60440	3205	21W-9S	D4
900	CLLK	60014	2693	37W-23N	C1
Whitehaven Ln					
-	LKPT	60441	3419	21W-20S	E5
Whitehill Dr					
100	RMVL	60446	3339	27W-17S	B6
Whitehorse Ln					
1400	BRLT	60103	2910	30W-6N	B7
White Lake Dr					
-	ANTH	60002	2418	20W-40N	A3
White Mountain Dr					
1000	NHBK	60062	2756	11W-17N	D5
White Oak Cir					
2100	NHBK	60062	2756	11W-16N	C7
2200	AURA	60502	3139	32W-5S	C2
2600	NpvT	60502	3139	32W-5S	C2
3200	CPVL	60110	2747	35W-17N	C6
White Oak Ct					
-	NARA	60542	3077	38W-4S	B7
10	ALGN	60102	2747	36W-19N	A2
100	SMBG	60195	2859	23W-12N	A1
200	BRTN	60010	2751	24W-20N	D1
300	GRNE	60031	2535	14W-33N	D2
2800	BFGV	60089	2701	17W-23N	B2
4600	PRGV	60012	2641	32W-27N	B1
11600	BRRG	60527	3208	14W-9S	D2
18300	TYPK	60487	3424	11W-21S	A7
Whiteoak Ct					
2600	MHRY	60050	2527	35W-34N	B1
S White Oak Ct					
10	PSHT	60463	3274	9W-14S	C5
W White Oak Ct					
12800	HMGN	60491	3422	16W-19S	A2
White Oak Dr					
-	AntT	60002	2358		E4
-	BtlT	53104	2358		D3
-	BtlT	60002	2358		E4
10	NARA	60542	3137	37W-4S	B1
100	LNHT	60046	2418	20W-38N	A7
100	LNHT	60046	2476	19W-38N	B1
100	NARA	60542	3077	37W-3S	B7
100	WHTN	60187	3024	25W-0S	A7
200	NPVL	60540	3141	26W-6S	E6
200	WnfT	60185	3081	28W-1S	A1
300	WNVL	60555	3080	29W-3S	D6
400	ROSL	60172	2913	22W-6N	B6
1700	ALGN	60102	2747	36W-19N	A2
2100	NfdT	60062	2756	11W-16N	C7
2100	NHBK	60062	2756	11W-16N	C7
2200	NfdT	60062	2809	11W-15N	C1
2200	NHBK	60062	2809	11W-15N	C1
12100	PNFD	60585	3266	30W-14S	B7
Whiteoak Dr					
6000	MHRY	60050	2527	35W-34N	B1
6200	MHRY	60050	2470	35W-34N	B7
S White Oak Dr					
-	WKGN	60085	2536	13W-32N	A5
1200	WKGN	60085	2535	13W-32N	E5
White Oak Ln					
-	HFET	60120	2856	31W-12N	A1
-	HnrT	60120	2856	31W-12N	A1
10	CmpT	60175	2961	41W-6N	E1
10	ELGN	60123	2799	36W-13N	E7
100	WYNE	60184	2966	30W-4N	B3
200	WNKA	60093	2812	5W-15N	A2
300	LKBN	60010	2643	26W-24N	D6
400	RVWD	60015	2755	13W-20N	D1
500	BtvT	60510	3077	37W-2S	B4
600	BRLT	60103	2856	29W-9N	C7
600	BRLT	60103	2910	29W-9N	C1
800	UYPK	60466	3684	3W-30S	B2
1300	WCHI	60185	2966	30W-2N	C7
1300	WCHI	60185	3022	30W-2N	C1
1300	WynT	60185	3022	30W-2N	C1
1400	WDSK	60098	2582	40W-30N	B1
1600	HFET	60192	2856	31W-12N	A1
1600	SMBG	60195	2859	23W-12N	A1
2500	LSLE	60532	3142	24W-7S	D6
3000	OKBK	60523	3084	18W-3S	E5
3100	DRGV	60515	3084	18W-3S	E5
3100	OKBK	60515	3084	18W-3S	E5
18300	TYPK	60487	3424	11W-22S	A7
N White Oak Ln					
34000	WrnT	60031	2534	17W-34N	B2
S White Oak Ln					
24900	CteT	60417	3686	2E-30S	D3
White Oak Rd					
500	BGBK	60440	3269	21W-11S	D1
1400	LKFT	60045	2703	12W-24N	B1
White Oak St					
200	HPSR	60140	2796	46W-16N	A2
E White Oak St					
10	ANHT	60005	2861	18W-12N	A1
W White Oak St					
10	ANHT	60005	2861	18W-12N	A1
500	ANHT	60005	2860	19W-12N	D1
1700	ANHT	60008	2860	19W-12N	D1
1700	RGMW	60008	2860	19W-12N	D1
2100	MPPT	60005	2861	17W-12N	B1
2100	MPPT	60056	2861	17W-12N	B1
White Oak Tr					
25900	CNHN	60410	3672	33W-31S	C6
White Oak Wy					
600	YKVL	60560	3333	43W-15S	B2
White Oaks Cir					
10	SCRL	60174	3020	35W-2N	B2
White Oaks Ct					
-	GwdT	60097	2469	37W-36N	B3
-	WRLK	60097	2469	37W-36N	C3
5300	JLET	60586	3496	30W-21S	B1
White Oaks Dr					
400	CRY	60013	2642	30W-24N	B7
Whiteoaks Ln					
700	HDPK	60035	2704	8W-21N	E6
White Oaks Rd					
10	FXLK	60020	2473	27W-37N	A3
10	MTSN	60443	3505	7W-24S	C5
7900	MchT	60097	2469	37W-37N	C3
7900	WRLK	60097	2469	37W-37N	C3
8000	GwdT	60097	2469	37W-37N	C3
White Owl Ln					
500	OSWG	60543	3262	39W-11S	E2
White Pigeon Rd					
700	BfdT	53147	2351		C1
White Pine Ct					
1200	YKVL	60560	3260	44W-14S	E7
15600	HMGN	60491	3422	15W-18S	C1
20000	FftT	60448	3502	14W-24S	E5
20000	MKNA	60448	3502	14W-24S	E5
White Pine Dr					
10	SMBG	60193	2858	23W-10N	E5
10	SMBG	60193	2859	23W-10N	A5
800	CRY	60013	2642	30W-24N	B7
900	ANTH	60002	2358	22W-42N	B6
2800	NHBK	60062	2756	11W-16N	D7
White Pine Ln					
10	LKVL	60046	2475	22W-37N	A2
800	CmpT	60175	2962	39W-4N	E3
1400	BGBK	60490	3267	26W-13S	E4
4100	ZION	60099	2421	12W-41N	B1
W White Pine Pl					
7600	PSHT	60463	3274	9W-15S	D7
White Pine Rd					
10	AddT	60106	2971	17W-4N	C3
400	BFGV	60089	2754	17W-18N	B4
500	ADSN	60106	2971	17W-4N	B3
500	BNVL	60106	2971	17W-4N	C3
W White Pine Rd					
21200	KLDR	60047	2699	22W-21N	B7
22000	ElaT	60074	2699	21W-21N	C7
22000	KLDR	60074	2699	21W-21N	C7
White Pine Tr					
1000	PGGV	60140	2797	42W-15N	E4
6800	DRN	60561	3145	17W-7S	B7
12100	HMGN	60491	3422	15W-18S	C1
12200	HMGN	60491	3344	15W-18S	C7
White Pine Wy					
-	PNFD	60585	3337	33W-15S	A2
6500	GRNE	60048	2534	16W-32N	C6
White Pines Cir					
600	LIHL	60156	2693	37W-22N	B4
White Pines Ct					
300	OSWG	60543	3263	37W-13S	C6
600	LIHL	60156	2693	37W-22N	B4
1600	NPVL	60563	3141	28W-4S	A2
White Pines Dr					
10	LKBN	60010	2643	26W-24N	C6
10	TRLK	60010	2643	26W-24N	C6
White Pines Ln					
10	HshT	60140	2796	44W-14N	E5
300	OSWG	60543	3263	37W-13S	C6
White Rabbit Tr					
-	GrtT	60051	2472	28W-34N	E7
Whitesail Dr					
700	SMBG	60194	2859	22W-10N	C5
White Sands Bay					
500	ROSL	60172	2913	22W-8N	B3
N White Sands Bay					
1700	PLTN	60074	2753	18W-18N	D4
S Whiteside Ct					
500	JLET	60435	3497	27W-23S	C4
Whiteside Dr					
300	JLET	60435	3497	27W-23S	C4
Whitespire Ct					
1400	NPVL	60565	3204	25W-8S	B2
White Tail Cir					
-	MRGO	60152	2634	49W-27N	C1
Whitetail Cir					
500	HPSR	60140	2795	47W-15N	D3
Whitetail Cross					
200	OSWG	60543	3263	38W-11S	B2
White Tail Ct					
800	MRGO	60152	2634	49W-27N	D1
4100	JLET	60431	3496	29W-23S	E4
20100	ELWD	60421	3675	25W-30S	C5
White Tail Dr					
-	MRGO	60152	2634	49W-27N	D1
300	HNVL	60030	2532	21W-33N	C3
2600	SPGV	60081	2413	31W-40N	D3
Whitetail Dr					
2000	AURA	60503	3201	33W-10S	B6
3400	WRLK	60097	2469	38W-35N	A5
White Tail Ln					
300	FXLK	60041	2473	27W-35N	C6
300	GrtT	60041	2473	27W-35N	C6
12100	HTLY	60142	2744	42W-18N	E4
Whitetail Ln					
10	PltT	60010	2751	23W-18N	D3
900	SDWH	60548	3258	51W-14S	A7
Whitetail Pl					
-	MRGO	60152	2634	49W-27N	D1
White Tail Run					
10600	ODPK	60467	3423	13W-20S	A5
Whitetail Tr					
10	CbaT	60010	2643	26W-25N	E5
10	TRLK	60010	2643	26W-25N	E5
White Tail Wy					
14900	LKPT	60441	3342	21W-17S	A5
14900	LktT	60441	3342	21W-17S	A6
White Tailed Ln					
6700	TYPK	60477	3425	8W-21S	B7
White Thorn Av					
2800	NPVL	60564	3202	29W-10S	C5
White Thorn Dr					
2000	AURA	60503	3201	31W-10S	D6

STREET Block	City	ZIP	Map#	CGS	Grid
White Thorne Rd					
10	SchT	60184	2964	34W-4N	E3
200	WYNE	60174	2964	34W-5N	E3
200	WYNE	60184	2964	34W-5N	E3
500	SchT	60174	2965	33W-5N	A2
500	SchT	60184	2965	33W-5N	A2
500	SCRL	60174	2965	33W-5N	A2
500	WYNE	60174	2965	33W-5N	A2
500	WYNE	60184	2965	33W-5N	A2
White Water Ct					
10	NLNX	60451	3500	19W-24S	D6
Whitewater Dr					
200	BGBK	60440	3268	24W-11S	D1
300	BGBK	60440	3204	24W-11S	D7
Whitewater Ln					
300	OSWG	60543	3263	38W-12S	A2
900	NPVL	60540	3202	28W-8S	E1
E White Water Ln					
1200	PLTN	60074	2753	19W-18N	C4
Whiteway Ct					
2500	AURA	60504	3201	32W-8S	C2
S White Willow Bay					
700	PLTN	60067	2805	22W-15N	B3
Whitewood Dr					
200	SMWD	60107	2857	27W-10N	C5
Whitfield Dr					
100	GNVA	60134	3020	33W-1N	E3
100	GnvT	60134	3020	33W-1N	E4
200	SRGV	60554	3135	42W-6S	D5
Whitfield Rd					
900	NHBK	60062	2757	8W-17N	E5
1100	NHBK	60062	2758	8W-17N	A5
6500	FoxT	60541	3331	48W-17S	A6
6500	FoxT	60545	3331	48W-17S	A6
Whitier Pl					
-	CmpT	60175	2962	39W-3N	D6
Whiting Ct					
100	VNHL	60061	2647	17W-26N	C4
2700	MHRY	60050	2470	34W-34N	C7
Whiting Dr					
5600	MHRY	60050	2470	34W-34N	B7
W Whiting Ln					
600	ANHT	60004	2753	18W-18N	E3
Whiting Wy					
26000	MONE	60449	3682	7W-31S	D6
Whitingham Cir					
1200	NPVL	60540	3142	25W-7S	A6
Whitingham Ln					
1800	HFET	60169	2858	26W-12N	A1
Whitley Av					
500	JLET	60433	3499	23W-24S	B5
E Whitley Av					
700	JLET	60433	3499	22W-24S	C5
Whitley Rd					
1500	NPVL	60563	3140	29W-5S	D3
Whitlock Av					
700	AraT	60506	3198	38W-8S	E2
800	AraT	60538	3198	38W-8S	E2
Whitlock Ct					
600	AraT	60506	3198	39W-8S	D2
Whitlock Dr					
2700	DRN	60561	3206	19W-9S	C2
Whitman Av					
17100	HLCT	60429	3427	3W-20S	A4
Whitman Ct					
800	LbvT	60048	2592	15W-29N	B4
1400	SMBG	60173	2859	21W-10N	E5
Whitman Dr					
10	SMBG	60173	2859	21W-10N	E5
100	SMBG	60193	2859	21W-10N	E6
2100	GLHT	60139	2969	23W-4N	A4
Whitman Ln					
1500	WHTN	60187	3082	24W-1S	C2
18000	LNSG	60438	3429	2E-21S	C6
Whitman Pl					
1100	VNHL	60061	2647	17W-27N	C1
Whitman Ter					
10	HNWD	60047	2645	22W-25N	B5
W Whitmore Ct					
1200	LKFT	60045	2649	12W-27N	B2
Whitmore Dr					
1900	RMVL	60446	3339	27W-17S	C6
Whitmore Ln					
300	LNSH	60045	2702	14W-23N	C1
1000	GNEN	60137	3025	21W-0S	E7
1000	MltT	60148	3025	21W-0S	E7
Whitmore Tr					
200	MHRY	60050	2527	34W-32N	C5
Whitmore Wy					
5400	LIHL	60156	2692	38W-21N	D6
Whitney Av					
500	WPHR	60096	2363	9W-42N	B6
21200	MTSN	60443	3593	7W-25S	C1
N Whitney Av					
300	JLET	60435	3498	24W-23S	D4
Whitney Ct					
600	GRNE	60031	2534	16W-33N	D2
1400	NARA	60542	3077	37W-3S	B7
Whitney Dr					
100	BRTN	60010	2751	25W-20N	B2
1700	HRPK	60133	2967	27W-5N	D1
Whitney Ln					
10	DGvT	60439	3270	20W-12S	C3
1300	BFGV	60089	2701	16W-21N	C6
Whitney Pl					
100	VNHL	60061	2647	17W-26N	B3
Whitney Rd					
10	CmpT	60175	2962	41W-5N	A2
100	WynT	60185	2966	30W-4N	B4
200	LKZH	60047	2698	24W-22N	C3
3000	AURA	60502	3139	31W-5S	D3
Whitney St					
1600	WKGN	60087	2479	11W-37N	E3
N Whitney St					
10	GYLK	60030	2532	20W-33N	E4
S Whitney St					
10	GYLK	60030	2532	20W-33N	E4
Whitney Ter					
400	JLET	60435	3498	24W-23S	D4
Whitney Wy					
10	OswT	60538	3199	36W-10S	E6
E Whitson St					
200	MHTN	60442	3678	19W-31S	A5
Whitt Ct					
1700	WHTN	60187	3082	23W-2S	E3
Whitten St					
500	FXLK	60041	2473	26W-35N	C5
Whittier Av					
400	GNEN	60137	3025	21W-0N	D5
400	MltT	60137	3025	21W-0N	D5
500	DRFD	60015	2703	10W-20N	E7
500	DRFD	60015	2704	10W-20N	A7
17100	HLCT	60429	3427	3W-20S	B4
N Whittier Av					
300	JLET	60435	3498	24W-23S	D4
Whittier Ct					
200	SMBG	60193	2858	25W-10N	A6
Whittier Dr					
7200	DRN	60561	3207	18W-8S	A1
Whittier Ln					
400	MDLN	60060	2646	18W-26N	E2
400	NHFD	60093	2811	7W-15N	A2
1500	WHTN	60187	3082	24W-1S	C2
1800	SMBG	60193	2858	25W-10N	A6
Whittingham Cir					
-	DRN	60561	3207	17W-9S	C3
Whittingham Ln					
13600	HTLY	60142	2744	43W-18N	B4
Whittington Ct					
300	LslT	60540	3205	23W-8S	A2
1000	GRNE	60031	2477	17W-35N	B6
Whittington Dr					
900	GNVA	60134	3020	34W-1N	E2
7800	TYPK	60477	3424	9W-19S	C2
Whittington Ln					
400	WldT	60564	3202	29W-10S	E6
400	WldT	60564	3266	29W-11S	E1
Whittington Course					
10	SCRL	60174	2964	34W-4N	D4
W Whytecliff Rd					
1000	PLTN	60067	2805	22W-15N	A2
1300	IVNS	60067	2805	22W-15N	B2
Whytegate Ct					
300	LNSH	60045	2702	14W-23N	D2
Wianno Ln					
200	SMBG	60194	2858	24W-10N	C5
Wiant Rd					
10	WynT	60185	2966	30W-4N	B4
100	WCHI	60185	2966	30W-3N	C6
100	WYNE	60184	2966	30W-4N	B4
100	WYNE	60185	2966	30W-4N	B4
Wichman Rd					
-	BNHL	60118	2802	29W-14N	C5
-	HFET	60118	2802	29W-14N	C5
-	HFET	60192	2802	29W-13N	C5
Wick Dr					
4800	OKLN	60453	3276	6W-11S	A1
4900	OKLN	60453	3211	6W-11S	E7
5000	OKLN	60453	3275	6W-11S	E1
Wick Wy					
-	MTGY	60506	3198	40W-9S	B4
-	MTGY	60538	3198	40W-9S	B4
Wicke Av					
900	DSPN	60018	2862	13W-10N	E6
1300	DSPN	60018	2863	12W-10N	A5
Wickenden Av					
-	ElgT	60124	2853	38W-11N	B5
Wicker Av					
600	SMWD	60107	2857	28W-9N	B7
600	SMWD	60107	2911	28W-9N	B1
Wicker Dr					
200	DRPK	60010	2699	22W-20N	B7
200	DRPK	60010	2752	22W-20N	B1
Wicker St					
700	WDSK	60098	2524	42W-31N	C6
N Wicker Park Av					
1400	CHCG	60622	3033	2W-1N	C1
Wickfield Ct					
1100	NPVL	60563	3142	25W-5S	A3
Wickham Av					
100	BMDL	60108	2968	24W-5N	C2
Wickham Ct					
1000	NPVL	60540	3142	24W-7S	D7
1100	NPVL	60540	3204	24W-8S	D1
1600	GNOK	60048	2592	14W-30N	C3
Wickham Dr					
200	SMBG	60194	2858	25W-10N	C5
W Wicklow Ln					
2000	RDLK	60073	2531	25W-33N	A3
2100	GrtT	60073	2531	25W-33N	A3
Wicklow Rd					
500	DRFD	60015	2757	9W-20N	B1
600	DRFD	60015	2704	10W-20N	B7
1800	NPVL	60564	3266	29W-12S	E3
Wicks St					
100	GYLK	60030	2532	20W-32N	E5
400	GYLK	60030	2533	20W-32N	A5
Widgeon Dr					
700	ANHT	60004	2754	16W-17N	D5
700	WLNG	60004	2754	16W-17N	D5
700	WLNG	60090	2754	16W-17N	D5
Widgeon Ln					
10	BmdT	60108	2967	26W-5N	E2
10	BmdT	60108	2968	26W-5N	A2
Widmayer Rd					
10	HPSR	60140	2743	46W-17N	B7
10	HshT	60140	2743	46W-17N	B7
700	HPSR	60140	2796	46W-16N	B1
700	HshT	60140	2796	46W-16N	B1
Widows Rd					
700	WMTN	60481	3853	28W-37S	A5
1000	WmTp	60481	3853	28W-37S	B5
Wieboldt Dr					
200	DSPN	60016	2862	14W-11N	D3
Wiedrich Rd					
100	RcmT	60071	2412	35W-38N	B7
N Wieland St					
1400	CHCG	60610	2978		D7
1400	CHCG	60610	3034	0W-1N	B1
1400	CHCG	60614	2978		D7
Wienecke Ct					
23100	LKBN	60010	2697	26W-23N	C2
Wiesbrock Ln					
1700	BTVA	60510	3078	34W-2S	E5
1700	BtvT	60510	3078	34W-3S	E5
Wiesbrook Rd					
-	OSWG	60538	3200	35W-10S	A6
-	OswT	60538	3200	35W-10S	A6
1900	OSWG	60543	3200	35W-10S	B6
S Wiesbrook Rd					
400	MltT	60187	3081	26W-2S	D4
400	WHTN	60187	3081	27W-2S	D4
400	WnfT	60187	3081	27W-2S	D4
500	WnfT	60555	3081	27W-2S	D4
W Wiesbrook Rd					
300	MltT	60187	3081	26W-2S	E3
300	WHTN	60187	3081	26W-2S	E3
1500	WHTN	60187	3082	25W-1S	A2
Wigeon Ct					
22900	PNFD	60585	3339	28W-15S	A2
Wiggington Dr					
700	CLLK	60014	2639	37W-24N	B7
Wight St					
10200	WSTR	60154	3087	12W-1S	A1
Wigtown Ct					
1000	WHTN	60187	3082	24W-1S	E2
W Wigwam Tr					
1400	MPPT	60056	2861	16W-12N	C1
Wilber St					
500	ELGN	60123	2854	34W-10N	E6
Wilbrandt St					
100	ALGN	60102	2747	33W-20N	D2
Wilbur Av					
500	WnfT	60555	3081	27W-3S	C6
500	WNVL	60555	3081	27W-3S	C6
Wilbur Ct					
500	GRNE	60031	2534	15W-33N	E3
600	GRNE	60031	2535	15W-33N	A3
Wilco Blvd					
500	CTHL	60441	3418	24W-18S	D2
500	RMVL	60441	3418	24W-18S	D2
Wilco Dr					
14900	ODPK	60467	3344	15W-17S	C6
15000	HMGN	60491	3344	15W-17S	C6
Wilcox Av					
10	ELGN	60123	2854	34W-11N	D5
700	MDLN	60060	2590	18W-27N	E7
800	MDLN	60060	2591	18W-27N	A7
2900	BLWD	60104	3029	12W-0S	B5
3800	OKBK	60523	3084	18W-3S	E6
3800	YkTp	60515	3084	18W-3S	E6
3800	YkTp	60523	3084	18W-3S	E6
3900	BLWD	60162	3029	12W-0S	A5
3900	HLSD	60162	3029	12W-0S	A5
4900	DRGV	60515	3144	18W-5S	E2
5500	DRGV	60516	3144	18W-6S	E4
7000	DRN	60561	3144	18W-8S	E7
Wilcox Ct					
200	BRLT	60103	2911	28W-7N	A5
Wilcox Dr					
100	BRLT	60103	2910	29W-7N	E5
100	BRLT	60103	2911	28W-7N	A5
Wilcox St					
10	MYWD	60153	3030	10W-0S	A5
700	MYWD	60153	3029	10W-0S	E5
1600	CTHL	60403	3498	24W-21S	D1
1600	JLET	60435	3498	24W-21S	D1
1700	CTHL	60403	3418	24W-21S	D7
7600	FTPK	60130	3030	9W-0S	C5
E Wilcox St					
-	HMND	46320	3352		D5
N Wilcox St					
100	JLET	60435	3498	24W-23S	D4
W Wilcox St					
2300	CHCG	60612	3033	2W-0S	B5
2800	CHCG	60612	3032	3W-0S	E5
3800	CHCG	60624	3032	5W-0S	B5
4500	CHCG	60644	3032	5W-0S	A5
Wild Wy					
-	HNWD	60047	2646	20W-24N	A6
Wild Ash Ln					
5700	NndT	60012	2584	34W-28N	B5
Wild Berry Ct					
-	SRWD	60404	3584	31W-25S	A2
Wildberry Ct					
100	AURA	60504	3202	31W-8S	A1
300	SMBG	60193	2859	22W-9N	D7
1100	WLNG	60090	2754	16W-18N	D3
36900	WrnT	60046	2476	18W-36N	D3
Wildberry Dr					
1700	GNVW	60025	2810	8W-15N	D3
1700	NHFD	60025	2810	8W-15N	E3
1700	NHFD	60093	2810	8W-15N	E3
Wild Berry Ln					
11200	MKNA	60448	3502	14W-24S	E4
11300	FftT	60448	3502	14W-24S	E4
Wildberry Ln					
300	BRLT	60103	2967	28W-5N	B2
6500	AlqT	60013	2642	29W-25N	B4
Wild Briar Ln					
600	PltT	60124	2852	40W-10N	B6
Wild Cat Wy					
-	NPVL	60564	3202	29W-11S	D7
Wild Cherry Ct					
2400	AURA	60506	3136	39W-6S	E5
Wild Cherry Ln					
10	PSPK	60464	3273	12W-14S	C7
100	NpvT	60540	3141	28W-7S	B6
600	NPVL	60540	3141	28W-7S	B6
9600	PlsT	60464	3273	12W-14S	C7
Wild Cherry Rd					
4600	NndT	60012	2640	35W-27N	A1
Wild Dunes Cir					
2400	AURA	60503	3201	32W-11S	C7
2500	AURA	60503	3265	31W-11S	D1
Wild Dunes Ct					
700	RVWD	60015	2703	13W-20N	A7
2000	GNVA	60134	3019	36W-0S	D6
2500	AURA	60503	3201	32W-11S	D7
Wilder Ct					
1100	NPVL	60540	3202	28W-8S	E1
Wilder Ln					
200	EMHT	60126	3027	16W-1N	E2
Wilder St					
100	AURA	60506	3138	35W-7S	A7
600	ELGN	60123	2854	34W-11N	D3
1300	EVTN	60202	2867	3W-10N	A4
3300	SKOK	60076	2866	4W-10N	D4
Wilderness Ct					
4800	LGGV	60047	2700	18W-23N	E2
S Wilderness Ct					
25200	CNHN	60410	3672	32W-30S	C5
Wilderness Rdg					
3800	NndT	60012	2584	35W-28N	B6
Wilderness Tr					
20200	OMFD	60461	3507	4W-24S	A5
Wildewoode Wy					
17000	CCHL	60478	3426	4W-20S	D4
Wild Fire Dr					
-	VLPK	60181	3027	18W-2N	A1
Wildflower Cir					
-	SRWD	60404	3496	31W-22S	A2
100	BFGV	60089	2701	16W-20N	C7
700	NPVL	60540	3140	29W-7S	D7
Wildflower Ct					
-	SPGV	60072	2413	33W-39N	A5
100	RLKB	60073	2475	22W-36N	A3
600	NPVL	60540	3140	29W-7S	D7
1700	SMBG	60173	2860	21W-10N	A5
2200	GNVA	60134	3019	36W-0S	E6
2800	NHBK	60025	2809	11W-15N	D1
5100	JLET	60586	3496	30W-21S	B1
W Wildflower Ct					
1000	VNHL	60061	2646	18W-24N	E7
Wildflower Dr					
-	FftT	60477	3504	11W-24S	A4
-	TroT	60404	3496	31W-22S	A3
900	SRWD	60404	3496	31W-22S	A3
1600	JLET	60586	3496	30W-21S	B1
19900	FKFT	60423	3504	11W-24S	A5
Wild Flower Ln					
500	WynT	60185	2966	29W-3N	D5
1700	AURA	60504	3201	33W-9S	A3
Wildflower Ln					
-	SMBG	60173	2859	21W-10N	E6
-	SMBG	60193	2859	21W-10N	E6
10	SMBG	60173	2860	20W-10N	A6
100	CLLK	60014	2640	33W-26N	D3
100	RLKB	60073	2475	22W-36N	B3
200	WLSP	60525	3208	13W-8S	E2
1000	DYR	46311	3510		D7
6200	GRNE	60031	2534	16W-34N	C2
6400	WrnT	60031	2534	16W-34N	C1
12100	HTLY	60142	2744	43W-19N	B2
24700	MHTN	60442	3677	19W-30S	E3
Wildflower Rd					
10500	ODPK	60462	3345	13W-17S	B5
21600	MTSN	60443	3594	4W-26S	E2
Wildflower Wy					
10	HnrT	60107	2856	30W-10N	C6
10	HnrT	60120	2856	30W-10N	C6
10	SMWD	60107	2856	30W-10N	B5
300	BGBK	60440	3268	23W-12S	E3
300	BGBK	60440	3269	23W-12S	A3
500	SMWD	60120	2856	30W-10N	B5
12300	HBRN	60034	2350	41W-41N	D7
18700	WrnT	60046	2476	18W-36N	D4
Wild Ginger Rd					
700	SRGV	60554	3135	41W-5S	E2
700	SRGV	60554	3136	41W-5S	A2
Wild Ginger Tr					
900	WCHI	60185	3022	29W-2N	D2
900	WnfT	60185	3022	29W-2N	D2
Wildhorse Dr					
2100	AURA	60503	3201	33W-10S	B6
Wild Indigo Av					
600	RMVL	60446	3340	25W-15S	C1
Wild Indigo Rd					
1300	GYLK	60030	2533	19W-31N	C7
Wild Iris Ln					
1400	GYLK	60030	2533	19W-32N	C5
Wildlife Wy					
10	LGGV	60047	2646	19W-24N	C7
Wildmeadow Dr					
500	BGBK	60490	3267	26W-13S	D4
1200	RDLK	60073	2531	23W-31N	E6
1200	RDLK	60073	2532	23W-31N	A6
Wild Meadow Ln					
3000	AURA	60504	3201	31W-8S	D1
Wildmere Dr					
10	ELGN	60123	2853	36W-12N	D3
10	ElgT	60123	2853	36W-12N	D3
800	ElgT	60124	2853	36W-12N	D3
Wildmint Tr					
1400	ELGN	60123	2907	36W-8N	E3
Wild Oak Ct					
10	LMNT	60439	3271	18W-14S	B6
3200	JLET	60431	3497	28W-23S	B3
Wild Oak Dr					
1000	LMNT	60439	3271	18W-14S	A6
Wild Olive Ln					
5700	NndT	60012	2584	34W-28N	B5
Wildplum Ct					
10	LMNT	60439	3271	18W-14S	A6
Wild Plum Dr					
5900	NndT	60014	2641	33W-26N	A3
Wild Plum St					
2700	WDRG	60517	3143	22W-7S	D7
Wild Prairie Ln					
3400	GNVA	60134	3019	37W-0N	B5
Wild Prairie Pointe					
-	HPSR	60140	2795	47W-16N	D1
Wildridge St					
11200	WSTR	60154	3086	14W-2S	D3
Wild Rock Ter					
300	RchT	60443	3593	8W-26S	B1
Wild Rose Cir					
-	LKVL	60046	2474	23W-37N	D3
Wild Rose Ct					
1700	NPVL	60565	3204	24W-10S	D5
Wildrose Ct					
-	CPVL	60110	2748	33W-17N	A6
-	DRPK	60010	2699	23W-21N	A7
10	HnrT	60107	2856	29W-9N	E7
10	SMWD	60107	2856	29W-9N	E7
300	BGBK	60440	3269	23W-12S	A2
1700	HDPK	60035	2704	10W-22N	A3
S Wildrose Ct					
200	RDLK	60073	2531	23W-33N	E4
Wildrose Dr					
800	CRY	60013	2642	30W-24N	B7
1900	CTHL	60403	3417	27W-21S	D7
11400	HTLY	60142	2691	41W-20N	C7
11600	HTLY	60142	2744	42W-20N	C1
N Wildrose Dr					
20700	DRPK	60010	2698	23W-20N	E7
21000	DRPK	60010	2699	23W-21N	A7
W Wild Rose Dr					
26300	CNHN	60410	3672	33W-31S	C7
Wild Rose Ln					
300	RMVL	60446	3340	25W-16S	C3
300	SchT	60174	2963	36W-3N	E5
1200	LKFT	60045	2703	12W-24N	B1
1500	AURA	60504	3200	33W-9S	E3
4900	LGGV	60047	2700	19W-23N	C2
15600	ODPK	60462	3346	9W-18S	E7
Wild Rose Rd					
10	SchT	60174	2963	36W-4N	E4
100	BfdT	53128	2353		C2
100	GNCY	53128	2353		C2
100	RdlT	53128	2353		C2
100	RdlT	53181	2353		C2
Wildrose Springs Dr					
800	SCRL	60174	2964	36W-4N	A5
Wild Rye Ct					
-	PNFD	60585	3337	33W-15S	A1
Wildspring Ct					
200	ITSC	60143	2914	19W-7N	C5
Wildspring Dr					
5300	LIHL	60142	2692	39W-22N	C3
Wildspring Ln					
6900	LGGV	60047	2646	18W-25N	D5
6900	LGGV	60060	2646	18W-25N	D5
S Wildspring Rd					
200	RDLK	60073	2531	23W-32N	E4
W Wildspring Rd					
300	RDLK	60073	2531	23W-33N	E3
Wild Timothy Ct					
2700	NPVL	60564	3266	29W-13S	C5
Wild Timothy Rd					
2100	NPVL	60564	3266	29W-13S	C5
Wildwood Av					
-	CHCG	60613	2977	1W-5N	D1
600	GrtT	60041	2473	26W-35N	D6
600	MDLN	60060	2590	18W-28N	E6
17800	LNSG	60438	3430	3E-21S	A6
18800	LNSG	60438	3510	3E-22S	A1
19300	LNSG	60411	3510	3E-22S	A2
19300	LYWD	60411	3510	3E-22S	A2
N Wildwood Av					
6700	CHCG	60646	2919	7W-8N	B1
Wildwood Cir					
1900	GLHT	60139	2969	23W-3N	A5
Wildwood Ct					
-	ANTH	60002	2358	22W-42N	C6
10	VNHL	60061	2647	16W-24N	E7
100	WNVL	60555	3080	30W-2S	B4
200	BMDL	60108	2969	22W-4N	C3
400	RMVL	60446	3269	23W-14S	A6
800	OKBK	60523	3086	15W-1S	B1
800	SMWD	60107	2857	27W-9N	B7
900	BRLT	60103	2911	28W-7N	B5
900	SchT	60174	2963	36W-3N	D6
900	SCRL	60174	2963	36W-3N	D6
1600	HMGN	60491	3421	16W-19S	E2
1700	GNVW	60025	2810	8W-14N	E4
2100	HRPK	60133	2967	27W-5N	C3
4400	HFET	60192	2804	24W-15N	C2
6600	LSLE	60532	3142	24W-7S	D7
7700	DRN	60561	3207	18W-8S	B2
S Wildwood Ct					
24500	CteT	60417	3687	3E-29S	E6
W Wildwood Ct					
15300	LbvT	60048	2592	15W-30N	A3
Wildwood Dr					
-	PGGV	60140	2797	42W-14N	D5
10	CbaT	60010	2644	25W-25N	B5
10	NLNX	60451	3501	18W-25S	B7
10	RLKB	60073	2475	22W-35N	A7
10	ROSL	60172	2912	24W-7N	E5
10	SgrT	60506	3136	40W-6S	C5
100	FXLK	60041	2473	27W-35N	C6
300	NARA	60542	3077	36W-3S	E7
300	PKFT	60466	3594	4W-26S	E3
300	PKFT	60466	3595	4W-26S	A2
500	ElgT	60124	2907	37W-8N	B3
600	JLET	60431	3497	28W-23S	A3
600	NLNX	60451	3589	18W-25S	A1
700	MNKA	60447	3672	34W-29S	A2
700	TroT	60431	3497	28W-23S	A3
900	NlxT	60451	3589	18W-25S	A1
4100	NndT	60014	2586	30W-27N	A7
4400	NndT	60014	2642	30W-27N	A1
4700	NndT	60051	2642	29W-27N	B1
10500	PlsT	60464	3273	13W-14S	A7
13400	HTLY	60142	2744	42W-20N	B1
N Wildwood Dr					
36200	LkvT	60046	2475	21W-36N	E4
S Wildwood Dr					
10	PTHT	60070	2754	15W-16N	E7
10	PTHT	60070	2755	14W-16N	B7
Wildwood Dr E					
900	PTHT	60070	2755	15W-16N	A7
Wildwood Dr N					
10	PTHT	60070	2754	15W-16N	E7
10	PTHT	60070	2755	14W-16N	B7
Wildwood Dr W					
900	PTHT	60070	2754	15W-16N	E7
Wildwood Ln					
-	LKMR	60051	2529	29W-32N	D4
10	JltT	60433	3587	23W-25S	A1
100	FRGV	60021	2696	29W-23N	C2
100	NARA	60542	3077	36W-4S	E7
500	WCHI	60185	3022	29W-2N	D1
700	SMWD	60107	2857	28W-9N	B7
900	HDPK	60035	2705	7W-21N	B7
900	NHBK	60062	2757	8W-17N	D6
1100	GNVW	60025	2811	7W-14N	A4
1600	DGvT	60516	3206	18W-9S	E3
1600	DRN	60516	3206	18W-9S	E3
1600	HRPK	60133	2967	27W-5N	C2
2600	WdfT	60015	2703	11W-23N	D3
2700	LKFT	60045	2703	11W-23N	D2
2700	WdfT	60045	2703	11W-23N	D3
4100	LGGV	60047	2700	18W-21N	E5
6100	BRRG	60527	3146	15W-6S	A5
8000	DRN	60561	3206	18W-9S	E3
8000	DRN	60561	3207	18W-9S	A3
16000	HMGN	60491	3421	16W-19S	E2
E Wildwood Ln					
1200	MPPT	60056	2808	14W-13N	C6
W Wildwood Ln					
13800	HMGN	60491	3421	17W-19S	D2
Wildwood Pl					
10	EGVV	60007	2861	18W-9N	A6
Wildwood Rd					
-	AlqT	60102	2695	33W-21N	A5
10	ALGN	60102	2695	33W-21N	A6
10	CTCY	60409	3430		C1
10	EGVV	60007	2861	18W-10N	A6
10	HMND	46320	3430		D1
10	HMND	46324	3430		C1
10	LKFT	60045	2650	10W-26N	B4
10	RGMW	60008	2806	19W-14N	B4
Wildwood St					
100	VLPK	60181	3027	17W-0N	B4
200	BDWD	60408	3942	30W-41S	B4
200	RedT	60481	3942	30W-41S	B4
500	RedT	60408	3942	30W-41S	B4
34100	WslT	60481	3943	27W-41S	E6
Wildwood Ter					
-	GNVW	60025	2810	8W-14N	E5
Wild Wood Tr					
10	PSPK	60464	3272	13W-14S	E7
10	PSPK	60464	3273	13W-15S	A7
Wildwood Tr					
10	CRY	60013	2641	31W-24N	C7
S Wildwood Tr					
24500	CteT	60417	3687	3E-29S	B2
Wildwood Lane G					
10	BGBK	60440	3269	22W-12S	D2
Wildwood Lane H					
-	BGBK	60440	3269	22W-12S	D2
Wildwood Lane Lot H					
10	BGBK	60440	3269	23W-11S	A1
Wildy Rd					
300	MNKA	60447	3583	34W-26S	A3
300	SwdT	60447	3583	34W-26S	A3
300	TroT	60404	3583	33W-26S	E3
Wileden Ln					
100	WldT	60564	3203	28W-10S	A5
Wiley Rd					
1000	SMBG	60173	2859	22W-12N	C1
N Wiley Rd					
1100	SMBG	60173	2859	22W-12N	D1
Wiley Farm Ct					
700	SMBG	60173	2859	22W-12N	C1
Wilhelm Ct					
300	JltT	60433	3499	23W-24S	B6
Wilhelm Rd					
1200	MDLN	60060	2647	17W-25N	A4
Wilhelmi Dr					
25400	CNHN	60410	3672	31W-30S	E3
Wilke Rd					
200	ANHT	60005	2806	19W-13N	D6
200	ANHT	60008	2806	19W-14N	D4
200	RGMW	60008	2806	19W-13N	D6

Chicago 7-County Street Index

STREET Block	City	ZIP	Map#	CGS	Grid
Wilke Rd					
1800	BfdT	53128	2351		E2
2300	RGMW	60005	2806	19W-13N	D6
N Wilke Rd					
-	ElaT	60004	2753	19W-18N	D2
-	ElaT	60047	2753	19W-18N	D2
-	PltT	60074	2753	19W-17N	D5
-	VrnT	60004	2753	19W-18N	D2
-	VrnT	60047	2753	19W-18N	D2
10	ANHT	60004	2806	19W-16N	D1
10	ANHT	60074	2806	19W-16N	D1
10	PLTN	60074	2753	19W-16N	D7
10	PLTN	60074	2806	19W-16N	D1
600	ANHT	60005	2806	19W-14N	D4
600	ANHT	60008	2806	19W-14N	D4
600	RGMW	60005	2806	19W-14N	D4
600	RGMW	60008	2806	19W-14N	D4
1600	PLTN	60004	2806	18W-15N	D2
3100	PltT	60004	2753	18W-18N	D3
3200	ANHT	60004	2753	18W-17N	D4
Wilkening Ct					
1500	SMBG	60173	2859	23W-12N	A1
Wilkening Rd					
1200	HFET	60169	2859	23W-12N	B2
1200	SMBG	60169	2859	23W-12N	B2
1200	SMBG	60173	2859	23W-12N	B1
Wilkens Dr					
200	DSPN	60016	2862	15W-11N	B3
200	MPPT	60016	2862	15W-11N	B3
200	MPPT	60056	2862	15W-11N	B3
W Wilkens Ln					
10	PNFD	60544	3338	29W-17S	D6
10	PnfT	60544	3338	29W-17S	D6
N Wilkens Pl					
1200	PNFD	60544	3338	29W-17S	D6
1200	PnfT	60544	3338	29W-17S	D6
Wilker Dr					
17800	LKPT	60441	3419	22W-20S	C5
Wilkes Dr					
3300	AURA	60564	3201	31W-9S	E5
Wilkes Ln					
1100	LKZH	60047	2699	22W-21N	A5
Wilkinson Ln					
800	NARA	60542	3077	37W-3S	B6
Wilkinson Pkwy					
700	PKRG	60068	2863	11W-9N	E6
Will Dr					
1200	LKPT	60441	3420	21W-19S	A3
Will Rd					
-	AxST	60450	3761	33W-34S	C5
-	AxST	60481	3761	33W-34S	C5
-	CLCY	60416	3941	33W-39S	C1
-	CNHN	60481	3761	33W-34S	C5
-	CnhT	60481	3761	33W-34S	C5
-	DMND	60416	3941	33W-39S	C1
-	GlkT	60416	3761	32W-35S	C7
-	GlkT	60450	3761	32W-34S	C5
-	GlkT	60481	3761	33W-34S	C5
-	WmTp	60416	3941	33W-39S	C1
-	WmTp	60481	3761	33W-34S	C5
S Will Rd					
-	BvlT	60407	3941	33W-41S	C6
10	DMND	60416	3941	33W-41S	C5
300	BDWD	60408	3941	33W-41S	C5
300	BvlT	60416	3941	33W-41S	C5
300	DMND	60408	3941	33W-41S	C5
300	RedT	60408	3941	33W-41S	C5
Will St					
500	PKCY	60085	2536	13W-33N	A3
N Will St					
10	PLNO	60545	3259	47W-13S	D6
S Will St					
100	PLNO	60545	3259	47W-13S	D6
Will Wy					
10	WYNE	60184	2965	32W-5N	D2
Willams Ln					
-	CRTE	60417	3597	0E-29S	A7
-	CRTE	60417	3686	0E-29S	A1
Willard Av					
10	ELGN	60120	2855	32W-10N	C5
15700	HRVY	60426	3428	1W-18S	A1
Willard Ct					
100	BmdT	60188	3024	23W-2N	E1
1100	NPVL	60540	3202	29W-8S	E1
N Willard Ct					
100	CHCG	60607	3033	1W-0N	E4
900	CHCG	60622	3033	1W-1N	D2
Willard Ln					
16300	LKPT	60441	3420	20W-21S	B6
Willard Pl					
200	WTMT	60559	3145	18W-4S	A1
1400	DRGV	60516	3206	20W-8S	B1
N Willard St					
300	JLET	60432	3499	23W-23S	B4
S Willard St					
24700	CNHN	60410	3672	31W-30S	E3
Willard Wy					
10	WNFD	60190	3023	27W-0N	C5
Willardshire Rd					
3000	JLET	60435	3417	28W-20S	B5
3000	PnfT	60431	3417	28W-20S	B5
3000	PnfT	60435	3417	28W-20S	B5
S Will Center Rd					
25100	MonT	60449	3683	5W-30S	B3
25100	UYPK	60449	3683	5W-30S	B3
25100	UYPK	60466	3683	5W-30S	B2
25500	MONE	60449	3683	6W-32S	B7
Will Cook Rd					
10	LMNT	60439	3272	15W-13S	C4
10	LmnT	60464	3272	15W-13S	C4
10	PlsT	60439	3272	15W-13S	C4
10	PlsT	60464	3272	15W-13S	C4
1200	HMGN	60467	3422	14W-19S	C2
1200	HMGN	60491	3422	14W-19S	C2
1200	ODPK	60467	3422	14W-20S	D4
1200	OrlT	60467	3422	14W-20S	D4
S Will Cook Rd					
-	LmnT	60439	3344	14W-16S	C2
-	LmnT	60464	3272	14W-14S	C7
-	LmnT	60464	3344	14W-15S	C1
-	LmnT	60467	3344	14W-15S	C1
-	LmnT	60491	3344	14W-16S	C2
-	PlsT	60464	3344	14W-15S	C1
-	PlsT	60467	3344	14W-16S	C2
11700	LMNT	60439	3272	14W-14S	C6
11700	PlsT	60439	3272	14W-14S	C6
11700	PlsT	60464	3272	14W-14S	C6
11800	PSPK	60439	3272	14W-14S	C7
13500	HMGN	60491	3344	15W-18S	C7
13500	OrlT	60467	3344	15W-15S	C2
14100	ODPK	60467	3344	14W-16S	C4
15600	HMGN	60491	3422	15W-18S	C1
15600	ODPK	60467	3422	15W-18S	C1
15600	OrlT	60467	3422	15W-18S	C1
Willcrest Rd					
1400	NPVL	60540	3140	28W-7S	E6
1400	NPVL	60540	3141	28W-7S	A6
Wille Av					
10	WLNG	60090	2755	14W-17N	D5
Wille Rd					
-	DSPN	60018	2861	16W-9N	E6
10	DSPN	60018	2862	15W-9N	B6
10	EGvT	60018	2862	15W-9N	B6
N Wille St					
10	MPPT	60056	2808	15W-13N	A6
S Wille St					
10	MPPT	60056	2808	15W-12N	A7
200	MPPT	60056	2862	15W-12N	A1
Willet Wy					
10	TVLY	60013	2695	31W-23N	D2
N Willetts Ct					
2500	CHCG	60647	2976	3W-3N	E5
Willey Ln					
10	BTVA	60510	3077	36W-1S	E1
Willey St					
10	GLBT	60136	2799	39W-16N	A1
Willgate Ter					
500	GLNC	60022	2758	6W-17N	E5
N William					
100	NHLK	60164	2972	13W-2N	E7
100	NHLK	60164	3028	13W-2N	E1
William Av					
800	DndT	60118	2801	33W-15N	A3
800	EDND	60118	2801	33W-15N	A3
2500	MaiT	60025	2864	9W-12N	B1
N William Av					
20500	BFGV	60069	2754	15W-20N	E1
20500	BFGV	60089	2754	15W-20N	E1
20500	VrnT	60069	2754	15W-20N	E1
20700	VrnT	60069	2701	15W-20N	E7
William Ct					
-	ODPK	60462	3345	11W-16S	E3
E William Ct					
100	PnfT	60544	3338	29W-16S	D4
William Dr					
-	MTGY	60538	3198	39W-10S	D5
100	ELGN	60123	2853	36W-11N	E4
100	ElgT	60123	2853	36W-11N	E4
600	DGvT	60527	3207	16W-9S	D4
1200	LKZH	60047	2699	21W-22N	C4
1600	RMVL	60446	3339	26W-18S	D7
1600	RMVL	60446	3417	27W-18S	D1
1900	CTHL	60403	3417	26W-21S	E7
14000	ODPK	60462	3345	11W-16S	E3
William Ln					
10	LtRT	60548	3258	50W-13S	B6
1200	BtnT	60081	2414	30W-40N	B3
William Pl					
-	GrtT	60081	2472	28W-37N	E1
William St					
-	FSMR	60422	3506	4W-23S	E3
-	RchT	60430	3506	4W-23S	E3
200	BNVL	60106	2971	16W-3N	D4
400	FTPK	60130	3030	9W-0N	D4
1200	RVFT	60305	3030	9W-1N	D1
1500	EDPK	60707	3030	9W-1N	D1
1500	RVFT	60707	3030	9W-1N	D1
4600	JNBG	60050	2472	30W-36N	B3
4600	MchT	60050	2472	30W-36N	B4
10100	RHMD	60071	2353	34W-41N	C7
10300	RcmT	60071	2353	34W-42N	C7
17000	LNSG	60438	3430	4E-20S	B4
18700	LNSG	60438	3510	4E-22S	C1
N William St					
10	JLET	60436	3498	25W-23S	C5
10	MPPT	60056	2808	15W-13N	B7
900	JLET	60435	3498	25W-22S	C1
1500	CTHL	60403	3498	25W-22S	C1
S William St					
10	JLET	60435	3498	25W-24S	C5
10	JLET	60436	3498	25W-24S	C5
10	MPPT	60056	2808	15W-12N	B7
200	MPPT	60056	2862	15W-12N	B1
900	DSPN	60016	2862	15W-11N	B2
900	DSPN	60056	2862	15W-11N	B2
W William St					
-	MONE	60449	3682	7W-31S	E6
William Wy					
200	BMDL	60108	2912	24W-5N	D7
200	BMDL	60108	2968	24W-5N	E1
William Clifford Ln					
1400	EGVV	60007	2914	21W-8N	A3
William Cullen Bryant St					
200	CmpT	60175	2962	40W-4N	C5
E William L McFetridge Dr					
400	CHCG	60605	3034	0E-1S	D7
William Penn Dr					
1500	NPVL	60563	3141	28W-5S	B2
Williams Av					
1100	DRFD	60015	2703	11W-21N	D5
1300	RLKB	60073	2475	22W-35N	C6
1500	SCRL	60174	3020	34W-2N	E1
S Williams Av					
400	PLTN	60074	2806	19W-15N	C2
9100	CHCG	60619	3214	0E-10S	D5
Williams Ct					
10	WDRG	60517	3143	22W-7S	D7
400	WNVL	60555	3080	29W-3S	E6
600	GRNE	60031	2534	16W-33N	E3
800	SMBG	60193	2858	24W-10N	D6
1500	CRTE	60417	3685	1W-30S	A3
4100	HFET	60192	2804	23W-15N	D3
Williams Dr					
-	HTLY	60142	2691	40W-22N	E4
100	SMBG	60193	2858	24W-10N	D6
500	SEGN	60177	2908	34W-7N	E4
2800	WDRG	60517	3143	22W-7S	D7
3200	FNPK	60131	2973	13W-4N	A4
7900	DGvT	60527	3207	16W-9S	D3
7900	WLBK	60527	3207	16W-9S	D3
E Williams Dr					
1000	PLTN	60074	2806	19W-16N	B1
1100	PLTN	60074	2753	19W-16N	C7
N Williams Dr					
10	PLTN	60074	2806	19W-16N	B1
1200	PLTN	60074	2753	19W-17N	C5
Williams Ln					
3500	CRTE	60417	3597	0E-28S	A6
Williams Pl					
200	EDND	60118	2801	33W-15N	A3
4400	OKLN	60453	3212	5W-11S	B7
Williams Rd					
-	HFET	60010	2751	24W-16N	C7
-	WCHI	60185	3022	29W-1N	E3
10	WnfT	60185	3080	29W-2S	E3
10	WnfT	60555	3080	29W-2S	E4
10	WNVL	60555	3080	29W-3S	D6
100	BfdT	53128	2353		B3
100	GNCY	53128	2353		B3
200	HFET	60192	2804	24W-15N	C1
200	IVNS	60010	2751	24W-16N	C7
200	IVNS	60067	2804	24W-15N	C1
200	WnfT	60185	3022	29W-1N	E3
700	CPVL	60110	2747	34W-17N	E7
700	CPVL	60110	2748	34W-18N	A6
700	DndT	60110	2748	34W-18N	A6
800	DndT	60102	2748	34W-18N	A6
2500	BTVA	60510	3077	37W-1S	C2
Williams St					
-	NLNX	60451	3501	17W-25S	D7
-	RSMT	60018	2917	11W-6N	C5
10	CPVL	60110	2747	34W-17N	E7
10	WNFD	60190	3023	27W-0S	C7
100	NlxT	60451	3501	17W-25S	D7
200	AURA	60506	3138	35W-7S	B6
300	ANTH	60002	2357	23W-42N	E6
300	NlxT	60451	3589	17W-25S	D1
300	ROSL	60172	2912	23W-7N	E4
600	SMBG	60172	2912	23W-7N	E4
600	WMTN	60481	3853	27W-39S	D7
700	WMTN	60481	3943	27W-39S	D1
800	CTCY	60409	3430	3E-19S	A1
1300	FDHT	60411	3509	1E-25S	B7
1400	WTMT	60559	3145	18W-7S	A6
2100	MltT	60187	3023	26W-0S	E7
2100	WHTN	60187	3023	26W-0S	E7
3500	CteT	60417	3595	1W-28S	E6
3500	CteT	60475	3595	1W-28S	E6
3500	STGR	60417	3595	1W-28S	E6
3500	STGR	60475	3595	1W-28S	E6
3900	DRGV	60515	3085	18W-4S	A7
3900	YkTp	60515	3085	18W-4S	A7
3900	YkTp	60559	3085	18W-4S	A7
4100	WTMT	60515	3085	18W-4S	A7
4100	WTMT	60559	3085	18W-4S	A7
5100	DRGV	60515	3145	18W-5S	A3
5100	DRGV	60559	3145	18W-5S	A3
5200	WTMT	60515	3145	18W-5S	A3
7500	DGvT	60561	3145	18W-7S	A7
7500	DRN	60561	3145	18W-8S	A7
E Williams St					
10	CTCY	60409	3352		C7
10	HMND	46320	3352		C7
N Williams St					
10	CLLK	60014	2640	34W-25N	B4
10	DRGV	60515	3145	18W-5S	A2
10	WTMT	60515	3145	18W-5S	A2
10	WTMT	60559	3145	18W-5S	A2
100	TNTN	60476	3428	0E-20S	D5
400	TNTN	60473	3428	0E-20S	D5
3800	DRGV	60515	3085	18W-3S	A6
3800	OKBK	60515	3085	18W-3S	A6
3800	OKBK	60523	3085	18W-3S	A6
3800	OKBK	60559	3085	18W-3S	A6
3800	YkTp	60515	3085	18W-3S	A6
3800	YkTp	60559	3085	18W-3S	A6
S Williams St					
10	CLLK	60014	2640	35W-25N	B4
100	TNTN	60476	3428	0E-21S	D7
200	DRGV	60515	3145	18W-5S	A3
200	WTMT	60515	3145	18W-5S	A3
300	DRGV	60559	3145	18W-5S	A3
400	WTMT	60516	3145	18W-6S	A5
400	WTMT	60559	3145	18W-6S	A5
7500	DRGV	60516	3207	18W-8S	A2
7500	DRN	60516	3207	18W-8S	A2
7500	DRN	60561	3207	18W-8S	A2
17500	BlmT	60425	3428	0W-21S	D7
17500	BlmT	60476	3428	0W-21S	D7
Williams Wy					
500	VNHL	60061	2647	17W-24N	A6
10500	MKNA	60448	3503	13W-23S	B4
Williamsburg Av					
300	GNVA	60134	3019	37W-1N	C3
600	GRNE	60031	2535	14W-33N	C3
Williamsburg Cir					
10	SKOK	60203	2866	4W-11N	C3
1000	GYLK	60030	2532	20W-34N	E1
Williamsburg Ct					
-	GNVW	60025	2809	11W-13N	D7
10	SKOK	60203	2866	4W-11N	C3
200	MTGY	60538	3200	36W-10S	A5
200	RMVL	60446	3340	25W-16S	C4
200	YkTp	60523	3084	19W-3S	D5
500	WLNG	60090	2754	15W-18N	E3
1600	WHTN	60187	3082	24W-2S	E3
4100	NfdT	60025	2809	11W-13N	D7
4400	RGMW	60008	2805	21W-14N	D4
4400	RGMW	60008	2806	20W-15N	A3
21500	FKFT	60423	3591	13W-26S	B1
W Williamsburg Ct					
21300	KLDR	60047	2699	21W-23N	D2
Williamsburg Dr					
10	ElgT	60124	2853	37W-10N	C5
100	BRLT	60103	2910	29W-8N	E3
300	ELGN	60124	2853	37W-10N	C5
800	NPVL	60540	3203	27W-8S	C1
1000	NHBK	60062	2757	9W-18N	D3
1200	SMBG	60193	2859	21W-10N	D6
1700	HFET	60169	2858	26W-12N	A1
1800	SMWD	60107	2857	26W-11N	E4
1900	WKGN	60085	2479	11W-35N	D5
2000	HFET	60169	2857	26W-11N	E4
2600	ALGN	60102	2746	36W-20N	D2
N Williamsburg Dr					
1900	PLTN	60074	2753	20W-20N	B1
S Williamsburg Dr					
2300	JLET	60586	3415	32W-21S	D6
2300	PnfT	60586	3415	32W-21S	D6
Williamsburg Ln					
-	LNSH	60069	2702	15W-23N	A2
10	SKOK	60203	2866	4W-11N	C3
10	YkTp	60181	3085	18W-1S	A1
100	BGBK	60440	3269	22W-13S	C4
400	PTHT	60070	2808	14W-14N	B3
1100	CLLK	60014	2693	37W-22N	B3
Williamsburg Pk					
900	BRTN	60010	2698	25W-20N	A7
Williamsburg Rd					
10	SKOK	60203	2866	4W-11N	C3
1100	CCHL	60478	3506	5W-22S	C1
1100	HLCT	60429	3506	5W-22S	C1
Williamsburg St					
1000	WTMT	60559	3085	17W-3S	C6
N Williamsburg St					
2200	ANHT	60004	2753	18W-16N	D7
Williamsburg Ter					
10	SKOK	60203	2866	4W-11N	C3
Williamsburg Tr					
10400	FKFT	60423	3591	13W-25S	B1
Williamsburgh Rd					
400	GNEN	60137	3083	22W-1S	B2
E Williamson Av					
1000	JLET	60432	3499	22W-22S	C2
N Williams Park Rd					
27000	ISLK	60084	2643	27W-27N	B1
27000	WcnT	60084	2643	27W-27N	B1
Williams Port Dr					
1200	WTMT	60559	3145	18W-7S	A5
Williamstown Ct					
2400	NPVL	60564	3202	29W-10S	D6
Williamstown Dr					
700	CLSM	60188	2967	27W-3N	D5
William Wood Ln					
300	BTVA	60510	3078	34W-1S	C2
Willida Av					
1200	WMTN	60481	3943	27W-39S	D2
Willigan Rd					
-	ThtT	60476	3429	1E-21S	A6
Willington Dr					
400	SMBG	60194	2858	25W-11N	A4
Willington Wy					
200	OSWG	60543	3263	36W-12S	E3
200	OSWG	60543	3264	35W-12S	A3
Willis Av					
1100	WLNG	60090	2755	14W-16N	B7
Willis Cir					
100	BbyT	60134	3018	39W-0S	D6
Willis St					
500	ELGN	60123	2855	33W-10N	A6
700	GNEN	60137	3025	22W-0N	C5
Williston Ct					
5100	JLET	60586	3496	30W-22S	C2
N Williston St					
200	WHTN	60187	3024	23W-0S	E6
S Williston St					
100	WHTN	60187	3024	23W-0S	E7
700	WHTN	60187	3082	23W-1S	E1
Willoby Ct					
200	SMBG	60173	2859	21W-11N	E3
Willoby Ln					
1000	ELGN	60120	2855	32W-12N	D1
Willoughby Ct					
10	ALGN	60102	2747	36W-19N	A2
Willoughby Ln					
100	AURA	60502	3079	32W-3S	D6
100	WnfT	60502	3079	32W-3S	C6
Willow					
-	ITSC	60143	2914	20W-6N	B6
Willow Av					
-	AntT	60002	2357	25W-43N	A4
-	LMNT	60439	3343	18W-15S	B2
10	DRFD	60015	2756	11W-20N	D1
200	FmtT	60060	2646	19W-26N	D3
600	WKGN	60085	2536	12W-33N	C3
1200	LYVL	60048	2591	17W-28N	B5
1300	DSPN	60016	2862	13W-11N	E2
1300	DSPN	60016	2863	13W-11N	A2
2000	HRPK	60133	2911	27W-8N	C3
2500	WDRG	60517	3205	21W-8S	D1
10400	MKNA	60448	3503	13W-23S	B4
10700	FftT	60448	3503	13W-23S	A4
17500	CCHL	60478	3426	5W-21S	C6
18500	CCHL	60478	3506	5W-22S	C1
E Willow Av					
100	WDSK	60098	2524	41W-32N	D5
1600	WHTN	60187	3024	23W-0S	E7
1600	WHTN	60187	3025	23W-0S	A7
1800	GNEN	60137	3025	23W-0S	A7
1800	GNEN	60187	3025	23W-0S	A7
S Willow Av					
100	JLET	60436	3498	24W-24S	D5
W Willow Av					
100	WDSK	60098	2524	41W-32N	D5
100	WHTN	60187	3024	24W-0S	C7
Willow Blvd					
-	WLSP	60480	3209	13W-10S	B4
Willow Bnd					
100	BGBK	60490	3267	27W-12S	B3
Willow Cir					
10	CRY	60013	2641	31W-24N	C6
Willow Ct					
-	CTHL	60403	3418	25W-21S	C7
10	BGBK	60440	3205	22W-10S	D5
10	CTCY	60409	3429	2E-18S	D1
10	CTSD	60525	3147	12W-6S	C4
10	WDRG	60517	3205	21W-8S	D2
10	WNVL	60555	3080	29W-1S	C2
100	MTSN	60443	3505	7W-24S	C5
100	SMWD	60107	2857	27W-10N	C5
400	DRPK	60010	2752	22W-20N	B1
500	RMVL	60446	3269	23W-14S	A6
500	WKGN	60085	2479	12W-33N	C7
500	WKGN	60085	2536	12W-33N	C1
700	BRLT	60103	2910	29W-6N	D6
700	ITSC	60143	2914	19W-7N	B5
800	SRWD	60404	3495	31W-25S	E7
1000	AURA	60504	3201	32W-9S	C3
5200	GRNE	60031	2478	14W-35N	C6
5800	DrrT	60014	2639	38W-26N	A3
9400	MaiT	60016	2863	11W-12N	D1
15500	HMGN	60491	3344	16W-18S	A7
15500	HMGN	60491	3422	16W-18S	A1
18800	CCHL	60478	3506	5W-22S	C2
E Willow Ct					
10	CTCY	60409	3352		D6
10	HMND	46320	3352		D6
500	PLTN	60074	2753	20W-16N	A7
Willow Dr					
-	LMNT	60439	3342	20W-15S	B1
10	SchT	60175	2964	35W-6N	B1
10	WKGN	60087	2480	10W-36N	B4
100	SchT	60175	2908	35W-6N	B7
600	CHHT	60411	3507	1W-24S	E6
600	CLSM	60188	2967	26W-3N	D5
800	CHHT	60411	3508	1W-24S	A6
4900	MchT	60097	2469	36W-37N	D3
8100	PSHL	60465	3274	10W-13S	B4
8700	JSTC	60458	3210	10W-8S	A1
20100	LYWD	60411	3509	3E-24S	E4
E Willow Dr					
10	RLKP	60073	2532	22W-33N	A3
300	HNVL	60030	2532	22W-33N	B3
W Willow Dr					
10	RLKP	60073	2532	23W-33N	A3
21200	KLDR	60047	2699	21W-20N	D7
Willow Dr E					
100	PNFD	60544	3338	31W-17S	A7
1700	PNFD	60544	3337	31W-18S	E7
Willow Dr W					
100	PNFD	60544	3337	31W-18S	E7
100	PNFD	60544	3415	31W-18S	E1
Willow Ln					
-	BtlT	60545	3333	43W-14S	A1
-	BtlT	60560	3333	43W-14S	A1
-	TYPK	60448	3504	11W-23S	B3
-	TYPK	60477	3504	11W-23S	B3
10	BtlT	60512	3198	40W-11S	B7
10	BtlT	60512	3262	40W-11S	B1
10	WDRG	60517	3205	21W-8S	D1
10	WnfT	60185	3080	29W-1S	C2
10	WnfT	60555	3080	29W-1S	C2
10	WNVL	60555	3080	30W-1S	C2
100	EGVV	60007	2861	18W-9N	A6
100	SchT	60174	2964	35W-5N	B3
100	WLSP	60480	3209	11W-9S	D3
200	BMDL	60108	2969	22W-4N	B3
200	GNVA	60134	3020	36W-1N	A3
200	NLNX	60451	3501	18W-23S	B4
400	DYR	46311	3598		D3
500	BCHR	60401	3864	0W-36S	C1
500	WDND	60118	2800	34W-15N	D3
600	SCRL	60134	3020	36W-1N	A3
600	SCRL	60174	3020	36W-1N	A3
800	SRWD	60404	3495	31W-25S	E7
800	WLBK	60527	3145	16W-7S	E6
900	ElgT	60124	2907	38W-8N	B3
900	SRWD	60404	3583	31W-25S	E1
900	SYHW	60118	2800	35W-15N	C3
1000	BTVA	60510	3078	34W-2S	E3
1000	DRN	60561	3207	17W-8S	B1
1100	LynT	60458	3209	11W-8S	D2
1100	NHBK	60062	2757	8W-17N	D6
1200	DGvT	60561	3207	18W-8S	B1
1200	GRNE	60031	2478	15W-35N	A6
1300	WTMT	60559	3145	18W-7S	B6
1500	CRTE	60417	3685	1W-30S	B3
2200	RGMW	60008	2806	19W-12N	C7
2900	ZION	60099	2421	11W-41N	D1
3300	ISLK	60042	2586	28W-28N	E5
3300	MKHM	60428	3348	4W-18S	E7
3600	GNVW	60025	2809	11W-15N	E2
4500	MHRY	60050	2527	33W-33N	D2
8900	FftT	60448	3504	11W-23S	A3
8900	MKNA	60448	3504	11W-23S	A3
9100	BGVW	60455	3210	8W-10S	E5
9200	FftT	60448	3503	12W-23S	D3
9200	MKNA	60448	3503	12W-23S	D3
14000	CTWD	60445	3348	5W-16S	A3
15100	BmnT	60452	3347	8W-18S	B6
15100	OKFT	60452	3347	8W-18S	B6
15300	MKHM	60426	3348	4W-18S	E7
18300	LNSG	60438	3430	4E-21S	C7
23700	CnhT	60447	3672	32W-28S	D1
26000	WmTp	60481	3761	32W-34S	C5
26200	GlkT	60481	3761	32W-34S	C5
N Willow Ln					
10	GNWD	60425	3508	0E-22S	E2
2200	MchT	60050	2527	34W-34N	D1
9200	NLES	60714	2864	10W-11N	B3
37000	GRNE	60031	2478	15W-37N	A3
37000	WDWH	60031	2478	15W-37N	A3
39100	AntT	60002	2415	26W-39N	D5
S Willow Ln					
10	GNWD	60425	3508	0E-22S	E2
W Willow Ln					
1000	MPPT	60056	2861	16W-11N	D3
1800	ANHT	60005	2861	17W-11N	B3
1800	ANHT	60056	2861	17W-11N	B3
Willow Pkwy					
-	VrnT	60089	2701	16W-22N	D3
300	BFGV	60089	2701	16W-22N	C3
Willow Rd					
-	NfdT	60062	2809	11W-15N	E2
-	NfdT	60062	2810	9W-15N	B2
-	NfdT	60090	2809	11W-15N	E2
-	NHFD	60093	2810	8W-15N	E2
10	MTSN	60443	3505	7W-24S	C6
10	MTSN	60477	3505	7W-24S	D4
10	RchT	60477	3505	7W-24S	D4
10	WLNG	60090	2808	14W-15N	B2
100	BRTN	60010	2751	25W-20N	B1
100	FXLK	60041	2473	27W-35N	B6
100	SMWD	60107	2857	27W-10N	C5
200	LKMR	60051	2529	29W-32N	D5
300	MltT	60187	3024	25W-0N	A5
300	WCDA	60084	2587	26W-27N	C7
300	WCDA	60084	2643	26W-27N	C1
400	MRGO	60152	2634	50W-26N	B2
400	NlxT	60451	3500	19W-24S	E5
400	NlxT	60451	3501	18W-24S	A5
600	NPVL	60540	3141	26W-7S	D7
600	WNKA	60093	2812	5W-15N	A2
1100	WNKA	60093	2811	5W-15N	E2
1300	GNVW	60025	2810	8W-15N	E2
1300	GNVW	60062	2810	9W-15N	C2
1300	NHBK	60025	2810	10W-15N	A2
1300	NHBK	60062	2810	8W-15N	E2
1300	NHFD	60093	2811	8W-15N	A2
1300	NtrT	60093	2811	6W-15N	D2
1400	SMBG	60173	2859	21W-10N	E4
1500	HMWD	60430	3507	2W-22S	D1
1500	TNLK	53181	2354		A3
1600	TNLK	53181	2353		E3
1900	RdlT	53181	2353		D3
2600	GNVW	60025	2809	10W-15N	E2
2600	NHBK	60025	2809	10W-15N	E2
2600	NHBK	60062	2809	10W-15N	E2
2700	GNVW	60062	2809	10W-15N	E2
3100	SCHT	60411	3595	1W-27S	E4
3700	FNPK	60131	2973	11W-4N	D2
3700	FNPK	60176	2973	11W-4N	D2
3700	SRPK	60176	2973	11W-4N	D2
8700	HYHL	60457	3209	11W-10S	E4
8700	HYHL	60457	3210	11W-10S	A4
E Willow Rd					
10	PTHT	60070	2808	15W-15N	A2
N Willow Rd					
100	EMHT	60126	3028	15W-1N	A1
400	EMHT	60126	2972	15W-2N	A7
26100	WcnT	60010	2642	28W-26N	E3
W Willow Rd					
10	PTHT	60070	2808	15W-15N	A2
100	PTHT	60070	2807	16W-15N	D2
100	WLNG	60090	2808	14W-15N	C2
500	ANHT	60004	2807	16W-15N	D2
700	PTHT	60004	2807	16W-15N	D2
21200	ElaT	60047	2699	21W-23N	D1
21200	KLDR	60047	2699	21W-23N	D1
Willow Run					
2000	WHTN	60187	3081	26W-1S	E2
Willow St					
-	FNPK	60131	2973	11W-4N	D4
-	NndT	60010	2586	30W-27N	B7
-	WslT	60481	3943	27W-41S	D6
10	ALGN	60102	2747	33W-20N	D1
10	BmdT	60172	2913	23W-7N	A5
100	IVNS	60010	2751	23W-16N	D7
100	NndT	60010	2642	29W-26N	D2
100	NndT	60051	2642	29W-26N	D2
100	PKFT	60466	3595	3W-26S	A3
100	ROSL	60172	2913	23W-7N	A5
200	FKFT	60423	3503	12W-25S	D7
200	FKFT	60423	3591	12W-25S	D1
300	AddT	60126	2972	15W-3N	A5
300	IVNS	60067	2751	23W-16N	E7

STREET Block	City	ZIP	Map#	CGS	Grid
Willow St					
300	NlxT	60451	3501	18W-24S	A5
300	WcnT	60010	2642	29W-26N	D2
400	LIHL	60156	2694	34W-22N	B5
600	FftT	60423	3503	12W-25S	D7
600	SRGV	60554	3135	42W-4S	D2
900	ITSC	60143	2914	20W-7N	B5
1400	LKFT	60045	2594	10W-27N	A7
1400	WNSP	60558	3086	14W-4S	C7
3500	FSMR	60422	3506	4W-22S	E2
6200	BtnT	60081	2414	29W-38N	D7
14500	ODPK	60462	3345	11W-17S	E5
14500	OrlT	60462	3345	11W-17S	E5
E Willow St					
10	ANHT	60004	2807	17W-14N	A3
10	LMBD	60148	3026	19W-0N	B4
200	ELBN	60119	3017	43W-2N	A2
N Willow St					
200	ITSC	60143	2914	20W-6N	B6
42300	AntT	60002	2356	26W-42N	D6
S Willow St					
200	GNWD	60425	3508	0E-23S	E3
W Willow St					
300	LMBD	60148	3026	20W-0N	A4
400	ANHT	60004	2807	18W-14N	A3
600	CHCG	60614	2978	0W-2N	A7
800	CHCG	60614	2977	1W-2N	E7
800	PLTN	60067	2752	22W-16N	B7
900	PltT	60067	2752	22W-16N	B7
1400	CHCG	60622	2977	1W-2N	D7
2000	CHCG	60647	2977	2W-2N	B7
21600	LkvT	60046	2417	21W-38N	D6
Willow Ter					
10	LKZH	60047	2698	24W-23N	C1
Willow Tr					
10	WLNG	60090	2754	15W-17N	E4
Willow Wy					
-	AvnT	60030	2533	19W-33N	C2
-	GYLK	60030	2533	19W-34N	C2
10	WTMT	60559	3145	18W-7S	B6
500	LNHT	60046	2476	19W-37N	C3
1200	BtlT	60545	3260	44W-14S	D7
1200	YKVL	60545	3260	44W-14S	D7
1200	YKVL	60560	3260	44W-14S	D7
N Willow Wy					
10	NARA	60542	3077	36W-4S	E7
10	NARA	60542	3137	36W-4S	E1
S Willow Wy					
10	NARA	60542	3137	36W-4S	E1
Willoway Dr					
200	NPVL	60540	3141	28W-6S	B6
300	BGBK	60440	3205	21W-11S	E7
Willow Bay					
1000	ELGN	60123	2907	36W-9N	D1
1000	ELGN	60123	2908	36W-9N	A1
Willow Bay Dr					
10	SBTN	60010	2803	27W-13N	C5
Willowbend Dr					
4400	JLET	60586	3416	29W-21S	D7
Willowbridge Wy					
10	BMDL	60108	2969	22W-4N	C3
Willow Brook Ct					
100	SMBG	60195	2859	23W-12N	B1
Willowbrook Ct					
700	CmpT	60175	2906	40W-7N	B6
E Willow Brook Ct					
2800	CteT	60417	3687	3E-30S	A3
Willowbrook Dr					
10	CmpT	60175	2906	40W-6N	B6
800	WLNG	60090	2755	15W-16N	A6
S Willow Brook Tr					
24500	CteT	60417	3687	3E-29S	A2
Willowbrook Wy					
200	GNVA	60134	3019	37W-1N	B2
Willowbrook Centre Pkwy					
500	DGvT	60527	3208	16W-8S	A1
500	WLBK	60527	3207	16W-8S	E1
500	WLBK	60527	3208	16W-8S	A1
Willow Brooke Dr					
-	WDSK	60098	2581	40W-29N	E4
-	WDSK	60098	2582	40W-29N	A4
Willowbrook Woods					
4300	LGGV	60047	2700	18W-22N	D3
Willowby Ct					
200	GYLK	60030	2532	21W-33N	D2
Willow Cir Dr					
1600	CTHL	60403	3418	26W-21S	A7
1600	CTHL	60403	3498	25W-21S	B1
Willow Creek Ct					
600	BbyT	60119	3075	43W-2S	A3
Willowcreek Ct					
-	DGvT	60514	3145	16W-6S	D4
500	CNHL	60514	3145	16W-6S	D4
Willow Creek Dr					
10	BbyT	60119	3075	43W-2S	A4
6100	RSMT	60018	2917	11W-7N	C3
Willow Creek Ln					
100	WLSP	60480	3209	13W-10S	A5
1500	DRN	60561	3207	18W-9S	A4
11200	ODPK	60467	3344	14W-18S	E7
S Willow Creek Ln					
25500	MonT	60449	3682	8W-31S	B5
W Willow Creek Ln					
12800	HTLY	60142	2744	41W-20N	C1
Willow Creek Rd					
900	WCHI	60185	3022	30W-2N	C1
2300	PRGV	60050	2585	31W-28N	D5
2500	NndT	60012	2585	31W-28N	D5
Willow Creek Church Dr					
-	BrnT	60010	2803	25W-14N	E3
-	BrnT	60010	2804	25W-14N	A3
-	SBTN	60010	2803	25W-14N	E3
-	SBTN	60010	2804	25W-14N	A3
Willow Crest Ct					
14900	MDLN	60445	3348	5W-17S	C6
Willowcrest Ct					
1200	AURA	60504	3202	31W-9S	A4
Willow Crest Dr					
-	BtnT	60099	2362	11W-42N	C7
-	MDLN	60445	3348	5W-17S	C6
100	ZION	60099	2362	12W-42N	C7
Willowcrest Dr					
-	WTMT	60523	3085	17W-3S	B5
-	WTMT	60559	3085	17W-3S	B5
300	VLPK	60181	3027	18W-0S	A6
Willow Crest Ln					
11200	MKNA	60448	3502	14W-23S	E4
Willowfield Ct					
700	NLNX	60451	3589	16W-25S	E1
19500	MKNA	60448	3503	13W-23S	B3
Willowfield Dr					
800	NLNX	60451	3589	16W-25S	E1
Willowgate Ln					
1100	SCRL	60174	3020	35W-2N	C1
S Willowgate Ln					
-	PNFD	60543	3337	33W-14S	B1
Willow Glen Ct					
3100	LSLE	60563	3142	25W-5S	B2
W Willow Glen St					
400	ADSN	60101	2970	19W-4N	D3
Willow Hill Ct					
1800	NHFD	60093	2811	7W-15N	B2
Willowhill Rd					
6100	WLBK	60527	3145	16W-6S	D5
Willow Hills Ln					
800	PTHT	60070	2808	14W-14N	C3
Willow Hollow Ln					
43200	BtnT	53158	2362	11W-43N	E4
43200	BtnT	60096	2362	11W-43N	E4
43200	PTPR	53158	2362	11W-43N	E4
43200	WPHR	53158	2362	11W-43N	E4
43200	WPHR	60096	2362	11W-43N	E4
Willowick Dr					
16000	OKFT	60452	3426	5W-19S	B3
Willow Lake Rd					
1100	ELGN	60123	2801	33W-14N	B6
Willow Lakes Ct					
2300	JLET	60586	3416	30W-21S	A6
Willow Lakes Dr					
2100	JLET	60586	3416	31W-21S	A6
Willow Ln Dr					
6300	TYPK	60477	3425	8W-20S	B3
Willowmere Dr					
10	SBTN	60010	2803	25W-15N	E3
10	SBTN	60010	2804	25W-15N	A2
Willowood Ct					
7400	ODPK	60462	3346	9W-18S	E6
W Willowood Ct					
7500	ODPK	60462	3346	9W-18S	D6
Willowood Ln					
300	WLBK	60527	3145	17W-6S	C5
Willow Pass					
-	SRWD	60404	3583	31W-25S	E2
W Willow Point Ct					
18800	WrnT	60030	2533	18W-33N	D3
Willow Point Dr					
18500	WrnT	60030	2533	18W-33N	E3
Willow Ridge Dr					
1900	RLKB	60073	2474	23W-35N	E5
2600	NPVL	60564	3203	28W-10S	A7
2900	NPVL	60564	3202	28W-11S	E7
9000	WLSP	60480	3208	14W-10S	C5
9000	WLSP	60527	3208	14W-10S	C5
11900	BRRG	60527	3208	14W-10S	C5
11900	DGvT	60527	3208	14W-10S	C5
Willows Edge Ct					
100	PlsT	60480	3209	13W-10S	A5
100	WLSP	60480	3209	13W-10S	A5
Willow Springs Ln					
10	LtRT	60545	3332	46W-15S	A3
Willow Springs Rd					
10	LGNG	60525	3087	13W-4S	A7
10	WNSP	60525	3087	13W-4S	A7
10	WNSP	60558	3087	13W-4S	A7
4400	LGNG	60525	3147	13W-5S	A2
4400	WNSP	60558	3147	13W-5S	A2
5300	LynT	60525	3147	13W-7S	A5
5300	WNSP	60525	3147	13W-7S	A5
5400	CTSD	60525	3147	13W-5S	A3
6400	IHPK	60525	3147	13W-7S	A6
7200	CTSD	60525	3209	13W-8S	A1
7200	LynT	60525	3209	13W-9S	A2
7400	HGKN	60525	3209	13W-9S	A2
7500	WLSP	60525	3209	13W-9S	A2
7900	HGKN	60480	3209	13W-9S	A2
7900	WLSP	60480	3209	13W-9S	A2
N Willow Springs Rd					
25500	LGGV	60047	2646	18W-25N	D5
25500	LGGV	60060	2646	18W-25N	D5
25800	MDLN	60060	2646	18W-25N	D4
Willow Terrace Dr					
8800	ODHL	60487	3424	11W-19S	A1
Willow Tree Av					
22200	SLVL	60411	3598	3E-26S	A3
Willow Tree Ct					
10	EMHT	60126	3027	16W-0S	E7
300	HFET	60169	2858	23W-11N	E3
Willow Tree Dr					
1400	CLLK	60014	2693	36W-23N	C2
Willow Tree Ln					
600	GLNC	60022	2758	7W-17N	B4
Willow Valley Rd					
3500	KLDR	60047	2700	20W-21N	A7
3500	LGGV	60047	2700	20W-21N	A7
Willowview Ct					
3400	AURA	60504	3201	31W-8S	E2
Willow View Dr					
3800	LIHL	60156	2693	37W-22N	B4
Willow View Ln					
300	OKBK	60523	3085	16W-1S	E1
Willowview Ter					
1800	NHFD	60093	2811	7W-15N	B2
Willow Walk Dr					
16400	LKPT	60441	3420	20W-21S	B6
S Willow Walk Dr					
800	PLTN	60067	2805	22W-14N	A3
Willow West Dr					
8300	WLSP	60480	3208	13W-9S	E4
8300	WLSP	60480	3209	13W-9S	A3
8300	WLSP	60525	3209	13W-9S	A3
Willowwood Ct					
-	DRGV	60516	3144	18W-7S	E6
Willow Wood Dr					
500	CLSM	60188	3024	24W-1N	D2
7900	WDRG	60517	3205	21W-9S	E3
Willowwood Dr					
100	OSWG	60543	3263	39W-12S	A2
200	OSWG	60543	3262	39W-12S	E3
N Willow Wood Dr					
300	PLTN	60074	2753	20W-16N	A7
W Willow Wood Dr					
6300	PSHT	60463	3275	7W-14S	B6
6300	WthT	60463	3275	7W-14S	B6
Willowwood Dr N					
100	OSWG	60543	3262	39W-11S	E2
100	OSWG	60543	3263	38W-11S	A2
Willow Wy Ln					
7200	WLBK	60527	3145	16W-7S	E7
7200	WLBK	60527	3207	16W-8S	E1
Wills St					
200	SEGN	60177	2908	34W-8N	C3
Will Scarlet Ln					
100	HnrT	60120	2856	31W-10N	A7
Willshire Ln					
200	LKWD	60014	2639	37W-25N	C5
400	CLLK	60014	2639	37W-25N	C6
1100	LKVL	60046	2474	23W-36N	E3
Willson Dr					
800	DSPN	60016	2862	15W-10N	A5
Willy Av					
10700	ALGN	60102	2694	34W-21N	C6
Wilma Ln					
900	EGVV	60007	2914	21W-8N	A2
Wilma Pl					
100	PKRG	60068	2864	9W-9N	C6
Wilmar Ct					
500	WNFD	60190	3023	27W-0S	B7
Wilmette Av					
10	WLMT	60091	2811	6W-13N	D6
100	GNVW	60025	2811	6W-13N	C6
500	CPVL	60110	2748	33W-17N	A7
500	CPVL	60110	2801	33W-16N	A1
500	CPVL	60118	2801	33W-16N	A1
500	EDND	60118	2801	33W-16N	A1
1000	WLMT	60091	2812	4W-13N	D6
4300	RGMW	60008	2806	20W-14N	A3
4400	RGMW	60008	2805	20W-14N	E3
10100	AlqT	60102	2694	33W-21N	E5
E Wilmette Av					
10	PLTN	60067	2805	20W-14N	E3
100	PLTN	60008	2805	20W-14N	E3
100	RGMW	60008	2805	20W-14N	E3
N Wilmette Av					
300	CNHL	60514	3145	17W-4S	B1
300	CNHL	60559	3145	17W-4S	B1
300	WTMT	60514	3145	17W-4S	B1
300	WTMT	60559	3145	17W-4S	B1
500	WTMT	60559	3085	17W-4S	B7
S Wilmette Av					
10	WTMT	60559	3145	17W-6S	B4
400	DRN	60561	3207	17W-9S	B4
6700	DRN	60527	3145	17W-7S	B7
6700	DRN	60561	3145	17W-7S	B7
Wilmette Ct					
200	SMBG	60193	2859	21W-10N	D6
1800	WHTN	60187	3024	23W-0N	E4
E Wilmette Rd					
600	PLTN	60074	2806	20W-15N	B2
Wilmette St					
-	WHTN	60187	3025	23W-0N	A5
10	OSWG	60543	3263	37W-13S	C4
1300	WHTN	60187	3024	23W-0N	E5
Wilmette Ter					
900	LKZH	60047	2698	24W-23N	B2
Wilmington Av					
10	FXLK	60020	2473	28W-37N	A2
Wilmington Ct					
100	BLVY	60098	2526	36W-32N	C5
100	MchT	60098	2526	36W-32N	C5
2300	NPVL	60565	3203	27W-10S	C6
Wilmington Dr					
300	BRLT	60103	2911	28W-8N	A3
Wilmington Ln					
1000	HFET	60169	2858	24W-11N	C3
W Wilmington Rd					
500	PtnT	60468	3860	9W-38S	E4
500	PTON	60468	3860	10W-37S	C4
Wilmor					
21500	AvnT	60030	2532	21W-34N	D1
Wilmore Dr					
700	OSWG	60543	3264	35W-12S	B2
Wilmot Av					
1600	TNLK	53181	2354		D1
Wilmot Av CO-Z					
1600	TNLK	53181	2354		D1
N Wilmot Av					
1700	CHCG	60647	2977	2W-2N	B7
Wilmot Ct					
4500	JNBG	60050	2472	30W-36N	A4
Wilmot Ln					
1600	DRFD	60015	2703	12W-21N	C7
Wilmot Rd					
-	RdlT	53181	2355	29W-43N	D4
-	RdlT	60002	2355	29W-43N	D4
10	DRFD	60015	2756	12W-20N	C1
100	WdfT	60015	2756	12W-20N	C2
600	DRFD	60015	2703	12W-20N	C7
1400	WdfT	60015	2703	12W-21N	C5
1500	BKBN	60015	2703	12W-21N	C7
7300	BtnT	60081	2414	30W-39N	B5
7600	SPGV	60081	2414	29W-40N	C3
7700	FXLK	60081	2414	29W-39N	B4
9500	FXLK	60081	2355	29W-43N	D4
10000	BtnT	60081	2355	29W-42N	C6
10900	AntT	60002	2355	29W-43N	D4
10900	FXLK	60002	2355	29W-43N	D4
24300	SlmT	53179	2357		A2
27200	SlmT	53179	2356		D2
30800	RdlT	53192	2355		E1
30800	SlmT	53192	2355		E1
30800	SlmT	53192	2356		A1
35600	RdlT	53181	2354		D3
35600	TNLK	53181	2354		D3
Wilmot Rd CO-B					
30000	SlmT	53179	2356		B1
Wilmot Rd CO-C					
24300	SlmT	53179	2357		A2
27200	SlmT	53179	2356		D2
30800	RdlT	53192	2355		E1
30800	SlmT	53192	2355		E1
30800	SlmT	53192	2356		A1
31200	RdlT	53181	2355		E1
Wilmot Rd CO-HM					
35600	RdlT	53181	2354		D3
35600	TNLK	53181	2354		D3
Wilmot Rd CO-V44					
7300	BtnT	60081	2414	30W-39N	B5
7600	SPGV	60081	2414	29W-40N	C3
7700	FXLK	60081	2414	29W-39N	B4
9500	FXLK	60081	2355	29W-41N	C7
10000	BtnT	60081	2355	29W-42N	C6
10900	AntT	60002	2355	29W-43N	D4
10900	FXLK	60002	2355	29W-43N	D4
W Wilmot Rd					
26300	AntT	60002	2356	27W-43N	B4
43400	AntT	53179	2356	27W-43N	B4
43400	SlmT	53179	2356	27W-43N	B4
Wilmot Farms Ln					
700	FXLK	60081	2414	29W-41N	C1
700	SPGV	60081	2414	30W-41N	B1
Wilmslow Ln					
100	SMBG	60194	2858	25W-10N	A5
Wilrose Ct					
13700	ODPK	60467	3344	13W-16S	E3
Wilshire Av					
500	WHTN	60137	3025	23W-0S	A6
900	EGVV	60007	2915	18W-8N	A1
2900	MKHM	60428	3427	3W-19S	A2
N Wilshire Av					
1700	ANHT	60004	2807	16W-15N	C1
Wilshire Blvd					
4800	CCHL	60478	3426	6W-21S	A5
Wilshire Ct					
-	LMNT	60439	3270	20W-14S	A7
10	VNHL	60061	2647	17W-26N	C3
100	SMWD	60107	2856	29W-10N	E5
700	WMTN	60481	3853	27W-39S	E7
700	WMTN	60481	3943	27W-39S	E1
900	LYVL	60048	2591	17W-29N	C4
1900	BFGV	60089	2701	17W-22N	B4
2200	AvnT	60030	2475	20W-35N	E6
2200	GYLK	60030	2475	20W-35N	E6
2700	AURA	60502	3079	32W-4S	C7
2900	MKHM	60428	3427	3W-19S	A2
5800	HRPK	60133	2911	26W-7N	E4
13600	HTLY	60142	2744	42W-20N	B1
19800	MKNA	60448	3502	15W-23S	C4
19800	MKNA	60451	3502	15W-23S	C4
N Wilshire Ct					
300	PLTN	60074	2753	20W-16N	B7
Wilshire Dr					
-	WLMT	60091	2812	5W-13N	A6
100	WLNG	60090	2755	15W-18N	A4
300	SDWH	60548	3330	51W-15S	A2
400	BGBK	60440	3268	24W-12S	E3
900	LYVL	60048	2591	17W-29N	B4
900	WLNG	60090	2754	15W-18N	E4
1200	NPVL	60540	3141	28W-6S	A5
3400	HFET	60067	2804	23W-14N	E4
3500	HFET	60192	2804	23W-14N	E4
6300	LslT	60517	3143	22W-7S	C6
15300	ODPK	60462	3345	12W-18S	D7
N Wilshire Dr					
600	MPPT	60056	2808	15W-13N	B5
W Wilshire Dr					
400	HFET	60067	2804	23W-14N	E4
400	HFET	60192	2804	23W-14N	E4
Wilshire Dr E					
300	WLMT	60091	2812	5W-13N	A7
Wilshire Dr W					
300	WLMT	60091	2812	5W-13N	A7
Wilshire Ln					
800	CRTE	60417	3596	0W-28S	C6
2700	NHBK	60062	2756	10W-18N	E4
N Wilshire Ln					
200	ANHT	60004	2807	16W-14N	C4
3000	ANHT	60004	2754	16W-17N	C5
S Wilshire Ln					
-	ANHT	60005	2807	16W-13N	C6
100	ANHT	60004	2807	16W-13N	C5
Wilshire Rd					
400	LKFT	60045	2649	11W-24N	D7
2700	PnfT	60435	3417	27W-20S	B6
2800	JLET	60435	3417	27W-20S	B6
2800	PnfT	60431	3417	27W-20S	B6
Wilshire St					
300	PKFT	60466	3594	4W-26S	E3
400	RNPK	60471	3594	4W-26S	E3
Wilshire Wy					
13500	HTLY	60142	2744	42W-20N	B1
Wilson Av					
10	JLET	60433	3499	23W-24S	B5
100	WCDA	60084	2643	26W-26N	D2
200	WCDA	60084	2644	25W-27N	A2
200	WcnT	60084	2644	25W-27N	A2
300	WCHI	60185	3022	29W-0N	C5
300	WPHR	60096	2363	9W-43N	C5
400	CTCY	60409	3352	3E-17S	A5
500	GNEN	60137	3083	22W-1S	B1
500	PKCY	60085	2535	14W-33N	D3
600	WKGN	60085	2535	14W-33N	D3
800	NPVL	60540	3141	27W-6S	B5
1000	WHTN	60187	3082	23W-1S	E1
1200	CHHT	60411	3507	2W-25S	D7
1300	CPVL	60110	2748	32W-17N	D7
1400	CHHT	60411	3595	2W-25S	D1
1400	CTCY	60409	3351	2E-17S	C5
1400	WKGN	60087	2479	11W-36N	E3
1600	WHTN	60187	3083	23W-1S	A1
1900	DLTN	60409	3351	2E-17S	C5
1900	DLTN	60419	3351	2E-17S	C5
4100	RGMW	60008	2805	20W-14N	E4
4100	RGMW	60008	2806	20W-14N	A4
4300	DRGV	60515	3144	21W-4S	A1
9900	SRPK	60176	2917	12W-5N	B7
9900	SRPK	60176	2973	12W-5N	B1
E Wilson Av					
10	LMBD	60148	3026	19W-0S	D6
N Wilson Av					
37800	BHPK	60087	2480	10W-38N	A1
38200	BHPK	60087	2422	10W-38N	A7
38200	BHPK	60099	2422	10W-38N	A7
W Wilson Av					
-	CHCG	60640	2922	0W-5N	A7
700	CHCG	60640	2921	2W-5N	B7
1900	CHCG	60625	2921	2W-5N	B7
3400	CHCG	60625	2920	4W-5N	C7
4000	CHCG	60630	2920	5W-5N	B7
5300	CHCG	60630	2919	6W-5N	D7
7200	HDHT	60706	2918	9W-5N	C7
7200	NRDG	60706	2918	9W-5N	C7
8400	CHCG	60656	2918	10W-5N	A7
8400	CHCG	60706	2918	10W-5N	A7
8600	CHCG	60656	2917	10W-5N	E7
25500	WCDA	60084	2644	25W-27N	A2
25500	WcnT	60084	2644	25W-27N	A2
Wilson Blvd					
35600	AvnT	60073	2474	24W-35N	B6
Wilson Ct					
-	PNFD	60586	3415	31W-19S	E4
10	PKFT	60466	3594	4W-26S	E3
10	PKFT	60466	3595	3W-26S	A2
100	BNVL	60106	2915	16W-6N	E7
1200	ZION	60099	2422	10W-41N	B2
1300	BtnT	60099	2422	10W-41N	B2
N Wilson Ct					
100	PLTN	60067	2752	22W-16N	C7
100	PLTN	60067	2805	22W-15N	B1
100	PltT	60067	2805	22W-15N	B1
S Wilson Dr					
1100	LKFT	60045	2649	13W-24N	A7
1700	LKFT	60045	2648	13W-24N	E7
Wilson Ln					
-	PNFD	60586	3415	31W-19S	E3
500	DSPN	60016	2863	12W-11N	B3
700	HNDL	60521	3146	14W-5S	C3
N Wilson Ln					
400	AddT	60101	2970	19W-4N	C4
400	ADSN	60101	2970	19W-4N	C4
Wilson Pl					
10	OSWG	60543	3263	37W-12S	B4
N Wilson Pl					
1800	ANHT	60004	2807	18W-15N	A1
Wilson Rd					
5600	RcmT	60071	2353	34W-43N	C4
5600	RHMD	60071	2353	34W-43N	C4
31600	GrtT	60030	2531	25W-31N	B7
31600	GrtT	60073	2531	25W-31N	B7
31600	RDLK	60073	2531	25W-31N	B7
31600	WcnT	60030	2531	25W-31N	B7
Wilson Rd CO-V58					
31600	GrtT	60030	2531	25W-31N	B7
31600	GrtT	60073	2531	25W-31N	B7
31600	RDLK	60073	2531	25W-31N	B7
31600	WcnT	60030	2531	25W-31N	B7
N Wilson Rd					
300	GrtT	60041	2530	26W-33N	E2
300	RDLK	60041	2530	26W-33N	E2
300	RDLK	60073	2530	26W-33N	E2
32500	GrtT	60030	2531	25W-32N	B5
32500	GrtT	60073	2531	25W-32N	A5
32500	RDLK	60073	2531	25W-32N	A5
32800	GrtT	60073	2530	26W-33N	E2
34600	GrtT	60041	2473	26W-34N	E7
N Wilson Rd CO-V58					
300	GrtT	60041	2530	26W-33N	E2
300	RDLK	60041	2530	26W-33N	E2
300	RDLK	60073	2530	26W-33N	E2
32500	GrtT	60030	2531	25W-32N	B5
32500	GrtT	60073	2531	25W-32N	A5
32500	RDLK	60073	2531	25W-32N	A5
32800	GrtT	60073	2530	26W-33N	E2
34600	GrtT	60041	2473	26W-34N	E7
W Wilson Rd					
10	LMBD	60148	3026	20W-0S	A6
300	LkvT	60002	2415	25W-38N	E6
300	LkvT	60002	2416	25W-38N	A6
400	YkTp	60148	3026	20W-0S	A6
600	LMBD	60148	3025	21W-0S	E6
600	MltT	60148	3025	21W-0S	E6
600	MltT	60148	3026	21W-0S	A6
25800	AntT	60002	2415	26W-38N	E6
Wilson St					
-	BtvT	60510	3079	32W-1S	B1
-	MONE	60449	3683	6W-31S	A5
-	WnfT	60510	3079	32W-1S	D1
10	WCHI	60185	3080	30W-1S	A1
10	WnfT	60185	3080	30W-1S	A1
10	WnfT	60510	3080	30W-1S	B1
10	WNKA	60093	2812	4W-15N	B2
100	PKFT	60466	3594	4W-26S	E3
100	PKFT	60466	3595	4W-26S	A3
200	AddT	60126	2972	15W-3N	A5
200	EMHT	60126	2972	15W-3N	A5
400	DRGV	60515	3144	19W-5S	D2
600	HRPK	60133	2912	26W-9N	A1
700	ELGN	60123	2854	34W-11N	D3
800	GNVA	60134	3020	35W-1N	B2
800	SCRL	60134	3020	35W-1N	B2
800	SCRL	60174	3020	35W-1N	B2
E Wilson St					
10	PLTN	60067	2805	20W-16N	E1
100	EMHT	60126	3027	16W-0N	E5
100	EMHT	60126	3028	15W-0N	A5
200	PTON	60468	3861	9W-37S	A3
400	PLTN	60067	2806	20W-16N	A1
400	PLTN	60074	2806	20W-16N	A1
1200	BTVA	60510	3078	33W-1S	E1
1500	BtvT	60510	3079	33W-1S	A1
1600	WnfT	60510	3079	33W-1S	B1
1700	BTVA	60510	3079	33W-1S	A1
E Wilson St SR-25					
100	BTVA	60510	3078	35W-1S	C2
S Wilson St					
10	JLET	60432	3499	23W-23S	B5
10	JLET	60433	3499	23W-23S	B5
W Wilson St					
-	MONE	60449	3683	5W-31S	B5
10	BTVA	60510	3078	36W-1S	A2
200	EMHT	60126	3027	16W-0N	D5
200	PTON	60468	3860	9W-37S	E3
200	PTON	60468	3861	8W-37S	B3
800	PLTN	60067	2805	22W-16N	B1
800	PltT	60067	2805	22W-16N	B1
2300	BTVA	60510	3077	36W-1S	E2
5600	MONE	60449	3682	7W-31S	E5
Wilson Ter					
4400	SKOK	60076	2866	5W-11N	A2
7900	MNGV	60053	2864	9W-11N	B2
7900	NLES	60053	2864	9W-11N	B2
7900	NLES	60714	2864	9W-11N	B2
Wilson Wy					
100	SEGN	60177	2908	34W-9N	D1
Wilson Creek Cir					
1900	AURA	60503	3201	33W-10S	B7
Wilson Hall Rd					
-	BtvT	60510	3079	33W-2S	B3
-	WnfT	60510	3079	33W-2S	B3
N Wilton Av					
2600	CHCG	60614	2977	1W-3N	E5
3500	CHCG	60613	2977	1W-4N	E3
3500	CHCG	60657	2977	1W-4N	E3
36900	LKVL	60046	2416	23W-38N	E6
36900	LkvT	60046	2416	23W-38N	E6
Wilton Ct					
-	OSWG	60543	3263	36W-12S	E3
1600	GNOK	60048	2592	14W-30N	D3
2400	YKVL	60560	3333	42W-17S	D6
7600	DRN	60561	3206	19W-8S	E2
E Wilton Ct					
600	PLTN	60074	2753	20W-16N	B7
Wilton Dr					
300	ANTH	60002	2357	23W-42N	E6
Wilton Ln					
10	MDLN	60060	2646	20W-27N	B1
300	SMBG	60193	2858	25W-10N	B6
2400	AURA	60502	3139	32W-4S	C1
Wilton Rd					
7500	DRN	60561	3206	19W-8S	E2
N Wilton Rd					
26500	WcnT	60084	2644	25W-26N	A3
Wilton Wy					
-	LkvT	60046	2416	23W-38N	E6
Wilton Croft Rd					
100	SchT	60175	2963	36W-5N	E3
Wiltse Dr					
10	NHLK	60164	3028	13W-2N	D1
Wiltshire Ct					
-	WYNE	60184	2966	30W-4N	B3
10	GRNE	60031	2535	14W-34N	B1
10	SMBG	60193	2859	23W-9N	A7
600	CLLK	60014	2640	35W-24N	A6
Wiltshire Dr					
10	LNSH	60069	2702	14W-22N	C3
800	MHRY	60050	2527	33W-32N	D4
Wiltshire Ln					
200	SgrT	60554	3134	44W-4S	E1
Wimbledon Cir					
500	PTHT	60070	2808	13W-15N	E2
Wimbledon Ct					
10	LNSH	60069	2702	15W-23N	A2
100	LKBF	60044	2593	11W-28N	E7
800	BGBK	60440	3205	22W-9S	D4
1600	LKFT	60045	2703	13W-23N	A2
Wimbledon Dr					
900	ISLK	60042	2586	30W-28N	B6

STREET Block	City	ZIP	Map#	CGS	Grid
Wimbledon Pl					
-	BMDL	60172	2912	24W-6N	D7
-	ROSL	60172	2912	24W-6N	D7
200	BMDL	60108	2912	24W-6N	D7
Wimbledon Rd					
10	LKBF	60044	2593	11W-28N	E7
Wimbleton Ln					
800	CLLK	60014	2639	36W-24N	C7
Wimbleton Tr					
400	MHRY	60050	2527	34W-32N	B5
W Wimbolton Dr					
10	MPPT	60056	2807	15W-14N	E4
10	MPPT	60056	2808	15W-14N	A4
Wimborne Av					
3600	JLET	60451	3500	19W-22S	E2
3600	NLNX	60451	3500	19W-22S	E2
Wimpole St					
-	MDLN	60061	2647	17W-25N	A5
-	VNHL	60060	2647	17W-25N	A5
-	VNHL	60061	2647	17W-25N	A5
1400	INCK	60060	2647	17W-25N	B5
1400	MDLN	60060	2647	17W-25N	B5
Winaki Tr					
1000	ALGN	60102	2747	34W-19N	D2
1000	DndT	60102	2747	34W-19N	E2
Winberie Av					
3900	AURA	60564	3202	30W-9S	B5
Winberie Ct N					
1500	AURA	60564	3202	30W-9S	A5
Winberie Ct S					
1600	AURA	60564	3202	30W-9S	B5
1600	NPVL	60564	3202	30W-9S	B5
Wincanton Dr					
1100	DRFD	60015	2703	10W-21N	E6
Wincanton Ln					
1600	HDPK	60035	2705	7W-22N	A5
Wincasset Ct					
-	BCHR	60401	3774	0W-35S	D6
Winchell Wy					
400	GNEN	60137	3083	22W-1S	B2
Winchester Av					
-	BLID	60827	3277	2W-15S	C7
-	CTPK	60827	3277	2W-15S	C7
4500	LSLE	60532	3142	23W-5S	C2
4500	LYNS	60534	3148	10W-4S	B1
4600	MCCK	60525	3148	10W-4S	B1
4600	MCCK	60534	3148	10W-4S	B1
12700	BLID	60406	3277	2W-15S	C7
12700	CTPK	60406	3277	2W-15S	C7
13100	BLID	60406	3349	2W-15S	C1
14100	DXMR	60426	3349	2W-16S	D4
14600	HRVY	60426	3349	2W-18S	D7
16100	MKHM	60428	3427	2W-20S	D4
16500	HLCT	60428	3427	2W-20S	D4
16500	HLCT	60429	3427	2W-20S	D4
17000	EHZC	60429	3427	2W-20S	D4
N Winchester Av					
800	CHCG	60622	3033	2W-1N	C2
1600	CHCG	60622	2977	2W-2N	C7
2300	CHCG	60614	2977	2W-3N	B5
4200	CHCG	60613	2977	2W-5N	C1
4400	CHCG	60613	2921	2W-5N	B7
4800	CHCG	60640	2921	2W-6N	B6
6000	CHCG	60660	2921	2W-7N	B3
6400	CHCG	60626	2921	2W-8N	B2
7300	CHCG	60626	2867	2W-9N	B7
7500	CHCG	60202	2867	2W-9N	B7
7500	EVTN	60202	2867	2W-9N	B7
S Winchester Av					
200	CHCG	60612	3033	2W-0S	C5
2300	CHCG	60608	3091	2W-2S	C2
3500	CHCG	60609	3091	2W-3S	C5
4700	CHCG	60609	3151	2W-5S	C2
5500	CHCG	60636	3151	2W-7S	C5
7500	CHCG	60620	3213	2W-9S	C3
9500	CHCG	60643	3213	2W-11S	C6
12400	BLID	60406	3277	2W-14S	C6
12400	BLID	60827	3277	2W-14S	C6
12400	CTPK	60406	3277	2W-14S	C6
12400	CTPK	60827	3277	2W-14S	C6
Winchester Cir E					
700	WNVL	60555	3080	29W-2S	D5
Winchester Cir N					
500	WNVL	60555	3080	29W-2S	D5
Winchester Cir S					
500	WNVL	60555	3080	29W-2S	D5
Winchester Cir W					
700	WNVL	60555	3080	29W-3S	D5
Winchester Ct					
300	LKBF	60044	2593	11W-29N	D5
600	BRLT	60103	2910	29W-6N	E7
600	LKVL	60046	2417	22W-39N	C4
800	CLSM	60188	2967	27W-3N	C5
1300	NPVL	60563	3140	29W-5S	E3
1600	SMBG	60193	2858	25W-10N	B6
6200	GRNE	60031	2534	16W-34N	D1
14200	HMGN	60491	3344	15W-16S	C4
W Winchester Ct					
400	RDLK	60073	2531	23W-32N	E5
Winchester Ct E					
3100	AURA	60504	3201	31W-9S	D4
Winchester Ct W					
3000	AURA	60504	3201	31W-9S	D4
Winchester Dr					
100	SMWD	60107	2856	29W-9N	E7
200	ALGN	60102	2694	35W-21N	A7
300	RDLK	60073	2531	23W-32N	E5
2800	ELGN	60124	2853	37W-11N	C3
22800	CNHN	60410	3584	29W-27S	D5
23900	CNHN	60436	3584	29W-27S	D5
S Winchester Dr					
700	RDLK	60073	2531	23W-32N	E5
Winchester Ln					
600	LKVL	60046	2417	22W-39N	C4
800	NHBK	60062	2756	11W-17N	D4
1600	SMBG	60193	2858	25W-10N	B6
2100	GNVW	60025	2810	10W-14N	A3
3400	GNVW	60025	2809	10W-14N	E3
Winchester Rd					
12000	HMGN	60491	3344	15W-16S	C4
E Winchester Rd					
100	LYVL	60048	2591	16W-29N	D3
N Winchester Rd					
39000	WDWH	60083	2420	13W-39N	E6
W Winchester Rd					
-	LbvT	60048	2591	17W-29N	B3
-	LYVL	60060	2591	17W-29N	A3
-	MDLN	60048	2591	17W-29N	A3
-	MDLN	60060	2591	17W-29N	A3
100	LYVL	60048	2591	17W-29N	A3
400	CHHT	60411	3507	2W-24S	D5
1400	LYVL	60048	2590	19W-30N	B3
1400	LYVL	60060	2590	19W-30N	B3
1400	MDLN	60048	2590	18W-29N	E3
1400	MDLN	60060	2590	18W-29N	E3
19100	FmtT	60048	2590	19W-30N	B3
W Winchester Rd					
19100	FmtT	60060	2590	19W-30N	B3
20500	RLKP	60030	2590	20W-30N	A3
W Winchester Rd CO-A34					
-	LbvT	60048	2591	17W-29N	B3
-	LYVL	60060	2591	17W-29N	A3
-	MDLN	60048	2591	17W-29N	A3
-	MDLN	60060	2591	17W-29N	A3
100	LYVL	60048	2591	17W-29N	A3
1400	LYVL	60048	2590	19W-30N	B3
1400	LYVL	60060	2590	19W-30N	B3
1400	MDLN	60048	2590	18W-29N	E3
1400	MDLN	60060	2590	18W-29N	E3
19100	FmtT	60048	2590	19W-30N	B3
19100	FmtT	60060	2590	19W-30N	B3
20000	RLKP	60030	2590	20W-30N	A3
Winchester Tr					
1900	RMVL	60446	3339	27W-17S	B7
Winchester Wy					
200	CmpT	60175	2962	40W-6N	B1
Windbrooke Dr					
1100	BFGV	60089	2701	16W-21N	E6
1100	VrnT	60089	2701	16W-21N	E6
Windbrooke Rd					
500	RMVL	60446	3339	27W-18S	C7
500	RMVL	60446	3417	27W-18S	C1
500	RMVL	60544	3339	27W-18S	C7
500	RMVL	60544	3417	27W-18S	C1
Windbury Ct					
1600	MTGY	60538	3199	36W-9S	E5
Windcrest Ct					
300	BGBK	60440	3269	22W-13S	D4
800	SYHW	60118	2800	36W-15N	A4
Windcrest Dr					
-	RMVL	60446	3339	27W-17S	C7
-	RMVL	60544	3339	27W-17S	C7
10	OSWG	60543	3263	36W-11S	D2
S Windcrest Dr					
400	RMVL	60446	3339	27W-18S	C7
400	RMVL	60544	3339	27W-18S	C7
Wind Crest Ln					
100	NLNX	60451	3500	19W-24S	D6
Windcrest Ln					
1700	AURA	60504	3201	33W-9S	A3
2000	JLET	60431	3417	28W-21S	B7
Windcrest Rd					
1400	DRFD	60015	2703	10W-21N	E6
Winddance Ct					
700	LKVL	60046	2474	23W-37N	E3
Wind Dance Dr					
11700	MKNA	60448	3502	14W-25S	D7
Winddance Dr					
10	LKVL	60046	2475	23W-37N	A3
200	LKVL	60046	2474	23W-37N	E3
Windemera Ct					
-	ODPK	60467	3344	14W-16S	C4
Windemere Av					
1200	NPVL	60564	3203	28W-10S	A7
8800	BKFD	60513	3087	11W-4S	D6
8800	BKFD	60513	3088	11W-4S	A6
8800	BKFD	60534	3088	11W-4S	A6
8800	LYNS	60534	3088	11W-4S	A6
Windemere Cir					
-	LKPT	60441	3419	21W-20S	E5
1100	GRNE	60031	2476	18W-35N	E6
1100	GRNE	60031	2477	18W-35N	A6
2000	SMBG	60194	2858	26W-12N	A2
Windemere Ct					
900	AURA	60504	3201	32W-9S	C3
1100	BRLT	60103	2910	29W-6N	E7
Windemere Dr					
10	GNEN	60137	3026	20W-0S	A7
Windemere Ln					
-	SBTN	60192	2804	24W-14N	C4
10	HFET	60010	2804	24W-14N	C3
10	HFET	60192	2804	24W-14N	C3
10	SBTN	60010	2804	24W-14N	C3
600	CLSM	60188	2967	26W-3N	D7
600	LKZH	60047	2699	22W-21N	B5
900	AURA	60504	3201	32W-9S	D4
Wind Energy Pass					
500	BTVA	60510	3078	34W-3S	D5
500	BTVA	60542	3078	34W-3S	C5
500	NARA	60542	3078	34W-3S	C5
1100	AURA	60510	3078	34W-3S	D5
1300	BtvT	60502	3078	33W-3S	E5
1300	BtvT	60510	3078	33W-3S	E5
Windermere Dr					
10	WNFD	60190	3023	27W-0N	C5
10	WnfT	60190	3023	27W-0N	B6
Windermere Wy					
300	LIHL	60156	2692	38W-21N	D5
Windermere on Duxbury					
10	RGMW	60008	2805	22W-13N	B6
Windett Ln					
500	GNVA	60134	3019	37W-1N	C2
Windette Dr					
1800	MTGY	60538	3198	40W-9S	A5
Windett Ridge Rd					
-	KdlT	60560	3333	42W-17S	C6
300	YKVL	60560	3333	42W-17S	D6
Windfield Ct					
1200	ROSL	60172	2912	25W-7N	A4
Windfield Wy					
1300	ROSL	60172	2912	25W-7N	B4
Windflower Ct					
10	RMVL	60446	3339	26W-17S	E5
1400	GYLK	60030	2533	19W-31N	C6
20300	FmtT	60060	2646	20W-26N	A3
Windgate Ct					
10	SMWD	60107	2857	27W-11N	B4
1000	NPVL	60540	3203	28W-8S	A1
1300	BRLT	60103	2966	30W-5N	B1
E Windgate Ct					
500	ANHT	60005	2861	17W-12N	B2
Windgate Wy					
5500	LIHL	60156	2692	38W-21N	D6
Windham Cir					
200	YKVL	60560	3332	44W-15S	E2
200	YKVL	60560	3333	43W-15S	A2
Windham Ct					
-	WDND	60118	2800	36W-16N	A2
-	WHTN	60187	3024	25W-0N	B4
1000	GNVA	60134	3020	36W-0N	A5
6500	LGGV	60047	2646	18W-24N	D6
N Windham Ct N					
2000	ANHT	60004	2807	17W-14N	C4
Windham Ct N					
1900	ANHT	60004	2807	17W-14N	B4
Windham Ln					
500	NPVL	60563	3141	26W-5S	E4
1100	EGVV	60007	2914	20W-8N	A2
6500	LGGV	60047	2646	18W-25N	D6
6500	LGGV	60060	2646	18W-25N	D6
N Windham Ln					
100	BMDL	60108	2968	24W-5N	C1
S Windham Ln					
100	BMDL	60108	2968	24W-5N	C1
Windham Pkwy					
1100	BGBK	60440	3268	24W-13S	D6
1100	RMVL	60446	3268	25W-14S	B7
1200	BGBK	60446	3268	25W-14S	A7
1200	BGBK	60490	3268	25W-14S	A7
Windham Tr					
400	CPVL	60110	2748	33W-17N	A7
Windham Cove Dr					
400	CLLK	60014	2693	36W-23N	E1
Windham Hill Ct					
10	LslT	60540	3142	25W-5S	B3
Windhaven Ct					
1000	LKFT	60045	2649	12W-24N	B7
N Windhaven Ct					
17500	WrnT	60030	2534	17W-32N	B4
S Windhaven Ct					
300	MHRY	60050	2527	34W-31N	C6
Windhaven Rd					
900	LYVL	60048	2591	17W-29N	A4
S Windhaven Tr					
400	MHRY	60050	2527	34W-31N	C6
W Windhaven Tr					
5500	MHRY	60050	2527	34W-31N	C6
S Windhill Dr					
1000	PLTN	60067	2805	22W-14N	B3
W Windhill Dr					
1200	PLTN	60067	2805	22W-14N	A4
1300	IVNS	60067	2805	22W-14N	A4
Windhill Ln					
2900	DYR	46311	3598		D4
3300	LIHL	60156	2692	39W-23N	C2
N Winding Ln					
28000	WcnT	60084	2587	25W-28N	E6
Winding Rd					
5600	NndT	60014	2641	32W-26N	B3
Winding Tr					
600	DndT	60118	2746	36W-17N	E7
600	DndT	60118	2747	36W-17N	A6
Winding Wy					
-	BGBK	60490	3267	28W-14S	A7
-	PNFD	60585	3267	28W-14S	A7
Winding Branch Rd					
10	ElaT	60047	2644	24W-25N	C4
10	HNWD	60047	2644	24W-25N	C4
Winding Canyon Ct					
10	ALGN	60102	2748	33W-19N	A2
Winding Canyon Wy					
100	ALGN	60102	2748	33W-19N	A2
Winding Creek Ct					
11400	ODPK	60467	3422	14W-20S	E4
Winding Creek Dr					
200	NPVL	60565	3203	26W-8S	D2
11300	ODPK	60467	3422	14W-20S	E4
W Winding Creek Dr					
5100	MHRY	60050	2527	33W-31N	D6
Winding Creek Lp					
12200	HTLY	60142	2744	42W-19N	D3
Winding Creek Rd					
-	PnfT	60586	3416	28W-20S	E4
10	OswT	60560	3334	40W-14S	C1
16300	PNFD	60586	3416	28W-19S	E4
16300	PNFD	60586	3417	28W-19S	A3
Winding Glen Ct					
1000	CLSM	60188	2967	27W-4N	C4
Winding Glen Dr					
1100	CLSM	60188	2967	27W-4N	C4
Winding Lakes Dr					
2000	JLET	60586	3416	31W-21S	A7
Winding Meadow Ln					
3400	GNVA	60134	3019	37W-0N	B5
W Winding Oak Ct					
26100	CNHN	60410	3672	32W-31S	C6
Winding Oak Ln					
200	BFGV	60089	2701	16W-21N	C7
Winding Oak Tr					
26300	CNHN	60410	3672	33W-31S	C7
W Winding Oak Tr					
26300	CNHN	60410	3672	32W-31S	C6
Winding Ridge Ct					
1800	RMVL	60446	3339	27W-17S	D6
Winding River Dr					
2100	NPVL	60564	3202	29W-10S	C5
Winding Run Ln					
10	SMWD	60107	2857	28W-12N	B1
W Winding Trail Cir					
200	RDLK	60073	2531	23W-31N	E6
Winding Trail Ln					
3600	HFET	60192	2804	25W-14N	A3
Winding Trails					
-	DMND	60416	3941	33W-39S	A2
Winding Trails Ct					
9100	WLSP	60480	3208	14W-10S	D5
Winding Trails Dr					
11700	WLSP	60480	3208	14W-10S	C6
Windjammer Ct					
10	TDLK	60030	2533	19W-34N	D1
Wind Jammer Ln					
400	WldT	60564	3202	29W-10S	D6
500	NPVL	60564	3202	29W-10S	D6
Windjammer Ln					
100	TDLK	60030	2533	19W-34N	D1
1200	HRPK	60133	2967	27W-4N	D3
Windlake Ct					
10	RVWD	60015	2703	12W-22N	A4
Windmere Cir					
-	ANTH	60002	2418	20W-40N	A3
N Windmere Cir					
100	RchT	60443	3593	8W-26S	B1
S Windmere Cir					
300	RchT	60443	3593	8W-26S	B2
Windmere Ct					
900	DRN	60527	3145	17W-7S	B6
900	DRN	60561	3145	17W-7S	B6
28500	GNOK	60044	2593	13W-28N	A6
Windmere Ln					
3600	JNBG	60050	2471	31W-35N	C5
Windmill Cir					
10	GLBT	60136	2798	39W-16N	E2
Windmill Ct					
-	PNFD	60544	3416	30W-18S	B2
W Windmill Ct					
1700	ADSN	60101	2970	20W-4N	A3
Windmill Dr					
1800	HRPK	60133	2967	27W-5N	C2
S Windmill Dr					
15900	HmrT	60491	3420	19W-19S	E2
W Windmill Dr					
7400	FftT	60423	3504	9W-24S	E5
Windmill Ln					
15700	PNFD	60544	3416	30W-18S	B1
Windmill Pl					
-	GLBT	60136	2798	39W-16N	E2
Windmill Rd					
-	FXLK	60041	2473	26W-36N	D4
Windmill Rd					
10	ODPK	60467	3344	14W-17S	D6
36200	GrtT	60041	2473	26W-36N	D4
Windmill Creek Dr					
200	ANTH	60002	2358	22W-42N	B6
Windmill Turn					
10	ODPK	60467	3344	14W-17S	D6
Windover Cir					
500	BFGV	60089	2754	17W-20N	C1
Wind Point Ct					
2700	LYWD	60411	3510	3E-23S	A3
Windridge Ct					
600	NPVL	60540	3140	28W-7S	E7
N Windridge Ct					
-	KLDR	60047	2699	21W-22N	D4
Windridge Dr					
100	MHRY	60050	2527	34W-32N	D5
200	RLKP	60073	2532	23W-33N	A2
1000	CLLK	60014	2639	37W-24N	B7
1800	LKFT	60045	2703	12W-23N	B2
Wind Ridge Rd					
10	SBTN	60010	2803	27W-15N	B1
Windrift Dr					
4200	AURA	60504	3202	30W-8S	B2
E Wind River Ter					
1200	PLTN	60074	2753	19W-18N	C3
Windrush Ln					
10	BNHL	60010	2750	26W-18N	C4
2500	NHBK	60062	2757	10W-18N	A4
Windscape Ln					
1600	BCHR	60401	3774	0W-35S	C6
Windslow Cir					
1000	CLLK	60014	2693	36W-23N	D1
5200	MHRY	60050	2527	34W-32N	D5
W Windslow Dr					
17300	WrnT	60030	2534	17W-33N	B3
Windsong Cir					
300	GLHT	60137	3025	23W-1N	A2
300	GLHT	60139	3025	23W-1N	A2
300	MltT	60137	3025	23W-1N	A2
300	MltT	60139	3025	23W-1N	A2
Windsong Ct					
300	BGBK	60440	3269	23W-12S	A2
2000	GRNE	60031	2477	16W-36N	E4
2300	SMBG	60194	2857	26W-11N	E3
Wind Song Dr					
1700	JLET	60435	3417	27W-21S	D7
1700	JLET	60435	3497	27W-21S	D1
Windsong Dr					
-	HFET	60169	2858	26W-12N	A3
-	SMBG	60169	2858	26W-12N	A3
1800	SMBG	60194	2857	26W-11N	E3
1900	SMBG	60194	2858	26W-11N	A3
Wind Song Ln					
1500	AURA	60504	3200	33W-9S	E3
Windsor Av					
100	WDDL	60191	2971	17W-5N	A1
300	GNEN	60137	3025	23W-0S	A6
900	AURA	60505	3200	34W-8S	D2
6400	BRWN	60402	3089	8W-3S	A4
6800	BRWN	60402	3088	8W-3S	E4
7000	BtnT	60081	2414	29W-39N	C6
7100	RVSD	60402	3088	8W-3S	E4
7100	RVSD	60546	3088	8W-3S	E4
E Windsor Av					
100	LMBD	60148	3026	19W-1N	C3
W Windsor Av					
400	LMBD	60148	3026	20W-1N	A3
700	CteT	60417	3685	1W-31S	B5
800	CHCG	60640	2921	1W-5N	E7
2100	CHCG	60625	2921	2W-5N	B7
2700	CHCG	60625	2920	3W-5N	E7
5100	CHCG	60630	2919	7W-5N	C7
7000	HDHT	60706	2918	8W-5N	D7
7000	NRDG	60706	2918	8W-5N	D7
8400	CHCG	60656	2918	10W-5N	A7
Windsor Cir					
10	SEGN	60177	2908	34W-8N	C4
200	SCRL	60175	2964	36W-4N	A3
500	FRGV	60021	2696	29W-23N	B2
500	IVNS	60067	2804	23W-15N	E3
1400	CPVL	60110	2748	32W-17N	D7
N Windsor Cir					
100	BMDL	60108	2968	25W-5N	B2
Windsor Ct					
10	ALGN	60102	2694	35W-21N	A6
10	SBTN	60010	2803	26W-14N	D3
10	SMWD	60107	2857	27W-11N	C4
100	DRFD	60015	2756	11W-20N	E2
200	SEGN	60177	2908	34W-8N	C4
200	SYHW	60118	2799	36W-15N	E3
300	CmpT	60175	2961	42W-4N	D4
300	LKVL	60046	2475	21W-37N	C2
600	LNHT	60046	2418	19W-39N	C5
800	WCHI	60185	3022	29W-0S	D7
800	WnfT	60185	3022	29W-0S	D7
1300	ELGN	60120	2855	31W-11N	E3
1300	GNVA	60134	3020	33W-1N	E3
1500	NPVL	60565	3204	25W-8S	C2
1600	WCHI	60185	3080	29W-1S	D1
1600	WnfT	60185	3080	29W-1S	D1
1800	DRGV	60516	3144	20W-7S	A6
1800	GRNE	60031	2477	16W-36N	E5
4400	RNPK	60471	3594	5W-26S	B3
5700	RGMW	60008	2805	21W-13N	C5
7900	DRN	60561	3206	19W-9S	C3
8200	BRRG	60527	3208	15W-9S	B3
11500	HTLY	60142	2691	42W-20N	A7
16600	LMNT	60439	3270	20W-14S	A7
16800	HMGN	60491	3422	15W-20S	B4
17300	SHLD	60473	3429	2E-20S	D4
E Windsor Ct					
10	SrgT	60506	3136	41W-6S	A4
10	SRGV	60506	3136	41W-6S	A4
S Windsor Ct					
600	LKFT	60045	2648	13W-25N	E6
1000	WKGN	60085	2535	14W-33N	C4
W Windsor Ct					
10	SrgT	60506	3136	41W-6S	A4
10	SRGV	60506	3136	41W-6S	A4
2200	ADSN	60101	2969	21W-3N	D5
22300	KLDR	60047	2699	21W-22N	D4
Windsor Dr					
10	DSPN	60018	2862	15W-10N	B5
10	EMHT	60126	3027	16W-0N	E4
10	LNSH	60069	2702	13W-22N	E3
10	LNSH	60069	2703	13W-22N	A4
10	OKBK	60523	3086	15W-2S	B4
10	RVWD	60015	2703	13W-22N	A4
10	RVWD	60069	2703	13W-22N	A4
100	EDND	60110	2801	32W-17N	D7
100	SchT	60175	2907	36W-7N	E5
100	VNHL	60061	2647	17W-26N	C4
200	BFGV	60089	2754	17W-18N	B3
200	BGBK	60440	3268	24W-11S	D1
200	BRLT	60103	2911	28W-6N	A6
Windsor Dr					
200	EGVV	60007	2914	19W-7N	C4
200	ITSC	60143	2914	19W-7N	C4
200	MltT	60137	3083	23W-2S	A4
200	ROSL	60172	2912	24W-7N	D5
300	WHTN	60187	3083	23W-2S	A4
400	OSWG	60543	3263	37W-14S	C6
500	FXLK	60020	2473	27W-35N	B5
500	GrtT	60020	2473	27W-35N	B5
600	CLLK	60014	2693	36W-24N	D1
600	SMBG	60193	2859	23W-9N	A7
700	SYHW	60118	2799	36W-15N	E3
900	SRWD	60404	3496	30W-24S	B6
900	WHTN	60187	3082	23W-2S	E4
1300	GYLK	60030	2475	21W-34N	C7
1300	GYLK	60030	2532	22W-34N	C1
2700	LSLE	60532	3142	24W-6S	C5
2800	NPVL	60540	3142	24W-6S	C5
7900	DRN	60561	3206	19W-9S	C3
9000	ODPK	60462	3346	11W-18S	A7
9000	PSHL	60465	3209	11W-11S	E7
9100	ODPK	60462	3345	11W-18S	E7
9100	PlsT	60465	3209	11W-11S	E7
9100	PlsT	60480	3209	11W-11S	E7
10400	WSTR	60154	3087	13W-2S	A3
10700	WSTR	60154	3086	13W-2S	E3
11400	HTLY	60142	2691	42W-20N	A7
11500	HTLY	60142	2744	42W-20N	A1
N Windsor Dr					
600	MPPT	60056	2808	15W-13N	A5
1200	PTHT	60004	2807	16W-15N	C3
1500	ANHT	60004	2807	17W-15N	C1
2000	ANHT	60004	2754	16W-16N	C7
3200	BFGV	60089	2754	17W-17N	C5
3200	WhlT	60004	2754	17W-17N	C5
3200	WhlT	60089	2754	17W-17N	C5
S Windsor Dr					
10	ANHT	60004	2807	16W-13N	C5
500	ANHT	60005	2807	16W-13N	C6
12500	PlsT	60464	3273	12W-14S	D7
12500	PSPK	60464	3273	12W-14S	D7
W Windsor Dr					
300	BMDL	60108	2968	25W-5N	C1
1000	MchT	60050	2472	29W-37N	B2
1800	RDLK	60073	2531	25W-33N	A3
21300	KLDR	60047	2699	21W-22N	D4
Windsor Ln					
-	LYWD	60411	3509	2E-23S	D4
10	GLHT	60139	3024	23W-2N	E1
10	GLHT	60139	3025	23W-2N	A1
100	WLBK	60527	3145	16W-6S	D5
200	OKTR	60181	3085	18W-1S	A1
200	YkTp	60181	3085	18W-1S	A1
300	IVNS	60010	2751	23W-16N	D6
400	ISLK	60042	2642	29W-27N	C1
500	BTVA	60510	3020	35W-0S	A7
700	RMVL	60446	3269	23W-14S	A6
900	DYR	46311	3510		E6
1100	HRPK	60133	2911	26W-9N	E1
1800	NLNX	60451	3500	19W-23S	D3
2200	CCHL	60478	3506	5W-22S	C1
2500	NHBK	60062	2810	10W-15N	A1
3200	JLET	60431	3497	28W-25S	B7
8800	BGVW	60455	3211	8W-10S	A5
S Windsor Ln					
16500	HmrT	60441	3421	18W-19S	A3
16500	LKPT	60441	3421	18W-19S	A3
Windsor Pkwy					
-	OrlT	60487	3423	11W-21S	E5
9200	TYPK	60487	3423	11W-21S	E5
Windsor Pl					
10200	MNSR	46321	3510		E4
N Windsor Pl					
10	MDLN	60060	2647	17W-27N	B1
Windsor Rd					
500	IVNS	60067	2804	23W-15N	E3
500	IVNS	60067	2805	23W-15N	A2
600	GNVW	60025	2811	7W-13N	B7
700	SgrT	60506	3135	41W-5S	D3
700	SgrT	60554	3135	42W-5S	D3
700	SRGV	60506	3135	41W-5S	D3
700	SRGV	60554	3135	42W-5S	D3
800	HDPK	60035	2704	9W-21N	B7
Windsor St					
300	PKFT	60466	3595	4W-27S	A4
Windsor Ter					
200	AntT	60002	2357	23W-41N	E7
400	LYVL	60048	2591	16W-28N	E6
23600	ANTH	60002	2357	23W-41N	E7
W Windsor Ter					
23500	ANTH	60002	2357	23W-41N	E7
23500	AntT	60002	2357	23W-41N	E7
Windsor Dalgaard Jr Ln					
42200	AntT	60002	2356	26W-42N	D6
Windsor Lake Ct					
16300	LktT	60403	3417	26W-19S	E3
Windsor Lake Ln					
21200	LktT	60403	3417	26W-19S	E3
Windsor Mall					
2300	PKRG	60068	2917	11W-8N	D2
Windsor Park Dr					
-	BmdT	60188	3024	26W-2N	A1
-	CLSM	60188	3024	26W-2N	A1
100	CLSM	60188	3023	26W-2N	E1
Windstar Cir					
4600	CPVL	60110	2747	36W-18N	A5
Windstone Ct					
900	LIHL	60156	2694	34W-21N	C5
7400	JLET	60586	3415	33W-21S	B7
Windstone Dr					
-	AraT	60542	3077	38W-4S	A7
-	AraT	60542	3137	38W-4S	B1
-	NARA	60542	3077	38W-4S	A7
-	SRGV	60554	3135	42W-4S	D2
1900	JLET	60586	3415	33W-21S	A7
Windstone Ln					
600	SRGV	60554	3135	41W-5S	E2
Windstream Ct					
300	AURA	60504	3140	31W-7S	A7
Windward					
100	LKMR	60051	2529	28W-33N	D4
Windward Av					
1600	NPVL	60563	3140	29W-6S	D4
Windward Ct					
-	LSLE	60532	3142	25W-5S	B2
1600	NPVL	60563	3140	29W-6S	D4
Windward Dr					
-	PGGV	60140	2797	42W-15N	C4
100	SMBG	60194	2859	22W-10N	C5
Windward Ln					
1700	HRPK	60133	2967	27W-4N	D3
Windward Rd					
-	LslT	60532	3142	24W-4S	C2
-	LslT	60563	3142	24W-4S	C2
4600	LSLE	60532	3142	25W-4S	C2

STREET Block	City	ZIP	Map#	CGS	Grid
Windward Tr					
13100	PlsT	60462	3346	10W-15S	B1
13100	PlsT	60464	3346	10W-15S	B1
Windwood Ct					
-	GRNE	60031	2478	14W-35N	C6
10	SgrT	60506	3135	41W-5S	E4
100	BFGV	60089	2701	16W-21N	C7
Windwood Dr					
10	SgrT	60506	3135	41W-5S	E4
Windy Ln					
-	NLNX	60451	3590	15W-26S	C1
N Windy Wy					
9900	NLES	60714	2864	10W-12N	A1
Windy Hill Ct					
200	NARA	60542	3077	37W-4S	C7
3700	AURA	60504	3202	30W-9S	A3
Windy Hill Dr					
-	FftT	60423	3592	10W-25S	B1
1500	NHBK	60062	2757	9W-16N	C6
21300	FKFT	60423	3504	10W-25S	B7
21300	FKFT	60423	3592	10W-25S	B1
Windy Hill Ln					
2000	HDPK	60035	2757	9W-20N	C1
Windy Hill Rd					
4200	DhmT	60033	2464	49W-36N	D4
Windy Knoll Dr					
1100	ALGN	60102	2694	34W-20N	B7
Windy Point Dr					
200	GLHT	60139	2969	23W-3N	A5
Windy Prairie Dr					
13300	HTLY	60142	2744	42W-18N	D4
Winesap Ct					
800	PTHT	60070	2808	13W-15N	E2
Winfal Dr					
800	SMBG	60173	2859	22W-10N	C5
Winfield Av					
-	MONE	60449	3682	8W-31S	C6
-	MonT	60449	3682	8W-31S	C6
Winfield Cir					
10	NHFD	60093	2811	6W-14N	E4
Winfield Ct					
200	VNHL	60061	2647	16W-24N	E6
300	SMBG	60194	2857	27W-10N	D5
Winfield Dr					
10	NHFD	60093	2811	6W-14N	D4
10	NtrT	60093	2811	6W-14N	E4
Winfield Ln					
400	IVNS	60010	2751	25W-16N	A7
Winfield Rd					
-	NPVL	60555	3141	28W-4S	B1
-	NPVL	60563	3141	28W-4S	B1
10	WNFD	60190	3023	27W-0N	C6
10	WnfT	60555	3081	28W-2S	B3
10	WNVL	60555	3081	28W-3S	B5
100	WNFD	60190	3081	27W-1S	C1
100	WnfT	60185	3081	28W-2S	B3
100	WnfT	60187	3081	27W-1S	B1
100	WnfT	60190	3081	27W-1S	C1
300	WNFD	60185	3023	27W-0N	C5
300	WnfT	60185	3023	27W-0S	C7
300	WnfT	60190	3023	27W-0S	C7
3600	WNVL	60555	3141	27W-4S	B1
16800	BtlT	53104	2359		B1
Winfield Rd CO-13					
-	NPVL	60555	3141	28W-4S	B1
-	NPVL	60563	3141	28W-4S	B1
10	WNFD	60190	3023	27W-0N	C6
10	WnfT	60555	3081	28W-2S	B3
10	WNVL	60555	3081	28W-3S	B5
100	WNFD	60190	3081	27W-1S	C1
100	WnfT	60185	3081	28W-2S	B3
100	WnfT	60187	3081	27W-1S	B1
100	WnfT	60190	3081	27W-1S	C1
300	WNFD	60185	3023	27W-0N	C5
300	WnfT	60185	3023	27W-0S	C7
300	WnfT	60190	3023	27W-0S	C7
3600	WNVL	60555	3141	27W-4S	B1
Winfield Rd CO-Q					
16800	BtlT	53104	2359		B1
S Winfield Rd					
26300	MONE	60449	3682	8W-32S	C7
26300	MonT	60449	3682	8W-32S	C7
Winfield Scott Dr					
10	WNFD	60190	3023	27W-0N	C5
Wing Av					
1000	SCRL	60174	2964	35W-3N	C6
Wing Ln					
400	SCRL	60174	2964	34W-3N	D6
Wing Rd					
1600	KdlT	60560	3333	41W-16S	E4
1600	KdlT	60560	3334	41W-16S	A5
1600	YKVL	60560	3333	41W-16S	E4
1600	YKVL	60560	3334	41W-16S	A5
Wing St					
600	ELGN	60123	2854	35W-12N	B2
2100	RGMW	60008	2806	19W-14N	C4
E Wing St					
100	ANHT	60004	2807	17W-14N	A5
W Wing St					
100	ANHT	60005	2807	18W-14N	A5
300	ANHT	60005	2806	18W-14N	E5
Wingate Cir					
10	CRTE	60417	3685	0W-29S	C1
Wingate Ct					
10	OSWG	60543	3200	34W-10S	E6
2600	AURA	60502	3139	32W-4S	B1
Wingate Dr					
-	MDLN	60060	2646	20W-27N	B1
10	OSWG	60543	3200	34W-10S	E7
200	SMBG	60193	2859	22W-9N	C7
300	CRTE	60417	3685	0W-29S	B1
6100	LSLE	60532	3142	23W-6S	E5
14900	HMGN	60491	3344	15W-17S	B6
Wingate Ln					
1800	WHTN	60187	3081	26W-2S	D4
Wingate Rd					
600	GNEN	60137	3025	22W-0S	C6
900	OMFD	60461	3506	4W-25S	D7
1000	MTSN	60443	3506	4W-25S	D7
6400	WLBK	60527	3146	15W-7S	A6
Winger Dr					
1700	JLET	60586	3415	32W-21S	C7
1700	JLET	60586	3495	32W-21S	C1
Wingfield Wy					
1300	BGBK	60490	3268	26W-12S	A3
Wing Foot Dr					
5000	MONE	60449	3683	6W-31S	A5
Wingfoot Dr					
500	NARA	60542	3078	35W-3S	B5
800	AURA	60510	3078	34W-3S	C6
800	NARA	60510	3078	34W-3S	C6
Wing Park Blvd					
200	ELGN	60123	2854	35W-11N	C3
Wing Pointe Dr					
10400	HTLY	60142	2745	39W-20N	B1
Wingpointe Dr					
500	AURA	60506	3198	39W-8S	E1
Wingstem St					
12500	PNFD	60585	3338	30W-14S	B1
Winhaven Dr					
10	ELGN	60124	2853	37W-11N	D4
10	ElgT	60124	2853	37W-11N	D3
2600	ELGN	60123	2853	37W-11N	D4
3300	WKGN	60087	2479	11W-37N	C1
Winifred Dr					
100	AURA	60506	3137	38W-7S	B7
Winifred St					
1400	JltT	60436	3586	24W-25S	D2
Winkleman Rd					
-	PTHT	60062	2809	12W-15N	B2
3800	NfdT	60062	2809	12W-15N	B2
Winkler Ct					
1800	LSLE	60532	3142	23W-6S	E5
Winmont Ct					
1800	MTGY	60538	3199	37W-10S	D5
Winmoor Ct					
1800	SYHW	60118	2800	35W-15N	C3
Winmoor Dr					
800	SYHW	60118	2800	35W-15N	B3
Winn Rd					
7600	SPGV	60081	2413	31W-40N	D2
7800	RcmT	60081	2413	31W-40N	D2
9700	RcmT	60071	2354	31W-41N	D7
9700	SPGV	60071	2354	31W-41N	D7
9700	SPGV	60081	2354	31W-41N	D7
Winn Rd CO-V40					
7600	SPGV	60081	2413	31W-40N	D2
7800	RcmT	60081	2413	31W-40N	D2
9700	RcmT	60071	2354	31W-41N	D7
9700	SPGV	60071	2354	31W-41N	D7
9700	SPGV	60081	2354	31W-41N	D7
N Winnebago Av					
1700	CHCG	60647	2977	2W-2N	A7
Winnebago Ct					
800	RMVL	60446	3340	24W-15S	C1
W Winnebago Ct					
33600	WrnT	60030	2534	17W-33N	B3
W Winnebago Dr					
17400	WrnT	60030	2534	17W-33N	B3
Winnebago Rd					
2200	WKGN	60087	2479	12W-36N	B4
4700	MchT	60097	2469	36W-36N	D4
4800	WRLK	60097	2469	36W-36N	D4
S Winnebago Rd					
12700	PSHT	60463	3274	9W-15S	D7
12800	PSHT	60463	3346	9W-15S	D1
Winnebago St					
-	WnfT	60510	3080	30W-1S	A2
300	PKFT	60466	3594	4W-26S	E2
300	PKFT	60466	3595	4W-26S	A2
400	PKFT	60471	3594	4W-26S	E2
400	RNPK	60471	3594	4W-26S	E2
Winnebago Tr					
600	BTVA	60510	3019	36W-0S	E7
1000	BTVA	60510	3020	36W-0S	A7
Winneberry Ln					
34100	GrtT	60073	2531	25W-34N	A1
W Winneconna Pkwy					
400	CHCG	60620	3214	0W-8S	B1
W Winnemac Av					
1400	CHCG	60640	2921	1W-6N	C6
1900	CHCG	60625	2921	3W-6N	A6
2700	CHCG	60625	2920	3W-6N	E6
4800	CHCG	60630	2919	6W-6N	E6
7400	HDHT	60706	2918	9W-6N	C6
7500	CHCG	60706	2918	9W-6N	C6
8000	NRDG	60706	2918	10W-6N	B6
8400	CHCG	60656	2918	10W-6N	A6
Winnemac St					
400	PKFT	60466	3594	4W-26S	E3
Winners Cir					
1100	LYVL	60048	2591	15W-27N	E7
1100	LYVL	60048	2647	15W-27N	E1
1400	RLKP	60030	2589	22W-31N	B1
W Winners Cir Ct					
24000	PNFD	60585	3266	30W-13S	C5
Winners Cup Cir					
10	WHTN	60187	3082	24W-2S	C3
1200	SCRL	60174	2964	34W-4N	D4
Winners Cup Ct					
800	GNVA	60134	3019	36W-0N	D4
900	NPVL	60564	3267	27W-11S	B1
900	WldT	60564	3267	27W-11S	B1
900	WldT	60565	3267	27W-11S	B1
1200	BRLT	60103	2910	29W-6N	E7
Winnetka Av					
100	KLWH	60043	2812	3W-15N	D3
100	WNKA	60093	2812	4W-14N	C3
500	NtrT	60093	2812	4W-14N	C3
3900	RGMW	60008	2806	20W-14N	A3
Winnetka Cir					
1600	RGMW	60008	2806	20W-14N	A3
Winnetka Ct					
-	GNVW	60025	2811	8W-15N	A3
2300	NHFD	60093	2811	8W-15N	A3
Winnetka Mw					
600	WNKA	60093	2812	5W-16N	A1
Winnetka Rd					
1300	NHFD	60093	2811	6W-15N	D3
1300	NtrT	60093	2811	6W-15N	E3
1300	WNKA	60093	2811	6W-15N	E3
1500	NHFD	60093	2810	8W-15N	E3
1800	NfdT	60093	2811	7W-15N	C3
2200	GNVW	60025	2811	6W-15N	D3
2200	NHFD	60025	2811	7W-15N	A3
3300	GNVW	60025	2809	10W-15N	E3
3300	GNVW	60025	2810	10W-15N	A3
W Winnetka St					
1200	PLTN	60067	2752	22W-17N	A5
Winnetka Ter					
900	LKZH	60047	2698	24W-23N	C2
Winnsboro Ct					
200	SMBG	60193	2857	27W-10N	D6
Winola Ct					
1700	NPVL	60565	3204	25W-9S	B3
Winona Av					
1300	AURA	60506	3137	37W-6S	C6
9400	SRPK	60176	2917	11W-6N	C6
Winona Ln					
5100	GRNE	60031	2478	15W-35N	B5
Winona Rd					
-	HDPK	60035	2757	8W-20N	E1
10	NfdT	60062	2757	8W-20N	E2
Winona St					
300	PKFT	60466	3594	4W-26S	E3
W Winona St					
1800	CHCG	60640	2921	2W-6N	B6
2200	CHCG	60625	2921	3W-6N	A6
2700	CHCG	60625	2920	3W-6N	E6
4900	CHCG	60630	2919	6W-6N	E6
7600	CHCG	60656	2918	9W-6N	C6
W Winona St					
7600	CHCG	60706	2918	9W-6N	C6
7600	HDHT	60706	2918	9W-6N	C6
7800	NRDG	60706	2918	9W-6N	C6
Winrock Rd					
10	OswT	60538	3199	36W-10S	E6
Winslow Av					
800	WDSK	60098	2581	42W-30N	B2
Winslow Cir					
900	GNEN	60137	3025	23W-1N	B3
900	MltT	60137	3025	23W-1N	A3
1300	WDSK	60098	2581	42W-30N	B2
Winslow Ct					
200	NPVL	60565	3204	26W-9S	A4
S Winslow Rd					
11900	PSPK	60464	3274	10W-14S	B5
W Winslow Rd					
8400	PSPK	60464	3274	10W-14S	B5
Winslow St					
10	PKFT	60466	3595	3W-26S	B2
Winslow Wy					
200	LIHL	60156	2692	38W-21N	E5
Winslowe Dr					
1400	PLTN	60074	2753	19W-17N	B4
E Winslowe Dr					
1500	PLTN	60074	2753	19W-17N	B4
Winsor Dr					
400	ANTH	60002	2357	23W-42N	D5
Winstead Ct					
-	LSLE	60532	3142	24W-6S	D6
Winstead Pl					
200	MDLN	60060	2646	19W-27N	C2
Winston Av					
400	JLET	60433	3499	23W-24S	B6
500	JltT	60433	3499	23W-24S	B6
S Winston Av					
9500	CHCG	60620	3213	1W-11S	D6
9500	CHCG	60643	3213	1W-11S	D6
W Winston Av					
23300	JLET	60586	3416	29W-21S	D7
23300	PnfT	60586	3416	29W-21S	D7
Winston Cir					
3500	HFET	60192	2804	23W-14N	D4
Winston Ct					
100	BGBK	60440	3205	22W-11S	B7
400	MLPK	60160	3030	10W-1N	A2
1600	MDLN	60060	2646	20W-26N	B2
17500	CCHL	60478	3426	4W-21S	D5
Winston Dr					
100	BGBK	60440	3205	22W-10S	C6
400	VrnT	60015	2755	14W-20N	B1
500	MLPK	60160	3030	10W-1N	A2
600	EGvT	60007	2860	19W-9N	C7
600	EGVV	60007	2860	19W-9N	C7
700	EGvT	60007	2914	19W-9N	B1
700	EGVV	60007	2914	19W-9N	B1
700	MLPK	60160	3029	10W-1N	E2
1400	BFGV	60089	2701	16W-21N	D5
3500	HFET	60192	2804	23W-15N	D3
6300	WDRG	60517	3143	22W-7S	C6
6800	TYPK	60477	3425	8W-19S	A3
17500	CCHL	60478	3426	4W-21S	D6
N Winston Dr					
10	PLTN	60074	2806	19W-16N	C1
100	PLTN	60074	2753	19W-16N	C7
S Winston Dr					
10	PLTN	60074	2806	19W-15N	C1
Winston Ln					
200	BMDL	60108	2969	23W-4N	A3
200	BRLT	60103	2967	28W-5N	A2
400	CHHT	60411	3507	2W-24S	D5
400	CHHT	60422	3507	2W-24S	D5
1900	SMBG	60193	2858	25W-10N	A6
3800	HFET	60192	2804	23W-14N	D3
S Winston Ln					
26000	CteT	60417	3685	1W-31S	B5
Winston Pl					
3600	HFET	60192	2804	23W-14N	D3
S Winston Rd					
10	LKFT	60045	2650	10W-25N	B4
Winston St					
700	WCHI	60185	3022	30W-2N	B1
Winter Av					
1900	NCHI	60064	2536	11W-31N	C7
Winter Ct					
1600	JLET	60431	3497	28W-21S	A1
Winterberry Ct					
10	BGBK	60440	3205	21W-10S	D5
10	SMWD	60107	2856	29W-9N	E7
600	JLET	60431	3497	28W-24S	B7
1300	NARA	60542	3078	34W-3S	C5
Winterberry Dr					
700	JLET	60431	3497	28W-24S	B7
Winterberry Ln					
1500	DRN	60561	3207	18W-9S	A4
11900	PNFD	60585	3266	31W-14S	A6
13400	HTLY	60142	2744	42W-20N	B1
16700	ODPK	60467	3423	13W-20S	B4
Winter Cir Dr					
7900	DGvT	60516	3206	19W-9S	D3
Wintercrag					
800	WDND	60118	2800	34W-15N	D4
Wintercress Cir					
2500	NHBK	60062	2756	11W-16N	D6
Wintercrest Ln					
1600	SRWD	60404	3495	31W-24S	E5
Winterfield Dr					
1700	AURA	60504	3200	34W-9S	E5
1700	AURA	60504	3201	33W-10S	A5
E Wintergreen Av					
2000	MPPT	60056	2808	13W-15N	E2
2000	MPPT	60056	2809	12W-15N	A2
Wintergreen Cir					
600	NPVL	60540	3140	29W-7S	D7
Wintergreen Ct					
10	WDRG	60517	3143	21W-7S	D7
700	AURA	60504	3201	33W-8S	B2
1100	BTVA	60510	3078	34W-1S	D2
Wintergreen Dr					
700	AURA	60504	3201	32W-8S	B3
9900	SPGV	60081	2355	30W-41N	B7
W Wintergreen Dr					
8200	FftT	60423	3504	10W-24S	C5
Wintergreen Ln					
1000	DRN	60561	3145	18W-7S	A7
Wintergreen Ter					
-	ALGN	60102	2746	37W-20N	B1
1000	BTVA	60510	3078	34W-1S	E2
3700	ALGN	60102	2693	37W-20N	B7
S Winterhaven Ct					
400	PLTN	60067	2805	22W-15N	C2
Winter Hill Cir					
10	MTGY	60538	3199	36W-10S	D5
Winter Hill Ct					
1600	MTGY	60538	3199	36W-10S	D5
Winter Park Ct					
2500	NPVL	60565	3203	27W-10S	C6
Winter Park Dr					
800	NLNX	60451	3589	18W-26S	A3
2600	NPVL	60565	3203	27W-10S	C6
10300	PSHL	60465	3274	10W-12S	A1
Winterport on Auburn					
10	RGMW	60008	2806	19W-15N	B3
W Winters Dr					
10	LydT	60164	2972	13W-3N	E5
10	NHLK	60164	2972	13W-3N	D5
Winterset Dr					
10700	ODPK	60467	3423	13W-19S	A3
Winterthur Grn					
-	YKVL	60560	3333	42W-17S	D6
Winterwood Ct					
800	ROSL	60172	2912	24W-6N	E7
Winterwood Dr					
400	ROSL	60172	2912	24W-6N	D6
Winthrop Av					
-	ADSN	60101	2970	21W-2N	A7
10	BmdT	60148	2970	21W-2N	A7
100	BmdT	60148	2969	21W-2N	E7
400	BmdT	60137	2969	22W-2N	B7
500	BmdT	60139	2969	22W-2N	C7
600	GLHT	60139	2969	22W-2N	C7
E Winthrop Av					
100	ADSN	60101	2971	18W-2N	A7
N Winthrop Av					
800	JLET	60435	3498	26W-22S	A2
5200	CHCG	60640	2921	1W-6N	E5
5500	CHCG	60660	2921	1W-6N	E5
6300	CHCG	60626	2921	1W-7N	D4
W Winthrop Av					
200	ADSN	60101	2970	19W-2N	D7
200	EMHT	60126	3027	16W-1N	D3
500	AddT	60101	2970	19W-2N	C7
Winthrop Ct					
10	DGvT	60516	3206	19W-8S	D1
800	ZION	60099	2422	9W-41N	C1
900	MDLN	60060	2646	18W-26N	E3
1300	BtnT	60099	2422	10W-41N	B1
1400	GLHT	60139	2969	22W-2N	C7
1700	SMBG	60193	2858	25W-10N	B6
Winthrop Dr					
-	OSWG	60543	3263	36W-12S	E3
1600	DSPN	60018	2862	14W-9N	C6
S Winthrop Dr					
100	RDLK	60073	2531	25W-33N	A4
Winthrop Ln					
10	GNVA	60134	3019	36W-1N	E4
100	OKTR	60181	3085	17W-1S	B1
100	YkTp	60181	3085	17W-1S	B1
1600	SMBG	60193	2858	25W-10N	B6
E Winthrop Ln					
100	LKFT	60045	2594	10W-27N	A7
W Winthrop Pl					
23900	LkvT	60046	2416	24W-38N	D6
Winthrop Rd					
1700	HDPK	60035	2704	9W-21N	C7
Winthrop Wy					
7200	DGvT	60516	3206	19W-8S	D1
7200	DRGV	60516	3206	19W-8S	D1
Winthrop New Rd					
10	SgrT	60506	3135	41W-5S	E4
10	SgrT	60506	3136	41W-5S	A4
10	SRGV	60506	3136	41W-5S	A4
Winton Ct					
2700	WDND	60118	2800	36W-16N	A2
Wintree Ln					
100	NLNX	60451	3500	20W-24S	B5
100	NlxT	60433	3500	20W-24S	B5
400	NLNX	60433	3500	20W-24S	B5
Winward Cir					
10	WLBK	60527	3145	16W-7S	D6
Winwood Dr					
1000	LKFT	60045	2649	12W-27N	B1
Winwood Wy					
7300	DRGV	60516	3206	19W-8S	D1
7400	DGvT	60516	3206	19W-8S	D1
Wirestem Ct					
5300	NPVL	60564	3266	29W-13S	D5
Wireton Rd					
2800	BLID	60406	3276	4W-15S	E7
2800	BLID	60406	3277	3W-15S	A7
2800	BLID	60406	3349	3W-15S	A1
2800	WthT	60406	3349	3W-15S	A1
Wirt Rd					
1200	JLET	60451	3500	19W-23S	E4
1200	NLNX	60451	3500	19W-23S	E4
1200	NlxT	60451	3500	19W-23S	E4
Wirth Dr					
7100	DRN	60561	3144	18W-8S	E7
7100	DRN	60561	3206	18W-8S	E1
S Wirth Ln					
22700	FftT	60423	3592	9W-27S	D5
22700	GGnT	60423	3592	9W-27S	D5
Wirth Tr					
3300	PRGV	60012	2585	32W-28N	A5
Wiscasset on Auburn					
10	RGMW	60008	2806	19W-14N	B3
Wisconsin Av					
-	NPVL	60563	3141	26W-5S	E3
10	LslT	60563	3142	26W-5S	A3
10	NPVL	60563	3142	26W-5S	A3
10	WKGN	60085	2536	11W-33N	D2
100	AddT	60181	3027	18W-2N	A1
300	OKPK	60302	3030	8W-0N	E5
1200	BRWN	60304	3030	8W-1S	E7
1200	BRWN	60402	3030	8W-1S	E7
1200	OKPK	60304	3030	8W-1S	E7
1400	BRWN	60402	3088	8W-1S	E1
3900	SKNY	60402	3088	8W-4S	E6
4400	FTVW	60402	3088	8W-4S	E7
4500	FTVW	60402	3148	8W-4S	E1
E Wisconsin Av					
100	BRTN	60010	2750	25W-18N	E3
200	BRTN	60010	2751	25W-18N	A3
300	LKFT	60045	2650	10W-27N	A2
N Wisconsin Av					
10	ADSN	60101	2971	18W-3N	A5
10	CPVL	60110	2800	34W-17N	E1
400	VLPK	60181	3027	18W-1N	A2
S Wisconsin Av					
10	ADSN	60101	2971	18W-3N	A6
100	VLPK	60181	3027	18W-0N	A4
800	AddT	60101	3027	17W-1N	B1
800	AddT	60181	3027	17W-1N	B1
800	ADSN	60101	3027	17W-1N	B1
1200	YkTp	60148	3027	18W-0S	A7
1200	YkTp	60181	3027	18W-0S	A7
1400	YkTp	60148	3085	18W-1S	A1
W Wisconsin Av					
600	JltT	60436	3586	24W-25S	D1
W Wisconsin Cir					
12900	HTLY	60142	2744	43W-18N	C4
Wisconsin Ct					
11100	ODPK	60467	3423	12W-20S	C5
Wisconsin Dr					
10	DSPN	60016	2808	14W-12N	C7
10	MPPT	60056	2808	14W-12N	B7
E Wisconsin Dr					
2900	NCHI	60088	2593	12W-30N	C2
W Wisconsin Dr					
2900	NCHI	60088	2593	12W-30N	C2
Wisconsin Ln					
800	EGVV	60007	2913	21W-8N	D2
Wisconsin Rd					
200	FKFT	60423	3503	12W-25S	D7
300	NLNX	60451	3501	18W-25S	B7
600	NlxT	60451	3501	18W-25S	B7
700	NLNX	60451	3589	18W-25S	B1
700	NlxT	60451	3589	18W-25S	B1
Wisconsin St					
100	GNCY	53128	2353		A4
1900	DRGV	60515	3143	21W-5S	E5
1900	DRGV	60515	3144	21W-5S	A3
1900	LslT	60515	3143	21W-5S	E5
E Wisconsin St					
1200	JLET	60432	3499	22W-22S	D2
1200	JltT	60432	3499	22W-22S	D2
N Wisconsin St					
100	CPVL	60110	2747	34W-17N	E7
500	GNCY	53128	2353		A3
S Wisconsin St					
10	CPVL	60110	2800	35W-16N	C1
W Wisconsin St					
200	CHCG	60614	2978	0W-2N	A7
800	CHCG	60614	2977	1W-2N	E7
1000	GNWD	60425	3508	1W-22S	A1
1000	HMWD	60425	3508	1W-22S	A1
1000	HMWD	60430	3508	1W-22S	A1
Wise Rd					
600	HRPK	60133	2912	25W-8N	A2
600	SMBG	60133	2912	25W-8N	A2
600	SMBG	60193	2912	25W-8N	A2
E Wise Rd					
-	EGVV	60007	2913	22W-8N	B1
-	EGVV	60193	2913	22W-8N	B1
-	SMBG	60007	2913	22W-9N	D1
-	SMBG	60193	2913	23W-9N	A1
W Wise Rd					
10	SMBG	60193	2913	23W-8N	A1
200	SMBG	60193	2912	24W-8N	E1
1200	SmbT	60193	2912	25W-9N	C1
1800	HRPK	60133	2912	25W-9N	A2
1800	SMBG	60133	2912	25W-9N	A2
Wise St					
900	ELBN	60119	3017	43W-0N	A5
W Wishing Well Dr					
7400	FftT	60423	3504	9W-24S	E6
Wishing Well Ln					
1100	NPVL	60564	3203	28W-10S	B6
3100	ISLK	60042	2586	28W-28N	E6
N Wisner Av					
2900	CHCG	60618	2976	4W-3N	D4
Wisner St					
10	PKRG	60068	2864	9W-9N	B7
10	PKRG	60068	2918	9W-8N	B1
N Wisner St					
8000	NLES	60068	2864	9W-10N	B6
8000	NLES	60714	2864	9W-10N	B5
8000	PKRG	60068	2864	9W-10N	B6
8200	MaiT	60714	2864	9W-10N	B5
Wissing Ln					
600	GNVW	60025	2810	9W-13N	C7
Wisteria Ct					
200	WDDL	60191	2971	17W-5N	C1
1900	NPVL	60565	3203	26W-9S	E3
1900	NPVL	60565	3204	26W-9S	A4
2600	PTBR	60010	2642	28W-26N	E2
3900	LIHL	60156	2693	37W-22N	B4
12600	PlsT	60464	3273	13W-14S	B7
Wisteria Dr					
300	SMWD	60107	2857	27W-10N	D7
1800	AURA	60503	3201	33W-10S	B6
3500	NndT	60012	2584	34W-28N	B5
3600	CLLK	60012	2584	34W-28N	B6
Wisteria Ln					
10	SMBG	60173	2859	21W-10N	E5
10	SMBG	60173	2860	20W-10N	A6
Wisteria Wy					
2700	PTBR	60010	2642	28W-26N	E2
E Wistoria Ct					
1800	MPPT	60056	2808	13W-14N	D4
E Witchie Dr					
9600	AlqT	60021	2695	30W-22N	E4
9600	FRGV	60021	2695	30W-22N	E4
W Witchie Dr					
9600	AlqT	60021	2695	30W-22N	E4
9600	FRGV	60021	2695	30W-22N	E4
Witchwood Ct					
1200	RLKB	60073	2475	23W-35N	A7
Witchwood Ln					
10	LNHT	60046	2476	20W-37N	B1
100	LNHT	60046	2418	20W-38N	A7
2900	WKGN	60087	2479	11W-37N	D2
E Witchwood Ln					
10	LKBF	60044	2593	11W-28N	C6
100	LKBF	60044	2594	10W-28N	A6
W Witchwood Ln					
100	LKBF	60044	2593	11W-28N	E6
Witham Ct					
8600	TYPK	60487	3424	10W-20S	B5
Witham Ln					
1500	WDRG	60517	3206	20W-11S	A7
Withorn Ln					
1500	IVNS	60067	2752	23W-16N	A6
W Withorn Ln					
200	MPPT	60056	2807	16W-13N	E6
Witt Ct					
1900	LMBD	60148	3083	21W-1S	E2
Witt Rd					
10	SBTN	60010	2803	26W-14N	C4
N Witt Rd					
42400	AntT	60002	2357	25W-42N	A6
N Wittenburg Dr					
39500	LkvT	60002	2417	21W-39N	D5
39500	LkvT	60046	2417	21W-39N	D5
Wittington Ct					
14200	ODPK	60462	3346	9W-16S	C4
Wium Rd					
8300	AlqT	60013	2696	29W-23N	D2
Wm Gooding Dr					
200	LKPT	60441	3419	22W-19S	B3
Wm Koepsel Dr					
-	GRNE	60031	2535	14W-34N	B2
-	WrnT	60031	2535	14W-34N	B2
Woburn Ct					
10300	ODPK	60462	3345	12W-17S	B5
Woburn Dr					
1200	LMNT	60439	3271	18W-14S	A6

Chicago 7-County Street Index

STREET Block	City	ZIP	Map#	CGS	Grid
Woburn Ln					
200	SMBG	60173	2859	21W-10N	E5
Woburn Rd					
17500	TYPK	60487	3424	11W-21S	A6
Wolcott Av					
-	BLID	60406	3277	2W-13S	C5
-	BLID	60643	3277	2W-13S	C5
-	CHCG	60643	3277	2W-13S	C5
-	ClmT	60406	3277	2W-13S	C5
-	ClmT	60643	3277	2W-13S	C5
16100	MKHM	60428	3427	2W-19S	D2
16500	HLCT	60428	3427	2W-19S	D3
16500	HLCT	60429	3427	2W-19S	D3
N Wolcott Av					
-	CHCG	60626	2921	2W-8N	B2
-	CHCG	60657	2977	2W-3N	C5
10	CHCG	60612	3033	2W-0N	C4
300	CHCG	60622	3033	2W-0N	C4
1600	CHCG	60622	2977	2W-2N	C7
2600	CHCG	60614	2977	2W-3N	C5
4200	CHCG	60613	2977	2W-5N	C1
4400	CHCG	60613	2921	2W-5N	C7
4400	CHCG	60640	2921	2W-5N	C7
6000	CHCG	60660	2921	2W-7N	C3
7400	CHCG	60626	2867	2W-9N	C7
7500	CHCG	60202	2867	2W-9N	C7
7500	EVTN	60202	2867	2W-9N	C7
S Wolcott Av					
200	CHCG	60612	3033	2W-0S	C5
1200	CHCG	60608	3033	2W-1S	C7
1600	CHCG	60608	3091	2W-1S	C1
3400	CHCG	60609	3091	2W-3S	C5
4700	CHCG	60609	3151	2W-5S	C2
5500	CHCG	60636	3151	2W-7S	C5
7500	CHCG	60620	3213	2W-9S	C3
Wolcott Ct					
100	SMBG	60193	2859	23W-10N	A5
N Wolcott St					
100	TNTN	60476	3428	0E-20S	D5
S Wolcott St					
100	TNTN	60476	3428	0E-21S	D6
Wolf Dr					
10600	HTLY	60142	2691	40W-21N	E6
S Wolf Dr					
11900	WldT	60564	3266	29W-14S	D6
11900	WldT	60585	3266	29W-14S	D6
Wolf Pl					
6800	DRGV	60516	3144	19W-7S	E7
Wolf Rd					
-	HLSD	60154	3086	14W-2S	D4
-	HLSD	60162	3086	14W-2S	D4
-	PlsT	60480	3208	14W-11S	E7
-	PlsT	60480	3272	14W-11S	E1
-	WLSP	60480	3208	14W-10S	E4
600	MTSN	60443	3505	7W-24S	C6
2500	WSTR	60154	3086	14W-2S	D4
2900	PvsT	60558	3086	14W-4S	E7
2900	WSTR	60558	3086	13W-2S	D4
3200	FNPK	60131	2972	14W-4N	D3
3200	FNPK	60164	2972	14W-4N	D4
3200	LydT	60164	2972	14W-4N	D4
3600	LydT	60131	2972	14W-4N	D3
3800	WNSP	60558	3086	14W-4S	E7
4500	WNSP	60558	3146	14W-5S	E2
5400	LynT	60525	3146	13W-5S	E3
5400	LynT	60558	3146	13W-5S	E3
5400	WNSP	60525	3146	13W-5S	E3
6000	IHPK	60525	3146	13W-6S	E5
6800	CTSD	60525	3146	13W-7S	E7
7000	BRRG	60525	3146	14W-8S	E7
7000	BRRG	60527	3146	14W-8S	E7
7000	IHPK	60527	3146	14W-8S	E7
7200	BRRG	60525	3208	14W-8S	E1
7200	BRRG	60527	3208	14W-8S	E1
7200	IHPK	60525	3208	14W-8S	E1
7200	IHPK	60527	3208	14W-8S	E1
7300	LynT	60525	3208	14W-8S	E1
7400	LynT	60527	3208	14W-8S	E1
7500	WLSP	60527	3208	14W-8S	E1
8000	WLSP	60525	3208	13W-9S	E3
8500	LynT	60480	3208	14W-10S	E4
9600	AlqT	60021	2695	30W-22N	E4
9600	FRGV	60021	2695	30W-22N	E4
9800	BNHL	60010	2695	30W-22N	E4
9800	BNHL	60021	2695	30W-22N	E4
13100	PlsT	60467	3344	14W-15S	E2
13200	OrlT	60467	3344	14W-15S	E2
13500	ODPK	60467	3344	14W-17S	E6
15600	ODPK	60467	3422	14W-21S	E7
15600	OrlT	60467	3422	14W-19S	E2
18300	FftT	60448	3422	14W-22S	E7
18300	FftT	60467	3422	14W-22S	E7
18300	MKNA	60467	3422	14W-22S	E7
18400	FftT	60448	3502	14W-22S	E1
18400	FftT	60467	3502	14W-22S	E1
18400	MKNA	60467	3502	14W-22S	E1
18500	MKNA	60448	3502	14W-23S	E4
20300	FftT	60448	3503	13W-24S	A6
20300	MKNA	60448	3503	13W-24S	A5
21000	FftT	60423	3591	13W-26S	A2
21000	FftT	60448	3591	13W-26S	A2
21000	FKFT	60423	3591	13W-26S	A2
21000	MKNA	60448	3591	13W-26S	A2
21700	MKNA	60423	3591	14W-26S	A2
23000	GGnT	60423	3591	13W-27S	A5
Wolf Rd SR-7					
14300	ODPK	60467	3344	14W-17S	E6
14300	OrlT	60467	3344	14W-17S	E6
15600	ODPK	60467	3422	14W-19S	E2
15600	OrlT	60467	3422	14W-19S	E2
Wolf Rd US-6					
15900	ODPK	60467	3422	14W-20S	E4
15900	OrlT	60467	3422	14W-20S	E4
N Wolf Rd					
-	BKLY	60160	3028	13W-1N	D3
-	MLPK	60160	3028	13W-1N	D3
-	MLPK	60163	3028	13W-1N	D3
10	HLSD	60162	3028	13W-0N	D4
10	NHLK	60164	3028	13W-2N	D1
10	PvsT	60162	3028	14W-0S	D6
100	DSPN	60016	2862	14W-12N	D1
200	NHLK	60164	2972	13W-2N	D7
300	DSPN	60016	2808	14W-13N	D6
300	DSPN	60056	2808	14W-13N	D6
300	MPPT	60016	2808	14W-13N	D6
300	MPPT	60056	2808	14W-13N	D6
500	WLNG	60090	2755	14W-18N	C2
800	LydT	60164	2972	14W-3N	D5
800	WhlT	60056	2808	14W-13N	D5
1200	BKLY	60163	3028	14W-0N	D3
1300	PTHT	60070	2808	14W-14N	D3
1500	BKLY	60162	3028	14W-0N	D4
3100	FNPK	60131	2972	14W-3N	D5
3100	FNPK	60164	2972	14W-3N	D5
S Wolf Rd					
10	HLSD	60162	3028	13W-0S	D7
10	NHLK	60164	3028	13W-1N	D1
10	PTHT	60070	2808	14W-15N	D2
10	PvsT	60162	3028	13W-0S	D7
10	WLNG	60090	2755	14W-16N	D7
100	DSPN	60016	2862	14W-9N	D6
100	MPPT	60056	2808	14W-14N	D3
300	HLSD	60154	3028	14W-0S	D7
1100	DSPN	60018	2862	14W-10N	D5
1200	WLNG	60070	2808	14W-15N	D1
1200	WLNG	60090	2808	14W-15N	D2
1400	HLSD	60154	3086	14W-1S	D2
1400	HLSD	60162	3086	14W-1S	D2
1400	PvsT	60162	3086	14W-1S	D2
1700	PTHT	60090	2808	14W-15N	D3
2100	DSPN	60018	2916	14W-8N	D2
2100	WSTR	60154	3086	13W-1S	D2
2400	CHCG	60018	2916	14W-8N	D1
12100	PlsT	60464	3272	13W-14S	E6
12100	PSPK	60464	3272	13W-14S	E6
12700	PSPK	60464	3344	13W-15S	E1
12900	PlsT	60464	3344	13W-15S	E1
12900	PlsT	60467	3344	13W-15S	E1
Wolf St					
200	YKVL	60560	3333	42W-16S	C4
Wolf Creek Ln					
11700	PNFD	60585	3266	30W-13S	B5
Wolfe Ct					
10	WDRG	60517	3143	21W-6S	D5
1000	JLET	60433	3499	23W-25S	A7
3100	NPVL	60564	3203	28W-11S	A7
Wolfe Dr					
2400	DRGV	60516	3143	21W-6S	D5
2400	DRGV	60517	3143	21W-6S	D5
2400	WDRG	60517	3143	21W-6S	D5
5100	OKLN	60453	3275	6W-12S	E2
Wolff Av					
1200	ELGN	60123	2854	35W-11N	B4
S Wolf Lake Blvd					
-	CHCG	60617	3280	4E-14S	B6
-	CHCG	60633	3280	4E-14S	B6
Wolf Lake Ct					
21500	LktT	60403	3417	26W-19S	D2
Wolf Lake Wy					
21400	LktT	60403	3417	26W-19S	D2
W Wolfram St					
1900	CHCG	60657	2977	2W-3N	B4
2300	CHCG	60618	2977	2W-3N	A4
3500	CHCG	60618	2976	4W-3N	C4
4800	CHCG	60641	2975	6W-3N	D4
6900	CHCG	60634	2974	8W-3N	E5
Wolf River Ct					
2700	NPVL	60565	3204	26W-10S	A6
W Wolfs Rd					
25700	AURA	60503	3265	32W-11S	B2
25700	AURA	60585	3265	32W-11S	B2
25700	WldT	60585	3265	32W-11S	B2
26100	OswT	60503	3265	32W-11S	B2
26100	OswT	60543	3265	32W-11S	B2
26100	WldT	60503	3265	32W-11S	B2
26100	WldT	60543	3265	32W-11S	B2
Wolf's Crossing Rd					
-	WldT	60564	3201	31W-10S	E6
Wolfs Crossing Rd					
10	AURA	60503	3265	33W-12S	A2
10	AURA	60585	3265	33W-12S	A2
10	OSWG	60543	3265	33W-11S	A2
10	OswT	60503	3265	33W-12S	A2
10	OswT	60543	3265	33W-12S	A2
10	WldT	60503	3265	33W-12S	A2
10	WldT	60543	3265	33W-12S	A2
10	WldT	60585	3265	33W-12S	A2
800	OSWG	60543	3264	35W-12S	C2
800	OswT	60543	3264	35W-12S	C2
2900	OSWG	60543	3263	36W-12S	D3
Wolf S Crossing Rd					
24800	NPVL	60564	3202	31W-11S	A7
24800	WldT	60564	3201	31W-11S	E7
24800	WldT	60564	3202	31W-11S	A7
24800	WldT	60564	3265	32W-11S	C2
24800	WldT	60585	3265	32W-11S	C2
25300	WldT	60503	3265	31W-11S	D1
25500	AURA	60503	3265	31W-11S	D1
25500	AURA	60585	3265	31W-11S	D1
Wollmington Dr					
200	OSWG	60543	3264	36W-11S	A1
Wolpers Rd					
2100	CteT	60417	3595	2W-29S	C7
2100	CteT	60466	3595	2W-29S	C7
2100	MonT	60466	3595	2W-29S	C7
Wolsfeld Dr					
200	HnrT	60120	2856	30W-11N	A3
Wolter Ln					
-	KLDR	60047	2699	21W-21N	D5
Wolverine Dr					
600	AURA	60502	3139	32W-7S	C7
2700	GNVW	60025	2810	9W-14N	B4
Wolverine Rd					
200	OSWG	60543	3262	39W-11S	E2
E Wonder Lake Dr					
4100	MchT	60097	2469	36W-36N	D4
W Wonder Lake Dr					
4400	WRLK	60097	2469	36W-36N	C4
4700	MchT	60097	2469	36W-36N	C4
E Wonder Lake Rd					
2200	MchT	60050	2526	36W-33N	D2
2200	MchT	60097	2526	36W-34N	D1
2200	MchT	60098	2526	36W-34N	D2
2700	MchT	60097	2469	36W-34N	D7
5300	WRLK	60097	2469	36W-37N	E2
W Wonder Lake Rd					
4600	WRLK	60097	2469	37W-36N	B4
4700	GwdT	60097	2469	37W-36N	C3
8500	GNWD	60097	2469	37W-36N	B4
9200	GNWD	60097	2468	38W-36N	E4
9200	GNWD	60098	2468	38W-36N	E4
Wondermere Rd					
8800	GNWD	60097	2469	38W-36N	A5
8800	WRLK	60097	2469	38W-36N	A5
9200	GNWD	60097	2468	38W-36N	E5
9200	WRLK	60097	2468	38W-36N	E5
9800	GNWD	60098	2468	38W-36N	E5
Wonder View Dr					
7600	MchT	60097	2469	37W-34N	C7
8000	GwdT	60097	2469	37W-34N	C7
8000	WRLK	60097	2469	37W-34N	C7
Wonder Woods Dr					
5100	WRLK	60097	2469	36W-37N	C3
5900	MchT	60097	2469	36W-37N	D2
S Wong Pkwy					
1800	CHCG	60616	3092		E1
Wood Av					
800	GNVA	60134	3019	37W-0N	C5
800	GnvT	60134	3019	37W-0N	C5
1400	DRGV	60515	3084	20W-3S	B6
E Wood Av					
10	BNVL	60106	2972	15W-5N	A2
S Wood Av					
5400	HMND	46320	3352		E6
W Wood Av					
10	BNVL	60106	2971	16W-5N	E2
1100	ADSN	60101	2970	19W-5N	C2
1100	WDDL	60106	2971	16W-5N	C2
1100	WDDL	60191	2971	16W-5N	C2
6400	ALSP	60803	3275	8W-13S	B4
6400	WRTH	60482	3275	8W-13S	B4
6400	WRTH	60803	3275	8W-13S	B4
Wood Ct					
10	BGBK	60440	3268	25W-11S	B1
10	LslT	60563	3142	25W-4S	B1
10	WYNE	60184	2966	30W-5N	C3
10	WynT	60103	2966	30W-5N	C3
10	WynT	60184	2966	30W-5N	C3
100	WNVL	60555	3080	30W-2S	C4
200	WLMT	60091	2812	3W-13N	E6
900	LslT	60532	3143	22W-6S	C5
Wood Dr					
-	TYPK	60477	3424	9W-21S	E6
100	ALGN	60102	2694	33W-20N	E7
1200	WDSK	60098	2581	41W-30N	D2
2200	NHBK	60062	2809	10W-16N	E1
2700	DYR	46311	3598		D4
6400	AlqT	60013	2641	31W-25N	D4
Wood Ln					
700	SchT	60175	2908	35W-6N	A7
700	SCRL	60175	2908	35W-6N	A7
5500	MchT	60097	2469	36W-37N	D2
E Wood Ln					
1700	MPPT	60056	2808	13W-14N	E3
S Wood Ln					
9900	PSHL	60465	3210	10W-11S	B7
Wood Rd					
500	OKBK	60521	3086	15W-3S	A6
500	OKBK	60523	3086	15W-3S	A6
Wood Row					
100	SEGN	60177	2908	34W-9N	D1
Wood St					
-	BLID	60406	3277	2W-14S	D5
-	BLID	60827	3277	2W-14S	D5
-	CTPK	60827	3277	2W-14S	D5
100	HFET	60010	2751	24W-16N	C7
100	IVNS	60010	2751	24W-16N	C7
100	WCHI	60185	3022	30W-0N	C5
200	IVNS	60067	2751	23W-16N	E7
200	WHTN	60187	3024	23W-0S	E6
200	WslT	60481	3943	27W-40S	D4
400	CHHT	60411	3507	2W-24S	D5
800	AURA	60505	3138	34W-6S	D5
1200	CRTE	60417	3685	0W-30S	B2
1200	DRFD	60015	2703	11W-21N	D6
1500	CteT	60417	3685	0W-30S	B3
1600	RLKB	60073	2475	21W-35N	D6
3900	PKCY	60085	2535	13W-33N	E3
12700	CTPK	60406	3277	2W-15S	D7
13000	BLID	60406	3349	2W-15S	D1
14000	DXMR	60426	3349	2W-17S	D5
14400	HRVY	60426	3349	2W-18S	D7
15600	HRVY	60426	3427	2W-20S	D4
16000	MKHM	60426	3427	2W-19S	D2
16000	MKHM	60428	3427	2W-19S	D2
16500	HLCT	60428	3427	2W-19S	D3
16500	HLCT	60429	3427	2W-19S	D3
17000	EHZC	60429	3427	2W-20S	D4
17400	EHZC	60430	3427	2W-20S	D5
17400	HLCT	60430	3427	2W-20S	D5
17400	HMWD	60430	3427	2W-20S	D5
E Wood St					
10	PLTN	60067	2752	20W-16N	E7
100	NLNX	60451	3501	17W-24S	C5
200	PLTN	60067	2753	20W-16N	A7
300	NlxT	60451	3501	17W-24S	C5
300	PLTN	60074	2753	20W-16N	A7
N Wood St					
-	CHCG	60614	2977	2W-2N	C6
10	CHCG	60612	3033	2W-0N	C4
100	ELWD	60421	3675	25W-31S	C7
1400	CHCG	60622	3033	2W-1N	C1
1600	CHCG	60622	2977	2W-2N	C7
2400	RVGV	60171	2974	10W-3N	A5
2900	CHCG	60657	2977	2W-3N	C4
S Wood St					
100	ELWD	60421	3675	25W-31S	C7
400	CHCG	60612	3033	2W-1S	C7
1100	CHCG	60608	3033	2W-1S	C7
1600	CHCG	60608	3091	2W-2S	C2
3400	CHCG	60609	3091	2W-3S	C5
4700	CHCG	60609	3151	2W-6S	C3
5500	CHCG	60636	3151	2W-8S	C7
7500	CHCG	60620	3213	2W-10S	C4
9500	CHCG	60643	3213	2W-11S	D7
11900	BLID	60406	3277	2W-14S	D5
11900	BLID	60643	3277	2W-14S	D5
11900	BLID	60827	3277	2W-14S	D5
11900	CHCG	60643	3277	2W-14S	D5
11900	CTPK	60643	3277	2W-14S	D5
11900	CTPK	60827	3277	2W-14S	D5
12600	CTPK	60406	3277	2W-14S	D7
W Wood St					
100	NLNX	60451	3501	18W-24S	B5
200	NlxT	60451	3501	18W-24S	B5
300	PLTN	60067	2752	21W-16N	C7
300	PTON	60468	3860	9W-37S	E3
700	NndT	60051	2586	29W-28N	B5
900	PltT	60067	2752	22W-16N	B7
1100	IVNS	60067	2752	22W-16N	B7
Wood Tr					
1200	EGVV	60007	2914	21W-8N	A3
Woodale St					
20100	LYWD	60411	3509	3E-23S	E4
Woodard St					
100	ELGN	60123	2854	34W-11N	E5
N Woodard St					
2800	CHCG	60618	2976	4W-3N	D4
Woodberry Rd					
10	DRPK	60010	2751	23W-20N	E1
10	ElaT	60010	2751	23W-20N	E1
Woodbine Av					
100	EVTN	60091	2812	3W-13N	E7
100	EVTN	60201	2812	3W-13N	E7
100	WLMT	60091	2812	3W-13N	E7
1100	ISLK	60042	2586	28W-28N	E6
N Woodbine Av					
42200	AntT	60002	2356	26W-42N	E6
Woodbine Av N					
1000	OKPK	60302	3030	8W-1N	E1
1200	CHCG	60302	3030	8W-1N	E1
1200	CHCG	60707	3030	8W-1N	E1
Woodbine Cir					
800	LKZH	60010	2699	22W-21N	B6
800	LKZH	60047	2699	22W-21N	B6
W Woodbine Cir					
15600	VNHL	60061	2648	15W-24N	A7
15600	VrnT	60061	2647	15W-24N	E7
15600	VrnT	60061	2648	15W-24N	A7
Woodbine Ct					
300	WDDL	60191	2971	17W-4N	C2
800	NPVL	60540	3142	25W-7S	B7
1500	BKBN	60015	2703	11W-21N	D5
1500	DRFD	60015	2703	11W-21N	D5
8800	TYPK	60487	3424	11W-22S	A7
8900	TYPK	60487	3504	11W-22S	A1
Woodbine Dr					
10	CLLK	60014	2639	37W-25N	A4
100	ELWD	60421	3675	25W-31S	B6
100	JknT	60421	3675	25W-31S	B6
300	WDDL	60191	2971	17W-4N	B2
600	MRGO	60152	2578	49W-27N	C7
1400	RLKB	60073	2475	23W-35N	A6
Woodbine Ln					
400	FRGV	60021	2696	29W-22N	C3
800	LKFT	60045	2650	9W-27N	B2
800	NHBK	60062	2757	10W-17N	A5
1000	DRN	60561	3145	18W-7S	A7
3100	LGGV	60047	2700	19W-21N	C5
Woodbine Pl					
200	NBRN	60010	2697	25W-23N	E1
800	LKFT	60045	2650	9W-27N	B2
Woodbine Rd					
10	RGMW	60008	2806	19W-14N	C4
300	AlqT	60013	2696	29W-23N	C1
800	HDPK	60035	2704	9W-21N	C7
10400	GfnT	60014	2638	39W-25N	C5
10400	GfnT	60142	2638	39W-25N	C5
10400	LKWD	60014	2638	39W-25N	C5
10400	LKWD	60142	2638	39W-25N	C5
22100	RNPK	60471	3594	5W-26S	C3
Woodbine Ter					
600	RchT	60443	3593	8W-26S	B2
S Woodbriar Ln					
26800	CNHN	60410	3672	33W-31S	C6
Woodbridge Av					
15700	HRVY	60426	3428	1W-19S	B1
Woodbridge Ct					
600	LKBN	60010	2643	26W-24N	D6
Woodbridge Dr					
200	BCHR	60401	3774	0W-35S	D6
600	ELGN	60124	2853	36W-10N	E7
900	CRY	60013	2695	32W-22N	A3
21100	FKFT	60423	3504	11W-25S	A7
Wood Bridge Ln					
500	PltT	60124	2905	43W-8N	B3
Woodbridge Ln					
2400	HDPK	60035	2704	8W-22N	E3
Woodbridge Rd					
200	DSPN	60016	2862	14W-11N	D3
1400	JLET	60436	3498	25W-24S	B5
Woodbrook Ct					
10	LslT	60540	3142	25W-6S	C5
10	NPVL	60540	3142	25W-6S	C5
800	SRWD	60404	3496	30W-23S	B5
Woodbrook Ln					
17400	LktT	60441	3341	21W-17S	D5
Woodburn Ct					
1100	IVNS	60067	2751	24W-17N	D5
Woodbury Cir					
1400	GRNE	60031	2477	18W-35N	A6
Woodbury Ct					
10	SBTN	60010	2803	27W-15N	B2
10	SMWD	60107	2857	26W-11N	E4
300	SMBG	60193	2859	21W-10N	D6
700	SRGV	60554	3135	41W-5S	E3
9200	ODPK	60462	3345	11W-16S	E3
W Woodbury Ct					
21000	ElaT	60047	2645	21W-25N	E5
E Woodbury Dr					
2700	ANHT	60004	2754	16W-16N	E7
Woodbury Ln					
100	NCHI	60044	2593	12W-30N	B3
1100	WLNG	60090	2754	15W-18N	E3
1700	AURA	60503	3201	32W-10S	C5
E Woodbury Ln					
1200	PLTN	60074	2753	19W-17N	D5
1200	PltT	60074	2753	19W-17N	C5
Woodbury Rd					
400	BFGV	60089	2754	16W-20N	D1
Woodbury St					
10	SEGN	60177	2908	34W-8N	D3
Woodbury Bend Dr					
300	BCHR	60401	3774	0W-35S	D6
Woodchuck Ln					
1300	NPVL	60563	3140	28W-6S	E4
Woodchuck Tr					
600	OSWG	60543	3262	39W-11S	E2
600	OSWG	60543	3263	39W-11S	A2
Woodcliff Ct					
2500	LSLE	60532	3142	24W-7S	D6
4800	RGMW	60067	2805	21W-13N	E6
Woodcliff Dr					
800	SchT	60177	2908	34W-7N	D4
Woodcliff Ln					
4700	RGMW	60008	2805	20W-13N	E6
4700	RGMW	60067	2805	20W-13N	E6
Woodcliff Rd					
10	OswT	60538	3199	37W-10S	D6
Wood Creek Ct					
200	NPVL	60565	3203	26W-8S	E2
700	ISLK	60042	2586	28W-29N	E4
700	ISLK	60042	2587	28W-28N	A6
Woodcreek Ct					
100	SCRL	60174	2964	36W-3N	A5
6100	BRRG	60527	3146	15W-6S	A5
8100	DGvT	60516	3206	19W-9S	D3
Wood Creek Dr					
500	ANTH	60002	2357	24W-42N	D5
500	ISLK	60042	2586	28W-28N	E6
Woodcreek Dr					
200	JLET	60432	3499	21W-23S	E4
200	JltT	60432	3499	21W-23S	E4
300	BGBK	60440	3269	23W-13S	A4
2900	DRGV	60515	3084	21W-2S	A4
3000	DRGV	60515	3083	21W-3S	E5
6000	BRRG	60527	3146	15W-6S	A5
11600	HTLY	60142	2745	40W-20N	A1
E Woodcreek Dr					
11600	HTLY	60142	2745	40W-20N	A1
S Woodcreek Dr					
11600	HTLY	60142	2745	40W-20N	A1
Woodcreek Ln					
10	WynT	60185	2967	28W-3N	B7
100	CLSM	60185	2967	28W-3N	B7
100	CLSM	60188	2967	28W-3N	B7
100	WynT	60188	2967	28W-3N	B7
1100	HFET	60169	2858	25W-11N	B3
Wood Creek Rd					
10	BNHL	60010	2802	29W-15N	D2
1100	SMBG	60173	2805	21W-13N	D6
Woodcreek Rd					
200	WLNG	60090	2808	14W-15N	B1
300	PTHT	60070	2808	14W-15N	B1
300	PTHT	60090	2808	14W-15N	B1
Wood Creek Tr					
1500	BRLT	60103	2966	29W-5N	C2
S Woodcrest Av					
14700	HMGN	60491	3344	15W-17S	B6
Woodcrest Cir					
100	SMWD	60107	2856	29W-10N	E5
1600	MDLN	60060	2590	20W-28N	B7
Woodcrest Ct					
10	CmpT	60119	2961	42W-3N	D7
10	LMNT	60439	3271	18W-14S	B6
100	BMDL	60108	2913	23W-6N	A7
500	CLSM	60188	2968	25W-3N	A6
1400	AURA	60502	3139	32W-5S	C3
4000	GRNE	60031	2535	14W-34N	D2
Woodcrest Ct E					
300	LslT	60540	3143	23W-7S	A7
Woodcrest Ct W					
300	LslT	60540	3143	23W-7S	A7
Woodcrest Dr					
10	WCHI	60185	2966	29W-2N	C7
10	WynT	60185	2966	29W-2N	C7
10	WynT	60185	3022	29W-2N	D1
500	LslT	60540	3142	24W-6S	C4
500	MDLN	60060	2590	20W-28N	B7
1000	DGvT	60516	3206	20W-10S	B5
1000	DRN	60516	3206	20W-10S	B5
1000	DRN	60561	3206	20W-10S	B5
1000	WDRG	60517	3206	20W-10S	B5
Woodcrest Ln					
10	EGVV	60007	2861	18W-10N	A6
500	DndT	60118	2747	35W-18N	C4
500	LMNT	60439	3271	18W-14S	A6
N Woodcrest Ln					
22900	KLDR	60047	2699	21W-22N	E3
S Woodcrest Ln					
22700	KLDR	60047	2699	21W-22N	E3
Woodcroft Ct					
400	SMBG	60173	2859	22W-11N	C4
Woodcroft Dr					
10	MltT	60137	3083	23W-2S	A4
Woodcroft Ln					
400	SMBG	60173	2859	22W-10N	C4
Woodcutter Ln					
1300	WHTN	60187	3082	25W-1S	A1
Wooddale Dr					
-	YKVL	60560	3333	42W-15S	D2
N Wooddale Ln					
28300	LbvT	60048	2592	15W-28N	B6
Wood Dale Rd					
-	AddT	60101	2971	17W-3N	B5
-	ADSN	60101	2971	17W-3N	B5
Wood Dale Rd CO-28					
-	AddT	60101	2971	17W-3N	A5
-	ADSN	60101	2971	17W-3N	A5
N Wood Dale Rd					
-	EGvT	60007	2915	18W-7N	A4
-	EGVV	60007	2915	18W-7N	A4
-	WDDL	60007	2915	18W-7N	A4
10	AddT	60101	2971	17W-5N	A2
10	AddT	60191	2971	17W-4N	B2
10	ADSN	60101	2971	17W-4N	B4
10	ADSN	60191	2971	17W-5N	B2
10	WDDL	60191	2971	17W-5N	B2
100	AddT	60106	2971	17W-5N	A2
200	WDDL	60191	2915	18W-7N	A4
400	AddT	60191	2915	17W-6N	A6
500	ADSN	60106	2971	17W-5N	A2
1400	EGVV	60191	2915	18W-7N	A4
N Wood Dale Rd CO-28					
-	EGvT	60007	2915	18W-7N	A4
-	EGVV	60007	2915	18W-7N	A4
-	WDDL	60007	2915	18W-7N	A4
10	AddT	60101	2971	17W-5N	A2
10	AddT	60191	2971	17W-4N	B2
10	ADSN	60101	2971	17W-4N	B4
10	ADSN	60191	2971	17W-5N	B2
10	WDDL	60191	2971	17W-5N	B2
100	AddT	60106	2971	17W-5N	A2
200	WDDL	60191	2915	18W-7N	A4
400	AddT	60191	2915	17W-6N	A6
500	ADSN	60106	2971	17W-5N	A2
1400	EGVV	60191	2915	18W-7N	A4
Wooddale Tr					
18700	WrnT	60046	2476	18W-37N	D3
N Wooddale Tr					
18700	WrnT	60046	2476	18W-37N	D2
Wood Duck Ct					
400	GYLK	60030	2533	20W-32N	A5
14600	HMGN	60491	3344	15W-17S	C5
Wood Duck Dr					
13100	PNFD	60585	3339	28W-15S	A2
13300	PNFD	60544	3339	28W-15S	A3
Woodduck Dr					
1600	ANHT	60004	2754	16W-17N	C6
1600	ANHT	60090	2754	16W-17N	C6
1600	WLNG	60090	2754	16W-17N	C6
Wood Duck Ln					
-	OrlT	60467	3423	13W-20S	B4
1400	JLET	60586	3496	29W-22S	D1
5100	RcmT	60071	2353	34W-42N	D5
5100	RHMD	60071	2353	34W-42N	D5
10500	ODPK	60467	3423	13W-20S	B4
14900	HMGN	60491	3343	16W-16S	A4
15000	HMGN	60491	3342	18W-16S	E4
Woodduck Ln					
1600	WLNG	60090	2754	16W-17N	D5
8500	GLkT	60481	3761	33W-34S	C5
8500	WmTp	60481	3761	33W-34S	C5
Wooded Ln					
10	FmtT	60084	2644	24W-26N	C4
10	HNWD	60047	2644	24W-26N	C4
10	LKFT	60045	2650	10W-25N	B4
200	NBRN	60010	2697	26W-23N	E1
2800	MchT	60051	2472	29W-34N	C7
Wooded Cove Dr					
21100	ELWD	60421	3675	25W-30S	C4
21100	JknT	60421	3675	25W-30S	C4
Woodedcreek Dr					
-	JLET	60431	3497	28W-22S	B3
Woodedge Ln					
19400	NlxT	60448	3502	15W-23S	B3
N Wooded Glen Dr					
33800	WrnT	60030	2533	18W-33N	E2
33800	WrnT	60030	2534	18W-33N	A2
Wooded Knoll Dr					
300	CRY	60013	2642	30W-24N	A7
Wooded Path Dr					
-	HMWD	60429	3428	1W-20S	A5
-	HMWD	60430	3428	1W-20S	A5
9000	PSHL	60465	3209	11W-11S	E6
17300	EHZC	60429	3428	1W-20S	A5

STREET Block City ZIP Map# CGS Grid

Wooded Path Ln
8400 ODPK 60462 3346 10W-17S B4
W Wooded Ridge Dr
- DRPK 60047 2699 22W-20N B7
- ElaT 60047 2699 22W-20N B7
22200 DRPK 60010 2699 22W-20N B7
22200 KLDR 60047 2699 22W-20N B7
22300 KLDR 60010 2699 22W-20N B7
Wooded Shore Dr
7600 WRLK 60097 2469 36W-35N D6
E Woodedshore Dr
- MchT 60097 2469 36W-35N D6
7300 WRLK 60097 2469 36W-35N D7
Wooden Bridge Dr
10 KdlT 60560 3333 42W-16S C4
Woodewind Dr
600 NpvT 60563 3140 30W-6S A4
Wood Farm Rd
14700 PNFD 60544 3338 30W-17S B6
14700 PnfT 60544 3338 30W-17S B6
Woodfern Dr
700 PGGV 60140 2797 41W-15N E4
700 PGGV 60140 2798 41W-15N A4
Woodfield Ct
- TYPK 60477 3504 9W-23S E3
1900 NPVL 60565 3203 26W-9S E4
Woodfield Ln
1000 GNOK 60048 2592 15W-29N B5
1000 LYVL 60048 2592 15W-29N B5
E Woodfield Rd
- EGvT 60007 2860 21W-11N A3
- EGvT 60173 2860 21W-11N A3
- SMBG 60007 2860 21W-11N A3
800 SMBG 60173 2859 22W-11N D3
1700 SMBG 60173 2860 21W-11N A3
E Woodfield Tr
400 ROSL 60172 2913 22W-8N B3
N Woodfield Tr
500 ROSL 60172 2913 22W-8N B3
700 SmbT 60172 2913 22W-8N B2
700 SmbT 60193 2913 22W-8N B2
Woodfield Mall
- SMBG 60173 2859 21W-11N E2
E Woodfield Office Ct
800 SMBG 60173 2859 22W-11N C3
Woodford Dr
3200 JLET 60431 3417 28W-21S B7
E Woodford Pl
1200 ANHT 60004 2807 17W-13N C5
Woodgate Ct
400 WLBK 60527 3146 15W-7S A6
Woodgate Dr
10 BRRG 60527 3146 15W-6S C5
5600 MTSN 60443 3505 7W-24S D4
Woodgate Rd
100 CmpT 60175 2962 39W-3N E6
700 SchT 60175 2963 37W-5N C2
Woodglen Ct
2300 AURA 60502 3139 32W-5S B3
Woodglen Dr
2300 AURA 60502 3139 32W-5S C3
Wood Glen Ln
200 OKBK 60523 3028 15W-1S B7
200 OKBK 60523 3086 15W-1S B1
Woodglen Ln
7900 DGvT 60516 3206 19W-9S D2
7900 DRN 60516 3206 19W-9S D2
7900 DRN 60561 3206 19W-9S D2
11400 BRRG 60527 3208 14W-8S D2
Woodgrove Dr
12700 HTLY 60142 2744 43W-19N B3
Woodhall Ct
600 WNFD 60190 3023 26W-1N E2
24200 WldT 60564 3266 30W-12S B3
Woodhall Dr
24200 WldT 60564 3266 30W-12S B3
Woodhaven Ct
1600 MDLN 60060 2590 20W-28N B7
Woodhaven Dr
10 SBTN 60010 2803 27W-13N A5
500 MDLN 60060 2590 20W-28N B7
1700 CLLK 60014 2693 37W-22N C3
1900 BRLT 60103 2909 32W-8N C3
19900 FftT 60448 3502 14W-24S D5
19900 MKNA 60448 3502 14W-24S D5
Woodhaven Ln
10 BNHL 60010 2749 30W-20N A1
10 DndT 60118 2747 35W-18N B5
2900 DYR 46311 3598 D4
Woodhaven St
1500 WHTN 60187 3081 27W-1S D2
Woodhead Dr
10 LKVL 60046 2417 21W-38N C7
10 LKVL 60046 2475 21W-38N C1
3400 NHBK 60062 2756 12W-18N C3
Woodhill Ct
800 LKVL 60046 2475 22W-36N B3
1000 ELGN 60120 2855 32W-12N C2
2300 JLET 60586 3416 29W-21S E6
Wood Hill Dr
- RMVL 60446 3339 26W-18S E7
Woodhill Dr
300 BmdT 60188 2967 26W-4N E4
400 CLSM 60188 2967 27W-4N C4
1400 NHBK 60062 2757 9W-17N C5
W Woodhill Dr
5500 GRNE 60031 2478 15W-35N A6
5600 GRNE 60031 2477 15W-35N E6
Woodhill Ln
300 LKVL 60046 2475 22W-36N B3
300 SchT 60175 2907 38W-6N A7
1300 LKFT 60045 2649 12W-24N A7
1300 LKFT 60045 2703 12W-24N B1
Woodhills Bay Rd
10 FXLK 60020 2473 27W-37N B2
Woodhollow Ct
1100 HFET 60192 2804 24W-15N C1
Woodhollow Dr
- RchT 60430 3506 4W-23S E3
1400 FSMR 60422 3506 4W-23S E3
1400 RchT 60422 3506 4W-23S E3
Wood Hollow Ln
1400 LbvT 60048 2590 18W-31N E1
Woodhollow Ln
300 BRLT 60103 2911 28W-7N B5
600 BFGV 60089 2701 17W-20N B7
Woodiris Dr
1000 JLET 60447 3495 33W-22S A2
Woodlake Blvd
10 GRNE 60031 2535 15W-34N A2
Woodlake Ct
2400 NPVL 60564 3202 29W-10S D7
Woodlake Dr
- CLSM 60133 2967 27W-4N C4
1000 CLSM 60188 2967 27W-4N C4
3800 HRPK 60133 2967 27W-4N C4
Woodlake Ln
- OrlT 60467 3344 14W-17S D5
Woodland Av
- AntT 60002 2416 25W-40N A2
- CHCG 60613 2977 1W-5N D1
10 AddT 60101 2971 18W-4N A4
10 AddT 60106 2971 17W-4N C4
10 ELGN 60123 2854 34W-11N D4
10 FXLK 60020 2473 27W-36N B4
10 WnfT 60185 3022 29W-1N E3
10 WynT 60185 2966 30W-3N B6
100 AURA 60505 3139 33W-7S A7
100 AURA 60505 3201 33W-7S A1
100 BNVL 60106 2971 16W-4N E3
100 WCHI 60185 2966 30W-2N B7
100 WNKA 60093 2812 4W-15N C3
300 WCDA 60084 2644 25W-27N B1
400 AddT 60101 2970 19W-4N C4
400 ADSN 60106 2971 17W-4N B4
400 WCDA 60084 2588 25W-27N B7
400 WCHI 60185 3022 30W-2N B1
400 WynT 60185 3022 30W-2N B1
500 ADSN 60101 2970 19W-4N C4
500 ADSN 60101 2971 17W-4N B4
500 HNDL 60521 3146 14W-5S C3
700 ShdT 60044 2593 12W-28N B5
800 BTVA 60510 3078 35W-2S B4
1400 AntT 60081 2415 27W-38N B6
1500 DSPN 60016 2863 13W-11N A2
1700 PKRG 60068 2863 11W-10N D5
3800 PvsT 60558 3086 14W-4S D7
3800 WDWH 60083 2420 13W-38N E7
3800 WNSP 60558 3086 14W-4S D7
4400 WNSP 60558 3146 14W-4S D1
14300 ODPK 60462 3345 12W-17S C5
N Woodland Av
21000 CbaT 60010 2698 25W-21N A6
24200 CbaT 60013 2642 28W-24N E7
39400 AntT 60002 2416 25W-39N B5
W Woodland Av
400 LMBD 60148 3026 20W-1N A3
1400 AddT 60101 2970 20W-4N B4
1400 ADSN 60101 2970 20W-4N B4
1600 BmdT 60101 2970 20W-4N A4
10500 BHPK 60087 2480 10W-38N A1
20500 LkvT 60046 2476 20W-36N A3
25200 AntT 60002 2416 25W-39N B5
26600 AntT 60002 2415 26W-38N D7
Woodland Cir
100 NARA 60542 3078 35W-3S A7
2200 NPVL 60565 3203 26W-10S D5
N Woodland Cir
20100 FftT 60448 3502 14W-24S E5
20100 MKNA 60448 3502 14W-24S E5
S Woodland Cir
20100 FftT 60448 3502 14W-24S E5
Woodland Cir N
3300 ISLK 60042 2586 28W-28N E5
Woodland Cir S
3500 ISLK 60042 2586 28W-28N E6
Woodland Ct
10 LMBD 60148 3026 20W-1N A3
10 PKFT 60466 3595 3W-28S B6
10 SEGN 60177 2908 36W-8N A2
10 WYNE 60185 2966 31W-4N A5
100 CPVL 60110 2748 33W-17N B7
100 CPVL 60118 2748 33W-17N B7
100 EDND 60118 2748 33W-17N B7
200 PltT 60067 2806 20W-13N A6
400 GNVW 60025 2811 7W-12N B7
700 WNVL 60555 3080 28W-4S E7
800 MRGO 60152 2634 49W-27N C1
800 SchT 60175 2963 36W-5N D2
1200 JLET 60436 3498 25W-24S B6
1300 RVWD 60015 2703 13W-21N A6
3400 OMFD 60461 3506 4W-25S E6
4700 RGMW 60008 2805 20W-13N E5
4700 RGMW 60067 2805 20W-13N E5
7500 BRRG 60527 3208 14W-8S D1
10300 DrrT 60098 2525 39W-31N C7
24900 CteT 60417 3686 2E-30S C3
W Woodland Ct
26000 CNHN 60410 3761 32W-32S D2
Woodland Ct E
10 RVWD 60015 2702 13W-21N E6
Woodland Ct W
1300 RVWD 60015 2702 13W-21N E6
Woodland Dr
- SHLD 60473 3350 0W-17S D6
- VOLO 60041 2530 27W-33N C3
10 CmpT 60175 2961 41W-6N E1
10 CTSD 60525 3147 12W-7S B6
10 KdlT 60560 3333 42W-15S D3
10 LKBN 60010 2697 27W-23N B2
10 LMNT 60439 3343 18W-15S A1
10 LtRT 60545 3258 49W-13S D6
10 OKBK 60523 3027 16W-1S E7
10 OKBK 60523 3085 16W-1S E1
10 RLKB 60073 2532 23W-34N A1
100 RLKB 60073 2531 23W-34N E1
200 MltT 60187 3024 25W-0N A5
200 MNKA 60447 3583 32W-28S D7
200 NBRN 60010 2697 26W-23N E1
300 GYLK 60030 2532 21W-33N D3
300 SEGN 60177 2908 36W-8N A2
500 CLLK 60014 2639 36W-25N D4
500 GNVW 60025 2811 7W-12N A7
500 RDLK 60073 2531 23W-34N E1
700 ANTH 60002 2357 24W-41N C7
700 ANTH 60002 2416 24W-41N C1
700 DrrT 60098 2525 39W-31N D7
800 CmpT 60175 2905 41W-6N E7
800 GLF 60025 2811 7W-12N B7
800 GNEN 60137 3025 21W-0N D4
900 WLNG 60090 2754 15W-18N E4
900 WLNG 60090 2755 15W-18N A4
1200 DRFD 60015 2703 11W-21N C5
1200 JLET 60436 3498 25W-24S B6
1300 AraT 60504 3138 34W-5S D4
1500 WdfT 60015 2703 11W-21N C5
1700 RGMW 60008 2860 21W-12N A1
1700 RGMW 60173 2860 21W-12N A1
1700 SMBG 60173 2859 21W-12N E1
1700 SMBG 60173 2860 21W-12N A1
2500 NHBK 60062 2809 10W-16N E1
2500 NHBK 60062 2810 10W-16N A1
3100 ZION 60099 2421 11W-40N D3
3400 OMFD 60461 3506 4W-25S E7
5200 OKFT 60452 3347 6W-18S E7
5500 WNSP 60558 3146 14W-6S D4
8200 DGvT 60561 3207 17W-9S C4
8200 DRN 60561 3207 17W-9S C4
8200 TYPK 60477 3424 10W-19S C2
9000 HYHL 60457 3209 11W-10S E5
9100 HYHL 60480 3209 11W-10S E5
9100 PlsT 60480 3209 11W-10S E5
Woodland Dr
10000 HBRN 60034 2351 40W-41N A7
12800 HMGN 60491 3344 16W-18S A7
13100 HMGN 60491 3343 16W-18S E7
E Woodland Dr
300 CmpT 60175 2906 41W-6N A7
400 CmpT 60175 2961 41W-6N E1
600 CmpT 60175 2905 41W-6N E7
N Woodland Dr
200 MPPT 60056 2808 13W-13N E5
200 WhlT 60056 2808 13W-13N E5
5600 MchT 60050 2472 29W-37N C1
9200 NLES 60714 2864 10W-11N B2
W Woodland Dr
- GrtT 60041 2530 25W-34N E1
- GrtT 60073 2530 25W-34N E1
- RDLK 60041 2530 25W-34N E1
- RDLK 60073 2530 25W-34N E1
5300 MchT 60050 2527 34W-34N C1
17000 WrnT 60030 2534 17W-33N B3
17000 WrnT 60048 2534 17W-33N C3
25700 GrtT 60073 2531 25W-34N A1
Woodland Gln
10 PKFT 60466 3595 3W-28S B6
Woodland Hllw
4300 PRGV 60012 2585 32W-27N B7
Woodland Ln
- LGGV 60047 2700 19W-21N B7
- SRWD 60404 3495 31W-24S E7
700 MRGO 60152 2634 49W-27N C1
1200 GwdT 60098 2525 38W-33N E3
1300 RVWD 60015 2702 13W-21N E5
1400 MchT 60051 2528 31W-33N D3
1500 BGBK 60490 3267 26W-13S D4
3600 DRGV 60515 3084 19W-3S D6
3600 YkTp 60515 3084 19W-3S D6
7500 BRRG 60527 3208 14W-8S D1
13600 VrnT 60045 2648 13W-25N E5
22300 FKFT 60423 3592 10W-27S C3
N Woodland Ln
1900 ANHT 60004 2807 16W-16N D1
Woodland Ln N
10 RVWD 60015 2703 12W-22N A4
500 NHFD 60093 2811 7W-15N B1
2100 LNSH 60015 2703 12W-22N A4
2100 LNSH 60069 2703 12W-22N A4
2100 RVWD 60069 2703 12W-22N A4
Woodland Ln S
500 NHFD 60093 2811 7W-15N B1
Woodland Pkwy
1400 BtnT 60081 2414 30W-39N A4
N Woodland Pl
42500 AntT 60002 2356 27W-42N B6
Woodland Rd
10 LIHL 60156 2694 35W-22N A5
100 LYVL 60048 2591 17W-28N B5
200 HDPK 60035 2758 7W-20N B1
400 WNVL 60555 3080 28W-4S E7
400 WNVL 60555 3081 28W-4S A7
700 WCDA 60084 2588 25W-28N B7
2700 EVTN 60201 2866 4W-11N D2
E Woodland Rd
10 LKBF 60044 2593 10W-28N E5
10 LKFT 60045 2649 10W-27N E2
100 LKBF 60044 2594 10W-28N A5
200 LKFT 60045 2650 10W-27N A1
W Woodland Rd
10 NndT 60013 2641 31W-26N D4
100 AlqT 60013 2641 31W-26N D4
100 ODHL 60013 2641 31W-26N D4
900 ShdT 60044 2593 12W-28N A5
Woodland St
600 PltT 60074 2752 21W-18N C2
N Woodland Ter
33100 WrnT 60030 2533 18W-33N E3
W Woodland Ter
18200 GRNE 60031 2477 18W-36N A5
18200 WrnT 60031 2477 18W-36N A5
18400 WrnT 60031 2476 18W-36N E5
25200 LkvT 60046 2474 25W-37N B2
Woodland Tr
- LkvT 60046 2417 21W-38N E6
- LNHT 60046 2417 21W-38N E6
- WDSK 60098 2581 41W-28N D6
12800 HTLY 60142 2744 43W-19N B3
N Woodland Tr
10 PSPK 60464 3274 10W-14S B6
S Woodland Tr
12200 PSPK 60464 3274 10W-14S B6
Woodland Tr S
100 WYNE 60185 2966 31W-4N A4
Woodland Tr W
100 WYNE 60185 2966 31W-4N A4
100 WynT 60185 2966 31W-4N A4
200 WYNE 60185 2965 31W-4N E4
Woodland Wy
200 BMDL 60108 2968 24W-5N D1
500 OSWG 60543 3263 37W-13S D6
21200 SRWD 60404 3584 31W-25S A1
Woodland Heights Blvd
700 SMWD 60107 2857 28W-10N B6
Woodland Hills Ct
- LKWD 60142 2638 39W-25N C5
Woodland Hills Dr
- BRLT 60103 2910 30W-6N B7
- BRLT 60103 2966 30W-6N B1
- LKWD 60142 2638 39W-25N C5
Woodland Hills Pkwy
1300 BRLT 60103 2966 30W-5N C1
Woodland Hills Rd
10 BTVA 60510 3078 34W-2S E3
E Woodland Park Av
600 CHCG 60616 3092 0E-3S D4
Woodland Park Cir
10 GLBT 60136 2799 38W-14N A5
Woodland Park Clb
- HNDL 60521 3146 15W-6S C4
Woodland Park Ct
100 GLBT 60136 2799 38W-14N A5
Woodlands Pkwy
600 VNHL 60061 2702 15W-23N A1
600 VrnT 60061 2702 15W-23N A1
1000 VNHL 60061 2701 16W-23N E1
Woodlane Ct
300 WDDL 60191 2971 17W-5N C2
Woodlane Dr
1900 LNHT 60046 2476 20W-37N A1
5500 MchT 60097 2469 36W-37N D2
Wood Lark Dr
10 MltT 60188 3023 26W-1N E3
10 MltT 60188 3024 26W-1N A3
Woodlark Dr
1500 NHBK 60062 2757 8W-17N D6
Woodlawn
- ELGN 60120 2855 32W-10N C6
Woodlawn Av
- BlmT 60411 3509 1E-24S B5
- LYWD 60411 3509 1E-24S B5
10 SchT 60174 2908 35W-6N B6
100 AURA 60506 3138 36W-7S A7
100 GLNC 60093 2759 5W-17N A6
200 AURA 60506 3199 36W-8S E1
200 GLNC 60093 2758 5W-17N E6
300 GLNC 60022 2758 6W-16N E6
400 AlqT 60021 2696 29W-22N C4
400 RMVL 60446 3340 24W-15S C2
500 WNVL 60555 3081 28W-3S A6
600 JltT 60433 3587 23W-25S B2
600 LKFT 60045 2650 10W-26N B4
700 FDHT 60411 3509 1E-25S B7
700 LslT 60540 3141 26W-7S E7
700 NPVL 60540 3141 26W-7S E7
800 DSPN 60016 2862 13W-11N D3
900 WKGN 60085 2479 11W-35N E6
900 WKGN 60085 2480 10W-35N A6
1300 GNVW 60025 2810 8W-14N E4
1300 GNVW 60025 2811 8W-14N A4
1400 FDHT 60411 3597 1E-25S B1
1500 SLVL 60411 3597 1E-25S B1
3400 GRNE 60031 2536 13W-34N A1
3400 WkgT 60031 2536 13W-34N A1
3400 WkgT 60085 2536 13W-34N A1
3500 GRNE 60031 2479 13W-34N A7
4100 GRNE 60031 2478 14W-34N D7
7000 HMND 46324 3430 E4
8100 MNSR 46321 3430 E6
11300 LMNT 60439 3272 16W-13S A4
14200 DLTN 60419 3351 1E-17S B6
15200 SHLD 60419 3351 1E-17S B6
22700 BlmT 60411 3597 1E-27S B5
22700 STGR 60475 3597 1E-27S B5
E Woodlawn Av
1000 LGPK 60525 3087 12W-3S C6
1100 BKFD 60513 3087 12W-3S C6
1100 BKFD 60525 3087 12W-3S C6
N Woodlawn Av
10 JLET 60435 3498 25W-23S B5
10 JLET 60436 3498 25W-23S B5
S Woodlawn Av
4400 CHCG 60653 3093 1E-4S A7
4600 CHCG 60615 3093 1E-4S A7
4700 CHCG 60615 3153 1E-6S A3
7100 CHCG 60619 3153 1E-8S A7
7100 CHCG 60637 3153 1E-8S A7
7800 CHCG 60619 3215 1E-9S A2
9500 CHCG 60628 3215 1E-11S A6
10300 CHCG 60628 3279 1E-12S A1
13300 RBBN 60472 3348 3W-15S E2
13300 WthT 60406 3348 3W-15S E2
13300 WthT 60472 3348 3W-15S E2
26200 CteT 60417 3686 1E-32S B7
W Woodlawn Av
10 LGPK 60525 3087 12W-3S B6
25500 AntT 60002 2357 25W-43N A4
Woodlawn Av W
15300 SHLD 60473 3350 0E-17S D6
Woodlawn Cir
1100 WKGN 60085 2479 11W-35N E6
Woodlawn Ct
16600 SHLD 60473 3429 1E-19S A3
S Woodlawn Ct
20700 FftT 60423 3504 9W-25S E7
20700 FftT 60423 3505 8W-24S A6
Woodlawn Dr
- NARA 60542 3078 35W-3S C6
10 MDLN 60060 2646 19W-27N D1
3800 ISLK 60042 2586 28W-28N D6
W Woodlawn Dr
7300 FftT 60423 3504 9W-25S E6
Woodlawn Rd
900 GNVW 60025 2811 7W-14N A4
2000 NHBK 60062 2757 10W-16N A6
2500 NHBK 60062 2756 10W-16N E6
E Woodlawn Rd
100 NlxT 60451 3589 17W-25S C1
200 NLNX 60451 3589 17W-25S C1
W Woodlawn Rd
500 NLNX 60451 3589 18W-25S A1
500 NlxT 60451 3589 18W-25S A1
Woodlawn St
10 GNVA 60134 3020 34W-1N D4
500 MltT 60187 3024 25W-0N A4
600 HFET 60169 2858 24W-11N D4
600 MltT 60188 3024 25W-0N A4
N Woodlawn St
1500 MltT 60187 3024 25W-0N A4
1500 WHTN 60187 3024 25W-0N A4
S Woodlawn St
100 WHTN 60187 3024 25W-0S A7
Woodlawn East Av
15400 SHLD 60419 3351 1E-18S B7
15400 SHLD 60473 3351 1E-18S B7
15800 SHLD 60473 3429 1E-19S B2
N Woodlawn Park Av
1600 MHRY 60051 2528 31W-33N D2
2100 MchT 60051 2528 31W-34N D2
2200 LKMR 60051 2528 31W-34N E2
Woodlawn West Av
15700 SHLD 60473 3350 0E-18S D7
15700 SHLD 60473 3428 0E-18S D1
Woodleigh Av
800 HDPK 60035 2704 9W-23N C2
Woodlet Ln
100 BGBK 60490 3267 27W-11S C2
Woodley Mnr
10 NtrT 60091 2811 5W-14N E4
10 NtrT 60093 2811 5W-14N E4
10 WLMT 60091 2811 5W-14N E4
Woodley Rd
10 NtrT 60093 2811 5W-14N E3
10 NtrT 60093 2812 5W-14N A3
10 WNKA 60093 2812 5W-14N A3
100 NtrT 60091 2812 5W-14N A4
100 WLMT 60091 2812 5W-14N A4
100 WLMT 60093 2812 5W-14N A4
Woodley Woods
400 NtrT 60091 2811 5W-14N E4
400 NtrT 60093 2811 5W-14N E4
400 WLMT 60091 2811 5W-14N E4
Woodlily Ct
1400 JLET 60447 3495 33W-22S A1
Woodlock St
200 FXLK 60020 2473 27W-36N C4
200 FXLK 60041 2473 27W-36N C5
Woodlyn Dr
300 AraT 60504 3138 35W-5S C2
300 AURA 60504 3138 35W-5S B2
2500 WDRG 60517 3205 21W-9S E3
Woodmar Av
15200 ODPK 60462 3346 10W-18S C7
Woodmar Ct
10 SMWD 60107 2857 27W-11N C4
5200 MHRY 60050 2527 34W-32N D5
Woodmar Dr
700 CLLK 60014 2639 36W-24N D7
Woodmar Ter
500 CLLK 60014 2639 36W-24N D7
Woodmere Ct
2800 NHBK 60062 2756 11W-16N E7
5000 JLET 60586 3496 30W-22S B1
Woodmere Dr
2600 DRN 60561 3206 19W-9S C3
2700 DRN 60517 3206 19W-9S C3
2700 WDRG 60517 3206 19W-9S C3
2800 NHBK 60062 2756 11W-16N D7
5800 HNDL 60521 3146 15W-6S B4
Woodmere Ln
100 WYNE 60184 2909 33W-6N B7
200 WLNG 60090 2755 14W-18N C4
600 GNVW 60025 2811 7W-13N B7
W Woodmere Ter
19700 AntT 60002 2359 20W-41N B7
19700 AntT 60002 2418 19W-41N C1
W Woodmill Ct
13900 HMGN 60491 3343 17W-17S C4
Woodmoor Dr
400 RLKB 60073 2475 22W-35N B7
Woodoak Ct
2100 RLKB 60046 2475 21W-36N D5
2100 RLKB 60073 2475 21W-36N D5
Woodoak Dr
2000 RLKB 60046 2475 21W-35N D5
2100 RLKB 60073 2475 21W-36N D4
Wood Oaks Dr
- BrnT 60010 2802 28W-14N E3
- BrnT 60010 2803 28W-14N A4
- BrnT 60118 2802 28W-14N E4
- SBTN 60010 2803 28W-14N A4
Woodpath Ln
2300 HDPK 60035 2704 8W-22N E3
Woodpecker Cor
3100 LGGV 60047 2700 19W-21N D5
Woodpecker Rd
- DhmT 60033 2464 50W-36N B3
Wood Rayne Rd
- HDPK 60035 2704 9W-21N C7
Woodridge Cir
200 SchT 60177 2908 34W-7N C4
200 SEGN 60177 2908 34W-7N C4
Wood Ridge Ct
600 ELGN 60123 2854 36W-12N A2
Woodridge Ct
1400 DRFD 60015 2704 10W-21N A6
N Woodridge Ct
30300 LbvT 60048 2592 15W-30N A2
Wood Ridge Dr
- HTLY 60142 2744 42W-19N D3
Woodridge Dr
- SRGV 60506 3136 40W-5S B3
10 OKBK 60523 3086 15W-1S B1
1300 RLKB 60073 2474 24W-35N D7
1500 RLKH 60073 2474 24W-35N D7
2600 WDRG 60517 3143 22W-7S D7
7000 WDRG 60517 3205 22W-8S D2
7400 LslT 60517 3205 22W-8S D1
Woodridge Ln
10 BFGV 60089 2701 16W-20N D7
10 SMWD 60107 2857 28W-10N B5
700 GLNC 60022 2758 7W-17N B5
3000 GNVW 60062 2809 11W-15N D3
3000 NfdT 60062 2809 11W-15N D3
13700 ODPK 60462 3346 11W-16S A3
S Woodridge Ln
10 ANHT 60004 2807 17W-14N C5
Woodridge Rd
10 OswT 60538 3199 37W-10S D6
Woodridge Tr
500 MchT 60050 2526 36W-32N E5
500 MHRY 60050 2526 36W-32N E4
Woodridge Wy
2300 LMBD 60148 3084 19W-2S C3
W Woodridge Wy
24400 TroT 60404 3584 30W-26S B3
W Woodriver Dr
6600 MNGV 60053 2865 8W-9N A6
6600 MNGV 60714 2865 8W-9N A6
6600 NLES 60714 2865 8W-9N A6
Woodrock Rd
10 BNHL 60010 2748 32W-19N E3
Woodrow Av
4800 MchT 60050 2472 29W-36N C3
E Woodrow Av
1000 LMBD 60148 3026 18W-0N E5
1100 LMBD 60181 3026 18W-0N E5
1100 VLPK 60181 3026 18W-0N E5
Woodrow Ln
800 PltT 60124 2852 40W-10N B5
Woodrow St
10 MHTN 60442 3677 19W-30S D4
W Woodrow St
200 VLPK 60181 3027 18W-0N A5
300 LMBD 60148 3026 19W-0S D6
300 LMBD 60181 3026 19W-0S D6
300 VLPK 60181 3026 19W-0S D6
Woodruff Av
500 JltT 60436 3586 24W-25S D1
1200 DRFD 60015 2703 11W-21N D6
S Woodruff Ct
19700 FftT 60423 3504 9W-23S C4
Woodruff Dr
7800 ODPK 60462 3346 9W-18S C7
E Woodruff Rd
400 JLET 60432 3499 22W-22S C2
1400 JltT 60432 3499 22W-22S D2
Woodruff St
300 AURA 60505 3138 34W-7S D7
Woodrush Ln
1000 DRN 60561 3145 17W-7S B6
S Woodrush Wy
25600 CNHN 60410 3672 32W-31S C5
Woods Av
10 MltT 60187 3023 26W-0N D4
10 MltT 60188 3023 26W-0N D4
S Woods Av
- ISLK 60042 2586 30W-28N A5
- NndT 60042 2586 30W-28N A5
3000 NndT 60051 2586 30W-28N A5
W Woods Av
- LkvT 60046 2417 21W-38N E6
800 JLET 60436 3498 25W-24S C7
S Woods Ct
10 FoxT 60560 3332 46W-16S A4
Woods Dr
- FftT 60423 3504 11W-24S A5
- FKFT 60423 3504 11W-24S A5
- LKPT 60441 3419 23W-20S B5

STREET Block City ZIP Map# CGS Grid

Woods Dr
9800 SKOK 60077 2865 6W-12N D1
N Woods Dr
42300 AntT 60002 2357 25W-42N B6
W Woods Dr
1400 ANHT 60004 2753 18W-17N D6
1400 PltT 60004 2753 18W-17N D6
Woods Ln
9600 HBRN 60034 2350 41W-41N E7
E Woods Ln
100 LKPT 60441 3419 22W-20S C5
Woods Rd
400 DSPN 60016 2863 12W-11N C3
Woods St
600 FKFT 60423 3503 12W-24S C6
W Woods St
700 MHRY 60050 2528 33W-32N A4
Woods Wy
- PNFD 60585 3337 32W-15S C2
N Woods Wy
1600 VNHL 60061 2647 16W-27N D2
Woodsage Av
- YKVL 60560 3333 43W-16S B4
Woods Briar Ct
6400 LSLE 60532 3142 24W-6S D5
Woods Chapel St
10 PltT 60067 2806 19W-14N C4
10 RGMW 60008 2806 19W-14N C4
Woodscreek Cir
1400 CLLK 60014 2693 37W-23N C2
Woods Creek Ct
10 ALGN 60102 2693 36W-20N D7
Woods Creek Ln
500 ALGN 60102 2693 36W-20N C7
Woods End Rd
3800 LGGV 60047 2700 19W-22N C3
4000 NndT 60012 2583 36W-28N E7
Woodside Av
500 HNDL 60521 3146 14W-5S C2
1100 LGPK 60525 3087 12W-2S B4
3500 BKFD 60513 3088 10W-3S B5
3800 BKFD 60534 3088 10W-3S A6
3800 LYNS 60534 3088 10W-3S A6
N Woodside Av
39400 AntT 60002 2416 25W-39N B5
Woodside Ct
200 WCHI 60185 3022 30W-2N B1
1300 GYLK 60030 2532 21W-34N D1
1300 SMBG 60193 2859 22W-10N C6
1600 GwdT 60098 2524 40W-32N E5
1600 WDSK 60098 2524 40W-32N E5
2300 CPVL 60110 2746 37W-18N D6
2700 AURA 60506 3198 39W-8S D1
3500 JLET 60431 3417 28W-20S A4
11700 BRRG 60527 3208 14W-9S C2
N Woodside Ct
500 LKPT 60441 3420 21W-18S A1
Woodside Dr
- DGvT 60517 3270 19W-12S C2
- GwdT 60098 2524 40W-32N E4
- WDSK 60098 2524 40W-32N E4
10 OKBK 60523 3086 15W-1S B1
200 WCHI 60185 3022 30W-2N B1
300 AddT 60106 2971 17W-4N C2
300 BMDL 60108 2968 24W-5N C1
300 WDDL 60106 2971 17W-4N C2
300 WDDL 60191 2971 17W-4N C2
400 ADSN 60106 2971 17W-4N C3
400 ADSN 60191 2971 17W-4N C3
700 ROSL 60172 2912 24W-6N D6
1000 NlxT 60451 3501 16W-23S E4
2000 GwdT 60098 2525 40W-32N A4
2000 RLKB 60073 2475 23W-35N A5
2200 CPVL 60110 2746 37W-18N C5
2300 CPVL 60118 2746 37W-18N D5
2900 JLET 60431 3417 28W-20S A4
22500 CNHN 60410 3584 29W-27S D5
Woodside Ln
200 SchT 60175 2907 38W-6N B7
800 ROSL 60172 2912 24W-6N C7
1900 GLHT 60139 2969 23W-3N B5
7900 BRRG 60527 3208 14W-9S C3
Woodside Rd
10 RVSD 60546 3088 10W-3S B4
200 NRIV 60546 3088 9W-3S B4
Woodside Ter
600 HPSR 60140 2795 47W-15N D3
Wood Sorrel Pl
10 WDRG 60517 3143 21W-7S E6
Woodstock Av
100 KLWH 60043 2812 4W-14N D4
200 CNHL 60514 3085 17W-4S C7
200 CNHL 60514 3145 17W-4S C1
200 CNHL 60559 3085 17W-4S C7
200 GNEN 60137 3025 21W-0S E6
200 WTMT 60559 3085 17W-4S C7
Woodstock Ct
200 LslT 60540 3142 25W-6S B4
Woodstock Dr
7700 TYPK 60477 3424 9W-20S D4
11000 ODPK 60467 3344 13W-16S E3
11000 ODPK 60467 3345 13W-16S A3
11000 OrlT 60467 3345 13W-16S A3
24600 PNFD 60585 3266 30W-13S A5
Woodstock Ln
1800 JLET 60586 3416 29W-21S D7
Woodstock Rd
700 OMFD 60461 3506 4W-25S D7
Woodstock St
3700 WRLK 60097 2469 37W-35N C5
E Woodstock St
10 CLLK 60014 2640 35W-26N B3
N Woodstock St
10700 HTLY 60142 2692 40W-21N A6
W Woodstock St
10 CLLK 60014 2640 35W-26N A3
200 CLLK 60014 2639 36W-26N E3
Woodstone Cir
200 BFGV 60089 2754 16W-20N D1
Woodstone Ct
10 BFGV 60089 2754 16W-20N D1
Woodstone Dr
10 BFGV 60089 2754 16W-20N D1
Woodstone Ln
- BLVY 60098 2525 38W-31N E6
- BLVY 60098 2526 38W-31N A6
Woodstream Ct
800 LKFT 60045 2649 11W-24N D6
Woodvale Av
300 DRFD 60015 2704 10W-21N A5
1500 DRFD 60015 2703 10W-21N E5
Woodvale Ct
500 MltT 60190 3023 26W-0N D5
Woodvale Dr
8500 DRN 60561 3206 20W-9S B4
8600 WDRG 60517 3206 20W-10S B4

Woodvale Dr
8600 WDRG 60561 3206 20W-9S B4
W Woodvale Rd
7800 FftT 60423 3592 10W-25S C1
7800 FKFT 60423 3592 9W-25S D1
Woodvale St
10 MltT 60190 3023 26W-0S D6
200 WNFD 60190 3023 26W-0N D5
Woodview Av
300 EGvT 60007 2861 18W-9N A7
300 EGVV 60007 2861 18W-9N A7
400 EGvT 60007 2915 17W-8N B1
400 EGVV 60007 2915 17W-8N B1
1300 CTCY 60409 3430 3E-19S A2
Woodview Cir
300 ELGN 60120 2855 32W-10N C5
Woodview Ct
10 SMWD 60107 2857 27W-9N C7
100 SchT 60175 2963 36W-6N E1
200 SchT 60175 2907 36W-6N E7
300 OKBK 60523 3086 15W-1S B1
1000 AURA 60502 3139 32W-6S C5
1800 DRN 60561 3206 19W-9S E4
2200 NPVL 60565 3203 26W-10S D5
2600 WKGN 60087 2478 14W-36N D3
2600 WrnT 60031 2478 14W-36N D3
5300 LGGV 60047 2701 17W-22N A4
Woodview Dr
10 BmdT 60143 2914 21W-6N A6
10 BmdT 60157 2913 22W-6N C6
10 ELGN 60120 2855 32W-11N D4
10 GNEN 60137 3025 21W-0S D7
10 ITSC 60143 2914 21W-6N A6
10 WynT 60185 2967 27W-3N B6
100 SMWD 60107 2857 27W-9N C7
200 BmdT 60143 2913 21W-6N E6
400 PTHT 60070 2754 16W-16N D6
1000 GNOK 60048 2535 11W-31N B7
2100 WslT 60481 3943 27W-41S D4
2800 SPGV 60081 2413 31W-40N D2
7600 WDRG 60517 3205 22W-8S D2
E Woodview Dr
2000 MPPT 60056 2808 13W-15N E2
2000 MPPT 60056 2809 13W-15N A3
2000 WhlT 60056 2809 13W-15N A3
2000 WhlT 60062 2809 13W-15N A3
Woodview Ln
- DRFD 60015 2703 12W-20N B7
- RVWD 60015 2703 12W-20N B7
- WdfT 60015 2703 12W-20N B7
10 ALGN 60102 2747 33W-20N E1
10 ALGN 60102 2748 33W-20N A1
10 IVNS 60067 2804 23W-15N D1
10 LmnT 60439 3272 15W-13S B4
10 LMNT 60464 3272 15W-13S B4
10 SchT 60175 2963 38W-6N A1
1300 GNVW 60025 2810 8W-13N D5
2100 MaiT 60016 2863 11W-11N E3
2100 MaiT 60068 2863 11W-11N E3
2100 PKRG 60016 2863 11W-11N E3
2100 PKRG 60068 2863 11W-11N E3
2200 NPVL 60565 3203 26W-10S D5
Woodview Pkwy
10 HshT 60140 2743 46W-19N A3
W Woodview Pkwy
7600 HshT 60140 2743 46W-19N A3
Woodview Rd
200 LKBN 60010 2643 26W-24N E7
1000 BRRG 60521 3146 14W-6S C3
1000 HNDL 60521 3146 14W-6S C3
Woodview St
12300 PLNO 60545 3332 45W-14S C1
Woodville Ln
200 SMBG 60193 2859 23W-10N A6
Woodward Av
- DGvT 60439 3270 20W-11S B1
- WDRG 60439 3206 20W-11S B7
100 GNVA 60134 3020 34W-1N D3
100 DPgT 60440 3206 20W-10S A6
200 BGBK 60440 3206 20W-10S A6
200 DPgT 60440 3206 20W-10S A6
200 DPgT 60517 3206 20W-10S A6
200 WDRG 60440 3206 20W-10S A6
800 DRFD 60015 2703 11W-21N D7
800 JLET 60432 3499 22W-22S C2
4300 DRGV 60515 3144 21W-5S A2
5500 DGvT 60515 3144 21W-6S A4
5500 DGvT 60516 3144 21W-7S A6
5500 LslT 60515 3144 21W-6S A4
5500 LslT 60516 3144 21W-7S A6
6100 DRGV 60516 3144 21W-7S A6
6400 HMND 46324 3430 E2
6600 WDRG 60516 3144 21W-7S A6
6600 WDRG 60517 3144 21W-7S A6
6800 DRGV 60517 3144 21W-7S A7
7100 WDRG 60516 3206 21W-8S A2
7100 WDRG 60517 3206 20W-10S A6
8300 DRN 60517 3206 20W-9S A4
8300 DRN 60561 3206 20W-9S A4
10000 WDRG 60439 3270 20W-11S B1
10000 WDRG 60517 3270 20W-11S B1
Woodward Av CO-56
7500 WDRG 60517 3206 20W-10S A6
8300 DRN 60517 3206 20W-9S A4
8300 DRN 60561 3206 20W-9S A4
Woodward Ct
400 LKFT 60045 2648 13W-25N E5
Woodward Dr
- SCRL 60175 2963 37W-3N B6
14000 ODPK 60462 3346 10W-16S C4
S Woodward Dr
10 CHCG 60624 3032 4W-0S C5
S Woodward St
200 BCHR 60401 3864 0W-37S B2
Woodwind Dr
700 NpvT 60563 3140 30W-5S A4
1100 PLNO 60545 3259 48W-12S B4
N Woodwork Ln
200 PLTN 60067 2752 21W-16N C7
Woodworth Av
- WDSK 60098 2581 41W-28N D5
300 JLET 60435 3498 24W-23S D4
Woodworth Pl
400 BmdT 60172 2913 23W-7N A5
500 BmdT 60172 2912 23W-7N E5
500 ROSL 60172 2912 23W-7N E5
2600 HLCT 60429 3427 3W-20S B5
2600 HLCT 60430 3427 3W-20S B5
3200 HLCT 60429 3426 4W-20S E5
E Woodworth Pl
10 ROSL 60172 2913 23W-7N A5
Woodworth St
300 BtlT 60560 3333 42W-15S D2
300 YKVL 60560 3333 42W-15S D2
Woody Tr
8800 GwdT 60097 2469 37W-35N A6
8800 WRLK 60097 2469 37W-35N A6

Woody Wy
10 AlqT 60013 2641 31W-26N E3
10 LIHL 60156 2694 35W-21N A5
10 ODHL 60013 2641 31W-26N E3
Wool St
100 BRTN 60010 2751 25W-18N A2
Wooley Rd
600 OswT 60543 3264 36W-13S A5
600 OswT 60543 3265 33W-13S A5
3000 OSWG 60543 3263 36W-13S E5
3000 OSWG 60543 3264 36W-13S A5
3000 OswT 60543 3263 36W-13S E5
W Wooly Hill Ct
12000 HMGN 60491 3344 15W-16S C3
S Wooly Hill Dr
13500 HMGN 60491 3344 15W-16S C3
Woonsocket Ct
1000 SMBG 60193 2912 24W-9N C1
Wooster Ct
1900 CHHT 60411 3595 2W-26S C2
3000 NPVL 60565 3204 24W-10S C5
W Wooster Ln
26700 FXLK 60041 2530 26W-34N C1
26700 GrtT 60041 2530 26W-34N C1
26700 VOLO 60041 2530 26W-34N C1
W Wooster Lake Av
26300 GrtT 60041 2473 26W-34N D7
26600 FXLK 60041 2473 26W-34N D7
Worack Pl
10 WKGN 60085 2536 11W-34N E2
Worbler Ln
- YKVL 60560 3333 42W-17S D6
Worcester Ct
400 SMBG 60193 2912 24W-9N E1
Worcester Ln
2800 AURA 60504 3201 32W-9S D3
Worchester Av
700 WSTR 60154 3029 12W-0S A7
Worden Wy
1400 EGVV 60007 2913 21W-8N E3
1400 EGVV 60007 2914 21W-8N A3
Worsley St
100 YKVL 60560 3333 42W-15S D2
N Worth Av
10 ELGN 60123 2854 34W-11N C4
S Worth Av
10 ELGN 60123 2854 35W-11N C4
10500 CHRG 60415 3274 8W-12S E2
10500 CHRG 60482 3274 8W-12S E2
10500 WRTH 60482 3274 8W-12S E2
11500 WRTH 60482 3275 8W-13S A4
Wortham Ct
600 MDLN 60060 2646 20W-27N B2
Wortham Dr
600 MDLN 60060 2646 20W-26N B2
800 LGGV 60047 2646 20W-26N B2
Worthing Dr
2200 NPVL 60565 3203 26W-10S E5
Worthington Dr
1000 HFET 60169 2858 24W-11N C3
2400 AURA 60506 3136 39W-6S E6
Worthington Ln
3300 LIHL 60156 2692 39W-23N C2
Wortman Dr
700 RKDL 60436 3498 25W-24S C7
Wren Av
8700 HGKN 60525 3147 11W-7S D6
N Wren Av
600 PLTN 60067 2752 20W-16N E6
Wren Cir
18700 FftT 60448 3503 13W-22S A1
18700 MKNA 60448 3503 13W-22S A1
Wren Ct
- SPGV 60081 2413 32W-39N C5
10 WDRG 60517 3143 21W-7S E7
100 GLHT 60139 2968 23W-4N E4
200 BMDL 60108 2969 23W-4N A2
800 NLNX 60451 3589 18W-27S A4
3900 RGMW 60008 2806 19W-13N D7
W Wren Ct
4500 WKGN 60048 2535 14W-31N C6
Wren Dr
200 BMDL 60108 2969 23W-4N A3
Wren Ln
400 VrnT 60015 2755 15W-20N B1
2100 RGMW 60008 2806 19W-14N C4
4100 ANHT 60005 2806 19W-13N D7
4100 ANHT 60008 2806 19W-13N D7
4200 ZION 60099 2362 12W-42N B7
Wren Rd
- KdlT 60560 3334 41W-16S A5
- YKVL 60560 3334 41W-16S A5
10 CPVL 60110 2748 32W-17N C6
25200 TRLK 60010 2643 27W-25N C5
Wren St
10 WDRG 60517 3143 21W-7S E7
Wrendale Av
100 HIWD 60040 2704 9W-23N D3
Wren's Gate
1000 MDLN 60060 2590 19W-28N B6
Wright Av
- ELGN 60120 2855 32W-10N C6
700 ISLK 60042 2642 29W-27N C1
700 ISLK 60051 2642 29W-27N C1
700 NndT 60042 2642 29W-27N C1
700 NndT 60051 2642 29W-27N C1
1900 NCHI 60064 2536 11W-31N D7
2300 NCHI 60064 2593 12W-31N C1
2300 NCHI 60088 2593 12W-31N C1
N Wright Av
34000 TDLK 60030 2533 18W-34N E2
34000 WrnT 60030 2533 18W-34N E2
Wright Blvd
1200 SMBG 60193 2912 24W-8N D3
2000 BFGV 60089 2701 16W-22N D4
2000 VrnT 60089 2701 16W-22N D4
Wright Ct
- PLNO 60545 3259 48W-13S B5
10 LIHL 60156 2692 38W-21N D5
200 AURA 60505 3139 33W-7S B7
300 LYVL 60048 2591 16W-29N D5
400 BGBK 60440 3205 22W-11S C7
Wright Dr
100 LIHL 60156 2692 38W-21N E5
Wright Ln
10 OKPK 60302 3031 8W-0N A4
1800 HRPK 60133 2967 27W-5N D1
25000 PNFD 60564 3265 31W-13S E5
25000 PNFD 60585 3265 31W-13S E5
Wright Rd
700 UYPK 60466 3684 3W-29S B2
S Wright Rd
3100 NndT 60014 2586 30W-28N A5
3100 NndT 60050 2586 30W-28N A5
3400 NndT 60012 2586 30W-28N A5
W Wright Rd
1700 NndT 60050 2586 30W-29N A5

W Wright Rd
1800 NndT 60050 2585 31W-29N D5
2100 PRGV 60050 2585 31W-29N E5
2500 PRGV 60012 2585 31W-29N D5
18600 WrnT 60030 2533 18W-34N E2
Wright St
- ELBN 60119 3017 43W-2N A1
17500 LNSG 60438 3430 4E-20S B5
N Wright St
10 NPVL 60540 3141 26W-6S E5
900 LslT 60563 3141 26W-5S E3
900 NPVL 60563 3141 26W-5S E3
S Wright St
10 NPVL 60540 3141 26W-7S E7
Wright Ter
3700 SKOK 60076 2866 4W-10N C4
4800 SKOK 60076 2865 6W-10N E4
4900 SKOK 60077 2865 6W-10N D4
W Wright Ter
7100 NLES 60714 2864 8W-10N D4
Wrightwood Av
- FNPK 60131 2973 12W-3N B5
- LydT 60131 2973 13W-3N A5
400 AddT 60101 2971 17W-3N B6
400 AddT 60126 2972 15W-3N A6
400 EMHT 60126 2972 15W-3N A6
10400 LydT 60164 2973 13W-3N A5
10600 LydT 60164 2972 13W-3N E5
10800 NHLK 60164 2972 13W-3N E5
E Wrightwood Av
- AddT 60126 2972 15W-3N A6
10 ADSN 60101 2970 18W-3N E6
10 ADSN 60101 2971 18W-3N A6
10 GLHT 60139 2968 23W-3N E6
200 EMHT 60126 2972 15W-3N A6
200 GLHT 60139 2969 23W-3N A6
W Wrightwood Av
10 GLHT 60139 2968 24W-3N D6
200 EMHT 60126 2971 16W-3N E5
400 CHCG 60614 2978 0W-3N A5
600 ADSN 60101 2970 19W-3N D6
800 CHCG 60614 2977 2W-3N C5
3200 CHCG 60647 2976 5W-3N B5
3900 CHCG 60639 2976 5W-3N B5
4700 CHCG 60639 2975 6W-3N E5
6600 CHCG 60707 2975 8W-3N A5
6700 CHCG 60707 2974 8W-3N E5
7200 EDPK 60707 2974 9W-3N D5
8200 RVGV 60171 2974 10W-3N A5
8700 RVGV 60171 2973 11W-3N E5
Wrightwood Ct
1600 GLHT 60139 2968 24W-3N D6
W Wrightwood Ct
1500 ADSN 60101 2970 20W-3N A6
Wrightwood Ter
400 LYVL 60048 2591 16W-28N E6
Wright Woods
28100 VrnT 60045 2648 14W-24N B7
28100 VrnT 60069 2648 14W-24N B7
28100 VrnT 60069 2702 14W-24N B1
E Writer Ct
- VNHL 60061 2701 16W-23N E1
N Wulff St
10 CRY 60013 2695 31W-23N D1
S Wulff St
10 CRY 60013 2695 31W-23N D2
Wurtsbaugh St
100 NCHI 60088 2593 10W-30N E2
S Wurtz Rd
34700 WslT 60481 3943 27W-42S E7
N Wyandot Ct
16200 LKPT 60441 3420 20W-20S C4
W Wyandot Dr
6600 PSHT 60463 3275 8W-14S A7
Wyandotte Av
2600 NndT 60051 2585 31W-30N D1
Wyatt Dr
- BbyT 60510 3076 39W-1S D2
15300 BbyT 60134 3076 39W-1S D2
Wyatt Ln
2100 GLHT 60139 2969 23W-4N B4
Wychwood Ln
10 SBTN 60010 2804 25W-15N A1
Wyckwood Ct
2500 AURA 60506 3198 39W-7S E1
Wyckwood Dr
2200 AURA 60506 3198 39W-7S D1
2200 AURA 60506 3199 38W-7S A1
Wycliffe Dr
100 WCHI 60185 3022 29W-0S C7
100 WnfT 60185 3022 29W-0S C7
W Wycombe Ct
14300 GNOK 60048 2592 14W-31N C1
Wydown Ct
1100 NPVL 60540 3204 25W-8S B1
Wydown Ln
2300 AURA 60502 3079 32W-4S C7
Wye Ct
1300 WLNG 60090 2754 16W-18N D2
Wyer St
- BHPK 60087 2421 12W-38N B7
- WKGN 60087 2421 12W-38N B7
W Wyer St
10000 BHPK 60087 2422 10W-38N B7
Wyeth Cir
400 BGBK 60440 3205 22W-11S C7
Wyeth Dr
2400 WCHI 60185 2965 32W-4N C4
Wyman Dr
8500 TYPK 60487 3424 10W-21S B7
N Wyncroft Pl
800 ADSN 60101 2970 21W-4N A3
Wyndance Wy
2200 NHBK 60062 2810 9W-15N B1
Wyndemere Cir
- WHTN 60187 3023 26W-0S E7
Wyndham Cir
1800 GNVW 60025 2810 8W-15N D2
E Wyndham Cir
1300 PLTN 60074 2753 19W-17N C4
1300 PltT 60074 2753 19W-17N C4
Wyndham Ct
10 OKBK 60523 3084 18W-2S E3
1200 PLTN 60074 2753 19W-17N C4
2300 AURA 60504 3201 32W-8S B2
Wyndham Dr
- SEGN 60177 2908 34W-9N E1
- SEGN 60177 2909 33W-9N A1
10 OswT 60538 3199 36W-10S D7
1200 PLTN 60074 2753 19W-17N C4
Wyndham Ln
1200 PLTN 60074 2753 19W-17N C4
Wyndham Cove Ln
1400 SMBG 60173 2859 21W-10N E5
Wyndmuir Ct
600 CLLK 60012 2640 33W-26N D2

Wyndmuir Dr
- NndT 60012 2640 33W-26N D2
600 CLLK 60012 2640 34W-26N D2
Wyndsong Ct
2600 NndT 60012 2584 34W-29N B4
Wyndstone Dr
100 ELWD 60421 3675 25W-31S B6
100 JknT 60421 3675 25W-31S B6
Wyndwood Dr
3900 AlqT 60014 2641 33W-25N A5
N Wyndwood Dr
6100 AlqT 60014 2641 32W-25N B4
6100 NndT 60014 2641 32W-25N B4
Wyngate Ct
10 CmpT 60175 2962 39W-4N E5
Wyngate Dr
100 BRTN 60010 2751 24W-18N C2
Wyngate Ln
500 BFGV 60089 2701 17W-20N B7
Wyngate Rd
10 CmpT 60175 2962 39W-4N E5
Wynham Lakes Ct
2100 JLET 60586 3416 30W-20S B5
Wynn Av
400 CLSM 60188 2967 28W-3N A6
400 WynT 60185 2966 29W-3N D6
400 WynT 60185 2967 28W-3N A6
400 WynT 60188 2967 28W-3N A6
Wynn Ct
500 WLNG 60090 2754 16W-18N E3
Wynncrest Dr
2600 LGGV 60047 2700 19W-20N B7
Wynnfield Ct
1000 ELGN 60120 2855 32W-10N D5
Wynnfield Dr
1200 ALGN 60102 2747 36W-19N A2
Wynstone Dr
- SRWD 60404 3495 31W-23S E5
- SRWD 60404 3583 31W-25S E1
- TroT 60404 3495 31W-23S E5
- TroT 60404 3583 31W-25S E2
800 SRWD 60404 3496 31W-25S A7
25100 SRWD 60404 3584 31W-25S A1
N Wynstone Dr
10 NBRN 60010 2644 24W-24N C6
S Wynstone Dr
- ElaT 60047 2644 24W-24N C7
- NBRN 60047 2644 24W-24N C7
10 NBRN 60010 2644 24W-24N C7
Wynstone Ln
- NBRN 60010 2644 24W-24N C7
- NBRN 60047 2644 24W-24N C7
Wynstone Wy
10 ElaT 60010 2644 25W-24N B7
10 ElaT 60010 2698 25W-24N B1
10 NBRN 60010 2644 25W-24N B7
10 NBRN 60010 2698 25W-24N B1
S Wynstone Park Dr
10 NBRN 60010 2644 25W-24N A6
Wynwood Ln
2200 AURA 60506 3137 38W-7S A7
Wynwood Rd
10 WNFD 60190 3023 28W-0S B6
600 WNFD 60190 3081 28W-1S B1
600 WnfT 60190 3023 28W-0S B7
600 WnfT 60190 3081 28W-1S B1
Wyoma Ln
200 SMBG 60193 2858 26W-10N A6
Wyoming Av
500 SchT 60174 2908 34W-6N D7
2900 NCHI 60088 2593 12W-30N B2
N Wyoming Av
1200 JLET 60435 3498 25W-22S B2
Wyoming Ct
3600 NCHI 60088 2593 12W-30N C2
10400 ODPK 60467 3423 13W-21S B7
10400 OrlT 60467 3423 13W-21S B7
10400 OrlT 60487 3423 13W-21S B7
Wyoming Wy
4600 NndT 60012 2641 33W-27N A1
Wysteria Dr
- CHHT 60411 3507 2W-24S C5
10 OMFD 60461 3507 2W-24S C5
Wythe Pl
2400 YKVL 60560 3333 42W-17S C6

X

Xavier Ct
2200 NPVL 60565 3204 24W-10S C5

Y

Yacht Club Dr
10 WPHR 60096 2363 8W-43N E5
Yackley Av
600 LslT 60565 3204 23W-8S E3
600 NPVL 60565 3204 23W-8S E3
4300 LSLE 60532 3142 24W-6S E4
Yackley Av CO-40
4300 LSLE 60532 3142 24W-6S E4
Yager Av
1300 HDPK 60035 2704 9W-21N C6
Yakima Dr
17400 LKPT 60441 3420 20W-20S B5
Yale Av
10 BNHL 60010 2750 25W-18N E4
10 BrnT 60010 2750 25W-18N E4
100 BrnT 60010 2751 25W-18N A4
1900 CHHT 60411 3595 2W-26S D2
N Yale Av
10 ANHT 60005 2806 18W-14N D4
10 VLPK 60181 3027 18W-1N A3
1000 VLPK 60181 2971 18W-2N A7
1100 ADSN 60101 2971 18W-2N A7
1100 ADSN 60181 2971 18W-2N A7
1100 VLPK 60101 2971 18W-2N A7
1900 ANHT 60004 2806 18W-16N D1
4100 ANHT 60004 2753 18W-18N E2
S Yale Av
10 ANHT 60005 2806 18W-13N D5
100 VLPK 60181 3027 18W-0N A4
200 ADSN 60101 2971 18W-3N A6
1300 ANHT 60005 2860 19W-12N D1
5900 CHCG 60621 3152 0W-7S B5
8800 CHCG 60620 3214 0W-10S B4
9500 CHCG 60628 3214 0W-11S B6
11300 CHCG 60628 3278 0W-13S B3
W Yale Av
1400 BHPK 60099 2422 10W-39N B5
1400 ZION 60099 2422 10W-39N B5
Yale Cir
2100 HFET 60192 2802 30W-12N B7
2100 HnrT 60192 2802 30W-12N B7
Yale Ct
10 HNWD 60047 2645 20W-25N E5

STREET Block	City	ZIP	Map#	CGS	Grid
Yale Ct					
100	GNVW	60025	2810	10W-15N	B2
100	SRWD	60404	3496	30W-24S	B6
600	DSPN	60016	2862	14W-12N	D2
1400	NPVL	60565	3204	24W-8S	C2
1500	EGVV	60007	2859	21W-9N	D7
1600	LKFT	60045	2649	13W-26N	A3
N Yale Ct					
1600	ANHT	60004	2806	18W-15N	D1
W Yale Ct					
1000	PLTN	60067	2805	22W-14N	B3
Yale Dr					
1700	MDLN	60060	2590	19W-29N	C4
Yale Ln					
500	ISLK	60042	2586	29W-28N	C5
600	MTSN	60443	3505	6W-24S	E6
800	HDPK	60035	2704	9W-22N	D4
1400	SMBG	60193	2912	25W-9N	B1
5200	MTSN	60443	3506	6W-24S	A6
17700	CCHL	60429	3426	4W-21S	E6
17700	CCHL	60478	3426	4W-21S	E6
17700	HLCT	60429	3426	4W-21S	E6
17700	HLCT	60478	3426	4W-21S	E6
Yale Rd					
1700	FSMR	60422	3507	2W-23S	D4
Yale St					
500	WCHI	60185	3022	30W-1N	C3
900	WLMT	60091	2812	4W-14N	B5
Yamma Rdg					
1000	NLNX	60451	3588	19W-27S	E5
1000	NLNX	60451	3589	19W-27S	A4
Yankee Ridge Ct					
10400	FKFT	60423	3591	13W-25S	B1
Yankee Ridge Dr					
10400	FKFT	60423	3591	13W-25S	B1
S Yard Dr					
-	CHCG	60629	3150	4W-7S	D6
Yardley Ct					
10	GLHT	60139	2968	24W-4N	E4
Yardley Dr					
400	BmdT	60188	2967	26W-4N	E4
400	CLSM	60188	2967	26W-4N	E4
9900	HTLY	60142	2692	38W-22N	D4
Yardley Ln					
10	SMBG	60194	2858	26W-10N	A5
600	HFET	60169	2858	25W-11N	C4
Yardley Tr					
500	MDLN	60060	2646	20W-27N	B2
Yarmouth Ct					
1300	SMBG	60193	2858	25W-10N	C6
E Yarmouth Ct					
2600	ANHT	60004	2807	16W-15N	D2
Yarmouth Ln					
100	SMBG	60193	2858	25W-10N	C6
N Yarmouth Pl					
1400	MPPT	60056	2807	16W-14N	D4
Yarmouth Rd					
200	EGVV	60007	2914	19W-8N	C2
Yarrow Ct					
100	RGMW	60008	2805	21W-13N	E5
100	RMVL	60446	3340	26W-17S	A6
Yarrow Ln					
2400	RGMW	60008	2805	21W-14N	D5
Yarwood St					
300	ELGN	60120	2855	33W-10N	A5
Yasgur Dr					
-	GwdT	60098	2525	40W-32N	A4
1800	GwdT	60098	2524	40W-32N	E4
Yates Av					
200	BNHM	60409	3351	2E-17S	D6
200	BNHM	60633	3351	2E-17S	D6
200	CTCY	60409	3351	2E-17S	D6
200	CTCY	60633	3351	2E-17S	D6
700	RMVL	60446	3340	24W-15S	C2
22100	SLVL	60411	3597	2E-27S	D4
S Yates Av					
-	CHCG	60633	3351	2E-15S	D2
7900	CHCG	60649	3215	2E-9S	D2
9500	CHCG	60617	3215	3E-11S	D7
10500	CHCG	60617	3279	2E-12S	D1
14300	BNHM	60633	3351	2E-16S	D4
14300	CTCY	60409	3351	2E-16S	D4
14300	CTCY	60633	3351	2E-16S	D4
14500	BNHM	60409	3351	2E-16S	D4
S Yates Blvd					
7100	CHCG	60649	3153	2E-8S	D7
7500	CHCG	60649	3215	2E-8S	D1
7800	CHCG	60617	3215	3E-8S	D1
N Yates Ln					
100	MPPT	60056	2808	14W-13N	D6
Yates Pl					
100	BbyT	60134	3018	39W-0N	D6
Yates St					
17100	SHLD	60473	3429	2E-20S	D4
Yaupon Ct					
200	ElgT	60175	2907	38W-7N	A4
200	SchT	60175	2907	38W-7N	A4
Yeadon Rd					
10	OSWG	60543	3263	37W-11S	D1
10	OswT	60538	3263	37W-11S	D1
Yeager Dr					
4000	NCHI	60088	2593	11W-30N	D1
Yearling Dr					
17000	WrnT	60083	2477	17W-36N	C3
Yearling Crossing Dr					
10600	ODPK	60467	3423	13W-20S	A4
Yellow Avens Ct					
-	RtdT	60140	2798	40W-14N	B6
Yellow Daisy Ct					
2000	NPVL	60563	3140	30W-5S	B4
Yellow Finch Ln					
21700	FKFT	60423	3591	13W-26S	A2
Yellowhead Ct					
1500	WDSK	60098	2582	39W-30N	C2
Yellow Pine Dr					
200	BGBK	60440	3268	24W-11S	D1
25400	CNHN	60410	3672	33W-30S	A5
Yellowpine Dr					
1200	AURA	60506	3137	37W-6S	C4
S Yellow Pine Dr					
-	AxST	60410	3672	33W-31S	A6
-	AxST	60447	3672	33W-31S	A6
25700	CNHN	60410	3672	33W-31S	A6
Yellow Star Ct					
10	WDRG	60517	3143	21W-7S	D7
Yellowstar Ct					
2000	NPVL	60564	3266	29W-13S	E4
Yellowstar Ln					
2100	NPVL	60564	3266	29W-13S	D4
Yellow Star St					
2500	WDRG	60517	3143	21W-7S	D7
Yellowstone					
1900	NPVL	60563	3081	26W-4S	E7
Yellowstone Cir					
1400	CLLK	60014	2693	36W-23N	D3
Yellowstone Ct					
1600	CLLK	60014	2693	36W-23N	D2
Yellow Stone Dr					
2700	AURA	60503	3265	32W-11S	D1
Yellowstone Dr					
500	ELGN	60123	2853	36W-12N	E2
1400	HnrT	60107	2856	30W-9N	B7
10500	HTLY	60142	2745	39W-20N	C1
Yellowstone Ln					
500	YKVL	60560	3261	43W-13S	B5
900	HRVD	60033	2406	49W-38N	C7
Yellowstone Pkwy					
1200	ALGN	60102	2748	32W-20N	B1
Yellowstone St					
800	CLSM	60188	2967	26W-3N	E5
Yender Av					
4400	LSLE	60532	3142	24W-5S	D2
Yender Ln					
4300	LSLE	60532	3142	24W-4S	E1
Yeoman St					
400	WKGN	60085	2536	11W-34N	E1
500	WKGN	60085	2479	11W-35N	E7
2000	WKGN	60087	2479	11W-36N	E4
Yew Ct					
1100	ELGN	60120	2855	32W-11N	D4
1400	GRNE	60031	2478	15W-35N	A5
1700	JltT	60433	3587	21W-26S	E3
1700	JltT	60433	3588	21W-26S	A3
Yew Tree Dr					
36200	WrnT	60031	2476	18W-36N	E3
36200	WrnT	60046	2476	18W-36N	E3
YMCA Rd					
-	LkvT	60046	2417	21W-38N	E7
-	LNHT	60046	2417	21W-38N	E7
Yoakum Blvd					
-	OSWG	60543	3264	34W-11S	D1
Yolane Ct					
10	SRGV	60554	3135	42W-7S	C7
Yolane St					
200	SRGV	60554	3135	43W-7S	B7
E York Av					
100	WCHI	60185	3022	29W-1N	C4
S York Av					
10	FXLK	60020	2473	27W-36N	B3
10	JLET	60433	3499	23W-24S	A5
W York Av					
100	WCHI	60185	3022	30W-1N	C4
York Cir					
1000	CPVL	60110	2748	32W-18N	D5
York Ct					
-	FmtT	60060	2645	21W-26N	D3
100	NPVL	60540	3142	25W-6S	B5
700	NHBK	60062	2757	8W-17N	E4
700	ROSL	60172	2913	22W-6N	B6
1200	AURA	60502	3139	33W-5S	B4
1500	MDLN	60060	2646	20W-26N	B2
2600	WDRG	60517	3143	21W-7S	D6
22400	RNPK	60471	3594	4W-27S	D4
W York Ct					
21300	KLDR	60047	2699	21W-20N	D7
York Dr					
-	LYWD	60411	3509	2E-23S	D4
300	GYLK	60030	2533	20W-33N	B3
500	MTGY	60543	3263	37W-11S	B2
500	OSWG	60543	3263	37W-11S	B2
700	WcnT	60084	2644	25W-26N	B3
1300	CPVL	60110	2748	32W-18N	D5
19300	MKNA	60448	3503	12W-23S	D3
York Ln					
300	DGvT	60516	3206	20W-10S	B6
300	DGvT	60517	3206	20W-10S	B6
500	ElgT	60124	2853	37W-11N	C5
1800	HDPK	60035	2704	10W-21N	A5
3300	ISLK	60042	2586	30W-28N	B5
E York Ln					
1800	GNEN	60137	3025	23W-0S	A7
1800	GNEN	60187	3025	23W-0S	A7
1800	WHTN	60187	3025	23W-0S	A7
W York Ln					
1600	WHTN	60187	3024	23W-0S	E7
1600	WHTN	60187	3025	23W-0S	A7
York Pl					
200	NLNX	60451	3500	20W-24S	C5
York Rd					
-	EMHT	60523	3086	15W-1S	A1
-	HTLY	60142	2692	39W-22N	D4
-	YkTp	60523	3086	15W-1S	A1
200	EMHT	60126	3027	16W-2N	E1
400	BRWN	60402	3088	9W-3S	D4
400	EMHT	60126	2971	16W-2N	E7
400	RVSD	60402	3088	9W-3S	D4
400	RVSD	60546	3088	9W-3S	D4
600	GNVW	60025	2811	8W-13N	A7
1700	OKBK	60523	3086	15W-2S	B4
3600	HNDL	60521	3086	15W-3S	B6
3700	OKBK	60521	3086	15W-3S	B6
7300	DRGV	60516	3206	19W-8S	D1
York Rd CO-8					
2700	OKBK	60523	3086	15W-2S	B3
3600	HNDL	60521	3086	15W-3S	B6
3700	OKBK	60521	3086	15W-3S	B6
N York Rd					
10	BNVL	60106	2971	16W-5N	E1
200	BNVL	60106	2915	16W-6N	E7
300	CHCG	60106	2915	16W-6N	E7
500	HNDL	60521	3086	15W-4S	B7
800	EGVV	60007	2915	16W-6N	E7
800	EGVV	60106	2915	16W-6N	E7
N York Rd CO-8					
200	BNVL	60106	2915	16W-6N	E7
300	CHCG	60106	2915	16W-6N	E7
800	EGVV	60007	2915	16W-6N	E7
800	EGVV	60106	2915	16W-6N	E7
S York Rd					
10	BNVL	60106	2971	16W-4N	E3
1000	EMHT	60106	2971	15W-3N	E5
1000	EMHT	60126	2971	15W-3N	E5
York St					
-	BDVW	60155	3029	12W-0S	C6
-	CTPK	60827	3277	1W-15S	D7
-	EMHT	60523	3028	15W-1S	A7
-	EMHT	60523	3086	15W-1S	A1
-	OKBK	60523	3086	15W-1S	A1
-	WSTR	60154	3029	12W-0S	C6
-	WSTR	60155	3029	12W-0S	C6
-	YkTp	60523	3028	15W-1S	A7
-	YkTp	60523	3086	15W-1S	A1
400	BGBK	60440	3205	23W-11S	A7
1800	BLID	60406	3277	2W-15S	C7
7600	FTPK	60130	3030	9W-0S	C6
N York St					
10	FXLK	60020	2473	27W-36N	B3
100	EMHT	60126	3027	16W-1N	E2
600	EMHT	60126	2971	16W-3N	E6
1000	BNVL	60106	2971	15W-3N	E5
1000	EMHT	60106	2971	15W-3N	E5
S York St					
-	EMHT	60523	3028	15W-1S	A7
100	EMHT	60126	3027	16W-1N	E3
600	EMHT	60126	3028	15W-0S	A5
1000	YkTp	60126	3028	15W-0S	A6
E Yorkfield Av					
200	EMHT	60126	3028	15W-0S	A6
York House Rd					
9800	BHPK	60087	2480	9W-37N	B2
W Yorkhouse Rd					
1200	BHPK	60087	2479	11W-37N	E2
1200	WKGN	60087	2479	13W-37N	A2
2500	WkgT	60087	2479	12W-37N	C2
3300	WKGN	60087	2478	13W-38N	E1
3300	WrnT	60087	2479	13W-37N	A2
3500	NptT	60083	2478	13W-38N	E1
10000	BHPK	60087	2480	10W-37N	A2
13900	WDWH	60083	2478	14W-38N	C1
13900	WDWH	60087	2478	13W-38N	D1
13900	WKGN	60083	2478	14W-38N	D1
W Yorkhouse Rd CO-A15					
1200	BHPK	60087	2479	11W-37N	E2
1200	WKGN	60087	2479	13W-37N	A2
2500	WkgT	60087	2479	12W-37N	C2
3300	WKGN	60087	2478	13W-38N	E1
3300	WrnT	60087	2479	13W-37N	A2
3500	NptT	60083	2478	13W-38N	E1
10000	BHPK	60087	2480	10W-37N	A2
13900	WDWH	60083	2478	14W-38N	D1
13900	WDWH	60087	2478	13W-38N	D1
13900	WKGN	60083	2478	14W-38N	D1
York Lake Ct					
10	OKBK	60523	3086	15W-3S	B5
Yorkshire Ct					
-	JLET	60431	3495	33W-22S	B1
10	ALGN	60102	2747	36W-18N	A4
10	ALGN	60118	2747	36W-18N	A4
10	SEGN	60177	2908	35W-8N	B3
10	SgrT	60506	3136	40W-5S	A4
200	GRNE	60031	2535	14W-34N	B1
400	GYLK	60030	2533	20W-32N	A5
1100	ELGN	60120	2855	32W-10N	D5
2700	AURA	60502	3139	32W-4S	C1
3300	HFET	60067	2804	23W-14N	E4
8000	HRPK	60133	2858	26W-9N	A7
Yorkshire Dr					
10	LNSH	60069	2702	14W-22N	D3
200	FRGV	60021	2696	29W-22N	B4
300	MDLN	60060	2590	20W-27N	A7
700	HRPK	60133	2858	26W-9N	A7
700	SMBG	60133	2858	25W-9N	A7
700	SMBG	60193	2858	25W-9N	A7
900	HRPK	60133	2857	26W-9N	E7
1200	NPVL	60563	3142	25W-5S	A3
1300	SMWD	60107	2857	27W-9N	D7
1500	SMWD	60133	2857	26W-9N	D7
7000	WDRG	60517	3143	21W-7S	E7
12400	HMGN	60491	3344	15W-17S	B6
19400	FftT	60448	3502	14W-23S	D3
19400	MKNA	60448	3502	14W-23S	D3
W Yorkshire Dr					
3500	MchT	60050	2471	32W-37N	B3
12600	HMGN	60491	3344	15W-17S	A6
20500	KLDR	60047	2699	20W-22N	E4
20500	KLDR	60047	2700	20W-22N	A4
Yorkshire Ln					
500	PGGV	60140	2797	41W-15N	E4
500	PGGV	60140	2798	41W-15N	A4
600	DSPN	60016	2808	14W-12N	D7
800	CLLK	60014	2639	35W-24N	E7
1200	CLSM	60188	2967	28W-3N	B6
1200	LKZH	60010	2698	24W-21N	D6
1400	SMBG	60194	2858	25W-10N	B5
2600	LSLE	60532	3142	24W-7S	C6
4000	NHBK	60062	2756	12W-17N	B5
15300	ODPK	60462	3345	11W-18S	E7
W Yorkshire Ln					
13000	BHPK	60083	2421	13W-39N	A5
13000	BHPK	60099	2421	13W-39N	A5
Yorkshire Pl					
200	WLNG	60090	2755	15W-18N	B3
Yorkshire Sq					
400	BGBK	60440	3269	22W-12S	B3
Yorkshire St					
-	JLET	60431	3495	33W-22S	B1
Yorkshire Ter					
800	CRTE	60417	3596	0W-28S	C6
Yorkshire Woods					
10	OKBK	60523	3086	15W-1S	A1
Yorkshire Woods Ct					
1200	WHTN	60187	3081	26W-1S	E2
Yorktown Av					
1800	NCHI	60088	2593	11W-30N	D1
Yorktown Ct					
10	SBTN	60010	2803	27W-14N	B4
400	AURA	60504	3140	30W-7S	A7
9100	ODPK	60462	3345	11W-16S	E3
Yorktown Dr					
700	ALGN	60102	2694	34W-20N	C7
700	ALGN	60102	2747	34W-20N	B1
9100	ODPK	60462	3345	11W-16S	E4
Yorktown Ln					
500	GRNE	60031	2535	14W-33N	D3
Yorktown Rd					
500	CHHT	60411	3507	2W-24S	C6
7300	FKFT	60423	3592	9W-25S	E1
7300	FKFT	60423	3593	8W-25S	A1
Yorktowne Ln					
400	LKFT	60045	2649	12W-25N	C5
Yorktown Shopping Ctr					
10	LMBD	60148	3084	19W-2S	D3
Yorkville Rd					
10	BtlT	60560	3334	41W-15S	A2
Yosemite					
600	NPVL	60563	3081	26W-4S	E7
Yosemite Ct					
-	LKMR	60051	2530	28W-31N	A6
500	ROSL	60172	2913	22W-8N	C3
Yosemite Dr					
2700	AURA	60503	3265	32W-11S	D1
Yosemite Pkwy					
1200	ALGN	60102	2748	32W-20N	C1
Yosemite Tr					
400	ROSL	60172	2913	22W-8N	C3
Yost Av					
10	CHCG	60068	2918	9W-7N	C3
10	CHCG	60631	2918	9W-7N	C3
10	PKRG	60068	2918	9W-7N	B3
Youghall St					
100	WNVL	60555	3080	30W-3S	B5
Young Av					
500	BTVA	60510	3078	34W-1S	C3
1500	AURA	60505	3200	33W-7S	E1
Young Cir					
1500	EGVV	60007	2914	21W-9N	A1
Young Ct					
2700	WDRG	60517	3143	22W-7S	D7
Young Dr					
700	NLNX	60451	3589	18W-25S	A1
1600	LYVL	60048	2591	17W-30N	C2
Young Ln					
-	JLET	60586	3415	32W-21S	C7
Young St					
-	LtRT	60545	3259	47W-13S	D5
-	PLNO	60545	3259	47W-13S	D5
800	LMNT	60439	3271	18W-14S	A6
S Young St					
10	GNWD	60425	3508	0E-22S	D2
W Young St					
3600	MHRY	60050	2528	32W-32N	B5
N Youngs Av					
100	JLET	60432	3499	23W-23S	B4
S Youngs Rd					
21300	CNHN	60410	3585	28W-28S	A6
21300	CnhT	60410	3585	28W-28S	A6
21300	JLET	60410	3585	28W-28S	A6
23200	CnhT	60410	3674	28W-28S	A1
23200	JLET	60410	3674	28W-28S	A1
Youth Camp Rd					
38700	MLTT	60555	3081	27W-3S	D6
38700	WnfT	60555	3081	27W-3S	D6
Yuba St					
7600	FTPK	60130	3030	9W-0S	C7
Yukon Ct					
10	BGBK	60490	3267	27W-12S	C2
Yukon Dr					
1900	BGBK	60490	3267	27W-12S	C2
Yuma Ln					
100	CLSM	60188	2968	25W-2N	A7
100	CLSM	60188	3024	25W-2N	A1
E Yuma Ln					
1900	MPPT	60056	2808	13W-15N	E3
Yuma Tr					
900	NndT	60051	2528	31W-31N	D7
900	NndT	60051	2585	31W-31N	D1
Yvonne Ct					
200	RLKB	60073	2474	23W-36N	E5
200	RLKB	60073	2475	23W-35N	A5
Yvonne Ln					
10	WnfT	60187	3081	27W-2S	C3
Yy Rd					
-	CteT	60417	3685	0E-29S	E2
Z					
Zachary Dr					
-	HPSR	60140	2796	46W-15N	A3
600	RMVL	60446	3418	26W-18S	A1
700	LktT	60441	3418	26W-18S	A2
700	RMVL	60441	3418	26W-18S	A2
6900	CPVL	60110	2747	36W-17N	A6
Zaininger Av					
600	NPVL	60563	3141	27W-5S	B3
Zange Dr					
600	ALGN	60102	2747	34W-20N	B1
Zapata Ln					
100	MNKA	60447	3672	32W-29S	C2
Zarley Blvd					
-	JltT	60436	3586	24W-25S	D2
E Zarley Blvd					
10	JltT	60433	3587	23W-26S	A2
10	JltT	60436	3587	23W-25S	A2
W Zarley Blvd					
10	JltT	60436	3586	24W-25S	E2
10	JltT	60436	3587	23W-26S	B2
400	JLET	60436	3586	24W-25S	E2
Zarnstorff Rd					
10700	BtnT	60071	2354	31W-42N	E5
10700	RcmT	60071	2354	31W-42N	E5
11000	BtnT	53181	2354	30W-43N	E4
11000	RcmT	53181	2354	30W-43N	E4
11000	RdlT	53181	2354	30W-43N	E4
W Zauratsky Rd					
-	CNHN	60410	3584	30W-28S	D6
24000	CnhT	60410	3584	30W-28S	C7
Zausa Dr					
16300	LktT	60403	3418	26W-19S	A3
16600	CTHL	60403	3418	26W-19S	A4
Zee Ct					
1300	WLNG	60090	2754	16W-18N	D2
Zelinger Ln					
10	ANTH	60002	2358	23W-43N	A4
W Zelinger Ln					
23200	ANTH	60002	2357	23W-43N	E4
23200	ANTH	60002	2358	23W-43N	A4
Zemke Blvd					
-	CHCG	60666	2917	13W-7N	A3
Zenda Rd					
300	LinT	53147	2349		E2
Zengele Av					
200	AURA	60505	3138	35W-6S	C5
Zenith Dr					
-	GNVW	60025	2809	11W-13N	C6
500	MaiT	60016	2809	12W-12N	C7
500	MaiT	60025	2809	12W-12N	C7
Zenner St					
900	AURA	60505	3138	35W-6S	C5
Zepher St					
12700	BHPK	60087	2479	12W-38N	B1
12700	WKGN	60087	2479	12W-38N	B1
Zephyr Rd					
500	NPVL	60563	3140	30W-6S	C4
Zeppelin Dr					
4600	HRPK	60133	2967	27W-5N	C1
Zerfas Dr					
2300	TNLK	53181	2354		A2
W Zermatt Dr					
8400	PSHL	60465	3274	10W-12S	B2
Ziegemeier St					
2300	LkeC	60088	2594	10W-30N	B1
2300	NCHI	60088	2537	10W-31N	B7
2300	NCHI	60088	2594	10W-30N	B1
Ziegler Av					
800	AURA	60505	3200	34W-8S	D2
1200	AraT	60504	3200	34W-8S	E2
Ziegler Dr					
10	AvnT	60030	2533	20W-33N	A3
10	GYLK	60030	2533	20W-33N	A3
Zilm Rd					
34300	CstT	60481	3943	28W-42S	C7
Zimmer Dr					
9600	AlqT	60102	2695	31W-22N	C5
Zimmerman Rd					
800	DrrT	60098	2582	40W-30N	A1
800	WDSK	60098	2582	40W-30N	A1
Zinnia Dr					
200	RMVL	60446	3339	26W-17S	D7
E Zinnia Ln					
800	PLTN	60074	2753	19W-18N	B3
Zion Ln					
-	PHNX	60426	3350	0W-17S	B6
-	SHLD	60426	3350	0W-17S	B6
Zipf Rd					
100	JltT	60433	3587	23W-27S	A4
100	JltT	60436	3587	23W-27S	A4
Zoumar Dr					
25100	PNFD	60586	3415	31W-19S	E2
Zuck Ct					
15000	HmrT	60491	3420	18W-19S	E2
15000	HmrT	60491	3421	18W-19S	A2
Zuelke Dr					
200	BLWD	60104	3029	12W-0N	B4
Zurich Ct					
10	CRTE	60417	3596	0E-28S	E6
2600	WDRG	60517	3205	21W-9S	D3
6800	TYPK	60477	3425	8W-22S	A7
Zurich Dr					
100	LYWD	60411	3510	4E-25S	C7
100	LYWD	60411	3598	4E-25S	C1
Zurich Ln					
2700	WDRG	60517	3205	21W-9S	D3
6800	TYPK	60477	3425	8W-22S	A7
18400	TYPK	60477	3505	8W-22S	A1
Zurich Rd					
-	JltT	60433	3587	23W-26S	A2
10	JltT	60436	3587	23W-26S	B3
100	JLET	60436	3586	24W-26S	E2
100	JltT	60436	3586	24W-26S	D2
S Zurich Rd					
-	JltT	60436	3586	24W-26S	E2
#					
1st Av					
-	FTPK	60130	3030	10W-1S	A7
-	FTPK	60153	3030	10W-1S	A7
-	LKBF	60044	2593	11W-29N	E4
-	MRGO	60152	2634	49W-27N	B1
-	MYWD	60130	3088	10W-1S	A1
-	MYWD	60153	3088	10W-1S	A1
-	NCHI	60044	2593	11W-29N	E4
-	NCHI	60088	2593	11W-29N	E4
-	NRIV	60141	3088	10W-1S	A2
-	NRIV	60546	3088	10W-1S	A2
-	PvsT	60130	3088	10W-1S	A1
-	PvsT	60141	3088	10W-1S	A1
-	PvsT	60153	3030	10W-1S	A7
-	PvsT	60153	3088	10W-1S	A1
-	ShdT	60044	2593	11W-29N	E4
-	ShdT	60088	2593	11W-29N	E4
10	BRLT	60103	2909	31W-8N	E3
10	EGvT	60005	2861	16W-10N	D6
10	MPPT	60005	2861	16W-10N	D6
10	MTGY	60538	3199	36W-9S	D4
100	NLNX	60451	3501	18W-25S	B7
400	DSPN	60016	2862	13W-11N	E3
1900	MLPK	60160	3030	10W-1N	A1
1900	MLPK	60171	3030	10W-1N	A1
1900	PvsT	60160	3030	10W-1N	A1
1900	RVGV	60160	3030	10W-1N	A1
1900	RVGV	60171	3030	10W-1N	A1
2100	MYWD	60130	3030	10W-1S	A7
2100	MYWD	60153	3030	10W-1S	A7
2100	PvsT	60130	3030	10W-1S	A7
3300	MchT	60050	2528	32W-33N	B3
3300	MHRY	60050	2528	32W-33N	B3
3900	BKFD	60513	3088	10W-4S	A7
3900	LYNS	60534	3088	10W-4S	A7
3900	RVSD	60513	3088	10W-4S	A7
3900	RVSD	60546	3088	10W-4S	A7
4500	LYNS	60534	3148	10W-4S	A1
4600	MCCK	60525	3148	10W-4S	A1
4600	MCCK	60534	3148	10W-4S	A1
9400	ALGN	60102	2694	33W-22N	E4
9400	AlqT	60013	2694	33W-22N	E4
9400	AlqT	60102	2694	33W-22N	E4
14400	ODPK	60462	3345	12W-17S	C4
15100	PHNX	60426	3350	0W-18S	B6
1st Av SR-171					
-	FTPK	60130	3030	10W-1S	A7
-	FTPK	60153	3030	10W-1S	A7
-	MYWD	60130	3088	10W-1S	A1
-	MYWD	60153	3088	10W-1S	A1
-	NRIV	60141	3088	10W-1S	A2
-	NRIV	60546	3088	10W-1S	A2
-	PvsT	60130	3088	10W-1S	A1
-	PvsT	60141	3088	10W-1S	A1
-	PvsT	60153	3030	10W-1S	A7
-	PvsT	60153	3088	10W-1S	A1
1900	MLPK	60160	3030	10W-1N	A1
1900	MLPK	60171	3030	10W-1N	A1
1900	PvsT	60160	3030	10W-1N	A1
1900	RVGV	60160	3030	10W-1N	A1
1900	RVGV	60171	3030	10W-1N	A1
2100	MYWD	60130	3030	10W-1S	A7
2100	MYWD	60153	3030	10W-1S	A7
2100	PvsT	60130	3030	10W-1S	A7
3900	BKFD	60513	3088	10W-4S	A7
3900	LYNS	60534	3088	10W-4S	A7
3900	RVSD	60513	3088	10W-4S	A7
3900	RVSD	60546	3088	10W-4S	A7
E 1st Av					
800	JLET	60433	3499	22W-24S	C5
N 1st Av					
10	MYWD	60153	3030	10W-0N	A4
10	SCRL	60174	2964	35W-3N	B6
200	AddT	60101	2970	19W-4N	D3
200	ADSN	60101	2970	19W-4N	D3
700	MLPK	60153	3030	10W-1N	A2
700	RVFT	60305	3030	10W-1N	A3
1600	MLPK	60160	2974	10W-2N	A7
1600	MLPK	60160	3030	10W-2N	A1
1600	MLPK	60171	3030	10W-2N	A1
1600	PvsT	60160	3030	10W-0N	A3
1600	RVGV	60160	2974	10W-2N	A7
1600	RVGV	60160	3030	10W-2N	A1
1600	RVGV	60171	2974	10W-2N	A6
1600	RVGV	60171	3030	10W-2N	A1
35300	GrtT	60041	2473	27W-35N	B6
38100	AntT	60081	2415	27W-38N	B7
42100	AntT	60002	2357	25W-42N	B6
N 1st Av SR-171					
10	MYWD	60153	3030	10W-0N	A4
700	MLPK	60153	3030	10W-1N	A2
700	RVFT	60305	3030	10W-1N	A3
1600	MLPK	60160	2974	10W-2N	A7
1600	MLPK	60160	3030	10W-2N	A1
1600	MLPK	60171	3030	10W-2N	A1
1600	PvsT	60160	3030	10W-0N	A3
1600	RVGV	60160	2974	10W-2N	A7
1600	RVGV	60160	3030	10W-2N	A1
1600	RVGV	60171	2974	10W-2N	A6
1600	RVGV	60171	3030	10W-2N	A1
S 1st Av					
-	BKFD	60513	3088	10W-3S	B6
-	LYNS	60534	3088	10W-3S	B6

STREET Block	City	ZIP	Map#	CGS	Grid
S 1st Av					
-	PvsT	60130	3030	10W-0S	A7
-	PvsT	60153	3030	10W-0S	A7
-	RVSD	60546	3088	10W-3S	B6
10	SCRL	60174	2964	35W-3N	B7
100	MYWD	60153	3030	10W-0S	A5
100	RVFT	60305	3030	10W-0S	A5
1700	FTPK	60130	3030	10W-0S	A6
1700	FTPK	60153	3030	10W-0S	A6
1700	MYWD	60130	3030	10W-0S	A6
2200	NRIV	60141	3088	10W-2S	A3
2200	NRIV	60546	3088	10W-2S	A3
2200	PvsT	60141	3088	10W-2S	A3
2500	BKFD	60546	3088	10W-2S	A3
3500	RVSD	60546	3088	10W-3S	B6
S 1st Av SR-171					
-	BKFD	60513	3088	10W-2S	A3
-	LYNS	60534	3088	10W-3S	B6
-	PvsT	60130	3030	10W-0S	A7
-	PvsT	60153	3030	10W-0S	A7
-	RVSD	60513	3088	10W-3S	B6
100	MYWD	60153	3030	10W-0S	A5
100	RVFT	60305	3030	10W-0S	A5
1700	FTPK	60130	3030	10W-0S	A6
1700	FTPK	60153	3030	10W-0S	A6
1700	MYWD	60130	3030	10W-0S	A6
2200	NRIV	60141	3088	10W-2S	A3
2200	NRIV	60546	3088	10W-2S	A3
2200	PvsT	60141	3088	10W-2S	A3
2500	BKFD	60546	3088	10W-2S	A3
3500	RVSD	60546	3088	10W-3S	B6
W 1st Av					
21700	LkvT	60046	2417	21W-38N	C7
21700	LNHT	60046	2417	21W-38N	C7
1st Ct					
200	CLLK	60014	2640	35W-25N	A5
800	MHTN	60442	3678	18W-31S	B5
10600	MKNA	60448	3503	13W-23S	B3
11300	PTPR	53158	2363		D2
1st Pl					
600	GRNE	60031	2478	14W-34N	D7
1st St					
-	HIWD	60037	2704	9W-23N	D1
-	HIWD	60040	2704	9W-23N	D1
-	MhtT	60442	3678	18W-31S	B5
-	MmT	60037	2704	9W-23N	D1
-	VrnT	60069	2701	16W-23N	D3
10	CRY	60013	2695	30W-23N	E1
10	MltT	60137	3025	22W-1N	C2
100	BMDL	60108	2969	23W-5N	A1
100	BTVA	60510	3078	36W-1S	A2
100	CLLK	60014	2640	35W-26N	B3
100	ITSC	60143	2914	19W-6N	C6
200	MHTN	60442	3677	19W-31S	D5
200	MHTN	60442	3678	19W-31S	A5
200	WLNG	60090	2755	14W-18N	C3
400	ANTH	60002	2357	24W-42N	D5
400	CRTE	60417	3685	1W-29S	A2
400	CRY	60013	2641	31W-24N	E7
400	LMNT	60439	3271	18W-14S	A6
400	LYVL	60048	2591	16W-29N	E4
500	GNCY	53128	2353		A3
500	GYLK	60030	2532	21W-33N	E3
500	WKGN	60085	2537	10W-34N	A1
600	HRVD	60033	2406	50W-38N	B6
700	NndT	60051	2586	29W-29N	C4
900	AlqT	60013	2641	31W-24N	E7
1000	BTVA	60510	3077	36W-1S	E2
1100	ELGN	60120	2855	32W-12N	B1
1200	NHBK	60062	2757	10W-17N	B5
1600	HDPK	60035	2704	8W-22N	E5
1900	GNVW	60025	2810	10W-14N	A4
3100	AlqT	60102	2695	32W-22N	C4
3800	PKCY	60085	2535	13W-33N	E3
10800	MKNA	60448	3503	13W-23S	A4
11200	FftT	60448	3502	14W-23S	E4
11200	MKNA	60448	3502	14W-23S	E4
11700	HTLY	60142	2692	40W-21N	A6
E 1st St					
-	ELBN	60119	3017	43W-2N	A1
10	HNDL	60521	3146	15W-5S	B1
100	BDWD	60408	3942	31W-41S	B5
100	EDND	60118	2801	34W-16N	A2
100	EMHT	60126	3027	17W-1N	C2
100	EMHT	60126	3028	15W-1N	A2
300	CPVL	60118	2801	34W-16N	A1
600	LKPT	60441	3419	21W-19S	D2
600	LktT	60441	3419	21W-19S	E2
800	CLCY	60416	3941	34W-39S	A2
N 1st St					
-	ELBN	60119	3017	43W-2N	A1
10	GNVA	60134	3020	35W-1N	C3
10	GRNE	60031	2535	14W-34N	D1
100	PTON	60468	3860	9W-37S	E3
100	WDND	60118	2801	34W-16N	A2
100	WLNG	60090	2755	14W-18N	C3
100	WMTN	60481	3853	28W-38S	C7
500	GRNE	60031	2478	14W-34N	D7
500	SCRL	60174	3020	35W-1N	C3
41000	ANTH	60002	2416	23W-41N	E2
41000	AntT	60002	2416	23W-41N	E2
N 1st St SR-31					
10	GNVA	60134	3020	35W-1N	C3
500	SCRL	60174	3020	35W-1N	C3
S 1st St					
10	ELBN	60119	3017	43W-1N	A3
10	GNVA	60134	3020	35W-1N	C4
10	GRNE	60031	2535	14W-34N	D2
10	SCRL	60174	2964	35W-2N	B7
100	PTON	60468	3860	9W-37S	E3
100	WDND	60118	2801	34W-15N	A3
100	WMTN	60481	3853	28W-39S	C7
S 1st St SR-31					
10	GNVA	60134	3020	35W-0N	C4
W 1st St					
10	HNDL	60521	3146	15W-5S	A2
10	SRGV	60554	3135	42W-7S	C7
100	BDWD	60408	3942	31W-41S	A5
100	EMHT	60126	3027	16W-1N	E2
100	MHTN	60442	3677	19W-31S	D5
300	BDWD	60408	3941	32W-41S	E5
25000	ANTH	60002	2357	25W-43N	B5
25000	AntT	60002	2357	25W-43N	B5
N 1st Bank Dr					
500	PLTN	60067	2753	20W-16N	A6
500	PLTN	60074	2753	20W-16N	A6
1st Park Av					
-	DSPN	60018	2917	11W-7N	D3
1st Private Rd					
2600	FSMR	60422	3507	3W-23S	B3
2nd Av					
-	JLET	60433	3499	21W-24S	E5
-	LKBF	60044	2593	11W-29N	E3
-	LKBF	60088	2593	11W-29N	E3
-	NCHI	60044	2593	11W-29N	E3
-	NCHI	60088	2593	11W-29N	E3
10	AddT	60191	2971	17W-4N	C2
10	EGvT	60005	2861	16W-10N	D6
10	MPPT	60005	2861	16W-10N	D6
10	NCHI	60064	2537	10W-31N	A7
10	NCHI	60088	2537	10W-31N	A7
10	WDDL	60106	2971	17W-4N	C2
10	WDDL	60191	2971	17W-4N	C2
100	BRLT	60103	2909	31W-8N	E3
100	MTGY	60538	3199	36W-9S	D5
200	LYVL	60048	2591	16W-28N	E6
200	MRGO	60152	2634	49W-27N	B1
300	AddT	60101	2970	19W-4N	D3
300	ADSN	60101	2970	19W-4N	D3
400	LMBD	60148	3026	18W-0N	E5
500	AddT	60106	2971	16W-4N	D2
500	AURA	60505	3200	34W-8S	D1
500	BNVL	60106	2971	16W-4N	C2
900	AURA	60504	3200	34W-8S	D1
1100	AraT	60504	3200	34W-8S	D1
1600	JltT	60433	3499	21W-24S	E5
3300	MchT	60050	2528	32W-33N	B3
3300	MHRY	60050	2528	32W-33N	B3
9400	ALGN	60013	2694	33W-22N	E4
9400	ALGN	60102	2694	33W-22N	E4
9400	AlqT	60013	2694	33W-22N	E4
11300	PTPR	53158	2363		D2
14400	ODPK	60462	3345	12W-17S	C4
15100	PHNX	60426	3350	0W-18S	B6
E 2nd Av					
100	NLNX	60451	3501	17W-25S	C7
600	NlxT	60451	3501	17W-25S	D7
1400	JLET	60433	3499	22W-24S	D5
1500	JltT	60433	3499	22W-24S	D5
N 2nd Av					
10	DSPN	60016	2862	13W-12N	D2
10	LMBD	60148	3026	18W-1N	E3
10	LMBD	60181	3026	18W-1N	E3
10	MYWD	60153	3030	10W-0N	A3
10	VLPK	60181	3026	18W-1N	E3
900	SCRL	60174	2964	35W-3N	B5
35400	FXLK	60041	2473	27W-35N	B6
35400	GrtT	60041	2473	27W-35N	B6
38100	AntT	60081	2415	27W-38N	B7
42100	AntT	60002	2357	25W-42N	B6
S 2nd Av					
10	SCRL	60174	2964	35W-3N	C6
200	MYWD	60153	3030	10W-0N	A5
400	DSPN	60016	2862	13W-10N	E4
1200	DSPN	60018	2862	13W-10N	E5
2200	NRIV	60141	3088	10W-2S	A2
2200	NRIV	60546	3088	10W-2S	A3
2200	PvsT	60141	3088	10W-2S	A3
2500	BKFD	60546	3088	10W-2S	A3
W 2nd Av					
100	NLNX	60451	3501	18W-25S	B7
21700	LkvT	60046	2417	21W-38N	C7
21700	LNHT	60046	2417	21W-38N	C7
2nd Ct					
300	CLLK	60014	2640	35W-25N	A5
400	AddT	60106	2971	16W-4N	D3
400	BNVL	60106	2971	16W-4N	D3
2nd Pl					
-	GLHT	60137	3025	23W-1N	B2
-	MltT	60137	3025	22W-1N	B2
-	MltT	60139	3025	22W-1N	B2
400	GLHT	60139	3025	23W-1N	B2
1800	GNVA	60134	3020	34W-2N	C2
1800	SCRL	60134	3020	34W-2N	C2
1800	SCRL	60174	3020	34W-2N	C2
S 2nd Pl					
1600	SCRL	60174	3020	34W-2N	C2
2nd St					
-	BDWD	60408	3942	30W-41S	B6
-	HDPK	60037	2704	8W-23N	D1
-	HIWD	60037	2704	9W-23N	D1
-	MmT	60037	2704	8W-23N	D1
-	RedT	60408	3942	30W-41S	B6
10	CLLK	60014	2640	35W-26N	B3
10	DRGV	60515	3145	18W-5S	A2
10	DRGV	60559	3145	18W-5S	A2
10	ELGN	60123	2854	36W-11N	A5
10	WTMT	60559	3145	18W-5S	A2
100	AURA	60506	3199	36W-8S	E1
100	DRGV	60515	3144	18W-5S	E3
100	GLHT	60137	3025	23W-1N	B2
100	GLHT	60139	3025	23W-1N	A2
100	LYVL	60048	2591	16W-29N	E5
100	MltT	60137	3025	23W-1N	A2
100	MltT	60139	3025	23W-1N	A2
100	VLPK	60181	3027	17W-1N	B2
100	YkTp	60181	3027	17W-1N	B2
200	MHTN	60442	3678	19W-31S	A5
200	WLNG	60090	2755	14W-18N	C3
300	ANTH	60002	2357	23W-42N	E5
300	ElgT	60123	2854	36W-10N	A6
300	OSWG	60543	3263	37W-11S	C2
400	WNVL	60555	3081	28W-3S	B6
500	CRTE	60417	3685	1W-29S	A1
500	GYLK	60030	2532	21W-33N	E3
500	HRVD	60033	2406	50W-38N	B6
500	LMNT	60439	3271	18W-14S	A6
500	WKGN	60085	2480	10W-34N	A7
1600	HDPK	60035	2704	8W-22N	E4
2000	NHBK	60062	2757	10W-16N	B7
2000	NHBK	60062	2810	10W-16N	B1
2000	WPHR	60096	2363	10W-43N	B4
3100	LKBF	60044	2593	10W-30N	E2
3100	LKBF	60088	2593	10W-30N	E2
3100	NCHI	60088	2593	10W-30N	E2
11000	MKNA	60448	3503	13W-23S	A4
11600	HTLY	60142	2692	40W-21N	A6
E 2nd St					
100	BDWD	60408	3942	31W-41S	A5
100	LKPT	60441	3419	22W-19S	D2
200	EDND	60118	2801	34W-16N	A2
200	EMHT	60126	3028	15W-1N	A2
300	CPVL	60118	2801	34W-16N	A2
600	SDWH	60548	3330	51W-14S	A1
900	CLCY	60416	3941	34W-39S	A2
N 2nd St					
10	CRY	60013	2695	30W-23N	E1
10	GNVA	60134	3020	35W-1N	C3
10	SCRL	60174	2964	35W-3N	A6
100	ELBN	60119	3017	43W-1N	A2
100	PTON	60468	3861	9W-37S	A3
100	WDND	60118	2801	34W-16N	A2
2700	SchT	60174	2964	35W-4N	A3
2700	SCRL	60175	2964	35W-4N	A3
33700	WrnT	60030	2533	18W-33N	E2
41000	AntT	60002	2416	23W-41N	E2
N 2nd St SR-31					
10	SCRL	60174	2964	35W-3N	A6
2700	SchT	60174	2964	35W-4N	A3
2700	SCRL	60175	2964	35W-4N	A3
S 2nd St					
10	CRY	60013	2695	30W-23N	E1
10	GNVA	60134	3020	35W-1N	C4
10	LMBD	60148	3026	18W-0N	E4
10	SCRL	60174	2964	35W-2N	B7
100	PTON	60468	3861	9W-37S	A4
100	WDND	60118	2801	34W-15N	A3
200	ELBN	60119	3017	43W-1N	A3
600	SCRL	60174	3020	35W-2N	B1
1400	SCRL	60134	3020	35W-2N	B2
S 2nd St SR-31					
10	SCRL	60174	2964	35W-2N	B7
W 2nd St					
10	HNDL	60521	3146	15W-5S	A2
100	EMHT	60126	3027	16W-1N	D2
200	BDWD	60408	3942	31W-41S	A5
300	LKPT	60441	3419	22W-18S	C2
400	BDWD	60408	3941	32W-41S	E5
500	HNDL	60521	3145	16W-5S	E2
25000	ANTH	60002	2357	25W-42N	B5
25000	AntT	60002	2357	25W-42N	B5
2nd Park Av					
-	DSPN	60018	2917	11W-7N	D3
2nd Private Rd					
2600	FSMR	60422	3507	3W-23S	B3
3rd Av					
-	BtlT	53104	2358		E3
-	LKBF	60044	2593	11W-29N	E3
-	LKBF	60088	2593	11W-29N	E3
-	MYWD	60141	3088	10W-1S	A1
-	MYWD	60153	3088	10W-1S	A1
-	NCHI	60088	2593	11W-29N	E3
-	PvsT	60141	3088	10W-1S	A1
10	EGvT	60005	2861	16W-10N	D6
10	MPPT	60005	2861	16W-10N	D6
10	MTGY	60538	3199	36W-9S	D5
100	BRLT	60103	2909	31W-8N	E3
100	MRGO	60152	2634	49W-27N	C1
300	AddT	60101	2970	19W-4N	C3
300	ADSN	60101	2970	19W-4N	C3
400	LMBD	60148	3026	18W-0N	E5
500	AddT	60106	2971	16W-4N	D3
500	BNVL	60106	2971	16W-4N	D3
600	AddT	60191	2971	16W-4N	D3
800	GNVA	60134	3020	34W-1N	C2
800	SCRL	60134	3020	34W-1N	C2
800	SCRL	60174	3020	34W-1N	C2
900	ShdT	60044	2593	11W-29N	E3
900	ShdT	60088	2593	11W-29N	E3
1600	JltT	60433	3499	21W-24S	E5
1900	JltT	60433	3500	21W-24S	A5
3300	MchT	60050	2528	32W-33N	B2
3300	MHRY	60050	2528	32W-33N	B2
9400	ALGN	60102	2694	33W-22N	E4
9400	AlqT	60013	2694	33W-22N	E4
10500	PTPR	53158	2363		C1
14400	ODPK	60462	3345	12W-17S	D4
15100	PHNX	60426	3350	0W-18S	B6
E 3rd Av					
10	JLET	60436	3499	23W-24S	A5
100	JLET	60433	3499	23W-24S	A5
1400	JltT	60433	3499	22W-24S	D5
N 3rd Av					
10	MYWD	60153	3030	10W-0N	A3
10	SCRL	60174	2964	35W-3N	B6
200	DSPN	60016	2862	13W-12N	D1
300	VLPK	60181	3026	18W-1N	E2
500	DSPN	60016	2808	13W-12N	D7
800	FXLK	60041	2473	27W-35N	B6
800	GrtT	60041	2473	27W-35N	B6
38100	AntT	60081	2415	27W-38N	B7
42100	AntT	60002	2357	25W-42N	B6
S 3rd Av					
10	SCRL	60174	2964	35W-2N	B7
200	MYWD	60153	3030	10W-0S	A5
400	DSPN	60016	2862	13W-10N	D5
1200	DSPN	60018	2862	13W-10N	D5
2200	NRIV	60141	3088	10W-2S	A2
2200	NRIV	60546	3088	10W-2S	A2
2200	PvsT	60141	3088	10W-2S	A2
2500	BKFD	60546	3088	10W-2S	A3
W 3rd Av					
100	NLNX	60451	3501	18W-25S	B7
21800	LkvT	60046	2417	21W-38N	C6
21800	LNHT	60046	2417	21W-38N	D6
3rd Ct					
10	BRLT	60103	2909	31W-8N	E3
S 3rd Pl					
1600	SCRL	60174	3020	34W-2N	D2
1800	GNVA	60134	3020	34W-2N	C2
1800	SCRL	60134	3020	34W-2N	C2
3rd St					
-	HDPK	60037	2704	9W-23N	D1
-	HIWD	60037	2704	9W-23N	D1
-	OSWG	60543	3263	37W-12S	C2
10	GLHT	60137	3025	23W-1N	A2
10	GLHT	60139	3025	23W-1N	A2
10	MltT	60137	3025	23W-1N	A2
10	PKRG	60068	2918	10W-8N	A1
10	YkTp	60148	3026	18W-1S	E7
10	YkTp	60148	3084	18W-1S	E1
100	BMDL	60108	2969	23W-5N	A1
100	EVTN	60091	2813	2W-13N	A7
100	EVTN	60201	2813	2W-13N	A7
100	MHTN	60442	3678	18W-31S	A5
200	AURA	60506	3199	36W-8S	E1
200	CLLK	60014	2640	35W-26N	B3
200	DRGV	60515	3144	18W-5S	E3
200	WLNG	60090	2755	14W-18N	C3
300	GNVW	60093	2810	8W-15N	E2
300	WLMT	60091	2813	2W-13N	A6
500	CRTE	60417	3685	1W-29S	B1
500	LMNT	60439	3271	18W-14S	A6
500	LYVL	60048	2591	16W-29N	E4
600	WMTN	60481	3853	28W-39S	C7
1000	HRVD	60033	2406	50W-38N	A6
2000	WPHR	60096	2363	10W-43N	B5
3100	LKBF	60044	2594	10W-30N	A2
3100	LKBF	60088	2594	10W-30N	A2
3100	NCHI	60044	2594	10W-30N	A2
3100	NCHI	60088	2594	10W-30N	A2
10600	MKNA	60448	3503	13W-23S	A3
11600	HTLY	60142	2692	40W-21N	A6
12000	HBRN	60034	2350	40W-41N	E7
12000	HBRN	60034	2351	40W-41N	A7
E 3rd St					
-	RedT	60481	3942	31W-41S	B4
10	EDND	60118	2801	33W-16N	A2
100	BDWD	60408	3942	31W-41S	B4
100	EMHT	60126	3027	16W-1N	E1
100	EMHT	60126	3028	15W-1N	A1
100	LKPT	60441	3419	22W-19S	D2
300	CPVL	60118	2801	34W-16N	A1
500	HNDL	60521	3146	14W-5S	C2
700	SDWH	60548	3330	51W-15S	A1
900	CLCY	60416	3941	34W-39S	A2
N 3rd St					
10	GNVA	60134	3020	35W-1N	C3
10	SCRL	60174	2964	35W-3N	B7
100	WDND	60118	2801	34W-16N	A2
200	ELBN	60119	3017	43W-2N	A2
900	MHRY	60050	2528	32W-32N	B4
41000	AntT	60002	2416	23W-41N	D2
S 3rd St					
10	GNVA	60134	3020	35W-1N	B4
10	LMBD	60148	3026	18W-0N	E4
10	SCRL	60174	2964	35W-2N	B7
100	ELBN	60119	3017	43W-1N	A3
100	PTON	60468	3861	9W-37S	A4
100	WDND	60118	2801	34W-15N	A3
500	PtnT	60468	3861	9W-37S	A4
600	SCRL	60174	3020	35W-2N	B1
1400	SCRL	60134	3020	35W-2N	B2
W 3rd St					
10	HNDL	60521	3146	15W-5S	A2
100	BDWD	60408	3942	31W-41S	A4
100	EMHT	60126	3027	16W-1N	E1
400	BDWD	60408	3941	32W-41S	E5
600	VLPK	60126	3027	17W-1N	C1
600	VLPK	60181	3027	17W-1N	C1
600	YkTp	60126	3027	17W-1N	C1
11300	BtnT	60096	2362	11W-43N	E5
11300	BtnT	60099	2362	11W-43N	D5
11300	WPHR	60099	2362	11W-43N	D5
25000	AntT	60002	2357	25W-42N	B5
3rd Park Av					
-	DSPN	60018	2917	11W-7N	D3
4th Av					
-	BtlT	53104	2358		E3
-	LKBF	60044	2593	11W-30N	E3
-	LKBF	60088	2593	11W-30N	E3
-	NCHI	60088	2593	11W-30N	E3
-	ShdT	60088	2593	11W-30N	E3
10	EGvT	60005	2861	16W-10N	D6
10	MPPT	60005	2861	16W-10N	D6
100	BRLT	60103	2909	31W-8N	E2
100	MRGO	60152	2634	49W-27N	C1
500	AddT	60101	2970	19W-4N	C4
500	AURA	60505	3200	35W-8S	B2
600	ADSN	60101	2970	19W-4N	C4
800	GNVA	60134	3020	34W-1N	D2
800	GNVA	60174	3020	34W-1N	D2
800	SCRL	60174	3020	34W-1N	D2
1400	JLET	60433	3499	22W-24S	D6
1400	JltT	60433	3499	22W-24S	D6
2000	JltT	60433	3500	21W-24S	A6
10500	PTPR	53158	2363		C1
15100	PHNX	60426	3350	0W-18S	B7
15100	SHLD	60426	3350	0W-18S	B7
E 4th Av					
-	JLET	60436	3499	23W-24S	A6
10	JLET	60433	3499	23W-24S	A6
200	NlxT	60451	3501	17W-25S	C7
200	NPVL	60540	3141	26W-6S	E4
600	NLNX	60451	3501	17W-25S	D7
N 4th Av					
-	AntT	60081	2473	27W-38N	B1
10	BvlT	60416	3941	34W-39S	A2
10	MYWD	60153	3030	10W-0N	A3
100	AddT	60101	2970	19W-4N	C4
100	ADSN	60101	2970	19W-4N	C4
300	DSPN	60016	2862	14W-12N	D1
500	CLCY	60416	3941	34W-39S	A1
500	DSPN	60016	2808	14W-12N	D7
900	SCRL	60174	2964	35W-3N	B6
38300	AntT	60081	2415	27W-38N	B7
42100	AntT	60002	2357	25W-42N	B6
S 4th Av					
10	SCRL	60174	2964	35W-2N	B7
100	LYVL	60048	2591	15W-27N	E7
200	MYWD	60153	3030	10W-0S	A5
400	DSPN	60016	2862	14W-11N	D3
1100	LYVL	60048	2647	15W-27N	E1
1200	DSPN	60018	2862	13W-10N	D6
2100	MYWD	60141	3030	10W-0S	A7
2100	PvsT	60141	3030	10W-0S	A7
2100	PvsT	60153	3030	10W-0S	A7
2200	NRIV	60141	3088	10W-2S	A3
2200	NRIV	60546	3088	10W-2S	A3
2200	PvsT	60141	3088	10W-2S	A3
2500	BKFD	60513	3088	10W-2S	A3
2500	BKFD	60546	3088	10W-2S	A3
W 4th Av					
100	NLNX	60451	3501	18W-25S	B7
21800	LkvT	60046	2417	21W-38N	C6
S 4th Pl					
1600	SCRL	60174	3020	34W-2N	D2
1800	GNVA	60134	3020	34W-2N	D2
1800	GNVA	60174	3020	34W-2N	D2
4th St					
-	BtlT	53104	2358		E3
-	BtnT	60096	2362	11W-43N	E5
-	HDPK	60037	2704	8W-23N	D1
-	HIWD	60037	2704	9W-23N	D1
10	DRGV	60515	3145	18W-5S	A3
10	WTMT	60515	3145	18W-5S	A3
10	WTMT	60559	3145	18W-5S	A3
100	DRGV	60515	3144	18W-5S	E3
100	EVTN	60091	2813	2W-13N	A7
100	EVTN	60201	2813	2W-13N	A7
100	LYVL	60048	2591	16W-29N	E5
100	WLMT	60091	2813	2W-13N	A7
200	AURA	60502	3139	31W-6S	D5
200	NpvT	60502	3139	31W-6S	D5
300	LMNT	60439	3271	18W-13S	A5
300	WKGN	60085	2480	10W-34N	A7
300	WNVL	60555	3081	28W-3S	A6
400	GNVW	60093	2810	8W-15N	E3
500	HRVD	60033	2406	50W-38N	A6
2300	WPHR	60096	2363	10W-43N	B5
3100	LKBF	60044	2594	10W-30N	A2
3100	LKBF	60088	2594	10W-30N	A2
3100	NCHI	60044	2594	10W-30N	A2
3100	NCHI	60088	2594	10W-30N	A2
4600	BtnT	60099	2362	11W-43N	D5
4600	WPHR	60099	2362	11W-43N	D5
11900	HTLY	60142	2691	40W-21N	E6
12000	HBRN	60034	2350	41W-41N	E7
12000	HBRN	60034	2351	40W-41N	A7
E 4th St					
10	HNDL	60521	3146	15W-5S	B2
100	LKPT	60441	3419	22W-19S	D2
200	EDND	60118	2801	33W-16N	A2
600	SDWH	60548	3330	51W-14S	A1
900	CLCY	60416	3941	34W-39S	A1
N 4th St					
10	GNVA	60134	3020	35W-1N	B3
10	SCRL	60174	2964	35W-3N	A6
100	PTON	60468	3861	9W-37S	A3
100	WDND	60118	2800	34W-16N	E2
200	AURA	60505	3138	35W-7S	C7
300	ELBN	60119	3017	43W-1N	A2
900	MHRY	60050	2528	32W-32N	B4
S 4th St					
10	AURA	60505	3200	35W-9S	A4
10	SCRL	60174	2964	35W-2N	B7
100	GNVA	60134	3020	35W-1N	B4
100	PTON	60468	3861	9W-37S	A4
100	WDND	60118	2800	34W-16N	E3
600	SCRL	60174	3020	35W-2N	B1
1300	MTGY	60505	3200	35W-9S	A4
1300	MTGY	60538	3200	35W-9S	A4
1300	SCRL	60134	3020	35W-2N	B2
W 4th St					
10	HNDL	60521	3146	15W-5S	A2
500	HNDL	60521	3145	16W-5S	E2
4th Park Av					
-	DSPN	60018	2917	11W-7N	D3
5th Av					
-	BtlT	53104	2358		E3
-	LKBF	60044	2593	11W-30N	E3
-	LKBF	60088	2593	11W-30N	E3
-	MYWD	60141	3088	10W-1S	A1
-	MYWD	60153	3030	10W-1S	A7
-	MYWD	60153	3088	10W-1S	A1
-	PvsT	60141	3030	10W-1S	A7
-	PvsT	60141	3088	10W-1S	A1
-	PvsT	60153	3030	10W-1S	A7
-	PvsT	60153	3088	10W-1S	A1
10	EGvT	60005	2861	16W-10N	D6
10	JLET	60433	3499	23W-24S	A6
10	JLET	60436	3499	23W-24S	A6
10	MPPT	60005	2861	16W-9N	D6
100	AddT	60101	2970	19W-4N	C4
100	ADSN	60101	2970	19W-4N	C4
100	BRLT	60103	2909	31W-8N	E2
100	MRGO	60152	2634	49W-27N	C1
500	AURA	60505	3200	35W-8S	C2
800	GNVA	60134	3020	34W-1N	D2
800	GNVA	60174	3020	34W-1N	D2
800	LYVL	60048	2591	16W-28N	E7
800	SCRL	60174	3020	34W-1N	D2
1000	AraT	60504	3200	35W-8S	C2
1000	AraT	60505	3200	34W-8S	E2
1000	NCHI	60088	2593	11W-30N	E3
1000	ShdT	60088	2593	11W-30N	E3
1100	CHHT	60411	3508	0W-25S	C7
1400	AURA	60504	3200	34W-8S	E2
1400	AURA	60505	3201	33W-8S	A2
1400	CHHT	60411	3596	0W-25S	C1
1400	JltT	60433	3499	22W-24S	D6
4300	AURA	60502	3201	33W-8S	A2
4300	AURA	60504	3201	33W-8S	A2
15100	PHNX	60426	3350	0W-18S	B7
15100	SHLD	60426	3350	0W-18S	B7
E 5th Av					
10	NPVL	60563	3141	26W-6S	E4
600	LslT	60563	3141	26W-6S	E4
N 5th Av					
-	BvlT	60416	3941	34W-39S	A2
-	MLPK	60171	3030	10W-2N	A1
-	RVGV	60160	3030	10W-2N	A1
-	RVGV	60171	3030	10W-2N	A1
10	DMND	60416	3941	34W-39S	A2
10	MYWD	60153	3030	10W-0N	A3
10	SCRL	60174	2964	35W-4N	B4
300	DSPN	60016	2862	14W-12N	D1
500	DSPN	60016	2808	14W-12N	D7
600	CLCY	60416	3941	34W-39S	A1
600	FlxT	60416	3941	34W-39S	A1
1100	MLPK	60160	3030	10W-1N	A2
1100	MYWD	60160	3030	10W-1N	A2
1700	MLPK	60160	2974	10W-2N	A7
1700	MLPK	60171	2974	10W-2N	A7
1700	PvsT	60160	3030	10W-1N	A1
1700	RVGV	60160	2974	10W-2N	A7
1700	RVGV	60171	2974	10W-2N	A7
38400	AntT	60081	2415	27W-38N	A7
42100	AntT	60002	2357	25W-42N	A6
N 5th Av SR-25					
10	SCRL	60174	2964	35W-4N	B4
S 5th Av					
10	MYWD	60153	3030	10W-0N	A4
10	SCRL	60174	2964	35W-2N	C7
500	DSPN	60016	2862	14W-11N	D3
1000	HMND	46320	3280		D3
1200	DSPN	60018	2862	14W-10N	D5
2100	PvsT	60141	3030	10W-0S	A7
2100	PvsT	60153	3030	10W-0S	A7
2200	NRIV	60141	3088	10W-2S	A2
2200	NRIV	60546	3088	10W-2S	A3
2200	PvsT	60141	3088	10W-2S	A3
2500	BKFD	60513	3088	10W-2S	A3
S 5th Av SR-25					
10	SCRL	60174	2964	35W-2N	C7
W 5th Av					
10	JLET	60433	3499	22W-24S	C6
10	JLET	60436	3498	24W-24S	E6
10	JLET	60436	3499	22W-24S	C6
1000	NPVL	60563	3141	28W-6S	B4
2800	CHCG	60612	3032	4W-0S	D5
3400	CHCG	60624	3032	4W-0S	D5
4500	CHCG	60644	3032	5W-0S	A6
21800	LkvT	60046	2417	21W-38N	C6
E 5th Ct					
400	DSPN	60016	2862	14W-11N	D3
S 5th Pl					
1600	SCRL	60174	3020	34W-2N	D2
1800	GNVA	60134	3020	34W-1N	D2
1800	GNVA	60174	3020	34W-2N	D2
5th St					
-	HDPK	60037	2704	8W-23N	D1
-	LKBF	60044	2594	10W-30N	A2
-	LKBF	60088	2594	10W-30N	A2
-	NCHI	60044	2594	10W-30N	A2
-	NCHI	60088	2594	10W-30N	A2
-	OSWG	60543	3264	34W-11S	D2
-	OswT	60543	3264	34W-11S	D2
10	OSWG	60538	3200	35W-10S	B5
10	OSWG	60543	3200	35W-10S	B6
100	AURA	60505	3200	35W-8S	B2
100	EVTN	60091	2813	3W-13N	A7
100	EVTN	60201	2813	3W-13N	A7
100	LYVL	60048	2591	15W-28N	E5
100	WLMT	60091	2813	3W-13N	A6
100	WLMT	60201	2813	3W-13N	A7
200	DRGV	60515	3144	18W-5S	E3
200	WLNG	60090	2755	14W-18N	C3
400	LMNT	60439	3271	18W-14S	A6
500	CRTE	60417	3685	1W-29S	B1
500	GNVW	60093	2810	8W-15N	E3
500	HRVD	60033	2406	50W-38N	A6
1100	AraT	60505	3200	35W-9S	B4
1200	MTGY	60505	3200	35W-9S	B4
1300	MTGY	60538	3200	35W-9S	B4
1800	WPHR	60096	2363	10W-43N	B5
4600	BtnT	60099	2362	11W-43N	D5

Chicago 7-County Street Index

STREET Block	City	ZIP	Map#	CGS	Grid
5th St					
4600	WPHR	60096	2362	11W-43N	D5
4600	WPHR	60099	2362	11W-42N	D5
31900	WMTN	60481	3853	28W-39S	B7
32000	WMTN	60481	3943	28W-39S	B1
32200	CstT	60481	3943	28W-39S	B2
E 5th St					
10	HNDL	60521	3146	15W-5S	B2
100	LKPT	60441	3419	22W-19S	D2
800	SDWH	60548	3330	51W-14S	A1
900	CLCY	60416	3941	34W-39S	A1
N 5th St					
10	GNVA	60134	3020	35W-1N	B3
10	SCRL	60174	2964	35W-3N	A7
100	WDND	60118	2800	34W-16N	E2
200	BCVL	60407	4030	34W-44S	A3
400	BvlT	60407	4030	34W-44S	A3
S 5th St					
10	GNVA	60134	3020	35W-1N	B4
10	SCRL	60174	2964	35W-2N	A7
100	WDND	60118	2800	34W-15N	E3
400	SCRL	60174	3020	35W-2N	B1
1300	SCRL	60134	3020	35W-2N	B2
W 5th St					
-	LKPT	60441	3419	22W-19S	C2
10	HNDL	60521	3146	15W-5S	A2
5th Av Cto					
10000	CTSD	60525	3147	12W-8S	C7
10200	CTSD	60525	3209	13W-8S	A1
10700	LynT	60525	3209	13W-8S	A1
5th Park Av					
-	DSPN	60018	2917	11W-7N	D3
6th Av					
-	BvlT	60416	3941	34W-39S	A2
-	CLCY	60416	3941	34W-39S	A2
-	DMND	60416	3941	34W-39S	A2
10	EGvT	60005	2861	16W-10N	D6
10	LGNG	60525	3087	12W-4S	C7
10	MPPT	60005	2861	16W-10N	D6
100	AddT	60101	2970	19W-4N	C4
100	ADSN	60101	2970	19W-4N	C4
100	BRLT	60103	2909	31W-8N	E2
100	MRGO	60152	2634	49W-27N	B1
500	AURA	60505	3200	35W-8S	C2
500	LGNG	60525	3147	12W-5S	C2
800	GNVA	60134	3020	34W-1N	D2
800	GNVA	60174	3020	34W-1N	D2
800	SCRL	60174	3020	34W-1N	D2
900	LKBF	60044	2593	11W-30N	E2
900	LKBF	60088	2593	11W-30N	E2
900	NCHI	60088	2593	11W-30N	E2
1000	AraT	60505	3200	34W-8S	D2
1000	ShdT	60088	2593	11W-30N	E3
1100	AraT	60504	3200	34W-8S	D2
5600	CTSD	60525	3147	12W-6S	C3
15100	PHNX	60426	3350	0W-18S	B7
15100	SHLD	60426	3350	0W-18S	B7
E 6th Av					
10	NPVL	60563	3141	26W-6S	D4
N 6th Av					
10	CLCY	60416	3941	34W-39S	A2
10	MYWD	60153	3030	10W-0N	A3
400	ADSN	60101	2970	19W-4N	C4
400	DSPN	60016	2808	14W-12N	D7
400	DSPN	60016	2862	14W-12N	D1
900	SCRL	60174	2964	35W-3N	B5
1100	MLPK	60160	3030	10W-1N	A2
1100	MYWD	60160	3030	10W-1N	A3
38200	AntT	60081	2415	27W-38N	A7
42100	AntT	60002	2357	25W-42N	A6
S 6th Av					
100	MYWD	60153	3030	10W-0S	A5
100	SCRL	60174	2964	35W-3N	C7
600	DSPN	60016	2862	14W-11N	D4
800	SCRL	60174	3020	35W-2N	C1
1200	DSPN	60018	2862	14W-10N	D5
2100	PvsT	60141	3030	10W-0S	A7
2100	PvsT	60153	3030	10W-0S	A7
2200	NRIV	60141	3088	10W-2S	A2
2200	NRIV	60546	3088	10W-2S	A3
2200	PvsT	60141	3088	10W-2S	A3
2500	BKFD	60513	3088	10W-2S	A3
W 6th Av					
10	NPVL	60563	3141	27W-6S	D4
21900	LkvT	60046	2417	22W-38N	C6
6th Ct					
10	BRLT	60103	2909	31W-8N	E2
6th St					
-	HDPK	60037	2704	8W-23N	D1
10	DRGV	60515	3145	18W-5S	A3
10	WTMT	60515	3145	18W-5S	A3
10	WTMT	60559	3145	18W-5S	A3
100	DRGV	60515	3144	18W-5S	E3
100	EVTN	60201	2813	3W-13N	A7
100	WLMT	60091	2813	3W-13N	A6
100	WLMT	60201	2813	3W-13N	A7
100	WLNG	60090	2755	14W-18N	C3
200	NCHI	60088	2594	10W-30N	A2
500	LMNT	60439	3271	18W-14S	A6
600	GNVW	60093	2810	8W-15N	E3
1300	HRVD	60033	2406	50W-39N	A5
1700	WKGN	60085	2536	11W-33N	D3
1800	WPHR	60096	2363	10W-42N	B5
3100	LKBF	60044	2594	10W-30N	A2
3100	LKBF	60088	2594	10W-30N	A2
E 6th St					
100	LKPT	60441	3419	22W-19S	D2
500	HNDL	60521	3146	14W-5S	C2
1300	SDWH	60548	3330	50W-14S	B1
N 6th St					
10	GNVA	60134	3020	35W-1N	B3
10	SCRL	60174	2964	36W-3N	A7
100	WDND	60118	2800	34W-16N	E2
300	PTON	60468	3861	8W-37S	B3
400	CPVL	60110	2800	34W-16N	E2
400	CPVL	60118	2800	34W-16N	E2
S 6th St					
10	SCRL	60174	2964	35W-2N	A7
100	WDND	60118	2800	34W-16N	E3
1300	GNVA	60134	3020	35W-2N	A2
1300	SCRL	60134	3020	35W-2N	A2
1300	SCRL	60174	3020	35W-2N	A2
W 6th St					
10	HNDL	60521	3146	15W-5S	A2
300	BDWD	60408	3941	31W-40S	E4
300	LKPT	60441	3419	22W-19S	C2
300	RedT	60408	3941	31W-40S	E4
500	HNDL	60521	3145	16W-5S	E2
600	BDWD	60408	3942	31W-40S	A4
7th Av					
10	EGvT	60005	2861	16W-10N	D6
10	LGNG	60525	3087	12W-4S	C7
10	MPPT	60005	2861	16W-9N	D6
100	BRLT	60103	2909	31W-8N	E2
100	MRGO	60152	2634	49W-27N	B1
200	LYVL	60048	2591	15W-28N	E6

STREET Block	City	ZIP	Map#	CGS	Grid
7th Av					
500	AURA	60505	3200	35W-8S	B2
500	LGNG	60525	3147	12W-5S	C2
1100	LKBF	60044	2593	11W-30N	E2
1100	LKBF	60088	2593	11W-30N	E2
1100	NCHI	60088	2593	11W-30N	E2
1100	ShdT	60088	2593	11W-30N	E2
1200	AraT	60504	3200	34W-8S	E2
1300	AURA	60504	3200	34W-8S	E2
2100	AraT	60505	3200	34W-8S	D2
5500	CTSD	60525	3147	12W-6S	C3
15100	PHNX	60426	3350	0W-18S	C7
15100	PHNX	60473	3350	0W-18S	C7
15100	SHLD	60426	3350	0W-18S	C7
E 7th Av					
10	NPVL	60563	3141	26W-6S	D4
N 7th Av					
10	MYWD	60153	3030	10W-0N	A3
10	SCRL	60174	2964	35W-3N	C7
100	AddT	60101	2970	19W-4N	C4
100	ADSN	60101	2970	19W-4N	C4
400	DSPN	60016	2808	14W-12N	D7
400	DSPN	60016	2862	14W-12N	D1
900	MYWD	60153	3029	10W-1N	E2
1100	MLPK	60160	3029	10W-1N	E2
38300	AntT	60081	2415	28W-38N	A7
38300	FXLK	60081	2415	28W-38N	A7
42100	AntT	60002	2357	25W-42N	A6
S 7th Av					
10	SCRL	60174	2964	35W-2N	C7
100	MYWD	60153	3030	10W-0S	A5
900	SCRL	60174	3020	34W-2N	D1
1800	GNVA	60134	3020	34W-2N	D2
1800	GNVA	60174	3020	34W-2N	D2
1800	SCRL	60134	3020	34W-1N	D2
2100	PvsT	60141	3030	10W-0S	A7
2100	PvsT	60153	3030	10W-0S	A7
2200	NRIV	60141	3088	10W-2S	A2
2200	NRIV	60546	3088	10W-2S	A3
2200	PvsT	60141	3088	10W-2S	A3
2500	BKFD	60513	3088	10W-2S	A3
W 7th Av					
21900	LkvT	60046	2417	21W-38N	C6
7th Cir					
500	MRGO	60152	2578	49W-27N	C7
500	MRGO	60152	2634	49W-27N	C1
7th Ct					
10	BRLT	60103	2909	31W-8N	E2
S 7th Ct					
1300	SCRL	60174	3020	35W-2N	A2
1400	GNVA	60134	3020	35W-2N	A2
1400	GNVA	60174	3020	35W-2N	A2
7th Pl					
100	CHHT	60411	3508	0W-24S	B6
100	GNVA	60134	3020	35W-1N	B3
7th St					
-	CteT	60417	3685	1W-30S	A4
-	HDPK	60037	2704	8W-23N	D1
-	LKBF	60044	2594	10W-30N	A2
-	LKBF	60088	2594	10W-30N	A2
-	NCHI	60088	2594	10W-30N	A2
10	DRGV	60515	3145	18W-5S	A3
10	WTMT	60515	3145	18W-5S	A3
10	WTMT	60559	3145	18W-5S	A3
100	DRGV	60515	3144	18W-5S	E3
200	WLNG	60090	2755	14W-18N	C3
300	WLMT	60091	2812	3W-13N	E6
700	GNVW	60093	2810	8W-15N	E3
1300	HRVD	60033	2406	50W-39N	A5
2500	WPHR	60096	2363	10W-42N	A6
2600	WKGN	60085	2536	12W-33N	C3
3100	PKCY	60085	2536	12W-33N	A3
E 7th St					
100	LKPT	60441	3419	22W-19S	C2
700	HNDL	60521	3146	14W-5S	C2
1100	LKPT	60441	3420	21W-19S	A3
N 7th St					
10	SCRL	60174	2964	36W-3N	A7
100	WDND	60118	2800	34W-16N	E2
S 7th St					
10	SCRL	60174	2964	36W-2N	A7
100	WDND	60118	2800	34W-15N	E3
1300	GNVA	60134	3020	35W-2N	A2
1300	GNVA	60174	3020	35W-2N	A2
1300	SCRL	60174	3020	35W-2N	A2
W 7th St					
-	LKPT	60441	3419	22W-19S	C2
10	HNDL	60521	3146	15W-5S	A2
300	BDWD	60408	3941	31W-40S	E4
300	BDWD	60408	3942	31W-40S	A4
300	RedT	60408	3941	31W-40S	E4
500	HNDL	60521	3145	16W-5S	E2
8th Av					
10	EGvT	60005	2861	16W-10N	D6
10	MPPT	60005	2861	16W-10N	D6
100	BRLT	60103	2909	31W-8N	E2
100	LGNG	60525	3087	12W-4S	C7
100	MRGO	60152	2578	49W-27N	B7
300	LGNG	60525	3147	12W-4S	C1
1000	CTSD	60525	3147	12W-5S	C2
1100	LKBF	60044	2593	11W-30N	E2
1100	LKBF	60088	2593	11W-30N	E2
1100	NCHI	60044	2593	11W-30N	E2
1100	NCHI	60088	2593	11W-30N	E2
1200	ShdT	60088	2593	11W-30N	E2
11000	PTPR	53158	2363		C2
15100	PHNX	60426	3350	0W-18S	C7
15100	PHNX	60473	3350	0W-18S	C7
15100	SHLD	60473	3350	0W-18S	C7
E 8th Av					
10	NPVL	60563	3141	26W-6S	D4
N 8th Av					
10	MYWD	60153	3029	10W-0N	E3
10	SCRL	60174	2964	35W-3N	C6
100	DSPN	60016	2862	14W-12N	D1
200	AddT	60101	2970	19W-4N	C3
900	ADSN	60101	2970	19W-4N	C2
38200	AntT	60081	2415	28W-38N	A7
38200	FXLK	60081	2415	28W-38N	A7
S 8th Av					
10	SCRL	60174	2964	35W-3N	C7
1800	MYWD	60153	3029	10W-0S	E6
2100	PvsT	60141	3029	10W-0S	E7
2100	PvsT	60153	3029	10W-0S	E7
2200	NRIV	60141	3088	10W-2S	A2
2200	NRIV	60546	3088	10W-2S	A3
2200	PvsT	60141	3088	10W-2S	A3
2500	BKFD	60513	3088	10W-2S	A3
W 8th Av					
10	NPVL	60563	3141	27W-6S	D4
8th Ct					
400	SCRL	60174	2964	36W-2N	A7
400	SCRL	60174	3020	36W-2N	A1
8th Pkwy					
1900	WKGN	60085	2536	12W-33N	C4

STREET Block	City	ZIP	Map#	CGS	Grid
8th Pl					
400	HNDL	60521	3146	15W-5S	A3
800	FDHT	60411	3509	1E-24S	B6
8th St					
-	HDPK	60037	2704	8W-23N	D2
-	OMFD	60461	3507	2W-24S	C6
10	DRGV	60515	3145	18W-5S	A3
10	NCHI	60088	2594	10W-30N	A2
10	WTMT	60515	3145	18W-5S	A3
10	WTMT	60559	3145	18W-5S	A3
100	DRGV	60515	3144	18W-5S	E3
100	LKBF	60044	2594	10W-30N	A2
100	LKBF	60088	2594	10W-30N	A2
200	WKGN	60085	2537	10W-33N	A4
200	WLNG	60090	2755	14W-18N	B3
300	CHHT	60411	3507	2W-24S	C6
400	WLMT	60091	2812	3W-14N	E5
500	BlmT	60411	3507	2W-24S	C6
800	GNVW	60093	2810	8W-15N	E3
800	HRVD	60033	2406	50W-38N	A6
900	WKGN	60085	2536	10W-33N	E4
1000	BlmT	60411	3509	1E-24S	A6
1000	FDHT	60411	3509	1E-24S	A6
1400	WPHR	60096	2363	9W-42N	C6
3100	PKCY	60085	2536	12W-33N	A4
E 8th St					
10	CHCG	60605	3034	0E-0S	C6
100	LKPT	60441	3419	22W-19S	C3
400	HNDL	60521	3146	15W-5S	B3
N 8th St					
100	WDND	60118	2800	34W-16N	E2
400	CPVL	60110	2800	34W-16N	E2
400	CPVL	60118	2800	34W-16N	E2
400	WDND	60110	2800	34W-16N	E2
N 8th St SR-31					
100	WDND	60118	2800	34W-16N	E2
400	CPVL	60110	2800	34W-16N	E2
400	CPVL	60118	2800	34W-16N	E2
400	WDND	60110	2800	34W-16N	E2
S 8th St					
-	DndT	60118	2800	34W-15N	E4
100	WDND	60118	2800	34W-15N	E5
300	SCRL	60174	2964	36W-2N	A7
500	GNVA	60134	3020	35W-0N	B4
600	SCRL	60174	3020	36W-2N	A1
S 8th St SR-31					
-	DndT	60118	2800	34W-15N	E4
100	WDND	60118	2800	34W-15N	E5
W 8th St					
-	PKCY	60085	2536	12W-33N	B4
10	HNDL	60521	3146	15W-5S	A3
500	HNDL	60521	3145	16W-5S	E3
600	LKPT	60441	3419	22W-19S	C2
3000	WKGN	60085	2536	12W-33N	B4
9th Av					
10	BRLT	60103	2909	31W-8N	E2
10	EGvT	60005	2861	16W-10N	D6
10	MPPT	60005	2861	16W-10N	D6
200	AddT	60101	2970	19W-4N	C4
200	ADSN	60101	2970	19W-4N	C4
200	LGNG	60525	3087	12W-4S	C7
900	NCHI	60044	2593	11W-30N	E2
1200	NCHI	60088	2593	11W-30N	E2
1200	ShdT	60088	2593	11W-30N	E2
5300	CTSD	60525	3147	12W-5S	C3
5300	LGNG	60525	3147	12W-5S	C3
11100	PTPR	53158	2363		C1
15100	PHNX	60426	3350	0W-18S	C7
15100	PHNX	60473	3350	0W-18S	C7
15100	SHLD	60473	3350	0W-18S	C7
15200	SHLD	60426	3350	0W-18S	C7
N 9th Av					
-	MLPK	60153	3029	10W-0N	E3
-	MLPK	60160	2973	10W-2N	E7
10	MLPK	60160	3029	10W-0N	E3
10	MYWD	60153	3029	10W-0N	E3
10	MYWD	60160	3029	10W-0N	E3
10	SCRL	60174	2964	35W-3N	C6
700	ADSN	60101	2970	19W-4N	C3
1300	AddT	60101	2970	19W-5N	C2
38300	AntT	60081	2415	28W-38N	A7
38300	FXLK	60081	2415	28W-38N	A7
S 9th Av					
10	MLPK	60153	3029	10W-0N	E3
10	MLPK	60160	3029	10W-0N	E3
10	MYWD	60153	3029	11W-1S	E7
10	MYWD	60160	3029	10W-0N	E3
500	SCRL	60174	2964	35W-2N	C7
2100	BDVW	60153	3029	11W-1S	E7
2100	BDVW	60155	3029	11W-1S	E7
2100	PvsT	60141	3029	11W-1S	E7
2100	PvsT	60153	3029	11W-1S	E7
2200	NRIV	60141	3087	11W-2S	E2
2200	NRIV	60155	3087	11W-2S	E2
2200	NRIV	60546	3087	11W-2S	E2
2200	PvsT	60155	3029	10W-1S	E7
2400	BDVW	60141	3087	11W-1S	E1
2400	BDVW	60155	3087	11W-1S	E1
2400	PvsT	60141	3087	11W-1S	E1
2500	PvsT	60546	3087	10W-2S	E3
9th Ct					
200	HNDL	60521	3146	15W-5S	B3
800	PTPR	53158	2363		C2
S 9th Ct					
300	SCRL	60174	2964	36W-2N	A7
9th Pkwy					
1900	WKGN	60085	2536	11W-33N	D4
9th St					
-	HDPK	60037	2704	8W-23N	D2
10	NCHI	60088	2594	10W-30N	A2
100	EVTN	60201	2812	3W-13N	E7
100	WLMT	60201	2812	3W-13N	E7
200	WKGN	60085	2537	10W-33N	A4
200	WLNG	60090	2755	14W-18N	B3
300	HIWD	60037	2704	9W-23N	D2
400	WLMT	60091	2812	3W-13N	E5
900	GNVW	60093	2810	8W-15N	E3
1100	FDHT	60411	3509	1E-24S	B6
1300	HRVD	60033	2406	50W-39N	A5
1400	WPHR	60096	2363	9W-42N	C6
2800	WKGN	60085	2536	12W-33N	B4
3100	BtnT	60096	2363	10W-42N	B6
3400	BtnT	60096	2362	11W-42N	E6
3400	WPHR	60096	2362	11W-42N	E6
9th St CO-A4					
1900	WPHR	60096	2363	10W-42N	B6
3100	BtnT	60096	2363	10W-42N	B6
3400	BtnT	60096	2362	11W-42N	E6
3400	WPHR	60096	2362	11W-42N	E6
E 9th St					
-	LKPT	60441	3420	21W-19S	A2
10	CHCG	60605	3034	0E-0S	C6
100	LKPT	60441	3419	22W-19S	D3
400	HNDL	60521	3146	15W-5S	B3
1100	LktT	60441	3419	21W-19S	E2

STREET Block	City	ZIP	Map#	CGS	Grid
E 9th St SR-7					
-	LKPT	60441	3420	21W-19S	A2
100	LKPT	60441	3419	22W-19S	D3
1100	LktT	60441	3419	21W-19S	E2
N 9th St					
10	SCRL	60174	2964	36W-2N	A7
S 9th St					
10	GNVA	60134	3020	35W-1N	B3
300	SCRL	60174	2964	36W-2N	A7
1300	SCRL	60174	3020	36W-2N	A2
1400	SCRL	60134	3020	36W-2N	A2
W 9th St					
-	RMVL	60441	3419	23W-19S	B2
10	CHCG	60605	3034	0W-0S	B6
10	LKPT	60441	3419	22W-19S	C3
100	HNDL	60521	3146	15W-5S	A3
500	LktT	60441	3419	23W-19S	B2
600	HNDL	60521	3145	16W-5S	E3
11400	BtnT	60096	2362	11W-42N	D6
11400	WPHR	60096	2362	11W-42N	D6
11600	BtnT	60099	2362	11W-42N	D6
11600	WPHR	60099	2362	11W-42N	D6
11700	ZION	60099	2362	11W-42N	D6
13000	BtnT	60099	2361	13W-42N	E6
13000	ZION	60099	2361	13W-42N	E6
13800	NptT	60099	2361	14W-42N	D6
13800	WDWH	60099	2361	14W-42N	D6
W 9th St CO-A4					
11400	BtnT	60096	2362	11W-42N	D6
11400	WPHR	60096	2362	11W-42N	D6
11600	BtnT	60099	2362	11W-42N	D6
11600	WPHR	60099	2362	11W-42N	D6
11700	ZION	60099	2362	11W-42N	D6
W 9th St SR-7					
-	RMVL	60441	3419	23W-19S	B2
10	LKPT	60441	3419	22W-19S	C3
500	LktT	60441	3419	23W-19S	B2
10th Av					
-	NCHI	60088	2593	11W-30N	E2
10	BRLT	60103	2909	31W-8N	E2
10	EGvT	60005	2861	16W-10N	D6
11100	PTPR	53158	2363		C1
N 10th Av					
-	AntT	60081	2415	28W-38N	A7
-	FXLK	60081	2415	28W-38N	A7
700	ADSN	60101	2970	19W-4N	B3
900	MLPK	60160	3029	11W-1N	E2
S 10th Av					
10	SCRL	60174	2964	35W-3N	C7
500	LGNG	60525	3147	12W-5S	C1
1000	SCRL	60174	3020	34W-2N	C1
1800	MYWD	60153	3029	11W-0S	E6
2100	BDVW	60153	3029	11W-0S	E7
2100	BDVW	60155	3029	11W-0S	E7
2200	NRIV	60155	3087	11W-2S	E2
2200	NRIV	60546	3087	11W-2S	E2
2400	BDVW	60155	3087	11W-1S	E1
W 10th Av					
10	NPVL	60563	3141	27W-5S	D3
10th Ct					
1600	WKGN	60085	2536	11W-32N	E4
S 10th Ct					
400	SCRL	60174	3020	36W-2N	A1
10th Pl					
800	FDHT	60411	3509	1E-25S	A6
10th St					
-	HDPK	60037	2704	8W-23N	D2
-	LKBF	60044	2594	10W-30N	A2
-	LKBF	60088	2594	10W-30N	A2
10	CHHT	60411	3508	1W-25S	A6
100	CHHT	60411	3507	1W-24S	E6
200	WLNG	60090	2755	14W-18N	B3
300	NCHI	60064	2537	10W-33N	A4
300	WKGN	60085	2537	10W-33N	A4
500	BlmT	60411	3507	2W-24S	D6
1000	FDHT	60411	3509	1E-24S	A6
1000	GNVW	60093	2810	8W-15N	E3
1000	NCHI	60064	2536	11W-33N	E4
1000	WKGN	60085	2536	11W-33N	D4
1300	HRVD	60033	2406	50W-39N	A5
1400	KLWH	60043	2812	3W-14N	E5
1400	WLMT	60043	2812	3W-14N	E5
1400	WLMT	60091	2812	3W-14N	E5
1600	KLWH	60091	2812	3W-14N	E5
2200	WPHR	60096	2363	10W-42N	B6
2400	WKGN	60064	2536	11W-33N	D4
3100	LkeC	60088	2594	10W-30N	A1
3100	NCHI	60088	2594	10W-30N	A1
3400	WPHR	60096	2362	10W-42N	E6
E 10th St					
100	CHHT	60411	3508	0W-24S	B6
100	LKPT	60441	3419	22W-19S	D3
S 10th St					
10	SCRL	60174	2964	36W-2N	A7
400	SCRL	60174	3020	36W-2N	A1
1300	GNVA	60134	3020	36W-2N	A2
1300	SCRL	60134	3020	36W-2N	A2
W 10th St					
400	LKPT	60441	3419	22W-19S	C3
4600	BtnT	60099	2362	11W-42N	D6
4600	WPHR	60099	2362	11W-42N	D6
11th Av					
10	BRLT	60103	2909	31W-8N	E2
10	EGvT	60005	2861	16W-10N	D6
300	LslT	60563	3141	26W-5S	E3
300	NPVL	60563	3141	26W-5S	E3
700	LGNG	60525	3147	12W-5S	C2
800	CTSD	60525	3147	12W-5S	C2
900	NCHI	60088	2593	11W-30N	E1
11100	PTPR	53158	2363		C1
E 11th Av					
10	NPVL	60563	3141	26W-5S	D3
400	LslT	60563	3141	26W-5S	D3
N 11th Av					
100	MLPK	60160	3029	11W-0N	E3
100	SCRL	60174	2964	35W-3N	C6
700	ADSN	60101	2970	19W-4N	B3
38300	AntT	60081	2415	28W-38N	A7
S 11th Av					
10	SCRL	60174	2964	34W-2N	C7
1000	SCRL	60174	3020	34W-2N	D1
1800	MYWD	60153	3029	11W-1S	E7
2100	BDVW	60153	3029	11W-1S	E7
2100	BDVW	60155	3029	11W-1S	E7
2200	NRIV	60155	3087	11W-1S	E2
2200	NRIV	60546	3087	11W-2S	E2
2400	BDVW	60155	3087	11W-1S	E1
2400	PvsT	60546	3087	11W-2S	E3
W 11th Av					
10	NPVL	60563	3141	27W-5S	D3
11th Ct					
1600	WKGN	60085	2536	11W-32N	D4
11th Pl					
800	FDHT	60411	3509	1E-25S	A7
W 11th Pl					
300	CHHT	60411	3507	2W-25S	E7

STREET Block	City	ZIP	Map#	CGS	Grid
11th St					
-	CHHT	60411	3509	1E-25S	A6
-	HDPK	60037	2704	8W-23N	D2
-	LKPT	60441	3419	22W-19S	C3
-	NCHI	60064	2536	12W-32N	B4
200	WLNG	60090	2755	14W-18N	B3
400	NCHI	60064	2537	10W-32N	A4
800	FDHT	60411	3509	1E-25S	A6
800	WLMT	60091	2812	3W-14N	E5
1100	GNVW	60093	2810	8W-15N	E3
1100	WKGN	60085	2536	11W-32N	E4
1400	WPHR	60096	2363	9W-42N	C7
111th St					
2000	NPVL	60564	3266	29W-12S	E4
11th St					
2800	WPHR	60096	2362	11W-42N	E7
2900	NCHI	60088	2594	10W-30N	A2
3600	BtnT	60096	2362	11W-42N	E7
4200	BtnT	60099	2362	11W-42N	E7
4200	ZION	60096	2362	11W-42N	E7
4200	ZION	60099	2362	11W-42N	E7
E 11th St					
10	CHCG	60605	3034	0E-0S	C6
100	LKPT	60441	3419	22W-19S	D3
200	CHHT	60411	3508	0W-25S	C7
900	FDHT	60411	3509	1E-25S	A6
N 11th St					
10	SCRL	60174	2963	36W-3N	E7
S 11th St					
10	SCRL	60174	2963	36W-2N	E7
400	SCRL	60174	3020	36W-2N	A1
W 11th St					
10	LKPT	60441	3419	22W-19S	C2
11400	BtnT	60096	2362	11W-42N	D7
11400	BtnT	60099	2362	11W-42N	D7
11400	WPHR	60096	2362	11W-42N	D7
11400	ZION	60096	2362	11W-42N	D7
11400	ZION	60099	2362	11W-42N	D7
12 Lakes Ct					
10	LIHL	60156	2693	36W-22N	C4
12th Av					
10	BRLT	60103	2909	31W-8N	E2
10	EGvT	60005	2861	16W-10N	D6
700	LGNG	60525	3147	12W-5S	D2
800	CTSD	60525	3147	12W-5S	D2
1000	NCHI	60088	2593	11W-31N	E1
E 12th Av					
10	NPVL	60563	3141	26W-5S	D3
400	LslT	60563	3141	26W-5S	D3
N 12th Av					
10	SCRL	60174	2964	35W-3N	C6
700	MLPK	60160	3029	11W-1N	E2
S 12th Av					
300	SCRL	60174	2964	34W-2N	C7
1000	SCRL	60174	3020	34W-2N	D1
1800	MYWD	60153	3029	11W-0S	E7
2100	BDVW	60153	3029	11W-0S	E7
2100	BDVW	60155	3029	11W-0S	E7
2200	BDVW	60155	3087	11W-2S	E2
2200	NRIV	60155	3087	11W-2S	E2
2200	NRIV	60546	3087	11W-2S	E2
W 12th Av					
10	NPVL	60563	3141	27W-5S	D3
W 12th Pl					
600	CHCG	60607	3034	0W-1S	A7
2600	CHCG	60608	3033	3W-1S	A7
2700	CHCG	60623	3033	3W-1S	A7
3400	CHCG	60623	3032	4W-1S	D7
4600	CCRO	60804	3032	5W-1S	A7
12th St					
-	NCHI	60064	2536	12W-32N	B4
10	WLNG	60090	2755	14W-18N	B3
300	SCRL	60174	2963	36W-3N	E6
500	NCHI	60064	2537	10W-32N	A5
700	WLMT	60091	2812	3W-14N	D5
1000	FDHT	60411	3509	1E-25S	A7
1100	WKGN	60085	2536	11W-32N	E5
1200	GNVW	60093	2810	8W-15N	D3
2800	WPHR	60096	2363	10W-42N	A7
E 12th St					
10	CHHT	60411	3508	0W-25S	B7
100	LKPT	60441	3419	22W-19S	C3
N 12th St					
10	SCRL	60174	2963	36W-3N	E7
S 12th St					
10	SCRL	60174	2963	36W-2N	E7
300	SCRL	60174	3019	36W-2N	E1
1400	GNVA	60134	3019	36W-2N	E2
1400	SCRL	60134	3019	36W-2N	E2
W 12th St					
10	LKPT	60441	3419	22W-19S	C2
300	CHHT	60411	3507	2W-25S	D7
11500	BtnT	60099	2362	11W-42N	D7
11500	WPHR	60096	2362	11W-42N	D7
11500	ZION	60096	2362	11W-42N	D7
11800	ZION	60099	2362	11W-42N	D7
W 12th Place Dr					
2800	CHCG	60608	3033	2W-1S	B7
2800	CHCG	60623	3032	3W-1S	E7
2800	CHCG	60623	3033	2W-1S	B7
N 13th Av					
10	SCRL	60174	2964	34W-3N	C6
700	MLPK	60160	3029	11W-1N	E2
S 13th Av					
10	SCRL	60174	2964	34W-3N	C7
1300	SCRL	60174	3020	34W-2N	D1
1800	BDVW	60153	3029	11W-1S	E7
1800	BDVW	60155	3029	11W-1S	E7
1800	MYWD	60153	3029	11W-1S	E7
1800	MYWD	60155	3029	11W-0S	E7
2200	NRIV	60155	3087	11W-2S	E2
2200	NRIV	60546	3087	11W-2S	E2
2400	BDVW	60155	3087	11W-1S	E1
2400	PvsT	60546	3087	11W-2S	E3
W 13th Av					
10	NPVL	60563	3141	27W-5S	D3
13th Pl					
1400	FDHT	60411	3509	1E-25S	B7
E 13th Pl					
10	LMBD	60148	3084	19W-1S	C1
10	YkTp	60148	3084	19W-1S	C1
W 13th Pl					
2600	CHCG	60608	3033	3W-1S	A7
3400	CHCG	60623	3032	4W-1S	D7
13th St					
-	BDVW	60155	3029	11W-1S	D7
-	BRTN	60010	2697	26W-20N	D7
-	CbaT	60010	2697	26W-20N	D7
-	MYWD	60130	3030	10W-1S	A7
-	MYWD	60153	3030	10W-1S	A7
-	PvsT	60130	3030	10W-1S	A7
-	PvsT	60141	3029	11W-1S	E7
-	PvsT	60141	3030	10W-1S	A7
-	PvsT	60153	3030	10W-1S	A7
-	PvsT	60155	3029	11W-1S	E7
100	EVTN	60091	2812	3W-13N	D7

STREET Block	City	ZIP	Map#	CGS	Grid
13th St					
100	EVTN	60201	2812	3W-13N	D7
600	NCHI	60064	2537	10W-32N	A5
700	LMBD	60148	3084	19W-1S	B1
700	YkTp	60148	3084	19W-1S	B1
800	CHHT	60411	3509	1E-25S	A7
800	FDHT	60411	3509	1E-25S	A7
900	WLMT	60091	2812	3W-14N	D5
1000	NCHI	60064	2536	10W-32N	E5
1700	WKGN	60085	2536	11W-32N	D5
3400	WPHR	60096	2363	10W-42N	A7
3600	WPHR	60096	2362	11W-41N	E7
3700	ZION	60099	2362	11W-41N	E7
6200	BRWN	60402	3031	8W-1S	A7
6200	CCRO	60402	3031	7W-1S	B7
6200	CCRO	60804	3031	7W-1S	A7
6800	BRWN	60402	3030	9W-1S	D7
7100	BRWN	60130	3030	9W-1S	D7
7100	FTPK	60130	3030	9W-1S	D7
E 13th St					
10	CHCG	60605	3034	0E-1S	C7
10	LMBD	60148	3084	19W-1S	C1
10	YkTp	60148	3084	19W-1S	C1
100	LKPT	60441	3419	22W-19S	D4
200	CHHT	60411	3508	0W-25S	C7
1200	VLPK	60181	3085	18W-1S	A1
1200	YkTp	60148	3085	18W-1S	A1
1200	YkTp	60181	3085	18W-1S	A1
S 13th St					
10	SCRL	60174	2963	36W-2N	E7
300	SCRL	60174	3019	36W-2N	E1
W 13th St					
10	CHCG	60605	3034	0W-1S	B7
10	LKPT	60441	3419	22W-19S	C2
100	CHHT	60411	3507	2W-25S	D7
100	CHHT	60411	3508	1W-25S	A7
1000	CHCG	60608	3033	1W-1S	D7
3100	CHCG	60623	3032	4W-1S	D7
4600	CCRO	60804	3032	5W-1S	A7
4800	CCRO	60804	3031	6W-1S	E7
6100	BRWN	60402	3031	7W-1S	B7
6100	CCRO	60402	3031	7W-1S	B7
11400	WPHR	60096	2362	11W-41N	D7
11400	ZION	60099	2362	11W-42N	D7
11800	BtnT	60099	2362	11W-41N	D7
14th Av					
800	MTGY	60538	3200	34W-9S	D4
11200	PTPR	53158	2363		B2
E 14th Av					
10	NPVL	60563	3141	26W-5S	D3
500	LslT	60563	3141	26W-5S	E3
N 14th Av					
1500	MLPK	60160	3029	11W-1N	E1
S 14th Av					
500	SCRL	60174	2964	34W-3N	C7
1200	MYWD	60153	3029	11W-0S	E6
1500	MYWD	60155	3029	11W-0S	E6
1800	BDVW	60155	3029	11W-0S	E6
2000	BDVW	60153	3029	11W-0S	E7
2200	NRIV	60155	3087	11W-2S	E2
2200	NRIV	60546	3087	11W-2S	E2
2400	BDVW	60155	3087	11W-1S	E1
W 14th Av					
10	NPVL	60563	3141	27W-5S	D3
14th Ct					
-	MLPK	60160	3029	11W-1N	D1
10900	PTPR	53158	2363		B1
14th Pl					
1400	FDHT	60411	3509	1E-25S	B7
1400	SLVL	60411	3509	1E-25S	B7
E 14th Pl					
-	YkTp	60148	3084	19W-1S	D1
10	CHCG	60605	3034	0E-1S	C7
10	LMBD	60148	3084	19W-1S	C1
W 14th Pl					
100	CHHT	60411	3507	1W-25S	E7
100	CHHT	60411	3508	1W-25S	A7
400	CHCG	60607	3034	0W-1S	A7
700	CHCG	60608	3034	0W-1S	A7
1300	CHCG	60608	3033	1W-1S	D7
14th St					
-	BRTN	60010	2697	26W-21N	D7
-	CbaT	60010	2697	26W-21N	D7
10	YkTp	60181	3085	18W-1S	A1
100	EVTN	60091	2812	4W-13N	D7
100	EVTN	60201	2812	4W-13N	D7
100	WLMT	60091	2812	3W-13N	D7
100	WLMT	60201	2812	4W-13N	D7
600	NCHI	60064	2537	10W-32N	A5
600	OKTR	60181	3085	17W-1S	B1
1000	NCHI	60064	2536	11W-32N	D5
1100	WKGN	60085	2536	11W-32N	D5
2200	WPHR	60096	2363	10W-41N	B7
6200	BRWN	60402	3031	8W-1S	A7
6200	CCRO	60402	3031	7W-1S	B7
6200	CCRO	60804	3031	7W-1S	B7
6800	BRWN	60402	3030	9W-1S	D7
7100	BRWN	60130	3030	9W-1S	D7
7100	FTPK	60130	3030	9W-1S	D7
14th St CO-A29					
600	NCHI	60064	2537	10W-32N	A5
1000	NCHI	60064	2536	11W-32N	D5
1100	WKGN	60085	2536	11W-32N	D5
E 14th St					
10	CHCG	60605	3034	0E-1S	C7
10	CHHT	60411	3508	0W-25S	C7
10	LMBD	60148	3084	19W-1S	C1
100	LKPT	60441	3419	22W-19S	C3
300	BlmT	60411	3508	0W-25S	C7
1000	YkTp	60148	3084	18W-1S	E1
1200	YkTp	60148	3085	18W-1S	A1
1200	YkTp	60181	3085	18W-1S	A1
E 14th St US-30					
10	CHHT	60411	3508	0W-25S	C7
300	BlmT	60411	3508	0W-25S	C7
S 14th St					
-	LMBD	60148	3084	19W-1S	D1
10	SCRL	60174	2963	36W-2N	E7
300	SCRL	60174	3019	36W-2N	E1
600	YkTp	60148	3084	18W-1S	E1
W 14th St					
-	PvsT	60141	3029	11W-1S	E7
-	PvsT	60155	3029	11W-1S	E7
10	CHCG	60605	3034	0W-1S	C7
10	CHHT	60411	3508	1W-25S	A7
10	LKPT	60441	3419	22W-19S	C3
100	CHHT	60411	3507	2W-25S	E7
700	CHCG	60607	3034	0W-1S	A7
700	CHCG	60608	3034	0W-1S	A7
700	OMFD	60461	3507	2W-25S	C7
1000	CHCG	60608	3033	1W-1S	E7
2200	BDVW	60155	3029	11W-1S	D7
2700	CHCG	60623	3033	3W-1S	A7
3800	CHCG	60623	3032	5W-1S	B7
4600	CCRO	60804	3032	5W-1S	A7
4800	CCRO	60804	3031	6W-1S	E7
W 14th St					
6100	BRWN	60402	3031	7W-1S	B7
6100	CCRO	60402	3031	7W-1S	B7
W 14th St US-30					
10	CHHT	60411	3508	1W-25S	A7
100	CHHT	60411	3507	2W-25S	E7
700	OMFD	60461	3507	2W-25S	C7
N 15th Av					
-	MYWD	60153	3029	11W-0N	E3
1500	MLPK	60160	3029	11W-1N	D1
1900	MLPK	60160	2973	11W-2N	D7
S 15th Av					
-	MLPK	60160	3029	11W-0N	D3
10	MYWD	60153	3029	11W-0N	E5
1500	MYWD	60155	3029	11W-0S	E6
1800	BDVW	60155	3029	11W-1S	E7
2200	NRIV	60155	3087	11W-2S	E2
2200	NRIV	60546	3087	11W-2S	E2
2400	BDVW	60155	3087	11W-1S	E1
S 15th Ct					
500	SCRL	60174	3019	36W-2N	E1
15th Pl					
1400	FDHT	60411	3597	1E-25S	B1
1400	SLVL	60411	3597	1E-25S	B1
3000	NCHI	60064	2536	12W-32N	B5
E 15th Pl					
200	CHCG	60605	3034	0E-1S	C7
400	YkTp	60148	3084	19W-1S	C1
W 15th Pl					
-	CHCG	60623	3090	5W-1S	A1
100	CHHT	60411	3595	2W-25S	D1
800	CHCG	60607	3034		E7
800	CHCG	60608	3033	1W-1S	E7
800	CHCG	60608	3034		E7
2700	CHCG	60623	3033	3W-1S	A7
3100	CHCG	60623	3032	3W-1S	E7
4600	CCRO	60804	3090	5W-1S	A1
5500	CCRO	60804	3089	6W-1S	D1
15th St					
-	BDVW	60141	3087	11W-1S	E1
-	BDVW	60155	3087	11W-1S	D1
-	PvsT	60141	3087	11W-1S	E1
100	EVTN	60201	2812	4W-13N	D7
100	WLMT	60091	2812	4W-13N	D6
100	WLMT	60201	2812	4W-13N	D7
700	NCHI	60064	2537	10W-32N	A5
900	FDHT	60411	3509	1E-25S	A7
1000	FDHT	60411	3597	1E-25S	A1
1400	SLVL	60411	3597	1E-25S	B1
1400	WPHR	60096	2422	9W-41N	C1
2800	BtnT	60099	2422	10W-41N	A1
3000	NCHI	60064	2536	12W-32N	C5
6200	BRWN	60402	3031	8W-1S	A7
6200	CCRO	60402	3031	7W-1S	B7
6200	CCRO	60804	3031	7W-1S	B7
6800	BRWN	60402	3030	8W-1S	E7
6900	BRWN	60402	3088	9W-1S	D1
7100	BRWN	60130	3088	9W-1S	D1
7100	FTPK	60130	3088	9W-1S	D1
E 15th St					
10	LMBD	60148	3084	19W-1S	C1
100	CHHT	60411	3596	0W-25S	B1
100	LKPT	60441	3419	22W-19S	C4
200	CHCG	60605	3034	0E-1S	C7
1000	YkTp	60148	3084	18W-1S	E1
1200	YkTp	60148	3085	18W-1S	A1
1200	YkTp	60181	3085	18W-1S	A1
N 15th St					
10	SCRL	60174	2963	36W-3N	E7
S 15th St					
200	SCRL	60174	2963	36W-2N	E7
200	SCRL	60174	3019	36W-2N	E1
W 15th St					
10	CHCG	60605	3034	0W-1S	B7
10	CHHT	60411	3596	1W-25S	A1
10	LKPT	60441	3419	22W-19S	C4
100	CHHT	60411	3595	1W-25S	E1
700	CHCG	60607	3034	0W-1S	A7
700	CHCG	60608	3034	0W-1S	A7
700	OMFD	60411	3595	2W-25S	C1
700	OMFD	60461	3595	2W-25S	C1
700	OMFD	60466	3595	2W-25S	C1
700	PKFT	60411	3595	2W-25S	C1
700	PKFT	60466	3595	2W-25S	C1
1300	CHCG	60608	3033	1W-1S	D7
3100	CHCG	60623	3032	3W-1S	E7
4800	CCRO	60804	3031	6W-1S	E7
6100	BRWN	60402	3031	7W-1S	B7
6100	CCRO	60402	3031	7W-1S	B7
W 15th Place Dr					
2800	CHCG	60608	3033	2W-1S	B7
2800	CHCG	60623	3033	2W-1S	B7
N 16th Av					
10	MLPK	60160	3029	11W-0N	D3
S 16th Av					
10	MYWD	60153	3029	11W-0N	D5
1500	MYWD	60155	3029	11W-0S	D6
1800	BDVW	60155	3029	11W-1S	D7
2400	BDVW	60155	3087	11W-1S	D1
16th Pl					
3000	NCHI	60064	2536	12W-32N	C6
E 16th Pl					
100	CHHT	60411	3596	0W-25S	B1
W 16th Pl					
10	CHHT	60411	3596	1W-25S	A1
500	CHHT	60411	3595	2W-25S	C1
16th St					
-	BRTN	60010	2697	26W-20N	D7
-	LMBD	60148	3084	20W-1S	A1
10	OKBK	60181	3085	17W-1S	C1
10	OKTR	60181	3085	17W-1S	C1
10	YkTp	60148	3084	19W-1S	D1
10	YkTp	60181	3085	18W-1S	A1
100	EVTN	60201	2812	4W-13N	C7
100	WLMT	60201	2812	4W-13N	C7
200	YkTp	60148	3085	18W-1S	A1
400	WLMT	60091	2812	4W-13N	C6
600	NCHI	60064	2537	10W-32N	A6
900	FDHT	60411	3597	1E-25S	A1
1200	KLWH	60043	2812	4W-13N	C5
1300	SLVL	60411	3597	1E-25S	B1
1400	OKBK	60523	3085	16W-1S	D1
1600	OKTR	60523	3085	16W-1S	D1
3000	NCHI	60064	2536	12W-32N	B6
3100	ZION	60099	2421	11W-41N	D1
6200	BRWN	60402	3089	8W-1S	A1
6200	CCRO	60402	3089	7W-1S	B1
6200	CCRO	60804	3089	7W-1S	B1
6800	BRWN	60402	3088	8W-1S	E1
7100	BRWN	60130	3088	8W-1S	E1
7100	FTPK	60130	3088	8W-1S	D1
7100	NRIV	60130	3088	8W-1S	D1
7300	PvsT	60130	3088	9W-1S	D1
E 16th St					
-	LMBD	60148	3084	19W-1S	C1
10	CHCG	60605	3034	0E-1S	C7
E 16th St					
10	CHCG	60616	3034	0E-1S	C7
10	CHHT	60411	3596	0W-25S	C1
100	LKPT	60441	3419	22W-20S	C4
300	BlmT	60411	3596	0W-25S	C1
1000	YkTp	60148	3084	18W-1S	E1
S 16th St					
500	SCRL	60174	3019	36W-2N	E1
W 16th St					
-	BDVW	60141	3087	11W-1S	E1
-	BDVW	60155	3087	11W-1S	E1
-	PvsT	60141	3087	11W-1S	E1
10	CHCG	60605	3034	0W-1S	C7
10	CHCG	60616	3034	0W-1S	B7
10	CHHT	60411	3596	1W-25S	A1
100	CHHT	60411	3595	2W-25S	D1
400	CHCG	60607	3034	0W-1S	A7
700	CHCG	60608	3034	0W-1S	A7
800	CHCG	60608	3033	1W-1S	E7
1300	CHCG	60608	3091	2W-1S	C1
2700	CHCG	60623	3091	3W-1S	A1
3100	CHCG	60623	3090	5W-1S	E1
4500	CCRO	60804	3090	5W-1S	A1
4800	CCRO	60804	3089	6W-1S	E1
6100	BRWN	60402	3089	7W-1S	B1
6100	CCRO	60402	3089	7W-1S	B1
9500	BtnT	60099	2422	9W-41N	C1
N 17th Av					
10	MLPK	60160	3029	11W-0N	D3
1900	MLPK	60160	2973	11W-2N	D7
2000	FNPK	60131	2973	11W-2N	D7
2000	MLPK	60131	2973	11W-2N	D7
S 17th Av					
-	PvsT	60513	3087	11W-2S	D2
-	PvsT	60525	3087	11W-2S	D2
10	MYWD	60153	3029	11W-0N	D4
1600	BDVW	60153	3029	11W-0S	D7
1600	BDVW	60155	3029	11W-0S	D7
1600	MYWD	60155	3029	11W-0S	D5
2200	BDVW	60155	3087	11W-1S	D2
2200	NRIV	60155	3087	11W-1S	D2
2200	NRIV	60546	3087	11W-1S	D2
17th Pl					
10	YkTp	60148	3084	19W-1S	D2
100	LMBD	60148	3084	19W-1S	D2
W 17th Pl					
10	LMBD	60148	3084	20W-1S	B2
10	YkTp	60148	3084	20W-1S	B2
700	CHCG	60608	3092	0W-1S	A1
700	CHCG	60616	3092	0W-1S	A1
17th St					
-	KLWH	60043	2812	4W-14N	C5
-	KLWH	60091	2812	4W-14N	C5
-	MLPK	60131	2973	11W-2N	D7
-	MLPK	60160	2973	11W-2N	D7
-	MYWD	60130	3088	10W-1S	A1
-	MYWD	60141	3088	10W-1S	A1
-	MYWD	60153	3088	10W-1S	A1
-	PvsT	60130	3088	10W-1S	A1
-	PvsT	60141	3088	10W-1S	A1
-	PvsT	60153	3088	10W-1S	A1
100	EVTN	60201	2812	4W-13N	C7
100	WLMT	60201	2812	4W-13N	C7
300	YkTp	60148	3084	19W-1S	C2
400	BtnT	60099	2422	9W-41N	D1
400	WLMT	60091	2812	4W-14N	C5
500	ZION	60099	2422	9W-41N	C1
700	NCHI	60064	2537	10W-32N	A6
800	CHHT	60411	3597	1E-25S	A1
800	FDHT	60411	3597	1E-25S	A1
1300	SLVL	60411	3597	1E-25S	B1
2300	FNPK	60131	2973	11W-2N	D7
2500	ZION	60099	2421	11W-41N	E1
3000	NCHI	60064	2536	12W-32N	C6
36500	SchT	60174	2963	36W-3N	E6
36500	SCRL	60174	2963	36W-3N	E6
E 17th St					
10	CHHT	60411	3596	0W-25S	B1
10	LMBD	60148	3084	19W-1S	C2
10	YkTp	60148	3084	19W-1S	C2
100	LKPT	60441	3419	22W-20S	C4
N 17th St					
10	SCRL	60174	2963	36W-3N	E7
S 17th St					
10	SCRL	60174	2963	36W-2N	E7
200	SCRL	60174	3019	36W-2N	E1
W 17th St					
10	LMBD	60148	3084	20W-1S	B2
10	YkTp	60148	3084	20W-1S	B2
200	CHHT	60411	3595	2W-25S	D1
300	LKPT	60441	3419	22W-20S	B4
700	CHCG	60608	3092	0W-1S	A1
700	CHCG	60616	3092	0W-1S	A1
1100	CHCG	60608	3091	1W-1S	E1
4200	CHCG	60623	3090	5W-1S	B1
9500	BtnT	60099	2422	9W-41N	C1
9500	ZION	60099	2422	10W-41N	B1
N 18th Av					
-	MYWD	60153	3029	11W-0N	D3
1900	MLPK	60160	2973	11W-2N	D7
1900	MLPK	60160	3029	11W-2N	D1
2000	FNPK	60131	2973	11W-2N	D7
2000	MLPK	60131	2973	11W-2N	D7
S 18th Av					
10	MYWD	60153	3029	11W-0N	D5
1900	BDVW	60153	3029	11W-0S	D6
1900	BDVW	60155	3029	11W-1S	D7
2200	NRIV	60155	3087	11W-2S	D2
2200	NRIV	60546	3087	11W-2S	D2
2400	BDVW	60155	3087	11W-1S	D1
E 18th Dr					
400	CHCG	60616	3092	0E-1S	D1
W 18th Dr					
2800	CHCG	60608	3091	3W-1S	A1
2800	CHCG	60623	3091	3W-1S	A1
18th Pl					
10	LMBD	60148	3084	19W-1S	D2
10	YkTp	60148	3084	19W-1S	D2
2900	NCHI	60064	2536	12W-31N	C6
W 18th Pl					
900	CHCG	60608	3091	1W-1S	E1
4300	CHCG	60623	3090	5W-1S	B1
18th St					
-	KLWH	60043	2812	4W-14N	C5
-	WLMT	60091	2812	4W-14N	C5
400	OKTR	60181	3084	18W-1S	E2
400	YkTp	60148	3084	18W-1S	E2
400	YkTp	60181	3084	18W-1S	E2
600	NCHI	60064	2537	10W-32N	A6
800	ZION	60099	2422	9W-41N	C1
1200	BtnT	60099	2422	10W-41N	B1
2800	NCHI	60064	2536	12W-31N	C6
2800	ZION	60099	2421	11W-41N	D1
6200	BRWN	60402	3089	8W-1S	A1
6200	CCRO	60402	3089	7W-1S	B1
6200	CCRO	60804	3089	7W-1S	B1
18th St					
6800	BRWN	60402	3088	8W-1S	E1
7100	BRWN	60130	3088	8W-1S	E1
7100	NRIV	60130	3088	8W-1S	D1
E 18th St					
10	CHCG	60616	3092	0E-1S	C1
100	LKPT	60441	3419	22W-20S	C4
300	LMBD	60148	3084	19W-1S	C2
300	YkTp	60148	3084	19W-1S	C2
N 18th St					
21000	BRTN	60010	2697	26W-21N	C7
21000	CbaT	60010	2697	26W-21N	C7
S 18th St					
100	SCRL	60174	2963	36W-2N	E7
200	SCRL	60174	3019	36W-2N	E1
W 18th St					
10	CHCG	60616	3092	0W-1S	B1
10	LMBD	60148	3084	20W-1S	B2
10	YkTp	60148	3084	20W-1S	B2
100	LKPT	60441	3419	22W-20S	C4
800	CHCG	60608	3091	2W-1S	B1
800	CHCG	60608	3092	1W-1S	A1
900	BDVW	60141	3087	11W-1S	E1
900	BDVW	60155	3087	11W-1S	E1
900	PvsT	60141	3087	11W-1S	E1
2700	CHCG	60623	3091	3W-1S	A1
3400	CHCG	60623	3090	4W-1S	D1
4700	CCRO	60804	3090	5W-1S	A1
4800	CCRO	60804	3089	6W-1S	E1
6100	BRWN	60402	3089	7W-1S	B1
6100	CCRO	60402	3089	7W-1S	B1
S 19th Av					
-	MLPK	60160	3029	11W-0N	D3
10	MYWD	60153	3029	11W-0N	D4
1900	BDVW	60153	3029	11W-0S	D6
1900	BDVW	60155	3029	11W-1S	D7
2200	NRIV	60155	3087	11W-2S	D2
2200	NRIV	60546	3087	11W-2S	D2
2400	BDVW	60155	3087	11W-1S	D1
19th Pl					
2900	NCHI	60064	2536	12W-31N	C6
E 19th Pl					
10	CHHT	60411	3596	1W-26S	A1
W 19th Pl					
700	CHCG	60608	3092	0W-1S	A1
700	CHCG	60616	3092	0W-1S	A1
900	CHCG	60608	3091	1W-1S	E1
19th St					
-	ZION	60099	2421	11W-41N	D2
1300	BtnT	60099	2422	10W-41N	B2
2100	ZION	60099	2422	10W-41N	A2
6200	BRWN	60402	3089	8W-1S	A1
6200	CCRO	60402	3089	7W-1S	B1
6200	CCRO	60804	3089	7W-1S	B1
6800	BRWN	60402	3088	8W-1S	E1
7100	BRWN	60130	3088	8W-1S	E1
7100	NRIV	60130	3088	8W-1S	D1
E 19th St					
100	LKPT	60441	3419	22W-20S	C4
N 19th St					
21000	BRTN	60010	2697	26W-21N	C7
21000	CbaT	60010	2697	26W-21N	C6
S 19th St					
10	SCRL	60174	2963	36W-2N	E7
100	SCRL	60174	3019	36W-2N	E1
W 19th St					
10	CHHT	60411	3596	1W-26S	A1
10	LMBD	60148	3084	20W-1S	B2
10	YkTp	60148	3084	20W-1S	B2
100	LKPT	60441	3419	22W-20S	B4
700	CHCG	60608	3092	0W-1S	A1
700	CHCG	60616	3092	0W-1S	A1
800	CHCG	60608	3091	1W-1S	E1
900	BDVW	60155	3087	11W-1S	E1
2700	CHCG	60623	3091	3W-1S	A1
2800	CHCG	60623	3090	4W-1S	D1
4600	CCRO	60804	3090	5W-1S	A1
6000	CCRO	60804	3089	7W-1S	B1
6100	BRWN	60402	3089	7W-1S	B1
6100	CCRO	60402	3089	7W-1S	B1
N 20th Av					
10	MLPK	60160	3029	11W-1N	D2
S 20th Av					
10	MYWD	60153	3029	11W-0N	D5
1900	BDVW	60153	3029	11W-0S	D6
1900	BDVW	60155	3029	11W-1S	D7
2400	BDVW	60155	3087	11W-1S	D1
E 20th Ct					
200	LKPT	60441	3419	22W-20S	C4
20th Pl					
600	YkTp	60148	3084	18W-1S	E2
2900	NCHI	60064	2536	12W-31N	B7
W 20th Pl					
500	CHCG	60616	3092	0W-1S	A1
900	CHCG	60608	3091	1W-1S	E1
20th St					
700	WLMT	60091	2812	4W-13N	C6
1200	ZION	60099	2422	10W-41N	A2
2900	NCHI	60064	2536	12W-31N	C7
3100	ZION	60099	2421	11W-41N	D2
E 20th St					
10	LMBD	60148	3084	19W-1S	C2
10	YkTp	60148	3084	19W-1S	C2
N 20th St					
21000	BRTN	60010	2697	26W-21N	C7
21000	CbaT	60010	2697	26W-21N	C7
W 20th St					
10	LMBD	60148	3084	20W-1S	B2
10	YkTp	60148	3084	20W-1S	B2
4600	CCRO	60804	3090	5W-1S	A1
N 21st Av					
10	MLPK	60160	3029	11W-0N	D3
S 21st Av					
10	MYWD	60153	3029	11W-0N	D5
1900	BDVW	60153	3029	11W-0S	D6
1900	BDVW	60155	3029	11W-1S	D7
2400	BDVW	60155	3087	11W-1S	D1
21st Pl					
100	LMBD	60148	3084	19W-1S	D2
100	YkTp	60148	3084	19W-1S	D2
2700	BDVW	60154	3087	12W-1S	C2
2700	BDVW	60155	3087	11W-1S	C2
2700	WSTR	60154	3087	12W-1S	C2
2900	NCHI	60064	2536	12W-31N	C7
W 21st Pl					
700	CHCG	60608	3092		E2
700	CHCG	60616	3092		E2
1300	CHCG	60608	3091	1W-1S	D1
2800	CHCG	60623	3091	3W-1S	A2
2900	CHCG	60623	3090	3W-1S	E2
4600	CCRO	60804	3090	5W-1S	A2
4800	CCRO	60804	3089	6W-1S	E2
21st St					
-	BtnT	60099	2422	9W-41N	D2
800	ZION	60099	2422	10W-41N	A2
1200	WLMT	60091	2812	4W-14N	B5
21st St					
2700	ZION	60099	2421	11W-41N	D2
2800	NCHI	60064	2536	12W-31N	C7
3600	BHPK	60099	2421	11W-41N	D2
4600	BtnT	60099	2421	11W-41N	D2
4800	WDWH	60099	2421	11W-41N	D2
6200	BRWN	60402	3089	8W-1S	A1
6200	CCRO	60402	3089	7W-1S	B1
6200	CCRO	60804	3089	7W-1S	B1
6800	BRWN	60402	3088	8W-1S	E2
7100	BRWN	60130	3088	8W-1S	D2
7100	NRIV	60130	3088	8W-1S	D2
21st St CO-A6					
2700	ZION	60099	2421	11W-41N	D2
3600	BHPK	60099	2421	11W-41N	D2
4600	BtnT	60099	2421	11W-41N	D2
4800	WDWH	60099	2421	11W-41N	D2
21st St SR-173					
1200	ZION	60099	2422	10W-41N	A2
E 21st St					
10	CHCG	60616	3092	0E-1S	C1
10	CHHT	60411	3596	1W-26S	A2
N 21st St					
21000	CbaT	60010	2697	26W-21N	C7
W 21st St					
-	BDVW	60155	3087	11W-1S	E2
10	CHHT	60411	3596	1W-26S	A2
600	CHCG	60616	3092	0W-1S	A1
700	CHCG	60608	3092	0W-1S	A1
1200	CHCG	60608	3091	3W-1S	A1
2700	CHCG	60623	3091	3W-1S	A1
2800	CHCG	60623	3090	3W-1S	E1
4600	CCRO	60804	3090	5W-1S	A1
4800	CCRO	60804	3089	6W-1S	E1
6100	BRWN	60402	3089	7W-1S	B1
6100	CCRO	60402	3089	7W-1S	B1
12800	BHPK	60099	2421	12W-41N	B2
12800	BtnT	60099	2421	12W-41N	B2
12800	WDWH	60083	2421	13W-40N	A2
12800	WDWH	60099	2421	12W-41N	A2
13200	ZION	60099	2421	13W-40N	A2
13400	BtnT	60083	2420	13W-41N	E2
13400	BtnT	60099	2420	13W-41N	E2
13400	WDWH	60083	2420	14W-41N	C2
13400	ZION	60099	2420	13W-41N	E2
13800	NptT	60083	2420	14W-41N	C2
15300	NptT	60099	2420	15W-41N	A1
W 21st St CO-A6					
12800	BHPK	60099	2421	12W-41N	B2
12800	BtnT	60099	2421	12W-41N	B2
12800	WDWH	60083	2421	13W-40N	A2
12800	WDWH	60099	2421	12W-41N	A2
13200	ZION	60099	2421	13W-40N	A2
13400	BtnT	60083	2420	13W-41N	E2
13400	BtnT	60099	2420	13W-41N	E2
13400	WDWH	60083	2420	13W-41N	E2
13400	ZION	60099	2420	13W-41N	E2
13800	NptT	60083	2420	14W-41N	D2
22nd Av					
100	BLWD	60104	3029	11W-0N	D5
1100	BLWD	60153	3029	11W-0S	D6
10400	PTPR	53158	2363		A1
N 22nd Av					
10	MLPK	60160	3029	11W-0N	D3
S 22nd Av					
1800	MYWD	60153	3029	11W-0S	D7
1900	BDVW	60153	3029	11W-0S	D6
2400	BDVW	60155	3029	11W-1S	D7
2400	BDVW	60155	3087	11W-1S	D1
22nd Pl					
2800	NCHI	60064	2536	12W-31N	B7
W 22nd Pl					
200	CHCG	60616	3092	0W-2S	B2
800	CHCG	60608	3091	1W-2S	E2
800	CHCG	60608	3092	1W-2S	A2
2700	CHCG	60623	3091	3W-2S	A2
2800	CHCG	60623	3090	3W-2S	E2
4800	CCRO	60804	3089	6W-2S	E2
4800	CCRO	60804	3090	5W-2S	A2
9000	NRIV	60546	3087	11W-2S	E2
22nd St					
-	ZION	60099	2421	11W-40N	E2
-	ZION	60099	2422	9W-40N	B2
10	MltT	60137	3083	22W-2S	D3
10	MltT	60148	3083	21W-2S	E3
10	MltT	60148	3084	21W-2S	A3
10	YkTp	60148	3084	19W-1S	D2
200	GNEN	60137	3083	23W-1S	A2
300	GNEN	60187	3083	23W-2S	A3
300	WHTN	60187	3083	23W-2S	A3
400	LMBD	60148	3084	20W-2S	A2
600	OKTR	60181	3084	19W-1S	D2
600	YkTp	60181	3084	19W-1S	D2
900	WHTN	60187	3082	23W-1S	E2
E 22nd St					
10	CHHT	60411	3596	0W-26S	C2
10	LMBD	60148	3084	19W-1S	C2
10	YkTp	60148	3084	19W-1S	C2
N 22nd St					
21000	CbaT	60010	2697	27W-21N	C7
W 22nd St					
10	LMBD	60148	3084	20W-1S	B2
100	OKBK	60181	3085	17W-1S	C2
100	OKBK	60523	3085	17W-1S	C2
100	OKBK	60523	3086	15W-1S	B2
100	OKTR	60181	3085	17W-1S	C2
100	OKTR	60523	3085	17W-2S	C2
400	YkTp	60148	3084	20W-2S	A3
23rd Av					
100	BLWD	60104	3029	11W-0N	D5
1100	BLWD	60153	3029	11W-0S	D6
11200	PTPR	53158	2363		A2
N 23rd Av					
10	MLPK	60160	3029	11W-1N	C2
S 23rd Av					
1800	MYWD	60153	3029	11W-0S	D6
1900	BDVW	60153	3029	11W-0S	D6
2400	BDVW	60155	3029	11W-1S	D7
23rd Pl					
2500	BDVW	60155	3087	12W-2S	C2
2500	BDVW	60525	3087	12W-2S	C2
2500	PvsT	60155	3087	12W-2S	C2
2500	PvsT	60525	3087	12W-2S	C2
2900	NCHI	60064	2536	12W-31N	C7
W 23rd Pl					
200	CHCG	60616	3092	0W-2S	B2
2100	CHCG	60608	3091	2W-2S	C2
2700	CHCG	60623	3091	3W-2S	A2
2800	CHCG	60623	3090	3W-2S	E2
4800	CCRO	60804	3089	7W-2S	C2
4800	CCRO	60804	3090	5W-2S	A2
9000	NRIV	60546	3087	11W-2S	E2
23rd St					
1400	ZION	60099	2422	9W-40N	B2
2300	ZION	60099	2421	11W-40N	E2
2500	BDVW	60155	3087	12W-2S	C2

STREET Block	City	ZIP	Map#	CGS	Grid
23rd St					
2900	NCHI	60064	2536	12W-31N	C7
6200	BRWN	60402	3089	8W-2S	A2
6200	CCRO	60402	3089	7W-2S	B2
6200	CCRO	60804	3089	7W-2S	B2
6800	BRWN	60402	3088	8W-2S	E2
E 23rd St					
10	CHCG	60616	3092	0E-2S	C2
200	CHHT	60411	3596	0W-26S	C2
N 23rd St					
21100	CbaT	60010	2697	27W-21N	C6
W 23rd St					
-	BRWN	60402	3088	9W-2S	D2
-	BRWN	60546	3088	9W-2S	D2
-	CHCG	60616	3092	0W-2S	C2
-	NRIV	60546	3088	9W-2S	D2
10	CHHT	60411	3596	1W-26S	A2
800	CHCG	60608	3092	1W-2S	A2
1800	CHCG	60608	3091	2W-2S	C2
2700	CHCG	60623	3091	3W-2S	A2
2800	CHCG	60623	3090	4W-2S	D2
4800	CCRO	60804	3089	7W-2S	B2
4800	CCRO	60804	3090	5W-2S	A2
6100	BRWN	60402	3089	7W-2S	B2
6100	CCRO	60402	3089	7W-2S	B2
8700	NRIV	60546	3087	11W-2S	E2
9200	BDVW	60155	3087	11W-2S	D2
24th Av					
200	BLWD	60104	3029	11W-0N	C5
1100	BLWD	60153	3029	11W-0S	C6
N 24th Av					
100	MLPK	60160	3029	11W-0N	C3
S 24th Av					
1800	MYWD	60153	3029	11W-0S	C7
1900	BDVW	60153	3029	11W-0S	C6
1900	BDVW	60155	3029	11W-0S	C6
3000	BDVW	60155	3087	11W-2S	D2
W 24th Blvd					
2800	CHCG	60623	3090	3W-2S	E2
24th Ct					
11900	PTPR	53158	2363		A3
24th Pl					
2400	NCHI	60064	2593	11W-31N	C1
E 24th Pl					
10	CHCG	60616	3092	0E-2S	C2
W 24th Pl					
-	CCRO	60804	3090	5W-2S	A2
200	CHCG	60616	3092	0W-2S	B2
2600	CHCG	60608	3091	3W-2S	A2
4000	CHCG	60623	3090	5W-2S	B2
4800	CCRO	60804	3089	6W-2S	B2
24th St					
-	NCHI	60064	2593	10W-31N	E1
-	NCHI	60064	2594	10W-31N	A1
-	ZION	60099	2421	11W-40N	E3
-	ZION	60099	2422	10W-40N	A3
1400	NCHI	60088	2593	11W-31N	E1
6200	BRWN	60402	3089	8W-2S	A2
6200	CCRO	60402	3089	7W-2S	B2
6200	CCRO	60804	3089	7W-2S	B2
6900	BRWN	60402	3088	8W-2S	E2
E 24th St					
10	CHCG	60616	3092	0E-2S	C2
300	CHHT	60411	3596	0W-26S	C2
N 24th St					
21100	CbaT	60010	2697	27W-21N	C7
W 24th St					
10	CHCG	60616	3092	0W-2S	C2
10	CHHT	60411	3596	1W-26S	A2
2100	CHCG	60608	3091	3W-2S	A2
2700	CHCG	60623	3091	3W-2S	A2
2800	CHCG	60623	3090	5W-2S	B2
4800	CCRO	60804	3089	7W-2S	B2
4800	CCRO	60804	3090	5W-2S	A2
6100	BRWN	60402	3089	7W-2S	B2
6100	CCRO	60402	3089	7W-2S	B2
7200	BRWN	60402	3088	9W-2S	D2
7200	BRWN	60546	3088	9W-2S	D2
7200	NRIV	60546	3088	9W-2S	D2
8700	NRIV	60546	3087	11W-2S	E2
25th Av					
-	BDVW	60153	3029	11W-0S	C6
-	BDVW	60155	3029	11W-0S	C6
-	BLWD	60153	3029	11W-0S	C6
-	BLWD	60155	3029	11W-0S	C6
-	MYWD	60153	3029	11W-0S	C6
100	BLWD	60104	3029	11W-0N	C5
100	BLWD	60160	3029	11W-0N	C3
100	MLPK	60104	3029	11W-0N	C3
100	MLPK	60160	3029	11W-0N	C3
3800	SRPK	60176	2973	12W-5N	C2
4500	SRPK	60176	2917	12W-5N	B7
11400	PTPR	53158	2363		A2
N 25th Av					
100	BLWD	60104	3029	12W-1N	C3
100	BLWD	60160	3029	12W-1N	C3
100	MLPK	60104	3029	12W-1N	C3
100	MLPK	60160	3029	12W-1N	C3
1900	FNPK	60131	2973	12W-2N	C7
1900	FNPK	60160	2973	12W-2N	C7
1900	MLPK	60131	2973	12W-2N	C7
1900	MLPK	60160	2973	12W-2N	C7
2000	FNPK	60164	2973	12W-2N	C7
2000	LydT	60164	2973	12W-2N	C7
2000	MLPK	60164	2973	12W-2N	C7
S 25th Av					
1800	BDVW	60153	3029	12W-0S	C7
1800	BDVW	60155	3029	12W-0S	C7
1800	MYWD	60153	3029	12W-0S	C7
1900	MYWD	60155	3029	11W-0S	C6
2400	BDVW	60155	3087	12W-1S	C2
3100	BDVW	60525	3087	11W-2S	C2
3100	PvsT	60155	3087	11W-2S	C2
3100	PvsT	60525	3087	11W-2S	C2
25th Ct					
11800	PTPR	53158	2363		A3
W 25th Pl					
-	CHCG	60616	3092	0W-2S	B2
2600	CHCG	60608	3091	3W-2S	A2
2800	CHCG	60623	3090	3W-2S	E3
2800	CHCG	60623	3091	3W-2S	A3
5000	CCRO	60804	3089	6W-2S	E3
25th St					
-	CbaT	60010	2697	27W-21N	B6
6200	BRWN	60402	3089	8W-2S	A2
6200	CCRO	60402	3089	7W-2S	B2
6200	CCRO	60804	3089	7W-2S	B2
6800	BRWN	60402	3088	8W-2S	E3
E 25th St					
10	CHCG	60616	3092	0E-2S	C2
300	CHHT	60411	3596	0W-26S	C2
W 25th St					
10	CHCG	60616	3092	0W-2S	A2
10	CHHT	60411	3596	1W-26S	A2
2300	CHCG	60608	3091	3W-2S	A2
2800	CHCG	60623	3090	4W-2S	D2
W 25th St					
2800	CHCG	60623	3091	3W-2S	A2
4800	CCRO	60402	3089	7W-2S	B3
4800	CCRO	60804	3090	5W-2S	A2
6100	BRWN	60402	3089	7W-2S	B2
6100	CCRO	60402	3089	7W-2S	B2
7200	BRWN	60402	3088	9W-2S	D2
7200	BRWN	60546	3088	9W-2S	D2
7200	NRIV	60546	3088	9W-2S	D2
8700	NRIV	60546	3087	11W-2S	E3
8800	PvsT	60546	3087	11W-2S	E3
26th Av					
200	BLWD	60104	3029	12W-0N	C4
11600	PTPR	53158	2363		A3
S 26th Av					
3000	BDVW	60155	3087	12W-2S	C2
3100	PvsT	60155	3087	12W-2S	C2
3100	PvsT	60525	3087	12W-2S	C2
26th Pkwy					
7000	BRWN	60402	3088	8W-2S	E3
26th Pl					
6400	BRWN	60402	3089	8W-2S	A3
7000	BRWN	60402	3088	8W-2S	E3
9000	BKFD	60513	3087	11W-2S	E3
9100	LGPK	60513	3087	11W-2S	D3
9100	LGPK	60525	3087	11W-2S	D3
W 26th Pl					
-	CHCG	60608	3091	3W-2S	A3
10	CHCG	60616	3092	0W-2S	B3
26th St					
-	SCHT	60411	3595	2W-26S	E2
-	SCHT	60466	3595	2W-26S	E2
100	BlmT	60466	3595	2W-26S	C2
100	PKFT	60466	3595	2W-26S	C2
300	CHHT	60411	3595	2W-26S	E2
400	LGPK	60525	3087	12W-2S	C3
1000	PvsT	60525	3087	12W-2S	C3
1900	BKFD	60513	3087	12W-2S	C3
1900	LGPK	60513	3087	12W-2S	C3
1900	PvsT	60513	3087	12W-2S	C3
2300	ZION	60099	2421	11W-40N	D3
2300	ZION	60099	2422	10W-40N	A3
6200	BRWN	60402	3089	7W-2S	B3
6200	CCRO	60402	3089	7W-2S	B3
6200	CCRO	60804	3089	7W-2S	B3
6800	BRWN	60402	3088	8W-2S	E3
7100	BRWN	60546	3088	8W-2S	D3
7100	NRIV	60546	3088	8W-2S	D3
7100	RVSD	60546	3088	8W-2S	D3
E 26th St					
10	BlmT	60411	3596	0W-26S	C2
10	CHCG	60616	3092	0E-2S	C3
10	CHHT	60411	3596	0W-26S	C2
10	SCHT	60411	3596	1W-26S	B2
W 26th St					
-	CHCG	60608	3091	1W-2S	E3
10	CHCG	60616	3092	0W-2S	A3
10	CHHT	60411	3596	1W-26S	A2
10	SCHT	60411	3596	1W-26S	A2
200	BlmT	60466	3595	2W-26S	E2
200	CHHT	60411	3595	1W-26S	E2
200	SCHT	60411	3595	1W-26S	E2
200	SCHT	60466	3595	2W-26S	E2
700	CHCG	60608	3092	0W-2S	A2
2800	CHCG	60623	3090	4W-2S	C3
2800	CHCG	60623	3091	3W-2S	A3
4800	CCRO	60804	3089	6W-2S	D3
4800	CCRO	60804	3090	5W-2S	A3
6100	BRWN	60402	3089	7W-2S	B3
6100	CCRO	60402	3089	7W-2S	B3
7200	BRWN	60402	3088	9W-2S	D3
7200	BRWN	60546	3088	9W-2S	D3
7200	NRIV	60546	3088	9W-2S	C3
7200	RVSD	60546	3088	9W-2S	B3
8100	BKFD	60546	3088	10W-2S	A3
8500	BKFD	60546	3088	10W-2S	A3
8700	BKFD	60513	3087	11W-2S	E3
8700	NRIV	60546	3087	11W-2S	E3
8700	PvsT	60546	3087	11W-2S	E3
27th Av					
200	BLWD	60104	3029	12W-0N	C4
N 27th Av					
1100	MLPK	60160	3029	12W-1N	C2
S 27th Av					
2300	BDVW	60155	3087	12W-1S	C1
27th Pl					
6400	BRWN	60402	3089	8W-2S	A3
W 27th Pl					
100	SCHT	60411	3596	1W-26S	A3
12600	BHPK	60099	2421	12W-40N	B4
12900	WDWH	60099	2421	12W-40N	A4
27th St					
-	ZION	60099	2421	12W-40N	B4
500	ZION	60099	2422	10W-40N	A4
3200	BHPK	60099	2421	11W-40N	D4
6200	BRWN	60402	3089	8W-2S	A3
6200	CCRO	60402	3089	7W-2S	B3
6200	CCRO	60804	3089	7W-2S	B3
6800	BRWN	60402	3088	8W-2S	E3
9000	BKFD	60513	3087	11W-2S	E3
9100	LGPK	60513	3087	11W-2S	D3
9100	LGPK	60525	3087	11W-2S	D3
E 27th St					
10	SCHT	60411	3596	1W-26S	B3
500	CHCG	60616	3092	0E-2S	D3
W 27th St					
10	SCHT	60411	3596	1W-26S	A3
400	CHCG	60616	3092	0W-2S	A3
800	CHCG	60608	3091	1W-2S	E3
800	CHCG	60608	3092	0W-2S	A3
2700	CHCG	60623	3091	3W-2S	A3
3000	CHCG	60623	3090	5W-2S	B3
5800	CCRO	60804	3089	7W-2S	B3
6100	BRWN	60402	3089	7W-2S	B3
6100	CCRO	60402	3089	7W-2S	B3
8000	NRIV	60546	3088	10W-2S	B3
8000	RVSD	60546	3088	10W-2S	B3
12700	BHPK	60099	2421	12W-40N	B4
28th Av					
200	BLWD	60104	3029	12W-0N	C4
11300	PTPR	53158	2363		A3
28th Pl					
6400	BRWN	60402	3089	8W-2S	A3
E 28th Pl					
100	CHCG	60616	3092	0E-2S	C3
W 28th Pl					
10	SCHT	60411	3596	1W-26S	A3
200	CHCG	60616	3092	0W-2S	B3
4900	CCRO	60804	3089	6W-2S	E3
12900	BHPK	60099	2421	13W-40N	A4
12900	WDWH	60099	2421	13W-40N	A4
28th St					
-	ZION	60099	2421	10W-40N	E4
-	ZION	60099	2422	9W-40N	B4
1000	LGPK	60525	3087	12W-2S	C3
1900	BKFD	60513	3087	11W-2S	D3
28th St					
1900	LGPK	60513	3087	11W-2S	D3
6200	BRWN	60402	3089	7W-2S	B3
6200	CCRO	60402	3089	7W-2S	B3
6200	CCRO	60804	3089	7W-2S	B3
7100	BRWN	60402	3088	8W-2S	E3
E 28th St					
10	CHCG	60616	3092	0E-2S	C3
10	SCHT	60411	3596	1W-26S	B3
W 28th St					
-	CHCG	60608	3091	3W-2S	A3
100	SCHT	60411	3596	1W-26S	A3
300	CHCG	60616	3092	0W-2S	A3
700	CHCG	60608	3092	0W-2S	A3
3000	CHCG	60623	3090	3W-2S	E3
4800	CCRO	60804	3089	6W-2S	E3
4800	CCRO	60804	3090	5W-2S	A3
6100	BRWN	60402	3089	7W-2S	B3
6100	CCRO	60402	3089	7W-2S	B3
8000	NRIV	60546	3088	10W-2S	B3
8000	RVSD	60546	3088	10W-2S	B3
12600	BHPK	60099	2421	12W-40N	B4
12700	WDWH	60099	2421	12W-40N	B4
29th Av					
200	BLWD	60104	3029	12W-0N	C4
W 29th Ct					
8000	NRIV	60546	3088	10W-2S	B3
8000	RVSD	60546	3088	10W-2S	B3
29th Pl					
6800	BRWN	60402	3088	8W-2S	E3
6800	BRWN	60402	3089	8W-2S	A3
E 29th Pl					
400	CHCG	60616	3092	0E-2S	D3
W 29th Pl					
10	SCHT	60411	3596	1W-26S	A3
300	CHCG	60616	3092	0W-2S	B3
4900	CCRO	60804	3089	6W-2S	D3
29th St					
-	BlmT	60475	3597	1E-27S	B4
-	STGR	60475	3597	1E-27S	B4
10	PvsT	60525	3087	12W-2S	B3
400	BtnT	60099	2422	9W-40N	C4
600	ZION	60099	2422	9W-40N	C4
900	LGPK	60525	3087	12W-2S	C3
1900	BKFD	60513	3087	11W-2S	E3
1900	LGPK	60513	3087	11W-2S	E3
2400	ZION	60099	2421	11W-40N	D4
2700	BHPK	60099	2421	11W-40N	E4
6200	BRWN	60402	3089	7W-2S	B4
6200	CCRO	60402	3089	7W-2S	B4
6200	CCRO	60804	3089	7W-2S	B4
6900	BRWN	60402	3088	8W-2S	E3
7100	RVSD	60402	3088	8W-2S	D3
7100	RVSD	60546	3088	8W-2S	D3
8600	BKFD	60513	3088	10W-2S	A3
E 29th St					
200	CHCG	60616	3092	0E-2S	C3
W 29th St					
10	SCHT	60411	3596	1W-26S	A3
400	CHCG	60616	3092	0W-2S	A3
700	CHCG	60608	3092	0W-2S	A3
800	CHCG	60608	3091	1W-2S	E3
4800	CCRO	60804	3089	6W-2S	E3
4800	CCRO	60804	3090	5W-2S	A3
8000	NRIV	60546	3088	10W-2S	B3
8000	RVSD	60546	3088	10W-2S	B3
11600	BHPK	60099	2421	12W-40N	C4
11600	ZION	60099	2421	11W-40N	D4
12800	WDWH	60099	2421	12W-40N	A4
30th Av					
200	BLWD	60104	3029	12W-0N	C4
N 30th Av					
1700	MLPK	60160	3029	12W-1N	C1
1700	MLPK	60165	3029	12W-1N	C1
1700	SNPK	60165	3029	12W-1N	C1
30th Pl					
500	MNSR	46321	3430		D6
6800	BRWN	60402	3088	8W-2S	E4
6800	BRWN	60402	3089	8W-2S	A4
E 30th Pl					
10	STGR	60475	3596	1W-27S	B4
W 30th Pl					
10	SCHT	60411	3596	1W-27S	A3
10	STGR	60475	3596	1W-27S	B4
300	CHCG	60616	3092	0W-2S	B3
4900	CCRO	60804	3089	6W-2S	E4
30th St					
-	PvsT	60525	3087	12W-2S	B4
-	STGR	60475	3597	1E-27S	B4
-	ZION	60099	2422	9W-39N	B4
500	MNSR	46321	3430		D6
1000	LGPK	60525	3087	12W-2S	C4
1900	BKFD	60513	3087	11W-2S	D4
1900	BKFD	60525	3087	11W-2S	D4
2500	BHPK	60099	2421	11W-39N	E4
2500	ZION	60099	2421	11W-39N	E4
6800	BRWN	60402	3088	8W-2S	E4
7100	RVSD	60402	3088	8W-2S	D4
7100	RVSD	60546	3088	8W-2S	D4
E 30th St					
400	CHCG	60616	3092	0E-2S	D3
W 30th St					
-	SCHT	60411	3595	1W-27S	E3
10	SCHT	60411	3596	1W-26S	A3
10	SCHT	60475	3596	1W-27S	A4
10	STGR	60475	3596	1W-27S	A4
400	CHCG	60616	3092	0W-2S	A3
700	CHCG	60608	3092	0W-2S	A3
2700	CHCG	60608	3091	3W-2S	A3
2700	CHCG	60623	3091	3W-2S	A3
3100	CHCG	60623	3090	5W-2S	B3
4800	CCRO	60804	3089	6W-2S	D4
4800	CCRO	60804	3090	5W-2S	A3
8000	NRIV	60546	3088	10W-2S	B3
8000	RVSD	60546	3088	10W-2S	B4
31st Av					
300	BLWD	60104	3029	12W-0N	C4
N 31st Av					
1100	MLPK	60160	3029	12W-1N	B2
W 31st Blvd					
2700	CHCG	60608	3091	3W-2S	A3
E 31st Pl					
10	STGR	60475	3596	1W-27S	B5
400	CHCG	60616	3092	0E-3S	D4
W 31st Pl					
10	STGR	60475	3596	1W-27S	B5
900	CHCG	60608	3091	1W-3S	E4
4900	CCRO	60804	3089	6W-3S	E4
31st St					
500	DRGV	60515	3084	19W-2S	C4
500	DRGV	60523	3084	19W-2S	C4
500	OKBK	60523	3084	19W-2S	C4
500	YkTp	60515	3084	19W-2S	C4
500	YkTp	60523	3084	19W-2S	C4
1000	ZION	60099	2422	9W-39N	B5
2400	ZION	60099	2421	11W-39N	E5
31st St					
2600	BHPK	60099	2421	11W-39N	E5
6400	BRWN	60402	3089	8W-2S	A4
6800	BRWN	60402	3088	8W-2S	E4
7100	RVSD	60402	3088	8W-3S	D4
8400	BKFD	60513	3088	10W-2S	A4
8400	BKFD	60546	3088	10W-2S	A4
8400	NRIV	60546	3088	10W-2S	A4
8400	RVSD	60546	3088	10W-2S	A4
8800	BKFD	60513	3087	11W-2S	E4
9100	BKFD	60525	3087	11W-2S	D4
10600	LGPK	60525	3087	13W-3S	A4
10600	WSTR	60154	3087	13W-3S	A4
10600	WSTR	60525	3087	13W-3S	A4
10700	LGPK	60154	3086	13W-3S	E4
10700	LGPK	60525	3086	13W-3S	E4
10700	PvsT	60154	3086	13W-3S	E4
10700	PvsT	60525	3086	13W-3S	E4
10700	PvsT	60558	3086	13W-3S	E4
10700	WSTR	60154	3086	13W-3S	E4
10800	WSTR	60558	3086	13W-3S	E4
31st St CO-34					
500	DRGV	60515	3084	19W-2S	C4
500	DRGV	60523	3084	19W-2S	C4
500	OKBK	60523	3084	19W-2S	C4
500	YkTp	60515	3084	19W-2S	C4
500	YkTp	60523	3084	19W-2S	C4
E 31st St					
10	CHCG	60616	3092	0E-2S	C3
10	LGPK	60525	3087	11W-3S	D4
10	PvsT	60525	3087	12W-2S	B4
10	STGR	60475	3596	1W-27S	B5
1100	BKFD	60513	3087	11W-3S	D4
1100	BKFD	60525	3087	11W-3S	D4
1100	LGPK	60513	3087	11W-3S	D4
W 31st St					
10	BlmT	60475	3596	1W-27S	A5
10	CHCG	60616	3092	0W-2S	B3
10	SCHT	60411	3596	1W-27S	A4
10	STGR	60475	3596	1W-27S	A5
300	LGPK	60525	3087	12W-2S	B4
300	PvsT	60525	3087	12W-2S	B4
400	WSTR	60525	3087	12W-2S	A4
700	CHCG	60608	3092	0W-2S	A3
800	CHCG	60608	3091	1W-3S	E4
1000	WSTR	60154	3087	12W-2S	A4
2700	CHCG	60623	3091	3W-3S	A4
2800	CHCG	60623	3090	5W-3S	B4
4600	CCRO	60804	3090	5W-3S	A4
4800	CCRO	60804	3089	7W-2S	B4
6100	BRWN	60402	3089	7W-2S	B4
6100	CCRO	60402	3089	7W-2S	B4
8000	NRIV	60546	3088	10W-3S	B4
8000	RVSD	60546	3088	10W-3S	B4
32nd Av					
200	BLWD	60104	3029	12W-0N	B4
1700	MLPK	60160	3029	12W-1N	B1
1700	SNPK	60160	3029	12W-1N	B1
1700	SNPK	60165	3029	12W-1N	B1
10400	PTPR	53158	2362		E1
N 32nd Av					
1700	MLPK	60160	3029	12W-1N	B1
1700	SNPK	60160	3029	12W-1N	B1
1700	SNPK	60165	3029	12W-1N	B1
E 32nd Pl					
10	STGR	60475	3596	0W-27S	B5
500	CHCG	60616	3092	0E-3S	D4
W 32nd Pl					
10	STGR	60475	3596	1W-27S	B5
900	CHCG	60608	3091	1W-3S	E4
4900	CCRO	60804	3089	6W-3S	E4
32nd St					
-	SCHT	60411	3596	0W-27S	C4
-	SCHT	60475	3596	0W-27S	C4
-	STGR	60411	3596	0W-27S	D4
-	STGR	60475	3596	0W-27S	D4
6200	BRWN	60402	3089	8W-3S	A4
6200	CCRO	60402	3089	7W-3S	B4
6200	CCRO	60804	3089	7W-3S	B4
6800	BRWN	60402	3088	8W-3S	E4
7100	RVSD	60402	3088	8W-3S	E4
7100	RVSD	60546	3088	8W-3S	E4
E 32nd St					
400	SCHT	60411	3596	0E-27S	D4
400	SCHT	60475	3596	0E-27S	D4
400	STGR	60411	3596	0E-27S	D4
400	STGR	60475	3596	0E-27S	D4
500	CHCG	60616	3092	0E-3S	D4
1000	STGR	60475	3597	1E-27S	A5
W 32nd St					
10	STGR	60475	3596	1W-27S	A5
100	BlmT	60475	3596	1W-27S	A5
800	CHCG	60608	3091	1W-3S	E4
800	CHCG	60608	3092	0W-3S	A4
800	CHCG	60616	3092	0W-3S	A4
3100	CHCG	60623	3090	5W-3S	B4
4800	CCRO	60804	3089	6W-3S	E4
4800	CCRO	60804	3090	5W-3S	A4
6100	BRWN	60402	3089	7W-3S	B4
6100	CCRO	60402	3089	7W-3S	B4
33rd Av					
10600	PTPR	53158	2362		E1
N 33rd Av					
1100	MLPK	60160	3029	12W-1N	B1
1400	MLPK	60165	3029	12W-1N	B1
1400	SNPK	60165	3029	12W-1N	B1
1700	SNPK	60160	3029	12W-1N	B1
E 33rd Blvd					
10	CHCG	60616	3092	0E-3S	C4
33rd Ct					
12200	PTPR	53158	2362		E3
E 33rd Pl					
10	STGR	60475	3596	0W-27S	B5
600	CHCG	60616	3092	0E-3S	D4
W 33rd Pl					
10	STGR	60475	3596	1W-27S	B5
800	CHCG	60608	3091	1W-3S	E4
800	CHCG	60608	3092	1W-3S	A4
800	CHCG	60616	3092	1W-3S	A4
33rd St					
-	DRGV	60515	3084	19W-3S	C5
-	STGR	60475	3596	0W-27S	C5
1100	ZION	60099	2422	9W-39N	B5
2300	ZION	60099	2421	11W-39N	E5
2400	BHPK	60099	2421	11W-39N	E5
6200	BRWN	60402	3089	7W-3S	B4
6200	CCRO	60402	3089	7W-3S	B4
6200	CCRO	60804	3089	7W-3S	B4
33rd St CO-A8					
1200	ZION	60099	2422	10W-39N	A5
2300	ZION	60099	2421	11W-39N	E5
2400	BHPK	60099	2421	11W-39N	E5
E 33rd St					
10	STGR	60475	3596	0W-27S	B5
300	CHCG	60616	3092	0E-3S	D4
W 33rd St					
10	SCHT	60411	3596	1W-27S	B4
10	STGR	60475	3596	1W-27S	A5
100	BlmT	60475	3596	1W-27S	A5
800	CHCG	60608	3092	1W-3S	A4
800	CHCG	60616	3092	1W-3S	A4
1500	CHCG	60608	3091	2W-3S	B4
3700	CHCG	60623	3090	4W-3S	C4
4800	CCRO	60804	3089	6W-3S	E4
11500	BHPK	60099	2421	12W-39N	C5
11500	ZION	60099	2421	12W-39N	C5
12000	BHPK	60087	2421	12W-39N	C5
W 33rd St CO-A8					
11500	BHPK	60099	2421	12W-39N	C5
11500	ZION	60099	2421	12W-39N	C5
12000	BHPK	60087	2421	12W-39N	C5
34th Av					
10800	PTPR	53158	2362		E1
N 34th Av					
1200	MLPK	60160	3029	12W-1N	B2
1500	MLPK	60165	3029	12W-1N	B2
1500	SNPK	60165	3029	12W-1N	B2
E 34th Pl					
10	STGR	60475	3596	0E-27S	D4
W 34th Pl					
10	STGR	60475	3596	1W-28S	B5
800	CHCG	60608	3091	1W-3S	E4
800	CHCG	60608	3092	1W-3S	A4
800	CHCG	60616	3092	1W-3S	A4
34th St					
10	SCHT	60475	3596	0E-27S	D4
10	STGR	60475	3596	0E-27S	D4
1200	BHPK	60099	2422	10W-39N	B5
2000	ZION	60099	2422	10W-39N	A5
6200	BRWN	60402	3089	7W-3S	B5
6200	CCRO	60402	3089	7W-3S	B5
6200	CCRO	60804	3089	7W-3S	B5
6800	BRWN	60402	3088	8W-3S	E5
7100	RVSD	60402	3088	8W-3S	E5
7100	RVSD	60546	3088	8W-3S	E5
E 34th St					
10	SCHT	60411	3596	0W-27S	C4
10	SCHT	60475	3596	1W-27S	B4
10	STGR	60411	3596	0W-27S	C4
10	STGR	60475	3596	0W-27S	C4
100	CRTE	60417	3596	0W-27S	C5
400	CHCG	60616	3092	0E-3S	D4
W 34th St					
-	BHPK	60099	2421	11W-39N	E5
-	ZION	60099	2421	11W-39N	E5
10	STGR	60475	3596	1W-27S	B5
100	BlmT	60475	3596	1W-27S	A5
200	CHCG	60616	3092	0W-3S	B4
300	BlmT	60466	3595	1W-27S	E5
300	BlmT	60475	3595	1W-27S	E5
300	CteT	60475	3595	1W-27S	E5
300	STGR	60475	3595	1W-27S	E5
800	CHCG	60608	3091	1W-3S	E4
800	CHCG	60608	3092	1W-3S	A4
2200	MonT	60466	3595	2W-27S	C5
2200	MonT	60475	3595	2W-27S	C5
2200	PKFT	60466	3595	2W-27S	C5
3700	CHCG	60623	3090	4W-3S	C4
4600	CCRO	60804	3090	5W-3S	A4
5200	CCRO	60804	3089	7W-3S	B4
6100	BRWN	60402	3089	7W-3S	B4
6100	CCRO	60402	3089	7W-3S	B4
10800	BHPK	60099	2422	10W-39N	A5
10800	ZION	60099	2422	10W-39N	A5
35th Av					
10700	PTPR	53158	2362		E1
N 35th Av					
1200	MLPK	60160	3029	12W-1N	B2
1500	SNPK	60160	3029	12W-1N	B2
1500	SNPK	60165	3029	12W-1N	B2
35th Pl					
-	CCRO	60804	3090	5W-2S	A3
E 35th Pl					
10	STGR	60475	3596	1W-28S	B6
W 35th Pl					
10	STGR	60475	3596	1W-28S	B6
800	CHCG	60609	3092	1W-3S	A5
900	CHCG	60609	3091	1W-3S	E5
2600	CHCG	60632	3091	3W-3S	A5
4100	CHCG	60623	3090	5W-3S	B4
4100	CHCG	60632	3090	5W-3S	B4
35th St					
1000	DRGV	60515	3084	20W-3S	B5
1000	OKBK	60523	3085	16W-3S	D5
2200	OKBK	60559	3085	18W-3S	A5
2200	WTMT	60523	3085	18W-3S	A5
2200	WTMT	60559	3085	18W-3S	A5
2800	OKBK	60523	3084	18W-3S	E5
3100	YkTp	60523	3084	18W-3S	E5
6200	BRWN	60402	3089	8W-3S	A5
6200	CCRO	60402	3089	7W-3S	B5
6200	CCRO	60804	3089	7W-3S	B5
6800	BRWN	60402	3088	8W-3S	E5
7100	RVSD	60546	3088	8W-3S	E5
E 35th St					
10	CHCG	60609	3092	0E-3S	C4
10	CHCG	60616	3092	0E-3S	D4
10	CHCG	60653	3092	0E-3S	D4
10	STGR	60475	3596	1W-28S	B6
100	CRTE	60417	3596	0W-28S	C6
100	CRTE	60475	3596	0W-28S	C6
W 35th St					
10	CHCG	60609	3092	0W-3S	A4
10	CHCG	60616	3092	0W-3S	A4
10	CHCG	60653	3092	0W-3S	A4
10	STGR	60475	3596	1W-28S	A6
200	STGR	60475	3595	2W-28S	E6
500	CteT	60475	3595	2W-28S	E6
700	CHCG	60608	3092	0W-3S	A4
800	CHCG	60608	3091	3W-3S	A5
800	CHCG	60609	3091	3W-3S	A5
2400	CHCG	60632	3091	3W-3S	A5
2700	CHCG	60623	3091	3W-3S	A5
2800	CHCG	60632	3090	3W-3S	E5
3700	CHCG	60623	3090	4W-3S	C5
5200	CCRO	60804	3089	7W-3S	B5
5200	SKNY	60804	3089	6W-3S	D5
6100	BRWN	60402	3089	7W-3S	B5
6100	CCRO	60402	3089	7W-3S	B5
36th Av					
12200	PTPR	53158	2362		E3
N 36th Av					
1200	MLPK	60160	3029	12W-1N	B2
1400	MLPK	60165	3029	12W-1N	B2
1400	SNPK	60165	3029	12W-1N	B2
36th Ct					
10800	PTPR	53158	2362		E1
E 36th Pl					
10	CHCG	60609	3092	0E-3S	C5
10	STGR	60475	3596	1W-28S	B6
500	CHCG	60653	3092	0E-3S	D5

STREET Block	City	ZIP	Map#	CGS	Grid
W 36th Pl					
10	STGR	60475	3596	1W-28S	B6
1200	CHCG	60609	3091	1W-3S	E5
2600	CHCG	60632	3091	3W-3S	A5
2800	CHCG	60632	3090	3W-3S	E5
36th St					
400	DRGV	60515	3084	19W-3S	D5
400	DRGV	60523	3084	19W-3S	D5
400	OKBK	60515	3084	19W-3S	D5
400	OKBK	60523	3084	19W-3S	D5
400	YkTp	60515	3084	19W-3S	D5
400	YkTp	60523	3084	19W-3S	D5
6200	BRWN	60402	3089	8W-3S	A5
6200	CCRO	60402	3089	7W-3S	B5
6200	CCRO	60804	3089	7W-3S	B5
7000	BRWN	60402	3088	8W-3S	E5
7100	BRWN	60546	3088	8W-3S	E5
7100	RVSD	60546	3088	8W-3S	E5
E 36th St					
10	CHCG	60609	3092	0W-3S	C5
10	CHCG	60653	3092	0W-3S	C5
10	STGR	60475	3596	0W-28S	B6
100	CRTE	60417	3596	0W-28S	B6
100	CRTE	60475	3596	0W-28S	B6
100	STGR	60417	3596	0W-28S	B6
W 36th St					
-	CHCG	60616	3092	0W-3S	B5
10	STGR	60475	3596	1W-28S	A6
500	CHCG	60609	3092	0W-3S	A5
1000	CHCG	60609	3091	1W-3S	E5
2400	CHCG	60632	3091	3W-3S	A5
2800	CHCG	60632	3090	3W-3S	E5
4000	CHCG	60623	3090	5W-3S	B5
5200	CCRO	60804	3089	7W-3S	C5
5200	SKNY	60804	3089	6W-3S	D5
6100	BRWN	60402	3089	7W-3S	B5
6100	CCRO	60402	3089	7W-3S	B5
37th Av					
100	SCRL	60174	2965	33W-3N	A7
12100	PTPR	53158	2362		E3
N 37th Av					
1200	MLPK	60160	3029	12W-1N	B2
1200	MLPK	60165	3029	12W-1N	B2
1200	SNPK	60160	3029	12W-1N	B2
1200	SNPK	60165	3029	12W-1N	B2
E 37th Pl					
10	CHCG	60609	3092	0E-3S	C5
500	CHCG	60653	3092	0E-3S	D5
W 37th Pl					
100	STGR	60475	3596	1W-28S	A6
800	CHCG	60609	3092	1W-3S	A5
900	CHCG	60609	3091	1W-3S	E5
2600	CHCG	60632	3091	3W-3S	A5
3000	CHCG	60632	3090	4W-3S	E5
37th St					
400	OKBK	60515	3084	19W-3S	D6
400	OKBK	60523	3084	19W-3S	D6
400	YkTp	60515	3084	19W-3S	D6
6200	BRWN	60402	3089	8W-3S	A5
6200	CCRO	60402	3089	7W-3S	B5
6200	CCRO	60804	3089	7W-3S	B5
6800	BRWN	60402	3088	8W-3S	E5
E 37th St					
10	CHCG	60609	3092	0E-3S	C5
10	CHCG	60653	3092	0E-3S	C5
10	CRTE	60417	3596	0W-28S	B6
10	STGR	60475	3596	0W-28S	B6
W 37th St					
10	STGR	60475	3596	1W-28S	A6
800	CHCG	60609	3092	0W-3S	A5
900	CHCG	60609	3091	1W-3S	E5
5200	CCRO	60804	3089	7W-3S	B5
5200	SKNY	60804	3089	6W-3S	D5
6100	BRWN	60402	3089	7W-3S	B5
6100	CCRO	60402	3089	7W-3S	B5
38th Av					
100	SCRL	60174	2965	33W-3N	B6
10700	PTPR	53158	2362		E1
N 38th Av					
1700	SNPK	60165	3029	12W-1N	B1
38th Pl					
7200	BRWN	60402	3088	9W-3S	D6
7200	LYNS	60402	3088	9W-3S	D6
7200	LYNS	60534	3088	9W-3S	D6
E 38th Pl					
800	CHCG	60653	3092	1E-3S	E5
W 38th Pl					
200	CHCG	60609	3092	0W-3S	B5
800	CHCG	60609	3091	1W-3S	E5
2700	CHCG	60632	3091	3W-3S	A5
2800	CHCG	60632	3090	4W-3S	E5
38th St					
400	OKBK	60523	3084	19W-3S	D6
400	YkTp	60515	3084	19W-3S	D6
400	YkTp	60523	3084	19W-3S	D6
2900	OKBK	60515	3084	18W-3S	E6
6200	BRWN	60402	3089	8W-3S	A6
6200	CCRO	60402	3089	7W-3S	B5
6200	CCRO	60804	3089	7W-3S	B6
6800	BRWN	60402	3088	8W-3S	E6
7100	LYNS	60402	3088	8W-3S	E6
7100	LYNS	60534	3088	8W-3S	E6
E 38th St					
10	CHCG	60609	3092	0E-3S	C5
900	CHCG	60653	3092	1E-3S	E5
W 38th St					
10	CHCG	60609	3092	0W-3S	C5
900	CHCG	60609	3091	1W-3S	E5
2400	CHCG	60632	3091	3W-3S	A5
2900	CHCG	60632	3090	4W-3S	C5
5200	CCRO	60804	3089	6W-3S	D6
5200	SKNY	60804	3089	6W-3S	D5
6100	BRWN	60402	3089	7W-3S	B6
6100	CCRO	60402	3089	7W-3S	B6
39th Av					
10400	PTPR	53158	2362		D1
12600	BtnT	53158	2362		E4
12600	BtnT	60096	2362		E4
12600	BtnT	60099	2362		E4
39th Av CO-EZ					
10400	PTPR	53158	2362		D1
12600	BtnT	53158	2362		E4
12600	BtnT	60096	2362		E4
12600	BtnT	60099	2362		E4
N 39th Av					
1500	MLPK	60160	3029	12W-1N	A2
1500	SNPK	60160	3029	12W-1N	A2
1500	SNPK	60165	3029	12W-1N	A2
W 39th Pl					
2500	CHCG	60632	3091	3W-4S	A6
2800	CHCG	60632	3090	3W-4S	E6
39th St					
10	DGvT	60515	3084	18W-3S	E6
10	DGvT	60559	3085	18W-4S	A6
10	DRGV	60515	3084	19W-3S	C6
10	DRGV	60515	3085	18W-3S	A6
39th St					
10	LGNG	60525	3087	13W-3S	A5
10	LGPK	60525	3087	13W-3S	A5
10	WNSP	60525	3087	13W-3S	A5
10	WNSP	60558	3086	13W-3S	E6
10	WNSP	60558	3087	13W-3S	A5
10	WTMT	60559	3085	18W-4S	A6
10	YkTp	60515	3084	18W-3S	E6
10	YkTp	60515	3085	18W-3S	A6
10	YkTp	60559	3085	18W-3S	A6
100	MltT	60563	3082	25W-3S	B6
7300	LYNS	60534	3088	9W-4S	D6
7300	LYNS	60546	3088	9W-4S	D6
7300	RVSD	60546	3088	9W-4S	D6
W 39th St					
100	DGvT	60559	3085	18W-4S	A6
100	YkTp	60559	3085	18W-3S	A6
300	DRGV	60515	3085	18W-3S	A6
300	YkTp	60515	3085	18W-3S	A6
N 40th Av					
1500	MLPK	60160	3029	12W-1N	A2
1500	SNPK	60160	3029	12W-1N	A2
1500	SNPK	60165	3029	12W-1N	A1
40th Ct					
18300	CCHL	60478	3426	5W-22S	D7
18300	HLCT	60429	3426	5W-22S	D7
40th Pl					
300	DRGV	60515	3084	18W-4S	E7
7000	SKNY	60402	3088	8W-4S	E6
7100	LYNS	60402	3088	8W-4S	E6
7100	LYNS	60534	3088	8W-4S	E6
E 40th Pl					
-	CHCG	60653	3092	1E-4S	E6
W 40th Pl					
300	CHCG	60609	3092	0W-4S	A6
2800	CHCG	60632	3090	3W-4S	E6
2800	CHCG	60632	3091	3W-4S	A6
40th St					
10	LGNG	60525	3087	13W-3S	A6
10	WNSP	60525	3087	13W-3S	A6
10	WNSP	60558	3086	13W-4S	E6
10	WNSP	60558	3087	13W-3S	A6
400	DRGV	60515	3084	19W-4S	D7
6400	SKNY	60402	3089	8W-4S	A6
6800	SKNY	60402	3088	8W-4S	E6
7200	LYNS	60402	3088	9W-4S	D6
7200	LYNS	60534	3088	9W-4S	D6
8700	BKFD	60513	3088	10W-4S	A6
8700	BKFD	60534	3088	10W-4S	A6
E 40th St					
10	CHCG	60609	3092	0E-4S	C6
400	CHCG	60653	3092	0E-4S	D6
W 40th St					
10	CHCG	60609	3092	0W-4S	C6
10	CHCG	60653	3092	0W-4S	C6
10	DGvT	60559	3085	18W-4S	A7
10	WTMT	60559	3085	18W-4S	A7
300	DRGV	60515	3085	18W-4S	A7
2400	CHCG	60609	3091	3W-4S	A6
2400	CHCG	60632	3091	3W-4S	A6
2800	CHCG	60632	3090	3W-4S	E6
41st Av					
10700	PTPR	53158	2362		D1
41st Ct					
7800	LYNS	60534	3088	9W-4S	C7
41st Pl					
7600	LYNS	60534	3088	9W-4S	C6
E 41st Pl					
1000	CHCG	60653	3092	1E-4S	E6
1100	CHCG	60653	3093	1E-4S	A6
W 41st Pl					
3000	CHCG	60632	3090	3W-4S	E6
41st St					
-	DGvT	60559	3085	18W-4S	A7
10	DRGV	60515	3085	18W-4S	A7
10	LGNG	60525	3087	13W-4S	A7
10	WNSP	60525	3087	13W-4S	A7
10	WNSP	60558	3086	13W-4S	E7
10	WNSP	60558	3087	13W-4S	A7
800	DRGV	60515	3084	19W-4S	C7
6300	SKNY	60402	3089	8W-4S	A6
6800	SKNY	60402	3088	8W-4S	E6
7100	LYNS	60402	3088	8W-4S	E6
7100	LYNS	60534	3088	8W-4S	E6
E 41st St					
10	CHCG	60609	3092	0E-4S	C6
800	CHCG	60653	3092	1E-4S	E6
W 41st St					
10	DGvT	60559	3085	18W-4S	A7
10	WTMT	60559	3085	18W-4S	A7
300	DRGV	60515	3085	18W-4S	A7
600	CHCG	60609	3092	0W-4S	A6
2200	CHCG	60609	3091	2W-4S	B6
2700	CHCG	60632	3091	3W-4S	A6
3000	CHCG	60632	3090	3W-4S	E6
4800	CHCG	60804	3089	6W-4S	E7
4800	CHCG	60804	3090	5W-4S	A6
4800	SKNY	60804	3089	6W-4S	E7
4900	FTVW	60402	3089	6W-4S	E7
42nd Av					
11000	PTPR	53158	2362		D2
42nd Ct					
1400	SNPK	60165	3029	13W-1N	A2
8000	LYNS	60534	3088	10W-4S	B7
42nd Pl					
7800	LYNS	60534	3088	9W-4S	C7
E 42nd Pl					
800	CHCG	60653	3092	1E-4S	E6
1100	CHCG	60653	3093	1E-4S	A6
W 42nd Pl					
300	CHCG	60609	3092	0W-4S	B6
2300	CHCG	60609	3091	2W-4S	B6
3100	CHCG	60632	3090	3W-4S	E6
42nd St					
10	LGNG	60525	3087	13W-3S	A6
10	WNSP	60525	3087	13W-3S	A6
10	WNSP	60558	3086	13W-4S	E7
10	WNSP	60558	3087	13W-3S	A6
6400	SKNY	60402	3089	8W-4S	A7
6800	SKNY	60402	3088	8W-4S	E7
8600	LYNS	60534	3088	10W-4S	A7
8700	BKFD	60513	3088	10W-4S	A7
8700	BKFD	60534	3088	10W-4S	A7
E 42nd St					
10	CHCG	60609	3092	0E-4S	C6
10	CHCG	60653	3092	0E-4S	C6
W 42nd St					
300	CHCG	60609	3092	0W-4S	B6
1600	CHCG	60609	3091	2W-4S	D6
2400	CHCG	60632	3091	3W-4S	A6
3000	CHCG	60632	3090	3W-4S	E6
43rd Av					
-	SNPK	60160	3029	13W-1N	A2
200	NHLK	60164	3029	13W-1N	A2
200	NHLK	60165	3029	13W-1N	A2
200	SNPK	60165	3029	13W-1N	A2
43rd Av					
1400	MLPK	60160	3029	13W-1N	A2
1400	MLPK	60165	3029	13W-1N	A2
1800	MLPK	60164	3029	13W-1N	A1
1800	SNPK	60164	3029	13W-1N	A1
10700	PTPR	53158	2362		D1
43rd Ct					
1400	MLPK	60160	3029	13W-1N	A2
1400	MLPK	60165	3029	13W-1N	A2
1400	SNPK	60165	3029	13W-1N	A2
43rd Pl					
8200	LYNS	60534	3088	10W-4S	B7
W 43rd Pl					
700	CHCG	60609	3092	0W-4S	A7
43rd St					
400	WNSP	60558	3086	13W-4S	E7
6400	SKNY	60402	3089	8W-4S	A7
6400	StkT	60402	3089	8W-4S	A7
6800	SKNY	60402	3088	8W-4S	E7
7100	SKNY	60534	3088	8W-4S	E7
7800	LYNS	60534	3088	9W-4S	C7
8700	BKFD	60513	3088	10W-4S	A7
8700	BKFD	60534	3088	10W-4S	A7
E 43rd St					
10	CHCG	60609	3092	0E-4S	C6
10	CHCG	60653	3092	0E-4S	D6
1100	CHCG	60653	3093	1E-4S	A6
W 43rd St					
-	CHCG	60632	3091	2W-4S	B7
10	CHCG	60609	3092	0W-4S	B6
10	CHCG	60653	3092	0W-4S	B6
1000	CHCG	60609	3091	2W-4S	C7
3200	CHCG	60632	3090	4W-4S	D7
4700	CHCG	60638	3090	5W-4S	A7
4800	CHCG	60638	3089	6W-4S	E7
44th Av					
200	NHLK	60165	3029	13W-1N	A1
1400	MLPK	60160	3029	13W-1N	A2
1400	MLPK	60165	3029	13W-1N	A2
1500	NHLK	60164	3029	13W-1N	A2
1500	SNPK	60165	3029	13W-1N	A2
11000	PTPR	53158	2362		D1
S 44th Av					
300	NHLK	60164	3029	13W-1N	A2
300	NHLK	60165	3029	13W-1N	A2
300	SNPK	60165	3029	13W-1N	A2
44th Ct					
1400	MLPK	60160	3029	13W-1N	A2
1400	MLPK	60165	3029	13W-1N	A2
1400	SNPK	60165	3029	13W-1N	A2
8000	LYNS	60534	3088	10W-4S	B7
S 44th Ct					
12300	ALSP	60803	3276	5W-14S	B6
44th Pl					
8500	BKFD	60534	3088	10W-4S	A7
8500	LYNS	60534	3088	10W-4S	A7
8800	BKFD	60513	3087	11W-4S	E7
8800	BKFD	60513	3088	10W-4S	A7
E 44th Pl					
500	CHCG	60653	3092	0E-4S	D7
1200	CHCG	60653	3093	1E-4S	A7
S 44th Pl					
-	ALSP	60655	3276	5W-13S	B4
-	ALSP	60803	3276	5W-13S	B4
-	CHCG	60655	3276	5W-13S	B4
W 44th Pl					
200	CHCG	60609	3092	0W-4S	B7
4100	CHCG	60632	3090	5W-4S	B7
4800	CHCG	60638	3089	6W-4S	E7
44th St					
6800	SKNY	60402	3088	8W-4S	E7
6800	SKNY	60402	3089	8W-4S	A7
7100	SKNY	60534	3088	8W-4S	E7
8000	LYNS	60534	3088	10W-4S	B7
8700	BKFD	60513	3088	10W-4S	A7
8700	BKFD	60534	3088	10W-4S	A7
E 44th St					
10	CHCG	60609	3092	0E-4S	C7
10	CHCG	60653	3092	0E-4S	D7
1100	CHCG	60653	3093	1E-4S	A7
W 44th St					
400	CHCG	60609	3092	0W-4S	A7
1200	CHCG	60609	3091	1W-4S	D7
2400	CHCG	60632	3091	3W-4S	A7
4300	CHCG	60632	3090	5W-4S	B7
4800	CHCG	60638	3089	6W-4S	E7
4800	CHCG	60638	3090	6W-4S	A7
5100	FTVW	60638	3089	6W-4S	E7
45th Av					
10	LNSG	60438	3510		C2
10	MNSR	46321	3510		D2
200	NHLK	60164	3029	13W-1N	A2
400	MLPK	60164	3029	13W-1N	A2
1400	MLPK	60160	3029	13W-1N	A2
1400	MLPK	60165	3029	13W-1N	A2
11600	PTPR	53158	2362		D3
S 45th Av					
12200	ALSP	60803	3276	5W-14S	B6
45th Ct					
8000	LYNS	60534	3088	10W-4S	B7
45th Pl					
8200	LYNS	60534	3148	10W-4S	B1
8500	LYNS	60534	3088	10W-4S	A7
8700	BKFD	60513	3148	10W-4S	A1
8700	LYNS	60513	3148	10W-4S	A1
8800	BKFD	60513	3147	11W-5S	E1
E 45th Pl					
400	CHCG	60653	3092	0E-4S	D7
N 45th Pl					
1400	MLPK	60160	3029	13W-1N	A2
W 45th Pl					
200	CHCG	60609	3092	0W-4S	B7
2300	CHCG	60609	3091	2W-4S	B7
2400	CHCG	60632	3091	3W-4S	A7
3800	CHCG	60632	3090	4W-4S	C7
45th St					
10	LGNG	60525	3147	13W-4S	A1
10	WNSP	60525	3147	13W-4S	A1
10	WNSP	60558	3146	13W-4S	E1
10	WNSP	60558	3147	13W-4S	A1
800	MNSR	46321	3510		E2
6800	FTVW	60402	3088	8W-4S	E7
6800	FTVW	60402	3089	8W-4S	A7
6800	SKNY	60402	3088	8W-4S	E7
6800	SKNY	60402	3089	8W-4S	A7
7100	FTVW	60534	3088	8W-4S	E7
7100	SKNY	60534	3088	8W-4S	E7
8000	LYNS	60534	3088	10W-4S	B7
8700	BKFD	60513	3088	10W-4S	A7
8700	LYNS	60513	3088	10W-4S	A7
E 45th St					
10	CHCG	60609	3092	0E-4S	C7
200	CHCG	60653	3092	0E-4S	C7
1100	CHCG	60653	3093	1E-4S	A7
W 45th St					
200	CHCG	60609	3092	0W-4S	B7
W 45th St					
800	CHCG	60609	3091	1W-4S	E7
2400	CHCG	60632	3091	3W-4S	A7
2800	CHCG	60632	3090	3W-4S	E7
4700	CHCG	60638	3090	5W-4S	A7
4800	CHCG	60638	3089	6W-4S	E7
5100	FTVW	60638	3089	6W-4S	E7
46th Av					
10	BLWD	60104	3029	13W-0N	A4
200	MLPK	60160	3029	13W-1N	A1
200	MLPK	60164	3029	13W-1N	A1
200	NHLK	60164	3029	13W-1N	A1
300	NHLK	60160	3029	13W-1N	A1
500	BLWD	60162	3029	13W-0N	A5
500	HLSD	60104	3029	13W-0N	A5
500	HLSD	60162	3029	13W-0N	A5
N 46th Av					
1400	MLPK	60160	3029	13W-1N	A2
S 46th Ct					
1600	CCRO	60804	3090	5W-1S	A1
E 46th Pl					
400	CHCG	60653	3092	0E-4S	D7
W 46th Pl					
100	CHCG	60609	3092	0W-4S	C7
2400	CHCG	60609	3091	3W-4S	A7
2400	CHCG	60632	3091	3W-4S	A7
3800	CHCG	60632	3150	4W-5S	D1
46th St					
-	NPVL	60563	3141	27W-4S	C1
10	LGNG	60525	3147	13W-4S	A1
10	WNSP	60525	3147	13W-4S	A1
10	WNSP	60558	3146	13W-4S	E1
10	WNSP	60558	3147	13W-4S	A1
400	MLPK	60160	3029	13W-1N	A2
400	MLPK	60164	3029	13W-1N	A2
400	NHLK	60160	3029	13W-1N	A2
400	NHLK	60164	3029	13W-1N	A2
6800	FTVW	60402	3148	8W-4S	E1
6800	FTVW	60402	3149	8W-4S	A1
7100	FTVW	60534	3148	8W-4S	E1
7600	LYNS	60534	3148	10W-4S	B1
E 46th St					
10	CHCG	60609	3092	0E-4S	C7
900	CHCG	60653	3092	1E-4S	E7
1200	CHCG	60653	3093	1E-4S	A7
W 46th St					
200	CHCG	60609	3092	0W-4S	B7
1200	CHCG	60609	3091	1W-4S	E7
2400	CHCG	60632	3091	3W-4S	A7
2800	CHCG	60632	3090	4W-4S	D7
4700	CHCG	60638	3090	5W-4S	A7
4800	CHCG	60638	3089	6W-4S	E7
5100	FTVW	60638	3089	6W-4S	E7
47th Av					
-	BKLY	60163	3028	14W-1N	C2
-	BKLY	60164	3028	14W-1N	C2
-	NHLK	60164	3028	14W-1N	C2
10	BLWD	60104	3028	13W-0N	E4
10700	PTPR	53158	2362		C2
12200	BtnT	53158	2362		D4
12200	BtnT	60099	2362		D4
N 47th Av					
1400	MLPK	60160	3028	13W-1N	E2
S 47th Av					
1200	CCRO	60804	3032	5W-1S	A7
1200	CHCG	60644	3032	5W-1S	A7
1200	CHCG	60804	3032	5W-1S	A7
1900	CCRO	60804	3090	5W-1S	A1
S 47th Ct					
1600	CCRO	60804	3090	5W-1S	A1
E 47th Pl					
800	CHCG	60615	3152	0E-5S	E1
1300	CHCG	60615	3153	1E-5S	A1
W 47th Pl					
600	CHCG	60609	3152	1W-5S	A1
1000	CHCG	60609	3151	1W-5S	E1
2400	CHCG	60632	3151	3W-5S	B1
3200	CHCG	60632	3150	4W-5S	D1
47th St					
10	WNSP	60525	3147	13W-4S	A1
10	WNSP	60558	3146	14W-4S	D1
10	WNSP	60558	3147	13W-4S	A1
7200	FTVW	60402	3148	9W-4S	E1
7200	FTVW	60534	3148	9W-4S	E1
7200	LYNS	60534	3148	10W-4S	A1
7400	MCCK	60534	3148	10W-4S	A1
8000	MCCK	60525	3148	10W-4S	B1
8700	BKFD	60513	3148	10W-4S	A1
8700	BKFD	60534	3148	10W-4S	A1
8700	MCCK	60513	3148	10W-4S	A1
8800	BKFD	60513	3147	11W-5S	D1
8800	MCCK	60513	3147	11W-5S	D1
8800	MCCK	60525	3147	11W-5S	D1
9200	BKFD	60525	3147	11W-4S	D1
9500	LGNG	60513	3147	11W-4S	D1
9500	LGNG	60525	3147	11W-4S	D1
E 47th St					
10	CHCG	60609	3092	0E-4S	C7
10	CHCG	60615	3092	0E-4S	C7
10	CHCG	60653	3092	0E-4S	C7
10	LGNG	60525	3147	12W-4S	C1
700	BKFD	60513	3147	12W-4S	C1
700	BKFD	60525	3147	12W-4S	C1
700	LGNG	60513	3147	12W-4S	C1
700	MCCK	60525	3147	12W-4S	C1
1100	CHCG	60615	3093	1E-5S	A7
1100	CHCG	60653	3093	1E-5S	A7
W 47th St					
10	CHCG	60609	3092	0W-4S	B7
10	CHCG	60615	3092	0W-4S	C7
10	CHCG	60653	3092	0W-4S	C7
10	LGNG	60525	3147	13W-4S	A1
500	CHCG	60609	3152	0W-5S	A1
800	CHCG	60609	3151	1W-5S	D1
1400	WNSP	60525	3147	13W-4S	A1
1400	WNSP	60558	3147	13W-4S	A1
2400	CHCG	60632	3151	3W-4S	B1
2900	CHCG	60632	3150	5W-4S	B1
4700	CHCG	60638	3150	5W-4S	A1
4800	CHCG	60638	3149	6W-4S	D1
5100	FTVW	60638	3149	6W-4S	E1
5300	StkT	60638	3149	6W-4S	E1
48th Av					
10	BLWD	60104	3028	13W-0N	E4
10600	PTPR	53158	2362		C1
S 48th Ct					
1200	CCRO	60644	3031	6W-1S	E7
1200	CCRO	60804	3031	6W-1S	E7
1200	CHCG	60644	3031	6W-1S	E7
1500	CCRO	60804	3089	6W-1S	E1
8900	OKLN	60453	3212	6W-10S	A4
E 48th Pl					
400	CHCG	60615	3152	0E-5S	D1
W 48th Pl					
600	CHCG	60609	3152	0W-5S	A1
2200	CHCG	60609	3151	2W-5S	B1
W 48th Pl					
2800	CHCG	60632	3151	3W-5S	A1
3200	CHCG	60632	3150	4W-5S	D1
48th St					
-	LGNG	60525	3147	13W-5S	A1
-	WNSP	60525	3147	13W-5S	A1
-	WNSP	60558	3147	13W-5S	A1
500	WNSP	60558	3146	14W-5S	D1
E 48th St					
10	CHCG	60609	3152	0E-5S	C1
10	LGNG	60525	3147	12W-5S	C1
900	CHCG	60615	3152	1E-5S	E1
1100	CHCG	60615	3153	1E-5S	A1
W 48th St					
10	LGNG	60525	3147	12W-5S	B1
100	NPVL	60563	3141	27W-5S	D2
100	NpvT	60563	3141	27W-5S	D2
600	CHCG	60609	3152	0W-5S	A1
700	LynT	60525	3147	12W-5S	B1
1300	WNSP	60558	3146	14W-5S	D1
2300	CHCG	60609	3151	2W-5S	B1
2700	CHCG	60632	3151	3W-5S	A1
3800	CHCG	60632	3150	5W-5S	B1
4700	CHCG	60638	3150	5W-5S	A1
4800	CHCG	60638	3149	6W-5S	E1
5100	StkT	60638	3149	6W-5S	E1
49th Av					
10	BLWD	60104	3028	13W-0N	E4
S 49th Av					
1200	CCRO	60644	3031	6W-1S	E7
1200	CCRO	60804	3031	6W-1S	E7
1200	CHCG	60644	3031	6W-1S	E7
1500	CCRO	60804	3089	6W-2S	E2
8900	OKLN	60453	3212	6W-10S	A5
S 49th Ct					
1200	CCRO	60644	3031	6W-1S	E7
1200	CCRO	60804	3031	6W-1S	E7
1200	CHCG	60644	3031	6W-1S	E7
1500	CCRO	60804	3089	6W-1S	E1
8700	BRBK	60459	3211	6W-10S	E4
8700	OKLN	60453	3211	6W-10S	E4
8700	OKLN	60459	3211	6W-10S	E4
9000	OKLN	60453	3212	6W-10S	A5
49th Ct N					
1400	WNSP	60558	3146	14W-5S	D2
49th Ct S					
1400	WNSP	60558	3146	14W-5S	D2
W 49th Pl					
-	CHCG	60609	3151	3W-5S	B1
-	CHCG	60632	3151	3W-5S	B1
700	CHCG	60609	3152	1W-5S	A1
3000	CHCG	60632	3150	3W-5S	E1
49th St					
100	NpvT	60563	3141	27W-5S	D2
800	WNSP	60558	3146	14W-5S	D2
E 49th St					
10	CHCG	60615	3152	0E-5S	C1
10	LGNG	60525	3147	12W-5S	C1
700	MCCK	60525	3147	12W-5S	C1
1100	CHCG	60615	3153	1E-5S	A1
8400	MCCK	60525	3148	10W-5S	B1
W 49th St					
10	LGNG	60525	3147	12W-5S	B2
600	CHCG	60609	3152	0W-5S	A1
700	LynT	60525	3147	12W-5S	B2
1100	CHCG	60609	3151	2W-5S	B1
3700	CHCG	60632	3150	4W-5S	C1
4700	CHCG	60638	3150	5W-5S	A1
4800	CHCG	60638	3149	6W-5S	D1
5100	StkT	60638	3149	6W-5S	E1
50th Av					
10	BLWD	60104	3028	13W-0N	E3
500	HLSD	60104	3028	13W-0N	E5
500	HLSD	60162	3028	13W-0N	E5
S 50th Av					
1200	CCRO	60644	3031	6W-1S	E7
1200	CCRO	60804	3031	6W-1S	E7
1200	CHCG	60644	3031	6W-1S	E7
1500	CCRO	60804	3089	6W-2S	E2
8700	BRBK	60459	3211	6W-10S	E5
8700	OKLN	60453	3211	6W-10S	E5
8700	OKLN	60459	3211	6W-10S	E5
S 50th Ct					
1200	CCRO	60644	3031	6W-1S	E7
1200	CCRO	60804	3031	6W-1S	E7
1200	CHCG	60644	3031	6W-1S	E7
1500	CCRO	60804	3089	6W-1S	E1
9500	OKLN	60453	3211	6W-11S	E6
50th Pl					
200	WNSP	60558	3146	13W-5S	E2
E 50th Pl					
500	CHCG	60615	3152	0E-5S	D1
1600	CHCG	60615	3153	2E-5S	B1
W 50th Pl					
700	CHCG	60609	3152	0W-5S	A1
900	CHCG	60609	3151	1W-5S	E1
1400	LGNG	60525	3147	13W-5S	A2
1400	WNSP	60525	3147	13W-5S	A2
1400	WNSP	60558	3147	13W-5S	A2
3700	CHCG	60632	3150	4W-5S	C2
50th St					
800	WNSP	60558	3146	14W-5S	D2
E 50th St					
10	LGNG	60525	3147	12W-5S	C2
900	CHCG	60615	3152	1E-5S	E1
1000	MCCK	60525	3147	12W-5S	C2
1600	CHCG	60615	3153	2E-5S	B1
8400	MCCK	60525	3148	10W-5S	B2
W 50th St					
10	LGNG	60525	3147	12W-5S	B2
200	CHCG	60609	3152	0W-5S	B1
700	LynT	60525	3147	12W-5S	B2
900	CHCG	60609	3151	2W-5S	B1
2400	CHCG	60632	3151	3W-5S	A1
4000	CHCG	60632	3150	5W-5S	B1
4700	CHCG	60638	3150	5W-5S	A1
4800	CHCG	60638	3149	6W-5S	E1
5100	StkT	60638	3149	6W-5S	E1
8900	LGNG	60525	3147	11W-5S	E2
8900	MCCK	60525	3148	10W-5S	A2
51st Av					
400	HLSD	60162	3028	13W-0N	E5
S 51st Av					
1200	CCRO	60644	3031	6W-1S	E7
1200	CCRO	60804	3031	6W-1S	E7
1200	CHCG	60644	3031	6W-1S	E7
1500	CCRO	60804	3089	6W-2S	E2
8700	BRBK	60459	3211	6W-10S	E5
8700	OKLN	60453	3211	6W-10S	E5
8700	OKLN	60459	3211	6W-10S	E5
51st Av S					
10	BKLY	60104	3028	13W-0N	E3
10	BKLY	60163	3028	13W-0N	E3
10	BLWD	60104	3028	13W-0N	E3
10	BLWD	60163	3028	13W-0N	E3

Block	City	ZIP	Map#	CGS	Grid
S 51st Ct					
1200	CCRO	60644	3031	6W-1S	E7
1200	CCRO	60804	3031	6W-1S	E7
1200	CHCG	60644	3031	6W-1S	E7
1500	CCRO	60804	3089	6W-1S	E1
10300	OKLN	60453	3275	6W-12S	E1
51st Pl					
100	WNSP	60558	3146	13W-5S	E2
100	WNSP	60558	3147	13W-5S	A2
W 51st Pl					
300	CHCG	60609	3152	0W-5S	B2
900	CHCG	60609	3151	1W-5S	E2
7000	CHCG	60638	3148	8W-5S	E2
51st St					
10	LGNG	60525	3147	13W-5S	A2
10	WNSP	60525	3147	13W-5S	A2
10	WNSP	60558	3147	13W-5S	A2
100	WNSP	60558	3146	14W-5S	D2
E 51st St					
10	CHCG	60609	3152	0E-5S	C1
10	CHCG	60615	3152	0E-5S	D1
10	LGNG	60525	3147	12W-5S	C2
400	CTSD	60525	3147	12W-5S	C2
W 51st St					
10	CHCG	60609	3152	0W-5S	A1
10	CHCG	60615	3152	0W-5S	A1
700	LynT	60525	3147	12W-5S	B2
900	CHCG	60609	3151	2W-5S	B2
1400	LGNG	60525	3147	13W-5S	A2
1400	WNSP	60525	3147	13W-5S	A2
1400	WNSP	60558	3147	13W-5S	A2
2400	CHCG	60632	3151	3W-5S	B2
2900	CHCG	60632	3150	4W-5S	D2
4700	CHCG	60638	3150	5W-5S	A2
4800	CHCG	60638	3149	7W-5S	C2
5100	StkT	60638	3149	6W-5S	E2
6400	FTVW	60638	3149	7W-5S	C2
6800	CHCG	60638	3148	8W-5S	E2
6800	StkT	60638	3148	8W-5S	E2
52nd Av					
10	BKLY	60163	3028	13W-0N	E3
10	BLWD	60104	3028	13W-0N	E3
10	BLWD	60163	3028	13W-0N	E3
500	HLSD	60104	3028	13W-0N	E5
S 52nd Av					
8700	BRBK	60459	3211	6W-10S	E4
8700	OKLN	60453	3211	6W-10S	E4
8700	OKLN	60459	3211	6W-10S	E4
10100	OKLN	60453	3275	6W-11S	E1
S 52nd Ct					
3100	CCRO	60804	3089	6W-3S	D4
9100	OKLN	60453	3211	6W-10S	E5
52nd Pl					
-	LynT	60525	3147	13W-5S	A3
-	WNSP	60525	3147	13W-5S	A3
-	WNSP	60558	3147	13W-5S	A3
300	WNSP	60558	3146	13W-5S	E3
E 52nd Pl					
1500	CHCG	60615	3153	1E-5S	B2
W 52nd Pl					
300	CHCG	60609	3152	0W-5S	B2
1300	LynT	60525	3147	13W-5S	A3
1300	WNSP	60525	3147	13W-5S	A3
1300	WNSP	60558	3147	13W-5S	A3
2000	CHCG	60609	3151	2W-5S	C2
4000	CHCG	60632	3150	5W-5S	B2
52nd St					
800	WNSP	60558	3146	14W-5S	E2
E 52nd St					
10	LGNG	60525	3147	12W-5S	C2
800	CHCG	60615	3152	1E-5S	E2
1300	CHCG	60615	3153	1E-5S	A2
W 52nd St					
10	LGNG	60525	3147	12W-5S	B2
200	CHCG	60609	3152	0W-5S	B2
700	LynT	60525	3147	12W-5S	B2
900	CHCG	60609	3151	2W-5S	C2
2400	CHCG	60632	3151	3W-5S	A2
2800	CHCG	60632	3150	4W-5S	D2
5000	CHCG	60638	3149	8W-5S	B2
6800	CHCG	60638	3148	8W-5S	E2
53rd Av					
400	BLWD	60104	3028	13W-0N	E4
500	HLSD	60104	3028	13W-0N	E5
500	HLSD	60162	3028	13W-0N	E5
S 53rd Av					
2200	CCRO	60804	3089	6W-2S	D2
9100	OKLN	60453	3211	6W-10S	E5
10100	OKLN	60453	3275	6W-11S	E1
S 53rd Ct					
2900	CCRO	60804	3089	6W-2S	D3
8700	BRBK	60459	3211	6W-10S	E4
8700	OKLN	60453	3211	6W-10S	E4
8700	OKLN	60459	3211	6W-10S	E4
W 53rd Pl					
800	CHCG	60609	3152	1W-5S	A2
900	CHCG	60609	3151	1W-5S	E2
1200	LynT	60525	3147	13W-5S	A3
1200	WNSP	60525	3147	13W-5S	A3
1200	WNSP	60558	3147	13W-5S	A3
3000	CHCG	60632	3150	3W-5S	E2
5200	CHCG	60638	3149	6W-5S	D2
53rd St					
10	WNSP	60558	3147	13W-5S	A3
600	WNSP	60558	3146	14W-5S	D3
E 53rd St					
10	CHCG	60609	3152	0E-5S	C2
900	CHCG	60615	3152	1E-5S	E2
1100	CHCG	60615	3153	1E-5S	A2
W 53rd St					
10	CHCG	60609	3152	0W-5S	B2
10	CTSD	60525	3147	12W-5S	B3
10	LGNG	60525	3147	12W-5S	B3
700	LynT	60525	3147	12W-5S	B3
1000	CHCG	60609	3151	1W-5S	E2
2400	CHCG	60632	3151	3W-5S	A2
2900	CHCG	60632	3150	4W-5S	D2
4700	CHCG	60638	3150	5W-5S	A2
5600	CHCG	60638	3149	7W-5S	C2
6800	CHCG	60638	3148	8W-5S	E2
7100	CHCG	60501	3148	8W-5S	E2
7200	SMMT	60501	3148	9W-5S	D2
8400	MCCK	60525	3148	10W-5S	A2
S 54th Av					
1200	CCRO	60644	3031	6W-1S	D7
1200	CCRO	60804	3031	6W-1S	D7
1200	CCRO	60804	3089	6W-2S	D2
1200	CHCG	60644	3031	6W-1S	D7
9100	OKLN	60453	3211	6W-11S	D7
S 54th Ct					
3100	CCRO	60804	3089	6W-3S	D4
9100	OKLN	60453	3211	6W-10S	D5
54th Pl					
-	LynT	60525	3146	13W-5S	E3
-	LynT	60558	3146	13W-5S	E3
-	WNSP	60558	3146	13W-5S	E3
E 54th Pl					
900	CHCG	60615	3152	1E-5S	E2
1400	CHCG	60615	3153	1E-5S	A2
W 54th Pl					
500	CHCG	60609	3152	1W-5S	A2
900	CHCG	60609	3151	1W-5S	E2
1200	LynT	60525	3147	13W-5S	A3
1600	LynT	60525	3146	13W-5S	E3
1700	LynT	60558	3146	13W-5S	E3
1700	WNSP	60558	3146	13W-5S	E3
3000	CHCG	60632	3150	3W-5S	E2
5800	CHCG	60638	3149	7W-5S	C3
54th St					
800	WNSP	60558	3146	14W-5S	D3
E 54th St					
10	CHCG	60609	3152	0E-5S	C2
900	CHCG	60615	3152	1E-5S	E2
1300	CHCG	60615	3153	1E-5S	A2
W 54th St					
10	CHCG	60609	3152	0W-5S	C2
300	CTSD	60525	3147	12W-5S	B3
300	LGNG	60525	3147	12W-5S	B3
1000	CHCG	60609	3151	1W-5S	E2
1300	LynT	60525	3147	13W-5S	A3
1600	LynT	60525	3146	13W-5S	E3
1600	LynT	60558	3146	13W-5S	E3
1600	WNSP	60558	3146	13W-5S	E3
2400	CHCG	60632	3151	3W-5S	A2
2900	CHCG	60632	3150	4W-5S	D2
4600	CHCG	60638	3150	5W-5S	A2
5200	CHCG	60638	3149	6W-5S	D2
6800	CHCG	60638	3148	8W-5S	E3
7100	CHCG	60501	3148	8W-5S	E3
7100	SMMT	60501	3148	8W-5S	E3
S 55th Av					
1600	CCRO	60804	3089	6W-1S	D1
8700	BRBK	60459	3211	6W-10S	D4
8700	OKLN	60453	3211	6W-10S	D4
8700	OKLN	60459	3211	6W-10S	D4
S 55th Ct					
1200	CCRO	60804	3031	6W-1S	D7
1400	CCRO	60804	3089	6W-1S	D1
8700	BRBK	60459	3211	6W-10S	D4
8700	OKLN	60453	3211	6W-10S	D4
8700	OKLN	60459	3211	6W-10S	D4
55th Pl					
100	DRGV	60516	3144	18W-6S	E3
1900	DGvT	60515	3144	20W-6S	A4
1900	LslT	60515	3144	20W-6S	A4
E 55th Pl					
200	CHCG	60637	3152	0E-6S	D3
1300	CHCG	60615	3153	1E-6S	A2
1300	CHCG	60637	3153	1E-6S	A2
W 55th Pl					
10	WTMT	60559	3145	18W-6S	A3
1000	CTSD	60525	3147	13W-6S	A3
1600	LynT	60525	3146	13W-6S	E3
1600	LynT	60525	3147	13W-6S	A3
2000	WNSP	60525	3146	13W-6S	E3
2000	WNSP	60558	3146	13W-6S	E3
3600	CHCG	60629	3150	4W-6S	C3
7300	SMMT	60501	3148	9W-6S	D3
55th St					
-	CNHL	60521	3145	16W-6S	E3
-	DGvT	60521	3145	16W-6S	E3
-	DRGV	60515	3145	18W-5S	A3
-	DRGV	60559	3145	18W-5S	A3
-	HNDL	60521	3145	16W-6S	E3
-	WTMT	60559	3145	18W-5S	A3
100	CNHL	60514	3145	17W-5S	D3
100	DRGV	60515	3144	20W-5S	B3
100	DRGV	60516	3144	20W-5S	B3
100	DRGV	60559	3144	20W-5S	B3
100	WTMT	60559	3144	20W-5S	B3
200	DGvT	60514	3145	17W-5S	D3
800	LynT	60525	3146	14W-5S	D3
800	LynT	60558	3146	14W-5S	D3
800	WNSP	60525	3146	14W-5S	D3
800	WNSP	60558	3146	14W-5S	D3
1100	HNDL	60521	3146	14W-5S	D3
55th St CO-35					
-	CNHL	60521	3145	16W-6S	E3
-	DGvT	60521	3145	16W-6S	E3
-	DRGV	60515	3145	18W-5S	A3
-	DRGV	60559	3145	18W-5S	A3
-	HNDL	60521	3145	16W-6S	E3
-	WTMT	60559	3145	18W-5S	A3
100	CNHL	60514	3145	17W-5S	C3
100	DRGV	60515	3144	20W-5S	B3
100	DRGV	60516	3144	20W-5S	B3
100	DRGV	60559	3144	20W-5S	B3
100	WTMT	60559	3144	20W-5S	B3
200	DGvT	60514	3145	17W-5S	D3
E 55th St					
-	WNSP	60558	3146	15W-5S	B3
10	WTMT	60559	3145	17W-5S	B3
300	CNHL	60514	3145	17W-5S	B3
300	WTMT	60514	3145	17W-5S	B3
400	HNDL	60521	3146	15W-5S	B3
500	BRRG	60521	3146	14W-5S	C3
800	CHCG	60615	3152	1E-6S	E2
800	CHCG	60637	3152	1E-6S	E2
1100	CHCG	60615	3153	1E-5S	A2
1100	CHCG	60637	3153	1E-5S	A2
9000	MCCK	60525	3147	11W-5S	D3
9500	CTSD	60525	3147	11W-5S	E3
E 55th St CO-35					
10	WTMT	60559	3145	17W-5S	B3
300	CNHL	60514	3145	17W-5S	B3
300	WTMT	60514	3145	17W-5S	B3
400	HNDL	60521	3146	15W-5S	C3
W 55th St					
-	CNHL	60514	3145	16W-6S	E3
-	CNHL	60521	3145	16W-6S	E3
-	HNDL	60521	3145	16W-6S	E3
10	CTSD	60525	3147	13W-5S	A3
10	HNDL	60521	3146	15W-6S	A3
10	WTMT	60559	3145	18W-6S	A3
300	DRGV	60515	3145	18W-5S	A3
300	DRGV	60559	3145	18W-5S	A3
300	WTMT	60515	3145	18W-5S	A3
400	LGNG	60525	3147	12W-5S	B3
500	DGvT	60521	3146	16W-5S	E3
800	LynT	60525	3147	13W-5S	A3
1500	LynT	60525	3146	13W-5S	E3
1700	LynT	60558	3146	13W-5S	E3
1700	WNSP	60558	3146	13W-5S	E3
1900	WNSP	60525	3146	13W-5S	E3
2400	CHCG	60609	3151	3W-5S	B3
2400	CHCG	60629	3151	3W-5S	A3
2400	CHCG	60632	3151	3W-5S	A3
2900	CHCG	60629	3150	4W-5S	C3
2900	CHCG	60632	3150	5W-5S	B3
4500	CHCG	60638	3150	5W-5S	B3
4800	CHCG	60638	3149	6W-5S	D3
W 55th St CO-35					
-	CNHL	60514	3145	16W-6S	E3
-	CNHL	60521	3145	16W-6S	E3
10	HNDL	60521	3146	15W-6S	A3
10	WTMT	60559	3145	18W-6S	A3
300	DRGV	60515	3145	18W-5S	A3
300	DRGV	60559	3145	18W-5S	A3
300	WTMT	60515	3145	18W-5S	A3
500	DGvT	60521	3145	16W-5S	E3
500	HNDL	60521	3145	16W-5S	E3
56th Ct					
100	DRGV	60516	3144	18W-6S	E4
S 56th Ct					
1200	CCRO	60644	3031	7W-1S	C7
1200	CCRO	60804	3031	7W-1S	C7
1200	CHCG	60644	3031	7W-1S	C7
1500	CCRO	60804	3089	7W-1S	C1
3800	SKNY	60402	3089	7W-3S	C6
56th Pl					
10	WTMT	60559	3145	17W-6S	B4
600	CNHL	60514	3145	16W-6S	D4
600	DGvT	60514	3145	16W-6S	D4
E 56th Pl					
700	CHCG	60637	3152	0E-6S	E3
W 56th Pl					
10	WTMT	60559	3145	18W-6S	A4
300	CHCG	60621	3152	0W-6S	B3
3600	CHCG	60629	3150	4W-6S	C3
7300	SMMT	60501	3148	9W-6S	D3
56th St					
100	CNHL	60514	3145	16W-6S	D3
100	DRGV	60516	3144	18W-6S	E4
300	DGvT	60514	3145	17W-6S	C4
400	WTMT	60514	3145	17W-6S	C4
400	WTMT	60559	3145	17W-6S	C4
E 56th St					
10	CHCG	60621	3152	0E-6S	C3
10	CHCG	60637	3152	0E-6S	C3
10	WTMT	60559	3145	17W-6S	B4
100	HNDL	60521	3146	15W-6S	B3
300	WTMT	60514	3145	17W-6S	B4
1100	CHCG	60637	3153	1E-6S	A3
9500	CTSD	60525	3147	12W-6S	C3
9500	MCCK	60525	3147	12W-6S	C3
W 56th St					
-	CTSD	60525	3147	12W-6S	C3
10	WTMT	60559	3145	18W-6S	A4
400	CHCG	60621	3152	0W-6S	A3
500	DGvT	60521	3145	16W-6S	E4
500	DGvT	60521	3146	16W-6S	A3
500	HNDL	60521	3146	16W-6S	A3
900	CHCG	60621	3151	1W-6S	D3
1900	LynT	60525	3146	13W-6S	E4
2400	CHCG	60629	3151	3W-6S	A3
2400	CHCG	60636	3151	3W-6S	A3
2900	CHCG	60629	3150	4W-6S	D3
5600	CHCG	60638	3149	7W-6S	D3
7200	CHCG	60501	3148	9W-6S	D3
7200	CHCG	60638	3148	9W-6S	D3
7200	SMMT	60501	3148	9W-6S	D3
S 57th Av					
1200	CCRO	60644	3031	7W-1S	C7
1200	CCRO	60804	3031	7W-1S	C7
1200	CHCG	60644	3031	7W-1S	C7
1500	CCRO	60804	3089	7W-2S	C2
3800	SKNY	60402	3089	7W-3S	C6
S 57th Ct					
1200	CCRO	60644	3031	7W-1S	C7
1200	CCRO	60804	3031	7W-1S	C7
1200	CHCG	60644	3031	7W-1S	C7
1500	CCRO	60804	3089	7W-1S	C1
3800	SKNY	60402	3089	7W-3S	C6
W 57th Pl					
10	CHCG	60621	3152	0W-6S	C3
10	CHCG	60637	3152	0W-6S	C3
3500	CHCG	60629	3150	4W-6S	D3
5700	CHCG	60638	3149	7W-6S	C3
7200	CHCG	60501	3148	9W-6S	D3
7200	CHCG	60638	3148	9W-6S	D3
7200	SMMT	60501	3148	9W-6S	D3
57th St					
100	CNHL	60514	3145	16W-6S	D4
300	DGvT	60514	3145	17W-6S	C4
400	DRGV	60516	3144	19W-6S	D4
400	WTMT	60559	3144	19W-6S	D4
E 57th St					
10	CHCG	60621	3152	0E-6S	C3
10	HNDL	60521	3146	15W-6S	B4
200	WTMT	60559	3145	17W-6S	B4
700	CHCG	60637	3152	1E-6S	E3
1100	CHCG	60637	3153	1E-6S	A3
9600	CTSD	60525	3147	12W-6S	C4
9600	MCCK	60525	3147	12W-6S	C4
W 57th St					
-	LynT	60525	3146	13W-6S	E4
-	LynT	60525	3147	13W-6S	A4
10	CHCG	60621	3152	0W-6S	A3
10	CHCG	60637	3152	0W-6S	C3
10	CTSD	60525	3147	12W-6S	B4
10	HNDL	60521	3146	15W-6S	A4
10	WTMT	60559	3145	18W-6S	A4
300	DGvT	60521	3146	16W-6S	A4
900	CHCG	60621	3151	1W-6S	D3
1100	CHCG	60636	3151	2W-6S	C3
2300	CHCG	60629	3151	3W-6S	A3
2900	CHCG	60629	3150	3W-6S	E3
5600	CHCG	60638	3149	7W-6S	D3
7200	CHCG	60501	3148	9W-6S	D3
7200	CHCG	60638	3148	9W-6S	D3
7200	SMMT	60501	3148	9W-6S	D3
S 58th Av					
1200	CCRO	60644	3031	7W-1S	C7
1200	CCRO	60804	3031	7W-1S	C7
1200	CHCG	60644	3031	7W-1S	C7
1500	CCRO	60804	3089	7W-2S	C3
3800	SKNY	60402	3089	7W-3S	C6
S 58th Ct					
1200	CCRO	60644	3031	7W-1S	C7
1200	CCRO	60804	3031	7W-1S	C7
1200	CHCG	60644	3031	7W-1S	C7
1500	CCRO	60804	3089	7W-2S	C3
3800	SKNY	60402	3089	7W-3S	C6
58th Pl					
100	DGvT	60514	3145	16W-6S	D4
100	WLBK	60514	3145	16W-6S	D4
400	DGvT	60521	3146	15W-6S	A4
400	HNDL	60521	3146	15W-6S	A4
E 58th Pl					
200	WTMT	60559	3145	17W-6S	B4
W 58th Pl					
500	DGvT	60521	3145	16W-6S	E4
500	DGvT	60521	3146	16W-6S	A4
1800	LynT	60525	3146	13W-6S	E4
3500	CHCG	60629	3150	4W-6S	D4
7200	CHCG	60501	3148	9W-6S	D4
7200	CHCG	60638	3148	9W-6S	D4
7200	SMMT	60501	3148	9W-6S	D4
58th St					
200	CNHL	60514	3145	16W-6S	D4
200	WLBK	60514	3145	16W-6S	D4
500	DGvT	60514	3145	16W-6S	D4
E 58th St					
10	CHCG	60621	3152	0E-6S	C3
10	HNDL	60521	3146	15W-6S	B4
400	CNHL	60514	3145	17W-6S	C4
400	DGvT	60514	3145	17W-6S	C4
400	WTMT	60559	3145	17W-6S	C4
800	CHCG	60637	3152	1E-6S	E3
1000	CHCG	60637	3153	1E-6S	A3
W 58th St					
10	WTMT	60559	3145	18W-6S	B4
400	CHCG	60621	3152	0W-6S	A3
500	DGvT	60521	3145	16W-6S	E4
500	DGvT	60521	3146	16W-6S	A4
500	HNDL	60521	3146	16W-6S	A4
600	WTMT	60559	3144	18W-6S	E4
700	DRGV	60516	3144	18W-6S	E4
700	WTMT	60516	3144	18W-6S	E4
800	LynT	60525	3147	13W-6S	B4
900	CHCG	60621	3151	1W-6S	E3
1100	CHCG	60636	3151	2W-6S	C3
2300	CHCG	60629	3151	3W-6S	A3
2900	CHCG	60629	3150	5W-6S	B3
5600	CHCG	60638	3149	7W-6S	D4
7200	CHCG	60501	3148	9W-6S	D4
7200	CHCG	60638	3148	9W-6S	D4
7200	SMMT	60501	3148	9W-6S	D4
9600	CTSD	60525	3147	12W-6S	C4
9600	MCCK	60525	3147	12W-6S	C4
S 59th Av					
1200	CCRO	60644	3031	7W-1S	C7
1200	CCRO	60804	3031	7W-1S	C7
1200	CHCG	60644	3031	7W-1S	C7
1500	CCRO	60804	3089	7W-2S	C2
3800	SKNY	60402	3089	7W-3S	C6
S 59th Ct					
1200	CCRO	60644	3031	7W-1S	C7
1200	CCRO	60804	3031	7W-1S	C7
1200	CHCG	60644	3031	7W-1S	C7
3200	CCRO	60804	3089	7W-3S	C5
3800	SKNY	60402	3089	7W-3S	C6
59th Pl					
900	DRGV	60516	3144	19W-6S	C4
1200	LynT	60525	3147	13W-6S	A4
1500	LynT	60525	3146	13W-6S	E4
W 59th Pl					
200	CHCG	60621	3152	0W-6S	B4
3300	CHCG	60629	3150	4W-6S	D4
7400	SMMT	60501	3148	9W-6S	D4
59th St					
10	WLBK	60514	3145	17W-6S	C4
10	WLBK	60527	3145	17W-6S	C4
100	DGvT	60514	3145	16W-6S	D4
100	DRGV	60516	3143	21W-6S	E4
100	LslT	60516	3143	21W-6S	E4
200	WTMT	60516	3144	19W-6S	D4
200	WTMT	60559	3144	18W-6S	E4
300	DRGV	60516	3144	20W-6S	C4
400	DGvT	60559	3145	17W-6S	C4
400	LslT	60532	3143	22W-6S	C5
400	WLBK	60559	3145	17W-6S	C4
400	WTMT	60559	3145	17W-6S	C4
900	LSLE	60532	3143	23W-6S	B5
1600	DGvT	60516	3144	21W-6S	A4
1900	LslT	60516	3144	20W-6S	A4
2400	LslT	60517	3143	21W-6S	D4
2400	WDRG	60517	3143	21W-6S	D4
2500	WDRG	60516	3143	21W-6S	D4
E 59th St					
10	BRRG	60527	3146	15W-6S	B4
10	CHCG	60621	3152	0E-6S	C3
10	WTMT	60559	3145	17W-6S	B4
300	BRRG	60521	3146	15W-6S	B4
300	HNDL	60521	3146	15W-6S	B4
400	DGvT	60559	3145	17W-6S	B4
400	WLBK	60527	3145	17W-6S	B4
400	WLBK	60559	3145	17W-6S	B4
800	CHCG	60637	3152	1E-6S	E3
1000	CHCG	60637	3153	1E-6S	A3
W 59th St					
10	BRRG	60521	3146	15W-6S	A4
10	BRRG	60527	3146	15W-6S	A4
10	CHCG	60621	3152	0W-6S	A4
10	CHCG	60637	3152	0W-6S	C3
10	HNDL	60521	3146	15W-6S	A4
10	WTMT	60559	3145	18W-6S	A4
200	WTMT	60516	3145	18W-6S	A4
300	WTMT	60559	3144	18W-6S	E4
400	CTSD	60525	3147	13W-6S	B4
500	WTMT	60516	3144	18W-6S	E4
700	DGvT	60521	3146	15W-6S	A4
700	DGvT	60527	3146	15W-6S	A4
700	LynT	60525	3147	12W-6S	B4
900	CHCG	60621	3151	1W-6S	D4
1100	CHCG	60636	3151	2W-6S	B4
1900	LynT	60525	3146	13W-6S	E4
2000	LynT	60558	3146	13W-6S	E4
2000	WNSP	60525	3146	13W-6S	E4
2000	WNSP	60558	3146	13W-6S	E4
2300	CHCG	60629	3151	3W-6S	A4
2900	CHCG	60629	3150	4W-6S	E4
4600	CHCG	60629	3150	5W-6S	A4
5700	CHCG	60638	3149	8W-6S	A4
7200	CHCG	60501	3148	9W-6S	C4
7200	CHCG	60638	3148	9W-6S	C4
7200	SMMT	60501	3148	9W-6S	C4
60th Ct					
300	WLBK	60527	3145	17W-6S	D5
S 60th Ct					
1200	CCRO	60304	3031	7W-1S	B7
1200	CCRO	60804	3031	7W-1S	B7
1200	OKPK	60304	3031	7W-1S	B7
1500	CCRO	60804	3089	7W-2S	B3
3800	SKNY	60402	3089	7W-3S	B6
60th Pl					
10	CTSD	60525	3147	12W-6S	C4
400	BRRG	60527	3146	15W-6S	A5
800	DRGV	60516	3144	19W-6S	D5
W 60th Pl					
200	CHCG	60621	3152	0W-6S	B4
3300	CHCG	60629	3150	4W-6S	D4
6800	CHCG	60638	3148	8W-6S	E4
6800	CHCG	60638	3149	8W-6S	A4
7100	CHCG	60501	3148	9W-6S	D4
7100	SMMT	60501	3148	9W-6S	D4
60th St					
10	BRRG	60527	3146	15W-6S	B4
10	HNDL	60521	3146	15W-6S	B4
10	WTMT	60516	3144	18W-6S	E5
10	WTMT	60516	3145	18W-6S	A5
10	WTMT	60559	3144	18W-6S	E5
10	WTMT	60559	3145	18W-6S	A5
1100	DRGV	60516	3144	19W-6S	C5
1200	LynT	60525	3147	13W-6S	A4
1500	LynT	60525	3146	13W-6S	E5
2300	DRGV	60516	3143	21W-6S	E5
2300	LslT	60516	3143	21W-6S	E5
E 60th St					
10	CHCG	60621	3152	0E-6S	C4
10	CHCG	60637	3152	0E-6S	C4
10	WTMT	60559	3145	17W-6S	B5
1000	CHCG	60637	3153	1E-6S	A4
W 60th St					
10	CHCG	60621	3152	0W-6S	C4
10	CHCG	60637	3152	0W-6S	C4
10	WTMT	60559	3145	18W-6S	A5
200	WTMT	60516	3145	18W-6S	A5
900	CHCG	60621	3151	1W-6S	D4
1100	CHCG	60636	3151	2W-6S	C4
2400	CHCG	60629	3151	3W-6S	A4
2900	CHCG	60629	3150	5W-6S	B4
5600	CHCG	60638	3149	8W-6S	A4
6900	CHCG	60638	3148	8W-6S	E4
7100	CHCG	60501	3148	8W-6S	E4
7600	SMMT	60501	3148	9W-6S	C4
61st Av					
11100	PTPR	53158	2362		B2
S 61st Av					
1200	CCRO	60304	3031	7W-1S	B7
1200	CCRO	60804	3031	7W-1S	B7
1200	OKPK	60304	3031	7W-1S	B7
1500	CCRO	60804	3089	7W-2S	B2
3800	SKNY	60402	3089	7W-3S	B6
S 61st Ct					
1200	CCRO	60304	3031	7W-1S	B7
1200	CCRO	60804	3031	7W-1S	B7
1200	OKPK	60304	3031	7W-1S	B7
1500	CCRO	60804	3089	7W-2S	B3
3800	SKNY	60402	3089	7W-3S	B6
61st Pl					
300	BRRG	60527	3146	15W-6S	B5
600	CTSD	60525	3147	12W-6S	B5
1400	LynT	60525	3147	13W-6S	A5
E 61st Pl					
1400	CHCG	60637	3153	1E-6S	A4
W 61st Pl					
400	CHCG	60621	3152	0W-6S	A4
3200	CHCG	60629	3150	4W-6S	D4
7200	CHCG	60501	3148	9W-6S	D4
7200	CHCG	60638	3148	9W-6S	D4
7200	SMMT	60501	3148	9W-6S	D4
61st St					
-	BRRG	60527	3146	15W-6S	B5
300	DGvT	60516	3144	20W-6S	B5
300	WLBK	60527	3145	17W-6S	C5
300	WTMT	60527	3145	17W-6S	C5
400	CTSD	60525	3147	13W-6S	B5
400	DGvT	60527	3145	17W-6S	C5
400	DGvT	60559	3145	17W-6S	C5
400	WTMT	60559	3145	17W-6S	C5
500	DRGV	60516	3144	19W-6S	D5
500	LslT	60532	3143	22W-6S	B5
1000	LSLE	60532	3143	22W-6S	B5
1200	LynT	60525	3147	13W-6S	A5
1900	LslT	60516	3144	20W-6S	A5
2100	DRGV	60516	3143	21W-6S	E5
2100	LslT	60516	3143	21W-6S	E5
E 61st St					
10	CHCG	60621	3152	0E-6S	C4
10	CHCG	60637	3152	0E-6S	C4
1000	CHCG	60637	3153	1E-6S	A4
W 61st St					
10	CHCG	60637	3152	0W-6S	C4
10	WTMT	60516	3144	18W-6S	E5
10	WTMT	60516	3145	18W-6S	A5
10	WTMT	60559	3144	18W-6S	E5
10	WTMT	60559	3145	18W-6S	A5
200	CHCG	60621	3152	0W-6S	A4
500	DRGV	60516	3144	18W-6S	E5
900	CHCG	60621	3151	1W-6S	D4
1100	CHCG	60636	3151	2W-6S	C4
2400	CHCG	60629	3151	3W-6S	A4
2900	CHCG	60629	3150	5W-6S	B4
4700	CHCG	60638	3150	5W-6S	A4
5600	CHCG	60638	3149	8W-6S	A4
7100	CHCG	60501	3148	9W-6S	D4
7100	CHCG	60638	3148	9W-6S	D4
7100	SMMT	60501	3148	9W-6S	D4
62nd Av					
17600	BmnT	60477	3425	7W-21S	C6
17600	TYPK	60477	3425	7W-21S	C6
62nd Ct					
1000	DRGV	60516	3144	19W-6S	C5
62nd Pl					
1000	DRGV	60516	3144	19W-6S	C5
1200	LynT	60525	3147	13W-6S	A5
E 62nd Pl					
1400	CHCG	60637	3153	1E-6S	A4
W 62nd Pl					
-	CHCG	60638	3148	8W-6S	E5
3200	CHCG	60629	3150	4W-6S	D5
7200	SMMT	60501	3148	9W-6S	C5
62nd St					
200	BRRG	60527	3146	15W-6S	B5
500	LslT	60532	3143	22W-6S	C5
600	DRGV	60516	3144	19W-6S	C5
800	CTSD	60525	3147	13W-6S	A5
1200	LynT	60525	3147	13W-6S	A5
2400	DRGV	60516	3143	21W-6S	E5
10900	LynT	60525	3146	13W-6S	E5
E 62nd St					
400	CHCG	60637	3152	0E-6S	D4
1100	CHCG	60637	3153	1E-6S	A4
W 62nd St					
400	CHCG	60621	3152	0W-6S	A4
900	CHCG	60621	3151	1W-6S	E4
1100	CHCG	60636	3151	1W-6S	E4
2300	CHCG	60629	3151	3W-6S	A4
2900	CHCG	60629	3150	3W-6S	E4
5600	CHCG	60638	3149	7W-6S	C5
6800	CHCG	60638	3148	8W-6S	E5
7100	CHCG	60501	3148	9W-6S	D5
7100	SMMT	60501	3148	9W-6S	D5
63rd Av					
11100	PTPR	53158	2362		B1
63rd Ct					
10	WDRG	60517	3143	22W-6S	C5
E 63rd Dr					
-	CHCG	60637	3153	2E-6S	B4
-	CHCG	60649	3153	2E-6S	B4
W 63rd Pkwy					
800	CHCG	60621	3151	1W-6S	E4
800	CHCG	60621	3152	1W-6S	A4
63rd Pl					
900	LynT	60525	3147	13W-7S	A5

STREET Block	City	ZIP	Map#	CGS	Grid
E 63rd Pl					
800	CHCG	60637	3152	1E-7S	E5
1400	CHCG	60637	3153	1E-7S	A5
W 63rd Pl					
-	BDPK	60501	3148	9W-7S	E5
-	BDPK	60638	3148	9W-7S	E5
-	CHCG	60501	3148	9W-7S	E5
400	CHCG	60621	3152	0W-7S	A5
3200	CHCG	60629	3150	4W-7S	D5
5000	CHCG	60638	3149	6W-7S	E5
6800	CHCG	60638	3148	8W-7S	E5
7200	SMMT	60501	3148	9W-7S	E5
63rd St					
-	CTSD	60525	3147	12W-6S	C5
-	HGKN	60525	3147	12W-6S	C5
10	DGvT	60527	3145	16W-6S	E5
10	DGvT	60527	3146	16W-7S	A5
10	WLBK	60527	3145	16W-6S	E5
400	BRRG	60527	3146	15W-6S	A5
400	DGvT	60559	3145	17W-6S	C5
400	WLBK	60527	3146	15W-6S	A5
400	WTMT	60527	3145	17W-6S	C5
400	WTMT	60559	3145	17W-6S	C5
600	LslT	60517	3143	21W-7S	D6
800	DRGV	60516	3144	19W-6S	C5
800	LynT	60525	3147	13W-6S	A5
1400	DGvT	60516	3144	20W-7S	B5
1900	LslT	60516	3144	20W-7S	A5
2100	DRGV	60516	3143	21W-6S	E5
2100	LslT	60516	3143	21W-6S	E5
2200	WDRG	60517	3143	22W-7S	D6
2700	WDRG	60516	3143	21W-7S	E5
10800	IHPK	60525	3147	13W-7S	A5
63rd St CO-38					
-	LslT	60517	3143	21W-6S	E5
10	DGvT	60527	3145	16W-6S	E5
10	DGvT	60527	3146	16W-7S	A5
10	WLBK	60527	3145	16W-6S	E5
10	WLBK	60527	3146	16W-7S	A5
400	DGvT	60559	3145	17W-6S	C5
400	WTMT	60527	3145	17W-6S	C5
400	WTMT	60559	3145	17W-6S	C5
800	DRGV	60516	3144	19W-6S	C5
1400	DGvT	60516	3144	20W-7S	B5
1900	LslT	60516	3144	20W-7S	A5
2100	DRGV	60516	3143	21W-6S	E5
2100	LslT	60516	3143	21W-6S	E5
2200	WDRG	60516	3143	21W-7S	E5
2700	WDRG	60517	3143	21W-7S	E5
E 63rd St					
10	CHCG	60621	3152	0E-7S	C4
10	CHCG	60637	3152	1E-6S	E4
10	WTMT	60527	3145	17W-7S	B5
10	WTMT	60559	3145	17W-7S	B5
1100	CHCG	60637	3153	1E-6S	A4
E 63rd St CO-38					
10	WTMT	60527	3145	17W-7S	B5
10	WTMT	60559	3145	17W-7S	B5
W 63rd St					
10	CHCG	60621	3152	0W-6S	B5
10	CHCG	60637	3152	0W-6S	C4
10	WTMT	60559	3145	18W-6S	A5
400	DGvT	60516	3144	19W-6S	E5
400	DRGV	60516	3144	19W-6S	E5
400	WTMT	60516	3144	19W-6S	E5
400	WTMT	60559	3144	19W-6S	E5
900	CHCG	60621	3151	2W-6S	D5
1100	CHCG	60636	3151	3W-6S	C5
2300	CHCG	60629	3151	3W-6S	A5
2900	CHCG	60629	3150	4W-6S	C5
4700	CHCG	60638	3150	5W-6S	A5
4900	CHCG	60638	3149	8W-6S	A5
6900	CHCG	60638	3148	8W-6S	E5
7100	CHCG	60501	3148	8W-6S	E5
7200	SMMT	60501	3148	9W-6S	C5
W 63rd St CO-38					
10	WTMT	60559	3145	18W-6S	A5
400	DGvT	60516	3144	19W-6S	E5
400	DRGV	60516	3144	19W-6S	E5
400	WTMT	60516	3144	19W-6S	E5
400	WTMT	60559	3144	19W-6S	D5
64th Av					
-	BtnT	60099	2362		B4
-	PTPR	60099	2362		B4
12700	PTPR	53158	2362		B4
64th Ct					
16300	TYPK	60477	3425	8W-19S	B2
E 64th Pl					
800	CHCG	60637	3152	1E-7S	E5
W 64th Pl					
3200	CHCG	60629	3150	4W-7S	D5
5400	CHCG	60638	3149	7W-7S	B5
6800	CHCG	60638	3148	8W-7S	E5
7200	BDPK	60638	3148	9W-7S	E5
7400	BDPK	60501	3148	9W-7S	D5
7400	SMMT	60501	3148	9W-7S	D5
64th St					
10	DGvT	60527	3146	16W-7S	A5
10	WLBK	60527	3146	16W-7S	A5
200	DRGV	60516	3143	21W-7S	E6
200	DRGV	60517	3143	21W-7S	E6
200	WDRG	60517	3143	21W-7S	E6
500	DGvT	60527	3145	17W-7S	B6
500	WTMT	60527	3145	17W-7S	B6
900	CTSD	60525	3147	13W-7S	A5
900	LynT	60525	3147	13W-7S	A5
E 64th St					
400	CHCG	60637	3152	0E-7S	D5
1100	CHCG	60637	3153	1E-7S	A5
W 64th St					
10	CHCG	60637	3152	0W-7S	C5
10	WTMT	60559	3145	18W-7S	B6
200	CHCG	60621	3152	0W-7S	B5
900	CHCG	60621	3151	1W-7S	D5
2200	CHCG	60636	3151	2W-7S	B5
2400	CHCG	60629	3151	3W-7S	B5
2900	CHCG	60629	3150	4W-7S	D5
4700	CHCG	60638	3150	5W-7S	A5
4900	CHCG	60638	3149	6W-7S	E5
6800	CHCG	60638	3148	8W-7S	E5
7100	BDPK	60638	3148	8W-7S	E5
7400	SMMT	60501	3148	9W-7S	D5
W 64th Lake Dr					
10	WTMT	60559	3145	18W-7S	A6
65th Av					
16300	TYPK	60477	3425	8W-19S	B2
65th Ct					
16300	TYPK	60477	3425	8W-19S	B2
65th Pl					
1500	CTSD	60525	3147	13W-7S	A6
1500	IHPK	60525	3147	13W-7S	A6
1700	IHPK	60525	3146	13W-7S	E6
E 65th Pl					
1400	CHCG	60637	3153	1E-7S	B5
W 65th Pl					
400	CHCG	60621	3152	0W-7S	B5
3200	CHCG	60629	3150	4W-7S	D5
7600	BDPK	60501	3148	9W-7S	C6
65th St					
200	DGvT	60527	3145	17W-7S	C6
200	WLBK	60527	3145	17W-7S	C6
500	DGvT	60516	3144	19W-7S	D6
500	DRGV	60516	3144	19W-7S	D6
500	WTMT	60527	3145	17W-7S	B6
600	WTMT	60559	3145	17W-7S	B6
1500	CTSD	60525	3147	13W-7S	A6
1500	IHPK	60525	3147	13W-7S	A6
1500	LynT	60525	3147	13W-7S	A6
E 65th St					
400	CHCG	60637	3152	0E-7S	D5
1300	CHCG	60637	3153	1E-7S	B5
W 65th St					
10	CHCG	60637	3152	0W-7S	C5
10	WTMT	60559	3145	18W-7S	A6
200	CHCG	60621	3152	0W-7S	B5
400	WTMT	60559	3144	18W-7S	E6
500	DGvT	60516	3144	18W-7S	E6
500	WTMT	60516	3144	18W-7S	E6
900	CHCG	60621	3151	1W-7S	E5
1400	CHCG	60636	3151	2W-7S	B5
2600	CHCG	60629	3151	3W-7S	A5
2900	CHCG	60629	3150	5W-7S	B5
4700	BDPK	60638	3150	5W-7S	A5
4700	CHCG	60638	3150	5W-7S	A5
4900	BDPK	60638	3149	7W-7S	D5
4900	CHCG	60638	3149	7W-7S	D5
6800	BDPK	60638	3148	8W-7S	E5
6800	CHCG	60638	3148	8W-7S	E5
7200	SMMT	60501	3148	9W-7S	E5
7600	BDPK	60501	3148	9W-7S	C5
66th Av					
16300	TYPK	60477	3425	8W-19S	B2
18300	RchT	60477	3425	8W-22S	B7
66th Ct					
14500	BmnT	60452	3347	8W-17S	B5
14600	OKFT	60452	3347	8W-17S	B5
16300	TYPK	60477	3425	8W-19S	B2
18200	RchT	60477	3425	8W-21S	B7
E 66th Pl					
10	CHCG	60621	3152	0E-7S	C5
10	CHCG	60637	3152	0E-7S	C5
1400	CHCG	60637	3153	1E-7S	B5
W 66th Pl					
400	CHCG	60621	3152	0W-7S	B5
3200	CHCG	60629	3150	4W-7S	D6
5200	BDPK	60638	3149	6W-7S	E6
7000	BDPK	60638	3148	8W-7S	E6
7600	BDPK	60501	3148	9W-7S	C6
7800	BDPK	60455	3148	9W-7S	C6
66th St					
400	DRGV	60516	3144	19W-7S	D6
E 66th St					
10	CHCG	60621	3152	0E-7S	C5
400	CHCG	60637	3152	0E-7S	D5
W 66th St					
10	WTMT	60559	3145	18W-7S	A6
100	CHCG	60621	3152	0W-7S	B5
900	CHCG	60621	3151	1W-7S	E5
1400	CHCG	60636	3151	2W-7S	C5
2300	CHCG	60629	3151	3W-7S	A5
2900	CHCG	60629	3150	5W-7S	B5
4700	BDPK	60638	3150	5W-7S	A5
4700	CHCG	60638	3150	5W-7S	A5
4800	BDPK	60638	3149	6W-7S	E6
7200	BDPK	60638	3148	9W-7S	E6
7600	BDPK	60501	3148	9W-7S	C6
67th Av					
17200	TYPK	60477	3425	8W-20S	B4
67th Ct					
400	DRGV	60516	3144	19W-7S	D6
400	DRN	60516	3144	19W-7S	D6
400	DRN	60561	3144	19W-7S	D6
16300	TYPK	60477	3425	8W-19S	A3
67th Pl					
500	WLBK	60527	3145	16W-7S	E6
500	WLBK	60527	3146	16W-7S	A6
1300	DRGV	60516	3144	20W-7S	B7
E 67th Pl					
1400	CHCG	60637	3153	1E-7S	B6
1500	CHCG	60649	3153	1E-7S	B6
W 67th Pl					
2000	CHCG	60636	3151	2W-7S	C6
3600	CHCG	60629	3150	4W-7S	C6
67th St					
10	DRN	60527	3145	17W-7S	C6
10	DRN	60561	3145	17W-7S	C6
10	WLBK	60527	3145	17W-7S	C6
10	WLBK	60561	3145	16W-7S	D6
600	DRGV	60516	3144	19W-7S	D6
8600	HGKN	60525	3147	12W-7S	C6
9200	CTSD	60525	3147	12W-7S	C6
E 67th St					
500	CHCG	60637	3152	1E-7S	E5
500	DRN	60527	3145	17W-7S	B6
500	DRN	60561	3145	17W-7S	B6
600	WTMT	60559	3145	17W-7S	B6
600	WTMT	60561	3145	17W-7S	B6
1100	CHCG	60637	3153	2E-7S	C5
1500	CHCG	60649	3153	2E-7S	C5
W 67th St					
-	DRN	60561	3145	18W-7S	A6
-	WTMT	60561	3145	18W-7S	A6
10	WTMT	60559	3145	18W-7S	A6
4800	BDPK	60638	3150	6W-7S	A6
4800	CHCG	60629	3150	6W-7S	A6
4800	CHCG	60638	3150	6W-7S	A6
4900	BDPK	60638	3149	6W-7S	E6
68th Ct					
17100	TYPK	60477	3425	8W-20S	A4
S 68th Ct					
9400	OKLN	60453	3211	8W-10S	A6
11900	PSHT	60463	3275	8W-14S	A6
68th Pl					
700	WLBK	60527	3145	16W-7S	E7
1300	DRGV	60516	3144	20W-7S	B7
W 68th Pl					
2000	CHCG	60636	3151	2W-7S	C6
3600	CHCG	60629	3150	4W-7S	C6
68th St					
100	DRN	60561	3145	16W-7S	D7
400	DRGV	60516	3144	19W-7S	D7
400	DRN	60516	3144	19W-7S	D7
400	DRN	60561	3144	19W-7S	D7
500	WLBK	60527	3145	16W-7S	E6
500	WLBK	60527	3146	16W-7S	A6
800	WLBK	60561	3145	16W-7S	E6
E 68th St					
500	CHCG	60637	3152	0E-7S	E6
1300	CHCG	60637	3153	1E-7S	A6
2000	CHCG	60649	3153	2E-7S	C6
W 68th St					
10	CHCG	60621	3152	0W-7S	C6
900	CHCG	60621	3151	1W-7S	D6
1100	CHCG	60636	3151	1W-7S	D6
2300	CHCG	60629	3151	3W-7S	A6
3600	CHCG	60629	3150	4W-7S	C6
6600	BDPK	60638	3148	8W-7S	E6
6600	BDPK	60638	3149	8W-7S	A6
69th Av					
17100	TYPK	60477	3425	8W-20S	A5
S 69th Av					
9300	BGVW	60455	3211	8W-10S	A6
9300	OKLN	60453	3211	8W-10S	A6
9300	OKLN	60455	3211	8W-10S	A6
11900	PSHT	60463	3275	8W-14S	A7
S 69th Ct					
9300	BGVW	60455	3211	8W-10S	A6
9300	OKLN	60453	3211	8W-10S	A6
9300	OKLN	60455	3211	8W-10S	A6
11900	PSHT	60463	3275	8W-14S	A6
E 69th Pl					
200	CHCG	60637	3152	0E-7S	C6
1400	CHCG	60637	3153	1E-7S	B6
1500	CHCG	60649	3153	1E-7S	B6
W 69th Pl					
2000	CHCG	60636	3151	2W-7S	C6
4100	CHCG	60629	3150	5W-7S	B6
69th St					
10	DRN	60561	3145	16W-7S	E7
10	WLBK	60527	3145	16W-7S	E7
10	WLBK	60561	3145	16W-7S	E7
1000	DRN	60559	3145	17W-7S	B7
E 69th St					
500	CHCG	60637	3152	0E-7S	E6
1400	CHCG	60637	3153	1E-7S	B6
1500	CHCG	60649	3153	1E-7S	B6
W 69th St					
10	CHCG	60621	3152	0W-7S	B6
10	CHCG	60637	3152	0W-7S	C6
900	CHCG	60621	3151	1W-7S	D6
1100	CHCG	60636	3151	2W-7S	B6
2300	CHCG	60629	3151	2W-7S	B6
3600	CHCG	60629	3150	4W-7S	C6
5800	BDPK	60638	3149	7W-7S	C6
70th Av					
17100	TYPK	60477	3425	8W-20S	A5
S 70th Av					
11900	PSHT	60463	3275	8W-15S	A7
70th Ct					
-	TYPK	60477	3425	8W-21S	A7
S 70th Ct					
11900	PSHT	60463	3274	8W-14S	E6
12900	PSHT	60463	3275	8W-15S	A7
12900	PSHT	60463	3347	8W-15S	A1
13000	WthT	60463	3347	8W-15S	A1
15200	ODPK	60462	3347	8W-18S	A7
15200	OKFT	60462	3347	8W-18S	A7
70th Pl					
11200	IHPK	60525	3146	14W-7S	D7
E 70th Pl					
300	CHCG	60637	3152	0E-7S	D6
2200	CHCG	60649	3153	2E-7S	D6
W 70th Pl					
300	CHCG	60621	3152	0W-7S	B6
2000	CHCG	60636	3151	2W-7S	C7
3600	CHCG	60629	3150	4W-7S	C7
5100	BDPK	60638	3149	6W-7S	D7
70th St					
400	DRN	60561	3145	17W-7S	C7
E 70th St					
10	CHCG	60637	3152	0E-7S	C6
1200	CHCG	60637	3153	1E-7S	A6
2000	CHCG	60649	3153	2E-7S	C6
W 70th St					
100	CHCG	60621	3152	1W-7S	A6
900	CHCG	60621	3151	1W-7S	D6
1100	CHCG	60636	3151	1W-7S	D6
2300	CHCG	60629	3151	3W-7S	A6
4100	CHCG	60629	3150	5W-7S	C6
7900	BGVW	60455	3148	9W-7S	C7
7900	BGVW	60458	3148	9W-7S	C7
71st Av					
17100	TYPK	60477	3425	8W-20S	A5
S 71st Av					
11900	PSHT	60463	3274	8W-14S	E6
12800	PSHT	60463	3346	8W-15S	E1
12900	WthT	60463	3346	8W-15S	E1
71st Ct					
17200	TYPK	60477	3425	8W-20S	A5
S 71st Ct					
10800	WRTH	60482	3274	8W-12S	E2
11900	PSHT	60463	3274	8W-14S	E6
13000	PSHT	60463	3346	8W-15S	E1
13000	WthT	60463	3346	8W-15S	E1
15500	ODPK	60462	3346	8W-18S	E7
15700	ODPK	60462	3424	8W-18S	E1
15800	ODPK	60462	3425	8W-18S	A1
15800	TYPK	60477	3425	8W-18S	A1
71st Pl					
10200	CTSD	60525	3147	12W-8S	B7
E 71st Pl					
1300	CHCG	60619	3153	1E-8S	A7
1900	CHCG	60649	3153	2E-8S	C7
W 71st Pl					
1200	CHCG	60621	3151	1W-8S	E7
1200	CHCG	60636	3151	1W-8S	E7
3400	CHCG	60629	3150	4W-8S	D7
7000	BDPK	60638	3148	8W-8S	E7
7100	BDPK	60455	3148	8W-8S	E7
7100	BGVW	60455	3148	8W-8S	E7
71st St					
10	DGvT	60561	3145	18W-8S	A7
10	DRN	60561	3145	18W-8S	A7
300	LslT	60517	3205	22W-8S	C1
300	LslT	60540	3205	22W-7S	C1
300	WDRG	60517	3205	22W-8S	C1
700	BRRG	60527	3146	16W-7S	A7
700	DGvT	60527	3146	16W-7S	A7
700	WLBK	60527	3146	16W-7S	A7
1400	DRGV	60516	3144	20W-7S	B7
1600	DRN	60561	3144	18W-8S	E7
1800	WDRG	60516	3144	20W-8S	A7
1900	DRN	60516	3144	18W-8S	E7
2000	DRGV	60517	3144	21W-7S	A7
2000	WDRG	60517	3144	21W-7S	A7
2100	WDRG	60517	3143	21W-7S	E7
2900	WDRG	60540	3205	22W-8S	C1
10800	CTSD	60525	3147	13W-7S	A7
11200	IHPK	60525	3146	14W-8S	D7
11200	IHPK	60527	3146	14W-8S	D7
E 71st St					
10	CHCG	60619	3152	0E-7S	C6
10	CHCG	60621	3152	0E-7S	C6
10	CHCG	60637	3152	0E-7S	C6
1000	CHCG	60619	3153	1E-7S	A6
1000	CHCG	60637	3153	1E-7S	A6
2500	CHCG	60649	3153	3E-7S	D6
W 71st St					
10	CHCG	60619	3152	0W-7S	C6
10	CHCG	60621	3152	0W-7S	B7
10	CHCG	60637	3152	0W-7S	C6
900	CHCG	60621	3151	2W-7S	C7
1100	CHCG	60636	3151	1W-7S	E7
2300	CHCG	60629	3151	2W-7S	B7
2900	CHCG	60629	3150	4W-7S	E7
7100	BDPK	60455	3148	8W-7S	E7
7100	BDPK	60638	3148	8W-7S	E7
7100	BGVW	60455	3148	9W-7S	D7
7900	JSTC	60455	3148	9W-7S	C7
8600	BDPK	60458	3148	10W-7S	B7
8600	BDPK	60501	3148	10W-7S	A7
8600	BGVW	60458	3148	10W-7S	A7
8600	BGVW	60501	3148	10W-7S	A7
8600	JSTC	60458	3148	10W-7S	A7
8600	JSTC	60501	3148	10W-7S	A7
71st Ter					
1500	DRGV	60516	3144	20W-7S	B7
72nd Av					
10400	PTPR	53158	2361		E1
72nd Ct					
600	DRGV	60516	3206	19W-8S	D1
700	DRN	60527	3207	16W-8S	E1
700	WLBK	60527	3207	16W-8S	E1
N 72nd Ct					
1600	EDPK	60707	3030	9W-2N	D1
1600	RVFT	60305	3030	9W-2N	D1
1600	RVFT	60707	3030	9W-2N	D1
2400	EDPK	60707	2974	9W-3N	D5
2900	CHCG	60707	2974	9W-3N	D5
S 72nd Ct					
5300	SMMT	60501	3148	9W-6S	E3
12000	PSHT	60463	3274	9W-14S	E6
15200	ODPK	60462	3346	9W-18S	E6
E 72nd Pl					
1300	CHCG	60619	3153	1E-8S	A7
2500	CHCG	60649	3153	3E-8S	D7
W 72nd Pl					
1200	CHCG	60621	3151	1W-8S	D7
1200	CHCG	60636	3151	1W-8S	D7
3400	CHCG	60629	3150	4W-8S	D7
7000	BDPK	60638	3148	8W-8S	E7
7100	BDPK	60455	3148	8W-8S	E7
7100	BGVW	60455	3148	8W-8S	E7
72nd St					
100	BRRG	60527	3146	15W-8S	B7
400	DRN	60561	3145	17W-8S	C7
500	DRGV	60516	3206	19W-8S	D1
700	DGvT	60527	3146	15W-8S	A7
700	WLBK	60527	3146	15W-8S	A7
1900	DRN	60516	3206	18W-8S	E1
1900	DRN	60561	3206	18W-8S	E1
11200	BRRG	60525	3146	14W-8S	D7
11200	IHPK	60525	3146	14W-8S	D7
11200	IHPK	60527	3146	14W-8S	D7
E 72nd St					
10	CHCG	60621	3152	0E-8S	C7
900	CHCG	60619	3152	1E-8S	E7
1000	CHCG	60619	3153	1E-8S	A7
1500	CHCG	60649	3153	2E-8S	B7
W 72nd St					
10	CHCG	60621	3152	0W-8S	B7
900	CHCG	60621	3151	1W-8S	E7
1100	CHCG	60636	3151	2W-8S	C7
2300	CHCG	60629	3151	3W-8S	A7
2900	CHCG	60629	3150	4W-8S	D7
4400	BDPK	60638	3150	5W-8S	A7
4400	CHCG	60638	3150	5W-8S	A7
7000	BDPK	60638	3148	9W-8S	E7
7100	BDPK	60455	3148	9W-8S	E7
7100	BGVW	60455	3148	9W-8S	E7
7900	JSTC	60455	3148	9W-8S	C7
8600	JSTC	60458	3148	10W-8S	A7
N 73rd Av					
1600	EDPK	60707	3030	9W-2N	D1
1600	RVFT	60305	3030	9W-2N	D1
1600	RVFT	60707	3030	9W-2N	D1
2400	EDPK	60707	2974	9W-3N	D5
2900	CHCG	60707	2974	9W-3N	D5
S 73rd Av					
5300	SMMT	60501	3148	9W-5S	D3
10300	BGVW	60455	3274	9W-12S	E1
10300	PSHL	60455	3274	9W-12S	E1
10300	PSHL	60465	3274	9W-12S	E1
12000	PSHT	60463	3274	9W-14S	E6
15100	ODPK	60462	3346	9W-18S	E6
15100	OrlT	60462	3346	9W-18S	E6
73rd Ct					
700	DRN	60527	3207	16W-8S	E1
700	WLBK	60527	3207	16W-8S	E1
N 73rd Ct					
1600	EDPK	60707	3030	9W-2N	D1
1600	RVFT	60305	3030	9W-2N	D1
1600	RVFT	60707	3030	9W-2N	D1
2400	EDPK	60707	2974	9W-3N	D5
2900	CHCG	60707	2974	9W-3N	D5
S 73rd Ct					
5200	SMMT	60501	3148	9W-5S	D2
10300	BGVW	60455	3274	9W-12S	E1
10300	PSHL	60455	3274	9W-12S	E1
10300	PSHL	60465	3274	9W-12S	E1
12000	PSHT	60463	3274	9W-14S	E6
73rd Pl					
10	DGvT	60561	3207	18W-8S	A1
11200	BRRG	60525	3208	14W-8S	E1
11200	BRRG	60527	3208	14W-8S	D1
11200	IHPK	60525	3208	14W-8S	E1
11200	LynT	60525	3208	14W-8S	E1
E 73rd Pl					
1500	CHCG	60619	3153	1E-8S	B7
2500	CHCG	60649	3153	3E-8S	D7
W 73rd Pl					
1200	CHCG	60621	3151	1W-8S	D7
1200	CHCG	60636	3151	1W-8S	D7
3400	CHCG	60629	3150	4W-8S	D7
7000	BDPK	60638	3148	8W-8S	E7
7100	BDPK	60455	3148	8W-8S	E7
7100	BGVW	60455	3148	8W-8S	E7
7800	BGVW	60455	3210	9W-8S	C1
7900	JSTC	60455	3210	9W-8S	C1
8500	JSTC	60458	3210	10W-8S	A1
8900	JSTC	60458	3209	11W-8S	E1
73rd St					
10	DGvT	60561	3207	18W-8S	A1
10	BRRG	60527	3208	15W-8S	B1
500	DRN	60561	3207	17W-8S	C1
700	DGvT	60527	3208	15W-8S	A1
700	WLBK	60527	3208	15W-8S	A1
800	DGvT	60516	3206	19W-8S	C1
800	DRGV	60516	3206	19W-8S	C1
1700	DRN	60561	3206	18W-8S	E1
E 73rd St					
10	CHCG	60619	3152	0E-8S	C7
10	CHCG	60621	3152	0E-8S	C7
1000	CHCG	60619	3153	1E-8S	A7
1500	CHCG	60649	3153	1E-8S	A7
W 73rd St					
10	CHCG	60621	3152	0W-8S	B7
900	CHCG	60621	3151	1W-8S	E7
1100	CHCG	60636	3151	2W-8S	C7
2300	CHCG	60629	3151	3W-8S	A7
2900	CHCG	60629	3150	4W-8S	D7
4800	BDPK	60638	3149	6W-8S	E7
4800	BDPK	60638	3150	6W-8S	A7
4800	CHCG	60638	3150	6W-8S	A7
6900	CHCG	60638	3148	8W-8S	E7
7100	BDPK	60455	3148	9W-8S	D7
7100	BGVW	60455	3148	9W-8S	D7
7900	JSTC	60455	3148	9W-8S	C7
8600	JSTC	60458	3148	10W-8S	A7
N 74th Av					
1600	EDPK	60707	3030	9W-2N	D1
1600	RVFT	60305	3030	9W-2N	D1
1600	RVFT	60707	3030	9W-2N	D1
2400	EDPK	60707	2974	9W-3N	D5
2900	CHCG	60707	2974	9W-3N	D5
S 74th Av					
5300	SMMT	60501	3148	9W-5S	D3
6400	BDPK	60501	3148	9W-7S	D5
10300	BGVW	60455	3274	9W-12S	D1
10300	PSHL	60455	3274	9W-12S	D1
10300	PSHL	60465	3274	9W-12S	D1
11900	PSHT	60463	3274	9W-14S	E6
15200	ODPK	60462	3346	9W-18S	E6
N 74th Ct					
1600	EDPK	60707	3030	9W-2N	D1
1600	RVFT	60305	3030	9W-2N	D1
1600	RVFT	60707	3030	9W-2N	D1
2500	EDPK	60707	2974	9W-3N	D5
2900	CHCG	60707	2974	9W-3N	D5
S 74th Ct					
6000	SMMT	60501	3148	9W-6S	D4
15100	OrlT	60462	3346	9W-18S	E6
E 74th Pl					
1500	CHCG	60619	3153	1E-8S	B7
2600	CHCG	60649	3153	3E-8S	E7
W 74th Pl					
1200	CHCG	60621	3151	1W-8S	E7
1700	CHCG	60636	3151	2W-8S	D7
5300	BDPK	60638	3211	6W-8S	D1
7000	BDPK	60638	3210	8W-8S	E1
7100	BGVW	60638	3210	8W-8S	E1
7800	BGVW	60455	3210	9W-8S	C1
7900	JSTC	60455	3210	9W-8S	C1
7900	JSTC	60458	3210	9W-8S	C1
74th St					
-	WLBK	60527	3207	16W-8S	E1
10	DRN	60527	3207	16W-8S	E1
10	DRN	60561	3207	16W-8S	E1
10	WLBK	60527	3207	16W-8S	E1
400	DRGV	60516	3206	19W-8S	E1
600	DGvT	60527	3208	15W-8S	A1
600	WLBK	60527	3208	15W-8S	A1
10500	CTSD	60525	3209	13W-8S	A1
11200	BRRG	60525	3208	14W-8S	D1
11200	BRRG	60527	3208	14W-8S	D1
11200	LynT	60525	3208	14W-8S	D1
E 74th St					
10	CHCG	60619	3152	0E-8S	C7
10	CHCG	60621	3152	0E-8S	C7
1200	CHCG	60619	3153	1E-8S	A7
1500	CHCG	60649	3153	1E-8S	A7
W 74th St					
10	CHCG	60621	3152	0W-8S	C7
900	CHCG	60621	3151	1W-8S	E7
2200	CHCG	60636	3151	3W-8S	B7
2300	CHCG	60629	3151	3W-8S	B7
3400	CHCG	60629	3150	4W-8S	D7
3700	CHCG	60629	3212	4W-8S	C1
6100	BDPK	60638	3211	8W-8S	B1
7000	BDPK	60638	3210	9W-8S	E1
7100	BGVW	60455	3210	9W-8S	E1
7100	BGVW	60638	3210	9W-8S	E1
7900	JSTC	60455	3210	9W-8S	C1
7900	JSTC	60458	3210	9W-8S	C1
N 75th Av					
1600	EDPK	60707	3030	9W-2N	C1
1600	RVFT	60305	3030	9W-2N	C1
1600	RVFT	60707	3030	9W-2N	C1
1700	EDPK	60707	2974	9W-2N	C7
2900	CHCG	60707	2974	9W-3N	C5
S 75th Av					
6000	SMMT	60501	3148	9W-6S	D4
6400	BDPK	60501	3148	9W-7S	D5
10300	BGVW	60455	3274	9W-12S	D1
10300	PSHL	60455	3274	9W-12S	D1
10300	PSHL	60465	3274	9W-12S	D1
11900	PSHT	60463	3274	9W-14S	D6
75th Ct					
15900	ODPK	60462	3424	9W-19S	D1
15900	ODPK	60477	3424	9W-19S	D1
15900	TYPK	60477	3424	9W-19S	D1
N 75th Ct					
1600	EDPK	60707	3030	9W-2N	C1
1600	RVFT	60305	3030	9W-2N	C1
1600	RVFT	60707	3030	9W-2N	C1
2500	EDPK	60707	2974	9W-3N	C5
2900	CHCG	60707	2974	9W-3N	C5
S 75th Ct					
6000	SMMT	60501	3148	9W-6S	D4
10300	BGVW	60455	3274	9W-12S	D1
10300	PSHL	60455	3274	9W-12S	D1
10300	PSHL	60465	3274	9W-12S	D1
15100	ODPK	60462	3346	9W-18S	D6
75th Pl					
10	WLBK	60527	3207	16W-8S	E1
E 75th Pl					
1500	CHCG	60619	3215	1E-8S	B1
1500	CHCG	60649	3215	1E-8S	B1
2700	CHCG	60649	3153	3E-8S	E7
S 75th Pl					
15100	ODPK	60462	3346	9W-17S	D6
15100	OrlT	60462	3346	9W-17S	D6
W 75th Pl					
1600	CHCG	60620	3213	2W-8S	D1
3700	CHCG	60652	3212	4W-8S	C1
3900	CHCG	60629	3212	4W-8S	C1
5200	BDPK	60459	3211	6W-8S	E1
5200	BDPK	60638	3211	6W-8S	E1
5600	BRBK	60459	3211	7W-8S	D1
75th St					
-	AURA	60504	3202	30W-8S	A2
-	LynT	60525	3209	13W-8S	A1
-	NPVL	60565	3203	27W-8S	D2
-	NpvT	60564	3203	27W-8S	B2
10	LslT	60540	3204	24W-8S	D2
10	LslT	60565	3204	25W-8S	A2
10	NPVL	60540	3204	24W-8S	D2

STREET Block	City	ZIP	Map#	CGS	Grid
75th St					
10	NPVL	60565	3204	24W-8S	D2
10	WLBK	60527	3207	16W-8S	E1
100	DRN	60527	3207	16W-8S	D1
200	DRN	60561	3206	18W-8S	E1
300	WLBK	60561	3207	17W-8S	D1
400	DGvT	60516	3206	19W-8S	C1
400	DRGV	60561	3206	19W-8S	E1
400	DRN	60561	3207	16W-8S	D1
400	LslT	60540	3205	23W-8S	A2
400	LslT	60565	3205	23W-8S	A2
400	NPVL	60540	3202	29W-8S	D2
400	NPVL	60564	3202	30W-8S	A2
400	NpvT	60564	3202	30W-8S	A2
500	DRGV	60516	3206	19W-8S	D1
500	DRN	60516	3206	19W-8S	D1
600	AURA	60540	3202	30W-8S	C2
600	AURA	60564	3202	30W-8S	C2
600	DGvT	60527	3208	15W-8S	A1
600	NpvT	60504	3202	30W-8S	C2
700	WLBK	60527	3208	15W-8S	A1
1000	WDRG	60516	3206	20W-8S	C1
1100	NPVL	60540	3203	28W-8S	A2
1100	NPVL	60564	3203	28W-8S	A2
1500	DRGV	60516	3207	18W-8S	A1
1500	DRN	60516	3207	18W-8S	A1
1700	WDRG	60517	3206	20W-8S	A1
2100	WDRG	60517	3205	22W-8S	D1
2900	LslT	60517	3205	22W-8S	D2
9800	HGKN	60480	3209	12W-8S	B1
9800	HGKN	60525	3209	13W-8S	A1
11200	BRRG	60525	3208	14W-8S	D1
11200	BRRG	60527	3208	14W-8S	D1
11200	LynT	60525	3208	14W-8S	D1
11200	LynT	60527	3208	14W-8S	D1
75th St CO-33					
-	NPVL	60565	3203	27W-8S	C2
-	NpvT	60504	3202	30W-8S	B2
-	NpvT	60564	3203	27W-8S	B2
10	LslT	60540	3204	24W-8S	D2
10	LslT	60565	3204	24W-8S	D2
10	NPVL	60540	3204	24W-8S	D2
10	NPVL	60565	3204	24W-8S	D2
10	WLBK	60527	3207	16W-8S	E1
100	DRN	60527	3207	16W-8S	D1
200	DRN	60516	3206	18W-8S	E1
300	WLBK	60561	3207	17W-8S	D1
400	DGvT	60516	3206	19W-8S	C1
400	DRGV	60516	3206	20W-8S	A1
400	DRGV	60561	3206	19W-8S	E1
400	DRN	60561	3206	19W-8S	E1
400	DRN	60561	3207	16W-8S	D1
400	LslT	60540	3205	23W-8S	A2
400	LslT	60565	3205	23W-8S	A2
400	NPVL	60540	3202	29W-8S	D2
400	NPVL	60564	3202	30W-8S	A2
400	NpvT	60564	3202	30W-8S	A2
500	WDRG	60516	3206	19W-8S	C1
600	AURA	60504	3202	30W-8S	C2
600	AURA	60540	3202	30W-8S	C2
600	AURA	60564	3202	30W-8S	C2
1000	WDRG	60517	3206	20W-8S	C1
1100	NPVL	60540	3203	28W-8S	A2
1100	NPVL	60564	3203	28W-8S	A2
1500	DRGV	60516	3207	18W-8S	A1
1500	DRN	60516	3207	18W-8S	A1
2100	WDRG	60517	3205	22W-8S	D1
2900	LslT	60517	3205	22W-8S	D2
E 75th St					
10	CHCG	60619	3152	0E-8S	E7
1000	CHCG	60619	3153	1E-8S	A7
1500	CHCG	60649	3153	3E-8S	E7
W 75th St					
-	CHCG	60629	3212	5W-8S	C1
-	CHCG	60629	3213	3W-8S	A1
10	CHCG	60619	3214	0W-8S	C1
800	CHCG	60620	3214	1W-8S	A1
800	CHCG	60621	3152	1W-8S	A7
800	CHCG	60621	3214	1W-8S	A1
900	CHCG	60621	3151	1W-8S	E7
900	CHCG	60621	3213	1W-8S	E1
2700	CHCG	60620	3213	2W-8S	B1
2700	CHCG	60636	3213	2W-8S	B1
2700	CHCG	60652	3213	2W-8S	B1
3400	CHCG	60652	3212	4W-8S	D1
5200	BDPK	60459	3211	6W-8S	D1
5200	BDPK	60638	3211	6W-8S	D1
5200	BRBK	60459	3211	6W-8S	D1
5200	BRBK	60638	3211	6W-8S	D1
7000	BDPK	60638	3210	8W-8S	E1
7000	BGVW	60638	3210	8W-8S	E1
7300	BGVW	60455	3210	9W-8S	D1
7900	JSTC	60455	3210	9W-8S	C1
8600	JSTC	60458	3210	11W-8S	A1
8900	JSTC	60458	3209	11W-8S	E1
76th Av					
15900	ODPK	60462	3424	9W-19S	D1
15900	TYPK	60477	3424	9W-19S	D2
18300	TYPK	60477	3504	9W-22S	D1
18700	FftT	60477	3504	9W-22S	E2
N 76th Av					
1600	EDPK	60707	3030	9W-2N	C1
1600	RVFT	60305	3030	9W-2N	C1
1600	RVFT	60707	3030	9W-2N	C1
2800	EDPK	60707	2974	9W-3N	C4
2900	CHCG	60707	2974	9W-3N	C4
3100	CHCG	60634	2974	9W-3N	C4
S 76th Av					
-	OrlT	60462	3346	9W-15S	D2
-	OrlT	60463	3346	9W-15S	D2
6000	SMMT	60501	3148	9W-6S	D4
6400	BDPK	60501	3148	9W-7S	D5
7300	BGVW	60455	3148	9W-8S	D7
8200	BGVW	60455	3210	9W-9S	D3
9300	HYHL	60455	3210	9W-10S	D6
9600	BGVW	60457	3210	9W-11S	D7
9600	HYHL	60457	3210	9W-11S	D7
10000	BGVW	60455	3274	9W-11S	D1
10000	PSHL	60455	3274	9W-11S	D1
10000	PSHL	60465	3274	9W-11S	D1
10800	PSHL	60482	3274	9W-12S	D3
10800	WRTH	60482	3274	9W-12S	D3
10900	WRTH	60465	3274	9W-12S	D3
11900	PSHT	60463	3274	9W-15S	D7
12800	PSHT	60463	3346	9W-15S	D2
12900	PlsT	60463	3346	9W-15S	D2
13300	PSHT	60462	3346	9W-15S	D2
15700	ODPK	60462	3424	9W-18S	D1
15800	TYPK	60477	3424	9W-18S	D1
N 76th Ct					
1600	EDPK	60707	3030	9W-2N	C1
1600	RVFT	60305	3030	9W-2N	C1
1600	RVFT	60707	3030	9W-2N	C1
2600	EDPK	60707	2974	9W-3N	C4
3100	CHCG	60634	2974	9W-3N	C4
S 76th Ct					
9300	BGVW	60457	3210	9W-10S	D6
9300	HYHL	60457	3210	9W-10S	D6
E 76th Pl					
1500	CHCG	60619	3215	1E-8S	B1
1500	CHCG	60649	3215	1E-8S	B1
W 76th Pl					
2100	CHCG	60620	3213	2W-8S	B1
3400	CHCG	60652	3212	4W-8S	D1
5700	BRBK	60459	3211	7W-8S	C1
8800	JSTC	60458	3209	11W-8S	E1
8800	JSTC	60458	3210	11W-8S	A1
76th St					
2900	LslT	60517	3205	22W-8S	C2
2900	WDRG	60517	3205	22W-8S	C2
E 76th St					
10	CHCG	60619	3214	0E-8S	C1
10	CHCG	60620	3214	0E-8S	C1
1000	CHCG	60619	3215	1E-8S	A1
1500	CHCG	60649	3215	1E-8S	A1
2800	CHCG	60649	3153	3E-8S	E7
W 76th St					
-	CHCG	60619	3214	0W-8S	C1
10	CHCG	60620	3214	1W-8S	A1
1000	CHCG	60620	3213	2W-8S	C1
2300	CHCG	60652	3213	2W-8S	B1
3400	CHCG	60652	3212	4W-8S	D1
5100	BDPK	60459	3211	6W-8S	E1
5100	BDPK	60638	3211	6W-8S	E1
5100	BRBK	60638	3211	6W-8S	E1
5800	BRBK	60459	3211	7W-8S	C1
7200	BGVW	60455	3210	9W-8S	D1
7900	BGVW	60458	3210	9W-8S	C1
7900	JSTC	60455	3210	9W-8S	C1
7900	JSTC	60458	3210	9W-8S	C1
77th Av					
400	DYR	46311	3598		E4
400	SjnT	46311	3598		E4
N 77th Av					
1600	EDPK	60707	3030	9W-2N	C1
1600	RVFT	60305	3030	9W-2N	C1
1600	RVFT	60707	3030	9W-2N	C1
2700	EDPK	60707	2974	9W-3N	C4
3100	CHCG	60634	2974	9W-3N	C4
S 77th Av					
6500	BDPK	60501	3148	9W-7S	C6
6700	BGVW	60455	3148	9W-7S	D6
8700	BGVW	60455	3210	9W-10S	D4
9000	BGVW	60457	3210	9W-10S	D6
9000	HYHL	60457	3210	9W-10S	D6
15600	ODPK	60462	3346	9W-18S	D7
15600	ODPK	60462	3424	9W-18S	D1
15800	TYPK	60462	3424	9W-18S	D1
15800	TYPK	60477	3424	9W-18S	D1
N 77th Ct					
1600	EDPK	60707	3030	9W-2N	C1
1600	RVFT	60305	3030	9W-2N	C1
1600	RVFT	60707	3030	9W-2N	C1
2800	EDPK	60707	2974	9W-3N	C4
3100	CHCG	60634	2974	9W-3N	C4
S 77th Ct					
6500	BDPK	60501	3148	9W-7S	C5
8300	BGVW	60455	3210	9W-9S	C3
9300	HYHL	60457	3210	9W-10S	D6
77th Pl					
-	PSHT	60462	3346	9W-15S	D2
-	PSHT	60463	3346	9W-15S	D2
E 77th Pl					
2800	CHCG	60649	3215	3E-8S	E1
W 77th Pl					
10	CHCG	60620	3214	0W-8S	C1
2100	CHCG	60620	3213	2W-8S	B1
4000	CHCG	60652	3212	5W-8S	C1
5200	BRBK	60459	3211	6W-8S	E1
77th St					
10	DRGV	60516	3207	18W-8S	A2
10	DRN	60516	3207	18W-8S	A2
10	DRN	60561	3207	18W-8S	A2
10	LslT	60565	3204	24W-8S	E2
500	NPVL	60565	3204	24W-8S	D2
11200	BRRG	60525	3208	14W-8S	D2
11200	BRRG	60527	3208	14W-8S	D2
11200	LynT	60525	3208	14W-8S	D2
11200	WLSP	60527	3208	14W-8S	D2
E 77th St					
10	CHCG	60619	3214	0E-8S	C1
10	CHCG	60620	3214	0E-8S	C1
1400	CHCG	60619	3215	1E-8S	B1
1600	CHCG	60649	3215	2E-8S	B1
W 77th St					
10	CHCG	60620	3214	0W-8S	B1
900	CHCG	60620	3213	2W-8S	C1
2300	CHCG	60652	3213	3W-8S	B1
2900	CHCG	60652	3212	4W-8S	D1
5000	BRBK	60459	3211	6W-8S	E1
6300	BDPK	60638	3211	7W-8S	B1
6300	BRBK	60638	3211	7W-8S	B1
6900	BRBK	60459	3210	8W-8S	E1
6900	BDPK	60638	3210	8W-8S	E1
6900	BRBK	60459	3210	8W-8S	E1
6900	BRBK	60638	3210	8W-8S	E1
7200	BGVW	60455	3210	9W-8S	D1
7900	BGVW	60458	3210	9W-8S	C1
8800	JSTC	60458	3209	11W-8S	D1
8800	JSTC	60458	3210	11W-8S	A2
78th Av					
15900	ODPK	60462	3424	9W-19S	D1
15900	TYPK	60477	3424	9W-19S	D1
N 78th Av					
1600	EDPK	60707	3030	9W-2N	C1
1600	RVFT	60305	3030	9W-2N	C1
1600	RVFT	60707	3030	9W-2N	C1
2800	EDPK	60707	2974	9W-3N	C4
3100	CHCG	60634	2974	9W-3N	C4
S 78th Av					
6500	BDPK	60501	3148	9W-7S	C6
6700	BGVW	60455	3148	9W-7S	C6
7300	BGVW	60455	3210	9W-10S	C4
8200	BGVW	60458	3210	9W-10S	C4
8200	JSTC	60455	3210	9W-10S	C4
8200	JSTC	60458	3210	9W-10S	C4
9900	HYHL	60457	3210	9W-11S	D7
9900	HYHL	60465	3210	9W-11S	D7
9900	PSHL	60465	3210	9W-11S	D7
10000	PSHL	60457	3274	9W-11S	C7
10100	PSHL	60465	3274	9W-11S	D1
15700	ODPK	60462	3424	9W-18S	D1
15800	TYPK	60462	3424	9W-18S	D1
15800	TYPK	60477	3424	9W-18S	D1
20700	FftT	60423	3504	9W-25S	D7
20700	FKFT	60423	3504	9W-25S	D7
21200	FftT	60423	3592	9W-25S	D1
21200	FKFT	60423	3592	9W-25S	D1
N 78th Ct					
1600	EDPK	60707	3030	9W-2N	C1
1600	RVFT	60305	3030	9W-2N	C1
1600	RVFT	60707	3030	9W-2N	C1
2900	EDPK	60707	2974	9W-3N	C4
3100	CHCG	60634	2974	9W-3N	C4
S 78th Ct					
7500	BGVW	60455	3210	9W-8S	C1
8300	JSTC	60455	3210	9W-9S	C3
8300	JSTC	60458	3210	9W-9S	C3
8600	BGVW	60458	3210	9W-9S	C4
9300	HYHL	60457	3210	9W-10S	C6
12900	PSHT	60463	3346	9W-15S	D1
E 78th Pl					
2900	CHCG	60649	3215	3E-8S	E1
W 78th Pl					
10	CHCG	60620	3214	0W-8S	C1
1200	CHCG	60620	3213	1W-8S	E1
3700	CHCG	60652	3212	4W-8S	C2
5200	BRBK	60459	3211	6W-8S	E2
E 78th St					
10	CHCG	60619	3214	0E-8S	C1
10	CHCG	60620	3214	0E-8S	C1
1200	CHCG	60619	3215	1E-8S	A1
2200	CHCG	60649	3215	2E-8S	D1
3000	CHCG	60649	3216	3E-8S	A1
W 78th St					
-	CHCG	60620	3214	0W-8S	B1
2100	CHCG	60620	3213	2W-8S	B1
2300	CHCG	60652	3213	2W-8S	B1
4100	CHCG	60652	3212	5W-8S	C1
4700	BRBK	60459	3212	6W-8S	A1
4700	CHCG	60459	3212	6W-8S	A1
4900	BRBK	60459	3211	6W-8S	E2
6900	BDPK	60459	3210	8W-8S	E2
6900	BDPK	60638	3210	8W-8S	E2
7200	BGVW	60455	3210	9W-8S	D2
7200	BRBK	60455	3210	9W-8S	D2
7200	BRBK	60459	3210	9W-8S	D2
7900	BGVW	60458	3210	9W-8S	C2
7900	JSTC	60458	3210	9W-8S	C2
79th Av					
-	TYPK	60477	3424	9W-21S	D5
N 79th Av					
1600	EDPK	60707	3030	9W-2N	B1
1600	RVFT	60305	3030	9W-2N	B1
1600	RVFT	60707	3030	9W-2N	B1
2900	EDPK	60707	2974	9W-3N	B4
3100	CHCG	60634	2974	9W-3N	B4
S 79th Av					
6700	BGVW	60455	3148	9W-7S	C6
8300	BGVW	60455	3210	9W-10S	C4
8300	BGVW	60458	3210	9W-9S	C3
8300	JSTC	60458	3210	9W-10S	C4
8800	HYHL	60457	3210	9W-10S	C5
12300	PSPK	60464	3274	9W-14S	C6
12900	PSHT	60463	3346	9W-15S	C1
21100	FftT	60423	3504	9W-25S	D7
21100	FftT	60423	3592	9W-25S	D1
N 79th Ct					
1700	EDPK	60707	2974	9W-2N	B7
S 79th Ct					
8300	BGVW	60455	3210	9W-9S	C3
8300	JSTC	60455	3210	9W-9S	C3
8300	JSTC	60458	3210	9W-9S	C3
9300	HYHL	60457	3210	9W-10S	C6
79th Pl					
300	DGvT	60527	3207	17W-9S	D2
600	DGvT	60516	3206	19W-9S	D2
E 79th Pl					
1100	CHCG	60619	3215	1E-9S	A2
3000	CHCG	60617	3215	3E-9S	E2
3000	CHCG	60617	3216	3E-9S	A1
W 79th Pl					
400	CHCG	60620	3214	0W-9S	B2
2000	CHCG	60620	3213	2W-9S	C2
2500	CHCG	60652	3213	3W-9S	A2
4200	CHCG	60652	3212	5W-9S	B2
5000	BRBK	60459	3211	6W-9S	E2
7700	BGVW	60455	3210	9W-9S	C2
7800	BGVW	60458	3210	9W-9S	C2
8800	JSTC	60458	3210	11W-9S	A2
79th St					
-	LslT	60565	3204	23W-8S	E3
-	NPVL	60565	3204	23W-8S	E3
10	DGvT	60527	3207	16W-8S	D2
100	BRRG	60527	3208	15W-8S	C2
200	DGvT	60527	3208	15W-8S	B2
200	LslT	60565	3205	23W-8S	A3
200	WLBK	60527	3207	16W-9S	E2
400	DRN	60561	3207	17W-8S	B2
700	AURA	60564	3202	29W-8S	C3
700	NpvT	60564	3202	29W-8S	C3
10900	LynT	60525	3209	13W-8S	A2
10900	WLSP	60525	3208	14W-8S	E2
10900	WLSP	60525	3209	13W-8S	A2
11100	BRRG	60525	3208	13W-8S	E2
11100	LynT	60525	3208	13W-9S	E2
E 79th St					
10	CHCG	60619	3214	0E-8S	E1
10	CHCG	60620	3214	0E-8S	C2
1000	CHCG	60619	3215	1E-8S	A1
1500	CHCG	60617	3215	1E-8S	A1
1500	CHCG	60649	3215	1E-8S	A1
3000	CHCG	60617	3216	3E-8S	A1
3000	CHCG	60649	3216	3E-8S	A1
W 79th St					
-	CHCG	60619	3214	0W-8S	C2
10	CHCG	60620	3214	0W-8S	B2
1000	CHCG	60620	3213	1W-8S	E2
2400	CHCG	60652	3213	3W-8S	A2
2900	CHCG	60652	3212	5W-8S	B2
4700	BRBK	60459	3212	5W-8S	A2
4700	CHCG	60459	3212	5W-8S	A2
4900	BRBK	60459	3211	6W-8S	E2
6900	BRBK	60455	3210	8W-8S	E2
6900	BDPK	60459	3210	8W-8S	E2
6900	BRBK	60455	3210	8W-8S	E2
6900	BRBK	60459	3210	10W-8S	B2
7000	BGVW	60459	3210	10W-8S	B2
7400	BGVW	60455	3210	9W-8S	D2
7900	BGVW	60458	3210	9W-8S	C2
8800	JSTC	60458	3209	11W-8S	E2
8800	JSTC	60458	3210	11W-8S	A2
9100	LynT	60458	3209	11W-8S	E2
9200	WLSP	60458	3209	11W-8S	E2
9200	WLSP	60480	3209	11W-8S	E2
80th Av					
-	FftT	60448	3504	9W-22S	D2
-	TYPK	60448	3504	9W-22S	D2
10700	PTPR	53158	2361		D1
15900	ODPK	60462	3424	10W-19S	C1
15900	TYPK	60477	3424	10W-20S	C3
17300	OrlT	60477	3424	9W-20S	C3
18000	FftT	60487	3424	10W-21S	C7
18400	FftT	60477	3424	9W-22S	C7
18600	FftT	60477	3504	9W-22S	C1
18600	FftT	60487	3504	9W-22S	C1
18600	TYPK	60477	3504	9W-22S	D2
18700	MKNA	60448	3504	9W-22S	D1
18700	MKNA	60477	3504	9W-22S	D2
18700	MKNA	60487	3504	9W-22S	D2
N 80th Av					
2600	EDPK	60171	2974	9W-3N	B5
2600	EDPK	60707	2974	9W-3N	B5
3100	CHCG	60634	2974	9W-3N	B5
S 80th Av					
-	FftT	60448	3504	9W-23S	D2
-	PlsT	60464	3274	10W-15S	C7
-	TYPK	60448	3504	9W-23S	D2
11900	PSPK	60464	3274	10W-14S	C7
12100	PSHT	60463	3274	10W-14S	C7
12100	PSPK	60463	3274	9W-14S	C6
12200	PSHT	60464	3274	10W-14S	C7
12900	PlsT	60464	3346	9W-15S	C1
13000	PlsT	60463	3346	10W-15S	C1
13500	ODPK	60462	3346	9W-17S	C4
13500	PSHT	60463	3346	10W-16S	C4
13500	PSHT	60464	3346	10W-16S	C4
14800	OrlT	60462	3346	10W-18S	C7
15600	ODPK	60462	3424	10W-18S	C1
15800	TYPK	60477	3424	10W-18S	C1
19700	FftT	60423	3504	9W-25S	D7
19700	FftT	60477	3504	9W-23S	D4
19700	TYPK	60423	3504	9W-23S	D4
19700	TYPK	60477	3504	10W-23S	D3
21000	FftT	60423	3592	10W-25S	D1
21900	FKFT	60423	3592	9W-27S	D4
23100	GGnT	60423	3592	10W-28S	D7
S 80th Ct					
8700	HYHL	60457	3210	10W-10S	C4
10000	PSHL	60465	3210	10W-11S	C7
10000	PSHL	60465	3274	10W-11S	C1
13100	PlsT	60464	3346	10W-15S	C1
80th Pl					
-	DGvT	60527	3207	16W-9S	D3
700	DGvT	60516	3206	18W-9S	E3
11000	LynT	60525	3208	13W-9S	E3
11100	BRRG	60525	3208	13W-9S	E3
11100	BRRG	60527	3208	13W-9S	E3
E 80th Pl					
2900	CHCG	60617	3215	3E-9S	E2
3000	CHCG	60617	3216	3E-9S	A2
W 80th Pl					
-	CHCG	60620	3214	0W-9S	A2
2000	CHCG	60620	3213	2W-9S	C2
2500	CHCG	60652	3213	3W-9S	A2
3500	CHCG	60652	3212	4W-9S	D2
5100	BRBK	60459	3211	6W-9S	E2
7600	BGVW	60455	3210	9W-9S	C2
7800	BGVW	60458	3210	9W-9S	C2
80th St					
10	BRRG	60527	3208	15W-9S	C3
10	DGvT	60527	3208	15W-9S	C3
10	NPVL	60565	3203	27W-9S	C3
10	NpvT	60565	3203	27W-9S	C3
200	DGvT	60527	3207	16W-9S	D3
700	DGvT	60516	3206	19W-9S	D3
E 80th St					
10	CHCG	60619	3214	0E-9S	C2
10	CHCG	60620	3214	0E-9S	C2
1100	CHCG	60619	3215	1E-9S	A2
2600	CHCG	60617	3215	3E-9S	E2
3000	CHCG	60617	3216	3E-9S	A2
W 80th St					
10	CHCG	60620	3214	1W-9S	A2
900	CHCG	60620	3213	2W-9S	C2
2300	CHCG	60652	3213	3W-9S	A2
2900	CHCG	60652	3212	4W-9S	E2
5600	BRBK	60459	3211	7W-9S	B2
6900	BRBK	60459	3210	8W-9S	E2
7200	BGVW	60455	3210	9W-9S	D2
7200	BRBK	60459	3210	9W-9S	D2
7800	BGVW	60458	3210	9W-9S	C2
8000	JSTC	60458	3210	10W-9S	B2
81st Av					
13900	SjnT	46311	3598		C5
14400	DYR	46311	3598		C5
15700	BlmT	60411	3598		C5
16000	CteT	60417	3598		C5
16800	TYPK	60477	3424	10W-20S	C3
18500	TYPK	60487	3504	10W-22S	C1
S 81st Av					
7900	BGVW	60458	3210	10W-9S	C2
7900	JSTC	60458	3210	10W-9S	C2
8700	HYHL	60457	3210	10W-10S	C4
9700	HYHL	60465	3210	10W-11S	C7
9700	PSHL	60465	3210	10W-11S	C7
10000	PSHL	60465	3274	10W-12S	C1
12300	PSPK	60464	3274	10W-14S	C6
14900	ODPK	60462	3346	10W-17S	C6
14900	OrlT	60462	3346	10W-17S	C6
81st Ct					
16800	TYPK	60477	3424	10W-20S	C3
S 81st Ct					
8700	HYHL	60457	3210	10W-10S	B4
9700	HYHL	60465	3210	10W-11S	C7
9700	PSHL	60465	3210	10W-11S	C7
10100	PSHL	60465	3274	10W-12S	C1
12700	PSPK	60464	3274	10W-15S	C7
12800	PlsT	60464	3274	10W-15S	C7
14900	ODPK	60462	3346	10W-17S	C6
14900	OrlT	60462	3346	10W-17S	C6
E 81st Pl					
1100	CHCG	60619	3215	1E-9S	A2
2900	CHCG	60617	3215	3E-9S	E2
W 81st Pl					
500	CHCG	60620	3214	0W-9S	B2
2200	CHCG	60620	3213	2W-9S	B2
2500	CHCG	60652	3213	3W-9S	A2
3500	CHCG	60652	3212	4W-9S	D2
5500	BRBK	60459	3211	7W-9S	C2
7000	BRBK	60459	3210	8W-9S	E2
7100	BRBK	60455	3210	8W-9S	E2
7900	BGVW	60455	3210	9W-9S	C3
7900	JSTC	60455	3210	9W-9S	C3
7900	JSTC	60458	3210	9W-9S	C3
81st St					
-	BGVW	60455	3210	9W-9S	D2
-	DGvT	60527	3207	16W-9S	D3
-	NPVL	60565	3203	26W-9S	D3
100	DGvT	60527	3208	15W-9S	C3
200	BRRG	60527	3208	15W-9S	B3
700	DGvT	60516	3206	19W-9S	D3
700	NpvT	60564	3202	29W-9S	C3
10300	NpvT	60565	3203	27W-9S	C3
E 81st St					
10	CHCG	60619	3214	0E-9S	C2
10	CHCG	60620	3214	0E-9S	C2
1100	CHCG	60619	3215	1E-9S	A2
1800	CHCG	60617	3215	2E-9S	C2
3000	CHCG	60617	3216	3E-9S	A2
W 81st St					
10	CHCG	60620	3214	0W-9S	A2
900	CHCG	60620	3213	2W-9S	C2
2300	CHCG	60652	3213	3W-9S	A2
2900	CHCG	60652	3212	4W-9S	E2
4700	BRBK	60459	3212	5W-9S	A2
4700	CHCG	60459	3212	5W-9S	A2
5200	BRBK	60459	3211	7W-9S	D2
6900	BRBK	60459	3210	8W-9S	E2
7100	BGVW	60459	3210	8W-9S	E2
7800	BGVW	60455	3210	9W-9S	C2
7900	BGVW	60458	3210	9W-9S	C2
8200	JSTC	60458	3210	10W-9S	B3
8800	JSTC	60458	3209	11W-9S	E3
9100	JSTC	60480	3209	11W-9S	E3
9100	WLSP	60458	3209	11W-9S	E3
9100	WLSP	60480	3209	11W-9S	E3
82nd Av					
14800	SjnT	46311	3598		D5
16700	TYPK	60477	3424	10W-20S	C4
18800	MKNA	60448	3504	10W-22S	C2
S 82nd Av					
7900	JSTC	60458	3210	10W-9S	B3
8600	HYHL	60457	3210	10W-9S	B4
9700	PSHL	60457	3210	10W-11S	B7
9800	PSHL	60465	3210	10W-11S	B7
9900	HYHL	60465	3210	10W-11S	B7
10200	PSHL	60465	3274	10W-12S	B1
11600	PSPK	60464	3274	10W-13S	C4
12800	PlsT	60464	3274	10W-15S	C7
12900	PlsT	60464	3346	10W-15S	C1
13300	PlsT	60462	3346	10W-15S	C2
13300	PSHT	60462	3346	10W-15S	C2
13300	PSHT	60464	3346	10W-15S	C2
13500	ODPK	60462	3346	10W-18S	C7
13500	OrlT	60462	3346	10W-17S	C5
13500	OrlT	60464	3346	10W-16S	C2
15600	ODPK	60462	3424	10W-18S	C1
20800	FftT	60423	3504	10W-25S	C7
S 82nd Ct					
7900	JSTC	60458	3210	10W-9S	B3
8400	HYHL	60457	3210	10W-9S	B4
9900	HYHL	60465	3210	10W-11S	B7
9900	PSHL	60465	3210	10W-11S	B7
10000	PSHL	60465	3274	10W-11S	B1
11600	PSPK	60464	3274	10W-13S	C5
12900	PlsT	60462	3346	10W-15S	C1
12900	PlsT	60464	3346	10W-15S	C1
12900	PSPK	60464	3346	10W-15S	C1
82nd Pl					
-	NpvT	60564	3203	27W-9S	B4
-	NpvT	60565	3203	27W-9S	B4
13600	ODPK	60462	3346	10W-16S	C3
E 82nd Pl					
1100	CHCG	60619	3215	1E-9S	A2
2900	CHCG	60617	3215	3E-9S	E2
W 82nd Pl					
2000	CHCG	60620	3213	2W-9S	C2
2400	CHCG	60652	3213	3W-9S	B2
3400	CHCG	60652	3212	4W-9S	D3
5100	BRBK	60459	3211	6W-9S	E3
7100	BGVW	60459	3210	8W-9S	E3
7100	BRBK	60455	3210	8W-9S	E3
7100	BRBK	60459	3210	8W-9S	E3
7700	BGVW	60455	3210	9W-9S	C3
7800	BGVW	60458	3210	9W-9S	C3
7800	JSTC	60455	3210	9W-9S	C3
8700	JSTC	60458	3210	10W-9S	A3
82nd St					
600	BRRG	60527	3208	15W-9S	A3
10200	NPVL	60565	3203	27W-9S	D4
10200	NpvT	60565	3203	27W-9S	D4
E 82nd St					
10	CHCG	60619	3214	0E-9S	C2
10	CHCG	60620	3214	0E-9S	C2
1000	CHCG	60619	3215	1E-9S	A2
1900	CHCG	60617	3215	2E-9S	C2
3000	CHCG	60617	3216	3E-9S	A2
W 82nd St					
10	CHCG	60620	3214	0W-9S	C2
900	CHCG	60620	3213	2W-9S	C2
2400	CHCG	60652	3213	3W-9S	A2
2900	CHCG	60652	3212	4W-9S	D2
4900	BRBK	60459	3211	6W-9S	E2
4900	BRBK	60459	3212	6W-9S	A2
6900	BRBK	60459	3210	8W-9S	E3
7300	BGVW	60455	3210	9W-9S	D3
8000	JSTC	60455	3210	10W-9S	C3
8200	JSTC	60458	3210	10W-9S	B3
83rd Av					
13300	PlsT	60462	3346	10W-15S	C2
13700	ODPK	60462	3346	10W-16S	B3
S 83rd Av					
7900	JSTC	60458	3210	10W-9S	B3
8400	HYHL	60457	3210	10W-9S	B4
10000	PSHL	60465	3210	10W-11S	B7
10000	PSHL	60465	3274	10W-11S	B1
12400	PSPK	60464	3274	10W-14S	B7
83rd Ct					
-	DGvT	60516	3206	19W-9S	C4
-	DGvT	60561	3206	19W-9S	C4
-	DRN	60516	3206	19W-9S	C4
-	DRN	60561	3206	19W-9S	C4
8300	ODPK	60462	3346	10W-16S	B3
S 83rd Ct					
7900	JSTC	60458	3210	10W-9S	B2
8300	HYHL	60457	3210	10W-9S	B3
10000	PSHL	60465	3210	10W-11S	B7
10000	PSHL	60465	3274	10W-11S	B1
12700	PSPK	60464	3274	10W-15S	B7
12900	PlsT	60464	3346	10W-15S	B1
12900	PSPK	60464	3346	10W-15S	B1
E 83rd Pl					
600	CHCG	60619	3214	0E-9S	E3
1500	CHCG	60619	3215	1E-9S	B3
3000	CHCG	60617	3215	3E-9S	E3
3100	CHCG	60617	3216	3E-9S	A3
W 83rd Pl					
2600	CHCG	60652	3213	3W-9S	A3
3000	CHCG	60652	3212	4W-9S	E3
5400	BRBK	60459	3211	7W-9S	D3
7300	BGVW	60455	3210	9W-9S	D3
8000	JSTC	60458	3210	10W-9S	C3
8800	HYHL	60457	3209	11W-9S	E3
8800	JSTC	60457	3209	11W-9S	E3
8800	JSTC	60458	3209	11W-9S	E3
83rd St					
-	LslT	60517	3205	22W-9S	C4
-	LslT	60565	3205	22W-9S	C4
10	BRRG	60527	3208	16W-9S	A3
10	DRN	60517	3206	21W-9S	A3
10	DRN	60561	3206	21W-9S	A3
10	NPVL	60564	3202	29W-9S	C4
10	NpvT	60564	3202	29W-9S	C4
10	WDRG	60517	3206	21W-9S	A3
100	BRRG	60527	3207	16W-9S	E3

STREET Block	City	ZIP	Map#	CGS	Grid
83rd St					
100	DGvT	60527	3207	16W-9S	E3
100	WLBK	60527	3207	16W-9S	E3
300	BGBK	60440	3205	22W-9S	C4
300	BGBK	60517	3205	22W-9S	C4
300	DGvT	60561	3206	20W-9S	B3
300	WDRG	60516	3206	20W-9S	B3
300	WDRG	60517	3205	22W-9S	D3
300	WDRG	60561	3206	20W-9S	B3
600	DGvT	60516	3206	18W-9S	E3
600	WDRG	60440	3205	21W-9S	E3
700	AURA	60564	3202	29W-9S	C4
1000	DGvT	60517	3206	20W-9S	C3
1000	DRN	60516	3206	20W-9S	C3
E 83rd St					
10	CHCG	60619	3214	0E-9S	E2
10	CHCG	60620	3214	0E-9S	C3
1000	CHCG	60619	3215	1E-9S	A2
1900	CHCG	60617	3215	3E-9S	E2
3000	CHCG	60617	3216	3E-9S	A2
W 83rd St					
-	CHCG	60619	3214	0W-9S	C3
10	CHCG	60620	3214	1W-9S	A3
900	CHCG	60620	3213	2W-9S	B3
2100	CHCG	60652	3213	2W-9S	B3
2900	CHCG	60652	3212	4W-9S	D3
4700	BRBK	60459	3212	6W-9S	A3
4700	CHCG	60459	3212	6W-9S	A3
4900	BRBK	60459	3211	7W-9S	B3
6800	BGVW	60455	3211	8W-9S	A3
6800	BGVW	60459	3211	8W-9S	A3
6800	BRBK	60455	3211	8W-9S	A3
6900	BGVW	60455	3210	9W-9S	D3
6900	BGVW	60459	3210	8W-9S	E3
6900	BRBK	60459	3210	8W-9S	E3
7000	BRBK	60455	3210	8W-9S	E3
7700	BGVW	60458	3210	9W-9S	C3
7700	JSTC	60455	3210	10W-9S	B3
7700	JSTC	60458	3210	10W-9S	B3
8400	HYHL	60457	3210	10W-9S	B3
8400	JSTC	60457	3210	10W-9S	A3
8800	HYHL	60457	3209	11W-9S	E3
8800	JSTC	60457	3209	11W-9S	E3
8800	JSTC	60458	3209	11W-9S	E3
84 Ct					
10	BmdT	60133	2968	25W-4N	A4
10	BmdT	60188	2968	25W-4N	A4
500	BmdT	60108	2968	25W-4N	A4
84th Av					
-	PSPK	60464	3274	10W-13S	B4
15900	ODPK	60462	3424	10W-19S	B1
15900	TYPK	60477	3424	10W-19S	B2
15900	TYPK	60487	3424	10W-19S	B2
16800	OrlT	60477	3424	10W-20S	B4
16800	OrlT	60487	3424	10W-20S	B4
S 84th Av					
-	FftT	60423	3592	10W-25S	C1
-	FKFT	60423	3504	10W-25S	C7
-	HYHL	60465	3210	10W-11S	B7
-	PSHL	60465	3210	10W-11S	B7
7900	JSTC	60458	3210	10W-9S	B2
8300	HYHL	60457	3210	10W-9S	B3
8300	JSTC	60457	3210	10W-9S	B3
10000	PSHL	60465	3274	10W-11S	B1
11800	PSPK	60464	3274	10W-13S	B5
13300	PlsT	60464	3346	10W-15S	B2
13500	ODPK	60462	3346	10W-16S	B3
13500	PlsT	60462	3346	10W-16S	B3
20500	FftT	60423	3504	10W-24S	C6
84th Ct					
16500	TYPK	60487	3424	10W-19S	B3
S 84th Ct					
7900	JSTC	60458	3210	10W-9S	B2
8300	JSTC	60457	3210	10W-9S	B4
8700	HYHL	60457	3210	10W-10S	B5
13200	PlsT	60464	3346	10W-15S	B1
W 84th Ct					
14700	SjnT	46311	3598		E6
84th Pl					
11000	WLSP	60480	3208	14W-9S	E2
16000	TYPK	60487	3424	10W-19S	B2
E 84th Pl					
900	CHCG	60619	3214	1E-9S	E3
1500	CHCG	60617	3215	1E-9S	B3
1500	CHCG	60619	3215	1E-9S	B3
W 84th Pl					
2600	CHCG	60652	3213	3W-9S	A3
4800	BRBK	60459	3212	6W-9S	A3
4800	CHCG	60459	3212	6W-9S	A3
4800	CHCG	60652	3212	6W-9S	A3
4900	BRBK	60459	3211	6W-9S	E3
7100	BGVW	60455	3210	8W-9S	E3
7100	BRBK	60459	3210	8W-9S	E3
8000	JSTC	60458	3210	10W-9S	C3
8800	HYHL	60457	3209	11W-9S	E3
8800	JSTC	60457	3209	11W-9S	E3
8800	JSTC	60458	3209	11W-9S	E3
E 84th St					
10	CHCG	60619	3214	0E-9S	C3
10	CHCG	60620	3214	0E-9S	C3
1400	CHCG	60619	3215	1E-9S	B3
2100	CHCG	60617	3215	2E-9S	D3
3200	CHCG	60617	3216	4E-9S	A3
W 84th St					
10	CHCG	60620	3214	0W-9S	C3
900	CHCG	60620	3213	1W-9S	E3
2600	CHCG	60652	3213	3W-9S	A3
3000	CHCG	60652	3212	4W-9S	E3
4800	BRBK	60459	3212	6W-9S	A3
4800	CHCG	60459	3212	6W-9S	A3
4900	BRBK	60459	3211	6W-9S	E3
6900	BRBK	60459	3210	9W-9S	E3
7000	BGVW	60455	3210	9W-9S	E3
7000	BGVW	60459	3210	9W-9S	E3
7700	BGVW	60458	3210	9W-9S	C3
7700	JSTC	60458	3210	10W-9S	C3
8800	HYHL	60457	3209	11W-9S	E3
8800	JSTC	60457	3209	11W-9S	E3
8800	JSTC	60458	3209	11W-9S	E3
S 84th Ter					
9900	PSHL	60465	3210	10W-11S	B7
10100	PSHL	60465	3274	10W-11S	B1
85th Av					
-	PSPK	60464	3274	10W-13S	B4
12200	PTPR	53158	2361		D3
16100	TYPK	60487	3424	10W-19S	B2
S 85th Av					
7900	JSTC	60458	3210	10W-9S	B2
8200	JSTC	60457	3210	10W-9S	B3
8700	HYHL	60457	3210	10W-10S	B5
11100	PSHL	60465	3274	10W-13S	B3
11700	PSPK	60464	3274	10W-13S	B5
13000	PlsT	60464	3346	10W-15S	B2
13500	PlsT	60462	3346	10W-16S	B2
14000	ODPK	60462	3346	10W-16S	B4

STREET Block	City	ZIP	Map#	CGS	Grid
85th Ct					
1100	DGvT	60516	3206	19W-9S	C4
1100	DGvT	60561	3206	19W-9S	C4
1100	DRN	60561	3206	19W-9S	C4
16000	TYPK	60487	3424	10W-19S	B1
19100	MKNA	60448	3504	10W-22S	B2
S 85th Ct					
8200	JSTC	60458	3210	10W-9S	A3
8300	JSTC	60457	3210	10W-9S	A4
8700	HYHL	60457	3210	10W-10S	A4
11500	PSPK	60464	3274	10W-13S	B4
12900	PlsT	60464	3346	10W-15S	B1
W 85th Ct					
14600	SjnT	46311	3598		E6
85th Pl					
11200	WLSP	60480	3208	14W-9S	E4
14500	SjnT	46311	3598		D6
16000	TYPK	60487	3424	10W-19S	B1
E 85th Pl					
1500	CHCG	60617	3215	2E-9S	B3
1500	CHCG	60619	3215	1E-9S	B3
S 85th Pl					
19100	MKNA	60448	3504	10W-23S	B2
W 85th Pl					
2600	CHCG	60652	3213	3W-9S	A3
4800	BRBK	60459	3212	6W-9S	A3
4800	CHCG	60459	3212	6W-9S	A3
4800	CHCG	60652	3212	6W-9S	A3
4900	BRBK	60459	3211	6W-9S	E3
7100	BRBK	60459	3210	8W-9S	E4
7300	BGVW	60455	3210	9W-9S	D4
8000	JSTC	60458	3210	10W-9S	C4
8800	HYHL	60457	3209	11W-9S	E4
8800	JSTC	60457	3209	11W-9S	E4
8800	JSTC	60458	3209	11W-9S	E4
13900	SJHN	46373	3598		E6
85th St					
10900	WLSP	60480	3208	14W-9S	E4
10900	WLSP	60480	3209	13W-9S	A4
E 85th St					
10	CHCG	60620	3214	0E-9S	C3
800	CHCG	60619	3214	1E-9S	E3
1300	CHCG	60619	3215	1E-9S	B3
2200	CHCG	60617	3215	2E-9S	D3
3200	CHCG	60617	3216	4E-9S	A3
E 85th St US-41					
3200	CHCG	60617	3216	4E-9S	A3
W 85th St					
10	CHCG	60620	3214	0W-9S	C3
1000	CHCG	60620	3213	2W-9S	C3
2600	CHCG	60652	3213	3W-9S	A3
2900	CHCG	60652	3212	4W-9S	E3
4700	BRBK	60459	3212	6W-9S	A3
4700	CHCG	60459	3212	6W-9S	A3
4900	BRBK	60459	3211	8W-9S	E3
6900	BRBK	60459	3210	9W-9S	E3
7100	BGVW	60455	3210	9W-9S	E3
7100	BGVW	60459	3210	9W-9S	E3
7100	BRBK	60459	3210	9W-9S	E3
7700	JSTC	60455	3210	9W-9S	C3
8200	HYHL	60457	3210	10W-9S	B3
8600	HYHL	60458	3210	10W-9S	A3
8600	JSTC	60457	3210	10W-9S	A3
8600	JSTC	60458	3210	10W-9S	A3
8800	HYHL	60457	3209	11W-9S	E3
8800	JSTC	60457	3209	11W-9S	E3
8800	JSTC	60458	3209	11W-9S	E3
86th Av					
13300	ODPK	60462	3346	10W-15S	B2
13300	PlsT	60462	3346	10W-15S	B2
15700	ODPK	60462	3424	10W-18S	B1
15800	TYPK	60462	3424	10W-18S	B1
15800	TYPK	60477	3424	10W-18S	B1
15800	TYPK	60487	3424	10W-18S	B1
S 86th Av					
-	PSHL	60465	3274	10W-13S	B3
7100	JSTC	60458	3148	10W-8S	A7
8300	HYHL	60457	3210	10W-9S	A3
8300	JSTC	60457	3210	10W-9S	A3
8600	HYHL	60458	3210	10W-9S	A4
8600	JSTC	60458	3210	10W-9S	A4
9900	HYHL	60465	3210	10W-11S	A7
9900	PSHL	60457	3210	10W-11S	A7
9900	PSHL	60465	3210	10W-11S	A7
11500	PlsT	60464	3274	10W-14S	B7
11500	PSPK	60464	3274	10W-14S	B7
12900	PlsT	60464	3346	10W-15S	B1
12900	PSPK	60464	3346	10W-15S	B1
13000	PlsT	60462	3346	10W-15S	B1
13100	ODPK	60462	3346	10W-15S	B1
86th Ct					
8600	SjnT	46311	3598		D6
14000	ODPK	60462	3346	10W-16S	B4
S 86th Ct					
7100	JSTC	60458	3148	10W-8S	A7
7900	JSTC	60458	3210	10W-9S	A3
9100	HYHL	60457	3210	10W-10S	A6
9900	PSHL	60465	3210	10W-11S	A7
10100	PSHL	60465	3274	10W-11S	A1
86th Pl					
600	DGvT	60516	3206	19W-9S	D4
14500	SjnT	46311	3598		E6
E 86th Pl					
500	CHCG	60619	3214	0E-9S	D3
1500	CHCG	60617	3215	1E-9S	B3
1500	CHCG	60619	3215	1E-9S	B3
W 86th Pl					
800	CHCG	60620	3214	1W-9S	A3
2600	CHCG	60652	3213	3W-9S	A4
2900	CHCG	60652	3212	3W-9S	E4
4800	BRBK	60459	3212	6W-9S	A4
6200	BRBK	60459	3211	7W-9S	B4
7000	BRBK	60459	3210	8W-9S	E4
8700	JSTC	60458	3210	10W-9S	A4
86th St					
400	DRN	60561	3206	19W-9S	E4
900	DGvT	60516	3206	19W-9S	C4
1100	DRN	60516	3206	19W-9S	C4
11300	WLSP	60480	3208	14W-9S	E4
E 86th St					
10	CHCG	60620	3214	0E-9S	C3
800	CHCG	60619	3214	1E-9S	E3
1400	CHCG	60619	3215	1E-9S	B3
2400	CHCG	60617	3215	3E-9S	E3
3200	CHCG	60617	3216	4E-9S	A3
W 86th St					
-	BGVW	60455	3210	9W-9S	D4
800	CHCG	60620	3214	1W-9S	A3
900	CHCG	60620	3213	2W-9S	C3
2900	CHCG	60652	3213	3W-9S	A3
2900	WLSP	60480	3208	13W-9S	E4
3200	CHCG	60652	3212	4W-9S	E3
4700	BRBK	60459	3212	6W-9S	A4
4700	CHCG	60459	3212	6W-9S	A4
4900	BRBK	60459	3211	6W-9S	E4
6900	BRBK	60459	3210	9W-9S	E4
7100	BGVW	60459	3210	8W-9S	E4
7100	BRBK	60455	3210	8W-9S	E4

STREET Block	City	ZIP	Map#	CGS	Grid
W 86th St					
7700	JSTC	60455	3210	9W-9S	C4
8600	LynT	60480	3208	14W-9S	E4
8700	JSTC	60458	3210	10W-9S	A4
8800	HYHL	60457	3209	11W-9S	E4
8800	HYHL	60457	3210	11W-9S	A4
8800	HYHL	60458	3209	11W-9S	E4
8800	HYHL	60458	3210	11W-9S	A4
8800	JSTC	60457	3209	11W-9S	E4
8800	JSTC	60457	3210	11W-9S	A4
8800	JSTC	60458	3209	11W-9S	E4
S 86th Ter					
9900	PSHL	60465	3210	10W-11S	B7
10100	PSHL	60465	3274	10W-11S	B1
87th Av					
-	HYHL	60457	3210	10W-9S	A4
-	HYHL	60458	3210	10W-9S	A4
-	JSTC	60457	3210	10W-9S	A4
-	JSTC	60458	3210	10W-9S	A4
12200	PTPR	53158	2361		D3
14800	SjnT	46311	3598		C6
15500	CteT	60417	3598		C6
S 87th Av					
7100	JSTC	60458	3148	10W-8S	A7
7900	JSTC	60458	3210	10W-9S	A2
8600	HYHL	60457	3210	10W-9S	A3
8600	HYHL	60458	3210	10W-9S	A4
9600	HYHL	60465	3210	10W-11S	A6
9600	PSHL	60465	3210	10W-11S	A6
9900	PSHL	60465	3274	10W-11S	A1
12100	PSPK	60464	3274	10W-14S	A6
14000	ODPK	60462	3346	10W-17S	A4
87th Ct					
14100	ODPK	60462	3346	10W-16S	A4
17100	TYPK	60487	3424	10W-20S	A4
S 87th Ct					
7100	JSTC	60458	3148	10W-8S	A7
7900	JSTC	60458	3210	10W-9S	A2
9100	HYHL	60457	3210	10W-10S	A5
9900	PSHL	60465	3210	10W-11S	A7
10100	PSHL	60465	3274	10W-11S	A1
E 87th Pl					
400	CHCG	60619	3214	0E-10S	E4
1200	CHCG	60619	3215	1E-10S	A4
1600	CHCG	60617	3215	2E-10S	B4
W 87th Pl					
4100	HMTN	60456	3212	5W-10S	A4
5600	OKLN	60453	3211	7W-10S	C4
7200	BGVW	60455	3210	9W-10S	E4
7900	HYHL	60457	3210	9W-10S	C4
87th St					
-	AURA	60564	3202	29W-10S	D5
-	WldT	60503	3201	32W-10S	C5
-	WldT	60564	3201	32W-10S	C5
10	BRRG	60527	3208	15W-9S	A4
10	DGvT	60527	3207	16W-9S	D4
10	DGvT	60527	3208	15W-9S	A4
10	LynT	60527	3208	15W-9S	A4
10	NpvT	60564	3203	28W-9S	A5
10	NpvT	60565	3203	28W-9S	A5
10	WldT	60564	3203	28W-9S	A5
10	WldT	60565	3203	28W-9S	A5
100	AURA	60504	3201	32W-10S	C5
100	DRN	60527	3207	17W-9S	C4
100	NPVL	60565	3204	26W-9S	A4
200	NPVL	60564	3203	28W-9S	A5
200	NPVL	60565	3203	27W-9S	C5
400	NpvT	60564	3202	28W-9S	E5
400	WldT	60564	3202	28W-9S	E5
600	DGvT	60516	3206	20W-10S	A5
600	DRN	60516	3206	20W-10S	A5
600	DRN	60561	3206	20W-10S	A5
600	NPVL	60564	3202	29W-10S	D5
1600	DGvT	60517	3206	20W-10S	B4
1600	DGvT	60561	3206	20W-10S	B4
1600	WDRG	60517	3206	20W-10S	B4
1600	WDRG	60561	3206	20W-10S	B4
2000	BGBK	60440	3206	20W-10S	A5
2000	WDRG	60440	3206	20W-10S	A5
2200	AURA	60503	3201	32W-9S	B5
3200	AURA	60564	3201	32W-10S	C5
3200	DRN	60517	3206	20W-10S	B4
3200	NpvT	60504	3201	32W-10S	C5
87th St CO-31					
1600	DGvT	60516	3206	20W-10S	A5
1600	DGvT	60517	3206	20W-10S	B4
1600	DGvT	60561	3206	20W-10S	B4
1600	DRN	60561	3206	20W-10S	A5
1600	WDRG	60517	3206	20W-10S	B4
1600	WDRG	60561	3206	20W-10S	B4
2800	DRN	60516	3206	20W-10S	A5
3200	DRN	60517	3206	20W-10S	B4
E 87th St					
-	BGBK	60440	3204	24W-10S	D5
-	BGBK	60565	3204	24W-10S	D5
-	LslT	60565	3204	24W-10S	D5
10	CHCG	60619	3214	0E-9S	E3
10	CHCG	60620	3214	0E-9S	C4
10	NPVL	60565	3204	24W-10S	D5
1000	CHCG	60619	3215	1E-9S	A3
1500	CHCG	60617	3215	2E-9S	C3
3000	CHCG	60617	3216	3E-10S	A3
E 87th St US-41					
3200	CHCG	60617	3216	4E-9S	A3
W 87th St					
-	CHCG	60619	3214	0W-9S	C4
-	HYHL	60455	3210	9W-9S	C4
10	CHCG	60620	3214	0W-10S	A4
900	CHCG	60620	3213	1W-9S	E4
1000	PlsT	60480	3209	12W-9S	C4
1000	WLSP	60480	3209	12W-9S	C4
2300	CHCG	60652	3213	2W-9S	B4
2300	CHCG	60805	3213	2W-9S	B4
2400	ENGN	60805	3213	3W-9S	A4
2900	CHCG	60652	3212	4W-9S	C4
2900	CHCG	60805	3212	4W-9S	C4
2900	ENGN	60805	3212	4W-9S	C4
3000	ENGN	60652	3212	3W-9S	E4
3900	CHCG	60456	3212	4W-9S	C4
4200	HMTN	60456	3212	5W-10S	B4
4600	HMTN	60652	3212	5W-10S	B4
4700	BRBK	60459	3212	6W-9S	A4
4700	CHCG	60459	3212	6W-9S	A4
4700	HMTN	60453	3212	6W-9S	A4
4700	HMTN	60459	3212	6W-9S	A4
4700	OKLN	60453	3212	6W-9S	A4
4700	OKLN	60459	3212	6W-9S	A4
4900	BRBK	60459	3211	7W-9S	B4
4900	OKLN	60453	3211	7W-9S	B4
4900	OKLN	60459	3211	7W-9S	B4
7000	BGVW	60453	3210	8W-9S	E4
7000	BGVW	60459	3210	8W-9S	E4
7000	BRBK	60459	3210	8W-9S	E4
7000	OKLN	60453	3210	8W-9S	E4
7000	OKLN	60459	3210	8W-9S	E4
7600	BGVW	60458	3210	9W-9S	C4

STREET Block	City	ZIP	Map#	CGS	Grid
W 87th St					
7600	JSTC	60458	3210	9W-9S	C4
7700	BGVW	60455	3210	9W-9S	C4
7700	JSTC	60455	3210	9W-9S	C4
8000	HYHL	60457	3210	10W-9S	C4
8500	HYHL	60458	3210	10W-9S	A4
8500	JSTC	60457	3210	10W-9S	A4
8900	HYHL	60457	3209	11W-9S	E4
9100	LynT	60457	3209	11W-9S	E4
9100	LynT	60480	3209	12W-9S	C4
9100	PlsT	60457	3209	11W-9S	E4
11200	LynT	60480	3208	14W-9S	E4
11300	WLSP	60480	3208	14W-9S	E4
S 87th Ter					
-	HYHL	60457	3210	10W-9S	A4
-	HYHL	60458	3210	10W-9S	A4
8700	JSTC	60458	3210	10W-9S	A4
88th Av					
10500	PTPR	53158	2361		D3
12200	NptT	60099	2361		D4
12200	PTPR	60099	2361		D4
13900	ODPK	60462	3346	10W-16S	A3
17100	ODHL	60487	3424	11W-21S	A5
17100	ODPK	60462	3424	11W-21S	A5
17100	ODPK	60487	3424	11W-21S	A5
17100	TYPK	60487	3424	11W-21S	A5
88th Av CO-H					
10500	PTPR	53158	2361		D3
12200	NptT	60099	2361		D4
12200	PTPR	60099	2361		D4
88th Av CO-ML					
11600	PTPR	53158	2361		D2
S 88th Av					
8300	JSTC	60458	3210	10W-9S	A3
9500	HYHL	60457	3210	11W-11S	A7
9500	HYHL	60465	3210	11W-11S	A7
9500	PSHL	60457	3210	11W-11S	A7
9500	PSHL	60465	3210	11W-11S	A7
10100	PSHL	60465	3274	10W-12S	A2
11900	PlsT	60464	3274	10W-14S	A6
11900	PSPK	60464	3274	10W-14S	A6
13100	ODPK	60462	3346	10W-16S	A2
13100	PlsT	60462	3346	11W-15S	A1
13100	PlsT	60464	3346	11W-15S	A1
15600	ODPK	60462	3424	10W-18S	A1
15900	ODHL	60462	3424	10W-20S	A4
15900	ODHL	60487	3424	10W-20S	A4
15900	ODPK	60487	3424	10W-19S	A2
17000	TYPK	60487	3424	11W-20S	A4
19000	MKNA	60448	3504	11W-23S	B3
19200	MKNA	60477	3504	10W-23S	B3
19200	TYPK	60448	3504	11W-23S	B3
19200	TYPK	60477	3504	11W-23S	B3
19400	FftT	60448	3504	10W-23S	B3
19500	FftT	60477	3504	10W-23S	B3
19700	FKFT	60423	3504	10W-23S	B4
20000	FftT	60423	3504	10W-24S	B4
23100	FftT	60423	3592	11W-28S	B6
23100	GGnT	60423	3592	11W-28S	B6
29700	PtnT	60468	3860	11W-38S	B5
W 88th Av					
15200	SjnT	46311	3598		D7
88th Ct					
14000	ODPK	60462	3346	10W-16S	A3
16700	ODHL	60487	3424	11W-20S	A3
S 88th Ct					
9100	HYHL	60457	3210	11W-10S	A5
E 88th Pl					
300	CHCG	60619	3214	0E-10S	D4
1200	CHCG	60619	3215	1E-10S	A4
W 88th Pl					
4500	HMTN	60456	3212	5W-10S	A4
6600	OKLN	60455	3211	8W-10S	A4
6800	BGVW	60453	3211	8W-10S	A4
6800	BGVW	60455	3211	8W-10S	A4
6800	OKLN	60453	3211	8W-10S	A4
6900	BGVW	60453	3210	8W-10S	E4
6900	BGVW	60455	3210	8W-10S	E4
6900	OKLN	60453	3210	8W-10S	E4
E 88th St					
10	CHCG	60620	3214	0E-10S	C4
300	CHCG	60619	3214	0E-10S	D4
1200	CHCG	60619	3215	1E-10S	A4
2500	CHCG	60617	3215	3E-10S	D4
3200	CHCG	60617	3216	4E-10S	A4
W 88th St					
200	CHCG	60620	3214	1W-10S	A4
900	CHCG	60620	3213	2W-10S	D4
2600	ENGN	60805	3213	3W-10S	A4
2900	ENGN	60805	3212	3W-10S	E4
4500	HMTN	60456	3212	5W-10S	A4
4700	HMTN	60453	3212	6W-10S	A4
4700	OKLN	60453	3212	6W-10S	A4
4900	OKLN	60453	3211	6W-10S	E4
7700	BGVW	60455	3210	9W-10S	C4
7900	HYHL	60457	3210	9W-10S	C4
S 88th Ter					
8500	JSTC	60458	3210	10W-9S	A4
89th Av					
16700	ODHL	60487	3424	11W-20S	A3
S 89th Av					
9100	HYHL	60457	3210	11W-10S	A5
9500	HYHL	60465	3210	11W-11S	A6
9500	PSHL	60465	3210	11W-11S	A6
10200	PSHL	60465	3274	11W-11S	A1
12100	PSPK	60464	3274	11W-14S	A6
16400	ODPK	60462	3424	11W-19S	A2
89th Ct					
16600	ODHL	60487	3424	11W-19S	A3
S 89th Ct					
9200	HYHL	60457	3210	11W-10S	A6
11900	PlsT	60464	3274	11W-14S	A5
11900	PSPK	60464	3274	11W-14S	A5
16400	ODPK	60462	3424	11W-19S	A2
89th Pl					
600	DGvT	60527	3207	16W-10S	D5
E 89th Pl					
10	CHCG	60619	3214	0E-10S	C4
10	CHCG	60620	3214	0E-10S	C4
1300	CHCG	60619	3215	1E-10S	A4
W 89th Pl					
-	CHCG	60620	3213	2W-10S	C4
2600	CHCG	60805	3213	3W-10S	A4
2600	ENGN	60805	3213	3W-10S	A4
4000	CHCG	60456	3212	5W-10S	C4
4700	HMTN	60453	3212	6W-10S	A4
4700	OKLN	60453	3212	6W-10S	A4
5700	OKLN	60453	3211	7W-10S	C4
6600	BGVW	60455	3211	8W-10S	A4
6600	OKLN	60455	3211	8W-10S	A4
7800	HYHL	60457	3210	10W-10S	C5
14100	SJHN	46373	3598		E7
89th St					
10	DGvT	60527	3208	16W-10S	A5
400	BRRG	60527	3208	15W-10S	A5

STREET Block	City	ZIP	Map#	CGS	Grid
E 89th St					
10	CHCG	60619	3214	0E-10S	C4
10	CHCG	60620	3214	0E-10S	C4
1300	CHCG	60619	3215	1E-10S	B4
2600	CHCG	60617	3215	3E-10S	E4
3100	CHCG	60617	3216	4E-10S	A4
W 89th St					
400	CHCG	60620	3214	1W-10S	A4
1000	CHCG	60620	3213	2W-10S	D4
2600	CHCG	60805	3213	3W-10S	A4
2600	ENGN	60805	3213	3W-10S	A4
2900	ENGN	60805	3212	3W-10S	E4
4800	HMTN	60453	3212	6W-10S	A4
4800	HMTN	60456	3212	6W-10S	A4
4800	OKLN	60453	3212	6W-10S	A4
4900	OKLN	60453	3211	6W-10S	E4
7800	HYHL	60457	3210	10W-10S	A4
8900	HYHL	60457	3209	11W-10S	E5
8900	HYHL	60480	3209	11W-10S	E5
8900	PlsT	60480	3209	11W-10S	E5
90th Av					
14500	SjnT	46311	3598		E7
15900	ODHL	60487	3424	11W-19S	A1
S 90th Av					
8300	HYHL	60457	3209	11W-9S	E3
8300	JSTC	60457	3209	11W-9S	E3
8300	JSTC	60458	3209	11W-9S	E3
8500	HYHL	60458	3209	11W-9S	E4
9500	HYHL	60465	3209	11W-11S	E7
9500	PSHL	60465	3209	11W-11S	E7
10000	PSHL	60465	3273	11W-11S	E1
10300	PSHL	60465	3274	11W-12S	A1
11900	PSPK	60464	3274	11W-14S	A5
16400	ODHL	60462	3424	11W-19S	A2
16400	ODHL	60487	3424	11W-19S	A2
16400	ODPK	60462	3424	11W-19S	A2
W 90th Av					
14000	SJHN	46373	3598		E7
90th Ct					
14700	SjnT	46311	3598		D7
S 90th Ct					
12000	PSPK	60464	3273	11W-14S	E5
14400	ODPK	60462	3345	11W-17S	E4
W 90th Ct					
14100	SJHN	46373	3598		E7
90th Pl					
14700	SjnT	46311	3598		D7
E 90th Pl					
500	CHCG	60619	3214	0E-10S	D4
1400	CHCG	60619	3215	1E-10S	A4
W 90th Pl					
200	CHCG	60620	3214	0W-10S	B4
1700	CHCG	60620	3213	2W-10S	D5
2600	ENGN	60805	3213	3W-10S	A5
4000	CHCG	60456	3212	5W-10S	C5
4000	CHCG	60805	3212	5W-10S	C5
4000	HMTN	60456	3212	5W-10S	B5
5700	OKLN	60453	3211	7W-10S	C5
7200	BGVW	60455	3210	9W-10S	E5
7900	HYHL	60457	3210	9W-10S	C5
90th St					
600	BRRG	60527	3208	15W-10S	A5
600	DGvT	60527	3207	16W-10S	D5
600	DGvT	60527	3208	15W-10S	A5
E 90th St					
10	CHCG	60620	3214	0E-10S	C4
900	CHCG	60619	3214	1E-10S	E4
1300	CHCG	60619	3215	1E-10S	B4
2800	CHCG	60617	3215	3E-10S	E4
3000	CHCG	60617	3216	3E-10S	A4
W 90th St					
400	CHCG	60620	3214	0W-10S	B4
900	CHCG	60620	3213	1W-10S	E4
2600	CHCG	60805	3213	3W-10S	A4
2600	ENGN	60805	3213	3W-10S	A4
2900	ENGN	60805	3212	3W-10S	E4
4700	HMTN	60453	3212	5W-10S	A5
4700	HMTN	60456	3212	6W-10S	A5
4700	OKLN	60456	3212	6W-10S	A5
4800	OKLN	60453	3212	6W-10S	A5
6700	BGVW	60453	3211	8W-10S	A5
6700	BGVW	60455	3211	8W-10S	A5
6700	OKLN	60453	3211	8W-10S	A5
7200	BGVW	60455	3210	9W-10S	D5
7900	HYHL	60457	3210	9W-10S	C5
91st Av					
-	TYPK	60487	3424	11W-21S	A7
15900	ODHL	60487	3424	11W-19S	A1
15900	ODPK	60462	3424	11W-19S	A1
S 91st Av					
12300	PSPK	60464	3273	11W-14S	E6
13900	ODPK	60462	3345	11W-16S	E3
13900	OrlT	60462	3345	11W-16S	E3
W 91st Av					
14200	SJHN	46373	3687		E1
15200	SjnT	46311	3598		D7
15700	CteT	60417	3598		C7
E 91st Pl					
-	CHCG	60619	3214	1E-10S	E5
1600	CHCG	60617	3215	2E-10S	B5
W 91st Pl					
100	CHCG	60620	3214	0W-10S	C5
1700	CHCG	60620	3213	2W-10S	D5
4000	ENGN	60805	3212	5W-10S	C5
4000	OKLN	60453	3212	5W-10S	B5
4900	OKLN	60453	3211	6W-10S	E5
6600	BGVW	60455	3211	8W-10S	A5
6600	OKLN	60455	3211	8W-10S	A5
8800	HYHL	60457	3210	11W-10S	A5
8900	HYHL	60457	3209	11W-10S	E5
9100	HYHL	60480	3209	11W-10S	E5
9100	PlsT	60480	3209	11W-10S	E5
91st St					
10	BRRG	60527	3208	16W-10S	A5
10	DGvT	60527	3207	17W-10S	E5
10	DGvT	60527	3208	16W-10S	A5
10	NPVL	60564	3202	31W-10S	A6
10	WldT	60564	3201	31W-10S	E6
10	WldT	60564	3202	31W-10S	A6
10	WLSP	60527	3208	16W-10S	A5
100	BRRG	60527	3207	16W-10S	E5
300	AURA	60503	3201	31W-10S	E6
300	WldT	60503	3201	31W-10S	E6
400	DGvT	60439	3206	18W-10S	E5
400	DGvT	60439	3207	18W-10S	A5
1300	NPVL	60565	3204	24W-10S	C6
11300	LynT	60480	3208	14W-10S	C5
11400	WLSP	60480	3208	14W-10S	D5
E 91st St					
10	CHCG	60620	3214	0E-10S	C5
300	CHCG	60619	3214	0E-10S	E4
1000	CHCG	60619	3215	1E-10S	A4
1500	CHCG	60617	3215	1E-10S	B4
3000	CHCG	60617	3216	4E-10S	A4
W 91st St					
-	CHCG	60619	3214	0W-10S	C5

STREET Block City ZIP Map# CGS Grid

W 91st St
10 CHCG 60620 3214 0W-10S B5
900 CHCG 60620 3214 2W-10S D5
2300 CHCG 60805 3213 3W-10S A5
2300 ENGN 60620 3213 3W-10S A5
2300 ENGN 60805 3213 3W-10S A5
2900 ENGN 60805 3212 4W-10S D5
3500 CHCG 60805 3212 4W-10S D5
4500 HMTN 60456 3212 5W-10S A5
4500 OKLN 60453 3212 6W-10S A5
4500 OKLN 60456 3212 5W-10S A5
4600 HMTN 60453 3212 5W-10S A5
4900 OKLN 60453 3211 8W-10S A5
6700 BGVW 60455 3211 8W-10S A5
6700 OKLN 60455 3211 8W-10S A5
6900 BGVW 60455 3210 8W-10S E5
7700 HYHL 60457 3210 10W-10S B5
92nd Av
16100 ODHL 60487 3423 11W-19S E2
17300 TYPK 60487 3423 11W-20S E5
18300 TYPK 60487 3503 11W-22S E1
21300 FftT 60423 3592 11W-25S A1
21300 FKFT 60423 3592 11W-25S A1
S 92nd Av
11900 PlsT 60464 3273 11W-14S E5
11900 PSPK 60464 3273 11W-14S E5
13600 ODPK 60462 3345 11W-16S E3
S 92nd Ct
14300 ODPK 60462 3345 11W-17S E4
14300 OrlT 60462 3345 11W-17S E4
W 92nd Ln
14000 SJHN 46373 3687 E1
92nd Pl
15600 CteT 60417 3687 C1
15600 SjnT 46311 3687 C1
E 92nd Pl
900 CHCG 60619 3214 1E-10S E5
1300 CHCG 60619 3215 1E-10S A5
2200 CHCG 60617 3215 2E-10S D5
W 92nd Pl
- ENGN 60620 3213 2W-10S B5
- ENGN 60805 3213 2W-10S B5
1000 CHCG 60620 3213 1W-10S E5
6200 OKLN 60453 3211 7W-10S B5
7200 BGVW 60455 3210 9W-10S E5
7600 BGVW 60457 3210 9W-10S D5
7600 HYHL 60457 3210 9W-10S D5
9000 HYHL 60457 3209 11W-10S E5
9000 PlsT 60457 3209 11W-10S E5
9000 PlsT 60480 3209 11W-10S E5
E 92nd St
10 CHCG 60620 3214 0E-10S C5
900 CHCG 60619 3214 1E-10S E5
1400 CHCG 60619 3215 1E-10S B5
1500 CHCG 60617 3215 1E-10S B5
3000 CHCG 60617 3216 3E-10S A5
W 92nd St
- BGVW 60455 3210 9W-10S D5
10 CHCG 60620 3214 0W-10S C5
1000 CHCG 60620 3213 2W-10S D5
2800 ENGN 60805 3213 3W-10S A5
2900 ENGN 60805 3212 4W-10S E5
4600 OKLN 60453 3212 6W-10S A5
5300 OKLN 60453 3211 7W-10S D5
6600 BGVW 60455 3211 8W-10S A5
6600 OKLN 60455 3211 8W-10S A5
7700 BGVW 60457 3210 9W-10S C5
8500 HYHL 60457 3210 10W-10S A5
9000 HYHL 60457 3209 11W-10S E5
9100 HYHL 60480 3209 11W-10S E5
9100 PlsT 60480 3209 11W-10S E5
93rd Av
16700 ODHL 60487 3423 11W-20S E4
S 93rd Av
11900 PlsT 60464 3273 11W-14S E6
11900 PSPK 60464 3273 11W-14S E6
21100 FftT 60423 3503 11W-25S E7
21100 FftT 60423 3591 11W-25S E1
21100 FKFT 60423 3503 11W-25S E7
W 93rd Av
14000 SJHN 46373 3687 E1
14000 SjnT 46311 3687 E1
14000 SjnT 46373 3687 E1
93rd Ln
14500 SjnT 46311 3687 E1
W 93rd Ln
14300 SJHN 46373 3687 E1
93rd Pl
- ODPK 60462 3345 11W-16S E4
200 BRRG 60527 3207 16W-10S E6
200 DGvT 60527 3207 16W-10S E6
14400 SjnT 46311 3687 E1
W 93rd Pl
200 CHCG 60620 3214 0W-10S B5
1600 CHCG 60620 3213 2W-10S D5
2600 ENGN 60805 3213 3W-10S A5
4000 OKLN 60453 3212 5W-10S C5
6200 OKLN 60453 3211 7W-10S B5
7100 OKLN 60453 3210 8W-10S E5
8500 HYHL 60457 3210 10W-10S A6
8800 HYHL 60457 3209 11W-10S E5
14000 SjnT 46311 3687 E1
93rd St
- DGvT 60527 3207 16W-10S D6
- NPVL 60564 3202 29W-10S C6
- WldT 60564 3202 29W-10S C6
E 93rd St
10 CHCG 60620 3214 0E-10S C5
600 CHCG 60619 3214 0E-10S E5
1500 CHCG 60617 3215 1E-10S B5
1500 CHCG 60619 3215 1E-10S B5
3000 CHCG 60617 3216 3E-10S A5
W 93rd St
10 CHCG 60620 3214 0W-10S C5
1000 CHCG 60620 3213 2W-10S D5
2800 ENGN 60805 3213 3W-10S A5
2900 ENGN 60805 3212 4W-10S E5
3900 OKLN 60453 3212 5W-10S B5
5800 OKLN 60453 3211 8W-10S A5
6600 BGVW 60455 3211 8W-10S A5
6600 OKLN 60455 3211 8W-10S A5
6900 BGVW 60455 3210 8W-10S E5
6900 OKLN 60453 3210 8W-10S E5
6900 OKLN 60455 3210 8W-10S E5
7600 BGVW 60457 3210 9W-10S D5
7600 HYHL 60455 3210 9W-10S D5
7600 HYHL 60457 3210 10W-10S C5
8900 HYHL 60457 3209 11W-10S E5
9000 PlsT 60457 3209 11W-10S E6
9000 PlsT 60480 3209 11W-10S E6
94th Av
16700 ODHL 60467 3423 11W-21S E6
16700 ODHL 60487 3423 11W-20S E4
16700 ODPK 60467 3423 11W-21S E6
16700 ODPK 60487 3423 11W-21S E6
17000 TYPK 60487 3423 11W-21S E7
94th Av
17300 OrlT 60487 3423 11W-21S E7
18200 FftT 60448 3423 11W-21S E7
18200 FftT 60487 3423 11W-21S E7
S 94th Av
12800 PlsT 60462 3345 11W-15S E1
12800 PlsT 60464 3273 11W-15S E7
12800 PlsT 60464 3345 11W-15S E1
14400 ODPK 60462 3345 11W-17S E5
14400 OrlT 60462 3345 11W-17S E4
15500 ODPK 60462 3423 11W-18S E1
15800 ODPK 60467 3423 11W-19S E2
15900 ODHL 60462 3423 11W-19S E1
15900 ODHL 60487 3423 11W-19S E2
16200 ODPK 60487 3423 11W-19S E2
16600 ODHL 60467 3423 11W-19S E3
21100 FftT 60423 3503 11W-25S E7
21100 FftT 60423 3591 11W-25S E1
21100 FKFT 60423 3503 11W-25S E7
21100 FKFT 60423 3591 11W-25S E1
W 94th Av
14000 SjnT 46311 3687 E1
94th Ct
17200 TYPK 60487 3423 11W-20S E5
W 94th Ct
13900 SjnT 46311 3687 E1
94th Pl
200 BRRG 60527 3207 16W-10S E6
200 DGvT 60527 3207 16W-10S E6
14600 SjnT 46311 3687 E1
W 94th Pl
300 CHCG 60620 3214 0W-10S B5
2400 CHCG 60620 3213 3W-10S B6
2400 CHCG 60805 3213 3W-10S B6
2400 ENGN 60805 3213 3W-10S B6
6400 CHRG 60453 3211 8W-10S B6
6400 OKLN 60453 3211 8W-10S B6
7000 OKLN 60453 3210 8W-10S E6
8600 HYHL 60457 3210 10W-11S A6
14100 SjnT 46311 3687 E1
94th St
- DGvT 60439 3207 18W-10S B6
200 BRRG 60527 3207 16W-10S E6
200 DGvT 60527 3207 16W-10S E6
700 BRRG 60527 3208 15W-10S A6
E 94th St
10 CHCG 60619 3214 0E-10S C5
10 CHCG 60620 3214 0E-10S C5
1100 CHCG 60619 3215 1E-10S A5
2000 CHCG 60617 3215 3E-10S D5
3500 CHCG 60617 3216 4E-10S B5
W 94th St
- CHCG 60805 3213 2W-10S B5
- ENGN 60620 3213 2W-10S B5
10 CHCG 60620 3214 0W-10S B5
1000 CHCG 60620 3213 1W-10S D5
2600 ENGN 60805 3213 3W-10S A5
2900 ENGN 60805 3212 4W-10S D5
3900 ENGN 60453 3212 4W-10S D5
4500 OKLN 60453 3212 5W-10S B5
6000 OKLN 60453 3211 7W-10S C6
6900 OKLN 60453 3210 8W-10S E6
7600 BGVW 60455 3210 9W-10S D6
7600 HYHL 60455 3210 9W-10S D6
7600 HYHL 60457 3210 10W-10S B6
S 95th Av
100 FKFT 60423 3591 11W-25S E1
200 FKFT 60423 3503 11W-25S E7
95th Pl
200 BRRG 60527 3207 16W-11S E6
200 DGvT 60527 3207 16W-11S E6
E 95th Pl
1200 CHCG 60628 3215 1E-11S A6
2500 CHCG 60617 3215 3E-11S D6
W 95th Pl
- ENGN 60805 3212 4W-11S D6
400 CHCG 60628 3214 0W-11S B6
1100 CHCG 60643 3213 1W-11S E6
2700 ENGN 60805 3213 3W-11S A6
6800 OKLN 60453 3211 8W-11S A6
6900 OKLN 60453 3210 8W-11S E6
95th St
- HYHL 60457 3209 11W-10S E6
- PlsT 60457 3209 11W-10S E6
- PlsT 60465 3209 11W-10S E6
- PlsT 60480 3208 13W-11S E6
- PlsT 60480 3209 12W-10S B6
- PSHL 60457 3209 11W-10S E6
- PSHL 60465 3209 11W-10S E6
400 NPVL 60564 3203 28W-10S A7
600 NPVL 60565 3203 28W-10S A7
600 WldT 60564 3203 28W-10S A7
600 WldT 60565 3203 28W-10S A7
1800 NPVL 60564 3202 30W-10S A7
3000 WldT 60564 3202 30W-10S C7
95th St US-12
- HYHL 60457 3209 11W-10S E6
- PlsT 60457 3209 11W-10S E6
- PlsT 60465 3209 11W-10S E6
- PlsT 60480 3209 11W-10S E6
- PSHL 60457 3209 11W-10S E6
- PSHL 60465 3209 11W-10S E6
95th St US-20
- HYHL 60457 3209 11W-10S E6
- PlsT 60457 3209 11W-10S E6
- PlsT 60465 3209 11W-10S E6
- PlsT 60480 3209 11W-10S E6
- PSHL 60457 3209 11W-10S E6
- PSHL 60465 3209 11W-10S E6
E 95th St
10 CHCG 60619 3214 1E-10S E5
10 CHCG 60620 3214 0E-10S C6
10 CHCG 60628 3214 1E-10S E5
900 CHCG 60619 3215 1E-10S A5
900 CHCG 60628 3215 1E-10S A5
1500 CHCG 60617 3215 2E-10S D5
3000 CHCG 60617 3216 3E-10S A5
E 95th St US-12
10 CHCG 60619 3214 1E-10S E5
10 CHCG 60620 3214 0E-10S C6
10 CHCG 60628 3214 1E-10S E5
900 CHCG 60619 3215 1E-10S A5
900 CHCG 60628 3215 1E-10S A5
1500 CHCG 60617 3215 2E-10S D5
3000 CHCG 60617 3216 3E-10S A5
E 95th St US-20
10 CHCG 60619 3214 1E-10S E5
10 CHCG 60620 3214 0E-10S C6
10 CHCG 60628 3214 1E-10S E5
900 CHCG 60619 3215 1E-10S A5
900 CHCG 60628 3215 1E-10S A5
1500 CHCG 60617 3215 2E-10S D5
3000 CHCG 60617 3216 3E-10S A5
W 95th St
- BGVW 60453 3210 8W-10S E6
- BGVW 60455 3210 10W-10S A6
W 95th St
- BGVW 60457 3210 9W-11S D6
- CHCG 60619 3214 0W-10S C6
- HYHL 60455 3210 10W-10S A6
- OKLN 60455 3210 8W-10S E6
10 CHCG 60620 3214 0W-10S B6
10 CHCG 60628 3214 0W-10S B6
700 CHCG 60643 3214 0W-10S A6
900 CHCG 60620 3213 1W-10S D6
2400 CHCG 60643 3213 3W-10S B6
2400 CHCG 60805 3213 3W-10S B6
2400 ENGN 60805 3213 3W-10S B6
2700 NPVL 60564 3202 29W-11S C7
2700 WldT 60564 3202 29W-11S C7
2900 ENGN 60805 3212 4W-10S E6
3900 ENGN 60453 3212 4W-10S C6
3900 OKLN 60453 3212 4W-10S C6
4900 OKLN 60453 3211 7W-11S D6
6300 CHRG 60415 3211 7W-10S B6
6300 CHRG 60453 3211 7W-10S B6
6300 OKLN 60415 3211 7W-10S B6
7000 OKLN 60453 3210 8W-10S E6
7600 HYHL 60457 3210 9W-11S D6
8700 HYHL 60465 3210 10W-10S A6
8700 PSHL 60457 3210 10W-10S A6
8700 PSHL 60465 3210 10W-10S A6
8900 HYHL 60457 3209 11W-10S E6
8900 HYHL 60465 3209 11W-10S E6
8900 PSHL 60465 3209 11W-10S E6
9000 PlsT 60457 3209 11W-10S E6
9000 PlsT 60465 3209 11W-10S E6
9000 PlsT 60480 3209 11W-10S E6
9000 PSHL 60457 3209 11W-10S E6
W 95th St US-12
- BGVW 60453 3210 8W-10S E6
- BGVW 60455 3210 10W-10S A6
- BGVW 60457 3210 9W-11S D6
- CHCG 60619 3214 0W-10S C6
- HYHL 60455 3210 10W-10S A6
- OKLN 60453 3210 8W-10S E6
- OKLN 60455 3210 8W-10S E6
10 CHCG 60620 3214 0W-10S B6
10 CHCG 60628 3214 0W-10S B6
700 CHCG 60643 3214 0W-10S A6
900 CHCG 60620 3213 1W-10S D6
900 CHCG 60643 3213 1W-10S D6
2400 CHCG 60805 3213 3W-10S B6
2400 ENGN 60805 3213 3W-10S B6
2900 ENGN 60805 3212 4W-10S E6
3900 ENGN 60453 3212 4W-10S C6
3900 OKLN 60453 3212 4W-10S C6
4900 OKLN 60453 3211 7W-11S C6
6300 CHRG 60415 3211 7W-10S B6
6300 CHRG 60453 3211 7W-10S B6
6300 OKLN 60415 3211 7W-10S B6
7600 HYHL 60457 3210 9W-11S D6
8700 HYHL 60465 3210 10W-10S A6
8700 PSHL 60457 3210 10W-10S A6
8700 PSHL 60465 3210 10W-10S A6
8900 HYHL 60457 3209 11W-10S E6
8900 HYHL 60465 3209 11W-10S E6
8900 PSHL 60465 3209 11W-10S E6
9000 PlsT 60457 3209 11W-10S E6
9000 PlsT 60465 3209 11W-10S E6
9000 PlsT 60480 3209 11W-10S E6
9000 PSHL 60457 3209 11W-10S E6
W 95th St US-20
- BGVW 60453 3210 8W-10S E6
- BGVW 60455 3210 10W-10S A6
- BGVW 60457 3210 9W-11S D6
- CHCG 60619 3214 0W-10S C6
- HYHL 60455 3210 10W-10S A6
- OKLN 60453 3210 8W-10S E6
- OKLN 60455 3210 8W-10S E6
10 CHCG 60620 3214 0W-10S B6
10 CHCG 60628 3214 0W-10S B6
700 CHCG 60643 3214 0W-10S A6
900 CHCG 60620 3213 1W-10S D6
900 CHCG 60643 3213 1W-10S D6
2400 CHCG 60805 3213 3W-10S B6
2400 ENGN 60805 3213 3W-10S B6
2900 ENGN 60805 3212 4W-10S E6
3900 ENGN 60453 3212 4W-10S C6
3900 OKLN 60453 3212 4W-10S C6
4900 OKLN 60453 3211 7W-11S C6
6300 CHRG 60415 3211 7W-10S B6
6300 CHRG 60453 3211 7W-10S B6
6300 OKLN 60415 3211 7W-10S B6
7600 HYHL 60457 3210 9W-11S D6
8700 HYHL 60465 3210 10W-10S A6
8700 PSHL 60457 3210 10W-10S A6
8700 PSHL 60465 3210 10W-10S A6
8900 HYHL 60457 3209 11W-10S E6
8900 HYHL 60465 3209 11W-10S E6
8900 PSHL 60465 3209 11W-10S E6
9000 PlsT 60457 3209 11W-10S E6
9000 PlsT 60465 3209 11W-10S E6
9000 PlsT 60480 3209 11W-10S E6
9000 PSHL 60457 3209 11W-10S E6
96th Av
- PlsT 60464 3273 12W-13S D4
- PlsT 60465 3273 12W-13S D3
- PlsT 60480 3273 12W-13S D3
- SjnT 46311 3687 E2
96th Av US-45
- PlsT 60464 3273 12W-13S D4
- PlsT 60465 3273 12W-13S D3
- PlsT 60480 3273 12W-13S D3
W 96th Av
14100 SjnT 46311 3687 E2
96th Ct
100 WldT 60565 3203 27W-11S C7
E 96th Pl
1200 CHCG 60628 3215 1E-11S A6
2700 CHCG 60617 3215 3E-11S E6
W 96th Pl
400 CHCG 60628 3214 0W-11S B6
2600 ENGN 60805 3213 3W-11S A6
3000 ENGN 60805 3212 3W-11S E6
4800 OKLN 60453 3212 6W-11S A6
6800 OKLN 60453 3211 8W-11S A6
6900 CHRG 60415 3210 8W-11S E6
6900 OKLN 60453 3210 8W-11S E6
7700 HYHL 60457 3210 9W-11S D6
8600 PSHL 60465 3210 10W-11S A6
E 96th St
100 CHCG 60628 3214 0E-11S D6
900 CHCG 60628 3215 1E-11S A6
2400 CHCG 60617 3215 3E-11S D6
3400 CHCG 60617 3216 4E-10S B6
W 96th St
800 CHCG 60628 3214 1W-11S A6
800 CHCG 60643 3214 1W-11S A6
1700 CHCG 60643 3213 2W-11S C6
2300 CHCG 60805 3213 3W-11S B6
2600 ENGN 60805 3213 3W-11S A6
W 96th St
2900 ENGN 60805 3212 3W-11S E6
4000 OKLN 60453 3212 5W-11S B6
6100 OKLN 60453 3211 7W-11S B6
6300 OKLN 60415 3211 7W-11S B6
6600 CHRG 60415 3211 8W-11S A6
6600 CHRG 60453 3211 8W-11S A6
6900 OKLN 60453 3210 8W-11S E6
7000 OKLN 60415 3210 8W-11S E6
8600 HYHL 60457 3210 10W-11S A6
8600 HYHL 60465 3210 10W-11S A6
8600 PSHL 60465 3210 10W-11S A6
8700 PSHL 60457 3210 10W-11S A6
97th Av
19400 MKNA 60448 3503 12W-23S D3
S 97th Av
16400 ODPK 60467 3423 12W-19S D2
97th Ct
15800 SjnT 46311 3687 C2
97th Ln
15400 SjnT 46311 3687 D2
97th Pl
6800 CHRG 60415 3211 8W-11S A6
6800 OKLN 60415 3211 8W-11S A6
6800 OKLN 60453 3211 8W-11S A6
15400 SjnT 46311 3687 D2
E 97th Pl
1200 CHCG 60628 3215 1E-11S A6
2500 CHCG 60617 3215 3E-11S D6
W 97th Pl
400 CHCG 60628 3214 0W-11S B6
1200 CHCG 60643 3213 1W-11S E6
2800 ENGN 60805 3213 3W-11S A6
2900 ENGN 60805 3212 3W-11S E6
4600 OKLN 60453 3212 5W-11S A6
6900 CHRG 60453 3210 8W-11S E6
6900 CHRG 60415 3211 8W-11S A6
7700 HYHL 60457 3210 9W-11S C7
7700 HYHL 60465 3210 9W-11S C7
7700 PSHL 60465 3210 9W-11S C7
97th St
- BRRG 60527 3208 16W-11S A7
- DGvT 60527 3208 16W-11S A7
10 DGvT 60439 3206 20W-11S C7
200 BRRG 60527 3207 16W-11S E7
200 DGvT 60527 3207 16W-11S E7
600 DRN 60439 3206 19W-11S C7
E 97th St
100 CHCG 60628 3214 0E-11S D6
1000 CHCG 60628 3215 1E-11S A6
2700 CHCG 60617 3215 3E-11S E6
3400 CHCG 60617 3216 4E-10S B6
W 97th St
- ENGN 60805 3212 3W-11S E6
800 CHCG 60628 3214 1W-11S A6
800 CHCG 60643 3214 1W-11S A6
1100 CHCG 60643 3213 1W-11S E6
2300 CHCG 60805 3213 2W-11S B6
2500 ENGN 60805 3213 3W-11S B6
3900 OKLN 60453 3212 5W-11S B6
6300 OKLN 60415 3211 7W-11S B6
6600 CHRG 60415 3211 8W-11S A6
6600 CHRG 60453 3211 8W-11S A6
6600 OKLN 60453 3211 8W-11S A6
6900 CHRG 60415 3210 8W-11S E6
6900 CHRG 60453 3210 8W-11S E6
6900 OKLN 60415 3210 8W-11S E6
6900 OKLN 60453 3210 8W-11S E6
7700 HYHL 60457 3210 10W-11S C6
7800 HYHL 60465 3210 10W-11S C6
8600 PSHL 60465 3210 10W-11S A6
8900 PSHL 60465 3209 11W-11S D7
98th Av
14500 SjnT 46311 3687 D2
98th Pl
10 DGvT 60439 3206 20W-11S C7
15300 SjnT 46311 3687 D2
E 98th Pl
800 CHCG 60628 3214 1E-11S E6
1400 CHCG 60628 3215 1E-11S B6
2000 CHCG 60617 3215 2E-11S C6
W 98th Pl
200 CHCG 60628 3214 0W-11S B6
800 CHCG 60643 3214 1W-11S A6
1300 CHCG 60643 3213 1W-11S E6
2600 ENGN 60805 3213 3W-11S A7
3300 ENGN 60805 3212 4W-11S E6
4600 OKLN 60453 3212 6W-11S A7
5600 OKLN 60453 3211 7W-11S D7
7500 BGVW 60455 3210 9W-11S D7
7500 HYHL 60455 3210 9W-11S D7
7800 HYHL 60457 3210 9W-11S C7
7800 PSHL 60457 3210 9W-11S C7
7800 PSHL 60465 3210 9W-11S C7
8800 PSHL 60465 3209 11W-11S E7
98th St
10 DGvT 60439 3206 20W-11S C7
6800 CHRG 60415 3211 8W-11S A7
6800 OKLN 60415 3211 8W-11S A7
6800 OKLN 60453 3211 8W-11S A7
7000 CHRG 60415 3210 8W-11S E7
E 98th St
800 CHCG 60628 3214 1E-11S E6
1000 CHCG 60628 3215 1E-11S A6
2600 CHCG 60617 3215 3E-11S E6
3500 CHCG 60617 3216 4E-10S B6
W 98th St
200 CHCG 60628 3214 0W-11S B6
700 CHCG 60643 3214 1W-11S A6
1300 CHCG 60643 3213 1W-11S E6
2400 CHCG 60805 3213 3W-11S B6
2400 ENGN 60805 3213 3W-11S B6
3500 ENGN 60805 3212 4W-11S D6
4900 OKLN 60453 3212 6W-11S A7
6200 OKLN 60415 3211 7W-11S B7
6600 CHRG 60415 3211 8W-11S A7
6600 CHRG 60453 3211 8W-11S A7
6700 OKLN 60415 3211 8W-11S A7
7600 HYHL 60457 3210 9W-11S D7
7800 HYHL 60465 3210 9W-11S C7
8000 PSHL 60457 3210 10W-11S C7
8600 PSHL 60465 3210 11W-11S A7
8700 PSHL 60465 3209 11W-11S E7
99th Pl
- CteT 60417 3687 C3
6500 CHRG 60415 3211 8W-11S A7
6500 OKLN 60415 3211 8W-11S A7
6500 OKLN 60453 3211 8W-11S A7
7000 CHRG 60415 3210 8W-11S E7
15900 SjnT 46311 3687 C3
W 99th Pl
400 CHCG 60628 3214 0W-11S B7
2600 CHCG 60655 3213 3W-11S A7
2800 ENGN 60655 3213 3W-11S A7
2800 ENGN 60805 3213 3W-11S A7
4000 CHCG 60453 3212 5W-11S B7
W 99th Pl
4000 CHCG 60655 3212 5W-11S B7
4000 OKLN 60453 3212 5W-11S B7
5400 OKLN 60453 3211 6W-11S D7
6300 CHRG 60415 3211 7W-11S B7
6300 CHRG 60453 3211 7W-11S B7
7800 HYHL 60457 3210 9W-11S C7
7800 HYHL 60465 3210 9W-11S C7
7800 PSHL 60465 3210 9W-11S C7
8800 PSHL 60465 3209 11W-11S D7
99th St
10 DGvT 60439 3206 20W-11S C7
6400 CHRG 60415 3211 8W-11S A7
6400 CHRG 60453 3211 8W-11S B7
6400 OKLN 60453 3211 8W-11S B7
6700 OKLN 60415 3211 8W-11S A7
7000 CHRG 60415 3210 8W-11S E7
7100 BGVW 60415 3210 8W-11S E7
7100 BGVW 60455 3210 8W-11S E7
E 99th St
800 CHCG 60628 3214 1E-11S E7
1000 CHCG 60628 3215 1E-11S A7
1900 CHCG 60617 3215 2E-11S C6
3600 CHCG 60617 3216 4E-11S B6
W 99th St
10 CHCG 60628 3214 0W-11S B7
800 CHCG 60643 3214 1W-11S A7
1100 CHCG 60643 3213 2W-11S C7
2300 CHCG 60655 3213 3W-11S A7
2300 CHCG 60805 3213 3W-11S A7
2300 ENGN 60805 3213 3W-11S A7
2700 ENGN 60655 3213 3W-11S A7
2900 ENGN 60805 3212 4W-11S D7
3600 CHCG 60655 3212 5W-11S B7
3900 CHCG 60453 3212 5W-11S B7
3900 OKLN 60453 3212 6W-11S A7
4900 OKLN 60453 3211 7W-11S D7
6300 CHRG 60415 3211 7W-11S B7
6300 CHRG 60453 3211 7W-11S B7
7500 BGVW 60455 3210 9W-11S D7
7600 HYHL 60457 3210 10W-11S B7
7600 HYHL 60465 3210 9W-11S C7
7600 PSHL 60457 3210 10W-11S B7
7600 PSHL 60465 3210 11W-11S A7
8800 PSHL 60465 3209 11W-11S E7
W 99th Ter
8400 PSHL 60465 3210 10W-11S B7
S 100th Av
12500 PlsT 60464 3273 12W-14S C7
12500 PSPK 60464 3273 12W-14S C7
E 100th Dr
3800 CHCG 60617 3216 4E-11S C6
100th Pl
15900 SjnT 46311 3687 C3
E 100th Pl
700 CHCG 60628 3214 1E-11S E7
1100 CHCG 60628 3215 1E-11S A7
W 100th Pl
300 CHCG 60628 3214 0W-11S B7
1200 CHCG 60643 3213 2W-11S D7
2600 CHCG 60655 3213 3W-11S A7
2800 ENGN 60655 3213 3W-11S A7
2800 ENGN 60805 3213 3W-11S A7
3000 ENGN 60805 3212 3W-11S E7
4400 OKLN 60453 3212 5W-11S B7
5600 OKLN 60453 3211 7W-11S D7
5800 CHRG 60415 3211 7W-11S C7
7200 BGVW 60415 3210 9W-11S D7
7200 CHRG 60415 3210 9W-11S D7
7600 BGVW 60455 3210 9W-11S D7
7800 PSHL 60465 3210 9W-11S C7
100th St
7000 CHRG 60415 3210 8W-11S E7
E 100th St
- CHCG 60628 3215 1E-11S B7
10 CHCG 60628 3214 0E-11S C7
2000 CHCG 60617 3215 3E-11S B7
3600 CHCG 60617 3216 4E-11S B7
W 100th St
10 CHCG 60628 3214 0W-11S B7
700 CHCG 60643 3214 1W-11S A7
1000 CHCG 60643 3213 1W-11S E7
2300 CHCG 60655 3213 3W-11S B7
2700 ENGN 60655 3213 3W-11S A7
2700 ENGN 60805 3213 3W-11S A7
3200 ENGN 60805 3212 4W-11S D7
4000 CHCG 60453 3212 5W-11S C7
4000 CHCG 60655 3212 5W-11S C7
4500 OKLN 60453 3212 5W-11S A7
5600 OKLN 60453 3211 7W-11S C7
5800 CHRG 60415 3211 7W-11S C7
5800 CHRG 60453 3211 7W-11S C7
7800 HYHL 60457 3210 9W-11S C7
7800 HYHL 60465 3210 9W-11S C7
7800 PSHL 60457 3210 9W-11S C7
8800 PSHL 60465 3209 11W-11S E7
W 100th Ter
- PSHL 60465 3210 10W-11S B7
W 101st Av
13600 HnrT 46311 3687 D3
13600 SjnT 46311 3687 D3
15800 CteT 60417 3687 D3
E 101st Pl
600 CHCG 60628 3214 0E-11S E7
W 101st Pl
300 CHCG 60628 3214 0W-11S B7
1200 CHCG 60643 3213 1W-11S D7
2600 CHCG 60655 3213 3W-11S A7
2800 ENGN 60655 3213 3W-11S A7
2800 ENGN 60805 3213 3W-11S A7
3000 ENGN 60805 3212 3W-11S E7
3900 CHCG 60655 3212 4W-11S C7
4500 CHCG 60453 3212 5W-11S B7
5700 OKLN 60453 3211 7W-11S D7
7800 PSHL 60465 3274 9W-11S C1
101st St
300 DGvT 60439 3270 20W-11S C1
300 WDRG 60439 3270 20W-11S B1
300 WDRG 60517 3270 20W-11S B1
E 101st St
700 CHCG 60628 3214 0E-11S E7
900 CHCG 60628 3215 1E-11S A7
2800 CHCG 60617 3215 3E-11S E7
3500 CHCG 60617 3216 4E-11S B7
W 101st St
10 CHCG 60628 3214 1W-11S A7
700 CHCG 60643 3214 1W-11S A7
1000 CHCG 60643 3213 1W-11S E7
2600 CHCG 60655 3213 3W-11S A7
2700 ENGN 60655 3213 3W-11S A7
2700 ENGN 60805 3213 3W-11S A7
3200 ENGN 60805 3212 4W-11S D7
3900 CHCG 60655 3212 4W-11S C7
4000 CHCG 60453 3212 5W-11S B7
4000 OKLN 60453 3212 5W-11S B7
6100 CHRG 60415 3211 7W-11S B7

STREET Block City ZIP Map# CGS Grid

W 101st St
6100 OKLN 60415 3211 7W-11S B7
6100 OKLN 60453 3211 7W-11S B7
7800 PSHL 60465 3210 9W-11S C7
8700 PSHL 60465 3274 11W-11S A1
W 101st Ter
8400 PSHL 60465 3210 10W-11S B7
8500 PSHL 60465 3274 10W-11S B1
102nd Ct
- PlsT 60464 3273 12W-14S C7
102nd Pl
6400 CHRG 60415 3275 8W-11S A1
E 102nd Pl
600 CHCG 60628 3214 0E-11S E7
W 102nd Pl
300 CHCG 60628 3214 0W-11S B7
1200 CHCG 60643 3213 1W-11S D7
1500 CHCG 60643 3277 1W-11S D1
2600 CHCG 60655 3277 3W-11S A1
2800 CHCG 60805 3277 3W-11S A1
2800 ENGN 60655 3277 3W-11S A1
2800 ENGN 60805 3277 3W-11S A1
3900 CHCG 60655 3276 4W-11S C1
4500 OKLN 60453 3276 5W-11S A1
8300 PSHL 60465 3274 10W-11S B1
E 102nd St
10 CHCG 60628 3214 0E-11S C7
2800 CHCG 60617 3215 3E-11S E7
3400 CHCG 60617 3216 4E-11S B7
W 102nd St
10 CHCG 60628 3214 0W-11S B7
700 CHCG 60643 3214 1W-11S A7
1000 CHCG 60643 3213 1W-11S E7
2300 CHCG 60655 3213 3W-11S B7
2700 ENGN 60655 3213 3W-11S A7
2700 ENGN 60805 3213 3W-11S A7
3100 ENGN 60805 3212 3W-11S E7
3900 CHCG 60655 3212 4W-11S C7
3900 OKLN 60655 3212 4W-11S C7
4500 OKLN 60453 3276 5W-11S B1
4800 OKLN 60453 3212 6W-11S A7
5200 OKLN 60453 3275 7W-11S D1
5800 CHRG 60415 3275 7W-11S C1
5800 OKLN 60415 3275 7W-11S C1
8800 PSHL 60465 3274 11W-11S A1
W 102nd Ter
8500 PSHL 60465 3274 10W-11S B1
E 103rd Pl
700 CHCG 60628 3278 0E-12S E1
W 103rd Pl
400 CHCG 60628 3278 0W-12S B1
1000 CHCG 60643 3278 1W-12S A1
1400 CHCG 60643 3277 1W-12S D1
2500 CHCG 60655 3277 3W-12S B1
5500 OKLN 60453 3275 6W-12S D1
8800 PSHL 60465 3274 11W-12S A1
103rd St
- WldT 60564 3265 31W-11S E2
- WldT 60585 3265 31W-11S E2
10 NPVL 60564 3266 29W-11S D2
10 WldT 60564 3266 29W-11S D2
6000 CHRG 60415 3275 7W-11S B1
6000 OKLN 60415 3275 7W-12S C1
6000 OKLN 60453 3275 7W-12S C1
7000 BGVW 60415 3274 8W-11S E1
7000 BGVW 60455 3274 8W-11S E1
7000 CHRG 60415 3274 8W-11S E1
7000 PSHL 60415 3274 8W-11S E1
7000 PSHL 60455 3274 8W-11S E1
7000 PSHL 60465 3274 8W-11S E1
15700 WDRG 60517 3270 20W-11S C1
16100 DGvT 60439 3270 20W-11S C1
16100 WDRG 60439 3270 20W-11S C1
E 103rd St
10 CHCG 60628 3278 0E-12S C1
800 CHCG 60628 3214 1E-11S E7
1000 CHCG 60628 3215 1E-11S A7
1600 CHCG 60617 3215 2E-11S D7
3200 CHCG 60617 3216 4E-11S B7
W 103rd St
10 CHCG 60628 3278 0W-12S B1
700 CHCG 60643 3278 1W-11S A1
1000 CHCG 60643 3277 1W-11S D1
2300 CHCG 60655 3277 1W-11S E1
2900 CHCG 60655 3276 4W-11S E1
3100 CHCG 60805 3276 3W-11S E1
3100 ENGN 60805 3276 3W-11S E1
3900 OKLN 60453 3276 4W-11S C1
3900 OKLN 60655 3276 4W-11S C1
4900 OKLN 60453 3275 6W-11S E1
5800 CHRG 60415 3275 7W-12S C1
5800 CHRG 60453 3275 7W-12S C1
5800 OKLN 60415 3275 7W-12S C1
7200 BGVW 60415 3274 9W-11S C1
7200 BGVW 60455 3274 9W-11S C1
7200 CHRG 60415 3274 9W-11S C1
7200 PSHL 60415 3274 9W-11S C1
7200 PSHL 60455 3274 9W-11S C1
7200 PSHL 60465 3274 9W-11S C1
8800 PSHL 60465 3273 11W-11S E1
9000 PlsT 60465 3273 11W-12S E1
9000 PlsT 60480 3273 11W-12S E1
W 103rd Ter
8400 PSHL 60465 3274 10W-11S B1
104th Av
- PlsT 60464 3273 13W-13S B3
- PlsT 60480 3273 12W-12S B3
15900 ODPK 60462 3423 12W-19S B1
15900 ODPK 60467 3423 13W-20S B4
15900 OrlT 60462 3423 12W-19S B1
15900 OrlT 60467 3423 13W-20S B4
17700 ODPK 60487 3423 12W-21S B6
17700 OrlT 60487 3423 12W-21S B6
19100 FftT 60448 3503 12W-22S C2
19100 MKNA 60448 3503 12W-22S C2
S 104th Av
- PlsT 60480 3273 13W-13S B3
12500 PlsT 60464 3273 13W-14S B7
12800 PlsT 60464 3345 13W-15S B2
13000 PlsT 60462 3345 13W-15S B2
22100 FKFT 60423 3591 13W-27S C4
23100 FftT 60423 3591 13W-28S C6
23100 GGnT 60423 3591 13W-28S C6
104th Pl
6600 CHRG 60415 3275 8W-12S A1
6700 WRTH 60415 3275 8W-12S A1
6700 WRTH 60482 3275 8W-12S A1
E 104th Pl
700 CHCG 60628 3278 0E-12S E1
W 104th Pl
10 CHCG 60628 3278 0W-12S C1
1000 CHCG 60643 3278 1W-12S A1
1600 CHCG 60643 3277 2W-12S D1
2600 CHCG 60655 3277 3W-12S A1
3900 CHCG 60453 3276 4W-12S C1
3900 CHCG 60655 3276 4W-12S C1

W 104th Pl
3900 OKLN 60453 3276 4W-12S C1
7900 PSHL 60465 3274 9W-12S C1
104th St
100 NPVL 60564 3267 28W-12S A2
300 NPVL 60564 3266 28W-12S E2
300 WldT 60564 3266 28W-12S E2
6600 CHRG 60415 3275 8W-12S A1
E 104th St
700 CHCG 60628 3278 0E-12S E1
800 CHCG 60628 3279 1E-12S A1
2500 CHCG 60617 3279 3E-11S E1
3300 CHCG 60617 3280 4E-11S B1
W 104th St
10 CHCG 60628 3278 0W-12S C1
700 CHCG 60643 3278 1W-12S A1
1600 CHCG 60643 3277 2W-12S D1
2300 CHCG 60655 3277 2W-12S B1
3600 CHCG 60655 3276 5W-12S C1
3900 CHCG 60453 3276 5W-12S C1
3900 OKLN 60453 3276 5W-12S C1
4900 OKLN 60453 3275 6W-12S E1
5900 CHRG 60415 3275 7W-12S C1
5900 OKLN 60415 3275 7W-12S C1
8000 PSHL 60465 3274 10W-12S C1
105th Ct
16300 ODPK 60467 3423 13W-19S B2
E 105th Pl
600 CHCG 60628 3278 0E-12S E1
W 105th Pl
200 CHCG 60628 3278 0W-12S B1
1400 CHCG 60643 3277 1W-12S D1
4000 CHCG 60453 3276 5W-12S C1
4000 CHCG 60655 3276 5W-12S C1
4000 OKLN 60453 3276 5W-12S C1
4900 OKLN 60453 3275 6W-12S E1
6900 WRTH 60482 3275 8W-12S A2
105th St
6300 CHRG 60415 3275 7W-12S B1
6700 WRTH 60415 3275 8W-12S A1
6700 WRTH 60482 3275 8W-12S A1
E 105th St
10 CHCG 60628 3278 0E-12S C1
2400 CHCG 60617 3279 3E-11S E1
3300 CHCG 60617 3280 4E-11S B1
W 105th St
10 CHCG 60628 3278 0W-12S C1
800 CHCG 60643 3278 1W-12S A1
1000 CHCG 60643 3277 1W-12S E1
2300 CHCG 60655 3277 3W-12S B1
3000 CHCG 60655 3276 4W-12S D1
3900 CHCG 60453 3276 4W-12S C1
3900 OKLN 60453 3276 6W-12S A1
5000 OKLN 60453 3275 6W-12S E1
5600 CHRG 60415 3275 7W-12S C1
5900 OKLN 60415 3275 7W-12S C1
7200 CHRG 60415 3274 9W-12S D1
7200 PSHL 60415 3274 9W-12S D1
7200 PSHL 60465 3274 9W-12S D1
106th Ct
- ODPK 60467 3423 13W-19S B3
106th Pl
3100 PTPR 53158 2362 E1
6700 CHRG 60415 3275 8W-12S A2
6700 WRTH 60415 3275 8W-12S A2
6700 WRTH 60482 3275 8W-12S A2
W 106th Pl
10 CHCG 60628 3278 0W-12S B1
1700 CHCG 60643 3277 2W-12S D2
2600 CHCG 60655 3277 3W-12S A2
4000 CHCG 60453 3276 5W-12S C2
4000 CHCG 60655 3276 5W-12S C2
4000 OKLN 60453 3276 5W-12S C2
4900 OKLN 60453 3275 6W-12S E2
6900 WRTH 60482 3275 8W-12S A2
106th St
100 PTPR 53158 2363 D1
5600 OKLN 60453 3275 7W-12S D2
6100 CHRG 60415 3275 7W-12S B2
6700 WRTH 60415 3275 8W-12S A2
6700 WRTH 60482 3275 8W-12S A2
E 106th St
600 CHCG 60628 3278 0E-12S E1
2400 CHCG 60617 3279 3E-11S E1
2800 CHCG 60617 3280 3E-11S A1
4000 HMND 46320 3280 4E-11S C1
W 106th St
200 CHCG 60628 3278 0W-12S B1
700 CHCG 60643 3278 1W-12S A1
1100 CHCG 60643 3277 1W-12S E1
2300 CHCG 60655 3277 3W-12S B1
3000 CHCG 60655 3276 3W-12S E1
3900 CHCG 60453 3276 5W-12S C1
3900 OKLN 60453 3276 5W-12S C1
4900 OKLN 60453 3275 6W-12S E2
8000 PSHL 60465 3274 10W-12S B2
107th Av
16300 ODPK 60467 3423 13W-19S B2
107th Pl
4900 PTPR 53158 2362 C1
5800 CHRG 60415 3275 7W-12S C2
W 107th Pl
200 CHCG 60628 3278 0W-12S B2
1000 CHCG 60643 3277 1W-12S E2
1000 CHCG 60643 3278 1W-12S A2
2200 CHCG 60655 3277 2W-12S B2
3800 CHCG 60655 3276 4W-12S C2
4300 OKLN 60453 3276 5W-12S B2
6900 WRTH 60482 3275 8W-12S A2
107th St
- PlsT 60465 3273 11W-12S E2
- PlsT 60480 3272 14W-12S C2
- PlsT 60480 3273 13W-12S A2
100 PTPR 53158 2363 D1
5600 CHRG 60415 3275 7W-12S D2
5600 OKLN 60453 3275 7W-12S D2
5900 PTPR 53158 2362 B1
6300 CHRG 60482 3275 7W-12S B2
6300 WRTH 60415 3275 7W-12S B2
6300 WRTH 60482 3275 7W-12S B2
12800 LmnT 60439 3272 15W-12S B2
12800 LmnT 60480 3272 15W-12S B2
E 107th St
10 CHCG 60628 3278 0E-12S D2
600 BGBK 60440 3269 21W-12S E2
600 WDRG 60440 3269 21W-12S E2
2500 CHCG 60617 3279 2E-12S D1
3200 CHCG 60617 3280 3E-12S A1
4000 HMND 46320 3280 4E-12S C1
W 107th St
10 CHCG 60628 3278 0W-12S B2
700 CHCG 60643 3278 1W-12S A2
1000 CHCG 60643 3277 2W-12S C2
2300 CHCG 60655 3277 2W-12S B2
3000 CHCG 60655 3276 5W-12S B2
3900 OKLN 60453 3276 6W-12S A2

W 107th St
3900 OKLN 60655 3276 5W-12S B2
5200 OKLN 60453 3275 6W-12S D2
6400 CHRG 60415 3275 8W-12S A2
6400 CHRG 60482 3275 8W-12S B2
6400 WRTH 60415 3275 8W-12S A2
6400 WRTH 60482 3275 8W-12S A2
6900 WRTH 60482 3274 9W-12S E2
7500 PSHL 60465 3274 9W-12S D2
8800 PlsT 60465 3273 11W-12S E2
8800 PlsT 60480 3273 11W-12S E2
8800 PSHL 60465 3273 11W-12S E2
108th Av
13000 PlsT 60462 3345 13W-15S A2
13000 PlsT 60464 3345 13W-15S A2
13000 PlsT 60467 3345 13W-15S A2
13900 ODPK 60462 3345 13W-18S A7
13900 ODPK 60467 3345 13W-18S A7
13900 OrlT 60462 3345 13W-16S A4
13900 OrlT 60467 3345 13W-16S A4
15600 ODPK 60462 3423 13W-18S A1
15600 ODPK 60467 3423 13W-20S A4
15700 OrlT 60462 3423 13W-18S A1
15700 OrlT 60467 3423 13W-20S A4
S 108th Av
21200 FKFT 60423 3591 13W-26S B2
21500 FftT 60423 3591 13W-26S B2
108th Pl
3200 PTPR 53158 2362 E1
5800 CHRG 60415 3275 7W-12S C2
W 108th Pl
10 CHCG 60628 3278 0W-12S B2
1000 CHCG 60643 3278 1W-12S A2
2000 CHCG 60643 3277 2W-12S C2
2300 CHCG 60655 3277 2W-12S B2
3200 CHCG 60655 3276 4W-12S E2
4200 OKLN 60453 3276 5W-12S B2
5200 OKLN 60453 3275 6W-12S D2
7200 WRTH 60482 3274 9W-12S E2
108th St
100 PTPR 53158 2363 C1
4200 OKLN 60453 3276 5W-12S B2
5700 CHRG 60415 3275 7W-12S D2
6300 WRTH 60415 3275 7W-12S B2
6300 WRTH 60482 3275 7W-12S B2
7200 PTPR 53158 2361 E1
7200 PTPR 53158 2362 A1
E 108th St
10 CHCG 60617 3278 4E-12S B2
10 HMND 46320 3280 C2
600 CHCG 60628 3278 0E-12S E2
2500 CHCG 60617 3279 2E-12S D2
W 108th St
10 CHCG 60628 3278 0W-12S C2
900 CHCG 60643 3278 1W-12S A2
1000 CHCG 60643 3277 1W-12S E2
2400 CHCG 60655 3277 3W-12S B2
3000 CHCG 60655 3276 4W-12S E2
4700 OKLN 60453 3276 6W-12S A2
4900 OKLN 60453 3275 6W-12S E2
6400 CHRG 60415 3275 8W-12S B2
6400 WRTH 60415 3275 8W-12S B2
6400 WRTH 60482 3275 8W-12S B2
7000 WRTH 60482 3274 8W-12S E2
7900 PSHL 60465 3274 9W-12S C2
109th Av
12900 HnrT 46311 3687 D5
15100 ODPK 60467 3345 13W-18S A6
15100 OrlT 60467 3345 13W-18S A7
109th Pl
5800 CHRG 60415 3275 7W-12S C2
25300 SlmT 53179 2357 B1
W 109th Pl
10 CHCG 60628 3278 0W-12S C2
900 CHCG 60643 3278 1W-12S A2
1600 CHCG 60643 3277 2W-12S D2
2500 CHCG 60655 3277 3W-12S B2
3800 CHCG 60655 3276 4W-12S C2
6800 WRTH 60482 3275 8W-12S A2
7100 WRTH 60482 3274 8W-12S E3
7500 PSHL 60465 3274 9W-12S D3
7500 WRTH 60465 3274 9W-12S D3
109th St
600 DGvT 60439 3270 19W-12S C3
600 LMNT 60439 3270 19W-12S C3
5600 CHRG 60415 3275 7W-12S C2
5600 OKLN 60453 3275 7W-12S C2
6000 PTPR 53158 2362 A1
6300 CHRG 60482 3275 7W-12S B2
6300 WRTH 60482 3275 7W-12S B2
8000 PTPR 53158 2361 D1
26700 SlmT 53179 2357 A1
E 109th St
10 CHCG 60628 3278 0E-12S D2
2500 CHCG 60617 3279 2E-12S D2
3200 CHCG 60617 3280 4E-12S B2
4000 HMND 46320 3280 4E-12S C2
W 109th St
10 CHCG 60628 3278 1W-12S A2
700 CHCG 60643 3278 1W-12S A2
1200 CHCG 60643 3277 1W-12S E2
2300 CHCG 60655 3277 2W-12S B2
4000 CHCG 60453 3276 5W-12S B2
4000 CHCG 60655 3276 5W-12S B2
4000 OKLN 60453 3276 5W-12S B2
4900 OKLN 60453 3275 6W-12S E2
6400 CHRG 60415 3275 8W-12S B2
6400 CHRG 60482 3275 8W-12S B2
6400 WRTH 60482 3275 8W-12S B2
7400 WRTH 60482 3274 9W-12S D2
7500 PSHL 60482 3274 9W-12S D2
7500 WRTH 60465 3274 9W-12S D2
8500 PSHL 60465 3274 10W-12S B2
110th Av
13000 PlsT 60467 3345 13W-15S A1
13500 ODPK 60467 3345 13W-16S A3
13500 OrlT 60467 3345 13W-16S A3
110th Ct
17200 ODPK 60467 3423 13W-20S A5
17200 OrlT 60467 3423 13W-20S A5
E 110th Pl
10 CHCG 60628 3278 0E-12S C2
W 110th Pl
10 CHCG 60628 3278 0W-12S C2
1000 CHCG 60643 3278 1W-12S A2
1100 CHCG 60643 3277 1W-12S E2
2500 CHCG 60655 3277 3W-12S B3
3800 CHCG 60655 3276 4W-12S C3
4500 OKLN 60453 3276 5W-12S B3
7200 WRTH 60482 3274 9W-12S E3
110th St
100 PTPR 53158 2363 D1
5600 CHRG 60415 3275 7W-12S C3
5600 OKLN 60453 3275 7W-12S C3
6300 CHRG 60482 3275 7W-12S B3
6300 WRTH 60482 3275 7W-12S B3

110th St
6400 PTPR 53158 2362 A1
11400 PTPR 53158 2360 E1
25600 SlmT 53179 2357 A1
34000 RdlT 53181 2354 E1
34000 RdlT 53181 2355 A1
34000 TNLK 53181 2354 E1
34000 TNLK 53181 2355 A1
39500 TNLK 53128 2353 E1
39500 TNLK 53181 2353 E1
40000 BfdT 53128 2353 D1
40000 BfdT 53128 2353 D1
110th St CO-C
34000 RdlT 53181 2354 E1
34000 RdlT 53181 2355 A1
34000 TNLK 53181 2354 E1
34000 TNLK 53181 2355 A1
110th St CO-O
39500 RdlT 53128 2353 D1
39500 TNLK 53128 2353 E1
39500 TNLK 53181 2353 E1
40000 BfdT 53128 2353 D1
E 110th St
- CHCG 60617 3279 2E-12S D2
300 HMND 46320 3280 D2
700 CHCG 60628 3278 0E-12S E2
3200 CHCG 60617 3280 4E-12S C2
W 110th St
10 CHCG 60628 3278 0W-12S C2
1000 CHCG 60643 3278 1W-12S A2
2000 CHCG 60643 3277 2W-12S B2
2400 CHCG 60655 3277 3W-12S B2
3200 CHCG 60655 3276 4W-12S C2
3900 OKLN 60453 3276 4W-12S C2
3900 OKLN 60655 3276 4W-12S C2
5200 OKLN 60453 3275 6W-12S E3
5400 CHRG 60415 3275 6W-12S D3
5400 CHRG 60453 3275 6W-12S D3
6400 WRTH 60415 3275 8W-12S B3
6800 WRTH 60482 3275 8W-12S A3
7100 WRTH 60482 3274 9W-12S E3
111th Pl
- PSHL 60465 3274 9W-13S C3
23200 SlmT 53179 2358 A1
26800 SlmT 53179 2357 A1
E 111th Pl
400 CHCG 60628 3278 0E-13S D3
W 111th Pl
10 CHCG 60628 3278 0W-13S B3
1000 CHCG 60643 3277 1W-13S E3
2200 CHCG 60655 3277 2W-13S B3
6500 WRTH 60482 3275 8W-13S B3
7200 WRTH 60482 3274 8W-13S E3
7900 PSHL 60465 3274 9W-13S C3
111th St
- PlsT 60464 3272 14W-12S E3
- PlsT 60464 3273 13W-13S A3
- PlsT 60480 3273 13W-13S A3
800 PTPR 53158 2363 C1
6100 PTPR 53158 2362 B1
12200 LMNT 60439 3272 15W-12S A3
12200 LmnT 60464 3272 14W-12S E3
22400 BGBK 60564 3267 28W-12S A4
22400 BGBK 60585 3267 28W-12S A4
22400 WldT 60490 3267 28W-12S A4
22400 WldT 60564 3266 28W-13S E4
22400 WldT 60564 3267 28W-12S A4
22400 WldT 60585 3267 28W-12S A4
23300 SlmT 53179 2357 E1
24800 WldT 60564 3265 31W-12S E4
24900 WldT 60585 3265 31W-12S E4
30600 SlmT 53192 2356 A1
111th St SR-83
- PlsT 60464 3272 14W-12S E3
- PlsT 60464 3273 13W-13S A3
- PlsT 60480 3273 13W-13S A3
12200 LMNT 60439 3272 15W-12S A3
12200 LmnT 60464 3272 14W-12S E3
E 111th St
- CHCG 60628 3279 1E-13S A3
10 CHCG 60628 3278 1E-12S E2
3300 CHCG 60617 3280 4E-12S B2
4000 HMND 46320 3280 4E-12S C2
W 111th St
- OswT 60543 3265 32W-12S B4
- WldT 60543 3265 32W-12S C4
- WldT 60564 3265 32W-12S C4
10 CHCG 60628 3278 0W-12S B3
700 CHCG 60643 3278 1W-13S A3
1000 CHCG 60643 3277 1W-12S E3
2300 CHCG 60655 3277 2W-12S B3
3000 CHCG 60655 3276 4W-12S E3
3900 OKLN 60453 3276 4W-12S C3
4300 CHCG 60453 3276 5W-12S B3
4300 OKLN 60655 3276 5W-12S B3
4800 ALSP 60453 3276 6W-12S A3
4800 ALSP 60655 3276 6W-12S A3
4800 ALSP 60803 3276 6W-12S A3
5000 ALSP 60453 3275 6W-12S E3
5000 ALSP 60803 3275 6W-12S E3
5000 OKLN 60453 3275 6W-12S E3
5400 ALSP 60482 3275 6W-12S D3
5400 CHRG 60415 3275 6W-12S D3
5400 CHRG 60453 3275 6W-12S D3
5400 CHRG 60482 3275 6W-12S D3
6100 WRTH 60482 3275 8W-12S A3
6300 WRTH 60415 3275 7W-12S B3
7000 WRTH 60482 3274 9W-12S D3
7400 PSHL 60465 3274 10W-12S A3
7400 WRTH 60465 3274 9W-12S D3
9000 PlsT 60465 3273 11W-13S E3
9000 PSHL 60465 3273 11W-13S E3
9200 PlsT 60480 3273 11W-13S D3
24100 AURA 60585 3265 32W-12S D4
24100 WldT 60585 3265 32W-12S C4
112th Ct
15500 ODPK 60467 3344 14W-18S E7
15500 OrlT 60467 3344 14W-18S E7
15600 OrlT 60467 3422 14W-18S E1
15700 ODPK 60467 3422 14W-18S E1
112th Pl
- PSHL 60465 3274 9W-13S C3
28600 SlmT 53179 2356 C1
E 112th Pl
10 CHCG 60628 3278 0E-13S C3
W 112th Pl
10 CHCG 60628 3278 0W-13S C3
1000 CHCG 60643 3277 1W-13S E3
1000 CHCG 60643 3278 1W-13S A3
2300 CHCG 60655 3277 2W-13S B3
3200 CHCG 60655 3276 4W-13S D3
4900 ALSP 60803 3276 6W-13S A3
6500 WRTH 60482 3275 8W-13S A3
7700 PSHL 60482 3274 9W-13S D3
7700 WRTH 60482 3274 9W-13S D3
7900 PSHL 60465 3274 9W-13S C3

112th St
1200 PTPR 53158 2363 B2
23200 SlmT 53179 2357 E1
29000 SlmT 53179 2356 C1
30600 SlmT 53192 2356 A1
E 112th St
- CHCG 60617 3279 3E-12S E3
100 CHCG 46320 3280 C3
100 CHCG 60617 3280 C3
100 HMND 46320 3280 D3
800 CHCG 60628 3278 1E-13S E3
W 112th St
10 CHCG 60628 3278 0W-13S B3
700 CHCG 60643 3278 1W-13S A3
1000 CHCG 60643 3277 1W-13S E3
2600 CHCG 60655 3277 3W-13S A3
3000 CHCG 60655 3276 3W-13S E3
6400 WRTH 60482 3275 8W-13S B3
7100 WRTH 60482 3274 8W-13S E3
7900 PSHL 60465 3274 9W-13S C3
113th Av
15500 OrlT 60467 3344 14W-18S E7
15700 OrlT 60467 3422 14W-18S E1
15800 ODPK 60467 3422 14W-18S E1
18800 FftT 60448 3502 14W-22S E2
18800 MKNA 60448 3502 14W-22S E2
S 113th Av
12300 PSPK 60464 3272 14W-14S E6
W 113th Av
14300 HnrT 46311 3687 D6
15900 CteT 60417 3687 D6
113th Ct
15700 OrlT 60467 3422 14W-18S E1
15800 ODPK 60467 3422 14W-18S E1
W 113th Ct
5100 ALSP 60803 3276 6W-13S A3
E 113th Pl
10 CHCG 60628 3278 0E-13S C3
W 113th Pl
10 CHCG 60628 3278 0W-13S C3
1000 CHCG 60643 3278 1W-13S A3
2300 CHCG 60643 3277 2W-13S B3
2300 CHCG 60655 3277 2W-13S B3
3000 CHCG 60655 3276 3W-13S E3
3000 MTPK 60655 3276 3W-13S E3
3000 MTPK 60803 3276 3W-13S E3
5100 ALSP 60803 3276 6W-13S A3
6700 WRTH 60482 3275 8W-13S A4
6900 WRTH 60482 3274 9W-13S E4
7900 PSHL 60465 3274 9W-13S C4
113th St
100 PTPR 53158 2363 D1
6100 PTPR 53158 2362 B1
8800 PTPR 53158 2361 C1
26800 SlmT 53179 2357 A1
28600 SlmT 53179 2356 D1
30500 SlmT 53192 2356 A1
113th St CO-C
30500 SlmT 53179 2356 A1
30500 SlmT 53192 2356 A1
E 113th St
- CHCG 60617 3279 3E-12S E3
800 CHCG 60628 3278 1E-13S E3
3300 CHCG 60617 3280 4E-12S B3
W 113th St
10 CHCG 60628 3278 0W-13S C3
700 CHCG 60643 3278 0W-13S A3
2200 CHCG 60643 3277 2W-13S B3
2400 CHCG 60655 3277 3W-13S B3
3000 CHCG 60655 3276 3W-13S E3
3000 MTPK 60655 3276 3W-13S E3
3000 MTPK 60803 3276 3W-13S E3
5000 ALSP 60803 3276 6W-13S A3
5100 ALSP 60803 3275 6W-13S E3
6400 WRTH 60482 3275 8W-13S B3
6900 WRTH 60482 3274 9W-13S E3
7900 PSHL 60465 3274 9W-13S C3
114th Av
15600 OrlT 60467 3422 14W-18S E1
15800 ODPK 60467 3422 14W-18S E1
19700 FftT 60448 3502 14W-23S E4
20000 MKNA 60448 3502 14W-24S E5
S 114th Av
12300 PlsT 60464 3272 14W-14S E6
12300 PSPK 60464 3272 14W-14S E6
114th Ct
15700 ODPK 60467 3422 14W-18S E1
15700 OrlT 60467 3422 14W-18S E1
114th Pl
- PSHL 60465 3274 9W-13S D4
- PSHT 60465 3274 9W-13S D4
E 114th Pl
500 CHCG 60628 3278 0E-13S D3
W 114th Pl
10 CHCG 60628 3278 0W-13S C3
900 CHCG 60643 3277 1W-13S E3
900 CHCG 60643 3278 1W-13S A3
3000 MTPK 60803 3276 3W-13S E4
3100 MTPK 60655 3276 3W-13S E4
3600 CHCG 60655 3276 4W-13S D4
5100 ALSP 60803 3276 6W-13S A4
6700 WRTH 60482 3275 8W-13S A4
6900 WRTH 60482 3274 9W-13S E4
114th St
- PSHL 60465 3274 9W-13S C4
600 HMND 46394 3280 E3
800 PTPR 53158 2363 C2
4100 PTPR 53158 2362 D2
25800 SlmT 53179 2357 B1
28600 SlmT 53179 2356 D1
30600 SlmT 53192 2356 A1
114th St CO-C
30700 SlmT 53192 2356 A1
E 114th St
500 CHCG 60628 3278 0E-13S E3
800 HMND 46394 3280 E3
2600 CHCG 60617 3279 3E-13S E3
3400 CHCG 60617 3280 4E-13S B3
W 114th St
10 CHCG 60628 3278 0W-13S C3
700 CHCG 60628 3278 0W-13S A3
2400 CHCG 60643 3277 3W-13S B3
2400 CHCG 60655 3277 3W-13S B3
3000 MTPK 60655 3276 3W-13S E3
3000 MTPK 60803 3276 3W-13S E3
3200 CHCG 60655 3276 4W-13S E3
5100 ALSP 60803 3276 6W-13S A4
6400 WRTH 60482 3275 7W-13S B4
6900 WRTH 60482 3274 9W-13S E4
115th Av
- ODPK 60467 3502 14W-22S E1
11400 ODPK 60448 3422 14W-22S E7
11400 ODPK 60467 3422 14W-22S E7
15800 OrlT 60467 3422 14W-18S E1
19500 FftT 60448 3502 14W-23S E4
19500 MKNA 60448 3502 14W-24S E4

STREET Block City ZIP Map# CGS Grid

S 115th Av
12300 PlsT 60464 3272 14W-14S D6
12300 PSPK 60464 3272 14W-14S D6
115th Ct
15500 OrlT 60467 3422 14W-18S D1
15700 ODPK 60467 3422 14W-18S D1
115th Pl
28600 SlmT 53179 2356 D1
W 115th Pl
900 CHCG 60643 3278 1W-13S A4
2500 CHCG 60655 3277 3W-13S B4
3400 CHCG 60655 3276 4W-13S C4
3400 MTPK 60655 3276 4W-13S C4
3400 MTPK 60803 3276 4W-13S C4
3600 CHCG 60803 3276 4W-13S D4
3600 WthT 60803 3276 4W-13S D4
4300 ALSP 60803 3276 5W-13S B4
6800 WRTH 60482 3275 8W-13S A4
7000 WRTH 60482 3274 8W-13S E4
115th St
- BGBK 60490 3267 26W-13S D5
- BGBK 60490 3268 26W-13S A5
- DPgT 60490 3268 26W-13S A5
- PSPK 60464 3274 10W-13S B4
10 LMNT 60439 3272 15W-13S A4
800 PTPR 53158 2363 C2
3100 PTPR 53158 2362 E2
12300 LmnT 60464 3272 15W-13S B4
26800 SlmT 53179 2357 A2
28600 SlmT 53179 2356 D1
E 115th St
10 CHCG 60628 3278 0E-13S D4
600 HMND 46394 3280 E3
3600 CHCG 60617 3280 4E-13S B3
W 115th St
- RMVL 60446 3268 25W-13S A5
- RMVL 60490 3268 25W-13S A5
10 CHCG 60628 3278 0W-13S B4
700 CHCG 60643 3278 0W-13S A4
1000 CHCG 60643 3277 1W-13S E4
1100 BGBK 60490 3268 25W-13S B5
1100 DPgT 60490 3268 25W-13S B5
2300 CHCG 60655 3277 3W-13S A4
2900 MTPK 60803 3277 3W-13S A4
3000 MTPK 60803 3276 4W-13S C4
3100 CHCG 60655 3276 E4
3100 MTPK 60655 3276 3W-13S E4
3200 CHCG 60803 3276 4W-13S E4
3600 WthT 60655 3276 4W-13S D4
3600 WthT 60803 3276 4W-13S D4
3800 ALSP 60655 3276 4W-13S C4
4200 ALSP 60803 3276 5W-13S B4
5000 ALSP 60803 3275 8W-13S A4
5300 OKLN 60453 3275 6W-13S D4
5300 OKLN 60803 3275 6W-13S D4
5400 ALSP 60453 3275 6W-13S D4
5400 ALSP 60482 3275 6W-13S D4
6000 WRTH 60482 3275 7W-13S C4
6000 WRTH 60803 3275 7W-13S C4
6900 WRTH 60482 3274 9W-13S E4
116th Av
- ODPK 60448 3422 14W-22S D7
- ODPK 60467 3422 14W-22S D7
- ODPK 60467 3502 14W-22S D1
- PTPR 53158 2360 E1
15500 OrlT 60467 3344 14W-18S D7
15600 OrlT 60467 3422 14W-18S D1
19200 FftT 60448 3502 14W-23S E4
19200 MKNA 60448 3502 14W-23S E4
22300 FftT 60423 3590 14W-26S E3
22300 FftT 60448 3590 14W-26S E3
22300 FKFT 60423 3590 14W-27S E5
22300 MKNA 60448 3590 14W-26S E3
22800 GGnT 60423 3590 14W-27S E5
S 116th Av
12300 PlsT 60464 3272 14W-14S D6
12300 PSPK 60464 3272 14W-14S D6
15500 OrlT 60467 3344 14W-18S D7
116th Ct
15500 OrlT 60467 3344 14W-18S D7
15600 OrlT 60467 3422 14W-18S D1
116th Pl
23900 SlmT 53179 2357 E2
W 116th Pl
600 CHCG 60628 3278 0W-13S A4
900 CHCG 60643 3278 1W-13S A4
2200 CHCG 60643 3277 2W-13S B4
2500 CHCG 60655 3277 3W-13S B4
3400 CHCG 60655 3276 4W-13S D4
3400 MTPK 60655 3276 4W-13S D4
3400 MTPK 60803 3276 4W-13S D4
3600 WthT 60655 3276 4W-13S D4
3600 WthT 60803 3276 4W-13S D4
4400 ALSP 60803 3276 5W-13S B4
116th St
- CHCG 60617 3279 2E-13S D4
- PlsT 60464 3274 10W-13S B4
100 PTPR 53158 2363 B2
2800 PTPR 53158 2362 D2
8000 PTPR 53158 2361 D2
8400 PSPK 60464 3274 10W-13S B4
12000 BtlT 53142 2360 C2
18200 BtlT 53104 2359 A2
18800 BtlT 53104 2358 B2
21600 SlmT 53104 2358 B2
22800 SlmT 53179 2358 A2
28500 SlmT 53179 2356 D2
31600 RdlT 53181 2355 A2
31800 TNLK 53181 2355 A2
35000 RdlT 53181 2354 E2
35000 TNLK 53181 2354 E2
116th St CO-C
31600 RdlT 53181 2355 D2
31800 TNLK 53181 2355 C2
116th St CO-HM
33600 RdlT 53181 2355 A2
33600 TNLK 53181 2355 A2
35000 RdlT 53181 2354 E2
35000 TNLK 53181 2354 E2
116th St CO-ML
8000 PTPR 53158 2361 D2
116th St CO-V
18200 BtlT 53104 2359 A2
18800 BtlT 53104 2358 B2
21600 SlmT 53104 2358 B2
E 116th St
- CHCG 60617 3280 3E-13S A4
10 CHCG 60628 3278 0E-13S C4
600 HMND 46394 3280 E4
W 116th St
600 CHCG 60628 3278 0W-13S A4
800 CHCG 60643 3278 1W-13S A4
1900 CHCG 60643 3277 2W-13S C4
2400 CHCG 60655 3277 3W-13S B4
3100 CHCG 60655 3276 4W-13S C4
3100 MTPK 60655 3276 4W-13S C4

W 116th St
3100 MTPK 60803 3276 4W-13S C4
3600 WthT 60655 3276 4W-13S D4
3600 WthT 60803 3276 4W-13S D4
4800 ALSP 60803 3276 6W-13S A4
5000 ALSP 60803 3275 6W-13S E4
6800 WRTH 60482 3275 8W-13S A4
7000 WRTH 60482 3274 8W-13S E4
117th Av
15500 OrlT 60467 3344 14W-18S D7
15600 OrlT 60467 3422 14W-18S D1
W 117th Av
13400 HnrT 46303 3687 E7
13400 HnrT 46311 3687 E7
117th Ct
15500 OrlT 60467 3344 14W-18S D7
15600 OrlT 60467 3422 14W-18S D1
117th Pl
600 HMND 46394 3280 D4
24000 SlmT 53179 2357 D2
E 117th Pl
10 CHCG 60628 3278 0E-13S C4
W 117th Pl
600 CHCG 60628 3278 0W-13S A4
700 CHCG 60643 3278 0W-13S A4
2100 CHCG 60643 3277 2W-13S C4
2500 CHCG 60655 3277 3W-13S B4
5800 ALSP 60803 3275 7W-13S C5
117th St
- PSHT 60463 3274 9W-13S C4
- PSHT 60465 3274 9W-13S C4
- PSPK 60464 3274 10W-13S B5
600 HMND 46394 3280 E4
1100 LMNT 60439 3271 18W-13S B5
21500 BtlT 53104 2358 B2
22000 SlmT 53104 2358 B2
22900 SlmT 53179 2358 A2
28400 SlmT 53179 2356 D2
30600 SlmT 53192 2356 A2
33400 RdlT 53181 2355 C2
E 117th St
10 CHCG 60628 3278 0E-13S C4
2600 CHCG 60617 3279 3E-13S E4
3600 CHCG 60617 3280 4E-13S B4
W 117th St
600 CHCG 60628 3278 0W-13S A4
800 CHCG 60643 3278 1W-13S A4
1900 CHCG 60643 3277 2W-13S C4
2400 CHCG 60655 3277 3W-13S B4
3400 MTPK 60655 3276 4W-13S D4
3500 CHCG 60655 3276 4W-13S C4
3500 MTPK 60803 3276 4W-13S C4
3500 WthT 60655 3276 4W-13S C4
3500 WthT 60803 3276 4W-13S C4
4900 ALSP 60803 3276 6W-13S A4
5000 ALSP 60803 3275 6W-13S E4
118th Av
15500 OrlT 60467 3344 14W-18S D7
15900 OrlT 60467 3422 14W-19S D1
16000 ODPK 60467 3422 14W-19S D2
118th Pl
- OrlT 60467 3422 14W-19S D3
25000 SlmT 53179 2357 C2
E 118th Pl
10 CHCG 60628 3278 0E-13S C4
W 118th Pl
700 CHCG 60628 3278 0W-13S A4
700 CHCG 60643 3278 0W-13S A4
2500 CHCG 60655 3277 3W-13S B5
4100 ALSP 60803 3276 5W-13S B5
118th St
- PlsT 60464 3274 10W-13S B5
- PSPK 60464 3274 10W-13S B5
1100 LMNT 60439 3271 18W-13S B5
4500 PTPR 53158 2362 D2
21100 BtlT 53104 2358 C2
21600 SlmT 53104 2358 B2
22800 SlmT 53179 2358 A2
24300 SlmT 53179 2357 D2
30600 SlmT 53192 2356 A2
31500 RdlT 53181 2355 E2
E 118th St
10 CHCG 60628 3278 0E-13S C4
600 HMND 46394 3280 E4
3400 CHCG 60617 3280 4E-13S B4
W 118th St
10 CHCG 60628 3278 0W-13S A4
700 CHCG 60643 3278 0W-13S A4
2100 CHCG 60643 3277 2W-13S C4
2400 CHCG 60655 3277 3W-13S B4
3600 MTPK 60803 3276 4W-13S C4
3600 WthT 60803 3276 4W-13S C4
4300 ALSP 60803 3276 5W-13S B5
5000 ALSP 60803 3275 6W-13S E5
8200 PSPK 60464 3274 10W-13S B5
11800 PlsT 60464 3272 14W-13S D5
11900 LMNT 60439 3272 14W-13S C5
11900 PlsT 60439 3272 14W-13S C5
119th Pl
2000 BLID 60406 3277 2W-14S B5
E 119th Pl
300 CHCG 60628 3278 0E-14S D5
W 119th Pl
4200 ALSP 60803 3276 5W-14S B5
7200 PSHT 60463 3274 9W-14S E5
8400 PSPK 60464 3274 10W-14S B5
119th St
200 PTPR 53158 2363 D3
1000 LMNT 60439 3271 18W-13S A5
7400 PSHT 60463 3274 9W-13S D5
7900 PSHT 60464 3274 9W-13S C5
7900 PSPK 60464 3274 9W-13S C5
18200 BtlT 53104 2359 A2
21100 BtlT 53104 2358 C2
23300 SlmT 53179 2357 E2
23300 SlmT 53179 2358 A2
30600 SlmT 53192 2356 A2
40000 BfdT 53128 2353 D2
40000 GNCY 53128 2353 D2
40000 RdlT 53128 2353 D2
40000 RdlT 53181 2353 D2
119th St CO-JF
23800 SlmT 53179 2357 C2
119th St SR-83
7400 PSHT 60463 3274 9W-13S C5
7900 PSHT 60464 3274 9W-13S C5
7900 PSPK 60464 3274 9W-13S C5
E 119th St
10 CHCG 60628 3278 0E-13S C5
600 HMND 46394 3280 E4
W 119th St
10 CHCG 60628 3278 0W-13S B5
700 CHCG 60643 3278 0W-13S A5
1000 CHCG 60643 3277 1W-13S E5
1500 CTPK 60643 3277 1W-13S D5
1600 CTPK 60827 3277 2W-13S D5

W 119th St
1800 BLID 60406 3277 3W-13S A5
1800 BLID 60643 3277 2W-13S D5
1800 BLID 60827 3277 2W-13S D5
1800 ClmT 60406 3277 2W-13S C5
1800 ClmT 60643 3277 2W-13S C5
2300 BLID 60655 3277 3W-13S A5
2300 CHCG 60655 3277 3W-13S A5
2600 MTPK 60655 3277 3W-13S A5
2600 MTPK 60803 3277 3W-13S A5
2600 WthT 60406 3277 3W-13S A5
2600 WthT 60655 3277 3W-13S A5
2600 WthT 60803 3277 3W-13S A5
3000 MTPK 60655 3276 3W-14S E5
3000 MTPK 60803 3276 4W-14S D5
3000 WthT 60655 3276 4W-14S D5
3000 WthT 60803 3276 4W-14S D5
4700 ALSP 60803 3276 6W-14S A5
5000 ALSP 60803 3275 6W-14S E5
8000 PSPK 60464 3274 10W-14S C5
8500 PlsT 60464 3274 10W-13S B5
8900 PlsT 60464 3273 11W-13S E5
8900 PSPK 60464 3273 11W-13S E5
22600 BGBK 60585 3267 28W-13S A6
22600 PNFD 60585 3267 28W-13S A6
22600 WldT 60564 3266 29W-13S C6
22600 WldT 60564 3267 28W-13S A6
22600 WldT 60585 3266 29W-13S C6
22600 WldT 60585 3267 28W-13S A6
24000 PNFD 60585 3266 29W-13S C6
24800 PNFD 60585 3265 31W-13S E6
25000 WldT 60585 3265 31W-13S E6
26000 WldT 60543 3265 32W-13S C6
26100 OswT 60543 3265 32W-13S B6
120th Av
10600 BtlT 53142 2360 D2
10600 PTPR 53142 2360 D1
10800 PTPR 53158 2360 E3
12500 BtlT 60099 2360 D2
12500 NptT 60099 2360 D2
120th Ct
11800 PTPR 53158 2360 E3
120th Pl
2000 BLID 60406 3277 2W-14S B5
3400 PTPR 53158 2362 E3
E 120th Pl
10 CHCG 60628 3278 0E-14S C5
W 120th Pl
3600 ALSP 60803 3276 4W-14S D5
3600 WthT 60803 3276 4W-14S D5
5000 ALSP 60803 3275 6W-14S E5
8800 PSPK 60464 3274 11W-14S A5
120th St
2000 BLID 60406 3277 2W-14S B5
4300 PTPR 53158 2362 D3
18200 BtlT 53104 2359 A2
21100 BtlT 53104 2358 C2
22100 SlmT 53104 2358 B2
22900 SlmT 53179 2358 A2
25700 SlmT 53179 2357 B2
32800 RdlT 53181 2355 C2
E 120th St
700 CHCG 60628 3278 0E-13S E5
700 HMND 46394 3280 E5
W 120th St
10 CHCG 60628 3278 0W-14S C5
700 CHCG 60643 3278 1W-14S A5
1000 CHCG 60643 3277 1W-14S E5
1600 CTPK 60643 3277 2W-14S D5
1600 CTPK 60827 3277 2W-14S D5
1800 BLID 60406 3277 2W-13S D5
1800 BLID 60827 3277 2W-14S D5
3600 WthT 60803 3276 4W-14S D5
4000 ALSP 60803 3276 5W-14S C5
5600 ALSP 60803 3275 7W-14S D5
6800 PSHT 60463 3275 8W-14S A5
7000 PSHT 60463 3274 9W-14S E5
7900 PSPK 60464 3274 9W-14S E5
9100 PSPK 60464 3273 11W-14S E5
121st Pl
2100 BLID 60406 3277 2W-14S B5
3200 PTPR 53158 2362 E3
21600 SlmT 53104 2358 B2
24600 SlmT 53179 2357 D3
32800 RdlT 53181 2355 C3
E 121st Pl
10 CHCG 60628 3278 0E-14S D5
W 121st Pl
3800 ALSP 60803 3276 4W-14S C5
5000 ALSP 60803 3275 6W-14S E5
121st St
- BLID 60827 3277 2W-14S D5
- BtlT 53104 2359 B3
- BtlT 53142 2359 B3
- CTPK 60827 3277 2W-14S D5
100 PTPR 53158 2363 D3
1100 LMNT 60439 3271 18W-14S B6
2300 BLID 60406 3277 3W-14S A5
4400 PTPR 53158 2362 D3
21100 BtlT 53104 2358 C2
21600 SlmT 53104 2358 B2
25000 SlmT 53179 2357 C3
E 121st St
10 CHCG 60628 3278 0E-14S C5
700 HMND 46394 3280 E5
W 121st St
10 CHCG 60628 3278 0W-14S C5
1400 CHCG 60643 3277 1W-14S D5
1600 CTPK 60643 3277 2W-14S D5
1600 CTPK 60827 3277 2W-14S D5
3600 ALSP 60803 3276 4W-14S D5
3600 WthT 60803 3276 4W-14S D5
5000 ALSP 60803 3275 6W-14S E5
6800 PSHT 60463 3275 8W-14S A5
7200 PSHT 60463 3274 9W-14S E5
7800 PSPK 60464 3274 10W-14S C5
9000 PSPK 60464 3273 11W-14S E6
9300 PlsT 60464 3273 11W-14S E6
122nd Pl
2600 BLID 60406 3277 3W-14S A6
25000 SlmT 53179 2357 E3
E 122nd Pl
10 CHCG 60628 3278 0E-14S C5
W 122nd Pl
3600 ALSP 60803 3276 4W-14S D6
8400 PSPK 60464 3274 10W-14S B6
122nd St
- BtlT 53142 2360 E3
- LMNT 60439 3272 16W-14S A6
100 PTPR 53158 2363 D3
2400 BLID 60406 3277 3W-14S A5
3900 PTPR 53158 2362 D3
8400 PTPR 53158 2361 A3
9100 PTPR 53158 2360 E3
18300 BtlT 53104 2359 A3
21100 BtlT 53104 2358 C3

122nd St
21900 SlmT 53104 2358 A3
22300 SlmT 53179 2358 B3
25700 SlmT 53179 2357 A3
26000 SlmT 53179 2356 E3
122nd St CO-ML
- BtlT 53142 2360 E3
8800 PTPR 53158 2361 A3
9100 PTPR 53158 2360 E3
E 122nd St
10 CHCG 60628 3278 0E-14S C5
800 HMND 46320 3280 E5
900 HMND 46394 3280 E5
1600 CHCG 60633 3279 2E-14S C5
1900 CHCG 60617 3279 2E-13S D5
W 122nd St
- BLID 60406 3277 2W-14S D5
10 CHCG 60628 3278 1W-14S A5
700 CHCG 60628 3278 1W-14S A5
1000 CHCG 60643 3277 1W-14S E5
1600 BLID 60643 3277 2W-14S D5
1600 BLID 60827 3277 2W-14S D5
1600 CTPK 60643 3277 2W-14S D5
1600 CTPK 60827 3277 2W-14S D5
4400 ALSP 60803 3276 5W-14S A5
5000 ALSP 60803 3275 6W-14S E6
6400 PSHT 60463 3275 8W-14S B6
7000 PSHT 60463 3274 9W-14S E6
7900 PSPK 60463 3274 9W-14S C6
7900 PSPK 60464 3274 9W-14S C6
9300 PSPK 60464 3273 11W-14S E6
123rd Pl
2200 BLID 60406 3277 2W-14S B6
6100 PTPR 53158 2362 A3
W 123rd Pl
3400 ALSP 60803 3276 4W-14S D6
3400 WthT 60803 3276 4W-14S D6
5200 ALSP 60803 3275 6W-14S E6
7600 PSHT 60463 3274 9W-14S D6
7700 PSPK 60464 3274 9W-14S D6
11400 PSPK 60464 3272 14W-14S D6
11500 PlsT 60464 3272 14W-14S D6
123rd St
2000 BLID 60406 3277 3W-14S A6
2800 ALSP 60655 3277 3W-14S A6
2800 ALSP 60803 3277 3W-14S A6
2800 BLID 60655 3277 3W-14S A6
2800 BLID 60803 3277 3W-14S A6
2800 WthT 60655 3277 3W-14S A6
3000 ALSP 60655 3276 3W-14S E6
3000 ALSP 60803 3276 3W-14S E6
3000 WthT 60655 3276 3W-14S E6
3000 WthT 60803 3276 3W-14S E6
4200 PTPR 53158 2362 D3
23500 SlmT 53179 2357 E3
E 123rd St
10 CHCG 60628 3278 0E-14S C6
W 123rd St
10 CHCG 60628 3278 1W-14S A6
700 CHCG 60643 3278 1W-14S A6
700 CTPK 60628 3278 1W-14S A6
700 CTPK 60643 3278 1W-14S A6
700 CTPK 60827 3278 1W-14S A6
1000 CHCG 60643 3277 1W-14S D6
1000 CTPK 60643 3277 1W-14S D6
1000 CTPK 60827 3277 1W-14S D6
1400 CHCG 60827 3277 1W-14S D6
1600 BLID 60643 3277 2W-14S D6
1600 BLID 60827 3277 2W-14S D6
3200 ALSP 60803 3276 6W-14S A6
3200 WthT 60655 3276 4W-14S D6
3200 WthT 60803 3276 4W-14S D6
5000 ALSP 60803 3275 6W-14S E6
6000 WthT 60803 3275 7W-14S C6
6100 PSHT 60463 3275 7W-14S C6
6400 WthT 60463 3275 8W-14S B6
7000 PSHT 60463 3274 9W-14S E6
8100 PSPK 60464 3274 10W-14S A6
9000 PSPK 60464 3273 11W-14S E6
9300 PlsT 60464 3273 11W-14S E6
124th Pl
23300 SlmT 53179 2357 E3
E 124th Pl
10 CHCG 60628 3278 0W-14S C6
W 124th Pl
3400 ALSP 60406 3276 4W-14S E6
3400 ALSP 60803 3276 4W-14S E6
3400 WthT 60406 3276 4W-14S E6
3400 WthT 60803 3276 4W-14S E6
5800 ALSP 60803 3275 7W-14S C6
6200 PSHT 60803 3275 7W-14S B6
7600 PSHT 60463 3274 9W-14S D6
124th St
6600 PTPR 53158 2362 A3
20800 BtlT 53104 2358 C3
23300 SlmT 53179 2357 E3
E 124th St
- CHCG 60628 3278 0E-14S E6
W 124th St
10 CHCG 60628 3278 0W-14S B6
700 CTPK 60628 3278 1W-14S A6
700 CTPK 60827 3278 1W-14S A6
1600 CTPK 60827 3277 2W-14S C6
1800 BLID 60406 3277 2W-14S C6
1800 BLID 60827 3277 2W-14S C6
1800 CTPK 60406 3277 2W-14S C6
3400 ALSP 60803 3276 4W-14S E6
3400 WthT 60803 3276 4W-14S D6
5300 ALSP 60803 3275 6W-14S E6
5800 WthT 60463 3275 7W-14S C6
5800 WthT 60803 3275 7W-14S C6
6100 PSHT 60463 3275 7W-14S C6
7000 PSHT 60463 3274 9W-14S E6
8000 PSPK 60464 3274 10W-14S C6
9100 PSPK 60464 3273 11W-14S E6
125th Pl
6600 PTPR 53158 2362 A4
E 125th Pl
10 CHCG 60628 3278 0W-14S C6
W 125th Pl
10 CHCG 60628 3278 0W-14S C6
5800 ALSP 60463 3275 7W-14S C7
5800 ALSP 60803 3275 7W-14S C7
5800 WthT 60463 3275 7W-14S C7
6100 PSHT 60463 3275 7W-14S B7
125th St
- PTPR 53158 2362 E3
- PTPR 53158 2363 D4
23400 SlmT 53179 2357 E3
32000 RdlT 53181 2355 C3
40400 GNCY 53128 2353 D3
40400 RdlT 53128 2353 C3
40400 RdlT 53181 2353 D3
40400 TNLK 53128 2353 C3
40400 TNLK 53181 2353 C3

125th St CO-CK
32000 RdlT 53181 2355 C3
W 125th St
10 CHCG 60628 3278 0W-14S B6
700 CTPK 60628 3278 0W-14S A6
1000 CTPK 60643 3277 1W-14S E6
1000 CTPK 60643 3278 1W-14S A6
1000 CTPK 60827 3277 2W-14S D6
1000 CTPK 60827 3278 1W-14S A6
1900 BLID 60406 3277 2W-14S C6
1900 CTPK 60406 3277 2W-14S C6
3400 ALSP 60406 3276 4W-14S E6
3400 ALSP 60803 3276 4W-14S E6
3600 BLID 60406 3276 4W-14S D6
6000 ALSP 60803 3275 7W-14S C6
6000 WthT 60463 3275 7W-14S C6
6000 WthT 60803 3275 7W-14S C6
6200 PSHT 60463 3275 8W-14S B6
7000 PSHT 60463 3274 8W-14S E6
8000 PSPK 60464 3274 10W-14S C6
9100 PSPK 60464 3273 11W-14S E7
126th Pl
6500 PTPR 53158 2362 A4
23400 SlmT 53179 2357 E3
E 126th Pl
100 CHCG 60628 3278 0W-14S D7
W 126th Pl
10 CHCG 60628 3278 0W-14S C6
5800 ALSP 60803 3275 7W-14S C7
6400 PSHT 60463 3275 8W-14S B7
126th St
- ALSP 60803 3276 3W-14S E6
- ALSP 60803 3277 3W-14S A6
1100 PTPR 53158 2363 C4
6500 PTPR 53158 2362 A4
22700 SlmT 53104 2358 A3
23700 SlmT 53179 2357 E3
E 126th St
10 CHCG 60628 3278 0W-14S C6
2600 CHCG 60633 3279 3E-14S E6
2600 CHCG 60633 3280 3E-14S A6
W 126th St
- PlsT 60464 3273 12W-14S C7
- PSPK 60464 3273 12W-14S C7
200 CHCG 60628 3278 0W-14S B6
700 CHCG 60643 3278 0W-14S A6
700 CTPK 60643 3278 0W-14S A6
1200 CTPK 60643 3277 1W-14S D6
1200 CTPK 60827 3277 1W-14S D6
1900 BLID 60406 3277 2W-14S C6
1900 BLID 60827 3277 2W-14S C6
4000 ALSP 60803 3276 5W-14S C7
5600 WthT 60463 3275 7W-14S D6
5700 ALSP 60463 3275 7W-14S D6
5800 ALSP 60803 3275 7W-14S C7
6800 PSHT 60463 3275 8W-14S A7
7200 PSHT 60463 3274 9W-14S E7
8000 PSPK 60464 3274 10W-14S C7
127th Pl
23400 SlmT 53179 2357 E3
W 127th Pl
500 CHCG 60628 3278 0W-15S B7
4900 ALSP 60803 3276 6W-15S A7
6000 WthT 60463 3275 7W-15S C7
6300 PSHT 60463 3275 7W-15S B7
W 127th Rd
- OswT 60543 3337 33W-14S A1
- OswT 60585 3337 33W-14S A1
- PNFD 60543 3337 33W-14S A1
- PNFD 60585 3337 33W-14S A1
- WldT 60585 3337 33W-14S A1
127th St
6400 PTPR 53158 2362 A4
23400 SlmT 53179 2357 E3
E 127th St
10 CHCG 60628 3278 0W-14S C7
2600 CHCG 60633 3279 3E-14S E6
2900 CHCG 60633 3280 3E-14S A6
W 127th St
- PNFD 60543 3337 32W-14S B1
10 CHCG 60628 3278 0W-14S B7
10 LMNT 60439 3270 20W-14S B7
700 CHCG 60628 3278 0W-14S A7
700 CTPK 60643 3278 0W-14S A7
1000 CTPK 60643 3277 1W-14S E7
1000 CTPK 60827 3277 1W-14S E7
1000 CTPK 60827 3278 1W-14S A7
3600 ALSP 60803 3276 6W-14S A7
3600 WthT 60406 3276 4W-14S C7
5100 ALSP 60803 3275 7W-14S C7
5200 ALSP 60445 3275 6W-14S E7
5200 CTWD 60445 3275 6W-14S E7
5500 CTWD 60463 3275 6W-14S D7
5500 CTWD 60803 3275 6W-14S D7
5600 WthT 60445 3275 7W-14S D7
5600 WthT 60463 3275 7W-14S D7
5700 ALSP 60463 3275 7W-14S D7
5900 WthT 60803 3275 7W-14S C7
6200 PSHT 60463 3275 7W-14S B7
7000 PSHT 60463 3274 9W-14S E7
7600 PSPK 60463 3274 9W-14S C7
7600 PSPK 60464 3274 9W-14S C7
10000 PlsT 60464 3273 12W-14S C7
10000 PSPK 60464 3273 12W-14S C7
14500 LMNT 60439 3271 18W-14S A7
16800 DPgT 60441 3341 21W-15S E1
16800 DPgT 60441 3342 21W-15S A1
16800 LMNT 60439 3342 21W-15S A1
23000 BGBK 60490 3338 28W-14S E1
23000 PNFD 60585 3338 30W-14S A1
23000 WldT 60585 3338 29W-14S E1
24800 PNFD 60585 3337 31W-14S E1
24800 WldT 60585 3337 31W-14S D1
W 127th St SR-83
4800 ALSP 60803 3276 6W-14S A7
5100 ALSP 60803 3275 7W-14S C7
5200 ALSP 60445 3275 6W-14S E7
5200 CTWD 60445 3275 6W-14S E7
128th Pl
- ALSP 60803 3276 5W-15S B7
5400 CTWD 60445 3275 7W-15S D7
W 128th Pl
400 CHCG 60628 3278 0W-15S A7
700 CHCG 60643 3278 0W-15S A7
3600 ALSP 60803 3276 4W-15S D7
6000 WthT 60463 3275 7W-15S C7
6300 PSHT 60463 3275 7W-15S B7
8000 PSPK 60464 3274 10W-15S C7
128th St
- BtlT 53142 2360 16W-43N E4
- BtlT 60099 2360 16W-43N E4
- NptT 60099 2360 16W-43N E4
10 SlmT 53104 2358 A4
2800 BLID 60406 3277 3W-15S A7
5700 CTWD 60445 3275 7W-15S D7
5700 WthT 60445 3275 7W-15S D7

STREET Block	City	ZIP	Map#	CGS	Grid
128th St					
5700	WthT	60463	3275	7W-15S	D7
15100	LMNT	60439	3342	18W-15S	E1
17900	AntT	60002	2359		A4
17900	BtlT	53104	2359		A4
17900	BtlT	53142	2359		A4
18100	AntT	60002	2359		A4
18400	AntT	53104	2358		E4
18400	AntT	53104	2359	20W-43N	A4
18400	AntT	60002	2358		E4
18400	BtlT	53104	2358		E4
22800	ANTH	60002	2358	23W-43N	A4
22800	SlmT	60002	2358	23W-43N	A4
23400	SlmT	53179	2357		E4
128th St CO-A2					
18100	AntT	60002	2359		A4
18100	BtlT	53104	2359		A4
18100	BtlT	53142	2359		A4
18100	BtlT	60002	2359		A4
18400	AntT	53104	2358		E4
18400	AntT	53104	2359	20W-43N	A4
18400	AntT	60002	2358		E4
18400	BtlT	53104	2358		E4
128th St CO-WG					
-	BtlT	53142	2360	16W-43N	E4
-	BtlT	60099	2360	16W-43N	E4
-	NptT	60099	2360	16W-43N	E4
17900	AntT	60002	2359		B4
17900	BtlT	53104	2359		B4
17900	BtlT	53142	2359		B4
E 128th St					
2600	CHCG	60633	3279	3E-14S	E7
W 128th St					
400	CHCG	60628	3278	0W-15S	B7
1200	CTPK	60827	3277	1W-15S	E7
1700	BLID	60406	3277	2W-15S	D7
1700	BLID	60827	3277	2W-15S	D7
1700	CTPK	60406	3277	2W-15S	D7
4500	ALSP	60803	3276	5W-15S	A7
6000	WthT	60463	3275	7W-15S	C7
7600	PSHT	60463	3274	9W-15S	D7
8300	PSPK	60464	3274	10W-15S	B7
26200	WldT	60585	3337	32W-15S	B1
129th Pl					
5400	CTWD	60445	3347	6W-15S	D1
W 129th Pl					
400	CHCG	60628	3278	0W-15S	A7
700	CHCG	60643	3278	0W-15S	A7
900	CTPK	60827	3278	1W-15S	A7
1100	CTPK	60827	3277	1W-15S	E7
6000	WthT	60463	3275	7W-15S	C7
6300	PSHT	60463	3347	7W-15S	B1
6300	WthT	60463	3347	7W-15S	B1
8000	PlsT	60464	3346	10W-15S	C1
129th St					
-	PNFD	60585	3337	32W-15S	C2
-	WldT	60585	3337	32W-15S	C2
100	HMND	46320	3280		E7
100	HMND	46327	3280		E7
5700	CTWD	60445	3275	7W-15S	D7
5700	WthT	60445	3275	7W-15S	D7
5700	WthT	60463	3275	7W-15S	D7
15100	LMNT	60439	3342	19W-15S	E1
E 129th St					
800	HMND	46320	3280		E7
800	HMND	46327	3280		E7
800	HMND	46394	3280		E7
2600	CHCG	60633	3279	3E-14S	E7
2900	CHCG	60633	3280	3E-14S	A7
W 129th St					
4000	ALSP	60803	3276	5W-15S	C7
4400	ALSP	60803	3348	5W-15S	B1
5700	CTWD	60445	3275	7W-15S	C7
5700	WthT	60445	3275	7W-15S	C7
6000	WthT	60463	3275	7W-15S	C7
7800	PSHT	60463	3274	9W-15S	C7
7800	PSPK	60463	3274	9W-15S	C7
8000	PlsT	60464	3274	10W-15S	C7
8000	PSPK	60464	3274	10W-15S	C7
8200	PlsT	60464	3346	10W-15S	B1
8200	PSPK	60464	3346	10W-15S	B1
129th Infantry Dr					
10	JLET	60435	3497	27W-22S	C3
10	JLET	60436	3497	27W-23S	C5
S 129th Infantry Dr					
-	JLET	60431	3497	27W-24S	C5
100	JLET	60435	3497	27W-24S	C6
100	JLET	60436	3497	27W-24S	C6
E 130th Av					
-	CHCG	60827	3279	1E-15S	A7
W 130th Ct					
4600	ALSP	60803	3348	5W-15S	A1
130th Pl					
15300	LMNT	60439	3342	19W-15S	D1
E 130th Pl					
-	CHCG	60628	3279	1E-14S	A7
-	CHCG	60827	3279	1E-14S	A7
600	CHCG	60827	3278	0E-15S	E7
W 130th Pl					
6000	WthT	60463	3347	7W-15S	C1
130th St					
-	RVDL	60827	3350	1W-15S	A1
E 130th St					
-	CHCG	60628	3279	2E-14S	D7
-	CHCG	60827	3279	2E-14S	D7
-	RVDL	60628	3278	0E-14S	D7
-	RVDL	60827	3278	0E-14S	D7
200	CHCG	60628	3278	0E-14S	D7
200	CHCG	60827	3278	0E-14S	D7
1400	CHCG	60633	3279	3E-14S	E7
2900	CHCG	60633	3280	3E-14S	A7
W 130th St					
4300	ALSP	60803	3348	5W-15S	C1
5400	CTWD	60445	3347	6W-15S	D1
7000	PSHT	60463	3346	8W-15S	E1
7000	PSHT	60463	3347	8W-15S	A1
8000	PlsT	60464	3346	10W-15S	C1
131st Ct					
1200	LMNT	60439	3342	20W-15S	C2
131st Pl					
3100	WthT	60406	3348	3W-15S	E1
3100	WthT	60406	3349	3W-15S	A1
E 131st Pl					
200	CHCG	60827	3350	0E-15S	D1
600	HMND	46320	3352		E1
600	HMND	46327	3352		E1
W 131st Pl					
8800	PlsT	60462	3346	11W-15S	A1
131st St					
2900	BLID	60406	3349	3W-15S	A1
2900	WthT	60406	3349	3W-15S	A1
3000	WthT	60406	3348	4W-15S	E1
3200	ALSP	60803	3348	4W-15S	E1
3200	WthT	60803	3348	4W-15S	E1
5100	CTWD	60445	3347	6W-15S	D1
5500	WthT	60445	3347	6W-15S	D1

STREET Block	City	ZIP	Map#	CGS	Grid
131st St					
5500	WthT	60463	3347	6W-15S	D1
E 131st St					
500	CHCG	60827	3278	0E-15S	E7
700	CHCG	60827	3279	0E-15S	A7
1100	CHCG	60827	3351	1E-15S	A1
2700	CHCG	60633	3279	3E-15S	E7
3000	CHCG	60633	3280	3E-15S	A7
W 131st St					
3400	WthT	60406	3348	4W-15S	D1
3400	WthT	60803	3348	4W-15S	D1
4100	ALSP	60803	3348	5W-15S	B1
6600	PSHT	60463	3347	8W-15S	A1
6600	WthT	60463	3347	8W-15S	A1
7000	PSHT	60463	3346	8W-15S	E1
7000	WthT	60463	3346	8W-15S	E1
7200	PlsT	60463	3346	9W-15S	E1
7900	PlsT	60464	3346	11W-15S	A1
8100	PlsT	60462	3346	11W-15S	A1
8800	PSPK	60462	3346	11W-15S	A1
8800	PSPK	60464	3346	11W-15S	A1
9000	ODPK	60462	3346	11W-15S	A1
9500	PlsT	60462	3345	13W-15S	A1
9500	PlsT	60464	3345	11W-15S	E1
9500	PSPK	60462	3345	13W-15S	A1
9500	PSPK	60464	3345	13W-15S	A1
10700	PlsT	60467	3345	13W-15S	A1
11000	PlsT	60467	3344	14W-15S	D1
12200	LmnT	60439	3344	15W-15S	B1
12200	LmnT	60464	3344	15W-15S	C1
12200	LmnT	60467	3344	15W-15S	C1
12200	PlsT	60464	3344	15W-15S	C1
13000	LMNT	60439	3343	18W-15S	A1
15000	LMNT	60439	3342	18W-15S	E1
26200	WldT	60585	3337	32W-15S	C2
26300	PNFD	60585	3337	32W-15S	B2
132nd Ct					
1200	LMNT	60439	3342	20W-15S	C2
5100	CTWD	60445	3347	6W-15S	E1
E 132nd Pl					
300	CHCG	60827	3350	0E-15S	D1
900	CHCG	60827	3351	1E-15S	A1
W 132nd Pl					
8500	ODPK	60462	3346	10W-15S	B1
8500	PlsT	60462	3346	10W-15S	B1
8500	PlsT	60464	3346	10W-15S	B1
132nd St					
1200	LMNT	60439	3342	19W-15S	C2
3100	WthT	60406	3348	3W-15S	E1
5500	CTWD	60445	3347	6W-15S	D1
5500	WthT	60445	3347	6W-15S	D1
5500	WthT	60463	3347	6W-15S	D1
E 132nd St					
700	CHCG	60827	3350	0E-15S	E1
800	CHCG	60827	3351	1E-15S	A1
2800	CHCG	60633	3351	3E-15S	E1
3000	CHCG	60633	3352	3E-15S	A1
W 132nd St					
8300	PlsT	60462	3346	10W-15S	B1
8300	PlsT	60464	3346	10W-15S	B1
133rd Ct					
1200	LMNT	60439	3342	20W-15S	C2
E 133rd Pl					
700	CHCG	60827	3350	0E-15S	E1
133rd St					
-	LMNT	60439	3343	18W-15S	A2
5100	CTWD	60445	3347	6W-15S	E1
E 133rd St					
100	RVDL	60827	3350	0W-15S	D1
700	CHCG	60827	3350	0E-15S	E1
800	CHCG	60827	3351	1E-15S	A1
2900	CHCG	60633	3351	2E-15S	D1
2900	CHCG	60633	3352	4E-15S	B1
W 133rd St					
8200	PlsT	60462	3346	10W-15S	B2
8200	PSHT	60462	3346	10W-15S	B2
8200	PSHT	60464	3346	10W-15S	B2
8300	PlsT	60464	3346	10W-15S	B2
8500	ODPK	60462	3346	10W-15S	B2
10800	PlsT	60462	3345	13W-15S	A2
10800	PlsT	60467	3345	13W-15S	A2
134th Ct					
4900	CTWD	60445	3348	6W-15S	A2
134th Pl					
4900	CTWD	60445	3348	6W-15S	A2
5000	CTWD	60445	3347	6W-15S	E2
E 134th Pl					
500	CHCG	60827	3350	0E-15S	E1
134th St					
-	RVDL	60827	3350	0W-15S	C1
4900	CTWD	60445	3348	6W-15S	A2
E 134th St					
100	CHCG	60827	3350	0E-15S	D1
100	RVDL	60827	3350	0W-15S	C1
1600	CHCG	60827	3351	2E-15S	C1
2300	CHCG	60633	3351	2E-15S	D1
3000	CHCG	60633	3352	4E-15S	B1
3600	HMND	46327	3352	4E-15S	C1
3600	HMND	60633	3352	4E-15S	C1
W 134th St					
3000	RBBN	60406	3348	3W-15S	E1
3000	RBBN	60472	3348	3W-15S	E1
3000	WthT	60406	3348	3W-15S	E1
3000	WthT	60472	3348	3W-15S	E1
4300	CTWD	60445	3348	5W-15S	B2
4300	RBBN	60445	3348	5W-15S	B2
10400	PlsT	60462	3345	13W-15S	B2
10400	PlsT	60464	3345	13W-15S	B2
S 135th Av					
14400	HmrT	60441	3342	20W-17S	B5
135th Ct					
-	BmnT	60445	3347	6W-16S	E2
5400	CTWD	60445	3347	6W-16S	E2
135th Pl					
2000	BLID	60406	3349	2W-16S	B2
4900	CTWD	60445	3348	6W-16S	A2
E 135th Pl					
200	CHCG	60827	3350	0E-15S	D2
200	RVDL	60827	3350	0E-15S	D2
W 135th Pl					
3400	RBBN	60472	3348	4W-16S	E2
4000	CTWD	60472	3348	5W-16S	C2
135th St					
-	CHCG	60633	3351	2E-15S	C1
-	CHCG	60827	3351	2E-15S	C1
-	CTWD	60445	3348	5W-15S	B2
-	CTWD	60472	3348	6W-15S	A2
-	RBBN	60445	3348	6W-15S	A2
-	RBBN	60472	3348	6W-15S	A2
2400	BLID	60406	3349	3W-16S	B2
2800	RBBN	60406	3349	3W-15S	A2
5000	CTWD	60445	3347	7W-15S	C2
5200	WthT	60445	3347	7W-15S	C2
5500	BmnT	60445	3347	7W-15S	D2
5500	WthT	60463	3347	7W-15S	C2
9100	HMGN	60439	3343	17W-15S	B2

STREET Block	City	ZIP	Map#	CGS	Grid
135th St					
9100	HMGN	60491	3343	17W-15S	B2
9100	LMNT	60439	3343	17W-15S	B2
9100	LMNT	60491	3343	18W-15S	B2
15800	HMGN	60439	3342	19W-15S	D2
15800	HMGN	60441	3342	19W-15S	D2
15800	HMGN	60491	3342	19W-15S	D2
15800	HmrT	60441	3342	20W-15S	B2
15800	LMNT	60439	3342	20W-15S	B2
16700	DPgT	60441	3342	20W-16S	A3
16700	LktT	60441	3342	20W-16S	A3
E 135th St					
900	CHCG	60827	3350	0E-15S	E1
900	CHCG	60827	3351	0E-15S	A1
2400	CHCG	60633	3351	2E-15S	D1
3100	CHCG	60633	3352	4E-15S	B1
W 135th St					
-	BmnT	60445	3346	9W-15S	E2
-	BmnT	60462	3346	10W-15S	C2
-	DPgT	60441	3342	21W-16S	A3
-	HMGN	60491	3344	14W-15S	C2
-	HmrT	60441	3342	21W-16S	A3
-	LktT	60441	3342	21W-16S	A3
-	LMNT	60439	3342	21W-16S	A3
-	LmnT	60439	3344	14W-15S	C2
-	LmnT	60491	3344	14W-15S	C2
-	OrlT	60467	3345	13W-15S	A2
-	PlsT	60467	3345	13W-15S	A2
-	RMVL	60544	3340	25W-15S	A3
-	WthT	60445	3346	10W-15S	C2
-	WthT	60462	3346	10W-15S	C2
-	WthT	60463	3346	10W-15S	C2
10	PNFD	60544	3338	30W-15S	B3
10	PNFD	60585	3338	30W-15S	B3
10	PnfT	60544	3338	29W-15S	D3
10	PnfT	60585	3338	29W-15S	D3
10	WldT	60544	3338	29W-15S	D3
10	WldT	60585	3338	29W-15S	D3
100	HMGN	60439	3343	18W-15S	A2
100	HMGN	60491	3343	18W-15S	A2
100	LMNT	60439	3343	18W-15S	A2
600	RMVL	60446	3340	25W-15S	B3
1000	RMVL	60441	3340	25W-15S	B3
1400	BGBK	60544	3339	27W-15S	B3
1400	PNFD	60544	3339	27W-15S	B3
1800	PNFD	60544	3337	32W-15S	C3
2000	PnfT	60585	3337	31W-16S	D3
2900	BLID	60406	3349	3W-15S	A2
2900	BLID	60472	3349	3W-15S	A2
2900	RBBN	60406	3349	3W-15S	A2
2900	RBBN	60472	3349	3W-15S	A2
3000	RBBN	60406	3348	4W-15S	E2
3000	RBBN	60472	3348	4W-16S	C2
3700	CTWD	60472	3348	4W-15S	D2
4200	CTWD	60445	3348	5W-15S	C2
4200	RBBN	60445	3348	5W-15S	C2
6200	BmnT	60445	3347	8W-15S	A2
6200	PSHT	60445	3347	8W-15S	A2
6200	PSHT	60463	3347	8W-15S	A2
6200	WthT	60445	3347	8W-15S	A2
6200	WthT	60463	3347	8W-15S	A2
7200	OrlT	60462	3346	10W-15S	C2
7200	OrlT	60463	3346	9W-15S	D2
7200	PlsT	60462	3346	10W-15S	C2
7200	PlsT	60463	3346	10W-15S	C2
7200	PSHT	60462	3346	9W-15S	D2
7200	PSHT	60463	3346	9W-15S	D2
7700	ODPK	60462	3346	9W-15S	D2
7900	PSHT	60464	3346	9W-15S	C2
8000	OrlT	60464	3346	10W-15S	C2
8100	PlsT	60464	3346	10W-15S	C2
9000	ODPK	60462	3345	11W-15S	E2
9000	PlsT	60462	3345	11W-15S	E2
9100	OrlT	60462	3345	11W-15S	E2
11300	OrlT	60467	3344	14W-15S	D2
11300	PlsT	60467	3344	14W-15S	D2
17200	DPgT	60441	3341	21W-15S	E3
17200	LktT	60441	3341	21W-15S	E3
17200	RMVL	60441	3341	21W-15S	E3
21600	PNFD	60585	3339	28W-16S	B3
21600	PnfT	60544	3339	27W-15S	C3
21600	WldT	60544	3339	27W-15S	C3
25900	NasT	60544	3337	32W-15S	B3
25900	PNFD	60543	3337	32W-15S	B3
25900	PNFD	60585	3337	32W-15S	B3
136th Av					
10400	BtlT	53142	2360		C2
12600	NptT	53142	2360		B4
12600	NptT	60002	2360		B4
136th Av CO-U					
10400	BtlT	53142	2360		C2
12600	NptT	53142	2360		B4
12600	NptT	60002	2360		B4
S 136th Av					
14400	HmrT	60441	3342	20W-17S	B5
W 136th Av					
14400	HMGN	60439	3343	18W-16S	B3
14400	HMGN	60491	3343	18W-16S	B3
136th Ct					
4300	CTWD	60445	3348	5W-16S	B2
136th Pl					
5200	CTWD	60445	3347	6W-16S	E2
E 136th Pl					
200	CHCG	60827	3350	0E-15S	D2
200	RVDL	60827	3350	0E-15S	D2
W 136th Pl					
400	RVDL	60827	3350	0W-15S	B2
4100	RBBN	60472	3348	5W-16S	C2
136th St					
-	CHCG	60633	3351	2E-15S	C2
-	CHCG	60827	3351	2E-15S	C2
2100	BLID	60406	3349	2W-16S	B2
4600	CTWD	60445	3348	5W-16S	A2
9000	ODPK	60462	3345	11W-16S	E2
9300	OrlT	60462	3345	11W-16S	E2
E 136th St					
10	CHCG	60633	3352		D2
10	CHCG	60827	3350	0W-15S	D2
10	HMND	46327	3352		D2
10	HMND	60633	3352		D2
10	RVDL	60827	3350	0W-15S	D2
2500	CHCG	60633	3351	2E-15S	D2
W 136th St					
-	CTWD	60472	3348	4W-16S	C2
-	RBBN	60472	3348	4W-16S	E2
400	RVDL	60827	3350	0W-15S	B2
137th Pl					
4300	CTWD	60445	3348	5W-16S	B2
5200	CTWD	60445	3347	6W-16S	E2
E 137th Pl					
10	CHCG	60827	3350	0W-15S	D2
10	RVDL	60827	3350	0W-15S	D2
W 137th Pl					
400	RVDL	60827	3350	0W-15S	B2
4100	RBBN	60472	3348	5W-16S	C2

STREET Block	City	ZIP	Map#	CGS	Grid
137th St					
-	CHCG	60633	3351	2E-15S	C2
-	CHCG	60827	3351	2E-15S	C2
4200	CTWD	60472	3348	5W-16S	C2
4200	RBBN	60445	3348	5W-16S	C2
4200	RBBN	60472	3348	5W-16S	C2
4500	CTWD	60445	3348	6W-16S	A2
5400	CTWD	60445	3347	6W-16S	D2
7900	ODPK	60462	3346	9W-16S	C2
7900	OrlT	60462	3346	10W-16S	C2
9100	ODPK	60462	3345	11W-16S	E3
E 137th St					
10	CHCG	60827	3350	0W-15S	C2
10	RVDL	60827	3350	0W-15S	C2
100	HMND	46327	3352		D2
W 137th St					
-	BLID	60406	3349	3W-16S	A2
-	BLID	60472	3349	3W-16S	A2
-	RBBN	60406	3349	3W-16S	A2
-	RBBN	60472	3349	3W-16S	A2
10	RVDL	60827	3350	0W-15S	C2
4000	CTWD	60472	3348	5W-16S	C2
4100	CTWD	60445	3348	5W-16S	C2
4100	RBBN	60472	3348	5W-16S	C2
138th Ct					
4800	CTWD	60445	3348	6W-16S	A3
138th Pl					
4800	CTWD	60445	3348	6W-16S	A3
5200	CTWD	60445	3347	6W-16S	E3
8200	ODPK	60462	3346	10W-16S	B3
E 138th Pl					
500	DLTN	60419	3350	0E-16S	E2
2700	BNHM	60633	3352	3E-16S	A2
W 138th Pl					
3800	RBBN	60472	3348	4W-16S	D3
138th St					
-	BNHM	60633	3351	3E-16S	E2
-	CTCY	60409	3351	2E-16S	C2
600	HMND	46327	3352		D2
2000	BLID	60406	3349	2W-16S	C2
4600	CTWD	60445	3348	5W-16S	A2
5200	CTWD	60445	3347	6W-16S	E3
8200	ODPK	60462	3346	10W-16S	B3
9100	ODPK	60462	3345	11W-16S	E3
9200	OrlT	60462	3345	11W-16S	E3
E 138th St					
10	RVDL	60827	3350	0W-15S	C2
100	HMND	46327	3352		D2
200	CHCG	60419	3350	0E-16S	E2
200	CHCG	60827	3350	0E-16S	E2
200	DLTN	60419	3350	0E-16S	E2
200	RVDL	60419	3350	0E-15S	D2
600	CHCG	60827	3351	1E-16S	A2
600	DLTN	60419	3351	1E-16S	A2
W 138th St					
10	RVDL	60827	3350	0W-16S	B2
900	RVDL	60827	3349	1W-16S	E2
2900	BLID	60406	3349	3W-16S	A2
2900	BLID	60472	3349	3W-16S	A2
2900	RBBN	60472	3349	3W-16S	A2
3100	RBBN	60472	3348	4W-16S	E2
15600	HMGN	60491	3342	19W-16S	D3
16600	HmrT	60441	3342	20W-16S	A3
16600	LktT	60441	3342	20W-16S	A3
139th Pl					
2400	DXMR	60406	3349	3W-16S	B3
2400	POSN	60406	3349	3W-16S	B3
2800	BLID	60406	3349	3W-16S	A3
2800	BLID	60469	3349	3W-16S	A3
2800	POSN	60469	3349	3W-16S	A3
4900	CTWD	60445	3348	6W-16S	A3
5000	BmnT	60445	3348	6W-16S	A3
5100	BmnT	60445	3347	6W-16S	E3
5100	CTWD	60445	3347	6W-16S	E3
W 139th Pl					
3100	RBBN	60472	3348	3W-16S	E3
139th St					
-	BLID	60472	3349	3W-16S	A3
-	BNHM	60633	3352	3E-16S	A2
-	CTWD	60445	3348	4W-16S	C3
-	CTWD	60472	3348	4W-16S	C3
-	RBBN	60472	3348	4W-16S	C3
1800	BLID	60406	3349	3W-16S	B3
1800	DXMR	60406	3349	3W-16S	B3
2200	POSN	60406	3349	2W-16S	B3
2500	POSN	60469	3349	3W-16S	B3
2700	BLID	60469	3349	3W-16S	A3
2900	RBBN	60406	3349	3W-16S	A3
2900	RBBN	60472	3349	3W-16S	A3
5200	BmnT	60445	3347	6W-16S	E3
5200	CTWD	60445	3347	6W-16S	E3
10800	ODPK	60467	3345	13W-16S	A3
10800	OrlT	60467	3345	13W-16S	A3
11000	ODPK	60467	3344	14W-16S	C3
11000	OrlT	60467	3344	14W-16S	C3
11900	HMGN	60491	3344	14W-16S	C3
E 139th St					
10	RVDL	60827	3350	0W-16S	C2
100	DLTN	60419	3350	0W-16S	D2
100	HMND	46327	3352		D2
2600	BNHM	60633	3351	3E-16S	E2
W 139th St					
-	RBBN	60472	3349	3W-16S	A3
10	RVDL	60827	3350	0W-16S	C2
3000	RBBN	60472	3348	4W-16S	D3
3800	CTWD	60445	3348	4W-16S	C3
3800	CTWD	60472	3348	4W-16S	C3
7800	OrlT	60462	3346	9W-16S	C3
8400	ODPK	60462	3346	10W-16S	B3
9100	OrlT	60462	3345	11W-16S	E3
9200	ODPK	60462	3345	11W-16S	E3
14800	HMGN	60491	3343	18W-16S	A3
15000	HMGN	60491	3342	19W-16S	E3
15600	HmrT	60491	3342	19W-16S	D3
16000	HmrT	60441	3342	20W-16S	C3
E 140th Ct					
10	RVDL	60827	3350	0W-16S	C3
100	DLTN	60419	3350	0W-16S	C3
100	DLTN	60827	3350	0W-16S	C3
W 140th Ct					
-	RVDL	60827	3350	0W-16S	B3
140th Pl					
2800	BLID	60406	3349	3W-16S	A3
2800	POSN	60406	3349	3W-16S	A3
2800	POSN	60469	3349	3W-16S	A3
5200	CTWD	60445	3347	6W-16S	E3
5200	MDLN	60445	3347	6W-16S	E3
E 140th Pl					
200	DLTN	60419	3350	0E-16S	D3
200	DLTN	60827	3350	0E-16S	D3
200	RVDL	60827	3350	0E-16S	D3
W 140th Pl					
2400	DXMR	60406	3349	3W-16S	B3
2400	POSN	60406	3349	3W-16S	B3
2400	POSN	60469	3349	3W-16S	B3
3600	RBBN	60472	3348	4W-16S	D3

STREET Block	City	ZIP	Map#	CGS	Grid
W 140th Pl					
3700	CTWD	60472	3348	4W-16S	D3
16400	HmrT	60441	3342	20W-16S	B4
140th St					
-	BNHM	60633	3352	3E-16S	A3
-	HMND	46327	3352		D3
2800	BLID	60406	3349	3W-16S	A3
2800	POSN	60406	3349	3W-16S	A3
2800	POSN	60469	3349	3W-16S	A3
E 140th St					
10	RVDL	60827	3350	0W-16S	C3
100	DLTN	60419	3350	0W-16S	C3
100	DLTN	60827	3350	0W-16S	C3
200	HMND	46327	3352		D3
2400	BNHM	60633	3351	3E-16S	E3
3300	BNHM	60633	3352	4E-16S	B3
W 140th St					
10	RVDL	60827	3350	0W-16S	C3
2400	DXMR	60406	3349	3W-16S	B3
2400	POSN	60406	3349	3W-16S	B3
2400	POSN	60469	3349	3W-16S	B3
3600	RBBN	60472	3348	4W-16S	D3
3700	CTWD	60472	3348	4W-16S	D3
3800	CTWD	60445	3348	4W-16S	C3
3800	RBBN	60445	3348	4W-16S	C3
8200	ODPK	60462	3346	10W-16S	B3
9000	ODPK	60462	3345	11W-16S	E3
10900	ODPK	60467	3345	13W-16S	A3
16700	HmrT	60441	3342	20W-16S	A4
16700	LktT	60441	3342	20W-16S	A4
141st Pl					
2800	BLID	60406	3349	3W-16S	A3
2800	POSN	60406	3349	3W-16S	A3
2800	POSN	60469	3349	3W-16S	A3
2900	BLID	60406	3348	3W-16S	E3
2900	RBBN	60406	3348	3W-16S	E3
4400	CTWD	60445	3348	5W-16S	B4
E 141st Pl					
200	DLTN	60419	3350	0E-16S	D3
200	DLTN	60827	3350	0E-16S	D3
200	RVDL	60827	3350	0E-16S	D3
W 141st Pl					
8700	ODPK	60462	3346	10W-16S	A4
9300	ODPK	60462	3345	11W-16S	E4
141st St					
-	DXMR	60406	3349	3W-16S	B3
-	POSN	60469	3349	3W-16S	B3
2200	POSN	60406	3349	2W-16S	C4
2800	BLID	60406	3349	3W-16S	A3
3000	BLID	60406	3348	3W-16S	E3
3000	RBBN	60406	3348	3W-16S	E3
4600	CTWD	60445	3348	6W-16S	A3
4900	BmnT	60445	3348	6W-16S	A3
5200	CTWD	60445	3347	6W-16S	E3
5200	MDLN	60445	3347	6W-16S	E3
E 141st St					
-	HMND	46320	3352		E3
10	HMND	46327	3352		D3
10	RVDL	60827	3350	0W-16S	C3
100	DLTN	60419	3350	0W-16S	C3
100	DLTN	60827	3350	0W-16S	C3
2400	BNHM	60633	3351	3E-16S	E3
3300	BNHM	60633	3352	3E-16S	A3
W 141st St					
200	RVDL	60827	3350	0W-16S	B3
1800	DXMR	60426	3349	2W-16S	D4
3700	CTWD	60472	3348	4W-16S	D3
3700	RBBN	60472	3348	4W-16S	D3
8600	ODPK	60462	3346	10W-16S	A3
15400	HMGN	60441	3342	19W-16S	D4
15400	HMGN	60491	3342	19W-16S	E4
16400	HmrT	60441	3342	20W-16S	B4
142nd Pl					
8500	ODPK	60462	3346	10W-16S	A4
E 142nd Pl					
200	DLTN	60419	3350	0E-16S	D3
200	DLTN	60827	3350	0E-16S	D3
200	RVDL	60827	3350	0E-16S	D3
142nd St					
-	CTWD	60445	3347	6W-16S	E4
-	DXMR	60406	3349	3W-16S	B3
-	MDLN	60445	3347	6W-16S	E4
-	POSN	60406	3349	3W-16S	B3
-	POSN	60469	3349	3W-16S	B3
4000	CTWD	60445	3348	5W-16S	C4
4800	BmnT	60445	3348	6W-16S	A4
4900	MDLN	60445	3348	6W-16S	A4
E 142nd St					
10	RVDL	60827	3350	0W-16S	C3
100	DLTN	60419	3350	0W-16S	C3
100	DLTN	60827	3350	0W-16S	C3
300	HMND	46327	3352		D3
2300	BNHM	60633	3351	2E-16S	E3
3300	BNHM	60633	3352	3E-16S	B3
W 142nd St					
10	RVDL	60827	3350	0W-16S	C3
1800	DXMR	60426	3349	2W-16S	D4
2100	DXMR	60406	3349	2W-16S	C4
3700	CTWD	60472	3348	4W-16S	D3
3700	RBBN	60472	3348	4W-16S	D3
8500	ODPK	60462	3346	10W-16S	B4
9100	ODPK	60462	3345	11W-16S	E4
10800	ODPK	60467	3345	13W-16S	A4
143rd Pl					
2800	BmnT	60406	3349	3W-17S	A4
4800	CTWD	60445	3348	6W-17S	A4
4800	MDLN	60445	3348	6W-17S	A4
W 143rd Pl					
8000	ODPK	60462	3346	10W-17S	C4
9900	ODPK	60462	3345	12W-17S	C4
143rd St					
600	PnfT	60544	3337	32W-16S	C4
700	PNFD	60543	3337	32W-16S	C4
2300	DXMR	60406	3349	2W-17S	C4
2300	POSN	60406	3349	2W-17S	C4
2800	BmnT	60406	3349	3W-16S	A4
2800	BmnT	60469	3349	3W-16S	A4
2800	PNFD	60544	3337	32W-17S	D5
2800	POSN	60469	3349	3W-16S	A4
3000	BmnT	60406	3348	3W-16S	E4
3100	MDLN	60406	3348	3W-16S	E4
3100	MDLN	60445	3348	3W-16S	E4
3100	RBBN	60406	3348	3W-16S	E4
3100	RBBN	60445	3348	3W-16S	E4
3900	CTWD	60445	3348	6W-16S	A4
5500	BmnT	60445	3347	7W-16S	D4
5500	MDLN	60445	3347	7W-16S	D4
6100	BmnT	60452	3347	8W-16S	A4
6900	BmnT	60445	3346	8W-16S	E4
6900	BmnT	60452	3346	8W-16S	E4
6900	OrlT	60445	3346	8W-16S	E4
6900	OrlT	60452	3346	8W-16S	E4
6900	OrlT	60462	3346	8W-16S	E4
E 143rd St					
10	RVDL	60827	3350	0W-16S	C3
100	DLTN	60827	3350	0W-16S	D3

STREET Block	City	ZIP	Map#	CGS	Grid
E 143rd St					
200	DLTN	60419	3350	0E-16S	D3
400	PnfT	60544	3338	28W-17S	E5
400	PnfT	60544	3339	28W-16S	A5
700	DLTN	60419	3351	1E-16S	A3
900	HMND	46327	3352		E3
2700	BNHM	60633	3351	3E-16S	E3
3300	BNHM	60633	3352	3E-16S	B3
W 143rd St					
10	DXMR	60426	3349	2W-16S	D4
10	RVDL	60827	3350	0W-16S	C3
600	PNFD	60544	3338	30W-16S	A5
600	PnfT	60544	3338	30W-16S	C5
1800	PNFD	60544	3337	31W-16S	E5
1800	PnfT	60544	3337	31W-16S	D5
2400	POSN	60469	3349	3W-16S	B4
2700	BmnT	60406	3349	3W-16S	A4
2700	BmnT	60469	3349	3W-16S	A4
7200	BmnT	60445	3346	10W-16S	B4
7200	BmnT	60452	3346	10W-16S	B4
7200	ODPK	60462	3346	10W-16S	B4
7200	OrlT	60445	3346	10W-16S	B4
7200	OrlT	60452	3346	10W-16S	B4
7200	OrlT	60462	3346	10W-16S	B4
9100	ODPK	60462	3345	13W-16S	A4
9100	OrlT	60462	3345	11W-16S	D4
10700	ODPK	60467	3345	13W-16S	A4
10700	OrlT	60467	3345	13W-16S	A4
10900	ODPK	60467	3344	14W-17S	E4
10900	OrlT	60467	3344	14W-17S	E4
11900	HMGN	60491	3344	14W-16S	C4
12400	HmrT	60491	3344	15W-16S	B4
12900	HMGN	60491	3343	18W-16S	A4
14800	HmrT	60491	3343	18W-16S	A4
15000	HMGN	60491	3342	20W-16S	B4
15000	HmrT	60491	3342	19W-16S	E4
15300	HMGN	60441	3342	20W-16S	B4
15700	HmrT	60491	3342	20W-16S	B4
16800	LktT	60441	3342	20W-16S	A5
17200	LktT	60441	3341	21W-16S	E5
W 143rd St SR-7					
9800	ODPK	60462	3345	13W-16S	A4
10600	OrlT	60462	3345	13W-16S	B4
10700	ODPK	60467	3345	13W-16S	A4
10700	OrlT	60467	3345	13W-16S	A4
10900	ODPK	60467	3344	13W-16S	E4
10900	OrlT	60467	3344	13W-16S	E4
144th Ct					
4800	MDLN	60445	3348	6W-17S	A4
E 144th Ct					
100	DXMR	60406	3349	2W-17S	C5
100	HRVY	60426	3349	1W-17S	E5
W 144th Ln					
16800	HmrT	60441	3342	21W-17S	A5
16800	LktT	60441	3342	21W-17S	A5
144th Pl					
4900	MDLN	60445	3348	6W-17S	A4
E 144th Pl					
600	DLTN	60419	3350	0E-16S	E4
W 144th Pl					
2300	DXMR	60406	3349	2W-17S	B4
2300	POSN	60406	3349	2W-17S	B4
2300	POSN	60469	3349	2W-17S	B4
8400	ODPK	60462	3346	10W-17S	B4
9300	OrlT	60462	3345	11W-17S	E4
10200	ODPK	60462	3345	12W-17S	C5
16400	HmrT	60441	3342	20W-17S	B5
144th St					
-	BNHM	60633	3351	2E-16S	D4
-	CTCY	60409	3351	2E-16S	D4
-	CTCY	60633	3351	2E-16S	D4
2900	BmnT	60406	3349	3W-17S	A4
3100	BmnT	60469	3348	3W-17S	E4
3100	MDLN	60469	3348	3W-17S	E4
3400	MDLN	60445	3348	4W-17S	E4
E 144th St					
10	DXMR	60426	3349	1W-17S	E4
10	HRVY	60426	3349	1W-17S	E4
200	DLTN	60419	3350	0E-16S	D4
200	DLTN	60827	3350	0E-16S	D4
200	RVDL	60827	3350	0E-16S	D4
800	DLTN	60419	3351	1E-16S	B4
W 144th St					
-	DXMR	60426	3349	2W-17S	D5
-	HRVY	60426	3349	2W-17S	E4
10	RVDL	60827	3350	0W-16S	C4
2000	DXMR	60406	3349	2W-17S	C4
2300	POSN	60406	3349	3W-17S	B4
2300	POSN	60469	3349	3W-17S	B4
2700	BmnT	60406	3349	3W-17S	A4
2700	BmnT	60469	3349	3W-17S	A4
8500	ODPK	60462	3346	10W-17S	B4
9800	ODPK	60462	3345	12W-17S	C4
145th Ct					
4900	MDLN	60445	3348	6W-17S	A4
W 145th Pl					
300	RVDL	60827	3350	0W-16S	B4
3000	POSN	60469	3349	3W-17S	A4
8200	OrlT	60462	3346	10W-17S	B5
8500	ODPK	60462	3346	10W-17S	B5
9600	ODPK	60462	3345	12W-17S	D5
16400	HmrT	60441	3342	20W-17S	B5
16600	LktT	60441	3342	20W-17S	A5
145th St					
-	BNHM	60633	3351	2E-16S	D4
-	CTCY	60409	3351	2E-16S	D4
-	CTCY	60633	3351	2E-16S	D4
-	HRVY	60426	3349	1W-17S	E5
2100	DXMR	60406	3349	2W-17S	C5
2100	DXMR	60426	3349	2W-17S	C5
2100	POSN	60406	3349	2W-17S	C5
2100	POSN	60469	3349	2W-17S	C5
3200	MDLN	60445	3348	4W-17S	E4
3200	POSN	60445	3348	4W-17S	E4
3200	POSN	60469	3348	4W-17S	E4
5500	BmnT	60445	3347	6W-17S	D4
5500	MDLN	60445	3347	6W-17S	D4
E 145th St					
10	HRVY	60426	3349	1W-17S	E5
10	RVDL	60827	3350	0W-16S	C4
100	DLTN	60827	3350	0W-16S	D4
100	HRVY	60426	3350	1W-17S	A5
700	DLTN	60419	3350	0E-16S	E4
800	DLTN	60419	3351	1E-16S	B4
W 145th St					
10	DXMR	60426	3349	2W-17S	E5
10	HRVY	60426	3349	2W-17S	E5
200	RVDL	60827	3350	0W-16S	C4
2300	DXMR	60406	3349	3W-17S	A4
2300	POSN	60406	3349	3W-17S	A4
2300	POSN	60469	3349	3W-17S	A4
3100	MDLN	60445	3348	3W-17S	E4
3100	POSN	60445	3348	3W-17S	E4
3100	POSN	60469	3348	3W-17S	E4
8500	ODPK	60462	3346	10W-17S	B4
9100	ODPK	60462	3345	11W-17S	E5
W 145th St					
9100	OrlT	60462	3345	11W-17S	E5
17000	LktT	60441	3341	21W-17S	E5
17000	LktT	60441	3342	21W-17S	A5
W 146th Pl					
16300	HmrT	60441	3342	20W-17S	B5
16600	LktT	60441	3342	20W-17S	A5
146th St					
-	POSN	60469	3349	3W-17S	A4
3200	MDLN	60445	3348	4W-17S	D5
3200	POSN	60445	3348	4W-17S	E5
3200	POSN	60469	3348	4W-17S	E5
E 146th St					
10	DLTN	60827	3350	0W-17S	C4
10	HRVY	60426	3349	1W-17S	E5
10	RVDL	60827	3350	0W-17S	C4
100	HRVY	60426	3350	1W-17S	A5
100	RVDL	60419	3350	0W-17S	C4
700	DLTN	60419	3350	0E-17S	E4
700	DLTN	60419	3351	0E-16S	A4
W 146th St					
10	DLTN	60419	3350	0W-17S	C4
10	DLTN	60827	3350	0W-16S	C4
10	HRVY	60426	3349	2W-17S	D5
10	RVDL	60827	3350	0W-16S	C4
100	DXMR	60426	3349	2W-17S	C5
400	HRVY	60426	3350	0W-17S	B4
400	HRVY	60827	3350	0W-17S	B4
2000	DXMR	60406	3349	2W-17S	C5
10000	ODPK	60462	3345	12W-17S	C5
147th Ct					
4900	MDLN	60445	3348	6W-17S	A5
5000	OKFT	60452	3348	6W-17S	A5
5100	MDLN	60452	3347	6W-17S	E5
5100	OKFT	60452	3347	6W-17S	E5
147th Pl					
3200	MDLN	60445	3348	4W-17S	E5
E 147th Pl					
-	SHLD	60426	3350	0W-17S	C5
500	HRVY	60426	3350	0W-17S	C5
500	SHLD	60473	3350	0W-17S	C5
600	DLTN	60419	3350	0E-17S	E5
W 147th Pl					
16400	HmrT	60441	3342	20W-17S	B5
16600	LktT	60441	3342	20W-17S	A5
147th St					
3200	MDLN	60445	3348	5W-17S	C5
3200	POSN	60445	3348	5W-17S	C5
3200	POSN	60469	3348	5W-17S	C5
4900	MDLN	60452	3348	6W-17S	A5
5000	MDLN	60445	3347	8W-17S	B5
5000	MDLN	60452	3347	8W-17S	B5
5100	OKFT	60452	3347	6W-17S	E5
5400	OKFT	60445	3347	6W-17S	E5
5500	BmnT	60445	3347	6W-17S	D5
5500	BmnT	60452	3347	6W-17S	D5
147th St SR-83					
3200	MDLN	60445	3348	5W-17S	C5
3200	POSN	60445	3348	5W-17S	C5
3200	POSN	60469	3348	5W-17S	C5
E 147th St					
10	DLTN	60419	3350	0W-17S	C4
1200	DLTN	60419	3351	1E-17S	B4
W 147th St					
-	LKPT	60441	3342	19W-17S	D5
10	DLTN	60419	3350	0W-17S	C4
2300	DXMR	60426	3349	2W-17S	C5
2300	HRVY	60426	3349	2W-17S	C5
2300	POSN	60426	3349	3W-17S	C5
2300	POSN	60469	3349	3W-17S	A5
3100	MDLN	60445	3348	3W-17S	E5
3100	POSN	60445	3348	3W-17S	E5
3100	POSN	60469	3348	3W-17S	E5
8800	ODPK	60462	3346	11W-17S	A5
8900	ODPK	60462	3345	11W-17S	E5
14400	HMGN	60491	3343	18W-17S	A5
14600	HMGN	60491	3342	19W-17S	D5
15300	HmrT	60491	3342	19W-17S	D5
15500	HmrT	60441	3342	19W-17S	D5
17000	LktT	60441	3341	21W-17S	E6
17000	LktT	60441	3342	21W-17S	A6
W 147th St SR-83					
2300	DXMR	60426	3349	2W-17S	C5
2300	HRVY	60426	3349	2W-17S	C5
2300	POSN	60426	3349	3W-17S	A5
2300	POSN	60469	3349	3W-17S	A5
3100	MDLN	60445	3348	3W-17S	E5
3100	POSN	60445	3348	3W-17S	E5
3100	POSN	60469	3348	3W-17S	E5
148th Ct					
5100	MDLN	60452	3347	6W-17S	E5
148th Pl					
3600	MDLN	60445	3348	4W-17S	D5
E 148th Pl					
200	HRVY	60426	3350	1W-17S	A6
500	SHLD	60473	3350	0W-17S	C6
W 148th Pl					
200	DLTN	60419	3350	0W-17S	C5
200	HRVY	60426	3349	2W-17S	C6
148th St					
3400	MDLN	60445	3348	4W-17S	D5
4800	MDLN	60452	3348	6W-17S	A5
5100	MDLN	60452	3347	6W-17S	E5
5100	OKFT	60452	3347	6W-17S	E5
E 148th St					
10	DLTN	60419	3350	0W-17S	C5
10	HRVY	60426	3349	1W-17S	E5
500	HRVY	60426	3350	0W-17S	C5
1200	DLTN	60419	3351	1E-17S	B5
W 148th St					
-	MDLN	60445	3348	3W-17S	E5
-	POSN	60445	3348	3W-17S	E5
-	POSN	60469	3348	3W-17S	E5
10	DLTN	60419	3350	0W-17S	C5
10	HRVY	60426	3349	2W-17S	D5
2500	POSN	60469	3349	3W-17S	B5
2800	BmnT	60469	3349	3W-17S	A5
W 149th Pl					
200	HRVY	60426	3349	2W-17S	C6
149th St					
-	MKHM	60428	3348	4W-17S	E5
-	MKHM	60469	3348	4W-17S	E5
-	ODPK	60462	3345	12W-17S	D6
-	POSN	60445	3348	4W-17S	E5
-	POSN	60469	3348	4W-17S	E5
3200	MDLN	60426	3348	4W-17S	D5
3200	MDLN	60445	3348	4W-17S	E5
3200	MKHM	60426	3348	4W-17S	E5
3200	MKHM	60445	3348	4W-17S	E5
4700	OKFT	60452	3348	6W-17S	A5
5000	MDLN	60452	3348	6W-17S	A5
5100	MDLN	60452	3347	6W-17S	E5
5100	OKFT	60452	3347	6W-17S	E5
E 149th St					
-	SHLD	60473	3350	0W-17S	C6
10	DLTN	60419	3350	0W-17S	C5
E 149th St					
10	HRVY	60426	3349	1W-17S	E6
200	HRVY	60426	3350	1W-17S	A6
500	SHLD	60426	3350	0W-17S	B6
800	HMND	46327	3352		E5
900	DLTN	60419	3351	1E-17S	A5
W 149th St					
10	DLTN	60419	3350	0W-17S	C5
10	HRVY	60426	3349	2W-17S	D6
300	HRVY	60469	3349	3W-17S	B6
400	BmnT	60426	3349	3W-17S	B6
2600	POSN	60426	3349	3W-17S	B5
2600	POSN	60469	3349	3W-17S	B5
2800	BmnT	60469	3349	3W-17S	A5
2900	MKHM	60428	3349	3W-17S	A5
2900	MKHM	60469	3349	3W-17S	A5
3000	POSN	60428	3349	3W-17S	A5
3100	MDLN	60445	3348	3W-17S	E5
3100	MKHM	60426	3348	3W-17S	E5
3100	MKHM	60428	3348	3W-17S	E5
3100	MKHM	60445	3348	3W-17S	E5
3100	MKHM	60469	3348	3W-17S	E5
3100	POSN	60445	3348	3W-17S	E5
3100	POSN	60469	3348	3W-17S	E5
150th Pl					
5700	OKFT	60452	3347	7W-17S	D6
E 150th Pl					
800	SHLD	60473	3351	1E-17S	A5
1000	DLTN	60419	3351	1E-17S	A5
1000	SHLD	60419	3351	1E-17S	A5
W 150th Pl					
200	HRVY	60426	3349	2W-17S	C6
150th St					
-	MKHM	60428	3348	4W-17S	E6
3600	MDLN	60445	3348	4W-17S	D6
3600	MKHM	60426	3348	4W-17S	E6
3600	MKHM	60445	3348	4W-17S	D6
5700	OKFT	60452	3347	7W-17S	D6
E 150th St					
800	HMND	46327	3352		E5
W 150th St					
2600	BmnT	60426	3349	3W-17S	B5
2600	BmnT	60469	3349	3W-17S	B5
2600	POSN	60426	3349	3W-17S	B5
2800	POSN	60469	3349	3W-17S	A6
2900	BmnT	60428	3349	3W-17S	A5
2900	MKHM	60428	3349	3W-17S	A5
2900	MKHM	60469	3349	3W-17S	A5
151st Pl					
3900	BmnT	60426	3348	4W-18S	C6
3900	MDLN	60426	3348	4W-18S	C6
3900	MDLN	60445	3348	4W-18S	C6
E 151st Pl					
900	PHNX	60426	3350	0W-18S	C6
900	PHNX	60473	3350	0W-18S	C6
900	SHLD	60473	3350	0W-18S	C6
W 151st Pl					
300	HRVY	60426	3349	2W-18S	C6
151st St					
-	CTCY	60409	3351	2E-17S	C5
-	CTCY	60419	3351	2E-17S	C5
-	DLTN	60409	3351	2E-17S	C5
-	DLTN	60419	3351	2E-17S	C5
-	MKHM	60428	3348	4W-17S	E6
3600	MKHM	60426	3348	4W-17S	D6
3600	MKHM	60445	3348	4W-17S	D6
4200	BmnT	60426	3348	5W-17S	B6
4200	MDLN	60426	3348	5W-17S	B6
4200	MDLN	60445	3348	6W-17S	A6
4500	MDLN	60452	3348	5W-17S	B6
4500	OKFT	60452	3348	6W-17S	A6
4600	OKFT	60445	3348	6W-17S	A6
5100	OKFT	60452	3347	6W-17S	E6
6000	BmnT	60452	3347	7W-18S	C6
E 151st St					
10	HRVY	60426	3349	1W-17S	E6
100	HRVY	60426	3350	1W-18S	A6
300	PHNX	60426	3350	0W-17S	B6
500	DLTN	60419	3350	0E-17S	E5
500	SHLD	60419	3350	0E-17S	E5
600	SHLD	60426	3350	0W-17S	B6
800	DLTN	60473	3351	0E-17S	A5
800	PHNX	60473	3350	0W-17S	B6
800	SHLD	60473	3350	0W-17S	B6
800	SHLD	60473	3351	0E-17S	A5
1000	DLTN	60419	3351	1E-17S	B6
1000	SHLD	60419	3351	1E-17S	A5
W 151st St					
-	BmnT	60452	3346	9W-17S	E6
-	BmnT	60462	3346	9W-17S	E6
10	HRVY	60426	3349	2W-17S	C6
900	LKPT	60441	3341	21W-17S	E7
1200	LKPT	60441	3342	21W-17S	A7
1300	LktT	60441	3342	21W-17S	A7
3100	MKHM	60426	3348	3W-17S	E6
3100	MKHM	60428	3348	3W-17S	E6
3100	MKHM	60428	3349	3W-17S	A6
7200	ODPK	60462	3346	10W-17S	C6
7200	OrlT	60462	3346	10W-17S	B6
9000	ODPK	60462	3345	12W-17S	C6
11200	ODPK	60467	3344	15W-17S	B6
11200	OrlT	60467	3344	15W-17S	B6
12000	HMGN	60491	3344	15W-17S	C6
12800	HMGN	60491	3343	18W-17S	A6
14700	HMGN	60441	3342	19W-17S	D6
14700	HMGN	60491	3342	19W-17S	D6
14700	HmrT	60441	3342	20W-17S	B6
15600	HmrT	60491	3342	20W-17S	B6
15700	LKPT	60491	3342	20W-17S	B6
W 151st Ter					
-	HRVY	60426	3349	2W-18S	C6
152nd Av					
10400	BtlT	53142	2360		A1
11700	BtlT	60002	2360		A4
11700	NptT	60002	2360		A4
152nd Av CO-MB					
10400	BtlT	53142	2360		A1
11700	BtlT	60002	2360		A4
11700	NptT	60002	2360		A4
W 152nd Ct					
7200	ODPK	60462	3346	9W-18S	E6
152nd Pl					
300	CTCY	60409	3352	4E-17S	B6
3600	MDLN	60445	3348	4W-18S	D6
E 152nd Pl					
900	PHNX	60426	3350	0W-18S	C7
900	SHLD	60426	3350	0W-18S	C7
900	SHLD	60473	3350	0W-18S	C7
W 152nd Pl					
7200	ODPK	60462	3346	9W-18S	E6
152nd St					
-	MKHM	60426	3348	4W-18S	E6
-	MKHM	60428	3348	4W-18S	E6
3900	BmnT	60426	3348	4W-18S	C6
3900	MDLN	60426	3348	4W-18S	C6
4300	BmnT	60445	3348	5W-18S	B6
152nd St					
4300	MDLN	60445	3348	5W-18S	B6
4500	OKFT	60445	3348	5W-18S	B6
4600	MDLN	60452	3348	5W-18S	B6
5000	OKFT	60452	3348	6W-18S	A6
5100	OKFT	60452	3347	6W-18S	E6
E 152nd St					
10	HRVY	60426	3349	1W-18S	E6
10	SHLD	60473	3350	0E-17S	D6
100	HRVY	60426	3350	1W-18S	A6
500	PHNX	60426	3350	0W-18S	B6
600	DLTN	60419	3350	0E-17S	E6
600	SHLD	60419	3350	0E-17S	E6
800	DLTN	60473	3351	1E-17S	A6
900	PHNX	60473	3350	0W-18S	C6
900	SHLD	60473	3351	1E-17S	A6
1100	SHLD	60419	3351	1E-17S	A6
1200	DLTN	60419	3351	1E-17S	B6
W 152nd St					
10	HRVY	60426	3349	2W-18S	D6
10	SHLD	60473	3350	0W-17S	D6
7200	ODPK	60462	3346	9W-18S	E6
7300	OrlT	60462	3346	9W-18S	E6
E 153rd Ct					
-	SHLD	60473	3351	1E-17S	A6
W 153rd Ct					
7200	ODPK	60462	3346	9W-18S	E7
153rd Pl					
200	CTCY	60409	3352	4E-17S	B6
3600	MDLN	60445	3348	4W-18S	D7
E 153rd Pl					
1000	SHLD	60473	3351	1E-17S	A6
W 153rd Pl					
10	SHLD	60473	3350	0W-17S	C6
7200	ODPK	60462	3346	9W-18S	E7
7300	OrlT	60462	3346	9W-18S	E7
153rd St					
-	CTCY	60409	3351	2E-17S	D6
-	MKHM	60426	3348	4W-18S	E6
-	MKHM	60428	3348	4W-18S	E6
10	CTCY	60409	3352	4E-17S	B6
10	HMND	46320	3352	4E-17S	C6
3600	MDLN	60445	3348	4W-18S	D7
3900	BmnT	60426	3348	4W-18S	C7
3900	MDLN	60426	3348	4W-18S	C7
4600	OKFT	60452	3348	6W-18S	A6
5100	OKFT	60452	3347	6W-18S	E6
E 153rd St					
-	DLTN	60419	3351	1E-17S	B6
10	HRVY	60426	3349	1W-18S	E7
100	HRVY	60426	3350	1W-18S	A7
500	DLTN	60419	3350	0E-17S	E6
500	PHNX	60426	3350	0W-18S	B7
500	SHLD	60419	3350	0E-17S	E6
700	DLTN	60473	3351	1E-17S	A6
700	SHLD	60473	3351	1E-17S	A6
900	SHLD	60426	3350	0W-18S	C7
900	SHLD	60473	3350	0W-18S	C7
W 153rd St					
2500	HRVY	60426	3349	3W-18S	B7
3100	MKHM	60426	3348	3W-18S	E6
3100	MKHM	60428	3348	3W-18S	E6
3100	MKHM	60428	3349	3W-18S	A6
7000	ODPK	60462	3346	9W-18S	E6
7000	OKFT	60452	3346	9W-18S	E6
7000	OKFT	60462	3347	8W-18S	A6
7300	OrlT	60462	3346	9W-18S	E6
9600	ODPK	60462	3345	13W-18S	A7
10100	ODPK	60467	3345	12W-18S	C7
10600	OrlT	60462	3345	13W-18S	A7
10600	OrlT	60467	3345	13W-18S	A7
11000	ODPK	60467	3344	13W-18S	E7
11000	OrlT	60467	3344	13W-18S	E7
154th Pl					
10	CTCY	60409	3352	4E-18S	C6
10	HMND	46320	3352	4E-18S	C6
6900	OKFT	60452	3347	8W-18S	A7
E 154th Pl					
500	HRVY	60426	3350	0W-18S	B7
500	PHNX	60426	3350	0W-18S	B7
600	SHLD	60473	3350	0E-18S	E6
600	SHLD	60473	3351	0E-18S	A6
700	SHLD	60419	3351	1E-18S	A6
1400	DLTN	60419	3351	1E-18S	B6
1600	DLTN	60473	3351	2E-18S	C6
W 154th Pl					
100	HRVY	60426	3349	2W-18S	C7
3700	BmnT	60426	3348	4W-18S	D7
3700	MKHM	60426	3348	4W-18S	D7
3700	MKHM	60428	3348	4W-18S	D7
7300	ODPK	60462	3346	9W-18S	E7
7300	OrlT	60462	3346	9W-18S	E7
154th St					
4800	OKFT	60452	3348	6W-18S	A7
5100	OKFT	60452	3347	6W-18S	E7
E 154th St					
10	HRVY	60426	3349	1W-18S	E7
500	HRVY	60426	3350	0W-18S	B7
500	PHNX	60426	3350	0W-18S	B7
600	DLTN	60419	3350	0E-17S	E6
600	SHLD	60419	3350	0E-17S	E6
600	SHLD	60473	3350	0E-17S	E6
700	DLTN	60419	3351	1E-17S	A6
700	DLTN	60473	3351	1E-17S	A6
700	SHLD	60419	3351	1E-18S	A6
700	SHLD	60473	3351	1E-18S	A6
1600	ThtT	60473	3351	1E-17S	A6
1700	CTCY	60409	3351	1E-17S	A6
1700	ThtT	60409	3351	1E-17S	A6
W 154th St					
-	BmnT	60426	3348	4W-18S	C7
-	MDLN	60426	3348	4W-18S	C7
-	MDLN	60445	3348	4W-18S	D7
-	MKHM	60428	3348	4W-18S	D7
-	MKHM	60445	3348	4W-18S	D7
-	OKFT	60462	3346	9W-18S	E7
10	HRVY	60426	3349	2W-18S	C7
10	SHLD	60473	3350	0W-17S	C6
100	PHNX	60426	3350	0W-17S	C6
100	PHNX	60473	3350	0W-17S	C6
3800	MDLN	60428	3348	4W-18S	C7
7300	ODPK	60462	3346	9W-18S	E7
7300	OrlT	60462	3346	9W-18S	E7
9700	ODPK	60462	3345	12W-18S	D7
E 155th Ct					
700	PHNX	60426	3350	0W-18S	B7
155th Pl					
10	CTCY	60409	3352	4E-18S	B7
10	HMND	46320	3352	4E-18S	C7
6800	OKFT	60452	3347	8W-18S	A7
E 155th Pl					
-	SHLD	60473	3351	1E-18S	B7
10	SHLD	60473	3350	0E-18S	D7
500	PHNX	60426	3350	0W-18S	B7
700	DLTN	60473	3351	0E-18S	A7
1400	DLTN	60419	3351	1E-18S	B7
W 155th Pl					
10	SHLD	60473	3350	0W-18S	D6
100	HRVY	60426	3349	2W-18S	D7
155th St					
600	CTCY	60409	3352	3E-18S	A6
4500	OKFT	60452	3348	6W-18S	A7
5100	OKFT	60452	3347	6W-18S	E7
E 155th St					
10	HRVY	60426	3349	1W-18S	E7
100	HRVY	60426	3350	1W-18S	A7
500	PHNX	60426	3350	0W-18S	B7
500	SHLD	60473	3350	0E-18S	E6
800	DLTN	60419	3351	1E-18S	A6
800	DLTN	60473	3351	1E-18S	A6
800	SHLD	60419	3351	1E-18S	A6
800	SHLD	60473	3351	1E-18S	A6
900	PHNX	60473	3350	0W-18S	C7
900	SHLD	60426	3350	0W-18S	C7
W 155th St					
-	OrlT	60467	3344	14W-18S	D7
10	SHLD	60473	3350	0W-17S	C6
2400	HRVY	60426	3349	3W-18S	B7
2400	MKHM	60426	3349	3W-18S	B7
3100	MKHM	60428	3349	3W-18S	A7
3400	MKHM	60428	3348	4W-18S	D7
3800	BmnT	60426	3348	4W-18S	C7
3800	MKHM	60426	3348	4W-18S	C7
7300	ODPK	60462	3346	9W-18S	E7
7300	OrlT	60462	3346	9W-18S	E7
11200	ODPK	60467	3344	14W-18S	E7
156th Pl					
10	CTCY	60409	3352	4E-18S	C7
10	HMND	46320	3352	4E-18S	C7
1000	CTCY	60409	3351	3E-18S	E7
6800	OKFT	60452	3347	8W-18S	A7
E 156th Pl					
600	SHLD	60473	3350	0E-18S	E7
700	SHLD	60419	3351	0E-18S	A7
700	SHLD	60473	3351	0E-18S	A7
1000	DLTN	60419	3351	1E-18S	A7
W 156th Pl					
100	HRVY	60426	3427	2W-18S	D1
200	HRVY	60428	3427	2W-18S	C1
200	MKHM	60428	3427	2W-18S	C1
156th St					
10	CTCY	60409	3352	4E-18S	B7
10	HMND	46320	3352	4E-18S	C7
1000	CTCY	60409	3351	3E-18S	E7
4700	OKFT	60452	3348	6W-18S	A7
5100	OKFT	60452	3347	6W-18S	E7
6800	BmnT	60452	3347	8W-18S	A7
7100	ODPK	60462	3346	9W-18S	E7
11200	OrlT	60467	3344	14W-18S	E7
E 156th St					
10	HRVY	60426	3349	1W-18S	E7
10	SHLD	60473	3350	0E-18S	D7
100	HRVY	60426	3350	1W-18S	A7
700	SHLD	60419	3351	0E-18S	A7
800	SHLD	60473	3351	1E-18S	A7
1400	DLTN	60419	3351	1E-18S	B7
W 156th St					
10	HRVY	60426	3349	2W-18S	C7
200	HRVY	60428	3349	2W-18S	C7
3200	MKHM	60428	3349	3W-18S	A7
3600	MKHM	60428	3426	4W-18S	D1
3700	BmnT	60426	3426	4W-18S	C1
3700	MKHM	60426	3426	4W-18S	C1
157th Pl					
6200	OKFT	60452	3347	7W-18S	B7
6800	BmnT	60452	3425	8W-18S	A1
6800	BmnT	60477	3425	8W-18S	A1
6800	OKFT	60452	3425	8W-18S	A1
6900	ODPK	60462	3425	8W-18S	A1
6900	ODPK	60477	3425	8W-18S	A1
E 157th Pl					
400	SHLD	60473	3350	0E-18S	E7
600	HRVY	60426	3428	0W-18S	B1
700	DLTN	60419	3351	0E-18S	A7
700	SHLD	60419	3351	0E-18S	A7
700	SHLD	60426	3428	0W-18S	B1
700	SHLD	60473	3351	0E-18S	A7
700	SHLD	60473	3428	0W-18S	B1
W 157th Pl					
100	HRVY	60426	3427	2W-18S	C1
100	HRVY	60428	3427	2W-18S	C1
100	MKHM	60428	3427	2W-18S	C1
2300	MKHM	60426	3427	2W-18S	C1
7600	ODPK	60462	3424	9W-18S	D1
157th St					
10	CTCY	60409	3352	4E-18S	C7
10	HMND	46320	3352	4E-18S	C7
4800	OKFT	60452	3348	6W-18S	A7
6000	OKFT	60452	3347	8W-18S	B7
6800	BmnT	60452	3347	8W-18S	A7
6800	BmnT	60477	3347	8W-18S	A7
E 157th St					
-	ThtT	60473	3351	2E-18S	C7
10	HRVY	60426	3427	1W-18S	E1
100	HRVY	60426	3428	0W-18S	B1
400	SHLD	60473	3350	0E-18S	E7
700	SHLD	60419	3351	0E-18S	A7
700	SHLD	60473	3351	0E-18S	A7
1600	DLTN	60419	3351	2E-18S	C7
W 157th St					
10	SHLD	60473	3350	0W-18S	C7
100	PHNX	60426	3350	0W-18S	C7
100	SHLD	60426	3350	0W-18S	C7
200	HRVY	60428	3427	2W-18S	C1
300	HRVY	60426	3427	3W-18S	B1
300	MKHM	60426	3427	3W-18S	B1
300	MKHM	60428	3427	3W-18S	B1
3300	MKHM	60428	3426	4W-18S	E1
7000	ODPK	60462	3347	8W-18S	A7
7100	ODPK	60462	3346	9W-18S	E7
7400	ODPK	60462	3424	10W-18S	B1
11200	ODPK	60467	3422	14W-18S	E1
11200	OrlT	60467	3422	14W-18S	D1
W 158th Ct					
7700	ODPK	60462	3424	9W-18S	D1
158th Pl					
10	CTCY	60409	3429	2E-18S	C1
5800	OKFT	60452	3425	7W-18S	C1
E 158th Pl					
10	SHLD	60473	3350	0E-18S	D7
W 158th Pl					
10	HRVY	60426	3427	2W-18S	D1
158th St					
600	CTCY	60409	3352	3E-18S	A7
4800	OKFT	60452	3426	6W-18S	A1
5100	OKFT	60452	3425	6W-18S	E1
7100	ODPK	60462	3424	9W-18S	E1
11200	ODPK	60467	3422	14W-18S	E1
11200	OrlT	60467	3422	14W-18S	E1
E 158th St					
10	HRVY	60426	3427	1W-18S	E1
100	HRVY	60426	3428	1W-18S	A1

STREET Block	City	ZIP	Map#	CGS	Grid
E 158th St					
400	SHLD	60473	3350	0E-18S	E7
700	DLTN	60419	3351	0E-18S	A7
700	HRVY	60473	3428	0W-18S	B1
700	SHLD	60419	3351	0E-18S	A7
700	SHLD	60473	3428	0W-18S	B1
1200	SHLD	60473	3351	1E-18S	B7
1600	DLTN	60473	3351	2E-18S	C7
1800	ThtT	60473	3351	2E-18S	C7
1900	CTCY	60409	3351	2E-18S	C7
1900	ThtT	60409	3351	2E-18S	C7
W 158th St					
-	SHLD	60473	3350	0W-18S	C7
10	HRVY	60426	3427	2W-18S	D1
2100	HRVY	60428	3427	2W-18S	C1
2100	MKHM	60428	3427	2W-18S	C1
2300	MKHM	60426	3427	2W-18S	C1
3400	MKHM	60428	3426	4W-18S	E1
159th Ct					
-	BmnT	60428	3427	3W-19S	B1
E 159th Ct					
600	SHLD	60473	3350	0E-18S	E7
159th Pl					
7400	TYPK	60477	3424	9W-19S	D1
9000	ODHL	60487	3424	11W-19S	A1
E 159th Pl					
600	SHLD	60473	3428	0E-18S	E1
900	SHLD	60473	3429	1E-18S	A1
1100	SHLD	60473	3351	1E-18S	A7
W 159th Pl					
3800	MKHM	60428	3426	4W-19S	D1
3900	BmnT	60426	3426	4W-19S	D1
3900	MKHM	60426	3426	4W-19S	D1
159th St					
-	SHLD	60409	3429	1E-19S	C1
-	SHLD	60473	3429	1E-19S	C1
200	CTCY	60409	3430	4E-18S	B1
1400	CTCY	60409	3429	2E-18S	D1
2400	BmnT	60428	3427	3W-19S	B1
2400	ThtT	60428	3427	3W-19S	B1
4700	BmnT	60426	3426	5W-18S	A1
4700	BmnT	60452	3426	5W-18S	A1
4700	OKFT	60426	3426	5W-18S	A1
4700	OKFT	60452	3426	5W-18S	A1
5100	OKFT	60452	3425	6W-18S	E1
5400	BmnT	60452	3425	6W-18S	D1
5400	BmnT	60477	3425	6W-18S	D1
6400	TYPK	60477	3425	8W-19S	B1
6700	TYPK	60452	3425	8W-19S	A1
6900	ODPK	60462	3425	8W-19S	A1
6900	ODPK	60477	3425	8W-19S	A1
159th St US-6					
-	SHLD	60409	3429	1E-19S	C1
-	SHLD	60473	3429	1E-19S	C1
1400	CTCY	60409	3429	2E-18S	D1
4700	BmnT	60426	3426	5W-18S	A1
4700	BmnT	60452	3426	5W-18S	A1
4700	OKFT	60426	3426	5W-18S	A1
4700	OKFT	60452	3426	5W-18S	A1
5100	OKFT	60452	3425	6W-18S	E1
5400	BmnT	60452	3425	6W-18S	D1
5400	BmnT	60477	3425	6W-18S	D1
6400	TYPK	60477	3425	8W-19S	B1
6700	TYPK	60452	3425	8W-19S	A1
6900	ODPK	60462	3425	8W-19S	A1
6900	ODPK	60477	3425	8W-19S	A1
E 159th St					
10	HRVY	60426	3427	1W-19S	E1
10	SHLD	60473	3350	0E-18S	D7
100	HRVY	60426	3428	1W-18S	A1
300	HRVY	60473	3428	1W-18S	A1
300	SHLD	60426	3428	1W-18S	A1
300	SHLD	60473	3428	1W-18S	A1
1200	LKPT	60441	3420	21W-19S	A2
1200	LktT	60441	3420	21W-19S	A2
1300	HmrT	60441	3420	21W-18S	A2
E 159th St SR-7					
1200	LKPT	60441	3420	21W-19S	A2
1200	LktT	60441	3420	21W-19S	A2
1300	HmrT	60441	3420	21W-18S	A2
E 159th St US-6					
10	HRVY	60426	3427	1W-19S	E1
100	HRVY	60426	3428	1W-18S	A1
300	HRVY	60473	3428	1W-18S	A1
300	SHLD	60426	3428	1W-18S	A1
300	SHLD	60473	3428	1W-18S	A1
W 159th St					
-	OKFT	60426	3426	5W-18S	B1
-	OKFT	60452	3426	5W-18S	B1
10	HRVY	60426	3427	2W-18S	D1
200	HRVY	60428	3427	2W-18S	C1
200	MKHM	60428	3427	2W-18S	C1
200	ThtT	60428	3427	2W-18S	C1
2300	BmnT	60428	3427	3W-18S	C1
2300	MKHM	60426	3427	2W-18S	C1
3300	MKHM	60428	3426	5W-18S	B1
3800	BmnT	60426	3426	5W-18S	B1
3800	MKHM	60426	3426	5W-18S	B1
7000	ODPK	60462	3425	8W-18S	A1
7000	ODPK	60477	3425	8W-18S	A1
7000	TYPK	60477	3425	8W-18S	A1
7100	ODPK	60462	3424	9W-18S	D1
7100	TYPK	60477	3424	9W-18S	D1
7200	ODPK	60477	3424	9W-19S	E1
7600	TYPK	60462	3424	9W-18S	D1
8000	TYPK	60487	3424	10W-19S	B1
8700	ODHL	60462	3424	10W-19S	A1
8700	ODHL	60487	3424	10W-19S	A1
8700	ODPK	60487	3424	10W-19S	A1
9100	ODHL	60487	3423	12W-18S	B1
9100	ODPK	60462	3423	12W-18S	B1
9200	ODHL	60462	3423	11W-19S	E1
9300	ODPK	60467	3423	11W-19S	E1
9900	OrlT	60462	3423	12W-18S	C1
9900	OrlT	60467	3423	12W-18S	C1
10800	ODPK	60467	3422	15W-18S	C1
10800	OrlT	60467	3422	15W-18S	C1
11800	HMGN	60491	3422	14W-18S	E1
13000	HMGN	60491	3421	16W-18S	E1
13900	HmrT	60491	3421	17W-18S	C1
14800	HmrT	60491	3420	20W-18S	C1
15400	HmrT	60441	3420	19W-19S	C1
16000	LKPT	60441	3420	20W-19S	C2
16000	LKPT	60491	3420	20W-19S	C2
16600	LktT	60441	3420	20W-18S	A2
W 159th St SR-7					
11200	ODPK	60467	3422	14W-18S	E1
11200	OrlT	60467	3422	14W-18S	E1
11800	HMGN	60491	3422	14W-18S	E1
13000	HMGN	60491	3421	16W-18S	E1
13900	HmrT	60491	3421	17W-18S	C1
14800	HmrT	60491	3420	20W-18S	C1
15400	HmrT	60441	3420	19W-19S	C1
16000	LKPT	60441	3420	20W-19S	C2
16000	LKPT	60491	3420	20W-19S	C2
16600	LktT	60441	3420	20W-18S	A2
W 159th St US-6					
-	OKFT	60426	3426	5W-18S	B1
-	OKFT	60452	3426	5W-18S	B1
10	HRVY	60426	3427	2W-18S	D1
200	HRVY	60428	3427	2W-18S	C1
200	MKHM	60428	3427	2W-18S	C1
200	ThtT	60428	3427	2W-18S	C1
2300	BmnT	60428	3427	3W-18S	C1
2300	MKHM	60426	3427	2W-18S	C1
3300	MKHM	60428	3426	5W-18S	B1
3800	BmnT	60426	3426	5W-18S	B1
3800	MKHM	60426	3426	5W-18S	B1
7000	ODPK	60462	3425	8W-18S	A1
7000	ODPK	60477	3425	8W-18S	A1
7000	TYPK	60477	3425	8W-18S	A1
7100	ODPK	60462	3424	9W-18S	D1
7100	TYPK	60477	3424	9W-18S	D1
7200	ODPK	60477	3424	9W-19S	E1
7600	TYPK	60462	3424	9W-18S	D1
8000	TYPK	60487	3424	10W-19S	B1
8700	ODHL	60462	3424	10W-19S	A1
8700	ODHL	60487	3424	10W-19S	A1
8700	ODPK	60487	3424	10W-19S	A1
9100	ODHL	60487	3423	12W-18S	B1
9100	ODPK	60462	3423	12W-18S	B1
9200	ODHL	60462	3423	11W-19S	E1
9300	ODPK	60467	3423	11W-19S	E1
9900	OrlT	60462	3423	12W-18S	C1
9900	OrlT	60467	3423	12W-18S	C1
10800	ODPK	60467	3422	15W-18S	C1
10800	OrlT	60467	3422	15W-18S	C1
E 160th Ct					
600	SHLD	60473	3428	0E-18S	E1
160th Pl					
900	CTCY	60409	3430	3E-19S	A2
8200	TYPK	60477	3424	10W-19S	B1
8300	TYPK	60487	3424	10W-19S	B1
9000	ODHL	60487	3424	11W-19S	A2
E 160th Pl					
300	HRVY	60426	3428	0W-19S	B2
300	SHLD	60426	3428	0W-19S	B2
400	SHLD	60473	3428	0E-18S	E1
1100	SHLD	60473	3429	1E-18S	B1
160th St					
600	CTCY	60409	3430	3E-19S	B1
4800	BmnT	60426	3426	6W-19S	A1
4800	BmnT	60452	3426	6W-19S	A1
5000	OKFT	60452	3425	6W-19S	E1
5000	OKFT	60452	3426	6W-19S	A1
7900	TYPK	60477	3424	10W-19S	C1
10700	ODPK	60467	3423	13W-19S	A2
E 160th St					
10	HRVY	60426	3427	1W-19S	E1
200	HRVY	60426	3428	1W-19S	A1
200	SHLD	60426	3428	0E-18S	D1
700	SHLD	60473	3429	0E-18S	A1
W 160th St					
-	SHLD	60473	3350	0W-18S	C7
-	SHLD	60473	3428	0W-18S	C1
10	HRVY	60426	3427	2W-19S	D2
2100	HRVY	60428	3427	2W-19S	C1
2100	ThtT	60428	3427	2W-19S	C2
2300	BmnT	60428	3427	2W-19S	C1
3200	MKHM	60428	3427	3W-19S	A1
3300	MKHM	60428	3426	4W-19S	E1
161st Pl					
8000	TYPK	60477	3424	10W-19S	C2
8400	TYPK	60487	3424	10W-19S	B2
9000	ODHL	60487	3424	11W-19S	A2
9100	ODHL	60487	3423	11W-19S	E2
E 161st Pl					
200	SHLD	60473	3428	0E-18S	E1
1100	SHLD	60473	3429	1E-18S	B1
W 161st Pl					
8700	ODHL	60487	3424	10W-19S	A2
8700	ODPK	60462	3424	10W-19S	A2
8700	ODPK	60487	3424	10W-19S	A2
161st St					
-	ODPK	60467	3423	12W-19S	D2
-	TYPK	60477	3425	8W-19S	A2
200	CTCY	60409	3430	4E-19S	B2
4800	BmnT	60426	3426	6W-19S	A1
4800	BmnT	60452	3426	6W-19S	A1
4800	OKFT	60452	3426	6W-19S	A1
5300	OKFT	60452	3425	6W-19S	E1
7800	TYPK	60477	3424	9W-19S	C1
8400	TYPK	60487	3424	10W-19S	B2
E 161st St					
-	HRVY	60426	3428	0W-19S	B2
600	SHLD	60473	3428	0E-18S	E1
600	SHLD	60473	3429	0E-18S	A1
W 161st St					
-	SHLD	60473	3428	0W-18S	C1
1700	HRVY	60426	3427	2W-19S	D2
1700	MKHM	60426	3427	2W-19S	D2
1800	HRVY	60428	3427	2W-19S	D2
1900	ThtT	60426	3427	2W-19S	D2
2200	MKHM	60428	3427	2W-19S	C2
2200	ThtT	60428	3427	2W-19S	C2
3300	MKHM	60428	3426	4W-19S	E2
162nd Pl					
10	CTCY	60409	3430	4E-19S	C2
7400	TYPK	60477	3424	9W-19S	D2
8400	TYPK	60487	3424	10W-19S	B2
E 162nd Pl					
10	SHLD	60473	3428	0E-19S	D1
900	SHLD	60473	3429	1E-19S	A1
W 162nd Pl					
3700	MKHM	60428	3426	4W-19S	D2
162nd St					
100	CTCY	60409	3430	4E-19S	C2
4800	BmnT	60426	3426	6W-19S	A2
4800	BmnT	60452	3426	6W-19S	A2
4800	OKFT	60452	3426	6W-19S	A2
5200	OKFT	60452	3425	6W-19S	E2
7400	TYPK	60477	3424	9W-19S	D2
8400	TYPK	60487	3424	10W-19S	B2
9000	ODHL	60487	3423	11W-19S	E2
9000	ODHL	60487	3424	11W-19S	A2
9400	ODPK	60467	3423	11W-19S	E2
E 162nd St					
10	SHLD	60473	3428	0E-18S	D1
200	HRVY	60426	3428	1W-19S	A2
700	SHLD	60473	3429	1E-18S	A1
E 162nd St US-6					
10	SHLD	60473	3428	0E-18S	D1
700	SHLD	60473	3429	1E-18S	A1
W 162nd St					
10	SHLD	60473	3428	0W-19S	C1
500	HRVY	60426	3428	0W-18S	B1
500	HRVY	60473	3428	0W-18S	B1
500	SHLD	60426	3428	0W-18S	B1
1400	HRVY	60426	3427	2W-19S	E2
1400	HRVY	60428	3427	2W-19S	C2
1400	MKHM	60428	3427	2W-19S	C2
2500	BmnT	60428	3427	3W-19S	B2
W 162nd St					
3300	MKHM	60428	3426	4W-19S	E2
8700	ODHL	60487	3424	10W-19S	A2
8700	ODPK	60462	3424	10W-19S	A2
8700	ODPK	60487	3424	10W-19S	A2
W 162nd St US-6					
10	SHLD	60473	3428	0W-19S	C1
500	HRVY	60426	3428	0W-18S	B1
500	HRVY	60473	3428	0W-18S	B1
500	SHLD	60426	3428	0W-18S	B1
163rd Ct					
7900	TYPK	60477	3424	9W-19S	C2
E 163rd Ct					
10	SHLD	60473	3428	0E-19S	D2
163rd Pl					
10	CTCY	60409	3430	4E-19S	C2
10	HMND	46324	3430	4E-19S	C2
6400	TYPK	60477	3425	8W-19S	B2
7900	TYPK	60477	3424	9W-19S	C2
10400	ODPK	60467	3423	13W-19S	B2
10400	OrlT	60467	3423	13W-19S	B2
E 163rd Pl					
700	SHLD	60473	3428	0E-19S	E2
700	SHLD	60473	3429	0E-19S	A2
W 163rd Pl					
2100	MKHM	60428	3427	2W-19S	C2
163rd St					
-	ODHL	60487	3423	11W-19S	E2
-	ODPK	60467	3423	11W-19S	E2
-	ODPK	60487	3423	11W-19S	E2
-	TYPK	60477	3424	9W-19S	E2
-	TYPK	60477	3425	8W-19S	A2
10	HMND	46324	3430	4E-19S	C2
700	CTCY	60438	3430	3E-19S	A2
700	LNSG	60438	3430	3E-19S	A2
800	CTCY	60409	3430	3E-19S	A2
4000	BmnT	60428	3426	5W-19S	C2
4000	MKHM	60426	3426	5W-19S	C2
4000	MKHM	60428	3426	5W-19S	C2
4800	BmnT	60426	3426	6W-19S	A2
4800	BmnT	60452	3426	6W-19S	A2
4800	OKFT	60452	3426	6W-19S	A2
5400	BmnT	60477	3425	6W-19S	D2
5400	OKFT	60452	3425	6W-19S	D2
5400	OKFT	60477	3425	6W-19S	D2
8300	TYPK	60487	3424	10W-19S	B2
8500	ODPK	60462	3424	10W-19S	B2
8500	ODPK	60487	3424	10W-19S	B2
E 163rd St					
10	SHLD	60473	3428	0E-19S	D1
200	HRVY	60426	3428	1W-19S	A2
300	SHLD	60426	3428	0W-19S	B2
1100	SHLD	60473	3429	1E-19S	B1
W 163rd St					
-	HRVY	60426	3427	1W-19S	E2
1400	HRVY	60428	3427	2W-19S	E2
1400	MKHM	60428	3427	2W-19S	D2
3300	MKHM	60428	3426	4W-19S	E2
4200	BmnT	60426	3426	5W-19S	C2
8600	ODPK	60462	3424	10W-19S	B2
8600	ODPK	60487	3424	10W-19S	B2
8600	TYPK	60487	3424	10W-19S	B2
8800	ODHL	60462	3424	11W-19S	A2
8800	ODHL	60487	3424	11W-19S	A2
13500	HMGN	60491	3421	16W-19S	D2
14100	HmrT	60441	3421	18W-19S	A2
14100	HmrT	60491	3421	18W-19S	A2
14100	LKPT	60441	3421	18W-19S	A2
15200	HmrT	60491	3420	19W-19S	C2
15600	HmrT	60441	3420	19W-19S	C2
15600	LKPT	60441	3420	20W-19S	B3
15600	LKPT	60491	3420	19W-19S	B3
164th Ct					
8200	TYPK	60477	3424	10W-19S	C3
E 164th Ct					
800	SHLD	60473	3429	1E-19S	A2
164th Pl					
10	CTCY	60409	3430	4E-19S	C3
10	HMND	46324	3430	4E-19S	C3
6400	TYPK	60477	3425	8W-19S	B2
7900	TYPK	60477	3424	9W-19S	C2
10400	ODPK	60467	3423	13W-19S	B3
10400	OrlT	60467	3423	13W-19S	B3
E 164th Pl					
200	SHLD	60473	3428	0E-19S	D2
1100	SHLD	60473	3429	1E-19S	B2
W 164th Pl					
8600	ODPK	60462	3424	10W-19S	B2
164th St					
10	CTCY	60409	3430	4E-19S	C2
10	HMND	46324	3430	4E-19S	C2
6600	TYPK	60477	3425	8W-19S	A2
8200	TYPK	60477	3424	10W-19S	C2
E 164th St					
10	SHLD	60473	3428	0E-19S	D2
300	HRVY	60426	3428	0W-19S	B2
1200	SHLD	60473	3429	1E-19S	B2
W 164th St					
1400	HRVY	60426	3427	1W-19S	E2
1400	HRVY	60428	3427	1W-19S	E2
1400	MKHM	60428	3427	1W-19S	E3
3300	MKHM	60428	3426	4W-19S	E2
8700	ODPK	60462	3424	11W-19S	A2
8900	ODHL	60462	3424	11W-19S	A2
8900	ODHL	60487	3424	11W-19S	A2
165th Av					
9600	ODPK	60467	3423	12W-19S	D3
165th Pl					
10	CTCY	60409	3430	4E-19S	C3
10	HMND	46324	3430	4E-19S	C3
6600	TYPK	60477	3425	8W-19S	A3
7900	TYPK	60477	3424	9W-19S	C3
8400	TYPK	60487	3424	10W-19S	B3
E 165th Pl					
300	SHLD	60473	3428	0E-19S	D2
800	SHLD	60473	3429	1E-19S	A2
W 165th Pl					
8600	ODPK	60462	3424	10W-19S	B3
8600	TYPK	60487	3424	10W-19S	B3
165th St					
10	CTCY	60409	3430		D2
10	HMND	46324	3430		D2
4000	MKHM	60428	3426	5W-19S	C3
4000	MKHM	60452	3426	5W-19S	C3
4000	OKFT	60428	3426	5W-19S	C3
4000	OKFT	60452	3426	5W-19S	C3
6600	TYPK	60477	3425	8W-19S	A2
7400	TYPK	60477	3424	9W-19S	D3
10700	ODPK	60467	3423	13W-19S	A4
E 165th St					
200	HRVY	60426	3428	1W-19S	B3
200	SHLD	60473	3428	0E-19S	D2
800	SHLD	60473	3429	1E-19S	A2
W 165th St					
1500	HRVY	60426	3427	2W-19S	D2
1500	HRVY	60428	3427	2W-19S	D3
W 165th St					
1500	MKHM	60428	3427	2W-19S	D3
3300	MKHM	60428	3426	4W-19S	E3
W 166th Ct					
9400	ODPK	60467	3423	11W-19S	E3
166th Pl					
10	CTCY	60409	3430	4E-19S	C3
10	HMND	46324	3430	4E-19S	C3
7900	TYPK	60477	3424	9W-19S	C3
E 166th Pl					
400	SHLD	60473	3428	0E-19S	E2
1200	SHLD	60473	3429	1E-19S	B2
W 166th Pl					
3800	MKHM	60428	3426	4W-19S	D3
3800	MKHM	60452	3426	4W-19S	D3
8700	ODHL	60487	3424	10W-19S	A3
8700	ODPK	60462	3424	10W-19S	A3
8700	ODPK	60487	3424	10W-19S	A3
9400	ODHL	60487	3423	11W-19S	E3
9400	ODPK	60467	3423	11W-19S	E3
9400	ODPK	60487	3423	11W-19S	E3
166th St					
-	MKHM	60428	3427	3W-19S	B3
10	CTCY	60409	3430	4E-19S	B3
10	HMND	46324	3430	4E-19S	C3
4100	OKFT	60452	3426	5W-19S	C3
6000	BmnT	60477	3425	7W-19S	C3
6000	TYPK	60477	3425	7W-19S	C3
7100	OrlT	60477	3424	8W-19S	E3
7600	TYPK	60477	3424	9W-19S	D3
E 166th St					
200	HRVY	60426	3428	1W-19S	A3
200	SHLD	60473	3428	0E-19S	E2
700	SHLD	60473	3429	1E-19S	A2
W 166th St					
3000	MKHM	60428	3427	3W-19S	A3
3600	MKHM	60428	3426	4W-19S	D3
8700	ODHL	60487	3424	10W-19S	A3
8700	ODPK	60462	3424	10W-19S	A3
8700	ODPK	60487	3424	10W-19S	A3
167th Pl					
10	CTCY	60409	3430	4E-20S	C3
3700	CCHL	60478	3426	4W-20S	D3
7900	TYPK	60477	3424	10W-20S	C3
8800	ODHL	60487	3424	11W-20S	A3
8800	ODPK	60462	3424	11W-20S	A3
8800	ODPK	60487	3424	11W-20S	A3
10900	ODPK	60467	3423	13W-20S	A3
E 167th Pl					
400	SHLD	60473	3428	0E-19S	E3
1300	SHLD	60473	3429	1E-19S	B3
W 167th Pl					
800	HRVY	60426	3428	1W-20S	A3
8600	ODPK	60462	3424	10W-20S	B3
8700	ODHL	60487	3424	10W-20S	A3
8700	ODPK	60487	3424	10W-20S	A3
167th St					
-	BmnT	60478	3426	5W-19S	C3
-	CCHL	60477	3426	5W-19S	C3
10	CTCY	60409	3430	4E-20S	C3
800	HMND	46324	3430		E2
4000	CCHL	60452	3426	5W-19S	C3
4000	CCHL	60478	3426	5W-19S	D3
4000	MKHM	60428	3426	5W-19S	D3
4000	MKHM	60452	3426	5W-19S	D3
4000	OKFT	60452	3426	6W-19S	A3
4200	BmnT	60477	3426	5W-19S	C3
4200	OKFT	60477	3426	5W-19S	C3
4500	BmnT	60452	3426	5W-20S	B3
5000	BmnT	60452	3425	8W-19S	B3
5000	BmnT	60477	3425	8W-19S	B3
5000	OKFT	60452	3425	8W-19S	B3
5600	TYPK	60477	3425	7W-20S	D3
7100	TYPK	60477	3424	9W-19S	E3
7400	OrlT	60477	3424	10W-20S	B3
8300	TYPK	60487	3424	10W-20S	B3
9000	ODHL	60487	3423	11W-19S	D3
9000	ODHL	60487	3424	11W-20S	A3
9300	ODHL	60467	3423	11W-20S	E3
9300	ODPK	60467	3423	11W-20S	E3
9300	ODPK	60487	3423	11W-20S	E3
9400	OrlT	60467	3423	11W-20S	D3
9400	OrlT	60487	3423	11W-20S	D3
E 167th St					
200	HRVY	60426	3428	0W-20S	B3
300	SHLD	60426	3428	0W-19S	B3
400	SHLD	60473	3428	0E-19S	E2
700	SHLD	60473	3429	0E-19S	A2
W 167th St					
400	SHLD	60473	3428	0W-19S	B2
1500	HLCT	60428	3427	2W-19S	D3
1500	HLCT	60429	3427	3W-19S	A3
1500	HRVY	60426	3427	2W-19S	E3
1500	HRVY	60428	3427	2W-19S	E3
1500	HRVY	60429	3427	2W-19S	E3
1500	MKHM	60428	3427	3W-19S	A3
1600	MKHM	60429	3427	2W-19S	D3
3300	HLCT	60428	3426	4W-19S	D3
3300	HLCT	60429	3426	4W-19S	D3
3300	MKHM	60428	3426	4W-19S	D3
3600	CCHL	60429	3426	4W-19S	D3
3600	CCHL	60478	3426	4W-19S	D3
3900	CCHL	60452	3426	4W-19S	D3
3900	MKHM	60452	3426	4W-19S	D3
8500	ODPK	60462	3424	11W-19S	A3
8500	ODPK	60487	3424	11W-19S	A3
8500	TYPK	60487	3424	11W-19S	A3
8700	ODHL	60462	3424	10W-20S	A3
8700	ODHL	60487	3424	10W-20S	A3
9600	ODHL	60467	3423	12W-19S	B3
9600	ODHL	60487	3423	12W-19S	B3
9600	ODPK	60467	3423	12W-19S	B3
9600	ODPK	60487	3423	12W-19S	B3
9600	OrlT	60467	3423	12W-19S	B3
9600	OrlT	60487	3423	12W-19S	B3
11100	ODPK	60467	3422	14W-19S	D3
11100	OrlT	60467	3422	14W-19S	D3
11800	HMGN	60467	3422	14W-19S	C3
12800	HMGN	60491	3421	16W-19S	E3
12800	HMGN	60491	3422	16W-19S	B3
14300	LKPT	60441	3421	18W-19S	B3
14600	HMGN	60491	3421	18W-19S	A3
14600	HmrT	60441	3421	18W-19S	A3
14600	LKPT	60491	3421	18W-19S	A3
14900	HmrT	60441	3420	19W-20S	E4
14900	HmrT	60491	3420	19W-19S	D3
14900	LKPT	60441	3420	19W-20S	E4
14900	LKPT	60491	3420	19W-19S	D3
16500	LktT	60441	3420	20W-19S	A4
E 168th Ct					
-	SHLD	60473	3428	0E-19S	E3
168th Pl					
3700	CCHL	60478	3426	4W-20S	D4
8100	TYPK	60477	3424	10W-20S	C3
8400	TYPK	60487	3424	10W-20S	B4
E 168th Pl					
600	SHLD	60473	3428	0E-19S	E3
700	SHLD	60473	3429	0E-19S	A3
W 168th Pl					
300	HRVY	60426	3428	1W-20S	B4
168th St					
1600	HLCT	60429	3427	2W-20S	D3
3700	CCHL	60429	3426	4W-20S	D3
3700	CCHL	60478	3426	4W-20S	D3
3700	HLCT	60429	3426	4W-20S	D3
6800	TYPK	60477	3425	8W-20S	A3
7100	TYPK	60477	3424	9W-20S	E3
8400	TYPK	60487	3424	10W-20S	B3
10900	ODPK	60467	3423	13W-20S	A4
E 168th St					
400	SHLD	60473	3428	0E-19S	E3
800	SHLD	60473	3429	1E-19S	A3
W 168th St					
10	SHLD	60473	3428	0W-19S	C3
800	HRVY	60426	3428	1W-20S	A3
8600	ODPK	60462	3424	10W-20S	B3
8600	TYPK	60462	3424	10W-20S	B3
8600	TYPK	60487	3424	10W-20S	B3
8700	ODHL	60487	3424	10W-20S	A3
8700	ODPK	60487	3424	10W-20S	A3
169th Ct					
3400	LNSG	60438	3430	4E-19S	B3
E 169th Ct					
900	SHLD	60473	3429	1E-19S	A3
169th Pl					
800	HMND	46324	3430		E3
8900	ODHL	60487	3424	11W-20S	A4
9200	ODHL	60487	3423	11W-20S	E4
9300	ODPK	60487	3423	11W-20S	E4
E 169th Pl					
200	SHLD	60473	3428	0E-19S	D3
800	SHLD	60473	3429	1E-19S	A3
169th St					
10	CTCY	60409	3430		C3
10	HMND	46324	3430	4E-20S	C4
1600	HLCT	60429	3427	2W-20S	D4
3700	CCHL	60478	3426	4W-20S	D4
5200	BmnT	60452	3425	6W-20S	E3
5200	BmnT	60477	3425	6W-20S	E3
5200	OKFT	60452	3425	6W-20S	E3
5200	OKFT	60477	3425	6W-20S	E3
6800	TYPK	60477	3425	8W-20S	A3
8000	TYPK	60477	3424	10W-20S	C4
8300	OrlT	60477	3424	10W-20S	B4
8300	OrlT	60487	3424	10W-20S	B4
8500	TYPK	60462	3424	10W-20S	B4
8500	TYPK	60487	3424	10W-20S	B4
8800	ODHL	60487	3424	11W-20S	A4
8800	ODPK	60462	3424	11W-20S	A4
8800	ODPK	60487	3424	11W-20S	A4
E 169th St					
600	SHLD	60473	3428	0E-19S	E3
800	SHLD	60473	3429	1E-19S	A3
W 169th St					
10	SHLD	60473	3428	0W-19S	B3
8600	ODPK	60462	3424	10W-20S	B4
8600	TYPK	60462	3424	10W-20S	B4
8600	TYPK	60487	3424	10W-20S	B4
8700	ODHL	60487	3424	10W-20S	A4
8700	ODPK	60487	3424	10W-20S	A4
170th Pl					
1000	HMND	46324	3430		E3
3400	LNSG	60438	3430	4E-20S	B3
5200	OKFT	60452	3425	6W-20S	E4
7200	TYPK	60477	3424	9W-20S	D4
8100	OrlT	60477	3424	10W-20S	C4
8400	TYPK	60487	3424	10W-20S	B4
8500	ODPK	60462	3424	10W-20S	B4
8500	TYPK	60462	3424	10W-20S	B4
9200	ODHL	60487	3423	11W-20S	E4
E 170th Pl					
200	SHLD	60473	3428	0E-20S	D3
1400	SHLD	60473	3429	1E-20S	B3
W 170th Pl					
-	HLCT	60429	3427	3W-20S	A4
8600	ODPK	60462	3424	10W-20S	B4
8600	TYPK	60462	3424	10W-20S	B4
8600	TYPK	60487	3424	10W-20S	B4
8700	ODHL	60487	3424	10W-20S	A4
8700	ODPK	60487	3424	10W-20S	A4
170th St					
800	HMND	46324	3430		E3
1700	HLCT	60429	3427	2W-20S	D4
5200	BmnT	60477	3425	6W-20S	E4
5200	OKFT	60452	3425	6W-20S	E4
5200	OKFT	60477	3425	6W-20S	E4
6800	TYPK	60477	3425	8W-20S	A4
7400	TYPK	60477	3424	9W-20S	E4
8300	OrlT	60477	3424	10W-20S	B4
8300	OrlT	60487	3424	10W-20S	B4
8500	TYPK	60462	3424	10W-20S	B4
8500	TYPK	60487	3424	10W-20S	B4
8800	ODPK	60462	3424	11W-20S	A4
8800	ODPK	60487	3424	11W-20S	A4
8900	ODHL	60487	3424	11W-20S	A4
9100	ODHL	60487	3423	11W-20S	E4
E 170th St					
200	SHLD	60473	3428	0E-20S	D3
700	SHLD	60473	3429	1E-20S	A3
1600	CTCY	60409	3429	2E-20S	E3
1600	CTCY	60438	3429	2E-20S	E3
1600	LNSG	60409	3429	2E-20S	D3
1600	LNSG	60438	3429	3E-20S	E3
2100	LNSG	60473	3429	2E-20S	D3
2100	SHLD	60409	3429	2E-20S	D3
2600	LNSG	60438	3430	3E-19S	A3
W 170th St					
8600	ODPK	60462	3424	10W-20S	B4
8600	TYPK	60462	3424	10W-20S	B4
8600	TYPK	60487	3424	10W-20S	B4
8700	ODHL	60487	3424	10W-20S	A4
8700	ODPK	60487	3424	10W-20S	A4
11400	ODPK	60467	3422	14W-20S	E4
E 171st Ct					
2000	SHLD	60473	3429	2E-20S	D3
171st Pl					
3700	CCHL	60478	3426	4W-20S	D4
5600	BmnT	60477	3425	7W-20S	D4
5600	OKFT	60452	3425	7W-20S	D4
5600	OKFT	60477	3425	7W-20S	D4
7700	TYPK	60477	3424	9W-20S	D4
8500	TYPK	60487	3424	10W-20S	B4
E 171st Pl					
200	SHLD	60473	3428	0E-20S	D4
1800	SHLD	60473	3429	2E-20S	D4
171st St					
-	CCHL	60478	3426	4W-20S	D5
-	HLCT	60429	3426	4W-20S	D5
-	HLCT	60478	3426	4W-20S	D5
-	OrlT	60487	3423	11W-20S	D4
-	TNTN	60476	3428	0E-20S	D4

STREET Block	City	ZIP	Map#	CGS	Grid
171st St					
500	HMND	46324	3430		D3
800	EHZC	60426	3428	1W-20S	A4
800	EHZC	60429	3428	1W-20S	A4
800	EHZC	60473	3428	1W-20S	B4
800	HRVY	60426	3428	1W-20S	A4
800	HRVY	60429	3428	1W-20S	A4
800	SHLD	60426	3428	1W-20S	B4
800	SHLD	60473	3428	1W-20S	B4
1300	EHZC	60429	3427	2W-20S	D4
1300	HRVY	60426	3427	1W-20S	E4
1300	HRVY	60429	3427	2W-20S	D4
2600	HLCT	60430	3427	3W-20S	B4
2900	LNSG	60438	3430	3E-20S	A3
3000	HLCT	60429	3427	3W-20S	A4
4800	BmnT	60478	3426	6W-20S	A4
4800	CCHL	60477	3426	6W-20S	A4
5000	BmnT	60452	3426	6W-20S	A4
5000	BmnT	60477	3426	6W-20S	A4
5000	OKFT	60452	3426	6W-20S	A4
5000	OKFT	60477	3426	6W-20S	A4
6500	TYPK	60477	3425	8W-20S	A4
7200	TYPK	60477	3424	10W-20S	C4
8100	OrlT	60477	3424	10W-20S	C4
8300	TYPK	60487	3424	10W-20S	B4
8500	ODPK	60462	3424	10W-20S	B4
8500	ODPK	60487	3424	10W-20S	B4
8700	ODHL	60487	3424	10W-20S	A4
9000	ODHL	60487	3423	11W-20S	E4
9000	TYPK	60487	3423	11W-20S	E4
9200	ODPK	60487	3423	11W-20S	E4
E 171st St					
300	SHLD	60473	3428	0E-20S	E3
1900	SHLD	60473	3429	2E-20S	D3
W 171st St					
11400	ODPK	60467	3422	14W-20S	E4
172nd Pl					
-	SHLD	60473	3429	2E-20S	C4
10	CTCY	60409	3430		C4
10	HMND	46324	3430		C4
1700	EHZC	60429	3427	2W-20S	D4
3400	LNSG	60438	3430	4E-20S	B4
4000	CCHL	60478	3426	5W-20S	C5
7900	TYPK	60477	3424	9W-20S	C4
172nd St					
-	TNTN	60476	3428	0E-20S	D4
10	CTCY	60409	3430		C4
10	HMND	46324	3430		C4
1000	EHZC	60429	3428	1W-20S	A4
1800	EHZC	60429	3427	2W-20S	D5
2200	LNSG	60438	3429	3E-20S	E4
2800	HLCT	60429	3427	3W-20S	A4
3600	LNSG	60438	3430	4E-20S	C4
3700	CCHL	60478	3426	4W-20S	D5
3700	HLCT	60429	3426	4W-20S	D5
3700	HLCT	60478	3426	4W-20S	D5
6800	TYPK	60477	3425	8W-20S	A4
7900	TYPK	60477	3424	9W-20S	C4
8800	TYPK	60487	3424	11W-20S	A4
10900	ODPK	60467	3423	13W-20S	A4
E 172nd St					
1100	SHLD	60473	3429	1E-20S	B4
W 172nd St					
-	EHZC	60426	3428	0W-20S	B4
-	HRVY	60426	3428	0W-20S	B4
-	SHLD	60426	3428	0W-20S	B4
400	TNTN	60476	3428	0W-20S	B4
500	SHLD	60473	3428	0W-20S	B4
500	SHLD	60476	3428	0W-20S	B4
500	TNTN	60473	3428	0W-20S	B4
700	EHZC	60429	3428	0W-20S	B4
700	EHZC	60473	3428	0W-20S	B4
700	SHLD	60429	3428	0W-20S	B4
173rd Ct					
3700	LNSG	60438	3430	4E-20S	C4
173rd Pl					
800	HMND	46324	3430		E4
3400	LNSG	60438	3430	4E-20S	B4
6500	TYPK	60477	3425	8W-20S	B5
7200	TYPK	60477	3424	9W-20S	E5
9200	TYPK	60487	3423	11W-20S	E5
E 173rd Pl					
200	SHLD	60473	3428	0E-20S	E4
1100	SHLD	60473	3429	1E-20S	B4
173rd St					
1000	EHZC	60429	3428	1W-20S	A5
1900	EHZC	60429	3427	2W-20S	D5
1900	HLCT	60430	3427	2W-20S	D5
2200	LNSG	60438	3429	2E-20S	E4
2800	HLCT	60429	3427	4W-20S	A5
3200	HLCT	60429	3426	4W-20S	E5
3400	LNSG	60438	3430	4E-20S	B4
4800	BmnT	60478	3426	6W-20S	A5
4800	CCHL	60478	3426	6W-20S	A5
5600	BmnT	60477	3425	7W-20S	D4
6600	TYPK	60477	3425	8W-20S	B4
7200	TYPK	60477	3424	9W-20S	D5
9400	TYPK	60487	3423	11W-20S	E5
E 173rd St					
10	HMND	46324	3430		D4
10	SHLD	60473	3428	0E-20S	D4
10	SHLD	60476	3428	0E-20S	D4
10	TNTN	60473	3428	0E-20S	D4
10	TNTN	60476	3428	0E-20S	D4
1300	SHLD	60473	3429	1E-20S	B4
174th Ct					
3600	LNSG	60438	3430	4E-20S	C4
174th Pl					
800	HMND	46324	3430		E4
6600	TYPK	60477	3425	8W-20S	B5
7200	TYPK	60477	3424	9W-20S	E5
174th St					
500	HMND	46324	3430		D4
800	EHZC	60429	3428	1W-20S	A5
800	HMWD	60429	3428	1W-20S	A5
800	HMWD	60430	3428	1W-20S	A5
1000	EHZC	60430	3428	1W-20S	A5
1900	EHZC	60429	3427	2W-20S	D5
1900	HLCT	60429	3427	2W-20S	D5
1900	HLCT	60430	3427	2W-20S	D5
5400	BmnT	60477	3425	6W-21S	E5
6400	TYPK	60477	3425	8W-20S	B5
7200	TYPK	60477	3424	9W-20S	D5
8800	TYPK	60487	3424	11W-20S	A5
9400	TYPK	60487	3423	11W-20S	E5
175th Pl					
800	HMND	46324	3430		E5
3600	CCHL	60478	3426	4W-21S	D5
3600	HLCT	60429	3426	4W-21S	D5
3600	HLCT	60478	3426	4W-21S	D5
6600	TYPK	60477	3425	8W-21S	B5
175th St					
-	HMWD	60476	3428	0W-20S	B5
-	TNTN	60476	3428	0W-20S	B5
500	HMND	46324	3430		D4
800	EHZC	60429	3428	1W-21S	A5
175th St					
800	EHZC	60430	3428	1W-21S	A5
800	HMWD	60429	3428	1W-21S	A5
800	HMWD	60430	3428	1W-21S	A5
1200	EHZC	60429	3427	1W-20S	E5
1200	HMWD	60429	3427	1W-20S	E5
1200	HMWD	60430	3427	1W-20S	E5
2000	EHZC	60430	3427	2W-20S	D5
2000	HLCT	60430	3427	2W-20S	C5
2500	HLCT	60429	3427	4W-20S	A5
2500	LNSG	60438	3429	3E-20S	E5
2500	LNSG	60438	3430	3E-20S	A4
3200	CCHL	60478	3426	6W-20S	A5
3200	HLCT	60429	3426	4W-20S	E5
3200	HLCT	60478	3426	4W-20S	E5
3600	MNSR	46321	3430	4E-20S	C5
4800	BmnT	60478	3426	6W-20S	A5
5300	BmnT	60477	3425	7W-20S	C5
5300	LNSG	60478	3426	6W-20S	A5
6800	TYPK	60477	3425	8W-21S	A5
7200	TYPK	60477	3424	11W-20S	A5
8300	TYPK	60487	3424	11W-20S	A5
9100	TYPK	60487	3423	11W-20S	D5
9400	OrlT	60487	3423	11W-20S	D5
11100	ODPK	60467	3422	13W-20S	E5
11100	ODPK	60467	3423	13W-20S	A5
11100	OrlT	60467	3422	13W-20S	E5
11100	OrlT	60467	3423	13W-20S	A5
14400	HMGN	60491	3421	18W-20S	B5
14400	HmrT	60491	3421	18W-20S	B5
176th Ct					
400	HMND	46324	3430		D5
176th Pl					
800	HMND	46324	3430		E5
2100	ThtT	60438	3429	2E-20S	D5
2400	LNSG	60438	3429	3E-20S	E5
3600	HLCT	60429	3426	4W-21S	E6
3600	HLCT	60478	3426	4W-21S	E6
3600	LNSG	60438	3430	4E-20S	C5
3700	CCHL	60478	3426	4W-21S	D6
3700	MNSR	46321	3430	4E-20S	C5
6800	TYPK	60477	3425	8W-21S	A5
176th St					
-	HLCT	60429	3426	4W-21S	E5
-	HLCT	60429	3427	4W-21S	A5
-	HLCT	60478	3426	4W-21S	E5
-	TYPK	60487	3423	11W-21S	E5
800	HMND	46324	3430		E5
3100	LNSG	60438	3430	3E-20S	B5
3600	CCHL	60478	3426	4W-21S	D5
6600	TYPK	60477	3425	8W-21S	A5
8700	TYPK	60487	3424	11W-21S	A5
177th Pl					
-	TYPK	60477	3424	9W-21S	E6
800	HMND	46324	3430		E5
2200	LNSG	60438	3429	2E-20S	D5
2200	ThtT	60438	3429	2E-20S	D5
3600	LNSG	60438	3430	4E-20S	C5
4300	CCHL	60478	3426	5W-21S	B6
7000	TYPK	60477	3425	8W-21S	A6
177th St					
-	LNSG	60438	3429	2E-20S	D5
800	HMND	46324	3430		E5
1900	ThtT	60438	3429	2E-20S	D5
2700	LNSG	60438	3430	3E-20S	A5
3200	HLCT	60429	3426	4W-21S	E6
3200	HLCT	60429	3427	4W-21S	A6
3300	HLCT	60478	3426	4W-21S	E6
3700	MNSR	46321	3430	4E-20S	C5
4000	CCHL	60478	3426	5W-21S	B6
5400	BmnT	60477	3425	6W-21S	E5
6200	TYPK	60477	3425	8W-21S	B5
178th Pl					
3100	LNSG	60438	3430	3E-21S	B5
3700	CCHL	60478	3426	4W-21S	D6
178th St					
2200	LNSG	60438	3429	2E-21S	E5
3100	LNSG	60438	3430	3E-20S	B5
4500	CCHL	60478	3426	5W-21S	B6
6600	TYPK	60477	3425	8W-21S	A6
8800	TYPK	60487	3424	11W-21S	A6
9100	TYPK	60487	3423	11W-21S	E6
179th Pl					
4600	CCHL	60478	3426	5W-21S	B6
6800	TYPK	60477	3425	8W-21S	A6
179th St					
-	TYPK	60477	3424	10W-21S	C6
-	TYPK	60487	3423	13W-21S	A6
-	TYPK	60487	3424	10W-21S	B6
2600	LNSG	60438	3429	3E-21S	E5
2700	LNSG	60438	3430	3E-21S	A5
3500	BmnT	60430	3426	4W-21S	D6
3500	CCHL	60430	3426	4W-21S	D6
4200	CCHL	60478	3426	5W-21S	B6
6200	BmnT	60477	3425	8W-21S	A6
6200	TYPK	60477	3425	8W-21S	A6
9900	ODPK	60467	3423	12W-21S	B6
9900	ODPK	60467	3423	12W-21S	B6
9900	OrlT	60467	3423	12W-21S	B6
9900	OrlT	60487	3423	13W-21S	A6
11100	ODPK	60467	3422	14W-21S	D6
11100	OrlT	60467	3422	13W-21S	E6
W 179th St					
12000	HMGN	60491	3422	15W-21S	C6
12000	ODPK	60467	3422	15W-21S	C6
13500	HMGN	60448	3421	17W-21S	D6
13500	HMGN	60491	3421	17W-21S	D6
13500	HmrT	60448	3421	17W-21S	D6
180th Ct					
6800	TYPK	60477	3425	8W-21S	A6
180th Pl					
1800	LNSG	60438	3429	2E-21S	C6
1800	ThtT	60438	3429	2E-21S	C6
6400	BmnT	60477	3425	8W-21S	B6
6400	TYPK	60477	3425	8W-21S	B6
180th St					
-	TYPK	60487	3424	11W-21S	A6
1600	ThtT	60438	3429	2E-21S	C6
2500	LNSG	60438	3429	3E-21S	E6
2700	LNSG	60438	3430	3E-21S	A6
4300	CCHL	60478	3426	5W-21S	C6
6500	TYPK	60477	3425	8W-21S	A6
181st Pl					
1500	LNSG	60438	3429	1E-21S	C6
3300	LNSG	60438	3430	4E-21S	B6
4500	CCHL	60478	3426	5W-21S	B7
6400	TYPK	60477	3425	8W-21S	B7
181st St					
-	LNSG	60438	3429	1E-21S	B6
-	ThtT	60438	3429	1E-21S	B6
2700	LNSG	60438	3430	3E-21S	A6
4700	BmnT	60478	3426	5W-21S	B7
4800	CCHL	60478	3426	6W-21S	A7
6200	TYPK	60477	3425	8W-21S	B6
182nd Av					
11800	BtlT	53104	2359		B2
182nd Pl					
1800	HMWD	60430	3427	2W-21S	D7
1900	LNSG	60438	3429	2E-21S	C6
3000	LNSG	60438	3430	3E-21S	A6
4500	CCHL	60478	3426	5W-21S	B7
4700	BmnT	60478	3426	5W-21S	B7
6400	TYPK	60477	3425	8W-21S	B7
182nd St					
1400	ThtT	60438	3429	2E-21S	C6
1500	LNSG	60438	3429	1E-21S	B6
4400	CCHL	60478	3426	5W-21S	B7
6400	TYPK	60477	3425	8W-21S	B7
183rd Av					
11900	BtlT	53104	2359		A2
183rd Pl					
2600	LNSG	60438	3429	3E-21S	E7
8200	TYPK	60487	3424	10W-22S	C7
8200	TYPK	60487	3504	10W-22S	B1
11200	FftT	60448	3422	14W-22S	D7
11200	FftT	60467	3422	14W-22S	D7
11200	MKNA	60467	3422	14W-22S	D7
11300	ODPK	60448	3422	14W-22S	E7
11300	ODPK	60467	3422	14W-22S	E7
W 183rd Pl					
1900	LNSG	60438	3429	2E-21S	D7
183rd St					
-	BlmT	60425	3428	0W-21S	C7
-	BlmT	60425	3429	1E-21S	A7
-	BlmT	60438	3429	1E-21S	A7
-	BlmT	60476	3428	0W-21S	C7
-	BlmT	60476	3429	1E-21S	A7
-	ThtT	60476	3429	1E-21S	A7
-	TNTN	60425	3428	0W-21S	C7
-	TNTN	60476	3428	0W-21S	C7
800	GNWD	60425	3428	1W-21S	B7
800	HMWD	60425	3428	1W-21S	A7
800	HMWD	60430	3428	1W-21S	A7
1200	HMWD	60430	3427	2W-21S	C7
1800	ThtT	60438	3429	2E-21S	C6
2400	LNSG	60438	3429	3E-21S	E6
2800	LNSG	60438	3430	3E-21S	A6
3000	HLCT	60429	3427	3W-21S	A7
3000	HLCT	60430	3427	3W-21S	A7
3200	HLCT	60429	3426	4W-21S	D7
3200	HLCT	60430	3426	4W-21S	D7
3200	HMWD	60430	3426	4W-21S	D7
3500	BmnT	60429	3426	4W-21S	E7
3500	BmnT	60430	3426	4W-21S	E7
3900	CCHL	60430	3426	4W-21S	D7
3900	CCHL	60478	3426	6W-21S	A7
4800	BmnT	60478	3426	6W-21S	A7
4900	RchT	60478	3426	6W-21S	A7
5100	BmnT	60477	3426	6W-21S	A7
5100	RchT	60477	3426	6W-21S	A7
5200	BmnT	60477	3425	6W-21S	E7
5200	RchT	60477	3425	8W-21S	A7
5900	TYPK	60477	3425	8W-21S	A7
7200	TYPK	60477	3424	9W-21S	D7
7600	FftT	60487	3424	9W-21S	C7
8000	TYPK	60487	3424	10W-22S	B7
9200	TYPK	60487	3423	11W-22S	E7
9300	FftT	60448	3423	11W-21S	E7
9300	FftT	60487	3423	11W-21S	E7
9500	TYPK	60448	3423	11W-21S	D7
10700	FftT	60467	3423	13W-22S	B7
10700	ODPK	60467	3423	13W-21S	A7
11100	FftT	60448	3422	14W-21S	D7
11100	FftT	60467	3422	14W-21S	E7
11100	ODPK	60467	3422	14W-21S	D7
11300	ODPK	60448	3422	14W-21S	E7
15500	OrlT	60467	3423	13W-21S	A7
184th Av					
11500	ODPK	60467	3502	14W-22S	D1
184th Ct					
4900	CCHL	60478	3506	6W-22S	A1
184th Pl					
1600	HMWD	60430	3507	2W-22S	D1
2200	LNSG	60438	3429	2E-21S	D7
4700	CCHL	60478	3426	5W-22S	B7
4700	CCHL	60478	3506	5W-22S	B1
13000	NlxT	60448	3422	16W-22S	A7
13100	NlxT	60448	3421	16W-22S	E7
13100	NlxT	60448	3501	16W-22S	E1
184th St					
2400	LNSG	60438	3429	3E-21S	E7
2800	LNSG	60438	3430	3E-21S	A7
3200	HMWD	60430	3426	4W-22S	E7
3200	HMWD	60430	3427	4W-22S	A7
3200	HMWD	60430	3506	4W-22S	E2
4700	CCHL	60478	3426	5W-22S	B7
185th Av					
12000	BtlT	53104	2359		A3
185th Ct					
2300	LNSG	60438	3429	2E-21S	E7
4900	CCHL	60478	3506	6W-22S	A1
185th Pl					
1000	HMWD	60430	3508	1W-22S	A1
2200	LNSG	60438	3429	2E-21S	D7
3200	HMWD	60430	3506	4W-22S	E1
3200	HMWD	60430	3507	4W-22S	A1
4200	CCHL	60478	3506	5W-22S	C1
185th St					
1000	HMWD	60430	3508	1W-22S	A1
1600	LNSG	60438	3429	2E-21S	C7
2800	LNSG	60438	3430	3E-21S	A7
4400	CCHL	60478	3506	5W-22S	B1
7600	TYPK	60477	3504	10W-22S	B1
7700	FftT	60477	3504	10W-22S	C1
7700	FftT	60487	3504	10W-22S	B1
8000	TYPK	60487	3504	10W-22S	B1
13000	NlxT	60448	3502	16W-22S	A1
13400	NlxT	60448	3501	16W-22S	D1
186th Pl					
1000	HMWD	60430	3508	1W-22S	A1
1500	HMWD	60430	3507	2W-22S	D1
2400	BlmT	60411	3429	3E-22S	E7
2400	LNSG	60411	3429	3E-22S	E7
2400	LNSG	60438	3429	3E-22S	E7
4100	CCHL	60478	3506	5W-22S	C1
186th St					
1000	HMWD	60430	3508	1W-22S	A1
1400	BlmT	60438	3429	2E-21S	D7
1400	LNSG	60438	3429	3E-21S	E7
1400	ThtT	60438	3429	2E-21S	D7
1600	BlmT	60411	3429	3E-21S	E7
2100	LNSG	60411	3429	2E-21S	E7
2700	BlmT	60411	3430	3E-21S	A7
2700	LNSG	60438	3430	3E-21S	A7
3200	FSMR	60422	3507	4W-22S	A1
3200	HMWD	60422	3507	4W-22S	A1
3200	HMWD	60430	3506	4W-22S	E1
3200	HMWD	60430	3507	4W-22S	A1
4300	CCHL	60478	3506	5W-22S	C1
8000	FftT	60477	3504	10W-22S	C1
8000	FftT	60487	3504	10W-22S	C1
8000	TYPK	60487	3504	10W-22S	C1
187th Av					
11600	BtlT	53104	2359		A2
187th Ct					
3200	LNSG	60438	3510	4E-22S	B1
187th Pl					
2400	LNSG	60411	3509	3E-22S	E1
2400	LNSG	60438	3509	3E-22S	E1
4000	CCHL	60478	3506	5W-22S	C1
187th St					
-	FftT	60448	3504	11W-22S	A1
-	GNWD	60430	3508	1W-22S	A1
-	HMWD	60425	3508	1W-22S	B1
300	MKNA	60448	3504	10W-22S	B1
800	GNWD	60425	3508	1W-22S	A1
800	HMWD	60430	3508	1W-22S	A1
1200	HMWD	60430	3507	2W-22S	D1
1900	FSMR	60422	3507	2W-22S	D1
1900	HMWD	60422	3507	2W-22S	D1
2400	BlmT	60411	3429	3E-22S	E7
2400	LNSG	60411	3429	3E-22S	E7
2400	LNSG	60438	3429	3E-22S	E7
3400	LNSG	60438	3430	4E-22S	B7
3900	CCHL	60422	3506	5W-22S	D1
3900	CCHL	60429	3506	5W-22S	D1
3900	FSMR	60422	3506	5W-22S	D1
3900	FSMR	60429	3506	5W-22S	D1
3900	HLCT	60422	3506	4W-22S	D1
3900	HLCT	60429	3506	5W-22S	D1
4300	CCHL	60478	3506	6W-22S	A1
9200	FftT	60448	3503	11W-22S	E1
10300	MKNA	60448	3503	13W-22S	A1
11100	FftT	60448	3502	14W-22S	E1
11100	MKNA	60448	3502	14W-22S	E1
W 187th St					
500	GNWD	60425	3508	0W-22S	B1
900	HMWD	60425	3508	0W-22S	B1
900	HMWD	60430	3508	0W-22S	B1
188th Pl					
-	FftT	60448	3503	13W-22S	A1
2900	LNSG	60438	3510	3E-22S	A1
4200	CCHL	60478	3506	5W-22S	C2
188th St					
2400	BlmT	60411	3509	3E-22S	E1
2400	LNSG	60411	3509	3E-22S	E1
2400	LNSG	60438	3509	3E-22S	E1
2800	LNSG	60438	3510	3E-22S	A1
3800	FSMR	60422	3506	4W-22S	D2
3900	CCHL	60422	3506	4W-22S	D2
3900	CCHL	60478	3506	5W-22S	C1
8100	MKNA	60448	3504	10W-22S	C1
189th Pl					
2800	LNSG	60438	3510	3E-22S	A1
4100	CCHL	60478	3506	5W-22S	C2
W 189th Pl					
11100	FftT	60448	3502	14W-22S	E2
11100	MKNA	60448	3502	14W-22S	E2
11100	MKNA	60448	3503	13W-22S	A2
189th St					
-	FftT	60448	3503	12W-22S	D2
2800	LNSG	60438	3510	3E-22S	A1
3800	FSMR	60422	3506	4W-22S	D2
4000	CCHL	60478	3506	5W-22S	C2
8000	MKNA	60448	3503	11W-22S	E2
8000	MKNA	60448	3504	10W-22S	C2
8000	TYPK	60477	3504	10W-22S	C2
11200	FftT	60448	3502	14W-22S	E2
11200	MKNA	60448	3502	14W-22S	E2
190th Pl					
-	FftT	60448	3503	12W-22S	C2
3400	LNSG	60438	3510	4E-22S	B1
4900	CCHL	60478	3506	6W-22S	A2
190th St					
-	MKNA	60448	3504	10W-22S	B2
1200	HMWD	60430	3508	1W-22S	A2
1400	BlmT	60430	3507	1W-22S	E2
1400	HMWD	60430	3507	1W-22S	E2
2800	LNSG	60438	3510	3E-22S	A1
3900	FSMR	60422	3506	5W-22S	D2
4900	CCHL	60478	3506	6W-22S	A2
9900	FftT	60448	3503	12W-22S	C2
9900	MKNA	60448	3503	12W-22S	C2
191st Ct					
4100	CCHL	60478	3506	5W-23S	C2
191st Pl					
3400	LNSG	60438	3510	4E-22S	B1
3600	BlmT	60438	3510	4E-22S	C2
4000	CCHL	60478	3506	5W-23S	C2
8400	MKNA	60448	3504	10W-23S	B2
E 191st Pl					
400	BlmT	60425	3508	0E-23S	E2
400	GNWD	60425	3508	0E-22S	E1
1000	GNWD	60425	3509	1E-23S	B2
191st St					
1100	HMWD	60430	3508	1W-22S	A2
1200	HMWD	60430	3507	1W-22S	E2
1300	BlmT	60430	3507	1W-22S	E2
3400	LNSG	60438	3510	4E-22S	B1
9600	FftT	60448	3503	12W-22S	C2
9600	MKNA	60448	3503	13W-22S	B2
11200	FftT	60448	3502	14W-23S	E2
11200	MKNA	60448	3502	14W-23S	E2
W 191st St					
-	FftT	60477	3505	8W-23S	A2
-	TYPK	60477	3505	8W-23S	A2
7500	FftT	60477	3504	9W-22S	E2
7500	TYPK	60477	3504	9W-22S	E2
7800	FftT	60448	3504	9W-23S	D2
7800	TYPK	60448	3504	9W-23S	D2
8000	MKNA	60448	3504	9W-22S	E2
9200	MKNA	60448	3503	11W-22S	E2
9300	FftT	60448	3503	11W-22S	E2
192nd Ct					
-	CCHL	60478	3506	5W-23S	C3
192nd Pl					
-	CCHL	60478	3506	5W-23S	C3
3500	LNSG	60438	3510	4E-22S	C2
4000	RchT	60430	3506	5W-23S	D3
4000	RchT	60478	3506	5W-23S	D3
8500	MKNA	60448	3504	10W-23S	B2
E 192nd Pl					
900	GNWD	60425	3509	1E-23S	B3
192nd St					
3200	FSMR	60422	3507	4W-23S	A2
3200	FSMR	60430	3507	4W-23S	A2
3200	RchT	60430	3507	4W-23S	A3
3300	RchT	60430	3506	4W-23S	E3
3400	LNSG	60438	3510	4E-22S	B2
3800	RchT	60478	3506	4W-23S	D3
4100	CCHL	60478	3506	5W-23S	C3
8400	MKNA	60448	3504	10W-23S	B2
11200	FftT	60448	3502	14W-23S	E2
11200	MKNA	60448	3502	14W-23S	E2
E 192nd St					
400	BlmT	60425	3508	0E-23S	E3
400	GNWD	60425	3508	0E-23S	E3
500	GNWD	60425	3509	1E-23S	A3
W 192nd St					
8400	MKNA	60448	3504	11W-23S	A2
193rd Ct					
3600	LNSG	60438	3510	4E-22S	C2
4100	CCHL	60478	3506	5W-23S	C3
193rd Pl					
800	BlmT	60411	3508	1W-23S	A3
900	CHHT	60411	3508	1W-23S	A3
3600	LNSG	60438	3510	4E-22S	C2
4100	CCHL	60478	3506	5W-23S	C3
E 193rd Pl					
600	GNWD	60425	3509	1E-23S	B3
193rd St					
-	CCHL	60478	3506	5W-23S	C3
3600	LNSG	60438	3510	4E-22S	C2
4000	FSMR	60422	3506	5W-23S	D3
8500	MKNA	60448	3504	10W-23S	B2
11200	FftT	60448	3502	14W-23S	E3
11600	MKNA	60448	3502	14W-23S	D3
E 193rd St					
700	GNWD	60425	3509	1E-23S	B3
194th Ct					
4100	CCHL	60478	3506	5W-23S	C3
194th Pl					
800	BlmT	60411	3508	1W-23S	A3
900	CHHT	60411	3508	1W-23S	A3
3000	LNSG	60411	3510	3E-23S	A2
4100	CCHL	60478	3506	5W-23S	C3
E 194th Pl					
1000	GNWD	60425	3509	1E-23S	B3
194th St					
800	BlmT	60411	3508	1W-23S	A3
900	CHHT	60411	3508	1W-23S	A3
2800	LNSG	60438	3510	3E-22S	A2
3200	FSMR	60422	3506	4W-23S	E3
3200	FSMR	60422	3507	4W-23S	A3
3200	RchT	60422	3507	4W-23S	A3
3200	RchT	60430	3506	4W-23S	E3
3200	RchT	60430	3507	4W-23S	A3
3300	RchT	60422	3506	4W-23S	E3
4100	CCHL	60478	3506	5W-23S	C3
7200	FftT	60477	3505	9W-23S	A3
7200	RchT	60423	3505	9W-23S	A3
7200	TYPK	60477	3505	9W-23S	A3
7300	TYPK	60477	3504	9W-23S	E3
9600	FftT	60448	3503	12W-23S	D3
9600	MKNA	60448	3503	12W-23S	D3
11200	FftT	60448	3502	14W-23S	D3
11200	MKNA	60448	3502	14W-23S	D3
E 194th St					
600	GNWD	60425	3509	1E-23S	A3
W 194th St					
300	CHHT	60411	3508	0W-23S	C3
300	GNWD	60411	3508	0W-23S	C3
300	GNWD	60425	3508	0W-23S	C3
195th Ct					
3000	LNSG	60411	3510	3E-23S	A2
195th Pl					
-	LYWD	60411	3510	3E-23S	A3
195th St					
700	BlmT	60411	3508	0W-23S	B3
700	BlmT	60425	3508	0W-23S	B3
700	CHHT	60411	3508	0W-23S	B3
700	CHHT	60425	3508	0W-23S	B3
700	GNWD	60425	3508	0W-23S	B3
2900	LYWD	60411	3510	3E-23S	A2
3200	FSMR	60422	3506	4W-23S	E3
3200	FSMR	60422	3507	4W-23S	A3
3200	RchT	60422	3506	4W-23S	E3
3200	RchT	60422	3507	4W-23S	A3
4100	CCHL	60478	3506	5W-23S	C3
7200	FftT	60423	3505	9W-23S	A3
7200	RchT	60423	3505	9W-23S	A3
9800	MKNA	60448	3503	12W-23S	C3
11200	FftT	60448	3502	14W-23S	E3
11200	MKNA	60448	3502	14W-23S	D3
W 195th St					
300	BlmT	60411	3508	0W-23S	C3
300	BlmT	60425	3508	0W-23S	C3
300	CHHT	60411	3508	0W-23S	C3
300	CHHT	60425	3508	0W-23S	C3
300	GNWD	60411	3508	0W-23S	C3
300	GNWD	60425	3508	0W-23S	C3
196th St					
700	BlmT	60411	3508	0W-23S	B4
700	CHHT	60411	3508	0W-23S	B4
3000	LNSG	60411	3510	3E-23S	A3
3000	LYWD	60411	3510	3E-23S	A3
3300	FSMR	60422	3506	4W-23S	E3
3300	FSMR	60422	3507	3W-22S	A2
3300	RchT	60422	3506	4W-23S	E3
3300	RchT	60422	3507	3W-22S	A2
3400	RchT	60430	3506	4W-23S	E4
9600	FftT	60448	3503	12W-23S	D3
9600	MKNA	60448	3503	12W-23S	D3
197th Pl					
-	LYWD	60411	3510	3E-23S	A3
100	CHHT	60411	3508	1W-23S	B4
197th St					
700	CHHT	60411	3508	0W-23S	B4
3000	LYWD	60411	3510	3E-23S	A3
9600	FftT	60448	3503	12W-23S	D4
9600	MKNA	60448	3503	12W-23S	D4
11400	FftT	60448	3502	14W-23S	E4
11400	MKNA	60448	3502	14W-23S	D4
198th Pl					
-	LYWD	60411	3510	3E-23S	A3
2000	LYWD	60411	3509	2E-23S	D3
198th St					
2400	BlmT	60411	3509	3E-23S	E3
2400	LYWD	60411	3509	3E-23S	E3
2700	LYWD	60411	3510	3E-23S	A3
3300	FSMR	60422	3506	4W-23S	E4
3600	RchT	60422	3506	4W-23S	D4
3600	RchT	60443	3506	4W-23S	D4
199th St					
2200	LYWD	60411	3509	2E-23S	D4
200th Pl					
2900	LYWD	60411	3510	3E-23S	A4
200th St					
2400	LYWD	60411	3509	3E-23S	E4
2600	LYWD	60411	3510	3E-23S	A4
201st Pl					
2600	LYWD	60411	3509	3E-23S	E4
2600	LYWD	60411	3510	3E-23S	A4
201st St					
2400	LYWD	60411	3509	3E-23S	E4
2700	LYWD	60411	3510	3E-23S	A4
202nd St					
200	CHHT	60411	3507	2W-24S	E5
2900	LYWD	60411	3510	3E-24S	A4
203rd St					
3200	LYWD	60411	3510	4E-24S	B4
3600	OMFD	60461	3506	4W-24S	D5
4600	MTSN	60443	3506	5W-24S	B5
10900	FftT	60448	3503	13W-24S	A5

STREET Block	City	ZIP	Map#	CGS	Grid
203rd St					
10900	MKNA	60448	3503	13W-24S	A5
204th St					
3100	OMFD	60461	3507	4W-24S	A6
3200	BlmT	60411	3510	4E-24S	B5
3200	LYWD	60411	3510	4E-24S	B5
4000	MTSN	60443	3506	5W-24S	C6
4000	OMFD	60461	3506	5W-24S	C6
10900	FftT	60448	3503	13W-24S	A5
10900	MKNA	60448	3503	13W-24S	A5
205th Pl					
500	DYR	46311	3510		D5
205th St					
2200	LYWD	60411	3509	2E-24S	E5
3200	OMFD	60461	3506	4W-24S	E6
3200	OMFD	60461	3507	4W-24S	A6
4000	MTSN	60443	3506	5W-24S	C6
206th Pl					
500	DYR	46311	3510		D5
4200	MTSN	60443	3506	5W-24S	C6
206th St					
600	DYR	46311	3510		E5
4000	MTSN	60443	3506	5W-24S	C6
4000	OMFD	60461	3506	5W-24S	C6
207th Pl					
2200	LYWD	60411	3509	2E-24S	D6
207th St					
2400	BlmT	60411	3507	3W-24S	B6
2400	OMFD	60461	3507	3W-24S	B6
4000	MTSN	60443	3506	6W-24S	A6
4000	OMFD	60461	3506	5W-24S	D6
4400	RchT	60443	3506	6W-24S	A6
E 207th St					
2300	LYWD	60411	3509	2E-24S	E5
W 207th St					
2200	BlmT	60411	3507	2W-25S	C6
2200	CHHT	60411	3507	2W-24S	D6
2300	OMFD	60461	3507	2W-24S	C6
208th Av					
11600	BtlT	53104	2358		C3
209th Ct					
700	DYR	46311	3510		E6
209th St					
500	CHHT	60411	3507	2W-25S	C7
600	DYR	46311	3510		E6
2200	BlmT	60411	3507	2W-25S	C7
2300	OMFD	60461	3507	2W-25S	C7
210th Av					
12600	AntT	60002	2358		C4
12600	BtlT	53104	2358		C4
12600	BtlT	60002	2358		C4
210th Pl					
600	DYR	46311	3510		D6
210th St					
700	DYR	46311	3510		E6
211th Pkwy					
5600	MTSN	60443	3505	7W-25S	D7
211th Pl					
600	DYR	46311	3510		E7
3600	MTSN	60443	3506	4W-25S	D7
211th St					
600	DYR	46311	3510		E6
3200	LYWD	60411	3510	4E-25S	B7
212th Av					
11700	BtlT	53104	2358		C2
212th Pl					
500	DYR	46311	3510		D7
3800	MTSN	60443	3594	4W-25S	D1
212th St					
600	DYR	46311	3510		E7
213th Av					
11600	BtlT	53104	2358		C2
213th Pl					
500	DYR	46311	3510		D7
3500	MTSN	60443	3594	4W-25S	D1
213th St					
400	DYR	46311	3510		E7
3900	MTSN	60443	3594	4W-25S	D1
214th Av					
11600	BtlT	53104	2358		C2
214th Pl					
3600	MTSN	60443	3594	4W-25S	D1
214th St					
500	DYR	46311	3510		D7
3900	MTSN	60443	3594	4W-25S	D1
215th Pl					
1600	SLVL	60411	3597	2E-26S	C2
2200	BlmT	60411	3597	2E-26S	D2
215th St					
400	DYR	46311	3510		C7
3600	MTSN	60443	3594	4W-26S	D1
216th Av					
11600	BtlT	53104	2358		C2
S 216th Av					
31600	WMTN	60481	3853	27W-38S	E6
216th Ct					
2000	SLVL	60411	3597	2E-26S	D2
216th Pl					
1600	SLVL	60411	3597	2E-26S	C2
3600	MTSN	60443	3594	4W-26S	D2
216th St					
1600	SLVL	60411	3597	2E-26S	C2
3600	MTSN	60443	3594	5W-26S	C1
217th Av					
12000	SlmT	53104	2358		B2
217th Ct					
11700	BtlT	53104	2358		B2
11700	SlmT	53104	2358		B2
217th Pl					
1600	SLVL	60411	3597	2E-26S	C2
217th St					
500	BlmT	60411	3596	0E-26S	E2
500	BlmT	60411	3597	0E-26S	A2
500	SLVL	60411	3597	0E-26S	A2
3600	MTSN	60443	3594	4W-26S	D2
218th Av					
11800	SlmT	53104	2358		B2
218th Pl					
2000	SLVL	60411	3597	2E-26S	D2
3400	MTSN	60443	3594	4W-26S	E2
218th St					
1700	SLVL	60411	3597	2E-26S	C2
3400	MTSN	60443	3594	4W-26S	E2
3400	PKFT	60466	3594	4W-26S	E2
219th Av					
12100	SlmT	53104	2358		B3
219th Pl					
1800	SLVL	60411	3597	2E-26S	D3
219th St					
500	BlmT	60411	3596	0E-26S	E2
500	BlmT	60411	3597	0E-26S	A2
500	SLVL	60411	3596	0E-26S	E2
500	SLVL	60411	3597	0E-26S	A2
3900	MTSN	60443	3594	4W-26S	D2
3900	RNPK	60443	3594	4W-26S	D2
3900	RNPK	60471	3594	4W-26S	D2
220th Av					
12100	SlmT	53104	2358		B3
220th Ct					
12000	SlmT	53104	2358		B2
220th St					
2200	SLVL	60411	3597	2E-26S	D3
221st Av					
11600	SlmT	53104	2358		B2
221st St					
1800	SLVL	60411	3597	2E-26S	D3
222nd Av					
12100	SlmT	53104	2358		B3
222nd Pl					
1600	SLVL	60411	3597	2E-26S	C3
222nd St					
2400	SLVL	60411	3597	2E-26S	D3
223rd Av					
11600	SlmT	53104	2358		B2
223rd Pl					
2200	BlmT	60411	3597	2E-27S	D3
2800	SLVL	60411	3597	3E-27S	E3
2800	SLVL	60411	3598	3E-27S	A3
E 223rd St					
1900	SLVL	60411	3597	2E-27S	D3
2400	BlmT	60411	3597	2E-27S	D3
2800	BlmT	60411	3598	3E-26S	B3
2800	SLVL	60411	3598	3E-26S	A3
224th Av					
11000	SlmT	53104	2358		A3
12100	SlmT	53179	2358		B3
12800	ANTH	60002	2358		B4
12800	AntT	60002	2358		B4
12800	SlmT	60002	2358		B4
224th Av CO-V					
11000	SlmT	53104	2358		B1
224th Ct					
1600	SLVL	60411	3597	2E-27S	C3
224th Pl					
2800	SLVL	60411	3597	3E-27S	E4
2800	SLVL	60411	3598	3E-27S	A4
224th St					
2800	SLVL	60411	3597	3E-27S	E4
2800	SLVL	60411	3598	3E-27S	A3
225th Pl					
2800	SLVL	60411	3597	3E-27S	E4
2900	SLVL	60411	3598	3E-27S	A4
225th St					
2800	SLVL	60411	3597	3E-27S	E4
2800	SLVL	60411	3598	3E-27S	A4
226th Pl					
2800	SLVL	60411	3597	3E-27S	E4
2800	SLVL	60411	3598	3E-27S	A4
228th Av					
-	ANTH	60002	2358		A4
12600	SlmT	53104	2358		A3
229th Av					
12700	SlmT	53104	2358		A3
231st Av					
12000	SlmT	53179	2358		A3
231st Ct					
11700	SlmT	53179	2358		A2
232nd Av					
11900	SlmT	53179	2358		A3
233rd Av					
11100	SlmT	53179	2357		E1
234th Av					
12400	SlmT	53179	2357		E3
12800	ANTH	53179	2357		E4
12800	ANTH	60002	2357		E4
235th Av					
11100	SlmT	53179	2357		E1
237th Pl					
11100	SlmT	53179	2357		E1
240th Av					
12500	SlmT	53179	2357		D3
241st Av					
11600	SlmT	53179	2357		D2
242nd Av					
11600	SlmT	53179	2357		D2
242nd Ct					
11600	SlmT	53179	2357		D2
243rd Av					
11800	SlmT	53179	2357		D2
246th Ct					
11600	SlmT	53179	2357		D2
247th Av					
11900	SlmT	53179	2357		D2
248th Av					
-	NPVL	60564	3202	31W-11S	A7
-	WldT	60564	3201	31W-11S	E7
-	WldT	60564	3202	31W-11S	A7
S 248th Av					
9100	WldT	60564	3202	31W-10S	A7
9600	NPVL	60564	3202	31W-10S	A7
9600	NPVL	60564	3266	30W-11S	A1
9600	WldT	60564	3266	31W-11S	A1
11100	PNFD	60564	3266	30W-13S	A5
11100	PNFD	60585	3266	30W-13S	A5
11300	WldT	60585	3266	30W-13S	A6
12200	PNFD	60585	3338	30W-14S	A1
12200	WldT	60585	3338	30W-14S	A1
249th Av					
12600	SlmT	53179	2357		C3
249th Cir					
12500	SlmT	53179	2357		C3
250th Av					
11500	SlmT	53179	2357		C2
251st Av					
11200	SlmT	53179	2357		C1
252nd Av					
11900	SlmT	53179	2357		C2
253rd Av					
11900	SlmT	53179	2357		C2
253rd Ct					
10900	SlmT	53179	2357		C1
254th Av					
10900	SlmT	53179	2357		C1
254th Ct					
12600	SlmT	53179	2357		C3
255th Av					
10900	SlmT	53179	2357		C1
255th Ct					
12500	SlmT	53179	2357		C3
256th Av					
10900	SlmT	53179	2357		B1
S 256th Av					
11900	WldT	60585	3265	31W-14S	D6
257th Av					
11900	SlmT	53179	2357		B2
258th Av					
11000	SlmT	53179	2357		B1
258th Ct					
11000	SlmT	53179	2357		B1
259th Av					
11400	SlmT	53179	2357		B1
260th Av					
11900	SlmT	53179	2357		B1
260th Av CO-JF					
-	SlmT	53179	2357		B2
263rd St					
900	CteT	60417	3686	1E-31S	B6
264th Av					
10600	SlmT	53179	2357		A1
265th St					
900	CteT	60417	3686	1E-32S	B7
267th Av					
10800	SlmT	53179	2357		A1
268th Av					
11000	SlmT	53179	2357		A1
268th Ct					
11100	SlmT	53179	2357		A1
269th Av					
10800	SlmT	53179	2357		A1
270th Av					
11000	SlmT	53179	2356		E1
11000	SlmT	53179	2357		A1
271st Av					
11300	SlmT	53179	2357		A1
272nd Av					
11300	SlmT	53179	2357		A1
273rd Av					
11300	SlmT	53179	2356		E1
274th Av					
11300	SlmT	53179	2356		E1
275th Av					
-	SlmT	53179	2356		E1
276th Av					
11400	SlmT	53179	2356		E2
277th Av					
11400	SlmT	53179	2356		E2
280th Av					
12000	AntT	53179	2356		D3
12000	AntT	60002	2356		D3
12000	SlmT	53179	2356		D3
286th Av					
10900	SlmT	53179	2356		D1
288th Av					
11200	SlmT	53179	2356		C1
290th Av					
11200	SlmT	53179	2356		C1
304th Av					
11500	AntT	53179	2356		B3
11500	AntT	60002	2356		B3
11500	SlmT	53179	2356		B3
304th Av CO-B					
11500	AntT	53179	2356		B3
11500	AntT	60002	2356		B3
11500	SlmT	53179	2356		B3
306th Av					
11100	SlmT	53192	2356		A1
306th Ct					
11300	SlmT	53192	2356		A2
308th Av					
11100	SlmT	53192	2356		A1
313th Av					
11400	RdlT	53181	2355		E2
11400	RdlT	53192	2355		E1
314th Av					
11700	RdlT	53181	2355		E2
316th Av					
11800	RdlT	53181	2355		E2
318th Av					
11600	RdlT	53181	2355		E2
330th Av					
12000	RdlT	53181	2355		C2
333rd Av					
11600	RdlT	53181	2355		C2
11600	TNLK	53181	2355		C2
334th Av					
11700	RdlT	53181	2355		C2
336th Av					
9800	RdlT	53181	2355		B1
9800	TNLK	53181	2355		B1
12700	BtnT	60081	2355		B4
12700	RdlT	60081	2355		B4
336th Av CO-C					
11000	RdlT	53181	2355		B2
11000	TNLK	53181	2355		B1
336th Av CO-CK					
12500	RdlT	53181	2355		B4
12700	BtnT	60081	2355		B4
12700	RdlT	60081	2355		B4
336th Av CO-KD					
9800	RdlT	53181	2355		B1
9800	TNLK	53181	2355		B1
12700	BtnT	60081	2355		B4
12700	RdlT	60081	2355		B4
342nd Av					
11600	RdlT	53181	2355		B2
11600	TNLK	53181	2355		B2
344th Av					
11600	RdlT	53181	2355		A3
11600	SPGV	60081	2355		A3
11600	TNLK	53181	2355		A3
347th Av					
11300	RdlT	53181	2355		A1
11300	TNLK	53181	2355		A1
360th Av					
-	RdlT	53181	2354		D2
-	TNLK	53181	2354		D1
360th Av CO-Z					
-	RdlT	53181	2354		D2
-	TNLK	53181	2354		D1
374th Av					
12600	RcmT	60081	2354		C4
12600	RdlT	53181	2354		C4
12600	RdlT	60081	2354		C4
374th Av CO-HM					
12600	RcmT	60081	2354		C4
12600	RdlT	53181	2354		C4
12600	RdlT	60081	2354		C4
395th Av					
10300	RdlT	53128	2353		E1
10300	TNLK	53128	2353		E1
10300	TNLK	53181	2353		E1
400th Av					
2800	RdlT	53181	2353		D3
2800	TNLK	53181	2353		D3
10400	RdlT	53128	2353		D1
N 4650th Rd					
2900	FoxT	60541	3330	51W-17S	A6
2900	FoxT	60548	3330	51W-17S	A6
2900	KdlC	60541	3330	51W-17S	A6
2900	KdlC	60548	3330	51W-17S	A6
2900	NvlT	60548	3330	51W-17S	A6
N 4750th Rd					
2900	FoxT	60548	3330	51W-16S	A4
2900	NvlT	60548	3330	51W-16S	A4
N 16000W Rd					
6700	EsxT	60481	4031	30W-46S	D7
6700	EsxT	60935	4031	30W-46S	D7
6700	RedT	60481	4031	30W-46S	D7
N 16000W Rd CO-41					
6700	EsxT	60481	4031	30W-46S	D7
6700	EsxT	60935	4031	30W-46S	D7
6700	RedT	60481	4031	30W-46S	D7
N 17000W Rd					
5000	EsxT	60935	4031	30W-46S	B7
5000	RedT	60481	4031	30W-46S	B7

Airports

FEATURE NAME	MAP#	CGS	GRID
Aero Estates, NpvT	3202	29W-8S	C3
Aurora Municipal, SgrT	3135	43W-6S	A6
Brookeridge Air Park, DGvT	3206	19W-9S	D4
Campbell, FmtT	2532	22W-31N	B6
Chicago Executive, WLNG	2755	13W-16N	E7
Chicago Midway, CHCG	3150	5W-6S	A3
Chicago O'Hare International, CHCG	2916	13W-6N	D5
Clow International, BGBK	3268	26W-12S	A2
Dacy, DhmT	2463	51W-37N	E2
DuPage, WynT	2965	32W-3N	D7
Esser Landing Strip, HshT	2743	45W-18N	C5
FBM Company Landing Strip, MonT	3684	4W-29S	A2
Frankfort, FKFT	3591	11W-27S	E4
Gade Landing Strip, AntT	2418	20W-41N	A1
Galt, GwdT	2468	38W-37N	E3
Haedtler Landing Strip, UYPK	3594	5W-28S	B6
Johnson Landing Strip, MhtT	3767	17W-33S	E3
Joliet Regional, JLET	3497	28W-24S	A5
Lake In the Hills, LIHL	2694	35W-23N	B1
Landings Condominiums Landing Field, RtdT	2745	40W-19N	C3
Landing Strip, FmtT	2588	23W-29N	E5
Lansing Municipal, LNSG	3510	4E-23S	B2
Lewis University, RMVL	3340	24W-18S	E7
Maas Landing Strip, NptT	2361	14W-42N	D7
Northern Pump Airstrip, MchT	2470	35W-35N	B6
Oak Knoll Landing Strip, WcnT	2587	28W-29N	A3
Olson Landing Strip, PltT	2905	43W-9N	B1
Richardsons Landing Strip, BtnT	2414	30W-41N	A1
Schaumburg Regional, SMBG	2912	24W-8N	D3
Waukegan Regional, WKGN	2479	12W-38N	C1
Westosha, RdlT	2355		D1
Wilhelmi, JLET	3587	23W-26S	A3

Beaches, Harbors & Water Rec

FEATURE NAME	MAP#	CGS	GRID
12th Street Beach, CHCG	3034		E7
A1 Millennium Marina, BNHM	3351	2E-16S	D3
Ardmore Hollywood Beach, CHCG	2921		E4
Bald Knob Marina, JNBG	2472	29W-35N	C5
Beach, CbaT	2696	28W-23N	D2
Beach, SBTN	2803	26W-14N	C4
Beach Park, WCDA	2643	26W-27N	E1
Belmont Harbor, CHCG	2978	0W-4N	B3
Bob's Marina, AntT	2357	25W-42N	A6
Carol Beach, PTPR	2363		E3
Charles & Sons Resort & Marina, AntT	2415	26W-39N	E4
Chicago Yacht Club, CHCG	3034	0E-0S	D4
Chicago Yacht Club, CHCG	2978	0W-4N	A3
Clark Street Beach, EVTN	2867	2W-11N	C2
Columbia Yacht Club, CHCG	3034	0E-0N	D4
Croissant Marina, BNHM	3351	2E-16S	D3
Crowleys Yacht Yard, CHCG	3091	1W-2S	E2
Dempster Street Beach, EVTN	2867		C3
Foster Avenue Beach, CHCG	2922		A5
Hammond Marina, HMND	3280		E2
Illinois Beach Resort, BtnT	2422	8W-38N	D6
Indian Trail Beach, LIHL	2694	35W-22N	A5
Inland Harbor Marina, AntT	2415	26W-38N	E6
Lake Elizabeth Manor Marina, TNLK	2354		A3
Lee Street Beach, EVTN	2867		C4
Loyola Avenue Beach, CHCG	2921		E2
Loyola Beach, CHCG	2921	1W-8N	D1
Main Beach, CLLK	2639	36W-25N	D5
Montrose Harbor, CHCG	2922	0W-5N	A7
Montrose-Wilson Beach, CHCG	2922	0W-5N	B7
North Avenue Beach, CHCG	2978	0E-2N	C7
North Point Marina, WPHR	2363	8W-43N	E5
Oak Street Beach, CHCG	3034		C2
Ohio Street Beach, CHCG	3034		D3
Palm Beach, MchT	2472	29W-35N	D6
Port Barrington Marina, NndT	2642	30W-27N	B1
Prairie Harbor Yacht Club, PTPR	2363		D4
Public Beach, GLNC	2758		E4
Public Beach, KLWH	2812		D3
Public Beach & Campground, BtnT	2422	9W-39N	D5
Sequoit Harbor Marina, ANTH	2357	25W-42N	B6
South Boulevard Beach, EVTN	2867		C5
South Pier, CHCG	3034		D3
Spiros East Marina, AntT	2356	26W-41N	E7
Spivey Marine & Harbor, JLET	3498	24W-25S	D7
Sunset Bay Marina, CHCG	3351	2E-15S	D2
Triplex Marina, RVDL	3350	0W-15S	A1
Waukegan Yacht Club, WKGN	2537		C1
Webb's Boat Service & Marina, AntT	2357	25W-42N	A6
West Shore Beach, MHRY	2527	34W-34N	D1
Wonder Lake Marina, MchT	2469	36W-36N	D5
Yacht Harbor, CHCG	3153	2E-7S	C5

Buildings

FEATURE NAME	Address City ZIP Code	MAP#	CGS	GRID
80th Avenue Industrial Park	MKNA, 60448	3504	10W-22S	C1
Abbott Laboratories	1 E 95th St, CHCG, 60628	3214	0E-11S	C6
Abbott Laboratories	100 Abbott Park Rd, LbvT, 60064	2593	13W-30N	A2
Airport Industrial Park	FKFT, 60423	3591	11W-27S	E4
Allanson Industrial Park	Allanson Rd, MDLN, 60060	2646	18W-27N	E1
Allstate	2775 Sanders Rd, NfdT, 60062	2809	12W-15N	B2
Amendodge Industrial Park	SRWD, 60404	3496	30W-24S	C6
Ameritech	12601 S Pulaski Rd, ALSP, 60803	3276	4W-14S	C7
Amoco Oil	2939 S Calumet Av, HMND, 46320	3352		E1
Annico Business Park	HMGN, 60491	3422	16W-18S	A1
Argonne National Laboratory	9700 S Cass Av, DGvT, 60439	3207	17W-11S	C7
Arrowhead Industrial Park	WldT, 60585	3265	31W-11S	D2
AT&T Bell Laboratories	1200 E Warrenville Rd, NPVL, 60563	3082	25W-4S	A7
AT&T Corporate Center	227 W Monroe St, CHCG, 60606	3034	0W-0S	B5
Baxter Healthcare	25212 Belvidere Rd, GrtT, 60073	2531	25W-32N	A5
Baxter Healthcare	1500 S Waukegan Rd, WrnT, 60085	2535	13W-32N	E6
Baxter International	1 Baxter Pkwy, WdfT, 60015	2756	12W-20N	B1
Baxter Technology Park	GrtT, 60073	2531	25W-32N	A5
Braidwood Nuclear Plant	RedT, 60407	4030	32W-44S	D5
Braidwood Nuclear Plant	RedT, 60408	4031	31W-44S	B4
Brainerd Building	416 W Park Av, LYVL, 60048	2591	16W-28N	D5
Brewster Creek Business Park	BRLT, 60120	2910	31W-7N	A4
Carbide & Carbon Building	230 N Michigan Av, CHCG, 60601	3034	0E-0N	C4
Carlow Corporate Center	BGBK, 60490	3268	26W-14S	A7
Cedar Industrial Park	NlxT, 60451	3589	18W-26S	B2
Centex Industrial Park	Lunt Av, EGVV, 60007	2915	16W-8N	D2
Central Square Building	E 9th St, LKPT, 60441	3419	22W-19S	D3
Chase Tower	21 S Clark St, CHCG, 60603	3034	0W-0S	B4
Cherry Hill Industrial Park	NlxT, 60433	3500	20W-24S	B6
Chicago Board of Trade Building	141 W Jackson Blvd, CHCG, 60604	3034	0W-0S	B5
Clow Creek Industrial Park	WldT, 60585	3265	31W-11S	E1
Commercial Park	CLLK, 60014	2639	36W-26N	D3
Commonwealth Edison Nuclear Power-Plant	101 Shiloh Blvd, ZION, 60099	2422	8W-40N	E3
Conway Office & Research Park	W Kennedy Rd, LKFT, 60045	2648	13W-26N	E4
Corporate Corridors	W 191st St, MKNA, 60448	3504	11W-23S	A2
Corporate Crossing	BGBK, 60440	3269	22W-12S	D3
Crossroads Business Center	PNFD, 60544	3338	30W-17S	B5
Crossroads Business Park	BGBK, 60440	3269	23W-13S	A5
Crown Trygg Industrial Park	JLET, 60436	3585	27W-26S	D2
Donohue Building	711 S Dearborn St, CHCG, 60605	3034	0W-0S	B6
Equitable Building	401 N Michigan Av, CHCG, 60611	3034	0E-0N	C3
Federal Center & Plaza	219 S Dearborn St, CHCG, 60604	3034	0W-0S	B5
Fermi National Accelerator-Laboratory	Main Entrance Rd, WnfT, 60510	3079	32W-2S	C3
Ferro Industrial Park	NLNX, 60451	3500	19W-24S	D6
Fine Arts Building	410 S Michigan Av, CHCG, 60605	3034	0E-0S	C5
First National Bank Plaza	1 W Monroe St, CHCG, 60603	3034	0W-0S	B5
Fisher Building	343 S Dearborn St, CHCG, 60604	3034	0W-0S	B5
Flat Iron Building	1581 N Milwaukee Av, CHCG, 60622	3033	2W-1N	C1
Ford Motor Company-Assembly Plant	CHCG, 60633	3279	2E-14S	D6
Ford Motor Stamping Plant	CHHT, 60411	3596	0E-25S	E1
Fox Bluff Corporate Center	ELGN, 60123	2908	35W-9N	B1
Fox River Business Park	ELGN, 60123	2800	34W-14N	E6
Franklin Building	720 S Dearborn St, CHCG, 60605	3034	0W-0S	B6
Gaylord Building	200 W 8th St, LKPT, 60441	3419	22W-19S	C2
General Motors Electro-Motive	MCCK, 60525	3147	11W-5S	D2
Geneva Industrial Park	Averill Rd, GNVA, 60134	3021	33W-1N	B3
Governors Gateway Industrial Park	UYPK, 60466	3682	7W-30S	D3
Grand Tri-State Business Park	Tri State Pkwy, GRNE, 60031	2477	16W-35N	D6
Hampton Industrial Park	RMVL, 60446	3341	23W-15S	A1
Higgins Industrial Park	Brummel Dr, EGVV, 60007	2861	17W-9N	C6
Hilton Chicago & Towers	720 S Michigan Av, CHCG, 60605	3034	0E-0S	C6
Hoffman Tower	3910 Riverwald Dr, LYNS, 60534	3088	10W-4S	B6
Illinois Center	N Michigan Av, CHCG, 60601	3034	0E-0N	C4
Illinois Science & Technology Park	SKOK, 60077	2865	6W-10N	E5
Industrial Area	CLLK, 60012	2583	38W-28N	A6
Industrial Area	CRY, 60014	2641	33W-25N	A5
Industrial Area	MHRY, 60050	2584	33W-30N	E1
Industrial Area	RHMD, 60071	2353	34W-42N	C5
Industrial Area	SPGV, 60081	2413	31W-39N	E5
Industrial Center	ELWD, 60421	3763	28W-33S	B2
Internationale Centre	WDRG, 60517	3270	20W-12S	A2
Internationale Centre Business Park	WDRG, 60517	3270	20W-12S	B2
Jaynes Industrial Park	Holmes Rd, ELGN, 60123	2800	36W-14N	A6
Jewel Food Stores	1955 W North Av, MLPK, 60160	3029	11W-1N	D1
John Hancock Center	875 N Michigan Av, CHCG, 60611	3034	0E-1N	C2
Johnsburg Industrial Park	RGWD, 60072	2470	34W-37N	C3
Kraft General Foods	555 Three Lakes Dr, NHFD, 60093	2810	8W-16N	E1
Kraft General Foods	1555 Ogden Av, NPVL, 60540	3140	29W-6S	E5
Lake Business Center	MNSR, 46321	3510		E1
Lincolnshire Corporate Center	LNSH, 60069	2702	15W-22N	A4
Lombard Industrial Park	LMBD, 60148	3026	19W-2N	B1
Marengo Industrial Park	MRGO, 60152	2634	48W-26N	D3
Marquette Building	140 S Dearborn St, CHCG, 60603	3034	0W-0S	B5
Marquette Business Park	RMVL, 60446	3269	23W-14S	B6
McDonald Plaza	1 McDonalds Dr, OKBK, 60523	3085	16W-1S	D2
McGaw Park	WrnT, 60085	2535	13W-32N	E5
Merchandise Mart	222 W North Bank Dr, CHCG, 60606	3034	0W-0N	A4
Mi-Jack Corporation	HLCT, 60429	3427	3W-20S	A3
Mobil Oil	CnhT, 60421	3674	29W-31S	A5
Mokena Crossings Business Park	191st St, MKNA, 60448	3503	12W-22S	C2
Motorola	HRVD, 60033	2406	49W-39N	C4
Motorola Corporate Headquarters	1303 E Algonquin Rd, SMBG, 60173	2805	21W-13N	D7
Motorola Corporate Office Tower	Tower Cir Dr, SMBG, 60173	2805	22W-12N	D7
Navistar International	1901 S Meyers Rd, OKTR, 60181	3084	18W-1S	E2
NBC Tower	455 N Cityfront Plaza Dr, CHCG, 60611	3034	0E-0N	C3
Normal Towers Industrial Park	MKNA, 60448	3503	12W-23S	D3
North Elgin Industrial Park	Tollgate Rd, ELGN, 60123	2800	35W-14N	D6
Northern Illinois Gas	1844 W Ferry Rd, NPVL, 60563	3080	29W-4S	C7
Northwest Business Park	Galvin Dr, ELGN, 60124	2799	37W-16N	D2
Northwest Corporate Park	Technology Dr, ELGN, 60124	2799	37W-15N	D3
Northwest Tower Building	1600 N Milwaukee Av, CHCG, 60647	2977	2W-2N	B7
Oakbrook Terrace Tower	1 Butterfield Rd, OKTR, 60181	3085	16W-1S	D1
Oak Leaf Center Business Park	JLET, 60436	3498	26W-24S	A6
Olivieri Business Park	190th Pl, FftT, 60448	3503	12W-22S	C2
One Financial Place	440 S Lasalle St, CHCG, 60605	3034	0W-0S	B5
One South Dearborn	1 S Dearborn St, CHCG, 60603	3034	0W-0S	B5
Park 55	RMVL, 60446	3268	24W-14S	D7
Pontiac Building	542 S Dearborn St, CHCG, 60605	3034	0W-0S	B5
Prudential Building	130 E Randolph St, CHCG, 60601	3034	0E-0N	C4
Rand McNally Corporate Headquarters	8255 Central Park Av, SKOK, 60076	2866	4W-10N	C5
Reliance Building	32 N State St, CHCG, 60602	3034	0W-0N	C4
Remington Lake Business Center	BGBK, 60440	3268	25W-13S	C4
River East Center	E Illinois St, CHCG, 60611	3034	0E-0N	D3
Rock Run Business Park	JLET, 60431	3585	28W-25S	A2
Santa Fe Building	224 S Michigan Av, CHCG, 60604	3034	0E-0S	C5
Sears Merchandise Headquarters	Sears Pkwy, HFET, 60192	2802	29W-13N	B5
Sears Tower	233 S Wacker Dr, CHCG, 60606	3034	0W-0S	A5
Shorewood Industrial Park	SRWD, 60404	3496	30W-24S	B5
Sky Corp Industrial Park	NlxT, 60451	3589	18W-26S	B2
South Barrington Executive Center	Executive Ct, SBTN, 60010	2803	26W-13N	E5
South Barrington Office Center	W Higgins Rd, SBTN, 60010	2803	27W-13N	A7
Southfield Business Park	JLET, 60431	3585	28W-25S	B1
Stone Container Building	150 N Michigan Av, CHCG, 60601	3034	0E-0N	C4
The Chicago Sun-Times	401 N Wabash Av, CHCG, 60611	3034	0E-0N	C4
The Rookery Building	209 S Lasalle St, CHCG, 60604	3034	0W-0S	B5
Timber Ridge Business Park	JLET, 60431	3496	29W-24S	D6
Time Life Building	303 E Ohio St, CHCG, 60611	3034	0E-0N	C3
Tootsie Roll Industries	7401 S Cicero Av, CHCG, 60629	3150	5W-8S	A7
Tribune Tower	435 N Michigan Av, CHCG, 60611	3034	0E-0N	C3
Trompe L'Oeil Building	1207 W Division St, CHCG, 60622	3033	1W-1N	D2
Underwriters Laboratories	NHBK, 60062	2756	10W-18N	E3
United Airlines	1200 E Algonquin Rd, EGvT, 60005	2861	16W-10N	D4
Walgreen Company Corporate-Headquarters	200 Wilmot Rd, WdfT, 60015	2756	12W-20N	C2
Waterfall Glen Industrial Park	Westgate Rd, DRN, 60439	3206	19W-11S	D7

Chicago 7-County Points of Interest Index

FEATURE NAME Address City ZIP Code	MAP#	CGS	GRID
Water Filtration Plant 200 Park Dr, CHCG, 60611	3034	0E-0N	E2
Water Filtration Plant CHCG, 60649	3216	4E-8S	A1
Water Tower Place 835 N Michigan Av, CHCG, 60611	3034	0E-1N	C2
Wauconda Industrial Park Industrial Dr, WCDA, 60084	2587	26W-28N	D5
Westinghouse Nuclear Plant Shiloh Blvd, ZION, 60099	2422	9W-40N	D3
Wheatland Industrial Park WldT, 60564	3201	31W-10S	E5
William Wrigley Jr Company 3535 S Ashland Av, CHCG, 60609	3091	1W-3S	D5
Windham Lakes RMVL, 60446	3268	25W-14S	B6
Wolf Creek Industrial Park WldT, 60585	3266	29W-14S	D7
Woodridge Medical Arts Building Hobson Rd, WDRG, 60517	3143	22W-7S	B7
Wrigley Building 400 N Michigan Av, CHCG, 60611	3034	0E-0N	C3
WW Grainger 100 Grainger Pkwy, VrnT, 60045	2648	14W-25N	C4
Zenith Electronics 1000 Milwaukee Av, GNVW, 60025	2809	11W-13N	C6

Buildings - Governmental

FEATURE NAME Address City ZIP Code	MAP#	CGS	GRID
Addison Twp Office 401 N Addison Rd, ADSN, 60101	2971	18W-3N	A4
Addison Village Hall 1 W Lake St, ADSN, 60101	2970	18W-3N	E4
Administration Building S Cicero Av, CHCG, 60638	3150	5W-6S	A4
Administrative Office Ill Court 222 N Lasalle St, CHCG, 60601	3034	0W-0N	B4
Algonquin Twp Office 3702 Northwest Hwy, AlqT, 60014	2641	32W-24N	B6
Algonquin Village Hall 2200 Harnish Dr, ALGN, 60102	2694	35W-20N	A7
Alsip Village Hall 4500 W 123rd St, ALSP, 60803	3276	5W-14S	B6
Antioch Village Hall 874 Main St, ANTH, 60002	2357	23W-42N	E6
Appellate Court 1st District 160 N Lasalle St, CHCG, 60601	3034	0W-0N	B4
Appellate Court 2nd District 55 Symphony Wy, ELGN, 60120	2854	34W-11N	E3
Arlington Heights Vil Hall & Vil-Board 3436 N Kennicott Av, ANHT, 60004	2753	18W-17N	E4
Aurora Branch Courthouse 350 N River St, AURA, 60506	3138	35W-7S	B7
Aurora City Hall 44 S Broadway, AURA, 60505	3138	35W-7S	B7
Bannockburn Village Hall 2275 Telegraph Rd, BKBN, 60015	2703	12W-22N	C3
Barrington Hills Village Hall 112 Algonquin Rd, BNHL, 60010	2750	28W-16N	A7
Barrington Twp Office 620 S Hough St, BRTN, 60010	2750	25W-18N	E3
Barrington Village Hall 200 S Hough St, BRTN, 60010	2750	25W-18N	E2
Bartlett Village Hall 228 S Main St, BRLT, 60103	2910	29W-8N	E3
Batavia City Hall 100 N Island Av, BTVA, 60510	3078	35W-1S	B1
Beach Park Village Hall 11270 W Wadsworth Rd, BHPK, 60099	2421	11W-39N	E6
Bedford Park Village Hall 6701 S Archer Rd, BDPK, 60501	3148	9W-7S	C6
Beecher Village Hall 724 Penfield St, BCHR, 60401	3864	0W-36S	C2
Bellwood Village Hall 3200 Washington Blvd, BLWD, 60104	3029	12W-0N	B4
Benjamin Sch Dist 25 Administration-Building St. Charles Rd, WynT, 60185	2967	28W-2N	B7
Bensenville Village Hall 12 S Center St, BNVL, 60106	2971	16W-5N	E1
Benton Twp Building 40020 W 29th St, BHPK, 60099	2421	12W-40N	B4
Berkeley Village Hall 5819 Electric Av, BKLY, 60163	3028	14W-0N	C4
Berwyn City Hall 6700 26th St, BRWN, 60402	3089	8W-2S	A3
Bloomingdale Twp Office 123 Rosedale Av, BmdT, 60108	2912	23W-6N	E7
Bloomingdale Village Hall 201 S Bloomingdale Rd, BMDL, 60108	2969	23W-5N	A2
Bloom Twp Municipal Office 21460 E Lincoln Hwy, LYWD, 60411	3510	4E-25S	B7
Blue Island City Hall 13051 Vermont St, BLID, 60406	3349	3W-15S	B1
Bolingbrook Branch Court 375 W Briarcliff Rd, BGBK, 60440	3269	23W-12S	A2
Bolingbrook Village Hall 375 W Briarcliff Rd, BGBK, 60440	3269	23W-12S	A2
Braceville City Hall 102 N Mitchell St, BCVL, 60407	4030	34W-44S	A4
Braidwood Branch Court 440 N Division St, BDWD, 60408	3941	32W-41S	E4
Braidwood City Hall 141 W Main St, BDWD, 60408	3942	31W-41S	A5
Bremen Twp Hall Kedzie Av, MKHM, 60428	3427	3W-19S	A3
Bridgeview 5th District Court 10220 S 76th Av, BGVW, 60455	3274	9W-11S	D1
Bridgeview Village Hall 7500 S Oketo Av, BGVW, 60455	3210	9W-8S	D1
Broadview Village Hall 2350 S 25th Av, BDVW, 60155	3029	12W-1S	C7
Brookfield Village Hall 8820 Brookfield Av, BKFD, 60513	3088	10W-3S	A5
Buffalo Grove Village Hall 50 Raupp Blvd, BFGV, 60089	2754	17W-18N	C2
Bull Valley Village Hall & Stickney-House 1904 S Cherry Valley Rd, BLVY, 60098	2583	36W-30N	C2
Burbank City Hall 6530 W 79th St, BRBK, 60459	3211	8W-8S	A2
Burr Ridge Village Hall 7660 S County Line Rd, BRRG, 60527	3208	15W-8S	C2
Calumet City Hall 204 Pulaski Rd, CTCY, 60409	3352	4E-17S	C6
Calumet Park Village Hall 12409 S Throop St, CTPK, 60827	3277	1W-14S	E6
Campton Twp Hall 4N498 Town Hall Rd, CmpT, 60175	2961	41W-4N	E4
Carol Stream Village Hall 500 Gary Av, CLSM, 60188	2968	25W-2N	B7
Carpentersville Village Hall 1200 LW Besinger Dr, CPVL, 60110	2748	33W-17N	B7
Cary Village Hall 655 Village Hall Dr, CRY, 60013	2695	31W-23N	C2
Chicago City Hall 121 N Lasalle St, CHCG, 60602	3034	0W-0N	B4
Chicago Heights City Hall 1601 Chicago Rd, CHHT, 60411	3596	1W-25S	A1
Chicago Public School Administration-HQs W Pershing Rd, CHCG, 60609	3091	2W-4S	C6
Chicago Ridge Village Hall 10455 Ridgeland Av, CHRG, 60415	3275	7W-12S	B1
Chicago Youth Center 100 N Western Av, CHCG, 60612	3033	3W-0N	A4
Cicero Town Hall 4936 W 26th St, CCRO, 60804	3089	6W-2S	E2
Circuit Court Clerk 2245 W Ogden Av, CHCG, 60612	3033	2W-0S	B6
Circuit Court Clerk 9511 Harrison St, MaiT, 60016	2863	11W-12N	C1
Circuit Court Clerk 200 E Wood St, PLTN, 60067	2752	20W-16N	E7
Civic Center Glen Ellyn Rd, BMDL, 60108	2969	22W-4N	C4
Civic Center Paul Av, GLHT, 60139	2969	23W-3N	A6
Civic Center Fairfield Rd, LNHT, 60046	2476	20W-37N	A1
Civic Center Plaza Symphony Wy, ELGN, 60120	2854	34W-11N	E3
Clarendon Hills Village Hall 1 N Prospect Av, CNHL, 60514	3145	16W-5S	D2
Clerk Office Ridge Rd, LNSG, 60438	3430	3E-21S	A6
Clerk of the Circuit Court 28 N Clark St, CHCG, 60602	3034	0W-0N	B4
Clerk of the Circuit Courts 5555 W Grand Av, CHCG, 60639	2975	6W-2N	D6
Clerk's Office 1500 Maybrook Dr, MYWD, 60153	3030	10W-0S	B5
Comm Unit Sch District 300 Board of-Edu 300 Cleveland Av, CPVL, 60110	2801	33W-16N	A1
Cook County Building 118 N Clark St, CHCG, 60602	3034	0W-0N	B4
Cook County Circuit Court 55 W Randolph St, CHCG, 60602	3034	0W-0N	B4
Cook County Circuit Court 1121 S State St, CHCG, 60605	3034	0E-0S	C6
Cook County Circuit Court 155 W 51st St, CHCG, 60609	3152	0W-5S	B2
Cook County Circuit Court 321 N Lasalle Blvd, CHCG, 60610	3034	0W-0N	B4
Cook County Circuit Court 3150 W Flournoy St, CHCG, 60612	3032	3W-0S	E6
Cook County Circuit Court 2452 W Belmont Av, CHCG, 60618	2977	3W-4N	A3
Cook County Circuit Court 937 N Wood St, CHCG, 60622	3033	2W-1N	C2
Cook County Circuit Court 2600 S California Av, CHCG, 60623	3091	3W-2S	A3
Cook County Circuit Court 727 E 111th St, CHCG, 60628	3278	0E-13S	E3
Cook County Circuit Court 5555 W Grand Av, CHCG, 60639	2975	6W-2N	D6
Cook County Criminal Court 2600 S California Blvd, CHCG, 60608	3091	3W-2S	A3
Cook County Department of Health 1010 Lake St, OKPK, 60301	3030	8W-0N	E3
Coral Twp Hall Jefferson St, CrlT, 60180	2635	46W-25N	E5
Country Club Hills Village Hall 4200 183rd St, CCHL, 60478	3426	5W-21S	C7
Countryside City Hall 5550 East Av, CTSD, 60525	3147	12W-6S	D3
County Clerk N Meadow Dr, WLMT, 60091	2812	5W-13N	A6
Court of Appeals-Province Chicago 20 N Wacker Dr, CHCG, 60606	3034	0W-0N	B4
Crest Hill City Hall 1610 Plainfield Rd, CTHL, 60403	3498	26W-21S	A1
Crestwood Village Hall 13840 Cicero Av, CTWD, 60445	3348	5W-16S	A3
Crete Village Hall 524 W Exchange St, CRTE, 60417	3685	1W-29S	B2
Crossroads Adult Transition Center 3210 W Arthington St, CHCG, 60624	3032	4W-0S	D6
Crystal Lake City Hall 100 W Municipal Complex, CLLK, 60014	2640	35W-26N	A3
Daley Civic Center 50 W Washington St, CHCG, 60602	3034	0W-0N	B4
Darien City Hall 1702 Plainfield Rd, DRN, 60516	3207	18W-8S	A2
Deerfield Village Hall 850 Waukegan Rd, DRFD, 60015	2703	10W-21N	E7
Deer Park Village Office 23680 Cuba Rd, DRPK, 60010	2698	23W-21N	E6
Department Adm Hearings 400 W Superior St, CHCG, 60610	3034	0W-0N	A3
Department of Justice 230 S Wood St, CHCG, 60612	3033	2W-0S	C5
Des Plaines City Hall 1420 Miner St, DSPN, 60016	2863	13W-11N	A3
Diamond Village Hall 1750 E Division St, DMND, 60416	3941	33W-39S	B2
Dixmoor Village Hall 170 W 145th St, HRVY, 60426	3349	2W-17S	E5
Dolton Village Hall 14014 Park Av, DLTN, 60419	3350	0E-16S	D3
Downers Grove Village Hall 801 Burlington Av, DRGV, 60515	3144	19W-5S	C2
DuPage Area Occupation Education-System North-South Tollway, ADSN, 60101	2969	21W-3N	E6
DuPage County Board of Education Stonewall Av, DRGV, 60516	3144	21W-6S	A5
DuPage County Circuit Court WHTN, 60187	3023	26W-0S	E6
DuPage County Courthouse WHTN, 60187	3023	26W-0S	E6
DuPage County Health Department W Lake St, ADSN, 60101	2970	20W-4N	B3
DuPage County Health Department 111 N County Farm Rd, WHTN, 60187	3023	26W-0S	E7
DuPage County Probation Court-Service WHTN, 60187	3023	26W-0S	E6
DuPage Twp Office 241 Canterbury Ln, BGBK, 60440	3269	23W-12S	A2
Dyer Town Hall Hart St, DYR, 46311	3598		D2
East Dundee Village Hall 120 Barrington Av, EDND, 60118	2801	33W-16N	A2
East Hazel Crest City Hall 1904 174th St, EHZC, 60429	3427	2W-20S	D5
Ela Twp Offices 95 E Main St, LKZH, 60047	2698	23W-22N	E3
Elburn Village Hall 301 E North St, ELBN, 60119	3017	43W-1N	A3
Elgin Branch Courthouse 150 Dexter Ct, ELGN, 60120	2854	34W-11N	E3
Elgin City Hall 150 Dexter Av, ELGN, 60120	2854	34W-11N	E3
Elgin Twp Office 164 Division St, ELGN, 60120	2854	34W-11N	E4
Elk Grove Twp Hall 2400 S Arlington Heights Rd, ANHT, 60005	2861	18W-11N	A3
Elk Grove Village Hall 901 Wellington Av, EGVV, 60007	2914	19W-8N	C2
Elmhurst City Hall 209 N York St, EMHT, 60126	3028	15W-1N	A1
Elmwood Park Village Hall 11 W Conti Pkwy, EDPK, 60707	2974	9W-3N	C5
Elwood Village Hall 100 N Matteson St, ELWD, 60421	3675	25W-32S	C7
Evanston City Hall 1200 Ridge Av, EVTN, 60201	2867	2W-12N	B1
Evergreen Park Village Hall 9418 S Kedzie Av, ENGN, 60805	3212	4W-10S	E5
FAA Administration Office Indian Trail Rd, AURA, 60506	3137	36W-5S	E4
Federal Court 194 E Delaware Pl, CHCG, 60611	3034	0E-1N	C2
Flossmoor Village Hall 2800 Flossmoor Rd, FSMR, 60422	3507	3W-23S	B2
Ford Heights Village Hall 1343 Ellis Av, FDHT, 60411	3509	1E-25S	A7
Forest Park City Hall 517 Des Plaines Av, FTPK, 60130	3030	9W-0S	C5
Forest View Village Hall 7000 46th St, FTVW, 60402	3088	8W-4S	E7
Fox Lake Village Hall 66 E Grand Av, FXLK, 60020	2473	27W-36N	A3
Fox River Grove Village Hall 305 Northwest Hwy, FRGV, 60021	2696	29W-23N	B3
Frankfort Village Hall 432 W Nebraska St, FKFT, 60423	3591	12W-26S	C2
Franklin Park Village Hall 9545 W Belmont Av, FNPK, 60131	2973	11W-3N	C4
Geneva City Hall 22 S 1st St, GNVA, 60134	3020	35W-1N	C3
Genoa City Courthouse 170 S Carter St, GNCY, 53128	2353		A3
Genoa City Municipal Court 715 Walworth St, GNCY, 53128	2353		A3
Genoa City Village Hall 715 Freeman St, GNCY, 53128	2353		A3
Gilberts Village Hall 87 Railroad St, GLBT, 60136	2799	38W-16N	A1
Glencoe Village Hall 325 Hazel Av, GLNC, 60022	2758	6W-17N	D5
Glendale Heights Village Hall 300 E Fullerton Av, GLHT, 60139	2969	23W-3N	A6
Glen Ellyn Village Hall 535 Duane St, GNEN, 60137	3025	22W-0N	B5
Glenview Village Hall 1225 Waukegan Rd, GNVW, 60025	2810	8W-13N	E5
Glenwood Village Hall 13 S Rebecca St, GNWD, 60425	3508	0E-22S	D2
Godley Village Hall 150 S Kankakee St, GDLY, 60407	4030	32W-43S	C2
Golf Village Hall 1 Briar Rd, GLF, 60029	2864	8W-12N	E1
Grafton Twp Office 10109 Vine St, HTLY, 60142	2691	40W-21N	E5
Grant Twp Office 26725 W Molidor Rd, GrtT, 60041	2530	26W-33N	D3
Grayslake Branch Court 1845 W Belvidere Rd, GYLK, 60030	2533	18W-32N	D4
Grayslake Village Hall 10 S Seymour Av, GYLK, 60030	2532	20W-33N	E4
Green Oaks Village Hall 2020 Oplaine Rd, GNOK, 60048	2592	14W-30N	C2
Greenwood Town Hall Greenwood Rd, GNWD, 60098	2468	38W-36N	E4
Greenwood Twp Office 5211 Miller Rd, GwdT, 60098	2468	39W-37N	D2
Gurnee Village Hall 325 N Oplaine Rd, GRNE, 60031	2535	14W-34N	C1
Hainesville Village Hall 100 N Hainesville Rd, HNVL, 60073	2532	22W-33N	C3
Hammond City Court 5925 S Calumet Av, HMND, 46320	3430		E1
Hammond City Hall 5925 S Calumet Av, HMND, 46320	3430		E1
Hampshire Twp Office 193 S State St, HPSR, 60140	2795	47W-16N	E2
Hampshire Village Hall 234 S State St, HPSR, 60140	2795	47W-16N	E2
Hanover Park Village Hall 2121 W Lake St, HRPK, 60133	2911	27W-8N	C3
Harvard City Hall 201 W Front St, HRVD, 60033	2406	50W-38N	A7

FEATURE NAME Address City ZIP Code	MAP#	CGS	GRID
Harvey City Hall 15320 Broadway Av, HRVY, 60426	3350	1W-18S	A7
Harwood Heights Village Hall 7300 W Wilson Av, HDHT, 60706	2918	9W-5N	D7
Hawthorn Woods Village Hall 2 Lagoon Dr, HNWD, 60047	2645	21W-24N	D7
Hazel Crest City Hall 3000 W 170th Pl, HLCT, 60429	3427	3W-20S	A4
Health Department N Cass Av, WTMT, 60559	3145	18W-4S	A1
Hickory Hills Village Hall 8652 W 95th St, HYHL, 60457	3210	10W-10S	A6
Highland Park City Hall 1707 St. John's Av, HDPK, 60035	2704	8W-22N	E5
Highwood City Hall 17 Highwood Av, HIWD, 60040	2704	9W-23N	D2
Hillside Village Hall 425 N Hillside Av, HLSD, 60162	3028	14W-0N	D5
Hinsdale Village Hall 19 W Chicago Av, HNDL, 60521	3146	15W-4S	B1
Hodgkins Village Hall 8990 Lyons St, HGKN, 60525	3147	11W-7S	D6
Hoffman Estates Village Hall 1900 Hassell Rd, HFET, 60169	2804	25W-12N	A7
Holiday Hills Village Hall 1304 Sunset Dr, HHLL, 60051	2586	30W-29N	B3
Homer Glen Village Hall 14331 S Golden Oak Dr, HMGN, 60491	3343	16W-17S	E4
Homer Twp Hall 16057 S Cedar Rd, HmrT, 60491	3421	18W-19S	A2
Homer TWP Administration Center W 151st St, HMGN, 60491	3343	18W-17S	B6
Hometown City Hall 4331 Southwest Hwy, HMTN, 60456	3212	5W-10S	B5
Homewood Village Hall 2020 Chestnut Rd, HMWD, 60430	3427	2W-21S	D6
House Of Corrections S California Av, CHCG, 60623	3091	3W-2S	A3
Huntley City Hall 11704 E Coral St, HTLY, 60142	2692	40W-21N	A6
Illinois Appellate 3rd District 300 E 5th Av, NPVL, 60563	3141	26W-6S	D4
Illinois Forest District Appellate-Court 160 N Lasalle St, CHCG, 60601	3034	0W-0N	B4
Illinois Judicial Courts 100 W Roosevelt Rd, WHTN, 60187	3082	24W-1S	C1
Illinois State Boy's Detention-Center McDonough St, JLET, 60436	3497	27W-24S	C6
Illinois Supreme Court 160 N Lasalle St, CHCG, 60601	3034	0W-0N	B4
Illinois Youth Center-Warrenville Ferry Rd, WNVL, 60563	3080	30W-4S	B7
Indian Head Park Village Hall 201 Acacia Dr, IHPK, 60525	3146	13W-7S	E6
Inverness Village Hall 1400 Baldwin Rd, IVNS, 60067	2752	22W-17N	A6
Island Lake Village Hall 3720 Greenleaf Av, ISLK, 60042	2586	28W-28N	E6
Itasca Village Hall 100 N Walnut Av, ITSC, 60143	2914	19W-6N	C6
Jessie Houston Adult Transition-Center 14127 Leavitt Av, DXMR, 60406	3349	2W-16S	C4
Johnsburg Village Hall 1515 Channel Beach Av, JNBG, 60050	2472	30W-36N	A4
Joliet City Hall 150 W Jefferson St, JLET, 60432	3498	24W-23S	E5
Joliet State Corrections Center 1125 Collins St, JLET, 60432	3499	23W-22S	A2
Joliet Twp Office 175 W Jefferson St, JLET, 60432	3498	24W-23S	E5
Judicary Courts of the State Ill 222 N Lasalle St, CHCG, 60601	3034	0W-0N	B4
Justice Village Hall 78 S Archer Rd, JSTC, 60458	3210	11W-8S	A2
Juvenile Justice Center SchT, 60175	3019	37W-2N	C1
Kane County Adult Correction-Complex E Fabyan Pkwy, GnvT, 60510	3020	34W-0N	D6
Kane County Circuit Court 301 W Fabyan Pkwy, GNVA, 60134	3020	35W-0S	B7
Kane County Court Service 122 W Downer Pl, AURA, 60506	3138	35W-7S	A7
Kane County Government Center 719 S Batavia Av, GNVA, 60134	3020	35W-0N	B4
Kane County Health Department 210 S 6th St, GNVA, 60134	3020	35W-1N	B4
Kane County Judicial Center SchT, 60175	3019	37W-2N	C1
Kendall County Circuit Court 110 W Ridge St, YKVL, 60560	3333	43W-15S	C2
Kendall County Courthouse 807 W John St, YKVL, 60560	3261	43W-14S	A7
Kendall County Department of Health 500 Countryside Ctr, YKVL, 60560	3261	43W-14S	C7
Kendall County Government Center 111 W Fox St, YKVL, 60560	3333	42W-15S	C3
Kenilworth Village Hall 419 Richmond Rd, KLWH, 60043	2812	4W-14N	C4
Kildeer Village Hall 21911 Quentin Rd, KLDR, 60047	2699	21W-21N	D6
La Grange Park Village Hall 447 N Catherine Av, LGPK, 60525	3087	12W-3S	B6
La Grange Village Hall 53 S La Grange Rd, LGNG, 60525	3087	12W-4S	C7
Lake Barrington Village Hall 23860 N Old Barrington Rd, LKBN, 60010	2697	27W-23N	B1
Lake Bluff Village Hall 40 E Center Av, LKBF, 60044	2593	10W-28N	E6
Lake County Circuit Court Branch 5 3050 N Main St, BFGV, 60089	2701	16W-23N	D2
Lake County Courthouse 18 N County St, WKGN, 60085	2537	10W-34N	B1
Lake County Health Department 3010 Grand Av, WKGN, 60085	2479	12W-35N	B7
Lake County Superior Court 232 Russell St, HMND, 46320	3352		D6
Lake Forest City Hall 220 E Deerpath Rd, LKFT, 60045	2650	10W-26N	A2
Lakehurst Branch Court 430 Lakehurst Rd, WKGN, 60085	2535	13W-33N	D4
Lake in the Hills Village Hall 600 Harvest Gate, LIHL, 60156	2693	36W-21N	D5
Lakemoor Village Hall 234 W Rand Rd, LKMR, 60051	2529	29W-32N	D5
Lake Villa Village Hall 65 Cedar Av, LKVL, 60046	2475	22W-38N	A1
Lakewood City Hall 2500 Lake Av, LKWD, 60014	2639	37W-25N	B5
Lake Zurich Village Hall 70 E Main St, LKZH, 60047	2698	23W-23N	E3
Lansing Village Hall 18200 Chicago Av, LNSG, 60438	3430	3E-21S	A6
Lemont Twp Office 16020 W 127th St, LMNT, 60439	3342	20W-15S	C1
Lemont Village Hall 418 Main St, LMNT, 60439	3270	19W-13S	D5
Libertyville Twp Hall W Linden Ln, GNOK, 60048	2592	14W-28N	D7
Libertyville Twp Hall 359 Merrill Ct, LYVL, 60048	2591	16W-29N	D4
Libertyville Village Hall 118 E Cook Av, LYVL, 60048	2591	16W-29N	D4
Lincolnshire Village Hall 1 Old Half Day Rd, LNSH, 60069	2702	15W-23N	B2
Lincolnwood Village Hall 6900 N Lincoln Av, LNWD, 60712	2920	5W-8N	B1
Lindenhurst Village Hall 2301 E Sand Lake Rd, LNHT, 60046	2476	20W-37N	B2
Linn Town Hall W3728 Franklin Walsh St, LinT, 53147	2349		E1
Lisle Village Hall 925 Burlington Av, LSLE, 60532	3143	22W-5S	B2
Lockport Branch Court 222 E 9th St, LKPT, 60441	3419	22W-19S	C3
Lockport City Hall 220 E 9th St, LKPT, 60441	3419	22W-19S	C3
Lombard Village Hall 255 E Wilson Av, LMBD, 60148	3026	19W-0S	C6
Long Grove Village Hall 3110 Twin Knolls Dr, LGGV, 60047	2700	18W-21N	D5
Lyons Village Hall 7801 Ogden Av, LYNS, 60534	3088	9W-4S	C6
Maine Twp Hall 1700 W Ballard Rd, MaiT, 60068	2863	11W-11N	E3
Manhattan Village Hall 245 S State St, MHTN, 60442	3677	19W-31S	E5
Marengo City Hall 132 E Prairie St, MRGO, 60152	2634	49W-26N	B2
Markham 6th District Court 16501 Kedzie Av, MKHM, 60428	3427	3W-19S	A3
Markham City Hall 16313 Kedzie Av, MKHM, 60428	3427	3W-19S	A2
Matteson Village Hall 4900 Village Coms, MTSN, 60443	3506	6W-24S	A6
Maywood 4th District Court 1500 Maybrook Dr, MYWD, 60153	3030	10W-0S	B5
Maywood Village Hall 40 Madison St, MYWD, 60153	3030	10W-0S	B5
McCook Village Hall 5000 Glencoe Av, MCCK, 60525	3148	10W-5S	B2
McCullom Lake Village Hall 4811 W Orchard Dr, MCLK, 60050	2470	33W-34N	E7
McHenry Branch Courts 333 S Green St, MHRY, 60050	2528	32W-31N	B6
McHenry City Hall 333 S Green St, MHRY, 60050	2528	32W-31N	B6
McHenry County Courthouse 2200 N Seminary Av, WDSK, 60098	2524	41W-32N	D4
McHenry County Department of Health 2200 N Seminary Av, WDSK, 60098	2524	41W-32N	D4
McHenry County Government Center 2200 N Seminary Av, WDSK, 60098	2524	41W-32N	D4
McHenry Twp Office 3703 N Richmond Rd, JNBG, 60050	2471	32W-35N	B6
Melrose Park Village Hall 1000 N 25th Av, MLPK, 60160	3029	12W-1N	C2
Merrionette Park Village Hall 11720 S Kedzie Av, MTPK, 60803	3276	4W-13S	E4
Midlothian Village Hall 14801 Pulaski Rd, MDLN, 60445	3348	4W-17S	C5
Minooka Village Hall 121 McEvilly Rd, MNKA, 60447	3672	33W-28S	B1
Mokena Village Hall 11004 Carpenter St, MKNA, 60448	3503	13W-23S	A3
Monee Branch Court 5130 W Court St, MONE, 60449	3683	6W-31S	A5
Monee Village Hall 5130 W Court St, MONE, 60449	3683	6W-31S	A5
Montgomery Village Hall 1300 SE River Rd, MTGY, 60538	3199	36W-9S	E4
Morton Grove Village Hall 6101 Capulina Av, MNGV, 60053	2865	7W-10N	B4
Mt Prospect Village Hall 100 S Emerson St, MPPT, 60056	2808	15W-12N	A7
Mundelein Village Hall 440 E Hawley St, MDLN, 60060	2590	18W-28N	E7
Municipal Building W Jefferson St, SRWD, 60404	3496	30W-24S	B5
Munster Town Hall 1005 Ridge Rd, MNSR, 46321	3430		E7
Naperville City Hall 400 S Eagle St, NPVL, 60540	3141	27W-6S	C6
Naperville Twp Office 139 S Main St, NPVL, 60540	3141	27W-6S	D6
National Safety Council 1121 Spring Lake Dr, ITSC, 60143	2914	20W-6N	A7
Native American Education Service 2838 W Peterson Av, CHCG, 60659	2920	3W-7N	E4
New Lenox Village Hall 701 W Haven Av, NLNX, 60451	3501	18W-24S	A6
Niles Twp Hall 5255 Main St, SKOK, 60077	2865	6W-10N	D5
Niles Village Hall 1000 Civic Center Dr, NLES, 60714	2864	8W-9N	E6
Norridge Village Hall 4020 N Olcott Av, NRDG, 60706	2974	9W-5N	C2
North Aurora Village Hall 25 E State St, NARA, 60542	3078	36W-4S	A7
North Barrington Village Hall 111 N Old Barrington Rd, NBRN, 60010	2697	26W-22N	D3
Northbrook Village Hall 1225 Cedar Ln, NHBK, 60062	2757	10W-17N	B5
North Chicago City Hall 1850 Lewis Av, NCHI, 60064	2536	11W-31N	D6
Northfield Village Hall 361 S Happ Rd, NHFD, 60093	2811	6W-15N	C2
Northlake City Hall 55 E North Av, NHLK, 60164	3028	13W-1N	D1
North Lawndale Adult Transition-Center 2839 W Fillmore St, CHCG, 60612	3032	3W-0S	E6
North Riverside Village Hall 2401 Des Plaines Av, NRIV, 60546	3088	9W-2S	C2
North Twp Hall 5947 S Hohman Av, HMND, 46320	3430		D1
Nunda Twp Office 3510 Bay Rd, PRGV, 60012	2584	34W-28N	D6
Oakbrook Terrace City Hall 17W275 Butterfield Rd, OKTR, 60181	3085	17W-1S	C1
Oak Brook Village Hall 1200 Oak Brook Rd, OKBK, 60523	3085	16W-2S	E4
Oak Forest City Hall 15440 Central Av, OKFT, 60452	3347	7W-18S	D7
Oak Lawn Village Hall 5252 Dumke Dr, OKLN, 60453	3211	6W-10S	E6
Oak Park Village Hall 1 Madison St, OKPK, 60304	3031	7W-0S	B5
Oakwood Hills Village Hall 3020 N Park Dr, ODHL, 60013	2641	31W-26N	C2
Old Mill Creek Village Hall 40870 N Hunt Club Rd, OMCK, 60083	2419	17W-40N	B2
Olympia Fields Village Hall 20701 Governors Hwy, OMFD, 60461	3506	4W-25S	D6
Orland Hills Village Hall 16033 S 94th Av, ODHL, 60487	3423	11W-19S	E2
Orland Park Village Hall 14700 S Ravinia Av, ODPK, 60462	3345	12W-17S	D5
Oswego Village Hall 113 S Main St, OSWG, 60543	3263	37W-12S	C4
Palatine Village Hall 200 E Wood St, PLTN, 60067	2752	20W-16N	E7
Palos Heights City Hall 7607 119th St, PSHT, 60463	3274	9W-14S	D5
Palos Hills City Hall 10335 S Roberts Rd, PSHL, 60465	3274	9W-12S	C1
Palos Park Village Hall 8999 W 123rd St, PSPK, 60464	3274	11W-14S	A6
Park City City Hall 3420 Kehm Blvd, PKCY, 60085	2536	13W-33N	A3
Park Forest Village Hall 350 Victory Dr, PKFT, 60466	3595	3W-27S	B4
Park Ridge City Hall 505 Butler Pl, PKRG, 60068	2918	10W-8N	B1
Peotone Village Hall 208 E Main St, PTON, 60468	3861	9W-37S	A3
Phoenix Village Hall 633 E 151st St, PHNX, 60426	3350	0W-18S	B6
Plainfield Twp Hall 24401 W Lockport Rd, PnfT, 60544	3339	28W-18S	B7
Plainfield Village Hall 530 W Lockport St, PNFD, 60544	3338	30W-18S	C7
Plano City Hall 17 E Main St, PLNO, 60545	3259	47W-13S	D6
Port Barrington Village Hall 69 S Circle Av, PTBR, 60010	2642	29W-26N	C4
Posen Village Hall 2440 W 147th St, POSN, 60469	3349	3W-17S	B5
Prairie Grove Village Hall 3125 Barreville Rd, PRGV, 60012	2585	32W-28N	C5
Prospect Heights City Hall 8 E Camp McDonald Rd, PTHT, 60070	2808	15W-15N	A3
Public Safety Building Deerfield Rd, HDPK, 60035	2704	9W-21N	B6
Public Services Building Underwood Pl, HDPK, 60035	2704	9W-23N	B3
Public Works N Skokie Hwy, GRNE, 60031	2478	14W-35N	C6
Public Works Facilities Bittersweet Dr, BRLT, 60103	2911	28W-6N	B6
Richmond Village Hall 5600 Hunter Dr, RHMD, 60071	2412	34W-41N	C1
Richton Park Village Hall 4455 Sauk Tr, RNPK, 60471	3594	5W-27S	C3
Ringwood Village Hall 6000 Inmans Wy, RGWD, 60072	2470	34W-36N	C3
Riverdale Village Hall 157 W 144th St, RVDL, 60827	3350	0W-16S	C4
River Forest Twp Hall 8020 Madison St, RVFT, 60305	3030	10W-0N	B5
River Forest Village Hall 400 Park Av, RVFT, 60305	3030	9W-0N	C4
River Grove Village Hall 2621 N Thatcher Av, RVGV, 60171	2974	10W-3N	A5
Riverside Village Hall 27 Riverside Rd, RVSD, 60546	3088	9W-3S	C5
Riverwoods Village Hall 300 Portwine Rd, RVWD, 60015	2755	13W-20N	E1
Robbins Village Hall 3327 W 137th St, RBBN, 60472	3348	4W-16S	E2
Robert W Depke Juvenile Justice-Complex 24647 N Milwaukee Av, VrnT, 60061	2648	15W-24N	A7
Rockdale Village Hall 79 Moen Av, RKDL, 60436	3498	25W-25S	C7
Rolling Meadows 3rd District Court 2121 W Euclid Av, RGMW, 60008	2806	19W-14N	D4
Rolling Meadows City Hall 3600 Kirchoff Rd, RGMW, 60008	2806	20W-13N	B5
Romeoville Village Hall 13 Montrose Dr, RMVL, 60446	3341	23W-15S	A2
Roselle Village Hall 31 S Prospect St, ROSL, 60172	2913	23W-7N	A4
Rosemont Village Hall 9501 E Devon Av, RSMT, 60018	2917	11W-7N	C3
Round Lake Beach Village Hall 1937 N Municipal Wy, RLKB, 60073	2475	22W-35N	B5
Round Lake Heights Village Hall 619 Pontiac Ct, RLKH, 60073	2474	23W-35N	D5
Round Lake Park Village Hall 203 E Lake Shore Dr, RLKP, 60073	2532	22W-34N	A2
Round Lake Village Hall 442 N Cedar Lake Rd, RDLK, 60073	2531	23W-33N	E2

FEATURE NAME Address City ZIP Code	MAP#	CGS	GRID
Safety & Justice Building S Halsted St, CHHT, 60411	3596	0W-25S	B1
St. Charles Village Hall 2 E Main St, SCRL, 60174	2964	35W-3N	B7
Sauk Village Town Hall 21701 Torrence Av, SLVL, 60411	3597	3E-26S	E2
Schaumburg Village Hall 101 Schaumburg Ct, SMBG, 60193	2859	22W-10N	B5
Schiller Park Village Hall 9526 Irving Park Rd, SRPK, 60176	2973	11W-5N	C1
Shorewood Village Hall 903 W Jefferson St, SRWD, 60404	3496	30W-24S	C5
Skokie 2nd District Court 5600 Old Orchard Rd, SKOK, 60077	2811	7W-12N	C7
Skokie Court House 5600 Old Orchard Rd, SKOK, 60077	2811	6W-12N	C7
Skokie Village Hall 5127 Oakton St, SKOK, 60077	2865	6W-9N	D6
Sleepy Hollow Village Hall 1 Thorobred Ln, SYHW, 60118	2800	35W-15N	B3
South Barrington Village Hall 30 S Barrington Rd, SBTN, 60010	2803	26W-13N	E6
South Chicago Heights Village Hall 3317 Chicago Rd, SCHT, 60411	3596	1W-27S	B4
South Elgin Village Hall 10 N Water St, SEGN, 60177	2908	34W-8N	D3
South Holland Village Hall 16226 Wausau Av, SHLD, 60473	3428	0E-19S	D1
Spring Grove Village Hall 7401 Meyer Rd, SPGV, 60081	2413	31W-39N	E5
State Of Illinois Youth Center Lincoln Hwy, SCRL, 60175	3019	38W-2N	A1
Stateville Correctional Center Broadway St, CTHL, 60441	3418	24W-20S	E4
Steger Village Hall 35 W Steger Rd, STGR, 60475	3596	1W-27S	A5
Stickney Village Hall 6533 Pershing Rd, SKNY, 60402	3089	8W-4S	A6
Stone Park Village Hall 1629 N Mannheim Rd, SNPK, 60165	3029	12W-1N	A2
Streamwood Village Hall 301 E Irving Park Rd, SMWD, 60107	2857	28W-9N	A7
Sugar Grove Village Hall 10 Municipal Dr, SRGV, 60554	3135	43W-7S	B6
Summit Village Hall 5810 S Archer Rd, SMMT, 60501	3148	9W-6S	D4
Third Lake Village Hall 87 S Lake Av N, TDLK, 60030	2476	19W-35N	C6
Thornton Twp Hall 333 E 162nd St, SHLD, 60473	3428	0E-19S	E1
Thornton Village Hall 115 E Margaret St, TNTN, 60476	3428	0E-21S	D6
Tinley Park Village Hall 16250 Oak Park Av, TYPK, 60477	3425	8W-19S	A2
Tower Lakes Village Hall TRLK, 60010	2643	26W-25N	D5
Union Village Hall 6606 N Union Rd, UNON, 60180	2635	46W-25N	D4
United States Courthouse 219 S Dearborn St, CHCG, 60604	3034	0W-0S	B5
United States District Court 507 E State St, HMND, 46320	3352		D6
University Park Village Hall 698 Burnham Dr, UYPK, 60466	3684	3W-29S	A1
Valley View School District-Administration 755 Luther Dr, RMVL, 60446	3268	24W-14S	E7
Vernon Hills Village Hall 290 Evergreen Dr, VNHL, 60061	2647	17W-24N	B6
Vernon Twp Office 3050 N Main St, BFGV, 60089	2701	16W-23N	D2
Villa Park Village Hall 20 S Ardmore Av, VLPK, 60181	3027	18W-0N	A3
Wadsworth Village Hall 14155 W Wadsworth Rd, WDWH, 60083	2420	14W-38N	D6
Warren Twp Hall 17801 W Washington St, WrnT, 60031	2534	17W-34N	A1
Warrenville City Hall 3S258 Stafford Pl, WNVL, 60555	3080	28W-3S	E5
Wauconda Village Hall 101 N Main St, WCDA, 60084	2643	26W-27N	E1
Waukegan City Hall 100 N Martin Luther King Jr Av, WKGN, 60085	2537	10W-34N	A1
Wayne Village Hall 5N430 Railroad St, WYNE, 60184	2965	32W-5N	D2
Westchester Village Hall 10300 W Roosevelt Rd, WSTR, 60154	3029	12W-0S	B7
West Chicago City Hall 475 Main St, WCHI, 60185	3022	29W-0N	D4
West Dundee Village Hall 102 S 2nd St, WDND, 60118	2801	34W-16N	A2
Western Springs Village Hall 740 Hillgrove Av, WNSP, 60558	3086	13W-4S	E7
Westmont Village Hall 31 W Quincy St, WTMT, 60559	3145	18W-5S	B2
West Side Adult Transition Center 121 N Campbell Av, CHCG, 60612	3033	3W-0N	A4
Wheaton City Hall 303 W Wesley St, WHTN, 60187	3024	24W-0S	C6
Wheeling Village Hall 255 W Dundee Rd, WLNG, 60090	2755	14W-18N	B4
Will County Clerk Main Office 302 N Chicago St, JLET, 60432	3499	23W-23S	A4
Will County Courthouse 14 W Jefferson St, JLET, 60432	3498	24W-23S	E5
Will County Health Department 501 Ella Av, JLET, 60433	3499	23W-25S	B7
Willowbrook Village Hall 7760 S Quincy St, WLBK, 60527	3207	16W-8S	E2
Willow Springs Village Hall 1 Archer Av, WLSP, 60480	3209	12W-9S	C3
Wilmette Village Hall 1200 Wilmette Av, WLMT, 60091	2812	3W-13N	D6
Wilmington Branch Court 1165 S Water St, WMTN, 60481	3943	27W-39S	D1
Wilmington City Hall 1165 S Water St, WMTN, 60481	3943	27W-39S	D1
Winfield Village Hall 27W465 Jewell Rd, WNFD, 60190	3023	27W-0S	C6
Winnetka Village Hall 510 Green Bay Rd, WNKA, 60093	2812	5W-15N	B2
Winthrop Harbor Village Hall 830 Sheridan Rd, WPHR, 60096	2363	9W-42N	C6
Wonder Lake Village Hall 4200 Thompson Rd, WRLK, 60097	2469	37W-36N	B4
Wood Dale City Hall 404 N Wood Dale Rd, WDDL, 60191	2915	18W-6N	A7
Woodridge Village Hall 5 Plaza Dr, WDRG, 60517	3205	21W-8S	D1
Woodstock City Hall 121 W Calhoun St, WDSK, 60098	2581	41W-31N	D1
Worth Twp Hall 11601 S Pulaski Rd, ALSP, 60803	3276	4W-13S	C4
Worth Village Hall 7112 W 111th St, WRTH, 60482	3274	8W-12S	E3
Yorkville City Hall 800 Game Farm Rd, YKVL, 60560	3333	43W-14S	B1
Zion City Hall 2828 Sheridan Rd, ZION, 60099	2422	10W-40N	B4

Cemeteries

FEATURE NAME	MAP#	CGS	GRID
Abraham Lincoln National Veteran's Cem, CnhT	3763	27W-33S	E3
Acacia Cem, CHCG	2974	10W-5N	B1
Adams Cem, CRTE	3685	1W-29S	A2
Alden Cem, AdnT	2349	45W-41N	B7
Allerton Ridge Cem, LMBD	3084	19W-2S	C3
All Saints Cem, CHCG	2917	11W-7N	D4
All Saints Cem, DSPN	2808	13W-12N	E7
Angola Cem, LKVL	2475	22W-37N	B1
Antioch Hillside Cem, ANTH	2357	24W-42N	D6
Archer Woods Cem, HYHL	3209	11W-9S	E3
Arlington Cem, EMHT	2972	15W-2N	B7
Arlington Heights Cem, ANHT	2807	16W-14N	D4
Ascension Cem, GNOK	2592	14W-30N	B1
Assumption Cem, BlmT	3508	0E-23S	E4
Assumption Cem, WnfT	3081	28W-1S	B2
Avon Centre Cem, AvnT	2475	21W-35N	D7
Barber's Corners Cem, BGBK	3205	22W-10S	C6
Barrett Cem, LKPT	3420	20W-20S	C5
Benton Greenwood Cem, BHPK	2421	12W-39N	B5
Bethania Cem, JSTC	3210	10W-8S	A2
Bethel & Ridgeland Cem, CHCG	2920	5W-7N	B4
Beverly Cem, WthT	3276	3W-14S	E5
Blackberry Cem, BbyT	3017	43W-1N	A4
Bluff City Cem, ELGN	2855	32W-10N	D7
Bohemian Cem, RedT	3942	30W-42S	D7
Bohemian National Cem, CHCG	2920	4W-6N	C5
Bronswood Cem, OKBK	3085	16W-3S	E6
Burr Oak Cem, ALSP	3276	5W-14S	A6
Calvary Cem, AURA	3138	35W-6S	B4
Calvary Cem, BlmT	3595	2W-27S	C5
Calvary Cem, EVTN	2867	2W-9N	C6
Calvary Cem, LKPT	3341	22W-18S	D7
Calvary Cem, WCHI	3022	29W-0N	D4
Calvary Cem, WDSK	2524	42W-31N	B7
Campton Cem, CmpT	2962	40W-2N	C7
Carr Harrison Cem, RGWD	2470	34W-36N	B3
Cary Cem, CRY	2695	30W-23N	E1
Cedar Park Cem, CTPK	3278	1W-14S	A6
Cedarvale Cem, RcmT	2413	32W-39N	A5
Chapel Hill Gardens Cem, YkTp	3085	17W-1S	C1
Chapel Hill Gardens South Cem, OKLN	3275	6W-13S	D3
Christ the King Cem, MchT	2469	36W-36N	E3
Church Of St. Mary Cem, MHRY	2528	32W-33N	B2
Clarendon Hills Cem, DRN	3145	18W-7S	A7
Concordia Cem, FTPK	3030	9W-0S	B5
Concordia Cem, HMND	3430		E2
Coral Cem, CrlT	2635	47W-24N	B7
Cotton Cem, BCVL	4030	33W-44S	A3
County Cem, BmnT	3426	5W-19S	C1
County Farm Cem, JLET	3497	27W-24S	C7
Crete Cem, CRTE	3685	1W-29S	B2
Crystal Lake Cem, CLLK	2639	36W-25N	E5
Crystal Lake Memorial Park, NndT	2639	36W-27N	C1
Danish Cem, LMNT	3342	20W-15S	C1
Deerfield Cem, DRFD	2756	10W-20N	E1
Dundee Twp Cem East, EDND	2801	32W-15N	C3
Dundee Twp Cem West, WDND	2800	34W-16N	E2
Dunham-Chemung Cem, DhmT	2463	53W-37N	A1
East Aurora Cem, AURA	3138	35W-7S	B7
East Batavia Cem, BTVA	3020	35W-0S	C7
East Fox Lake Cem, LkvT	2474	24W-36N	C3
Eckert Cem, GwdT	2525	40W-34N	B1
Eden Memorial Park, SRPK	2973	12W-5N	B1
Elemwood Cem, YKVL	3333	43W-14S	B1
Elk Grove Cem, EGVV	2861	18W-11N	A4
Elmhurst Cem, JltT	3499	22W-24S	D6
Elm Lawn Mausoleum & Cem, EMHT	2972	15W-2N	B7
Elmwood Memorial Cem, RVGV	2974	10W-3N	A4
English Prairie Cem, BtnT	2355	29W-41N	B7
Evergreen Cem, BRTN	2750	26W-18N	E3
Evergreen Cem, ENGN	3212	4W-9S	D4
Evergreen Hills Memorial Gardens, - CteT	3596	1W-28S	A7
Fairfield Cem, ElaT	2645	21W-24N	D7
Fairmount-Willow Hills Cem, PlsT	3209	13W-10S	A6
Fairview Cem, GwdT	2525	39W-32N	D4
Fairview Memorial Park Cem, NHLK	2972	14W-3N	D6
First Evangelical Lutheran Cem, ALSP	3276	5W-15S	C7
Forest Hill Cem, MltT	3025	22W-1N	D3
Forest Home Cem, FTPK	3030	10W-0S	B6
Fort Sheridan Cem, LKFT	2650	9W-24N	C6
Frankfort Cem, FKFT	3503	11W-25S	E7
Fredens Cem, BNVL	2971	16W-4N	E3
French Cem, MTGY	3199	36W-9S	D4
Fullersburg Cem, HNDL	3086	15W-4S	A7
Glencoe Pioneer Cem, HDPK	2758	7W-20N	C2
Glen Oak Cem, PvsT	3029	13W-1S	A7
Glen Oak Cem, WCHI	3022	30W-1N	C2
Graceland Cem, CHCG	2977	1W-5N	D1
Grant Cem, GrtT	2530	26W-33N	D3
Grass Lake Cem, AntT	2415	26W-39N	E5
Greenwood Cem, GNWD	2468	38W-35N	D5
Griswald Cem, LtRT	3332	46W-15S	A2
Hadley Cem, HMGN	3421	17W-21S	D6
Hampshire Center Cem, HshT	2795	47W-16N	D1
Hebrew Cem, CHCG	2977	1W-4N	D2
Hebron Cem, HBRN	2351	40W-41N	A7
Hickory Union Cem, AntT	2359	19W-42N	C6
Highland Memorial Park Cem, WrnT	2534	17W-33N	C4
Hillcrest Cem, BGBK	3205	22W-10S	C6
Hillside Cem, GNCY	2353		B2
Hills of Rest Cem, TroT	3497	28W-23S	B5
Holy Cross Cem, CTCY	3430	3E-18S	A1
Holy Cross Cem, CTHL	3497	26W-22S	E1
Holy Sepulchre Cem, ALSP	3275	7W-13S	C3
Home Oaks Cem, LkvT	2417	22W-39N	C4
Huntley Cem, HTLY	2692	40W-20N	A7
Immanuel Cem, HLSD	3086	13W-2S	D2
Irving Park Boulevard Cem, CHCG	2974	9W-4N	B2
Ivanhoe Cem, MDLN	2589	21W-28N	D6
Jericho Cem, SgrT	3197	43W-9S	A5
Jerome Cem, DhmT	2464	49W-37N	C2
Jewish Cemeteries, FTPK	3030	9W-1S	C7
Jewish Waldheim Cem, NRIV	3088	9W-1S	D1
Klinger Cem, MhtT	3766	20W-33S	B3
Knopf Cem, BFGV	2754	17W-20N	A1
Lake Forest Cem, LKFT	2594	10W-27N	B7
Lake Mound Cem, ZION	2422	10W-39N	B4
Lakeside Cem, LYVL	2591	16W-29N	C4
Lakewood Memorial Park, HnrT	2856	30W-10N	A7
Lake Zurich Cem, LKZH	2698	23W-23N	E2
Lawrence Cem, CmgT	2405	51W-39N	C5
Lincoln Cem, WthT	3276	4W-14S	E6
Lincoln Memorial Park Cem, OswT	3200	34W-10S	E7
Linn-Hebron Cem, HbnT	2350	42W-42N	B5
Lisle Cem, LSLE	3143	22W-4S	B1
Lithuanian National Cem, JSTC	3209	11W-9S	E3
Little Rock Twp Cem, LtRT	3259	47W-13S	C5
Little Woods Cem, WYNE	2909	33W-7N	B5
Lockport Cem, LKPT	3419	22W-19S	D3
Lutheran Cem, NLES	2864	8W-10N	D4
Lutheran Cem, TYPK	3425	7W-20S	C3
Maine Cem, PKRG	2917	11W-8N	D1
Maple Hill Cem, ELWD	3674	26W-32S	E7
Maplewood Cem, NLNX	3501	18W-24S	B6
Marengo City Cem, MRGO	2634	49W-26N	C2
Marshall Cem, NlxT	3502	15W-23S	B3
Mary Hill Cem, MaiT	2864	10W-10N	B4
McHenry County Memorial Park, DrrT	2582	40W-29N	B4
Memorial Park Cem, SKOK	2866	5W-12N	A1
Memory Gardens Cem, ANHT	2807	16W-14N	D4
Menorah Gardens Cem, BDVW	3087	11W-1S	D1
Millburn Cem, OMCK	2418	18W-38N	E7
Montrose Cem, CHCG	2920	5W-6N	B5
Mooney Cem, HDPK	2704	9W-21N	B6
Mound Cem, JltT	3500	21W-23S	A4
Mt Auburn Cem, DhmT	2464	49W-37N	D1
Mt Auburn Cem, SKNY	3089	8W-4S	A7
Mt Calvary Cem, LktT	3499	22W-21S	C1
Mt Carmel Cem, PvsT	3028	14W-0S	C7
Mt Emblem Cem, EMHT	2972	15W-3N	B5
Mt Forest Cem, ThtT	3428	0E-20S	E5
Mt Glenwood Cem, BlmT	3428	0E-22S	D7
Mt Greenwood Cem, CHCG	3277	3W-12S	A2
Mt Hope Cem, CHCG	3277	3W-13S	A4
Mt Hope Cem, ELGN	2855	32W-10N	C6
Mt Mayriv Cem, CHCG	2975	8W-4N	A2
Mt Moriah Cem, JLET	3498	24W-22S	D1
Mt Olive Cem, CHCG	2975	8W-4N	A2
Mt Olive Cem, WMTN	3943	27W-39S	D1
Mt Olivet Cem, AURA	3200	36W-8S	A3
Mt Olivet Cem, CHCG	3277	3W-13S	A3
Mt Olivet Cem, JltT	3499	22W-23S	D4
Mt Olivet Cem, RedT	4031	30W-43S	B1
Mt Olivet Memorial Park Cem, ZION	2362	12W-41N	C7
Mt Rest Cem, WDWH	2360	16W-42N	E6
Mt Vernon Memorial Estates, LMNT	3271	16W-14S	D6
Naperville Cem, NPVL	3141	27W-7S	C6
North Cem, SCRL	2964	35W-4N	B5
Northshore Cem, NCHI	2536	12W-32N	C6
Oakdale Cem, ZION	2362	13W-42N	A7
Oak Glen Lutheran Cem, LNSG	3429	2E-21S	D6
Oak Grove Cem, BtlT	3261	42W-12S	E4
Oak Hill Cem, GNVA	3020	34W-1N	C2
Oak Hill Cem, HMND	3430		D2
Oak Hill Cem, PSPK	3346	11W-15S	A1
Oak Hill Cem, WthT	3276	4W-14S	D5
Oakland Cem, DLTN	3351	2E-17S	C6
Oakland Cem, WDSK	2524	42W-31N	B7
Oak Lawn Cem, CstT	4031	29W-42S	D1
Oak Lawn Cem, TNTN	3428	0W-21S	B6
Oak Ridge Cem, LNSG	3429	2E-21S	C6
Oak Ridge Cem, PvsT	3086	13W-1S	E1
Oakwood Cem, WCHI	3022	29W-1N	D3
Oakwood Cem, WKGN	2537	10W-33N	B4
Oakwood Cem, WMTN	3853	27W-39S	C7
Oakwoods Cem, CHCG	3152	1E-7S	E6
Orland-Tinley Park Cem, TYPK	3424	10W-20S	B4
Ostend Cem, MHRY	2526	36W-34N	E2
Oswego Prairie Cem, OswT	3264	34W-13S	D4
Parkholm Cem, LGPK	3087	12W-2S	B3
Peace Cem, OSWG	3263	37W-12S	D3
Peotone Cem, WllT	3861	8W-37S	B3
Pineview Memorial Park Cem, BHPK	2422	10W-38N	A7
Plainfield Cem, PNFD	3416	29W-18S	C1
Pleasant Hill Cem, FKFT	3591	12W-25S	C1
Prairie Grove Cem, PRGV	2641	31W-27N	C1
Queen of Heaven Cem, PvsT	3086	14W-1S	C1
Randhill Park Cem, PltT	2753	18W-17N	D5
Resthaven Cem, CHCG	2916	15W-5N	B7
Restvale Cem, ALSP	3275	6W-13S	E4
Resurrection Cem, GnvT	3019	37W-0S	C6
Resurrection Cem, JSTC	3210	10W-8S	B1
Resurrection Cem, RMVL	3340	24W-15S	E2
Richmond Cem, RHMD	2353	34W-42N	C6
Ridgefield Cem, CLLK	2639	37W-27N	C1
Ridgewood Cem, MaiT	2863	11W-12N	D1
Ringwood Cem, RGWD	2470	34W-36N	D4
River Hills Memorial Park, BtvT	3078	35W-2S	B4
Riverside Cem, MTGY	3199	36W-9S	D4
River Valley Memorial Gardens Cem, - WDND	2800	34W-14N	E5
Rosehill Cem, CHCG	2921	2W-7N	A4
Rose Hill Cem, GGnT	3591	12W-28S	D7
Rosemont Cem, CHCG	2975	8W-4N	A2
Russian Cem, LKPT	3419	22W-20S	C4
Sacred Heart Cem, MRGO	2634	50W-27N	B1
Sacred Heart Cem, NHBK	2757	8W-18N	D4
Sacred Heart Cem, PlsT	3209	11W-11S	E7
St. Adalbert Cem, NLES	2918	8W-8N	E1
St. Alphonsus Cem, LMNT	3270	19W-14S	D7
St. Anne's Cem, PKFT	3595	4W-27S	A4

Chicago 7-County Points of Interest Index

FEATURE NAME Address City ZIP Code	MAP#	CGS	GRID
St. Benedict Catholic Cem, CTWD	3348	5W-15S	B2
St. Boniface Cem, CHCG	2921	1W-6N	D6
St. Casimir Lithuanian Cem, CHCG	3276	5W-13S	B3
St. Gabriel Cem, BmnT	3426	5W-19S	A2
St. Gall Cem, ELBN	3017	43W-2N	A2
St. Isidore Cem, BMDL	2968	25W-4N	B3
St. James Cem, LmnT	3272	15W-12S	A2
St. James Cem, SLVL	3597	2E-26S	C3
St. John's Cem, BNHL	2695	31W-22N	E4
St. John's Cem, FftT	3503	13W-24S	A5
St. John's Cem, HGKN	3147	12W-7S	C6
St. John's Cem, JLET	3498	24W-22S	D3
St. John's Cem, WshT	3864	0E-37S	E4
St. John the Baptist Cem, JNBG	2471	31W-35N	E5
St. Joseph Cem, AURA	3138	35W-5S	B3
St. Joseph Cem, HRVD	2464	50W-37N	B1
St. Joseph Cem, JLET	3498	24W-22S	D1
St. Joseph Cem, MhtT	3677	19W-30S	D3
St. Joseph's Cem, RHMD	2353	34W-43N	C4
St. Joseph's Cem, RVGV	2974	10W-3N	A4
St. Lucas Cem, CHCG	2920	5W-6N	B5
St. Luke's Cem, ITSC	2969	21W-5N	E1
St. Luke's Cem, WshT	3864	0W-37S	D3
St. Mary's Cem, CHCG	3212	4W-10S	C4
St. Mary's Cem, CTHL	3418	24W-21S	D6
St. Mary's Cem, EMHT	3027	16W-1N	D2
St. Mary's Cem, HTLY	2745	40W-20N	A1
St. Mary's Cem, LKFT	2594	10W-27N	A7
St. Mary's Cem, MKNA	3503	13W-23S	A3
St. Mary's Cem, MNKA	3583	33W-28S	A7
St. Mary's Cem, PnfT	3338	29W-16S	D5
St. Mary's Cem, RtdT	2799	38W-15N	B4
St. Mary's Cem, WKGN	2537	10W-33N	B3
St. Mathew Cem, LMNT	3270	20W-14S	C7
St. Michael Cem, AURA	3138	35W-6S	B4
St. Michael's Cem, WHTN	3082	25W-1S	C1
St. Michael the Archangel Cem, PLTN	2805	22W-13N	B6
St. Nicholas Cem, AURA	3138	34W-7S	D7
St. Nicholas Cem, CHCG	2917	11W-7N	E4
St. Patrick Cem, LKFT	2649	12W-24N	B7
St. Patrick's Cem, DGvT	3271	18W-11S	A1
St. Patrick's Cem, JLET	3498	24W-23S	D5
St. Patrick's Cem, WDWH	2419	16W-40N	E2
St. Paul Cem, BlmT	3507	2W-23S	C4
St. Paul Lutheran Cem, MPPT	2807	15W-13N	E7
St. Paul Lutheran Cem, MTGY	3200	35W-9S	A5
St. Paul's Cem, ADSN	2970	19W-4N	D4
St. Paul's Cem, BMDL	2969	22W-5N	B1
St. Paul's Cem, MONE	3683	6W-31S	A6
St. Paul's Cem, SKOK	2865	6W-10N	D4
St. Paul's Cem, WshT	3774	1W-36S	A7
St. Peter & Paul Cem, NPVL	3141	26W-6S	E4
St. Peter's Cem, GGnT	3592	9W-29S	D7
St. Peter's Cem, SKOK	2865	6W-10N	E5
Saints Cyril & Methodius Cem, JltT	3499	21W-22S	E2
Sand Lake Cem, LkvT	2475	21W-37N	D1
Scandinavian Cem, GwdT	2524	41W-34N	D1
Scottish Cem, MngT	2578	49W-28N	B5
Serbian National Cem, WrnT	2534	16W-32N	D5
Skyline Memorial Park, MonT	3683	6W-30S	A2
Smyna German Cem, HRPK	2911	27W-7N	D5
South Cem, SCRL	2964	35W-2N	C7
Spring Lake Memorial Garden, AURA	3199	36W-8S	E3
SS Cyril & Methodius Cem, LMNT	3270	19W-14S	D7
Sugar Grove Cem, SRGV	3135	42W-5S	D2
Sunset Memorial Lawns, GNVW	2810	10W-15N	A3
Transfiguration Cem, FmtT	2644	24W-27N	C1
Trinity Cem, CteT	3685	0W-30S	B3
Troutman Grove Cem, JLET	3674	26W-28S	E1
Union Cem, BNHL	2749	30W-17N	B6
Union Cem, CLLK	2640	35W-26N	A3
Union Cem, CrlT	2635	47W-25N	C5
Union Cem, SCRL	2964	35W-4N	B5
Union Ridge Cem, CHCG	2918	8W-6N	E5
Vermont Cem, WldT	3265	31W-11S	E1
Vernon Cem, LNSH	2702	15W-23N	B2
Village Cem, SEGN	2908	33W-8N	E3
Village Of Algonquin Cem, ALGN	2694	33W-21N	E6
Waldheim Cem, FTPK	3030	10W-0S	B6
Warren Cem, GRNE	2477	16W-35N	D6
Washington Cem, RcmT	2354	32W-42N	C6
Washington Church Cem, PltT	2798	39W-13N	D7
Washington Memory Gardens, TNTN	3428	0W-21S	B7
Washington Street Cem, LMBD	3026	20W-0N	B5
Wayne Center Cem, WynT	2966	29W-4N	E3
West Aurora Cem, AURA	3138	35W-6S	B6
West Batavia Cem, BTVA	3078	35W-1S	B3
Westlawn Cem, CHCG	2974	10W-5N	B1
Westside Cem, GNVA	3020	35W-1N	C3
Wheaton Cem, WHTN	3082	25W-1S	B1
White Memorial Cem, CbaT	2697	26W-21N	D6
Whitney Cem, CmpT	2962	40W-5N	C2
Willow Lawn Cem, VNHL	2647	16W-24N	C7
Windridge Cem, AlqT	2642	29W-24N	B6
Woodlawn Cem, FTPK	3088	9W-1S	C1
Woodlawn Memorial Park Cem, TroT	3497	28W-23S	A5
Wray-Imeson Cem, BtnT	2414	30W-41N	A1
Wunders Cem, CHCG	2977	1W-4N	D2
Zion Cem, BNVL	2971	16W-4N	D4
Zion Cem, CteT	3685	0W-30S	B4
Zion Lutheran Cem, OMFD	3506	4W-25S	E7
Zion Luthern Cem, OKBK	3086	15W-3S	A6

Colleges & Universities

FEATURE NAME Address City ZIP Code	MAP#	CGS	GRID
Aurora University 374 S Gladstone Av, AURA, 60506	3199	37W-7S	C1
Benedictine University 5700 College Rd, LSLE, 60532	3142	24W-6S	D5
Catholic Theological Union Chicago 5401 S Cornell Av, CHCG, 60615	3153	2E-5S	B2
Chicago City Wide College 226 W Jackson Blvd, CHCG, 60606	3034	0W-0S	B5
Chicago State University 9501 S Dr Martin L King Jr Dr, CHCG, 60628	3214	0E-11S	D6
City College of Chicago-Harold Wash-College 30 E Lake St, CHCG, 60601	3034	0E-0N	C4
City College of Chicago-Kennedy King-College 6800 S Wentworth Av, CHCG, 60621	3152	0W-7S	B6
CIty Coll of Chicago-Richard J Daley-Coll 7500 S Pulaski Rd, CHCG, 60652	3212	5W-8S	B1
City College of Chicago-West Side-Tech Inst 2800 S Western Av, CHCG, 60608	3091	3W-2S	A3
City Coll of Chicago-Wilbur Wright-Coll 4300 N Narragansett Av, CHCG, 60634	2975	8W-5N	A1
College of DuPage 425 Fawell Blvd, GNEN, 60137	3083	22W-2S	B3
College of DuPage-Naperville 1223 Rickert Dr, NPVL, 60540	3203	28W-8S	A2
College of Lake County-Lakeshore 111 N Genesee St, WKGN, 60085	2537	10W-34N	B1
College of Lake Co-Southlake Edual-Campus 1120 Milwaukee Av, VNHL, 60061	2702	15W-23N	A2
Columbia College 600 S Michigan Av, CHCG, 60605	3034	0E-0S	C6
Concordia University-River Forest 7400 Augusta St, RVFT, 60305	3030	9W-1N	D2
DePaul University-Lincoln Park-Campus 2250 N Kenmore Av, CHCG, 60614	2977	1W-2N	E6
DePaul University-Naperville 150 W Warrenville Rd, NPVL, 60563	3081	27W-4S	D7
DePaul University-Oak Forest Campus 16333 Kilbourn Av, OKFT, 60452	3426	5W-19S	C2
DePaul University-O'Hare Campus 3166 River Rd, DSPN, 60018	2917	11W-8N	D3
DePaul University-Rolling Meadows-Campus 2550 Golf Rd, RGMW, 60008	2860	19W-12N	C2
DePaul University-The Loop 1 E Jackson Blvd, CHCG, 60604	3034	0E-0S	C5
Dominican University 7900 Division St, RVFT, 60305	3030	9W-1N	B2
Dominican University-Priory Campus 7200 Division St, RVFT, 60305	3030	9W-1N	D1
East-West University 816 S Michigan Av, CHCG, 60605	3034	0E-0S	C6
Elgin Community College 1700 Spartan Dr, ELGN, 60123	2854	35W-10N	A6
Elmhurst College 190 S Prospect Av, EMHT, 60126	3027	16W-1N	E2
Erikson University 420 N Wabash Av, CHCG, 60611	3034	0W-0N	C3
Fox College 4201 W 93rd St, OKLN, 60453	3212	5W-10S	B5
Governors State University 1 University Pkwy, UYPK, 60466	3683	5W-29S	C1
Harper College 1200 W Algonquin Rd, PLTN, 60067	2805	22W-13N	B5
Harry S Truman College 1145 W Wilson Av, CHCG, 60640	2921	1W-5N	D7
Hebrew Theological College 7135 Carpenter Rd, SKOK, 60077	2919	6W-8N	D1
IBEW-NECA Technical Institute 6201 W 115th St, ALSP, 60803	3275	7W-13S	B4
Illinois College of Optometry 3241 S Michigan Av, CHCG, 60616	3092	0E-3S	C4
Illinois Institute of Art-Chicago 350 N Orleans St, CHCG, 60606	3034	0W-0N	A4
Illinois Institute of Art-Schaumburg 1000 N Plaza Dr, SMBG, 60173	2859	21W-11N	E3
Illinois Institute of Technology 3300 S Federal St, CHCG, 60616	3092	0W-3S	C4
Joliet Junior College 1215 Houbolt Rd, JLET, 60431	3585	28W-25S	A1
Joliet Junior College-City Center-Campus 214 N Ottawa St, JLET, 60432	3498	24W-23S	E4
Joliet Junior College-North Campus 1125 W 135th St, RMVL, 60441	3340	25W-16S	B3
Judson College 1151 N State St, ELGN, 60123	2854	34W-13N	D1
Kaes College 5909 N Rogers Av, CHCG, 60646	2920	5W-7N	B4
Kendall College-Evanston 2408 Orrington Av, EVTN, 60201	2867	2W-12N	B1
Lake Forest College 555 N Sheridan Rd, LKFT, 60045	2650	10W-26N	B2
Lake Forest Graduate School of-Management 1905 N Field Ct, LKFT, 60045	2649	13W-26N	A3
Lewis University 1 University Dr E, RMVL, 60441	3341	23W-18S	A7
Lewis University-Hickory Hills 9634 S Roberts Rd, HYHL, 60457	3210	10W-11S	B6
Lewis University-Oak Brook 2122 York Rd, OKBK, 60523	3086	15W-1S	A2
Lewis University-Shorewood 247 Brook Forest Av, SRWD, 60404	3496	30W-23S	C5
Lewis University-Tinley Park Maple Creek Dr, TYPK, 60477	3424	9W-22S	E7
Loyola University Chicago-Lakeshore-Campus 6525 N Sheridan Rd, CHCG, 60626	2921	1W-8N	D2
Loyola University Chicago-Maywood-Campus 2160 S 1st Av, MYWD, 60153	3030	10W-0S	A6
Loyola University Chicago-Water Tower-Campus 820 N Michigan Av, CHCG, 60611	3034	0E-1N	C2
MacCormac College 29 E Madison St, CHCG, 60603	3034	0E-0S	C4
Malcolm X College 1900 W Van Buren St, CHCG, 60612	3033	2W-0S	C5
McHenry County College CLLK, 60012	2639	37W-27N	B1
Meadville Lombard Theological-School 5701 S Woodlawn Av, CHCG, 60637	3153	1E-6S	A3
Midwestern University 555 31st St, YkTp, 60515	3084	19W-3S	D5
Moraine Valley Community College 10900 S 88th Av, PSHL, 60465	3274	11W-12S	A2
Morton College 3801 S Central Av, CCRO, 60804	3089	6W-3S	D5
NAES College 2838 W Peterson Av, CHCG, 60659	2920	3W-7N	E3
National College of Naprapathic-Method 3330 N Milwaukee Av, CHCG, 60641	2976	5W-4N	B3
National Louis University 122 S Michigan Av, CHCG, 60603	3034	0E-0S	C5
National-Louis University-Elgin 620 Tollgate Rd, ELGN, 60123	2800	34W-14N	D6
National-Louis University-Evanston 2840 Sheridan Rd, EVTN, 60201	2813	2W-13N	B7
National-Louis University-Lisle 850 Warrenville Rd, LSLE, 60532	3083	22W-4S	B7
National-Louis University-Wheeling 1000 Capitol Dr, WLNG, 60090	2808	14W-16N	C1
North Central College 30 N Brainard St, NPVL, 60540	3141	26W-6S	D5
Northeastern Illinois University 5500 N St. Louis Av, CHCG, 60625	2920	4W-6N	C5
Northern Illinois Univ-Hoffman-Estates Camp 5555 Trillium Blvd, HFET, 60192	2802	29W-13N	B6
North Park University Chicago 3225 N Spaulding Av, CHCG, 60625	2920	4W-6N	D6
Northwestern Bus College-Bridgeview-Campus 7725 S Harlem Av, BGVW, 60455	3210	8W-8S	E1
Northwestern Business College-Chicago-Campus 4939 N Lipps Av, CHCG, 60630	2919	6W-6N	D6
Northwestern University-Chicago 710 N Lake Shore Dr, CHCG, 60611	3034		D2
Northwestern University-Evanston-Campus 633 Clark St, EVTN, 60201	2867	2W-11N	B2
Oakton Community College-Des Plaines-Campus 1600 E Golf Rd, DSPN, 60016	2863	13W-12N	A1
Oakton Comm College-Ray Hartstein-Campus 7701 Lincoln Av, SKOK, 60077	2865	6W-9N	E6
Olive Harvey College 10001 S Woodlawn Av, CHCG, 60628	3215	1E-11S	A7
Olive-Harvey College-South Chicago 3055 E 92nd St, CHCG, 60617	3216	3E-10S	A5
Olivet-Nazarene Univ-Rolling Meadows-Campus 3601 Algonquin Rd, RGMW, 60008	2860	20W-12N	B1
Prairie State College 202 S Halsted St, CHHT, 60411	3508	1W-24S	B4
Robert Morris College-Bensenville-Campus 1000 Tower Ln, BNVL, 60106	2915	17W-7N	C4
Robert Morris College-Chicago 401 S State St, CHCG, 60605	3034	0E-0S	C5
Robert Morris College-DuPage Campus 905 Meridian Lakes Dr, AURA, 60504	3140	30W-6S	B5
Robert Morris College-Lake County-Campus 1507 S Waukegan Rd, WrnT, 60085	2535	13W-32N	E5
Robert Morris College-Orland Park-Campus 82 Orland Square Dr, ODPK, 60462	3345	11W-17S	E6
Roosevelt University 430 S Michigan Av, CHCG, 60605	3034	0E-0S	C5
Roosevelt University-Schaumburg-Campus 1400 N Roosevelt Blvd, SMBG, 60173	2859	21W-12N	E2
Rosalind Franklin Univ of Med &-Science 3333 Green Bay Rd, NCHI, 60088	2593	11W-30N	D3
Rush University 600 W Congress Pkwy, CHCG, 60612	3033	2W-0S	C6
St. Augustine College 1345 W Argyle St, CHCG, 60640	2921	1W-6N	D6
St. Xavier University-Chicago 3700 W 103rd St, CHCG, 60655	3276	4W-11S	C1
St. Xavier University-Orland Park 18230 Orland Pkwy, ODPK, 60467	3423	12W-21S	D7
Shimer College 414 N Sheridan Rd, WKGN, 60085	2537	10W-34N	B1
Southern Illinois University-Great-Lakes 2221 Macdonough St, NCHI, 60088	2537	10W-31N	B7
South Suburban College 15800 State St, SHLD, 60473	3350	0W-18S	C7
Telshe Yeshiva-Chicago 3535 W Foster Av, CHCG, 60625	2920	4W-6N	C6
The School of the Art Institute of-Chicago 37 S Wabash Av, CHCG, 60603	3034	0E-0S	C5
Trinity Christian College 6601 W College Dr, PSHT, 60463	3275	8W-14S	A5
Trinity International University 2065 Half Day Rd, BKBN, 60015	2703	12W-23N	B3
Triton College 2000 N 5th Av, RVGV, 60171	2974	10W-2N	A7
Univ Ctr of Lake County-Grayslake-Campus 1200 University Center Dr, GYLK, 60030	2533	19W-34N	C1
University of Chicago 5801 S Ellis Av, CHCG, 60637	3152	1E-6S	E3
University of Illinois at Chicago 601 S Morgan St, CHCG, 60607	3033	1W-0S	E6
University of St. Francis-Joliet 500 N Wilcox St, JLET, 60435	3498	24W-23S	D3
Vander Cook College of Music 3140 S Federal St, CHCG, 60616	3092	0W-2S	B3
Waubonsee Community College-Aurora 5 E Galena Blvd, AURA, 60506	3138	35W-7S	B7
Waubonsee Community College-Copley-Campus 2060 Ogden Av, AURA, 60504	3201	33W-9S	A4
Waubonsee Community College-Sugar-Grove SgrT, 60554	3135	43W-4S	B2
Westwood College-DuPage Campus 7155 Janes Av, WDRG, 60517	3205	21W-8S	E1
Wheaton College 501 College Av, WHTN, 60187	3024	24W-0S	D6

Entertainment & Sports

FEATURE NAME Address City ZIP Code	MAP#	CGS	GRID
A Crew of Patches Theatre Company 1337 W Fargo Av, CHCG, 60626	2867		D7
Alexian Field Baseball Stadium 1999 S Springinsguth Rd, SMBG, 60193	2912	25W-8N	B3
Allstate Arena 6920 Mannheim Rd, RSMT, 60018	2917	13W-8N	A1
Aon Center 200 E Randolph St, CHCG, 60601	3034	0E-0N	C4
Apollo Theatre 2540 N Lincoln Av, CHCG, 60614	2977	1W-3N	E5
Appetite Theatre 900 W Ainslie St, CHCG, 60640	2921	1W-6N	E6
Aragon Ballroom 1106 W Lawrence Av, CHCG, 60640	2921	1W-6N	D6
Arctic Ice Arena 10700 160th St, ODPK, 60467	3423	13W-19S	A1
Arie Crown Theatre 2301 S Lake Shore Dr, CHCG, 60616	3092	0E-2S	D1
Arlington Park 2200 W Euclid Av, ANHT, 60005	2806	19W-14N	C4
Athenaeum Theatre 2936 N Southport Av, CHCG, 60657	2977	2W-3N	C4
Auditorium Theatre 50 E Congress Pkwy, CHCG, 60605	3034	0E-0S	C5
Balmoral Park Race Track 26435 S Dixie Hwy, CteT, 60417	3685	0W-32S	C6
Benedetti-Wehrli Stadium NPVL, 60540	3141	26W-7S	D6
Biograph Theater 2433 N Lincoln Av, CHCG, 60614	2977	1W-3N	E5
Briar Street Theatre 3133 N Halsted St, CHCG, 60657	2977	1W-3N	E4
Bridgeview Stadium W 71st St, BGVW, 60455	3148	9W-7S	D7
Brookfield Zoo-Chicago Zoological-Park 8401 31st St, BKFD, 60513	3088	10W-3S	A4
Cadillac Palace Theatre 151 W Randolph St, CHCG, 60602	3034	0W-0N	B4
Cantigny Park Gardens 1S151 Winfield Rd, WnfT, 60187	3081	27W-1S	B1
Cascade Mountain Ski & Snowboard-Area 28W545 W Ogden Av, NPVL, 60563	3141	28W-6S	A4
Center Ice of DuPage 450 Highland Av, MltT, 60137	3025	22W-1N	B2
Chicago Blaze Rugby Club 13011 Smith Rd, LMNT, 60439	3342	20W-15S	A1
Chicago Botanical Garden 1000 Lake Cook Rd, NTrT, 60062	2758	7W-18N	A2
Chicago Center for Performing Arts 777 N Green St, CHCG, 60622	3033	1W-1N	E2
Chicago Indoor Racing 301 Hastings Ln, BFGV, 60089	2755	15W-20N	A1
Chicagoland Speedway 500 Speedway Blvd, JLET, 60433	3587	23W-27S	B6
Chicago Motor Speedway 3301 S Laramie Av, CCRO, 60804	3089	6W-3S	E4
Chicago Symphony Orchestra Hall 220 S Michigan Av, CHCG, 60604	3034	0E-0S	C5
Chicago Theatre 175 N State St, CHCG, 60601	3034	0E-0N	C4
Chicago Theatre for Young Audiences 2625 N Clark St, CHCG, 60614	2978	0W-3N	A5
Children's Theater of Elgin 1700 Spartan Dr, ELGN, 60123	2854	36W-10N	A7
Chopin Theatre 1543 W Division St, CHCG, 60622	3033	2W-1N	C2
Christian Community Theater 700 Industrial Dr, CRY, 60013	2641	32W-24N	C7
Cicero Stadium 1909 S Laramie Av, CCRO, 60804	3089	6W-1S	E1
Civic Opera House 20 N Wacker Dr, CHCG, 60606	3034	0W-0N	A4
Clearwater Theater 96 W Main St, WDND, 60118	2801	33W-16N	A2
Congress Theater 2135 N Milwaukee Av, CHCG, 60647	2977	3W-2N	A6
Convention Center Indian Trail Rd, AURA, 60506	3138	35W-6S	A4
Convention Center University Pkwy, UYPK, 60466	3683	5W-29S	D2
Coral Cove Water Park 849 Lies Rd, CLSM, 60188	2967	27W-4N	D5
Cosley Zoo 1356 N Gary Av, WHTN, 60187	3024	25W-0N	B5
Court Theatre-University of Chicago 5535 S Ellis Av, CHCG, 60637	3152	1E-6S	E3
Curious Theatre Branch 3502 N Elston Av, CHCG, 60618	2976	4W-4N	D3
Cutting Hall 150 E Wood St, PLTN, 60067	2752	20W-16N	E7
Cypress Cove Aquatic Park 8301 N Janes Av, WDRG, 60517	3205	21W-9S	E4
David Adler Cultural Center 1700 N Milwaukee Av, LYVL, 60048	2591	16W-30N	D2
DePaul University Concert Hall 800 W Belden Av, CHCG, 60614	2977	1W-2N	E6
Dinorex Amusement Park 6250 Northwest Hwy, CLLK, 60014	2640	35W-25N	B5
Dinorex Amusement Park 1227 E Rand Rd, PTHT, 60004	2807	16W-15N	C3
Dolphin Cove Family Aquatic CPVL, 60110	2801	33W-16N	C1
Donald E Stephens Convention Center 5555 N River Rd, RSMT, 60018	2917	11W-6N	C5
Downers Grove Ice Arena 5501 Walnut Av, DRGV, 60515	3143	21W-5S	D3
Drury Lane Convention Center 100 Drury Ln, OKTR, 60181	3027	16W-1S	D7
DuPage County Fairgrounds 2015 Manchester Rd, WHTN, 60187	3023	26W-0S	E6
Eckersall Stadium 2423 E 82nd St, CHCG, 60617	3215	3E-9S	D2
Elfstrom Stadium 34W002 Cherry Ln, GnvT, 60134	3020	34W-0N	E4
Empress Casino-Joliet 2300 Empress Dr, JLET, 60436	3585	27W-26S	C4
Expo Center Apparel Center 350 N Orleans St, CHCG, 60606	3034	0W-0N	B4
Expo Center International-Amphitheatre 350 N Orleans St, CHCG, 60606	3034	0W-0N	B3
Ford Ctr for Perf Arts & Oriental-Theatre 24 W Randolph St, CHCG, 60601	3034	0W-0N	B4
Four Lakes Village Ski Area 5790 Lakeside Dr, LslT, 60532	3142	23W-6S	E4
Fox Valley Ice Arena & Fitness-Center 1996 Kirk Rd, GnvT, 60134	3020	34W-0N	E5
Free Associates Theater 1633 N Halsted St, CHCG, 60614	2978	0W-2N	A7
Freedom Hall Nathan Manilow Theatre 410 Lakewood Blvd, PKFT, 60466	3595	3W-26S	A3
Frontier Sports Complex 2720 95th St, NPVL, 60564	3202	29W-11S	C7
Genesee Theater 203 N Genesee St, WKGN, 60085	2537	10W-34N	B1
Glacier Ice Arena 670 Lakeview Pkwy, VNHL, 60061	2647	16W-25N	D5
Goodman Theatre 170 N Dearborn St, CHCG, 60601	3034	0W-0N	B4
Grand Victoria Casino 250 S Grove Av, ELGN, 60120	2855	33W-11N	A5
Harrah's Joliet 151 N Joliet St, JLET, 60432	3498	24W-23S	E4
Hawthorne Race Course 3501 S Laramie Av, SKNY, 60804	3089	6W-3S	E5
Hemmens Auditorium 150 Dexter Ct, ELGN, 60120	2854	34W-11N	E3
Hollywood Casino-Aurora 49 W Galena Blvd, AURA, 60506	3138	35W-7S	A7
Horseshoe Casino 777 Casino Center Dr, HMND, 46320	3280		E2
House Theatre of Chicago 4700 N Ravenswood Av, CHCG, 60640	2921	2W-5N	C7
Illinois Philharmonic Orchestra 377 Indianwood Blvd, PKFT, 60466	3595	3W-27S	B4
Illinois Theatre Center 371 Main St, PKFT, 60466	3595	3W-27S	B3
Inland Meeting & Expo Center 400 E Ogden Av, WTMT, 60559	3085	17W-4S	C7
Jack Benny Center for the Arts 39 Jack Benny Dr, WKGN, 60087	2480	10W-36N	B5
John G Shedd Aquarium 1200 S Lake Shore Dr, CHCG, 60605	3034	0E-0S	D6
Joliet Memorial Stadium 3000 W Jefferson St, JLET, 60435	3497	27W-24S	C5
Kane County Events Center 33W848 Cherry Ln, GnvT, 60134	3020	34W-0N	E4
Kane County Fairgrounds 525 S Randall Rd, SCRL, 60175	3019	37W-2N	D1
Kenosha County Fairgrounds 30820 111th St, SlmT, 53192	2356		A1
Kiddieland 8400 W North Av, MLPK, 60160	3030	10W-2N	A1
Kingsbridge Arboretum S Surrey Ln, ANHT, 60005	2860	18W-12N	E2
Ladd Arboretum 2024 McCormick Blvd, EVTN, 60201	2866	3W-12N	E1
Lake County Fairgrounds 19200 E Belvidere Rd, GYLK, 60030	2533	19W-32N	D4
Lakeshore Theater 3175 N Broadway St, CHCG, 60657	2978	0W-3N	A3
Lakeside Center at McCormick Place 2301 S Lake Shore Dr, CHCG, 60616	3092	0E-2S	D2
Lasalle Bank Theatre 18 W Monroe St, CHCG, 60603	3034	0W-0S	B5
Libertyville Sports Complex LYVL, 60048	2590	18W-30N	D1
Lifeline Theatre 6912 N Glenwood Av, CHCG, 60626	2921	1W-8N	C1
Lincoln Park Zoo 2001 N Cannon Dr, CHCG, 60614	2978	0W-2N	B6
Mandel Hall-University of Chicago 1131 E 57th St, CHCG, 60637	3153	1E-6S	A3
Mary Arrchie Theatre 735 W Sheridan Rd, CHCG, 60613	2977	0W-4N	E2
Maywood Park Race Track 8600 W North Av, PvsT, 60160	3030	10W-1N	A1
McCormick Place North 2301 S Dr Martin L King Jr Dr, CHCG, 60616	3092	0E-2S	C1
McCormick Place South 2301 S Dr Martin L King Jr Dr, CHCG, 60616	3092	0E-2S	D2
McHenry County Fairgrounds Country Club Rd, DrrT, 60098	2581	40W-30N	E1
McHenry County Fairgrounds WDSK, 60098	2524	40W-31N	E7
McHenry County Music Center 401 Country Club Rd, CLLK, 60014	2639	36W-25N	D5
Medinah Temple Theater 600 N Wabash Av, CHCG, 60611	3034	0E-0N	C3
Memorial Auditorium E Chicago St, ELGN, 60120	2855	32W-11N	D5
Millennium Park Bandshell N Columbus Dr, CHCG, 60603	3034	0E-0N	C4
Morton Arboretum LslT, 60532	3083	22W-4S	B7
Navy Pier Exhibit Complex 600 N Streeter Dr, CHCG, 60611	3034		E3
New Regal Theatre 1645 E 79th St, CHCG, 60617	3215	2E-8S	B1
Norris Cultural Arts Center 1040 Dunham Rd, SCRL, 60174	2964	34W-3N	E5
North Shore Center for Performing-Arts 9501 Skokie Blvd, SKOK, 60076	2865	6W-11N	E2
North Shore Theater of Wilmette 3000 Glenview Rd, WLMT, 60091	2811	5W-13N	E6
Northwestern University-Ryan Field 1501 Central St, EVTN, 60201	2813	2W-13N	A7
Oak Brook Polo Grounds 23700 W 119th St, WldT, 60564	3266	29W-13S	D6
Oak Park Conservatory 615 Garfield St, OKPK, 60304	3031	8W-0S	A6
Oasis Theater 12952 Western Av, BLID, 60406	3277	3W-15S	B7
Odeum Sports & Expo Center Arena 1033 N Villa Av, VLPK, 60101	2971	17W-2N	B7
Odyssey Fun World-Naperville 3440 Odyssey Ct, NPVL, 60563	3140	30W-4S	C1
Odyssey Fun World-Tinley Park 19111 Oak Park Av, TYPK, 60477	3505	8W-23S	A2
Orland Park Civic Center 14750 S Ravinia Av, ODPK, 60462	3345	12W-17S	D5
Paramount Theatre 23 E Galena Blvd, AURA, 60505	3138	35W-7S	B7
Petrillo Music Shell 235 S Columbus Dr, CHCG, 60603	3034	0E-0S	C5
Pfeifer Theatre-North Central-College 310 N Brainard St, NPVL, 60540	3141	26W-6S	D5
Pheasant Run Resort & Convention-Center 4051 E Main St, SCRL, 60174	2965	32W-3N	C6
Phillips Park Zoo 900 Ray C Moses Dr, AURA, 60505	3200	34W-9S	D3
Pick-Staiger Concert Hall 50 Arts Cir Dr, EVTN, 60201	2867	2W-11N	C2
Q Center Conference Center 1405 N 5th Av, SCRL, 60174	2964	35W-4N	B4
Raceway Park Ashland Av, CTPK, 60827	3277	1W-15S	D7
Raue Center 26 N Williams St, CLLK, 60014	2640	35W-26N	B4
Raven Theatre 6157 N Clark St, CHCG, 60660	2921	2W-7N	C3
Ravinia Festival Music Center 418 Lambert Tree Av, HDPK, 60035	2758	7W-20N	B1
Rialto Square Theatre 15 E Van Buren St, JLET, 60432	3499	23W-23S	A4
Riviera Theatre 4750 N Racine Av, CHCG, 60640	2921	1W-5N	D7
Rocket Ice Arena 180 Canterbury Ln, BGBK, 60440	3269	23W-12S	A2
Rosemont Theatre 5400 N River Rd, RSMT, 60018	2917	11W-6N	C5
Route 66 Raceway 500 Speedway Blvd, JLET, 60421	3587	23W-28S	B6
Royal George Theatre 1641 N Halsted St, CHCG, 60614	2978	0W-2N	A7
Schaumburg Convention Center N Thoreau Dr, SMBG, 60173	2859	21W-12N	E1
Schaumburg Prairie Center for the-Arts 201 Schaumburg Ct, SMBG, 60193	2859	22W-10N	C5
Sea Lion Aquatic Park 1825 Short St, LSLE, 60532	3143	23W-5S	A3
Sears Centre 5333 Prairie Stone Pkwy, HFET, 60192	2802	29W-13N	C6
Seascape Aquatic Park Moon Lake Blvd, HFET, 60169	2858	26W-12N	A2
Second City 1616 N Wells St, CHCG, 60614	2978	0W-2N	B7
Six Flags Great America 542 N Riverside Dr, GRNE, 60031	2535	15W-34N	B1
Six Flags Hurricane Harbor Great America, GRNE, 60031	2478	15W-35N	A6
Skyline Stage CHCG, 60611	3034		E3
Soldier Field 1410 E William L McFetridge Dr, CHCG, 60605	3034	0E-1S	D7
Splash Country 195 S Barnes Rd, AURA, 60506	3136	39W-7S	C6
Splash Station Waterpark 2780 Channahon Rd, JLET, 60436	3585	27W-26S	D2
Stage Left Theatre 3408 N Sheffield Av, CHCG, 60657	2977	1W-4N	E3
Theatre Building Chicago 1225 W Belmont Av, CHCG, 60657	2977	1W-3N	D4
The Edge Ice Arena 545 John St, BNVL, 60106	2972	15W-4N	B3
Thillens Stadium W Devon Av, LNWD, 60712	2920	4W-8N	D2
Tweeter Center 19100 Ridgeland Av, TYPK, 60477	3505	8W-22S	B2
UIC Pavilion 1150 W Harrison St, CHCG, 60607	3033	1W-0S	E5
United Center 1901 W Madison St, CHCG, 60612	3033	2W-0S	C5
US Cellular Field 333 W 35th St, CHCG, 60616	3092	0W-3S	B5
Uptown Theatre 4816 N Broadway St, CHCG, 60640	2921	1W-6N	D6
Vernon Hills Memorial Arbor Theater 50 N Fairway Dr, VNHL, 60061	2647	16W-25N	D6
Vic Theatre 3154 N Sheffield Av, CHCG, 60657	2977	1W-3N	E4
Victory Gardens Theater 2257 N Lincoln Av, CHCG, 60614	2978	0W-2N	A6
Villa Olivia Ski Area Naperville Rd, BRLT, 60103	2856	30W-9N	B7
Welsh-Ryan Arena 2705 Ashland Av, EVTN, 60201	2813	2W-13N	A7
Westin North Shore Hotel and Conv-Center 601 N Milwaukee Av, WLNG, 60090	2755	14W-18N	C2
White Water Canyon Water Park 8221 171st St, TYPK, 60477	3424	10W-20S	C4
Will County Fairgrounds 710 S West St, PTON, 60468	3860	9W-37S	E4
Wilmette Theatre 1122 Central Av, WLMT, 60091	2812	3W-13N	E5
Wilmot Mountain Ski Hill 11931 Fox River Rd, RdlT, 53181	2355		E2
Wilmot Speedway 30820 111th St, SlmT, 53192	2356		A1
Wrigley Field 1060 W Addison St, CHCG, 60613	2977	1W-4N	E2
Zimmerman Baseball Field NPVL, 60540	3141	26W-7S	D6
Zion Conservancy of Music Dowie Memorial Dr, ZION, 60099	2422	10W-40N	A3

Golf Courses

FEATURE NAME	MAP#	CGS	GRID
Addison GC, AddT	2970	19W-3N	D5
Addison Links & Tees, ADSN	2970	19W-4N	C3
Anetsberger GC, NHBK	2757	9W-16N	B6
Anetsberger Park & GC, NHBK	2757	9W-16N	B6
Antioch GC, AntT	2416	24W-40N	C3

FEATURE NAME Address City ZIP Code	MAP#	CGS	GRID
Apple Orchard GC, BRLT	2910	29W-7N	D5
Arboretum GC, BFGV	2701	17W-22N	C3
Arlington Lakes GC, ANHT	2806	19W-12N	D7
Arrowhead GC, MltT	3081	26W-2S	E4
Aurora CC, AURA	3199	37W-8S	C1
Balmoral Woods CC, CteT	3685	0E-32S	D7
Barrington Hills CC, BNHL	2750	27W-20N	B2
Barrington Park District GC, BRTN	2750	26W-20N	E1
Bartlett Hills GC, BRLT	2910	29W-8N	D3
Beverly CC, CHCG	3213	3W-10S	B4
Big Oaks GC, PTPR	2362		B3
Big Run GC, LktT	3341	21W-16S	E3
Billy Caldwell GC, CHCG	2919	6W-7N	D3
Biltmore CC, NBRN	2698	25W-23N	A3
Bittersweet GC, GRNE	2477	17W-35N	A7
Blackberry Oaks GC, BtlT	3262	40W-12S	B3
Black Sheep GC, BbyT	3075	41W-2S	E4
Bliss Creek GC, SRGV	3136	41W-6S	A4
Bloomingdale GC, BMDL	2969	22W-5N	C2
Bob-O-Link GC, HDPK	2704	8W-21N	E6
Bolingbrook GC, BGBK	3267	27W-14S	D6
Bonnie Brook GC, WKGN	2479	11W-37N	D3
Bonnie Dundee GC, EDND	2801	32W-16N	C1
Boone Creek GC, NndT	2583	35W-30N	E2
Boughton Ridge GC, BGBK	3205	22W-10S	C6
Boulder Ridge CC, LIHL	2693	37W-21N	C5
Brae Loch GC, AvnT	2533	19W-33N	D3
Braidwood Fairways GC, RedT	4031	30W-43S	D2
Briar Ridge CC, DYR	3510		E7
Briarwood CC, DRFD	2704	10W-20N	A7
Broken Arrow GC, LKPT	3420	20W-20S	B5
Bryn Mawr CC, LNWD	2920	5W-8N	B2
Buffalo Grove GC, BFGV	2754	17W-18N	C2
Bull Valley GC, WDSK	2582	39W-30N	B1
Burnham Woods GC, BNHM	3352	4E-16S	B3
Butler National GC, OKBK	3086	15W-2S	A3
Butterfield CC, YkTp	3085	17W-2S	B4
Calumet CC, HLCT	3427	2W-20S	C5
Cantigny GC, WnfT	3081	27W-1S	C2
Cardinal Creek GC, BCHR	3864	0W-36S	C2
Carillon North of Grayslake, GYLK	2476	20W-35N	A6
Carriage Greens CC, DRN	3206	18W-9S	E4
Cary CC, AlqT	2695	31W-22N	D3
Cedardell GC, LtRT	3259	47W-14S	D7
Chalet Hills GC, ODHL	2642	30W-26N	A3
Chapel Hill CC, MchT	2528	31W-34N	E1
Chicago GC, MltT	3082	25W-1S	B2
Chicago Heights GC East, CHHT	3508	0W-24S	B4
Chicago Heights Park West Course, - CHHT	3507	2W-25S	E7
Chick Evans GC, MNGV	2865	7W-11N	B2
Cinder Ridge Golf Links, WmTp	3942	31W-39S	A1
Cog Hill Golf & CC, LMNT	3271	17W-14S	C6
Columbus Park GC, CHCG	3031	7W-0S	C5
Conway Farms GC, LKFT	2648	13W-25N	E5
Country Lakes GC, NPVL	3140	30W-5S	B2
Countryside GC, FmtT	2589	20W-27N	E7
Coyote Run GC, RchT	3506	4W-22S	E2
Craig Woods Executive GC, DrrT	2638	40W-26N	A3
Crane's Landing GC, LNSH	2702	14W-22N	B3
Cress Creek CC, NPVL	3141	27W-5S	B3
Crystal Highlands, GfnT	2693	37W-23N	A2
Crystal Lake CC, CLLK	2639	36W-24N	D6
Crystal Tree Golf & CC, ODPK	3345	13W-17S	B4
Crystal Woods GC, DrrT	2638	40W-26N	A3
Deer Creek GC, UYPK	3684	2W-30S	C3
Deerfield GC, RVWD	2703	12W-21N	B6
Deerpath GC, LKFT	2649	11W-26N	D3
Deer Valley GC, BRkT	3196	46W-8S	A3
Downers Grove GC, DRGV	3143	21W-5S	E2
Eagle Brook CC, GNVA	3019	36W-0N	E5
Eaglewood Resort & Spa, ITSC	2969	21W-5N	E1
Edgebrook GC, CHCG	2919	6W-7N	C3
Edgewood Valley CC, LynT	3209	13W-8S	A1
Elgin CC, ElgT	2853	37W-11N	D4
Evanston GC, SKOK	2866	5W-10N	A4
Evergreen CC, ENGN	3213	3W-10S	B5
Exmoor CC, HDPK	2704	9W-22N	D3
Flagg Creek GC, IHPK	3146	13W-7S	E7
Flossmoor CC, FSMR	3507	2W-23S	C3
Foss Park GC, NCHI	2536	12W-31N	B6
Fountain Hills GC, ALSP	3276	3W-14S	E6
Four Winds GC, FmtT	2589	23W-27N	A7
Fox Bend GC, OSWG	3263	36W-12S	E2
Foxford Hills GC, CRY	2642	29W-25N	B5
Fox Lake CC, FXLK	2414	28W-39N	D5
Fox Run Golf Links, EGVV	2859	22W-9N	C7
Fox Valley GC, NARA	3078	35W-3S	A5
Fresh Meadows GC, PvsT	3086	14W-1S	D2
Geneva GC, GNVA	3020	35W-1N	B4
George W Dunne National GC, BmnT	3425	7W-19S	D2
Glencoe GC, GLNC	2758	7W-18N	B3
Glendale Lakes GC, GLHT	2968	24W-2N	E7
Gleneagles CC, LMNT	3272	16W-14S	A7
Glen Flora CC, WKGN	2480	10W-36N	B4
Glen Oak CC, MltT	3025	21W-0N	E5
Glen View Club, GLF	2865	7W-12N	B1
Glenview National 9 GC, GNVW	2810	9W-14N	B3
Glenview Park GC, GNVW	2810	9W-13N	C7
Glenwoodie GC, BlmT	3508	0E-23S	D3
Golf Center, DSPN	2863	13W-12N	A1
Golf Club of Illinois, ALGN	2747	35W-20N	B1
Golf Vista Estates, MONE	3683	6W-31S	B5
Graystone Golf Links, TYPK	3504	9W-22S	D2
Green Acres CC, NHBK	2757	8W-18N	E4
Green Meadows GC, WTMT	3145	18W-7S	A6
Greenshire GC, BHPK	2421	11W-38N	D7
Harborside International GC, CHCG	3279	1E-13S	A3
Hawthorn Woods CC, HNWD	2645	22W-26N	B3
Heather Ridge GC, GRNE	2534	16W-33N	E3
Hickory Hills CC, HYHL	3210	10W-11S	B6
Hickory Knoll GC, LkvT	2474	24W-36N	C3
Highland Park CC, HDPK	2704	9W-22N	C4
Highland Woods GC, PltT	2804	23W-13N	E6
Hillcrest CC, LGGV	2700	19W-21N	D6
Hilldale GC, HFET	2858	25W-12N	B1
Hinsdale GC, CNHL	3145	17W-4S	D1
Hughes Creek GC, ELBN	3017	42W-0N	C6
Hunter CC, RHMD	2353	34W-42N	D6
Idlewild CC, BlmT	3507	2W-23S	D2
Indian Boundary GC, CHCG	2973	10W-4N	E3
Indian Hill CC, NtrT	2812	4W-14N	B3
Indian Lakes CC, BMDL	2968	24W-5N	D2
Inverness GC, IVNS	2752	22W-16N	A7
Inwood GC, JLET	3497	27W-24S	C5
Itasca CC, ITSC	2914	19W-6N	C6
Ivanhoe GC, FmtT	2589	21W-28N	C6
Jackson Park GC, CHCG	3153	2E-7S	B5
Joe Louis the Champ GC, RVDL	3350	1W-15S	A1
Joliet CC, JLET	3587	22W-25S	C2
Kemper Lakes GC, KLDR	2700	20W-23N	A1
Ken Loch Golf Links, YkTp	3084	20W-1S	B2
Klein Creek GC, WNFD	3023	26W-1N	E3
Knollwood CC, LKFT	2593	12W-28N	B6
La Grange CC, LynT	3147	13W-5S	B2
Lake Barrington Shores GC, LKBN	2697	26W-24N	D1
Lake Bluff GC, LKBF	2593	11W-28N	D5
Lakemoor GC, LKMR	2529	28W-32N	E4
Lake Park GC, DSPN	2862	13W-9N	E7
Lake Shore CC, GLNC	2758	6W-18N	D2
Lake Zurich GC, LKZH	2698	24W-23N	D2
Lansing CC, LNSG	3430	4E-22S	C7
Lansing CC, MNSR	3510		D1
Legends of Bensenville GC, AddT	2972	15W-3N	B5
Leisure Village GC, FXLK	2414	28W-39N	E5
Libertyville GC, LYVL	2592	15W-28N	A7
Lincoln Oaks GC, CRTE	3596	0E-28S	E7
Lincolnshire CC, CRTE	3596	0E-28S	E7
Links at Carillon, LktT	3339	26W-16S	E3
Lockport Golf & Recreation Club, - LktT	3341	22W-17S	D6
Longwood CC, CteT	3598	4E-28S	C5
Lost Marsh GC, HMND	3280		E7
Makray Memorial GC, BRTN	2751	24W-18N	C4
Maple Meadows GC, WDDL	2970	18W-4N	E2
Marquette Park GC, CHCG	3150	4W-7S	E6
McHenry CC, MHRY	2528	32W-32N	C4
Meadowlark GC, PvsT	3086	14W-3S	C4
Meadows GC, BLID	3277	3W-14S	A6
Medinah CC, BmdT	2913	21W-6N	D7
Michael Jordan Golf Center, AURA	3140	30W-6S	B6
Mid Iron GC, LMNT	3272	16W-15S	A7
Midlane CC, WKGN	2478	14W-37N	C1
Midlothian CC, MDLN	3348	6W-17S	A5
Mill Creek GC, BbyT	3018	39W-0N	E5
Mission Hills CC, NfdT	2756	12W-16N	B6
Mistwood GC, RMVL	3417	27W-18S	D2
Mt Prospect GC, MPPT	2861	16W-12N	D2
Naperbrook GC, WldT	3267	27W-12S	C4
Naperville CC, LslT	3142	25W-6S	A5
Nickol Knoll GC, ANHT	2753	18W-18N	E3
Northmoor CC, HDPK	2705	8W-20N	A7
North Shore CC, GNVW	2811	8W-13N	A6
Oak Brook GC, OKBK	3086	15W-2S	A3
Oak Grove GC, AdnT	2349	45W-41N	A7
Oak Hills CC, PSHT	3346	9W-15S	D1
Oak Meadows GC, ADSN	2971	18W-4N	A3
Oak Park CC, RVGV	2974	10W-2N	B7
Odyssey CC, TYPK	3505	8W-23S	B2
Old Elm Club, HDPK	2650	10W-24N	B7
Old Oak CC, HMGN	3343	17W-16S	D4
Old Orchard CC, MPPT	2807	15W-14N	E4
Old Top Farm GC, NndT	2584	34W-29N	B3
Old Wayne GC, WCHI	2966	29W-2N	E7
Olympia Fields CC, RchT	3507	3W-24S	B5
Onwentsia Club, LKFT	2650	10W-26N	A4
Orchard Hills GC, WKGN	2421	12W-38N	B7
Orchard Valley GC, AURA	3136	39W-6S	E5
Palatine Hills GC, PLTN	2752	21W-17N	D5
Palos CC, PlsT	3345	11W-15S	E1
Palos Hills Municipal GC, PSHL	3274	9W-12S	E1
Park Ridge CC, PKRG	2864	10W-9N	B6
Peter N Jans Community GC, EVTN	2813	2W-12N	B7
Pheasant Run GC, SCRL	2965	32W-3N	C6
Phillips Park GC, AURA	3200	34W-9S	D3
Pinecrest GC, HTLY	2692	40W-21N	B6
Pine Meadow GC, MDLN	2591	18W-29N	A4
Pistakee CC, MchT	2529	29W-34N	C1
Plum Tree National GC, HtdT	2464	48W-34N	E7
Poplar Creek CC, HFET	2857	26W-12N	E2
Pottawatomie GC, SCRL	2964	35W-3N	B6
Prairie Bluff GC, CTHL	3418	24W-19S	E2
Prairie Isle GC, PRGV	2585	31W-27N	E7
Prairie Landing GC, WCHI	3021	32W-1N	C4
Prestwick CC, FKFT	3592	9W-26S	D1
Randall Oaks GC, WDND	2746	37W-17N	D7
Ravinia Green CC, RVWD	2703	12W-21N	A6
Ravisloe CC, HMWD	3427	2W-21S	C7
Red Tail GC, LKWD	2639	37W-24N	A7
Renwood GC, RLKB	2475	22W-35N	C6
Rich Harvest Links, SgrT	3196	44W-7S	D1
Ridge CC, CHCG	3277	3W-12S	A1
Ridgemoor CC, HDHT	2919	8W-6N	A7
River Bend GC, LSLE	3143	23W-6S	B5
River Forest CC, AddT	2972	15W-3N	A4
River Oaks GC, CTCY	3429	2E-19S	C1
Riverside GC, NRIV	3088	10W-2S	B3
Robert A Black GC, CHCG	2921	2W-8N	B1
Rob Roy GC, PTHT	2808	14W-14N	B3
Rolling Green CC, ANHT	2807	16W-14N	D3
Rolling Knolls CC, HnrT	2856	31W-11N	A4
Royal Fox GC, SCRL	2965	33W-5N	A2
Royal Hawk CC, SchT	2963	38W-5N	B2
Royal Melbourne CC, LGGV	2700	18W-23N	E2
Ruffled Feathers GC, LMNT	3271	17W-14S	C7
Ruth Lake CC, DGvT	3146	16W-6S	A5
St. Andrews Golf & CC, WCHI	2966	30W-3N	C6
St. Charles CC, SCRL	2964	34W-4N	C3
Salt Creek GC, AddT	2914	18W-7N	D4
Sanctuary GC, NLNX	3501	16W-24S	E5
Schaumburg GC, SMBG	2859	23W-11N	A4
Settler's Hill GC, GnvT	3020	34W-0N	D6
Seven Bridges GC, WDRG	3143	23W-7S	A6
Shepherd's Crook GC, ZION	2362	13W-43N	A5
Shiloh Park GC, ZION	2422	10W-40N	A3
Shore Acres CC, LKBF	2594	10W-30N	A3
Silver Lake CC, ODPK	3346	10W-17S	B5
Silver Oaks GC, RedT	3942	30W-40S	D4
Skokie CC, GLNC	2758	6W-17N	D6
South Shore GC, CHCG	3153	3E-7S	D6
Sportsman's CC, NHBK	2756	11W-17N	C4
Springbrook GC, NPVL	3202	29W-9S	D4
Spring Valley CC, SlmT	2357		E1
Square Links, FftT	3504	9W-24S	D5
Steeple Chase GC, MDLN	2645	21W-27N	D1
Stonebridge CC, AURA	3139	32W-5S	C3
Stonehenge GC, LKBN	2697	27W-22N	C4
Stonewall Orchard GC, WcnT	2588	25W-31N	A1
Stony Creek GC, CHRG	3275	7W-11S	C1
Streamwood Oaks GC, SMWD	2856	29W-10N	D6
Sugar Creek GC, VLPK	3027	17W-0S	C6
Sunset Ridge CC, NHFD	2811	8W-16N	A1
Sunset Valley GC, HDPK	2704	9W-21N	D6
Sydney R Marovitz GC, CHCG	2978	0W-4N	A2
Tamarack GC, WldT	3266	30W-12S	C3
Tam O' Shanter GC, NLES	2864	8W-9N	E6
Tanna Farms GC, BbyT	3018	39W-0S	D7
Terrace Hill GC, ALGN	2693	37W-21N	B6
The Glen Club, GNVW	2810	9W-14N	B4
The Highlands of Elgin, ELGN	2854	36W-10N	A7
The Merit Club, GRNE	2534	16W-32N	D5
Thunderhawk GC, BHPK	2421	11W-39N	D4
Traditions at Chevy Chase, BFGV	2755	14W-20N	C1
Turnberry CC, LKWD	2638	38W-24N	E6
Twin Lakes GC, PLTN	2806	19W-15N	C2
Twin Lakes GC, WTMT	3145	18W-6S	A4
Twin Orchard CC, VrnT	2700	18W-22N	D5
University GC, PKFT	3594	5W-28S	D7
Valley Green GC, NARA	3137	36W-4S	E1
Valley Lo Sports Club, GNVW	2810	8W-14N	D3
Vernon Hills GC, VNHL	2647	17W-24N	C7
Village Green CC, MDLN	2590	19W-29N	C3
Village Greens GC, WDRG	3206	20W-8S	B2
Village Links of Glen Ellyn, GNEN	3083	22W-1S	B1
Villa Olivia CC, BRLT	2856	30W-9N	B7
Walnut Greens GC, SMBG	2858	25W-11N	A3
Waters Edge GC, MRGO	2578	50W-28N	B6
Water's Edge GC, WRTH	3274	9W-13S	E4
Weber Park GC, SKOK	2865	6W-11N	E2
Wedgewood GC, JLET	3416	30W-20S	C6
Western Acres GC, MltT	3083	21W-2S	D4
Westmoreland CC, WLMT	2812	5W-13N	A7
Whisper Creek GC, HTLY	2744	42W-19N	C3
White Deer Run GC, VNHL	2647	17W-27N	C2
White Eagle GC, NPVL	3202	30W-10S	B5
White Mountain GC, ODPK	3423	12W-21S	D6
White Pines GC, BNVL	2971	16W-4N	E3
Willow Crest GC, WTMT	3085	17W-3S	B5
Willow Glen GC, NCHI	2593	12W-30N	C1
Willow Hill GC, NHBK	2810	9W-15N	C2
Willow Run GC, NlxT	3502	15W-22S	B1
Wilmette GC, WLMT	2811	6W-14N	C5
Wing Park GC, ELGN	2854	35W-12N	C2
Winnetka GC, WNKA	2811	6W-15N	E2
Wolf Run GC, AraT	3199	37W-8S	B2
Woodbine GC, HMGN	3343	17W-17S	C6
Woodruff GC, JLET	3500	20W-23S	C3
Woodstock CC, BLVY	2582	39W-30N	D1
Wynstone GC, NBRN	2644	24W-24N	B7
Zigfield Troy Golf, WDRG	3206	20W-8S	B1

Historic Sites

FEATURE NAME Address City ZIP Code	MAP#	CGS	GRID
Aurora Historical Museum 317 Cedar St, AURA, 60506	3138	35W-7S	A6
Charles Gates Dawes House 225 Greenwood St, EVTN, 60201	2867	2W-11N	C3
Cheney Mansion 220 N Euclid Av, OKPK, 60302	3031	8W-0N	A3
Chicago Avenue Water Tower & Pumping-Station 806 N Michigan Av, CHCG, 60611	3034	0E-1N	C2
Chicago Portage Historical Monument 4898 Harlem Av, LYNS, 60534	3148	9W-5S	D1
Colonial Palmer House 600 E Terra Cotta Av, CLLK, 60012	2640	34W-26N	D2
Dearborn Station 47 W Polk St, CHCG, 60605	3034	0W-0S	B6
Dresden Station Nuclear Power-Station N Dresden Rd, GLkT, 60450	3761	34W-33S	A2
Dunham Castle Dunham Rd, WYNE, 60184	2965	33W-5N	A2
Durant Peterson House SchT, 60175	2963	37W-4N	D5
Elks National HQs & Memorial-Building 2750 N Lakeview Av, CHCG, 60614	2978	0W-3N	B4
Ernest Hemingway Birthplace 339 N Oak Park Av, OKPK, 60302	3030	8W-0N	E3
Fitzpatrick House Broadway St, RMVL, 60441	3419	23W-19S	A2
Frederick C Robie House 5757 S Woodlawn Av, CHCG, 60637	3153	1E-6S	A3
Governor Oglesby Monument N Cannon Dr, CHCG, 60614	2978	0W-3N	B5
Haymarket Martyrs' Monument 863 Des Plaines Av, FTPK, 60130	3030	9W-0S	C6
Heller House 5132 S Woodlawn Av, CHCG, 60615	3153	1E-5S	A2
Historical Society 499 Biesterfield Rd, EGVV, 60007	2914	19W-8N	C2
Historic Pleasant Home 217 Home Av, OKPK, 60302	3030	8W-0N	E4
Hyde Park Historical Society 5529 S Lake Park Av, CHCG, 60637	3153	1E-6S	B3
Joliet Iron Works Historic Site E Columbia St, JLET, 60432	3499	23W-23S	A3
Lincoln Monument W La Salle Dr, CHCG, 60614	2978	0W-2N	B7
Logan Monument S Michigan Av, CHCG, 60605	3034	0E-0S	C6
Louis Sullivan Row Houses 1826 N Lincoln Pk W, CHCG, 60614	2978	0W-2N	B7
Martin Mitchell Mansion Aurora Av, NPVL, 60540	3141	27W-7S	C6
McGuire House Villa Maria Rd, SchT, 60174	2908	35W-6N	C7
Mother Rudd Home 4690 Old Grand Av, GRNE, 60031	2478	14W-35N	C7
Naper Settlement 523 S Webster St, NPVL, 60540	3141	27W-7S	D6
Patrick C Haley Mansion JLET, 60436	3498	24W-24S	D5
Prairie Avenue Historic District 2200 S Prairie Av, CHCG, 60616	3092	0E-1S	C1

Chicago 7-County Points of Interest Index

FEATURE NAME Address City ZIP Code	MAP#	CGS	GRID
Pullman Historic District E 111th St, CHCG, 60628	3278	0E-12S	E2
Streamwood Historical Society 777 W Irving Park Rd, HnrT, 60107	2856	29W-10N	D6
Tanner House 305 Cedar St, AURA, 60506	3138	35W-7S	A7
The History Makers 1900 S Michigan Av, CHCG, 60616	3092	0E-1S	C1
US Customs House 610 S Canal St, CHCG, 60607	3034	0W-0S	A6
Unity Temple 875 Lake St, OKPK, 60301	3030	8W-0N	E4
Woodstock Opera House 121 W Van Buren St, WDSK, 60098	2524	41W-31N	D7

Hospitals

FEATURE NAME Address City ZIP Code	MAP#	CGS	GRID
Adventist Glenoaks Hosp 701 Winthrop Av, GLHT, 60139	2969	22W-2N	C7
Adventist Hinsdale Hosp 120 N Oak St, HNDL, 60521	3146	15W-4S	B1
Adventist La Grange Memorial Hosp 5101 Willow Springs Rd, LGNG, 60525	3147	13W-5S	A2
Advocate Bethany Hosp 3435 W Van Buren St, CHCG, 60624	3032	4W-0S	D5
Advocate Christ Med Ctr 4440 W 95th St, OKLN, 60453	3212	5W-10S	B6
Advocate Good Samaritan Hosp 3815 Highland Av, DRGV, 60515	3084	19W-3S	C6
Advocate Good Shepherd Hosp CbaT, 60010	2697	27W-22N	A3
Advocate Hope Children's Hosp 4440 W 93rd St, OKLN, 60453	3212	5W-10S	B5
Advocate Illinois Masonic Med Ctr 836 W Wellington Av, CHCG, 60657	2977	1W-3N	D4
Advocate Lutheran General Hosp 1775 Dempster St, PKRG, 60068	2863	11W-10N	E4
Advocate South Suburban Hosp 17800 Kedzie Av, HLCT, 60429	3426	4W-21S	E6
Advocate Trinity Hosp 2320 E 93rd St, CHCG, 60617	3215	2E-10S	D5
Alexian Brothers Behavioral Health-Hosp 1650 Moon Lake Blvd, HFET, 60169	2857	26W-12N	E1
Alexian Brothers Med Ctr 800 Biesterfield Rd, EGVV, 60007	2914	19W-8N	C2
Bolingbrook Med Ctr 400 S Schmidt Rd, BGBK, 60440	3268	23W-13S	E4
Centegra Memorial Med Ctr 3701 Doty Rd, WDSK, 60098	2582	39W-28N	C6
Centegra Northern Illinois Med Ctr 4201 W Medical Center Dr, MHRY, 60050	2528	33W-31N	A7
Central DuPage Hosp 25 Winfield Rd, WNFD, 60190	3023	27W-0N	C5
Chicago Lakeshore Hosp 4840 N Marine Dr, CHCG, 60640	2921	1W-6N	E6
Chicago Osteopathic Hosp & Med Ctr 5200 S Ellis Av, CHCG, 60615	3152	1E-5S	E1
Chicago-Read Mental Health Center 4200 N Oak Park Av, CHCG, 60634	2974	8W-5N	E1
Chicago Shriners Hosp 2211 N Oak Park Av, CHCG, 60707	2974	8W-2N	E6
Chicago-South Loop River City Med-Ctr 800 S Wells St, CHCG, 60607	3034	0W-0S	B6
Children's Memorial Hosp 2300 N Childrens Plz, CHCG, 60614	2978	0W-3N	A5
Community Hosp-Munster 901 MacArthur Blvd, MNSR, 46321	3510		E1
Condell Med Ctr 801 Garfield Av, LYVL, 60048	2591	16W-28N	D7
Delnor Community Hosp 300 Randall Rd, GNVA, 60134	3019	37W-1N	D3
Edward Hosp 801 S Washington St, NPVL, 60540	3141	27W-7S	C7
Edwards Med Ctr 130 N Weber Rd, BGBK, 60440	3268	25W-11S	A2
Elgin Mental Health Center 750 S State St, ELGN, 60123	2854	34W-10N	E7
Elizabeth Ludeman Development-Center 114 N Orchard Dr, PKFT, 60466	3595	3W-26S	A2
Elmhurst Center for Health 1200 S York St, EMHT, 60126	3028	15W-0S	A7
Elmhurst Memorial Hosp 200 N Berteau Av, EMHT, 60126	3028	15W-1N	A1
Evanston Hosp 2650 Ridge Av, EVTN, 60201	2813	2W-13N	B7
Forest Med Ctr 9050 W 81st St, JSTC, 60458	3209	11W-9S	E3
Glenbrook Hosp 2100 Pfingsten Rd, GNVW, 60025	2809	11W-14N	D3
Gottlieb Memorial Hosp 701 W North Av, MLPK, 60160	3029	10W-1N	E1
Hartgrove Hosp 520 N Ridgeway Av, CHCG, 60624	3032	4W-0N	C3
Highland Park Hosp 718 Homewood Av, HDPK, 60035	2704	9W-22N	D4
Holy Cross Hosp 2701 W 68th St, CHCG, 60629	3151	3W-7S	A6
Holy Family Med Ctr 100 N River Rd, DSPN, 60016	2863	13W-12N	A1
Howe Development Center 7600 Tiger Ln, TYPK, 60477	3424	9W-21S	D7
Ingalls Memorial Hosp 1 Ingalls Dr, HRVY, 60426	3349	2W-18S	D7
Jackson Park Hosp & Med Ctr 7531 S Stony Island Av, CHCG, 60649	3215	2E-8S	B1
Jesse Brown VA Med Ctr 820 S Damen Av, CHCG, 60612	3033	2W-0S	B6
John H Stroger Jr Hosp 1901 W Harrison St, CHCG, 60612	3033	2W-0S	C6
Kindred Chicago Central Hosp 4058 N Pulaski Rd, CHCG, 60641	2976	5W-4N	B3
Kindred Hosp Chicago-Lakeshore 6130 N Sheridan Rd, CHCG, 60660	2921	1W-7N	E3
Kindred Hosp Chicago-North Campus 2544 W Montrose Av, CHCG, 60625	2921	3W-5N	A7
Kindred Hosp Chicago Northlake 365 E North Av, NHLK, 60164	3029	13W-1N	A1
Lake Forest Hosp 660 N Westmoreland Rd, LKFT, 60045	2649	11W-26N	C2
La Rabida Childrens Hosp & Research-Center S Promontory Dr, CHCG, 60637	3153		C5
Lincoln Park Hosp 550 W Webster Av, CHCG, 60614	2978	0W-2N	A6
Little Co of Mary Hosp & Health Care-Ctr 2800 W 95th St, ENGN, 60805	3213	3W-10S	A5
Loretto Hosp 645 S Central Av, CHCG, 60644	3031	7W-0S	C6
Louis A Weiss Memorial Hosp 4646 N Marine Dr, CHCG, 60640	2921	1W-5N	E7
Loyola University Med Ctr 2160 1st Av, MYWD, 60153	3030	10W-1S	A7
MacNeal Hosp 3249 Oak Park Av, BRWN, 60402	3089	8W-3S	A4
Mercy Harvard Hosp 901 Grant St, HRVD, 60033	2406	49W-38N	C6
Mercy Health Care & Rehabilitation-Center 19000 S Halsted St, HMWD, 60430	3508	1W-22S	A2
Mercy Hosp & Med Ctr 2525 S Michigan Av, CHCG, 60616	3092	0E-2S	C2
Methodist Hosp of Chicago 5025 N Paulina St, CHCG, 60640	2921	2W-6N	C6
Michael Reese Hosp & Med Ctr 2929 S Ellis Av, CHCG, 60616	3092	0E-2S	D3
Midwestern Regional Med Ctr 2520 Emmaus Av, ZION, 60099	2422	10W-40N	B3
Mt Sinai Hosp 1501 S California Av, CHCG, 60608	3033	3W-1S	A7
Northwest Community Hosp 800 W Central Rd, ANHT, 60005	2806	18W-13N	E7
Northwestern Memorial Hosp 251 E Huron St, CHCG, 60611	3034	0E-0N	C3
Norwegian American Hosp 1044 W Cortez St, CHCG, 60622	3032	3W-1N	E2
Oak Forest Hosp of Cook County 15900 Cicero Av, BmnT, 60426	3426	5W-19S	B1
Our Lady of Resurrection Med Ctr 5645 W Addison St, CHCG, 60634	2975	6W-4N	C3
Palos Community Hosp 12251 S 80th Av, PSHT, 60463	3274	9W-14S	C6
Prairie Med Ctr S Wolf Rd, WSTR, 60154	3086	14W-2S	D2
Provena Mercy Center 1325 N Highland Av, AURA, 60506	3138	36W-5S	A3
Provena St. Joseph Hosp 77 N Airlite St, ELGN, 60123	2854	36W-11N	A4
Provena St. Joseph Med Ctr 333 Madison St, JLET, 60435	3497	26W-23S	E4
Provident Hosp of Cook County 500 E 51st St, CHCG, 60615	3152	0E-5S	D1
Rehabilitation Institute of Chicago 345 E Huron St, CHCG, 60611	3034	0E-0N	C3
Resurrection Med Ctr 7435 W Talcott Av, CHCG, 60631	2918	9W-7N	C4
Riveredge Hosp 8311 Roosevelt Rd, FTPK, 60130	3030	10W-0S	B7
RML Specialty Hosp 5601 S County Line Rd, HNDL, 60521	3146	14W-6S	C3
Roseland Community Hosp 45 W 111th St, CHCG, 60628	3278	0W-12S	C2
Rush-Copley Med Ctr 2000 Ogden Av, AURA, 60504	3201	33W-9S	A4
Rush North Shore Med Ctr 9600 Gross Point Rd, SKOK, 60076	2866	5W-12N	A1
Rush Oak Park Hosp 520 S Maple Av, OKPK, 60304	3030	8W-0S	E5
Rush University Med Ctr 1653 W Congress Pkwy, CHCG, 60612	3033	2W-0S	C6
Sacred Heart Hosp 3240 W Franklin Blvd, CHCG, 60624	3032	4W-0N	D3
St. Alexius Med Ctr 1555 Barrington Rd, HFET, 60169	2857	26W-12N	E2
St. Anthony Hosp 2875 W 19th St, CHCG, 60623	3090	3W-1S	E1
St. Bernard Hosp & Health Care-Center 326 W 64th St, CHCG, 60621	3152	0W-7S	B5
St. Francis Hosp 355 Ridge Av, EVTN, 60202	2867	2W-9N	B6
St. Francis Hosp & Health Center 12935 Gregory St, BLID, 60406	3277	2W-15S	B7
St. James Hosp 1251 E Richton Rd, CRTE, 60417	3597	1E-28S	B7
St. James Hosp & Health Center 1423 Chicago Rd, CHHT, 60411	3508	1W-25S	A7
St. James Hosp & Health Ctrs-Olympia-Campus 20201 Crawford Av, OMFD, 60461	3506	4W-24S	D5
St. Joseph Hosp 2900 N Lake Shore Dr W, CHCG, 60657	2978	0W-3N	B4
St. Joseph Immediate Care 2250 W Algonquin Rd, LIHL, 60156	2694	35W-21N	A5
St. Margaret Mercy Healthcare-Center 24 Joliet St, DYR, 46311	3598	4E-26S	C2
St. Margaret Mercy Healthcare-Center 5454 S Hohman Av, HMND, 46320	3352		C6
St. Mary & Elizabeth's Med Ctr-Claremont Av 1431 N Claremont Av, CHCG, 60622	3033	3W-1N	A1
St. Mary & Elizabeth's Med Ctr-Div-Street 2233 W Division St, CHCG, 60622	3033	2W-1N	B2
Salem Med Ctr S Rowell Av, JLET, 60433	3587	22W-25S	C1
Schwab Rehabilitation Hosp 1401 S California Av, CHCG, 60608	3033	3W-1S	A7
Sherman Family Health Care Hosp 600 S Randall Rd, ALGN, 60102	2693	36W-20N	E7
Sherman Family Health Care Hosp CLLK, 60012	2640	33W-27N	E1
Sherman Hosp 934 Center St, ELGN, 60120	2854	34W-12N	E1
Silver Cross Hosp 1200 Maple Rd, JLET, 60432	3499	22W-23S	D3
South Shore Hosp 8012 S Crandon Av, CHCG, 60617	3215	2E-9S	D2
Streamwood Behavioral Health Center 1400 East Av, SMWD, 60107	2911	27W-9N	C1
Suburban Health Center Quadrangle Dr, BGBK, 60440	3269	23W-12S	A3
Swedish Covenant Hosp 5145 N California Av, CHCG, 60625	2920	3W-6N	E6
The Neurologic & Orthopedic Inst of-Chicago 4501 N Winchester Av, CHCG, 60640	2921	2W-5N	B7
Thorek Memorial Hosp 850 W Irving Park Rd, CHCG, 60613	2977	1W-5N	E1
University of Chicago Med Ctr 5841 S Maryland Av, CHCG, 60637	3152	1E-6S	E3
University of Illinois Med Ctr 1740 W Taylor St, CHCG, 60612	3033	2W-0S	C6
Valley West Community Hosp 604 Center Pkwy, YKVL, 60560	3261	43W-14S	B6
Veterans Affairs Edward Hines Jr-Hosp W Roosevelt Rd, PvsT, 60141	3030	10W-1S	A7
Veterans Affairs Med Ctr 3001 Green Bay Rd, NCHI, 60088	2593	11W-30N	D2
Veterans Lakeside Med Ctr 333 E Huron St, CHCG, 60611	3034	0E-0N	D3
Vista Health St. Therese Med Ctr 2615 Washington St, WKGN, 60085	2536	12W-33N	C2
Vista Health Victory Memorial Hosp 1324 N Sheridan Rd, WKGN, 60085	2480	10W-35N	A6
Westlake Hosp 1225 W Lake St, MLPK, 60160	3029	11W-0N	E3
West Suburban Med Ctr 3 Erie St, OKPK, 60302	3031	7W-0N	B3

Law Enforcement

FEATURE NAME Address City ZIP Code	MAP#	CGS	GRID
Addison Police Dept 131 W Lake St, ADSN, 60101	2970	18W-3N	E4
Algonquin Police Dept 2200 Harnish Dr, ALGN, 60102	2694	35W-20N	A7
Alsip Police Dept 4500 W 123rd St, ALSP, 60803	3276	5W-14S	B6
Antioch Police Dept 882 Main St, ANTH, 60002	2357	23W-42N	E6
Arlington Heights Police Dept 33 S Arlington Heights Rd, ANHT, 60005	2807	17W-14N	A5
Aurora Police Dept 350 N River St, AURA, 60506	3138	35W-7S	B7
Bannockburn Police Dept 2275 Telegraph Rd, BKBN, 60015	2703	11W-22N	C3
Barrington Hills Police Dept 112 Algonquin Rd, BNHL, 60010	2750	28W-16N	A7
Barrington Police Dept 400 W Station St, BRTN, 60010	2750	25W-18N	E2
Bartlett Police Dept 228 S Main St, BRLT, 60103	2910	29W-8N	E3
Batavia Police Dept 100 N Island Av, BTVA, 60510	3078	35W-1S	B1
Bedford Park Police Dept 6701 S Archer Rd, BDPK, 60501	3148	9W-7S	C6
Beecher Police Dept 724 Penfield St, BCHR, 60401	3864	0W-36S	C2
Bellwood Police Dept 3200 Washington Blvd, BLWD, 60104	3029	12W-0N	B4
Bensenville Police Dept 100 N Church Rd, BNVL, 60106	2971	16W-5N	D1
Berkeley Police Dept 5819 Electric Av, BKLY, 60163	3028	14W-0N	C4
Berwyn Police Dept 6401 31st St, BRWN, 60402	3089	8W-2S	A4
Bloomingdale Police Dept 201 S Bloomingdale Rd, BMDL, 60108	2969	23W-5N	A2
Blue Island Police Dept 13031 Greenwood Av, BLID, 60406	3349	3W-15S	B1
Bolingbrook Police Dept 375 W Briarcliff Rd, BGBK, 60440	3269	23W-12S	A2
Braidwood Police Dept 141 W Main St, BDWD, 60408	3942	31W-41S	A5
Bridgeview Police Dept 7500 S Oketo Av, BGVW, 60455	3210	9W-8S	D1
Broadview Police Dept 2350 S 25th Av, BDVW, 60155	3029	12W-1S	C7
Brookfield Police Dept 8820 Brookfield Av, BKFD, 60513	3088	10W-3S	A6
Buffalo Grove Police Dept 46 Church Rd, BFGV, 60089	2754	17W-20N	C2
Burnham Police Dept 14450 Hammond Av, BNHM, 60633	3351	3E-16S	E4
Burr Ridge Police Dept 7660 S County Line Rd, BRRG, 60527	3208	15W-8S	C2
Calumet City Police Dept 1200 Pulaski Rd, CTCY, 60409	3351	3E-17S	E6
Calumet Park Police Dept 12409 S Throop St, CTPK, 60827	3277	1W-14S	E6
Carol Stream Police Dept 500 Gary Av, CLSM, 60188	2968	25W-2N	B7
Cary Police Dept 255 Village Hall Dr, CRY, 60013	2695	31W-23N	C2
Chicago Heights Police Dept 1601 S Halsted St, CHHT, 60411	3596	1W-25S	B1
Chicago Police Dept 1300 W Jackson Blvd, CHCG, 60607	3033	1W-0S	D5
Chicago Police Dept 1718 S State St, CHCG, 60616	3092	0W-1S	C1
Chicago Police-District 1 Central 11 E 11th St, CHCG, 60605	3034	0E-0S	C6
Chicago Police-District 2 Wentworth 5101 S Wentworth Av, CHCG, 60609	3152	0W-5S	B2
Chicago Police-District 3 Grand-Crossing 7040 S Cottage Grove Av, CHCG, 60637	3152	0E-7S	E6
Chicago Police-District 4 South-Chicago 2255 E 103rd St, CHCG, 60617	3279	2E-11S	D1
Chicago Police-District 5 Calumet 727 E 111th St, CHCG, 60628	3278	0E-13S	E3
Chicago Police-District 6 Gresham 819 W 85th St, CHCG, 60620	3214	1W-9S	A3
Chicago Police-District 7 Englewood 6120 S Racine Av, CHCG, 60636	3151	1W-6S	E4
Chicago Police-District 8 Chicago-Lawn 3515 W 63rd St, CHCG, 60629	3150	4W-7S	D5

Chicago 7-County Points of Interest Index

FEATURE NAME	Address City ZIP Code	MAP#	CGS	GRID
Chicago Police-District 9 Deering	3501 S Lowe Av, CHCG, 60609	3092	0W-3S	A5
Chicago Police-District 10-Marquette	2259 S Damen Av, CHCG, 60608	3091	2W-2S	C2
Chicago Police-District 11 Harrison	3151 W Harrison St, CHCG, 60612	3032	3W-0S	E6
Chicago Police-District 12 Monroe	100 S Racine Av, CHCG, 60607	3033	1W-0S	D5
Chicago Police-District 13 Wood	937 N Wood St, CHCG, 60622	3033	2W-1N	C2
Chicago Police-District 14-Shakespeare	2150 N California Av, CHCG, 60647	2976	3W-2N	E6
Chicago Police-District 15 Austin	5327 W Chicago Av, CHCG, 60644	3031	6W-0N	D3
Chicago Police-District 16 Jefferson-Park	5151 N Milwaukee Av, CHCG, 60630	2919	6W-6N	C5
Chicago Police-District 17 Albany-Park	4461 N Pulaski Rd, CHCG, 60625	2920	4W-5N	B7
Chicago Police-District 18 East-Chicago	1160 N Larrabee St, CHCG, 60610	3034	0W-1N	A2
Chicago Police-District 19 Belmont	2452 W Belmont Av, CHCG, 60618	2977	3W-4N	A3
Chicago Police-District 20 Foster	1940 W Foster Av, CHCG, 60640	2921	2W-6N	B5
Chicago Police-District 21 Prairie	300 E 29th St, CHCG, 60616	3092	0E-2S	C3
Chicago Police-District 22 Morgan-Park	1830 W Monterey Av, CHCG, 60643	3277	2W-13S	C3
Chicago Police-District 23 Town-Hall	3600 N Halsted St, CHCG, 60613	2977	1W-4N	E2
Chicago Police-District 24 Rogers-Park	6464 N Clark St, CHCG, 60626	2921	2W-8N	C2
Chicago Police-District 25 Central	5555 W Grand Av, CHCG, 60639	2975	6W-2N	C6
Chicago Ridge Police Dept	10501 Oxford Av, CHRG, 60415	3275	7W-12S	B1
Cicero Police Dept	4932 W 26th St, CCRO, 60804	3089	6W-2S	E2
Clarendon Hills Police Dept	448 Park Av, CNHL, 60514	3145	17W-5S	C2
Cook County Sheriff's Dept	1401 Maybrook Dr, MYWD, 60153	3030	10W-0S	B5
Country Club Hills Police Dept	3700 175th Pl, CCHL, 60478	3426	4W-21S	D5
Countryside Police Dept	5550 East Av, CTSD, 60525	3147	12W-6S	D3
Crest Hill Police Dept	1610 Plainfield Rd, CTHL, 60403	3498	26W-21S	A1
Crestwood Police Dept	13840 Cicero Av, CTWD, 60445	3348	5W-16S	A3
Crete Police Dept	1370 Benton St, CRTE, 60417	3685	1W-29S	B2
Crystal Lake Police Dept	121 W Woodstock St, CLLK, 60014	2640	35W-26N	A3
Darien Police Dept	1710 Plainfield Rd, DRN, 60516	3207	18W-8S	A2
Deerfield Police Dept	850 Waukegan Rd, DRFD, 60015	2703	10W-21N	E7
Des Plaines Police Dept	1420 Miner St, DSPN, 60016	2863	13W-11N	A3
Dixmoor Police Dept	170 W 145th St, HRVY, 60426	3349	2W-17S	E5
Dolton Police Dept	14030 Park Av, DLTN, 60419	3350	0E-16S	D3
Downers Grove Police Dept	825 Burlington Av, DRGV, 60515	3144	19W-5S	D2
DuPage County Sheriff's Dept	WHTN, 60187	3023	26W-0S	E6
Dyer Police Dept	230 Schulte St, DYR, 46311	3598		D2
East Dundee Police Dept	120 Barrington Av, EDND, 60118	2801	34W-16N	A2
East Hazel Crest Police Dept	17223 Throop St, EHZC, 60429	3427	1W-20S	E5
Elgin Police Dept	150 Dexter Av, ELGN, 60120	2854	34W-11N	E3
Elk Grove Village Police Dept	901 Wellington Av, EGVV, 60007	2914	19W-8N	C2
Elmhurst Police Dept	125 E 1st St, EMHT, 60126	3028	15W-1N	A2
Elmwood Park Police Dept	11 W Conti Pkwy, EDPK, 60707	2974	9W-3N	C5
Evanston Police Dept	1454 Elmwood Av, EVTN, 60201	2867	2W-11N	B3
Evergreen Park Police Dept	9420 S Kedzie Av, ENGN, 60805	3212	4W-10S	E6
Flossmoor Police Dept	2800 Flossmoor Rd, FSMR, 60422	3507	3W-23S	B2
Ford Heights Police Dept	1343 Ellis Av, FDHT, 60411	3509	1E-25S	A7
Forest Park Police Dept	517 Des Plaines Av, FTPK, 60130	3030	9W-0S	C5
Forest View Police Dept	7000 46th St, FTVW, 60402	3088	8W-4S	E7
Fox Lake Police Dept	FXLK, 60041	2473	26W-36N	C4
Fox River Grove Police Dept	408 Northwest Hwy, FRGV, 60021	2696	30W-23N	B3
Frankfort Police Dept	14 N Hickory St, FKFT, 60423	3591	12W-26S	D1
Franklin Park Police Dept	9545 W Belmont Av, FNPK, 60131	2973	11W-3N	C4
Genoa City Police Dept	715 Walworth St, GNCY, 53128	2353		A3
Gilberts Police Dept	86 Railroad St, GLBT, 60136	2799	39W-16N	A1
Glencoe Police Dept	325 Hazel Av, GLNC, 60022	2758	6W-17N	D5
Glendale Heights Police Dept	300 Civic Center Plz, GLHT, 60139	2969	23W-3N	A6
Glen Ellyn Police Dept	535 Duane St, GNEN, 60137	3025	22W-0N	B5
Glenview Police Dept	1215 Waukegan Rd, GNVW, 60025	2810	8W-13N	E6
Glenwood Police Dept	1 S Rebecca St, GNWD, 60425	3508	0E-22S	D2
Golf Police Dept	1 Briar Rd, GLF, 60029	2864	8W-12N	E1
Grayslake Police Dept	151 Hawley St, GYLK, 60030	2532	20W-33N	E3
Gurnee Police Dept	100 N Oplaine Rd, GRNE, 60031	2535	14W-34N	C1
Hainesville Police Dept	83 W Belvidere Rd, HNVL, 60030	2532	22W-33N	B4
Hammond Police Dept	5925 S Calumet Av, HMND, 46320	3430		E1
Hampshire Police Dept	234 S State St, HPSR, 60140	2795	47W-16N	E2
Hanover Park Police Dept	2121 W Lake St, HRPK, 60133	2911	27W-8N	C3
Harvard Police Dept	201 W Front St, HRVD, 60033	2406	50W-38N	A6
Harvey Police Dept	15301 Dixie Hwy, HRVY, 60426	3349	2W-18S	C7
Harwood Heights Police Dept	7300 W Wilson Av, HDHT, 60706	2918	9W-5N	D7
Hawthorn Woods Police Dept	2 Lagoon Dr, HNWD, 60047	2645	21W-24N	D7
Hebron Police Dept	10315 Freeman Rd, HBRN, 60034	2350	40W-42N	E6
Hickory Hills Police Dept	8652 W 95th St, HYHL, 60457	3210	10W-10S	A6
Highland Park Police Dept	1677 Old Deerfield Rd, HDPK, 60035	2704	9W-21N	C6
Highwood Police Dept	17 Highwood Av, HIWD, 60040	2704	9W-23N	D2
Hillside Police Dept	425 N Hillside Av, HLSD, 60162	3028	14W-0N	D5
Hinsdale Police Dept	121 Symonds Dr, HNDL, 60521	3146	15W-4S	B1
Hodgkins Police Dept	6015 Lenzi Av, HGKN, 60525	3147	11W-6S	D4
Hoffman Estates Police Dept	1200 Gannon Dr, HFET, 60169	2858	24W-12N	C2
Hometown Police Dept	4331 Southwest Hwy, HMTN, 60456	3212	5W-10S	B5
Homewood Police Dept	17950 Dixie Hwy, HMWD, 60430	3427	2W-21S	D6
Huntley Police Dept	11351 Allison Ct, HTLY, 60142	2745	41W-19N	A2
Indian Head Park Police Dept	201 Acacia Dr, IHPK, 60525	3146	13W-7S	E6
Island Lake Police Dept	3720 Greenleaf Av, ISLK, 60042	2586	28W-28N	E6
Itasca Police Dept	411 N Prospect Av, ITSC, 60143	2914	18W-6N	E5
Johnsburg Police Dept	3611 N Chapel Hill Rd, JNBG, 60050	2471	31W-35N	E6
Joliet Police Dept	150 W Jefferson St, JLET, 60432	3498	24W-23S	E5
Justice Police Dept	7800 S Archer Rd, JSTC, 60458	3210	11W-8S	A2
Kane County Sheriff	777 E Fabyan Pkwy, GnvT, 60510	3020	34W-0S	D6
Kendall County Sheriff	1102 Cornell Ln, YKVL, 60560	3261	43W-14S	A7
Kenilworth Police Dept	419 Richmond Rd, KLWH, 60043	2812	4W-14N	C4
Kildeer Police Dept	Quentin Rd, KLDR, 60047	2699	21W-21N	D6
La Grange Park Police Dept	447 N Catherine Av, LGPK, 60525	3087	12W-3S	B6
La Grange Police Dept	304 W Burlington Av, LGNG, 60525	3087	12W-4S	B7
Lake Bluff Police Dept	45 E Center Av, LKBF, 60044	2593	10W-28N	E6
Lake County Sheriff's Dept	25 S Martin Luther King Jr Av, WKGN, 60085	2537	10W-34N	B2
Lake Forest Police Dept	255 W Deerpath Rd, LKFT, 60045	2649	11W-26N	D3
Lake in the Hills Police Dept	1115 Crystal Lake Rd, LIHL, 60156	2693	35W-22N	E4
Lakemoor Police Dept	234 W Rand Rd, LKMR, 60051	2529	29W-32N	D5
Lake Villa Police Dept	65 Cedar Av, LKVL, 60046	2475	22W-38N	A1
Lakewood Police Dept	2500 Lake Av, CLLK, 60014	2639	37W-25N	B5
Lake Zurich Police Dept	200 Mohawk Tr, LKZH, 60047	2699	23W-22N	A3
Lansing Police Dept	2710 E 170th St, LNSG, 60438	3430	3E-19S	A3
Lemont Police Dept	416 Main St, LMNT, 60439	3270	19W-13S	D5
Libertyville Police Dept	200 E Cook Av, LYVL, 60048	2591	16W-29N	D4
Lincolnshire Police Dept	1 Old Half Day Rd, LNSH, 60069	2702	15W-23N	B2
Lincolnwood Police Dept	6900 N Lincoln Av, LNWD, 60712	2920	5W-8N	B1
Lindenhurst Police Dept	2301 E Sand Lake Rd, LNHT, 60046	2476	20W-37N	B2
Linn Police Dept	N556 Mill Rd, LinT, 53147	2349		E1
Lisle Police Dept	5040 Lincoln Av, LSLE, 60532	3143	23W-5S	A2
Lockport Police Dept	915 S State St, LKPT, 60441	3419	22W-19S	C3
Lombard Police Dept	235 E Wilson Av, LMBD, 60148	3026	19W-0S	C6
Lynwood Police Dept	21460 E Lincoln Hwy, LYWD, 60411	3510	4E-25S	B7
Lyons Police Dept	7801 Ogden Av, LYNS, 60534	3088	9W-4S	C6
Manhattan Police Dept	245 S State St, MHTN, 60442	3677	19W-31S	E5
Marengo Police Dept	142 E Prairie St, MRGO, 60152	2634	49W-26N	B2
Markham Police Dept	16313 Kedzie Av, MKHM, 60428	3427	3W-19S	A2
Matteson Police Dept	20500 Cicero Av, MTSN, 60443	3506	6W-24S	B6
Maywood Police Dept	125 S 5th Av, MYWD, 60153	3030	10W-0N	A4
McHenry Police Dept	333 S Green St, MHRY, 60050	2528	32W-31N	B6
Melrose Park Police Dept	101 Broadway St, MLPK, 60160	3029	11W-0N	D3
Merrionette Park Police Dept	11750 S Kedzie Av, MTPK, 60803	3276	4W-13S	E4
Midlothian Police Dept	14801 Pulaski Rd, MDLN, 60445	3348	4W-17S	C5
Minooka Police Dept	121 McEvilly Rd, MNKA, 60447	3672	33W-28S	B1
Mokena Police Dept	10907 Front St, MKNA, 60448	3503	13W-23S	A4
Montgomery Police Dept	1460 SE River Rd, MTGY, 60538	3199	37W-9S	D4
Morton Grove Police Dept	6101 Capulina Av, MNGV, 60053	2865	7W-10N	B4
Mt Prospect Police Dept	112 E Northwest Hwy, MPPT, 60056	2808	15W-12N	A7
Mundelein Police Dept	221 N Lake St, MDLN, 60060	2590	18W-27N	D7
Munster Police Dept	1007 Ridge Rd, MNSR, 46321	3430		E7
Naperville Police Dept	1350 Aurora Av, NPVL, 60540	3141	28W-7S	A6
New Lenox Police Dept	701 W Haven Av, NLNX, 60451	3501	18W-24S	A6
Niles Police Dept	7200 N Milwaukee Av, NLES, 60714	2864	8W-9N	E7
Norridge Police Dept	4020 N Olcott Av, NRDG, 60706	2974	9W-5N	C2
North Aurora Police Dept	25 E State St, NARA, 60542	3078	36W-4S	A7
Northbrook Police Dept	1401 Landwehr Rd, NHBK, 60062	2756	11W-17N	D6
North Chicago Police Dept	1850 Lewis Av, NCHI, 60064	2536	11W-31N	D6
Northfield Police Dept	350 Walnut Av, NHFD, 60093	2811	6W-15N	C2
Northlake Police Dept	55 E North Av, NHLK, 60164	3028	13W-1N	E1
North Riverside Police Dept	2359 Des Plaines Av, NRIV, 60546	3088	9W-2S	C2
Oak Brook Police Dept	1200 Oak Brook Rd, OKBK, 60523	3085	16W-2S	E4
Oakbrook Terrace Police Dept	17W275 Butterfield Rd, OKTR, 60181	3085	17W-1S	C1
Oak Forest Police Dept	15440 Central Av, OKFT, 60452	3347	7W-18S	D7
Oak Lawn Police Dept	9446 Raymond Av, OKLN, 60453	3211	6W-10S	E6
Oak Park Police Dept	1 Madison St, OKPK, 60304	3031	7W-0S	B5
Olympia Fields Police Dept	20701 Governors Hwy, OMFD, 60461	3506	4W-25S	D6
Orland Hills Police Dept	16039 S 94th Av, ODHL, 60487	3423	11W-19S	E2
Orland Park Police Dept	14600 S Ravinia Av, ODPK, 60462	3345	12W-17S	D5
Oswego Police Dept	OSWG, 60543	3263	36W-11S	E2
Palatine Police Dept	200 E Wood St, PLTN, 60067	2752	20W-16N	E7
Palos Heights Police Dept	7607 119th St, PSHT, 60463	3274	9W-14S	D5
Palos Hills Police Dept	8555 W 103rd St, PSHL, 60465	3274	10W-12S	B1
Palos Park Police Dept	12301 S 90th Av, PSPK, 60464	3274	11W-14S	A6
Park City Police Dept	3420 Kehm Blvd, PKCY, 60085	2536	13W-33N	A3
Park Forest Police Dept	200 Lakewood Blvd, PKFT, 60466	3595	3W-26S	B3
Park Ridge Police Dept	200 Vine Av, PKRG, 60068	2918	10W-8N	B1
Peotone Police Dept	208 E Main St, PTON, 60468	3861	9W-37S	A3
Phoenix Police Dept	15240 Vincennes Rd, PHNX, 60426	3350	0W-18S	B7
Plainfield Police Station	14300 Coil Plus Dr, PNFD, 60544	3338	30W-17S	B5
Plano Police Dept	9 E North St, PLNO, 60545	3259	47W-13S	D6
Posen Police Dept	2440 W Walter Zimny Dr, POSN, 60469	3349	3W-17S	B5
Prairie Grove Police Dept	3125 Barreville Rd, PRGV, 60012	2585	32W-28N	C5
Prospect Heights Police Dept	14 E Camp McDonald Rd, PTHT, 60070	2808	15W-15N	A3
Richmond Police Dept	5600 Hunter Dr, RHMD, 60071	2412	34W-41N	C1
Richton Park Police Dept	4455 Sauk Tr, RNPK, 60471	3594	5W-27S	C3
Riverdale Police Dept	14140 S Emerald Av, RVDL, 60827	3350	1W-16S	A2
River Forest Police Dept	7810 Central Av, RVFT, 60305	3030	9W-0N	C4
River Grove Police Dept	2621 N Thatcher Av, RVGV, 60171	2974	10W-3N	A5
Riverside Police Dept	31 Riverside Rd, RVSD, 60546	3088	9W-3S	C5
Robbins Police Dept	3323 W 137th St, RBBN, 60472	3348	4W-16S	E2
Rolling Meadows Police Dept	3600 Kirchoff Rd, RGMW, 60008	2806	20W-13N	B5
Romeoville Police Dept	10 Montrose Dr, RMVL, 60446	3341	23W-15S	A2
Roselle Police Dept	103 S Prospect St, ROSL, 60172	2913	23W-7N	A5
Rosemont Police Dept	9501 E Devon Av, RSMT, 60018	2917	11W-7N	C3
Round Lake Beach Police Dept	1947 N Municipal Wy, RLKB, 60073	2475	22W-35N	B5
Round Lake Heights Police Dept	629 Pontiac Ct, RLKH, 60073	2474	23W-35N	D5
Round Lake Park Police Dept	215 E Main St, RLKP, 60073	2532	22W-33N	A3
Round Lake Police Dept	430 N Cedar Lake Rd, RDLK, 60073	2531	23W-33N	E2
St. Charles Police Dept	2 State Av, SCRL, 60174	2964	35W-3N	B7
Sauk Village Police Dept	21701 Torrence Av, SLVL, 60411	3597	3E-26S	E2
Schaumburg Police Dept	1000 W Schaumburg Rd, SMBG, 60194	2858	24W-10N	D5

FEATURE NAME Address City ZIP Code	MAP#	CGS	GRID
Schiller Park Police Dept 9526 Irving Park Rd, SRPK, 60176	2973	11W-5N	C1
Shorewood Police Dept 903 W Jefferson St, SRWD, 60404	3496	30W-24S	B5
Skokie Police Dept 8350 Laramie Av, SKOK, 60077	2865	6W-10N	D5
South Chicago Heights Police Dept 2729 Jackson Av, SCHT, 60411	3596	1W-26S	B3
South Elgin Police Dept 111 W Spring St, SEGN, 60177	2908	34W-8N	D3
South Holland Police Dept 16220 Wausau Av, SHLD, 60473	3428	0E-19S	D1
Steger Police Dept 35 W Steger Rd, STGR, 60475	3596	1W-27S	B5
Stickney Police Dept 6533 Pershing Rd, SKNY, 60402	3089	8W-4S	A6
Stone Park Police Dept 1629 N Mannheim Rd, SNPK, 60165	3029	12W-1N	A2
Streamwood Police Dept 401 E Irving Park Rd, SMWD, 60107	2857	28W-9N	A7
Sugar Grove Police Dept 10 Municipal Dr, SRGV, 60554	3135	43W-7S	B6
Summit-Argo Police Dept 5810 S Archer Rd, SMMT, 60501	3148	9W-6S	D4
Thornton Police Dept 700 Park Av, TNTN, 60476	3428	0E-20S	D5
Tinley Park Police Dept 17355 68th Ct, TYPK, 60477	3425	8W-20S	A5
Union Police Dept 6606 N Union Rd, UNON, 60180	2635	46W-25N	D4
University Park Police Dept 698 Burnham Dr, UYPK, 60466	3684	3W-29S	A1
Vernon Hills Police Dept 754 Lakeview Pkwy, VNHL, 60061	2647	16W-25N	D4
Villa Park Police Dept 11 W Home Av, VLPK, 60181	3027	18W-0N	A3
Warrenville Police Dept 3S245 Warren Av, WNVL, 60555	3081	28W-3S	A5
Wauconda Police Dept 311 S Main St, WCDA, 60084	2643	25W-27N	E1
Waukegan Police Dept 420 Robert V Sabonjian Pl, WKGN, 60085	2537	10W-34N	A1
Wayne Police Dept 5N430 Railroad St, WYNE, 60184	2965	32W-5N	D2
Westchester Police Dept 10300 W Roosevelt Rd, WSTR, 60154	3029	12W-0S	A7
West Chicago Police Dept 325 Clayton St, WCHI, 60185	3022	29W-0N	D5
West Dundee Police Dept 555 S 8th St, WDND, 60118	2800	34W-15N	E3
Western Springs Police Dept 740 Hillgrove Av, WNSP, 60558	3086	13W-4S	E7
Westmont Police Dept 500 N Cass Av, WTMT, 60559	3145	18W-4S	B1
Wheaton Police Dept 900 W Liberty Dr, WHTN, 60187	3024	25W-0S	B7
Wheeling Police Dept 255 W Dundee Rd, WLNG, 60090	2755	14W-18N	B4
Will County Sheriff's Dept 14 W Jefferson St, JLET, 60432	3498	24W-23S	E5
Willowbrook Police Dept 7760 S Quincy St, WLBK, 60527	3207	16W-8S	E2
Willow Springs Police Dept 8480 Archer Av, WLSP, 60480	3209	12W-9S	B3
Wilmette Police Dept 710 Ridge Rd, WLMT, 60091	2812	4W-13N	C6
Wilmington Police Dept 120 N Main St, WMTN, 60481	3853	27W-38S	D6
Winfield Police Dept 27W463 Jewell Rd, WNFD, 60190	3023	27W-0S	C6
Winnetka Police Dept 410 Green Bay Rd, WNKA, 60093	2812	4W-15N	B2
Winthrop Harbor Police Dept 830 Sheridan Rd, WPHR, 60096	2363	9W-42N	C6
Wood Dale Police Dept 404 N Wood Dale Rd, WDDL, 60191	2915	18W-6N	A7
Woodridge Police Dept 1 Plaza Dr, WDRG, 60517	3205	21W-8S	E1
Woodstock Police Dept 121 W Calhoun St, WDSK, 60098	2581	41W-31N	C1
Yorkville Police Dept 804 Game Farm Rd, YKVL, 60560	3333	43W-14S	B1
Zion Police Dept 2101 Salem Blvd, ZION, 60099	2422	10W-40N	A3

Libraries

FEATURE NAME Address City ZIP Code	MAP#	CGS	GRID
95th Street 3015 Cedar Glade Dr, NPVL, 60564	3202	29W-10S	C7
Acorn Public 15624 Central Av, OKFT, 60452	3347	7W-18S	D7
Addison Public 235 N JF Kennedy Dr, ADSN, 60101	2970	18W-3N	E4
Alsip Merrionette Park 11960 S Pulaski Rd, ALSP, 60803	3276	5W-14S	C5
Antioch Public 757 Main St, ANTH, 60002	2357	23W-42N	E5
Arlington Heights Memorial 500 N Dunton Av, ANHT, 60004	2807	17W-14N	A4
Aurora Public 233 S Constitution Dr, AURA, 60506	3137	38W-7S	A7
Barrington Area 505 N Northwest Hwy, BRTN, 60010	2751	25W-20N	A1
Bartlett Public 800 S Bartlett Rd, BRLT, 60103	2910	29W-7N	E5
Batavia Public 399 W Wilson St, BTVA, 60510	3078	35W-1S	B2
Bedford Park Public 7816 W 65th Pl, BDPK, 60501	3148	9W-7S	C5
Bellwood Public 600 Bohland Av, BLWD, 60104	3029	12W-0N	B5
Bensenville Public 200 S Church Rd, BNVL, 60106	2971	16W-5N	D2
Berkeley Public 1637 N Taft Av, BKLY, 60163	3028	14W-0N	C4
Berwyn Public 2701 Harlem Av, BRWN, 60402	3088	8W-2S	E3
Bloomingdale Public 101 E Fairfield Wy, BMDL, 60108	2969	23W-5N	A2
Blue Island 2433 York St, BLID, 60406	3277	3W-15S	B7
Bradford Anderson Oblesby 16640 Kedzie Av, MKHM, 60428	3427	4W-19S	A3
Bridgeview Public 7840 W 79th St, BGVW, 60455	3210	9W-8S	C2
Broadview Public 2226 S 16th Av, BDVW, 60155	3029	11W-1S	D7
Brookfield 3609 Grand Blvd, BKFD, 60513	3087	11W-3S	E5
Calumet City 660 Manistee Av, CTCY, 60409	3351	3E-17S	E6
Carol Stream Village 616 Hiawatha Dr, CLSM, 60188	2968	25W-3N	A6
Cary Public 1606 Three Oaks Rd, CRY, 60013	2642	30W-24N	A7
Chicago-Albany Park 5150 N Kimball Av, CHCG, 60625	2920	4W-6N	D6
Chicago-Altgeld 950 E 132nd Pl, CHCG, 60827	3351	1E-15S	A1
Chicago-American 50 E Huron St, CHCG, 60611	3034	0E-0N	C3
Chicago-Archer Heights 5148 S Archer Av, CHCG, 60632	3150	5W-5S	B2
Chicago-Austin 5615 W Race Av, CHCG, 60644	3031	7W-0N	C3
Chicago-Austin Irving 6110 W Irving Park Rd, CHCG, 60634	2975	7W-5N	B2
Chicago-Back of the Yards 4650 S Damen Av, CHCG, 60609	3091	2W-4S	C7
Chicago-Bessie Coleman 731 E 63rd St, CHCG, 60637	3152	0E-7S	E5
Chicago-Beverly 2121 W 95th St, CHCG, 60643	3213	2W-11S	C6
Chicago-Bezazian 1226 W Ainslie St, CHCG, 60640	2921	1W-6N	D6
Chicago-Blackstone 4904 S Lake Park Av, CHCG, 60615	3153	1E-5S	B1
Chicago-Brainerd 8945 S Loomis St, CHCG, 60620	3213	1W-10S	E4
Chicago-Brighton Park 4314 S Archer Av, CHCG, 60632	3090	3W-4S	E7
Chicago-Canaryville 642 W 43rd St, CHCG, 60609	3092	0W-4S	A6
Chicago-Chicago Lawn 6120 S Kedzie Av, CHCG, 60629	3150	4W-6S	E4
Chicago-Chinatown 2353 S Wentworth Av, CHCG, 60616	3092	0W-2S	B2
Chicago-Clearing 6423 W 63rd Pl, CHCG, 60638	3149	8W-7S	B5
Chicago-Damen Avenue 2056 N Damen Av, CHCG, 60647	2977	2W-2N	B6
Chicago-Dirkwales 345 W Fullerton Pkwy, CHCG, 60614	2978	0W-2N	A5
Chicago-Douglas 3353 W 13th St, CHCG, 60623	3032	4W-1S	D7
Chicago-Eckhart Park 1371 W Chicago Av, CHCG, 60622	3033	1W-0N	D3
Chicago-Edgebrook 5426 W Devon Av, CHCG, 60646	2919	6W-8N	D2
Chicago-Edgewater 1210 W Elmdale Av, CHCG, 60660	2921	1W-7N	D3
Chicago-Gage Park 2807 W 55th St, CHCG, 60629	3151	3W-6S	A3
Chicago-Galewood/Mont Clare 6969 W Grand Av, CHCG, 60707	2974	8W-2N	E6
Chicago-Hall 4801 S Michigan Av, CHCG, 60615	3152	0E-5S	C1
Chicago-Hansberry 4314 S Cottage Grove Av, CHCG, 60653	3092	0E-4S	E6
Chicago-Harold Ickes 2420 S State St, CHCG, 60616	3092	0W-2S	C2
Chicago-Harper 1116 E 59th St, CHCG, 60637	3153	1E-6S	A3
Chicago-Hegewisch 3048 E 130th St, CHCG, 60633	3280	3E-14S	A7
Chicago Heights Public 25 W 15th St, CHHT, 60411	3596	1W-25S	A1
Chicago-Humbolt 1605 N Troy St, CHCG, 60647	2976	3W-2N	E7
Chicago-Independence 3548 W Irving Park Rd, CHCG, 60618	2976	4W-5N	C1
Chicago-Jefferson Park 5363 W Lawrence Av, CHCG, 60630	2919	6W-5N	D7
Chicago-Jeffery Manor 2435 E 100th St, CHCG, 60617	3215	3E-11S	D7
Chicago-Kelly 6151 S Normal Av, CHCG, 60621	3152	0W-6S	B4
Chicago-Lincoln Belmont W Belmont Av, CHCG, 60657	2978	0W-4N	A3
Chicago-Lincoln Park 1150 W Fullerton Av, CHCG, 60614	2977	1W-3N	D5
Chicago-Mabel Manning 6 S Hoyne Av, CHCG, 60612	3033	2W-0S	B5
Chicago-Marshall Square 2724 W Cermak Rd, CHCG, 60608	3091	3W-1S	A2
Chicago-Martin Luther King Jr 3436 S Dr Martin L King Jr Dr, CHCG, 60616	3092	0E-3S	D4
Chicago-Mayfair 4400 W Lawrence Av, CHCG, 60630	2920	5W-6N	A6
Chicago-Mayfield 4200 W Lawrence Av, CHCG, 60630	2920	5W-6N	B6
Chicago-McKinley Park 1915 W 35th St, CHCG, 60609	3091	2W-3S	C5
Chicago-Midwest 2335 W Chicago Av, CHCG, 60612	3033	2W-0N	B3
Chicago-Mt Greenwood 11010 S Kedzie Av, CHCG, 60655	3276	4W-12S	E3
Chicago-Near North Branch 310 W Division St, CHCG, 60610	3034	0W-1N	B1
Chicago-North Austin 5724 W North Av, CHCG, 60639	3031	7W-2N	C1
Chicago-North Lake View 3754 N Southport Av, CHCG, 60613	2977	1W-4N	D2
Chicago-Northtown 6435 N California Av, CHCG, 60645	2920	3W-8N	E2
Chicago-Portage-Cragin 5108 W Belmont Av, CHCG, 60641	2975	6W-4N	D4
Chicago Public-Avalon Branch 8828 S Stony Island Av, CHCG, 60619	3215	1E-10S	B4
Chicago Public-Budlong Woods Branch 5630 N Lincoln Av, CHCG, 60625	2921	3W-6N	A5
Chicago Public-Garfield 6348 S Archer Av, CHCG, 60638	3149	7W-5S	B3
Chicago Public-Logan Square 3030 W Fullerton Av, CHCG, 60647	2976	3W-3N	E5
Chicago Public-Roden 6083 N Northwest Hwy, CHCG, 60631	2918	8W-7N	E3
Chicago Public-T. Roosevelt 1101 W Taylor St, CHCG, 60607	3033	1W-0S	E6
Chicago Public-Toman 4005 W 27th St, CHCG, 60623	3090	5W-2S	C3
Chicago-Pullman 11001 S Indiana Av, CHCG, 60628	3278	0E-12S	D2
Chicago-Richard J Daley 3400 S Halsted St, CHCG, 60608	3092	1W-3S	A4
Chicago Ridge 10400 Oxford Av, CHRG, 60415	3275	7W-12S	B1
Chicago-Robert Taylor 5120 S Federal St, CHCG, 60609	3152	0W-5S	B2
Chicago-Rogers Park 6907 N Clark St, CHCG, 60626	2921	2W-8N	C1
Chicago-Rudy Lozano 1805 S Loomis St, CHCG, 60608	3091	1W-1S	D1
Chicago-Scottsdale 4101 W 79th St, CHCG, 60652	3212	5W-9S	C2
Chicago-Sherman Park 5440 S Racine Av, CHCG, 60609	3151	1W-5S	E2
Chicago-South Chicago 9055 S Houston Av, CHCG, 60617	3216	3E-10S	A4
Chicago-Stateway 3647 S State St, CHCG, 60653	3092	0E-3S	C5
Chicago-Sulzer Regional 4455 N Lincoln Av, CHCG, 60625	2921	2W-5N	B7
Chicago-Thurgood Marshall 7506 S Racine Av, CHCG, 60620	3213	1W-8S	E1
Chicago-Tuley Park 501 E 90th Pl, CHCG, 60619	3214	0E-10S	D4
Chicago-Uptown 929 W Buena Av, CHCG, 60613	2977	1W-5N	E1
Chicago-Vodak-East Side Branch 3710 E 106th St, CHCG, 60617	3280	4E-11S	B1
Chicago-Walker 11071 S Hoyne Av, CHCG, 60643	3277	2W-12S	C3
Chicago-West Addison 7536 W Addison St, CHCG, 60634	2974	9W-4N	C3
Chicago-West Belmont 3104 N Narragansett Av, CHCG, 60634	2975	8W-3N	A4
Chicago-West Lawn 4020 W 63rd St, CHCG, 60629	3150	5W-6S	C5
Chicago-Whitney M Young Jr 7901 S Dr Martin L King Jr Dr, CHCG, 60619	3214	0E-9S	D2
Chicago-Woodson Regional 9525 S Halsted St, CHCG, 60628	3214	0W-11S	A6
Chicago-Wrightwood 2519 W 79th St, CHCG, 60652	3213	3W-9S	B2
Christian Lending 1025 Pleasant Pl, OKPK, 60302	3030	8W-0N	E4
Cicero Public 5225 W Cermak Rd, CCRO, 60804	3089	6W-2S	D2
Clarendon Hills Public 7 N Prospect Av, CNHL, 60514	3145	16W-5S	D2
Cook Memorial Public 413 N Milwaukee Av, LYVL, 60048	2591	16W-29N	D4
Crest Hill-Des Plaines Valley 1298 Theodore St, CTHL, 60403	3498	25W-21S	B1
Crestwood Public 4955 135th St, CTWD, 60445	3348	6W-16S	A2
Crete Public 1177 Main St, CRTE, 60417	3685	0W-29S	B1
Crystal Lake 126 W Paddock St, CLLK, 60014	2640	35W-25N	A4
Deerfield Public 920 Waukegan Rd, DRFD, 60015	2703	10W-21N	E7
Des Plaines Public 1501 E Thacker St, DSPN, 60016	2862	13W-10N	E4
Dolton Public 14037 Lincoln Av, DLTN, 60419	3350	0E-16S	D3
Downers Grove Public 1050 Curtiss St, DRGV, 60515	3144	19W-5S	C2
Dundee Twp 555 Barrington Av, EDND, 60118	2801	33W-16N	B2
Eisenhower Public 4652 N Olcott Av, HDHT, 60706	2918	9W-5N	C7
Ela Area Public 275 Mohawk Tr, LKZH, 60047	2698	23W-22N	E3
Elk Grove Village Public 1001 Wellington Av, EGVV, 60007	2914	19W-8N	C2
Ella Johnson Public 109 S State St, HPSR, 60140	2795	46W-16N	E2
Elmhurst Public 125 S Prospect Av, EMHT, 60126	3027	16W-1N	E2
Elmwood Park Public 1 W Conti Pkwy, EDPK, 60707	2974	9W-3N	C5
Eola Road Branch 555 S Eola Rd, AURA, 60504	3201	32W-8S	D2
Evanston-Main 1703 Orrington Av, EVTN, 60201	2867	2W-11N	B2
Evanston Public-North 2026 Central St, EVTN, 60201	2812	3W-12N	E7
Evanston-South Branch 949 Chicago Av, EVTN, 60202	2867	2W-10N	B4
Evergreen Park Public 9400 S Troy St, ENGN, 60805	3212	3W-10S	E5
Flossmoor Public 1000 Sterling Av, FSMR, 60422	3507	3W-22S	B2
Forest Park Public 7555 Jackson Blvd, FTPK, 60130	3030	9W-0S	C5
Fountaindale Public 300 W Briarcliff Rd, BGBK, 60440	3269	23W-11S	A2
Fox Lake Public 255 E Grand Av, FXLK, 60020	2473	27W-36N	C4
Frankfort Public 21119 Pfeiffer Rd, FKFT, 60423	3504	10W-25S	B7
Franklin Park Public 10311 Grand Av, FNPK, 60131	2973	12W-3N	A5
Fremont Public 470 N Lake St, MDLN, 60060	2590	19W-28N	D7
Geneva Public 127 James St, GNVA, 60134	3020	35W-1N	C4
Glencoe Public 320 Park Av, GLNC, 60022	2758	6W-17N	D5
Glen Ellyn Public 400 Duane St, GNEN, 60137	3025	22W-0N	B5
Glenside Public 25 E Fullerton Av, GLHT, 60139	2968	23W-2N	E7

FEATURE NAME Address City ZIP Code	MAP#	CGS	GRID
Glenview Public 1930 Glenview Rd, GNVW, 60025	2810	8W-13N	D6
Glenwood-Lynwood Public 320 E Glenwood Lansing Rd, GNWD, 60425	3508	0E-23S	E2
Grande Prairie Public 3479 183rd St, HLCT, 60429	3426	4W-22S	E7
Grayslake Public 100 Library Ln, GYLK, 60030	2533	20W-33N	A3
Green Hills Public 8611 W 103rd St, PSHL, 60465	3274	10W-12S	A1
Hammond-Lincoln 3835 S Hohman Av, HMND, 46327	3352		D2
Hammond-Main 564 E State St, HMND, 46320	3352		D6
Hammond-Rupp 847 117th St, HMND, 46394	3280		E4
Hammond-Sawyer 649 Mulberry St, HMND, 46324	3430		E2
Harold Washington Center 400 S State St, CHCG, 60605	3034	0W-0S	C5
Harvey Public 15447 Turlington Av, HRVY, 60426	3350	1W-18S	A7
Helen M Plum Memorial 110 W Maple St, LMBD, 60148	3026	20W-0N	B4
Highland Park 494 Laurel Av, HDPK, 60035	2704	8W-22N	E5
Highwood Public 102 Highwood Av, HIWD, 60040	2704	9W-23N	D2
Hillside Public 405 N Hillside Av, HLSD, 60162	3028	14W-0S	D5
Hinsdale Public 20 E Maple St, HNDL, 60521	3146	15W-4S	B1
Hodgkins Public 6500 Wenz Av, HGKN, 60525	3147	11W-7S	D6
Hoffman Estates-Main 1890 Hassell Rd, HFET, 60169	2804	25W-12N	B7
Homer Twp Public 14320 W 151st St, HMGN, 60491	3343	17W-17S	B6
Homewood Public 17917 Dixie Hwy, HMWD, 60430	3427	2W-21S	D6
Huntley 11000 Ruth Rd, HTLY, 60142	2692	39W-21N	B7
Indian Prairie Public 337 W Irving Park Rd, WDDL, 60191	2914	18W-6N	E7
Itasca Community 500 W Irving Park Rd, ITSC, 60143	2914	20W-6N	B6
John Crerar Science 5730 S Ellis Av, CHCG, 60637	3152	1E-6S	E3
Johnsburg Public 3000 N Johnsburg Rd, JNBG, 60050	2471	30W-35N	E5
John T Richardson 2350 N Kenmore Av, CHCG, 60614	2977	1W-2N	E6
Joliet Public 3340 Ring Rd, JLET, 60431	3417	28W-20S	B4
Joliet Public 150 N Ottawa St, JLET, 60432	3498	24W-23S	E4
Joseph Regenstein 1100 E 57th St, CHCG, 60637	3153	1E-6S	A3
Justice 7641 Oak Grove Av, JSTC, 60458	3210	11W-8S	A1
La Grange Park 555 N La Grange Rd, LGPK, 60525	3087	12W-3S	B5
La Grange Public 10 W Cossitt Av, LGNG, 60525	3087	12W-4S	C7
Lake Bluff Public 123 E Scranton Av, LKBF, 60044	2594	10W-28N	A6
Lake County-Dyer 2005 Hart St, DYR, 46311	3598		D2
Lake Forest 360 E Deerpath Rd, LKFT, 60045	2650	10W-26N	A2
Lake View Public W Belmont Av, CHCG, 60657	2977	2W-4N	C3
Lake Villa District 1001 E Grand Av, LKVL, 60046	2475	21W-37N	D1
Lansing Public 2750 Indiana Av, LNSG, 60438	3430	3E-21S	A6
Lemont Village of Public 50 E Wend St, LMNT, 60439	3270	19W-14S	D7
Lincolnwood Public 4000 W Pratt Av, LNWD, 60712	2920	5W-8N	B1
Lisle 777 Front St, LSLE, 60532	3143	22W-5S	B2
Lockport-Des Plaines Valley 121 E 8th St, LKPT, 60441	3419	22W-19S	C3
Lyons Public 4209 Joliet Av, LYNS, 60534	3088	9W-4S	C7
Manhattan Public 240 E Whitson St, MHTN, 60442	3678	19W-31S	A5
Marengo Public 200 S State St, MRGO, 60152	2634	50W-26N	B2
Matteson Public 801 School Av, MTSN, 60443	3506	5W-25S	B6
Maywood Public 121 S 5th Av, MYWD, 60153	3030	10W-0N	A4
McHenry Nunda Public 813 W Rand Rd, MchT, 60051	2529	29W-32N	C5
McHenry Public 809 N Front St, MHRY, 60050	2528	32W-32N	A4
Melrose Park Public 801 Broadway St, MLPK, 60160	3029	11W-1N	D3
Messenger Public 113 Oak St, NARA, 60542	3077	36W-4S	E7
Metropolitan-Calumet Park 1500 W 127th St, CTPK, 60827	3277	1W-14S	D7
Midlothian Public 14701 Kenton Av, MDLN, 60445	3348	5W-17S	B5
Mokena Community 11327 195th St, MKNA, 60448	3502	14W-23S	E3
Morton Grove Public 6140 Lincoln Av, MNGV, 60053	2865	7W-10N	B4
Mt Prospect Public 10 S Emerson St, MPPT, 60056	2808	15W-12N	A7
Munster-Lake County 8701 Calumet Av, MNSR, 46321	3510		E1
Naperville Boulevard 2035 Naper Blvd, NPVL, 60565	3204	25W-9S	B4
Naperville-Nichols Branch 200 W Jefferson Av, NPVL, 60540	3141	27W-6S	C5
Naperville Public 3015 Cedar Glade Dr, WldT, 60564	3202	29W-11S	C7
Newberry 60 W Walton St, CHCG, 60610	3034	0W-1N	B2
New Lenox Public 120 Veterans Pkwy, NLNX, 60451	3501	18W-24S	A6
Nippersink Public 5418 Hill Rd, RcmT, 60071	2412	34W-41N	D1
Northbrook Public 1201 Cedar Ln, NHBK, 60062	2757	10W-17N	B5
North Chicago Public 2100 Argonne Dr, NCHI, 60064	2536	11W-31N	D6
Northfield-Winnetka 1785 Orchard Ln, NHFD, 60093	2811	7W-15N	C2
Northlake Public 231 N Wolf Rd, NHLK, 60164	2972	13W-2N	D7
North Pulaski Branch 4330 W North Av, CHCG, 60639	3032	5W-2N	A1
North Riverside 2501 Des Plaines Av, NRIV, 60546	3088	9W-2S	C3
Oak Brook Public 600 Oak Brook Rd, OKBK, 60523	3086	15W-2S	A4
Oak Lawn Public 9427 Raymond Av, OKLN, 60453	3211	6W-10S	E6
Oak Park Public 834 Lake St, OKPK, 60301	3030	8W-0N	E3
Oak Park Public-Dole 255 Augusta St, OKPK, 60302	3031	7W-1N	B2
Oak Park Public-Maze Branch 845 Gunderson Av, OKPK, 60304	3031	8W-0S	A6
Oriole Park Branch 7454 W Balmoral Av, CHCG, 60656	2918	9W-6N	C5
Orland Park Public 14921 S Ravinia Av, ODPK, 60462	3345	12W-17S	D6
Oswego Public 32 W Jefferson St, OSWG, 60543	3263	37W-12S	C3
Palatine Branch 1230 Freeman Rd, HFET, 60192	2804	24W-15N	C2
Palatine Branch 1585 N Rand Rd, PLTN, 60074	2753	19W-17N	B4
Palatine Public 700 N North Ct, PLTN, 60067	2753	20W-16N	A6
Palos Heights Public 12501 W 125th St, PSHT, 60463	3274	8W-14S	E6
Palos Park Public 12330 S Forest Glen Blvd, PSPK, 60464	3274	11W-14S	A6
Park Forest 400 Lakewood Blvd, PKFT, 60466	3595	3W-26S	B3
Park Ridge Public 20 S Prospect Av, PKRG, 60068	2918	10W-8N	B1
Peotone Public 515 N 1st St, PTON, 60468	3861	9W-37S	A2
Plainfield Public 705 N Illinois St, PNFD, 60544	3338	30W-17S	C7
Plano Community 15 W North St, PLNO, 60545	3259	47W-13S	C6
Poplar Creek Public 4300 Audrey Ln, HRPK, 60133	2967	27W-5N	C2
Prairie Trails 8449 Moody Av, BRBK, 60459	3211	7W-9S	C3
Prospect Heights Public 12 Elm St, PTHT, 60070	2807	15W-15N	E3
Richton Park Public 4155 Sauk Tr, RNPK, 60471	3594	5W-27S	C3
Riverdale Public 208 W 144th St, RVDL, 60827	3350	0W-16S	C4
River Forest Public 735 Lathrop Av, RVFT, 60305	3030	9W-0N	C3
River Grove Public 8638 W Grand Av, RVGV, 60171	2973	10W-3N	E5
Riverside Public 1 Burling Rd, RVSD, 60546	3088	9W-3S	C5
Rolling Meadows Public 3110 Martin Ln, RGMW, 60008	2806	19W-13N	B5
Romeoville-Des Plaines 318 N Independence Blvd, RMVL, 60446	3341	23W-16S	A3
Romeoville-Fountaindale 201 W Normantown Rd, RMVL, 60446	3340	24W-15S	E1
Roselle Public 40 S Park St, ROSL, 60172	2913	23W-7N	A4
Round Lake Area 906 Hart Rd, RDLK, 60073	2531	24W-34N	D2
Saint Charles Public 1 E Main St, SCRL, 60174	2964	35W-3N	B7
Schaumburg Public 130 S Roselle Rd, SMBG, 60193	2859	23W-10N	A6
Schiller Park Public 4200 Old River Rd, SRPK, 60176	2973	11W-5N	D1
Shakespeare Data Bank 1217 Ashland Av, EVTN, 60202	2867	3W-10N	A4
Shorewood-Troy 650 Deerwood Dr, SRWD, 60404	3496	30W-23S	C5
Skokie Public 5215 Oakton St, SKOK, 60077	2865	6W-9N	D6
South Holland 16250 Wausau Av, SHLD, 60473	3428	0E-19S	D1
Steger-South Chicago Heights 54 E 31st St, STGR, 60475	3596	0W-27S	B5
Stickney-Forest View 6800 43rd St, SKNY, 60402	3089	8W-4S	A7
Streamwood-Poplar Creek 1405 S Park Av, SMWD, 60107	2911	28W-9N	A1
Sugar Grove Public 2 Snow St, SRGV, 60554	3135	42W-7S	C7
Summit Public 6233 S Archer Rd, SMMT, 60501	3148	9W-6S	C5
Thomas Ford Memorial 800 Chestnut St, WNSP, 60558	3086	14W-4S	E7
Thornton Public 111 E Margaret St, TNTN, 60476	3428	0E-21S	D6
Three Rivers-Minooka 109 N Wabena Av, MNKA, 60447	3583	33W-28S	B7
Tinley Park Public 7851 Timber Dr, TYPK, 60477	3424	9W-21S	D6
University Park Public 1100 Blackhawk Dr, UYPK, 60449	3684	3W-30S	B4
Vernon Area Public 300 Old Half Day Rd, LNSH, 60069	2702	15W-23N	A3
Vernon Hills Public 23184 N Indian Creek Rd, LNSH, 60069	2702	15W-23N	A3
Villa Park Public 305 S Ardmore Av, VLPK, 60181	3027	17W-0N	A4
Warren Newport Public 224 N Oplaine Rd, GRNE, 60031	2535	14W-34N	C1
Warrenville Public 28W751 Stafford Pl, WNVL, 60555	3080	28W-3S	E5
Wauconda Area Public 801 N Main St, WCDA, 60084	2587	26W-27N	E7
Wauconda Twp 212 Osage St, WCDA, 60084	2643	26W-27N	E1
Waukegan Public 128 N County St, WKGN, 60085	2537	10W-34N	B1
Westchester Public 10700 Canterbury St, WSTR, 60154	3087	13W-1S	A1
West Chicago Public 118 W Washington St, WCHI, 60185	3022	30W-0N	C4
Westmont Public 428 N Cass Av, WTMT, 60559	3145	18W-4S	B1
Wheaton Public 225 N Cross St, WHTN, 60187	3024	24W-0S	C6
Wheeling-Buffalo Grove 355 Schoenbeck Rd, WLNG, 60090	2754	15W-17N	E5
Wheeling-North Suburban 200 W Dundee Rd, WLNG, 60090	2755	14W-18N	C4
William Leonard Public 13822 Central Park Av, RBBN, 60472	3348	4W-16S	D3
Wilmette Public 1242 Wilmette Av, WLMT, 60091	2812	3W-13N	D6
Wilmington Public 201 S Kankakee St, WMTN, 60481	3853	27W-38S	D7
Winfield Public 0S291 Winfield Rd, WNFD, 60190	3023	27W-0S	C6
Winnetka Public 768 Oak St, WNKA, 60093	2812	5W-15N	B2
Wood Dale Public 520 N Wood Dale Rd, WDDL, 60191	2915	18W-6N	A6
Woodridge Public 3 Plaza Dr, WDRG, 60517	3205	21W-8S	E1
Woodstock Public 414 W Judd St, WDSK, 60098	2524	41W-31N	C7
Worth Public 6917 W 111th St, WRTH, 60482	3275	8W-13S	A3
Yorkville Public 902 Game Farm Rd, YKVL, 60560	3333	43W-14S	B1
Zion-Benton Public 2400 Gabriel Av, ZION, 60099	2422	10W-40N	A3

Military Installations

FEATURE NAME Address City ZIP Code	MAP#	CGS	GRID
Air National Guard 5400 W 63rd St, CHCG, 60638	3149	6W-6S	D5
Armory N Broadway St, CHCG, 60660	2921	1W-7N	D4
Aurora Armory 102 N River St, AURA, 60506	3138	35W-7S	B7
Coast Guard Station S Coast Guard Dr, CHCG, 60637	3153	2E-7S	C4
Coast Guard Station N Lake Shore Dr, CokC, 60601	3034		D4
Crestwood Armory 13838 Springfield Av, CTWD, 60445	3348	4W-16S	C3
Donnelley Armory 1901 S Calumet Av, CHCG, 60616	3092	0E-1S	C1
Elgin Armory 254 Raymond St, ELGN, 60120	2855	33W-11N	A4
Fort Sheridan HDPK, 60037	2704	8W-23N	E2
General Jones Armory 5200 S Cottage Grove Av, CHCG, 60615	3152	0E-5S	D2
Great Lakes Naval Station 2601 Paul Jones St, NCHI, 60088	2594	10W-31N	A1
Illinois National Guard 8660 W Cermak Rd, PvsT, 60141	3088	10W-1S	A2
Joliet Armory 2900 W Jefferson St, JLET, 60435	3497	27W-24S	C5
Joliet Army Training Area CnhT, 60421	3674	27W-30S	C4
National Guard S La Grange Rd, ODPK, 60462	3345	12W-18S	D7
National Guard Armory CHCG, 60612	3033	3W-0S	A5
Northwest Armory 1551 N Kedzie Av, CHCG, 60622	3032	3W-1N	D1
O'Hare Air Force Base & Air National-Guard Bessie Coleman Dr, CHCG, 60666	2917	13W-7N	A3
US Army Reserve Center ANHT, 60005	2806	18W-12N	D7
US Army Reserves AURA, 60506	3137	36W-5S	E3
United States Army Reserve Training-Center WKGN, 60087	2479	11W-36N	C5
US Coast Guard 4001 E 98th St, CHCG, 60617	3216	4E-10S	B6
US Coast Guard 1011 W Ogden Av, NPVL, 60563	3141	28W-5S	A4
US Coast Guard 9 N Harbor Pl, WKGN, 60085	2537		C1
US Coast Guard Marine Safety 83rd St, DGvT, 60527	3207	16W-9S	E3
US Coast Guard Station 10 Harbor Dr, WLMT, 60091	2813	2W-13N	B6
US Naval Reserve Training Center Howell Pl, AURA, 60505	3200	34W-9S	C4
Waukegan Armory 1600 W Glen Flora Av, WKGN, 60085	2479	11W-35N	E6
Woodstock Armory 1301 Sunset Ridge Rd, WDSK, 60098	2524	43W-31N	A6

Museums

FEATURE NAME Address City ZIP Code	MAP#	CGS	GRID
4art 1932 S Halsted St, CHCG, 60608	3092	1W-1S	A1
African American Heritage Mus 126 S Kendall St, AraT, 60504	3200	34W-8S	E1
Air Classics Mus SgrT, 60554	3135	43W-6S	A6
American Police Center & Mus 1717 S State St, CHCG, 60616	3092	0W-1S	C1
Arlington Heights Historical Mus 110 W Fremont St, ANHT, 60004	2807	18W-14N	A4
Aurora Regional Fire Mus 53 N Broadway, AURA, 60505	3138	35W-7S	B7
Balzekas Mus of Lithuanian Culture 6500 S Pulaski Rd, CHCG, 60629	3150	5W-7S	B5
Batavia Depot Mus 155 Houston St, BTVA, 60510	3078	35W-1S	B1

Chicago 7-County Points of Interest Index

FEATURE NAME Address City ZIP Code	MAP#	CGS	GRID
Beacon Street Gallery 4131 N Broadway St, CHCG, 60613	2977	1W-5N	E1
Beith House Mus 8 W Indiana St, SCRL, 60174	2964	35W-3N	B7
Billy Graham Center Mus 500 College Av, WHTN, 60187	3024	24W-0S	D6
Bloomingdale Park District Mus 108 S Bloomingdale Rd, BMDL, 60108	2969	23W-5N	A1
Cabin Nature Program Center 111 N Wood Dale Rd, WDDL, 60191	2971	17W-5N	A1
Campbell House Art Gallery 33W848 Cherry Ln, GnvT, 60134	3020	33W-0N	E4
Cernan Earth & Space Center 2000 N 5th Av, RVGV, 60171	2974	10W-2N	A7
Chester Gould-Dick Tracy Mus Main St, WDSK, 60098	2524	41W-31N	D7
Chicago Academy of Sciences 2060 N Clark St, CHCG, 60614	2978	0W-2N	B6
Chicago Architecture Foundation 224 S Michigan Av, CHCG, 60604	3034	0E-0S	C5
Chicago Athenaeum Mus 190 S Roselle Rd, SMBG, 60193	2859	23W-10N	A6
Chicago Children's Mus 700 E Grand Av, CHCG, 60611	3034	0E-0N	E3
Chicago Cultural Center 78 E Washington St, CHCG, 60602	3034	0E-0N	C4
Chicago Historical Society Mus 1601 N Clark St, CHCG, 60614	2978	0W-2N	B7
Cuneo Mus & Gardens 1350 S Milwaukee Av, VNHL, 60061	2647	16W-26N	E3
Des Plaines Historical Mus 789 Pearson St, DSPN, 60016	2863	13W-10N	A4
Door County Maritime Mus 120 N Madison Av, LGNG, 60525	3087	12W-3S	B6
Downers Grove Historical Mus 831 Maple Av, DRGV, 60515	3144	19W-5S	D3
Dundee Twp Historical Society Mus 426 Highland Av, WDND, 60118	2800	34W-16N	E2
Dunham Hunt Mus 302 Cedar Av, SCRL, 60174	2964	35W-3N	B7
DuPage Children's Mus 301 N Washington St, NPVL, 60540	3141	27W-6S	C4
DuPage County Historical Mus 102 E Wesley St, WHTN, 60187	3024	24W-0S	C7
Du Sable Mus of African American-History 740 E 56th Pl, CHCG, 60637	3152	0E-6S	D3
Elgin Area Mus 360 Park St, ELGN, 60120	2855	33W-11N	A3
Elgin Public Mus 225 Grand Blvd, ELGN, 60120	2855	32W-11N	B3
Elmhurst Art Mus 150 S Cottage Hill Av, EMHT, 60126	3027	16W-1N	E2
Elmhurst Historical Mus 120 E Park Av, EMHT, 60126	3027	16W-1N	E2
Ernest Hemingway Mus 200 N Oak Park Av, OKPK, 60302	3030	8W-0N	E3
Evanston Art Center 2603 Sheridan Rd, EVTN, 60201	2813	2W-13N	C7
Farmhouse Mus 499 Biesterfield Rd, EGVV, 60007	2914	19W-8N	C2
Farnsworth House 14520 River Rd, LtRT, 60545	3331	47W-15S	D3
Field Mus of Natural History 1200 S Lake Shore Dr, CHCG, 60605	3034	0E-1S	D7
Fire Barn Mus & Park 533 St. Charles St, ELGN, 60120	2855	33W-10N	A5
First Division Mus 1S151 Winfield Rd, WnfT, 60187	3081	27W-1S	C1
Frank Lloyd Wright Home & Studio 951 Chicago Av, OKPK, 60302	3030	8W-1N	E3
Gallery 500 Wells 500 N Wells St, CHCG, 60610	3034	0W-0N	B3
Gallery Romain 1478 N Milwaukee Av, CHCG, 60622	3033	2W-1N	C1
Geneva Historical Mus 113 S 3rd St, GNVA, 60134	3020	35W-1N	B3
George S Clayson House Mus 224 E Palatine Rd, PLTN, 60067	2805	20W-16N	E1
Glencoe Historical Society Mus 377 Park Av, GLNC, 60022	2758	6W-17N	D5
Glen Ellyn Historic Society 800 N Main St, GNEN, 60137	3025	22W-1N	C3
Glessner House Mus 1800 S Prairie Av, CHCG, 60616	3092	0E-1S	C1
Grand Army of the Republic Mus 23 E Downer Pl, AURA, 60505	3138	35W-7S	B7
Granite Gallery 111 E Townline Rd, VNHL, 60061	2647	16W-25N	C4
Granite Gallery 952 Green Bay Rd, WNKA, 60093	2759	5W-16N	A7
Grant Hall Mus 411 Washington St, FXLK, 60041	2473	26W-36N	D5
Graue Mill & Mus 3770 York Rd, OKBK, 60523	3086	15W-3S	A6
Gregg House Mus 117 S Linden Av, WTMT, 60559	3145	17W-5S	B2
Haegar Pottery Factory S Van Buren St, EDND, 60118	2801	33W-16N	A3
Haines House Mus 1917 N Sheridan Rd, WKGN, 60087	2480	10W-36N	B5
Hellenic Mus & Cultural Center W Kinzie St, CHCG, 60610	3034	0W-0N	B3
Hinsdale Historical Society 15 S Clay St, HNDL, 60521	3146	15W-4S	A1
Historical Society Kenilworth Av, KLWH, 60043	2812	4W-14N	D4
Hoosier Grove Mus 700 W Irving Park Rd, HnrT, 60107	2856	29W-10N	D7
Illinois & Michigan Canal Mus 803 S State St, LKPT, 60441	3419	23W-19S	B3
Illinois Art Gallery 100 W Randolph St, CHCG, 60601	3034	0W-0N	B4
Illinois Aviation Mus 130 S Clow International Pkwy, BGBK, 60490	3268	26W-12S	A2
Illinois Railway Mus 7000 Olson Rd, CrlT, 60180	2635	45W-25N	E5
Illinois State Mus S State St, LKPT, 60441	3419	23W-19S	B3
International Cinema Mus 319 W Erie St, CHCG, 60610	3034	0W-0N	B3
International Mus of Surgical-Science 1524 N Lake Shore Dr, CHCG, 60610	3034	0E-1N	C1
Isle A La Cache Mus 501 E Romeo Rd, RMVL, 60446	3341	23W-16S	B3
Jane Addams Hull-House Mus 800 S Halsted St, CHCG, 60607	3034	1W-0S	A5
Joliet Area Historical Society Mus 204 N Ottawa St, JLET, 60432	3498	24W-23S	E4
Jurica Nature Mus Maple Av, LSLE, 60532	3142	24W-6S	D4
Kenosha Military Mus 11114 120th Av, PTPR, 53142	2360		D1
Kohl Children's Mus 2100 Patriot Blvd, GNVW, 60025	2810	9W-14N	B3
Kruse House Mus 527 Main St, WCHI, 60185	3022	29W-0N	D4
Lake Bluff Mus 127 E Scranton Av, LKBF, 60044	2594	10W-28N	A5
Lake County Mus 27277 N Forest Preserve Rd, FmtT, 60084	2644	24W-27N	C1
Lansing Veterans Memorial Mus Burnham Av, LNSG, 60411	3510	4E-23S	B2
Lemont Historical Society Mus 306 Lemont St, LMNT, 60439	3270	19W-13S	D5
Lisle Station Mus 921 School St, LSLE, 60532	3143	22W-5S	B2
Little White School Mus 2 Polk St, OSWG, 60543	3263	37W-12S	C4
Lizzadro Mus of Lapidary Art 220 S Cottage Hill Av, EMHT, 60126	3027	16W-1N	E3
Lombard Historical Mus 23 W Maple St, LMBD, 60148	3026	19W-0N	B4
Mary & Leigh Block Mus of Art 40 S Campus Dr, EVTN, 60201	2867	2W-11N	C2
McCormick Tribune Freedom Mus 445 N Michigan Av, CHCG, 60611	3034	0E-0N	C3
McDonald's Mus 400 Mannheim Rd, DSPN, 60016	2863	13W-11N	A3
McHenry County Mus 6422 Main St, UNON, 60180	2635	46W-25N	D4
Mexican Fine Arts Center Mus 1852 W 19th St, CHCG, 60608	3091	2W-1S	C1
Midwest Carvers Mus 16236 Vincennes Rd, SHLD, 60473	3428	0W-19S	B1
Mitchell Mus of the American Indian 2600 Central Park Av, EVTN, 60201	2812	4W-13N	C7
Morton B Weiss Mus of Judaica 1100 E Hyde Park Blvd, CHCG, 60615	3153	1E-5S	A1
Morton Grove Historical Mus 6240 Dempster St, MNGV, 60053	2865	7W-11N	A3
Motorola Mus of Electronics 1297 E Algonquin Rd, SMBG, 60173	2805	21W-13N	D6
Mt Prospect Historical Society 101 S Maple St, MPPT, 60056	2808	15W-12N	A7
Museum of Broadcast Communications 78 E Washington St, CHCG, 60602	3034	0E-0N	C4
Museum of Contemporary Art 220 E Chicago Av, CHCG, 60611	3034	0E-1N	C2
Museum of Holography 1134 W Washington Blvd, CHCG, 60607	3033	1W-0N	E4
Museum of Science & Industry 5700 S Lake Shore Dr, CHCG, 60637	3153	2E-6S	B3
National Italian Amer Sports Hall of-Fame 1431 W Taylor St, CHCG, 60607	3033	1W-0S	D6
National Jazz Mus 1727 S Indiana Av, CHCG, 60616	3092	0E-1S	C1
National Vietnam Veterans Mus 1801 S Indiana Av, CHCG, 60616	3092	0E-1S	C1
Oak Lawn Children's Mus Edison Av, OKLN, 60453	3211	6W-11S	D6
Oakview Mus Kilpatrick Av, OKLN, 60453	3276	5W-12S	A3
Open Door Gallery 1630 N Milwaukee Av, CHCG, 60647	2977	2W-2N	B7
Oriental Institute Mus 1155 E 58th St, CHCG, 60637	3153	1E-6S	A3
Peace Mus 314 W Institute Pl, CHCG, 60610	3034	0W-1N	B2
Peck Farm Park 38W199 Kaneville Rd, GnvT, 60134	3019	38W-0S	A6
Peggy Notebaert Nature Mus 2430 N Cannon Dr, CHCG, 60614	2978	0W-3N	B5
Pioneer Settlement S State St, LKPT, 60441	3419	22W-19S	C3
Pioneer Sholes School SchT, 60175	2963	37W-3N	D5
Polish Mus of America 984 N Milwaukee Av, CHCG, 60622	3033	1W-1N	D2
Power House Energy Mus 100 Shiloh Blvd, ZION, 60099	2422	9W-40N	D3
Raupp Memorial Mus 901 Dunham Ln, BFGV, 60089	2701	17W-21N	A7
Round Barn Farm & Mus MhtT, 60442	3677	20W-29S	D1
St. Charles History Mus 2 E Main St, SCRL, 60174	2964	35W-3N	B7
Skokie Heritage Mus 8031 Floral Av, SKOK, 60077	2865	6W-10N	E5
Swedish American Mus Center 5211 N Clark St, CHCG, 60640	2921	1W-6N	D5
Terra Mus of American Art 664 N Michigan Av, CHCG, 60611	3034	0E-0N	C3
The Art Institute of Chicago 111 S Michigan Av, CHCG, 60603	3034	0E-0S	C5
The Grove 1421 Milwaukee Av, GNVW, 60025	2809	11W-14N	C5
Tinley Park Historical Society 6727 174th St, TYPK, 60477	3425	8W-20S	B5
Trailside Mus 738 Thatcher Av, RVFT, 60305	3030	10W-0N	B3
Ukrainian Institute of Modern Art 2320 W Chicago Av, CHCG, 60622	3033	2W-1N	B2
Ukrainian National Mus 721 N Oakley Blvd, CHCG, 60612	3033	2W-0N	B3
Vietnam War Mus 954 W Carmen Av, CHCG, 60640	2921	1W-6N	E5
Villa Park Historical Mus 220 S Villa Av, VLPK, 60181	3027	17W-0N	B4
Volo Auto Mus 27582 Volo Village Rd, VOLO, 60041	2530	27W-31N	B6
Walter Payton Mus 205 N Broadway, AURA, 60505	3138	35W-7S	B7
Warren Tavern 3S540 2nd St, WNVL, 60555	3081	28W-3S	A6
West Chicago City Mus 132 Main St, WCHI, 60185	3022	29W-1N	C4
Wheaton History Center 606 N Main St, WHTN, 60187	3024	25W-0S	C6
Willard House-WCTU Mus 1730 Chicago Av, EVTN, 60201	2867	2W-11N	B2
Will County Historical Society 803 S State St, LKPT, 60441	3419	22W-19S	C2
Wilmette Historical Mus 609 Ridge Rd, WLMT, 60091	2812	4W-13N	C6
Winnetka Historical Mus 411 Linden St, WNKA, 60093	2812	5W-15N	B2
Woman Made Gallery 685 N Milwaukee Av, CHCG, 60622	3033	1W-0N	E3

Open Space

FEATURE NAME	MAP#	CGS	GRID
26th Street Woods Forest Preserve, - PvsT	3087	11W-2S	D3
Alden Sedge Meadow, AdnT	2349	44W-41N	C7
Alessio Prairie Preserve, CTHL	3418	26W-21S	A7
Alexander Stillman Nature Center, - SBTN	2803	27W-14N	B3
Allyson Woods Forest Preserve, NfdT	2809	12W-15N	A1
Almond Marsh Forest Preserve, WrnT	2534	18W-32N	A5
Arboretum Woods Pk, LSLE	3083	23W-4S	A7
Arie Crown Woods Forest Preserve, - CTSD	3147	13W-7S	B7
Army Trail Nature Center, AddT	2970	20W-3N	B4
Ashbury Greenway, NPVL	3267	28W-11S	A1
Atkinson Forest Preserve, LbvT	2592	13W-30N	D2
Aurora West Forest Preserve, SgrT	3136	40W-5S	B4
Avery Preserve, PnfT	3339	28W-17S	A6
Bachelor Grove Forest Preserve, BmnT	3347	8W-16S	B3
Baker's Lake Forest Preserve, BRTN	2751	24W-18N	B4
Bannockburn Forest Preserve, BKBN	2703	12W-22N	B5
Barrington Bog Nature Preserve, LKBN	2643	25W-24N	E6
Beaubien Woods Forest Preserve, CHCG	3351	1E-15S	A1
Beck's Woods Conservation Area, CmgT	2405	52W-38N	B6
Belleau Lake Forest Preserve, PKRG	2863	12W-10N	C5
Belleau Woods Forest Preserve, WHTN	3081	26W-1S	D1
Bemis Woods Forest Preserve, PvsT	3086	14W-3S	C5
Bensenville Ditch Forest Preserve, - BNVL	2972	15W-4N	B3
Berkeley Prairie Forest Preserve, - HDPK	2704	10W-21N	A5
Beulah Pk Nature Area, ZION	2422	10W-41N	A1
Big Rock Forest Preserve, BRkT	3196	46W-8S	A3
Big Woods Forest Preserve, AURA	3079	31W-3S	D6
Binnie Woods Forest Preserve, RtdT	2746	38W-17N	B6
Blackberry Maples Forest Preserve, - BbyT	3075	43W-1S	B3
Bliss Woods Forest Preserve, SgrT	3135	42W-5S	D3
Braidwood Dunes & Savanna, RedT	4031	30W-42S	C1
Braidwood Dunes & Savanna, RedT	3942	30W-42S	C7
Brezina Woods Forest Preserve, PvsT	3087	12W-2S	A3
Brookfield Woods Forest Preserve, - BKFD	3088	10W-2S	A4
Brookwood Forest Preserve, WDDL	2970	19W-5N	D2
Brownell Woods Forest Preserve, TNTN	3428	0E-21S	D7
Buffalo Creek Forest Preserve, ElaT	2753	19W-20N	C2
Buffalo Pk Forest Preserve, DndT	2747	24W-19N	D3
Buffalo Woods Forest Preserve, LynT	3209	11W-9S	D3
Bunker Hill Woods Forest Preserve, - NLES	2919	8W-8N	A1
Burlington Pk Forest Preserve, NPVL	3141	27W-6S	B5
Burnham Woods Forest Preserve, BNHM	3352	4E-16S	B2
Burnidge-Paul Wolff Forest Preserve, - RtdT	2799	38W-14N	A6
Burr Oak Forest Preserve, BRRG	3208	15W-8S	B1
Burr Oak Woods Forest Preserve, OrlT	3346	9W-16S	D3
Butternut Preserve, CLLK	2639	38W-25N	A4
Calumet City Forest Preserve, CTCY	3430	4E-18S	B1
Calumet Woods Forest Preserve, RVDL	3349	2W-16S	D2
Campground Road Forest Preserve, - CHCG	2863	12W-10N	B5
Camp Pine Woods Forest Preserve, - NfdT	2809	12W-13N	B6
Campton Forest Preserve, CmpT	2962	41W-4N	A4
Cantigny Woods Forest Preserve, CTSD	3147	13W-8S	A7
Cap Sauers Holdings Forest Preserve, - PlsT	3272	14W-13S	D4
Catherine Chevalier Forest Preserve, - SRPK	2917	11W-6N	D5
Cedar Lake Bog Nature Preserve, LkvT	2416	24W-38N	D7
Center Point Recreation & Preserve, - NHLK	2972	14W-2N	C7
Cermak Woods Forest Preserve, RVSD	3088	9W-4S	C6
Che-Che-Pin-Qua Woods Forest Preserve, - CHCG	2974	10W-4N	A2
Cherry Hill Woods Forest Preserve, - PlsT	3273	12W-14S	B5
Chicago Portage Woods Forest Preserve, - LYNS	3148	9W-5S	C1
Chipilly Woods Forest Preserve, NHBK	2757	8W-17N	D5
Chippewa Woods Forest Preserve, CHCG	2917	11W-8N	C1
Chiwaukee Prairie Nature Preserve, - PTPR	2363		D3
Churchill Woods Forest Preserve, - MltT	3025	21W-0N	E4
Clayhole Woods Forest Preserve, CTCY	3429	3E-18S	E1
Columbia Woods, WLSP	3208	13W-10S	E4
Conservation Area, GNEN	3025	22W-1N	C3
Coral Woods, CrlT	2634	48W-24N	E6
County Forest Preserve, CmpT	2962	41W-6N	A1
County Forest Preserve, OrlT	3346	9W-17S	D5
County Forest Preserve, OrlT	3423	12W-20S	C5
Crabtree Forest Preserve, BrnT	2803	26W-15N	D1
Cranberry Lake Wetland Preserve &- Wildlife, HNVL	2532	22W-33N	B2
Cricket Creek Forest Preserve, ADSN	2971	17W-2N	B6
Crooked Creek Woods Forest Preserve, - PlsT	3273	11W-12S	D2
Cuba Marsh Forest Preserve, DRPK	2698	24W-21N	C7
Culver Forest Preserve, AURA	3136	39W-6S	D5
Dam No 1 Woods Forest Preserve, WLNG	2755	13W-17N	E4
Dam No 4 Forest Preserve, PKRG	2917	11W-7N	D3
Danada Forest Preserve, MltT	3082	25W-3S	B6

FEATURE NAME Address City ZIP Code	MAP#	CGS	GRID
Dan Ryan Woods Forest Preserve, CHCG	3213	2W-9S	B3
Darien Chestnut Forest Preserve, DRN	3206	19W-8S	C2
Deer Creek Forest Preserve, CteT	3684	2W-29S	D1
Deer Creek Open Space, WTMT	3144	18W-6S	E4
Deer Grove Forest Preserve, PltT	2752	22W-18N	A3
Dick Young Forest Preserve, BbyT	3076	39W-2S	D3
Duck Farm Forest Preserve, LkvT	2475	21W-37N	D2
DuPage River Confluence Preserve, - BGBK	3204	26W-11S	A7
DuPage River Preserve, BGBK	3267	27W-11S	C1
East Branch Forest Preserve, BmdT	2969	21W-2N	D6
Edgebrook Woods Forest Preserve, - CHCG	2919	6W-7N	D4
Eggers Woods Forest Preserve, CHCG	3280	4E-13S	C4
Elizabeth A Conkey Forest Preserve, - WthT	3347	7W-15S	C1
Elm Roads Forest Preserve, VrnT	2648	14W-24N	C7
Emily Oaks Nature Center, SKOK	2866	5W-9N	A6
Ethel's Woods Forest Preserve, NptT	2418	18W-40N	E2
Fabyan East Windmill Forest Preserve, - GNVA	3020	35W-0N	C5
Fairfield Nature Preserve, RDLK	2531	24W-33N	C2
Ferson Creek Fen Nature Preserve, - SchT	2964	35W-4N	A4
Fischer Woods Forest Preserve, AddT	2971	16W-3N	C4
Fitchie Creek Forest Preserve, PltT	2852	39W-10N	E6
Florsheim Nature Preserve, LNSH	2702	13W-24N	E1
Forest Glen Woods Forest Preserve, - CHCG	2919	6W-6N	D5
Forest Preserve, BLID	3349	2W-15S	D1
Forest Preserve, DSPN	2862	13W-12N	E2
Forest Preserve, JLET	3584	29W-28S	E7
Forest Preserve, PlsT	3273	11W-14S	E7
Forest Preserve, RVFT	3030	9W-0N	D3
Forest Preserve, SHLD	3351	1E-18S	B7
Forked Creek Preserve, WslT	3943	26W-40S	E2
Forty Acre Woods Forest Preserve, - PlsT	3273	11W-14S	D5
Fourth Lake Forest Preserve, LkvT	2476	20W-37N	A3
Fox Hollow Forest Preserve, DGvT	3206	20W-8S	C2
Fox River Bluff Forest Preserve East, - SchT	2964	35W-5N	B1
Fox River Bluff Forest Preserve West, - SchT	2964	35W-5N	B1
Fox River Forest Preserve, PTBR	2642	28W-25N	E4
Fox River Shores Forest Preserve, - CPVL	2747	34W-18N	E6
Freeman Kane Nature Preserve, RtdT	2745	40W-18N	D5
Friendship Pk Conservatory, DSPN	2862	15W-10N	A5
Fullersburg Woods Forest Preserve, - OKBK	3086	15W-3S	A5
Fullerton Pk Forest Preserve, AddT	2970	19W-2N	C6
Fullerton Woods Forest Preserve, - RVGV	2973	11W-3N	E4
Gander Mountain Forest Preserve, - AntT	2355	28W-43N	E4
GAR Woods Forest Preserve, RVFT	3030	10W-0N	B4
Gateway Wetlands, BGBK	3205	21W-10S	D5
Gensburg-Markham Prairie Nature-Preserve, MKHM	3349	3W-18S	A7
Glenwood Pk Forest Preserve, BtvT	3078	35W-2S	B4
Glenwood Woods Forest Preserve, BlmT	3508	0W-23S	D3
Goodrich Forest Preserve, LslT	3204	25W-8S	B1
Goose Lake Natural Area, HbnT	2351	39W-42N	D6
Grainger Woods Forest Preserve, MTWA	2648	14W-25N	C6
Granger Forest Preserve, BRLT	2966	29W-6N	C1
Grant Woods Forest Preserve, LkvT	2474	24W-37N	B2
Grassy Lake Forest Preserve, LKBN	2643	27W-24N	B6
Greenbelt Forest Preserve, WKGN	2536	12W-32N	C4
Greene Valley Forest Preserve, LslT	3205	23W-9S	B3
Gunnar Anderson Forest Preserve, - GNVA	3020	35W-0N	B5
Gurnee Woods Forest Preserve, WrnT	2535	15W-33N	A3
Half Day Forest Preserve, VrnT	2702	15W-23N	A1
Hammel Woods Forest Preserve, SRWD	3496	29W-23S	D4
Hampshire Forest Preserve, HshT	2796	44W-16N	D1
Hannaford Woods Forest Preserve, - SgrT	3135	42W-4S	B2
Harms Woods Forest Preserve, GLF	2865	7W-12N	C1
Harris Forest Preserve, KdlT	3333	43W-17S	B6
Hastings Lake Forest Preserve, LkvT	2417	21W-39N	E6
Hawk Hollow Forest Preserve, WynT	2911	28W-6N	A7
Heartland Meadows Dentention Area, - ELGN	2908	36W-9N	A1
Helm Woods Forest Preserve, BNHL	2748	32W-18N	D6
Henry DeTonty Woods Forest Preserve, - LmnT	3272	15W-11S	A1
Heron Creek Forest Preserve, ElaT	2700	19W-22N	B4
Herrick Lake Forest Preserve, MltT	3081	26W-3S	D6
Hickory Creek Forest Preserve, NlxT	3502	14W-24S	D5
Hickory Grove Conservation Area, - AlqT	2642	29W-25N	C5
Hickory Grove Forest Preserve, LslT	3142	23W-7S	E6
Hickory Grove-Lyons Prairie & Marsh-Cons, NndT	2642	30W-26N	B3
Hickory Hills Woods Forest Preserve, - HYHL	3210	10W-11S	B6
Hidden Lake Forest Preserve, MltT	3083	22W-3S	C6
Hidden Pond Woods Forest Preserve, - PlsT	3209	11W-10S	E5
Higginbotham Woods Forest Preserve, - JLET	3500	19W-23S	D4
Hobson Grove, NPVL	3204	25W-7S	A1
Hunters Woods Forest Preserve, FftT	3592	9W-25S	D1
Independence Grove Forest Preserve, - LbvT	2591	16W-30N	E1
Indian Hill Woods Forest Preserve, - CHHT	3595	1W-26S	E1
Iroquois Woods Forest Preserve, CHCG	2863	12W-9N	C7
Isle A La Cache Forest Preserve, - RMVL	3341	23W-15S	B2
Joe Orr Woods Forest Preserve, CHHT	3508	0W-24S	B5
John J Duerr Forest Preserve, SchT	2908	34W-7N	C6
John J Duffy Preserve, LmnT	3344	15W-15S	C1
Johnson's Mound Forest Preserve, - BbyT	3017	41W-0N	E6
Jurgensen Woods Forest Preserve, - BlmT	3509	1E-22S	A1
Kane County Forest Preserve, BbyT	3076	40W-3S	C5
Keepataw Forest Preserve, DPgT	3269	21W-13S	E5
Kenyon Farm Forest Preserve, ElgT	2908	33W-8N	E2
Kickapoo Meadows Forest Preserve, - RVDL	3350	1W-16S	A4
Kildeer Nature Center, KLDR	2699	21W-21N	D6
Kings Grove Forest Preserve, BlmT	3595	2W-27S	D5
Kishwaukee Fen Nature Preserve, LKWD	2692	38W-23N	D1
Koenick Grove Preserve, BGBK	3204	24W-10S	D6
La Bagh Woods Forest Preserve, CHCG	2920	5W-6N	A5
La Grange Pk Woods Forest Preserve, - LGPK	3087	12W-3S	B4
Lake Avenue Woods Forest Preserve, - NfdT	2809	12W-14N	A4
Lake Bluff Forest Preserve, LKBF	2593	11W-28N	D7
Lake Carina Forest Preserve, WrnT	2535	15W-33N	A2
Lake Forest Nature Preserve, LKFT	2650	9W-25N	B6
Lakefront Pk & Sanctuary, HMND	3280		D2
Lake Katherine Nature Preserve, PSHT	3275	8W-14S	A5
Lake Renwick Heron Rookery Nature-Preserve, PNFD	3416	29W-18S	E1
Lakewood Forest Preserve, FmtT	2644	24W-26N	C2
Lambs Woods Forest Preserve, LktT	3420	21W-20S	A5
Lansing Woods Forest Preserve, BlmT	3509	2E-22S	D1
Larsen Nature Preserve, WKGN	2479	11W-35N	E5
Laughton Preserve, WltT	3767	17W-35S	D6
Leroy Oakes Forest Preserve, SchT	2963	37W-3N	C5
Les Arends Forest Preserve, BtvT	3078	36W-3S	A5
Lincoln Marsh Natural Area, WHTN	3024	25W-0S	A6
Linne Woods Forest Preserve, MNGV	2865	7W-11N	B3
Lion Nature Preserve, OswT	3334	41W-15S	A2
Lion Woods Forest Preserve, DSPN	2863	13W-11N	A2
Lockport Prairie Nature Preserve, - LktT	3419	23W-19S	A3
Lower Plum Creek Preserve, CteT	3598	3E-28S	A6
Lower Rock Run Forest Preserve, JLET	3497	28W-24S	A6
Lower Rock Run Preserve, TroT	3585	28W-26S	A4
Lower Spring Creek Forest Preserve, - JltT	3499	21W-22S	E1
Lyman Woods Forest Preserve, DRGV	3084	19W-3S	C5
Lyons Prairie & Marsh Nature Preserve, - CbaT	2643	28W-25N	A5
Lyons Woods Forest Preserve, WkgT	2480	10W-37N	A3
MacArthur Woods Forest Preserve, - MTWA	2648	15W-26N	A3
Mallard Lake Forest Preserve, BmdT	2911	26W-6N	E7
Maloney Farm Preserve, KLWH	2812	3W-14N	E4
Maple Grove Forest Preserve, DRGV	3144	20W-5S	B3
Maramach Forest Preserve, LtRT	3331	47W-15S	C2
Marengo Ridge Conservation Area, - MngT	2578	49W-29N	C4
Marl Flat Forest Preserve, GrtT	2530	26W-32N	D5
Max McGraw Wildlife Foundation, DndT	2801	33W-15N	B4
Mays Lake Forest Preserve, OKBK	3085	17W-3S	C5
Mazonia-Braidwood State Fish & Wildlife-Area, BvlT	4030	34W-45S	A6
McClaughry Springs Woods Forest-Preserve, PlsT	3273	11W-13S	D4
McCormick Woods Forest Preserve, - NRIV	3088	10W-2S	B3
McDonald Woods Forest Preserve, LNHT	2418	19W-38N	C7
McDowell Grove Forest Preserve, NPVL	3140	29W-4S	E1
McGinnis Forest Preserve, OrlT	3345	12W-15S	C2
McHenry County Conservation Area Forest Pres, RcmT	2354	33W-43N	A4
McKinley Woods Forest Preserve, CnhT	3761	32W-32S	E1
McMahon Woods Forest Preserve, PlsT	3273	12W-12S	C3
Meacham Grove Forest Preserve, BMDL	2913	23W-6N	A7
Meagher Forest Preserve, RtdT	2745	40W-18N	C5
Memorial Parkway, RVFT	3030	9W-0N	D4
Messenger Woods Forest Preserve, - HMGN	3421	16W-20S	E4
Messenger Woods Nature Preserve, - HMGN	3421	17W-20S	C4
Miami Woods Forest Preserve, MNGV	2865	8W-10N	A5
Middlefork Savanna Forest Preserve, - LKFT	2649	13W-27N	A2
Middle Plum Creek Preserve, CteT	3686	1E-31S	C5
Midewin National Tallgrass Prairie, - WmTp	3763	27W-35S	D6
Midlothian Meadow Forest Preserve, - BmnT	3348	5W-18S	B7
Miller Meadows Forest Preserve, PvsT	3088	10W-1S	B1
Miller Woods Forest Preserve, RVSD	3088	9W-3S	D5
Misty Meadows Natural Area, WYNE	2965	33W-5N	B1
National Grove Woods Forest Preserve, - NRIV	3088	10W-2S	B3
Ned Brown Forest Preserve, EGvT	2860	19W-10N	D4
Nippersink Forest Preserve, RDLK	2531	24W-33N	C4
Norris Woods Forest Preserve, SCRL	2964	35W-4N	B4
Northwestern Woods Forest Preserve, - DSPN	2863	12W-10N	B4
Oakhurst Forest Preserve, AURA	3201	33W-8S	A1
Oak Ridge Marsh Nature Pk, LKZH	2698	23W-23N	E2
Oakwood Hills Fen Conservation Area, - NndT	2642	30W-27N	A1
O'Hara Woods Nature Preserve, RMVL	3340	25W-15S	C2
Old School Forest Preserve, MTWA	2592	14W-28N	B7
Open Space Preserve, LGGV	2646	20W-26N	A4
Ottawa Trail Woods Forest Preserve, - LYNS	3088	9W-4S	D7
Otter Forest Creek Preserve, ElgT	2907	37W-9N	B2
Paddock Woods Forest Preserve, PlsT	3274	11W-13S	A4
Palos Pk Woods Forest Preserve, PlsT	3273	11W-13S	E4
Papoose Lake Forest Preserve, PlsT	3273	12W-14S	C6
Paul Douglas Forest Preserve, HFET	2804	24W-13N	C5
Paw Paw Woods Forest Preserve, PlsT	3208	13W-10S	E6
Peat Lake State Natural Area, SlmT	2356		C3
Pine Dunes Forest Preserve, NptT	2360	17W-43N	B4
Pioneer Woods Forest Preserve, PlsT	3209	12W-11S	C7
Pistakee Bog Nature Preserve, GrtT	2529	28W-34N	D2
Plum Creek Forest Preserve, BlmT	3598	4E-27S	B4
Plum Grove Forest Preserve, CteT	3774	0W-33S	C2
Poplar Creek Forest Preserve, HFET	2857	27W-12N	C2
Possum Hollow Woods Forest Preserve, - WSTR	3087	13W-2S	A4
Potawatomi Woods Forest Preserve, - WhlT	2755	13W-18N	D3
Potawatomi Woods Preserve, NlxT	3500	19W-24S	D5
Prairie Kame Forest Preserve, SgrT	3134	44W-4S	D1
Prairie Wolf Forest Preserve, LKFT	2703	11W-23N	D1
Pratt's Wayne Woods Forest Preserve, - WynT	2909	32W-6N	C6
Pulaski Woods Forest Preserve, PlsT	3208	14W-11S	D7
Raceway Woods Forest Preserve, CPVL	2747	35W-17N	C6
Raven Glen Forest Preserve, AntT	2418	19W-40N	B3
Rays Lake Forest Preserve, FmtT	2589	22W-29N	A4
Red Gate Woods Forest Preserve, LmnT	3272	15W-11S	B1
Red Wing Marsh Forest Preserve, AntT	2417	21W-41N	C1
Richard Winters Conservation Area, - WDDL	2915	18W-6N	A6
Riegel Farm & Conservation Center, - UYPK	3684	3W-30S	C4
Riverview Farm Forest Preserve, NPVL	3266	29W-13S	E5
Rock Run Forest Preserve, SRWD	3584	30W-25S	B2
Rock Run Preserve, TroT	3497	28W-22S	A2
Rollins Savanna Forest Preserve, - AvnT	2476	20W-35N	B6
Romeoville Prairie Nature Preserve, - DPgT	3269	22W-14S	B6
Romeoville Prairie Nature Preserve, - RMVL	3341	23W-15S	B2
Roy C Blackwell Forest Preserve, - WnfT	3080	29W-1S	D2
Rubio Woods Forest Preserve, BmnT	3347	7W-16S	C3
Rush Creek Conservation Area, DhmT	2464	49W-37N	D2
Rutland Forest Preserve, RtdT	2798	41W-16N	A1
Ryerson Woods Conservation Area, - VrnT	2755	14W-20N	D1
St. Mihiel Forest Preserve, BmnT	3425	6W-20S	E3
St. Paul Woods Forest Preserve, MNGV	2865	8W-10N	A4
Salt Creek Forest Preserve, EMHT	3027	17W-1N	C2
Salt Creek Forest Preserve, WDDL	2971	18W-5N	A1
Salt Creek Marsh Forest Preserve, - ITSC	2914	18W-6N	E6
Sam & Dorothy Dean Nature Sanctuary, - OKBK	3086	15W-3S	B5
Sand Ridge Savanna Preserve, CstT	3943	28W-41S	B5
Sauk Trail Forest Preserve, FKFT	3592	9W-27S	E3
Sauk Trail Woods Forest Preserve, - BlmT	3595	2W-26S	D3
Saw Wee Hee Nature Preserve, OswT	3262	40W-13S	C5
Schiller Woods Forest Preserve, CHCG	2973	11W-5N	D1
Schuberts Woods Forest Preserve, - BlmT	3595	2W-27S	D4
Sequoit Creek Forest Preserve, AntT	2417	23W-41N	A1
Seymour Simon Forest Preserve, CHCG	2973	11W-4N	E2
Shabbona Woods Forest Preserve, CTCY	3351	2E-18S	D7
Shag Lake Nature Preserve Pk, RLKH	2474	24W-35N	D5
Shoe Factory Road Woods, HnrT	2856	30W-11N	C3
Sidney Yates Flatwoods Forest Preserve,- CHCG	2919	7W-8N	B2
Singing Hills Forest Preserve, WcnT	2587	26W-30N	E1
Somme Woods Forest Preserve, NHBK	2757	9W-18N	B4
Songbird Slough Forest Preserve, - ADSN	2970	19W-5N	C1
Spears Woods Forest Preserve, PlsT	3209	12W-10S	C5
Spring Bluff Forest Preserve, WPHR	2363	9W-43N	D5
Spring Brook Nature Center, ITSC	2914	20W-6N	B6
Springbrook Prairie Forest Preserve, - NpvT	3202	29W-8S	D3
Spring Creek Valley Forest Preserve, - BNHL	2749	29W-17N	C4
Springfield Pk Wetlands Nature Area, - BMDL	2968	24W-5N	D1
Spring Hill Farm Fen Forest Preserve, - LIHL	2694	35W-22N	A3
Spring Valley Nature Sanctuary, SMBG	2859	22W-10N	D6
Stickney Run Conservation Area, NndT	2585	32W-30N	C2
Subat Forest Preserve, LtRT	3332	45W-14S	C1
Sugar Ridge Wetland Detention Area, - SEGN	2908	35W-7N	C4
Sun Lake Forest Preserve, LKVL	2417	22W-39N	B5
Sunset Ridge Woods Forest Preserve, - NHBK	2758	8W-17N	A6
Swallow Cliff Woods Forest Preserve, - PlsT	3273	12W-14S	C5
Swanson & Trigg Conservation Area, - GRNE	2478	14W-34N	D7
Sweet Woods Forest Preserve, BlmT	3508	0E-22S	D1
Swift Prairie Forest Preserve, BmdT	2969	21W-4N	D4
Teasons Woods Forest Preserve, PlsT	3273	12W-13S	C4
Thatcher Woods Forest Preserve, RVFT	3030	10W-1N	B1
The Hollows Conservation Area, AlqT	2641	32W-25N	B5
Theodore Marsh Preserve, CTHL	3417	26W-21S	E7
Theodore Stone Forest Preserve, HGKN	3147	12W-7S	C5
The Wetlands Forest Preserve, WrnT	2478	15W-37N	B3
Thomas Jefferson Woods Forest Preserve,- MYWD	3030	10W-0N	B4
Thorn Creek Woods Nature Preserve, - MonT	3684	4W-29S	A1
Thornwood Retention, SEGN	2907	37W-7N	B5
Timber Ridge Forest Preserve, WnfT	3023	27W-1N	B2
Tinley Creek Forest Preserve, RchT	3505	7W-23S	D2
Tinley Creek Woods Forest Preserve, - BmnT	3347	8W-16S	A3
Turnbull Woods Forest Preserve, GLNC	2758	7W-18N	B3
Tyler Creek Forest Preserve, ELGN	2800	34W-13N	D7
Van Horne Woods Forest Preserve, - FftT	3503	12W-24S	C5
Van Horn Woods, PnfT	3416	29W-20S	E5
Van Patten Woods Forest Preserve, - NptT	2361	15W-42N	B5
Veteran Woods Forest Preserve, DPgT	3269	22W-13S	C6
Village Wildlife Refuge, NBRN	2697	26W-22N	D3
Volo Bog State Natural Area, GrtT	2530	27W-33N	A3
Voyageur Landing Forest Preserve, - DndT	2801	33W-14N	A6
Wadsworth Prairie Forest Preserve, - NptT	2420	15W-40N	A4
Walter E Heller Nature Preserve, - HDPK	2704	10W-23N	A2
Wampum Lake Woods Forest Preserve, - ThtT	3429	1E-20S	A5
Warrenville Grove Forest Preserve, - WNVL	3081	28W-3S	A5
Waterfall Glen Forest Preserve, DGvT	3206	19W-11S	D7
Waukegan Savanna Forest Preserve, - WKGN	2478	13W-37N	E1
Wayne Grove Forest Preserve, WynT	2910	29W-7N	D5
Wayside Woods Forest Preserve, MNGV	2865	8W-11N	A3
Wedgewood Creek Recreation Preserve, - GRNE	2478	14W-35N	C5
Weingart Road Sedge Meadow, JNBG	2472	29W-35N	B5
Weisbrook Access Preserve, WldT	3265	31W-13S	E4
Wentworth Woods Forest Preserve, - CTCY	3430	4E-19S	B1

Chicago 7-County Points of Interest Index

FEATURE NAME Address City ZIP Code	MAP#	CGS	GRID
West Branch Reservoir Forest Preserve, - BRLT	2966	29W-5N	E2
West Branch Reservoir Forest Preserve, - WynT	2967	28W-4N	A4
Westchester Woods Forest Preserve, - PvsT	3087	12W-2S	B2
West Chicago Prairie Forest Preserve, - WCHI	3022	31W-1N	A3
West DuPage Woods Forest Preserve, - WnfT	3023	28W-0S	A6
Westgate Nature Preserve, GRNE	2477	16W-36N	D4
Whistler Woods Forest Preserve, RVDL	3350	1W-15S	B1
White Eagle Woods Forest Preserve, - LYNS	3088	9W-4S	D6
Wildwood Nature Center, PKRG	2863	11W-9N	D7
Will County Preserve, PNFD	3417	28W-18S	B1
William N Erickson Forest Preserve, - GLNC	2758	7W-17N	B6
Willowbrook Wildlife Center, GNEN	3083	22W-2S	C3
Wilmot Woods Forest Preserve, LbvT	2592	15W-30N	A3
Winding Trails Detention, HnrT	2856	30W-12N	B3
Winfield Mounds Forest Preserve, - WnfT	3023	28W-0N	B4
WM Powers State Conservation Area, - CHCG	3280	4E-14S	B6
Wolfe State Wildlife Refuge, OKLN	3275	6W-12S	E2
Wolf Road Woods Forest Preserve, - PlsT	3273	13W-12S	A2
Wood Dale Grove Forest Preserve, - AddT	2971	17W-4N	B2
Woodland Meadows, EGvT	2914	21W-9N	A1
Wood Oaks Green Forest Preserve, - NHBK	2756	12W-17N	A5
Woodridge Forest Preserve, DGvT	3270	20W-13S	B4
Woodrow Wilson Forest Preserve, CHHT	3508	1W-25S	A7
Wright Woods Forest Preserve, VrnT	2702	14W-24N	B1
Yankee Woods Forest Preserve, BmnT	3425	7W-19S	D2
York-High Ridge Forest Preserve, - YkTp	3026	18W-0S	E7
York Woods Forest Preserve, EMHT	3028	15W-1S	A7
Zalar Woods Forest Preserve, JltT	3587	22W-26S	D3
Zander Woods Forest Preserve, ThtT	3429	1E-21S	A6
Zoo Woods Forest Preserve, RVSD	3088	10W-3S	A5

Other

FEATURE NAME Address City ZIP Code	MAP#	CGS	GRID
87th Street Auto Center W 87th St, BGVW, 60455	3210	9W-10S	D4
Adler Planetarium 1300 E Solidarity Dr, CHCG, 60605	3034	0E-1S	E7
AERO Center Pinehurst Ct, BRBK, 60459	3211	7W-8S	C1
Albanian Cultural Center 5825 St. Charles Rd, BKLY, 60163	3028	14W-0N	C3
American Legion Hall Century Ln, AURA, 60505	3200	34W-7S	D1
American Legion Hall E Main St, RLKP, 60073	2532	22W-33N	A3
Aquatic Center 327 W Dundee Rd, WLNG, 60090	2755	14W-17N	B4
Arlington in Waukegan 630 S Green Bay Rd, WKGN, 60085	2536	12W-33N	B3
Art-Centric 307 Division St, OKPK, 60302	3031	7W-1N	A2
Aurora Art & History Center W Benton St, AURA, 60506	3200	35W-7S	A1
Baha'i Place of Worship 112 Linden Av, WLMT, 60091	2813	2W-13N	B6
Band Shell Concert Ln, NPVL, 60540	3141	26W-6S	D5
Barr Yard Jackson St, ClmT, 60827	3349	1W-15S	E1
Batavia Riverwalk 100 N Island Av, BTVA, 60510	3078	35W-1S	B1
Bird Sanctuary Belmont Harbor Dr, CHCG, 60613	2978	0W-4N	A2
Blackberry Farm's Pioneer Village 100 S Barnes Rd, AURA, 60506	3136	39W-7S	D6
Blue Island Yard Ashland Av, RVDL, 60426	3349	2W-16S	E3
Bowman Russell Art Advisory 311 W Superior St, CHCG, 60610	3034	0W-0N	B3
Bristol Renaissance Faire 12550 120th Av, BtlT, 53142	2360		D3
Buckingham Memorial Fountain &- Garden 1001 S Columbus Dr, CHCG, 60605	3034	0E-0S	C5
Calumet Yard S Oglesby Av, CHCG, 60617	3279	2E-12S	C2
Camp Greenwood DuPage Girl Scout- Council LslT, 60540	3205	22W-8S	C1
Centennial Fountain & Arc 300 N McClurg Ct, CHCG, 60611	3034	0E-0N	D3
Challenge Park Schweizer Rd, TroT, 60421	3585	27W-27S	D6
Chicago Mercantile Exchange 30 S Wacker Dr, CHCG, 60606	3034	0W-0S	A4
Chicago Post Office 437 W Van Buren St, CHCG, 60607	3034	0W-0S	A5
Chicago Temple 77 W Washington St, CHCG, 60602	3034	0W-0N	B4
Cicero Yard W 26th St, CCRO, 60804	3089	7W-2S	C3
Commercial Center W 33rd St, CHCG, 60608	3091	1W-3S	D4
Commonwealth Edison Power Station E Greenwood Av, WKGN, 60085	2480	9W-35N	C5
Corwith Yard S Kedzie Av, CHCG, 60632	3090	4W-4S	D6
Country Farm Center HRPK, 60133	2967	27W-4N	C3
Courthouse Place 54 W Hubbard St, CHCG, 60610	3034	0W-0N	B3
Crabtree Nature Center 3 Stover Rd, BrnT, 60010	2803	27W-16N	C1
Dammrich Rowing Center 3220 Oakton St, SKOK, 60076	2866	4W-10N	D5
Darien Sports Plex Brookdale Dr, DRN, 60561	3207	17W-8S	C1
Dartmoor Plaza McHenry Av, CLLK, 60014	2693	36W-24N	E1
Dearborn Observatory 2131 Sheridan Rd, EVTN, 60201	2867	2W-12N	C1
Delaney Business Center Swanson Ct, GRNE, 60031	2478	13W-36N	E4
District 56 Office Kilbourn Rd, GRNE, 60031	2478	14W-35N	C6
Dominican Conference Center 7200 Division St, RVFT, 60305	3030	8W-1N	D2
DuPage Flight Center 2700 International Dr, WynT, 60185	3021	32W-2N	C1
Easter Seal Center E Madison St, VLPK, 60181	3026	18W-0S	E5
Eisenhower Center 178th St, LNSG, 60438	3429	3E-20S	E5
Elgin U-46 Planetarium 312 Watch St, ELGN, 60120	2855	33W-10N	A5
Environmental Learning Center Briarwood Ln, FftT, 60448	3503	13W-25S	A7
Fairway Plaza S Western Av, ENGN, 60805	3213	3W-10S	B5
Farm in the Zoo N Stockton Dr, CHCG, 60614	2978	0W-2N	B7
Fine Arts Center 508 N Center St, NPVL, 60563	3141	26W-6S	D4
Four Seasons-Ritz Carlton Chicago 160 E Pearson St, CHCG, 60611	3034	0E-1N	C2
Freedom Walk State Av, SCRL, 60174	2964	35W-3N	B6
Garfield Park Conservatory 300 N Conservatory Dr, CHCG, 60624	3032	4W-0N	C4
Glencoe Community Center Green Bay Rd, GLNC, 60022	2758	6W-18N	C3
Glendale Plaza GLHT, 60139	3025	22W-2N	B1
Glenn Yard S Central Av, StkT, 60638	3149	7W-5S	C1
Glen Palmer Game Farm Game Farm Rd, BtlT, 60560	3261	43W-14S	B7
Graham Center W Madison St, EMHT, 60126	3027	16W-0S	D5
Greater Harvard Area Historical- Society Church Blvd, HRVD, 60033	2406	50W-38N	B7
Gurnee Center for Commerce &- Industry N Delany Rd, GRNE, 60031	2478	14W-35N	D5
Harpo Studios 1058 W Washington Blvd, CHCG, 60607	3033	1W-0N	E4
Haverton Conservation Area N Hough St, NBRN, 60010	2697	26W-22N	E4
Heritage Falls Water Park Taylor Rd, RMVL, 60446	3340	24W-16S	E4
Hickory Hills Rod & Gun Club Pilcher Rd, PNFD, 60544	3339	28W-16S	A3
Historical Society 172nd Pl, SHLD, 60473	3429	2E-20S	D4
Holy Trinity Cathedral 1121 N Leavitt St, CHCG, 60622	3033	2W-1N	B2
International House 1414 E 59th St, CHCG, 60637	3153	1E-6S	A3
Irish American Heritage Center W Leland Av, CHCG, 60630	2920	5W-5N	A7
Irondale Yard S Torrence Av, CHCG, 60617	3279	3E-13S	E4
JFK Health World S Barrington Rd, BRTN, 60010	2750	25W-17N	E5
John E Egan Water Reclamation Plant S Meacham Rd, SmbT, 60193	2859	21W-9N	E6
Kane County Flea Market S Randall Rd, SCRL, 60175	3019	37W-2N	D1
Kensington Yard S Cottage Grove Av, CHCG, 60628	3278	0E-13S	D4
Kline Creek Farm 1N600 County Farm Rd, WnfT, 60185	3023	27W-1N	D2
Lake Forest Waterworks Spruce Av, LKFT, 60045	2594		B7
Lake Shore Drive Synagogue 70 E Elm St, CHCG, 60611	3034	0E-1N	C1
Lake Villa Rescue Squad N Deep Lake Rd, LKVL, 60046	2475	21W-38N	D1
Lake Wood Center Ravine Rd, EDND, 60118	2748	33W-17N	B7
Lambs Farm E Park Av, GNOK, 60048	2592	14W-28N	D6
Leaning Tower Replica W Touhy Av, NLES, 60714	2865	7W-9N	A7
Leisure Lake Family Resort SW Frontage Rd, TroT, 60404	3584	30W-26S	C3
Lincoln Center Dist 60 Admin Center Amstutz Expwy, WKGN, 60085	2480	10W-35N	B6
Lincoln Park Conservatory 2400 N Stockton Dr, CHCG, 60614	2978	0W-3N	A5
Lithuanian World Center LMNT, 60439	3271	18W-14S	A7
Little Red School House Nature- Center Flavin Rd, PlsT, 60480	3209	13W-11S	A7
Loews-House of Blues Hotel 333 N Dearborn St, CHCG, 60610	3034	0W-0N	B4
Long Grove Village Robert Parker Coffin Rd, LGGV, 60047	2700	18W-21N	E6
Lutheran Home Luther Ln, ANHT, 60004	2806	18W-15N	E2
Marina City 300 N State St, CHCG, 60610	3034	0W-0N	B4
Markham Yard 171st St, HRVY, 60429	3427	1W-20S	E4
Marytown-St. Maximilian Kolbe- Shrine 1600 W Park Av, LYVL, 60048	2591	17W-28N	A6
Mayslake Retirement Village 35th St, WTMT, 60559	3085	17W-3S	C5
Merner Fieldhouse NPVL, 60540	3141	26W-7S	D6
Midway Studios 6016 S Ingleside Av, CHCG, 60637	3152	1E-6S	E4
Midwest Buddhist Temple 435 W Menomonee St, CHCG, 60614	2978	0W-2N	A7
Midwest Stock Exchange W Van Buren St, CHCG, 60605	3034	0W-0S	B5
Moore-Dugal Residence 333 Forest Av, OKPK, 60302	3030	8W-0N	E3
Mother Teresa Home St. Joseph Ct, LMNT, 60439	3271	18W-13S	B4
Nature Center N Main St, CLLK, 60014	2640	35W-26N	B2
Nature Center 2501 Highland Park Dr, JLET, 60432	3500	20W-23S	B4
Nature Center Illinois St, SchT, 60174	2908	34W-6N	C6
Navy Pier 600 N Streeter Dr, CHCG, 60611	3034	0E-0N	D3
Norge Ski Club Ski Hill Rd, FRGV, 60021	2696	29W-23N	C2
Noyes Culture Arts Center 927 Noyes St, EVTN, 60201	2867	2W-12N	B1
Oak Park Sportsmen Club PnfT, 60544	3339	28W-17S	A6
Oak Park Yards Franklin St, FTPK, 60130	3030	9W-0N	C4
Old Court House Arts Center 101 N Johnson St, WDSK, 60098	2524	41W-31N	C7
Our Lady of Mt Carmel Church 690 W Belmont Av, CHCG, 60657	2978	0W-4N	A3
Palatine Stables W Dundee Rd, PLTN, 60067	2751	23W-17N	E5
Pavilion Longford Dr, JLET, 60431	3497	28W-25S	B7
Pioneer Landing RcmT, 60071	2412	34W-39N	D6
Pirate's Cove Children's Theme Park 901 Leicester Rd, EGVV, 60007	2914	19W-8N	C2
Port of Chicago Lake Calumet Harbor- Fclts S Doty Av, CHCG, 60633	3279	1E-13S	A5
Presbyterian Home Golf Rd, EVTN, 60201	2866	4W-12N	B1
Printer's Square 640 S Federal St, CHCG, 60605	3034	0W-0S	B6
Pure Rod & Gun Club 260 W Lockport Rd, PnfT, 60544	3338	29W-17S	E7
Quaker Oats Building 321 N Clark St, CHCG, 60610	3034	0W-0N	B3
Ray Graham Association for- Handicapped E Wilson Av, LMBD, 60148	3026	19W-0S	D6
Red Oak Nature Center N River Rd, NARA, 60542	3078	36W-3S	A6
Regency Point Plaza W 119th St, CHCG, 60643	3277	2W-13S	D4
Rescue Squad 110 Telegraph St, MRGO, 60152	2634	50W-27N	B1
Rinkside Family Entertainment- Center Tri-State Tollway, GRNE, 60031	2477	16W-35N	D5
Rose Garden Payne Dr, CHCG, 60637	3152	0E-6S	D2
St. Clement's Church 642 W Deming Pl, CHCG, 60614	2978	0W-3N	A5
St. Gabriel Church 4522 S Wallace St, CHCG, 60609	3092	0W-4S	A7
St. Michael's Church 1633 N Cleveland Av, CHCG, 60614	2978	0W-2N	A7
St. Nicholas Ukrainian Catholic- Cathedral 2238 W Rice St, CHCG, 60622	3033	2W-1N	B2
Sand Ridge Nature Center 15890 Paxton Av, CTCY, 60409	3429	2E-18S	D1
Second Presbyterian Church 1936 S Michigan Av, CHCG, 60616	3092	0E-1S	C1
SEDOL Administration 18160 W Gages Lake Rd, WrnT, 60030	2534	18W-33N	A2
Shakespeare Garden 2121 Sheridan Rd, EVTN, 60201	2867	2W-12N	B1
Shiloh House 1300 Shiloh Blvd, ZION, 60099	2422	10W-40N	B3
Skybridge 1 N Halsted St, CHCG, 60661	3034	1W-0N	A4
Slovenian Cultural Center Main St, LmnT, 60439	3271	17W-13S	B4
Smuggler's Cove 4400 Westbrook Dr, AURA, 60504	3202	30W-8S	B1
South Water Market W South Water Market, CHCG, 60608	3033	1W-1S	E7
Sports Hub Bloomingdale Rd, GLHT, 60139	2969	23W-3N	A6
Springbrook Nature Center 130 W Grove St, ITSC, 60143	2914	20W-6N	B6
Spring Valley Nature Sanctuary 1111 E Schaumburg Rd, SMBG, 60193	2859	22W-10N	D5
Stolp Island E Downer Pl, AURA, 60505	3138	35W-7S	B7
Sunny Acres Sanitarium JLET, 60433	3499	23W-25S	B7
The Cenacle Retreat Center Morris Ct, WNVL, 60555	3080	28W-2S	E4
The Palmer House Hilton 17 E Monroe St, CHCG, 60603	3034	0E-0S	C5
The Tempel Lipizzans 17000 W Wadsworth Rd, OMCK, 60083	2419	17W-39N	C6
Thorn Creek Woods Nature Center Old Monee Rd, MonT, 60466	3594	4W-28S	E7
Train Depot W Depot St, ANTH, 60002	2357	23W-42N	E6
Tyner Interpretive Center Compass Rd, GNVW, 60025	2810	9W-15N	C2
Union Station 225 S Canal St, CHCG, 60606	3034	0W-0S	A5
University Of Illinois Experimental- Station Finley Rd, LslT, 60532	3083	21W-4S	E7
Veteran's Memorial Penfield St, BCHR, 60401	3864	1W-36S	B2
Vogt Visual Arts Center 17420 67th Ct, TYPK, 60477	3425	8W-20S	A5
Walter E Heller Nature Center 2821 Ridge Rd, HDPK, 60035	2703	10W-23N	E2
Windy City Balloon Port 100 Ski Hill Rd, FRGV, 60021	2696	29W-23N	C2
Winston Plaza W North Av, MLPK, 60160	3029	11W-1N	E1
Wood Street Gallery & Sculpture- Garden 1239 N Wood St, CHCG, 60622	3033	2W-1N	C1

Chicago 7-County Points of Interest Index

FEATURE NAME / Address City ZIP Code	MAP#	CGS	GRID
Yard Center, Indiana Av, DLTN, 60419	3350	0E-17S	D5
YMCA, AURA, 60506	3138	36W-7S	A7

Park & Ride

FEATURE NAME / Address City ZIP Code	MAP#	CGS	GRID
Park & Ride CTA, CHCG	3150	5W-6S	A4
Park & Ride-CTA-Cumberland, CHCG	2918	10W-7N	A4
Park & Ride-CTA-Pulaski, CHCG	3150	5W-5S	C2
Park & Ride-CTA-Rosemont, RSMT	2917	11W-7N	D4
Park & Ride-Genoa City, GNCY	2353		C3
Park & Ride-South Holland, SHLD	3428	0W-19S	C2

Parks & Recreation

FEATURE NAME / Address City ZIP Code	MAP#	CGS	GRID
4-H Field, NlxT	3501	17W-23S	D4
63rd Street Pk, WDRG	3143	22W-6S	C5
75th Street Pk, WDRG	3205	22W-8S	D2
Abbott Pk, CHCG	3214	0E-11S	C6
Abbott Pk, ELGN	2854	35W-11N	B5
Abraham Lincoln Pk, AURA	3199	36W-7S	D1
Abrahamsen Pk, SMBG	2859	22W-10N	B6
Ackerman Pk, GNEN	3025	22W-1N	D3
Adam Perry Pk, EVTN	2866	3W-11N	E2
Adams Pk, CHCG	3215	1E-8S	A1
Adam's Pk, WHTN	3024	24W-0S	C6
Ada Pk, CHCG	3277	1W-13S	E3
Addams Pk, CHCG	3033	1W-1S	D7
Addison Community Pk, ADSN	2971	18W-4N	A4
Adelphi Pk, WKGN	2479	12W-36N	B3
Adlai E Stevenson Special Use Area, - MTWA	2648	15W-25N	A6
Adler Memorial Pk, LYVL	2591	16W-30N	D2
Aerohaven Pk, NLNX	3589	18W-25S	A1
AF Hill Pk, LktT	3499	23W-21S	B1
Ahlstrand Pk, HRPK	2911	27W-8N	C2
Aiello Pk, CHCG	2975	7W-2N	B6
Aintree Pk, SCRL	2964	34W-4N	E4
Air Station Prairie, GNVW	2810	9W-15N	C2
Albert A Adam's Pk, JNBG	2471	32W-35N	A5
Albright Pk, WHTN	3083	23W-3S	A6
Alcott Center & Pk, BFGV	2754	17W-18N	B3
Alexander Pk, EVTN	2867	3W-11N	A3
Algonquin Lakes Pk, ALGN	2748	33W-19N	A3
Algonquin Pk, PKFT	3595	2W-26S	C2
Allan Weissburg Pk, SKOK	2866	5W-12N	B1
Allemong Pk, MTSN	3505	7W-24S	C5
Almond Pk, CHCG	3277	2W-13S	B4
Altgeld Pk, CHCG	3033	3W-0S	A6
Altman Pk, PSHT	3274	9W-13S	D4
Amarias Pk, RDLK	2531	23W-31N	E7
Amberwood Pk, AURA	3202	31W-8S	A2
American Lane Pk, SMBG	2859	22W-11N	D2
Amundsen Pk, CHCG	2975	7W-2N	B7
Ancient Oaks Pk, BRLT	2910	30W-6N	B7
Andersen Pk, OKPK	3031	7W-1N	B2
Anderson Pk, CHCG	3092	0E-3S	C5
Anderson Pk, HMTN	3212	5W-10S	B5
Andover Pk, AURA	3201	31W-9S	E5
Andres Pk, CPVL	2748	33W-18N	B5
Andrews Pk, EGVV	2861	18W-9N	A6
Angel Pk, NCHI	2593	11W-31N	C1
Anniversary Pk, SMWD	2856	29W-9N	E7
Antioch Centennial Pk, ANTH	2358	23W-42N	A5
Antler Pk, HNVL	2532	21W-33N	C3
Apollo Pk, ALSP	3276	5W-14S	B6
Apollo Pk, BLWD	3029	12W-0S	B5
Apollo Pk, HMWD	3508	1W-22S	A2
Apollo Pk, SMBG	2859	22W-9N	B6
Appleby Pk, WHTN	3082	23W-3S	E5
Applegate Pk, SMBG	2859	23W-10N	A6
Apple Hill Pk, BFGV	2701	16W-22N	E4
Apple Orchard Greenway Pk, BRLT	2910	29W-6N	D6
Apple Orchard Pk, WynT	2910	29W-7N	E5
Appleseed Pk, EGVV	2860	18W-9N	E7
Aptakisic Pk, BFGV	2701	16W-21N	E6
Aquarius Pk, SMWD	2856	29W-10N	E6
Aquatic Pk, ALSP	3276	5W-14S	B5
Arbor Day Pk, PlsT	3345	12W-15S	D2
Arboretum Mews Pk, WHTN	3082	24W-3S	D6
Arbor Hills Pk, ALGN	2693	35W-21N	E6
Arbor Pk, WKGN	2535	14W-32N	D4
Arbor View Pk, LSLE	3143	22W-4S	C1
Arbor Way Pk, NPVL	3203	26W-9S	E4
Arcade Pk, CHCG	3278	0E-13S	E3
Arcadia Pk, OMFD	3506	4W-24S	E6
Archer Pk, CHCG	3150	5W-5S	A1
Argyle-Keeler Pk, CHCG	2920	5W-6N	B6
Arlington Pk, RMVL	3340	24W-15S	E1
Armory Pk, WKGN	2479	11W-35N	D6
Armour Square Pk, CHCG	3092	0W-3S	B4
Armstrong Pk, CLSM	2968	26W-3N	A6
Armstrong Pk, HFET	2858	25W-12N	B2
Arndt Pk, DSPN	2863	13W-9N	A7
Arne & Mary Oldberg Pk, EVTN	2867	2W-11N	B2
Arnie Gunther Sports Fields, TYPK	3424	9W-20S	D4
Arquilla Pk, GNWD	3508	0W-22S	C1
Arrigo Pk, CHCG	3033	1W-0S	D6
Arrowhead Pk, MltT	3082	26W-2S	A3
Arrowhead Pk, NPVL	3141	26W-5S	E2
Arrowhead Pk, RLKH	2474	23W-35N	D6
Arrow Wood Pk, AURA	3137	37W-6S	D4
Artisan Lake Pk, LKBF	2593	10W-28N	E6
Asbury Pk, AURA	3139	32W-6S	C6
Asbury Pk, MDLN	2590	19W-29N	B4
Asbury Pk, NndT	2640	34W-26N	C3
Ashburn Pk, CHCG	3212	3W-9S	E3
Ashbury Pk, NPVL	3266	28W-11S	E1
Ashmore Pk, CHCG	2919	6W-6N	E6
Ashwood Pk, PLTN	2752	20W-16N	E6
Aspen Drive Pk, VNHL	2647	17W-25N	B5
Aspen Trails Pk, MPPT	2808	13W-15N	E2
Atcher Pk, SMBG	2858	25W-9N	B7
Atchley Pk, RMVL	3340	24W-16S	D3
Athletic Field, LKPT	3419	22W-19S	D3
Athletic Field Pk, CHCG	2976	4W-4N	C2
Athletic Field Pk, TroT	3584	30W-26S	B3
Athletic Pk, CLLK	2640	35W-25N	A4
Atkin Pk, CCHL	3426	5W-21S	C6
Atten Pk, WHTN	3081	26W-2S	D3
Auburn Pk, CHCG	3214	0W-8S	B1
Audubon Pk, EGVV	2914	18W-8N	E1
Augusta Lake Pk, MTGY	3263	38W-11S	B1
Augusta Pk, VNHL	2647	17W-25N	C5
Austin-Foster Playlot Pk, CHCG	2919	7W-6N	B5
Austin Gardens Pk, OKPK	3030	8W-0N	E3
Austin Pk, CHCG	3031	7W-0N	B4
Austin Pk, MNGV	2865	7W-10N	B5
Austin Town Hall Pk, CHCG	3031	7W-0N	C4
Austin View Pk, WthT	3275	7W-14S	C6
Avalon Pk, CHCG	3215	1E-9S	A3
Avalon Pk, LIHL	2692	39W-23N	C2
Avon Community Pk, HNVL	2532	22W-33N	C2
Avondale Pk, CHCG	2976	4W-4N	C3
Babcock Grove Pk, GNEN	3025	23W-0N	A4
Babe Ruth Pk, BLWD	3029	11W-0S	C5
Bailey Hobson Woods Pk, NPVL	3204	25W-8S	A1
Bainbridge Greens Pk, NPVL	3140	29W-5S	D3
Baker Field Pk, SCRL	3020	35W-2N	B1
Baker Memorial Pk, SCRL	2964	35W-3N	B7
Baker Pk, EVTN	2867	2W-10N	C5
Ballard Pk, NLES	2864	10W-11N	A3
Balstrode Pk, BGBK	3268	25W-12S	B2
Balzer Pk, LNSH	2703	13W-22N	A3
Bambrick Pk, DPgT	3342	21W-15S	A2
Banford Rd Pk, WDSK	2525	40W-32N	B5
Barbara Key Pk, LIHL	2694	34W-22N	B3
Barclay Pk, ELGN	2854	34W-11N	E3
Barnard Pk, CHCG	3277	2W-12S	C1
Barnes Pk, ALSP	3276	5W-13S	B4
Barrie Pk, OKPK	3031	7W-0S	B6
Bartlett Pk, BRLT	2910	29W-8N	E3
Bartlett Pk, SMWD	2857	28W-9N	A7
Bartrum Pk, EGVV	2915	18W-9N	A1
Bataan Pk, MLPK	3029	11W-1N	E2
Batavia Riverwalk, BTVA	3078	35W-1S	B1
Bates Pk, WDSK	2524	41W-32N	D5
Bauler Pk, CHCG	2978	0W-2N	A7
Bayview Pk, LkvT	2474	25W-37N	A2
Beach Oak Pk, LGPK	3087	12W-3S	C5
Beach Pk, WKGN	2537	9W-34N	C1
Beaubien Pk, LSLE	3142	24W-4S	C2
Beau Drive Pk, DSPN	2862	15W-11N	A3
Beau Ridge Pk, AURA	3137	36W-5S	E4
Beaver Pond Pk, BRLT	2910	29W-7N	C5
Beck Pk, EVTN	2866	4W-11N	D2
Bedrosian Pk, WKGN	2537	10W-33N	A2
Beilfuss Pk, CHCG	2976	4W-2N	C7
Bel-Aire Pk, MKHM	3349	3W-18S	B7
Bellerive Pk, WTMT	3145	18W-7S	A6
Bell Pk, CHCG	2974	8W-3N	E6
Belmont Prairie Pk, DRGV	3143	21W-5S	D2
Belvidere Pk, WKGN	2536	11W-33N	D3
Ben Allison Pk, EMHT	3027	17W-0N	C4
Ben Diamond Pk, WKGN	2479	11W-36N	D4
Bengson Pk, RLKP	2532	22W-34N	A1
Bennett Pk, GNVA	3020	35W-1N	C2
Bennett Pk, RHMD	2353	34W-41N	B7
Bennity Pk, JLET	3498	26W-23S	A4
Bensley Pk, CHCG	3215	3E-11S	D6
Bent Pk, EVTN	2812	4W-12N	C7
Berbecker Pk, ANHT	2807	16W-14N	C4
Berger Beach & Pk, CHCG	2921	1W-7N	E3
Berguin Recreation & Field Pk, BRWN	3089	8W-2S	A4
Berkeley Community Pk, BKLY	3028	14W-0N	C4
Besley Pk, WKGN	2537	10W-34N	A2
Bessemer Pk, CHCG	3215	3E-10S	E4
Bethel Pk, BHPK	2422	10W-39N	A5
Betsey Warrington Pk, GfnT	2691	41W-20N	E7
Bettenhausen Pk, TYPK	3424	9W-19S	D2
Betty Limbrunner Pk, PKCY	2536	12W-33N	A2
Betty Russell Community Pk, GRNE	2478	15W-36N	A5
Beverly Pk, BDVW	3087	11W-2S	D2
Beverly Pk, CHCG	3213	3W-11S	B7
Bevier Pk, WKGN	2479	11W-37N	D2
Bicentennial Pk, JLET	3498	24W-23S	E4
Bicentennial Pk, LNSH	2702	13W-22N	D5
Bicentennial Pk, OMFD	3506	4W-24S	E5
Bicentennial Pk, TYPK	3425	8W-19S	A2
Bickerdike Square Pk, CHCG	3033	1W-0N	B3
Bierman Pk, CLSM	2967	27W-4N	C4
Big Sky Pk, LIHL	2693	36W-22N	E4
Big Woods Pk, BTVA	3078	34W-2S	D3
Bill Young Pk, ODPK	3345	12W-18S	C7
Birch Pk, FNPK	2973	11W-3N	D4
Birch Pk, HFET	2859	23W-11N	B3
Birchwood Pk, DRN	3207	18W-8S	A1
Birchwood Pk, PLTN	2805	21W-14N	D3
Birchwood South Pk, PLTN	2805	21W-14N	D3
Bird Haven Pk, JLET	3500	20W-23S	C4
Birmingham Pk, AURA	3139	33W-5S	B3
Bison Pk, BFGV	2754	17W-17N	B4
Bixler Pk, CHCG	3153	1E-6S	A3
Black Bear Pk, HFET	2856	31W-12N	A1
Blackhawk Pk, CHCG	2975	6W-2N	E6
Blackhawk Pk, CNHL	3145	17W-5S	B2
Blackhawk Pk, DSPN	2862	14W-11N	B2
Black Hawk Pk, IHPK	3146	13W-7S	E6
Blackhawk Pk, WTMT	3085	17W-4S	B6
Blackhawk Pond, BGBK	3268	24W-11S	D1
Blacksmith Pk, WHTN	3083	23W-3S	A5
Blackstone Pk, DLTN	3351	1E-17S	B4
Black Walnut Pk, SRGV	3136	41W-4S	A2
Blackweider Pk, CHCG	3277	2W-13S	C4
Blasius Schwer Pk, ENGN	3212	4W-10S	D5
Block Pk, CHCG	3278	0W-12S	B1
Bluedingen Pk, TYPK	3424	10W-19S	B3
Blue Prairie Pk, LIHL	2693	36W-22N	D5
Blue Star Memorial Woods, GNVW	2811	7W-13N	C6
Bluestone Bay Pk, NLNX	3590	15W-25S	B1
Bluett Pk, MPPT	2808	14W-13N	C6
Boak Pk, NCHI	2536	11W-31N	E6
Bob Fowler Memorial Soccer Fields, - JLET	3498	26W-22S	A3
Bob Woodard Pk, WKGN	2536	11W-33N	E3
Bock Pk, SMBG	2858	25W-10N	C6
Bogan Pk, CHCG	3212	4W-9S	C2
Bohn Pk, CHCG	3277	2W-12S	C3
Bonnie Brae Pk, LktT	3419	21W-18S	E1
Borhart Family Pk, HTLY	2692	40W-22N	A4
Bosley Pk, CHCG	3091	1W-2S	E3
Boulder Creek Pk, MHRY	2528	32W-31N	B7
Boundary Hill Woods, WDRG	3205	22W-8S	C2
Bowen Pk, WKGN	2480	10W-36N	B5
Boy Scout Island, SCRL	2964	35W-3N	A6
Bradford Pk, BGBK	3268	25W-13S	A4
Bradford Place Pk, RDLK	2532	23W-32N	A4
Braeburn Pk, BTVA	3019	36W-0S	E7
Braemar Pk, LKZH	2698	24W-21N	D5
Braewood Pk, ALGN	2747	35W-19N	B2
Braidwood City Pk, BDWD	3942	31W-41S	A5
Brainerd Pk, CHCG	3213	1W-10S	E5
Brandenberry Pk, ANHT	2807	16W-15N	D3
Brandenburg Pk, SMBG	2857	26W-11N	E4
Brands Pk, CHCG	2976	3W-4N	E3
Brandt Pk, OKLN	3211	6W-10S	E4
Breckenridge Pk, AURA	3201	32W-8S	C2
Brees Pk, NHBK	2757	9W-17N	C6
Breezewald Pk, LKZH	2698	23W-23N	D3
Bremen Heights Pk, MDLN	3348	5W-17S	B4
Brentwood Pk, DSPN	2862	15W-11N	B3
Brentwood Pk, ODPK	3346	11W-16S	A2
Bretman Pk, BNVL	2972	15W-5N	A1
Briarcliff Woods Pk, MTGY	3199	37W-10S	D5
Briar Knoll Pk, WHTN	3082	24W-1S	D2
Briar Patch Pk, WHTN	3082	23W-2S	E3
Briar Pointe Pk, SMBG	2912	25W-8N	A3
Briarwood Pk, DRFD	2757	9W-20N	B1
Bricher Pk, GNVA	3019	36W-1N	D2
Brickyard Pk, DRFD	2756	11W-20N	E1
Brierwood Estates Pk, HNWD	2644	24W-25N	D4
Briggs Ellis Pk, ThtT	3349	1W-16S	E4
Bright Meadows Pk, RDLK	2531	23W-33N	E3
Brighton Pk, WHTN	3082	25W-2S	A4
Brighton Ridge Pk, NPVL	3203	27W-8S	C2
Brisbin Pk, LktT	3418	26W-19S	A2
Bristol Pk, TYPK	3424	9W-21S	D5
Bristol Trails Pk, LKZH	2699	22W-22N	C4
Brittany Pk, CRY	2641	31W-25N	D6
Brittany Pk, HNVL	2532	21W-33N	C3
Broadview Slough, LMBD	3026	20W-1N	A2
Brook Crossing Pk, NPVL	3203	28W-10S	B7
Brook Pk, HNDL	3146	14W-5S	C2
Brookrose Pk, ROSL	2912	24W-7N	D5
Brookside Pk, JLET	3415	31W-20S	E6
Brooks Pk, CHCG	2918	9W-8N	D1
Brookwood Pk, WDDL	2970	19W-5N	D1
Brown Pk, HDPK	2705	7W-20N	A7
Brown Pk, ODPK	3345	13W-17S	B5
Bruce Ponti Community Pk, PnfT	3339	27W-16S	C4
Bruce Ream Memorial Pk, HPSR	2795	47W-16N	D2
Brush Hill Pk, NPVL	3140	28W-6S	E5
Buckthorn Pk, HDPK	2704	10W-22N	B4
Budler Pk, RMVL	3339	27W-17S	C6
Buena Pk, LKFT	2649	10W-24N	E7
Buffalo Pk, CHCG	2920	3W-5N	E7
Bulger Pk, MLPK	3029	11W-1N	D1
Bulldog Pk, BGBK	3269	23W-11S	A1
Burbank Pk, EGVV	2914	18W-8N	E2
Burlington Pk, HNDL	3146	15W-5S	A1
Burlington Square Pk, NPVL	3141	26W-6S	D5
Burnham Pk, BNHM	3352	3E-16S	A2
Burnham Pk, CHCG	3092	0E-1S	D1
Burnham Shores Pk, EVTN	2867	1W-10N	C4
Burnidge Woods Pk, ELGN	2799	36W-13N	E7
Burning Bush Trail Pk, MPPT	2808	13W-14N	E4
Burns Field, HNDL	3146	15W-4S	A1
Burnside Pk, CHCG	3215	1E-10S	A5
Burr Oak Pk, NPVL	3141	26W-7S	E7
Burr Ridge District Pk, DGvT	3208	16W-10S	A5
Busch Grove Community Pk, BFGV	2701	17W-21N	B6
Bush Hill Pk, HNDL	3146	15W-4S	B1
Buske Pk, MKNA	3502	14W-22S	E2
Busse Pk, MPPT	2808	15W-13N	B7
Busse Pk, SMBG	2859	21W-10N	E5
Butler Lake Pk, LYVL	2591	17W-29N	C4
Butler Pk, EVTN	2866	3W-11N	E2
Butterfield Pk, AURA	3079	32W-4S	C7
Butterfield Pk, EMHT	3028	15W-0S	B6
Butterfield Pk, HMWD	3508	1W-23S	A3
Butterfly Pk, SMWD	2857	27W-10N	C7
Buttonwood Pk, NPVL	3141	28W-7S	A7
Buzz 'N Bloom Prairie Pk, PSHT	3274	9W-13S	E5
Byron Pk, ADSN	2970	18W-4N	E3
Cachey Pk, ODPK	3346	10W-18S	B7
Ca-Crest Pk, SRWD	3496	30W-23S	B4
Caddie Corner Pk, WDRG	3142	23W-7S	E6
California Pk, CHCG	2976	3W-4N	E2
Callahan Pk, WKGN	2479	12W-37N	C2
Calumet Pk, CHCG	3216	4E-10S	C6
Calumet Pk, HRVY	3350	1W-17S	A4
Calvary Pk, PSHL	3274	9W-13S	C3
Calvin Spencer Pk, MRGO	2634	49W-26N	B2
Camberley Pk, PvsT	3086	14W-2S	C3
Cambria Pk, CRY	2695	32W-24N	A1
Cambridge Country Pk, MDLN	2646	19W-27N	B1
Cambridge Pk, BFGV	2754	16W-17N	D4
Cambridge Pk, CLSM	2967	27W-4N	D4
Cambridge Pk, GYLK	2533	19W-33N	B3
Cambridge Pk, SCRL	3020	34W-2N	E1
Camelot Corner Pk, BFGV	2701	17W-21N	B5
Camelot Pk, ANHT	2754	17W-16N	B6
Cameno Real Pk, ODPK	3345	12W-18S	C6
Campanelli Pk, SMBG	2858	24W-9N	C6
Campbell Pk, RGMW	2806	19W-14N	B4
Campton Hills Pk, SCRL	2963	38W-2N	A7
Campton Pk, CmpT	2961	41W-5N	E3
Campus Greens Pk, NPVL	3204	25W-8S	C2
Campus Pk, ELGN	2855	31W-10N	E5
Candlewood Pk, BFGV	2755	15W-20N	A1
Candlewood Pk, CRY	2642	30W-24N	A7
Candlewood Pk, LSLE	3142	24W-5S	D3
Candy Cane Pk, BKFD	3087	11W-2S	E3
Candy Cane Pk, ENGN	3212	3W-11S	E7
Cannan Pk, ZION	2421	11W-39N	E6
Cannon Crossings Pk, HnrT	2856	30W-12N	B1
Canterbury Fields Pk, HFET	2855	32W-12N	D1
Canterbury Pk, BFGV	2701	17W-23N	B2
Canterbury Pk, CLLK	2640	35W-24N	B7
Canterbury Pk, GYLK	2533	19W-32N	B4
Canterbury Pk Place, HFET	2855	32W-12N	D2
Cantigny Pk, WnfT	3081	27W-1S	C1
Cardinal Pk, PLTN	2805	21W-14N	D3
Carefree Pk, ANHT	2861	17W-12N	B1
Carleton Rogers Pk, ELGN	2854	34W-11N	E4

FEATURE NAME Address City ZIP Code	MAP#	CGS	GRID
Carl Sands Pk, CRY	2696	30W-23N	A1
Carmel Pk, ZION	2422	9W-39N	B5
Carmen Garcia Memorial Arboretum Pk, - DndT	2801	33W-16N	B2
Carousel Pk, ANHT	2754	16W-16N	D6
Carpenter Pk, CPVL	2800	34W-16N	E1
Carriage Crest Pk, BTVA	3020	36W-0S	A7
Carriage Green Pk, VNHL	2647	18W-25N	A4
Carriage Walk Pk, ANHT	2807	17W-14N	C3
Carroll Pk, OKPK	3030	8W-0S	E6
Carson Pk, EGVV	2913	21W-8N	E3
Carson Slough Pk, SgrT	3136	40W-5S	A2
Carver Pk, CHCG	3351	0E-15S	A1
Cary-Grove Pk, AlqT	2641	30W-24N	E6
Cary Veterans Pk, CRY	2695	31W-23N	E1
Castaldo Pk, WDRG	3143	22W-7S	C7
Caterbury Woods, PNFD	3265	31W-14S	E7
Caton Ridge Pk, JLET	3415	31W-21S	E6
Ceaser Pk, CTWD	3348	5W-16S	B3
Cedar Lake Pk, LKVL	2474	23W-37N	E1
Cedar Pk, GRNE	2478	15W-35N	A6
Cedar Pk, PKFT	3595	2W-27S	C3
Cedar Pk, PLTN	2805	21W-15N	D1
Cedar Valley Pk, RDLK	2531	23W-33N	E2
Celtic Pk, PLTN	2753	19W-17N	B4
Centennial Pk, ADSN	2970	20W-4N	A3
Centennial Pk, ANHT	2754	17W-17N	C5
Centennial Pk, BLID	3277	2W-15S	C7
Centennial Pk, CHCG	2918	8W-7N	E3
Centennial Pk, EVTN	2867	2W-11N	C3
Centennial Pk, LMNT	3342	20W-15S	C1
Centennial Pk, NPVL	3141	27W-6S	C6
Centennial Pk, ODPK	3345	12W-18S	C7
Centennial Pk, OKLN	3211	8W-10S	A5
Centennial Pk, PKRG	2917	11W-8N	E1
Centennial Pk, RVFT	3030	9W-0N	C3
Centennial Pk, TYPK	3424	9W-20S	D3
Centennial Pk, WLMT	2812	5W-13N	B7
Center Street Pk, MHRY	2528	32W-32N	B4
Central Pk, AddT	2915	17W-6N	B6
Central Pk, BGBK	3269	22W-12S	C2
Central Pk, BLID	3277	2W-15S	C7
Central Pk, CHCG	3032	4W-0N	C3
Central Pk, DSPN	2863	13W-10N	A4
Central Pk, ELGN	2854	34W-11N	E5
Central Pk, GNVW	2810	8W-13N	E7
Central Pk, GYLK	2533	20W-33N	A3
Central Pk, HDPK	2705	8W-22N	A4
Central Pk, LNWD	2920	4W-8N	C2
Central Pk, NPVL	3141	26W-6S	D5
Central Pk, OKBK	3085	16W-2S	D3
Central Pk, OKFT	3347	6W-18S	D7
Central Pk, OKLN	3212	5W-10S	A5
Central Pk, PKFT	3595	3W-26S	A3
Central Pk, SKOK	2866	4W-11N	C2
Central Pk, WHTN	3024	24W-0S	C7
Century Pk, BGBK	3267	26W-12S	D3
Century Pk, RMVL	3340	26W-17S	A5
Century Pk, VNHL	2647	16W-26N	C3
Cerny Pk, WNVL	3081	28W-4S	A7
Chain O' Lakes State Pk, AntT	2415	27W-40N	B2
Champion Creek Pk, PNFD	3266	30W-13S	B5
Championship Pk, FNPK	2973	11W-4N	D3
Champions Pk, BGBK	3267	26W-11S	E1
Chandler Pk, EVTN	2867	2W-12N	A1
Chaney Field, CTHL	3418	24W-21S	D7
Channahon State Pk, CNHN	3672	31W-31S	E5
Channel Runne Pk, LNWD	2920	4W-8N	D1
Channelside Pk, SKOK	2866	4W-10N	D5
Charlemagne Kingswood Pk, SCRL	2965	33W-3N	B5
Charlemagne Pk, HFET	2804	24W-14N	B4
Charles Brown Pk, LYVL	2591	17W-27N	C7
Chase Avenue Beach & Pk, CHCG	2867	1W-9N	D7
Chase Pk, CHCG	2921	1W-5N	C7
Chatburg Pk, ROSL	2912	25W-7N	C5
Chatham Lions Pk, BFGV	2754	17W-18N	B3
Chatham Pk, WHTN	3082	25W-2S	B4
Chelsea Pk, SRGV	3135	42W-7S	D7
Cherbourg Pk, BFGV	2701	16W-21N	C7
Cherokee Pk, ADSN	2971	18W-3N	A5
Cherokee Pk, DSPN	2863	13W-10N	A5
Cherry Creek Pk, GYLK	2533	20W-33N	B2
Cherry Hill Pk, AURA	3136	39W-7S	E7
Cherry Hill Pk, NLNX	3500	20W-24S	B5
Cherrywood Pk, PLTN	2752	20W-17N	E5
Chesapeake Trail Pk, RLKH	2474	24W-36N	C5
Chesterfield Pk, NARA	3138	35W-4S	B1
Chestnut Corners-Hunters Creek Pk, - LKZH	2699	22W-22N	C4
Chestnut Pk, DRN	3145	17W-7S	C6
Chestnut Pk, FNPK	2973	12W-3N	B5
Chestnut Pk, HFET	2858	25W-11N	C3
Chestnut Pk, PLTN	2806	19W-16N	C1
Cheyenne Pk, DSPN	2808	14W-12N	D7
Chicago Blaze Rugby, LMNT	3342	20W-15S	A1
Childerly Pk, WLNG	2755	15W-18N	A3
Children's Pk, BFGV	2701	18W-21N	A6
Chino Pk, HFET	2859	23W-11N	A4
Chippewa Pk, CHCG	2920	3W-8N	D2
Chippewa Pk, DSPN	2862	14W-12N	D1
Chittenden Pk, GRNE	2478	13W-35N	D6
Chopin Pk, CHCG	2975	6W-4N	D3
Churchill Hunt Pk, GRNE	2478	15W-37N	A3
Churchill Pk, BFGV	2701	17W-22N	C4
Churchill Pk, CHCG	2977	2W-2N	C7
Churchill Pk, MltT	3025	23W-1N	A3
Church Pk, LslT	3143	22W-6S	C5
Church Road Pk, AURA	3138	34W-5S	D3
Cider Creek Pk, BGBK	3267	27W-12S	C3
Circle Pk, BMDL	2969	23W-5N	B2
Citizen's Pk, BRTN	2751	25W-20N	B1
City Pk, BGBK	3205	21W-11S	E7
City Pk, CHCG	3150	5W-6S	B4
City Pk, CTSD	3147	12W-6S	B5
City Pk, ELGN	2855	33W-11N	A4
City Pk, HMND	3430		E1
City Pk, NPVL	3202	30W-10S	B5
City Pk, RMVL	3340	24W-16S	E3
City Pk, SHLD	3351	1E-17S	A6
Civic Center Pk, OSWG	3263	37W-11S	C1
C Kelly Franson Pk, RVDL	3350	0W-16S	B4
Claire Lane Pk, PTHT	2808	14W-15N	C2
Claremont Pk, CHCG	3033	2W-0S	B6
Clarendon Pk, CHCG	2921	1W-5N	E7
Clark Pk, CHCG	3032	5W-0S	A5
Clark Pk, EGVV	2913	21W-8N	D1
Clarkson Pk, NHFD	2811	7W-15N	B2
Clark Square Pk, EVTN	2867	1W-10N	C5
Clauss Rec Area, ROSL	2912	24W-6N	E6
Clavey Pk, DRFD	2703	12W-21N	B7
Clear Brook Pk, MDLN	2646	18W-26N	E3
Clearview Pk, WKGN	2479	11W-35N	C5
Clearwater Springs Pk, JLET	3415	32W-20S	C5
Clearwood Pk, AURA	3201	31W-8S	E3
Clemente Pk, CHCG	3033	2W-1N	B1
Clifford-Owasco Pk, ELGN	2854	34W-12N	D2
Clocktower Commons, WHTN	3024	24W-0S	D7
Cloverdale Pk, HDPK	2704	10W-22N	A5
Clover Hills Pk, GnvT	3019	38W-0S	B7
Clyde Pk, CCRO	3089	7W-2S	C3
Clydesdale Pk, WHTN	3083	23W-3S	A5
Coast Guard Pk, NHBK	2757	10W-18N	A4
Cold Springs Pk, MHRY	2527	33W-32N	E5
Cole Pk, GNVW	2811	7W-14N	B4
Cole Pk, NCHI	2536	11W-32N	D5
College Green Pk, ELGN	2854	36W-9N	A7
College Pk, ELGN	2853	36W-10N	E6
College Pk, GLHT	2969	23W-4N	B3
College Pk, JLET	3497	28W-25S	B7
College Road Pk, LSLE	3142	24W-7S	D6
College Trail Pk, GYLK	2533	19W-33N	C3
College View Pk, RMVL	3340	24W-17S	E6
Colonial Pk, ODPK	3345	11W-16S	E3
Colony Lake Pk, SMBG	2858	24W-11N	C3
Colony Pk, EGVV	2913	22W-9N	C1
Colony Pk, HFET	2751	24W-16N	C7
Columbia Avenue Beach & Pk, CHCG	2921	1W-8N	E2
Columbia Commons, NPVL	3204	25W-8S	A2
Columbia Estates Pk, NPVL	3141	26W-6S	E4
Columbus Manor Pk, OKLN	3211	7W-11S	C6
Columbus Pk, CCRO	3089	6W-3S	D4
Columbus Pk, CHCG	3031	7W-0S	C5
Com Ed Greenway, BGBK	3204	24W-11S	D7
Commissioners Pk, WldT	3266	30W-13S	A4
Commissioner's Pk, ALSP	3276	4W-14S	E6
Commissioner's Pk, BGVW	3210	9W-9S	D2
Commissioner's Pk, CHHT	3508	1W-23S	A3
Commissioner's Pk, CHRG	3275	7W-12S	C2
Commissioner's Pk, CTCY	3352	3E-17S	A6
Commissioner's Pk, JSTC	3210	11W-8S	A1
Commissioner's Pk, TYPK	3424	10W-19S	C2
Commons Pk, BFGV	2754	17W-20N	C1
Commons Pk, NRIV	3088	9W-2S	C2
Community Pk, BGBK	3268	24W-12S	D3
Community Pk, CCHL	3426	5W-20S	C5
Community Pk, CLSM	3024	24W-1N	D3
Community Pk, CNHN	3584	29W-27S	E5
Community Pk, FftT	3504	9W-24S	D5
Community Pk, FKFT	3592	10W-26S	C3
Community Pk, GnvT	3019	38W-0N	A5
Community Pk, HFET	2858	23W-11N	E3
Community Pk, LKZH	2698	23W-21N	E6
Community Pk, PLTN	2806	20W-16N	A1
Community Pk, PSHT	3274	9W-14S	D5
Community Pk, PTON	3860	9W-37S	E4
Community Pk, TYPK	3424	10W-20S	C4
Community Pk, WSTR	3087	12W-1S	A2
Concord Oaks Pk, GRNE	2477	17W-35N	A6
Concord Pk, SEGN	2908	35W-8N	B4
Concord Square Pk, DRGV	3144	20W-7S	B7
Conrad Fischer Pk, EMHT	2972	15W-3N	A5
Conservation Pk, RMVL	3340	24W-15S	D2
Constitution Field, NCHI	2537	10W-31N	A7
Constitution Pk, DRGV	3144	19W-5S	C3
Constitution Pk, RVFT	3030	9W-1N	C1
Container Pk, DLTN	3350	0E-16S	D4
Continental Pk, ELGN	2854	34W-10N	E7
Convent Pk, OKFT	3347	7W-17S	D5
Converse Pk, ISLK	2586	28W-27N	E7
Conway Farms Pk, LKFT	2648	13W-25N	E6
Cooney Meadow, EGVV	2859	22W-9N	D7
Cooper Pk, BFGV	2754	17W-18N	A2
Cooper Pk, CHCG	3277	1W-13S	E4
Cooper Pk, HRVY	3349	2W-17S	C6
Copley Island Pk, AURA	3199	36W-8S	D2
Copley Pk, SMBG	2859	23W-12N	B2
Copperfield Pk, HNWD	2645	23W-25N	A5
Cornell Pk, CHCG	3153	2E-5S	B2
Cornell Pk, DSPN	2862	14W-12N	C1
Cornell Square Pk, CHCG	3151	2W-5S	C1
Cornerstone Lakes Pk, WCHI	2965	32W-4N	D4
Cornet Pk, CHHT	3595	2W-25S	D1
Corrine Deinert Pk, TYPK	3424	10W-20S	B5
Cotting Pk, RHMD	2353	34W-42N	C5
Cotton Tail Pk, CHCG	3034	0W-1S	B7
Cottonwood Pk, HFET	2804	25W-12N	B7
Cottonwood Pk, RGMW	2805	21W-13N	C5
Country Aire Pk, MKHM	3348	4W-18S	D6
Country Club Estates Pk, ODPK	3346	10W-17S	B5
Country Club Pk, ITSC	2914	19W-7N	D5
Country Commons Pk, NPVL	3141	26W-6S	E5
Country Creek Community Pk, NlxT	3589	18W-26S	A2
Country Gardens Pk, PTHT	2754	15W-16N	E7
Country Lakes Pk, NPVL	3140	30W-6S	B4
Country Lane Pk, WKGN	2478	15W-37N	B1
Country Ridge Pk, WCDA	2587	26W-27N	D7
Countryside Pk, CTSD	3147	12W-6S	B4
Countryside Pk, GNVW	2809	10W-13N	E6
Countryside Pk, MPPT	2862	15W-11N	A2
Countryside Pk, NfdT	2757	10W-18N	B3
Countryside Pk, RGMW	2805	20W-14N	E4
Countryside Pk, SMWD	2857	28W-10N	A5
Countryside West Pk, LKZH	2699	22W-21N	B7
Countryview Pk, NLNX	3588	19W-27S	D4
Country Walk Pk, RLKB	2475	23W-36N	A5
Country West Pk, SRWD	3496	30W-23S	B4
Coventry Pk, CLLK	2640	35W-24N	A7
Cove Pk, SMBG	2912	24W-9N	E1
Covington Knolls Pk, LMNT	3270	18W-14S	E7
Crabtree Creek Pk, WDRG	3205	22W-8S	C2
Cragin Pk, CHCG	2975	6W-3N	D5
Craig Manor Pk, DSPN	2808	13W-13N	D7
Cranberry Lake Pk, RLKP	2532	22W-33N	B3
Cranston Meadows Pk, SchT	2907	38W-7N	A4
Crawford Pk, PSHT	3346	9W-15S	D1
Creekside, PNFD	3415	31W-18S	E1
Creekside Pk, ALSP	3276	6W-13S	A3
Creekside Pk, GYLK	2533	20W-33N	A3
Creekside Pk, MHRY	2528	32W-31N	C7
Creekside Pk, MTSN	3505	7W-24S	C6
Creekside Pk, RGMW	2806	20W-13N	A6
Creekside Pk, TYPK	3424	9W-19S	D3
Creekside Pk, WLBK	3146	15W-7S	A5
Creekside Pk, WNFD	3023	27W-0S	C6
Creekside West Pk, ANHT	2753	18W-18N	D2
Crescent Pk, AURA	3201	32W-9S	B4
Crescent Pk, CHCG	3277	2W-12S	B2
Crescent Pk, EMHT	3028	15W-0N	A4
Crescent Pk, LMBD	3026	20W-0N	A4
Cress Creek Pk, NPVL	3141	27W-5S	B3
Cress Creek Property, CLLK	2639	36W-24N	D6
Crest Hill Community Pk, CTHL	3418	25W-21S	C7
Crestview Pk, EMHT	2972	15W-2N	A6
Crestwood Pk, NHBK	2757	9W-17N	B4
Crete Pk, CRTE	3685	1W-29S	B1
Crombie Pk, JLET	3499	23W-24S	B5
Cronin Pk, ANHT	2807	18W-13N	A5
Crossing Pond Pk, LGGV	2700	18W-21N	E6
Crow Island Woods, WNKA	2811	5W-15N	E2
Cubs Care Pk, CHCG	3034	0W-1N	A1
Cullen Pk, GYLK	2532	21W-32N	E5
Culver Pk, HMGN	3343	17W-17S	D5
Cumberland Pk, AURA	3201	32W-9S	B4
Cumberland Pk, PKRG	2918	10W-8N	A1
Cumberland Terrace Pk, DSPN	2862	14W-11N	C3
Cunliff Pk, GNVW	2811	7W-12N	C7
Curie Pk, CHCG	3150	4W-5S	C1
Cynthia Pk, WNVL	3080	30W-2S	B4
Cypress Pk, ANHT	2807	18W-12N	A7
Cypress Pk, FSMR	3506	4W-23S	D3
Dalenberg Pk, SHLD	3428	0E-19S	D3
Danby Pk, GNEN	3025	23W-0N	A5
Daniel Pk, ZION	2422	10W-39N	A4
Danny Cunniff Pk, HDPK	2704	10W-24N	A1
Darien Community Pk, DRN	3145	17W-8S	D7
Dauphin Pk, CHCG	3214	1E-10S	E4
David Pk, ZION	2421	11W-40N	D2
Davis Pk, CHCG	3031	6W-1N	D2
Davis Pk, SCRL	3020	36W-2N	A1
Davis Square Pk, CHCG	3091	2W-4S	C7
Dawes Pk, CHCG	3213	2W-9S	C2
Dawes Pk, EVTN	2867	2W-11N	C3
Dearborn Pk, CHCG	3034	0W-0S	B6
Debra Pk, EGVV	2914	21W-8N	A1
Decorah Pk, GrtT	2474	25W-34N	B7
Dedra Pk, SMBG	2858	26W-10N	A6
Dee Pk, MaiT	2863	11W-11N	D2
Deer Haven Pk, FXLK	2473	26W-36N	D4
Deering Estate Pk, EVTN	2813	2W-13N	C7
Deerpath Community Pk, LKFT	2649	11W-26N	E3
Deerpath Pk, BTVA	3077	37W-1S	D2
Deerpath Pk, VNHL	2647	16W-25N	D5
Deer Point Estates Pk, ODPK	3423	13W-20S	A5
Deer Spring Pk, DRFD	2704	10W-21N	A7
Deicke Pk, HTLY	2691	40W-20N	E7
Della Pk, GfnT	2639	38W-25N	A4
Dellwood Pk, LKPT	3419	22W-20S	C5
Dellwood West Pk, LKPT	3419	23W-20S	B5
Delnor Woods Pk, SCRL	2964	35W-3N	C6
Denning Pk, LGNG	3147	13W-5S	A1
Depot Pk, BCHR	3864	0W-36S	B2
Devonshire Pk, DSPN	2862	15W-10N	B5
Devonshire Pk, HDPK	2704	9W-21N	C7
Devonshire Pk, SKOK	2866	5W-11N	A3
De Youngs Grove Pk, SHLD	3350	0E-18S	D7
Diana Street Pk, SRWD	3496	29W-24S	D6
Dickinson Pk, CHCG	2975	6W-5N	E1
Dick Tracy Way Pk, WDSK	2581	41W-30N	D1
Diedrich Pk, GLF	2864	8W-12N	E1
Dietz Pk, HNDL	3145	16W-5S	E3
Dillion Pk, OKLN	3211	6W-11S	E7
Dimucci Pk, DSPN	2862	14W-12N	B1
Diorio Pk, BNVL	2971	16W-5N	E2
Discovery Pk, HRPK	2967	27W-6N	D1
Discovery Pk, ODPK	3422	14W-20S	E5
Diversity Pk, WKGN	2535	14W-33N	C4
Doerhoefer Pk, DRGV	3084	20W-4S	B7
Doherty Pk, SMBG	2859	22W-9N	B7
Dolores A Austin Memorial Pk, MTGY	3199	36W-9S	D4
Dolphin Lake Pk, HMWD	3427	3W-21S	B7
Dolphin Pk, SMWD	2857	28W-10N	B6
Dolton Pk, DLTN	3350	0E-17S	E4
Dominic J Sesto Pk, CHHT	3595	2W-25S	C1
Donald A Bejek Pk, ENGN	3212	3W-10S	E4
Don Burns Pk, OKFT	3426	6W-20S	A3
Don Forni Pk, GNVA	3019	37W-1N	C3
Donovan Pk, CHCG	3091	1W-3S	E5
Doogan Pk, ODPK	3345	12W-17S	C5
Dooley Pk, SMBG	2858	24W-9N	C7
Doolittle Pk, GYLK	2532	21W-34N	E1
Dorothy Drennon Pk, OKTR	3085	17W-1S	B2
Dorset Pk, WHTN	3082	25W-2S	A5
Dougherty Pk, CHCG	3215	3E-10S	D5
Douglas Avenue Pk, ELGN	2854	34W-11N	E3
Douglas Pk, CHCG	3032	3W-1S	E7
Doug Lindberg Pk, PLTN	2753	19W-16N	C6
Dove Pk, PLTN	2753	19W-18N	C3
Dover Pond Pk, DRPK	2752	22W-20N	B1
Downey Pk, CTCY	3351	2E-17S	C4
Drafke Pk, BGBK	3268	25W-13S	B4
Drake Field, ELGN	2855	33W-10N	B6
Drake Pk, LNWD	2920	4W-8N	C2
Dr Edwin B Tharp Pk, TYPK	3424	9W-21S	D5
Dresser Pk, MKHM	3349	3W-18S	A7
Drexel Square Pk, CHCG	3152	0E-5S	E1
Drury Lane Pk, WSTR	3029	12W-1S	C7
Dryden Pk, ANHT	2807	17W-13N	B7
Dryden Pk, GNVA	3020	35W-0N	A4
Dubkin Pk, CHCG	2867	2W-9N	C7
Duffy Pk, ENGN	3212	4W-10S	D5
Dugan Pk East, SRGV	3134	44W-7S	E7
Dugan Pk West, SRGV	3134	44W-7S	D7
Dugdale Pk, WKGN	2536	11W-33N	E3
Dunbar Pk, CHCG	3092	0E-2S	C3
Dunham Pk, CHCG	2919	7W-5N	A7
Dunham Place Pk, DRGV	3144	20W-7S	B7

FEATURE NAME Address City ZIP Code	MAP#	CGS	GRID
Dunmore Estates, PNFD	3337	32W-15S	C3
DuPage Rec Area, DPgT	3204	26W-11S	A7
DuPage River Greenway, BGBK	3205	23W-10S	B6
DuPage River Pk, NPVL	3204	25W-10S	B6
Durkin Pk, CHCG	3212	5W-9S	B3
Durso Pk, CHCG	3034	0W-1N	A2
Dusable Pk, CHCG	3034	0E-0N	D3
Duxbury Pk, SMBG	2858	24W-9N	C7
Dvorak Pk, CHCG	3091	1W-1S	E1
Dwyer Pk, WNKA	2812	5W-15N	A2
Eagle Brook Pk, GNVA	3019	36W-0N	D6
Eagle Heights Pk, ELGN	2854	36W-12N	A2
Eagle Pk, NPVL	3204	25W-8S	B3
Eagle Pk, PLTN	2752	20W-17N	E4
Eagle Pk, SMBG	2858	24W-9N	D7
Eagle Ridge II Pk, ODPK	3422	14W-21S	E5
Eagle Ridge Pk, ODPK	3423	13W-21S	A7
East Avenue Pk, SEGN	2908	34W-8N	E3
East Beach Pk, MHRY	2527	33W-34N	E2
East End Pk, EMHT	3028	15W-1N	B1
Eastgate Pk, PKFT	3595	2W-26S	C2
East Greens Pk, NPVL	3141	26W-6S	E5
East Harbor Pk, HRPK	2967	27W-5N	C3
East Lake Farms Pk, GYLK	2533	20W-32N	A4
Easton Pk, WCHI	3022	29W-0N	E4
East River Pk, CHCG	2920	3W-6N	E6
East Street Pk, WNFD	3023	27W-0S	D6
Eastview Terrace Pk, LMBD	3026	19W-0N	B5
Eaton Field Pk, DSPN	2917	12W-8N	C2
Eaton Preserve, PnfT	3338	29W-16S	D3
Ebersold Pk, DRGV	3144	19W-6S	C5
Echo Point Pk, WDRG	3205	21W-9S	D3
Echo Ridge Pk, LIHL	2693	36W-22N	D4
Eckersall Pk, CHCG	3215	3E-9S	D2
Eckhart Pk, CHCG	3033	1W-1N	D2
Edgebrook Pk, CHCG	2919	6W-8N	D2
Edge Brook Pk, HRPK	2911	26W-8N	E2
Edgewater Pk, LKWD	2639	37W-25N	B4
Edgewood School, WDRG	3205	21W-9S	D3
Edina Pk, ZION	2422	9W-40N	C3
Edison Pk, CHCG	2918	9W-8N	C1
Edison Pk, HMND	3430		D3
Edna M Rollins Pk, AURA	3138	34W-7S	D7
Edson Pk, LMBD	3026	20W-0S	B7
Edward Mraz Pk, ROSL	2913	22W-8N	B2
Egan Pk, CTCY	3430	4E-19S	C2
Ehler Pk, CHCG	2977	2W-2N	B7
Ehlert Pk, BKFD	3087	11W-4S	E7
Ehret Pk, HNDL	3145	16W-5S	E2
Einstein Pk, DSPN	2862	15W-10N	A4
Eisenhower Pk, HLSD	3028	13W-0N	D4
Elaine Bond Pk, SMBG	2858	25W-10N	B6
Elder Lane Pk, WNKA	2812	4W-15N	D3
Eldridge Pk, EMHT	3027	16W-0S	D6
Eleanor Pk, HNDL	3146	15W-5S	A1
Elgin Sports Complex, ELGN	2854	35W-10N	C7
Elizabeth Pk, ZION	2422	9W-41N	C2
Elks Pk, EVTN	2867	2W-9N	B6
Elliot Pk, EVTN	2867	1W-10N	C4
Elliot Woods Pk, OMFD	3506	4W-25S	D7
Ellis Pk, CHCG	3092	0E-3S	D5
Ellis Pk, RLKB	2474	23W-34N	D7
El Morro Pk, OKFT	3347	7W-18S	C7
Elm Pk, GNVA	3020	34W-1N	D2
Elm Pk, GNVW	2810	9W-12N	D7
Elm Pk, LGNG	3087	12W-4S	B7
Elnora Smith Pk, EVTN	2867	3W-11N	A2
Emerson Pk, MPPT	2808	15W-13N	A6
Emerson Pk, SKOK	2865	6W-11N	E2
Emmerich East Pk, BFGV	2754	16W-18N	C2
Emmerich Pk, BFGV	2754	17W-18N	C2
Emmerson Pk, CHCG	2921	2W-7N	B3
Emricson Pk, WDSK	2581	42W-30N	B1
Engle Memorial Pk, LNHT	2418	20W-39N	B5
Engstrom Family Pk, BTVA	3077	36W-1S	E2
Enneth B Shipley Memorial Field, - STGR	3596	0W-28S	B6
Equestrian Pk, OrlT	3423	13W-18S	A1
Erfert Pk, LNSG	3510	3E-22S	A1
Erickson Pk, BGBK	3269	23W-11S	A2
Eric Nasebandt Pk, TYPK	3424	9W-20S	E5
Esmeralda Pk, ELGN	2854	34W-12N	E2
Esper Petersen Pk, GRNE	2478	14W-35N	C7
Essey Pk, CHCG	3215	1E-8S	A1
Estates Pk, HMWD	3428	1W-22S	A7
Eton Pk, NBRN	2697	25W-23N	E1
Euclid Pk, CHCG	3214	0W-11S	B6
Euclid Pk, CHHT	3596	1W-26S	A2
Euclid Square, OKPK	3031	8W-0S	A7
Eugene A Cernan Pk, BLWD	3029	12W-0S	B6
Eugene Field Pk, CHCG	2920	4W-6N	C6
Eugene Matanky Pk, CHCG	2921	2W-8N	B1
Everett Pk, LKFT	2649	12W-24N	B7
Evergreen Lakes Recreational Pk, - CLSM	2967	27W-3N	C6
Evergreen Pk, ANHT	2807	16W-13N	C5
Evergreen Pk, HFET	2858	24W-11N	D4
Evergreen Trails Pk, MPPT	2808	15W-14N	A5
Facoln Pk, PLTN	2753	20W-18N	A2
Fairchild Pk, EGVV	2915	18W-8N	A2
Fair Oaks Pk, CLSM	2967	28W-3N	B6
Fairview Pk, MPPT	2807	16W-13N	E6
Fairview Pk, RLKB	2475	23W-35N	A6
Fairview Pk, SCRL	3019	36W-2N	D1
Falcon Pk, ANHT	2861	17W-11N	B3
Falcon Ridge Pk, ALGN	2694	35W-21N	A6
Falconridge Pk, BGBK	3205	21W-9S	E4
Falk Pk, SMBG	2912	25W-9N	C1
Fargo Avenue Beach & Pk, CHCG	2867	1W-9N	D7
Fargo Pk, GNVA	3020	36W-0N	A5
Farmington Commons Pk, NPVL	3204	25W-10S	B6
Farmington Pk, NPVL	3204	25W-10S	B5
Farmstone Ridge, PNFD	3339	28W-15S	A2
Farmwood Pk, ADSN	2970	19W-5N	C2
Farnsworth Pk, AURA	3200	33W-8S	E1
Fawn Pk, SRWD	3495	31W-25S	E7
Fedor Pk, BGVW	3148	9W-8S	C7
Feinberg Pk, CLLK	2640	33W-25N	D5
Fenhouse Pk, BLWD	3029	12W-0N	B4
FE Peacock Pk, ITSC	2914	19W-6N	C5
Fernwood Pk, CHCG	3278	0W-12S	A1
Fernwood Pkway Pk, CHCG	3214	0W-11S	B6
Ferson Creek Pk, SchT	2964	35W-4N	A5
Fetzner Pk, CLLK	2693	36W-23N	D2
Fiddler Farm Pk, AURA	3079	33W-3S	A6
Fiddler's Oak Pk, AURA	3079	33W-3S	A6
Fieldbrook Pk, WCDA	2588	24W-30N	B2
Fieldcrest Pk, OKFT	3426	5W-19S	B2
Field Pk, HFET	2858	24W-12N	E1
Field Pk, OKPK	3030	8W-1N	E2
Field Pk, WNSP	3086	13W-4S	E7
Fieldstone Pk, NLNX	3500	19W-24S	D6
Filson Pk, TYPK	3424	9W-19S	E2
Finch Pk, HFET	2804	23W-14N	E4
Finneran Pk, CTCY	3430	4E-19S	B2
Fippinger Pk, BLWD	3029	11W-0S	C5
Firefighters Pk, WHTN	3023	26W-0S	E7
Fireman's Memorial Pk, NPVL	3141	27W-6S	B5
Fireman's Pk, MONE	3683	6W-31S	A5
Firemen's Memorial Pk, WKGN	2479	11W-37N	D1
Firemen's Pk, EVTN	2867	2W-11N	B1
Firemen's Pk, STGR	3596	1W-27S	A4
Fischel Pk, DRGV	3144	19W-5S	C3
Fisher Family Pk, WcnT	2587	28W-30N	A1
Fishhook Pk, WCDA	2588	25W-29N	B3
Fitzgerald Pk, BRBK	3211	8W-9S	A3
Flanagan Pk, BLWD	3029	13W-0N	A4
Flentie Pk, ANHT	2807	16W-16N	C1
Flick Pk, GNVW	2809	10W-13N	E6
Flora Pk, ALGN	2694	35W-20N	A7
Flossmore Pk, FSMR	3507	3W-22S	B2
Ford School Pk, LIHL	2694	35W-21N	A6
Forest & Iowa Triangle, RVFT	3030	9W-1N	B2
Forest Glen Pk, CHCG	2919	6W-6N	E5
Forest Glen Pk, OKBK	3086	15W-1S	B1
Forest Hills Pk, WNSP	3146	14W-5S	D2
Forest Pk, GNWD	3508	0E-22S	E1
Forest Pk, LKFT	2650	9W-27N	C2
Forest Trails Pk, WCHI	3022	29W-2N	E1
Forest View Pk, DGvT	3270	20W-12S	B3
Forest View Pk, LNHT	2418	19W-38N	C6
Forestview Pk, NPVL	3140	29W-5S	E3
Forsythe Pk, HMND	3280		D4
Fossland Pk, WPHR	2363	10W-43N	B5
Foss Pk, NCHI	2537	10W-31N	A6
Foss Pk, WKGN	2536	11W-32N	E5
Foster Pk, CHCG	3213	1W-9S	D3
Founders Pk, BGVW	3210	9W-9S	C3
Founders Pk, HDPK	2758	7W-20N	C2
Founders Pk, WNFD	3023	27W-0N	D6
Foundry Pk, ELGN	2854	34W-11N	D3
Fountain Square Pk, EGVV	2859	21W-9N	D7
Four Colonies Pk, CLLK	2639	37W-24N	C7
Four Seasons Pk, LMBD	3084	20W-1S	B1
Four Seasons Pk, ROSL	2912	24W-6N	D6
Four Seasons Pk, SRWD	3495	31W-24S	E6
Four Seasons Pk Sports Complex, PNFD	3339	28W-17S	A7
Fox Chase Pk, RLKB	2475	21W-36N	C4
Fox Chase Pk, SCRL	2964	34W-4N	D5
Foxcroft Pk, AURA	3137	38W-5S	A3
Foxdale Pk, ADSN	2970	20W-5N	B1
Foxford Hills Pk, CRY	2642	30W-25N	A5
Fox Glen Pk, RLKH	2474	23W-36N	D4
Fox Hill Greens Pk, NPVL	3140	29W-5S	D3
Fox Lake Veterans Memorial Pk, FXLK	2473	26W-36N	C4
Fox Meadow Pk, NHFD	2810	8W-15N	E2
Fox Meadow School Pk, SEGN	2908	35W-9N	A2
Fox Pk, HRPK	2912	26W-9N	A1
Fox Pk, OKPK	3030	8W-0S	E5
Fox Ridge Pk, MHRY	2527	34W-32N	C4
Fox River Pk, TVLY	2695	31W-22N	C3
Fox River Valley Gardens 1 Pk, PTBR	2642	29W-26N	C3
Fox Trail Pk, BTVA	3078	35W-2S	C4
Fox Trail Pk, PTBR	2642	29W-26N	C2
Francione Pk, SNPK	3029	12W-1N	B1
Frankfort Prairie Pk, FKFT	3591	11W-25S	E1
Frank K Burgess Pk, GNVA	3019	37W-1N	C3
Franklin Pk, CHCG	3032	5W-1S	B7
Franklin Pk, VLPK	3026	18W-1N	E3
Frankowiak Pk, DRGV	3144	20W-6S	C4
Franzen Grove Pk, WDDL	2915	18W-6N	A5
Franzen Pk, ITSC	2914	20W-7N	B5
Frederick Beach Pk, BTVA	3078	35W-1S	B2
Freedom Pk, ALSP	3348	5W-15S	A1
Freedom Pk, BGBK	3267	26W-13S	D5
Freedom Pk, BRWN	3089	8W-3S	A5
Freedom Pk, CHRG	3275	7W-12S	B1
Freedom Pk, SMBG	2912	25W-9N	C1
Frenchmens Cove Pk, ANHT	2754	17W-17N	B4
Freund Field, MHRY	2528	32W-33N	A3
Friendly Oaks Pk, OKFT	3425	6W-19S	E2
Friendship Pk, CLSM	2967	26W-3N	D6
Friendship Pk, NHLK	3028	13W-1N	D1
Friendship Pk USA, SMWD	2857	27W-10N	C6
Fritz Werley Pk, WTMT	3145	17W-4S	B1
Frontier Pk, ANHT	2806	18W-16N	E1
Frontier Pk, ODPK	3345	12W-17S	D4
Frost Pk, MLPK	3028	13W-1N	E2
Fuller Pk, CHCG	3092	0W-4S	B7
Ful-Roy Pk, NHLK	2972	13W-3N	E6
Fulton Pk, CHCG	3032	5W-0N	A4
Gabriel Pk, ZION	2422	10W-39N	A5
Gaelic Pk, OKFT	3347	7W-17S	C5
Gage Pk, CHCG	3151	3W-6S	B3
Gale Moore Pk, WRTH	3274	8W-12S	E2
Galewood Pk, CHCG	2975	7W-2N	C7
Gallery Pk, GNVW	2810	9W-14N	B3
Gano Pk, CHCG	3277	1W-13S	E4
Gardens Pk, BGVW	3148	9W-7S	C6
Garfield Pk, AURA	3138	34W-6S	D5
Garfield Pk, CHCG	3032	4W-0S	C5
Garfield Square, CHCG	3032	4W-0N	C3
Garibaldi Pk, CHCG	3033	1W-0S	D6
Garnsey Pk, JLET	3498	24W-22S	D1
Gartner Pk, NPVL	3203	27W-8S	C2
Gasior Pk, TYPK	3423	11W-20S	E6
Gaslight Pk, ALGN	2694	34W-20N	B7
Gateley Stadium Pk, CHCG	3214	0E-11S	E7
Gateway Pk, RLKB	2475	22W-35N	C6
Gene Leonard Pk, MDLN	3347	6W-17S	E5
General Fry's Landing, LMNT	3270	19W-13S	D5
George Ball Pk, GNEN	3025	22W-0N	C3
George Geracie Pk, MDLN	3348	5W-17S	B4
Georgetown Pk, RMVL	3340	25W-16S	C3
Gerald L Walter Pk, CLSM	2967	27W-3N	C5
Gerald Weeks Pk, MltT	3024	25W-1N	B3
German Pk, TYPK	3424	9W-19S	D2
Gifford Pk, ELGN	2855	33W-11N	A4
Gilberto Pk, GLHT	2968	24W-3N	D6
Gilbert Pk, DRGV	3144	20W-5S	B2
Gilbert Pk, EVTN	2867	3W-11N	A2
Gilbert Pk, LGNG	3087	13W-4S	A7
Gilbert Stiles Pk, LYVL	2591	17W-30N	C2
Gill Pk, CHCG	2977	1W-4N	E2
Gillson Pk, WLMT	2813	2W-14N	A5
Glacial Pk, RcmT	2412	35W-39N	B6
Gladstone Pk, CHCG	2919	7W-6N	B5
Gladstone Pk, GLHT	2969	23W-4N	A4
Gladstone Pk, WSTR	3029	12W-0S	B7
Glaeser Pk, RNPK	3594	5W-26S	B3
Gleiss Pk, SKOK	2866	5W-11N	B2
Glenbrook Pk, SMWD	2857	27W-11N	B4
Glendale Pk, HMND	3430		C1
Glen Ellyn Manor Pk, GNEN	3025	23W-0S	A7
Glen Hill Pk, GLHT	3025	23W-2N	A1
Glen Oak Pk, GNEN	3025	21W-0S	D6
Glos Pk, EMHT	3028	15W-1N	A2
Golden Gate Pk, CHCG	3278	0E-15S	D7
Golden Meadows, PNFD	3338	30W-15S	B3
Golden Meadows 4, PNFD	3338	30W-15S	C2
Golden Meadows Pk, EMHT	3028	15W-1N	B2
Golf Mill Pk, NLES	2864	10W-11N	A3
Golf Road Pk, HFET	2856	31W-12N	A3
Golfview Pk, CPVL	2801	32W-17N	C1
Golfview Pk, RLKB	2474	23W-35N	E6
Gompers Pk, CHCG	2920	5W-6N	A5
Gonin Pk, FNPK	2973	12W-3N	B6
Goodenow Grove, CteT	3686	0E-32S	A7
Goodrich School, WDRG	3143	22W-7S	C7
Good Temple Pk, GNVA	3020	34W-1N	D2
Goodway Pk, NARA	3137	37W-4S	C1
Goose Lake Pk, ROSL	2912	24W-7N	C5
Gordon Ray Pk, MDLN	2646	18W-26N	D3
Gouwens Pk, SHLD	3429	1E-18S	B1
Governors Trail Pk, MTSN	3594	5W-25S	C1
Graf Pk, WHTN	3024	25W-0S	A6
Graham Pk, WKGN	2422	10W-38N	A6
Grand Crossing Pk, CHCG	3214	1E-8S	E1
Grande Pk, PNFD	3337	33W-15S	B2
Grand Pk, CHCG	3032	4W-1N	D2
Grant Pk, CHCG	3034	0E-0S	C6
Grasmere Pk, MKNA	3503	12W-23S	C4
Grasslands Pk, ODPK	3422	14W-20S	D4
Graver Pk, CHCG	3213	1W-11S	D7
Gray Farm Pk, SMBG	2858	26W-10N	A5
Green Briar Pk, CHCG	2921	3W-7N	A3
Green Briar Pk, GLHT	3025	22W-1N	B2
Greenbriar Pk, NLNX	3501	18W-24S	A6
Greenbrier Pk, ANHT	2753	18W-16N	D7
Greenebaum Pk, CHCG	2976	5W-2N	B7
Greene Field Pk, AURA	3137	36W-6S	E6
Greenfield Pk, NHBK	2756	11W-18N	D3
Greenfields Pk, CRY	2695	32W-23N	C2
Green Lake Pk, BFGV	2701	17W-21N	B6
Greenman School Pk, AURA	3137	36W-7S	D7
Green Meadow Pk, ADSN	2970	18W-4N	E3
Green Meadows Pk, BRLT	2910	30W-7N	B5
Green Meadows Pk, MKNA	3503	13W-23S	B4
Green Slopes Pk, ANHT	2807	17W-15N	B2
Greens Pk, ANHT	2807	17W-15N	B2
Green Tree Pk, LYVL	2647	16W-27N	C1
Greenview Pk, NHBK	2810	10W-15N	A1
Greenview Pk, RLKB	2474	23W-35N	D6
Greenwood Pk, RLKP	2532	22W-33N	A2
Gregg Pk, NCHI	2593	11W-30N	E2
Gregory Pk, MPPT	2808	15W-13N	A6
Greg Pappas Pk, MDLN	3348	5W-17S	B4
Grennan Heights Pk, NLES	2864	9W-10N	D5
Grey Pk, EVTN	2867	2W-10N	B4
Grosse Pointe Pk, VNHL	2646	18W-25N	E5
Gross Pk, CHCG	2920	3W-6N	E6
Gross Point Pk, SKOK	2865	6W-11N	E3
Groveland Pk, CHCG	3092	0E-3S	D4
Grove Pk, HDPK	2704	9W-21N	C7
Grow Pk, SMWD	2857	28W-10N	A5
Gus Bock Pk, LNSG	3430	3E-20S	A5
Guy Patrarca Pk, CHHT	3596	0W-26S	B2
Hale Pk, CHCG	3149	7W-6S	B5
Haley Meadows Pk, RMVL	3340	25W-15S	C1
Haley Pk, NlxT	3502	15W-22S	B1
Hall School Pk, AURA	3137	38W-6S	B5
Hamilton Pk, CHCG	3152	0W-8S	B7
Hamilton Pk, DRPK	2698	23W-21N	E5
Hamlet Pk, BTVA	3078	34W-1S	D1
Hamlet Pk, NCHI	2536	12W-31N	B6
Hamlin Pk, CHCG	2977	2W-3N	B4
Hamlin Pk, SKOK	2866	4W-9N	C6
Hampe Pk, CLSM	2968	25W-4N	A4
Hampshire Pk, EGVV	2859	21W-9N	D7
Hampton Pk, CLLK	2693	37W-22N	B3
Hampton Pk, CRY	2695	32W-23N	B1
Hampton Pk, RDLK	2532	23W-32N	A6
Hanesworth Pk, LGPK	3087	12W-2S	C3
Hanover Community Pk, HRPK	2911	27W-8N	C3
Hanover Pk, SMMT	3148	9W-5S	D2
Hanrahan Pk, MDLN	2591	18W-27N	A7
Hansen Pk, NHLK	3029	13W-1N	A1
Hanson Pk, CHCG	2975	6W-2N	D6
Hanson Pk, EGVV	2914	20W-8N	A3
Happiness Pk, ANHT	2753	18W-16N	D7
Harding Pk, CHCG	3032	4W-1N	C2
Harmon Pk, HRVY	3350	1W-17S	A6
Harnew Pk, OKLN	3211	7W-10S	C5
Harold A Reskin Pk, GLHT	2969	22W-2N	B6
Harold Hecht Pk, BlmT	3596	1W-27S	A5
Harper Playground Pk, CHCG	3153	1E-7S	B4
Harrer Pk, MNGV	2865	7W-11N	B3
Harris Fawell Pk, NPVL	3202	29W-8S	D1
Harrison-Benwell Pk, McHT	2469	35W-35N	E5
Harrison Pk, CHCG	3091	2W-1S	C1
Harrison Pk, HMND	3352		D7
Harr Pk, BRBK	3211	6W-9S	E3
Hartfield Pk, NARA	3078	35W-3S	C5
Hartigan Pk & Beach, CHCG	2921		E2
Hartmann Pk, VNHL	2647	17W-24N	A6
Hart Pk, BLID	3277	2W-14S	B6

Chicago 7-County Points of Interest Index

FEATURE NAME Address City ZIP Code	MAP#	CGS	GRID
Harts Hill Pk, RDLK	2531	24W-33N	D2
Harts Woods Pk, RDLK	2531	24W-33N	D1
Harvester Pk, BRRG	3146	15W-8S	B7
Harvest Glen, PNFD	3338	31W-16S	A4
Harvest Hills Pk, SCRL	3019	37W-2N	C1
Hasan Pk, CHCG	3153	2E-7S	D6
Hasbrook Pk, ANHT	2807	18W-15N	A2
Hathaway Pk, BbyT	3018	39W-0S	D6
Hawaii Pk, DSPN	2808	14W-12N	D7
Hawthorne Glen Pk, GNVW	2809	11W-15N	D2
Hawthorne Hill Woods, LslT	3205	22W-8S	C1
Hawthorne Junction Pk, WHTN	3024	24W-0N	D5
Hawthorne Pk, CCRO	3089	6W-2S	D3
Hawthorne Pk, CHCG	3213	1W-8S	E1
Hawthorne Pk, PLTN	2805	21W-15N	E2
Hawthorn Hills Pk, ELGN	2853	36W-11N	D4
Hawthorn Mellody Pk, VNHL	2591	17W-27N	B7
Hawthorn Woods Community Pk, HNWD	2645	21W-24N	C6
Heartland Pk, ANTH	2417	21W-40N	D2
Heatherwood Pk, RLKB	2475	21W-35N	C7
Hebron Pk, ZION	2421	11W-40N	E2
Hecht Pk, MKNA	3503	11W-23S	E3
Heggie Pk, JLET	3499	23W-22S	B2
Helen Pk, ODPK	3346	11W-18S	A7
Helmut Berens Pk, EMHT	2971	16W-2N	D7
Henry J Kalk Pk, GLNC	2758	6W-17N	D5
Henry Proesel Pk, LNWD	2920	5W-8N	A1
Heritage Green, PNFD	3266	30W-14S	B6
Heritage Meadows, PNFD	3266	30W-14S	B7
Heritage Oaks, PNFD	3266	31W-14S	A7
Heritage Pk, ANHT	2860	18W-12N	E1
Heritage Pk, BGBK	3204	24W-10S	E5
Heritage Pk, CRTE	3685	1W-30S	A3
Heritage Pk, ELBN	3017	42W-0N	C5
Heritage Pk, GLHT	2969	23W-3N	B5
Heritage Pk, HRPK	2911	26W-6N	E6
Heritage Pk, ODPK	3345	11W-16S	E4
Heritage Pk, OKFT	3347	6W-17S	E5
Heritage Pk, OSWG	3263	37W-12S	C4
Heritage Pk, WLNG	2755	14W-17N	B4
Heritage Pleasant Hill Pk, MltT	3023	26W-1N	E3
Hermitage Pk, CHCG	3151	2W-6S	C4
Hermits Pk, HMND	3352		C3
Hermon Pk, ZION	2421	11W-40N	E4
Hermosa Pk, CHCG	2976	5W-2N	A6
Heron Pk, PLTN	2805	22W-15N	B2
Heron View Pk, RDLK	2531	25W-33N	A2
Herrick Pk, MltT	3024	25W-0N	A5
Hessler Pk, BRWN	3088	8W-3S	E5
Hiawatha Pk, CHCG	2974	10W-4N	B3
Hibbard Pk, WLMT	2811	5W-13N	E6
Hickory Glen Pk, GNWD	3509	1E-23S	B2
Hickory Meadows Pk, ANHT	2807	17W-15N	B2
Hickory Pk, MDLN	2646	18W-26N	D3
Hidden Creek Aquapark, HDPK	2704	9W-21N	D6
Hidden Lakes Historic Trout Farm, - BGBK	3204	23W-11S	E7
Hidden Lakes Pk, BGBK	3204	24W-11S	E7
Hidden Pond Pk, HRPK	2967	27W-4N	D4
Hidden River, PNFD	3416	30W-19S	A3
High Hill Pk, ALGN	2694	35W-20N	A7
Highland Pk, FSMR	3507	3W-23S	A4
Highland Pk, HFET	2858	24W-12N	D1
Highland Pk, HNDL	3146	15W-4S	B1
Highland Pk, JLET	3500	21W-23S	A3
Highland Pk, RLKB	2475	23W-35N	A7
Highland Point Pk, BFGV	2701	16W-21N	D7
Highlands Pk, BTVA	3020	35W-0S	C6
Highlands Pk, NARA	3077	37W-4S	D7
Highmoor Pk, HDPK	2704	10W-22N	A3
High Point Pk, HFET	2858	25W-12N	C1
Highridge Pk, WSTR	3086	13W-1S	E1
Highview Pk, ADSN	2970	18W-3N	E5
Highview Pk, HNWD	2645	20W-24N	E6
Hilbert Siemsen Meadow, OrlT	3424	9W-19S	E3
Hill Crest Pk, HLCT	3427	3W-21S	B6
Hiller Pk, MchT	2472	30W-37N	A2
Hill Farm Pk, CLLK	2639	36W-24N	D7
Hillhurst Pk, CRY	2696	30W-23N	A1
Hillside Commons Pk, HLSD	3028	14W-0N	D5
Hilltop Pk, SMBG	2858	25W-11N	B3
Hinckly Pk, PKRG	2864	10W-9N	A7
Hinkston Pk, WKGN	2479	12W-35N	B7
Hirsch Pk, TYPK	3425	8W-21S	B6
Hitchcock Woods, LSLE	3142	24W-5S	D3
H Michael Wild Pk, BTVA	3078	34W-1S	D2
Hoard Pk, CHCG	3153	1E-8S	A7
Hobson Corner Pk, WDRG	3143	22W-7S	C6
Hobson West Pk, NPVL	3141	27W-7S	C7
Hobson Woods Pk, NPVL	3203	26W-7S	E1
Hodgkins Pk, HGKN	3147	11W-7S	D5
Hoffman Estates Community Center & Ice-Arena, HFET	2858	25W-12N	B2
Hoffman Pk, AlqT	2695	32W-23N	A2
Hoffman Pk, FftT	3504	9W-24S	D5
Hoffman Pk, HFET	2858	23W-11N	E4
Hoffman Pk, MltT	3083	21W-2S	D2
Hoffman Pk, WHTN	3025	23W-0S	A6
Holder Memorial Pk, ALGN	2695	32W-20N	A7
Hollandale Pk, SHLD	3428	0E-19S	D2
Holly Pk, DRN	3144	18W-7S	E7
Hollywood Pk, CHCG	2920	4W-7N	D4
Holstein Pk, CHCG	2977	2W-2N	B6
Homerding Pk, WRTH	3275	8W-13S	A4
Homer T Cook Memorial Pk, WCDA	2587	26W-27N	E7
Homewood Estates Pk, HMWD	3427	3W-21S	A7
Honore Pk, HRVY	3349	2W-17S	D6
Hooper's Hollow Pk, DRGV	3144	20W-4S	A1
Hoosier Grove Pk, HnrT	2856	29W-10N	D6
Hoover Pk, SMBG	2858	25W-10N	B5
Hope Pk, CHCG	3152	0W-6S	A3
Horan Pk, CHCG	3032	3W-0S	E5
Horizon Pk, WLNG	2754	15W-17N	E5
Horizon Village Pk, ZION	2421	12W-41N	C1
Horner Pk, CHCG	2977	3W-5N	A1
Horner Pk, LIHL	2694	34W-21N	B5
Horse Fair Pk, SPGV	2413	31W-40N	E3
Hosek Pk, CNHL	3145	17W-5S	C3
Houston Pk, CHCG	3152	0E-5S	E1
Howard Pk, WLMT	2812	4W-13N	C5
Howard Street Beach & Pk, CHCG	2867	1W-9N	D6
Hoyne Pk, CHCG	3091	2W-3S	B4
Hubbard Pk, CHCG	3031	6W-0N	E3
Huber Lane Pk, GNVW	2810	10W-13N	A7
Hull Pk, WHTN	3082	23W-3S	E5
Humboldt Pk, CHCG	3032	3W-1N	E2
Humbracht Pk, BRLT	2967	28W-5N	A1
Hummer Pk, DRGV	3144	18W-5S	E2
Hummingbird Pk, PLTN	2752	22W-17N	A5
Humphrey Complex, ODPK	3345	12W-17S	C5
Hunt Club Community Pk, GRNE	2477	17W-35N	C7
Hunt Club Pk, SCRL	2964	34W-3N	C6
Hunt Club Wetlands, SCRL	2964	34W-4N	D5
Hunter Prairie Pk, FftT	3504	9W-24S	E6
Hunter's Cove Pk, GYLK	2533	19W-33N	B4
Hunters Ridge Pk, HFET	2856	30W-12N	B2
Hunters Woods Pk, NPVL	3204	25W-9S	B4
Huntington Chase Pk, EGVV	2914	20W-8N	A2
Huntington Commons Pk, NPVL	3142	25W-6S	B5
Huntington Estates Parkway, NPVL	3142	25W-7S	B7
Huntington Pk, HFET	2804	25W-15N	B3
Huntington Ridge Pk, NPVL	3142	25W-7S	C7
Hurley Gardens, WHTN	3081	26W-1S	E1
Hurley Pk, CHCG	3213	2W-11S	C7
Husky Pk, WLNG	2754	15W-17N	E4
Hyacinth Pk, CHCG	3092	1E-4S	E7
I&M Canal State Trail Pk, CNHN	3672	31W-30S	E5
Ide's Grove East Pk, WDRG	3206	20W-9S	B2
Ide's Grove West Pk, WDRG	3206	20W-9S	A3
Idlewild Pk, HDPK	2705	7W-21N	A6
Idlewild Pk, RLKB	2474	23W-34N	E7
Idlewild Pk, WrnT	2533	18W-33N	E3
Illinois Avenue Pk, AURA	3138	35W-6S	B5
Illinois Beach State Pk North, ZION	2422	9W-40N	D2
Illinois Beach State Pk South, BtnT	2422	9W-39N	D5
Illinois Beach State Pk South, WkgT	2480	9W-37N	D3
Illinois Pk, PKFT	3595	3W-25S	B1
Independence Pk, CCHL	3426	4W-21S	D5
Independence Pk, CHCG	2976	4W-4N	C2
Independence Pk, RMVL	3339	27W-17S	D6
Independence Square, CHCG	3032	4W-1S	C7
Indiana-Illinois Pk, HMND	3430		C3
Indiana Pk, PKFT	3595	3W-25S	A1
Indian Boundary North Pk, FftT	3504	9W-23S	D4
Indian Boundary Pk, BGBK	3204	25W-11S	B7
Indian Boundary Pk, CHCG	2921	3W-8N	A1
Indian Boundary South Pk, FftT	3504	9W-24S	D4
Indian Chase Meadows, BGBK	3267	26W-12S	E3
Indian Creek Pk, AURA	3139	33W-5S	A2
Indian Hill Pk, WNKA	2812	4W-15N	C3
Indian Lakes Pk, BMDL	2968	24W-4N	E3
Indian Oaks Pk, MRGO	2634	50W-26N	A3
Indian Oaks Pk, PNFD	3416	31W-18S	A1
Indian Prairie Pk, CLLK	2693	36W-22N	D3
Indian Prairie State Pk, BGBK	3267	27W-12S	C3
Indian Ridge Pk, GNVW	2809	11W-15N	C2
Indian Road Pk, CHCG	2919	7W-7N	B3
Indian Trail Island Pk, AURA	3138	35W-5S	B4
Indian Trail Pk, GNVW	2809	12W-14N	B5
Indian Trails Pk, ElaT	2646	19W-25N	D4
Indian Train Pk, ElaT	2646	19W-25N	C5
Indian Woods Pk, PSHL	3210	10W-11S	C7
Indigo Bird Pk, CHCG	3034	0W-1S	B7
Internationale Estates Pk, WDRG	3270	20W-12S	C2
Inwood Pk, JLET	3497	28W-24S	B5
Iron Oaks Pk, FSMR	3507	3W-23S	C4
Ishnala Pk, ODPK	3346	10W-16S	B2
Ishnala Woods Pk, ODPK	3346	10W-16S	C2
Island Pk, BTVA	3078	35W-1S	B2
Island Pk, GNVA	3020	35W-1N	C4
Island Pk, NARA	3138	36W-4S	A1
Ivanhoe Pk, BGBK	3205	22W-11S	B7
Ivanhoe Pk, RVDL	3350	0W-16S	C3
Ivy Hall Pk, BFGV	2701	17W-20N	A7
Izaak Walton Pk, PTHT	2808	15W-15N	A2
Jack & Bob Tures Pk, HTLY	2692	39W-20N	D7
Jackman Pk, GNVW	2810	9W-13N	D6
Jackson Pk, CHCG	3153	2E-6S	B4
Jackson Pk, SCHT	3596	1W-26S	B3
Jacob Pk, CHCG	2920	3W-5N	E7
Jacobson Pk, WRLK	2469	37W-36N	B5
Jacobs Pk, MNGV	2865	8W-11N	A2
James A Malecky Pk, OKFT	3425	6W-20S	E4
James C Mitchell Pk, DRFD	2703	11W-21N	C7
James E Clayson Pk, ITSC	2914	19W-6N	C5
James J Kamradt Recreation Area, - HRPK	2911	27W-6N	D6
James Knight Pk, SDWH	3258	51W-14S	A7
James O Setnes Pk, HLCT	3427	3W-20S	B3
James O Setnes Sport Center, HLCT	3427	3W-20S	B3
James Pate Phillip State Pk, BRLT	2909	32W-7N	B4
James Pk, EVTN	2866	3W-9N	E6
James Pk, FNPK	2973	13W-3N	A4
Jamesway Pk, CRY	2641	31W-24N	D7
James W Jesk Pk, OKFT	3347	8W-18S	B7
Janes Avenue Pk, WDRG	3205	21W-9S	E3
Janes Avenue Soccer Field, WDRG	3205	21W-9S	E3
Jan Smith Pk, CLSM	2967	26W-4N	E4
Janura Pk, BRWN	3089	8W-2S	A3
Jarvis Avenue Beach & Pk, CHCG	2867	1W-9N	D7
Jaycee Field Pk, ALGN	2694	34W-21N	B7
Jaycee Grove Pk, TYPK	3424	9W-20S	C4
Jaycee Memorial Pk, DRFD	2703	12W-21N	C6
Jaycee Pk, AURA	3137	36W-6S	E5
Jaycee Pk, BGBK	3268	24W-12S	E3
Jaycee Pk, CRY	2641	31W-24N	D7
Jaycee Pk, DSPN	2863	13W-10N	A5
Jaycee Pk, EGVV	2914	18W-8N	E1
Jaycee Pk, GYLK	2533	20W-32N	A4
Jaycee Pk, OSWG	3200	35W-11S	A7
Jaycee Pk, PKRG	2918	9W-7N	B3
Jaycee Pk, PTHT	2808	15W-14N	A3
Jaycee Pk, RMVL	3340	25W-16S	C3
Jaycee Pk, SMBG	2912	25W-9N	C1
Jay-Cee Pk, GNVA	3020	34W-1N	E3
Jaycees Bicentennial Pk, BFGV	2701	18W-21N	A6
Jaycees Pk, MHRY	2527	33W-31N	E6
Jefferson Jr High, WDRG	3205	21W-8S	D1
Jefferson Pk, AURA	3137	37W-7S	C6
Jefferson Pk, CHCG	3092	0W-1S	A1
Jefferson Pk, SMWD	2856	29W-10N	E6
Jehsen Pk, CHCG	2920	4W-5N	C7
Jennifer Ann Voots Pk, JLET	3497	26W-22S	E2
Jennings Pk, GNVW	2810	10W-15N	A3
Jensen Pk, ANTH	2357	23W-42N	D5
Jensen Pk, EGVV	2913	22W-8N	D2
Jensen Pk, HRPK	2911	27W-8N	D2
Jensen Pk South, EGVV	2913	22W-8N	D3
Jensen Toboggan Slides, CHCG	2919	8W-8N	A2
Jens Jensen Pk, HDPK	2705	7W-20N	B7
Jericho Lake Pk, MTGY	3198	39W-9S	D4
Jewett Pk, DRFD	2703	11W-21N	E7
Jirsa Pk, CLSM	2967	28W-3N	B5
Jirtle Pk, CHHT	3596	0W-26S	B2
Joanna Pk, ZION	2421	11W-41N	E2
Joe Sisolack Pk, WKGN	2480	10W-36N	A3
Johansen Farm Pk, BGBK	3204	25W-11S	C7
John A Bannes Pk, TYPK	3424	10W-19S	C3
John Gage Pk, GYLK	2533	19W-32N	D5
John H Leach Pk, JLET	3497	27W-23S	C3
John Jack Hill Memorial Pk, CPVL	2800	34W-16N	E2
John Janega Memorial Pk, LNHT	2417	20W-38N	E7
John Leach Memorial Pk, JLET	3417	27W-21S	C7
Johnsburg Community Club, JNBG	2471	31W-35N	D5
Johnson Pk, EGVV	2914	21W-8N	A2
Jones Island Pk, GYLK	2532	21W-33N	D3
Jones Meadow Pk, NARA	3077	38W-3S	A6
Jon Paul Pk, SNPK	3029	13W-1N	A2
Jonquil Pk, CHCG	2977	1W-3N	E5
Jonquil Terrace Pk, NLES	2864	9W-9N	C6
Jozwiak Pk, NLES	2918	8W-8N	E1
Juneway Terrace Beach & Pk, CHCG	2867	1W-9N	D6
Juniper Pk, HFET	2804	24W-16N	D1
Kamen East Pk, EVTN	2867	2W-10N	A5
Kamen West Pk, EVTN	2867	3W-10N	A5
Kandy Kane Pk, DLTN	3351	1E-16S	A4
Karl Krueger Pk, HYHL	3210	11W-10S	A5
Kasey Meadow Pk, HYHL	3210	10W-10S	C5
Katherine Legge Memorial Pk, HNDL	3146	14W-6S	C4
Kay Lovett Pk, GNVA	3019	37W-1N	B4
Kedron Pk, ZION	2421	11W-41N	E1
Kehoe Pk, SCRL	3020	36W-2N	A1
Keith Mione Community Pk, MDLN	2590	19W-29N	C5
Keller Pk, DRFD	2756	11W-20N	D1
Kelliher Pk, ALGN	2693	37W-20N	A7
Kelly Pk, CHCG	3091	3W-4S	A6
Kelly Pk, WHTN	3082	24W-1S	C1
Kelvyn Pk, CHCG	2976	5W-3N	A5
Kemmerling Pk, ROSL	2913	23W-6N	A6
Kemper Pk, CPVL	2748	32W-17N	D6
Ken Bird Pk, CLLK	2693	36W-22N	C3
Kendall Pk, NPVL	3141	27W-6S	D4
Kennedy Pk, CHCG	3277	3W-13S	B3
Kennedy Pk, HDPK	2758	7W-20N	A1
Kennedy Pk, ROSL	2912	25W-6N	B6
Kennicott Pk, CHCG	3093	1E-4S	A7
Kenroy Pk, ADSN	2969	21W-4N	D4
Kensington Pk, CHCG	3278	0E-13S	D4
Kensington Pk, MltT	3083	21W-2S	E3
Kensington Pk, PNFD	3338	30W-15S	C1
Ken-Wel Pk, CHCG	2976	5W-3N	B4
Kenwood Community Pk, CHCG	3153	1E-5S	A1
Keokuk Pk, PKFT	3594	4W-27S	E4
Kessell Pk, SMBG	2858	24W-12N	D1
Ketelaar Pk, ALSP	3276	4W-14S	C6
Keystone & Augusta Triangle, RVFT	3030	10W-1N	B2
Keystone Pk, CHCG	2976	5W-2N	B7
Keystone Pk, RVFT	3030	9W-0N	B4
Kich Pk, HRVY	3349	2W-18S	C7
Kiddieland Pk, MLPK	3030	10W-2N	A1
Kilbourn Pk, CHCG	2976	5W-4N	A3
Kilmer Pk, BFGV	2754	16W-18N	C4
Kimball Hill Pk, RGMW	2806	19W-14N	B5
King Pk, WKGN	2537	10W-33N	A3
Kingsbury Pk, RLKP	2532	23W-33N	A2
Kings Crossing, PNFD	3338	31W-15S	A1
Kingshill Pk, AURA	3202	30W-9S	B4
Kings Pk, GRNE	2535	14W-33N	C3
Kings Pk, NPVL	3141	26W-6S	E6
Kingsport East Pk, SMBG	2913	22W-9N	C1
Kingsport Lake Pk, SMBG	2859	23W-9N	A7
Kingsport Pk, SMBG	2859	23W-9N	A7
Kingsport Terrace Pk, SMBG	2859	23W-9N	A6
Kingsport Villages Pk, SEGN	2908	36W-8N	A2
Kingston Pk, FftT	3504	9W-24S	D5
Kingston Pk, HFET	2751	24W-16N	B7
Kingston Pk, LslT	3143	22W-6S	B4
Kingswood Wetland, SCRL	2965	33W-4N	B3
Kinzie Pkway Pk, CHCG	3031	6W-0N	D3
Kirk Pk, WKGN	2537	10W-33N	A2
Kit's Korner Pk, SRWD	3496	31W-23S	A4
Kiwanis Pk, ALSP	3275	6W-14S	E5
Kiwanis Pk, BKFD	3088	10W-3S	A5
Kiwanis Pk, CHCG	2920	4W-6N	D6
Kiwanis Pk, DSPN	2863	12W-10N	A6
Kiwanis Pk, EMHT	3028	15W-0N	B5
Kiwanis Pk, FftT	3504	10W-24S	C5
Kiwanis Pk, HRVY	3427	1W-18S	E1
Kiwanis Pk, LNSG	3429	2E-21S	D6
Kiwanis Pk, TYPK	3424	10W-21S	B5
Kiwanis Pk, WnfT	3080	29W-3S	D5
Kiwanis Pk, WTMT	3145	18W-5S	A2
Kjar Pk, BRLT	2910	30W-8N	B2
Klawitter Pk, RNPK	3594	6W-27S	A4
Klehm Pk, ANHT	2807	16W-14N	C4
Klein Pk, ENGN	3212	4W-11S	D6
K Mine Pk, GDLY	4030	32W-43S	C3
Knaack Pk, CLLK	2639	36W-24N	E7
Knights of Columbus Pk, BGBK	3269	22W-11S	B1
Knoch Knolls Pk, DPgT	3203	26W-11S	D7
Knoch Pk, NPVL	3141	27W-7S	C7
Knolls Pk, YkTp	3084	18W-1S	E1
Knollwood Pk, ShdT	2593	12W-28N	A5
Knollwood Pk, SMBG	2857	26W-11N	E3
Knotty Pines Pk, CRY	2642	30W-24N	A7
Knox Pk, LKZH	2699	22W-22N	B3
Knox Pk, MHRY	2528	32W-31N	B6
Kolar Pk, CCRO	3089	7W-3S	B5
Kollar Pk, SMWD	2911	28W-9N	B1
Kolmar Pk, CHCG	2976	5W-5N	A1
Kopp Pk, MPPT	2861	16W-11N	D4
Kosciuszko Pk, CHCG	2976	4W-3N	B5
Kostner Pk, MDLN	3348	5W-17S	B6
Kracklauer Pk, MDLN	2646	18W-27N	D1
Krasowski Pk, PSHL	3274	9W-12S	C1
Krempels Pk, BNVL	2972	15W-4N	A3

Chicago 7-County Points of Interest Index

FEATURE NAME Address City ZIP Code	MAP#	CGS	GRID
Kristina Pk, RDLK	2588	23W-30N	E1
Kroehler Pk, NPVL	3141	26W-6S	D4
Krotiak Pk, PKFT	3595	3W-26S	B3
Krug School Pk, MTGY	3200	36W-9S	A4
Kuechmann Pk, LKZH	2698	23W-23N	E2
Lacrosse Pk, ALSP	3276	6W-15S	A7
Lacy Pk, SMWD	2911	27W-9N	B1
Ladd Pk, CLLK	2640	35W-24N	A6
Ladendorf Pk, GNVW	2864	9W-12N	C1
Lafferty Pk, NBRN	2698	25W-22N	B3
La Follette Pk, CHCG	3031	6W-1N	E1
Lagoon Pk, OKFT	3425	6W-19S	D1
Lagoon Pk, WCDA	2587	27W-28N	C7
LaidLaw Pk, WNSP	3086	14W-4S	D7
Lake Arlington Pk, ANHT	2754	16W-16N	D7
Lake Charles Pk, VNHL	2647	16W-27N	C1
Lake Ellyn Pk, GNEN	3025	22W-0N	C4
Lake Foxcroft Pk, MltT	3083	23W-2S	A4
Lakefront Pk, GLNC	2758	5W-17N	E4
Lake Harriet Pk, WDRG	3143	21W-7S	D7
Lake Killarney Pk, AlqT	2641	31W-25N	C4
Lakeland Pk, MHRY	2527	34W-33N	C2
Lake Manor Pk, ADSN	2970	18W-3N	D6
Lake Meadows Pk, CHCG	3092	0E-3S	D3
Lake Pk, DSPN	2862	13W-9N	E7
Lake Shore Pk, CHCG	3034	0E-1N	D2
Lake Shore Pk, OKLN	3211	6W-11S	D6
Lake Terramere Pk, ANHT	2753	18W-18N	E2
Lakeview Community Pk, LYWD	3510	3E-23S	A3
Lakeview Pk, BMDL	2913	22W-5N	B7
Lakeview Pk, OSWG	3263	37W-13S	C5
Lakewood County Line Estates Pk, -BRRG	3208	15W-9S	B3
Lakewood Estates Pk, RMVL	3340	24W-15S	C1
Lakewood Grove Pk, RDLK	2588	23W-30N	E1
Lakewood Heights Pk, MDLN	2646	18W-27N	D1
Lakewood Pk, JLET	3416	30W-20S	A5
Lakewood Pk, LNHT	2418	20W-39N	B5
Lakewood Pk, MNSR	3510		E3
Lakewood Pk, RLKB	2474	23W-35N	E6
Lamb Pk, CHCG	3277	1W-12S	E2
Lamplighter Pk, SHLD	3351	0E-17S	A6
Lancaster Woods Pk, TYPK	3425	7W-20S	C4
Lancer Creek Pk, SMBG	2859	23W-9N	A7
Lane Beach & Pk, CHCG	2921	1W-7N	E4
Langendorf Pk, BRTN	2750	25W-20N	E1
Langum Pk, SCRL	3020	35W-2N	C1
Lan-Oak Pk, LNSG	3429	3E-21S	E5
Lappins Pk, AlqT	2640	33W-25N	E4
Laramie Pk, ALSP	3275	6W-14S	E5
Laramie Pk, SKOK	2865	6W-9N	D7
Larimer Pk, EVTN	2867	2W-10N	A4
Larkdale Pk, WCDA	2587	26W-27N	C7
Larry Fink Memorial Pk, HDPK	2757	8W-20N	E1
Larry Sabatino Jr Memorial Pk, SYHW	2800	35W-15N	B3
Lathrop Pk, PLNO	3259	47W-13S	D6
Laurel Hill Pk, ODPK	3423	13W-20S	A4
Laurel Pk, HDPK	2704	8W-22N	E5
Laurel Pk, PKFT	3595	2W-28S	C6
Laurel Wood Pk, BTVA	3020	35W-0S	B7
Laurence Roesner Pk, MDLN	3348	4W-17S	D5
Lauth Pk, SKOK	2866	5W-10N	B5
Lawler Pk, CHCG	3149	6W-7S	E5
Lawler Pk, SKOK	2811	6W-12N	E7
Lawn Manor Pk, OKLN	3276	5W-12S	B2
Lawson Field, WHTN	3024	24W-0N	D5
Leahy Pk, EVTN	2867	2W-12N	B1
Leavitt Avenue Pk, FSMR	3507	3W-22S	B2
Lebanon Pk, AURA	3200	35W-9S	A3
Lebanon Pk, ZION	2421	11W-39N	E4
Lebeck Pk, WTMT	3145	18W-5S	A3
Leclaire Hearst Pk, CHCG	3089	6W-4S	E7
Lee & Grant Pk, DRGV	3144	20W-4S	A1
Legion Pk, BDVW	3029	11W-1S	E7
Legion Pk, CHCG	2920	3W-6N	D5
Legion Pk, LktT	3419	22W-18S	D1
Leisberg Pk, BRLT	2911	28W-7N	A4
Leisure Center Hockey & Ice Skating, -ZION	2422	10W-40N	B3
Lemm Pk, BLWD	3029	11W-0N	C4
Leo Leathers Pk, MDLN	2590	20W-28N	A6
Leonardi Pk, HDPK	2704	10W-22N	A3
Leonard Pk, NBRN	2698	25W-23N	A1
Leone Pk & Beach, CHCG	2867	1W-9N	D7
Lerner Pk, CHCG	2920	3W-8N	E1
Leroy Guy Pk, LIHL	2692	38W-21N	E6
Leslie Pk, BMDL	2968	23W-5N	E2
Levi Newton Pk, BbyT	3076	39W-0S	D1
Levin Pk, CHCG	3031	6W-0N	D4
Levitt Pk, HFET	2858	25W-11N	C4
Lewandowski Pk, OKLN	3212	6W-10S	A4
Lewis Pk, LNHT	2418	20W-38N	B7
Lewis Pk, TYPK	3425	8W-20S	B3
Lexington Pk, HRVY	3349	1W-17S	E6
Lexington Woods Pk, GYLK	2475	21W-34N	D7
Liberty Memorial Pk, LYWD	3510	3E-25S	A7
Liberty Pk, BGBK	3268	24W-11S	C1
Liberty Pk, ELBN	3017	43W-0N	A4
Liberty Pk, HRPK	2911	26W-9N	E2
Liberty Pk, ODPK	3346	11W-18S	A7
Lilacia Pk, LMBD	3026	20W-0N	B4
Lilac Pk, BGBK	3267	26W-12S	E2
Lily Cache Greenway, BGBK	3267	26W-13S	E4
Lily Cache Sportsfields, BGBK	3268	26W-13S	A4
Lily Gardens Pk, CHCG	3152	0W-8S	A7
Limas Pig Pk, CHCG	3090	4W-2S	D2
Lincoln Meadows Pk, FKFT	3591	12W-25S	D1
Lincoln Mini Pk, AURA	3138	35W-7S	C7
Lincoln Pk, CHCG	2978	0E-2N	C7
Lincoln Pk, CHHT	3508	0W-25S	C7
Lincoln Pk, HDPK	2704	8W-21N	E6
Lincoln Pk, HFET	2804	25W-14N	A3
Lincoln Pk, HRVY	3427	2W-18S	D1
Lincoln Pk, MDLN	2590	19W-28N	D6
Lincoln Pk, NPVL	3141	26W-7S	D7
Lincoln Pk, SCRL	2964	35W-3N	A7
Lincoln Pk, WHTN	3082	24W-1S	D2
Lincoln Place Pk, HDPK	2705	8W-21N	A5
Lincolnshire East, CRTE	3597	1E-28S	A6
Lindbergh Pk, EGVV	2913	21W-8N	E1
Lindberg Pk, OKPK	3030	8W-1N	E1
Lindblom Pk, CHCG	3151	2W-6S	C4

FEATURE NAME Address City ZIP Code	MAP#	CGS	GRID
Linden Pk, CHCG	3032	4W-1N	B2
Linden Pk, GLNC	2758	6W-17N	E6
Linden Pk, GnvT	3019	38W-0S	A7
Lindenwood Pk, DRN	3207	17W-8S	B2
Lion Field, CHCG	3278	0W-14S	C6
Lions Club Pk & Pool, HMWD	3428	1W-21S	A7
Lions Den Pk, NLNX	3501	17W-25S	C7
Lions Field, MDLN	2646	18W-27N	E1
Lions Pk, BCHR	3864	1W-36S	B1
Lions Pk, BGBK	3269	23W-11S	A2
Lions Pk, BNVL	2971	16W-5N	E1
Lions Pk, CRY	2641	31W-24N	D6
Lions Pk, DndT	2801	33W-16N	B2
Lions Pk, EGVV	2914	18W-9N	D1
Lions Pk, FRGV	2696	30W-23N	A2
Lions Pk, GNVA	3020	34W-1N	E2
Lions Pk, HRPK	2967	28W-4N	B3
Lions Pk, HRVD	2406	49W-38N	C6
Lions Pk, LKZH	2698	23W-22N	E3
Lions Pk, LNSG	3429	3E-21S	E7
Lions Pk, MNKA	3672	33W-28S	B1
Lions Pk, MPPT	2862	15W-12N	B1
Lions Pk, PTHT	2807	15W-15N	E3
Lions Pk, ROSL	2913	22W-7N	B4
Lions Pk, SEGN	2908	34W-8N	D3
Lions Pk, VLPK	3027	17W-0N	B3
Lions Pk, WLSP	3209	12W-9S	C3
Lions Pk, WTMT	3145	17W-4S	B1
Lions Pk Pool, CNHL	3145	16W-5S	D2
Lionwood Pk, WDDL	2915	18W-5N	A7
Lippold Pk, CLLK	2639	37W-26N	C3
Lisle Community Pk, LSLE	3143	23W-5S	A3
Lisle Station Pk, LSLE	3143	22W-5S	B2
Little Calumet Pk, SHLD	3351	1E-18S	B7
Little Coyote Pk, SRWD	3496	30W-24S	C5
Little Creek Pk, SMWD	2856	30W-10N	B5
Lloyd Bate Pk, PTON	3861	8W-37S	B3
Lloyd Pk, WNKA	2759	4W-16N	B7
Lockwood Pk, SKOK	2865	6W-10N	D4
Locust Pk, HFET	2858	23W-12N	E1
Locust Pk, PLTN	2753	20W-16N	B7
Logan Pk, PKFT	3595	3W-25S	B1
Logan Square, CHCG	2976	3W-3N	D5
Lomar Pk, EVTN	2867	3W-9N	A6
Lombard Common Pk, LMBD	3026	19W-0N	D4
Lombard Lagoon Pk, LMBD	3026	19W-1N	C1
Longcommon Pk, RVSD	3088	9W-3S	C4
Longfellow Pk, BFGV	2754	18W-18N	A3
Longfellow Pk, OKPK	3031	7W-0S	A5
Long Lake Pk, RLKB	2474	24W-35N	B7
Long Meadow Pk, MDLN	2590	20W-29N	A5
Longview Pk, HDPK	2705	8W-21N	A6
Lords Pk, ELGN	2855	32W-11N	B3
Lorelie Acres Pk, ZION	2362	12W-42N	B6
Lorel Pk, SKOK	2865	6W-10N	D5
Louis Pk, ADSN	2971	18W-3N	A5
Lovelace Pk, EVTN	2812	4W-13N	B7
Loveland Pk, PSHL	3274	10W-12S	B2
Lowe Pk, CHCG	3152	0W-5S	A2
Loyola Pk, CHCG	2921	1W-8N	D1
Loy Pk, DRGV	3144	21W-5S	A2
Lufkin Pk, VLPK	3027	18W-0S	A6
Lyle Pk, CHCG	3214	0W-8S	A1
Lyle Thomas Pk, BtnT	2414	29W-38N	C7
Lyon Pk, SKOK	2866	5W-9N	A6
Mabel Avenue Pk, ELGN	2854	34W-12N	D1
MacArthur Pk, BRBK	3211	7W-9S	B3
MacArthur Pk, SHLD	3428	0E-19S	E3
Madden Pk, CHCG	3092	0E-3S	D5
Madin Pk, BKFD	3087	11W-3S	D5
Madison Meadow Pk, LMBD	3026	19W-0S	D6
Madison Pk, CHCG	3153	1E-5S	A1
Madison Pk, WHTN	3082	26W-1S	A2
Maggie Cosme Pk, CHCG	3213	2W-10S	C5
Maggie Rogers Pk, IVNS	2751	23W-16N	D7
Magnolia Pk, HDPK	2757	9W-20N	C1
Maicach Pk, SHLD	3429	1E-19S	A2
Maiman's Lake Shore Pk, WCDA	2588	25W-27N	B7
Main Beach Pk, CLLK	2639	36W-25N	D5
Majestic Oaks Pk, SCRL	2965	33W-4N	A4
Majestic Oaks Wetland, SCRL	2965	33W-4N	A4
Malibu Pk, RMVL	3340	25W-16S	B3
Mallard Landings Pk, ODPK	3423	13W-20S	B4
Mallard Pk, PLTN	2805	22W-15N	B3
Mallard Pk, SRGV	3197	42W-8S	D1
Manary Pk, ROSL	2913	22W-7N	C5
Manchester Pk, WHTN	3024	25W-0S	B6
Mandrake Pk, CHCG	3092	0E-4S	D6
Manhattan Community Pk, MHTN	3677	19W-31S	E5
Mann Pk, CHCG	3280	3E-15S	A7
Manor Pk, CCRO	3089	7W-3S	C4
Manor Pk, DSPN	2862	14W-11N	C3
Manor Pk, GNVW	2864	9W-12N	D1
Manor Pk, LKZH	2698	24W-23N	C1
Mansfield Pk, MNGV	2865	7W-11N	C2
Manville Oaks Pk, WnfT	3080	30W-0S	C1
Maple Pk, CHCG	2976	4W-2N	D6
Maple Pk, HFET	2858	24W-10N	E5
Maple Pk, OKPK	3030	8W-0S	C7
Maple Pk, PLTN	2753	19W-16N	C7
Maple Pk, WLMT	2813	2W-13N	A6
Maple Street Pk, WNKA	2812	4W-16N	B1
Maple Trails Pk, MPPT	2808	14W-13N	B6
Maple Trail Woods Pk, EMHT	3027	16W-0N	D5
Maplewood Pk, CHCG	2977	3W-2N	A7
Maplewood Pk, DRFD	2703	11W-21N	D7
Mar-Duke Pk, DRGV	3144	19W-7S	C7
Margaret A Connelly Pk, SMBG	2859	21W-10N	E5
Marie Grolich Pk, ELGN	2855	33W-10N	A6
Marimac Pk, VNHL	2647	17W-24N	C7
Marimal Pk, VNHL	2647	16W-24N	C6
Marion Pk, ROSL	2913	23W-7N	A4
Marjorie Davis Pk, EMHT	3027	16W-2N	D1
Marjorie Murray School Pk, GNVA	3020	36W-1N	A2
Mark Gorski Pk, ROSL	2913	22W-6N	B6
Markham Memorial Pk, MKHM	3426	4W-19S	D2
Marley Creek Pk, MKNA	3503	13W-22S	B2
Marley Creek Pk, ODPK	3422	14W-21S	E7
Marquette Pk, CHCG	3150	4W-7S	D7
Marquette Pk, PKFT	3595	3W-27S	A4
Marshall Pk, EGVV	2914	19W-8N	C1
Marshfield Pk, CHCG	3213	2W-10S	C4

FEATURE NAME Address City ZIP Code	MAP#	CGS	GRID
Marsh Pk, EGVV	2913	21W-9N	E1
Martin F Peccia Pk, SKOK	2865	6W-9N	D6
Martin Luther King Jr Pk, HMND	3430		E1
Martin Luther King Pk, MKHM	3427	1W-19S	E2
Martin Pk, HYHL	3210	9W-10S	C5
Marty Ptacek Pk, HYHL	3210	9W-11S	C6
Marvin A Weiss Pk, HTLY	2692	39W-22N	C4
Marvin Dunteman Pk, SBTN	2803	26W-14N	C3
Mary D Ayer Pk, HRVD	2406	50W-38N	A7
Maryknoll Pk, GNEN	3083	21W-1S	D1
Mary's Pk, ANTH	2359	20W-41N	A7
Mary Stephens Community Pk, PnfT	3416	29W-19S	D4
Mason Pk, CHCG	3032	5W-0N	B4
Mason Pk, EVTN	2867	3W-11N	A3
Mather Pk, CHCG	2920	3W-7N	E4
Mather Pk, EGVV	2913	21W-8N	E2
Mather Woods, PnfT	3416	31W-18S	A2
Maurice A Noll Pk, MDLN	2647	18W-27N	A1
Mawman Pk, LKBF	2593	11W-28N	E6
Max Freeman Memorial Pk, EDND	2801	33W-16N	A2
Mayfair Pk, CHCG	2920	5W-5N	A7
Mayfair Pk, JLET	3415	32W-20S	C5
Mayfair Pk, WSTR	3086	13W-2S	E3
Mayfair Station Pk, HRPK	2967	27W-5N	C1
Maynegaite Pk, OMFD	3507	3W-25S	A7
May Street Pk, AURA	3137	36W-6S	E6
May T Watts Pk, HDPK	2705	7W-20N	B7
May Watts Pk, NPVL	3203	28W-7S	A1
Maywood Pk, MYWD	3030	10W-0N	A4
Maywood Sportsman's Club, AddT	2972	15W-2N	B6
McCarty Pk, AURA	3200	35W-7S	B1
McCaslin Pk, WynT	2967	27W-2N	B7
McCleery School Pk, AURA	3137	37W-6S	D6
McCollum Pk, DRGV	3144	19W-7S	C7
McConnell Road Pk, WDSK	2582	39W-29N	C3
McCormick Pk, CLLK	2639	36W-25N	E5
McCulloch Pk, EVTN	2812	3W-13N	E7
McCullom Lake Beach Pk, MCLK	2470	33W-34N	D7
McCullough Pk, AURA	3138	35W-6S	B6
McDolo Pk, SRGV	3136	40W-5S	B2
McGee Pk, EGVV	2913	21W-8N	D2
McGuane Pk, CHCG	3092	1W-2S	A3
McHenry Pk, CHCG	3092	0W-4S	A7
McKenna Woods Pk, PnfT	3416	30W-20S	B5
McKinley Pk, CHCG	3091	2W-3S	B5
McKinley Pk, JLET	3498	24W-25S	E7
McLemore Pk, SMBG	2858	25W-11N	B4
McNally Pk, SKOK	2866	4W-10N	C5
McNeil Pk, MKHM	3426	4W-18S	E1
Meadowalk Pk, RMVL	3269	23W-14S	A6
Meadowbrook Pk, AURA	3202	30W-9S	A4
Meadow Brook Pk, RLKB	2474	23W-35N	E6
Meadow Glens Pk, NPVL	3204	25W-8S	C2
Meadowhill Pk, NHBK	2757	9W-17N	C6
Meadowlane Pk, DLTN	3351	1E-17S	B5
Meadows Center Pk, LslT	3143	22W-6S	C4
Meadows Pk, GNVA	3020	35W-0S	A6
Meadows Pk, MPPT	2807	16W-13N	D6
Meadows Pk, SMWD	2857	27W-10N	C6
Meadowview Pk, RDLK	2531	25W-33N	A3
Meadowview Pk, WCDA	2643	26W-26N	C2
Meadowview Woods Pk, GYLK	2532	21W-34N	D1
Meadow Wood Pk, WCHI	2966	29W-3N	E5
Mead Pk, EGVV	2913	22W-9N	D1
Medgar Evers Pk, HRVY	3349	1W-17S	E6
Medgar Evers Pk, MKHM	3427	2W-19S	D2
Medinah Pk, BmdT	2913	22W-7N	D5
Meidell Pk, CHHT	3507	2W-24S	D5
Meineke Recreation Center, SMBG	2859	23W-9N	B6
Melas Pk, MPPT	2807	16W-13N	C7
Melin Pk, HNDL	3145	16W-5S	E3
Memorial Pk, BLID	3277	3W-15S	A7
Memorial Pk, BtnT	2414	30W-39N	A4
Memorial Pk, BTVA	3078	35W-0S	A1
Memorial Pk, CHCG	3152	0W-8S	B7
Memorial Pk, CTCY	3352	4E-17S	C6
Memorial Pk, CTSD	3147	12W-6S	B3
Memorial Pk, DRGV	3144	20W-5S	A3
Memorial Pk, GLBT	2799	38W-15N	C3
Memorial Pk, GNEN	3025	22W-0N	C5
Memorial Pk, GYLK	2532	20W-32N	E4
Memorial Pk, HDPK	2704	8W-22N	E5
Memorial Pk, HYHL	3210	9W-10S	D6
Memorial Pk, LGPK	3087	12W-3S	C5
Memorial Pk, LNSH	2702	14W-23N	D2
Memorial Pk, MDLN	2590	19W-27N	C7
Memorial Pk, MDLN	3348	4W-17S	E4
Memorial Pk, MTSN	3594	4W-25S	D1
Memorial Pk, MYWD	3029	11W-0N	E4
Memorial Pk, OKLN	3275	7W-11S	C1
Memorial Pk, PKFT	3595	2W-27S	C4
Memorial Pk, POSN	3349	3W-16S	B4
Memorial Pk, TYPK	3425	8W-20S	B4
Memorial Pk, WCDA	2643	25W-27N	E1
Memorial Pk, WDRG	3205	21W-8S	E1
Memorial Pk, WHTN	3024	24W-0S	C6
Memorial School Pk, TYPK	3425	8W-21S	B6
Mending Wall Pk, WDRG	3205	22W-9S	D4
Merchants Pk, HMWD	3427	2W-22S	C7
Merrill Pk, CHCG	3215	2E-11S	C6
Merrimac Pk, CHCG	2975	7W-4N	A2
Mertz Memorial Pk, WTMT	3145	17W-6S	B5
Messiah Pk, PKRG	2863	11W-10N	E4
Metcalfe Pk, CHCG	3092	0W-4S	C6
Methodist Pk, ANHT	2807	16W-14N	C4
Metro-Majeski Athletic Fields, DSPN	2862	15W-9N	A7
Meyering Pk, CHCG	3152	0E-8S	D7
Meyers Pk, PSHT	3275	8W-15S	A7
Micek Pk, CHCG	3151	2W-5S	B2
Michael Arbizzani Pk, BTVA	3077	37W-1S	C1
Michael Camera Pk, GLHT	2968	23W-2N	E7
Michael D' Angelo Pk, DRPK	2752	22W-20N	C1
Michael Drive Pk, PSHL	3274	9W-12S	C1
Michael E Craig Pk, UYPK	3684	3W-30S	B2
Michael P Doherty Pk, SMBG	2913	23W-9N	B1
Michael Pk, PSHL	3274	9W-12S	D2
Michelle Bingham Memorial Pk, FKFT	3591	12W-26S	C1
Midlothian Reservoir, BmnT	3425	6W-19S	E2
Midway Plaisance Pk, CHCG	3153	1E-6S	B3
Milky Way Pk, HRVD	2405	51W-38N	E7
Millard Pk, HDPK	2705	7W-21N	B5
Millcreek Pk, BFGV	2754	17W-17N	A5

Chicago 7-County Points of Interest Index

Parks & Recreation

FEATURE NAME Address City ZIP Code	MAP#	CGS	GRID
Mill Creek Pk, GYLK	2533	19W-34N	B2
Millennium Pk, CHCG	3034	0E-0S	C4
Millennium Pk, GLHT	2968	23W-4N	E3
Millennium Pk, LNHT	2476	19W-37N	C2
Millennium Pk, TNLK	2354		B3
Miller Riverfront Pk, MHRY	2528	31W-31N	C6
Millette Memorial Pk, BGVW	3210	9W-9S	E3
Mill Meadows Pk, ADSN	2970	19W-3N	C5
Mill Pond Pk, GLHT	2968	24W-4N	D4
Mill Pond Pk South, GLHT	2968	24W-3N	D5
Mills Pk, OKPK	3030	8W-0N	E4
Mill Street Pk, NPVL	3141	27W-5S	C3
Millview Pk, BTVA	3077	36W-2S	E4
Milness Family Pk, DRGV	3144	19W-6S	D5
Minear Pk, LYVL	2592	15W-29N	A4
Minuteman Pk, CHCG	3149	7W-6S	C4
Mirador Pk, NARA	3076	39W-3S	E6
Mirielle Pk, BFGV	2701	16W-22N	D4
Mitchell Lakes Pk, CLSM	2968	25W-3N	A6
Mohawk Pk, AddT	2915	17W-6N	C5
Mohawk Pk, RVDL	3350	0W-15S	C2
Mokena Community Pk, MKNA	3503	13W-24S	A5
Montgomery Pk, MTGY	3199	36W-9S	D4
Monticello Pk, CHCG	2976	4W-2N	C7
Monument Pk, CHCG	2918	9W-8N	C2
Moody Pk, SCRL	3020	35W-2N	B1
Mooney Pk, HDPK	2704	9W-21N	B6
Moore Pk, CHCG	3031	6W-0S	E5
Moore Pk, GNVA	3020	34W-1N	D2
Moose Field, HRVD	2406	50W-38N	A6
Moraine Hills State Pk, NndT	2529	30W-31N	A7
Moraine Pk, HDPK	2704	8W-23N	E3
Moran Pk, CHCG	3151	1W-6S	E3
Morgan Field Pk, CHCG	3278	1W-13S	A4
Morgan Pk, PKRG	2864	10W-9N	B7
Morningside Pk, LIHL	2693	35W-22N	E4
Morrison Pk, LKMR	2529	29W-32N	C6
Morris Pk, HmrT	3420	19W-19S	E3
Morton Pk, CCRO	3089	6W-2S	E2
Morton Pk, EGVV	2914	18W-8N	E2
Mosgrove Pk, NndT	2585	32W-30N	B2
Mountain View Pk, DSPN	2862	14W-10N	C5
Mt Greenwood Pk, CHCG	3276	4W-13S	D3
Mt St. Mary Pk, SCRL	3020	35W-2N	B1
Mt Vernon Pk, CHCG	3278	1W-12S	A1
Mozart Pk, CHCG	2976	4W-2N	C6
Mraz Pk, BRWN	3088	8W-2S	E2
Muddy Waters Pk, WTMT	3145	18W-7S	A5
Muehe Pk, BGVW	3210	8W-10S	E4
Muir Pk, EGVV	2915	18W-8N	A3
Muir Pk, PTHT	2755	15W-16N	A7
Mulberry Pk, PLTN	2752	22W-16N	C6
Municipal Pk, SHLD	3428	0E-19S	E2
Munroe Pk, CHCG	3277	3W-12S	A1
Munster Community Pk, MNSR	3430		E7
Murphy Pk, PKFT	3595	2W-27S	C4
Murphy Pk, RMVL	3341	23W-15S	A2
Murphy School, WDRG	3205	21W-8S	E2
Murray Pk, CHCG	3151	2W-8S	C7
MWRD Pk, HRPK	2911	26W-8N	D2
Myrtle Grove Pk, CHCG	2918	8W-7N	D3
Narragansett Pk, BDPK	3211	8W-8S	A1
National Pk, MNGV	2864	8W-11N	D2
Nat King Cole Pk, CHCG	3214	0E-9S	D3
Nautilus Pk, HRPK	2967	26W-4N	D3
Nazos Pk, GLHT	2969	22W-2N	D7
Needles Pk, DLTN	3351	1E-16S	A3
Nelson Pk, CHCG	2976	3W-3N	E4
Neville Pk, NCHI	2536	11W-32N	E5
Newberry Pk, EGVV	2859	22W-9N	C7
Newcastle Pk, BRBK	3211	8W-9S	A2
New Holmes Pk, HRVY	3428	1W-19S	A2
Newman Pk, MHRY	2528	32W-33N	B3
Newport Pk, BRLT	2911	28W-7N	B4
Newsome Pk, ELGN	2854	33W-11N	E3
Newton Pk, GNEN	3025	22W-0S	C7
Nicholas-Dowden Pk, LYVL	2591	17W-28N	C6
Nichols Pk, CHCG	3153	1E-5S	A2
Nick Corwin Pk, WNKA	2758	6W-16N	D7
Nickol Knoll Pk, ANHT	2753	18W-18N	E3
Nico Pk, NLES	2864	8W-10N	E5
Nike Pk, ADSN	2970	20W-3N	A6
Nike Pk, NPVL	3141	27W-4S	D2
Nippersink Pk, RHMD	2353	34W-41N	D7
Nockels Pk, LIHL	2694	35W-22N	A4
Nordic Pk, BmdT	2969	21W-5N	E1
Norfolk Pk, DRGV	3144	20W-7S	C6
Norfolk Pk, WSTR	3029	12W-0S	B7
Normal Pk, CHCG	3152	0W-7S	A6
Normandie Pk, SgrT	3136	41W-6S	A4
Normandy Pk, CHCG	3149	8W-5S	A2
Norman Greenway, PNFD	3337	31W-15S	E3
Norman Schack Pk, SKOK	2919	6W-8N	D1
Norridge Pk, HDHT	2918	9W-5N	C7
Northampton Pk, OSWG	3263	37W-11S	D2
North Aurora Shoreline Pk, NARA	3078	36W-3S	A6
North Beach Pk, WKGN	2537	9W-34N	C1
North Central College Athletic Complex,- NPVL	3141	26W-6S	D6
North Clyde Pk, CCRO	3089	7W-1S	B2
Northcroft Pk, LKFT	2703	11W-24N	E1
Northeast Pk, ENGN	3213	3W-10S	A4
Northeast Pk, EVTN	2813	2W-13N	B7
Northeast Pk, PKRG	2864	9W-9N	B6
Northerly Island Pk, CHCG	3092	0E-1S	E1
Northfield Pk, HRVD	2406	50W-38N	A5
Northfield Pk, NHFD	2811	6W-15N	D3
Northgate Community Pk, DYR	3510		E5
North Island Pk, WMTN	3853	28W-38S	C6
North Mayfair Pk, CHCG	2920	5W-6N	A6
North Pk, ANTH	2357	24W-43N	D4
North Pk, FNPK	2973	12W-4N	B3
North Pk, IVNS	2751	23W-16N	E7
North Pk, PKRG	2863	11W-10N	E4
North Pk, VrnT	2648	13W-24N	D7
North Pk Villlage, CHCG	2920	4W-7N	C4
North Ridge Pk, PKRG	2864	10W-10N	A5
North River Street Pk, AURA	3138	35W-7S	B6
North Salk Pk, RGMW	2806	19W-13N	B6
Northshire Pk, DSPN	2862	14W-12N	B2
North Shore Avenue Beach & Pk, CHCG	2921	1W-8N	E2
Northside Pk, DRGV	3084	20W-3S	B5
Northside Pk, WHTN	3024	24W-0N	C5
North Side Pk, WLNG	2755	14W-18N	C3
North Terrace Pk, VLPK	3026	18W-1N	E3
North Twin Pk, HFET	2804	24W-12N	D7
Northview Pk, LMNT	3271	18W-14S	A5
North Warren Pk, CCRO	3031	7W-1S	C7
Northwest Community Pk, PNFD	3337	31W-15S	D1
Northwest Pk, PKRG	2863	11W-10N	D5
Northwood Pk, BFGV	2754	16W-20N	E1
Norwood Circle Pk, CHCG	2918	8W-7N	D4
Norwood Pk, CHCG	2919	8W-7N	A4
Norwood Playground Pk, CHCG	2918	8W-8N	E2
Notre Dame Pk, MTSN	3505	6W-25S	E6
Novotny Pk, WPHR	2363	10W-43N	B5
Nowell Pk, JLET	3587	23W-25S	A1
Oakdale Pk, CHCG	3213	1W-11S	E6
Oak Grove Pk, BRLT	2910	29W-8N	D3
Oak Grove Pk, WcnT	2643	26W-26N	D3
Oak Hill Pk, LSLE	3142	24W-5S	D3
Oak Hill Pk East, HLCT	3427	3W-20S	B4
Oak Hollow Pk, SMBG	2858	24W-10N	E6
Oakhurst Community Pk, AURA	3201	32W-8S	C2
Oak Knoll Pk, ADSN	2971	17W-3N	B5
Oak Lane Pk, NHBK	2757	8W-17N	E5
Oak Lawn Community Athletic Fields, - OKLN	3212	5W-10S	B5
Oakley Pk, CHCG	3151	2W-5S	B2
Oak Meadow Pk, OKLN	3211	6W-11S	E7
Oak Pk, HFET	2858	25W-12N	A1
Oak Pk, NLES	2864	9W-10N	C4
Oak Pk, PLTN	2753	19W-16N	C7
Oakridge Parkway, NPVL	3204	25W-9S	A5
Oak Ridge Pk, SMWD	2856	29W-9N	D7
Oaks Pk, NCHI	2593	11W-30N	D1
Oakton Pk, PKRG	2863	11W-10N	C5
Oakton Pk, SKOK	2866	5W-9N	A6
Oak Tree Pk, RLKB	2475	21W-35N	D5
Oak Valley Pk, SPGV	2413	31W-40N	D2
Oakwood Hills Pk, ODHL	2641	31W-26N	D2
Oakwood Pk, HRPK	2911	27W-6N	D6
Oakwood Pk, LNSG	3510	3E-22S	A1
Oakwood Pk, MTSN	3506	5W-25S	B6
Oakwood Pk, WNFD	3023	27W-0N	C4
Oakwood Pk, WTMT	3085	17W-3S	C6
O'Brien Pk, DRGV	3144	20W-7S	B7
Observatory Pk, ELGN	2855	33W-11N	A5
Odlum NE Pk, SMBG	2857	26W-10N	E5
Odlum NW Pk, SMBG	2857	27W-10N	D5
Odlum Pk, ROSL	2912	25W-7N	B4
Odlum SE Pk, SMBG	2857	26W-10N	E6
Odlum SW Pk, SMBG	2857	27W-10N	C6
O'Donnell Pk, AURA	3139	33W-5S	A3
Ogden Pk, CHCG	3151	1W-7S	E5
O'Hallaren Pk, CHCG	3213	2W-9S	C3
Ohio 8 Harding Pk, CHCG	3032	5W-0N	B3
Ohio Pk, BtvT	3077	36W-2S	E5
Oketo Pk, MNGV	2864	9W-11N	D3
Old Elm Pk, HDPK	2650	9W-24N	B7
Olde Mill Pk, LNSH	2702	13W-23N	D2
Olde Nantucket Pk, SMBG	2913	23W-9N	A1
Olde Salem Pk, HRPK	2912	25W-9N	A1
Old Farm Greenway, NPVL	3203	26W-9S	E4
Old Farm Pk, BFGV	2701	16W-21N	D6
Old Grove Pk, LMBD	3026	19W-0S	D7
Old Mill Grove Pk, LKZH	2699	22W-22N	B3
Old Mill Pk, ADSN	2970	19W-4N	D3
Old Mill Pk, GNVA	3020	35W-1N	C3
Old Plank Pk, NPVL	3142	26W-6S	A4
Old Renwick Trail Pk, JLET	3417	27W-19S	C2
Old Sawmill Pk, NPVL	3203	27W-10S	C6
Old Tavern Road Pk, LSLE	3142	24W-4S	C1
Old Timers Sports Complex, LNSG	3430	3E-19S	A2
Old Town Pk, BMDL	2969	23W-5N	A1
Oleson Farm Pk, NPVL	3142	25W-7S	B6
Olive Pk, CHCG	3034	0E-0N	D3
Ollman Pk, GLHT	2969	23W-3N	A5
Olmstead Pk, EGVV	2914	18W-8N	E1
Olson Pk, HDPK	2704	10W-22N	A4
Olson Pk, WDSK	2524	41W-31N	D6
Ol' Timers Pk, HTLY	2692	40W-21N	A6
Olympia Pk, CHCG	2918	9W-8N	C2
Olympic Pk, ANHT	2806	18W-14N	E4
Olympic Pk, SMBG	2860	21W-10N	A6
Onarga Pk, PKFT	3595	3W-27S	B5
Onbridge Pk, ALGN	2747	35W-20N	A1
Ontarioville Pk, HRPK	2911	27W-7N	C4
Ophir Pk, ZION	2422	10W-39N	B5
O'Plaine Community Pk, GRNE	2535	14W-34N	C2
O'Rahilly Volunteer Pk, CLSM	2967	27W-2N	D7
Orchard Brook Pk, DRGV	3084	20W-3S	C5
Orchard Hills Pk, WCDA	2588	24W-29N	B4
Orchard Pk, LkvT	2474	25W-37N	A2
Orchard Pk, WHTN	3082	26W-2S	A4
Orchard View Pk, MDLN	2646	20W-27N	B2
Oriole Pk, CHCG	2918	9W-6N	C5
Oriole Pk, MNGV	2864	9W-11N	C3
Orlandino Pk, BLWD	3029	13W-0N	A3
Orland Park Sportsplex, ODPK	3422	14W-19S	E1
Orland Woods Pk, ODPK	3422	14W-21S	D5
Orr Pk, CHCG	3032	5W-0N	B3
Osage Pk, PLTN	2753	19W-18N	B2
Osage Pk, WCDA	2643	26W-27N	E1
Osborne Pk, HYHL	3210	10W-10S	B6
Osborne Pk, PSHL	3274	10W-12S	B1
Osborn Pk, EGVV	2861	18W-10N	A6
Osgood Pk, JLET	3499	23W-24S	A5
Osteopathic Hospital Medical Pk, - OMFD	3506	4W-24S	D5
O'Toole Athletic Field, CHCG	3152	0W-5S	A1
Ottawa Pk, PNFD	3338	29W-18S	C7
Otter Creek Bend Wetland Pk, SchT	2907	37W-6N	C7
Overhalser Pk, LYVL	2591	18W-30N	A3
Overhill Pk, MNGV	2864	9W-11N	C2
Owen Pk, MPPT	2808	15W-12N	A7
Oxford Pk, BFGV	2701	17W-21N	A5
Oz Pk, CHCG	2978	0W-2N	A6
Paarlberg Pk, SHLD	3429	2E-20S	C4
Pacesetter Pk, SHLD	3351	1E-18S	B7
Pacific Pk, RMVL	3340	25W-16S	C4
Palatine Hills Pk, PLTN	2752	21W-17N	C6
Palisades Pk, BRRG	3208	15W-10S	B5
Palma Lane Pk, MNGV	2865	8W-11N	A2
Palmer Pk, CHCG	3278	0E-13S	D3
Palmer Pk, PSHT	3274	9W-14S	E6
Palmer Pk, UYPK	3684	3W-31S	C4
Palmer Square Pk, CHCG	2976	3W-2N	E6
Panfish Pk, GNEN	3083	22W-1S	C1
Papoose Pk, SHLD	3428	0E-20S	D3
Paradise Pk, LYVL	2591	17W-29N	B5
Parisek Pk, HTLY	2692	39W-21N	B6
Park 289, CHCG	3214	0E-9S	E3
Park 386, CHCG	3214	0W-9S	A3
Park 462, CHCG	2921	1W-7N	D4
Park 484, CHCG	3150	5W-7S	A6
Park 492, CHCG	3092	0E-4S	D7
Park 495, CHCG	3276	4W-13S	C3
Park 503, CHCG	3216	4E-10S	B4
Park 511, CHCG	3034	0W-0N	A3
Park 518, CHCG	2867	2W-9N	C6
Park 523, CHCG	3216	4E-10S	C3
Park 528, CHCG	3150	5W-7S	A5
Park & Rec Area, CHCG	3279	1E-12S	C2
Park Avenue Beach, HDPK	2705	8W-22N	A4
Park Av Pk, CNHL	3145	17W-5S	C2
Park Beach, RLKB	2475	23W-34N	A7
Park Center, GNVW	2810	9W-14N	C4
Parkchester Pk, BFGV	2701	16W-20N	E7
Park Forest Aqua Center, PKFT	3595	3W-26S	B3
Park Hill Pk, ODPK	3423	11W-18S	E1
Parkholme Pk, CCRO	3089	6W-1S	E1
Park in the Glen, WKGN	2536	12W-33N	C2
Parkside Pk, RDLK	2531	23W-32N	E5
Parkside Pk, ROSL	2913	23W-7N	B5
Parkview Meadows East, PNFD	3416	29W-19S	C4
Parkview Meadows West, PNFD	3416	29W-19S	D3
Parkview Pk, CHCG	2976	4W-4N	C3
Partridge Pk, PLTN	2805	22W-14N	B3
Paschen Pk, CHCG	2921	2W-8N	B1
Passarelli Pk, PSHT	3275	8W-14S	A6
Pasteur Pk, CHCG	3150	5W-6S	B3
Pasture Pk, WrnT	2477	16W-36N	D3
Pathways Pond, BGBK	3268	24W-11S	E1
Patriots Pk, ANHT	2807	16W-15N	D1
Patriots Pk, DRGV	3144	19W-6S	D4
Patriot's Pk, SDWH	3258	51W-14S	A7
Patterson Pk, HMTN	3212	5W-10S	C4
Paul E Briese Pk, JLET	3497	27W-22S	C2
Paulus Pk, LKZH	2698	24W-22N	C3
Payne Woods Pk, BTVA	3078	34W-3S	E5
Peach Creek Pk, LSLE	3142	25W-5S	B3
Peaks Pk, WRTH	3275	8W-12S	A2
Pebble Creek Pk, MHRY	2528	32W-31N	B7
Peck Farm Pk, GnvT	3019	38W-0N	B6
Pedersen Pk, ANTH	2357	24W-42N	D6
Peirce Pk, HNDL	3146	14W-4S	C1
Pembroke Pk, NPVL	3142	25W-6S	A5
Pembrook Woods, GRNE	2478	15W-36N	A4
Penny Pk, EVTN	2867	3W-11N	A3
People's Pk, CHCG	2977	3W-2N	A7
People's Pk, HMND	3352		D5
Peregrine Pk, PLTN	2805	22W-14N	B4
Perkins Woods, EVTN	2866	4W-12N	D1
Perminas Pk, ODPK	3346	10W-16S	B4
Persimmon Woods, SCRL	2964	34W-4N	C5
Pete Muscarella Field, OKFT	3347	7W-17S	D5
Peter J Exner Marsh, GfnT	2692	38W-22N	E4
Peterson Pk, CHCG	2920	4W-7N	C4
Peterson Pk, LKMR	2529	29W-32N	C4
Peterson Pk, MchT	2528	33W-34N	A2
Peterson Pk Beach, MHRY	2528	33W-34N	A1
Petkiewitz Pk, HYHL	3210	10W-10S	A4
Pheasant Hills Pk, DYR	3598		D3
Pheasant Ridge Pk, GLHT	2969	23W-3N	A6
Pheasant Trail Pk, FSMR	3507	2W-23S	D4
Pheasant Valley Pk, MHRY	2527	34W-33N	D3
Philbrick Pk, EVTN	2867	2W-12N	B1
Phillips Pk, AURA	3200	34W-9S	D3
Phillips Pk, OKLN	3211	6W-10S	D4
Phoenix Pk District, PHNX	3350	0W-18S	C7
Phoenix Pk District, SHLD	3428	0W-18S	C1
Picnic Grove Pk, FRGV	2696	29W-23N	B2
Pierce Pk, MTGY	3200	35W-9S	B4
Pierce Pk, RNPK	3594	5W-27S	B4
Pigeon Hill Pk, AURA	3138	34W-6S	C5
Pilcher Pk, JLET	3500	20W-23S	B3
Pine Creek Pk, NARA	3078	35W-3S	B7
Pine Knoll Pk, AraT	3199	38W-8S	B2
Pine Lake Pk, UYPK	3683	4W-29S	D2
Pine Pk, HFET	2804	23W-14N	D4
Pines Pk, BNVL	2971	16W-4N	D3
Pine Street Pk, DRFD	2756	11W-20N	D1
Pinewood Pk, DRN	3207	17W-9S	C3
Pioneer Pk, ANHT	2806	18W-13N	E6
Pioneer Pk, AURA	3136	39W-7S	D6
Pioneer Pk, BDVW	3029	11W-1S	C7
Pioneer Pk, EMHT	3027	16W-0N	E4
Pioneer Pk, NLES	2918	8W-8N	D1
Pioneer Pk, NPVL	3203	26W-7S	E1
Pioneer Pk, SHLD	3429	1E-19S	B2
Pioneer Pk, WCHI	3022	30W-0N	B6
Piotrowski Pk, CHCG	3090	5W-3S	B4
Plainfield Fishing Resort, PnfT	3417	28W-18S	B2
Playdale Pk, BDVW	3029	11W-0S	E6
Playfield Pk, CTWD	3275	6W-15S	D7
Play Haven Pk, BDVW	3029	11W-0S	C7
Pleasant Pkway Pk, CHCG	3213	2W-10S	C4
Pleasant Run Pk, WLNG	2755	15W-16N	B7
Plecas Pk, BLWD	3028	13W-0N	E3
Plimmer Pk, BGBK	3268	23W-12S	E3
Plonien Pk, WKGN	2536	11W-33N	E2
Plum Grove Reservoir Pk, RGMW	2805	22W-13N	C5
Plum Grove Village Pk, SMBG	2859	22W-10N	D5
Plunket Pk, EMHT	3027	17W-1N	C2
Pochet Pk, SMBG	2858	24W-10N	D6
Poet's Pk, CmpT	2962	39W-4N	D5
Pohatan Pk, LNWD	2919	6W-8N	E1
Point Pk, NLES	2864	8W-10N	E5
Pokey Oats Pk, ALSP	3276	6W-14S	A6
Polk Branch Pk, SMBG	2859	22W-10N	C4
Polley Field, LKVL	2417	21W-39N	C4
Poplar Pk, BGBK	3268	24W-11S	C2
Poplar Pk, BNVL	2915	17W-6N	C7
Poplar Pk, HFET	2804	25W-12N	A7
Portage Pk, CHCG	2975	6W-5N	C1

Chicago 7-County Points of Interest Index

FEATURE NAME Address City ZIP Code	MAP#	CGS	GRID
Port Clinton Pk, HDPK	2704	8W-23N	D3
Potomac Pk, EGVV	2913	21W-9N	D1
Pottawatomie Pk, SCRL	2964	35W-3N	B6
Pottawatomie Pk, TYPK	3424	11W-21S	A6
Pottawattomie Pk, CHCG	2867	2W-9N	B7
Potts Pk, LNSG	3430	3E-20S	A4
Powder River Pk, ELGN	2854	36W-12N	A3
Powell Pk, EGVV	2859	21W-9N	E7
Powell Pk, WKGN	2537	10W-34N	A1
Pow Wow Pk, SHLD	3428	0E-19S	E2
Prairie Knoll, PNFD	3337	31W-16S	E4
Prairie Lakes Pk, DSPN	2862	14W-10N	C4
Prairie-Lathem Pk, BTVA	3020	34W-0S	C7
Prairie Path Pk, BTVA	3078	34W-2S	D4
Prairie Path Pk, WHTN	3082	25W-1S	B1
Prairie Pk, ANHT	2861	17W-12N	B2
Prairie Pk, BFGV	2701	17W-21N	B5
Prairie Pk, NPVL	3142	25W-7S	A6
Prairie Pk, SMBG	2858	26W-11N	A4
Prairie Towne Pk, GYLK	2533	19W-32N	C4
Prairie Trail Pk, WLBK	3145	16W-6S	D4
Prairie Trail Pk, WNFD	3023	27W-1N	D3
Prairie Trails Pk, BGBK	3339	28W-15S	A2
Prairie View Pk, ALSP	3276	5W-14S	B5
Prairieview Pk, BRLT	2967	28W-5N	A1
Prairie View Pk, HYHL	3210	10W-9S	B4
Prairie View Pk, MNGV	2864	8W-11N	E3
Prairieview Pk, OSWG	3263	37W-13S	B5
Prairie View Pk, VNHL	2701	16W-23N	C1
Prairie Walk Pk, RDLK	2532	23W-31N	A6
Pratt Boulevard Beach & Pk, CHCG	2921	1W-8N	E1
Preservation Pk, JLET	3498	24W-23S	D4
Presidential Pk, ALGN	2695	32W-21N	A6
Presidents Pk, WHTN	3083	23W-1S	A1
President's Pk, GNEN	3025	21W-0S	D6
Preston Pk, BbyT	3018	39W-0S	E7
Prime Pk, GNCY	2353		A3
Primrose-Bode Pk, SMBG	2858	26W-11N	A4
Prince Pk, DRGV	3144	20W-5S	B2
Princeton Pk, CHCG	3214	0W-10S	B5
Princeton Pk, HnrT	2802	30W-12N	B7
Princeton Wetlands Pk, HnrT	2802	30W-12N	B7
Priory Pk, RVFT	3030	9W-1N	D2
Progress Pk, ALSP	3276	4W-14S	C5
Proksa Pk, BRWN	3088	8W-2S	E4
Prospect Meadow Pk, ANHT	2807	16W-14N	E4
Prospect Pk, CHCG	3277	2W-12S	C2
Prospect Pk, CNHL	3145	17W-5S	C1
Providence Pk, GRNE	2535	14W-33N	C3
Pulaski Pk, CHCG	3033	1W-1N	D1
Pulaski Pk, CTCY	3352	4E-18S	B6
Quail Run, PNFD	3338	30W-16S	B4
Quail Run Pk, LKZH	2698	23W-21N	E5
Queensbury Greens Pk, NPVL	3140	29W-5S	D4
Quinlan Pk, EVTN	2866	3W-12N	D1
Radio Station Pk, MKHM	3427	3W-18S	B1
Rahlfs Woods Pk, SMWD	2911	28W-9N	A1
Rainbow Pk, LYWD	3509	2E-24S	E6
Rainbow Pk & Beach, CHCG	3216	3E-8S	A1
Rainey Pk, CHCG	3212	5W-8S	B2
Raintree Pk, WDSK	2581	41W-30N	D1
Ralph Tredup Pk East, SEGN	2908	35W-7N	B5
Rambling Hills Pk, HNWD	2700	20W-24N	B1
Ranch View Pk, NPVL	3204	24W-9S	D3
Randall Oaks Pk, WDND	2746	37W-17N	E7
Randall Pk, AURA	3137	37W-5S	C4
Randall Pk, DRGV	3144	19W-5S	D3
Randall Square Pk, GNVA	3019	37W-0N	C6
Ranger Pk, HRPK	2911	26W-9N	D1
Rathje Pk, WHTN	3024	25W-0S	B7
Rauhoff Pk, TYPK	3425	8W-21S	A6
Raupp Memorial Pk, BFGV	2701	17W-21N	B7
Raven Pk, ANHT	2754	18W-17N	A6
Ravenswood Manor Pk, CHCG	2920	3W-5N	E7
Ravine Pk, LKBF	2594	10W-28N	A6
Ravinia Pk, GRNE	2476	18W-35N	E7
Ray Bradbury Pk, WKGN	2537	10W-34N	A1
Raymond Benson Pk, ITSC	2970	19W-5N	D1
Raymond Pk, EVTN	2867	2W-11N	B3
Raymond Pk, FmtT	2589	23W-30N	A2
RC Hill Pk, RMVL	3340	23W-15S	E1
Recreation Center Pk, DRGV	3143	21W-4S	E1
Recreation Pk, ANHT	2807	17W-14N	B5
Recreation Pk, CnhT	3584	31W-28S	A6
Redfield Commons, NPVL	3140	29W-5S	D2
Red Gate Pk, SCRL	2964	36W-5N	A2
Red Hawk Pk, CLSM	3023	26W-2N	D1
Redmond Pk, BNVL	2972	15W-4N	A3
Redwood Pk, MPPT	2861	16W-11N	C4
Reed Pk, WCHI	3022	30W-1N	C3
Rehm Pk, OKPK	3031	8W-0S	A6
Remington Lakes Sport Complex, BGBK	3268	24W-13S	D5
Renwick Community Pk, PNFD	3416	30W-18S	B2
Renwick Pk, MRGO	2634	49W-27N	C1
Reservation & Rec Area, PLTN	2806	19W-15N	B2
Revere Pk, CHCG	2977	3W-4N	A2
Rice Pk, BRBK	3211	7W-8S	D1
Richard Clark Pk, CHCG	2977	3W-4N	A3
Richard F Kelly Pk, ODHL	3423	11W-19S	E3
Richard H Klatt Memorial Field, PLNO	3259	47W-13S	E6
Richard M Gory Pk, TYPK	3424	10W-19S	B2
Richard Taylor Soccer Field, LIHL	2693	35W-22N	E4
Ridge Acres Pk, WNSP	3147	13W-4S	A1
Ridgeland Common Pk, OKPK	3031	8W-0N	A4
Ridgeland Pk, BRBK	3211	7W-8S	B1
Ridge Pk, AURA	3201	32W-9S	C4
Ridge Pk, CHCG	3213	2W-11S	C6
Ridge Pk, EGVV	2914	18W-9N	E1
Ridge Pk, SMWD	2857	27W-10N	C5
Ridge Pk, WHTN	3082	25W-2S	B5
Ridge Road Sports Center, NasT	3415	33W-19S	A3
Ridge Steamwood Pk, SMWD	2857	27W-10N	C6
Ridgeville Pk, EVTN	2867	2W-10N	B5
Ridgeway Pk, MNSR	3430		E6
Ridgewood Pk, JltT	3499	22W-23S	C4
Ridgewood Pk, WNSP	3146	14W-6S	D3
Riemer Reservoir Pk, PLTN	2752	21W-16N	C7
Riis Pk, CHCG	2975	7W-3N	B5
Rima Pk, BmdT	2913	22W-6N	C6
Ringneck Pk, GLHT	2968	24W-3N	D6
Ringwood Commons Pk, RGWD	2470	34W-36N	D4
Rivals Pk, JLET	3498	24W-22S	E1

FEATURE NAME Address City ZIP Code	MAP#	CGS	GRID
Riverbend Pk, BGBK	3267	27W-12S	C2
River Crest Estates Pk, WldT	3267	27W-11S	D1
Riverdale Pk, RVDL	3350	0W-15S	C2
Riverfront Pk, ALGN	2694	33W-20N	E7
Riverfront Pk, DLTN	3351	1E-18S	A7
Riverfront Pk, NndT	2528	31W-31N	D6
Riverfront Pk, SHLD	3429	2E-19S	C2
River Hills Pk, BGBK	3339	28W-14S	A1
River Oaks Pk, SRWD	3496	30W-24S	B6
River Point Estates, PNFD	3416	31W-19S	A3
River Ridge Pk, SEGN	2908	34W-7N	C5
Rivershire Pk, LNSH	2702	14W-22N	C4
Riverside Parkway, JLET	3416	29W-21S	E6
Riverside Pk, GNVW	2810	8W-13N	E7
Riverside Pk, HMND	3430		E5
Riverside Pk, SHLD	3350	0W-17S	C6
Riverside Pk, WNFD	3023	27W-0S	B6
Riverview, PNFD	3338	29W-17S	C6
Riverview Pk, SHLD	3351	0E-18S	A7
Riverwalk Pk, JLET	3416	29W-20S	D5
Riverwalk Pk, NPVL	3141	27W-6S	C5
Robbins Pk, HNDL	3146	15W-5S	A2
Robert Crown Pk, EVTN	2866	3W-10N	E4
Robert I Stuart Sports Complex, MTGY	3198	39W-8S	D3
Roberts Pk, SMBG	2912	23W-9N	E1
Robert Square Pk, CHCG	2919	6W-6N	D6
Robert T Jackson Clearwater Pk, MPPT	2861	17W-11N	C2
Robert W Depke Center Pk, WrnT	2534	17W-34N	A1
Robichaux Pk, CHCG	3214	0W-10S	B5
Robin Hood Pk, LGPK	3087	12W-2S	C4
Robin Pk, PltT	2805	22W-16N	B1
Robinson Pk, RVSD	3088	9W-3S	D5
Rob Roy Pk, AURA	3137	37W-6S	C5
Rock Run Pk, ROSL	2912	24W-6N	D6
Rockwell Pk, CHCG	3033	3W-0S	A5
Roesner Pk, MKHM	3427	3W-19S	A1
Rogen Pk, GNVW	2864	10W-12N	B1
Rogers Avenue Beach & Pk, CHCG	2867	1W-9N	D6
Rogers School Pk, CHCG	2867	3W-9N	A7
Rohrssen Pk, HFET	2856	31W-12N	A2
Rolling Hills North Pk, BFGV	2701	17W-22N	B4
Rolling Hills Pk, BFGV	2701	17W-22N	B5
Rolling Oaks Pk North, SRGV	3197	42W-8S	D1
Rolling Oaks Pk South, SRGV	3197	42W-8S	D2
Ronald Centanni Pk, TYPK	3424	10W-20S	B5
Ronan Pk, CHCG	2920	3W-6N	E6
Ron Beese Pk, BRTN	2751	25W-17N	B4
Ronnetree Pk, ALSP	3276	5W-15S	B7
Roosevelt Pk, EGVV	2914	19W-8N	C3
Roosevelt Pk, GNVW	2810	9W-13N	C6
Roosevelt Pk, SHLD	3428	0E-18S	D1
Roosevelt Pk, WKGN	2537	10W-33N	A3
Roosevelt Road Pk, CHCG	3034	0W-0S	B6
Rosedale Pk, CHCG	2919	7W-7N	A4
Rose Hill Farms Pk, NPVL	3267	28W-11S	A1
Rosemblum Pk, CHCG	3215	2E-8S	C1
Rose Pk, BNVL	2972	15W-4N	A4
Rosewood Pk & Beach, HDPK	2705	7W-21N	C7
Ross Field, NCHI	2594	10W-31N	A1
Rotary Pk, BGBK	3269	22W-11S	D1
Rotary Pk, HMND	3430		E1
Rotary Pk, LNSG	3510	4E-22S	B2
Rotary Pk, RMVL	3339	27W-17S	C6
Rotary Pk, SCRL	2964	34W-2N	C7
Rotary Pk, VLPK	3027	17W-0N	C3
Roth Pk, PTHT	2808	15W-14N	A4
Route 60 Pk, LKFT	2649	12W-25N	A4
Rowan Pk, CHCG	3280	4E-13S	B3
Royce Homestead Pk, BGBK	3204	25W-11S	B7
RS Corcoran Pk, NLNX	3501	18W-24S	B6
Rudd Farm Pk, WKGN	2535	14W-32N	D6
Russell Pk, CHCG	3216	3E-9S	A2
Russ Pker Pk, SMBG	2859	21W-10N	D4
Rutgers Site, WDRG	3206	20W-10S	A5
Rutherford Pk, CHCG	2974	8W-2N	E6
Ruth Family Pk, HTLY	2692	39W-21N	C5
Ruth K Powers Pk, DRGV	3144	20W-7S	B6
Ruth MacIntyre Pk, SMBG	2858	24W-9N	D7
Ruzicka Memorial Pk, BRLT	2911	28W-7N	B4
Ryder Pk, LIHL	2694	35W-22N	A4
Ryders Woods, WDSK	2581	41W-30N	D1
Sacajawea Pk, IHPK	3146	14W-7S	D5
Sacramento Pk, CHCG	2976	3W-4N	E3
Saddle Brook Pk, OKBK	3085	18W-3S	A5
Saddle Oaks Pk, AlqT	2642	29W-24N	C6
Saddlewood Pk, WCDA	2643	26W-26N	C2
Safari Springs Family Aquatic Center, - HRPK	2911	27W-7N	D5
Safety Town Pk, GLHT	2969	23W-3N	B6
Saganashkee Slough, PlsT	3272	15W-12S	B3
St. Boniface Pk, TYPK	3425	8W-19S	A2
St. Claire Pk, SMBG	2859	22W-10N	D4
St. Francis Pk, BGBK	3268	24W-11S	D1
St. Francis Pk, ELGN	2854	34W-12N	E2
St. Joseph Pk, JLET	3498	24W-22S	D1
Salceda Pk, NHBK	2756	13W-18N	A2
Salk Pk, SMBG	2858	24W-10N	D5
Salt Creek Pk, EGVV	2914	19W-8N	D2
Salt Creek Pk, EMHT	3027	17W-1N	C2
Sam Johns Pk, CLLK	2693	36W-23N	D1
Sanctuary Pk, LKBF	2593	12W-29N	B4
Sandburg Pk, HRVY	3349	1W-17S	E4
Sandburg Pk, MDLN	2590	19W-27N	C7
Sanders Pk, EGVV	2861	18W-9N	A7
Sandholm Woods Pk, GNVA	3020	34W-1N	D4
Sands Main Street Pk, AlqT	2696	29W-23N	B1
Sangamon Pk, CHHT	3508	1W-24S	A5
Sarah Adams Pk, LKZH	2699	22W-22N	B4
Sarah's Grove Pk, SMBG	2859	23W-10N	A5
Saratoga Pk, BTVA	3077	36W-1S	E1
Sauganash Pk, CHCG	2920	5W-7N	A4
Sauk School Pk, RNPK	3594	5W-26S	C3
Savannah Pk, SMBG	2912	26W-8N	A2
Sayre Pk, CHCG	2974	8W-2N	E6
Schiller Pk, ITSC	2914	19W-6N	D6
Schiller Pk, SRPK	2973	12W-5N	B2
Schneider School Pk, NARA	3078	35W-3S	B6
Schoolhouse Manor Pk, NLNX	3502	16W-25S	A7
School Pk, RMVL	3268	23W-14S	E7
School Trail, GYLK	2532	21W-33N	D3
Schoppe Pk, BRLT	2911	28W-8N	A2
Schrader Pk, BRLT	2967	28W-5N	A2

FEATURE NAME Address City ZIP Code	MAP#	CGS	GRID
Schraeder Pk, BGBK	3269	22W-12S	D2
Schreiber Pk, CHCG	2921	2W-8N	C2
Schroeder Pk, BDVW	3087	11W-1S	E1
Schultz Pk, LNSG	3430	4E-21S	B7
Schussler Pk, ODPK	3346	11W-17S	A5
Schuster Pk, BNVL	2972	15W-5N	B1
Scott Brown Pk, MDLN	2646	20W-27N	A1
Scottdale Pk, WHTN	3083	23W-3S	A5
Scotts Cove Pk, WHTN	3083	23W-3S	A5
Scottsdale Pk, CHCG	3212	5W-9S	A3
Scout Pk, MDLN	3348	5W-17S	B5
Scoville Pk, OKPK	3030	8W-0N	E3
Seager Pk, NPVL	3142	25W-5S	A3
Searle Pk, SKOK	2865	6W-10N	E5
Sears Pk, ALSP	3276	4W-14S	D6
Seba Pk, SEGN	2908	34W-8N	D2
Sedgewick Pk, LGNG	3147	12W-5S	C1
Seeser Pk, JLET	3498	24W-24S	D5
Seifer Pk, CHHT	3596	0W-25S	C1
Seminole Pk, DSPN	2917	12W-8N	B2
Seminole Pk, HFET	2804	25W-14N	A3
Seneca Pk, CHCG	3034	0E-1N	C2
Seneca Pk, SKOK	2866	5W-10N	B4
Senior Citizens Memorial Pk, CHCG	2977	2W-2N	A6
Senka Pk, CHCG	3150	4W-6S	D3
Senn Pk, CHCG	2921	1W-7N	C4
Sentinel Pk, WTMT	3145	18W-4S	A1
Sequoya Pk, SKOK	2865	6W-11N	D2
Serenity Pk, WKGN	2535	14W-32N	D5
Sergeant Mean's Pk, OMFD	3507	3W-25S	B6
Sesquintennial Pk, DSPN	2863	12W-11N	A2
Sesqui Pk, WNVL	3080	29W-3S	E6
Settlers Pk, PNFD	3416	30W-18S	B1
Seven Bridges Pk, WDRG	3143	23W-7S	A6
Seven Gables Pk, WHTN	3082	25W-2S	C3
Seward Pk, CHCG	3034	0W-1N	A2
Shabbona Pk, CHCG	2974	8W-4N	E3
Shabbona Pk, PKFT	3595	3W-28S	A5
Shabonee Pk, SKOK	2866	5W-12N	B1
Shady Oaks Pk, SMWD	2857	28W-10N	A6
Shamrock Farm Pk, MHRY	2527	35W-32N	A5
Shana Elman Pk, DRFD	2757	10W-20N	B2
Shanahan Grove Pk, BTVA	3078	34W-1S	D2
Shannon Pk, BbyT	3076	39W-1S	E1
Sharon Pk, ZION	2422	10W-39N	A5
Sharp Pk, MLPK	3029	12W-1N	B2
Shawmut Pk, LGNG	3087	12W-4S	C6
Shaw Pk, GRNE	2479	13W-35N	A6
Sheed Pk, CHCG	3090	4W-2S	C2
Sheffield Pk, HFET	2858	25W-12N	A2
Sheffield Plains Pk, SRGV	3135	42W-7S	D7
Sheffield Ridge Pk, SMBG	2858	26W-11N	A3
Sheil Pk, CHCG	2977	1W-4N	D3
Shelton Pk, GLNC	2758	5W-17N	E6
Shenandoah Pk, EGVV	2913	21W-8N	E3
Shepard Pk, DRFD	2756	11W-20N	D1
Sheridan Pk, CHCG	3033	1W-0S	E6
Sheridan Pk, HDPK	2650	9W-24N	C7
Sherman Pk, CHCG	3151	1W-5S	D2
Shermer Pk, MNGV	2864	9W-11N	D2
Sherwin Avenue Beach & Pk, CHCG	2867	1W-9N	D7
Sherwood Pk, CHCG	3152	0W-6S	B3
Sherwood Pk, HDPK	2704	9W-21N	B5
Shiloh Pk, ZION	2422	10W-40N	B3
Shining Waters Pk, CLSM	2967	27W-3N	D6
Shorewood Pk, SRWD	3496	30W-24S	C7
Sidney Pk, GLHT	3025	22W-2N	C1
Siems Pk, GLHT	2968	24W-4N	D4
Silver Cross Baseball Field, JLET	3499	23W-23S	A4
Silver Oaks Pk, RLKB	2475	22W-36N	B4
Silver Springs State Pk, FoxT	3331	47W-16S	D4
Simkus Recreation Center, CLSM	2967	27W-4N	D4
Simmons Pk, CHCG	2976	4W-2N	D7
Simmons School Pk, AURA	3138	34W-6S	D4
Sioux Pk, DSPN	2808	14W-12N	C7
Sipley School Pk, WDRG	3205	22W-9S	D3
Sippel Memorial Field, BCHR	3864	0W-36S	C2
Site 21 Pk, BFGV	2754	17W-20N	A1
Skinner Pk, CHCG	3033	1W-0S	D5
Skokie Pk Tennis Center, SKOK	2865	6W-10N	E5
Skokie Sculpture Pk, SKOK	2866	4W-11N	D3
Skokie Sports Pk, SKOK	2866	4W-9N	C6
Slade Avenue Pk, ELGN	2854	34W-12N	E1
Sleepy Hollow Pk, EMHT	3027	16W-0N	C5
Sleepy Hollow Pk, GNVW	2810	8W-13N	E5
Sleepy Hollow Pk, HDPK	2704	10W-23N	B2
Slepicka Homestead Pk, CLSM	2967	28W-3N	B5
Slinglerland Pk, SMBG	2913	23W-9N	A1
Sloan Pk, HFET	2858	24W-11N	D3
Smart Oaks Pk, DRN	3207	18W-9S	A4
Smirz Pk, BRWN	3089	7W-3S	B5
Smith Memorial Pk, CHHT	3507	2W-25S	E7
Smith Pk, CHCG	3214	0W-11S	B7
Smith Pk, LYNS	3088	10W-4S	B7
Smith Pk, WKGN	2537	10W-33N	A3
Snapper Field Pk, ALGN	2747	33W-20N	E1
Soehrman Pk, CTSD	3147	13W-7S	A7
Solfisburg Pk, AURA	3138	34W-7S	D6
Somerset Pk, BbyT	3076	39W-0S	E1
Somonauk Pk, PKFT	3594	4W-27S	E5
South Broadway Pk, AURA	3199	36W-8S	E2
South End Pk, WDND	2801	34W-15N	A4
Southfield Knoll Pk, BCHR	3864	0W-37S	C3
South Grove Pk, DRN	3206	20W-9S	B4
Southland Pk, LMBD	3026	19W-0S	C7
South Mill Creek Community Pk, BbyT	3076	39W-1S	E2
South Pk, DRFD	2756	11W-20N	C1
South Pk, GRNE	2478	15W-34N	B7
South Pk, IVNS	2804	23W-14N	E3
South Pk, LKFT	2650	10W-25N	A4
South Pk, PKRG	2918	10W-8N	A3
South Pointe Pk, NPVL	3266	29W-13S	D5
South Ridge Lake Pk, HFET	2804	24W-15N	B3
Southridge Pk, GRNE	2534	16W-34N	D2
South Twin Pk, HFET	2804	24W-12N	D7
Southwest Pk, PKRG	2917	10W-7N	E3
Spalding Pk, MltT	3025	22W-1N	C2
Sparrow Pk, PLTN	2805	22W-15N	B2
Sparrow Ridge Pk, LKZH	2699	22W-21N	A5
Spirit Creek Pk, ODPK	3344	14W-18S	E6
Spirit Trail Pk, OMFD	3506	4W-25S	E7
Spoerl Pk, AlqT	2640	33W-24N	D7

Parks & Recreation

Chicago 7-County Points of Interest Index

Parks & Recreation

FEATURE NAME Address City ZIP Code	MAP#	CGS	GRID
Sports Center, SMBG	2912	24W-8N	C3
Sprenger Pk, ANTH	2359	20W-41N	A7
Springbrook Parkway-Cedar Glen, AURA	3202	31W-9S	A5
Spring Creek Pk, FRGV	2695	30W-22N	E3
Spring Creek Reservoir, BMDL	2969	22W-5N	D1
Spring Dale Pk, SPGV	2413	31W-41N	E1
Springdale Pk, WNSP	3146	13W-5S	E3
Springfield Pk, NPVL	3203	26W-9S	D4
Springhill Pk, NPVL	3142	25W-6S	A4
Springhill Pk, ROSL	2913	22W-7N	C5
Spring Lake Pk, AURA	3202	30W-7S	A1
Spring Lake Pk, LNSH	2702	14W-23N	C3
Spring Pk, DRGV	3144	19W-7S	D6
Spring Rock Pk, WNSP	3146	14W-4S	D1
Spring Street Pond, SEGN	2908	36W-8N	A2
Spring Valley Pk, CLSM	2967	28W-4N	B3
Spruce Pk, CHCG	3153	1E-5S	A2
Squaw Creek Property, NndT	2584	34W-27N	C7
Squire Pk, DRPK	2698	23W-21N	E6
Stacy Pk, GNEN	3025	22W-1N	B3
Stahlak Pk, WRTH	3275	8W-13S	B3
Stanford Meadows Pk, NPVL	3204	25W-9S	C4
Stanger Pk, FRGV	2696	30W-22N	A4
Stanley A Esping Pk, GNVA	3020	34W-0N	D4
Stanton Schiller Pk, CHCG	3034	0W-1N	A1
Stars & Stripes Pk, CHCG	3148	8W-5S	E2
State Game & Wildlife Pk, WMTN	3853	28W-37S	B3
Stateway Pk, CHCG	3092	0W-3S	B5
Station Pk, FTPK	3030	9W-0S	D6
Steck Pk, AURA	3200	36W-7S	A1
Steeves Pk, CNHL	3145	16W-5S	D3
Sterling Manor Pk, GNVA	3019	37W-0N	C4
Sterling North Pk, DRGV	3144	20W-5S	A3
Sterne's Pk, CLLK	2640	34W-27N	C1
Steven Sherwood Memorial Pk, LKVL	2475	23W-37N	A1
Stevenson Pk, BLWD	3029	12W-0N	B4
Stevenson Pk, BRBK	3211	7W-9S	C3
Stevenson Pk, OKPK	3031	7W-0N	B4
Stevens Pk, BRRG	3208	15W-9S	B4
Stevens Pk, WHTN	3024	25W-0S	B6
Stillers Pk, FRGV	2696	30W-23N	A3
Stonebridge Pk, CLSM	2967	27W-3N	C5
Stonebridge Pk, NLNX	3588	19W-26S	E3
Stone Fence Pk, VNHL	2647	16W-24N	C6
Stonegate Pk, NHBK	2809	11W-16N	C1
Stonegate Pk, OSWG	3263	37W-12S	C3
Stone Hollow Pk, HLCT	3427	3W-21S	A6
Stone Monroe Pk, LGPK	3087	12W-3S	B5
Stoneybrook Pk, ALGN	2694	34W-21N	C6
Stoney Island Pk, CHCG	3215	2E-10S	C4
Stough Pk, HNDL	3145	16W-5S	E2
Stout Pk, CHCG	3152	1E-5S	E2
Stratford Pk, BMDL	2968	24W-4N	C3
Streamside Pk, HRVY	3350	1W-17S	A4
Strohacker Pk, CHCG	3150	5W-5S	B3
Strubler Pk, SRGV	3135	42W-7S	D6
Struckman Basin, BRLT	2910	29W-6N	E7
Sugar Grove Sports Complex, SRGV	3134	44W-5S	D3
Sullivan and Aquatic Center, VNHL	2647	17W-25N	C4
Sullivan Pk, OKLN	3212	5W-11S	B7
Sullivan Woods Pk, VNHL	2701	16W-23N	C1
Summerfield Lake Pk, NPVL	3202	29W-9S	C4
Summerhill Pk, WDRG	3143	22W-6S	B5
Summer Lakes Pk, WNVL	3080	30W-3S	B5
Summit Pk, SMMT	3148	9W-6S	C4
Sundance Pk, CLSM	2967	26W-4N	E4
Sundance Pk, HFET	2804	24W-15N	C2
Sunken Gardens Pk, CHCG	2921	3W-5N	A7
Sunnydale Pk, SMWD	2911	27W-9N	B1
Sunnydale Pk, WDRG	3144	21W-7S	A7
Sunnyside Memorial Pk, JNBG	2472	30W-35N	A5
Sunnyside Pk, BMDL	2969	22W-4N	C3
Sunny Side Pk, ODPK	3346	10W-16S	A2
Sunnyside Pk, WDSK	2581	41W-30N	C1
Sunnyside Pk, WHTN	3082	23W-1S	E1
Sunrise Pk, BNVL	2972	15W-4N	A2
Sunrise Pk, BRLT	2910	29W-6N	D7
Sunrise Pk, GNVA	3020	33W-1N	E3
Sunrise Pk, GYLK	2475	20W-35N	E7
Sunrise Pk, LKBF	2594	10W-28N	B6
Sunrise Pk, MPPT	2862	15W-11N	B2
Sunset Knoll Pk, LMBD	3026	20W-0S	A6
Sunset Meadows Pk, ANHT	2806	18W-13N	D6
Sunset Pk, ADSN	2970	21W-4N	A4
Sunset Pk, ANHT	2753	18W-18N	E2
Sunset Pk, BGBK	3267	26W-13S	E5
Sunset Pk, BNVL	2971	16W-5N	E1
Sunset Pk, BRLT	2910	29W-6N	D7
Sunset Pk, GNEN	3025	22W-0S	B7
Sunset Pk, GNVA	3020	36W-0N	A4
Sunset Pk, LIHL	2692	39W-22N	D3
Sunset Pk, MPPT	2861	16W-11N	E2
Sunset Pk, RLKB	2474	23W-35N	D6
Sunset Pk, RMVL	3340	24W-16S	D4
Sunset Pk, SMBG	2913	22W-8N	B1
Sunset Pkway Pk, JLET	3496	29W-21S	E1
Sunset Ridge Pk, CCHL	3426	6W-21S	A6
Sunset Woods Pk, HDPK	2704	8W-22N	D4
Sunshine Pk, BRWN	3088	8W-2S	E3
Sunshine Pk, DLTN	3350	0E-16S	E2
Superior Pk, CHCG	3033	2W-0N	B3
Surkey Wood Pk, SMWD	2856	29W-11N	D4
Surrey Hill Pk, SCRL	2964	34W-3N	D6
Surrey Ridge Pk, LSLE	3142	24W-6S	C6
Susan John Pk, OswT	3199	37W-10S	D7
Sweet Briar Pk, WSTR	3086	14W-2S	D3
Swenson Pk, GNVW	2810	9W-13N	C6
Swiss Valley, CRTE	3596	0E-28S	E5
Sycamore Pk, HFET	2858	23W-12N	E1
Sycamore Pk, PLTN	2753	19W-17N	B6
Sycamore Trails Pk, MPPT	2808	14W-14N	C5
Taft Pk, HRVY	3428	0W-19S	B2
Tallgrass Lakes Pk, NPVL	3266	30W-11S	B2
Tall Grass Pk, BRLT	2911	28W-7N	B5
Tallmadge Pk, EVTN	2867	2W-12N	B1
Tall Oaks Pk, HFET	2856	31W-12N	A2
Tall Tree Pk, GNVW	2810	8W-14N	E5
Taly Pk, SchT	2908	34W-7N	D6
Tamarack Trails Pk, MPPT	2808	13W-14N	E5
Tamara Heights Pk, ADSN	2970	19W-4N	D2
Tanglewood Hills Pk, BTVA	3077	37W-2S	D3
Tanglewood Pk, FKFT	3503	13W-25S	C6
Tanner Pk, NARA	3076	39W-3S	E7
Tartan Pk, BFGV	2701	16W-20N	D7
Tate Woods Pk, LSLE	3142	23W-4S	E1
Taylor-Lauridsen Pk, CHCG	3092	0W-4S	A6
Taylor Pk, CHCG	3152	0W-5S	C1
Taylor Pk, OKPK	3031	8W-1N	A2
Techny Prairie Pk, NHBK	2757	9W-16N	C7
Tedrahn Pk, CLSM	2967	28W-3N	B5
Ted Spella Pk, ALGN	2746	36W-20N	C1
Tekakwitha Woods, SchT	2908	35W-6N	C7
Terada Pk, SMBG	2858	24W-10N	D6
Terminal Pk, SKOK	2866	5W-11N	A2
Terney Pk, BbyT	3018	39W-0N	D5
Terrace Pk, BNVL	2915	17W-7N	C3
Terrace View Pk, LMBD	3026	20W-1N	B2
Terrace View Pk, OKTR	3085	17W-1S	C2
Terrace View Pk, SHLD	3429	1E-19S	B3
Terry Steczo Pk, OKFT	3347	7W-17S	C5
The Bowl, LMNT	3270	19W-13S	D5
The Forest, BGBK	3268	26W-11S	A1
The Grove, GNVW	2809	11W-14N	D5
The Pk at Auburn Lakes, PNFD	3266	31W-13S	A6
The Pk Of River Oaks, CTCY	3429	2E-19S	C2
The Ponds, PNFD	3338	29W-15S	D2
The Reserve, PNFD	3339	28W-16S	A5
Thiele Pk, HLSD	3028	13W-0S	E5
Thomas T Hamilton Pk, PLTN	2752	21W-17N	E5
Thornbark Pk, HFET	2804	24W-15N	C2
Thorncreek Pk, SHLD	3429	1E-20S	A4
Thorndale Pk, SHLD	3428	0E-20S	E4
Thornwood Pk, SEGN	2907	37W-7N	C6
Thornwood Pk, SHLD	3428	0E-20S	D4
Thornwood Pk, WLMT	2812	5W-14N	A4
Three Meadows Pk, LslT	3204	25W-8S	C1
Three Oaks Pk, CRY	2642	30W-24N	A7
Throop Pk, CHCG	3151	1W-5S	D1
Tilton Pk, CHCG	3032	5W-0N	B4
Timber Creek Pk, WldT	3203	27W-11S	B7
Timbercrest Pk, SMBG	2859	23W-10N	A6
Timberlake Pk, DGvT	3207	16W-10S	D4
Timberline Pk, LMNT	3270	20W-14S	B6
Timber Pk, LSLE	3142	24W-6S	E5
Timber Ridge Pk, SKOK	2866	4W-11N	C3
Timber Trails Pk, SCRL	2963	36W-3N	E6
Timber Woods Pk, GRNE	2477	18W-34N	A7
Timothy Pk, ZION	2362	12W-42N	C6
Tinley Gardens Pk, TYPK	3423	11W-22S	E7
Titsworth Mini Pk, AURA	3200	35W-8S	A1
Tolentine Pk, OMFD	3506	4W-24S	D6
Tomahawk Pk, DSPN	2862	14W-11N	B3
Tomahawk Pk, SHLD	3350	0W-18S	C6
Tom Ping Memorial Pk, CHCG	3092	0W-1S	B1
Tompkins Pk, BMDL	2969	23W-4N	A2
Toohey Pk, WHTN	3082	25W-2S	A4
Tooterville Pk, GYLK	2533	20W-32N	A5
Torrey Pines Pk, VNHL	2647	17W-26N	B2
Touhy Herbert Pk, CHCG	3033	2W-0S	B5
Touhy Pk, CHCG	2867	2W-9N	C7
Tower Pk, CCHL	3426	4W-20S	D4
Tower Pk, HRPK	2967	27W-5N	C1
Tower Pk, WDND	2800	34W-16N	E2
Tower Road Pk, WNKA	2759	5W-16N	B7
Town & Country Pk, DLTN	3350	0W-17S	B5
Town Center Pk, HMGN	3343	17W-17S	B5
Towne Pk, ALGN	2694	33W-20N	D7
Town Pointe Pk, TYPK	3424	10W-21S	B6
Township Pk Hampshire, HPSR	2796	46W-16N	A2
Trails End Pk, BRLT	2911	27W-7N	C5
Trail Tree Pk, DRFD	2757	9W-20N	B1
Travelers Pk, BlmT	3507	2W-25S	C6
Trebes Pk, CHCG	2977	1W-2N	D6
Tree Nursery Pk, SMWD	2856	28W-10N	E6
Treetop Pk, ODPK	3345	12W-18S	C7
Triangle Pk, CHCG	3032	5W-0N	B3
Triangle Pk, DLTN	3351	1E-17S	B6
Triangle Pk, HRVY	3428	1W-19S	A3
Triangle Pk, LKFT	2650	10W-26N	A2
Triangle Pk, WDRG	3143	22W-6S	C6
Triangle Pk, WHTN	3024	23W-0S	E6
Trinity Blumberg Pk, DRFD	2703	11W-22N	E5
Trinity Terrace Pk, ELGN	2853	36W-12N	E2
Trout Pk, ELGN	2801	33W-13N	B7
Trumbull Pk, CHCG	3279	2E-11S	D1
Tuley Pk, CHCG	3214	0E-10S	D4
Turner Pk, HMND	3352		E5
Turner Pk, ROSL	2913	23W-7N	A4
Twiggs Pk, EVTN	2866	3W-12N	E1
Twin Creek Pk, JLET	3497	27W-22S	D2
Twin Creeks Pk, BFGV	2701	17W-21N	C5
Twin Lakes Pk, HMGN	3344	15W-18S	B7
Twin Lakes Pk, VLPK	3027	18W-2N	A1
Twin Lakes Pk, WrnT	2534	18W-32N	A4
Twin Lakes Pk, WTMT	3145	18W-6S	A4
Twin Lakes West Side Pk, TNLK	2354		A1
Twin Lakes Woods, WTMT	3145	18W-6S	A3
Ty Warner Pk, WTMT	3085	17W-4S	B7
Udall Pk, EGVV	2861	17W-9N	B6
Ulrich Pk, BGVW	3210	9W-8S	D1
Union Creek Community Pk, FftT	3504	10W-23S	C4
Union Pk, CHCG	3033	1W-0N	D4
Union Square Pk, HNVL	2532	22W-33N	C2
Unity Pk, CHCG	2976	4W-3N	D5
University Heights Pk, NPVL	3204	24W-9S	C3
University Pk, GRNE	2478	13W-34N	E7
Upton Pk, WKGN	2480	10W-35N	B7
Valley Forge Pk, CHCG	3148	8W-6S	E4
Valley Forge Pk, GYLK	2533	19W-34N	C1
Valley Pk, BmdT	2912	23W-6N	E5
Valley Pk, HFET	2804	23W-15N	D2
Van Buren Pk, BTVA	3078	35W-1S	C2
Van Laten Pk, LNSG	3429	2E-21S	C7
Van Oostenbrugge Pk, SHLD	3350	0E-18S	E7
Van Voorst Pk, EMHT	3028	15W-0N	B5
Vasa Pk, SchT	2908	35W-7N	C6
Vattmann Pk, WLMT	2812	4W-13N	C5
Veeck Pk, HNDL	3146	14W-4S	C1
Verne Gowe Memorial Pk, GRNE	2535	14W-34N	C1
Vernon Hills Athletic Complex, VNHL	2647	16W-24N	D6
Veteran Pk, SMBG	2857	26W-10N	E5
Veterans Acres Pk, CLLK	2640	35W-26N	B2
Veterans Memorial Pk, AURA	3138	35W-6S	B6
Veterans Memorial Pk, GLNC	2758	6W-17N	D4
Veterans Memorial Pk, GNCY	2353		A2
Veterans Memorial Pk, LNSG	3430	4E-19S	B3
Veterans Memorial Pk, MHRY	2528	32W-33N	C3
Veterans Memorial Pk, PKFT	3595	3W-26S	B3
Veterans Memorial Pk, SHLD	3428	0E-18S	E1
Veterans Memorial Pk, STGR	3596	0W-28S	B6
Veterans Memorial Pk, WTMT	3145	17W-5S	B3
Veterans Memorial Pk, ZION	2422	10W-40N	B3
Veteran's Memorial Pk, SKNY	3089	7W-4S	B6
Veterans Pk, BFGV	2701	16W-21N	E6
Veterans Pk, CHCG	3215	3E-11S	E6
Veterans Pk, CTCY	3430	3E-19S	B3
Veterans Pk, GLHT	2969	23W-3N	A6
Veterans Pk, NPVL	3141	26W-7S	E7
Veterans Pk, NRIV	3088	9W-2S	C3
Veterans Pk, ODPK	3346	9W-18S	D7
Veterans Pk, SKOK	2865	6W-10N	D5
Veterans Pk, SMWD	2857	28W-10N	B5
Veterans Pk, TYPK	3424	9W-19S	D1
Veteran's Pk, BNVL	2971	16W-5N	E1
Veteran's Pk, CLSM	2968	25W-3N	A5
VFW Little League Pk, HMWD	3428	1W-21S	A6
Victoria Pk, HFET	2858	25W-11N	B3
Victory Pk, ANHT	2860	18W-12N	D1
Victory Pk, WKGN	2480	10W-35N	A6
Viking Pk, GRNE	2478	14W-35N	C7
Viking Pk, RDLK	2531	24W-33N	D2
Village Green, PNFD	3338	30W-18S	C7
Village Green Pk, CTCY	3429	2E-18S	C1
Village Green Pk, GNEN	3083	23W-1S	A1
Village Green Pk, NHBK	2757	9W-17N	B5
Village Green Pk, WNKA	2812	4W-15N	B2
Village in the Pk, SMBG	2858	23W-12N	E1
Village Pk, ANTH	2417	21W-41N	E2
Village Pk, RMVL	3340	25W-15S	C3
Village Pk, WPHR	2363	10W-42N	B6
Village Square Pk, ODPK	3345	11W-18S	E7
Villa Pk, VLPK	3026	19W-1N	D1
Vine Pk, SMWD	2857	28W-9N	B7
Vineyard Pk, GRNE	2476	18W-35N	E5
Vintage Harvest, PNFD	3416	30W-19S	B3
Violet Patch Pk, OswT	3263	37W-11S	C1
Virginia Terrace Pk, ANHT	2806	18W-15N	D2
Vista Pond Pk, LMBD	3026	19W-1N	D3
Vittum Pk, CHCG	3149	6W-5S	E1
Vogelei Pk, HFET	2858	24W-12N	D2
Vogt Woods Community Pk, TYPK	3425	8W-20S	B4
Volbrecht Pk, SHLD	3429	1E-20S	B4
Volkening Pk, SMBG	2858	24W-10N	C5
Volunteer Pk, BGBK	3268	25W-12S	C2
Volunteer Pk, SRGV	3135	42W-7S	C6
Volunteer Pk, TYPK	3424	10W-21S	C5
Volz Pk, ANHT	2806	18W-14N	E4
Wacker Pk, CHHT	3508	0W-25S	B6
Wadsworth Community Pk, WDWH	2420	14W-38N	D6
Wagner Pk, CHCG	3151	1W-5S	E1
Waiola Pk, LGNG	3147	12W-5S	B1
Waitcus Pk, GLBT	2799	39W-16N	A1
Wales S Stamper Pk, OMFD	3507	3W-24S	A5
Walker Pk, CNHL	3145	17W-5S	D3
Walker Pk, CTWD	3347	6W-16S	E3
Walker Pk, LynT	3208	13W-8S	E1
Walkers Grove Pk, PNFD	3337	31W-15S	E3
Walkers Grove School, PNFD	3338	31W-15S	A3
Wallace Pk, CHCG	3214	0W-10S	A5
Wallingford Pk, DRGV	3084	19W-4S	D7
Wally Degner Pk, PltT	2805	22W-15N	B1
Walnut Glen Pk, GNEN	3025	21W-0N	D5
Walnut Grove Pond Pk, HFET	2856	30W-12N	B1
Walnut Pk, BTVA	3078	35W-1S	A2
Walnut Ridge Pk, NPVL	3204	25W-10S	C5
Walnut Ridge Woods, NPVL	3204	24W-10S	C5
Walnut Woods, PTHT	2808	15W-15N	B1
Walnut Woods Pk, SRGV	3136	40W-4S	B2
Walona Athletic Pk, NLNX	3501	17W-25S	D7
Walter Carroll Pk, DRGV	3144	20W-6S	B4
Walton Island Pk, ELGN	2854	34W-11N	E3
Warren Pk, CCRO	3089	7W-1S	C1
Warren Pk, CHCG	2921	2W-8N	A2
Warren Shadron Pk, WrnT	2533	18W-33N	E3
Warwick Pk, LKZH	2699	21W-21N	C5
Washburn Pk, BbyT	3018	39W-0N	E6
Washington Circle Pk, HNDL	3146	15W-5S	A3
Washington Commons Pk, RVFT	3030	9W-0N	B4
Washington Pk, AURA	3137	38W-7S	A7
Washington Pk, BTVA	3078	35W-1S	B1
Washington Pk, CHCG	3152	0E-6S	D3
Washington Pk, DRGV	3144	19W-5S	C2
Washington Pk, EMHT	3028	15W-0N	A4
Washington Pk, HMWD	3428	1W-21S	A5
Washington Pk, ITSC	2914	19W-6N	C7
Washington Pk, WKGN	2537	10W-34N	A2
Washington Square Pk, CHCG	3034	0W-1N	B2
Washington Square Pk, RVFT	3030	9W-0N	B4
Washington Triangle Pk, RVFT	3030	9W-0N	C4
Washtenaw Pk, CHCG	2977	3W-3N	A4
Wastenaw Pk, CHCG	3091	3W-2S	A2
Waterford Pk, WLBK	3146	15W-7S	A6
Water Pk, BNVL	2971	16W-5N	D2
Water Spray Pk, LMBD	3026	20W-0N	B4
Water's Ridge, PNFD	3339	28W-16S	A4
Waterstone Pk, WCDA	2588	25W-28N	B5
Water Tower Pk, BCHR	3864	1W-36S	B2
Watts Pk, GLNC	2758	6W-17N	D6
Waubonsie Lake Pk, AURA	3201	32W-8S	C2
Waveland Pk, LKFT	2650	10W-25N	A5
Waverly Creekside Pk, OKFT	3348	5W-18S	A7
Waverly Pk, MDLN	3348	4W-17S	D4
Wayside Pk, NLNX	3501	18W-24S	B6
Weaver Pk, BbyT	3018	39W-0N	E5
Weber Pk, SKOK	2865	6W-11N	E2
Wedgewood Commons Pk, ODPK	3346	10W-16S	C4
Wedgewood Estates Pk, ODPK	3346	10W-17S	B4
Wedgewood Pk, MPPT	2808	15W-14N	A4
Weeks Pk, MltT	3024	25W-1N	B3
We Go Pk, MPPT	2807	16W-12N	D7
Weidner Pk, BFGV	2754	17W-18N	B2
Weigand Riverfront Pk, NPVL	3203	26W-10S	E5
Weiss Field, WKGN	2536	11W-34N	D1
Wellers Creek Pk, MPPT	2861	16W-12N	E2
Welles Pk, CHCG	2921	2W-5N	A7
Wentland Athletic Field, MLPK	3029	11W-1N	E3

Chicago 7-County Points of Interest Index

FEATURE NAME Address City ZIP Code	MAP#	CGS	GRID
Wentworth Gardens Pk, CHCG	3092	0W-3S	B5
Wentworth Pk, CHCG	3149	7W-6S	B3
Wentworth Pk, CRY	2642	30W-25N	B5
Wescott Pk, NHBK	2757	10W-16N	A6
Wesglen Pk, RMVL	3339	26W-17S	E6
Weslake Pk, RMVL	3339	27W-17S	C5
Weslake Pk West, RMVL	3339	27W-17S	B5
Wesley G Usher Memorial Pk, ITSC	2914	19W-6N	C6
Wesmere Pk, JLET	3416	30W-21S	B7
West Beach Pk, MHRY	2527	33W-33N	D2
West Branch Parkway, NPVL	3204	25W-8S	A3
West Branch Riverway, NPVL	3204	26W-9S	A4
Westbury Lake Pk, HFET	2804	24W-15N	C2
West Chatham Pk, CHCG	3214	0W-9S	B2
Westchester Pk, BFGV	2701	16W-21N	C6
Westdale Pk, LydT	2972	14W-3N	D4
West Elm Street Pk, WNKA	2811	5W-15N	E1
Western Avenue Pk, GNVA	3020	36W-0N	A6
Western Pk, CHCG	3033	2W-1N	B2
Westfield Pk, DSPN	2862	14W-10N	C4
West Fork Pk, GNVW	2810	8W-15N	D2
Westgate Pk, GRNE	2477	16W-36N	E5
Westgate Valley Pk, PSHT	3347	8W-15S	A1
Westglen Commons, NPVL	3203	27W-8S	D2
Westglen Pk, NPVL	3203	27W-8S	C3
West Harbor Pk, HRPK	2967	27W-4N	B3
Westhaven Pk, WHTN	3082	25W-1S	A1
West Hobson Ponds, NPVL	3203	27W-8S	B1
West Lake Pk, BMDL	2969	22W-4N	B2
Westlands Pk, VLPK	3027	17W-0S	C7
West Lawn Pk, CHCG	3150	5W-7S	B5
West Main Community Pk, BbyT	3076	40W-1S	C2
Westminster Pk, WDRG	3206	20W-10S	B6
Westmore Woods Pk, LMBD	3026	18W-0N	E4
West Morton Pk, CCRO	3089	6W-2S	D2
West Pk, DSPN	2862	14W-11N	D3
West Pk, JLET	3498	25W-24S	C7
West Pk, LKFT	2649	10W-27N	E2
West Pk, NHBK	2756	11W-16N	D6
West Pullman Pk, CHCG	3278	0W-14S	B6
Westridge Pk, HDPK	2757	9W-20N	C1
West River Pk, CHCG	2920	3W-6N	E6
West Shore Pk, SRWD	3496	30W-24S	C6
West Side Pk, LKPT	3419	22W-19S	C2
West Side Pk, SchT	2963	37W-3N	C6
West Trail Pk, GYLK	2532	21W-33N	D4
Westview Pk, ADSN	2971	18W-2N	A7
Westview Pk, WDDL	2970	18W-5N	E1
Westwood Pk, ADSN	2970	20W-4N	B4
Westwood Pk, AraT	3199	37W-8S	C2
Westwood Pk, DRN	3206	18W-8S	E1
Wetlands Pk, LKBF	2593	11W-28N	E7
Wexford Pk, WHTN	3081	26W-1S	E2
Whealan Pool, CHCG	2919	7W-8N	B2
Wheatland Pk, AURA	3201	31W-9S	D3
Wheeler Pk, GNVA	3020	35W-1N	C2
Wheeler Pk, MHRY	2528	32W-31N	B6
Whihala Beach County Pk, HMND	3280		E3
Whipple O'Parrot Pk, RLKP	2532	22W-33N	B2
Whippoorwill Pk, PLTN	2805	22W-14N	B3
Whispering Oaks Pk, MHRY	2527	33W-33N	E3
Whispering Willow Pk, HGKN	3147	12W-7S	C6
White Ash, PNFD	3265	31W-14S	E7
White Oak Pk, WDDL	2971	17W-5N	B1
White Oaks Pk, CRY	2642	30W-24N	B6
White Pk, CHCG	3277	1W-14S	E5
White Tail Pk, SRWD	3496	31W-25S	A7
Whitewood Pk, AvnT	2474	24W-35N	C6
Whitlock Pk, DRGV	3084	18W-4S	E7
Whittaker Pk, BRRG	3208	15W-8S	B2
Whyte Gate Pk, LNSH	2702	14W-23N	D2
Wicker Pk, CHCG	3033	2W-1N	C1
Wierzba Pk, BGVW	3210	9W-8S	D2
Wigwam Pk, SHLD	3350	0E-18S	D7
Wilbur M Kent Pk, CLSM	2967	27W-4N	C4
Wilderness Pk, ADSN	2970	20W-3N	B4
Wilder Pk, AURA	3138	35W-7S	B7
Wilder Pk, EMHT	3027	16W-1N	E2
Wild Meadow Pk, EMHT	3028	15W-0N	B4
Wildwood Pk, ANHT	2754	16W-16N	D7
Wildwood Pk, CHCG	2919	7W-8N	B1
Wildwood Pk, WrnT	2533	18W-33N	D3
Wilkins Pk, ALSP	3276	5W-15S	B7
William Aldis Sr Pk, WDND	2801	34W-15N	A3
William Friedrich Pk, NPVL	3141	27W-7S	D6
William G Yena Pk, LGPK	3087	11W-2S	D3
William H Althoff Pk, MHRY	2527	33W-33N	E2
William Kaper Sr Pk, CRY	2641	32W-24N	B7
William Kelly, PNFD	3338	30W-16S	C4
Williamsburg Pk, GNVA	3019	36W-1N	E3
Williamsburg Pk, NHBK	2757	9W-18N	D3
Williams Cove Pk, WTMT	3145	18W-7S	A6
Williams Pk, ANTH	2357	23W-42N	E5
Williams Pk, CHCG	3092	0W-2S	B3
Williams Pk, OKLN	3212	5W-11S	B7
Williams Wetlands, SCRL	2964	34W-4N	D4
Willoughby Farms Pk, ALGN	2747	36W-19N	A2
Willow Bend Pk West, NpvT	3140	30W-5S	C3
Willow Brook Community Pk, WLBK	3207	16W-8S	D1
Willowbrook Pk, SHLD	3428	0E-19S	D2
Willowbrook Pk, VLPK	3027	18W-0S	A6
Willow Glen Pk, LSLE	3142	25W-5S	B3
Willow Lake Pk, AURA	3201	31W-8S	E1
Willow Lake Pk, NARA	3077	37W-3S	C7
Willow Pk, ANHT	2807	17W-16N	C1
Willow Pk, CHCG	3152	1E-5S	E2
Willow Pk, DSPN	2863	13W-11N	A2
Willow Pk, GNVW	2810	10W-15N	A2
Willow Pk, HFET	2804	24W-14N	C4
Willow Pk, NHFD	2811	7W-15N	B2
Willow Pk, PLTN	2753	20W-16N	A6
Willow Point, MltT	3024	25W-0N	A4
Willow Stream Pk, BFGV	2754	17W-20N	B1
Willow Trails Pk, PTHT	2808	13W-15N	E1
Willowview Pk, MKNA	3502	14W-23S	E4
Wilmington Island Pk, WMTN	3853	27W-39S	C7
Wilmington Pk, HFET	2858	24W-11N	C2
Wilmot Pk, DRFD	2703	11W-20N	C7
Wil-O-Way Pk, NPVL	3141	28W-6S	A6
Wilson Pk, CHCG	3091	1W-3S	E4
Windemere Pk, EGVV	2913	22W-8N	C2
Windemere Pk, NLNX	3589	17W-25S	C1
Wind Energy Pk, BTVA	3078	34W-3S	D5
Windermere West Pk, NLNX	3500	20W-24S	B5
Winding Creek Pk, BRLT	2911	28W-7N	A5
Winding Creek Pk, CLLK	2693	36W-23N	D3
Winding Creek Pk, NPVL	3203	26W-9S	E3
Windsor Pkway Pk, ANHT	2807	17W-13N	C5
Windsor Pointe Pk, SRGV	3135	41W-6S	E5
Windsor Pointe Pk North, SRGV	3135	41W-6S	E4
Windsor Pointe Pk South, SRGV	3135	42W-6S	D5
Windsor Ridge Pk, BFGV	2754	17W-18N	B4
Windsor West Pk, SRGV	3135	42W-6S	C5
Windy Oaks Pk, BRLT	2910	30W-9N	B1
Windy Point Pk, WDRG	3206	21W-9S	A3
Winfield Estates Pk, WNFD	3023	27W-0N	D4
Winfield Pk, BFGV	2754	18W-18N	A3
Wingfoot Pk, NARA	3078	35W-3S	B6
Wing Pk, ELGN	2854	34W-12N	C2
Wing Street Pk, ELGN	2854	34W-12N	D3
Winnebago Pk, PKFT	3595	4W-26S	A2
Winnebago Pk, SKOK	2866	5W-10N	A5
Winnemac Pk, CHCG	2921	2W-6N	B6
Winrock Pk, OswT	3200	36W-10S	A6
Winston Pk, PLTN	2806	19W-15N	C1
Winston Woods, BGBK	3205	22W-10S	B6
Wintercrag Pk, WDND	2800	34W-15N	D4
Winterhoff Pk, LNSG	3430	3E-21S	B6
Wipfler Pk, BGBK	3269	21W-11S	D1
Wlodarski Pk, ODPK	3424	10W-19S	A3
Wolf Lake Pk, HMND	3280		D6
Wolf Pk, CCHL	3506	5W-22S	B1
Wolf Pk, CHCG	3280	3E-12S	A2
Womens Welfare Pk, BCHR	3864	1W-36S	B1
Woodborough Pk, HMWD	3508	1W-22S	A1
Wood Dale Community Pk, WDDL	2915	18W-7N	A5
Woodgate Pk, MTSN	3505	7W-24S	D5
Woodglen Pk, LSLE	3142	24W-7S	E6
Woodhull Pk, CHCG	3153	2E-8S	B7
Wood Land Estates Pk, NndT	2640	35W-27N	A1
Woodland Hills Pk, BTVA	3078	34W-1S	E2
Woodland Pk, BFGV	2701	17W-22N	B3
Woodland Pk, CHCG	3092	0E-3S	D4
Woodland Pk, DRFD	2703	11W-21N	C6
Woodland Pk, HYHL	3209	11W-10S	E5
Woodland Pk, PKRG	2863	11W-10N	E5
Woodland Pk, SMWD	2857	27W-10N	C7
Woodland Pk, WynT	2966	30W-3N	B5
Woodlands Pk, FmtT	2589	21W-29N	E5
Woodlands Pk, LktT	3420	21W-18S	A1
Woodland Trails Pk, MPPT	2808	14W-14N	C4
Woodlawn Pk, FftT	3504	9W-25S	E7
Woodlawn Pk, GRNE	2479	13W-34N	A7
Woodridge Pk, HDPK	2757	8W-20N	D2
Woodscreek Pk, CLLK	2693	36W-23N	C2
Woodstock Pk, SMBG	2858	24W-9N	E7
Woodstock Square Pk, WDSK	2524	41W-31N	D7
Wortham Pk, MDLN	2646	20W-26N	B2
Worthbrook Pk, OKLN	3211	7W-10S	B4
Worth Woods Pk, WRTH	3274	9W-12S	D3
Worthy Pk, HRVY	3349	3W-18S	B6
Wright Pk, ELGN	2855	32W-10N	C6
Wright Pk, SKOK	2865	6W-10N	E4
Wrightwood Pk, CHCG	2977	1W-3N	D5
WR Keck Pk, SRGV	3135	42W-7S	B7
Wyndwood Pk, AlqT	2641	33W-25N	A5
Yangas Pk, HMGN	3344	15W-16S	C3
Yellowstone Pk, ALGN	2748	32W-20N	B1
Yeoman Pk, WKGN	2479	11W-34N	E7
Yogi Bear Pk, GYLK	2532	20W-34N	E1
York Commons, EMHT	3028	15W-0N	A5
Yorkshire Manor Pk, NPVL	3142	25W-5S	A3
Young Pk, CHCG	3033	1W-0S	D5
Youth Pk, BLWD	3029	12W-0N	B4
Yukich Pk, ENGN	3212	4W-10S	E4
Yunker Pk, FftT	3503	13W-23S	A4
Ziebell Pk, HRVY	3349	3W-17S	B6
Zocher Pk, SMBG	2858	24W-11N	D3
Zurites Pk, LKZH	2698	24W-23N	B3

Post Offices

FEATURE NAME Address City ZIP Code	MAP#	CGS	GRID
Addison Main 175 S Lincoln Av, ADSN, 60101	2970	18W-3N	E5
Algonquin 801 W Algonquin Rd, ALGN, 60102	2694	33W-21N	D6
AMF O'Hare Finance 11600 W Irving Park Rd, CHCG, 60666	2972	14W-5N	D2
Antioch Main 420 Orchard St, ANTH, 60002	2357	23W-42N	E6
Argonne Branch 9700 S Cass Av, DGvT, 60439	3207	17W-11S	C7
Arlington Heights Main 909 W Euclid Av, ANHT, 60005	2806	18W-14N	E4
Ashburn 3639 W 79th St, CHCG, 60652	3212	4W-9S	D2
Auburn Park 8345 S Ashland Av, CHCG, 60620	3213	1W-9S	D3
Aurora East Station 3900 Gabrielle Ln, AURA, 60504	3140	30W-7S	A7
Aurora Main 525 N Broadway, AURA, 60505	3138	35W-7S	B6
Barrington Main 1515 S Grove Av, BRTN, 60010	2751	25W-17N	A5
Bartlett 160 W Railroad Av, BRLT, 60103	2910	29W-8N	E3
Batavia Main 500 N Randall Rd, BTVA, 60510	3019	36W-0S	D7
Bedford Park 6801 W 73rd St, BDPK, 60638	3149	8W-8S	A7
Beecher 712 Penfield St, BCHR, 60401	3864	0W-36S	C2
Bellwood Main 2800 St. Charles Rd, BLWD, 60104	3029	12W-0N	C4
Bensenville Main 303 E Green St, BNVL, 60106	2972	15W-5N	A1
Berwyn 6625 Cermak Rd, BRWN, 60402	3089	8W-2S	A2
Bloomingdale Main 108 W Schick Rd, BMDL, 60108	2969	23W-5N	A1
Blue Island Main 2441 Vermont St, BLID, 60406	3349	3W-15S	B1
Bolingbrook Main 105 Canterbury Ln, BGBK, 60440	3269	23W-12S	A2
Braceville Main 106 N Mitchell St, BCVL, 60407	4030	34W-44S	A4
Braidwood Main 280 W Main St, BDWD, 60408	3942	31W-41S	A5
Bridgeview 7401 W 100th Pl, BGVW, 60455	3210	9W-11S	D7
Bristol 11 N Cannonball Tr, BtlT, 60512	3261	41W-12S	E3
Broadview 2131 S 17th Av, BDVW, 60155	3029	11W-0S	D7
Brookfield Main 3731 Prairie Av, BKFD, 60513	3087	11W-3S	E5
Buffalo Grove 255 N Buffalo Grove Rd, BFGV, 60089	2754	16W-20N	C1
Calumet City Main 1200 159th St, CTCY, 60409	3429	2E-19S	D1
Cardiss Collins 433 W Harrison St, CHCG, 60607	3034	0W-0S	B6
Carol Stream Main 550 E Fullerton Av, CLSM, 60188	2968	24W-2N	D7
Carpentersville Main 100 N Kennedy Dr, CPVL, 60110	2748	33W-18N	C5
Cary Main 2707 Three Oaks Rd, CRY, 60013	2641	31W-24N	D7
Charles A Hayes 7436 S Exchange Av, CHCG, 60649	3153	3E-8S	D7
Chicago Heights 1333 W End Av, CHHT, 60411	3508	0W-25S	B7
Chicago Lawn 6037 S Kedzie Av, CHCG, 60629	3150	4W-6S	E4
Chicago Ridge Main 10525 Ridgeland Av, CHRG, 60415	3275	7W-12S	B1
Chinatown 2345 S Wentworth Av, CHCG, 60616	3092	0W-2S	B2
Cicero 2440 S Laramie Av, CCRO, 60804	3089	6W-2S	D2
Clarendon Hills 312 Park Av, CNHL, 60514	3145	17W-5S	D2
Clearing 5645 S Archer Av, CHCG, 60638	3149	6W-5S	E2
Country Club Hills Branch 4053 183rd St, CCHL, 60478	3426	5W-22S	C7
Cragin 5100 W Grand Av, CHCG, 60639	2975	6W-2N	E7
Crete Main 515 Cass St, CRTE, 60417	3685	0W-29S	B2
Crystal Lake Main 301 E Congress Pkwy, CLLK, 60014	2640	34W-25N	C5
Daniel Doffyn 3750 N Kedzie Av, CHCG, 60618	2976	4W-4N	D2
Deerfield Main 707 Osterman Av, DRFD, 60015	2703	10W-20N	E7
Des Plaines Downtown Station 601 Mannheim Rd, DSPN, 60016	2863	13W-11N	A3
Des Plaines Main 1000 E Oakton St, DSPN, 60018	2862	13W-10N	E6
Dolton Main 14212 Cottage Grove Av, DLTN, 60419	3351	0E-16S	A3
Downers Grove Main 920 Curtiss St, DRGV, 60515	3144	19W-5S	C2
Dundee Main 611 S 8th St, WDND, 60118	2800	34W-15N	E3
Edgebrook 5424 W Devon Av, CHCG, 60646	2919	6W-8N	C2
Edison Square Station 1519 N Lewis Av, WKGN, 60085	2479	11W-35N	D6
Elburn 815 N Main St, ELBN, 60119	3017	43W-2N	A1
Elgin Main 66 Grove Ct, ELGN, 60120	2854	34W-11N	E4
Elgin West Side 208 S Randall Rd, ELGN, 60124	2853	36W-10N	D5
Elk Grove Village Branch 611 Landmeier Rd, EGVV, 60007	2861	17W-9N	B7
Elmhurst 154 W Park Av, EMHT, 60126	3027	16W-1N	E2
Elmwood Park 7300 W Fullerton Av, EDPK, 60707	2974	9W-3N	D6
Elwood Main 303 E Mississippi Av, ELWD, 60421	3675	25W-32S	C7
Eola N Eola Rd, NpvT, 60502	3139	31W-6S	D5
Evanston Main 1101 Church St, EVTN, 60201	2867	2W-11N	A2
Evanston North 1929 Central St, EVTN, 60201	2812	3W-13N	E7
Evanston South 701 Main St, EVTN, 60202	2867	2W-10N	B5
Evergreen Park 9359 S Kedzie Av, ENGN, 60805	3212	3W-10S	E5
Flossmoor 1020 Park Dr, FSMR, 60422	3507	3W-22S	B2
Forest Park Main 417 Des Plaines Av, FTPK, 60130	3030	9W-0S	C5
Fox Lake Main 33 E Grand Av, FXLK, 60020	2473	28W-36N	A3
Fox River Grove Main 938 Ski Hill Rd, FRGV, 60021	2696	29W-22N	C3
Frankfort Main 21201 S Elsner Rd, FKFT, 60423	3503	12W-25S	C7
Franklin Park Main 9760 Franklin Av, FNPK, 60131	2973	12W-4N	C4
Geneva Main 26 S 3rd St, GNVA, 60134	3020	35W-1N	B3
Genoa City Main 742 Walworth St, GNCY, 53128	2353		A3
Gilberts Main 57 Railroad St, GLBT, 60136	2799	38W-16N	A1
Glencoe Main 336 Hazel Av, GLNC, 60022	2758	6W-17N	D5
Glendale Heights 1950 Bentley Ct, GLHT, 60139	2969	23W-3N	A5
Glen Ellyn Downtown Station 528 Pennsylvania Av, GNEN, 60137	3025	22W-0N	B5
Glen Ellyn Main 757 DuPage Blvd, GNEN, 60137	3025	22W-0S	D7
Glenview Main 1919 Prairie St, GNVW, 60025	2810	8W-13N	D6
Glenwood Main 19 W Main St, GNWD, 60425	3508	0E-22S	D2
Golf 1 Briar Rd, GLF, 60029	2864	8W-12N	E1

Chicago 7-County Points of Interest Index

FEATURE NAME Address City ZIP Code	MAP#	CGS	GRID
Grayslake Main 75 Commerce Dr, GYLK, 60030	2533	19W-33N	B4
Great Lakes 525 Bronson Av, NCHI, 60088	2594	10W-31N	A1
Great Lakes Branch 525 Bronson Av, NCHI, 60088	2594	10W-31N	A1
Gurnee Main 1 N Oplaine Rd, GRNE, 60031	2535	14W-34N	C1
Hammond Main 5530 S Sohl Av, HMND, 46320	3352		D6
Hampshire Main 196 E Washington Av, HPSR, 60140	2795	46W-16N	E2
Harvard Main 300 N Eastmann St, HRVD, 60033	2406	50W-38N	B6
Harvey 15441 Center Av, HRVY, 60426	3350	1W-18S	A7
Harwood Heights 7101 W Gunnison St, HDHT, 60706	2918	8W-6N	D7
Haymarket 168 N Clinton St, CHCG, 60661	3034	0W-0N	A4
Hazel Crest Main 17541 Kedzie Av, HLCT, 60429	3427	3W-21S	A5
Hebron Main 9912 Illinois St, HBRN, 60034	2351	40W-41N	A7
Hegewisch 13234 S Baltimore Av, CHCG, 60633	3352	3E-15S	A1
Highland Park Main 833 Central Av, HDPK, 60035	2704	8W-22N	D5
Highwood 130 Highwood Av, HIWD, 60040	2704	9W-23N	D2
Hillside Branch 505 N Wolf Rd, HLSD, 60162	3028	13W-0N	D5
Hines Main 220 1st Av, MYWD, 60153	3088	10W-1S	A1
Hinsdale Main 1314 Kensington Rd, OKBK, 60523	3085	16W-2S	D3
Hoffman Estates Branch 1255 Gannon Dr, HFET, 60169	2858	24W-12N	C2
Homewood Main 1921 Ridge Rd, HMWD, 60430	3427	2W-21S	D7
Hubbard Wood 1052 Gage St, WNKA, 60093	2759	5W-16N	A7
Huntley Main 11013 N Woodstock St, HTLY, 60142	2692	40W-21N	A6
Ingleside Main 604 Rollins Rd, FXLK, 60041	2473	26W-35N	D5
Irving Park N Cicero Av, CHCG, 60641	2975	6W-4N	E3
Island Lake Main 129 E State Rd, ISLK, 60042	2586	28W-28N	D6
Itasca Main 1050 W Irving Park Rd, ITSC, 60143	2914	20W-6N	A6
Jefferson Park 5401 W Lawrence Av, CHCG, 60630	2919	6W-5N	D7
Joliet Downtown Station 51 E Clinton St, JLET, 60432	3499	23W-23S	A4
Joliet Main 2000 McDonough St, JLET, 60436	3497	26W-24S	E6
Kenilworth Main 408 Green Bay Rd, KLWH, 60043	2812	4W-14N	C4
Lafox 279 Lafox Rd, BbyT, 60119	3018	40W-1N	B4
La Grange Branch 701 E 31st St, LGPK, 60525	3087	12W-2S	C4
La Grange Main 121 W Hillgrove Av, LGNG, 60525	3087	12W-4S	B6
Lake Bluff 26 E Scranton Av, LKBF, 60044	2593	10W-28N	E6
Lake Forest Carrier Annex 27848 N Bradley Rd, GNOK, 60048	2592	14W-27N	D7
Lake Forest Main 230 Northgate St, LKFT, 60045	2650	10W-26N	A2
Lakeview Postal Office W Irving Park Rd, CHCG, 60613	2977	1W-4N	D2
Lake Villa Main 206 Cedar Av, LKVL, 60046	2417	22W-38N	A7
Lake Zurich Main 380 Surryse Rd, LKZH, 60047	2699	23W-22N	A4
Lansing Main 18125 Roy St, LNSG, 60438	3430	4E-21S	B6
Lansing Torrence Avenue 18525 Torrence Av, LNSG, 60438	3429	3E-21S	E7
Lemont Annex 15871 W 127th St, LMNT, 60439	3270	19W-14S	C7
Lemont Branch 42 Stephen St, LMNT, 60439	3270	19W-13S	D5
Libertyville Main 1520 Artaius Pkwy, LYVL, 60048	2647	16W-27N	E1
Lincoln Park Carrier Annex W Diversey Pkwy, CHCG, 60614	2978	0W-3N	A5
Lincolnshire Main 125 Schelter Rd, LNSH, 60069	2702	15W-22N	A3
Lincolnwood Carrier Annex 6500 N Lincoln Av, LNWD, 60712	2920	4W-8N	C2
Lisle Main 817 Ogden Av, LSLE, 60532	3143	22W-4S	B1
Lockport Finance 1059 E 9th St, LKPT, 60441	3419	21W-19S	E2
Lombard Main 380 E St. Charles Rd, LMBD, 60148	3026	19W-1N	C3
Lombard Yorktown 226 Yorktown Shopping Ctr, LMBD, 60148	3084	19W-2S	C3
Lyons Main 7836 Ogden Av, LYNS, 60534	3088	9W-4S	C6
Manhattan Main 185 S State St, MHTN, 60442	3677	19W-31S	E5
Marengo Main 223 E Grant Hwy, MRGO, 60152	2634	49W-26N	B2
Markham 16011 Kedzie Av, MKHM, 60428	3427	3W-19S	A1
Matteson Main 20650 Cicero Av, MTSN, 60443	3506	6W-24S	B6
Maywood 415 S 5th Av, MYWD, 60153	3030	10W-0N	A4
McHenry Main 4530 W Crystal Lake Rd, MHRY, 60050	2527	33W-32N	E4
Medinah Main 736 Medinah Rd, BmdT, 60157	2913	22W-7N	D5
Melrose Park Main 1824 N 25th Av, MLPK, 60160	3029	12W-1N	C1
Midlothian Main 14722 Pulaski Rd, MDLN, 60445	3348	5W-17S	C5
Milton Brunson 324 S Laramie Av, CHCG, 60644	3031	6W-0S	D5
Minooka Main 301 W Mondamin St, MNKA, 60447	3583	33W-28S	A7
Mokena 19934 Wolf Rd, MKNA, 60448	3502	14W-24S	E4
Monee Main 5410 W Main St, MONE, 60449	3683	6W-31S	A5
Montgomery Main 1899 Village Center Pkwy, MTGY, 60538	3200	36W-10S	A5
Morgan Park 1805 W Monterey Av, CHCG, 60643	3277	2W-13S	C3
Morton Grove 9114 Waukegan Rd, MNGV, 60053	2864	8W-11N	E3
Mt Greenwood 3349 W 111th St, CHCG, 60655	3276	4W-13S	E3
Mt Prospect 300 W Central Rd, MPPT, 60056	2807	15W-13N	E7
Mundelein Main 435 E Hawley St, MDLN, 60060	2590	18W-27N	E7
Munster Branch 917 Ridge Rd, MNSR, 46321	3430		E7
Nancy B Jefferson 2419 W Monroe St, CHCG, 60612	3033	3W-0S	A5
Naperville Finance 5 S Washington St, NPVL, 60540	3141	27W-6S	D5
Naperville Main 1750 Ogden Av, NPVL, 60540	3140	28W-7S	E7
New Lenox Main 300 Vine St, NLNX, 60451	3501	18W-24S	B6
Niles Branch 6977 W Oakton St, NLES, 60714	2864	8W-9N	E6
North Aurora Main 65 N Randall Rd, NARA, 60542	3077	37W-4S	C7
Northbrook 2460 Dundee Rd, NHBK, 60062	2757	10W-18N	A4
North Chicago Main 1514 Sheridan Rd, NCHI, 60064	2537	10W-32N	A5
Northfield 1787 Orchard Ln, NHFD, 60093	2811	7W-15N	C2
Northlake 47 W North Av, NHLK, 60164	3028	14W-1N	D1
North Riverside BMC Branch 7300 W 25th St, NRIV, 60546	3088	9W-2S	D2
Northtown 3401 W Devon Av, CHCG, 60659	2920	4W-7N	D3
Norwood Park 6300 N Northwest Hwy, CHCG, 60631	2918	8W-7N	D3
Oak Brook 109 Symonds Dr, HNDL, 60521	3146	15W-4S	B1
Oak Forest Main 15811 Central Av, OKFT, 60452	3425	6W-18S	D1
Oak Park 901 Lake St, OKPK, 60301	3030	8W-0N	E4
Oak Park South 1116 Garfield St, OKPK, 60304	3030	8W-0S	E6
Ogden Park 6559 S Ashland Av, CHCG, 60636	3151	2W-7S	D5
Old Orchard Station 9318 Skokie Blvd, SKOK, 60077	2865	6W-11N	E2
Olympia Fields Main 3033 Edmund M Burke Rd, OMFD, 60461	3507	3W-24S	A5
Orland Park Main 9500 W 144th Pl, ODPK, 60462	3345	11W-17S	D4
Orland Park Retail Branch 15128 S La Grange Rd, ODPK, 60462	3345	12W-18S	D6
Oswego 26 S Madison St, OSWG, 60543	3263	37W-12S	C3
Otis Grant Collins 2302 S Pulaski Rd, CHCG, 60623	3090	5W-2S	C2
Otto Mall Finance Station 1601 Otto Blvd, CHHT, 60411	3596	1W-25S	B1
Palatine Main 440 W Colfax St, PLTN, 60067	2752	21W-16N	D7
Palos Heights Main 12238 S Harlem Av, PSHT, 60463	3274	9W-14S	E6
Palos Park Main 12100 S 80th Av, PSPK, 60464	3274	10W-14S	C6
Park Forest Main 123 Indianwood Blvd, PKFT, 60466	3595	3W-27S	B4
Park Ridge Main 333 Busse Hwy, PKRG, 60068	2864	10W-9N	A7
Peotone Main 117 S West St, PTON, 60468	3860	9W-37S	E3
Pilsen 1859 S Ashland Av, CHCG, 60608	3091	1W-1S	D1
Plainfield Main 14855 S Van Dyke Rd, PnfT, 60544	3338	30W-17S	B7
Plano Main 102 E North St, PLNO, 60545	3259	47W-13S	D6
Posen Main 2720 W 147th St, POSN, 60469	3349	3W-17S	A5
Prospect Heights Main 9 S Elmhurst Rd, PTHT, 60070	2808	15W-14N	A3
Ravenswood 2522 W Lawrence Av, CHCG, 60625	2921	3W-6N	A6
Ravinia Station 582 Roger Williams Av, HDPK, 60035	2705	7W-20N	A7
Richmond Main 5510 Mill St, RHMD, 60071	2353	34W-42N	C6
Richton Park 22332 Governors Hwy, RNPK, 60471	3594	5W-27S	D3
Ringwood Main 5016 Barnard Mill Rd, RGWD, 60072	2470	33W-36N	D4
Riverdale 661 W 138th St, RVDL, 60827	3350	1W-15S	B2
River Forest 401 William St, RVFT, 60305	3030	9W-0N	D4
River Grove Main 2728 N Clinton St, RVGV, 60171	2974	10W-3N	B5
Robbins Main 3447 W 137th St, RBBN, 60472	3348	4W-16S	E2
Roger P Mcauliffee 6441 W Irving Park Rd, CHCG, 60634	2975	8W-4N	A2
Rogers Park 1723 W Devon Av, CHCG, 60660	2921	2W-7N	C2
Rolling Meadows Branch 3266 Kirchoff Rd, RGMW, 60008	2806	19W-13N	B5
Romeoville 315 E Romeo Rd, LktT, 60446	3341	23W-16S	B3
Romeoville W Romeoville Rd, RMVL, 60446	3340	24W-16S	E3
Roseland 11033 S State St, CHCG, 60628	3278	0E-12S	C2
Roselle Branch 256 Central Av, ROSL, 60172	2912	23W-7N	E4
Rosemont Branch 6153 Gage St, RSMT, 60018	2917	11W-7N	C3
Round Lake Main 1940 N Municipal Wy, RLKB, 60073	2475	22W-35N	B5
Russell 43410 N Kilbourne Rd, NptT, 60099	2361	14W-43N	D4
St. Charles 2600 Oak St, SCRL, 60175	2963	37W-3N	C7
St. Charles East Side 616 E Main St, SCRL, 60174	2964	35W-3N	C7
Saint Charles Main 1405 W Main St, SCRL, 60174	2963	36W-2N	E7
Schaumburg Main 450 W Schaumburg Rd, SMBG, 60194	2858	24W-10N	E5
Schiller Park Branch 9460 Irving Park Rd, SRPK, 60176	2973	11W-5N	C1
Skokie Main 4950 Madison St, SKOK, 60077	2865	6W-10N	E5
South Calumet Avenue 5530 S Sohl Av, HMND, 46320	3352		D6
South Elgin Carrier Annex 164 N Gilbert St, SEGN, 60177	2908	34W-8N	D2
South Elgin Main 310 N La Fox St, SEGN, 60177	2908	34W-8N	D2
South Holland Main 16260 Louis Av, SHLD, 60473	3428	0E-19S	E1
Spring Grove Main 2410 Westward Dr, SPGV, 60081	2413	31W-39N	E4
Station F Finance 7056 N Clark St, CHCG, 60626	2921	2W-8N	C1
Station H Finance 10238 S Vincennes Av, CHCG, 60643	3213	1W-11S	E7
Station K Finance 3933 W North Av, CHCG, 60647	3032	4W-2N	C1
Station M Finance 7617 N Paulina St, CHCG, 60626	2867	2W-9N	C6
Station Q Finance 4749 N Bernard St, CHCG, 60625	2920	4W-5N	D7
Station T Finance 2011 W Montrose Av, CHCG, 60625	2921	2W-5N	B7
Station W Finance 10422 S Ewing Av, CHCG, 60617	3280	4E-11S	B1
Steger Main 23 W Steger Rd, STGR, 60475	3596	1W-27S	B5
Streamwood 115 E Irving Park Rd, SMWD, 60107	2856	28W-9N	E7
Sugar Grove Main 45 E Cross St, SRGV, 60554	3135	42W-7S	D7
Summit Argo Main 7415 W 63rd St, SMMT, 60501	3148	9W-7S	D5
Techny Main 2001 Waukegan Rd, NHBK, 60062	2810	8W-16N	E1
Terminal Two O'Hare Airport 11600 W Irving Park Rd, CHCG, 60666	2972	14W-5N	D2
Thornton Main 103 E Eleanor St, TNTN, 60476	3428	0E-21S	D5
Tinley Park Main 7230 171st St, TYPK, 60477	3424	9W-20S	E4
Trevor 25930 Wilmot Rd, SlmT, 53179	2357		B1
Union Main 17803 Depot St, UNON, 60180	2635	46W-25N	D4
US Postal Facility FTPK, 60130	3030	9W-1S	C7
Vernon Hills Branch 675 Lakeview Pkwy, VNHL, 60061	2647	16W-25N	D4
Villa Park Main 1415 S Ardmore Av, VLPK, 60181	3027	17W-0S	B7
Wacker Drive 233 S Wacker Dr, CHCG, 60606	3034	0W-0S	B5
Wadsworth 39067 N Caroline Av, WDWH, 60083	2420	15W-39N	B6
Warrenville 101 Rockwell St, WNVL, 60555	3080	28W-3S	E5
Wasco CmpT, 60175	2962	40W-4N	C3
Wauconda 539 W Liberty St, WCDA, 60084	2643	26W-27N	D1
Waukegan 326 N Genesee St, WKGN, 60085	2537	10W-34N	B1
Wayne Main 431 Railroad St, WYNE, 60184	2965	32W-5N	D2
Wentworth Avenue Station 680 Wentworth Av, CTCY, 60409	3352	4E-17S	C6
Westchester 10240 W Roosevelt Rd, WSTR, 60154	3029	12W-0S	B7
West Chicago Main 1130 W Washington St, WCHI, 60185	3022	31W-0N	A5
Western Springs 4479 Lawn Av, WNSP, 60558	3146	14W-4S	D1
Westmont 5707 S Cass Av, WTMT, 60559	3145	17W-6S	B4
Wheaton 46 Danada Sq W, WHTN, 60187	3082	24W-2S	C4
Wheaton Main 122 N Wheaton Av, WHTN, 60187	3024	24W-0S	C7
Wheeling Main 250 W Dundee Rd, WLNG, 60090	2755	14W-18N	B4
Wicker Park W Division St, CHCG, 60622	3033	2W-1N	C1
Willow Springs 8448 Archer Av, WLSP, 60480	3209	12W-9S	C3
Wilmette Main 1241 Central Av, WLMT, 60091	2812	3W-13N	D6
Wilmington Main 301 N Water St, WMTN, 60481	3853	27W-38S	D6
Wilmot Main 30725 113th St, SlmT, 53192	2356		A1
Winfield Main 525 Highlake Rd, WNFD, 60190	3023	27W-0S	C6
Winnetka 512 Chestnut St, WNKA, 60093	2812	5W-15N	A2
Winthrop Harbor Main 1706 7th St, WPHR, 60096	2363	9W-42N	C6
Wonder Lake Main E Wonder Lake Rd, MchT, 60097	2469	36W-35N	D5
Wood Dale 270 N Wood Dale Rd, WDDL, 60191	2915	18W-5N	A7

Chicago 7-County Points of Interest Index

FEATURE NAME Address City ZIP Code	MAP#	CGS	GRID
Woodfield Station 651 Mall Dr, SMBG, 60173	2859	21W-11N	E3
Woodridge Branch 2 Plaza Dr, WDRG, 60517	3205	21W-8S	E1
Woodstock Main 1050 S Country Club Rd, DrrT, 60098	2583	37W-29N	A3
Worth Main 11114 S Harlem Av, WRTH, 60482	3274	9W-13S	E3
Yorkville Main 201 W Hydraulic Av, YKVL, 60560	3333	43W-15S	C2
Zion 1225 Shiloh Blvd, ZION, 60099	2422	10W-40N	B3

Schools

FEATURE NAME Address City ZIP Code	MAP#	CGS	GRID
7th Avenue Elementary School 701 7th Av, LGNG, 60525	3147	12W-5S	C2
21st Century Preparatory Center 240 S Orchard Dr, PKFT, 60466	3595	3W-27S	B4
Abbott Elementary School 3630 S Wells St, CHCG, 60609	3092	0W-3S	B5
Abbott Middle School 949 Van St, ELGN, 60123	2854	34W-11N	C4
Abbott Middle School 1319 Washington St, WKGN, 60085	2536	11W-34N	E2
Abraham Lincoln Elementary School 380 Greenfield Av, GNEN, 60137	3025	23W-0S	B6
Academy of Our Lady School 510 Grand Av, WKGN, 60085	2537	10W-34N	A1
Academy of St. Benedict-Honore 7033 S Honore St, CHCG, 60636	3151	2W-7S	C6
Academy of St. Benedict-Laflin 6020 S Laflin St, CHCG, 60636	3151	1W-6S	D4
Academy of St. Benedict-Stewart 6547 S Stewart Av, CHCG, 60621	3152	0W-7S	B5
Academy of Scholastic Achievement 4651 W Madison St, CHCG, 60644	3032	5W-0S	A5
ACE Technical Charter High School 5410 S State St, CHCG, 60609	3152	0E-5S	C2
Addams Elementary School 10810 S Avenue H, CHCG, 60617	3280	4E-12S	B2
Addams Junior High School 700 S Springinsguth Rd, SMBG, 60193	2858	25W-9N	B7
Addison Trail High School 213 N Lombard Rd, ADSN, 60101	2970	20W-3N	B5
Adlai E Stevenson High School 1 Stevenson Dr, LNSH, 60069	2701	16W-23N	E3
Adler Park Elementary School 1740 N Milwaukee Av, LYVL, 60048	2591	16W-30N	D2
AF Ames Elementary School 86 Southcote Rd, RVSD, 60546	3088	9W-2S	C3
Agassiz Elementary School 2851 N Seminary Av, CHCG, 60657	2977	1W-3N	E4
Akiba-Schechter Jewish Day School 5235 S Cornell Av, CHCG, 60615	3153	2E-5S	B2
Albany Park Multicultural Academy 4929 N Sawyer Av, CHCG, 60625	2920	4W-6N	D6
Albright Middle School 1110 S Villa Av, VLPK, 60181	3027	17W-0S	B6
Alcott Elementary School 2625 N Orchard St, CHCG, 60614	2978	0W-3N	A5
Alcuin Montessori School 324 N Oak Park Av, OKPK, 60302	3030	8W-0N	E3
Alden Hebron Junior-Senior High-School 9604 Illinois St, HBRN, 60034	2350	41W-41N	E7
Aldridge Elementary School 630 E 131st St, CHCG, 60827	3278	0E-15S	E7
Aldrin Elementary School 617 Boxwood Dr, SMBG, 60193	2858	24W-9N	D7
Alexander Graham Bell Regional Elem-School 3730 N Oakley Av, CHCG, 60618	2977	2W-4N	B2
Algonquin Elementary School 170 Algonquin St, PKFT, 60466	3595	2W-26S	D2
Algonquin Lakes Elementary School 1401 Compton Dr, ALGN, 60102	2748	33W-19N	A2
Algonquin Middle School 520 Longwood Dr, ALGN, 60102	2695	33W-20N	A7
Algonquin Middle School 767 E Algonquin Rd, DSPN, 60018	2862	14W-10N	D5
Algonquin Road Elementary School 975 Algonquin Rd, FRGV, 60021	2696	30W-22N	A4
Alice Barnard Math & Science Center 10354 S Charles St, CHCG, 60643	3277	1W-12S	D1
Alphonsus Academy 1439 W Wellington Av, CHCG, 60657	2977	1W-3N	D4
Altgeld Elementary School 1340 W 71st St, CHCG, 60636	3151	1W-7S	D7
Americana Intermediate School 1629 President St, GLHT, 60139	2968	23W-3N	E6
Ames Middle School 1920 N Hamlin Av, CHCG, 60647	2976	4W-2N	C7
Amos Alonzo Stagg High School 8015 W 111th St, PSHL, 60465	3274	10W-13S	C3
Amundsen High School 5110 N Damen Av, CHCG, 60625	2921	2W-6N	B6
Andersen Elementary School 1148 N Honore St, CHCG, 60622	3033	2W-1N	C2
Anderson Elementary School 35W071 Villa Maria Rd, SchT, 60174	2908	35W-6N	C7
Andrew High School 9001 171st St, TYPK, 60487	3424	11W-20S	A4
Anna McDonald Elementary School 200 2nd St, MHTN, 60442	3678	19W-31S	A5
Anne M Jeans Elementary School 16W631 91st St, DGvT, 60527	3207	16W-10S	D5
Anne Sullivan School 700 N Schoenbeck Rd, PTHT, 60070	2807	16W-15N	E1
Annunciata School 3750 E 112th St, CHCG, 60617	3280	4E-12S	B3
Annunciation of the BVM School 1840 Church Rd, AURA, 60505	3138	34W-5S	D2
Antioch Community High School 1133 Main St, ANTH, 60002	2357	23W-41N	E7
Antioch Elementary School 817 Main St, ANTH, 60002	2357	23W-42N	E6
Antioch Upper Grade School 800 Highview Dr, ANTH, 60002	2357	24W-42N	C6
Apollo Elementary School 10100 Dee Rd, MaiT, 60016	2809	11W-12N	D7

FEATURE NAME Address City ZIP Code	MAP#	CGS	GRID
Aptakisic Junior High School 1231 Weiland Rd, BFGV, 60089	2701	16W-21N	E6
AQSA School 7361 W 92nd St, BGVW, 60455	3210	9W-10S	E5
Arbor View Elementary School 22W430 Ironwood Dr, MltT, 60137	3083	22W-3S	C5
Arbury Hills Elementary School 19651 Beechnut Dr, FftT, 60448	3503	11W-23S	E4
Arcadia Elementary School 20519 Arcadian Dr, OMFD, 60461	3506	4W-24S	E6
Archbishop Quigley Seminary School 103 E Chestnut St, CHCG, 60611	3034	0E-1N	C2
Archbishop Romero School 312 High St, AURA, 60505	3138	35W-7S	C7
Ardmore Elementary School 225 S Harvard Av, VLPK, 60181	3027	18W-0N	A4
Argo Community High School 7329 W 63rd St, SMMT, 60501	3148	9W-7S	D5
Arie Crown Hebrew Day School 4600 Main St, SKOK, 60076	2866	5W-10N	A4
Ariel Community Academy School 1119 E 46th St, CHCG, 60653	3093	1E-4S	A7
Armour Branch School 911 W 32nd Pl, CHCG, 60608	3091	1W-3S	E4
Armour Elementary School 950 W 33rd Pl, CHCG, 60608	3091	1W-3S	E4
Armstrong Math Science Spclty-School 5345 W Congress Pkwy, CHCG, 60644	3031	6W-0S	D6
Armstrong School 1320 Kingsdale Rd, HFET, 60169	2858	25W-12N	B2
Army Trail Elementary School 346 W Army Trail Blvd, ADSN, 60101	2970	18W-3N	E4
Arnold Mireles Academy 9000 S Exchange Av, CHCG, 60617	3215	3E-10S	E4
Arthur Ashe Elementary School 8505 S Ingleside Av, CHCG, 60619	3214	1E-9S	E3
Ascension School 601 Van Buren St, OKPK, 60304	3031	8W-0S	A6
Ashburn Community Elementary School 8300 S St. Louis Av, CHCG, 60652	3212	4W-9S	D3
Ashburn Lutheran School 3345 W 83rd St, CHCG, 60652	3212	4W-9S	D3
Attucks Elementary School 3813 S Dearborn St, CHCG, 60609	3092	0W-3S	C5
Audubon Elementary School 3500 N Hoyne Av, CHCG, 60618	2977	2W-4N	B3
Augustus H Burley Elementary School 1630 W Barry Av, CHCG, 60657	2977	2W-3N	C4
Aurora Central Catholic High School 1255 N Edgelawn Dr, AURA, 60506	3137	37W-5S	B4
Aurora Christian Elementary School 801 W Illinois Av, AURA, 60506	3137	36W-6S	E5
Aurora Christian Middle-High School 2255 Sullivan Rd, AURA, 60506	3137	38W-5S	A3
Austin Career Education Center 5352 W Chicago Av, CHCG, 60651	3031	6W-1N	D3
Austin Community Academy High-School 231 N Pine Av, CHCG, 60644	3031	6W-0N	D4
Avalon Park Elementary School 8045 S Kenwood Av, CHCG, 60619	3215	1E-9S	A2
Avery Coonley School 1400 Maple Av, DRGV, 60515	3144	20W-5S	B3
A Vito Martinez Middle School 590 Belmont Dr, RMVL, 60446	3340	24W-15S	D3
Avoca West Elementary School 235 Beech Dr, GNVW, 60025	2811	6W-13N	C6
Avon Center Elementary School 1617 Route 83, RLKB, 60046	2475	21W-35N	D6
Avondale Elementary School 2945 N Sawyer Av, CHCG, 60618	2976	4W-3N	D4
Bais Yaakov High School 3333 W Peterson Av, CHCG, 60659	2920	4W-7N	D4
Baker Demonstration School 2840 Sheridan Rd, EVTN, 60201	2813	2W-13N	B7
Balmoral Elementary School 1124 W New Monee Rd, CteT, 60417	3685	1W-31S	A5
Bannes Elementary School 16835 O'Dell Av, TYPK, 60477	3424	9W-20S	E3
Bannockburn Elementary School 2165 Telegraph Rd, BKBN, 60015	2703	11W-22N	C4
Barbara A Sizemore Charter Academy 1540 W 84th St, CHCG, 60620	3213	1W-9S	D3
Barbara B Rose Elementary 61 W Penny Rd, SBTN, 60010	2803	27W-14N	A3
Barrington High School 616 W Main St, BRTN, 60010	2750	26W-20N	D2
Barrington Middle School-Prairie 40 E Dundee Rd, BRTN, 60010	2751	24W-17N	B5
Barrington Middle School-Station 215 Eastern Av, BRTN, 60010	2751	24W-18N	B2
Bartlett Elementary School 111 E North Av, BRLT, 60103	2910	28W-8N	E3
Bartlett High School 701 W Schick Rd, BRLT, 60103	2966	29W-5N	D2
Barton Elementary School 7650 S Wolcott Av, CHCG, 60620	3213	2W-8S	C1
Bass Elementary School 1140 W 66th St, CHCG, 60621	3151	1W-7S	E5
Batavia High School 1200 W Wilson St, BTVA, 60510	3077	36W-1S	E2
Beach Park Middle School 40667 N Green Bay Rd, BHPK, 60099	2421	12W-40N	B3
Beacon Hill Elementary School 401 Concord Dr, CHHT, 60411	3595	2W-26S	D1
Beardsley Middle School 515 E Crystal Lake Av, CLLK, 60014	2640	34W-25N	C4
Beasley Academic Magnet School 5255 S State St, CHCG, 60615	3152	0E-5S	C2
Beaubien Elementary School 5025 N Laramie Av, CHCG, 60630	2919	6W-6N	D6
Beaupre Elementary School 954 E Benton St, AURA, 60505	3200	34W-8S	D1
Bednarcik Junior High School 10250 Heggs Rd, AURA, 60585	3265	32W-11S	C2
Beebe Elementary School 110 E 11th Av, NPVL, 60563	3141	26W-5S	D3
Beecher Elementary School 629 Penfield St, BCHR, 60401	3864	0W-36S	C2
Beecher High School 538 Miller St, BCHR, 60401	3864	0W-36S	C1

FEATURE NAME Address City ZIP Code	MAP#	CGS	GRID
Beecher Junior High School 629 Penfield St, BCHR, 60401	3864	0W-36S	C2
Beethoven Elementary School 25 W 47th St, CHCG, 60609	3152	0W-5S	C1
Belle Aire Elementary School 3935 Belle Aire Ln, DRGV, 60515	3084	20W-4S	B7
Bell-Graham Elementary School 4N505 Fox Mill Blvd, CmpT, 60175	2962	39W-4N	D4
Belmont-Cragin Community School 2456 N Mango Av, CHCG, 60639	2975	7W-3N	C6
Benet Academy 2200 Maple Av, LSLE, 60532	3142	24W-6S	D4
Benjamin Franklin Elementary School 350 Bryant Av, GNEN, 60137	3025	22W-0S	D6
Benjamin Franklin Elementary School 2401 Manor Ln, PKRG, 60068	2863	11W-10N	D5
Benjamin Middle School 28W300 St. Charles Rd, WynT, 60185	2967	28W-2N	B7
Bennett Elementary School 10115 S Prairie Av, CHCG, 60628	3214	0E-11S	D7
Benny Middle School 1401 Montesano Av, WKGN, 60087	2479	11W-36N	E4
Benson Primaryschool 301 E Washington St, ITSC, 60143	2914	19W-6N	C7
Bentley Elementary School 513 E Illinois Hwy, NLNX, 60451	3589	17W-25S	D1
Berger-Vandenberg Elementary School 14833 Avalon Av, DLTN, 60419	3351	1E-17S	B5
Bernard J Ward Elementary School 200 Recreation Dr, BGBK, 60440	3269	22W-12S	C2
Bernard Zell-Anshe Emet Day 3751 N Broadway St, CHCG, 60613	2978	0W-4N	A2
Bernhard Moos Elementary School 1711 N California Av, CHCG, 60647	2976	3W-2N	E7
Bessie Rhodes Magnet School 3701 Davis St, SKOK, 60076	2866	4W-11N	C3
BEST Academy 2719 E 89th St, CHCG, 60617	3215	3E-10S	E4
Bethany Lutheran School 1550 Modaff Rd, NPVL, 60565	3203	26W-8S	D2
Bethel Christian School 4215 W West End Av, CHCG, 60624	3032	5W-0N	B4
Bethune Elementary School 3030 W Arthington St, CHCG, 60612	3032	3W-0S	E6
Betsy Ross Elementary School 6059 S Wabash Av, CHCG, 60637	3152	0E-6S	C4
Betsy Ross Elementary School 1315 Marengo Av, FTPK, 60130	3030	9W-1S	D7
Betsy Ross Elementary School 700 N Schoenbeck Rd, PTHT, 60070	2807	16W-15N	E1
Beulah Park Elementary School 1910 Gilboa Av, ZION, 60099	2422	10W-41N	A2
Beverly Skoff Elementary School 775 W Normantown Rd, RMVL, 60446	3340	25W-16S	C3
Beye Elementary School 230 N Cuyler Av, OKPK, 60302	3031	7W-0N	B3
Bibich Elementary School 14600 81st Av, DYR, 46311	3598		E5
Bible Baptist Christian Academy 301 W Normantown Rd, RMVL, 60446	3340	24W-15S	E1
Big Hollow Elementary School 34699 N US Highway 12, FXLK, 60041	2473	27W-34N	B7
Big Hollow Primary School 33335 N Fish Lake Rd, GrtT, 60041	2530	26W-33N	E3
Birth to Kindergarten Center 15121 Dorchester Av, DLTN, 60419	3351	1E-17S	B6
BJ Hooper Elementary School 2400 E Sand Lake Rd, LNHT, 60046	2476	19W-37N	B2
Blackberry Creek Elementary School 1122 Anderson Rd, ELBN, 60119	3017	43W-0N	B5
Black Hawk Elementary School 2101 Gladstone Dr, GLHT, 60139	2969	23W-4N	A4
Blackhawk Intermidiate Center 130 Blackhawk Dr, PKFT, 60466	3595	3W-27S	A5
Blackhawk Middle School 250 S Church Rd, BNVL, 60106	2971	16W-5N	D2
Bloom Twp High School 101 W 10th St, CHHT, 60411	3508	1W-24S	A6
Bloom Trail High School 22331 Cottage Grove Av, STGR, 60411	3597	1E-26S	A3
Blythe Park Elementary School 735 Leesley Rd, RVSD, 60546	3088	9W-2S	D4
Bogan Computer Technical High-School 3939 W 79th St, CHCG, 60652	3212	4W-9S	C2
Bolingbrook High School 365 Raider Way, BGBK, 60440	3268	24W-12S	D3
Bond Elementary School 7050 S May St, CHCG, 60621	3151	1W-7S	E6
Bontemps Elementary School 1241 W 58th St, CHCG, 60636	3151	1W-6S	E3
Booth Central Elementary School 201 N Kankakee St, WMTN, 60481	3853	27W-38S	D6
Bouchet Academy 7355 S Jeffery Blvd, CHCG, 60649	3153	2E-8S	C7
Bouchet Branch Elementary School 7401 S Chappel Av, CHCG, 60649	3153	2E-8S	C7
Boulder Hill Elementary School 163 Boulder Hill Pass, OswT, 60538	3199	36W-10S	D7
Bowen Environmental Studies High-School 2710 E 89th St, CHCG, 60617	3215	3E-10S	E4
Bower Elementary School 4s241 River Rd, WNVL, 60555	3081	28W-4S	A7
Braceville Elementary School 209 N Mitchell St, BCVL, 60407	4030	33W-44S	A4
Bradwell Math-Science-Tech School 7736 S Burnham Av, CHCG, 60649	3215	3E-8S	E1
Braeside Elementary School 150 Pierce Rd, HDPK, 60035	2758	7W-20N	C2
Bremen High School 15203 Pulaski Rd, MDLN, 60445	3348	4W-18S	C6
Brennemann Elementary School 4251 N Clarendon Av, CHCG, 60613	2977	0W-5N	E1
Brentano Elementary Math & Science-Academy 2723 N Fairfield Av, CHCG, 60647	2977	3W-3N	A5
Brentwood Baptist Christian Academy 588 Dara James Rd, DSPN, 60016	2862	15W-11N	A3
Brentwood Elementary School 260 Dulles Rd, DSPN, 60016	2862	15W-11N	B3

Chicago 7-County Points of Interest Index

FEATURE NAME Address City ZIP Code	MAP#	CGS	GRID
Briargate Elementary School 100 S Wulff St, CRY, 60013	2695	31W-23N	D1
Briar Glen Elementary School 1800 Briarcliffe Blvd, WHTN, 60187	3082	23W-2S	E3
Brickton Montessori School 8622 W Catalpa Av, CHCG, 60656	2917	10W-6N	E5
Bridgeport Catholic Academy 3700 S Lowe Av, CHCG, 60609	3092	0W-3S	A5
Bridges Montessori Academy 716 Oak St, SCRL, 60174	2964	36W-2N	A7
Bridgeview Elementary School 7800 Thomas Av, BGVW, 60455	3210	9W-8S	D2
Bright Elementary School 10740 S Calhoun Av, CHCG, 60617	3279	2E-12S	D2
Brighton Park Elementary School 3825 S Washtenaw Av, CHCG, 60632	3091	3W-3S	A5
Bristol Grade School 23 Hunt St, BtlT, 60512	3261	42W-12S	E3
British School of Chicago 1643 W Bryn Mawr Av, CHCG, 60640	2921	2W-6N	C4
Broadview Academy 41W501 Keslinger Rd, BbyT, 60119	3017	41W-0N	E4
Brodnicki Elementary School 8641 W 75th St, JSTC, 60458	3210	10W-8S	A1
Bronzeville Lighthouse Charter-School 8 W Root St, CHCG, 60609	3092	0W-4S	C6
Brookdale Elementary School 1200 Redfield Rd, NPVL, 60563	3140	29W-5S	E3
Brook Forest Elementary School 60 Regent Dr, OKBK, 60523	3085	17W-2S	C3
Brook Park Elementary School 1214 Raymond Av, LGPK, 60525	3087	11W-2S	D4
Brooks College Prep Academy 250 E 111th St, CHCG, 60628	3278	0E-12S	D2
Brooks Elementary School 2700 Stonebridge Blvd, AURA, 60502	3139	32W-5S	C3
Brooks Middle School 350 Blair Ln, BGBK, 60440	3269	23W-11S	A1
Brookwood Elementary School 630 Kossuth St, GNCY, 53128	2353		A3
Brookwood Junior High School 201 E Glenwood Lansing Rd, GNWD, 60425	3508	0E-22S	E2
Brookwood Middle School 1020 Hunters Ridge Dr, GNCY, 53128	2353		B1
Brookwood Middle School 200 E Glenwood Lansing Rd, GNWD, 60425	3508	0E-23S	E2
Brother Rice High School 10001 S Pulaski Rd, CHCG, 60655	3212	4W-11S	C7
Bruning Elementary School 1910 Bruning Dr, WslT, 60481	3943	27W-40S	D3
Brunson Elementary School 932 N Central Av, CHCG, 60651	3031	7W-1N	C2
Bryan Middle School 111 W Butterfield Rd, EMHT, 60126	3027	16W-0S	E6
Bryant Elementary School 14730 Main St, HRVY, 60426	3350	1W-17S	A5
Buffalo Grove High School 1100 W Dundee Rd, BFGV, 60089	2754	17W-18N	A4
Builta Elementary School 1835 Apple Valley Rd, BGBK, 60490	3267	27W-12S	C3
Burnham Branch Elementary School 9800 S Torrence Av, CHCG, 60617	3215	3E-11S	E6
Burnham Elementary Inclusive-Academy 1903 E 96th St, CHCG, 60617	3215	2E-11S	C6
Burnham Elementary School 13945 S Green Bay Av, BNHM, 60633	3352	3E-16S	B3
Burnham Elementary School 1630 S 59th Av, CCRO, 60804	3089	7W-1S	C1
Burnside Scholastic Academy 650 E 91st Pl, CHCG, 60619	3214	0E-10S	E5
Burr Oak Academy 1441 W 124th St, CTPK, 60827	3277	1W-14S	D6
Burr Oak Elementary School 1440 W 125th St, CTPK, 60827	3277	1W-14S	D6
Burr Ridge Middle School 15W451 91st St, BRRG, 60527	3208	15W-10S	B5
Bush Elementary School 2117 Church St, JNBG, 60050	2471	31W-35N	E5
Butler Junior High School 2801 York Rd, OKBK, 60523	3086	15W-2S	B3
Butterfield Elementary School 1441 Lake St, LYVL, 60048	2591	17W-29N	A4
Butterfield Elementary School 2S500 Gray Av, MltT, 60148	3083	21W-2S	E4
Byrd Elementary School 265 Wellington Av, EGVV, 60007	2914	19W-8N	C3
Caldwell Elementary School 8546 S Cregier Av, CHCG, 60617	3215	2E-9S	B3
Calumet Academy High School 8131 S May St, CHCG, 60620	3213	1W-9S	E2
Calumet Elementary School 1440 W Vermont Av, CTPK, 60827	3277	1W-15S	E7
Calvary Academy 16300 State St, SHLD, 60473	3428	0W-19S	D1
Calvin Christian School 528 E 161st Pl, SHLD, 60473	3428	0E-18S	E1
Cambridge Lakes Charter School 900 Wester Blvd, PGGV, 60140	2797	41W-15N	E4
Cameron Elementary School 1234 N Monticello Av, CHCG, 60651	3032	4W-1N	C1
Campanelli Elementary School 310 S Springinsguth Rd, SMBG, 60193	2858	25W-10N	B6
Canterbury Elementary School 875 Canterbury Dr, CLLK, 60014	2640	35W-24N	B7
Canter Middle School 4959 S Blackstone Av, CHCG, 60615	3153	1E-5S	A1
Canton Middle School 1100 Sunset Cir, SMWD, 60107	2857	27W-10N	C5
Canty Elementary School 3740 N Panama Av, CHCG, 60634	2974	10W-4N	B2
Cardenas Elementary School 2345 S Millard Av, CHCG, 60623	3090	4W-2S	D2
Cardinal Bernardin Early Childhood-Center 1651 W Diversey Pkwy, CHCG, 60614	2977	2W-3N	C5
Carleton Washburne Middle School 515 Hibbard Rd, WNKA, 60093	2811	5W-15N	E2
Carl Sandburg Elementary School 1100 Lilac Ln, JLET, 60435	3497	26W-22S	E2
Carl Sandburg High School 13300 S La Grange Rd, PlsT, 60462	3345	12W-15S	D2
Carl Sandburg Junior High School 2600 Martin Ln, RGMW, 60008	2806	19W-13N	C6
Carl Von Linne Elementary School 3221 N Sacramento Av, CHCG, 60618	2976	3W-4N	E3
Carman-Buckner Elementary School 520 Helmholz Av, WKGN, 60085	2537	10W-33N	A3
Carmel High School 1 Carmel Pkwy, MDLN, 60060	2591	18W-28N	A7
Carnegie Elementary School 1414 E 61st Pl, CHCG, 60637	3153	1E-6S	A4
Caroline Sibley Elementary School 1550 Sibley Blvd, CTCY, 60409	3351	2E-17S	D5
Carol Mosely Braun Elementary-School 1655 153rd St, CTCY, 60409	3351	2E-17S	D6
Carol Stream Elementary School 422 Sioux Ln, CLSM, 60188	2967	26W-2N	E7
Carpenter Elementary School 1250 W Erie St, CHCG, 60622	3033	1W-0N	D3
Carpentersville Middle School 100 Cleveland Av, CPVL, 60110	2800	34W-16N	E1
Carroll Elementary School 2929 W 83rd St, CHCG, 60652	3212	3W-9S	E3
Carson Elementary School 5516 S Maplewood Av, CHCG, 60629	3151	3W-6S	A3
Carter Elementary School 5740 S Michigan Av, CHCG, 60637	3152	0E-6S	C3
Caruso Middle School 1801 Montgomery Rd, DRFD, 60015	2703	12W-21N	B7
Carver Middle School 801 E 133rd Pl, CHCG, 60827	3350	0E-15S	E1
Carver Military Academy High School 13100 S Doty Av, CHCG, 60827	3279	1E-15S	A7
Carver Primary School 901 E 133rd Pl, CHCG, 60827	3350	0E-15S	E1
Cary-Grove Community High School 2208 Three Oaks Rd, AlqT, 60013	2641	30W-24N	E6
Cary Junior High School 2109 Crystal Lake Rd, CRY, 60013	2641	31W-25N	E5
Cassell Elementary School 11314 S Spaulding Av, CHCG, 60655	3276	4W-13S	E3
Cass Junior High School 8502 Bailey Rd, DRN, 60561	3207	18W-9S	A4
Cathedral of St. Raymond School 713 Douglas St, JLET, 60435	3498	24W-23S	D3
Cather Elementary School 2908 W Washington Blvd, CHCG, 60612	3032	3W-0N	E4
Catherine Cook School 226 W Schiller St, CHCG, 60610	3034	0W-1N	B1
Centennial Elementary School 14101 Creek Crossing Dr, ODPK, 60467	3344	14W-16S	E4
Centennial Elementary School 800 S West St, PLNO, 60545	3259	47W-14S	C7
Centennial School 234 E Stearns Rd, BRLT, 60103	2911	27W-6N	B6
Central Elementary School 620 Greenwood Av, GLNC, 60022	2758	6W-17N	D5
Central Elementary School 400 N Division St, HRVD, 60033	2406	50W-38N	B6
Central Elementary School 350 W Washington Av, LKBF, 60044	2593	11W-29N	D5
Central Elementary School 61 Woodside Rd, RVSD, 60546	3088	9W-3S	C5
Central Elementary School 900 Central Av, WLMT, 60091	2812	3W-13N	E6
Central Junior High School 9400 S Sawyer Av, ENGN, 60805	3212	4W-10S	E5
Central Junior High School 1716 27th St, ZION, 60099	2422	10W-40N	A4
Central Middle School 18146 Oak Park Av, TYPK, 60477	3425	8W-21S	A7
Central Park Elementary School 3621 151st St, MDLN, 60445	3348	4W-18S	D6
Central Road Elementary School 3800 Central Rd, RGMW, 60008	2806	20W-13N	B7
Central School 1526 E Thacker St, DSPN, 60016	2863	13W-10N	A4
Central School 410 McCarthy Rd, LMNT, 60439	3270	19W-13S	D5
Century Junior High School 10801 W 159th St, ODPK, 60467	3423	13W-19S	A1
Century Oaks Elementary School 1235 Braeburn Dr, ELGN, 60123	2800	35W-13N	B7
Chalmers Speciality School 2745 W Roosevelt Rd, CHCG, 60608	3033	3W-1S	A7
Chaney Elementary School 400 Elsie Av, CTHL, 60403	3418	24W-21S	D7
Channing Memorial Elementary School 63 S Channing St, ELGN, 60120	2855	33W-11N	A4
Chappell Elementary School 2135 W Foster Av, CHCG, 60625	2921	2W-6N	B6
Charles E Hughes Elementary School 4247 W 15th St, CHCG, 60623	3032	5W-1S	B7
Charles J Sahs Elementary School 5001 S Long Av, StkT, 60638	3149	6W-5S	D2
Charles Quentin Elementary School 21250 W Shirley Rd, ElaT, 60074	2752	21W-20N	E1
Charles S Brownell Elementary-School 6741 S Michigan Av, CHCG, 60637	3152	0E-7S	C6
Charles W Earle Elementary School 6121 S Hermitage Av, CHCG, 60636	3151	2W-6S	C4
Chase Elementary School 2021 N Point St, CHCG, 60647	2977	3W-2N	A6
Chateaux School 3600 Chambord Ln, HLCT, 60429	3426	4W-21S	E6
Chauncy H Duker Elementary School 3711 W Kane Av, MHRY, 60050	2528	32W-32N	B4
Chavez Multicultural Academy Center 4747 S Marshfield Av, CHCG, 60609	3151	2W-5S	D1
Chavez Upper Grade Center 4831 S Hermitage Av, CHCG, 60609	3151	2W-5S	C1
Cheder Lubavitch School 5201 Howard St, SKOK, 60077	2865	6W-9N	D7
Chelsea Intermediate School 601 Willow St, FKFT, 60423	3503	12W-25S	D7
Cherokee Elementary School 475 Cherokee Rd, LKFT, 60045	2650	10W-25N	A6
Chesterbrook Academy 1571 Oswego Rd, NPVL, 60540	3140	28W-7S	E7
Chiaravalle Montessori School 425 Dempster St, EVTN, 60201	2867	2W-11N	B3
Chicago Academy 3400 N Austin Av, CHCG, 60634	2975	7W-4N	B3
Chicago Academy for the Arts 1010 W Chicago Av, CHCG, 60622	3033	1W-1N	E2
Chicago Academy High School 3400 N Austin Av, CHCG, 60634	2975	7W-4N	B3
Chicago City Day School 541 W Hawthorne Pl, CHCG, 60657	2978	0W-4N	A3
Chicago Discovery Academy 2710 E 89th St, CHCG, 60617	3215	3E-10S	E4
Chicago High School for Agri-Sciences 3857 W 111th St, CHCG, 60655	3276	4W-13S	C3
Chicago Int'l Charter Sch-Basil-Campus 1816 W Garfield Blvd, CHCG, 60609	3151	2W-5S	C3
Chicago International Charter Sch-Bucktown 2235 N Hamilton Av, CHCG, 60647	2977	2W-2N	B6
Chicago International Charter Sch-Longwood 1309 W 95th St, CHCG, 60643	3213	1W-11S	D6
Chicago International Charter School-Prairie 11530 S Prairie Av, CHCG, 60628	3278	0E-13S	D4
Chicago Int'l Charter Sch-St.-Edmunds 6105 S Michigan Av, CHCG, 60637	3152	0E-6S	C4
Chicago Math & Science Academy 1705 W Lunt Av, CHCG, 60626	2921	2W-8N	C1
Chicago Military Academy 3519 S Giles Av, CHCG, 60653	3092	0E-3S	C5
Chicago Vocational Career Academy 2100 E 87th St, CHCG, 60617	3215	2E-9S	C3
Chicago Waldorf School 1300 W Loyola Av, CHCG, 60626	2921	1W-8N	D2
Chicago West Side Christian School 1240 S Pulaski Rd, CHCG, 60623	3032	5W-1S	B7
Children of Peace-Holy Trinity 1900 W Taylor St, CHCG, 60612	3033	2W-0S	C6
Childs Elementary School 14123 S Lydia Av, RBBN, 60472	3348	4W-16S	E3
Chippewa Elementary School 322 S York Rd, BNVL, 60106	2971	16W-4N	E2
Chippewa Elementary School 12425 S Austin Av, WthT, 60803	3275	7W-14S	C6
Chippewa Middle School 123 N 8th Av, DSPN, 60016	2862	14W-12N	D2
Choir Academy 3737 S Paulina St, CHCG, 60609	3091	2W-3S	C5
Chopin Elementary School 2450 W Rice St, CHCG, 60622	3033	3W-1N	A2
Christian Ebinger Elementary School 7350 W Pratt Av, CHCG, 60631	2918	9W-8N	D1
Christian Heritage Academy 315 Waukegan Rd, NHFD, 60093	2810	8W-15N	E2
Christian Hills School 9001 159th St, ODHL, 60487	3424	11W-19S	A1
Christian Liberty Academy 502 W Euclid Av, ANHT, 60004	2806	18W-14N	E4
Christopher Columbus Elementary-School 1003 N Leavitt St, CHCG, 60622	3033	2W-1N	B2
Christ Our Savior School-E Campus 320 156th St, CTCY, 60409	3352	4E-18S	B7
Christ Our Savior School-West-Campus 900 E 154th St, SHLD, 60473	3351	1E-17S	A6
Christ the King School 9240 S Hoyne Av, CHCG, 60620	3213	2W-10S	C5
Christ the King School 115 E 15th St, YkTp, 60148	3084	19W-1S	C1
Churchill Elementary School 240 Geneva Rd, GNEN, 60137	3025	23W-1N	A3
Churchill Elementary School 520 Secretariat Ln, OSWG, 60543	3264	34W-12S	C2
Chute Middle School 1400 Oakton St, EVTN, 60202	2867	3W-9N	A6
Cicero East Elementary School 2324 S 49th Av, CCRO, 60804	3089	6W-2S	E2
Cicero West Elementary School 4937 W 23rd St, CCRO, 60804	3089	6W-2S	E2
CICS West Belden Campus 2245 N McVicker Av, CHCG, 60639	2975	7W-2N	B6
CI Johnson Elementary School 1934 Liberty St, AraT, 60505	3139	33W-7S	A6
Circle Center Grade School 901 Mill St, YKVL, 60560	3333	42W-15S	C3
Circle Rock Prep School 118 N Central Av, CHCG, 60644	3031	7W-0N	C4
City Baptist Schools 4925 S Sohl Av, HMND, 46327	3352		E5
Claremont Academy 2300 W 64th St, CHCG, 60636	3151	2W-7S	B5
Clarendon Hills Middle School 301 Chicago Av, CNHL, 60514	3145	17W-5S	C1
Clark Academic Prep High School 5101 W Harrison St, CHCG, 60644	3031	6W-0S	E6
Clark Elementary School 601 Blanchard Rd, WKGN, 60087	2480	10W-36N	A3
Clark Middle-High School 1921 Davis Av, HMND, 46394	3280		E4
Clay Elementary School 13231 S Burley Av, CHCG, 60633	3352	3E-15S	A1
Clay Elementary School 112 Grove St, WDSK, 60098	2524	41W-31N	D6
Clearmont Elementary School 280 Clearmont Dr, EGVV, 60007	2914	18W-8N	E2
Clearview Elementary School 1700 Delaware Rd, WKGN, 60087	2479	11W-36N	D5
Clemente Community Academy High-School 1147 N Western Av, CHCG, 60622	3033	2W-1N	B1
Cleveland Elementary School 3121 W Byron St, CHCG, 60618	2976	3W-4N	D2
Clinton Elementary School 770 Mill St, SEGN, 60177	2908	34W-8N	E3
Cloverdale School 1182 Merbach Dr, CLSM, 60188	2968	26W-4N	A4

Chicago 7-County Points of Interest Index

FEATURE NAME Address City ZIP Code	MAP#	CGS	GRID
Clow Elementary School 1301 Springdale Cir, NPVL, 60564	3203	28W-10S	A6
CM Bardwell Elementary School 550 S Lincoln Av, AURA, 60505	3200	35W-8S	A2
Coleman Elementary School 1220 Dundee Av, ELGN, 60120	2855	33W-13N	B1
Colemon Academy 1441 W 119th St, CHCG, 60643	3277	1W-14S	D5
Coles Language Academy 8441 S Yates Blvd, CHCG, 60617	3215	3E-9S	D3
College Prep School of America 331 W Madison St, LMBD, 60148	3026	20W-0S	A5
Collins Elementary School 407 Summit Dr, SMBG, 60193	2859	22W-9N	B6
Collins High School 1313 S Sacramento Dr, CHCG, 60623	3032	3W-1S	E7
Columbia Explorers Academy 4520 S Kedzie Av, CHCG, 60632	3090	4W-4S	E7
Columbia School 94 Richton Rd, CRTE, 60417	3596	1W-28S	B7
Columbus East Elementary School 3100 S 54th Av, CCRO, 60804	3089	6W-3S	D4
Columbus Manor Elementary School 9700 Mayfield Av, OKLN, 60453	3211	7W-11S	C6
Columbus West Elementary School 5425 W 31st St, CCRO, 60804	3089	6W-3S	D4
Community High School 326 Joliet St, WCHI, 60185	3022	30W-0N	C5
Concord Elementary School 1019 Concord Pl, DRN, 60561	3207	17W-9S	B2
Concord Lutheran School 865 S Church Rd, BNVL, 60106	2971	16W-4N	D4
Congregation Betham School 225 McHenry Rd, BFGV, 60089	2754	16W-20N	C2
Congress Park Elementary School 9311 Shields Av, BKFD, 60513	3087	11W-4S	D7
Conley Elementary School 750 Academic Dr, ALGN, 60102	2746	38W-20N	A1
Connor Shaw Center 212 W Wilson St, PTON, 60468	3860	9W-37S	E3
Conrad Fischer Elementary School 888 N Wilson St, EMHT, 60126	2972	15W-3N	A5
Conrady Junior High School 7950 W 97th St, HYHL, 60457	3210	9W-11S	C6
Cooke Magnet Elementary School 522 Belvidere St, WKGN, 60085	2537	10W-33N	A2
Coolidge Elementary School 17845 Henry St, LNSG, 60438	3430	4E-21S	B5
Coolidge Middle School 155th St, PHNX, 60426	3350	0W-18S	C7
Cooper Dual Language Academy 1624 W 19th St, CHCG, 60608	3091	2W-1S	C1
Cooper Middle School 1050 Plum Grove Cir, BFGV, 60089	2754	17W-18N	A2
Copeland Manor Elementary School 801 7th Av, LYVL, 60048	2591	15W-28N	E6
Copernicus Elementary School 6010 S Throop St, CHCG, 60636	3151	1W-6S	E4
Corkery Elementary School 2510 S Kildare Av, CHCG, 60623	3090	5W-2S	B2
Corliss High School 821 E 103rd St, CHCG, 60628	3278	1E-12S	E1
Cossitt Elementary School 115 W Cossitt Av, LGNG, 60525	3087	12W-4S	B7
Costello School 4632 Clyde Av, LYNS, 60534	3148	10W-4S	B1
Cottage Grove Middle School 800 E Lincoln Hwy, FDHT, 60411	3509	1E-25S	A7
Cotton Creek Elementary School 545 Newport Ct, ISLK, 60042	2586	29W-28N	C5
Coultrap Elementary School 1113 Peyton St, GNVA, 60134	3020	35W-1N	A3
Country Meadows Montessori School 6151 Washington St, GRNE, 60031	2534	16W-34N	D1
Countryside Elementary School 205 W County Line Rd, BNHL, 60010	2750	27W-18N	A2
Countryside Montessori School 1985 Pfingsten Rd, NHBK, 60062	2756	10W-16N	E7
Courtenay Language Arts Center 1726 W Berteau Av, CHCG, 60613	2977	2W-5N	C1
Coventry Elementary School 820 Darlington Ln, CLLK, 60014	2640	35W-24N	A7
Covington Elementary School 9130 S 52nd Av, OKLN, 60453	3211	6W-10S	E5
Cowherd Middle School 441 N Farnsworth Av, AURA, 60505	3138	33W-7S	E7
Cowlishaw Elementary School 1212 Sanctuary Ln, NPVL, 60540	3202	29W-8S	D1
Crane Achievement Academy High-School 2245 W Jackson Blvd, CHCG, 60612	3033	2W-0S	B5
Creekside Elementary School 655 N Airlite St, ELGN, 60123	2854	36W-12N	A2
Creekside Elementary School 13909 S Budler Rd, PnfT, 60544	3339	27W-16S	C4
Crete Elementary School 435 North St, CRTE, 60417	3685	0W-29S	B2
Crete Lutheran School 448 Cass St, CRTE, 60417	3685	0W-29S	B2
Crete-Monee High School 760 W Exchange St, CRTE, 60417	3685	1W-29S	A2
Crete-Monee Intermediate Center 1124 W New Monee Rd, CteT, 60417	3685	1W-31S	A5
Crete-Monee Middle School 635 Olmstead Ln, UYPK, 60449	3684	3W-31S	B4
Cristo Rey Jesuit High School 1852 W 22nd Pl, CHCG, 60608	3091	2W-2S	C2
Crone Middle School 4020 111th St, WldT, 60564	3266	31W-13S	A4
Crow Island Elementary School 1112 Willow Rd, WNKA, 60093	2811	5W-15N	E2
Crown Community Academy 2128 S St. Louis Av, CHCG, 60623	3090	4W-1S	D1
Crystal Lake Central High School 45 W Franklin Av, CLLK, 60014	2640	35W-25N	A4
Crystal Lake Montessori School 3013 S Country Club Rd, DrrT, 60098	2583	37W-29N	A5
Crystal Lake South High School 1200 S McHenry Av, CLLK, 60014	2693	36W-23N	D1
Crystal Lawns Elementary School 2544 Crystal Dr, PnfT, 60435	3417	27W-20S	C5
Cuffe Math-Science-Tech Academy 8324 S Racine Av, CHCG, 60620	3213	1W-9S	E3
Culbertson Elementary School 1521 E Washington St, JLET, 60433	3499	22W-24S	D5
Cullen Elementary School 10650 S Eberhart Av, CHCG, 60628	3278	0E-12S	D1
Culver School 6901 W Oakton St, NLES, 60714	2864	8W-9N	E6
Cumberland Elementary School 700 E Golf Rd, DSPN, 60016	2862	14W-12N	D2
Cunningham Elementary School 500 Moran St, JLET, 60435	3498	24W-22S	D2
Curie Metropolitan High School 4959 S Archer Av, CHCG, 60632	3150	4W-5S	C1
Currier Elementary School 800 Garys Mill Rd, WnfT, 60185	3080	29W-0S	D1
Curtis Elementary School 32 E 115th St, CHCG, 60628	3278	0E-13S	C4
Dan H Pietrini Elementary School 9750 Fullerton Av, FNPK, 60131	2973	11W-3N	C6
Daniel Boone Elementary School 6710 N Washtenaw Av, CHCG, 60645	2920	3W-8N	E2
Daniel Wright Junior High School 1370 N Riverwoods Rd, LNSH, 60069	2702	14W-24N	D1
Darwin Elementary School 3116 W Belden Av, CHCG, 60647	2976	3W-2N	E6
Davinci Academy 37w080 Hopps Rd, ELGN, 60123	2854	36W-11N	A4
Davis Elementary School 3014 W 39th Pl, CHCG, 60632	3090	3W-4S	E6
Davis Elementary School 1125 S 7th St, SCRL, 60174	3020	35W-2N	A1
Dawes Elementary School 3810 W 81st Pl, CHCG, 60652	3212	4W-9S	C2
Dawes Elementary School 440 Dodge Av, EVTN, 60202	2866	3W-9N	E6
Dayspring Christian Academy 5133 W Fullerton Av, CHCG, 60639	2975	6W-3N	D5
DD Eisenhower High School 12700 Sacramento Av, BLID, 60406	3277	3W-14S	A7
Dean Street Elementary School 600 Dean St, WDSK, 60098	2581	41W-30N	C1
Decatur Classical Elementary School 7030 N Sacramento Av, CHCG, 60645	2920	3W-8N	E1
De Diego Community Academy 1313 N Claremont Av, CHCG, 60622	3033	2W-1N	B1
Deer Creek Christian School 425 University Pkwy, UYPK, 60466	3684	3W-29S	B1
Deerfield High School 1959 Waukegan Rd, DRFD, 60015	2703	11W-22N	D4
Deer Path Elementary School 2211 Crystal Lake Rd, CRY, 60013	2641	31W-25N	E5
Deer Path Middle School East 95 W Deerpath Rd, LKFT, 60045	2649	11W-26N	E3
Deer Path Middle School West 155 W Deerpath Rd, LKFT, 60045	2649	11W-26N	E3
Delano Elementary School 3937 W Wilcox St, CHCG, 60624	3032	4W-0S	C5
De La Salle Institute-Main Campus 3455 S Wabash Av, CHCG, 60616	3092	0E-3S	C4
De La Salle Institute-West Campus 1040 W 32nd Pl, CHCG, 60608	3091	1W-3S	D4
Deneen Elementary School 7240 S Wabash Av, CHCG, 60619	3152	0E-8S	C7
Depriest Elementary School 139 S Parkside Av, CHCG, 60644	3031	7W-0S	C5
Dett Elementary School 2306 W Maypole Av, CHCG, 60612	3033	2W-0N	B4
Dever Elementary School 3436 N Osceola Av, CHCG, 60634	2974	9W-4N	C3
Devonshire Elementary School 1401 Pennsylvania Av, DSPN, 60018	2862	15W-10N	B5
Devonshire Elementary School 9040 Kostner Av, SKOK, 60076	2866	5W-11N	A3
Devry University Academy 3300 N Campbell Av, CHCG, 60618	2977	3W-4N	A3
Dewey Academy of Fine Arts 5415 S Union Av, CHCG, 60609	3152	0W-5S	A2
Dewey Elementary School 1551 Wesley Av, EVTN, 60201	2867	3W-11N	A3
DeWitt Clinton Elementary School 6110 N Fairfield Av, CHCG, 60659	2920	3W-7N	E3
Diamond Lake Elementary School 25807 N Diamond Lake Rd, VrnT, 60060	2646	18W-25N	D4
Diekman Elementary School 15121 Dorchester Av, DLTN, 60419	3351	1E-17S	B6
Dirksen Elementary School 8601 W Foster Av, CHCG, 60656	2918	10W-6N	A6
Dirksen Elementary School 116 W Beech Dr, SMBG, 60193	2859	23W-10N	A6
Dirksen Junior High School 203 S Midland Av, JLET, 60436	3498	25W-24S	B5
Dirksen Middle School 1650 Pulaski Rd, CTCY, 60409	3351	2E-17S	D6
Disney Magnet Elementary School 4140 N Marine Dr, CHCG, 60613	2978	0W-5N	A1
Divine Infant Jesus School 1640 Newcastle Av, WSTR, 60154	3087	12W-1S	B1
Divine Providence School 2500 Mayfair Av, WSTR, 60154	3086	13W-2S	E3
Dixon Elementary School 8306 S St. Lawrence Av, CHCG, 60619	3214	0E-9S	D3
Dodge Renaissance Academy 2651 W Washington Blvd, CHCG, 60612	3033	3W-0N	A4
Dooley Elementary School 622 Norwood Ln, SMBG, 60193	2858	24W-9N	D7
Doolittle East School 535 E 35th St, CHCG, 60653	3092	0E-3S	D4
Dore Elementary School 6108 S Natoma Av, CHCG, 60638	3149	8W-6S	A4
Dorn Primary Center 7840 W 92nd St, HYHL, 60457	3210	9W-10S	C5
Douglass Junior High Academy 543 N Waller Av, CHCG, 60644	3031	7W-0N	C3
Downers Grove Christian School 929 Maple Av, DRGV, 60515	3144	19W-5S	C3
Downers Grove North High School 4436 Main St, DRGV, 60515	3144	19W-4S	C1
Downers Grove South High School 1436 Norfolk St, DRGV, 60516	3144	20W-7S	B6
Drauden Point Middle School 1911 Drauden Rd, JLET, 60586	3415	31W-21S	E7
Dr Charles E Gavin Elementary-School 280 E 12th St, CHHT, 60411	3508	0W-25S	C7
Drexel Elementary School 5407 W 36th St, CCRO, 60804	3089	6W-3S	D5
Driscoll Catholic High School 555 N Lombard Rd, ADSN, 60101	2970	20W-4N	B4
Dr Julian Rogus Elementary School 20027 S 88th Av, FftT, 60477	3504	10W-23S	B4
Dryden Elementary School 722 S Dryden Pl, ANHT, 60005	2807	17W-13N	B6
Du Jardin Elementary School 166 Euclid Av, BMDL, 60108	2969	22W-5N	C2
Dulles Elementary School 6311 S Calumet Av, CHCG, 60637	3152	0E-7S	D5
Dumas Elementary School 6650 S Ellis Av, CHCG, 60637	3152	1E-7S	E5
Dundee-Crown High School 1 Charger Country Dr, CPVL, 60110	2748	33W-18N	A5
Dundee Highlands Elementary School 407 S 5th St, WDND, 60118	2800	34W-15N	E3
Dundee Middle School 37W450 Route 72, DndT, 60118	2799	37W-16N	D2
Dunne Elementary School 10845 S Union Av, CHCG, 60628	3278	0W-12S	A2
DuPage Montessori School 24W500 Maple Av, LSLE, 60532	3142	24W-6S	C4
Durkin Park Elementary School 8445 S Kolin Av, CHCG, 60652	3212	5W-9S	B3
Du Sable High School 4934 S Wabash Av, CHCG, 60615	3152	0E-5S	C1
Dvorak Math-Science Tech Academy 3615 W 16th St, CHCG, 60623	3090	4W-1S	D1
Dwight D Eisenhower School 700 N Schoenbeck Rd, PTHT, 60070	2807	16W-15N	E1
Dyett Academic Center 555 E 51st St, CHCG, 60615	3152	0E-5S	D2
Eads Elementary School 8000 Jackson Av, MNSR, 46321	3430		D6
Eagle Point Elementary School 24562 Norwood Dr, PNFD, 60585	3338	30W-15S	B2
Eagles Wings Urban Academy 2447 W Granville Av, CHCG, 60659	2921	3W-7N	A3
Earhart Elementary School 1710 E 93rd St, CHCG, 60617	3215	2E-10S	B5
Early Education Center 882 Nippersink Av, RDLK, 60073	2531	24W-33N	D3
East Aurora High School 500 Tomcat Ln, AURA, 60505	3200	34W-8S	C2
East Elementary School 121 E Sheridan Pl, LKBF, 60044	2593	10W-28N	E6
East Elementary School 2913 Elim Av, ZION, 60099	2422	9W-39N	C4
East Leyden High School 3400 Rose St, FNPK, 60131	2973	12W-4N	C3
East Middle School 201 N Butrick St, WKGN, 60085	2536	11W-34N	E1
East Prairie Elementary School 3907 Dobson St, SKOK, 60076	2866	4W-9N	B6
Eastview Elementary School 540 Longwood Dr, ALGN, 60102	2695	33W-20N	A7
Eastview Elementary School 3411 Hopkins St, CRTE, 60417	3596	0W-28S	C5
East View Elementary School 4209 State Route 71, OSWG, 60543	3263	37W-12S	D3
Eastview Middle School 321 N Oak Av, BRLT, 60103	2910	28W-8N	E2
Echo Early Childhood Program 640 E 168th Pl, SHLD, 60473	3428	0E-19S	E3
Edgar Allen Poe Classical School 10538 S Langley Av, CHCG, 60628	3278	0E-12S	E1
Edgar A Poe Elementary School 2800 N Highland Av, ANHT, 60004	2754	18W-17N	A6
Edgebrook Elementary School 6525 N Hiawatha Av, CHCG, 60646	2919	6W-8N	D2
Edgebrook Elementary School 701 N Green St, MHRY, 60050	2528	32W-32N	B4
Edgewood Elementary School 7900 Woodridge Dr, WDRG, 60517	3205	21W-8S	D2
Edgewood Middle School 929 Edgewood Rd, HDPK, 60035	2704	8W-21N	E7
Edison Elementary School 246 S Fair Av, EMHT, 60126	3028	15W-1N	B3
Edison Elementary School 7025 Madison Av, HMND, 46324	3430		E3
Edison Elementary School 4100 Scoville Av, SKNY, 60402	3089	8W-4S	A6
Edison Middle School 1125 S Wheaton Av, WHTN, 60187	3082	24W-1S	C1
Edison Regional Gifted Center 6220 N Olcott Av, CHCG, 60631	2918	9W-7N	C3
Edmond H Taveirne Middle School 34699 N US Highway 12, FXLK, 60041	2473	27W-34N	B7
Edmund Burke Elementary School 5356 S King Dr, CHCG, 60615	3152	0E-5S	D2
Edna Keith Elementary School 400 4th Av, JLET, 60433	3499	23W-24S	B6
Edward Everett Elementary School 3419 S Bell Av, CHCG, 60608	3091	2W-3S	B4
Eggers Middle School 5825 Blaine Av, HMND, 46320	3352		D7
Einstein Academy 747 Davis Rd, ELGN, 60123	2800	34W-13N	C7
Einstein Elementary School 1100 Laurie Ln, HRPK, 60133	2857	26W-9N	E7
Eisenhower Academy 406 Burke Dr, JltT, 60433	3499	21W-24S	E6
Eisenhower Elementary School 16001 Minerva Av, SHLD, 60473	3429	1E-18S	B1
Eisenhower Junior High School 1410 75th St, DRN, 60561	3207	18W-8S	A1
Eisenhower Junior High School 800 Hassell Rd, HFET, 60169	2804	24W-12N	D7
Elgin Academy 350 Park St, ELGN, 60120	2855	33W-11N	A3
Elgin High School 1200 Maroon Dr, ELGN, 60120	2855	32W-10N	D5
Eli Whitney Elementary School 2815 S Komensky Av, CHCG, 60623	3090	5W-2S	C3
Elizabeth Blackwell School 345 N Walnut Ln, SMBG, 60194	2858	26W-10N	A5

Chicago 7-County Points of Interest Index

Schools

FEATURE NAME Address City ZIP Code	MAP#	CGS	GRID
Elizabeth Ide Elementary School 2000 Manning Rd, DRN, 60516	3206	18W-8S	E2
Elizabeth Meyer School 8100 Tripp Av Tripp Av, SKOK, 60076	2866	5W-10N	B5
Elk Grove High School 500 W Elk Grove Blvd, EGVV, 60007	2860	18W-9N	D7
Ellington Branch Elementary School 243 N Parkside Av, CHCG, 60644	3031	7W-0N	C4
Ellington Elementary School 243 N Parkside Av, CHCG, 60644	3031	7W-0N	C4
Ellis Middle School 225 S Liberty St, ELGN, 60120	2855	33W-11N	B4
Ellsworth Elementary School 145 N Sleight St, NPVL, 60540	3141	26W-6S	E5
Elm Elementary School 15w201 60th St, BRRG, 60527	3146	15W-6S	B4
Elmer G Kich Elementary School 191 W 155th Pl, HRVY, 60426	3349	2W-18S	D7
Elm Middle School 7607 W Cortland St, EDPK, 60707	2974	9W-2N	C7
Elm Place Middle School 2031 Sheridan Rd, HDPK, 60035	2704	8W-22N	E4
Elmwood Elementary School 2319 N 76th Av, EDPK, 60707	2974	9W-2N	C6
Elmwood Elementary School 1024 Magnolia Ln, NPVL, 60540	3203	27W-7S	D1
Elmwood Elementary School 3025 Ezra Av, ZION, 60099	2422	10W-39N	A4
Elmwood Park High School 8201 W Fullerton Av, RVGV, 60171	2974	10W-2N	B6
Elsie Johnson Elementary School 1380 Nautilus Ln, HRPK, 60133	2967	26W-4N	E3
El Sierra Elementary School 6835 Fairmount Av, DRGV, 60516	3144	19W-7S	D7
Elwood Community Consolidated-School 409 N Chicago St, ELWD, 60421	3675	25W-32S	B7
Emerson Elementary School 3105 Clinton Av, BRWN, 60402	3088	8W-3S	E4
Emerson Elementary School 400 N West Av, EMHT, 60126	3027	17W-2N	C1
Emerson Elementary School 311 Washington Blvd, MYWD, 60153	3030	10W-0N	A4
Emerson Elementary School 119 S Woodlawn St, WHTN, 60187	3024	25W-0S	A7
Emerson Middle School 8101 N Cumberland Av, NLES, 60714	2864	10W-10N	A5
Emmanuel Christian School 8301 S Damen Av, CHCG, 60620	3213	2W-9S	C3
Emmettill Elementary School 6543 S Champlain Av, CHCG, 60637	3152	0E-7S	E5
Emmons Grade School 24226 W Beach Grove Rd, AntT, 60002	2416	24W-41N	D2
Enders-Salk Elementary School 345 N Salem Dr, SMBG, 60194	2858	24W-10N	D4
Englewood Academy High School 6201 S Stewart Av, CHCG, 60621	3152	0W-6S	B4
Entrepreneurship School 7627 S Constance Av, CHCG, 60649	3215	2E-8S	C1
Epiphany School 4223 W 25th St, CHCG, 60623	3090	5W-2S	B2
Erickson Elementary School 277 Springfield Dr, BMDL, 60108	2968	24W-4N	C3
Ericson Scholastic Academy 3600 W 5th Av, CHCG, 60624	3032	4W-0S	C5
Erie Charter Elementary School 2510 W Cortez St, CHCG, 60622	3033	3W-1N	A2
Esmond Elementary School 1865 W Montvale Av, CHCG, 60643	3277	2W-13S	C3
Euclid Elementary School 1211 N Wheeling Rd, MPPT, 60056	2808	14W-14N	B4
Eugene Field Elementary School 7019 N Ashland Blvd, CHCG, 60626	2921	1W-8N	C1
Eugene Field Elementary School 707 Wisner St, PKRG, 60068	2864	9W-9N	B6
Eugene Field Elementary School 51 St. Armand Ln, WLNG, 60090	2754	15W-18N	E4
Evangelical Christian School 9130 S Vincennes Av, CHCG, 60620	3213	1W-10S	E5
Evangelic Assembly of God Academy 5100 W Diversey Av, CHCG, 60641	2975	6W-3N	E5
Evanston Twp High School 1600 Dodge Av, EVTN, 60201	2866	3W-11N	E3
Everett Elementary School 1111 Everett School Rd, LKFT, 60045	2649	12W-24N	B7
Everett F Kerr Middle School 12915 Maple Av, BLID, 60406	3277	3W-15S	B7
Evergreen Elementary School 1041 Evergreen Dr, CLSM, 60188	2967	27W-3N	C6
Evergreen Middle Academy 3537 S Paulina St, CHCG, 60609	3091	2W-3S	C5
Evergreen Park High School 9901 S Kedzie Av, ENGN, 60805	3212	3W-11S	E7
Evers Elementary School 9811 S Lowe Av, CHCG, 60628	3214	0W-11S	A6
Fairfield Academy 6201 S Fairfield Av, CHCG, 60629	3151	3W-6S	A4
Fairhaven School 634 Countryside Hwy, MDLN, 60060	2646	18W-27N	E1
Fairmont School District 89 745 Green Garden Pl, LktT, 60441	3419	22W-21S	B6
Fairmount Elementary School 6036 Blodgett Av, DRGV, 60516	3144	19W-6S	D5
Fairview Elementary School 7301 Fairview Av, DRN, 60561	3206	18W-8S	E1
Fairview Elementary School 375 Arizona Blvd, HFET, 60169	2859	23W-11N	B4
Fairview Elementary School 300 N Fairview Av, MPPT, 60056	2807	15W-13N	E6
Fairview South Elementary School 7040 Laramie Av, SKOK, 60077	2919	6W-8N	D1
Faith Christian Elementary School 1745 Kaneville Rd, GNVA, 60134	3020	36W-1N	A3
Faith Evangelical Lutheran School 1275 Main St, ANTH, 60002	2357	23W-41N	E7
Falconer Elementary School 3020 N Lamon Av, CHCG, 60641	2975	6W-3N	E4
Faraday Elementary School 3250 W Monroe St, CHCG, 60624	3032	4W-0S	D5
Farnsworth Elementary School 5414 N Linder Av, CHCG, 60630	2919	6W-6N	C5
Farragut Career Academy 2345 S Christiana Av, CHCG, 60623	3090	4W-2S	D2
Farragut Elementary School 701 Glenwood Av, JLET, 60435	3498	24W-23S	D4
Faulkner School 7110 S Coles Av, CHCG, 60649	3153	3E-8S	D6
FB McCord Elementary School 8450 Nashville Av, BRBK, 60459	3211	8W-9S	A3
Fearn Elementary School 1600 Hawksley Ln, NARA, 60542	3077	38W-3S	B7
Fenger Academy High School 11220 S Wallace St, CHCG, 60628	3278	0W-13S	A3
Fenton High School 1000 W Green St, BNVL, 60106	2971	16W-5N	D1
Fenwick High School 505 Washington Blvd, OKPK, 60302	3031	8W-0N	A5
FE Peacock Middle School 301 E North St, ITSC, 60143	2914	19W-6N	C5
Fermi Elementary School 1415 E 70th St, CHCG, 60637	3153	1E-7S	A6
Fernway Park Elementary School 16600 S 88th Av, ODPK, 60462	3424	11W-19S	A3
Fernwood Elementary School 10041 S Union Av, CHCG, 60628	3214	0W-11S	A7
Ferson Creek Elementary School 38W160 Bolcum Rd, SchT, 60175	2963	38W-6N	B1
Fieldcrest Elementary School 4100 Wagman St, OKFT, 60452	3426	5W-19S	C2
Field Elementary School 295 N Emroy Av, EMHT, 60126	3028	15W-1N	A1
Field Middle School 2055 Landwehr Rd, NHBK, 60062	2756	11W-16N	D7
Field Park Elementary School 4335 Howard Av, WNSP, 60558	3086	13W-4S	E7
Field-Stevenson Elementary School 925 Beloit Av, FTPK, 60130	3030	9W-0S	D6
Fierke Elementary School 6535 Victoria Dr, OKFT, 60452	3347	8W-18S	B7
Finkl Elementary School 2332 S Western Av, CHCG, 60608	3091	3W-2S	B2
Finley Junior High School 10835 Lombard Av, CHRG, 60415	3275	7W-12S	C2
Fiske Elementary School 6145 S Ingleside Av, CHCG, 60637	3152	1E-6S	E4
Fleming Branch Elementary School 4918 W 64th St, CHCG, 60638	3149	6W-7S	E5
Flossmoor Hills Elementary School 3721 Beech St, FSMR, 60422	3506	4W-22S	D1
Foreman High School 3235 N Leclaire Av, CHCG, 60641	2975	6W-4N	E4
Forest Elementary School 1375 S 5th Av, DSPN, 60018	2862	14W-10N	D5
Forest Glen Elementary School 561 Elm St, GNEN, 60137	3025	22W-0N	B3
Forest Hills Elementary School 5020 Central Av, WNSP, 60558	3146	14W-5S	D2
Forest Park Elementary School 1220 California Av, JLET, 60432	3499	22W-22S	C1
Forest Park Middle School 925 Beloit Av, FTPK, 60130	3030	9W-0S	D6
Forest Road Elementary School 901 Forest Rd, LGPK, 60525	3087	12W-3S	C4
Forest Trail Middle School 215 Wilson St, PKFT, 60466	3594	4W-26S	E3
Forest View Elementary School 1901 W Estates Dr, MPPT, 60056	2861	17W-12N	C2
Forrestal Elementary School 2833 E Washington Av, NCHI, 60088	2593	11W-30N	C3
Fort Dearborn Elementary School 9025 S Throop St, CHCG, 60620	3213	1W-10S	E4
Foster Elementary School 5931 School St, OKFT, 60452	3347	7W-18S	C6
Foster Park Elementary School 8530 S Wood St, CHCG, 60620	3213	2W-9S	C3
Foundations Elementary School 2040 W Adams St, CHCG, 60612	3033	2W-0S	B5
Four Winds Waldorf School 30W160 Calumet Av W, WNVL, 60555	3080	30W-3S	C5
Fox Chase Elementary School 260 Fox Chase Dr N, OSWG, 60543	3263	38W-11S	B2
Fox Elementary School 1035 Parkview Dr, HRPK, 60133	2911	26W-9N	E1
Fox Meadow Elementary School 1275 Jenna Dr, SEGN, 60177	2908	35W-9N	A1
Fox Ridge Elementary School 1905 E Tyler Rd, SCRL, 60174	3020	33W-2N	E1
Fox River Christian School 3450 Swenson Av, SCRL, 60174	3021	33W-2N	A1
Fox River Country Day School 1600 Dundee Av, DndT, 60118	2801	33W-14N	B7
Fox River Grove Middle School 401 Orchard St, FRGV, 60021	2696	29W-22N	B3
Fox Valley Montessori School 850 N Commonwealth Av, AURA, 60506	3137	37W-6S	D5
Frances Xavier Warde School-Hnc 751 N State St, CHCG, 60611	3034	0E-0N	C2
Francis Parker School 2233 N Clark St, CHCG, 60614	2978	0W-2N	B6
Frank C Whitely Elementary School 4335 Haman Av, HFET, 60192	2804	24W-15N	D2
Frankfort Square Elementary School 7710 W Kingston Dr, FftT, 60423	3504	9W-24S	D5
Frank Hall Elementary School 2001 Heather Dr, AURA, 60506	3137	38W-6S	B5
Franklin Elementary School 14701 Chicago Rd, DLTN, 60419	3350	0E-17S	E5
Franklin Elementary School 1000 116th St, HMND, 46394	3280		E4
Franklin Fine Arts Center 225 W Evergreen Av, CHCG, 60610	3034	0W-1N	B1
Franklin Middle School 211 E Franklin St, WHTN, 60187	3024	24W-0S	C6
Franzen Intermediate School 730 Catalpa Av, ITSC, 60143	2914	20W-7N	B5
Frazier Elementary School 4027 W Grenshaw St, CHCG, 60624	3032	5W-0S	B7
Frederick School 595 Friederick Rd, GYLK, 60030	2533	20W-33N	B2
Freedom Middle School 3016 Ridgeland Av, BRWN, 60402	3089	8W-2S	B4
Freeman Elementary School 153 S Randall Rd, AURA, 60506	3137	37W-7S	C7
Fremont Elementary School 28908 N Fremont Center Rd, FmtT, 60060	2589	22W-28N	B5
Fremont Middle School 28855 N Fremont Center Rd, FmtT, 60060	2589	22W-28N	B5
Friendship Junior High School 550 Elizabeth Ln, DSPN, 60018	2862	15W-10N	A5
Frost Junior High School 320 W Wise Rd, SMBG, 60193	2912	23W-9N	E1
Fry Elementary School 3204 Tall Grass Dr, NPVL, 60564	3202	30W-11S	B7
Fuller Elementary School 4214 S St. Lawrence Av, CHCG, 60653	3092	0E-4S	D6
Fullerton Elementary School 400 S Michigan Av, ADSN, 60101	2971	18W-2N	A6
Fulton Elementary School 5300 S Hermitage Av, CHCG, 60609	3151	2W-5S	C2
Fulton School 6601 171st St, TYPK, 60477	3425	8W-20S	B4
Funston Elementary School 2010 N Central Park Av, CHCG, 60647	2976	4W-2N	C7
Gage Park High School 5630 S Rockwell St, CHCG, 60629	3151	3W-6S	A3
Gale Community Academy 1631 W Jonquil Ter, CHCG, 60626	2867	2W-9N	C6
Galileo Scholastic Academy 820 S Carpenter St, CHCG, 60607	3033	1W-0S	E6
Gallistel Branch School 10200 S Avenue J, CHCG, 60617	3216	4E-11S	B7
Gallistel Language Academy 10347 S Ewing Av, CHCG, 60617	3280	4E-11S	B1
Garfield Elementary School 140 E 23rd St, CHHT, 60411	3596	0W-26S	B2
Garfield Elementary School 420 May St, ELGN, 60120	2855	33W-10N	A5
Garfield Elementary School 543 Hannah Av, FTPK, 60130	3030	9W-0S	D5
Garfield Elementary School 1514 S 9th Av, MYWD, 60153	3029	11W-0S	E6
Garrett A Morgan Elementary School 8407 S Kerfoot Av, CHCG, 60620	3214	0W-9S	A3
Garvy Elementary School 5225 N Oak Park Av, CHCG, 60656	2918	8W-6N	E5
Gary Elementary School 130 E Forest Av, WCHI, 60185	3022	29W-0S	C6
Gavin Central School 36414 N Ridge Av, GrtT, 60041	2473	26W-36N	E4
Gavin South Junior High School 25775 W Route 134, GrtT, 60041	2474	25W-34N	A7
Gemini Junior High School 8955 N Greenwood Av, NLES, 60714	2864	10W-11N	A3
General Patton Elementary School 13700 S Stewart Av, RVDL, 60827	3350	0W-15S	B2
Geneva Community High School 416 McKinley Av, GNVA, 60134	3020	35W-1N	A2
Geneva Middle School South 1415 Viking Dr, GnvT, 60134	3019	37W-0S	C6
George Armstrong Elementary School 2110 W Greenleaf Av, CHCG, 60645	2921	2W-8N	B1
George Carpenter Elementary School 300 N Hamlin Av, PKRG, 60068	2863	11W-9N	E7
George R Clark Elementary School 1045 S Monitor Av, CHCG, 60644	3031	7W-0S	C6
George Schneider Elementary School 2957 N Hoyne Av, CHCG, 60618	2977	2W-3N	B4
Georgetown Elementary School 995 Long Grove Dr, AURA, 60504	3201	31W-8S	D3
George Washington Elementary School 12545 S Homan Av, ALSP, 60406	3276	4W-14S	E6
George Washington Elementary School 3611 E 114th St, CHCG, 60617	3280	4E-13S	B3
George Washington Elementary School 1500 Stewart Av, PKRG, 60068	2917	11W-8N	E1
George Washington Elementary School 4835 Michigan Av, SRPK, 60176	2917	12W-6N	C7
George Washington High School 3535 E 114th St, CHCG, 60617	3280	4E-13S	B3
George Washington Middle School 4040 Joliet Av, LYNS, 60534	3088	10W-4S	C6
Gifford Elementary School 240 S Clifton Av, ELGN, 60123	2854	35W-10N	B5
Gillespie Elementary School 9301 S State St, CHCG, 60619	3214	0E-10S	C5
G Kerkstra Elementary School 14950 Laramie Av, OKFT, 60452	3347	6W-17S	E6
Glacier Ridge Elementary School 1120 Village Rd, CLLK, 60014	2693	37W-22N	B3
Gladstone Elementary School 1231 S Damen Av, CHCG, 60608	3033	2W-1S	C7
Glenbard East High School 1014 S Main St, LMBD, 60148	3026	20W-0S	B7
Glenbard North High School 990 Kuhn Rd, CLSM, 60188	2967	26W-3N	D5
Glenbard South High School 23W200 Butterfield Rd, MltT, 60137	3083	22W-2S	B4
Glenbard West High School 670 Crescent Blvd, GNEN, 60137	3025	22W-0N	C5
Glenbrook Elementary School 315 Garden Cir, SMWD, 60107	2857	27W-11N	C4
Glenbrook North High School 2300 Shermer Rd, NHBK, 60062	2810	10W-16N	B1
Glenbrook South High School 4000 W Lake Av, GNVW, 60025	2809	11W-14N	D4
Glen Crest Middle School 725 Sheehan Av, GNEN, 60137	3083	22W-1S	C2
Glen Flora Elementary School 1110 Chestnut St, WKGN, 60085	2480	10W-35N	A6
Glen Grove Elementary School 3900 Glenview Rd, GNVW, 60025	2809	11W-13N	E6
Glen Hill Primary School 1324 Bloomingdale Rd, GLHT, 60139	3025	23W-2N	A1
Glenn Westlake Middle School 1514 S Main St, LMBD, 60148	3084	20W-1S	B1
Glen Oaks Elementary School 9045 S 88th Av, HYHL, 60457	3210	10W-10S	A5
Glenside Middle School 1560 Bloomingdale Rd, GLHT, 60139	2969	23W-2N	A7
Glenwood Elementary School 2500 Northmoor Av, WKGN, 60085	2479	11W-35N	C6
Glenwood School 500 W 187th St, HMWD, 60430	3508	1W-22S	B1
Global Visions Academy 2710 E 89th St, CHCG, 60617	3215	3E-10S	E4

Chicago 7-County Points of Interest Index

FEATURE NAME Address City ZIP Code	MAP#	CGS	GRID
GN Dieterich Elementary School 1141 Jackson St, AURA, 60505	3200	35W-9S	B4
Goethe Elementary School 2236 N Rockwell St, CHCG, 60647	2977	3W-2N	A6
Goldblatt Elementary School 4257 W Adams St, CHCG, 60624	3032	5W-0S	B5
Golf Middle School 9401 Waukegan Rd, MNGV, 60053	2864	8W-11N	E2
Golfview Elementary School 124 Golfview Ln, CPVL, 60110	2801	32W-17N	D1
Gombert Elementary School 2707 Ridge Rd, AURA, 60504	3201	32W-9S	C4
Gompers Elementary School 12302 S State St, CHCG, 60628	3278	0W-14S	C6
Gompers Junior High School 1501 Copperfield Av, JLET, 60432	3499	22W-23S	D3
Goodings Grove Elementary School 12914 W 143rd St, HmrT, 60491	3344	16W-16S	A4
Goodlow Magnet Elementary School 2040 W 62nd St, CHCG, 60636	3151	2W-6S	C4
Goodrich Elementary School 3950 Hobson Road, WDRG, 60517	3143	22W-7S	C7
Good Shepherd Lutheran School 1111 Van St, ELGN, 60123	2854	35W-11N	C4
Goodwin Elementary School 2625 S Austin Blvd, CCRO, 60804	3089	7W-2S	C3
Goodwin Elementary School 18 Poplar Pl, NARA, 60542	3137	37W-4S	D1
Gordon School 14100 S Harrison Av, POSN, 60469	3349	3W-16S	A3
Gordon Tech High School 3633 N California Av, CHCG, 60618	2976	3W-4N	E2
Goudy Elementary School 5120 N Winthrop Av, CHCG, 60640	2921	1W-6N	D6
Gower Middle School 7941 S Madison St, BRRG, 60527	3208	15W-9S	A2
Gower West Elementary School 7650 Clarendon Hills Rd, WLBK, 60527	3207	17W-8S	D2
Grace Lutheran School 4106 W 28th St, CHCG, 60623	3090	5W-2S	B3
Grace Lutheran School 7300 Division St, RVFT, 60305	3030	9W-1N	D2
Grace McWayne Elementary School 3501 Hapner Way, BTVA, 60510	3077	37W-1S	B2
Graham Elementary School 4436 S Union Av, CHCG, 60609	3092	0W-4S	A7
Graham Elementary School 2315 High Meadow Rd, NPVL, 60564	3266	29W-13S	D4
Grand Prairie Elementary School 10480 Nebraska St, FKFT, 60423	3591	13W-26S	B2
Grand Prairie Elementary School 3300 Caton Farm Rd, JLET, 60431	3417	28W-21S	B6
Granger Middle School 2721 Stonebridge Blvd, AURA, 60502	3139	32W-5S	C3
Grant Community High School 285 E Grand Av, FXLK, 60020	2473	26W-36N	C4
Grant Elementary School 1300 N 34th Av, MLPK, 60160	3029	12W-1N	B2
Grant Elementary School 2712 Miller Av, SCHT, 60411	3596	1W-26S	A3
Grant-White Elementary School 147 Circle Av, FTPK, 60130	3030	9W-0N	D4
Grass Lake Elementary School 26177 W Grass Lake Rd, AntT, 60002	2415	25W-39N	E4
Graves Elementary School 6021 S 74th Av, SMMT, 60501	3148	9W-6S	D4
Gray Elementary School 3730 N Laramie Av, CHCG, 60641	2975	6W-4N	D2
Gray M Sanborn Elementary School 101 N Oak St, PLTN, 60067	2805	20W-16N	E1
Grayslake Community High School-Central 400 N Lake St, GYLK, 60030	2532	21W-33N	E3
Grayslake Community High School-North 1925 N Route 83, GYLK, 60046	2475	21W-35N	D6
Grayslake Middle School 440 Barron Blvd, GYLK, 60030	2533	20W-33N	A3
Greeley Elementary School 275 Fairview Av, WNKA, 60093	2812	4W-15N	C3
Greeley Regional Gifted Center 832 W Sheridan Rd, CHCG, 60613	2977	1W-4N	E2
Green Bay Elementary School 2100 Green Bay Rd, NCHI, 60064	2536	12W-31N	C7
Greenbriar Elementary School 101 W Greenbriar Av, CHHT, 60411	3508	1W-24S	A5
Greenbriar Elementary School 1225 Greenbriar Ln, NHBK, 60062	2757	10W-17N	A5
Greenbrier Elementary School 2330 N Verde Dr, ANHT, 60004	2753	18W-16N	D7
Greenbrook Elementary School 5208 Arlington Cir, HRPK, 60133	2911	26W-6N	E6
Greene Elementary School 3525 S Honore St, CHCG, 60609	3091	2W-3S	C5
Greenman Elementary School 729 W Galena Blvd, AURA, 60506	3137	36W-7S	E7
Greenwood Elementary School 4618 Greenwood Rd, GNWD, 60097	2468	38W-36N	E3
Greenwood Elementary School 16801 Greenwood Av, SHLD, 60473	3429	1E-19S	A3
Greenwood Elementary School 1919 North Av, WKGN, 60087	2480	10W-36N	A5
Gregory Elementary School 3715 W Polk St, CHCG, 60624	3032	4W-0S	C6
Gregory Middle School 2621 Springdale Cir, NPVL, 60564	3203	28W-10S	A6
Gresham Elementary School 8524 S Green St, CHCG, 60620	3214	1W-9S	A3
Grimes Elementary School 5450 W 64th Pl, CHCG, 60638	3149	6W-7S	D5
Grissom Elementary School 12810 S Escanaba Av, CHCG, 60633	3279	3E-14S	E7
Grissom Middle School 17000 80th Av, TYPK, 60477	3424	10W-20S	C4
Gross Middle School 3524 Maple Av, BKFD, 60513	3087	11W-3S	D5
Grove Avenue Elementary School 900 S Grove Av, BRTN, 60010	2751	25W-18N	A3
Grove Elementary School 1000 Pfingsten Rd, NHBK, 60062	2756	11W-17N	E5
G Stanley Hall Elementary School 1447 Wayne Av, GLHT, 60139	2969	22W-2N	D7
Guerin Prep High School 8001 Belmont Av, RVGV, 60171	2974	10W-3N	B4
Guggenheim Elementary School 7141 S Morgan St, CHCG, 60621	3151	1W-8S	E7
Gunsaulus Scholastic Academy 4420 S Sacramento Av, CHCG, 60632	3090	3W-4S	E7
Gurnee Grade School 940 Kilbourne Rd, GRNE, 60031	2478	14W-35N	C7
Gurrie Middle School 1001 S Spring Av, LGNG, 60525	3147	12W-5S	B2
Gustafson Elementary School 905 Carlisle Rd, BTVA, 60510	3078	36W-2S	A3
Gwendolyn Brooks Middle School 14741 Wallace St, HRVY, 60426	3350	0W-17S	B5
Hadley Junior High School 240 Hawthorne Blvd, GNEN, 60137	3025	23W-0N	A4
Hadley Middle School 15731 S Bell Rd, HMGN, 60491	3422	15W-18S	A1
Haines Elementary School 247 W 23rd Pl, CHCG, 60616	3092	0W-2S	B2
Haines Elementary School 155 Haines Av, NLNX, 60451	3501	18W-24S	B5
Haines Middle School 305 S 9th St, SCRL, 60174	2964	36W-2N	A7
Hale Elementary School 6140 S Melvina Av, CHCG, 60638	3149	7W-6S	B4
Hale Elementary School 1300 W Wise Rd, SMBG, 60193	2912	25W-9N	C1
Hales Franciscan High School 4930 S Cottage Grove Av, CHCG, 60615	3152	0E-5S	E1
Haley Elementary Academy 11411 S Eggleston Av, CHCG, 60628	3278	0W-13S	B3
Half Day School 239 Olde Half Day Rd, LNSH, 60069	2702	15W-23N	A3
Hamilton Elementary School 1650 W Cornelia Av, CHCG, 60657	2977	2W-4N	C3
Hamline Branch Elementary School 1548 W 48th St, CHCG, 60609	3151	1W-5S	D1
Hamline Elementary School 4747 S Bishop St, CHCG, 60609	3151	1W-5S	D1
Hamlin Upper Grade Center 12150 S Hamlin Av, ALSP, 60803	3276	4W-14S	D5
Hammerschmidt Elementary School 617 Hammerschmidt Av, LMBD, 60148	3026	19W-0S	C5
Hammond Elementary School 2819 W 21st Pl, CHCG, 60623	3090	3W-1S	E2
Hammond High School 5926 S Calumet Av, HMND, 46320	3430		E1
Hampshire Elementary School 321 Terwilliger Av, HPSR, 60140	2795	47W-15N	D3
Hampshire Middle-High School 560 S State St, HPSR, 60140	2795	47W-15N	E3
Hampton Fine & Performing Arts-School 3434 W 77th St, CHCG, 60652	3212	4W-8S	D1
Hancock College Prep 4034 W 56th St, CHCG, 60629	3150	5W-6S	B3
Hancock High School 4350 W 56th St, CHCG, 60629	3150	5W-6S	B3
Hannah Martin Elementary School 10920 Reed Rd, LIHL, 60142	2692	39W-22N	B5
Hanna Sacks Bais Yaakov High School 3021 W Devon Av, CHCG, 60659	2920	3W-8N	E2
Hannum Elementary School 9800 S Tripp Av, OKLN, 60453	3212	5W-11S	B7
Hanover Countryside Elementary-School 6 S Bartlett Rd, SMWD, 60107	2857	28W-10N	A5
Hanover Highlands Elementary School 1451 Cypress Av, HRPK, 60133	2911	26W-8N	E2
Hanson Park Elementary School 5411 W Fullerton Av, CHCG, 60639	2975	6W-2N	D6
Harlan Community Academy High-School 9652 S Michigan Av, CHCG, 60628	3214	0E-11S	C6
Harnew Elementary School 9101 Meade Av, OKLN, 60453	3211	7W-10S	C5
Harold Washington Elementary School 9130 S University Av, CHCG, 60619	3215	1E-10S	A5
Harper Elementary School 1101 Dartmouth St, WLMT, 60091	2812	5W-14N	A5
Harper High School 6520 S Wood St, CHCG, 60636	3151	2W-7S	C5
Harriet Tubbman Elementary School 333 E 142nd St, DLTN, 60419	3350	0E-16S	D3
Harrison Elementary School 6809 McCullom Lake Rd, MchT, 60097	2470	35W-35N	A5
Harrison Street Elementary School 201 N Harrison St, GNVA, 60134	3020	34W-1N	D3
Harte Elementary School 1556 E 56th St, CHCG, 60637	3153	2E-6S	B3
Hart Elementary School 1110 18th St, NCHI, 60064	2536	10W-32N	E6
Harvard Elementary School 7525 S Harvard Av, CHCG, 60620	3214	0W-8S	B1
Harvard High School 1103 N Jefferson St, HRVD, 60033	2406	50W-38N	B6
Harvard Junior High School 1301 Garfield St, HRVD, 60033	2406	49W-39N	B5
Harvest Christian Academy 1000 N Randall Rd, ELGN, 60124	2853	36W-12N	D2
Hatch Elementary School 1000 N Ridgeland Av, OKPK, 60302	3031	7W-1N	B1
Haugan Elementary School 4540 N Hamlin Av, CHCG, 60625	2920	4W-5N	C7
Haven Middle School 2417 Prairie Av, EVTN, 60201	2866	3W-12N	E1
Havlicek Elementary School 6401 15th St, BRWN, 60402	3089	8W-1S	A1
Hawk Hollow Elementary School 235 Jacaranda Dr, BRLT, 60103	2967	28W-5N	A2
Hawthorn Aspen Elementary School 500 Aspen Dr, VNHL, 60061	2647	17W-25N	B5
Hawthorne Elementary School 145 W Arthur St, EMHT, 60126	3027	16W-1N	E2
Hawthorne Elementary School 334 Wakeman Av, WHTN, 60187	3024	24W-0N	D5
Hawthorn Elementary School-North 301 W Hawthorn Pkwy, VNHL, 60061	2647	17W-26N	B4
Hawthorn Elementary School-South 430 Aspen Dr, VNHL, 60061	2647	17W-25N	B5
Hawthorne Scholastic Academy 3319 N Clifton Av, CHCG, 60657	2977	1W-4N	E3
Hawthorn Middle North School 201 W Hawthorn Pkwy, VNHL, 60061	2647	17W-26N	B4
Hawthorn Middle South School 600 Aspen Dr, VNHL, 60061	2647	17W-25N	B4
Hawthorn Townline Elementary School 810 Aspen Dr, VNHL, 60061	2647	17W-26N	B4
Hayt Elementary School 1518 W Granville Av, CHCG, 60660	2921	1W-7N	C3
Hazelgreen Elementary School 11751 S Lawler Av, ALSP, 60803	3275	6W-13S	E4
HD Jacobs High School 2601 Bunker Hill Dr, ALGN, 60102	2693	36W-20N	D7
Healy Elementary School 3010 S Parnell Av, CHCG, 60616	3092	0W-2S	A3
Healy Elementary School Annex 3040 S Parnell Av, CHCG, 60616	3092	0W-2S	A3
Hearst Elementary School 4640 S Lamon Av, CHCG, 60638	3149	6W-4S	E1
Heartland Elementary School 3300 Heartland Dr, GNVA, 60134	3019	37W-1N	C3
Heather Hill Elementary School 1439 Lawrence Cres, FSMR, 60422	3507	3W-23S	B3
Hedges Branch Elementary School 1954 W 48th St, CHCG, 60609	3151	2W-5S	C1
Hedges Elementary School 4747 S Winchester Av, CHCG, 60609	3151	2W-5S	C1
Hefferan Elementary School 4409 W Wilcox St, CHCG, 60624	3032	5W-0S	A5
Heineman Middle School 725 Academic Dr, ALGN, 60102	2693	38W-20N	A7
Helen Keller Elementary School 7846 163rd St, TYPK, 60477	3424	9W-19S	D2
Henderson Elementary School 5650 S Wolcott Av, CHCG, 60636	3151	2W-6S	C3
Hendricks Community Academy 4316 S Princeton Av, CHCG, 60609	3092	0W-4S	B7
Henking Elementary School 2941 Linneman St, GNVW, 60025	2810	10W-13N	B7
Henry D Lloyd Elementary School 2103 N Lamon Av, CHCG, 60639	2975	6W-2N	E6
Henry H Nash Elementary School 4837 W Erie St, CHCG, 60644	3031	6W-0N	E3
Henry Puffer Elementary School 2220 Haddow Av, DRGV, 60515	3143	21W-5S	E2
Henry R Clissold Elementary School 2350 W 110th Pl, CHCG, 60643	3277	2W-12S	B2
Henry Winkelman Elementary School 1919 Landwehr Rd, GNVW, 60025	2809	11W-14N	D4
Henson Elementary School 1326 S Avers Av, CHCG, 60623	3032	4W-1S	C7
Herbert Elementary School 2131 W Monroe St, CHCG, 60612	3033	2W-0S	B5
Herget Middle School 1550 Deerpath Rd, SgrT, 60506	3136	39W-5S	E3
Heritage Elementary School 507 Arnold Av, SMWD, 60107	2911	28W-9N	B1
Heritage Grove Middle School 12450 S Van Dyke Rd, PNFD, 60544	3338	30W-18S	B7
Heritage Lakes Elementary School 925 Woodhill Dr, CLSM, 60188	2967	27W-4N	C4
Heritage Middle School 6850 31st St, BRWN, 60402	3088	8W-3S	E4
Heritage Middle School 19250 Burnham Av, LNSG, 60438	3510	3E-22S	B2
Heritage Middle School 6021 S 74th Av, SMMT, 60501	3148	9W-6S	D4
Herrick Middle School 4435 Middaugh Av, DRGV, 60515	3144	20W-4S	B1
Herzl Elementary School 3711 W Douglas Blvd, CHCG, 60623	3032	4W-1S	C7
Hester Junior High School 2836 Gustav St, FNPK, 60131	2973	12W-3N	C5
Hiawatha Elementary School 6539 26th St, BRWN, 60402	3089	8W-2S	A3
Hibbard Elementary School 3244 W Ainslie St, CHCG, 60625	2920	4W-6N	D6
Hickory Bend Elementary School 600 E 191st Pl, GNWD, 60425	3509	1E-23S	A2
Hickory Creek Middle School 22265 S 80th Av, FKFT, 60423	3592	9W-26S	D3
Hickory Elementary School 1009 Blackhawk Dr, UYPK, 60466	3684	3W-30S	B3
Hickory Point School 500 Laburnum Dr, NHBK, 60062	2756	12W-18N	C3
Higgins Community Academy 11710 S Morgan St, CHCG, 60643	3278	1W-13S	A4
Highcrest Middle School 569 Hunter Rd, WLMT, 60091	2812	5W-13N	B6
Highland Christian Academy 2250 W Highland Av, ELGN, 60123	2853	36W-12N	E3
Highland Elementary School 3935 Highland Av, DRGV, 60515	3084	19W-4S	C7
Highland Elementary School 190 N Melrose Av, ELGN, 60123	2854	35W-11N	C4
Highland Elementary School 9700 Crawford Av, SKOK, 60076	2866	5W-12N	B1
Highland Middle School 310 W Rockland Rd, LYVL, 60048	2591	16W-28N	D6
Highland Park High School 433 Vine Av, HDPK, 60035	2704	8W-22N	E3
Highlands Elementary School 3420 Laurel Ln, HLCT, 60429	3426	4W-20S	E4
Highlands Elementary School 5850 Laurel Av, LynT, 60525	3146	13W-6S	E4
Highlands Elementary School 525 S Brainard St, NPVL, 60540	3141	26W-7S	D6
Highlands Middle School 1850 W Plainfield Rd, LynT, 60525	3146	13W-6S	E4
High Point Elementary School 14825 West Av, ODPK, 60462	3345	12W-17S	C5
High School of the Arts 7529 S Constance Av, CHCG, 60649	3215	2E-8S	C1
Hillcrest Elementary School 433 E Depot St, ANTH, 60002	2358	22W-42N	C6
Hillcrest Elementary School 1435 Jefferson Av, DRGV, 60516	3144	20W-6S	B4
Hillcrest Elementary School 80 N Airlite St, ELGN, 60123	2853	36W-11N	E4
Hillcrest High School 17401 Crawford Av, CCHL, 60478	3426	4W-20S	D5

FEATURE NAME Address City ZIP Code	MAP#	CGS	GRID
Hill Elementary School 724 Pennsylvania Av, AURA, 60506	3138	36W-6S	A5
Hillel Torah North Day School 7120 Laramie Av, SKOK, 60077	2919	6W-8N	D1
Hille Middle School 5800 151st St, OKFT, 60452	3347	7W-17S	D6
Hill Middle School 1836 Brookdale Rd, NPVL, 60563	3140	29W-5S	D3
Hillside Academy 431 N Hillside Av, HLSD, 60162	3028	14W-0N	C5
Hillside Elementary School 4804 Harrison St, HLSD, 60162	3028	14W-0S	D6
Hilltop Elementary School 2615 W Lincoln Rd, MHRY, 60051	2528	31W-33N	D3
Hinsdale Adventist Academy 631 E Hickory St, HNDL, 60521	3146	14W-4S	C1
Hinsdale Middle School 100 S Garfield Av, HNDL, 60521	3146	15W-5S	B2
Hinsdale South High School 7401 Clarendon Hills Rd, DRN, 60561	3207	16W-8S	D1
Hinton Elementary School 644 W 71st St, CHCG, 60621	3152	0W-7S	A6
Hiram H Belding Elementary School 4257 N Tripp Av, CHCG, 60641	2976	5W-5N	B1
Hirsch Metropolitan High School 7740 S Ingleside Av, CHCG, 60619	3214	1E-8S	E1
Hitch Elementary School 5625 N McVicker Av, CHCG, 60646	2919	7W-7N	B4
H McNelty School 2100 Main St, MLPK, 60160	3029	11W-0N	D3
Hodgkins Elementary School 6516 Kane Av, HGKN, 60525	3147	11W-7S	D6
Hoffman Elementary School 2000 Harrison St, GNVW, 60025	2810	9W-12N	D7
Hoffman Estates High School 1100 W Higgins Rd, HFET, 60169	2858	24W-12N	C2
Holden Elementary School 1104 W 31st St, CHCG, 60608	3091	1W-2S	E3
Hollywood Elementary School 3423 Hollywood Av, BKFD, 60513	3088	10W-3S	A5
Holmes Elementary School 16000 Carse Av, HRVY, 60426	3428	1W-19S	B2
Holmes Elementary School 508 N Kenilworth Av, OKPK, 60302	3030	8W-1N	E3
Holmes Elementary School 5800 Holmes Av, WLBK, 60514	3145	16W-6S	D4
Holmes Junior High School 1900 W Lonnquist Blvd, MPPT, 60056	2861	17W-12N	C2
Holmes Middle School 221 S Wolf Rd, WLNG, 60090	2755	14W-17N	C4
Holy Angels School 720 Kensington Pl, AURA, 60506	3137	36W-7S	E7
Holy Angels School 545 E Oakwood Blvd, CHCG, 60653	3092	0E-4S	D6
Holy Cross School 720 Elder Ln, DRFD, 60015	2703	10W-21N	E7
Holy Family Catholic Academy 2515 Palatine Rd, HFET, 60192	2804	24W-15N	C1
Holy Family Lutheran School 4256 W Walton St, CHCG, 60651	3032	5W-1N	B2
Holy Family School 600 Brook Forest Av, SRWD, 60404	3496	29W-23S	C3
Holy Ghost School 260 N Wood Dale Rd, WDDL, 60191	2915	18W-5N	A7
Holy Trinity High School 1443 W Division St, CHCG, 60622	3033	1W-1N	D2
Holy Trinity School 108 S Linden Av, WTMT, 60559	3145	17W-5S	B3
Home Elementary School 4400 Home Av, SKNY, 60402	3088	8W-4S	E7
Homer Junior High School 15711 S Bell Rd, HMGN, 60491	3422	15W-18S	A1
Homestead Elementary School 2830 Hillsboro Blvd, AURA, 60503	3201	31W-10S	D7
Hometown Elementary School 8870 S Duffy Av, HMTN, 60456	3212	5W-10S	B4
Homewood Community Academy 18620 Kedzie Av, HMWD, 60430	3507	4W-22S	A1
Homewood-Flossmoor High School 999 Kedzie Av, FSMR, 60422	3507	3W-22S	A2
Hoover Elementary School 1259 Superior Av, CTCY, 60409	3430	3E-19S	A1
Hoover Elementary School 315 N Springinsguth Rd, SMBG, 60194	2858	25W-10N	B5
Hoover Wood School 1640 Wagner Rd, BTVA, 60510	3078	34W-2S	E4
Hope College Preparatory High-School 5515 S Lowe Av, CHCG, 60621	3152	0W-6S	A3
Hope Lutheran School 6416 S Washtenaw Av, CHCG, 60629	3151	3W-7S	A5
Horace Mann Elementary School 8050 S Chappel Av, CHCG, 60617	3215	2E-9S	C2
Horace Mann Elementary School 921 N Kenilworth Av, OKPK, 60302	3030	8W-1N	E2
Horizon Elementary School 1701 Greenbrook Blvd, HRPK, 60133	2911	27W-6N	D6
Hough Street Elementary School 310 S Hough St, BRTN, 60010	2750	25W-18N	E2
Howe Elementary School 10271 W Beach Rd, BHPK, 60087	2422	10W-38N	B7
Hoyne School 8905 S Crandon Av, CHCG, 60617	3215	2E-10S	D4
Hubbard High School 6200 S Hamlin Av, CHCG, 60629	3150	4W-6S	C4
Hubbard Woods Elementary School 1110 Chatfield Rd, WNKA, 60093	2758	5W-16N	E7
Hubble Middle School 603 S Main St, WHTN, 60187	3024	24W-0S	D7
Hubert H Humphrey Middle School 777 Falconridge Wy, BGBK, 60440	3205	21W-11S	E7
Huff Elementary School 801 Hastings St, ELGN, 60120	2855	32W-10N	B6
Hufford Junior High School 1125 N Larkin Av, JLET, 60435	3498	26W-22S	A2
Humboldt Community Christian School 1847 N Humboldt Blvd, CHCG, 60647	2976	3W-2N	E7
Hunting Ridge Elementary School 1105 W Illinois Av, PLTN, 60067	2805	22W-14N	B3
Huntley High School 13719 Harmony Rd, HTLY, 60142	2691	42W-20N	B7

FEATURE NAME Address City ZIP Code	MAP#	CGS	GRID
Hurley Elementary School 3849 W 69th Pl, CHCG, 60629	3150	4W-7S	C6
Husmann Elementary School 131 W Paddock St, CLLK, 60014	2640	35W-25N	A4
Hyde Park Academy High School 6220 S Stony Island Av, CHCG, 60637	3153	1E-6S	B4
Hyde Park Elementary School 1525 Hyde Park Av, WKGN, 60085	2536	11W-34N	E1
Hynes Elementary School 9000 Belleforte Av, MNGV, 60053	2864	8W-11N	E3
Ida Crown Jewish Academy 2828 W Pratt Blvd, CHCG, 60645	2920	3W-8N	E1
Ideal Elementary School 9901 W 58th St, CTSD, 60525	3147	12W-6S	C4
Illiana Christian High School 2261 Indiana Av, LNSG, 60438	3429	2E-21S	D6
Illinois School 210 Illinois St, PKFT, 60466	3595	3W-25S	B1
Immaculate Conception Grade School 132 W Arthur St, EMHT, 60126	3027	16W-1N	E2
Immaculate Conception High School 217 S Cottage Hill Av, EMHT, 60126	3027	16W-1N	E3
Immaculate Conception School 1431 N North Park Av, CHCG, 60610	3034	0W-1N	B1
Immaculate Conception School 8739 S Exchange Av, CHCG, 60617	3215	3E-10S	E3
Immaculate Conception School 7263 W Talcott Av, CHCG, 60631	2918	9W-7N	D4
Immaculate Heart of Mary High-School 10900 W Cermak Rd, WSTR, 60154	3086	13W-1S	E2
Immanuel Evang Lutheran School 1310 N Frolic Av, WKGN, 60085	2479	12W-35N	B6
Immanuel Lutheran School 950 Hart Rd, BTVA, 60510	3078	34W-2S	C3
Immanuel Lutheran School 5 S Van Buren St, EDND, 60118	2801	33W-16N	A2
Immanuel Lutheran School 148 E 3rd St, EMHT, 60126	3028	15W-1N	A1
Immanuel Lutheran School 200 N Plum Grove Rd, PLTN, 60067	2752	21W-16N	E7
Incarnation School 5705 W 127th St, WthT, 60463	3275	7W-15S	D7
Independence Junior High School 6610 W Highland Dr, PSHT, 60463	3275	8W-15S	A7
Indiana Elementary School 165 Indiana St, PKFT, 60466	3595	3W-25S	A1
Indian Grove Elementary School 1340 N Burning Bush Ln, MPPT, 60056	2808	13W-14N	E4
Indian Hill Elementary School 1920 Lotus Dr, RLKH, 60073	2474	24W-35N	D5
Indian Knoll Elementary School 0N645 Indian Knoll Rd, WnfT, 60185	3023	28W-0N	A4
Indian Prairie Elementary School 651 Village Rd, CLLK, 60014	2693	36W-22N	D3
Indian Trail Elementary School 6235 Stonewall Av, DRGV, 60516	3144	20W-6S	A5
Indian Trail Elementary School 20912 S Frankfort Square Rd, FftT, 60423	3504	9W-25S	D7
Indian Trail Elementary School 2075 St. Johns Av, HDPK, 60035	2704	8W-22N	E4
Indian Trail Junior High School 222 N JF Kennedy Dr, ADSN, 60101	2970	18W-3N	E4
Indian Trail Middle School 1005 N Eastern Av, PNFD, 60544	3338	29W-17S	D6
Infant Jesus of Prague School 1101 Douglas Av, FSMR, 60422	3507	3W-23S	B2
Infinity High School 3120 S Kostner Av, CHCG, 60623	3090	5W-3S	A4
Inter-American Magnet School 919 W Barry Av, CHCG, 60657	2977	1W-3N	E4
Ira Jones Middle School 15320 W Wallin Dr, PNFD, 60544	3338	31W-18S	A7
Irene H King Elementary School 301 Eaton Av, RMVL, 60446	3340	24W-16S	E3
Iroquois Community School 1836 E Touhy Av, DSPN, 60018	2917	12W-9N	B1
Irving Elementary School 3501 Clinton Av, BRWN, 60402	3088	8W-3S	E5
Irving Elementary School 4727 S Pine Av, HMND, 46327	3352		E4
Irving Elementary School 805 S 17th Av, MYWD, 60153	3029	11W-0N	D5
Irving Park Middle School 3815 N Kedvale Av, CHCG, 60641	2976	5W-4N	B2
Isaac Fox Elementary School 395 W Cuba Rd, LKZH, 60010	2699	23W-21N	A6
Islamic Foundation School 300 W Highridge Rd, VLPK, 60181	3027	18W-0S	A6
Ivy Hall Elementary School 1072 Ivy Hall Ln, BFGV, 60089	2701	17W-21N	A7
Ivy Hill Elementary School 2211 N Burke Dr, ANHT, 60004	2754	17W-16N	B7
Jackson Elementary School 925 S Swain Av, EMHT, 60126	3027	16W-0S	E6
Jackson Language Academy 1340 W Harrison St, CHCG, 60607	3033	1W-0S	D5
Jackson Middle School 301 W Jackson St, VLPK, 60181	3027	18W-0S	A6
Jacob Beidler Elementary School 3151 W Walnut St, CHCG, 60612	3032	3W-0N	E4
Jacqueline B Kennedy School 7644 Central Av, BRBK, 60459	3211	7W-8S	D1
Jahn Elementary School 3149 N Wolcott Av, CHCG, 60657	2977	2W-3N	C4
James B Conant High School 700 E Cougar Trl, HFET, 60169	2859	22W-11N	C4
James G Blaine Elementary School 1420 W Grace St, CHCG, 60613	2977	1W-4N	D2
James Hart School 18220 Morgan St, HMWD, 60430	3428	1W-21S	A7
James Johnson Elementary School 1420 S Albany Av, CHCG, 60623	3032	3W-1S	E7
James Madison Elementary School 7433 S Dorchester Av, CHCG, 60619	3153	1E-8S	A7
James Monroe Elementary School 3651 W Schubert Av, CHCG, 60647	2976	4W-3N	C5
James R Lowell Elementary School 3320 W Hirsch St, CHCG, 60651	3032	4W-1N	D1
James Shields Elementary School 4250 S Rockwell St, CHCG, 60632	3091	3W-4S	A6

FEATURE NAME Address City ZIP Code	MAP#	CGS	GRID
Jamie McGee Elementary School 179 Commonwealth Dr, BGBK, 60440	3268	25W-11S	B2
Jamieson Elementary School 5650 N Mozart St, CHCG, 60659	2920	3W-7N	E4
Jane Addams Elementary School 910 Division St, MLPK, 60160	3029	11W-1N	E2
Jane Addams Elementary School 1020 E Sayles Dr, PLTN, 60074	2753	19W-16N	C6
Jane Addams Middle School 905 Lily Cache Ln, BGBK, 60440	3268	25W-12S	C3
Jane A Neil Elementary School 8555 S Michigan Av, CHCG, 60619	3214	0E-9S	C3
Jane Stenson Elementary School 9201 Lockwood Av, SKOK, 60077	2865	6W-11N	D2
Jay Stream Middle School 283 El Paso Ln, CLSM, 60188	2968	25W-2N	A7
J Calhoun North Elementary School 2833 W Adams St, CHCG, 60612	3032	3W-0S	E5
Jefferson Elementary School 225 46th Av, BLWD, 60104	3029	13W-0N	A4
Jefferson Elementary School 7035 16th St, BRWN, 60402	3088	8W-1S	E1
Jefferson Elementary School 176 E 11th St, CHHT, 60411	3508	0W-25S	B7
Jefferson Elementary School 360 E Crescent Av, EMHT, 60126	3028	15W-0N	A5
Jefferson Elementary School 1200 N Jefferson St, HRVD, 60033	2406	50W-38N	B6
Jefferson Junior High School 1525 N Loomis St, NPVL, 60563	3141	26W-5S	D2
Jefferson Junior High School 7200 Janes Av, WDRG, 60517	3205	21W-8S	E1
Jefferson Middle School 1151 Plum St, AURA, 60506	3137	37W-6S	D6
Jefferson Middle School 255 W Vermont St, VLPK, 60181	3027	18W-1N	A2
Jefferson Middle School 600 S Lewis Av, WKGN, 60085	2536	11W-33N	D3
Jenner Academy of the Arts 1119 N Cleveland Av, CHCG, 60610	3034	0W-1N	A2
Jensen Scholastic Academy 3030 W Harrison St, CHCG, 60612	3032	3W-0S	E6
Jerling Junior High School 8851 W 151st St, ODPK, 60462	3346	11W-18S	A6
Jesse Sherwood Elementary School 245 W 57th St, CHCG, 60621	3152	0W-6S	B3
Jewel Middle School 1501 Waterford Rd, NARA, 60542	3077	38W-4S	B7
JFH Educational Academy 7642 W Irving Park Rd, NRDG, 60706	2974	9W-5N	C2
J Giles Elementary School 4251 N Oriole Av, NRDG, 60706	2974	9W-5N	C1
J Leigh Elementary School 8151 W Lawrence Av, NRDG, 60706	2918	10W-5N	B7
Joan Dachs Bais Yaakov 3200 W Peterson Av, CHCG, 60659	2920	3W-7N	D3
John Barry Elementary School 2828 N Kilbourn Av, CHCG, 60641	2976	5W-3N	A4
John B Drake Elementary School 2722 S King Dr, CHCG, 60616	3092	0E-2S	D3
John C Burroughs Elementary School 3542 S Washtenaw Av, CHCG, 60632	3091	3W-3S	A5
John C Coonley Elementary School 4046 N Leavitt St, CHCG, 60618	2977	2W-5N	B1
John F Eberhart Elementary School 3400 W 65th Pl, CHCG, 60629	3150	4W-7S	D5
John F Kennedy Elementary School 3945 Wehrman Av, SRPK, 60176	2973	12W-4N	B2
John F Kennedy High School 6325 W 56th St, CHCG, 60638	3149	8W-6S	A3
John Hay Community Acadamey 1018 N Laramie Av, CHCG, 60651	3031	6W-1N	D2
John Hersey High School 1900 E Thomas St, ANHT, 60004	2807	16W-15N	D2
John Jay Elementary School 1835 W Pheasant Tr, MPPT, 60056	2861	17W-11N	C3
John Laidlaw Elementary School 4072 Forest Av, WNSP, 60558	3086	14W-4S	D7
John L Marsh Elementary School 9810 S Exchange Av, CHCG, 60617	3215	3E-11S	E6
John Middleton Elementary School 8300 St. Louis Av, SKOK, 60076	2866	4W-10N	C5
John Mills Elementary School 2824 N 76th Av, EDPK, 60707	2974	9W-3N	C5
John Muir Literacy Academy 1973 Kensington Ln, HFET, 60169	2858	25W-12N	A1
John R Tibbott Elementary School 520 Gary Dr, BGBK, 60440	3269	21W-11S	D1
Johnsburg High School 2002 W Ringwood Rd, JNBG, 60050	2471	31W-37N	E2
Johnsburg Junior High School 2220 Church St, JNBG, 60050	2471	31W-35N	E5
Johnson Elementary School 2s700 Continental Dr, WNVL, 60555	3080	30W-2S	C5
John W Cook Elementary School 8150 S Bishop St, CHCG, 60620	3213	1W-9S	D2
Joliet Catholic Academy 1200 N Larkin Av, JLET, 60435	3498	26W-22S	A2
Joliet Central High School 201 E Jefferson St, JLET, 60432	3499	23W-23S	A4
Joliet Montessori School 1600 Root St, CTHL, 60403	3418	26W-21S	A6
Joliet West High School 401 N Larkin Av, JLET, 60435	3498	26W-23S	A4
Jonas E Salk Elementary School 500 King Arthur Way, BGBK, 60440	3205	21W-11S	D7
Jonathan Burr Elementary School 1621 W Wabansia Av, CHCG, 60622	2977	2W-2N	C7
Jones College Prep High School 606 S State St, CHCG, 60605	3034	0W-0S	B6
Jordan Community School 7414 N Wolcott Av, CHCG, 60626	2867	2W-9N	B7
Josephine Perry Elementary School 251 Amarillo Dr, CPVL, 60110	2748	33W-18N	B4
Josephinum Academy 1501 N Oakley Blvd, CHCG, 60622	3033	2W-1N	B1
Joseph J Pleviak Elementary School 304 E Grand Av, LKVL, 60046	2475	22W-38N	B1
Joseph Sears Elementary School 542 Abbotsford Rd, KLWH, 60043	2812	4W-14N	C4
JS Morton East High School 2423 S Austin Blvd, CCRO, 60804	3089	7W-2S	C2

Chicago 7-County Points of Interest Index

FEATURE NAME	Address City ZIP Code	MAP#	CGS	GRID
JS Morton West High School	2400 Home Av, BRWN, 60402	3088	8W-2S	E2
Juarez Community Academy	2150 S Laflin St, CHCG, 60608	3091	1W-1S	D1
Julian High School	10330 S Elizabeth St, CHCG, 60643	3277	1W-12S	E1
Julia Ward Howe Elementary School	720 N Lorel Av, CHCG, 60644	3031	6W-0N	D3
Juliette Low Elementary School	1530 S Highland Av, ANHT, 60005	2861	18W-12N	A1
Jungman Elementary School	1746 S Miller St, CHCG, 60608	3091	1W-1S	E1
JW Gates Elementary School	800 7th Av, AURA, 60505	3200	35W-8S	C2
JW James Christian School	911 S 6th Av, MYWD, 60153	3030	10W-0N	A5
Kahler Middle School	600 Joliet St, DYR, 46311	3598		D2
Kaneland John Shields Elementary-School	85 S Main St, SRGV, 60554	3135	42W-7S	C7
Kaneland-John Stewart Elementary-School	817 Prairie Valley St, ELBN, 60119	3017	43W-2N	B2
Kanoon Magnet Elementary School	2233 S Kedzie Av, CHCG, 60623	3090	3W-2S	E2
Katzenmaier Elementary School	1829 Kennedy Dr, NCHI, 60064	2536	11W-31N	D6
Kellar School	14123 S Lydia Av, RBBN, 60472	3348	4W-16S	E3
Keller Junior High School	820 Bode Rd, SMBG, 60194	2858	24W-11N	D3
Keller Regional Gifted Center	3020 W 108th St, CHCG, 60655	3276	3W-12S	E2
Kellman Corp Community School	751 S Sacramento Blvd, CHCG, 60612	3032	3W-0S	E6
Kellogg Elementary School	9241 S Leavitt St, CHCG, 60620	3213	2W-10S	C5
Kelly High School	4136 S California Av, CHCG, 60632	3091	3W-4S	A6
Kelvin Grove Junior High School	808 Adams St, LKPT, 60441	3419	21W-19S	E3
Kelvyn Park High School	4343 W Wrightwood Av, CHCG, 60639	2976	5W-3N	B5
Kendall Elementary School	2408 Meadow Lake Dr, NPVL, 60564	3266	29W-12S	D3
Kennedy Elementary School	1013 Division St, CHHT, 60411	3507	2W-25S	D6
Kennedy Junior High School	2929 Green Trails Dr, LSLE, 60532	3142	24W-7S	C6
Kenneth L Hermansen Elementary-School	101 Wesglen Pkwy, RMVL, 60446	3339	26W-17S	E5
Kenneth Murphy Elementary School	11315 W Wadsworth Rd, BHPK, 60099	2421	11W-39N	E6
Kenwood Academy	5015 S Blackstone Av, CHCG, 60615	3153	1E-5S	A1
Kenwood Academy High School	5015 S Blackstone Av, CHCG, 60615	3153	1E-5S	A1
Kenwood Elementary School	6416 Hohman Av, HMND, 46324	3430		C2
Kenyon Woods Middle School	1515 Raymond St, SEGN, 60177	2908	33W-9N	E1
Kershaw Elementary School	6450 S Lowe Av, CHCG, 60621	3152	0W-7S	A5
Key Elementary School	517 N Parkside Av, CHCG, 60644	3031	7W-0N	C3
Keystone Montessori School	7415 North Av, RVFT, 60305	3030	9W-1N	D1
Kildeer Countryside Elementary-School	3100 Old McHenry Rd, LGGV, 60047	2700	18W-21N	D5
Kilmer Elementary School	655 Golfview Ter, BFGV, 60089	2754	16W-18N	C4
Kilmer Elementary School	6700 N Greenview Av, CHCG, 60626	2921	1W-8N	C2
Kimball Hill Elementary School	2905 Meadow Dr, RGMW, 60008	2806	19W-13N	C5
Kimball Middle School	451 N McLean Blvd, ELGN, 60123	2854	35W-11N	B3
King College Prep High School	4445 S Drexel Blvd, CHCG, 60653	3092	1E-4S	E7
King Elementary School	740 S Campbell Av, CHCG, 60612	3033	3W-0S	A6
Kingsley Elementary School	6509 Powell St, DRGV, 60516	3144	20W-7S	B6
Kingsley Elementary School	2300 Green Bay Rd, EVTN, 60201	2867	3W-12N	A1
Kingsley Elementary School	2403 Kingsley Dr, NPVL, 60565	3203	26W-10S	E5
Kingswood Academy	1501 N Frontage Rd, DRN, 60561	3207	18W-9S	A4
Kinzie Elementary School	5625 S Mobile Av, CHCG, 60638	3149	7W-6S	B3
Kipling Elementary School	9351 S Lowe Av, CHCG, 60620	3214	0W-10S	A5
Kipling Elementary School	700 Kipling Pl, DRFD, 60015	2704	10W-20N	A7
KIPP Ascend Charter School	715 S Kildare Av, CHCG, 60624	3032	5W-0S	B6
KIPP Chicago Youth Academy	2710 S Dearborn St, CHCG, 60616	3092	0W-2S	C3
Kohn Elementary School	10414 S State St, CHCG, 60628	3278	0W-12S	C1
Kolb Elementary School	9620 Normandy Av, OKLN, 60453	3211	8W-11S	A6
Kolmar Avenue Elementary School	10425 S Kolmar Av, OKLN, 60453	3276	5W-12S	B1
Kolmar Elementary School	4500 143rd St, CTWD, 60445	3348	5W-16S	B4
Komarek Elementary School	8940 W 24th St, NRIV, 60546	3087	11W-2S	E2
Komensky Elementary School	2515 Cuyler Av, BRWN, 60402	3089	7W-2S	B3
Koraes Elementary School	11025 S Roberts Rd, PSHL, 60465	3274	9W-12S	C3
Kozminski Community Academy	936 E 54th St, CHCG, 60615	3152	1E-5S	E2
Kruse Education Center	7617 Hemlock Dr, ODPK, 60462	3346	9W-18S	D7
Lace Elementary School	7414 S Cass Av, DRN, 60561	3207	18W-8S	B1
Lafayette Elementary School	2714 W Augusta Blvd, CHCG, 60622	3033	3W-1N	A2
Lafayette Elementary School	856 E Sibley St, HMND, 46320	3352		E6
Lake Bluff Middle School	31 E Sheridan Pl, LKBF, 60044	2593	10W-28N	E6
Lake County Baptist School	1550 W Yorkhouse Rd, WKGN, 60087	2479	11W-37N	E2
Lake Forest Academy	1500 W Kennedy Rd, LKFT, 60045	2649	13W-26N	A3
Lake Forest Country Day School	145 S Green Bay Rd, LKFT, 60045	2650	10W-25N	A4
Lake Forest High School	1285 N McKinley Rd, LKFT, 60045	2650	10W-27N	A1
Lake In the Hills Elementary School	519 Willow St, LIHL, 60156	2694	34W-22N	B5
Lake Louise Elementary School	500 N Jonathan Dr, PLTN, 60074	2753	19W-16N	D7
Lake Park Elementary School	330 W Lake Park Dr, ADSN, 60101	2970	18W-3N	D6
Lake Park High School East Campus	600 Medinah Rd, ROSL, 60143	2913	22W-6N	C6
Lake Park High School West Campus	500 W Bryn Mawr Av, ROSL, 60172	2912	24W-7N	D5
Lakes Community High School	1600 Eagle Wy, LKVL, 60002	2417	21W-39N	C4
Lake Shore School	6759 N Greenview Av, CHCG, 60626	2921	1W-8N	C2
Lake Shore School	5611 N Clark St, CHCG, 60660	2921	1W-7N	C4
Lakeview Elementary School	615 Lakeview Ln, HFET, 60169	2858	24W-11N	E4
Lake View High School	4015 N Ashland Av, CHCG, 60613	2977	2W-5N	C1
Lakeview Junior High School	701 Plainfield Rd, DGvT, 60516	3206	19W-9S	D3
Lakewood Creek Elementary School	2301 Lakewood Crk, MTGY, 60538	3199	36W-10S	D5
Lakewood Falls Elementary School	14050 S Budler Rd, PnfT, 60544	3339	27W-16S	C4
Lakewood School	1651 Ravine Ln, CPVL, 60110	2748	33W-17N	C7
Lake Zurich High School	300 Church St, LKZH, 60047	2698	23W-23N	E2
Lake Zurich Middle School-North	95 Hubbard Ln, LKZH, 60047	2698	23W-23N	E3
Lake Zurich Middle School-South	435 W Cuba Rd, LKZH, 60010	2699	23W-21N	A6
Landmark Elementary School	3614 Waukegan Rd, MHRY, 60050	2528	32W-33N	B4
Lane Elementary School	4600 W 123rd St, ALSP, 60803	3276	5W-14S	B6
Lane Technical High School	2501 W Addison St, CHCG, 60618	2977	3W-4N	A3
Langston Hughes Elementary School	226 W 104th St, CHCG, 60628	3278	0W-12S	B1
Lansing Christian School	3660 Randolph St, LNSG, 60438	3430	4E-21S	C6
Lara Academy	4619 S Wolcott Av, CHCG, 60609	3091	2W-4S	C7
Laraway Elementary School	275 W Laraway Rd, JltT, 60436	3586	24W-26S	E4
Larkin High School	1475 Larkin Av, ELGN, 60123	2854	35W-11N	B4
Larsen Middle School	665 Dundee Av, ELGN, 60120	2855	33W-12N	A2
Lasalle Language Academy	1734 N Orleans St, CHCG, 60614	2978	0W-2N	B7
Lathrop Elementary Academy	1440 S Christiana Av, CHCG, 60623	3032	4W-1S	D7
Latin School of Chicago	59 W North Blvd, CHCG, 60610	2978	0W-2N	B7
Latin School of Chicago	1531 N Dearborn Pkwy, CHCG, 60610	3034	0W-1N	B1
Laura Sprague Elementary School	2425 Riverwoods Rd, LNSH, 60069	2702	13W-22N	D3
Laura S Ward Elementary School	410 N Monticello Av, CHCG, 60624	3032	4W-0N	C3
Laurel Hill Elementary School	1750 Laurel Av, HRPK, 60133	2911	27W-9N	D2
Lavizzo Elementary School	138 W 109th St, CHCG, 60628	3278	0W-12S	C2
Lawndale Community Academy	3500 W Douglas Blvd, CHCG, 60623	3032	4W-1S	D7
Lawn Manor Primary Center	4300 W 108th Pl, OKLN, 60453	3276	5W-12S	B2
Lawrence Elementary School	9928 S Crandon Av, CHCG, 60617	3215	2E-11S	D7
LD Brady Elementary School	600 Columbia St, AURA, 60505	3138	35W-7S	C7
Lee Elementary School	6448 S Tripp Av, CHCG, 60629	3150	5W-7S	B5
Leggee Elementary School	13723 Harmony Rd, HTLY, 60142	2691	42W-20N	B7
Leland Elementary School	5221 W Congress Pkwy, CHCG, 60644	3031	6W-0S	D6
Lemont High School	800 Porter St, LMNT, 60439	3270	19W-13S	E5
Lemoyne Elementary School	851 W Waveland Av, CHCG, 60613	2977	1W-4N	E2
Lenart Regional Gifted Center	8101 S la Salle St, CHCG, 60620	3214	0W-9S	B2
Leo High School	7901 S Sangamon St, CHCG, 60620	3214	1W-9S	A2
Leslie Lewis Elementary School	1431 N Leamington Av, CHCG, 60651	3031	6W-1N	E1
Lester Elementary School	236 Indianapolis Av, DRGV, 60515	3144	18W-4S	E1
Lexington Elementary School	415 Lexington St, MYWD, 60153	3030	10W-0S	A6
LH Day School	1720 W 87th St, CHCG, 60620	3213	2W-9S	D4
Libby Elementary School	5300 S Loomis Blvd, CHCG, 60609	3151	1W-5S	D2
Liberty Elementary School	121 Naperville Rd, BRLT, 60103	2910	30W-8N	B3
Liberty Elementary School	4946 W 13th St, CCRO, 60804	3031	6W-1S	E7
Liberty Elementary School	6500 Miller Rd, CPVL, 60110	2747	36W-17N	A6
Liberty Elementary School	8801 W 151st St, ODPK, 60462	3346	10W-18S	A6
Liberty Junior High School	5900 W 81st St, BRBK, 60459	3211	7W-9S	C2
Liberty Junior High School	151 Lenox St, NLNX, 60451	3501	17W-23S	C3
Liberty Temple Academy	2255 W 79th St, CHCG, 60620	3213	2W-9S	B2
Libertyville High School	708 W Park Av, LYVL, 60048	2591	17W-28N	C5
Lieb Elementary School	9101 Pembroke Ln, BGVW, 60455	3211	8W-10S	A5
Lincoln Elementary School	720 N Lincoln Av, ADSN, 60101	2970	18W-4N	E3
Lincoln Elementary School	641 S Lake St, AURA, 60506	3199	36W-8S	E1
Lincoln Elementary School	4300 Grove Av, BKFD, 60513	3087	11W-4S	E7
Lincoln Elementary School	3420 Jackson St, BLWD, 60104	3029	12W-0S	B5
Lincoln Elementary School	3545 S 61st Av, CCRO, 60804	3089	7W-3S	B5
Lincoln Elementary School	615 W Kemper Pl, CHCG, 60614	2978	0W-2N	A6
Lincoln Elementary School	1520 Center Av, CHHT, 60411	3596	0W-25S	B1
Lincoln Elementary School	410 157th St, CTCY, 60409	3352	4E-18S	B7
Lincoln Elementary School	14151 Lincoln Av, DLTN, 60419	3350	0E-16S	E3
Lincoln Elementary School	14100 Honore Av, DXMR, 60426	3349	2W-16S	D4
Lincoln Elementary School	565 S Fairfield Av, EMHT, 60126	3027	16W-0N	D4
Lincoln Elementary School	910 Forest Av, EVTN, 60202	2867	2W-10N	C4
Lincoln Elementary School	711 Lincoln Av W, HDPK, 60035	2704	8W-21N	E6
Lincoln Elementary School	1650 Maureen Dr, HFET, 60192	2855	31W-12N	D1
Lincoln Elementary School	4221 S Towle Av, HMND, 46327	3352		D3
Lincoln Elementary School	200 W Maple Av, MDLN, 60060	2590	19W-28N	D6
Lincoln Elementary School	811 Chicago Av, MYWD, 60153	3029	10W-1N	E3
Lincoln Elementary School	1111 S Grove Av, OKPK, 60304	3030	8W-0S	E6
Lincoln Elementary School	1021 N Ridgewood Ln, PLTN, 60067	2753	20W-17N	A5
Lincoln Elementary School	14740 Meadow Ln, PNFD, 60544	3337	31W-17S	E6
Lincoln Elementary School	511 Park Av, RVFT, 60305	3030	9W-0N	C3
Lincoln Elementary School	211 S 6th Av, SCRL, 60174	2964	35W-3N	C7
Lincoln Elementary School	630 Dawes Av, WHTN, 60187	3082	24W-1S	D1
Lincoln Hall Middle School	6855 N Crawford Av, LNWD, 60712	2920	4W-8N	B1
Lincoln Junior High School	14151 Lincoln Av, DLTN, 60419	3350	0E-16S	E3
Lincoln Junior High School	700 W Lincoln St, MPPT, 60056	2861	16W-12N	E1
Lincoln Junior High School	1320 Olympus Dr, NPVL, 60565	3203	26W-8S	E2
Lincoln Junior High School	7839 Lincoln Av, SKOK, 60077	2865	6W-9N	E6
Lincoln Middle School	6432 16th St, BRWN, 60402	3089	8W-1S	A1
Lincoln Middle School	200 S Lincoln Av, PKRG, 60068	2917	10W-8N	E1
Lincoln Middle School	4050 Wagner Av, SRPK, 60176	2973	12W-5N	C2
Lincoln Park High School	2001 N Orchard St, CHCG, 60614	2978	0W-2N	A6
Lincoln Prairie Elementary School	500 Hillcrest Blvd, HFET, 60169	2858	24W-12N	E1
Lincoln Prairie Elementary School	500 Harvest Gate, LIHL, 60156	2693	36W-21N	D5
Lincoln School	2140 Broadway St, BLID, 60406	3349	2W-15S	C1
Lincoln-Way Central High School	1801 E Lincoln Hwy, NlxT, 60451	3502	16W-25S	A7
Lincoln-Way East High School	201 Colorado Av, FKFT, 60423	3503	12W-25S	D7
Lincolnwood Elementary School	2600 Colfax St, EVTN, 60201	2866	4W-12N	D1
Lindblom College Prep High School	6130 S Wolcott Av, CHCG, 60636	3151	2W-6S	C4
Lindop Elementary School	2400 S 18th Av, BDVW, 60155	3029	11W-1S	D7
Lines Elementary School	217 Eastern Av, BRTN, 60010	2751	24W-18N	B2
Link Elementary School	900 W Glenn Tr, EGVV, 60007	2913	21W-8N	E1
Lions Park Elementary School	300 E Council Tr, MPPT, 60056	2862	15W-12N	A1
Lisle High School	1800 Short St, LSLE, 60532	3143	23W-5S	A3
Lisle Junior High School	5207 Center Av, LSLE, 60532	3143	22W-5S	B3
Little Fort Elementary School	1775 Blanchard Rd, WKGN, 60087	2479	11W-36N	D3
Little Village Academy	2620 S Lawndale Av, CHCG, 60623	3090	4W-2S	C3
Living Word Christian Academy	501 Bellwood Av, BLWD, 60104	3029	12W-0N	B4
LJ Hauser Junior High School	65 Woodside Rd, RVSD, 60546	3088	9W-3S	C5
LJ Stevens Middle School	221 Ryan St, WMTN, 60481	3853	27W-39S	D7
Locke 21st Century School	3141 W Jackson Blvd, CHCG, 60612	3032	3W-0S	E5
Locke Elementary School	2828 N Oak Park Av, CHCG, 60634	2974	8W-3N	E5
Lockport Twp High School-Central	1333 E 7th St, LKPT, 60441	3419	22W-19S	C3
Lockport Twp High School-East	1333 E 7th St, LKPT, 60441	3420	21W-19S	A3
Locust Elementary School	539 Locust St, MRGO, 60152	2634	49W-26N	C3
Logandale Middle School	3212 W George St, CHCG, 60618	2976	4W-3N	D4

Chicago 7-County Points of Interest Index

FEATURE NAME Address City ZIP Code	MAP#	CGS	GRID
London Middle School 1001 W Dundee Rd, WLNG, 60090	2754	15W-18N	E4
Long Beach Elementary School 67 Long Beach Rd, OswT, 60538	3199	36W-10S	E7
Longfellow Elementary School 501 Arlington Heights Rd, BFGV, 60089	2754	17W-18N	A3
Longfellow Elementary School 715 Highland Av, OKPK, 60304	3031	7W-0S	B5
Longfellow Elementary School 311 W Seminary Av, WHTN, 60187	3024	24W-0S	C6
Longwood Elementary School 441 N Longwood Dr, GNWD, 60425	3508	0W-22S	B1
Longwood Elementary School 30W240 Bruce Ln, NpvT, 60563	3140	30W-5S	B3
Lords Park Elementary School 323 Waverly Dr, ELGN, 60120	2855	32W-11N	C3
Lotus School 29067 W Grass Lake Rd, FXLK, 60081	2414	28W-39N	D6
Louise White Elementary School 800 N Prairie St, BTVA, 60510	3020	34W-0S	C7
Lovett Elementary School 6333 W Bloomingdale Av, CHCG, 60639	2975	7W-2N	B7
Lowell Elementary School 312 S President St, WHTN, 60187	3024	24W-0S	E7
Lowell-Longfellow Elementary School 15636 Lexington Av, HRVY, 60426	3427	1W-18S	E1
Lowrie Elementary School 264 Oak St, ELGN, 60123	2854	34W-10N	E5
Loyola Academy 1100 Laramie Av, WLMT, 60091	2811	6W-14N	D5
Lozano Bilingual-International-Center 1424 N Cleaver St, CHCG, 60622	3033	1W-1N	D1
Ludwig School 710 N State St, LKPT, 60441	3341	22W-18S	D7
Lundahl Middle School 560 Nash Rd, CLLK, 60014	2639	36W-24N	E6
Lutheran School of St. Luke 410 S Rush St, ITSC, 60143	2914	19W-6N	C7
Luther Burbank Elementary School 8235 Linder Av, BRBK, 60459	3211	6W-9S	D3
Luther Burbank Elementary School 2035 N Mobile Av, CHCG, 60639	2975	7W-2N	B7
Luther East High School 2750 Glenwood Lansing Rd, LNSG, 60438	3510	3E-22S	A2
Luther High School North 5700 W Berteau Av, CHCG, 60634	2975	7W-5N	C1
Luther High School South-Junior High-School 3130 W 87th St, CHCG, 60652	3212	3W-9S	E3
Luther J Schilling Elementary-School 16025 S Cedar Rd, HmrT, 60491	3421	18W-19S	A2
Lycee Francais de Chicago 613 W Bittersweet Pl, CHCG, 60613	2978	0W-5N	A1
Lyle Elementary School 7801 W 75th St, BGVW, 60455	3210	9W-8S	C1
Lyman A Budlong Elementary School 2701 W Foster Av, CHCG, 60625	2920	3W-6N	E6
Lynne Thigpen Elementary School 207 S Midland Av, JLET, 60436	3498	25W-24S	B5
Lyon Elementary School 1335 Waukegan Rd, GNVW, 60025	2810	8W-13N	E5
Lyon Magnet Elementary School 800 S Elmwood Av, WKGN, 60085	2536	11W-33N	D4
Lyons Twp High School-North 100 S Brainard Av, LGNG, 60525	3087	13W-4S	A7
Lyons Twp High School-South 100 S Brainard Av, WNSP, 60558	3147	13W-5S	A2
Mabel O'Donnell Elementary School 1640 Reckinger Rd, AURA, 60505	3139	33W-5S	A4
MacArthur Elementary School 1800 Chippendale Rd, HFET, 60169	2858	24W-12N	C1
MacArthur Middle School 1310 N Wolf Rd, BKLY, 60163	3028	14W-0N	D3
MacArthur Middle School 700 N Schoenbeck Rd, PTHT, 60070	2807	16W-15N	E1
Mackeben Elementary School 800 Academic Dr, ALGN, 60102	2746	38W-20N	A1
Maddock Elementary School 8258 Sayre Av, BRBK, 60459	3210	8W-9S	E3
Madero Middle School 3202 W 28th St, CHCG, 60623	3090	4W-2S	E3
Madison Elementary School 611 S Madison St, HNDL, 60521	3146	15W-5S	A2
Madison Elementary School 150 W Madison St, LMBD, 60148	3026	20W-0N	B5
Madison Elementary School 15700 Orchid Dr, SHLD, 60473	3350	0E-18S	E7
Madison Elementary School 5100 Madison St, SKOK, 60077	2865	6W-10N	D5
Madison Elementary School 1620 Mayo Av, WHTN, 60187	3082	25W-1S	A2
Madison Junior High School 1000 River Oak Dr, NPVL, 60565	3204	25W-9S	C3
Mae Jemison School 3450 W 177th St, HLCT, 60429	3426	4W-21S	E6
Maercker Elementary School 5827 S Cass Av, WTMT, 60559	3145	17W-6S	B4
Mahalia Jackson Elementary School 917 W 88th St, CHCG, 60620	3214	1W-10S	A4
Maine East High School 2601 Dempster St, PKRG, 60068	2863	11W-10N	D4
Maine South High School 1111 S Dee Rd, PKRG, 60068	2917	11W-8N	D2
Maine West High School 1755 S Wolf Rd, DSPN, 60018	2862	14W-9N	D6
Manhattan Junior High School 15606 W Smith Rd, MHTN, 60442	3677	19W-29S	D2
Manierre Elementary School 1420 N Hudson Av, CHCG, 60610	3034	0W-1N	A1
Manley Career Academy High School 2935 W Polk St, CHCG, 60612	3032	3W-0S	E6
Mannheim Middle School 2600 Hyde Park Av, LydT, 60164	2973	13W-3N	A5
Manning Elementary School 200 N Linden Av, WTMT, 60559	3145	17W-5S	B2
Manor Hill Elementary School 1464 S Main St, LMBD, 60148	3084	20W-1S	B1
Maplebrook Elementary School 1630 Warbler Dr, NPVL, 60565	3203	26W-9S	E3

FEATURE NAME Address City ZIP Code	MAP#	CGS	GRID
Maple Middle School 2370 Shermer Rd, NHBK, 60062	2810	10W-16N	B1
Maplewood Elementary School 422 Krenz Av, CRY, 60013	2695	31W-23N	D1
Maranatha Christian Academy 115 W 108th St, CHCG, 60628	3278	0W-12S	C2
Marconi Community Academy 230 N Kolmar Av, CHCG, 60624	3032	5W-0N	A4
Marcus M Garvey Elementary School 10309 S Morgan St, CHCG, 60643	3278	1W-12S	A1
Marengo High School 110 Franks Rd, MRGO, 60152	2634	49W-26N	D3
Marengo Middle School 816 E Grant Hwy, MRGO, 60152	2634	49W-26N	C3
Maria High School 6727 S California Av, CHCG, 60629	3151	3W-7S	A6
Marian Catholic High School 700 Ashland Av, CHHT, 60411	3507	2W-24S	D5
Marian Central Catholic High School 1001 McHenry Av, WDSK, 60098	2524	40W-31N	E6
Marie Murphy Middle School 2921 Illinois Rd, WLMT, 60091	2811	5W-14N	E4
Marion Jordan Elementary School 100 N Harrison Av, PLTN, 60067	2805	22W-16N	B1
Marist High School 4200 W 115th St, CHCG, 60655	3276	5W-13S	C4
Mark Delay Elementary School 6801 Wilmette Av, DRN, 60561	3145	17W-7S	B7
Markham Park Elementary School 16239 Lawndale Av, MKHM, 60428	3426	4W-19S	D2
Mark Sheridan Academy 533 W 27th St, CHCG, 60616	3092	0W-2S	A3
Mark Twain Elementary School 515 Merle Ln, WLNG, 60090	2755	15W-17N	A5
Marmion Academy 1000 Butterfield Rd, AURA, 60502	3078	34W-3S	D7
Marquardt Middle School 1912 Glen Ellyn Rd, GLHT, 60139	2969	22W-3N	C5
Marquette Elementary School 6550 S Richmond St, CHCG, 60629	3150	3W-7S	E5
Marquette Manor Baptist Academy 333 75th St, DRGV, 60516	3206	19W-8S	E1
Marshall Elementary School 2501 Oak St, BLWD, 60104	3029	12W-0N	C4
Marshall Elementary School 319 Harwood St, JLET, 60432	3499	22W-23S	D4
Marshall Metropolitan High School 3250 W Adams St, CHCG, 60624	3032	4W-0S	D5
Marshall Middle School 3900 N Lawndale Av, CHCG, 60618	2976	4W-4N	C2
Marti Bilingual Education Center 5126 N Kenmore Av, CHCG, 60640	2921	1W-6N	E6
Martin Luther King Elementary-School 14600 Seeley Av, DXMR, 60426	3349	2W-17S	C5
Martino Junior High School 731 E Joliet Hwy, NLNX, 60451	3501	17W-25S	D7
Marva Collins Preparatory School 8035 S Honore St, CHCG, 60620	3213	2W-9S	C2
Marya Yates Elementary School 6131 Allemong Dr, MTSN, 60443	3505	7W-24S	C5
Mary Endres Elementary School 2181 N Seminary Av, WDSK, 60098	2524	41W-32N	D4
Mary Lyon Elementary School 2941 N McVicker Av, CHCG, 60634	2975	7W-3N	B4
Mary Seat of Wisdom School 1352 S Cumberland Av, PKRG, 60068	2918	10W-7N	A3
Mason Elementary School 4217 W 18th St, CHCG, 60623	3090	5W-1S	B1
Maternity BVM School 1537 N Lawndale Av, CHCG, 60651	3032	4W-1N	C1
Mather High School 5835 N Lincoln Av, CHCG, 60659	2920	3W-7N	E4
Matteson Elementary School 21245 Main St, MTSN, 60443	3594	4W-25S	E1
Maya Angelou Elementary School 15748 Page Av, HRVY, 60426	3427	2W-18S	D1
May Chesak Elementary School 10910 Reed Rd, LIHL, 60142	2692	39W-22N	B5
May Community Academy 512 S Lavergne Av, CHCG, 60644	3031	6W-0S	E6
Mayer Elementary School 2250 N Clifton Av, CHCG, 60614	2977	1W-2N	D6
Mayo Elementary School 249 E 37th St, CHCG, 60653	3092	0E-3S	C5
May Whitney Elementary School 120 Church St, LKZH, 60047	2698	23W-23N	E2
Maywood Elementary School 1001 165th St, HMND, 46324	3430		E2
McAuliffe Elementary School 1841 N Springfield Av, CHCG, 60647	2976	4W-2N	C7
McAuliffe Elementary School 8944 174th St, TYPK, 60487	3424	11W-20S	A5
McCall Elementary School 3215 N McAree Rd, WKGN, 60087	2479	11W-37N	C2
McCarty Elementary School 3000 Village Green Dr, AURA, 60504	3201	31W-8S	D2
McCleery Elementary School 1002 W Illinois Av, AURA, 60506	3137	36W-6S	D6
McClellan Elementary School 3527 S Wallace St, CHCG, 60609	3092	0W-3S	A5
McClure Junior High School 4225 Wolf Rd, WNSP, 60558	3086	13W-4S	E7
McCorkle Elementary School 4421 S State St, CHCG, 60653	3092	0E-4S	C7
McCormick Elementary School 2712 S Sawyer Av, CHCG, 60623	3090	4W-2S	D3
MCC School 8601 Menard Av, MNGV, 60053	2865	7W-10N	C4
McCutcheon Branch Elementary School 4850 N Kenmore Av, CHCG, 60640	2921	1W-6N	E6
McCutcheon Elementary School 4865 N Sheridan Rd, CHCG, 60640	2921	1W-6N	E6
McDade Classical Elementary School 8801 S Indiana Av, CHCG, 60619	3214	0E-10S	C4
McDole Elementary School 2901 Foxmoor Dr, MTGY, 60538	3198	40W-9S	C5
McDowell Elementary School 1419 E 89th St, CHCG, 60619	3215	1E-10S	B4
McHenry High School East 1012 N Green St, MHRY, 60050	2528	32W-32N	B4

FEATURE NAME Address City ZIP Code	MAP#	CGS	GRID
McHenry High School West 4724 W Crystal Lake Rd, MHRY, 60050	2527	33W-32N	E4
McHenry Middle School 2120 W Henry Rd, MHRY, 60051	2528	31W-33N	E2
McKay Elementary School 6901 S Fairfield Av, CHCG, 60629	3151	3W-7S	A6
McKenzie Elementary School 649 Prairie Av, WLMT, 60091	2812	3W-13N	D6
McKinley Elementary School 3317 Butterfield Rd, BLWD, 60104	3029	12W-0N	B4
McKinley Elementary School 5900 W 14th St, CCRO, 60804	3031	7W-1S	C7
McKinley Elementary School 25 W 16th Pl, CHHT, 60411	3596	1W-25S	A1
McKinley Elementary School 258 Lovell St, ELGN, 60120	2854	33W-12N	E2
McKinley Elementary School 850 E 170th St, SHLD, 60473	3429	1E-19S	A3
McKinley Junior High School 16949 Cottage Grove Av, SHLD, 60473	3429	1E-19S	A3
McKinley Park Elementary School 2744 W Pershing Rd, CHCG, 60632	3091	3W-3S	A6
McPherson Elementary School 4728 N Wolcott Av, CHCG, 60640	2921	2W-5N	C7
Mead Junior High School 1765 Biesterfield Rd, EGVV, 60007	2913	22W-9N	D1
Meadowbrook Elementary School 1600 Walters Av, NHBK, 60062	2757	9W-17N	C6
Meadowdale Elementary School 14 Ash St, CPVL, 60110	2748	32W-17N	C6
Meadow Glens Elementary School 1150 Muirhead Av, NPVL, 60565	3204	25W-8S	C2
Meadow Lane Intr Center 11800 S Meadow Lane Dr, MTPK, 60803	3276	3W-13S	E5
Meadow Ridge School 10959 W 159th St, ODPK, 60467	3423	13W-19S	A1
Meadowview Elementary School 4701 179th Pl, CCHL, 60478	3426	5W-21S	B6
Meadow View Elementary School 2501 Mirage Av, JLET, 60586	3415	32W-20S	C6
Meadowview Elementary School 2525 Mitchell Dr, WDRG, 60517	3143	21W-7S	D6
Meadowview School 291 Lexington Ln, GYLK, 60030	2532	21W-34N	D1
Meca Elementary Christian Academy 425 Bohland Av, BLWD, 60104	3029	12W-0N	B4
Mechanics Grove Elementary School 1200 N Midlothian Rd, MDLN, 60060	2590	19W-28N	B5
Medgar Evers Primary Academy Center 1101 E 10th St, FDHT, 60411	3509	1E-24S	B6
Medill Elementary School 1301 W 14th St, CHCG, 60608	3033	1W-1S	D7
Medinah Christian School 900 Foster Av, ROSL, 60157	2913	22W-6N	C6
Medinah Intermediate School 7n330 Medinah Rd, BmdT, 60157	2913	22W-7N	D5
Medinah Middle School 700 E Granville Av, ROSL, 60172	2913	22W-7N	C4
Medinah Primary School 22W300 Sunnyside Rd, BmdT, 60157	2913	22W-6N	C5
Melody Elementary School 412 S Keeler Av, CHCG, 60624	3032	5W-0S	B5
Melrose Park Elementary School 1715 W Lake St, MLPK, 60160	3029	11W-1N	D3
Melzer School 9400 Oriole Av, MNGV, 60053	2864	9W-11N	C2
Memorial Elementary School 6701 179th St, TYPK, 60477	3425	8W-21S	B6
Memorial Junior High School 2721 Ridge Rd, LNSG, 60438	3430	3E-21S	A6
Meridian Middle School 2195 Brandywyn Ln, BFGV, 60089	2701	16W-22N	D4
Metcalfe Community Academy 12339 S Normal Av, CHCG, 60628	3278	0W-14S	B6
Metro Prep School 2525 E Oakton St, EGvT, 60005	2861	16W-9N	E6
Michael M Byrne Elementary School 5329 S Oak Park Av, CHCG, 60638	3149	8W-5S	A2
Middlefork Primary School 405 Wagner Rd, NHFD, 60093	2811	7W-15N	B2
Midway Academy 5434 S Lockwood Av, CHCG, 60638	3149	6W-5S	D3
Midwestern Christian Academy 3465 N Cicero Av, CHCG, 60641	2975	5W-4N	E3
Mighty God Christian Academy 6740 S South Shore Dr, CHCG, 60649	3153	3E-7S	D5
Millburn Community Consolidated-School 18550 W Millburn Rd, OMCK, 60083	2418	18W-38N	E7
Millburn School 640 Freedom Wy, LNHT, 60046	2418	19W-39N	C5
Millburn West Elementary School 640 Freedom Way, ANHT, 60004	2807	17W-16N	A1
Mill Creek Elementary School 0N900 Brundige Dr, BbyT, 60119	3018	39W-1N	D2
Millennium Elementary School 17830 84th Av, TYPK, 60487	3424	10W-21S	B6
Millennium School 18211 Aberdeen St, HMWD, 60430	3428	1W-21S	A7
Miller Elementary School 125 W Traube Av, WTMT, 60559	3145	18W-4S	A1
Mill Street Elementary School 1300 N Mill St, NPVL, 60563	3141	27W-5S	C3
Milne Grove Elementary School 565 E 7th St, LKPT, 60441	3419	22W-19S	D3
Minooka Community High School 301 S Wabena Av, MNKA, 60447	3672	33W-28S	A1
Minooka Elementary School 400 W Coady Dr, MNKA, 60447	3583	33W-28S	B6
Minooka Intermediate School 305 W Church St, MNKA, 60447	3583	33W-28S	A7
Minooka Junior High School 333 McEvilly Rd, MNKA, 60447	3672	33W-28S	A1
Mitchell Branch Elementary School 2315 W Erie St, CHCG, 60612	3033	2W-0N	B3
Mitchell Elementary School 2233 W Ohio St, CHCG, 60612	3033	2W-0N	B3
ML King Junior Lab School 2424 Lake St, EVTN, 60201	2866	3W-11N	D3
M Moody Christian School 3811 W 139th St, RBBN, 60472	3348	4W-16S	D3

FEATURE NAME Address City ZIP Code	MAP#	CGS	GRID
Mohawk Elementary School 917 W Hillside Dr, BNVL, 60106	2915	16W-6N	D7
Mohawk Elementary School 301 Mohawk St, PKFT, 60466	3595	4W-27S	A4
Mokena Elementary School 11244 Willow Crest Ln, MKNA, 60448	3502	14W-23S	E4
Mokena Intermediate School 11331 195th St, MKNA, 60448	3502	14W-23S	E3
Mokena Junior High School 19815 Kirkstone Wy, MKNA, 60448	3503	12W-23S	C4
Mollison Elementary School 4415 S King Dr, CHCG, 60653	3092	0E-4S	D7
Monee Elementary School 5154 W Main St, MONE, 60449	3683	6W-31S	A5
Monge Junior High School 400 Elsie Av, CTHL, 60403	3418	24W-21S	D7
Monroe Elementary School 210 N Madison St, HNDL, 60521	3146	16W-4S	A1
Monroe Middle School 1855 Manchester Rd, WHTN, 60187	3024	26W-0S	A6
Montessori Academy 595 S River St, BTVA, 60510	3078	35W-1S	C3
Montessori School House 5935 S Hohman Av, HMND, 46320	3430		D1
Montessori School of Lake Forest 13700 W Laurel Dr, LbvT, 60045	2592	13W-28N	E7
Montessori School of Long Grove 1115 Robert Parker Coffin Rd, LGGV, 60047	2700	18W-21N	D6
Montini Catholic High School 19W070 16th St, YkTp, 60148	3084	19W-1S	D1
Montini Middle School 1405 N Richmond Rd, MHRY, 60050	2528	32W-33N	B3
Montini Primary Center 3504 Washington St, MHRY, 60050	2528	32W-33N	B3
Morgan Park Academy 2153 W 111th St, CHCG, 60643	3277	2W-12S	B2
Morgan Park High School 1744 W Pryor Av, CHCG, 60643	3277	2W-12S	D3
Morrill Elementary Math & Science-School 6011 S Rockwell St, CHCG, 60629	3151	3W-6S	A4
Morse Elementary Tech School 620 N Sawyer Av, CHCG, 60624	3032	4W-0N	D3
Morton Career Academy 431 N Troy St, CHCG, 60612	3032	3W-0N	E3
Morton-Gingerwood Elementary School 16936 Forest Av, OKFT, 60452	3426	6W-20S	A4
Mose Vines Prep Academy 730 N Pulaski Rd, CHCG, 60624	3032	5W-0N	B3
Most Holy Redeemer School 9536 S Millard Av, ENGN, 60805	3212	4W-11S	D6
Mother McAuley Liberal Arts High-School 3737 W 99th St, CHCG, 60655	3212	4W-11S	D7
Mt Assisi Academy 13860 Main St, LmnT, 60439	3271	17W-13S	C4
Mt Carmel Academy-East Lakeview 720 W Belmont Av, CHCG, 60657	2978	0W-4N	A3
Mt Carmel High School 6410 S Dante Av, CHCG, 60637	3153	1E-7S	B5
Mt Greenwood Elementary School 10841 S Homan Av, CHCG, 60655	3276	4W-12S	E2
Mount Vernon Elementary School 10540 S Morgan St, CHCG, 60643	3278	1W-12S	A1
Mozart Elementary School 2200 N Hamlin Av, CHCG, 60647	2976	4W-2N	C6
Mundelein High School 1350 W Hawley St, MDLN, 60060	2590	19W-28N	B7
Munhall Elementary School 1400 S 13th Av, SCRL, 60174	3020	34W-2N	D1
Murphy Elementary School 3539 W Grace St, CHCG, 60618	2976	4W-4N	C2
Murphy Elementary School 7700 Larchwood Ln, WDRG, 60517	3205	21W-8S	E2
Murray Language Academy 5335 S Kenwood Av, CHCG, 60615	3153	1E-5S	A2
NA Hermes Elementary School 1000 Jungles Av, AURA, 60505	3138	34W-6S	D5
Namaste Charter School 3540 S Hermitage Av, CHCG, 60609	3091	2W-3S	C5
Naper Elementary School 39 S Eagle St, NPVL, 60540	3141	27W-6S	C5
Naperville Central High School 440 Aurora Av, NPVL, 60540	3141	27W-7S	C6
Naperville North High School 899 N Mill St, NPVL, 60563	3141	27W-5S	C4
Nathan Hale Elementary School 19055 Burnham Av, LNSG, 60438	3510	4E-22S	B1
Nathan Hale Intermediate School 5312 135th St, CTWD, 60445	3347	6W-15S	E2
Nathan Hale Middle School 5220 135th St, CTWD, 60445	3347	6W-15S	E2
Nathan Hale Primary School 5324 135th St, CTWD, 60445	3347	6W-15S	E2
National Teacher's Academy 55 W Cermak Rd, CHCG, 60616	3092	0W-2S	B1
Nativity BVM School 6820 S Washtenaw Av, CHCG, 60629	3151	3W-7S	A6
Nature Ridge Elementary School 1899 Westridge Blvd, BRLT, 60103	2909	32W-8N	D3
Navajo Heights Elementary School 12401 S Oak Park Av, PSHT, 60463	3275	8W-14S	A6
Nazareth Academy 1209 W Ogden Av, LGPK, 60525	3087	13W-3S	A6
Neal Math Science Academy 1905 Argonne Dr, NCHI, 60064	2536	11W-31N	D6
Near North Montessori School 1434 W Division St, CHCG, 60622	3033	1W-1N	D1
Neil Armstrong Elementary School 5030 Imperial Dr, RNPK, 60471	3594	6W-27S	A4
Nelson Elementary School 334 William Wood Ln, BTVA, 60510	3078	34W-1S	C2
Nelson Elementary School 8901 N Ozanam Av, NLES, 60714	2864	9W-11N	C3
Nelson Prairie Elementary School 2366 Nelson Rd, NLNX, 60451	3589	18W-27S	A4
Nelson Ridge Elementary School 2470 Nelson Rd, NLNX, 60451	3589	18W-27S	A5
Nettelhorst Elementary School 3252 N Broadway St, CHCG, 60657	2978	0W-4N	A3
Neubert Elementary School 1100 Huntington Dr, ALGN, 60102	2694	34W-21N	C7
Neuqua Valley High School 2360 95th St, NPVL, 60564	3202	29W-11S	D7
New Beginnings Christian School 151 E Briarcliff Rd, BGBK, 60440	3269	22W-12S	B2
Newberry Math-Science Academy 700 W Willow St, CHCG, 60614	2978	0W-2N	A7
New Covenant Christian Academy 15213 5th Av, PHNX, 60426	3350	0W-18S	B6
New Field Primary School 1707 W Morse Av, CHCG, 60626	2921	2W-8N	C1
New Millennium Health High School 2710 E 89th St, CHCG, 60617	3215	3E-10S	E4
Newport Elementary School 15872 W 21st St, NptT, 60083	2420	15W-41N	A1
New Sullivan Elementary School 8331 S Mackinaw Av, CHCG, 60617	3216	4E-9S	A2
Newton Bateman Elementary School 4220 N Richmond St, CHCG, 60618	2976	3W-5N	E1
Newton Bateman Elementary School 4220 N Richmond St, CHCG, 60649	3153	3E-8S	D6
New Trier High School Northfield-Campus 7 Happ Rd, NHFD, 60093	2811	6W-14N	C4
New Trier Twp Winnetka Campus 7 Happ Rd, WNKA, 60093	2812	4W-15N	C3
Nicholas Senn High School 5900 N Glenwood Av, CHCG, 60660	2921	1W-7N	C4
Nichols Middle School 800 Greenleaf St, EVTN, 60202	2867	2W-10N	B4
Nicholson Elementary School 649 N Main St, MTGY, 60538	3199	37W-9S	D4
Nicholson Specialty School 6006 S Peoria St, CHCG, 60621	3152	1W-6S	A4
Nightingale Elementary School 5250 S Rockwell St, CHCG, 60632	3151	3W-5S	A2
Niles North High School 9800 Lawler Av, SKOK, 60077	2865	6W-12N	E1
Niles West High School 5701 Oakton St, SKOK, 60077	2865	7W-9N	C6
Ninos Heros Community Academy 8344 S Commercial Av, CHCG, 60617	3215	3E-9S	E2
Nippersink Middle School 10006 N Main St, RHMD, 60071	2353	34W-41N	C7
Nixon Elementary School 2121 N Keeler Av, CHCG, 60639	2976	5W-2N	B6
Nobel Elementary School 4127 W Hirsch St, CHCG, 60651	3032	5W-1N	B1
Nob Hill Elementary School 3701 168th St, CCHL, 60478	3426	4W-20S	D4
Noble Street Charter School 1012 N Noble St, CHCG, 60622	3033	1W-1N	D2
Noonan Elementary Academy 19131 Henry Dr, MKNA, 60448	3503	11W-23S	E2
Norman Bridge School 3800 N New England Av, CHCG, 60634	2974	8W-4N	E2
North Barrington Elementary School 310 N Route 59, NBRN, 60010	2697	26W-24N	E1
Northbrook Junior High School 1475 Maple Av, NHBK, 60062	2757	9W-17N	C6
North Chicago Community High School 1717 17th St, NCHI, 60064	2536	11W-32N	D6
Northeast Elementary School 9058 S California Av, ENGN, 60805	3213	3W-10S	A5
North Elementary School 500 W Woodstock St, CLLK, 60014	2639	36W-26N	E3
North Elementary School 1789 Rand Rd, DSPN, 60016	2863	12W-11N	B3
North Elementary School 9500 Gage Av, FNPK, 60131	2973	11W-4N	C4
North Elementary School 1210 Adams St, NCHI, 60064	2537	10W-32N	A5
North Elementary School 150 W Sunset Av, VLPK, 60181	3027	18W-1N	A2
North Elementary School 410 Franklin St, WKGN, 60085	2480	10W-34N	A7
North Grand High School 4338 W Wabansia Av, CHCG, 60639	2976	5W-2N	A7
North Kenwood Charter School 1119 E 46th St, CHCG, 60653	3093	1E-4S	A7
Northlake Middle School 202 S Lakewood Av, NHLK, 60164	3028	13W-1N	D2
North Lawndale Charter High School 1616 S Spaulding Av, CHCG, 60623	3090	4W-1S	D1
North Park Elementary School 2017 W Montrose Av, CHCG, 60618	2977	2W-5N	B1
North Prarie Junior High School 500 North Av, WPHR, 60096	2363	10W-42N	A5
Northridge Prep School for Boys 8320 W Ballard Rd, NLES, 60714	2864	10W-11N	A3
North River Elementary School 4416 N Troy St, CHCG, 60625	2920	3W-5N	D7
North Shore Country Day School 310 Green Bay Rd, WNKA, 60093	2812	5W-15N	B2
North Shore Junior Academy 5220 N California Av, CHCG, 60625	2920	3W-6N	E5
Northside Academy-St. Gertrude C 6216 N Glenwood Av, CHCG, 60660	2921	1W-7N	D3
Northside Catholic Academy-St. Ita 5525 N Magnolia Av, CHCG, 60640	2921	1W-6N	D5
Northside College Prep High School 5501 N Kedzie Av, CHCG, 60625	2920	3W-6N	D5
Northwest Academy 301 S Swift Rd, ADSN, 60101	2969	21W-3N	E5
Northwest Baptist Academy 9N889 Nesler Rd, PltT, 60124	2852	39W-9N	D7
Northwest Elementary School 3630 W 92nd St, ENGN, 60805	3212	4W-10S	D5
Northwest Institute Learning-Academy 5108 W Division St, CHCG, 60651	3031	6W-1N	E2
Northwest Middle School 5252 W Palmer St, CHCG, 60639	2975	6W-2N	D6
Northwest Suburban Christian-Academy 255 Quentin Rd, WCDA, 60084	2587	26W-28N	E6
Northwood Junior High School 945 North Av, HDPK, 60035	2704	9W-23N	B2
Northwood Middle School 2121 N Seminary Av, WDSK, 60098	2524	41W-32N	D4
Norwood Park Elementary School 5900 N Nina Av, CHCG, 60631	2918	8W-7N	E4
Notre Dame High School 3000 N Mango Av, CHCG, 60634	2975	7W-3N	C4
Notre Dame High School 7655 W Dempster St, NLES, 60714	2864	9W-10N	C4
Notre Dame School 66 Norfolk Av, CNHL, 60514	3145	16W-5S	D1
Novak-King 6th Grade Center 1500 Kemble Av, NCHI, 60064	2536	11W-32N	D5
Oakbrook Elementary School 170 S Wood Dale Rd, WDDL, 60191	2971	18W-5N	A1
Oak Crest Elementary School 38550 N Lewis Av, BHPK, 60099	2421	11W-38N	D7
Oakdale Christian Academy 9440 S Vincennes Av, CHCG, 60620	3213	1W-10S	E5
Oakdale Elementary School 2230 N McAree Rd, WKGN, 60087	2479	12W-36N	C4
Oak Elementary School 950 S Oak St, HNDL, 60521	3146	15W-5S	B3
Oak Forest High School 15201 Central Av, OKFT, 60452	3347	6W-18S	D6
Oak Glen Elementary School 2101 182nd St, LNSG, 60438	3429	2E-21S	D6
Oak Grove Elementary School 1700 Oplaine Rd, GNOK, 60048	2592	14W-30N	C2
Oakhill Elementary School 502 S Oltendorf Rd, SMWD, 60107	2857	28W-10N	A6
Oakland Grade School 22018 W Grass Lake Rd, LkvT, 60002	2417	22W-39N	C4
Oak Lawn Community High School 9400 Southwest Hwy, OKLN, 60453	3211	7W-10S	C5
Oaklawn Hometown Middle School 5345 W 99th St, OKLN, 60453	3211	6W-11S	D7
Oak Park Christian School 931 Lake St, OKPK, 60301	3030	8W-0N	E4
Oak Park Elementary School 1200 Front St, AURA, 60505	3138	34W-7S	E6
Oak Park-River Forest High School 201 N Scoville Av, OKPK, 60302	3031	8W-0N	A3
Oak Prairie Junior High School 15161 S Gougar Rd, HmrT, 60491	3342	19W-18S	C7
Oak Ridge Elementary School 8791 W 103rd St, PSHL, 60465	3274	10W-12S	A1
Oak Terrace Elementary School 240 Prairie Av, HIWD, 60040	2704	9W-23N	C3
Oakton Elementary School 436 Ridge Av, EVTN, 60202	2867	2W-9N	B6
Oak View Elementary School 150 N Schmidt Rd, BGBK, 60440	3268	23W-11S	E1
Oakwood Elementary School 1130 Kim Pl, LMNT, 60439	3270	19W-14S	D7
OC Allen Elementary School 700 S Farnsworth Av, AURA, 60504	3200	33W-8S	E2
Octavio Paz Charter School-Congress 2401 W Congress Pkwy, CHCG, 60612	3033	3W-0S	A5
Ogden Avenue Elementary School 501 W Ogden Av, LGNG, 60525	3087	12W-4S	B6
Ogden Elementary School 24 W Walton St, CHCG, 60610	3034	0W-1N	B2
Oglesby Elementary School 7646 S Green St, CHCG, 60620	3214	1W-8S	A1
O'Keeffe Elementary School 6940 S Merrill Av, CHCG, 60649	3153	2E-7S	C6
Old Orchard Junior High School 9310 Kenton Av, SKOK, 60076	2866	5W-11N	A2
Old Post Elementary School 100 Old Post Rd, OSWG, 60543	3199	36W-11S	E7
Old Quarry Middle School 16100 127th St, LMNT, 60439	3342	20W-15S	C1
Old School Montessori 144 Commerce Dr, GYLK, 60030	2533	19W-33N	B4
Olive C Martin Elementary School 24750 W Dering Ln, LkvT, 60046	2416	24W-38N	C6
Olive-Mary Stitt Elementary School 303 E Olive St, ANHT, 60004	2807	17W-15N	B2
Oliver McCracken Middle School 8000 E Prairie Rd, SKOK, 60076	2866	4W-10N	B5
Oliver Windows Holmes Elementary-School 955 W Garfield Blvd, CHCG, 60621	3151	1W-6S	E3
Olson Middle School 720 W Judd St, WDSK, 60098	2524	42W-31N	C7
OL Westside-Presentation School 3900 W Lexington St, CHCG, 60624	3032	4W-0S	C6
Onahan Elementary School 6634 W Raven St, CHCG, 60631	2919	8W-7N	A3
O'Neill Middle School 635 59th St, DRGV, 60516	3144	19W-6S	D4
O'Plaine Campus 500 N Oplaine Rd, GRNE, 60031	2478	14W-34N	C7
Oplaine School 333 N Oplaine Rd, GRNE, 60031	2535	14W-34N	C1
Orchard Hill Farm School 16800 Kilpatrick Av, BmnT, 60477	3426	5W-20S	B3
Orchard Place Elementary School 2727 Maple St, DSPN, 60018	2917	12W-8N	B2
Oriole Park Elementary School 5424 N Oketo Av, CHCG, 60656	2918	9W-6N	D5
Orland Center Elementary School 9407 W 151st St, ODPK, 60462	3345	11W-18S	E6
Orland Junior High School 14855 West Av, ODPK, 60462	3345	12W-17S	C6
Orland Park Elementary School 9960 W 143rd St, ODPK, 60462	3345	12W-16S	C4
Orozco Elementary School 1940 W 18th St, CHCG, 60608	3091	2W-1S	C1
Orrington Elementary School 2636 Orrington Av, EVTN, 60201	2813	2W-13N	B7
Ortiz de Dominguez Elementary-School 3000 S Lawndale Av, CHCG, 60623	3090	4W-2S	C3
Oster-Oakview School 809 N Cedar Rd, NLNX, 60451	3501	18W-24S	B5
Oswego East High School 2510 Harvey Rd, OswT, 60543	3265	33W-11S	A1
Oswego High School 4250 State Route 71, OSWG, 60543	3263	37W-12S	D3
Otis Elementary School 525 N Armour St, CHCG, 60622	3033	1W-0N	D3
O'Toole Elementary School 6550 S Seeley Av, CHCG, 60636	3151	2W-7S	C5
Otter Creek Elementary School 2701 Hopps Rd, ELGN, 60124	2907	37W-8N	D3

FEATURE NAME Address City ZIP Code	MAP#	CGS	GRID
Our Lady of Charity School 3620 S 57th Ct, CCRO, 60804	3089	7W-3S	C5
Our Lady of Destiny S Campus 1880 Ash St, DSPN, 60018	2862	13W-9N	E6
Our Lady of Good Counsel School 601 Talma St, AURA, 60505	3200	35W-8S	B2
Our Lady of Grace School 2446 N Ridgeway Av, CHCG, 60647	2976	4W-3N	C5
Our Lady of Guadalupe School 9050 S Burley Av, CHCG, 60617	3216	4E-10S	A4
Our Lady of Humility School 10601 W Wadsworth Rd, BHPK, 60099	2422	10W-39N	A6
Our Lady of Loretto School 9003 S Kostner Av, HMTN, 60456	3212	5W-10S	B5
Our Lady of Tepeyac High School 2228 S Whipple St, CHCG, 60623	3090	3W-2S	E2
Our Lady of Tepeyac School 2235 S Albany Av, CHCG, 60623	3090	3W-2S	E2
Our Lady of the Gardens School 13300 S Langley Av, CHCG, 60827	3350	0E-15S	E1
Our Lady of the Ridge School 10859 Ridgeland Av, CHRG, 60415	3275	7W-12S	B2
Our Lady of the Snows School 4810 S Leamington Av, CHCG, 60638	3149	6W-5S	E1
Our Lady of the Wayside School 432 S Mitchell Av, ANHT, 60005	2807	18W-13N	A5
Our Lady of Peace School 709 Plainfield Rd, DRN, 60561	3207	17W-8S	C1
Our Lady of Perpetual Help School 1123 Church St, GNVW, 60025	2810	8W-13N	E6
Our Lady of Victory School 4434 N Laramie Av, CHCG, 60630	2919	6W-5N	D7
Overton Elementary School 221 E 49th St, CHCG, 60615	3152	0E-5S	C1
Owen Elementary School 1560 Westglen Dr, NPVL, 60565	3203	27W-8S	C3
Owen Scholastic Academy 8247 S Christiana Av, CHCG, 60652	3212	4W-9S	E3
Owens Community Academy 12450 S State St, CHCG, 60628	3278	0W-14S	C6
OW Huth Middle School 3718 213th Pl, MTSN, 60443	3594	4W-25S	D1
Pablo Casals Elementary School 3501 W Potomac Av, CHCG, 60651	3032	4W-1N	D1
Paderewski Learning Academy 2221 S Lawndale Av, CHCG, 60623	3090	4W-2S	C2
Palatine High School 1111 N Rohlwing Rd, PLTN, 60074	2753	20W-17N	B5
Palmer Elementary School 5051 N Kenneth Av, CHCG, 60630	2920	5W-6N	A6
Palos East Elementary School 7700 W 127th St, PSHT, 60463	3274	9W-14S	D7
Palos South Middle School 13100 S 82nd Av, PlsT, 60464	3346	10W-15S	C1
Palos West Elementary School 12700 S 104th Av, PlsT, 60464	3273	13W-14S	B7
Parker Community Academy 6800 S Stewart Av, CHCG, 60621	3152	0W-7S	B6
Parker Junior High School 2810 School St, FSMR, 60422	3507	3W-22S	B2
Park Forest Academy 375 Oswego St, PKFT, 60466	3595	3W-27S	A5
Park Junior High School 325 N Park Rd, LGPK, 60525	3087	12W-3S	B6
Parkland School 1802 N Ringwood Rd, MHRY, 60050	2527	34W-33N	C2
Parkman Elementary School 245 W 51st St, CHCG, 60609	3152	0W-5S	B2
Park Manor Elementary School 7037 S Rhodes Av, CHCG, 60637	3152	0E-7S	D6
Park School 14200 S Wentworth Av, RVDL, 60827	3350	0W-16S	C3
Parkside Community Academy 6938 S East End Av, CHCG, 60649	3153	2E-7S	B6
Parkview Elementary School 122 Carpenter Blvd, CPVL, 60110	2800	34W-16N	E1
Park View Elementary School 250 S Park Blvd, GNEN, 60137	3083	22W-1S	C2
Park View Elementary School 341 N Elizabeth St, LMBD, 60148	3026	20W-1N	B3
Park View School 6200 Lake St, MNGV, 60053	2865	7W-11N	B3
Parkwood Elementary School 2150 Laurel Av, HRPK, 60133	2911	27W-9N	C2
Partnership School 407 S Calumet Av, AURA, 60506	3199	37W-7S	C1
Passages Charter School 1447 W Montrose Av, CHCG, 60613	2921	1W-5N	D7
Passow Elementary School 2838 Calwagner St, FNPK, 60131	2973	12W-3N	C5
Pasteur Elementary School 5825 S Kostner Av, CHCG, 60629	3150	5W-6S	B4
Patrick Henry Elementary School 4250 N St. Louis Av, CHCG, 60618	2976	4W-5N	C1
Patterson Elementary School 3731 Lawrence Dr, NPVL, 60564	3266	28W-11S	E2
Patton Elementary School 1616 N Patton Av, ANHT, 60004	2806	18W-15N	E1
Paul Revere Intermediate School 12331 Gregory St, BLID, 60406	3277	2W-14S	B6
Paul Revere Primary School 2300 123rd Pl, BLID, 60406	3277	2W-14S	B6
Peabody Elementary School 1444 W Augusta Blvd, CHCG, 60622	3033	1W-1N	D2
Peck Elementary School 3826 W 58th St, CHCG, 60629	3150	4W-6S	C3
Peirce International Studies School 1423 W Bryn Mawr Av, CHCG, 60640	2921	1W-6N	D4
Penn Elementary School 1616 S Avers Av, CHCG, 60623	3090	4W-1S	C1
Pennoyer Elementary School 5200 N Cumberland Av, NRDG, 60706	2918	10W-6N	A6
Peotone Elementary School 426 N Conrad St, PTON, 60468	3860	9W-37S	E3
Peotone High School 605 W North St, PTON, 60468	3860	9W-37S	D3
Peotone Junior High School 1 Blue Devil Dr, PTON, 60468	3860	9W-37S	E4
Percy Julian Middle School 416 S Ridgeland Av, OKPK, 60302	3031	7W-0N	A5
Perez Elementary School 1241 W 19th St, CHCG, 60608	3091	1W-1S	D1
Perez Elementary School Annex 2001 S Throop St, CHCG, 60608	3091	1W-1S	D1
Pershing Elementary School 6537 37th St, BRWN, 60402	3089	8W-3S	A5
Pershing Elementary School 251 N Midland Av, JLET, 60435	3498	25W-23S	B4
Pershing Magnet E Humanities School 3113 S Rhodes Av, CHCG, 60616	3092	0E-3S	D3
Pershing West Middle School 3200 S Calumet Av, CHCG, 60616	3092	0E-3S	D4
Peter J Palombi Middle School 133 McKinley Av, LKVL, 60046	2475	22W-37N	A1
Peterson Elementary School 5510 N Christiana Av, CHCG, 60625	2920	4W-6N	D5
Pheasant Ridge Primary School 43 E Stevenson Dr, GLHT, 60139	2968	23W-3N	E6
Philip Rogers Elementary School 7345 N Washtenaw Av, CHCG, 60645	2866	3W-9N	E7
Phillips Academy High School 244 E Pershing Rd, CHCG, 60653	3092	0E-3S	C5
PH Miller Elementary School 904 N Lew St, PLNO, 60545	3259	47W-13S	D5
Piccolo Specialty School 1040 N Keeler Av, CHCG, 60651	3032	5W-1N	B2
Pickard Elementary School 2301 W 21st Pl, CHCG, 60608	3091	2W-1S	B1
Pierce Downer Elementary School 1436 Grant St, DRGV, 60515	3144	20W-4S	B1
Pilgrim Lutheran School 4300 N Winchester Av, CHCG, 60613	2977	2W-5N	B1
Pilsen Community Academy 1420 W 17th St, CHCG, 60608	3091	1W-1S	D1
Pioneer Elementary School 1470 Raven Dr, BGBK, 60490	3267	26W-12S	E3
Pioneer Elementary School 615 Kenwood Av, WCHI, 60185	3022	30W-0N	B5
Pioneer Path School 24920 S Sage St, CNHN, 60410	3672	31W-30S	E4
Piper Elementary School 2435 Kenilworth Av, BRWN, 60402	3088	8W-2S	E2
Pirie Magnet Elementary School 650 E 85th St, CHCG, 60619	3214	0E-9S	E3
Plainfield Elementary School 1850 Plainfield Dr, DSPN, 60018	2862	13W-9N	D6
Plainfield High School Central-Cmpus 611 Fort Beggs Dr, PNFD, 60544	3416	30W-18S	B1
Plainfield North High School 12005 S 248th Av, PNFD, 60585	3266	30W-14S	A7
Plainfield South High School 7800 Caton Farm Rd, JLET, 60586	3415	33W-21S	A6
Plamondon Elementary School 2642 W 15th Pl, CHCG, 60608	3033	3W-1S	A7
Plank Junior High School 510 Secretariat Ln, OSWG, 60543	3264	34W-11S	C2
Plano High School 704 W Abe St, PLNO, 60545	3259	48W-13S	B6
Plano Middle School 804 S Hale St, LtRT, 60545	3259	47W-14S	D7
Plato Academy 8535 Georgiana Av, MNGV, 60053	2865	7W-10N	B4
Player Primary Center 8600 S Roberts Rd, JSTC, 60458	3210	10W-9S	C4
Pleasantdale Elementary School 8100 School St, WLSP, 60525	3208	13W-9S	E3
Pleasantdale Middle School 7450 Wolf Rd, BRRG, 60527	3208	14W-8S	E1
Pleasant Hill Elementary School 434 W Illinois Av, PLTN, 60067	2805	21W-15N	D3
Pleasant Hill Elementary School 1N220 Pleasant Hill Rd, WNFD, 60188	3023	26W-1N	E3
Pleasant Lane Elementary School 401 N Main St, LMBD, 60148	3026	19W-1N	B2
Pleasant Ridge School 1730 Sunset Ridge Rd, GNVW, 60025	2811	8W-14N	A4
Plum Grove Junior High School 2600 Plum Grove Rd, RGMW, 60008	2805	21W-14N	E5
Pope Elementary School 1852 S Albany Av, CHCG, 60623	3090	3W-1S	E1
Pope John Paul II School 4325 S Richmond St, CHCG, 60632	3090	3W-4S	E7
Pope John XXIII School 1120 Washington St, EVTN, 60202	2867	2W-10N	A5
Portage Park Elementary School 5330 W Berteau Av, CHCG, 60641	2975	6W-5N	D1
Posen School 14545 S California Av, POSN, 60469	3349	3W-17S	A4
Powell Academy 7530 S South Shore Dr, CHCG, 60649	3153	3E-8S	E7
Prairie Elementary School 1530 Brandywyn Ln, BFGV, 60089	2701	17W-21N	B5
Prairie Elementary School 500 S Charles Av, NPVL, 60540	3142	25W-7S	A6
Prairie Grove Elementary School 3223 Route 176, PRGV, 60014	2641	32W-27N	C1
Prairie Hill School 233 E Oriole Tr, CRY, 60013	2641	30W-24N	E7
Prairie-Hills Junior High School 3035 W 163rd St, MKHM, 60428	3427	3W-19S	A2
Prairie Junior High School 11910 S Kostner Av, ALSP, 60803	3276	5W-14S	B5
Prairie Lane Elementary School 10717 47th Av, PTPR, 53158	2362		D1
Prairie Oak Elementary School 1427 Oak Park Av, BRWN, 60402	3031	8W-1S	A7
Prairie Point Elementary School 3650 Grove Rd, OSWG, 60543	3263	37W-13S	C5
Prairie Ridge High School 6000 Dvorak Dr, CLLK, 60012	2584	34W-28N	B6
Prairie School 14200 S 82nd Av, ODPK, 60462	3346	10W-16S	C4
Prairieview Elementary School 285 Mayflower Ln, BRLT, 60103	2967	28W-5N	B1
Prairieview Elementary School 699 Plainfield Rd, DGvT, 60516	3206	19W-9S	D3
Prairie View Grade School 10n630 Nesler Rd, PltT, 60124	2852	39W-10N	E5
Prairie View Middle School 8500 175th St, TYPK, 60487	3424	10W-20S	B5
Prarie Grove Middle School 3225 Route 176, PRGV, 60014	2641	32W-27N	C1
Prescott Elementary School 1632 W Wrightwood Av, CHCG, 60614	2977	2W-3N	C5
Price Elementary School 4351 S Drexel Blvd, CHCG, 60653	3092	1E-4S	E7
Prichett Elementary School 200 Horatio Blvd, BFGV, 60089	2754	16W-20N	E1
Primary Academic Center 3055 W 163rd St, MKHM, 60428	3427	3W-19S	A2
Prince of Peace School 135 S Milwaukee Av, LKVL, 60046	2475	22W-37N	B1
Princeton AC Elementary School 5125 S Princeton Av, CHCG, 60609	3152	0W-5S	B2
Pritzker Elementary School 2009 W Schiller St, CHCG, 60622	3033	2W-1N	B1
Prologue Alt High School 640 W Irving Park Rd, CHCG, 60613	2978	0W-4N	A2
Prospect Elementary School 100 N Prospect Av, CNHL, 60514	3145	16W-5S	D2
Prospect High School 801 W Kensington Rd, MPPT, 60056	2807	15W-13N	E5
Protestant Reformed School 16511 S Park Av, SHLD, 60473	3428	0E-19S	E2
Protsman Elementary School 1121 Harrison Av, DYR, 46311	3510		D7
Providence Catholic High School 1800 W Maple St, NLNX, 60451	3500	19W-24S	D5
Providence St. Mel School 119 S Central Park Blvd, CHCG, 60624	3032	4W-0S	D5
Proviso East High School 807 S 1st Av, MYWD, 60153	3030	10W-0N	A5
Proviso West High School 4701 Harrison St, HLSD, 60162	3028	13W-0S	D6
Prussing Elementary School 4650 N Menard Av, CHCG, 60630	2919	7W-5N	C7
Pulaski Community Academy 2230 W McLean Av, CHCG, 60647	2977	2W-2N	B6
Pullman Elementary School 11311 S Forrestville Av, CHCG, 60628	3278	0E-13S	E3
Queen of All Saints School 6230 N Lemont Av, CHCG, 60646	2920	5W-7N	A3
Queen of Angels School 4520 N Western Av, CHCG, 60625	2921	3W-5N	A7
Queen of Martyrs School 3550 W 103rd St, ENGN, 60805	3276	4W-11S	D1
Queen of the Rosary School 690 W Elk Grove Blvd, EGVV, 60007	2914	18W-9N	E1
Queen of the Universe School 7130 S Hamlin Av, CHCG, 60629	3150	4W-8S	C7
Queen of Peace High School 7659 Linder Av, BRBK, 60459	3211	6W-8S	D1
Quentin Road Christian School 60 Quentin Rd, HNWD, 60047	2699	21W-24N	C1
Quest Academy 500 N Benton St, PLTN, 60067	2752	20W-16N	E7
Ralph J Bunche Elementary School 16500 Park Av, MKHM, 60428	3427	1W-19S	E3
Ranch View Elementary School 1651 Ranchview Dr, NPVL, 60565	3204	24W-9S	D3
Randolph Magnet Elementary School 7316 S Hoyne Av, CHCG, 60636	3151	2W-8S	C7
Rauner College Prep Charter School 1337 W Ohio St, CHCG, 60622	3033	1W-0N	E3
Ravenswood Baptist Christian School 4437 N Seeley Av, CHCG, 60625	2921	2W-5N	B7
Ravenswood Elementary School 4332 N Paulina St, CHCG, 60613	2977	2W-5N	C1
Ravinia Elementary School 763 Dean Av, HDPK, 60035	2705	7W-20N	B7
Ray Elementary School 5631 S Kimbark Av, CHCG, 60637	3153	1E-6S	A3
Raymond Ellis Elementary School 720 Central Park Dr, RLKB, 60073	2474	23W-34N	D7
Reavis Elementary School 834 E 50th St, CHCG, 60615	3152	1E-5S	E1
Reavis Elementary School 17121 Roy St, LNSG, 60438	3430	4E-20S	B4
Reavis High School 6034 W 77th St, BRBK, 60459	3211	7W-8S	B1
Red Oak Elementary School 530 Red Oak Ln, HDPK, 60035	2757	9W-20N	C1
Reed-Custer High School 249 Comet Dr, BDWD, 60408	3942	30W-42S	B6
Reed Custer Intermediate School 162 S School St, BDWD, 60408	3942	31W-41S	A6
Reed-Custer Middle School 407 Comet Dr, RedT, 60408	4031	30W-42S	B1
Reed Elementary School 6350 S Stewart Av, CHCG, 60621	3152	0W-7S	B5
Reed Elementary School 14939 W 143rd St, HmrT, 60491	3343	18W-17S	A4
Regina Dominican High School 701 Locust Rd, WLMT, 60091	2812	5W-13N	A6
Reilly Elementary School 3650 W School St, CHCG, 60618	2976	4W-4N	C3
Reinberg Elementary School 3425 N Major Av, CHCG, 60634	2975	7W-4N	C3
Reskin Elementary School 1555 Ardmore Av, GLHT, 60139	2969	22W-2N	B7
Resurrection High School 7500 W Talcott Av, CHCG, 60631	2918	9W-7N	C3
Revere Elementary School 1010 E 72nd St, CHCG, 60619	3152	1E-8S	E7
Rhodes Elementary School 8931 Fullerton Av, RVGV, 60171	2973	11W-3N	E6
Richard Byrd Elementary School 8259 Lavergne Av, BRBK, 60459	3211	6W-9S	E3
Richard Daley Academy 5024 S Wolcott Av, CHCG, 60609	3151	2W-5S	C1
Richard Edwards Elementary School 4815 S Karlov Av, CHCG, 60632	3150	5W-5S	B1
Richard F Bernotas Middle School 170 N Oak St, CLLK, 60014	2639	36W-26N	E3
Richards Career Academy 5009 S Laflin St, CHCG, 60609	3151	1W-5S	D1
Rich Central High School 3600 W 203rd St, OMFD, 60461	3506	4W-24S	D5
Rich East High School 300 Sauk Tr, PKFT, 60466	3595	3W-27S	A4
Richland Grade School 1919 Caton Farm Rd, CTHL, 60403	3418	26W-21S	A6
Richmond-Burton County High School 8311 N Route 31, RHMD, 60071	2412	34W-40N	C3

Chicago 7-County Points of Interest Index

FEATURE NAME Address City ZIP Code	MAP#	CGS	GRID
Richmond Elementary School 5815 Broadway St, RHMD, 60071	2353	34W-42N	C6
Richmond Elementary School 300 S 12th St, SCRL, 60174	2963	36W-2N	E7
Rich South High School 5000 Sauk Trl, RNPK, 60471	3594	6W-26S	A3
Rickover Junior High School 22151 Torrence Av, SLVL, 60411	3597	3E-26S	E3
Rickover Navy Academy High School 5900 N Glenwood Av, CHCG, 60660	2921	1W-7N	D4
Ridge Central Elementary School 10800 Lyman Av, CHRG, 60415	3275	7W-12S	C2
Ridge Circle Elementary School 420 Ridge Cir, SMWD, 60107	2857	27W-10N	C6
Ridge Elementary School 1900 Caton Ridge Dr, JLET, 60586	3415	31W-21S	E7
Ridge Family Center for Learning 650 Ridge Av, EGVV, 60007	2914	18W-9N	E1
Ridge Lawn Elementary School 5757 105th St, CHRG, 60415	3275	7W-12S	C1
Ridgewood Baptist Academy 1968 Hillcrest Rd, JltT, 60433	3500	21W-23S	A4
Ridgewood Community High School 7500 W Montrose Av, NRDG, 60706	2974	9W-5N	C1
Riley Elementary School 1209 E Burr Oak Dr, ANHT, 60004	2754	17W-17N	C5
Riley Elementary School 123 S Wolf Rd, NHLK, 60164	3028	13W-1N	D1
Ringwood School Primary Center 4700 School Rd, RGWD, 60072	2470	34W-36N	D3
River Grove Elementary School 2650 Thatcher Av, RVGV, 60171	2974	10W-3N	A5
Riverside-Brookfield Twp High-School 160 Ridgewood Rd, RVSD, 60546	3088	10W-3S	B5
River Trails Middle School 1000 N Wolf Rd, MPPT, 60056	2808	14W-14N	D5
River View Elementary School 2097 S Bronk Rd, JLET, 60586	3416	29W-21S	D7
Riverwood Elementary School 300 S Driftwood Tr, MHRY, 60050	2527	33W-31N	D6
River Woods Elementary School 2607 River Woods Dr, NPVL, 60565	3204	25W-10S	A6
Robert A Black Magnet School 9101 S Euclid Av, CHCG, 60617	3215	2E-10S	C4
Robert C Hill Elementary School 616 Dalhart Av, RMVL, 60446	3340	23W-15S	E1
Robert Crown Elementary School 620 W Bonner Rd, WCDA, 60084	2587	26W-28N	C6
Robert Emmet Elementary School 5500 W Madison St, CHCG, 60644	3031	6W-0N	D5
Robert Frost Elementary School 1805 N Aspen Dr, MPPT, 60056	2808	13W-15N	E2
Robert Frost Middle School 2206 W 167th St, MKHM, 60428	3427	2W-19S	C3
Robeson High School 6835 S Normal Blvd, CHCG, 60621	3152	0W-7S	B6
Robinson Elementary School 4225 S Lake Park Av, CHCG, 60653	3093	1E-4S	A6
Robinson Elementary School 4431 Gage Av, LYNS, 60534	3088	9W-4S	C7
Rockdale Elementary School 715 Meadow Av, RKDL, 60436	3498	25W-25S	B7
Rockland Elementary School 160 W Rockland Rd, LYVL, 60048	2591	16W-28N	D6
Rolling Meadows High School 2901 Central Rd, RGMW, 60008	2806	19W-12N	C7
Rollins Elementary School 950 Kane St, AURA, 60505	3138	34W-7S	D7
Romeoville High School 100 N Independence Blvd, RMVL, 60446	3341	23W-16S	A4
Romona Elementary School 600 Romona Rd, WLMT, 60091	2811	5W-13N	E6
Ronald Brown Academy 12607 S Union Av, CHCG, 60628	3278	0W-14S	A6
Ronald E McNair Academic Center 4820 W Walton St, CHCG, 60651	3031	6W-1N	E2
Rondout Elementary School 28593 N Bradley Rd, LbvT, 60045	2592	13W-28N	D6
Roosevelt Elementary School 1927 S 15th Av, BDVW, 60155	3029	11W-0S	E6
Roosevelt Elementary School 1500 S 50th Av, CCRO, 60804	3031	6W-1S	E7
Roosevelt Elementary School 1345 Sunnyside Av, CHHT, 60411	3507	1W-25S	E7
Roosevelt Elementary School 111 W 146th St, DLTN, 60419	3350	0W-17S	C4
Roosevelt High School 3436 W Wilson Av, CHCG, 60625	2920	4W-5N	C7
Roosevelt Junior High School 111 W 146th St, DLTN, 60419	3350	0W-17S	C4
Roosevelt Middle School 2500 Oak St, BLWD, 60104	3029	12W-0N	C4
Roosevelt Middle School 7560 Oak Av, RVFT, 60305	3030	9W-0N	C3
Roque de Du Prey Elementary School 1405 N Washtenaw Av, CHCG, 60622	3033	3W-1N	A1
Rosa Parks Middle School 14700 Robey Av, HRVY, 60426	3349	2W-17S	D5
Rosario Castellanos Middle School 2524 S Central Park Av, CHCG, 60623	3090	4W-2S	D2
Rosary High School 901 N Edgelawn Dr, AURA, 60506	3137	37W-6S	B5
Rose E Krug Elementary School 240 Melrose Av, AURA, 60505	3200	36W-9S	A4
Roseland Christian School 314 W 108th St, CHCG, 60628	3278	0W-12S	B2
Roselle Middle School 500 S Park St, ROSL, 60172	2913	23W-6N	A6
Rosemont Elementary School 6101 Ruby St, RSMT, 60018	2917	12W-7N	C3
Rosenwald Branch Elementary School 2601 W 80th St, CHCG, 60652	3213	3W-9S	A2
Rosenwald-Carroll School 2601 W 80th St, CHCG, 60652	3213	3W-9S	A2
Roslyn Road Elementary School 224 Roslyn Rd, BRTN, 60010	2697	25W-20N	E7
Rotolo Middle School 1501 S Raddant Rd, BTVA, 60510	3078	34W-2S	D4
Round Lake Beach Elementary School 1421 Ardmore Dr, RLKB, 60073	2475	23W-35N	A6
Round Lake Middle School 2000 Lotus Dr, RLKH, 60073	2474	24W-35N	D5
Round Lake Senior High School 800 High School Dr, RDLK, 60073	2531	23W-34N	E1
Roycemore School 640 Lincoln St, EVTN, 60201	2867	2W-12N	B1
Roy de Shane Elementary School 475 Chippewa Tr, CLSM, 60188	2967	26W-3N	E6
Roy Elementary School 533 N Roy Av, NHLK, 60164	2972	13W-2N	E6
Ruben Salazar Bilingual Center 160 W Wendell St, CHCG, 60610	3034	0W-1N	B2
Ruggles Elementary School 7831 S Prairie Av, CHCG, 60619	3214	0E-8S	D1
Ruiz Elementary School 2410 S Leavitt St, CHCG, 60608	3091	2W-2S	B2
Rupley Elementary School 305 Oakton St, EGVV, 60007	2861	18W-9N	A6
Rutledge Hall Elementary School 6850 N East Prairie Rd, LNWD, 60712	2920	4W-8N	B1
Ryder Elementary School 8716 S Wallace St, CHCG, 60620	3214	0W-10S	A4
Ryerson Elementary School 646 N Lawndale Av, CHCG, 60624	3032	4W-0N	C3
Sabin Magnet School 2216 W Hirsch St, CHCG, 60622	3033	2W-1N	B1
Sacred Heart School 2906 E 96th St, CHCG, 60617	3215	3E-11S	E6
Sacred Heart School 6250 N Sheridan Rd, CHCG, 60660	2921	1W-7N	E3
Sacred Heart School 322 W Maple St, LMBD, 60148	3026	20W-0N	B4
Sacred Heart School 815 N 16th Av, MLPK, 60160	3029	11W-1N	D3
Sacred Heart School 1095 Gage St, WNKA, 60093	2758	5W-16N	E7
St. Agnes of Bohemia School 2643 S Central Park Av, CHCG, 60623	3090	4W-2S	D3
St. Agnes School 1501 Chicago Rd, CHHT, 60411	3596	1W-25S	A1
St. Ailbe School 9037 S Harper Av, CHCG, 60619	3215	1E-10S	B4
St. Albert the Great School 5535 State Rd, BRBK, 60459	3211	6W-9S	D2
St. Alexander School 136 S Cornell Av, VLPK, 60181	3027	17W-0N	A4
St. Alphonsus Liguori School 411 N Wheeling Rd, WLNG, 60090	2808	14W-15N	B2
St. Anastasia School 629 W Glen Flora Av, WKGN, 60085	2480	10W-35N	A6
St. Andrew Lutheran School 3659 S Honore St, CHCG, 60609	3091	2W-3S	C5
St. Andrew School 1710 W Addison St, CHCG, 60613	2977	2W-4N	C2
St. Andrew's Lutheran School 260 N Northwest Hwy, PKRG, 60068	2864	10W-9N	A7
St. Andrew the Apostle School 505 Kingston Dr, RMVL, 60446	3340	24W-15S	E2
St. Angela School 1332 N Massasoit Av, CHCG, 60651	3031	7W-1N	C1
St. Anne School 319 Franklin St, BRTN, 60010	2751	25W-20N	A2
St. Ann School 2211 W 18th Pl, CHCG, 60608	3091	2W-1S	B1
St. Ann School 3014 Ridge Rd, LNSG, 60438	3430	3E-21S	A6
St. Athanasius School 2510 Ashland Av, EVTN, 60201	2813	3W-12N	A7
St. Barbara School 8900 Windemere Av, BKFD, 60513	3087	11W-4S	E6
St. Barbara School 2867 S Throop St, CHCG, 60608	3091	1W-2S	E3
St. Barnabas School 10121 S Longwood Dr, CHCG, 60643	3213	2W-11S	C7
St. Bartholomew School 4941 W Patterson Av, CHCG, 60641	2975	6W-4N	E2
St. Beatrice School 4141 Atlantic Av, SRPK, 60176	2973	12W-5N	C1
St. Bede School 36399 N Wilson Rd, GrtT, 60041	2473	25W-36N	E4
St. Bede the Venerable School 4440 W 83rd St, CHCG, 60652	3212	5W-9S	B3
St. Benedict High School 3900 N Leavitt St, CHCG, 60618	2977	2W-4N	A2
St. Benedict School 2324 New St, BLID, 60406	3349	2W-15S	B1
St. Benedict School 3920 N Leavitt St, CHCG, 60618	2977	2W-4N	B2
St. Bernadette School 9311 S Francisco Av, ENGN, 60805	3213	3W-10S	A5
St. Bernardine School 815 Elgin Av, FTPK, 60130	3030	9W-0S	D6
St. Bruno School 4839 S Harding Av, CHCG, 60632	3150	4W-5S	C1
St. Cajetan School 2447 W 112th St, CHCG, 60655	3277	3W-13S	B3
St. Casimir School 4329 S Cameron Av, HMND, 46327	3352		D3
St. Catherine Laboure School 3425 Thornwood Av, GNVW, 60025	2809	10W-14N	E5
St. Catherine of Alexandria School 10621 Kedvale Av, OKLN, 60453	3276	5W-12S	C2
St. Catherine of Siena School 845 W Main St, WDND, 60118	2800	34W-16N	E2
St. Catherine-St. Lucy School 27 Washington Blvd, OKPK, 60302	3031	7W-0N	B4
St. Celestine School 3017 N 77th Av, EDPK, 60707	2974	9W-3N	C4
St. Charles Borromeo School 145 E Grand Av, BNVL, 60106	2972	15W-3N	A4
St. Charles Borromeo School 288 E Jefferson Av, HPSR, 60140	2795	46W-16N	E2
St. Charles East High School 1020 Dunham Rd, SCRL, 60174	2964	34W-3N	E5
St. Charles North High School 255 Red Gate Rd, SCRL, 60175	2964	36W-5N	A2
St. Christina School 3333 W 110th St, CHCG, 60655	3276	4W-12S	E3
St. Christopher School 14611 Keeler Av, MDLN, 60445	3348	5W-17S	C5
St. Clement School 2524 N Orchard St, CHCG, 60614	2978	0W-3N	A5
St. Cletus School 700 W 55th St, LGNG, 60525	3147	12W-5S	B3
St. Colette School 3900 Pheasant Dr, RGMW, 60008	2806	19W-13N	C6
St. Columbanus School 7120 S Calumet Av, CHCG, 60619	3152	0E-8S	D7
St. Constance School 5841 W Strong St, CHCG, 60630	2919	7W-6N	B6
St. Cornelius School 5252 N Long Av, CHCG, 60630	2919	6W-6N	D5
St. Cyprian School 2561 Clinton St, RVGV, 60171	2974	10W-3N	B5
St. Damian School 5300 155th St, OKFT, 60452	3347	6W-18S	E7
St. Daniel the Prophet School 5337 S Natoma Av, CHCG, 60638	3149	8W-5S	A2
St. Dennis School 1201 S Washington St, LKPT, 60441	3419	22W-19S	C3
St. Dominic School 420 E Briarcliff Rd, BGBK, 60440	3269	22W-11S	D2
St. Domitilla School 605 N Hillside Av, HLSD, 60162	3028	14W-0N	D5
St. Dorothy School 7740 S Eberhart Av, CHCG, 60619	3214	0E-8S	D1
St. Edmund School 200 S Oak Park Av, OKPK, 60302	3030	8W-0N	E4
St. Edward Central Catholic High-School 335 Locust St, ELGN, 60123	2854	34W-11N	D4
St. Edward School 4343 W Sunnyside Av, CHCG, 60630	2920	5W-5N	A7
St. Elizabeth School 4052 S Wabash Av, CHCG, 60653	3092	0E-4S	C6
St. Emily School 1400 E Central Rd, MPPT, 60056	2808	14W-13N	C7
St. Ethelreda School 8734 S Paulina St, CHCG, 60620	3213	2W-10S	D4
St. Eugene School 7930 W Foster Av, CHCG, 60656	2918	9W-6N	B6
St. Ferdinand School 3131 N Mason Av, CHCG, 60634	2975	7W-3N	B4
St. Florian School 13110 S Baltimore Av, CHCG, 60633	3280	3E-15S	A7
St. Frances of Rome School 1401 S Austin Blvd, CCRO, 60804	3031	7W-1S	C7
St. Francis Borgia School 3535 N Panama Av, CHCG, 60634	2974	10W-4N	B3
St. Francis de Sales High School 10155 S Ewing Av, CHCG, 60617	3216	4E-11S	B7
St. Francis de Sales School 11 S Buesching Rd, LKZH, 60047	2699	23W-22N	A3
St. Francis High School 2130 W Roosevelt Rd, WHTN, 60187	3081	26W-1S	E1
St. Francis Xavier School 145 N Waiola Av, LGNG, 60525	3087	12W-4S	B6
St. Francis Xavier School 808 Linden Av, WLMT, 60091	2812	3W-13N	E6
St. Gabriel School 607 W 45th St, CHCG, 60609	3092	0W-4S	A7
St. Gall School 5515 S Sawyer Av, CHCG, 60629	3150	4W-6S	E3
St. Genevieve School 4854 W Montana St, CHCG, 60639	2975	6W-3N	E5
St. George School 6700 176th St, TYPK, 60477	3425	8W-21S	B5
St. Gerald School 9320 S 55th Ct, OKLN, 60453	3211	6W-10S	D5
St. Germaine School 9735 S Kolin Av, OKLN, 60453	3212	5W-11S	B6
St. Gilbert School 231 E Belvidere Rd, HNVL, 60030	2532	21W-33N	C4
St. Giles School 1034 Linden Av, OKPK, 60302	3031	8W-1N	A1
St. Gregory High School 1677 W Bryn Mawr Av, CHCG, 60640	2921	2W-7N	C4
St. Helena of the Cross School 10115 S Parnell Av, CHCG, 60628	3214	0W-11S	B7
St. Helen School 2347 W Augusta Blvd, CHCG, 60622	3033	2W-1N	B2
St. Hilary School 5614 N Fairfield Av, CHCG, 60659	2920	3W-7N	E4
St. Hubert School 255 Flagstaff Ln, HFET, 60169	2858	23W-11N	E3
St. Hyacinth School 3640 W Wolfram St, CHCG, 60618	2976	4W-3N	C4
St. Ignatius College Prep School 1076 W Roosevelt Rd, CHCG, 60607	3033	1W-0S	E6
St. Irene School 3s601 Warren Av, WNVL, 60555	3081	28W-3S	A6
St. Isaac Jogues School 421 S Clay St, HNDL, 60521	3146	15W-5S	A2
St. Isidore School 431 W Army Trail Rd, BMDL, 60108	2968	25W-4N	B3
St. James Lutheran School 2101 N Fremont St, CHCG, 60614	2977	1W-2N	E6
St. James School 821 N Arlington Heights Rd, ANHT, 60004	2807	17W-14N	A3
St. James School 140 North Av, HIWD, 60040	2704	9W-23N	D2
St. James the Apostle School 490 S Park Blvd, GNEN, 60137	3083	22W-2S	C3
St. Jane de Chantal School 5201 S McVicker Av, CHCG, 60638	3149	7W-5S	C2
St. Jerome School 2801 S Princeton Av, CHCG, 60616	3092	0W-2S	B3
St. Joan of Arc 4913 Columbia Av, LSLE, 60532	3143	22W-5S	B2
St. Joan of Arc School 9245 Lawndale Av, SKOK, 60203	2866	4W-11N	C2
St. John Berchmans School 2509 W Logan Blvd, CHCG, 60647	2977	3W-3N	A5
St. John Brebeuf School 8301 N Harlem Av, NLES, 60714	2864	8W-10N	D5
St. John de La Salle Elementary-School 10212 S Vernon Av, CHCG, 60628	3214	0E-11S	D7
St. John Fisher School 10200 S Washtenaw Av, CHCG, 60655	3213	3W-11S	A7
St. John Lutheran School 305 Circle Av, FTPK, 60130	3030	9W-0N	D5
St. John Lutheran School 125 E Seminary Av, WHTN, 60187	3024	24W-0S	C6

Chicago 7-County Points of Interest Index

FEATURE NAME Address City ZIP Code	MAP#	CGS	GRID
St. John of the Cross School 708 51st St, WNSP, 60558	3146	13W-5S	E2
St. John's Lutheran School 300 Jefferson St, ALGN, 60102	2694	33W-20N	D7
St. John's Lutheran School 4231 183rd St, CCHL, 60478	3426	5W-22S	C7
St. John's Lutheran School 4939 W Montrose Av, CHCG, 60641	2975	6W-5N	E1
St. John's Lutheran School 109 N Spring St, ELGN, 60120	2854	33W-11N	E4
St. John's Lutheran School 505 S Park Rd, LGNG, 60525	3147	13W-5S	B1
St. John's Lutheran School 215 S Lincoln St, LMBD, 60148	3026	20W-0N	B4
St. John's Lutheran School 18100 Wentworth Av, LNSG, 60438	3430	4E-21S	C6
St. John's Lutheran School 501 W Park Av, LYVL, 60048	2591	16W-28N	C5
St. John the Baptist School 2304 Church St, JNBG, 60050	2471	31W-35N	E5
St. John the Baptist School 0S259 Church St, WNFD, 60190	3023	27W-0S	C6
St. John the Evangelist School 513 Parkside Cir, SMWD, 60107	2857	28W-10N	B6
St. John Vianney School 27 N Lavergne Av, NHLK, 60164	3028	14W-2N	D1
St. Josaphat School 2245 N Southport Av, CHCG, 60614	2977	1W-2N	D6
St. Joseph Catholic School 201 N Division St, HRVD, 60033	2406	50W-38N	B7
St. Joseph High School 1840 Mayfair Av, WSTR, 60154	3086	13W-1S	E2
St. Joseph School 330 E Fullerton Av, ADSN, 60101	2971	18W-3N	A6
St. Joseph School 706 High St, AURA, 60505	3138	35W-6S	C5
St. Joseph School 430 Joliet St, DYR, 46311	3598		D2
St. Joseph School 274 Division St, ELGN, 60120	2854	33W-11N	E4
St. Joseph School 17949 Dixie Hwy, HMWD, 60430	3427	2W-21S	D6
St. Joseph School 409 N Scott St, JLET, 60432	3499	23W-23S	A4
St. Joseph School 529 Madison St, LKPT, 60441	3419	22W-19S	D2
St. Joseph School 221 Park Pl, LYVL, 60048	2591	16W-28N	D5
St. Joseph School 275 W North St, MHTN, 60442	3677	19W-30S	E4
St. Joseph School 118 Lincoln Av, RDLK, 60073	2531	23W-33N	E3
St. Joseph School 5641 S 73rd Av, SMMT, 60501	3148	9W-6S	D3
St. Joseph School 1740 Lake Av, WLMT, 60091	2812	4W-14N	C5
St. Jude Parish School 241 W 2nd Av, NLNX, 60451	3501	18W-25S	B7
St. Jude School 2204 McDonough St, JLET, 60436	3497	26W-24S	E6
St. Juliana School 7400 W Touhy Av, CHCG, 60631	2918	9W-8N	D1
St. Kieran School 700 195th St, CHHT, 60411	3508	0W-23S	B3
St. Ladislaus Catholic School 3330 N Lockwood Av, CHCG, 60641	2975	6W-4N	D3
St. Laurence High School 5556 W 77th St, BRBK, 60459	3211	6W-8S	D1
St. Laurence School 572 Standish St, ELGN, 60123	2854	34W-11N	D5
St. Lawrence O'Toole School 4101 St. Lawrence Av, MTSN, 60443	3594	5W-25S	C1
St. Leonard School 3322 Clarence Av, BRWN, 60402	3089	8W-3S	A4
St. Liborius School 24201 S Kings Rd, CRTE, 60417	3684	2W-29S	D1
St. Liborius School 3440 Halsted Blvd, STGR, 60475	3596	1W-28S	A5
St. Linus School 10400 Lawler Av, OKLN, 60453	3275	6W-12S	E1
St. Louis de Montfort School 8840 Ridgeland Av, OKLN, 60453	3211	8W-10S	B4
St. Louise de Marillac School 1125 Harrison Av, LGPK, 60525	3087	11W-2S	D4
St. Luke Academy 1500 W Belmont Av, CHCG, 60657	2977	1W-4N	D3
St. Luke School 519 Ashland Av, RVFT, 60305	3030	9W-0N	C3
St. Lukes Lutheran School 11 Pembrooke Rd, OswT, 60538	3199	36W-10S	D6
St. Malachy School 2252 W Washington Blvd, CHCG, 60612	3033	2W-0N	B4
St. Margaret Mary School 119 S Hubbard St, ALGN, 60102	2694	33W-20N	E7
St. Margaret Mary School 7318 N Oakley Av, CHCG, 60645	2867	2W-9N	A7
St. Margaret of Scotland School 9833 S Throop St, CHCG, 60643	3213	1W-11S	E7
St. Maria Goretti School 10050 Ivanhoe Av, SRPK, 60176	2973	12W-4N	B2
St. Mary Immaculate School 15629 S Route 59, PNFD, 60544	3416	29W-18S	C1
St. Mary Magdalene School 201 S Briggs St, JLET, 60433	3499	22W-24S	D5
St. Mary Nativity School 702 N Broadway St, JLET, 60435	3498	24W-23S	E3
St. Mary of Annunciation School 22277 W Erhart Rd, FmtT, 60060	2589	22W-29N	B3
St. Mary of Czestochowa School 3001 S 49th Av, CCRO, 60804	3089	6W-2S	E3
St. Mary of Gostyn School 440 Prairie Av, DRGV, 60515	3144	19W-5S	E2
St. Mary of the Angels School 1810 N Hermitage Av, CHCG, 60622	2977	2W-2N	C7
St. Mary of the Lake School 1026 W Buena Av, CHCG, 60613	2977	1W-5N	E1
St. Mary of the Woods School 7033 N Moselle Av, CHCG, 60646	2919	7W-8N	B1
St. Mary School 50 N Buffalo Grove Rd, BFGV, 60089	2754	16W-20N	C2
St. Mary School 103 S Gifford St, ELGN, 60120	2855	33W-11N	A4
St. Mary School 11409 195th St, MKNA, 60448	3502	14W-23S	E3
St. Mary School 227 Monee Rd, MonT, 60466	3594	4W-28S	E6
St. Mary School 817 N Center St, PLNO, 60545	3259	47W-13S	C5
St. Mary School 97 Herrick Rd, RVSD, 60546	3088	9W-3S	C5
St. Mary School 147 Garden St, WCHI, 60185	3022	29W-1N	D4
St. Mary School 313 N Tryon St, WDSK, 60098	2524	41W-31N	C7
St. Mary Star of the Sea School 6424 S Kenneth Av, CHCG, 60629	3150	5W-7S	B5
St. Matthew Lutheran School 24480 N Old McHenry Rd, ElaT, 60047	2645	21W-24N	D7
St. Matthew School 1555 Glen Ellyn Rd, GLHT, 60139	2969	22W-2N	C6
St. Matthias School 4910 N Claremont Av, CHCG, 60625	2921	2W-6N	A6
St. Michael School 14355 Highland Av, ODPK, 60462	3345	12W-17S	C4
St. Michael School 314 W Willow Av, WHTN, 60187	3024	24W-0S	C7
St. Michael the Archangel School 8231 S South Shore Dr, CHCG, 60617	3216	3E-9S	A2
St. Monica School 5115 N Mont Clare Av, CHCG, 60656	2918	8W-6N	D6
St. Nicholas of Tolentine School 3741 W 62nd St, CHCG, 60629	3150	4W-6S	C4
St. Nicholas Ukrainian Catholic-School 2200 W Rice St, CHCG, 60622	3033	2W-1N	B2
St. Norbert School 1817 Walters Av, NHBK, 60062	2757	9W-17N	B6
St. Odilo Elementary School 6617 23rd St, BRWN, 60402	3089	8W-2S	A2
St. Pascal School 6143 W Irving Park Rd, CHCG, 60634	2975	7W-4N	B2
St. Patricia School 9000 S 86th Av, HYHL, 60457	3210	10W-10S	A5
St. Patrick High School 5900 W Belmont Av, CHCG, 60634	2975	7W-4N	B3
St. Patrick School 110 Willow Av, JLET, 60436	3498	24W-24S	D5
St. Patrick School 118 N 5th St, SCRL, 60174	2964	35W-3N	A7
St. Patrick School 15020 W Wadsworth Rd, WDWH, 60083	2420	15W-39N	B6
St. Paul Lutheran Academy 5201 Galitz St, SKOK, 60077	2865	6W-9N	D6
St. Paul Lutheran School 846 N Menard Av, CHCG, 60651	3031	7W-1N	C2
St. Paul Lutheran School 1025 W Lake St, MLPK, 60160	3029	11W-0N	E3
St. Paul Lutheran School 8601 Harrison Av, MNSR, 46321	3430		D7
St. Paul Lutheran School 18 S School St, MPPT, 60056	2808	15W-12N	A7
St. Paul Lutheran School 5650 N Canfield Av, NpkT, 60631	2918	9W-7N	B5
St. Paul Lutheran School 4660 W 94th St, OKLN, 60453	3212	5W-10S	A5
St. Paul of the Cross School 140 S Northwest Hwy, PKRG, 60068	2918	10W-8N	B1
St. Paul-Our Lady of Vilna School 2114 W 22nd Pl, CHCG, 60608	3091	2W-2S	B2
St. Paul's Christian School 5323 W Margaret St, MONE, 60449	3683	6W-31S	A6
St. Paul's Lutheran School 550 2nd Av, AURA, 60505	3200	35W-8S	C1
St. Paul's Lutheran School 330 W Highland Dr, CHHT, 60411	3507	2W-24S	E6
St. Paul the Apostle School 130 Woodlawn Av, JLET, 60435	3498	25W-23S	B5
St. Peter Lutheran School 111 W Olive St, ANHT, 60004	2807	17W-15N	A2
St. Peter Lutheran School 208 E Schaumburg Rd, SMBG, 60194	2859	23W-10N	B5
St. Peter School 900 St. Peter St, ANTH, 60002	2357	24W-42N	D6
St. Peter School 1881 Kaneville Rd, GNVA, 60134	3019	36W-1N	E4
St. Peter School 8140 Niles Center Rd, SKOK, 60077	2865	6W-10N	E5
St. Peter the Apostle School 500 N Cherry St, ITSC, 60143	2914	19W-6N	C5
St. Petronille School 425 Prospect Av, GNEN, 60137	3025	22W-0N	B5
St. Philip Lutheran School 2500 W Bryn Mawr Av, CHCG, 60659	2921	3W-7N	A4
St. Philip Neri School 2110 E 72nd St, CHCG, 60649	3153	2E-8S	C7
St. Philip the Apostle School 1233 W Holtz Av, ADSN, 60101	2970	20W-4N	B3
St. Pius V School 1919 S Ashland Av, CHCG, 60608	3091	1W-1S	D1
St. Pius X School 601 Westmore Meyers Rd, LMBD, 60148	3026	18W-0S	E5
St. Priscilla School 7001 W Addison St, CHCG, 60634	2974	8W-4N	E3
St. Procopius School 1625 S Allport St, CHCG, 60608	3091	1W-1S	E1
St. Raphael School 1215 Modaff Rd, NPVL, 60540	3203	27W-8S	D1
St. Raymond School 300 S Elmhurst Av, MPPT, 60056	2861	16W-12N	E1
St. Rene Goupil School 6340 S New England Av, CHCG, 60638	3148	8W-7S	E5
St. Richard School 5025 S Kenneth Av, CHCG, 60632	3150	5W-5S	B2
St. Rita of Cascia High School 7740 S Western Av, CHCG, 60652	3213	3W-8S	B1
St. Rita of Cascia School 770 W Old Indian Tr, AURA, 60506	3137	36W-6S	E4
St. Robert Bellarmine School 6036 W Eastwood Av, CHCG, 60630	2919	7W-5N	B7
St. Rose School 626 S Kankakee St, WMTN, 60481	3853	27W-39S	D7
St. Sabina Academy 7801 S Throop St, CHCG, 60620	3213	1W-8S	E1
St. Scholastica Academy 7416 N Ridge Blvd, CHCG, 60645	2867	2W-9N	B7
St. Scholastica School 7720 Janes Av, WDRG, 60517	3205	21W-8S	E2
Sts. Cyril & Methodius School 607 Sobieski St, LMNT, 60439	3270	19W-14S	E5
Sts. Faith Hope & Charity School 180 Ridge Av, WNKA, 60093	2812	5W-15N	B3
Sts. Peter & Paul School 416 1st St, CRY, 60013	2641	31W-24N	E7
Sts. Peter & Paul School 201 E Franklin Av, NPVL, 60540	3141	26W-6S	D5
St. Stanislaus Bishop-Martyr School 14418 S McKinley Av, POSN, 60469	3349	3W-17S	B4
St. Stanislaus Kostka School 1255 N Noble St, CHCG, 60622	3033	1W-1N	D1
St. Sylvester School 3027 W Palmer Blvd, CHCG, 60647	2976	3W-2N	E6
St. Symphorosa School 6125 S Austin Av, CHCG, 60638	3149	7W-6S	C4
St. Tarcissus School 6040 W Ardmore Av, CHCG, 60646	2919	7W-7N	B4
St. Thecla School 6323 N Newcastle Av, CHCG, 60631	2918	8W-7N	E3
St. Theresa School 445 N Benton St, PLTN, 60067	2752	20W-16N	E7
St. Therese School 247 W 23rd St, CHCG, 60616	3092	0W-2S	B2
St. Thomas More School 1625 W Highland Av, ELGN, 60123	2854	35W-11N	B3
St. Thomas More School 8435 Calumet Av, MNSR, 46321	3430		E7
St. Thomas of Canterbury School 4827 N Kenmore Av, CHCG, 60640	2921	1W-6N	E6
St. Thomas of Villanova School 1141 E Anderson Dr, PLTN, 60074	2753	19W-16N	C7
St. Thomas the Apostle School 5467 S Woodlawn Av, CHCG, 60615	3153	1E-5S	A2
St. Thomas the Apostle School 265 King St, CLLK, 60014	2639	36W-25N	E5
St. Turibius School 4120 W 57th St, CHCG, 60629	3150	5W-6S	B3
St. Viator High School 1213 E Oakton St, ANHT, 60004	2807	17W-14N	B3
St. Viator School 4140 W Addison St, CHCG, 60641	2976	5W-4N	B3
St. Vincent Ferrer School 1515 Lathrop Av, RVFT, 60305	3030	9W-1N	C1
St. Walter School 11741 S Western Av, CHCG, 60643	3277	2W-13S	B4
St. Walter School 201 W Maple Av, ROSL, 60172	2912	23W-7N	E5
St. William School 2559 N Sayre Av, CHCG, 60707	2974	8W-3N	E5
St. Zachary School 567 W Algonquin Rd, DSPN, 60018	2862	15W-10N	A5
Salem Christian Academy 11816 S Indiana Av, CHCG, 60628	3278	0E-13S	D4
Salem Christian School 2845 W McLean Av, CHCG, 60647	2976	3W-2N	E6
Salt Creek Elementary School 65 JF Kennedy Blvd, EGVV, 60007	2914	19W-8N	D2
Salt Creek Primary School 980 S Riverside Dr, EMHT, 60126	3027	17W-0S	C6
Sandburg Elementary School 14500 Myrtle Av, HRVY, 60426	3349	1W-17S	E5
Sandburg Elementary School 1345 Jewell Rd, WHTN, 60187	3024	25W-0N	A5
Sandburg Middle School 345 E St. Charles Rd, EMHT, 60126	3028	15W-0N	B3
Sandburg Middle School 855 W Hawley St, MDLN, 60060	2590	19W-27N	C7
Sanders Academy of Excellence 1425 W 112th St, CHCG, 60643	3277	1W-13S	D3
Sandidge Elementary School 16600 66th Av, TYPK, 60477	3425	8W-19S	B3
Sandoval Elementary School 5534 S St. Louis Av, CHCG, 60629	3150	4W-6S	D3
Sandridge Elementary School 2950 Glenwood Dyer Rd, BlmT, 60411	3510	3E-24S	A6
San Miguel-Gary Comer School 819 N Leamington Av, CHCG, 60651	3031	6W-1N	E3
Santa Lucia School 3017 S Wells St, CHCG, 60616	3092	0W-2S	B3
Santa Maria del Popolo School 126 N Lake St, MDLN, 60060	2646	19W-27N	D1
Sarah Adams Elementary School 555 Old Mill Grove Rd, LKZH, 60047	2699	22W-22N	B4
Sator Sanchez Elementary School 1101 Harrison Av, JLET, 60432	3499	23W-22S	B2
Saucedo Scholastic Academy 2850 W 24th Blvd, CHCG, 60623	3091	3W-2S	A2
Sauganash Elementary School 6040 N Kilpatrick Av, CHCG, 60646	2919	5W-7N	E3
Sauk Elementary School 4435 S Churchill Dr, RNPK, 60471	3594	5W-26S	C3
Saukview Elementary School 3341 Miller Av, SCHT, 60411	3596	1W-27S	A4
Sawyer Elementary School 5248 S Sawyer Av, CHCG, 60632	3150	4W-5S	E2
Sayre Language Academy 1850 N Newland Av, CHCG, 60707	2974	8W-2N	E7
Scammon Elementary School 4201 W Henderson St, CHCG, 60641	2976	5W-4N	B3
Scarlet Oak Elementary School 5731 Albert Dr, OKFT, 60452	3347	7W-18S	D7
Schafer Elementary School 700 E Pleasant Ln, LMBD, 60148	3026	19W-1N	D2
Schaumburg Christian School 200 N Roselle Rd, SMBG, 60194	2859	23W-10N	A4
Schaumburg High School 1100 W Schaumburg Rd, SMBG, 60194	2858	24W-10N	C5
Schiesher Elementary School 5205 Kingston Av, LSLE, 60532	3143	22W-5S	B3
Schiller Middle School 640 W Scott St, CHCG, 60610	3034	0W-1N	A1
Schmid Elementary School 9755 S Greenwood Av, CHCG, 60628	3215	1E-11S	A6
Schneider Elementary School 304 Banbury Rd, NARA, 60542	3078	35W-3S	B7
School of Navy Science & Tech 821 E 103rd St, CHCG, 60628	3278	1E-12S	E1

FEATURE NAME Address City ZIP Code	MAP#	CGS	GRID
School of Tech High School 7529 S Constance Av, CHCG, 60649	3215	2E-8S	B1
School of St. Mary-Primary Center 900 W Everett Rd, LKFT, 60045	2649	12W-24N	C6
School of St. Mary-Upper Grade-Center 185 E Illinois Rd, LKFT, 60045	2650	10W-26N	A3
Schrum Memorial School 485 165th St, CTCY, 60409	3430	4E-19S	B3
Schubert Elementary School 2727 N Long Av, CHCG, 60639	2975	6W-3N	D5
Schurz High School 3601 N Milwaukee Av, CHCG, 60641	2976	5W-4N	B2
Science & Arts Academy 1825 Miner St, DSPN, 60016	2863	12W-11N	B4
Science Academy of Chicago 2601 N Meade Av, CHCG, 60639	2975	7W-3N	B5
Scott Elementary School 2250 Scott St, LydT, 60164	2973	12W-2N	B6
Scott Elementary School 500 Warwick Dr, NPVL, 60565	3204	25W-9S	B4
Scott Joplin Elementary School 7931 S Honore St, CHCG, 60620	3213	2W-9S	C2
Scullen Middle School 2815 Mistflower Ln, NPVL, 60564	3266	30W-11S	B2
Serena Hills Elementary School 255 Pleasant Dr, CHHT, 60411	3507	1W-23S	E4
Seth Paine Elementary School 50 Miller Rd, LKZH, 60047	2698	24W-24N	D1
Seward Arts Academy 4600 S Hermitage Av, CHCG, 60609	3091	2W-4S	C7
Seward Branch Academy 4541 S Wood St, CHCG, 60609	3091	2W-4S	C7
Sexton Elementary School 6020 S Langley Av, CHCG, 60637	3152	0E-6S	E4
Shabonee School 2929 Shabonee Trl, NHBK, 60062	2756	11W-17N	E5
Shedd Branch of Bennett School 200 E 99th St, CHCG, 60628	3214	0E-11S	D6
Sheila Daniels Christian Academy 2313 Washington St, WKGN, 60085	2536	11W-34N	D2
Shepard High School 13049 S Ridgeland Av, WthT, 60463	3347	7W-15S	B1
Shepard Middle School 440 Grove Av, DRFD, 60015	2756	11W-20N	E1
Sheridan Elementary School 510 Franklin Blvd, ELGN, 60120	2855	33W-11N	B3
Sheridan Elementary School 1360 N Sheridan Rd, LKFT, 60045	2650	10W-27N	A1
Sherlock Elementary School 5347 W 22nd Pl, CCRO, 60804	3089	6W-2S	D2
Sherwood Elementary School 1900 Stratford Rd, HDPK, 60035	2704	9W-20N	C7
Shiloh Park Elementary School 2635 Gabriel Av, ZION, 60099	2422	10W-40N	A3
Shoesmith Elementary School 1330 E 50th St, CHCG, 60615	3153	1E-5S	A1
Shoop Academy of Math Science &-Technology 1460 W 112th St, CHCG, 60643	3277	1W-13S	D3
Sieden Prairie School 725 Notre Dame Dr, MTSN, 60443	3505	6W-25S	E6
Simmons Middle School 1130 Sheffer Rd, AURA, 60505	3138	34W-6S	D5
Simmons Middle School 6450 W 95th St, CHRG, 60453	3211	8W-10S	B6
Sipley Elementary School 2806 83rd St, WDRG, 60517	3205	22W-9S	D3
Sir Miles Davis Academy 6723 S Wood St, CHCG, 60636	3151	2W-7S	C6
Skinner Classical Elementary School 111 S Throop St, CHCG, 60607	3033	1W-0S	D5
Skokie School 520 Glendale Av, WNKA, 60093	2811	5W-15N	E1
Sleepy Hollow Elementary School 898 Glen Oak Dr, SYHW, 60118	2800	35W-15N	B4
Smith Elementary School 1332 Robinwood Dr, AURA, 60506	3137	36W-5S	E3
Smith Elementary School 744 E 103rd St, CHCG, 60628	3214	0E-11S	E7
Smyser Elementary School 4310 N Melvina Av, CHCG, 60634	2975	7W-5N	B1
Smyth Elementary School 1059 W 13th St, CHCG, 60608	3033	1W-1S	E7
Socrates Greek School 5701 N Redwood Dr, CHCG, 60631	2918	10W-7N	B5
Solomon Elementary School 6206 N Hamlin Av, CHCG, 60659	2920	4W-7N	C3
Solomon Schechter Day School 3210 Dundee Rd, NHBK, 60062	2756	11W-18N	D4
Solomon Schechter Day School 9301 Gross Point Rd, SKOK, 60076	2865	5W-11N	E2
South Chicago Community Area Elem-School 8255 S Houston Av, CHCG, 60617	3216	3E-9S	A2
Southeast Elementary School 9800 S Francisco Av, ENGN, 60805	3213	3W-11S	A6
South Elementary School 601 Golf Rd, CLLK, 60014	2639	36W-25N	D5
South Elementary School 1535 Everett Av, DSPN, 60018	2863	13W-9N	A6
South Elementary School 266 Linden Av, GLNC, 60022	2758	5W-17N	E6
South Elementary School 1812 Morrow Av, NCHI, 60064	2536	11W-31N	D7
South Elementary School 133 S Grant St, WTMT, 60559	3145	18W-5S	A3
South Elgin High School 760 E Main St, SEGN, 60177	2908	34W-8N	E2
South Loop Elementary School 1212 S Plymouth Ct, CHCG, 60605	3034	0W-1S	B7
South Middle School 400 S Highland Av, ANHT, 60005	2807	18W-13N	A5
South Park Elementary School 1421 Hackberry Rd, DRFD, 60015	2756	11W-20N	C1
South Side Baptist School 5220 W 105th St, OKLN, 60453	3211	6W-11S	E7
Southwest Christian School 17171 84th Av, TYPK, 60477	3424	10W-20S	B4
Southwest Elementary School 9900 S Central Park Av, ENGN, 60805	3212	4W-11S	D7
Southwood Middle School 18635 Lee St, CCHL, 60478	3426	5W-21S	C7
Spaulding Elementary School 2000 Belle Plaine Av, GRNE, 60031	2479	13W-36N	A5
Spaulding Elementary School 14811 Turner Av, MDLN, 60445	3348	4W-17S	E5
Speed Therapeutic Elementary School 16121 Central Park Av, MKHM, 60428	3426	4W-19S	E2
Spencer Math-Science Academy 214 N Lavergne Av, CHCG, 60644	3031	6W-0N	E4
Spencer Pointe Elementary School 1721 Spencer Road, NLNX, 60451	3589	16W-26S	E3
Spring Avenue Elementary School 1001 S Spring Av, LGNG, 60525	3147	12W-5S	B2
Spring Bluff Elementary School 628 College Av, WPHR, 60096	2363	10W-42N	B5
Spring Brook Elementary School 2700 Seiler Dr, NPVL, 60565	3203	27W-10S	C6
Springfield Elementary School 14620 Springfield Av, MDLN, 60445	3348	4W-17S	C5
Spring Grove Elementary School 2018 Main St Rd, SPGV, 60081	2413	31W-40N	E4
Spring Hills Elementary School 560 Pinecroft Dr, ROSL, 60172	2913	22W-6N	B6
Springman Middle School 2701 Central Rd, GNVW, 60025	2810	9W-12N	B7
Spring Trail Elementary School 1384 Spring Valley Dr, CLSM, 60188	2967	28W-4N	B3
Spring Wood Middle School 5540 Arlington Dr E, HRPK, 60133	2912	25W-6N	A6
Spry Elementary School 2400 S Marshall Blvd, CHCG, 60623	3090	3W-2S	E2
SS Alphonsus-Patrick School 20W145 Davey Rd, LMNT, 60439	3270	19W-13S	D5
Stagg Elementary School 7424 S Morgan St, CHCG, 60621	3151	1W-8S	E7
Stanton School 101 Hawthorne Ln, FXLK, 60041	2473	27W-36N	C4
Steck Elementary School 460 Inverness Dr, AURA, 60504	3201	32W-8S	C2
Steeple Run Elementary School 6S151 Steeple Run Dr, LslT, 60540	3142	24W-6S	C4
Steinmetz Academic Center High-School 3030 N Mobile Av, CHCG, 60634	2975	7W-3N	A4
Stella May Swartz Elementary School 17W160 16th St, OKTR, 60181	3085	17W-1S	C1
Stevenson Elementary School 8010 S Kostner Av, CHCG, 60652	3212	5W-9S	B2
Stevenson Elementary School 1414 Armstrong Ln, EGVV, 60007	2913	21W-8N	E2
Stevenson Elementary School 9000 Capitol Dr, MaiT, 60016	2863	11W-11N	D3
Stevenson Elementary School 1630 N 20th Av, MLPK, 60160	3029	11W-1N	D1
Stevenson Elementary School 18W331 15th St, YkTp, 60148	3085	18W-1S	A1
Stevenson Middle School 4350 W 79th St, CHCG, 60652	3212	5W-8S	B2
Stewart Elementary School 4525 N Kenmore Av, CHCG, 60640	2921	1W-5N	E7
Still Middle School 787 Meadowridge Dr, AURA, 60504	3202	30W-8S	A3
Stockton Specialty School 4420 N Beacon St, CHCG, 60640	2921	1W-5N	D7
Stone Church Christian Academy 6330 W 127th St, PSHT, 60463	3275	7W-14S	B7
Stone Elementary School 1404 W Stone Av, ADSN, 60101	2970	20W-4N	B4
Stone Scholastic Academy 6239 N Leavitt St, CHCG, 60659	2921	2W-7N	B3
Stony Creek Elementary School 11700 S Kolin Av, ALSP, 60803	3276	5W-13S	B4
Storm Elementary School 305 N Van Nortwick Av, BTVA, 60510	3078	36W-1S	A1
Stowe Elementary School 3444 W Wabansia Av, CHCG, 60647	2976	4W-2N	D7
Strassburg Elementary School 2002 223rd St, SLVL, 60411	3597	2E-27S	D3
Stratford Middle School 251 Butterfield Dr, BMDL, 60108	2968	24W-4N	C3
Streamwood High School 701 W Schaumburg Rd, SMWD, 60107	2856	29W-10N	D5
Stuart R Paddock Elementary School 225 W Washington St, PLTN, 60067	2805	21W-15N	E1
Suder Montessori School 2022 W Washington Blvd, CHCG, 60612	3033	2W-0N	B4
Sullivan High School 6631 N Bosworth Av, CHCG, 60626	2921	1W-8N	C2
Summit Academy 333 W River Rd, ELGN, 60123	2800	33W-13N	E7
Summit Hill Junior High School 20130 S Rosewood Dr, FftT, 60423	3504	10W-24S	C5
Summit School 611 E Main St, EDND, 60118	2801	33W-15N	B3
Sumner Elementary School 4320 W 5th Av, CHCG, 60624	3032	5W-0S	B6
Sunnydale Elementary School 716 Sunnydale Blvd, SMWD, 60107	2857	27W-9N	C7
Sunny Hill Elementary School 2500 Helm Rd, CPVL, 60110	2748	32W-18N	C5
Sunnyside Elementary School 5412 St. Charles Rd, BKLY, 60163	3028	14W-0N	D3
Sunset Ridge Elementary School 525 Sunset Ridge Rd, NHFD, 60093	2811	7W-15N	A1
Sutherland Elementary School 10015 S Leavitt St, CHCG, 60643	3213	2W-11S	C7
Sward Elementary School 9830 Brandt Av, OKLN, 60453	3211	6W-11S	E7
SW Chicago Christian School 10110 Central Av, OKLN, 60453	3211	7W-11S	D7
Swift Specialty School 5900 N Winthrop Av, CHCG, 60660	2921	1W-7N	D4
Sycamore Trails Elementary School 1025 Sycamore Ln, BRLT, 60103	2910	29W-6N	D6
Sykuta School 4301 180th St, CCHL, 60478	3426	5W-21S	C6
Tabernacle Christian Academy 1233 W 109th Pl, CHCG, 60643	3277	1W-12S	E2
Taft Elementary School 393 E 163rd St, HRVY, 60426	3428	0W-19S	B2
Taft Elementary School 1125 Oregon St, JLET, 60435	3498	25W-22S	B2
Taft Grade School 1605 S Washington St, LKPT, 60441	3419	22W-20S	C4
Taft High School 6530 W Bryn Mawr Av, CHCG, 60631	2919	8W-7N	A4
Talala Elementary School 430 Talala St, PKFT, 60466	3595	4W-28S	A6
Talcott Elementary School 1840 W Ohio St, CHCG, 60622	3033	2W-0N	C3
Talman Community Elementary School 5450 S Talman Av, CHCG, 60632	3151	3W-5S	A2
Tanner Elementary School 7350 S Evans Av, CHCG, 60619	3152	0E-8S	E7
Tarkington Elementary School 310 Scott St, WLNG, 60090	2754	16W-17N	D5
Tarkington School of Excel 3330 W 71st St, CHCG, 60629	3150	4W-7S	E7
Tate Woods Elementary School 1736 Middleton Av, LSLE, 60532	3142	23W-4S	E1
Taylor Elementary School 9912 S Avenue H, CHCG, 60617	3216	4E-11S	B6
Tefft Middle School 1100 Shirley Av, SMWD, 60107	2911	27W-9N	B1
Telpochcalli Elementary School 2832 W 24th Blvd, CHCG, 60623	3091	3W-2S	A2
Terrace Elementary School 735 S Westgate Rd, DSPN, 60016	2862	14W-11N	C4
The Ancona School 4770 S Dorchester Av, CHCG, 60615	3153	1E-5S	A1
The Lane Elementary School 500 N Elm St, HNDL, 60521	3086	15W-4S	B7
Theodore Roosevelt Elementary-School 1001 S Fairview Av, PKRG, 60068	2918	10W-8N	A2
The Willows Academy 1012 E Thacker St, DSPN, 60016	2862	13W-10N	E4
Thomas Drummond Elementary School 1845 W Cortland St, CHCG, 60622	2977	2W-2N	C7
Thomas Edison Elementary School 8200 Gross Point Rd, MNGV, 60053	2865	6W-10N	C5
Thomas Jefferson Elementary School 3805 Winston Dr, HFET, 60192	2804	23W-14N	D3
Thomas Jefferson Elementary School 2651 Glenwood Av, JLET, 60435	3497	27W-23S	D4
Thomas Middle School 1430 N Belmont Av, ANHT, 60004	2807	17W-15N	B2
Thompson Junior High School 440 Boulder Hill Pass, OSWG, 60543	3263	36W-11S	D2
Thompson Middle School 705 W Main St, SCRL, 60174	2964	36W-2N	A7
Thornridge High School 15000 Cottage Grove Av, DLTN, 60419	3351	1E-17S	A5
Thornton Fractional North High-School 755 Pulaski Rd, CTCY, 60409	3352	3E-18S	A6
Thornton Fractional South High-School 18500 Burnham Av, LNSG, 60438	3430	3E-21S	A7
Thornton Twp High School 15001 Broadway Av, HRVY, 60426	3350	1W-17S	A6
Thornwood High School 17101 S Park Av, SHLD, 60473	3428	0E-20S	E3
Thorp Elementary School 8914 S Buffalo Av, CHCG, 60617	3216	4E-10S	A4
Thorp Scholastic Academy 6024 W Warwick Av, CHCG, 60634	2975	7W-4N	B2
Three Oaks Elementary School 1514 Three Oaks Rd, AlqT, 60013	2642	30W-24N	A7
Three Rivers School 24150 Minooka Rd, CNHN, 60410	3672	32W-29S	E2
Tilden Achievement Academy 4747 S Union Av, CHCG, 60609	3152	0W-5S	A1
Tilton Elementary School 223 N Keeler Av, CHCG, 60624	3032	5W-0N	B4
Timber Ridge Middle School 2101 S Bronk Rd, JLET, 60586	3416	29W-21S	D7
Timber Trails Elementary School 1675 McDonough Rd, HFET, 60192	2856	30W-12N	B1
Timothy Christian Elementary-Middle-School 188 W Butterfield Rd, EMHT, 60126	3027	16W-0S	E6
Timothy Christian High School 1061 S Prospect Av, EMHT, 60126	3027	16W-0S	E7
Timothy Lutheran School 1700 W 83rd St, CHCG, 60620	3213	2W-9S	D3
Tinley Park High School 6111 175th St, TYPK, 60477	3425	7W-21S	C5
Tioga Elementary School 212 W Memorial Rd, BNVL, 60106	2971	16W-4N	E2
Tobin Elementary School 8501 Narragansett Av, BRBK, 60459	3211	7W-9S	B3
Todd Hall Elementary School 3925 W Lunt Av, LNWD, 60712	2920	4W-8N	B1
Tonti Branch Elementary School 4950 S Laporte Av, CHCG, 60638	3149	6W-5S	E1
Tonti Elementary School 5815 S Homan Av, CHCG, 60629	3150	4W-6S	D3
Transfiguration School 316 W Mill St, WCDA, 60084	2643	26W-27N	E1
Traughber Junior High School 61 Franklin St, OSWG, 60543	3263	37W-12S	C4
Trevor Grade School 26325 Wilmot Rd, SlmT, 53179	2357		B2
Trinity Christian School 901 Shorewood Dr, SRWD, 60404	3496	30W-22S	C3
Trinity College Prep High School 7574 Division St, RVFT, 60305	3030	9W-1N	C2
Trinity Lutheran School 448 Cass St, CRTE, 60417	3685	0W-29S	B2
Trinity Lutheran School 18144 Glen Ter, LNSG, 60438	3429	3E-21S	E6
Trinity Lutheran School 405 Rush St, ROSL, 60172	2913	23W-6N	B5
Trinity Lutheran School 6850 159th St, TYPK, 60477	3425	8W-18S	A1
Trinity Lutheran School 11503 German Church Rd, WLSP, 60480	3208	14W-9S	D3
Trinity Lutheran School 1008 E Roosevelt Rd, YkTp, 60148	3026	18W-0S	E7
Trinity Oaks Christian Academy 409 1st St, CRY, 60013	2641	30W-24N	E7

Schools

Chicago 7-County Points of Interest Index

Schools

FEATURE NAME Address City ZIP Code	MAP#	CGS	GRID
Tripp School 850 Highland Grove Dr, BFGV, 60089	2701	16W-21N	D7
Troy Craughwell Elementary School 3333 Black Rd, JLET, 60431	3497	28W-22S	B3
Troy Crossroads Elementary School 210 E Black Rd, SRWD, 60404	3496	29W-23S	D3
Troy Heritage Trail Elementary 3389 Longford Dr, JLET, 60431	3497	28W-25S	B7
Troy Middle School 5800 Theodore Dr, JLET, 60586	3496	31W-22S	A1
Troy Shorewood Elementary School 210 School Rd, SRWD, 60404	3496	29W-24S	D5
Trumbull Elementary School 5200 N Ashland Av, CHCG, 60640	2921	2W-6N	C5
Turner-Drew Language Academy 9300 S Princeton Av, CHCG, 60620	3214	0W-10S	B5
Turner Elementary School 3847 W 135th St, CTWD, 60472	3348	4W-16S	D2
Turner Elementary School 750 Ingalton Av, WCHI, 60185	3022	29W-1N	D2
Twain Elementary School 5131 S Linder Av, CHCG, 60638	3149	6W-5S	D2
Twain Elementary School 9401 N Hamlin Av, NLES, 60714	2863	11W-11N	E2
Twin Groves Middle School 2600 N Buffalo Grove Rd, BFGV, 60089	2701	17W-22N	B3
Tyler Elementary School 511 E Illinois Hwy, NLNX, 60451	3589	17W-25S	D1
Union Elementary School 1661 Cherry Hill Rd, JLET, 60433	3588	21W-25S	B1
Union Ridge Elementary School 4600 N Oak Park Av, HDHT, 60706	2918	8W-5N	E7
Unity Junior High School East-Campus 2100 S Laramie Av, CCRO, 60804	3089	6W-1S	D2
Unity Junior High School West-Campus 2115 S 54th Av, CCRO, 60804	3089	6W-1S	D1
Universal School 7350 W 93rd St, BGVW, 60455	3210	9W-10S	E5
Uplift Community High School 900 W Wilson Av, CHCG, 60640	2921	1W-5N	E7
Uplift Community School 900 W Wilson Av, CHCG, 60640	2921	1W-5N	E7
Valley View Elementary School 6515 W Illinois, MHRY, 60050	2527	35W-33N	A2
Vanderpoel Humanities Academy 9510 S Prospect Av, CHCG, 60643	3213	2W-11S	D6
Vernon Hills High School 145 Lakeview Pkwy, VNHL, 60061	2647	16W-25N	E6
Vernon Johns Middle Academy 6936 S Hermitage Av, CHCG, 60636	3151	2W-7S	C6
Veterans Memorial Middle School 12320 Greenwood Av, BLID, 60406	3277	3W-14S	B6
Viking School 4460 Old Grand Av, GRNE, 60031	2478	14W-35N	C7
Village Elementary School 880 Nippersink Av, RDLK, 60073	2531	24W-33N	D2
Virginia Lake Elementary School 925 N Glenn Dr, PLTN, 60074	2753	19W-17N	B6
Visitation School 900 W Garfield Blvd, CHCG, 60609	3151	1W-5S	E2
Visitation School 851 S York St, EMHT, 60126	3028	15W-0S	A6
Volta Elementary School 4950 N Avers Av, CHCG, 60625	2920	4W-6N	C6
Von Humboldt Elementary School 2620 W Hirsch St, CHCG, 60622	3033	3W-1N	A1
Von Steuben Metropolitan High-School 5039 N Kimball Av, CHCG, 60625	2920	4W-6N	D6
Wacker Elementary School 9746 S Morgan St, CHCG, 60643	3213	1W-11S	E6
Wadsworth Elementary School 6420 S University Av, CHCG, 60637	3153	1E-7S	A5
Wagoner Elementary School 1831 215th Pl, SLVL, 60411	3597	2E-26S	C2
WA Johnson Elementary School 252 Ridgewood Av, BNVL, 60106	2971	16W-4N	D2
Walden Elementary School 630 Essex Ct, DRFD, 60015	2704	10W-21N	A6
Waldo Middle School 56 Jackson St, AURA, 60505	3200	35W-8S	B1
Walker Elementary School 7735 W 66th Pl, BDPK, 60501	3148	9W-7S	C6
Walker Elementary School 120 Walker Ave, CNHL, 60514	3145	16W-5S	D3
Walker Elementary School 3601 Church St, SKOK, 60203	2866	4W-11N	C3
Walker Intermediate School 19900 80th Av, FftT, 60423	3504	10W-23S	D4
Walkers Grove Elementary School 24810 W 135th St, PNFD, 60585	3338	31W-15S	A3
Wallace Elementary School 6235 Jefferson Av, HMND, 46324	3430		E1
Walnut Trails Elementary School 301 Wynstone Dr, SRWD, 60404	3495	31W-24S	E6
Walsh Elementary School 2015 S Peoria St, CHCG, 60608	3092	1W-1S	A1
Walsh Elementary School 514 MacGregor Rd, LKPT, 60441	3419	21W-18S	E1
Walsh Elementary School 5640 S 75th Av, SMMT, 60501	3148	9W-6S	D3
Walter Payton Coll Prep High School 1034 N Wells St, CHCG, 60610	3034	0W-1N	B2
Walter R Sundling Junior High-School 1100 N Smith St, PLTN, 60067	2752	21W-17N	D5
Walther Lutheran High School 900 Chicago Av, MLPK, 60160	3029	11W-1N	E3
Ward Elementary School 2701 S Shields Av, CHCG, 60616	3092	0W-2S	B3
Warren Elementary School 9239 S Jeffery Av, CHCG, 60617	3215	2E-10S	C5
Warren Palm Academy 1910 170th St, HLCT, 60429	3427	2W-20S	D4
Warren Park Elementary School 1225 S 60th Ct, CCRO, 60804	3031	7W-1S	B7
Washington Elementary School 819 W Chicago St, ELGN, 60123	2854	34W-11N	D4
Washington Elementary School 914 Ashland Av, EVTN, 60202	2867	3W-10N	A4
Washington Elementary School 15248 Lincoln Av, HRVY, 60426	3349	2W-18S	D7
Washington Elementary School 2710 Golf Rd, MaiT, 60025	2864	9W-12N	B1
Washington Elementary School 122 S Garfield Av, MDLN, 60060	2646	19W-27N	D1
Washington Elementary School 1111 Washington Blvd, MYWD, 60153	3029	11W-0N	E4
Washington Elementary School 13900 S School St, RVDL, 60827	3350	0W-16S	B2
Washington Elementary School 911 Bridle Ln, WHTN, 60187	3024	24W-0N	E4
Washington Elementary School 110 S Orchard Av, WKGN, 60085	2536	11W-34N	D2
Washington Irving Elementary School 749 S Oakley Blvd, CHCG, 60612	3033	2W-0S	B6
Washington Irving Elementary School 1125 S Cuyler Av, OKPK, 60304	3031	7W-0S	B6
Washington Junior High School 402 Richards St, JLET, 60433	3499	23W-24S	A6
Washington Junior High School 201 N Washington St, NPVL, 60540	3141	27W-6S	D5
Washington Middle School 231 S Constitution Dr, AURA, 60506	3137	38W-7S	A7
Washington School 25 W 16th Pl, CHHT, 60411	3596	1W-25S	A1
Waterbury Elementary School 355 Rodenburg Rd, ROSL, 60172	2912	25W-7N	C5
Waters Fine Arts Elementary School 4540 N Campbell Av, CHCG, 60625	2921	3W-5N	A7
Watts Elementary School 800 S Whispering Hills Dr, NPVL, 60540	3203	28W-7S	A1
Waubonsie Valley High School-Gold 1305 Long Grove Dr, AURA, 60504	3201	31W-9S	D3
Waubonsie Valley High School-Green 2590 Ogden Av, AURA, 60504	3201	32W-8S	C3
Wauconda Elementary School 225 Osage St, WCDA, 60084	2643	26W-27N	D1
Wauconda High School 555 N Main St, WCDA, 60084	2587	26W-27N	D7
Wauconda Middle School 215 Slocum Lake Rd, WCDA, 60084	2643	26W-27N	D1
Waukegan High School 2325 Brookside Av, WKGN, 60085	2536	11W-34N	C1
Waukegan High School Ninth Grade-Center 1011 Washington St, WKGN, 60085	2536	11W-34N	E2
Wayne Elementary School 5n443 School St, WYNE, 60184	2965	32W-5N	D2
Wayne Thomas Elementary School 2939 Summit Av, HDPK, 60035	2704	9W-23N	B2
WC Petty Elementary School 850 Highview Dr, ANTH, 60002	2357	24W-42N	C6
Webster Elementary School 4055 W Arthington St, CHCG, 60624	3032	5W-0S	B6
Webster Middle School 930 New York St, WKGN, 60085	2479	11W-35N	E7
Wegner Elementary School 1180 Marcella Ln, WCHI, 60185	3022	30W-2N	C1
Welch Elementary School 2620 Leverenz Rd, NPVL, 60564	3202	29W-10S	D6
Wells Community Academy High School 936 N Ashland Av, CHCG, 60622	3033	2W-1N	C2
Wells Preparatory Academy 244 E Pershing Rd, CHCG, 60653	3092	0E-3S	C5
Wendell E Green Elementary School 1150 W 96th St, CHCG, 60643	3213	1W-11S	E6
Wentworth Elementary School 6950 S Sangamon St, CHCG, 60621	3151	1W-7S	E6
Wentworth Intermediate School 530 Superior Av, CTCY, 60409	3352	3E-17S	A5
Wentworth Junior High School 560 Superior Av, CTCY, 60409	3352	3E-17S	A6
Wescott Elementary School 1820 Western Av, NfdT, 60062	2756	12W-16N	C7
Wesley Elementary School 1111 W Westwood Tr, ADSN, 60101	2970	19W-4N	C4
Wesmere Elementary School 2001 Wesmere Pkwy, JLET, 60586	3416	30W-21S	B7
Westbrook Elementary School 1333 Greenwood Rd, GNVW, 60025	2810	10W-13N	A5
Westchester Middle School 1620 Norfolk Av, WSTR, 60154	3087	12W-1S	B1
Westchester Primary School 2400 Downing Av, WSTR, 60154	3087	13W-2S	A3
West Chicago Middle School 238 E Hazel St, WCHI, 60185	3022	29W-0N	C5
Westcott Elementary School 409 W 80th St, CHCG, 60620	3214	0W-9S	B2
Westdale Elementary School 99 Diversey Av, NHLK, 60164	2972	14W-3N	D5
West Elementary School 100 Briarwood Dr, CLLK, 60014	2639	38W-25N	A4
West Elementary School 2412 Jethro Av, ZION, 60099	2421	11W-40N	E3
Western Avenue Elementary School 940 Western Av, FSMR, 60422	3507	3W-22S	C2
Western Avenue Elementary School 1500 Western Av, GNVA, 60134	3020	36W-0N	A5
Western Trails Elementary School 860 Idaho St, CLSM, 60188	2968	25W-3N	A5
Westfield Community School 2100 Sleepy Hollow Rd, ALGN, 60102	2747	36W-19N	A3
Westfield Elementary School 2S125 Mayfield Ln, MltT, 60137	3083	21W-2S	E3
Westfield Middle School 149 Fairfield Way, BMDL, 60108	2969	23W-5N	B2
Westfield School 2309 9th St, WPHR, 60096	2363	10W-42N	B6
Westgate Elementary School 500 S Dwyer Av, ANHT, 60005	2806	18W-13N	E6
Westlake Christian Academy 275 S Lake St, GYLK, 60030	2532	21W-32N	E4
West Leyden High School 1000 N Wolf Rd, NHLK, 60164	2972	14W-3N	D5
Westminster Christian School 2700 W Highland Av, ELGN, 60124	2853	37W-12N	D2
Westmont High School 909 Oakwood Dr, WTMT, 60559	3085	17W-3S	C6
Westmont Junior High School 944 Oakwood Dr, WTMT, 60559	3085	17W-3S	C6
Westmoor Elementary School 2500 Cherry Ln, NHBK, 60062	2757	10W-17N	A5
Westmore Elementary School 340 S School St, LMBD, 60148	3026	18W-0N	E5
West Oak Middle School 500 Acorn Ln, FmtT, 60060	2646	19W-26N	C4
West Park Academy 1425 N Tripp Av, CHCG, 60651	3032	5W-1N	B1
West Pullman Elementary School 11941 S Parnell Av, CHCG, 60628	3278	0W-14S	B5
West School 1010 Forestway Dr, GLNC, 60022	2758	7W-17N	B4
West Senior High School 1201 W New York St, AURA, 60506	3137	37W-7S	D6
Westview Elementary School 200 N Addison Rd, WDDL, 60191	2970	18W-5N	E1
Westview Hills Middle School 630 65th St, WTMT, 60527	3145	17W-7S	B6
Westwood Elementary School 14124 W South St Rd, WDSK, 60098	2581	43W-30N	A2
Wharton Elementary School 7555 W 64th St, SMMT, 60501	3148	9W-7S	D5
Wheaton Christian Grammar School 530 E Harrison Av, WHTN, 60187	3024	24W-0S	D6
Wheaton North High School 701 W Thomas Rd, WHTN, 60187	3024	25W-0N	B4
Wheaton Warrenville South High-School 1993 Tiger Trl, WHTN, 60187	3081	27W-2S	D4
Wheeling High School 900 S Elmhurst Rd, WLNG, 60090	2755	15W-17N	A6
Whistler Elementary School 11533 S Ada St, CHCG, 60643	3277	1W-13S	E4
White Career Academy 1136 W 122nd St, CHCG, 60643	3277	1W-14S	E5
White Eagle Elementary School 1585 White Eagle Dr, AURA, 60564	3202	30W-9S	A5
Whitman Elementary School 133 Wille Av, WLNG, 60090	2755	14W-17N	D4
Whitney Young Magnet High School 211 S Laflin St, CHCG, 60607	3033	1W-0S	D5
Whittier Elementary School 1900 W 23rd St, CHCG, 60608	3091	2W-2S	C2
Whittier Elementary School 536 Hill St, DRGV, 60515	3144	19W-5S	D3
Whittier Elementary School 71 E 152nd St, HRVY, 60426	3349	1W-18S	E6
Whittier Elementary School 338 Whitehall Dr, NHLK, 60164	2972	13W-2N	E7
Whittier Elementary School 715 N Harvey Av, OKPK, 60302	3031	7W-1N	B2
Whittier Elementary School 218 W Park Av, WHTN, 60187	3082	24W-1S	C1
Whittier School 13043 Maple Av, BLID, 60406	3349	3W-15S	B1
Wiesbrook Elementary School 2160 Durfee Rd, WHTN, 60187	3081	26W-2S	E3
Wild Rose Elementary School 36w730 Red Haw Ln, SchT, 60174	2963	36W-3N	E5
Wildwood Elementary School 6950 N Hiawatha Av, CHCG, 60646	2919	7W-8N	B1
Wilkins Elementary School 8001 S 82nd Av, JSTC, 60458	3210	10W-9S	B2
Wilkins Junior High School 8001 S 82nd Av, JSTC, 60458	3210	10W-9S	B2
Willard Elementary School 2700 Hurd Av, EVTN, 60201	2812	4W-13N	C7
Willard Elementary School 1250 Ashland Av, RVFT, 60305	3030	9W-1N	C2
Willard Elementary School 370 W Spring St, SEGN, 60177	2908	34W-8N	C3
William B Orenick Intr School 5800 Theodore Dr, JLET, 60586	3496	31W-22S	A1
William Dubois Elementary School 330 E 133rd St, CHCG, 60827	3350	0E-15S	D1
William Fremd High School 1000 S Quentin Rd, PLTN, 60067	2805	22W-14N	C3
William H Brown Elementary School 54 N Hermitage Av, CHCG, 60612	3033	2W-0N	C4
William J Attea Middle School 2500 Chestnut Av, GNVW, 60025	2810	9W-14N	C4
William J Butler Elementary School 1900 S Farrell Rd, LKPT, 60441	3420	20W-20S	A5
Williams Elementary School 2710 S Dearborn St, CHCG, 60616	3092	0W-2S	B3
Williams Preparatory Academy 2710 S Dearborn St, CHCG, 60616	3092	0W-2S	C3
William Thompson Elementary School 515 Thompson Ln, LKVL, 60046	2474	23W-37N	E2
William T Sherman Elementary School 1000 W 52nd St, CHCG, 60609	3151	1W-5S	E2
Willow Bend Elementary School 4700 Barker Av, RGMW, 60008	2806	19W-12N	B7
Willowbrook Elementary School 2500 Happy Hollow Rd, GNVW, 60025	2809	10W-15N	E2
Willowbrook High School 1250 S Ardmore Av, VLPK, 60181	3027	18W-0S	A6
Willow Creek Elementary School 2901 Jackson Dr, WDRG, 60517	3143	22W-6S	D5
Willow School 1804 Willow Rd, HMWD, 60430	3507	2W-22S	D1
Willow Springs Elementary School 8345 Archer Av, WLSP, 60480	3209	12W-9S	C3
Wilmette Junior High School 620 Locust Rd, WLMT, 60091	2812	5W-13N	A6
Wilmington High School 715 S Joliet St, WMTN, 60481	3853	27W-39S	D7
Wilmot Elementary School 795 Wilmot Rd, DRFD, 60015	2703	11W-20N	C7
Wilmot Union High School 11112 308th Av, SlmT, 53192	2356		A1
Wilson Elementary School 1136 24th Av, BLWD, 60104	3029	11W-0S	C6
Wilson Elementary School 2310 S 57th Av, CCRO, 60804	3089	7W-2S	C2
Wilson Elementary School 422 W 16th Pl, CHHT, 60411	3595	2W-25S	D1
Wilson Elementary School 560 Wentworth Av, CTCY, 60409	3352	4E-17S	C6
Windsor Elementary School 1315 E Miner St, ANHT, 60004	2807	17W-14N	C4

FEATURE NAME Address City ZIP Code	MAP#	CGS	GRID
Winfield Central School 0S150 Park St, WNFD, 60190	3023	27W-0S	C6
Winfield Primary School 0S150 Winfield Rd, WNFD, 60190	3023	27W-0S	C6
Winnebago Elementary School 195 Greenway Dr, BMDL, 60108	2969	22W-4N	B3
Winston Campus Elementary-Junior High-School 900 E Palatine Rd, PLTN, 60074	2806	19W-16N	B1
Winston Churchill Elementary School 1520 Jones Rd, SMBG, 60195	2858	24W-12N	D1
Winston Churchill School 1300 190th St, HMWD, 60430	3508	1W-22S	A2
WJ Murphy Elementary School 220 Greenwood Dr, RLKP, 60073	2532	23W-33N	A2
Wolcott School 200 N Wolcott St, TNTN, 60476	3428	0E-21S	D5
Woodbine Elementary School 3003 S 50th Ct, CCRO, 60804	3089	6W-2S	E3
Wood Dale Junior High School 655 N Wood Dale Rd, WDDL, 60191	2915	17W-6N	A5
Woodgate Elementary School 101 Central Av, MTSN, 60443	3505	6W-24S	E5
Woodland Elementary-East 17261 W Gages Lake Rd, WrnT, 60030	2534	17W-33N	C2
Woodland Elementary School 16900 Western Av, HLCT, 60429	3427	3W-20S	C4
Woodland Elementary School 701 3rd Av, JLET, 60433	3499	23W-24S	B5
Woodland Elementary School-West 17371 W Gages Lake Rd, WrnT, 60030	2534	17W-33N	C2
Woodland Intermediate School 1115 N Hunt Club Rd, GRNE, 60031	2477	16W-35N	C6
Woodland Middle School 7000 Washington St, WrnT, 60031	2534	17W-34N	B1
Woodlands Academy Sacred Heart 760 E Westleigh Rd, LKFT, 60045	2650	10W-25N	B5
Woodlawn Community Academy 6657 S Kimbark Av, CHCG, 60637	3153	1E-7S	A5
Woodlawn Middle School 6362 Gilmer Rd, HNWD, 60060	2645	21W-25N	D4
Wood Oak Junior High School 1250 Sanders Rd, NHBK, 60062	2756	12W-17N	B5
Woods Academy 6206 S Racine Av, CHCG, 60636	3151	1W-6S	E4
Woods Creek Elementary School 1100 Alexandra Blvd, CLLK, 60014	2693	37W-23N	B2
Woodson South Elementary School 4414 S Evans Av, CHCG, 60653	3092	0E-4S	E7
Woodstock High School 501 W South St, WDSK, 60098	2581	42W-30N	C1
Wood View Elementary School 197 Winston Dr, BGBK, 60440	3205	22W-10S	C6
Woodview School 340 N Alleghany Rd, GYLK, 60030	2532	21W-33N	D3
Worth Elementary School 11158 S Oak Park Av, WRTH, 60482	3275	8W-13S	A3
Worth Junior High School 11151 S New England Av, WRTH, 60482	3275	8W-13S	A3
Worthwoods School 11000 S Oketo Av, WRTH, 60482	3274	9W-12S	D3
Wredling Middle School 1200 Dunham Rd, SCRL, 60174	2964	34W-4N	E5
Yale Elementary School 7025 S Princeton Av, CHCG, 60621	3152	0W-7S	B6
Yates Elementary School 1839 N Richmond St, CHCG, 60647	2976	3W-2N	E7
Yeshiva Shearis Yisroel 2620 W Touhy Av, CHCG, 60645	2867	3W-9N	A7
Yeshiva Tiferes Tzvi 6122 N California Av, CHCG, 60659	2920	3W-7N	E3
York Center Elementary School 18w701 14th St, YkTp, 60148	3084	18W-1S	E1
York Community High School 355 W St. Charles Rd, EMHT, 60126	3027	16W-1N	D3
Yorkville Grade School 201 W Somonauk St, YKVL, 60560	3333	43W-14S	C1
Yorkville High School 797 Game Farm Rd, YKVL, 60560	3333	43W-14S	B1
Yorkville Intermediate School 103 E Schoolhouse Rd, YKVL, 60560	3333	43W-15S	C3
Yorkville Middle School 702 Game Farm Rd, YKVL, 60560	3333	43W-14S	B1
Young Elementary School 800 Asbury Dr, AURA, 60502	3139	32W-7S	C6
Young Elementary School 1434 N Parkside Av, CHCG, 60651	3031	7W-1N	C1
Zapata Academy 2728 S Kostner Av, CHCG, 60623	3090	5W-2S	B3
Ziebell Elementary School 14900 S Rockwell Av, POSN, 60469	3349	3W-17S	B6
Zion-Benton Twp High School 3901 W 21st St, ZION, 60099	2421	12W-40N	C2
Zion Lutheran School 540 Oak Park Av, BCHR, 60401	3864	1W-36S	B2
Zion Lutheran School 125 S Vine St, HNDL, 60521	3146	15W-5S	A2
Zion Lutheran School 408 Jackson St, MRGO, 60152	2634	49W-26N	B2
Zion Lutheran School 3840 216th St, MTSN, 60443	3594	4W-26S	D1

Shopping Centers

FEATURE NAME Address City ZIP Code	MAP#	CGS	GRID
33rd Street Shopping Center Sheridan Rd, ZION, 60099	2422	9W-39N	B5
Addison Commons Shopping Center W Lake St, ADSN, 60101	2970	19W-4N	D4
Addison Mall W Addison St, CHCG, 60618	2976	3W-4N	E3
Algonquin Commons S Randall Rd, ALGN, 60102	2746	37W-19N	E2
Almar Plaza E 154th St, DLTN, 60419	3351	1E-18S	A6
Alsip Plaza S Pulaski Rd, ALSP, 60803	3276	4W-14S	C5
Annex of Arlington Shopping Center N Arlington Heights Rd, ANHT, 60004	2807	17W-16N	A1
Arlington Heights Town Square S Arlington Heights Rd, ANHT, 60005	2807	17W-14N	B5
Arlington Market Shopping Center E Kensington Rd, ANHT, 60004	2807	17W-14N	B5
Arlington Plaza Shopping Center N Arlington Heights Rd, ANHT, 60004	2754	17W-16N	A7
Arlington Promenade Shopping Center N Arlington Heights Rd, ANHT, 60004	2807	17W-16N	B1
Arlington Towne Square S Arlington Heights Rd, ANHT, 60005	2861	18W-11N	A2
Army Trail Plaza W Army Trail Blvd, ADSN, 60101	2970	19W-3N	D4
Aurora Commons Shopping Center Indian Trail Rd, AURA, 60506	3138	36W-5S	A4
Aurora Marketplace AURA, 60504	3202	30W-8S	C1
Baker Hill Shopping Center Roosevelt Rd, GNEN, 60137	3025	21W-0S	D7
Bannockburn Green Shopping Center Waukegan Rd, BKBN, 60015	2703	11W-23N	D3
Barrington Commons Shopping Center N Hough St, BRTN, 60010	2750	25W-20N	E1
Barrington Ice House Mall Garfield St, BRTN, 60010	2750	25W-20N	E2
Barrington Square Mall W Higgins Rd, HFET, 60169	2857	26W-12N	E1
Bartlett Commons Shopping Center Sutton Rd, BRLT, 60103	2910	30W-7N	C5
Bedford City Square S Cicero Av, BDPK, 60638	3150	6W-8S	A7
Belvidere Mall 2101 Belvidere St, WKGN, 60085	2536	11W-33N	D3
Big Oak Shopping Center W Chicago St, ELGN, 60123	2854	34W-11N	D4
Bloomingdale Court Shopping Center W Army Trail Rd, BMDL, 60108	2968	24W-4N	C4
Bolingbrook Commons S Bolingbrook Dr, BGBK, 60440	3269	22W-12S	B3
Boone Creek Plaza 4222 W Elm St, MHRY, 60050	2528	33W-33N	A3
Brandenberry Park Shopping Center W Camp McDonald Rd, ANHT, 60004	2807	16W-15N	D3
Brementowne Mall 6813 159th St, TYPK, 60477	3425	8W-19S	A1
Brentwood Commons Shopping Center E Grand Av, BNVL, 60106	2972	15W-3N	A4
Brentwood Square E Kensington Rd, MPPT, 60056	2808	13W-14N	D5
Briar Square N Bolingbrook Dr, BGBK, 60440	3269	22W-11S	B2
Bricktown Square Shopping Center N Narragansett Av, CHCG, 60707	2975	8W-3N	A5
Bridgeview Court S Harlem Av, BGVW, 60455	3210	9W-9S	D2
Bridgeview Shopping Center S Harlem Av, CHRG, 60415	3274	8W-12S	E1
Broadview Village Square Shopping-Center S 17th Av, BDVW, 60155	3087	11W-1S	D1
Brookhaven Shopping Center S Cass Av, DRN, 60561	3207	18W-8S	A2
Buffalo Grove Town Center McHenry Rd, BFGV, 60089	2754	16W-20N	D2
Burbank Station Shopping Center S Cicero Av, BRBK, 60459	3212	5W-8S	A2
Burbank Town Center S Cicero Av, BRBK, 60459	3212	6W-8S	A1
Butterfield Plaza Butterfield Rd, MltT, 60137	3083	22W-2S	C4
Butterfield Plaza Shopping Center Butterfield Rd, DRGV, 60515	3084	20W-2S	B4
Butterfield Square 1413 Peterson Rd, LYVL, 60048	2591	17W-30N	A2
Cadwell's Corners Shopping Center Waukegan Rd, DRFD, 60015	2757	10W-20N	A2
Calumet Center 80 River Oaks Dr, CTCY, 60409	3430	3E-18S	A1
Calumet Shopping Center 8001 Calumet Av, MNSR, 46321	3430		E6
Cambridge Plaza 820 S Milwaukee Av, LYVL, 60048	2591	16W-28N	D6
Canterbury Shopping Center Kedzie Av, MKHM, 60428	3427	3W-19S	A1
Carriage Way Shopping Center Rockland Rd, LKBF, 60044	2593	12W-28N	B6
Cary Square Northwest Hwy, CRY, 60013	2641	32W-24N	C7
Cass Harbor Shopping Center S Cass Av, WTMT, 60559	3145	17W-7S	B5
Caton Crossing Towne Square JLET, 60586	3416	29W-21S	C6
Centennial Plaza Lake St, ADSN, 60101	2970	20W-4N	A2
Centerpointe Of Woodridge Shopping-Center Woodward Av, WDRG, 60517	3206	20W-8S	A1
Central Maywood Shopping Center Washington Blvd, MYWD, 60153	3030	10W-0N	A4
Century Plaza W Northwest Hwy, PLTN, 60067	2752	21W-16N	D6
Century Plaza S 8th St, WDND, 60118	2800	34W-15N	D4
Century Shopping Center 2828 N Clark St, CHCG, 60657	2978	0W-3N	A4
Century Tile Plaza Cicero Av, MTSN, 60443	3506	5W-25S	B7
Cermak Plaza Shopping Center Cermak Rd, BRWN, 60402	3088	8W-2S	E2
Charlestowne Mall 3800 E Main St, SCRL, 60174	2965	33W-3N	B6
Chase Plaza N Arlington Heights Rd, BFGV, 60089	2754	17W-20N	A2
Cherry Creek Shopping Center Governors Hwy, HMWD, 60430	3427	3W-21S	B7
Chestnut Court Shopping Center 75th St, DRN, 60516	3206	19W-8S	C2
Chicago Place Mall 700 N Michigan Av, CHCG, 60611	3034	0E-0N	C3
Chicago Premium Outlets N Farnsworth Av, AURA, 60502	3138	33W-4S	E1
Church Street Plaza Church St, EVTN, 60201	2867	2W-11N	A3
Cicero Marketplace Shopping Center S Cicero Av, CCRO, 60804	3090	5W-2S	A3
City Park At Lincolnshire Shopping-Center 215 Parkway Dr, LNSH, 60069	2702	15W-21N	B5
Civic Center Plaza N Waukegan Rd, NLES, 60714	2864	8W-9N	E6
Clock Tower Shopping Center National St, ELGN, 60120	2855	33W-10N	A5
Clock Tower Square Shopping Center Plainfield-Naperville Rd, NpvT, 60564	3203	28W-8S	A2
Cobblers Crossing Shopping Center Summit St, ELGN, 60120	2855	32W-12N	C2
College Square Shopping Center College Rd, LSLE, 60532	3142	24W-7S	D6
Colony Square Shopping Center W Camp McDonald Rd, PTHT, 60070	2808	15W-15N	A3
Commons Of Chicago Ridge Commons Dr, CHRG, 60415	3211	8W-11S	B7
Concorde Green Shopping Center Bloomingdale Rd, GLHT, 60139	3025	23W-1N	A2
Country Aire Commons Shopping-Center N Weber Rd, BGBK, 60490	3268	26W-11S	A1
Country Club Plaza 167th St, CCHL, 60478	3426	5W-20S	C3
Country Corners Shopping Center W Virginia St, CLLK, 60014	2640	35W-25N	A5
Country Court Shopping Center W Dundee Rd, BFGV, 60089	2754	16W-17N	C4
Countryside Center W Veterans Pkwy, YKVL, 60560	3261	42W-14S	C7
Countryside Court Shopping Center S Elmhurst Rd, MPPT, 60056	2861	16W-11N	E3
Countryside Plaza S La Grange Rd, CTSD, 60525	3147	12W-6S	B4
Countryview Plaza Willow Springs Rd, LynT, 60525	3147	13W-6S	A4
Cress Creek Shopping Center 790 Royal St. George Dr, NPVL, 60563	3141	27W-5S	B4
Crossing Shopping Center Frankfort S La Grange Rd, FKFT, 60423	3503	12W-25S	D7
Crossroads Shopping Center Skokie Valley Rd, HDPK, 60035	2757	8W-20N	D2
Crystal Court Northwest Hwy, CLLK, 60014	2640	34W-24N	C6
Crystal Court Shopping Center W Algonquin Rd, MPPT, 60056	2861	17W-10N	C4
Crystal Lake Plaza Northwest Hwy, CLLK, 60014	2640	35W-25N	A6
Crystal Point Mall Crystal Point Dr, CLLK, 60014	2640	34W-25N	B5
Danada Square East Shopping Center Butterfield Rd, WHTN, 60187	3082	24W-2S	D4
Danada Square West Shopping Center Butterfield Rd, WHTN, 60187	3082	24W-2S	C4
Darien Towne Center 75th St, DRN, 60561	3206	19W-8S	D1
Deerbrook Mall S Waukegan Rd, DRFD, 60062	2757	10W-18N	A2
Deerfield Square Deerfield Rd, DRFD, 60015	2703	11W-20N	E7
Deer Grove Centre N Rand Rd, PLTN, 60074	2753	20W-18N	A3
Deer Grove Crossing E Dundee Rd, PLTN, 60074	2753	20W-17N	B4
Deer Park Town Center N Rand Rd, DRPK, 60074	2752	21W-20N	D1
Deerpath Court Shopping Center S Rand Rd, LKZH, 60047	2698	23W-22N	E4
Delco Plaza Of Waukegan 3232 N Lewis Av, WKGN, 60087	2479	11W-37N	D1
Dempster Plaza Dempster St, NLES, 60714	2864	10W-10N	A4
Diamond Lake Shopping Center S Lake St, MDLN, 60060	2646	18W-26N	D2
Douglas Shopping Center Grand Av, WKGN, 60085	2479	12W-33N	C7
Downers Grove Center Lemont Rd, DRGV, 60516	3206	19W-8S	C1
Downers Grove Marketplace Ogden Av, DRGV, 60515	3085	18W-4S	A7
Downtown Oak Park N Harlem Av, OKPK, 60301	3030	8W-0N	D3
Dundee Point Shopping Center W Dundee Rd, BFGV, 60089	2754	16W-18N	C4
Dunhurst Plaza S Elmhurst Rd, WLNG, 60090	2755	15W-17N	A4
Eaglecrest Shopping Center E Chicago Av, NPVL, 60540	3142	25W-6S	B5
East Gate Commons E Main St, SCRL, 60174	2965	33W-3N	B6
Eastgate Shopping Center S Westmore-Meyers Rd, LMBD, 60148	3026	18W-0S	E6
Edens Plaza Lake Av, WLMT, 60091	2811	6W-14N	D5
Elk Crossing Biesterfield Rd, EGVV, 60007	2914	19W-8N	D1
Elk Grove Annex S Arlington Heights Rd, EGVV, 60007	2914	19W-8N	D2
Eurofresh Plaza W Northwest Hwy, PLTN, 60067	2752	21W-16N	D6
Evanston Center W Howard St, CHCG, 60645	2867	3W-9N	A7
Evanston Galleria Church St, EVTN, 60201	2867	2W-11N	B2
Evanston Plaza Shopping Center Dempster St, EVTN, 60202	2866	3W-10N	E4
Fairview Plaza Shopping Center Fairview Av, DRGV, 60516	3206	19W-8S	D1
Farmwood Plaza W Surrey Rd, ADSN, 60101	2970	20W-4N	B2
Finley Square Mall Butterfield Rd, DRGV, 60515	3084	20W-2S	B4
Flossmoor Commons Shopping Center Governors Hwy, FSMR, 60422	3506	4W-23S	E4
Ford City Mall 7601 S Cicero Av, CHCG, 60652	3212	5W-8S	A1
Ford City North S Cicero Av, CHCG, 60652	3212	5W-8S	A1
Fountainbleau Court Shopping Center Kedzie Av, HLCT, 60429	3427	3W-21S	A7
Fountain Square Shopping Center S Meyers Rd, YkTp, 60181	3084	18W-2S	E2

Chicago 7-County Points of Interest Index

FEATURE NAME Address City ZIP Code	MAP#	CGS	GRID
Foxboro Plaza 2400 E Main St, SCRL, 60174	2964	34W-3N	E6
Foxfield Commons E Main St, SCRL, 60174	2965	33W-3N	A5
Fox Lake Commons Plaza Lake St, ADSN, 60101	2970	20W-5N	B2
Fox Lake Crossing Frontage Rd, FXLK, 60041	2473	27W-34N	B7
Fox River Commons Shopping Center Ogden Av, NPVL, 60540	3202	29W-7S	C1
Fox River Plaza Shopping Center Airport Rd, ELGN, 60123	2800	34W-14N	E6
Fox Run Square Shopping Center 75th St, NPVL, 60540	3204	25W-8S	B2
Frankfort Town Center N La Grange Rd, FKFT, 60423	3503	11W-25S	E7
French Village Shopping Center 183rd St, HLCT, 60429	3427	3W-21S	A7
Fresh Farms Plaza E Dundee Rd, WLNG, 60090	2755	14W-18N	C4
Garden Market Shopping Center 47th St, WNSP, 60558	3146	13W-5S	E1
Gary At North Center Gary Av, CLSM, 60188	3024	25W-2N	A1
Geneva Commons Lincoln Hwy, SCRL, 60175	3019	37W-2N	D2
Geneva Crossing Shopping Center Geneva Rd, MltT, 60188	3024	24W-1N	C3
Georgetown Square Shopping Center George St, WDDL, 60191	2914	18W-6N	E7
Glenwood Plaza S Halsted St, GNWD, 60425	3428	0W-22S	B7
Golf Center N Roselle Rd, HFET, 60169	2859	23W-11N	A2
Golf Flaggs Shopping Center N Milwaukee Av, NLES, 60714	2864	10W-11N	A2
Golf Glen Mart Shopping Center W Golf Rd, NLES, 60714	2863	11W-12N	D2
Golf Mill Shopping Center 239 Golf Mill Ctr, NLES, 60714	2864	10W-11N	A2
Golf Milwaukee Plaza W Golf Rd, NLES, 60714	2864	10W-12N	A1
Golf Plaza W Golf Rd, MPPT, 60056	2861	17W-11N	C3
Golf Plaza II W Golf Rd, MPPT, 60056	2861	16W-11N	E3
Governors Plaza Sauk Tr, RNPK, 60471	3594	4W-27S	D3
Grand Avenue Shopping Center Grand Av, WKGN, 60085	2479	12W-35N	C7
Grand Hunt Shopping Center 6525 Grand Av, GRNE, 60031	2477	17W-35N	C5
Grand Mill Plaza Fuller Rd, GRNE, 60031	2478	15W-35N	B6
Grand Plaza Grand Av, FNPK, 60131	2973	12W-3N	A5
Grandview Court Shopping Center Grand Av, WKGN, 60085	2479	13W-35N	A7
Grant Square W Chicago Av, HNDL, 60521	3146	15W-4S	A1
Green Knolls Shopping Center 63rd St, DRGV, 60516	3144	19W-6S	C5
Green Meadow Shopping Center N Addison Rd, ADSN, 60101	2970	18W-4N	E4
Green Oaks Shopping Center S Cicero Av, OKLN, 60453	3212	5W-11S	A6
Green Trails Shopping Center Maple Av, LSLE, 60532	3142	24W-6S	C4
Greentree Plaza Shopping Center Green Tree Pkwy, LYVL, 60048	2647	16W-27N	D1
Grenoble Square Shopping Center 183rd St, HLCT, 60429	3426	4W-21S	E7
Gurnee Mills Mall 6170 W Edwards Ct, GRNE, 60031	2477	16W-36N	C4
Gurnee Plaza Fuller Rd, GRNE, 60031	2478	15W-35N	B6
Halsted Indoor Mall 11444 S Halsted St, CHCG, 60643	3278	1W-13S	A3
Harlem-Foster Shopping Center N Harlem Av, CHCG, 60656	2918	9W-6N	D5
Harlem-Irving Plaza 4200 N Harlem Av, NRDG, 60706	2974	9W-5N	D1
Harvard Shopping Center S Division St, HRVD, 60033	2464	50W-37N	B2
Harwood Commons N Harlem Av, HDHT, 60706	2918	9W-6N	D7
Hawthorne Square Shopping Center S Washington St, NPVL, 60565	3204	26W-9S	A3
Hawthorne Village Commons N Milwaukee Av, VNHL, 60061	2647	16W-25N	E4
Hawthorne Works Shopping Center S Cicero Av, CCRO, 60804	3090	5W-2S	A2
Hawthorn Hills Fashion Square 700 N Milwaukee Av, VNHL, 60061	2647	16W-25N	E4
Hazel Crest Center 175th St, HLCT, 60429	3427	3W-21S	A5
Heritage Plaza 175th St, CCHL, 60478	3426	5W-21S	C5
Heritage Plaza N County Farm Rd, CLSM, 60188	2967	27W-4N	D3
Heritage Square Shopping Center Aurora Av, NPVL, 60540	3140	29W-7S	C6
Hickory Creek Center La Grange Rd, MKNA, 60448	3503	12W-22S	D2
Hickory Creek Marketplace La Grange Rd, FKFT, 60423	3503	11W-24S	E4
Hickory Palos Shopping Center W 95th St, HYHL, 60457	3210	10W-11S	B6
High Point Shopping Center E Roosevelt Rd, LMBD, 60148	3026	19W-1S	D7
Hill Creek Shopping Center S 88th Av, HYHL, 60457	3210	11W-11S	A6
Hillcrest Shopping Center 1701 N Larkin Av, CTHL, 60403	3498	26W-21S	A1
Hoffman Plaza N Roselle Rd, HFET, 60169	2859	23W-11N	A2
Hoffman Village Shopping Center Barrington Rd, HFET, 60194	2857	26W-11N	E3
Holiday Plaza Shopping Center N Harlem Av, HDHT, 60706	2918	8W-5N	D7
Homewood Square 17715 Halsted St, HMWD, 60430	3428	0W-21S	B6
Huntington Plaza Charlemagne Dr W, HFET, 60192	2804	24W-14N	B3
Huntington Shopping Center E Chicago Av, NPVL, 60540	3142	25W-6S	B5
Indian Trails E Indian Tr, AURA, 60504	3138	35W-6S	B4
Indian Trails Shopping Center W 127th St, PSHT, 60463	3275	8W-15S	B7
International Plaza Shopping Center E Golf Rd, ANHT, 60005	2861	17W-12N	B2
Iroquois Shopping Center E Ogden Av, NPVL, 60563	3142	25W-5S	A2
Jewel/Osco Shopping Center 2963 W 95th St, NPVL, 60564	3202	29W-10S	C7
Jewel Plaza State St, LMNT, 60439	3342	19W-15S	D1
Kmart Plaza E Sibley Blvd, DLTN, 60419	3351	1E-17S	A5
Lake Addison Plaza Shopping Center 1038 Lake St, ADSN, 60101	2970	21W-5N	A2
Lake Cook Plaza Lake Cook Rd, DRFD, 60062	2757	10W-18N	A2
Lake Mill Shopping Plaza W Lake St, ADSN, 60101	2970	19W-4N	D3
Lake Plaza Shopping Center Belvidere St, WKGN, 60085	2536	12W-33N	C3
Lake Street Plaza W Lake St, ADSN, 60101	2970	18W-4N	E4
Lake View Plaza W 159th St, ODPK, 60462	3423	12W-18S	D1
Lansing Commons Torrence Av, LNSG, 60438	3429	2E-20S	E4
Lansing Square 176th Pl, LNSG, 60438	3429	3E-20S	E5
Lemont Plaza Weimer Av, LMNT, 60439	3270	19W-14S	D7
Liberty Mill Shopping Center Valley Park Dr, LYVL, 60048	2591	16W-28N	E7
Lincoln Crossing Shopping Center W 14th St, CHHT, 60411	3507	2W-25S	C7
Lincoln Mall 208 Lincoln Mall Dr, MTSN, 60443	3506	5W-25S	B7
Lincolnshire-Riverwoods Schelter Rd, LNSH, 60069	2701	15W-22N	E3
Lincoln Way Center W Lincoln Hwy, NLNX, 60451	3501	18W-24S	A6
Lincolnwood Town Center 3333 W Touhy Av, LNWD, 60712	2920	4W-8N	D1
Linden Plaza Shopping Center 2000 E Grand Av, LNHT, 60046	2476	20W-37N	A1
Lombard Pines Shopping Center E Roosevelt Rd, LMBD, 60148	3026	19W-0S	B7
Long Run Marketplace 13460 S Archer Av, LMNT, 60439	3342	19W-15S	D2
Lynwood Center Torrence Av, LYWD, 60411	3509	3E-23S	E3
Main Place Mall W 143rd St, ODPK, 60462	3345	11W-16S	D4
Main Street Commerce Shopping-Center W Main St, SCRL, 60174	2963	36W-3N	D7
Main Street Commons E Main St, SCRL, 60174	2965	33W-3N	A6
Main Street Plaza N Main St, WHTN, 60187	3024	24W-0N	C4
Mainstreet Square Shopping Center Butterfield Rd, DRGV, 60515	3084	20W-2S	A4
Mallard Creek Shopping Center 722 E Rollins Rd, RLKB, 60073	2475	22W-35N	C5
Market Meadows Shopping Center 75th St, NPVL, 60540	3204	25W-8S	B2
Market Park Place W Boughton Rd, BGBK, 60490	3268	26W-11S	A1
Market Place Golf Rd, RGMW, 60008	2860	18W-12N	E2
Marketplace at Barbers Corners W Boughton Rd, BGBK, 60440	3205	23W-11S	A7
Market Place At Vernon Hills Shopping-Center 413 N Milwaukee Av, VNHL, 60061	2647	15W-25N	E4
Marketplace of Matteson Crawford Av, MTSN, 60443	3506	5W-25S	C7
Market Place of Oak Lawn W 87th St, OKLN, 60453	3212	6W-10S	A4
Market Plaza Shopping Center Roosevelt Rd, GNEN, 60137	3083	22W-1S	C1
Market Square 901 Ridge Rd, MNSR, 46321	3430		E7
Market Square Shopping Center S Bolingbrook Dr, BGBK, 60440	3269	22W-12S	B2
Matteson Plaza Governors Hwy, MTSN, 60443	3506	4W-25S	D7
Matteson Town Center Cicero Av, MTSN, 60443	3594	6W-25S	A1
Maycrest Shopping Center W Jefferson St, JLET, 60436	3497	26W-24S	E5
McHenry Commons 2000 N Richmond Rd, MHRY, 60050	2528	32W-33N	B2
McHenry East & West 2461 N Richmond Rd, MHRY, 60050	2528	32W-34N	B1
McHenry Shopping Center 4310 W Elm St, MHRY, 60050	2528	33W-33N	A3
Meadowbrook Shopping Center Woodward Av, DRGV, 60516	3144	21W-7S	A6
Meadowdale Shopping Center Lake Marian Rd, CPVL, 60110	2748	33W-17N	C6
Melrose Crossing Shopping Center N Mannheim Rd, MLPK, 60160	3029	13W-2N	A1
Melrose Park Venture Shopping-Center 1st Av, MLPK, 60160	3030	10W-1N	A1
Meridian Retail Center AURA, 60504	3140	30W-6S	C6
Meridian Towne Center AURA, 60504	3140	30W-6S	C5
Merrionette Park Shopping Center W 115th St, MTPK, 60803	3276	4W-13S	E4
Mid Oak Plaza Cicero Av, MDLN, 60445	3348	6W-17S	A5
Midway Square S Pulaski Rd, CHCG, 60632	3150	4W-5S	C2
Mt Prospect Plaza Mt Prospect Plz, MPPT, 60056	2808	14W-13N	B7
Mundelein Shopping Center E Crystal St, MDLN, 60060	2646	18W-27N	D1
Nantucket Square E Wise Rd, SMBG, 60193	2913	23W-9N	A1
Naperville Plaza Shopping Center W Gartner Rd, NPVL, 60540	3203	26W-8S	D1
Naper West Plaza Aurora Av, NPVL, 60540	3140	29W-7S	C7
Nelson Plaza W Lincoln Hwy, NLNX, 60451	3501	18W-24S	A6
New York Square E New York St, AURA, 60504	3140	30W-7S	C7
Norridge Commons N Harlem Av, NRDG, 60706	2974	8W-5N	D1
North & 9th Shopping Center W North Av, MLPK, 60160	3029	11W-2N	E1
North Bridge E Ohio St, CHCG, 60611	3034	0E-0N	C3
Northbrook Court 2171 Northbrook Ct, NHBK, 60062	2757	9W-18N	C2
Northgate Plaza W North Av, LMBD, 60148	3026	21W-2N	A1
Northgate Shopping Center 970 N Lake St, AURA, 60506	3138	35W-6S	A5
North Lake Commons Shopping Center S Rand Rd, LKZH, 60047	2698	24W-22N	C4
Northlake Commons Shopping Center S Hillside Av, NHLK, 60164	3028	14W-1N	D1
Northland Mall N Main St, CLSM, 60188	3024	24W-1N	C3
North Park Mall 270 W North Av, VLPK, 60181	3027	18W-2N	A1
North Pier 435 E Illinois St, CHCG, 60611	3034		D3
Northpoint Shopping Center N Arlington Heights Rd, ANHT, 60004	2754	17W-16N	A7
North Quentin Center N Quentin Rd, PLTN, 60067	2752	22W-16N	C6
North Ridge Plaza 6401 Grand Av, GRNE, 60031	2478	15W-35N	A6
North Ridge Plaza N Larkin Av, JLET, 60435	3498	26W-22S	A1
North Riverside Park Mall 7501 W Cermak Rd, NRIV, 60546	3088	9W-2S	D2
North Riverside Plaza W Cermak Rd, NRIV, 60546	3088	9W-2S	D2
Northwest Shopping Center E Dundee Rd, PLTN, 60074	2753	20W-17N	A4
Norwood Square Shopping Center Norwood Square Dr, PKFT, 60466	3595	3W-26S	B2
Oakbrook Court Kingery Hwy, OKBK, 60523	3085	16W-1S	D1
Oakbrook Shopping Center OKBK, 60523	3085	16W-1S	D2
Oak Creek Plaza Townline Rd, MDLN, 60060	2646	18W-25N	E4
Oak Creek Shopping Center 159th St, OKFT, 60452	3425	7W-18S	D1
Oak Forest Commons Shopping Center Central Av, OKFT, 60452	3425	6W-18S	D1
Oak Lawn Shopping Center W 95th St, OKLN, 60453	3212	5W-11S	C6
Oak Mill Mall W Oakton St, NLES, 60714	2864	9W-9N	C6
Ogden Mall E Ogden Av, NPVL, 60563	3142	25W-5S	A2
Old Church Plaza Old Church Rd, SMWD, 60107	2857	27W-11N	D4
Olde Church Centre Old Church Rd, SMWD, 60107	2857	27W-11N	C5
Old Farm Market S Washington St, NPVL, 60565	3203	26W-9S	E5
Old Towne Shopping Center E Lake St, BMDL, 60108	2969	23W-5N	A1
Olympia Corners Lincoln Hwy, OMFD, 60461	3507	2W-25S	C7
Olympia Glen Shopping Center Vollmer Rd, OMFD, 60461	3507	3W-24S	A4
Olympia Plaza Dixie Hwy, CHHT, 60411	3507	1W-24S	E5
Olympia Square Shopping Center Governors Hwy, OMFD, 60461	3506	4W-24S	E4
One Milwaukee Place Shops N Milwaukee Av, WLNG, 60090	2755	14W-18N	D4
Orland Consumer Square Shopping-Center W 159th St, ODPK, 60462	3424	9W-18S	E1
Orland Greens Shopping Center S La Grange Rd, ODPK, 60462	3345	12W-17S	D6
Orland Park Place Shopping Center 1400 Orland Park Pl, ODPK, 60462	3345	11W-18S	D7
Orland Park Shopping Plaza S La Grange Rd, ODPK, 60462	3345	12W-16S	D4
Orland Plaza S 94th Av, ODPK, 60462	3423	11W-18S	E1
Orland Square Shopping Center S 94th Av, ODPK, 60462	3345	11W-17S	E6
Orland Towne Center W 159th St, ODHL, 60487	3423	11W-19S	E1
Oswego Commons Douglas Rd, OSWG, 60543	3264	35W-11S	B1
Otter Creek Shopping Center S Randall Rd, ELGN, 60124	2853	36W-10N	D5
Pacesetter Park Plaza E 162nd St, SHLD, 60473	3429	1E-18S	A1
Palatine Centre E Northwest Hwy, PLTN, 60067	2753	20W-16N	A7
Palatine Mall N Hicks Rd, PLTN, 60074	2753	20W-16N	A6
Palatine Plaza E Northwest Hwy, PLTN, 60067	2752	20W-16N	E7
Palatine Windsor Shopping Center N Windsor Dr, ANHT, 60004	2807	17W-15N	C1
Park Center Harlem Av, TYPK, 60477	3424	9W-19S	E1
Park Place Harlem Av, TYPK, 60477	3424	9W-19S	E2
Park Place Plaza Ridge Rd, HMWD, 60430	3428	1W-21S	B6

Chicago 7-County Points of Interest Index

FEATURE NAME Address City ZIP Code	MAP#	CGS	GRID
Park Place Shopping Center E Dundee Rd, PLTN, 60074	2753	19W-17N	C4
Park St. Claire Plaza N Meacham Rd, SMBG, 60173	2859	21W-11N	D4
Parkside Plaza 80th Av, TYPK, 60477	3424	9W-20S	C3
Pebblewood Plaza Shopping Center NPVL, 60563	3140	29W-5S	C2
Pembrook Corners Shopping Center Grand Av, GRNE, 60031	2478	15W-35N	A6
Pheasant Hill Plaza Lily Cache Ln, BGBK, 60440	3269	23W-12S	B2
Pickwick Place N Park Blvd, GNEN, 60137	3025	22W-0S	C7
Plaza Del Lago Sheridan Rd, WLMT, 60091	2812	3W-14N	E4
Plaza Del Prado Pfingsten Rd, GNVW, 60025	2809	10W-15N	E2
Plaza Westlake Shopping Center E Army Trail Rd, GLHT, 60139	2969	23W-4N	A4
Pointe Plaza W Touhy Av, NLES, 60714	2865	7W-9N	C7
Poplar Creek Plaza W Golf Rd, SMBG, 60194	2858	25W-11N	A3
Prairie Street Plaza S Randall Rd, SCRL, 60174	3019	36W-2N	D1
Prairie Town Center S Barrington Rd, SMBG, 60194	2857	26W-10N	E5
Prairie View Plaza Waukegan Rd, MNGV, 60053	2864	8W-10N	E4
Prime Outlets At Pleasant Prairie 11211 120th Av, PTPR, 53158	2360		E1
Prime Outlets-Huntley 11800 Factory Shops Blvd, HTLY, 60142	2744	41W-17N	E6
Prospect Crossing Shopping Center E Rand Rd, ANHT, 60004	2807	17W-15N	C2
Prospect Heights Plaza S Elmhurst Rd, PTHT, 60070	2808	15W-14N	A3
Quentin Corners N Quentin Rd, PLTN, 60067	2752	21W-17N	C6
Randall Square Shopping Center Fargo Blvd, GNVA, 60134	3019	37W-0N	D5
Randhurst Commons W Rand Rd, MPPT, 60056	2807	15W-14N	E5
Randhurst Shopping Center 999 N Elmhurst Rd, MPPT, 60056	2808	15W-14N	A5
Ravinia Plaza W 153rd St, ODPK, 60462	3345	12W-18S	D7
Red Top Plaza Shopping Center 1300 S Milwaukee Av, LYVL, 60048	2647	16W-27N	E1
Regency Plaza W Euclid Av, PLTN, 60067	2805	21W-14N	C4
Rice Lake Square Butterfield Rd, WHTN, 60187	3082	24W-2S	D4
Ridge Plaza Shopping Center W Dundee Rd, BFGV, 60089	2754	18W-18N	A4
Riverbrook Shopping Center Raymond Dr, NPVL, 60563	3140	29W-6S	E4
Rivercrest Center Cicero Av, CTWD, 60445	3348	6W-15S	A1
Rivercrest Shopping Center Cicero Av, CTWD, 60445	3348	5W-16S	A2
River Oaks Shopping Center 1201 River Oaks Dr, CTCY, 60409	3429	3E-19S	E1
River Oaks West Shopping Center 1451 159th St, CTCY, 60409	3429	2E-19S	D1
River Place Shop Center Torrence Av, LNSG, 60438	3429	3E-19S	E3
River Pointe Of Algonquin S Randall Rd, ALGN, 60102	2693	35W-21N	E6
Riverside Plaza S Milwaukee Av, WLNG, 60090	2755	13W-18N	D4
River Square E Chicago Av, NPVL, 60540	3141	26W-6S	D5
Rivertree Court At Hawthorn 701 N Milwaukee Av, VNHL, 60061	2647	15W-25N	E4
River Valley Square E Main St, EDND, 60118	2801	33W-15N	C3
Riverwoods Plaza W Boughton Rd, BGBK, 60440	3204	23W-11S	E7
Rolling Meadows Shopping Center Kirchoff Rd, RGMW, 60008	2806	19W-13N	B5
Rollins Crossing Shopping Center 400 E Rollins Rd, RLKB, 60073	2475	22W-35N	B5
Roosevelt Plaza S Finley Rd, LMBD, 60148	3084	20W-1S	B1
Round Lake Commons Shopping Center 965 E Rollins Rd, RLKB, 60046	2475	21W-35N	C6
St. Charles Mercantile W Main St, SCRL, 60175	2963	37W-3N	D7
St. Charles Place Mall S Randall Rd, SCRL, 60175	3019	37W-2N	D1
St. James Crossing E Ogden Av, WTMT, 60559	3085	16W-4S	D7
Salem Square S Brainard Av, CTSD, 60525	3147	12W-6S	B3
Scharrington Square S Barrington Rd, SMBG, 60193	2857	26W-10N	E6
Schaumburg Corners Shopping Center E Golf Rd, SMBG, 60173	2859	23W-12N	A2
Schaumburg Town Center W Wise Rd, SMBG, 60193	2913	23W-9N	A1
Settlers Landing Mall Douglas Rd, OSWG, 60543	3200	35W-10S	A6
Shiloh Village Shopping Center Sheridan Rd, ZION, 60099	2422	9W-40N	B4
Shoppes At Mill Creek W 131st St, PSPK, 60464	3345	12W-15S	D1
Shopping Center Rohlwing Rd, ADSN, 60143	2970	20W-5N	A2
Shopping Center Townes Cir, AURA, 60502	3139	32W-6S	D4
Shopping Center Lakewood Rd, LIHL, 60156	2692	38W-22N	E3
Shopping Center N Front St, MHRY, 60050	2528	33W-32N	A5
Shops At Coopers Grove Pulaski Rd, CCHL, 60478	3426	5W-21S	C7
Shops At Schaumburg Court W Schaumburg Rd, SMBG, 60194	2857	27W-10N	D5
Shorewood Marketplace W Black Rd, SRWD, 60404	3496	29W-22S	D3

FEATURE NAME Address City ZIP Code	MAP#	CGS	GRID
Shorewood Plaza W Jefferson St, SRWD, 60404	3496	30W-23S	C5
Sibley Crossing Shopping Center E Sibley Blvd, DLTN, 60419	3351	1E-17S	B5
Southfield Plaza S Harlem Av, BGVW, 60455	3210	8W-10S	E4
South Holland Plaza E 163rd St, SHLD, 60473	3428	0E-19S	D2
Southpoint Shopping Center E Palatine Rd, ANHT, 60004	2807	17W-15N	A1
South Point Shopping Center E Camp McDonald Rd, WLNG, 60090	2808	14W-15N	D3
Southwest Square Dixie Hwy, HRVY, 60426	3349	2W-17S	C6
Spinney Run Shopping Center S Riverside Dr, GRNE, 60031	2534	16W-33N	E3
Springbrook Shopping Center E Lake St, BMDL, 60108	2969	23W-5N	B1
Spring Hill Fashion Corner N 8th St, WDND, 60118	2800	34W-16N	E2
Spring Hill Mall 801 Springhill Ring Rd, WDND, 60118	2800	34W-16N	D2
State Road Plaza Shopping Center W 87th St, OKLN, 60453	3211	7W-10S	B4
Stearns Crossing W Stearns Rd, BRLT, 60103	2910	30W-7N	C6
Stonebrook Commons Plaza 6655 Grand Av, GRNE, 60031	2477	17W-35N	B5
Stonebrook Plaza W 115th St, MTPK, 60803	3276	4W-13S	E4
Stonehill Center 980 Northwest Hwy, FRGV, 60021	2696	29W-22N	C3
Stratford Plaza Shopping Center Schick Rd, BMDL, 60108	2968	25W-5N	A2
Stratford Square Mall 152 Stratford Dr, BMDL, 60108	2968	25W-5N	B2
Streamwood Market Square E Irving Park Rd, SMWD, 60107	2911	27W-9N	C1
Stuarts Crossing Shopping Center N Kirk Rd, SCRL, 60174	2965	33W-3N	A6
Summit Shopping Center S Cicero Av, BRBK, 60459	3212	6W-9S	A2
Summit Square Shopping Center Summit St, ELGN, 60120	2855	32W-12N	C2
Sunset Corners Shopping Center S Waukegan Rd, LKFT, 60045	2649	12W-25N	B6
Sunset Plaza 422 S Governors Hwy, PTON, 60468	3861	8W-37S	A4
Surrey Ridge Shopping Center W Algonquin Rd, ANHT, 60005	2860	18W-12N	E2
The Brickyard 6465 W Diversey Av, CHCG, 60707	2975	8W-3N	A5
The Commons Of Crystal Lake Northwest Hwy, CLLK, 60014	2640	35W-25N	A5
The Commons Shopping Center W 159th St, ODPK, 60462	3424	9W-18S	E1
The Depot Division St, WDDL, 60191	2915	17W-5N	B7
The Foundry Of Barrington Shopping-Center W Northwest Hwy, BRTN, 60010	2697	26W-21N	C7
The Franklin Park Mall Mannheim Rd, FNPK, 60131	2973	12W-3N	A4
The Glen Town Center Patriot Blvd, GNVW, 60025	2810	9W-14N	B4
The Grove S Meacham Rd, RGMW, 60067	2805	21W-14N	E5
The Grove Shopping Center McHenry Rd, BFGV, 60089	2754	16W-20N	C2
The Grove Shopping Center Lemont Rd, DRGV, 60516	3206	20W-8S	B1
The Hall Plaza W Diversey Av, CHCG, 60641	2976	5W-3N	A4
The Landings Torrence Av, LNSG, 60438	3429	3E-19S	E2
The Market Place Shoreline Rd, LKBN, 60010	2643	26W-25N	E5
The Market Place At Six Corners-Shopping Ctr N Milwaukee Av, CHCG, 60641	2975	6W-5N	D1
The Oaks Of Des Plaines Shopping-Center Mannheim Rd, DSPN, 60018	2862	13W-10N	E5
The Plaza 9730 S Western Av, ENGN, 60805	3213	3W-11S	B6
The Quarry Joliet Rd, HGKN, 60525	3147	12W-6S	C5
The Shoppes At Windmill Place N Randall Rd, BTVA, 60510	3077	37W-1S	D1
The Shops At North Bridge E Illinois St, CHCG, 60611	3034	0E-0N	C3
The Shops At Oak Brook Midwest Rd, OKBK, 60523	3085	17W-2S	B2
The Shops of Kildeer N Rand Rd, KLDR, 60047	2752	21W-20N	D1
The Streets of Woodfield 601 N Martingale Rd, SMBG, 60173	2860	21W-11N	A4
The Village Centre E 162nd St, SHLD, 60473	3428	0E-18S	E1
The Village Market N La Grange Rd, LGPK, 60525	3087	12W-3S	B6
The Vineyards Shopping Center S La Grange Rd, FKFT, 60423	3503	11W-24S	E6
Thornwood Mall UYPK, 60466	3684	3W-29S	B1
Tiffany Square Shopping Center W College Dr, PSHT, 60463	3274	9W-13S	E5
Tin Cup Pass E Main St, SCRL, 60174	2964	34W-3N	D6
Tinley Downs Shopping Center 171st St, TYPK, 60477	3424	9W-20S	D4
Tinley Park Commons Shopping Center 171st St, TYPK, 60477	3425	8W-20S	A4
Tinley Park Plaza Harlem Av, TYPK, 60477	3424	9W-19S	E1
Tower Crossing Shopping Center N Naper Blvd, NPVL, 60563	3142	25W-5S	B2
Town & Country Mall 301 E Palatine Rd, ANHT, 60004	2807	17W-15N	B1
Town & Country Plaza S McLean Blvd, ELGN, 60123	2854	35W-10N	B5

FEATURE NAME Address City ZIP Code	MAP#	CGS	GRID
Town Center Shopping Mall Garden Ct, RVFT, 60305	3030	9W-0N	D3
Towne Centre Plaza Rollins Rd, FXLK, 60020	2473	27W-36N	A3
Townes Crossing OSWG, 60543	3200	35W-10S	A6
Townline Commons Shopping Center 555 E Townline Rd, VNHL, 60061	2647	16W-25N	D4
Townline Square S Lake St, MDLN, 60060	2646	18W-26N	E4
Town Square Schaumburg S Roselle Rd, SMBG, 60193	2859	23W-10N	A5
Town Square Wheaton S Naperville Rd, WHTN, 60187	3082	24W-2S	D4
Tri City Shopping Center Randall Rd, SCRL, 60174	3019	36W-2N	D2
Two Rivers Plaza W Boughton Rd, BGBK, 60440	3268	25W-11S	B1
Tyler Creek Plaza Shopping Center N McLean Blvd, ELGN, 60123	2854	35W-13N	A1
United Plaza W Algonquin Rd, MPPT, 60056	2861	16W-10N	C4
University Commons Villanova Dr, NPVL, 60565	3204	24W-9S	C3
University Park Town Center University Pkwy, UYPK, 60466	3684	3W-29S	A1
Valley Creek Shopping Center N Randall Rd, ELGN, 60123	2853	36W-12N	E1
Valley Plaza Shopping Center W 111th St, PSHL, 60465	3274	10W-13S	C3
Valley Shopping Center W Main St, SCRL, 60174	2963	36W-2N	E7
Vernon Plaza W Townline Rd, VNHL, 60061	2647	17W-25N	C4
Villa DuPage Shopping Center N Westmore Av, VLPK, 60181	3026	19W-1N	D1
Village Commons Shopping Center 3567 Grand Av, GRNE, 60031	2479	13W-34N	A7
Village Crossing Shopping Center Touhy Av, SKOK, 60077	2919	6W-8N	D1
Village Green Old Half Day Rd, LNSH, 60069	2702	15W-23N	B2
Village Green Shopping Center Long Grove Dr, AURA, 60504	3201	31W-8S	D3
Village Green Shopping Center Old Half Day Rd, LNSH, 60069	2702	15W-23N	A2
Village Green Shopping Center N Greenwood Av, PKRG, 60068	2864	10W-9N	A6
Village Oasis W Northwest Hwy, PLTN, 60067	2752	21W-16N	D6
Village Square Of Northbrook 243 Skokie Blvd, NHBK, 60062	2757	8W-18N	E2
Village Square Shopping Center S Rand Rd, LKZH, 60047	2698	24W-22N	C4
Villa Oaks Shopping Center W Roosevelt Rd, VLPK, 60181	3027	18W-0S	A7
Wal-Mart S Bolingbrook Dr, BGBK, 60440	3269	22W-12S	B2
Washington Commons N Washington St, MNGV, 60053	2864	9W-11N	B2
Waukegan Shopping Plaza 1325 N Lewis Av, WKGN, 60085	2479	11W-35N	D6
Weber Plaza Rodeo Dr, BGBK, 60490	3268	26W-13S	A6
Wedgewood Corners W Caton Farm Rd, JLET, 60586	3416	30W-21S	C6
Wentworth Woods Shopping Center River Oaks Dr, CTCY, 60409	3430	4E-19S	B1
West Aurora Plaza Shopping Center W Galena Blvd, AURA, 60506	3137	38W-7S	B6
Westbrook Commons Shopping Center 31st St, WSTR, 60154	3086	13W-2S	E4
Westfield Chicago Ridge 6501 W 95th St, CHRG, 60415	3211	8W-11S	A6
Westfield Fox Valley 4199 Fox Valley Center Dr, AURA, 60504	3202	30W-7S	B1
Westfield Hawthorn 122 Ring Rd, VNHL, 60061	2647	16W-26N	E3
Westfield Louis Joliet Mall 3340 Mall Loop Dr, JLET, 60431	3417	28W-20S	B4
Westfield Old Orchard Skokie Blvd, SKOK, 60077	2865	6W-12N	E1
West Gate Shopping Center Peck Rd, SCRL, 60175	2963	37W-3N	B6
Westmont Village Shopping Center W 63rd St, WTMT, 60559	3145	18W-6S	A5
West Point Plaza 101 N Wolf Rd, HLSD, 60162	3028	13W-0S	D6
Westridge Court Shopping Center 2603 Aurora Av, NPVL, 60540	3140	29W-7S	C6
Westriver Crossing Essington Rd, JLET, 60435	3417	27W-21S	B6
Westview Center S Barrington Rd, SMWD, 60107	2857	27W-9N	D7
Westview North Plaza S Cass Av, WTMT, 60559	3145	18W-6S	A5
Westview South Plaza S Cass Av, WTMT, 60559	3145	18W-6S	B5
Wheatland Marketplace 95th St, NPVL, 60564	3202	30W-10S	B7
Willow Plaza Willow Springs Rd, CTSD, 60525	3147	13W-7S	A6
Wind Point Center 381 N Randall Rd, BTVA, 60510	3077	36W-0S	D1
Wingren Plaza Shopping Center Kingery Hwy, WLBK, 60527	3207	16W-8S	E1
Wood Dale Center W Irving Park Rd, WDDL, 60191	2914	18W-6N	E7
Woodfield Mall 5 Middle Dr, SMBG, 60173	2859	21W-11N	E2
Woodfield Village Green Shopping-Center N Meacham Rd, SMBG, 60173	2859	21W-12N	E1
Woodgrove Festival Shopping Center Lemont Rd, WDRG, 60517	3206	20W-8S	B2
Woodland Commons Shopping Center N Buffalo Grove Rd, BFGV, 60089	2701	17W-23N	C3
Woodland Heights Shopping Center E Irving Park Rd, SMWD, 60107	2857	28W-9N	A7
Yards Plaza S Seeley Av, CHCG, 60643	3213	2W-11S	C6

Chicago 7-County Points of Interest Index

FEATURE NAME / Address City ZIP Code	MAP#	CGS	GRID
Yorkhouse Commons Shopping Center 3050 N Lewis Av, WKGN, 60087	2479	11W-37N	D2
Yorkshire Plaza Shopping Center 4412 E New York St, AURA, 60504	3140	30W-7S	B7
Yorktown Shopping Center LMBD, 60148	3084	19W-2S	D3

Subdivisions & Neighborhoods

FEATURE NAME / Address City ZIP Code	MAP#	CGS	GRID
Altgeld Gardens, CHCG	3350	0E-15S	E1
Andersonville, CHCG	2921	1W-6N	D5
Argo, BGVW	3210	9W-8S	C2
Ashburn, BRBK	3211	7W-9S	D2
Ashland Avenue, CHCG	3213	1W-8S	D1
Auburn Park, CHCG	3213	1W-9S	E2
Auburn Woods, PLTN	2752	21W-17N	D6
Austin, CHCG	3031	6W-0S	E5
Austin View, ALSP	3275	7W-14S	C6
Barrington Center, BNHL	2802	28W-16N	D1
Beau Bien, DRGV	3143	21W-5S	E3
Belmont, DRGV	3143	21W-5S	E3
Bernice, LNSG	3430	3E-20S	A4
Bishop Quarter Lane, OKPK	3031	8W-0N	A4
Blackhawk, ELGN	2855	32W-12N	C1
Blodgett, HDPK	2704	9W-22N	B3
Burnside, CHCG	3215	1E-11S	A6
Cantera Village, WNVL	3081	28W-4S	B7
Carol Stream Main, CLSM	2968	24W-2N	C7
Central Street, EVTN	2812	3W-13N	E7
Chatham Manor, BFGV	2754	17W-18N	B4
Chatham Square, PNFD	3337	32W-14S	B1
Cherrywood, BGBK	3269	23W-11S	A1
Chicago Lawn, CHCG	3150	3W-6S	E4
Churchville, AddT	2971	16W-3N	D4
Cinnamon Creek, BGBK	3268	24W-12S	C2
Clearing, BDPK	3149	6W-7S	D5
College Green, ELGN	2853	36W-9N	E7
Countryside, YKVL	3261	43W-13S	C6
Covington Manor, WhlT	2754	16W-17N	C4
Cragin, CHCG	2975	6W-2N	E7
Crawford Countryside, OMFD	3506	5W-24S	C6
Crystal Gardens, GfnT	2638	38W-25N	E5
Crystal Manor, AlqT	2640	33W-24N	D6
Crystal Vista, CLLK	2639	37W-25N	A4
Division Street, CHCG	3031	6W-1N	E2
Downey, NCHI	2593	11W-30N	D2
Dunmoor Estates, PNFD	3337	32W-15S	C3
Dunning, CHCG	2974	8W-4N	E2
East Joliet, JLET	3499	22W-23S	C3
East Side, CHCG	3216	4E-11S	B7
Edgebrook, CHCG	2919	6W-8N	D2
Edison Square, WKGN	2536	11W-34N	D1
Eileen, CLCY	3941	34W-39S	A1
Elsdon, CHCG	3150	4W-5S	C3
Englewood, CHCG	3152	0W-7S	A5
Evanston North, EVTN	2812	3W-12N	D7
Evanston South, EVTN	2867	2W-10N	B4
Expo Park, HFET	2802	29W-13N	D6
Flossmoor Highlands, FSMR	3506	4W-22S	D2
Forest Park, JLET	3499	22W-22S	C2
Fort Dearborn, CHCG	3034	0W-1N	B2
Fox Chase, SCRL	2964	34W-4N	E4
Fox Point, BRTN	2751	24W-18N	B2
Fox Valley East, AURA	3140	30W-7S	B7
Garfield Park, CHCG	3032	4W-0S	C5
Glengarry, GNVA	3020	34W-1N	D4
Glenview Woodlands, GNVW	2810	10W-13N	A6
Golden Acres, GNVW	2810	10W-13N	A6
Grand Crossing, CHCG	3214	1E-8S	E1
Grande Park, PNFD	3337	32W-15S	C2
Hawthorne, CHCG	3090	5W-1S	B2
Haymarket, CHCG	3034	0W-0N	A4
Hazelgreen, ALSP	3275	6W-13S	E4
Heartland Meadows, ElgT	2908	35W-9N	B1
Heatherlea, PLTN	2752	20W-17N	E5
Hegewisch, CHCG	3352	3E-15S	A1
Highland Glen, ELGN	2853	37W-12N	C1
Holbrook, CHHT	3508	1W-23S	A3
Hubbard Woods, WNKA	2759	5W-16N	A7
Hyde Park, CHCG	3092	0E-4S	E7
Indian Hill, CHHT	3596	1W-25S	A1
Inverness on the Ponds, IVNS	2805	22W-16N	A1
Irving Park, CHCG	2975	6W-4N	E2
Jackson Park, CHCG	3152	0E-6S	D4
Jefferson Park, CHCG	2919	6W-6N	C6
Kedzie Grace, CHCG	2976	4W-4N	D2
Kenilwicke, PLTN	2752	21W-17N	D5
Kensington, CHCG	3278	0E-14S	E5
Kimberly Heights, OKFT	3347	8W-18S	B7
King's Bridge Estates, PNFD	3337	32W-14S	D1
Kings Island, FXLK	2473	28W-35N	A5
Lake Briarwood, MPPT	2861	17W-11N	B4
Lakeland Park, MHRY	2527	34W-34N	C1
Lakeview, CHCG	2977	1W-4N	D2
Lidice, CTHL	3418	24W-21S	E7
Lincoln Park, CHCG	2978	0W-3N	A5
Logan Square, CHCG	2976	3W-3N	E5
Loop, CHCG	3034	0W-0S	B5
Main Street, EVTN	2867	2W-10N	B4
Maple Hill, WNVL	3080	30W-1S	C2
McHenry Shores, MHRY	2528	32W-31N	C7
Merchandise Mart, CHCG	3034	0W-0N	B3
Middlebury, BNHL	2749	30W-18N	A3
Midwest, CHCG	3033	2W-0S	B5
Miller Woods, CHHT	3596	0W-26S	C2
Moraine Valley Facility, BGVW	3210	9W-11S	D7
Morgan Park, CHCG	3277	2W-13S	C3
Mount Greenwood, CHCG	3276	4W-13S	E3
Nature's Crossing, PNFD	3337	31W-15S	D3
Nineteenth Avenue, MLPK	3029	11W-0N	D3
North Center, CHCG	2977	2W-4N	A2
Northfield Woods, GNVW	2809	12W-14N	B4
North Shore, CLLK	2639	37W-25N	B4
Northtown, CHCG	2920	4W-7N	C4
Norwood Park, CHCG	2918	8W-7N	E3
Nottingham Park, BGVW	3210	9W-8S	D1
Oak Glen, LNSG	3429	3E-21S	E6
Oak Park South, OKPK	3030	8W-0S	E6
Ogden Park, CHCG	3151	1W-7S	D5
Olympia Gardens, FSMR	3507	3W-23S	B4
Ontario Street, CHCG	3034	0E-0N	C3
Pam Anne Estates, GNVW	2809	10W-13N	E6
Peterson Avenue, CHCG	2920	5W-7N	A4
Pilsen, CHCG	3091	2W-1S	C1
Pleasant Dale, BRRG	3208	15W-8S	B1
Pottawatami Highlands, TYPK	3424	10W-21S	C6
Prairie Ponds, PNFD	3337	32W-15S	D3
Prospect Meadows, MPPT	2807	15W-14N	E4
Pullman, CHCG	3278	0E-12S	E2
Randall Ridge, ELGN	2853	37W-11N	C4
Ravenswood, CHCG	2921	2W-6N	B6
Ravinia, HDPK	2705	7W-20N	A7
Raynor Park, JLET	3498	24W-22S	D1
Ridgewood, BRRG	3146	14W-6S	C3
Ridgewood, JltT	3499	21W-23S	E3
Ridgewood West, OKFT	3347	8W-18S	A6
Robertsdale, HMND	3280		E4
Roby, HMND	3280		D4
Rockdale Junction, CTHL	3418	25W-21S	C6
Rogers Park, CHCG	2921	2W-7N	C3
Roseland, CHCG	3278	0E-12S	C3
Sauganash, CHCG	2920	5W-7N	A4
Shenandoah, PNFD	3337	32W-15S	C2
Shires of Inverness, IVNS	2805	22W-14N	A4
South Addison, VLPK	3026	18W-1N	E1
South Calumet Avenue, HMND	3430		E3
South Chicago, CHCG	3216	4E-10S	B5
South Deering, CHCG	3279	3E-12S	E3
South Lockport, LKPT	3419	22W-20S	D5
South Shore, CHCG	3153	2E-8S	C7
State Line, WPHR	2363	9W-43N	C4
Stewart Ridge, PNFD	3265	32W-14S	C7
Stock Yards, CHCG	3092	0W-4S	A6
Stone Avenue, LGNG	3087	12W-4S	B7
Sugar Brook, BGBK	3268	24W-12S	E2
Sunnyside, JNBG	2472	30W-36N	A4
Tanbark, TYPK	3424	10W-19S	B3
Techny, NfdT	2757	9W-16N	D7
Thornton Junction, SHLD	3428	0E-19S	E3
Turtle Farm, PNFD	3337	31W-15S	D2
Twenty-Second Street, CHCG	3092	0E-1S	C1
Uptown, CHCG	2921	1W-6N	D6
Valley Creek, ELGN	2853	36W-12N	E3
Village Green, NPVL	3081	27W-4S	C7
Villa West, PSPK	3274	11W-14S	A7
Walker's Grove, PNFD	3337	31W-15S	E3
Warrenhurst, WnfT	3080	30W-3S	A5
Waycinden Park, DSPN	2862	15W-10N	A4
Wentworth Avenue, CTCY	3352	4E-18S	C6
West Lake Forest, LKFT	2649	12W-24N	C7
West Pullman, CHCG	3278	0W-13S	A4
Wheatland Plains, WldT	3337	32W-15S	B1
Wheaton South, WHTN	3082	24W-2S	C4
Wicker Park, CHCG	3033	2W-1N	C2
Wilson Avenue, CHCG	2921	2W-5N	C7
Winston Village, BGBK	3205	22W-10S	B6
Winston Woods, BGBK	3205	23W-10S	B6
Woodbridge, ELGN	2853	37W-10N	D7
Woodland Hills, BTVA	3078	34W-1S	E2

Transportation

FEATURE NAME / Address City ZIP Code	MAP#	CGS	GRID
Amtrak-Chicago Station, CHCG	3034	0W-1S	B7
Amtrak-Glenview Station, GNVW	2810	8W-13N	D6
Amtrak-Hammond-Whiting Station, HMND	3280		E3
Amtrak-Joliet Union Station, JLET	3499	23W-23S	A5
Amtrak-La Grange Station, LGNG	3087	12W-4S	C6
Chicago Union Station, CHCG	3034	0W-0S	A5
CTA-Adams Station, CHCG	3034	0E-0S	C5
CTA-Armitage Station, CHCG	2977	1W-2N	E6
CTA-Ashland Branch-Ashland Station, - CHCG	3151	1W-7S	D5
CTA-Ashland Branch-Halsted Station, - CHCG	3152	0W-7S	A5
CTA-Belmont Station, CHCG	2977	1W-3N	D4
CTA-Blue Line-Addison Station, CHCG	2976	4W-4N	C3
CTA-Blue Line-Belmont Station, CHCG	2976	4W-3N	D4
CTA-Blue Line-California Station, - CHCG	2976	3W-2N	E6
CTA-Blue Line-Chicago Station, CHCG	3033	1W-0N	E3
CTA-Blue Line-Clark Station, CHCG	3034	0W-0N	B4
CTA-Blue Line-Clinton Station, CHCG	3034	0W-0S	A5
CTA-Blue Line-Cumberland, CHCG	2918	10W-7N	A5
CTA-Blue Line-Damen Station, CHCG	3033	2W-1N	B1
CTA-Blue Line-Division Station, CHCG	3033	1W-1N	D1
CTA-Blue Line-Grand Station, CHCG	3034	0W-0N	A3
CTA-Blue Line-Harlem Station, CHCG	2918	8W-6N	D5
CTA-Blue Line-Irving Park Station, - CHCG	2976	5W-5N	B1
CTA-Blue Line-Jackson Station, CHCG	3034	0W-0S	B5
CTA-Blue Line-Jefferson Park Station, - CHCG	2919	6W-6N	D6
CTA-Blue Line-Kedzie/Holman Station, - CHCG	3032	4W-0S	D5
CTA-Blue Line-Logan Square, CHCG	2976	3W-3N	E5
CTA-Blue Line-Monroe Station, CHCG	3034	0W-0S	B4
CTA-Blue Line-Montrose Station, CHCG	2920	5W-5N	A7
CTA-Blue Line-O'Hare Station, CHCG	2916	13W-6N	D5
CTA-Blue Line-Racine Station, CHCG	3033	1W-0S	E5
CTA-Blue Line-Rosemont Station, RSMT	2917	11W-7N	D4
CTA-Blue Line-UIC Halsted Station, - CHCG	3033	1W-0S	E5
CTA-Blue Line-Washington Station, - CHCG	3034	0W-0N	B4
CTA-Blue Line-Western Station, CHCG	2977	3W-2N	A7
CTA-Brown Line-Addison Station, CHCG	2977	2W-4N	C2
CTA-Brown Line-Chicago Station, CHCG	3034	0W-1N	B2
CTA-Brown Line-Damen Station, CHCG	2921	2W-5N	B7
CTA-Brown Line-Francisco Station, - CHCG	2920	3W-5N	E7
CTA-Brown Line-Irving Park Station, - CHCG	2977	2W-5N	B1
CTA-Brown Line-Kedzie Station, CHCG	2920	4W-5N	D7
CTA-Brown Line-Kimball Station, CHCG	2920	4W-5N	D7
CTA-Brown Line-Montrose Station, - CHCG	2921	2W-5N	C7
CTA-Brown Line-Paulina Station, CHCG	2977	2W-4N	C3
CTA-Brown Line-Rockwell Station, - CHCG	2921	3W-5N	A7
CTA-Brown Line-Southport Station, - CHCG	2977	1W-4N	D3
CTA-Brown Line-Western Station, CHCG	2921	3W-5N	A7
CTA-Cermak Branch-18th Station, CHCG	3091	2W-1S	C1
CTA-Cermak Branch-54-Cermak Station, - CCRO	3089	6W-1S	D1
CTA-Cermak Branch-California Station, - CHCG	3091	3W-1S	A1
CTA-Cermak Branch-Central Park Station,- CHCG	3090	4W-1S	C1
CTA-Cermak Branch-Cicero Station, - CCRO	3090	5W-1S	A2
CTA-Cermak Branch-Damen Station, - CHCG	3091	2W-1S	C1
CTA-Cermak Branch-Kedzie Station, - CHCG	3090	4W-1S	E1
CTA-Cermak Branch-Kostner Station, - CHCG	3090	5W-1S	B1
CTA-Cermak Branch-Polk Station, CHCG	3033	2W-0S	C6
CTA-Cermak Branch-Pulaski Station, - CHCG	3090	4W-1S	C1
CTA-Cermak Branch-Western Station, - CHCG	3091	2W-1S	B1
CTA-Diversey Station, CHCG	2977	1W-3N	E4
CTA-Forest Park Branch-Austin Station, - CHCG	3031	7W-0S	B6
CTA-Forest Park Branch-Cicero Station, - CHCG	3031	6W-0S	E6
CTA-Forest Park Branch-Forest Park-Station, FTPK	3030	9W-0S	C5
CTA-Forest Park Branch-Harlem Station, - FTPK	3030	9W-0S	D6
CTA-Forest Park Branch-Medical Ctr-Station, CHCG	3033	2W-0S	C5
CTA-Forest Park Branch-Oak Park-Station, OKPK	3030	8W-0S	E6
CTA-Forest Park Branch-Pulaski Station,- CHCG	3032	5W-0S	B6
CTA-Forest Park Branch-Western Station,- CHCG	3033	3W-0S	A5
CTA-Fullerton Station, CHCG	2977	1W-2N	E6
CTA-Green Line-43rd Station, CHCG	3092	0E-4S	C6
CTA-Green Line-47th Station, CHCG	3092	0E-4S	D7
CTA-Green Line-51st Station, CHCG	3152	0E-5S	D2
CTA-Green Line-Ashland Station, CHCG	3033	2W-0N	C4
CTA-Green Line-Austin Station, CHCG	3031	7W-0N	B4
CTA-Green Line-Bronzeville, CHCG	3092	0E-3S	C5
CTA-Green Line-California Station, - CHCG	3032	3W-0N	E4
CTA-Green Line-Central Station, CHCG	3031	7W-0N	C4
CTA-Green Line-Cicero Station, CHCG	3031	6W-0N	E4
CTA-Green Line-Clinton Station, CHCG	3034	0W-0N	A4
CTA-Green Line-Conservatory/Central-Park Sta, CHCG	3032	4W-0N	C4
CTA-Green Line-E 63rd-Cottage Grove-Station, CHCG	3152	0E-6S	D4
CTA-Green Line-Garfield Station, - CHCG	3152	0E-6S	D3
CTA-Green Line-Harlem-Lake Station, - OKPK	3030	8W-0N	D4
CTA-Green Line-Indiana Station, CHCG	3092	0E-4S	C6
CTA-Green Line-Kedzie Station, CHCG	3032	4W-0N	D4
CTA-Green Line-King Drive Station, - CHCG	3152	0E-6S	D4
CTA-Green Line-Laramie, CHCG	3031	6W-0N	D4
CTA-Green Line-Oak Park Station, - OKPK	3030	8W-0N	E4
CTA-Green Line-Pulaski Station, CHCG	3032	5W-0N	B4
CTA-Green Line-Ridgeland Station, - OKPK	3031	7W-0N	A4
CTA-Howard Station, CHCG	2867	2W-9N	C7
CTA-Jackson Station, CHCG	3034	0W-0S	B5
CTA-LaSalle Station, CHCG	3034	0W-0S	B5
CTA-Library Station, CHCG	3034	0W-0S	C5
CTA-Madison Station, CHCG	3034	0E-0N	C4
CTA-Orange Line-35-Archer Station, - CHCG	3091	2W-3S	B5
CTA-Orange Line-Ashland Station, - CHCG	3091	2W-2S	C3
CTA-Orange Line-Halsted Station, - CHCG	3091	1W-2S	E2
CTA-Orange Line-Kedzie Station, CHCG	3150	4W-5S	D1
CTA-Orange Line-Midway Station, CHCG	3150	5W-6S	A4
CTA-Orange Line-Pulaski Station, - CHCG	3150	5W-5S	C2
CTA-Orange Line-Western Station, - CHCG	3151	2W-5S	B1
CTA-Purple Line-Central Station, - EVTN	2813	2W-13N	B7
CTA-Purple Line-Davis Station, EVTN	2867	2W-11N	A3
CTA-Purple Line-Dempster Station, - EVTN	2867	2W-11N	B3
CTA-Purple Line-Foster Station, EVTN	2867	2W-11N	B2
CTA-Purple Line-Linden Station, WLMT	2813	2W-13N	A6
CTA-Purple Line-Main Station, EVTN	2867	2W-10N	B5
CTA-Purple Line-Noyes Station, EVTN	2867	2W-12N	B1
CTA-Purple Line-South Blvd Station, - EVTN	2867	2W-10N	B5
CTA-Quincy Station, CHCG	3034	0W-0S	B5
CTA-Randolph Station, CHCG	3034	0E-0N	C4
CTA-Red Line-47th Station, CHCG	3092	0W-4S	B7
CTA-Red Line-63rd Station, CHCG	3152	0W-6S	B4
CTA-Red Line-69th Station, CHCG	3152	0E-7S	C6
CTA-Red Line-79th Station, CHCG	3214	0W-9S	C2
CTA-Red Line-87th Station, CHCG	3214	0W-10S	C4
CTA-Red Line-95th/Dan Ryan Station, - CHCG	3214	0E-10S	C5
CTA-Red Line-Addison Station, CHCG	2977	1W-4N	E2
CTA-Red Line-Argyle Station, CHCG	2921	1W-6N	D6
CTA-Red Line-Berwyn Station, CHCG	2921	1W-6N	D5
CTA-Red Line-Bryn Mawr Station, CHCG	2921	1W-6N	D4
CTA-Red Line-Cermak-Chinatown Station, CHCG	3092	0W-1S	B1
CTA-Red Line-Chicago Station, CHCG	3034	0W-0N	B2
CTA-Red Line-Clark-Division Station, - CHCG	3034	0W-1N	B1
CTA-Red Line-Garfield Station, CHCG	3152	0W-5S	B2
CTA-Red Line-Grand Station, CHCG	3034	0W-0N	B3
CTA-Red Line-Granville Station, CHCG	2921	1W-7N	D3
CTA-Red Line-Harrison Station, CHCG	3034	0E-0S	C6
CTA-Red Line-Jackson Station, CHCG	3034	0W-0S	C5
CTA-Red Line-Jarvis Station, CHCG	2867	2W-9N	C7
CTA-Red Line-Lake Station, CHCG	3034	0W-0N	B4
CTA-Red Line-Lawrence Station, CHCG	2921	1W-5N	E6
CTA-Red Line-Loyola Station, CHCG	2921	1W-8N	D2
CTA-Red Line-Monroe Station, CHCG	3034	0W-0S	C5

FEATURE NAME Address City ZIP Code	MAP#	CGS	GRID
CTA-Red Line-Morse Station, CHCG	2921	1W-8N	D1
CTA-Red Line-North-Clybourn Station, - CHCG	2977	1W-2N	E7
CTA-Red Line-Roosevelt Station, CHCG	3034	0W-0S	B6
CTA-Red Line-Sheridan Station, CHCG	2977	1W-4N	E1
CTA-Red Line-Sox-35th Station, CHCG	3092	0W-3S	B4
CTA-Red Line-Thorndale Station, CHCG	2921	1W-7N	D3
CTA-Red Line-Washingon Station, CHCG	3034	0W-0N	B4
CTA-Red Line-Wilson Station, CHCG	2921	1W-5N	D7
CTA-Sedgwick Station, CHCG	3034	0W-1N	B1
CTA-State Station, CHCG	3034	0W-0N	B4
CTA-Washington Station, CHCG	3034	0W-0N	B4
CTA-Wellington Station, CHCG	2977	1W-3N	E4
CTA-Yellow Line-Skokie Station, SKOK	2865	6W-10N	E4
Greyhound-Chicago, CHCG	3034	0W-0S	A5
Greyhound-Chicago, CHCG	3091	3W-1S	A2
Greyhound-Chicago-95th & Dan Ryan, - CHCG	3214	0W-10S	C5
Greyhound-Chicago-Cumberland Av, - CHCG	2918	10W-7N	A4
Greyhound-Chicago Heights, CHHT	3596	1W-26S	A1
Greyhound-Forest Park, FTPK	3030	9W-0S	C5
Greyhound-Hammond, HMND	3352		E3
Greyhound-Joliet, JLET	3498	24W-23S	E3
Greyhound-Markham, MKHM	3427	3W-19S	A2
Greyhound-Melrose Park, MLPK	3029	12W-1N	B2
Greyhound-Northbrook, NHBK	2758	8W-17N	A4
Greyhound-Oak Brook, OKBK	3085	16W-1S	D1
Greyhound-Skokie, SKOK	2865	6W-10N	E4
Greyhound-Waukegan, WKGN	2479	11W-34N	C7
Metra-18th Street Station, CHCG	3092	0E-1S	C1
Metra-23rd Street Station, CHHT	3596	0W-26S	D2
Metra-27th Street Station, CHCG	3092	0E-2S	D3
Metra-47th Street Station, CHCG	3093	1E-5S	A7
Metra-53rd St Station, CHCG	3153	2E-5S	B2
Metra-55th-56th-57th Street Station, - CHCG	3153	1E-6S	B3
Metra-59th Street Station, CHCG	3153	1E-6S	B3
Metra-63rd Street Station, CHCG	3153	1E-7S	A5
Metra-75th Street Station, CHCG	3153	1E-8S	A7
Metra-79th Street Station, CHCG	3215	1E-9S	A2
Metra-83rd Street Station, CHCG	3215	3E-9S	E2
Metra-87th Street Station, CHCG	3216	3E-9S	A3
Metra-87th Street Station, CHCG	3214	1E-9S	E3
Metra-91st Street Station, CHCG	3214	1E-10S	E4
Metra-91st Street Station, CHCG	3213	2W-10S	D5
Metra-95th Street Station, CHCG	3213	2W-10S	C5
Metra-99th Street Station, CHCG	3213	2W-11S	D7
Metra-103rd Street Station, CHCG	3214	0E-11S	E7
Metra-103rd St Station, CHCG	3277	2W-12S	C1
Metra-107th Street Station, CHCG	3278	0E-12S	D2
Metra-107th Street Station, CHCG	3277	2W-12S	C2
Metra-111th Street Station, CHCG	3277	2W-12S	C2
Metra-115th Street Station, CHCG	3277	2W-13S	C3
Metra-119th Street Station, CHCG	3277	2W-13S	C5
Metra-123rd Street Station, BLID	3277	2W-14S	C6
Metra-143rd Street Station, ODPK	3345	12W-16S	C4
Metra-147th St Station, HRVY	3350	0W-17S	B5
Metra-179th Street Station, ODPK	3422	14W-21S	D6
Metra-211th Street Station, MTSN	3506	4W-25S	E7
Metra-Antioch Station, ANTH	2357	23W-42N	E6
Metra-Arlington Heights Station, - ANHT	2807	17W-14N	A5
Metra-Arlington Park Station, ANHT	2806	19W-14N	C3
Metra-Ashburn Station, CHCG	3212	4W-9S	D3
Metra-Ashland Station, CTPK	3277	1W-14S	D6
Metra-Aurora Station, AURA	3138	35W-7S	B7
Metra-Barrington Station, BRTN	2751	25W-18N	A2
Metra-Bartlett Station, BRLT	2910	29W-8N	E3
Metra-Bellwood Station, BLWD	3029	12W-0N	A3
Metra-Belmont Station, DRGV	3143	21W-5S	E2
Metra-Belmont Station, FNPK	2973	11W-4N	D4
Metra-Bensenville Station, BNVL	2971	16W-5N	E1
Metra-Berkeley Station, BKLY	3028	14W-1N	C2
Metra-Berwyn Station, BRWN	3089	8W-3S	A4
Metra-Big Timber Rd Station, ELGN	2854	36W-13N	A1
Metra-Blue Island-Grove Street Station,- BLID	3349	2W-15S	B1
Metra-Blue Island-Vermont Street-Station, BLID	3349	2W-15S	C1
Metra-Blue Line-LaSalle Station, - CHCG	3034	0W-0S	B5
Metra-Braeside Station, HDPK	2758	7W-20N	C2
Metra-Brainerd Station, CHCG	3213	1W-10S	E4
Metra-Brookfield Station, BKFD	3087	11W-3S	E6
Metra-Bryn Mawr Station, CHCG	3153	2E-8S	B6
Metra-Buffalo Grove Station, BFGV	2701	15W-21N	E7
Metra-Burr Oak Station, BLID	3277	2W-15S	C7
Metra-Calumet Station, EHZC	3427	2W-20S	D5
Metra-Cary Station, CRY	2695	31W-23N	E1
Metra-Central Street Station, EVTN	2812	3W-12N	E7
Metra-Cheltenham Station, CHCG	3215	3E-8S	E1
Metra-Chicago Ridge Station, CHRG	3275	8W-12S	B1
Metra-Chicago Station, CHCG	3034	0W-0S	B5
Metra-Cicero Station, CCRO	3089	6W-2S	E3
Metra-Clarendon Hills Station, CNHL	3145	16W-5S	D2
Metra-Clybourn Station, CHCG	2977	1W-2N	D6
Metra-College Av Station, WHTN	3024	23W-0S	E6
Metra-Congress Park Station, BKFD	3087	11W-4S	D6
Metra-Crystal Lake Station, CLLK	2640	35W-26N	B3
Metra-Cumberland Station, DSPN	2862	14W-11N	C2
Metra-Dee Rd Station, PKRG	2863	11W-9N	D6
Metra-Deerfield Station, DRFD	2703	11W-21N	E7
Metra-Des Plaines Station, DSPN	2863	13W-11N	A4
Metra-Downers Grove Fairview Av-Station, DRGV	3144	18W-5S	E2
Metra-Downers Grove Main Street-Station, DRGV	3144	19W-5S	C2
Metra-Edgebrook Station, CHCG	2919	6W-8N	C2
Metra-Edison Park Station, CHCG	2918	9W-8N	C2
Metra-Elgin Station, ELGN	2854	34W-11N	D4
Metra-Elmhurst Station, EMHT	3027	16W-1N	E2
Metra-Elmwood Park Station, EDPK	2974	9W-3N	C5
Metra-Evanston/Davis Street Station, - EVTN	2867	2W-11N	B3
Metra-Flossmoor Station, FSMR	3507	3W-22S	B2
Metra-Forest Glen Station, CHCG	2919	6W-6N	D5
Metra-Fort Sheridan Station, HIWD	2650	9W-24N	B7
Metra-Fox Lake Station, FXLK	2473	28W-36N	A3
Metra-Fox River Grove Station, FRGV	2696	30W-22N	A3
Metra-Franklin Park Station, FNPK	2973	12W-3N	C4
Metra-Galewood Station, CHCG	2975	8W-2N	A6
Metra-Geneva Station, GNVA	3020	35W-0N	B4
Metra-Gladstone Park Station, CHCG	2919	7W-6N	B5
Metra-Glencoe Station, GLNC	2758	6W-17N	D4
Metra-Glen Ellyn Station, GNEN	3025	22W-0N	C5
Metra-Glenview Station, GNVW	2810	8W-13N	D6
Metra-Golf Station, GLF	2864	8W-12N	E1
Metra-Grand/Cicero Station, CHCG	2975	6W-2N	E7
Metra-Grayland Station, CHCG	2976	5W-4N	A2
Metra-Grayslake Station, GYLK	2532	20W-32N	E5
Metra-Grayslake Washington Street-Station, GYLK	2532	21W-34N	D2
Metra-Great Lakes Station, NCHI	2593	11W-30N	E2
Metra-Gresham Station, CHCG	3214	1W-9S	A3
Metra-Halsted Station, CHCG	3034	0W-1S	A7
Metra-Hanover Park Station, HRPK	2911	27W-8N	D4
Metra-Hanson Park Station, CHCG	2975	7W-2N	C7
Metra-Harlem Avenue Station, BRWN	3088	8W-3S	E4
Metra-Harvard Station, HRVD	2406	50W-38N	A7
Metra-Harvey Station, HRVY	3350	1W-18S	A7
Metra-Hazel Crest Station, HLCT	3427	2W-20S	E4
Metra-Healy Station, CHCG	2976	5W-3N	B5
Metra-Hegewisch Station, CHCG	3352	3E-15S	A2
Metra-Hickory Creek Station, MKNA	3503	11W-22S	E2
Metra-Highland Park Station, HDPK	2704	8W-22N	E5
Metra-Highlands Station, HNDL	3146	14W-4S	C1
Metra-Highwood Station, HIWD	2704	9W-23N	D2
Metra-Hinsdale Station, HNDL	3146	15W-5S	B1
Metra-Hollywood Station, BKFD	3088	10W-3S	A5
Metra-Homewood Station, HMWD	3427	2W-21S	C7
Metra-Hubbard Woods Station, WNKA	2759	5W-16N	A7
Metra-Indian Hill Station, WNKA	2812	4W-15N	B3
Metra-Ingleside Station, FXLK	2473	26W-35N	D5
Metra-Irving Park Station, CHCG	2976	5W-5N	A1
Metra-Itasca Station, ITSC	2914	19W-6N	C6
Metra-Ivanhoe Station, RVDL	3350	0W-16S	B4
Metra-Jefferson Park Station, CHCG	2919	6W-6N	D6
Metra-Joliet Station, JLET	3499	23W-23S	A5
Metra-Kedzie Station, CHCG	3032	4W-0N	D4
Metra-Kenilworth Station, KLWH	2812	4W-14N	C4
Metra-Kensington-115th Street Station, - CHCG	3278	0E-13S	D3
Metra-Lafox Station, BbyT	3018	40W-1N	B3
Metra-La Grange Road Station, LGNG	3087	12W-4S	C6
Metra-Lake Bluff Station, LKBF	2593	11W-28N	E5
Metra-Lake Cook Station, DRFD	2757	10W-18N	A2
Metra-Lake Forest Station, LKFT	2649	12W-24N	B6
Metra-Lake Villa Station, LKVL	2475	22W-38N	A1
Metra-Lavergne Station, BRWN	3089	8W-3S	B4
Metra-Lemont Station, LMNT	3270	19W-13S	D5
Metra-Libertyville Station, LYVL	2591	16W-29N	C4
Metra-Lisle Station, LSLE	3143	22W-5S	B2
Metra-Lockport Station, LKPT	3419	22W-19S	C3
Metra-Lombard Station, LMBD	3026	19W-0N	C4
Metra-Long Lake Station, GrtT	2474	25W-34N	A7
Metra-Longwood Station, CHCG	3214	1E-10S	E5
Metra-Main Street Station, EVTN	2867	2W-10N	B5
Metra-Mannheim Station, FNPK	2973	12W-4N	A3
Metra-Mars Station, CHCG	2974	8W-2N	E6
Metra-Matteson Station, MTSN	3594	4W-25S	E1
Metra-Mayfair Station, CHCG	2975	5W-5N	E1
Metra-Maywood Station, MYWD	3030	10W-0N	A4
Metra-McCormick Place Station, CHCG	3092	0E-2S	D2
Metra-McHenry Station, MHRY	2528	32W-33N	A4
Metra-Medinah Station, BmdT	2913	22W-7N	D5
Metra-Melrose Park Station, MLPK	3029	11W-0N	D3
Metra-Midlothian Station, MDLN	3348	4W-17S	D5
Metra-Millennium Station, CHCG	3034	0E-0N	C4
Metra-Mokena Station, MKNA	3503	13W-23S	A4
Metra-Mont Clare Station, CHCG	2974	8W-2N	E6
Metra-Morton Grove Station, MNGV	2865	7W-10N	A4
Metra-Mt Prospect Station, MPPT	2808	15W-12N	A7
Metra-Mundelein Station, MDLN	2590	18W-27N	E7
Metra-Naperville Station, NPVL	3141	26W-6S	D4
Metra-National Street Station, ELGN	2854	33W-10N	E5
Metra-New Lenox Station, NLNX	3501	17W-24S	C6
Metra-Northbrook Station, NHBK	2757	9W-17N	B6
Metra-North Chicago Station, NCHI	2537	10W-32N	A6
Metra-North Glenview Station, GNVW	2810	9W-15N	C3
Metra-Norwood Park Station, CHCG	2918	8W-7N	E3
Metra-Oak Forest Station, OKFT	3426	6W-18S	A1
Metra-Oak Lawn Station, OKLN	3211	6W-11S	E6
Metra-Oak Park Station, OKPK	3030	8W-0N	E4
Metra-Ogilvie Transportation Center, - CHCG	3034	0W-0N	A4
Metra-O'Hare Transfer Station, CHCG	2917	12W-7N	A3
Metra-Olympia Fields Station, OMFD	3507	3W-24S	A5
Metra-Orland Park-153rd Street Station,- ODPK	3345	13W-18S	B7
Metra-Palatine Station, PLTN	2805	21W-16N	E1
Metra-Palos Heights Station, PSHT	3274	9W-13S	D4
Metra-Palos Park Station, PSPK	3274	10W-14S	C6
Metra-Park Ridge Station, PKRG	2918	10W-8N	B1
Metra-Pingree Road Station, CLLK	2640	34W-25N	D5
Metra-Prairie Crossing Station, LYVL	2533	19W-31N	C7
Metra-Prairie Street Station, BLID	3277	2W-15S	C7
Metra-Prairie View Station, VrnT	2701	16W-22N	D3
Metra-Prospect Heights Station, PTHT	2808	14W-14N	C3
Metra-Pullman-111th Street Station, - CHCG	3278	0E-13S	D3
Metra-Racine Avenue Station, CHCG	3277	1W-14S	E5
Metra-Ravenswood Station, CHCG	2921	2W-5N	C7
Metra-Ravinia Station, HDPK	2705	7W-20N	B7
Metra-Richton Park Station, RNPK	3594	4W-26S	D3
Metra-Riverdale Station, RVDL	3350	0W-15S	C2
Metra-River Forest Station, RVFT	3030	10W-0N	B4
Metra-River Grove Station, RVGV	2974	10W-3N	A5
Metra-Riverside Station, RVSD	3088	10W-3S	B5
Metra-Robbins Station, RBBN	3349	3W-16S	A3
Metra-Rogers Park Station, CHCG	2921	2W-8N	C1
Metra-Roosevelt Road Station, CHCG	3034	0E-1S	C6
Metra-Roselle Station, ROSL	2913	22W-7N	B5
Metra-Rosemont Station, RSMT	2917	12W-6N	B5
Metra-Round Lake Beach Station, RLKB	2475	22W-35N	C5
Metra-Round Lake Station, RDLK	2531	23W-33N	E2
Metra-Route 59 Station, NPVL	3140	30W-6S	C5
Metra-Schaumburg Station, ROSL	2912	25W-8N	B3
Metra-Schiller Park Station, SRPK	2917	12W-5N	B7
Metra-South Chicago Station, CHCG	3216	3E-10S	A5
Metra-South Shore Station, CHCG	3153	3E-8S	D6
Metra-State Street Station, CHCG	3278	0E-14S	C5
Metra-Stewart Ridge Station, CHCG	3278	0W-14S	B5
Metra-Stone Av Station, LGNG	3087	12W-4S	B7
Metra-Stony Island Station, CHCG	3153	1E-8S	A7
Metra-Summit Station, SMMT	3148	9W-5S	C2
Metra-Tinley Park-80th Av Station, - TYPK	3424	9W-21S	D6
Metra-Tinley Park Station, TYPK	3425	8W-20S	A5
Metra-University Park Station, MonT	3594	5W-28S	C6
Metra-Van Buren Street Station, CHCG	3034	0E-0S	C5
Metra-Vernon Hills Station, VNHL	2647	17W-24N	C7
Metra-Villa Park Station, VLPK	3027	17W-1N	B2
Metra-Washington Heights Station, - CHCG	3277	1W-12S	E1
Metra-Waukegan Station, WKGN	2537	10W-34N	B2
Metra-West Chicago Station, WCHI	3022	29W-0N	D4
Metra-Western Avenue Station, CHCG	3091	2W-1S	B1
Metra-Western Av Station, CHCG	3033	3W-0N	A3
Metra-Western Springs Station, WNSP	3086	14W-4S	D7
Metra-West Hinsdale Station, HNDL	3145	16W-5S	E2
Metra-Westmont Station, WTMT	3145	18W-5S	B2
Metra-West Pullman Station, CHCG	3278	1W-14S	A5
Metra-Wheaton Station, WHTN	3024	25W-0S	B7
Metra-Wheeling Station, WLNG	2755	15W-17N	B4
Metra-Willow Springs Station, WLSP	3209	13W-9S	B4
Metra-Wilmette Station, WLMT	2812	3W-13N	D6
Metra-Windsor Park Station, CHCG	3153	3E-8S	E7
Metra-Winfield Station, WNFD	3023	27W-0S	C6
Metra-Winnetka Station, WNKA	2812	5W-15N	B2
Metra-Winthrop Harbor Station, WPHR	2363	9W-42N	D6
Metra-Wood Dale Station, WDDL	2915	17W-6N	B7
Metra-Woodstock Station, WDSK	2524	41W-31N	D7
Metra-Worth Station, WRTH	3274	8W-12S	E3
Metra-Wrightwood Station, CHCG	3212	3W-8S	E2
Metra-Zion Station, ZION	2422	9W-40N	C3
NICTD-Hammond Station, HMND	3352		D4

Visitor Information

FEATURE NAME Address City ZIP Code	MAP#	CGS	GRID
Chicago Convention & Visitors-Bureau 2301 S Lake Shore Dr, CHCG, 60616	3092	0E-2S	D2
Chicago Southland Conv & Visitors-Bureau 2304 173rd St, LNSG, 60438	3429	2E-20S	E4
Convention & Visitors Bureau W State St, SCRL, 60174	2964	35W-3N	B7
DuPage Convention & Visitors Bureau 915 Harger Rd, OKBK, 60523	3085	16W-1S	E2
Illinois & Michigan Canal Visitor-Center 200 W 8th St, LKPT, 60441	3419	22W-19S	C2
Illinois Tourism Information Center 78 E Washington St, CHCG, 60602	3034	0E-0N	C4
Joliet Tourism Bureau 30 N Bluff St, JLET, 60435	3498	24W-24S	E5
Oak Park Visitors Center 158 Forest Av, OKPK, 60301	3030	8W-0N	E3
Tourist Information E Grand Av, CHCG, 60611	3034	0E-0N	E3
Tourist Information LslT, 60532	3083	22W-4S	B7
Tourist Information Park Blvd, MltT, 60137	3083	23W-3S	B6
Woodfield Convention & Visitors-Bureau 1450 E Woodfield Rd, SMBG, 60173	2859	21W-11N	D3

CUT ALONG DOTTED LINE

RAND McNALLY

Thank you for purchasing this Rand McNally Street Guide! We value your comments and suggestions.

Please help us serve you better by completing this postage-paid reply card.
This information is for internal use ONLY and will not be distributed or sold to any external third party.

Missing pages? Maybe not... Please refer to the "Using Your Street Guide" page for further explanation.

Street Guide Title: Chicago 7-County **ISBN-13#** 978-0-5288-6089-8 **MKT:** CHG

Today's Date: ____________ Gender: ☐M ☐F Age Group: ☐18-24 ☐25-31 ☐32-40 ☐41-50 ☐51-64 ☐65+

1. What type of industry do you work in?
   ☐Real Estate ☐Trucking ☐Delivery ☐Construction ☐Utilities ☐Government
   ☐Retail ☐Sales ☐Transportation ☐Landscape ☐Service & Repair
   ☐Courier ☐Automotive ☐Insurance ☐Medical ☐Police/Fire/First Response
   ☐Other, please specify: ____________
2. What type of job do you have in this industry? ____________
3. Where did you purchase this Street Guide? (store name & city) ____________
4. Why did you purchase this Street Guide? ____________
5. How often do you purchase an updated Street Guide? ☐Annually ☐2 yrs. ☐3-5 yrs. ☐Other: ____________
6. Where do you use it? ☐Primarily in the car ☐Primarily in the office ☐Primarily at home ☐Other: ____________
7. How do you use it? ☐Exclusively for business ☐Primarily for business but also for personal or leisure use
   ☐Both work and personal evenly ☐Primarily for personal use ☐Exclusively for personal use
8. What do you use your Street Guide for?
   ☐Find Addresses ☐In-route navigation ☐Planning routes ☐Other: ____________
   Find points of interest: ☐Schools ☐Parks ☐Buildings ☐Shopping Centers ☐Other: ____________
9. How often do you use it? ☐Daily ☐Weekly ☐Monthly ☐Other: ____________
10. Do you use the internet for maps and/or directions? ☐Yes ☐No
11. How often do you use the internet for directions? ☐Daily ☐Weekly ☐Monthly ☐Other: ____________
12. Do you use any of the following mapping products in addition to your Street Guide?
    ☐Folded paper maps ☐Folded laminated maps ☐Wall maps ☐GPS ☐PDA ☐In-car navigation ☐Phone maps
13. What features, if any, would you like to see added to your Street Guide? ____________
14. What features or information do you find most useful in your Rand McNally Street Guide? (please specify)
15. Please provide any additional comments or suggestions you have. ____________

We strive to provide you with the most current updated information available if you know of a map correction, please notify us here.

Where is the correction? Map Page #: ____________ Grid #: ____________ Index Page #: ____________

Nature of the correction: ☐Street name missing ☐Street name misspelled ☐Street information incorrect
☐Incorrect location for point of interest ☐Index error ☐Other: ____________

Detail: ____________

I would like to receive information about updated editions and special offers from Rand McNally
☐via e-mail E-mail address: ____________
☐via postal mail
Your Name: ____________ Company (if used for work): ____________
Address: ____________ City/State/ZIP: ____________

Thank you for your time and help. We are working to serve you better.
This information is for internal use ONLY and will not be distributed or sold to any external third party.

CUT ALONG DOTTED LINE

SG-noCD.06

TAPE SHUT TAPE SHUT

get directions at
randmcnally.com

CUT ALONG DOTTED LINE

2ND FOLD LINE

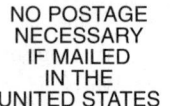

NO POSTAGE
NECESSARY
IF MAILED
IN THE
UNITED STATES

BUSINESS REPLY MAIL
FIRST-CLASS MAIL PERMIT NO. 388 CHICAGO IL
POSTAGE WILL BE PAID BY ADDRESSEE

RAND MCNALLY
CONSUMER AFFAIRS
PO BOX 7600
CHICAGO IL 60680-9915

1ST FOLD LINE

The most trusted name on the map.

You'll never need to ask for directions again with these Rand McNally products!

- EasyFinder® Laminated Maps
- Folded Maps
- Street Guides
- Wall Maps
- CustomView Wall Maps
- Road Atlases
- Motor Carriers' Road Atlases

CUT ALONG DOTTED LINE

SGTG_07